Who's Who
Among American
High School Students®
Honoring Tomorrow's Leaders Today®

1985-86
Twentieth Annual Edition
Volume I

WHO'S WHO AMONG AMERICAN HIGH SCHOOL STUDENTS® is a publication of Educational Communications, Inc. of Lake Forest, Illinois and has no connection with "Who's Who In America" and its publisher, Marquis — Who's Who, Inc. Students featured in this volume attended school in the following states: Connecticut, Foreign, Maine, Massachusetts, New Hampshire, New York, Puerto Rico, Rhode Island, Vermont and the Virgin Islands.

Compilation of the copyright matter published in this volume has required considerable time, and has been carried out only at great expense. The copyright matter contained herein is intended for the exclusive use of our subscribers. No information contained in this volume may be key-punched, entered into a computer, or photocopied in any manner for any purpose what-soever. The use of any such information as a mailing list, either in whole or in part, is strictly forbidden unless authorized in writing by the publishers. The contents have been coded, and cannot be copied without detection. Infringements will be prosecuted.

TABLE OF CONTENTS

* *Wherever students attend school out of state they will be listed in
  the state where they attend school.*

IN MEMORIUM:

Salvatore R. Salato
1925 - 1985

This book is dedicated to the memory of Salvatore R. Salato who served WHO'S WHO AMONG AMERICAN HIGH SCHOOL STUDENTS as a member of the Ethics, Standards and Practices Committee for six years. His untimely death in November, 1985, saddened all who came into contact with this warm, caring, compassionate human being. Sal had a long and distinguished career in public and private schools. At the time of his death, he was Principal of Thornridge High School, a school with 2,050 students, in Dolton, Illinois. He held that position since 1976. He joined the Thornridge faculty in 1961 as a physical education teacher and assistant varsity football coach. Recognizing his skills in working with adolescents, he was appointed Dean of Students in 1964 and then Assistant Principal at Thornridge in 1968.

Before coming to Thornridge High School, Sal taught and was head football coach at St. Mel High School in Chicago. A former Crane Technical High School and Drake University football player, he continued his interest in sports and young people by promoting and developing youth football. Starting in 1970 he served as the coach of the 7th and 8th grade football team at Holy Ghost Parish. Principal Salato received his bachelor's degree from Drake University and earned his master's degree from Purdue University.

Sal was the devoted husband of Mary Lou and father of four children and grandfather of five. As he dedicated his life to the development of youth, we respectfully dedicate the twentieth edition of WHO'S WHO AMONG AMERICAN HIGH SCHOOL STUDENTS to Sal Salato, professional educator, husband, father, coach, teacher and friend.

PUBLISHER'S CORNER:

After 20 years, some things are still the same.

Welcome to the 20th Annual Edition of WHO'S WHO AMONG AMERICAN HIGH SCHOOL STUDENTS. This is a very special, exciting anniversary edition.

In twenty years we have honored and recognized just under 5,000,000 students. We have helped over 700 students go to college by awarding over $800,000 in scholarships. We have made 2,000,000 referrals to colleges and universities through our College Referral Service and sponsored seventeen Annual Surveys of High Achievers.

Over the past twenty years we have witnessed and observed a multitude of changes and a few consistencies — through the end of the 60's, the entire 70's and now into the mid-80's. Much has changed including styles, music, politics, national leadership, morals, values, national interests, priorities, strengths and weaknesses. Big wars have ended, skirmishes and conflicts continue. Terrorism incidents startled us all when they first occurred and now they rarely make the front page of most of our newspapers. Our nation's morale reached an all-time low in the early 70's only to see a re-birth of patriotism and pride in the past few years, peaking perhaps as we celebrated Miss Liberty's 100th birthday this past summer.

Yet, through all this turbulence and change, one thing has remained conspicuously the same —the pursuit of academic excellence by a substantial percentage of American high school students. And, academic excellence is even more respected today than it was twenty years ago because educational reforms and higher standards have become a national priority resulting from several major reports issued in the past several years.

Historically we have been a nation which has honored, sometimes even worshiped, athletes, movie stars, politicians and celebrities of every ilk. From time-to-time we have gone overboard in this fanaticism. While we still reserve a special place in our collective hearts for those media marvels, we are finally coming to grips with the importance of recognizing and rewarding our best students, teachers and educational administrators.

At WHO'S WHO AMONG AMERICAN HIGH SCHOOL STUDENTS we are proud to be counted as one of the many organizations in the educational community which has always recognized the significance of spotlighting students who achieve excellence. For twenty years we have witnessed a constant and growing parade of outstanding young men and women who have been committed to achievement. Day in and day out they grind out their work, master their lessons, find time to contribute to their schools, communities and families. They may have stumbled and even fallen sometimes, but they persevered and never gave up their pursuit for excellence. To us, these students have always been heroes worthy of the applause usually reserved for individuals of lesser talent, but greater visibility.

To these students, their teachers, administrators and families we say congratulations for a job well done. The students we recognized twenty years ago, fifteen years ago and even ten years ago are already taking their rightful places of leadership in our nation's businesses, industries, professions, schools and the arts. We are confident that the students now being recognized on the following pages will similarly follow in their footsteps. We are proud of all of you.

Who's Who Review

A Summary of the Objectives, Programs, Policies for
WHO'S WHO AMONG AMERICAN HIGH SCHOOL STUDENTS®

Since 1967, WHO'S WHO AMONG AMERICAN HIGH SCHOOL STUDENTS® has been committed to celebrating outstanding students for their positive achievements in academics, athletics, school and community service. Our first edition recognized 13,000 students from 4,000 high schools; the current, 20th edition, published in ten regional volumes, honors over 440,000 junior and senior class high school students representing 18,000 public, private, and parochial high schools nationwide.

As our publication has grown and matured over the years, we have expanded the scope and depth of the services and benefits provided for listed students and refined our policies and procedures in response to the needs of the schools and youth organizations who share our objectives.

Commencing with the 1986-87 academic year, we have expanded eligibility for recognition in WHO'S WHO to freshman and sophomore class students. This policy change was in direct response to educators who requested the opportunity to nominate younger students at a crucial point in their academic careers and reward those who excel through listing in the publication.

In our view, the growth, acceptance, and preeminence of WHO'S WHO AMONG AMERICAN HIGH SCHOOL STUDENTS as the leading student recognition publication in the nation, can be attributed to the involvement of educators in the policy-making areas of our programs.

During the past several years, we have hosted over 90 day-long reviews with key educational association executives to exchange ideas and perspectives regarding our standards, criteria, and services.

Most importantly, we must acknowledge the contributions of our Committee on Ethics, Standards and Practices, a group of distinguished educators representing relevant areas in secondary and post-secondary education. The committee was created in 1979 in order to formalize appropriate standards for our program which could be used as a guide for all student recognition programs. These standards are distributed to 80,000 high school principals, guidance counselors, and other faculty members each year.

It is a tribute to the committee that the standards they developed have been used as a model by several educational associations who have created their own guidelines for evaluating student recognition programs on a uniform basis. WHO'S WHO is proud of its well documented leadership role in promoting standards and ethics for all student recognition programs.

The committee meets each year and reviews literature, policies, programs, and services. They bring a perspective to the company which assures students and school administrators that WHO'S WHO policies and programs are in compliance and compatible with the standards and objectives of the educational community.

Major Policies and Procedures

Free Book Program—*Guarantees extensive recognition through wide circulation*

WHO'S WHO sponsors the largest Free Book Program of any publisher in any field. The book is automatically sent free to all participating high schools and youth organizations and offered free to all 7,500 libraries and 3,000 colleges and universities. Up to 15,000 complimentary copies are distributed each year.

The major purposes of this extensive free distribution system are to provide meaningful, national recognition for listed students among insitutions traditionally concerned with student achievement, and to make it convenient and easy for these students to view their published biography without purchasing the book.

For students who cannot locate an inspection copy of the book in their community, a listing of libraries within their state which received the most current edition is available upon request.

The recognition and reference purpose(s) of WHO'S WHO AMONG AMERICAN HIGH SCHOOL STUDENTS® have been acknowledged in the favorable review of the publication by the Reference and Subscription Books Reviews Committee of the American Library Association (*Booklist*, 3/1/82).

Financial Policies—*Legitimate honors do not cost the recipient money*

There are no financial requirements whatsoever contingent upon recognition in WHO'S WHO AMONG AMERICAN HIGH SCHOOL STUDENTS. The vast majority of students featured in all past editions have not purchased the book, but have received the recognition they have earned and deserve.

For those students who do purchase the publication or any related award insignia, satisfaction is guaranteed. Refunds are always issued on request.

Nominating Procedures—*Representation from all areas of student achievement*

Each year all 22,000 public, private, and parochial high schools are invited to nominate junior and senior class students who have achieved a "B" grade point average or better and demonstrated leadership in academics, athletics, or extracurricular activities. On rare occasions, students with slightly under a "B" average have been included when their achievements in non-academic areas were extraordinary. Nominators are requested to limit selections to 15% of their eligible students. Most nominate less.

Approximately 13,500 high schools participate in our program by nominating students. An additional 5,000-7,500 schools are represented by their outstanding students as a result of nominations received from bona fide youth organizations, churches with organized youth activities, scholarship agencies, civic and service groups. Most of our nation's major youth groups participate in our program by nominating their meritorious student leaders.

Editing—*Maintains the integrity of the honor*

Occasionally, nominators recommend students who are not qualified for recognition. When these students receive our literature and forms, there may be confusion concerning our standards and criteria. When biography forms are submitted for publication, they are all reviewed and edited to monitor compliance with our high standards. In the past ten years, approximately 167,300 students were disqualified by our editors because they did not meet our standards, including several thousand who ordered the publication. More than $1,106,500 in orders were returned to these students. Our standards are never compromised by the profit motive. (Auditor's verification available upon request.)

Verification of Data—*A continuous safety check on the effectiveness of our procedures*

To monitor the accuracy and integrity of data submitted by students, a nationally respected accounting firm conducts annual, independent audits of published biographical data. Previous audits reveal that up to 97.2% of the data published was substantially accurate. (Complete studies available upon request.)

Educational Communications Scholarship Foundation Committee members meet to select 50 scholarship winners for the 1983-84 academic year. Each winner receives a $1,000 award. Left: Dr. Norman Feingold, President, National Career & Counseling Services; Morton Temsky, Educator; Lester Benz, Executive Secretary Emeritus, Quill & Scroll Society; Wally Wikoff, Former Director, National Scholastic Press Association; Lily Rose, Scholarship Committee Chairperson and Director of Admissions, Roosevelt University; Fred Brooks, Asst. VP for Enrollment Services & Management, SUNY at Binghamton; Aline Rivers, 1979-80 Executive Board, National Association of College Admissions Counselors, Robert MacVicar, President Emeritus, Oregon State University; and Dr. James Schelhammer, Dean of Admissions, Austin Peay State University. Committee members not shown: Neill Sanders, Associate Director of Admissions, Washington State University and Dr. Hilda Minkoff, 1983-84 President, American School Counselor's Association.

Programs, Services and Benefits for Students

Scholarship Awards—*From $4,000 in 1968 to $100,000 annually since 1982*

The Educational Communications Scholarship Foundation®, a not-for-profit organization which is funded by the publishing company, now sponsors three separate scholarship award programs, which award over $100,000 in college scholarships each year. Over $800,000 has been funded to date.

Through the general high school program, 65 awards of $1,000 each are awarded to students by a committee of knowledgeable educators on the basis of grade point average, class rank, test scores, activities, an essay and financial need. An additional $15,000 in scholarships is funded through grants to youth organizations where we sponsor awards for their officers or contest winners. For students already in college, $25,000 in scholarships is awarded through THE NATIONAL DEAN'S LIST® Program.

Our research indicates that the Educational Communications Scholarship Foundation's programs represent one of the 10 largest scholarship programs in the nation funded by a single private sector organization. The Foundation is listed in numerous government and commercial directories on financial aid and scholarships.

Grants-In-Aid—*Financial support for organizations who work with or for students*

Since 1975, we have funded grants to youth and educational organizations to support their programs and/or services on behalf of high school students. The stipends fund scholarships or subsidize research, educational publications or competitive events, and programs. A brief summary of grants issued or committed to date, totaling approximately $346,000 appears in this review.

The College Referral Service (CRS)® — *Links students with colleges*

WHO'S WHO students receive a catalog listing all 3,000 colleges and universities. They complete a form indicating which institutions they wish us to notify of their honorary award. This service links interested students with colleges and universities and serves as a "third party" reference.

Certainly, listing in WHO'S WHO will not assure a student of admission into the college of his or her choice any more than any other award or honor society. Most selective colleges rely almost exclusively on grade point average, class rank, and test scores. Nevertheless, several hundred colleges have indicated that the CRS and/or the publication is a valuable reference source in their recruitment programs. (Letters from colleges available for inspection.)

17th Annual Survey of High Achievers™ —*The views of student leaders are as important as their achievements*

Since 1969, we have polled the attitudes and opinions of WHO'S WHO students on timely issues of interest. This study provides students with a collective voice otherwise not available to them. As young voters and future leaders, their views are important. Therefore, survey results are sent to the President, all members of Congress, state Governors, educational agencies, high school administrators, and the press.

Each year, survey results are widely reported in the press and have been utilized in academic studies and research indicating the educational value of this program.

WHO'S WHO Spokesteen Panel™— *Another voice for student leaders and a service for media*

Because WHO'S WHO has become an authoritative source on high school students, we receive frequent inquiries from reporters when they are preparing special features on teen views, lifestyles, etc. To assist reporters and to assure teens of appropriate representation of their views, we have created a network of articulate and well-informed students, nationwide, who are made available to the press for interviews of local and national coverage. WHO'S WHO Spokesteens have appeared on the "CBS Morning News," NBC "Today Show," "Merv Griffin Show," "Hour Magazine," and numerous other broadcasts, newspaper and magazine stories.

College-Bound Digest®—*What students need to know*

A compilation of articles written by prominent educators covering the various opportunities available to college-bound students, i.e., financial aid opportunities, the advantages of large schools, small schools, research universities, achievement test usage, and preparation and numerous other topics of similar relevancy. The Digest appears in the introductory section of this publication and is offered as a separate publication, free of charge, to 20,000 high school guidance offices, 20,000 principals, and 3,000 college admissions offices.

Local Newspaper Publicity—*Additional recognition for honored students*

Consistent with our primary purpose of providing recognition for meritorious students, we routinely provide over 2,000 newspapers nationwide with rosters of their local students featured in the publication with appropriate background information. (Students must authorize this release.)

Other Publications

Who's Who Among Black Americans®

This publication has been extremely well received by librarians, government agencies, educational institutions, and major corporations. All four major library trade journals reviewed and recommended earlier editions for their subscribers. The book was selected by the American Library Association as one of the "Outstanding Reference Books of the Year" and by *Black Scholar* as "A Notable Book," one of only 19 publications to receive this distinction.

WHO'S WHO AMONG BLACK AMERICANS was one of 380 titles chosen by the Library of Congress to be exhibited at The White House Conference on Library & Information Services held in November, 1979 and was selected for inclusion in the Presidential Library at Camp David.

William C. Matney, of WHO'S WHO AMONG BLACK AMERICANS, was introduced on the "Today Show" by book and theatre critic Gene Shalit. The publication has received numerous awards and honors.

The National Dean's List®

The ninth edition of THE NATIONAL DEAN'S LIST® recognizes 94,000 outstanding students representing 2,500 colleges and universities. All students were selected by their respective deans or registrars because of their academic achievements. This year, $25,000 in scholarships were distributed to twenty-five students. For 1986-87, a minimum of $25,000 in scholarships will again be awarded.

Memberships

Educational Communications, Inc. or its publisher is a member of the following organizations:
American Association of Higher Education
American Association of School Administrators
Chicago Metropolitan Better Business Bureau
Distributive Education Clubs of America,
    National Advisory Board
Educational Press Association
Future Farmers of America, Executive Sponsor
National Association of Financial Aid Administrators
National School Public Relations Association
Office Education Association,
    National Business Advisory Council

Profile of Who's Who Student

(Statistics From 1986 Edition)

General Listing
Total Number of Students 440,000
WHO'S WHO Students as Percentage of 6,500,000
    Juniors and Seniors Enrolled Nationwide 6½%
Females (%) 61%
Males (%) 39%

Academics
Grade Point Average (%)
    "A" 70%
    "B" 29%
    "C" .... less than 1%
Local Honor Roll 203,025
National Honor Society 133,597
Valedictorian/Salutatorian 9,836

Leadership Activities/Clubs
Student Council 80,740
Boys State/Girls State 35,672
Senior Class Officers 35,159
Junior Class Officers 47,713
Key Club 27,876

Major Vocational Organizations
Future Homemakers of America 30,655
4-H 30,473
Junior Achievement 23,156
Future Farmers of America 15,577
Distributive Education Clubs of America 9,663
Office Education Association 6,447

Varsity Athletics
Basketball 79,238
Track 66,706
Cheerleading/Pom Pon 59,390
Football 52,476
Volleyball 39,969
Soccer 30,085
Baseball 28,307
Tennis 27,300
Cross Country 22,450
Wrestling 12,386

Music/Performing Arts
Orchestra/Band 91,555
Chorus 66,629
Drama 43,744

Miscellaneous
Church/Temple Activities 162,913
Yearbook 89,455
School Paper 68,727
Students Against Driving Drunk 43,776
Community Worker 32,161
Fellowship of Christian Athletes 28,930

Grants to Youth and Educational Organizations

American Association for Gifted Children
$2,000, 1 Grant
To sponsor a conference for educators concerning "The Gifted Child, the Family and the Community."

American Children's Television Festival
$2,000, 1 Grant
To promote excellence in television programming for our nation's youth. Founded by the Central Educational Network.

American Council on the Teaching of Foreign Language
$500, 1 Grant
To support the general goals and objectives in the field of foreign language.

American Legion Auxiliary Girls Nation
$20,000, 8 Grants
Scholarships for Vice President and Outstanding Senator of program where students participate in mock government structure.

American Legion Boys Nation
$21,000, 9 Grants
Scholarships for President and Vice President of program where students learn about government through participation.

Animal Welfare Institute
$1,582, 2 Grants
For biology textbook on experiments which do not involve cruelty towards animals. Second grant to fund convention booth equipment.

Black United Fund
$5,000, 1 Grant
Scholarships for Black students selected by BUF Committee.

Colorado Forum of Educational Leaders
$1,000, 1 Grant
To fund a series of quarterly activities regarding the educational successes of Colorado Schools.

Contemporary-Family Life Curriculum
$1,500, 1 Grant
Funded formal grant request, resulting in $100,000 grant from government to test this contemporary curriculum.

Distributive Education Clubs of America (DECA)
$42,800, 12 Grants
ECI serves on the National Advisory Board for this major vocational/educational organization and sponsors scholarships for national officers.

Earthwatch
$3,000, 3 Grants
Scholarships for students conducting scientific expeditions with scientists, researchers.

Education Roundtable
$5,000, 1 Grant
To fund the creation of a committee of representatives from government, education, private industry, and the general public to support and improve education in America.

Fellowship of Christian Athletes
$12,800, 5 Grants
Original stipend funded seminar of athletic directors. Subsequent grants for scholarships for coaches' conferences concerning spiritual, professional and family growth.

Joint Council on Economic Education
$11,000, 4 Grants
Funds ongoing economic education program for students and educators from elementary school to college level.

Junior Achievement
$14,000, 7 Grants
Scholarship for the winner of the WHO'S WHO Essay Contest.

Junior Classical League
$6,000, 6 Grants
Funds a scholarship to the outstanding member selected by an educational committee for this organization whose members study the civilizations of Greece and Rome to provide a better understanding of our culture, literature, language and arts.

Junior Engineering Technical Society
$6,000, 2 Grants
Stipends were used to help revise the National Engineering Aptitude Search Test.

Key Club International
$1,000, 1 Grant
For two scholarships of $500 each for two outstanding Key Clubbers.

Law & Economic Center, University of Miami Law School
$4,500, 1 Grant
Funded study on use of media to effectively communicate economic issues and policies to general public.

Miss Teenage America Scholarship Program
$33,000, 8 Grants
Currently funds a $5,000 scholarship for student selected as Miss Teenage America; previously funded four $1,000 awards for each of the semifinalists.

Modern Miss
$1,000, 2 Grants
Scholarship for the National Academic Winner.

Modern Music Masters
$4,500, 2 Grants
For chapter expansion program of this national music honor society, high school level.

Mr. U.S.A. Teen Program
$5,500, 4 Grants
Scholarships for outstanding student selected on basis of leadership, citizenship, academics, and community involvement.

National Cheerleaders Association
$8,100, 8 Grants
Scholarships for winners of state drill team contests.

National Federation for Catholic Youth Ministry
$3,000, 2 Grants
Funds a scholarship of $1,000 for the student elected President of the National Youth Council and a $500 scholarship for another Catholic Teen Leader selected by the National organization.

National Forensic League
$10,000, 5 Grants
For two scholarships of $1,000 each to the members of the first place National Debate Team.

National Foundation for Advancement in the Arts
$3,000, 3 Grants
For general support for the Arts, Recognition, and Talent Search Program of this Foundation.

National 4-H Council
$21,500, 8 Grants
Grants are used for scholarships for outstanding 4-H students.

National Future Farmers of America (FFA)
$29,000, 10 Grants
Grants are used for scholarships for outstanding FFA students.

Office Education Association (OEA)
$44,000, 11 Grants
ECI serves on the National Business Advisory Council and sponsors scholarship program for national officers.

Performing & Visual Arts Society (PAVAS)
$4,000, 2 Grants
To conduct expansion program for high school chapters.

The President's Committee on the Employment of the Handicapped
$5,000, 5 Grants
Scholarship for the winner of the President's Committee National Poster contest, high school division.

Quill & Scroll Society
$10,000, 5 Grants
For two scholarships of $1,000 each to students who apply as contestants in Quill & Scroll's Current Events Quiz and National Writing/Photography Contest.

Soroptimist International of the Americas, Inc.
$4,000, 4 Grants
Scholarship for organization's Youth Citizenship Award Winner.

Special Olympics, Inc.
$1,000, 1 Grant
Scholarship for outstanding student volunteer and direct mail promotion to high school athletic directors requesting volunteers to work with handicapped children.

Standards for
Who's Who Among American High School Students and Other Recognition Programs and Societies

1. Nominations will be from established organizations that work with and for the benefit of high school aged youth. Under no circumstances will recommendations be accepted from students, their parents or solicited from standard commercial lists.

2. Criteria for students to be selected will be clearly defined and reflect high personal achievement.

3. Listing in "Who's Who" will not require purchase of any items or payments of any fees.

4. Additional programs and services which are available to those listed in "Who's Who" at cost to the students, will be clearly described in the literature provided.

5. A refund policy will be clearly stated in all literature.

6. Nominators will be able to recommend students without releasing confidential data or fear of having confidential data released by program sponsors.

7. Student information will be confidential and will not be released except where authorized by the student.

8. Home addresses will not be published in the book or made public in any way.

9. Under no circumstances will "Who's Who" sell student information or lists.

10. The publisher will describe, disseminate and verify the methods employed to assure national/regional recognition to students listed.

11. The publisher will respond to all inquiries, complaints and requests for relevant background information.

12. The basis for the scholarship program competition will be defined. Number and amount of awards will be stated, lists of previous winners will be available. Finalist selection process and funding method will be clearly defined. Employees' or their relatives will not be eligible for scholarships.

13. There will be an advisory council (external to the organization) to review and make recommendations regarding the policies, procedures, and evaluation process of the "Who's Who" programs.

14. The publisher will set forth in writing and make publicly known the policies and procedures it follows in the implementation of these standards.

Our company's adherence to the above standards has been attested to by an independent public accounting firm. A copy of their report is available upon request.

Members of the Committee on Ethics, Standards and Practices:

Dr. Wesley Apker
Executive Director
Association of California
School Administrators
Sacramento, CA

James T. Barry
Assoc. Vice President
for College Relations
St. Ambrose College
Davenport, IA

Phyllis Blaunstein
Executive Director
National Association of State
Boards of Education
Alexandria, VA

Dr. Harold Crosby
Regents Professor
University of West Florida
Pensacola, FL

Dr. S. Norman Feingold
President
National Career &
Counseling Services
Washington, DC

Charles R. Hilston
Executive Director
Association of Wisconsin
School Administrators
Madison, WI

Dr. Betty James
Assoc. Dean for
Academic Affairs
Livingstone College
Salisbury, NC

Dr. John Lucy
Asst. Superintendent for
Curriculum & Instruction
Downers Grove Public School
District 58
Downers Grove, IL

Paul Masem
Superintendent
Ames Community
School Dist.
Ames, IA

Dr. Edward J. Rachford
Superintendent
Homewood-Flossmoor
Community High School
Flossmoor, IL

Dr. Vincent Reed
Vice President for
Communications
The Washington Post
Washington, DC

David Hartman, host of ABC's "Good Morning America" (right), interviewed WHO'S WHO Spokesteen Shannin Mealiffe from LaCanada High School, LaCanada, CA (second from left) with two authorities on teen suicide.

On the NBC "Today Show," host Tom Brokow (center) interviews WHO'S WHO Spokesteens (left) Burnell Newsome, Hazelhurst, Mississippi, Amy Krentzman, Deerfield Beach, Florida, Tari Marshall, ECI Representative, and Mike McGriff, Chicago, Illinois.

Merv Griffin interviews WHO'S WHO Spokesteen Steven Silver from South Shore High School, Brooklyn, New York on the nationally televised talk show.

WHO'S WHO Spokesteens are interviewed by Gary Collins, host of the popular, nationally syndicated TV talk show, "Hour Magazine."

President Reagan greets Miss Teenage America, Amy Sue Brenkacz in the Oval Office. WHO'S WHO sponsors a $5,000 scholarship for Miss Teenage America and listed Amy Sue in the publication.

Bill Kurtis, host of the "CBS Morning News," interviews WHO'S WHO Spokesteens Stephanie Woolwich, Long Beach, New Jersey and Alex Tachmes, Miami Beach, Florida.

A group of 12 WHO'S WHO Spokesteens appear with host Pat Robertson (center) on the popular TV magazine program, "700 Club" (CBN) to present teen leaders' views on America's future in a special 7 part, 8 hour debate.

WHO'S WHO sponsors $1,500 and $1,000 scholarships for the president and vice-president of the American Legion Boy's Nation program. (Left to right) Marcus R. Dilworth, Jr., 1985 Boy's Nation President; Mike Ayers, Director, Americanism and Children & Youth Division; and Daniel Bricken, 1985 Boy's Nation Vice-President.

Penni Ann McClean, right, Congress delegate advisor from North Carolina, presents a citation to Mrs. Jackie McGuinn, assistant to the publisher of WHO'S WHO, for five years support of the 4-H Citizenship-Washington Focus program.

Right to left: Debbie Moyer from Allentown, PA pointing to her prize winning poster in the high school category with Harold Russell, Chairman, President's Committee on Employment of the Handicapped. WHO'S WHO sponsors a $1,000 college scholarship for this annual contest.

College-Bound Digest®

As a public service to the 96% of WHO'S WHO students who will continue their education after graduation from high school, we have invited a group of distinguished educators to use our publication as a forum to inform and assist students through the articles in this section.

While we do not presume that these articles contain "everything you need to know" about preparing for college, we believe you will find they will be helpful in learning "some of the things you need to know."

We wish to acknowledge the special contribution of Robert McLendon, Executive Director, Brookstone College of Business, High Point, North Carolina, who was instrumental in selecting appropriate topics and authors for this section.

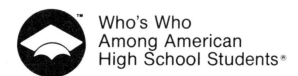

Who's Who
Among American
High School Students®

Getting the most from your high school counselor

By James Warfield

A high school counselor, helping you apply to college, is able to provide a wide variety of services tailored to your needs. The nature of this assistance will depend upon your abilities and achievement as well as the nature and quality of the colleges to which you apply. Effective use of the counselor's services will require you to have frequent discussions. Although your ideas about which colleges to apply to will change often, the more closely you work with your counselor the more valuable he/she will be to you.

Finding, selecting and applying to the colleges that are right for you is a long and studied process. It involves a lot of letter-writing, telephoning, research, weighing alternatives, and just plain old thinking. It's a decision-making process.

Your counselor makes recommendations as to which courses you should be taking in high school. These recommendations should be based upon your academic abilities and goals. This is a critical issue because the appropriateness of this advice is determined by the consistency between your aspirations and aptitudes. Verifying the accuracy of your self-perceptions is important in order to avoid sudden surprises caused by false hopes or unrealistic expectations. The reason why your counselor exists, is to help you become everything you are capable of within a realistic framework.

For many students, the college selection process begins with the PSAT, taken in the fall of the junior year. Your counselor should advise you which of the college entrace tests to take, SAT, ACT, ACH and AP, and when to take them. The type of college you apply to will determine which tests to take. The quality of the college, or the quality of your own academic program, and whether or not you plan to apply Early Decision, will determine when you should take such tests. Many students don't know in their junior year to which schools they'd like to apply, so advance planning is necessary in order to maintain open options.

Finding the right college will require you to know yourself, your likes and dislikes. In what kind of environment do you see yourself being most comfortable? Can you picture yourself at a small college or a mid-size or large university setting? Do you want a school to be in a rural community, a suburb or to be in an urban environment? Do you want to be in a different geographic part of the country or is being close to home important to you? What are some of your academic areas of interest? What kind of extra curricular offering do you want to participate in? As you answer these questions the attributes of your ideal college will become more clear. Through discussion with your counselor you'll be able to assess your needs, and more clearly focus your perceptions of yourself and of the schools you will be researching.

Your counselor should help generate a list of colleges that meet your requirements by drawing upon his/her own wealth of knowledge or utilizing the many reference materials available.

Many counselors have access to computers that will provide a list of colleges for you to investigate, once you have determined the characteristics you are looking for. If the guidance office does not have a computer, the same information can be obtained, with a little effort, from the commercially published reference books that are available through your counselor. After generating a list of perhaps twelve to twenty schools, your research really begins.

Resource books provide a wealth of statistical and narrative descriptions on virtually every college. The counseling office is likely to have college catalogs as well as files on each college containing brochures, view books and leaflets of the various academic and extracurricular offerings available at that particular school. Although college catalogs are boring reading material, information relating to admission procedures and requirements, course offerings and requirements for each of the academic majors are outlined. In addition, course prerequisites and methods of exempting yourself from some prerequisites are also indicated. As your research continues, you'll be able to eliminate schools and determine some colleges in which you are seriously interested.

Many high schools set up procedures whereby students may meet with representatives from colleges to obtain more information or answer individual questions. These representatives may be the Director of Admission, Admissions officers, or personnel hired to represent the college. Of course, the more you know about the college, before talking with the college representative, the more value they will be to you. Some colleges require an interview either by the representative, an alumni, or by an admissions officer. Your counselor should help you determine if an interview is necessary in your situation.

Campus visits are the most effective means to determine if the college is right for you. When to visit is a matter of individual taste or need. A school you casually visit during a summer vacation will serve a different purpose, and have different flavor, than a visit made in the fall after you have applied. It is also difficult to compare schools that are on break from those in session. Keep in mind that as you visit more schools your observational skills will become more sophisticated and your reflections of each will be altered. It may be more prudent to visit only those schools to which you have been accepted, after you have received all your admissions decisions.

As you narrow your choice of colleges, your counselor should review with you the possibilities of acceptance or rejection at each. At least one of your choices should be a safety choice, one in which you are almost guaranteed of being admitted.

After the list of colleges to which you are going to apply has been determined, it is your responsibility to obtain the application and meet deadline dates. Many colleges require a counselor's recommendation or a Secondary School Reference. Some require additional recommendations from specific teachers. Establish application procedures with your counselor so that he/she, the teacher, and school have adequate time to do their part in order to meet your deadline dates. If you are required to write an essay, or personal statement, discuss this with your counselor. These discussions serve several purposes: help you generate ideas and narrow topics that you wish to write about; provide you with suggestions that will enhance your applications; and provide the counselor with insights that will compliment your application.

It is your responsibility to file your applications on time, see that your test scores are sent to the admissions office, and file the financial aid applications. Your counselor will help you determine which scores to send, which financial aid form is required and how to fulfill these requirements.

Selecting and applying to a college is a decision-making process. The truly wise decision maker knows that he must clarify questions, obtain the most information possible, and probe until no new information becomes evident. Generally, the more information obtained, the better the decision, and the happier the college experience.

Jim Warfield is Director of Guidance at Lake Forest High School, Lake Forest, Illinois. Jim is currently involved and active in a number of professional organizations, and presently serving on the National Advisory Council for The Educational Records Bureau, Wellesley, Massachusetts.

The use of the SAT at selective colleges

By Dr. Judith Gatlin

For many students the numbers — from 200 to 800 on the verbal and on the quantitative sections of the College Board examination — seem to be the voice of doom; for others, they announce the possibility of admission into the nation's most selective colleges. But just how important, really, are those scores, and how will college admissions committees interpret them?

It is important to remember that the SAT (or ACT) is only one part of your total record. Your rank in your high school class, your grades, extracurricular activities which show leadership potential, and your recommendations are all extremely important. In addition, some colleges will consider your geographic location (it may be easier for the valedictorian of a South Dakota high school to enter Harvard than for the top student in a Connecticut prep school), your relationship with alumni, your religious preference at some denominational colleges, and the success of other graduates from your school at the institution.

Colleges treat scores, grades, rank, activities and recommendations in a variety of ways, but very few use arbitrary cut-off scores to determine acceptance. Every selective college or university attempts to select a class which will be successful (they don't want you to flunk out after your first year). Students who are admitted are those who they can predict will do well; and admissions staff experience with standardized tests suggests that certain levels of achievement, can be predicted with a fair degree of accuracy when used in conjunction with the high school record.

Often the total score on the SAT is less important than the individual score on either the verbal or the quantitative aptitude section. While colleges and universities may publish their average SAT as a combination, many liberal arts colleges believe that the verbal score is a particularly good indicator of ability, and many technically oriented engineering programs will be impressed with a very good quantitative score. A pre-engineering student with an 1150 SAT may be a very good candidate if his scores are 450 on the verbal section and 700 in the quantitative area; he might be substantially less impressive with 650/500.

One of the problems that many students confront when they first look at their scores is a sinking feeling that their numbers do not match their high school achievement level. The 'A' student who is third in her class and barely makes a 450/450 on the SAT is disappointed for days afterwards. It is important, however, to understand what your scores mean. The national average on the verbal section of the SAT is 427; on the mathematics section it is 467. Clearly, many college bound students will have a total score under 900. Many colleges and most state universities have average scores at this level or below it; more selective institutions will generally have average scores that are substantially higher, but even among these colleges there will be a number of students whose scores are at this level if their grades and rank indicate a strong chance of success.

But how can you explain or understand an average score when you have been an excellent student? It may be that you had a bad day (or a bad night before); a headache, too little sleep, a testing environment that is too hot or too cold may cause your scores to be less than your best. It may be that the scores are an accurate indicator of your aptitude and that you are a high achiever. Or it may mean that your grades have

been inflated and that you have not been challenged by teachers or peers. One way that you can determine if it was just the specific test day is to compare your scores on the SAT with your PSAT. If you scored, for example, 48/50 on the PSAT and have a combined total on the SAT of from 970 to 1020 your test is probably valid. If, on the other hand, your PSAT was 55/58 and you scored 1020 on the SAT, you probably should plan to retake the examination to see if the second time might show real improvement.

In addition to the "bad day" low score there are other reasons that good students do not do well on standardized tests. It may be that they panic under time pressure, that they are unfamiliar with national tests and the testing environment, or that their skills and abilities cannot be shown on such tests. Really creative students, those with talents in the arts, and those who work very slowly through a problem, analyzing as they go, are sometimes at a disadvantage. If you fall in one of these categories, it is especially useful for a teacher whose recommendation you have requested be asked to discuss your other strengths in an admissions letter.

Some students retake the SAT two or three times to see if they can improve their overall scores, and it is important to realize that scores will vary slightly every time you take a Scholastic Aptitude Test. A variation of 30 points in either direction is normal; more than 50 points, unusual. How worthwhile is it to retake the SAT if your scores are under the average published by the college of your choice? Some schools, like Furman, accept your best scores from each test. Others may average your test results. It is probably true that you can improve your quantitative score with tutoring over several months; improving verbal scores is far more difficult. You should remember, however, that while selective colleges have many high-scoring students, their *average* SAT is just that: there have been many others whose scores are under the average but who have the proven achievement to be admitted.

Suppose, however, that you are very interested in an institution which indicates an average SAT of 1275; your score is 1050, but your parents are alumni, you graduated in the top 20% of your class, and you have been an outstanding high school leader. Academically you would be in the bottom quarter of your class, yet you may well be admitted because of your parents and your activities. Should you attend such a college? Will you be able to compete at a level comfortable for you with students whose high school backgrounds may be substantially superior? Are you ready to make a number of "C's" or to study harder and longer than your roommates?

You should consider, too, that very high scores do not necessarily mean admission to the college of your choice. Several years ago a young man with an SAT score of 1440 applied to a selective Southeastern liberal arts college. He had graduated in the lower half of his high school class and although he had been involved in some extracurricular activities, he also had been a discipline problem in high school. After substan-

tial discussion, he was not admitted, but the college admissions office was interested enough to trace his career several years later. He had flunked out of two other colleges. SAT scores indicate aptitude — the ability to learn — not achievement. They do not show the desire to learn, the ambition to succeed or the perserverance necessary for academic excellence. College admissions officers are aware of these facts and they will read your entire application with an awareness that you are more than a score on a computer printout.

Dr. Judith Gatlin is the Director of Educational Services and Assistant Professor of English at Furman University, Greenville, South Carolina. She has authored various articles for the *Journal of College Placement* and is a former columnist for the *Charlotte Observer*.

Tips on taking the SAT

By Dr. Ernest W. Beals

If you are college-bound or plan to be, chances are that you will be required to take a college admissions test such as the Scholastic Aptitude Test (SAT) of The College Board or the American College Testing Program's assessment test (ACT).

The SAT's format and content have changed enormously over its 55 years of existence, and is now designed to measure the extent to which your reasoning abilities, that is skill with verbal expressions and mathematical concepts, have been developed up to the time you take the test.

It is important to realize that students are neither accepted nor denied admission to an institution solely on the basis of SAT or other test scores. When looking at prospective students, institutions of higher learning also stress to varying degrees such factors as your high school record (including courses taken, grade patterns, and class rank or high school average) and extracurricular activities. Other factors may be the outcome of personal interviews and teacher or counselor recommendations, as well as the student body needs of the college or university itself.

Students frequently ask: What can I do about raising my SAT scores or about making them better than they would be otherwise? The answer is: Quickly and immediately, probably not much. Over longer periods it depends on how much time, effort and concentration goes into the preparation. The abilities measured by the test are related to academic success in college. These abilities grow over a period of time through learning experiences such as those encountered in the family, in the classroom, with your friends and associates, and in reading and independent study.

The best preparation for the SAT is to have had varied opportunities of this kind and to have made the most of them. The contents of the tests cover such a broad area that trying to "cram" for it has never been found to yield validly measurable results. You may, however, find it useful to review some of the fundamental principles of algebra and geometry in order to refresh your memory for the mathematical section of the test.

In order to reduce anxiety and increase confidence when test time arrives, here are some valuable tips: First, become familiar with the format of the test. Obtain a copy of the informative booklet, *Taking the SAT*, from your guidance counselor. This free booklet describes the nature and components of the SAT and, provides a full sample SAT which you can administer and score yourself. By taking this sample test, you will familiarize yourself with the directions and the format of the questions. You will also gain valuable practice in allocating your time to each item.

You will also learn that, as a rule, the easier questions of each section come at the beginning of that section, with the questions growing progressively more difficult to the end of the section. Use your time wisely. If you find the individual items of a particular section are extremely difficult for you, read quickly through the remaining questions in the group, answering only those that you feel you know. You should then begin work on the next set of questions, returning to the omitted questions in that section if you have time. You receive as much credit for answering correctly the questions you find easy as you get for answering the hard ones. Above all, don't panic. You receive one point for each question correctly answered; you lose a fraction of a point for each item incorrectly answered. You neither gain nor lose points for omitted questions. Therefore, keep in mind that random guessing on questions will rarely increase your scores, and might even have the effect of reducing your raw score. However, some selective guessing can pay off for you: If you can confidently eliminate as incorrect at least two of the possible four or five answers to a question, then it would be to your advantage to take a stab at one of the remaining answers to that question.

Your raw score on the SAT is determined by adding up all correct answers and subtracting from that total the sum of the fractions for all incorrect answers. The raw score is then converted to the College Board scale ranging from a low of 200 to a high of 800 on the verbal and mathematics sections of the SAT.

The Test of Standard Written English (TSWE) is a 30-minute multiple-choice test administered with the SAT. The questions evaluate your ability to recognize standard written English, the language of most college textbooks and the English you will be expected to use in the papers you write for college courses. The scores may be used to place you in a freshman English course that is appropriate for you.

Contrary to the anxiety-ridden expectations of students taking the SAT and TSWE for the first time, these tests do not require specialized knowledge in science, social sciences, literature, or any other field.

In brief summary, the best strategies to follow in order to prepare yourself for taking the SAT include: enroll in college preparatory courses that your school offers, maintain good solid and consistent effort in your everyday classroom work and classroom tests, force yourself to read as many and varied outside readings as possible, brush up on your algebra and geometry lessons, become familiar with the SAT format, content, directions, etc. (obtain a copy of *Taking the SAT* booklet from your counselor and take the sample SAT test, score it yourself, and read the suggestions and explanations included with it), get a good night's sleep the night before the examination and take a positive attitude with you to the test center. If you do all of the above, you will be putting your best foot forward and enhancing your chances of obtaining good test scores. Good luck to you.

Dr. Ernest W. Beals is Association Director of the Southern Regional Office of The College Board. Dr. Beals has worked in the field of education for the past 26 years at the high school and college level including 13 years in college admissions.

Can you prepare for the SAT?

By Stanley H. Kaplan

The discussion of the issue of preparation for the SAT has come full circle since the 1950's. In the 1957 Bulletin, issued to the students, the College Board stated, "Coaching may be a sound and rewarding method. If coaching means an honest effort, under the guidance of a good teacher, over an extended period of time, to improve those skills in which you are weak, then it can be recommended as effective study." In the 1960's, the statement about the possible positive effects of coaching was withdrawn. The reason, I was told, was the proliferation of cram schools that preyed on students' (and parents') anxieties and offered little of educational value and little possibility of an improvement on the SAT. And now in the 1980's, the College Board and ETS which constructs the SAT, once again are distinguishing between cramming and long-term coaching which is now looked upon as "supplementary education."

Can one be prepared for the SAT? My answer is an emphatic yes. Some students can prepare by self-study. There are many materials, including tests released by the College Board and SAT review books available at bookstores.

My organization has been preparing students for the SAT for more than thirty years. Actually — and this is important — we are not preparing for the SAT per se. Rather, we are working to improve a student's basic math, verbal, and reasoning skills. The SAT does not measure a scholastic aptitude — if by aptitude we mean an innate, unchangeable indication of academic potential. The SAT measures the level of verbal and mathematical achievement, including the ability to handle innovative, non-routine approaches in these areas. The SAT evaluates the learning experiences of students in and out of school. The more the experience, the higher the level of achievement and therefore the higher the SAT score. Only an improved student can achieve an improved score. It seems that many students and parents still believe that all a test preparation program has to do is teach a few test techniques and strategies, wave a magic wand, and presto — a higher score. The goal of an SAT preparation program should go beyond that of improved SAT scores. It should provide improved skills to insure better performance at the college level. In fact, parents are beginning to realize the valuable long-range effects of SAT preparation. When reports of declining SAT scores made a big splash in the press, several years ago, the enrollments in our programs increased dramatically, despite the decreasing importance of SAT scores in the college admissions process. Declining SAT scores indicate a deficiency in basic skills which in turn could mean a poorer performance at the college level. Years of experience have convinced me that the "specter" of the SAT is an excellent device in motivating students toward working and improving these skills necessary for success at the college level.

Unfortunately, too many students memorize facts that teachers and textbooks provide, regurgitate this information on a test, and then promptly proceed to forget. A review can be of immense value in "bringing it all back," in making what one has learned more meaningful, and in giving the student an opportunity to think more creatively. This does not mean that every student should enroll in an SAT preparation program. Certainly, you should take at least one of the released exams to become familiar with the instructions, format, content, and time pressures of the test. If you feel, however, that you would like to enroll in a structured program of preparation, here are some tips you might follow in choosing a legitimate program that could give you the maximum benefit:

1) The program should be a long-range one — extending over a period of at least several months. Cram courses are of little value. The lessons should be held weekly with home-study assignments in between to reinforce what has been taught in class.

2) The classes should be small — not seminars of 100 or so. A class size should not exceed 25.

3) There should be an opportunity to make up missed lessons. Very frequently, you might miss a lesson because of illness or other commitments. Certainly,

you should not give up studying for an important school exam in order to attend a class session.

4) The program should offer you the option of continuing your study for the SAT if you choose to take the exam for a second time.

5) Most important, the school should have a *permanent* location where you might look at the materials and be able to talk in depth with a person in charge. Beware of fly-by-night programs that advertise by box numbers, have telephone answering services, hold classes in hotels or other meeting rooms, and silently steal away when the course is over.

6) The better programs offer scholarship assistance if you cannot afford to pay for the program.

7) You should check a program out with others who have taken it previously. Their experiences as to the quality of the teaching, the adequacy of the materials, and most important, the improvement they have achieved, can be most helpful in making your decision.

Be suspicious of high pressure tactics designed to corral you as a student — such as statements that the SAT is the most important exam you will ever take, claims of fantastic improvements, and guarantees of improved scores. Avoid correspondence courses. They are often expensive — almost as much as a course with live class programs. Usually the purchase of an SAT review book and use of materials supplied by the College Board itself is just as helpful.

Remember, the SAT is *not* the most important exam you'll ever be taking. It is only one of many criteria used by admissions officers to make a decision. Certainly your high school record is more important than the SAT score you will get.

Perhaps one of the best reasons for some kind of preparation is to make sure that the SAT score evaluates your achievement as reliably as possible. After all, you wouldn't enter a tennis tournament cold. I've seen hundreds of cases of underachievers or poor "test-takers" whose self-images have been enhanced by improved scores that more accurately evaluated this academic achievement.

Remember, there is much you can do on your own long before you take a preprartion course or even decide to do so. You can start reading — newspapers, magazines, best-sellers, — read something that interests you, but read! At the same time, you'll be improving your vocabulary and the ability to integrate ideas. In math, as well as in science, don't just memorize rules and standard ways of attacking problems. Try to reason things through and find out the why as well as the how as well as the what. Then, when the time comes to review for the SAT, you will have done most of your preparation already. Good luck!

Stanley H. Kaplan is Executive Director of the Stanley H. Kaplan Educational Center, Ltd., New York, New York with offices nationwide and abroad. Kaplan has been featured in numerous articles including *Time*, *Newsweek*, and the *New York Times*. He has also appeared on numerous public radio and television programs as an authority on test preparation.

Searching for student financial aids

By S. Norman Feingold and Marie Feingold

The purpose of this article is to suggest practical techniques and pathways for gathering accurate information about financial aids that are available and to indicate time frames within which it is advisable to initiate financial aid seeking efforts.

1. Start Early

The high school student should begin not later than the beginning of the junior year of high school. Many scholarships require that the student have taken the Scholastic Aptitude Test or the Preliminary SAT. The National Merit Scholarship competitions start the beginning of the junior year in high school. Many organizations use the results of this exam for the selection of their recipients; and this includes some companies which provide scholarships for the children of its employees. Some colleges select student aid recipients from National Merit competitors. Some competitions for research fellowships, overseas grants may close a year before recipients are announced.

2. Federal Publications

A. The U.S. Department of Education publishes two helpful pamphlets, that are revised annually. They are *Five Federal Financial Aid Programs: A Student Consumer's Guide* and *Federal Financial Aid for Men and Women Resuming Their Education or Training.* They are both available without cost from Federal Financial Aid, Box 84, Washington, DC 20044.

B. Veterans Administration each January publishes *Federal Benefits for Veterans and Dependents*. It contains details of educational assistance and is available from the Superintendent of Documents, U.S. Printing Office, Washington, DC 20402. Cost $1.50.

C. The Department of Defense. Each of the armed forces has ROTC programs and annually revises its pamphlets about programs.

Achievement through Education, Air Force ROTC is obtained from the Department of the Air Force, Air Force Reserve Officers Training Corps, Maxwell Air Force Base, AL 36112.

Navy-Marine Corps Scholarship Programs. U.S. Department of the Navy, Navy Recruiting Command, 4015 Wilson Boulevard, Arlington, VA 22203.

Information about Army ROTC scholarships can be obtained by writing to:

Army ROTC, P.O. Box 7000
Larchmont, NY 10538.

D. The U.S. Department of Health and Human Services, Washington, DC 20201 maintains up-to-date publications about social security benefits. Details should be obtained from the local Social Security office. Generally dependents of deceased or disabled contributors to Social Security are eligible for benefits while they are full-time elementary or high school students under the age of 19. Until April, 1985, there is a phasing out of the benefits as they existed until August, 1981.

Information about financial aid for students in the health and allied health professions is available from the U.S. Public Health Service, Bureau of Health Manpower, Student Assistance Branch, Center Building, Room G-23, 3700 East-West Highway, Hyattsville, MD 20782.

E. The U.S. Department of the Interior, Bureau of Indian Affairs, Washington, DC 20245 publishes pamphlets about educational assistance for native Americans.

If you are having difficulty locating information about Federal financial assistance for training and education, write to your Congressman or Senator at either his local office or at his Washington, DC office in the House of Representatives of the Senate.

3. State Publications

Most if not all states publish booklets or flyers about the student financial aid programs they administer. *Five Federal Financial Aid Programs: A Student Consumer's Guide* lists the names, addresses and telephone numbers of every state agency that provides information on the Guaranteed Student Loan Program and *Federal Financial Aid for Men and Women Resuming Their Education or Training* lists the names and addresses of each state scholarship agency. For details write to the state scholarship agency of the state in which you are a resident.

States also publish material on scholarships for special groups within the state such as veterans and their dependents, policemen, prison guards and firemen. It is likely that the state scholarship agency can give you the name and address you need.

Your state Senator can help you locate state aids.

4. Local Publications
(City and County)

Many communities have a printed or typed listing of student aids available to their residents. Your counselor may be helpful in directing you to these sources.

5. Know the ethnic, religious, and place origins of your family.

A fairly large amount of student financial aid is awarded by private organizations to persons of specific origin. Consult *Scholarships, Fellowships and Loans, Volumes VI and VII*, by S. Norman Feingold and Marie Feingold, and the *Scholarships, Fellowships, and Loans News Service and Counselors Information Services*, Bellman Publishing Company, P.O. Box 164, Arlington, MA 02174-0164.

6. Know for whom your parents or guardian work.

Some corporations and labor unions provide awards for their employees and members respectively. Have your parents speak to the personnel department of the company and the steward of the labor union for details. Company and union newspapers/magazines are good sources of keeping abreast of these financial aids.

7. As soon as practical for you, try to determine a **field of interest and hobby.** Some aids are given for majoring or studying certain subjects or having engaged in specific activities.

8. Enter Contests.

There are many different kinds of contests. The National Federation of Music Clubs, 310 South Michigan Ave., Suite 1936, Chicago, IL 60604 publishes scholarships and awards charts for two-year periods.

9. Get your own work experience.

Students who have been caddies or delivered newspapers or worked in other capacities are often eligible for scholarship competitions. Tuition refunds from the company for which you work cover a part or all of the fees for courses. Generally, the course must be related to your work and permission must be obtained.

10. Attend free post-secondary institutions of education and training.

The military academies and the Webb Institute of Naval Architecture are schools for which there are no tuition or room and board fees.

11. Consider scholarship loans.

In areas of work in which there are manpower shortages, it is possible to convert a loan to a scholarship by working in a given geographical area or in a specific subject matter field. Teaching the handicapped and working in rural poverty areas where there are shortages of specific personnel are two ways. Generally these programs are federally or state sponsored.

12. Loans to parents, to children of employees, to residents of service areas.

Such loans may be administered and awarded by business, foundations, banks, non-profit corporations. Two programs for which you should write for information are those of the United Student Aid Funds, Inc., 200 East 42nd St., New York, NY 10017 and Richard C. Knight Insurance Agency, Inc., 53 Beacon St., Boston, MA 02108.

13. Attend Cooperative or Work-Study Schools.

Your earnings will cover much if not all of your tuition and living expenses. More than 200,000 college students are enrolled in cooperative education pro grams. In the "typical" co-op program, students alternate semesters of study and supervised paid work. More than 1,000 colleges now offer co-op programs. Request *Undergraduate Programs of Cooperative Programs in the United States and Canada* which is available at no cost from the National Commission for Cooperative Education, 360 Huntington Ave., Boston, MA 02115.

14. Apprenticeship Training

In the skilled trades this is a way to learn and earn. Details are available from the following four sources: State Bureau of Apprenticeship and Training (one office is located in each state capital); a network of approximately 2,300 local and state employment offices; in a number of states there is a state apprenticeship council; U.S. Department of Labor, Bureau of Apprenticeship and Training, 601 D St., N.W., Washington, DC 20213.

15. Teachers, principals, ministers, lawyers, bankers, business people, counselors may know of individuals who anonymously assist deserving individuals to obtain the training and education they are seeking.

16. How do you locate the donors and administrators of financial aid programs?

There are a number of publications that should either be in the public library, school library, or college library. If not, request the library to order them. Some are:

Need a Lift, American Legion, P.O. Box 1055, Indianapolis, IN 46206. Revised every fall.

Scholarships, Fellowships and Loans, Volumes VI and VII, S. Norman Feingold and Marie Feingold. Bellman Publishing Company, P.O. Box 164, Arlington, MA 02174-0164, 1977 and 1982 respectively.

Scholarships, Fellowships and Loans News Service and Counselors Information Services, quarterly newsletter. Bellman Publishing Company, P.O. Box 164, Arlington, MA 02174-0164.

Don't Miss Out. The Ambitious Student's Guide to Scholarships and Loans, 5th ed., 1980/82, Robert Leider, Octameron Associates, Alexandria, VA. Published biennially.

Financial Aids for Higher Education 1980-81 Catalog, 9th ed., 1980, Wm. Brown Publisher, Dubuque, IA.

AFL-CIO Guide to Union Sponsored Scholarships, Awards, and Student Financial Aid, 1981. AFL-CIO Department of Education, 815 16th St., N.W., Washington, DC 20006.

Additionally, there are local newspapers, particularly suburban ones. They generally announce who won what and provide a name or address you can contact.

Local banks, community foundations, and social service agencies are aware of funds about which there is little or no publicity.

Usually there is less competition for local student aid funds in comparison with those available to candidates on a national level.

Many states publish directories of local aids. Your guidance counselor or public librarian will know how to obtain a copy or will have a copy for you to read.

17. The financial aid office of the institution you wish to attend or are attending.

Many funds are administered by the schools themselves, and you must let the financial aids officer know of your need for assistance. Many schools and colleges and universities publish a directory of their aids; they are usually free.

18. Answer all letters and application forms with great care.

Be certain that you have answered *every* question; for those not applicable, write N/A. If at all possible, type; be certain of accuracy and neatness. Meet all deadline dates. Deadline dates may change from those listed in directories. You need enough time to edit your answers several times. The quality of essays when they are required with the application blank is an important screening device. Be certain you remind your references and schools you've attended to submit requested material on time.

19. If you try each one of the methods described above and have ability and potential, you have a good chance of getting student aid. A study by the authors showed that with students of equal ability, the ones who applied to more resources were more successful in obtaining assistance. You may get a scholarship on your second try from the same fund.

Good luck. Don't let the lack of money deter you from seeking further education and training. Your post-secondary education can open up rewarding careers to which you otherwise would not have access.

Dr. S. Norman Feingold is President, National Career and Counseling Services, Washington, DC; Honorary National Director of B'nai B'rith Career and Conseling Services; Past-President of the American Personnel and Guidance Association and the author of several publications including seven volumes of *Scholarships, Fellowships and Loans.* Marie Feingold is a Rehabilitation Counselor, Washington, DC and co-author of volumes six and seven of *Scholarships, Fellowships and Loans.*

Tough questions to ask any admissions officer

By Robert G. McLendon

As a college admissions officer for the past fouteen years, it is clear to me that today's prospective students are carefully comparing colleges and striving to learn all they can about the colleges to which they apply. The age group of 18 to 24 year olds is declining in the United States, and this is creating a type of "buyer's market" in the market place of higher education.

In order to assure yourself that your expectations of a college are met, you, the student consumer, need not hesitate to ask admissions officers some "tough questions." This article will offer you a few suggestions of some tough questions that I hope will help you make the right choice when selecting a college.

Academic Questions

1. How many students in last year's

freshman class returned for their sophomore year?

2. What percent of the freshman class obtained a 2.00 (C) average or above last year?

3. If accepted, will you tell me my predicted freshman grade-point average?

Many colleges use a mathematical formula based on studies of currently enrolled students to predict an applicant's freshman grade average.

4. What is the college's procedure for class placement?

This is especially important in the areas of English and mathematics because freshmen often vary significantly in their ability to handle these important academic skills.

5. What procedure is used to assign a faculty advisor when the student is undecided as to the major area of study?

6. What type of additional academic services does your college offer at no additional cost to the student (e.g., tutoring, career or personal counseling, study-skills workshops, improving reading speed, etc.)?

7. How effective is your college's honor code? What is the penalty for cheating?

Social Questions

1. What is the average age of your student body and what percent resides on campus?

Many colleges today have a large and increasing population of commuting part-time adult students and a dwindling enrollment of 17 to 18 year old full-time, degree-seeking students residing on campus.

2. Is your college a "suitcase college" on the weekends? If not, what are some typical weekend activities for students on your campus?

3. What procedure is used to select roommates if no preference is listed?

4. What are some of the causes of students being suspended or dismissed from your college? Is there a system of appeal for those who have been dismissed?

5. How can a prospective student arrange a campus visit?

Clearly the best possible way to evaluate a college socially is to plan a visit to the campus. When you visit, try not to be shy. After your talk and tour with the admissions officer, walk around by yourself and informally ask students their opinions. A good place to chat with students is in the college's student center or at the dining hall.

6. What are some of the rules and regulations that govern residence hall life? Are there coeducational residence halls?

Financial Questions

1. What percent of your students received financial aid based on financial need?

2. What percent of your students received scholarships based on academic ability?

3. What percent of a typical financial aid offer is in the form of a loan?

4. How much did your college increase cost (room, board, tuition, and fees) from last year to current year?

5. If an accepted student must submit a room deposit, when is the deposit due, and when is it refundable?

The deposit should be refundable in full up to May 1, if the college or university is a member of the National Association of College Admissions Counselors.

6. If my family demonstrates a financial need on the FAF or FFS forms; what percent of the established need will typically be awarded? When can I expect to receive an official financial aid award letter?

The distinguishing quality of any person is the quality of the mind, and the college you select will have a long-lasting impact on your career and life. I realize that you are painfully aware of the need to make the right college choice because most high school students realize that the college years are often the most productive stage of life. Knowing what questions to ask an admissions officer is an important part of this decision-making process. Most admissions officers want you to ask "tough questions" because if you make the wrong choice we, too, have failed in our job.

Bob McLendon is Executive Director, Brookstone College of Business, High Point, North Carolina. He served on the Admissions Practices Committee of the National Association of College Admissions Counselors and has been Chairman of the Admissions Practices Committee of the Southern Association of College Admissions Counselors. He is a member of the Executive Board of SACAC and President-Elect of the Carolinas Association of Collegiate Registrars and Admissions Officers.

Common mistakes students make in selecting a college

By William B. Stephens, Jr.

The process of choosing a college can be a rewarding, worthwhile experience or it can be an endless, frustrating series of mistakes. Those mistakes are common and are usually the result of inadequate research and preparation — both characteristics you will need as a successful college student. The selection of a college is a good place to begin developing those virtues.

Begin the process with a series of questions. Am I most interested in a small, medium, or large college? Do I want to stay close to home or go away? What will be my major? Does the college have a broad curriculum if my major is undecided? How academically competi-

tive do I want my college to be? What are the costs? Is financial aid available? Which extracurricular activities are the most important to me? When these questions are satisfactorily answered, it is time to begin the next stage.

Research is of primary importance in selecting a college. Do not make the mistake of choosing a college simply because your friends go there. List priorities. Be willing to invest time and effort in investigating colleges which share these priorities.

In writing to colleges for information, be neat, concise, and accurate in providing information about yourself. Many students forget to include the address to which the college should send material. Also include your high school graduation date, the high school you attend, your anticipated major (if that has been decided), and any pertinent information regarding grades and test scores. Decisions are made about students on the basis of their initial contact with the college. Do not be careless in this important decision.

There are numerous publications which are helpful in gathering information. These publications may be located in school and public libraries, bookstores, and guidance offices. Many are cross-referenced according to majors offered, geographic locations, costs, and sizes. Once familiar with college publications, the task of choosing a college becomes an easier one. Do not make the mistake of floundering with too many college options.

Your school guidance office can offer an abundance of information. Among the many contributions of guidance counselors is the provision of data concerning financial aid, college representatives scheduled to visit the school and/or vicinity, College Fairs, and testing for college entrance. In addition, most schools provide counseling to help students choose colleges compatible with their scholastic aptitudes, personality, financial means, and extracurricular interests. Often these guidance resources are not tapped, yet they can be among the most beneficial that you could explore.

Do not neglect the value of contacting alumni, college representatives, and currently enrolled students. Alumni can provide firsthand accounts of life at college while representatives will have the current facts about admissions requirements, new majors offered, scholarships, sports, and campus activities. Students who are currently enrolled in a particular college can provide additional insight into the actual experiences you can expect at the institution.

It is important that you visit the colleges which are your first preferences. Never will catalogs, counseling, or recommendations from alumni replace an actual visit to the campus. Much can be learned from sitting in on a few classes, walking through dormitories, and talking to faculty and staff. It is extremely risky to choose a college without personal observation.

Many colleges have orientation programs to acquaint students and their parents with the facilities and various aspects of student and faculty involvement. Investigate the colleges being considered to discover their plans for orientation programs. Do not fail to be present at the programs in which you are most interested.

Since the cost of attending college can be one of the greatest factors determining your choice, the possibility of obtaining financial aid is to be taken into careful consideration. Watch for the deadlines in applying for financial assistance, and have the appropriate forms completed well in advance. If financial aid is offered, be certain to compare the amount of aid offered and the total cost of attending that particular college. Remember that the matter of final importance is in determining the amount which has to be paid by you and your family.

College preparations should begin in the ninth grade. Solid academic courses (usually beyond the minimum required for high school graduation) should be completed each year. Four years of English is normally expected. Most colleges expect a student to complete at least three years of math, including two years of algebra and one of geometry. Although requirements vary from college to college, it is generally advantageous to have a sound background in biology, chemistry, physics, history, and a foreign language.

High schools administer PSAT, SAT, and ACT exams to juniors and seniors. It is wise to plan to take a College Board exam more than once. As these exams take four to six weeks to be graded, you should allow plenty of time so as not to delay the application process. Your score on a college board exam will further indicate the type of college to attend. Colleges vary considerably in their College Board score requirements.

By October of your senior year, choices should be narrowed to two or three prospective colleges. You should be aware of all admission requirements for each institution considered. Do not delay the application process until after Christmas. Many colleges begin waiting lists very soon after the beginning of each new year. Your application and all required documents should be on file by November 1 at each college considered. Do not expect high schools to send transcripts or teachers to send recommendations the day the request is made. Allow a couple of weeks for these items to be completed and mailed to the college.

Incomplete or illegible applications will greatly diminish the opportunity for rapid processing. These types of delays can mean the difference between being able to attend your first choice of colleges and having to wait another full academic year to enroll.

College-bound students should never hesitate to ask questions. Begin early and be organized. Parental involvement is essential in choosing a college that will meet the need of you and your family. Diligent research and careful planning are the keys to the prevention of the most common mistakes made by college applicants today.

Bill Stephens is Director of Admissions at Florida Southern College, Lakeland, Florida and has worked in the Admissions field for ten years. Stephens is a member of the National Association of Admissions Counselors, the Southern Association of Admissions Counselors, the American Association of Collegiate Admissions and Registrar Officers, and the Southern and Florida Associations of Collegiate Admissions and Registrars Officers.

The advantages and pitfalls of advanced placement and credit by examination for the freshman year of college

By Carl D. Lockman

I think we all agree that gifted young people need help in order to recognize their potential role in society. Through advanced placement and credit by examination programs, secondary school systems and universities alike are making a bona fide effort to encourage the development of academic talent, thus helping students to better understand their contributions to society and self.

Perhaps an explanation of the main difference between advanced placement and credit by examination is appropriate at this point. Both programs serve the purpose of awarding the student college course credit for acceptable scores on examinations. However, the Advanced Placement Program is a function of the College Entrance Examination Board. It is a formally structured program of instruction culminating with an examination. Institutions also may give departmental examinations which may be referred to as advanced placement. Credit by examination may or may not be a formally structured program. The College Level Examination Program (CLEP) is an example of the former, through which a student can receive credit for non-traditional (learning outside the classroom) educational experiences by presenting satisfactory scores on examinations.

All programs designed to award credit at the university level have advantages that are worth the student's consideration. Credit programs complement conventional instruction by allowing students to begin academic study at a level appropriate to their experience. They require students to demonstrate that they have achieved at a level equal to college experience. By being given this opportunity, the student can save both time and money.

A second advantage is that studies indicate that advanced placement continues throughout the undergraduate years. Quantitatively and qualitatively the student benefits. Course credit granted through advanced placement generally allows for increased hours to be completed in a four-year program, much of which may be completed at the junior level and above. This certainly allows for greater flexibility and versatility in designing one's curriculum. Somewhat the opposite has shown up in early studies of CLEP credit. Students with CLEP credit tend to graduate earlier. However, this still permits the student the advantages of having saved money and time and allows the opportunity to move into graduate studies at an earlier date. The challenge for the student is brought to the front when he/she is placed into courses recognizing achievement when his/her ability surpasses basic proficiency level courses.

Another advantage to the participation in and the receiving of credit through these programs is the quality of instruction associated with advanced placement. Generally speaking, it is safe to say that some of the best secondary instructors are asked to conduct the advanced courses. These instructors will stretch to stay ahead of these bright students who comprise the classes. Also, students in these programs not only benefit from the quality of instruction, but from the fact that most schools set up programs by drawing on the experiences of other school systems. In effect, students are being exposed to highly researched programs that have been trial tested for years by many systems.

A closer look at these programs reveals additional advantages. Many advanced placement programs borrow lectures, lab facilities, and equipment from local businesses and universities to accelerate their programs. Schools sometimes pool courses to give a wider curriculum offering. Credit programs allow secondary schools and colleges to articulate their programs, thus helping to bridge the curriculum gap that has been prevalent for years. In bridging this gap the student with an outstanding background can be recognized.

The advantages far outweigh the disadvantages when studying advanced placement and credit by examination programs. Two negative comments might be made at this point. There is always the possibility that students entering these programs do not have a thorough understanding of the extra demands that will be placed on them. Remember that the courses offered in the secondary schools are rigorous college-level courses. College credit granted may result in the student being placed in upper-level courses, which in turn will demand more effort on the student's part. It is not a bad idea either that parents be made aware of what is to be expected of students involved in advanced placement programs and of those having received credit by examination.

Secondly, uninformed secondary and college personnel cause very definite problems. After a student has participated in an advanced placement program or has the experience to achieve credit through examination, it is imperative that the secondary counselors advise students and their parents of colleges that have established policies that would meet the needs of the student. I can think of few things more disappointing than for a student to miss the opportunity to have more flexibility in his courses and to avoid repetition. The other fears are that the college officials may not have required faculty members in the subject areas covered by the tests to review the examinations and that the procedures and practices of the college regarding credit have not been carefully studied. As you can see, such omissions by the institution in establishing policies could lead to improper credit and, even worse, improper placement in courses "over the head" of the student.

In conclusion, whether a student goes through the CEEB Advanced Placement Program, participates in the institution's own advanced placement program by taking departmental examinations, or receives credit for life experiences, the importance of the programs is that they are attempts to equate classroom and/or non-classroom experience to college-level learning. The programs are models of learning closely conforming with college courses. Placement and credit programs are relatively new opportunities which each year seem to become more and more accepted by the academic communities. These are ways to recognize the individual differences in students, an attempt to confront the age-long problems of recognizing the variety of experiences students bring to college, and a breaking from the tradition that all students need to enroll in core curricula.

For students with exceptional learning experiences and/or intellectual talents, advanced placement and credit by examination programs are recommended. The rewards for such accomplishments are great.

Carl D. Lockman is Assistant Director of Admissions at Georgia Institute of Technology, Atlanta, Georgia. Lockman serves on the Admissions Practices Committee of the Southern Association for College Admissions Counselors and is a member of the American and Georgia Associations of Collegiate Registrars and Admissions Officers. He was appointed to the Governor's Committee to study recruitment techniques and is a board member of the Middle Georgia Drug Council.

The academic and social benefits of large American universities

By James C. Blackburn

There is no type of collegiate experience which is most appropriate for all students. The purpose(s) of this essay are to identify and discuss the academic and social benefits of large universities.

In almost every state in the union, there is at least one large university whose enrollment exceeds 10,000 persons. More than a score of states have within their borders, universities enrolling more than 30,000 students. There are several community colleges whose enrollments meet the criterion of having 10,000+ enrollments. Those institutions are not included within the scope of this essay.

A substantial number of large universities are state-supported. However, more than a few large universities are private institutions of higher education. Such universities are more common in the more populous regions of the nation, e.g. the East Coast and upper Midwest. The tuition prices of large universities vary from nominal charges to $10,000 per year. It is, therefore, possible to select a large university from any price range. Some of America's most expensive and least costly institutions can be classified as large universities.

Large universities are located in large cities such as New York, Boston, and Los Angeles, as well as in small towns, e.g. Bloomington, Indiana and Tuscaloosa, Alabama. The selectivity of admission to large universities is also quite varied. Some universities admit as few as one in five of its applicants. Other moderately large institutions offer admission to more than 90% of their applicant pools.

In short, the diversity between and among large universities makes it possible for almost every student who desires to attend such an institution. Enrollment at a large university is not the private privilege of any socio-economic or intellectual sub-segment of American society. That being the case, there must be some good reasons for matriculation at and graduation from a large university.

There are academic benefits which apply to each size and type of college or university. The academic benefits of enrolling at a large university are especially striking.

Few freshmen actually complete the academic major which they begin. At a large university, the available academic majors often number in the hundreds, not dozens. If a student changes his or her major or career choice, the large university is most likely to be able to accommodate that change.

As a result of the "knowledge explosion," many undergraduate *curricula* now require extensive equipment and large library resources. Because of their graduate and professional schools, large universities tend to offer more sophisticated laboratory equipment and libraries of considerable size. So called "economies of scale" seem likely to perpetuate this circumstance. At a large university, undergraduates often compete with others for these resources. The point is that the equipment and libraries are available.

For most students, post-graduate employment is a major reason for college enrollment. Large universities typically offer a multiplicity of services designed to help students in the identification and pursuit of career options. Selecting a career and finding a job are not often easy; it may be well to get as much help as possible.

There is an additional "job search" benefit to holding a degree from a large university. Most such institutions are well known on at least a regional basis. Assuming the reputation of a given institution is good, the employer or graduate school may be more impressed if they are familiar with an applicant's university.

Each type and size of college and university has academic benefits to offer. Ony a few of the academic benefits of the large university have been addressed here. There are other benefits related to the academic learning environment of each large university. Academic learning is clearly the primary reason for the existence of colleges and universities. It would be foolish to suggest that all of the benefits of college attendance happen inside the classroom, laboratory, and library. Many of the non-academic benefits of college attendance are social in nature. It is well that those benefits be discussed.

The typical ages of college attendance (18-22) constitute an important period of intellectual and social development. It is important that these changes take place in the most nearly appropriate environment possible. Intellectual development is obviously an academic enterprise. Social development, which means more than just dating, parties, and football games, happens throughout the campus environment. As with the academic areas, each type of college or university has social benefits to offer prospective students. The social benefits of large universities are significant; those benefits should be considered carefully by aspiring freshmen.

It is reasonable to state that larger universities offer more student activities and more varied opportunities to associate with other students. In fact, many freshmen who enroll at the largest university find themselves inundated with opportunities for social involvement, community service, etc. It may be difficult to select the activities, clubs, and personal associations which are most appropriate for individual students.

The variety of opportunities for student involvement at a large university are often more impressive than the sheer number of such involvements, activities, clubs, etc. Many larger universities offer organizations which cater to a plethora of interests ranging from handicrafts to hang gliding. There are often religious organizations for many faiths and denominations. The opportunities for political involvement are often wide ranging. From the most serious of religious or political convictions to the desire for big or small parties, large universities can frequently provide activities which meet the needs of all their students.

As universities grow, the size of the student services staffs also grow. With regard to academics, this growth in student services results in improved opportunities for career identification and job seeking. In the arena of social development, this growth means more opportunities for personal counseling and other activities which are designed to help a person to improve their social awareness and skills.

A final social benefit of large universities has to do with one's classmates.

Because of their size, large universities often enroll students whose backgrounds present a wide variety of experiences, values, and perspectives. Exceptions to this rule do exist, but is is generally true that one's classmates at a large university will be less homogeneous than might be the case at smaller colleges and universities.

There is an important social benefit in this lack of sameness among a student's classmates. Most students will study, work, and live out their lives in a world composed of a huge variety of persons. Our society has become more pluralistic in recent years. It seems, therefore, likely that there is a good in being able to live and work with a wide variety of persons. College is an excellent place to gain experience in dealing with people whose backgrounds and perspectives may be different from your own. Large universities offer many opportunities for such experiences.

By way of the above, it is hoped the nature(s) and benefits of large universities may be better understood by qualified prospective students. The more important points of this essay are that American higher education is quite varied and that no type of colleges or universities is inherently superior to any other type or types. Each student must make his or her own decisions about the appropriateness of small colleges, community colleges, church affiliated colleges, and large universities.

This writer's bias for large universities should be obvious. Huge varieties of academic and social opportunities are available at large universities. Those varieties serve to make such institutions an excellent choice for many aspiring freshmen. Large universities, although varied themselves, are not for everyone. They do present very appropriate choices for many prospective students.

Jim Blackburn is Director of Admissions at the University of Northern Colorado, Greeley, Colorado and has been involved in the college admissions process for over ten years. He has conducted a number of conference presentations for admissions personnel at various association meetings.

The academic and social advantages of a private church-related college or university

By A. Mitchell Faulkner

Many educators in recent days are concerned that moral and ethical matters have been so largely excluded from the educational experience. Under the influence of a technology expanding beyond all expectations, the demands placed upon most professions, including the social and natural sciences, have worked to exclude serious consideration of moral and ethical concerns inseparably bound up in that expanding technology.

But the assumption that our complex society can be safely led by technicians untrained in the making of serious ethical decisions affecting our corporate well being is totally unacceptable to any thinking person.

As Bruce Haywood has written in *The Chronicle of Higher Education,* "too many of our colleges and universities have become vocational schools... Whereas once they offered our children avenues to a larger sense of their humanity, they now direct them to the market place. Instead of seeing themselves enlarged under the influence of great minds and grand ideas, students find themselves shrunken to fit the narrowing door of the graduate school or tailored to a job description. It is time for our colleges and universities to talk again about the worth of a free life, time while we are still able to distinguish between the *training* of young people and their *education.*" (1/8/79)

Young people are not born with moral and ethical convictions. They are learned in the educational process, if learned at all, by precept and by example, by being in the presence of people with convictions. Healthy self identity, says Lloyd Averill, emerges out of an environment which has convictional distinctiveness, in which the maturing self has access to a range of clear and competing values where the competition serves to sharpen and enliven the options rather than to subjugate or obliterate them.

A subtle but pervasive element emerging in our day is what Archibald MacLeish has called the diminution of man, the "long diminishment of value put upon the idea of man" in our society. Why has this happened now at the moment of our greatest intellectual triumphs, our never equalled technological mastery, our electronic miracles? "Man was a wonder to Sophocles when he could only sail and ride horseback and plow; now that he knows the whole of modern science he is a wonder to no one," says MacLeish.

At least part of this loss of the humane is caused by the knowledge explosion, the sheer weight of information in the print and electronic media, so that man despairs of any cognitive wholeness and surrenders ever increasing areas of knowledge to a vast array of experts.

Earl McGrath, former Commissioner of Education, says on the other hand, that this vast array of facts and theories needs to be collated and evaluated within the framework of philosophic convictions and religious beliefs in order for the wisdom of the ages to again invest dehumanizing facts with meaning for man.

One further point of definition needs stating. Our sense of community has well nigh been lost, and every social philosopher recognizes the need to restore it. What is at stake here, says John Gardner, is the individual's sense of responsibility for something beyond the self. The "me" generation threatens the cohesiveness of our social fabric, and a spirit of concern and caring is virtually impossible to sustain in a vast, impersonal society.

All of the above points directly to the purpose of the church-related liberal arts college. The essence of the liberal arts is the passion for man, the development of the humane values in literature, philosophy, history, and religion; and the great ideas of the race, such as truth, justice, love, beauty, honor, and wisdom are precisely the vehicles through which the deepest purposes of religion are served. Religion is only secondarily a matter of creeds and rituals. At its heart it is a matter of meaning, and this meaning is conveyed most effectively through the wisdom of the ages, the liberal arts.

Education is more than a learned set of mental exercises, the ability to respond properly to fixed mental inquiries. A computer does this admirably. To be fully human is to add to this a capacity for imagination, the ability to feel reverence and awe in the presence of mystery, a capacity for caring and compassion, and appreciation for the mixed grandeur and misery of the human experience. These represent the uniquely human accomplishment and point the direction for the church-related liberal arts college.

Further, the church-related college, usually smaller, offers a community in which students have more opportunity to learn through experience the interpersonal skills so necessary to effective participation in today's society. The development of the whole person involves taking responsibility for the care of the community, its governance, its social life, its ethical and moral tone, its operative effectiveness. A broad participation in all aspects of the campus community should mark the church-related college.

Students are not uniformly at the same place in their development, and ought not to be coerced to march lock step through some standardized program. The undergraduate program, through flexibility made possible by forms of governance and individual care, ought to allow as much as possible for diversity of interest and differences in development as the student progresses. A college ought to find ways to encourage each student to develop to the fullest potential his individual gifts and educational aspirations. A student's goals ought to be headed by the desire not only to master the curriculum but to develop himself. The church-related college will seek to aid this through the total experience, intellectual, social, cultural and religious.

The church-related college, if dedicated to the fully human development of its students, will retain a healthy respect for the vocational skills. In order to fully *be,* a person must be able to *do.* Life cannot be divorced from work, and a healthy self identity depends in part upon the ability to make some significant contribution to society. Thus the great truths of the liberal arts must be brought to focus and a point of service through competency in a chosen area of the world's work, where one may serve and fully live.

After all, as Montaigne said a long time ago, the purpose of education is not to make a scholar but a man.

A. Mitchell Faulkner is the former Executive Director, Council for Higher Education, Western North Carolina Conference, The United Methodist Church. He is on the Board of Trustees for Pfeiffer, Greensboro, High Point and Brevard Colleges, and is a member of many educational associations including the North Carolina Association of Independent Colleges and Universities, Secretary, S.E. Jurisdictional Commission on Higher Education.

Advantage of attending a state university

By Stanley Z. Koplik

For most students and their families, the cost of a four-year college education is an important consideration, and for this reason alone, many choose state colleges and universities. These institutions are usually considerably less expensive than private institutions and in many cases provide students with the option of living at home while pursuing a degree.

State scholarship programs are frequently available providing monetary incentives even to those who attend state institutions. Some families appreciate the opportunity of utilizing a system they continue to support with their tax dollars. But state universities are a wise choice for the college bound for many reasons other than simply economics. For young people growing toward independence, the proximity of the state college or university to parents, friends and home communty can provide the firm base of support students need as they adjust to the academic, social and emotional pressures of a more demanding way of life.

High school graduates seeking to continue their education in an atmosphere of intellectual challenge and academic diversity should also look to the state universities and colleges. With a wide range of courses and curricula from which to choose, state institutions of higher education provide a solid grounding in most fields from vocational and technical training to liberal arts education. No longer stereotyped as teacher training schools, state colleges and universities now emphasize engineering, computer technology, business, and science as well as teacher education and the humanities.

As a first step for those seeking professional careers, state institutions offer programs in such fields as medicine, dentistry, law and architecture. Virtually, any area of academic interest can be satisfied through state college programs. At the University of Kansas, for example, there are 112 degree programs offered; the University of Missouri offers approximately 125. Other states offer an equally broad array of programs. With outstanding faculties in many disciplines, and national reputations in many areas, state institutions have developed into comprehensive universities where intellectual inquiry and academic excellence flourish.

A large number of state colleges and universities are equipped with fine research facilities and outstanding libraries providing unlimited opportunities for questioning and stimulating creative minds. In some areas the most complete and comprehensive library in the state thrives on the campus of the state university, while inter-library loan systems enhance access of all state residents to study and research materials.

For those who are concerned about "being lost in the crowd," state higher education systems usually provide a variety of campus sizes ranging from the very samll school with 1-2,000 students to the "mega-campus" with a student population of 25,000 or more. Attendance at a smaller campus does not imply inferior educational quality or diminished services. Excellent instruction, stimulating classroom discussion and challenging extracurricular activities can be found on all state college campuses regardless of size.

Providing an integrated educational program with a maximum of flexibility is the goal of many state systems. To facilitate student choice, states such as Kansas and Missouri have developed clear articulation or transfer agreements with junior college for a senior institution. Many junior college graduates enter four-year institutions as juniors with legitimate standing.

Continuous attendance at college or university is ideal for those pursuing a degree but it is not always possible. When attendance must be interrupted, many state universities provide cooperative extension programs and programs of continuing education for those who cahnot attend classes full-time on campus. State higher education institutions also use sophisticated telecommunications systems to bring the university and its courses to the most outlying areas of the state.

The college years are, for many, a time to develop relationships which will provide a source of friendships and professional contacts for a lifetime. Attending college in one's home state increases opportunities to establish such long-lasting relationships and to be woven more fully into the fabric of state life.

Young people are increasingly aware of significant roles they will play in the social, political and economic life of this country. A college education in the state in which they are most likely to live can provide students with early involvement in the complexities of state activity. Increasingly, states are encouraging participation by student government groups in legislative activities. Some states, including Kansas, have authorized the appointment of a Student Advisory Committee to the Board of Regents, thus ensuring direct student participation in the decision making process.

State universities have long been known for athletic as well as academic excellence, and this continues to be true. On many campuses, intramural sports along with intercollegiate sports, enable large numbers of students to develop athletic prowess. As early responders to the growing need for quality in women's athletics, state universities provide equal opportunity in such sports as basketball, volleyball, swimming and tennis. Large multipurpose buildings springing up on many campuses indicate a dedication of state institutions to physical development and the cultural development of both campus and community. In some areas, the state college campus is the site of important cultural events, bringing lecturers, exhibits and the performing arts to an entire region. Attention must be given to the academic interest, the scholastic ability and the social and emotional maturity of the student as well as to the range of curricula, quality of instruction and extracurricular activities of the institution. A close examination of state university systems in the United States will indicate that there is virtually around every corner a quality institution of higher education solidly grounded in academics and attuned to the social and cultural needs of both students and community. State colleges and universities are a vital link in the network of public educational services and as such, merit serious consideration by the college bound.

Stanley Z. Koplik is Executive Officer of the Kansas Board of Regents, the governing body of public higher education in Kansas. Prior to assuming his current duties, Koplik served as Commissioner of Higher Education for the State of Missouri, where he directed activities of the Coordinating Board for Higher Education.

Advantages of a women's college

By Dr. Julia McNamara

Women's colleges are alive and well, even in 1982's all-too-realistic environment which predicts financial aid cuts, decreasing numbers of traditional college-age students, and a tight job market. Today, the mission and goals of 117 women's colleges in the United States matches neatly and clearly those of thousands of young women precisely because of these realities which they must face.

Women's colleges affirm and strengthen a woman's talent and ability; they exist specifically to develop the potential of their students; they demand and expect student participation and involvement. Women's colleges implant in women an attitude that is invaluable for success and achievement: "I can accomplish this task *and* I am a woman," not "even though" or "because" one is a woman. Rather the emphasis is on the fact that being a woman *and* accomplishing the task are quite compatible. Women's colleges instill in students the attitude that there is no sex-based limit to their potential for success. "I've lost that 'If-you're-a-woman-maybe-you-can't' attitude," said a 1982 women's college graduate who was also a student governor.

At a women's college, women learn that they can handle things because they have to handle them. They run the show; they exert influence; they wield power in student organizations which are exclusively their own. No one ever tells them that a particular leadership role is inappropriate for a woman. They can become properly aggressive and assertive without fear of seeming unattractive to men.

They learn to compete intellectually in an environment that consciously prepares them to realize that, if they seek it, the opportunity is there to excel. Their femininity will not be a deterrent at a women's college. Thus, women in leadership roles are not conspicuous at a women's college. Theirs is the only leadership that will occur, and they become comfortable with it. Women have to be in front of and behind all campus activities and events through which they learn to expect the best of themselves and of one another.

One woman, slightly overwhelmed by the extent of her responsibilities as student government treasurer, a task which involved budgets and planning, told me that she learned more from that experience than from some of her accounting classes, because she had final responsibility, and she had to make hard and unpopular decisions. She also said that her shyness and timidity would, in another setting, have prevented her from running for that office. "I would have thought some sharp guy could do it better."

When considering a women's college, it is important to understand several facts: First, women's colleges are not havens for people who could not survive elsewhere. Challenges and difficulties are just as much a part of this educational scene as any other, but there is emphasis on assisting women to meet the challenges which are special to them. Second, traditional views of women's colleges as protective shelters for innocent girls just do not pertain in 1982. Women's colleges are usually exciting places where learning and living mesh to create a viable educational and human experience. Third, women's colleges are not islands or ivory towers which exist by themselves, tiny spheres of influence which no other form of life can touch. Today, women's colleges often share facilities, faculty, and activities with neighboring schools so that students do participate in other educational environments. Thus, women's colleges can and do enjoy the benefits of co-education while maintaining their basic identity. This identity distinguishes her college and gives the young woman a chance to become a competitor, an achiever, a doer in an environment that is specifically concerned with her own development as a woman.

If women's colleges do not apologize for their *raison d'etre* of being for and about women's education, neither do they ignore men. Quite the contrary: women at a college for women, know well that this environment is only a temporary one, a step on the way to fuller participation in the human, common endeavor. If the college does its job well, the woman will realize that this environment prepares her for the next move and, indeed, sets the pace for it.

"You probably won't find your husband at a women's college," said one admissions counselor to a roomful of high school juniors, "but you will find out a lot about yourself, and about the kind of man you may want to marry." In considering a college, a woman needs to be clear about the reason for attendance at *any* college. Social life and experience are part of the rationale, but her intellectual development, the best and most comprehensive of which she is capable, is the key factor. To honor a woman's desire for quality education and self-development is the mission of a college which proclaims that it is *for* women.

Both academic and student services programs at women's colleges are consciously designed to achieve this mission. The opportunity to be leaders increases a student's self-awareness and inculcates a sense of feminine identity, preparing women for participation in every area of endeavor. No matter how secure or talented they are, young women do need affirmation and assistance in developing self-confidence. For example, two young women on my campus participated recently in the management of a political campaign. They were hired as business manager and associate to the candidate who was a woman. Because of specific communication skills that they had learned while working in a college office where the woman supervisor constantly exemplified a serious professional relationship with them, they succeeded admirably in a tough task. Of course, such training could occur on any college campus, but the point is that on a women's college campus specific efforts to develop a young woman's potential are a priority in all aspects of campus life from residence hall to classroom.

At women's colleges, career development offices train women for the competitive environment of the job market. Internship programs established in cooperation with local business and professional offices give students initial experience in administration or management or one of the professions, and provides a bridge between the world of academe and the business scene. When academic credit is linked with direct work experience a student's incentive increases; so does her personal satisfaction. And before she started out for the office, the student learned in a seminar room or through directed role-play what would be expected of her as a woman in the internship environment.

Faculties and administrative staffs at women's colleges are aware of their responsibility to develop young women's awareness of problems which she may face because she is a woman in a particular environment. The realities of discrimination and sexual harassment, can be a shock for the individual who needs to learn to deal with them effectively and, above all, to move beyond them.

When considering a women's college, these are questions which an applicant may want to ask during interviews:

1. Do the college's representatives seem to value their institution's specific identity as a women's college?
2. Does the college offer career guidance and advice for women?
3. Does the college have an internship program for its women?
4. What rapport has this institution established with neighboring universities and colleges?
5. What do students there say about their experience at a women's college?
6. Does the social life there give them a chance to meet men?

Responses to such questions give the prosepctive student a clear picture of the institution's commitment to the specific and unique character of a women's college. Certainly, a women's college is not for every woman. But equally as certain is the fact that these colleges continue to be extremely advantageous to the women who choose them.

Note: For more information on women's colleges, see: "A Profile of Women's Colleges" Women's College Coalition, Suite 1003, 1725 K St. N.W. Washington, DC 20006.

Dr. Julia McNamara is President of Albertus Magnus College in New Haven, Connecticut where she is also adjunct assistant professor of French literature. Dr. McNamara has also served as Dean of Students at this women's college. As an undergraduate she attended two women's colleges, Marymount Manhattan in New York City and St. Mary of the Springs, now Ohio Dominican, Columbus, Ohio and holds a Master's degree from Middlebury College and a Ph.D. from Yale University. She has been a Fulbright scholar and has studied for two years in Paris.

Opportunities at independent research universities

By F. Gregory Campbell

The diversity in American higher education is one of the greatest glories of our culture. No where else in the world does a prospective student enjoy such a wide range of choice. Public or private, large or small, urban or rural, secular or religiously oriented — American universities and colleges vary so greatly that any student should be able to find an institution seemingly tailor-made for that individual.

The major independent research universities constitute an important segment of American higher education. Frequently, they are considered primarily graduate or professional centers, and it is true that many students would be well advised to spend their undergraduate years elsewhere. But those universities typically possess vital undergraduate colleges offering a highly stimulating intellectual and extracurricular environment. For the right kind of student there is no better place.

In academic circles, the independent research universities enjoy an extraordinary reputation. That image depends on the quality of the faculty, and research is normally the means by which a scholar is evaluated. No one has yet devised a reliable method of measuring, comparing, and publicizing good teachers across the country. Good researchers are easy to spot, however, for they publish their discoveries for their colleagues around the world to evaluate. The research universities boast outstanding faculties containing highly innovative scholars with world-wide reputations.

But do they — or can they — teach? In ideal circumstances, the answer is yes. A standard view is that teachers are best when they continue to discover knowledge in their respective fields of scholarship. Conversely, the challenge of sharing their discoveries with critical young minds makes researchers better as a result of their also being teachers. Clearly, this ideal is not always realized. No university can guarantee that its most recent Nobel-prize winner will be teaching freshman chemistry, but such does happen.

The hope of learning from such scholars lures top-notch students to the research universities. Indeed, those institutions would have to do very little in order to produce outstanding graduates. Most college students quickly discover that they learn as much, or more, from their fellow students as from their professors. Inasmuch as the research universities serve as a meeting point for many bright young people, much of the intellectual stimulation on the campuses is provided by the students themselves. Compatibility with others who take their studies seriously is an essential prerequisite for prospective students.

But college life cannot be all work and pressure. There have been persistent efforts over the past fifteen years or so to reduce intellectual competition among students. Professorial complaints about "grade inflation" reflect the fact that it is much easier for a student to stay in the universities than to get into them to begin with. The dropout rate is low, the failure rate even lower.

The learning experience extends beyond classrooms, libraries, and laboratories, and cannot be measured by grades alone. Extracurricular opportunities for learning and growth are central to a college experience. Most of the independent research universities seek to encourage informal association between professors and students. Professors may be encouraged to eat meals regularly with students in the dining halls. Leaders in public affairs or the arts and sciences may be invited to the campuses in order to engage in informal meetings with students. How does one measure the worth to a pre-law student of a breakfast conversation with a Supreme Court justice?

The independent research universities almost never appear on the list of major NCAA powers in football or basketball. Their teams normally compete at a lower level. But their programs do offer opportunities to participate in intercollegiate athletics to many young men and women who could not make the teams of the major powers. In addition, the intra-mural programs typically attract the vast majority of students on campus. The schools do not figure prominently in the sports pages, but the student communities are active and vigorous.

The undergraduate colleges within the independent research universities are normally quite small. Whereas they enroll more students than a typical liberal arts college, they have many fewer students than the state universities. That size both provides a critical mass for a wide variety of activities and allows for a sense of community and personal identity in a manageable environment.

The student bodies themselves are quite diverse. Admissions officers try hard to insure a nationally representative student body — including students from various regions of the country, diverse ethnic groups, and economic levels. There is also a significant number of foreign students. This intimate exposure to differences among people is a key element in the growth to adulthood.

The kind of education that is offered in the independent research universities is expensive, and tuition levels are high. Yet, since the 1960's, those institutions have tried to provide sufficient amounts of aid to enable students to matriculate regardless of financial need. It is an open question whether that policy can be maintained, even formally, in a more difficult economic environment.

The concept of a "University College" is the most apt way of thinking about undergraduate programs in an independent research university. Students find a relatively small college with a distinct identity of its own. Yet that college lives within a much larger institution possessing resources available for undergraduates to exploit. Those "University Colleges" are not appropriate for everyone, and there are many other excellent institutions from which to choose. But, when the match is right, a "University College" can offer gifted and serious young people opportunities seldom found elsewhere.

F. Gregory Campbell is Secretary of the Board of Trustees and Special Assistant to the President at The University of Chicago. He is a historian specializing in the history of international relations and Central and Eastern European history. In addition to administrative duties, he teaches in the college and the Graduate Divisions at Chicago.

Choosing the right college major

By James E. Moore

Implicit in this analysis is the assumption that there are some important decisions to make before choosing a major. A brief look at these is in order. First is the decision to enroll in a college or university. There is much rewarding and lucrative work in the world which does not require a college education. Furthermore, a wealth of adult programs have sprung up in the last decade, making the college education readily available later on to those who for a variety of reasons do not attend on a full-time basis immediately after high school. While there is immense peer and parental pressure in favor of college directly after grade twelve, there are many fascinating people who can attest to the value of travel or work after twelve years of formal schooling; these experiences shape and enrich the college experience when it is finally pursued.

Once the decision to go to college is made, one must choose the right college in order to be able to choose the right major. Not all schools teach everything, nor do they all teach as well as one another in a particular area. Obviously, the school should offer a program in what is the applicant's current major interest. Then, with some agressive questioning of students, faculty, and admissions personnel, the applicant can get a sense of how well the school does in that area and what, if any, particular perspective on the discipline is represented by that department.

The choosing of the major — in educational parlance, it is called "declaring the major" — is something which usually occurs toward the end of the sophomore year. While colleges and universities are interested in knowing what a prospective student intends to study and generally solicit that information on the application, that designation is neither binding nor necessary. Admissions officers and academic advisors are understanding of the many freshmen who simply do not know in what field they will concentrate, and it is not uncommon for a person to change directions a number of times during the first two years of college. It is, however, difficult to change majors as a junior or senior and still complete degree requirements in four years.

How does one determine what should be the major area of interest? A critical look at the high school record and aptitude and preference tests is a good way to start. What were the courses that proved exciting? In what did the student excel? Are the verbal or the quantitative skills more highly developed? The Kuder Preference Test asks the taker to respond to a variety of hypothetical situations and, by patterns that emerge from the responses, is a decent indicator of the general kind of work that will be congruent with the sense of self and others that is reflected in a person's answers.

Most colleges and universities require all students to complete course work in a variety of broad areas regardless of the intended major. This work commences during the freshman year and can be a useful way to further define the primary interest. Colleges offer courses in subjects that most high schools cannot or do not. In the process of meeting course requirements in the humanities, social sciences, and natural sciences or math, students expose themselves to new disciplines, one of which might well become the major.

In recent years, along with curricular development, there has been much interest and innovation in the issue of modes of learning. While the conventional classroom-lecture-textbook-test method of teaching and learning remains prevalent, the opportunity of "learning by doing" has become a widespread option. Some high schools offer their seniors the opportunity to do volunteer work for a variety of agencies, businesses, and charities. This work often evolves into summer employment for high school students. At the college level, the programs are more comprehensive, often involving both college credit and remuneration. Internships and cooperative education placements are an excellent way for students to discover exactly what a particular workplace is like and to determine just how suitable their preparation for that career is.

In addition to faculty, libraries, and laboratories, one of the most important resources for the undergraduate is the student who lives two doors down the hall. He or she probably studies in an area far removed from one's own or comes to the same interests for entirely different reasons. That person has parents who may well have had professional experiences and can share a sense of that professionalism from a perspective more personal than one that is offered in the classroom. The "bull session" is both misnamed and underestimated; these hours of informal exchange are often fundamental in shaping the direction and quality of life for many college students.

These are times when choosing the right major entails a gamble, regardless of how one sees it. The numbers of options are mind-boggling. The lack of certainty about the usefulness of a particular degree is a reality which should not be ignored, given rapid and constant change in the nature and needs of the workplace. Perhaps more than ever there is a case to be made for seeing the undergraduate years as ones for refining skills in reading, writing, and reasoning well, whichever department serves as the context for such endeavors. The risks are substantially reduced if the student is realistic about his or her capabilities and commitments, and thorough in exposure to the wealth of opportunity and resources colleges and universities offer. Above all, choosing the right major is cast in an

appropriate light when seen as but one milestone of many in the process of learning, a venture which lasts a lifetime.

Jim Moore is an Admissions Officer at The American University in Washington, DC and previously worked in admissions at Aurora College, Aurora, Illinois; Goddard College, Plainfield, Vermont; and The New England Graduate Center of Antioch College, Keene, New Hampshire.

A yearn to earn

By Lawrence B. Durham

Throughout the 1970's much was made over the fact that the earnings differential between those with college degrees and those with only high school diplomas had shrunk. Many sought to interpret this statistical fact as evidence of the lessened worth of a college education. In the latter part of the decade, spiraling inflation and unemployment rates combined to produce a generation of college-bound young people more dedicated than ever to securing degrees which would assure them of employment upon graduation.

High school graduates of the early 1980's have thus been conditioned towards a very pragmatic view of the value of a college education. Yet, while post-college employment should be enhanced by this credentialing process, there is a real danger of overlooking the far more important and life-spanning aspects of the collegiate experience.

Indeed, many college faculties have contributed to this trend since the Russians launched their first Sputnik in 1957. Now, increasing numbers of these unwitting advocates of vocationalism are breathing fresh life into timeproven concepts such as core curricula and general education programs. Thus, the student entering college in the early 1980's faces the perplexing efforts of college faculties and our national economy as both seek to regain lost equilibrium through seemingly contradictory means.

In order to plot a realistic and rewarding course through the uncharted waters of higher education in this decade, students should be careful to expect neither too much nor too little from their collegiate experience. In an era where many college graduates may have to accept employment in jobs which had typically been filled by persons without degrees, certainly one would be unwise to expect a guaranteed position upon graduation. On the other hand, the rate of change in our society and in technological development is so rapid that a significant portion of the jobs in the next decade are non-existent at the present time. Consequently, one

must seek to attain preparation for the unknown.

Education at its best results in the participant learning *how to learn* and *how to cope with change*. Given these two skills, the future can be faced with confidence. "Educational experiences" not producing these skills would better be labeled "training." And, it is crucial to note that such skills cannot be *taught*, they must be *learned*. As a result, the burden is on the student, not the teacher!

How then should one pursue such lofty goals? First, and foremost, there should be a commitment made to be an active participant in the educational process rather than to be satisfied as a passive subject. Then, a process of exploration should ensue during which the fear of the unknown is overcome by the excitement of discovery. In short, courage will lead to adventure!

Perhaps it would be useful at this point to emphasize the scope of these considerations. During the course of a life's work, a person may well change jobs eight to ten times. While several jobs may be in the same field, such as engineering, others may be in another field altogether, such as education. Generally, the different jobs are referred to as vocations, while the different fields are spoken of as careers. Thus an engineer might have several jobs within the field of engineering and then change careers to education where his vocation might be teaching in a particular college. In today's world and even more so in the future, students can ill afford to prepare for only a single career, let alone for a single vocation!

In this context, this author submits that the academic debate between specialized curricula and liberal arts programs is little more than a semantic exercise if the importance of developing both useful skills and broad perspectives is recognized. Just as an engineering program can include courses in the humanities, so can a liberal arts program include basic business courses. Studies continue to show that those who communicate effectively (orally as well as in writing), reason analytically, work well with others, and understand basic business principles find their respective pursuits far more rewarding.

A word of caution is in order, too, lest the reader fail to acknowledge consciously that the most important "rewards" are not financial. Over the years, studies of worker attitudes and values have increasingly revealed that pay ranks below other aspects of work such as the nature of the job environment the degree of individual autonomy, and the self-esteem derived from performing the work. Therefore, students should be careful not to choose a career path for purely financial reasons.

The process of choosing a course of study is no mean feat! Unless one has a burning desire to qualify for a particular profession, it is quite likely that several fields are of interest. Naturally, in the former case, the student would follow that academic track leading to certification in the chosen field. However, even in such cases, sampling courses in other fields and apprenticeships in the field of primary interest will often pay unexpected dividends. A person who is undecided should not develop an inferiority complex and go through senior high school and college apologizing! Rather, that individual should seek counsel and work experiences in areas of interest and engage in a sound, broadly-based course of study up to the point where declaration of a major field is required.

As of this writing, energy and computer science head the list of promising fields with other engineering and business areas and health services close behind. As we become more and more dependent on information exchange, related vocations in that field will increase in their attractiveness. And who knows where we are headed in the fields of microelectronics and genetic engineering. Yet, the reader who selected a course of collegiate study based solely on this or any similar listing would have missed the real point of this article. The true value of a college education cannot be quantified. To the contrary, its qualitative dimensions transcend the relatively narrow considerations of vocation and career to affect our entire lives.

Yearn to learn and you will learn to live. Live to learn and you will learn to earn.

Dr. Lawrence B. Durham is Dean of Admission Services, The University of Alabama. He holds memberships in many associations including the American, Southeastern and Alabama Associations of Collegiate Registrars and Admissions Officers. He has published numerous articles in the field of education.

The two-year experience

By Dr. Jacob C. Martinson, Jr.

It is a difficult adjustment for a student to go from a high school, sometimes a small high school at that, directly into a multi-complex university often with thousands and thousands of other students. Are the majority of high school graduates equipped for this kind of transition? The answer, of course, is that some are, and some are not. There is an alternative approach.

There is a wide range of academic programs available among two-year colleges today. There are many accredited institutions which offer outstanding two-year terminal programs in areas such as business arts, computer science, and medical arts. This article, however, will focus on the two-year colleges that are designed to prepare the students for continuation at a four-year college or university. It will address the belief that, in many cases, the pursuit of the baccalaureate degree is greatly enhanced by "The Two-Year Experience."

When it comes to the role of a college education in career performance, an academically recognized two-year college can provide the essential foundations of undergraduate training often better than the best universities. After all, it doesn't take an expert to see that faculty qualifications are not that different from one center of learning to another. For example, a survey of the educational credentials of faculty members at good two-year colleges reveals that they have received their graduate training at the finest colleges and universities in the country.

The advantages of getting a good start at a two-year college are numerous. I will cite some reasons why a two-year college program should be considered.

1. Access to the Faculty

A faculty member ordinarily does not choose to teach at a two-year college unless he/she is specifically dedicated to teaching. Those faculty members who are interested in publishing or research usually go to the multi-complex universities where much of their undergraduate teaching responsibilities are delegated to graduate assistants. Classes in two-year colleges are generally taught by first-line faculty members.

Students have a right to expect some time with their professors who have spent many hours embodying much of the knowledge in which the students are interested. In the smaller two-year colleges, the opportunity is provided to know professors on a one-to-one basis. It is not uncommon to observe ballgames between faculty and students, or for faculty to invite students to their homes for refreshments.

2. A Good Beginning

The first two years of college are probably the most important of a student's college career. With the exception of kindergarten and first grade, they are all-important to the pursuance of formal education. Statistics show that when a students does well in an academically sound two-year college, he/she seldom does poorly academically anywhere else. A good start can make the difference.

3. Budget Appropriations

Many multi-complex universities give the "lion's share" of the funds to the upper-level undergraduate courses and to the graduate programs. Two-year colleges, on the other hand, give their entire budget to those critical first two undergraduate years.

4. Less Expense to the Student

One can attend a fine two-year college with a superb academic reputation for less than one can attend most universities. The community colleges are less expensive to the student, but even the private residential two-year colleges are relatively inexpensive. Of course, if commuting is possible, the expense is even less. Since the private college also wants to serve the surrounding community, special scholarships to commuting area residents are offered by some colleges.

5. Opportunities for Leadership and Participation

The freshmen and sophomores at a two-year college will have no juniors and seniors to compete with in extra-curricular activites for campus leadership roles, team sport participation, and faculty time. The individual has an opportunity to become involved more quickly and more deeply in the total life of the college. Where else could a student be a representative to the college committees and the Board of Trustees at the age of 18? In short, there is no "sophomore slump" in the two-year college.

6. Vocational Future

The two-year college can enrich one's vocational future. The fact is that too many college graduates today are ignorant of the English language, history, science, and math. Many are deficient in their ability to get along with others and in that all-important skill of communication. One need only watch a nationally televised athletic event to observe the inability of some students from the so-called "prestigious" centers of learning to speak proper English. This is not to imply that the two-year college student will consistently perform any better; however, at good two-year colleges, there is a concerted effort to start wherever a student is academically and teach him/her to read and write effectively. For example, some of the better two-year colleges have 3 or 4 different levels of beginning English. The same is true of math. These schools place great emphasis on English and math with the conviction that if one can read and write and add and subtract, one has the educational foundation to function in the world. The hallmark of the best two-year colleges is that of toughness with caring. Such colleges encourage the formulation of long-range educational goals and positive views on how education can assist one in meeting vocational objectives. Obviously, there are some limitations to the depth to which one can pursue objectives in a two-year setting, but the seeds are planted and the incentives aroused.

7. The Best of Both Worlds

A student can have the best of the two-year and the four-year educational systems. During those critical first two years of college, a fine two-year school can provide an excellent academic program and curriculum, caring faculty members, and a concerned college community, all of which prepare the student to transfer to the larger college or university.

There are those in educational circles who would have one believe that transferring is dangerous to one's educational future. In most cases this belief is unfounded. On the contrary, it is sometimes easier to get into the best four-year schools after a two-year Associate of Arts/Science/Fine Arts degree than to apply right out of high school. Academic credits from a good, academically sound, two-year college are accepted by most of the finest universities. In fact, transfer students are not only accepted, they are actively recruited because of the natural attrition in the senior colleges and universities after the first and second years. Also, some students perform better in a two-year college than they did in high school; therefore, these students are more likely to have their application accepted when they leave the two-year college than when they graduated from high school. Further, there are certain rights and responsibilities which are uniquely applicable to the transferring student. A statement of these rights and responsibilities has been approved by the NACAC (National Association of College Admissions Counselors) in 1980 and revised in 1982.

In conclusion, today's two-year college generally offers a university-parallel curriculum. It is nearly always designed for the brilliant as well as the average student. The task is to successfully meet and challenge each student where he/she is academically despite varying aptitudes, dispositions, and outlooks.

The two-year college experience is not for everyone, but it certainly fills a need. It is a good place to start in higher educational pursuits — a good place to begin on the way toward the baccalaureate degree.

Jake Martinson is President of Brevard College, Brevard, North Carolina. Before going to Brevard in 1976, he was President of Andrew College in Cuthbert, Georgia. Dr. Martinson holds degrees from Huntingdon College, Duke University, and Vanderbilt University. Beyond serving Brevard College, he has been President of the Brevard Chamber of Commerce and Secretary of the Independent College Fund of North Carolina and is an elected Board member of the National Association of Schools and Colleges of the United Methodist Church. Born of Norwegian-American lineage, he is an honorary member of the American-Scandinavian Foundation.

The value of a liberal arts education

By Dr. David Maxwell

We are in the midst of a crisis that threatens the very fabric of higher education in America today, and that endangers the quality of education that we all desire for our children. The crisis centers on the relationship between undergraduate education and the so-called "real world": What are we preparing our students for? The resolution of this crisis has serious implications for the undergraduate curriculum, for the nature of the demands placed on our students by the institutions, by their parents and by themselves — and profound consequences for the continuing health and vitality of our nation.

A liberal education has always been measured in terms of its relevance to society's needs, and there is no reason that it should not continue to be; the notion of utility is firmly ingrained in our national character. The crisis to which I refer lies in the determination of precisely what those needs are, for it is in those "needs" that we express the relationship between education and the "real world."

I have witnessed a trend in American

College students that I find particularly disturbing. An increasingly large number of students are demanding what they term "relevance" in their studies. Clearly, I feel that liberal education has profound relevance to the "real world," but these students have a definition of that term that is different from mine. By "relevance," they often mean professional training; training not for the future, but for jobs. With an entirely justifiable concern for their future economic well-being, they are making — I am afraid — a terrible and potentially devastating error of logic.

Although few of our students would accept the state of our "reality" as ideal, many are allowing the priorities of that reality — as expressed in economic terms — to dictate the priorities of their education. They are mistaking financial reward, prestige, and excitement for genuine intellectual interest. Many, I fear, view the undergraduate experience as a "credentialling" process, rather than as an education that will make them productive, fulfilled adults. I am not suggesting that our students do have neither genuine intellectual curiosity nor the thirst for pure knowledge, for they have ample supplies of both. But they are subjected to enormous pressures from the outside: the fear that the field in which they are truly interested will not provide them with a comfortable income; the fear that their parents (often professionals themselves) will not approve of their interests; the fear that their ambitions are not sufficiently "prestigious" in the eyes of their peers. These are all very real fears and pressures that must be recognized as valid, but they have two important — and destructive — consequences. It is my sense that many of our students go on to careers in the so-called "professions" with very little idea of what these professions entail and, what is worse, they have tailored their entire undergraduate education to fit what they feel is appropriate preparation for those professions.

We are engaging in the process of creating many unhappy adults as such students grow up to find that they have no real intellectual investment in the occupation toward which they have aspired since they were teenagers. Having focused their education at an early stage, with the mistaken impression that you have to major in economics to go into business, in political science to enter law school, or in biology to be a physician, they will be plagued with the gnawing feeling that they have missed something — but without knowing quite what it was that they have missed.

Furthermore, the misplaced emphasis on grades caused by the intense competition for professional schools discourages many students from their natural inclination to question, to challenge, to experiment, to take risks. Rather than risk the uncharted waters of their own ideas and their own imagination, many students choose the safe route of repeating what they've heard and read as they write their examinations and papers.

Clearly, it is our responsibility to find ways to encourage our students to follow their natural inclinations, to resist the pressures — we must make it clear to them that, as teachers, we will reward initiative, originality, and risk-taking. Perhaps most important is that we must convince them that it is precisely these skills that are the most "pre-professional," that no business ever grew without developing original ideas, that every physician must take calculated risks daily, and that the practice of law rests on the principle of challenge to ideas.

Most people with professional aspirations hope to advance beyond entry-level positions into managerial or executive roles; positions in which they can assume responsibility, control, and authority and positions in which they can implement their own visions. It is precisely these roles that demand breadth of education — not only in subject matter, but breadth in the range of personal and intellectual skills that the student acquires in his/her studies.

There is growing evidence that the "real world" is taking notice of the correlation between liberal arts skills at the professions. For the past twenty-nine years, AT&T has been conducting longitudinal studies of its managers, correlating field of undergraduate major to career advancement and managerial skills. The AT&T study showed clearly that those with non-technical majors (humanities and the social sciences) were "clearly superior in administrative and interpersonal skills." (Robert E. Beck, *The Liberal Arts Major in Bell System Management*, [Washington, D.C.: 1981], pp. 6, 8). Significantly, "Nearly half of the humanities and social science majors were considered to have potential for middle management, compared to only thirty-one percent of the business majors . . ." (p. 12) Within eight years of employment, the average management level of humanities and social science majors was significantly higher than that of other groups. As the author of the Bell report states: "One overall conclusion from these data is that there is no need for liberal arts majors to lack confidence in approaching business careers." (p. 13) It is interesting to note that this affirmation of the professional value of a liberal education comes from the experience of one of the world's largest high-tech corporations!

I am not presenting this evidence to argue that those who genuinely love engineering and the sciences should not pursue them, for their love is the best reason to enter those fields. Rather, the evidence presents a powerful argument for those whose interests lie elsewhere to *follow* their interests without fearing that their skills and knowledge will not be needed.

Not long ago, I had a meeting with several people who work in admissions at the Harvard Business School. We discussed the criteria for evaluating applicants, and they stressed that the single most important criterion was academic excellence at a respected, selective institution. Certainly, a few courses in economics and a familiarity with mathematics were an advantage, but the field of undergraduate major was not significant. As do the law and medical schools, they stress breadth of excellence and potential ability as reflected in the quality of the student's educational experience. It is significant that at Harvard, like many of the nation's best business schools, ninety-seven percent of their admitted applicants have had at least one year of full-time work experience before applying.

It should be clear from what I've said that liberal education *is* valued in certain segments of the "real world," and that there is often no correlation between choice of major and choice of career. Therefore we must encourage our students to spend their first year or more exploring, taking courses in a broad range of fields; courses in which they suspect they might be interested because of previous experience, courses in which they might be interested because they sound fascinating, courses in subjects that they know nothing about.

They should talk with their teachers, their advisors, their deans, their fellow students, with their parents, with other adults. In this process of exploration —if they are allowed to explore without pressure — they will find something in which they are genuinely fascinated. Pursuit of that fascination will lead them not only to sophisticated knowledge of a particular field, but to the development of intellectual and personal skills that will enable them to survive, happily and productively, as adults. The fascination will lead them to accept challenges, exercise their creativity, to take risks in the name of learning, to find out what they are good at and what to avoid, to be critical rather than accepting, and to be pathfinders rather than followers. It will also lead them, the evidence suggests, to a career that will allow them to use what they've learned in the broadest sense; one which they will find rewarding, interesting and challenging. To put it simply, they should decide *who* they want to be when they grow up, not just *what* they want to be.

David Maxwell has been the Dean of Undergraduate Studies at Tufts University since 1981. Formerly the Director of the Program in Russian at Tufts, he has been teaching Russian language and literature nearly fifteen years, and in 1979 was the recipient of the Lillian Leibner Award for Distinguished Teaching and Advising. A Fulbright Fellow in Moscow in 1970-71, Dean Maxwell is the author of numerous scholarly articles on Russian literature. He is active in a number of organizations concerned with liberal arts education, and is a charter member of the Council on Liberal Learning.

Preparing for a career in the arts

By Gene C. Wenner

Although the notion that there is no future in a career in the arts is still espoused by many, the number and quality of opportunities in the arts has dramatically increased in the past ten years. Not every vocational opportunity is with the Metropolitan Opera, Carnegie Hall or on Broadway but nationally the growth of the arts organization and career opportunities is much improved.

Many colleges and universities are responding to this trend, by greatly expanding their programs in the arts (music, dance, theater, visual arts and writing) that develop performers, creative artists, arts educators and arts administrators. In addition, there are many course offerings in the arts for those students less determined to pursue a career in the arts, but who also desire further training and experience in the arts.

Many young people are able to combine their artistic and academic skills in preparation for the demands of being an artist. Combination of skills are also necessary for careers in the management of artists or arts organizations.

If you are seriously considering further training and education in either music, dance, theater, visual arts or writing, you should be aware of a program designed to assist young artists.

The Arts Recognition and Talent Search (ARTS) program of the National Foundation for Advancement in the Arts is a national program to recognize and support excellence in the arts. Over 5,000 high school seniors from every state participate in ARTS nationally every year.

The Educational Testing Service (ETS) of Princeton, N.J. administers the screening and adjudication activities of ARTS for the Foundation. Applications received from aspiring young artists include; a video tape of performance in dance and theater, an audio tape of solo music performance, a slide portfolio for visual artists and a portfolio of compositions by writers.

Each year, students with ability in the arts who will be high school seniors register for the ARTS program by these two dates: a regular registration deadline, May 15, (as a junior) and a late registration deadline, October 15 (as a senior).

The decisions made by panels of expert judges in each art field made solely on the basis of the artistic content of the student's performances as submitted. No other criteria, such as grades or academic standing have any bearing on their decisions.

As the result of these judgements four categories are selected: Finalists, awarded $3,000 in cash, Semifinalists, awarded $1,500, Merits, awarded $500 and Honorable Mention, a non-cash award. In addition, the registrants and award winners are recruited by leading colleges, universities and professional arts organizations who offer over 3 million dollars in scholarships and internships.

The Foundation recommends their top artistically talented students to the Presidential Commission on Scholars each year and twenty are selected as Presidential Scholars in the Arts. These young artists are presented in concert at the John F. Kennedy Center for the Performing Arts in Washington, D.C.

If you aspire to a creative career, you need to be realistic about your talent, for that is what is most important in getting a job in the arts or establishing a reputation. Practical experience outside of the school environment — with local theaters, music and dance groups, galleries and community newspapers — can give you an extra edge. Even the most talented artist must be willing to spend years of their lives mastering their skills so it is not too early to develop that necessary sense of dedication.

A life in the arts can be very rewarding because you give of yourself to others and what you get in return makes it more than worth the hard work and dedication.

Gene Wenner is the Vice President of Programs for the National Foundation for the Advancement in the Arts.

Guide to guides for high-school students

Reprinted with permission from the "Chronicle of Higher Education."

The Best Buys in College Education, by Edward B. Fiske (Times Books; 393 pages). Mr. Fiske, the education

editor of the New York *Times,* has published his *Selective Guide to Colleges* since 1982. This fall he released *Best Buys,* which lists 200 colleges — both public and private — that are identified as particularly good values. The institutions range from Pratt Institute ($10,088 tuition) to Cooper Union ($300). Included are statistics (including admissions and financial-aid figures), and essays describing what Mr. Fiske calls "the academic and social climate" of the institutions.

The Insider's Guide to the Colleges, by the staff of the Yale *Daily News* (St. Martin's Press; 568 pages). "Obviously," the editors say in their preface, "it's impossible to capture the full scope and breadth of any institution in two or three pages of text." The editors of the Yale *Daily News* — and student correspondents on more than 150 campuses — offer readers, according to the book's cover, an account of "what . . . colleges are really like."

The brief descriptive sections tend to give colleges labels, provide a sweeping sense of the atmosphere, and describe campus social life. The book also provides an introduction to college "trends in the Eighties" and includes lists of colleges in categories such as "liberal arts colleges with an emphasis on pre-professionalism," and "colleges de-emphasizing varsity sports."

100 Top Colleges, by John McClintock (John Wiley & Sons, Inc.; 225 pages). In addition to its statistical descriptions of what it calls "America's best" institutions, *100 Top Colleges* suggests a systematic method for selecting a college. By answering a series of multiple-choice questions and plugging the answers into boxes, students may narrow their choice of institutions to conform to the qualities they value. "Choosing a college may never become a strictly scientific process," writes Mr. McClintock, "but it can be rational." The profiles of institutions rely heavily on statistics of all kinds, including ratings for "personal life," "mix of students," and "student motivation."

Rugg's Recommendations on the Colleges, by Frederick E. Rugg (Whitebrook Books; 65 pages). Mr. Rugg, a high-school guidance counselor, organizes his book by academic majors, from agriculture to zoology. In each section, the book recommends several colleges whose departments are felt to be among the best in the country. Within majors, the lists are divided into three categories: "most selective," "very selective," and "selective." Information about the colleges was obtained primarily through random interviews with students and others affiliated with institutions, according to the book.

"I even did weird things like interview the scorer and timer at the halftime of a basketball game at Williams College," Mr. Rugg writes. "We ended up discussing the classics department there (small, but good)." Mr. Rugg rates William's classics department among the best in the nation.

Lisa Birnbach's College Book, by Lisa Birnbach (Ballantine Books; 515 pages). Lake Forest College has the best salad bar of any College. The most promiscuous students are at Boston University. Connoisseurs of such information will find plenty of it in Ms. Birnbach's book, which describes student life at 186 colleges. "This is the inside scoop," writes Ms. Birnbach, "the juicy stuff you can only learn by visiting the campuses, by going to school there. This is the real thing." Entries place little emphasis on statistics and list such categories as "best professors," "gay situation," and "best thing about school."

The Public Ivys: A Guide to America's Best Public Undergraduate Colleges and Universities, by Richard Moll (Viking; 289 pages) "Even the parents with ready cash are wondering if Olde Ivy is worth two or three times the price of a thoroughly respectable public institution," Mr. Moll writes. His book contains lengthy narrative and statistical descriptions of 17 public institutions he says are comparable to Ivy League universities. Mr. Moll chose the 17 based on admissions selectivity, "quality" of "undergraduate experience," institutions' financial resources, and prestige.

America's Lowest Cost Colleges, by Nicholas A. Ross (Freundlich Books; 253 pages). North Carolina residents will be delighted to learn that, according to Mr. Ross's book, 13 institutions in their state charge $150 or less for one year's tuition. Californians have more reason to celebrate: 36 colleges are identified here as charging $100.

"This book was written," Mr. Ross writes, "because too many parents have been forced to sacrifice for their children's education. . . . Worst of all, too many young people have decided not to go to college, because they think they can't afford it." The book includes brief descriptions of more than 700 colleges with annual tuitions of less than $1,500.

The College Handbook, 1985-86 (College Entrance Examination Board; 1,900 pages). The College Board's guide is filled with facts and figures that answer any basic question a prospective student might have about more than 3,000 institutions: number of students, a description of the location ("city," "small town," etc.), major fields of study, and special programs. It also gives a brief "class profile" and statistics on the number of applicants admitted from the most recent pool. The introduction offers students advice on how to choose a college.

Selective Guide to Colleges, by Edward B. Fiske (Times Books; 482 pages). "If you are wondering whether to consider a particular college," Mr. Fiske writes, "it is logical to seek out friends or acquaintances who go there and ask what it's like. What we have done is exactly this. . . ." Mr. Fiske has written brief, general descriptions of what the book calls "the 275 colleges you are most likely to consider." The descriptions tend to emphasize various components of student life, as well as the academic reputations of institutions. In addition to the narrative descriptions, Mr. Fiske rates three qualities — "Academics," "Social Life," and "Quality of Life," on a subjective one-to-five scale.

GENERAL CATALOGUES

Barron's Guide to the Two-Year Colleges (Barron's Educational Series, Inc.; volume one: 319 pages; volume two: 282 pages). The first volume of this two-volume set lists facilities, costs, programs and admissions requirements of more than 1,500 two-year institutions. Using charts, the second volume identifies institutions offering programs in five general categories: business and commerce; communications, media, and

public services; health services; agricultural and environmental management; engineering and technologies. It also provides a separate list of institutions offering liberal-arts programs.

Barron's Profiles of American Colleges (Barron's Educational Series, Inc.; 1,151 pages). In addition to providing statistical information — including median S.A.T. scores, student-faculty ratio, and tuition costs — Barron's ranks each college on a scale from "most competitive" to "non-competitive." The book's introduction says the rankings are determined by a combination of the institution's rate of acceptance and the average high-school grade-point average and median S.A.T. scores of students who are accepted.

Comparative Guide to American Colleges, by James Cass and Max Birnbaum (Harper & Row; 706 pages). While it includes many of the statistical laundry lists of other fact-filled guides, Cass and Birnbaum's book also throws in an introductory paragraph giving a general description of each institution. Each entry also includes sections on "academic environment," "religious orientation," and "campus life" and information on the proportion of degrees conferred in various departments. Like Barron's, the book uses what it calls a "selectivity index," rating institutions with competitive admissions from "selective" to "among the most selective in the country."

Lovejoy's College Guide, edited by Charles Straughn and Barbarasue Lovejoy Straughn (Monarch Press; 604 pages). Listing more than 2,500 colleges and universities, Lovejoy's is concise and informative but offers less statistical material than do some of the other catalogues. Its descriptions are much briefer than those in most of the other guides, such as Barron's and Cass and Birnbaum.

Peterson's Competitive Colleges, Karen C. Hegener, editor (Peterson's Guides; 358 pages). In its fourth edition, it includes one-page profiles of 301 "selective" institutions — those whose students do well on standarized tests and which consistently have more applicants who meet entrance standards than are admitted. The book contains lists of the colleges and universities by cost, size, religious affiliation, and other factors. It also includes one-paragraph profiles of selective arts colleges and conservatories.

Peterson's Four-Year Colleges 1986, Andrea E. Lehman, editor (Peterson's Guides; 2,237 pages). In a volume larger than the Manhattan telephone directory, Peterson's, which is updated annually, provides general information about more than 3,000 institutions. It also includes a section of two-page "messages from the colleges," profiles provided by institutions that each pay $895 for the space. In addition, the book provides a chart with a state-by-state breakdown of colleges, listings of institutions organized by majors offered, difficulty of admission, and costs.

Lovejoy's Concise College Guide, edited by Charles Straughn and Barbarasue Lovejoy Straughn (Monarch Press; 375 pages). "The criteria used for the selection of the 370 institutions are varied to include the most diverse selection of schools for you to choose from," says the introduction. The book never explains those criteria, but the editors

seem to have included the most selective institutions. The descriptions of the colleges are slightly abbreviated selections from the larger Lovejoy's, including information on enrollment, cost, academic majors, and student life.

SPECIALIZED GUIDES

Who Offers Part-Time Degree Programs? edited by Karen C. Hegener (Peterson's Guides; 417 pages). The listings include more than 2,500 institutions offering part-time undergraduate and graduate degree programs. The guide also includes separate directories of colleges with evening, summer, and weekend programs.

The Black Student's Guide to Colleges, edited by Barry Beckham (Beckham House Publishers; 495 pages). Mr. Beckham, a professor of English at Brown University, writes in his introduction that he wishes to provide information "in both objective and subjective terms" to help black students choose among colleges. Each campus profile is based on information supplied by the institution and by five of its students, whose individual statements are often noted. In narrative form, the book provides details on topics including race relations, support services, cultural opportunities, and black organizations.

Everywoman's Guide to Colleges and Universities, edited by Florence Howe, Suzanne Howard, and Mary Jo Boehm Strauss (Feminist Press; 512 pages). For each of the 600 colleges it evaluates, Everywoman's Guide provides a ranking — on a three-star scale — for each of several categories: "students," "faculty," "administrators," "women and the curriculum," and "women and athletics." An introduction notes that those are areas of "special importance." In narrative form, each entry provides additional material under such headings as "policies to ensure fairness to women," "women in leadership positions," and "special services and programs for women."

A Guide to Colleges for Learning Disabled Students, edited by Mary Ann Liscio (Academic Press, Inc.; 490 pages). In addition to some basic information about admissions requirements and tuition, each entry lists services for learning disabled students, "modifications to the traditional learning environment" (including such details as tape recorders provided to tape lectures, and "longer time to complete exams"), and a person on campus for learning-disabled students to contact.

Learning a new role

By Paul and Ann Krouse

Most literature directed to parents of college-bound students focuses on financial matters, an area of great

(Continued next column)

interest and concern to most of us. Yet there are other roles besides bankrolls which require attention and involvement. Some are obvious and others more subtle. Having just completed the college admissions process with our eldest daughter, my wife and I would like to share our experiences and views.

Be involved.

Selecting a college is just one more experience in the parenting process with the usual mixture of risks, rewards, joys, and uncertainties. You will find yourself pouring over directories, college catalogs, counselor recommendations, applications, and financial aid forms. The more you do together, the less tedious the tasks and the more enlightening the process becomes. We found ourselves engaged in a very productive cycle which started with counselor/student meetings. From this counselor-to-parent shuttle which was repeated several times over a period of a few weeks, our daughter developed a list of six or seven college choices. We visited several of her college choices on a 4-day car trip and ultimately she selected a college which happily accepted her. Waiting for the acceptance letter was agonizing, receiving it was joyous. The family celebration which followed was memorable.

Our experiences were undoubtedly quite common. The subtleties merit equal awareness.

Listen to your child.

Most of us have our own preferences of where we would like our children to go to school, but we've had our chance(s) and now it's their turn. Certainly your guidance, opinions, and views are important. You may have some inflexible requirements which your child must be responsive to such as financial limitations. Nevertheless, it is imperative that you listen to your child's preferences and to the best of your ability and with your best judgement encourage your child to fulfill his or her dreams, not yours.

Be patient and "tune-in."

The separation between child and family is beginning and it impacts on everyone involved in different ways and at different times. So much of the college admissions process requires that the children initiate action which will cause separation that there is frequently a reluctance to complete a task which can easily be misinterpreted as laziness or irresponsibility. An application may remain untouched, an essay delayed, a conference postponed. You must "tune-in" to your child's emotions and try to determine when he or she is being lax and when normal anxieties are rising to the surface, slowing down progress. Try to be patient, guide instead of push and acknowledge your mutual feelings instead of hiding them. The closer the family is, the more pronounced these experiences may be.

Respect your child's privacy.

Social gatherings will undoubtedly bring you into contact with other parents of college-bound students and the plans and experiences of your children will become timely topics of conversation. Sharing experiences with other parents can be mutually beneficial.

But, revealing your child's exact SAT scores, GPA, class rank and similar information is an invasion of privacy. If your child wants to announce this information to friends, relatives or other parents, that's his or her business and choice — not yours. Certainly you wouldn't want your child publicizing your income or other personal information to outsiders. Similarly, your child probably would prefer that some aspects of this process remain within the family. You will be amazed at what remarkably bad taste some parents exhibit in discussing their children's experiences.

Shop carefully.

As adults, you are undoubtedly a more experienced and sophisticated shopper than your child and your experience can be significant as your child shops for a college. Most colleges are very ethical and professional in their recruitment practices, but remember they are "selling." At college fairs, admissions officers can be persuasive which is not to their discredit. College catalogs can be slick and attractive which is also understandable and acceptable. But remember, most colleges are selling a package that can cost $5,000 to $15,000 per year or $20,000 to $60,000 over four years. They need from 100 to 10,000 new students each year to keep their doors open. That's not an indictment of their motives, but simply a representation of their realities. Read between the lines and beyond the pretty pictures. Don't hesitate to confer with your child's counselors about the choices and options available — counselors are generally objective and committed to serving the student, not a particular institution. When you visit campuses allow enough time to wander on your own *after* your formal tour, usually conducted by the admissions office. Walk into the library, dormitories, student union and even classrooms, if possible. Talk to students around the campus and observe as much as you can. Virtually all college admissions officials will encourage such "investigations" on your part since they don't want your child to make a mistake and stay for one year or less anymore than you do.

Naturally, each family's experiences will be a little different. The process is not very scientific yet, inspite of computerbanks, search services, video presentations, etc. Like looking for a house, there is more emotion in the process than some are ready to acknowledge. Nevertheless, as we look back, it was another enjoyable family experience where the rewards far outweigh the risks.

Paul and Ann Krouse are the publishers of WHO'S WHO AMONG AMERICAN HIGH SCHOOL STUDENTS and the parents of four delightful children. This article was written shortly after they completed the college selection/admissions process for the first time with their eldest daughter Amy who entered the freshman class at Tufts University, Medford, Massachusetts in the fall of 1983. WHEW!

THE EDUCATIONAL COMMUNICATIONS SCHOLARSHIP FOUNDATION®

During the 1985-86 academic year, approximately 20,000 students competed for scholarship awards sponsored by the Educational Communications Scholarship Foundation® which is funded by the publishing company. Students competed by completing an application which requested data regarding aptitude test scores, grade point average, extracurricular activities, work experience and general background information. Semifinalists were selected based on careful examination of all this information and were then requested to provide information regarding financial need. In addition, semifinalists were asked to write an essay from which the Scholarship Awards Committee attempted to evaluate the overall maturity of the students.

Fifty winners were selected and a total of $50,000 was awarded. Over $800,000 has been distributed through the Scholarship Foundation to date.

1985-86 SCHOLARSHIP WINNERS

Susan Lynn Abbott
Greens Farms Academy
Southport, CT
Williams College
Williamstown, MA

Katherine Chen
Lowell High School
San Francisco, CA
Stanford University
Stanford, CA

Amy Ferry
Gowanda Central School
Perrysburg, NY
SUNY University at
    Buffalo
Buffalo, NY

Preetinder Bharara
The Ranney School
Eatontown, NJ
Harvard University
Cambridge, MA

Kenneth C. Chern
W.T. Woodson High
    School
Annandale, VA
Northwestern University
Evanston, IL

Mei-Ling Fong
Putnam City High
    School
Oklahoma City, OK
Pepperdine University
Malibu, CA

Philip T. Blazek
St. John High School
Ennis, TX
Harvard University
Cambridge, MA

William Lance Conn
McComb High School
McComb, MS
Princeton University
Princeton, NJ

Richard Gay
Rich East High School
Park Forest, IL
University of
    Pennsylvania
Philadelphia, PA

David Yu Sam Chang
H.S. for the Performing
    and Visual Arts
Houston, TX
Standford University
Stanford, CA

Ross Dickerson
York High School
York, NE
University of Iowa
Iowa City, IA

Leon L. Gebhardt
Charter Oak-Ute
    Community High
Charter Oak, IA
The University of Iowa
Iowa City, IA

Nancy S. Chang
Niles North
Morton Grove, IL
Northwestern University
Evanston, IL

Patrick Spencer Egan
Neah-Kah-Nie High
    School
Nehalem, OR
Williamette University
Monmouth, OR

Sabrina J. Goodman
Marina High School
Huntington Beach, CA
Massachusetts Institute
    of Technology
Cambridge, MA

1985-86 SCHOLARSHIP WINNERS

Robert A. Grothe, Jr.
St. Louis University
   High School
St. Louis, MO
California Institute
   of Technology
Pasadena, CA

Molly Ann McMahon
Marian High School
Troy, MI
University of
   Notre Dame
Notre Dame, IN

Margaret S. Oertling
Trinity Episcopal High
   School
Natchez, MS
Trinity University
San Antonio, TX

Elizabeth Marie Gruca
Bishop McCort High
   School
Johnstown, PA
Penn State University
University Park, PA

Frances Mikasa
Orosi High School
Orosi, CA
College of the Sequoias
Visalia, CA

Lisa Patnode
Banning High School
Banning, CA
Ithaca College
Ithaca, NY

Liane Adele Hancock
Mary Institute
St. Louis, MO
Massachusetts Institute
   of Technology
Cambridge, MA

Michele Chiyomi
   Mitsumori
Waiakea High School
Hilo, HI
Yale University
New Haven, CT

Charles F. Pazdernik
Breckenridge Senior
   High
Ithaca, NY
Cornell University
Ithaca, NY

Joseph Scott Howlett
Forest High School
Ocala, FL
Massachusetts Institute
   of Technology
Cambridge, MA

Charles Wallace Moniak
Garden Grove High
   School
Garden Grove, CA
University of California
Berkeley, CA

Krystle Quynh Pham
Redlands Senior High
   School
Redlands, CA
Stanford University
Stanford, CA

Andrew Thomas Hudak
Greenway High School
Grand Rapids, MN
Itasca Community
   College
Grand Rapids, MN

John S. Monical
Pontiac Township High
Pontiac, IL
University of Illinois
Champaign, IL

Gregory Randal Ralph
Wheeler High School
Hobart, IN
California Institute of
   Technology
Pasadena, CA

Darin Scott Katz
George Washington
   High School
Philadelphia, PA
Pennsylvania State
   University
University Park, PA

John S. Neville
Miami Beach Senior
   High
Surfside, FL
Dartmouth College
Hanover, NH

Todd H. Rider
Ole Main High School
N. Little Rock, AR
Massachusetts Institute
   of Technology
Cambridge, MA

1985-86 SCHOLARSHIP WINNERS

Kevin Paul Schutz
Andrean High School
Schererville, IN
University of Chicago
Chicago, IL

Roger Dale Shipplett
Tennessee High School
Bristol, TN
Princeton University
Princeton, NJ

Karla Elizabeth Usalis
Thayer Academy
Hanover, MA
Princeton University
Princeton, NJ

Jay Bertram Seliber
Stoughton High School
Stoughton, MA
University of
   Pennsylvania
Philadelphia, PA

David M. Stevens
Soldotna High School
Soldotna, AK
California Institute
   of Technology
Pasadena, CA

Timothy Ray Vollbrecht
LaFollette High School
Madison, WI
University of Wisconsin
Madison, WI

Juan Pablo Semidey
Colegio San Ignacio
   de Loyola
Guaynobo, PR
Massachusetts Institute
   of Technology
Cambridge, MA

Adam Franklin
   Strassberg
Ramapo Senior High
   School
Monsey, NY
Harvard University
Cambridge, MA

Michael Edwin Wall
Santa Monica High
   School
Malibu, CA
Harvard University
Cambridge, MA

James Eric Sims
Jersey Village
Houston, TX
Rice University
Houston, TX

Ali Tabatabai
Lower Merion High
   School
Narberth, PA
Stanford University
Stanford, CA

Tracey Rae Winters
Robertsdale High School
Silverhill, AL
Rockford College
Rockford, IL

Volney Leo Sheen
Henry Clay High School
Lexington, KY
The John Hopkins
   University
Baltimore, MD

Roxanne Tapia
Los Lunas High School
Los Lunas, NM
Adams State College
Alamosa, CO

Joseph T. Woods
Chicopee Comprehensive
   High School
Chicopee, MA
Rensellaer Polytechnic
   Institute
Troy, NJ

Irene Shih
Calabasas High School
Calabasas, CA
Harvard University
Cambridge, MA

Cynthia A. Tarkowski
Carmel High School
   for Girls
Wauconda, IL
Northwestern University
Evanston, IL

GLOSSARY OF ABBREVIATIONS

Acpl Chr ....Acappella Choir
AFS ....American Field Service
Am Leg Boys St........ American Legion Boys State
Am Leg Aux Girls St ....American Legion
Auxiliary Girls State
Aud/Vis ....Audio-Visual
Awd ....Award

Badmtn .... Badminton
Bsbl .... Baseball
Basktbl .... Basketball
Btty Crckr Awd .... Betty Crocker Award
Bus .... Business
Bwlng................................. Bowling

C of C Awd........... Chamber of Commerce Award
Camp Fr Inc .... Camp Fire, Inc.
CAP................................. Civil Air Patrol
Capt......................................Captain
Cit Awd .... Citizenship Award
Clb .... Club
Cmnty Wkr .... Community Worker
Coach Actv .... Coaching Activities
Crs Cntry .... Cross Country

DAR Awd .... Daughters of the American
Revolution Award
DECA ....Distributive Education Clubs of America
Dnfth Awd............Danforth (I Dare You) Award
Drm & Bgl .... Drum & Bugle Corps
Drm Mjr(t) ....Drum Major(ette)

Ed-Chief ....Editor-In-Chief

FBLA .... Future Business Leaders of America
FCA ....Fellowship of Christian Athletes
FFA .... Future Farmers of America
FHA............... Future Homemakers of America
Fld Hcky ....Field Hockey
FNA................... Future Nurses of America
FTA .... Future Teachers of America
Ftbl .... Football

GAA................... Girls Athletic Association
Gov Hon Prg Awd ....Governors Honor
Program Award
Gym .... Gymnastics

Hist .... Historian
Hon .... Honor
Hosp Aide.......................... Hospital Aide

Ice Hcky .... Ice Hockey
Intnl Clb .... International Club

JA................................Junior Achievement
JC Awd ....Jaycees Award
JCL .... Junior Classical League
JETS Awd .... Junior Engineering Technical
Society Award
JP Sousa Awd .... John Philip Sousa Award
Jr NHS.............. Junior National Honor Society
JV................................. Junior Varsity

L ....Letter
Lcrss .... Lacross
Lion Award.....................Lions Club Award
Lit Mag .... Literary Magazine

Mgr(s) .... Manager(s)
MMM .... Modern Music Masters
Mrchg Band....................... Marching Band

NCTE Awd ....National Council of Teachers
of English Award
NEDT Awd ...... National Educational Development
Test Award
NFL .... National Forensic League
NHS...................... National Honor Society
Ntl ....National
Nwsp.....................................Newspaper

OEA................... Office Education Association
Opt Clb Awd .... Optimist Club Award
Orch ....Orchestra

PAVAS ....Performing & Visual Arts Society
Phtg.................................. Photographer
Pres..................................... President
Prfct Atten Awd ....Perfect Attendance Award

Rep...................................Representative
Rptr .... Reporter
ROTC .... Reserve Officer Training Corps

XXXV

S.A.D.D.	Students Against Driving Drunk		Trea	Treasurer
Sal	Salutatorian		Trk	Track
SAR Awd	Sons of the American Revolution Award		Twrlr	Twirler
Schol	Scholarship			
Sec	Secretary		V	Varsity
SF	Semifinalist		Val	Valedictorian
Sftbl	Softball		VICA	Vocational Industrial Clubs of America
Socr	Soccer		Vllybl	Volleyball
Sprt Ed	Sports Editor		Voice Dem Awd	Voice of Democracy Award
St Schlr	State Scholar		VP	Vice President
Stf	Staff			
Stu Cncl	Student Council			
Swmmng	Swimming		Wrstlng	Wrestling
Symp Band	Symphonic Band		Wt Lftg	Weight Lifting
Tm	Team			
Thesps	Thespians		Yrbk	Yearbook

Sample Biography

This sample is presented to familiarize the reader with the format of the biographical listings. Students are identified by name, school, home, city and state. In order to protect the privacy and integrity of all students, home addresses are not published.

KEY

1 Name
2 High School
3 Home, City and State
4 Nomination Source*
5 Class Rank (when given)
6 Accomplishments
7 Future Plans

*(S) = School Nomination
 (Y) = Youth Organization Nomination

1 Wolk, Sheffield L.; **2** Normandy Isle H.S.; **3** Miami, FL; **4** (S); **5** 10-350; **6** Pres Stu Cncl; VP Sr Cls; Ftbl; 4-H; NHS; Cit Awd; Am Leg Awd; **7** Harvard University; Biochemist

STUDENT BIOGRAPHIES

CONNECTICUT

ABATE, KRISTEN; Southington HS; Southington, CT; (Y); 9/600; Ski Clb; VP Spanish Clb; Rep Stu Cncl; Cheerleading; High Hon Roll; NHS; Bus.

ABBOTT, GINA; Sacred Heart Acad; New Haven, CT; (Y); Cmnty Wkr; Hosp Aide; Spanish Clb; Church Choir; Orch; Yrbk Stf; High Hon Roll; NHS; NEDT Awd; Spanish NHS; Scared Hrt Acad Endowmng Schlrshp 84-85; Psychlgy.

ABBOTT, SUSAN L; Greens Farms Acad; Southport, CT; (Y); 2/50; Church Yth Grp; Hosp Aide; Co-Capt Math Tm; Church Choir; Ed Nwsp Stf; Ed Yrbk Stf; High Hon Roll; Ntl Merit SF; Wagner Awd Hghst Avg 83 & 85; Bus.

ABELARDO, ANABELA; Stamford Catholic HS; Stamford, CT; (Y); 25/150; Church Yth Grp; Drama Clb; JA; PAVAS; Red Cross Aide; Teachers Aide; Chorus; Church Choir; School Musical; School Play; John Carroll Awd 85; St Maurice Chrch Fr Holleran Schlrshp 86; U Of CT; Law.

ABRAHAMIAN, RACHEL; Newington HS; Newington, CT; (S); Church Yth Grp; SADD; Drill Tm; Flag Corp; Orch; School Musical; Variety Show; High Hon Roll; NHS; Dance Clb.

ACAMPORA, MARY; Bristol Central HS; Britol, CT; (Y); 2/281; GAA; Latin Clb; Ski Clb; Sec Frsh Cls; Pres Soph Cls; Sec Jr Cls; Pres Sr Cls; Var L Swmmng; Var L Tennis; DAR Awd; Schlr Athlt Awd 86; Yale Book Prz 85; Dghtrs Amrcn Rvltn Good Ctznshp Awd 86; U Of Notre Dame; Librl Arts.

ACERBI, JENNIFER L; Litchfield HS; Litchfield, CT; (Y); 13/87; Art Clb; Church Yth Grp; Girl Scts; SADD; Variety Show; Yrbk Stf; Cheerleading; Trk; Cit Awd; High Hon Roll; Dghtrs Isabella Ctznshp Awd 85; Edward L Mabry Art Awd 85; Marn Bio.

ACHEYCHEK, SANDI; Foran HS; Milford, CT; (Y); Yrbk Stf; Cheerleading; Hon Roll; Katherine Gibb Schl; Exec Sec.

ACHILLES, BETH; Danbury HS; Danbury, CT; (Y); Hosp Aide; JA; SADD; Chorus; Stu Cncl; Cheerleading; Trk; Hon Roll; 2nd Pl Cty Wd Spllg Bee 84; Hnr Rll 84-85; Penn ST; Psych.

ACHILLI, BETH; Lewis S Mills HS; Burlington, CT; (Y); 8/176; Model UN; Sec Band; Concert Band; Mrchg Band; Stage Crew; Yrbk Stf; Trs Frsh Cls; High Hon Roll; Hon Roll; NHS; Bus.

ACTON, REGINA; Ridgefield HS; Ridgefield, CT; (Y); Church Yth Grp; Cmnty Wkr; Var L Swmmng; JV Trk; Hon Roll; Safe Rides For Teens; Psych.

ADAE, NANA; Shelton HS; Shelton, CT; (Y); Art Clb; JCL; Speech Tm; Ed Yrbk Stf; Cit Awd; High Hon Roll; VP NHS; Trs Latin Clb; Rep Stu Cncl; Tennis; 2nd Pl ST Lvl Am Leg Oratrcl Cntst 86; Treas Latin Ntl Hnr Soc 85-86; Coombs Awd 86; Engrng.

ADAM, DANIEL; Conard HS; W Hartford, CT; (Y); 41/308; Cmnty Wkr; German Clb; Political Wkr; Teachers Aide; Mgr(s); Swmmng; Vllybl; Hon Roll; NHS; Spanish NHS; Boston U; Secndry Ed.

ADAMCZYK, DONNA L; North Branford HS; Northford, CT; (Y); 19/148; Church Yth Grp; Cmnty Wkr; Dance Clb; Hosp Aide; Chorus; Variety Show; Var Vllybl; Var Hon Roll; NHS; CT Schltc Achvt 86; H S Schlrshp 86; U Of CT; Nrsng.

ADAMO, M LISS; St Bernard HS; Westerly, RI; (Y); 5/289; Library Aide; Yrbk Stf; Sec Frsh Cls; Stu Cncl; Mgr(s); High Hon Roll; NHS; Pres Schlr; Cheerleading; Acdmc All Am 85-86; Rollns Coll; Premed.

ADAMS, CHRISTOPHER; Wilton HS; Wilton, CT; (Y); 140/360; Ski Clb; Varsity Clb; Bsbl; Var L Lcrss; Im Wt Lftg; Hon Roll; Prfct Atten Awd; Ski Tm-Ltr 85 & 86.

ADAMS, JOHN; Norwalk HS; Norwalk, CT; (Y); Band; Concert Band; Mrchg Band; Pep Band; School Musical; Symp Band; Crs Cntry; Tennis; Hon Roll; Bnkng.

ADAMS, MICHAEL B; The Hotchkiss Schl; Rye, NY; (Y); Pres Model UN; Band; Mrchg Band; Orch; Nwsp Bus Mgr; Nwsp Rptr; Nwsp Stf; Lit Mag; Im Socr; JV L Trk.

ADAMS, PAULENE; W F Kaynor Technical HS; Waterbury, CT; (Y); Pep Clb; SADD; VICA; Variety Show; Yrbk Stf; Rep Sr Cls; Stu Cncl; Hon Roll; NHS; Prfct Atten Awd; Wstrn CT ST U; Med Tech.

ADDESSO, JOHN; Brien Mc Mahon HS; Norwalk, CT; (Y); 32/289; Key Clb; Ski Clb; Lcrss; High Hon Roll; Hon Roll; UCSD; Comp Sci.

ADKINS, MERLE; Ridgefield HS; Ridgefield, CT; (Y); 111/380; DECA; SADD; Ftbl; Golf; Hon Roll; Wrkg Supr Danc MDA 86; U Of NC Chapel Hill; Orthodnts.

ADSHADE, GORDON; Southington HS; Milldale, CT; (Y); 119/600; DECA; JV Bsbl; High Hon Roll; Hon Roll; Central CT; Biochem.

AGARWAL, POORNIMA; Tolland HS; Tolland, CT; (Y); 24/160; Intnl Clb; Spanish Clb; SADD; School Musical; Capt Var Tennis; Hon Roll; NHS; U CT; Intl Bus.

AGASI, DAVID; Manchester HS; Manchester, CT; (Y); Aud/Vis; Church Yth Grp; Cmnty Wkr; Drama Clb; Intnl Clb; School Play; Stage Crew; Variety Show; Hon Roll; U Hrtfrds Rad Sta Anncr WWUH 85-86; Anncr Rad Trinity Coll Rad Sta WRTC 86; Arts.

AGRAWAL, HANS; Simsbury HS; Simsbury, CT; (Y); 2/410; Pres Debate Tm; Math Tm; Quiz Bowl; L Orch; JV Socr; High Hon Roll; NHS; Drtmth Bk Awd 85-86; Ltn Cm Dgnt Awd 84-86; Smsbry Schlr 83-86; Exclnc Engl Awd 85-86.

AGRIA, CAROLYN M; Bunnell HS; Stratford, CT; (Y); Concert Band; Orch; School Musical; Symp Band; High Hon Roll; Trs Church Yth Grp; Band; Church Choir; Hon Roll; Bridgprt Symphny Yng Arts Comptn Fin & Hnrb Mntn 85 & 86; All ST Orch 86, Band 85; Wstrn CT Orch 86; Juilliard Curtis; Music Perfrmn.

AHLGREN, SCOTT D; Glastonbury HS; Glastonbury, CT; (Y); 8/420; Key Clb; Math Tm; Scholastic Bowl; Concert Band; Mrchg Band; Orch; School Musical; High Hon Roll; Ntl Merit SF; Spanish NHS.

AIELLO, CHRIS; East Catholic HS; E Hartford, CT; (Y); 18/270; Lit Mag; Bsbl; Golf; Socr; DAR Awd; High Hon Roll; Hon Roll; NHS; Honore E Awd 85; 1st Hnrs 85-86; Arch.

AIKEN, JOHN M; Fairfield College Preparatory Schl; Shelton, CT; (Y); Key Clb; Model UN; Political Wkr; Chorus; Yrbk Phtg; Ed Yrbk Stf; Sec Stu Cncl; Trk; Cit Awd; Hon Roll; Ordr Dmly Pst Mstr Cnclr Merit Svc Awd, Rep Dmly Awd 86; ST Mstr Cnclr CT ST Chptr Odr Dmly 86-87; Law.

AIRES, IRENE; Danbury HS; Danbury, CT; (Y); 42/577; JA; Varsity Clb; Variety Show; Yrbk Stf; Off Frsh Cls; Off Soph Cls; Off Jr Cls; Off Sr Cls; Cheerleading; DAR Awd; Princeton Book Awd; U RI; Bus Admin.

AKERLIND, KRIS; Avon HS; Avon, CT; (Y); Church Yth Grp; PAVAS; Band; Chorus; Church Choir; Madrigals; Mrchg Band; School Musical; Hon Roll; Al-ST Chorus 86; U Of Hartford; Music Ed.

AKERS, FELICIA; Kolbe-Cathedral HS; Bridgepor T, CT; (Y); VP Church Yth Grp; Hosp Aide; Yrbk Stf; Bsktbl; Hon Roll; Prfct Atten Awd; Nrsg.

AKERS, LITA; Kolbe-Cathedral HS; Bridgeport, CT; (Y); Computer Clb; Drama Clb; Sec Exploring; Hosp Aide; Yrbk Stf; Cheerleading; Hon Roll; NHS; Prfct Atten Awd; VP Spanish NHS; Med.

AKERSON, VALERIE; Bethel HS; Bethel, CT; (Y); 14/250; AFS; Variety Show; Yrbk Stf; JV Mgr Bsbl; L Var Crs Cntry; Trk; High Hon Roll; Kiwanis Awd; NHS; Pres Schlr; Wellsley Book Awd 85; Jr Marshall 85; IN U; Pol Sci.

AKOURY, LISA; Masuk HS; Monroe, CT; (Y); AFS; Ski Clb; Spanish Clb; Hon Roll; Cedar Crest Coll; Engnrng.

AKUMBAK, ROBERT; V F Kaynor Technical Schl; Waterbury, CT; (Y); Drftg.

ALASCIA, VINCENT; Bullard Havens Tech HS; Bridgeport, CT; (S); High Hon Roll; NHS; U Hartford; Music.

ALBERT, MICHAEL; Wilcox Tech HS; Meriden, CT; (Y); SADD; Var Bsbl; Var Bsktbl; Im Bowling; Hon Roll; Rep Jr Cls.

ALBRIGHT, WENDY; Norwich Free Acad; Brooklyn, CT; (Y); Church Yth Grp; Cmnty Wkr; FHA; Hosp Aide; Math Clb; Office Aide; Spanish Clb; Trk; Vllybl; ST Ofc FHA 84-87; Mormn Yth Ldr 83-87; Yth Cmp Cnslr 84-87; Brigham Young U; Math.

ALBRO, KAREN; Watertown HS; Watertown, CT; (Y); 43/250; Pres Trs AFS; Cmnty Wkr; Chorus; Off Soph Cls; Hon Roll; NHS; Dartmouth Bk Clb Awd Of NE Ct; Phys Therapy.

ALCAZAR, NICOLE; Greenwich HS; Greenwich, CT; (Y); Chorus; Orch; High Hon Roll; Hon Roll; Audio Engrng.

ALDO, ALICIA; Shelton HS; Shelton, CT; (Y); Drama Clb; JA; SADD; JV Cheerleading; JV Sftbl; Hon Roll.

ALDSWORTH, SCOTT; Notre Dame HS; Hamden, CT; (Y); 30/232; Computer Clb; Math Clb; Pep Clb; Ski Clb; Spanish Clb; Yrbk Ed-Chief; Lit Mag; Ice Hcky; High Hon Roll; Hon Roll; Babson Coll; Investmnts.

ALEJANDRO, MARTHA; Bassick HS; Bridgeport, CT; (Y); 6/200; Exploring; Hosp Aide; Band; Yrbk Phtg; Sec Sr Cls; Rep Stu Cncl; Var Co-Capt Sftbl; NHS; Pres Schlr; Rotary Awd; Futuro Inc $2000 Schlrshp Awd Hispanic Stu 86; Schlstc Achvmnt Awd $1500 86; Queen & Teen Pgnt 86; Fairfield U; Nrsng.

ALEKSHUN, MICHAEL; Holy Cross HS; Waterbury, CT; (Y); 163/380; Var JV Bsbl; Capt Var Bsktbl; Sci.

ALESSANDRO, JOSEPH; New Fairfield HS; New Fairfld, CT; (Y); 40/240; Cmnty Wkr; Varsity Clb; School Play; Variety Show; Yrbk Sprt Ed; Im Coach Actv; Var Capt Ftbl; Im Wt Lftg; Var Wrstlng; Hon Roll; Washington & Jefferson; Pre-Med.

ALESSI, FRANCENE; Middletown HS; Middletown, CT; (Y); 30/180; Sec French Clb; Teachers Aide; Varsity Clb; Pres Sr Cls; VP Stu Cncl; Capt Cheerleading; Mgr(s); DAR Awd; Hon Roll; Kiwanis Awd; Assumptn Coll; Pol Sci.

ALEXANDER, BRUCE; New Canaan HS; New Canaan, CT; (Y); Church Yth Grp; Debate Tm; NFL; Nwsp Rptr; Yrbk Stf; Pres Sr Cls; L Lcrss; NHS; Boy Scts; French Clb; Eagle Scout 85; Cert Of Achvmnt Sci 84; Lived & Studied In Europe 84; Pre-Med.

ALEXANDER, DAVID; Joseph A Foran HS; Milford, CT; (Y); Key Clb; Stu Cncl; JV Var Bsbl; Wt Lftg; High Hon Roll; Hon Roll; NHS; Frnch II Hnrs Awd 84-85; Hist Awd 84; Stu Cncl 85-86; Engrng.

ALEXANDER, EMILY; Miss Porters Schl; Geneva, IL; (Y); Drama Clb; GAA; School Play; Rep Stu Cncl; Var Capt Socr; 4-H; French Clb; Math Clb; Math Tm; Model UN; Head Of New Girls 86; 10th Pl Chlds Div-IL Hunter & Jmpr Assn 83; Co-Head Stu Guides-Jan 86.

ALEXANDER JR, JOSEPH; Shelton HS; Shelton, CT; (Y); 90/334; Computer Clb; Drama Clb; Ski Clb; SADD; Nwsp Rptr; Var L Socr; Var Trk; High Hon Roll; Hon Roll; Boys Clb Am; Seton Hall U; Comp Pro.

ALEXANDER, SUPRINA; Weaver HS; Hartford, CT; (Y); Computer Clb; JA; Teachers Aide; Rep Stu Cncl; Sftbl; Tchg.

ALEXOPOULOS, EVELYN S; New Britain HS; New Britain, CT; (Y); 1/335; Drama Clb; Math Tm; SADD; Church Choir; Madrigals; Swing Chorus; Church Yth Grp; French Clb; Office Aide; Acpl Chr; Wesleyan U.

ALIANO, JENNIFER; Seymour HS; Oxford, CT; (S); 4/220; AFS; Teachers Aide; Variety Show; Yrbk Stf; Tennis; High Hon Roll; NHS; Southern CT ST U In Fall Hnrs Course Crtcl Inqry 86; Yales Frontiers Appld Sci Semnrs 86.

ALIX, CHRISTYANN; East Catholic HS; Marlborough, CT; (Y); 62/294; Church Yth Grp; Teachers Aide; Band; Svc Awd-H S 86; Saint Joseph Coll; Spcl Ed Tchr.

ALLARD, KELLY; Montville HS; Oakdale, CT; (Y); 14/165; Cmnty Wkr; Rep Soph Cls; Trs Jr Cls; Pres Sr Cls; Rep Stu Cncl; Cit Awd; French Hon Soc; Hon Roll; NHS; Pres Schlr; U Of CT Awd Acdmc Achvmnt 86; Clark U; Intl Affrs.

ALLEN, BETH ANN; St Joseph HS; Ansonia, CT; (Y); 42/220; Drama Clb; Hosp Aide; VP Spanish Clb; Stage Crew; Nwsp Rptr; Lit Mag; Hst Socr; High Hon Roll; Spanish NHS; Schltc Acvht Schlrshp 86; Syracuse U Schlrshp; Syracuse U; Socl Wrk.

ALLEN, JEANNIE; Seymour HS; Seymour, CT; (Y); Variety Show; Nwsp Rptr; Pres Jr Cls; VP Stu Cncl; Capt Twrlr; Hon Roll; Cmmnctns.

ALLEN, TRACY; East Hartford HS; E Hartford, CT; (Y); 80/408; Southenr VT Coll Schlrshp 86; Southern VT Coll; Soc Wrk.

ALLEN, TRACY; West Haven HS; West Haven, CT; (Y); Computer Clb; JA; Q&S; Chorus; Nwsp Stf; Yrbk Stf; Lit Mag; Cit Awd; Hon Roll; Jr NHS; Sthrn CT ST U; Comp Sci.

ALLEN, V M CHRISTY; Wamago Regional HS; Warren, CT; (Y); 15/85; Trs Pres AFS; Am Leg Aux Girls St; Sec Band; Ed Yrbk Ed-Chief; Var JV Tennis; Hon Roll; NHS; Exc Engl,Theater 84-86; Outstndng Effort Chem 85-86; Med.

ALLING, R DOUGLAS; The Gilbert Schl; Torrington, CT; (Y); 2/100; Am Leg Boys St; VP Key Clb; Science Clb; Ski Clb; Spanish Clb; Band; Jazz Band; Capt Socr; Capt Swmmng; Sal; Hrvrd-Rdclff Bk Prz 84-85; O G Williams Schlrshp 86; Cornell U; Engrng.

ALLINSON, DEIRDRE; East Catholic HS; Coventry, CT; (Y); 19/280; Computer Clb; VP French Clb; Math Tm; Band; Church Choir; Pep Band; Yrbk Stf; Rptr Lit Mag; Hon Roll; NHS; Semifnlst US Senate Japan Schlrshp Pgm 84; Smith Coll; Psych.

ALOI JR, JOSEPH ALLEN; Hamden HS; Hamden, CT; (Y); 213/419; Camera Clb; Computer Clb; FCA; JA; Letterman Clb; Ski Clb; SADD; Golf; All Tourn 1st Team Hcky 86; Jr Olympic Selective Camp 85-86; New England Jr Olympics 84-85; Prof Hockey.

ALONZO, JUSTINE; Southington HS; Southington, CT; (Y); 30/600; Latin Clb; Ski Clb; School Play; Nwsp Rptr; Rep Stu Cncl; L Swmmng; Var Trk; Hon Roll; NHS; Hnrb Mntn ST Lat Exam 85; Head Tutorl Pgm Natl Hnr Soc 86-87.

ALVES, LUCIA; Bassick HS; Bridgeport, CT; (Y); 2/190; Key Clb; Yrbk Rptr; Yrbk Stf; High Hon Roll; Hon Roll; Jr NHS; NHS; Schltc Achvt Grant 86; Presdntl Acad Ftns Awd 86; Yale Book Awd 85; Fairfield U; Comp Sci.

ALVORD, LINNEA K; Conard HS; W Hartford, CT; (Y); 8/345; Spanish Clb; Band; Concert Band; Drm & Bgl; Mrchg Band; Orch; Pep Band; School Musical; School Play; Symp Band; Wesleyan Bk Prz 86; All CT Band & Orch 85-86; All New England Band 84-85.

AMADOR, ELIZABETH; Stratford HS; Stratford, CT; (Y); 13/235; Pres JA; Nwsp Stf; Lit Mag; Pres Frsh Cls; Pres Soph Cls; Pres Jr Cls; Pres Sr Cls; Capt Pom Pon; Cit Awd; Hon Roll; Peace Corps Schlrshp To Columbia As Exc Stu 85; Intl Rltns.

AMAIO, RUTH; Southington HS; Southington, CT; (Y); 30/550; Sec Church Yth Grp; SADD; Band; Concert Band; Jazz Band; Mrchg Band; School Musical; Sec Soph Cls; VP Sr Cls; Rep Stu Cncl.

AMATO, ALAN; Seymour HS; Seymour, CT; (S); Wt Lftg; Hon Roll; NHS; Karate Black Belt 84; Annapolis Naval Acad; Law.

AMATO, CHERYLE; Seymour HS; Seymour, CT; (S); 19/192; AFS; Rep Jr Cls; Rep Sr Cls; Rep Stu Cncl; Crs Cntry; High Hon Roll; Hon Roll; NHS; Stage Crew; Nwsp Stf; MA Coll Of Pharmacy; Pharm.

AMATO, JIM; Emmett Obrien RV Tech Schl; Bethany, CT; (Y); Boy Scts; Church Yth Grp; Debate Tm; Ski Clb; Variety Show; Rep Sr Cls; Rep Stu Cncl; Mgr Bsktbl; Socr; Futr Problm Slvrs 86; Laser Tech.

AMBROSE, COLIN; Wethersfield HS; Wethersfield, CT; (Y); 7/289; Am Leg Boys St; Church Yth Grp; Var Bsbl; Var L Bsktbl; High Hon Roll; NHS; NEDT Awd; Prfct Atten Awd; Princeton U Bk Awd 86.

AMICUCCI, MARY; Stamford Catholic HS; Stamford, CT; (Y); 20/156; GAA; Pep Clb; Varsity Clb; Var L Bsktbl; Coach Actv; Var Sftbl; Var Trk; Var Capt Vllybl; High Hon Roll; Hon Roll; Vllybl Ath Scholar 86; U CT; Telecmmnctns.

AMILL, SALLY; Weston HS; Weston, CT; (Y); 61/154; Intnl Clb; Key Clb; Latin Clb; Spanish Clb; Yrbk Stf; Var Stat Bsktbl; Mgr(s); Var JV Powder Puff Ftbl; JV Vllybl; Hon Roll; George Washington U; Intl Affrs.

AMIR-ARJOMAND, KEYVAN; Greenwich HS; Cos Cob, CT; (Y); Am Leg Boys St; Cmnty Wkr; Rep Stu Cncl; Var Swmmng; French Hon Soc; NCTE Awd; NHS; Boys Clb Am; Boy Scts; Church Yth Grp; Yale Alumni Assn Book Awd 86; Math/Sci Achvt Awd 86; Wshngtn Intrn Prgm 86.

AMODEO, MICHAEL; Warren F Kaynor Tech Schl; Naugatuck, CT; (Y); Church Yth Grp; SADD; VICA; Rep Jr Cls; Waterbury ST Tech Coll; Engr.

AMOS, DANNY; New Britain HS; New Britain, CT; (Y); Boys Clb Am; Church Yth Grp; Im Bsbl; Im Bsktbl; Im Ftbl; Capt Mgr(s); Var Score Keeper; Im Vllybl; Im Wt Lftg; Hon Roll; Acctng.

ANCONA, JAMES; Ridgefield HS; Ridgefield, CT; (S); 57/387; Band; Concert Band; Jazz Band; Mrchg Band; Orch; School Musical; Symp Band; Variety Show; Outstndng Musicn Awd 85; Accptnc Wstrn Regnl Symphnc Band 85; Studio Musicn.

ANCONA, JENNIFER; Bristol Eastern HS; Bristol, CT; (Y); Computer Clb; Var Sftbl; High Hon Roll; Hon Roll; Shop Exclnc Awd-Indus Elec 84-85; Comp Sci.

ANDERSON, EDWARD; Fitch SR HS; Groton, CT; (Y); Ftbl.

ANDERSON, JOHN; Bethel HS; Bethel, CT; (Y); 25/245; AFS; Boy Scts; Church Yth Grp; Band; Chorus; Jazz Band; Mrchg Band; High Hon Roll; NHS; Pres Schlr; Century III Ldrs Awd Finlst 86; Widener U 4 Yr Music Schlrhsp 86; Widener U; Mech Engrng.

ANDERSON, KAREN; Newington HS; Newington, CT; (Y); 14/365; Off Church Yth Grp; Pep Clb; Ski Clb; Chorus; Drill Tm; Madrigals; Yrbk Stf; Var Trk; Lion Awd; NHS; Civitan Awd 86; Frfld U; Spch Pthlgy.

ANDERSON, LAURA; Stamford HS; Stamford, CT; (Y); Church Yth Grp; Church Choir; Concert Band; Mrchg Band; Yrbk Stf; Var Capt Cheerleading; Hon Roll; Katharine Gibbs Schl Ldrshp Awd-Future Secy 86; Mst Spirited Chrldr Trophy 85; Coaches Awd Chrldng 86.

ANDERSON, MELANIE; Southington HS; Plantsville, CT; (Y); Latin Clb; Ski Clb; Chorus; High Hon Roll; Hon Roll.

ANDERSON, MICHELE G; Mercy HS; Middletown, CT; (Y); 32/178; Church Yth Grp; Dance Clb; Hosp Aide; Chorus; School Musical; Yrbk Stf; Stat Vllybl; Hon Roll; Pres Schlrshp 86; Fairleigh Dickinson U; Phy Thrp.

ANDERSON, RUDD; Weston HS; Weston, CT; (Y); Dance Clb; Drama Clb; Band; Chorus; Jazz Band; Mrchg Band; School Musical; School Play; Stage Crew; Variety Show; Schlrshp At Amer Ballet Acad 85; NY U; Prfmg Arts.

ANDRE, CHRIS; Weston HS; Weston, CT; (Y); 16/150; Latin Clb; Capt Var Crs Cntry; Var Lcrss; Swmmng; Tennis; Trk; High Hon Roll; NHS; Ntl Merit Ltr; Duke U.

ANDREANA, CRISTINA; Sacred Heart Acad; Stamford, CT; (Y); Sec Church Yth Grp; Girl Scts; Service Clb; Stage Crew; Nwsp Stf; Lit Mag; VP Soph Cls; French Hon Soc; NHS; Variety Show; Socty Of Wmn Engrs Citation 86.

ANDREW, TARA; Franics T Maloney HS; Meriden, CT; (Y); DECA; Hosp Aide; Key Clb; Spanish Clb; Yrbk Stf; Rep Frsh Cls; Rep Soph Cls; Rep Jr Cls; Var Trk; Hon Roll.

ANDREWS, SHERRI; St Marys HS; New Haven, CT; (Y); Church Yth Grp; Cmnty Wkr; Office Aide; Political Wkr; Ski Clb; Spanish Clb; Teachers Aide; Rep Stu Cncl; Bowling; Tennis; Albertus Magnus Coll; Pre Law.

ANDREWS, SUSAN; Nonnewaug HS; Woodbury, CT; (Y); School Play; Stu Cncl; Cheerleading; Gym; Sftbl; Tennis; High Hon Roll; Frnch.

ANGELASTRO, TERESE MARIE; Kent HS; W Nyack, NY; (Y); Nwsp Ed-Chief; Rep Sr Cls; Var Bsktbl; Socr; Sftbl; DAR Awd; High Hon Roll; Pres Schlr; Church Yth Grp; Latin Clb; Rdrs Dgst Schlrshp 84-86; NY ST Rgnts Schlrshp Wnnr 86; WNEPS Bsktbl-Wstrn Nw Englnd Prep Schl 85; Cornell U; Cmnctns.

ANGELINI, MICHELLE; Norwalk HS; Norwalk, CT; (Y); 34/456; Church Yth Grp; Key Clb; Spanish Clb; SADD; Capt Color Guard; Capt Flag Corp; Mrchg Band; Yrbk Stf; Mgr(s); Powder Puff Ftbl; Sci Fair 2nd Pl Chem 86; CT Enrgy Pstr Cont 2nd Pl 84; U Richmond; Bus Math.

ANGELO, DEBBIE; East Haven HS; E Haven, CT; (Y); 38/270; Latin Clb; Ski Clb; Sec Jr Cls; VP Stu Cncl; NHS; CSS Achvt Awd 86; U Of CT; Bio.

ANGLACE, TRACI; Emmett O Brien RVTS HS; Derby, CT; (Y); Church Yth Grp; Library Aide; Ski Clb; Rep Stu Cncl; Var Cheerleading; Var Sftbl; Norwalk ST Tech.

ANGLACE, WAYNE; St Joseph HS; Ansonia, CT; (Y); 44/257; Ski Clb; Spanish Clb; Varsity Clb; Golf; Hon Roll; NEDT Awd; Spanish NHS; Engrng.

ANGLEMYER, CRAIG; Pomperaug HS; Southbury, CT; (Y); Boy Scts; Concert Band; Mrchg Band; Pep Band; JV Var Bsbl; Im Stat Bsktbl; Golf; Mgr(s); U Of CT; Bus.

ANNETT, MICHELLE LOUISE; Immaculate HS; Newtown, CT; (Y); 7/137; Hosp Aide; Ed Yrbk Stf; Rep Stu Cncl; Capt Var Fld Hcky; Var Sftbl; High Hon Roll; Pres NHS; VFW Awd; Church Yth Grp; Cmnty Wkr; Am Optical Yth Undrstndng Schlrshp Finland 85; Yth Sftbl Assoc & Visiting Nurse Assoc Schlrshps 86; Boston Coll; Bio.

ANNICK, JENNIFER; Trumbull HS; Trumbull, CT; (Y); 5/503; Mrchg Band; Ed Nwsp Rptr; Trs Frsh Cls; Var Bsktbl; Var Tennis; Var Capt Vllybl; VP NHS; Ntl Merit Ltr; AFS; Church Yth Grp; Schl Rep CIAC Schlr Athl Awd 86; Gen Elec Stu Tchr Achvt Recog Schlrp 86; Boosters Clb Schlrp 86; GA U; Intl Econ.

ANNINO, JIM; Vinal Regional Vo Tech HS; Haddam, CT; (Y); Yrbk Stf; Rep Stu Cncl; JV Bsbl; Bsktbl; Hon Roll; Elec.

ANNINO, ROB; Coventry HS; Coventry, CT; (Y); Boy Scts; Church Yth Grp; Radio Clb; Teachers Aide; Var L Crs Cntry; Var Golf; Aud/Vis; Drama Clb; Stage Crew; Im Mgr Bsktbl; SR Ptrl Ldr Awd 83; Stu Frgn Exchng Pgm 83; Gudng Eyes Blnd 84; Vet Med.

ANNUNZIATA, CHRISTINA M; Cheshire Acad; Cheshire, CT; (Y); 8/60; Key Clb; VP Jr Cls; Pres Sr Cls; VP Sec Stu Cncl; Stat Bsbl; Stat Bsktbl; Stat Socr; Var Capt Sftbl; DAR Awd; Hon Roll; Boston U; Educ.

ANNUNZIATA, CHRISTOPHER; East Haven HS; E Haven, CT; (Y); 6/250; Am Leg Boys St; Pres Frsh Cls; Pres Soph Cls; Pres Jr Cls; Pres Sr Cls; VP L Ice Hcky; High Hon Roll; NHS; Pres Schlr; U S Army Schlr Athlt Awd 86; Bausch & Comb Sci Awd 86; HOBY Ldrshp Fndtn 84; Boston Coll; Bio.

ANSART, JOHN; Simsbury HS; Simsbury, CT; (Y); Letterman Clb; Varsity Clb; Golf; Lcrss; Lbrl Arts.

ANSTETT, CHRISTINA; East Hapton HS; East Hampton, CT; (Y); Drama Clb; School Musical; Rep Chrmn Stu Cncl; Var Cheerleading; Var Trk; Hon Roll; Tap Dancer In Closing Ceremonies For Liberty Weekend 86; Dance.

ANTALIK, EILEEN; Joseph A Foran HS; Milford, CT; (Y); 7/225; Church Yth Grp; Keywanettes; Yrbk Stf; Rep Stu Cncl; High Hon Roll; Hon Roll; NHS; Gnr Guard 86; 4.0 GPA Cert Of Achvt 86; Elem Ed.

ANTELL, MATT; Staples HS; Westport, CT; (Y); Key Clb; Radio Clb; Yrbk Stf; Im Bsktbl; Ftbl; Lcrss; Var Trk; Bausch & Lomb Sci Awd; Hon Roll; Bus.

ANTONUCCI, BRIAN; Vinal Regional Vocational Tech; Portland, CT; (Y); Library Aide; Ski Clb; Trk; Hon Roll; All-Conf 4x100 Meter Tm 86; ST Open 4x400 Meter Tm 86; Arch Drftsmn.

ANTOSIAK, HANKA; New Britain HS; New Britain, CT; (Y); Var Crs Cntry; Var Trk; Nrsg.

ANTOSIAK, HANNAH; New Britain SR HS; New Britain, CT; (Y); Var Crs Cntry; Var Trk; Nrsng.

ANZIVINE, DEANNA; Crosby HS; Waterbury, CT; (Y); Church Yth Grp; FHA; Hosp Aide; Key Clb; Spanish Clb; SADD; School Musical; Yrbk Stf; Stu Cncl; Hon Roll; Tracy O Day Mrl Awd 86; Otstndng Bus Stu 86; Sec Law.

APICE, ANTHONY D; Fairfield Prep; Fairfield, CT; (Y); Boy Scts; Key Clb; Yrbk Stf; JV Var Crs Cntry; Hon Roll; NHS; Spanish NHS; Scout Of Yr 84 & 85; Sci Fair Hon Mntn 85; Bus.

APPLEBY, JACKIE; St Bernard HS; Old Lyme, CT; (Y); 60/287; Teachers Aide; Yrbk Stf; Var JV Tennis; Hon Roll; Pres Schlr; Hollins Coll Roanoke; Pol Sci.

APREA, NICK; Shelton HS; Shelton, CT; (Y); Var Bsbl; JV Ftbl; Hon Roll; Itln Ntl Hnr Soc 86; Med Tech.

ARAYA, ARTURO O; Christian Heritage HS; Bridgeport, CT; (Y); Pep Clb; Q&S; Soph Cls; Socr; Sftbl; Prfct Atten Awd; TX A & M; Engrng.

ARCHER, SUZANNE; Ridgefield HS; Ridgefield, CT; (S); 58/400; Church Yth Grp; Cmnty Wkr; SADD; Orch; School Musical; Sec Frsh Cls; Rep Stu Cncl; Hon Roll; Pres NHS; Dance Clb; Music Achvt Awd 84; Princpl Flute 83-84; Typng Awd 84; Spec Ed.

ARCIOLA III, SAMUEL P; Staples HS; Westport, CT; (Y); JV Capt Bsbl; Var L Ftbl; Var L Lcrss; Hon Roll; Peter B Weisman Mem Awd 86; Dean JC; Crimnlgy.

ARCOVITCH, HEATHER; Joseph A Foran HS; Milford, CT; (Y); Red Cross Aide; SADD; Lit Mag; Capt L Swmmng; Hon Roll; Jr NHS; NEDT Awd; Art Clb; Church Yth Grp; Girl Scts; Full Tuitn Schlrshp Ed Ctr Arts 86-87; Red Cross Yth Ldrshp Dv Schrlshp 85; Cty Rep Gov Conf 85.

ARIYAN, STEPHAN A; Branford HS; Branford, CT; (Y); Latin Clb; Stu Cncl; Var Capt Swmmng; Hon Roll; All State Swmmng 86.

ARMSTRONG, KRISTIN; Manchester HS; Manchester, CT; (Y); AFS; 4-H; French Clb; Coach Actv; Fld Hcky; Score Keeper; AFS Exchng Stu Dnmrk 86; Bus.

ARMSTRONG, LEIGH A; Greenwich Acad; Greenwich, CT; (Y); Drama Clb; Stage Crew; Nwsp Ed-Chief; Stu Cncl; Var Bsktbl; Var Crs Cntry; JV Fld Hcky; Lcrss; Hon Roll; Ntl Merit SF; Wall Awd Exclnce Am Hist 85; New England Classics Soc Latin Awd 85; Blazer Awd 84 & 85; Jrnlsm.

ARNING, LISA; Greenwich HS; Cos Cob, CT; (Y); Church Yth Grp; Cmnty Wkr; Service Clb; SADD; Chorus; School Musical; Var Mgr(s); High Hon Roll; Hon Roll.

ARNOLD, MICHELE; Rham HS; Marlborough, CT; (Y); Church Yth Grp; Dance Clb; Ski Clb; Variety Show; Var Cheerleading; Im Vllybl; Im Wt Lftg; High Hon Roll; Hon Roll; Jr NHS; MIP Jazz Dance 84; :Dance.

ARROYO, JOSE; Bullard Haven Ruts HS; Bridgeport, CT; (Y); 8/22; Y-Teens; Rep Stu Cncl; Sacred Heart U; Bus Adm.

ARTER, DARLENE; Farmington HS; Hartford, CT; (Y); Bus.

ASCH, DAVID; Brookfield HS; Brookfield Ctr, CT; (Y); 6/220; Math Clb; VP Stu Cncl; Var L Socr; Var L Trk; High Hon Roll; NHS; Harvard Book Awd; Alliance Francaise Awd.

ASCIONE, JOSEPH; Holy Cross HS; Waterbury, CT; (Y); 138/380; Boys Clb Am; Church Yth Grp; SADD; Hon Roll; Elec Contractor.

ASHBY, KAREN; The Masters Schl; West Hartford, CT; (Y); Drama Clb; Pres Exploring; Model UN; School Play; Rep Sr Cls; Var Capt Socr; Var Capt Sftbl; High Hon Roll; NHS; Oberlin Coll.

ASHE, SUSAN; Newington HS; Newington, CT; (S); 11/365; Am Leg Aux Girls St; Band; Chorus; Church Choir; Madrigals; School Musical; Variety Show; Mgr(s); High Hon Roll; NHS; Musicl Productn Awd 84; Annl Schlrs Brkfst 83 & 85.

ASSELIN, LIONEL; Oliver Nolcott Tech; Winsted, CT; (Y); Capt Var Bsbl; Hon Roll; Chess Clb; Varsity Clb; Off Soph Cls; Off Jr Cls; Stu Cncl; Boston Coll; Engrng.

ASSELIN, PHIL; Oliver Wolcott RVTS HS; Winsted, CT; (Y); JV Bsbl; High Hon Roll; Hon Roll; Carpntr.

ATREE, SUSHEEL; East Lyme HS; Niantic, CT; (Y); 1/300; Math Tm; Quiz Bowl; Scholastic Bowl; High Hon Roll; NHS; Ntl Merit Ltr; Rep Stu Cncl; Im Bsktbl; Im Tennis; Med.

AUCOIN, MELISSA; Putnam HS; Putnam, CT; (Y); Chorus; Church Choir; Color Guard; Concert Band; Drm Mjr(t); VP Jr Cls; Off Stu Cncl; Jr NHS; NHS; Twrlr; 1st Pl Drmjr Trphy Hrtg Fstvl 86; Wntrgrd Awd 85; Band Awd 85; Flagler; Tv Brdcstng.

AUDET, CYNTHIA; O H Platt HS; Meriden, CT; (Y); VP Service Clb; Band; Concert Band; Yrbk Stf; Sec Soph Cls; Sec Jr Cls; Sec Sr Cls; Mgr(s); Powder Puff Ftbl; Var Capt Trk; Pblc Rltns.

AUERBACH, JOSHUA D; Greens Farms Acad; Norwalk, CT; (Y); 3/49; Nwsp Stf; Yrbk Stf; Ed Lit Mag; Pres Frsh Cls; Pres Soph Cls; Off Stu Cncl; Ntl Merit Schol.

AUERBACH, RICHARD; Andrew Warde HS; Fairfield, CT; (Y); French Clb; Hosp Aide; Math Clb; Math Tm; Yrbk Stf; Socr; French Hon Soc; High Hon Roll; Chemc Soc Awd 85; Natl JR Sci Sympsm 85-86; Williams/Tufts; Vet Med.

AUGLIERA, KELLY; St Mary HS; New Haven, CT; (Y); Bsktbl; Hon Roll; Class Speakr Awd 86; Optomtrst.

AUGUSTINE, TRACY; St Joseph HS; Stratford, CT; (Y); 170/253; Var Sftbl.

AULT, JONATHAN; Farmington HS; Farmington, CT; (Y); 7/204; Church Yth Grp; Teachers Aide; Mrchg Band; Nwsp Rptr; Ed Nwsp Sprt Ed; Nwsp Stf; High Hon Roll; NHS; Ntl Merit Ltr; Math Achvt Awd; Trinity Coll Bk Awd-Hgh Schltc Stndg & Svc To Schl; Jrnlsm Awd; Fairfield U; Amer Hstry.

AUREA, FIGUERUA; Bassick HS; Bpt, CT; (Y); Computer Clb; Chorus; Sftbl; Vllybl; Hon Roll; Schlstc Achvt Awd 85; Blck Hstry Quz 85; Sthrn CT ST U; Wrd Prcssng.

AUSMUS, BRAD; Cheshire HS; Cheshire, CT; (Y); 11/300; Am Leg Boys St; Var Capt Bsbl; Var Capt Bsktbl; High Hon Roll; Kiwanis Awd; NHS; St Schlr; All ST Bsbl Tm 86; Yale Bk Awd 86.

AUSTIN, BONNIE; Joseph A Foran HS; Milford, CT; (Y); Cmnty Wkr; Drama Clb; JCL; Sec Keywanettes; SADD; Co-Capt Color Guard; School Play; Nwsp Rptr; Yrbk Stf; Stat Swmmng; Comm.

AUSTIN, JOHN A; Northwestern Regional HS; New Hartford, CT; (Y); 15/147; Aud/Vis; Church Yth Grp; 4-H; Ski Clb; Spanish Clb; Frsh Cls; Stu Cncl; Bsbl; Socr; Hon Roll; Winsted Ath Clb Ath Mnth Awd 85; Bst Def Bsbl 85, Soccr 85; Pacholski Mem Awd 86; Fairfield U; Mth.

AUSTIN, SHERRAL; William H Hall HS; W Hartford, CT; (Y); 28/329; Church Yth Grp; Girl Scts; Hosp Aide; Pep Clb; Lit Mag; Capt Lcrss; Socr; High Hon Roll; NHS; Margeret Bollier Awd 86; Pres Acdmc Fit Awd 86; De Paw U; Equine Vet.

AVANZINO JR, KENNETH C; New Canaan HS; New Canaan, CT; (Y); Ski Clb; Coach Actv; Var Ftbl; Var Lcrss; Powder Puff Ftbl; Im Wt Lftg; High Hon Roll; Hon Roll; Iron Man Wghtlftng Awd 85; NCHS; Petroleum Gelgy.

AVERY JR, ROBERT C; F T Maloney HS; Meriden, CT; (Y); Am Leg Boys St; JV Var Bsbl; Var Capt Stu Cncl; Hon Roll.

AVERY, WILL; Granby HS; Granby, CT; (Y); Church Yth Grp; Political Wkr; Hon Roll; Bus.

AVILA, MARITZA; Bulkeley HS; Hartford, CT; (Y); FBLA; Latin Clb; Yrbk Phtg; Rep Stu Cncl; Hon Roll; Upward Bound Wesleyan Coll Prep Pgm Awd 85; NYU; Psych.

AVILES, CARMEN; Hartford Public HS; Hartford, CT; (Y); Bus Wrkr.

AVITABILE, CHRISTOPHER G; West Haven HS; West Haven, CT; (S); DECA; Intnl Clb; Teachers Aide; Var Bsktbl; Hon Roll; Schlstc Exc Awds US Hist, Itln 85; Schlstc Exc Awd DECA 86; Hnr ST Rprtr DECA 86; Food Mktg Awd 86; UNH; Cmnctns.

AVITABILE, VINCENT; Nonnewaug HS; Bethlehem, CT; (Y); Am Leg Boys St; Orch; School Play; Stage Crew; Rep Frsh Cls; Rep Jr Cls; Rep Stu Cncl; Var Capt Bsktbl; Capt Crs Cntry; Var Trk; Washington DC; Pol Sci.

AWLASEWICZ, ANNA; Brookfield HS; Brookfield, CT; (Y); 23/243; AFS; Varsity Clb; School Play; Socr; Var Trk; Capt Vllybl; High Hon Roll; NHS; Certs Achvt 84.

AYAZIDES, ALEXANDRA; Torrington HS; Torrington, CT; (Y); 25/278; Church Yth Grp; Spanish Clb; Varsity Clb; Stage Crew; JV Bsktbl; Var L Socr; Mgr Sftbl; Hon Roll; NHS; Prfct Atten Awd; Marian Awd 84; Math.

AYLES, F MICHAEL; Guilford HS; Guilford, CT; (Y); 60/288; Var L Bsbl; High Hon Roll; Hon Roll; Schltc Achvt Awd-Drftng 83-84; Guilfrd Schlrshp/Guilfrd Bsbl Lge Schlrshp 86; 2nd Tm-All Shrln Bsbl 86; Roger Williams Coll; Arch.

AZIERE, DENISE; Newtown HS; Newtown, CT; (Y); 79/310; VP 4-H; VP FHA; Capt Cheerleading; 4-H Awd; Hon Roll; Western CT ST U.

BAB, EMILY; The Hotchkiss Schl; New York City, NY; (Y); Key Clb; Acpl Chr; Chorus; Madrigals; School Musical; Nwsp Rptr; Var Bsktbl; Var Tennis; Hon Roll; Ntl Merit SF; Spec Faclty Cmmndtn 83.

BABINEAU, ANDREA; Crosby HS; Waterbury, CT; (Y); DECA; Trs JA; Spec Educ.

BACIK, TIMOTHY; Shelton HS; Shelton, CT; (Y); Am Leg Boys St; Spanish Clb; Var L Bsbl; JV Bsktbl; Var Ftbl; High Hon Roll; Spanish NHS.

BACKMAN, AUTUMN; The Masters Schl; Canton, CT; (S); Church Yth Grp; Drama Clb; Pres Girl Scts; Model UN; School Play; Yrbk Phtg; Var L Socr; Var L Sftbl; High Hon Roll; Govt Sci.

BAER, KEVIN; Hopkins Gramor Schl; Woodbridge, CT; (S); JV Bsktbl; Var Capt Golf; CT ST Glf Assoc Jr Chmpn 85; Nw Engld Glft Assoc Jr Chmpnshp 85.

BAGINSKI, ANDREW G; Wolcott HS; Wolcott, CT; (Y); 2/263; Civic Clb; Sec French Clb; Pres Math Clb; Pres Band; School Musical; High Hon Roll; NHS; Ntl Merit Ltr; Pres Schlr; Sal; KC Schlrshp 86; Am Leg Schlrshp 86; CT Schlstc Achvt Awd 86; Wesleyan U; Math.

BAILEY, SUE; Lyme-Old Lyme HS; Old Lyme, CT; (Y); 15/110; AFS; Chess Clb; Dance Clb; Intnl Clb; Variety Show; Stu Cncl; Vllybl; High Hon Roll; Hon Roll; Spanish NHS; Spnsh Hnr Soc 84-86; Intl Bus.

BAINBRIDGE, KATIE; Westover HS; Carmel, IN; (Y); Drama Clb; School Musical; School Play; Lit Mag; Off Jr Cls; Off Sr Cls; JV Lcrss; Church Yth Grp; Dance Clb; PAVAS; Litry Excllnc 86; Eng.

BAKER, AMANDA; Ridgefield HS; Ridgefield, CT; (Y); Aud/Vis; Ski Clb; Swmmng; Trk; UNC Charlotte; Htl Clb Mgmt.

BAKER III, ARTHUR; New Britain HS; New Britain, CT; (Y); 15/375; Church Yth Grp; Chorus; Rep Frsh Cls; Rep Stu Cncl; Var JV Bsbl; Im Bsktbl; Pres Bowling; Var Socr; High Hon Roll; Hon Roll; Naval Acad; Bio.

BAKER, BECKIE J; New Britain HS; New Britain, CT; (Y); 69/306; Church Yth Grp; Hosp Aide; Office Aide; Q&S; Teachers Aide; Nwsp Ed-Chief; Nwsp Rptr; Nwsp Stf; Lit Mag; Hon Roll; Creative Wrtng Awd New Britain Schl Dist 84-86; Utica COLL Syracuse ; Cmmnctns.

BAKER, COURTNEY; Manchester HS; Manchester, CT; (Y); Drama Clb; French Clb; FBLA; Hon Roll.

BAKER, ERIK; Seymour HS; Seymour, CT; (S); 1/200; JV Bsbl; Var Bsktbl; Var Ftbl; Var Trk; Var Wt Lftg; High Hon Roll; NHS; U PA; Engrng.

BAKER, KRISTEN; Norwich Free Acad; Norwich, CT; (Y); Church Yth Grp; Cmnty Wkr; English Clb; Hosp Aide; Letterman Clb; Science Clb; Varsity Clb; Sec Soph Cls; Pres Stu Cncl; Var L Sftbl; Wellesley Bk Awd Hgh Schlstc Achvt 86; Newton Perkins Mdl Awd Excel Frnch 84; Mrshl Cls 86 Grad 86; Med.

BAKER, MEREDITH; Lyme-Old Lyme HS; Old Lyme, CT; (Y); 38/105; Vllybl; Excellnc Engl 83-84; Psych.

BAKER, SARAH; Greenwich HS; Old Greenwich, CT; (Y); AFS; Cmnty Wkr; Band; Hon Roll; U S Air Force Mst Outstndg Sci Prjct 86; SEER Fnlst SR Div ST Sci Fair; U S Dept Of Enrgy Spcl Awd.

BAKER, TODD; Wethersfield HS; Wethersfield, CT; (Y); Church Yth Grp; Ski Clb; Off Stu Cncl; Var Diving; Var L Socr; Var L Swmmng; Var L Trk; Hon Roll; Econ.

BALDO, RENEE; North Haven HS; N Haven, CT; (Y); 65/287; Drama Clb; French Clb; L JA; Variety Show; Hon Roll; Exc In Scl Studies & Viedo Prod 86; Exc In Media Clb; Quinnipiac Coll; Physcl Thrpy.

BALDWIN, ANGELA; Hamden HS; Hamden, CT; (Y).

BALDWIN, LISA; Warren F Kaynor Tech; Wolcott, CT; (Y); VICA; Stat Bsbl; Var Capt Bsktbl; Mgr(s); Score Keeper; Stat Socr; Hon Roll; Most Agresv Bsktbl Plyr Awd; Most Athletic Ad; Mattatuck CC; Legal Assist.

BALINSKAS, BETH; Southington HS; Southington, CT; (Y); 42/550; Hosp Aide; Key Clb; Ski Clb; Yrbk Stf; Var L Tennis; High Hon Roll; Hon Roll; NHS; Jaycees Mem Schlrshp 86; Mitchell J Porydzy II Mem Schlrshp 86; U CT; Bus.

BALL, JONATHAN S; Conard HS; West Hartford, CT; (Y); 70/320; Boy Scts; Jazz Band; Socr; Hon Roll; JP Sousa Awd; Church Yth Grp; Band; Church Choir; Concert Band; Mrchg Band; Hartford Jazz Soc 85; Berklee Coll Jazz Perf 85; Western MI U 86; Western MI U; Bus.

BALOGH, PATRICIA; Sacred Heart Acad; New Haven, CT; (Y); 40/122; Church Yth Grp; Cmnty Wkr; French Clb; Hosp Aide; Latin Clb; Pep Clb; Stage Crew; Variety Show; Im Vllybl; Computer Clb; U Of CT; Pre-Bus.

BANATOSKI, JILL; Lewis S Mills HS; Burlington, CT; (Y); 1/172; Am Leg Aux Girls St; Church Yth Grp; Pres Exploring; Model UN; Church Choir; Color Guard; Sec Frsh Cls; Twrlr; Bausch & Lomb Sci Awd; Dnfth Awd; Harvard Bk Awd 86; H O Brien Ldrshp Smnr Ambssdr & Jr Cnslr 85-86; Advncd Jr Miss Mjrtte Ne 86; Med.

BANKS, TERI; New Canaan HS; New Canaan, CT; (Y); Var Fld Hcky; Im Powder Puff Ftbl; Var Sftbl; Hon Roll.

BANTON, JENNIFER; Bassick HS; Bridgeport, CT; (Y); Church Yth Grp; Red Cross Aide; Spanish Clb; Chorus; Church Choir; School Musical; Prfct Atten Awd; MAT Impvmnt Awd 86; Fairfld U Upwrd Bnd Prog 85; Blck Hstry Cntst 85; Pharmacy.

BARAN, ALLISON; Windsor Locks HS; Windsor Locks, CT; (Y); 11/169; Church Yth Grp; VP JA; Model UN; Office Aide; Nwsp Rptr; Nwsp Stf; Var Capt Cheerleading; Mgr Gym; Hon Roll; 3rd Rnnr Up JR Prom 86; Bus Admin.

BARAN, LISA; Southington HS; Plantsville, CT; (Y); Sec DECA; Pep Clb; Var Trk; Bus.

BARBIERI, JANET; Watertown HS; Oakville, CT; (Y); Art Clb; FBLA; Physcl Thrpy.

BARDELL, KRISTIN; Griswold HS; Groton, CT; (Y); 8/79; Sec GAA; Varsity Clb; Yrbk Phtg; Yrbk Stf; Chrmn Sr Cls; JV Vllybl; Cit Awd; High Hon Roll; Pres Schlr; UN Pilgrimage For Yth 85; U Of CT; Engl.

BARILLARO, RONALD; H C Wilcox Reg Voc Tech School; Meriden, CT; (Y); Exploring; SADD.

BARIS, DAWN; Danbury HS; Danbury, CT; (Y); 65/481; Trk; Hon Roll; Law.

BARKER, JULIE; Guilford HS; Guilford, CT; (Y); 32/300; VP Church Yth Grp; Drama Clb; French Clb; Co-Capt Flag Corp; School Play; Variety Show; Yrbk Stf; French Hon Soc; Hon Roll; Vrsty Fncng Ltr 85-86; JR Sci & Hmnts Sym 86; 3rd Awd SR Div CT Sci Fair 84; SCI.

BARLOW, SARA; St Joseph HS; Stratford, CT; (Y); Drama Clb; Hosp Aide; Ski Clb; Spanish Clb; Stage Crew; JV Swmmng; JV Trk; Hon Roll; Nrsg.

BARNARD, DAVID; Fairfield College Preparatory Schl; New Canaan, CT; (Y); VP Key Clb; Stu Cncl; Var Ftbl; Var Capt Lcrss; High Hon Roll; NHS; Hist.

BARNES, KIM; Glastonbury HS; Glastonbury, CT; (Y); Ski Clb; SADD; Yrbk Stf; Rep Soph Cls; Rep Jr Cls; Rep Stu Cncl; Var Cheerleading; Mgr Socr; Hon Roll; Mrktg.

BARNES, LAURI; Greenwich HS; Saugerties, NY; (Y); Church Yth Grp; GAA; Girl Scts; Sec JA; Library Aide; Church Choir; High Hon Roll; Hon Roll; Ulster County CC.

BARNES, MALCOLM; W F Keynor Tech; Waterbury, CT; (Y); Drama Clb; Yrbk Stf; Crs Cntry; U Of CT; Elec Engr.

BARONE, DEBORAH; Holy Cross HS; Prospect, CT; (Y); 116/380; Yrbk Stf; Pres Frsh Cls; Pres Soph Cls; VP Jr Cls; VP Sr Cls; JV Var Bsktbl; Capt Var Cheerleading; JV Var Sftbl; Hon Roll; Church Yth Grp; Bus Admnstrtn.

BARR, KENYA; Joseph A Foran HS; Orange, CT; (Y); 23/240; Trs Church Yth Grp; JCL; Letterman Clb; Stu Cncl; Var L Gym; Var L Trk; Var L Vllybl; Hon Roll; Ntl Merit Schol; St Schlr; Outstndng Sci Awd 82; U Of VA; Chld Psych.

BARRETT, ANDREW C; Roger Ludlowe HS; Fairfield, CT; (Y); Church Yth Grp; Trs Soph Cls; Trs Jr Cls; Trs Sr Cls; JV Socr; Var Trk; High Hon Roll; NHS; Holy Crs Bk Awd 86; Aviatn.

BARRY, CHRIS; Simsbury HS; West Simsbury, CT; (Y); 126/405; JA; Varsity Clb; JV Var Bsbl; JV Var Ftbl; Powder Puff Ftbl; Hon Roll; JC Awd; U IA; Mech Engrng.

BARRY, CHRISTOPHER J; St Bernard HS; Preston, CT; (Y); 49/287; Bsbl; Bsktbl; Acad Hnrs 84-86; Fine Art Awd 83; Worcester Poly Tech Inst; Engr.

BARRY, ERIC; Weaver HS; Hartford, CT; (Y); Aud/Vis; Boy Scts; JA; Church Choir; Lit Mag; Accntng.

BARRY, KEVIN; Fairfield College Preparatory Schl; Easton, CT; (Y); Am Leg Boys St; Key Clb; SADD; Chorus; Ed Nwsp Stf; Rep Sr Cls; Sec Stu Cncl; JV Lcrss; High Hon Roll; School Play; Chaplncy Tm 84-85; Spcl Olympcs 84-85; Chrstn Life Cmnties 85-86; Advrtsng.

BARRY, WILLIAM J; Daniel Hand HS; Madison, CT; (Y); 42/276; Church Yth Grp; French Clb; Model UN; Ski Clb; Concert Band; Jazz Band; Mrchg Band; Var L Socr; Band; Natl Soc Stds Olympd Hons Awd 85; Syracuse U; Poltcl Sci.

BARSTOW, MICHAEL; Housatonic Valley Regional HS; Sharon, CT; (Y); Ski Clb; JV Var Bsbl; JV Var Ftbl; High Hon Roll; Hon Roll; Peer Ed Counseling 85-86; Outstndg Citizen HVRHS 86; Hon Ment Bi Valley Ftbll Leag 85; Bus.

BARTINIK, JENNIFER; St Bernard HS; Groton, CT; (Y); 40/265; French Clb; Ski Clb; SADD; Acpl Chr; Chorus; Rep Frsh Cls; Rep Soph Cls; Rep Jr Cls; Stat Socr; Hon Roll; Bus Admn.

BARTLETT, DENISE; RHAM HS; Marlborough, CT; (Y); Am Leg Aux Girls St; JCL; Latin Clb; Co-Capt Math Tm; Trs Spanish Clb; High Hon Roll; NHS; Ntl Merit Ltr; Scty Of Women Engr Cert Of Merit 86; Pre-Med.

BARTLETT, VALERIE; East Hartford HS; E Hartford, CT; (Y); 36/445; Trs Sec JA; Quiz Bowl; Spanish Clb; Yrbk Phtg; Yrbk Stf; Rep Soph Cls; Hon Roll; NHS; Crmnl Jstc.

BARTLEY, NEAL; Wamogo Regional HS; Goshen, CT; (Y); 1/85; Computer Clb; French Clb; Stat Bsbl; Stat Bsktbl; L Mgr(s); Score Keeper; High Hon Roll; Hon Roll; NHS; SAR Awd; Citation From Wmns Leag Of Engrs 86; MIT; Comp Sci.

BARTNER, NICOLE; Brookfield HS; Brookfield, CT; (Y); 10/276; SADD; Varsity Clb; Orch; Nwsp Stf; Ed Lit Mag; Capt Crs Cntry; Trk; High Hon Roll; VP NHS; Ntl Merit SF; Bst Stu Frnch III; Bst Stu Crtv Wrtng; Cornell U; Vet Med.

BARTOLOTTA, LISA; St Joseph HS; Ansonia, CT; (Y); 21/220; Cmnty Wkr; Drama Clb; Rep Spanish Clb; Stage Crew; Nwsp Rptr; Yrbk Rptr; Ed Lit Mag; High Hon Roll; NEDT Awd; Spanish NHS; U CT; Lib Arts.

BARTON, GLEN; Mark T Sheehan HS; Wallingford, CT; (Y); 81/197; Pres VP AFS; VP Pres Church Yth Grp; German Clb; Chorus; School Musical; School Play; Variety Show; Hon Roll; US Navy; Hosp Corp.

BARTON, LISA; Manchester HS; Manchester, CT; (Y); VP AFS; Drama Clb; FBLA; Girl Scts; School Play; JV Socr; Hon Roll; Awd Excllnt Wrk Guid Aide 84; Culinary Inst; Chef.

BARTON, LORI; Conard HS; West Hartford, CT; (Y); 35/315; Church Yth Grp; Pep Clb; Rep Sr Cls; Capt Cheerleading; Var Gym; JV Trk; High Hon Roll; Hon Roll; NHS; Hartwick Coll.

BARTONE, LISA; Shelton HS; Shelton, CT; (Y); 66/315; Art Clb; Sacred Heart U; Lgl Asst.

BARTYZEL, HELEN B; Newington HS; Newington, CT; (Y); 30/363; Key Clb; Intnl Clb; Political Wkr; JV Bsktbl; High Hon Roll; Hon Roll; Var Tennis; Magna Cum Laude Natl Latn Exm 83-84; U Of CT; Dietcs.

BASCHE, DAVID; William H Hall HS; W Hartford, CT; (Y); Cmnty Wkr; Drama Clb; School Play; Bsbl; JV Capt Socr; High Hon Roll; Thtr Awd 86; Emerson Coll; Comm.

BASSETT, JENNIFER; Danbury HS; Danbury, CT; (Y); Cmnty Wkr; Hosp Aide; Acpl Chr; Band; Chorus; Concert Band; Jazz Band; Mrchg Band; Pep Band; Stage Crew; Med.

BASSETT, TAMMY; Maloney HS; Meriden, CT; (Y); Ed Key Clb; Yrbk Stf; Rep Frsh Cls; Rep Soph Cls; Rep Jr Cls; Stu Cncl; Capt Fld Hcky; Stu Cncl; High Hon Roll; Hon Roll; Soc Wmn Engrs Merit Awd 86; Athltc Jckt Awd 86.

BATCHELOR, SHAWN; Fairfield Prep; Shelton, CT; (Y); Chess Clb; Drama Clb; Math Tm; High Hon Roll; NHS; Spanish NHS; Overall Wnnr Sci Fair 84; Hnrb Mntn Sci Fair 85; 2nd Pl Overall Strength Bridge Bldg Sci Fair 86; Elec Engrng.

BATES, SUSAN M; Lyman Hall HS; Wallingford, CT; (Y); 4-H; Trs FBLA; Girl Scts; JA; Office Aide; SADD; Teachers Aide; Chorus; Stu Cncl; Bowling; Spnsh Awd 82; JR Achvt Awd 82; Ftr Bus Ldrs Amer; Quinnipiac Coll; Fnc.

BATISTA, MIRIAM; Stratford HS; Stratford, CT; (Y); 11/257; Cmnty Wkr; Drama Clb; Spanish Clb; Lit Mag; Hon Roll; NHS; Wnnr Bst Essy Army Rsrv Essy Cntst 85; Psychlgy.

BATTAGLIA, DAWN; Berlin HS; Berlin, CT; (Y); 9/200; Var Capt Socr; Var L Sftbl; Var L Trk; Hon Roll; Amer H S Athl 84-85; All Conf Selctn Sccr & Trck 85-86; Outstndng Achvt Awd Sccr Goalie 83-84; Phy Thrpst.

BATTALIN, JUNE; Farmington HS; Farmington, CT; (Y); 55/240; Ski Clb; Spanish Clb; SADD; Chorus; Yrbk Stf; Powder Puff Ftbl; Bus.

BATTS, TARA; R E Fitch SR HS; Groton, CT; (Y); Keywanettes; High Hon Roll; Hon Roll; Excllnc Sci 83-84; Excllnc Math 83-84; GIA; Gmlgy.

BAYENDOR, HOLLY; Greenwich HS; Old Greenwich, CT; (Y); 2/764; Cmnty Wkr; Color Guard; Yrbk Phtg; Yrbk Sprt Ed; Var Stat Bsbl; Score Keeper; DAR Awd; NHS; Church Yth Grp; Varsity Clb; GASFA 86; CT Schlstc Achvmnt Grnt 86; Bio Awd 83; Hmpshr Coll; Vsl Cmmnctns.

BAYSINGER, HEINRICH; Joseph A Foran HS; Milford, CT; (Y); Ski Clb; Spanish Clb; Yrbk Stf; Ftbl; Hon Roll; TX A&M; Comm Pilot.

BAZAKAS, TODD; Westhill HS; Stamford, CT; (Y); 31/409; German Clb; JA; Ski Clb; Nwsp Stf; Stu Cncl; Hon Roll; NHS; Pres Schlr; U Of CA Berkeley; Bus.

BAZZANO, KIM; Orville H Platt HS; Meriden, CT; (Y); Trk; Hon Roll; UCONN; Soc.

BEAUCHENE, CATHLEEN; New Britain HS; New Britain, CT; (Y); Church Yth Grp; Drama Clb; JA; SADD; Chorus; Hon Roll; St Joseph; Nrsg.

BEAUDOIN, LISA; St Bernard HS; North Franklin, CT; (Y); 38/297; Cmnty Wkr; Exploring; FNA; Hosp Aide; Red Cross Aide; Yrbk Stf; Stu Cncl; Hon Roll; Awds Acadmc Excllnc 84-86; Presdntl Acadmc Ftns Awd 86; Spnsh IV Awd 86; St Joseph Coll; Nrsng.

BEAUDREAU, ELIZABETH; Simsbury HS; Simsbury, CT; (Y); 70/410; Church Yth Grp; Yrbk Sprt Ed; Var Capt Socr; Var Capt Trk; Hon Roll; Ntl Merit Ltr; CT ST Slct Sccr Tm 85-86; 6th Pl Mdl Rly Cls Meet 86.

BEAULAC, BETH ANN; Tolland HS; Tolland, CT; (Y); Camera Clb; Church Yth Grp; French Clb; Yrbk Stf; Lit Mag; High Hon Roll; Hon Roll; Outstndng Acadmc Achvt Art Awd 86; CT Indpnt Coll Schlrshp 86-87; Eng Awd 83-84; Hartford Art Schl; Graphic Dsgn.

BECHER, THOMAS; Greenwich HS; Greenwich, CT; (Y); Pres JA; Pres Radio Clb; Nwsp Ed-Chief; Nwsp Rptr; Nwsp Sprt Ed; Nwsp Stf; JV Socr; Hon Roll; Natl HS Jrnlst Yr-Fnlst 86; Northwestrn U; Jrnlsm.

BECK, DAVID; Naugatuck HS; Naugatuck, CT; (Y); 56/309; Trs Drama Clb; Chorus; Drm & Bgl; Drm Mjr(t); Jazz Band; Madrigals; Orch; Sec Symp Band; Tennis; Hon Roll; Kollege Kappers Schlrshp 86; Audrey Thayers Schlrshp Music 86; Keilocker Schlrshp 86; Ithaca Coll; Music Ed.

BECK, JOHN D; Windsor HS; Windsor, CT; (Y); 10/315; Church Yth Grp; VP Drama Clb; FBLA; Quiz Bowl; Scholastic Bowl; Drm & Bgl; School Play; JC Awd; NHS; Ntl Merit SF; Econ.

BECK, STACY; Plainfield HS; Moosup, CT; (Y); 7/127; Am Leg Aux Girls St; Model UN; Pres Frsh Cls; Pres Soph Cls; Pres Jr Cls; Pres Sr Cls; Rep Stu Cncl; Im Powder Puff Ftbl; Im Trk; DAR Awd; Internatl Youth Yr Essay Cntst Wnnr 85; CT U; Political Sci.

BECKENSTEIN, MICHELE; Guilford HS; Guilford, CT; (Y); Key Clb; Ski Clb; Temple Yth Grp; Orch; Nwsp Rptr; Nwsp Stf; Badmtn; Crs Cntry; Fld Hcky; Golf; Northeastern U; Mrktng.

BECKER, DIRK; Ridgefield HS; Ridgefield, CT; (Y); 78/380; Cmnty Wkr; Letterman Clb; Ski Clb; SADD; Varsity Clb; Band; Concert Band; Mrchg Band; Pep Band; Symp Band; Ski Tm Cpt, 3 Hr Ltrmn 83-87; Grmn Awd 86; Hnr Rll 86-87; Rensselaer Polytech Inst; Engrg.

BECKER, LIBBE; Brien Mc Mahon HS; Norwalk, CT; (Y); Exploring; Stat Ice Hcky; Hon Roll; Silvermine Guild Smmr Schrlshps 85; Hickory Hill Figure Sktng Clb Achvt Certf 83-84.

BECKERER, TARA; Lauralton Hall HS; Milford, CT; (Y); 20/119; Math Clb; Model UN; Trs Service Clb; Acpl Chr; Chorus; School Musical; School Play; Stu Cncl; NHS; NEDT Awd; Spain Sngng Grp 85; Dncd In MTV Video 86; Awd For Excep Prfrmnc On Natl Latin Exam 84; Phys Thrpy.

BECKERLEG, ANNE MARIE S; Canton HS; Canton, CT; (Y); Chorus; Madrigals; School Musical; Lit Mag; High Hon Roll; Hon Roll; Wellesley Bk Awd 86; Frgn Lang.

BECKING, ALEXANDER; Southington HS; Southington, CT; (Y); 39/600; Am Leg Boys St; Aud/Vis; Pres Church Yth Grp; Key Clb; Im Bsktbl; JV Crs Cntry; L Trk; Hon Roll; NHS; Dist Yth Cncl Pres 86-87.

BECKMANN, DEBORAH E; Guilford HS; Guilford, CT; (Y); Yrbk Phtg; Yrbk Stf; Pres Frsh Cls; Trs Soph Cls; Rep Stu Cncl; Hon Roll; NHS; Ntl Merit Ltr; Brd Of Drctrs Gulfrd Yth Srv Bureau 85; A Btr Chnc Clb 84; Exc In Lng Arts Awd 85 & 86.

BECOTTE, DONNA; St Bernard HS; Bozrah, CT; (Y); 27/289; French Clb; Flag Corp; Off Jr Cls; DAR Awd; Hon Roll; Chapman Fndtn Scholar 86; Bozrah Town Scholar 86; Band Awds 86; U CT; Chem Engrng.

BEDARD, MICHELLE; Berlin HS; Berlin, CT; (Y); 3/220; Am Leg Aux Girls St; Sec Frsh Cls; VP Jr Cls; VP Sr Cls; Powder Puff Ftbl; Sftbl; Vllybl; High Hon Roll; Hon Roll; NHS; HOBY Ldrshp 85; Pres Prom Comm 86; Bus.

BEELER, BRIAN; Putnam HS; Pomfret Center, CT; (Y); Cmnty Wkr; Brynt Coll; Bus Mgmt.

BEERS, JULIE; Oliver Wolcott Tech; Cornwall Bridge, CT; (Y); Art Clb; VICA; Band; Mrchg Band; Yrbk Stf; Hon Roll; NHS; Cosmetldy.

BEINEKE, SARAH; Windsor HS; Windsor, CT; (Y); 30/330; Pres Church Yth Grp; 4-H; Intnl Clb; Chorus; Church Choir; Concert Band; Pep Band; Cit Awd; 4-H Awd; Hon Roll; Concordia Coll; Elem Ed.

BELFIORE, TODD; Oliver Wolcott Tech HS; Kent, CT; (Y); Boy Scts; Ski Clb; Hon Roll; NHS; Engr.

BELIASOV, PAUL J; Hartford Christian Acad; Manchester, CT; (Y); 1/5; Acpl Chr; School Play; Yrbk Ed-Chief; Pres Sr Cls; Var Bsktbl; Cit Awd; Hon Roll; Val; Church Yth Grp; Chorus; Bob Jones U.

BELL, HEATHER; Northhaven HS; North Haven, CT; (Y); 23/299; Art Clb; Aud/Vis; PAVAS; Ski Clb; Nwsp Phtg; Nwsp Rptr; Yrbk Stf; High Hon Roll; Hon Roll; Spanish NHS; Fairfield U; Law.

BELL, JEREMY; Marianapolis Prep Schl; Brooklyn, CT; (Y); 12/47; Church Yth Grp; High Hon Roll; Hon Roll; Whenton Coll; Bus.

BELL, LOUANN; Farmington HS; Unionville, CT; (Y); 18/230; Church Yth Grp; Cmnty Wkr; Hosp Aide; Ski Clb; Spanish Clb; Band; Yrbk Stf; NHS; Spanish NHS.

BELL, MARY; Wethersfield HS; Wethersfield, CT; (Y); 75/350; Letterman Clb; Nwsp Rptr; Cheerleading; Co-Capt Gym; Swmmng; Hon Roll; Merrimac Coll Boston MA; Bus.

BELLEFONTAINE, JOAN; East Lyme HS; Salem, CT; (Y); 78/257; FHA; VP Frsh Cls; Pres Soph Cls; Pres Jr Cls; Stu Cncl; JV Var Cheerleading; Var L Crs Cntry; Var Powder Puff Ftbl; Var L Sftbl; High Hon Roll; Lawrence & Memorial Hosp; Nuclr.

BELLITTO JR, ROBERT B; Fairfield Prep; Fairfield, CT; (Y); Church Yth Grp; Q&S; Spanish Clb; Nwsp Rptr; Nwsp Stf; JV Crs Cntry; JV Trk; Spanish NHS; Mark Walinowski Awd Bsbl 84; Frfld U; Attrny.

BELLOCK, SANDRA; Brookfield HS; Brookfield, CT; (Y); 9/218; Church Yth Grp; Drama Clb; Pres Girl Scts; Math Tm; Chorus; Var L Trk; High Hon Roll; Lion Awd; Pres NHS; Ntl Merit Ltr; Girl Scout Silver,Gold Awd 84-85; U CT Alumni Assoc Awd 86; U CT; Puppetry.

BELMONTE, SUSAN; Torrington HS; Torrington, CT; (Y); 27/283; Drama Clb; Latin Clb; Varsity Clb; Chorus; Stage Crew; Stat Bsbl; Stat Bsktbl; Score Keeper; High Hon Roll; Hon Roll; Med Tech.

BELOIN, DAN; South Windsor HS; S Windsor, CT; (Y); 90/290; Cmnty Wkr; Math Tm; Im Bsbl; Im Bsktbl; Im Sftbl; Im Wt Lftg; Hon Roll; Prfct Atten Awd; U Of CT; Math.

BELSITO, KARIN; Tolland HS; Tolland, CT; (Y); 8/175; Band; Jazz Band; Madrigals; Mrchg Band; School Musical; Stage Crew; Rep Sr Cls; JV Var Vllybl; High Hon Roll; NHS; Tolland Schrlshp 86; U Hartford Hnrs Piano Recitl 86; NCCC Chorus Band 84-85; Holy Cross Coll; Pre-Med.

BEMBERIS, KIMBERLY; Ridgefield HS; Ridgefield, CT; (Y); 24/381; Hosp Aide; Scholastic Bowl; SADD; Capt Tennis; High Hon Roll; NHS; Yale Smmr Pgm Gftd JR 86; Pre-Med.

BENAMATI, SUSAN A; Torrington HS; Torrington, CT; (Y); 29/280; Cmnty Wkr; Trs Exploring; Hosp Aide; Model UN; Ski Clb; Stage Crew; Trs Sr Cls; High Hon Roll; NHS; Candystriper Svc 86; Wesminister Sem Term Paper Pblshd 85 & 86; Intl Law.

BENAVIDES, LISA M; Coginchaug Regional HS; Durham, CT; (Y); 6/135; Am Leg Aux Girls St; Hosp Aide; Yrbk Ed-Chief; Sec Stu Cncl; Var Cheerleading; Var Tennis; Cit Awd; High Hon Roll; Sec NHS; Pres Schlr; Centry III Ldrshp Awd 86; Brown U; Poli Sci.

BENDER, BETH; Fitch SR HS; Groton, CT; (Y); Cmnty Wkr; Hosp Aide; Intnl Clb; Library Aide; Office Aide; Red Cross Aide; Science Clb; Yrbk Rptr; Stu Cncl; Powder Puff Ftbl; Psych.

BENDZA, SHIRLEY; Miss Porters HS; Kensington, CT; (Y); Cmnty Wkr; GAA; Spanish Clb; Nwsp Rptr; Yrbk Stf; Off Frsh Cls; JV Co-Capt Fld Hcky; Cit Awd; Hon Roll; Latin Awd 84; Sci Awd 84; Music Awd 84; PSYCH.

BENEDETTO, LOUIS; Fairfield Preparatory Schl; Fairfield, CT; (Y); Church Yth Grp; Spanish Clb; Var L Bsbl; Im Bsktbl; JV Ftbl; Var L Tennis; Hon Roll; Spanish NHS; USTA Natl Ranked Ten Plyr 84; NELTA 3rd 84; Law.

BENITEZ, MARIA D; Wilbur L Cross HS; New Haven, CT; (S); 31/265; Sec Church Yth Grp; French Clb; Library Aide; Pres Spanish Clb; Hmntrn Awd 84-85; Spc Olympc Vlntr 82-83; Quinnipiac Coll; Intl Bus.

BENNETT, AMY; East Lyme HS; E Lyme, CT; (Y); 50/250; Church Yth Grp; Ski Clb; SADD; Varsity Clb; Color Guard; Flag Corp; Mrchg Band; Hon Roll; Cmnty Wkr; Spanish Clb; Zoology.

BENNETT, JOSEPH; Enrico Fermi HS; Enfield, CT; (Y); 38/339; Am Leg Boys St; VP Drama Clb; School Musical; Rep Stu Cncl; High Hon Roll; NHS; Pres Schlr; U Of CT.

BENNETT, SCOTT; Branford HS; Branford, CT; (Y); Rep Stu Cncl; Var L Bsktbl; JV Golf; Hon Roll; All ST Clss L Bskbtl Tm 85-86; All Cnty Bsktbl Tm 85-86; All Housatonic Lg Bskbl Tm 85-86; Bus Adm.

BENNETT, TAMMY; Maloney HS; Meriden, CT; (Y); UCONN; Bus Admin.

BENNETT, YVONNE; Weaver HS; Hartford, CT; (Y); Cmnty Wkr; JA; Teachers Aide; School Musical; Rep Stu Cncl; Var Trk; Capt Vllybl; Interacl Schlrshp 86; Weaver Hi Cls 1948 Schlrshp 86; Alpha House Schlrshp 86; U Of Hartford; Psych.

BENNI, BILL; Branford HS; Branford, CT; (Y); 74/320; Band; Concert Band; Jazz Band; Mrchg Band; Pep Band; Var JV Bsbl; Crs Cntry; Var Ice Hcky; Hon Roll; Northeastern; Mgmt.

BENOIT, DAWN M; Putnam HS; Putnam, CT; (Y); Church Yth Grp; Ed Yrbk Bus Mgr; Yrbk Stf; Rep Frsh Cls; Rep Jr Cls; Rep Stu Cncl; Co-Capt Cheerleading; Trk; Jr NHS; Intr Arch Dsgn.

BENTZ, STEPHEN; Southington HS; Plantsville, CT; (Y); 70/550; Library Aide; Spanish Clb; Var Bsbl; JV Bsktbl; Ftbl; Hon Roll; Cmmnctns.

BENWAY, PENNIE; Windham HS; W Willington, CT; (Y); 4-H; U Of CT.

BENYSEK, KRISTINA; Brookfield HS; Brookfield Center, CT; (Y); Band; Concert Band; Mrchg Band; Lit Mag; High Hon Roll; Hon Roll; Microbio.

BERGLUND, HANS; Hopkins Grammar Day Schl; Branford, CT; (S); Boy Scts; Service Clb; Ed Yrbk Phtg; Lit Mag; Var Capt Lcrss; Socr; Var Capt Swmmng; Eagle Scout Awd 83; Yale U Frntrs Of Apld Sci Prgm 85; Archtctr.

BERMAN, JANETTE; Thomaston HS; Thomaston, CT; (Y); 11/67; Spanish Clb; JV Bsktbl; JV Sftbl; Hon Roll; Spnsh Heritage 3 Wk Exchng Prog To Spain 85; Hosted Stu From Spain 84-85; Fash Merch.

BERNDT, MATTHEW; Fairfield College Prepartory Schl; Norwalk, CT; (Y); Cmnty Wkr; Im Bsktbl; Var Golf; High Hon Roll; Hon Roll; Golf Clb 85.

BERNIER, NEIL; Southington HS; Southington, CT; (Y); Yrbk Ed-Chief; Yrbk Stf; Golf; Hon Roll; Tunxis CC; Graphic Arts.

BERNITZKI, SASCHA; East Granby HS; E Granby, CT; (Y); Boy Scts; JA; Trk; Sls.

BERNSTEIN, ANYA; Guilford HS; Guilford, CT; (Y); 23/320; Church Yth Grp; Cmnty Wkr; Hosp Aide; Model UN; Quiz Bowl; Chorus; VP Stu Cncl; DAR Awd; Hon Roll; NHS; Yth Yr Awd 86; Exc Soc Sci Awd 86; Colby Bk Awd 86; Barnard Coll; Prof.

BERRY, DAWN MARIE; St Bernard HS; Norwich, CT; (Y); Church Yth Grp; Cmnty Wkr; Pres French Clb; Hosp Aide; Yrbk Stf; Rep Jr Cls; Rep Sr Cls; Chrmn Stu Cncl; Var Tennis; Hon Roll; Acdmc Exc For Hnr Roll 86; Inst Of Food Tech Schlrshp 86; U RI; Bio Chmcl Engrng.

BERTOLA, JOHN; Southington HS; Southington, CT; (Y); Ski Clb; Stage Crew; Bsbl; L Ftbl; L Wrstlng; Hon Roll; Crim Justc.

BERUBE, TARA; Southington HS; Southington, CT; (Y); Concert Band; Mrchg Band; School Play; Stu Cncl; Var Trk; Hon Roll; NHS; Discvry III Giftd/Tlntd Stu 85; Nrsng.

BESSETTE, DEBRA; Plainfield HS; Plainfield, CT; (Y); 36/169; Hon Roll; Nrsg.

BEST, MONA; James Hillhouse HS; New Haven, CT; (Y); Art Clb; Drama Clb; Library Aide; Math Tm; Chorus; Church Choir; Yrbk Stf; Rep Frsh Cls; JV Gym; High Hon Roll; Marines; Nrsng.

BETZ, KAREN; Sacred Heart Academy; Stamford, CT; (Y); Art Clb; Yrbk Stf; Sftbl; Trk; Advncd Art Awd 85 & 86; Outstndng H S Athlts Of Amer 85; Fairchstr Leag-All Leag Sftbl Awd 85; Southwest TX ST U; Grphc Dsgn.

BEUST, LESLIE; Stratford HS; Stratford, CT; (Y); 8/257; JA; Spanish Clb; Rep Soph Cls; Rep Jr Cls; High Hon Roll; Hon Roll; Awd Of Merit Spnsh 86.

BEZIO, TWILA; Bristol Central HS; Bristol, CT; (Y); Hosp Aide; Ski Clb; Band; Concert Band; Mrchg Band; Symp Band; Socr; Phys Ftnss Awd 83-86; CPR 85-86; U CT; Vet.

BIANCHI, MARK; Amity Regional SR HS; Woodbridge, CT; (Y); 143/388; Boy Scts; Band; Concert Band; Mrchg Band; Orch; U Of New Haven; Engr.

BIANCO, DANIELLE; Trumbull HS; Trumbull, CT; (Y); Church Yth Grp; Spanish Clb; Band; Mgr(s); Score Keeper; High Hon Roll; HS Athletic Awd Sccr 84-85.

BIBEAU, PAULA; Windham Vo Tech; Willimantic, CT; (Y); Church Yth Grp; Hosp Aide; VICA; Church Choir; Yrbk Stf; High Hon Roll; Hon Roll; NHS; Prfct Atten Awd; Outstndng-Arch Drftng-2nd 86; Schlrhsp Awd 86; 3rd Pl-Arch Drftng-CT Skll Olympcs 86; Hrtfrd ST Tech Coll; Cvl Engr.

BIEBEL, JOHN T; Frank Scott Bunnell HS; Stratford, CT; (Y); 49/260; French Clb; JA; Yrbk Stf; Lit Mag; Hon Roll; Cooper Union Schl Art Scholar 86; CT Yth Issues Town Rep 85; PBS Stu Art Fest Fin 86; Cooper Union; Graphic Desgn.

BIELAK, BEN; Lyman Hall HS; Wallingford, CT; (Y); 3/287; Quiz Bowl; Off Stu Cncl; Var L Tennis; High Hon Roll; Pres NHS; Brian Faustman Memrl Awd Excllnc Hnrs Bio 85; MENSA 86; Plntry Soc 85; MIT; Physcs.

BIELLO, DOM; Watertown HS; Oakville, CT; (Y); 26/260; NHS; Attrny.

BIERMAN, TIM; Fairfield College Prep Schl; Greens Farms, CT; (Y); Key Clb; Service Clb; Chorus; Var Capt Socr; Var Tennis; High Hon Roll; NHS; Liberal Arts.

BILELLO, KRISTINA; Shelton HS; Shelton, CT; (Y); Latin Clb; Spanish Clb; Hon Roll; NHS; Ntl Merit Ltr; Spanish NHS; Latin Natl Hnr Soc 85; 1st Pl Statue Of Liberty Essay Cont 85; Biology.

BILLINGS, LISA; Norwalk HS; Norwalk, CT; (Y); 12/456; Trs French Clb; Trs Key Clb; Ski Clb; Mrchg Band; School Musical; Nwsp Rptr; VP Soph Cls; JV Tennis; High Hon Roll; NHS; Prncpls Advsry Cmmtee 84-85.

BILOTTA, JASON; Holy Cross HS; Woodbury, CT; (Y); 10/392; Concert Band; Jazz Band; School Musical; Var Ftbl; Var Lcrss; Var Swmmng; French Hon Soc; High Hon Roll; NHS; Latin Clb; Vocal Jazz Ensmbl; Pre-Med.

BINDER, DARREN TODD; Avon HS; Avon, CT; (Y); 29/172; JA; Political Wkr; Ski Clb; Temple Yth Grp; Nwsp Ed-Chief; High Hon Roll; NHS; Safe Rides 84-86; Exc Awd Analytic Geo 85; Pres Acad Ftns Awd 86; U Connecticut; Math.

BINGHAM, MARY JANE; Avon HS; Avon, CT; (Y); Chorus; JV Cheerleading; Var Crs Cntry; Var Trk; Hon Roll; VP NHS; Church Yth Grp; French Clb; Math Tm; Band; Bus Wk Schlrshp 86; Cls Rep Avon Safe Rides 85-86; Kids For Kids 86; Close Up Schlrshp Wnnr 86; Pol Sci.

BIRCHENOUGH, PAM; Farmington HS; Farmington, CT; (Y); #32 In Class; Ski Clb; Capt Crs Cntry; Capt Trk; Hon Roll; ST Sci Fair Awd 86; Mt Holyoke Coll; Bio.

BIRDSELL, MARY; Seymour HS; Seymour, CT; (S); 5/194; Church Yth Grp; JA; Yrbk Ed-Chief; Rep Frsh Cls; Rep Soph Cls; High Hon Roll; Sec NHS; Yth Yr 86; U MD.

BIRMINGHAM, SUSAN; Pomperaug HS; Southbury, CT; (Y); 14/202; Sec Church Yth Grp; Library Aide; Concert Band; Mrchg Band; Orch; Symp Band; Capt Socr; Trk; NHS; Natl Sci Olympiad 1st Pl Bio 85; U Of CT; Bio.

BISHOP, JENNIFER; Torrington HS; Torrington, CT; (Y); GAA; Spanish Clb; Stat Bsktbl; Mgr(s); Score Keeper; Sftbl; High Hon Roll; Hon Roll; Prfct Atten Awd; Var Ltr Bsktbl & Sftbl; 1st Pl Trnmnt Tr Phy Sftbl 84 & 85; Accntnt.

BISHOP, LESLEY; Simsbury HS; Simsbury, CT; (Y); 80/352; AFS; Church Yth Grp; German Clb; Key Clb; Ski Clb; Concert Band; Mrchg Band; Pep Band; Hon Roll; Jr NHS; Penn ST; Aerospc Engr.

BISO, CHRISTINE; Ansonia HS; Ansonia, CT; (Y); French Clb; Yrbk Stf; Pom Pon; Hon Roll; The Briarwood Book Awd 86; Bay Path JC Alumnae Assn Awd 86; Acctng.

BITTNER, PATTY; Berlin HS; Berlin, CT; (Y); 10/200; Nwsp Stf; Var Powder Puff Ftbl; Var Socr; Var Trk; High Hon Roll; NHS; Occptnl Thrpy.

BLACK, CAROLYN; East Catholic HS; Marlborough, CT; (Y); 20/300; Chess Clb; Computer Clb; Math Tm; Rep Jr Cls; High Hon Roll; NHS; Schlrshp Hnr Awd 86; U CT Cprtv Prgm Awd For Supr Acad Achvt 86; 2nd Pl Wnnr In Hartford Crnt 86; Bryant Clg; Comp Info Systms.

BLACK, GWEN; Putnam HS; Pomfret Center, CT; (Y); Computer Clb; High Hon Roll; Hon Roll; Dudley Hall; Exec Sec.

BLACK, MATTHEW; Hopkins Grammar Schl; New Haven, CT; (S); Nwsp Rptr; Nwsp Sprt Ed; Nwsp Stf; Var L Ftbl; Var Trk; Var Wrstlng; Mrt Brwstr Thmpsn Schlr; Krby Sci Prz; Teacher.

BLACKIE, LINDA; Griswold HS; Glasgo, CT; (Y); 30/79; Girl Scts; Hon Roll; Psych.

BLACKWOOD IV, ANDREW W; Amity Regional HS; Orange, CT; (Y); 102/388; Band; Mrchg Band; Orch; School Musical; Symp Band; Ntl Merit Ltr; Music Scholar Boston U; Music.

BLAIR, TRACIE; Bristol Central HS; Bristol, CT; (Y); GAA; Varsity Clb; Yrbk Stf; Off Sr Cls; Bsktbl; Sftbl; Vllybl; Hon Roll; Rookie Of The Year 84-85; All Confrnc Sftbll 86; Hon Mntn Vllybll 85; Bus.

BLAIS, GRETCHEN; Watertown HS; Watertown, CT; (Y); AFS; Computer Clb; Hosp Aide; VP Spanish Clb; Pres SADD; Band; Yrbk Sprt Ed; Off Frsh Cls; Off Soph Cls; Trk; Proj Sage; Bio.

BLAKE, CHARLIE; Berlin HS; Berlin, CT; (Y); Nwsp Phtg; Nwsp Stf; Yrbk Phtg; JV Var Bsktbl; JV Var Ftbl; Var Capt Tennis; Aerontcl Sci.

BLAKE, DIANE; Seymour HS; Oxford, CT; (Y); 26/186; Trs Church Yth Grp; Drama Clb; Hosp Aide; Office Aide; Band; Concert Band; Mrchg Band; Orch; Stage Crew; Hon Roll; Oxford Jr Women Club Schlrshp 86; VT Coll-Norwich U; Nrsng.

BLAKE, FREDERICK G; The Hotchkiss Schl; Baldwin, NY; (Y); Band; Church Choir; Concert Band; Mrchg Band; Orch; JV Bsbl; JV Bsktbl; Im Coach Actv; Im Socr; Cit Awd; Lehigh; Astrphycs.

BLAKE, SUSAN; Southington HS; Southington, CT; (Y); 81/601; FBLA; Key Clb; Red Cross Aide; Stage Crew; Yrbk Stf; Mgr Cheerleading; Mgr(s); Powder Puff Ftbl; High Hon Roll; Jr NHS; Outstndng Svc Awd Of Key Clb 85-86; Schl Of Hartford Hosp; Rdlgc.

BLANCHARD, BRUCE; Tourtellotte Memorial HS; N Grosvenordale, CT; (Y); 2/95; Am Leg Boys St; Yrbk Ed-Chief; Var Bsbl; Var Bsktbl; High Hon Roll; NHS; Prfct Atten Awd; Sal; Drama Clb; Church Yth Grp; CT Schlr-Ath Awd 86; Amer Opticl Scholar Awd 86; U CT; Med Tech.

BLANCHARD, MARIANNE; Holy Cross HS; Waterbury, CT; (Y); 160/380; Church Yth Grp; 4-H; Var Cheerleading; Grammar Schl CYO 82 & 84-86; New Englnd Champs Chrldng Trophies 83 & 85; Hrsbck Rdng 1st Pl 76-78; ST Tech Coll; Comp.

BLANCO, MARIA; The Taft Schl; Watertown, CT; (Y); Dance Clb; Debate Tm; French Clb; GAA; Intnl Clb; Spanish Clb; School Play; Stage Crew; Nwsp Rptr; Yrbk Rptr; Bst Athl Awd 84; Taft Schl; Econ.

BLANK, RANDALL; Cheshire HS; Cheshire, CT; (Y); 20/287; School Musical; Stage Crew; Mgr Ed Nwsp Stf; Yrbk Stf; High Hon Roll; Sec NHS; Ntl Merit Ltr; Debate Tm; Science Clb; Stu Cncl; Hampshire Coll; Cmnctns.

BLANKER, CHRIS; Robert E Fitch SR HS; Groton, CT; (Y); 28/370; Cmnty Wkr; Intnl Clb; Science Clb; Band; Nwsp Ed-Chief; Nwsp Rptr; VP Stu Cncl; Bsbl; Crs Cntry; Hon Roll; Columbia U; Poly Sci.

BLAYDES, MARGARET; Miss Porters Schl; Lexington, KY; (Y); French Clb; Hosp Aide; Service Clb; Nwsp Stf; Yrbk Bus Mgr; Socr; Capt Var Tennis; Hon Roll; Ntl Merit Ltr; Usher 86-87; Dorm Rep 85-86; Stu Actvts Committee 84-87.

BLAYNEY, MICHELLE; Danbury HS; Danbury, CT; (Y); Church Yth Grp; Hosp Aide; Ski Clb; Yrbk Stf; George W Perry Awd Frgn Lang/Spnsh 85; Ntl Fed Of Music Piano Solo 83; Nrs.

BLEYLE, JODY; Staples HS; Westport, CT; (Y); Aud/Vis; Pres Church Yth Grp; German Clb; Radio Clb; Acpl Chr; Church Choir; Jazz Band; School Musical; Symp Band; Nwsp Bus Mgr.

BLINSTRUBAS, THOMAS; Holy Cross HS; Waterbury, CT; (Y); 34/346; JV Bsbl; Var Bsktbl; Hon Roll; NHS; Ntl Merit SF; Pres Schlr; U CT; Bus Fnc.

BLODGET JR, HUGH R; Manchester HS; Manchester, CT; (Y); Am Leg Boys St; German Clb; School Musical; L Var Crs Cntry; L Var Ice Hcky; L Var Trk; NHS; Ntl Merit Schol; Cngrs Bndstg Yth Exchng Schlrshp 85-86; Nvl Acad Smmr Smnr 85; Cornell U; Engrng.

BLOOM, ALLISON; Joel Barlow HS; Easton, CT; (Y); Aud/Vis; Cmnty Wkr; Drama Clb; Teachers Aide; Thesps; Chorus; School Musical; School Play; Stage Crew; Yrbk Stf; ST Cert Emergncy Med Tech; Lwyr.

BLOOM, ERICA; Trumbull HS; Trumbull, CT; (Y); AFS; Latin Clb; Library Aide; Office Aide; VP Spanish Clb; Yrbk Stf; Sec Stu Cncl; Mgr(s); High Hon Roll; Hon Roll.

BLUM, DENA; Amity Regional SR HS; Orange, CT; (Y); 47/388; Cmnty Wkr; Drama Clb; FBLA; Latin Clb; Pep Clb; SADD; Temple Yth Grp; Band; Concert Band; Mrchg Band; Yrbk Sls 85-86; Cum Laude Natl Latn Exm 84-85; Clark U; Law.

BOARDMAN, DOUGLAS; East Granby HS; E Granby, CT; (Y); 7/57; Drama Clb; Band; Chorus; School Musical; Variety Show; VP Frsh Cls; Var L Bsbl; Var L Socr; High Hon Roll; NHS.

BOBBITT III, JOHN T; Ridgefield HS; Ridgefield, CT; (Y); 34/376; Aud/Vis; Boy Scts; German Clb; Trs Radio Clb; Pres Stage Crew; JV Crs Cntry; Hon Roll; Eagle Scout With Gld, Brnz & Slvr Mdls 83; Grmn-Amer Exch 84 & 86; Order Of Arrow 83; Aerospace Engrng.

BOCK, MICHELLE; Naugatuck HS; Naugatuck, CT; (Y); 82/300; Church Yth Grp; Chorus; Church Choir; Hon Roll; Mattatuck CC; Accntng.

BODAK, MICHELLE; St Joseph HS; Ansonia, CT; (Y); Girl Scts; Hosp Aide; JA; Spanish Clb; Yrbk Stf; Hon Roll; NEDT Awd; Comm.

BODIE, BETH; Branford HS; Branford, CT; (Y); 101/320; Church Yth Grp; Latin Clb; Office Aide; Yrbk Stf; Rep Stu Cncl; Stat Bsktbl; Var Cheerleading; JV Fld Hcky; JV Mgr(s); Feat Artcl Seventeen Maz Chrldng 84-85; Mst Imprvd Awd Chrldng 84; JR Prom; Ed.

BOEHM, MELISSA; Windsor HS; Windsor, CT; (Y); Intnl Clb; Model UN; Yrbk Stf; Var L Socr; Var L Sftbl; Spanish NHS; Spanish Clb; Trk; Hon Roll; Prfct Atten Awd; Comm.

BOGAN, CHRISTOPHER; Hopkins HS; Branford, CT; (S); Art Clb; Boy Scts; Chess Clb; Drama Clb; Nwsp Stf; Yrbk Stf; Lit Mag; Rep Jr Cls; Var Trk; Area HS Art Show Paint & Clay Clb Awd 82; Engnrng.

BOGAN, JACK; Ridgefield HS; Ridgefield, CT; (Y); Church Yth Grp; Spanish Clb; Var L Bsktbl; High Hon Roll; Spnsh Bk Awd; Outstdng Achvt Bio & Adv Math.

BOGANSKI, CHRISTINE; Horace Wilcox Technical Schl; Meriden, CT; (Y); 52/220; Art Clb; Computer Clb; English Clb; Teachers Aide; Variety Show; Yrbk Rptr; Yrbk Stf; Rep Frsh Cls; Rep Soph Cls; Rep Jr Cls; Waterbury CT; Intr Dsgn.

BOGARDUS, KATHLEEN; East Granby HS; E Granby, CT; (Y); 19/62; Dance Clb; Band; Chorus; Yrbk Stf; Capt L Bsktbl; Var L Socr; Var Capt Sftbl; High Hon Roll; Hon Roll; Prfct Atten Awd; Spnsh I & Engl II Excel 84 & 85; Intr Dsgn.

BOGART, KRIS; The Morgan HS; Clinton, CT; (Y); 14/160; AFS; French Clb; Girl Scts; Quiz Bowl; SADD; Chorus; Stage Crew; Yrbk Stf; Stu Cncl; Var L Trk; Psychlgy.

BOGNAR, CHRISTINE; Saint Joseph HS; Shelton, CT; (Y); Dance Clb; Drama Clb; Hon Roll; Jill Chase Dance Studio 5 Yr Awd 83; Bronze Mdl In Dance Mstrs Of Amer Cmpttn 83.

BOHL, DOUG; Norwalk HS; Norwalk, CT; (Y); 3/450; Computer Clb; German Clb; Chorus; School Musical; High Hon Roll; NHS; Yth Rep Parsh Cncl 85; Brwn Bk Awd, JR Outstndng Eng 86; Aerosp Engrg.

BOHLMAN, STEPHEN; Southington HS; Plantsville, CT; (Y); Ski Clb; JV Bsbl; JV Bsktbl; Var L Ftbl; High Hon Roll; Hon Roll; NHS; Engrng.

BOISSONEAU, MICHELLE; Berlin HS; Kensington, CT; (Y); 23/220; 4-H; Hosp Aide; Band; Concert Band; JV Bsktbl; Powder Puff Ftbl; Socr; Var Capt Trk; Hon Roll; NHS; Phy Thrpy.

BOISVERT, RONALD; Morgan HS; Clinton, CT; (Y); 28/143; French Clb; High Hon Roll; Hon Roll; Aeronautical Engr.

BOIUCANER, ANCA; Farmington HS; Farmington, CT; (Y); 30/230; Band; Mrchg Band; Nwsp Phtg; Nwsp Rptr; Nwsp Stf; Rep Soph Cls; Fld Hcky; Tennis; French Hon Soc; High Hon Roll.

BOIVIN, DENISE; St Joseph HS; Stratford, CT; (Y); 20/250; French Clb; Ski Clb; Nwsp Rptr; Yrbk Stf; Stu Cncl; Var JV Cheerleading; Var Trk; French Hon Soc; High Hon Roll; NHS; Wellesley Book Awd 86; Engrng.

BOLAND, JEFF; Farmington HS; Burlington, CT; (Y); 66/200; Hon Roll; Art.

BOLBROCK, MARYPAT; Manchester HS; Manchester, CT; (Y); Church Yth Grp; SADD; Teachers Aide; Orch; High Hon Roll; Hon Roll; Law.

BOLDUC, JOEL; Windham HS; Willimantic, CT; (Y); 37/280; Am Leg Boys St; High Hon Roll; Prsdntl Acdmc Ftnss Awd 86; U Of CT; Engnrng.

BOLES, TAMMY; East Lynne HS; Salem, CT; (Y); 42/280; Key Clb; Cheerleading; Fld Hcky; Gym; Mgr(s); Powder Puff Ftbl; Trk; Hon Roll; Eastern CT ST U; Bus Trvl.

BONADIES, TRACEY LYN; Farmington HS; Unionville, CT; (Y); 38/206; Ed Yrbk Bus Mgr; Yrbk Stf; High Hon Roll; Hgst Avg Accntng I Awd 86; U CT Storrs; Accntng.

BONATO, DONNA JEAN; Farmington HS; Farmington, CT; (Y); 25/217; Am Leg Aux Girls St; Church Yth Grp; Math Tm; Spanish Clb; Varsity Clb; Chorus; Yrbk Ed-Chief; Rep Frsh Cls; Rep Soph Cls; Rep Jr Cls; Hugh O Brien Ldrshp 85; Boston Coll; Archtctr.

BONHAGE, JOHN; Brien Mc Mahon HS; Norwalk, CT; (Y); 29/300; Am Leg Boys St; Church Yth Grp; JA; Mrchg Band; Symp Band; Rep Jr Cls; Var L Socr; Var L Trk; Hon Roll; NHS; Norden Systms Essay Cntst; Wilderness Chl Summer 85; Polt.

BONIN, DAVID; East Lyme HS; Niantic, CT; (Y); 8/275; Boy Scts; Church Yth Grp; Drama Clb; School Musical; Stage Crew; JV Golf; High Hon Roll; Hon Roll; NHS; Bob Strecker Mem Sprtsmnshp Awd Babe Ruth 85; Pre Med.

BONITO, RONALD R; Derby HS; Derby, CT; (Y); Ski Clb; Varsity Clb; VP Soph Cls; Rep Stu Cncl; JV Bsbl; JV Bsktbl; Var Capt Ftbl; Psych.

BONTEMPO, PAMELA MARIE; Daniel Hand HS; Madison, CT; (Y); 24/272; Church Yth Grp; French Clb; Nwsp Stf; High Hon Roll; Hon Roll; NHS; Principals Sem 86; Ladies Auxialary NMVFD Schlrshp 86; Boston U; Phychology.

BONTRAGER, JAMES; Seymour HS; Seymour, CT; (Y); Computer Clb; Debate Tm; Swmmng; Valparaiso U; Mech Engr.

BOOK, JAMES; Wilton HS; Wilton, CT; (Y); 104/356; Pep Clb; Varsity Clb; Mrchg Band; Rep Stu Cncl; Capt L Crs Cntry; Var Lcrss; Hon Roll; Cross Cntry 4 Yr Varsty 2 Yr Capt Ldrshp Awd 85.

BOOKER, DOROTHEA; E Hartford HS; East Hartford, CT; (Y); 39/384; Co-Capt Drill Tm; Rep Sr Cls; Rep Stu Cncl; Var Tennis; High Hon Roll; Hon Roll; Sec NHS; Aud/Vis; Drama Clb; FBLA; Princpls Achvt Awd; Outstndng Svc Stu Cncl; Outstndng Eng Stu; Child Psychlgy.

BOOS, SCOTT; Fairfield College Preparatory Schl; Fairfield, CT; (Y); Debate Tm; Exploring; Model UN; Service Clb; Im Socr; Var Trk; JV Wrstlng; High Hon Roll; Hon Roll; NHS; Internatl Studies.

BORCHETTA, PETER M; St Marys HS; Greenwich, CT; (Y); 8/52; Am Leg Boys St; Boys Clb Am; Capt Var Bsbl; Capt JV Bsktbl; Capt Var Ftbl; Var Golf; Score Keeper; Hon Roll; NHS; Yale Cup Awd; Med Rsrch.

BORGES, AGOSTINHO; Crosby HS; Waterbury, CT; (Y); Var Socr; Hon Roll; Elec Engr.

BORGHESI, LISA; Torrington HS; Torrington, CT; (Y); 35/283; FBLA; Key Clb; Ski Clb; Spanish Clb; Thesps; Pep Band; Stage Crew; Nwsp Phtg; High Hon Roll; NEDT Awd; Physics.

BORLA, CATHY; Torrington HS; Torrington, CT; (Y); 2/270; Pres Drama Clb; Latin Clb; Model UN; Sec Thesps; School Musical; School Play; Nwsp Rptr; Yrbk Stf; Pres NHS; Pres Frsh Cls; Hgh O Brn Yth Ldrshp Orgnztn; Ctr Crtv Yth Wslyn U; Cert Excllnc Soc Wmn Engnrs.

BOROVY, DENISE; Oliver Wolcott Tech Schl; Torrington, CT; (S); 39/147; VICA; Nwsp Ed-Chief; Rep Jr Cls; Sec Stu Cncl; Var Co-Capt Sftbl; Hon Roll; MI ST U; Hortculture.

BORRELLI, LAIRD; William H Hall HS; W Hartford, CT; (Y); 18/324; Church Choir; Nwsp Stf; Yrbk Bus Mgr; Stu Cncl; Capt Crs Cntry; High Hon Roll; Hon Roll; NHS; Spanish NHS; Dartmouth Bk Club Awd 85; NHS Merit Awd/Schlrshp 86; Michaels Jewlers Awd 86; Unesco Schlrshp 86; Boston Coll; Intl Bus.

BOSCH, MEGAN; Pomperaug HS; Southbury, CT; (Y); Math Tm; SADD; Concert Band; Var Socr; JV Sftbl; Hon Roll; Pub Lib Cultural Essay Awd 86; Lib Arts.

BOSMA, LISA; Southington HS; Southington, CT; (Y); Church Yth Grp; Key Clb; Spanish Clb; Chorus; Church Choir; Hon Roll; New England Singing Awd 85; MA Church Choir Awd 84; Music Awd 86; Acad Of Business Careers; Nrsng.

BOSSONE, VIRGINIA; Brien Mc Mahon HS; S Norwalk, CT; (Y); Pres FBLA; GAA; Rep Frsh Cls; Rep Soph Cls; Rep Jr Cls; Var Powder Puff Ftbl; Var JV Sftbl; High Hon Roll; Hon Roll; NHS; Ldrshp Awd Katherine Gibbs 86; Miss Teen Pangt 86; U Connecticut; Bus Adm.

BOTET, ALFREDO; Bullard Hayens Tech; Bridgeport, CT; (S); 7/150; Exploring; Var L Crs Cntry; Var L Socr; Var L Trk; High Hon Roll; Pres Racqtbl Clb 85-86; Engrng.

BOTTICELLO, JULIE; East Hartford HS; E Hartford, CT; (Y); 5/400; Spanish Clb; SADD; Nwsp Stf; Yrbk Ed-Chief; Yrbk Stf; Diving; High Hon Roll; NHS; Pres Schlr; Outstndng 4 Yr Stdnt Forgn Lang Spnsh, Engl 86; Yrbk Awd 86; Fordham U; Mktg.

BOUCHER, GREGORY; Rham HS; Andover, CT; (Y); 4/158; AFS; FBLA; Math Tm; Ski Clb; Capt Crs Cntry; Capt Trk; High Hon Roll; Hon Roll; Jr NHS; NHS; CT Schlr Athl Awd 86; All COC 800 M & 4x400 M Tm 86; Excllnc Engl 86; Coll Voltaire Switzrlnd; Stdnt.

BOUCHER, MAURA; East Windsor HS; Broad Brook, CT; (Y); Am Leg Aux Girls St; Church Yth Grp; Pep Clb; Nwsp Rptr; Yrbk Ed-Chief; Rep Frsh Cls; Rep Soph Cls; Rep Jr Cls; Rep Sr Cls; Rep Stu Cncl; Wslyn U Ctr For Crtv Yth 85; Close Up 86; Mgzn Drive 86-87; Syracuse U RI; Vsl Arts.

BOUCHER, SCOTT; Plainfield HS; Wauregan, CT; (Y); Boy Scts; Varsity Clb; JV Ftbl; Var L Trk; Hon Roll; Voice Dem Awd; Annapolis; Aero Engr.

BOUDREAU, DEIRDRE; East Catholic HS; S Windsor, CT; (Y); 28/279; Drama Clb; Chorus; Church Choir; School Musical; School Play; Variety Show; Lit Mag; Var Twrlr; High Hon Roll; Prncpls Awd Ctznshp & Schlrhshp 86; Cmmnctns.

BOUDREAU, DENISE; Southington HS; Plantsville, CT; (Y); 112/570; Cmnty Wkr; Pep Clb; Ski Clb; Fld Hcky; Sftbl; Hon Roll; Northeastern U.

BOUDREAU, SCOTT; Guilford HS; Guilford, CT; (Y); Hst Boy Scts; Bsbl; Tennis; S CT; Acctg.

BOUFFARD, STEVEN; Rham HS; Andover, CT; (Y); 37/194; JV Bsbl; Hon Roll; Hova U; Comp Prgmr.

BOULANGER, TODD; Holy Cross HS; Waterbury, CT; (Y); 51/380; Church Yth Grp; Cmnty Wkr; SADD; School Musical; Var L Lcrss; Hon Roll; NHS; Spanish NHS.

BOULDREAU, DENISE; Southington HS; Pantsville, CT; (Y); 112/570; Cmnty Wkr; Ski Clb; Fld Hcky; Var Sftbl; Hon Roll; Nrtheastrn; Pharm.

BOULE, MICHELE; East Hampton HS; E Hampton, CT; (Y); Girl Scts; Band; Concert Band; Mrchg Band; Rep Stu Cncl; Var Bsktbl; Var Capt Socr; Var Capt Sftbl; Hon Roll; Mst Offnsv Soccer Plyr 85; Jr All Amer Band Hnrs 85; Amer Musical Fndtn Band Hnrs 85; Phy Therapy.

BOURBEAU, LISA; Putnam HS; Putnam, CT; (Y); Chess Clb; Spanish Clb; Teachers Aide; Band; Concert Band; Mrchg Band; High Hon Roll; Hon Roll; Jr NHS; NHS; Bus Mgt.

BOURNE, KATHRYN; Greenwich HS; Cos Cob, CT; (Y); Church Yth Grp; JA; Chorus; School Musical; Swing Chorus; Variety Show; Var Badmtn; Mgr(s); Powder Puff Ftbl; Merit In Music Cert 83; Musical Achvt Cert 86; Mt St Mary Coll; Nrs.

BOWEN, MELISSA; Seymour HS; Seymour, CT; (Y); 34/192; High Hon Roll; Hon Roll; Most Outstndng Bus Stu 85; Briarwood Bk Ad 85; Stone Schl; Acctng.

BOWEN, SUZANNE; Sacred Heart Acad; West Haven, CT; (Y); French Clb; FBLA; Var Capt Bsktbl; Var Capt Sftbl; Hon Roll; NHS; NEDT Awd; Natl Sci Olympd Chem 86; Stu Of 86 Jr Olympcs Bsktbl Tm; All-CT Conf 1st Tm Bsktbl 86; Pre Law.

BOWERS, RAY K; Derby HS; Derby, CT; (Y); 13/106; Am Leg Boys St; Church Yth Grp; Computer Clb; JA; VP Jr Cls; VP Sr Cls; JV Var Bsbl; JV Ftbl; Hon Roll; JA Schlrshp Dale Carnegie Crse Pblc Spkng & Hmn Rltns 84-85; Polc Union Schlr/Athlt Awd Bsbl 86; Central CT ST U; Bus Mgmt.

BOWLER, CELESTE; Branford HS; Branford, CT; (Y); Library Aide; PAVAS; Yrbk Phtg; Hon Roll; RI Schl Of Photo; Photo.

BOYCE, MICHAEL; Southington HS; Southington, CT; (Y); 200/600; Aud/Vis; FBLA; Key Clb; Ski Clb; Yrbk Stf; Rep Stu Cncl; Socr; Var Trk; High Hon Roll; Hon Roll; Accntng.

BOYDEN, KARA; Windham HS; Willimantic, CT; (Y); Church Yth Grp; Ski Clb; Varsity Clb; Bsktbl; Var Socr; Hon Roll.

BOYER, DANIEL; Shelton HS; Shelton, CT; (Y); Boy Scts; Computer Clb; Exploring; BSA Mdl Merit 81; Air Force; Elec.

BOYNTON, DREW R; E Windsor HS; Warehouse Point, CT; (Y); 3/86; VICA; Var Crs Cntry; Mgr(s); Var Trk; High Hon Roll; Hon Roll; Lion Awd; NHS; Prfct Atten Awd; Pres Schlr; Worcester Inst; Mech Engrng.

BRADFORD, KRISTEN; Guilford HS; Guilford, CT; (Y); 47/315; Pres Church Yth Grp; Cmnty Wkr; Pres Model UN; Political Wkr; Red Cross Aide; Madrigals; School Musical; Sec Jr Cls; Var Capt Crs Cntry; High Hon Roll; All Shoreline Crs Cntry 85; Outstndg Achvt Soc Stud 86; Northfield Mt Hermon.

BRADLEY, CHERYL; Southington HS; Southington, CT; (Y); Yrbk Sprt Ed; Yrbk Stf; JV Var Bsktbl; Var L Sftbl; 2yr Strtng Outfldr ST Champnshp Sftbll 85-86; Math.

BRADLEY, MARK; Central HS; Bridgeport, CT; (Y); 50/238; Debate Tm; JA; Latin Clb; SADD; Y-Teens; Sr Cls; VP Stu Cncl; U Connecticut; Phrmcy.

BRADLEY, YVONNE RENEE; Richard C Lee HS; New Haven, CT; (Y); Dance Clb; Girl Scts; Nwsp Ed-Chief; Nwsp Stf; Yrbk Stf; Hampton Inst; Accntng.

BRADSHAW, CHARMAINE; Farmington HS; Hartford, CT; (Y); 41/219; Girl Scts; Hon Roll; Cert Achvt 86; Ldrshp Awd 86.

BRADY, ANDREA; Holy Cross HS; Waterbury, CT; (Y); Civic Clb; Girl Scts; Service Clb; Spanish Clb; SADD; Crs Cntry; Trk; Hon Roll; Msc Awd 83; Jr Vrsty Ltr Trck 85; U Of CT; Nrsng.

BRADY, DEBORAH; East Hampton HS; E Hampton, CT; (Y); 2/95; Am Leg Aux Girls St; Lib Band; Nwsp Ed-Chief; VP Soph Cls; Rep Stu Cncl; Model UN; Jazz Band; Var Trk; Hon Roll; Hrvrd Bk Prz 86; Ntl Hstry Day Comptr 85; Engl.

BRAGG, DAVID C; Choate Rosemary Hall; Elon College, NC; (S); Church Yth Grp; French Clb; Acpl Chr; Chorus; Church Choir; School Musical; School Play; Variety Show; Nwsp Rptr; Nwsp Stf; Bnjmn Duke Ldrshp Schlrshp 86; Trnty Coll, Duke U Schlrshp 86; Duke U; Psycho Bio.

BRANDOLINI, JODI; Cheshire HS; Cheshire, CT; (Y); Dance Clb; SADD; Variety Show; Yrbk Stf; JV Vllybl; Awd Dancing 84; Tremaine Dance Conventns Merit Awd 86; Mrktng.

BRANDON, CYNTHIA A; Thomas Snell Weavee HS; Hartford, CT; (Y); 32/322; JA; Library Aide; Teachers Aide; Sec Sr Cls; Hon Roll; Hrtfrd Fdrtn Of Tchrs Schlrshp 86; Hrtfrd Coll For Wmn; Ed.

BRAUN, KIM; Branford HS; Branford, CT; (Y); 120/315; Red Cross Aide; SADD; Yrbk Stf; Stu Cncl; JV Var Bsktbl; JV Var Vllybl; Hon Roll; Prncpls Advsry Cmmtee 85-86; Bently Coll; Bus Admin.

BRAY, KELLY; Torrington HS; Torrington, CT; (Y); Trs Thesps; Acpl Chr; Chorus; School Musical; School Play; Stage Crew; Sec Frsh Cls; Sec Soph Cls; Sec Jr Cls; VP Sr Cls; Outstndng Fresh Choral Grp Awd 83; Yth Ldrshp Devel Cntr-Red Crss Cmp 85; Commnctns.

BRAYTON, JAMES; Southington HS; Marion, CT; (Y); VP Church Yth Grp; Computer Clb; Pres JA; Latin Clb; Math Clb; Stu Cncl; Var L Bsktbl; Var L Socr; Var L Tennis; High Hon Roll; Bus.

BREAULT, MICHELLE A; Tourtellotte Memorial HS; Putnam, CT; (Y); 5/95; Am Leg Aux Girls St; Pep Clb; Nwsp Stf; Trs Yrbk Stf; Dnfth Awd; Hon Roll; NHS; Pres Acdmc Ftns Awd 86; Keene ST Coll; Educ.

BRECHER, JENNIFER; Greenwich HS; Greenwich, CT; (Y); Hosp Aide; Temple Yth Grp; Yrbk Stf; Tennis; French Hon Soc; High Hon Roll; Hon Roll; NHS.

BRECHER, VALERIE; Lauraeton Hall HS; Shelton, CT; (Y); Drama Clb; French Clb; Model UN; Pep Clb; Service Clb; Yrbk Sprt Ed; Yrbk Stf; Pres Frsh Cls; Var Capt Crs Cntry; NHS; Bus.

BREINES, STACY; Stamford HS; Stamford, CT; (Y); Cmnty Wkr; Pep Clb; Science Clb; Ski Clb; Varsity Clb; Stu Cncl; Fld Hcky; Tennis; Hon Roll; NHS.

BREIVE, STACY; Watertown HS; Watertown, CT; (Y); Yrbk Sprt Ed; Var Bsktbl; Var L Trk; Var L Vllybl; DECA Pres 86-87; USC; Marine Bio.

BREMER, JENNIFER LYNN; East Granby HS; East Granby, CT; (Y); 21/61; AFS; Church Yth Grp; Drama Clb; Chorus; Church Choir; School Musical; Stage Crew; Hon Roll; Greater Hartford Yth Chorale U Of Hartford 84-86; GHYC Conert Tour Great Britain 86; Music.

BRENNAN, KARA; Bristol Central HS; Bristol, CT; (Y); GAA; Var Capt Cheerleading; Hon Roll; U Of CT; Lbrl Arts.

BRENNAN, KATIE; Lauralton Hall HS; Fairfield, CT; (Y); Cmnty Wkr; Science Clb; Service Clb; Spanish Clb; Yrbk Stf; Im Fld Hcky; Im Socr; Bus.

BRETON, CHRISTINE; Stratford HS; Stratford, CT; (Y); 23/230; Drama Clb; French Clb; Drill Tm; Variety Show; Off Soph Cls; Off Jr Cls; Off Sr Cls; Pom Pon; French Hon Soc; High Hon Roll; PTSAS Schlrshp 86; Fairfield U; Bus.

BRETON, STEVEN; St Paul Catholic HS; Bristol, CT; (Y); 5/246; Am Leg Boys St; Boy Scts; School Musical; Var Crs Cntry; Elks Awd; VP French Hon Soc; VP NHS; Ordr Arrw Sectn Chf 86-87; Army ROTC Schlrshp; CT Smmr Intrnshp Prog 85; Fordham U; Publ Adm.

BREUNIG, DARCY; Francis T Maloney HS; Meriden, CT; (Y); Key Clb; Spanish Clb; Yrbk Stf; Rep Jr Cls; Rep Stu Cncl; Var Fld Hcky; Var Trk; High Hon Roll; NHS; Pres Schlr; Acctng.

BREYAN, CHRIS; Fairfield Prep; Easton, CT; (Y); Church Yth Grp; JV Crs Cntry; Var Golf; JV Socr; JV Swmmng; Comm.

BREZICKI, SANDRA; Southington HS; Southington, CT; (Y); #15 In Class; Girl Scts; Key Clb; Latin Clb; Teachers Aide; Nwsp Stf; DAR Awd; High Hon Roll; NHS; Visual Arts.

BRIGANDI, KRISTIN; Berlin HS; Berlin, CT; (Y); Sec Church Yth Grp; Drama Clb; Service Clb; Teachers Aide; Sec Chorus; School Musical; Nwsp Stf; Mgr(s); High Hon Roll; Stu Cndctr Pres Of Chorus 86; Keene ST Clg; Psych.

BRIGANTI, MARIANN; St Marys HS; New Haven, CT; (Y); 5/102; Service Clb; Trk; High Hon Roll; Hon Roll; Itln Hnr Soc 85; U Of RI; Marine Bio.

BRIGGS, WILLIAM; Maloney HS; Meriden, CT; (Y); Drama Clb; Thesps; School Play; Yrbk Rptr; Yrbk Stf; Im Vllybl; Hon Roll; NHS; Upwrd Bnd Stu Cncl 83 & 87; Mrne Bio.

BRINKLEY, PAUL; Tourtellotte Memorial HS; N Crosvnordal, CT; (Y); 20/105; Am Leg Boys St; Cmnty Wkr; Debate Tm; Sec Frsh Cls; Sec Soph Cls; Stu Cncl; Var L Bsbl; JV Bsktbl; Prfct Atten Awd; Physcl Ed.

BRIONES, EDWARD; East Lyme HS; Salem, CT; (Y); Ftbl; Wrstlng; Hon Roll; Oustndng Achvt Earth Sci 84; Aero Engrng.

BRISTOL, HILARY; Nathan Hale-Ray HS; East Haddam, CT; (S); 2/66; Math Tm; Nwsp Stf; Yrbk Stf; Var Capt Bsktbl; VP Capt Sftbl; Var Capt Vllybl; High Hon Roll; Hon Roll; NHS; Harvard Bk Clb Awd; Schlr-Ath Awd; All ST Vllybl Class S; Marietta Coll; Sprts Med.

BRKIC, CHRISTINE; Academy Of Our Lady Of Mercy; Bridgeport, CT; (Y); 20/117; Pres Drama Clb; French Clb; Math Clb; Model UN; School Play; Ed Lit Mag; Rep Stu Cncl; Mu Alp Tht; NHS; Bst Typst 83-84; Polka Dot Drama Awd 85-86; Fairfield U; Bus.

BROADNAX, ANTHONY; Bassick HS; Bridgeport, CT; (Y); Computer Clb; DECA; Stage Crew; Variety Show; Yrbk Stf; Rep Sr Cls; Rep Stu Cncl; Crs Cntry; Ftbl; Trk; CT Schlr 85; Psych.

BRODT, SONJA; Amity Regional HS; Woodbridge, CT; (Y); 1/388; VP German Clb; High Hon Roll; NHS; Ntl Merit Ltr; Prfct Atten Awd; Val; Ntl French Cont 83; Brown U Book Awd 85; 4th Rnnr Up CT St Jr Miss Comp 86; Randolph Macon Womans Coll; Bio.

BROMKAMP, ANGELA; East Lyme HS; E Lyme, CT; (Y); Key Clb; Office Aide; Variety Show; Var Crs Cntry; Mgr Gym; Mgr(s); Powder Puff Ftbl; Trk; Hon Roll; New London Schl; Comp Off.

BRONICO, CHRISTINE; Danbury HS; Danbury, CT; (Y); 35/462; Camp Fr Inc; Church Yth Grp; Drama Clb; Key Clb; School Musical; Lit Mag; Rep Soph Cls; Rep Jr Cls; Hon Roll; Sec NHS; Creative Yth 86.

BRONKE, PATTI; Rham HS; Andover, CT; (Y); 6/154; Am Leg Aux Girls St; Church Yth Grp; Acpl Chr; Chorus; Church Choir; Yrbk Stf; Stat Bsbl; JV Bsktbl; Capt Cheerleading; NHS; Amer Bus Wmns Assn Scholar; Amer Lg Aux Scholar; Pres Acad Fit Awd; U CT; Banking.

BROOKS, CHARLENE; Brien Mc Mahon HS; Norwalk, CT; (Y); Church Yth Grp; Dance Clb; Spanish Clb; Chorus; Church Choir; School Musical; School Play; Yrbk Stf; Var Bsktbl; Var Sftbl; Awd Wnnr Iona Lang Cntst 86; Trphy Awd Physcl Ftnss Athlt 84; U Of SC; Bus Educ.

BROOKS, LORI L; Emmanuel Christian Acad; Hartford, CT; (Y); 2/21; Church Yth Grp; Chorus; Church Choir; Orch; School Musical; School Play; Trs Frsh Cls; Trs Soph Cls; Sec Trs Jr Cls; JV Var Vllybl; 2nd Pl Clsscl Piano 84; Piano Schlrshp Hart Schl Mus 84-85; Piano.

BROOKS, SHARON M; Cromwell HS; Cromwell, CT; (Y); 4/84; Am Leg Aux Girls St; Spanish Clb; Yrbk Stf; Rep Stu Cncl; Var L Cheerleading; High Hon Roll; Lion Awd; VP NHS; JV Sftbl; Natl Latin Exam Maxima Cum Laude Awd; Prsdntl Acdmc Ftns Awd; Outstndng Acdmc Achvmnt Advncd Math; Quinnipiac Coll; Legal Studies.

BROSNAN, BRUCE; New Britain HS; New Britain, CT; (Y); French Clb; Key Clb; Variety Show; Lbrl Arts.

BROUGHTON, JACQULYNN M; F T Maloney HS; Meriden, CT; (S); 8/265; Trs VP DECA; Exploring; 4-H; JA; Latin Clb; Chorus; Yrbk Phtg; Yrbk Stf; Rep Sr Cls; Rep Stu Cncl; Rotary Clb Stu Of Mnth 85; U CT Day Of Pride Schlrshp 85; Briarwood Bk Awd 85.

BROVERO, MICHAEL; Griswold HS; Norwich, CT; (Y); Boy Scts; Varsity Clb; Stu Cncl; Var JV Ftbl; Var Tennis; JV Trk; Hon Roll; Fclty Awd, Newsgm Awd & Spnsh Hnrs 86; Cong Cert Of Merit & Micrblgy Hnrs 84; BSA Cert Of Merit 85; CT U; Physcl Thrpy.

BROWN, ANDREA; St Josephs HS; Stratford, CT; (Y); Church Yth Grp; Hst Drama Clb; English Clb; Thesps; Chorus; School Musical; School Play; Variety Show; Nwsp Stf; Lit Mag; U CO; Psychlgy.

BROWN, ANNE; Windham HS; Willington, CT; (Y); Trs Drama Clb; 4-H; Concert Band; Jazz Band; Orch; Pep Band; School Musical; Stage Crew; 4-H Awd; Hon Roll; Ldrshp Mdl 4-H 84; Hmemkr/Yr 4-H 84; Hnr Drama Cert 84-85; Costume Dsgn.

BROWN, DAVID; The Cheshire Acad; Valley Stream, NY; (Y); 8/64; Computer Clb; Intnl Clb; JV Crs Cntry; JV Tennis; Hon Roll; SUNY Bflo; Bus Adm.

BROWN, DOUGLAS; Robert E Fitch SR HS; Mystic, CT; (Y); 3/278; Am Leg Boys St; Pres Exploring; VP Key Clb; Yrbk Bus Mgr; Capt Socr; Var Tennis; NHS; Ntl Merit Schol; Bsbl; Im Vllybl; CT Schlr Athlete; Indoor Soccer Capt/Mgr; Princeton U; Ecnmcs.

BROWN, ELIZABETH; Lyme-Old Lyme HS; Lyme, CT; (Y); Pres Soph Cls; Pres Jr Cls; Pres Sr Cls; Var Capt Bsktbl; Var Capt Socr; Var Sftbl; Hugh O Brien Ldrshp Awd 84-85; Principles Awd-Outstndng Ldrshp 86; Hnrbl Mntn All-Shoreline Sccr 85-86; Educ.

BROWN, JIM; Branford HS; Branford, CT; (Y); Church Yth Grp; Computer Clb; Debate Tm; Church Choir; Stage Crew; Ice Hcky; Hon Roll; Bio Awd Excllnce; U CT; Elec Engrng.

BROWN, KIM; Danbury HS; Danbury, CT; (Y); 41/481; Church Yth Grp; Key Clb; Ski Clb; Yrbk Ed-Chief; Yrbk Stf; JV Trk; Hon Roll; NHS; Bus.

BROWN, KIMBERLY; Saint Joseph HS; Trumbull, CT; (Y); Church Yth Grp; Drama Clb; Ski Clb; Yrbk Bus Mgr; Crs Cntry; Mgr(s); High Hon Roll; Hon Roll; Bus.

BROWN, LEANNE; Amity HS; Bethany, CT; (Y); 71/388; Drama Clb; Hosp Aide; Spanish Clb; SADD; Chorus; School Musical; School Play; Yrbk Stf; Stu Cncl; Cheerleading; PA ST U; Pblc Rltns.

BROWN, MATT; East Lyme HS; Niantic, CT; (Y); Boy Scts; Band; Concert Band; Jazz Band; Mrchg Band; Orch; Pep Band; School Musical; Variety Show; All ST Band 85; All New England Orchestra 85-86; Most Valuable Soph & JR ELHS Band 85-86; Law.

BROWN, MICHAEL; Windsor HS; Windsor, CT; (Y); 55/365; Church Yth Grp; Civic Clb; Cmnty Wkr; Model UN; SADD; Church Choir; Concert Band; Jazz Band; Pep Band; Hon Roll; Natl Sci Olympiad 84-85; Elec Engr.

BROWN, RAY; Farmington HS; Farmington, CT; (Y); Boy Scts; Church Yth Grp; Cmnty Wkr; Political Wkr; Varsity Clb; Bsbl; Socr; Wrstlng; Hon Roll; Arch.

BROWN, ROBYN L; The Hotchkiss Schl; Decatur, GA; (Y); Drama Clb; Hosp Aide; Library Aide; Band; Stage Crew; Var Mgr Bsktbl; Cmnty Wkr; Trs Frsh Cls; JV Mgr Ftbl; JV Sftbl; Proctor 86; Play Flute; Chem Tutor; Minority & Frgn Stu Union; Rice U; Chem.

BROWN, SEAN; Bassick HS; Bridgeport, CT; (Y); 5/300; Camera Clb; SADD; Varsity Clb; Stu Cncl; Bsktbl; Ftbl; Cit Awd; Hon Roll; Howard U; Psychlgy.

BROWNING, KATHLEEN; Killingly HS; Danielson, CT; (Y); 27/295; Drama Clb; Sec SADD; Capt Flag Corp; Symp Band; Yrbk Ed-Chief; Var Cheerleading; Cit Awd; French Hon Soc; High Hon Roll; NHS; Outstndg Effrt Algbra II 86; Spch Pthlgy.

BRUCK, NICOLE; Greenwich HS; Riverside, CT; (Y); Pres Dance Clb; German Clb; Stage Crew; Bsktbl; Fld Hcky; Lcrss; High Hon Roll; Hon Roll; Sp Shttle Stdnt Invol Prj 84.

BRUDER, ERIC; Shelton HS; Shelton, CT; (Y); Am Leg Boys St; JA; Spanish Clb; Bsktbl; Trk; Spanish NHS; Bus.

BRUENN, ERICA; O H Platt HS; Meriden, CT; (Y); Color Guard; Hon Roll; Summit Clb; Bus Adm.

BRUMFIELD, HEATHER; Plainfield HS; Central Vlg, CT; (Y); 20/142; GAA; Varsity Clb; Nwsp Rptr; Nwsp Stf; Yrbk Stf; Stu Cncl; Bsktbl; Powder Puff Ftbl; Socr; Hon Roll; Rotary Club Bk Awd 86; Chmbr Of Cmmrc Schlrshp 86; HS Fac Schlrshp 86; Northeastern U.

BRUNETTI, MARC; Stratford HS; Stratford, CT; (Y); 3/257; JA; Trs Library Aide; Varsity Clb; Rep Jr Cls; Rep Sr Cls; Var L Crs Cntry; Var L Trk; High Hon Roll; Sec NHS; Church Yth Grp; Rep Sc Natl Hnrs Semnr 86; Columbia Bk Awd 86; Acctg.

BRUNO, STEPHEN; Wilton HS; Wilton, CT; (Y); 100/350; Boy Scts; Ed Yrbk Stf; Im Mgr Bsktbl; Im Mgr Golf; Im Mgr Socr; Hon Roll; Eagl Sct 83; Ad Altare Dei BSA Relgs Awd 82; CA Schlrshp Fdrtn 84-85; U Of MD Coll Pk; Mech Engr.

BRYAN, AMY E; Wilton HS; Wilton, CT; (Y); Pres VP Drama Clb; French Clb; Model UN; School Musical; School Play; Swing Chorus; Lit Mag; VP Frsh Cls; Pres Soph Cls; Rep Jr Cls; U Of TX; Psych.

BRYAN, JO ANN; Brien Mc Mahon HS; Darien, CT; (Y); 16/288; Ski Clb; Rep Soph Cls; Rep Jr Cls; Rep Sr Cls; Fld Hcky; Powder Puff Ftbl; Swmmng; High Hon Roll; Hon Roll; NHS; U Of CT; Mech Engrng.

BRYANT, MELINDA; Staples HS; Westport, CT; (Y); 3/250; Key Clb; Var Fld Hcky; Lcrss; Powder Puff Ftbl; Var Trk; 2nd Hnrs Acadmc Yr 84-85.

BUCCIERI, CHRISTOPHER; St Joseph HS; Trumbull, CT; (Y); 11/253; French Clb; Quiz Bowl; Scholastic Bowl; Rep Stu Cncl; Var Ftbl; Var Wt Lftg; French Hon Soc; High Hon Roll; NHS; Holy Cross Book Prize 86; Medicine.

BUCHER, OLIVIA; Shelton HS; Shelton, CT; (Y); Teachers Aide; Church Choir; Stage Crew; Socr; Hon Roll; Central CT ST U; Elem Ed.

BUCK, DANIEL; Wethersfield HS; Wethersfield, CT; (Y); 2/300; Am Leg Boys St; Church Yth Grp; Church Choir; JV Bsktbl; High Hon Roll; NHS; NEDT Awd; Allnc Frncs Awd 3rd Pl; Crnll Bk Awd; Bio Awd.

BUCK, MARIA; Edwin O Smith HS; Storrs, CT; (Y); 21/174; Cmnty Wkr; Dance Clb; Political Wkr; SADD; Teachers Aide; Rep Stu Cncl; L Cheerleading; U Of CT Coop Prgm For Sup HS Stu 86; Sclgy.

BUCKANAVAGE, ROSANNE; Avon HS; Avon, CT; (Y); Church Yth Grp; Ski Clb; Sec Stu Cncl; Var Crs Cntry; Var Trk; Hon Roll; All ST Hnrs Crs Cntry 84-85; All Conf Crs Cntry 83-85, Trck 85-86.

BUCKHEIT, JANET; Holy Cross HS; Cheshire, CT; (Y); Church Yth Grp; Cmnty Wkr; Pep Clb; Church Choir; JV Var Bsktbl; Var L Sftbl; Hon Roll; Frshmn All Str Lg Vrsty Sftbl 83-84; All Cty Tm Sphmr & JR Yrs 84-86; Yth Sptlght Of Wk 84; Chldhd Educ.

BUCKLEY, SCOTT; Berlin HS; Berlin, CT; (Y); 20/200; Am Leg Boys St; Boy Scts; Church Yth Grp; Drama Clb; Radio Clb; Science Clb; Ski Clb; Band; Concert Band; Drm Mjr(t); Outstndng Lab Rsrch 86; Advncd Math Hnrs Awd 86; Biomedcl Engrng.

BUCKMAN, JOHN; Cheshire HS; Cheshire, CT; (Y); Mrchg Band; JV Bsbl; JV Im Bsktbl; Im Fld Hcky.

BUCZAK, MARY; Holy Cross HS; Waterbury, CT; (Y); 37/342; Hon Roll; NHS; St Schlr; Pres Acadmc Fitnss Awd 86; Fairfield U.

BUDIHAS, ALEXA A; Glastonbury HS; Glastonbury, CT; (Y); 28/413; Church Yth Grp; Band; Orch; School Musical; Off Frsh Cls; Gym; Vllybl; High Hon Roll; NHS; Alumni Reg Schlrshp Acad 86; CT Vlly Wind Ensmbl 1st Flure Natly Recgnzd 85-86; U Of Rochester.

BUDZ, PENNY; Griswold HS; Jewett City, CT; (Y); 2/100; Girl Scts; Hosp Aide; Chorus; Capt Bowling; Tennis; High Hon Roll; NHS; VFW Awd; VFW Vol Awd Backus Hosp 85; Pre-Med.

BUE, ONDINE; Staples HS; Westport, CT; (Y); Acpl Chr; Chorus; Cheerleading; Powder Puff Ftbl; Law.

BUEHLER, LAUREN; Stamford HS; Stamford, CT; (Y); Drama Clb; Library Aide; Ski Clb; Teachers Aide; VP Temple Yth Grp; School Play; Yrbk Stf; Hon Roll; NHS; Humanities.

BUFFO, KERRY; Branford HS; Branford, CT; (Y); 19/315; Drama Clb; Trs PAVAS; Acpl Chr; School Play; Twrlr; Hon Roll; CT All ST Chr, S CT Reg Chr Fstvl 86; Frnch & Spnsh Excllnc Rec Awds 86; Shrln Allnc Arts Schlrshp; Music.

BUGBEE, DEBBY; East Hartford HS; E Hartford, CT; (Y); Church Yth Grp; Drama Clb; Hosp Aide; Chorus; Flag Corp; School Musical; School Play; Yrbk Stf; Frsh Cls; Soph Cls; Dynamic Tm Perfrmnce Awd; NYU; Drama.

BUGG, STEVEN; The Morgan Schl; Clinton, CT; (Y); 31/155; Capt Var Golf; JV Wrstlng; Bus.

BUI, CHUNG; Wilbur Cross HS; New Haven, CT; (S).

BUITRAGO, EDWIN; New Britain HS; New Britain, CT; (Y); Boy Scts; Church Yth Grp; FCA; SADD; Drill Tm; Gym; Wt Lftg; Hon Roll; Hartford Tech; Compu Elec.

BUKOWINSKI, ANNA; Windsor Locks HS; Windsor Locks, CT; (Y); 14/155; Model UN; Chorus; Church Choir; Color Guard; Flag Corp; JV Tennis; High Hon Roll; Hon Roll; NHS.

BULLOCK, JENNIFER; The Masters Schl; Collinsville, CT; (S); Church Yth Grp; Model UN; Chorus; Church Choir; Yrbk Rptr; Yrbk Stf; Mgr(s); JV Socr; High Hon Roll; Music Awd 84; Nrsng.

BURDETTE, JEFF; Greenwich HS; Greenwich, CT; (Y); Boys Clb Am; Band; Concert Band; Jazz Band; Mrchg Band; Ice Hcky; Hon Roll; Aviation.

BURDICK, BECKY; Holy Cross HS; Waterbury, CT; (Y); 121/380; Art Clb; Latin Clb; Im Tennis; JV Trk; High Hon Roll; Hon Roll; Acctg.

BURDICK, SARAH; Fitch SR HS; Noank, CT; (Y); Chorus; Crs Cntry; Trk; Hon Roll; Church Yth Grp; Girl Scts; Spanish Clb; Sec Frsh Cls; Spanish NHS.

BURDICK, SUSAN; Killingly HS; Danielson, CT; (Y); Trs Church Yth Grp; Capt Color Guard; Flag Corp; Mrchg Band; Rep Jr Cls; Stat Bsbl; Stat Socr; Trk; Hon Roll; Johnson & Wales; Clnry Arts.

BURDO, MICHAEL; Bullard Havens R V T S HS; Bridgeport, CT; (S); Yrbk Stf; Stu Cncl; Hon Roll; Culinary Inst Of Amer; Food Trd.

BURGESS, LAWRENCE; Sheehan HS; Wallingford, CT; (Y); Hosp Aide; Var L Crs Cntry; JV Var Socr; Capt L Swmmng; Capt L Trk; High Hon Roll; Hon Roll; Marine Corps Schrlshp; Emblen Cub Schlrshp 86; Yth Soccer League Schrlshp; Barrett Delea Hnr Schrlshp; Western CT ST U; Bus Mgmt.

BURGESS, LYNN; Miss Porters Schl; Plainfield, NJ; (Y); Computer Clb; French Clb; Model UN; Band; Concert Band; Mrchg Band; High Hon Roll; Hon Roll; ABC Schlrshp Pgm 83-86; LEAD Pgm Bus 85; U Of PA; Comm.

BURKE, COLLEEN E; Andrew Warde HS; Fairfield, CT; (Y); 1/323; VP Trs AFS; Church Yth Grp; Dance Clb; Hosp Aide; VP Pres JA; Spanish Clb; Lit Mag; Elks Awd; NHS; Spanish NHS; Mrqt Vldctrn Schlrshp 86; CT Schlr 86; Chmpn Irsh Stpdncr 84-86; Marquette U; Biomed.

BURKE, ELIZABETH; East Lyme HS; Salem, CT; (Y); 6/252; Church Yth Grp; Key Clb; Teachers Aide; JV Var Fld Hcky; Powder Puff Ftbl; Var Capt Trk; Lion Awd; Trs NHS; Pres Schlr; Im Bsktbl; Art Wrk In Art Shws 83-86; Gbbns Hnr Schlrshp 86; Catholic U Of Amer; Bio-Med.

BURKE, KATHLEEN; Sacred Heart Acad; N Haven, CT; (Y); Church Yth Grp; Hosp Aide; School Musical; Lit Mag; Rep Sr Cls; Var Tennis; Var Vllybl; French Hon Soc; High Hon Roll; NHS; Mt Holyoke Bk Awd Ldrshp 86.

BURLEIGH, SCOTT; Southington HS; Plantsville, CT; (Y); Ski Clb; Var L Crs Cntry; Var L Wrstlng; Hon Roll; Math.

BURLINGTON, JENNIFER; Westover HS; Middlebury, CT; (Y); Church Yth Grp; Pep Clb; School Musical; Rep Bsktbl; Rep Jr Cls; Rep Stu Cncl; JV Capt Fld Hcky; JV Tennis; Mgr(s); Smith Coll Bk Awd 86; Head Admssns Guide 86; Htl Adm.

BURNOSKY, JEFF; Wethersfield HS; Wethersfield, CT; (Y); 29/300; Var L Tennis; Hon Roll; Ntrtnl Sci.

BURNS, HEIDI; Killingly HS; Danielson, CT; (Y); 50/294; Church Yth Grp; Girl Scts; SADD; Color Guard; JV Bsktbl; JV Var Cheerleading; JV Var Sftbl; Hon Roll; Stu Govt Awd 82-83; Physcl Ed Awd 82-83; St Josephs Coll; Accntng.

BURNS, JENNIFER; Seymour HS; Seymour, CT; (S); 12/194; Var Bsktbl; Var Sftbl; High Hon Roll; Hon Roll; NHS; Pres Schlr; Sacred Heart U; Lgl Asst.

BURNS, JOEL E; Seymour HS; Oxford, CT; (S); 13/192; JA; Mgr Stage Crew; Yrbk Sprt Ed; Yrbk Stf; Rep Frsh Cls; Rep Soph Cls; Rep Jr Cls; Rep Sr Cls; JV Capt Bsktbl; Crs Cntry; Typng Awd 85; Spn Awd 85; UMO; Anml Sci.

BURNS, JOHN PAUL; Rham HS; Hebron, CT; (Y); Aud/Vis; 4-H; Spanish Clb; Band; Mrchg Band; Nwsp Rptr; Ed Nwsp Stf; Golf; Trk; Hon Roll; U CT; Bus.

BURNS, MOIRA; Nonnewaug HS; Woodbury, CT; (Y); Church Yth Grp; Latin Clb; Chorus; Swing Chorus; Capt Sftbl; Capt Vllybl; High Hon Roll; Hon Roll; Math.

BURR, JOHN; Wilton HS; Wilton, CT; (Y); Varsity Clb; Ftbl; Trk; Hon Roll.

BURRELL, TISHEMA; Cooperative HS; New Haven, CT; (Y); Rep Stu Cncl; Hon Roll; Excllnce Frnch I & II 84-85; Excllnce Spn I 86; Acctg.

BURROUGHS, KELVIN; James Hillhouse HS; New Haven, CT; (Y); 31/259; Church Yth Grp; Computer Clb; Math Tm; Red Cross Aide; Science Clb; Chorus; Church Choir; School Musical; Yrbk Stf; Rep Soph Cls; Alld Hlth Clb; Pace U; Medcl Tech.

BUSCH, GWENDOLYN; Acad Of Our Lady Of Mercy; W Haven, CT; (Y); 29/117; Church Yth Grp; Church Choir; Nwsp Bus Mgr; Yrbk Stf; Lit Mag; Rep Frsh Cls; Pres Soph Cls; VP Sr Cls; Rep Stu Cncl; Mu Alp Tht; Alpa Phi Alpa Frat Inc 86; Top 100 Minorty Stu CT 85; U CT; Acctng.

BUTERA, SUSAN; Stamford HS; Stamford, CT; (Y); Drama Clb; Thesps; School Musical; School Play; Stage Crew; Diving; Sftbl; Hon Roll; Rep Soph Cls; Rep Sr Cls; Itln Clb Pres 86; Outstndng Ldrshp Itln Clb 86; Bst Spprtng Actrss Schl Drama 86; U RI; Thtr.

BUTKIEWICZ, KRISTIN; West Haven HS; W Haven, CT; (Y); Church Yth Grp; DECA; US Hist Excllnc Awd 85; Southern CT ST U; Elem Ed.

BUTLER, CHERELLE; Bulkeley HS; Hartford, CT; (Y); Drama Clb; 4-H; FHA; Girl Scts; JA; Church Choir; Insrnc.

BUTLER, JOS; Maloney HS; Meriden, CT; (Y); Boys Clb Am; Bsbl; Bsktbl; Hon Roll; All St Bsbl, All Conf Bsbl 84-86.

BUTTERMAN, HOWIE; Stamford HS; Stamford, CT; (Y); 66/400; JA; Ski Clb; Varsity Clb; Lit Mag; Stu Cncl; JV Socr; Capt Wrstlng; Hon Roll; NHS; Lehigh U.

BYAM, LORRAINE; Holly Cross HS; Naugatuck, CT; (Y); Dance Clb; Teachers Aide; Concert Band; Drm Mjr(t); Mrchg Band; Pep Band; Debutante 86; Miss Bobbi Thlnd Awd 86; 1st Pl Afro-Latin Fstvl Essy Cmptn 86; Spec Educ.

BYERLY, LYNN M; Windsor HS; Windsor, CT; (Y); 11/360; Cmnty Wkr; Girl Scts; Science Clb; French Hon Soc; High Hon Roll; NHS; Intnl Clb; Stage Crew; Nwsp Stf; JV Socr; Schl Jacket & Ltr Hgh Schltc Achvt 85; Pre-Med.

BYRNE, MONICA; Jonathan Law HS; Milford, CT; (Y); 6/240; Am Leg Aux Girls St; Sec Frsh Cls; Trs Soph Cls; VP Jr Cls; Var Capt Bsktbl; Var L Tennis; Var Capt Vllybl; NHS; NEDT Awd; Church Yth Grp; Smth Bk Awd 86; Kolbe Bk Awd 86; Excllnc Hstry Awd 86; Ecnmcs.

BYSTREK, BONNIE; East Hampton HS; Cobalt, CT; (Y); 11/110; Am Leg Aux Girls St; Drama Clb; Pres Model UN; Ski Clb; Band; Nwsp Stf; Yrbk Phtg; Stat Bsktbl; Var Crs Cntry; Var Trk; HS Schlrs Pgm; Ntl Hstry Day; Mst Vlbl Rnr Trk; Bus.

CADETT, BEVERLY; Mark T Sheehan HS; Wallingford, CT; (Y); 32/207; Cmnty Wkr; Hosp Aide; Teachers Aide; Chorus; School Musical; School Play; Nwsp Rptr; Nwsp Stf; Hon Roll; Southern U; Elem Educ.

CADRAIN, SARA; Southington HS; Southington, CT; (Y); Drama Clb; Madrigals; Swing Chorus; Hon Roll; SADD; Chorus; School Musical; Bus.

CADRIN, LISA; Bullard Havens Tech; Bridgeport, CT; (Y); FNA; Hosp Aide; Library Aide; Office Aide; Ski Clb; Bsktbl; Sftbl; High Hon Roll; Hon Roll; Sec NHS; Nrsng.

CAHALAN, EVA; Wilton HS; Wilton, CT; (Y); 74/306; Church Yth Grp; Key Clb; Orch; JV Var Bsktbl; JV Var Lcrss; Var Socr; Hon Roll; Varsity Clb; Co-Capt Powder Puff Ftbl; All-Frfld Cnt Intr-Schlstc Cnfrnc Wmns Lcrs 85-86; CT ST Slct Sccr Tm 84-85; Rsn Clb Vstd USSR 86.

CAHILL, DEBBIE; Morgan HS; Clinton, CT; (Y); 42/167; Church Yth Grp; Spanish Clb; Acpl Chr; Chorus; School Musical; School Play; Stage Crew; Score Keeper; Vllybl; Hon Roll; Brown Schl Bus; Acctng.

CAHILL, KRISTI; Windsor HS; Windsor, CT; (S); Sec DECA; Chorus; High Hon Roll; Hon Roll; Outstndng Bus Stud Awd Bay Path JR Coll 86; Dist Ed Clbs Of Amer Stud Of The Yr 86; DECA 86; Sales Rep.

CAHILL, MICHAEL; Emmett Obrien Vo Tech Schl; Naugatuck, CT; (Y); Band; High Hon Roll; Hon Roll; Electrcl.

CALABRO, MARIA; Bristol Central HS; Bristol, CT; (Y); Latin Clb; Math Clb; Math Tm; Stu Cncl; Gym; High Hon Roll; Hon Roll; NHS; Yth Ftns Achvt Awd 84-86; Math Leag Cert; Latin Test 86; Nrsng.

CALAFIORE, RICHARD; Kingswood-Oxford HS; Hartford, CT; (Y); French Clb; Model UN; Pep Clb; Political Wkr; Service Clb; Pres SADD; Concert Band; Trs Jazz Band; VP Sr Cls; Var L Bsktbl.

CALCAGNO, MARGHERITA; Sacred Heart Acad; Hamden, CT; (Y); Hosp Aide; Spanish Clb; School Musical; Bowling; Im Vllybl; High Hon Roll; Spanish NHS; Fairfield U; Biolgy.

CALDAROLA, CHARLES; St Mary HS; Greenwich, CT; (Y); 3/40; Church Yth Grp; Computer Clb; NFL; Spanish Clb; Yrbk Stf; Woodsmn Awd Cvc Oration 1st Pl 84; Comp Prog Consdrd For Pub By Run Computer Mag 86; Fordham U; Comp Sci.

CALLAHAN, DEBBIE; Jonathan Law HS; Milford, CT; (Y); 40/211; Camera Clb; Drama Clb; Keywanettes; Ski Clb; Color Guard; Nwsp Rptr; Yrbk Stf; Tennis; High Hon Roll; Hon Roll; Schlrshp Outstndng Chrctr 86; Excllence In Mthds & Media 86; Cntrl CT ST U; Psych.

CALLAN, ELIZABETH; Weston HS; Weston, CT; (Y); Dance Clb; French Clb; Intnl Clb; Key Clb; Chorus; Madrigals; School Musical; Nwsp Stf; NHS; Ntl Merit SF; Le Grand Coneours 82; Mc Gill U; Lib Arts.

CALLIS, PAUL; Wethersfield HS; Wethersfield, CT; (Y); Am Leg Boys St; Cmnty Wkr; Yrbk Stf; Stu Cncl; Im Badmtn; Mgr(s); Var L Swmmng; Steven R Shults Swmmng Awd 86; CT Clss M Mst Outstndg Swmmr 86; Top 10 CT ST Opn Swm Champ 84-86.

CALO, THOMAS; W F Kaynor RVTS; Oakville, CT; (Y); Church Yth Grp; SADD; Pres VICA; Stage Crew; Rep Frsh Cls; Var L Crs Cntry; Var L Trk; High Hon Roll; Trs NHS; Mst Dsrvng Frshmn 84; VICA Ldrshp Cert 86; U Of CT; Pol Sci.

CALVO, LINDA; Rham HS; Hebron, CT; (Y); 10/158; AFS; Am Leg Aux Girls St; Church Yth Grp; Sec FBLA; Acpl Chr; Chorus; Yrbk Stf; High Hon Roll; Hon Roll; Sec NHS; Credit Assn Schlrshp For Wmn In Bus 86; U Of CT; Finance.

CAMARCO, MICHELE; Jonathan Law HS; Milford, CT; (Y); 24/249; Band; Ed Yrbk Stf; Sec Soph Cls; Rep Stu Cncl; Var Capt Cheerleading; Mgr(s); Hon Roll; NEDT Awd 84; Acctng.

CAMERON, WILLIAM; Staples HS; Westport, CT; (Y); Church Yth Grp; French Clb; Key Clb; Varsity Clb; Acpl Chr; Yrbk Stf; Rep Sr Cls; Ftbl; Capt Swmmng; Trk; Cnty & LL Div Champ & 3rd In ST-100 Yd Breastroke 86; 22nd Pl-YMCA Natls 85; 18th Pl-YMCA Natls 86; Denison U.

CAMEROTA, MICHELE; South Windsor HS; S Windsor, CT; (Y); 54/300; Band; Concert Band; Mrchg Band; School Musical; Mgr(s); Hon Roll; Legal Assist.

CAMP, DEDRA; Crosby HS; Waterbury, CT; (S); FHA; JA; Spanish Clb; Chorus; Drill Tm; School Play; Hon Roll; St Schlr; Waterbury ST Tech Coll; Comp.

CAMPAIGNE, CATHERINE; Guilford HS; Guilford, CT; (Y); 12/300; Church Yth Grp; Model UN; Trs Band; Stage Crew; High Hon Roll; NHS; Ntl Merit Ltr; AFS; Drama Clb; Trs Concert Band; Calcls Awd 86; Music Awd Bnd & Jazz Vcl Grp 86; Excllnce Lang Arts Awd 83-85; Dartmouth Coll; Law.

CAMPAILLA, MELINDA; Mary Immaculate Acad; New Britain, CT; (Y); Nwsp Rptr; Rep Jr Cls; Badmtn; Bsktbl; Hon Roll; Mrt Awd Chem 85-86; Schlrshp Awds Relgn,Hstry,Latin,Math,En 83-86; U Of CT; Pre-Law.

CAMPANA, PAUL; Platt HS; Meriden, CT; (Y); Varsity Clb; Stage Crew; Bsktbl; Socr; Sftbl; Hon Roll; NHS; Ntl Ldrshp Cnfrnc 85; Upwrd Bnd Prgm 83; Engr.

CAMPANELLI, RICK; Oliver Wollcott Technical HS; Torrington, CT; (Y); 4/143; VICA; Nwsp Stf; Stu Cncl; Bsbl; Golf; Socr; High Hon Roll; Hon Roll; Lion Awd; NHS; Anthoy Arnista Schlrshp 86; Frank Albreda Schlrshp 86; VP Stu Cong 86; Waterbury ST; Elect Engr.

CAMPBELL, ANGELA; Wilby HS; Waterbury, CT; (Y); 10/237; Church Yth Grp; FHA; Church Choir; Vllybl; Bausch & Lomb Sci Awd; French Hon Soc; High Hon Roll; Hon Roll; Michael Jeweler Awd; Med.

CAMPBELL, CAROLYN; Bethel HS; Bethel, CT; (Y); Camp Fr Inc; Church Yth Grp; Ski Clb; Band; Concert Band; Mrchg Band; School Play; JV Bsktbl; JV Tennis; High Hon Roll; Grassy Plains Drum & Bugle Corp Awd 86; Band Awd 86; U W Ontario; Polit Sci.

CAMPBELL, CARRIE; Torrington HS; Torrington, CT; (Y); 24/300; Thesps; Chorus; Yrbk Stf; Var L Swmmng; High Hon Roll; Hon Roll; NHS; Rep Jr Cls; Church Yth Grp; Drama Clb; Vlntr Awd 84; Pres Of Ldrs Clb At YMCA 86-87.

CAMPBELL, COLLEEN; Bukard Haven R V T S HS; Bridgeport, CT; (Y); GAA; JA; Model UN; Pep Clb; Scholastic Bowl; Var Cheerleading; Hon Roll; Ntl Merit Schol; Fash Merch.

CAMPBELL, GEO; Hartford Public HS; Hartford, CT; (Y); Boys Clb Am; FBLA; Comp Sci.

CAMPBELL, SEAN MICHAEL; Avon Old Farms Schl; Avon, CT; (Y); 1/101; Sec French Clb; Radio Clb; Nwsp Stf; JV Bsktbl; Var Crs Cntry; Var JV Golf; Bausch & Lomb Sci Awd; Pres Schlr; Val; Avon Chapter Cum Laude Soc 86; Cornell U; Engrng.

CAMPION, DAN; Stamford HS; Stamford, CT; (Y); VP JA; Library Aide; Varsity Clb; VP Sr Cls; Stu Cncl; Trk; Hon Roll; NHS; Hnrbl Mntn City Sci Fair 84; Prm King 86.

CAMUSO, MATTHEW; Kent Schl; Ridgefield, CT; (Y); 6/154; Debate Tm; Latin Clb; Letterman Clb; Varsity Clb; Band; Chorus; Nwsp Sprt Ed; Nwsp Stf; Yrbk Stf; Pres Frsh Cls; Decemvir Soc-Top 10 Stu 83; Albrt T Mrrll Prz-Cntrbtng Mst To Schl 83; Almni Hnr Cup 83.

CANALES, CARMEN R; Richard C Lee HS; New Haven, CT; (Y); 4-H; Hosp Aide; Office Aide; Red Cross Aide; Yrbk Stf; 4-H Awd; High Hon Roll; Hon Roll; NHS; Yale U Schl Med Rsrch Pgm 86; Amrcn Red Crss Cmp Delegt 86; Brown U; Bio-Chem.

CANALIA, PAULA; O M Platt HS; Meriden, CT; (Y); 27/239; Boys Clb Am; Church Yth Grp; Powder Puff Ftbl; High Hon Roll; Hon Roll; Adv Gen Bus Awd 84; Pres Acadmc Fit Awd 86; Outstndng Excllnc Typg 2 84; Quinnipac Coll; Bus.

CANAVAN, SUSAN; Woodstock Acad; E Woodstock, CT; (Y); 1/75; Am Leg Aux Girls St; Sec Mathletes; Band; Chorus; Trs Frsh Cls; Trs Soph Cls; Trs Jr Cls; Trs Sr Cls; JV Var Socr; Sec NHS; Yale Hnr Cup Awd & Lions Clb Schlrshp 86; ST CT Gnrl Asmbly Ctns For Vldctrn 86; Bates Coll.

CANDELORA, JOHN; Shelton HS; Shelton, CT; (Y); 9/600; Am Leg Boys St; Chess Clb; JA; Political Wkr; SADD; Band; Concert Band; Mrchg Band; High Hon Roll; NHS; Am Lgn Boys ST; Engrg.

CANER, ROY; Emmett O Brien HS; Derby, CT; (Y); Church Yth Grp; Coach Actv; Wt Lftg; Cit Awd; Hon Roll; NHS; Schlrshp & Comm 86; Outstndng Plumbg Awd 86.

CANIZARES, MONICA; Lauralton Hall HS; Fairfield, CT; (Y); 45/112; Cmnty Wkr; Debate Tm; GAA; JA; Model UN; Service Clb; School Play; Var Diving; NHS; Spanish NHS; Bus.

CAOUETTE, MARC; Bulkeley HS; Hartford, CT; (Y); 45/316; Boy Scts; Trs French Clb; JA; SADD; Ed Yrbk Ed-Chief; Trs Stu Cncl; Var Ftbl; Hon Roll; Ntl Merit Ltr; Trs Jr Cls; Frnch Hnr Awd; HOBY Ldrshp Awd; U MA; Mech Engr.

CAPASSO JR, ANGELO; Torrington HS; Torrington, CT; (Y); Art Clb; Band; Concert Band; Drm & Bgl; Jazz Band; Mrchg Band; Pep Band; Soph Cls; Socr; Hon Roll; Bnd Awd Drms; Waterbury ST Tech; Engr.

CAPASSO, KAREN; St Joseph HS; Trumbull, CT; (Y); 56/253; Church Yth Grp; Pep Clb; Spanish Clb; Yrbk Stf; Rep Frsh Cls; Rep Soph Cls; Rep Stu Cncl; Hon Roll; Jr NHS; San Giuseppe Fstvl Qun 84.

CAPLICE, SEAN; Simsbury HS; W Simsbury, CT; (Y); 33/410; Am Leg Boys St; Boy Scts; VP JA; Yrbk Stf; Var L Ftbl; Var Capt Lcrss; Var L Wrstlng; High Hon Roll; NHS; Hon Roll; Harvard U Book Awd 86; Natrl Sci.

CAPONE, TAMMY; St Marys HS; E Haven, CT; (Y); Church Yth Grp; School Musical; School Play; Stage Crew; Sr Cls; Trk; Hon Roll; Aviatn.

CAPOZZI, KAREN; Holy Cross HS; Prospect, CT; (Y); 46/380; Cmnty Wkr; Pep Clb; Political Wkr; Spanish Clb; Varsity Clb; JV Var Cheerleading; High Hon Roll; Hon Roll; NHS; Spanish NHS; Lbrl Arts.

CARBERRY, ANDREW; Oliver Wolcott Regional Vo-Tech; Sharon, CT; (S); 7/167; Math Clb; Pres Soph Cls; Rep Pres Stu Cncl; High Hon Roll; Hon Roll; Elctrnc Engrng.

CARBERRY, EDWARD J; Joseph A Foran HS; Milford, CT; (Y); 3/300; Am Leg Boys St; Cmnty Wkr; JCL; Key Clb; Political Wkr; Sec Yrbk Ed-Chief; Stu Cncl; High Hon Roll; VP NHS; NEDT Awd; Bio Awd; Stats Awd; Michaels Jwlrs Awd Schlrshp.

CARBONE, GREG; Mark T Sheehan HS; Wallingford, CT; (Y); 16/203; Yrbk Phtg; Pres Frsh Cls; Pres Soph Cls; Pres Jr Cls; Pres Sr Cls; Rep Stu Cncl; Var L Ftbl; Var L Swmmng; Hon Roll; Physcl Thrpy.

CARDARELLI, MICHAEL; Branford HS; Branford, CT; (Y); 180/360; Latin Clb; Ski Clb; VP SADD; Var Capt Ftbl; Var Trk; Wt Lftg; Var Wrstlng; Mst Outstndng Wrstlr Awd 84; Schl Rcrd Relay Hnrs, MVP Awd, Housatonic Leag Hnrbl Ment 86; Norwich U; Phy Ed.

CARDELLA, ANDREA; Torrington HS; Torrington, CT; (Y); Drama Clb; FBLA; Key Clb; Pep Clb; Ski Clb; Thesps; Stage Crew; Nwsp Rptr; Nwsp Stf; Hon Roll.

CARDINALI, JOHN; West Haven HS; W Haven, CT; (Y); Exploring; JA; Var Swmmng; High Hon Roll; Hon Roll; NHS; Rotary Awd; Central CT ST U; Bus Admn.

CARDOZA, PAULA; Wilby HS; Wtby, CT; (Y); VP FHA; FHA Schlrshp 86; Recog Awd-Cert FHA 85; Mattuck CC; Erly Chldhd Ed.

CAREY, MICHELLE; Joseph A Foran HS; Milford, CT; (Y); 20/275; Hosp Aide; Hst Keywanettes; Service Clb; Spanish Clb; Yrbk Stf; Stu Cncl; Swmmng; Hon Roll; NHS.

CARLASCIO, KEITH; Kaynor Tech Schl; Waterbury, CT; (Y); SADD; Hon Roll; Clnary Inst Of Amer; Clnry Arts.

CARLSON, ALLEN; Cheshire HS; Cheshire, CT; (Y); School Play; Rep Frsh Cls; Rep Soph Cls; Rep Jr Cls; Rep Sr Cls; Var Socr; Capt Trk; DAR Awd; Hon Roll; WA Wrkshps Cngrsnl Smnr 86; All ST Class L Trck & All League Soccer; Pltcl Sci.

CARLSON, CYNTHIA; Berlin HS; Kensington, CT; (Y); 4-H; Hosp Aide; Sec JA; Yrbk Stf; JV Vllybl; High Hon Roll; Hon Roll; NHS.

CARLSON, JANE; Nathan Hale-Ray SR HS; East Haddam, CT; (S); 6/70; Drama Clb; Rptr Trs Political Wkr; School Musical; Yrbk Stf; Stu Cncl; JV Bsktbl; Var Capt Socr; Hon Roll; NHS; Chorus; U S Pony Clb 83-86; Colby Sawyer Coll; Nrsng.

CARLSON, KARIN; East Hampton HS; Marlborough, CT; (Y); Band; Mrchg Band; Var Cheerleading; Var Socr; Var Sftbl; Hon Roll; Jr NHS; Med.

CARMICHAEL, NEVIN; Wilton HS; Wilton, CT; (Y); Boy Scts; Cmnty Wkr; Letterman Clb; SADD; Varsity Clb; Var Crs Cntry; Var Capt Swmmng; Hon Roll; Captn YMCA Swim Tm 85-86; Ltr Man Vrsty Clb 87; Boy Scouts Am Awd Eagle 86; Engrng.

CARNESE, CHRISTOPHER E; Andrew Warde HS; Fairfield, CT; (Y); Var L Bsktbl; Hon Roll; Bus Admn.

CARNEY, CHRIS; Cheshire HS; Appleton, WI; (Y); Boy Scts; French Clb; Pep Clb; Ski Clb; Band; Jazz Band; Pep Band; Var Crs Cntry; Var Capt Diving; Var Trk; Mst Valubl Appltn W Dvng Team 86; Bus Mgmt.

CAROLLA, MICHELE; Hamden HS; Hamden, CT; (Y); Church Yth Grp; Hosp Aide; Band; Concert Band; Ed Lit Mag; Rep Soph Cls; Rep Jr Cls; Art Awd 83-84; Engl Awd 84-85.

CARON, SONIA; Plainfield HS; Plainfield, CT; (Y); Dance Clb; Exploring; French Clb; SADD; Stu Cncl; Gov Hon Prg Awd; St Schlr; Val; Awd French 1,2,3 & Cnvrstnl; Rep Town Comm, Griswold Rubber Co & Alumni Assoc John L Chapman Shrlrshp; U CT; Clncl Dietetics.

CAROTENUTO, LAURA; Sacred Heart Acad; Hamden, CT; (Y); Art Clb; Church Yth Grp; Cmnty Wkr; Spanish Clb; Stage Crew; Yrbk Ed-Chief; Yrbk Stf; Im Vllybl; High Hon Roll; NHS; Natl Sci Olympd Awd Chem 86; Psychol.

CARPENTER, LISA A; Enfield HS; Enfield, CT; (Y); 4/228; Drama Clb; Girl Scts; Science Clb; Ski Clb; Spanish Clb; Sec Trs Band; Concert Band; Mrchg Band; Stage Crew; Variety Show; Advncd Biolgy Awd 86; CT Schlstc Achvmnt Sch 86; Prsdntl Acdmc Ftns Awd 86; U Of NH; Anml Sci.

CARR, DANA; Brien Mc Mahon HS; Norwalk, CT; (Y); Drama Clb; Band; Chorus; Concert Band; Mrchg Band; School Play; Stage Crew; Variety Show; Var Powder Puff Ftbl; Hon Roll; 4 Gld Cup Awds-Schubert Clb Amer/Piano 81-86; Music Ed.

CARRERAS, ISMAEL; William H Hall HS; West Hartford, CT; (Y); 26/331; Church Yth Grp; Rep Sr Cls; Var Bsbl; Var L Socr; High Hon Roll; NHS; Pres Spanish NHS; Ntl Hspnc Schlr Awds 86; Bates Coll.

CARRINGTON, ELIZABETH; Holy Cross HS; Waterbury, CT; (Y); 66/352; Church Yth Grp; Cmnty Wkr; Latin Clb; Trs Band; Church Choir; Concert Band; Mrchg Band; Variety Show; Mgr(s); Score Keeper; MVP Awd Swmmng 86; Mst Hardwrkg Swmmr Awd 85; Clark U; Lib Art.

CARRINGTON III, HIRAM; Amity Regional HS; Bethany, CT; (Y); Am Leg Boys St; Boy Scts; Church Yth Grp; Drama Clb; Acpl Chr; Chorus; Madrigals; School Musical; School Play; Stage Crew; Bethony Lions Clb Schlrshp 86; Norwich U.

CARRION, WILLIAM; Orville Platt HS; Meriden, CT; (Y).

CARROLL, JONATHAN; Fairfield College Prep; Shelton, CT; (Y); Church Yth Grp; Drama Clb; Pres Key Clb; Chorus; Church Choir; School Play; Yrbk Phtg; High Hon Roll; NHS; Spanish NHS; Fairfield Prep Ldrshp Wkdn 85; Outward Bound 83; Bus.

CARROLL, KEITH; St Josephs HS; Stratford, CT; (Y); 27/253; French Clb; Nwsp Sprt Ed; Yrbk Sprt Ed; JV Bsbl; Var Socr; Var Trk; Trs French Hon Soc; High Hon Roll; NHS.

CARSTEN, MIKE; Branford HS; Branford, CT; (Y); Hon Roll; Typng Awd 84-85; Comp.

CARTER, ALLISON; Andrew Warde HS; Fairfield, CT; (Y); Church Yth Grp; Drama Clb; Key Clb; Band; Concert Band; Mrchg Band; School Play; Stu Cncl; Bsktbl; Engl.

CARTER, HEIDI; The Williams Schl; Waterford, CT; (Y); 6/38; School Play; Yrbk Bus Mgr; Pres Jr Cls; Pres Sr Cls; Var L Fld Hcky; Var L Tennis; High Hon Roll; VP Temple Yth Grp; Nwsp Stf; Rep Frsh Cls; Stdnt Cncl Schlrshp 85; Yale Sci Lctr Srs 86.

CARTER, KELLI; Joseph A Foran HS; Milford, CT; (Y); Church Yth Grp; Dance Clb; Keywanettes; Hon Roll; Bus.

CARTIER, MONIQUE; Putnam HS; Woodstock, CT; (Y); Chess Clb; Cmnty Wkr; Yrbk Stf; Cheerleading; Hon Roll.

CARTY, THOMAS; The Williams Schl; Waterford, CT; (Y); Nwsp Sprt Ed; Yrbk Stf; Bsbl; Bsktbl; Crs Cntry; Hon Roll; Prfct Atten Awd; Marshall 85-86; Uppr Schl Athlt 85-87.

CARUSO, ANGELA; Ridgefield HS; Ridgefield, CT; (Y); 76/387; DECA; Flag Corp; JV Sftbl; High Hon Roll; Hon Roll; U Of CT; Accntng.

CASABLANCA, KAREN; Lauralton Hall HS; Huntington, CT; (Y); 38/111; Service Clb; Ed Yrbk Stf; NHS; Drama Clb; Latin Clb; Spanish Clb; School Musical; School Play; Piano Awds 83 & 84; Natl Latin Exam Awd 84; Pre-Med.

CASALE, DOUGLAS; Kingswood Oxford HS; W Hartford, CT; (Y); Rep Frsh Cls; JV Ftbl; Var Ice Hcky; Bus Mgmt.

CASAVANT, MICHELE; Torrington HS; Torrington, CT; (Y); 76/270; Varsity Clb; Chorus; Yrbk Stf; Var L Mgr(s); Var Stat Trk; Hon Roll; Elem Eductn.

CASCIA, JONA; Enfield HS; Enfield, CT; (S); 35/245; DECA; Spanish Clb; Variety Show; Yrbk Stf; Pres Jr Cls; Sec Pres Stu Cncl; CC Awd; Cit Awd; DAR Awd; Hon Roll; DECA Stu Yr 85-86; Bryant Coll; Accntng.

CASCIANO, SCOTT; Mark T Sheehan HS; Wallingford, CT; (Y); 67/237; Church Yth Grp; Variety Show; Var Capt Ftbl; Var Capt Tennis; Hon Roll; US Mrne Corps Dist Athl & Mark T Sheehan HS Bstr Clb Sr Athl Awds 86; M T Sheehan Stu Cncl Schlrshp; Quinnipiac Coll; Mass Comm.

CASCIO, LAUREN; St Bernard HS; New London, CT; (Y); 27/265; Ski Clb; Yrbk Stf; Sec Jr Cls; Sec Sr Cls; Chrmn Stu Cncl; Cheerleading; Hon Roll; Pre-Law.

CASE, DARCY; Suffield HS; W Suffield, CT; (Y); 12/143; Ski Clb; Chorus; Madrigals; School Musical; School Play; VP Frsh Cls; Pres Soph Cls; Rep Stu Cncl; Co-Capt Cheerleading; Pres Schlr; Stu Cncl Ldrshp Awd 84 & 86; Bryant Coll; Fshn Rtlng.

CASEY, LORI; Avon HS; Avon, CT; (Y); Church Yth Grp; JA; Yrbk Stf; Var Vllybl; Stat Wrstlng; High Hon Roll; Hon Roll; Rep Close Up Pgm; Hotel Adm.

CASEY, MARGARET; Ridgefield HS; Ridgefield, CT; (Y); 12/387; German Clb; Service Clb; Chorus; Nwsp Rptr; Nwsp Stf; JV Fld Hcky; Im Lcrss; High Hon Roll; Hon Roll; NHS; Holy Crs Bk Awd 85-86; Grmn Cnslt Bk Prz 83-86; Pltcl Sci.

CASEY, MARY; Sacred Heart Acad; New Haven, CT; (Y); Exploring; FBLA; Library Aide; Political Wkr; Vllybl; Hon Roll; 3 Yr Hnr Awd 86; Chem Awd-Natl Sci Olympiad 86.

CASSARINO, ANTHONY; St Bernard HS; Colchester, CT; (Y); VP Drama Clb; Var L Socr; Finance.

CASSELLA, JENNIFER; North Branford HS; North Branford, CT; (Y); Band; Chorus; Concert Band; Madrigals; Mrchg Band; Variety Show; JV Bsktbl; Var Capt Sftbl; High Hon Roll; Hon Roll; Music Excllnc 84-85; Outstdng Svc Chorus 85-86; UCONN; Psych.

CASSIDY, KEVIN; Lyman Hall HS; Wallingford, CT; (Y); 11/200; Church Yth Grp; VP JA; Pres Spanish Clb; Varsity Clb; Stu Cncl; Var L Socr; Dnfth Awd; NHS; Prfct Atten Awd; Voice Dem Awd; Schlr-Athlete Awd 86; Amer Legion Schl Awd 86; Pres Acad Ftnss Awd 86; Fairfield U; Comp Sci.

CASTRO, DEBORAH LYNN; Bassick HS; Bridgeport, CT; (Y); Church Yth Grp; DECA; JA; Teachers Aide; Church Choir; Lit Mag; Hon Roll; Prfct Atten Awd; Girl Scts; Variety Show; Prfct Atten JA 85-86; Sls Clb In JA 85-86; Butler Bus Schl; Data Entry Op.

CATANZARO, RUTH; The Morgan Schl; Clinton, CT; (Y); 34/167; AFS; Pep Clb; Band; Chorus; School Musical; Yrbk Stf; VP Stu Cncl; Capt Cheerleading; High Hon Roll; Hon Roll; Keen ST; Elem Ed.

CATERSON, SUZANNE; Danbury HS; Danbury, CT; (Y); 93/577; Varsity Clb; Band; Rep Stu Cncl; Capt Cheerleading; Tennis; Hon Roll; French Clb; Hosp Aide; Office Aide; Variety Show; Western Rgnl H S Band 85; Hmcmng Queen 85; Finance.

CATES, JESSICA; Trumbull HS; Trumbull, CT; (Y); Chorus; Color Guard; Nwsp Stf; Fld Hcky; Mgr(s); Score Keeper; Mgr Sftbl; High Hon Roll; Hon Roll; NHS; Hlth.

CAVALERI, ROBERT; Joseph A Foran HS; Milford, CT; (Y); Computer Clb; Key Clb; Spanish Clb; SADD; Crs Cntry; Var Trk; U Connecticut; Comp Sci.

CAVALIERE, KRISTEN A; Newtown HS; Newtown, CT; (Y); 16/288; Office Aide; SADD; Teachers Aide; Nwsp Ed-Chief; High Hon Roll; Hon Roll; NHS; Pres Schlr; Trs Spanish NHS; Holy Cross Schlrshp 86; Newtown Schlrshp 86; Coll Of Holy Cross; Pltcl Sci.

CAVANAUGH, CATHERINE; Simsbury HS; Simsbury, CT; (Y); 31/410; Drama Clb; FBLA; JA; Chorus; Var L Crs Cntry; JV Fld Hcky; Var L Trk; High Hon Roll; NHS; CT ST Chmpn Acctng I FBLA 86; Bus Adm.

CAVANAUGH, MAUREEN; Conard HS; W Hartford, CT; (Y); 4/345; Cmnty Wkr; Math Tm; Var Bsktbl; JV Trk; Capt Vllybl; Var High Hon Roll; NHS; Ntl Merit Ltr; Spanish NHS; Church Yth Grp; Marion Jones Prz Outstndng Stu 86; Math.

CAVOLI, JOANNE; Rham HS; Marlborough, CT; (Y); 38/200; Var Capt Bsktbl; JV Var Sftbl; Var Tennis; Hon Roll; Jr NHS.

CEDERSTAV, ANNA; Greenwich HS; Cos Cob, CT; (Y); Exploring; Acpl Chr; Chorus; Concert Band; Jazz Band; Mrchg Band; School Musical; Variety Show; NHS; Ntl Merit Ltr; Top 5 Pct CT Chemtn 84; 3rd Awd CT ST Sci Fair 85; Yale U; Chem Engrng.

CELELLO, LISA; Holy Cross HS; Watertown, CT; (Y); 58/380; Am Leg Aux Girls St; French Clb; Latin Clb; SADD; JV Trk; Stat Vllybl; Cit Awd; NHS.

CELENTANO, MICHAEL; Notre Dame HS; New Haven, CT; (Y); Boy Scts; Church Yth Grp; Political Wkr; Var L Trk; High Hon Roll; Vrsty Jckt In Trk 86; U Of CT; Psych.

CELTRUDA, CHRISTOPHER R; St Bernard HS; Mystic, CT; (Y); 49/289; Boy Scts; Ski Clb; Var L Crs Cntry; Var Trk; U Of ME Orono; Forest Engrng.

CENCE, SANDRA; Southington HS; Southington, CT; (Y); 42/548; Am Leg Aux Girls St; Nwsp Ed-Chief; Nwsp Phtg; Nwsp Rptr; Nwsp Sprt Ed; L Swmmng; Capt L Tennis; High Hon Roll; Hon Roll; NHS; Recrd-Jrnl Schlrshp 86; New Britain Herald Bk Prz 86; Boston U; Prnt Jrnlsm.

CEPPETELLI, JILL; Tolland HS; Tolland, CT; (Y); 37/150; Am Leg Aux Girls St; School Musical; Yrbk Stf; Lit Mag; Var Cheerleading; Hon Roll; Bryant Coll; Mktg.

CERASULO, TOM; Holy Cross HS; Waterbury, CT; (Y); 190/380; Latin Clb; Political Wkr; SADD; JV L School Musical; JV L School Play; Nwsp Stf; JV Lcrss; Hon Roll; Art Clb; Drama Clb; NY U; Film Wrtg.

CERINO, SCOTT; Trumbull HS; Trumbull, CT; (Y); Boy Scts; Church Yth Grp; Chorus; Nwsp Ed-Chief; Nwsp Stf; Rotary Awd; Treas-Italn Clb 85-86; Manhattanville Coll; Bus Mgmt.

CERVERO, KIM; Kolbe-Cathedral HS; Naugatuck, CT; (Y); Hosp Aide; Yrbk Stf; Science Clb; Nwsp Phtg; Yrbk Phtg; Yrbk Rptr; Mattatuck Coll; Nrsng.

CESTARO, APRIL; Chesshire HS; Cheshire, CT; (Y); Cmnty Wkr; Hosp Aide; Library Aide; Red Cross Aide; Bus.

CHABINA, LARA; Brookfield HS; Brookfield Center, CT; (Y); Varsity Clb; Mrchg Band; Rep Frsh Cls; Rep Soph Cls; Cheerleading; Fld Hcky; Tennis; Trk; High Hon Roll; NHS; Natl Pop Warner Schlr Chrldr 82; Typng Awd 84; U Of San Diego; Aviatn.

CHAFFEE JR, DON J; Newington HS; Newington, CT; (Y); 64/352; Church Yth Grp; Ski Clb; Band; Jazz Band; School Musical; Pres Symp Band; Variety Show; Co-Capt Crs Cntry; Hon Roll; NHS; Music Dirctrs Awd 86; Northrn Regnl Band 86; Frank Roswell Fuller Schlrshp 86; Bryant Coll; Accntng.

CHALFANT, JOYCE; Southington HS; Plantsville, CT; (Y); Church Yth Grp; Cmnty Wkr; Band; Church Choir; Color Guard; Concert Band; Mrchg Band; Capt Twrlr; Hon Roll; Intrr Desgn.

CHAMIDES, DARCY; Wilton HS; Wilton, CT; (Y); 39/354; Church Yth Grp; Cmnty Wkr; Drama Clb; Ski Clb; School Play; Stage Crew; Lit Mag; Rep Frsh Cls; High Hon Roll; NHS; Natl Latin Exam 84.

CHAN, ALBERT; Stamford HS; Stamford, CT; (Y); Cmnty Wkr; Key Clb; Science Clb; Orch; Stu Cncl; JV Crs Cntry; Trk; High Hon Roll; NHS; CT Al-ST Orchstra 1st Violin 85; CT Schlrs Pgm 86; Aerospc.

CHAN, ANGEL; Norwalk HS; Norwalk, CT; (Y); 7/420; Office Aide; Band; Concert Band; Mrchg Band; Symp Band; High Hon Roll; NHS; Nrowalk Sci Fair 1st Pl 86; Holy Cross Bk Awd Exc Engl 86; Yale U; Sci.

CHANDRA, SUMEET; Kingswood Oxford HS; W Hartford, CT; (Y); Intnl Clb; JV Var Tennis; Hon Roll; Ntl Merit Ltr; Engr.

CHAPMAN, YOLANDA; Stamford HS; Stamford, CT; (Y); Color Guard; Drill Tm; Mrchg Band; Bsktbl; Hon Roll; Church Yth Grp; 4-H; Pep Clb; Political Wkr; Sftbl; Bsktbl Vrsty Awd 83-84 & 85-86; Cinderella Ball Schlrshp 83-84; Psychology.

CHARLES, STEPHANIE; Miss Porters Schl; Salisbury, CT; (Y); Cmnty Wkr; Head Ushers-Schl Orgnztn 86-87; RISD; Art.

CHARNEY, APRIL; Shelton HS; Shelton, CT; (Y); Drama Clb; Spanish Clb; Band; Concert Band; Mrchg Band; Orch; Pep Band; Hon Roll; Spanish NHS; Htl Mgmt.

CHARTIER, DANIEL; Killingly HS; Brooklyn, CT; (Y); 60/325; Var Bsktbl; Var Socr; Var Trk; DAR Awd; Hon Roll; Indoor Sccr 85-86; Prom Committee 85-86; Ski Clb 84-86; UCONN.

CHASSE, MICHELE; Seymour HS; Seymour, CT; (Y); Church Yth Grp; Yrbk Stf; Pom Pon; Hon Roll; Cert Outstndng Achvt Accntng I, Typng I 84-86; Bus.

CHEMACKI, TIM; Daniel Hand HS; Madison, CT; (Y); 18/229; Boy Scts; Church Yth Grp; JCL; Quiz Bowl; School Play; L Var Crs Cntry; JV Trk; High Hon Roll; Hon Roll; NHS; Aeronautcl Engrng.

CHEN, ELEANOR; Amity Regional HS; Orange, CT; (Y); 3/388; Am Leg Aux Girls St; Church Yth Grp; French Clb; Mrchg Band; Symp Band; Ed Nwsp Ed-Chief; Stu Cncl; Swmmng; High Hon Roll; NHS; All Hstnc Leag Swmng Team; Crnll Bk Awd; Laurel Girls ST; Wharton Schl Finance; Bus Admn.

CHEN, IVAN; Choate Rosemary Hall HS; Dartmouth, MA; (Y); Debate Tm; Math Clb; Orch; Lit Mag; Rep Frsh Cls; Rep Soph Cls; Rep Jr Cls; JV Var Tennis; NHS; Ntl Merit Ltr; All-Natl HS Orch 85; All-Eastern HS Orch 84; MA SR High Dist Orch 83-85; Dartmouth Coll.

CHEN, JULIE; Greenwich HS; Greenwich, CT; (Y); Debate Tm; Service Clb; Nwsp Ed-Chief; French Hon Soc; High Hon Roll; JETS Awd; NHS; Ntl Merit Ltr; Am Leg Aux Girls St; Quiz Bowl; Coll Of Holy Cross Book Awd 86; Odyssey Of Mind Ranatra Fusca Creativity Awd 86; Harvard; Mathematics.

CHENG, LESLIE; Trumbull HS; Trumbull, CT; (Y); AFS; French Clb; Key Clb; Orch; Lit Mag; French Hon Soc; High Hon Roll; NHS; Latn Hnr Soc 84; Elizabeth Leete Awd-Hghst Acadmc Avg Entire Schl 83-84; Oberlin Coll Bk Awd 86.

CHETCUTI, MARGARET; Brien Mc Mahon HS; Norwalk, CT; (Y); Band; Concert Band; Mrchg Band; Orch; High Hon Roll; NHS; Ct All St Fstvl 84-86; Ct Wstrn Rgnl Band Fstvl 84-86; M L Kellog Schlrshp, E J Partridge Schlrshp 84; NYSU; Music Tchr.

CHIANG, DARRYL D; Edwin O Smith Schl; Mansfield Center, CT; (Y); 2/169; VP Drama Clb; School Play; Yrbk Stf; Ed Trs Lit Mag; Var Tennis; NCTE Awd; Pres NHS; Ntl Merit Ltr; Harvard-Radcliffe Clb Nrthrn CT Bk Prz 85; Ctr Creatv Yth Visl Arts Stu 85; CT ST Msc Tchrs Assn 85; Princeton U.

CHIAPPINELLI, JOHN P; Central Catholic HS; S Norwalk, CT; (Y); 4/78; Cmnty Wkr; Var L Bsbl; High Hon Roll; NHS; Prfct Atten Awd; St Schlr; U Of CT Almni Assn Bk Awd 85-86; Firefghtrs Lcl 830 Schlrshp 85-86; Excllnc-Trig 85-86; U Of CT; Accntng.

CHILTON, RALPH; Conard HS; W Htfd, CT; (Y); 30/357; Church Yth Grp; Political Wkr; Concert Band; Jazz Band; Rep Jr Cls; Rep Sr Cls; Stu Cncl; Var L Lcrss; Var L Swmmng; High Hon Roll; James J Stewert Swmng Awd 85; Official Citation Achvt From ST Of Ct Genrl Assmbly 86; Hstry.

CHIN, LARRY; Norwalk HS; Norwalk, CT; (Y); 19/456; Computer Clb; Spanish Clb; Yrbk Stf; High Hon Roll; Rep Soph Cls; Rep Jr Cls.

CHIRICO, MIRIAM; East Hartford HS; E Hartford, CT; (Y); Am Leg Aux Girls St; Pres Church Yth Grp; Dance Clb; Political Wkr; Pres SADD; School Musical; Nwsp Ed-Chief; Lit Mag; High Hon Roll; NHS; Spnsh Spkg Cntst Awd 84&85; Hrtfrd Wllsly Clb Bk Awd 86; E Hrtfrd Hstrcl Soc Awd 86; Engl.

CHISHOLM, BRIDGET; Wilbur Cross HS; New Haven, CT; (Y); 4-H; Girl Scts; Spanish Clb; Teachers Aide; Band; 4-H Awd; Bus Adm.

CHIU, JEANNIE Y; Watertown HS; Watertown, CT; (Y); 1/216; Am Leg Aux Girls St; English Clb; Co-Capt Scholastic Bowl; Orch; Variety Show; Nwsp Rptr; Rep Frsh Cls; Rep Jr Cls; Rep Sr Cls; JV Trk; Cornell U; Bio.

CHMIELEWSKI, KAREN; St Bernard HS; Norwich, CT; (Y); 43/280; Chess Clb; Stage Crew; JV Im Bsktbl; JV Var Sftbl; Im Wt Lftg; Hon Roll; A Avg Fres Yr In Fine Arts 84; Renssalear Poly Tech; Sci.

CHO, ME YOUNG; Hotchkiss Schl; Voorhees, NJ; (Y); VP Church Yth Grp; Band; Orch; School Musical; Lit Mag; Hon Roll; Ntl Merit Schol; Columbia U; Pltcl Sci.

CHOI, SUENHEE; Trumbull HS; Trumbull, CT; (Y); Library Aide; Color Guard; Mrchg Band; Rep Frsh Cls; Var L Vllybl; Prfct Atten Awd; Peer Tutrng 86; U CT; Bus.

CHOLAK, DAVID; Stamford HS; Stamford, CT; (Y); Church Yth Grp; Yrbk Stf; JV Golf; Socr; Capt Trk; Hon Roll.

CHRISS, KIM; The Taft Schl; Woodbury, CT; (Y); 6/115; Church Yth Grp; Dance Clb; Band; Church Choir; Yrbk Stf; Var L Crs Cntry; JV Fld Hcky; Var L Trk; High Hon Roll; Hon Roll; Princetn-Yale-Brown; Math.

CHRISSOS, ELLEN; Enrico Fermi HS; Enfield, CT; (S); DECA; Office Aide; Hon Roll; Fshn Mrchndsr.

CHRISTENSEN, HEIDI; Wamogo Regional HS; Goshen, CT; (Y); 12/79; FBLA; Co-Capt Cheerleading; Trk; NHS; AFS; Church Yth Grp; Girl Scts; Pep Clb; High Hon Roll; Hon Roll; 3rd Pl Future Bus Ldrs Amer ST Ldrshp Cnfrnc 86; Stone School; Exec Secry.

CHRISTIAN, MELISSA; Torriington HS; Torrington, CT; (Y); 34/340; French Clb; Girl Scts; Band; Drm Mjr(t); Mrchg Band; School Musical; Stage Crew; High Hon Roll; NHS; Drama Clb; Itln-Amer Repb Schlrshp 86; Fairfield U; Law.

CHRISTIAN, RITA; Suffield HS; Suffield, CT; (Y); 36/143; Chorus; JV Capt Cheerleading; CC Awd; High Hon Roll; Hon Roll; Awd Excllnc Bus Educ 86; St Josephs Rosary Guild Schlrshp 86; Briarwood Coll Bk Prize 85; Albertus Magnus Coll; Acctg.

CHRISTIE, JEFFREY; Holy Cross HS; Watertown, CT; (Y); 12/347; Yrbk Stf; Rep Stu Cncl; JV Capt Socr; Capt Tennis; French Hon Soc; High Hon Roll; NHS; Ntl Merit Ltr; Pres Schlr; St Schlr; Seimon Co & Dr Edward Lewicki Memrl Schlrshps 86; Cert Hnr 86; Bowdoin Coll Brunswick ME.

CHRISTIE, STEPHEN; Trumbull HS; Trumbull, CT; (Y); High Hon Roll; NHS; Bus Admn.

CHRISTOS, CHRIS; Brookfield HS; Brookfield Center, CT; (Y); Church Yth Grp; Cmnty Wkr; Math Tm; Spanish Clb; Socr; Trk; Wt Lftg; High Hon Roll; Sci Awd 83; Spn II & III Achvt Awd 83-84; Engrng.

CHRZAN, DONALD; Putnam HS; Woodstock, CT; (Y); Band; School Play; Var Crs Cntry; Var Trk; Hon Roll; Johnson & Wales Coll; Mgmt.

CHRZANOWSKI, JON; Derby HS; Derby, CT; (Y); Ski Clb; Im Bsktbl; Im Vllybl; Im Wt Lftg; Im Wrstlng; Schlrshp Awd 82; Ind Arts Tchr.

CHUN, JENNIFER; Kent HS; Budd Lake, NJ; (Y); Chorus; Nwsp Rptr; Rep Frsh Cls; Rep Soph Cls; Rep Jr Cls; Off Sr Cls; Rep Stu Cncl; Var Capt Fld Hcky; Var Capt Lcrss; JV Score Keeper; Head Stdy Hall Mntr 85-86; All-Star Fld Hcky Tm 85; Sprts Updt Edtr 85-86.

CHUNG, DAVID; Amity Regional HS; Woodbridge, CT; (Y); Am Leg Boys St; German Clb; Pres Latin Clb; VP Science Clb; Band; Concert Band; Mrchg Band; Nwsp Stf; Capt L Crs Cntry; L Var Trk.

CHUPREVICH, SARAH; Southington HS; Southington, CT; (Y); 67/600; Latin Clb; Ski Clb; Concert Band; Var Trk; Hon Roll; Bentley; Acctg.

CHURCHILL, CINDY; Windham Regional Vo Tech; Lebaron, CT; (Y); Art Clb; Cheerleading; Sftbl; Hon Roll; Vermont Tech Coll; Archtctrl En.

CHWALEK, DAVID; Tourtellotte Memorial HS; Thompson, CT; (Y); 2/101; Am Leg Boys St; Band; Trs Frsh Cls; Trs Soph Cls; Trs Jr Cls; Trs Sr Cls; Var L Bsbl; L Capt Socr; DECA; Trs NHS; Hugh O Brian Yth Ldrshp Sem 85; Rensselaer Math/Sci Awd, Outstndng Achvt Am Studies 86.

CIAK, SHARI; Erkico Fermi HS; Enfield, CT; (S); Church Yth Grp; DECA; Drama Clb; Ski Clb; Vlntr Nrsng Home Aid 84 & 85; Bus.

CIANCHETTI, LISA; Plainville HS; Plainville, CT; (Y); #14 In Class; Bsbl; Var L Bsktbl; Var L Sftbl; Hon Roll; NHS; All NW Cnfrnce Sftbl 85; Rnnrup Cls M ST Fnls CT Sftbl 86; NW Cnfrnce Chmps Bsktbl 85; Springfield Coll; Physcl Thrpy.

CIANCI, DEBRA; Southington HS; Southington, CT; (Y); Ski Clb; Y-Teens; Stu Cncl; Gym; Hon Roll; Pres Physcl Fitnss Awd 84; Clss II Tm YMCA Gymnstcs ST Chmps 84/Brnz Mdl-Vaultng Slvr-Bm St Chmpns; FBI.

CIANCIULLI, JACQUELINE; Mark T Sheehan HS; Wallingford, CT; (Y); 20/207; Art Clb; JA; Powder Puff Ftbl; Swmmng; High Hon Roll; U Of CT; Bus.

CIARCIA, DONALD; Southington HS; Southington, CT; (Y); 260/580; Ski Clb; JV Bsbl; Var Ftbl; Bus.

CIERI, DEBRA; Morgan HS; Clinton, CT; (Y); 9/140; Spanish Clb; SADD; Yrbk Stf; Rep Stu Cncl; Var L Crs Cntry; Powder Puff Ftbl; Trk; Hon Roll; Phys Thrpst.

CIHOCKI, CONSTANCE; Lyme-Old Lyme HS; Old Lyme, CT; (Y); 10/110; Pres Intnl Clb; Jazz Band; Orch; School Musical; Lit Mag; VP Soph Cls; Stu Cncl; Var Tennis; NHS; AFS; Tri-M Music Hnr Soc 85.

CIMINO, RENEE; North Branford HS; North Branford, CT; (Y); 32/182; Cmnty Wkr; Hosp Aide; Pep Clb; SADD; Varsity Clb; Trs Frsh Cls; Trs Soph Cls; VP Jr Cls; Stu Cncl; Bsktbl; Spnsh Awd; All Shoreline & All ST Fld Hcky; Trck-3rd Pl In Shoreline; Scl Wrkr.

CIOPPA, JULIE LYNN; Wilton HS; Wilton, CT; (Y); Dance Clb; Drama Clb; GAA; Girl Scts; Library Aide; Pep Clb; Stage Crew; Rep Stu Cncl; JV Bsktbl; Hon Roll; Model.

CIOSEK, TRACY; Southington HS; Southington, CT; (Y); Var L Bsktbl; Var Capt Sftbl; High Hon Roll; NHS; Grls Bsktbl ST Trnmnt MVP 86; Grls Bsktbl Cntrl CT Cnfrnce Tm 85-86; Grls Sftbl CT Cnfnc Tm 86; Bus.

CIPRIANO, CHRISTINE; Watertown HS; Watertown, CT; (Y); 12/275; AFS; Computer Clb; Spanish Clb; SADD; Rep Jr Cls; Rep Stu Cncl; Var Socr; High Hon Roll; Hon Roll; Rep Soph Cls; Bus Admnst.

CIPRIANO, GIUSEPPE; Holy Cross HS; Waterbury, CT; (Y); Latin Clb; Elec.

CIPRIANO, JILL; Wilby HS; Waterbury, CT; (Y); 10/300; Rep Frsh Cls; Rep Soph Cls; Rep Jr Cls; Sec Trs Stu Cncl; Bsktbl; Crs Cntry; Swmmng; Tennis; Hon Roll; NHS.

CIPRIANO, MELISSA; Crosby HS; Waterbury, CT; (Y); Cmnty Wkr; Key Clb; Office Aide; Varsity Clb; School Play; Sec Jr Cls; Sec Sr Cls; Mgr(s); Swmmng; Hon Roll; Mt St Marys Coll; Nrsng.

CISLO, JENNIFER N; Portland HS; Portland, CT; (Y); 4/96; Art Clb; Drama Clb; English Clb; Lit Mag; High Hon Roll; Ntl Merit Ltr; NEDT Awd; U Of CT; Engl.

CISZEWSKI, JOEL; East Catholic HS; E Hartford, CT; (Y); 1/280; Rep Sr Cls; Socr; Pres NHS; Ntl Merit Schol; Val; Mst Vlbl Sccr Plyr Awd 86; U S Army Resrv Natl Schlr/Athlt Awd 86; Mcdonalds Schlr Athlt Awd 86; Yale U; Bio.

CIUCI, LYNN; St Joseph HS; Stratford, CT; (Y); 6/256; Church Yth Grp; Drama Clb; French Clb; Thesps; School Musical; School Play; Variety Show; French Hon Soc; High Hon Roll; Hon Roll; Frnch Awd Mst Outstndng Stu 84-85; Ed.

CLAFFEY III, CHARLES B; Conrad HS; W Htfd, CT; (Y); 8/345; Boys Clb Am; Church Yth Grp; JV Capt Bsktbl; Var Capt Golf; High Hon Roll; NHS; Smith Coll Book Awd Acdmc Achvt 86; Engrng.

CLAPP, JAMIE; Shelton HS; Shelton, CT; (Y); Dance Clb; Drama Clb; Office Aide; NHS; Ntl Merit SF; Mdl Effrt & Dedctn Jazz 84; Cert Mrt Prtcptng Mck Trl 86; Educ.

CLARK, ALICIA; Maloney HS; Meriden, CT; (Y); 28/253; Church Yth Grp; Band; Concert Band; Mrchg Band; Pep Band; Nwsp Stf; Powder Puff Ftbl; High Hon Roll; Excllnc Spnsh II; S CT ST Clg; Bio.

CLARK, ANDREW; Canton HS; Collinsville, CT; (Y); Rep Am Leg Boys St; VP Church Yth Grp; Cmnty Wkr; Ski Clb; Pres SADD; Stu Cncl; Var JV Socr; Hon Roll; Bio.

CLARK, BILLY; Oliver Wolcott Regional Votech Schl; Litchfield, CT; (Y); VICA; Hon Roll; 4th Pl ST Wide UICA Comp 86; Moore Awd Mach Tool & Die Trade JR Yr 86; Tool & Die Maker.

CLARK, CHRISTINE; Brookfield SR HS; Brookfield, CT; (Y); Church Yth Grp; Girl Scts; Yrbk Stf; Bsktbl; Var Tennis; Hon Roll; Grl Sct Slvr Awd 84; Asst Ldr 1st Grd Brwnie Trp 85-86; Trvl.

CLARK, DAWN; Kent Schl; New York, NY; (Y); 5/176; Spanish Clb; Pres Church Choir; Madrigals; Stat Bsktbl; JV Mgr(s); JV Socr; JV Capt Sftbl; God Cntry Awd; Ntl Merit Schol; R Lee Gilliam Choral Awd 85; Harvard; Bus Adm.

CLARK, FRANCIS; R E Fitch SR HS; Groton, CT; (Y); 93/306; FBLA; Intnl Clb; Science Clb; SADD; Swmmng; Hon Roll; Unit Commendation Ribbon Naval Sea Cadet Corps 84; MIT; Comp Sci.

CLARK, GERALD; New Britain HS; New Britain, CT; (Y); Camera Clb; Var L Crs Cntry; JV Ftbl; Var Trk; Capt Wt Lftg; Invtnl Track & Field Meet Pole Vault 2nd Pl 84; UCONN; Pol Sci.

CLARK, HEIDI; Foran HS; Milford, CT; (Y); Hosp Aide; Keywanettes; SADD; Yrbk Stf; Stu Cncl; Coach Actv; L Gym; Swmmng; Hon Roll; Lawyer.

CLARK, JENNY; Norwalk HS; Norwalk, CT; (Y); Church Yth Grp; Letterman Clb; Band; Concert Band; Mrchg Band; School Musical; Stage Crew; Symp Band; Yrbk Phtg; Sec Soph Cls; Librl Arts.

CLARK, KAREN; Westhaven HS; Cheshire, CT; (Y); 23/396; Intnl Clb; Spanish Clb; Acpl Chr; Chorus; Madrigals; Hon Roll; Jr NHS; NHS; Pres Schlr; Spanish NHS; U Of CT; Elem Ed.

CLARK, KATIE; Farmington HS; Farmington, CT; (Y); Church Yth Grp; Sec Drama Clb; Ski Clb; Chorus; School Play; Variety Show; JV Gym; JV Socr; Var Tennis; Simmons Of Boston; Pblc Rltns.

CLARK, STEPHEN; Norwalk HS; Norwalk, CT; (Y); 30/428; Ski Clb; Yrbk Phtg; Rep Frsh Cls; Rep Soph Cls; Rep Jr Cls; Rep Sr Cls; Var L Tennis; High Hon Roll; Pres NHS; Syracuse U; Arch.

CLARK, TODD C; Putnam HS; Putnam, CT; (Y); 37/145; Band; VP Chorus; Jazz Band; L JV Ftbl; L Var Trk; Chess Clb; Church Yth Grp; Pep Clb; Acpl Chr; Church Choir; Ptr Cpltt Awd Ftbl 85-86; Outstndng Fld Prfrmr Trck 85-86; Outstndng Chrl Svc Awd 85-86; Liberty Baptst U; Music.

CLARK, TRACY; Newington HS; Newington, CT; (S); 3/365; Am Leg Aux Girls St; Church Yth Grp; Cmnty Wkr; Pres Orch; School Musical; Var Trk; High Hon Roll; NHS; Drama Clb; School Play; Frgn Lang Clb Pres,Treas 84-85; CT Hnrs Sem 84; Schlr Brkfst 83-875; St Joseph Coll; Math.

CLARKIN, ELIZABETH; Our Lady Of The Angels Acad; Enfield, CT; (Y); 3/18; Nwsp Ed-Chief; Trs Frsh Cls; Trs Pres Stu Cncl; High Hon Roll; Prfct Atten Awd; 1st Pl Cert For Feature Wrtng Clmba U 84; 500 Hour Pin Johnson Mem Hosp 85; Ocptnl Thrpy.

CLARO, CAROLINE; Greenwich HS; Cos Cob, CT; (Y); Office Aide; JV Bsktbl; Var Tennis; JV Vllybl; Hon Roll; Fairfield U.

CLARO, VERONICA; Greenwich HS; Cos Cob, CT; (Y); JV Bsktbl; Var Tennis; JV Vllybl; Hon Roll.

CLAVETTE, JANET; East Hampton HS; E Hampton, CT; (Y); 9/90; Cmnty Wkr; Drama Clb; Hosp Aide; Office Aide; Political Wkr; Ski Clb; Stage Crew; Trk; Hon Roll; NHS; Bus Mgmt.

CLAYPOOLE, JOHN; Central Catholic HS; Norwalk, CT; (Y); Boy Scts; Math Tm; Ski Clb; Spanish Clb; Yrbk Bus Mgr; Lit Mag; Trs Stu Cncl; Ftbl; Bryant Coll; Acctg.

CLEARY, ERIKA; St Marys HS; New Haven, CT; (Y); 1/113; Pres PAVAS; School Musical; Lit Mag; Trs Jr Cls; Rep Stu Cncl; French Hon Soc; Mu Alp Tht; NHS; Church Yth Grp; Cmnty Wkr; Soc Wmn Engrs Awd; Ldrhsp Awd; Nwsp Column Schl Wrtr; Lib Arts.

CLEARY, MARIE; St Marys HS; New Haven, CT; (Y); Cmnty Wkr; Hosp Aide; Model UN; Ski Clb; School Musical; Stage Crew; Rep Jr Cls; Hon Roll; Taught 4th Grdrs Rlgn CCD 85; Model For Macys Dept Store 85; Chld Psych.

CLEMENS, DAVID; Fairfield College Prep; Fairfield, CT; (Y); Key Clb; Yrbk Sprt Ed; Im Bsktbl; JV Var Socr; JV Trk; Hon Roll; NHS; Sci Fair 1st Pl Bio Div 85; Pub Spkr Fairfield Safe Rides 86-87; Pk City Hosp Vlntr 85; Med.

CLEMENS, HOLLY; Trumbull HS; Trumbull, CT; (Y); Cmnty Wkr; Ski Clb; Teachers Aide; Chorus; Variety Show; Var Cheerleading; L Crs Cntry; Var L Gym; Score Keeper; Timer; Bus.

CLEMENTS, STEPHEN; North Haven HS; North Haven, CT; (Y); 70/299; Model UN; Ski Clb; Varsity Clb; Im Badmtn; Im Bsktbl; Im Ftbl; Im Golf; Var Socr; Im Sftbl; Im Vllybl; Var Ltr Soccr 85; Var Jacket 86; Pre-Med.

CLONEY, CINDY; Watertown HS; Oakville, CT; (Y); Pres Church Yth Grp; Cmnty Wkr; FBLA; Girl Scts; Spanish Clb; School Play; Sec Soph Cls; Trs Jr Cls; Hon Roll; Comm.

CLONMELL, MICHELLE; Lauralton Hall HS; Milford, CT; (Y); Drama Clb; Hosp Aide; JA; Math Tm; Model UN; Church Choir; Yrbk Stf; Rep Frsh Cls; Im Vllybl; Ntl Merit SF; Med.

CLOSE, KENNETH J; Guilford HS; Guilford, CT; (Y); 2/318; Math Tm; Capt Quiz Bowl; Lit Mag; Im Badmtn; Elks Awd; JETS Awd; NCTE Awd; NHS; Ntl Merit SF; Pres Spanish NHS; Rensselaer Medal 85; Hrvrd Bk Awd 85; Brn U; Engrng.

COADY, DENIS ROBBIE; New Canaan HS; New Canaan, CT; (Y); Science Clb; JV Bsktbl; Var Mgr(s); Var L Socr; High Hon Roll; Hon Roll; Best All Arnd Boy Awd; Capt JV Indr Soccr; Comptr Sci.

COAKLEY, RICHARD; Wilby HS; Waterbury, CT; (Y); 7/260; Aud/Vis; Yrbk Stf; Var Ftbl; Var Trk; Hon Roll; NHS; Cty Coachs Awd Ftbl 85; Waterbury ST Tech; Data Prcssg.

COATES, JOHN; Seymour HS; Seymour, CT; (Y); Pres VP Church Yth Grp; VP JA; High Hon Roll; Hon Roll; Prfct Atten Awd; Bio.

COBB, MICHELLE; Farmington HS; Farmington, CT; (Y); 23/204; Am Leg Aux Girls St; Pres Drama Clb; Model UN; Political Wkr; Ski Clb; Yrbk Stf; High Hon Roll.

COCHRANE, HEATHER; Ridgefield HS; Ridgefield, CT; (Y); 118/369; Church Yth Grp; Dance Clb; German Clb; Office Aide; Red Cross Aide; High Hon Roll; Hon Roll; Outstndg Achvt Geom 85; Pre-Vet.

COCKFIELD, CELIA; Staples HS; Westport, CT; (Y); Church Yth Grp; French Clb; VP Model UN; Orch; High Hon Roll; Hon Roll; Frnch Achvt Awd; Chamber Orch; Stu Ed Pgm.

COCO, AUDREY; Northwest Catholic HS; Hartford, CT; (Y); Chorus; JV Bsktbl; Religion Awd 85; Poli Sci.

COEN, FRAN; Staples HS; Westport, CT; (Y); 1/400; Church Yth Grp; Nwsp Rptr; Lit Mag; Var Socr; JV Tennis; CT Indus Arts Assoc Mrt Awd 85; CT Indus Arts Assoc 1st, Hnrbl Mntn 86; Arch.

COHAN, TAMARA; Branford HS; Branford, CT; (Y); Political Wkr; Hon Roll; Hnr Rl 83-85; Bio.

COHEN, HEIDI; Bethel HS; Bethel, CT; (Y); AFS; Dance Clb; Ski Clb; Temple Yth Grp; Color Guard; Var Socr; Var Tennis; Phila Coll Tex/Sci; Fash Merch.

COHEN, IRIS; Andrew Warde HS; Fairfield, CT; (Y); 1/323; Cmnty Wkr; Dance Clb; Temple Yth Grp; Rep Stu Cncl; French Hon Soc; High Hon Roll; NHS; Rotary Awd; Civtn Clb Civc Awd 86; Gould Found Schlrshp 86; Cornell U; Humn Devlpmnt.

COHEN, JEFF; Mark T Sheehan HS; Wallingford, CT; (Y); Boys Clb Am; JA; Letterman Clb; Temple Yth Grp; Var Bsbl; Var L Bsktbl; Hon Roll; All League Bsktbl Tm Selctn 85-86; Econ.

COHEN, KAREN B; Amity Regional SR HS; Orange, CT; (S); Cmnty Wkr; French Clb; Red Cross Aide; Yrbk Stf; Off Stu Cncl; NHS; Cls I Hnrs 84; Peer Tutrng Cnslng 86; Amty On The Air 86-87; Photo.

COHEN, KENNETH; Conard HS; W Hartford, CT; (Y); 2/300; Capt Math Tm; Model UN; Spanish Clb; Trs Temple Yth Grp; Jazz Band; Lit Mag; High Hon Roll; Pres NHS; Ntl Merit SF; Spanish NHS; 1st Pl ST Chmthn 85; Amer Legion Schl Awd 86; Yale Book Prize 85; Yale U.

COHEN, SHARON; Cooperative HS; New Haven, CT; (Y); 2/52; SADD; Nwsp Ed-Chief; Yrbk Phtg; Lit Mag; Sec Stu Cncl; JV L Tennis; Bausch & Lomb Sci Awd; Hon Roll; NHS; Sal; Black Stu Union Black Achvt Essay Awd; Womens Intl Leag Peace/Frdm; Cngrsnl Mdl Mrt; Albertus Magnus; Pre-Med.

COLE, HELENA; Wilbur Cross HS; New Haven, CT; (S); 3/264; Math Clb; Political Wkr; Teachers Aide; Nwsp Stf; Lit Mag; High Hon Roll; Ntl Merit Ltr; French Clb; Chem Awd 84; Engl Awd 83-84; Italian Awd 83-84; Politics.

COLELLA, DENISE; St Marys HS; New Haven, CT; (Y); Spanish Clb; Rep Stu Cncl; Hon Roll; Sis Elizabeth Seton Schlrshp 85-86; Bus Mngmnt.

COLEMAN, BETH; East Hartford HS; E Hartford, CT; (Y); Church Yth Grp; Chorus; School Musical; School Play; Nwsp Stf; Stat Wrstlng; High Hon Roll; Hon Roll; NHS; Fnlst Frnch Spkg Cntst.

COLEMAN, JULIA HEATH; Amity HS; Orange, CT; (Y); 11/388; Am Leg Aux Girls St; Cmnty Wkr; Hosp Aide; Yrbk Sprt Ed; Rep Frsh Cls; Rep Soph Cls; Rep Jr Cls; Rep Sr Cls; Rep Stu Cncl; Var L Sftbl; New Haven Rgster Yth Of The Yr 86; Stud Of The Mnth 86; Robert Pite Memrl Schlrshp 86; Haverford Coll.

COLETTI, BRIAN TODD; Berlin HS; Berlin, CT; (Y); Hosp Aide; Mgr JA; Quiz Bowl; Yrbk Phtg; Trs Jr Cls; Trs Sr Cls; Powder Puff Ftbl; JV Socr; Var Capt Trk; Hon Roll.

COLGAN, DANIELLE; Immaculate HS; Newtown, CT; (Y); 31/137; VP Church Yth Grp; Dance Clb; Drama Clb; Ski Clb; School Play; Yrbk Stf; Cheerleading; Hon Roll; NHS; Bus.

COLLA JR, RAYMOND A; Windsor HS; Windsor, CT; (Y); 14/319; Trs FBLA; High Hon Roll; Hon Roll; JC Awd; 1st ST Of CT Econ FBLA Cmptn 86; Hgh Dstnctn 86; Schlrshp To U Of CT 86; U Of CT; Bus Mgmt.

COLLEN, KEVIN; Oliver Wolcott RVTS HS; Harwinton, CT; (Y); 1/146; Am Leg Boys St; Math Clb; Hst VICA; Yrbk Stf; Bausch & Lomb Sci Awd; High Hon Roll; NHS; Val; Elctrncs Dept Awd, Wm E Kelvie Mem Schlrshp, CBIA Indstrl Educ Awd 86; Waterbury ST Tech; Elctrncs.

COLLINS, JENNIFER; Fitch SR HS; Groton, CT; (Y); Drama Clb; Intnl Clb; Thesps; Stage Crew; Lit Mag; JV Tennis; 1st Pl Shrt Stry Amphora Magz 86; Law.

COLLINS, LYNN; East Catholic HS; East Hartford, CT; (Y); Cmnty Wkr; Dance Clb; Math Clb; Band; Drm Mjr(t); Nwsp Phtg; Yrbk Phtg; Cit Awd; DAR Awd; Hon Roll; Otsndng Vlntr Yr Awd 85; Miss AM Coed ST Fnlst 86; Mss AM Coed Vlntr Awd 86; St Joseph Coll; Elem Ed.

COLLINS, MARY BETH; Simsbury HS; Simsbury, CT; (Y); 91/406; Trs FBLA; VP JA; Library Aide; Ski Clb; Nwsp Rptr; Yrbk Stf; JV Fld Hcky; Hon Roll; Ntl Merit Ltr; Powder Puff Ftbl; Jr Achvt Co Of The Yr 85; Young Life Work Crew 86; News Brdcstng.

COLLINS, VANESSA; Plainfield HS; Plainfield, CT; (Y); 28/162; Church Yth Grp; Band; Chorus; Stu Cncl; Hon Roll; Jr NHS.

COLON, CHARLES; Norwalk HS; Norwalk, CT; (Y); JA; SADD; Rep Frsh Cls; Rep Soph Cls; Rep Jr Cls; JV Lcrss; Bus Mgmt.

COLONNA, ANDREA; Sacred Heart Acad; New Haven, CT; (Y); Church Yth Grp; Chorus; School Musical; Capt Cheerleading; Prfct Atten Awd; St Aedans Chrch Schlrshp 83; Our Ldy Mt Carmel Alumni Schlrshp 85; Pro-Life Clb Treas 85-86; Pres 86-87; Bus.

COLONNESE, MELISSA; Sacred Heart Acad; New Haven, CT; (Y); Cmnty Wkr; French Clb; FBLA; Girl Scts; Stage Crew; Yrbk Stf; Capt Cheerleading; Im Vllybl; FBLA Bus Awd 86; NH Coll; Bus Admin.

COLUCCI, ANTHONY R; Saint Joseph HS; Ansonia, CT; (Y); 49/227; Spanish Clb; Var L Ftbl; Hon Roll; NEDT Awd; Merchnat Marine Acad 86; Schlstc Achvt Grant 86; US Merchant Marine Acad.

COLUCCI, KAREN M; Immaculate HS; Danbury, CT; (Y); 36/179; Cmnty Wkr; Spanish Clb; Rep Stu Cncl; JV Trk; High Hon Roll; Spnsh Hnr Socty 84-86; Cornell; Vet.

COLWELL, THOMAS; Hamden HS; Hamden, CT; (Y); Church Yth Grp; ROTC; Ski Clb; Varsity Clb; Orch; Nwsp Stf; Yrbk Stf; Crs Cntry; Trk; Hon Roll; ST Latin Exam Awd 86; U RI; Engrng.

COMAR, JENNIFER; Bloomfieldm SR HS; Bloomfield, CT; (Y); 19/235; Art Clb; Model UN; Flag Corp; Variety Show; Rep Soph Cls; Stu Cncl; Var Socr; Var Tennis; Hon Roll; NHS; Creatv Arts Pgm 2ndry Stu Schlrshp 85-87; Accptd U Of Hartford 85-86; Fshn Dsgn.

COMBS, CURTIS; Lyman Hall HS; Wallingford, CT; (Y); 54/253; Key Clb; Stu Cncl; JV Bsktbl; L Crs Cntry; Ftbl; L Trk; Key Clb Presf 86-87; Tutor 86-87; Pre Law.

COMERFORD, BRIAN; Nonnewaug HS; Woodbury, CT; (Y); Var Trk; JV Wrstlng; Hon Roll; Film Edtr.

COMSTOCK, LARA; Cromwell HS; Cromwell, CT; (Y); 4/86; FBLA; Hosp Aide; Spanish Clb; Variety Show; Soph Cls; Off Jr Cls; Off Sr Cls; Cheerleading; Socr; Chem Awd 85; Congrsnl Intern 85; Pre-Med.

COMSTOCK, STACEY M; Lyman Hall HS; South Meriden, CT; (Y); Sec FFA; Band; Concert Band; Mrchg Band; Powder Puff Ftbl; High Hon Roll; Hon Roll; De Cato Schlrshp 85-86fFFA Alumni Awd 85-86; Becker JC; Vtrny Asstnt.

CONCILIO, TERESA; Derby HS; Derby, CT; (Y); 7/130; Am Leg Aux Girls St; Pres Civic Clb; Pep Clb; Spanish Clb; Band; Yrbk Stf; High Hon Roll; Hon Roll; NHS; Spanish NHS; Nursing.

CONIFF, MELISSA ANN; Daniel Hand HS; Madison, CT; (Y); #26 In Class; Concert Band; Mrchg Band; Trs Stu Cncl; Capt Swmmng; NHS; Hosp Aide; Trk; High Hon Roll; Hon Roll.

CONLISK, KELLY ANNE; Our Lady Of Mercy Lauralton Hl Acad; Stratford, CT; (Y); 40/111; Church Yth Grp; Dance Clb; Drama Clb; French Clb; Service Clb; Chorus; School Play; Lit Mag; NHS; Mktg Mgmt.

CONNELL, CRAIG; Torrington HS; Torrington, CT; (Y); Church Yth Grp; Cmnty Wkr; Drama Clb; Latin Clb; School Musical; Stage Crew; Var Crs Cntry; Im Socr; JV Trk; Hon Roll; Lbrl Arts.

CONNELL, KIM O; Trumbull HS; Trumbull, CT; (Y); Ski Clb; Color Guard; Socr; Var Trk; High Hon Roll; Hon Roll; Bryant Coll; Htl Mgmt.

CONNELLY, CRISTIN; Convent Of The Sacred Heart; Bronxville, NY; (Y); Hosp Aide; Off Model UN; Lit Mag; JV Lcrss; Var Tennis; Hon Roll; Jr NHS; Dsgn Awds Effrt & Achvmnt 86; Intl Rltns Pgm 86; Intl Rltns.

CONNOR, BRIAN; East Catholic HS; Manchester, CT; (Y); 12/300; Cmnty Wkr; Lit Mag; Rep Frsh Cls; Rep Soph Cls; Rep Jr Cls; Rep Sr Cls; Var Trk; High Hon Roll; Ntl Merit SF; Hnrs E 84-86; Econ.

CONNOR, MARGOT; Newtown HS; Newtown, CT; (Y); 15/280; Debate Tm; NFL; Var L Bsktbl; Trk; Var Capt Vllybl; High Hon Roll; NHS; Century 21 Acctng Hgst Bus Awd 85; Pres Acad Ftns Awd 86; All Conf Vlybl 84-86; U RI; Textile Mrktng.

CONRAD, KIMBERLY; Southington HS; Southington, CT; (Y); Spanish Clb; SADD; Rep Frsh Cls; Trs Soph Cls; Rep Jr Cls; Rep Sr Cls; Sec Stu Cncl; Var Trk; Hon Roll; CT Coll; Bus.

CONRAD, PETER; Wilbur L Cross HS; New Haven, CT; (S); Church Yth Grp; French Clb; JA; Latin Clb; PAVAS; Church Choir; Lit Mag; ISSP Law Awd 83; Linguistics.

CONROY, CONSTANCE; Holy Cross HS; Naugatuck, CT; (Y); 20/347; Concert Band; Mrchg Band; Orch; Pep Band; Swing Chorus; Variety Show; High Hon Roll; Hon Roll; NHS; Prfct Atten Awd; Pres Acad Fit Awd; Soc Stds Hon Soc; All St Bnd 86; U CT; Psychlgst.

CONROY, MICHAEL; Lewis S Mills HS; Harwinton, CT; (Y); 10/200; Debate Tm; Model UN; Band; Concert Band; Jazz Band; Mrchg Band; School Musical; High Hon Roll; NHS; Chess Clb; Instrmntl Music Achvmnt Awd 86; Jazz Band Awd 84-86; Law.

CONROY, TIMOTHY; Xavier HS; Meriden, CT; (Y); Am Leg Boys St; Boy Scts; SADD; Church Choir; School Musical; Rep Soph Cls; Pres Jr Cls; Im Ice Hcky; Im Lcrss; Pep Band; Mdlsx Yth Assoc Rtrd Ctzns Vlntr 83-86; Tufts U; Phy Ther.

CONSIGLI, JOSEPH; Bethel HS; Bethel, CT; (Y); Church Yth Grp; JA; Ski Clb; Variety Show; Var L Bsbl; Var Trk; High Hon Roll; Hon Roll; U CT Storrs; Bus Econ.

CONSOLATI, EDDIE; Norwalk HS; Norwalk, CT; (Y); 10/450; Spanish Clb; Yrbk Stf; Rep Frsh Cls; Rep Soph Cls; Rep Jr Cls; Var Golf; DAR Awd; High Hon Roll; Ntl Merit Ltr; Yearbook Staff Awd 86.

CONSOLINI, TRACEY; Housatonic Valley Regional HS; Falls Village, CT; (Y); Chorus; Sec Frsh Cls; Rep Stu Cncl; Capt Cheerleading; High Hon Roll; Hon Roll; Library Aide; Nwsp Rptr; Yrbk Stf; Nuc Med.

CONTADINO, ANNA; Greenwich HS; Riverside, CT; (Y); Office Aide; Lit Mag; Jr NHS; Hon Roll; NHS; Cert Of Schlstc Achvt 83; Sci Ed Cntr Sci Stu Rcgntn Awd 85; Exclnc In Mthmtcs 86; Exclnc Itln Awd 86; Frfld U.

CONTINO, LISA; Norwich Free Acad; Bozrah, CT; (Y); JV Sftbl; Hon Roll; Med Tech.

CONTRACT, VICTOR ALAN; Westhill HS; Stamford, CT; (Y); 11/417; VP AFS; Hosp Aide; Pres Math Clb; Temple Yth Grp; Stu Cncl; Elks Awd; Hon Roll; NHS; Opt Clb Awd; Pres Science Clb; Japan-U S Senate Schlrshp Pgm 1st Alt CT 85; Dean Schlrshp Emry U 86; Emory U; Intl Law.

COOK, EMILY JANE; Low-Heywood Thomas Schl; Wellesley, MA; (Y); 7/40; Cmnty Wkr; JA; SADD; School Play; Rep Soph Cls; Sec Jr Cls; Im Crs Cntry; JV Var Fld Hcky; JV Capt Lcrss; Var Tennis.

COOK, PAUL; Wilton HS; Wilton, CT; (Y); Church Yth Grp; Varsity Clb; Band; Concert Band; Mrchg Band; Score Keeper; Timer; Im Wt Lftg; Var L Wrstlng; Hon Roll; Engnrng.

COOK, POLLY; Griswold HS; Jewett City, CT; (Y); GAA; Girl Scts; Chorus; Variety Show; Cheerleading; Tennis; Trk; Hon Roll; Comp.

COOKE, ELIZABETH; Old Saybrook HS; Old Saybrook, CT; (Y); Sec AFS; Drama Clb; Latin Clb; Scholastic Bowl; Chorus; School Musical; School Play; Rep Stu Cncl; High Hon Roll; U Of CT Sci Smmr Intrnshp 86; Latn Awd Hghst Avg 85-86; Sci.

COOKE, RACHEL F; Miss Porters HS; Ridgefield, CT; (Y); Art Clb; GAA; PAVAS; Stage Crew; Yrbk Stf; Ed Lit Mag; Var Bsktbl; Var JV Socr; Var Sftbl; Hon Roll; Paul & Audrey Fisher Art Awd 84; Phy Educ.

COON, ANDREA; Simsbury HS; W Simsbury, CT; (Y); 185/410; Church Yth Grp; Cmnty Wkr; VP GAA; JA; Sec Jr Cls; Rep Stu Cncl; JV Var Lcrss; JV Socr; Asstnt Coach Socr Tm 84; Mbr Of Twn Tsk Frce 85-86; Mbr Outng Club 84; Communications.

COOPER, BENJAMIN; Killingly HS; Danielson, CT; (Y); 15/275; Cmnty Wkr; Pres SADD; Mrchg Band; Symp Band; Rep Stu Cncl; JV Var Socr; French Hon Soc; Hon Roll; Lion Awd; NHS; Miltry Offcr.

COOPER, LISA; Killingly HS; Rogers, CT; (Y); Cmnty Wkr; Band; Drill Tm; Flag Corp; Mrchg Band; Yrbk Stf; Cheerleading; Coach Actv; Score Keeper; Sftbl; Bus Mgmt.

COOPER, MICHELE; Stamford HS; Stamford, CT; (Y); Sec Drama Clb; French Clb; Girl Scts; Ski Clb; Thesps; Varsity Clb; School Play; Yrbk Phtg; Yrbk Stf; Sec Jr Cls; Arts.

COPELAND, JOSEPHINE; Thomas Snell Weaver HS; Hartford, CT; (Y); 9/317; Pres Church Yth Grp; Ed FBLA; Pres Church Choir; Sr Cls; Cheerleading; Gym; Trk; High Hon Roll; JV Var NHS; Pres Schlr; Schlr Of The Mnth 84; Stu Of The Mnth 86; U Of MA; Corp Lawyer.

COPEN, RACHEL; Ridgefield HS; Ridgefield, CT; (Y); 26/385; Dance Clb; French Clb; Temple Yth Grp; Nwsp Stf; Yrbk Stf; High Hon Roll; NHS.

COPPOLA, SUZANNE; Holy Cross HS; Naugatuck, CT; (Y); 47/346; Church Yth Grp; Cmnty Wkr; VP JA; Var Cheerleading; High Hon Roll; Hon Roll; NHS; St Schlr; Itln Natl Hnr Soc 84-86; Pres Fit Awd 86; Du Quesne U Comp Scholar 86; Du Quesne U; Phrmcy.

COPPOLA, TAMMY; Lauralton Hall HS; W Haven, CT; (Y); 13/117; Cmnty Wkr; Latin Clb; Library Aide; Math Clb; Science Clb; Service Clb; Trs Spanish Clb; Nwsp Stf; Yrbk Stf; Lit Mag; Awds Exclnc ST & Ntl Math & Latin Exams 82-85; U Of CT.

CORDANI, JOE; Simsbury HS; Weatogue, CT; (Y); Nwsp Stf; Var Capt Golf; Hon Roll; Am Leg Awd 86; Lt Richard Kellaher Mem Schlrshp 86; U CT; Bus.

CORDELLA, LINDA L; Greenwich HS; Old Greenwich, CT; (Y); AFS; Service Clb; Nwsp Rptr; Hon Roll; NHS; Ntl Merit Ltr; Dundee Awd 86; Silver Maxima Cum Laude Mdl In Natl Latin Exam 86; Contntl Math Lgue Awd Comp Div 86; M Inst Of Tech; Astrophyscs.

CORDERY, JEREMY; Wilton HS; Wilton, CT; (Y); 65/352; AFS; Spanish Clb; Band; Concert Band; Jazz Band; Symp Band; Socr; Tennis; Hon Roll; Englsh.

CORDILICO, PAUL; Wethersfield HS; Wethersfield, CT; (Y); 8/299; Im Socr; Var L Tennis; High Hon Roll; Hon Roll; NHS; NEDT Awd; Prfct Atten Awd.

CORNELL, ASHLEY; Lyme-Old Lyme HS; Old Lyme, CT; (Y); SADD; Yrbk Stf; Stu Cncl; Var L Socr; Var Capt Trk; High Hon Roll; NHS; Computer Clb; Intnl Clb; Service Clb; Dan Moore Awd Ldrshp 86; MVP Track 85-86; Shoreline Champ Track 85.

COROLLA, MIKE; E Haven HS; E Haven, CT; (Y); Varsity Clb; Ftbl; Hon Roll; E Have Gridiron Clb Awd Outstndg Contribtn 85; Gr New Haven ST Tech Clg; Engr.

CORREIA, LOIS ANN; St Bernard HS; Mystic, CT; (Y); 10/277; Church Yth Grp; Dance Clb; Drama Clb; School Musical; Stage Crew; Rep Jr Cls; Stu Cncl; High Hon Roll; NHS; Tufts U; Phrmctcls.

CORYELL, MURALI; Staples HS; Westport, CT; (Y); French Clb; Im Bsktbl; Im Sftbl; Im Wt Lftg; Span Awd 85-86; French Awd 84-85; Bard Coll; Lang.

COSACCHI, TARA LYNN; New Milford HS; Sherman, CT; (Y); 5/295; Debate Tm; Math Tm; Nwsp Stf; Yrbk Ed-Chief; Pres Soph Cls; Var Tennis; Cit Awd; French Hon Soc; Hon Roll; Ntl Merit Ltr; U Notre Dame; Hist.

COSCIELLO, MATTHEW; St Joseph HS; Ansonia, CT; (Y); Spanish Clb; JV Bsbl; Acctng.

COSCO, KAREN ANN; Brien Mc Mahon HS; Rowayton, CT; (Y); Drama Clb; Latin Clb; Ski Clb; Chorus; Cheerleading; Treas Italian Club 84-85; Actng.

COSENTINO, JOSEPH D; Norwich Free Acad; N Franklin, CT; (Y); Boy Scts; Spanish Clb; High Hon Roll; Hon Roll; Nwsp Stf; VFW Awd; Penn ST U; Meterology.

COSKER, DIANE; Simsbury HS; Simsbury, CT; (Y); 56/410; Drama Clb; JA; School Play; Nwsp Stf; Var JV Mgr(s); Var JV Score Keeper; Var JV Socr; Hon Roll; Engl.

COSSETTE, MARTIN; John F Kennedy HS; Waterbury, CT; (Y); Aud/Vis; Stage Crew; Mgr Bsbl; Mgr Bsktbl; Mgr Ftbl; Var Socr; Cit Awd; Hon Roll; Political Wkr; Score Keeper; CT St Senate Page 86; Med.

COSTA, JOHN; Crosby HS; Waterbury, CT; (Y); Key Clb; Trs Jr Cls; Hon Roll.

COSTELLO, DONALD J; Killingly HS; Danielson, CT; (Y); 5/260; Tennis; High Hon Roll; Hon Roll; Prfct Atten Awd; Spanish NHS; Dentist.

COSTELLO, ELAINE; Farmington HS; Unionville, CT; (Y); 9/204; Church Yth Grp; Spanish Clb; Var Capt Fld Hcky; Trk; Hon Roll; NHS.

COTE, KAREN; Plainfield HS; Plainfield, CT; (Y); Hon Roll; Psych.

COTE, WENDY; East Hartford HS; E Hartford, CT; (Y); Spanish Clb; High Hon Roll; Hon Roll; NHS; Acctg.

COTTER, KATHLEEN; Newington HS; Newington, CT; (S); 22/365; Drama Clb; Pep Clb; Ski Clb; Madrigals; School Musical; Yrbk Sprt Ed; Var Capt Cheerleading; Hon Roll; NHS.

COTTO JR, WALBERTO; Bullard-Havens Tech Schl; Bridgeport, CT; (S); JA; JV Bsbl; Var Ftbl; High Hon Roll; Hon Roll; Culinary Inst Amer; Culinry Art.

COTTON, AIMEE; Southington HS; Southington, CT; (Y); 47/600; Am Leg Aux Girls St; Cmnty Wkr; Computer Clb; FBLA; Hosp Aide; JA; Key Clb; Political Wkr; Ski Clb; Capt Flag Corp; Pg At ST Cptl 85-86; Poli Sci.

COUGHLAN, JAMES M; Avon HS; Avon, CT; (Y); 1/172; Pres French Clb; Math Tm; Science Clb; Chorus; Bausch & Lomb Sci Awd; NHS; Val; High Hon Roll; Tied 1st Plc CT Chmthn 84; Rep Of CT Natl Chmstry Olympd 85-86; Prtcptd 86 All-ST Chrs; Harvard; Physcs.

COURCHESNE, RANDY; H C Wilcox Vo-Tech HS; Meriden, CT; (Y); Church Yth Grp; VICA; Var Golf; NHS.

COUTURE, ALAN; W F Kaynor RVT Schl; Waterbury, CT; (Y); 1/200; VP JA; SADD; VICA; VP Jr Cls; VP Sr Cls; Trs Stu Cncl; Pres NHS; Cmnty Wkr; Hosp Aide; Political Wkr; Mst Dsrvng Soph & Jr; V-Pres Stwd Stu Cngrs; Med Dctr.

COUTURE, BRIAN; Plainfield HS; Plainfield, CT; (Y); 2/167; Am Leg Boys St; Church Yth Grp; Model UN; High Hon Roll; NHS; Prfct Atten Awd; CT JR Sci, Humnts Sympsm 85; Schlrs Gftd-Tlntd Pgm 84-86; Psych.

COWENHOVEN JR, MICHAEL V; Fairfield College Prep Schl; Redding Ridge, CT; (Y); Camera Clb; Cmnty Wkr; Computer Clb; JA; Quiz Bowl; Scholastic Bowl; Service Clb; Spanish Clb; JV Bsbl; Im Bsktbl; Arch.

COX, ESTHER; R C Lee Education Center; New Haven, CT; (Y); Cmnty Wkr; Hosp Aide; Nwsp Stf; Var JV Sftbl; JV Vllybl; Hon Roll; NHS; Pre Med.

COYKENDALL, JOHN; Farmington HS; Unionville, CT; (Y); 7/207; Aud/Vis; Exploring; Ski Clb; Nwsp Bus Mgr; Nwsp Rptr; JV Golf; French Hon Soc; High Hon Roll; NHS; Ntl Merit Ltr; Fin CT ST Sci Fair 2nd Hnrs 86; Brown U; Pre-Law.

COYNE, DAVID; The Morgan Schl; Clinton, CT; (Y); 8/160; AFS; French Clb; Scholastic Bowl; SADD; Band; Orch; School Play; L Trk; Hon Roll; Concert Band; Natl Mrt Fnlst 86; Awd Excllnc Art 85; Cornell U; Intrnl Rltns.

COZZOLINO, SUSAN; St Bernard HS; Westerly, RI; (Y); 48/289; Teachers Aide; Yrbk Stf; Lit Mag; Off Jr Cls; Off Sr Cls; Hon Roll; Art Recgntn Awds 83 & 86; UAA Math Awd USNMA 83; NLSA Awd 84; Pratt Inst.

CRABB III, JAMES; St Basils Prep; Stamford, CT; (Y); 1/10; Yrbk Stf; VP Stu Cncl; Var Bsbl; High Hon Roll; NHS; Am Chem Soc Outstndng Chem Achvt; Graphic Arts Awd; Chem.

CRACCO, LARA; Torrington HS; Torrington, CT; (Y); 8/284; Drama Clb; Pep Clb; Ski Clb; Stage Crew; Trs Soph Cls; Twrlr; Cit Awd; DAR Awd; High Hon Roll; NHS; Fairfield U; Mth.

CRAGGETTI, GARDIE W; Choute Rosemary Hall HS; West Islip, NY; (Y); Boy Scts; French Clb; Intnl Clb; Model UN; Pep Clb; Political Wkr; Spanish Clb; Nwsp Rptr; Lit Mag; JV Socr; Chnce Schlr; Intl Reltn.

CRAIG, PETER; Fairfield College Prep; Norwalk, CT; (Y); 23/226; Cmnty Wkr; Yrbk Stf; High Hon Roll; Jr NHS; NHS; Spanish NHS; Engrng.

CRANE, AMANDA; Wethersfield HS; Wethersfield, CT; (Y); 34/319; Cmnty Wkr; Girl Scts; Chorus; Madrigals; Orch; School Musical; JV Diving; JV Trk; High Hon Roll; NHS; Ntl Schl Orch Awd 86; U CT.

CRANE, MARK; Holy Cross HS; Middlebury, CT; (Y); 250/400; Band; Var Crs Cntry; Var Trk; Bus.

CRAW III, KENNETH G; Norwalk HS; Norwalk, CT; (Y); 1/456; SADD; Trs Frsh Cls; Var Bsbl; Var Socr; Var Trk; High Hon Roll; NHS; Harvard Bk Awd 86; Yale Clb Darien-Norwlk Savngs Bond 86; Al-Expns Pd Trp Kennedy Spc Ctr 86; Bio.

CREAN, KELLEY; Southington HS; Southington, CT; (Y); Church Yth Grp; Cmnty Wkr; Pep Clb; Political Wkr; Varsity Clb; Band; Concert Band; Cheerleading; Acctnt.

CREW, JANET; Avon HS; Avon, CT; (Y); Church Yth Grp; Debate Tm; FCA; GAA; SADD; Nwsp Stf; Im Score Keeper; Var Socr; Var Tennis; JV Vllybl; Excllnce British Lit II 86; Short Story Phase 7 Cert Merit 86; All Conf Ten 86; Jrnlsm.

CREW, SHERI; Sheehan HS; Wallingford, CT; (Y); Key Clb; Varsity Clb; Chorus; Color Guard; Stu Cncl; Var L Ice Hcky; Var L Socr; Var Capt Trk; High Hon Roll; Hon Roll; 2nd Tm Al Housy Soccer 84&85; Co-Capt Sccr 86; Bus Admin.

CREWS, ALICIA; New Haven Cooperative HS; New Haven, CT; (Y); Office Aide; SADD; Teachers Aide; Chorus; Nwsp Rptr; Yrbk Phtg; Yrbk Stf; Lit Mag; Pres Frsh Cls; Off Soph Cls; Clark Coll; Psych.

CRIBBINS III, ALLAN J; Fairfield College Prep Schl; Huntington, CT; (Y); Boy Scts; JA; Key Clb; Math Tm; Yrbk Stf; Lit Mag; JV Socr; Var Wrstlng; NHS; Med.

CRISTOFARO, DOMINICK; Bulkeley HS; Hartford, CT; (Y); Computer Clb; Var Socr; Var Swmmng; Ntl Merit Ltr; Engrng.

CROMBIE, KAREN; East Catholi HS; Manchester, CT; (Y); Church Yth Grp; Yrbk Stf; Swmmng; High Hon Roll; Hon Roll; Hnrs 85-86; Regina Cavagnaro Mem Awd 86; Fairfield U; Nrsng.

CROSS, SCOTT; Marianapolis Prep; Brooklyn, CT; (Y); 8/50; Hon Roll; Ntl Merit Ltr; NEDT Awd; Physics.

CROSSMAN, STEVEN; Wethersfield HS; Wethersfield, CT; (Y); #24 In Class; Ski Clb; JV Var Socr; High Hon Roll; Hon Roll; Bryant Coll; Accntng.

CROWLEY, ROBERT; Staples HS; Westport, CT; (Y); Key Clb; Model UN; Yrbk Phtg; Yrbk Stf; JV Ftbl; Purdue; Ecnmcs.

CRUMMEY, CATHERINE C; Staples HS; Westport, CT; (Y); Exploring; Hosp Aide; Key Clb; Latin Clb; SADD; Var Socr; Pres Safe Rides 85-87; Lat Awd 83-84; Bryer Bk Awd Outstndg Achvt Bus 85-86.

CRUMRINE, DAVID; Cheshire HS; Cheshire, CT; (Y); Jazz Band; Variety Show; Trk; Hon Roll; Music.

CRUZ, ALVIN P; Manchester HS; Manchester, CT; (Y); Aud/Vis; Camera Clb; Math Tm; Model UN; Orch; High Hon Roll; Church Yth Grp; Nwsp Phtg; Yrbk Phtg; Hon Roll.

CSER, KATHRYN; Oliver Wolcott Technical Schl; Litchfield, CT; (Y); 40/175; Church Yth Grp; Girl Scts; VICA; Nwsp Stf; Yrbk Stf; Trs Jr Cls; Rep Stu Cncl; JV Cheerleading; Grphc Comm.

CUBETA, KAREN; Newington HS; Newington, CT; (Y); 1/365; Key Clb; Teachers Aide; Socr; High Hon Roll; NHS; Pres Schlr; Val; U S Hstry Awd; Sophmr Schlr Awd; Grnd Mrshll-Grad 85; Saint Joseph Coll; Elem Educ.

CUCCINELLO, LISA M; Newtown HS; Sandy Hook, CT; (Y); 2/292; Cmnty Wkr; Chorus; Madrigals; School Musical; Pres NHS; Ntl Merit SF; Sal; Sec Spanish NHS; AFS; Drama Clb; Vassar Bk Prz For Excllnc In Humnts 85; Womens Engrng Scty Awd 85; Western CT Rgnl Choir 84; Lbrl Arts.

CUEVAS, ELIZABETH; Bullard Havens Regional Vo Tec Schl; Bridgeport, CT; (Y); JA; Library Aide; Office Aide; Church Choir; Drill Tm; Sacred Heart U; Bus Adm.

CULOTTA, THOMAS; Holy Cross HS; Waterbury, CT; (Y); 240/380; Boys Clb Am; Red Cross Aide; Var Diving; Var Ftbl; JV Trk; Hon Roll; Bus.

CUMMINGS, CHRISTINE; Sacred Heart Acad; Hamden, CT; (Y); 4/122; Pres French Clb; Yrbk Ed-Chief; Lit Mag; French Hon Soc; High Hon Roll; NHS; Ntl Merit Ltr; Hosp Aide; Science Clb; Stage Crew; Yale Frontiers Appld Sci; Japan U S Senate Scholar Schl Rep; 3rd Pl Nation Fr Creat Wrtg Cont; NYU; Intl Rel.

CUMMINGS, KIRBY; Morgan HS; Clinton, CT; (Y); 18/143; JV Bsktbl; Var Capt Socr; Hon Roll; Engl.

CUNHA, TODD; Rockville HS; Vernon, CT; (Y); 85/340; Church Yth Grp; Rep Stu Cncl; VP Socr; VP Trk; Boston College; Marine Biology.

CUNNINGHAM, JOHN; The Taft School; Watertown, CT; (Y); Church Yth Grp; School Play; Yrbk Stf; Jr Cls; Sr Cls; JV Bsbl; L Var Ftbl; Capt Var Trk; Jr NHS; Epis Yth Comm Diocese Of CT 85-87; Co Edof CT Episcopal Yth Nwslttr 86-87.

CUNNINGHAM, MARK; Norwich Free Acad; Voluntown, CT; (Y); 45/512; Computer Clb; Exploring; Rep Sr Cls; High Hon Roll; Worcester Poly Tech; Comp Sci.

CURETON II, JOHN P; Fairfield College Prep; Shelton, CT; (Y); Church Yth Grp; Cmnty Wkr; Key Clb; Pep Clb; Lit Mag; Pres Frsh Cls; Pres Soph Cls; Rep Jr Cls; Var Ftbl; Var L Trk; Cum Laude Hnrs 83-84; Hgh Hnrs Essay Comprehnsn Exam 84-85; Engl.

CURI, SARAH E; The Taft Schl; Goshen, CT; (Y); Camera Clb; Cmnty Wkr; Girl Scts; Intnl Clb; Office Aide; Chorus; Yrbk Phtg; Var L Bsktbl; Var L Trk; Hon Roll; Coleco Adam Schlrshp 85; Charlotte Hungerford Hlth Schlrshp 86; Wellesley Coll; Psychology.

CURRY, SCOTT; Guilford HS; Guilford, CT; (Y); Church Yth Grp; High Hon Roll; Hon Roll; Vrsty Lttr-Fncng Tm 84-85; Comp Sci.

CURSEADEN, KEVIN; Joseph A Foran HS; Milford, CT; (Y); 15/293; Am Leg Boys St; Key Clb; SADD; VP Sr Cls; VP Stu Cncl; Hon Roll; Pres Jr NHS; NHS; JV Bsbl; Var Crs Cntry; Bobby Orr Nabisco Sprtsmnshp Awd 84; Bio Awd 85; Mbr Of Mdgt ST Chmpnshp Hcky Team 85; US Nvl Acad; Pilot.

CUSACK, WILLIAM; Branford HS; Branford, CT; (Y); Boy Scts; Political Wkr; Rep Sr Cls; L Swmmng; Hon Roll; Rotc.

CUSANO, EDWARD; Bolton HS; Bolton, CT; (Y); Model UN; Spanish Clb; Varsity Clb; Rep Stu Cncl; Var L Bsbl; Var L Bsktbl; JV Ftbl; Var L Socr; Im Wt Lftg; Hon Roll; Instrctr Handicapped 86; U CT; Real Est.

CUSHEN, RENEE; Francis T Maloney HS; Meriden, CT; (Y); Cmnty Wkr; Dance Clb; Debate Tm; Political Wkr; Red Cross Aide; Service Clb; SADD; Band; Chorus; Variety Show; Bus.

CUTLER, DAWN; Tourkellotte Memorial HS; N Grosvenordale, CT; (Y); 12/92; 4-H; Sec Library Aide; Pep Clb; Flag Corp; Yrbk Stf; Rep Jr Cls; Rep Stu Cncl; Dnfth Awd; Elks Awd; 4-H Awd; Soc Profsnl Estimators-Schlrshp 86; Roger Williams Coll; Arch.

CZARNATY, CHERYL; Southington HS; Southington, CT; (Y); 14/550; Sec FBLA; Hosp Aide; Sec JA; Band; Drm Mjr(t); Mrchg Band; Nwsp Stf; Ed Yrbk Stf; High Hon Roll; NHS; Alg I Prz Exam 84; Lat I Hghst Avg 84; Bus Fld.

CZARNIK, CORY; Ridgefield HS; Ridgefield, CT; (Y); 16/400; Church Yth Grp; School Musical; School Play; Stage Crew; Mgr Lit Mag; High Hon Roll; NHS.

CZECZOTKA, STEFANIE; Plainfield HS; Plainfield, CT; (Y); Cmnty Wkr; FBLA; Library Aide; Yrbk Stf; High Hon Roll; Hon Roll; VP NHS; Voice Dem Awd; Schlrs Progrm 86-87; FBLA Typing Comp 85.

CZECZOTKO, YOLANDA; Bullard Havens RVT Schl; Bridgeport, CT; (Y); Library Aide; Office Aide; Yrbk Stf; Cit Awd; Hon Roll; Prfct Atten Awd; Air Force; Compu.

CZERWINSKI, CHRISTOPHER; Shelton HS; Shelton, CT; (Y); 11/334; Am Leg Boys St; JA; Band; Cit Awd; Elks Awd; High Hon Roll; NHS; Spanish NHS; Pres Acad Ftns Awd 86; Vitramon Fndtn SR Sci Awd 86; Earnest Blackman Meml Schlrshp 86; U Of CT; Elec Engrng.

D ADDIO, GINA; St Marys HS; New Haven, CT; (Y); Service Clb; High Hon Roll; Ski Clb; Stage Crew; Lit Mag; Tennis; Hon Roll; Typng Awd 85; Bus Schlrshp Eileen Kernon 86; Ntl Hnr Bus Soc 86; Acad For Bus Careers; Exec Sec.

D AMATO, ELIZABETH; Wilby HS; Waterbury, CT; (Y); 2/250; Aud/Vis; Church Yth Grp; Church Choir; Yrbk Stf; Rep Jr Cls; High Hon Roll; Jr NHS; NHS; Oratorl Awd Prtcptn Gttysbrg Awd 82&83; Awds Frnch I-84 & Frnch II-85; Comp.

D AMORE, GINA; Southington HS; Plantsville, CT; (Y); 63/600; Ski Clb; Color Guard; School Musical; Stage Crew; Nwsp Rptr; Stat Fld Hcky; Mgr(s); Score Keeper; Timer; High Hon Roll.

D ANDREA, CHRISTINE; Torrington HS; Torrington, CT; (Y); 18/282; Church Yth Grp; Cmnty Wkr; Drama Clb; 4-H; Girl Scts; Sec Latin Clb; Nwsp Rptr; High Hon Roll; Hon Roll; NHS; Chester Edward Bufferd Latin Prz 86; Cls Schlrshp 86; Hnr Stu Medallion 86; Smith Coll; Comm.

D ANDREA, JODY; Sacred Heart Acad; North Haven, CT; (Y); Art Clb; Dance Clb; FBLA; Hosp Aide; Office Aide; Nwsp Rptr; NHS; Spanish NHS; Fairfield U; Bus Admin.

D ANGELO, WILLIAM ROBERT; Newington HS; Newington, CT; (Y); 31/350; Am Leg Boys St; Church Yth Grp; VP Math Tm; Rep Stu Cncl; Var Ftbl; Var Trk; Hon Roll; Ntl Merit SF; Yale U Math & Sci Frntrs Prog 85; Worcester Poly Tech; Bio Engr.

D AUTEUIL, MONIQUE L; William H Hall HS; West Hartford, CT; (Y); 78/324; Art Clb; Church Yth Grp; Cmnty Wkr; Yrbk Stf; High Hon Roll; Hon Roll; NHS; Outstndg Art Awd 83; One Person Art Exhbt 85; Hall Juried Art Show 85; U Of Hartford; Art.

D EMIDIO, PATRIZIA; Brien Mc Mahon HS; Norwalk, CT; (Y); Rep Jr Cls; High Hon Roll; Hon Roll; Italian Clb Pres,Treas 84-86; Iona Coll Lang Cntst 86; Katharine Gibbs; Sec.

D ONFRO, DAVE; Cheshire HS; Cheshire, CT; (Y); Dance Clb; Radio Clb; SADD; Yrbk Phtg; Stu Cncl; Bsktbl; Prfct Atten Awd; Radio Brdcstng.

D ONOFRIO, DINA; Joseph A Foran HS; Milford, CT; (Y); 50/240; Dance Clb; Pres Keywanettes; Red Cross Aide; Service Clb; Spanish Clb; NEDT Awd; Skidmore Coll.

DABKOWSKI, CYNTHIA; Bristol Central HS; Bristol, CT; (Y); GAA; Trs Frsh Cls; VP Sr Cls; Var Capt Diving; Var Score Keeper; DAR Awd; High Hon Roll; NHS; Trinity Bk Awd 85; U Of Pittsburgh.

DACRUZ, JOHN B; Amity SR HS; Orange, CT; (Y); 171/388; Art Clb; School Musical; Variety Show; Nwsp Stf; Socr; Natla Art Hnrs Soc 83; Arts Recog & Tlnt Srch 85; U Of CT; Comp Grphcs.

DACUNTO, KEN; Vinal Vo Tech; Northford, CT; (Y); Auto Mech.

DAKE, ROBIN; Staples HS; Westport, CT; (Y); JV Sftbl; Hon Roll; Bus.

DALAKU, ALAN; Derby HS; Derby, CT; (Y); Band; Concert Band; Nwsp Rptr; Im Trk; High Hon Roll; Hon Roll; U Of CT; Comp Prgrmg.

DALESIO, SCOTT; Holy Cross HS; Waterbury, CT; (Y); 240/390; Var Capt Bsktbl; Var Golf; 1st Flght Wtrbry Rep & Amer Champ 84; Sammy Davis Jr G H O Jr 1st Low Grs Champ 85; HS Golf Mvp 85-86.

DALEY, BRIAN C; Conard HS; W Hartford, CT; (Y); 13/308; Acpl Chr; School Musical; Yrbk Sprt Ed; Rep Stu Cncl; Lcrss; Wrstlng; High Hon Roll; NHS; Ntl Merit Ltr; Pres Schlr; Trinity Bk Prize 85; Am Leg Aux Mem Schlrshp & Natl Pres Cert, Instrmnt Soc Am Schlrshp 86; MA Inst Tech; Engrng.

DALEY, JOANNE; St Joseph HS; Huntington, CT; (Y); Dance Clb; Drama Clb; Teachers Aide; Stage Crew; Bus Adm.

DALEY, JULIE; RHAM HS; Andover, CT; (Y); 4-H; FBLA; JV Bsktbl; Var Cheerleading; L Crs Cntry; L Trk; 4-H Awd; Hon Roll; U CT; Bio.

DALPE, KYLE; South Windsor HS; S Windsor, CT; (Y); 48/283; Church Yth Grp; 4-H; Ski Clb; Band; School Musical; School Play; 4-H Awd; Hon Roll; Aviatn.

DALRYMPLE, SUSAN; New Canaan HS; New Canaan, CT; (Y); Church Yth Grp; Cmnty Wkr; French Clb; Service Clb; Teachers Aide; Nwsp Rptr; Ed Nwsp Stf; Mgr(s); Var Trk; High Hon Roll; Engl.

DALTON, JOHN; Shelton HS; Shelton, CT; (Y); 5/315; Bsbl; High Hon Roll; Spanish NHS; Shelton Fed Tchrs SR Math Scholar 86; Shelton Jaycees Scholar Comp Sci 86; Bst Work Math 86; U CT; Comp Sci.

DAMARJIAN, BETH; The Morgan HS; Clinton, CT; (Y); 13/180; AFS; Am Leg Aux Girls St; Drama Clb; Pres Spanish Clb; SADD; Band; Chorus; Concert Band; Mrchg Band; Rep Stu Cncl; Schlr Athlt Awd 86; Engl Awd 86; Soc Studs Awd 86; Beton Hall U; Commnctns.

DAMATO, LYNN; Morgan HS; Clinton, CT; (Y); 59/160; Color Guard; Yrbk Stf; JV Bsktbl; Hon Roll; Industrial Arts Awd; TCI; Arch.

DAMATO, ROBIN; Norwalk HS; Norwalk, CT; (Y); 22/459; Church Yth Grp; Ski Clb; SADD; Orch; School Musical; Stu Cncl; Var Cheerleading; Stat Lcrss; JV Powder Puff Ftbl; High Hon Roll; Med.

DAMIA, JEFFREY DOUGLAS; Danbury HS; Danbury, CT; (Y); 100/481; Cmnty Wkr; JA; Ski Clb; Band; Concert Band; Jazz Band; Mrchg Band; Stage Crew; Symp Band; Variety Show; CT Clbrtn 350 Inc Hmtwn Hero 86; Accntng.

DAMICO, MIKE; Emmet O Brien Reg Voc Tech; Shelton, CT; (Y); Hon Roll; NHS; Rep Stu Cncl; Electrical.

DAMJANOVICH, DAJANA; Seymour HS; Seymour, CT; (Y); Rep Church Yth Grp; VP Rep Jr Cls; JV Var Cheerleading; :Art.

DAMMERMAN, DAVID; Fairfield College Prep Schl; Monroe, CT; (Y); 15/240; Sec Key Clb; Yrbk Stf; Mgr(s); Capt Swmmng; High Hon Roll; NHS.

DANAHY, KAREN; Coventry HS; Coventry, CT; (Y); 1/100; Drama Clb; Teachers Aide; School Play; Yrbk Ed-Chief; Lit Mag; Rep Soph Cls; Var Cheerleading; Bausch & Lomb Sci Awd; High Hon Roll; Pres NHS; Brown U Bk Awd 86.

DANCSAK, SUSAN; Southington HS; Plantsville, CT; (Y); 173/600; Church Yth Grp; Stage Crew; Var Socr; Hon Roll; Nrsng.

DANIEL, SHERRY C; Choate Rosemary Hall; Poughkeepsie, NY; (Y); 7/292; JA; Natl Beta Clb; Stage Crew; Yrbk Ed-Chief; Swmmng; Im Tennis; High Hon Roll; Ntl Merit Ltr; Rassweiler Awd 86; Cum Laude Grad 86; IBM Watson Schlrshp 86; Brown U.

DANIELLO, CARMELA; New Fairfield HS; New Fairfield, CT; (Y); 12/237; Math Tm; Spanish Clb; Nwsp Ed-Chief; Rep Stu Cncl; High Hon Roll; Hon Roll; NHS; Ntl Merit Ltr; Spanish NHS; Drama Clb; Natl Latin Awd 84-85 & 85-86; St Latin Awd 84-85; Constitutional Conv II 85-86; Nrsng.

DANIELS, KATHI; Bethel HS; Bethel, CT; (Y); AFS; FBLA; Ski Clb; Variety Show; Capt Cheerleading; Mgr Ftbl; Mgr(s); Var Capt Trk; Hon Roll; Natl Chrldr Assoc All Amer 85; Exch Club Yth Mnth 86; U Of CT; Ntrtnl Sci.

DANIELS, LIANNE; East Catholic HS; Vernon, CT; (Y); Church Yth Grp; Hosp Aide; Pep Clb; Rep Jr Cls; Rep Sr Cls; Rep Stu Cncl; Hon Roll; Hnrs E; Schlrshps; NH Tech Inst; Dntl Hygn.

DANKO, CHERYL; Southington HS; Plantsville, CT; (Y); Girl Scts; Band; Concert Band; Mrchg Band; Var Sftbl; Var Vllybl; High Hon Roll; Hon Roll; Jr NHS; NHS; Marion Mdl 84; Slvr Awd 84; Gld Ldrshp Awd 86; Accntng.

DAPSIS, JENNIFER; Killingly HS; Danielson, CT; (Y); 40/311; Yrbk Stf; JV Crs Cntry; Hon Roll; Spanish NHS; Nrsng.

DARR, ASHLEY; Wamogo Regional HS; Goshen, CT; (Y); 3/80; AFS; Am Leg Aux Girls St; Pres Church Yth Grp; Girl Scts; School Play; Yrbk Stf; Var Capt Cheerleading; High Hon Roll; NHS; Harvard Bk Awd 86; Stu Mnth Mar 86; Grad Usher 86; Acadmc Awds; Engr.

DARRAGH, STACEY; Norwalk HS; E Norwalk, CT; (Y); Ski Clb; Chorus; Rep Frsh Cls; Rep Soph Cls; Rep Jr Cls; Stu Cncl; Cheerleading; Powder Puff Ftbl; Swmmng; Hon Roll; Cnfrmtn Spec Dlgt Bshp 85; Skidmore U; Spnsh Tchr.

DART, DIANA; Morgan HS; Clinton, CT; (Y); 3/150; VP Church Yth Grp; Sec French Clb; School Musical; High Hon Roll; NCTE Awd; NHS; Ntl Merit Ltr; SADD; Chorus; Nwsp Rptr; Shorline Alliance For Arts Schlrshp-Dance 86; Harvard Bk Awd 86; Colby Coll Bk Awd 86; Danc Ther.

DARYL, SMITH; Greenwich HS; Old Greenwich, CT; (Y); Am Leg Boys St; Boy Scts; Church Yth Grp; Var L Swmmng; Hon Roll; NHS; Ntl Merit Ltr; U Of NC Chapel Hill.

DATE, HARI; Trumbull HS; Trumbull, CT; (Y); Band; Chorus; Concert Band; Jazz Band; Mrchg Band; Orch; Symp Band; Nwsp Stf; Yrbk Ed-Chief; Yrbk Stf; PA ST U; Mech Engrng.

DAUGHERTY, TRACEY; Farmington HS; Farmington, CT; (Y); Church Yth Grp; Cmnty Wkr; DECA; Ski Clb; Chorus; Variety Show; Yrbk Stf; Fld Hcky; Gym; Gymnstcs NW Conf 85-86; CT Interschlstc Athlt Conf Awd 86; Vrsty Fld Hcky 85; Katheryn Gibbs; Secy.

DAUGHTERS, CAROLINE; Ridgefield HS; Ridgefield, CT; (Y); 135/387; Church Yth Grp; FHA; Political Wkr; Varsity Clb; Sec Soph Cls; Sec Jr Cls; VP Stu Cncl; Fld Hcky; Powder Puff Ftbl; Trk; Ldrshp To Clss Of 87 Class Sec 85; Jr Clss Sec 86; FHA Awd 85; Ec.

DAUM JR, JAMES R; Ridgefield HS; Ridgefield, CT; (Y); Boy Scts; Cmnty Wkr; German Clb; Stage Crew; Im Mgr Bsktbl; Var Diving; High Hon Roll; Hon Roll; VA Commonwealth U; Bio.

DAVIDSON, JEAN; Old Saybrook SR HS; Old Saybrook, CT; (Y); AFS; Art Clb; French Clb; Hon Roll; Art Achvt Awd 84; Encllnc World Geo Awd 84; Rhode Island Schl; Fshn Dsgn.

DAVIDSON III, WILLIAM F; Faifield College Prep Schl; Stratford, CT; (Y); Key Clb; Rep Jr Cls; Rep Sr Cls; JV Ftbl; Var Trk; Pres Wt Lftg; NHS; Pres Schlr; VP Spanish NHS; Acad Excllnc Bio & Hstry 86; Cornell U; Aerntcl Engrng.

DAVINO II, GERALD; Seymour HS; Oxford, CT; (S); Church Yth Grp; Variety Show; JV Bsktbl; JV Crs Cntry; Hon Roll; Pres Jr NHS; NHS; Essay Wnr Intl Yr Of Youth 85; Forn Sci.

DAVIS, AMY; Norwalk HS; Norwalk, CT; (Y); AFS; German Clb; Hosp Aide; Service Clb; Spanish Clb; SADD; Teachers Aide; Tchr.

DAVIS, CARLA ANN; Sacred Heart Acad; New Haven, CT; (Y); 15/122; Spanish Clb; Im Vllybl; High Hon Roll; NHS; Spanish NHS; St Schlr; Manhattanville Coll Schlrshp 86; 4 Yr Hnrs Awd 86; CT Schltc Achvt Grnt 86; Fairfield U; Bio.

DAVIS, DARLENE; Robert E Fitch SR HS; Groton, CT; (Y); 35/327; Church Yth Grp; Drama Clb; Office Aide; Pep Clb; SADD; Church Choir; Variety Show; Nwsp Ed-Chief; Nwsp Rptr; Pres Frsh Cls; Trk, Fld Grad Nbrs; Good Ctzn Wheeler; Bus Admn.

DAVIS, MARK; Brien Mc Mahon HS; Norwalk, CT; (Y); Boy Scts; Latin Clb; Varsity Clb; Band; Concert Band; Drm Mjr(t); Jazz Band; Mrchg Band; Orch; Pep Band; Cty Wghtlftng 1st Pl 85-86; U Of PA; Finance.

DAVIS, MARY; Notre Dame Catholic HS; Trumbull, CT; (Y); Cmnty Wkr; Dance Clb; Hosp Aide; Pep Clb; Spanish Clb; Yrbk Phtg; Rep Frsh Cls; Rep Soph Cls; Cheerleading; Mst Improvmnt In Alg II Awd 86; Nrsng.

DAVIS, MARY-BETH; Bulkeley HS; Hartford, CT; (Y); 5/300; Sec Church Yth Grp; Pres Computer Clb; Ed Yrbk Ed-Chief; Var L Mgr(s); Var L Socr; Var L Sftbl; JV L Swmmng; Cit Awd; High Hon Roll; NHS; Hly Cross Bk Awd; Boston Coll; Educ.

DAWKINS, ABIGAIL; Kingswood-Oxford Schl; W Hartford, CT; (Y); French Clb; Orch; Hon Roll; Ntl Merit Ltr.

DAY, JONATHAN; Oliver Wolcott RVTS HS; New Hartford, CT; (Y); 10/153; Art Clb; Boy Scts; Math Clb; Nwsp Stf; Yrbk Stf; Socr; Hon Roll; NHS; Oliver Wolcott Almn Schlrshp 86; Schltc Achvt Awd 83-86; MVP Sccr Awd; Waterbury Sst Tech; Elec Engrng.

DAYO, SONDRA; Joseph A Foran HS; Milford, CT; (Y); Church Yth Grp; Pres DECA; Varsity Clb; Yrbk Stf; JV Bsktbl; Var L Sftbl; Var L Vllybl; Hon Roll; Jr NHS; Sec Ntl Hnr Soc 82-83; Schlstc Achvt Subj Awds 85-86; 2nd Pl Local DECA Conf 85-86; Mgmt.

DAYS, EWEEKA; Bullard Havens Tech; Bridgeport, CT; (Y); JA; Library Aide; Hon Roll; Bus.

DE ANGELO, DEANN; Ansonia HS; Ansonia, CT; (Y); 20/140; Hosp Aide; VP JA; Spanish Clb; Teachers Aide; Drill Tm; Variety Show; Nwsp Stf; Yrbk Stf; Rep Soph Cls; Pom Pon; Hosp Volunteer Work; Jr Achvt Sales Club Awd; Catholic Religion Teacher; Management.

DE BIASE, SABRINA; Norwalk HS; Norwalk, CT; (Y); 25/422; Art Clb; JV Var Sftbl; High Hon Roll; Gould Found Schlrshp 86; 1st Prz Holiday Card Comptn 85-86; Italian Clb Pres 84-86; RI Schl Design; Fash Design.

DE CAPUA, SARAH; Shelton HS; Shelton, CT; (Y); 53/334; Church Yth Grp; Drama Clb; Key Clb; Ski Clb; Spanish Clb; SADD; School Musical; Nwsp Ed-Chief; Yrbk Bus Mgr; Pom Pon; Emerson Coll; Brdcst Jrnlsm.

DE CARO, LYNN M; New Milford HS; New Milford, CT; (Y); 7/295; Church Yth Grp; Concert Band; Jazz Band; Mrchg Band; School Musical; Yrbk Stf; VP Frsh Cls; Stat Bsktbl; NHS; Ntl Merit SF.

DE CONTI, CHRIS A; Daniel Hand HS; Madison, CT; (Y); 6/269; Civic Clb; Cmnty Wkr; Debate Tm; Pres Drama Clb; JCL; Model UN; Capt Quiz Bowl; Capt Scholastic Bowl; School Play; Stage Crew; Hugh O Brien Yth Ldrshp Awd 84; Intl Bus.

DE COSTA, DAWN; Ledyard HS; Galesferry, CT; (Y); Art Clb; Camera Clb; Church Yth Grp; Girl Scts; Letterman Clb; Varsity Clb; Band; JV Bsktbl; Var Sftbl; Im Vllybl; Estrn CT ST U; Sclgy.

DE FELICE, JENNIFER; Shelton HS; Shelton, CT; (Y); Ski Clb; Rep Stu Cncl; Pom Pon; Hon Roll; Spanish NHS; Itln Clb 85-86; Southern CC; Phy Thrpy.

DE FRANCO, SUSAN; Immaculate HS; Danbury, CT; (Y); Ski Clb; School Play; Sec Jr Cls; Var Cheerleading; Var Tennis; Hon Roll; Comm.

DE FREITAS, SCOTT; King Schl; Darien, CT; (Y); Boy Scts; Church Yth Grp; Drama Clb; Letterman Clb; PAVAS; School Musical; School Play; Variety Show; L Golf; Capt Socr; Drama.

DE GRAY, ANN; East Lyme HS; Niantic, CT; (Y); 55/257; Church Yth Grp; Key Clb; Band; Church Choir; Mrchg Band; JV Fld Hcky; Powder Puff Ftbl; Hon Roll; New London Schl Bus Schlrshp 86; Edwaard W Rice Schrlshp 86; New London Schl Bus; Comp Pgmr.

DE JESUS, ROSALINDA; Bulkeley HS; Hartford, CT; (Y); 3/350; Am Leg Aux Girls St; JA; Variety Show; Nwsp Rptr; Yrbk Stf; VP Jr Cls; Twrlr; High Hon Roll; NHS; Computer Clb; Wise Travel Awd 86; Brown U; Psych.

DE LIETO, AMY; West Woods Christian Acad; Ansonia, CT; (Y); Church Yth Grp; Cmnty Wkr; French Clb; Library Aide; Teachers Aide; Church Choir; Nwsp Rptr; Yrbk Stf; Aca Achvt Awd-Trphy 84; Excllnc Spch Cert 84; Gordon Coll Wenham MO; Spec Ed.

DE LUCA, LAURA; Brien Mcmahon HS; Norwalk, CT; (Y); 6/257; Key Clb; Ski Clb; Tennis; High Hon Roll; NHS; Excllnc Awd-Lang Stdy 86; IA Lang Cntst-2nd Hnrs 86; Southern CT ST U; Elem Ed.

DE LUCIA, ANITA; Sacred Heart Acad; New Haven, CT; (Y); Aud/Vis; Hosp Aide; School Musical; Sftbl; Vllybl; Hon Roll; Prfct Atten Awd; Mem Schrlshp 85; Endwnmnt Schrlshp 86; Hnrs 83-84; Physcl Thrpy.

DE MATTEO, TERRI; North Haven HS; North Haven, CT; (Y); 20/280; Pres Church Yth Grp; Church Choir; Stage Crew; Yrbk Stf; Rep Stu Cncl; JV Cheerleading; JV Score Keeper; JV Trk; Hon Roll; NHS; Bus.

DE MEOLA, KAREN; St Marys HS; Branford, CT; (Y); 10/113; Var L Bsktbl; Im Bowling; Mgr(s); Var Capt Sftbl; High Hon Roll; Latn Awd 86; Acdmc Achvt Awd 86; Outstndng H S Athl Amer 86; Bio.

DE PALMA, MARK; St Paul Catholic HS; Bristol, CT; (Y); Boy Scts; Exploring; Math Clb; Science Clb; School Musical; Variety Show; Trk; Elks Awd; Eagle Scout 85; Chptr Chief-Order Of The Arrow 85; Amer Legion Schlrshp; Worcester Polytech Inst; Comp.

DE PAOLI, YVONNE; Torrington HS; Torrington, CT; (Y); Cmnty Wkr; Dance Clb; PAVAS; Varsity Clb; Rep Jr Cls; Var Cheerleading; Coach Actv; Gym; High Hon Roll; Ntl Chrldng Assn Awd 86; Sthrn CT ST U; Fitness.

DE PODESTA, CRAIG; Hamden HS; Hamden, CT; (Y); Cmnty Wkr; French Clb; Var L Crs Cntry; Var L Ice Hcky; Var L Trk; Hon Roll; NHS; SADD; Varsity Clb; Natl Latin Test Slr Medlst 86; Co-Pres Future Med Careers Clb 85-86; Stu Athlt Awd 86; Premed.

DE VITO, JOHN; Danbury HS; Danbury, CT; (Y); Church Yth Grp; JV Socr; L Trk; Hon Roll; Jr NHS; Perry Awd For Math 85; Accntng.

DEAK, PATRICK; Masuk HS; Monroe, CT; (Y); JV Socr; Hon Roll; Ntl Merit Ltr; Natl Mrt Schlrhsp Qlfng Awd 86; Awd Mntng 3.o-3.8 Avg 86; U Of CT.

DEAN, ADRIENNE; Sacred Heart HS; Waterbury, CT; (Y); 36/220; Cmnty Wkr; Yrbk Stf; Rep Frsh Cls; Rep Soph Cls; Rep Jr Cls; Trs Sr Cls; JV Var Cheerleading; Hon Roll; NHS; Villanova U; Pre-Law.

DEAN, DENISE R; Holy Cross HS; Oxford, CT; (Y); 30/380; Civic Clb; Library Aide; Sec Spanish Clb; Teachers Aide; School Musical; School Play; Hon Roll; Jr NHS; NHS; Spanish NHS; Chptr Pres Oxford Jrettes 85-86; Soc Studies Hnr Soc 85 & 86; Spanish.

DEAN, KAREN M; Holy Cross HS; Waterbury, CT; (Y); Civic Clb; Cmnty Wkr; SADD; Stu Cncl; JV Var Cheerleading; Hon Roll; VP Italian Clb; Miss Teen All Am,USA; Chiropractice.

DEARBORN, LESLEY; Staples HS; Westport, CT; (Y); Church Yth Grp; French Clb; Ntl Merit Ltr; U Of CT.

DEAVENPORT, JOSEPH; East Lyme HS; E Lyme, CT; (Y); Church Yth Grp; Math Tm; Trk; Hon Roll; Top Scr Adv Stu Lcl Physcs Olympd 86; Abilene Christian U; Chmstry.

DEBO, SYLVIA; Mary Immaculate Acad; New Britain, CT; (Y); Service Clb; Chorus; Pres Stu Cncl; Var Cheerleading; Cit Awd; DAR Awd; Prfct Atten Awd; Drama Clb; School Musical; School Play; US Army Rsrv Ntl Schlr Athlt Awd 85-86; Cvtn Clb Awd 85-86; Miss Grtr Nw Brtn 1st Rnr Up 86-87; U Of Connecticut; Pre-Med.

DECHESSER, MICHELLE; Suffield HS; W Suffield, CT; (Y); 13/143; AFS; Chorus; Stage Crew; Yrbk Stf; High Hon Roll; Hon Roll; N Cntrl Connecticut Rltrs Schlrshp 86; Stfld Rtry Schlrshp 86; U Of Connecticut; Lbrl Arts.

DEDONATO, FRANK; Shelton HS; Shelton, CT; (Y); Latin Clb; NHS; Fince.

DEELEY, KATHY; Holy Cross HS; Waterbury, CT; (Y); 241/380; Church Yth Grp; Hosp Aide; Chorus; Acctng.

DEEN, FEROZE A; Bolton HS; Bolton, CT; (Y); 1/70; Am Leg Boys St; Model UN; Nwsp Ed-Chief; Pres Jr Cls; VP Sr Cls; Trs Stu Cncl; Bausch & Lomb Sci Awd; VP NHS; Val; Boy Scts; Rensselaer Math & Sci Awd 85; Yale Clb Bk Awd 85; MIT; Engrng.

DEERY, JENNIFER; Greenwich HS; Greenwich, CT; (Y); AFS; Hosp Aide; Trs Service Clb; Rep Stu Cncl; Bsktbl; Cheerleading; Fld Hcky; Var Capt Socr; Tennis; U Of Vermont; Fshn Mrchndsng.

DEFAZIO, ITALIA; Torrington HS; Torrington, CT; (Y); 62/270; Aud/Vis; French Clb; Library Aide; Yrbk Stf; High Hon Roll; Hon Roll; Itln Clb 83-87; Finance.

DEFEO, RENEE; Windham HS; W Willington, CT; (Y); 14/285; Chess Clb; Nwsp Stf; Yrbk Stf; Rep Jr Cls; Rep Sr Cls; Im Socr; Var Trk; Hon Roll; Pres Schlr; U-Conn Co-Op Bio/Chem 85-86; Boston U; Med.

DEGNAN, KEVIN MICHAEL; St Joseph HS; Monroe, CT; (Y); 5/230; Am Leg Boys St; Debate Tm; Ed Nwsp Rptr; Rep Soph Cls; Rep Sr Cls; Trk; French Hon Soc; VP NHS; Church Yth Grp; Drama Clb; Scty Engrs Citatn Exclnc Math & Sci; 3rd ST Intl Frnch Tst; TSSMA Msc Cntst Vocl; Pltcs.

DEGRAW, RONALD P; Joel Barlow HS; West Redding, CT; (Y); Boy Scts; Church Yth Grp; Cmnty Wkr; FCA; Science Clb; Varsity Clb; Variety Show; JV Bsktbl; Var L Socr; Hon Roll; High Avrg Alg I; Engrg.

DEITERT, KIMBERLY; Killingly HS; Dayville, CT; (Y); Art Clb; Camera Clb; Church Yth Grp; Cmnty Wkr; Pep Clb; Spanish Clb; Varsity Clb; Yrbk Stf; Var Cheerleading; Var Coach Actv; ECC Chrldng Chmpns 86; Art Achvt Ad 86; Ntl Chrldng Awd Of Encllnc 86; Fshn.

DEL BUONO, JOSEPH; Southington HS; Southington, CT; (Y); 225/600; FCA; Band; Concert Band; Drm & Bgl; Jazz Band; Mrchg Band; Orch; Pep Band; School Musical; School Play; CT Bus & Indstry Assn Schlrshp 85; 3rd Pl Poetry Cntst 84; Benito Perone Schlrshp 86; Central CT ST U; Acctg.

DEL VECCHIO, ANDREA; Holy Cross HS; Waterbury, CT; (Y); 38/380; Art Clb; Service Clb; Hon Roll; Spanish NHS; Socl Studs Hnr Soc 84; Ophelia Actvty Awd 85; Vrsty Ltr Acadmcs 86; Alld Hlth Flds.

DEL VECCHIO, ANDREA; Lauralton Hall HS; New Haven, CT; (Y); 76/111; GAA; Model UN; Pep Clb; Science Clb; Service Clb; Spanish Clb; Yrbk Stf; Rep Frsh Cls; VP Soph Cls; Pres Jr Cls; U Of CT; Bus Mgmt.

DELAGE, DOREEN; Holy Cross HS; Prospect, CT; (Y); French Clb; Sec Frsh Cls; Sec Soph Cls; Sec Jr Cls; Sec Sr Cls; Var JV Bsktbl; Var JV Sftbl; Hon Roll; Natl JR Honor Society; Commercial Art.

DELANEY, LAURIE; E Hartford HS; E Hartford, CT; (Y); Am Leg Aux Girls St; French Clb; Sec Concert Band; Sec Mrchg Band; Lit Mag; Twrlr; High Hon Roll; NHS; Church Yth Grp; Drama Clb; U Of MI Bk Awd 86; 1st Pl Wnnr Natl Yth Yr Essy Cntst 85; Law.

DELGRECO, DEB; William H Hall HS; W Hartford, CT; (Y); 167/349; JV Fld Hcky; Acctng.

DELIO, KARLA; Central Catholic HS; Norwalk, CT; (Y); 11/78; Ski Clb; Spanish Clb; Yrbk Stf; Stu Cncl; Vllybl; High Hon Roll; Hon Roll; NHS; Pres Schlr; St Schlr; U S Fig Sktg Tests 82-86; Providence Coll; Lwyr.

DELLA ROCCO, JULIE; Amity Regional SR HS; Orange, CT; (Y); Lit Mag; Cheerleading; Sftbl; Hon Roll; Peer Tutor & Cnslng 86; U Bridgeport; Fshn Merch.

DELNEGRO, CHRISTOPHER; Pomperaug HS; Southbury, CT; (Y); 40/236; Church Yth Grp; Cmnty Wkr; Ski Clb; SADD; Teachers Aide; Varsity Clb; Variety Show; Swmmng; High Hon Roll; Hon Roll; Ntl Sci Olympd 85 & 86.

DELUCIA, JOANNA; Ellington HS; Ellington, CT; (Y); 6/140; Drama Clb; FBLA; Latin Clb; Ski Clb; School Play; Var L Crs Cntry; Var Capt Trk; High Hon Roll; NHS; Ntl Merit Ltr; Ellington Cmmnty Schlrhsp 86; Englsh IV Awd 85; Wrtng Awd 85; Wellesley Coll.

DELVENTHAL, LISA; Shelton HS; Shelton, CT; (S); DECA; Hon Roll; Finance.

DEMARS, ELIZABETH; St Bernard HS; Norwich, CT; (Y); Church Yth Grp; Varsity Clb; VP Frsh Cls; VP Soph Cls; VP Jr Cls; Stat Bsbl; Var Cheerleading; Cit Awd; DAR Awd; Knghts Columbus Schlrshp 86; Hugh O Brien Yth Ldrshp Awd 84; Christopher Awd Yng Christ Bearer 86; St Joseph Coll; Nrsg.

DEMCE, ASLAN; Plainfield HS; Moosup, CT; (Y); 10/162; Am Leg Boys St; Hon Roll; Jr NHS; Gifted Ed Prg; Poli Sci.

DEMETER, ANNA; Bassick HS; Bridgeport, CT; (Y); 1/190; Computer Clb; Drama Clb; French Clb; JA; Key Clb; Office Aide; Spanish Clb; Teachers Aide; Yrbk Stf; Lit Mag; All MBIAC 2nd Bsmn Sftbl Tm 85-86; Fair Housg Create A Comercl Cntst Wnnr 84-85; U Of Bridgeport; Dntl Hyg.

DEMILO, JUSTINE; Sacred Heart Acad; New Haven, CT; (Y); 23/123; Spanish Clb; Vllybl; Hon Roll; Spanish NHS; CT ST Schlrp 86; Mc Donalds Schlrp 86; U CT; Biol.

DEMIRALI, ELIZABETH; Notre Dame Acad; Waterbury, CT; (Y); Church Yth Grp; Office Aide; SADD; Chorus; Orch; Variety Show; Hon Roll; Jr NHS; NEDT Awd; Govt.

DEMPSEY, DAWN; Torrington HS; Torrington, CT; (Y); 26/282; Cmnty Wkr; French Clb; Trs Key Clb; Varsity Clb; Nwsp Stf; Var L Tennis; High Hon Roll; NHS; Prfct Atten Awd; Rory Hatch Meml Fund Engrng 86; Syracuse U; Engrng.

DEMPSEY, JENNIFER; Berlin HS; Kensington, CT; (Y); 32/208; Church Yth Grp; Girl Scts; Service Clb; Band; Concert Band; Mrchg Band; Hon Roll; Silver Awd Girl Scouts 86; Elem Educ.

DEMPSEY, KATHERINE; Miss Porters Schl; Avon, CT; (Y); Intnl Clb; Latin Clb; SADD; Chorus; JV Socr; Swmmng; High Hon Roll; Hon Roll; Ntl Merit Ltr; AFS; Cum Laude Natl Latin Exam 86; Lbrl Arts.

DEMPSEY, RAYMOND; Fairfield Prep; Weston, CT; (Y); Hosp Aide; Chorus; NHS.

DEMSKY, BONNIE; New Fairfield HS; New Fairfld, CT; (Y); 10/240; Latin Clb; School Play; Nwsp Rptr; Mgr(s); Swmmng; French Hon Soc; High Hon Roll; Hon Roll; NHS; Psych.

DENNIN, AMY P; Brien Mcmahon HS; Norwalk, CT; (Y); 1/270; Nwsp Ed-Chief; Tennis; Vllybl; Hon Roll; NHS; Ntl Merit Ltr; Rotary Awd; Val; NHS Scholar 86; Yale U.

DENOTO, ROB; Morgan HS; Clinton, CT; (Y); 33/145; JV Ftbl; JV Socr; Var L Wrstlng; Hon Roll; Communications.

DENTE, MARCELLO; East Haven HS; East Haven, CT; (Y); Concert Band; Socr; S Cntrl CC.

DEPASCALE, MICHAEL; St Joseph HS; Huntington, CT; (Y); 73/257; Chess Clb; Computer Clb; Letterman Clb; Varsity Clb; Crs Cntry; Trk; High Hon Roll; Hon Roll; Acctg.

DEPTULA, MATTHEW; Ansonia HS; Ansonia, CT; (Y); 17/144; Rep Am Leg Boys St; Rep Frsh Cls; Rep Soph Cls; Rep Jr Cls; Rep Sr Cls; Var Bsktbl; JV Ftbl; Capt Golf; Cit Awd; Hon Roll; Glf Tm Lwst Scrs Awd 85-86; Accntng.

DEQUATTRO, JOHN; Kingswood-Oxford Schl; Manchester, CT; (Y); Ed Hosp Aide; Intnl Clb; Band; Jazz Band; Variety Show; Bsktbl; Ftbl; Im Tennis; Im Wt Lftg; Hon Roll.

DERMODY, DOREEN; Pomperang HS; Middlebury, CT; (Y); Girl Scts; Var JV Cheerleading; JV Vllybl; High Hon Roll; Hon Roll; Outstndng Geo Achvt 84; Pblc Lbry Cltrl Essy Awd 86; Comp.

DEROSA, JENNY; South Windsor HS; S Windsor, CT; (Y); Gov Hon Prg Awd; High Hon Roll; Manchester CC; Bus.

DEROSIER, LISA; Southington HS; Southington, CT; (Y); 46/560; FBLA; Key Clb; Math Tm; Ski Clb; High Hon Roll; NHS; Fairfield U; Acctg.

DEROUIN, STEPHANIE; Weston HS; Weston, CT; (Y); 14/277; Church Yth Grp; Drama Clb; Spanish Clb; Chorus; School Musical; School Play; Capt Cheerleading; Var Powder Puff Ftbl; High Hon Roll; Hon Roll; Best Suprtng Actrs 84; Most Vlbl Chrldr 84-85; Med.

DERRIG, ELIZABETH; East Lyme HS; E Lyme, CT; (Y); Church Yth Grp; Var Capt Cheerleading; Hon Roll; Vet Sci.

DERY, KELLY; Putnam HS; Putnam, CT; (Y); Hosp Aide; Varsity Clb; Band; Chorus; Color Guard; Concert Band; Mrchg Band; Yrbk Stf; Sec Frsh Cls; Var Bsktbl; MVP Grls Bsktbl 85-86; Natl JR Olympcs Grls Bsktbl Champ Gms 86; Bus.

DESANTO, DANA; Wilby HS; Waterbury, CT; (Y); School Play; Var Cheerleading; Dance Clb; Drama Clb; Girl Scts; Chorus; Rep Jr Cls; Rep Sr Cls; Hon Roll; X Ray Tech.

DESCAULT, DEBBIE; Holy Cross HS; Naugatuck, CT; (Y); 8/392; Art Clb; Exploring; DAR Awd; High Hon Roll; Jr NHS; Maria & Claire Schfllt Awd 83; Psychlgy.

DESENA, PAUL; Holy Cross HS; Waterbury, CT; (Y); 78/389; Church Yth Grp; Ski Clb; Spanish Clb; SADD; JV Golf; High Hon Roll; Spanish NHS; Soc Stud Hnr Scty.

DESIDERIO, STEPHEN; Crosby HS; Waterbury, CT; (Y); Church Yth Grp; Ski Clb; Band; Concert Band; Mrchg Band; Lit Mag; Golf; Hon Roll; Voice Dem Awd; CT Bus Wk 85; YMCA Pr Edctrs 85; Bentley Coll; Bus Law.

DESILETS, DANNY; Putnam HS; Putnam, CT; (Y); Chess Clb; Hosp Aide; Ftbl; Socr; Vllybl; Wt Lftg; Voice Dem Awd; U Of S Calif; Wrtr.

DESMANGLES, MICHELLE; Conard HS; W Htfd, CT; (Y); 134/345; Art Clb; Band; Color Guard; Jazz Band; Pep Band; School Musical; Stage Crew; PA ST U; Vet Med.

DESPATHY, DANIELLE; St Bernard HS; Norwich, CT; (Y); Ski Clb; Yrbk Stf; Var Capt Cheerleading; Var Sftbl; Var Capt Tennis; Var Trk; High Hon Roll; Hon Roll; Stu Govt Awd; Chrldng Sftbl Athltc Awd; FCC ST Tnns MVP HCC Semi-Fnls; U Of MA Long Island; Mrine Bio.

DESPER, RICHARD M; William H Hall HS; W Hartford, CT; (Y); 2/329; Math Tm; Capt Model UN; Jazz Band; Symp Band; JV Socr; JV Trk; French Hon Soc; High Hon Roll; NHS; Ntl Merit Schol; John Hays Fllws Bk Awd Excllnce Hstry; Top Ind Scorer New Englnd Mth Lg; Schl Match Wits Tm; Georgetown U; Intl Affrs.

DESROCHERS, KIM; Stratford HS; Stratford, CT; (Y); 108/240; Office Aide; SADD; Gym; JV Swmmng; High Hon Roll; Hon Roll; Southrn CT ST U; Elem Ed.

DESRUISSEAUX, CORINNE; Windham Technical Schl; Tolland, CT; (Y); Yrbk Stf; High Hon Roll; Hon Roll; NHS; Stu Rcgntn Awd 86; Elec Awd 86; U Of ME; Elec Engrng.

DEVINE, MARY KATHERINE; Mark T Sheenan HS; Wallingford, CT; (Y); 29/250; Church Yth Grp; Hosp Aide; Chorus; Mgr Powder Puff Ftbl; High Hon Roll; Hon Roll; Lion Awd; NHS; Rotary Awd; Rotary Schlrshp 86; Chldrn Of Mary Pres 82-86; Saint Anselm NH; Nrs.

DEVINE, REBECCA E; Shepaug Valley HS; Bridgewater, CT; (Y); 3/70; Art Clb; Debate Tm; Band; Concert Band; Pep Band; Powder Puff Ftbl; NHS; Lit Intrprtn Awd; Excl German; Modrn Mus Mastrs; Ithaca Schl Of Mus; Mus Ed.

DEYOE, GRANT C; Trumbull HS; Trumbull, CT; (Y); AFS; Boy Scts; Church Yth Grp; JA; Science Clb; Spanish Clb; Nwsp Rptr; Yrbk Stf; High Hon Roll; NHS; Sct Ldrshp Corps; Ntl Histry Day 85; US Presdntl Schlrs Prog 86.

DHARMSHI, SAPNA; Kobe-Catherdral HS; Bridgeport, CT; (Y); Computer Clb; Nwsp Phtg; Sacred Heart U.

DI BENEDETTO, KATE; Southington HS; Southington, CT; (Y); 70/600; Cmnty Wkr; Key Clb; Latin Clb; Ski Clb; Trs Spanish Clb; SADD; Rep Frsh Cls; Rep Soph Cls; Rep Jr Cls; Rep Sr Cls.

DI CAMILLO, STEPHEN R; Bloomfield HS; Bloomfield, CT; (Y); 3/236; French Clb; Capt Math Tm; Concert Band; Jazz Band; Capt Golf; French Hon Soc; High Hon Roll; NHS; Ntl Merit Ltr; Rotary Awd; Cornell U; Elec Engrng.

DI COCCO, LYNN; Conard HS; W Hartford, CT; (Y); 76/345; Cmnty Wkr; Chorus; School Musical; VP Jr Cls; Rep Stu Cncl; Var Bsktbl; Var Capt Socr; Var Capt Sftbl; Hon Roll; NHS.

DI DOMINIC JR, DOMINIC; Joseph F Foran HS; Milford, CT; (Y); 56/240; Letterman Clb; Yrbk Sprt Ed; L Var Bsbl; L Var Tennis; Drama Clb; Stage Crew; Yrbk Stf; Var Bsktbl; Score Keeper; Timer; Prnts Clb Awd 86; Cmpltd Pilots Crs 85; Cert Umprs Bsbl Gms NY Schl Umprng 86; Bethany Coll Bethany; Bus Admn.

DI DONNO, LAURA; Southington HS; Southington, CT; (Y); 9/600; FBLA; Math Tm; High Hon Roll; Sec NHS; 5th In ST Bus Law Awd FBLA 86; Outstndg Achvt Hm Econ 83; P Hutton & Son Schlrshp Awd 86; Hartford Coll/Women; Law.

DI GIORGIO, RAY J; King School; Stamford, CT; (Y); 12/40; Art Clb; Cmnty Wkr; JA; Model UN; School Musical; School Play; Nwsp Stf; Yrbk Phtg; Yrbk Stf; Bsbl; Bus.

DI GIROLAMO, THERESA; Weston HS; Weston, CT; (Y); 5/152; Girl Scts; Hosp Aide; Concert Band; Mrchg Band; School Musical; JV Vllybl; Hon Roll; Spnsh Exc Stu 84; Beaver Coll; Hstry.

DI MATTEO, PASQUALE; Bristol Central HS; Bristol, CT; (Y); Church Yth Grp; Yrbk Stf; Bowling; Socr; High Hon Roll; NHS; Smnr Wrld Affrs Awd-Reprt On S Africa 86; Frgn Cultr Clb 83-87; Athl Assn 83-87; Engrng.

DI PIETRO, LISA MARIE; Southington HS; Southington, CT; (Y); 8/600; Cmnty Wkr; Hosp Aide; Latin Clb; Capt Quiz Bowl; Powder Puff Ftbl; High Hon Roll; Hon Roll; Jr NHS; NHS; New Britain Gen Hosp Aux Schrlshp 86; Bradley Mem Hosp Schrlshp 86; Mary Our Queen Chrch Schlrshp 86; Fairfield U; Nrsng.

DI TULLIO, GINA; Brookfield HS; Brookfield, CT; (Y); AFS; Acpl Chr; Chorus; Rep Soph Cls; Sec Jr Cls; JV Cheerleading; Var JV Fld Hcky; JV Trk; High Hon Roll; NHS; Rcgntn Cert Of Awd Spcl Chorus 85-86; Awd For COLT Frgn Lang Ptry Cntst 85; Bus & Trvl.

DIAZ, PEGGY; Miss Porters HS; Wethersfield, CT; (Y); Latin Clb; Ski Clb; Spanish Clb; Im Socr; Im Wt Lftg; High Hon Roll; Hon Roll; Exc Hist,Religion 84; Intl Law.

DIAZ, WILFRED; New Britain HS; New Britain, CT; (Y); SADD; Capt Crs Cntry; Capt Trk; Wt Lftg; Vrsty Ltr Awd 84; Most Imprvd Awd 86; Vrsty Ltr Awd Trk 85; MIT; Engrng.

DICKEY, RANDY; Warren F Kaynor Technical Schl; Waterbury, CT; (Y); Red Cross Aide; Trs VICA; Rep Frsh Cls; Rep Soph Cls; Rep Jr Cls; Var Bsbl; Cit Awd; Hon Roll; NHS; Voc Nd Clbs Am Skill Olympics; All Inter Cty Athletic Conf 86; Carpenter.

DICKINSON, PAGE; Kent Schl; Cheriton, VA; (Y); Church Yth Grp; Girl Scts; Latin Clb; Library Aide; Teachers Aide; Church Choir; Nwsp Stf; Var Lcrss; JV Var Socr; DAR Awd; Libr Proctor 86-87; Duke U; Frgn Svc.

DICKS, DAVID; Holy Cross HS; Southbury, CT; (Y); 207/380; Hon Roll.

DICKSON, SEAN; Tolland HS; Tolland, CT; (Y); Im Ice Hcky; Im Socr; Yale U Sci Lectrs 85; Water Sfty Instr Red Crss 85; Advncd Lfsvng Red Crss 84; Wentworth Inst Of Tech; Ag Engr.

DICKSON, WILLIAM; South Windsor HS; S Windsor, CT; (Y); Computer Clb; Drama Clb; Thesps; Chorus; School Musical; School Play; Swing Chorus; Stu Cncl; Hon Roll; Ntl Merit Ltr; Cltrl Arts Awd 86; CT Estrn Rgnl Chrs 84-86; CT All ST Chrs 85 & 86; U Of Hartford; Engl.

DIDIER, ELLEN M; St Bernard HS; Gales Ferry, CT; (Y); 23/298; AFS; Girl Scts; School Musical; School Play; Lit Mag; Ftbl; Mgr(s); Score Keeper; Stat Sftbl; Hon Roll; Girl Sct Gld Awd 86; Poem Pblshd Amer Anthlgy & Ptry 86; Schlrshp Ntl Assn Wmn Cnstrctn 86; Carnegie-Mellon U; Arch.

DIES, JASON; Fairfield College Prep; Fairfield, CT; (Y); Church Yth Grp; Cmnty Wkr; SADD; Lit Mag; Im Bsktbl; JV Trk.

DIETLIN, NANCY; Simsbury HS; Simsbury, CT; (Y); Chorus; School Play; Var Cheerleading; Trk; Advrtsng.

DILLANE, TIM; Central Catholic HS; Norwalk, CT; (Y); 1/76; VP Frsh Cls; VP Soph Cls; Pres Jr Cls; Pres Sr Cls; Capt Bsbl; High Hon Roll; NHS; St Schlr; Val; Mrchnts Bnk Schlrshp 86; Dailey Memrl Schlrshp 86; Coll Hly Crs Bk Awd 85; U Of Notre Dame; Bus.

DILLON, PETER; Ledyard HS; Gales Ferry, CT; (Y); Dance Clb; German Clb; Band; Jazz Band; Pep Band; Symp Band; Var Lcrss; Var Socr; Var Trk; Hon Roll; Mech Engnrg.

DILLON, THOMAS; Watertown HS; Oakville, CT; (Y); 18/260; Am Leg Boys St; Spanish Clb; Trs SADD; Chorus; Yrbk Stf; Rep Soph Cls; Rep Jr Cls; Rep Sr Cls; Hon Roll; NHS; Central CT ST U; Elem Ed.

DIMITRATOS, ANDREW; Bristol Central HS; Bristol, CT; (Y); Drama Clb; Letterman Clb; Varsity Clb; School Play; Var L Ftbl; Hon Roll; Northeastern U; Intl Bus.

DION, RENEE; Plainfield HS; Wauregan, CT; (Y); Boy Scts; GAA; Varsity Clb; Stage Crew; Nwsp Stf; Bsktbl; Hon Roll; Voice Dem Awd; Eastern CT ST U; Physcl Educ.

DIONE, JANINE; The Morgan Schl; Clinton, CT; (Y); 6/160; AFS; French Clb; Chrmn SADD; Chorus; Stage Crew; Nwsp Rptr; Rep Stu Cncl; Var L Tennis; Var L Trk; Sec NHS; Hnrs Pgm Stu; Acad Awd Mth, Comp.

DISBROW, MICHAEL; Bullard Havens HS; Bridgeport, CT; (Y); Aud/Vis; Library Aide; Office Aide; Yrbk Stf; Cit Awd; High Hon Roll; Sacred Heart U; Sci.

DISISTO, DANIELLE; Trumbull HS; Trumbull, CT; (Y); French Clb; JV Capt Fld Hcky; Var Trk; High Hon Roll; Hon Roll; Sec Ed.

DISTASIO, GARY; Branford HS; Branford, CT; (Y); Am Leg Boys St; Church Yth Grp; VP Soph Cls; Var Bsbl; Var Bsktbl; Var Ftbl; Hon Roll; Bus Adm.

DISTASIO, KAREN; Branford HS; Branford, CT; (Y); 16/264; Am Leg Aux Girls St; Nwsp Stf; Lit Mag; VP Soph Cls; Off Stu Cncl; Capt Cheerleading; High Hon Roll; Hon Roll; NHS; Fairfield U; Comm.

DIXON, CRAIG; Bulkeyley HS; Hartford, CT; (Y); Boy Scts; Church Yth Grp; FHA; JV Var Bsktbl; Var Capt Ftbl; Var Trk; Prfct Atten Awd; MVP Ftbl Tm 85-86; Crmnl Just.

DIXON, SAGE; Westmont HS; Campbell, CA; (Y); French Clb; Yrbk Phtg; Trs Jr Cls; Mgr Stu Cncl; Var JV Bsktbl; JV Crs Cntry; French Hon Soc; Hon Roll; Cert Merit Natl Fr Exam 84-86; USAFA; Aero.

DIZENZO, SUSAN; Southington HS; Southington, CT; (Y); FCA; Pep Clb; School Play; Var L Fld Hcky; Var L Gym; Trk; Hon Roll; Relig Stud Mdl & Cert 83; Cert Outstndg Achvt Americanism 83; Schl Rcd Brkr Cert 83; Corp Law.

DOBBINS, KELLEY; Watertown HS; Watertown, CT; (Y); 58/256; Chorus; Capt Color Guard; Drm & Bgl; Nrsng.

DOBKINS, DAVID; Watertown HS; Oakville, CT; (Y); Am Leg Boys St; Math Clb; JV Var Ftbl; JV Trk; High Hon Roll; Pres Schlr; Mst Imprvd SR 86; Cls Entcr 85-86; Waterbury ST Tech; Chem Engrng.

DOBORWICZ, GAIL; Derby HS; Derby, CT; (Y); 9/110; Pep Clb; Spanish Clb; Varsity Clb; Var Capt Bsktbl; JV Sftbl; Im Vllybl; Hon Roll; NHS; Spanish NHS; Katharine Gibbs; Secy.

DOBRATZ, JEFFREY; Horace C Wilcox Tech; Meriden, CT; (Y); Sec Stu Cncl; Capt L Bsktbl; JV Socr; Var L Trk; Hon Roll; Vlbl Plyr Vrsty Bsktbl 85-86; Printg Indstry CT 85-86.

DODAJ, VJOLLCA; Sacred Heart Acad; Stamford, CT; (Y); Cmnty Wkr; Dance Clb; Library Aide; Chorus; Nwsp Rptr; Lit Mag; Sec Frsh Cls; Sec Soph Cls; Off Stu Cncl; Office Aide; Cert Of Recog-Sci 84-85; U CT; Gynclgst.

DODSON, JOE; New Canaan HS; New Canaan, CT; (Y); 120/300; Boy Scts; Church Yth Grp; Band; Concert Band; Jazz Band; School Musical; Symp Band; Nwsp Rptr; Nwsp Stf; Hon Roll; Ftr Edtr HS Paper 86-87; Crtv Wrtng.

DOERR, DANIEL; Morgan HS; Clinton, CT; (Y); 13/140; Pep Clb; Var L Tennis; High Hon Roll; Hon Roll.

DOERR, JENNIFER; The Morgan School HS; Clinton, CT; (Y); 25/160; Library Aide; Pep Clb; Band; Chorus; School Musical; Nwsp Ed-Chief; Yrbk Ed-Chief; High Hon Roll; Hon Roll; NHS; Engl Merit Awd 84; Engl Dept Rcgntn Of Merit 86; Skidmore Coll; Engl Mjr.

DOHERTY, SARAH; Windsor HS; Windsor, CT; (Y); 26/383; Dance Clb; Intnl Clb; Yrbk Stf; Var L Mgr(s); Var L Score Keeper; Var Capt Swmmng; High Hon Roll; Hon Roll; NCTE Awd; Spanish NHS; Economic Dev Commission For Town Of Windsor 85-87; Economics.

DOIRON, ROBBIN; Nathan Hale Ray HS; E Haddam, CT; (Y); Am Leg Aux Girls St; Drama Clb; Ski Clb; School Play; Yrbk Stf; Sec Jr Cls; Golf; High Hon Roll; Hon Roll; Fashion Desng.

DOKLA, MICHAEL ANDREW; Shelton HS; Shelton, CT; (Y); 93/314; Boys Clb Am; Latin Clb; Letterman Clb; Ski Clb; Pres Varsity Clb; Var Coach Actv; Var Ftbl; Var Wt Lftg; Hon Roll; Frederick B Silliman Schlrshp 86; Shelton Educ Fund Schlrshp 86; Pr Ttr 2 Spcl Accmdtns Chem 85-86; U Of CT; Liberal Arts.

DOLIVEIRA, ROBERTA; Holy Cross HS; Waterbury, CT; (Y); 190/392; Hosp Aide; Hon Roll.

DOLLAK, MELISSA; William H Hall HS; W Hartford, CT; (Y); Cit Awd; High Hon Roll; Bay Path JC Bus Awd 85; Home Ec Awd 86; Amer Lgn Ctznshp Awd 86; Cazenovia Coll; Chldhd Ed.

DOMBROWSKI, LISA; Southington HS; Plantsville, CT; (Y); Am Leg Aux Girls St; Girl Scts; Key Clb; Band; Concert Band; Mrchg Band; Stu Cncl; JV Var Fld Hcky; Trk; Hon Roll; Slvr Awd Girl Scouts 84; Physcl Thrpy.

DOMBROWSKI, WALTER; St Bernard HS; Jewett City, CT; (Y); Hon Roll; Woodwind Schlrshp 4 Yr Partcl Tuitn 86-90; Berklee Coll; Prof Musician.

DOMINELLO, JOANNE; Cromwell HS; Cromwell, CT; (Y); 17/80; Art Clb; FBLA; Drm Mjr(t); School Play; Variety Show; Socr; Sftbl; Trk; High Hon Roll; Hon Roll; Keene ST Coll; Cmmrcl Artst.

DONAGHER, KELLY; Farmington HS; Farmington, CT; (Y); Ski Clb; Nwsp Stf; Yrbk Phtg; Yrbk Stf; Lit Mag; Bsktbl; Tennis; 2nd Pl Floor Hcky Girls Div 86; Adv Plcmnt Hstry & Coop Engl 86-87; Adv Spn 87; Emerson Coll; Cmmnctns.

DONAHUE, MARY-LEA; East Hartford HS; E Hartford, CT; (Y); JA; Ski Clb; Bsktbl; Crs Cntry; Socr; Sftbl; High Hon Roll; Hon Roll; Equine Studies.

DONAHUE, MAURINE; Ansonia HS; Ansonia, CT; (Y); 18/145; Computer Clb; French Clb; FHA; Yrbk Stf; VP Frsh Cls; Rep Soph Cls; Stu Cncl; Capt Var Sftbl; Capt Var Vllybl; Hon Roll; Sftbl Coach Awd 85; Mst Imprvd Plyr Sftbl 86; Phy Thrpy.

DONAHUE, NORINE; Ansonia HS; Ansonia, CT; (Y); 17/146; Church Yth Grp; Computer Clb; Spanish Clb; Yrbk Stf; JV Sftbl; JV Var Vllybl; Hon Roll; Spanish NHS; Comp Sci.

DONAHUE, PATRICIA; East Windsor HS; Broadbrook, CT; (Y); Drama Clb; Chorus; School Musical; School Play; Sec Frsh Cls; Sec Soph Cls; Var Fld Hcky; Trk; Hon Roll; Psychiatric Nurse.

DONALDSON, MICHELLE; St Marys HS; W Haven, CT; (Y); 62/108; Church Yth Grp; Cmnty Wkr; Intnl Clb; JA; Service Clb; Yrbk Stf; Sec Stu Cncl; Hon Roll; Ntl Merit Ltr; U Bridgeport; Soclgy.

DONATO, DAVID; Bassick HS; Bpt, CT; (Y); 30/205; Computer Clb; Radio Clb; Band; Concert Band; Jazz Band; Mrchg Band; Orch; Hon Roll; CT Schltc Achvt Grant 86; Norwalk ST Tech Clg; Arch.

DONATO, DEANNA M; Holy Cross HS; Oxford, CT; (Y); 82/396; Church Yth Grp; Hosp Aide; Spanish Clb; SADD; Capt Cheerleading; Trk; Hon Roll; NHS; Spanish NHS; Schlrshp Eckend Coll Wnng Ldrshp 86; U Of CT; Math.

DONNELLY, CARRIE; West Haven HS; W Haven, CT; (Y); Drama Clb; PAVAS; Thesps; Acpl Chr; Madrigals; School Musical; School Play; Stage Crew; Hon Roll; Jr NHS; Schltc Excllnc Awd 86; U Of CT; Drama.

DONNELLY, JOHN; Loomis Chaffee HS; Kensington, CT; (Y); Pep Clb; Ski Clb; Rep Frsh Cls; Rep Soph Cls; Stu Cncl; Ftbl; Golf; Coachs Awd Ski Tm 85-86; Ftbl Awds 84-86.

DONOHUE, KERRY; Danbury HS; Danbury, CT; (Y); Chorus; Swing Chorus; Variety Show; Nwsp Stf; Yrbk Stf; Rep Stu Cncl; Mgr Var Socr; JV Sftbl; Hon Roll; Jr NHS; Ltr Mgr Sccr 85-86; Psych.

DONOVAN, DENISE; Norwich Free Acad; Norwich, CT; (Y); 33/515; Church Yth Grp; VP Cmnty Wkr; Letterman Clb; Model UN; VP Pres Science Clb; Spanish Clb; Teachers Aide; Varsity Clb; Rep Frsh Cls; Rep Soph Cls.

DONOVAN, KATHRYN; Southington HS; Southington, CT; (Y); Cmnty Wkr; Hosp Aide; Pep Clb; Ski Clb; Spanish Clb; Trs Band; Chorus; Concert Band; Mrchg Band; Rep Stu Cncl; U Hartford Ct Hart Summer Youth Music Prog Partial Schlrshp 86.

DONOVAN, SANDRA; Norwich Free Acad; Norwich, CT; (Y); Office Aide; Science Clb; Spanish Clb; Church Choir; Sec Stu Cncl; Stat Bsktbl; Var JV Tennis; Hon Roll; Manwaring Awd Reprt Hstry Of Norwich 86; Awd Dedctn & Actn Stdnt Advsry Brd 85-86; Fmly Psych.

DOOHAN, JOSEPH; Fairfield College Prep; Stratford, CT; (Y); 45/250; Church Yth Grp; Cmnty Wkr; Political Wkr; Coach Actv; Ntl Merit Ltr; Ultmt Frisbee Clb Pres 86; Racqtbl Clb Pres 86; Judo Champ 86; Miami U; Bus.

DORCHINSKY, STEVEN; Trumbull HS; Trumbull, CT; (Y); Trs Temple Yth Grp; Band; Concert Band; Mrchg Band; Symp Band; Var L Swmmng; High Hon Roll; Hon Roll; Bus.

DORIA, DAMIAN; Holy Cross HS; Waterbury, CT; (Y); 25/380; Teachers Aide; Concert Band; Jazz Band; School Musical; High Hon Roll; NHS; Ntl Merit Ltr; Cmnty Wkr; Library Aide; Office Aide; Svc Awd Msc Lbry Wrk; Svc Awd Msc Tutrng; Fltn Amer Cmnty Bnd 1st Flute; Elec Engr.

DORR, MARSHALL M; Kingswood-Oxford Schol; Simsbury, CT; (Y); Art Clb; Trs Service Clb; Pres Spanish Clb; Lit Mag; Rep Frsh Cls; Rep Trs Soph Cls; JV Ice Hcky; JV Lcrss; JV Socr; Miami U Of OH; Bus.

DORRICO, STACEY; Mt Sheehan HS; Wallingford, CT; (Y); 28/205; Key Clb; Varsity Clb; Variety Show; Yrbk Phtg; Yrbk Stf; Capt Cheerleading; Powder Puff Ftbl; L Sftbl; Hon Roll; Math Awd 84; Bus.

DOUGHERTY, JOE; East Lyme HS; Niantic, CT; (Y); JV Var Bsbl; Var Ftbl; Prfct Atten Awd.

DOUGLAS, KATHY; Westhill HS; Stamford, CT; (Y); Outstndng JR Bus Dept 85; Hnrbl Mentn Ldrshp Ablty 85; Outstndng Achvt Awd Alpha Kappa Alpha 86; Katharine Gibbs; Sec Arts.

DOUGLAS, PAM; The Taft School; Morristown, NJ; (Y); Dance Clb; Office Aide; Spanish Clb; School Musical; School Play; Yrbk Stf; Mgr(s); JV Tennis; JV Capt Vllybl; Hon Roll; Math.

DOUGLAS, STEVEN; Wilby HS; Waterbury, CT; (Y); Rep Soph Cls; Rep Jr Cls; Stu Cncl; JV Ftbl; Var L Swmmng; Var Trk; Hon Roll; Spnsh II Awd 86.

DOUGLAS, TRACIE; Wilby HS; Waterbury, CT; (Y); 14/240; Drama Clb; VP FHA; Chorus; Drm Mjr(t); Nwsp Stf; Yrbk Stf; Rep Jr Cls; Rep Sr Cls; Rep Stu Cncl; Hon Roll; Robert Donaldson Awd 86; Hampton U; Nrsng.

DOUGLASS, LINDA; Windsor Locks HS; Windsor Locks, CT; (Y); 32/155; Church Yth Grp; Girl Scts; Flag Corp; Var L Tennis; Hon Roll; Mth.

DOUKAS, DAVID; Mark T Sheehan HS; Wallingford, CT; (Y); 68/212; Variety Show; Stu Cncl; Var L Bsbl; Var Capt Bsktbl; Var L Ftbl; Hon Roll; Hnr Mntn Al Housatonic Lge Ftbl 85; Southern CT ST U; Inds Psych.

DOVER, TIFFANY V; Choate Rosemary Hall; Atlanta, GA; (Y); Pep Clb; Spanish Clb; Co-Capt Capt Sftbl; Vllybl; Hon Roll; Margaret Brampton Harvey Prz Grl For Excllnc 84-85; Katherine Carlebach Prz Grl For Excllnc 85-86; Intl Bus.

DOWD, JACKEY; Torrington HS; Torrington, CT; (Y); 53/287; Dance Clb; Sec FHA; Chorus; Nwsp Stf; Fld Hcky; Cit Awd; Hon Roll; U CT; Crmnl Law.

DOWD, JENNIFER; Torrington HS; Torrington, CT; (Y); 2/282; Am Leg Aux Girls St; Rep Frsh Cls; Trs Jr Cls; Trs Stu Cncl; Var Capt Crs Cntry; Var Capt Trk; VP NHS; Sal; Latin Clb; Rep Soph Cls; Harvard Bk Prz 85; Svc Clb Cup Awd 85; CIACC Schlr/Athl Awd 86; Boston Coll; Cmmnctn.

DOWDEN, NATE; Granby Memorial HS; Granby, CT; (Y); School Play; Hon Roll; Var L Socr; Var L Trk; Soccer Tm ST Champ 84-85; Outstndng Achvci 83; Best Actor 1 Act Ply Awd 85; Boston Coll; Mrktng.

DOWER, JOHN; East Catholic HS; Vernon Rockville, CT; (Y); 132/300; Boy Scts; Stockbroker.

DOWIE, MEGHAN; The Morgan Schl; Clinton, CT; (Y); 33/160; AFS; SADD; Band; Chorus; Concert Band; Mrchg Band; School Musical; Stage Crew; Variety Show; Rep Stu Cncl; Field Hockey Coaches Awd 85; U NH; Bus Adm.

DOWNEY, JOHN; Ocginchaug Regional HS; Durham, CT; (Y); Acpl Chr; Chorus; Yrbk Stf; Jr Cls; Elec Engr.

DOWNEY, MAUREEN; Sacred Heart Acad; West Haven, CT; (Y); Dance Clb; Spanish Clb; Lit Mag; Rep Frsh Cls; Hon Roll; NEDT Awd.

DOYLE, ELIZABETH; St Marys HS; West Haven, CT; (Y); Ski Clb; Spanish Clb; Speech Tm; Acpl Chr; Chorus; Church Choir; Madrigals; School Musical; School Play; Swing Chorus; Albertus Magnus; Tchr.

DOYLE, MARGARET; Danbury HS; Danbury, CT; (Y); 25/457; AFS; Camp Fr Inc; Math Tm; Band; Mrchg Band; Orch; Lit Mag; Hon Roll; NHS; Ntl Merit Ltr; Hugh Obrien Ldrshp Rep85; Choate Rsmry Hall-Hmnties Schlr 86; Fed Of Music Fstvl 84-86.

DRAGON, JENNIFER; Killingly HS; Dayville, CT; (Y); 67/267; Library Aide; Hon Roll; Outstndng Svc Awd Lib 86; Bus.

DRAPER, MARY LYNN; Branford HS; Branford, CT; (Y); Rep Church Yth Grp; FCA; French Clb; Hosp Aide; Ski Clb; Band; Chorus; Mrchg Band; Lit Mag; Cheerleading.

DRECHSLER, ANA; The Taft Schl; New Canaan, CT; (Y); Pres Spanish Clb; Yrbk Stf; Var Ice Hcky; Capt Lcrss; Capt Socr; U Of VT; Arts.

DRESELLY, JIM; Bolton HS; Bolton, CT; (Y); Am Leg Boys St; Latin Clb; School Musical; Var L Bsbl; Var L Socr; Hon Roll; NHS; TV.

DRESEN, JOE; Wilton HS; Wilton, CT; (Y); 20/347; Boy Scts; SADD; Lit Mag; Var L Ftbl; Hon Roll; NHS; Ntl Merit SF; Lbrl Arts.

DREVER III, PETER G; Tourtellotte Memorial HS; Thompson, CT; (Y); Am Leg Boys St; Debate Tm; French Clb; Model UN; School Musical; Nwsp Rptr; Yrbk Stf; VP Stu Cncl; Im Ice Hcky; Hon Roll.

DREW, DAVID; Avon Old Farms Schl; Avon, CT; (Y); Ski Clb; Nwsp Stf; JV Bsbl; JV Bsktbl; Var Socr; Hon Roll; Hnrbl Ment Hist Awd 85; Hist.

DREZEK, DAWN; Windsor Locks HS; Windsor Locks, CT; (Y); 15/157; Church Yth Grp; Band; Concert Band; Mrchg Band; Stage Crew; Yrbk Stf; Hon Roll; NHS; Mazie S Green Awd 86; Theodore Malec Bus Awd 86; Post Coll-Waterbury CT; CPA.

DRINKARD, LISA J; Waterford HS; Waterford, CT; (Y); 62/248; Church Yth Grp; Cmnty Wkr; Sec Trs Drama Clb; Pres VP SADD; Chorus; School Musical; School Play; Yrbk Ed-Chief; Yrbk Phtg; Hon Roll; Nrsng.

DRISCOLL, ANNE; The Williams HS; Westerly, RI; (Y); GAA; Office Aide; Teachers Aide; Sec Yrbk Stf; Sec Trs Frsh Cls; Var Fld Hcky; Lcrss; Var Sftbl; Hon Roll; Athltc Assn Williams Chptr Pres 85-87; Outstndg Contr Schl Athltcs Awd 85-86; Athltc Ldrshp Awd 85-86; Wrd Proc.

DROPICK, CHRISTOPHER M; Simsbury HS; Simsbury, CT; (Y); 62/410; Church Yth Grp; SADD; Rep Stu Cncl; Var L Lcrss; Var L Wrstlng; Hon Roll; Simsbury Yth Recrtn Council 85-86; Safe Rides; US Naval Acad; Law.

DROUIN, KAREN; Enrico Fermi HS; Enfield, CT; (Y); JA; Variety Show; Yrbk Stf; Lit Mag; Sftbl; Hon Roll; Amer Lgn Schl Awd 86; Hstry Tchr.

DRUGAN, DANIELLE ELIZABETH; Lyme-Old Lyme HS; Old Lyme, CT; (Y); 41/125; Art Clb; Key Clb; Service Clb; SADD; Nwsp Stf; Trs Jr Cls; Bowling; Crs Cntry; High Hon Roll; Hon Roll; Prom Qn; Engl & Art Awds; June Dow Erly Chldhd Educ Schlrshp; Mac Curdy-Salisbury Fndtn Schlrshp; Lesley Coll; Psych.

DRUGAN, MARGARET M; Lyme-Old Lyme HS; Old Lyme, CT; (Y); 15/110; Am Leg Aux Girls St; Band; School Musical; Yrbk Ed-Chief; VP Jr Cls; Bsktbl; Sftbl; Cit Awd; NHS; Summer Exchange With AFS To Brazil 85; Intl Lawyer.

DRYBURGH, DOUGLAS; Staples HS; Westport, CT; (Y); Church Yth Grp; Pres Key Clb; Red Cross Aide; Chorus; JV Crs Cntry; JV Var Socr; Var JV Trk; Spanish NHS; Stu Orntnt Comm; Key Clb Pres; Law.

DSUPIN, SHELLY; Guilford HS; Guilford, CT; (Y); 52/316; Church Yth Grp; Cmnty Wkr; GAA; Latin Clb; Pep Clb; Ski Clb; Spanish Clb; Varsity Clb; Chorus; Rep Frsh Cls; Clark U; Med.

DU BAY, PAULETT; Stamford HS; Stamford, CT; (Y); Church Yth Grp; JA; Ski Clb; Spanish Clb; Church Choir; Var Crs Cntry; JV Fld Hcky; Var Trk; High Hon Roll; Hon Roll; U CT.

DU QUETTE, JOHN; East Hartford HS; E Hartford, CT; (Y); Math Tm; Ski Clb; High Hon Roll; NCTE Awd; Ewnaawlwe Poly Math & Sci Awd 86.

DUBAUSKAS, LEIGH ANN; Holy Cross HS; Waterbury, CT; (Y); 34/346; Hosp Aide; Trs Service Clb; Yrbk Stf; Capt Crs Cntry; Trk; High Hon Roll; NHS; St Schlr; Fairfield U; Bus.

DUBIEL, CATHERINE; Manchester HS; Manchester, CT; (Y); AFS; Drama Clb; French Clb; Hosp Aide; Teachers Aide; Concert Band; Mrchg Band; School Musical; High Hon Roll; NHS; Lwyr.

DUBNICKA, PAUL; West Haven HS; W Haven, CT; (Y); 21/398; Var L Tennis; High Hon Roll; Hon Roll; Jr NHS; NHS; CT Schlstc Achvt Awd 86; Schlstc Excllnc Pre-Calcls, US Hstry, Comp Pgm, Contmpry Issues 85-86; U Of New Haven; Elec Engr.

DUBOS, KRISTINA MARIE; Parish Hill HS; Chaplin, CT; (Y); 6/48; Church Yth Grp; Drama Clb; Library Aide; PAVAS; Chorus; Church Choir; Swing Chorus; NHS; Trinity Bk Awd 86; Smith Coll; Theatr.

DUCHARME, KELLY; Parish Hill HS; N Windham, CT; (Y); Teachers Aide; Yrbk Stf; Var JV Cheerleading; Score Keeper; Hon Roll; Office Aide; Red Cross Aide; Nwsp Stf; U Of CT; Chld Psych.

DUCHESNEAU, NICOLE; Windham HS; Willimantic, CT; (Y); Cmnty Wkr; Teachers Aide; Var L Crs Cntry; Var L Trk; Hon Roll; City Sftbll All Star Tm 83-85; B Bell Cir Excllnc Crss Cntry 86; Cntrl CT Conf Tm Crss Cntry 84; Eastern CT; Law.

DUCHESNEAU, RITA; Manchester HS; Manchester, CT; (Y); Cmnty Wkr; French Clb; Nwsp Stf; Yrbk Stf; Mgr(s); High Hon Roll; Adelphi U; Scl Wrk.

DUCRET, MARC L; Greenwich HS; Old Greenwich, CT; (Y); Boy Scts; Church Yth Grp; Debate Tm; Exploring; Eagle Sct 86; Fairfield U; Mech Engrng.

DUDA, MARY BETH; St Bernard HS; Jewett City, CT; (Y); Cmnty Wkr; Frsh Cls.

DUENKEL, AMY; Morgan HS; Clinton, CT; (Y); Office Aide; Yrbk Stf; Rep Stu Cncl; Var L Cheerleading; Var L Fld Hcky; Powder Puff Ftbl; Hon Roll; Stu Cncl Rep-St Stu Cncl Convtn 86; Hmcmn Comm 83-86; Prom Comm 86; Lib Arts.

DUER, KELLY; Holy Cross HS; Wolcott, CT; (Y); Cmnty Wkr; Teachers Aide; High Hon Roll; Hon Roll; Spanish NHS; JV Var Cheerleading; Mst Imprvd Chrldr Awd 86; Salve Regina Coll; Spec Ed.

DUFFY, STEPHEN; Wilton HS; Wilton, CT; (Y); Drama Clb; Varsity Clb; School Play; Stage Crew; Nwsp Stf; Crs Cntry; Trk; Hon Roll; Ntl Merit Ltr.

DUFOUR, MICHELLE; Windsor HS; Windsor, CT; (Y); Girl Scts; Intnl Clb; Ski Clb; JV Bsktbl; Var JV Sftbl; French Hon Soc; High Hon Roll; GAA; Hon Roll; Top Bus Stu Awd 84; Top Acctg I Stu Awd 85; Top Acctg Ii Stu Awd 86; New Hampshire Coll; Acctg.

DUGAN, SEAN; Southington HS; Southington, CT; (Y); FCA; Letterman Clb; Ski Clb; Varsity Clb; Var Capt Socr; Hon Roll; NE Slct Sccr Team 86; Law.

DUGGAN, MARNIE; East Hartford HS; East Hartford, CT; (Y); DECA; French Clb; Varsity Clb; Chorus; Drill Tm; Hon Roll; NHS; JV Bsktbl; JV Var Mgr(s); Var Pom Pon; Yth In Am Essy Twn Awd 86.

DULIN, DAVID; Stratford HS; Stratford, CT; (Y); 20/250; Camera Clb; Yrbk Phtg; Yrbk Stf; Cmmnctns.

DUMAS, MARCO; Windham Reg Voc Technical Schl; Stafford Spgs, CT; (Y); Computer Clb; VICA; Yrbk Stf; Stu Cncl; Swmmng; High Hon Roll; Hon Roll; NHS; Exlnc In Electrncs Schlrshp 86; Contnung Of Schl Schlrshp 86; Coll Of Boca Raton; Comp Sci.

DUMIN, JO ANN; Southington HS; Southington, CT; (Y); 10/600; Aud/Vis; Stage Crew; Stu Cncl; Var L Bsktbl; Var Sftbl; High Hon Roll; NHS; Prfct Atten Awd; CT JR Olympic Bsktbl 86; Coaches Awds Bskbl & Sftbl 84; Bio Sci.

DUNN, ELIZABETH; Westover Schl; Middlebury, CT; (Y); Art Clb; French Clb; Model UN; Pep Clb; Ski Clb; Spanish Clb; JV Fld Hcky; Im Tennis; JV Vllybl; Law.

DUNN, MARIE; Conard HS; W Hartford, CT; (Y); 110/330; Art Clb; Church Yth Grp; Civic Clb; Cmnty Wkr; Spanish Clb; Church Choir; Yrbk Stf; Rep Frsh Cls; Rep Soph Cls; Stu Cncl.

DUNN, PATRICK; Suffield HS; Suffield, CT; (Y); 40/123; Ski Clb; Yrbk Stf; Ftbl; Var Gym; Var Trk; Hon Roll; Rdng Curriclum Revw Cncl 86; Sat Schlrs Coll Of Engrng U Of Hartford 86; Engrng.

DUNNACK, KERRY CHRISTINE; R H A M SR HS; Andover, CT; (Y); Sec English Clb; FBLA; Nwsp Stf; Yrbk Stf; Pom Pon; High Hon Roll; Hon Roll; Art Clb; Dance Clb; Drill Tm; 1st,2nd Pl Hebron Harvest Fair Art Show 85; Cert Achvt Exc Mural Design 86; Fine Arts.

DUONG, DUC MINH; Hartford Public HS; Hartford, CT; (Y); Trs FNA; Socr; Cit Awd; High Hon Roll; NHS; Prfct Atten Awd; St Schlr; Intrcl Schlrshp, Jcb L & Lws Fox Fndtn Schlrp 86; Pres Acdmc Ftns Awds Pgm 86; Clarkson U; Elec Engr.

DUPONT, ANDREA; Southington HS; Southington, CT; (S); Rptr DECA; Ski Clb; High Hon Roll; Hon Roll; 3rd Pl Rest Mrktng Human Rel 86; ST Conf In Waterbury Ct Local Reprtr For Dist Educ Clbs Of Am; Hotel Motel Mgmt.

DUPONT, SUSANNE; Thomaston HS; Thomaston, CT; (Y); 10/67; Spanish Clb; School Play; Stage Crew; Mgr(s); High Hon Roll; Hon Roll; Fshn Mrch.

DUPONT, WES; Kellingly HS; Danielson, CT; (Y); 32/375; Hst Frsh Cls; VP Soph Cls; Hst Sr Cls; Stu Cncl; Im Golf; Var Socr; Var Capt Trk; Im Wt Lftg; High Hon Roll; NHS.

DUPUIS, KIM; Southington HS; Southington, CT; (Y); 21/600; Hosp Aide; Band; Concert Band; Drm Mjr(t); Mrchg Band; Ed Yrbk Phtg; High Hon Roll; Hon Roll; NHS; Chld Psych.

DURKIN, RACHEL; Conard HS; W Hartford, CT; (Y); Church Yth Grp; Cmnty Wkr; Drama Clb; Thesps; Acpl Chr; VP Chorus; Church Choir; School Musical; School Play; Swing Chorus; Frank H Scheekl Schlrshp Fund 86; Berkshire Chrstian Coll; Mnstry.

DURSO, JENNIFER; Thomaston HS; Thomaston, CT; (Y); Spanish Clb; Sec Jr Cls; Trk; High Hon Roll; Hon Roll; NHS.

DUSCHANG, JOHN; Fairfield College Prepatory Schl; Monroe, CT; (Y); Key Clb; Lit Mag; JV Lcrss; Hon Roll; NHS; Spanish NHS.

DWYER, KRISTIN; Cheshire HS; Cheshire, CT; (Y); Church Yth Grp; Hosp Aide; Pep Clb; Mrchg Band; Stage Crew; Rep Sr Cls; Hon Roll.

DZIERZBINSKI, MARGARET; Mary Immaculate Acad; New Britain, CT; (S); 7/48; Dance Clb; Drama Clb; Pres JA; Chorus; School Play; Pres Soph Cls; Trs Jr Cls; VP Sr Cls; Var Capt Cheerleading; Hon Roll; Myr/Day Pgm 85; Psychlgy.

EARLY, RENEE J; Shelton HS; San Diego, CA; (Y); 8/315; Am Leg Aux Girls St; Drama Clb; Exploring; Pres French Clb; Trs Soph Cls; Rep Sr Cls; Stu Cncl; Sec French Hon Soc; Hon Roll; NHS; U CA; Pol Sci.

EASTON, LISA; Coginchaug Regional HS; Durham, CT; (Y); #2 In Class; Art Clb; Drama Clb; Math Tm; Teachers Aide; Concert Band; Mrchg Band; Pep Band; Var L Sftbl; NHS; Prfct Atten Awd; Attnded U Conn Hnrs Smnr 86; Qst Awd-Qst Pgm Tutrng Elem Chldrn 85-86; Chldrns Elem Educ.

EBBSON, JENNIFER; Foran HS; Milford, CT; (Y); Keywanettes; Ski Clb; Spanish Clb; Teachers Aide; Yrbk Stf; Hon Roll; Accntng.

ECHAVARRIA, NORA; Brien Mc Mahon HS; S Norwalk, CT; (Y); Spanish Clb; High Hon Roll; Frgn Lang.

ECKERSLEY, PEIR; Cheshire HS; Cheshire, CT; (Y); VP SADD; Yrbk Phtg; Rep Jr Cls; Rep Sr Cls; Sec Stu Cncl; Var L Diving; Var L Trk; French Hon Soc; Hon Roll; Intl Rel.

ECKERT, JOHN; Jonathan Law HS; Milford, CT; (Y); Am Leg Boys St; Computer Clb; Yrbk Stf; Var Bsktbl; Var Crs Cntry; Var L Trk; High Hon Roll; Hon Roll; NHS; Ntl Merit Ltr; Bus Law.

EDGERTON, SUSAN; Manchester HS; Manchester, CT; (Y); Church Yth Grp; Drama Clb; French Clb; Band; Concert Band; Mrchg Band; Pep Band; Stu Cncl; Hon Roll; Illng Jr HS Sci Fr Hnrbl Mntn 83-84; Intr Archtctr.

EDGEWORTH, DOROTHY; Joseph A Foran HS; Milford, CT; (Y); DECA; Keywanettes; Ski Clb; Varsity Clb; Ed Yrbk Stf; Sec Jr Cls; Var L Cheerleading; Var L Gym; Var Tennis; Fshn Mrchndsng.

EDMONDS, SHARON; Coventry HS; Coventry, CT; (Y); Church Yth Grp; Girl Scts; Teachers Aide; Band; Hon Roll; NHS; Psychlgy.

EDMONDSON, STEPHANIE; Torrington HS; Torrington, CT; (Y); 22/256; AFS; Pep Clb; Ski Clb; Spanish Clb; JV Fld Hcky; JV Sftbl; JV Tennis; High Hon Roll; Psych.

EDWARDS, JENINE; James Hillhouse HS; New Haven, CT; (Y); 21/270; Debate Tm; French Clb; Yrbk Rptr; Rep Soph Cls; Var Sftbl; JV Vllybl; NHS; COLT Poetry Cntst Frnch 2nd Pl 85 & 3rd Pl 86; CT Pep Upwrd Bnd; Vassar Coll; Frnch.

EHRHARDT, LAURENCE W; New Canaan HS; New Canaan, CT; (Y); Band; Jazz Band; Orch; School Play; Nwsp Stf; Concert Band; Mrchg Band; School Musical; High Hon Roll; Ntl Merit SF.

EICKMEYER, DAVID; Saint Josephs HS; Shelton, CT; (Y); Pres Church Yth Grp; Drama Clb; Ski Clb; Bowling; Mltry Sci.

EIGEL, CHRISTINA; Ridgefield HS; Ridgefield, CT; (Y); Church Yth Grp; Debate Tm; Intnl Clb; Service Clb; Mgr(s); JV Trk; High Hon Roll; Value 100 Hrs Srvc 86; German Bk Awd 86; Hist Achvt 85; Aerntcl Engr.

EIGEN, MIKE; Wethersfield HS; Wethersfield, CT; (Y); 34/300; Cmnty Wkr; Nwsp Rptr; Var Capt Bsktbl; High Hon Roll; Hon Roll; NHS; Intl Bus.

EITEL, PATTY; Manchester HS; Manchester, CT; (Y); 21/572; AFS; Dance Clb; Drama Clb; French Clb; German Clb; Hosp Aide; Stage Crew; High Hon Roll; Hon Roll; NHS; Boston Coll; Law.

EKEDAHL, JIM; Stamford HS; Stamford, CT; (Y); Church Yth Grp; Cmnty Wkr; JA; Science Clb; Lit Mag; Var Gym; Capt Var Ice Hcky; Trk; Hon Roll; NHS; Engr.

ELBAUM, PATTY; Kingswood-Oxford HS; W Hartford, CT; (Y); Art Clb; Cmnty Wkr; Red Cross Aide; Service Clb; Pres Spanish Clb; Temple Yth Grp; Nwsp Rptr; Yrbk Rptr; Var Socr; Capt Var Trk; Track Awd 86; Merit Awd Vol Soc Wrk 85-86; Track Awds 84-86.

ELDRIDGE, TRICIA; Killingly HS; Sterling, CT; (Y); 20/278; Church Yth Grp; Teachers Aide; Band; Concert Band; Mrchg Band; Symp Band; High Hon Roll; NHS; Hnr Schlrshp From ENC 86; E Nzrn Coll; Bus Adm.

ELENGO, CHRISTINA; Holy Cross HS; Cheshire, CT; (Y); 71/380; Church Yth Grp; Trs French Clb; Concert Band; Jazz Band; Mrchg Band; Pep Band; High Hon Roll; Hon Roll; NHS; Socl Studs Hnr Soc 85-86.

ELLIOTT, TISHA; Waterford HS; Waterford, CT; (Y); Bus.

ELLIS, DEBBIE; Danbury HS; Danbury, CT; (Y); Hon Roll; Camp Fr Inc; Dance Clb; Law.

ELLSWORTH, JEFFREY; Lyme-Old Lyme HS; Hadlyme, CT; (Y); 29/110; Letterman Clb; Ski Clb; Yrbk Stf; Var Bsktbl; Im Bowling; Var Crs Cntry; JV Tennis; Im Vllybl; Hon Roll; Smmr Intrnshp Prog 86.

ELSINGER, ELISABETH; Southington HS; Southington, CT; (Y); 22/600; German Clb; Hosp Aide; Key Clb; Latin Clb; Yrbk Phtg; High Hon Roll; Jr NHS; Pres NHS; Dscvr III Gftd & Tlntd 84-86; Med.

EMBARDO, LISA; Holy Cross HS; Waterbury, CT; (Y); 4/347; Am Leg Aux Girls St; Cmnty Wkr; Pres Service Clb; High Hon Roll; NHS; Ntl Merit Ltr; Pres Schlr; St Schlr; U Of CT.

EMRO, SHARON; Wilton HS; Wilton, CT; (Y); 94/365; Pres Church Yth Grp; Hosp Aide; SADD; Madrigals; Symp Band; Hon Roll; Pre Med.

ENG, DAVID L; Westhill HS; Stamford, CT; (Y); 1/409; VP JA; Capt Quiz Bowl; Yrbk Ed-Chief; Rep Frsh Cls; Rep Soph Cls; Rep Jr Cls; Rep Sr Cls; High Hon Roll; NHS; Ntl Merit SF; Harvard Bk Awd 85; Iona Lang Cntst 2nd Hnrs Spnsh 84-85.

ENGEL, JOE; Brien Mc Mahon HS; Norwalk, CT; (Y); Church Yth Grp; Red Cross Aide; Pringting.

ENGELS, SHANNON; The Taft Schl; Greenwich, CT; (Y); Chorus; Nwsp Stf; Stu Cncl; Var Fld Hcky; Var Ice Hcky; Var Capt Lcrss; Hon Roll; U Of VA.

EPPINGER, ERIC; Rham HS; Marlborough, CT; (Y); 40/190; Am Leg Boys St; Ski Clb; Yrbk Phtg; JV Bsktbl; Var Socr; Capt Tennis; Capt Vllybl; Hon Roll; WA D C Internshp 85; Purdue U; Econ.

EPPRIGHT, ELIZABETH A; Ledyard HS; Gales Ferry, CT; (Y); 6/215; JV Bsktbl; Powder Puff Ftbl; Hon Roll; Med.

EPSTEIN, DANA; Miss Porters Schl; Las Vegas, NV; (Y); Art Clb; Cmnty Wkr; Computer Clb; Debate Tm; GAA; Spanish Clb; School Play; Nwsp Ed-Chief; Nwsp Rptr; Nwsp Stf; Hurrican Island Outwrd Bnd Awd Ovrly Commttd 85; SR Clss Ush 86; Boston Interestedin U; Commnctn.

EPSTEIN, HOLLY; Manchester HS; Manchester, CT; (Y); Drama Clb; French Clb; Hosp Aide; Band; Yrbk Stf; Stu Cncl; Cheerleading; Socr; Hon Roll; NHS; Pre-Law.

EPSTEIN, STEVEN; Conard HS; West Hartford, CT; (Y); 15/300; Am Leg Boys St; Drama Clb; Acpl Chr; Chorus; School Musical; School Play; Mgr Bsbl; High Hon Roll; NHS; Pres Schlr; U Of Rochester; Psych.

EQUALE, PAUL; Wilton HS; Wilton, CT; (Y); 4/300; Varsity Clb; Rep Soph Cls; Rep Jr Cls; Rep Sr Cls; Var Ice Hcky; Tennis; High Hon Roll; NHS; Socr; CT Cup Hocky Tm 86; Dartmouth Bk Awd 86.

ERDA, ELIZABETH; Guilford HS; Guilford, CT; (Y); 14/300; Pres Church Yth Grp; Rep Cmnty Wkr; Chorus; Pres Stu Cncl; Capt L Fld Hcky; Var L Trk; French Hon Soc; High Hon Roll; Hon Roll; NHS; Frshmn Soc Stds Awd 83-84; US Hstry Awd 84-85; CT Assoc Wmns Dns Cnslrs Awd 85-86.

ERDMAN, JOHN; Lewis S Mills HS; Harwinton, CT; (Y); Debate Tm; DECA; Latin Clb; Model UN; VP Political Wkr; School Musical; School Play; Hon Roll; Ntl Merit Ltr; Crtv Wrtng Awd 84; Deb Tm Champs 85-86; Hist.

ERICKSON, AMY; Berlin HS; Kensington, CT; (Y); 42/164; Church Yth Grp; Drama Clb; FHA; SADD; Color Guard; School Musical; School Play; Powder Puff Ftbl; Socr; Hon Roll; Bryant Coll; Advrtsng.

ERICKSON, DOUGLAS; Windham HS; Columbia, CT; (Y); Am Leg Boys St; Church Yth Grp; Band; Concert Band; Jazz Band; Var L Crs Cntry; Var L Trk; High Hon Roll; Hon Roll; U Of CT; Engrng.

ERICKSON, JOHN; Plainfield HS; Plainfield, CT; (Y); Bsbl; Bsktbl; Ftbl; Cit Awd; Schlr Athlete Awd 84.

ERICKSON, TROY; Wethersfield HS; Wethersfield, CT; (Y); 30/315; Am Leg Boys St; Church Yth Grp; Civic Clb; Cmnty Wkr; Intnl Clb; Ski Clb; Spanish Clb; SADD; Variety Show; Nwsp Stf; Duke Univ; Business Pre Law.

ESCUDERO, MARIA DEL PILAR; Mary Immaculate Acad; New Britain, CT; (Y); 3/43; Church Yth Grp; Trs French Clb; Hosp Aide; Rep Stu Cncl; High Hon Roll; Hon Roll; Prfct Atten Awd; Cert Accmplshmnt Prjct Bus 83-84; Cert Schlrshp Frnch Ii 84-85; Awd Mrt Engl Ii, Rlgn Ii Typng I 84-85; Med.

ESHOO, MARLENE MARIE; Berlin HS; Kensington, CT; (Y); 30/183; Church Yth Grp; Hosp Aide; Band; Concert Band; Jazz Band; Mrchg Band; Pep Band; School Musical; JV Cheerleading; Var Socr; Laura Ann Downer Art Awd 86; Music Cup Medal 86; Spcl Berlin Schrlshp 86; U RI; Graphic Desgn.

ESPINOZA, SHEILA JEANETTE; New Britain HS; New Britain, CT; (Y); Camera Clb; FBLA; JA; Key Clb; Office Aide; Ski Clb; Spanish Clb; Rep Sr Cls; Rep Stu Cncl; Hon Roll; Mayor For Day 85-86; Prgm Initiating Careers 86; U CT; Bus Adm.

ESPOSITO, DAVID; Joseph A Foran HS; Milford, CT; (Y); 1/240; Am Leg Boys St; Pres JCL; Pres Soph Cls; Pres Jr Cls; Pres Sr Cls; Var Bsbl; Var Ftbl; Chrmn Capt Wrstlng; St Schlr; Val; Harvard Bk Awd 85; UICO Ntl Schlr, CIAC Schlr Athl 86; Yale U; Med.

ESPOSITO, JILL; Jonathan Law HS; Milford, CT; (Y); Pres Church Yth Grp; Drama Clb; Girl Scts; Keywanettes; PAVAS; Ski Clb; Chorus; Church Choir; Hon Roll; Educ Cntr For Arts Schlrshp 85-87; Cinderella Girl Schlrshp Pgnt 84; Vcl Cmptn 1st Pl Wnnr 84-85; Stud Art.

ESPOSITO, SALLY ANN; Sacred Heart Acad; New Haven, CT; (Y); Art Clb; Camera Clb; Pep Clb; Im Vllybl; High Hon Roll; 3 Yr Hnr Awd 86; Endwmnt Cmmt Schlrshp 86; Schlrshp Scrd Hrt Acad 85; Scl Wrk.

ESTES, MELANIE; R H A M HS; Marlborough, CT; (Y); 8/173; AFS; Math Tm; Acpl Chr; School Musical; Nwsp Stf; Crs Cntry; Twrlr; NHS; Ntl Merit Ltr; Green Blt Karate 84-86; U CT; Creat Wrtng.

ESTEVES, ANTONIO; Naugatuck HS; Naugatuck, CT; (Y); 34/320; Science Clb; Spanish Clb; NHS; Teen Mnth; Waterbury ST Tech; Elec Engr.

ETIENNE JR, GABRIEL; King Schl; Stamford, CT; (Y); Chess Clb; Drama Clb; JA; Thesps; School Musical; School Play; Var Bsbl; Var L Bsktbl; Var L Socr; Tennis; Englsh.

EVANS, ERIC; St Bernard HS; Norwich, CT; (Y); Exploring; Rep Stu Cncl; JV Ftbl; Var Wrstlng; Law.

EVELAND, JEFFREY; Greenwich HS; Riverside, CT; (Y); Am Leg Boys St; Var Bsktbl; Var Capt Socr; Var Trk; High Hon Roll; NHS; Ntl Merit Ltr; Church Yth Grp; Math Tm; Band; Yng Am Awd 86; Coach Bsbl 83-86; Comm Chrch Prod Sweeney Todd 83-86; U VA; Engr.

EVERETT, JEFF; The Taft Schl; New Orleans, LA; (Y); Var Ftbl; Var Ice Hcky; Var Trk; High Hon Roll; Hon Roll.

EVERITT, KATIE; Low Heywood Thomas HS; Wilton, CT; (Y); 3/38; Art Clb; Yrbk Ed-Chief; Yrbk Stf; Rep Frsh Cls; Var Gym; Var Tennis; High Hon Roll; NHS.

EWCHUK, STACEY; North Haven HS; N Haven, CT; (Y); 63/280; Church Yth Grp; Church Choir; Variety Show; Mgr(s); Score Keeper; Sftbl; Vllybl; Hon Roll; Lab Tech.

EZA, LESLIE; New Britain HS; New Britain, CT; (Y); JV Sftbl; Var L Vllybl; Cert Hnr Excllnc Frnch 85; Central CT ST U; Accntng.

FADOR, TARA; Torrington HS; Torrington, CT; (Y); Church Yth Grp; FHA; Post Coll; Acctg.

FAFARD, KYLE H; Tourtellotte Memorial HS; Thompson, CT; (Y); 10/93; Church Yth Grp; Yrbk Rptr; Yrbk Stf; Hon Roll; Ntl Merit SF; Harvard Radcliffe Clb Bk Awd 85; Ntl Merit Fnlst; CT U; Comp Engr.

FAGAN, CAROLYN; Orville H Platt HS; Meriden, CT; (Y); Drama Clb; Sec Key Clb; Yrbk Phtg; Off Jr Cls; US Navy; Radiolgy.

FAGAN, MICHAEL; Xavier HS; Middletown, CT; (Y); 15/200; Boy Scts; Var Crs Cntry; Var Trk; Liberty Bk Schlrshp 86; Trinity Coll.

FAHEY, CAROLYN; Manchester HS; Manchester, CT; (Y); 10/581; Sec AFS; Sec French Clb; Band; Mrchg Band; Jr Cls; Sr Cls; Stu Cncl; Capt Var Crs Cntry; L Trk; High Hon Roll.

FAHEY, ERIN; Compenaug HS; Southbury, CT; (Y); 45/160; Church Yth Grp; School Play; Yrbk Stf; JV Tennis; Hon Roll.

FAIRFAX, BETH; The Masters Schl; Winsted, CT; (S); 1/19; Model UN; Chorus; School Play; Yrbk Stf; Var Bsktbl; Var Sftbl; High Hon Roll; FCA; School Musical; Stage Crew; Greater Hartford Area Yth Chorale 84-85; Vocal Schlrshp 85-86; Varsity Sftbl MVP 84-85; Lawyer.

FALES, EMERSON; Pomfret Schl; Miami, FL; (Y); Letterman Clb; Varsity Clb; Nwsp Rptr; JV Ice Hcky; JV Socr; Capt L Tennis; Colgate U.

FALLON, FRANCES; Manchester HS; Manchester, CT; (Y); Church Yth Grp; Hon Roll; Morse Schl Of Bus; Fshn Merch.

FALSEY, ELLEN; Sacred Heart Acad; New Haven, CT; (Y); Cmnty Wkr; French Clb; Political Wkr; Variety Show; Crs Cntry; NEDT Awd; Psych.

FALVO, MELISSA; Wethersfield HS; Wethersfield, CT; (Y); 15/298; Cmnty Wkr; Dance Clb; Red Cross Aide; Ski Clb; Yrbk Stf; Stu Cncl; JV Bsktbl; Var Sftbl; Var Vllybl; High Hon Roll; Biochemistry.

FALZARANO, CAREN; Putnam HS; Putnam, CT; (Y); Am Leg Aux Girls St; Band; Var JV Cheerleading; Var Sftbl; Hon Roll.

FANELLI, DENISE; Wethersfield HS; Wethersfield, CT; (Y); 33/299; Rep Frsh Cls; Rep Soph Cls; Hon Roll; Early Chld Cr.

FARAH, TERESA; Masuk HS; Danbury, CT; (Y); Church Yth Grp; Latin Clb; Political Wkr; Ski Clb; Chorus; Nwsp Stf; Yrbk Stf; Rep Frsh Cls; Bsktbl; High Hon Roll; Ltn 85-86; Cls-Up Fndtn Pgm 85-86; Outstndg Chorus Stu 83-84; U Of Houston; Intl Rltns.

FARFAN, JORGE; Ft Maloney HS; Meriden, CT; (Y); Key Clb; Yrbk Stf; Lit Mag; Socr; Hon Roll; Sketchbook Contest 1st & 2nd Pl 85-86; Comm Art.

FARKAS, LINDA; Trumbull HS; Trumbull, CT; (Y); Church Yth Grp; Debate Tm; Trs Pres Exploring; Library Aide; Band; Concert Band; Jazz Band; JV Trk; Hon Roll; CT Bus Week 86; PTSA Recording Sec; Accntng.

FARMER, COLIN; Danbury HS; Danbury, CT; (Y); 90/630; Boy Scts; Church Yth Grp; Socr; Tennis; Arch.

FARNEN, JIM; St Josephs HS; Shelton, CT; (Y); Debate Tm; Varsity Clb; Var Bsbl; Capt Ftbl; Capt Wt Lftg; Hon Roll; Sportsmnshp Awd-Ftbl 85; U CT; Pre-Law.

FARRELL, JO ANN; Plainfield HS; Moosup, CT; (Y); 1/154; Am Leg Aux Girls St; GAA; Varsity Clb; Stu Cncl; Var Bsktbl; L Var Sftbl; High Hon Roll; Lion Awd; NHS; Voice Dem Awd; Outstndng Schlr/Athltc 83-84; Renssealer Mdl 85-86; Hghst Bttng Avg Vrsty Sftbl 85-86; Pre Med.

FARRELL, KAREN; Rham HS; Hebron, CT; (Y); 21/218; AFS; Church Yth Grp; French Clb; Girl Scts; Yrbk Stf; Stat Bsbl; Var L Cheerleading; JV Score Keeper; Hon Roll; NHS; Accounting.

FASSIO, TERRI; Torrington HS; Torrington, CT; (Y); 92/300; Pep Clb; Chorus; Stage Crew; Nwsp Rptr; Yrbk Bus Mgr; Yrbk Rptr; High Hon Roll; Hon Roll; South End Comm Schlrshp 86; Castleton ST Coll; Comm.

FAUSEY, JOY; Windham HS; Willimantic, CT; (Y); 2/283; Am Leg Aux Girls St; Cmnty Wkr; Ski Clb; SADD; Capt Cheerleading; Capt Tennis; Pres Mu Alp Tht; NHS; Sal; Boston Coll; Chem.

FAUXBEL, SHANNON; Plainfield HS; Plainfield, CT; (Y); Cmnty Wkr; Drama Clb; SADD; Band; Concert Band; High Hon Roll; Hon Roll; Voice Dem Awd; Outstndng Achvmnt In French III 86; Excllnce In Algebra II 85; Community Coll; Psych.

FAZIO, RAFFAELE; St Bernard HS; Groton, CT; (Y); 88/265; Boy Scts; Hon Roll; Spec Hnr Awd In Italian 84-85; Law.

FAZZARI, KIRSTEN; Wilton HS; Wilton, CT; (Y); 49/450; Computer Clb; Pres Debate Tm; German Clb; Girl Scts; Chorus; Var Trk; High Hon Roll; Hon Roll; NHS; Ntl Merit Ltr; Silver Awd 83; Fife Drum Corps 84; FBS 2nd Pl ST Bowl 84; Comp Sci.

FAZZINO, CATHLEEN; Holy Cross HS; Waterbury, CT; (Y); 89/388; Church Yth Grp; Dance Clb; Capt Var Gym; Hon Roll; Trs NHS; Girls Clb Am Capt Gym Tm 85; Camp Laurel Vol Pgm 84; Ed.

FECTEAU, JULIE; St Bernard HS; Norwich, CT; (Y); Hosp Aide; JV Crs Cntry; Stat Ftbl; JV Trk; Explrs Prgm; Peer Mnstry Prgm; YMCA Cnclr Outdr Ctr; Psych.

FEDAK, MARY; Shelton HS; Shelton, CT; (Y); 55/323; JCL; Latin Clb; Var L Bsktbl; Var L Socr; Var L Sftbl; Hon Roll; Natl Phys Ed Awd Wnnr 83; Lat Natl Hnr Soc 85-86; Guildo Pastore Schlr/Ath Scholar 86; URI; Comp Sci.

FEDELI, KIMBERLY; St Bernard HS; Norwich, CT; (Y); 38/264; Teachers Aide; Yrbk Stf; Stu Cncl; Bsbl; JV Tennis; Hon Roll; Invlvd Peer Mnstry For SR Yr; Spndng 1 Mnth Frnce Prt Of Ncl Intl Cltrl Exchnge; VA Poly Tech; Engrng.

FEDIRKO, JOHN; West Haven HS; West Haven, CT; (Y); 27/396; Am Leg Boys St; Math Tm; Nwsp Sprt Ed; Pres Soph Cls; Var Capt Tennis; Hon Roll; Jr NHS; NHS; Hosp Aide; Q&S; Schlr Athlt 85; U Of CT; Mech Engrg.

FEDOR, MARK; Bristol Central HS; Bristol, CT; (Y); Boys Clb Am; Cmnty Wkr; Cit Awd; Hon Roll; NHS; Sec Jr Cls; Var Capt Bsktbl; Var Capt Ftbl.

FEENEY, KATHLEEN; East Catholic HS; Coventry, CT; (Y); 106/298; Stu Cncl; JV Bsktbl; Var L Golf; JV Sftbl; High Hon Roll; Hon Roll; Mercy Schlrshp Awd 86; St Joseph CT; Spcl Ed.

FEGLER, DEBORAH; Maloney HS; Meriden, CT; (Y); Church Yth Grp; Key Clb; Spanish Clb; Chorus; Nwsp Rptr; Yrbk Stf; Lit Mag; Hon Roll; Sec NHS.

FEINBERG, PAUL; Hopkins Grammar Day Prspct Hll Schl; New Haven, CT; (S); SADD; Teachers Aide; Yrbk Stf; Var JV Lcrss; Var JV Socr; JV Wrstlng; Bowdorn Coll; Sci.

FEINSTEIN, BRETT; Kingswood Oxford Schl; W Hartford, CT; (Y); Debate Tm; Drama Clb; Hosp Aide; Intnl Clb; Model UN; Science Clb; Thesps; School Musical; School Play; Nwsp Rptr; Foreign Svc.

FEIST, SAM; Ridgefield HS; Ridgefield, CT; (Y); 57/387; Pres Aud/Vis; Pres Scholastic Bowl; Service Clb; Pres Temple Yth Grp; Nwsp Rptr; Nwsp Stf; Rep Stu Cncl; Hon Roll; NHS; Lcl Repblcn Wshngtn Intrnshp 86; Pltcl Sci.

FELDMAN, RACHEL; Hamden HS; Hamden, CT; (Y); VP Boy Scts; Drama Clb; Temple Yth Grp; Stage Crew; JV Crs Cntry; Hon Roll; Safe Rides VP & Treas 85-86; Rotary Clb Exchng Stu 86; Bio.

FELSEN, BRIAN H; Andrew Warde HS; Fairfield, CT; (Y); 1/350; Chess Clb; French Clb; Math Clb; Math Tm; Scholastic Bowl; Pres Science Clb; Band; Trs Soph Cls; French Hon Soc; High Hon Roll; Colby Coll Bk Prz-Achvt & Invlvmnt 85; Amer Chem Soc Chem Awd 84; Symphny Orch Cmptn 84; U Of PA; Sci.

FENN, MEG; Holy Cross HS; Watertown, CT; (Y); Concert Band; Jazz Band; Var L Bsktbl; Var L Sftbl; Var L Trk; Var L Vllybl; High Hon Roll; Hon Roll; All City Bsktbl Hon Men 86; All Naugatuck Vly Lg Bsktbl Hon Men 86; CT JR Olympc Regnl Tm Bsktbl 86; Nrsg.

FERBES, DIANA; Bulkeley HS; Hartford, CT; (Y); Art Clb; FHA; Teachers Aide; VICA; Nwsp Bus Mgr; Lit Mag; Gym; Socr; Sftbl; Vllybl; Kndgtn Tchr.

FERGUSON, BRIAN; St Mary HS; Greenwich, CT; (Y); 17/67; Spanish Clb; Pres Stu Cncl; Capt Ftbl; Var Lcrss; NHS; Alumni Assoc Schlrshp 86; S CT ST U.

FERGUSON, LAURA; Coventry HS; Coventry, CT; (Y); 10/75; Band; Rep Frsh Cls; Rep Soph Cls; VP Jr Cls; Rep Sr Cls; NHS; Pres Schlr; Perry S Ury WTIC FM Schlrhsp 86; Pres Acd Ftns Awd 86; E Connecticut ST U; Comp Sci.

FERGUSON, MICHELE; Stamford HS; Stamford, CT; (Y); Trs Girl Scts; Letterman Clb; Red Cross Aide; Ski Clb; Varsity Clb; Concert Band; Mrchg Band; Gym; Hon Roll; NHS; Slvr Awd Girl Sctng 10 Yr In Sctng 86; Phlsphy.

FERGUSON, MIKE; Stamford HS; Stamford, CT; (Y); Science Clb; Meteorlgy.

FERGUSON, SCOTT; Holy Cross HS; Southbury, CT; (Y); PAVAS; Variety Show; Hon Roll; Physcn.

FERGUSON, SUSAN; Nonnewaug HS; Woodbury, CT; (Y); Pep Clb; School Play; Variety Show; Sec Frsh Cls; Sec Soph Cls; Off Jr Cls; Pres Sr Cls; JV Var Cheerleading; JV Fld Hcky; Mgr(s); Bst Tp 10 Bus Stu Hnr 84; Hm Ec Awd 85; Outstndng Keybrdng 84; Psych.

FERLAND, JENNIFER; Loomis Chaffee Schl; Windsor, CT; (Y); Drama Clb; SADD; Teachers Aide; Concert Band; School Musical; School Play; Stage Crew; Rep Stu Cncl; Var L Trk; Thesps; Frdrck G Torrey Schlrshp; Law.

FERLUZZO, AMY; Ridgefield HS; Ridgefield, CT; (S); 7/388; Spanish Clb; Orch; Lit Mag; JV Fld Hcky; Var Vllybl; High Hon Roll; Bio.

FERNANDEZ, EVA; Academy Of Our Lady Of Mercy; Fairfield, CT; (Y); 11/111; Church Yth Grp; Debate Tm; French Clb; JA; Latin Clb; Model UN; Spanish Clb; Acpl Chr; Chorus; Madrigals; D E La Macchia Mem Music Awd 86; Magna Cum Laude Ntl Latn Exm 84, 86; Frgn Lagn.

FERNANDEZ, JOSEPH; Shelton HS; Shelton, CT; (Y); Chess Clb.

FERRANTE JR, JOHN J; Notre Dame HS; Milford, CT; (Y); 16/207; Church Yth Grp; Variety Show; Nwsp Rptr; Lit Mag; High Hon Roll; NHS; Peer Cnslrs Pgm 86; Music 1st Pl Awd 85; Adv.

FERRARO, ROSANNA; St Mary HS; New Haven, CT; (Y); Chorus; Church Choir; School Musical; Lit Mag; Soph Cls; Vllybl; Hon Roll; Stone Schl Acad Schlrshp 86; Forgn Lang Poetry Cont 3r Pl Italian I & II 85 & 86; Stone Schl; Word Procsr.

FERREIRA, MARTA; Conard HS; W Htfd, CT; (Y); 66/345; German Clb; Spanish NHS; Art.

FERRERA, EVANA; Bulkeley HS; Hartford, CT; (Y); Band; High Hon Roll; Hon Roll; NHS; Bus.

FERRI, JEFFREY; Amity SR HS; W Haven, CT; (Y); 89/414; Ski Clb; Band; Concert Band; Jazz Band; Mrchg Band; Orch; Symp Band; Variety Show; Var Capt Socr; Hon Roll; New Haven U; Music.

FERRILLO, HEATHER ANN; Holy Cross HS; Oxford, CT; (Y); 105/398; Cmnty Wkr; Hosp Aide; Spanish Clb; Teachers Aide; Var L Trk; High Hon Roll; Hon Roll; Law Enfrcmnt.

FESKO, NICK; Greenwich HS; Greenwich, CT; (Y); Key Clb; Chorus; Variety Show; JV Capt Bsbl; L Bsktbl; JV Var Ftbl; High Hon Roll; Hon Roll; Bus Adm.

FESTA, LYNN M; Hamden HS; Hamden, CT; (Y); 4/319; Church Yth Grp; Orch; School Musical; School Play; Stage Crew; Nwsp Ed-Chief; Nwsp Rptr; Rep Stu Cncl; High Hon Roll; Ntl Merit SF; Dept Hnrs Eng, Scl Sci, Theatre, Math, & French 83-85; English.

FIACCO, DOUG; Ridgefield HS; Ridgefield, CT; (Y); 151/387; Radio Clb; Ski Clb; Sec Stage Crew; Nwsp Rptr; Nwsp Stf; Lit Mag; Jrnlsm.

FIEDOROWICZ, TODD; Torrington HS; Torrington, CT; (Y); 50/277; Var Golf; High Hon Roll; Hon Roll; Bus Admin.

FIERTEK, CHRIS; Newington HS; Newington, CT; (Y); 80/364; Boys Clb Am; Math Clb; Cntrl CT ST U; Bus Mgmt.

FIFIELD, STEPHANIE; Nonnewaug HS; Woodbury, CT; (Y); AFS; Church Yth Grp; Trs FBLA; Office Aide; Ski Clb; Chorus; Variety Show; JV Fld Hcky; Var Gym; Hon Roll; Cert Of Merit-FBLA 86; Cert Of Aprciatn-FBLA 86; Bus Educ Awd-FBLA 86; Accntnt.

FILINGERI, DEBORAH-LEE; St Joseph HS; Huntington, CT; (Y); 76/221; Camera Clb; VP Church Yth Grp; Drama Clb; Hosp Aide; Spanish Clb; Nwsp Stf; Yrbk Stf; Var L Swmmng; Var L Trk; High Hon Roll; Villanova U; Law.

FILIPPONE, MICHAEL; Holy Cross HS; Waterbury, CT; (Y); 10/346; High Hon Roll; NHS; Ntl Merit Ltr; Pres Schlr; Stp & Shp Co Schrlshp 86; CT ST Schlr 86; Unico Clb Schlrshp 86; U Of CT; Chem Engnr.

FILOSA, KURT A; East Catholic HS; Glastonbury, CT; (Y); 16/278; Cmnty Wkr; VP Key Clb; Ski Clb; Stage Crew; Var L Bsbl; Var L Crs Cntry; Jr NHS; NHS; Im Lcrss; High Hon Roll; Var Crew Tm 85; Princpls Awd Ctznshp & Scholar 86; Arch Engrng.

FINCKE, KIM; Ridgefield HS; Ridgefield, CT; (Y); 207/381; Church Yth Grp; Ski Clb; Chorus; Cheerleading; Hon Roll.

FINELLI, LISA; Watertown HS; Oakville, CT; (Y); Church Yth Grp; DECA; Drm & Bgl; Rep Stu Cncl; Bsktbl; Stat Mgr(s); Score Keeper; Socr; High Hon Roll; Hon Roll; Comp Tech.

FINKE, STACY; Holy Cros HS; Watertown, CT; (Y); Speech Tm; Teachers Aide; Acpl Chr; Chorus; Madrigals; Swing Chorus; Rep Soph Cls; Hon Roll; Ntl Merit Schol; Cncrt Choir 84-86; Mck Trl Ntl Merit Schlrshp 85; Post Coll; Physhlgy.

FIORELLA, RONDA; Norwalk HS; E Norwalk, CT; (Y); 59/495; Rep Soph Cls; Rep Jr Cls; Rep Stu Cncl; Im Powder Puff Ftbl; Var Swmmng; Var Trk; Hon Roll; Schlrshp For Silvermine Guild Schl Of Art Ctr 86; Pratt Inst; Int Dsn.

FIRGELESKI, MICHELE LEE; Trumbull HS; Trumbull, CT; (Y); Church Yth Grp; Dance Clb; Band; Concert Band; Mrchg Band; Symp Band; High Hon Roll; NHS; Library Aide; Office Aide; Dr Richard Simses Memrl Schlrshp 86; ST Fnlst Miss Southern New England Pagnt 86; U Of CT; Nrsg.

FISCH JR, GENE; Maruk HS; Monroe, CT; (Y); School Musical; School Play; Yrbk Stf; JV Var Socr; Var Swmmng; JV Var Trk; Hon Roll; Boy Scts; Drama Clb; Band; Smr Wesleyan Schlrhsp Crtvly Gftd Yths 86; Ref Scr Bys Lttle Lge Grls Sftbl 85-86; Bus.

FISCHER, ELIZABETH; Avon HS; Avon, CT; (Y); Church Yth Grp; Ski Clb; SADD; Var Sftbl; Vllybl; High Hon Roll; NHS; Natl Scis.

FISCHER, JULIA; Ridgefield HS; Ridgefield, CT; (Y); Art Clb; Pres Political Wkr; Mrchg Band; Ed Lit Mag; Hon Roll; Ntl Merit SF; Frnch Bk Awd 84-86; Wellesley Bk Awd 85-86; Studio Art.

FISCO, APRIL; Sacred Heart Acad; New Haven, CT; (Y); Computer Clb; Dance Clb; FBLA; School Musical; Scungilli Intl Schlrshp 85-6 & 86-7; Endowment Schlrshp 84-5; Providence Coll; Accntng.

FISHBERG, MITCHELL; Newington HS; Newington, CT; (Y); 40/365; Cmnty Wkr; Var L Tennis; High Hon Roll; Hon Roll; Nw Englnd Lwn Tnns Assn Sprtsmnshp Awd 83; Arthr Frdmn Mem Schlrshp Awd 86; Lafayette Coll; Law.

FISHER, JILL; Stanford HS; Stamford, CT; (Y); Hosp Aide; JA; Acpl Chr; Church Choir; Rep Frsh Cls; Var JV Fld Hcky; Trk; Hon Roll; NHS; Vrsty Let In Field Hcky 86; Psych.

FITTS, ANDREW; Kingswood-Oxford HS; Farmington, CT; (Y); Debate Tm; Spanish Clb; Var Capt Ftbl; Im Wt Lftg; Var Capt Wrstlng.

FITZ, JEFFREY W; Masuk HS; Monroe, CT; (Y); 93/290; Spanish Clb; Nwsp Rptr; Nwsp Sprt Ed; Nwsp Stf; Yrbk Stf; JV Bsbl; Var Capt Bsktbl; JV Var Ftbl; Lw Enfrcmnt Schlrshp 86; Vrsty Bsktbl Tm Cptns Awd 86; S CT ST U; Bus.

FITZGERALD, JOHN G; Fairfield Prep; Norwalk, CT; (Y); Ed Yrbk Stf; Var Crs Cntry; Var Trk; High Hon Roll; NHS; Ntl Merit SF; Brown U Bk Awd 85; Tchr.

FITZPATRICK, PAUL; New Canaan HS; New Canaan, CT; (Y); Church Yth Grp; FBLA; Sec Sr Cls; Var Ftbl; Var Wrstlng; Hon Roll; Jr NHS; Ntl Merit SF; JR Clss V Chrmn County SAC.

FITZPATRICK, SEAN; Staples HS; Westport, CT; (Y); VP Pres Key Clb; Yrbk Phtg; JV Socr; Var Capt Wrstlng; Hon Roll.

FLANAGAN, WILLIAM; Griswold HS; Jewett City, CT; (Y); Hon Roll; Mst Imprvd Sci 83; Cert Microbio Lab Asst 85; Tchr.

FLAWS, DESIREE; Kolbe-Cathedral HS; Bridgeport, CT; (Y); JA; Hon Roll; S Prestly Blake Schlrshp 86; Bay Path Presdntl Schlrshp 86; Kolloe-Cathdrl Schlstc Awd-Plaq 86; Bay Path JC; Arts.

FLAY, HEATHER; Canton HS; Collinsville, CT; (Y); 17/95; 4-H; Girl Scts; Concert Band; Bsktbl; High Hon Roll; Hon Roll; Girl Sct Slvr Awd 85; Girl Sct Slvr Ldrshp Pin 85; Central CT ST U; Elem Ed.

FLEMING, KIMBERLY; Daniel Hand HS; Madison, CT; (Y); 60/262; FCA; GAA; Pep Clb; SADD; Band; Trs Frsh Cls; Var Cheerleading; Var Capt Sftbl; MVP Sftbl 86; U VT; Bus Adm.

FLEXNER, JENNIFER; Greenwich HS; Greewnich, CT; (Y); Hosp Aide; Service Clb; Chorus; School Musical; Stage Crew; Im L Badmtn; High Hon Roll; Hon Roll; Poli Sci.

FLOREK, JOHN; Naugatuck HS; Naugatuck, CT; (Y); Boy Scts; Latin Clb; Ski Clb; Spanish Clb; Capt Crs Cntry; Var Trk; Hon Roll; U Of ME Orono; Engr.

FLORES, ALBERTO; Watkinson HS; Hartford, CT; (Y); Aud/Vis; Cmnty Wkr; Dance Clb; Radio Clb; Chorus; School Musical; Nwsp Stf; JV Socr; Hon Roll; Hartford Bllt Schl Schlrshp 82-86; Arts Recog Tlnt Srch Mrt Awd 86; Watkinson Schl Schlrshp 83-86; Dance.

FLORIO, LISA; Wilton HS; Wilton, CT; (Y); 126/354; Chorus; Hon Roll; Comp.

FLOTTE, HOLLI; Granby Memorial HS; Granby, CT; (Y); Church Yth Grp; Drama Clb; Office Aide; Teachers Aide; Acpl Chr; Chorus; School Musical; School Play; Nwsp Stf; Hon Roll; Cert Of Awd Velvet Voices & Chorus 85-86; Music Fsvl 85-86; Mst Imprvd Stu In Chorus 85-86; Elem Ed.

FLOWERS, ANTHONY; Central HS; Bridgeport, CT; (Y); Church Yth Grp; JA; Church Choir; Nwsp Stf; Chrch Yth Grp 85; Jr Achvt 85; Nwspapr Stff 85; Music.

FLUGEL, RUSSELL A; Enrico Fermi HS; Enfield, CT; (Y); 7/345; Boy Scts; Quiz Bowl; Rep Stu Cncl; Bsbl; Capt L Tennis; High Hon Roll; Trs NHS; Yth & Govt Pgm 83 & 85; Hstry Awd 85-86.

FLYNN, CHRIS; Fairfield College Preparatory Schl; Wilton, CT; (Y); Art Clb; Letterman Clb; Varsity Clb; Var L Lcrss; Hnrs Math Fairfld Pk 83-87.

FLYNN, COREEN; St Bernard HS; Uncasville, CT; (Y); 49/265; Church Yth Grp; French Clb; Girl Scts; Band; Off Jr Cls; Var L Crs Cntry; JV Trk; Hon Roll; Concert Band; Mrchg Band; Mst Val Frshmn Rnnr 84; Bonne Belle Circle Excllnc Cert Of Merit 85; UVM; Phys Therapy.

FOGARTY, HELEN; Westover Schl; Southport, CT; (Y); Ski Clb; Var Fld Hcky; Var Lcrss; Art Clb; Church Yth Grp; Church Choir; Stage Crew; Variety Show; Yrbk Stf; Lit Mag; Most Imprvd Fld Hcky Plyr 83; Art Awd 86.

FOGG, ERIC; Watertown HS; Oakville, CT; (Y); JA; Ski Clb; U Of CT; Accntng.

FOGG, KAREN; Fitch SR HS; Groton, CT; (Y); Church Yth Grp; Band; Church Choir; Concert Band; Mrchg Band; Orch; School Musical; Yrbk Stf; Swmmng; High Hon Roll; Soc Studies Exclnce Awd 84.

FORAN, SUSAN; St Marys HS; Hamden, CT; (Y); Church Yth Grp; Hosp Aide; Service Clb; Spanish Clb; Stage Crew; Lit Mag; Sec Trs Frsh Cls; VP Soph Cls; Trs Stu Cncl; Tennis; Wrld Hstry Awd; Ldrshp Awd; Rlgn Awd; Nrsng.

FORAND, PETER A; William H Hall HS; W Hartford, CT; (Y); 15/324; Pres VP JA; Model UN; Pep Band; Symp Band; Var Capt Crs Cntry; Var Capt Trk; Dnfth Awd; High Hon Roll; NHS; Amer Legion Mdl 86; Most Dedctd Athlete 86; Co Of Yr JR Achvmnt; Boston Coll; Ecnmcs.

FORD, ROBIN; Brian Mc Mahon HS; Norwalk, CT; (Y); 52/360; Girl Scts; Latin Clb; Chorus; Church Choir; Orch; Hon Roll; Hlth Sci Clustr Prog U Of CT 85; Satrdy Acdmy Prog Sci & Engrng 84; Yale U.

FORMAN, LISA; Amity Regional HS; Orange, CT; (S); Cmnty Wkr; French Clb; Pres Temple Yth Grp; Yrbk Bus Mgr; Lit Mag; Hon Roll; NHS; Hosp Aide; Pep Clb; Scholastic Bowl; Harvard Bk Awd 86; Hnrbl Mntn Frnch CT Concours 86; Peer Cnslng Tutrng 86; Bio Sci.

FORREST, KEN; Bristol Central HS; Bristol, CT; (Y); Latin Clb; Acpl Chr; Church Choir; Madrigals; Variety Show; Stu Cncl; Capt Crs Cntry; Socr; Capt Trk; Wrstlng; Outstndng Rnnr Awd Crs Cntry 84; Bst In Trk 85; 3rd L Div 5000 M ST Champnshp; Psych.

FORSTER, DAN; Southington HS; Southington, CT; (Y); 53/575; Church Yth Grp; Concert Band; Jazz Band; Mrchg Band; School Musical; Stage Crew; L Socr; Var L Swmmng; Var Trk; High Hon Roll; U New Haven Pgmmng Comptn 2nd Pl 86; New England Mth Lg 84-86; Comp.

FORSTER, JACQUELINE; Miss Porters Schl; The Woodlands, TX; (Y); Cmnty Wkr; Pres Debate Tm; Model UN; School Play; Var Badmtn; Im Pom Pon; Hon Roll; Art Clb; Church Yth Grp; JA; VP Stu Teachers Prevntn Neclear War 86-87; Sci Fair Wnnr 83-84; Watu Wazuri Minority Stu Clb 85-87; U Pennsylvania; Law.

FORTE, STEPHEN; Saint Joseph HS; Shelton, CT; (Y); Computer Clb; Trk; Bus.

FORTIER, JEFF; Warren F Kaynor Tech; Waterbury, CT; (Y); Aud/Vis; Rep Stu Cncl; Johnson & Wales; Bus.

FORTUNA, MIKE; Fairfield Prep; Fairfield, CT; (Y); Boy Scts; Red Cross Aide; JV Swmmng; Var Trk; Wt Lftg; Parks Coll; Arntcl Engrng.

FOSS, JULIE; Old Saybrook SR HS; Old Saybrook, CT; (Y); 1/120; French Clb; Latin Clb; Nwsp Phtg; Nwsp Rptr; Rep Stu Cncl; Tennis; Trk; High Hon Roll; Lion Awd; Ntl Merit Schol; Outstndng Math Stu 86; Acad Excllnc Chem & Frnch IV 86; Civil Engr.

FOSTER, KIMBERLY; Manchester HS; Manchester, CT; (Y); AFS; Church Yth Grp; Church Choir; Hon Roll; Prfct Atten Awd; Porter & Chester Inst; Arch.

FOUNTAIN, SHERYL; Lyman Hall HS; Wallingford, CT; (Y); 13/225; Church Yth Grp; Sec French Clb; Sec JA; Band; Chorus; School Musical; Lit Mag; Mgr Bsktbl; Tennis; Sec NHS; Voice Of Dmcrcy 84 & 86; High Hnr Roll; Syracuse; Advrtsng.

FOUQUETTE, ADRIENNE; East Catholic HS; East Windsor, CT; (Y); Cmnty Wkr; JA; Red Cross Aide; Chorus; Hon Roll; Excllnce Vocal Mus Awd 86; St Josephs Coll; Nrsng.

FOURNIER, NICOLE; Lyme-Old Lyme HS; Old Lyme, CT; (Y); 10/118; Sec AFS; Band; Nwsp Rptr; Trs Sr Cls; JV Capt Socr; Cit Awd; Elks Awd; High Hon Roll; Lion Awd; NHS; Tri-M Music Hnr Soc 85 & 86; Crw Slvr Wmns Ntls 85; Ithaca Coll; Phy Thrpy.

FOWLER, MATT; J A Foran HS; Milford, CT; (Y); DECA; Hon Roll; Physics.

FOWLER, TARA; Masuk HS; Monroe, CT; (Y); Cmnty Wkr; Drama Clb; Spanish Clb; Teachers Aide; Color Guard; Drill Tm; Twrlr; High Hon Roll; Hon Roll; Spanish NHS; Spnsh.

FOX, BENJAMIN; Brien Mc Mahon HS; Norwalk, CT; (Y); 19/350; Church Yth Grp; JV Var Bsbl; JV Bsktbl; JV Var Socr; JV Var Tennis; High Hon Roll; Hon Roll; NHS; Ntl Merit SF; NC Chapel Hill; Englsh Ed.

FOX, LE ANNE; Guilford HS; Guilford, CT; (Y); 9/300; Church Yth Grp; Cmnty Wkr; Sec Trs Latin Clb; Sec Band; French Hon Soc; High Hon Roll; NHS; Concert Band; Mrchg Band; Orch.

FOY, LAURA; Norwalk HS; E Norwalk, CT; (Y); JA; Key Clb; Spanish Clb; Rep Jr Cls; High Hon Roll; Commercial Art.

FRACCASCIA, CHARRISE; Acad Of Our Lady; Trumbull, CT; (Y); 3/118; GAA; Model UN; Service Clb; Spanish Clb; Sec Jr Cls; Sec Sr Cls; Var L Sftbl; NHS; Church Yth Grp; Cmnty Wkr; U S Army Awd Sci Proj CT ST Sci Fair 85; Magna Cum Laude 84 & 85; Cum Laude Lat Awd Natl Lat Exm 86.

FRAKLIN, JEFFREY; Crosby HS; Waterbury, CT; (S); Computer Clb; French Clb; JA; Nwsp Rptr; Im Ftbl; Hon Roll; Prfct Atten Awd; St Schlr; U Of CT Day Of Pride Top 100 Mnrty CT 86; U Of CT; Comp Sci.

FRANCO, JAMES; Notre Dame HS; Orange, CT; (Y); 57/238; Cmnty Wkr; Political Wkr; Hon Roll; SCSU; Math.

FRANK, JENNIFER; Housatonic Vly Regional HS; Lakeville, CT; (Y); Aud/Vis; FBLA; Library Aide; High Hon Roll; Hon Roll; Acctng.

FRATTAROLA, MARK W; Greenwich HS; Greenwich, CT; (Y); 5/764; Hst Key Clb; Am Leg Boys St; Boys Clb Am; Red Cross Aide; High Hon Roll; Kiwanis Awd; Pres Spanish NHS; Fencing 86; Red Cross Adv Lifesaver,Instructr 86; Harvard U; Bus Adm.

FRATTAROLI, VANESSA; Ridgefield HS; Ridgefield, CT; (Y); 56/387; Camp Fr Inc; Band; Concert Band; Mrchg Band; Orch; Symp Band; Var Cheerleading; Capt Var Gym; Hon Roll.

FRAY, CHRISTOPHER; Thomaston HS; Thomaston, CT; (Y); 2/64; Am Leg Boys St; Aud/Vis; Nwsp Stf; Yrbk Stf; Rep Stu Cncl; Crs Cntry; Trk; DAR Awd; High Hon Roll; Pres NHS; Excllnc Amer Hist Dghtrs Amer Rvltn 86; Outstndng Acad Achvt Awd 86; Yth Merit Awd Rotary Clb 86.

FREDERICK, ANNA; Tourtellotte Memorial HS; N Grosvnordal, CT; (Y); 6/102; Pep Clb; Chorus; Hon Roll.

FREDERICK, LORI; Orville H Platt HS; Meriden, CT; (Y); Yrbk Stf; Rep Frsh Cls; Rep Soph Cls; Rep Jr Cls; Rep Sr Cls; Powder Puff Ftbl; Capt Var Sftbl; Var L Vllybl; Hon Roll; Hosp Aide; Italian,Summit Clb.

FREED, PETER; Wilbur Cross HS; New Haven, CT; (S); 1/259; AFS; Cmnty Wkr; PAVAS; Political Wkr; Quiz Bowl; Nwsp Stf; Lit Mag; Rep Soph Cls; JV Crs Cntry; JV Lcrss; Brown U Bk Awd 85; Lit Awd 85; Eng Awd 84-85; Polit Sci.

FREEMAN JR, JEFFREY; Windham R V T S HS; Baltic, CT; (Y); 3/117; Am Leg Boys St; Chess Clb; Computer Clb; VICA; High Hon Roll; Hon Roll; NHS; Trk; Steven Anthony Bergeron Memrl Schlrshp Awd 86; Worcester Poly Inst; Elec Engrn.

FREIBOTT, PAUL; Saint Joseph HS; Stratford, CT; (Y); 42/227; Art Clb; Drama Clb; JA; Yrbk Stf; Lit Mag; Hon Roll; Ntl Merit Ltr; Fairfield U; Comp Sci.

FRENCH, GAILYNN; New Fairfield HS; New Fairfld, CT; (Y); 37/230; Cmnty Wkr; Hosp Aide; Office Aide; SADD; Hon Roll; U Of CT.

FRENCH, JONATHAN; Windsor HS; Windsor, CT; (Y); 7/360; Church Yth Grp; Intnl Clb; Library Aide; Model UN; Nwsp Rptr; Pres NHS; Eng Bk Awd JR Clss 85-86; Yale Bk Awd 85-86; Engr Physcs.

FRESA, DANIEL; Branford HS; Branford, CT; (Y); JV Bsbl; High Hon Roll; Hon Roll.

FREUNDLICH, JOEL S; Weston HS; Weston, CT; (Y); 1/167; Teachers Aide; Nwsp Stf; Trs Sr Cls; Var L Tennis; Var Trk; Bausch & Lomb Sci Awd; High Hon Roll; NHS; Val; Eng Schlr 85-86; NELTA Ranked Tennis 83-84; Engrng.

FRICKE, LAURA; Miss Porters Schl; Ridgefield, CT; (Y); Drama Clb; GAA; School Play; Yrbk Stf; Var Socr; Var Sftbl; JV Vllybl; Cmmndtn Excllnc Drama & Art 84.

FRIEDEL, STEPHAN; Trumbull HS; Trumbull, CT; (Y); Pres German Clb; Hon Roll; Chem Engrng.

FRIEDMAN, REBECCA; Nathan Hale-Ray HS; East Haddam, CT; (S); 1/70; Am Leg Aux Girls St; Drama Clb; Chorus; School Musical; Nwsp Bus Mgr; Yrbk Ed-Chief; Pres Stu Cncl; Var JV Sftbl; High Hon Roll; NHS; Skidmore Coll.

FRIEND, LESLEY M; Shelton HS; Shelton, CT; (Y); Am Leg Aux Girls St; Key Clb; Spanish Clb; Rep Stu Cncl; Var Capt Bsktbl; Var L Socr; Var Capt Trk; NHS; Trs Spanish NHS; Wellesley Bk Awd 86.

FRIEZ, STACEY; Rham HS; Hebron, CT; (Y); JCL; Dance Clb; Sec Latin Clb; Science Clb; Ski Clb; Hon Roll; Culnry Arts.

FRIGIANI, ANTHONY; Holy Cross HS; Watertown, CT; (Y); 152/380; Spanish Clb; Wrstlng; Leo Fbn Hstry Awd 83; PA ST; Engnrng.

FRINK, KRISTY; Griswold HS; Jewett City, CT; (Y); GAA; Varsity Clb; JV Bsktbl; JV Capt Sftbl; JV Var Vllybl; Hon Roll; Becker JC; Comp Sci.

FRISBIE, ELIZABETH; Miss Porters Schl; Edwardsville, IL; (Y); Cmnty Wkr; Drama Clb; School Play; Stage Crew; Mgr Vllybl; Hon Roll; Wellesley Coll Excllnc Prz-Eng & Socl Svc 85; J D Grey Drama Prz 86; S B Machennan Hmnts Awd 86; Oberlin Coll; Eng.

FRISK, RHONDA; Berlin HS; Kensington, CT; (Y); Key Clb; Service Clb; Band; Color Guard; Var Soph Cls; Cntrl CT ST U; Elem Ed.

FRITSCHE, CHERYL; Danbury HS; Danbury, CT; (Y); 4/400; Church Yth Grp; JA; Key Clb; Variety Show; Yrbk Stf; Var Tennis; Var Vllybl; High Hon Roll; Hon Roll; NHS; German Book Awd 86; Perry Awd German 85.

FRITZ, JENNIFER; Morgan HS; Clinton, CT; (Y); 42/130; Church Yth Grp; Chorus; Church Choir; Var Capt Crs Cntry; Powder Puff Ftbl; Var Trk; Hon Roll; All Shoreln Crss Cntry Tm 83 & 85; Christn Ed.

FRITZ, ROBERT; East Lyme HS; Niantic, CT; (Y); Var Bsktbl; Hon Roll; Accntng.

FRITZ, SUZANNE; Ridgefield HS; Ridgefield, CT; (Y); 87/390; VP Art Clb; Church Yth Grp; Cmnty Wkr; German Clb; Nwsp Bus Mgr; Nwsp Rptr; Nwsp Stf; Hon Roll; Young Life Guild Artists Art Shw 86; Outstndg Svc Awd RHS Voice 86; Vlntr Pgm Awd 84; Carnegie Mellon; Illustration.

FROELICK, TRACI ANN; Holy Cross HS; Naugatuck, CT; (Y); Service Clb; SADD; Chorus; Stu Cncl; High Hon Roll; NHS; Bus.

FRUSCIANTE, ANGELA K; Central HS; Bridgeport, CT; (Y); 1/300; Stage Crew; High Hon Roll; NHS; Val; Ushers Guild Head Usher 85-86; Crtve Yth Wesleyan U 84-85; Brown U Bk Awd Engl Exprsn 85; U Bridgeport; Interior Design.

FRYER, JEFFREY M; Holy Cross HS; Waterbury, CT; (Y); 158/380; Rep Boy Scts; French Clb; Latin Clb; Ski Clb; Nwsp Phtg; Lit Mag; Var Crs Cntry; Var Trk; Hon Roll; Bike Clb; Editor Newsltr 86; Soc Studies Hon Soc; Acctng.

FU, DANIEL D; Newington HS; Newington, CT; (Y); 20/370; Sec Aud/Vis; Hosp Aide; Sec Math Tm; Yrbk Sprt Ed; Hon Roll; NHS; Comp Sci Awd 86; Natl Hnr Soc Scholar 86; Cornell U; Engrng.

FUELLHART, KURT; Rockville HS; Vernon, CT; (Y); 37/308; Computer Clb; Tennis; Cntrl Ct All Str Tnns Tm,Coachs Awd Tnns 85; U Of VT; Bus Admin.

FUISTING, KIMBERLY; Fitch SR HS; Groton, CT; (Y); Drama Clb; Library Aide; Ski Clb; Varsity Clb; Chorus; School Play; Lit Mag; Var Swmmng; Var Capt Tennis; Cit Awd.

FULLER, KATRINA; Bassick HS; Bridgeport, CT; (Y); 4/200; Am Leg Aux Girls St; JA; Cheerleading; Var Trk; Hon Roll; NHS; Rotary Awd; Voice Dem Awd; Church Yth Grp; Gvrnrs SSACE 84-86; Jane Fndas Lrl Spgs Rnch Cmp For Prfrmng Arts Schlrshp 84; USA Teen Mss CT ST; U S Naval Acad Prep; Poly Sci.

FULLER, SUSAN; East Granby HS; E Granby, CT; (Y); Pep Clb; Yrbk Stf; Sec Soph Cls; Var L Bsktbl; Var L Socr; Stat Sftbl; Hon Roll; Bus Admn.

FULMORE, LASHONDA; James Hillhouse HS; New Haven, CT; (Y); Computer Clb; Dance Clb; 4-H; Girl Scts; JA; Rep Stu Cncl; High Hon Roll; Hon Roll; NHS; Prfct Atten Awd; Acad Hnrs 83; Sci,Math Hnrs 84-85; Comp Pgmr.

FULTON, BRIAN; Kent HS; Carbandale, CO; (Y); Capt Crs Cntry; JV Ice Hcky; Tennis; Wrstlng; Hon Roll.

FUNCH, LISA; Stamford HS; Stamford, CT; (Y); Cmnty Wkr; Varsity Clb; Bsktbl; Var Trk; Allan Mc Clelland Memrl Awd Excllnc Ed 86; Bus.

FURDAS, GREG; New Brtain HS; New Britain, CT; (Y); JA; Jazz Band; Orch; Stage Crew; Hon Roll; Gftd & Talntd Prgm 84; Bentley College; Bus Adm.

FUSCO, JOSEPH; Cross HS; New Haven, CT; (Y); Teachers Aide; Hon Roll; Black Belt 86; Mchnst.

FUTTNER, JEFF; East Hartford HS; E Hartford, CT; (Y); 57/406; Trs Am Leg Boys St; Nwsp Rptr; Nwsp Sprt Ed; Yrbk Phtg; Pres Sr Cls; Trs Stu Cncl; Capt Bsbl; Var Capt Ftbl; Cit Awd; DAR Awd; Safe Rides Stu 85-86; Weekly Schl Colmnst 81-86; Centennial Comm 85-86; Keene ST Coll; Pol Sci.

GABNER, DENISE; Valley Regional HS; Deep River, CT; (Y); Hon Roll.

GABOR, NATALIE; Griswold HS; Griswold, CT; (Y); GAA; Varsity Clb; Chorus; Color Guard; School Musical; Variety Show; Cheerleading; Score Keeper; DAR Awd; Hon Roll; U CT; Bio.

GADUE, LYNN M; William H Hall HS; West Hartford, CT; (Y); 61/342; Swmmng; Trk; High Hon Roll; Hon Roll; NHS; Spanish NHS; Safe Rides West Hartford 82-86; U CT; Psych.

GAGE, JENNIFER L; Wethersfield HS; Wethersfield, CT; (Y); 8/310; Church Yth Grp; Model UN; Quiz Bowl; Acpl Chr; Chorus; School Musical; Nwsp Stf; Yrbk Stf; Stu Cncl; Badmtn; Wesleyan JR Sci & Humnts Sympsm 85; Calvin Coll.

GAGLIARDI, BUDDY; Jonathan Law HS; Milford, CT; (Y); 42/257; Am Leg Boys St; Church Yth Grp; Key Clb; Sec Sr Cls; Stu Cncl; Var Capt Bsbl; Var Capt Socr; Var Tennis; Hon Roll; Prfct Atten Awd; Algbra Awd-Excllnc; King Of Dance; Bus.

GAGLIARDI, DAWN M; Southington HS; Southington, CT; (Y); 68/600; FBLA; Capt Color Guard; Flag Corp; Mrchg Band; School Play; High Hon Roll; 1st Pl St Confrnce FBLA 86; Miss TEEN CT Pgnt 86; Mst Outstndng Indvdl-Fred J Miller Clinics 85; Fisher JC; Lgl Executive.

GAGNE, ANDREA; Sacred Heart Acad; E Haven, CT; (Y); Dance Clb; Spanish Clb; School Musical; Variety Show; Vllybl; Hon Roll; NEDT Awd; Dance Comptn Gold & Silv Mdls 85 & 86; Frgn Lang Trnsltr.

GAGNE, BERNADETTE; Jonathan Law HS; Milford, CT; (Y); 11/211; Keywanettes; Ski Clb; Spanish Clb; Yrbk Stf; Mgr Swmmng; Hon Roll; Rtry Exchng Stu Bolivia 84-85; Sprntndnts Acdmc Awd 86; Crlyn Shnly Bryn Art Awd 86; The Art Inst Dallas; Advrtsng.

GAGNON, PAULA; Southington HS; Southington, CT; (Y); DECA; Latin Clb; Hon Roll; Bus.

GAGNON, TIMOTHY; Farmington HS; Farmington, CT; (Y); Church Yth Grp; Cmnty Wkr; English Clb; FCA; JA; Church Choir; Variety Show; JV Bsbl; Im Socr; Sftbl; Drftng Awd 86; Andrews U; Bldng Cnstrctn Tech.

GAJDA, NANCY; Berlin HS; Kensington, CT; (Y); 35/180; Band; Concert Band; Jazz Band; Mrchg Band; Pep Band; School Musical; School Play; Yrbk Stf; Hon Roll; Bus Clb Sec & Pres 83-86; Modern Hist Awd 84; U CT Hartford; Fashn Desgn.

GAJDA, PETER; The Taft Schl; Bethlehem, CT; (Y); Boy Scts; French Clb; Intnl Clb; Chorus; Church Choir; Im Bsktbl; Im Socr; JV Trk; Schrlshp Hamilton Coll 86; Tchr Polish Hamilton 86; Schrlshp Taft 82-86; Hamilton Coll; Econmcs.

GAJEWSKI, MARYANNE; Sacred Heart Acad; Chesire, CT; (Y); Computer Clb; Chorus; Variety Show; Yrbk Phtg; Im Vllybl; High Hon Roll; Acctng.

GALBERTH, DAWNA; Richard C Lee HS; New Haven, CT; (Y); Hosp Aide; Pep Clb; JV Im Sftbl; Im Vllybl; Medcl Tech.

GALLACHER, JAMES; Fairfield College Prep; E Norwalk, CT; (Y); Boy Scts; Church Yth Grp; Political Wkr; Bus Mgmt.

GALLAGHER, EDITH; Brookfield HS; Brookfield Ctr, CT; (Y); Sec DECA; Nwsp Ed-Chief; Yrbk Stf; Capt Var Bsktbl; Capt Var Fld Hcky; Capt Var Sftbl; High Hon Roll; Score Keeper; Coach Actv; Varsity Clb; DECA Schlrshp 86; Mst Imprvd Stu Awd 86; Mrn Corp Outst Athlt 86; Sr Athlt Awd 86; Hofstra U; Bus Mgmt.

GALLAGHER, GREGORY; Simsbury HS; Simsbury, CT; (Y); 100/352; VP Church Yth Grp; Exploring; JA; Ski Clb; VICA; Bsbl; Capt Bsktbl; Golf; Sftbl; Syracuse U; Arch.

GALLAGHER, KARYN; Sacred Heart Acad; West Haven, CT; (Y); Drama Clb; Latin Clb; School Play; Nwsp Stf; Crs Cntry; Crs Cntry Mst Imprvd Rnnr 85; Bio.

GALLAGHER, KATHY; Daniel Hand HS; Madison, CT; (Y); GAA; Yrbk Stf; Safe Rides Cls Rep 84-85.

GALLAGHER, KATHY; Jonathan Law HS; Milford, CT; (S); DECA; Color Guard; DECA 2nd Pl Trphy In Gnrl Merch 86; 2nd In ST DECA Buying & Prcng 86; Bus.

GALLAGHER, THERESA; Brookfield HS; Brookfield Center, CT; (Y); Chorus; Var Capt Crs Cntry; Var Capt Trk; High Hon Roll; Hon Roll.

GALLEGOS, NENA; Valley Regional HS; Deep River, CT; (Y); 22/130; Spanish Clb; Band; Mrchg Band; Nwsp Stf; Yrbk Sprt Ed; Pres Frsh Cls; Var Capt Bsktbl; Var L Cheerleading; Var Capt Vllybl; Wt Lftg; Deep River Rotry Schlrshp 86; John Aaron Joanson Schlrshp 86; Ann Hendershot Vickery Schlrshp 86; U Connecticut; Nrsng.

GALLERY, DANIELLE; East Hartford HS; E Hartford, CT; (Y); 14/469; JA; Spanish Clb; Yrbk Stf; Off Frsh Cls; Off Soph Cls; Rep Jr Cls; Rep Sr Cls; Rep Stu Cncl; High Hon Roll; Hon Roll; E Hrtsfrd Wmns Clb Schlrshp 86; Rtry Clb 86; Mark Antil Memrl Schlrshp 86; Pres Acdmc Ftns Awrd 86; Central CT ST U; Math.

GALLOP III, WILLIE E; Trumbull HS; Milford, CT; (Y); Church Yth Grp; FFA; Letterman Clb; Varsity Clb; Church Choir; Nwsp Rptr; Nwsp Stf; Var L Bsktbl; Var L Ftbl; Cit Awd.

GALLUP, MATTHEW; Saint Bernard HS; Willimantic, CT; (Y); 88/265; Church Yth Grp; Cmnty Wkr; Trk; Hon Roll; Psych.

GALUSHA, CHRISTINA; Lewis S Mills HS; Burlington, CT; (Y); 9/176; Church Yth Grp; Sec 4-H; Library Aide; Chorus; Co-Capt Color Guard; Flag Corp; Madrigals; Mrchg Band; School Play; High Hon Roll.

GALVIN, LAURA ANNE; Holy Cross HS; Waterbury, CT; (Y); 180/400; Art Clb; Cmnty Wkr; Var Capt Crs Cntry; Var Trk; Hon Roll; Southern CT; Sprts Nutrtnst.

GAMBACINI, EDWARD; West Haven HS; W Haven, CT; (Y); Intnl Clb; Q&S; Nwsp Ed-Chief; Nwsp Stf; High Hon Roll; Hon Roll; NHS; 3 Clg Credts For Engl Cours 86; Engl.

GAMBARDELLA, LEE; Sacred Heart Acad; Hamden, CT; (Y); Camera Clb; Church Yth Grp; Dance Clb; Intnl Clb; Stage Crew; Yrbk Phtg; High Hon Roll; NHS; NEDT Awd; Spanish NHS; Natl Sci Olympiad 86.

GAMBER, KIM; Southington HS; Southington, CT; (Y); 193/600; Variety Show; Rep Stu Cncl; L Bsktbl; Capt L Socr; Hon Roll; Jr NHS; Booster Clb Schlrshp 86; U CT; Mrktg.

GAMBER, PAUL; O H Platt HS; Meriden, CT; (Y); L Var Bsbl; Im Bsktbl; Capt L Ftbl; L Var Trk; Im Wt Lftg; Mvp Ftbl 85; West Point.

GAMBINO, LAURA; Andrew Warde HS; Fairfield, CT; (Y); Church Yth Grp; Chorus; Church Choir; School Play; Hon Roll; Soclgy.

GAMBINO, STEPHANIE; St Mary HS; Harrison, NY; (Y); 19/50; French Clb; Pep Clb; Var Bsktbl; Var Fld Hcky; Var Powder Puff Ftbl; Var Sftbl; Bus Adm.

GANS, LAURA; Robert E Fitch SR HS; Mystic, CT; (Y); 3/400; Drama Clb; Intnl Clb; Science Clb; Thesps; Stage Crew; Yrbk Stf; Ed Lit Mag; High Hon Roll; Hon Roll; NHS; Weslyan Sci & Human Symposm 86; Outstndg Wk Schl Literary Mag 85-86; Outstndng Frnch Stu 84.

GARALA, MIKE; Oliver Wolcott Technical Schl; Torrington, CT; (Y); Church Yth Grp; Y-Teens; Hon Roll; Waterbury ST Tech Schl; Electr.

GARAMELLA, CHRIS; Kolbe Cathedral HS; Bridgeport, CT; (Y); Yrbk Stf; Rep Soph Cls; Trs Civic Clb; JV Socr; Southern CT ST U; Brdcstng.

GARCEAU, ROBERTA J; Naugatuck HS; Naugatuck, CT; (Y); 1/306; Am Leg Aux Girls St; Scholastic Bowl; Madrigals; Swing Chorus; Variety Show; VP Stu Cncl; Co-Capt Cheerleading; Pres NHS; Ntl Merit Ltr; Val; Elks Ntl Schlrshp MV Stdnt; ARCO Metals Schlrshp; Uniroyal Schlrshp; Dartmouth Coll; Bio.

GARCIA, BEATRICE; Plainville HS; Plainville, CT; (Y); 64/184; Am Leg Aux Girls St; Key Clb; VP Service Clb; Ski Clb; Band; Yrbk Stf; Pres Frsh Cls; Sec Soph Cls; Trs Jr Cls; VP Sr Cls; Pre-Law.

GARCIA, NORMA; Bassick HS; Bridgept, CT; (Y); JA; Church Choir; Trs Jr Cls; Stu Cncl; Sftbl; Sacred Heart U; Lgl Sec.

GARCIA, RAUL; Bulkeley HS; Hartford, CT; (Y); Church Yth Grp; Computer Clb; Spanish Clb; Band; Yrbk Rptr; Lit Mag; JV Var Bsbl; Crs Cntry; Mst Imprvd Stu Trphy, Trnty Coll Upwrd Bnd Chem, Mst Imprvd Trphys Upwrd Bnd Bio,Rdng 84; Pre-Law.

GARDNER, CATHERINE; Cheshire HS; Cheshire, CT; (Y); #1 In Class; Cmnty Wkr; Hosp Aide; Yrbk Stf; Rep Frsh Cls; Rep Soph Cls; Rep Sr Cls; JV Fld Hcky; High Hon Roll; Jr NHS; NCTE Awd; Sci Olymp; Frng Lang Poetry Spkng Cntst.

GARG, MANOJ K; Greenwich HS; Greenwich, CT; (Y); Debate Tm; Scholastic Bowl; School Play; Nwsp Stf; Var Bsktbl; Im Bowling; Im Tennis; High Hon Roll; NHS; Med.

GARIBALDI, SUSANNE; William H Hall HS; W Hartford, CT; (Y); 49/340; VP Stu Cncl; Var Capt Socr; Var Capt Tennis; DAR Awd; NHS; Spanish NHS; Cit Awd; High Hon Roll; J Lublin Mem Schlrshp Awd 85-86;D Harper Complt Athlt Awd 85-86; JAYFRO Schlr Athlt Awd 85-86; Bowdoin Coll.

GARLITZ, KEITH; Naugatuck HS; Ellicott City, MD; (Y); Trs VP Band; Trs VP Concert Band; Jazz Band; Mrchg Band; Pep Band; Symp Band; HS Band Parents Awd 86; Western MD Coll; Ecnmcs.

GARNER, ALANA; Plainfield HS; Central Village, CT; (Y); 21/162; Am Leg Aux Girls St; JA; Model UN; Office Aide; Red Cross Aide; Stu Cncl; Hon Roll; Computer Clb; Library Aide; Band; GATE Pro Schlrs; Princpls Awd Outstndng Svc; Sec Young Voluntrs In Action; Legal Asst.

GAROFALO, JOLEEN; Immaculate HS; Danbury, CT; (Y); 59/132; Church Choir; Var Capt Cheerleading; High Hon Roll; Hon Roll; Hmcmg Qn 85-86; JR Prom Qns Ct 85; Schl Of Radiology Danbury Hosp.

GAROFALO, MARCI; Sacred Heart Acad; Derby, CT; (Y); Church Yth Grp; Dance Clb; Hosp Aide; Red Cross Aide; Chorus; School Musical; Stage Crew; Rep Jr Cls; Trs Sr Cls; Var JV Bsktbl; Holy Cross Bk Awd 86; Michaels Jewelers Wrstwtch Awd 86; Svc Awd 3 Yr Hnrs Awd 86; Med.

GARRIGAN, HEATHER; Canterbury Schl; Pensacola, FL; (Y); 9/88; Camera Clb; Chorus; School Musical; School Play; Stage Crew; JV Fld Hcky; Var JV Sftbl; JV Capt Vllybl; High Hon Roll; Hon Roll; Proctor 86; Adv.

GARRITY, JANE; Lewis S Mills HS; Burlington, CT; (Y); AFS; Model UN; Ski Clb; Nwsp Rptr; Var Fld Hcky; Var Tennis; Hon Roll; Pres Schlr; Lewis S Mills Schlrshp 86; Hartford Coll For Wmn; Librl.

GASKINS, RICHARD; Wilbur Cross HS; New Haven, CT; (Y); 120/300; Boys Clb Am; Band; Drm & Bgl; Pep Band; Im Bsktbl; Awd Mrt Outstndng Achvmnt Humn Psych 84-85; Army.

GASPARINO, SANDRA; Greenwich HS; Greenwich, CT; (Y); 5/730; Chorus; School Musical; School Play; Variety Show; High Hon Roll; Hon Roll; Tony Salerno Awd 86; GASFA Awd 86; Strght A Awd 86; Iona Coll; Mrktng.

GATELY, NOELLE; East Catholic HS; East Hartford, CT; (Y); Political Wkr; Science Clb; Ski Clb; Swmmng; Tennis; Lawyer.

GATISON, DEBRA; Lauralton Hall HS; West Haven, CT; (Y); 13/111; Cmnty Wkr; Hosp Aide; Math Tm; Model UN; Pep Clb; Variety Show; Nwsp Rptr; Yrbk Stf; Rep Stu Cncl; NHS; Engrng.

GATTI, VICTOR; Kingswood-Oxford HS; Glastonbury, CT; (Y); Quiz Bowl; Scholastic Bowl; Spanish Clb; JV Tennis; Hon Roll; Ntl Merit Ltr; CT ST Latin Test Letter Of Commndtn 86; Lbrl Arts.

GAUCHES, JOANNE; Hall HS; W Hartford, CT; (Y); Sec JA; Yrbk Stf; Rep Stu Cncl; Var Fld Hcky; Im Lcrss; Var Trk; Hon Roll; U Of ME Orono; Bio.

GAUDIOSI, MARC; Crosby HS; Waterbury, CT; (Y); Boy Scts; Church Yth Grp; Varsity Clb; Band; Hon Roll; Best Frshmn Crosby Rifle Tm 83-84; Cptn Crosby Rifle Tm 86-87; Elec Engrng.

GAUDREAU, MICHELLE; East Windsor HS; Broad Brook, CT; (Y); 12/95; Pres Band; Concert Band; Drm Mjr(t); Jazz Band; Mrchg Band; School Musical; Rep Sr Cls; Stu Cncl; Var L Cheerleading; Hon Roll; U CT; Med Tech.

GAULT, KEVIN DONALD FRANCAIS; St Lukes HS; Stamford, CT; (Y); Sec Stu Cncl; Var Bsbl; Capt Bsktbl; Capt Ftbl; JV Score Keeper; Im Vllybl; Var Wt Lftg; Im Wrstlng; Cmnty Wkr; Mst Imprvd Ftbl 83; Nrthrn Div Bsktbl Champs 85; UNC Chapel Hill; Phys Thrpy.

GAWEL, IRENE; Sacred Heart Acad; Stamford, CT; (Y); Aud/Vis; Drama Clb; French Clb; Political Wkr; School Musical; School Play; Stage Crew; Variety Show; Nwsp Rptr; Yrbk Stf; Gnrl Excllnc Awd 84 & 86; Natl Ltn Exm-Magn Cum Laud Awd-Slvr Mdl 84 & 85.

GAYDOS, SUSAN; Housatonic Valley Regional HS; Falls Village, CT; (Y); Aud/Vis; FBLA; Spanish Clb; High Hon Roll; Hon Roll; SS 9 Hghst Avg Out Of Cls 84; Wrld Hist 10-A Hghst Avg 85; US Hist 11-A Tied Hghst Avg 86; Pltcl Sci.

GEARY, MICHELLE; Francis T Maloney HS; Meriden, CT; (Y); Church Yth Grp; Var Cheerleading; High Hon Roll; Hon Roll; Excellence In Latin Awd 84; Intr Dsgn.

GEARY, NANCY; Sacred Heart HS; Oakville, CT; (Y); Yrbk Rptr; Yrbk Stf; JV Var Bsktbl; Capt L Sftbl; All City-Sfbl Plyr 86; Hnrb Mntn-NVL Sftbl 86; Central CT ST U; Chldhd Ed.

GEE, CAMMY; Bullard Havens Vo Tech; Bridgeport, CT; (S); 2/185; Drama Clb; Rep Stu Cncl; High Hon Roll; Pres NHS; Doctor.

GEETTER, JENNIFER; Simsbury HS; Simsbury, CT; (Y); 53/406; JA; SADD; VP Temple Yth Grp; Yrbk Stf; Hon Roll; Coachs Awd Smr Swm Lg 83.

GEFFERT, JAMES; Shelton HS; Shelton, CT; (Y); 20/235; Am Leg Boys St; Ski Clb; Spanish Clb; SADD; Var Capt Bsbl; Ftbl; High Hon Roll; Hon Roll; NHS; Spanish NHS; Schlr Athlt 86; Edward C Finn Schlrshp 86; Bill Benham Schlrshp 86; U Of CT; Engr.

GEMMA, MARIA; Robert E Fitch SR HS; Groton, CT; (Y); 16/350; Drama Clb; Thesps; Varsity Clb; School Musical; Swing Chorus; Sec Soph Cls; Pres Jr Cls; Sec Stu Cncl; Var Crs Cntry; NHS; Outstndng Acdmc Achvt Awd 84; Art.

GENDREAU, CHARLES; Plainfield HS; Moosup, CT; (Y); 21/150; Varsity Clb; Var JV Ftbl; Trk; Prfct Atten Awd; Thames Valley Tech School; Data.

GENDREAU, ROBERT; Coventry HS; Coventry, CT; (Y); 8/80; Band; Concert Band; Jazz Band; JV Socr; Hon Roll; NHS; Pres Schlr; VP Soph Cls; VP Jr Cls; All Eastern CT ST Band 86; U CT; Comp Sci.

GENERAL JR, LEROY; Choate Rosemary Hall HS; Branford, CT; (Y); VP JA; Model UN; Pres Radio Clb; Science Clb; Spanish Clb; School Play; Lit Mag; Rep Jr Cls; Rep Sr Cls; Var Ftbl; Ntl Negro Merit Schlr 86; Chmcl Engrng.

GENEST, SCOTT; Sheehan HS; Wallingford, CT; (Y); 40/200; Cmnty Wkr; Political Wkr; Ski Clb; Hon Roll; New Haven Rlty Schl; Rl Est.

GENOVA, CARRIE; Holy Cross HS; Waterbury, CT; (Y); 5/380; Trs French Clb; French Hon Soc; High Hon Roll; NHS; Frnch Awd-Level III & IV; Soc Wmn Engrs Awd; Soc Studies Hnr Soc; Poli Sci.

GENOVESE, LAURIE; New Fairfield HS; New Fairfield, CT; (Y); Cmnty Wkr; Science Clb; Variety Show; Nwsp Rptr; Yrbk Rptr; Yrbk Stf; Lit Mag; Rep Stu Cncl; Var Capt Fld Hcky; Hon Roll; Western CT; Psychology.

GENTILE, CARRIE; Seymour HS; Oxford, CT; (S); 12/220; Drm Mjr(t); Variety Show; Rep Frsh Cls; Rep Soph Cls; Rep Jr Cls; JV Sftbl; Capt Swmmng; Twrlr; Law.

GENTILE, SYLVIA; Holy Cross HS; Waterbury, CT; (Y); 212/380; Hosp Aide; Latin Clb; Political Wkr; Peer Minstry 86-87; Providence Coll; Pre-Law.

GEORGE, DARLENE; Cheshire HS; Cheshire, CT; (Y); SADD; Variety Show; JV Var Cheerleading; Hon Roll; Jr NHS.

GERARD, MICHELE; Sacred Heart Acad; Northford, CT; (Y); Dance Clb; FBLA; Hosp Aide; Library Aide; School Musical; Stage Crew; JV Crs Cntry; Hon Roll; Nrsng.

GERARDI, AMY; Putnam HS; Putnam, CT; (Y); Church Yth Grp; Cmnty Wkr; Hosp Aide; JA; Yrbk Rptr; Yrbk Stf; Im Badmtn; JV Bsktbl; Im Bowling; Im Fld Hcky; Phys Ed.

GERMAN, HEATHER; Valley Regional HS; Chester, CT; (Y); Chorus; Trk; Hon Roll; Intr Dsgn.

GERTNER, ABIGAIL; Guilford HS; Guilford, CT; (Y); Temple Yth Grp; Band; Orch; NHS; Ntl Merit Schol; Rotary Awd; Spanish NHS; Church Yth Grp; Cmnty Wkr; Red Cross Aide; Cornell Bk Awd 85; Amer HS Math Exam 86; Bausch & Lomb Sci Awd 86; Hrvrd; Bio Sci.

GESSECK, STEFANIE LYNN; St Margarets-Mc Ternan HS; Cheshire, CT; (Y); French Clb; Spanish Clb; Chorus; School Musical; Nwsp Ed-Chief; Nwsp Rptr; Sec Trs Stu Cncl; Gym; L Var Vllybl; Hon Roll; Mount Holyoke Coll.

GETSIE, PAMELA; Southington HS; Southington, CT; (Y); 14/600; Am Leg Aux Girls St; Church Yth Grp; Ski Clb; SADD; Trs Frsh Cls; Trs Soph Cls; Sec Stu Cncl; Var Cheerleading; High Hon Roll.

GHIO, BRYAN; Crosby HS; Waterbury, CT; (S); Church Yth Grp; Key Clb; Library Aide; Bsbl; Capt Crs Cntry; Trk; Hon Roll; Trs NHS; Prfct Atten Awd; St Schlr; Math.

GHIROLI, BETH; Branford HS; Branford, CT; (Y); Cmnty Wkr; Yrbk Stf; Hon Roll; Stu Ldr Pgm 85-86; Hlpd Brnfrd Police Wth Yng Stu On Bus 85-86; JR Prm Cmmtee 85-86; Lgl Asst.

GIACCONE, MARY BETH; Guilford HS; Guilford, CT; (Y); 96/300; 4-H; JV Crs Cntry; Var Powder Puff Ftbl; VP Capt Trk; 4-H Awd; High Hon Roll; Hon Roll; Acdmc Excllnc Engl 84; Trdy Kntz Mem Schlrshp 86; Quinnipiac Coll; Acctg.

GIAIMO JR, EDWARD M; North Haven HS; North Haven, CT; (Y); 60/300; Chess Clb; Band; Concert Band; Jazz Band; Mrchg Band; Variety Show; Hon Roll; Outstndng Achvt Musc 83; Electrncs Awd 83; CPR Sci Prgm Cert; U Of CT.

GIANDOMENICO, LAURIE; Berlin HS; Kensington, CT; (Y); 41/204; Powder Puff Ftbl; Tennis; Hon Roll; U Of CT.

GIANNATTASIO, SANDRA; St Mary HS; Old Greenwich, CT; (Y); 23/51; French Clb; Latin Clb; Yrbk Phtg; Yrbk Stf; JV Var Bsktbl; Var Fld Hcky; JV Var Sftbl; Phy Ed, Frnch & Latn 1st & 2nd Hnrs; Psychlgy.

GIANNELLI, DIANE; St Marys HS; New Haven, CT; (Y); 19/110; FBLA; Rep Soph Cls; Rep Jr Cls; JV Bsktbl; Vllybl; High Hon Roll; Hon Roll; Bus Adm.

GIANNELLI, KARA; Southington HS; Southington, CT; (Y); 53/600; Church Yth Grp; Computer Clb; Ski Clb; SADD; School Play; Rep Frsh Cls; Rep Soph Cls; Rep Jr Cls; Crs Cntry; Sftbl; Sftbl Awd 83-84; Bus.

GIANNELLI, MIKE; Southington HS; Southington, CT; (Y); Ski Clb; Trs Sr Cls; Stu Cncl; Wrstlng; Oceanography.

GIANNOTTI, VINCENT T; New Fairfield HS; New Fairfield, CT; (Y); Boy Scts; Church Yth Grp; French Clb; High Hon Roll; SAR Awd; Ordr Arrow 84; Arspc Engrng.

GIARDINA, HOLLY; O H Platt HS; Meriden, CT; (Y); Church Yth Grp; Service Clb; Chorus; Church Choir; Rep Jr Cls; Hon Roll; NHS; Cmnty Wkr; Lit Mag; Brd Ed Rep 86; Stu Drug/Alchl Abuse Comm 86; Shenandoah Coll Music & Dance Summr 84; Northeastern U; Med.

GIBB, JAMES; Greenwich HS; Greenwich, CT; (Y); Computer Clb; French Clb; JA; Key Clb; Varsity Clb; Crs Cntry; Golf; Var L Ice Hcky; JV Socr; U Of MI Ann Arbor; Pdtrcn.

GIBBONS, ANGIE; The Morgan Schl; Clinton, CT; (Y); Band; Color Guard; Mrchg Band; Rep Stu Cncl; Var L Trk; Hon Roll; Hon Roll; Church Yth Grp; Office Aide; Pep Clb; Hnbl Mntn All Shore Line Sccr 86; US Army Mst Vlbl Sccr Plyr Awd 86; Mst Goals Bst Frwrd 84; Wm & Mary; Phys Thrpst.

GIBILISCO, NOELLE; Bristol Central HS; Bristol, CT; (Y); Political Wkr; Sftbl; High Hon Roll; NHS.

GIGUERE, AMY; Manchester HS; Manchester, CT; (Y); 47/521; VP Drama Clb; Hosp Aide; Thesps; Band; Chorus; Church Choir; Concert Band; Mrchg Band; School Musical; School Play; U CT; Cmnctns.

GILBERT, MARK AL; Saint Bernard HS; Waterford, CT; (Y); Camera Clb; Computer Clb; Key Clb; Yrbk Phtg; Swmmng; Hon Roll; 16th Annl CT JR Intrn Prog In Washington DC 86; U Of CT; Bus.

GILBERT, NATALIE; New Britain HS; New Britain, CT; (Y); 10/390; Church Yth Grp; Var Capt Badmtn; High Hon Roll; Hon Roll; NHS; Amer H S Athl 84-85; Excllnc Frnch 84-85; Badmntn Rookie Yr & MVP 84 & 85; Central CT ST U; Math.

GILCHRIST, KRISTIN; Norwalk HS; Norwalk, CT; (Y); French Clb; Trs Key Clb; Jazz Band; Madrigals; Mrchg Band; School Musical; School Play; Nwsp Rptr; Stat Debate Tm; NCTE Awd.

GILDEA, KATHY; Shelton HS; Shelton, CT; (Y); Drama Clb; VP JA; Pres Frsh Cls; Pres Soph Cls; Pres Sr Cls; Stu Cncl; L Bsktbl; Capt Crs Cntry; Capt Trk; Cit Awd; Educ.

GILL, SHARI; Platt HS; Meriden, CT; (Y); Church Yth Grp; Cmnty Wkr; JA; Key Clb; Var Tennis; Hon Roll; All Conf For Grls Tnns 86; Accntng.

GILL, STEPHEN; Ridgefield HS; Ridgefield, CT; (Y); 35/381; Am Leg Boys St; Nwsp Stf; Lit Mag; Tennis; Hon Roll; NHS; Pres Saferides 86-87; Bus Mgr Litrary Mag 85-86; Poly Sci.

GILL, VIRGINIA; Bloomfield HS; Bloomfield, CT; (Y); 12/235; Trs Girl Scts; Church Choir; JV Var Cheerleading; Hon Roll; NHS; Girl Scout Silver Awd 84; Bus.

GILLETT, AMY; Wilton HS; Wilton, CT; (Y); AFS; VP French Clb; Pres Latin Clb; School Play; Ed Yrbk Stf; Lit Mag; Var Crs Cntry; High Hon Roll; NHS; Ntl Merit Ltr; Smith Coll Bk Awd 86; Yrbk Staff Recgntn Awd 86.

GILLETTE, KEVIN; Houstonic Valley Regional HS; Sharon, CT; (Y); Church Yth Grp; Computer Clb; 4-H; Varsity Clb; Variety Show; Lit Mag; Im Badmtn; Im Bsktbl; Im Gym; Var L Trk; Bus Adm.

GILLETTE, MATTHEW; Holy Cross HS; Watertown, CT; (Y); 40/380; Boy Scts; Church Yth Grp; Band; Concert Band; Mrchg Band; Var Ftbl; Var Trk; High Hon Roll; Hon Roll; NHS; Law.

GILLIN, PETER; Kingswood Oxford Schl; Avon, CT; (Y); Pres Debate Tm; Model UN; Spanish Clb; Nwsp Rptr; Rep Jr Cls; Var L Bsktbl; JV Ftbl; Var L Lcrss; Var L Socr; Hon Roll; 1st Yr Awd 83-84.

GILMORE, MELISSA; Foran HS; Milford, CT; (Y); 57/250.

GINSBURG, MITCHELL; Bloomfield HS; East Windsor, CT; (Y); 6/236; Church Yth Grp; VP JA; Model UN; Ski Clb; Yrbk Stf; Capt L Socr; Capt L Tennis; Trs French Hon Soc; High Hon Roll; VP NHS; Schlr-Ath 85-86; Johns Hopkins U; Intl Stud.

GIORDANO, ANTONIETTA; Ansonia HS; Ansonia, CT; (Y); FHA; Hosp Aide; Library Aide; Office Aide; Spanish Clb; Yrbk Bus Mgr; Yrbk Stf; Hon Roll; Spanish NHS; Lry Aid Spclst 86; R Vlntr Svc Awd 83-85; Spnsh Hnr Scty Awd 85-86; Law.

GIORDANO, SARAH; Kolbe Cathedral HS; Bridgeport, CT; (Y); JA; Yrbk Phtg; Yrbk Stf; Var Cheerleading; Var L Sftbl; High Hon Roll; Hon Roll; Treas Bd Achvrs 86-87; Religion Acad Awd 85; Pres Stu Schl Unity 86-87; Math.

GIRARD, KAREN; Granby Memorial HS; W Granby, CT; (Y); Church Yth Grp; Drama Clb; 4-H; Girl Scts; Hosp Aide; Library Aide; Office Aide; Teachers Aide; Band; Church Choir; Hartt Schl Music; Music.

GIRARD, VICTOR; Holy Cross HS; Seymour, CT; (Y); 37/395; Cmnty Wkr; SADD; Teachers Aide; Concert Band; Jazz Band; Mrchg Band; JV Lcrss; High Hon Roll; NHS; Scl Stud Hon Soc 85-86; Outdrs Clb 85-86; Peer Mnstry 86-87; Palmer U; Pre-Med.

GIRAUD, WENDY; Staples HS; Westport, CT; (Y); Art Clb; Cmnty Wkr; PAVAS; Cit Awd; Hon Roll; Ntl Merit Ltr; Westport Wmns Clb Art Scholar 86; Rotary Clb Scholar 86; Staples Tuition Grant Scholar 86; U SC; Grphc Dsgn.

GIUSEFFI, KEELY; Housatonic Valley Regional HS; Sharon, CT; (Y); Pres Soph Cls; JV Badmtn; Im Bsktbl; JV Fld Hcky; Im Sftbl; JV Trk; Im Vllybl; Hon Roll; Med.

GLADSTONE, BETH; Kingswood-Oxford HS; Newington, CT; (Y); Cmnty Wkr; Dance Clb; French Clb; Service Clb; Spanish Clb; Teachers Aide; Temple Yth Grp; Yrbk Stf; Im Gym; Im Ice Hcky; Outstndg Confrmnd 85; Outstndg JR CT Regn Untd Synagogue Yth 86; Abraham Joshua Heschel Hnr Soc.

GLASS, ANTONIO D; R C Lee HS; New Haven, CT; (Y); Chess Clb; Computer Clb; Science Clb; Teachers Aide; Rep Frsh Cls; Rep Jr Cls; Rep Stu Cncl; Electrical Engineering.

GLASS, SYLVESTER W; Kent Schl; Kent, CT; (Y); Aud/Vis; Debate Tm; Spanish Clb; Camera Clb; Chess Clb; Stage Crew; Im Bsktbl; JV Ftbl; Im Tennis; Hon Roll; PSAT/Nmsqt Top 7 Pct 85; Correll U; Comp Sci.

GLATT, BARBARA; The Taft Schl; Carmel, NY; (Y); Hosp Aide; Yrbk Phtg; Var Sftbl; Im Tennis; Var Vllybl; Jobs Pgm Inspctr; Frnch.

GLAZIER, JASON S; William H Hall HS; West Hartford, CT; (Y); 50/331; Pres Computer Clb; Concert Band; Jazz Band; Orch; Symp Band; Nwsp Phtg; Lit Mag; Wt Lftg; JV Wrstlng; High Hon Roll; Hartford Mutual Soc Schlrshp 86; CT ST Schrlshp 86; Johns Hopkins U; Elect Engr.

GLENN, GEOFRY; Shelton HS; Shelton, CT; (Y); Am Leg Boys St; Boy Scts; Church Yth Grp; Cmnty Wkr; Dance Clb; Drama Clb; Exploring; French Clb; Band; Concert Band; Yale Bk Awd; Eagle Scout Awd; Natl Eng Tchrs Awd Wrtng; Sci.

GLENN, JAY; New Haven Co-Op HS; New Haven, CT; (Y); 12/57; Boy Scts; Cmnty Wkr; Ski Clb; Varsity Clb; Nwsp Ed-Chief; Nwsp Rptr; Nwsp Sprt Ed; Yrbk Bus Mgr; Stu Cncl; Var Bsktbl; Engrng.

GLICK, CONNIE; Staples HS; Westport, CT; (Y); Cmnty Wkr; Key Clb; Service Clb; Ski Clb; Teachers Aide; Variety Show; Lit Mag; JV Sftbl; Hon Roll; Lib Arts; Frgn Lang.

GLIDDEN, THOMAS; Manchester HS; Manchester, CT; (Y); Boy Scts; Band; Concert Band; Mrchg Band; Im Var Bsbl; Im Ftbl; Im Socr; Deck-Hockey 81; Navy; Pilot.

GOBELI, CHARLENE; East Lyme HS; E Lyme, CT; (Y); AFS; Ed Key Clb; SADD; Yrbk Stf; Powder Puff Ftbl; Capt Trk; Hon Roll; All Eastern CT Conf Trck Tm 84; All ST Trck Tm 84; Northeastern U; Bio.

GODIN, JENNIFER; Bristol Central HS; Bristol, CT; (Y); Am Leg Aux Girls St; Cmnty Wkr; GAA; VP Ski Clb; Varsity Clb; Ed Yrbk Stf; Pres Soph Cls; Off Jr Cls; Capt Var Trk; Capt Var Vllybl; CT Bus Wk 85; Bristol Peer Edctr 85; Mst Insprtnl Plyr Vlybl Tm 85; Mktg.

GODLEY, MARK; Amity HS; Woodbridge, CT; (S); Am Leg Boys St; French Clb; Var L Bsktbl; Capt L Golf; Hon Roll; Prfct Atten Awd.

GODSIL, MICHELLE; Crosby HS; Waterbury, CT; (Y); DECA; Ski Clb; Hair Stylng.

GOLDBAUM, DAVID; West Haven HS; W Haven, CT; (Y); 28/397; Ski Clb; Band; Concert Band; Mrchg Band; Bsbl; Socr; Hon Roll; Jr NHS; NHS; Steel Drum Band 84-86; Ski Clb 85-86; PA ST U; Mtrlgy.

GOLDBERG, DONNA; New Fairfield HS; New Fairfield, CT; (Y); 19/233; Cmnty Wkr; Drama Clb; Latin Clb; Teachers Aide; Chorus; Stage Crew; French Hon Soc; High Hon Roll; NHS.

GOLDEN, THOMAS MATT; Danbury HS; Danbury, CT; (Y); Art Clb; Boy Scts; Hon Roll; Wslyn U Creative Yth Ctr 85; Artst.

GOLDIN, JOSHUA; Jonathan Law HS; Milford, CT; (Y); VP Camera Clb; Pres VP Computer Clb; Key Clb; SADD; Sec Band; Jazz Band; Nwsp Phtg; Yrbk Phtg; Capt Tennis; JV Trk; U Bridgeport; Comp Eng.

GOLDSMITH, WENDY; Branford HS; Branford, CT; (Y); 13/251; Computer Clb; Capt Color Guard; Yrbk Ed-Chief; Capt Ice Hcky; Hon Roll; NHS; Cntry III Ldr 85-86; MI Tech U; Chem Engrng.

GOLDSTEIN, DEIDRE J; Miss Porters Schl; Woodmere, NY; (Y); Drama Clb; French Clb; Latin Clb; School Musical; Yrbk Ed-Chief; Lit Mag; Stu Cncl; High Hon Roll; Hon Roll; Ntl Merit Ltr; Pre-Med.

GOLDSTEIN, LAURA; Ridgefield HS; Ridgefield, CT; (Y); 29/380; Cmnty Wkr; Off Intnl Clb; Service Clb; Sec Temple Yth Grp; Orch; High Hon Roll; Hon Roll; NHS; Latin Natl Hon Soc 85-86; Exc Advncd Math I 86; Frnch Bk Awd 85; Hist.

GOLDSTEIN, MARK; Norwalk HS; Norwalk, CT; (Y); 35/400; Drama Clb; Chorus; Madrigals; School Musical; School Play; Nwsp Stf; Trs Soph Cls; Pres Jr Cls; Amer Lgn Bys ST 86.

GOLLNICK, LISA; Berlin HS; Berlin, CT; (Y); 17/204; Stage Crew; Var Capt Cheerleading; Mgr(s); JV Vllybl; Hon Roll; NHS; Med.

GOLUB, NEIL; Norwalk HS; Norwalk, CT; (Y); 51/432; Cmnty Wkr; Temple Yth Grp; Orch; Cit Awd; Hon Roll; Pres Schlr; Bd Realters Schrlshp Awd 86; Glazer Found Schrlshp Awd 86; Cert Commendntn 84; U CT; Engrng.

GOMES, KELLY; Crosby HS; Waterbury, CT; (Y); Cmnty Wkr; JA; Key Clb; Latin Clb; Mrchg Band; Rep Frsh Cls; Stu Cncl; Var L Cheerleading; Var L Tennis; Twrlr; Ctznshp Awd 86; Peer Ed 86; Baton Twrlng Miss Mjrt CT; Soc Sci.

GOMOLAK, DEBBIE; Shelton HS; Huntington, CT; (Y); 33/446; VP Drama Clb; Trs SADD; Church Choir; Drill Tm; School Play; Trs VP Stu Cncl; JV Gym; Var Pom Pon; Hon Roll; NHS; H Obrien Ldrshp Awd; Ms Morgan Cnty Fair Queen; Homecmng Princss; Fashn.

GONCALVES, MARIA; Crosby HS; Waterbury, CT; (Y); Church Yth Grp; French Clb; JA; Ski Clb; Variety Show; Stu Cncl; Hon Roll; Rl Est.

GONDAR, KERI; St Joseph HS; Monroe, CT; (Y); Art Clb; Pres Trs Church Yth Grp; Cmnty Wkr; Drama Clb; Spanish Clb; Church Choir; School Musical; School Play; Stage Crew; Nwsp Stf; Accntng.

GONZALEZ, AUREA; Bullard Havens Tech; Stratford, CT; (Y); Girl Scts; Church Choir; Hon Roll; Acctng.

GONZALEZ, CARMEN; Bulkeley HS; Hartford, CT; (Y); Sns Am Revltn Awd 83; Nrsng.

GONZALEZ, EFRAIN; Bullard Havens Tech; Stratford, CT; (Y); Var JV Ftbl.

GONZALEZ, JOHN; Bullard-Havens RVTS HS; Bridgeport, CT; (Y); Hon Roll; Bus.

GONZALEZ, SONIA; Bassick HS; Bridgeport, CT; (Y); 27/200; Church Yth Grp; Cmnty Wkr; Key Clb; Church Choir; Hon Roll; Jr NHS; NHS; Schlstc Achvt Awd 84-85; Ed.

GONZALEZ, VANESSA; Shepaug Valley HS; Bridgewater, CT; (Y); 24/74; Art Clb; Church Yth Grp; French Clb; Spanish Clb; Nwsp Rptr; Stu Cncl; Var Trk; DAR Awd; Hon Roll; Natl Hispnc Schlr Awds Semi-Fnlst 86; Excllnc Art 84 & 85; Art.

GOOCH, JENNIFER; Greenwich HS; Old Greenwich, CT; (Y); Var Socr; Hon Roll; MVP Soccr Tm 85-86; Clark U.

GOOD, KELLY; Danbury HS; Danbury, CT; (Y); ROTC; High Hon Roll; Hon Roll; VFW Awd; Amer Lgn Schltc Achvt Awd 86; AF Acad; Engrng.

GOODRICH, SCOTT; Kingswood-Oxford School; Marlborough, CT; (Y); Aud/Vis; Q&S; Spanish Clb; Stage Crew; Nwsp Sprt Ed; Jr Cls; JV Bsbl; JV Stat Bsktbl; VP Crs Cntry; Hon Roll; Jrnlsm.

GOOLEY, MARK; Shelton HS; Shelton, CT; (Y); 25/322; Quiz Bowl; Ski Clb; Spanish Clb; Im Tennis; Hon Roll; Spanish NHS; Most Improved Stu 86; U Of CT; Business.

GOOLEY, RAYMOND; Fairfield Prep; West Haven, CT; (Y); Church Yth Grp; Spanish Clb; Rep Frsh Cls; JV Capt Bsbl; Hon Roll; NHS; Spanish NHS; Key Club 86-87.

GORALSKI, JOHN; Southington HS; Southington, CT; (Y); Ski Clb; School Play; Var Ftbl; High Hon Roll; Hon Roll; Frnch.

GORDON, CHERI ANN; Stratford HS; Stratford, CT; (Y); 50/257; Trs Church Yth Grp; Cmnty Wkr; Dance Clb; Pres Drama Clb; French Clb; Science Clb; Chorus; Church Choir; School Musical; School Play; CT All State Choir 85; Drama Awd 86; Dnc Awd Jazz, Tap, Ballet 83-86; Performing Arts.

GORDON, JULIE; Bethel HS; Bethel, CT; (Y); 2/248; Am Leg Aux Girls St; Math Tm; Quiz Bowl; Nwsp Ed-Chief; Yrbk Ed-Chief; Var Capt Crs Cntry; NHS; Ntl Merit Schol; Sal; AFS; Hgh O Brn Yth Fndtn Ldrshp Awd 84; CT Intrschlstc Athltc Cnfrnc Schlr-Athlt 86; Bthl Ed Assoc Schlrsp; Marist Coll; Jrnlsm.

GORDON, MARC; Ridgefield HS; Ridgefield, CT; (Y); 243/381; Cmnty Wkr; DECA; Exploring; PTSA Awd Excllnc Phys Ed 86; Natl Rfle Assoc Shrpshtr; Bus Admin.

GORNISH, ALANNA E; William Hall HS; W Hartford, CT; (Y); 85/340; Q&S; Drm Mjr(t); Yrbk Stf; Pom Pon; Hon Roll; Taksar Trphy Encllnc Fgr Sktng 84; Rnnr Up Taksar Trphy 85; US Fgr Sktng Assoc Gld Mdl 86; George Washington U; Comp Sci.

GOSLEE II, JAMES C; Litchfield HS; W Bantam, CT; (Y); 10/86; Art Clb; Debate Tm; Math Tm; Quiz Bowl; Variety Show; Bsbl; Trk; Cit Awd; Hon Roll; NHS; Boston U; Aerospc Engnrng.

GOSSELIN, MICHELLE; Canton HS; Collinsville, CT; (Y); 1/95; Math Tm; Concert Band; Nwsp Sprt Ed; Lit Mag; VP Stu Cncl; Var Bsktbl; Var Crs Cntry; Bausch & Lomb Sci Awd; NHS; Ntl Merit Ltr.

GOSTANIAN, DANIELLE; Ridgefield HS; Ridgefield, CT; (S); 3/394; Sec Trs Art Clb; Debate Tm; Intnl Clb; Temple Yth Grp; Chorus; Orch; School Musical; Lit Mag; High Hon Roll; Excllnce Biol 83-84; JR Sci & Humnties Symp Weselyan U 86; DR.

GOSTYLA, JEFFREY; Berlin HS; Berlin, CT; (Y); 43/183; Am Leg Boys St; Church Yth Grp; Stu Cncl; Bsktbl; Var L Ftbl; Var L Golf; Villanova U; Polit Sci.

GOULET, CHRISTINE M; Mosuk HS; Stevenson, CT; (Y); Cmnty Wkr; French Clb; Lib Chorus; Nwsp Stf; Hon Roll; Eastern CT ST U; Elem Educ.

GOUTHRO, LAURA; Bristol Central HS; Forestville, CT; (Y); #8 In Class; GAA; Rep Stu Cncl; Capt Var Sftbl; Var Capt Swmmng; High Hon Roll; NHS; Class L ST Champn Sftbl Tm Mdl 85.

GOZZO, PATRICIA; Berlin HS; Kensington, CT; (Y); GAA; Varsity Clb; Yrbk Stf; Trs Stu Cncl; Var Capt Bsktbl; Powder Puff Ftbl; Sftbl; Var Capt Vllybl; Cncl Of Yth 86; Stu Cncl Rep 85-86; Athltc Awd Bsktbl & Vlybl 84-86; U Of RI; Bus.

GRABSCH, LAURA; Mark T Sheehan HS; Wallingford, CT; (Y); 3/200; German Clb; High Hon Roll.

GRABSKI, STEPHEN; East Catholic HS; Somers, CT; (Y); JV Crs Cntry; Var Capt Swmmng; JV Trk; Hon Roll; Jr NHS; Athlt Of Seasn-Fels-Schl 86; All ST & All HCC Swmmr 86; Engrng.

GRACE, CLAUDIA; St Josephs HS; Trumbull, CT; (Y); Art Clb; JA; Rep Spanish Clb; JV Crs Cntry; JV Var Trk; Gldn Awd 86; Hnbl Mntn Poetry, Art Awd 85; Paier Coll Art; Intr Dec.

GRACE JR, EDMUND M; Holy Cross HS; Beacon Falls, CT; (Y); 26/347; Boy Scts; Service Clb; Ed Lit Mag; NHS; Drama Clb; French Clb; Political Wkr; Science Clb; Stage Crew; High Hon Roll; Soc Sci Fair Comp 1st Pl 84-85; Boston U; Comp Sci.

GRACE, KATHY; South Windsor HS; S Windsor, CT; (Y); 74/300; Hosp Aide; Office Aide; Ski Clb; Chorus; Nwsp Stf; Yrbk Stf; Var Capt Bsktbl; Var Capt Fld Hcky; Var Capt Sftbl; Hon Roll; All Conf Plyr-Fld Hockey 85; U Of CT All Star Fld Hockey 85 & 86.

GRADOWSKI, MICHAEL; Torrington HS; Torrington, CT; (Y); 72/284; Ski Clb; Varsity Clb; Var L Socr; Var L Swmmng; JV Trk; Hon Roll; Bus.

GRADY, AMY; New Fairfield HS; New Fairfld, CT; (Y); 52/225; Sec Computer Clb; DECA; Pres JA; Im Bsktbl; JV Fld Hcky; AFS; Latin Clb; Political Wkr; Chorus; School Musical; Jr Achvt Achvr Of Yr 86; Natl Jr Achvt Conf Delf 85 & 86; DECA Natl Conf Fnlst 86; U CT; Bus Mgmt.

GRADY, DIANE; Sacred Heart Acad; Wallingford, CT; (Y); Pres FBLA; Pro Lf Clb 85-86; Brianwood Bk Awd 85-86; Pres FBLA 86-87; Chrprsn JR SR Fstvty 85-86; Bus Math.

GRADY, TRICIA; Holy Cross HS; Middlebury, CT; (Y); Chorus; School Musical; Hon Roll.

GRAHAM, DIANE; Old Saybrook SR HS; Old Saybrook, CT; (Y); AFS; Drama Clb; SADD; Chorus; School Musical; Stu Cncl; Tennis; Hon Roll; Outstndng Achvt, Grade Math 86; CT Smr Intrn Pgm WA DC 86.

GRAHAM, JENNIFER; Berlin HS; Berlin, CT; (Y); 20/204; Service Clb; Hst Stu Cncl; Powder Puff Ftbl; Hon Roll; NHS; Comm Arts.

GRAN, JEFF; Waterford HS; Waterford, CT; (Y); Ftbl; Wrstlng; Excllnce Awd 86; Diesel Mechnc.

GRANDE, ELIZABETH; Newington HS; Newington, CT; (Y); 20/365; Church Yth Grp; Var Gym; Var Capt Socr; Var Capt Trk; Hon Roll; NHS; Treas Safe Rides 85-86; Schlr Athlete 86; Fairfield U; Math.

GRANDE JR, PHILIP W; West Haven HS; W Haven, CT; (Y); 1/400; Am Leg Boys St; Aud/Vis; Q&S; Scholastic Bowl; Band; Nwsp Ed-Chief; Pres Frsh Cls; JV Swmmng; High Hon Roll; NEDT Awd; Physcs Clb-Pres 85-86; Med.

GRANFORS, GAIL; Masok HS; Monroe, CT; (Y); VP Church Yth Grp; Hosp Aide; Spanish Clb; Ed Nwsp Stf; Mgr(s); Vllybl; Hon Roll; Gettysburg Coll; Bus Mgmnt.

GRANITTO, JOSEPH; W F Kaynor Technical Schl; Waterbury, CT; (Y); SADD; Yrbk Stf; Stu Cncl; JV Var Socr; High Hon Roll; Hon Roll; Am Lgn Awd Dstngshd Achvmnt 83; Elect.

GRANT, BETH; Berlin HS; Kensington, CT; (Y); 104/208; Band; Mrchg Band; Stat Im Bsktbl; JV Var Mgr(s); Powder Puff Ftbl; Score Keeper; Swmmng; Timer; Soclgy.

GRANT, JEANNE; Robert E Gitch HS; Groton, CT; (Y); Girl Scts; Capt Flag Corp; Mrchg Band; Hon Roll; George Washington U; Math.

GRANT, KATHY; New Fairfield HS; New Fairfield, CT; (Y); Pres Church Yth Grp; Drama Clb; Sec Girl Scts; Chorus; Church Choir; School Musical; School Play; U CT; Physcl Ther.

GRANT, RUTH; Norwich Free Acad; N Franklin, CT; (Y); Varsity Clb; Var L Bsktbl; Var Trk; Eastern Ct ST U.

GRANT, TARA; Holy Cross HS; Wolcott, CT; (Y); 78/380; Chorus; Hon Roll; Fine Arts Clb 85-86; Outdrs Clb 85-86; Lwyr.

GRASSO, CHRISTINA; Norwalk HS; Norwalk, CT; (Y); Am Leg Aux Girls St; GAA; Rep Frsh Cls; Rep Soph Cls; Trs Jr Cls; Pres Sr Cls; Powder Puff Ftbl; JV Var Sftbl; JV Vllybl; Hon Roll.

GRASSO, LISA M; East Hartford HS; E Hartford, CT; (Y); 103/348; Spanish Clb; Rep Jr Cls; Hon Roll; Central CT ST U; Acctg.

GRASWALD, RICHARD; Stratford HS; Stratford, CT; (Y); Var Bsbl; Var Ftbl; Var Golf; Prfct Atten Awd; U Of Maryland; Physcl Educ.

GRATRIX, ELAINE M; Trumbull HS; Trumbull, CT; (Y); Girl Scts; Spanish Clb; Church Choir; Nwsp Rptr; Var Fld Hcky; Var Sftbl; High Hon Roll; NHS; Spanish NHS; Church Yth Grp; Excllnc Art 84; Grl Sct Slvr Awd 85; Outstndng Achvt Wrtg 86.

GRATRIX, KAREN A; Trumbull HS; Trumbull, CT; (Y); Church Yth Grp; Girl Scts; Spanish Clb; Church Choir; Nwsp Rptr; Var Fld Hcky; Var Sftbl; High Hon Roll; NHS; Spanish NHS; Grl Sct Slvr Ldrshp Awd & Slvr Awd 85; Outstndng Achvt In Wrtng 86.

GRAVELLE, SHERRY; Bristol Central HS; Bristol, CT; (Y); Exploring; Library Aide; Band; Concert Band; Mrchg Band; Stu Cncl; Crs Cntry; Mgr(s); High Hon Roll; Hon Roll; Awd Intrn For City SR Ctr 86; Central CT ST U; Elem Educ.

GRAVES, CAMERON; Greenwich HS; Riverside, CT; (Y); Am Leg Aux Girls St; Art Clb; Church Yth Grp; PAVAS; Service Clb; Spanish Clb; SADD; Variety Show; Rep Stu Cncl; Capt Cheerleading; Congrssnl Art Comptn 85; Greenwich Art Soc Scholar Awd 86; Skidmore Book Awd 85; Princeton U; Engl.

GRAVES, DAVID; Southington HS; Plantsvill, CT; (Y); Boy Scts; Church Yth Grp; Band; Chorus; Church Choir; School Musical; School Play; Engr.

GRAVES, SHELLEY; St Bernard HS; Norwich, CT; (Y); 30/289; Library Aide; Rep Jr Cls; Hon Roll; Patrolmns Assoc Schlrp 86; Intl All-Amer Awd 85; U CT; Psychol.

GRAY, DIAN; Guilford HS; Brooklyn, NY; (Y); 10/317; Cmnty Wkr; High Hon Roll; NHS; Spanish NHS; Latin Hnr Soc 84; Spn Iii Awd 85; Wesleyan U; Pre Med.

GRAY, DONNA; Southington HS; Southington, CT; (Y); 241/600; School Play; Stage Crew; Nwsp Stf; Yrbk Stf; Lit Mag; Var JV Fld Hcky; Hon Roll; Ski Clb; Chorus; Acknwldgmt Awds Arts Cncl 83-85; Cert Partcptn CT Stdnt Plywrghts Comptn 86; Engl.

GRAY, JIMMIE; Griswold HS; Jewett City, CT; (Y); Church Yth Grp; Concert Band; Jazz Band; Mrchg Band; Orch; Pep Band; School Musical; Symp Band; Trk; NHS; All Eastern H S Bnd 85 & 86; Phila Coll Of Bible; Music.

GRAZIANO, KIM; Holy Cross HS; Oakville, CT; (Y); Cmnty Wkr; Hosp Aide; Flagler; Fashion.

GRAZIOSO, CLAUDIA; Hopkins Day Prospect Hill Schl; New Haven, CT; (S); Ed Yrbk Stf; Ed Lit Mag; Teen Connection; SHARE; Maroon Key Schl Svc Grp; Discplnry Comm; SR Afflts; Law.

GRECO, JOYCE; Crosby HS; Waterbury, CT; (Y); JA; Library Aide; Chorus; Stage Crew; Hon Roll; NHS; Sec Studies Awd Sacred Heart U 86; Piano Achvt Awd 86; 042; Accntng.

GRECO, NOELLE; Sacred Heart Acad; Hamden, CT; (Y); 10/100; Church Yth Grp; Cmnty Wkr; Dance Clb; French Clb; Ski Clb; Stage Crew; Nwsp Rptr; Crs Cntry; Tennis; High Hon Roll.

GRECO, SUSAN; Shelton HS; Shelton, CT; (Y); Drama Clb; French Clb; Ski Clb; Stu Cncl; French Hon Soc; Hon Roll; U Of CT; Law.

GREELEY, LEONORA; Sacred Heart Acad; Orange, CT; (Y); Computer Clb; Variety Show; Yrbk Phtg; Im Vllybl; NEDT Awd; Ntl Sci Olympiad 86; Prolife Clb 84-87; Zoolgy.

GREEN, ALFRED L; Bullard-Havens Tech; Bridgeport, CT; (Y); High Hon Roll; Hon Roll; ROTC; Elctrncs.

GREEN, HOLCOMBE; The Taft Schl; Atlanta, GA; (Y); Golf; Wrstlng; Ntl Merit Ltr.

GREEN, KELLY; Choate Rosemary Hall; Wallingford, CT; (Y); Camera Clb; GAA; JA; Latin Clb; Pep Clb; Varsity Clb; Yrbk Stf; Fld Hcky; Ice Hcky; Lcrss; Walter B Welch Schlrshp 85-86; Julle M Case Prize 83; Outstndng Perfmnce Field Hockey 83; Dartmouth; Pediatrician.

GREEN, LARA; Derby HS; Derby, CT; (Y); Debate Tm; FHA; Girl Scts; JA; Pep Clb; Craftworks FHA Conf 85; Mattatuck CC; Secry.

GREEN, TERESA; Richard C Lee HS; New Haven, CT; (Y); Church Yth Grp; Computer Clb; JA; Office Aide; Church Choir; Off Frsh Cls; Off Soph Cls; Stu Cncl; Hon Roll; Prfct Atten Awd; Quinnipiac Coll; Nrsng.

GREENE, BELINDA; Bassick HS; Bridgeport, CT; (Y); Hosp Aide; Teachers Aide; Color Guard; Drm Mjr(t); Mrchg Band; Nwsp Rptr; VP Jr Cls; Hon Roll; Band; Nwsp Stf; Am Hmcmng Queen USA CT Rep 85; Cert Nrsng Assist Awd & Cert 86; Chld Care Pgm 86; Sacred Heart U; Nrsng.

GREENE, CHRIS; East Catholic HS; Manchester, CT; (Y); 71/289; Quiz Bowl; JV Bsbl; Hon Roll; Accntng.

GREENE, LAUREN; St Josephs HS; Huntington, CT; (Y); Cmnty Wkr; Teachers Aide; Chorus; Church Choir; Paint Exhbt 83; Fnlst Miss Natl Teen Pgnt 85; Lwyr.

GREENHAGEN, SONIA; East Lyme HS; E Lyme, CT; (Y); Chorus; Color Guard; Flag Corp; Mrchg Band; High Hon Roll; Hon Roll; Bus Adm.

GREENSPAN, MELISSA; Andrew Warde HS; Fairfield, CT; (Y); Thesps; School Play; Yrbk Stf; Hon Roll; NHS; Dance Clb; Drama Clb; Key Clb; Spanish NHS; Bst Stu Actrss Awd 83-85; NY U; Thtre.

GREENWOOD, WENDY; Windham HS; Willimantic, CT; (Y); Hosp Aide; SADD; School Musical; Var L Fld Hcky; Hon Roll; Outstndng Achvt US Hstry 86; Pre-Law.

GREGORY, CARRIE; Robert E Fitche SR HS; Mystic, CT; (Y); Varsity Clb; Variety Show; Yrbk Stf; Var L Crs Cntry; Im Powder Puff Ftbl; Stat Score Keeper; JV Trk; Im Wt Lftg; Hon Roll; Mst Imprvd Plyr Awd Crs Cntry 86.

GREGORY, CHRISTOPHER; Seymour HS; Seymour, CT; (Y); Church Yth Grp; Teachers Aide; Hon Roll; Blk Belt In Karate 86; Pre-Law.

GREY, DELANDRA; James Hillhouse HS; New Haven, CT; (Y); Trk; Var Vllybl; NHS; Prfct Atten Awd; Compu Sci.

GRIEDER, JAMES; Morgan HS; Clinton, CT; (Y); Yrbk Phtg; Ftbl; Var Capt Wrstlng; Hon Roll; Sports Mgmt.

GRIFFIN, ED; South Windsor HS; S Windsor, CT; (Y); 87/300; Cmnty Wkr; 4-H; Political Wkr; Ski Clb; Varsity Clb; Rep Soph Cls; Var L Golf; Western New England Coll; Engr.

GRIFFIN, NEAL DAVID; Canterbury Schl; Brookfield Ctr, CT; (Y); Yrbk Stf; Stu Cncl; Var Bsbl; Var Bsktbl; Var Ftbl; U Of PA; Finance.

GRIFFITHS, BRIGITTE; Greenwich HS; Greenwich, CT; (Y); AFS; French Clb; Ski Clb; Spanish Clb; Stat Lcrss; Mgr(s); Score Keeper; French Hon Soc; Spanish NHS; Intl Bus.

GRIFFITHS, RICHARD; Guilford HS; Guilford, CT; (Y); 12/350; Church Yth Grp; Drama Clb; School Musical; School Play; Stage Crew; French Hon Soc; High Hon Roll; NHS; Ntl Merit SF; Prncpls Awd Acad Excllnce 80; Sci Awd 83; Med.

GRIMALDI, HEATHER; Southington HS; Southington, CT; (Y); Pep Clb; Ski Clb; Color Guard; Jazz Band; Mrchg Band; School Play; Variety Show; Stu Cncl; Cheerleading; Trk.

GRIMM, A; Guilford HS; Guilford, CT; (Y); Church Yth Grp; Dance Clb; Sftbl; Var Trk; Hon Roll; Hotel Mgr.

GRIMSHAW, TINA; Killingly HS; Rogers, CT; (Y); French Clb; Office Aide; SADD; Nwsp Rptr; Nwsp Stf; Yrbk Ed-Chief; Yrbk Stf; Score Keeper; Sftbl; Trk; Outstndng Bus Awd 85; Yuth Vlntr In Action 86-87; Journalism.

GRINDROD, SHANNON; Emmet O Brien RVTS HS; Seymour, CT; (Y); Church Yth Grp; Cmnty Wkr; Sec JA; Library Aide; Trs Stu Cncl; Sftbl; Vllybl; Wt Lftg; High Hon Roll; Hon Roll; Med.

GRISGRABER, DARYL; Watertown HS; Watertown, CT; (Y); 3/215; VP AFS; Pres French Clb; Yrbk Stf; Stu Cncl; Var Fld Hcky; Var Trk; NHS; Ntl Merit Ltr; Amer Legn Schlr Fld Hcky 85; Mst Outstndg Defensive Plyr Fld Hcky 85; CT Coll; French.

GROHE, PAMELA; Joseph A Foran HS; Milford, CT; (Y); 1/250; VP JCL; Keywanettes; Capt Color Guard; VP Soph Cls; Rep Stu Cncl; High Hon Roll; Sec NHS; Church Yth Grp; Drama Clb; Girl Scts; Hugh O Brian Yth Fndtn Ldrshp Sem 85; Harvard Bk Awd 86; Awd For Excllnc In Engl I, II, Wrting, Latin; Econ.

GROSS, CHRISTOPHER M; Brookfield HS; Brookfield, CT; (Y); Cmnty Wkr; Drama Clb; Science Clb; School Play; VP Stu Cncl; JV Trk; High Hon Roll; WPT; Mgmt Engrng.

GROTH, KATHLEEN; O H Platt HS; Meriden, CT; (Y); 4/239; Civic Clb; French Clb; Science Clb; Chorus; High Hon Roll; Hcks Mdlst 2nd Plc Essy Cntst 86; Art Exhbtns Incldg 1 Prsn Exhbtn 85-86; Ctrl CT ST U; Phrmcy.

GROVE, GLEN; North Haven HS; North Haven, CT; (Y); 95/280; Var JV Bsbl; Var JV Bsktbl; Hon Roll.

GROW, TOM S; South Kent HS; Chatham, NJ; (Y); Model UN; Service Clb; Spanish Clb; SADD; Varsity Clb; Nwsp Stf; Var Bsbl; Var Ftbl; High Hon Roll; NHS; Covetd Bell Achvt Awd-Sci 84; PSYCHIATRY.

GRUNBECK, ALICE; N Branford HS; Northford, CT; (Y); 15/154; Church Yth Grp; SADD; Yrbk Stf; Stu Cncl; Bsktbl; Fld Hcky; Powder Puff Ftbl; Sftbl; High Hon Roll; NHS; Merrimack Coll; Comp Engr.

GRYK, MICHAEL; St Thomas Aquinas HS; New Britain, CT; (Y); 2/154; Drama Clb; Im Golf; Bausch & Lomb Sci Awd; NHS; Ntl Merit Ltr; Pres Schlr; Sal; Chess Clb; Math Tm; Spanish Clb; Bruce H Mhn Schlrshp 86; CT ST Cncl Knghts Of Clmbs Schlrshp 86; New Brtn Dnry Schlrshp 86; U Of CT; Math.

GRZYBOWSKI, DONALD; Southington HS; Plantsville, CT; (Y); 81/625; Church Yth Grp; French Clb; Key Clb; Ski Clb; Band; Concert Band; Mrchg Band; Bsbl; Socr; High Hon Roll; MA Inst Tech; Aero Sp Engr.

GUERIN, PATTY; Holy Cross HS; Watertown, CT; (Y); 66/380; Art Clb; Church Yth Grp; Science Clb; Hon Roll; NHS; Pol Sci.

GUETZLOFF, TOM; Trumbull HS; Trumbull, CT; (Y); Church Yth Grp; Variety Show; Ftbl; Trk; Hon Roll; Ray Meyars Athletic Awd 86; Booster Clb Awd 86; All ST Defnsv End 85-86; St Norberts Coll; Sci.

GUGLIETTA, LISA; Trumbull HS; Trumbull, CT; (Y); French Clb; VP JA; Nwsp Stf; JV Bsktbl; Var Capt Socr; Var Sftbl; French Hon Soc; High Hon Roll; Hon Roll; Gldn Glv Awd 84; Rookie Of Yr 83; Mst Dedicated Plyr Sftbl 83; Prvdnc Coll; Jrnlsm.

GUIDI, CHRISTINA MARIE; The Morgan HS; Clinton, CT; (Y); 4/155; Am Leg Aux Girls St; Chorus; Yrbk Ed-Chief; Trs Soph Cls; Stat Bsktbl; JV Var Fld Hcky; High Hon Roll; Hon Roll; Jr NHS; NHS; CT Hnr Smnr Dy Dstngshd HS Stu 86; Bld Mbl Rd Crs Co Chrmn 87.

GUIEL, MINDY; Enrico Fermi HS; Enfield, CT; (Y); 69/300; Drama Clb; FBLA; Spanish Clb; Color Guard; Drm & Bgl; Drm Mjr(t); Yrbk Stf; Sr Cls; Bsktbl; JV Sftbl; Schlrp O Meara Fndtn 86; U CT; Pharm.

GUILD, ROGER; Vinal Regional Vo Tech; Haddam, CT; (Y); Ski Clb; Rep Frsh Cls; Rep Soph Cls; Rep Stu Cncl; JV Var Bsbl; Bsktbl; Var High Hon Roll; Var Hon Roll; CO ST.

GUINNESS, WILLIAM; Nathan Hale-Ray HS; E Haddam, CT; (Y); 15/58; Am Leg Boys St; Stage Crew; High Hon Roll; Hon Roll.

GUITE, JESSICA; Newington HS; Newington, CT; (S); Church Yth Grp; Hosp Aide; Key Clb; SADD; Teachers Aide; Madrigals; Orch; School Musical; Var Socr; Var Sftbl.

GUITERRERZ, MARGARITA; Stamford HS; Stamford, CT; (Y); French Clb; Crs Cntry; Trk; Jr NHS; Trck Coaches Awd, 3rd Crss Cntry 84; Michaelson Mem Trphy, Medl 85-86; U CT; Frnch.

GULICK, SHANNON; Nonnewaug HS; Woodbury, CT; (Y); Pep Clb; Varsity Clb; Stage Crew; Im Bsktbl; Var Capt Socr; Im Tennis; Im Vllybl; Hon Roll; Acadmc Achvmnt Awd In Arch Drwng 85-86; Acadmc Achvmnt Awd In Tech Drwng 84; Arch.

GULIUZZA, DAVID; Seymour HS; Seymour, CT; (Y); 72/184; Computer Clb; Drama Clb; JA; School Play; Stu Cncl; Persnlty Of Yr 86; Mattatuck CC; Food Mgmt.

GUNNING, KELLY A; Sacred Heart Acad; W Haven, CT; (Y); 47/122; Cmnty Wkr; FNA; Girl Scts; Hosp Aide; Pep Clb; Hon Roll; NHS; Scrd Hrt Acad Endwmnt Schlrshp 85; W Haven Cmbr Cmmrc Schlrshp 86; W Haven Indpndnt Insrs Schlr 86; U Of CT; Nrsng.

GUNTHER, BRENDAN; Jonathan Law HS; Milford, CT; (Y); Boy Scts; Intnl Clb; Latin Clb; Capt L Diving; Var Socr; Var Capt Swmmng; Douglas Romanchic Schlrshp Outstndng Ath & Acad 86; U CT; Comp Sci.

GUPTA, ANUJ; Glastonbury HS; Glastonbury, CT; (Y); 8/413; Pres Computer Clb; VP Debate Tm; Var Math Tm; High Hon Roll; NHS; Latin Natl Hnr Soc 83-8; Peer Tutoring 82-86; Dartmouth Coll; Med.

GUPTA, APARNA; The Hotchkiss Schl; Releigh, NC; (Y); French Clb; Orch; Nwsp Sprt Ed; Yrbk Stf; Lit Mag; Stu Cncl; JV Fld Hcky; Hon Roll; 9th Grd Math Awd 82-83; MIT; Comp Sci.

GUPTA, JULIE; Greenwich HS; Greenwich, CT; (Y); Am Leg Aux Girls St; Red Cross Aide; Science Clb; VP Service Clb; Chorus; School Musical; High Hon Roll; NHS; Ntl Merit SF; Spanish NHS; Black Hist Mnth Essay Awd 86; Outstndng Math Achvt Awd 86; Ntl Sci League Awd 86; Sci.

GUSTAFSON, BRITT; Manchester HS; Manchester, CT; (Y); 62/565; AFS; Church Yth Grp; FBLA; Spanish Clb; Stage Crew; Nwsp Ed-Chief; Yrbk Stf; Stu Cncl; Var Fld Hcky; JV Trk; Achvt Awd 86; Cmmnctns.

GUTFRAN, CORINNE; Simsbury HS; W Simsbury, CT; (Y); Church Choir; Yrbk Stf; JV Socr; Hon Roll; Bus Adm.

GUTIERREZ, ALINA; Killingly HS; Brooklyn, CT; (Y); 11/275; 4-H; Girl Scts; Red Cross Aide; Ski Clb; Varsity Clb; Band; Yrbk Stf; Stu Cncl; Var Bsktbl; Var Capt Fld Hcky; Slvr Awd 2nd Hghst Awd Grl Scts, Hghst Aver Awds Math 84, Spnsh 86; Math.

GUTTMANN, LILIAN; Staples HS; Westport, CT; (Y); Office Aide; SADD; Teachers Aide; Temple Yth Grp; Chorus; Hon Roll.

GUY, JUDITH; Westover Schl; Waterbury, CT; (Y); Dance Clb; VP Drama Clb; FHA; Latin Clb; Model UN; Pres Spanish Clb; JV Sftbl; High Hon Roll; Hon Roll; Natl Latin Awd 84; Awd Being Outstndg Dance 86; CT Coll; Cmmnctns.

GUZAUCKAS, JEFFREY; Southington HS; Southington, CT; (Y); 92/600; Band; Concert Band; Jazz Band; Mrchg Band; Var Computer Clb; Var Swmmng; Var Trk; N E Sccr Clb For Intl Play 86.

GUZZARDI, FRANK; Holy Cross HS; Waterbury, CT; (Y); 131/400; Church Yth Grp; Hon Roll; Soc Stds Hon Soc 85-86.

HAACK, AMY; Manchester HS; Mancester, CT; (Y); AFS; Drama Clb; French Clb; Hosp Aide; Orch; Swmmng; Instrctrs Of The Handicapped 85-86; PSYCH.

HABB, LATEEF; Central Catholic HS; Darien, CT; (Y); 1/82; Drama Clb; French Clb; Math Tm; Yrbk Stf; Lit Mag; Stu Cncl; Var Trk; French Hon Soc; High Hon Roll; NHS; Boston Coll; Med.

HABER, PAMELA H; Bloomfield HS; Bloomfield, CT; (Y); 17/250; JA; Spanish Clb; Temple Yth Grp; Hon Roll; NHS; Spanish NHS; Co Pres Of Spnsh Natl Hnr Soc 86; Union Coll; Finance.

HACHTEN, PAUL C; Guilford HS; Guilford, CT; (Y); Red Cross Aide; SADD; Var L Tennis; High Hon Roll; Safe Rides Vlntr 84-86; Genrl Excllnc Lang Arts Awd 86; Worcester Polytechnic; Bio Med.

HADDAD, WILLIAM; Windham HS; Willimantic, CT; (Y); Am Leg Boys St; Math Clb; Yrbk Stf; Rep Jr Cls; Trs Sr Cls; Var L Bsktbl; High Hon Roll; Mu Alp Tht; NHS; Athl Cncl; Med.

HADFIELD, ANDREW; Plainfield HS; Moosup, CT; (Y); 16/160; Church Yth Grp; VP Frsh Cls; VP Soph Cls; VP Jr Cls; Stu Cncl; Bsktbl; Ftbl; Golf; Hon Roll; Forestry.

HADMAN, JULIA; Vinal Regional Vo Tech; Cromwell, CT; (Y); 5/160; JA; Keywanettes; Nwsp Stf; Yrbk Stf; Sec Soph Cls; Sec Jr Cls; VP Stu Cncl; High Hon Roll; Hon Roll; NHS; U Of ME Machias; Marine Bio.

HAGEMAN, MARGARET; Lauralton Hall HS; Trumbull, CT; (Y); 16/111; Art Clb; Cmnty Wkr; Debate Tm; Intnl Clb; Model UN; Nwsp Stf; Lit Mag; NHS; Drama Clb; French Clb; Ntl Latn Awd 83-85; Thtre Co 84-86; Schlrshp Geo Wash U 86; Frgn Lang.

HALABY, KIM; Trumbull HS; Trumbull, CT; (Y); Chorus; Lit Mag; VP Frsh Cls; Trs Sr Cls; Co-Capt Cheerleading; Var Co-Capt Tennis; French Hon Soc; High Hon Roll; NHS; Peer Tutor 85-86.

HALBERT, LARA; Stratford HS; Ridgefield, CT; (Y); 8/230; VP Drama Clb; Ski Clb; Variety Show; Nwsp Rptr; Yrbk Stf; Off Stu Cncl; Capt Pom Pon; High Hon Roll; NHS; Boston U; Brdcst Jrnlst.

HALBROOKS, J F; Plainfield HS; Sterling, CT; (Y); 4/200; Am Leg Boys St; Cmnty Wkr; Model UN; JV Bsbl; Bausch & Lomb Sci Awd; High Hon Roll; NHS; Voice Dem Awd; Outstndng Achvt Comp Pgmg 86; Achvt In Chem 86; Excllnc In Advncd Mth 86.

HALE, CHRIS; Nonnewaug HS; Ansonia, CT; (Y); FFA; Var Bsbl; JV Wrstlng; Hon Roll; Vet.

HALES, SCOTT; New Fairfield HS; New Fairfield, CT; (Y); 2/249; Church Yth Grp; Scholastic Bowl; Pres Jr Cls; Var Capt Bsktbl; JV Var Socr; High Hon Roll; Pres NHS; Ntl Merit Ltr; St Schlr; CT JR Sci & Hmnts Sympsm Schl Dlgt 86; Acctng & Bus.

HALEY, MICHAEL; Fairfield Coll Prep; Milford, CT; (Y); Church Yth Grp; Hosp Aide; Pep Clb; JV Bsbl; Im Bsktbl; Var JV Socr; Prfct Atten Awd; Psych.

HALL, JENNIFER; Lyme-Old Lyme HS; Old Lyme, CT; (Y); Ski Clb; Yrbk Phtg; Yrbk Stf; Socr; JV Tennis; Var Trk; Phtgrphy.

HALL, LINDA; Staples HS; Westport, CT; (Y); Rptr Aud/Vis; Church Yth Grp; Library Aide; Radio Clb; SADD; Chorus; Orch; Nwsp Rptr; Hon Roll; Ntl Excllnc-Wrtg Cont 86; Brdcst Jrnlsm.

HALOTEK, CHRISTOPHER; Wethersfield HS; Wethersfield, CT; (Y); Cmnty Wkr; Ski Clb; Im Badmtn; Var Bsbl; Var Socr; Hon Roll; Sci.

HALSTEAD, SCOTT; Mark T Sheehan HS; Wallingford, CT; (Y); 13/212; AFS; German Clb; Scholastic Bowl; Off Frsh Cls; Bsktbl; Hon Roll; Bus Admn.

HAMES, MARY ELLEN; Shelton HS; Shelton, CT; (Y); Drama Clb; JA; Key Clb; Ski Clb; Spanish Clb; SADD; Rep Stu Cncl; JV Capt Cheerleading; Crs Cntry; Trk; Homecmng Qn 83; Boston Coll; Mrktng.

HAMILTON, DENNIS; Avon Old Farms HS; New Britain, CT; (Y); 4/101; Art Clb; Nwsp Stf; Lit Mag; Var Diving; Var Socr; High Hon Roll; Cum Laude Soc 86; Pres Acad Ftnss Awd 86; Fndrs Mdl 86; Tufts U; Lbrl Arts.

HAMILTON, JENNIFER; Lauralton Hall HS; Stratford, CT; (Y); GAA; Model UN; Pep Clb; Service Clb; SADD; School Play; Var L Cheerleading; ST Diving Qlfr CCIAC Fin 84-86; Econ.

HAMM, DOUGLAS; Andrew Warde HS; Fairfield, CT; (Y); AFS; Boy Scts; Trs Church Yth Grp; Trk; Hon Roll; Hon Ushr Grad 86; NASTAR Gld Mtl 86.

HAMMETT, PAULA; Windham HS; Windham, CT; (Y); High Hon Roll; Hon Roll; Ltn Awd 86; Quinnipiac Coll; Bio.

HANKINS, JAMES L; Notre Dame Catholic HS; Fairfield, CT; (Y); 126/227; Boy Scts; Key Clb; JV Bsktbl; Var Capt Crs Cntry; Var Trk; High Hon Roll; Hon Roll; Eagle Scout 86; Syrcs U; Cvl Engrng.

HANKOVSZKY, PETER; Danbury HS; Danbury, CT; (Y); 39/474; Ski Clb; Socr; Tennis; Wt Lftg; Hon Roll; Perry Awd Math 85; Engrng.

HANNAN JR, RAYMOND T; Notre Dame HS; W Haven, CT; (Y); 33/235; Church Yth Grp; Debate Tm; Concert Band; Jazz Band; Mrchg Band; Orch; Lit Mag; High Hon Roll; NHS; Ntl Merit Ltr; Harry Berman Mus Awd 86; Am Mus Fndtn Band Hnrs 85; Trinity Coll; Hist.

HANRAHAN, CATHERINE; New London HS; New London, CT; (S); DECA; Key Clb; Variety Show; VP Jr Cls; Stat Socr; Var Trk; U Of RI; Sclgy.

HANRATTY, MARK G; Greenwich HS; Greenwich, CT; (Y); 81/731; Am Leg Boys St; Radio Clb; Nwsp Rptr; Yrbk Stf; Hon Roll; NHS; Amax Inc Earth Sci Awd 86; New Lebanon Schl PTA Awd 86; Fordham U; Fin.

HANSCOM, DAN; W F Kaynor Regional Vo Tech; Naugatuck, CT; (Y); Boy Scts; Drama Clb; JA; VICA; Hon Roll; Tech Coll; Drftng.

HANSEN, JAMES C; Ellat Grasso-SE Reg Voc Tech Schl; Groton, CT; (Y); 17/165; Church Yth Grp; Cmnty Wkr; Debate Tm; Pep Clb; Service Clb; SADD; Pres VICA; Rep Stu Cncl; High Hon Roll; NHS; Mst Outstdng Bus Tu 84 & 86; Mst Imprvd Math Stu 86; Johnson & Wales Coll; Htl Mgmt.

HANSEN, KARIN; Miss Porters Schl; Greenwich, CT; (Y); Hosp Aide; Intnl Clb; Math Tm; Var Badmtn; JV Lcrss; High Hon Roll; Hon Roll; Ntl Merit Ltr; Cum Laude 86; Wellesly Coll Bk Awd 86; CT Chemathon 1st Pl 85.

HANSEN, MARTHA; Hamden HS; Hamden, CT; (Y); Pres VP Church Yth Grp; Letterman Clb; Varsity Clb; Yrbk Stf; Stu Cncl; Var L Sftbl; JV Vllybl; Hon Roll; Phys Ther.

HANSON, WILL; Loomis Chaffee HS; Greenwich, CT; (Y); Boys Clb Am; Chess Clb; Debate Tm; Math Tm; Stage Crew; Nwsp Stf; JV Bsbl; Diving; Lcrss; Math Clb; Dvng & Swm Tm Capt 85 & 86; Psych.

HANSTEIN, CHRISTOPHER; Seymour HS; Seymour, CT; (Y); Band; Concert Band; Jazz Band; Mrchg Band; Pep Band; School Play; Stage Crew; Rep Stu Cncl; Arion Fndtn Music Awd; Music.

HARAY, JAMIE; Kolbe Catherdral HS; Bridgeport, CT; (Y); JA; Service Clb; Cheerleading; Phy Therapist.

HARGRAVES, FRANK R; Norwich Free Acad; Voluntown, CT; (Y); Aud/Vis; PAVAS; Spanish Clb; Brdcstg Cmmnctns.

HARGROVE, SAMANTHA; New London HS; New London, CT; (S); 37/159; DECA; Yrbk Stf; VP Frsh Cls; VP Soph Cls; VP Jr Cls; VP Sr Cls; Stat Bsbl; Var Im Cheerleading; Hon Roll; FIT; Fshn Dsgn.

HARING, BARBARA; Valley Regional HS; Deep River, CT; (Y); FNA; Hosp Aide; Score Keeper; Sftbl; Hon Roll.

HARKINS, ANNE; Eastr Catholic HS; Tolland, CT; (Y); 1/297; Cmnty Wkr; Debate Tm; Drama Clb; Math Tm; School Musical; Nwsp Sprt Ed; Socr; Vllybl; High Hon Roll; NHS; Honors E Awd 84-86.

HARKINS, DAVID; East Lyme HS; Oakdale, CT; (Y); Boy Scts; Church Yth Grp; Varsity Clb; Yrbk Rptr; Yrbk Sprt Ed; Yrbk Stf; Crs Cntry; Trk; Hon Roll; SAR Awd; Eagle Sct 83; CT U Avery Point; Comp.

HARLAN, WENDY; Daniel Hand HS; Madison, CT; (Y); 2/250; Church Yth Grp; French Clb; JCL; Model UN; Concert Band; Mrchg Band; School Musical; Nwsp Ed-Chief; Nwsp Stf; High Hon Roll; Exchnge Clb Yth Of The Mnth 86; Math Awd 86; Wellesley Coll; Lbrl Arts.

HARLOW, JOYCE; Vinal Regional Voc Tech HS; Higganum, CT; (Y); Keywanettes; Yrbk Stf; Sftbl; Hon Roll; 5 Yrs Of Dance Haddam Dance Studio 86; Jr Hairdressing Comp 1s Tpl 86; Dance & Hairdressing.

HARLOW, ROB; Vinal Regional Tech Schl; Haddam, CT; (Y); Boy Scts; Var JV Bsbl; Var JV Bsktbl; Var JV Socr; Hon Roll; U CT; Engrng.

HARPER, KIM; Naugatuck HS; Naugatuck, CT; (Y); 33/300; Chorus; JV Sftbl; JV Trk; High Hon Roll; Hon Roll; NHS; Mattatuck CC; Radlgy.

HARPER, PHAIDRA; Thomaston HS; Thomaston, CT; (Y); Spanish Clb; Chorus; Concert Band; Mrchg Band; Yrbk Stf; High Hon Roll; Hon Roll; NHS; Pep Clb; Band; Middlebury Coll; Intl Bus.

HARRIMAN, PATRICK; Windham HS; Columbia, CT; (Y); Church Yth Grp; Drama Clb; Pep Clb; Acpl Chr; Band; Chorus; Concert Band; Jazz Band; Mrchg Band; Orch; All New Englnd Frnch Horn 85-86; All Eastern ST Chori 85-86; CT U; Biology.

HARRIOTT, SHAWN; Bassick HS; Bridgpt, CT; (Y); Rep Soph Cls; Stu Cncl; JA; Schlstc Achvmnt Awd 85; Rdng Imprvmnt MAT Scrs Awd 86; Excl Rdrshp Awd 86; Bus Adm.

HARRIS, DINA; Hillhouse HS; New Haven, CT; (Y); Computer Clb; FBLA; Math Clb; Church Choir; Cheerleading; High Hon Roll; Hon Roll; NHS; Labov Awd 86; Bio Awd 84; Hampton U; Arch Engrng.

HARRIS, JEANINE; Rockville HS; Somers, CT; (S); Chrmn FFA; Hosp Aide; High Hon Roll; Hon Roll; Creed Speaking Cntst 84; Pblc Speaking Cntst 85; Livestock Judging St Cntst 84-85; U CT; Vet Med.

HARRIS, LEIGH W; The Hotchkiss Schl; Lexington, KY; (Y); Drama Clb; Chorus; School Musical; School Play; Stage Crew; JV Fld Hcky; JV Mgr(s); Hon Roll; Ntl Merit SF.

HARRIS, LINDSEY; Brien Mc Mahon HS; Norwalk, CT; (Y); 21/330; Trs Temple Yth Grp; Var Tennis; High Hon Roll; Hon Roll; NHS; Math.

HARRIS, TIMOTHY; Salisbury HS; Governors Island, NY; (Y); 4/70; Pres Key Clb; Band; Sec Chorus; Mrchg Band; School Play; Variety Show; Nwsp Sprt Ed; Kiwanis Awd; NHS; Ntl Merit SF; Vrsty Squash; V Crew.

HARRIS, TINA; Guilford HS; Guilford, CT; (Y); 20/235; Church Yth Grp; Hosp Aide; SADD; Chorus; Sec Orch; School Musical; High Hon Roll; Hon Roll; NHS; Spanish NHS; Music Hnr Awd Outstndg Contrib 86; Schltc Achvt Acad Excllnce Lang Art 84; Pre-Med.

HARRIS, TRACY; Amity Regional SR HS; Orange, CT; (Y); Drama Clb; Hosp Aide; Drm Mjr(t); Jazz Band; Mrchg Band; Symp Band; Lit Mag; NHS; Ntl Merit Ltr; School Play; Colt Frgn Lang Poetry Cntst Spanish I 84.

HARRISON, PAUL; F Scott Bunnell HS; Stratford, CT; (Y); 2/260; French Clb; Ed Yrbk Stf; Var Capt Crs Cntry; Var L Trk; French Hon Soc; High Hon Roll; Pres NHS; Ntl Merit Ltr; Sal; Spanish NHS; Let Cmmndtn JETS Ntl Entrng Apttd Srch 84; Accptd Yales Series Applied Sci 85; Swarthmore Coll; Math.

HARRISON, VALERIE; Crosby HS; Waterbury, CT; (Y); FHA; Chorus; Bsktbl; Hon Roll.

HARRISON, WAYNE M; Nonnewaug HS; Woodbury, CT; (Y); 4-H; FFA; Hon Roll.

HART, DAVID; Manchester HS; Manchester, CT; (Y); Church Yth Grp; French Clb; Letterman Clb; Var Socr; Hon Roll; Ntl Merit Ltr; Acad Encllnc 3 Yr Hnr Rll 83; Manchester Schlrshp Awd 86; Merit Awd Frnch 84; Roger Williams Coll; Archtr.

HARTIGAN, DENNIS; The Hotchkiss Schl; Ormond Bch, FL; (Y); Dance Clb; Drama Clb; Model UN; Chorus; School Musical; School Play; Stage Crew; Lit Mag; JV Crs Cntry; High Hon Roll.

HARTMAN, THOMAS R C; Robert E Fitch SR HS; Mystic, CT; (Y); 50/250; Boy Scts; Ski Clb; Varsity Clb; Band; Mrchg Band; Capt Diving; Golf; Socr; Capt Swmmng; Wentwrth Boston; Arch.

HARTMANN, JENNIFER; Brookfield HS; Brookfield, CT; (Y); 11/210; Church Yth Grp; Chorus; Off Jr Cls; L Crs Cntry; L Trk; High Hon Roll; Colt Poetry Cntst 1st Pl Frnch I 84 & 2nd Pl Frnch II 85; Reads Jr Fshn Advsry Brd Mbr 86; Engl.

HARTRICK, LAURA; Wilton HS; Wilton, CT; (Y); 60/350; Girl Scts; Mrchg Band; Symp Band; Rep Frsh Cls; VP Soph Cls; Rep Jr Cls; Stat Ice Hcky; JV Tennis; Var Vllybl; Hon Roll.

HARTSHORNE, MANDY; Greenwich HS; Cos Cob, CT; (Y); Dance Clb; Service Clb; Rep Stu Cncl; Var Capt Cheerleading; Coach Actv; Var Crs Cntry; Var Capt Gym; Var Trk; High Hon Roll; Spanish NHS; MVP & MIP Gymnstcs 83&85-86; Schlr Athlete Awd 83; All Cnty & Hon Ment All ST Gymnstcs 85-86; CT Coll.

HASAKA, MICHELLE; Manchester HS; Manchester, CT; (Y); Art Clb; French Clb; Mgr JA; Chorus; Lit Mag; Tennis; High Hon Roll; Hon Roll; Rhode Isl Schl Of Dsn; Grphc Dn.

HASSELBERG, KATHERINE; Orville M Platt HS; Meriden, CT; (Y); 13/221; Pres VP Drama Clb; Chorus; School Play; Swing Chorus; Variety Show; Yrbk Ed-Chief; Yrbk Stf; NHS; Ntl Merit Ltr; Pres Schlr; JR Wmns Clb, Clark Fdtn Schlrshp, Pres Schlr Grant 86; Gettysburg Coll; Music.

HATHAWAY, KAREN; Kaynoy Tech; Waterbury, CT; (Y); JA; High Hon Roll; Hon Roll; NHS; Stu Cncl 85-86; Stu Fash Desgn 83-87; Intr Desgnr.

HATTENBACH, CHARLES; Saint Lukes Schl; Norwalk, CT; (Y); Cmnty Wkr; Teachers Aide; Temple Yth Grp; Yrbk Phtg; L Var Tennis; Hon Roll; Prfct Atten Awd.

HATZIKOSTANTIS, ANTONIA; Wethersfield HS; Wethersfield, CT; (Y); Church Yth Grp; FHA; Flag Corp; Hon Roll; Acctng.

HAUCK, WARREN; Trumbull HS; Trumbull, CT; (Y); AFS; Church Yth Grp; Drama Clb; German Clb; JA; Library Aide; Science Clb; School Play; Stage Crew; Nwsp Stf; Bio-Med.

HAUGHS, LISA; Greenwich HS; Cos Cob, CT; (Y); Service Clb; SADD; Var Cheerleading; Var Capt Tennis; High Hon Roll; NHS; Buteva Awd 86; Artwrk Dsplyd-Stwrt Mc Knny Art Exhbt 86; Bucknell U; Lbrl Arts.

HAUSMANN, DANIEL; East Granby HS; E Granby, CT; (Y); 1/60; JA; Math Clb; Radio Clb; Rep Frsh Cls; Rep Soph Cls; Rep Jr Cls; Stu Cncl; Mgr(s); Score Keeper; Stat Socr; Harvard Bk Awd 86; CT Hnrs Sem Dstngshd H S Stu 86.

HAVEY, KATHLEEN; Bethel HS; Bethel, CT; (Y); 5/240; Am Leg Aux Girls St; Church Yth Grp; Chorus; School Play; Yrbk Ed-Chief; JV Sftbl; Elks Awd; VP NHS; Ntl Merit Ltr; AFS; Notre Dame Schlr; Knghts Columbus Schlrshp; U Of Notre Dame; Chem.

HAVIRA, JILL; New Fairfield HS; New Fairfield, CT; (Y); 57/237; Dance Clb; Hosp Aide; Latin Clb; Off Jr Cls; JV Var Fld Hcky; JV Sftbl; Im Tennis; Hon Roll; Awd 12 Yr Stu Fanton Dnc Schl 85; Wstrn CT Conf 2nd Tm Fld Hcky 85; Mrktng.

HAVRANEK, BILL; Greenwich HS; Greenwich, CT; (Y); Church Yth Grp; Exploring; Key Clb; Var L Bsbl; JV Capt Lcrss; High Hon Roll; Outstndng Accomp Span 84; Safe Rides 86; Accntng.

HAWK, MARY ELLEN; Stamford Catholic HS; Stamford, CT; (Y); Yrbk Ed-Chief; High Hon Roll; NHS; Acdmc Schlrshp Johnson & Wales Coll 86; Johnson & Wales Coll; Fshn Mrch.

HAWKINS, CHRIS; Staples HS; Westport, CT; (Y); Am Leg Boys St; Cmnty Wkr; Debate Tm; Key Clb; Letterman Clb; SADD; Var L Crs Cntry; Var L Trk.

HAWKINS, LOU; Suffield HS; W Suffield, CT; (Y); Pres Aud/Vis; Drama Clb; Library Aide; Chorus; School Musical; Yrbk Stf; Rep Stu Cncl; Mgr(s); Prfct Atten Awd; Robert Alcorn Schlrshp 85; Emerson Coll; Actor.

HAWKINS, LYNLE; Westover Schl; Middlebury, CT; (Y); Pep Clb; Ski Clb; Chorus; School Musical; Mgr(s); JV Sftbl; JV Capt Vllybl; High Hon Roll; Hon Roll; Cmps Gdng 85-86; Proctor Of Prfct 85-86; Intr Desgn.

HAZEL, MICHAEL; Manchester HS; Manchester, CT; (Y); Red Cross Aide; VICA; Nwsp Rptr; Ftbl; High Hon Roll; Hon Roll; ST Champ Hum Rel Voc Ind Clbs Amer 86; Bus.

HAZYK, BRUCE; Branford HS; Branford, CT; (Y); 76/400; Aud/Vis; Boy Scts; Computer Clb; Crs Cntry; Trk; Comp Sci.

HEAD, DARLENE; James Hillhouse HS; New Haven, CT; (Y); #1 In Class; Church Yth Grp; Math Clb; Math Tm; Model UN; Teachers Aide; Yrbk Stf; Lit Mag; Cit Awd; High Hon Roll; NHS; Duke U; Pre-Med.

HEAD, LISA; St Marys HS; New Haven, CT; (Y); Art Clb; Church Yth Grp; Debate Tm; English Clb; French Clb; Girl Scts; Math Clb; Quiz Bowl; Ski Clb; Church Choir; Christ Schlrshp 86; Hampton Inst; Mass Media.

HEADLEY, NORA; Windsor HS; Windsor, CT; (Y); Church Yth Grp; Cmnty Wkr; Drama Clb; French Clb; Pep Clb; SADD; School Musical; School Play; Nwsp Stf; Yrbk Stf; Cls Wittiest 83-84; Comm.

HEALEY, JENNIFER; E O Smith HS; Mansfield, CT; (Y); 42/180; Drama Clb; Hosp Aide; Intnl Clb; Model UN; SADD; Yrbk Stf; Lit Mag; Pres Frsh Cls; Var L Crs Cntry; Political Wkr; Mock Trl Tm ST Smfnlst 86; Inter Rltns.

HEALY, TIMOTHY; Rham HS; Hebron, CT; (Y); 1/200; Pres SADD; Variety Show; Pres Frsh Cls; Rep Stu Cncl; Var L Bsbl; Var Capt Bsktbl; Var Capt Socr; Im Capt Vllybl; High Hon Roll; Jr NHS; Harvard Bk Awd Acdmc Excllnc & Achvmnt 86; HS Math Dept Outstndg Stu 86; Grad Hon Court 86; Ivy League Coll; Math.

HEARD, DEREK M; Fairfield Coll Preparatory Schl; Trumbull, CT; (Y); 111/243; Teachers Aide; Trs Church Yth Grp; Cmnty Wkr; Exploring; JA; Var L Bowling; Var L Ftbl; Cit Awd; Spanish NHS; Rugby; Natl Achvt Cmmnd Stdnt; Oratrcl & Essy Cntst Wnnr 1st Pl SR Div; Biomed Engrng.

HEATH, RANDALL; Southington HS; Southington, CT; (Y); 77/600; Church Yth Grp; Computer Clb; Ski Clb; Nwsp Stf; Yrbk Stf; Var L Bsktbl; DAR Awd; Masonic Awd; Ntl Merit SF; U Of VT; Comp Sci.

HEAVIN, PATRICIA; Southington HS; Southington, CT; (Y); Key Clb; Library Aide; Ski Clb; SADD; Stage Crew; Trs Stu Cncl; Hon Roll; U CT; Lib Art.

HEDDING, RICHARD J; Enfield HS; Enfield, CT; (Y); #55 In Class; Art Clb; Drama Clb; German Clb; Spanish Clb; Teachers Aide; School Play; Yrbk Stf; Hon Roll; Lebanon Vly Coll.

HEDENBERG, JANET; New Britain SR HS; New Britain, CT; (Y); 24/336; Sec Key Clb; Yrbk Stf; Badmtn; Var Tennis; Var Trk; Hon Roll; NHS.

HEDICK, CHRISTOPHER; Taft HS; New Hartford, CT; (Y); Camera Clb; Mgr Pres Radio Clb; Spanish Clb; Nwsp Phtg; Nwsp Rptr; Yrbk Phtg; JV Lcrss; Hon Roll; Commnctns.

HEENIE, ROBIN; West Haven HS; W Haven, CT; (Y); Church Yth Grp; Library Aide; Church Choir; Nwsp Stf; Yrbk Stf; High Hon Roll; NHS; NEDT Awd; Spanish NHS; Schltc Excllnc Awd-Spnsh I & Engl I 83-84; Schltc Excllnc Awd-Bkkpng I, Engl II, 84-85.

HELMECKI, TODD; Berlin HS; Kensington, CT; (Y); 21/183; Hosp Aide; Nwsp Stf; Lit Mag; Var JV Socr; Var JV Trk; Hon Roll; NHS; Cert Apprctn New Britain Gen Hosp JR Vlntr Svc 84; Bus Mgmt.

HELMERS, KRISTEN; Miss Porters Schl; Spartanburg, SC; (Y); Art Clb; Math Tm; Service Clb; Chorus; Latin Clb; High Hon Roll; Hon Roll; Nalt Schlstc Art Awd, Art Excllnce Awd, 3rd City Art Show 84; House Rep Cngrsnl Art Comp 86.

HEMSTREET, ROBERT; East Lyme HS; E Lyme, CT; (Y); Boy Scts; VP Drama Clb; Acpl Chr; Chorus; Church Choir; School Musical; JV Socr; High Hon Roll; NHS; Ntl Merit Ltr; All ST Chorus 86; Ministry.

HENCLIK, THERESA; Mark T Sheehan HS; Wallingford, CT; (Y); Trs AFS; Am Leg Aux Girls St; Pres Church Yth Grp; French Clb; FBLA; Math Tm; Acpl Chr; Chorus; Flag Corp; Hon Roll; Math Cntst Winning Team; Quinnipiac Coll; Med.

HENDERSON, LAURA; Wethersfield HS; Wethersfield, CT; (Y); 18/300; Band; Concert Band; Mrchg Band; Yrbk Stf; JV Socr; Sftbl; Var Trk; Var Vllybl; Hon Roll; NHS.

HENDERSON, LINDA; Kaynor Tech HS; Waterbury, CT; (Y); JA; SADD; Yrbk Stf; Rep Frsh Cls; Rep Soph Cls; Rep Jr Cls; Rep Stu Cncl; High Hon Roll; Hon Roll; Mst Dsrvng JR 86; 1st Pl In Schl Comptn 86; Csmtlgst.

HENDRICKS, MAUREEN; Academy Of Our Lady Of Mercy; Bridgeport, CT; (Y); 31/140; Church Yth Grp; Latin Clb; Quiz Bowl; Spanish Clb; Chorus; Church Choir; Nwsp Rptr; Achvt Awd For NEDT 84; Lbrl Arts.

HENDRICKSON, HEATHER; Staples HS; Westport, CT; (Y); French Clb; Pep Clb; Ski Clb; JV Cheerleading; Powder Puff Ftbl; Hon Roll; Ski Tm Vrsty 84-86; CO U.

HENNESSEY, MAURA; Lavralton Hall HS; Fairfield, CT; (Y); GAA; Service Clb; SADD; Varsity Clb; Acpl Chr; Chorus; Var Capt Swmmng; Acctng.

HENRICKS, SARAH; Farmington HS; Farmington, CT; (Y); 2/206; Math Tm; VP Soph Cls; Sec Jr Cls; Sec Sr Cls; Capt L Fld Hcky; Var Swmmng; Var Trk; Bausch & Lomb Sci Awd; High Hon Roll; NHS; Yale Bk Awd 86; Outstndg Sci Stu 86; UTC Acad Scholar 86; Amherst Coll; Spn.

HENRIQUES, KRISTINE; Branford HS; Branford, CT; (Y); Political Wkr; Chorus; Yrbk Rptr; Yrbk Stf; Mgr(s); Score Keeper; Timer; Soclgy.

HENRY, DANA; Immaculate HS; Bethel, CT; (Y); Yrbk Stf; Pres Jr Cls; Rep Stu Cncl; JV Bsktbl; Var Cheerleading; JV Sftbl; Im Vllybl; Hon Roll; Spanish NHS.

HENRY, LOREL; Shelton HS; Shelton, CT; (Y); Exploring; Sec 4-H; Pres FFA; JA; JCL; Sec Latin Clb; 4-H Awd; High Hon Roll; Hon Roll; NHS; Summa Cum Laude 85; Achvt Awd 83; Adelaide Coombs Awd 85; Hrs Jcky.

HENRY, SUSAN; East Hartford HS; E Hartford, CT; (Y); 46/369; Art Clb; VP Church Yth Grp; Drama Clb; VP French Clb; Stage Crew; NHS; Schlrps E Hartford Art Lg, Viola Anderson, Emblem Clb & E Hrtfrd HS Almni 86; Art Awds 85-86; Anna Maria Coll; Art Ther.

HENSCHEL, HEATHER; Watertown HS; Watertown, CT; (Y); Church Yth Grp; Band; Pres Chorus; Church Choir; Rep Jr Cls; Hon Roll; Musicon 84-86; Blue Nts 84-87; Elem.

HERBERT, ROYAN; Wamogo Regional HS; Warren, CT; (Y); 4/79; AFS; Am Leg Aux Girls St; Ed Yrbk Stf; High Hon Roll; NHS; Phys Ther.

HERNANDEZ, HELENA; Joseph A Foran HS; Milford, CT; (Y); Spanish Clb; Co-Capt Color Guard; Co-Capt Drill Tm; Yrbk Stf; Hon Roll; Poli Sci.

HERNANDEZ, JUAN; Bullard-Havens RTVS; Bridgeport, CT; (Y); Computer Clb; NHS; Elec Engr.

HEROLD, KAREN; East Catholic HS; Vernon, CT; (Y); 41/325; Church Yth Grp; Cmnty Wkr; Dance Clb; GAA; Hosp Aide; Ski Clb; Spanish Clb; Drill Tm; Nwsp Stf; Rep Frsh Cls; Natl Hnr Soc 81, 82, 84 & 85; Boston Coll; Educ.

HESSELBACH, CATHRINE; St Bernard HS; Norwich, CT; (Y); 27/300; Band; Concert Band; Jazz Band; Mrchg Band; School Musical; Rep Frsh Cls; Rep Soph Cls; Rep Jr Cls; JV Tennis; Hon Roll; Acad Excel 83-84; Musical Achvt 83-85; Peer Mnstry 86-87; Law.

HETZEL, ROD; Mark T Sheehan HS; Wallingford, CT; (Y); 13/200; Pres German Clb; Quiz Bowl; Band; Elks Awd; High Hon Roll; NHS; Rotary Awd; Scholastic Bowl; Concert Band; Jazz Band; CT All St Band; Bio Awd; Music Awds; De Pauw U; Pre-Vet.

HEUSER, TAMMY; Shelton HS; Shelton, CT; (Y); Spanish Clb; High Hon Roll; Hon Roll; NHS; Vitamen Inc Eleanor F Moor Bus Awd 86; Accntng.

HICKEY, SEAN; Wethersfield HS; Wethersfield, CT; (Y); 17/310; Rep Am Leg Boys St; Trs Church Yth Grp; Intnl Clb; Quiz Bowl; Nwsp Ed-Chief; Stu Cncl; JV Socr; High Hon Roll; Hon Roll; NHS; Pres Acad Fit Awd 86; Acad Promise Sci Awd 86; New Britain Herald Book Awd Jrnlstc Achvt 86; U Notre Dame; Engrng.

HICKMAN, SEAN; East Hartford HS; E Hartford, CT; (Y); 101/462; Computer Clb; Science Clb; Var Ftbl; Wt Lftg; JV Wrstlng; Hon Roll; Western CT ST U; Bus Adm.

HICKS JR, ROBERT S; Oliver Wolcott Vo Tech; South Kent, CT; (Y); 3/145; Exploring; High Hon Roll; Hon Roll; NHS; Jacksonville U; Aviation.

HIGGINSON, HADLEY; Miss Porters Schl; Woodstock, VT; (Y); Cmnty Wkr; Intnl Clb; JV L Fld Hcky; Lcrss; Tennis; Hon Roll; Engl.

HIGHSMITH, LISA; Wilbur Cross HS; New Haven, CT; (Y); Chess Clb; Computer Clb; French Clb; GAA; Pep Clb; Spanish Clb; Church Choir; School Play; Nwsp Rptr; Stu Cncl; Brkly Schl/Fshn Dsgn; Fshn Dsgn.

HILDEBRAND, GREGORY; R E Fitch SR HS; Mystic, CT; (Y); Drama Clb; French Clb; Thesps; School Play; Trs Stu Cncl; Hon Roll.

HILGER, FLORINDA; Sacred Heart Acad; New Haven, CT; (Y); Am Leg Aux Girls St; Drama Clb; Stu Cncl; Var Cheerleading; JV Crs Cntry; French Hon Soc; NHS; Church Yth Grp; French Clb; School Musical; Yale Frontiers Sci Pgm 86; Schl Svc Awd 86; Acad Achvt Awd 86; Lib Arts.

HILL, PAMELA; Thumbull HS; Trumbull, CT; (Y); Church Yth Grp; Cmnty Wkr; Hosp Aide; Chorus; Color Guard; High Hon Roll; NHS; Natl Hist Day 2nd Pl Dist Fnls 85; Outstndng Svc To Class Of 86 83; Peer Tutoring Awds 85-86; Syracus U; Comm.

HILL, SCOTT; Ridgefield HS; Ridgefield, CT; (Y); German Clb; Quiz Bowl; School Musical; School Play; Stage Crew; Hon Roll; Dungns And Dragns Clb 83-84; Orientation Sco 85-86; GA Inst Of Tech; Aerosp Engrg.

HILLMAN, REGINA L; Rockville HS; Vernon, CT; (Y); 30/320; Am Leg Aux Girls St; Church Yth Grp; JA; Yrbk Bus Mgr; Rep Sr Cls; JV Var Tennis; NHS; Cmnty Wkr; Mrchg Band; Yrbk Stf; U CT Hlth Sci Cluster Pgm; Outstndng Perfrmnce Bio Awd 84; LEAD Pgm 85; Bus.

HILTON, CHERYL; Southington HS; Southington, CT; (Y); Latin Clb; Library Aide; Ski Clb; Spanish Clb; Band; Concert Band; Drm & Bgl; Mrchg Band; School Musical; School Play; Psychlgy.

HINCKLEY, JULIE A; Suffield HS; Suffield, CT; (Y); 17/141; Girl Scts; Pep Clb; Yrbk Stf; Cheerleading; Fld Hcky; High Hon Roll; Hon Roll; Rotary Awd.

HINGORANI, SEEMA; Norwalk HS; Norwalk, CT; (Y); Key Clb; Spanish Clb; Concert Band; Nwsp Rptr; Ed Yrbk Stf; Pres Soph Cls; Var L Bsktbl; Var L Sftbl; High Hon Roll; NHS; Oberlin Coll Bk Awd 86; Ntl Iona Spnsh Cntst 86; All City Sftbl Tm 85; Law.

HINTZ, COLEEN; East Hampton HS; Middle Haddam, CT; (Y); 5/110; Model UN; Ski Clb; Band; Chorus; Pep Band; Yrbk Stf; Trs Stu Cncl; Var Trk; Hon Roll; NHS; Natl Hstry Day Fnlst CT 85; Acctg.

HIRTLE, ROBIN; Newington HS; Bloomfield, CT; (S); Church Yth Grp; Drama Clb; Pep Clb; Thesps; Acpl Chr; Chorus; Church Choir; Madrigals; School Musical; School Play; Divisnl ST Choir 85; Music Ed.

HITZ, ALEXANDER; Avon Old Farms Schl; Atlanta, GA; (Y); 7/101; Art Clb; School Play; Nwsp Rptr; Im Socr; JV Tennis; Engl Awd & Frnch Bk Prz & Algbr I Bk Prz; Finc.

HLOZEK, LAURA; Trumbull HS; Trumbull, CT; (Y); AFS; Church Yth Grp; Mrchg Band; Symp Band; High Hon Roll; Hon Roll; Natl Hist Day 2nd Pl In Dist; Bryant Coll; Acctnt.

HO, JAN; Stamford HS; Stamford, CT; (Y); French Clb; JA; Science Clb; Ski Clb; Stu Cncl; Crs Cntry; Trk; Hon Roll; NCTE Awd; NHS; Williams Coll Bk Awd 86; Harvard U; Corp Law.

HOAGLAND, JAMES; Manchester HS; Manchester, CT; (Y); Boys Clb Am; Trs Church Yth Grp; Band; Rep Frsh Cls; Off Soph Cls; Off Jr Cls; Rep Stu Cncl; Golf; Lcrss; Socr; Syracuse U; Arch.

HOBAN, HEATHER; Wykeham Rise Schl; West Haven, CT; (Y); Camera Clb; French Clb; Girl Scts; Ski Clb; School Musical; Yrbk Ed-Chief; Yrbk Phtg; Trs Sr Cls; Rep Stu Cncl; Vllybl; Prfct Of Drm Rsdnt Asst 85-86; Wvng Awd 84-85; Hdmstrs Hnr Rl 84-86; U Of Miami; Blgy.

HOBER, JENNIFER; Lyme-Old Lyme HS; Old Lyme, CT; (Y); 17/100; AFS; Church Yth Grp; Computer Clb; Ski Clb; Band; Concert Band; Mrchg Band; Yrbk Stf; Rep Stu Cncl; Hon Roll; Lndscpe Arch.

HOCHHOLZER, JANA; Guilford HS; Guilford, CT; (Y); 70/349; AFS; Church Yth Grp; Drama Clb; Model UN; Acpl Chr; Chorus; School Musical; Stage Crew; Swing Chorus; Auburn; Spch Ther.

HODER IV, STEPHEN M; Stamford Catholic HS; Stamford, CT; (Y); 85/180; John Carroll Awd 86; Antmy Exemptn Awd 86; Relgs Stds Exmptn Awd 86; St Francis Coll; Physcn.

HODGE, KIM; Coventry HS; Coventry, CT; (Y); Am Leg Aux Girls St; Band; Yrbk Sprt Ed; Rep Frsh Cls; Sec Jr Cls; Trs Stu Cncl; Var Capt Socr; Var Capt Trk; High Hon Roll; NHS; Hrvrd Rdclff Clb Bk Prz 86; Med.

HODGE, TRACEY; Daniel Hand HS; Madison, CT; (Y); 71/273; GAA; Pep Clb; SADD; Sec Frsh Cls; Rep Soph Cls; Var Capt Bsktbl; Var L Sftbl; Var L Trk; Hon Roll; Babe Ruth Sprtsmnshp Awd 86; Most Imprvd Bsktbl 85-86; Keene ST Coll; Elem Educ.

HODGE, YVETTE; Kolbe-Cathedral HS; Ansonia, CT; (Y); Cheerleading; Soclgy.

HOFFMAN, DAVE; Griswold HS; Jewett City, CT; (Y); Band; Concert Band; Jazz Band; Mrchg Band; Pep Band; Symp Band; Bsbl; Ftbl; High Hon Roll; Hon Roll.

HOFFMAN, HOLLY; Trumbull HS; Trumbull, CT; (Y); VP Intnl Clb; Temple Yth Grp; Acpl Chr; Chorus; Yrbk Stf; Socr; High Hon Roll; Jr NHS; Mgmt.

HOFFMANN, CARRIE; Brookfield HS; Brookfield, CT; (Y); Drama Clb; FBLA; Hosp Aide; Nwsp Stf; Yrbk Stf; Hon Roll; U Of CT; Comm.

HOLBROOK, SUSAN N; Holy Cross HS; Cheshire, CT; (Y); 5/350; Concert Band; Mrchg Band; School Musical; Stage Crew; Swing Chorus; Yrbk Stf; Ed Lit Mag; NHS; Ntl Merit SF; Latn Hnr Soc 83 To Presnt; Vet.

HOLCOMBE, CHRIS M; Ridgefield HS; Ridgefield, CT; (Y); ROTC; Trk.

HOLDEN, ELIZABETH; Guilford HS; Guilford, CT; (Y); Key Clb; Ski Clb; Var Socr; Var Trk; Hon Roll; Sec Spanish NHS; Math.

HOLDER, JOY; New London HS; New London, CT; (S); DECA; FBLA; Key Clb; Library Aide; Chorus; School Musical; Nwsp Bus Mgr; Yrbk Bus Mgr; Yrbk Stf; Sec Frsh Cls; Chorus/Choir Awds 83-84; FBLA 84-85; DECA/Music Theory 85-86; Hofstra U; Acctg.

HOLLAND, ALLYSON; St Mary HS; Riverside, CT; (Y); 5/52; Cmnty Wkr; Drama Clb; Hosp Aide; JA; Math Tm; VP Jr Cls; Sec Stu Cncl; JV Capt Cheerleading; Var Fld Hcky; NHS; Spcl Ed.

HOLLER, GEORGE; Joseph A Foran HS; Milford, CT; (Y); Am Leg Boys St; JCL; Key Clb; Ski Clb; Drm & Bgl; Jazz Band; Mrchg Band; Var Socr; Var Trk; High Hon Roll.

HOLMES, AUDRA ANGEL; High School In Cmnty; New Haven, CT; (Y); Dance Clb; 4-H; JA; Drill Tm; Gym; High Hon Roll; NHS; Prfct Atten Awd; Prfrmg Arts Indepndt Mdlg 83-86; Actvties Aerobcs YMCA 84-86; Nghbrhd Grp 85-86; UCLA; Pedtrcs.

HOLMES, HEATHER E; East Hartford HS; E Hartford, CT; (Y); 6/462; Church Yth Grp; Drama Clb; Pres French Clb; Ski Clb; Chorus; Church Choir; Drill Tm; Nwsp Rptr; NHS; Rotary Awd; Stevens Alumni Rgnl Schlrshp 86; Stevens Inst Tech; Matl Engrng.

HOLMES, WILLIAM; The Williams Schl; Uncasville, CT; (Y); Boy Scts; Varsity Clb; Nwsp Rptr; Rep Soph Cls; VP Jr Cls; Sec Sr Cls; Var L Bsktbl; Im Ice Hcky; JV Socr; Hon Roll; Elctrcl Engrng.

HOLMWOOD, SCOTT; East Lyme HS; Salem, CT; (Y); Temple Yth Grp; Yrbk Phtg; JV Bsbl; Var JV Ftbl; Var Wrstlng; Hon Roll; HS Athl Hnrs 84-85; Jr Intern Pgm 85; Hndcp Art Awd Poster Cntst 84-85; Law Enfrcmnt.

HOLOWATY, JUDITH; Griswold HS; Jewett City, CT; (Y); 26/83; Camera Clb; GAA; Library Aide; Office Aide; Chorus; Hon Roll.

HOLT, STEWART; Canton HS; N Canton, CT; (Y); 10/94; Boy Scts; Church Yth Grp; Political Wkr; Rep Jr Cls; Var Socr; Var Wrstlng; High Hon Roll; Hon Roll; CT JR Intrnshp 86; Alt Boys ST 86; Canton Saferides Chrtr 84-86; West Point; Law.

HOLTERMAN III, HENRY F; New Fairfield HS; New Fairfield, CT; (Y); 64/238; Art Clb; Latin Clb; Science Clb; School Musical; School Play; Stage Crew; Variety Show; Yrbk Stf; Lit Mag; Bsbl; Exclnc In Socl Stud; Awds State And Natl Latn Exams; Talntd Art Prog; W CT ST Univ; Free Lance Ills.

HOLYST, JODY; Southington HS; Plantsville, CT; (Y); 52/600; Am Leg Aux Girls St; Chess Clb; Church Yth Grp; Civic Clb; Computer Clb; FBLA; Key Clb; Ski Clb; Band; Concert Band; Minnie Wrinn Awd; Police Union Schlrshp; U CT; Psychlgy.

HOLZER, DEBBIE; Derby HS; Derby, CT; (Y); 5/111; Am Leg Aux Girls St; Pep Clb; Rep Soph Cls; JV Bsktbl; Var Pom Pon; Stat Score Keeper; Var Sftbl; Wt Lftg; High Hon Roll; Hon Roll; Tchg.

HOLZMAN, DARA; Stamford HS; Stamford, CT; (Y); 267/365; Trs Pres 4-H; JA; Temple Yth Grp; Chorus; Yrbk Stf; Rep Stu Cncl; JV Gym; Hon Roll; Outstndng Svc Awd 85; Bus Adm.

HOMAN, DONNA; Totland HS; Tolland, CT; (Y); Intnl Clb; Band; Yrbk Stf; George Washington U; Intl Bus.

HOMISKI, DAWN; Norwich Free Acad; Norwich, CT; (Y); Church Yth Grp; Cmnty Wkr; FHA; German Clb; Girl Scts; Hosp Aide; Political Wkr; SADD; JV Crs Cntry; Hon Roll; Psych.

HONAN, KELLY; Nonnewaug HS; Woodbury, CT; (Y); Chorus; School Play; VP Frsh Cls; Rep Soph Cls; Rep Jr Cls; Capt Cheerleading; Fld Hcky; Trk; Trs NHS; AFS; Co-Chrmn Prom Committee 87; Sentr Mc Laughlin-Campgn Wrkr 86.

HONG, L; Cheshire HS; Cheshire, CT; (Y); 5/287; Am Leg Aux Girls St; Scholastic Bowl; Sec Science Clb; Chorus; Sec Jr Cls; Sec Sr Cls; French Hon Soc; Math Tm; Quiz Bowl; Service Clb; Harvard Bood Awd 85; Amercn Assn U Wmn Awd 86; United Technlgs Schlrshp 86; Amherst Coll; Psych.

HOOD, HEIDI; Brookfield HS; Brookfield, CT; (Y); Church Yth Grp; Nwsp Stf; Yrbk Stf; Lit Mag; Rep Frsh Cls; Rep Soph Cls; Rep Jr Cls; Var Bsktbl; JV Cheerleading; JV Fld Hcky; Outstndng Achvt Spnsh II; U Of CT; Bus Admin.

HOOT, DARYL J; Shelton HS; Shelton, CT; (Y); #1 In Class; Am Leg Boys St; Art Clb; Boy Scts; Church Yth Grp; Computer Clb; Nwsp Rptr; Nwsp Stf; Ed Yrbk Bus Mgr; High Hon Roll; Sec Jr NHS; Engrng.

HOPCROFT, TONYA; Killingly HS; Danielson, CT; (Y); Drama Clb; Chorus; School Play; Variety Show; Yrbk Phtg; Yrbk Stf; Hon Roll; Jr NHS; All-ST Chorus 86; Thtre.

HOPKINS, ROBERT; Daniel Hand HS; Madison, CT; (Y); 115/217; Church Yth Grp; JV Bsktbl; JV Crs Cntry; Var JV Trk; Im Wt Lftg; Hon Roll; Wally Cataldo Achvmnt Awd 86; U Of CT; Bus Adm.

HORNUNG, ERICA; Ridgefield HS; Ridgefield, CT; (Y); 11/386; Aud/Vis; Lit Mag; High Hon Roll; JETS Awd; Cornell U Smmr Pgm Arch 86; GA Tech; Arch.

HOROWITZ, STEVE; New Fairfield HS; New Fairfield, CT; (Y); 24/330; Computer Clb; Key Clb; Chorus; School Musical; School Play; Crs Cntry; Wt Lftg; High Hon Roll; Hon Roll; Jr NHS; Original Sci Fiction Short Story Pblshd In New Fairfield Litry Annl 85-86; Comp Sci.

HORSEY, ERIKA; Avon HS; Avon, CT; (Y); VP French Clb; Acpl Chr; Jazz Band; Rep Jr Cls; Sec Sr Cls; Var Cheerleading; JV Swmmng; NHS; Church Yth Grp; Dance Clb; HOBY ST Ldrshp Sem Ambassador 85; All-ST CT Choir Alto 86; Northern Regional CT ST Choir 86; Liberal Arts.

HOSIG, AMY; Old Lyme HS; Old Lyme, CT; (Y); 15/110; Am Leg Aux Girls St; School Musical; Nwsp Rptr; Yrbk Stf; Lit Mag; Var Capt Bsktbl; Var Socr; Var Trk; High Hon Roll; NHS; All-Around Plyr Var Bsktbl 86.

HOSSLER, MIKE; Masuk HS; Monroe, CT; (Y); AFS; German Clb; Band; Socr; Swmmng; Tennis; NHS; Sccr Team Sprtmnshp Awd 85-86; PA ST Engr.

HOTALING, GREG A; Simsbury HS; W Simsbury, CT; (Y); Church Yth Grp; Cmnty Wkr; FCA; Ski Clb; Spanish Clb; School Play; Bsbl; Bsktbl; Ftbl; Hon Roll; Indstrl Engr.

HOWARD, CHRISTOPHER; Fairfield Coll Preparatory Schl; Darien, CT; (Y); Church Yth Grp; French Clb; JA; Ski Clb; Nwsp Stf; Yrbk Stf; Lit Mag; Im Bsktbl; JV Crs Cntry; Im Ftbl.

HOWE, ALBERTO; New London HS; New London, CT; (S); 20/180; Church Yth Grp; DECA; Pres Jr Cls; Pres Sr Cls; Capt Ftbl; Capt Trk; Cit Awd; Hon Roll; Barry U; Bus Adm.

HOWE, ALISON; Lyman Hall HS; Wallingford, CT; (Y); Spanish Clb; Sec Varsity Clb; Band; Sec Stu Cncl; Capt Cheerleading; Powder Puff Ftbl; High Hon Roll; Hon Roll; Concert Band; Mrchg Band; Bst Chrldng Awd 85-86; Music Prnts Assctn Awd 86; Providence Coll.

HOYT, LISA M; Enfield HS; Enfield, CT; (Y); 18/245; VP Pres JA; Mgr Band; Mgr Concert Band; Jazz Band; Mgr Mrchg Band; Orch; Mgr School Musical; Stage Crew; Trs Soph Cls; Var L Socr; Outstndng Erth Sci 83; Outstndng Bio 84; Outstndng SR In Band 86; Embry-Rdl Aerontcl U; Wrnt Ofcr.

HRACYK, TRACIE; St Bernard HS; Oakdale, CT; (Y); 49/265; Chorus; Off Jr Cls; Sftbl; Hon Roll; Law.

HRYNCHUK, CHRISTINE; New Britain HS; New Britain, CT; (Y); Church Yth Grp; Pres Girl Scts; Office Aide; Spanish Clb; Acpl Chr; Chorus; Madrigals; Swing Chorus; Var Badmtn; Hon Roll; New Britain H S SR Music Awd 86; Badminton Coaches Awd 85; Briarwood Coll; Trvl.

HU, YAN JING; New Milford HS; New Milford, CT; (Y); 58/295; AFS; Odd Fellows Schlrshp 86; A Russell Ayre Schlrshp 86; Outstndng Progrs Engl Awd, Coop Wrk Exp Awd 86; Wstrn CT ST U; Bus.

HUANG, JULIET; Daniel Hood HS; Madison, CT; (Y); 3/229; Jazz Band; Orch; School Musical; Yrbk Stf; Trk; High Hon Roll; Hon Roll; HS Exclnc Math 86.

HUBBARD, ARTHUR E; Oliver Wolcott Technical HS; Winsted, CT; (Y); Computer Clb; Hon Roll; Ntl Merit Ltr; Waterbury Sst Tech; Elec Engrng.

HUBBARD, CHRISTINA; Guilford HS; Guilford, CT; (Y); 82/317; Pres Civic Clb; Sec Band; Sec Concert Band; Sec Mrchg Band; Trk; Hon Roll; Guilford Hndcrfts Schlrshp 86; Cvc Actn Clb Schlrshp 86; U MA; Art.

HUBBARD, SUSAN; Guilford HS; Guilford, CT; (Y); 5/300; Sec Church Yth Grp; SADD; Concert Band; Orch; French Hon Soc; High Hon Roll; NHS; Band; School Musical; CT All ST Bnd 86; Nancy A Lathrop Awd Exclln Wmns Stds 86; Amrcn Mscl Foundtn Band Hons 84-86; Comp Sci.

HUDOCK, LARA; Rham HS; Marlborough, CT; (Y); 35/194; 4-H; VP Latin Clb; SADD; Stu Cncl; Var Capt Cheerleading; Coach Actv; Score Keeper; Sftbl; High Hon Roll; Hon Roll.

HUDSON, DANIELLE; Orville H Platt HS; Meriden, CT; (Y); 4-H; JA; Spanish Clb; Powder Puff Ftbl; 4-H Awd; High Hon Roll; Hon Roll; JC Awd; Awd Outstndng Cntrbtn Life Prog Platt 86; Accntnt.

HUDSON, DANNY; Canton HS; Canton, CT; (Y); Capt Var Crs Cntry; Capt Var Wrstlng; Hon Roll; Engrng Awd 86; Math Awd 82; Tech Drawing 86; David Lipscomb Coll; Engrng.

HUDSON, JOHN BARBOUR; Oliver Wolcott Tech Schl; Harwinton, CT; (Y); Church Yth Grp; VICA; Waterbury ST Tech; Elec Genrtn.

HUESTIS, CHRISTOPHER; Manchester HS; Manchester, CT; (Y); 12/541; Band; Concert Band; Jazz Band; Mrchg Band; School Musical; High Hon Roll; Hon Roll; NHS; U Of CT; Photo.

HUFFMAN, MARY JO; St Joseph HS; Trumbull, CT; (Y); 14/257; Drama Clb; Library Aide; Spanish Clb; Nwsp Stf; Yrbk Stf; Var Bsktbl; Var L Trk; High Hon Roll; Hon Roll; NHS; Engrng.

HUGHES, ANDREA; Sacred Heart Acad; Derby, CT; (Y); 29/122; Church Yth Grp; Dance Clb; Hosp Aide; Teachers Aide; Nwsp Rptr; Vllybl; High Hon Roll; Jr NHS; NHS; Art Clb; 3 Yr Hnrs Awd 83-86; Latin Hon Soc Awd 86; Quinnipiac Coll; Med Tech.

HUGHES, PEYTON; Greenwich HS; Greenwich, CT; (Y); Camp Fr Inc; Cmnty Wkr; 4-H; Hosp Aide; Pep Clb; Red Cross Aide; Service Clb; SADD; Varsity Clb; Chorus; Psych.

HUGHES, RENEE; Jonathan Law HS; Milford, CT; (Y); Church Yth Grp; Ski Clb; L Var Socr; Hon Roll; SECTY.

HUGHES, TONYA; Stamford HS; Stamford, CT; (Y); Church Yth Grp; French Clb; Pep Clb; Ski Clb; Varsity Clb; Rep Stu Cncl; Var L Cheerleading; Diving; Var L Swmmng; Hon Roll; A P Biol & Hist 85-86; A P Engl & Frnch 86-87; Bus.

HUGO, MARK E; M T Sheehan HS; Wallingford, CT; (Y); 70/213; Pres VP JA; Var Stat Mgr(s); Var L Swmmng; Middlesex CC.

HULME, DEBBIE; Acad Of Our Lady Of Mercy; Milford, CT; (Y); 47/110; Church Yth Grp; Drama Clb; Hosp Aide; Model UN; Stage Crew; Yrbk Stf; Im Vllybl; Psychol.

HULME, NANCY; Kingswood Oxford Schl; Manchester, CT; (Y); Cmnty Wkr; Drama Clb; French Clb; School Musical; School Play; Variety Show; Rep Frsh Cls; Rep Stu Cncl; JV Cheerleading; Var L Ftbl; Red Cross Advanced Lifesaving & Water Safty 84&86; Art.

HULSE, LESLIE; The Loomis Chaffee Schl; S Galstonbury, CT; (Y); Church Yth Grp; 4-H; French Clb; Ski Clb; Band; Concert Band; Lcrss; Socr; High Hon Roll; Hon Roll.

HUMMEL, KERRY; Middletown HS; Middletown, CT; (Y); Yrbk Stf; JV Var Cheerleading; Mgr(s); Var L Trk; High Hon Roll; Hon Roll; NHS; Outstndng Achvt-Spnsh Awd 85; U Of CT; Lwyr.

HUMPAGE, COREY; Francis T Maloney HS; Meriden, CT; (Y); Key Clb; Math Tm; Science Clb; Variety Show; Im Bowling; JV Socr; High Hon Roll; Ntl Merit Ltr; Stu Sci Trng Inst Ball ST U Muncie IN 86; Astronomy Clss Gftd & Tlntd Stu 86; Mechncl Engr.

HUNT, EILEEN; Immaculate HS; Danbury, CT; (Y); 9/137; AFS; Church Yth Grp; Spanish Clb; School Musical; School Play; Yrbk Stf; Var L Cheerleading; Im Vllybl; High Hon Roll; Hon Roll; Natl Fdrtns Fstvls Hnrs 83-85; Natl Piano Plyng Adtn Exclnt 83-85.

HUNT, TECIA-LUE; Emmett O Brien RVT Schl; Beacon Falls, CT; (Y); Church Yth Grp; Hosp Aide; Library Aide; Pep Clb; Ski Clb; Drill Tm; Rep Stu Cncl; Var Cheerleading; Mgr(s); Score Keeper; Yng Marine Of Yr 83; Crowned Statue Of Mary Good Shepherd Ch Seymour 86; Greater New Haven ST; Computer.

HUNTER, MARGARET; Shelton HS; Shelton, CT; (Y); Drama Clb; French Clb; Rep Stu Cncl; Mgr Bsktbl; Trk; French Hon Soc; Hon Roll; NHS.

HUNTER, MAUREEN; Rham HS; Amston, CT; (Y); Trs AFS; Church Yth Grp; 4-H; Pres FBLA; Red Cross Aide; Teachers Aide; Nwsp Rptr; Nwsp Stf; Sftbl; 4-H Awd; Central CT ST Su; Bus Mgt.

HUPE, KURT; The Taft School; New York, NY; (Y); Acpl Chr; Chorus; Madrigals; School Musical; Rep Frsh Cls; Pres Soph Cls; Pres Jr Cls; Rep Sr Cls; Im Wt Lftg; Var Wrstlng; Head Mntr Stdnt Bdy Pres 86; Head Ml Acapella Sng Clb 86-87; ROTC; Bus Adm.

HURD, CINDY; Central HS; Bridgeport, CT; (Y); Church Yth Grp; Debate Tm; Hosp Aide; JA; SADD; Church Choir; JV Tennis; Masonic Awd; Med Career.

HURLBERT, ELIZABETH; Coginchaug Regional HS; Durham, CT; (Y); 25/130; AFS; Church Yth Grp; Drama Clb; Pep Clb; Trs Sec SADD; Band; Concert Band; Capt Pep Band; School Musical; Swing Chorus; Phy Thrpy.

HURLBERT, LISA; Thomston HS; Thomaston, CT; (Y); 4/67; Am Leg Aux Girls St; Sec Rep Frsh Cls; Sec Rep Soph Cls; Rep Trs Stu Cncl; Var Capt Bsktbl; Var Capt Fld Hcky; Var Capt Sftbl; High Hon Roll; Hon Roll; NHS; Hrvrd Bk Awd 86; Coaches Awds-Fld Hcky, Bsktbl & Sftbl 86; Bus.

HURLBURT, EDWARD; H C Wilcox Tech; Wallingford, CT; (Y); 2/212; Boy Scts; Cmnty Wkr; VP JA; Hst Stu Cncl; High Hon Roll; Hon Roll; Rotary Club Schlrshp 86; Unity Coll; Environ Sci.

HURT, MARCUS; Branford HS; Branford, CT; (Y); 20/370; Band; Concert Band; Jazz Band; Mrchg Band; Yrbk Stf; Stu Cncl; Socr; Trk; Wt Lftg; Hon Roll; Exclinc Engl Compstn 86; Bus.

HURTA, GARY; Danbury HS; Danbury, CT; (Y); 7/474; Am Leg Boys St; Boy Scts; JV Crs Cntry; Var Trk; High Hon Roll; Hon Roll; NHS; Vassar Bk Prz Exclinc Hmnts 86; 3rd Pl CT Indstrl Arts Assn Stu Crfts & Tech Fair 86; Engrng.

HUTCHINSON, SCOTT; Windham HS; Columbia, CT; (Y); 20/300; Church Yth Grp; Math Clb; Concert Band; Madrigals; Orch; Pep Band; High Hon Roll; NHS; Ntl Merit Ltr; VFW Awd; 1st Plc Essy CT Intl Yth Yr Comptn 85; Air Force; Elec Engr.

HUTTON, JIM; Tolland HS; Tolland, CT; (Y); 30/175; Boy Scts; Church Yth Grp; Ski Clb; Var Capt Ice Hcky; Var JV Socr; Var Capt Tennis; JV Trk; Hon Roll; NHS; VA Tech; Landscape Arch.

HUYDIC, PAM; Stratford HS; Stratford, CT; (Y); 25/231; Church Yth Grp; Ski Clb; Concert Band; Yrbk Stf; Rep Sr Cls; Sec Stu Cncl; Capt Cheerleading; Trk; Hon Roll; Ntl Merit Schol; Unitd Way Yth Grp Agnst Substnc Abuse 85-86; Stratfrd Exchng Clb Yth Mnth 86; Intl Ordr Rainbw Grls 86; Bryant Coll; Bus.

HUYNH, PHUOC; Avon Old Farms HS; Hartford, CT; (Y); 2/104; Art Clb; Computer Clb; FNA; Red Cross Aide; Im Socr; JV Swmmng; Var Trk; High Hon Roll; Pres Schlr; Cum Laude, Latin Translation Awd 86; Walks Schlr 84-86; Wesleyan U; Bio-Chem.

HUZI, RICHARD; Seymour HS; Seymour, CT; (S); 4/192; Chess Clb; Computer Clb; Band; Concert Band; Mrchg Band; Var Swmmng; High Hon Roll; NHS; Arion Awd Music 85; Wstrn CT ST U; Acctng.

HWANG, HELEN; Glastonbury HS; Glastonbury, CT; (Y); 128/416; Chorus; Variety Show; Yrbk Phtg; Yrbk Stf; Capt Var Cheerleading; Hon Roll; U Of CT; Psych.

HYDE, KATHLEEN; Branford HS; Branford, CT; (Y); 35/300; Church Yth Grp; Chorus; Var Fld Hcky; Var Trk; Hon Roll; Arista Awd In Eng Lit 86; Nursing.

HYDE, YVONNE; Branford HS; Branford, CT; (Y); 22/315; Church Yth Grp; Cmnty Wkr; Dance Clb; Drama Clb; Hst PAVAS; Acpl Chr; Chorus; Church Choir; Sec Stu Cncl; Hon Roll; Brnz Mdl For Dance Comp 86; Pre Law.

HYLTON, MICHELE; Weaver HS; Hartford, CT; (Y); School Musical; School Play; London England; Fshn Mrchndsng.

HYSON, ROSEMARY; Greenwich HS; Cos Cob, CT; (Y); Church Yth Grp; Service Clb; Fld Hcky; Var L Tennis; High Hon Roll; NHS; Ntl Merit Ltr; Grls Tns Tm Cochs Awd 86; Engl, Geom, Bio, Wlrd Cultrs Awds 84; Econmcs.

HYZY, CHRISTOPHER M; Brien Mc Mahon HS; S Norwalk, CT; (Y); 12/365; Art Clb; Math Clb; Science Clb; Spanish Clb; Rep Frsh Cls; Rep Soph Cls; Var Bsbl; Ftbl; High Hon Roll; NHS; Arch Engr.

IACURCI, DIANE; Trumbull HS; Trumbull, CT; (Y); Church Yth Grp; Cmnty Wkr; Math Clb; High Hon Roll; Hon Roll; Acctng.

IAGUESSA, CRISTIN; Branford HS; Branford, CT; (Y); Art Clb; Dance Clb; Drama Clb; Stage Crew; Mgr(s); Hon Roll; Admsn Wesleyan U Cntr Yth Vsl Arts 86; Fshn Dsgn.

IANNINO, ROSE; Shelton HS; Shelton, CT; (Y); Drama Clb; Spanish Clb; Stu Cncl; High Hon Roll; Hon Roll; NHS; Spanish NHS; Phyciatry.

IANNUCCI, SHERRY; Sacred Heart Acad; W Haven, CT; (Y); Church Yth Grp; FBLA; Office Aide; Band; Stage Crew; Variety Show; Rep Frsh Cls; Rep Stu Cncl; Bowling; Cheerleading; Tlnt Show Wnnr 85&86; Dance Comp Awds 83; May Crowning Hnr Court 83; U RI; Psych.

IATOMASI, ALFONSINA; Hamden HS; Hamden, CT; (Y); Cmnty Wkr; SADD; Teachers Aide; High Hon Roll; Hon Roll; Poem Contst For Italian 84-85; Maint 96% Avr All-Yr Bus 84-85; Ms Tn Contestnt 85-86; Intl Bus.

IFFLAND, PAUL; Torrington HS; Torrington, CT; (Y); 20/300; Latin Clb; Ski Clb; Trs Spanish Clb; VP Thesps; Chorus; School Musical; Yrbk Stf; High Hon Roll; NHS; Drama Clb; CT ST Ltn Exm Cum Dgnt 84; Bus Admin.

ILARDO, MICHAEL; Fairfield College Prep Schl; Easton, CT; (Y); Church Yth Grp; Cmnty Wkr; Pep Clb; Spanish Clb; Varsity Clb; Nwsp Rptr; Nwsp Stf; JV Var Bsbl; Im Bsktbl; Hon Roll; Encmncs.

IMBIMBO, STEVEN; Holy Cross HS; Cheshire, CT; (Y); Art Clb; Church Yth Grp; Cmnty Wkr; Computer Clb; French Clb; Ski Clb; SADD; Chorus; School Musical; Variety Show; St Joseph Coll; Law.

IMPRONTO, TONY; O H Platt HS; Meriden, CT; (Y); Boys Clb Am; Church Yth Grp; Drama Clb; Latin Clb; School Play; Var L Ftbl; Var L Tennis; Wt Lftg; Var L Wrstlng; Hon Roll; Law.

INGER, TRACEY; Lymon Hall HS; Wallingford, CT; (Y); 9/246; AFS; Cmnty Wkr; JA; Key Clb; Lit Mag; Dnfth Awd; High Hon Roll; NHS; Voice Dem Awd; Physcl Thrpy.

INGERSOLL III, RICHARD W; East Lyme HS; E Lyme, CT; (Y); 39/280; Trs Church Yth Grp; Key Clb; Political Wkr; SADD; Im Bsbl; Capt Ice Hcky; Im Lcrss; Var L Tennis; Cit Awd; Hon Roll; U Of VT; Bus Mgmt.

INGRAHAM, CHRISTINE; Joseph A Foran HS; Milford, CT; (Y); 53/273; Church Yth Grp; Hosp Aide; Chorus; Church Choir; Drm & Bgl; Madrigals; JV Sftbl; Var Swmmng; Hon Roll; Alg Awd; Chem.

INKROTT, JULIE; Trumbull HS; Trumbull, CT; (Y); Church Yth Grp; Dance Clb; JCL; Key Clb; Latin Clb; Color Guard; Capt Drill Tm; Flag Corp; Mrchg Band; Cheerleading; Miami OH; Bus.

IORFINO, DOM; Stamford HS; Stamford, CT; (Y); Church Yth Grp; JA; Science Clb; Varsity Clb; Var Capt Crs Cntry; JV Socr; Var Trk; Cit Awd; Hon Roll; 3rd Pl Dsgn 85; Comp.

IOTOMASI, ALLIE; Hamden HS; Hamden, CT; (Y); Cmnty Wkr; SADD; Teachers Aide; Yrbk Stf; High Hon Roll; Hon Roll; Italian Poem Cnst 84-85; Intl Bus.

IOVINO, MIKE; Bullard Havens Tech; Bridgeport, CT; (Y); Bsbl; Capt Ftbl; U Of CT; Bus.

IRELAND, MATTHEW; Ridgefield HS; Ridgefield, CT; (Y); Church Yth Grp; German Clb; Pres Sr Cls; JV Var Bsbl; JV Var Bsktbl; NHS; Arch.

IRIARTE, CHRISTOPHER; Simsbury HS; West Simsbury, CT; (Y); AFS; Drama Clb; Thesps; Band; Jazz Band; School Play; Trk; Hon Roll; NHS; Ntl Merit SF; Ensgn Bickford Fdntn Awd 86; Ntl Hspnc Merit Semi Fnlst 86; U Of MA Lowell; Snd Rcrdng Tec.

IRISH, JULIE; Killingly HS; Brooklyn, CT; (Y); 14/317; Library Aide; High Hon Roll; Hon Roll; Jr NHS; Outstndng Comp Basics 85-86; Outstndng Achvt Frnch 84-85; Exclince Soc Studs 83-84; Acctng.

IRIZARRY, GLORIMAR; Hartford HS; Hartford, CT; (Y); Art Clb; Math Clb; Spanish Clb; Off Frsh Cls; Bsbl; Bsktbl; Vllybl; High Hon Roll; Hon Roll; Spanish NHS; Acad All Amer Awd Natl Sec Ed Cncl 84; Trinity Coll; Word Proc.

IRVIN, ZORIAN; Stamford HS; Stamford, CT; (Y); Boy Scts; JA; Ftbl; Wt Lftg; Wrstlng; Electrncs.

IRVINE, PAUL; The Morgan HS; Clinton, CT; (Y); 58/150; French Clb; JV Ftbl; Hon Roll; CPA.

IRVING, PAULA D; Ridgefield HS; Ridgefield, CT; (Y); 6/400; AFS; Church Yth Grp; Cmnty Wkr; Math Tm; Office Aide; High Hon Roll; Ntl Merit SF; Frnch Bk Awd 85; Chem Achvt Awd 84; Ltn Hnr Soc 83-84; Engrng.

ISAAC, PAUL; Shelton HS; Huntington, CT; (Y); 16/335; High Hon Roll; Hon Roll; U CT; Comp Sci.

ISFAHANI, KAZIM; Greenwich HS; Riverside, CT; (Y); 2/730; Im Capt Bsbl; Im Bsktbl; Im Ftbl; Var L Trk; Im Vllybl; High Hon Roll; Hon Roll; GASFA Acadmc Awd $1000 86; Cert Of Merit-Frnch 86; Cert Of Achvt-Frnch, Math, Hstr, Geo 84; Boston U; Fin.

ISLEIB, ANNE LOUISE; East Lyme HS; Niantic, CT; (Y); Church Yth Grp; Cmnty Wkr; Intnl Clb; Key Clb; Band; Color Guard; Flag Corp; Mrchg Band; Powder Puff Ftbl; Score Keeper; 2nd Pl Governors Essay Contest 86; Assumption Coll; Erly Chldhd Ed.

IVERSEN, LISA; Vinal Regional Vo-Tech Schl; Madison, CT; (Y); VICA; High Hon Roll; Hon Roll; NHS; Hdrsr.

IZZO, MARY; St Marys HS; New Haven, CT; (Y); #9 In Class; Church Yth Grp; Intnl Clb; JA; Teachers Aide; School Play; Variety Show; Lit Mag; Rep Stu Cncl; Vllybl; Hon Roll; U RI; Bus Mgmt.

JABLONKA, MARY; Ledyard HS; Ledyard, CT; (Y); 79/215; Band; Mrchg Band; Rep Frsh Cls; Rep Soph Cls; Rep Jr Cls; Mgr Crs Cntry; Var Socr; Var Trk; All Eastrn CT Conf Sccr Tm & Trck Tm 85; All ECC Indoor Trck Tm 86; Hlth.

JACKSON, BRIAN; Danbury HS; Danbury, CT; (Y); 109/465; Boy Scts; Math Tm; Science Clb; Yrbk Stf; 3rd Pl Sr Bio Div Sci Horizens Sci Fair 86; Comp.

JACKSON, NANCY; James Hillhouse HS; New Haven, CT; (Y); Church Yth Grp; FBLA; Pep Clb; Church Choir; Trk; Vllybl; Hon Roll; Prfct Atten Awd; Rotary Awd; Ms Mt Calvary Delivrnce Tabrncle 85-86; Bus.

JACOBSEN, JON; St Mary HS; Bedford, NY; (Y); Boy Scts; JV Var Bsbl; Eagle Scout 85; Randy Heerdt Memrl Awd 86.

JACOBSON, AMY; Berlin HS; Kensington, CT; (Y); Am Leg Aux Girls St; Church Yth Grp; Drama Clb; Key Clb; Thesps; VP Chorus; School Musical; School Play; Variety Show; Var Capt Bsktbl; Art Awd; Exclinc Frnch Studs; Bio Exclinc Lab Rsrch; Bates; Engl.

JACOBUCCI, CHUCK; Portland HS; Portland, CT; (Y); AFS; CAP; Cmnty Wkr; Exploring; ROTC; SADD; VICA; Y-Teens; Var Bsbl; Ftbl.

JADACH, MICHAEL; Derby HS; Derby, CT; (Y); 16/108; Am Leg Boys St; Boy Scts; Church Yth Grp; Computer Clb; Letterman Clb; Varsity Clb; Rep Frsh Cls; VP Soph Cls; Rep Jr Cls; Rep Sr Cls; Polish Wmns Clb Awd Hghst Acad Stu 86; Central CT ST U; Acctg.

JAHNCKE, ALISON; The Taft Schl; Chicago, IL; (Y); School Musical; Nwsp Stf; JV Bsktbl; JV Fld Hcky; Im Lcrss; Hon Roll; Ntl Merit Ltr; Allnce Frncs Frnch Awd 86.

JAKIELA, BETH; Lyman Hall HS; Wallingford, CT; (Y); Spanish Clb; Band; School Musical; Variety Show; Stu Cncl; Swmmng; High Hon Roll; Hon Roll; Awd High Achvmnt Chem 86; Chem.

JAKONCZUK, JEFF; Bethel HS; Cabot, AR; (Y); 45/270; Var Bsbl; Var Bsktbl; High Hon Roll; Hon Roll; Pres Schlr; AR U; Chem Engr.

JAMES, CHARISE; Hillhouse HS; New Haven, CT; (Y); Pep Clb; Rep Jr Cls; Var Cheerleading; U Of CT Pre-Coll Sumr Pgm 85-86; U Of CT Convctn For Distngshd HS Stu 86; Indpndnt Stdies Law 85-86; Pre-Med.

JAMISON, ADRIENNE; Stratford HS; Stratford, CT; (Y); 52/250; JA; Vllybl; Hon Roll; Norwalk St Tech Coll Saturday Acad Sci/Engrng 84; U Bridgeport :Edy Smmr Pgm 86; Comp Pgmr.

JANCIS, ERIK; Naugatuck HS; Naugatuck, CT; (Y); 6/310; Am Leg Boys St; Library Aide; Political Wkr; Red Cross Aide; Scholastic Bowl; Ski Clb; Stu Cncl; Bsbl; Var L Bsktbl; High Hon Roll; Boston Coll; Blgy Pre-Med.

JANDREAU, DANIELLE; Southington HS; Southington, CT; (Y); 49/600; VP Key Clb; Sec Spanish Clb; Flag Corp; Stage Crew; Rep Jr Cls; Rep Sr Cls; L Twrlr; Hon Roll; Jr NHS; NHS; Prm Chairprsn; Prm Cmmtte 85.

JANELLE, TRICIA; Torrington HS; Torrington, CT; (Y); 99/248; Exploring; Cheerleading; Bus.

JANESKI, JULIE; Granby Memorial HS; Granby, CT; (Y); Spanish Clb; SADD; Yrbk Stf; Var Fld Hcky; Var Sftbl; Hon Roll; Law.

JANKE, BOB; Fairfield College Prep; Fairfield, CT; (Y); Boy Scts; Cmnty Wkr; Drama Clb; JA; Red Cross Aide; Chorus; Eagl Sct 85; Dale Carnegie Schlrshp 85; Homecmng Chrmn 85; NAJAC Schlrshp 85; Chrmn W CT JA 86.

JANKOVICH, JENNIFER; Sacred Heart Acad; Hamden, CT; (Y); Church Yth Grp; Dance Clb; Stage Crew; Nwsp Phtg; Yrbk Phtg; Lit Mag; Vllybl; High Hon Roll; NEDT Awd; U CT; Med Tech.

JANKOWSKA, RENATA; Norwalk HS; Norwalk, CT; (Y); Church Yth Grp; German Clb; Intnl Clb; Office Aide; Vllybl; Hon Roll; Vllybl Awd 85 86; U CT; Comp Prog.

JANKOWSKI JR, RONALD L; Windsor HS; Windsor, CT; (Y); 20/319; Church Yth Grp; FCA; VP FBLA; Intnl Clb; Varsity Clb; Var L Ftbl; Sec French Hon Soc; High Hon Roll; Hon Roll; All Conf Ftbl Tm Offnsv Tckl 84; Bryant Coll; Bus Ldrshp.

JANOSKO JR, PAUL A; Fairfield Prep; Bridgeport, CT; (Y); JV Capt Bsbl; JV Ftbl; Law.

JANSUJWICZ, ALAN; Enrico Fermi HS; Enfield, CT; (Y); 4/352; Ski Clb; Concert Band; Mrchg Band; Rep Stu Cncl; Var Bsbl; High Hon Roll; NHS; Ntl Merit Ltr; RPI Mth & Sci Awd; Hrvrd-Rdclf Bk Awd; Chem Engrng.

JANUS, MICHAEL T; St Bernard HS; Uncasville, CT; (Y); 12/266; Library Aide; Teachers Aide; Rep Jr Cls; Stu Cncl; High Hon Roll; NHS; Yale Frontiers Applied Sci Awd 85; Acad Achvt Awd 84-86; Rifle Clb 83-86; Worcester Poly Tech Inst; Engr.

JANUSHA, SCOTT; Kolbe-Cathedral HS; Bridgeport, CT; (Y); Wt Lftg; Hon Roll; Natl Sci Merit Awd 85; Politcl Sci.

JARONCZYK, JENNIFER; Holy Cross HS; Ansonia, CT; (Y); Pres Church Yth Grp; Hosp Aide; Service Clb; Spanish Clb; Teachers Aide; Stage Crew; Yrbk Stf; Hon Roll; Southern CT ST U; Acctng.

JARRETT, CHRISTINE; Stamford HS; Stamford, CT; (Y); Band; Concert Band; Mrchg Band; School Musical; JV Fld Hcky; High Hon Roll; Hon Roll; NHS.

JARROLD, TOM; Fairfield Coll Prep; Easton, CT; (Y); Civic Clb; Cmnty Wkr; Exploring; JA; Key Clb; Pep Clb; Ski Clb; Spanish Clb; Acpl Chr; Church Choir; 3rd Pl Sci Fair Physcs 85; 1st Pl Sci Fair Brdg Bldg 86; 2nd Pl Triathln 85; Georgetown; Art.

JARVIS, KIMBERLY; Trumbull HS; Trumbull, CT; (Y); French Clb; Band; Mrchg Band; Symp Band; Nwsp Stf; Var Mgr Bsktbl; Var Mgr Sftbl; Var Mgr Vllybl; French Hon Soc; High Hon Roll; 2nd Pl Trumbull Lit Fest 85; U CT; Hist.

JASMINSKI, ROBERT; Wethersfield HS; Wethersfield, CT; (Y); 7/299; Boy Scts; SADD; Im Badmtn; JV Var Socr; Im Swmmng; Im Tennis; Im Wt Lftg; High Hon Roll; Hon Roll; NHS; Yale Bk Awd 86; Aerontcl Engr.

JEHALUDI, BIBI; Wilby HS; Waterbury, CT; (Y); Computer Clb; FNA; Hosp Aide; Library Aide; Office Aide; OEA; Red Cross Aide; SADD; Teachers Aide.

JELLIFFE, MARIE LOUISE; West Haven HS; W Haven, CT; (Y); 95/397; Chorus; Stu Cncl; Mgr(s); Score Keeper; Var Swmmng; High Hon Roll; Hon Roll; Jr NHS; Kic Kid Invstgtng Careers 82-83; SR Prom Comm & Grad Comm 85-86; Southern CT ST U; Spec Ed.

JENKIN, MARK C; The Morgan Schl; Clinton, CT; (Y); Civic Clb; Ski Clb; JV Var Wrstlng; Hon Roll; Ldrshp Awd Clinton Frotilla Sea Cdts 85 D Cndct Awd Frotilla Sea Cdts 84.

JENKINS, ANGELA; Bulkeley HS; Hartford, CT; (Y); FHA; Girl Scts; Yrbk Stf; Bsktbl; Cit Awd; High Hon Roll; Prfct Atten Awd; Sal; Val; Howard U; Lwyr.

JENKINS, FATICIA; Cooperative HS; New Haven, CT; (Y); Awd Of Recgntn 84.

JENKINS, GAYLE; Pompevalley Regionel HS; Southbury, CT; (Y); 8/193; Rep Stu Cncl; Var Capt Vllybl; High Hon Roll; NHS; Am Awd Schlr 86; Cert Of Merit Spnsh 86; Chapman Clg; Legl Stud.

JENKINS, JODI; Francis T Maloney HS; Meriden, CT; (Y); FBLA; Hosp Aide; Key Clb; Art Clb; Stu Cncl; Var Fld Hcky; JV Tennis; High Hon Roll; Hon Roll; NHS; Presdntl Clsrm Yng Amercns DC 86; Bus.

JENNINGS, GREGORY; Fairfield College Prep; Fairfield, CT; (Y); 15/226; Boy Scts; Cmnty Wkr; Variety Show; Yrbk Stf; Rep Jr Cls; JV Wrstlng; High Hon Roll; NHS; Schlr Athlt Awd Wrstlng Tm 85-86; Lwyr.

JENSEN, MELISSA; West Haven HS; W Haven, CT; (Y); 11/395; Pres Science Clb; Band; Concert Band; Jazz Band; Trk; Elks Awd; High Hon Roll; Sec NHS; Spanish NHS; Smith Clg; Comp Prgmmg.

JENSEN, SCOTT J; East Catholic HS; Glastonbury, CT; (Y); 80/278; Coach Actv; Var L Ice Hcky; Var L Socr; Var L Tennis; High Hon Roll; Hon Roll; Hnrs 85 Avg 84-85; Bus.

JEPSON, JENNIFER; Daniel Hand HS; Guilford, CT; (Y); #75 In Class; Church Yth Grp; Service Clb; Chorus; School Musical; Yrbk Stf; Stu Cncl; Bsktbl; Hon Roll; Rotary Awd; Natl Soc Stud Olympd 85; Outstndng Svc Sak Ride Pgm 85; CT U; Hist.

JEWETT, ANN; Lyme Old Lyme HS; Old Lyme, CT; (Y); 29/110; AFS; Church Yth Grp; Cmnty Wkr; Computer Clb; Band; Concert Band; Stu Cncl; High Hon Roll; Hon Roll; Exc Data Proc 86; Bus.

JEZIERNY, NICHOLAS; Stratford HS; Stratford, CT; (Y); 23/235; Am Leg Boys St; Ski Clb; Nwsp Ed-Chief; Nwsp Phtg; Nwsp Rptr; Nwsp Sprt Ed; Yrbk Sprt Ed; Yrbk Stf; Rep Frsh Cls; Rep Soph Cls; All CCIAC Crss Cntry 85-86; All Dist Crss Cntry 85-86; Barnum King Fest 86; OH U; Jrnlsm.

JODOIN, HOLLY; Griswold HS; Griswold, CT; (Y); Varsity Clb; Chorus; Stu Cncl; Stat Bsktbl; Var Cheerleading; Mgr(s); Score Keeper; Stat Sftbl; High Hon Roll; NHS; Jrnlsm.

JOHNS, MARNEE; Ridgefield HS; Ridgefield, CT; (Y); 76/369; Drama Clb; Exploring; VP Chorus; Madrigals; School Musical; High Hon Roll; NHS; Latin Book Awd 86; Outstndng Musician Awd 86; Earth Sci Achvt 84; Music.

JOHNS, SHARON; Manchester HS; Manchester, CT; (Y); Church Yth Grp; Dance Clb; French Clb; Variety Show; Capt Cheerleading; High Hon Roll; Hon Roll; NHS; Acad Exclinc Awd 84; Dancing.

JOHNSON, ALLISON B; Ridgefield HS; Danbury, CT; (Y); 3/340; Church Yth Grp; DECA; Sec German Clb; High Hon Roll; Ntl Merit SF; Bio.

JOHNSON, BRIAN; Northwestern Regional No 7 HS; New Hartford, CT; (Y); Spanish Clb; Varsity Clb; Band; Concert Band; Mrchg Band; Var Capt Bsbl; JV Bsktbl; Hon Roll; Hnrs Courses Engl,Math,Sci,Hist 84-86; Engrng.

JOHNSON, DWINETTE; The Loomis Chaffee Schl; West Hartford, CT; (Y); Drama Clb; Hosp Aide; Spanish Clb; Chorus; School Musical; School Play; Ed Yrbk Stf; JV Socr; Hon Roll; Ntl Merit SF; Natl Achvt Schlrshp Prog Outstndng Negro Stdnt Hnbl Mntn 85; Miss West Indian Socl Clb 84; Med.

JOHNSON, ELIZABETH; Plainfield HS; Central Village, CT; (Y); 37/167; GAA; Varsity Clb; Var JV Cheerleading; JV Mgr(s); Powder Puff Ftbl; JV Score Keeper; Hon Roll; Prfct Atten Awd; Young Volntrs In Action 84-85; Hghst Avg Engl 84-86; Hghst GPA Intr Dsgn 85-86; Bus.

JOHNSON, FERN; Danbury HS; Danbury, CT; (Y); Cmnty Wkr; Girl Scts; Hosp Aide; Ski Clb; Chorus; Nwsp Stf; Rep Stu Cncl; Var Bsktbl; JV Vllybl; Jr NHS; Perry Awd-Bio 85; Cmmnctns.

JOHNSON, GAVIN; Killingly HS; Brooklyn, CT; (Y); 70/285; VP Jr Cls; Off Stu Cncl; Var Bsbl; Var Bsktbl; Var Capt Ftbl; Hon Roll; Schlr Athl 83-84; Ftbl Awds 85-86; Law.

JOHNSON, JACQUELINE M; Windsor HS; Windsor, CT; (Y); 23/316; Church Yth Grp; Church Choir; Jazz Band; Mrchg Band; Pres Jr Cls; Stu Cncl; Hon Roll; NHS; Prfct Atten Awd; Top 100 Minority Stu In ST Of CT 85; Yale Bk Awd 85; Biol.

JOHNSON, JACQUELYN; Rham HS; Amston, CT; (Y); Church Yth Grp; Pres 4-H; Girl Scts; Quiz Bowl; Science Clb; Cit Awd; 4-H Awd; Hon Roll; VP AFS; 1st Pl Beef Cattle Jdgng 85; CT Lvstck Jdg Tm 84; U Of CT; Phy Thrpy.

JOHNSON, JENNIFER; Southington HS; New Britain, CT; (Y); 22/600; Church Yth Grp; Trs FFA; Pres Girl Scts; Band; Jr NHS; NHS; Chsmr Schlrshp, Shkspr Co Schlrshp, Frnk Rswl Fllr Schlrshp 86; Johnson ST Coll; Envir Sci.

JOHNSON, JENNIFER; Wilbur Cross HS; New Haven, CT; (Y); Co-Capt Pom Pon.

JOHNSON, KAREN; Rockville HS; Somers, CT; (S); 83/320; Sec Exploring; Pres FFA; Sec Girl Scts; Church Choir; Concert Band; Jazz Band; High Hon Roll; Hon Roll; FFA Natl Band Flute 85; Natl Poultry Judg Cntst Brnz Emblm 84; Ag Ed.

JOHNSON, KELLY; Our Lady Of The Angels Acad; Enfield, CT; (Y); 5/25; Church Yth Grp; Ed Nwsp Ed-Chief; Yrbk Stf; Sec Frsh Cls; Rep Stu Cncl; Var Cheerleading; Hon Roll; NHS; Lttr Cngrtltns Frm Bill Kiner Mntng Hnr Rll 3 Yrs 86; Phrmcy.

JOHNSON, KIMBERLY; Shelton HS; Shelton, CT; (Y); Trs Boy Scts; Drama Clb; Latin Clb; Trs Service Clb; Spanish Clb; SADD; Yrbk Stf; Hon Roll; NHS; Hstry.

JOHNSON, LEE; Branford HS; Reno, NV; (Y); 46/312; Ski Clb; Varsity Clb; Var Capt Socr; Tennis; Wt Lftg; Hon Roll.

JOHNSON, LESLIE; Manchester HS; Manchester, CT; (Y); 16/541; FBLA; German Clb; Hosp Aide; Var L Tennis; Hon Roll; NHS; U Of Chicago; Eco.

JOHNSON, LYNN; Farmington HS; Farmington, CT; (Y); 3/280; Church Yth Grp; Spanish Clb; Band; Concert Band; Mrchg Band; Nwsp Stf; Yrbk Stf; Im JV Fld Hcky; Im Tennis; High Hon Roll; Intl Rltns.

JOHNSON, MELODIE; Southington HS; Southington, CT; (Y); 28/600; Ski Clb; Var Capt Socr; Var L Sftbl; High Hon Roll; NHS; Schlr Athlt Awd 84.

JOHNSON, NAOMI; Watertown HS; Oakville, CT; (Y); 11/253; Am Leg Aux Girls St; Church Yth Grp; Drama Clb; Political Wkr; JV Bsktbl; DAR Awd; High Hon Roll; NHS; U CT Convctn Distngshd Stu 86; 1st Pl Persuasv Pblc Spkng-Mattatuck CC 86; Schlstc Excllnc Hnr 86; Messiah Coll; Poli Sci.

JOHNSON III, RALPH W; Central Catholic HS; Norwalk, CT; (Y); 2/78; Yrbk Ed-Chief; Trs Frsh Cls; Stu Cncl; Bsbl; Ftbl; Wt Lftg; High Hon Roll; JC Awd; VP NHS; Pres Schlr; Iona Coll; Pol Sci.

JOHNSON, SHARON; Stamford HS; Stamford, CT; (Y); Art Clb; Camera Clb; Church Yth Grp; JA; Yrbk Stf; Vllybl; Hon Roll; Miss Stamford Teen 2nd Rnr-Up 85; Comm.

JOHNSON, SUSAN; Branford HS; Branford, CT; (Y); 14/315; Lit Mag; Rep Stu Cncl; High Hon Roll; Hon Roll; Cert Awd Typ I 85; Bus Admin.

JOHNSON, TERRI; Wilby HS; Waterbury, CT; (Y); Church Yth Grp; FHA; JA; Church Choir; Stu Cncl; Hon Roll; Criminology.

JOHNSON, TROY; Danbury HS; Danbury, CT; (Y); 124/481; Rep Soph Cls; Rep Jr Cls; L Var Bsbl; L Var Bsktbl; L Var Trk; JV Wrstlng; Hnrs Achvt Awd-Math & Social Psych 85; Western NY MVP Awd-Baseball 85; Bus Mgt.

JOLIN, GARY; Plainfield HS; Plainfield, CT; (Y); 14/162; Var Golf; Hon Roll; St Schlr.

JOLY, MICHELLE; Killingly HS; Danielson, CT; (Y); Am Leg Aux Girls St; Concert Band; Mrchg Band; Symp Band; Var JV Cheerleading; Capt Twrlr; French Hon Soc; High Hon Roll; Jr NHS; NHS; All Am Chrldr Awd 85; Northeastern U; Phys Thrpy.

JONES, ALISON; Ridgefield HS; Ridgefield, CT; (Y); DECA; Red Cross Aide; Ski Clb; Variety Show; JV Fld Hcky; Var Score Keeper; Var Timer; Var Trk; Hon Roll; Cert Excllnc Ntl Career Dvlpmnt Cnfrnc 86; 1s Pl ST CT Achvt DECA 86; Sprts Med.

JONES, BRUCE A; Stamford HS; Stamford, CT; (Y); 26/354; JV Crs Cntry; Var L Trk; Hon Roll; NHS; Cmmnded Awd Natl Achvt Pgm 85; Cert Achvt U CT Pride Day 85; Biomed.

JONES, CAMILLA; Bulkeley HS; Hartford, CT; (Y); VP Church Yth Grp; Dance Clb; Chorus; Sec Church Choir; Drill Tm; VA ST U; Bus Mgmt.

JONES, HOWARD; West Haven HS; W Haven, CT; (Y); 90/400; Chorus; Rep Frsh Cls; Rep Soph Cls; Var Bsbl; JV Ftbl; Hon Roll; Schlrshp Awd From H S 86; U Of CT; Finc.

JONES, IVORYNE; Shelton HS; Shelton, CT; (Y); FHA; Hosp Aide; Hon Roll; Manhattanville Coll; Nrs.

JONES, JENNIFER; Torrington HS; Torrington, CT; (Y); 37/330; Drama Clb; French Clb; Varsity Clb; School Play; Rep Sr Cls; Var L Cheerleading; High Hon Roll; Sec NHS; NEDT Awd; Laurel Girls ST Rnnr Up 84.

JONES, LISA; New Britain HS; New Britain, CT; (Y); Church Yth Grp; Dance Clb; Drama Clb; Exploring; French Clb; Hosp Aide; Church Choir; U Of CT; Psychltrc Nrsng.

JONES, MICHELLE; Bacon Acad; Colchester, CT; (Y); Math Tm; Yrbk Stf; Trs Soph Cls; Trs Jr Cls; Cheerleading; Trk; Hon Roll; Math Awd 85; Chrldr Of Yr 85; Ntl Hnr Soc 86; Math.

JONES, SHARON; Berlin HS; Berlin, CT; (Y); Am Leg Aux Girls St; Sec Frsh Cls; Sec Soph Cls; Pres Jr Cls; Pres Sr Cls; VP Stu Cncl; High Hon Roll; Jr NHS; NHS; Pres Schlr; Stu Cncl Awd 86; Probe Schlrshp 86; U CT; Advrtsng.

JONES, SHERI; New Fairfield HS; New Fairfld, CT; (Y); 22/226; Church Yth Grp; Teachers Aide; Band; Concert Band; Mrchg Band; Var Mgr(s); Hon Roll; Chorus; Orch; Pep Band; Bnd Ad Awd 86; Smpr Fdls Awd Musical Excllnc 86; Spr Rtng Natl Music Fstvls 82-86; Houghton Coll; Music Educ.

JONES, TRINA; Bulkeley HS; Hartford, CT; (Y); DECA; Var L Trk; Hon Roll; Crtcl Thinking Talented & Gifted Clss 85-86; Law.

JORDAN, CHARLES LOUIS; Loomis Chaffee Schl; Charlotte, NC; (Y); Boy Scts; Chorus; VP Jr Cls; Pres Stu Cncl; JV Capt Bsbl; Var L Ftbl; JV Ice Hcky; God Cntry Awd; Russian Clb; Radio Sta WLCS VP; U Os St Andrews; Jrnlsm.

JORDAN, DEBORAH; William H Hall HS; W Hartford, CT; (Y); 74/329; Pep Clb; Yrbk Stf; Cheerleading; U Of CT.

JORDHAMO, EMILY; New Canaan HS; S Salem, NY; (Y); Church Yth Grp; Acpl Chr; Chorus; Madrigals; Mgr(s); Powder Puff Ftbl; Hon Roll; School Play; Landscape Arch.

JOSEPH, MICHAEL; Westhill HS; Stamford, CT; (Y); Church Yth Grp; Drama Clb; Thesps; School Play; Stage Crew; Hon Roll; Blackfrears Schlrshp-Providence Coll 86; Spnsh Awd 85; Providence; Theater Arts.

JOSEPHSON, PHILIP; Berlin HS; Berlin, CT; (Y); Am Leg Boys St; Drama Clb; School Play; JV Bsktbl; Var Golf.

JOSLIN, ELIZABETH S; Conard HS; W Hartford, CT; (Y); 3/304; Capt Math Tm; Church Choir; Yrbk Stf; Var L Fld Hcky; High Hon Roll; NHS; Ntl Merit SF; Latin Clb; Concert Band; Jazz Band; JR Classcl Lg Latin Awd Silv Mdl; A B Duke Scholar Duke U; Renssalaer Mdl Mth & Sci; Duke U; Med.

JOYCE, MARGOT; Cheshire HS; Cheshire, CT; (Y); 78/345; Church Yth Grp; Drama Clb; Pep Clb; Band; Mrchg Band; Stage Crew; Rep Soph Cls; Rep Jr Cls; Rep Sr Cls; Hon Roll; Bus.

JOYCE, PATRICK J; Fairfield College Prep Schl; Ridgefield, CT; (Y); Boy Scts; Key Clb; Stage Crew; Rep Stu Cncl; Ftbl; Var Wrstlng; Hon Roll; Eagle Sct Boy Scts Of Amer 85.

JUERGENS, MARIE; East Hartford HS; E Hartford, CT; (Y); 31/400; FBLA; Spanish Clb; Yrbk Stf; Stu Cncl; Var Trk; NHS; Pres Schlr; Off Church Yth Grp; Grls Trk Tm 85; 9th Pl Bst Grls Shtpttr In ST 85; Top 6 Bus Eng In FBLA Area Cnfrnc 86; St Jsph Coll; Dietetics.

JUNE, JENNIFER; Masuk HS; Monroe, CT; (Y); 42/278; Var Capt Crs Cntry; Stat Swmmng; Var Capt Trk; High Hon Roll; Hon Roll; NHS; Athltc Cnfrnc All-Cnfrnc Tm 84-86; Dnbry News-Times All-Area Tm 84-86.

JUSSAUME, JULIE; Killingly HS; Dayville, CT; (Y); Ski Clb; Yrbk Stf; Cheerleading; Bus Adm.

KACHEVSKY, RAISA; Danbury HS; Danbury, CT; (Y); 43/171; Drama Clb; JA; Key Clb; School Musical; Hon Roll; Coll Engrng; Mech Engrng.

KACZMARCZYK, DOROTHY; Mary Immaculate Acad; Plainville, CT; (Y); Chorus; School Musical; Rep Frsh Cls; Trs Soph Cls; Trs Jr Cls; Rep Stu Cncl; Hon Roll; Sci Fr 3rd Awd 83-84; Schl Schlrshps & Mrts All 3 Yrs; Schl Art Cntst 1st Plc 85-86; U Of CT; Archtctr.

KACZMAREK, MICHELE; Wilby HS; Waterbury, CT; (Y); Church Yth Grp; Drama Clb; Office Aide; Band; Concert Band; Mrchg Band; JV Cheerleading; Tennis; Hon Roll.

KACZOR, CHARLES; Berlin HS; Kensington, CT; (Y); 5/183; Math Tm; Concert Band; Mrchg Band; Var Trk; High Hon Roll; Hon Roll; NHS; Church Yth Grp; Band; NROTC Schlrshp 86; Pres Acad Fitness Awd 86; RPI; Chem.

KACZYNSKI, GEOFFREY; North Haven HS; N Haven, CT; (Y); 80/325; Exploring; Model UN; Ski Clb; Civl Engrng.

KAHN, ANDREW; Greenwich HS; Greenwich, CT; (Y); Art Clb; Cmnty Wkr; Nwsp Rptr; Nwsp Stf; Lit Mag; JV Lcrss; JV Socr; JV Tennis; High Hon Roll; Hon Roll; Philsphy.

KALAMA, LUANA; Windham Regional Voc Tech Schl; Amston Lake, CT; (Y); Am Leg Aux Girls St; VP VICA; Yrbk Ed-Chief; Trs Stu Cncl; Capt Trk; DAR Awd; Elks Awd; High Hon Roll; NHS; Prfct Atten Awd; QVC All Star 100 M Dash & 200 Dash 85-86; Trk MVP 84-85; Trk Most Outstndng Perfrmr 86; Intr Desgn.

KALJULAID, KAREN; Wm H Hall HS; W Hartford, CT; (Y); 28/329; Church Yth Grp; English Clb; Pres Concert Band; Jazz Band; Mrchg Band; Orch; Pep Band; Yrbk Stf; Var JV Crs Cntry; Im Vllybl; Solo W/ Town String Ensemble Flute 85-86; Aid Coll Chem W/Resrch Project 86; Wellesley MA Coll; Med.

KAMINSKI, PETER; Oliver Wolcott Regional Vo-Tech; Bethlehem, CT; (Y); 11/145; Hon Roll; Tech Coll; Prntng.

KAMM, DEBRA; East Hartford HS; E Hartford, CT; (Y); Church Yth Grp; Drama Clb; FBLA; JA; Q&S; Co-Capt Flag Corp; School Musical; Mgr Stage Crew; Nwsp Bus Mgr; Hon Roll; Phy Thrpy.

KANDEFER, MARY ALICE; Torrington HS; Torrington, CT; (Y); 19/270; Ski Clb; Spanish Clb; Varsity Clb; Bsktbl; Sftbl; Vllybl; High Hon Roll; NHS; All-Naugatuck Vly League Grls Sftbl Tm 86.

KANE, DARLENE; Derby HS; Derby, CT; (Y); 3/120; Church Yth Grp; Hosp Aide; Pep Clb; Spanish Clb; Flag Corp; High Hon Roll; Hon Roll; NHS; Spanish NHS; Bus Week Quinnipiac Coll 86; Accntnt.

KANE, GARY; W F Kaynor RVTS HS; Waterbury, CT; (Y); 4/200; SADD; VICA; Rptr Yrbk Stf; Off Stu Cncl; Var Capt Golf; High Hon Roll; Trs NHS; Pres ST Stdnt Cngrs 85-86; Mem ST Stdnt Advsry Cncl Educ 86; 2nd Pl ST VICA Mchn Drftng Comp 86; Wentworth Inst Of Tech; Arch.

KANE, SHEILA; Fitch SR HS; Groton, CT; (Y).

KANTHARAJ, DEVAPRASAD; Norwich Free Acad; Norwich, CT; (Y); Church Yth Grp; Hosp Aide; Orch; Stage Crew; Rep Stu Cncl; Hon Roll; Prfct Atten Awd; Outstndng Orch Music Prz 86; Med.

KAPLAN, ERIC M; Enrico Fermi HS; Enfield, CT; (Y); 31/330; Stu Cncl; Bsbl; Var Ice Hcky; JV Var Socr; Hon Roll; NHS; U Of CT; Engrng.

KAPLAN, WENDY; Francio T Maloney HS; Meriden, CT; (Y); Cmnty Wkr; Girl Scts; Spanish Clb; Yrbk Phtg; Rep Jr Cls; Var L Fld Hcky; JV Trk; Hon Roll; Towson U; Occupational Therapy.

KAPLIN, JUDY; Trubull HS; Trumbull, CT; (Y); Spanish Clb; Temple Yth Grp; Yrbk Stf; High Hon Roll; Mst Imprvd Gymnast Milford Jags Gym Tm 84-86; CT St Rgnl Champ Balance Beam Cls II 86.

KAPRAL, CINDY; Bullard-Havens Tech; Bridgeport, CT; (S); Church Yth Grp; Stu Cncl; Capt Sftbl; Vllybl; High Hon Roll; Hon Roll; Sacred Heart U; Acctng.

KAPTINSKI, NANCY; Lyman Hall HS; Wallingford, CT; (Y); 35/242; VP Varsity Clb; Pres Band; Color Guard; Sec Sr Cls; Stu Cncl; Capt Swmmng; Var L Trk; Hon Roll; Pep Clb; Pres Concert Band; Cvcs Dept Awd 85; Pres Ftnss Awd 86.

KARANIKOLAOU, MARIA; Killingly HS; Danielson, CT; (Y); SADD; Yrbk Stf; Off Jr Cls; Off Sr Cls; Off Stu Cncl; French Hon Soc; Jr NHS; Perf Attndnc Awd 84-85; Elctrcl Engrng.

KARAS, PAMELA; Watertown HS; Watertown, CT; (Y); 4/243; Computer Clb; Bsktbl; Var Mgr(s); Sftbl; High Hon Roll; NHS.

KARASEVICH, DAVID M; St Bernard HS; Uncasville, CT; (Y); 30/289; Cmnty Wkr; Rep Jr Cls; Im Bsktbl; Im Ftbl; Im Sftbl; Hon Roll; Prfct Atten Awd; Pres Schlr; KC Awd Patriotism 86; Geo Washington U; Mech Engrng.

KARAZIN, DEBORAH; Staples HS; Westport, CT; (Y); Church Yth Grp; Radio Clb; Acpl Chr; Nwsp Ed-Chief; Stu Cncl; JV Var Fld Hcky; JV Var Sftbl; Aud/Vis; JA; Political Wkr; JR Hnr Usher Grad 86; Sem Distngshd HS Stu U CT 86; Acad Mag Publctn 86; Engl.

KARCHER, COLLEEN; Shelton HS; Shelton, CT; (Y); #125 In Class; Cmnty Wkr; Hosp Aide; Pep Clb; Ski Clb; Spanish Clb; Varsity Clb; Capt Var Cheerleading; Cit Awd; Hon Roll; Salve Regina; Photo.

KARKOWSKI, AMY; Windsor HS; Windsor, CT; (Y); 4/400; Intnl Clb; Model UN; Scholastic Bowl; French Hon Soc; High Hon Roll; Hon Roll; NHS; Ntl Merit Ltr; Prfct Atten Awd; Engl Bk Awd 85; Wstmnstr Wrld Affr Smnr Awd 86; Futre Prblm Slvng Fnls 86; Engl.

KARLBERGS, MICHELLE; Staples HS; Westport, CT; (Y); 60/285; JA; Q&S; Spanish Clb; Yrbk Rptr; Yrbk Stf; Lit Mag; Off Soph Cls; JV Socr; Hon Roll; Church Yth Grp; Pre-Law.

KARSZES, JAMES; Rockville HS; Somers, CT; (S); FFA; Ftbl; Hon Roll; Frmr Beef.

KASPERSKI, JENNIFER LYNN; Holy Cross HS; Prospect, CT; (Y); 30/346; Mgr Wrstlng; French Hon Soc; High Hon Roll; Jr NHS; NHS; PA ST; Sci.

KASPERSKI, ROBERT; Holy Cross HS; Prosepct, CT; (Y); 152/380; School Musical; School Play; Stage Crew; Variety Show; JV Ftbl; L Wrstlng; Hon Roll; JC Awd; Jr NHS.

KATRECZKO, ALEXANDER J; St Joseph HS; Huntington, CT; (Y); 1/251; Pres Debate Tm; Drama Clb; Acpl Chr; School Musical; Stu Cncl; Var Trk; NHS; Spanish NHS; Exploring; Spanish Clb; Harvard Bk Awd 86; Diploma For Ukrainian Studies 85.

KATRICK, META; Joseph A Foran HS; Milford, CT; (Y); 18/300; Church Yth Grp; Keywanettes; Spanish Clb; Varsity Clb; Nwsp Rptr; Yrbk Stf; Var Bsktbl; Capt Trk; Capt Twrlr; NHS.

KATRICK, WENDY; Foran HS; Milford, CT; (Y); 60/275; Pres Girl Scts; Hosp Aide; Pres Keywanettes; Latin Clb; Spanish Clb; Trs Color Guard; Yrbk Sprt Ed; Stu Cncl; Hon Roll; Prfct Atten Awd; Keyette Of Yr 85-86; Spcl Ed.

KATSARAKES, LAURIE; Brookfield HS; Brookfield Center, CT; (Y); 38/230; Church Yth Grp; 4-H; Intnl Clb; Math Tm; Pep Clb; Acpl Chr; Chorus; Madrigals; Swing Chorus; Variety Show; Villanova:Math.

KATZ, DEBORAH L; William H Hall HS; West Hartford, CT; (Y); 96/320; Church Yth Grp; Cmnty Wkr; Red Cross Aide; Pres Service Clb; Spanish Clb; Pres SADD; Hon Roll; Var JV Vllybl; Schlrshp Qunnplc Coll 86-90; Qunnpc; Paralgl Stds.

KATZ, JAY; Staples HS; Westport, CT; (Y); Key Clb; Band; Mrchg Band; School Musical; Var Capt Socr; High Hon Roll; Hon Roll; Cornell Engrng; CAD Dsgn.

KAUFMAN, REBECCA; Miss Porters Schl; Ventnor, NJ; (Y); Dance Clb; GAA; Hosp Aide; School Musical; Nwsp Rptr; Hon Roll; Brown U Achvmnt Awd 86; ; Chemathon Part 86; ; Dorm Rep 85-86.

KAWECKI, LISA; Ft Maloney HS; Meriden, CT; (Y); Cmnty Wkr; DECA; Service Clb; Rep Frsh Cls; Rep Soph Cls; Trs Jr Cls; Trs Sr Cls; Sec Stu Cncl; Capt Var Cheerleading; Powder Puff Ftbl.

KAWESA, ANNE; Academy Of The Holy Family; Taylor, MI; (Y); Sec Art Clb; Office Aide; Red Cross Aide; Band; Im Crs Cntry; Hon Roll; Med.

KAZANJIAN, ABRHAM; Berlin HS; E Berlin, CT; (Y); 22/200; Nwsp Bus Mgr; Nwsp Ed-Chief; Nwsp Rptr; Nwsp Stf; Var Tennis; Hon Roll; Elected Boys ST 86; CT JR Intern Prg 86.

KAZLAUSKAS, KEVIN; Holy Cross HS; Watertown, CT; (Y); 93/380; Church Yth Grp; Lit Mag; Im Crs Cntry; Score Keeper; JV Wrstlng; Hon Roll; Hist Hnrs Soc Awd & Clb 86; Hist Fair Entry.

KEARNEY, JENNIFER; Lauralton Hall HS; Fairfield, CT; (Y); 77/111; Art Clb; Dance Clb; French Clb; Key Clb; Science Clb; Service Clb; Yrbk Stf; Cheerleading; Var Swmmng.

KEARNS, HEATHER; Rham HS; Hebron, CT; (Y); Church Yth Grp; Girl Scts; Gym; Var L Trk; Hon Roll; MVP Trk 83; Bst Trk Perfrmnce 85; Cls S ST Trk Mt 3rd 86; Manchster CC; Comp.

KEELING, CHARLENE; Miss Porters Schl; Bronx, NY; (Y); Model UN; Var Badmtn; Hon Roll; Ms Prts Schl Schlrshp 83-87; 1st Head Mnrty Stu Union 86-87; LEAD Bus Prgm At U VA 86; U PA; Bus & Cmnctns.

KEENEY, WILLIAM; William H Hall HS; W Hartford, CT; (Y); 6/331; Var Socr; High Hon Roll; NHS; Ntl Merit Ltr; Pres Schlr; Sec Spanish NHS; S D Fisher Schlrshp 86; W Hrtfrd Ed Fund Schlrshp 86; Pomona Coll.

KEETON, DANA; Shelton HS; Shelton, CT; (Y); French Clb; Latin Clb; Rep Stu Cncl; Hon Roll; Bus.

KEETON, EMILY; Miss Porters School; Houston, TX; (Y); Art Clb; Drama Clb; Model UN; Spanish Clb; Chorus; School Play; JV Fld Hcky; Var Sftbl; High Hon Roll; Hon Roll; Soph Cls Spch Awd 85.

KELLERS, CARL; Saint Bernard HS; Charlestown, RI; (Y); 27/265; Boy Scts; Church Yth Grp; Exploring; Ski Clb; God Cntry Awd; U RI; Mech Engrng.

KELLETT, MARY JANE; Shelton HS; Shelton, CT; (Y); 146/323; Sec Exploring; Nwsp Stf; Hon Roll; Explr Yr 85; Bst Avg Bus 85; Mst Prgrsv SR Stu 86; Jrnlsm.

KELLEY, BRIAN; Brookfield HS; Brookfield Center, CT; (Y); 21/230; French Clb; Var Golf; Var Capt Socr; High Hon Roll; Notre Dame; Bus Admin.

KELLEY, COURTNEY; Masuk HS; Monroe, CT; (Y); Drama Clb; French Clb; JCL; Swmmng; Tennis; Hon Roll; Rndlph-Mcn Coll; Intl Rltns.

KELLEY, EDWARD; Ridgefield HS; Ridgefield, CT; (Y); 16/329; Rep Am Leg Boys St; Off Church Yth Grp; Nwsp Ed-Chief; Nwsp Rptr; JV Socr; Var Capt Trk; High Hon Roll; Hon Roll; NHS; Ntl Merit SF; Lions Clb Schlrshp 86; NEA Schlrshp 86; Excllnc Engl 86; Dartmouth Coll; Engl.

KELLEY, HEDY; Oliver Wolcott RVTS HS; Thomaston, CT; (Y); Sec VICA; JV Var Cheerleading; Certfd Nrs Aid 85; Hotl Mgmt.

KELLEY, KATHLEEN; Mary Immaculate Acad; New Britain, CT; (Y); Cmnty Wkr; French Clb; Sec Jr Cls; JV Var Bsktbl; Hon Roll; Wstrn New England Coll; Lawyer.

KELLEY, MICHAEL; Ridgefield HS; Ridgefield, CT; (Y); 27/380; Am Leg Boys St; Off Church Yth Grp; Nwsp Rptr; Nwsp Sprt Ed; Nwsp Stf; Var Socr; JV Trk; High Hon Roll; Hon Roll; NHS; Arch.

KELLMEL, VICKI; East Hartford HS; E Hartford, CT; (Y); Ski Clb; Drm Mjr(t); Mrchg Band; Yrbk Stf; Rep Jr Cls; Var Capt Swmmng; Trk; High Hon Roll; NHS; Ntl Merit Ltr; Elem Ed.

KELLY, BRIAN; Fairfield Prep Schl; Southport, CT; (Y); Radio Clb; VP SADD; Im Bsktbl; Var L Lcrss; Smmr Ct Cngrssnl Intern Prog 86.

KELLY, GINA; Brookfield HS; Brookfield, CT; (Y); 21/250; Pep Clb; Varsity Clb; Variety Show; Yrbk Stf; Sec Frsh Cls; Rep Soph Cls; Rep Jr Cls; Var Cheerleading; High Hon Roll; Hon Roll; Peer Cnslng Committee 86-87.

KELLY, KATHLEEN A; Naugatuck HS; Union City, CT; (Y); 15/307; Chorus; Var Capt Crs Cntry; Var Capt Trk; Hon Roll; NHS; Amer HS Athlt 84; All-ST X-Cntry Tm 85; Mattatuck CC; Crimnl Justice.

KELLY, MARK; Wilton HS; Wilton, CT; (Y); Civic Clb; SADD; Rep Frsh Cls; Rep Soph Cls; JV Var Bsbl; JV Var Bsktbl; Coach Actv; Ftbl; High Hon Roll; Hon Roll; NHS 85; Ldrshp Awd Bsktbl 84; Duke; Bus Adm.

KENDALL, LEIGH; William H Hall HS; W Hartford, CT; (Y); JA; Ski Clb; Jazz Band; Orch; School Musical; Symp Band; Var Ftbl; Hon Roll; JP Sousa Awd; Berklee Coll Of Music Schlrshp 85; U Of Hartford; Accntng.

KENDALL, MICHAEL; West Haven HS; W Haven, CT; (Y); Cmnty Wkr; Science Clb; Nwsp Stf; Lit Mag; Jr NHS; Babson College; Acctg.

KENDRA, CARYN MARIE; Notre Dame Catholic HS; Fairfield, CT; (Y); 4/230; Trs French Clb; Hosp Aide; Yrbk Ed-Chief; Sr Cls; Twrlr; Dnfth Awd; Elks Awd; French Hon Soc; NHS; Rotary Awd; Hgh Hon Rl 82-86; Bys Var Bsktbl Scrkpr 83-86; Ky Clb 83-86; Georgetown U; Nrsng.

KENDRICK, JENETTE; St Joseph HS; Stratford, CT; (Y); 76/258; Drama Clb; Girl Scts; Ski Clb; Spanish Clb; Band; Concert Band; Orch; Stage Crew; Yrbk Stf; JV Bowling; Vetrnry Mdcn.

KENNAN, ROBERT T; Parish Hill HS; Hampton, CT; (Y); 9/38; Computer Clb; Band; Chorus; Church Choir; Concert Band; Jazz Band; Orch; School Musical; Swing Chorus; Boy Scts; Yth Amer Bnd 85 & 86; Shanandoah Coll; Music Thrpy.

KENNEDY, HEATHER; Andrew Warde HS; Fairfield, CT; (Y); Drama Clb; Varsity Clb; Band; Rep Jr Cls; Trs Sr Cls; Cheerleading; Var Tennis; Var Vllybl; High Hon Roll; Hon Roll; Librl Arts.

KENNEDY, KEVIN; Putnam HS; Putnam, CT; (Y); 3/125; Am Leg Boys St; Boy Scts; School Play; Yrbk Ed-Chief; VP Frsh Cls; Var Socr; Var Capt Trk; Pres NHS; Ntl Merit Ltr; Voice Dem Awd; Air Force ROTC & Navy ROTC Schlrshps 86; Trck MVP 85; U S Air Force Acad; Astrntcl En.

KENNEDY, SHANNON LEE; Mary Immaculate Acad; New Britain, CT; (Y); French Clb; Hosp Aide; Hon Roll; Jr NHS; Sec Soph Cls; Pres Jr Cls; JV Cheerleading; Outstndng Scholar Engl II Awd 85; Outstndng Scholar Geom Awd 85; Alg II Merit Awd 86; Bus.

KENNEY, ELIZABETH ANN; Holy Cross HS; Waterbury, CT; (Y); Church Yth Grp; Pres SADD; Rep Pres Stu Cncl; Stat Ftbl; Mgr(s); JV Sftbl; Hon Roll; NHS; Fn Arts Clb 85-86; Soc Stds Hnr Scty 85-86; Bus.

KENNEY, ROBIN; Maloney HS; Meriden, CT; (Y); Cmnty Wkr; Drama Clb; Nwsp Stf; Yrbk Stf; Off Jr Cls; Off Sr Cls; Trs Stu Cncl; Var L Swmmng; JV Tennis; Hon Roll; Elem Ed.

KENT, DEBORAH; Academy Of Our Lady Of Mercy; Milford, CT; (Y); 25/111; Church Yth Grp; French Clb; Girl Scts; Church Choir; Stage Crew; Yrbk Stf; Jr NHS; Psychlgy.

KENT, ROBERT; Oliver Wolcott Tech HS; Torrington, CT; (Y); Aud/Vis; VICA; Rep Soph Cls; Rep Jr Cls; Air Con/Refrgrtn Tech.

KENYON, KIMBERLY; Mark T Sheehan HS; Wallingford, CT; (Y); 1/238; Key Clb; Spanish Clb; Church Choir; Yrbk Stf; VP Frsh Cls; Trs Stu Cncl; Stat Ice Hcky; Var Capt Socr; High Hon Roll; NHS; Hrvd Bk Clb Awd 86; Otstndng Non-Ofcr Stu 86; ST Cptl 86; Pre-Law.

KEOGH, MAUREEN; Brien Mc Mahon HS; Norwalk, CT; (Y); 1/275; Am Leg Aux Girls St; Church Yth Grp; Band; Capt Powder Puff Ftbl; JC Awd; JP Sousa Awd; NHS; Debate Tm; Hosp Aide; Spanish Clb; Hrvrd U Bk Awd 85; Wstrn Rgnl Band 85 & 86; Obrln Coll Bk Awd 85; Duke U; Med.

KEOGH, PATRICIA; Brien Mcmahon HS; Norwalk, CT; (Y); 1/288; Am Leg Aux Girls St; Church Yth Grp; Sec Bsbl; Hosp Aide; Concert Band; Mrchg Band; Rep Stu Cncl; JC Awd; JP Sousa Awd; Sec NHS; Hrvrd Bk Awd 85; Hly Crss Bk Awd 85; Wstrn Ct Rgnl Band 84&85; Duke U; Pre-Med.

KERELEJZA, STEPHEN J; New Britain HS; New Britain, CT; (Y); Art Clb; Q&S; L Var Crs Cntry; JV Ftbl; Var L Trk; Hon Roll; Xavier Frshmn Invtnl Trck & Fld Meet 1st Pl 84; All State Track Tm 85-86; All State Track Tm Trpl Jmp.

KERNS, KATHLEEN; Southington HS; Marion, CT; (Y); FBLA; High Hon Roll; Hon Roll; Stone Schl Of Bus; Ex Sec.

KETT, DENISE; Laurelton Hall HS; Stratford, CT; (Y); 4/117; Math Clb; Math Tm; Service Clb; Spanish Clb; Teachers Aide; Chorus; Mu Alp Tht; NHS; Ntl Merit SF; Spanish NHS; Pre-Med.

KHALIFA, ALY G; Greenwich HS; Riverside, CT; (Y); Art Clb; Stage Crew; Ed Nwsp Stf; Var Socr; High Hon Roll; Robt W Amick Art Schlrshp 86; Sci Stu Rcgntn, 3rd Stu Exhib Energy Resources 85; NC ST U; Prod Dsgn.

KHANT, SANJAY; Windsor HS; Windsor, CT; (Y); 2/350; Math Clb; Math Tm; Quiz Bowl; Scholastic Bowl; High Hon Roll; Hon Roll; Ntl Merit Ltr; Prfct Atten Awd; Sal; Engl & Socl Stds Awds 84; Rensselaer Polytechnc Inst; Eng.

KIDA, TRACI; Seymour HS; Seymour, CT; (Y); Am Leg Aux Girls St; Church Yth Grp; SADD; Color Guard; School Play; Stage Crew; Nwsp Stf; Yrbk Stf; Jr Cls; Rep Stu Cncl.

KIELY, MEG; Sacred Heart Acad; Hamden, CT; (Y); School Musical; Rep Frsh Cls; Rep Soph Cls; Pres Jr Cls; VP Stu Cncl; Var Capt Tennis; Cit Awd; High Hon Roll; NHS; Spanish NHS; Chem Olympd Exm Awd; NEDT Awd; 3 Yrs Hnrs Awd; Lib Arts.

KIERAS, SCOTT; Shelton HS; Shelton, CT; (Y); VP Ski Clb; Spanish Clb; Stage Crew; Capt L Bsbl; Capt L Bsktbl; Wt Lftg; Hon Roll.

KIERNAN, BRIAN; Torrington HS; Torrington, CT; (Y); 24/284; Aud/Vis; Cmnty Wkr; Drama Clb; Library Aide; School Musical; School Play; Stage Crew; Ftbl; High Hon Roll; Hon Roll; Jhn D Hogan Schlrshp, Trrngtn Schlrshp, Grace Hand Kelly Schlrshp 86; U CT Elec Engrng.

KIERNAN, SARA; Ridgefield HS; Ridgefield, CT; (S); Church Yth Grp; Cmnty Wkr; Dance Clb; German Clb; Girl Scts; Intnl Clb; Political Wkr; Band; Jazz Band; Mrchg Band; Cngrss-Bundestag Yth Exch Recip 84-85; Cert Achvt Schl Int Trnng 84; Supr Ratg Natl Fed Music Fstvl 83; Intl Rel.

KIGANDA, MARY EDNA; Academy Of The Holy Family HS; Gaithersburg, MD; (Y); 2/29; Red Cross Aide; Chorus; School Musical; Stage Crew; Sec Sr Cls; Var L Bsktbl; Var Capt Sftbl; High Hon Roll; Hon Roll; NHS; Natl Hon Soc Of Art 85-86; CIAC & US Army Reserve Schlr Athl Awd 85-86; MVP Schls Var Bsbkbl & Sftb; Rosemont Coll; Bio Chem.

KILBRIDE, SEAN; Fairfield College Prep Schl; Fairfield, CT; (Y); Nwsp Rptr; Var Bsktbl; Lib Art.

KILLIAN, THOMAS C; Trumball HS; Trumbull, CT; (Y); 1/450; Trs French Clb; Scholastic Bowl; Thesps; Chorus; Madrigals; Pres Trs Stu Cncl; Var Capt Swmmng; Bausch & Lomb Sci Awd; NCTE Awd; NHS; Harvard Clb Book Awd 86; ST Wide Chemathon Wnnr 86; All CT Swim Tm 84; Physcs.

KILLIANY, MARY; Lewis S Mills HS; Burlington, CT; (Y); Ski Clb; Color Guard; Concert Band; Mrchg Band; Var L Fld Hcky; JV L Tennis; Hon Roll; Fld Hcky Mst Imprvd Plyr 84.

KIM, EDWARD; Greenwich HS; Greenwich, CT; (Y); Church Yth Grp; Debate Tm; Varsity Clb; Church Choir; Rep Soph Cls; JV Bsktbl; VP Trk; Var JV Vllybl; Gov Hon Prg Awd; NHS; CA Schlrshp Fdrtn 85.

KIMBALL, JAMES; Naugatuck HS; Naugatuck, CT; (Y); Boy Scts; Church Yth Grp; Cmnty Wkr; Library Aide; Nwsp Rptr; Yrbk Sprt Ed; Var L Crs Cntry; Var L Trk; Hon Roll; Gettysburg Coll.

KIMBLER, CAROLYN; Low Heywood Thomas HS; Stamford, CT; (Y); 1/38; Nwsp Stf; Yrbk Stf; JV Bsktbl; Var L Tennis; JV Vllybl; High Hon Roll; NHS; Vssr Bk Prz 86; Govt.

KING, ALISON; Stamford HS; Stamford, CT; (Y); German Clb; JA; Political Wkr; Band; Concert Band; Jazz Band; Mrchg Band; Hon Roll; NHS; Iona Coll Lang Cntst Grmn 85&86; Intl Rltns.

KING IV, GEORGE; Ridgefield HS; Ridgefield, CT; (Y); 25/350; Service Clb; Nwsp Stf; Pres Soph Cls; Pres Stu Cncl; Trk; Hon Roll; NHS; Ntl Merit Ltr; Pres Frsh Cls; Rep Jr Cls; Hugh O Brian Yth Found; Outstndng Ldr; SF Ntl Achvt Comptn; Stu Rep Bd Ed; Brown U; Neurosci.

KING, HILARY; Stamford HS; Stamford, CT; (Y); Ski Clb; Varsity Clb; Band; Concert Band; Mrchg Band; Rep Stu Cncl; Sftbl; Hon Roll; NHS.

KING, JENNIFER; Berlin HS; Kensington, CT; (Y); 2/198; Math Tm; Band; Mrchg Band; School Musical; Bausch & Lomb Sci Awd; High Hon Roll; NHS; Ctr For Creative Yth Wesleyan U 85; Hon Rsrh Prog A Brockhvn Ntl Lab 86; Molecular Bio.

KING, KATHY; Old Say Brook SR HS; Old Saybrook, CT; (Y); AFS; Church Yth Grp; Cmnty Wkr; Chorus; School Musical; Rep Stu Cncl; VP Crs Cntry; JV Trk; High Hon Roll; Hon Roll; Jr Internship To Washington DC 86.

KING, KRISTEN; Lauralton Hall HS; Trumbull, CT; (Y); Drama Clb; French Clb; Model UN; Science Clb; Ski Clb; Acpl Chr; Chorus; Stage Crew; Yrbk Stf; Lit Mag; Marine Bio.

KINKADE, CHRIS; Nonnewaug HS; Woodbury, CT; (Y); Computer Clb; Rep Soph Cls; Var Crs Cntry; JV Im Socr; Var Trk; Var Wrstlng; Hon Roll; Brkshr Leag All Star-Crss Cntry 85-86; Sprano Awd 85; MVP Crss Cntry 85-86; Elec Engrng.

KINKAID, TRACEY; New Fairfield HS; New Fairfield, CT; (Y); 1/230; School Musical; Cmnty Wkr; Pres French Hon Soc; High Hon Roll; NHS; Ntl Merit Ltr; Church Yth Grp; Drama Clb; Trs Girl Scts; Latin Clb; Sci Soc Of Wmn Engrs Awd 86 Rnsslr Paly 86; Lang Top Frnch & Ltn Stud 86; Music 86; Hrvrd Bk Clb Awd 86; Bio.

KINSELLA, LEANNE; Brookfield HS; Brookfield Ctr, CT; (Y); 13/202; Church Yth Grp; FBLA; Girl Scts; Math Clb; Math Tm; Red Cross Aide; Spanish Clb; Chorus; Nwsp Rptr; Lit Mag; Spnsh V Hnrs Awd 86; Brookfld Wmns Clb Awd 86; Chorus Awd 86; Alg IA Awd 83; Mary Washington Coll; Psych.

KIPP, CHRISTIAAN; Fairfield College Preparatory Schl; Fairfield, CT; (Y); Cmnty Wkr; Exploring; SADD; Im Fld Hcky; JV Golf; Var Swmmng; Wt Lftg; Mrktg.

KIRBY, SUSAN; Seymour HS; Beacon Falls, CT; (S); JA; School Play; Variety Show; Nwsp Rptr; Nwsp Stf; NHS; 2nd Pl 1st Annl Housatonic Leag Persuasive Pblc Spkng Cntst 85; Ntl Piano Plyng Audtns 84; Cmmcntns.

KIRSCHNER, PAUL; Torrington HS; Torrington, CT; (Y); Waterbury ST Tech; Air Cndtng.

KISSAM, BARBARA; Avon HS; Avon, CT; (Y); 3/145; Church Yth Grp; French Clb; Ski Clb; Chorus; Sec Sr Cls; Mgr Stat Ftbl; Pres NHS; Stat Bsbl; Stat Trk; DAR Awd; Soc Women Engrs Awd Exc 85; Weslyan Bk Awd 85-86; Close Up Pgm WA DC 85; U CT; Pre-Med.

KITTREDGE, COURTNEY; Southington HS; Southington, CT; (Y); 17/600; Church Yth Grp; Hosp Aide; Ski Clb; Color Guard; Drill Tm; Mrchg Band; School Musical; School Play; High Hon Roll; NHS.

KJOS, RACHEL; Norwich Free Acad; Canterbury, CT; (Y); 29/514; Var L Cheerleading; Intnl Clb; Letterman Clb; High Hon Roll; Hon Roll; NHS; Cmmrcl Art.

KLAUCK, MATTHEW; New Fairfield HS; New Fairfield, CT; (Y); Church Yth Grp; Latin Clb; Stage Crew; Hon Roll; Ntl Latin Exam Awd 85; Mech Engr.

KLEIN, JENNIFER; St Marys HS; New Haven, CT; (Y); 4/95; Spanish Clb; Church Choir; Gov Hon Prg Awd; Spanish NHS; Frsh Alg Awd 84.

KLEIN, MARY; St Marys HS; Branford, CT; (Y); Spanish Clb; School Musical; High Hon Roll; Law.

KLEIN, MICHELLE; Saint Lukes HS; Norwalk, CT; (Y); Temple Yth Grp; Var JV Fld Hcky; Var Sftbl; Hon Roll; Biolgy Awd 85; St Lukes Hnr Soc Awd 85.

KLEINSCHMIDT, ALLISON; Southington HS; Southington, CT; (Y); 4-H; Chorus; Jazz Band; School Musical; High Hon Roll; Hon Roll; NHS; Meridan Fed Musicians 2nd Pl Schlrshp 85-86; New Britain Musicl Clb Schlrshp 85-86; Acad Perform Arts; Music.

KLEKOTKA, PEGGIE; Bolton HS; Bolton, CT; (Y); Dance Clb; VP French Clb; Hosp Aide; Ski Clb; School Musical; VP Frsh Cls; Pres Soph Cls; Var L Cheerleading; NHS; Ntl Merit Ltr; Sprtswmn Awd, Jzz Trphy 85; Bst Vrsty Chrldr 86; PSAT Hgh Scorer 86; 150 Hrs Vlntrng 86; Pre-Med.

KLINE, ALLISON; Brookfield HS; Brookfield Center, CT; (Y); Drama Clb; Math Clb; School Play; Rep Frsh Cls; Var L Gym; Var Mgr Socr; High Hon Roll; NHS; Soc Of Women Engrs Awd 86; Creative Wrtng Awd 86; Dsgn Awd 85; Archtctr.

KLINE, JAMES; Wilbur Cross HS; New Haven, CT; (Y); Boy Scts; Ski Clb; Rep Frsh Cls; Rep Soph Cls; Var Capt Swmmng; Hon Roll; Northwestern; Crmnlgy.

KLINE, MATTHEW; Bloomfield HS; Bloomfield, CT; (Y); 5/250; Civic Clb; French Clb; Thesps; Concert Band; Var JV Socr; Capt Trk; Capt Wrstlng; Pres French Hon Soc; NHS; Ntl Merit Ltr.

KLING, KRISTEN CRATCH; Suffield HS; West Suffield, CT; (Y); 2/145; Drama Clb; Math Tm; Madrigals; School Play; Stu Cncl; Gym; Trk; NHS; Sal; Schlr Ath Awd 86; Colgate U.

KLUGER, BEN; Emmett O Brien RVST HS; Chesire, CT; (Y); 2/178; Ski Clb; Nwsp Rptr; Rep Jr Cls; Rep Stu Cncl; Var JV Crs Cntry; Var Trk; High Hon Roll; NHS; Outstndng Undrclssmn Engl 85-86; Finc.

KMETZ, JOY M; Morgan HS; Clinton, CT; (Y); 40/150; VP FBLA; Hosp Aide; Office Aide; Pep Clb; Powder Puff Ftbl; Btty Crckr Awd; Cit Awd; High Hon Roll; Hon Roll; Home Ec Dept Awd 83; Outstndg Bus Awd 86; Briarwood Coll Bk Awd 86; Becker JC; Bus Admin.

KNEELAND, KIMBERLY; East Hampton HS; E Hampton, CT; (Y); French Clb; FBLA; Band; Lit Mag; Hon Roll; Mst Hrd-Wrkng Frnch Stu 81-82; Hnr Rll Cert Awd 83-84; Jrnlsm.

KNICKERBOCKER, DEAN; Branford HS; Branford, CT; (Y); 12/315; Am Leg Boys St; Yrbk Sprt Ed; Var Ftbl; Var Trk; High Hon Roll; Prfct Atten Awd; Yrbk Stf; Im Bsktbl; Im Wt Lftg; Hon Roll; Proj AIM U S Coast Guard Acad 86; Mst Imprvd Plyr Ftbl 85; Amer H S Math Exam 3rd Pl 86; U S Naval Acad; Naval Aviation.

KNOWLTON, TARA; Watertown HS; Watertown, CT; (Y); 8/250; Church Yth Grp; Ski Clb; Church Choir; Variety Show; Rep Stu Cncl; High Hon Roll; NHS; Schlstc Excllnce Awd 86; Mst Outstndng Skr Awd Ski Team 84; Bus.

KNOX, KATHLEEN; Low-Heywood Thomas Schl; New Canaan, CT; (Y); Drama Clb; Pep Clb; Service Clb; School Musical; School Play; Yrbk Bus Mgr; Rep Jr Cls; High Hon Roll; Hon Roll; Cum Laude Ntl Ltn Exam 84; Yale Clb Awd 86.

KOCH, ANDREW; East Lyme HS; E Lyme, CT; (Y); Camp Fr Inc; School Musical; School Play; Stage Crew; Golf; JV Wrstlng; Hon Roll.

KOCH, PETER; Central HS; Bristol, CT; (Y); 2/356; Am Leg Boys St; Boy Scts; Church Yth Grp; Computer Clb; Band; Mrchg Band; Symp Band; Capt L Socr; Capt L Trk; Wrstlng; Comp Sci.

KOCH, SHARYON; Old Saybrook SR HS; Old Saybrook, CT; (Y); Exploring; Band; Mrchg Band; School Musical; Yrbk Stf; Im Badmtn; Var Mgr(s); JV Tennis; Im Vllybl; NHS; Tri-M Music Hnr Soc 86-87; Undrgrad Art Awd 86; Law.

KOCHANEK, KATHRYN; Tolland HS; Tolland, CT; (Y); 5/165; Debate Tm; Hosp Aide; Rep Frsh Cls; Rep Soph Cls; Rep Jr Cls; Rep Sr Cls; JV Bsktbl; Var Crs Cntry; High Hon Roll; VP NHS; William & Mary; Pre-Med.

KOCHISS, DARCY; Shelton HS; Shelton, CT; (Y); 23/327; Spanish Clb; Band; Hon Roll; Travel Clb 85-86; SADD 85-86; U Of MA; Psych.

KOCHOL, LISA; Southington HS; Southington, CT; (Y); 52/600; Key Clb; Sec Latin Clb; Church Choir; School Musical; School Play; Pres Stu Cncl; NHS; Church Yth Grp; Drama Clb; Ski Clb; Hstss Appl Hrvst Fest 86; Dscvr III Gftd & Tlnt Prog At SHS 84-86; Frsh Schlr Athlt 84.

KOERKEL, HOLLY; Seymour HS; Seymour, CT; (S); 9/194; Yrbk Bus Mgr; Rep Stu Cncl; JV Crs Cntry; Hon Roll; NHS; Bryant Coll Grant Awd 86; Bryant Coll; Bus Adm.

KOERNER, TRACEY; Greenwich HS; Riverside, CT; (Y); AFS; Hosp Aide; JA; Library Aide; Stu Cncl; Stat Bsktbl; Hon Roll; IL ST Spn Achvt Tst 84; Bus Mgmt.

KOGUT, BRIAN; Francis T Maloney HS; Meriden, CT; (Y); Am Leg Boys St; Key Clb; Yrbk Stf; Pres Frsh Cls; Pres Soph Cls; Pres Jr Cls; Pres Sr Cls; VP Stu Cncl; JV Bsbl; NHS; Hugh O Brien Yth Fndtn Dlgt; Yale Bk Awd Rcpnt; CT Schlr.

KOHLER, MARGARET; East Catholic HS; Manchester, CT; (Y); 36/283; Church Yth Grp; Hon Roll; Tap Lsns 83 84; Bstn U.

KOHMAN, PATTI; Wilton HS; Wilton, CT; (Y); 100/350; Church Yth Grp; Chorus; Drm Mjr(t); Gym; Twrlr; Hon Roll; Bio.

KOHN, JENNIFER L; Andrew Warde HS; Fairfield, CT; (Y); Political Wkr; Band; JV Var Bsktbl; Am Leg Aux Girls St; Teachers Aide; Drm Mjr(t); Mrchg Band; Stu Cncl; Cit Awd; High Hon Roll; Young Americans Awd 86; Century III Leaders 86; U Of VA; Pol Sci.

KOLESAR, KAREN D; Danbury HS; Danbury, CT; (Y); Cmnty Wkr; Drama Clb; JA; Ski Clb; Variety Show; Nwsp Rptr; Nwsp Stf; Soph Cls; Jr Cls; Sr Cls; Frnkln Mrshl Bk Prz For Exc In Hmnts; Perry Awd In Scl Studies; U CT; Law.

KOLESNIK, KELLIE; Holy Cross HS; Waterbury, CT; (Y); 9/380; Latin Clb; Political Wkr; High Hon Roll; NHS; Ltn Hnr Scyt 85; Law.

KOMARENKO, PAUL; East Haven HS; E Haven, CT; (Y); 2/200; Am Leg Boys St; Computer Clb; French Clb; Library Aide; Math Tm; Yrbk Stf; Var Swmmng; Var Tennis; NHS; Sal; Yale Bk Awd 85; Lee Hartstone Memrl Schlrshp 86; Mayo Schlrshp 86; Rensselaer Polytechnc Inst.

KOMAROWSKA, AGNIESZKA; Norwalk HS; Norwalk, CT; (Y); Cmnty Wkr; German Clb; Hosp Aide; Teachers Aide; High Hon Roll; NHS; Pres Schlr; Goethe Inst Awd 85-86; Math Achvt Awd 85; Fathers Clb Awd 86; Fairfield U; Engrng.

KOMAROWSKA, KASIA; Norwalk HS; Norwalk, CT; (Y); 13/500; German Clb; Hosp Aide; High Hon Roll; Goethe Inst 86; Math.

KONARKOWSKI, OLIVER; Daniel Hand HS; Madison, CT; (Y); Boy Scts; German Clb; Orch; JV Coach Actv; Socr; Capt Var Swmmng; JV Tennis; Var Vllybl; Grmn Spch Dplma, Grmn Grdtng Dplma 85.

KONWERSKI, PETER; Amity Regional SR HS; Woodbridge, CT; (Y); Boy Scts; SADD; Concert Band; Jazz Band; Mrchg Band; Yrbk Sprt Ed; Var Ftbl; Var Wt Lftg; Hon Roll; NHS; Egl Sct 85; All ST 84.

KOPERWHATS, KATHY; Stratford HS; Stratford, CT; (Y); Dance Clb; Drama Clb; Ski Clb; School Musical; School Play; Ed Nwsp Stf; Yrbk Stf; Rep Sr Cls; Rep Stu Cncl; Capt Cheerleading; Achvt Awrd 86; Natnl Ldrshp Svc Awrd 86; USA Honr Spirt Sqd 86; CT ST U Grant Awrd 86; Southern CT ST U; Commnctns.

KORDYS, CYNTHIA; Southington HS; Southington, CT; (Y); 22/550; Pres Debate Tm; French Clb; Math Clb; Math Tm; High Hon Roll; NHS; Key Clb; Stat Tennis; Italian Clb V-Pres 84-85; Dscvr 2II Gftd & Tlntd Prgrm 83-86; Tnns Tm Mgr 85-86; Gdng Knghts Clb 84-86; Smith Coll; Lbrl Arts.

KORMANIK, KELLEY; Brookfield HS; Brookfieldcenter, CT; (Y); 30/240; Church Yth Grp; French Clb; GAA; Pep Clb; Varsity Clb; Acpl Chr; Chorus; Swing Chorus; Variety Show; Trs Frsh Cls; Anatomy & Physlgy Sci Awd 86; PA ST; Phys Thrpy.

KORN, MICHELLE; Westhill HS; Stamford, CT; (Y); Computer Clb; Dance Clb; DECA; VP JA; Library Aide; Office Aide; Pep Clb; Fshn.

KORZON, GARY; Emmett O Brien Technical HS; Beacon Falls, CT; (Y); Church Yth Grp; JV Bsktbl; Tool/Die Trade.

KOSHA, TODD RICHARD; Holy Cross HS; Watertown, CT; (Y); 73/352; Band; Concert Band; Mrchg Band; Var L Diving; Var L Swmmng; Hon Roll; Jr NHS; Ntl Merit SF; Presdntl Acadmc Ftns Awd 86; Daniel Webster Coll; Aviatn.

KOST, CAROLYN; Trumbull HS; Trumbull, CT; (Y); Computer Clb; Pres FTA; Mgr JA; Sec Math Clb; Chorus; Ed Lit Mag; High Hon Roll; NCTE Awd; NHS; Sec Spanish NHS; Trumbull Adm Assn Awd 86; Audrey Toigo Scholar 86; Spn Awd 86; St Joseph Coll; Elem Ed.

KOSTEK, DAVID; Wethersfield HS; Wethersfield, CT; (Y); 21/299; Trs Science Clb; School Musical; Ed Nwsp Phtg; Ed Yrbk Phtg; Lit Mag; Var L Crs Cntry; Var L Trk; High Hon Roll; NHS; NEDT Awd; Schl Rock Band Bassist 86-87; Safe Rides Similiar To SADD 84-87; Rochester Inst Tech; Pro Photog.

KOUTROUBIS, CHRISTINA; Norwalk HS; Norwalk, CT; (Y); Trs Church Yth Grp; Latin Clb; School Musical; Mgr Stage Crew; Var L Trk; High Hon Roll; Hon Roll; Memorial Scholar Contemporary Issues 86; CT Indstrl Arts Assn Awd 1st & 3rd Pl 86; U CT; Med.

KOVACS, MARK; Bullard Havens Technical Schl; Fairfield, CT; (Y); JA; Hon Roll; Tool & Die Mkr.

KOWACK, ERIC P; St Bernard HS; N Stonington, CT; (Y); 16/297; Camera Clb; Church Yth Grp; Computer Clb; Math Clb; Teachers Aide; Variety Show; Stu Cncl; High Hon Roll; Hon Roll; Socr; Yale Frntrs In Sci 83-84; NROTC Schlrshp 86; U S Cst Brd Acad; Pdtrcn.

KOWALCHIK, RICHARD M; Trumbull HS; Trumbull, CT; (Y); Aud/Vis; Drama Clb; JA; Band; Concert Band; Mrchg Band; School Play; Symp Band; High Hon Roll; Hon Roll; Amherst; Bus.

KOZLOWSKI, LISA; Southington HS; Southington, CT; (Y); 5/550; Am Leg Aux Girls St; Church Yth Grp; Rep Key Clb; Pres Latin Clb; School Play; Ed Nwsp Stf; High Hon Roll; JC Awd; Cmnty Wkr; Red Cross Aide; Discover III-GIFTED & Talented Prgm 83-86; Outstndng Stu Of The Yr 85; Outstndng Svc In Key Clb 83-86; Northeastern U; Med Rsrch.

KOZLOWSKY, JOHN; The Kingswood-Oxford Schl; Newington, CT; (Y); Service Clb; Spanish Clb; Yrbk Stf; Rep Frsh Cls; JV Ice Hcky; Var Lcrss; Wt Lftg; USAF; Pilot.

KRALIK, STEPHEN; New Britain HS; New Britain, CT; (Y); 24/305; Boy Scts; High Hon Roll; Hon Roll; Ntl Merit SF; U CT; Engrng.

KRAMER, DAVID; Staples HS; Westport, CT; (Y); Drama Clb; Acpl Chr; Chorus; School Musical; School Play; Stage Crew; JV Ftbl; Awd Por Spnsh Excllence 85; NYU; Mstrs Degree In Flm.

KRAMER, STEVEN; New Fairfield HS; New Fairfield, CT; (Y); 54/240; Am Leg Boys St; Boy Scts; Civic Clb; Cmnty Wkr; Dance Clb; Debate Tm; Political Wkr; Varsity Clb; School Play; Stage Crew; Exch Stu Puerto Rico 85; Georgetown; Senator.

KRAUS, DANIEL; Holy Cross HS; Cheshire, CT; (Y); 64/386; Church Yth Grp; Var JV Socr; High Hon Roll; Hon Roll; NHS; Spanish NHS; Rnr Up ST Chmpnshp Sccr 85-86; Bus Admin.

KRAUS, GREGORY; Wilbur Cross HS; New Haven, CT; (S); 9/259; PAVAS; Political Wkr; Ed Lit Mag; Stu Cncl; Swmmng; Trk; Hon Roll; Ski Clb; Yrbk Stf; Crs Cntry; Essy Cntst Wnnr ST CT Govnrs Conf Yth 85; Schlrshp-Rep Yth Ldrshp Semnr 84; Hgh Hnr Achvt Awd-Psych; Psychlgcl Rsrch.

KRAUSS, STACEY; New Fairfield HS; New Fairfield, CT; (Y); 42/230; Latin Clb; Variety Show; Lit Mag; Stat Bsktbl; Capt Cheerleading; Trk; Hon Roll; Tlntd Wrtrs Pgm, Creatv Wrtng Clb 85-86; Penn ST; Advtsng.

KRAYESKI, SUSAN; Holy Cross HS; Naugatuck, CT; (Y); Pep Clb; Ski Clb; SADD; Crs Cntry; Gym; Hon Roll.

KREITLOW, STORMEY; Seymour HS; Seymour, CT; (S); 20/194; Church Yth Grp; Hosp Aide; VP JA; Church Choir; Pom Pon; Hon Roll; Russell Sage Coll; Phy Thrpst.

KREONIDES, NICHOLAS C; Litchfield HS; Litchfield, CT; (Y); Sec Trs AFS; Am Leg Boys St; Trs Sec 4-H; Rep Stu Cncl; Var L Bsktbl; DAR Awd; Hon Roll; Drama Clb; Math Tm; Radio Clb; St Anthnys Cir Dghtr Of Isabella 83-85; Frnc Gosinski Mem Awd 86; Ann Toohey Mem 86; Cntrl CT ST U.

KRISTAN, CHRIS; O H Platt HS; Meriden, CT; (Y); Am Leg Boys St; Drama Clb; Key Clb; Latin Clb; Crs Cntry; Swmmng; Tennis; Hon Roll; Nwsp Stf; YMCA Yth & Govt 85-86; Outstndng JR Boy Awd 86.

KRISTENSEN, SARAH; Simsbury HS; Simsbury, CT; (Y); Church Yth Grp; Rep Drama Clb; VP JA; L Chorus; Stage Crew; Yrbk Stf; Lit Mag; Var L Badmtn; Hon Roll; NHS; Wrtg.

KRIVANEC, LISA; Francis T Maloney HS; Meriden, CT; (Y); DECA; Key Clb; Yrbk Stf; Rep Frsh Cls; Rep Soph Cls; Rep Jr Cls; Rep Sr Cls; Var Socr; Var Trk; Var Hon Roll; Bus Admn.

KROCHTA, STEPHEN; Stratford HS; Stratford, CT; (Y); 13/231; Pres Church Yth Grp; Math Clb; Rep Jr Cls; Rep Sr Cls; Rep Stu Cncl; Var L Crs Cntry; Var L Trk; Hon Roll; Trs NHS; AZ ST U; Aerontcl Engnrng.

KROESE, MICHAEL; Southington HS; Southington, CT; (Y); 2/600; Math Tm; Quiz Bowl; Ski Clb; JV Socr; Bausch & Lomb Sci Awd; Pres NHS; Sal; 1st Prz Comp Sci-CT Sci Fair 86; Elks Clb Stu Of Mnth 85; Worcester Polytech Inst; Engrng.

KROKOSKY, RAYMOND; Emmett O Brien Tech; Beacon Falls, CT; (Y); High Hon Roll; Hon Roll; STAR Supply Co Awd 86; Waterbury ST Tech; Comp Pgmmr.

KROM, KYLE; East Lyme HS; Niantic, CT; (Y); 15/257; Math Tm; Acpl Chr; School Musical; Var Crs Cntry; Var Trk; NHS; Ntl Merit SF; Church Yth Grp; Drama Clb; Chorus; CASS CIAC/Armd Frcs Schlr Athlt; SR Math Awd; All ST Chrs; U Of CT; Math.

KROMISH, ZANE; Pham HS; Amston, CT; (Y); 40/210; Am Leg Boys St; Trs Sr Cls; Var Bsktbl; Hon Roll; Yale Frntiers Appld Sci Series 86; Statstcn.

KRONENWETTER, JOHN; East Catholic HS; South Windsor, CT; (Y); Rep Soph Cls; Rep Jr Cls; Var Socr; Im Wt Lftg; JV Wrstlng; Smmr Rec Dept Sccr Team MVP 83; Bus.

KRUEGER, LAURA; Acad Of Our Lady Of Mercy; Trumbull, CT; (Y); Drama Clb; Spanish Clb; School Play; Stage Crew; Yrbk Stf; Dance Clb; Math Clb.

KRUGER, KERI W; Coginchaug Regional HS; Middlefield, CT; (Y); 14/128; AFS; Pres Sec 4-H; Service Clb; 4-H Awd; Hon Roll; Yrbk Stf; Off Soph Cls; Off Jr Cls; Socr; Prfct Atten Awd; Englsh & Comp Awds; Algebra I; Bus Mngmnt.

KRUM, DARIN; Granby HS; Granby, CT; (Y); Band; Concert Band; Drm Mjr(t); Mrchg Band; School Play; Stage Crew; Symp Band; Sec Jr Cls; Sec Stu Cncl; Prfct Atten Awd; Most Colorful Drum Major; Meritorus Tech Assist Schl Prod 86.

KRUPKA, ROBERT; New Britain HS; New Britain, CT; (Y); 4/400; Church Yth Grp; High Hon Roll; NCTE Awd; Yale Bk Awd 86; Awd Excllnce Spn 84; Engrng.

KRUZEL, CHRISTINE; East Windsor HS; E Windsor, CT; (Y); Rep Soph Cls; Rep Jr Cls; Bsktbl; Fld Hcky; Trk; Hon Roll; Bsktbl Most Impvd Awd 86; Schl Shot Put Recd 32 Ft 7 In 86; U Of CT; Engrng.

KRYSIAK, KAREN; Platt Regional Vocational Tech Schl; Milford, CT; (Y); Rep Frsh Cls; Rep Soph Cls; Rep Jr Cls; Rep Stu Cncl; Var Cheerleading; Var Sftbl; High Hon Roll; Hon Roll; Jr NHS; NHS; Mech Engr.

KU, ALAN; Brookfield HS; Brookfield Center, CT; (Y); Math Clb; JV Socr; High Hon Roll; Hon Roll.

KUBECK, MICHAEL; O H Platt HS; S Meriden, CT; (Y); 24/240; French Clb; Pres Math Clb; Yrbk Stf; Stu Cncl; High Hon Roll; Hon Roll; PA ST U; Engrng.

KUBICKO, SHARON; Lauralton Hall HS; Shelton, CT; (Y); 21/111; Sec Church Yth Grp; Debate Tm; Drama Clb; Hosp Aide; Model UN; Yrbk Stf; Rep Frsh Cls; French Clb; JA; Latin Clb; NEDT Prfrmnc Awd 84; Boston Coll; Pre-Law.

KUGELMAN, KRISTEN; The Taft Schl; Chappaqua, NY; (Y); Nwsp Rptr; Yrbk Stf; Im Ice Hcky; JV Lcrss; Var L Socr; Hamilton Coll.

KUHN, SUSAN; Rockville HS; Vernon, CT; (Y); 9/342; Pres Church Yth Grp; Math Tm; Office Aide; SADD; Sftbl; High Hon Roll; Hon Roll; NHS; Ntl Merit Ltr; Lebbeus Bissel Schlrshp 86; MIT; Bio-Med.

KUHR, REBECCA; Southington HS; Southington, CT; (Y); VP Church Yth Grp; Sec VP FFA; Achvt Awd Extmprns Spkng 85; Greenhnd Degree FFA 83; Chptr Frmr Degree FFA 84; Ag Bus.

KULAS, DONALD; Granby Memorial HS; Granby, CT; (Y); 2/124; Drama Clb; Math Clb; Trs Jr Cls; High Hon Roll; Lion Awd; NHS; Pres Schlr; Sal; Aud/Vis; Red Cross Aide; Dept Schlr Englsh, Math & Sci 86; Excllnc Calculus, Comp Sci & Bio II 86; Exemplory Acvht Englsh 86; U Of VT; Biochem.

KULL, CHRISTIAN; Ridgefield HS; Ridgefield, CT; (Y); 4/387; Church Yth Grp; Cmnty Wkr; VP German Clb; Math Tm; Mrchg Band; Symp Band; High Hon Roll; Engl Dept Bk Awd 86; Earth Sci.

KULLBERG, ROBIN; Shelton HS; Shelton, CT; (Y); Art Clb; VP Church Yth Grp; Library Aide; Yrbk Phtg; Yrbk Stf; Stat Bsktbl; Mgr(s); High Hon Roll; Ntl Merit Ltr; Spanish NHS; Spnsh II Awd 85; Ctr For Creative Yth At Wesleyan U 85.

KUNZE, RONALD; Southington HS; Southington, CT; (Y); Church Yth Grp; Hosp Aide; Math Tm; Spanish Clb; Nwsp Rptr; Golf; Hon Roll; Pre-Med.

KUPPERMAN, CHARLES; Choate Rosemary Hall HS; Mansfield Ctr, CT; (S); Acpl Chr; Church Choir; Nwsp Stf; Lit Mag; JV Trk; Franklin Hstry Prize 85; Writer.

KUPSON, JONATHAN; Amity Regional SR HS; West Haven, CT; (Y); 28/388; Am Leg Boys St; Hst Latin Clb; Red Cross Aide; Chorus; Lit Mag; Var L Crs Cntry; Var L Trk; NHS; Ntl Merit Ltr; Colby Coll; Envirmntl Stud.

KUSHNER, STEPHANIE; Danbury HS; Danbury, CT; (Y); 11/483; Key Clb; Band; Concert Band; Jazz Band; Mrchg Band; Orch; Symp Band; High Hon Roll; Hon Roll; Ntl Merit Ltr; Perry Awd Achvt Engl 86; Sci.

KUSMIK, WILLIAM ALDO; E Catholic HS; Manchester, CT; (Y); 34/285; Ski Clb; Band; Pep Band; Variety Show; Lit Mag; Swmmng; Hon Roll; Ntl Merit Ltr; Engr.

KUZIAK, JACQUELYN; Shelton HS; Shelton, CT; (Y); French Clb; French Hon Soc; Hon Roll; Bus Admin.

KUZIAK, PAUL; Southington HS; Plantsville, CT; (Y); Key Clb; Math Tm; Ski Clb; Concert Band; Mrchg Band; Yrbk Phtg; Crs Cntry; Socr; Trk; Hon Roll; Wtrbry ST Tech; Elec Engrng.

KWAKYE, GLADYS; Hartofrd Public HS; Hartford, CT; (Y); FFA; Intnl Clb; Math Clb; Church Choir; Off Stu Cncl; Trk; High Hon Roll; Church Yth Grp; FNA; Tennis; Certfctn 82-83; Hartford Coll Women; Med.

KWAN, TANYA; Wilton HS; Wilton, CT; (Y); Trs Church Yth Grp; Hosp Aide; Key Clb; Pep Clb; Mgr Ski Clb; Acpl Chr; Jazz Band; Swing Chorus; Var Twrlr; Hon Roll.

KWASH, KRISTIN; Trumbull HS; Trumbull, CT; (Y); Dance Clb; VP Exploring; Hosp Aide; Library Aide; Spanish Clb; Chorus; Yrbk Stf; Mgr(s); Tennis; High Hon Roll; Villanova; Med.

KWESKIN, AMY; Stamford HS; Stamford, CT; (S); Debate Tm; Library Aide; Stage Crew; Rptr Nwsp Phtg; Nwsp Sprt Ed; Rep Frsh Cls; Stu Cncl; Capt Fld Hcky; Capt Trk; Hon Roll; 3rd Pl Hnrs Awd Annl CT Sci Fair 83; 2nd Pl Stamford Sci Fair 83; Comm.

KYLE, PAULA; Lyme-Old Lyme HS; Lyme, CT; (Y); 20/103; AFS; Church Yth Grp; Cmnty Wkr; VP Concert Band; Jazz Band; Mrchg Band; Yrbk Phtg; Yrbk Stf; Stu Cncl; Var Bsktbl; CT Jr Intern Schlrp Wash DC 86; Natl Wmns Rowg Chmpnshps 85; Inrschlstc Rowg Chmpshps 2nd Pl New Eng.

L HEUREUX, KIMBERLY; Southington HS; Southington, CT; (Y); 69/600; Pres Sec Church Yth Grp; FTA; Key Clb; Latin Clb; High Hon Roll; Hon Roll; Prfct Atten Awd; ST Ltn Awd Lvl 1 83-84; Philip G Goodrow Memrl Schlrshp 86; Reuben E Thalberg Schlrshp 86; Central CT ST U; Elem Educ.

LA BELLE, JOANNE; Putnam HS; Putnam, CT; (Y); 4/115; Lib Band; School Play; Yrbk Ed-Chief; Trs Sr Cls; Sftbl; High Hon Roll; Hon Roll; Sec NHS; Jazz Band; Mrchg Band; All-Amer Bnd Hnrs 86; Mst Vlable Bnd Mbr 86; All-Estrn Bnd 86; U Of CT; Music.

LA BRACK, JILL; Southington HS; Southington, CT; (Y); 95/600; FBLA.

LA CELLS, DIANE; Southington HS; Southington, CT; (Y); 12/600; Trs FBLA; High Hon Roll; NHS; Briarwood Coll Bk Awd 86; 1st Plc CT ST FBLA Shrthnd Cmptn 86; Schlrshp Attnd CT Bus Wk 86; Bus Mgmt.

LA FAYETTE, LYNN; Platt HS; Meriden, CT; (Y); Math Clb; Service Clb; Stu Cncl; Mgr Ftbl; Mgr(s); High Hon Roll; NHS; Elem Ed.

LA FONTANA, KATHRYN; East Catholic HS; Manchester, CT; (Y); 7/303; Church Yth Grp; Drama Clb; Hosp Aide; Ed Nwsp Stf; Lit Mag; Rep Frsh Cls; Rep Soph Cls; Rep Jr Cls; Hon Roll; Ntl Merit Ltr; Hrvrd Bk Awd 85-86; U Of Toronto; Lbrl Arts.

LA FOREST, BRAD; Putnam HS; Putnam, CT; (Y); 32/123; Ski Clb; Band; Concert Band; Mrchg Band; Stage Crew; Var Bsbl; JV Bsktbl; VP Jr NHS; Casimir Pulaski Schlrshp 86; Maintained 85% 4 Yrs 86; Northland Coll WI; Bio.

LA PLACA, MICHELLE; East Catholic HS; Vernon, CT; (Y); 12/300; Service Clb; Pres Frsh Cls; Soph Cls; Jr Cls; Sr Cls; Stu Cncl; Gym; High Hon Roll; Hon Roll; Jr NHS; Dartmouth Bk Awd; Hnr E Awd; Hugh O Brien Yth Ldrshp; Sci.

LA ROSA, CHANNELL P; Central HS; Bridgeport, CT; (Y); 23/258; Computer Clb; Stu Cncl; Hon Roll; Prfct Atten Awd; U Bridgeports Proj Choice Scholar 86; Minrty Achvt Awd 85; Pres Acad Fit Awd 86; U Bridgeport; Comp Sci.

LA VALLEY, BRIAN; Robert E Fitch SR HS; Groton, CT; (Y); 15/234; Science Clb; Capt Var Tennis; Deptmntl Awd Chem 86; Worcester Polytech; Chem Engrng.

LABONTE, GABRIELLE; Putnam HS; Woodstock Valley, CT; (Y); 4-H; Red Cross Aide; Chorus; Chorus; Color Guard; Concert Band; Jazz Band; Mrchg Band; JR All Amer Hall Of Fm Band Hnrs 85-86.

LABOWSKY, KATRINA; Shelton HS; Shelton, CT; (Y); Art Clb; Drama Clb; French Clb; Color Guard.

LACH, JENNIFER; Torrington HS; Torrington, CT; (Y); 1/278; Am Leg Aux Girls St; Math Tm; VP Spanish Clb; Nwsp Rptr; Rep Frsh Cls; Rep Soph Cls; Rep Jr Cls; Mgr(s); High Hon Roll; NHS; Westminster Sem Term Paper Publshd 85-86; Jrnlsm.

LADD, PAUL; Norwich Regional Vocatnl Tech Schl; Jewett City, CT; (Y); Church Yth Grp; Drama Clb; School Musical; School Play; Stat Bsktbl; Var Crs Cntry; Mgr(s); Score Keeper; Timer; NRVTS; Tool & Die.

LADD, ROBIN; Coventry HS; Coventry, CT; (Y); 10/100; Dance Clb; Drama Clb; Band; Concert Band; Rep Stu Cncl; High Hon Roll; Hon Roll; VP NHS; Arch.

LADYKA, MELISSA; Tourtellotte Memorial HS; N Grosvenbrdale, CT; (Y); 4/95; Church Yth Grp; Drama Clb; Chorus; School Musical; Symp Band; Stage Crew; Hon Roll; Pres Schlr; Nichols Coll; Acctg.

LAGE, DEIRDRE; Ridgefield HS; Ridgefield, CT; (Y); 145/380; DECA; Color Guard; Drill Tm; Mrchg Band; Yrbk Stf; Hon Roll; Gldn Poet Awd 85; Engl.

LAGO, ANTHONY; Wilbur Cross HS; New Haven, CT; (Y); 1/350; Boy Scts; Chess Clb; Debate Tm; Political Wkr; Ski Clb; Chorus; Drill Tm; Nwsp Rptr; Nwsp Sprt Ed; Nwsp Stf; Spch Awd 82; Amtr Bxng Chmpn 85; Yale.

LAHAIE, SHERRI; Plainfield HS; Sterling, CT; (Y); 32/160; Church Yth Grp; GAA; Office Aide; Varsity Clb; Yrbk Stf; Stat Bsktbl; Ftbl; Mgr(s); Hon Roll; Dntl Hyg.

LAHOSKI, ALEX; Windham HS; Windham Ctr, CT; (Y); 25/285; Boy Scts; Chess Clb; Computer Clb; Hosp Aide; Nwsp Stf; Var L Wrstlng; Hon Roll; Mu Alp Tht; NHS; Pres Schlr; CT U; Comp Engrng.

LAIRD, DONNA; Francis T Maloney HS; Meriden, CT; (Y); Exploring; SADD; Band; Concert Band; Drm & Bgl; Mrchg Band; Pep Band; Hon Roll; Tchr.

LAKE, DAVID; Maloney HS; Meriden, CT; (Y); Key Clb; Math Tm; Science Clb; Yrbk Phtg; Yrbk Stf; Var Crs Cntry; JV Socr; Var Stat Trk; Mgr(s); Photogrphy Awd 85; U CT; Phrmcy.

LALIBERTE, JOHN; Southington HS; Southington, CT; (Y); 20/550; Boy Scts; Cmnty Wkr; Key Clb; Capt Math Clb; Math Tm; Rep Frsh Cls; Var L Tennis; High Hon Roll; NHS; Elks Ntl Schlrshp Mst Vlbl Stu 86; U Of CT; Mdcl Rsrch.

LALLIER, MICHELLE; Conard HS; W Hartford, CT; (Y); 40/345; Office Aide; Red Cross Aide; Ed Yrbk Sprt Ed; Var Capt Crs Cntry; Var Trk; High Hon Roll; Hon Roll; NHS; Spanish NHS.

LALLY, PATRICIA; New Canaan HS; Ne Canaan, CT; (Y); Church Yth Grp; Dance Clb; Intnl Clb; Latin Clb; Ski Clb; SADD; Powder Puff Ftbl; JV Socr; JV Vllybl; Hon Roll; Bus Mgt.

LALONE, JENNIFER; Marianapolis Preparatory Schl; Oxford, MA; (Y); Sec 4-H; 4-H Awd; Hon Roll; Tufts U; Vet Sci.

LAM, REGGIE; Stratford HS; Stratford, CT; (Y); 5/257; Library Aide; Office Aide; High Hon Roll; Hon Roll; Prfct Atten Awd; Outstndng Svc Awd Libry Clb 84-86; Amrcn HS Math Exam Chllng Prblm Bk Awd 85-86; Summer Inst 86; Nrthestrn U Of CT; Engrng.

LAMARRE, MICHAEL A; Southington HS; Southington, CT; (Y); 91/548; FCA; Var L Bsbl; Elks Awd; Hon Roll; Northeastern U; Civil Engr.

LAMMIE, MARCIA A; Danbury HS; Danbury, CT; (Y); 230/590; DECA; Variety Show; Rep Stu Cncl; JV Trk; Hon Roll; Prfct Atten Awd; Rep Frsh Cls; Rep Soph Cls; Cmnty Wkr; JA; Perry Awd 84-85; Mktng Schlrshp 85-86; NAACP Schlrshp 86; Johnson & Wales Coll; Fshn Mrch.

LANDAURO, VICTOR; St Mary HS; Greenwich, CT; (Y); 6/50; Boys Clb Am; Cmnty Wkr; Drama Clb; Hosp Aide; Hon Roll; CT ST Yth Of Yr 86; Greenwich Yth Of Yr 86; United Way Volntr Of Yr 84-85; Educ.

LANDERS, DEIRDRE; Farmington HS; Farmington, CT; (Y); Yrbk Bus Mgr; Rep Frsh Cls; JV Bsktbl; JV Fld Hcky; Hon Roll; Peer Edctr 84-86; Safe Rides 83-85; Pre-Law.

LANDERS, WILLIAM M; Stamford HS; Stamford, CT; (Y); Computer Clb; JA; Trs Science Clb; Ski Clb; Varsity Clb; JV Bsktbl; Var Capt Socr; Var Trk; Pres NHS; Iona Coll Language Cont Spn Ii 4th Pl 86; Notre Dame U PA Geotwn; Financ.

LANDINO, LYNN; Sacred Heart Acad; E Haven, CT; (Y); Spanish Clb; Variety Show; High Hon Roll; Jr NHS; Spanish NHS; Ed.

LANDINO, SANDRA ELISE; Sacred Heart Acad; New Haven, CT; (Y); 21/135; Pep Clb; Variety Show; Bowling; Vllybl; High Hon Roll; Hon Roll; Spanish NHS; St Schlr; CT Schlr U RI 86; U RI; Pre-Law.

LANDRIE, BRIAN; Southington HS; Southington, CT; (Y); Ski Clb; Wrstlng; Hon Roll.

LANDRY, LAUREN; Lyme-Old Lyme HS; Old Lyme, CT; (Y); Yrbk Stf; Lit Mag; Bowling; Hon Roll; Briarwood Bk Awd-Most Outstndng Bus Stu, Acdmc Exclnce Keyboarding, Acdmc Exclnce Data Proc 86; Mktg Mgt.

LANDRY, ROSEANNE; Holy Cross HS; Waterbury, CT; (Y); 61/380; Hosp Aide; Service Clb; Chorus; Concert Band; Mrchg Band; Stage Crew; Lit Mag; Hon Roll; NHS; Var Ltr Stage Crw & Chorus 86.

LANDY, BRETT; Bethel HS; Bethel, CT; (Y); Spanish Clb; SADD; School Musical; School Play; Stage Crew; Var Ftbl; Var Mgr(s); Var Wrstlng; Ski Clb; Biol Fld Study Pgm 85; Chemathon CT 86; CT U; Sci, Chem, Bio.

LANE, JENNIFER; Lauralton Hall HS; Fairfield, CT; (Y); 10/111; French Clb; JA; Key Clb; Math Clb; Math Tm; French Hon Soc; NHS; Church Yth Grp; Chorus; Yrbk Stf; Ntl Ltn Exm Maxma Cum Laude 84 & 85; Bus.

LANE, TIM; Bullard-Havens Reg Vo-Tech; Stratford, CT; (S); 5/185; Cmnty Wkr; Band; Symp Band; Rep Jr Cls; Rep Sr Cls; JV Bsktbl; Var Capt Ftbl; Var Capt Trk; Hon Roll; Trs NHS; Coaches Awd Captn Track Tm 85; All MBIAC Offense Tm 85; Engrng.

LANG, MARCIA A; St Bernard HS; Lebanon, CT; (Y); 29/297; Cmnty Wkr; Band; Pep Band; Ed Yrbk Phtg; Rep Stu Cncl; Stat Sftbl; NHS; Pres Schlr; Hon Roll; Cntry 3 Ldrshp Awd 85; NRA Shrpshtr Awd 85, 86; Musicl & Acadmc Acht Awd 84, 85; Simmons Coll; Psychlgy.

LANGDON, WENDY; Farmington HS; Farmington, CT; (Y); 19/204; High Hon Roll; Hon Roll; NHS; Spanish Clb; Band; Mrchg Band; Fld Hcky; Vllybl; Trip To Spain With Upper Lvl Spnsh Cls 86; Sci.

LANGE, SHELLEY; Cheshire Acad; Wallingford, CT; (Y); Art Clb; Church Yth Grp; Key Clb; Yrbk Ed-Chief; Ed Lit Mag; Hon Roll.

LANGLOIS, MIKE; Marianapolis HS; Webster, MA; (Y); 7/49; Hosp Aide; Spanish Clb; Stage Crew; Nwsp Rptr; Nwsp Stf; Yrbk Rptr; Yrbk Stf; Var Crs Cntry; Var Trk; High Hon Roll; Psych.

LANGOU, VIVIANA; Amity Regional HS; Woodbridge, CT; (Y); Cmnty Wkr; Off Latin Clb; Spanish Clb; Chorus; Church Choir; Variety Show; Yrbk Stf; Cit Awd; Hon Roll; NHS; Yale Frontiers Appld Sci 85; Cert Recog Math Fair 83; Georgetown U; Frgn Lgs.

LANKARGE, JENNIFER; Morgan HS; Clinton, CT; (Y); Trs Church Yth Grp; Band; Hon Roll; AFS; Girl Scts; Chorus; Concert Band; Mrchg Band; Orch; School Musical; Mc Donald All Am HS Band Audition 86; All St Band Audition 84; Acctg.

LANNI, DAVID; West Haven HS; W Haven, CT; (Y); 10/396; JV Var Bsbl; Var Capt Ftbl; CC Awd; DAR Awd; High Hon Roll; Jr NHS; NHS; Natl Ftbl Fndtn Schlr Ath 86; All Dist Ftbl 86; Coaches All ST Tm 86; Worcester Polytech; Elec Engr.

LANZILOTTA, CHRISTINE; Danbury HS; Danbury, CT; (Y); 91/500; Church Yth Grp; Cmnty Wkr; Key Clb; Ski Clb; Band; Concert Band; Mrchg Band; Socr; Hon Roll; Symphnic Bnd Awd 83-84; Sphmore Bnd Rep 84-85; Psych.

LAROSSA, LAURA; Saint Mary HS; Cos Cob, CT; (Y); 2/60; Latin Clb; Spanish Clb; Variety Show; Yrbk Stf; Var Stu Cncl; Fld Hcky; Powder Puff Ftbl; Hon Roll; NHS; Pres Schlr; Fthr Gay Schlrsph; Boston Coll; Law.

LARRACUENTE, CARLA; Lauralton Hall HS; Stratford, CT; (Y); 43/111; Drama Clb; French Clb; Girl Scts; Hosp Aide; Math Clb; Service Clb; Chorus; School Musical; School Play; Yrbk Stf; Natl Fedn Of Music Clbs Piano Solo-Exclnt Rtng 83; Stratford Recreatn Dept Spec Recogn 83.

LARSEN, TONYA; Greenwich HS; Riverside, CT; (Y); Service Clb; Mgr(s); High Hon Roll; Hon Roll.

LARSON, HOLLY; Southington HS; Southington, CT; (Y); 108/600; Church Yth Grp; Cmnty Wkr; Drama Clb; Hosp Aide; Key Clb; Latin Clb; Acpl Chr; Chorus; School Play; Yrbk Stf; Hon Mntn ST Latin Exm 84; R E Thalberg Schlrp 86; Western CT ST U; Elem Ed.

LARSON, KRISTIN; Greenwich HS; Old Greenwich, CT; (Y); Church Yth Grp; Capt Flag Corp; Madrigals; Nwsp Stf; Hon Roll; Pres NHS; Ntl Merit SF; German Clb; Chorus; Church Choir; PA All ST Orchstr 84-85; PA Gov Schl Arts 84; Pres Schlrshp Wheaton 86; Wheaton Coll; Poli Sci.

LARSON, KRISTINE; Conard HS; W Htfd, CT; (Y); 54/331; Nwsp Rptr; Nwsp Stf; Yrbk Stf; Rep Jr Cls; Rep Sr Cls; L Var Cheerleading; JV Lcrss; Mgr(s); High Hon Roll; Hon Roll; Hnry Usher Grad Cls 86; Art Wrks At Local Shows 85-86.

LASHER, JENNIFER; Tolland HS; Tolland, CT; (Y); 13/166; Trs Church Yth Grp; French Clb; Ski Clb; Rep Band; Capt Color Guard; Mrchg Band; School Play; Sec Jr Cls; Var L Crs Cntry; Var L Swmmng; Schlrshp Untd Congregtnl Chch 86; Gettysburg Coll; Frnch.

LASHER, LAURA; Our Lady Of The Angels Acad; Enfield, CT; (Y); 1/17; Cmnty Wkr; Girl Scts; Quiz Bowl; Nwsp Ed-Chief; Yrbk Ed-Chief; VP Jr Cls; Rep Stu Cncl; Sftbl; High Hon Roll; Smith Book Clb Awd; Early Chldhd Ed.

LASKOS, PETER GUS; Derby HS; Derby, CT; (Y); 15/130; Trs Spanish Clb; Varsity Clb; Var Capt Crs Cntry; Var Capt Trk; Lamar U; Mech Engrg.

LASKOWSKI, KATHY; Southington HS; Southington, CT; (Y); 134/570; Rptr FBLA; High Hon Roll; Pres HS FBLA 86-87; Vet.

LATTA, LAURA; Wilton HS; Wilton, CT; (Y); 124/350; Ski Clb; Varsity Clb; Rep Frsh Cls; Rep Soph Cls; Var Capt Lcrss; Var L Socr; JV Swmmng; Var L Trk; Hon Roll.

LATTANZI, SUSAN; Sacred Heart Acad; Branford, CT; (Y); Art Clb; Church Yth Grp; Dance Clb; Hosp Aide; JA; Office Aide; Yrbk Stf; High Hon Roll; Hon Roll; NHS; Hnr Awds 85-86; Vlntr Svc Awd 83-86; Fairfield U; Nrsng.

LAVALLEE, RICHARD; St Joseph HS; Monroe, CT; (Y); 32/263; Art Clb; Drama Clb; French Clb; School Musical; School Play; Stage Crew; French Hon Soc; High Hon Roll; Hon Roll; U Of RI; Chem Engrng.

LAVIERO, DEBBIE; Bristol Central HS; Bristol, CT; (Y); Art Clb; Sec Soph Cls; Var Capt Swmmng; Var Capt Tennis; Hon Roll; Art.

LAVOIE, LISA; Canton HS; Canton, CT; (Y); 15/90; Girl Scts; JA; Model UN; Band; Chorus; School Musical; Nwsp Ed-Chief; Ed Yrbk Phtg; JV Capt Fld Hcky; High Hon Roll; Drexel U; Bus.

LAWLOR, JACKI; Stratford HS; Stratford, CT; (Y); 44/257; Drama Clb; FBLA; JA; Office Aide; Q&S; Variety Show; Nwsp Bus Mgr; Nwsp Rptr; Score Keeper; JV Vllybl; Certf Achvt Modern Miss 85; FL Southern; Elem Ed.

LAWLOR IV, JAMES R; Holy Cross HS; Waterbury, CT; (Y); 96/346; Church Yth Grp; Political Wkr; Badmtn; Wt Lftg; Hon Roll; NHS; Pres Acadmc Ftns Awd 85-86; Ralph Silvernail Memrl Schlrshp 85-86; Bentley Coll; Accntng.

LAWLOR, JOHN; Holy Cross HS; Waterbury, CT; (Y); 81/396; Boys Clb Am; Bsbl; Var L Bsktbl; JV L Crs Cntry; Hon Roll; NHS; Jr Schlr Athl 85-86; Capt Bsktbl Tm 86-87.

LAWLOR, MARY PATRICIA; Canterbury Schl; Waterbury, CT; (Y); 28/88; Cmnty Wkr; Debate Tm; Political Wkr; Nwsp Rptr; Lit Mag; VP Soph Cls; Var Stu Cncl; Var Diving; JV Lcrss; Hon Roll; Notre Dame Acad Schlrshp Awd 85; Political Science.

LAWLOR, THOMAS P; Wethersfield HS; Wethersfield, CT; (Y); 7/287; Am Leg Boys St; Church Yth Grp; VP Frsh Cls; Pres Soph Cls; Pres Jr Cls; Pres Sr Cls; Capt L Crs Cntry; Capt L Trk; NHS; Ntl Merit SF; Hugh O Brien Yth; Math.

LAWRENCE, TONYA; Pomfret Schl; Pomfret Center, CT; (Y); Nwsp Ed-Chief; Var L Bsktbl; Var L Lcrss; Var L Socr; NHS; Key Clb; Nwsp Rptr; Nwsp Stf; Lit Mag; Rep Frsh Cls; Mansfield Cup, Pomfred Bowl, 12 Letter Awd 86; All ST Sccr Plyr 85-86; All Amer Lax Plyr Bsktbll 86; Yale U.

LAWSON, CAROLYN L; New Britain HS; New Britain, CT; (Y); 15/325; Pres Church Yth Grp; Cmnty Wkr; Key Clb; Madrigals; VP Stu Cncl; Cit Awd; Elks Awd; Pres Schlr; Tomasso Fmly Fndtn Schlshp 1st Pl 86; Mary Bethune Mc Cloud Schlrshp 1st Pl 86; U Of CT; Hstry.

LAWTON, NOEL; Holy Cross HS; Middlebury, CT; (Y); 125/400; Band; Concert Band; Jazz Band; Mrchg Band; Pep Band; Mgr Stage Crew; JV Socr; St Schlr; Soc Stu Awd 86; U CT; Poli Sci.

LAZARUS, DAWN; Miss Porters Schl; Hartford, CT; (Y); French Clb; GAA; Hosp Aide; Model UN; Political Wkr; School Play; Yrbk Stf; Pres Stu Cncl; Bsktbl; Hon Roll; Jame O Henderson Bwl Sprtsmnshp 84; Merrill Lynch Pierce Fenner & Smith Awd 84; Pre-Med.

LAZEREN, CHERYL; Rockville HS; Vernon, CT; (Y); 36/374; Am Leg Aux Girls St; French Clb; Girl Scts; Service Clb; Chorus; Yrbk Phtg; High Hon Roll; Hon Roll; NHS.

LE, TRANG; Central HS; Bridgeport, CT; (Y); 8/258; Church Yth Grp; Office Aide; Red Cross Aide; Band; Concert Band; Mrchg Band; Rep Stu Cncl; High Hon Roll; Hon Roll; Jr NHS; Pres Schrslhp 86; Music Awd 86; Pres Acad Ftns Awd 86; U Bridgeport; Int Bus.

LE, TUAN; Conard HS; W Hartford, CT; (Y); 12/345; Socr; Tennis; High Hon Roll; Elec Engrng.

LE BLANC, CATHERINE E; Putnam HS; Putnam, CT; (Y); 17/113; Am Leg Aux Girls St; Acpl Chr; Chorus; Church Choir; Color Guard; Concert Band; Mrchg Band; School Play; Hon Roll; NHS; Natl Choral Awd 85-86; U CT; Music Educ.

LE BLANC, CHERIE; Te Williams Schl; Waterford, CT; (Y); School Musical; School Play; Stage Crew; Nwsp Stf; JV Bsktbl; JV Fld Hcky; JV Sftbl; Hon Roll; Margaret A Carter Mem Schlrshp 84; Alma Clarke Wies Dstngshd Alumna Schlrshp 85-86.

LE DONNE, JAMES; St Josephs HS; Shelton, CT; (Y); 69/250; Debate Tm; Spanish Clb; Wharton Schl Bus; Bus.

LE DUC, GISELE; Notre Dame Acad; Middlebury, CT; (Y); Exploring; SADD; Nwsp Rptr; Trs Soph Cls; Trs Jr Cls; Socr; Swmmng; Tennis; Hon Roll; NHS; Mrch Dime Smr Intrnshp 86; Pre-Med.

LE FORT, RENEE L; Southington HS; New Britain, CT; (Y); 39/600; FBLA; Ski Clb; Chorus; School Play; Yrbk Stf; Cheerleading; Sftbl; High Hon Roll; NHS; Southington Assn Ins Agents Scholar 86; Tunxis CC; Drug/Alch Rehab.

LEAHY, WENDY; Staples HS; Westport, CT; (Y); 3/408; Art Clb; Library Aide; PAVAS; Chorus; Orch; Nwsp Stf; Lit Mag; Hon Roll; Ctr Creative Yth 5 Wk Prg 86; Norwalk Yth Symphony Orchestra 85.

LEBOV, JENNIFER; HS In The Communty; New Haven, CT; (Y); Exploring; French Clb; Library Aide; Pres Ski Clb; Temple Yth Grp; Orch; Yrbk Stf; Im Bsktbl; Im Sftbl; Hon Roll; Phys Thrpy.

LEBUDZINSKI, THOMAS; Marianapolis Preparatory Schl; Webster, MA; (Y); 4/44; Office Aide; Yrbk Stf; Bsbl; Hon Roll.

LECHTRECKER, ELIZABETH; Danbury HS; Danbury, CT; (Y); Chorus; Stage Crew; Variety Show; Rep Frsh Cls; Rep Soph Cls; Rep Jr Cls; Swmmng; Rose Geary Cert Of Merit 84; Chnnl 13 Art Cntst 85; Fash Inst Of Tech; Art.

LECLAIR, DONNA M; Plainfield HS; Plainfield, CT; (Y); 3/164; Am Leg Aux Girls St; High Hon Roll; Hon Roll; NHS; Voice Dem Awd; Schlrs Prg & Harvard Bk Awd 85-86; Engr.

LEDERER, MARY BETH; Sacred Heart Acad; East Haven, CT; (Y); Art Clb; Church Yth Grp; Variety Show; Endwmnt Schlrshp 85-86.

LEDWITH, MISSY; Wethersfield HS; Wethersfield, CT; (Y); 81/299; Nwsp Stf; Cheerleading; JV Socr; JV Socr; Hon Roll; Prfct Atten Awd; Prsdntl Physcl Ftnss Awd 82.

LEE, ANGELA; Hamden HS; San Francisco, CA; (Y); German Clb; Orch; Yrbk Stf; High Hon Roll; NHS; Wnr Yng Muscns Awds Comptn SF Symph 84; New Haven Symph Solo Perf & Wnr Yng Artst Comptn 86; Yale U; Music.

LEE, ANJA; Tolland HS; Tolland, CT; (Y); Art Clb; Drama Clb; JA; Ski Clb; Chorus; School Musical; Yrbk Stf; Cheerleading; Hon Roll; Miss Southern New Englanc Co-Ed Schlrshp Pgnt 85; Simons Rock Of Bard Coll; Bus.

LEE, CHARLES; Shelton HS; Shelton, CT; (Y); Am Leg Boys St; Variety Show; Nwsp Ed-Chief; Pres Jr Cls; Stu Cncl; Ftbl; Var Socr; Var L Trk; Drama Clb; Spanish Clb; JR Hmcmng Prince 85; Mock Trial Tm 86; Lwyr.

LEE, ELIZABETH; Sacred Heart Acad; Hamden, CT; (Y); Church Yth Grp; Hosp Aide; Varsity Clb; School Musical; Stage Crew; Nwsp Phtg; JV Crs Cntry; Var Capt Tennis; High Hon Roll; NHS; 1st Plk Photo Cntst 85-86; Lbrl Arts.

LEE, HELYN; Bulkeley HS; Hartford, CT; (Y); FBLA; Girl Scts; JA; SADD; Drill Tm; Stu Cncl; Cheerleading; Cit Awd; Hon Roll; Prfct Atten Awd; Comp Pgm.

LEE, JASON; South Windsor HS; S Windsor, CT; (Y); 5/287; Computer Clb; Library Aide; Math Tm; Orch; JV Socr; Var Trk; Hon Roll; Ntl Merit Ltr; Hrvrd/Rdcliffe Coll Book Awd 86; RPI Math & Sci Awd 86; Aerontcl Engr.

LEE, JOSEPH; Windham HS; Willimantic, CT; (Y); 1/285; Math Tm; Var L Golf; Kiwanis Awd; Val; Pres Soph Cls; Bausch & Lomb Sci Awd; High Hon Roll; Hon Roll; Mu Alp Tht; NHS; Butleman Memrl Awd 86; Dr A K Buchbinder Schlrshp 86; W Mc Queen Hunter Awd 86; Harvrd-Rdclf Bk Awd 85; U Of PA.

LEE, LISA; Southington HS; Southington, CT; (Y); 13/548; Church Yth Grp; Hosp Aide; Trs Key Clb; Stat Bsktbl; Elks Awd; High Hon Roll; NHS; Merrimack Coll; Comp Sci.

LEE, N TANYA; Hamden HS; Hamden, CT; (Y); Cmnty Wkr; Political Wkr; Varsity Clb; Swing Chorus; Nwsp Stf; L Capt Crs Cntry; JV Trk; High Hon Roll; NHS; Yale Bk Awd 86; Columbia MO Tribune Wrtng Awd 84; Sociology.

LEE, RICHARD; East Catholic HS; S Windsor, CT; (Y); 20/280; Art Clb; Church Yth Grp; Pep Clb; Ski Clb; Nwsp Stf; Lit Mag; Rep Soph Cls; Pres Jr Cls; Rep Stu Cncl; JV Ftbl; 2x Mst Vlbl Wrstlr 85-86; 4th Plc ST Wrstlng Chmpnship 86; Simons Rock Of Bard Coll; Psych.

LEFKO, CHRISTINE; Low Heywood Thomas Schl; Stamford, CT; (Y); 18/38; Model UN; School Play; Nwsp Ed-Chief; Nwsp Rptr; Nwsp Stf; Lit Mag; Sec Sr Cls; JV Fld Hcky; Var Tennis; WA Wrkshps Cngrssnal Seminr 86; Politcl Sci.

LEFKOWITZ, EVA S; Wilton HS; Wilton, CT; (Y); 15/299; Drama Clb; JA; School Play; Hon Roll; NHS; Ntl Merit SF.

LEFRANCOIS, STEPHANIE; Hamden HS; Hamden, CT; (Y); CPA.

LEGGO, HEATHER; Ansonia HS; Ansonia, CT; (Y); Church Yth Grp; Computer Clb; JA; Hon Roll; Prfct Atten Awd; Hstry Clb Pres 85-86; Educ.

LEHENY, CARA; Ridgefield HS; Danbury, CT; (S); 16/387; Capt Debate Tm; Drama Clb; Chorus; Church Choir; Madrigals; Mrchg Band; Orch; School Musical; School Play; Lit Mag; Law.

LEIBOWITZ, ALICE; E O Smith HS; Storrs, CT; (Y); 26/178; Cmnty Wkr; Drama Clb; Math Tm; Chorus; School Play; Lit Mag; JV Vllybl; Ntl Merit SF; ST Latin Exam 2nd Pl 86; Natl Latin Exam Maxima Cum Laude 85-86; Psych.

LEICACH, SANDY; Berlin HS; Kensington, CT; (Y); Band; Capt Color Guard; Concert Band; Mrchg Band; Nwsp Stf; Yrbk Stf; Mgr(s); Twrlr; Lib Arts.

LEIPER, DAVID; Seymour HS; Seymour, CT; (Y); 28/196; JV Bsbl; Capt Bsktbl; JV Crs Cntry; JV Trk; Hon Roll; NHS; Pres Acad Ftnss Awd 85-86; U Of CT; Engrng.

LEMANOWICZ, KEVIN; Killingly HS; Danielson, CT; (Y); 4/275; VP SADD; Pres Frsh Cls; Pres Soph Cls; Pres Jr Cls; JV Var Bsbl; Bsktbl; JV Var Ftbl; Score Keeper; High Hon Roll; Hon Roll; Meteorolgy.

LEMOINE, PAUL; Danbury HS; Danbury, CT; (Y); 36/474; Boy Scts; Ski Clb; JV Tennis; Hon Roll.

LENIART, KAREN; East Hartford HS; E Hartford, CT; (Y); Spanish Clb; Var Swmmng; Hon Roll; NHS; Sec Frsh Cls; Rep Soph Cls; Rep Jr Cls; Educ.

LENNON, BONNIE; Windsor Locks HS; Windsor Locks, CT; (Y); Sec Civic Clb; Chorus; School Musical; Var Capt Cheerleading; High Hon Roll; Hon Roll; Prlgl Stds.

LENT, NANCY; Brien Mc Mahon HS; Norwalk, CT; (Y); 11/288; Church Yth Grp; Key Clb; Ski Clb; Spanish Clb; Band; Yrbk Stf; Rep Sr Cls; DAR Awd; Hon Roll; NHS; Frank James Schlrshp 86; Villanova U; Bus.

LENTZ, ROBERT; Brookfield HS; Brookfield Center, CT; (Y); 8/240; DECA; Math Tm; Spanish Clb; Rep Jr Cls; Sec Sr Cls; Var Capt Crs Cntry; Var Capt Trk; High Hon Roll; NHS; Ntl Merit Ltr; Schlr Athl Awd Trk 84; Mrktg, Dist Ed Awd, Hnrs Chem Awd 86; Engrng.

LEONARD, ANDREW J; Hamden HS; Hamden, CT; (Y); 56/419; School Musical; Var Trk; Hon Roll; Frontrs Of Sci Smnrs Yale U 85; Outstndg Achvt Mus 85; Hnrbl Mntn Ntl Fndtn Advcmt Arts 86; Hartt Schl Of Mus; Mus.

LEONARDI, LINDA; Hamden HS; Hamden, CT; (Y); U CT.

LEPOUTRE, CHRISTINE; Stamford Catholic HS; Stamford, CT; (Y); Church Yth Grp; Pres 4-H; Nwsp Rptr; Var Capt Crs Cntry; Var Capt Trk; 4-H Awd; NHS; Nwsp Stf; JV Fld Hcky; High Hon Roll; Crss Cntry All FCIAC 85; Indr Trck All FCIAC 86.

LESCHINSKI, SUSAN; Plainville HS; Plainville, CT; (Y); 3/184; Pep Clb; Varsity Clb; Band; Concert Band; Jazz Band; Mrchg Band; Pep Band; Symp Band; Yrbk Sprt Ed; Yrbk Stf; Yale Bk Awd 85; Rotary Clb Scholar 86; Bnd Scholar 86; Plainville Firemns ST 86; 2nd Pl Exch Clb Essy; Springfield Coll; Phys Ther.

LESNIAK, CINDY; Manchester HS; Manchester, CT; (Y); 17/580; Church Yth Grp; Drama Clb; FBLA; Band; Trk; High Hon Roll; NHS; Russell Wright Acctng I Awd 86; 2nd Pl Bus Math 85; Fnlst Bus Eng 86; Bus.

LESNICK, NANCY; Ansonia HS; Ansonia, CT; (Y); #30 In Class; Cmnty Wkr; Hosp Aide; Latin Clb; Office Aide; Yrbk Stf; Score Keeper; Var Sftbl; JV Vllybl; DAR Awd; Hon Roll; Nrsng.

LESPERANCE, MICHELLE; Ridgefield HS; Ridgefield, CT; (Y); 1/330; French Clb; Office Aide; Service Clb; Band; Concert Band; Mrchg Band; High Hon Roll; Ntl Merit Schol; St Schlr; Val; U VA.

LESSAND, SANDY; Bristol Central HS; Bristol, CT; (Y); Church Yth Grp; French Clb; Hosp Aide; Math Tm; Stu Cncl; Bowling; JV Cheerleading; High Hon Roll; NHS; Concours De Francais Du CT Cert D Honneur 86; Yth Ftnss Achvmnt Awd 84.

LESSARD, SANDY; Bristol Central HS; Bristol, CT; (Y); Sec Church Yth Grp; French Clb; GAA; Hosp Aide; Math Tm; Stu Cncl; Bowling; Cheerleading; High Hon Roll; NHS; Consours De Francais Du CT Certificat Dhonneur 86; Yth Ftns Achvmnt Awd 84; 1st Plc Bwlng Lge 84.

LESSNER, JILLIAN; Farmington HS; Farmington, CT; (Y); 22/206; Cmnty Wkr; Ski Clb; Varsity Clb; Yrbk Stf; Var L Fld Hcky; Hon Roll; MVP Fld Hcky-Bst Dfnsv Back 83; Mst Imprvd Plyr-Fld Hcky 84; U Of VT; Acctng.

LEV, ROSLYN; Cheshire HS; Cheshire, CT; (Y); Girl Scts; Hosp Aide; Ski Clb; SADD; Band; Chorus; Mrchg Band; Stage Crew; Off Jr Cls; Stu Cncl; Bates; Psych.

LEVESQUE, ANDREW; Holly Cross HS; Woodbury, CT; (Y); Yrbk Phtg; Im Coach Actv; JV Var Lcrss; Im Socr; French Hon Soc; Soc Stud Hnr Soc; Soc Stud Fine Arts Clb.

LEVETT, MATT D; King Schl; Stamford, CT; (Y); 3/30; Jazz Band; Pres Frsh Cls; Var Crs Cntry; Lcrss; Cit Awd; High Hon Roll; Ntl Merit SF; Model UN; Ski Clb; Band; Hugh O Brian Yth Ldrshp Rep 84-85; Iona Lang Cntst French 2nd Hnrs 84-85; Supr Rtng Piano Fstvl 83; Bus.

LEVINE, ERIC M; Stamford HS; Stamford, CT; (Y); 136/354; JA; Varsity Clb; Band; Concert Band; Jazz Band; Mrchg Band; Yrbk Bus Mgr; Yrbk Ed-Chief; Yrbk Stf; Pres Stu Cncl; U Of Miami; Bus.

LEVINE, ROBIN; Branford HS; Branford, CT; (Y); 3/312; Church Yth Grp; High Hon Roll; Hon Roll; Ntl Merit SF; RAH Awd; Stu Ldr Pgm; Bus.

LEVY, DAVID; Norwalk HS; Norwalk, CT; (Y); 21/489; Spanish Clb; SADD; Temple Yth Grp; Stage Crew; Var Golf; Var Capt Swmmng; Gov Hon Prg Awd; NHS; Bus.

LEWANDOWSKI, VERONICA; Rham HS; Amston, CT; (Y); Hosp Aide; Pres Soph Cls; Rep Stu Cncl; JV Var Bsktbl; Var L Crs Cntry; JV Var Sftbl; High Hon Roll; Hon Roll; Phys Thrpy.

LEWIS, DAWN LUCILLE; Henry Abbott Tech HS; Bethel, CT; (S); 2/155; Church Yth Grp; Church Choir; Yrbk Stf; Var Capt Bsktbl; Var Vllybl; High Hon Roll; NHS; Sal; Exchng Clb Yth Mth Awd 86; Mst Likly Succd 86; Arch.

LEWIS, JONATHAN; Southington HS; Southington, CT; (Y); 60/600; Am Leg Boys St; Boys Clb Am; Church Yth Grp; Var Bsktbl; High Hon Roll; Hon Roll; Discover III-GFTD & Tlnt Prog 83; Acad Intro Mission Finlst 86; USCG Acad; Engrng.

LEWIS, KIMBERLY; Baptist Bile Acad; Waterford, CT; (Y); Church Yth Grp; Cmnty Wkr; Variety Show; Yrbk Ed-Chief; Var Sftbl; Var Vllybl; High Hon Roll; Prfct Atten Awd; Val; 1st Pl Acctg CACS, 1st Pl Bible Quz Team CACS 86; Bob Jones U; Ofc Admn.

LEWIS, MAURA L; William H Hall HS; W Hartford, CT; (Y); Aud/Vis; Dance Clb; Drama Clb; PAVAS; Thesps; Chorus; Madrigals; Orch; School Musical; School Play; Drama Awd Outstndng Svc 86; Amer Acad Of Dramatic Arts.

LEYDEN, PATRICIA M; Acad Of Our Lady Of Mary; Westport, CT; (Y); Drama Clb; French Clb; Trs Model UN; Service Clb; Acpl Chr; School Musical; School Play; Yrbk Bus Mgr; Rep Stu Cncl; NHS.

LEYDON, BRENDEN P; Westhill HS; Stamford, CT; (Y); 26/409; Drama Clb; Stage Crew; Nwsp Bus Mgr; Capt Wrstlng; Hon Roll; NHS; Ntl Merit SF; FBI.

LEYDORF, MARK A; Choate Rosemary Hall HS; Akron, OH; (Y); Drama Clb; Chorus; School Musical; School Play; Nwsp Stf; Lit Mag; Rep Stu Cncl; Swmmng; Hon Roll; Ntl Merit SF; Stu Hlpng Stu Schlrshp; Cls Prz Genrl Excllnc; Hstrcl Schlrshp Awd; Excllnc Engl Exprssn; Memrl Schlrshp; Yale; Engl.

LI, JIAMING; Choate Rosemary Hall HS; Wallingford, CT; (Y); Dance Clb; French Clb; Intnl Clb; Orch; Variety Show; Rachael Austin Awd Hist 84; St John Schlr Yr 85-86; 3rd Prz CT Frnch Poetry Cntst 86; Mgmt.

LI VOLSI, AMY; Stamford HS; Stamford, CT; (Y); #15 In Class; Pep Clb; Varsity Clb; Band; Concert Band; Mrchg Band; Stu Cncl; Var L Cheerleading; Var JV Mgr(s); Socr; Sftbl; MV Chrldr Coachs Awd 86.

LIEBER, CAROLINE; Pomperaug HS; Southbury, CT; (Y); Church Yth Grp; Drama Clb; SADD; Stage Crew; Yrbk Stf; Rep Soph Cls; Socr; JV Mgr Trk; Lbrl Arts Coll; Lbrl Arts.

LIEBMANN, THEODOR S; Choate Rosemary Hall HS; Branford, CT; (Y); Orch; School Play; Ed Lit Mag; Pres Frsh Cls; JV Bsbl; JV Socr; Hon Roll; Lion Awd; Ntl Merit SF; Cornell Clb Prz Hnrb Mntn 85; Scintfc Rsrch.

LIEDER, COLLEEN; Seymour HS; Oxford, CT; (S); JA; Yrbk Stf; Soph Cls; Jr Cls; High Hon Roll; Hon Roll; NHS; JR Achvt Awd 85; Accntng.

LIGHT, ALLEN; Danbury HS; Danbury, CT; (Y); FBLA; JA; Hon Roll; Dnbry Area Wstrn CT JR Achvmnt Assn Coll Schlrshp 86; HS Spcl Educ Rcgntn Awd 86; JA PRES; Dean JC; Bus Admin.

LIGHT, ALLISON; Guilford HS; Guilford, CT; (Y); 14/390; AFS; Model UN; Band; Concert Band; Mrchg Band; School Musical; Symp Band; Hon Roll; NHS; Ntl Merit Ltr; Vassar Coll.

LIGHT, LAURA; Greenwich HS; Greenwich, CT; (Y); Cmnty Wkr; Hosp Aide; SADD; Yrbk Phtg; JV Sftbl; Hon Roll; NHS; Ntl Bio Achvt Awd 84; Atlantic Pacific Math Leag Awd 85; Cert Merit Math 86.

LIGUORI, CHRISTOPHER; St Bernard HS; Westerly, RI; (Y); Chess Clb; Yrbk Stf; Stu Cncl; Socr; JV Trk; JR Senate 85-86; Biomed Engrng.

LILLEY, ANTHONY; Thomas Snell Weaver HS; Hartford, CT; (Y); 14/317; Am Leg Boys St; Cmnty Wkr; Var Bsktbl; Var Ftbl; Hon Roll; Cls 48 Schlrshp 86; Bryant Coll.

LILLEY, DENISE; Housatonic Valley Regional HS; Falls Village, CT; (Y); Chorus; School Musical; Co-Capt Cheerleading; Gym; Music.

LILLIQUIST, ANNE; Farmington SR HS; Farmington, CT; (Y); Yrbk Phtg; High Hon Roll; Photo.

LILLIS, GERALDINE; St Marys HS; Hamden, CT; (Y); 34/108; Rep Church Yth Grp; Girl Scts; Science Clb; Service Clb; Ski Clb; Spanish Clb; School Musical; Trs Soph Cls; Rep Sr Cls; Var L Cheerleading; Forsyth Schlrshp 86; Eagl Crs-CYO Awd 86; Forsyth Schl Dntstry; Dntl Hygn.

LIMA, JOSEPH S; Berlin HS; Berlin, CT; (Y); Am Leg Boys St; Aud/Vis; Band; Concert Band; Mrchg Band; JV Crs Cntry; Var Trk; Hon Roll; NHS; Quiz Bowl; Pres Clsrm 87; Aerosp Engrng.

LIMATO, PAULETTE; Holy Cross HS; Cheshire, CT; (Y); 54/380; French Clb; Capt Var Gym; Var JV Vllybl; French Hon Soc; High Hon Roll; NHS; Soc Studies Hnr Soc 85-86; Most Imprvd Vlybl Plyr 84; Legal Studies.

LIMAURO, MICHELE; Branford HS; Branford, CT; (Y); 65/320; Office Aide; Frsh Cls; Soph Cls; Jr Cls; Sr Cls; Stu Cncl; Var Cheerleading; JV Fld Hcky; Hon Roll; Hlth.

LIMAURO, STACEY; Sacred Heart Acad; Woodbridge, CT; (Y); Church Yth Grp; FBLA; Hosp Aide; School Musical; Yrbk Phtg; Var Cheerleading; Im Vllybl; Hon Roll.

LINDEN, JULIE A; Plainfield HS; Plainfield, CT; (Y); 3/140; Chorus; Madrigals; Yrbk Stf; High Hon Roll; Hon Roll; Jr NHS; NHS; Ntl Merit Ltr; CT Yth Cnfrnc Essy Awd 85; U Of ST; Jrnlsm.

LINDEN, POLLY; Low-Heywood Thomas Schl; Stamford, CT; (Y); 9/37; AFS; Cmnty Wkr; Pep Clb; Var Bsktbl; Var Fld Hcky; Var Capt Sftbl; Hon Roll; Frnch Prz 86; All Leag Awd Sftbl 86; AIFS Cannes.

LINDGREN, DIANE; Farmington HS; Farmington, CT; (Y); DECA; JV Tennis; Cntrl CT ST U; Bus.

LINDINGER, ROSEMARY; Conard HS; W Hartford, CT; (Y); 86/331; Spanish Clb; High Hon Roll; Hon Roll; Church Yth Grp; Service Clb; Acctng.

LINDO, ERIC H; James Hillhouse HS; New Haven, CT; (Y); CAP; Chorus; Drill Tm; Jazz Band; JV Badmtn; Var Bsbl; JV Bsktbl; JV Lcrss; Var Socr; Var Sftbl; Math.

LINDSTROM, ALISSA; Masuk HS; Monroe, CT; (Y); 8/273; VP JA; JCL; Latin Clb; Spanish Clb; Band; Concert Band; Mrchg Band; Pep Band; Nwsp Rptr; Nwsp Stf; Outstndng Achvt Engl; Temple U; Engl.

LINER, ROBERT; Danbury HS; Danbury, CT; (Y); 31/474; Symp Band; Yrbk Stf; JV Socr; Hon Roll; George W Perry Awd Engl 86; Naval Acad.

LINSLEY, NANCY; Branford HS; Branford, CT; (Y); 41/253; DECA; Latin Clb; Rep Frsh Cls; Var Capt Bsktbl; Sftbl; Var Capt Vllybl; Cit Awd; Hon Roll; Vllybl 1st Tm 86; Hnrb Mntn All ST Vllybl 86; Tilcon/Tomasso Co Scholar 86; Bryant Coll; Finance.

LINSLEY, TRACEY; Branford HS; Branford, CT; (Y); #142 In Class; Latin Clb; SADD; Varsity Clb; Yrbk Stf; Rep Frsh Cls; Rep Soph Cls; Rep Jr Cls; JV Var Bsktbl; JV Var Vllybl; Hon Roll; Outstndng Stu Awd Acctg I 86; Acctg.

LIPELES, CHARLES; Masuk HS; Monroe, CT; (Y); 7/300; Boy Scts; Church Yth Grp; JCL; Latin Clb; Ski Clb; Spanish Clb; Off Sr Cls; Ice Hcky; Tennis; High Hon Roll; West Point; Engrng.

LIPSON, JEFF; Southington HS; Southington, CT; (Y); 87/600; Am Leg Boys St; Boy Scts; Key Clb; Math Clb; Concert Band; Mrchg Band; Bowling; Crs Cntry; Tennis; Hon Roll; Bus Adm.

LIPTROT, MELANIE; Richard C Lee HS; New Haven, CT; (Y); Hosp Aide; Band; Mrchg Band; Nwsp Stf; Sec Jr Cls; Sftbl; Vllybl; Bausch & Lomb Sci Awd; Pres NHS; Sec Spanish NHS; Yale Intrnshp Prg Yr Of Choate Rosemary Hall CT Schlr Summrs 85-87; Med Tech.

LISIEWSKI, MECHELLE; Norwich Regional Vo-Tech HS; Norwich, CT; (Y); SADD; Varsity Clb; VICA; Stu Cncl; Cheerleading; Sftbl; VFW Awd; Miss Prstn, Lylty Qn ST Of ST & Miss Sthrn New Englnd 86; Hrdrsr.

LISKA, ELISABETH; Stratford HS; Stratford, CT; (Y); 9/260; Cmnty Wkr; French Clb; Trs Band; Church Choir; Var L Socr; DAR Awd; French Hon Soc; High Hon Roll; Vsr Bk Awd 86; Otstndng Svc Awd Vlntr Tutoring Engl As 2nd Language 86; Physcl Thrpy.

LISKA, LYNN; Nathan Hale-Ray HS; Moodus, CT; (Y); 3/60; Drama Clb; Math Tm; School Musical; Yrbk Stf; Off Frsh Cls; Off Soph Cls; Off Jr Cls; Var JV Bsktbl; Var Co-Capt Vllybl; High Hon Roll; Math.

LISS, KATHLEEN; Windsor Locks HS; Windsor Locks, CT; (Y); 31/155; Chorus; Color Guard; Mrchg Band; School Musical; School Play; Swing Chorus; Golf; Swmmng; High Hon Roll; Hon Roll.

LITTLE, ADRIENNE; Richard C Lee Educational Ctr; New Haven, CT; (Y); Hosp Aide; Science Clb; Teachers Aide; Nwsp Stf; Rep Frsh Cls; Rep Soph Cls; Rep Jr Cls; High Hon Roll; NHS; Prfct Atten Awd; Briarwood Book Awd Bus 86; Conn Pep; Acctng.

LIVERMORE, ALLEN; Manchester HS; Manchester, CT; (Y); Drama Clb; English Clb; Band; Concert Band; Jazz Band; Orch; Stage Crew; Symp Band; Music Compstn.

LIVINGSTON, NEIL; Windsor HS; Windsor, CT; (Y); Sec Church Yth Grp; Mgr Drama Clb; Speech Tm; Band; Church Choir; Concert Band; JV Socr; Hon Roll; Bus Admn.

LIZDAS, DANIEL; East Granby HS; E Granby, CT; (Y); 5/60; Boy Scts; JV Bsktbl; Var L Crs Cntry; Var L Trk; High Hon Roll; NHS; CT JR Intrnshp Pgm- WA DC 86; Law.

LJUNGGREN, DEBORAH; St Marys HS; N Haven, CT; (Y); Church Yth Grp; Girl Scts; Ski Clb; Spanish Clb; School Musical; School Play; Off Sr Cls; Stu Cncl; Cheerleading; Rivier Coll Schlrshp 86; Rivier Coll; Surg Nrsng.

LLOYD, DEBBIE; Miss Porters HS; Wethersfield, CT; (Y); Computer Clb; Hosp Aide; JV Lcrss; Grant Prize 84; Med.

LLOYD, TANYA; Kolbe Cathedral HS; Bridgeport, CT; (Y); Cmnty Wkr; Yrbk Stf; VP Stu Cncl; High Hon Roll; NHS; Pres Schlr; Rotary Awd; St Schlr; Spk Up Amer III 86; St Jsph Coll; Ed.

LO, WENDY; Stamford HS; Stamford, CT; (S); 17/354; VP Sec JA; Sec Pres Key Clb; Science Clb; Nwsp Rptr; Nwsp Stf; Rep Sr Cls; Stu Cncl; Hon Roll; NHS; Tennis; Gold Cup Piano Solo 84; Awd Superior Rtng Piano Solo 82; Awd Excllnt Rtng Piano Solo 81-85; Aero Engr.

LO CASCIO, LOREN; Sacred Heart Acad; West Haven, CT; (Y); Church Yth Grp; FBLA; Spanish Clb; Yrbk Stf; Vllybl; High Hon Roll; NHS; NEDT Awd; Spanish NHS; Law.

LOCKE, ILENE; Low Heywood Thomas Schl; Norwalk, CT; (Y); 12/37; Art Clb; Pep Clb; Radio Clb; Pres Temple Yth Grp; School Musical; Ed Nwsp Phtg; Yrbk Stf; Mgr Lit Mag; Var Fld Hcky; JV Lcrss; Outstndng Art Exhbt At Met NY 84; Gllry Shw Stmfrd Art Assoc 3rd Plc Pntng 86; Outstndng Intrnshp Awd; Syracus U; Bus.

LOCKE, KEVIN; Emmett Obrien RUTS HS; Shelton, CT; (Y); Church Yth Grp; Tennis; Hon Roll; UMO; Chrstn Camp Cnslr.

LOCKE, SHARON DENISE; Wilbur Cross HS; New Haveon, CT; (Y); Math Clb; Science Clb; SADD; Band; Concert Band; Mrchg Band; Vllybl; Cit Awd; Hon Roll; Comp Splst.

LOCKETT, JEFFREY; Hillhouse HS; New Haven, CT; (Y); Camera Clb; Church Yth Grp; Teachers Aide; Chorus; Church Choir; Pres Soph Cls; Hon Roll; Comp.

LOCKWOOD, HOLLY; Seymour HS; Seymour, CT; (Y); JA; Yrbk Stf; Hon Roll; Htl Mngmnt.

LOHENITZ, SUSAN; Seymour HS; Oxford, CT; (S); 8/210; Cmnty Wkr; Variety Show; Rep Jr Cls; Stu Cncl; Pom Pon; High Hon Roll; Hon Roll; Jr NHS; NHS; Alg II Awd Hgh Achvt 85; Pom Pon Sqd Atten Awd 85; Mth Cont 85; Arch.

LOMBARDI, JOHN; Kaynor Technical HS; Waterbury, CT; (Y); Aud/Vis; Computer Clb; VP JA; Stage Crew; Hon Roll; NHS; 1st Pl VW Prdctn In JA & Wnt To NAJAC 85; Schlrshp To Bus Wk 86 86; Elctrnc Engr.

LOMBARDI, LISA; Amity Regional HS; Orange, CT; (Y); Church Yth Grp; Drama Clb; French Clb; Pep Clb; Ski Clb; Yrbk Stf; Fld Hcky; Sftbl; Cit Awd; Hon Roll; Physcl Thrpy.

LOMBARDIA, DEVEN; Stanford HS; Stamford, CT; (Y); 22/354; Cmnty Wkr; Hosp Aide; Latin Clb; Red Cross Aide; Varsity Clb; Capt L Crs Cntry; Stat Ftbl; Capt L Trk; High Hon Roll; NHS; Natl Hispanic Schlr Awd 86; All Cnty Cross Cntry 84-85; MVP X-Cntry 82-85; U Of PA; Bio.

LOMBARDO, KATHLEEN; Stamford HS; Stamford, CT; (Y); VP Church Yth Grp; Girl Scts; Hosp Aide; Hon Roll; NHS; Grl Scout Silv Ldrshp Awd 85; Candystripng Pin 85; Dance Scholar 85.

LOMBARDO, NANCY; New Britain HS; New Britain, CT; (Y); 23/385; German Clb; Key Clb; Political Wkr; Band; Concert Band; Mrchg Band; Orch; Jr Cls; Rep Stu Cncl; Hon Roll; Close Up Pgm DC 86; Politcs.

LOMBARDO, PHILIP; Wethersfield HS; Wethersfield, CT; (Y); 124/300; Aud/Vis; Boy Scts; Band; Concert Band; Mrchg Band; School Musical; School Play; Stage Crew; Symp Band; Hon Roll; Central CT ST U; Tech Theatre.

LONG, LISABETH; The Taft Schl; Watertown, CT; (Y); Spanish Clb; Yrbk Bus Mgr; Yrbk Ed-Chief; Yrbk Stf; Fld Hcky; Ice Hcky; Lcrss; Jr NHS; Sci.

LONGO, MARCO; Holy Cross HS; Naugatuck, CT; (Y); 197/380; School Play; Hon Roll; Business.

LONGSTREET, PATTY; East Granby HS; E Granby, CT; (Y); Church Yth Grp; Cmnty Wkr; Yrbk Stf; Lit Mag; Rep Jr Cls; Rep Sr Cls; Stu Cncl; Var Tennis; High Hon Roll; Hon Roll; Excllnc Creatv Wrtg 86; Excllnc Frnch 84-85; Jrnlsm.

LOPES, VITORINO; Danbury HS; Danbury, CT; (Y); 118/483; Boy Scts; Cmnty Wkr; Exploring; Church Choir; Yrbk Stf; Rep Soph Cls; Rep Jr Cls; Im Coach Actv; JV Crs Cntry; JV Trk; Intl Bus.

LOPEZ, BRUNILDA; Richard Clee HS; New Haven, CT; (Y); Church Yth Grp; Hosp Aide; Political Wkr; Red Cross Aide; Lit Mag; Trs Soph Cls; Hon Roll; Jr NHS; Comp Sci.

LOPEZ, FERNANDO; Avon Old Farms HS; Venezuela; (Y); 21/100; Aud/Vis; Radio Clb; Im Golf; Var Mgr(s); Im Socr; JV Swmmng; High Hon Roll; Hon Roll; Pres Schlr; Prjct Physcs Hnry Mntn 86; Comp Awd For Excllnc 86; Ecnmcs Hnry Mntn 86; Metropolitan U; Comp Engr.

LOPREIATO, MARIA; Berlin HS; Kensington, CT; (Y); Church Yth Grp; Cmnty Wkr; Dance Clb; FCA; FBLA; Hosp Aide; JA; Office Aide; Red Cross Aide; Service Clb; Idl Stu 83; Bus.

LORIMIER, KIMBERLY M; New Canaan HS; New Canaan, CT; (Y); 1/320; Church Yth Grp; Cmnty Wkr; French Clb; Chorus; Concert Band; Jazz Band; Orch; School Musical; Var L Trk; Cit Awd; Outstndng Musician 85; U MI; Flute Perf.

LOVETERE, CAROLINE; Glastonbury HS; Glastonbury, CT; (Y); 26/413; Church Yth Grp; Dance Clb; Drama Clb; FCA; Intnl Clb; School Play; Var Capt Cheerleading; Var L Fld Hcky; Var L Trk; NHS; U VT; Pol Sci.

LOVETT, BRIAN; Seymour HS; Oxford, CT; (Y); Boy Scts; Church Yth Grp; JA; Trk; Engrng.

LOWLES, CHRISTY; Hamden HS; Hamden, CT; (Y); Church Yth Grp; FBLA; Ski Clb; Varsity Clb; School Play; Yrbk Stf; JV Bsktbl; Var Socr; Var Trk; Im Wt Lftg; Var Soccr Ltr 84-85; V Trk Ltr 85-86; U Of CT; Psych.

LOWREY, JENNIFER K; Bristol Eastern HS; Bristol, CT; (Y); 10/350; Cmnty Wkr; GAA; Political Wkr; Red Cross Aide; Spanish Clb; SADD; Chorus; Madrigals; School Musical; Pres Frsh Cls; 1st Runnr-Up In Sthrn New Engl Miss Amer Co-Ed Pgnt 85; Trinity Coll Bk Awd 86; Prom Queen 86.

LOYD, AMY G; Greenwich Acad; Darien, CT; (Y); Art Clb; Debate Tm; Chorus; School Musical; Nwsp Rptr; Lit Mag; Crs Cntry; French Hon Soc; Hon Roll; SADD; La Prise Dexcellence Alliance Francais 86; Bowdoin Coll; Englsh.

LU, UT TINH; Branford HS; Branford, CT; (Y); Camera Clb; Chess Clb; Computer Clb; Exploring; Math Clb; Radio Clb; Bsktbl; Hon Roll; Perfect Attendance 85-86; Yale; Compu Sci.

LUBECK, CHRISTOPHER G; Fairfield College Prep; Fairfield, CT; (Y); Pres Church Yth Grp; Cmnty Wkr; Key Clb; Letterman Clb; Varsity Clb; Yrbk Sprt Ed; Rep Frsh Cls; Capt Swmmng; Hon Roll; Swmng All-St Of Conosince 79-86; Capt Of Swm Tm & Wtr Polo Tm 86; Swmng All-ST For HS 84-86; Bus Mgmt.

LUCAS, SUZANNE; Farmington HS; Unionville, CT; (Y); Dance Clb; Chorus; Rep Frsh Cls; The Greater Hartford Acad Of Performing Arts 84-86; Public Relations.

LUCCARO, MARY; Holy Cross HS; Watertown, CT; (Y); 160/380; Art Clb; Dance Clb; Hosp Aide; Spanish Clb; Variety Show; L Trk; High Hon Roll; Hon Roll; Church Yth Grp; Computer Clb; 12 Yr Dancing Awd 86; Tchrs Training Cert 86; Phys Thrpy.

LUCSKY, CHRISTY M; Stratford HS; Stratford, CT; (Y); 66/257; Church Yth Grp; FBLA; Band; Concert Band; Mrchg Band; Orch; Stage Crew; Rep Frsh Cls; Rep Stu Cncl; JV Sftbl; Bk Awds From Sacred Hrt U & Briarwood Coll For Outstndng JR Secy Stds 86; Bus Mgmt.

LUISI, THERESA; Berlin HS; Kensington, CT; (Y); JA; Service Clb; Sec Band; Concert Band; Mrchg Band; School Musical; Variety Show; Outstndng Band Stu 83-84; Bus Clb Treas 84-85; Bus Adm.

LUMIA, ROBERT; Holy Cross HS; Waterbury, CT; (Y); 69/380; Church Yth Grp; Cmnty Wkr; Service Clb; Var Crs Cntry; Var Trk; High Hon Roll; Elec Engrng.

LUMIERE, ERICA; Kent Schl; New York, NY; (Y); JV Lcrss; JV Socr; French Clb; Hon Roll; Bus Intl Law.

LUPIA II, RICHARD A; Holy Cross HS; Oxford, CT; (Y); 1/396; Quiz Bowl; Nwsp Stf; High Hon Roll; NHS; Spanish NHS; Harvard Clb Southern CT Bk Awd 86; Rensselaer Math & Sci Awd 86; Soc Stu Hnr Soc 85-86; Bio-Chem.

LUPICA, CHRISTINE; Notre Dame Acad; Waterbury, CT; (Y); Dance Clb; Hosp Aide; SADD; Nwsp Stf; Sec Jr Cls; Cheerleading; Swmmng; Hon Roll; NHS; NEDT Awd; Schl Schlrshp Awd; Fnance Mjr.

LUPO, SCOTT; St Joseph HS; Stratford, CT; (Y); Church Yth Grp; Drama Clb; Exploring; JA; Spanish Clb; Chorus; Church Choir; School Musical; School Play; Stage Crew; Kings Coll; FBI.

LUSSIER, HEATHER; Putham HS; Pomfret Center, CT; (Y); Church Yth Grp; Dance Clb; Girl Scts; Office Aide; Spanish Clb; Band; Color Guard; Drill Tm; Flag Corp; Mrchg Band; Bio.

LUSSIER, JENNIFER; Putnam HS; Pomfret Center, CT; (Y); Dance Clb; Office Aide; Band; Color Guard; Drill Tm; Flag Corp; Var Socr; Wt Lftg; Trvl & Trsm.

LUST, ASTRID R; Wilton HS; Wilton, CT; (Y); Church Yth Grp; Dance Clb; German Clb; Intnl Clb; Pep Clb; Spanish Clb; Teachers Aide; School Play; Yrbk Stf; Trk; Delta Epsilon Phi Ger Lang Awd 84; Tchr.

LUU, THUAN P; Hartford Public HS; Hartford, CT; (Y); Chess Clb; Computer Clb; Math Tm; High Hon Roll; Hon Roll; St Schlr; Jacob & Lewis Fox Schlrshp 86; Interracial Schlrshp 86; Edward Bode Fund Awd 86; Wesleyan U; Math.

LYAS, KENNY; W L Cross HS; New Haven, CT; (S); 7/258; Computer Clb; Mathletes; Spanish Clb; Teachers Aide; JV Bsbl; Comp Engrng.

LYDA, KENNETH E; Greenwich HS; Greenwich, CT; (Y); Camera Clb; Cmnty Wkr; Drama Clb; Exploring; Thesps; School Musical; School Play; Mgr Frsh Cls; Trk; Columbus Coll GA; Law.

LYDING, KRISTY; Middletown HS; Middletown, CT; (S); 26/207; DECA; Band; Nwsp Rptr; Yrbk Rptr; Lit Mag; High Hon Roll; MYCC; Bus Adm.

LYLE, ELIZABETH; Low-Heywood Thomas Schl; Darien, CT; (Y); 6/40; Model UN; Stage Crew; Yrbk Bus Mgr; Rep Frsh Cls; Rep Soph Cls; Pres Jr Cls; Var Fld Hcky; JV Lcrss; High Hon Roll; Hon Roll; Cls Awd 84; Latin Awd 85; Wllsly Book Awd 86; Clssics.

LYNAS III, ROBERT; Danbury HS; Danbury, CT; (Y); Boy Scts; Church Yth Grp; U Of CT; Asronaut.

LYNCH, DIANE; St Marys Catholic HS; No Haven, CT; (Y); 3/115; Nwsp Rptr; Yrbk Rptr; JV Vllybl; French Hon Soc; High Hon Roll; Mu Alp Tht; NHS; Ntl Merit Ltr; Pres Schlr; Church Yth Grp; Natl Sci Olympd Mrt Awd 82-83; Hgh Hnrs Awd Yr 82-83; Soph Englsh Awd 83-84; U Of CT; Mgmt.

LYNCH, GRETCHEN; Holy Cross HS; Waterbury, CT; (Y); 25/380; Drama Clb; Hosp Aide; SADD; Acpl Chr; Chorus; Stage Crew; Variety Show; Hon Roll; Sec NHS; Madrigals; Scl Stds Hon Soc 85-86; Foreign Lang Ntl Hon Soc Italian 84-86; Ed.

LYNCH, KARRIEANN; East Catholic HS; S Windsor, CT; (Y); 102/285; Cmnty Wkr; Dance Clb; Chorus; Rep Sr Cls; Rep Stu Cncl; Capt Cheerleading; Gym; Sftbl; High Hon Roll; Rep Soph Cls; Louise Sweetland Schlrshp 83-84; Ed.

LYNCH, PETER; Wilton HS; Wilton, CT; (Y); Boy Scts; Pres Drama Clb; Chorus; Madrigals; School Play; Stage Crew; Socr; Hon Roll; Theat.

LYNCH, RYAN; Maloney HS; Meriden, CT; (Y); Latin Clb; Scholastic Bowl; Spanish Clb; Lit Mag; JV Tennis; High Hon Roll; Hon Roll; U Of GA; Educ.

LYON, CHRISTOPHER; Masuk HS; Oxford, CT; (Y); 68/283; Boy Scts; JV Crs Cntry; JV Ftbl; Var Trk; Hugh O Brien Yth Ldrshp Awd 85; Outstndg Of Yr Awd 85; Pol Sci.

LYON, KRISTEN; Coginchaug Regional HS; Middlefield, CT; (Y); 6/13; AFS; Ski Clb; Varsity Clb; Chorus; Madrigals; School Musical; Swing Chorus; Sr Cls; JV Capt Sftbl; Var Tennis; Craig H Pearson Mem Awd 86; 1st Pl Poet Shoreline Wrtg Cont 83; Outstndg Achvt Spn II & IV 84 & 86; Providence Coll; Jrnlsm.

LYONS, ALISA; Ledyard HS; Ledyard, CT; (Y); 42/285; VP Church Yth Grp; SADD; Chorus; Stu Cncl; JV Fld Hcky; Mgr(s); High Hon Roll; Hon Roll; Nwspapr Arts Edtr; Safe Rds; Jrnlsm.

LYONS, JAMES; Fairfield College Prep; Darien, CT; (Y); Church Yth Grp; JA; Math Clb; Math Tm; Teachers Aide; Socr; Trk; Merchant Marine AcadENGRNG.

LYSKOWSKI, KEVIN; Fairfield College Preparatory Schl; Ansonia, CT; (Y); 1/226; Capt Debate Tm; Sec JA; Key Clb; Capt Quiz Bowl; Ed Lit Mag; Rep Sr Cls; NHS; Val; Chess Clb; Church Yth Grp; Yale Mdl UN Awd Mrt Rcgntn Excllnt Prprtn & Cntrbtn 84-86; Awd Mrt Rcgntn & Dstngshd Perf N Amer Inv; Pltcl Sci.

LYTTON, JENNIFER; Hopkins Grammar HS; Woodbridge, CT; (S); Ed Nwsp Phtg; Yrbk Phtg; Var Crs Cntry; JV Tennis; Mgr Wrstlng.

MAACK, ERIC; Maloney HS; Meriden, CT; (Y); Key Clb; Varsity Clb; Var JV Crs Cntry; Var JV Trk; Var JV Wrstlng; Hon Roll; CC Tom Smith Mem Awd 85; Wrstlng All Conf 86; Crs Cntry, Trk, Wrstlng Var Ltrs 85-86.

MABE, TODD; Ridgefield HS; Ridgefield, CT; (Y); 53/360; AFS; Trs German Clb; Pep Clb; Ski Clb; SADD; JV Var Socr; High Hon Roll; Hon Roll; Colgate; Sprts Med.

MAC CALMONT, TERRY L; Nathan Hale-Ray HS; Colchester, CT; (S); 9/70; AFS; Drama Clb; Band; Chorus; Drm & Bgl; School Musical; Nwsp Rptr; Nwsp Stf; Yrbk Stf; Stu Cncl; Boston Clg; Nrsg.

MAC DONALD, CURT; Canton HS; Collinsville, CT; (Y); 12/94; Boy Scts; Math Tm; Model UN; Yrbk Stf; Crs Cntry; Hon Roll; Ntl Merit Ltr.

MAC DOWELL, SCOTT; Southington HS; Southington, CT; (Y); 70/600; Rptr FBLA; JA; VP Key Clb; Variety Show; Nwsp Rptr; High Hon Roll; Hon Roll; NHS; Elks Stu Of Mnth 85; CT U; Psychlgy.

MAC FARLANE, PATRICIA; Avon HS; Avon, CT; (Y); Drama Clb; School Play; Mgr(s); Hon Roll; NHS; Schrlshp CCY 86; Chem Engr.

MAC KAY, GREGORY; Holy Cross HS; Waterbury, CT; (Y); 174/380; Boys Clb Am; Church Yth Grp; Letterman Clb; Varsity Clb; Var Swmmng; Hon Roll; Bryant Coll; Bus Adm.

MAC KAY, KERRY; East Lyme HS; Niantic, CT; (Y); Am Leg Aux Girls St; Church Yth Grp; Yrbk Stf; Rep Stu Cncl; Var Fld Hcky; Powder Puff Ftbl; NHS; Var Crew.

MAC NEAL, DEBORAH; Tolland HS; Tolland, CT; (Y); Madrigals; School Musical; Yrbk Bus Mgr; NHS; Church Yth Grp; Chorus; Church Choir; Yrbk Stf; Mgr(s); Hon Roll; Hnrs Chr Boston 86; All-ST Chr 85-86; U Of CT; Pre-Bus.

MACBRIEN, NATHAN; Pomperaug HS; Southbury, CT; (Y); 1/194; Math Tm; Band; Chorus; Jazz Band; Madrigals; JP Sousa Awd; NHS; Val; All-ST Band & Chorus; E US Music Awd; Oberlin Cnsrvtry; Music Hstry.

MACCHI, ANITA; East Hartford HS; E Hartford, CT; (Y); Trs Latin Clb; Rep Teachers Aide; Rep Drill Tm; Rep Yrbk Stf; Rep Soph Cls; Rep Stu Cncl; High Hon Roll; Hon Roll; Rep Nwsp Stf; DAR Awd; Mst Outstndng Stu Wk 85; Accntnt.

MACIEJAK, DONNA; East Haven HS; East Haven, CT; (Y); Church Yth Grp; Computer Clb; Office Aide; Cheerleading; Bus.

MACKAY, AUDREY; Academy Holy Family HS; Farmington, NH; (Y); Art Clb; Stage Crew; Yrbk Stf; 4-H Awd; Hon Roll; Kiwanis Awd; 3rd Pl Schl Art Shw 86; Spec Record Awd 86; Trebas Inst Record; Sngwrtg.

MACKAY, BRYAN; Holy Cross HS; Waterbury, CT; (Y); #8 In Class; Boys Clb Am; Church Yth Grp; Letterman Clb; Varsity Clb; School Musical; Var Capt Swmmng; Hon Roll; Prfct Atten Awd; GUTS Awd Swmng 86; Sthrn CT ST U; Physch.

MACKENZIE, CHERYL; East Haven HS; E Haven, CT; (Y); 7/257; Sec French Clb; Library Aide; Chorus; Yrbk Ed-Chief; Stu Cncl; High Hon Roll; Rotary Awd; Pres Acadmc Ftnss Awd 86; Frnch Awd 86; Alumni Assoc Bk Awd 86; U Of CT; Psych.

MACKENZIE, ROBERT; Putnam HS; Putnam, CT; (Y); Var Bsbl; Var JV Bsktbl; Var Capt Socr; Jrnlsm.

MACKEY, FIONNUALA; St Marys HS; New Haven, CT; (Y); 19/108; Drama Clb; Elks Awd; Hon Roll; Chorus; School Musical; Nwsp Stf; Cheerleading; French Hon Soc; Elks Mst Valbl Stu Awd 86; CT Schlstc Achvt Grnt 86; U Of CT; Bus Admin.

MACKNIAK, SUSAN; Choate Rosemary Hall; Wallingford, CT; (Y); Debate Tm; Latin Clb; Model UN; Spanish Clb; Rep Stu Cncl; Capt JV Bsktbl; L Var Crs Cntry; L Var Sftbl; High Hon Roll; 3rd Pl Novice Tm At CRH 85-86; Pres Of Used Bk Store 85-87; Med.

MACKO, STEPHANIE; New Fairfield HS; New Fairfield, CT; (Y); Church Yth Grp; Cmnty Wkr; Ski Clb; SADD; Band; Concert Band; Mrchg Band; Variety Show; Var Socr; Mst Imprvd Band 84-85; Keystone JC; Early Chldhd Dev.

MACLEOD, SCOT; Torrington HS; Torrington, CT; (Y); 14/278; Key Clb; Trs Latin Clb; Varsity Clb; Pres Stu Cncl; Var JV Ftbl; Var Capt Swmmng; JV Trk; High Hon Roll; Jr NHS; Var Wt Lftg; Tlntd & Gifted Prog 86; Bio.

MADDEN, ELIZABETH; East Catholic HS; Vernon, CT; (Y); 22/277; FBLA; Var JV Cheerleading; Crs Cntry; Trk; High Hon Roll; Hon Roll; NHS; CT Bus Wk 86; Princpls Awd Ctznshp & Scholar; Chase JR Fellow 86.

MADDEN, MARY; Southington HS; Plantsville, CT; (Y); 56/600; Church Yth Grp; FBLA; Pep Clb; Color Guard; Var Cheerleading; Hon Roll; Jr NHS; NHS; Law.

MADISON, DANA; Plainville HS; Plainville, CT; (Y); 6/184; Pres Science Clb; Yrbk Sprt Ed; Capt Ftbl; Capt Golf; DAR Awd; High Hon Roll; VP NHS; Yrbk Phtg; Elks Awd; Pres Schlr; Schlr Athlete Ntl Ftbl Found Hall Fame 86; CT Coll; Zoolgy.

MAGAC, NADINE J; Naugatick HS; Naugatuck, CT; (Y); 5/307; Var Capt Crs Cntry; Var L Trk; Hon Roll; NHS; Cornell U; Engr.

MAGALHAES, JOSE PAUL; Warren F Kaynor Tech HS; Waterbury, CT; (Y); SADD; Stu Cncl; Im Bsktbl; Var L Socr; Im Sftbl; Im Vllybl; High Hon Roll; NHS; U Of New Haven; Elec Engrng.

MAGDON, CHRISTINE; Acad Of Our Lady Of Mercy; Milford, CT; (Y); 23/117; Latin Clb; Spanish Clb; Yrbk Stf; NHS; Cert Awd Exclnce Latin, Cert Awd CT Classical Lg 83; Cert Hnbl Merit Cum Laude Am Clscl Lg 84; Dickinson Coll.

MAGER, CYNTHIA; Sacred Heart Acad; Hamden, CT; (Y); Aud/Vis; Cmnty Wkr; English Clb; Stage Crew; Nwsp Rptr; Ed Yrbk Stf; High Hon Roll; NHS; Yale Book Awd 86; Self Defnse Clb 84-85; Soc Stud.

MAGERA, EDWARD; Emmett O Brien Ruts HS; Bridgeport, CT; (Y); Boy Scts; Camera Clb; Ski Clb; Anapolis; Nvy Plt.

MAGID, CHERI A; Joel Barlow HS; Easton, CT; (Y); 4/165; Sec Trs French Clb; School Play; Yrbk Stf; Lit Mag; Rep Jr Cls; High Hon Roll; NHS; Gftd & Tlntd Crtv Wrtng CT ST 85; Joe Tremaine Dance Stu Schlrshp 86; Mikki Williams Dance Prfmng; Creative Wrtng.

MAGUBANE, ZINE; Edwin O Smith HS; Storrs, CT; (Y); Cmnty Wkr; Drama Clb; Model UN; SADD; Drm Mjr(t); Stage Crew; Nwsp Rptr; Yrbk Stf; Lit Mag; Law.

MAGUDER, JILL; Berlin HS; Kensington, CT; (Y); JA; Office Aide; Band; Drill Tm; Yrbk Stf; Trs Stu Cncl; Powder Puff Ftbl; Hon Roll; Stud Cncl 85 & 86; Dean JR Coll; Exctive Sec.

MAHON, COLLEEN; Maloney HS; Meriden, CT; (Y); AFS; Key Clb; VICA; Yrbk Phtg; Yrbk Stf; Fld Hcky; Powder Puff Ftbl; Sftbl; Trk; Hon Roll; RN.

MAHON, DAN; Canton HS; Collinsville, CT; (Y); 7/94; JA; Math Tm; Model UN; Nwsp Bus Mgr; Yrbk Bus Mgr; Tennis; High Hon Roll; Hon Roll; Bus.

MAHONEY, KARIN L; Amity Regional SR HS; Orange, CT; (Y); Trs Art Clb; Sec Church Yth Grp; Drama Clb; SADD; Acpl Chr; School Play; Stage Crew; Natl Art Hnr Soc 85-86; Invlvmnt Arts Recog & Tlnt Srch 85-86; Prfrmng Arts.

MAILHOT, ROSE; St Marys HS; New Haven, CT; (Y); 4/102; Chorus; School Musical; Lit Mag; High Hon Roll; Mu Alp Tht; NHS; Spanish NHS; Art Awd 84; Ltry Awd 86; Englsh.

MAIN, KEVIN; Oliver Wolcott Tec; Litchfield, CT; (Y); Yrbk Stf; Var Golf; Hon Roll; Timothy A Johnson Mem Schlrshp 86; Carpenter.

MAINI, BENNY; Trumbull HS; Bridgeport, CT; (Y); Coach Actv; Capt Var Socr; High Hon Roll; Hon Roll; Italian Clb Tres 86; Acctng Clb Mem 86; AKSO Sccr Ref 83-85; Acctng.

MAISANO, LISA; Bethel HS; Bethel, CT; (Y); 50/250; Boy Scts; Church Yth Grp; Hosp Aide; Chorus; School Musical; Variety Show; Yrbk Stf; Var L Crs Cntry; JV Trk; Hon Roll; Explrs Clb Dnbry Hsptl; E CT ST U; Physcl Thrpst.

MAJOCHN, BRIAN; Wilton HS; Wilton, CT; (Y); 104/354; Spanish Clb; JV Tennis; Trk; Hon Roll; Math.

MAKOWICZ, DAVID; Ellington HS; Rockville, CT; (Y); 1/137; Am Leg Boys St; Aud/Vis; CAP; Mgr Variety Show; Yrbk Ed-Chief; Var Bsbl; Bausch & Lomb Sci Awd; High Hon Roll; VP NHS; Val; Pres Acad Fit Awd 86; NROTC Schlrshp 86; ROTC Schlrshp 86; US Naval Acad; Pol Sci.

MALACHESKY, LYNDA; Daniel Hand HS; Madison, CT; (Y); Art Clb; Drama Clb; Jazz Band; Nwsp Rptr; Nwsp Stf; Lit Mag; Hon Roll; Flm Phtgrphy.

MALDONADO, JOSE; Wilcox Tech HS; Meriden, CT; (Y); Boy Scts; JA; VICA; Yrbk Stf; Rep Soph Cls; Hon Roll; VICA Awd 6th Pl ST 86; U Connecticut; Mech Engr.

MALEC, KIMBERLY; Sacred Heart Acad; Orange, CT; (Y); 7/122; Pres FBLA; Pep Clb; School Musical; Rep Stu Cncl; NHS; Ntl Merit Ltr; Spanish NHS; Briarwood Book Awd 85; Bus Awd In Bus Law 86; Entrepreneurship II-1ST Pl Awd 85; Fairfield U; Bus.

MALENDA, KATHY; Sacred Heart Acad; W Haven, CT; (Y); Church Yth Grp; Spanish Clb; Variety Show; Im Vllybl; Jrnlsm.

MALENDA, LORI; Holy Cross HS; Naugatuck, CT; (Y); 202/380; Aud/Vis; Trs Spanish Clb; SADD; Rep Stu Cncl; JV Crs Cntry; Hon Roll; Post Coll; Fash Merch.

MALERBA, KRISTINE L; Joseph A Foran HS; Milford, CT; (Y); 80/244; DECA; Hosp Aide; Yrbk Stf; Hon Roll; Jr NHS; Nrsg Art 84-85; 1st Pl Dist Conf DECA 85-86; ST Conf DECA 85-86; Quinnipiac Coll; Bus.

MALON, ALICIA; Kaynor Tech; Watebury, CT; (Y); Var Sftbl; Hon Roll; NHS; Prom Comm 86; Waterbury ST Tech; Elect Engr.

MALONEY, DARBY; Greenwich HS; Riverside, CT; (Y); Art Clb; Cmnty Wkr; Drama Clb; Pres Service Clb; School Play; JV Socr; Var Tennis; High Hon Roll; NHS; NW Ayer Mrt Schlrshp 86; Sherri Irons Lnk Srv Clb Schlrshp 86; Art Hnrs Scty 85; NW U.

MALTZAN, MARY KATE; RHAM HS; Marlborough, CT; (Y); 13/208; Church Yth Grp; SADD; Band; Chorus; VP Frsh Cls; VP Jr Cls; Rep Stu Cncl; Capt Var Socr; High Hon Roll; NHS.

MALUSZEWSKI, KATHY; Southington HS; Southington, CT; (Y); 120/600; Church Yth Grp; Hosp Aide; Key Clb; Latin Clb; Service Clb; Ski Clb; Church Choir; Cheerleading; Crs Cntry; Hon Roll; Central CT ST; Bus Adm.

MAMACLAY, ELEANOR; East Hartford HS; E Hartford, CT; (Y); SADD; Concert Band; Trs Frsh Cls; Trs Soph Cls; Trs Jr Cls; Trs Sr Cls; Stu Cncl; Var Capt Trk; NHS; Church Yth Grp; Most Imprvd On Otdr Trck 85-86; All Lg Trck Tm 85-86.

MANCHUCK, AMY MARIE; Sacred Heart Acad; Stamford, CT; (Y); 1/57; Yrbk Stf; Pres Frsh Cls; Pres Sr Cls; Var L Bsktbl; Var L Sftbl; Var L Vllybl; NHS; Val; Church Yth Grp; Pres French Clb; Thomas J Watson Mem Scholar 86; HOBY Ldrshp Awd 84; U CT Dstngshd Stu Awd 85; N Stamford Exch Clb Yth; Duke U; Forn Med.

MANCINI, DONNA; Notre Dame Catholic HS; Bridgeport, CT; (Y); 17/242; Rep Frsh Cls; Sec Soph Cls; Sec Jr Cls; VP Sr Cls; High Hon Roll; Hon Roll; NHS; Pres Schlr; Italian Clb VP,Pres 83-86; Italian Hnr Soc 85-86; Sacred Heart U; Para Legal.

MANCINI, LISA; South Windsor HS; S Windsor, CT; (Y); Cmnty Wkr; Letterman Clb; Varsity Clb; Chorus; Variety Show; JV Bsktbl; Var L Fld Hcky; Hon Roll; Video Tapd Vrsty Grls Bsktbl Gms 85-86; Fashn Merchnds.

MANCINI, MARIO; Holy Cross HS; Waterbury, CT; (Y); Var Socr.

MANCINI, STEVEN; Berlin HS; Berlin, CT; (Y); 6/183; Am Leg Boys St; Church Yth Grp; JA; Science Clb; Band; Concert Band; Mrchg Band; Tennis; High Hon Roll; NHS; Outstndg Prfrmnc Spnsh 84-85; Holy Cross; Bio.

MANDRONA, MELISSA; Heritage Christian Acad; Seymour, CT; (Y); Camera Clb; Church Yth Grp; Drama Clb; Acpl Chr; Chorus; School Play; Stage Crew; Variety Show; Stat Bsbl; Var Socr; Spirit Awd 83-85; Hghst Acad Awd 83-85; Cert Extrdnry Stu 83-85; Bob Jones U; Csmtlgy.

MANFREDA, MICHELE; Sacred Heart Acad; N Haven, CT; (Y); Church Yth Grp; Cmnty Wkr; JA; Pep Clb; Sec Soph Cls; Rep Jr Cls; Var Cheerleading; Im Vllybl; Hugh O Brian Yth Foundtn Semnr 85; Pre-Law.

MANGINI, DANIELLE; Brookfield HS; Brookfield, CT; (Y); Math Clb; Variety Show; JV Bsktbl; Var L Socr; JV Vllybl; French Hon Soc; High Hon Roll; Hon Roll; Frnch.

MANGLER, JEFF; The Morgan Schl; Clinton, CT; (Y); Boy Scts; Ski Clb; Spanish Clb; Capt Bsktbl; Hon Roll; Bus.

MANISCALCO, DAVID; Windsor HS; Windsor, CT; (Y); Math Clb; Math Tm; Model UN; Y-Teens; JV Bsbl; Var Golf; JV Mgr(s); Im Socr; Hon Roll; Actrl Sci.

MANNING, JOSPEH; Choate Rosemary Hall HS; S Yarmouth, MA; (Y); Model UN; Political Wkr; Ski Clb; VP Capt Bsbl; Var Bsktbl; Im Vllybl; Ntl Merit Ltr; Sci.

MANNUZZA, ROSS; Ridgefield HS; Ridgefield, CT; (Y); Boy Scts; Church Yth Grp; Varsity Clb; Drm Mjr(t); Jazz Band; Mrchg Band; Nwsp Phtg; Pres Sr Cls; Var Trk; Var Wrstlng; Outstndng Musician Awd 85 & 86; Eagle Sct 86; WA Intern Pgm 86; Mktg.

MANSKI, KAREN; Wolcott HS; Wolcott, CT; (Y); French Clb; Math Clb; Teachers Aide; High Hon Roll; NHS; Acad Excllnce Fr I II & III 84-86; Achvt Outstndg Stu Mth 84 & 85; Geol.

MANUELE, ANGELO; Southington HS; Southington, CT; (Y); Band; Concert Band; Mrchg Band; Hon Roll; Law.

MAPES, SHANNON LEIGH; Acad Of Holy Family; Brooklyn, CT; (Y); JA; Library Aide; Office Aide; Red Cross Aide; Teachers Aide; Chorus; Yrbk Phtg; Yrbk Stf; Lcrss; Socr; Greatest Imprvd Stu; Eastern CT U; Bio.

MARANE, KRISTINE; Daniel Hand HS; Madison, CT; (Y); Church Yth Grp; Drama Clb; JCL; Concert Band; Mrchg Band; Stage Crew; Yrbk Stf; Marine Sci.

MARATEA, KIMBERLY; Amity Regional SR HS; Orange, CT; (Y); 85/388; Art Clb; Church Yth Grp; Drama Clb; French Clb; Pep Clb; Ski Clb; Spanish Clb; SADD; Natl Art Hnr Soc Treas, Amity Educ Fund Schlrshp Grant; Boston U; Intl Rel.

MARCANTONIO, KIM; O H Platt HS; Meriden, CT; (Y); Hosp Aide; Ed Key Clb; Latin Clb; JV Crs Cntry; High Hon Roll; Hon Roll; Debate Tm; Stu Senate Secy; Yth In Govt Hnrs Sem; UCONN Hnrs Sem; Pre-Med.

MARCANTONIO, LISA; Torrington HS; Torrington, CT; (Y); 5/278; Latin Clb; Model UN; Varsity Clb; Nwsp Stf; Sec Stu Cncl; Mgr Swmmng; NHS; NEDT Awd; Art Clb; Cmnty Wkr; U Of CT Cooprtv Pgm Supr HS Stu 85-86; Tlntd-Gftd Stu Pgm 83-86; Econmcs.

MARCANTONIO, MICHELE; Low-Heywood Thomas HS; Darien, CT; (Y); 13/38; Model UN; Scholastic Bowl; School Musical; Stage Crew; Ed Yrbk Stf; JV Capt Fld Hcky; JV Lcrss; JV Var Tennis; Hon Roll; Art Shw 3rd Pl Watercolor 85.

MARCHESSEAULT, DONALD; South Windsor HS; South Windsor, CT; (Y); Boy Scts; Exploring; Ski Clb; Chorus; Yrbk Phtg; Im Bsbl; High Hon Roll; Hon Roll; Eagle Sct 86; Bill Fisher Mem Awd Cmmnty Svc 86; U CT; Bus Adm.

MARCHETTI, MARIA; Greenwich HS; Riverside, CT; (Y); Cmnty Wkr; Service Clb; Nwsp Stf; Yrbk Stf; Capt Bsktbl; Var Sftbl; Gov Hon Prg Awd; High Hon Roll; Hon Roll; NHS; U Of CT.

MARCHETTI, MICHELE; Torrington HS; Torrington, CT; (Y); Model UN; Spanish Clb; Sec Thesps; School Musical; School Play; Stage Crew; Nwsp Ed-Chief; Capt Twrlr; High Hon Roll; NEDT Awd; 2 1st Pl Trphys Team Twrlg NBTA Comp 85; Pre-Med.

MARCIL, JOSEPH; Holy Cross HS; Watertown, CT; (Y); Band; JV Bsbl; Var Ftbl; Var Capt Trk; Wt Lftg; Var Wrstlng; High Hon Roll; Hon Roll; Mthrs Clb Awd 86; Naugahuck Vlly Lg Ftbll 86; All Cty Trck 86; Boston U; Pre-Med.

MARCIL, LAURA; Holy Cross HS; Watertown, CT; (Y); Church Yth Grp; Band; Chorus; Crs Cntry; Mgr(s); Trk; Hon Roll; Advrtsng.

MARCIL, MARIA; Ridgefield HS; Ridgefield, CT; (S); 108/330; DECA; Fld Hcky; Powder Puff Ftbl; High Hon Roll; Hon Roll; DECA Natl Level Comptn 85-86; Bentley Coll; Bus.

MARCINKOWSKI, KEITH; Brookfiled HS; Brookfield, CT; (Y); Church Yth Grp; Cmnty Wkr; FBLA; Leo Clb; Acpl Chr; Chorus; Trs Sr Cls; Var Capt Bsktbl; Var Capt Bsktbl; Coach Actv; Bus.

MARCUCCI, JENNIFER; St Marys HS; E Haven, CT; (Y); 21/112; Hosp Aide; Math Clb; Math Tm; Service Clb; Yrbk Stf; High Hon Roll; Hon Roll; Jr NHS; Mu Alp Tht; S Prestley Blake Schlrshp 86; Bay Path JC; Med Assist.

MARDOIAN, RICHARD; New Canaan HS; New Canaan, CT; (Y); Church Yth Grp; Cmnty Wkr; Red Cross Aide; Spanish Clb; Jazz Band; Mrchg Band; Symp Band; Bsktbl; Coach Actv; Var Socr; Bsktbl Coach Of The Yr 85-86; Bus.

MARECKI, LISA; Torrington HS; Torrington, CT; (Y); GAA; Varsity Clb; Bsktbl; Socr; Sftbl; Cmnty Wkr; All Naugatuck Vlly Leag 3rd Bsmn Sftbl 84; 2nd Tm NVL 3rd Bs 85; Hon Mntn 3rd Bs 86; Bus.

MARGANSKI, KRISTIN; Sacred Heart Acad; Ansonia, CT; (Y); Aud/Vis; Church Yth Grp; Hosp Aide; Pep Clb; Var Cheerleading; Southern CT ST U; Nrsng.

MARGIOTTA, DANA; Reodeville HS; Vernon, CT; (Y); High Hon Roll; Hon Roll; Psychlgy.

MARINO, LISA; West Haven HS; W Haven, CT; (Y); Church Yth Grp; Civic Clb; Cmnty Wkr; Dance Clb; Drama Clb; Girl Scts; Pep Clb; Political Wkr; Ski Clb; Spanish Clb; Cls Vclst 86; Schlrshp Mst Invlvd 86; Hofstra U; Law.

MARINO, MARY ANN; St Paul Catholic HS; Farmington, CT; (Y); 13/257; Church Yth Grp; Drama Clb; Sec Ski Clb; Trs Spanish Clb; School Play; Variety Show; Yrbk Phtg; Lit Mag; Trs Stu Cncl; Powder Puff Ftbl; Frmngtn Exchng Clb 86; Sntr Lowell Weicker Frmntn Twn Rep Cncl Smmr Intrnshp 85; NY U; Jrnlsm.

MARKEY, JENNIFER; Pomperang HS; Southbury, CT; (Y); AFS; Drama Clb; Stage Crew; Jr Cls; Var Sftbl; High Hon Roll; NHS.

MARKS, CHERI-LYN; East Hartford HS; Hartford, CT; (Y); 27/463; Drama Clb; Nwsp Rptr; Sec Soph Cls; Sec Jr Cls; Sec Sr Cls; Rep Stu Cncl; Var Sftbl; Var Co-Capt Vllybl; NHS; Ski Clb; Hrtfrd Mutual Schlrshp Awd 86; Brnrd Dndly Mem Schlrshp 86; Outstndng Athlt Awd Slvr Mdlln 86; U CT; Psych.

MARKS, KAREN; Southington HS; Southington, CT; (Y); 124/600; Pres Aud/Vis; Pres Camera Clb; Pres Office Aide; Concert Band; Jazz Band; Mgr(s); Hon Roll; Ski Clb; Teachers Aide; Band; Med Tech.

MARMORA, STACEY; Shelton HS; Shelton, CT; (Y); JV Crs Cntry; JV Socr; Hon Roll; Central CT ST U; Polc Ofcr.

MAROTTO, KIMBERLY ANN; Norwalk HS; S Norwalk, CT; (Y); 50/430; Color Guard; School Musical; Yrbk Ed-Chief; Trs Soph Cls; Pres Jr Cls; Rep Sr Cls; Cheerleading; Powder Puff Ftbl; High Hon Roll; NHS; U Of CT; Engnrng.

MARR, SANDRA; East Lyme HS; E Lyme, CT; (Y); 56/280; Flag Corp; Mrchg Band; Yrbk Stf; Sec Frsh Cls; Stu Cncl; Var Bsktbl; Var Crs Cntry; Var Trk; Hon Roll; Rotary Awd.

MARSHALL, DAVID; Trumbull HS; Trumbull, CT; (Y); Chess Clb; VP Church Yth Grp; Computer Clb; Church Choir; Var L Bsktbl; Im Socr; Cit Awd; Hon Roll; Outstndng Achvt In Wrtg 86; Pilot.

MARSHALL, LESLIE; Greenwich HS; Riverside, CT; (Y); Art Clb; JA; Chorus; School Play; Nwsp Stf; Yrbk Stf; Bsktbl; Fld Hcky.

MARTIN, ANDREW; Kaynor RVTS HS; Waterbury, CT; (Y); Church Yth Grp; JA; SADD; Pres Jr Cls; VP Stu Cncl; Bsbl; Bsktbl; High Hon Roll; VP NHS; UCLA; Plumbng.

MARTIN, GLEN; Holy Cross HS; Waterbury, CT; (Y); 33/380; Art Clb; Varsity Clb; High Hon Roll; NHS; Var JV Ftbl; Amer Lgn Awd 83; Air Force Acad; Arch.

MARTIN, JENNIFER J; New Fairfield HS; New Fairfield, CT; (Y); 49/283; Drama Clb; PAVAS; Science Clb; Thesps; Chorus; School Musical; School Play; Variety Show; Yrbk Stf; Hon Roll; Arch.

MARTIN, KELLY; Housatonie Valley Regional HS; Falls Village, CT; (Y); AFS; French Clb; Ski Clb; Varsity Clb; Off Soph Cls; Socr; Trk.

MARTIN, RAYMOND; Morgan HS; Clinton, CT; (Y); 23/143; AFS; Am Leg Boys St; Drama Clb; French Clb; Pep Clb; SADD; Chorus; School Musical; School Play; Yrbk Stf; Intl Rltns.

MARTIN, SUZANNAH; Loomis Chaffee HS; Essex Jct, VT; (Y); Church Yth Grp; Dance Clb; Band; School Play; Nwsp Rptr; Nwsp Stf; Lbrl Arts.

MARTINEZ, ELISSA; New Fairfield HS; New Fairfield, CT; (Y); Church Yth Grp; CAP; Computer Clb; JA; Office Aide; Acpl Chr; Chorus; Church Choir; School Musical; Stage Crew; Hofstra U; Surgeon.

MARTINI, ROBERT; Trumbull HS; Trumbull, CT; (Y); Band; Jazz Band; School Musical; Variety Show; Trs Stu Cncl; Bsbl; Socr; Church Yth Grp; SADD; Mrchg Band; Symp Band; Trumbull Arts Cmmssn Schlrshp 84; PTSA Outstndng Musc Awd 84; Bus.

MARTINO, MICHAEL; Windsor HS; Windsor, CT; (Y); FCA; Intnl Clb; Latin Clb; Im Badmtn; JV Ftbl; Im Lcrss; Im Vllybl; Im Wt Lftg; Hon Roll; Outstndg Plyr Awd, Hghst Sav Goalie-La Crosse 86; Indstrl Engr.

MARTINO, SUSAN; North Branford HS; Northford, CT; (Y); 17/150; Trs AFS; Church Yth Grp; Drama Clb; FBLA; Chorus; Church Choir; Nwsp Rptr; Yrbk Stf; JV Sftbl; High Hon Roll; Assumption Coll; Elem Ed.

MARTINOLI, ANNE; St Bernard HS; Oakdale, CT; (Y); 24/289; Church Yth Grp; Drama Clb; Band; Concert Band; School Musical; Chrmn Stu Cncl; Hon Roll; JP Sousa Awd; NHS; Pres Schlr; Semper Fidelis Awd 86; Music Excllnce 86; Thomas Engelke Mem Awd 86; Catholic U Am; Music Ed.

MARTINS, STEVE; Vinal Regional Vo Tech Schl; Guilford, CT; (Y); VICA; Pres Frsh Cls; Pres Jr Cls; Trk; NHS; 2nd Pl VICA 86; Carpntr.

MARTONE, CHRIS; Bullard-Havens Regnl Vo-Tec Shcl; Shelton, CT; (Y); Church Yth Grp; VICA; Var Golf; High Hon Roll; NHS; Clnry Inst Of Amrca; Clnry Arts.

MARZANO, LISA; Conard HS; W Hartford, CT; (Y); 77/380; 4-H; Chorus; JV Bsktbl; Var L Swmmng; Var L Tennis; JR Ushr For Grad 86; SR Cls Brd 87; Engl.

MARZULLO, SCOTT; St Mary HS; Stamford, CT; (Y); Cmnty Wkr; Pres Exploring; VP JA; Spanish Clb; Stage Crew; Variety Show; Im Lcrss; Im Socr; Var Tennis; Hon Roll; ST U NY; Lbrl Arts.

MASON, CAROLE; Marianapolis Prep Schl; Danielson, CT; (Y); Church Yth Grp; Political Wkr; Flag Corp; School Play; Symp Band; Yrbk Stf; Sec Stu Cncl; Socr; High Hon Roll; Hon Roll; US Sen Page; Hghst Achvt Alg; Comm.

MASOTTI, JOHN; Bristol Central HS; Bristol, CT; (Y); 12/271; Church Yth Grp; Ski Clb; Variety Show; Var Capt Tennis; High Hon Roll; Hon Roll; NHS; G Buchanan Mem Schlrshp, U CT Bk Prz 86; U CT; Elec Engrng.

MASTO, JENNIFER A; Amity Regional SR HS; West Haven, CT; (Y); 198/413; Pep Band; School Play; Variety Show; Yrbk Stf; Lit Mag; Capt Fld Hcky; Cit Awd; Drama Clb; Girl Scts; Pep Clb; Field Hockey 2NC Tm 85-86; Ntl Art Hne Soc Awd 86; Ldrshp Cncl Awd; Emerson Coll; Arts.

MASTO, STEPHEN; Notre Dame HS; Orange, CT; (Y); 28/231; Boy Scts; Church Yth Grp; Varsity Clb; Nwsp Sprt Ed; Im Bsktbl; Var L Crs Cntry; Var L Trk; NHS; Italian Clb Scrtry; Math Hnr Soc; Villanova U; Bus.

MASTORS, ALYSSA; Wethersfield HS; Wethersfield, CT; (S); Church Yth Grp; DECA; JA; Im Badmtn; Var L Socr; Var L Tennis; High Hon Roll; Hon Roll; #6-18b Ctgry-New Englnd Tnns 86; Cash Awd-Outstndng DECA Stu 86; All Conf Tm-Grls Tnns 84-86; Central CT ST U.

MASTRIANO, CAROL; Sacred Heart Acad; East Haven, CT; (Y); Church Yth Grp; Variety Show; Nwsp Rptr; Rep Sr Cls; High Hon Roll; Jr NHS; Spanish NHS; Actvty CPB 85-86; U Of Bridgeport; Dntl Hygnst.

MASUCCI, JUDY P; Torrington HS; Torrington, CT; (Y); 25/286; Var Church Yth Grp; Cmnty Wkr; Drama Clb; Math Tm; Stage Crew; High Hon Roll; Hon Roll; NHS; Charlotte Hungerford Hosp Aux Schlrshp; Smith Coll; Gentc Engrng.

MATHEWS, KATHY; Watertown HS; Watertown, CT; (Y); 27/290; Church Yth Grp; Computer Clb; Ski Clb; Variety Show; Off Frsh Cls; Off Soph Cls; Off Jr Cls; Stu Cncl; Mgr(s); Score Keeper; Bus.

MATHEWS, SHANNON; Sacred Heart Acad; West Haven, CT; (Y); Church Yth Grp; Cmnty Wkr; Letterman Clb; Concert Band; Var L Tennis; Im Vllybl; High Hon Roll; Hon Roll; Jr NHS; NHS; Natl Fed Music Clubs Super Hon 83-85; Pre Med.

MATHEWSON, LISA; St Bernard HS; Windham, CT; (Y); 6/268; 4-H; Yrbk Stf; Stu Cncl; High Hon Roll; NHS; Ntl Merit Ltr; Dartmouth Bk Awd 86; Excllnc Spnsh 85; Biochem.

MATHIEU, RICHARD; Marianapolis Preparatory Schl; N Grosvenordale, CT; (Y); 8/42; Yrbk Sprt Ed; Yrbk Stf; Bsbl; High Hon Roll; Bus Adm.

MATIAS, LISA; Farmington HS; Farmington, CT; (Y); 14/206; Acpl Chr; Chorus; Madrigals; Var Capt Gym; Im Wt Lftg; High Hon Roll; Sec NHS; Spanish NHS; Dance Studio Ownr/Oper; Lisa Matias Dance Ctr Tchr; Studio Dncng; Trinity Coll; Dance Tchr.

MATON, ELIO; Kaynor Technical Schl; Naugatuck, CT; (Y); Hon Roll; Fd Svc.

MATTHEWS, KRISTIN; St Josephs HS; Trumbull, CT; (Y); 30/275; Debate Tm; Drama Clb; Hosp Aide; Thesps; School Musical; Nwsp Ed-Chief; Yrbk Stf; Hon Roll; NHS; NEDT Awd; Advncd Plcmnt Engl 86-87.

MATTHEWS, TANYA; Bloomfield HS; Bloomfield, CT; (Y); 41/236; Civic Clb; Hon Roll; Spanish NHS; FBLA; Hosp Aide; Pep Clb; Color Guard; UCONN Day Of Pride 85; Best Spnsh II Stu 84; Briarwood Bk Awd 85; CT U.

MATTSON, JOHN; East Haven HS; East Haven, CT; (Y); 21/245; Am Leg Boys St; PAVAS; Spanish Clb; Band; Jazz Band; Mrchg Band; Lit Mag; High Hon Roll; Hon Roll; NHS; Western CT ST U; Music.

MATUG, BOGDAN; New Britain HS; New Britain, CT; (Y); Hartfrd ST Tech Coll; Mech Eng.

MATURO, KIM; Longview Catholic HS; Braodbrook, CT; (Y); 4/16; VP Sec 4-H; Nwsp Rptr; Yrbk Stf; Pres Frsh Cls; Socr; Sftbl; 4-H Awd; Hon Roll; Cornell U; Vetrnrn Srgn.

MATUSOVICH, WENDY; Pomperaug Regional HS; Southbury, CT; (Y); 20/196; Model UN; SADD; Varsity Clb; Yrbk Stf; Rep Frsh Cls; Pres Soph Cls; Pres Jr Cls; Pres Sr Cls; Rep Stu Cncl; JV Bsktbl; Outstndng SR Athlt 86; Ftr Tchrs Awd Schlrshps; APNAS Bstrs Clb Awd Schlrshps; Hrtg Vlg Schlshp; Brown U; Educ.

MATZ, DAVID; Norwalk HS; Norwalk, CT; (Y); 39/495; Letterman Clb; Concert Band; Jazz Band; Mrchg Band; Rep Jr Cls; Capt Var Ice Hcky; Var Capt Lcrss; Powder Puff Ftbl; Hon Roll; S Dv La Crosse 86; All FCIAC Lacrosse 86; Physcl Thrpy.

MAURIELLO, MICA; West Haven HS; W Haven, CT; (Y); Camera Clb; Pep Clb; Science Clb; Ski Clb; SADD; Yrbk Phtg; Stu Cncl; JV Vllybl; Lab Sci.

MAXWELL, MICHELE; Holy Cross HS; Waterbury, CT; (Y); 103/380; Drama Clb; Latin Clb; SADD; Chorus; School Musical; Stage Crew; Hon Roll; Socl Stds Hnr Soc Cert Of Merit 85-86; Pol Sci.

MAYER, HELEN; Tolland HS; Tolland, CT; (Y); Pres 4-H; Ski Clb; Band; Rep Frsh Cls; Rep Soph Cls; Rep Jr Cls; Var L Crs Cntry; Var L Trk; Cit Awd; 4-H Awd; Phtgrphy.

MAYHEW, JOHN; Rockville HS; Vernon, CT; (Y); Rptr Pres 4-H; Church Choir; Nwsp Ed-Chief; 4-H Awd; Hon Roll; 4-H Ctznshp Wshngtn Fcs 85; 4-H Fr Brd 83-86 ; Elctrcl Cntrctr.

MAYOTTE, DAVID; Tourtellotte HS; Quinebaug, CT; (Y); 16/102; JV Var Bsbl; Hon Roll; Prfct Atten Awd; Acctnt.

MAZER, KAYLA; Trumbull HS; Trumbull, CT; (Y); Cmnty Wkr; Dance Clb; SADD; VP Temple Yth Grp; Mrchg Band; Symp Band; Yrbk Rptr; High Hon Roll; AFS; Spanish Clb; A J Heshel Hnrs Scty 85; Bio.

MAZZAFERRO, ELISA; Holy Cross HS; Waterbury, CT; (Y); 15/396; French Clb; Hosp Aide; SADD; Chorus; Nwsp Rptr; Nwsp Stf; VP Frsh Cls; Trk; French Hon Soc; Hon Roll; Vet Med.

MAZZALUPO, CHRISTY; Notre Dame Acad; Waterbury, CT; (Y); SADD; Nwsp Rptr; Nwsp Stf; Lit Mag; Pres Frsh Cls; Sec Soph Cls; VP Jr Cls; Stu Cncl; Var Bsktbl; Var Socr; Sports Awds; Bus Mgmt.

MAZZAMURRO, LAURIE; Wethersfield HS; Wethersfield, CT; (Y); Church Yth Grp; Cmnty Wkr; Acpl Chr; Band; Chorus; Church Choir; Concert Band; School Play; Lit Mag; Hon Roll; Sci Awd-Bio Invstgn; 2nd Pl St Poetry Wrtng; 2nd Pl Nation-Poetry Wrtng; Jrnlst.

MAZZARO, VINCENT; Shelton HS; Shelton, CT; (Y); Ski Clb; Var Ftbl; Var Wt Lftg; New Haven U; Police Officer.

MAZZONE, ALICIA; Bristol Central HS; Bristol, CT; (Y); Church Yth Grp; Library Aide; Teachers Aide; Yrbk Stf; Hon Roll; Prfct Atten Awd; New Rochelle Coll; Chld Psychrs.

MC ALLISTER, VALERIE; Wilcox Tech Reg Vo Tech; Albany, VT; (Y); Cmnty Wkr; JA; Library Aide; Nwsp Rptr; Nwsp Stf; High Hon Roll; Hon Roll; NHS; Pres Schlr; Fincng.

MC BARNETTE, ANDREA; Kent Schl; New York, NY; (Y); Chess Clb; Debate Tm; Spanish Clb; Church Choir; School Play; Nwsp Rptr; Bsktbl; Lcrss; Socr; Ntl Merit Ltr; Acad Hnr Rl 83-85.

MC BRIDE JR, DAVID F; St Bernard HS; Lisbon, CT; (Y); 158/285; Am Leg Boys St; Boy Scts; Chess Clb; Var L Bsbl; Var L Ftbl; Im Wt Lftg; Spec Olymp Volunteer; Wheelchr Games Volunteer.

MC CAIN, THOMAS; St Josephs HS; Trumbull, CT; (Y); Spanish Clb; Nwsp Rptr; JV Bsbl; Im Bsktbl; Var Ftbl; Var Wt Lftg; Hon Roll; Prfct Atten Awd; Bus.

MC CANN, AMY; Hamden HS; Hamden, CT; (Y); FNA; High Hon Roll; Hon Roll; Certified Nurses Asst 86; Nrsng.

MC CARRICK, JULIE; Joseph A Foran HS; Milford, CT; (Y); 33/293; Keywanettes; Spanish Clb; Yrbk Stf; Hon Roll; Acctg.

MC CART, MIKE; Fairfield College Prep Schl; Shelton, CT; (Y); JA; Math Tm; Lit Mag; Var L Bowling; JV Socr; High Hon Roll; NHS; Natl Merit Schlr 86; Engrng.

MC CARTHY, GABRIELLE; Daniel Hand HS; Madison, CT; (Y); Church Yth Grp; GAA; Office Aide; Orch; Cheerleading; Mst Imprvd Chrldng Awd 86.

MC CARTHY, KARA BETH; West Haven HS; W Haven, CT; (Y); 29/390; Intnl Clb; High Hon Roll; Hon Roll; Jr NHS; NHS; Pres Schlr; West Haven Yth Found Awd 86; Natl Hnr Scty Schlrshp 86; Schltc Excllnce Awds 82-86; Albertus Magnus Coll; Bio.

MC CARTHY, MAUREEN; St Bernard HS; Oakdale, CT; (Y); 14/265; Church Yth Grp; Hosp Aide; Off Band; Church Choir; Off Color Guard; Off Concert Band; Capt Flag Corp; Mrchg Band; High Hon Roll; Hon Roll; Engrg.

MC CARTHY, MEGHAN; Sacred Heart Acad; Stamford, CT; (Y); Drama Clb; Chorus; Church Choir; School Musical; School Play; Lit Mag; Pres Jr Cls; JV Vllybl; French Hon Soc; NHS; Holy Cross Bk Awd 86; Lib Arts.

MC CARTHY, NEIL; Brookfield HS; Brookfield, CT; (Y); Math Tm; Lit Mag; JV Crs Cntry; High Hon Roll; Hon Roll; CT HS Bowl 85; Schlrshp Ctr Creative Yth Wesleyan U 86; Fine Arts.

MC CARVILL, JOHN; Jonathan Lan HS; Milford, CT; (Y); 3/247; Am Leg Boys St; Key Clb; Rencalerr Polytech Inst; Engrng.

MC CAULEY, THERESA; West Haven HS; West Haven, CT; (Y); 3/390; Ski Clb; Mrchg Band; Var Capt Swmmng; Cit Awd; NHS; NEDT Awd; Pres Schlr; Spanish NHS; Cmnty Wkr; Intnl Clb; United Tech Scholar 86; Christa Mac Auliffe Scholar 86; Rensselaer Polytech Inst Scholar 86; Rensselaer Polytech; Biochem.

MC CLOSKEY, SEAN; Killingly HS; Danielson, CT; (Y); 1/230; Am Leg Boys St; Church Yth Grp; Band; VP Soph Cls; VP Jr Cls; Var L Bsbl; L Socr; Pres NHS; Pres Schlr; Val; Amer Lgn Boys Natn 85; Estrn CT Allstar Sccr Tm 84-85; Brown U Book Awd 85; Boston Clg; Law.

MC CLURE, MARVA; James Hillhouse HS; New Haven, CT; (Y); French Clb; Red Cross Aide; Rep Frsh Cls; Rep Jr Cls; JV Var Vllybl; Hon Roll; NHS; Prfct Atten Awd; Cert Of Adv Bio 86; Lawyer.

MC CLYMONT, PATRICK; Fairfield College Prep; Ridgefield, CT; (Y); Key Clb; Im Mgr Ftbl; Golf; Var Score Keeper; JV Wrstlng; NHS; Ntl Merit Ltr; Spanish NHS; Washington Intern 86; Bus.

MC CONNELL, MELANIE GWEN; Greenwich HS; Old Greenwich, CT; (Y); Church Yth Grp; JA; Service Clb; Band; Chorus; Concert Band; Mrchg Band; School Musical; Hon Roll; Outstndng Contrbtn Music 84; Princpls Recgntn 84.

MC CONNIN, MATTHEW; Greenwich HS; Greenwich, CT; (Y); Church Yth Grp; Spanish Clb; SADD; Capt L Ftbl; Capt L Trk; Capt L Wrstlng; NHS; Key Clb; Service Clb; Spanish NHS; Econ.

MC CORMACK, KELLY; Berlin HS; Kensington, CT; (Y); Art Clb; Service Clb; SADD; Capt Color Guard; Ed Nwsp Stf; Ed Lit Mag; Hon Roll; NHS; Pres Schlr; Calligrphy Awd 84; Creatv Art Hnr Awd 85; Colby Bk Awd 85; AAA Natl Sfty Pstr Contst 3rd 86; Bridgeport U; Advrtsng Art.

MC CORMACK, MAUREEN; Trumbull HS; Trumbull, CT; (Y); AFS; Church Yth Grp; Girl Scts; Hosp Aide; Spanish Clb; Chorus; Color Guard; Yrbk Stf; High Hon Roll; NHS; PTSA Schlrshp 86; Boston Coll; Nursing.

MC COTER, VALERIE; HS In The Comm; New Haven, CT; (Y).

MC COWN, TONIA; James Hillhouse HS; New Haven, CT; (Y); Camera Clb; VP Stu Cncl; Capt Var Bsktbl; Stat Ftbl; Capt Var Sftbl; Capt Var Vllybl; Hon Roll; Jr NHS; NHS; Prfct Atten Awd; Smith Book Awd 86; Soc Sci.

MC CROCKLIN, TOM; Torrington HS; Torrington, CT; (Y); 25/245; Latin Clb; Letterman Clb; Model UN; Varsity Clb; Var L Bsbl; Var L Bsktbl; JV Ftbl; High Hon Roll; NHS; Red Auerbach Bsktbl Cmp Schlrshp 85; U Of Notre Dame; Bus Law.

MC CULLAGH, SANDRA L; Trumbull HS; Trumbull, CT; (Y); AFS; Chorus; Capt Color Guard; Madrigals; Nwsp Rptr; High Hon Roll; Trumbull Arts Ltry Comptn Hon Mntn; Prnt Tchr Stdnt Asso Rcrdng Sec; PTSA 2dn Vice Presnt.

MC CULLOUGH, TAMMIE; Killingly HS; Danielson, CT; (Y); 44/316; Church Yth Grp; Hosp Aide; Off Mrchg Band; Stat Socr; High Hon Roll; Hon Roll; Jr NHS; Spanish Clb; SADD; Off Band; Var Pin-Soccer Statistician 85-86; Surg Tech.

MC CURDY, PATRICIA; New Britain HS; New Britain, CT; (Y); 43/335; Cmnty Wkr; Drama Clb; Exploring; Pres Y-Teens; Chorus; Church Choir; Yrbk Stf; Office Aide; Service Clb; School Play; Natl Hstry Day Competition 1st Pl Regnls 3rd ST 86; Schlrshp Wrld Camp 85; 2 Full Schlrships Ldrs Sch; Physical Thrpy.

MC CUTCHEON, SUSAN; Sacred Heart Acad; Branford, CT; (Y); Computer Clb; FBLA; Hosp Aide; Hon Roll; Spanish NHS; 3 Yr Hnr Awd 86; Bus Mgmt.

MC DERMOTT, LESLIE; Low-Heywood Thomas HS; Stamford, CT; (Y); Art Clb; Church Yth Grp; Cmnty Wkr; Debate Tm; Drama Clb; GAA; Intnl Clb; JA; Letterman Clb; Model UN; Drama Awd 86; MVP Vllybl 86; Cptn Vllybl Tm 86; Cls Prze 86; Hamilton Coll; Psych.

MC DONALD, DEBORAH; Farmington HS; Farmington, CT; (Y); 56/206; Church Yth Grp; Chorus; Madrigals; Hon Roll; Bus Ed Awd Achvt 85-86; U RI; Child Psych.

MC DONALD, FAY; Vinal Vocational Regional Tech Schl; Middletown, CT; (Y); VICA; Yrbk Stf; Crs Cntry; Trk; Cazenovia Coll; Fshn Dsgnng.

MC DONALD, MELINDA; Cheshire HS; Cheshire, CT; (Y); Drama Clb; Red Cross Aide; SADD; Nwsp Rptr; Hon Roll; Psych.

MC DONELL, AMY; Putnam HS; Pomfret Center, CT; (Y); Cmnty Wkr; JA; Acpl Chr; Band; Chorus; Church Choir; Color Guard; Concert Band; Flag Corp; Mrchg Band; Mrshl Graduation 86; Music.

MC DONNELL, JAMIE; Old Saybrook SR HS; Old Saybrook, CT; (Y); Exploring; FCA; Latin Clb; Letterman Clb; Ski Clb; Nwsp Rptr; Nwsp Sprt Ed; Yrbk Stf; Off Jr Cls; Var Bsbl; Sports Brdcstng.

MC DOUGALL, JERRY; St Lukes Schl; Trumbull, CT; (Y); Capt L Bsbl; L Var Bsktbl; L Var Ftbl; Hon Roll; All Lg Bsbl 86; Pat Thms Ftbl Bwl Awd 86; Bsbl All Star Gm 85-86.

MC ELDOWNEY, SARA; Lauralton Hall HS; Fairfield, CT; (Y); Boys Clb Am; French Clb; Science Clb; Service Clb; Chorus; Yrbk Stf; JV Crs Cntry; Hon Roll; Bio.

MC EWEN, RHONDA; Shelton HS; Shelton, CT; (Y); JCL; Pres Latin Clb; Yrbk Stf; Trk; High Hon Roll; Hon Roll; NHS; Rep Stu Cncl; Library Aide; Cmnty Wkr; Ltn Ntl Hnr Soc 84-86; Miss Adelaide Coombs Awd 84; Ltn III Awd Grt Dedctn Twd Cls 86; Med.

MC FARLAND, HEATHER; Stratford HS; Stratford, CT; (Y); 40/257; High Hon Roll; Hon Roll; Ushers Guild; Nrsng.

MC FARLAND, ROBERT; Simsbury HS; Simsbury, CT; (Y); 6/351; Am Leg Boys St; Sec Trs Church Yth Grp; Drama Clb; Church Choir; Yrbk Bus Mgr; Cit Awd; High Hon Roll; NHS; Ntl Merit Ltr; Pres Schlr; ITT Col Schrlshp 86; Humphrey Awd 86; Barbara N Heath Awd 86; U VA; Schlr.

MC GANN, PATRICK; Southington HS; Southington, CT; (Y); 161/600; Church Yth Grp; Var Bsktbl; Var Golf; Var Socr; Hon Roll; Poltcl Sci.

MC GEE, DANA R; Rockville HS; Vernon, CT; (Y); 13/320; Office Aide; Yrbk Stf; Ed Lit Mag; Sec Stu Cncl; High Hon Roll; NHS; Mgr Sftbl; Yth NAACP 84; Natl Achvt Cmmnded Schlr 85; AIC Mod Congress Co-Spnsr Bill 85; Tutor Spn & Alg 83-84; Atty.

MC GIRR, JOHN; Norwalk HS; Norwalk, CT; (Y); VP German Clb; JV Bsbl; High Hon Roll; Hon Roll; Acctg.

MC GOE, DAWN; Ansonia HS; Ansonia, CT; (Y); Church Yth Grp; Computer Clb; Latin Clb; Yrbk Stf; Var Capt Sftbl; JV Vllybl; NHS; Engrng.

MC GRATH, SCOTT; Manchester HS; Manchester, CT; (Y); Art Clb; Drama Clb; Spanish Clb; School Play; Stage Crew; Hon Roll.

MC GRATH, TODD; Vinal Tech; Middlefield, CT; (Y); Aud/Vis; Boy Scts; Hosp Aide; Elec Engr.

MC GRAW, PATRICK N; The Loomis Chaffee Schl; Maplewood, NJ; (Y); Boy Scts; VP Debate Tm; German Clb; Library Aide; Math Tm; Concert Band; Orch; Im Socr; Ntl Merit SF; Rensselaer Polytech Inst Mth/Sci Awd 85; Goethe Inst Germ Awd 84; Thomas L Hochwalt Chem Awd 83; Physics.

MC GREIVY, JESSE; The Taft Schl; Hollywood, CA; (Y); Hon Roll; Debate Tm; Math Tm; Chorus; JV Im Bsktbl; Var Crs Cntry; Im Socr; Var Trk; U Of Cal; Neurological Rsch.

MC GUINNESS, KATHERINE A; Central Catholic HS; Norwalk, CT; (Y); Am Leg Aux Girls St; Pres Drama Clb; Ski Clb; Yrbk Ed-Chief; Var Vllybl; French Hon Soc; NHS; NEDT Awd; Pres Schlr; St Schlr; Amer Lgn Schlrshp 86; Mensa Schlrshp 86; St Bonaventure U.

MC GUIRE, LAURA; Brien Mc Mahon HS; Norwalk, CT; (Y); 4-H; FBLA; Ski Clb; Band; Concert Band; Mrchg Band; Orch; Symp Band; Bowling; Powder Puff Ftbl; Bus Adm.

MC GUIRE, LAURA; St Bernard HS; Noank, CT; (Y); 10/300; VP Church Yth Grp; Chorus; Church Choir; Jazz Band; School Musical; Var Capt Gym; High Hon Roll; NHS; Natl Schl Chrl Awd 86; Pres Acad Ftnss Awd 86; Susan Mary O'connor Awd 86; Anna Maria Coll; Music Therapy.

MC GUIRE, MEGAN E; Gulford HS; Guilford, CT; (Y); Church Yth Grp; Ski Clb; SADD; Band; Concert Band; Mrchg Band; Off Frsh Cls; Sec Soph Cls; Pres Jr Cls; Pres Sr Cls; Providence Coll; Pol Sci.

MC GURK, JAMIE; Litchfield HS; Litchfield, CT; (Y); Camera Clb; Radio Clb; Scholastic Bowl; Variety Show; Yrbk Stf; Var L Socr; Var Capt Swmmng; Var L Trk; Hon Roll; Rotary Awd; Natl Merit Schlrshp Cmmdtn PSAT 85; ASVAB Awd Wnr 84; ST Fnlst Medley Relay Tm 86; Cinemtgrphy.

MC HALE, SHERI; Holy Cross HS; Watertown, CT; (Y); 70/400; Art Clb; Church Yth Grp; Drama Clb; French Clb; Latin Clb; Spanish Clb; SADD; School Musical; School Play; JV Vllybl; NY U; Intl Intrprtr.

MC HUGH, JOANNE P; Glatonbury HS; Glastonbury, CT; (Y); 61/415; Variety Show; Var L Lcrss; High Hon Roll; Hon Roll; Full Schlrshp Stu Hartford Acad Prffrmng Arts 85-86; Semi-Fnlst Natl Fndtn Advnmnt Arts 86; Theatre Arts.

MC INTYRE, KEVIN; Weston HS; Newkirk, OK; (Y); Church Yth Grp; Cmnty Wkr; VICA; JV Var Ftbl; JV Var Wrstlng; Hon Roll; ST Wrstlng Chmpnshp 185 Lb 85-86; Goldn Hmmr Awd 85-86; Wldng.

MC INTYRE, MICHELLE A; Danbury HS; Danbury, CT; (Y); 80/600; Drama Clb; Ski Clb; Acpl Chr; Variety Show; Var Fld Hcky; JV Trk; Hon Roll; Jr NHS; Excllnc In Hlth Awd 84.

MC KEE, BRAD; New Canaan HS; New Canaan, CT; (Y); Church Yth Grp; Debate Tm; Rep Frsh Cls; Rep Soph Cls; Rep Jr Cls; Rep Sr Cls; Var L Ftbl; JV Ice Hcky; Var L Lcrss; Hon Roll.

MC KEEN, AMY; Griswold HS; Jewett City, CT; (Y); 6/87; Trs Church Yth Grp; GAA; Varsity Clb; Chorus; VP Soph Cls; VP Jr Cls; JV Var Bsktbl; JV Var Sftbl; High Hon Roll; NHS.

MC KEEVER, KEVIN; Stamford Catholic HS; Stamford, CT; (Y); 2/150; Aud/Vis; Capt Math Tm; Capt Quiz Bowl; Nwsp Ed-Chief; Lit Mag; Rep Soph Cls; Var L Bsbl; Stat Mgr Vllybl; DAR Awd; High Hon Roll; Scripps Howard Fndtn Schlrshp 86-87; CT ST Wnr Natl Jrnlsm Cntst 86; The George Washington U.

MC KENNA, JOHN; St Bernard HS; Oakdale, CT; (Y); 52/300; Off Jr Cls; Off Sr Cls; Bsbl; Crs Cntry; Hon Roll; Ntl Merit SF; U CT; Chem Engrg.

MC KENZIE, LEROY; Central HS; Bridgeport, CT; (Y); French Clb; JA; Spanish Clb; Socr; Elec Engrng.

MC KNIGHT, JANE KATHRYN; Joseph A Foran HS; Milford, CT; (Y); 55/275; Church Yth Grp; Spanish Clb; SADD; Var Tennis; Hon Roll; Coaches Achvt & Sprtsmnshp Awds Tennis 85 & 86; Advrtsng.

MC LACHLAN, ANDREW; Roger Ludlowe HS; Fairfield, CT; (Y); Boy Scts; Church Yth Grp; Cmnty Wkr; Political Wkr; Yrbk Phtg; Yrbk Stf; Walkathon Clss Ofcr; Spec Olympcs; Bus Comm.

MC LAUGHLIN, CHRIS; New Milford HS; New Milford, CT; (Y); Boy Scts; Pres Exploring; Cit Awd; Eagl Sct 84.

MC LAUGHLIN, MICHELE D; Newtown HS; Sandy Hook, CT; (Y); 22/290; Drama Clb; Varsity Clb; Acpl Chr; Chorus; Madrigals; School Musical; School Play; Variety Show; Nwsp Stf; Lit Mag; Wstrn Rgnls Chr 83-84; All-CT ST Chr 85; Frnds Of Msc Schlrshp 86; Providence Coll; Pltcl Sci.

MC LAUGHLIN, TARA; Rockville HS; Rockville, CT; (Y); Band; Concert Band; Mrchg Band; Orch; Pep Band; School Musical; Lit Mag; Hon Roll; NHS; Church Yth Grp; Ntnl Hnr Scty 86; CT Gnrl Assmbly Citatn 86; Art.

MC LEOD, ROBERT; Morgan Schl; Clinton, CT; (Y); 15/150; VP AFS; Am Leg Boys St; School Musical; Pres Soph Cls; Pres Jr Cls; Pres Sr Cls; Socr; Capt Trk; Hon Roll; NHS.

MC LOUGHLIN JR, STEPHEN; Seymour HS; Seymour, CT; (S); 16/192; Church Yth Grp; Capt Bsbl; Cheerleading; Socr; Capt Swmmng; Hon Roll; Pres NHS; U Of CT.

MC MAHON, CHERYL; Vinal Regional Technical Schl; N Branford, CT; (Y); Keywanettes; VICA; Variety Show; Yrbk Stf; Rep Frsh Cls; Pres Soph Cls; Rep Jr Cls; Pres Sr Cls; Pres Stu Cncl; Var Cheerleading; Athltc Achvt Awd-Sftbl, Crss Cntry, & Trck; MVP-CRSS Cntry; Prom Queen.

MC MAHON, DEBORAH; St Joseph HS; Shelton, CT; (Y); 51/257; Dance Clb; Drama Clb; French Clb; Thesps; Chorus; School Musical; Variety Show; Nwsp Stf; Lit Mag; French Hon Soc; Phys Thrpy.

MC MANUS, STEPHEN M; Windsor HS; Windsor, CT; (Y); 1/314; Political Wkr; Trs Sr Cls; Var Capt Socr; Var L Tennis; Trs French Hon Soc; NCTE Awd; Sec NHS; Daniel Howard Schlr 85-86; Pltcl Sci.

MC MILLAN, MERYDITH C; The Hotchkiss Schl; Lakeville, CT; (Y); Pres Cmnty Wkr; SADD; School Musical; Nwsp Rptr; Lit Mag; Stu Cncl; Var Fld Hcky; Hon Roll; Ntl Merit SF; Pres Schlr; Ledr Those Girls 84-86; Dartmouth.

MC NAIR, LINDSAY A; St Margarets-Mc Ternan HS; Waterbury, CT; (Y); Drama Clb; Sec VP Latin Clb; Chorus; School Musical; School Play; Stage Crew; Var Socr; Var Tennis; JV Var Vllybl; Hon Roll; U CT Scholar 85.

MC NAMARA, MAUREEN; Ridgefield HS; Ridgefield, CT; (Y); 87/381; Varsity Clb; Bsktbl; Powder Puff Ftbl; Golf; Vllybl; Hon Roll.

MC NAMEE, JOHN; St Mary HS; Greenwich, CT; (Y); Drama Clb; Latin Clb; Spanish Clb; Band; Yrbk Phtg; Yrbk Sprt Ed; Var JV Bsktbl; Var JV Ftbl; Var Lcrss; Hon Roll; Awd High Scores NADTS 84-85; Awd High Achvt Hstry 85-86; Scored 1140 SAT Exam; Boston Coll; Intl Bus.

MC NEALY, MEGAN; Mis Porters Schl; Woodstock, IL; (Y); Cmnty Wkr; Spanish Clb; Pres Jr Cls; Pres Sr Cls; Pres Stu Cncl; Fld Hcky; Var Capt Tennis; High Hon Roll; Hon Roll; Head Schl Stu Bdy Pres Miss Porters Schl 86-87.

MC NEIL, SANJEE; Bossick HS; Bridgeport, CT; (Y); Church Yth Grp; FNA; Key Clb; Red Cross Aide; Chorus; Church Choir; Yrbk Stf; Hartford Coll; Med.

MC PHERSON, TAMMY; Middletown HS; Middletown, CT; (Y); Spanish Clb; Teachers Aide; Y-Teens; Var L Socr; Var L Sftbl; Hon Roll; Educ.

MC TIGUE, KEITH; Fairfield College Prep; Huntington, CT; (Y); 53/226; Exploring; Yrbk Stf; Im Bsktbl; JV Crs Cntry; Im Ftbl; JV Trk; Hon Roll.

MC WADE, FRANK; New Fairfield HS; New Fairfield, CT; (Y); 38/240; Boy Scts; Church Yth Grp; Latin Clb; Math Clb; Science Clb; Ski Clb; Drm & Bgl; Pep Band; Variety Show; Wrstlng; Magna Cm Ld Ntl Ltn Exm 86; Chem Engrng.

MEADE, MICHELLE; Ansonia HS; Ansonia, CT; (Y); Girl Scts; Science Clb; Yrbk Ed-Chief; Yrbk Stf; Score Keeper; Hon Roll; Spanish NHS; Spec Ed.

MEADE, PATRICIA; Ansonia HS; Ansonia, CT; (Y); 5/150; Girl Scts; OEA; Yrbk Stf; Score Keeper; High Hon Roll; NHS; Spanish NHS; Mrt Dplma In Spnsh 84-85.

MECCA, SCOTT; Holy Cross HS; Prospect, CT; (Y); 116/380; Chorus; School Musical; School Play; Bsbl; Hon Roll; Bryant Coll; Bus.

MEDINA, NORA; Bassick HS; Bridgeport, CT; (Y); Drm Mjr(t); Mrchg Band; Hon Roll; NHS; Christa Mc Auliffe Schlrshp 86; Philip Holzer Schlrshp 86; Amer Assn Of Univ Women 86; U Of Bridgeport; Music Eductn.

MEEHAN, KEVIN; Holy Cross HS; Waterbury, CT; (Y); 181/380; Art Clb; Var L Bsbl; Sci.

MEIMAN, MARGARET; Andrew Warde HS; Fairfield, CT; (Y); Cmnty Wkr; Pres Thesps; Orch; Pres Stage Crew; NHS; Drama Clb; Chorus; Frfld Wmns Clb Drama Awd 86; Frfld PTA Drama Awd Plq 86; Albertus Magnus Coll; Lbrl Arts.

MEJIA, OMAR; Wilbur Cross HS; New Haven, CT; (Y); 93/270; Intnl Clb; JV Trk; U New Haven Pgmmg Comptn 3rd Pl 85-86; Aerospc Engrng.

MELENDEZ, DEAN; Hartford Public HS; Manati, PR; (Y); 20/308; Am Leg Boys St; Church Yth Grp; VP Computer Clb; Ed Lit Mag; Trs Church Yth Grp2; Pres Stu Cncl; Crs Cntry; Cit Awd; DAR Awd; Hon Roll; PR Coll; Med.

MELILLO, CHRISTOPHER; Mark T Sheehan HS; Wallingford, CT; (Y); Am Leg Boys St; Varsity Clb; Yrbk Stf; JV Bsbl; Capt Ftbl.

MELILLO, LISA; Shelton HS; Shelton, CT; (Y); JA; Spanish Clb; Nwsp Rptr; Rep Jr Cls; Stu Cncl; Cheerleading; High Hon Roll; NHS; VP Spanish NHS; Miguel De Unamuna Awd Excllnce Spn III 85; Outstndng Stu Cncl Svc Awd 84 & 85; Pre-Law.

MELO, VERA; Hartford Public HS; Hartford, CT; (Y); Cmnty Wkr; DECA; Drama Clb; Chorus; Mgr(s); Swmmng; Tennis; Hon Roll; Acad Drmtc Arts; Actg.

MELVIN, GREG; Taft Schl; Brookfield, CT; (Y); AFS; Yrbk Stf; Ed Lit Mag; L Var Crs Cntry; L Var Tennis; High Hon Roll; Georgetown U; Bus Admin.

MENCEL, TERESA; St Joseph HS; Bridgeport, CT; (Y); 85/257; JA; Church Choir; Bsktbl; Var L Trk; Bus.

MENCIO, AMANDA; Holy Cross HS; Waterbury, CT; (Y); 75/380; Art Clb; VP Latin Clb; Hon Roll; SADD; Stat Trk; Hist Hon Soc 85-87; Downhill Ski Tm JV Lttr 85-87; JR Apprctn Night Committee 86; Law.

MENDEZ, MARIA; New London HS; Waterford, CT; (Y); 14/180; Key Clb; Stu Cncl; Im Badmtn; High Hon Roll; Hon Roll; NHS; SF Natl Hspnc Merit Schlrshp 85-86; U Of CT; Engrng.

MENDOZA, LISA; Bullard Havens Tech; Bpt, CT; (Y); Girl Scts; SADD; Rep Jr Cls; Rep Stu Cncl; Sftbl; Hon Roll; Post Coll; Bus Mngmnt.

MENNA, JULIE; Brien Mc Mahon HS; Norwalk, CT; (Y); FBLA; Concert Band; Jazz Band; Mrchg Band; Symp Band; Rep Soph Cls; High Hon Roll; Hon Roll; Jr NHS; NHS; Briarwood Coll Awd Mst Outstndg Bus Stu 86; FBLA Schlrp 86; Pres Gold Seal Acad Achvt Awd 86; Katherine Gibbs Norwalk; Secy.

MERCADO, RONALD; Bullard Havens Tech; Bridgeport, CT; (Y); 1/153; Church Yth Grp; VP JA; Bausch & Lomb Sci Awd; High Hon Roll; NHS; Hghst GPA; Norwalk ST Tech; Elec Tech.

MERISOTIS, EMANUEL; Manchester HS; Manchester, CT; (Y); 17/490; Am Leg Boys St; Pres French Clb; Capt Math Tm; Nwsp Stf; Sec Sr Cls; Pres NHS; Voice Dem Awd; JV Bsktbl; JV Crs Cntry; Schlr Grad 86; Bates Coll; Math.

MERLINO, THOMAS; Fairfield Coll Prep Schl; W Redding, CT; (Y); Computer Clb; Ski Clb; Yrbk Stf; Hon Roll; Boston Coll; Bus.

MERRITT, KRISTIN; Staples HS; Westport, CT; (Y); English Clb; Natl Beta Clb; Service Clb; Spanish Clb; Church Choir; Yrbk Stf; Rep Frsh Cls; Sec Soph Cls; Rep Jr Cls; Rep Stu Cncl; Annual Hnr Awd Engl 85; Annual Hnr Awd Yrbk 85; Awd Excllnc Spansh 86; Mt Holyoke Coll.

MERRITT, ROBERT; Southington HS; Southington, CT; (Y); Hon Roll; Hnr Art 84-85; Writer.

MERTL, GREG; Greenwich HS; Greenwich, CT; (Y); Am Leg Boys St; Quiz Bowl; JV Tennis; High Hon Roll; NCTE Awd; NHS; Ntl Merit Ltr; CT Music Compstn Fest Wnnr 85-86; Rockefeller Awd 85; Greenwich Cncl Arts Creatvty Awd 86; Music Compstn.

MERTON, JENNIFER; Rockville HS; Rockville, CT; (Y); Church Yth Grp; Dance Clb; Variety Show; JV Vllybl; Hon Roll; 2nd Pl Rgnl Dance Comp 85; Vsvl & Perf Arts.

METZ, SUZANNE; Westover Schl; Salisbury, CT; (Y); Camera Clb; Cmnty Wkr; Varsity Clb; Stage Crew; Nwsp Phtg; Yrbk Phtg; Var L Bsktbl; Var L Fld Hcky; Var L Sftbl; 4-H Awd; Resident Proctor 85-86; Vet.

METZGER, KATHY; Jonathan Law HS; Milford, CT; (Y); Ski Clb; Sftbl; Hon Roll; All St Jr Rifle Tm 84.

MEYER, GARY; Ridgefield HS; Ridgefield, CT; (Y); DECA; Ski Clb; JV Bsbl; Var JV Ftbl; Bus Admin.

MEYER, MARTIN; W F Kaynor Tech HS; Waterbury, CT; (Y); Pres SADD; Rep Jr Cls; Pres Stu Cncl; JV Crs Cntry; Hon Roll; U Of CT; Elec.

MEYER, OLIVIER S; Stamford HS; Stamford, CT; (Y); 36/365; Aud/Vis; Var Tennis; Hon Roll; NHS; IONA Lang Cont 1st Pl Fr III 84; IONA Lang Cont 1st Pl Native 86; Henry W Bartnikowski Crftsmn Awd; Rensellaer Polytech; Comp Sci.

MICACCI, ANNMARIE; Southington HS; Southington, CT; (Y); 26/600; Key Clb; Color Guard; Concert Band; School Play; Variety Show; Rep Soph Cls; Twrlr; High Hon Roll; NHS; Atndnc Awd; Frfld U; Acntng.

MICCIULLA, MIKE; E Hartford HS; E Hartford, CT; (Y); Chess Clb; Drama Clb; Concert Band; Mrchg Band; School Musical; Nwsp Stf; Lit Mag; Hon Roll; NCTE Awd; NHS; Biol Flds.

MICHALEK, JOHN; Torrington HS; Torrington, CT; (Y); French Clb; Key Clb; Model UN; Stage Crew; Ftbl; Wt Lftg; Hon Roll; U CT; Chem Engr.

MICHAUD, BRIAN; Kaynor Tech; Prospect, CT; (Y); Aud/Vis; High Hon Roll; Hon Roll; Jr NHS; NHS; 2nd Pl In Sci Fair; U Hartford; Elec Engrng.

MICHAUD, GLENN; Southington HS; Southington, CT; (Y); Am Leg Boys St; JA; VP Pres Key Clb; Quiz Bowl; Chorus; Nwsp Ed-Chief; Elks Awd; Gov Hon Prg Awd; NHS; Hrvrd Bk Prz 86; JR Ply 86; Acctng.

MICHAUD, JAMIE; Lewis S Mills HS; Burlington, CT; (Y); 7/125; Chorus; Jazz Band; Mrchg Band; School Musical; Symp Band; High Hon Roll; NHS; NEDT Awd; Girl Scts; Church Choir; Grl Sct Slvr Awd 84; UCONN Med Cntr Cncr Rsrch Vrty Shw 83; Vet Sci.

MICHAUD, LOUISE; Manchester HS; Manchester, CT; (Y); AFS; FBLA; Hosp Aide; JA; Bsktbl; Central CT ST U; Ed.

MICHAUD, PAUL; East Catholic HS; E Hartford, CT; (Y); Chess Clb; CAP; Yrbk Phtg; Lit Mag; E Catholic Serv Awd 86; Hnry Recrutr Awd 86; Bill Mitchell Awd 86; Centrl CT ST U; Pwr Plnt Mec.

MICHEK, BOB; Norwalk HS; Norwalk, CT; (Y); 86/465; Church Yth Grp; SADD; Band; Concert Band; Drm & Bgl; Mrchg Band; Orch; Pep Band; School Musical; Symp Band; Music.

MICHELLE, DEADRIANE; Bullard Havens RVTS HS; Bridgeport, CT; (Y); Church Yth Grp; JA; SADD; Church Choir; Sacred Heart U; Acctng.

MIDDLETON, JEANINE; West Haven HS; W Haven, CT; (Y); Cmnty Wkr; Band; Concert Band; Mrchg Band; Variety Show; Nwsp Stf; Rep Soph Cls; Capt Bsktbl; Capt Sftbl; Var L Vllybl; W Haven Fire Fghtrs Athl Sprtsmnshp Awd 86; W Haven Elks Yth Day Partcpnt 86; AZ ST U; Wldlf Bio.

MIERZEJEWSKI, KEVIN; Canton HS; Collinsville, CT; (Y); Boy Scts; Model UN; Red Cross Aide; SADD; Yrbk Stf; Golf; Socr; Hon Roll; Schl Trip France Spain 86; Engrng.

MIGLIACCIO, KRISTEN; Conard HS; West Hartford, CT; (Y); 77/331; Service Clb; Orch; Yrbk Stf; Var Cheerleading; Fld Hcky; JV Var Gym; JV Tennis; Hon Roll.

MIHALY, MATTHEW; Trumball HS; Trumbull, CT; (Y); Trs Church Yth Grp; L Ftbl; Co-Capt Trk; Cit Awd; High Hon Roll; NHS; Ntl Merit SF; Spanish NHS; CT ST Schlr Ath Awd 86; NY U; Bus Adm.

MIHOK, SCOTT; Parish Hill HS; Scotland, CT; (Y); Var L Bsbl; Var L Bsktbl; Im JV Socr; Hon Roll; Hartford U; Crimnl Justc.

MIKAN, SUSAN; Ridgefield HS; Ridgefield, CT; (S); Band; Mrchg Band; Orch; School Musical; Wstrn Rgnl Bnd 85.

MIKSOVSKY, JAN T; Choate Rosemary Hall HS; Maplewood, NJ; (Y); Boy Scts; Pres Computer Clb; Math Tm; Nwsp Ed-Chief; JV Crs Cntry; Hon Roll; Ntl Merit SF; 1st Pl CT ST Comp Cntst 85; Magna Cum Laude Natl Ltn Cntst 85; 1st Pl NJ Yng Flmmkrs Fstvl 83; Comp Sci.

MIKULAK, JASON; Windham HS; Stafford Spgs, CT; (Y); 22/280; Off Sr Cls; JV Capt Socr; Hon Roll; NHS; Willington PTA Awd 86; Embry-Riddle; Prof Pilot.

MILDREN, KEITH; Cromwell HS; Cromwell, CT; (Y); 15/78; Am Leg Boys St; Church Yth Grp; Rep Jr Cls; Rep Sr Cls; VP Stu Cncl; Bsktbl; Socr; Capt Trk; Gov Hon Prg Awd; NHS; Stanadyne Found Schlrshp 86; Hofstra U; Bus Comp.

MILEWSKI, YVONNE; Nonnwauge HS; Bethlehem, CT; (Y); Dance Clb; VP FFA; Yrbk Stf; Stu Cncl; Sftbl; Hon Roll; Horse Profncy Awd 85-86; FFA Mem Of Mth 85-86; Pre Law.

MILEWSKI, YVONNE; Stamford Catholic HS; Stamford, CT; (Y); 5/160; Trs FBLA; Red Cross Aide; Chorus; Nwsp Bus Mgr; Yrbk Stf; High Hon Roll; NHS; Prfct Atten Awd; St Schlr; Dance Clb; Amer Cyanamid Co Sci Ed Awd 86; Coll Atlantic; Marn Bio.

MILICI, WILLIAM; Hamden HS; Hamden, CT; (Y); Ftbl; Air Force Plt.

MILLER, BRYAN; Simsbury HS; Simsbury, CT; (Y); 74/410; Boy Scts; High Hon Roll; Hon Roll; FBI.

MILLER, CANDACE; East Lyme HS; Niantic, CT; (Y); 39/260; JV Capt Socr; Tennis; Villanova; Engr.

MILLER, DENYSE; Holy Cross HS; Seymour, CT; (Y); 171/380; Church Yth Grp; Cmnty Wkr; PAVAS; Spanish Clb; Hon Roll; Spec Educ.

MILLER, JENNIFER; Newington HS; Newington, CT; (S); 91/365; Drama Clb; Chorus; Jazz Band; Madrigals; Mrchg Band; Orch; School Musical; School Play; Symp Band; Variety Show; Lavon Lach Awd-Outstndng Prtcptn In Prodctn 84; Outstndng All Arnd Plyr 85; Theater Arts.

MILLER, JEREMY; Danbury HS; Danbury, CT; (Y); 32/538; Boy Scts; Church Yth Grp; Math Tm; Yrbk Phtg; Var Ftbl; Var Capt Trk; Var Wt Lftg; High Hon Roll; NHS; Safe Rides Of Danbury; Engrng.

MILLER, JODY; Stamford HS; Stamford, CT; (Y); Church Yth Grp; Hosp Aide; VP JA; Varsity Clb; Rep Frsh Cls; Trs Soph Cls; Rep Jr Cls; Stu Cncl; Crs Cntry; Trk; 1st Pl Outdr Cities Trk Meet Hgh Jmp 86; Art Advrtsg.

MILLER, JON; Greenwich HS; Greenwich, CT; (Y); Var L Swmmng; All Amercn Water Polo 2nd Tm 86; US Naval Acadmy.

MILLER, MICHELLE; Stamford Catholic HS; Stamford, CT; (Y); Art Clb; Church Yth Grp; Cmnty Wkr; Dance Clb; Pep Clb; PAVAS; Red Cross Aide; Rep Frsh Cls; Rep Soph Cls; JV Cheerleading; ST Wnnr Ms Lvs Baby Sft Cnsts 86; Ms YM Cvr Girl Srch Fnlst 84; Schl Spnsrd 24 Hr Dance Mrthn 83-86; U CT Storrs; Advrtsng.

MILLER, SETH; Plainville HS; Plainville, CT; (Y); JV Ftbl; Var L Swmmng; Var Trk; Im Wt Lftg; Hon Roll.

MILLER, SHARON; Shelton HS; Shelton, CT; (Y); Church Yth Grp; Drama Clb; French Clb; VP Key Clb; Latin Clb; Mrchg Band; School Play; Sec Frsh Cls; Sec Soph Cls; Sec Stu Cncl; Latn Ntl Hon Sco.

MILLER, SUSAN; Central Catholic HS; S Norwalk, CT; (Y); Drama Clb; School Musical; School Play; Stage Crew; Variety Show; Lit Mag; Hon Roll; NHS; Pres Schlr; Laux-Lajoie Scholar 82-83; Home-Schl Assn Scholar 83-84 & 84-85; U CT; Law.

MILLER, THOMAS; Fairfield College Preparatory School; Norwalk, CT; (Y); Church Yth Grp; Var Bsbl; JV Bsktbl; Wt Lftg; High Hon Roll; NHS.

MILLS, ALDEN M; Kent Schl; Southbridge, MA; (Y); Nwsp Sprt Ed; JV Crs Cntry; Var Wrstlng; Hon Roll; Bus.

MILLS, MICHAEL; Bristol Eastern HS; Bristol, CT; (Y); 2/282; Am Leg Boys St; Model UN; Crs Cntry; Ftbl; Trk; NHS; Sal; US Senate Page 84-85; Yale Bk Awd 85; All Conf Cross Cty 85; Pomona Coll; Intl Rel.

MILNE, JENNIFER; Joseph A Foran HS; Milford, CT; (Y); #9 In Class; Am Leg Aux Girls St; Hosp Aide; JCL; Keywanettes; Nwsp Rptr; Yrbk Stf; Trs Stu Cncl; Tennis; High Hon Roll; Hon Roll; ST Student Advisory Council On Educ 85-87; Stdnt Mem Of Governors Task Force Substance Abuse 86-87; Econ.

MINAHAN, TIMOTHY; Danbury HS; Danbury, CT; (Y); Civic Clb; Letterman Clb; Red Cross Aide; Teachers Aide; Varsity Clb; Acpl Chr; Chorus; Stage Crew; Yrbk Phtg; Yrbk Rptr; Marine Sci.

MINELLI, JENNIFER; Torrington HS; Torrington, CT; (Y); 43/283; Varsity Clb; Chorus; Rep Soph Cls; Trs Jr Cls; Sec Sr Cls; Var Score Keeper; Socr; High Hon Roll; Hon Roll; NHS; Psychrc Nrsng.

MINICHINO, DONNA; Guilford HS; Guilford, CT; (Y); 28/315; Hosp Aide; VP Key Clb; Latin Clb; Red Cross Aide; Teachers Aide; Var Trk; Hon Roll; NHS; Spanish NHS; Russell Sage Coll Fndrs Schlr 86-87; Russell Sage Coll; Phys Ther.

MINKOFF, CHARLES; Kent Schl; Ft Barrington, MA; (Y); Aud/Vis; Camera Clb; Nwsp Phtg; Yrbk Phtg; Yrbk Stf; JV Swmmng; Bio.

MINNICK, SCOTT; East Hampton HS; East Hampton, CT; (Y); 11/81; Am Leg Boys St; Church Yth Grp; Drama Clb; Model UN; School Musical; Yrbk Bus Mgr; Yrbk Ed-Chief; Yrbk Phtg; Var Capt Crs Cntry; Var Capt Tennis; Prncpls Awd 86; Long Island U; Marine Bio.

MINOPLI, MARY; Bullard Haven Tech; Bridgeport, CT; (S); Church Yth Grp; Girl Scts; Church Choir; Yrbk Ed-Chief; Off Frsh Cls; Off Soph Cls; Sec Sr Cls; Rep Stu Cncl; Vllybl; High Hon Roll.

MINOR, STEPHANY; Sacred Heart Acad; New Haven, CT; (Y); Art Clb; Church Yth Grp; Drama Clb; FBLA; Nwsp Rptr; Lit Mag; Rep Frsh Cls; Rep Stu Cncl; High Hon Roll; NHS; N E Dist NANBPW Achvr Pin 86; 1st Pl Prlmntry Precdr ST Ldrshp Cnfrnc FBLA 86; Cmmnctns.

MINOR, TAMMY; Saint Bernard HS; Preston, CT; (Y); 59/290; Church Yth Grp; Cmnty Wkr; Girl Scts; Church Choir; Color Guard; Lit Mag; Var Cheerleading; Hon Roll; Art Clb; Schlrsp To Cntr Fr Crtv Yth Wslyan U 86; Noteable Achvmnt-Art 86; Grace V Small Awd 86; Engnrng.

MIRANDO, RICHARD; H C Wilcox Technical Schl; Plantsville, CT; (Y); 10/221; Boy Scts; Church Yth Grp; Capt Var Wt Lftg; High Hon Roll; Hon Roll; NHS; Immclt Wmns Clb Schlrshp Awd 86; David T Zdunczyk Mem Schlrshp 86; Waterbury ST Tech; Elec Engrng.

MIREK, STEPHEN J; Brien Mcmahon HS; Norwalk, CT; (Y); Spanish Clb; C T Coll; Psych.

MIRMINA, GLEN; Joseph A Foran HS; Milford, CT; (Y); 15/280; Chess Clb; Key Clb; Spanish Clb; Stu Cncl; Hon Roll; Trs NHS; 2nd Pl Nw Englnd Dist Key Clb Essy Cntst; NEDT Tst Score Awd; Cvl Engrng.

MIRTO, WENDY; Lauralton Hall HS; Huntington, CT; (Y); 42/111; Cmnty Wkr; Drama Clb; Pep Clb; Service Clb; Spanish Clb; Stage Crew; Stat Bsktbl; Mgr(s); Hon Roll; NHS.

MISHRA, VIBHA R; Newington HS; Newington, CT; (Y); 4/352; Pres JA; Key Clb; Office Aide; Rep Frsh Cls; Rep Soph Cls; High Hon Roll; Ntl Merit Ltr; Plaq Hghst Ovrll GPA That Prtclr Yr 85-86; Plaq Hghst Avgs Spnsh II III IV 84-86; Ss Avg 4 Yr 86; U Of CT; Intl Bus.

MISTRETTA, GREGORY; East Lyme HS; Madison, CT; (Y); 18/280; Am Leg Boys St; Church Yth Grp; Yrbk Stf; Pres Frsh Cls; Pres Soph Cls; Pres Jr Cls; Rep Stu Cncl; Var Bsktbl; Var Tennis; NHS.

MITCHELL, ANDREW; Wilton HS; Wilton, CT; (Y); 75/364; Drama Clb; Exploring; Intnl Clb; VP SADD; Band; Concert Band; Mrchg Band; Pep Band; School Play; Symp Band; Prvt Stu Tour Grp-Australia, New Zealnd 86.

MITCHELL, DEBBIE ANN; Seymour HS; Seymour, CT; (Y); 118/194; Church Yth Grp; Dance Clb; Drama Clb; English Clb; French Clb; Pep Clb; Red Cross Aide; SADD; Acpl Chr; Chorus; Rep Southern CT ST Rgnl Choir 81-86; Rnnr Up Rep Girls All ST 85; Beacon Flls JR Miss Sprt Awd 86; Cntrl CT ST U; Nrsng.

MITCHELL, JEFF; Wilton HS; Wilton, CT; (Y); 71/355; Camera Clb; SADD; Hon Roll; Prfct Atten Awd; Gftd & Tlntd Prgm 86; Bus.

MITCHELL, PATRICIA; Ansonia HS; Ansonia, CT; (Y); Church Yth Grp; Girl Scts; JA; Trs Service Clb; Yrbk Stf; Hon Roll; Education.

MITCHELL, TAMARA; Berlin HS; E Berlin, CT; (Y); Dance Clb; Drama Clb; Girl Scts; Pep Clb; Red Cross Aide; Service Clb; Chorus; Drill Tm; School Musical; Nwsp Stf; Svc Awd 86.

MITCHELL, WENDY; East Haven HS; E Haven, CT; (Y); 9/370; Am Leg Aux Girls St; Latin Clb; Band; Nwsp Stf; Yrbk Stf; Mat Maids; JV Sftbl; Hon Roll; NHS; Math Tm.

MIZESKI, SUZANNE; Naugatuck HS; Union City, CT; (Y); 19/300; Church Yth Grp; Teachers Aide; Church Choir; Var L Swmmng; Var Tennis; Elks Awd; High Hon Roll; NHS; Prfct Atten Awd; Prjct SAGE 84-85; U Connecticut; Acctg.

MLOGANOSKI, SUSAN; Tolland HS; Tolland, CT; (Y); 22/165; Dance Clb; School Play; Sec Soph Cls; VP Capt Socr; Var Capt Trk; Hon Roll; Sec NHS; Wmns Forum Schlrhsp 86; Hartford Courant All St Girls Soccer Team 85; St Matthews Schlrshp 86; U Of CT; Phy Therapist.

MOHR, KELLY; Lauralton Hall; Fairfield, CT; (Y); 56/111; Boy Scts; Exploring; French Clb; GAA; Service Clb; Varsity Clb; Var Vllybl; Exec Comm Bd 86; Crew Ldr 84; MIP Vlybl 85; Bus.

MOLINARO, GIOIA; Conard HS; Farmington, CT; (Y); JA; Service Clb; Spanish Clb; Chorus; School Musical; Yrbk Stf; NHS; Spanish NHS.

MOLL, PATIENCE; Lyme-Old Lyme HS; Old Lyme, CT; (Y); 11/110; AFS; Church Yth Grp; 4-H; Ski Clb; Band; Chorus; Concert Band; Mrchg Band; School Musical; Stu Cncl; AFS Exchng Stu 86-87; Spnsh IV Acdmc Awd, Spnsh II, III, Ltn II, Ltn I Acdmc Awd 84-86.

MONACO, CARLA; Ansonia HS; Ansonia, CT; (Y); 4/144; Am Leg Aux Girls St; Church Yth Grp; Computer Clb; Ski Clb; Hon Roll; NHS; Trs Frsh Cls; Trs Soph Cls; Trs Jr Cls; VP Sr Cls; RI Coll; Med Tech.

MONDE, RITA-ANN; Wethersfield HS; Wethersfield, CT; (Y); 24/299; Yrbk Sprt Ed; Rep Frsh Cls; Var Fld Hcky; JV Socr; JV Trk; High Hon Roll; NHS; Rcgntn Outstndg Prfrmnc NEDTS 84-85; Rcgntn Acdmc Prms Sci 86; Biochem.

MONDELLO, KRISTINE; Wilton HS; Wilton, CT; (Y); 96/566; Cmnty Wkr; Dance Clb; French Clb; SADD; Varsity Clb; Variety Show; Gym; NHS.

MONGILLO, TERESA; Holy Cross HS; Waterbury, CT; (Y); Am Leg Aux Girls St; PAVAS; Band; Concert Band; Mrchg Band; Pep Band; Stage Crew; Rep Jr Cls; Rep Stu Cncl; Hon Roll; Social Stds Hnr Society Awd 86; Ct Laurel Grls St 86.

MONKS, MAX; Staples HS; Westport, CT; (Y); 190/550; Boy Scts; Church Yth Grp; Library Aide; Acpl Chr; Chorus; Church Choir; School Musical; School Play; Var Stu Cncl; Im Bsktbl; Fin.

MONNIER, MELISSA; Masuk HS; Monroe, CT; (Y); 12/272; JA; Spanish Clb; Trk; High Hon Roll; NHS; Pres Schlr; $2,500 Schlrshp 86; Salem Coll; Pre-Med.

MONROE, ANDREA; Wilton HS; Wilton, CT; (Y); 1/340; Church Yth Grp; Pres Key Clb; Varsity Clb; JV Lcrss; Var Capt Swmmng; Var Trk; High Hon Roll; NHS; Amer Chmcl Scty Otstndng Chem Stu 84-85; Amer Physcs Tchrs Otstndng Physcs Stu 85-86; Hrvrd Prz Bk 85.

MONTALBO, INEABELL; Hartford HS; Hartford, CT; (Y); FBLA; GAA; Jazz Band; Nwsp Phtg; Nwsp Rptr; Gym; Swmmng; Tennis; Vllybl; 4-H Awd.

MONTALTO, MARC M; Holy Cross HS; Waterbury, CT; (Y); 76/380; Service Clb; School Musical; JV Im Bsbl; Hon Roll; NHS; Achvt 90 4 Qtrs Ltr 85; Law.

MONTANARO, MAURIZIO; Bullard-Havens RVTS; Bridgeport, CT; (Y); Art Clb; Computer Clb; Rep Frsh Cls; Norwalk ST Tech; Indstrl.

MONTEI, KRISTI; Conard HS; W Hartford, CT; (Y); 10/345; Service Clb; Spanish Clb; Chorus; School Musical; Yrbk Stf; High Hon Roll; NHS; Spanish NHS; Holy Cross Bk Prz 86.

MONTGOMERY, JASON; Heritage Christian Acad; Cheshire, CT; (Y); Church Yth Grp; School Play; Stu Cncl; Socr; Hon Roll; US Army Spc Frcs.

MONTGOMERY, RIKI; Torrington HS; Torrington, CT; (Y); Drama Clb; French Clb; PAVAS; VICA; School Play; Stage Crew; Variety Show; Var Cheerleading; Im Mgr(s); Trk; Cert Prof Vica 86; NY Inst Tech; Sports Med.

MONTIGNY, JESSICA A; Norwich Free Acad; Norwich, CT; (Y); Trs Art Clb; German Clb; Trs Church Choir; School Play; Hon Roll; Schltc SR Gold Key Art 85; Most Impvd Uppr Fine Arts Awd 85; Grphc Dsgn.

MOODY, MICHAEL; Kent Schl; Goshen, CT; (Y); Boy Scts; Socr; Var Wrstlng; Coaches Cup-Most Improved Wrestler 83-84; Comp Engrng.

MOORE, ALISSA; Taft Schl; Cortland, NY; (Y); Cmnty Wkr; Dance Clb; Ski Clb; School Play; Capt Fld Hcky; Mgr L Ice Hcky; JV Lcrss; Mgr(s); Score Keeper; JV Trk.

MOORE, CHERYL; East Hartford HS; E Hartford, CT; (Y); 136/462; French Clb; Spanish Clb; Varsity Clb; Yrbk Sprt Ed; Yrbk Stf; Swmmng; Trk; French Hon Soc; High Hon Roll; Hon Roll; Manchester CC; Lang.

MOORE, DEBORAH; O H Platt HS; Meriden, CT; (Y); 3/240; Debate Tm; Sec French Clb; Intnl Clb; Key Clb; Math Tm; Political Wkr; Ski Clb; Nwsp Rptr; Yrbk Rptr; Rep Stu Cncl; Brown U; Intl Law.

MOORE, DENNIS; ST Bernard HS; Waterford, CT; (Y); 9/297; Stage Crew; Capt L Golf; JV Socr; High Hon Roll; Hon Roll; Trs NHS; Pres Schlr; U MI-ANN Arbor; Econ.

MOORE, KIM; Orville H Platt HS; Meriden, CT; (Y); Rep Key Clb; Pres Math Clb; Rep Soph Cls; Rep Jr Cls; Rep Sr Cls; Rep Stu Cncl; Var L Crs Cntry; Var L Tennis; High Hon Roll; NHS; Soc Wmn Engrs Mth-Sci Awd 85-86; 4th Plc AHSME Mth Tst 84-85; 2nd Plc AHSME Mth Tst 85-86.

MOORE, TRACEY; New Milford HS; New Milford, CT; (Y); 56/295; Dance Clb; Office Aide; School Musical; Ed Yrbk Stf; JV Trk; Hon Roll; Odd Flws Schlrshp 86; Salem Col; Tv Brdcstng.

MORAN, CHRISTIAN J; Fairfield College Prep Schl; Milford, CT; (Y); 20/237; Debate Tm; Key Clb; Latin Clb; Model UN; Im Bsktbl; JV Var Crs Cntry; Mgr(s); JV Var Trk; High Hon Roll; NHS; Poli Sci.

MORAN, DEBORAH; Holy Cross HS; Watertown, CT; (Y); 39/346; Drama Clb; Spanish Clb; Chorus; School Musical; Variety Show; High Hon Roll; Jr NHS; NHS; Pres Schlr; Spanish NHS; Sr Margaret Bamon CND Serv Awd 86; U Of CT; Tchg.

MORAN, LAURA; Sacred Heart Acad; Hamden, CT; (Y); Hosp Aide; Spanish Clb; Stage Crew; Nwsp Rptr; Rep Frsh Cls; Rep Soph Cls; JV Bsktbl; High Hon Roll; NHS; Spanish NHS; 3 Yrs Hnr Stu Awd 86; Cert Rcgntn Superior Prfrmncc NEDT 85; Ec.

MORDARSKI, TERESA I; Lyman Hall HS; Wallingford, CT; (Y); 29/198; L Trk; JV Var Vllybl; Hon Roll; Yale-Brown Schlrp 86; Polish Natl Allnc Schlrp 86; Hon Awd Physcs 86; Northwestern Coll IA; Pre-Med.

MORETTI, CHERYL; Greenwich HS; Greenwich, CT; (Y); Service Clb; Band; Concert Band; Drm Mjr(t); Mrchg Band; Variety Show; Yrbk Ed-Chief; Var L Fld Hcky; Capt Sftbl; NHS; Acad Achfvt Geo 83-84; Acad Achvt 85-86; Hnr Rl 83-86; Med.

MORETZ, JONATHAN; Joseph A Foran HS; Milford, CT; (Y); 4/300; Am Leg Boys St; Boy Scts; Church Yth Grp; Key Clb; Band; Jazz Band; High Hon Roll; NHS; NEDT Awd; Grmn Awd 84 & 86; Band Awd 84-86; Hnr Guard 86; Econmcs.

MORGAN, JASON WILLIAM; Simsbury HS; Simsbury, CT; (Y); 52/352; Pres SADD; VP Soph Cls; Stu Cncl; L Lcrss; Capt Socr; Wrstlng; All Conf Tm Ct Soccer Tm 85; Amer Soccer Tour Eurpn Games 86; William & Mary; Pre-Law.

MORGAN, JULIE; Ajon HS; Avon, CT; (Y); Dance Clb; Band; Chorus; Orch; School Musical; Variety Show; Acdmclly Tlntd & Gftd 83-86; Chem Engr.

MORGAN, LEE A; St Mary HS; Bethel, CT; (Y); Cmnty Wkr; JA; Service Clb; Spanish Clb; Stage Crew; Variety Show; VP Jr Cls; Var JV Cheerleading; Fld Hcky; FIT; Fash Merch.

MORIN, CYNTHIA; Bristol Central HS; Bristol, CT; (Y); Church Yth Grp; French Clb; Band; Color Guard; Mrchg Band; Symp Band; Yrbk Stf; Rep Jr Cls; Hon Roll; NHS; Tchng.

MORIN, KELLY ANNE; Litchfield HS; Litchfield, CT; (Y); 3/86; AFS; Am Leg Aux Girls St; Sec Trs Band; Concert Band; Yrbk Stf; Capt Crs Cntry; Capt Trk; Pres French Hon Soc; High Hon Roll; NHS; All-ST X-Cntry & Trck 83-86; Var Ltr In X-Cntry & Trck 82-86; RI U; Soclgy.

MORIN, MIKE; Oliver Wolcott RVTS; Litchfield, CT; (Y); Am Leg Boys St; Math Clb; VICA; Var Crs Cntry; Hon Roll; Archtctr.

MORMINO, RICHARD PAUL; Enrico Fermi HS; Enfield, CT; (Y); 3/339; Boy Scts; Ski Clb; Teachers Aide; Stu Cncl; Var Capt Swmmng; High Hon Roll; Trs NHS; Ntl Merit Ltr; Pres Schlr; Rensselaer Math,Sci Awd; Schlr Athlete Awd; Math,Sci Dept Awds; Rensselaer Poly Tech; Engrng.

MOROCHNIK, PAUL J; Newington HS; Newington, CT; (Y); 90/365; Boy Scts; Temple Yth Grp; Chorus; Jazz Band; Mrchg Band; School Musical; Symp Band; Variety Show; Var Capt Socr; Hon Roll; All Conf Goalkpr Sccr 85; Hofstra U.

MORREY, GARY; Windsor Locks HS; Windsor Locks, CT; (Y); 9/151; Am Leg Boys St; Drama Clb; School Musical; School Play; Nwsp Ed-Chief; Hon Roll; NHS; Ntl Merit Schol; Pres Schlr; Voice Dem Awd; Wm Connor Schlrshp; U CT; Comp Sci.

MORRIS, ELIZABETH; Sacred Heart Acad; Guilford, CT; (Y); Church Yth Grp; Sec French Clb; Thesps; Chorus; School Musical; School Play; Swing Chorus; Variety Show; Vllybl; Lbrl Arts.

MORRIS, KATHRYN S; Windsor Locks HS; Windsor Locks, CT; (Y); 20/169; Church Yth Grp; French Clb; Pres JA; Model UN; Acpl Chr; Chorus; School Musical; Swing Chorus; Variety Show; Sec Jr Cls; 2nd Rnr-Up Miss S NE Co-Ed Pgnt 85; Slctd Nrthrn Rgnl Chrs CT 84-86; Slctd Crtv Ctr Yth Weslyn U 86; Theatre.

MORRISON, PATRICIA; Lauralton Hall HS; Milford, CT; (Y); 29/111; GAA; Pep Clb; Sec Service Clb; Spanish Clb; Yrbk Stf; Var Bsktbl; Var Sftbl; NHS; Church Yth Grp; Yrbk Bus Mgr; Cncl Cathlc Wmn Schlrshp 83-84; All City Sftbl 84-86; MIP Awd Sftbl 85; CCIAC Sftbl Hnrbl Mntn 85-86.

MORRISON, PETER; Southington HS; Southington, CT; (Y); 75/580; Latin Clb; JV Var Bsktbl; L Tennis.

MORRISSETTE, SUSAN; Conard HS; W Hartford, CT; (Y); 7/345; Q&S; Orch; Nwsp Ed-Chief; Var Capt Crs Cntry; High Hon Roll; NHS; Spanish NHS; Cit Awd; JV Trk; Cit Awd; All-ST Orchstra Asst Prncpl Violst 86; Trnty Clb Hrtfrd Bk Awd 86; I Giovani Solisti Prncpl Violst; Cmmnctns.

MORRISSEY, KRISTEN; North Haven HS; N Haven, CT; (Y); 90/290; Political Wkr; Yrbk Stf; Hon Roll; Church Yth Grp; Red Cross Aide; Achvt Frgn Lgn 86; Advsl Brd 85-86; Prm Cmmttee Chrprsn Entrtnmnt 86; Bus.

MORTALI, KATIE; Old Saybrook SR HS; Old Saybrook, CT; (Y); Church Yth Grp; Sec Latin Clb; Chorus; Nwsp Stf; Rep Stu Cncl; High Hon Roll; Hon Roll; Drama Clb; School Musical; Cheerleading; Bio Awd 84; Tri-M Muscl Hnr Soc 85-87; Per Awds 86; Intrptr.

MORUS, MEREDITH; Greenwich HS; Greenwich, CT; (Y); Badmtn; High Hon Roll; Hon Roll; Prfct Atten Awd.

MOSES, DAVID; New Britain HS; New Britain, CT; (Y); Jazz Band; Orch; School Musical; Var Golf; Hon Roll; Physcs.

MOSIMANN, KRISTIN; Thomaston HS; Thomaston, CT; (Y); 9/66; Camera Clb; Pres Spanish Clb; Band; Mrchg Band; Yrbk Stf; Stu Cncl; Capt Var Cheerleading; Trk; Hon Roll; Mgr(s); Brkshr League Bnd Cncrt 84 & 85; Sthrn CT ST U; Intl Bus.

MOSKAL, MICHELLE E; Mary Immaculate Acad; New Britain, CT; (Y); 8/48; Church Yth Grp; Dance Clb; Pres French Clb; Chorus; Church Choir; School Musical; Var Cheerleading; Hon Roll; Prfct Atten Awd; Cmnty Wkr; Tunxis Cmmnty Coll Alumni Assoc HS Stu Schlrshp 86; Tunxis Cmmnty Coll; Dntl Hygn.

MOSMAN JR, RICHARD; Crosby HS; Waterbury, CT; (Y); Computer Clb; SADD; Bsktbl; Bowling; Ftbl; Golf; Wrstlng; Hon Roll; Prfct Atten Awd; Waterbury ST Tech; Mfg Engrng.

MOUNTAIN, KIMBERLY; Canton HS; Collinsville, CT; (Y); 13/89; Cmnty Wkr; Model UN; Concert Band; JV Var Bsktbl; JV Score Keeper; Hon Roll; Math.

MOURA, MARIA; Kolbe-Cathedral HS; Bridgeport, CT; (Y); 1/87; JA; Math Clb; Political Wkr; Nwsp Ed-Chief; Nwsp Rptr; Yrbk Ed-Chief; Yrbk Phtg; Pres Jr Cls; Stu Cncl; High Hon Roll; Partial Schrlshp; Hugh O Brien Yth Ldrshp 84; Hnrs Symp U CT 85; Fairfield U; Psychlgy.

MOY, WAYNE; Danbury HS; Danbury, CT; (Y); Boy Scts; Computer Clb; Math Tm; Nwsp Rptr; Lit Mag; Mgr(s); Var Stat Trk; High Hon Roll; Hon Roll; Pres Schlr; Sci & Envrnmntl Cnfrnce 84; Vrsty Athltc Awd 85; Perry Awd Drftng 86; Syracuse U; Arch.

MOYE, KASANDRA; Farmington HS; Hartford, CT; (Y); Yrbk Stf; Trk; Hon Roll; MIP Track 85; Schlrshp Bus Wk Sem Hartford 84-85; Outstndng Achvt Steno 86; Bay Path Jr Coll Alum Awd; Lib Arts.

MOYHER, SUSAN; Shelton HS; Shelton, CT; (Y); Sec Trs Exploring; Band; Color Guard; JV Trk; High Hon Roll; NHS; Spanish NHS; Drama Clb; Spanish Clb; Concert Band; Awd Scty Wmn Wngrs 86; Engr.

MUCHA, GREG; Kingswood Oxford HS; W Hartford, CT; (Y); Art Clb; Camera Clb; Debate Tm; German Clb; Intnl Clb; Latin Clb; Lit Mag; JV Ice Hcky; JV Lcrss; JV Socr; Bus.

MUDRICK, MARYELLEN; St Joseph HS; Stratford, CT; (Y); 25/240; Church Yth Grp; Cmnty Wkr; Drama Clb; Spanish Clb; JV Crs Cntry; High Hon Roll; Hon Roll; Spanish NHS; Engrng.

MUELLER, EMILY; Loomis Chaffee Schl; Hartford, CT; (Y); Key Clb; Chorus; Madrigals; Nwsp Bus Mgr; Stu Cncl; JV Fld Hcky; JV Lcrss; Socr; Most Insprng JV La Crosse Tm 86; Bst Attd JV La Crosse Tm 86; Architct.

MUELLER, LYNN; Danbury HS; Danbury, CT; (Y); 59/471; JA; Ski Clb; Varsity Clb; Variety Show; Yrbk Phtg; Yrbk Stf; JV Sftbl; Var Tennis; JV Var Vllybl; Hon Roll; Loyola Of MD; Acctg.

MUHL, ADEL-MARIE; The Morgan Schl; Clinton, CT; (Y); 5/150; AFS; FBLA; Chorus; Yrbk Stf; Var Cheerleading; High Hon Roll; Hon Roll; NHS; Acad Distnctn Math 83-85; Bentley Coll; Acctng.

MUIK, SUSAN; Torrington HS; Torrington, CT; (Y); 22/300; Church Yth Grp; Cmnty Wkr; Drama Clb; 4-H; VP French Clb; Thesps; Varsity Clb; Chorus; School Musical; School Play; Tlntd & Gftd Prgm THS 85-86; U Hartford Satrdy Schlr Prgm Hnr Cert 85-86; Worcester Plytech Inst; Mchncl.

MUIRHEAD, MELISSA; Manchester HS; Manchester, CT; (Y); AFS; Intnl Clb; Band; Concert Band; Mrchg Band; Yrbk Stf; JV Socr; Hon Roll.

MULDER, TARA S; Bristol Central HS; Bristol, CT; (Y); VP Art Clb; Church Yth Grp; Latin Clb; Chorus; Church Choir; Hon Roll; NHS; Cum Laude Latin Exam; Amer JR Classcl Lg 86; CT ST Schltc 1st Pl 3-D Desgn 85; 1st Pl Printmkng 86; Rochester Inst Tech; Prntmkng.

MULHERN, JEANNIE; Stamford HS; Stamford, CT; (Y); Sec Church Yth Grp; JA; Science Clb; Spanish Clb; JV Im Sftbl; Var Swmmng; Hon Roll; U CT; Vet.

MULLIGAN, ELIZABETH; Tolland HS; Tolland, CT; (Y); 11/166; Lit Mag; Rep Stu Cncl; Var Capt Cheerleading; Var L Socr; Var Capt Trk; 4-H Awd; High Hon Roll; Hon Roll; NHS; Central Ct St U Fndtn Schlr 86; Central CT ST U; Elem Ed.

MULREADY, GREGORY; William H Hall HS; W Hartford, CT; (Y); 152/349; Am Leg Boys St; Orch; Var Badmtn; Capt L Bsbl; Var Bsktbl; Var L Socr; Hon Roll; Character Awd To Sr Athl 86; MVP Soccer By US Army & Ntl Soccer Coach Assn 86; Suffield Acad.

MUNCH, LISA; Shelton HS; Shelton, CT; (Y); French Clb; Ski Clb; SADD; Nwsp Stf; Stu Cncl; Twrlr; French Hon Soc; Hon Roll; NHS; Phrmcy.

MUNDELL, MARIBETH; Kingswood-Oxford Schl; Wethersfld, CT; (Y); Pres Dance Clb; Drama Clb; PAVAS; Chorus; School Musical; School Play; Stage Crew; Hon Roll; Ntl Merit Ltr; Arts.

MUNRO, KENNETH; Daniel Hand HS; Madison, CT; (Y); 39/229; FCA; Band; JV Bsbl; Var Socr; JV Wrstlng; Hon Roll; Physcs Olypiad; Hgst Score Schl Tm 86; Mechncl Engr.

MURDOCH, DOUGLAS; South Windsor HS; S Windsor, CT; (Y); 17/300; Computer Clb; Drama Clb; Math Tm; School Musical; School Play; Stage Crew; Stu Cncl; Hon Roll.

MURDOCK, JEANNE; Litchfield HS; Northfield, CT; (Y); Red Cross Aide; Band; Chorus; Church Choir; Madrigals; Mgr Crs Cntry; Mgr Tennis; Cit Awd; NHS; Am Leg Aux Girls St; Edwrd L Maby Awd Music; Michaels Jwlrs Math Awd; Our Ldy Of Grc Chrch Awd; Mt Holyoke Coll; Chem.

MURILLO, CESAR; Brien Mc Mahon HS; Norwalk, CT; (Y); Boys Clb Am; Church Yth Grp; Cmnty Wkr; Dance Clb; French Clb; Key Clb; Ski Clb; School Play; Variety Show; Var JV Bsktbl; Science Fair; 1st Pl Leading Role School Play; 1st & 2nd Pl School Variety Show; Mech Engrng.

MURPHY, CINDY; St Joseph HS; Trumbull, CT; (Y); 10/257; Debate Tm; Drama Clb; French Clb; Nwsp Rptr; Yrbk Rptr; Yrbk Stf; French Hon Soc; High Hon Roll; NHS.

MURPHY, GEORGE; Holy Cross HS; Waterbury, CT; (Y); 44/380; Church Yth Grp; Cmnty Wkr; Pres French Clb; French Hon Soc; High Hon Roll; Jr NHS; NHS; Soc Stud Hnr Scty Awd Rcvd 85-86; French Clb Outstndng Svc Awd 85-86; Mattauck Social Sci Fair 85-86; Pre-Med.

MURPHY, JENNIFER; Bethel HS; Bethel, CT; (Y); AFS; Key Clb; Nwsp Stf; Stat Socr; Stat Sftbl; DAR Awd; Hon Roll; NHS; Boston U; Pre Law.

MURPHY, JERRY; East Catholic HS; Bolton, CT; (Y); 10/294; Boy Scts; Band; Var Trk; High Hon Roll; JP Sousa Awd; NHS; U CT Alumni Bk Awd 86; Trk Awds 82-86; U CT; Mech Engrng.

MURPHY, KATHERINE; Newington HS; Newington, CT; (S); 12/365; Church Yth Grp; Church Choir; Mrchg Band; Orch; School Musical; Symp Band; Mgr(s); High Hon Roll; Hon Roll; Pres NHS; Mscnshp Awd 85; Cntrl CT Div Bnd 85-86; U Of RI; Math.

MURPHY, MARY BETH; The Morgan HS; Clinton, CT; (Y); 22/145; AFS; Church Yth Grp; Cmnty Wkr; Girl Scts; SADD; Chorus; Church Choir; Hon Roll; FNA; Hosp Aide; Southern CT ST U; Nrsng.

MURPHY, MAUREEN; Southington HS; Southington, CT; (Y); 37/600; Am Leg Aux Girls St; Chorus; Church Choir; Mrchg Band; Symp Band; Variety Show; Yrbk Stf; L Var Trk; Hon Roll; NHS; Med.

MURPHY, RONNI; Holy Cross HS; Wolcott, CT; (Y); 184/380; Hon Roll; Mdcl.

MURPHY, SUZANNE; Daniel Hand HS; Madison, CT; (Y); Church Yth Grp; Drama Clb; GAA; Yrbk Sprt Ed; Yrbk Stf; Stu Cncl; Socr; Trk; Fshn.

MURPHY, TIMOTHY; Torrington HS; Torrington, CT; (Y); 7/310; Am Leg Boys St; Latin Clb; Math Tm; Varsity Clb; Mrchg Band; Swmmng; High Hon Roll; NHS; NEDT Awd; Naval Acad Smmr Smnr & Wrkshp 86; Worcstr Pol Tech; Engnrng.

MURRAY, LISA; Southington HS; Southington, CT; (Y); 18/600; Key Clb; Spanish Clb; SADD; Band; Yrbk Stf; Im Bsktbl; JV Sftbl; NHS; Chemathon 86.

MURRAY, TARA; Holy Cross HS; Naugatuck, CT; (Y); Trk; Bently Coll; Psychlgy.

MURRELL, NICOLE; Richard C Lee Education Ctr; New Haven, CT; (Y); GAA; Pep Clb; Spanish Clb; Yrbk Stf; Sftbl; Trk; Vllybl; Wt Lftg; Doctrs Asst.

MURZYNSKA, MONIKA; Crosby HS; Waterbury, CT; (S); Art Clb; French Clb; Varsity Clb; Capt Vllybl; Hon Roll; Ntl Merit Ltr; Quinnipiac; Nclr Med.

MURZYNSKI, MACIEK; Crosby HS; Waterbury, CT; (Y); Key Clb; Ftbl; Trk; Hon Roll; Waterbury ST Tech; Mfg Engrng.

MUSANTE, JESSICA; Seymour HS; Seymour, CT; (S); 13/170; Church Yth Grp; Cmnty Wkr; Pep Clb; Color Guard; Stage Crew; Variety Show; Nwsp Rptr; Yrbk Phtg; Yrbk Stf; Sec Jr Cls.

MUSHKIN, SCOTT; Kent HS; Bennington, RI; (Y); 25/215; Intnl Clb; Letterman Clb; Math Tm; SADD; Varsity Clb; Pres Frsh Cls; Pres Frsh Cls; Stu Cncl; Var L Ice Hcky; Golf; Gvnrs Awd For Drug & Alchl Awrns 86; Pres Physcl Ftns Awd 86; Sci.

MYERS, AMY; Shelton HS; Shelton, CT; (Y); Church Yth Grp; Sec Drama Clb; French Clb; Latin Clb; VP Stu Cncl; Var Mgr(s); Hon Roll; School Musical; School Play; Stage Crew; Latin Natl Hnr Soc 85.

MYERS, ANNA; Ridgefield HS; Ridgefield, CT; (Y); 2/337; Drama Clb; Scholastic Bowl; Service Clb; School Play; Nwsp Rptr; High Hon Roll; NHS; Stage Crew; Lit Mag; Harvard Bk Awd 86; CT Hnrs Smnr 86; Litrry Magazn Edtr In Chf 85-86; Psych.

MYERSON, NANCY; Kingswood-Oxford School; W Hartford, CT; (Y); Spanish Clb; Pres Temple Yth Grp; Pres Chorus; Madrigals; School Musical; Swing Chorus; Nwsp Rptr; Rep Jr Cls; Ice Hcky; Var Score Keeper; CA College; Dntstry.

MYJAK, JEFFREY; Old Saybrook SR HS; Old Saybrook, CT; (Y); 2/120; Boy Scts; Math Tm; Scholastic Bowl; Band; Jazz Band; School Musical; Yrbk Bus Mgr; High Hon Roll; NHS; Ntl Merit Ltr; Hrvrd Bk Prz 86; Tri-M Music Hnr Soc 86; Egl Sct 85; Engnrng.

MYOTT, TRACY L; Ellington HS; Ellington, CT; (Y); 16/137; Church Yth Grp; Dance Clb; Variety Show; Yrbk Stf; Sec Sr Cls; Var L Cheerleading; Var L Sftbl; Hon Roll; NHS; Pres Schlr; Pres Acdmc Ftns Awd 86; American U; Intl Bus.

NADEAU, NANCY; Central HS; Bristol, CT; (Y); FNA; Hosp Aide; Red Cross Aide; Nwsp Rptr; Off Sr Cls; Vllybl; Wt Lftg; Hon Roll; Vica Olympic Skill Awd 86; Newbury Coll; Physical Therapy.

NADLER, JEFF; Shelton HS; Huntington, CT; (Y); Exploring; Ski Clb; Bus Adm.

NADLER, MARC; Shelton HS; Shelton, CT; (Y); Boy Scts; Chess Clb; Church Yth Grp; Computer Clb; Exploring; Spanish Clb; Hon Roll; Spanish NHS; Comp Appl Awd ST CT Dprtmnt Hghr Educ Soc Sci Fr 86; Comp Sci.

NAJJAR, MICHELE; Holy Cross HS; Seymour, CT; (Y); 17/346; Spanish Clb; School Musical; High Hon Roll; NHS; Pres Schlr; Spanish NHS; Brother Francis Leary Schrlshp Awd 82; U CT; Acctnt.

NALLEY, KIM; Cooperative HS; New Haven, CT; (Y); Drama Clb; SADD; Chorus; Drm Mjr(t); Nwsp Rptr; Yrbk Stf; Trs Frsh Cls; Rep Stu Cncl; JV Tennis; Psych.

NARDI, RENEE; Wilcox Tech; Meriden, CT; (Y); 42/250; Art Clb; Yrbk Stf; Rep Stu Cncl; Capt Cheerleading; Socr; Hon Roll; Prfct Atten Awd; Tunxis Com Coll; Fshn Mrchnds.

NARO, TANYA; Plainfield HS; Plainfield, CT; (Y); 7/162; High Hon Roll; Hon Roll; NHS; Awd Mntng A Avg Algbra II 85; Awd Outstndng Achvt Latin I 84; Awd Exllnc Engl 86; Bus Admin.

NAUCK, MARGRET; Greenwich HS; Old Greenwich, CT; (Y); Chess Clb; German Clb; Service Clb; Var Trk; DAR Awd; High Hon Roll; Hon Roll; NHS; Awd ST Latin Comptn 86; Lit.

NAUM, THOMAS; Tourtellotte HS; N Grosvnordal, CT; (Y); Yrbk Stf; Bsbl; Bsktbl; Socr; Chem Engrng.

NAVAGE, MARGO; Loomis Chaffee Schl; Glastonbury, CT; (Y); Sec 4-H; Teachers Aide; Yrbk Stf; Pres Frsh Cls; Pres Soph Cls; Pres Jr Cls; Pres Sr Cls; JV Bsktbl; Var Socr; Var Trk; Ntl Hnr Soc Slavic Lang 85-86.

NAVICKAS, JOHN M; Rham HS; Marlborough, CT; (Y); 42/167; Am Leg Boys St; Ski Clb; VP Jr Cls; Pres Sr Cls; JV Bsbl; Var Wrstlng; Raymnd W Brunl III & Davd Sarnk Mem Schlrshps 86; Central CT ST U; Bus.

NAZZAL, JACKIE; Brien Mc Mahon HS; Norwalk, CT; (Y); Church Yth Grp; Chorus; Hon Roll; Csmtlgst.

NEE, CHRISTINE; Greenwich HS; Riverside, CT; (Y); Pres Church Yth Grp; Cmnty Wkr; Pres Drama Clb; Madrigals; School Play; Stage Crew; Socr; Hon Roll; Camera Clb; Acpl Chr; Obrln Coll Bk Awd 86; CT ST Drama Cmptn 1st Pl 86.

NEEDHAM, JENNIFER; Berlin HS; Kensington, CT; (Y); Drama Clb; Office Aide; Science Clb; School Musical; Yrbk Stf; Yng Writers Conf At Breadloaf 86; Arch.

NEEDS, PENNY; Farmington HS; Farmington, CT; (Y); 50/217; Church Yth Grp; Trs Drama Clb; Acpl Chr; Chorus; Church Choir; School Play; Var Swmmng; Hon Roll; CT All St Choir 86; Music.

NEES, ERIK; Brien Mcmahon HS; Darien, CT; (Y); 20/330; Church Yth Grp; Bsbl; Ftbl; Tennis; Trk; High Hon Roll; Hon Roll; NHS; Engrng.

NEIPP, KEVIN; New Britain HS; New Britain, CT; (Y); Var Crs Cntry; JV Ftbl; Var Golf; Im Trk; New Britain Dept Of Phys Educ Weight Lftng 86; Vrsty Letter Golf 86; Poem Pblshd Schl Lit Booklet 85; Civil Engrng.

NELSON, HEATHER; Greenwich HS; Riverside, CT; (Y); Civic Clb; Stat Bsktbl; Mgr(s); Score Keeper; Stat Sftbl; Hon Roll; YMCA Red Cross Life Svng 86; Bus Adm.

NELSON, MELISSA; Litchfield HS; Litchfield, CT; (Y); 14/86; Sec SADD; Yrbk Stf; Sec Soph Cls; JV Var Bsktbl; Var L Trk; French Hon Soc; High Hon Roll; NHS; NEDT Awd; Spanish NHS; Latin Hnr Soc 82-86; Excllnc-Spnsh Lang & Lit 86; Concrs De Frnsais-3rd-ST Lvl 1-A 86; Trinity Coll; Law.

NELSON, MICHAEL; Vinal Reg Voc Tech Schl; Middletown, CT; (Y); 79/150; Aud/Vis; Pres Computer Clb; VICA; Yrbk Stf; Rep Soph Cls; Rep Jr Cls; Hon Roll; Arch.

NELSON JR, RICHARD; Rham HS; Hebron, CT; (Y); 30/172; Church Yth Grp; Computer Clb; Chorus; Hon Roll; Aerodynmcs.

NELSON, ROBERT; Tourtellotte Memorial HS; Thompson, CT; (Y); 12/102; Nwsp Stf; Prfct Atten Awd; Aeronautical Engrng.

NEMETH, KRISTINE; Torrington HS; Torrington, CT; (Y); 66/278; Key Clb; Latin Clb; Pep Clb; Ski Clb; Thesps; Chorus; School Play; Stage Crew; Variety Show; Nwsp Stf; Thespian Troupe 86; Music Blue Rbbn Awd 86; Lip Sync Cntst 2nd Pl Trophy 86; U Hartford; TV Comm.

NEMETZ, LAURICE; Brookfield HS; Brookfield, CT; (Y); 8/239; Church Yth Grp; Math Tm; Jazz Band; Lit Mag; Gym; High Hon Roll; NHS; Wellesley Bk Awd 86; Cretive Yth Wesleyan U 85; ST Trvlng Art Show Local Photo Exhbtn 85-86.

NENNINGER, CRAIG; Orville Platt HS; Meriden, CT; (Y); Socr; Hon Roll.

NEPAUL, MICHAEL; Bulkeley HS; Hartford, CT; (Y); 20/360; Aud/Vis; Pres Church Yth Grp; Computer Clb; Quiz Bowl; Church Choir; Nwsp Stf; Lit Mag; JV Ftbl; Hon Roll; Embry-Rddl Arntcl U; Arspc Engr.

NESTIR, IRENE; Wilbur Cross HS; New Haven, CT; (Y); High Hon Roll; Hon Roll; NHS; Spn I Awd.

NEUMANN, ANN; Hamden HS; Hamden, CT; (Y); FNA; Hon Roll; Schlrshp To CT Bus Wk 86; Awd Outstndg Achvt Bus Educ Type 84; Bus Adm.

NEWMAN, CHRISTY; Griswold HS; Jewett City, CT; (Y); 15/83; VICA; Sec Frsh Cls; Pres Soph Cls; Rep Stu Cncl; Var Cheerleading; Var Trk; Hon Roll; Prfct Atten Awd; SADD; Yrbk Stf; Gregg Shrthnd Spd Tst 86; Mcrblgy Lbrtry Ast Awd 85; Awd NIKYU 2nd Judo 84.

NEWTH, MARK; Torrington HS; Torrington, CT; (Y); Camera Clb; Model UN; Golf; Hon Roll; Yth Awrns Wk Awd 85; Photo.

NEWTON, DERICK; Brien Mc Mahon HS; S Norwalk, CT; (Y); JV Stat Bsktbl; L Var Ftbl; Im Mgr(s); Stat Score Keeper; JV Var Trk; Hon Roll; Sci & Math Prblm 83-84; Chem Engr.

NEWTON, LAVINIA; Coginchaug HS; Durham, CT; (Y); 20/135; Sec Church Yth Grp; Varsity Clb; Concert Band; Flag Corp; Mrchg Band; Pep Band; Stage Crew; Nwsp Ed-Chief; Nwsp Rptr; Nwsp Sprt Ed; Harvard Book Awd 86; X-Cntry Mst Vlble Plyr 84 & 85; Spnsh Awd 86; Sec Ed.

NG, RICHMOND; Torrington HS; Torrington, CT; (Y); 14/230; Church Yth Grp; Key Clb; Model UN; Wt Lftg; High Hon Roll; Hon Roll; Chrs From Quad Awd Of Regntn 83; Wesleyan U; Engrng.

NGOV, SENGDAO; Danbury HS; Danbury, CT; (Y); 206/474; FBLA; Nwsp Bus Mgr; Yrbk Stf; Off Sr Cls; Bsbl; Bsktbl; Ftbl; Socr; Sftbl; Tennis; Perrya Awd 85; Bryant Coll; Accntng.

NGUYEN, DAVID QUAN; Old Saybrook SR HS; Old Saybrook, CT; (Y); Am Leg Boys St; Aud/Vis; Boy Scts; English Clb; Quiz Bowl; Scholastic Bowl; Science Clb; School Play; Stage Crew; Nwsp Ed-Chief; Outstndng Achvt Mod Europ Hist 84, Hist Pers 85, US Hist 86; Pre Med.

NGUYEN, TAM VAN; Hartford Public HS; Hartford, CT; (Y); 35/289; Church Yth Grp; FCA; Math Clb; Math Tm; Red Cross Aide; Varsity Clb; Socr; Swmmng; U CT; Elec Engrng.

NICHOLS, SANDI; Putnam HS; Putnam, CT; (Y); Hosp Aide; Band; Concert Band; Mrchg Band; Yrbk Stf; JV Capt Bsktbl; Hon Roll; Jr NHS; U Of CT; Phys Thrpy.

NICHOLS, TIMOTHY; Killingly HS; Dayville, CT; (Y); 8/275; SADD; Band; Chorus; Drm Mjr(t); High Hon Roll; NHS; CT All ST Chorus 85-86; All New England Chorus 85-86; CT Eastern Region Chorus 84-86; Communctns.

NICOLAYSEN, LUCY; Guilford HS; Guilford, CT; (Y); Drama Clb; English Clb; School Play; Nwsp Stf; Lit Mag; High Hon Roll.

NIELSEN, ARLA J; Amity Regional HS; Orange, CT; (Y); 49/388; Church Yth Grp; Cmnty Wkr; Drama Clb; Key Clb; Chorus; Madrigals; High Hon Roll; NHS; CT Al-ST Music Fstvl Choir 86; Ricks Coll.

NIERENBERG, TARA; Wilton HS; Wilton, CT; (Y); 103/352; Cmnty Wkr; Temple Yth Grp; Frsh Cls; Fld Hcky; Tennis; Hon Roll; Safe Rides; Stu Hlpng Stu Clb.

NIEVES, AZAREL; Bulard Havens R V T S; Bridgeport, CT; (Y); Exploring; Var Crs Cntry; Var Trk.

NIEVES, JULIAN; H C Wilcox Tech; Meriden, CT; (Y); Church Yth Grp; High Hon Roll; NHS; Prfct Atten Awd; Elec Trade Top Stu 84-85; Andrews U; Aircrft Tech.

NIEZELSKI, LAURA; Morgan HS; Clinton, CT; (Y); Church Yth Grp; Hosp Aide; PAVAS; Chorus; Color Guard; Pep Band; School Musical; Stage Crew; Mgr Crs Cntry; Mgr(s); Southern Music Fstvl 85-86; Bus.

NILSSON, APRIL; Windsor HS; Windsor, CT; (Y); 47/141; French Clb; SADD; Yrbk Stf; French Hon Soc; Hon Roll; Drama Clb; Hosp Aide; Latin Clb; Color Guard; Stage Crew; Cmmnctns.

NIQUETTE, LISA; Wilby HS; Waterbury, CT; (Y); Model UN; Band; Concert Band; Nwsp Ed-Chief; Rptr Nwsp Rptr; Lit Mag; Stu Cncl; High Hon Roll; Hon Roll; NHS; Mentor For Dr Michael Matzkin; U Of New Haven; Dental.

NISTA, SUZANNE; Conard HS; W Hartford, CT; (Y); 11/340; Church Yth Grp; Chorus; School Musical; School Play; High Hon Roll; NHS; Spanish NHS; Grtr Hrtfrd Acad Prfrmng Arts 84; Dnc Mstrs Amer Dnc Schlrshps 83-86; Prfrmng Arts.

NIXON, ANDREA; St Marys HS; New Haven, CT; (Y); Pep Clb; Bsktbl; Trk; MVP Bsktbl Awd 85; Boston Area; Comp.

NOBILE, FRANK; Bollard-Havens Tech HS; Stratford, CT; (Y); Var Ftbl; Var Trk; Hon Roll; NHS; Richard F Moore Awd 86.

NOBLES, TERRY; Platt HS; Meriden, CT; (Y); 32/283; Bsktbl; Powder Puff Ftbl; Sftbl; Vllybl; Hon Roll; 11th Varsity Ltr 86; All ST Tm Part Sftbll Ll Div 86; Henry Zaleski Mem Schlsrhp 86; U Of CT; Bus.

NOCERA, JODI; Bristol Central HS; Bristol, CT; (Y); 13/281; Latin Clb; Soph Cls; Jr Cls; Sr Cls; Cheerleading; Score Keeper; Tennis; Elks Awd; High Hon Roll; NHS; Fairfield U; Lib Arts.

NOCERA, VICKI; Central HS; Bristol, CT; (Y); Dance Clb; Drama Clb; Office Aide; Pep Clb; School Play; Variety Show; JV Var Cheerleading; Tennis; Schl Of Perfrmg Arts; Dance.

NOFI, SUSAN; Ansonia HS; Ansonia, CT; (Y); 13/145; Yrbk Ed-Chief; Yrbk Phtg; Yrbk Rptr; Rep Frsh Cls; Sec Soph Cls; Trs Sr Cls; High Hon Roll; NHS; Spanish NHS; Cmnctns.

NOGLES, SCOTT; New Fairfield HS; New Fairfield, CT; (Y); 32/257; VP Radio Clb; JV Bsbl; Hon Roll; Mech Engr.

NOLAN, KATHLEEN; East Catholic HS; Glastonbury, CT; (Y); 71/294; Cmnty Wkr; Service Clb; Yrbk Stf; Off Jr Cls; Off Sr Cls; High Hon Roll; NHS; Hon Roll; Acadmc Ltr Hnrs E 85; U Of CT; Bus Adm.

NOLAN, RACHEL; Holy Cross HS; Waterbury, CT; (Y); Civic Clb; Cmnty Wkr; Yrbk Stf; Var L Swmmng; JV L Trk; High Hon Roll; NHS; Spanish NHS; St Schlr; Providence Coll; Biol.

NOLAN, TRACY; Shelton HS; Shelton, CT; (Y); Cmnty Wkr; Dance Clb; Drama Clb; Latin Clb; School Play; Sec Stu Cncl; Cheerleading; Crs Cntry; Trk; Hon Roll; U Of CT; Spec Educ.

NOLL, BETH; Seymour HS; Oxford, CT; (Y); Church Yth Grp; JA; Chorus; Church Choir; Variety Show; Yrbk Stf; Hon Roll; Art.

NONNON, ANNIQUE; Watertown HS; Oakville, CT; (Y); Library Aide; Spanish Clb; Vllybl; Hon Roll; Oakwood Coll; Sci.

NOONAN, MARK; Old Saybrook HS; Old Saybrook, CT; (Y); 3/120; Drama Clb; Capt Quiz Bowl; School Play; Nwsp Stf; Yrbk Stf; Lit Mag; VP Frsh Cls; Pres Soph Cls; Pres Stu Cncl; Var L Bsbl; Jrnlstc Mrt Awd, CT Assc Stu Ldrshp Awd, Savage/Lorkas Mem Achvt Awd, Stu Rep Bd Ed, Coachs Awd 86; CT Coll.

NOPANEN, CRISSIE; Shelton HS; Shelton, CT; (Y); 10/400; Am Leg Aux Girls St; Pres Drama Clb; School Musical; Variety Show; Capt JV Bsktbl; Capt Var Socr; Cit Awd; High Hon Roll; JC Awd; Pres NHS; French & Geom Hghst Acadmc Avg; Soccer Mst Imprvd, All Housy 2nd Team, Track Mst Prmsng; UNC Chapel Hill; Bio.

NORARO, ELIZABETH; Brien Mc Mahon HS; S Norwalk, CT; (Y); Drama Clb; 4-H; Girl Scts; Intnl Clb; Ski Clb; Band; Color Guard; Drm & Bgl; Flag Corp; Mrchg Band; Scl Wrkr.

NORDIN, CHRISTINE; Shelton HS; Shelton, CT; (Y); French Clb; JCL; Off Stu Cncl; Capt Var Bsktbl; Capt Var Socr; Capt Var Sftbl; French Hon Soc; High Hon Roll; Hon Roll; NHS; Hrvrd Bk Prize 86; Ntl Merit Cmmndtn 86; 1st Tm All Hstnc Pick For Sftbl 85.

NORELLI, SALLY; Nonnewaug HS; Bethlehem, CT; (Y); Yrbk Ed-Chief; JV Capt Cheerleading; Mgr(s); Trk; Vllybl; High Hon Roll; Hon Roll; Eng Awd 86; Jwlry Awd 86.

NORMAN, KEVIN; Ledyard HS; Ledyard, CT; (Y); 32/220; Boy Scts; Church Yth Grp; Letterman Clb; Varsity Clb; Band; Var Ftbl; Var Trk; Wt Lftg; Var Wrstlng; Kenneth Wright Memrl Awd 86; All Eastern CT Conf Ftbl 86; Springfield Coll; Hlth.

NORMAN, TANYA; Loomis Chaffee Schl; S Windsor, CT; (Y); German Clb; Ski Clb; Chorus; Madrigals; School Musical; School Play; Stage Crew; Variety Show; Stu Cncl; Fld Hcky; Mst Outstndg Stu 83-84; Achvmnt Awd Bio 83-84; Bus.

NORMANDY, LISA; Francis T Maloney HS; Meriden, CT; (Y); 6/265; VICA; Stu Cncl; Powder Puff Ftbl; High Hon Roll; Hon Roll; Pres NHS; Excllnce Prfssnlsm VICA 85; Cert Stu Ldrshp 86; Northeastern U; Physcl Thrpy.

NORMILE, AMY E; Enfield HS; Enfield, CT; (S); 76/259; DECA; GAA; VP Jr Cls; Var Socr; Var Sftbl; Hon Roll; Dist & ST Awds DECA Comptn 85-86; Fmly Lvng Awd Chld Dvlpmnt 84-85; DECA Regntn Awd 85-86; Boston Coll; Jrnlsm.

NORRIS, CHRISTOPHER B; Nonnewaug HS; Woodbury, CT; (Y); Rptr FBLA; Ski Clb; Stage Crew; Rep Jr Cls; Rep Stu Cncl; Socr; Trk; Hon Roll; Hnrd Outstndng Jr 86; Jr Spirit Committee 85-86; Bus.

NORRIS, NEVA; James Hillhouse HS; New Haven, CT; (Y); Aud/Vis; Dance Clb; Drama Clb; French Clb; FBLA; Radio Clb; Spanish Clb; School Musical; Nwsp Bus Mgr; Yrbk Bus Mgr; Stone School; Bus Mngmnt.

NORTHROP, RITA; Danbury HS; Danbury, CT; (Y); JA; Orch; Perry Awd-Math 86; Bus.

NORTON, HEATHER; Southington HS; Southington, CT; (Y); 97/600; FBLA; Key Clb; Ski Clb; Stage Crew; Rep Soph Cls; Rep Jr Cls; Rep Stu Cncl; Capt Fld Hcky; Var Trk; High Hon Roll; Law.

NORTON, KELLY; Maloney HS; Meriden, CT; (Y); Cmnty Wkr; FNA; FTA; Teachers Aide; VICA; Hon Roll; Occuptnl Child Care Svc 85-86; Quinnipiac; Psychlgy.

NORTON, LAUREN; Simsbury HS; W Simsbury, CT; (Y); 11/410; Hosp Aide; Q&S; Teachers Aide; Sec Temple Yth Grp; Stage Crew; Yrbk Stf; Hon Roll; Ntl Merit Ltr; Simsbury Schlr 85; Latn Awd 85.

NOTARINO, CONNIE A; East Haven HS; E Haven, CT; (Y); Church Yth Grp; Civic Clb; Cmnty Wkr; Hosp Aide; Latin Clb; Office Aide; Political Wkr; Red Cross Aide; Teachers Aide; Yrbk Stf; Albertus Magnus Coll; Pre Med.

NOURIZADEH, KAREN; St Thomas Aquinas HS; New Britain, CT; (Y); 15/156; Spanish Clb; Teachers Aide; Chorus; Capt Vllybl; Hon Roll; NHS; Union Coll; Law.

NOVAK, ROBERT; St Josephs HS; Shelton, CT; (Y); Aud/Vis; Boy Scts; Cmnty Wkr; Drama Clb; VP Exploring; School Play; Stage Crew; Nwsp Rptr; Nwsp Stf; Eagle Scout 86; Psych.

NOVITCH, BENNETT; Waterford HS; Waterford, CT; (Y); 5/213; Ski Clb; Nwsp Rptr; Ed Yrbk Stf; Rep Soph Cls; Rep Sr Cls; Var Ftbl; JV Trk; High Hon Roll; NHS; Ntl Merit Ltr; Prtcptn Chemathn 86; Chem Olympd 86; Yale Frntrs Appld Sci-Engrng Series 86; Bio Sci.

NOWAK, EWA; Southington HS; Southington, CT; (Y); Sec FBLA; Key Clb; Ski Clb; SADD; Band; Mrchg Band; Yrbk Stf; High Hon Roll; Jr NHS; NHS; FBLA 3rd Pl Entreprenurshp 86; Engl Awd 84; 2nd Hgst Avg 84.

NOWELL, DAWN; Seymour HS; Seymour, CT; (S); AFS; Church Yth Grp; 4-H; Church Choir; Nwsp Stf; Swmmng; Tennis; High Hon Roll; Bus.

NUCIFORA, SALVATORE; Vinal Regional Vocational Tech Schl; East Hampton, CT; (Y); Am Leg Boys St; Aud/Vis; VICA; Yrbk Phtg; Off Sr Cls; Pres Stu Cncl; Trk; High Hon Roll; NHS; Mbr RSROA Rllrsktg-Svrl Plcmnts Rllrsktg Cmptn 81-86; Waterbury ST Tech; Elec Engr.

NUNEZ, KATHLEEN; Lauralton Hall HS; Fairfield, CT; (Y); 64/111; Art Clb; Cmnty Wkr; Hosp Aide; Spanish Clb; Y-Teens; Yrbk Stf; Crs Cntry; Hon Roll; Art Edtr Yrbk 86-87; Spn Clb 84-85; Art Staff 85-86; Art.

NUNZIANTE, FERDINANDO; Bristol Central HS; Bristol, CT; (Y); Library Aide; Pep Clb; Varsity Clb; Pep Band; Variety Show; Var Cheerleading; L Var Socr; Capt L Trk; Hon Roll; Frgn Culture Clb 84; Amer Chem Soc Of CT Vly Sect Olympd 85; Northeastern; Engrng.

NUNZIANTE JR, RICHARD J; Notre Dame HS; West Haven, CT; (Y); 21/252; Political Wkr; Spanish Clb; Teachers Aide; Lit Mag; CC Awd; High Hon Roll; NHS; Ntl Merit SF; Spanish NHS; Amity Clb Schlrshp Awd 86; Fairfield U; Intl Bus.

NYE, TINA; Coventry HS; Coventry, CT; (Y); Debate Tm; Teachers Aide; Var Socr; Hon Roll; PA ST; Legal.

NYQUIST, ERIC B; Frank Scott Bunnell HS; Stratford, CT; (Y); 31/260; Church Yth Grp; Trs Pres Drama Clb; Chorus; Church Choir; Mrchg Band; School Musical; Rep Frsh Cls; Rep Soph Cls; Rep Jr Cls; Rep Sr Cls; Amer Mus & Drama Acad; Mus Thtr.

NYREN, RONALD; Southington HS; Southington, CT; (Y); 1/600; Math Tm; Church Choir; Ed Nwsp Stf; High Hon Roll; NHS; Ntl Merit Ltr; Val; CT Stud Plywrght Cmptn Wnnr 86; Prsdntl Acad Ftnss Awd 86; Yale U; Engl.

O BRIEN, AMY; Ansonia HS; Ansonia, CT; (Y); 37/146; Computer Clb; Latin Clb; Library Aide; Rep Frsh Cls; Rep Soph Cls; Rep Jr Cls; Rep Sr Cls; Stu Cncl; JV Sftbl; JV Vllybl; Excllnt Mgr Awd Vllybl 86; Exec Sec.

O BRIEN, BARBARA; St Bernard HS; Westerly, RI; (Y); 21/265; Dance Clb; Ski Clb; Yrbk Stf; Stu Cncl; Trk; Hon Roll; Handicap Poster Awd Hnr Mntn 83-84.

O BRIEN, JAYE ELLEN; Tourtellotte HS; N Grosvenordale, CT; (Y); 5/102; Church Yth Grp; Girl Scts; Acpl Chr; Lib Band; Rep Stu Cncl; Dnfth Awd; High Hon Roll; Hon Roll; Jr NHS; NHS; Genetcs.

O BRIEN, KEVIN; Valley Regional HS; Deep River, CT; (Y); Boy Scts; Varsity Clb; VP Jr Cls; VP Sr Cls; Rep Stu Cncl; JV Bsktbl; Var Capt Ftbl; Var L Trk; Var L Wrstlng; Hon Roll.

O BRIEN, SEAN; Brookfield HS; Brookfield, CT; (Y); Computer Clb; Varsity Clb; Var Capt Socr; Var Trk; High Hon Roll; All Area Sccr Tm, Hon Mntn-All WCC & All ST 85-86; Chem Awd 85-86; Intrmdt Comp Awd 84-85; Duke U.

O BRYAN, JACQUELYN; Lewis S Mills HS; Burlington, CT; (Y); 2/170; Debate Tm; Capt Math Tm; Model UN; Ski Clb; Chorus; School Play; High Hon Roll; NHS; Ntl Merit Ltr; MVP Mth Tm 85-86; Excllnce Latin 84-86; Engr.

O CONNELL, DANIEL; Shelton HS; Shelton, CT; (Y); 17/323; Am Leg Boys St; Spanish Clb; Trs Jr Cls; Trs Sr Cls; High Hon Roll; Hon Roll; NHS; Spanish NHS; Spnsh Clb VP 85-86; Blk Karate 82-86; Bentley Coll; Acctg.

O CONNELL, KATHY; Glastonbury HS; Glastonbury, CT; (Y); 35/390; Cmnty Wkr; French Clb; Ski Clb; SADD; Rep Soph Cls; Rep Stu Cncl; JV Var Cheerleading; JV Coach Actv; High Hon Roll; Hon Roll; Psychlgy.

O CONNELL, SUSAN; Farmington HS; Unionville, CT; (Y); 11/219; Ski Clb; Chorus; Yrbk Stf; Capt Var Fld Hcky; Tennis; Trk; French Hon Soc; High Hon Roll; Hon Roll; NHS; CT JR Intrnshp Prgrm WA DC 86; Blgy.

O CONNOR, JENNIFER; New Fairfield HS; New Fairfield, CT; (Y); 52/236; Art Clb; Church Yth Grp; PAVAS; Stage Crew; Yrbk Phtg; Yrbk Stf; Lit Mag; VP Frsh Cls; VP Soph Cls; Bsktbl; Graphic Desgn.

O CONNOR, LAURA; The Morgan Schl; Clinton, CT; (Y); 8/200; AFS; Trs French Clb; SADD; Chorus; Trs Frsh Cls; Rep Stu Cncl; Fld Hcky; Powder Puff Ftbl; Hon Roll; NHS; Intl Bus.

O CONNOR, PATRICIA L; Sacred Heart Acad; West Haven, CT; (Y); Church Yth Grp; Cmnty Wkr; Computer Clb; French Clb; Office Aide; Scungilli Intl Schlrshp 84-86; Mthrs Clb Schlrshp 83; Bus.

O FARRELL, SUZANNE; St Bernard HS; Niantic, CT; (Y); 9/297; Church Yth Grp; Cmnty Wkr; Drama Clb; Hosp Aide; Library Aide; Scholastic Bowl; Band; Concert Band; Mrchg Band; School Play; Prnts Cncl Srvc Awd 86; Acad All Amrcn 85; Cngrssnl Schlr Yng Ldr Conf Rep 86; Boston Coll; Psychlgy.

O GRADY, THOMAS; Fairfield Prep; Ridgefield, CT; (Y); JA; Math Tm; Political Wkr; Nwsp Rptr; JV Golf; High Hon Roll; NHS; Ntl Merit Ltr; Pres Schlr; Spanish NHS; WA Smr Cngrssnl Intrn 85; Vanderbilt U; Cvl Engr.

O HEARN, MARY; Miss Porters Schl; New York, NY; (Y); GAA; Math Tm; Model UN; Ski Clb; Im Socr; Im Tennis; High Hon Roll; Ntl Merit SF; Cum Laude Soc 86.

O KEEFE, RYAN; Seymour HS; Seymour, CT; (S); 3/194; Chess Clb; Computer Clb; Math Clb; SADD; Jazz Band; Mrchg Band; Yrbk Stf; Pres Stu Cncl; Var Swmmng; NHS; Harvard Bk Prz Recpnt 85; All Housannic Leag Swmmr 85; Michaels Tenels Awd For Acad Achvt; U Of CT; Comp Sci.

O KEEFFE, SEAN; St Bernard HS; Uncasville, CT; (Y); 27/269; Band; Concert Band; Drm Mjr(t); Jazz Band; Mrchg Band; Orch; School Musical; School Play; Symp Band; Hon Roll; Excllnc Fld Music 86; Outstndng Drm Mjr 86; All Estrn CT ST Bnd 86; Music.

O LEARY, SHEILA; Hamden HS; Hamden, CT; (Y); School Musical; School Play; Stage Crew; Hon Roll; Outstndng Achvt Theatr 84 & 85; Outstndng Achvt Phy Ed 84; Poli Sci.

O NEIL, THOMAS; Ansonia HS; Ansonia, CT; (Y); 20/120; Var Ftbl; WPI; Actuarian.

O NEILL, DARREN; Holy Cross HS; Watebury, CT; (Y); 74/347; Capt Debate Tm; Nwsp Rptr; JV Bsbl; JV Im Bsktbl; High Hon Roll; Hon Roll; St Schlr; Asst Coach Waterbury Spec Olympcs Bsktbll 82; Micky Mantle Bsbl Wrld Series 84; Co Cpt CT Champ Tm 85; Mc Gill U Montreal Can; Pre Med.

O NEILL, JILL; Marianapolis Preparatory Schl; Woodstock, CT; (Y); 8/45; Church Yth Grp; Drama Clb; School Play; Stage Crew; JV Cheerleading; Var Ftbl; High Hon Roll; Hon Roll; NEDT Awd; Sci Fair Hon Mntn 85-86; Pol Sci.

O NEILL, MARY; New Fairfield HS; New Fairfield, CT; (Y); 79/235; Yrbk Stf; Var Cheerleading; Var Fld Hcky; Mgr(s); Wrstlng.

OAKLEY, CHRIS; Wilby HS; Waterbury, CT; (Y); Pres Church Yth Grp; Cmnty Wkr; Dance Clb; Drama Clb; Political Wkr; Stage Crew; Var Cheerleading; Stat Crs Cntry; Stat Sftbl; High Hon Roll; U CT; Psychlgy.

OAKLEY, ELIZABETH A; Avon HS; Avon, CT; (Y); 26/172; Chess Clb; Church Yth Grp; Dance Clb; Chorus; Hon Roll; NHS; ARTS Awd In ARTS Recgntn & Tnlt Srch 86; Mbr Of Tlntd & Gftd Prog 83-86; Hartford Ballet Co; Prof Bllt.

OATMAN, ANDREW J; Avon HS; Avon, CT; (Y); Drama Clb; Chorus; Vllybl; High Hon Roll; Hon Roll; NHS; Htl Mgt.

OBER, CHRISTINE; Simsbury HS; Simsbury, CT; (Y); JA; Yrbk Phtg; Sftbl; Hon Roll; U CT; Biophyscs.

OBOMA-LAYAT, GRACE; Suffield Acad; Suffield, CT; (Y); Church Yth Grp; Cmnty Wkr; Intnl Clb; School Musical; Nwsp Ed-Chief; VP Frsh Cls; Im Socr; High Hon Roll; Hon Roll; NHS; Schlrshp Suffield Acad 85-86; Yth Yr Awd Yth Grp 85; 1st Pl SUNL Spkrs Cntst 85; Cmmnctns.

OBRIEN, JAMES; Ridgefield HS; Ridgefield, CT; (Y); DECA; Ski Clb; Trs Frsh Cls; Trs Soph Cls; JV Socr; JV Trk; High Hon Roll; Hon Roll; Ntl Merit Ltr; Srvc To Clss; Aerospace Engr.

OCCULTO, MARY; Sacred Heart Acad; Stamford, CT; (Y); GAA; Girl Scts; Library Aide; Office Aide; Band; Chorus; Concert Band; Mrchg Band; Orch; School Musical; Engrng.

OCONNOR, MATTHEW; Mark T Sheehan HS; Wallingford, CT; (Y); Yrbk Stf; Stu Cncl; Bsktbl; Hon Roll; Jr NHS; Choate Rosemary Hall CT Schlr 86.

OGDEN, ROBIN; Putnam HS; Putnam, CT; (Y); Computer Clb; Chorus; Color Guard; Flag Corp; School Play; Stage Crew; Yrbk Stf; Hon Roll; Bus Adm.

OGORODNIK, CLAUDINE; Joseph A Foran HS; Milford, CT; (Y); 8/240; French Clb; Keywanettes; Spanish Clb; Var Trk; JV Im Vllybl; Im Mgr Wt Lftg; Cit Awd; Hon Roll; St Schlr; Audrey Degray Awd-Stu Who Hlps Othrs 86; Prsdntl Acad Ftns Awd 86; Northeastern U; Alld Hlth.

OGREN, KURT; Hamden HS; Hamden, CT; (Y); Var L Crs Cntry; Var L Trk; High Hon Roll; Hon Roll; Outstndng Achvt Awd Spnsh 84; Trk Most Points Clss 84-86; Outstndng Achvt Awd Soc Sci 85; Sprts Med.

OLANDER, MARK; Staples HS; Westport, CT; (Y); Boy Scts; Var Swmmng; High Hon Roll; Aerospace.

OLBRICH, GREGORY; Wilton HS; Wilton, CT; (Y); Church Yth Grp; Pep Clb; Varsity Clb; Y-Teens; Im Coach Actv; Stat Score Keeper; Im Socr; Var L Swmmng; Hon Roll; All Cnty Swmmng 85-86; Natl Team Y Wahoos 85-86; Bus.

OLDHAM, SHARON; Plainfield HS; Plainfield, CT; (Y); 22/160; FBLA; Office Aide; Y-Teens; High Hon Roll; Hon Roll; Sec NHS; Prfct Atten Awd; Voice Dem Awd; Katherine Gibbs Awd 86; 4th Pl ST CT Bus Mth 85; Local Comptn Awd Bus Mth 85; Bus.

OLEARCZYK, LISA; Pamperaug Regional HS; Southbury, CT; (Y); 17/200; Church Yth Grp; Cmnty Wkr; Library Aide; Red Cross Aide; Yrbk Stf; High Hon Roll; NHS; VFW Awd; Youth Vol Action Awd 85; Lions Club Schlrshp 86; Knights Columbus Schlrshp 86; U CT; Pharmacology.

OLECHNA, DAVID; Granby Memorial HS; Granby, CT; (Y); Scholastic Bowl; Trs Stu Cncl; Var L Socr; L Tennis; Capt L Trk; Hon Roll; AFS; Exemplry Achvt Soc Studs; Creatv Wrtng Awd; MVP Trk; U RI; Engl.

OLIVEA, PETER; Watertown HS; Watertown, CT; (Y); Rep Soph Cls; Rep Jr Cls; Rep Sr Cls; Rep Stu Cncl; Var L Ice Hcky; Var L Socr.

OLIVERI, JOHN; South Catholic HS; Hartford, CT; (Y); 65/200; Church Yth Grp; Cmnty Wkr; Letterman Clb; Band; Concert Band; Variety Show; Var L Ftbl; Hon Roll; NEDT Awd; U CT; Elec Engrng.

OLMSTED, ERIKA; Sacred Heart Acad; Ansonia, CT; (Y); School Musical; Nwsp Rptr; Nwsp Sprt Ed; Nwsp Stf; Yrbk Rptr; Yrbk Stf; Soph Cls; French Hon Soc; High Hon Roll; NHS; Sci Olympiad Awd 86; Soc Of Wmn Engrs Awd 86; Excllnc In Frnch 84 & 86; Scl Sci.

OLSEN, JENNIFER; St Bernard HS; Waterford, CT; (Y); 58/267; French Clb; Ski Clb; Stu Cncl; JV Cheerleading; Var L Sftbl; Hon Roll; Hugh O Brienldrshp Awd 85.

ONGCHIN, STEVEN; New Fairfield HS; New Fairfield, CT; (Y); 7/235; Math Tm; Ski Clb; Yrbk Stf; Lit Mag; Trs Stu Cncl; JV Tennis; JV Wrstlng; High Hon Roll; NHS; Spanish NHS; Math,Engl,Bio Awd 85-86; Bus.

ONOFRIO, THOMAS; O H Platt HS; Meriden, CT; (Y); DECA; Var L Ftbl; Var Trk; Var L Wt Lftg; Hon Roll; Trphy Frm Boys Clb Bktbl 78; Hon All Str JR Ftbl Tm 80; Cert Var Bktbl 81-82; Cmptr Engrng.

ONORATO, RICHARD; Brookfield HS; Brookfield Center, CT; (Y); 7/249; Hosp Aide; Math Tm; Stage Crew; Yrbk Stf; Trs Soph Cls; Trs Sr Cls; Var Wrstlng; High Hon Roll; Jr NHS; NHS; Sci Horizens Sci Fair Finalist 85.

OPATRNY, JOE; Shelton HS; Shelton, CT; (Y); Church Yth Grp; Drama Clb; Varsity Clb; Stu Cncl; Capt Ftbl; Wt Lftg; High Hon Roll; Hon Roll; NHS; Holy Cross Bk Awd 86; U Of AL; Cmmnctns.

OPPEDISANO, JAMES; Wilby HS; Waterbury, CT; (Y); Boys Clb Am; Church Yth Grp; JA; Stage Crew; Hon Roll; Mattatuck CC; Auto Tech.

ORAVEC, GLENN; Foran HS; Milford, CT; (Y); 2/300; Am Leg Boys St; Church Yth Grp; JCL; Key Clb; Latin Clb; Var L Tennis; High Hon Roll; NHS; NEDT Awd; Service Clb; Yale Book Awd 85-86; Bus.

OREE, LATRICE; East Hartford HS; East Hartford, CT; (Y); DECA; FBLA; Girl Scts; Nwsp Stf; Off Jr Cls; Stu Cncl; Var Cheerleading; Co-Capt Tennis; Cit Awd; Hon Roll; Recognition Cert, Internatl Yth Conf Christians & Jews 86; Outstndng Svc Awd FBLA 85; Best Mgrs Trphy; Mrktng.

ORLOSKI, STEVEN; Bullard Havens Tech HS; Stratford, CT; (Y); Boy Scts; Church Yth Grp; Varsity Clb; Bsbl; Ftbl; Sftbl; Swmmng; Trk; Wt Lftg; Hon Roll; All MBIAC Ftbl-MVP; Hnrb Mntn All-St Ftbl; U Of CT; Engr.

OROS, KIM; St Mary HS; Stamford, CT; (Y); 11/50; Church Yth Grp; Cmnty Wkr; JA; Yrbk Rptr; JV Powder Puff Ftbl; Score Keeper; Var Sftbl; JV Tennis; High Hon Roll; Hon Roll; 2nd Awd Spn Cls; 1st Awd Hstry Cls.

ORTEGA, DAMON; High School In The Communty; New Haven, CT; (Y); Aud/Vis; Latin Clb; Office Aide; Political Wkr; Wrstlng; Ntl Merit SF; Anthro.

ORTIZ, EDDIE; Bullard Havens Tech; Bridgeport, CT; (Y); VICA; Clnry Inst Of Amer; Chef.

OSBORN, NATASHA; Miss Porters Schl; Norwich, VT; (Y); French Clb; GAA; Varsity Clb; Variety Show; Frsh Cls; Stu Cncl; Lcrss; Socr; Vet Med.

OSBORN, ROBERT SCOTT; Joseph A Foran HS; Milford, CT; (Y); Letterman Clb; Varsity Clb; Stu Cncl; Bsbl; Cit Awd; Hon Roll; Prfct Atten Awd; Drafting Awd; Athletics Bsbl Ptchr,Tm MVP,City MVP,All Leag Selctn; NH Vo Tech Coll; Inds Arts.

OSENKOWSKI, DONNA; Bristol Central HS; Bristol, CT; (Y); Church Yth Grp; Ski Clb; Var Capt Crs Cntry; JV Var Trk; Hon Roll; NHS; Bristol Press Caries Month 86; Lbrl Arts.

OSHMAN, ANDRA; Brookfield HS; Brookfield, CT; (Y); Intnl Clb; Math Clb; Red Cross Aide; Spanish Clb; Teachers Aide; Temple Yth Grp; Chorus; High Hon Roll; Hon Roll; NHS; Dancng 5 & 6 Yr Awds 85-86; Cert Of Awd Algebra II 86; Med.

OSOWIECKI, BRIGITTE K; Thomaston HS; Thomaston, CT; (Y); 1/66; Church Yth Grp; French Clb; Office Aide; School Play; Variety Show; Yrbk Stf; Fld Hcky; Trk; NHS; Pres Schlr; Natl Ldrshp & Svc Awd 84-85; Harvard Book Clb Awd 84-85; Pres Phy Ftnss Awd 84-86; Southern CT ST U; Bus Mgmt.

OSTRANDER, ROGER; The Taft Schl; Watertown, CT; (Y); Hosp Aide; Science Clb; Yrbk Stf; JV Bsbl; JV Ftbl; JV Ice Hcky; JV Lcrss; High Hon Roll; All Western NEJV Tm 86; Math.

OSTREICHER, SARAH; Farmington HS; Farmington, CT; (Y); Church Yth Grp; Ski Clb; Band; Chorus; Mrchg Band; Rep Frsh Cls; Rep Soph Cls; Socr; Wt Lftg; NW Conf 85; Physcl Thrpy.

OSULLIVAN, DIANE; Lyman Hall HS; Wallingford, CT; (Y); 27/247; AFS; JA; Key Clb; SADD; Mgr(s); Trk; High Hon Roll; Hon Roll; Outstndng Achvt Accntng I & Chem A 85-86; Accntng.

OSULLIVAN, MAUREEN; Sacred Heart Acad; Hamden, CT; (Y); Cmnty Wkr; FBLA; Hosp Aide; Chorus; Stage Crew; Variety Show; JV Crs Cntry; Im Mgr Vllybl; Prfct Atten Awd; 1st Pl Parlmntry Procdrs ST Ldrshp Conf FBLA 86; Treas Pro-Life Clb 86-87.

OTERO, YVETTE; Bullard Havens Votech; Bridgeport, CT; (Y); Church Yth Grp; Church Choir; School Play; Yrbk Stf; Stu Cncl; Sftbl; Swmmng; Vllybl; Hon Roll; Prfct Atten Awd; Sacred Heart U; Computers.

OTTEN, ERICH; Putnam HS; Putnam, CT; (Y); Computer Clb; Ski Clb; Var Socr; JV Trk; JV Hon Roll; Trk; Eastern CT ST U; Accntng.

OTTO, CONNIESUE; Torrington HS; Torrington, CT; (Y); DECA; Exploring; Chorus; Var Sftbl; Plce Offcr.

OUDIN, CAROLINE A C; Pomfret HS; Pomfret, CT; (Y); 1/72; Chorus; Orch; School Musical; School Play; Nwsp Stf; Yrbk Ed-Chief; Ed Lit Mag; Off Soph Cls; Socr; Val; Cum Laude Socy 84-85; Brown U Awd-Engl & Citznshp 85; Intern In Washington DC Schlrshp 85; CT Coll; Psych.

OUELLETTE, BRENDA; East Hartford HS; E Hartford, CT; (Y); Chorus; Hon Roll; Bay Paty JC Alumanae Assc Awd 86; Bus.

OUELLETTE, CATHLEEN; Crsoby HS; Waterbury, CT; (Y); Hosp Aide; Key Clb; Latin Clb; Stu Cncl; Mgr(s); Swmmng; Hon Roll; Achvt Acad 83; Nrsng.

OUELLETTE, VICKI L; The Gilbert Schl; Winsted, CT; (Y); Pres Church Yth Grp; Computer Clb; Girl Scts; Chorus; School Play; Yrbk Stf; High Hon Roll; Hon Roll; NHS; Prfct Atten Awd; Coll Holy Cross; Acctg.

OVERGARD, ERIC; Wilton HS; Wilton, CT; (Y); School Play; Stage Crew; Crs Cntry; Socr; Trk; Wt Lftg; Slctd To Prtcpate In A Gftd Pgm 85; Physcs.

PACCHIANA, PHILIP; New Canaan HS; New Canaan, CT; (Y); JCL; Band; Concert Band; Mrchg Band; Pep Band; Trk; High Hon Roll; Hon Roll; Med.

PAGE, ANDREW; Southington HS; Southington, CT; (Y); 13/602; Church Yth Grp; Ski Clb; Band; Concert Band; Jazz Band; Mrchg Band; School Musical; Symp Band; Trk; High Hon Roll; Comp Sci.

PAGE, SANDRA J; Guilford SR HS; Kissimmee, FL; (Y); Church Yth Grp; Cmnty Wkr; SADD; Hon Roll; VFW Awd; Briarwood Book Awd 85; Velencia Coll; Bnkg Mgmt.

PAGLIARO, PETREA; Central Catholic HS; Norwalk, CT; (Y); Cheerleading; Trk; Ice Sktng 83-86; Itln Clb-Treas 83-85; Chld Psych.

PAHAHAM, CHERYL; Wooster Schl; Danbury, CT; (Y); Variety Show; Yrbk Bus Mgr; Rep Frsh Cls; Off Jr Cls; Capt JV Bsktbl; Var Socr; Sftbl; French Hon Soc; Readers Digest Endwd Scholar 85; 2nd Pl LE BEPC France 85; Corp Lwyr.

PAINTER, ELLEN E; Conard HS; West Hartford, CT; (Y); 4/315; Chorus; Church Choir; School Musical; School Play; Yrbk Stf; Lit Mag; French Hon Soc; High Hon Roll; Sec NHS; Ntl Merit Ltr; Janice Debbie Aaron Awd Outstndng SR 86; PTO Schlrshp 86; Soc Studies Awd 86; William & Mary Coll.

PALADINO, SCOTT; Greenwich HS; Greenwich, CT; (Y); Var Bsbl; Var Ftbl; Outstndg Achvt Engl & Phys Educ 84; Hon Pass 84.

PALAIA, KEVIN; Farming HS; Farmington, CT; (Y); 13/219; Pres Church Yth Grp; Ski Clb; Varsity Clb; Band; Jazz Band; Var Tennis; Scholastic Bowl; NHS; Spanish NHS; Pre-Med.

PALERMINO, GIANNA; Wethersfield HS; Wethersfield, CT; (Y); 45/300; Dance Clb; Ski Clb; Jazz Band; Yrbk Stf; Rep Frsh Cls; Rep Soph Cls; Rep Jr Cls; Rep Sr Cls; High Hon Roll; Hon Roll; Bus Mgmt.

PALEY, SARAH; Housatonic Valley Regional HS; Sharon, CT; (Y); Cmnty Wkr; Rep Soph Cls; JV Socr; U Of KS; Physcl Thrpy.

PALMER, DAWNA J; Rham HS; Hebron, CT; (Y); Cmnty Wkr; Hosp Aide; Office Aide; Science Clb; Spanish Clb; SADD; Mgr(s); JR Prom Cmmtte 86; Jukido Clb 84; Bus Admin.

PALMER, DONALD; Emmett O Brien RUTS; Shelton, CT; (Y); 12/146; Pres Church Yth Grp; Rep Stu Cncl; Capt Bsktbl; High Hon Roll; Hon Roll; NHS.

PALMER, DOUGLAS; St Mary HS; Pt Chester, NY; (Y); Boy Scts; VP JA; Yrbk Ed-Chief; Yrbk Stf; JV Bsbl; JV Ftbl; Var JV Golf; NEDT Awd; Nvl Arch.

PALMER, LAURIE ANNE; Suffield HS; W Suffield, CT; (Y); 3/141; Symp Band; Mgr(s); High Hon Roll; Hon Roll; NHS; Pres Schlr; Rotary Awd; Ruth Morse Latin Awd 85; Suffield Womens Clb Future Teacher Awd 86; Latin Book Awd 86; Boston Coll; Elem Edu.

PALMER, SHAWN; Rocky Hill HS; Rocky Hill, CT; (Y); 33/115; Rep Am Leg Boys St; Church Yth Grp; Drama Clb; Ski Clb; Teachers Aide; Concert Band; Mrchg Band; School Play; Variety Show; Yrbk Bus Mgr; Providence Coll; Med.

PALMER, TIMOTHY; Hamden HS; Hamden, CT; (Y); 129/419; Band; Chorus; Concert Band; Mrchg Band; Pep Band; Variety Show; Rep Stu Cncl; Stat Bsktbl; Mgr(s); Hon Roll; NE U; Engrng.

PALMIERI, CHERYL; Southington HS; Southington, CT; (Y); Gym; Hon Roll; Briarwood Coll.

PALMIERI, KATHY; Southington HS; Southington, CT; (Y); Pres FBLA; Key Clb; Latin Clb; High Hon Roll; NHS; Mss Future Bus Ldr Awd 3rd Pl 87; Comp Prgmmr.

PALMIERI, KIM TRACY; Southington HS; Plantsville, CT; (Y); 85/600; Sec VP Church Yth Grp; Chorus; School Play; Yrbk Stf; Sec Sr Cls; Rep Stu Cncl; Var L Cheerleading; Var L Vllybl; High Hon Roll; FCA; Gifted & Talented Program 83-86; U Of MA; Communications.

PALONEN, MEG; Griswold HS; Jewett City, CT; (Y); Church Yth Grp; Chorus; Stat Bsktbl; Score Keeper; Hon Roll.

PALUMBO, MICHAEL; Holy Cross HS; Southington, CT; (Y); 42/380; Church Yth Grp; Latin Clb; Service Clb; VP Concert Band; Jazz Band; Madrigals; Mrchg Band; School Musical; Hon Roll; NHS; Biomed Engr.

PALUMBO, TRACEY; St Thomas Aquinas HS; New Britain, CT; (Y); 6/154; Drama Clb; SADD; Lit Mag; Trs Stu Cncl; Capt Vllybl; Hon Roll; NHS; Pres Schlr; JCL; School Musical; Unico Ntl Schlrshp 86; Rev John T Shegrue Awd 86; Ntl Hnr Soc Schlrshp 85; Northeastern U; Med Tech.

PANARONI, DONNA; Seymour HS; Seymour, CT; (S); 2/192; AFS; Am Leg Aux Girls St; Hosp Aide; Stage Crew; Variety Show; JV Crs Cntry; NHS; High Hon Roll; Sal; Hugh O Brien Yth Ldrshp Smnr Dlgte 84; Yale U Bk Awd 86; Wheelock Coll; Erly Chldhd Educ.

PANAYOTOU, NICK; New Fairfield HS; New Fairfield, CT; (Y); 32/238; Boy Scts; JV Ftbl; Im Wt Lftg; Var Wrstlng; Hon Roll; U Of Connecticut; Engrng.

PANICO, KRISTIE; Lauralton Hall HS; Orange, CT; (Y); 54/117; Church Yth Grp; French Clb; Science Clb; Service Clb; Chorus; Yrbk Phtg; Yrbk Stf; Bryant Coll; Bus.

PANNELLA, LEA; Sacred Heart Acad; Hamden, CT; (Y); Stage Crew; Nwsp Rptr; Yrbk Rptr; Lit Mag; Hon Roll; NHS; NEDT Awd; Prolife Clb; Prolife Essy Awd; Itln Clb; Tnns Clb; Social Studier.

PANTANO, EDWARD M; Fairfield Coll Prep Schl; Fairfield, CT; (Y); JA; Model UN; Chorus; Nwsp Ed-Chief; Nwsp Rptr; Rep Frsh Cls; Rep Soph Cls; Pres Jr Cls; Pres Stu Cncl; Var Trk.

PAPA, TRINA; Seymour HS; Seymour, CT; (S); Var Pom Pon; Hon Roll; 2nd Pl Stu Crftsmn Awd Drftng 84-85; Intr Dsgn.

PAPALLO, ANNE; Platt HS; Meriden, CT; (Y); 24/248; French Clb; Latin Clb; Rep Stu Cncl; Powder Puff Ftbl; NHS; St Legislature Yth, Govt 85-86; U CT; Eng.

PAPCIAK, JEFF; H C Wilcox Tech; Meriden, CT; (Y); Cmnty Wkr; Rep Frsh Cls; JV Var Bsbl; JV Ftbl; Im Vllybl; Hon Roll; Art Awd 84-85; Demolay 84; ST Tech Schl; Crpntry.

PAPIERSKI, KEVIN; Tourtellotte Memorial HS; N Grosvenordale, CT; (Y); 1/100; Debate Tm; Nwsp Rptr; Ed Nwsp Stf; Yrbk Rptr; Yrbk Sprt Ed; Yrbk Stf; High Hon Roll; Hon Roll; NHS; Ntl Merit Ltr; Harvard Radcliffe Clb Bk Awd; Outstndng Achvt Amer Stds; Schl Visual Arts; Artst.

PAPINEAU, ALICE; Avon HS; Avon, CT; (Y); Chorus; Var Capt Cheerleading; Hon Roll; NHS; Tlntd & Gftd Pgm; Arch.

PAPP, JENNIFER E; Plainfield HS; Moosup, CT; (Y); 1/143; Varsity Clb; Chorus; Var Capt Crs Cntry; Var Capt Trk; Bausch & Lomb Sci Awd; Elks Awd; Jr NHS; NHS; Pres Schlr; Val; Rsnsslr Mdl 85; Wrcster Plytech Inst; Chem Engr.

PAPP, JILL DENISE; Lyman Hall HS; Wallingford, CT; (Y); 2/198; Political Wkr; Pres Spanish Clb; Nwsp Rptr; Stat Ftbl; Var L Tennis; Bausch & Lomb Sci Awd; Elks Awd; High Hon Roll; Sec NHS; Ntl Merit Ltr; Vrsty Schlr 86; Cynmd Sci Awd; Boston Coll; Pre-Med.

PAPPALARDO, NELLA; East Hartford HS; E Hartford, CT; (Y); Drill Tm; Yrbk Stf; High Hon Roll; Hon Roll; NHS; Achvmnt Awd Italian 83-84; Hon Awd Making Hon Roll 3 Cnsctv Qrtrs 84-86.

PAPPANO, THERESE M; Simsbury HS; W Simsbury, CT; (Y); 26/410; Am Leg Aux Girls St; Church Yth Grp; FBLA; JV Crs Cntry; JV Socr; Hon Roll; NHS; Lbrl Arts.

PAPPAS, DIANA; New Fairfield HS; New Fairfield, CT; (Y); Church Yth Grp; Hosp Aide; Latin Clb; Variety Show; Var Swmmng; JV Trk; Hon Roll; Pace U; Crmnl Jstc.

PAQUETTE, MICHELE; Watertown HS; Oakville, CT; (Y); Art Clb; Spanish Clb; Teachers Aide; Varsity Clb; School Musical; Variety Show; Coach Actv; Gym; Score Keeper; Var Socr; 1st Prze Wtng Poem Library Media Wk, Watertown Pk & Rec Gynastics Tchr Of Spec Ed & K-5 Chldrn 85-86; Southern CT ST U; Phys Educ.

PAQUETTE, MICHELLE; Farmington HS; Farmington, CT; (Y); Hosp Aide; Band; Concert Band; Mrchg Band; Vllybl; Hon Roll; Church Yth Grp; Nrs.

PAQUIN, TODD; J M Wright Technical HS; Stamford, CT; (Y); 1/120; Var L Socr; Hon Roll; NHS; Val; Schlr Athl Awd, Outstndng Elec Stu Awd 86; Outstndng Stu Awd, Sprtsmnshp Awd.

PARADIS, JASON; New Britain HS; New Britain, CT; (Y); 74/380; Church Yth Grp; Band; Concert Band; Jazz Band; Madrigals; Mrchg Band; Pep Band; School Musical; Stage Crew; Hon Roll; Cvl Engr.

PARADIS, TIMOTHY; W F Kaynor Vocational Tech Schl; Wolcott, CT; (Y); Church Yth Grp; Church Choir; Army; Law Enfrcmnt.

PARENT, SCOTT; Fairfield College Prep; Fairfield, CT; (Y); 2/234; ROTC; Ftbl; Lcrss; High Hon Roll; NHS; Pres Schlr; Rotary Awd; Sal; Apptmnt To US Air Force Acad 86; Overall Sci Fair Winner 85; Suma Com Laude 86; USAFA Acad; Aero Space.

PARENTE, CIRO; Oliver Wolcott HS; Torrington, CT; (Y); Boy Scts; Varsity Clb; Nwsp Rptr; Var Capt Socr; Mst Imprvd Sccr Plyr 84-85; Watbury St Tech Coll; Elec.

PARENTEAU, LISA; Wolcott HS; Wolcott, CT; (Y); Hosp Aide; Spanish Clb; Hon Roll; Cert For Nrs Aide 86; Mattatuck; Nrsng.

PARHAM, DEANIA; Masuk HS; Monroe, CT; (Y); Teachers Aide; Chorus; School Musical; Nwsp Rptr; JV Cheerleading; Hon Roll; Outstndng Achvt Home Ec 84-86; Keene ST Coll; Home Ec.

PARISI, VICKI; Greenwich HS; Old Grwich, CT; (Y); AFS; Art Clb; Church Yth Grp; Cmnty Wkr; Powder Puff Ftbl; Trk; Hon Roll; Advrtsng.

PARK, CHRIS; Fairfield College Prep; Easton, CT; (Y); CAP; Exploring; Im Ftbl; Wt Lftg; NHS.

PARK, ERIC; F T Maloney HS; Meriden, CT; (Y); Computer Clb; Key Clb; Math Tm; Quiz Bowl; Ski Clb; Bsbl; Trk; High Hon Roll; NHS; Ntl Merit SF; Pre Vet Med.

PARKER, JEFFREY L; Staples HS; Westport, CT; (Y); 1/450; Boy Scts; Math Tm; Radio Clb; Trs Spanish Clb; Lit Mag; Hon Roll; Ntl Merit SF; Pres DBFC 84-86; Philosophy.

PARKER, JULIE; Glastonbury HS; Glast, CT; (Y); 152/416; Church Yth Grp; Hosp Aide; Ski Clb; Y-Teens; Church Choir; Var Cheerleading; JV Fld Hcky; JV Lcrss; Var Mgr(s); Hon Roll; Bus Adm.

PARKER, KIRSTEN; East Lyme HS; Niantic, CT; (Y); 9/257; Church Yth Grp; Drama Clb; Band; Concert Band; Mrchg Band; School Play; Im Powder Puff Ftbl; Score Keeper; Hon Roll; NHS; Edwin Damon Meml Awd 86; Harold Moran Meml Awd 86; Wesleyan U; Cmptr Sci.

PARKER, LESLIE; St Joseph HS; Shelton, CT; (Y); 45/257; Sec Drama Clb; Thesps; Chorus; School Musical; Variety Show; Capt Var Swmmng; High Hon Roll; Spanish NHS; Church Yth Grp; Cmnty Wkr; Swim Tm Coaches Awd 86; Drama Clb Tlnt Show 1st Pl 86.

PARKER, TIFFANY; James Hillhouse HS; New Haven, CT; (Y); FBLA; Yrbk Stf; Ntl Sci Merit Awd 85; Natl Ldrshp & Svc Awd 86; Accntnt.

PARKHURST, CATHERINE M; Ridgefield HS; Ridgefield, CT; (Y); 4/331; Drama Clb; Trs German Clb; School Play; Stage Crew; High Hon Roll; Hon Roll; Ntl Merit SF; Intl Thespian Soc 84; Chem Tchrs New Eng Assoc 84; Anderson Mem Awd Outstndng Achvt Sci 85; Comp Sci.

PARRA, VICTORIA; New Canaan HS; New Canaan, CT; (Y); Drama Clb; French Clb; Intnl Clb; Varsity Clb; Band; Concert Band; Mrchg Band; Orch; School Musical; Symp Band; Comptr For NCTE 85; Tri-M Music Hnr Scty 86; Most Impv Musicn Trphy 85; Hampshire Coll; Pre Law.

PARSA, TIM; New Canaan HS; New Canaan, CT; (Y); Art Clb; Nwsp Rptr; Nwsp Stf; Trs Frsh Cls; Rep Sr Cls; Var Socr; Var Capt Trk; Hon Roll; Ntl Merit SF; All Cnty Trl & Outdoor Trk 84; Yale U.

PARSELL, ERIC; Canton HS; Collinsville, CT; (Y); 3/94; Am Leg Boys St; Ski Clb; School Play; High Hon Roll; Hon Roll; FL Inst Of Tech; Marine Engrng.

PARSONS, SUSAN; Maloney HS; Meriden, CT; (Y); Church Yth Grp; Cmnty Wkr; Girl Scts; Key Clb; Service Clb; Spanish Clb; Yrbk Stf; Rep Frsh Cls; Rep Soph Cls; Rep Jr Cls; Spnsh.

PARUTA, TINA; Housatonic Valley Regional HS; E Canaan, CT; (Y); Am Leg Aux Girls St; Church Yth Grp; FBLA; Ski Clb; Varsity Clb; Im Coach Actv; Var Capt Crs Cntry; Var Capt Trk; Hon Roll; Girl Scts; Berkshire Lg Champ Trk 3200 M 84-85; MVP Var Crs Cntry 85-86; Berkshire Lg All Star Rm 4x100 M 85-86; Bus.

PASCARELLA, ROSA MARIA; Branford HS; Branford, CT; (Y); 4/312; Am Leg Aux Girls St; Pres PAVAS; Band; Pres Chorus; Madrigals; School Musical; Trs Sr Cls; Fld Hcky; High Hon Roll; Church Yth Grp; Hugh Obrien Yth Fndtn Outstndng 85; Regnl Choir 85-86; All ST Chr 86; Med.

PASCHALL, LAURA; Miss Porters Schl; Natchitoches, LA; (Y); Computer Clb; Lit Mag; Im Socr; Mary Parker Foss New Girl Awd 84; Schlstc Arts Awd Natl Cmpttn Gold Key 85; Art.

PASS, MONICA; Norwalk HS; Norwalk, CT; (Y); Church Yth Grp; Cmnty Wkr; Chorus; Church Choir; Var Crs Cntry; Trk; High Hon Roll; Hon Roll; Fairwood Bible Inst; RN.

PASSARELLI, JAMES; Southington HS; Southington, CT; (Y); 35/625; Am Leg Boys St; German Clb; SADD; Yrbk Stf; Off Jr Cls; Off Sr Cls; Stu Cncl; Var L Ftbl; Hon Roll; NHS; Wstpoint Miltry Acad; Polc Sci.

PASTORE, SHIRLEY; Seymour HS; Seymour, CT; (S); Church Yth Grp; JA; Variety Show; Nwsp Rptr; Nwsp Stf; High Hon Roll; Hon Roll; NHS; Bst Annl Rprt Jr Achvmnt 85; Rep CT 350 Winters Sympsm 86; Comm.

PASTORICK, DENISE; Cheshire HS; Cheshire, CT; (Y); Church Yth Grp; FCA; Stu Cncl; Var Bsktbl; Hon Roll; Jr NHS; All Lg Hnbl Mntn Bsktbl 84-85; Med.

PATON, THOMAS; St Basil College Preparatory Schl; Weston, CT; (Y); 5/11; Yrbk Stf; Wrstlng; Hon Roll; Hly Crs Bk Awd Ctznshp 86; St Basil Hgh Prncpls Awd 85; Pblc Spkng Sm Fnlst 84-85; U Of Bridgeport; Mech Engrng.

PATRICIA, FOY; Griswold HS; Jewett City, CT; (Y); 16/83; AFS; Church Yth Grp; Spanish Clb; Bsktbl; Mgr(s); Score Keeper; Tennis; Vllybl; Hon Roll; Med Tech.

PATRY, SHERRY; O H Platt HS; Meriden, CT; (S); 29/240; DECA; FBLA; Variety Show; Hon Roll; Dance Awd 82-86; Rcrd Jrnl DECA Scholar 86; Gen Bus/Recrdkeepng Awds 82-86; Centenary Coll; Dance.

PATTERSON, MICHELA; Low-Heywood Thomas Schl; Stamford, CT; (Y); Drama Clb; Hosp Aide; Pres Chorus; School Musical; Variety Show; VP Frsh Cls; Pres Stu Cncl; L Bsktbl; L Sftbl; Sweeny Todd Prfrmnce Awd 84; Intl Stud.

PAVANO, MICHELLE; Southington HS; Southington, CT; (Y); Ski Clb; Pres Frsh Cls; Rep Soph Cls; Rep Jr Cls; Rep Sr Cls; Rep Stu Cncl; JV Sftbl; Var L Trk; Hon Roll; Vrsty Ltr Trck Tm 86; Pres Fshmn Clss 81-82; Central U; Dntstry.

PAVLIK, ROBERT; Oliver Wolcott Technical HS; Torrington, CT; (Y); 2/167; High Hon Roll.

PAWLAK, JULIE; Holy Cross HS; Watertown, CT; (Y); Church Yth Grp; Service Clb; Chorus; Hon Roll; Jr NHS; NHS; Fin.

PAWLAK, VALERIE; Seymour HS; Seymour, CT; (Y); 32/200; SADD; Variety Show; Nwsp Rptr; Nwsp Stf; Rep Frsh Cls; Rep Soph Cls; Rep Jr Cls; Off Stu Cncl; Pom Pon; Var Sftbl; All Vly, All Housatonic, All ST Sftbl 86; Med.

PAWLOWSKI, PAULA; Holycross HS; Waterbury, CT; (Y); 50/380; French Clb; SADD; Drm & Bgl; Stage Crew; French Hon Soc; Hon Roll; NHS; Socl Stds Hnr Soc; Fife Srgnt 82-86; Spych.

PAYNE, MORGANNA; St Marys HS; New Haven, CT; (Y); 30/100; Spanish Clb; Chorus; Stage Crew; Lit Mag; Rep Stu Cncl; Mgr(s); Var L Trk; Vllybl; Hon Roll; Adv.

PEARSON, CAROLINE; Hamden HS; Hamden, CT; (Y); Quiz Bowl; Science Clb; Band; Concert Band; Mrchg Band; Orch; High Hon Roll; NHS; Rensselaer Medal 86; Chemathon 86; Hlth.

PECCERILLO, KIERSTEN; Derby HS; Derby, CT; (Y); 1/111; Church Yth Grp; Math Tm; Pep Clb; Trs Spanish Clb; Chorus; Sftbl; Vllybl; High Hon Roll; NHS; Trs Spanish NHS; Yale Bk Awd 86; UCONN Hnrs Sem 86; Fairfield U; Law.

PECHENUK, NATALIE; Conard HS; W Hartford, CT; (Y); 33/345; Drama Clb; Spanish Clb; Concert Band; Pep Band; School Play; Yrbk Stf; Mgr(s); JV Sftbl; Var Swmmng; High Hon Roll; U Rl; Oceanogrphy.

PECK, JASON; Trumbull HS; Trumbull, CT; (Y); Church Yth Grp; Cmnty Wkr; Mgr Ftbl; Bus.

PECK, RANDALL; Avon Old Farms Schl; Houston, TX; (Y); 1/105; Stage Crew; Rep Church Yth Grp; Rep Jr Cls; Trs Sr Cls; Stu Cncl; Capt Var Ftbl; Var L Trk; Var Capt Wrstlng; Bausch & Lomb Sci Awd; Cit Awd; Cum Laude 86; HOBY Ldrshp Conf 85; Congrssnl Ldrshp Conf 86.

PECK, TERRIE; Danbury HS; Danbury, CT; (Y); Capt Var Bsktbl; Capt Var Socr; Hon Roll; Jr NHS; Capt Var Sftbl; Capt Var Vllybl; Cntrl U; Phy Ed.

PECKHAM, NIOMI R; Nathan Hale Ray HS; East Haddam, CT; (S); 6/66; Sec FFA; Model UN; Political Wkr; Nwsp Stf; Stat Bsktbl; High Hon Roll; Hon Roll; NHS; Stu Tech Audit Team; U CT; Chem.

PEDERSEN, DEREK; Trumbull HS; Trumbull, CT; (Y); Church Yth Grp; Ski Clb; Diving; Ftbl; Ice Hcky; Socr; Trk; Wrstlng; Hon Roll; Pre Med.

PEEBLES, MARION; Trumbull HS; Bridgeport, CT; (Y); Drama Clb; FFA; Church Choir; School Play; High Hon Roll; CT Summer Intern Prog 86; Liberal Arts.

PEKAR, BROOKE; St Joseph HS; Huntington, CT; (Y); 97/260; Drama Clb; Hosp Aide; Ski Clb; Spanish Clb; School Play; Nwsp Ed-Chief; Yrbk Stf; Cheerleading; Hon Roll; Prfct Atten Awd; Pre Law.

PELAEZ, GINA L; Greenwich HS; Greenwich, CT; (Y); Am Leg Aux Girls St; Hosp Aide; Yrbk Stf; Mgr(s); High Hon Roll; Jr NHS; NHS.

PELIZZARI, ANNE; Ansonia HS; Ansonia, CT; (Y); 20/140; Hosp Aide; Spanish Clb; Yrbk Stf; Pom Pon; Stat Trk; Hon Roll; Spanish NHS; Mgmnt.

PELLEGRINI, CHRISTOPHER J; Enrico Fermi HS; Enfield, CT; (Y); 15/317; Rep Stu Cncl; Var Capt Bsbl; Var Capt Ice Hcky; High Hon Roll; Hon Roll; NHS; Sci Symp Weslyan U; Engrng.

PELLEGRINO, CHRISTINE; East Lyme HS; E Lyme, CT; (Y); Band; Concert Band; Mrchg Band; Pep Band; Off Frsh Cls; Off Soph Cls; Mgr Trk; Hon Roll.

PELLETIER, MAUREEN; W F Kaynor Regional Tech HS; Prospect, CT; (Y); Dance Clb; Drm & Bgl; Drm Mjr(t); Flag Corp; Stu Cncl; Capt Cheerleading; Mgr(s); Jb Skll Dmstrn Csmtlgy 2nd Pl; CT ST VICA 86; Hairshw 2nd Pl Trphy 86; Csmtlgy.

PELUSO, MARIE; Cheshire HS; Cheshire, CT; (Y); 20/400; Drama Clb; JCL; Latin Clb; Red Cross Aide; Chorus; School Musical; School Play; Nwsp Rptr; Yrbk Stf; Hon Roll; Cert Schlstc Achvt 85-86; Villanova U; Lib Arts.

PENSIERO, JOE; Stamford HS; Stamford, CT; (Y); Church Yth Grp; Varsity Clb; Stu Cncl; Var JV Ftbl; Var Wt Lftg; Hon Roll; Italian Clb 83-86; Elec Engr.

PENTZ, SHELLEY; Greenwich HS; Greenwich, CT; (Y); Church Yth Grp; Cmnty Wkr; French Clb; Intnl Clb; Office Aide; Red Cross Aide; Yrbk Phtg; Trk; High Hon Roll; Hon Roll; French Exlcenc Awd 85-86; Cmmrcl Art.

PEPE, JIM; Putnam HS; Abington, CT; (Y); Church Yth Grp; Debate Tm; 4-H; Ski Clb; Plnthlgy.

PEPE, KIMBERLY; Hamden HS; Hamden, CT; (Y); 142/419; Hon Roll; Quinnipiac Clg; Accntng.

PEPIN, DAVID; Lewis S Mills HS; Harwinton, CT; (Y); Am Leg Boys St; Boy Scts; Camera Clb; Computer Clb; School Musical; Stage Crew; Stu Cncl; Var Score Keeper.

PEPSOSKI, TONY; Daniel Hand HS; Madison, CT; (Y); 22/900; JA; Teachers Aide; Rep Frsh Cls; Var Bsbl; Var Tennis; Cit Awd; High Hon Roll; Jr NHS; NHS; Safe Rides; MVP Tnns 83; Yng Achvrs; U Of MI; Engnrng.

PEREIRA, ANTHONY; West Haven HS; West Haven, CT; (Y); 11/396; Am Leg Boys St; Intnl Clb; Jr Cls; Capt Ftbl; Capt Golf; Elks Awd; Jr NHS; NHS; Rotary Awd; Spanish NHS; Ftbl Vrsty Capt 85; La Crosse Vrsty Capt 86; Pres Acdmc Ftns Awd 86; Fordham U; Cvl Engr.

PEREIRA, JOSEPH; East Lyme HS; Niantic, CT; (Y); Church Yth Grp; Key Clb; ROTC; Science Clb; Var Socr; JV Var Tennis; Hon Roll; Lion Awd; East Lyme Lions Clb Awd 86; U Of CT; Engrng.

PERERIA, JOSEPH; Bullard Havens RVTS; Bridgeport, CT; (S); 1/185; Church Yth Grp; Var Mgr Bsktbl; Var Mgr Crs Cntry; High Hon Roll; NHS; Elec Engr.

PEREZ, RHONDA EVETTE; Bullard-Havesn RVT Schl; Bridgeport, CT; (Y); Church Yth Grp; 4-H; Girl Scts; JA; Math Clb; Office Aide; SADD; Varsity Clb; Rep Frsh Cls; Rep Soph Cls; Accntng.

PERGAMENT, NEIL; Joseph A Foran HS; Milford, CT; (Y); 10/300; Am Leg Boys St; Cmnty Wkr; JCL; Key Clb; Im Bsbl; Im Ftbl; Var Trk; Hnr Grad; Law.

PERINGER, JENNIFER; Bethel HS; Bethel, CT; (Y); 37/238; Church Yth Grp; FBLA; Variety Show; Capt Var Crs Cntry; Capt Var Trk; High Hon Roll; Hon Roll; NHS; Pres Schlr; James Madison U; Bus.

PERLOT, CHRISTINE; Southington HS; Southington, CT; (Y); 41/600; FTA; Hosp Aide; Key Clb; Church Choir; Color Guard; Nwsp Rptr; Tennis; High Hon Roll; NHS; Spnsh Awd 84; Elem Ed.

PERLOT, DAVID; Southington HS; Southington, CT; (Y); 61/600; Church Yth Grp; FBLA; Key Clb; Political Wkr; Red Cross Aide; Var Trk; High Hon Roll; New Englandc Math Leag 84-86; Most Hours Of Srv Key Club 85-86; Red Men Club 86; U Of CT; Compu Engrng.

PERNAL, STACEY; Thomaston HS; Thomaston, CT; (Y); 7/68; Spanish Clb; Trs Jr Cls; Trs Sr Cls; High Hon Roll; Hon Roll; Briarwd Bk Awd Achvt Bus Crrclm 86; Pres Physcl Ftns Awd 84-85; Accntng.

PERREAULT, DONNA; Southington HS; Plantsville, CT; (Y); Dance Clb; DECA; Chorus; Swing Chorus; Trk; Hon Roll; Bus.

PERREAULT, JANE MARY; Plainfield HS; Moosup, CT; (Y); FBLA; Girl Scts; Office Aide; God Cntry Awd; Hon Roll; Prfct Atten Awd; Voice Dem Awd; Rotary Clb, E/A Miller Mem Schlrshps, Perf Atten 5 Yrs 86; Quinebaug Valley CC; Exec Secy.

PERRI, KEVIN; Bristol Centeral HS; Bristol, CT; (Y); Church Yth Grp; Capt Crs Cntry; Trk; Hon Roll; Hrtfrd ST Tech Coll; Archt.

PERROTT, STEPHANIE; Nonnewaug HS; Seymour, CT; (Y); 86/157; FBLA; FFA; Red Cross Aide; Vllybl; Ag Awd 86; Stone Schl; Sec.

PERROTTI, MAUREEN; Acad Of Our Lady Of Mercy; New Haven, CT; (Y); Drama Clb; French Clb; JA; Model UN; School Play; Variety Show; Nwsp Stf; Yrbk Stf; Ed Lit Mag; Pep Clb; Outstndg Achvmnt Art 85-86; NY Inst Of Tech; Archtctr.

PERRY, COLLEEN; Trumbull HS; Trumbull, CT; (Y); Variety Show; Sec Frsh Cls; VP Soph Cls; Pres Jr Cls; Pres Sr Cls; Cheerleading; Var Capt Tennis; JV Trk; High Hon Roll; NHS; Harambee Open Newfield Ten Assoc 85; Bus.

PERRY, PATRICK; St Lukes HS; Norwalk, CT; (Y); Model UN; Yrbk Stf; Off Sr Cls; Off Stu Cncl; Lcrss; Socr; Hon Roll; Chem Awd 86; Spnsh Awd 86; Hist Awd 85.

PERRY, STACY; East Granby HS; E Granby, CT; (Y); 18/59; AFS; Math Tm; Ski Clb; Yrbk Stf; VP Jr Cls; Var Capt Bsktbl; JV Var Socr; Var Capt Sftbl; High Hon Roll; Hon Roll; Excllnc Spansh 84; Mst Imprvd Plyr 84; Fashn Mrchndsng.

PERRY, TERESA; Bassick HS; Bridgpt, CT; (Y); Varsity Clb; School Play; Var Capt Bsktbl; Gym; Sftbl; Prfct Atten Awd; Awd Bsktbl 85-86; Dbl Dutch 85; Awd Sftbl 84-86; US Army; Comm.

PERSCHINO, CHIP; Danbury HS; Danbury, CT; (Y); Ski Clb; Stage Crew; Rep Soph Cls; Rep Jr Cls; Rep Stu Cncl; JV Trk; Soph Yr Bd Of Fnce 85; Soph Float Comm 85; JR Prom King 86.

PERSSON, CHRISTINE; Shelton HS; Shelton, CT; (Y); 4-H; Spanish Clb; Bridgeport U; Atty.

PERTILLAR, TAMMY L; Loomis Chaffee HS; Hartford, CT; (Y); School Play; Variety Show; SF New Engl Wmns Poetry 84; Tp StdntWALKS Stdnt 85; DTAAA 82-84; Mount Holyoke Coll; Cret Wrtng.

PERUGINI, MARIA A; Sacred Heart HS; Prospect, CT; (Y); 5/217; Yrbk Ed-Chief; Var L Swmmng; L Trk; Elks Awd; High Hon Roll; Pres NHS; Ntl Merit Ltr; St Schlr; Providene Coll; Humanities.

PERUGINI, THOMAS; Holy Cross HS; Watertown, CT; (Y); 113/380; Var L Socr; Hon Roll; NHS; Spanish NHS.

PERUSSE, DIANE; Farmington HS; Farmington, CT; (Y); Church Yth Grp; Cmnty Wkr; Chorus; Hon Roll; Drftng.

PERUZZI, MICHELE; Jonathan Law HS; Milford, CT; (Y); 23/200; Drama Clb; Band; Concert Band; Drm Mjr(t); Jazz Band; Mrchg Band; School Musical; School Play; Yrbk Stf; Rep Jr Cls; Band Schlrshp 86; Superntndt Acadmc Awd 86; Southern CT; Elem Educ.

PETAJASOJA, NANCY; Putnam HS; Putnam, CT; (Y); VP Band; Chorus; Color Guard; VP Concert Band; School Play; Trs Frsh Cls; Trs Soph Cls; Trs Stu Cncl; Var Capt Cheerleading; NHS; Coll Schlrshp 86; Chrldng Awds 84-85 & 86; Adelphi U; Bio.

PETE, WILLIAM; Torrington HS; Torrington, CT; (Y); 7/280; Math Tm; Model UN; Ski Clb; JV Golf; Var L Socr; Var L Trk; NHS; NEDT Awd; High Hon Roll; U Of CT Coop Pgm For Superior Hgh Schl Stu Acad Achvt Awd 85-86; Stu Of Month 85.

PETERS, ALISON; East Haven HS; E Haven, CT; (Y); Church Yth Grp; Spanish Clb; Nwsp Stf; Yrbk Stf; High Hon Roll; Hon Roll; NHS; U Of New Haven; Crmnl Jstc.

PETERS, CRAIG; Trumbull HS; Trumbull, CT; (Y).

PETERS, MAUREEN; Stratford HS; Stratford, CT; (Y); 29/231; Church Yth Grp; Ski Clb; Rep Soph Cls; Rep Jr Cls; Rep Sr Cls; Var L Mgr(s); Var L Pom Pon; Hon Roll; Pres Acdmc Ftnss Awd 86; Hofstra U; Bus Mgmt.

PETERS, MICHELLE; Miss Porters Schl; Kensington, CT; (Y); Art Clb; Camera Clb; Cmnty Wkr; Drama Clb; Thesps; Chorus; School Musical; School Play; Stage Crew; Nwsp Stf; Jrnlsm.

PETERS, WALTER; Emmet Obrien R U T S; Shelton, CT; (Y); Nwsp Stf; Yrbk Stf; Socr; Hon Roll; NHS; Awd Mst Imprvd Sccr Plyr 85; Ntl Hnr Soc Secy 86-87; Arch.

PETERSON, KAREN; Conard HS; W Hartford, CT; (Y); 13/331; Latin Clb; Service Clb; Spanish Clb; Chorus; Church Choir; NHS; Ntl Merit Ltr; Spanish NHS.

PETERSON, RON; Pomerang HS; Southbury, CT; (Y); 27/184; Mgr Chess Clb; Var Math Tm; SADD; Rep Sr Cls; Rep Stu Cncl; JV Var Crs Cntry; Hon Roll; Rep Jr Cls; Head Delegate Harvard Model 85; Co-Coordntr Mock Trial Tm; Princpls Commtt On Hmwrk; CT U; Chem Engrng.

PETIT, LOU-ANNE E; Northwestern Reg School 7; New Hartford, CT; (Y); FHA; Chorus; Hmcmg Cmmttee 85; Prom Cmmttee 86; Concrt Chr Awd 86; Smmr Intrn For Sen Lowell Welcker DC 85; Northwestern CT CC; Crmnlgy.

PETRAFASSI, JOE; Thomaston HS; Thomaston, CT; (Y); 3/55; Trk; High Hon Roll; Hon Roll; NHS; Math.

PETRELLI, FELICIA; East Haven HS; East Haven, CT; (Y); Hosp Aide; Southern CT ST U; Engl.

PETROKAITIS, ELIZABETH; Holy Cross HS; Waterbury, CT; (Y); 63/346; Service Clb; Hon Roll; NHS; CT U.

PETRONI, KAREN; Stamford HS; Stamford, CT; (Y); Band; Concert Band; Jazz Band; Mrchg Band; High Hon Roll; Hon Roll; NHS; Ntl Merit Ltr; Unico Schlrshp 86; Rutgers Coll Eng.

PETROSSI, MICHELLE; Southington HS; Plantsville, CT; (Y); Church Yth Grp; Girl Scts; Key Clb; Library Aide; Pep Clb; Ski Clb; Chorus; Yrbk Stf; Jrnlsm.

PETROVITS, BRIAN; Wamago HS; Goshen, CT; (Y); 13/85; Yrbk Bus Mgr; Trs Frsh Cls; Trs Soph Cls; Trs Jr Cls; Im Golf; Var L Socr; Var L Tennis; Hon Roll; NHS; Acctng.

PETROVITS, WENDY; Torrington HS; Torrington, CT; (Y); Dance Clb; Yrbk Stf; Var Cheerleading; Hon Roll; Prfct Atten Awd; Fairfield U; Psychlgy.

PETROWSKI, JILL; Academy Of The Holy Family; Bozrah, CT; (Y); 4/40; Pres Frsh Cls; Var Crs Cntry; JV Sftbl; 1st Prz-Spring Art Show 86; RI Schl Of Dsgn; Grphc Dsgn.

PETRUZZELLI, CYNTHIA; Hamden HS; Hamden, CT; (Y); Church Yth Grp; GAA; Y-Teens; Var L Bsktbl; High Hon Roll; Spec Svc To The HFBA Clnc Awd 86; U Of Dayton; Chem.

PETRUZZI, DONALD; Kennedy HS; Waterbury, CT; (Y); Hosp Aide; Key Clb; SADD; Band; Concert Band; Jazz Band; Hon Roll; Jr NHS; Kiwanis Awd; NHS; Choate Rosemary Hall Schlrshp 84-85; Proj Sage 84; U Of CT; Pre Med.

PETRUZZI, JIM; Southington HS; Southington, CT; (Y); Chrmn Key Clb; Pres Latin Clb; Math Clb; Math Tm; Scholastic Bowl; Ski Clb; Chorus; School Musical; Nwsp Rptr; Nwsp Stf; Boston U; Eng Lit.

PETTERSON, SONJA; Tourtellotte Memorial HS; Quinebaug, CT; (Y); 26/93; Church Yth Grp; Pep Clb; Katharine Mangan Schlrshp Awd 86; Anna Maria Coll; Psychology.

PETTERSSON, JANICE; Old Saybrook SR HS; Old Saybrook, CT; (Y); Am Leg Aux Girls St; Concert Band; Drm Mjr(t); Jazz Band; Orch; NHS; Church Yth Grp; Cmnty Wkr; Spanish Clb; All ST Orchst 86; Mdrn Music Mstrs Music Hon Soc 86; Acdm Awds Englsh, Math, Soc Ctds, Spnsh 84 & 86; Music.

PETTINICO JR, GEORGE; Holy Cross HS; Waterbury, CT; (Y); 10/356; Boy Scts; PAVAS; Teachers Aide; Band; Mrchg Band; Pep Band; School Play; Hon Roll; NHS; St Schlr; Fordham U; Pltcl Sci.

PETTWAY, WAYNE; Bullard-Havens Tech; Bridgeport, CT; (Y); Exploring; Trs Jr Cls; Rep Stu Cncl; Engrng.

PETTY, CAROL; East Lyme HS; Salem, CT; (Y); Hon Roll; Sec.

PEZZELLO, DARYL ALAYNE; Saint Joseph HS; Trumbull, CT; (Y); 25/220; Art Clb; Drama Clb; French Clb; Hosp Aide; JA; Band; Chorus; Yrbk Sprt Ed; French Hon Soc; High Hon Roll; U VT; Biol.

PFAHLER, KRISTIN; Berlin HS; Kensington, CT; (Y); 12/175; Am Leg Aux Girls St; Drama Clb; Service Clb; VP Band; Capt Cheerleading; Lion Awd; VP NHS; Pres Schlr; Probe Awd 86; Fr Rbrt Caroll 1st Annual Schlrshp 86; Bryant Coll; Bus Commnctn.

PFANNKUCH, SEAN; Trumbull HS; Trumbull, CT; (Y); Church Yth Grp; Latin Clb; JV Bsktbl; Var L Ftbl; Var L Golf; Hon Roll; Bus.

PFISTNER, PAULA; Torrington HS; Torrington, CT; (Y); 30/273; Church Yth Grp; Varsity Clb; Var Diving; Var Swmmng; Var Trk; NHS; Ocngrphy.

PHANEUF, JOSEPH; Putnam HS; Putnam, CT; (Y); Am Leg Boys St; Church Yth Grp; Exploring; Hosp Aide; Office Aide; Red Cross Aide; Chorus; School Musical; School Play; Yrbk Stf; U Of Sthrn CA; Engrng.

PHELAN, PAMELA; Holy Cross HS; Waterbury, CT; (Y); 125/380; Church Yth Grp; Chorus; Diving; Gym; Hon Roll; Gymnstcs Instrtr Girls Clb Of Amer 84-86; Sec Ed.

PHILBRICK, LAURIE; Bolton HS; W Willington, CT; (Y); Church Yth Grp; Exploring; French Clb; Latin Clb; Teachers Aide; Chorus; Intrr Dsgnr.

PHILIPPOPOULOS, EVAN; St Basil Prep Schl; Stamford, CT; (Y); 3/10; Church Yth Grp; Yrbk Stf; Sec Jr Cls; Sec Stu Cncl; JV Var Socr; Im Sftbl; Im Vllybl; Hon Roll; Most Imprvd Stu 86; St Basil Spch Cntst SF 86; Lehigh U; Dentstry.

PHILLIPS, KEVIN; Jonathan Law HS; Milford, CT; (Y); 12/246; Am Leg Boys St; Latin Clb; Var Bsbl; L Var Bsktbl; L Var Crs Cntry; L Var Trk; Hon Roll; NHS; Hon Merit Awd Ntl Ltn Exm 84; Mdl Excllnc Hon Hstry, Econ 85 & 86; All ST 1st Team Bsktbl 86; Econ.

PHILPOTT, JILL; Ridgefield HS; Ridgefield, CT; (Y); Church Yth Grp; Sec Exploring; French Clb; Pep Clb; Drill Tm; Stage Crew; Mgr(s); Powder Puff Ftbl; Hon Roll; Martial Art Tae Kwon Do Hgh Rank Blt & Instr 83-86.

PHINNEY, WILLIAM; East Lyme HS; E Lyme, CT; (Y); 60/280; Yrbk Stf; Var Ftbl; Var Golf; Var Trk; Hon Roll; U Of CT; Nuclear Engrng.

PHOUTHASACK, NATHAYA; Hartford Public HS; Hartford, CT; (Y); AFS; Girl Scts; Rep Stu Cncl; Capt Tennis; Co-Capt Vllybl; Hon Roll; Prfct Atten Awd.

PICARD, JENNIFER; South Windsor HS; S Windsor, CT; (Y); 8/300; Library Aide; Trk; CC Awd; High Hon Roll; Bryant Coll; Bus Mgmt.

PICARD, KERRI; Holy Cross HS; Waterbury, CT; (Y); 67/360; Church Yth Grp; Chorus; Cheerleading; Swmmng; Hon Roll; NHS; Ed.

PICCARELLI, LISA; Wooster Schl; Danbury, CT; (Y); 5/43; Var Fld Hcky; Var Sftbl; Var Vllybl; Hon Roll; Ntl Merit SF; Concours Ntl De Francais Frnch 84-86; Coaches Awd Hockey 85-86; Tupts U.

PIEGER, DANA; Trumbull HS; Bridgeport, CT; (Y); Church Yth Grp; Cmnty Wkr; Dance Clb; FFA; Teachers Aide; School Musical; School Play; Gym; Swmmng; Vllybl; Briarwood Coll Awd Excllnce Bus 86; Northeastern U; Bus Mgt.

PIENKOWSKI, ALAN; Rockville HS; Vernon-Rockvill, CT; (Y); 18/334; Pres Chess Clb; Computer Clb; Math Tm; Jazz Band; Mrchg Band; Pep Band; School Musical; Symp Band; NHS; Vernon Jr Wmns Clb Schlrshp 86; St Lukes Chrch Schlrshp 86; Ernie Rock Memrl Music Awd 86; U Of CT; Math.

PIERSOL, WILLOW BRYN; Miss Porters Schl; Chicopee, MA; (Y); Art Clb; Intnl Clb; Fld Hcky; Var Lcrss; JV Socr; JV Var Vllybl.

PIERSON, MELISSA; Plainfield HS; Plainfield, CT; (Y); 23/123; Acpl Chr; Chorus; Frsh Cls; Bsktbl; Tennis; Trk; U CT.

PIERSON, RUSS; Guilford HS; Guilford, CT; (Y); Boy Scts; Church Yth Grp; Exploring; Band; Concert Band; Mrchg Band; Orch; Hon Roll; Music Awd For Comptn Williamsburg VA 86; Grad Wth Hnrs 86; U CT; Bus.

PIERZ, KRISTAN; Wethersfield HS; Wethersfield, CT; (Y); 1/299; Am Leg Aux Girls St; Sec Stu Cncl; Var Capt Socr; Bausch & Lomb Sci Awd; Pres NHS; Ntl Merit Ltr; Cmnty Wkr; Science Clb; Service Clb; Yrbk Stf; Rensselear Mth/Sci Mdl 86; Citvitan Awd Geom 85; HOBY Ldrshp Awd 85; Acad Promise Sci 84; Acad Excllnce; Med.

PIKE, SANDRA; East Lyme HS; Salem, CT; (Y); 86/263; Drama Clb; SADD; Mrchg Band; School Play; Stage Crew; Rep Soph Cls; Rep Jr Cls; Stu Cncl; Stat Bsktbl; Hon Roll; Manchester CC; Resprtry Thrpy.

PIKUL, DAWN; Danbury HS; Danbury, CT; (Y); 6/472; Rep Key Clb; Office Aide; ROTC; Drill Tm; Yrbk Phtg; Var Tennis; JV Trk; High Hon Roll; Hon Roll; NHS; Perry Awd For Coll Bio 85; Kitty Hawk Air Woc 86; Smith Coll Bk Awd 86; Aerosp.

PIKUL, JO ANNE; East Windsor HS; East Windsor, CT; (Y); 7/80; Varsity Clb; Chorus; Yrbk Stf; Rep Soph Cls; Rep Jr Cls; Rep Sr Cls; Var Cheerleading; Var Fld Hcky; Var Trk; Hon Roll; Pres Acad Fit Awd 86; Alumni Assn Scholar 86; Charles D Gerstein Scholar 86; Bryant Coll; Bus Mgmt.

PILLA, TONY; Lyman Hall HS; Wallingford, CT; (Y); 48/220; Camera Clb; FHA; Yrbk Phtg; Yrbk Rptr; Yrbk Stf; Frsh Cls; Soph Cls; Jr Cls; Sr Cls; Stu Cncl; Hero Clb Awd 86.

PILLAR, ROBT; Maloney HS; Meriden, CT; (Y); Office Aide; Quiz Bowl; Scholastic Bowl; Hon Roll; Penn ST; Indstrl Engr.

PINA, JAMIE; Norwich Free Acad; Preston, CT; (Y); JV Var Bsktbl; JV Sftbl; Hon Roll; U ME; Trainer Animls.

PINSKY, SHARI; Hamden HS; Hamden, CT; (Y); 32/419; VP Temple Yth Grp; Ed Yrbk Stf; High Hon Roll; NHS; CT ST Schlr 85-86; Jewish War Vet Ladies Aux Scholar 86; Acad Achvt Spn Soc Sci Hebrew & Art 85-86; Clark U.

PINTO, ANTONIO; Holy Cross HS; Waterbury, CT; (Y); 83/380; Church Yth Grp; Pres Science Clb; Crs Cntry; Trk; Hon Roll; Accntng.

PINTO, WILLIAM; Trumbull HS; Trumbull, CT; (Y); Church Yth Grp; Varsity Clb; Frsh Cls; Capt Var Ftbl; Var Trk; Wt Lftg; Bus.

PIOTROWSKI, NICHOLAS; Bristol Central HS; Bristol, CT; (Y); Computer Clb; German Clb; Ski Clb; High Hon Roll; Hon Roll; Engr.

PIPER, FRANCESCA L; Stamford HS; Stamford, CT; (Y); Art Clb; Church Yth Grp; Office Aide; Pep Clb; Ski Clb; Varsity Clb; Yrbk Stf; Var Fld Hcky; Hon Roll; Fiore Art Schlrshp 86; 1st-Natl Schlstc Art Cmptn 86; 1st-HS Art Fair 86; 2nd Art Assoc 86; Rhd Islnd Schl Dsgn; Fine Arts.

PIPKIN, GILLIAN; Hamden HS; Hamden, CT; (Y); Church Yth Grp; Chorus; Swmmng; Hon Roll.

PISACICH, KAREN E; St Bernard HS; Waterford, CT; (Y); 42/297; Church Yth Grp; Band; Concert Band; Mrchg Band; Bsktbl; Capt Sftbl; Fairfield U; Comp.

PISELLI, LAURA; Brien Mc Mahon HS; Norwalk, CT; (Y); Drama Clb; Ski Clb; Band; Mrchg Band; School Play; Symp Band; Cheerleading.

PITTACK, JEAN; Shelton HS; Shelton, CT; (S); Church Yth Grp; DECA; Girl Scts; Hosp Aide; JA; Office Aide; SADD; Teachers Aide; Color Guard; Drill Tm; 3rd Pl DECA Wrtn Evnt 86; St Ptrsbrg JR Coll; Bnkng.

PIVAR, DAVID; Bolton HS; Willington, CT; (Y); Ski Clb; Ed Lit Mag; JV Socr; High Hon Roll; Hon Roll; NHS; Spanish NHS; Conservation Educ & Firearms Safety Awd 84; Creative Writing Awd 86; Elec Engrng.

PIVARNIK JR, RONALD E; Pomperaug HS; Southbury, CT; (Y); Aud/Vis; Drama Clb; Science Clb; Teachers Aide; School Play; Stage Crew; Hon Roll; Drama Stage Crew 85-86; Drama Partcptn 86; Elec Engrng.

PIVNICK, SCOTT; Manchester HS; Manchester, CT; (Y); Aud/Vis; Boy Scts; Debate Tm; Drama Clb; Hst French Clb; Pres Intnl Clb; Library Aide; Ski Clb; Temple Yth Grp; School Musical; Arch.

PLACIDO, CLAUDIO; Central HS; Bridgeport, CT; (Y); Elec.

PLAZZA, AMY; Lyman Hall HS; Wallingford, CT; (Y); AFS; Church Yth Grp; VP Key Clb; Concert Band; Jazz Band; Mrchg Band; Pep Band; Variety Show; Pres Chess Clb; Powder Puff Ftbl; Middlesex CC; Telecomm.

PLODER, STEVE; Wilton HS; Wilton, CT; (Y); 60/360; Church Yth Grp; Cmnty Wkr; SADD; JV Bsktbl; JV Ftbl; Hon Roll; Bus.

PLOSKI, KATHLEEN; Holy Cross HS; Seymour, CT; (Y); 45/380; Art Clb; Hosp Aide; Stage Crew; High Hon Roll; U Of CT; Nrsng.

PODESZWA, CHRISTINE; Norwich Free Acad; Baltic, CT; (Y); Church Yth Grp; Office Aide; Science Clb; Trs Frsh Cls; Sec Jr Cls; Rep Stu Cncl; Bsktbl; JV Tennis; High Hon Roll; Hon Roll; Mthmtcs.

PODURGIEL, SUZANNE; The Williams Schl; Norwich, CT; (Y); 4/39; Hosp Aide; SADD; School Musical; Yrbk Stf; Pres Stu Cncl; Var L Fld Hcky; Var Sftbl; Cit Awd; High Hon Roll; Prfct Atten Awd; Clss Schlr 85; MVP Fld Hcky Awd 85; SR Mrshll 86; Bio.

POERSCHKE, HEIDI; Wethersfield HS; Wethersfield, CT; (Y); 41/300; Church Yth Grp; Hosp Aide; Ski Clb; JV Sftbl; Var Vllybl; Hon Roll; Scientists Of Tomorrow 84; Pblc Rel.

POHORYLO, BRIAN; Windsor Locks HS; Windsor Locks, CT; (Y); 7/151; Am Leg Boys St; Church Yth Grp; Co-Capt Math Tm; School Play; Nwsp Stf; Var Tennis; NHS; Ntl Merit Ltr; U Of CT Bk Awd 86; Pres Acadmc Ftnss Awd 86; Windsor Locks Tchrs Assoc Schlrshp 86; U Of CT; Cmptr Sci.

POIRIER, LISA; Brookfield HS; Brookfield Center, CT; (Y); Ski Clb; Chorus; Fld Hcky; Gym; Trk; Hon Roll; Photo Jrnlst.

POISSON, TODD; Frank Scott Bunnell HS; Stratford, CT; (Y); 3/260; Cmnty Wkr; Concert Band; Yrbk Stf; Var Capt Socr; Var Capt Swmmng; Var L Trk; Cit Awd; NHS; Schlt Athl Awd 86; Excllnc Engl 4 Yrs Awd 86; Excllnc Arch Drftg Medln 85 & 86; Cornell U; Arch.

POITRAS, DANIELLE; Farmington HS; Unionville, CT; (Y); Im Powder Puff Ftbl; JV Socr; Hon Roll; Mc Donalds Emplyee Yr 85; Blgy.

POITRAS, GREGORY; Francis T Maloney HS; Meriden, CT; (Y); 3/257; Am Leg Boys St; Latin Clb; Yrbk Stf; Pres Stu Cncl; Elks Awd; High Hon Roll; NHS; Pres Schlr; Var L Socr; Var L Tennis; Schlr Athl Awd 86; Pres Acdmc Fit Awd 86; Meriden Fndtn Schlrshp Awd 86; Trinity Coll; Ecnmcs.

POKLEMBA, AUDREY; Trumbull HS; Trumbull, CT; (Y); AFS; Church Yth Grp; Drama Clb; Red Cross Aide; Ski Clb; Varsity Clb; Concert Band; Mrchg Band; Orch; Yrbk Stf; Pediatrc Thrpy.

POKRAS, KAREN; Amity Regional SR HS; Orange, CT; (Y); 42/388; French Clb; FBLA; Key Clb; Ski Clb; Temple Yth Grp; Yrbk Stf; Hon Roll; NHS; Ithaca Coll; Bus.

POLAN, CINDY; Trumbull HS; Trumbull, CT; (Y); Exploring; Spanish Clb; Chorus; Color Guard; Madrigals; Mrchg Band; Bsktbl; Fld Hcky; Sftbl; High Hon Roll; Spnsh Stu Of Yr Awd 84; Dncng & Gymnstc Awd 86; Stu Rep Itln Ptry Cntst 85; Mth Sci.

POLGAR, DAVID S; Newtown HS; Newtown, CT; (Y); 8/278; Var Co-Capt Diving; Var Socr; Var Capt Trk; JETS Awd; Sec NHS; Pres Schlr; Pres Spanish NHS; AFS; Sec Exploring; Quiz Bowl; Sci Awd 86; Cntry III Ldr ST Fnlst 86; CT Schlr Athltc 86; Bowdoin Coll; Bio.

POLIDORO, DANIEL; Granby Memorial HS; Granby, CT; (Y); 15/130; Sec AFS; Am Leg Boys St; Pres Trs Drama Clb; Ski Clb; SADD; Yrbk Ed-Chief; JV Bsktbl; Hon Roll; Grnby Cmmnty Schlrshp 86; Elctd Clss 86 Reprsntv Schl Efftvnss 84-86; Acad Awds Blgy Art Spnsh II; CT Coll.

POLLACK, CALEB J; Ridgefield HS; Ridgefield, CT; (Y); 19/330; Math Tm; Ski Clb; Temple Yth Grp; High Hon Roll; Hon Roll; Ntl Merit SF; Comp Pgmng Awd 85; Math Tm Ltr 84; Engrng.

POLLACK, JENNY; Ridgefield HS; Ridgefield, CT; (Y); Trs Temple Yth Grp; JV Tennis; Hon Roll; Ntl Merit Ltr; Biophysics.

POLLACK, RONALD; Hartford Public HS; Hartford, CT; (Y); Leo Clb; Chorus; Nwsp Bus Mgr.

POLMATIER, MICHAEL H; Enrico Fermi HS; Enfield, CT; (Y); 37/341; Ski Clb; Stu Cncl; JV Bsktbl; Var Golf; Hon Roll; NHS; CT ST Champ AAU Tack Won Do Blue Blt & Green Blt 84-85; Mech Engrng.

POND, CHRISTINE; Platt RUTS HS; Milford, CT; (Y); Nwsp Rptr; Yrbk Stf; Hst Frsh Cls; Hst Soph Cls; JV Capt Cheerleading; NHS; Norwalk ST Tech Coll; Engrng.

POOLE, SHANNON A; Farmington HS; Hartford, CT; (Y); Bowling; Trs Chorus; Rep Frsh Cls; Rep Soph Cls; Rep Jr Cls; Stu Cncl; Var Capt Cheerleading; Prjct Cncrn Clb Chrmn 86-87; Attrny.

POPIELARCZYK, AMY; Farmington HS; Farmington, CT; (Y); 67/207; JA; Band; Jazz Band; Rep Jr Cls; Rep Stu Cncl; Var Bsktbl; Var Socr; High Hon Roll; Hon Roll; Bus.

PORADA, CHRIS; Southington HS; Plantsville, CT; (Y); 2/600; Am Leg Boys St; Boy Scts; Band; Orch; Yrbk Stf; High Hon Roll; NHS; Church Yth Grp; Latin Clb; Ski Clb.

PORTER, RICHARD A; Bethel HS; Bethel, CT; (Y); 9/268; Drama Clb; Math Tm; Capt Quiz Bowl; School Play; Variety Show; Nwsp Ed-Chief; Nwsp Rptr; Yrbk Stf; Trs Stu Cncl; Ntl Merit SF; Harvard Bk Awd 85; PA ST U; Med.

PORTNOY, RACHEL; Staples HS; Westport, CT; (Y); Radio Clb; Concert Band; Orch; Nwsp Stf; Lit Mag; Ed Yrbk Bus Mgr; Wesleyan U; Eng.

PORTO, MICHELE; Joseph A Foran HS; Milford, CT; (Y); 24/253; Keywanettes; Latin Clb; Spanish Clb; JV Sftbl; JV Vllybl; Hon Roll; Pre Med.

PORTO, PATTY; East Haven HS; E Haven, CT; (Y); 14/233; Ski Clb; Spanish Clb; High Hon Roll; Hon Roll; NHS; Pres Acad Fit Awd 86; Marion J Fusco Scholar 86; U CT; Med Tech.

POSKAS III, PETER E; Kent Schl; Washington, CT; (Y); Art Clb; French Clb; Varsity Clb; Lit Mag; Off Frsh Cls; Socr; Tennis; Alfred E Heart II Awd Five Arts 84; Art.

POSSO, JAMES; Greenwich HS; Riverside, CT; (Y); Boys Clb Am; JA; Key Clb; Science Clb; Band; Gym; Trk; Hon Roll; Varsty Gymnstcs Mst Imprvd Athlte 86; JR Achvmnt Salesmn Clb Indctrntn 85; Concerg Band Medal Wnr 84; U Of Miami; Marine Sci.

POTE, NICOLE; New Canaan HS; New Canaan, CT; (Y); Church Yth Grp; JA; Spanish Clb; SADD; JV Lcrss; JV Socr; Var Trk; Hon Roll.

POTTER, BONNIE; Housatonic Valley Regional HS; W Cornwall, CT; (Y); 7/108; French Clb; Ski Clb; Band; Nwsp Ed-Chief; Yrbk Phtg; Sec Sr Cls; Hon Roll; Church Yth Grp; Nwsp Phtg; Semper Fidelis Awd 86; Marist Coll; Prnt Journlsm.

POTTER, JAY; Torrington HS; Torrington, CT; (Y); Aud/Vis; Pres Latin Clb; Chrmn Model UN; Capt Quiz Bowl; Trs Thesps; School Musical; Pres Schlr; VP Church Yth Grp; Debate Tm; Drama Clb; Wesleyan U.

POTTER, LINDA; Seymour HS; Seymour, CT; (S); Stage Crew; Var Pom Pon; Hon Roll; Arch.

POULIOT, STEPHANIE; Windsor HS; Windsor, CT; (Y); 74/360; Church Yth Grp; Cmnty Wkr; Drama Clb; Intnl Clb; SADD; Stage Crew; Yrbk Stf; Im Mgr Tennis; Im Mgr Vllybl; Natl Sci Olympd 85; S CT U; Socl Wrkr.

POWELL, KARRON; West Haven HS; Brooklyn, NY; (Y); Drama Clb; Office Aide; Teachers Aide; Acpl Chr; Band; School Play; Gym; Wt Lftg; Fash Merch.

POWELL, ROBYN; Thomaston HS; Thomaston, CT; (Y); 2/62; Church Yth Grp; Band; Concert Band; Symp Band; Yrbk Stf; Sec Sr Cls; JV Sftbl; High Hon Roll; NHS.

POWELL, SIMONE; Thomas Snell Weaver HS; Hartford, CT; (Y); 64/317; Church Yth Grp; Drama Clb; FBLA; Intnl Clb; VP JA; Red Cross Aide; Band; Church Choir; Cit Awd; JC Awd; Stu Mnth 85; Data Pros Highest Av, Rhea Theicher Zipkin Mem Awd 86; U CT; Pol Sci.

POWERS, MICHELLE; Coventry HS; Coventry, CT; (Y); Church Yth Grp; Dance Clb; Letterman Clb; Varsity Clb; Band; Yrbk Bus Mgr; Yrbk Stf; JV Capt Cheerleading; NHS; Cmnty Wkr; CT JR Sci & Hnmnts Sympsm 86; Math.

POWERS, SHEILA C; Central Catholic HS; Westport, CT; (Y); Cmnty Wkr; French Clb; Math Clb; Math Tm; Ski Clb; Teachers Aide; Yrbk Stf; JV Bsktbl; Powder Puff Ftbl; Var Capt Trk; Harold Glazer Found Schrlshp 86; Diocese Bridgept Ed Assoc Awd 86; Southern CT ST U; Elem Ed.

POWERS, WILLIAM M; Ridgefield HS; Ridgefield, CT; (Y); 2/332; Band; Mrchg Band; Orch; Var Crs Cntry; JV Socr; Var Trk; High Hon Roll; Ntl Merit SF; Sal; CT Jr Sci & Humanities Symposium 85; Elec Engrng.

POYER, WENDY; Old Saybrook SR HS; Old Saybrook, CT; (Y); Church Yth Grp; Intnl Clb; Latin Clb; Spanish Clb; Band; School Musical; Yrbk Stf; NHS; Tri M Music Hnrs Soc 86; Encllnc Spnsh Ii, Iii & Iv 84-86.

PRAGANA, SANDRA; St Marys HS; New Haven, CT; (Y); FBLA; Lit Mag; Rep Jr Cls; Rep Sr Cls; JV Vllybl; Hon Roll; NHS; K Gibbs Ldrshp Awd Fut Sec, Bus Awd 86; Frnch Awd 85; Cmptr Sys Anlyst.

PRATVIEL, MARYALICE; Norwich Free Acad; Norwich, CT; (Y); Art Clb; Cmnty Wkr; Dance Clb; Drama Clb; Hosp Aide; Latin Clb; Q&S; School Musical; School Play; Nwsp Rptr; Creativ Yth Prog 84; Schltc Art Awds 85; Ceramcs.

PRAY, JUDY; Shelton HS; Shelton, CT; (Y); Cmnty Wkr; JA; Spanish Clb; Rep SADD; Rep Jr Cls; Rep Stu Cncl; Var Cheerleading; Cit Awd; Hon Roll; Voice Dem Awd; 3rd Pl Persuasv Publ Spkg Cntst 85; Bus Mgmt.

PREFONTAINE, KAREN; Berlin HS; Berlin, CT; (Y); 33/184; Hosp Aide; Trs Service Clb; SADD; Band; Drm Mjr(t); Mrchg Band; Sec Stu Cncl; Powder Puff Ftbl; Hon Roll; U CT; Anml Sci.

PRELESNIK, ANGELA; Manchester HS; Manchester, CT; (Y); 9/581; Am Leg Aux Girls St; Drama Clb; Thesps; Band; Chorus; School Musical; Var L Swmmng; High Hon Roll; NHS; French Clb; Stu Adv Bd; Anthrplgy.

PRESCOTT, ERIN; Manchester HS; Manchester, CT; (Y); 18/560; Pres Frsh Cls; Rep Jr Cls; Capt Bsktbl; Capt Socr; Sftbl; High Hon Roll; Hon Roll; NHS; AFS; Church Yth Grp; All Conf Goalkeepr Sccr 84-84; Yale Clb Bk Awd 86; All Conf Pitchr.

PRESSMAN, KAREN; Trumbull HS; Trumbull, CT; (Y); French Clb; Latin Clb; Office Aide; Temple Yth Grp; Chorus; Yrbk Stf; Mgr(s); High Hon Roll; Bus Mgmt.

PREUSS, LINDA; Wethersfield HS; Wethersfield, CT; (Y); Yrbk Stf; Sec Sr Cls; JV Bsktbl; Var Trk; Hon Roll; Tunxis CC; Dntl Hygn.

PREZIOSO, MICHELE; Jonathn Law HS; Milford, CT; (Y); Trs Drama Clb; Intnl Clb; Sec Keywanettes; Latin Clb; SADD; Capt Color Guard; School Musical; School Play; Stage Crew; Nwsp Rptr; Outstndng Keyett Awd 86; Engl.

PRICE, JACQUELINE; North Haven HS; N Haven, CT; (Y); 49/282; Church Yth Grp; Dance Clb; Band; Concert Band; Mrchg Band; Var L Bsktbl; Var L Trk; JV Vllybl; Fidle Scty 85-86; Wash Wrkshp Smnr 86; Crmnlgy.

PRIMEAU, MARK; Farmington HS; Unionville, CT; (Y); 31/220; DECA; Rep Jr Cls; Rep Sr Cls; Bsktbl; Ice Hcky; Socr; Wt Lftg; Hon Roll; All Conf, Tm Plyr Awd 85-86, Cpt Sccr 86-87.

PRIMINI, DAVID; Watertown HS; Oakville, CT; (Y); 90/262; Church Yth Grp; School Play; Variety Show; Rep Frsh Cls; Rep Soph Cls; Rep Jr Cls; Rep Stu Cncl; Var Capt Bsbl; Var Capt Bsktbl.

PRINDLE, DEBORAH; Housatonic Valley Regional HS; Sharon, CT; (Y); Art Clb; Computer Clb; Drama Clb; Girl Scts; Key Clb; Chorus; School Play; Yrbk Stf; Hon Roll; Art.

PRIOLEAU, CASSANDRA; Stratford HS; Stratford, CT; (Y); 11/233; Exploring; Library Aide; Variety Show; Cit Awd; High Hon Roll; Hon Roll; Pres Schlr; Delta Sigma Theta, Alpha Kappa Alpha 86; Lbry Aide Schlrshp 86; U CT; Med.

PRIOR, DAWN; Southington HS; Southington, CT; (Y); 73/600; Aud/Vis; French Clb; FTA; Pep Clb; High Hon Roll; Pres Physcl Ftns Awd 82; U Of CT.

PRISCSAK, AGNES; New Fairfield HS; New Fairfield, CT; (Y); Latin Clb; Stage Crew; Nwsp Rptr; Nwsp Stf; Lit Mag; JV Socr; JV Trk; Hon Roll; NHS; Tlntd Pgm Wrtng 83-87.

PROCTOR, COURTNEY; Ridgefield HS; Ridgefield, CT; (Y); 61/387; Church Yth Grp; Cmnty Wkr; Var Fld Hcky; Var Trk; Hon Roll; NHS; Co-Capt Indr-Outdr Trk 86-87; ST Indr Trk Champs CT 85-86.

PROCTOR, JONATHAN D; Trumbull HS; Trumbull, CT; (Y); Aud/Vis; JA; Varsity Clb; Band; Drm & Bgl; Symp Band; Trk; Hon Roll; Excllnc Woodwrkg Awd 84.

PRODAN, ANGELA JEAN; Shelton HS; Shelton, CT; (Y); 26/336; Am Leg Aux Girls St; Nwsp Sprt Ed; Yrbk Sprt Ed; Pres Frsh Cls; Pres Sr Cls; Var Capt Sftbl; NHS; Ski Clb; VP SADD; Rep Soph Cls; Yth Of Mnth-Exchng Clb Of Shelton CT; All-ST Sftbl Ptchr Cls LL; Pres Italian Natl Hnr Soc; Lehigh U; Intl Rel.

PROSNICK, RENEE; Ansonia HS; Ansonia, CT; (Y); Computer Clb; French Clb; Hosp Aide; Library Aide; Pep Clb; Yrbk Stf; Capt Pom Pon; JV Tennis; Hon Roll; Anml Sci.

PROTOPAPAS, ALEXANDER; Fairfield College Prep Schl; Huntington, CT; (Y); 6/231; Chess Clb; Church Yth Grp; Debate Tm; Pres Chrmn JA; Key Clb; Capt Math Tm; Model UN; Lit Mag; High Hon Roll; NHS; 2TT Schlrshp; J A Schrlshp; Century III Fnlst; Most Outstndng Stu; Acad Exc Math; Columbia U; Elect Engr.

PROTSKO, DEANNA; Masuk HS; Monroe, CT; (Y); 21/280; Drama Clb; Spanish Clb; Pres Chorus; Madrigals; School Musical; School Play; Mgr(s); High Hon Roll; NHS; Pres Schlr; Outstndng Chrl; All ST Chr 83-86; U Of CT.

PROVENCAL, ROBIN; Manchester HS; Manchester, CT; (Y); Church Yth Grp; Girl Scts; Spanish Clb; Band; Concert Band; Jazz Band; Mrchg Band; Orch; Pep Band; School Musical; U CT; Elm Ed.

PUCCI, KATHLEEN; Seymour HS; Oxford, CT; (S); 24/192; Am Leg Aux Girls St; Exploring; Chorus; Variety Show; Rep Soph Cls; Cit Awd; Voice Dem Awd; Intl Yth Yr Gvrnrs Conf Stu Wnnr 86; Wstrn CT ST U; Psycho-Bio.

PUCKETT, KELLEY B; Roger Ludlowe HS; Southport, CT; (Y); Church Yth Grp; Drama Clb; Chorus; School Musical; School Play; Stage Crew; Variety Show; Lit Mag; High Hon Roll; NHS; Rensselaer Medal Outstndng Sci & Math Stu 85.

PUDIMAT, GARY; Shelton HS; Shelton, CT; (Y); 30/450; Church Yth Grp; Sec German Clb; Rep Stu Cncl; Var Socr; Hon Roll; German Hnr Scty 83-84; Bst Dfndr 85-86; Southern Connecticut; Acctng.

PUDLINSKI, JILL; Torrington HS; Torrington, CT; (Y); 4/280; Drama Clb; Latin Clb; Math Tm; Ski Clb; Band; Drm Mjr(t); School Musical; Yrbk Stf; NHS; NEDT Awd; Harvard Bk Prz 85-86; 2nd Rnnr-Up Mdrn Ms Pgnt 85; CT Hnrs Semnr 85; Oceangrphy.

PUEBLA, AMY; Kolbe Cathedral Catholic HS; Bridgeport, CT; (Y); 24/97; Church Yth Grp; Hosp Aide; JA; VP Jr Cls; Var Capt Bsktbl; Coach Actv; Sftbl; S CT; Teacher.

PUGH, TRICIA; Norwalk HS; So Norwalk, CT; (Y); 162/456; FHA; Pep Clb; Chorus; Drill Tm; Nwsp Stf; Hon Roll; Hnrs Awd 84-85; Orgnztn Pblc Spkng Awd 85; Bus.

PULLIN, BRIAN; Wamogo Regional HS; Morris, CT; (Y); 11/80; AFS; Boy Scts; Band; VP Frsh Cls; Rep Soph Cls; Var L Bsbl; Var L Bsktbl; Var L Socr; Hon Roll; NHS; Highest Hstry Avg 84; Stu Of Mnth Mar 85-86; Cornell; Chem Engrng.

PUNSALAN, KIMBERLY M; St Bernard HS; Oakdale, CT; (Y); 8/270; Rep Frsh Cls; Sec Soph Cls; Sec Jr Cls; Pres Sr Cls; Stu Cncl; JV Cheerleading; Var Tennis; High Hon Roll; Hon Roll; NHS; Acadmc Awd 84-86.

PURCELL, EILEEN; Hamden HS; Hamden, CT; (Y); Church Yth Grp; Ski Clb; Band; Concert Band; Mrchg Band; Lit Mag; Crs Cntry; Capt Var Trk; Hon Roll; 6th Plc Awd Dist Trck Chmpnshps 86.

PURCELL, MARGARET; Maloney HS; Meriden, CT; (Y); 21/263; FBLA; Key Clb; Band; Yrbk Stf; Sec Jr Cls; Sec Sr Cls; Rep Stu Cncl; Var L Cheerleading; Hon Roll; NHS; U Of CT; Bus.

PURCER, KAREN; Northwest Catholic HS; East Granby, CT; (Y); 6/162; Sec French Clb; Hosp Aide; Pep Clb; Band; School Play; Var Cheerleading; High Hon Roll; VP NHS; Excllnc Awds Honr Math 84-86; Stu Asst Fresh Contact 86-87; Math.

PURDIE, ANDREW; Branford HS; Branford, CT; (Y); 29/315; Concert Band; Jazz Band; Mrchg Band; School Musical; Stat Bsktbl; Hon Roll; Cmptr Engr.

PUSKAS, ANNMARIE; Southington HS; Plantsville, CT; (Y); Church Yth Grp; Cmnty Wkr; Pep Clb; School Play; Capt Cheerleading; Hon Roll; Ansthlgy.

PUSSINEN, CINDY E; Plainfield HS; Plainfield, CT; (Y); 4/146; Am Leg Aux Girls St; Yrbk Stf; Tennis; Cit Awd; Elks Awd; Hon Roll; NHS; Pres Schlr; Rotary Awd; Voice Dem Awd; Thames Vly Tech; Engrng.

PYE, RICHARD; Plainfield HS; Moosup, CT; (Y); Var Bsbl; Var Bsktbl; Var Ftbl; Nmrs Sprts Awd.

QUERCIA, KALEEN; Marianapolis Prep; Thompson, CT; (Y); 11/43; Intnl Clb; School Musical; VP Frsh Cls; Trs Jr Cls; Var Capt Sftbl; High Hon Roll; NHS; NEDT Awd; Yrbk Rptr; Yrbk Stf; Soccer Conf All Star Tm ; Bsktbl MVP 85-86.

QUINLEY, MATTHEW; Coginchaug Regional HS; Durham, CT; (Y); 9/135; Am Leg Boys St; Band; Concert Band; Jazz Band; Pep Band; NHS; Ntl Merit Ltr; Math Tm; Mrchg Band; School Musical; Mrshl Hahn Engrng Merit Schlrshp 86; Stu Sthrn Div Music Fstvl Band 86; Acad Achvt Awd 86; VA Poly-Tech Inst; Engrng.

QUINN, JENNIFER; Daniel Hand HS; Madison, CT; (Y); 51/229; French Clb; Band; Concert Band; Mrchg Band; Stage Crew; Yrbk Stf; Var Cheerleading; Var Crs Cntry; JV Trk; Declamation Fnlst; Lbrl Arts.

QUINN, JOHN; Kingswood-Oxford HS; W Hartford, CT; (Y); Aud/Vis; Latin Clb; PAVAS; Spanish Clb; Band; Concert Band; Pep Band; Stage Crew; Symp Band; Variety Show; VP Film Clb.

QUINN, KATHY; Sacred Heart Acad; Hamden, CT; (Y); FBLA; Rep Frsh Cls; Pres Soph Cls; VP Jr Cls; Chrmn Sr Cls; High Hon Roll; NHS; NEDT Awd; Spanish NHS; Stu Cncl; Srv Awd; St Mary Madgeline Schlrshp Awd; Bus.

QUINN, LISA; North West Catholic HS; N Granby, CT; (Y); Cmnty Wkr; Pep Clb; Band; Lit Mag; Rep Stu Cncl; High Hon Roll; Hon Roll; NHS; Physician Asstnt.

QUINN, PAMELA MICHELE; Ridgefield HS; Ridgefield, CT; (Y); 1/330; Trs Stu Cncl; Capt Crs Cntry; Capt Trk; Dnfth Awd; NHS; Ntl Merit Ltr; Val; Cmnty Wkr; German Clb; Band; Sec Ridgefield ABC 84-86; Ridgefield Yth Comm 84-86; Safe Rides Stu; Brown U; Bio-Chem.

QUINN, THOMAS; Cheshire HS; Cheshire, CT; (Y); Boy Scts; School Play; JV Crs Cntry; L Capt Trk; Hon Roll; Kiwanis Awd; Indr Trck Fld MVP 86.

QUINT, KRIS; Nonnewaug HS; Woodbury, CT; (Y); Art Clb; Dance Clb; Girl Scts; JA; Ski Clb; School Musical; School Play; Yrbk Stf; Gym; Hon Roll; Typing Awd 83-84; Foods Awd 84-85; Art.

QUINT, TIMOTHY; Holy Cross HS; Thomaston, CT; (Y); Band; Concert Band; Jazz Band; Mrchg Band; Orch; Pep Band; School Musical; School Play; Jhnsn & Wls; Htl-Rstrnt Mgmt.

QUIRKE, JEFFREY; Pomperaug Regional HS; Southbury, CT; (Y); 4/194; Capt Chess Clb; Math Tm; Model UN; Mgr Bsktbl; Golf; Score Keeper; High Hon Roll; NHS; St Schlr; Quiz Bowl; Cunningham Math Awd 86; Wrocester Polytech; Mech Engrg.

QUSBA, SANDEEP; Avon Old Farms HS; Avon, CT; (Y); 4/105; Office Aide; Radio Clb; Yrbk Stf; Rep Frsh Cls; JV Bsktbl; JV Ftbl; Var Trk; Hon Roll; Frgn Lang Poetry Cont 83; Geom Bk Prz 85; Law.

RABASSA, ANA; Low Heywood Thomas HS; Stamford, CT; (Y); 4/38; AFS; Nwsp Ed-Chief; Rptr Yrbk Stf; Trs Jr Cls; Var Bsktbl; Var Fld Hcky; Var Capt Lcrss; Hon Roll; Spanish NHS; Mary Rodgers Rpr Schlrshp 86; Mst Imprvd Lacrosse 84; Mst Imprvd Bsktbl 85.

RABENOLD, CHRISTA; Brien Mc Mahon HS; Norwalk, CT; (Y); 4/288; VP Latin Clb; Ski Clb; Spanish Clb; Yrbk Stf; Trs Jr Cls; Trs Sr Cls; Powder Puff Ftbl; Trk; NHS; Sal; U NC-CHAPEL HILL.

RABIDEAU, DAVID; Ridgefield HS; Ridgefield, CT; (Y); 157/380; Boy Scts; Band; Jazz Band; Mrchg Band; Ftbl; High Hon Roll; Hon Roll; Algebr II Top Stu Awd 86; Bio Recgntn Awd 85; Bus.

RACZKA, LINDA; Southington HS; Southington, CT; (Y); 61/600; German Clb; L Socr; Hon Roll; NHS; Geothe Inst Grmn Awd Schlrshp 85; Poli Sci.

RADEMACHER, LAWRENCE R; Bristol Eastern HS; Bristol, CT; (Y); Pres Trs French Clb; Model UN; Political Wkr; SADD; Nwsp Phtg; VP Stu Cncl; Dnfth Awd; Hon Roll; NHS; Repub Congrssnl Page 85; Amer U; Politics.

RAFFAELE, MICHELE; North Haven HS; North Haven, CT; (Y); 10/280; Nwsp Stf; Yrbk Stf; Swmmng; Hon Roll; Fidle Socty Frgn Lang Clb 84-86; Pedtrcn.

RAFFIN, CHRISTINE; East Catholic HS; Marlborough, CT; (Y); 106/284; Church Yth Grp; Girl Scts; Band; Var Capt Bsktbl; Var Capt Socr; Var Capt Sftbl; High Hon Roll; Hon Roll; All ACC 1st Team All Lge Sftbl & Soccer 86; Hnbl Mntn All St Soccer 86; U Of CT; Anml Sci.

RAGAGLIA, JOSEPH; Holy Cross HS; Waterbury, CT; (Y); 18/380; Q&S; VP Service Clb; Nwsp Phtg; Nwsp Rptr; Yrbk Stf; Trs Soph Cls; High Hon Roll; VP NHS; Soc Studys Hnr Soc 86; Amer Legn Awd 83.

RAMIREZ, DAWN; Lauralton Hall HS; Bridgeport, CT; (Y); Drama Clb; Yrbk Stf; Rep Stu Cncl; Sacred Heart U; Advrstng Exec.

RANA, JEFFREY; St Bernard HS; Bradford, RI; (Y); 49/265; Engrng.

RANANDO, LYNNE; Holy Cross HS; Waterbury, CT; (Y); 29/346; Spanish Clb; JV Var Bsktbl; High Hon Roll; NHS; Sportsmans Clb Awd 86; Boston U Schrlshp Bsktbl; Boston U; Physcl Thrpy.

RANCIATO, STEPHANIE; Lyman Hall HS; Wallingford, CT; (Y); DECA; FBLA; Varsity Clb; Variety Show; Bsktbl; Cheerleading; Gym; Sftbl; CC Awd; Chmbr Comm Deca Srvyng Twn Wllngfrd 86; Albertus Magnus Coll; Fshn Merc.

RANDALL, DIANA LEE; Valley Regional HS; Deep River, CT; (Y); 13/130; Am Leg Aux Girls St; Spanish Clb; Nwsp Rptr; JV Var Sftbl; Var Capt Tennis; Mst Imprvd Tnns Plyr 84; Giardini Ctznshp Awd 86; Amer Lgn Pst Rsdnt Awd 86; Clark U.

RANERI, PATRICIA; Cheshire HS; Cheshire, CT; (Y); Pres Church Yth Grp; SADD; Chorus; School Musical; Lit Mag; Rep Soph Cls; Rep Jr Cls; Rep Sr Cls; JV Fld Hcky; Var Socr; Mst Vlbl Dbls Tm Girls Tnns 86; Mst Imprvd Girls Tnns 86; Englsh.

RANNIE, ROBERT; Wilby HS; Waterbury, CT; (Y); Art Clb; Band; Socr; Swmmng; Hon Roll; Accntng.

RASHBA, GARY; Amity Regional SR HS; Orange, CT; (Y); 26/388; Political Wkr; Pres Temple Yth Grp; Nwsp Bus Mgr; Pres Soph Cls; NHS; Pres Schlr; Am Leg Boys St; Camera Clb; French Clb; Model UN; Cert Merit Outstndng Svc Amer Pres Rgn 84; Syngge Yth Awd Outstndng Avc 86; Abrhm Jsha Hschl Hon Soc; Brandeis U; Govt.

RASTEN, PETER; Southington HS; Southington, CT; (Y); German Clb; Band; Concert Band; Bowling; Cmrcl Pilot.

RATKUS, CARRIE; Trumbull HS; Trumbull, CT; (Y); AFS; French Clb; Hosp Aide; JA; Stu Cncl; Fld Hcky; Swmmng; Trk; Cit Awd; Hon Roll; Cheseborough Ponds Art Awd 84; U Richmond; Pre-Law.

RAVIZZA, TRACEY; Berlin HS; Berlin, CT; (Y); 14/200; Girl Scts; Powder Puff Ftbl; Trk; Vllybl; Hon Roll; NHS; U CT; Med.

RAWSON, LESLEY; Southington HS; Southington, CT; (Y); Sftbl; Hon Roll; CCSU; Bus.

RAYMOND, DAVID; Holy Cross HS; Waterbury, CT; (Y); 88/396; Church Yth Grp; Latin Clb; Im Bsktbl; Capt Ftbl; Capt Var Lcrss; Im Vllybl; Hon Roll; NHS; ARCH.

RAZZANO, PASQUALE; Staples HS; Westport, CT; (Y); Ftbl; L Lcrss; Powder Puff Ftbl; Wrstlng; Psych.

REALE, ENZO J; Enrico Fermi HS; Enfield, CT; (Y); 3/341; Scholastic Bowl; Ski Clb; Stu Cncl; Tennis; High Hon Roll; Pres NHS; Yale Book Awd 86; History Awd 86; Engrng.

REARDON, GAIL; Windsor HS; Windsor, CT; (Y); 12/316; FBLA; Intnl Clb; Spanish Clb; Nwsp Rptr; Elks Awd; High Hon Roll; Pres Schlr; Spanish NHS; Harvard Bk Awd; Scholar Recog Prgm; Windsor Democ Wmns Clb Awd; Regis Coll; Comm.

REBSTOCK, STACY; Francis T Maloney HS; Meriden, CT; (Y); Key Clb; Nwsp Stf; Var Tennis; Hon Roll; Exclnc Spanch 85; Journlsm.

RECUPIDO, GINA; Stratford HS; Stratford, CT; (Y); 70/257; JA; Office Aide; Off Frsh Cls; Off Soph Cls; Off Jr Cls; Hon Roll; U Of New Haven; Hotel & Rest.

REDDEN, DENISE N; Naugatuck HS; Naugatuck, CT; (Y); 20/340; Drama Clb; Office Aide; Pres Spanish Clb; NHS; Church Yth Grp; Acpl Chr; Chorus; Church Choir; High Hon Roll; Police Mem Schlrshp 86; NHS Cls Poet 86; Walter Ruth Parsons Schrlsh P86; Bentley Coll; Econ.

REDEN, ROBERT; Jonathan Law HS; Milford, CT; (Y); Intnl Clb; Ski Clb; Spanish Clb; Band; Chorus; Concert Band; Jazz Band; Mrchg Band; Swmmng; Hon Roll; Spn Clb Awd 86; Band Awds 84-86; Alumni Support Grp 86; Sthrn CT ST U; Spn.

REDINGER, PAULA; Rockville HS; Vernon, CT; (Y); 4/320; Church Yth Grp; Jazz Band; Var Trk; JP Sousa Awd; NHS; Wm Oster Bio Awd 86; Am Assn Phsycs Tchrs Awd 86; All-ST, All N E Musi Fests 83-86; Boston U; Appld Music.

REDLICH, LISA; Brookfield HS; Brookfield, CT; (S); DECA; Hosp Aide; Nwsp Sprt Ed; Yrbk Stf; Var Capt Gym; High Hon Roll; FBLA; Service Clb; Temple Yth Grp; Variety Show; Apprl & Accessries 1st & 3rd Pl 85-86; Cert Of Achvt 84-85; U Of RI.

REDMAN, JENNIFER; East Hartford HS; E Hartford, CT; (Y); 3/396; Am Leg Aux Girls St; French Clb; Quiz Bowl; Band; Concert Band; Mrchg Band; Orch; School Musical; Capt Ed Yrbk Stf; Rep Frsh Cls; Naval Academy.

REDMAN, KRISTEN; Bristol Central HS; Bristol, CT; (Y); GAA; Sec Latin Clb; Yrbk Stf; Trs Soph Cls; Var Cheerleading; JV Swmmng; JV Trk; Hon Roll; Rcmmnd All Star Chrldng Camp Advisor JR; Pblc Rltns.

REED, APRIL; Trumbull HS; Trumbull, CT; (Y); AFS; Aud/Vis; Church Yth Grp; Drama Clb; Chorus; High Hon Roll; NHS; Ntl Merit Ltr; U Of CT; Humn Dvlpmt.

REELITZ, KATHRYN; St Bernard HS; Gales Ferry, CT; (Y); 6/289; Church Yth Grp; 4-H; Yrbk Ed-Chief; Chrmn Stu Cncl; Mgr Ftbl; JV Var Trk; 4-H Awd; NHS; Ntl Merit SF; Ledyard Lions Clb Schlrshp 86; George Washington U; Intl Bus.

REESE, DAVID; Pomperaug Regional HS; Middlebury, CT; (Y); 54/191; Debate Tm; Exploring; Model UN; Nwsp Rptr; Cert Merit Living Hist & Law Debat Pro 83; Natl Sci Olympiad Bio 84; ST Legisltve Explrng Actvts 85; Police Offcr.

REGAN, KATE; Choate Rosemary Hall HS; Katonah, NY; (S); Art Clb; Church Yth Grp; Acpl Chr; Chorus; Orch; School Musical; JV Fld Hcky; Var L Ice Hcky; JV Sftbl; Var Trk; Music Awd-Hrvy Schl NY 84; Outstndng Fresh Awd-Hrvy Schl 84.

REGAN, MEREDITH; Tolland HS; Tolland, CT; (Y); 16/165; Ski Clb; Band; Rep Frsh Cls; Rep Jr Cls; Rep Sr Cls; Cheerleading; Tennis; High Hon Roll; Hon Roll; NHS; Stonehill Coll; Math.

REGAN, MIKE; Derby HS; Ansonia, CT; (Y); 33/120; French Clb; Comm.

REH, MARY BETH; Saint Josephs HS; Shelton, CT; (Y); 96/275; Spanish Clb; Off Frsh Cls; Off Soph Cls; Stu Cncl; Crs Cntry; Trk; High Hon Roll; Hon Roll; Scndry Educ.

REID, MARK; Rockville HS; Manchester, CT; (S); 71/361; English Clb; FFA; Hon Roll; Natl Dairy Prdct Awd-Brnz 85; Vet.

REID, THOMAS; Holy Cross HS; Prospect, CT; (Y); 141/352; Church Yth Grp; PAVAS; Ftbl; Lcrss; Hon Roll; Jr NHS; Natl Achvt Schlrshp Pgm Achvt Awd; Bus.

REIL, JENNIFER; Lyme-Old Lyme HS; Old Lyme, CT; (Y); AFS; Chorus; School Musical; High Hon Roll; VP Church Yth Grp; Drama Clb; Hon Roll; Tri-M Muscic Hnr Soc 86; Art Schlrshp Lyme Acad Fine Arts 86; AFS Sumr Progrm Brazl 86; Art.

REILLY, JAMES; The Taft HS; Bloomfield, NJ; (Y); Chess Clb; German Clb; Varsity Clb; School Play; Lit Mag; Rep Frsh Cls; JV Bsbl; L Ftbl; L Ice Hcky; JV Lcrss.

REILLY, KIMBERLY; Sacred Heart Acad; Hamden, CT; (Y); FBLA; Sec School Musical; Ed Yrbk Stf; JV Bsktbl; Var Capt Sftbl; Im Swmmng; Im Vllybl; NHS; All Cnfrnc Sftbl Tm 2nd Tm 86.

REILLY, MARY; Holy Cross HS; Waterbury, CT; (Y); Scholastic Bowl; Spanish Clb; Var Crs Cntry; Var Trk; High Hon Roll; NHS; Spanish NHS; Awd-Hghst Avrg Spnsh Hnrs II & III 85 & 86.

REIMER, LISA; Manchester HS; Manchester, CT; (Y); 7/500; AFS; Cmnty Wkr; German Clb; Math Clb; Model UN; Office Aide; Spanish Clb; Socr; High Hon Roll; Hon Roll; Yale Book Adw 85; U Conn; Chem Engr.

REINHARD, DONNA; Southington HS; Southington, CT; (Y); 102/600; Pep Clb; Band; Chorus; Church Choir; Concert Band; Swing Chorus; Bowling; Mgr(s); Trk; Hon Roll; Briarwood Coll; Accntnt.

REINWARDT, SILKE; Brandford HS; West Germany; (Y); Drama Clb; PAVAS; Chorus; School Musical; School Play; Stage Crew; Stu Cncl; JV Vllybl; Hon Roll; JV Vllybl Ltr 85; Arista Frnch Frgn Lang Awd 86; Hnr Soc 86; Otto Yahn Schule; Engl.

REISNER, JENNIFER; Staples HS; Westport, CT; (Y); 3/408; Church Yth Grp; Sec Key Clb; Acpl Chr; Band; Chorus; Yrbk Stf; Jr NHS; Hon Ushr For Grad Cls Of 86.

REITENBACH, CLAUDIA; Greenwich HS; Cos Cob, CT; (Y); Church Yth Grp; Cmnty Wkr; Drama Clb; Hosp Aide; Service Clb; Chorus; School Musical; School Play; Variety Show.

REK, LAURA; Naugatuck HS; Naugatuck, CT; (Y); 17/309; Pres GAA; Sec Band; Jazz Band; Mrchg Band; Variety Show; Gym; Tennis; Hon Roll; NHS; Prfct Atten Awd; Amer Legn Auxlry Schlrshp 86; Fml Athltc Schlrshp 86; All Sthrn Band Regnls; U Of CT; Phrmcy.

REMISZEWSKI, CAROL; St Marys HS; New Haven, CT; (Y); 25/101; Ski Clb; Lit Mag; Rep Stu Cncl; Var Trk; JV Var Vllybl; Hon Roll; Peer Tutr Vlntr Awd 86; Itln Hnr Socty 86; U Of New Haven; Bus.

REMLIN, LISA; Staples HS; Westport, CT; (Y); Art Clb; VP Church Yth Grp; Cmnty Wkr; Radio Clb; Acpl Chr; Chorus; Church Choir; Yrbk Stf; Hon Roll; Exc Art 85-86; Assumption Coll.

RENDA, CRAIG; Danbury HS; Danbury, CT; (Y); Chorus; Variety Show; Var Bsbl; Var Ftbl; Hon Roll; Chrs Awd, Hnr Rll 83-84; Home Cmng King; Itln Clb Pres; Itln Clb Awd Schlrshp 85-86; Mt St Marys College; Acctg.

RENDA, JOHN; Robert E Fitch SR HS; Groton, CT; (Y); Drama Clb; Chrmn Intnl Clb; Rep Stu Cncl; JV Crs Cntry; JV Trk; High Hon Roll; Hon Roll; Comp Sci.

RENDOCK, DUSTIN; Windsor Public HS; Windsor, CT; (Y); 94/360; Boy Scts; Church Yth Grp; Cmnty Wkr; Im Badmtn; Im Bsbl; Im Vllybl; God Cntry Awd; Hon Roll; Yth In Govt Day 83-84; Crmnl Jstc.

RENOLA, MATTHEW EDWARD; Guilford HS; Guilford, CT; (Y); 60/350; Church Yth Grp; Letterman Clb; Varsity Clb; Nwsp Stf; Lit Mag; Rep Stu Cncl; JV Bsbl; Capt Ice Hcky; Capt Socr; Yale Frntrs Appld Sci Pgm 85-86; Safe Rdrs Mbr-Drvr 85-86.

RENZULLI, DAVID; Fairfield College Preparatory Schl; Southport, CT; (Y); Cmnty Wkr; Key Clb; Pep Clb; Service Clb; Spanish Clb; Yrbk Stf; Capt Bsktbl; Capt Golf; NHS; Pres Schlr; Acadmc Excllnc Awd 86; Wakemn Boys Clb Boy Of Yr 85; George B Thms Awd 86; U Of Richmond.

RESNISKY, PHILIP A; East Lyme HS; Niantic, CT; (Y); Cmnty Wkr; Wt Lftg; High Hon Roll; Hon Roll; William H Chapman Fndtn Schlrshp 86; U Of CT; Acctg.

REUTER, DEBORAH; Bethel HS; Bethel, CT; (Y); 18/240; AFS; Quiz Bowl; Stage Crew; Variety Show; Nwsp Sprt Ed; Yrbk Stf; Var L Crs Cntry; High Hon Roll; NHS; Bethel Wmns Clb Schlrshp; Prsdntl Acdmc Ftnss Awd; IN U; Poly Sci.

REYES, ELIZABETH; Stratford HS; Stratford, CT; (Y); 28/231; Sec FBLA; Girl Scts; Hosp Aide; Keywanettes; Hon Roll; Northeastern U; Physcl Thrpy.

REYNOLDS, DAWN; The Morgan Schl; Clinton, CT; (Y); 2/170; Church Yth Grp; FCA; Chorus; Church Choir; High Hon Roll; Eng Awd 83-86; Sci Awd 83-86; Mth Awd 83-85; Chrstn Educ.

REYNOLDS, LELAND THOMAS; Lyme-Old Lyme HS; Lyme, CT; (Y); 21/130; Church Yth Grp; Cmnty Wkr; Var L Bsktbl; Vllybl; Wt Lftg; Hon Roll; Vlntr Firemn 85; Crw Vrsty Lttr 85-87; 2nd Hd CT Regatta 85; Bus.

REYNOLDS JR, MICHAEL J; Oliver Wolcott Tech Schl; Warren, CT; (Y); Church Yth Grp; Exploring; Bsbl; Bsktbl; Ftbl; JV Var Socr; Swmmng; Trk; Hon Roll; Boys Clb Am; Abilene Christian U; Ind Tech.

REZNICEK, PETER; Berlin HS; Kensington, CT; (Y); Drama Clb; JA; Quiz Bowl; Ski Clb; School Musical; Var L Crs Cntry; JV Golf; Hon Roll; Bentley Coll; Econ.

REZNIK, DEIRDRE M; Sacred Heart Acad; Branford, CT; (Y); FBLA; Stage Crew; Yrbk Stf; Var Sftbl; Hon Roll; NHS; Computer Clb; Stat Bsktbl; Im Vllybl; FBLA 1st Pl Parl Procedures Ldrshp Convntn 86; Engr.

REZOSKI, LISA; East Catholic HS; Marlborough, CT; (Y); 76/281; Pres Art Clb; Church Yth Grp; Cmnty Wkr; Yrbk Stf; Lit Mag; High Hon Roll; Hon Roll; Syracuse U; Cmmnctns.

RHODES, JULIA A; Central HS; Bridgeport, CT; (Y); 4/250; JA; Spanish Clb; SADD; Color Guard; Nwsp Ed-Chief; Nwsp Rptr; VP Jr Cls; Cit Awd; High Hon Roll; Pres NHS; Hgst Spnsh Stu Awd; Negro Bus Prof Yth Clb Awd; Amherst Coll; Pol Sci.

RIBANDO JR, FRANK; Holy Cross HS; Woodbury, CT; (Y); 169/400; Teachers Aide; Yrbk Phtg; Var Capt Ftbl; JV Capt Lcrss; Hon Roll; 3rd Pl Schl Cndy Drv, 3rd Pl Chrty Wk 85; 3rd Pl Soc Sci Fair 85; 1st Pl Chrty Wk 86; Navel Acad; Pilot.

RICCARDINO, PATRICK; Marianapolis Prep; Plainfield, CT; (Y); 1/44; Quiz Bowl; Nwsp Stf; Bausch & Lomb Sci Awd; High Hon Roll; NHS; Ntl Merit Ltr; Boy Scts; NEDT Cert Of Awd; Hrvrd-Rdclff Bk Prz; Fthr Anthny Kacevivius Schlrshp; Quntl Schlrshp; Rensselaer Plytech; Nclr Physcs.

RICCI, SUSAN; Killingly HS; Danielson, CT; (Y); 29/297; Church Yth Grp; Latin Clb; Band; Pres Stu Cncl; Cheerleading; Crs Cntry; Socr; Sftbl; Hon Roll; NHS; All Amrcn Chrldr 86; CT Stu Ldrshp Awd 86; Rnnr Up All ECC Chrldr Awd 85; Pre Law.

RICCIARDI, TRICIA; Crosby HS; Waterbury, CT; (Y); Church Yth Grp; Key Clb; Political Wkr; Church Choir; Art Clb; Chess Clb; Drama Clb; French Clb; School Play; Nwsp Stf; JR Intern Pgm 86; Pre-Law.

RICCITELLI JR, JOSEPH; East Haven HS; East Haven, CT; (Y); CAP; Drama Clb; School Play; Nwsp Stf; Comp Sci.

RICE, BRENT; Masuk HS; Monroe, CT; (Y); 40/275; JV Socr; Var Capt Tennis; Hon Roll; NHS; Pres Schlr; NHS 86; Pres Schlr 86; Vrsty Capt Ten Tm 86; James Madison U; Chem.

RICE, ETTA; Oliver Wolcott Tech RV HS; Winsted, CT; (Y); 62/170; VICA; Nwsp Rptr; Nwsp Sprt Ed; Rep Soph Cls; Rep Jr Cls; Trs Stu Cncl; Var Capt Bsktbl; Var Sftbl; Elks Awd; Hrdrssng.

RICE, MARGARET; Holy Cross HS; Cheshire, CT; (Y); 51/380; French Clb; Var Capt Crs Cntry; Var Trk; French Hon Soc; High Hon Roll; NHS; Spg Trck-All ST, All Naugatuck Vly Leag, Most Impvd Rnnr 86; X-Cntry All Naugatuck Vly Leag 84 & 85; Nutrtn.

RICH, JILL; Old Saybrook SR HS; Old Saybrook, CT; (Y); AFS; French Clb; Latin Clb; School Musical; Stage Crew; Yrbk Stf; Rep Stu Cncl; High Hon Roll; Hon Roll; NHS; Tutor Elem Stu 83-84.

RICH, TAMMY; Cheshire HS; Cheshire, CT; (Y); 3/364; Service Clb; SADD; Temple Yth Grp; Yrbk Stf; Rep Frsh Cls; Rep Soph Cls; Rep Jr Cls; Rep Sr Cls; Stu Cncl; Var Gym; Twn Clrk For A Day Stdnt Govt Day 86; Hnrd Schlstc Banq 86; Pres New Haven Cncl BBYO Yth Grp 86-87; Pre-Law.

RICHARDSON, MICHELLE; Holy Cross HS; Waterbury, CT; (Y); Hosp Aide; JA; Spanish Clb; SADD; Rep Stu Cncl; Var JV Cheerleading; JV Crs Cntry; JV Trk; Hon Roll; Prfct Atten Awd; VP Finance Of Year JA 84 & 85; Bus Admn.

RICHARDSON, MICHELLE; Oliver Wolcott Tech; Harwinton, CT; (Y); Dance Clb; Library Aide; VICA; Chorus; Church Choir; Madrigals; Nwsp Phtg; Nwsp Rptr; Var Cheerleading; Var Pom Pon; Dance.

RICHER, DANIEL; Trumbull HS; Trumbull, CT; (Y); AFS; Boy Scts; Latin Clb; Spanish Clb; Temple Yth Grp; Yrbk Stf; High Hon Roll; NHS; Ntl Merit Ltr; Abraham Joshua Heschel Soc 86; Untd Synagogue Yth Rgnl Committee 86.

RICHEY, TOM; Darien HS; Darien, CT; (Y); 35/260; JA; Ski Clb; Nwsp Rptr; JV Var Socr; French Hon Soc; High Hon Roll; Hon Roll; Ntl Merit SF; Wesleyan U.

RICHTER, MARC; Ridgefield HS; Ridgefield, CT; (Y); 215/387; Drama Clb; Ski Clb; Temple Yth Grp; School Musical; School Play; Stage Crew; Variety Show; Yrbk Stf; JV Socr; Short Stories Piece-Lit Art Mag 83; Pottery Dsplyd Schl Art Shw 84-85; Psych.

RICKERD, NANCY; Amity Regional SR HS; Branford, CT; (Y); 138/388; French Clb; Office Aide; Political Wkr; Spanish Clb; Variety Show; JV Cheerleading; Stat Mgr(s); L Var Socr; L Var Trk; Cit Awd; Nrthstrn U; Bus Mntmnt.

RIDEOUT, BETHANY; Berlin HS; Kensington, CT; (Y); Church Yth Grp; Chorus; Church Choir; Hon Roll; Best Typing 1 Stu 84; French II Achvt Awd 86; U S Hist Achvt Awd 86; Missionary Trip Kingston Jamaica; Central Bible Coll; Music.

RIDER, LEANN; Wheeler HS; N Stonington, CT; (Y); Band; Var Sftbl; Var Vllybl; Cit Awd; High Hon Roll; Hon Roll; NHS.

RIEGEL, BRAD; Brookfield HS; Brookfield, CT; (Y); 1/176; Math Clb; Band; Concert Band; Jazz Band; Mrchg Band; Tennis; High Hon Roll; Trs NHS; Pres Schlr; Val; Arntcl Engrng.

RIGGIO, KENNETH C; St Lukes Schl; New Canaan, CT; (Y); Boy Scts; Church Yth Grp; JA; Band; Concert Band; Mrchg Band; Pep Band; Bsbl; Ftbl; Trk; Math.

RIGGS, ERICA; Ridgefield HS; Ridgefield, CT; (S); 62/387; Church Yth Grp; Cmnty Wkr; Hst DECA; Orch; School Musical; JV Sftbl; Hon Roll; Mrchg Band; Variety Show; All ST Orch 85; VALUE 84-86; Orientatn Soc 85-86.

RIGGS, PATRICK; Thomas Snell Weaver HS; Hartford, CT; (Y); Latin Clb; Spanish Clb; Church Choir; School Musical; Bsktbl; Trk; Hon Roll; Bus Admin.

RIGOGLIOSO, RAY; Brookfield HS; Brookfield, CT; (Y); Concert Band; Mrchg Band; Pep Band; Lit Mag; Trk; High Hon Roll; Outstndng JR Mrchng Band 85-86; Western CT ST U; Bus.

RIHM, LUCINDA; Rham HS; Marlborough, CT; (Y); 12/200; Church Yth Grp; Trs French Clb; Trs Band; Yrbk Ed-Chief; Trs Soph Cls; Pres Jr Cls; Pres Sr Cls; High Hon Roll; Jr NHS; Sec NHS; Elem Ed.

RIKER, KATHERINE; Westhill HS; Stamford, CT; (Y); 39/409; Hosp Aide; JA; Pep Clb; Soroptimist; Yrbk Stf; Hst Sr Cls; Chrmn Stu Cncl; Var Fld Hcky; Skidmore; Lbrl Arts.

RILEY, MARY CHRISTINE; Miss Porters Schl; Larchmont, NY; (Y); Computer Clb; Hosp Aide; School Play; Var Golf; Swmmng; Var Tennis; Hon Roll; NHS; 2nd Hon Roll 84-85; Magna Cum Laude 83; Afro-Asian Stds Cert Of Excllnc 83; U Of CA; Ecnmcs.

RILEY, MEGHAN; Staples HS; Santa Barbara, CA; (Y); Camera Clb; Dance Clb; Drama Clb; School Musical; Yrbk Phtg; JV Bsbl; Im Powder Puff Ftbl; NHS; Spanish NHS; Joe Trmne-1st Pl Dnc Awd Fnlst, 1/2 Fnlst 85, 86; Dnc Amer-1st Pl Dnc Awd 86; U Of CA-SAN Diego; Pre-Med.

RINALDI, FILOMENA; Holy Cross HS; Oakville, CT; (Y); 23/346; Art Clb; Drama Clb; School Musical; School Play; Stage Crew; High Hon Roll; NHS; Italian Hnr Scty 85; Coronas Clb Awd 86; Leavenworth Fndtn Schlrshp 86; U Of CT; Bus.

RINALDI, TERESA; Wethersfield HS; Wethersfield, CT; (Y); Church Yth Grp; Cmnty Wkr; Girl Scts; Hosp Aide; Gym; Mgr Socr; Hon Roll; Prfct Atten Awd.

RING, DAN; New Canaan HS; New Canaan, CT; (Y); French Clb; Var Ice Hcky; Var Lcrss; DAR Awd; Law.

RINGSTAD, CHRISTINE; Torringtron HS; Torrington, CT; (Y); 15/366; Art Clb; Girl Scts; Math Clb; Spanish Clb; Yrbk Stf; Var Swmmng; High Hon Roll; NHS; New England Math Lge, 3rd Hghst Scorer 86; ; U Of CT Co-Op Prog; Acdmc Achvmnt 85-86; Comm.

RIPPEL, CHARLIE; Seymour HS; Seymour, CT; (Y).

RISCH, JOLENE; Greenwich HS; Cos Cob, CT; (Y); Cmnty Wkr; Drama Clb; VP Service Clb; Temple Yth Grp; School Musical; School Play; Variety Show; Nwsp Bus Mgr; Nwsp Rptr; Badmtn; Brandes U.

RISH, MICHELLE; Amity Regional HS; Woodbridge, CT; (Y); 71/388; VP Drama Clb; Red Cross Aide; School Play; Variety Show; Yrbk Stf; Sec Frsh Cls; Rep Stu Cncl; JV Var Cheerleading; Hon Roll; NHS; Cum Laude Ntl Latin Exam; Psychlgy.

RISTOW, JAMES; Oliver Wolcot RVT HS; Thomaston, CT; (Y); Elect Engr.

RITCHIE, KRISTEN; Farmington HS; Farmington, CT; (Y); 22/210; Church Yth Grp; Rep Thesps; Sec Varsity Clb; Chorus; School Musical; Swing Chorus; Yrbk Sprt Ed; Var L Tennis; High Hon Roll; Hon Roll; 2nd Hnrs Spnsh Poetry Memorization Cont 84; Duke U; Intl Rltns.

RIVERA, CYNTHIA; Nonnewaug HS; Prospect, CT; (Y); Church Yth Grp; FFA; Girl Scts; Band; School Play; Yrbk Stf; Stu Cncl; Sftbl; Trk; Csmtlgy.

RIVERA, OMAYRA; Hartford HS; Hartford, CT; (Y); 9/300; AFS; Am Leg Aux Girls St; VP JA; Model UN; Rep Stu Cncl; JV Sftbl; Mgr Wrstlng; Prfct Atten Awd; Wm C Gease Ltn Prz 85; Hannah Co Flaherty Ltn III Awd 86; Intl Affrs.

RIVERS, MONA; Academy Of The Holy Family; Willimantic, CT; (Y); 1/44; Art Clb; Drama Clb; Red Cross Aide; Acpl Chr; Chorus; School Musical; School Play; Stage Crew; High Hon Roll; NHS; Pres Natl Hnr Socty 86-87; Natl Art Hnr Socty 86; Arch.

RIZZA, ROBERTA; Lyman Hall HS; Wallingford, CT; (Y); Drama Clb; FHA; Ed Key Clb; School Musical; Ed Lit Mag; Hon Roll; Prfct Atten Awd; Outstndng Englsh Awd 85; Childrens Lit Inst 86-88; Albentus Magnus Coll; Bio.

RIZZI, THOMAS; Torrington HS; Torrington, CT; (Y); 15/278; Church Yth Grp; Latin Clb; Model UN; High Hon Roll; NHS; Rep Soph Cls; Rep Jr Cls; Yrbk Stf; Pub Term Paper Westministes Sem 86; Aero Sp Engr.

RIZZO, LOUIS; St Joseph HS; Shelton, CT; (Y); 82/220; Pres Church Yth Grp; Drama Clb; Teachers Aide; Thesps; Band; Chorus; Concert Band; School Musical; Stage Crew; Hon Roll; Intl Thespian Soc 85; Fordham U; Cmnctns.

RIZZO, RENEE; Norwalk HS; Norwalk, CT; (Y); 19/422; FBLA; Spanish Clb; Yrbk Stf; Rep Frsh Cls; Rep Soph Cls; Rep Jr Cls; Rep Sr Cls; Capt Cheerleading; Powder Puff Ftbl; High Hon Roll; Engrng Physcs.

ROACH, KIMBERLY; Kingswood-Oxford School; Bristol, CT; (Y); 4-H; French Clb; Intnl Clb; Political Wkr; Service Clb; Chorus; JV Fld Hcky; Im Mgr(s); 4-H Awd; Hon Roll; Rensselear Mdl 86; Engrng.

ROBBINS, NICHOLAS; Avon Old Farms Schl; Avon, CT; (Y); 10/105; German Clb; Intnl Clb; Letterman Clb; Math Tm; Model UN; Color Guard; Nwsp Ed-Chief; Ed Lit Mag; Var Ice Hcky; Var Lcrss; Bio Awd; AP Hist Awd; Russn Hist Awd; CT College.

ROBERTS, DANIELLE; Maloney HS; Meriden, CT; (Y); Stu Cncl; Swmmng; DAR Awd; High Hon Roll; Hon Roll; Arch Engr.

ROBERTS, JENNIFER; Coginchaug HS; Durham, CT; (Y); Am Leg Aux Girls St; Yrbk Ed-Chief; Stu Cncl; Var L Cheerleading; Bausch & Lomb Sci Awd; NHS; Ntl Merit Ltr; AFS; Ski Clb; School Musical; HOBY Ldrshp Awd 85; Bishop Mc Farland K C Awd 86; Stu Cncl Merit Awd 86; Math.

ROBERTS JR, LEWIS CHARLES; East Hartford HS; E Hartford, CT; (Y); 23/441; Boy Scts; Pres Church Yth Grp; Church Choir; Var L Trk; God Cntry Awd; Hon Roll; NHS; Physcs.

ROBERTSON, KERRY; Wilton HS; Wilton, CT; (Y); Key Clb; Pep Clb; Rep Frsh Cls; Rep Soph Cls; Rep Stu Cncl; Var Crs Cntry; JV Fld Hcky; Var Trk; Hon Roll; Safe Rides Rep 84-87.

ROBINS, RACHEL; Norwalk HS; Norwalk, CT; (Y); 33/500; Cmnty Wkr; Red Cross Aide; Church Choir; Orch; Nwsp Stf; High Hon Roll; Hon Roll; NHS; Nwrlk Yth Symphny Yth Cmt 84-85; Ed.

ROBINSON, DARBY; Brookfield HS; Brookfield, CT; (Y); 31/210; AFS; Church Yth Grp; Hosp Aide; Math Tm; Chorus; Var Gym; Var Trk; Hon Roll; Pre-Med.

ROBINSON, DORI LEE; Farmington HS; Farmington, CT; (Y); FNA; Hosp Aide; VICA; Chorus; Yrbk Stf; Bsktbl; Cheerleading; Trk; Hon Roll; U CT; Nrs.

ROBINSON, ERIC; Torrington HS; Litchfield, CT; (Y); Church Yth Grp; Var Crs Cntry; JV Socr; Var Trk; Hon Roll; Bus.

ROBINSON, JAMES; St Joseph HS; Shelton, CT; (Y); Ftbl; Var Capt Socr; JV Var Trk.

ROBINSON, KESHIA; Jonathan Law HS; Milford, CT; (Y); Church Yth Grp; Intnl Clb; Pres Spanish Clb; Trs Jr Cls; Trs Sr Cls; Stu Cncl; Bowling; L Trk; High Hon Roll; Hon Roll; Frnch I Hgh Avg 86; Harvard; Intl Law.

ROBLES, SARA; St Bernard HS; Griswold, CT; (Y); 52/289; Church Yth Grp; Dance Clb; Drama Clb; Chorus; School Musical; School Play; Stage Crew; Stu Cncl; Hon Roll; Music Achvt Awd 83 & 84; Prfrmng Arts Awd 86; Northeastern U; Arch.

ROCCASECCA, DANTE; Berlin HS; Kensington, CT; (Y); Cmnty Wkr; Computer Clb; Exploring; Band; Concert Band; Mrchg Band; School Musical; Bowling; Fld Hcky; Golf; Bio.

ROCHELLE, DOUG; Norwalk HS; Norwalk, CT; (Y); 66/450; Boy Scts; Ski Clb; Yrbk Stf; VP Jr Cls; Var Ice Hcky; Var Lcrss; Bus Admin.

ROCHES, CATHERINE; Norwich Free Acad; Norwich, CT; (Y); Church Yth Grp; Drama Clb; German Clb; GAA; Girl Scts; Hosp Aide; PAVAS; SADD; Chorus; School Play; Boston U.

ROCKWELL II, ROGER; Mark T Sheehan HS; Chesire, CT; (Y); 17/207; Am Leg Boys St; High Hon Roll; Finc.

RODAS, MARTHA; Warren Harding HS; Bridgeport, CT; (Y); Church Yth Grp; Trs FBLA; Pres Intnl Clb; VP Sr Cls; Capt Vllybl; Hon Roll; NHS; Flag Corp; Stage Crew; Rep Soph Cls; Natl Hispanic Schlrshp Semi-Fin 85-86; Proj SEED Schlrshp 85; Northeastern U; Comp Sci.

RODKIN, JILL; Ridgefield HS; Ridgefield, CT; (Y); Pep Clb; Service Clb; Sec Spanish Clb; Yrbk Stf; Rep Jr Cls; Rep Stu Cncl; Var L Tennis; High Hon Roll; Hon Roll; Cmnty Wkr; Svc To Cls Awd 86; Pol Sci.

RODMAN, KIM ANNE; Kingswood-Oxford HS; Avon, CT; (Y); Church Yth Grp; Cmnty Wkr; Drama Clb; French Clb; Red Cross Aide; Church Choir; Concert Band; Mrchg Band; School Musical; School Play; USAA Awd-Sci 83; USAA Awd-Ldrshp 84; De Pauw U; Psy.

RODRIGUE, SUSAN; East Hartford HS; E Hartford, CT; (Y); 1/408; French Clb; Office Aide; Ski Clb; Variety Show; Yrbk Stf; Capt Cheerleading; Sftbl; High Hon Roll; NHS; Val; 4 Yr Eng Achvt Awd 86; 3 Yr Sci Achvt Awd 85; CIAC-CASS Schlr Ath 86; Wesleyan U; Med Sci.

RODRIGUES, ELIZABETH M; South Catholic HS; Rocky Hill, CT; (Y); 16/197; French Clb; Yrbk Stf; Lit Mag; Vllybl; High Hon Roll; Hon Roll; NHS; NEDT Awd; St Schlr; Chorus; Outstndng Svc Mntly Rtrded Awd 83; Assumption Coll; Social Svc.

RODRIGUES, LOU; Danbury HS; Danbury, CT; (Y); 123/500; Cmnty Wkr; Im Bsktbl; Var L Ftbl; Var Wt Lftg; Hon Roll; Mech Engr.

RODRIGUES, PAUL; Stratford HS; Stratford, CT; (Y); Computer Clb; JV Bsbl; JV Var Bsktbl; Accntng.

RODRIGUEZ, ANGEL; Notre Dame Catholic HS; Bridgeport, CT; (Y); #25 In Class; Boys Clb Am; Boy Scts; Exploring; Spanish Clb; Var Ftbl; Var Trk; High Hon Roll; Hon Roll; Spanish NHS; Eagle Scout 86; Ntl Hnr Hisp Schlr Semi-Fnlsts 85; U CT Day Of Pride Top 100 85; U Of CT; Psych.

RODRIGUEZ, FELIX; Sacred Heart HS; Waterbury, CT; (Y); 12/256; Boy Scts; Computer Clb; Var L Crs Cntry; Var Trk; High Hon Roll; Hon Roll; NHS; Spanish NHS; U CT; Comp Engrng.

RODRIGUEZ, LUZ; Richard C Lee HS; New Haven, CT; (Y); JA; Teachers Aide; Nwsp Stf; Awd Vlybl, Tnns; Awd Sthrn CT ST U; Comp.

ROELOFSEN, LORI; Haddam-Killingworth HS; Killingworth, CT; (Y); 8/111; Pres Church Yth Grp; Stu Cncl; Var Capt Fld Hcky; High Hon Roll; Lion Awd; Hst NHS; Pres Schlr; U CT Almni Assn Bk Awd, Excel Physcs.

ROGDAN, ANDREW; Greenwich HS; Greenwich, CT; (Y); Church Yth Grp; Key Clb; Spanish Clb; Band; Concert Band; Mrchg Band; Pep Band; School Play; Variety Show; Hon Roll; De Paul U; Engl.

ROGERS, AMY J; Robert E Fitch SR HS; Mystic, CT; (Y); 12/329; Drama Clb; Thesps; School Musical; Stage Crew; Nwsp Stf; Lit Mag; Pres Frsh Cls; Hon Roll; NCTE Awd; Pres NHS; Engl.

ROGERS, PAIGE; Holy Cross HS; Naugatuck, CT; (Y); Church Yth Grp; Drama Clb; PAVAS; Ski Clb; Spanish Clb; Varsity Clb; Band; Chorus; Concert Band; Mrchg Band; Holy Cross Grls Ski Tm Mst Val 86; Coach Of Lttl Lg Sccr Tm 86; Chld Study.

ROGERS, RITA-MARIE; Sacred Heart Acad; Hamden, CT; (Y); Church Yth Grp; Im Vllybl; Hon Roll; Prfct Atten Awd; Prft Atten 85-86; 1st Hnrs Awd Above 3.5 85-86; Nrsng.

ROGERS, TIM; New Canaan HS; New Canaan, CT; (Y); VP Church Yth Grp; Dance Clb; Var Capt Crs Cntry; Var Capt Trk; Hon Roll; Bus Adm.

ROHM, KIRA; Ledyard HS; Gales Ferry, CT; (Y); 11/261; AFS; Varsity Clb; Yrbk Stf; Off Soph Cls; Off Jr Cls; Var Capt Gym; High Hon Roll; Hon Roll; Trs NHS; Gymnstcs Cls M ST Chmpn & ST Opn Chmpn 86.

ROHR, KRISTINE; Tourtellotte HS; Webster, MA; (Y); #8 In Class; Drama Clb; Library Aide; VP Pep Clb; JV Bsktbl; High Hon Roll; Hon Roll; NHS.

ROJAS, MATIAS; Kent HS; Kent, CT; (Y); 1/180; Library Aide; Pres Frsh Cls; Rep Jr Cls; Sec Sr Cls; Sec Stu Cncl; High Hon Roll; Debate Tm; Acpl Chr; School Play; Cum Laude Soc 86; Editor The Kent Review 85-86; W Colored Bio Price & Chem Price 85-86; Poli Sci.

ROKE, IAN; Litchfield HS; Northfield, CT; (Y); Am Leg Boys St; Computer Clb; Math Tm; Radio Clb; Socr; High Hon Roll; NHS; Math.

ROLOFF, LOUIS; Stamford HS; Stamford, CT; (Y); French Clb; VP JA; Science Clb; Temple Yth Grp; JV Tennis; High Hon Roll; Hon Roll; Pres Stanford Leviticus AZA Yth Grp 85-86; Stanford Jew Ctr Teen Comm 85-86; Brdcstg.

ROLZHAUSEN, YVONNE; Academy Of Our Lady Of Mercy; Fairfield, CT; (Y); 27/111; Dance Clb; Drama Clb; French Clb; Latin Clb; Sec Model UN; Acpl Chr; Ed Lit Mag; Rep Stu Cncl; High Hon Roll; Sec NHS; Engl.

ROMAINE, ASHLEY; Miss Porters Schl; New York, NY; (Y); Dance Clb; Pres Latin Clb; Nwsp Phtg; Yrbk Stf; Rep Frsh Cls; Var Badmtn; JV Fld Hcky; Var Vllybl; High Hon Roll; Cert Honrbl Merit Cum Laude Natl Latn Exm 85; Cum Laude Soc 86; Cum Dignitate Societatis Classicae 86.

ROMAN, CHRISTINE; Old Saybrook SR HS; Old Saybrook, CT; (Y); AFS; Church Yth Grp; Latin Clb; SADD; Band; Jazz Band; Stage Crew; Nwsp Stf; Hon Roll; NEDT Awd; Stud Advsr Of Chrstn Ed At My Chrch 86; Elec Engr.

ROMAN, LYNDA; Mary Immaculate Acad; New Britain, CT; (S); Trs Girl Scts; Hosp Aide; VP Sec JA; Spanish Clb; Chorus; School Musical; JV Badmtn; Capt JV Bsktbl; Im Vllybl; Hon Roll; Englsh II Schlrshp Cert 85; Algbr I & Gemtry Schlrshp Cert 85; Spnsh I & II Schlrshp Cert 85; Math.

ROMANO, DAWN; Shelton HS; Huntington, CT; (Y); JA; Office Aide; Hon Roll; Nurses Aide Fshmn Yr; Fairfield U.

ROMANO, GAYLE; The Morgan Schl; Clinton, CT; (Y); Chorus; Rep Stu Cncl; Var Capt Cheerleading.

ROMARY, MARY ELLEN; Staples HS; Westport, CT; (Y); Key Clb; Acpl Chr; Chorus; Nwsp Rptr; Yrbk Stf; Hon Roll.

ROMEO, FRANK; Kingswood Oxford HS; Newington, CT; (Y); Service Clb; Spanish Clb; SADD; School Musical; School Play; Nwsp Stf; Rep Soph Cls; Rep Jr Cls; Var L Bsbl; Var L Bsktbl; Georgetown.

ROMMEY, TODD; Wilton HS; Wilton, CT; (Y); 76/352; Boy Scts; Church Yth Grp; Debate Tm; Band; Jazz Band; Mrchg Band; Symp Band; Trs Sr Cls; Tennis; Hon Roll.

RONVELWALA, LINA; Bullard Havens Tech; Shelton, CT; (S); Teachers Aide; Hon Roll; Prfct Atten Awd; Elec Stu Recvng Hnr Grds 84-85; Elec.

ROONEY, SUSAN; Canton HS; Collinsville, CT; (Y); 2/100; Am Leg Aux Girls St; Spanish Clb; Band; Concert Band; Nwsp Stf; Yrbk Bus Mgr; Rep Stu Cncl; JV Score Keeper; High Hon Roll; NHS; Trnty Coll Bk Awd 86; Bio.

ROOT, RENEE; Old Saybrook SR HS; Old Saybrook, CT; (Y); French Clb; SADD; Chorus; School Musical; Yrbk Bus Mgr; Yrbk Ed-Chief; Sec Jr Cls; Fld Hcky; Hon Roll; NHS; Awd For Excllnc In Hm Ecnmcs 85; Pre-Law.

ROPER, GREGORY B; Weaver HS; Hartford, CT; (Y); Art Clb; Teachers Aide; Swmmng; Wt Lftg; Prfct Atten Awd; Montserrat Coll Art; Illstrn.

ROSARBO, LOUISE; Sacred Heart Acad; New Haven, CT; (Y); 28/122; High Hon Roll; Msc Awd 86; Srv Awd 85-86; Prvdnc Coll; Pltcl Sci.

ROSE, ELLEN; Griswold HS; Jewett City, CT; (Y); GAA; Girl Scts; Hosp Aide; Band; Concert Band; Mrchg Band; Pep Band; Hon Roll; JP Sousa Awd; C Medbury Awd/Ldrshp 86; Medcl.

ROSE, JACKIE; Griswold HS; Norwich, CT; (Y); GAA; Basc Microbio Tech 84; Guilea Kenny Bk Awd 86.

ROSE, NICHOLE; St Marys HS; New Haven, CT; (Y); Church Yth Grp; French Clb; FBLA; Y-Teens; Church Choir; School Play; Variety Show; Trk; French Hon Soc; Hon Roll; Maryland U; Psych.

ROSE, PAULINE; Griswold HS; Voluntown, CT; (Y); 4-H; Girl Scts; Library Aide; Office Aide; High Hon Roll; Hon Roll; Steno 80 WPM; Sec.

ROSEBROOKS, EARL; Tourtellote Memorial HS; N Grosvenordale, CT; (Y); Church Yth Grp; Yrbk Stf; JV Bsbl; Var Bsktbl; MVP Var Bktbl 86; JR Prm Ct 86.

ROSEN, JENNIFER E; Weston HS; Weston, CT; (Y); 5/165; Sec Trs Debate Tm; Latin Clb; SADD; Temple Yth Grp; JV Sftbl; JV Vllybl; High Hon Roll; JETS Awd; Ntl Merit Ltr; Vsr Coll Bk Awd Exclnc Hmnts 86; Debt Clb Outstndng Plyr 86; 1st Pl Team Wnr ST CT Dbtng Awd 86; Bio.

ROSENBAUM, SUSAN B; Hamden HS; Hamden, CT; (Y); 3/450; Concert Band; Mrchg Band; Orch; School Musical; Nwsp Rptr; Nwsp Stf; Lit Mag; High Hon Roll; NHS; Ntl Merit Ltr; ARTS Merit Awd Wnnr In Music 86; All-ST & All-Eastern Band 83-86; Yale; Englsh.

ROSENBLATT, SARAH; Hall HS; W Hartford, CT; (Y); 118/342; Hosp Aide; Pep Clb; Varsity Clb; Var L Cheerleading; Fld Hcky; Var Capt Lcrss; Var Capt Swmmng; Hon Roll; CT Coll; Psych.

ROSENTHAL, LIZA; Stamford HS; Stamford, CT; (Y); Ski Clb; Temple Yth Grp; Varsity Clb; Stage Crew; Stu Cncl; Fld Hcky; Trk; Hon Roll; 3rd Pl Stamford Art Assn Art Show 84.

ROSLER, CRAIG; Holy Cross HS; Naugatuck, CT; (Y); 10/380; Boy Scts; Drama Clb; School Play; Yrbk Stf; Var Crs Cntry; JV Trk; High Hon Roll; NHS; Natl Latin Soc 85; Stu Theatre Bst Actor Fall Drama 85; Fine Arts Club 85; Intl Bus.

ROSS, BETSY; Danbury HS; Danbury, CT; (Y); 85/550; Office Aide; Varsity Clb; Variety Show; Yrbk Stf; Var L Cheerleading; Hon Roll; Jr NHS; NHS; Danbury Athltc Yth Orgnztn Schlrshp 86; Prsdntl Acad Ftns Awd 86; Western Ct ST U; Bus.

ROSS, JENNIFER; Greenwich HS; Greenwich, CT; (Y); Yrbk Stf; Mgr(s); Var Sftbl; JV Var Vllybl; Hon Roll.

ROSS JR, JONATHAN WOODMAN; Daniel Hand HS; Madison, CT; (Y); 12/276; Am Leg Boys St; VP FCA; Spanish Clb; Var L Crs Cntry; JV Socr; Var Tennis; Var L Trk; High Hon Roll; NHS; OHHS Art Show-Mixed Media 1st Pl 85; X-Cntry Jr Olympcs 85; Clemson U; Architctr.

ROSS, KIMBERLEY; Miss Porters Schl; Bristol, CT; (Y); Math Tm; Thesps; Band; Chorus; Orch; School Musical; School Play; Stage Crew; Frtzngr Music Schlrshp 85-86; JCSO Schlrshp 85-86; Tuition Schlrshp 85-87; Music.

ROSTOSKY, SHELLY; Middletown HS; Middletown, CT; (Y); AFS; FBLA; Sec Latin Clb; Q&S; Radio Clb; Nwsp Ed-Chief; Capt Cheerleading; Var L Socr; High Hon Roll; Sec NHS; Outstndng Achvt Itln 86; Gsppe Grbldi Schlrshp 85; Bst Stfr Schl Nwsppr 86; Med.

ROTH, AMY; Bethel HS; Bethel, CT; (Y); 6/250; Church Yth Grp; Computer Clb; Hosp Aide; Chorus; School Play; Variety Show; L Crs Cntry; High Hon Roll; NHS; Ntl Merit Cmnd Stu; Dart & Kfrt Schlrshp; Wlnt Hl Gnrl Str Schlrshp; Duke U; Gntcs.

ROTH, CYNTHIA; Trumbull HS; Trumbull, CT; (Y); Ski Clb; Band; Color Guard; Mrchg Band; Mgr(s); Sftbl; Hon Roll; Bus.

ROTHBERG, MADELEINE A; Hamden HS; Hamden, CT; (Y); 5/419; Drama Clb; Math Tm; Quiz Bowl; Temple Yth Grp; School Play; Stage Crew; Nwsp Rptr; Nwsp Stf; High Hon Roll; Ntl Merit SF; Holy Cross Coll Bk Awd 84-85; Sci.

ROTHSCHILD JR, J DAVID; Brookfield HS; Brookfield, CT; (Y); 3/218; Cmnty Wkr; Math Tm; JV Var Socr; High Hon Roll; NHS; Ntl Merit SF; Cert Awd Geo, Intro IA, Alg II, French III 83-84; Cert Awd Hnrs Thry Functn, Chem & Engl III 85; Elec Engr.

ROTMIL, RACHEL; Greenwich HS; Riverside, CT; (Y); Exploring; FHA; Pep Clb; Hon Roll; Sci.

ROTTENBERG, JONATHAN A; Ridgefield HS; Ridgefield, CT; (Y); 15/331; Lit Mag; Coach Actv; Var L Socr; Var L Tennis; High Hon Roll; Jr NHS; VP NHS; Ntl Merit SF; Harvard & Spnsh Bk Awds; Engl.

ROUCOULET, DAVID; Southington HS; Southington, CT; (Y); 141/600; Key Clb; Band; Mrchg Band; Hon Roll.

ROULEAU, JANETTE; Torrington HS; Torrington, CT; (Y); 132/178; Church Yth Grp; FHA; Spanish Clb; Stage Crew; 3rd Pl Synchrnzd Swmmng Comptn 86; Plcmnt Rbbns Sychrnzd Swmmng 85; Prschl Tchr.

ROURKE, REBECCA; St Bernard HS; Lisbon, CT; (Y); 7/297; Library Aide; Nwsp Ed-Chief; Rep Stu Cncl; Stat L Ftbl; NHS; Drctr Sgn Lnge Chr; Hstry Awd; Tutr Englsh & Algbr; Holy Cross Coll; Hstry.

ROUSSEAU JR, KENNETH C; Bloomfield HS; Bloomfield, CT; (Y); Math Tm; Thesps; Stage Crew; Lit Mag; NHS; Church Yth Grp; Library Aide; Brown Book Awd 86; Rensselaer Mdl 86.

ROUSSEAU, MICHAEL; Lewis S Mills HS; Burlington, CT; (Y); 3/160; Rep Am Leg Boys St; Math Tm; Nwsp Rptr; Ed Lit Mag; High Hon Roll; Hon Roll; NHS; NEDT Awd; Michaels Jewelers Awd Outstndng Soph 84; Frank Hayes Hist Achvt Awd 85; U CT; Bio Sci.

ROUSSIS, OREA V; Watkinson HS; West Hartford, CT; (Y); Aud/Vis; PAVAS; Orch; Var Bsktbl; Var Socr; Unsung Hero Awd 85; Berry Awd 86; Hampshire Coll.

ROVALDI, ALISON; Marianapolis Preparatory Schl; Brooklyn, CT; (Y); 19/43; Church Choir; Yrbk Stf; Sec Stu Cncl; Var Bsktbl; Var Capt Socr; Var Capt Sftbl; La Salle U; Law.

ROWE, EDWARD; Fairfield College Prep; Trumbull, CT; (Y); Church Yth Grp; Key Clb; Pep Clb; Nwsp Ed-Chief; Nwsp Sprt Ed; Yrbk Stf; Bsbl; Wt Lftg; Cit Awd; High Hon Roll; Engrng.

ROWE, GORDON; Avon HS; Avon, CT; (Y); Boy Scts; Ski Clb; JV Golf; U Of CT; Mech Engr.

ROWLAND, WENDY; Bethel HS; Southbury, CT; (Y); AFS; Church Yth Grp; Cmnty Wkr; DECA; Ski Clb; Church Choir; Yrbk Stf; High Hon Roll; Hon Roll; NHS; AARP Bethel Chptr 6; Southern CT ST U; Med Tech.

ROWLEY, MARK; Xavier HS; Killingworth, CT; (Y); 4/187; Boy Scts; Var Math Tm; Var L Crs Cntry; Var L Trk; High Hon Roll; NHS; Ntl Merit Ltr; Pres Schlr; CT All ST Tm 85-86; CT Indr Trck All St Tm 85-86; CT Crss Cntry All ST Tm 85; Duke U; Engr.

ROY, LANAY; Oliver Wolcott Technical Schl; Winsted, CT; (Y); Math Clb; Hon Roll; Acad Awd 85; Nrsng.

ROY, RICHARD; Bristol Central HS; Bristol, CT; (Y); Sec Boys Clb Am; Math Tm; Ski Clb; Hon Roll; Ntl Merit Ltr; Pres Boys Club Rifle Team 85-86; Nuclear Engr.

RUBLER, JOSEPH; Daniel Hand HS; Madison, CT; (Y); 21/229; Am Leg Boys St; Cmnty Wkr; L Ftbl; L Lcrss; JV Wrstlng; High Hon Roll; Hon Roll; VP NHS; Williams Coll Bk Awd-Ldrshp, Actv Extracrlr 86; USNA Annapolis; Aerntcl Engr.

RUCCI, MARGARITA; Crosby HS; Waterbury, CT; (S); Spanish Clb; Hon Roll; Prfct Atten Awd; Span IV Awd 85; Stone Bus Schl; Wrd Proc.

RUDNICK, CHERYL; Trumbull HS; Trumbull, CT; (Y); Key Clb; Temple Yth Grp; Concert Band; High Hon Roll; Hon Roll; Bus.

RUDOF, MICHAEL; Hopkins HS; Orange, CT; (S); Math Tm; Radio Clb; Ed Nwsp Stf; Rep Jr Cls; Rep Sr Cls; Sec Stu Cncl; Capt Var Tennis; Ntl Merit Ltr; Cum Laude Soc; David Sears Mem Awd.

RUGAR, BRETT; Wethersfield HS; Wethersfield, CT; (Y); Church Yth Grp; Cmnty Wkr; JV Bsbl; JV Socr; Hon Roll; Svngs Bnd Awd Atten 85; West Point; Cvl Engr.

RUGGIERO, KIMBERLY A; The Morgan Schl; Clinton, CT; (Y); 15/155; Spanish Clb; Chorus; School Musical; Yrbk Phtg; Yrbk Stf; Rep Stu Cncl; Stat Bsbl; JV Var Cheerleading; Var Trk; NHS; Prom Committee 85-86.

RULLI, KAREN; Bristol Central HS; Bristol, CT; (Y); Latin Clb; SADD; Yrbk Stf; Hon Roll; Med Tech.

RUMM, PETER; Bolton HS; Bolton, CT; (Y); 50/68; Art Clb; Church Yth Grp; Latin Clb; Ski Clb; Rep Jr Cls; Exclinc Art 86; RIT; Mdcl Illstrtn.

RUNG, CHRISTOPHER; Holy Cross HS; Naugatuck, CT; (Y); Church Yth Grp; Cmnty Wkr; SADD; Sec Frsh Cls; Sec Soph Cls; Pres Jr Cls; Pres Sr Cls; JV Bsktbl; Var Capt Lcrss; High Hon Roll; Ldrshp Awd 84-87; Bus Adm.

RUPE, VALERIE; Nonnewaug HS; Bethlehem, CT; (Y); 3/170; Am Leg Aux Girls St; 4-H; Off Frsh Cls; Off Soph Cls; Off Jr Cls; VP Sr Cls; Var Fld Hcky; Var Capt Trk; Cit Awd; Trs NHS; Ntl 4-H Cngrss Delg 84; 4-H Ldrshp Awd 85; Tufts U.

RUSSO, KELLEE; St Bernard HS; Norwich, CT; (Y); 68/265; Church Yth Grp; Cmnty Wkr; Computer Clb; Hosp Aide; Teachers Aide; Chorus; Yrbk Stf; Rep Jr Cls; JV Trk; Hon Roll; Math.

RUSSO JR, KENNETH J; Holy Cross HS; Waterbury, CT; (Y); 29/380; Cmnty Wkr; SADD; Var Capt Bsbl; JV Im Bsktbl; Im Sftbl; Im Vllybl; High Hon Roll; Hon Roll; NHS; Spanish NHS; Mst Athltc Soph Cert 85; Soc Stds Hon Soc Cert 86; Lmp Knwldg Pin 86; Notre Dame; Engrng.

RUSSO, MARC; Fairfield College Prep Schl; Easton, CT; (Y); Band; Chorus; Church Choir; School Musical; Rep Frsh Cls; Rep Soph Cls; Rep Jr Cls; Stu Cncl; Ftbl; Socr.

RUSSO, MONICA; Masuk HS; Monroe, CT; (Y); 10/277; Math Tm; Ski Clb; Spanish Clb; Chorus; Color Guard; Drm Mjr(t); Jazz Band; Dnfth Awd; High Hon Roll; NHS; Outstndng SR Achvt Band 85-86; Pres Acdmc Ftns Awd 85-86; Tufts U; Med.

RUSSO, NANCY; Wilton HS; Wilton, CT; (Y); Dance Clb; Pep Clb; Varsity Clb; Variety Show; Rep Frsh Cls; Pres Soph Cls; VP Jr Cls; Stu Cncl; Fld Hcky; Lcrss; La Crosse Hnrbl Mntn All FCIAC 85-86; La Crosse Vrsty Tm Cptn 86-87.

RUSSO, ROSEMARIE; Lauralton Hall HS; Milford, CT; (Y); 11/111; Church Yth Grp; Hosp Aide; Math Clb; Service Clb; Spanish Clb; Yrbk Stf; Mu Alp Tht; NHS; Lib Arts.

RUTHOWSKI, SANDY; East Haven HS; E Haven, CT; (Y); 2/300; Latin Clb; Mrchg Band; Trs Frsh Cls; Capt Crs Cntry; Var Trk; High Hon Roll; Jr NHS; Trs NHS; Rotary Awd; Rotary Yth Mnth Awd 86; Acctng.

RYAN, ANTHONY J; Staples HS; Westport, CT; (Y); Model UN; Radio Clb; Acpl Chr; Mrchg Band; School Musical; School Play; JV Bsbl; High Hon Roll; Aud/Vis; Dance Clb; Prog Dir WWPT 90.3 FM 86-87; Pres Norwalk Yth Symph 83-86; Minutemn Brass Quintet 85-86; Lbrl Arts; Drama.

RYAN, BRENT; Choate Rosemary Hall HS; Branford, CT; (Y); Math Clb; Radio Clb; JV Crs Cntry; Score Keeper; Im Swmmng; 3rd Frnch Poetry 86; Wrtr, Tech Ed Sch Sic Mag 84-86; Bio.

RYAN, CHRISTOPHER M; Robert E Fitch HS; Groton, CT; (Y); JV Bsbl; High Hon Roll; Hon Roll; Athletic Schlr 84; Pres Awd Physcl Ftns 84-86; CPA.

RYAN, DENISE; Cheshire HS; Cheshire, CT; (Y); 60/287; Church Yth Grp; GAA; Yrbk Stf; Stat Bsbl; JV Var Bsktbl; Stat Mgr(s); Var Trk; Cit Awd; High Hon Roll; Hon Roll; Central CT ST U; Bus.

RYAN, LYNN; Conard HS; West Hartford, CT; (Y); 24/314; Church Yth Grp; Chorus; School Musical; Rep Jr Cls; Rep Sr Cls; Rep Stu Cncl; Cheerleading; High Hon Roll; Hon Roll; NHS; Bus.

RYCHLIK, LAUREN; Sacred Heart Acad; Ridgefield, CT; (Y); Church Yth Grp; Drama Clb; Stage Crew; Lit Mag; Rep Jr Cls; Var Sftbl; Var Vllybl; French Hon Soc; Hon Roll; NHS; Ntl Ltn I & II Exam Magna Aim Laude Cert 84-86; Cert Of Exclinc Eng III 85-86; Psych.

RYKOSKI JR, TED; Holy Cross HS; Waterbury, CT; (Y); VP Pres JA; Im JV Wrstlng; Hon Roll; Pres JR Achvt 85-86; Bus.

SABA, CRAIG; Windham HS; Willington, CT; (Y); Varsity Clb; Var Bsbl; Im DECA; Var Socr; Hon Roll; All CCC E Conf Team Soccer 85-86; W Point; Engrng.

SABIA, DEANNE; Brien Mc Mahon HS; Darien, CT; (Y); Church Yth Grp; Ski Clb; Nwsp Stf; Powder Puff Ftbl; Var Swmmng; Var Tennis; High Hon Roll; Hon Roll; NHS; Trs Frsh Cls; Comm.

SABIA, SHARON; Westhill HS; Stamford, CT; (Y); Church Yth Grp; Computer Clb; Sec JA; Latin Clb; Math Clb; Science Clb; Orch; JV Bsktbl; JV Sftbl; Hon Roll; 2nd Pl City Wide Sci Fair 86; Best In Latin Awd 86; Womens Clb 86; U CT; Chem.

SABIO, LORI; Holy Cross HS; Naugatuck, CT; (Y); 104/346; Art Clb; Dance Clb; Band; Concert Band; Mrchg Band; Hon Roll; Pres Schlr; Chldrn Prfrmng Arts Trphy 85; Quinnipiac Coll; Acctg.

SABO, BARBARA A; Trumbull HS; Trumbull, CT; (Y); Church Yth Grp; German Clb; Chorus; Capt Var Bsktbl; Fld Hcky; Capt JV Sftbl; Var Vllybl; High Hon Roll; Hon Roll; Spanish Clb; Law.

SABO, MICHAEL; Joesph A Foran HS; Milford, CT; (Y); 35/240; VP Church Yth Grp; Capt Varsity Clb; Var L Bsktbl; Capt L Socr; Var L Trk; Hon Roll; St Schlr; Latin Clb; Eagle Of Crs Awd/ST Cthlc Yth Awd 86; T Parsons Awd 86; Nchls Coll Dudley MA.

SACKETT, WILLIAM; Oliver Walcott Tech; Norfolk, CT; (Y); Computer Clb; Ski Clb; Yrbk Stf; Var Jr Cls; JV Bsktbl; Var Golf; Hon Roll; Engrng.

SADLOWSKI, YOLANTA; Hartford Public HS; Hartford, CT; (Y); 10/300; AFS; FNA; Hosp Aide; Science Clb; Crs Cntry; High Hon Roll; Hon Roll; NHS; Alumni Assoc Earth Sci Prize, CT Sci Fair 3rd Sr Div, 1st HPHS Energy Fair 84; Mar Sci.

SAKAL, DEBORAH; Seymour HS; Seymour, CT; (S); Church Yth Grp; Band; Variety Show; Rep Soph Cls; Rep Jr Cls; High Hon Roll; NHS; Dance Clb; Church Choir; Amer HS Math Exm 85-86; Hugh O Brien Yth Ldrshp Fndtn 85; Bus.

SAKOWICZ, BRUCE; Stratford HS; Stratford, CT; (Y); 7/257; Library Aide; High Hon Roll; Hon Roll; Sci.

SAKSA, DAWN; Shelton HS; Shelton, CT; (Y); Drama Clb; Ski Clb; Art Clb; Band; Mrchg Band; Orch; Rep Frsh Cls; Rep Soph Cls; Rep Jr Cls; Rep Sr Cls; Pre-Law.

SALA, SCOTT; Greenwich HS; Greenwich, CT; (Y); Band; Concert Band; Jazz Band; Mrchg Band; School Musical; Hon Roll; Bus.

SALAZAR, FRANCISCO; Derby HS; Derby, CT; (Y); Boys Clb Am; Spanish Clb; Varsity Clb; Var Bsktbl; Var Ftbl; Var Trk; Central.

SALAZAR, MARCO; Emmett O Brien Tech; Ansonia, CT; (Y); Boys Clb Am; Ski Clb; Spanish Clb; Socr 87.

SALEM, TIMOTHY; Danbury HS; Danbury, CT; (Y); 139/500; Yrbk Stf; Rep Jr Cls; Rep Stu Cncl; JV Bsbl; Var L Bsktbl; Ftbl; Hon Roll; Sprtsmnshp Awd Bsktbl 84-85 & 85-86; Pre-Law.

SALOMON, DEIRDRE; Staples HS; Westport, CT; (Y); Camera Clb; Debate Tm; French Clb; Intnl Clb; Latin Clb; Ski Clb; Orch; Gym; Swmmng; Hon Roll; Staples Grant 86; George Washington U; Intl Bus.

SALTZMAN, SUSAN; Berlin HS; Berlin, CT; (Y); Service Clb; Color Guard; Mrchg Band; Powder Puff Ftbl; Hon Roll; Art Dept Achvt Awd 85-86; Cmmnctns.

SALVATORE, JENNIFER; Lewis S Mills HS; Burlington, CT; (Y); 13/172; Am Leg Aux Girls St; Drama Clb; Band; Chorus; School Musical; Pres Stu Cncl; Var Capt Fld Hcky; Co-Capt Var Tennis; Hon Roll; NHS; Intl Bus.

SALVESTRINI, MATTHEW; Fairfield College Prep Schl; Ridgefield, CT; (Y); Art Clb; Church Yth Grp; Exploring; Lit Mag; Trk; Archtctr.

SALVIN, AMY; The Morgan Schl; Clinton, CT; (Y); 2/144; Chorus; School Musical; Nwsp Ed-Chief; Pres Stu Cncl; Capt Cheerleading; Gym; NHS; Sal; Boston Coll; Pol Sci.

SALWIERZ JR, CHARLES P; Holy Cross HS; Southbury, CT; (Y); 189/380; Church Yth Grp; Jazz Band; Variety Show; Socr.

SAMAL, KATHLEEN; Torrington HS; Torrington, CT; (Y); Camera Clb; Yrbk Stf; Cheerleading; Trk; Nrsg.

SAMOK, KRISTYN; Litchfield HS; Bantam, CT; (Y); Chess Clb; FBLA; Latin Clb; Quiz Bowl; Spanish Clb; SADD; Teachers Aide; Bsktbl; Sftbl; NHS; Hotl/Restrnt Mgmt.

SAMOKAR, ROBERT; Notre Dame HS; W Haven, CT; (Y); 36/230; Math Clb; Ski Clb; High Hon Roll; NHS; Spanish NHS; Providence Coll; Engrng.

SAMPSON, ROBT; Maloney HS; Meriden, CT; (Y); Computer Clb; Latin Clb; Math Tm; Lit Mag; Hon Roll; Plcd 3rd Ntl Math Exm 86; SAT Scores Vrbl 570 Math 660 86; Rcrdng Engr.

SAMSEL, REGINA; St Marys HS; New Haven, CT; (Y); 28/97; School Musical; Lit Mag; Sec Sr Cls; Tennis; French Hon Soc; Hon Roll; Svc Awd 86.

SAMUL, CYNTHIA A; New London HS; New London, CT; (Y); 19/143; Drama Clb; Lit Mag; Wrld Hist Awd 83; Art Awd 84; 2nd Hrns 84-85; Illus.

SANANGELO, GINA; Holy Cross HS; Beacon Fals, CT; (Y); 148/380; Art Clb; Trk.

SANAULLA, ADIL; Windsor HS; Windsor, CT; (Y); Library Aide; Math Tm; Model UN; High Hon Roll; NHS; Scholastic Bowl; Hon Roll; Ntl Merit Ltr; Prfct Atten Awd; Blacks & Math Essay Awd; Harvard Bk Awd; Bown Bk Awd; Natl Hstry Day Cert; JR Sci & Humanties Sym Cert.

SANCHEZ, ALEX; Francis T Mabney HS; Meriden, CT; (Y); Boys Clb Am; Chess Clb; Church Yth Grp; Computer Clb; Socr; Hon Roll; U Bridgeport; Hlth.

SANCHEZ, TARA; Southington HS; Plantsville, CT; (Y); Church Yth Grp; Spanish Clb; JV L Fld Hcky; Hon Roll.

SANDERS, GRAIG; East Lyme HS; Niantic, CT; (Y); Church Yth Grp; Mgr(s); Med Tech.

SANDERS, JENNIFER; E C Goodwin Tech; Forestvile, CT; (Y); Red Cross Aide; Pres Soph Cls; Pres Jr Cls; Pres Sr Cls; Sec Stu Cncl; Capt Cheerleading; Sftbl; Richard F Moore Awd 86; PTO Shop Exclinc Awd 86; Mst Imprvd Machnst JR Clss 86; Waterbury ST Tech; Engrng.

SANFORD, GARY; Holy Cross HS; Naugatuck, CT; (Y); 71/380; Var Ftbl; Var Trk; Hon Roll; NHS; Accntng.

SANNA, KERRY; Brien Mc Mahon HS; Norwalk, CT; (Y); Spanish Clb; Mrchg Band; Symp Band; Stat Trk; High Hon Roll; NHS; Mst Promise Chem Awd 86; Engrng Awd Soc Wmn Engrng 86; Bio.

SANTA, KERSTIN; Academy Of Our Lady Of Mercy; Stratford, CT; (Y); 60/111; Debate Tm; Drama Clb; Model UN; Chorus; School Musical; School Play; Yrbk Stf; Off Frsh Cls; Im Fld Hcky; Marketing.

SANTANA, LISSETTE; Bassick HS; Bridgeport, CT; (Y); 7/268; DECA; Latin Clb; Office Aide; Nwsp Stf; Yrbk Ed-Chief; High Hon Roll; NHS; Prfct Atten Awd; Pres Schlr; Rotary Awd; Futoro Inc Schlrshp, Perf Atten Cert 4 Yrs 86; Southern CT ST U; Bus.

SANTANGELO, MELISSA A; Sacred Heart Acad; Ansonia, CT; (Y); 5/124; Hosp Aide; Chorus; Nwsp Rptr; Lit Mag; Im Vllybl; High Hon Roll; NHS; Ntl Merit SF; NEDT Awd; Spanish NHS; Yale Frontiers Of Appld Sci 84-85; SAT Hgh Scorer Ltr 84-85; Bus.

SANTARSIERO, GINA; Holy Cross HS; Waterbury, CT; (Y); 4-H; SADD; Rep Frsh Cls; Rep Soph Cls; Hon Roll; U Of Bridgeport; Dntl Hygn.

SANTERRE, DEANNE; Norwich Free Acad; Norwich, CT; (Y); Church Yth Grp; FHA; Girl Scts; Spanish Clb; High Hon Roll; Hon Roll; Proj Outrch; Med.

SANTIAGO, MELISSA; Bullard Havens Tech RVTS; Bpt, CT; (S); 3/200; AFS; Church Yth Grp; VICA; Stu Cncl; Var Cheerleading; Var Vllybl; High Hon Roll; Hon Roll; NHS; Hrdrssr.

SANTILLO, MICHELE; St Marys HS; New Haven, CT; (Y); Service Clb; Chorus; School Musical; School Play; Rep Jr Cls; Rep Sr Cls; Sftbl; Hon Roll; Vlntr Serv 86; Dntl Hygnst.

SANTINO, MICHELE; West Haven HS; W Haven, CT; (Y); 9/396; Church Yth Grp; Elks Awd; French Hon Soc; High Hon Roll; NHS; Humanities Awd 83-86; Helyn Georgia Mem Mth Awd; Cont Issuer Awd 86; Biol I Awds; Fr IV Awds 84-86; S CT ST U; Chldhd Ed.

SANTORO, STACEY; Wilby HS; Wtubry, CT; (Y); 6/270; Art Clb; Dance Clb; Drama Clb; Chorus; School Musical; School Play; Rep Jr Cls; Rep Sr Cls; Var Tennis; Mattatuck Coll; Radlgy.

SARACCO, PAULA; Sacred Heart Acad; New Haven, CT; (Y); Drama Clb; Spanish Clb; School Musical; Hon Roll; NEDT Awd; Langs.

SARNO, DEBBIE; Sacred Heart Acad; Hamden, CT; (Y); Hosp Aide; Spanish Clb; Teachers Aide; Stage Crew; Nwsp Rptr; High Hon Roll; Hon Roll; NHS; Spanish NHS; Hlth Prof.

SASKAL, RICHARD; Branford HS; Branford, CT; (Y); 12/250; Var L Socr; High Hon Roll; Hon Roll; NHS; French Certf Merit; Pres Acad Ftnss Awd; U CT.

SATTERLEE, KIMBERLY; Wethersfield HS; Wethersfield, CT; (Y); Hon Roll; Busnss.

SAUNDERS, SHANNON; E Hartford HS; E Hartford, CT; (Y); 94/445; Drama Clb; Pres VP FBLA; Girl Scts; JA; Science Clb; Capt Flag Corp; Stage Crew; Nwsp Rptr; Trk; Hon Roll; Greater Hartford CC; RN.

SAUTTER, ROBERT; Holy Cross HS; Oxford, CT; (Y); 4/392; Cmnty Wkr; Quiz Bowl; Service Clb; Spanish Clb; High Hon Roll; Jr NHS; NHS; Ntl Merit Ltr; Spanish NHS; Persuasvie Pub Spkng Awd 86; Soc Studies Hnr Soc Awd 86; Law.

SAVASTANO, JOE; Hamden HS; Hamden, CT; (Y); Ski Clb; School Musical; School Play; High Hon Roll; Hon Roll; Music.

SAVASTANO, LAURIE; Sacred Heart Acad; New Haven, CT; (Y); Cmnty Wkr; VP Spanish Clb; Variety Show; Nwsp Ed-Chief; Nwsp Rptr; Nwsp Stf; JV Crs Cntry; High Hon Roll; NHS; Spanish NHS; Hghst Grd Pt Aver 3 Yrs Of Spnsh Awd 86; Sacred Hrt Wrk Stdy Pgm 85-86; Sacred Hrt Schlrshp Awd 86; Langs.

SAVINELLI, CHRISTINE; Sacred Heart Acad; Northford, CT; (Y); 50/117; Art Clb; Dance Clb; Var Cheerleading; Im Civic Clb; God Cntry Awd; Spanish NHS; Mother C Merloni Schlrshp 84-85; Sacred Hrt Acad Endwmnt Schlrshp 86-87; U Of CT; Ntrtn.

SAVINO, DENISE; East Haven HS; E Haven, CT; (Y); 17/260; Library Aide; Spanish Clb; Yrbk Ed-Chief; Pom Pon; Trk; Hon Roll; NHS; Rotary Awd; Memrndm Schlrshp 85-86; Schlr Athl Awd 85-86; Sprtsmnshp Awd Pres Fit Awd 85-86; Aldelphi U.

SAVINO, TINA MARIE; Parish Hill HS; Hampton, CT; (Y); Spanish Clb; VP Stu Cncl; Var L Bsktbl; Var L Socr; Var Capt Trk; High Hon Roll; Hon Roll; Phys Ed.

SAVOCCHIA, DONNA; Torrington HS; Torrington, CT; (Y); 50/278; French Clb; Varsity Clb; Chorus; Rep Sr Cls; Stat Bsktbl; Var Tennis; High Hon Roll; Prfct Atten Awd.

SAWIN, BRIAN; Canton HS; Collinsville, CT; (Y); 9/100; Boy Scts; Model UN; Yrbk Ed-Chief; Lit Mag; Rep Stu Cncl; Var Capt Tennis; Hon Roll; Band; Rep Frsh Cls; Rep Soph Cls; Eagle Sct 85; Atheltc Cncl-Vp 85-86; Engrng.

SAWYER, TIMOTHY; Windsor Locks HS; Windsor Locks, CT; (Y); Boy Scts; Church Yth Grp; JV Var Bsbl; Hon Roll; Acadmc Schlrshp 86-87; Wesley Grnt & SEOG I Grnt 86-87; N Cntrl Conn Brd Of Reltrs Schlrshp Awd 86-87; Wesley Coll; Acctng.

SCALISE, JAMES; New Britain HS; New Britain, CT; (Y); Church Yth Grp; JA; Key Clb; Stage Crew; JV Bsbl; Var Ftbl; Im Wt Lftg; Hon Roll.

SCARANO, JANET; North Haven HS; N Haven, CT; (Y); 61/276; Trs Church Yth Grp; Nwsp Stf; Frsh Cls; Soph Cls; Jr Cls; Sr Cls; Sec Stu Cncl; Cheerleading; Hon Roll; Yrbk Stf; Fidle Soc; Central CT ST U; Acctg.

SCARINGE, LORI; Southington HS; Southington, CT; (Y); 16/600; Am Leg Aux Girls St; Key Clb; Var Bsktbl; Capt Vllybl; Elks Awd; Hon Roll; VP NHS; ELEET Schlrshp 86; Hnrbl Mntn In Vlybl 85-86; Sthnr CT ST U; Elem Ed.

SCAVETTA, JOE; Wilton HS; Wilton, CT; (Y); 15/354; Nwsp Stf; Trs Soph Cls; Rep Sr Cls; VP Stu Cncl; JV Crs Cntry; JV Trk; High Hon Roll; Hon Roll; NHS; Ntl Merit Ltr; Arch.

SCHAAF, KATY; Stratford HS; Stratford, CT; (Y); Exploring; Sec French Clb; Ski Clb; French Hon Soc; Hon Roll; Natural Resources.

SCHAEFER, KAREN; Conard HS; W Hartfo D, CT; (Y); 24/345; Church Yth Grp; Letterman Clb; Service Clb; Varsity Clb; Band; Pep Band; Var Swmmng; Var Timer; High Hon Roll; Spanish NHS.

SCHAFFNER, CHRIS; St Mary HS; Cos Cob, CT; (Y); 4/50; Am Leg Boys St; Cmnty Wkr; JA; Stage Crew; Var Capt Bsktbl; Score Keeper; High Hon Roll; NHS; Fr Gay Awd 86; Vrsty Ltr Bsktbl 86; Hnrs Mth, Hstry, Phys Ed 85; Hnrs Hstry 84.

SCHAIVER, VANESSA; Trumbull HS; Trumbull, CT; (Y); FFA; Hosp Aide; Hgh Nrs All SR Yr 85-86; Hghst 2nd Hnrs JR Yr 84-85; A Aver In Nrsg Crse 85-86; U Of CT; Nrsg.

SCHAPER, PETER; Plainfield HS; Moosup, CT; (Y); Thames Valley Tech Coll; Eng.

SCHAUB, FRED; Holy Cross HS; Oxford, CT; (Y); French Clb; School Play; Stage Crew; Bus.

SCHENA, PATRICE; Cheshire HS; Cheshire, CT; (Y); Yrbk Stf; Var L Bsktbl; Coach Actv; Capt Var Fld Hcky; Var L Trk; High Hon Roll; Hon Roll; All Housatonic Leag Trck & Fld Hcky 84-85; Schlstc Achvt Awd 86; Hlth Serv.

SCHENKEL, LISSA; Oliver Wolcott Technical HS; Thomaston, CT; (Y); 10/145; Art Clb; Math Clb; Yrbk Stf; Rep Soph Cls; Trs Jr Cls; Trs Sr Cls; Tennis; Hon Roll; Jr NHS; VP NHS; Waterbury ST Tech Coll; Drftg.

SCHERZINGER, KEITH; St Paul Catholic HS; Southington, CT; (Y); JV Var Crs Cntry; Hon Roll; Jr NHS; NHS; Acdmc Schlrshp U Of Hartford SAT 86; U Of Hartford; Cvl Engrng.

SCHILLING, DONALD; Bullard-Havens RVTS; Bridgeport, CT; (Y); Ski Clb; SADD; Hon Roll; Machnst.

SCHIMELMAN, BRAD; East Lyme HS; East Lyme, CT; (Y); 25/257; Boy Scts; Key Clb; Political Wkr; Hon Roll; Coll Holy Cross; Pre-Med.

SCHIPPER, KIM; Danbury HS; Danbury, CT; (Y); Trs German Clb; Band; Jazz Band; Pep Band; Variety Show; Mgr(s); Tennis; Hon Roll; Jr NHS; NHS.

SCHIPUL, RICH; Trumbull HS; Trumbull, CT; (Y); Boy Scts; Ski Clb; Spanish Clb; Concert Band; Var Trk; Hon Roll; Prfct Atten Awd; 4th FCIAC Fnls 100 M Dash, 3rd Finals 4 X 100 M Relay 85-86; Ornmtl Hort.

SCHLAUCH JR, ARTHUR C; O H Platt HS; Meriden, CT; (Y); #1 In Class; Pres German Clb; Trs Key Clb; Trs Stu Cncl; Swmmng; Tennis; High Hon Roll; NHS; Drama Clb; Pres Math Clb; Nwsp Stf; Hitchcock Sci Awd Chem 85; AHSME Math Awd 86; Yale Bk Awd 86; Astrphyscs.

SCHLEGEL, KRISTIN; Ridgefield HS; Ridgefield, CT; (Y); Rep Church Yth Grp; DECA; Letterman Clb; Varsity Clb; Chorus; Madrigals; School Musical; Off Jr Cls; JV Var Cheerleading; Var Vllybl; Schl Store Mgr 86-87; Dist Educ Local Food Mktg Competition 1st Pl 86; ST Mktg Competition 86; Dean; Fshn Merchandising.

SCHLESS, GARY; Trumbuu HS; Trumbull, CT; (Y); JV Bsbl; High Hon Roll; U Of CT; Bus.

SCHMEER, MICHAEL; Kaynor Tech HS; Waterbury, CT; (Y); SADD; High Hon Roll; Hon Roll; VFW Awd; Elctrncs Engnr.

SCHMERL, AMY; Edwin O Smith HS; Storrs, CT; (Y); 4/177; VP Art Clb; Cmnty Wkr; Exploring; Math Tm; Yrbk Stf; Var Tennis; Smith Coll Book Awd 86; 10th Pl ST Wide Natl Frnch Exam 86.

SCHMID, DAVID; Cathedral HS; Enfield, CT; (Y); Boy Scts; Math Clb; Rep Stu Cncl; Var L Swmmng; Egl Sct 84; U Of CT; Chem Engrng.

SCHMID, JENNIFER L; Weston HS; Weston, CT; (Y); 1/153; Church Yth Grp; Nwsp Stf; Var Crs Cntry; Var Trk; High Hon Roll; NHS; Ntl Merit SF; Val; Intnl Clb; Band; Japan-US Snt Schlrshp 85; JR Englsh Schlr 85; Intl Rltns.

SCHMIDT, GRETCHEN; Holy Cross HS; Waterbury, CT; (Y); 63/380; Exploring; Intnl Clb; Latin Clb; Chorus; Stage Crew; Yrbk Stf; Hon Roll; NHS; Ntl Latin Exm Cum Laude 83-84; Scl Stds Hnrs Soc 85-87; Prjct Sage Escl Pst Coll 84-85; Intl Finance.

SCHNEIDER, CHRISTINE; Denbury HS; Danbury, CT; (Y); 85/565; German Clb; Girl Scts; Ski Clb; Varsity Clb; Band; JV Sftbl; Var Trk; Var Vllybl; Hon Roll; NHS; Grl Scouts Gld Awd 86; Ithaca Coll; Sprts Med.

SCHNEIDER JR, DAVID E; Fairfield Prep; Monroe, CT; (Y); Chess Clb; Library Aide; Political Wkr; Var Capt Crs Cntry; Var Trk; High Hon Roll; Hon Roll; NHS; Exploring; Im Bsktbl; Frnch Exchng Stu; US Mrchnt Marine; Marine Trans.

SCHREIBER, CHRIS; Danbury HS; Danbury, CT; (Y); Varsity Clb; Chorus; Variety Show; Capt Socr; Capt Trk; Hon Roll; Rotary Awd; Sprtmnshp Trck 86; All Co 1st Tm Trck 86; All Co Hnrb Mntn Soccer 85; U Of CT; Lbrl Art.

SCHREIBER, STEPHANIE; Danbury HS; Danbury, CT; (Y); 109/536; Math Tm; Acpl Chr; JV Var Bsktbl; JV Var Sftbl; Hon Roll; Jr NHS; Perry Awd Italian 85; U Of CT; Psychlgy.

SCHUBERT, EMILY; Wilton HS; Wilton, CT; (Y); 35/356; Chorus; Swing Chorus; Yrbk Bus Mgr; Mgr Lit Mag; Fld Hcky; High Hon Roll; Hon Roll; Engl.

SCHUBERT, PAMELA; Berlin HS; Berlin, CT; (Y); Drama Clb; Exploring; SADD; Band; Concert Band; Capt Drill Tm; Mrchg Band; School Musical; Nwsp Rptr; Stu Cncl; Nrsg.

SCHUHL, MARK W; Manchester HS; Manchester, CT; (Y); 4/568; Cmnty Wkr; German Clb; Pres Spanish Clb; Nwsp Ed-Chief; High Hon Roll; NHS; Pres Schlr; Voice Dem Awd; AFS; Harvard-Radcliffe Bk Awd 85; Wesleyan JR Sci & Humanities Symposium 86; Uof PA; Lang Sci.

SCHULMAN, BRUCE; Staples HS; Westport, CT; (Y); Boy Scts; Yrbk Phtg; Socr; Var Tennis; Gov Hon Prg Awd; High Hon Roll; Hon Roll; Hrvrd Bk Awd 86; Brdgport Art Cncl Hoto Hnr 84; Chemathon 85.

SCHULMAN, HEIDI; Staples HS; Westport, CT; (Y); Var Capt Socr; Var Tennis; High Hon Roll; Crmlo & Mry Arcd Frgn Lang Schlrshp, Lfflr Schlrshp 86; CT Schlr Athlt Awd 86; Mst Vlbl Plyr Sccr 85; Yale U; Frgn Lang.

SCHULTZ, RICK; Ridgefield HS; Ridgefield, CT; (Y); 37/375; Church Yth Grp; Cmnty Wkr; Ski Clb; SADD; Mrchg Band; Symp Band; Nwsp Rptr; Lit Mag; Trk; Hon Roll; Commendable Volunteer 85; Notre Dame; Bus Admin.

SCHUSTER, BILL; Berlin HS; Berlin, CT; (Y); 65/210; Boys Clb Am; Var Bsbl; Var Ftbl; Golf; Hon Roll.

SCHUSTER, WENDI; Derby HS; Derby, CT; (Y); 7/110; Am Leg Aux Girls St; Pres Trs Church Yth Grp; Nwsp Ed-Chief; Yrbk Ed-Chief; Rep Frsh Cls; Fld Hcky; High Hon Roll; Hon Roll; NHS; Spanish NHS; Marine Corps Phys Ftns Awd 85; Hnbl Mntn CT Latin Test 85; CT Assn Sec Schls 86; Pre-Med.

SCHWARTZ, KAREN; Greenwich HS; Old Greenwich, CT; (Y); Hosp Aide; Service Clb; Chorus; School Play; Hon Roll; Hope Fut Clb.

SCHWARTZ, THEA; Amity Regional HS; Woodbridge, CT; (Y); Sec Latin Clb; Red Cross Aide; Symp Band; Nwsp Rptr; Lit Mag; Var Capt Crs Cntry; Var Capt Trk; Cit Awd; High Hon Roll; VP NHS; Red Cross Recgntn Awd 86; NHL Schlrshp 86; All-ST X-Cntry 84; Brown U; Env Sci.

SCHWEIGHOFER, PETER; Ridgefield HS; Ridgefield, CT; (S); 12/331; Church Yth Grp; Orch; School Musical; High Hon Roll; Hon Roll; NHS; CT Wstrn Regn Music Fest Orch; CT All ST Music Fest; Creatv Wrtng.

SCINTO, RONALD LOUIS; Shelton HS; Shelton, CT; (Y); DECA; Drama Clb; Hosp Aide; Ski Clb; School Musical; Stu Cncl; Hon Roll; Pres Distrbtve Ed 85-86; Elec Engrng.

SCIORTINO, MICHAEL J; Trumbull HS; Trumbull, CT; (Y); Am Leg Boys St; Var Capt Bsbl; JV Ftbl; All FCIAC Ptchr Bsbl 86; NY Daily Nws All Str Ptchr Bsbl 86; Barry K Oneil Memrl Sprtsmnshp Awd 86; Central CT ST U.

SCOTT, CHRIS; Canton HS; Collinsville, CT; (Y); 15/96; Political Wkr; High Hon Roll; Hon Roll; Engrng.

SCOTT, DONALD; Canton HS; Collinsville, CT; (Y); 34/96; Jazz Band; School Musical; Variety Show; Hon Roll; Jazz Bnd Awd 86; U Hrtfrd; Mscn.

SCOTT, JENNIFER; Mark T Sheehan HS; Wallingford, CT; (Y); 15/235; German Clb; Hosp Aide; Nwsp Ed-Chief; High Hon Roll; NHS; Cmnty Wkr; JA; Key Clb; Concert Band; Nwsp Stf; Vrsty Schlr 86; Natl Hnr Soc Inductn 86; Gaylor Hosp Scholar 86; Smith Coll; Psych.

SCOTT, LARA L; Greenwich Acad; Stamford, CT; (Y); Art Clb; Debate Tm; Drama Clb; School Play; Nwsp Rptr; Nwsp Stf; Lit Mag; Pres Stu Cncl; JV Var Bsktbl; Ntl Merit SF; Bonnett Art, Christina W Kelley Drama Awds 85.

SCOTT, RACHAEL; Stanford HS; Stamford, CT; (Y); Computer Clb; JA; Spanish Clb; Church Choir; Yrbk Stf; Var Sftbl; Hon Roll; Ntl Merit SF; Hofstra U; Acctng.

SCOTT, ROSE-MARIE; Torrington HS; Torrington, CT; (Y); VP Church Yth Grp; VP Exploring; Hosp Aide; Model UN; Chorus; Church Choir; Rep Frsh Cls; VP Jr Cls; Pres Sr Cls; High Hon Roll; High Hnr Roll 85; Wesleyan; Psychlgy.

SCRIVENER, MARC; Rham HS; Hebron, CT; (Y); Aud/Vis; Church Yth Grp; 4-H; Hon Roll; AIASA; Frstry.

SCULLY, MICHAEL; New Fairfield HS; New Fairfield, CT; (Y); Latin Clb; Office Aide; Ski Clb; Varsity Clb; JV Bsbl; Var L Bsktbl; U Of MD; Bus.

SEARS, CHRIS; Windsor HS; Windsor, CT; (Y); Varsity Clb; Band; Concert Band; Jazz Band; Mrchg Band; Orch; Pep Band; Symp Band; Var Socr; Berklee Music Fstvl 86; CT All ST Band 86; Nthrn Rgnl Orch 85; Music Pfrmnc.

SEASTEAD, KRIS; Stamford HS; Stamford, CT; (Y); Girl Scts; Nwsp Phtg; Nwsp Rptr; Nwsp Stf; Yrbk Phtg; Yrbk Rptr; Yrbk Stf; Trk; Grl Sct Slvr, Gld Awds 85 & 87; Photo.

SECREST, LAUREN; Ridgefield HS; Ridgefield, CT; (Y); 161/385; English Clb; Lit Mag; Rep Soph Cls; Rep Jr Cls; Rep Sr Cls; Rep Stu Cncl; Hon Roll; Nwsp Rptr; Nwsp Stf; Cheerleading; Awd RHS Voice 85; 1st Pl Lode Str Literary Mgzn Poetry Cntst 86; Svc Clss Of 87 Awd 86; Frnch.

SEEGER, MICHAEL; East Catholic HS; Glastonbury, CT; (Y); 48/290; Math Tm; Rep Jr Cls; VP Sr Cls; Rep Stu Cncl; Var L Bsktbl; Var L Ftbl; Var Capt Trk; Hon Roll; Ntl Merit Ltr; ST Of CT Hi-Achvmnt Grnt; Villanova U; Engrng.

SEIFERT, JOHN; Trumbull HS; Trumbull, CT; (Y); Im Bsktbl; Wrstlng; High Hon Roll; U Of Bridgeport Proj Choice Schlrshp 86-87; U Of Bridgeport; Mech Engrng.

SELMONT, LINDA; North Haven HS; N Haven, CT; (Y); Girl Scts; Flag Corp; Variety Show; Yrbk Ed-Chief; Stu Cncl; Hon Roll.

SEMENTINI, NANCY; Stamford HS; Stamford, CT; (Y); Dance Clb; JA; Key Clb; Lit Mag; High Hon Roll; NHS; Boston U; Phys Ther.

SEMLOW, MARK; Bunnell HS; Stratford, CT; (Y); 19/270; Varsity Clb; Yrbk Stf; Var Ftbl; Var Trk; Var Wrstlng; Hon Roll; NHS; All Leag Ftbll 85; ST Chmp Hvywght Wrstlr 86; Bio.

SEMNOSKI, DAVID; Choate Rosemary Hall HS; Southington, CT; (S); Im Socr; Im Wt Lftg; Hon Roll; US Coast Guard Acad; Marn Engr.

SEMSEL III, JOHN S; Greenwich HS; Greenwich, CT; (Y); Am Leg Boys St; Boy Scts; Church Yth Grp; Debate Tm; Exploring; Key Clb; Spanish Clb; Teachers Aide; Orch; Variety Show; Outstndg Sci Awd Biol/Physcs 83 & 84; BSA Eagle Sct, Brnze Palms 84 & 86; PTA Scholar; Boston U; Acctg.

SENF, STEPHANIE; Ridgefield HS; Ridgefield, CT; (Y); Pres AFS; Capt Color Guard; Concert Band; Capt Flag Corp; Mrchg Band; Symp Band; Hon Roll; Band; Stage Crew; Natl Ger Test Wnnr & Consulate Bk Prz 84; Outstndg Achvt Geom 85; AFS Svc 84-86; Bus.

SENGSTOCK, MICHAEL; H C Wilcox HS; Meriden, CT; (Y); 8/202; High Hon Roll; Hon Roll; Cvl Technen.

SEPPLES, CHRISTINE; Lewis S Mills HS; Harwinton, CT; (Y); 4/170; Am Leg Aux Girls St; Church Yth Grp; Math Tm; Model UN; Band; Concert Band; Jazz Band; Mrchg Band; High Hon Roll; NHS; Engrng.

SERIMONKON, SUSAN; Ellington HS; Ellington, CT; (Y); Exploring; Latin Clb; Sec Chorus; Variety Show; Yrbk Stf; Hon Roll; U Of CT Cert Of Achvt 85; Gld Music Awd 84-85; Solo & Ensmbl Fest Awd 84; Roger Williams Coll.

SERRAMBANA JR, VICTOR; East Catholic HS; Vernon, CT; (Y); 7/280; Nwsp Rptr; Lit Mag; Off Frsh Cls; Pres Jr Cls; Trs Stu Cncl; Cit Awd; High Hon Roll; Hon Roll; VP NHS; Var Capt Ice Hcky; Done Most For Class Awd 86; Svc Awd 86; Prncpls Awd 85; RPI; Engrng.

SERRANO, DREW; Kaynor Regional Technical Voc Schl; Waterbury, CT; (Y); Red Cross Aide; SADD; Bsbl; Hon Roll; NHS; Machnst.

SERRANO, RAQUEL; Central Magnet HS; Bridgeport, CT; (Y); Computer Clb; Spanish Clb; Comp Awd; Chem Engr.

SESTO, VINCENZO; Bristol Central HS; Bristol, CT; (Y); Am Leg Boys St; Boys Clb Am; Church Yth Grp; Cmnty Wkr; Library Aide; Red Cross Aide; Rptr VICA; Nwsp Sprt Ed; High Hon Roll; NHS; Carnegie Smnr 84-85; MA Inst Of Tech Awd Outstndg Ptntl Sci 85; Itln-Engl Trnsltr Cmmnty Svc Prjcts; Northeastern U; Elec Engnrng.

SETARO, NANCY; Holy Cross HS; Waterbury, CT; (Y); 53/346; Hon Roll; Jr NHS; NHS; Spanish NHS; Natl Italian Hnr Soc 84-86; Italian Lvl IV Awd 85-86; CT U; Educ Itln/Spnsh.

SEVERINO, DAVID; Cheshire HS; Cheshire, CT; (Y); Boy Scts; Church Yth Grp; Briarwood Coll; Accntng.

SEVERINO, DAVID; East Haven HS; E Haven, CT; (Y); 25/260; Spanish Clb; Hon Roll; Jr NHS; Pres Schlr.

SEWELL, MICHAEL S; Saint Joseph HS; Trumbull, CT; (Y); 39/260; Varsity Clb; Capt Crs Cntry; Capt Trk; High Hon Roll; Hon Roll; NEDT Awd; Engrng.

SEYMOUR, JONATHAN; Coventry HS; Coventry, CT; (Y); Symp Band; Rep Stu Cncl; Var Capt Bsktbl; Var Golf; Hon Roll; Law.

SHACKETT, HEATHER; Windsor Locks HS; Windsor Locks, CT; (Y); 3/150; Church Yth Grp; Trs Civic Clb; Stage Crew; Yrbk Stf; Hon Roll; NHS; Pres Schlr; Tlctt Mntn Sci Pgm 84; Amer Lgn Schlrshp 86; Jcksn Mem Schlrshp 86; Hrtwick Coll; Pre-Med.

SHAH, HEMAL; Danbury HS; Danbury, CT; (Y); 19/481; Cmnty Wkr; Hosp Aide; JA; Key Clb; Math Tm; Yrbk Stf; High Hon Roll; NHS; Hillside Sympsm Hnrbl Mntn 86; Perry Awd Bio 85; Soc Stud Plaque 84; Med.

SHALLIS, RENEE; Jonathan Law HS; Milford, CT; (Y); 14/198; Church Yth Grp; Spanish Clb; Band; Jazz Band; Nwsp Stf; Var L Trk; Prfct Atten Awd; Pres Schlr; St Schlr; Slvr Mdl Of Excllnc-Spnsh; Sacred Heart U; Bio.

SHANAHAN, WENDY ANNE; Wilby HS; Waterbury, CT; (Y); Art Clb; Dance Clb; Drama Clb; PAVAS; Chorus; Church Choir; School Musical; Nwsp Phtg; Nwsp Rptr; Nwsp Stf; Stdnt Weslyn U Ctr Creatv Yth 86; Awd Paintg H S Catgry NOW Afro Latn Fest 86; Visl Arts.

SHANNON, MICHAEL; Saint Joseph HS; Stratford, CT; (Y); 51/253; Bsbl; JV Var Bsktbl; High Hon Roll; Hon Roll; Fairfield U; Bus.

SHARNIK, SAM; Kingswood-Oxford HS; W Simsbury, CT; (Y); 16/145; Pres Latin Clb; Service Clb; Ski Clb; Spanish Clb; Ed Lit Mag; Var Socr; JV Tennis; Hon Roll; NHS; Natl Hnr Rll 85-86; Law.

SHARON, BESSER; Simsbury HS; W Simsbury, CT; (Y); 41/410; Church Yth Grp; Concert Band; Yrbk Phtg; High Hon Roll; Hon Roll.

SHARON, MICHELE; Farmington HS; Farmington, CT; (Y); 1/220; Math Tm; Band; Concert Band; Drm Mjr(t); Mrchg Band; Symp Band; Nwsp Phtg; Yrbk Stf; Swmmng; Trk; Harvard Radcliff Bk Awd 86; Frnch Bk Awd 86; Manchester Young Artists Comptn 85; Music.

SHARP, BENJAMIN; King HS; Stamford, CT; (Y); 3/35; Drama Clb; JA; Model UN; Scholastic Bowl; School Musical; School Play; Nwsp Rptr; Nwsp Sprt Ed; Yrbk Rptr; Var JV Bsbl; All Leag Ftbl 85-86; MVP Bsktbl 85-86; Comm.

SHARRARD, LAURA; Simsbury HS; Simsbury, CT; (Y); 6/410; Yrbk Stf; Var L Badmtn; JV Bsktbl; Var L Sftbl; Var L Vllybl; High Hon Roll; NHS; Simsbury Schlr Awd 84-87; Cntrl CT Conf All Conf Tm Awd Sftbll 86.

SHARRON, MICHELE; Seymour HS; Oxford, CT; (S); Hon Roll; Engr.

SHATAS, KAREN; Southington HS; Southington, CT; (Y); 176/600; DECA; Ski Clb; Capt Swmmng; Trk; Hon Roll; Cmptd YMCA Ntls Swmmng 84; Eckerd Coll; Bus.

SHAW, CHRISTINE; Enrico Fermi HS; Enfield, CT; (Y); Dance Clb; Band; Concert Band; Jazz Band; Mrchg Band; Pep Band; Variety Show; High Hon Roll; Hon Roll; Ntl Merit SF; U Of CT Top 100 Stus CT 85; U Of CT; Intl Bus.

SHAW, RICHARD; Emmett O Brien HS; Seymour, CT; (Y); Dance Clb; JA; Ski Clb; Band; Bsbl; Bsktbl; Ftbl; Wt Lftg; Hon Roll; Machnst Trade.

SHEA, CINDY; Seymour HS; Seymour, CT; (Y); 22/321; Church Yth Grp; Drama Clb; Teachers Aide; Drm Mjr(t); Nwsp Ed-Chief; Twrlr; Hon Roll; U Of Bridgeport; Journalism.

SHEA, COLLEEN; Holy Cross HS; Waterbury, CT; (Y); Hosp Aide; JA; School Play; Stage Crew; Variety Show; Yrbk Stf; Crs Cntry; VP Mgr(s); VP Score Keeper; Trk; Lbrl Arts.

SHEA, ELIZABETH; Southington HS; Southington, CT; (Y); 11/600; German Clb; Hosp Aide; Key Clb; Trs Pep Clb; Yrbk Stf; Mgr(s); Var L Vllybl; High Hon Roll; Jr NHS; NHS; Gftd & Tnltd Prgm 83-86; Latin Awd 84 & 85; Grmn Awds From Goethe Inst In Bstn 84 & 85; Coll Of Hly Cross; Doctor.

SHEA, KYLA; Holy Cross HS; Middlebury, CT; (Y); 40/350; Var Swmmng; Var Trk; High Hon Roll; Hon Roll; Spanish NHS; St Schlr; Presdntl Acadmc Ftns Awd 86; Fairfield U; Bio.

SHEARSTONE, ANGELINE; Southington HS; Plantsville, CT; (Y); Church Yth Grp; Library Aide; Ski Clb; Chorus; JV Bsktbl; High Hon Roll; Music.

SHEEHAN, KATHRYN; Hammonasset HS; Madison, CT; (Y); Dance Clb; Drama Clb; Hosp Aide; Latin Clb; Pep Clb; School Play; Stage Crew; Variety Show; Yrbk Stf; Score Keeper; Elizabethtown Coll; Chld Dvlpmt.

SHEFFIELD, GAIL; Manchester HS; Manchester, CT; (Y); Church Yth Grp; French Clb; Var L Tennis; Hon Roll; NHS; Ntl Merit Ltr; Psych.

SHEIDLEY, NATHANIEL J; Edwin O Smith HS; Storrs, CT; (Y); 2/160; Intnl Clb; Model UN; Nwsp Rptr; Lit Mag; Rep Stu Cncl; Var Crs Cntry; NHS; Cmnty Wkr; Political Wkr; Im Badmtn; 1st Congress-Bundestag Scholar Exch Germny 84-85; Stanford.

SHELDON, JOSLYN; Putnam HS; Putnam, CT; (Y); 2/150; Band; Sec Trs Concert Band; Jazz Band; Mrchg Band; School Play; Yrbk Stf; Co-Capt Sftbl; High Hon Roll; Sec NHS; Sal; Dr Robt E Johnston Mem Schlrshp, Stanley Thos Scraba Salutatorian Awd, Ella J Thayer Mem Schlrshp 86; U CT; Phys Ther.

SHEN, CINDY; The Academy Of Our Lady Of Mercy; Bridgeport, CT; (Y); 35/117; Debate Tm; Math Clb; Math Tm; Pres Model UN; Scholastic Bowl; Science Clb; Stage Crew; Ed Yrbk Phtg; NHS; French Clb; Bio.

SHERIDAN, LAURA; South Catholic HS; Hartford, CT; (Y); 33/251; Aud/Vis; Drama Clb; Exploring; School Musical; Trs Sr Cls; Rep Stu Cncl; Var Capt Cheerleading; Var L Crs Cntry; Var L Trk; Hon Roll; Outstndng Srv Cls 85; Finlst Miss Amercn Pagnt 85; Commentor Schl TV Pgm 87; Cmmnctns.

SHERIFF, EWAN A; Farmington HS; Farmington, CT; (Y); Boy Scts; DECA; Crs Cntry; Trk; Wt Lftg; Wrstlng; Bus Admin.

SHERMAN, CAROLYN E; Wilton HS; Wilton, CT; (Y); 10/300; Key Clb; Chorus; Swing Chorus; Sec Stu Cncl; Var Capt Fld Hcky; Var L Lcrss; DAR Awd; High Hon Roll; NHS; Ntl Merit Ltr; Wilton La Crosse Assn Outstdng SR Awd Scholar 86; Harvard Bk Awd 85; CT Smmr Intern Pgm 85; U PA.

SHERMAN, MERCEDES; Hopkins HS; New Haven, CT; (Y); Church Yth Grp; Girl Scts; Hosp Aide; Office Aide; Sec Church Choir; Capt Fld Hcky; Lcrss; Var L Vllybl; Ntl Merit Schol; Wellesley; Med.

SHERMAN, RODERICK; Suffield HS; Suffield, CT; (Y); 34/132; JA; Var L Trk; Hon Roll; JohnsonST UT; Bus Mngmnt.

SHERWILL, BARBARA; Mark T Sheehan HS; Yalesville, CT; (Y); 30/230; Spanish Clb; Powder Puff Ftbl; High Hon Roll; Hon Roll; Exclnce Span II 84; U CT; Elem Educ.

SHERWOOD, CHERYLANN; Rockville HS; Vernon, CT; (Y); 66/374; French Clb; Concert Band; Mrchg Band; Symp Band; Capt L Crs Cntry; Var L Trk; High Hon Roll; Hon Roll; NHS; Band; ST LL X-Cntry Chmpshp 85-86; Pre Med.

SHEWOKIS, CHRISTINE M; Enrico Fermi HS; Enfield, CT; (Y); 10/307; Hosp Aide; Ski Clb; Var Fld Hcky; Mgr Ice Hcky; JV Sftbl; CC Awd; High Hon Roll; NHS; Pres Schlr; Boostr Clb Awd 86; Enfield Polsh JR Leag Schlrshp, Wmns Clb Schlrshp 86; Syracuse U; Acctng.

SHILBERG, NATHAN; Bristol Central HS; Bristol, CT; (Y); 1/316; Drama Clb; JA; Math Tm; School Play; Ed Nwsp Rptr; JV Trk; Bausch & Lomb Sci Awd; High Hon Roll; Val; Schlstc Jrnlst Awd 86; Nancy Henderson Mem 86; Acad Ftnss Awd 86; Tufts U.

SHINN, WENDY; Hartford Christian Acad; Ellington, CT; (Y); 2/5; Church Yth Grp; Drama Clb; Speech Tm; Teachers Aide; Chorus; School Play; Stage Crew; Nwsp Rptr; Yrbk Stf; Sec Frsh Cls; SR Eng Wd 85-86; Bob Jones U.

SHIO, PAUL; Staples HS; Westport, CT; (Y); Computer Clb; Math Tm; ROTC; Acpl Chr; Chorus; Hon Roll; Yales Frontrs Appld Sci 86; U Bridgeport EDY Smmr Prog 85; Norwalk TECH Coll 84; Elec Engr.

SHIPPEE, DEBRA; Plainfield HS; Moosup, CT; (Y); 36/180; Pep Clb; Varsity Clb; Yrbk Phtg; Yrbk Stf; Sec Frsh Cls; Sec Soph Cls; Sec Jr Cls; Var Cheerleading; Trk; Hon Roll; Bus Adm.

SHIRLEY, NANETTE RAE; Bristol Central HS; Bristol, CT; (Y); Intnl Clb; Science Clb; Yrbk Stf; Mgr(s); Mat Maids; Score Keeper; Hon Roll; Mgr Sftbl; Mgr Wrstlng; Med Tech.

SHIRLING, AMY; Wilby HS; Waterbury, CT; (Y); Art Clb; JA; Var L Cheerleading; Var L Sftbl; Hon Roll; Clothng Desgnr.

SHIVELY, T DELOE; Avon Old Farms HS; Harwinton, CT; (Y); 22/101; Nwsp Rptr; Nwsp Sprt Ed; JV L Bsbl; Var L Bsktbl; Var L Ftbl.

SHOLA, LISA; Trumbull HS; Trumbull, CT; (Y); Dance Clb; Drama Clb; Hosp Aide; Color Guard; Mrchg Band; School Play; JV Mgr(s); Hon Roll; Awd Bst Italn Stu 84-85; Sci.

SHOLTIS, ADRIENNE; Lyme-Old Lyme HS; Old Lyme, CT; (Y); AFS; Computer Clb; Intnl Clb; Chorus; Cheerleading; High Hon Roll; Hon Roll; BUS.

SHOOK, JENNIFER; Oliver Wolcott Reg VT Schl; Kent, CT; (Y); Art Clb; Aud/Vis; Hosp Aide; Red Cross Aide; Library Aide; VICA; Yrbk Stf; RN.

SHORTELL, HEIDI; Farmington HS; Farmington, CT; (Y); Political Wkr; Chorus; Swing Chorus; Tunxis CC; Graphic Dsgn.

SHOTZ, GEOFF; Taft Schl; Tarzana, CA; (Y); Boy Scts; Radio Clb; Ski Clb; Orch; Nwsp Stf; JV Var Ice Hcky; Mgr(s); Mgr Socr; Hon Roll; Town Crier Schl Hons & Ldrshp Group 82-83; Art.

SHULAR, CAROL A; Norwalk HS; Norwalk, CT; (Y); 64/456; Pres VP Church Yth Grp; ROTC; Var L Bsktbl; Var L Sftbl; High Hon Roll; Hon Roll; All Cty Bsktbl Team 86; All Cty Sftbl Team 85; Math.

SIA, MICHAEL; Fairfield Prep; Fairfield, CT; (Y); Boy Scts; Nwsp Phtg; Yrbk Phtg; Yrbk Stf; Off Soph Cls; VP Bsbl; Stu Cncl; Spanish NHS; Comp Engr.

SIDELLA, LOUIS; Bristol Central HS; Bristol, CT; (Y); Boys Clb Am; Boy Scts; Latin Clb; Ski Clb; Varsity Clb; VP Soph Cls; Pres Jr Cls; VP Sr Cls; JV Bsktbl; Var Ftbl; Johnson & Wales; Htl Mgmt.

SIE, JACKSON; Staples HS; Westport, CT; (Y); Boy Scts; French Clb; Math Clb; Math Tm; Hon Roll; Excellence French 85 & 86; Comp Sci.

SIEBOLD, MEL; Manchester HS; Manchester, CT; (Y); Boy Scts; Yrbk Phtg; Crs Cntry; L Var Swmmng; L Var Trk; Timer; Schl Sci Fair 2nd Pl 84; Smmr Outdoor Advntrs 84; Ind Tech.

SIEDEL, MIKE; Southington HS; Southington, CT; (Y); Key Clb; Latin Clb; Concert Band; Jazz Band; Mrchg Band; Nwsp Stf; Capt Bsbl; Bsktbl; Ftbl; Hon Roll.

SIEFERT, PHIL; Fairfield College Prep Schl; Fairfield, CT; (Y); Im Socr; Fr Thomas Murphy Schlrshp 85; Princeton; Engrng.

SIEGLE, GREG; Stamford HS; Stamford, CT; (Y); Cmnty Wkr; Capt Debate Tm; Political Wkr; Science Clb; Temple Yth Grp; Stu Cncl; High Hon Roll; Hon Roll; NHS; W R Farrington Mem Schlrshp 85; Brown U Bk Awd 86; 1st Pl Amer Inst Chem Ngrs Physcs Cntst 86; Compu Sci.

SIEREJKO, DEANA; East Haven HS; East Haven, CT; (Y); Cheerleading; Legal Sec.

SIKORA, BETH; Old Saybrook HS; Old Saybrook, CT; (Y); AFS; Church Yth Grp; Cmnty Wkr; SADD; Band; Nwsp Rptr; JV Crs Cntry; Hon Roll; Hartford Courant Jrnlsm Awd Sprts Writg 84; Engl Dept Jrnlsm Awd 86; AFS Sch Yr Exch Stu Turkey 86-87; Jrnlsm.

SIKORSKI, PATRICK; Norwich Reg Voc Technical Schl; Norwich, CT; (Y); 2/136; Am Leg Boys St; Chess Clb; High Hon Roll; NHS; Prfct Atten Awd; Sal; Val; NE Utlties Awd & Fl Schlrshp 86; Englsh Awd 86; Zezulka Awd 86; Thames Vlly ST Tech Coll; Engr.

SILANO, CHRISTINE; St Joseph HS; Trumbull, CT; (Y); Church Yth Grp; Debate Tm; Drama Clb; Spanish Clb; Stage Crew; Yrbk Stf; JV Sftbl; High Hon Roll; Jr NHS; NHS; Awd For Hghst Grd Spnsh I, II 84-86; Lectr At Cathedrl 83-86; Pre-Law.

SILK, KELLY A; Kingswood-Oxford Schl; West Hartford, CT; (Y); Pres Art Clb; Camera Clb; French Clb; Intnl Clb; Latin Clb; Model UN; Service Clb; Chorus; School Musical; School Play; Katherine Day Awd-Facity Awd 85; 1st Pl-ST Comptn Model UN; Arts Studnt; Archeology.

SILL, BRUCE; Derby HS; Derby, CT; (Y); Am Leg Boys St; Boy Scts; VP Spanish Clb; Varsity Clb; Band; Concert Band; Mrchg Band; Ftbl; Capt Wrstlng; Hon Roll; Phrmcy.

SILVA, MICHELLE L; Henry Abbott RVTS HS; Danbury, CT; (S); 5/155; Church Yth Grp; Ski Clb; VICA; Yrbk Ed-Chief; VP Soph Cls; VP Jr Cls; VP Stu Cncl; Hon Roll; NHS; Daughters Amer Revltn-Good Ctzn Awd; Rifl Tm-Co-Capt, Capt; AZ ST U; Graphc Cmnctns.

SILVA, NANCY; Andrew Warde HS; Fairfield, CT; (Y); Trs Band; Orch; Lit Mag; Sec Soph Cls; Pres Jr Cls; Sec Sr Cls; JV Var Fld Hcky; High Hon Roll; Trs NHS; Spanish NHS; Vssr Bk Awd Excllnc Hmnts 86; Wstrn CT Reg Music Fstvl 84-85; Bus.

SILVA, ROSA M; South Catholic HS; Newington, CT; (Y); 4/191; Church Yth Grp; JA; Stage Crew; Nwsp Rptr; Nwsp Sprt Ed; Nwsp Stf; Yrbk Stf; Lit Mag; Pres Soph Cls; Rep Jr Cls; Schlr Athlt 86; D Hayes Schlrshp 86; Boston Clg; Mktg/Fnce.

SILVERMAN, ANDREA; Miss Porters Schl; Wilmington, VT; (Y); Cmnty Wkr; Debate Tm; German Clb; Model UN; Political Wkr; Ski Clb; Nwsp Rptr; Nwsp Stf; Var Badmtn; Swmmng; Pol Sci.

SILVERMAN, KIM; Stamford HS; Stamford, CT; (Y); JA; Yrbk Stf; Var L Sftbl; Hon Roll; NHS.

SILVERSTEIN, AMY; East Catholic HS; Bolton, CT; (Y); Pres Trs French Clb; Nwsp Rptr; Ed Nwsp Stf; Yrbk Ed-Chief; Sec VP Jr Cls; Hon Roll; Ski Clb; Off Soph Cls; Off Sr Cls; Stu Cncl; Clark U Alumni & Friends Schlrshp 86; Clark U; Intl Rel.

SILVESTRI, AMY; Holy Cross HS; Beacon Falls, CT; (Y); 103/380; Sec Church Yth Grp; L Concert Band; Jazz Band; Mrchg Band; Lit Mag; Hon Roll; Psych.

SIMARD, LAURA; R E Fitch SR HS; Groton, CT; (Y); 2/350; Intnl Clb; Pres Science Clb; Thesps; Chorus; Nwsp Ed-Chief; Bausch & Lomb Sci Awd; DAR Awd; NHS; Rotary Awd; Sal; Drtmth Coll; Math.

SIMMONS, ROBERT; Putnam HS; Putnam, CT; (Y); Band; Chorus; Concert Band; Jazz Band; Mrchg Band; Orch; Pep Band; Var Trk; Chess Clb; Church Yth Grp; All Amer Hall Fame Band Awd 86; U S Collegiate Wind Band 86; Comp.

SIMMONS, SHANNON; St Marys HS; New Haven, CT; (Y); Church Yth Grp; Cmnty Wkr; Church Choir; Variety Show; Stu Cncl; Hon Roll; Vlntr Svc 86; Psychol.

SIMMS, ROBYN; Southington HS; Southington, CT; (Y); Girl Scts; Rep Key Clb; Latin Clb; Chorus; Drill Tm; School Musical; Nwsp Bus Mgr; Nwsp Stf; Theatre.

SIMONE, ELIZABETH; Southington HS; Southington, CT; (Y); 7/600; German Clb; Latin Clb; Band; Concert Band; Mrchg Band; Nwsp Stf; Yrbk Stf; Hon Roll; NHS; Ntl Merit Ltr; Zoology.

SIMONOVICH, LAURA; Immaculate HS; Danbury, CT; (Y); 13/137; Church Yth Grp; Dance Clb; Spanish Clb; School Play; Yrbk Stf; Co-Capt Cheerleading; High Hon Roll; NHS; Spanish NHS; Irish Dancing Awds 78-85.

SIMONS, DEBORAH A; Danbury HS; Danbury, CT; (Y); 138/577; Cmnty Wkr; Drama Clb; Key Clb; Nwsp Stf; Hon Roll; Jr NHS; Excllnce Eng 82-83; U CT; Gen Drama.

SIMPLICIO, PHILIP; Wilton HS; Wilton, CT; (Y); 41/350; Cmnty Wkr; Pep Clb; Varsity Clb; Rep Stu Cncl; Var L Ftbl; Var Golf; Hon Roll; NHS; Ldrshp Awd Ski Tm, All ST Ski Tm 85-86; Pre-Med.

SIMPSON, ERIN K; Lyme/Old Lyme HS; Old Lyme, CT; (Y); 9/126; Art Clb; Church Yth Grp; Variety Show; Nwsp Stf; Lit Mag; Rep Stu Cncl; Cheerleading; DAR Awd; NHS; AFS; Schltc Art Awd Comp Gold Key 85; Fine Art.

SINGH, VEENA; Shelton HS; Shelton, CT; (Y); 10/327; French Clb; SADD; Yrbk Sprt Ed; Ed Yrbk Stf; Tennis; VP French Hon Soc; High Hon Roll; NHS; Pres Schlr; Gona Tichy Awd; L M Verdock Memrl Awd; Hghst Avg Frnch II-V; Rutgers U; Intl Bus.

SIPPEL, CHRISTINA L; Roger Ludlowe HS; Fairfield, CT; (Y); 1/345; French Clb; Math Tm; Ski Clb; Teachers Aide; Trs Band; Jazz Band; School Musical; Ed Yrbk Stf; Rep Frsh Cls; Rep Soph Cls; Mr & Mrs Gordon Biledes Scholar 86; NHS 85-86; Mod Music Masters Intl Hnr Soc 85-86; Bucknell U; Bio.

SIPPLES, TIMOTHY F; The Morgan Schl; Clinton, CT; (Y); 1/149; Trs AFS; Drama Clb; Capt Quiz Bowl; Spanish Clb; Band; Chorus; School Musical; Nwsp Rptr; Bausch & Lomb Sci Awd; Elks Awd; Harvard Coll; Econ.

SIRICO, ANITA; Danbury HS; Danbury, CT; (Y); Art Clb; Dance Clb; French Clb; PAVAS; Chorus; Stage Crew; Tennis; High Hon Roll; Pres Schlr; Ctr Creative Yth Wesleyan U 85; Western CT ST U; Graphic Dsgn.

SIROIS, KIM; East Hartford HS; E Hartford, CT; (Y); 38/369; Sec French Clb; Chorus; Nwsp Stf; Rep Soph Cls; Trs Jr Cls; Trs Sr Cls; Sec Stu Cncl; JV Cheerleading; Var Crs Cntry; Hon Roll; E Hartford Wmns Clb Schlrshp 86; CT ST Achvt Grnt 86; Dr Raymond Hoyle Schlrshp 86; Framingham ST Coll; Md Cmmnctn.

SIROWICH, SUE; Seymour HS; Beacon Falls, CT; (Y); 4-H; Girl Scts; Nwsp Stf; Yrbk Stf; Stu Cncl; JV Bsktbl; Stat Score Keeper; JV Var Sftbl; High Hon Roll; Hon Roll; S CT ST U; Englsh.

SISKO, CHERYL; Pomperaug HS; Southbury, CT; (Y); 34/194; Rep Frsh Cls; Rep Soph Cls; Rep Jr Cls; Trk; Hon Roll; Sthbry-Mdlbry Schlrshp 86; Wmns Clb Schlrshp 86; Grd Pnt Avrg & Cls Rnk Schlrshp 86; Ctrl CT ST U; Bus.

SIVERTSEN, ERIC; Mark T Sheehan HS; Yalesville, CT; (Y); Boys Clb Am; Cmnty Wkr; Key Clb; Political Wkr; Im Bsktbl; JV Var Socr; Hon Roll; Kiwanis Awd; Corp Law.

SIZEMORE, DAVID; Xavier HS; Northford, CT; (Y); 21/199; Nwsp Ed-Chief; Yrbk Stf; Rep Jr Cls; Var Capt Bsktbl; Var Capt Socr; All-Hartford Cnty Conf Goalkpr 85-86; All-Middlesex Cnty Goalkpr 85-86; All ST Cls LL Goalkper 85-86; Drew U; Econ.

SKABARDONIS, GEORGE; Holy Cross HS; Middlebury, CT; (Y); 24/392; Pres Church Yth Grp; Science Clb; Spanish Clb; Crs Cntry; NHS.

SKEENS, DIANE; West Haven HS; W Haven, CT; (Y); Church Yth Grp; Office Aide; SADD; Nwsp Stf; Kimberly Rassmussin Awd 80; Inds Arts Awd 86; U Of New Haven; Crim Jus.

SKRIPOL, LORI; Colchester Christian Acad; Marlborough, CT; (Y); Church Yth Grp; FCA; Chorus; Var Capt Bsktbl; Var Sftbl; Var Vllybl; Hon Roll; U Hartford; Pol Sci.

SKURAT, JENNIFER; Holy Cross HS; Seymour, CT; (Y); 113/380; Church Yth Grp; Chorus; Hon Roll; Church Yth Grp Chrldg Sqd; Church Yth Grp Chrldg Sqd Capt.

SKYERS, SHARON A; Notre Dame Catholic HS; Bridgeport, CT; (Y); 46/248; Sec VP JA; VP Spanish Clb; Church Choir; Ed Church Choir; Ed Nwsp Rptr; Lit Mag; Hon Roll; Prsdntl Acad Ftnss Awd 86; Duke U; Acctng.

SLADE, LISA MICHELLE; Kolbe-Cathedral HS; Bridgeport, CT; (Y); Church Yth Grp; FHA; JA; Band; Chorus; Church Choir; Variety Show; Nwsp Stf; Yrbk Stf; Hon Roll; Sacred Heart U; Psych.

SLATER, RUSSELL; Oliver Wolcott Tech; Riverton, CT; (Y); 26/146; Trs 4-H; Pres VICA; Rep Yrbk Stf; Rep Soph Cls; Rep Jr Cls; Rep Stu Cncl; Cheerleading; Var Socr; 4-H Awd; Hon Roll; 2nd Pl ST VICA Skill Olympcs 86; Bst 4-Her Clb Awd 84 & 85; 1st Pl Showmnshp 4-H Fair Awds 85; Elec Engr.

SLAVIK, KRISTA; New Fairfield HS; New Fairfield, CT; (Y); Church Yth Grp; VP Band; Chorus; Church Choir; School Musical; Variety Show; Var Mgr(s); Var Capt Swmmng; Var Trk; Hon Roll.

SLIPSKI, CHERYL; Berlin HS; E Berlin, CT; (Y); Cmnty Wkr; Drama Clb; SADD; Y-Teens; VP Band; Sec Concert Band; Mrchg Band; Pep Band; School Play; Variety Show; Outstndng Jr In Bnd 85-86; Yrbk Awd 85-86; Hstry Achvt Awd 85-86; Pre-Law.

SLOAN, SHARON; Manchester HS; Manchester, CT; (Y); AFS; Church Yth Grp; Cmnty Wkr; JA; Spanish Clb; Yrbk Ed-Chief; Yrbk Stf; Stu Cncl; Hon Roll; JR Achvt Sales Clb 84-86; Outstndng Wrk Yrbk Edtr 84-85; Law.

SLONSKI, KEITH M; Gr*iswold HS; Jewett City, CT; (Y); 1/86; Var Bsktbl; Var Capt Crs Cntry; Var Capt Trk; High Hon Roll; NHS; Acad All Amer 86; Engrng.

SLOSSBERG, MATTHEW; Brien Mc Mahon HS; Norwalk, CT; (Y); Ski Clb; Spanish Clb; Temple Yth Grp; Lcrss; Socr; Hon Roll.

SLOWIK, CHRISTOPHER E; Shelton HS; Shelton, CT; (Y); Tradesmn Awd 86; Tech Careers Inst; Htg.

SLOWIK, CRIS; Southington HS; Southington, CT; (Y); 6/600; Am Leg Boys St; Key Clb; Quiz Bowl; Nwsp Ed-Chief; DAR Awd; Hon Roll; NHS; Ntl Merit SF; Wnnr Nw Englnd Key Clbs Essy Cntst 84-86; Wnnr CT Yng Plywrts Cntst 86; Engl.

SLYWA, SUSAN; East Windsor HS; E Windsor, CT; (Y); 20/103; Band; Concert Band; Jazz Band; Mrchg Band; Rep Frsh Cls; Rep Soph Cls; Rep Jr Cls; Var Capt Cheerleading; Var Sftbl; VP NHS; U Of CT; Nrsng.

SMITH, ALITA D; Windsor SR HS; Windsor, CT; (Y); 29/315; VP Church Yth Grp; Hosp Aide; Church Choir; Nwsp Rptr; High Hon Roll; Hon Roll; Spanish NHS; U CT Schlrshp 85; Soc Wmn Engrs Cert Merit Math & Sci 85; Natl Achvt Commended Stu 85; Acctg.

SMITH, AMY; Windsor HS; Windsor, CT; (Y); 9/360; Pres Soph Cls; Pres Jr Cls; Rep Stu Cncl; JV Crs Cntry; Var Swmmng; JV Trk; French Hon Soc; High Hon Roll; NHS; U Of MI Bk Awd 86.

SMITH, BECKY A; Windsor Locks HS; Windsor Locks, CT; (Y); 69/160; Drama Clb; Teachers Aide; Chorus; Stage Crew; Variety Show; Hon Roll; Voice Dem Awd; 3rd Schl Poetry 83-84, 2nd 86; Manchester CC; Radio Tech.

SMITH, CHRISTINE; Manchester HS; Manchester, CT; (Y); Church Yth Grp; French Clb; High Hon Roll; Hon Roll; Wrld Of Poetry Cntst-3 Hnrb Mntns 85; NYU; Hotel Mgt.

SMITH, DIANE; St Marys HS; New Haven, CT; (Y); #8 In Class; Am Leg Aux Girls St; VP Church Yth Grp; Service Clb; Chorus; School Musical; Lit Mag; Pres Stu Cncl; Dnfth Awd; High Hon Roll; Mu Alp Tht; HOBY Ldrshp Awd 85; History.

SMITH, EDWARD C; Saint Bernard HS; Stonington, CT; (Y); 58/265; Church Yth Grp; Off Jr Cls; Socr; Hon Roll; Aerontcl Engnrng.

SMITH, ELIZABETH; Academy Of Our Lady Of Mercy; W Haven, CT; (Y); Church Yth Grp; Drama Clb; French Clb; Chorus; Church Choir; School Musical; Hon Roll; Elec Engrng.

SMITH, ERIC; Oliver Wolcott Regional Vo Tech; Canton, CT; (Y); Hon Roll; Mchncl Engr.

SMITH, EVERETT V; Norwich Free Acad; Canterbury, CT; (Y); Computer Clb; Var L Tennis; High Hon Roll; Syracuse U; Comp.

SMITH, GENEVIEVE; Coventry HS; Coventry, CT; (Y); Church Yth Grp; Chorus; Church Choir; Lit Mag; Hon Roll; U Of CT; Psychlgy.

SMITH, GERARD; New Fairfield HS; New Fairfield, CT; (Y); 13/242; Boy Scts; Chess Clb; Church Yth Grp; Latin Clb; Scholastic Bowl; Science Clb; High Hon Roll; NHS; Atten 11th Annl Convtn II 86; Un Crbd Sessn Wshngtn Wrkshp 86; Vassr Bk Prz 86.

SMITH, JESSICA; Amity Regional HS; Woodbridge, CT; (Y); Church Yth Grp; Model UN; Spanish Clb; Lit Mag; JV Trk; Hon Roll; JETS Awd; Cert Merit Gannon U Sci P Engrng Career Day 85; 2nd Pl Slippery Rock U Frgn Lang Cont 85.

SMITH, JILL; East Lyme HS; Oakdale, CT; (Y); 4-H; Trs Frsh Cls; Trk; High Hon Roll; Hon Roll; NHS; Scl Wk.

SMITH, KIMBLE; Cheshire HS; Cheshire, CT; (Y); SADD; School Play; Yrbk Stf; JV Bsktbl; Socr; Var Trk; Scl Wrkr.

SMITH, LAUREEN; Seymour HS; Seymour, CT; (S); 8/192; AFS; Church Yth Grp; Hosp Aide; Yrbk Stf; Cit Awd; Hon Roll; NHS; Womns Clg Clb Schlrhsp 86; U Of CT; Phy Thrpy.

SMITH, MARY; Sacred Heart Acad; N Branford, CT; (Y); FBLA; Hosp Aide; Spanish Clb; School Musical; Variety Show; Capt Var Crs Cntry; Vllybl; Hon Roll; NEDT Awd 86.

SMITH, MICHAEL; Wethersfield HS; Wethersfield, CT; (Y); 104/300; Church Yth Grp; Cmnty Wkr; Debate Tm; Exploring; Q&S; Ski Clb; SADD; Off Stu Cncl; JV Swmmng; Hon Roll; Bus.

SMITH, MICHELLE; Putnam HS; Putnam, CT; (Y); Aud/Vis; Office Aide; Stat Socr; Jr NHS.

SMITH, PATRICIA; Sacred Heart Acad; N Branford, CT; (Y); 86/105; Capt Drama Clb; FBLA; Pep Clb; Chorus; School Musical; School Play; Stage Crew; Nwsp Rptr; Yrbk Stf; Lit Mag; U Of CT; Art Hstry.

SMITH, PATRICK; Plainfield HS; Moosup, CT; (Y); 33/200; VP Varsity Clb; Var Bsbl; Var Bsktbl; Var Ftbl; Hon Roll; Voice Dem Awd.

SMITH, RANDI; Kingswood-Oxford HS; W Hartford, CT; (Y); Cmnty Wkr; Pres German Clb; Service Clb; Chorus; Madrigals; School Play; Ed Nwsp Stf; Var Crs Cntry; JV Tennis; Hon Roll; Psych.

SMITH, REGINA; Putnam HS; Putnam, CT; (Y); 5/113; Spanish Clb; Pres VP Band; Jazz Band; Yrbk Stf; High Hon Roll; NHS; Chorus; Concert Band; Mrchg Band; Pep Band; All Amer Hl Of Fm Band 86; All Estrn Band 85-86; MVP Band 85; U Of CT; Mech Engr.

SMITH, RICHARD C; Howell Cheney Tech Schl; Manchester, CT; (Y); Church Yth Grp; Library Aide; Office Aide; VICA; Yrbk Rptr; Yrbk Stf; Sec Jr Cls; Sec Sr Cls; Cit Awd; DAR Awd; News Media.

SMITH, SHARAI E; Amity Regional SR HS; Orange, CT; (Y); 130/388; Art Clb; PAVAS; Lit Mag; Cit Awd; High Hon Roll; Cert For Outstndng Artistic Achvt 85; Illustration.

SMITH III, SIDNEY S; New Canaan HS; New Canaan, CT; (Y); Math Tm; Radio Clb; Jazz Band; Mrchg Band; Pep Band; School Musical; Symp Band; Var Swmmng; Bausch & Lomb Sci Awd; NHS; Fairfield Cnty Med Assn Awd Schltc Excllnce 85; Bowdoin Coll.

SMITH, STACY; East Lyme HS; E Lyme, CT; (Y); Political Wkr; Band; Concert Band; Mrchg Band; Yrbk Stf; Sec Soph Cls; Sec Jr Cls; Rep Stu Cncl; Powder Puff Ftbl; Sec NHS; Intl Rel.

SMITH, STACY; New Britain SR HS; New Britain, CT; (Y); Church Yth Grp; Dance Clb; Key Clb; Madrigals; Nwsp Phtg; Nwsp Rptr; Rep Sr Cls; VP Stu Cncl; Var Capt Cheerleading; Hon Roll; Spnsh Exc Awd 84-85; Gftd/Tlntd Scl Sci Prgm 86-87; Pdtrcn.

SMITH, TARA; Miss Porters Schl; Keene, NH; (Y); VP JA; Latin Clb; Spanish Clb; Chorus; Color Guard; Stage Crew; Var Golf; Var Trk; JV Vllybl; Latin Awd 86.

SMOKO, ROBERT; Southington HS; Southington, CT; (Y); Chess Clb; High Hon Roll; Hon Roll; Locl Exm Awd 84; Engrng.

SMOLEN, PETER; Farmington HS; Unionville, CT; (Y); Variety Show; JV Var Ftbl; Var Lcrss; Wt Lftg; JV Var Wrstlng; Civil Engrng.

SMYERS, RICHARD; Wethersfield HS; Wethersfield, CT; (Y); 3/300; Am Leg Boys St; Ski Clb; Capt JV Socr; L Var Swmmng; L Var Trk; High Hon Roll; NHS; Cmnty Wkr; Yrbk Stf; Rep Stu Cncl; Awd Of Proms Fld Of Sci 84; All Leag Swmr 86; All ST 400 Free Rely Swmg 86.

SNIDER, MICHAEL; Rham HS; Hebron, CT; (Y); 11/204; Aud/Vis; Boy Scts; Chess Clb; Temple Yth Grp; Band; Jazz Band; Wrstlng; High Hon Roll; NHS; Talcott Mtn Sci Pgm Tlntd & Gifted 84-85; US Olympic Comm JR Kayak Tm 86; Mth.

SNIHUR, DARRIN; Bullaro Havens Ruts HS; Bridgeport, CT; (Y); Church Yth Grp; Dance Clb; Rep Stu Cncl; Hon Roll; Greater New Haven Tech; Comp Sc.

SNODGRASS, LAURA; Litchfield HS; Bantam, CT; (Y); 5/90; Art Clb; School Musical; Nwsp Ed-Chief; High Hon Roll; NHS; Writers Symposium Hartford Ct 86; Mock Trial Comp 84; High Achvt Eng 86; Boston U; Lib Arts.

SNYDER JR, CHARLES A; Oliver Wolcott Tech; Sharon, CT; (Y); Art Clb; Rep Jr Cls; Musc Snd Tech 85-86; Arch.

SOBANSKI, JENIFER; Foran HS; Milford, CT; (Y); Drama Clb; Keywanettes; Color Guard; School Play; Yrbk Stf; Stu Cncl; Hon Roll; NHS; Tchr.

SOBCZAK, DARYL; Berlin HS; E Berlin, CT; (Y); Chess Clb; Stu Cncl; JV Ftbl; L Var Golf; Var Ice Hcky; L Var Socr; Actrl Wrk.

SODEL, MELISSA; O H Platt HS; Meriden, CT; (S); Pres DECA; Girl Scts; JA; Band; Concert Band; Mrchg Band; Pep Band; Yrbk Stf; Var L Diving; Var Powder Puff Ftbl; DECA Schlrshp Fr Johnson & Wales Coll 86; Rcrd Jrnl DECA Schlrshp 86; Jhnsn & Wls Coll; Fshn Merch.

SODERBERG, ROBERT JOHN; Rham HS; Hebron, CT; (Y); 31/165; Am Leg Boys St; Var Bsbl; Capt Socr; Hon Roll; Pres Acadmc Ftnss Awd; Hebron Tri Centnnl Comm Schlrshp; Patricia Mulligan Meml Schlrshp; U Of Hartford; Math.

SODLOSKY, LEE-ANN; Sacred Heart Acad; West Haven, CT; (Y); 88/122; Church Yth Grp; Cmnty Wkr; Pres 4-H; Sec FBLA; Office Aide; Service Clb; Teachers Aide; Band; Concert Band; Jazz Band; Gregg Awd 84-85; Quinnipiac Coll; Accntg.

SOHN, ROBERT; Newington HS; Newington, CT; (Y); 10/365; Am Leg Boys St; Church Yth Grp; Cmnty Wkr; Ski Clb; Var Lcrss; High Hon Roll; Hon Roll; Pres Schlr; Schlr Athl Awd 86; Top Scholar For Boys 83; Top Scholar For Boys 86; Trinity Coll; Pre-Med.

SOL, ADAM; New Fairfield HS; New Fairfield, CT; (Y); 6/235; Latin Clb; VP Temple Yth Grp; School Musical; Lit Mag; Off Frsh Cls; Var L Tennis; French Hon Soc; High Hon Roll; Hon Roll; NHS; 1st In ST CT On ST Latin Exam 85; Brown; Author.

SOLINSKY, MERYL; William H Hall HS; W Hartford, CT; (Y); 136/349; French Clb; Pep Clb; Teachers Aide; Temple Yth Grp; Band; Drm Mjr(t); Jazz Band; Pom Pon; Twrlr; Hon Roll; Capt Of Majorettes Var Letter 85-87.

SOLOMON, JULIE; Cheshire HS; Cheshire, CT; (Y); 1/283; Am Leg Aux Girls St; Cmnty Wkr; Quiz Bowl; Service Clb; Temple Yth Grp; School Play; Stu Cncl; High Hon Roll; NHS; Ntl Merit SF; Colt Poetry Cntst Spnsh 1st Pl 83; Soc Sci Sympsm Hon Ment 85; Stu Rep Quiz Bowl 85; Anthrplgy.

SOLOWAY, BRETT; Amity Regional SR HS; Woodbridge, CT; (Y); 21/388; Model UN; Ed Yrbk Phtg; Ed Yrbk Stf; Rep Frsh Cls; Var L Swmmng; High Hon Roll; NHS; Pres Schlr; U Of MI; Pltcl Sc.

SOLTESZ, ANDREA; Masuk HS; Monroe, CT; (Y); 48/270; Variety Show; Yrbk Stf; JV Var Sftbl; Var Swmmng; Outstndng Achvt Bus 85; Eleanor F Moore Bus Awd 85; Briarwood Bk Awd 85; Fairfield U; Bus Mgmt.

SOMMA, NICOLE; Sacred Heart Acad; New Haven, CT; (Y); Trs FBLA; Hosp Aide; VP Chorus; School Musical; Im Vllybl; Hon Roll; Editer HS Vol Nwslttr Yale New Haven Hosp 85-87; HS Ldr Vlntr Prog YNHH 85-87; Awd Spkng FBLA Conv.

SOMODY, MICHELLE; Westhill HS; Stamford, CT; (Y); 35/409; JA; Rep Sr Cls; Var Capt Gym; Var Capt Vllybl; Hon Roll; NHS; Gettysburg Coll; Pre-Law.

SONNE, JONATHAN; Conard HS; W Hartford, CT; (Y); 14/345; Church Yth Grp; Concert Band; School Musical; Capt Var Swmmng; High Hon Roll; Trs NHS; Ntl Merit Ltr; Spanish NHS; All-Nw Englnd Music Fstvl 84-86; All-ST Music Fstvl 85-86.

SONNONE, STEPHEN T; South Catholic HS; Hartford, CT; (Y); 20/191; Letterman Clb; Yrbk Sprt Ed; Pres Frsh Cls; Pres Jr Cls; Rep Stu Cncl; Var Capt Ftbl; High Hon Roll; NHS; Pres Schlr; St Schlr; Intrcl Schlrshp Awd 86; Bus & Prof Wmns Clb Hrtfrd Schlrshp 86; Ftbl Mst Imprvd & All-Conf 86; Trinity Coll; Biolgy.

SORBO, MICHELE; Holy Cross HS; Waterbury, CT; (Y); 14/348; Church Yth Grp; VP Service Clb; High Hon Roll; NHS; CT ST Schlr 86; Unico Schlrshp 86; U Of CT; Alld Hlth Fld.

SORCE, MICHELLE; Seymour HS; Seymour, CT; (S); Hosp Aide; JA; Band; JV Swmmng; Var Tennis; L Twrlr; High Hon Roll; Hon Roll; Prfct Atten Awd; U Of CT; Med Field.

SORENSEN, HOLLY; Shelton HS; Shelton, CT; (Y); 9/334; Drama Clb; Hosp Aide; JA; Ski Clb; Spanish Clb; Rep Stu Cncl; Cheerleading; High Hon Roll; NHS; Spanish NHS; Anthony Muchado Awd 85; Boston Coll; Hlth.

SOSNOWSKI, DONALD; Danbury HS; Danbury, CT; (Y); AFS; Boy Scts; VP Church Yth Grp; VP JA; French Hon Soc; Hon Roll; Rep Stu Cncl; Ftbl; JV Tennis; JV Trk; Am Can Co Fdn Schlrshp Awd 86-87; Gordon Coll Deans Sclrshp 86-87; Egl Sct Bdg Awd 86; Gordon Coll; Thlgy.

SOUCY, AMY; East Catholic HS; E Hartford, CT; (Y); 32/300; Capt Var Socr; Sftbl; High Hon Roll; Hon Roll; Jr NHS; NHS; Providence Coll; Bus.

SOUCY, BRETT; Conard HS; W Htfd, CT; (Y); 198/331; Latin Clb; Library Aide; VP Capt Ice Hcky; Wt Lftg; Hartford Whlrs HS Plyr Of Mnth 85; All ST, All Conf,All Leag Goalie 85-86; Bus Admin.

SOUSA, CHERYL ANN; East Haven HS; E Haven, CT; (Y); 15/231; Am Leg Aux Girls St; Church Yth Grp; Model UN; Red Cross Aide; High Hon Roll; Hon Roll; Jr NHS; NHS; Pres Schlr; Rotary Awd; Social Stds Awd 86; Amity Schlr 86; U Of CT Awd For Acad Achvt 86; Fairfield U; Nrsng.

SPADA, WENDY; Marianapolis Prep; Brooklyn, CT; (Y); Pres Frsh Cls; Pres Soph Cls; Var Bsktbl; JV Cheerleading; Var Socr; Capt Sftbl; MIP 84-85, MVP 85-86 Sftbl; U CT.

SPAFFORD, MICHELLE; Sacred Heart Acad; Norwalk, CT; (Y); Variety Show; Var Vllybl; High Hon Roll; Hon Roll; NHS; Spanish NHS; Psych.

SPATAFORE, JILL; Holy Cross HS; Waterbury, CT; (Y); 160/380; JV Trk; Hon Roll; Business.

SPEIGEL, JEFFREY; Manchester HS; Manchester, CT; (Y); 2/550; French Clb; Capt Math Tm; PAVAS; Temple Yth Grp; Band; Nwsp Ed-Chief; High Hon Roll; VP NHS; Ntl Merit Ltr; Camera Clb; RPI Math & Sci Mdl 86.

SPEIGHT, KATRINA; Wilbur L Cross HS; New Haven, CT; (S); 34/253; French Clb; Teachers Aide; Church Choir; Nwsp Rptr; Stu Cncl; Hon Roll; Bus Adm.

SPELL, MIA; James Hillhouse HS; New Haven, CT; (Y); 14/260; High Hon Roll; Hon Roll; Jr NHS; NHS; Martin Luther King Essy Cntst Wnnr 82; Advnc Fnctns 2nd Pl Prz Exm 86; Yale Med Schl Pgm 85; Quinnipiac Coll; Fnc.

SPENCE, CARALANN; Hartford Public HS; Hartford, CT; (Y); 4-H; FBLA; Girl Scts; JA; JCL; Pep Clb; 4-H Awd; Hon Roll; Weslyan U; Sci Engr.

SPENCER, JOANNE; Southington HS; Meriden, CT; (Y); 110/600; Concert Band; Jazz Band; Mrchg Band; Nwsp Stf; Bsktbl; Sftbl; High Hon Roll; Pres Schlrshp-Franklin Pierce Coll 86; Secy-Band 86; Franklin Pierce Coll; Adv.

SPERDUTO, VITO; Greenwich HS; Greenwich, CT; (Y); Church Yth Grp; JV Trk; High Hon Roll; NHS; Ntl Merit Ltr; Spanish NHS; Comp Sci.

SPEZZANO, ELIZABETH; Andrew Warde HS; Stamford, CT; (Y); Key Clb; Rep Soph Cls; Rep Jr Cls; Cheerleading; Var Gym; Var L Sftbl; High Hon Roll; Hon Roll; NHS; Co-Fndr, Co-Pres Totl Cmnctns Clb 85-86; Al-FCIAC 1st Tm Sftbl 85-86; ACL NJCL Natl Ltm Exm Cert; Psych.

SPIEGELHALTER, CRAIG; Oliver Wolcott Tech Ruts HS; Torrington, CT; (Y); VICA; Nwsp Phtg; Yrbk Phtg; VP NHS; Bus Admin.

SPIELMAN, FRED; Rockville HS; Ellington, CT; (S); Pres 4-H; VP FFA; Quiz Bowl; 4-H Awd; Hon Roll; ST Dairy Judgng Tm 4-H 84; Brnz Awd Dairy Judgng FFA Natl Conv 85; UNY Cobleskill; Dairy.

SPINELLA, SUZANNE; Stamford HS; Stamford, CT; (Y); 86/399; Cmnty Wkr; DECA; FHA; Hosp Aide; Office Aide; Fld Hcky; Sftbl; Hon Roll; Wheelock Coll; Social Wrk.

SPINO, CARLA; Sacred Heart Acad; Hamden, CT; (Y); Hosp Aide; Trs Spanish Clb; Chorus; Church Choir; School Musical; School Play; Hon Roll; 1st Hnrs 85-86; Scrd Hrt Endwnmnt Fund 85-86; Nrsng.

SPONZA, JOHN; Wilton HS; Wilton, CT; (Y); 52/350; Church Yth Grp; Pep Clb; SADD; Variety Show; JV Ftbl; JV Lcrss; Im Wt Lftg; Hon Roll; Commendation Norwalk CT Mayor For Boarded Burning Sailboat Marina And Extingushing Fire 84; Bus.

SPRINGER, BRUCE; Berlin HS; Kensington, CT; (Y); 5/204; Am Leg Boys St; Drama Clb; Band; Chorus; Concert Band; Drm Mjr(t); Jazz Band; Mrchg Band; School Musical; School Play; Nrthrn Regl Music Fest Chorus 84-85; Cmmnctns.

SPURRIER, ANDREW; Farmington HS; Unionville, CT; (Y); 21/209; Am Leg Boys St; Drama Clb; Ski Clb; VP SADD; Nwsp Ed-Chief; Yrbk Stf; Rep Stu Cncl; French Hon Soc; High Hon Roll; Ntl Merit SF; Mst Promsng Writer 84 & 86; New Britain Herald Bk Awd Jrnlsm 86.

ST GEORGES III, GEORGE W; East Catholic HS; Broad Brook, CT; (Y); 11/290; Boy Scts; Drama Clb; Chorus; Jazz Band; Stage Crew; Variety Show; JP Sousa Awd; NHS; School Musical; School Play; Eagle Scout 86; Archbishop Henry J Obrien Schlr 86; PA ST U; Arch Engr.

ST JEAN, MELISSA; Tourtellotte Mem HS; N Grosvenordale, CT; (Y); 9/91; Am Leg Aux Girls St; Pres Pep Clb; Church Choir; Yrbk Phtg; Yrbk Stf; Rep Frsh Cls; Rep Soph Cls; Rep Jr Cls; Sec Stu Cncl; Stat Crs Cntry; CT Hnrs Smnr 86; Outstndng Amer Stds Awd 86; Finance.

ST LAWRENCE, KELLY; Norwich Free Acad; Norwich, CT; (Y); Var Crs Cntry; Var Trk.

STABACK, TRACEY; Cheshire Acad; Meriden, CT; (Y); 6/58; Computer Clb; Drama Clb; School Play; Nwsp Rptr; Yrbk Stf; Hon Roll; U Of New Haven; Htl/Rest Mgmt.

STABLER, DENISE; Shelton HS; Huntington, CT; (Y); VP Art Clb; French Clb; Quiz Bowl; Drill Tm; Stage Crew; Swmmng; French Hon Soc; NHS; Fathers Clb Awd 85-86; Cert Of Merit Frnch 85-86; Paier Coll Of Art; Intrior Dsgn.

STACK JR, RONALD W; Berlin HS; East Berlin, CT; (Y); 28/190; Aud/Vis; Boy Scts; Camera Clb; Radio Clb; Stage Crew; Lit Mag; Hon Roll; NHS; Egl Sct 85; Sci.

STAHOVEC, JEAN; Housatonic Valley Regional HS; Falls Village, CT; (Y); AFS; Science Clb; Chorus; Rep Frsh Cls; Rep Jr Cls; Sec Stu Cncl; JV Bsktbl; Var Cheerleading; JV Socr; Hon Roll; Nrsng.

STALEY, BETH A; Cheshire HS; Cheshire, CT; (Y); Pep Clb; SADD; Chorus; School Play; Yrbk Rptr; JV Capt Cheerleading; Hon Roll; Hotl Mgmt.

STALEY, LISA L; Enfield HS; Enfield, CT; (Y); 17/250; Girl Scts; Ski Clb; Variety Show; Yrbk Sprt Ed; Swmmng; High Hon Roll; NHS; Wmsn Clb Of Enfld Schlrshp 86; Soc Stds Acad Achvt Awd 84; U Of Dayton OH; Nclr Med Tech.

STAMILIO, MELINDA; Southington HS; Southington, CT; (Y); Church Yth Grp; JA; Pep Clb; School Musical; Yrbk Stf; Sec Frsh Cls; Rep Jr Cls; Var Fld Hcky; Var Gym; Var Trk; Law Stds.

STANEK, JANINA T; Mary Immaculate Acad; New Britain, CT; (Y); 1/40; Cmnty Wkr; Pres JA; Service Clb; Trs Spanish Clb; Chorus; Nwsp Rptr; Rep Frsh Cls; High Hon Roll; Hon Roll; NEDT Awd; Chr Lctr 83-86; U Of CT; Phrmcst.

STANEK, KRISTEN; Southington HS; Southington, CT; (Y); Am Leg Aux Girls St; School Play; VP Stu Cncl; Var L Crs Cntry; Capt L Gym; Wt Lftg; Hon Roll; NHS; Grls ST Alt 86; U CT; Bus Financng.

STANGE, GERALD W; Bristol Central HS; Bristol, CT; (Y); 20/317; Boys Clb Am; Church Yth Grp; Ski Clb; Var Socr; DAR Awd; High Hon Roll; NHS; Ntl Merit Ltr; Natl Hnr Socy Schlrshp 86; Grace Atkins Schlrshp 86; Northeastern U; Comp Sci.

STANISH, KIMBERLY; Plainfield HS; Plainfield, CT; (Y); Band; Concert Band; Mrchg Band; School Play; Hon Roll; Pre-Med.

STANKEWICH, PAUL; Robert E Fitch SR HS; Groton, CT; (Y); 1/329; Am Leg Boys St; Sec Trs Drama Clb; Trs Intnl Clb; Thesps; Var L Tennis; Elks Awd; Kiwanis Awd; NHS; Ntl Merit Ltr; Val; U CT; Law.

STANOWSKI, KIM; Berlin HS; Kensington, CT; (Y); 4/183; Am Leg Aux Girls St; Var Capt Bsktbl; Var Capt Sftbl; High Hon Roll; Lion Awd; NHS; Pres Schlr; Var Capt Powder Puff Ftbl; Var Socr; Jr NHS; C Howard Goding Schlstc Athltc Awd 85; SR Hnrs Englsh Awd 86; Tomasso Family Fndtn Schlrshp 86; Clark U.

STAPELL, DENNIS; New Britain SR HS; New Britain, CT; (Y); 65/329; Var Bsbl; Var Bsktbl; Var Capt Ftbl; Hon Roll; Midget Ftbl Awd 81; Ftbl Awd 82-83; U RI; Mech Engrg.

STAPLES, TRACY L; Litchfield HS; Litchfield, CT; (Y); AFS; Art Clb; VP Church Yth Grp; Civic Clb; Cmnty Wkr; Pep Clb; SADD; Capt Varsity Clb; Chorus; Variety Show; Chrldng Vrsty Ltr & Pin 83-85; Hartford U; Pre-Law.

STAPLETON, MICHAEL; East Catholic HS; Willington, CT; (Y); 137/300; Art Clb; Aud/Vis; Boy Scts; Drama Clb; Latin Clb; Ski Clb; Stage Crew; Pres Sec Stu Cncl; Hon Roll; Principals Awd For Citzenshp & Schlrshp; Egl Sct Awd BSA; Al-Altare-Dei Religious Awd BSA; Art.

STARKS, MARY E; Masuk HS; Monroe, CT; (Y); 24/320; Am Leg Aux Girls St; Boy Scts; Drama Clb; JA; Pres Chorus; Madrigals; School Musical; School Play; Rep Frsh Cls; Rep Soph Cls; Jrnlsm.

STARZEC, MICHELE; Nathan Hale-Ray HS; East Haddam, CT; (S); Drama Clb; Capt Math Tm; Chorus; School Musical; Nwsp Stf; Yrbk Stf; Rep Stu Cncl; High Hon Roll; Hon Roll; Sec NHS; Syracuse U; Art.

STEBEN, RON; Torrington HS; Torrington, CT; (Y); Boy Scts; 4-H; JV Capt Crs Cntry; JV Trk; Mngmnt.

STEC, RICHARD; Edwin O Smith HS; Storrs, CT; (Y); Nwsp Rptr; Yrbk Stf; Lit Mag; Tennis; Rhodes Coll; Intl Bus.

STEEVES, MARSHALL; Avon HS; Avon, CT; (Y); 11/172; Office Aide; Political Wkr; Nwsp Rptr; Nwsp Stf; High Hon Roll; Hon Roll; Jr NHS; NHS; Ntl Merit Ltr; Pres Schlr; Cert Merit Media & Cmmnctns 85; Cert Merit Frnch IV 85; NY U; Bus Adm.

STEIGERWALD, JESSICA G; Westhill HS; Stamford, CT; (Y); 17/400; German Clb; VP JA; Orch; Ed Yrbk Stf; Hon Roll; NHS; Ntl Merit Ltr; Computer Clb; Sec Math Clb; Pres Acadmc Ftns Awd 86; Goethe Inst Excllnc/German 86; Stamford Brd Ed Awd Acad Excllnc 85-86; Harvard U; Pre-Law.

STEINBERG, BRIAN; Stamford HS; Stamford, CT; (S); Off Radio Clb; Orch; Nwsp Ed-Chief; Nwsp Rptr; Lit Mag; Rep Soph Cls; Crs Cntry; Trk; NHS.

STEINEN, TONYA; Edwin O Smith HS; Mansfield Center, CT; (Y); 41/173; Church Yth Grp; Hosp Aide; Political Wkr; Ski Clb; SADD; Yrbk Stf; Rep Stu Cncl; Med.

STELLA, DONNA; Southington HS; Southington, CT; (Y); 153/600; Ski Clb; School Play; VP Frsh Cls; VP Stu Cncl; High Hon Roll.

STELLATO, CAROLYN; Sacred Heart Acad; New Haven, CT; (Y); Art Clb; Spanish Clb; Church Choir; Bowling; Hon Roll; 3 Yr Hnr Awd 83-86; Antoinette Barba Memrl Schlrshp 85-86; Louis A Sidoli Schlrshp 86-87; Nrsg.

STELLATO, FRANK; J A Foran HS; Milford, CT; (Y); 11/242; Church Yth Grp; JCL; Key Clb; Latin Clb; JV Ftbl; Hon Roll; Kiwanis Awd; NHS; Ntl Merit Ltr; Rensselaer Polytech Inst; Physc.

STELLER, YVONNE; Shelton HS; Shelton, CT; (Y); Spanish Clb; Band; Concert Band; Mrchg Band; Spanish NHS; Ed Fld.

STENZ, CHRISTOPHER; Fairfield College Prep Schl; Norwalk, CT; (Y); Computer Clb; Var Ice Hcky; Im Wt Lftg; Bus.

STEPHENS, LAURA; Southington HS; Southington, CT; (Y); Acpl Chr; Chorus; Swing Chorus; Trk; Pres Cmnty Wkr; Pres Ftnss Awd; UCON; PHD.

STEVENS, GERIN; Kingswood-Oxford HS; W Hartford, CT; (Y); French Clb; Hosp Aide; Service Clb; SADD; Temple Yth Grp; Chorus; School Musical; Capt Vllybl; Hon Roll; Ntl Merit Ltr; Abraham Joshua Heschel Hnr Scty 85-86; Med.

STEVENS, PHILIP; Wethersfield HS; Wethersfield, CT; (Y); Yrbk Ed-Chief; Rep Jr Cls; Stu Cncl; Var L Tennis; Hon Roll; NHS; Ntl Merit Ltr; NEDT Awd.

STEVENS, TAMMY; Wetersfield HS; Wethersfield, CT; (Y); 38/299; FHA; Concert Band; Mrchg Band; Symp Band; Ed Yrbk Stf; Hon Roll; NEDT Awd; Htl Mgmt.

STIEGLER, JILL; Lauralton Hall HS; Shelton, CT; (Y); 15/111; Pres Church Yth Grp; Off Drama Clb; Latin Clb; Science Clb; School Musical; School Play; Im Vllybl; NHS; Hosp Aide; Scholastic Bowl; Natl Latin Exam-Cum Laude-Amer Clsscl League 84-86; Societatis Classicae In Nova Anglia Pars Conn 84; Child Psych.

STOCKMAN, DEBORA; Bristol Central HS; Britol, CT; (Y); 7/317; Office Aide; Yrbk Bus Mgr; Ed Yrbk Stf; High Hon Roll; NHS; ST Latin Awd 83; St Joseph Coll Priv Donr Schlrshp 86; Guid Office Aide 84-86; St Joseph Coll; Psych.

STOCKWELL, TODD; West Haven HS; W Haven, CT; (Y); JA; Yrbk Stf; High Hon Roll; Hon Roll; NHS; Pres Schlr; SAR Awd; Drftg Achvt Awd 85; Plane Geom Hnrs Awd; 1/2 Yr Schlrp To U New Haven During SR Yr 86; U CT; Mech Engrg.

STODDARD, ANDREW; St Bernard HS; N Stoninston, CT; (Y); 160/289; Yrbk Stf; Rep Jr Cls; JV Socr; JV Trk; Hon Roll; Thames Vly ST Tech Coll; Engr.

STOKES, ETHEL LORRAINE; Brien Mc Mahon HS; Norwalk, CT; (Y); JA; Spanish Clb; Church Choir; School Play; Rep Frsh Cls; Rep Soph Cls; Fshn Mdsng.

STOLFI, DAWN M; Holy Cross HS; Waterbury, CT; (Y); 155/346; Service Clb; Chorus; Variety Show; Yrbk Stf; Lit Mag; Rep Stu Cncl; Cheerleading; Hon Roll; VFW Awd; Voice Dem Awd; Am Leg Schl Awd 84; St CT Genl Assy Ofcl Citation, HS Actvty Awd 86; Merrimack Coll; Pol Sci.

STOLFI, JANET; Southington HS; Southington, CT; (Y); 91/612; Church Yth Grp; Hosp Aide; Ski Clb; Color Guard; Mrchg Band; School Musical; School Play; Twrlr; Hon Roll; Accntng.

STORMONT, RANETTE; Housatonic Valley Regional HS; Sharon, CT; (Y); Church Yth Grp; Dance Clb; French Clb; Ski Clb; Tennis; Hon Roll; Art Clb; Hosp Aide; Library Aide; Im Mgr Fld Hcky; Partcptn Peer Educ Cnslng Grp 86; UCLA; Fshn Mrktng.

STORY, CHRIS; Nonnewaug HS; Woodbury, CT; (Y); AFS; Pep Clb; Ski Clb; Yrbk Stf; Rep Frsh Cls; Rep Soph Cls; Rep Jr Cls; Stu Cncl; Psychology.

STRATER, CHARLES; Choate Rosemary Hall HS; Philadelphia, PA; (S); Drama Clb; Political Wkr; Acpl Chr; Chorus; Jazz Band; School Musical; School Play; Nwsp Rptr; Nwsp Stf; Lit Mag; Lead All Schl Ply Godspell, Camelot, Grease 84-86; Jrnlsm.

STRATTON, STACEY; Brien Mc Mahon HS; Norwalk, CT; (Y); GAA; High Hon Roll; Hon Roll; Sec.

STRICKLAND, CONNIE; East Hartford HS; E Hartford, CT; (Y); Chorus; Rep Stu Cncl; Hon Roll; Manchester CC; Comptr Prgrmr.

STRICKLAND, ELAINE; Southington HS; Southington, CT; (Y); Cmnty Wkr; Ski Clb; Trs Y-Teens; Band; Mrchg Band; Orch; Yrbk Bus Mgr; Yrbk Stf; Hartt Schl Music Smmr Prgm Schlrshp 86; PSAT NMSQT Qrtr Fnlst 86; LABOR Relations.

STROINEY, RICHARD E; Enrice Fermi HS; Enfield, CT; (Y); 6/341; Am Leg Boys St; Stu Cncl; Bsbl; Pres Bowling; Crs Cntry; JV Var Trk; High Hon Roll; NHS; Grnd Mrshl 86; Math Awd 86; Engr.

STROMBERG, KERRY; Terryville HS; Terryville, CT; (Y); 10/162; School Musical; Yrbk Bus Mgr; Trs Soph Cls; Sec Stu Cncl; Cheerleading; DAR Awd; Hon Roll; NHS; Conn Assoc Past Pres Awd 86; Rhytmic Gym Rnkd 2nd New England 86; Olympic Camp Gym CO Sprgs CO 86; Intl Bus.

STUART, JAMES; Coventry HS; Coventry, CT; (Y); Boy Scts; Church Yth Grp; Concert Band; Jazz Band; JV Var Bsbl; Sftbl; Hon Roll.

STUPAK, DONNA; Trumbull HS; Trumbull, CT; (Y); VP Trs Girl Scts; Drm Mjr(t); Mrchg Band; Symp Band; Nwsp Stf; Stat Sftbl; JV Vllybl; High Hon Roll; Hon Roll; Gilr Sct Gold Awd 86; George W Kelso Schlrshp 86; Boston U; Bio.

SUBER, GAIL; West Haven HS; W Haven, CT; (Y); Church Yth Grp; Computer Clb; English Clb; Intnl Clb; JA; Office Aide; Pep Clb; Spanish Clb; Band; Chorus; Parsons; Spn.

SUHIE, KAREN; Manchester HS; Manchester, CT; (Y); Church Yth Grp; Yrbk Stf; Mgr(s); JV Socr; High Hon Roll; Hon Roll; Bus.

SULICK, NANCY; East Catholic HS; Manchester, CT; (Y); 45/294; Am Leg Aux Girls St; Chorus; Rep Frsh Cls; Pres Sr Cls; Rep Stu Cncl; L Bsktbl; JV Sftbl; Capt Var Tennis.

SULLIVAN, BRIAN; Holy Cross HS; Waterbury, CT; (Y); JA; SADD; Yrbk Stf; Trs Jr Cls; Trs Sr Cls; Var Lcrss; Socr; Var Wrstlng; Hon Roll; Gettysburg Coll; Ecnm.

SULLIVAN JR, CHARLES H; St Paul Catholic HS; Southington, CT; (Y); 18/257; Boy Scts; French Clb; Math Clb; VP Ski Clb; Yrbk Sprt Ed; Lit Mag; Stu Cncl; Var Socr; NHS; By Scts Ldr Of Arrw, Ldg & Sctn Offcr 82; Boston U; Engrng.

SULLIVAN, EMMETT; Morgan Schl; Clinton, CT; (Y); 21/143; AFS; Church Yth Grp; Quiz Bowl; Chorus; School Musical; Yrbk Stf; VP Soph Cls; Rep Stu Cncl; JV Var Socr; Hon Roll.

SULLIVAN, KATIE; Holy Cross HS; Middlebury, CT; (Y); 79/380; Church Yth Grp; Computer Clb; Office Aide; Ski Clb; Spanish Clb; Varsity Clb; Yrbk Ed-Chief; Var L Trk; High Hon Roll; Hon Roll; Spn I Hnr Awd 84; Ski Team JV Lttr 86; Mattatuck Soc Sci Fair 2nd Pl 85; Elem Ed.

SULLIVAN, KELLI; Robert E Fitch SR HS; Mystic, CT; (Y); 20/326; Girl Scts; Key Clb; Office Aide; Yrbk Stf; Stat Bsktbl; Score Keeper; NHS.

SULLIVAN, MICHAEL J; Wilton HS; Wilton, CT; (Y); 30/390; Concert Band; Mrchg Band; JV Crs Cntry; JV Trk; High Hon Roll; Hon Roll; NHS; Ntl Merit SF; Bio.

SUNEGA, WENDY; East Catholic HS; E Windsor, CT; (Y); Church Yth Grp; Cmnty Wkr; Church Choir; Rep Stu Cncl; Var Gym; High Hon Roll; Hon Roll; U Of CT; Fin.

SUPLICKI, ELAINE; Robert E Fitch SR HS; Mystic, CT; (Y); 18/323; Church Yth Grp; Sec Key Clb; Varsity Clb; Chorus; Yrbk Stf; Stat Bsktbl; L Mgr(s); Stat Trk; High Hon Roll; NHS.

SUPPA, SUE; Torrington HS; Torrington, CT; (Y); 45/285; FHA; Rep Soph Cls; Wt Lftg; Hon Roll; Prfct Atten Awd; Morse Schl Bus; Secrtrl.

SURANNA, KEITH; Newington HS; Newington, CT; (S); Drama Clb; Chorus; School Musical; Variety Show; Nwsp Stf; Rep Frsh Cls; Socr; Trk; Madrigals; School Play; Bst Actr Awd For Drama Clb 82-84; Lavon Loch Mem Awd Outstdng Achvt In Theatre 82; Actr.

SURGEON, KIRK; West Hill HS; Stamford, CT; (Y); Drama Clb; Acpl Chr; Concert Band; School Play; Variety Show; Tennis; Hon Roll; New England ST Chorus 86; Syracuse U; Intl Business.

SURPRENANT, PAULA; Harvard M Ellis R V T S HS; Plainfield, CT; (Y); SADD; VICA; School Play; Yrbk Stf; VP Stu Cncl; High Hon Roll; Hairdrssng.

SWAN, CHRIS; Simsbury HS; W Simsbury, CT; (Y); 50/350; FBLA; Pres SADD; Nwsp Rptr; Yrbk Stf; USA JR Natl Rowing Tm 85; Var Crew 84-86; Harvard Radcliffe Coll; Ecnmcs.

SWANBERY, BETH ANN; Andrew Warde HS; Fairfield, CT; (Y); FBLA; GAA; Yrbk Stf; Rep Frsh Cls; Rep Soph Cls; Rep Jr Cls; Rep Sr Cls; Var L Fld Hcky; Hon Roll; Achvt In Bus Crrclm Awd 84-85; Western New Engl Coll; Mktg.

SWANSON, BRETT; Bulkeley HS; Hartford, CT; (Y); Nwsp Stf; Var Swmmng; Cartooning.

SWANSON, PAUL; Glastonbury HS; Glastonbury, CT; (Y); 2/407; Am Leg Boys St; Jazz Band; Rep Soph Cls; Capt Socr; L Tennis; L Wrstlng; Cit Awd; NCTE Awd; Sal; Ski Clb; Frnch Bk Awd Bst Frnch Stu 86; Brown U; Chem.

SWARD, HOLLY; Windham HS; South Windham, CT; (Y); Girl Scts; Hosp Aide; Library Aide; JV Trk; High Hon Roll; Hon Roll; Physcl Thrpy.

SWEENEY, KATHRYN; Danbury HS; Danbury, CT; (Y); 32/481; Church Yth Grp; Key Clb; Math Tm; Office Aide; Ski Clb; Ed Yrbk Stf; Var Trk; Hon Roll; Trs NHS.

SWEENEY, TRICIA; The Taft Schl; Oakville, CT; (Y); Political Wkr; Spanish Clb; Yrbk Stf; JV Bsktbl; Im Socr; Var Sftbl; Im Tennis; High Hon Roll; Pres Schlr; St Schlr; Marguerite Magraw Trust Schlrshp 86; Dr Wm Dwyer Schlrshp 86; Unico Clb Schlrshp 86; Georgetown U; Govt.

SWEET, DONNA; Hartford Public HS; Hartford, CT; (S); Church Yth Grp; DECA; GAA; Church Choir; Variety Show; Nwsp Stf; Yrbk Stf; Bsktbl; Mgr Ftbl; 3rd Pl Trophy ST DECA Convntn 86; FL Inst Tech; Marine Bio.

SWEET, KEVIN; Morgan HS; Clinton, CT; (Y); 5/160; Am Leg Boys St; Boy Scts; Band; Concert Band; Jazz Band; Mrchg Band; School Musical; NHS; Pep Band; Hon Roll; Math, Physcs Awds; Physcs.

SWEET, MEGAN; St Bernard HS; North Stonington, CT; (Y); 25/263; Church Yth Grp; Cmnty Wkr; Ski Clb; Var Bsktbl; Var Socr; Var Sftbl; Var Trk; Hon Roll; NHS; All ACC Bsktbl & Trck 86; Hnbl Mntn All ST Bsktbl 86; 2nd Tm All Area Bsktbl 86; Pre-Med.

SWEETING, ANDREW C G; Avon Old Farms Schl; Bahamas; (Y); Off Jr Cls; Off Sr Cls; Var Crs Cntry; JV Lcrss; JV Swmmng; Var Wrstlng; Hon Roll; Founders Meda-Outstndng Svc In Stu Govt 86; Southrn Methodist U; Bus.

SWENSON, DANA; Daniel Hand HS; Madison, CT; (Y); 13/272; GAA; Political Wkr; SADD; Var L Cheerleading; JV Gym; Hon Roll; NHS; CT Bus Week Schlrshp 85; Villanova U; Bus Adm.

SWIATEK, MICHELE; Plainville HS; Plainville, CT; (Y); 34/235; Flag Corp; JV Crs Cntry; Var Tennis; Hon Roll; NHS; Schlrshp Bus Wk 86; Schlrshp Flag Camp 85; Western CT ST U; Accntng.

SWINDLE, HONEY; New London HS; New London, CT; (Y); Church Yth Grp; Chorus; Concert Band; Flag Corp; Mrchg Band; School Musical; School Play; Library Aide; Band; Color Guard; Music Apprctn Awd Estrn CT Symphny Orch 86; Cnwy Awd Futur Tchrs Schlshrp 86; Mitchell Coll; Chldhd Stds.

SYBRANDT, MARK; New Fairfield HS; New Fairfield, CT; (Y); Boy Scts; FCA; Chorus; L Bsbl; L Ftbl; Wt Lftg; Drftng.

SYKES, JOHN; Farmington HS; Hartford, CT; (Y); 118/207; Boys Clb Am; Church Yth Grp; Church Choir; Stage Crew; Var JV Bsktbl; Hon Roll; Pre-Law.

SYKES, JOS; Wilby HS; Waterbury, CT; (Y); Science Clb; Spanish Clb; Church Choir; Yrbk Stf; Stu Cncl; Bsktbl; Gym; Hon Roll; Prfct Atten Awd; Engrng.

SYRETT, CHERYL; Jonathan Law HS; Milford, CT; (Y); Intnl Clb; Keywanettes; Latin Clb; Hon Roll; NHS; Certo Awd 84; Accntng.

SZATKOWSKI, PAUL; Manchester HS; Manchester, CT; (Y); Var Crs Cntry; Var L Trk; Hon Roll; Ntl Merit Ltr; Pres Schlr; Most Sprtsmnlk Indr Trk 85-86; Rochester U; Phrmcy.

SZATKOWSKI, SUSAN; Bethel HS; Bethel, CT; (Y); 21/268; Church Yth Grp; Sec Band; Concert Band; Variety Show; Nwsp Stf; Fld Hcky; Tennis; High Hon Roll; NHS; Pres Schlr; Bethl Exchng Clb Stu Of Mnth & Yr 85-86; U Of CT; Phrmcy.

SZLACHETKA, MARGERY; The Loomis Chaffee Schl; Windsor, CT; (Y); Library Aide; Co-Capt Math Tm; Church Choir; Orch; Var Swmmng; Smith Clb Hartford Bk Awd 86; V Swmmng Coaches Awd 86; Math.

SZNAJDER, STEPHEN B; Suffield HS; W Suffield, CT; (Y); 33/133; Boy Scts; Church Yth Grp; 4-H; Library Aide; 4-H Awd; Hon Roll; Aud/Vis; Eagle Sct 85; Hnr Smth & Sci 83-85; Guid Eyes For Blind Raiser 83-85; USAF; Engrng.

SZULC, JOEL; Simsbury HS; Simsbury, CT; (Y); 5/410; Boy Scts; Band; School Musical; School Play; JV Wrstlng; Hon Roll; Ntl Merit SF; VP JA; Political Wkr; Concert Band; Cornell Bk Awd 86; Simsbury Schlr 85-86; Senate Intern 86; Dentstry.

SZYMANSKI, LYNDA; Torrington HS; Torrington, CT; (Y); 10/283; Cmnty Wkr; Key Clb; Latin Clb; Varsity Clb; Nwsp Stf; Rep Jr Cls; Capt Vllybl; High Hon Roll; NHS; Smith Coll Bk Awd 86; Psych.

TABER, ELIZABETH; Stratford HS; Stratford, CT; (Y); 35/367; French Clb; Hosp Aide; Ski Clb; Concert Band; Mgr(s); Var Capt Swmmng; Tennis; French Hon Soc; Phy Thrpy.

TABER, MATTHEW; Hotchkiss HS; Lakeville, CT; (Y); Camera Clb; Church Yth Grp; Cmnty Wkr; Drama Clb; Ski Clb; Band; Concert Band; School Musical; School Play; Stage Crew; Bauer Fndtn Schlrshp 86; Nrdc Ski Prz 85&86; Frnk Sprl Ctznshp Awd 86; Colby Coll; Engl Educ.

TACCHI JR, JOHN; Berlin HS; Kensington, CT; (Y); Hosp Aide; Quinnipiac Coll; Phys Thrpy.

TAIT, ANDREW; Masuk HS; Monroe, CT; (Y); 18/280; Latin Clb; Math Clb; Varsity Clb; Var Capt Ice Hcky; Var L Socr; Hon Roll; NHS; Bucknell U; Mech Engrng.

TAKACS, ROBERT; Torrington HS; Torrington, CT; (Y); 54/295; Church Yth Grp; Cmnty Wkr; Drama Clb; School Play; JV Socr; High Hon Roll; Hon Roll; NHS; Prfct Atten Awd; John Denza Chapter Natl Hon Soc Schlrshp 86; Embry-Riddle U; Engrng.

TALARICO, JOSEPH; New Britain SR HS; New Britain, CT; (Y); 23/430; Hon Roll; NEDT Awd; Prfct Atten Awd; U CT; Comp Sci.

TALIERCIO, ANN ELIZABETH; Central Catholic HS; Norwalk, CT; (Y); Drama Clb; French Clb; Library Aide; Spanish Clb; Chorus; French Hon Soc; High Hon Roll; NHS; Pres Schlr; St Schlr; Alexander Kipnis Prize Excllnce Vocl Perfrmc 83; CT ST Schlr Scholar 86; Jack Tolan Mem Scholar 86; Fairfield U; Lawyer.

TAN, JUDY; Danbury HS; Danbury, CT; (Y); 125/476; Cmnty Wkr; Acpl Chr; Variety Show; Yrbk Stf; JV Bsktbl; Var Trk; Cmmnctn Arts.

TAN, KATHY; Danbury HS; Danbury, CT; (Y); 44/476; Acpl Chr; Variety Show; Yrbk Stf; JV Bsktbl; Var Trk; Hon Roll; Typng Awd 83-84; Rutger U; Chinese.

TANGNEY, LISA; Southington HS; Southington, CT; (Y); 120/600; Aud/Vis; German Clb; Hosp Aide; Key Clb; Pep Clb; Ski Clb; School Play; JV Fld Hcky; Hon Roll; Cert Of Excllnc Germ 84; Cert Of Attndc Cilcl Sch 84; Apple Harvest Fest Host 85; U Of CT; Nrsg.

TANGUAY, ROBERT; Kaynor RVTS HS; Prospect, CT; (Y); Aud/Vis; Computer Clb; Library Aide; SADD; Yrbk Stf; High Hon Roll; Hon Roll; NHS; Hartford U; Elctrnc Engr.

TAO, LILLY; Wilton HS; Wilton, CT; (Y); Chorus; Orch; School Musical; School Play; Stage Crew; Lit Mag; High Hon Roll; Hon Roll; NHS; CT All-ST Orch 85 & 86; Wstrn Rgnls Orch 85 & 86.

TARINI, LISA; Seymour HS; Seymour, CT; (S); 17/194; Church Yth Grp; JA; Chorus; Yrbk Stf; Rep Frsh Cls; Rep Soph Cls; Rep Jr Cls; Rep Sr Cls; Trs Pom Pon; Hon Roll; Law.

TASKO, ANNE; Kingswood-Oxford HS; Granby, CT; (Y); Service Clb; Chorus; Var L Crs Cntry; Swmmng; Im Tennis; Im Trk; Hon Roll; Cmnty Wkr; Bio.

TATA, MICHAEL; Bristol Central HS; Bristol, CT; (Y); 5/270; Intnl Clb; Math Tm; Band; Concert Band; Mrchg Band; Orch; Symp Band; JV Tennis; High Hon Roll; NHS; Natl Sci Merit Awd 84; Brown; Pschtry.

TATSAPAUGH, HEATHER; Housatonic Valley Regional HS; Canaan, CT; (Y); French Clb; Off Jr Cls; Off Sr Cls; Socr.

TATTEN, DE-JO; Bullard-Havens Tech; Bridgeport, CT; (Y); Cazenovia Coll; Advrtsng.

TAURAS, JENNIFER; East Catholic HS; Tolland, CT; (Y); 8/250; Service Clb; Nwsp Rptr; Nwsp Stf; Off Frsh Cls; Off Soph Cls; Off Jr Cls; Off Sr Cls; Var Capt Crs Cntry; Var Trk; NHS; Pre-Med.

TAVARES, LISA; Joseph A Foran HS; Milford, CT; (Y); 35/254; Civic Clb; JCL; Color Guard; Nwsp Rptr; Yrbk Stf; Sec Jr Cls; Sec Sr Cls; Stu Cncl; Var Capt Cheerleading; Hon Roll; Spelman Coll; Pol Sci.

TAYLOR, ADRIANE; Joseph A Foran HS; Milford, CT; (Y); Service Clb; Varsity Clb; Color Guard; Drill Tm.

TAYLOR, AMANDA; Miss Porters HS; Atlanta, GA; (Y); Art Clb; French Clb; Chorus; School Play; Nwsp Ed-Chief; Nwsp Phtg; Nwsp Rptr; Yrbk Phtg; Lit Mag; JV Socr; Englsh-Jrnlsm.

TAYLOR, CHRISTOPHER; Choate Rosemary Hall HS; Nantucket, MA; (Y); Chorus; Concert Band; Var Crew Rowing; Mth Tutoring Soc; Russian Clb; Colby Coll; Govt.

TAYLOR, COLLEEN; Southington HS; Southington, CT; (Y); Church Yth Grp; Key Clb; Library Aide; Service Clb; Variety Show; Yrbk Stf; Im Bsktbl; Var Trk; Hon Roll; FHA.

TAYLOR, DAWN; Danbury HS; Danbury, CT; (Y); Trs Ski Clb; SADD; Varsity Clb; Concert Band; Mrchg Band; Symp Band; Yrbk Stf; Var Tennis; Hon Roll; Pres Jr NHS; Med.

TAYLOR, RICHARD; Wilton HS; Wilton, CT; (Y); Jazz Band; Mrchg Band; Orch; Stage Crew; Trk.

TEDESCHI, JAMES; Berlin HS; Kensington, CT; (Y); Computer Clb; Math Clb; Math Tm; Science Clb; Service Clb; Nwsp Bus Mgr; Nwsp Rptr; Nwsp Stf; Wocester Polytechnic Inst; Comp.

TEDESCO, LAURA; Stamford HS; Stamford, CT; (Y); DECA; Sec JA; Pep Clb; Hon Roll; Educ.

TEIXEIRA, MARCIA; Bullard-Havens Ruts HS; Bridgeport, CT; (S); Church Yth Grp; Hon Roll; Prfct Atten Awd; Electrncs; Electrncs.

TELFORD JR, BOB; Daniel Hand HS; Madison, CT; (Y); 4-H; Ski Clb; Im Badmtn; Im Sftbl; Im Vllybl; Exch Clb Wally Cataldo Achvt Awd 86; Betty Ann Islep Outdr Ed Awd 86; Sterling Coll; Rural Resrce.

TELLER, SCOTT; Joseph A Foran HS; Milford, CT; (Y); 40/200; Computer Clb; Sec Key Clb; Math Tm; Service Clb; Spanish Clb; Teachers Aide; Temple Yth Grp; Stu Cncl; Trk; Wrstlng; Comp Sci.

TENAGLIA, ANGELA; Stamford HS; Stamford, CT; (Y); Dance Clb; Girl Scts; Color Guard; Nwsp Rptr; Socr; Hon Roll; Jr NHS; NHS; U Of Miami; Intl Fin & Mktg.

TERELMES, MIKE; Hartford Christian Acad; West Hartford, CT; (S); 2/8; Pres Church Yth Grp; Band; Chorus; Concert Band; Pep Band; School Musical; Yrbk Ed-Chief; Trs Frsh Cls; Pres Jr Cls; Bsktbl; Bob Jones U; Accntng.

TERKELSEN, SANDRA; Greenwich HS; Greenwich, CT; (Y); Church Yth Grp; Band; Chorus; Church Choir; Concert Band; Mrchg Band; Rep Stu Cncl; High Hon Roll; Hon Roll; Word Of Life Bible Inst.

TERRY, BRETT C; The Williams Schl; Mansfield Ctr, CT; (Y); 3/28; Thesps; Chorus; Jazz Band; School Musical; School Play; Lit Mag; Ntl Merit Ltr; High Hon Roll; Jean M Watson Prz Excllnce Mth 86; Leonard J Bodenlos Prz Excllnce Phys Sci 86; Fecundity Prz Music 86; Wesleyan U; Chem.

TERRY, SETH S; The Hotchkiss Schl; Denver, CO; (Y); Church Yth Grp; French Clb; Chorus; School Musical; School Play; Variety Show; Stu Cncl; JV Crs Cntry; Var L Ftbl; JV Lcrss; Pre-Med.

TERZA, ANGELA; Manchester HS; Manchester, CT; (Y); Auto Mechnc.

TESEI, PETER; Greenwich HS; Greenwich, CT; (Y); Art Clb; Boy Scts; FBLA; Key Clb; Model UN; Political Wkr; Stage Crew; Hon Roll; U S Senate Pg 86; Pres Cert Svc U S Senate 86; Pol Sci.

TESSIER, SHAWN; A H Ellis Ruts HS; Putnam, CT; (Y); Cmnty Wkr; Yrbk Stf; US Navy; Auto Tech.

TESTA, TRACI; Holy Cross HS; Watertown, CT; (Y); 129/380; Church Yth Grp; Cmnty Wkr; Girl Scts; PAVAS; Sec Spanish Clb; Chorus; School Play; Hon Roll; Spec Ed Tchr For Rlgs Instrctn 84-86; Asstnt Drctr/Cnslr For Chldrns Cmp 85-86; Quinnipac Coll; Physcl Thrpy.

TETER, MELINDA; Orville H Platt HS; Meriden, CT; (Y); Sec Church Yth Grp; Sec Pres Drama Clb; Key Clb; Concert Band; Stu Cncl; Bsktbl; High Hon Roll; NHS; Hugh O Brian Yth Fndt Ambssdr 85; Rensselaer Polytchnc Inst Medal 86; Natl Drama & Speech Awd 86.

TETRAULT, RONALD; Windham Regnl Vocatnl Technel Schl; Storrs, CT; (Y); Boy Scts; Church Yth Grp; Hon Roll; NHS; Central CT ST U; Bus Adm.

TEWKSBURY, JOHN MICHAEL; Norwich Free Acad; Norwich, CT; (Y); Drama Clb; German Clb; Letterman Clb; Varsity Clb; School Play; Stage Crew; Nwsp Stf; Stu Cncl; JV Var Ftbl; Im Wt Lftg; Arts.

THEREAULT, JENNIFER; Nathan Hale-Ray HS; Moodus, CT; (Y); 22/65; AFS; Cmnty Wkr; Drama Clb; Band; School Musical; Nwsp Stf; Yrbk Stf; Cit Awd; Hon Roll; JP Sousa Awd; Cthrn M Shnagn Awd 86; CT Assn Of Scndry Schls-Lrdrshp 86; Central CT ST U; Elem Educ.

THERIAULT, NICOLE; Old Saybrook SR HS; Rockwood, ME; (Y); 16/130; Am Leg Aux Girls St; Cmnty Wkr; French Clb; Ski Clb; Chorus; Flag Corp; Nwsp Rptr; Rep Stu Cncl; Cheerleading; Crs Cntry; Math Awd Outstndng Achvt 86; Socl Stu Awd Excllnc In Soclgy 86; Colby College; Admn Sci.

THIBAULT, JAMES; Bullard Havens RVTS; Bridgeport, CT; (Y); Aud/Vis; Hosp Aide; Library Aide; Trvl Agnt.

THIBODEAU, DONNA M; East Catholic HS; Manchester, CT; (Y); 70/297; Church Yth Grp; 4-H; Nwsp Rptr; Nwsp Stf; Lit Mag; Vllybl; 4-H Awd; High Hon Roll; Hon Roll; Kiwanis Awd; CT Delg Natl 4-H Clb Cong 85; Cnty 4-H Fair Qn 85; ST CT Pub Spkg Awd 85; Bus Admin.

THIEDE, MICHELLE; Mark T Sheehan HS; Wallingford, CT; (Y); 4/215; Pres Church Yth Grp; Girl Scts; Hosp Aide; Key Clb; Math Tm; Spanish Clb; Chorus; Flag Corp; Mrchg Band; Variety Show; VFW Oratrcl 3rd Pl Rgnls 84; Choate Schlrp Smmr Sessn Humnts 86; Brigham Young U; Phys Ther.

THOMAS, ALISON; Nonnewaug HS; Bethlehem, CT; (Y); Cmnty Wkr; Pres Drama Clb; School Play; Stage Crew; Variety Show; Yrbk Phtg; Lit Mag; Off Frsh Cls; Off Soph Cls; Off Jr Cls; Vassar Coll; Theater Arts.

THOMAS, CHRIS; East Lyme HS; E Lyme, CT; (Y); 34/315; Rep Am Leg Boys St; Pres Key Clb; SADD; Yrbk Phtg; Rep Jr Cls; Lcrss; Powder Puff Ftbl; Var Socr; Hon Roll; Babson COLL; Intl Bus.

THOMAS, GARY; Brookfield HS; Brookfield, CT; (Y); JV Im Bsktbl; JV Ftbl; Im Vllybl; High Hon Roll; Hon Roll; UCLA.

THOMAS, JASON; Wilton HS; Wilton, CT; (Y); 159/364; Off Pep Clb; Off Ski Clb; Varsity Clb; Yrbk Sprt Ed; Coach Actv; JV Var Lcrss; Im Wt Lftg; Hon Roll; Cmmnctns.

THOMAS, LISA; Morgan Schl; Clinton, CT; (Y); 1/150; AFS; French Clb; SADD; Concert Band; Mrchg Band; Orch; School Musical; Nwsp Rptr; High Hon Roll; Hon Roll; Yale Book Awd 86; Acad Dstnctn In Math 84-86; Math.

THOMAS, RONALD; Fairfield College Preparatory Schl; Bridgeport, CT; (Y); Boys Clb Am; Boy Scts; Cmnty Wkr; JA; Psych.

THOMPSON, ANNETTE; Brien Mcmahon HS; Norwalk, CT; (Y); Church Yth Grp; Drama Clb; Spanish Clb; Chorus; School Play; Sec Jr Cls; Capt Cheerleading; Ntl Chrldng Assoc 85.

THOMPSON, BRADFORD; Old Saybrook SR HS; Old Saybrook, CT; (Y); 12/120; AFS; Latin Clb; SADD; Band; Jazz Band; School Play; Yrbk Stf; Capt JV Socr; Hon Roll; Concert Band; Tlntd & Acad Gftd In Cls 83-86.

THOMPSON, DAVID; Wethersfield HS; Wethersfield, CT; (Y); 11/299; Am Leg Boys St; Church Yth Grp; Capt Bsktbl; Capt Ftbl; NHS.

THOMPSON, DIAHANN; Wilbur Cross HS; New Haven, CT; (S); 21/265; FBLA; Nwsp Stf; Hon Roll; Ntl Merit Schol.

THOMPSON, JASON; Shelton HS; Shelton, CT; (Y); Church Yth Grp; Cmnty Wkr; Band; Mrchg Band.

THOMPSON II, RICHARD L; Xavier HS; Middletown, CT; (Y); 47/200; Yrbk Stf; Lit Mag; JV Var Bsktbl; Var L Ftbl; Var L Trk; Ntl Merit SF; Yale Appld Sci Frntrs 85; Mnrty Engrng Intro US Cst Grd Prjct 85; Dartmouth; Engrng.

THOMPSON, TERRY; Southington HS; Southington, CT; (Y); 60/600; Hosp Aide; Key Clb; Ski Clb; Church Choir; Concert Band; Mrchg Band; Var L Tennis; Hon Roll; Jr NHS; NHS; Nrsng.

THOMPSON, WILLIAM; Manchester HS; Manchester, CT; (Y); 40/571; Church Yth Grp; Cmnty Wkr; Rep Band; Concert Band; Jazz Band; Mrchg Band; Orch; School Musical; Var L Swmmng; Hon Roll; Mst Imprvd Plyr Concert Band 84; Adv.

THORBURN, LINDA ANN; Danbury HS; Danbury, CT; (Y); #132 In Class; Church Yth Grp; VP Exploring; Acpl Chr; Chorus; Color Guard; Nwsp Stf; Im Bsbl; Gym; Im Sftbl; Hon Roll; JR Vlntr 83-85; Russell Sage Coll; Phy Thrpy.

THORNTON, SHARLENE; Parish Hill HS; Hampton, CT; (Y); Library Aide; Office Aide; Chorus; Yrbk Phtg; Yrbk Stf; Lit Mag; Sec Sr Cls; 4-H Awd; Hon Roll; CT Bus Wk Sem 85; Achvt Awd Acad Excllnce Adv Engl 86; Breadloaf Yng Writers Conf 85; Publc Rltns.

THURZ, MICHAEL; East Catholic HS; Glastonbury, CT; (Y); 139/300; Church Yth Grp; Capt Exploring; Ski Clb; Hon Roll; St Anselms; Bus Admin.

THYNE III, JOHN JOSEPH; Ridgefield HS; Ridgefield, CT; (Y); 38/332; Boy Scts; Church Yth Grp; Cmnty Wkr; Drama Clb; Latin Clb; Library Aide; Math Tm; PAVAS; Teachers Aide; Thesps; Outstndng Ldrshp REACH 86; Latin Hnr Soc 84-86; Tutorng Frgn Stu Recgntn 82-84; U CT; Bio.

TIEZZI, CARA; Old Saybrook SR HS; Old Saybrook, CT; (Y); Pres AFS; Band; Concert Band; Mrchg Band; School Musical; Stu Cncl; Fld Hcky; Trk; Hon Roll; NHS; Modern European Hist Awd 83-84; Bus.

TIEZZI, LAURA; Maloney HS; Meriden, CT; (Y); DECA; Girl Scts; Rep Frsh Cls; Rep Soph Cls; Rep Jr Cls; Bsktbl; Mgr(s); Vllybl; Hon Roll; Bldrs Clb Svc Awd 82.

TILKI, JOHN; Derby HS; Derby, CT; (Y); 2/130; Am Leg Boys St; Computer Clb; Math Tm; Varsity Clb; Concert Band; Nwsp Ed-Chief; Pres Frsh Cls; Pres Soph Cls; Pres Jr Cls; Pres Sr Cls; Untd Tech Corp Schlrshp 86; Ntl Ftbl Fndtn & Hall Of Fame Schlr Athlt Awd 86; CIAT Schlr Athlt Awd 86; Wrcstr Poly Tech Inst; Engrng.

TILLEY, ANGELA; Miss Porters Schl; Ft Worth, TX; (Y); Debate Tm; Model UN; Yrbk Stf; Rep Soph Cls; Var Lcrss; Capt Var Socr; JV Tennis; Var Vllybl; High Hon Roll; Hon Roll; 2nd Head Of Newgrls 85-86; MPS Athltc & Languge Awd 86; Vanderbilt U; Linguistcs.

TILLEY, SUZANNE; Branford HS; Branford, CT; (Y); Office Aide; Yrbk Stf; Var Tennis; Var Trk; Var Vllybl; Hon Roll; Awd Merit Cert Hnbl Mntn Poem 83; Silvr Poet Awd 86; Excllnt Prfrmnc Acctg I 86; Acctg.

TINH, NGUYET; New Britain HS; New Britian, CT; (Y); 39/300; Key Clb; Nwsp Rptr; Yrbk Stf; Sec Jr Cls; Capt Tennis; Trk; Hon Roll; Librl Arts.

TINKER, JORDAN B; Ridgefield HS; Ridgefield, CT; (Y); Art Clb; Ed Yrbk Stf; Lit Mag; Cngrsnl Art Awd 85; PTSA Awd Exclnce Art, PTSA Awd Outstndng Stu Certain Categorie 86; Cooper Union.

TISDALE, PAMELA JANE; The Gilbert Schl; Winsted, CT; (Y); 5/115; Art Clb; Acpl Chr; Chorus; Stage Crew; Yrbk Stf; Stu Cncl; Var Capt Crs Cntry; Var Tennis; Var Trk; DAR Awd; Intl Yuth Yr Awd 1st Rgn 86; Hustlr Awd Trk 84; Music Fstvl Leag, Divsnl 84-86; U CT; Cmptr Sci.

TISLER, MATTHEW; Conard HS; W Hartfrod, CT; (Y); 90/345; Boy Scts; Letterman Clb; Temple Yth Grp; Varsity Clb; Chorus; School Musical; School Play; Yrbk Stf; Stu Cncl; Ftbl; CIAA Sprg Conf Stu Crftmns Fair 1st Pl 83-84; Graphic Comm.

TITUS, MARO; Farmington HS; Farmington, CT; (Y); Chrmn Church Yth Grp; Spanish Clb; Band; Church Choir; Nwsp Ed-Chief; Nwsp Rptr; JV Tennis; Hon Roll; Spanish NHS; Lwyr.

TKACZ, WILLIAM; Rham HS; Hebron, CT; (Y); 5/225; Am Leg Boys St; Aud/Vis; Cmnty Wkr; Spanish Clb; Teachers Aide; Crs Cntry; Trk; NHS; Peer Cnslr 86; LOC Jvln Chmpn 86; Trinity Coll; Psych.

TOBACK, LISA; Brookfield HS; Brookfield, CT; (Y); Library Aide; Office Aide; 2nd Hnrs 2nd Quarter 83-84; Airline Stewrds.

TOBELER, TRACY; East Catholic HS; Vernon Rockville, CT; (Y); 62/284; L Gym; Hon Roll; Trvl.

TOBIN, KIMBERLY; Watertown HS; Watertown, CT; (Y); Adlscnt Psychlgy.

TOBIN, RICHARD NEIL; Stamford Catholic HS; Stamford, CT; (Y); Boy Scts; Ski Clb; Yrbk Phtg; Yrbk Stf; Swmmng; Hon Roll; Prfct Atten Awd; Art Hnrs Awd 85; Pratt Inst; Ind Dsgnr.

TOIGO, CHRISTINA; Shelton HS; Shelton, CT; (Y); VP Exploring; Color Guard; School Play; Nwsp Rptr; Rep Jr Cls; Rep Stu Cncl; Ntl Merit Ltr; Spanish NHS; Drama Clb; Spanish Clb; Wrote Dedctn Poem Yrbk SR Clss; Wrote Dedctn Poem Prom; Advrtsng.

TOKARZ, CHRISTOPHER; Notre Dame HS; Seymour, CT; (Y); 44/231; Cmnty Wkr; Trs French Clb; Im Bsktbl; French Hon Soc; Hon Roll; Frnch Awd 86; U Of CT; Pre-Bus.

TOLE, JACQUELINE; Farmington HS; Unionville, CT; (Y); DECA; Var JV Bsktbl; Stat Fld Hcky; Var Capt Sftbl; 4th Pl DECA Compttn 86; BUS Admn.

TOLOMEO, ELVIRA; North Haven HS; North Haven, CT; (Y); Church Choir; Hon Roll; Italian Clb; Huntington Inst; Dentl Asst.

TOMAS, TRACEY; Bullard-Havens Rvts HS; Bridgeport, CT; (Y); Church Yth Grp; Cmnty Wkr; Exploring; Var Science Clb; Var Hon Roll; Tufts U; Vet Med.

TOMASCAK, ANDREA; Brookfield HS; Brookfield Center, CT; (Y); Art Clb; Cmnty Wkr; SADD; Chorus; School Musical; Stage Crew; Sec Jr Cls; Hon Roll; Gymnstcs, Swmmng 85-86; Pgm Dir Fshn Shw 85-86; Bus.

TOMATORE, KAREN; Shelton HS; Shelton, CT; (Y); French Clb; SADD; Nwsp Rptr; Nwsp Stf; Hon Roll.

TOMOLONIS, PAUL; East Windsor HS; Broad Brook, CT; (Y); 2/84; Church Yth Grp; Computer Clb; Intnl Clb; Office Aide; Crs Cntry; Trk; High Hon Roll; Lion Awd; NHS; Pres Schlr; E Windsor Educ Assn Awd 86; Comm Schlrshp Awd 86; Julie Ann Brady Meml Awd 86; U CT; Elec Engrng.

TOMPKINS, CHRIS; Trumbull HS; Trumbull, CT; (Y); Church Yth Grp; Latin Clb; Spanish Clb; Var Bsktbl; Var Sftbl; Var Vllybl; High Hon Roll; Spanish NHS; 1st Tm FCIAC Bsktbl 85-86; Engrng.

TOMPKINS, DANIEL; Robert E Fitch SR HS; Groton, CT; (Y); Pres Band; Concert Band; Jazz Band; Mrchg Band; Bsbl; Bsktbl; JV Socr; Cit Awd; Hon Roll; Exc Sci Awd 84; Alter Svc Awd 85; Cert Crediblty Band 84; U CT; Comp Engr.

TONER, CHRISTINE; St Bernard HS; Preston, CT; (Y); 91/300; Church Yth Grp; Cmnty Wkr; Hosp Aide; Stage Crew; Yrbk Stf; Rep Jr Cls; Rep Sr Cls; Hon Roll; Acad Achvt Awd 85; Hmcmng Ct 82-86; Fairfield U; Bus.

TONNER, KRISTOFER; Newfairfield HS; New Fairfld, CT; (Y); Boy Scts; Church Yth Grp; Computer Clb; Chorus; Church Choir; School Musical; School Play; Variety Show; Schlrshp Hartt Schl Of Music 83-4; All-St Choir CT 83-4; Western Rgnl Choir CT 83-86; Berkelee Coll; Prfssnl Music.

TORELLO, JEFF; Branford HS; Branford, CT; (Y); 45/312; Varsity Clb; Yrbk Sprt Ed; Yrbk Stf; VP Stu Cncl; JV Bsktbl; Var Tennis; Hon Roll; Prfct Atten Awd; Gvrnrs Yth Cnfrence 86; Stud Of The Mnth 85; Stud Ldr 86; Acctg.

TORNAY, KEVIN; Andrew Warde HS; Fairfield, CT; (Y); Hon Roll.

TORPEY, DIANE; Shelton HS; Shelton, CT; (Y); Cmnty Wkr; Dance Clb; Hosp Aide; Key Clb; Office Aide; Ski Clb; Spanish Clb; Mrchg Band; Pom Pon; Sftbl; Bus.

TORRANT, JENNIFER L; Torrington HS; Torrington, CT; (Y); 26/286; Am Leg Aux Girls St; Pres Church Yth Grp; Drama Clb; Ski Clb; Spanish Clb; Thesps; Y-Teens; School Musical; School Play; VP Soph Cls; U Of CT Coop Pgm For Calculus I 86; WPI Smmr Pgm-Frntrs In Sci 86; Chem Engnr.

TORTORA, KERRI; Glastonbury HS; Cullman, AL; (Y); 59/413; French Clb; Model UN; Yrbk Bus Mgr; Rep Sr Cls; Rep Stu Cncl; Var Capt Cheerleading; DAR Awd; High Hon Roll; Cmnty Wkr; Drama Clb; Best All Arnd Chrldr 85-86; Wlliams Coll Bk Awd 84-85; Intl Politics.

TORTORA, KERRI; Glastonbury HS; Glastonbury, CT; (Y); 59/413; French Clb; Intnl Clb; Model UN; Political Wkr; Service Clb; Varsity Clb; Acpl Chr; Swing Chorus; Yrbk Bus Mgr; Yrbk Stf; Chrldng Hartwell Awd 85-86; Rotary Club Prod Show Schlrshp Queen86; Stu Council Schlsrhp Awd 86; American U; Intl Pol.

TOSCANO, JOHN; Conard HS; W Hartford, CT; (Y); 15/331; Pres Concert Band; VP Jazz Band; Orch; High Hon Roll; NHS; Spanish NHS; Band; Mrchg Band; Pep Band; School Musical; U Of CT; Acctg.

TOSCARO, JOHN; Conard HS; W Hartford, CT; (Y); 15/331; Concert Band; Jazz Band; Orch; Stu Cncl; High Hon Roll; NHS; Spanish NHS; Band; Mrchg Band; Pep Band; U Of CT; Accntng.

TOTH, CHERYL ANN; New Britain HS; New Britain, CT; (Y); Cmnty Wkr; Sec Trs Exploring; Chorus; Nwsp Ed-Chief; Rep Jr Cls; Rep Sr Cls; JV L Vllybl; Church Yth Grp; Drama Clb; GAA; Quill & Scroll Awd 86; Music Clb Awd 86; Gtd & Tlntd 84-86; Hartford Coll For Women; Chd Ps.

TOTMAN, SERENA; Miss Porters Schl; Hamden, CT; (Y); 15/90; Cmnty Wkr; Intnl Clb; Nwsp Bus Mgr; Nwsp Stf; Rep Stu Cncl; Var JV Fld Hcky; JV Vllybl; Hon Roll; Latin Clb; Nwsp Rptr; Magna Cum Laude Natl Latn Exam 84; Eng.

TOTTE, JON; Guilford HS; Guilford, CT; (Y); Camera Clb; Letterman Clb; Yrbk Stf; Off Jr Cls; JV Bsktbl; Capt Var Ftbl; Capt Var Golf; Im Sftbl; Capt Wt Lftg; Hon Roll; All Shoreline Linebckr, MVP Def 85; All Shoreline Golf 86; MVP Golf 86; Sci.

TRACEY, ANDREA; Enrico Fermi HS; Enfield, CT; (Y); Exploring; Pep Clb; Sec Chorus; School Play; VP Frsh Cls; Rep Stu Cncl; Mgr Bsbl; Var Capt Cheerleading; Cit Awd; Hon Roll; Enfield Police Explorers 85-86; Mass Cmmnctns.

TRACY, JOHN; Brookfield HS; Brookfield, CT; (Y); AFS; Drama Clb; Math Clb; Math Tm; Political Wkr; Rep Sr Cls; JV Trk; High Hon Roll; School Play; Hon Roll; VP AFS 87; Nwtms Carrier Of Mnth 83; Air Force; Pilot.

TRACY, TODD; Lewis S Mills HS; Harwinton, CT; (Y); 2/172; Am Leg Boys St; Church Yth Grp; Model UN; Red Cross Aide; Rep Stu Cncl; JV Var Bsktbl; High Hon Roll; NHS; NEDT Awd; Michaels Jewlers Outstndg Stu Awd 84-85; Hstry Dept Awd 85-86; Analytic Wrtg Awd 84 & 86; Opthmlgy.

TRAISCI, LEIGH ANN; New Fairfield HS; New Fairfield, CT; (Y); 54/238; Church Yth Grp; Hosp Aide; Latin Clb; Chorus; School Musical; VP Frsh Cls; Off Sr Cls; Stu Cncl; Var L Socr; Sec French Hon Soc; Harding U; Bio.

TRALONGO, VICTORIA; Wethersfield HS; Wethersifld, CT; (Y); 34/301; Church Yth Grp; Drama Clb; Chorus; Church Choir; Madrigals; School Musical; School Play; JV Socr; High Hon Roll; Hon Roll; Ralph Baldwin Schlrshp Achvt 84-86; Hnry Schlrshp Cnsrvtry Music 84-85; Depauw U; Music.

TRAMONTANA, GINA; Ansonia HS; Ansonia, CT; (Y); 7/150; Hosp Aide; Science Clb; Spanish Clb; Yrbk Stf; Cit Awd; High Hon Roll; Hon Roll; NHS; Prfct Atten Awd; Spanish NHS; New England Schlstc Math Awd 84; U Conn; Med Tech.

TRAN, NUOI; Manchester HS; Manchester, CT; (Y); Computer Clb; OEA; VICA.

TRANBERG, LISA C; Choate Rosemary Hall HS; New York, NY; (Y); Church Yth Grp; French Clb; Math Clb; Pep Clb; Radio Clb; Spanish Clb; JV Gym; Var Mgr(s); Var Trk; Im Wt Lftg; Cmmnd Schlr Natl Achvt Schlrshp Prog For Outstdng Negro Stu 85; Lbrl Arts.

TRANTOLO, BETH; Farmington HS; Farmington, CT; (Y); 23/256; Hosp Aide; Chorus; School Musical; Var JV Fld Hcky; Mgr(s); Score Keeper; Var Mgr Trk; Im Vllybl; High Hon Roll; Hon Roll; Invtnl U Of Hartfrd Art Show 86; Ctr Crtv Yth Pgm Wesleyan 86; Peer Educ Prnt Wrkshps 83-87; Advrtsng.

TRAVERS, NATALIE; Canton HS; Canton, CT; (Y); Church Yth Grp; Lit Mag; Mc Gill; Pre-Law.

TRAVERS, REGINA; Miss Porkers Schl; Farmington, CT; (Y); French Clb; Model UN; Teachers Aide; Varsity Clb; JV Fld Hcky; JV Capt Lcrss; JV Mgr(s); Score Keeper; Im Tennis; Timer; Librl Arts.

TREADWELL, ANNE; Lyme-Old Lyme HS; Old Lyme, CT; (Y); Art Clb; Church Yth Grp; Library Aide; Ski Clb; SADD; Yrbk Phtg; Yrbk Stf; Lit Mag; Var L Tennis; Hon Roll; Ntl Schlstc Art Awd 86; Outstndng Artistc Achvt Awd 86; Lyme Acad Schrlshp 86.

TRELA, ARLENE; Bulkeley HS; Hartford, CT; (Y); DECA; High Hon Roll; Prfct Atten Awd; 2nd Pl Dist Conf 86; 3rd Pl Mini Awds DE ST Conf 86; Mrktng.

TREMBLE, ANGELIQUE; Windsor HS; Windsor, CT; (Y); Am Leg Aux Girls St; Church Yth Grp; Girl Scts; Hosp Aide; Intnl Clb; JA; Model UN; Spanish Clb; SADD; Church Choir; Chrmn Publcty Stdnt Cncl 86-87; Patnt Care Vlntr Locl Hosp 86; Pre-Med.

TREZISE, ELIZABETH; Ridgefield HS; Ridgefield, CT; (Y); 12/387; Cmnty Wkr; Sec French Clb; Hosp Aide; Service Clb; High Hon Roll; Hon Roll; NHS; Soc Wmn Engrs Ct Chptr-Engrng Awd 86; Latn Bk Awd 84 & 85; Ntl Latn Hon Soc 84 & 85; Bio.

TRICKETT, BARBARA; Lyman Hall HS; Wallingford, CT; (Y); 34/256; JA; VP Key Clb; Concert Band; Mrchg Band; School Musical; Bsktbl; Powder Puff Ftbl; Swmmng; Capt Tennis; Hon Roll; Pre-Med.

TRIMARCHI, DEBBIE; Wilton HS; Wilton, CT; (Y); Lit Mag; Var Chess Clb; Var Twrlr; Hon Roll; Ntl Merit Ltr.

TRINE, STEPHEN; Brookfield HS; Broofield Center, CT; (Y); 3/225; SADD; Variety Show; Lit Mag; Badmtn; Diving; Timer; Btty Crckr Awd; God Cntry Awd; NHS; Prfct Atten Awd.

TRIOMPO, DAVID; Terryville HS; Terryville, CT; (Y); 9/120; Am Leg Boys St; Band; Jazz Band; JV Bsktbl; JV Socr; DAR Awd; Hon Roll; Pres NHS; Pres Schlr; Louis Armstrng Jazz Awd 86; Syracuse U; Comp Sci.

TRIPP, MICHELLE D; Naugatuck HS; Naugatuck, CT; (Y); 65/310; Pres Art Clb; Teachers Aide; Thesps; Rep Jr Cls; Sftbl; Vllybl; Hon Roll; Southern CT ST; Art Ed.

TROCCIOLA, SUSAN; East Catholic HS; Glastonbury, CT; (Y); 4/297; Trs Camp Fr Inc; VP JA; Nwsp Ed-Chief; Lit Mag; Rep Stu Cncl; JV Var Socr; High Hon Roll; NHS; Rotary Awd; Yale Bk Awd 86; Pre-Med.

TROLL, STEVEN; New Fairfield HS; New Fairfield, CT; (Y); 25/239; Im Bsktbl; Hon Roll; NHS; Awd Outstndng Achvt Clg Prep Bio 85; W CT ST U; Bus.

TROPASSO, LORI; Holy Cross HS; Waterbury, CT; (Y); 16/380; Latin Clb; Var Trk; High Hon Roll; NHS; Soc Stds Hon Soc 85-86; Latin Hon Soc 84-85.

TROTTA, JILL; East Catholic HS; Coventry, CT; (Y); Church Yth Grp; Hosp Aide; Rep Frsh Cls; Rep Soph Cls; Rep Jr Cls; Sci.

TROTTA, RONALD J; Ledyard HS; Gales Ferry, CT; (Y); Spanish Clb; Temple Yth Grp; Hon Roll; U CT; Phrmcy.

TROWBRIDGE, DAVID; Conard HS; W Hartford, CT; (Y); 59/345; Church Yth Grp; Band; Socr.

TRUCKSESS, JEFF; Wilton HS; Wilton, CT; (Y); 16/365; AFS; Church Yth Grp; Varsity Clb; Ice Hcky; Socr; Tennis; High Hon Roll; JC Awd; Econ.

TSAI, NETTY H; The Taft Schl; Saudi Arabia; (Y); Church Yth Grp; Girl Scts; Intnl Clb; Acpl Chr; Chorus; Madrigals; Nwsp Stf; Yrbk Phtg; Yrbk Stf; Rep Sr Cls; Hgh Hnrs 82-83; Intl Bus.

TSARFATY, VERED; William H Hall HS; W Hartford, CT; (Y); 27/329; Church Yth Grp; Concert Band; Orch; Nwsp Stf; NHS; Pres Schlr; All Eastern Band 85; All New Englnd Band 86; All ST Band 86; Oberlin Coll.

TSOI, LOUISA; Greenwich HS; Greenwich, CT; (Y); Service Clb; School Musical; Badmtn; Mth & Sci Awd 86; Strght As 86; Excptnl Wrk Fr 85-86; Med.

TUBBS, DENISE; Windham HS; Windham, CT; (Y); FBLA; High Hon Roll; Hon Roll; Bus Ed.

TUCKER, ANDREA; Nathan Hale-Ray HS; East Haddam, CT; (S); 3/75; Am Leg Aux Girls St; Red Cross Aide; Varsity Clb; Sec Frsh Cls; Sec Stu Cncl; Var Capt Bsktbl; Var Capt Socr; Var Sftbl; High Hon Roll; Hon Roll; Most Imprvd-Bsktbl 83-84; Defnsv Speclst-Bsktbl 84-85; Leag All Star-Bsktbl 85-86; Central CT ST U; Bio Teachr.

TUELL, DAVE; Stratford HS; Stratford, CT; (Y); 34/257; JV Var Bsbl; French Hon Soc; High Hon Roll; Comp Sci.

TUFANO, PAMELA; Branford HS; Branford, CT; (Y); Church Yth Grp; Dance Clb; Band; Mrchg Band; Stu Cncl; Score Keeper; Hon Roll; Lib Arts.

TUFTS, DAVID; Southington HS; Southington, CT; (Y); Hon Roll; Cmnctns.

TUOZZOLA, JILL; Joseph Foran HS; Milford, CT; (Y); Spanish Clb; SADD; Band; Jazz Band; Nwsp Rptr; Nwsp Stf; Hon Roll.

TUPPONCE, DAVID; Rockville HS; Rockville, CT; (Y); Am Leg Boys St; Church Yth Grp; Hosp Aide; Symp Band; Var L Crs Cntry; Var L Crs Cntry; Var L Trk; High Hon Roll; JC Awd; NHS; George Washington U; Bio.

TURECEK, PATRICIA; Shelton HS; Shelton, CT; (Y); Art Clb; Church Yth Grp; JA; Ski Clb; Spanish Clb; SADD; School Play; JV Var Cheerleading; High Hon Roll; Hon Roll.

TUREK, DEBORAH A; Our Lady Of The Angels Acad; Suffield, CT; (Y); 1/24; VP Jr Cls; High Hon Roll; Prfct Atten Awd; Pres Schlr; Val; Hrvd-Rdclff Clb Of Nthrn CT Bk Prize For Acad Excllnc 84-85; Acad All-Amer Ntl Scndry Ed Cncl 86; Creighton U; Pre-Med.

TUREK, MICHELLE; Our Lady Of The Angels Acad; Enfield, CT; (Y); 1/18; Concert Band; Nwsp Stf; Off Stu Cncl; Cheerleading; Socr; High Hon Roll; Harvard Radcliff Clb Outstndng Awd 86.

TURI, GEOFFREY; Jonathan Law HS; Milford, CT; (Y); 34/246; Computer Clb; Intnl Clb; Scholastic Bowl; Yrbk Stf; Capt Var Tennis; Hon Roll; NCTE Essay Rep 86; Hist Awd 85; Wrtng.

TURNER, CHRISTIAN; Shelton HS; Shelton, CT; (Y); JA; Stu Cncl; JV Bsbl; JV Var Bsktbl; JV Crs Cntry; Hon Roll; U Of WI-MADISON; Poltcl Sci.

TURNER, MARK; Andrew Warde HS; Fairfield, CT; (Y); Church Yth Grp; Ftbl; Wt Lftg; High Hon Roll; Hon Roll; SR Grad Ushr 85-86; Bus Mgmt.

TURNQUIST, KIRSTEN; Stratford HS; Stratford, CT; (Y); Cmnty Wkr; Drama Clb; Exploring; Spanish Clb; Rep Stu Cncl; Var Diving; Var Tennis; High Hon Roll; Hon Roll; Anml Sci.

TURRO, SUSAN; Middletown HS; Middletown, CT; (S); 15/202; Pres DECA; Teachers Aide; Pres Frsh Cls; Pres Soph Cls; Sec Jr Cls; Rep Sr Cls; Capt Cheerleading; High Hon Roll; Hon Roll; NHS; Edward A Marszalek Mem Svc Awd 86; Schl Communty Svc; Nichols Coll; Acctng.

TWARDOSKI, DONNA; Griswold HS; Lisbon, CT; (Y); NHS; Model.

TWEED, CHRISTOPHER M; Howell Cheney Tech; Manchester, CT; (Y); 2/130; VICA; Im Bsktbl; NHS; Prnt Clb Schlrshp Awd 86; CT Bus & Indstry Assn 86; U Of CT; Elec Engrng.

TWIGG, JENNIFER; Branford HS; Branford, CT; (Y); 3/312; Hosp Aide; Ed Yrbk Stf; Ed Lit Mag; Stu Cncl; High Hon Roll; Ntl Merit Ltr; VFW Awd; Voice Dem Awd; Brown U Bk Awd; Lbrl Arts.

TWILLEY, SUE M; R E Fitch SR HS; Mystic, CT; (Y); Intnl Clb; Pres Key Clb; VP Science Clb; Acpl Chr; Chorus; Rep Stu Cncl; Rotary Awd; VFW Awd; Towson ST U; Bio.

TYCZ, PAM; Southington HS; Milldale, CT; (Y); 95/600; Pep Clb; Ski Clb; Var Mgr(s); Var Socr; JV Var Sftbl.

TYLER, SUSAN; East Windsor HS; Broad Brook, CT; (Y); 20/105; Church Yth Grp; Drama Clb; PAVAS; Q&S; Thesps; Chorus; Church Choir; Madrigals; School Musical; NHS; Engl.

TYRRELL, DEBORAH; R C Lee HS; New Haven, CT; (Y); Hosp Aide; Nwsp Stf; Vllybl; Hon Roll; NHS; Spanish NHS; Hrvrd Book Prz 86; Physcl Thrpst.

ULISSE, CHRISTIAN; Jonathan Law HS; Milford, CT; (Y); 4/280; Computer Clb; Intnl Clb; Latin Clb; Stat Bsktbl; Var Capt Tennis; Hon Roll; NHS; Prfct Atten Awd; Intermed Alg Hnrs Awd 85; Intro Anlys Hnrs Awd 86; Math.

UNDERKOFLER, DAN; North Haven HS; North Haven, CT; (Y); Debate Tm; FBLA; Latin Clb; Letterman Clb; Model UN; Ski Clb; SADD; Varsity Clb; School Play; JV Ftbl; All ST Soccer Tm; Fidle Soc Latin; Spcl Recgntn Comm Yth Actvty; Brown; Law.

UNGARO, MARC; Southington HS; Southington, CT; (Y); Art Clb; Cmnty Wkr; Key Clb; Ski Clb; Varsity Clb; Variety Show; Var Bsktbl; Hon Roll; Arts Cncl 84 & 86; Art Inst; Cmmrcl Art.

UNTO, LUCIA DELL; Wethersfield HS; Wethersfield, CT; (Y); Cmnty Wkr; Debate Tm; English Clb; French Clb; Orch; Hon Roll; SADD; School Musical; Capt Socr; 1st Pl Violin Comptn 85; 3rd Pl ST Music Comptn 86; Archlgst.

URBAN, DONNA; Ellington HS; Vernon, CT; (Y); 10/139; FBLA; Latin Clb; Band; Concert Band; Flag Corp; Mrchg Band; Yrbk Stf; Stu Cncl; Bsktbl; Sftbl; ARMA Schlrshp 86; Cmmnty Schlrshp 86; Ellington Faclty Schlr 86; Babson Coll; Intl Bus.

URSINI, KAREN; Holy Cross HS; Waterbury, CT; (Y); 46/390; Spanish Clb; Hon Roll; NHS; Spanish NHS; Soc Stud Hnr Soc Svc Awd; Hartford U; Crmnl Justc.

URSO, ROCCO; Berlin SR HS; Kensington, CT; (Y); 53/204; Am Leg Boys St; Drama Clb; Band; Concert Band; Mrchg Band; School Musical; School Play; Pres Jr Cls; Pres Sr Cls; Var Capt Ftbl; Yale Bk Awd 86.

URSO, SALVATORE; Berlin SR HS; Kensington, CT; (Y); 48/183; Am Leg Boys St; Band; Concert Band; Jazz Band; Mrchg Band; Orch; Pep Band; School Musical; School Play; Stage Crew; Natl Hon Soc Schlrshp 86; Italian Fraternl Bk Bnd Awd 86; Western New England MA; Bus.

USMAN, SAJID; Westhill HS; Stamford, CT; (Y); 57/409; AFS; Church Yth Grp; Cmnty Wkr; VP Computer Clb; Pres JA; Latin Clb; Rep Soph Cls; Rep Jr Cls; JV Bsbl; Ptny Bws Schlrshp 86; JA Pres Yr 84; JA Outstndng Yng Busmn 84; Boston Coll; Bio.

UTERSTAEDT, TODD; St Joseph HS; Ansonia, CT; (Y); 20/257; Am Leg Boys St; Trs Debate Tm; Drama Clb; Thesps; Chorus; School Musical; School Play; Stage Crew; Nwsp Phtg; Nwsp Rptr; Syracuse; Brdcst Jrnlsm.

VACCINO, DINNEEN; Sacred Heart Acad; West Haven, CT; (Y); Art Clb; Church Yth Grp; Pep Clb; Spanish Clb; Teachers Aide; Variety Show; High Hon Roll; Hon Roll; 2 Yr Hnr Awd 86; Teacher.

VAGTS JR, BRUCE; Southington HS; Southington, CT; (Y); Boys Clb Am; Boy Scts; Church Yth Grp; Latin Clb; Ski Clb; Band; Concert Band; Var JV Bsktbl; JV Crs Cntry; High Hon Roll; Air Force Acad; Eng.

VAICIULIS, AMY; St Bernard HS; Mystic, CT; (Y); 14/298; Cmnty Wkr; FNA; Library Aide; Red Cross Aide; Sec Jr Cls; Capt Gym; NHS; Church Yth Grp; Exploring; Hosp Aide; Schlt Athlete 86; Elec Boat Mngmnt Assn Gen Dynamics Corp Schlrshp Wnnr 86; Georgetown U; Nrsng.

VALDENTINE, LISA; Wethersfield HS; Wethersfield, CT; (Y); #9 In Class; Camp Fr Inc; Church Yth Grp; Dance Clb; FHA; Math Clb; School Play; Yrbk Stf; Var JV Vllybl; High Hon Roll; NHS; Acadmc Promise Sci 85; Bio.

VALENTE, MICHAEL; Notre Dame HS; New Haven, CT; (Y); 56/233; Pep Clb; Ski Clb; Rep Frsh Cls; Rep Jr Cls; Rep Sr Cls; JV Var Crs Cntry; JV Var Trk; High Hon Roll; Hon Roll; CT Schltc Achvt Schlrshp 86; Northeastern U; Engrg.

VALENTINE, WENDY A; Andrew Warde HS; Fairfield, CT; (Y); Dance Clb; JV Cheerleading; Hon Roll; NYU; Prof Dancr.

VALERIO, ALISON; Danbury HS; Danbury, CT; (Y); 98/550; Church Yth Grp; Yrbk Stf; Sr Cls; Var Tennis; Hon Roll; Jr NHS; Pres Schlr; Slvrmine Guild Of Art Schlrshp 85; Southern CT ST U; Cmmrcl Dsgn.

VALIANTE, DONNA; Staples HS; Westport, CT; (Y); Church Yth Grp; Cmnty Wkr; Spanish Clb; Teachers Aide; JV Var Bsktbl; JV Var Sftbl; JV Vllybl; Hon Roll; Var Lttr 85; Cert Athltc; Accounting.

VALLERIE, SARAH; St Lukes Schl; Ridgefield, CT; (Y); Fld Hcky; Lcrss; Score Keeper; Sftbl; Timer; U Of CT; Bus.

VALORIE, TRACY; Newington HS; Newington, CT; (S); 14/365; Church Yth Grp; VP Drama Clb; Hosp Aide; Chorus; Madrigals; School Musical; Pres Frsh Cls; Trs Sr Cls; Stu Cncl; Sec NHS; Hgh Hnr Roll; Stu Assist Bk Awd; Bio.

VALSECCHI, PATRICIA; Torrington HS; Torrington, CT; (Y); 11/280; Art Clb; Math Tm; Spanish Clb; Stage Crew; Nwsp Stf; Ed Yrbk Stf; High Hon Roll; Hon Roll; NHS; NEDT Awd; U CT Co-Op Prog Super HS Stus 85-86; Cart Part Pstr/Essay Cntst 85; Cert/Awd Contnentl Math Lg 83-84; Wrtng.

VALUCKAS, LAUREN; Farmington HS; Farmington, CT; (Y); 27/206; Hosp Aide; Ski Clb; Varsity Clb; Nwsp Phtg; Yrbk Phtg; Capt Var Crs Cntry; Var Socr; Var Tennis; Capt Var Trk; High Hon Roll; Helen Flood Beauchemin Schlrshp 86; Fllr Schlrshp 86; Grahm Schlrshp 86; Villanova U; Nrsng.

VALUS, SHARON; Lauralton Hall HS; Fairfield, CT; (Y); 4/111; French Clb; Service Clb; Chorus; Yrbk Stf; Capt Cheerleading; French Hon Soc; High Hon Roll; Pres NHS; Awd For Schlrshp, Citznshp & Comm Serv.

VAN ACHTE, JENNIFER; Brookfield HS; Brookfield Center, CT; (Y); 16/238; Math Tm; Concert Band; Mrchg Band; Var L Gym; High Hon Roll; NHS.

VAN BRAMER, AMY; Northwest Catholic HS; Windsor Locks, CT; (Y); Cmnty Wkr; Band; Concert Band; Jazz Band; Mrchg Band; Orch; Yrbk Stf; Var L Socr; JV Var Sftbl; Outstndng Perfrmnce Band 86; All Hartford Cnty Conf Soccr 85; Pre-Law.

VAN DER SLUYS, BONNIE; Trumbull HS; Trumbull, CT; (Y); Church Yth Grp; Ski Clb; Mrchg Band; Symp Band; High Hon Roll; NHS; CT Rgnl Bank 86; Supr Rating Flute Solo Free Church Natl Comp 85; Med.

VAN DER VEEN, KIRSTEN M; Valley Regional HS; Essex, CT; (Y); 5/126; Drama Clb; French Clb; Band; School Play; Stage Crew; High Hon Roll; NHS; Ntl Merit Ltr; Cheesebrgh Pnds Fmly Arts Comptn Reg 1st & Natl 2nd Prz 84; Schlstc Art Comptn Natl Hon Mntn 84; Yale U.

VAN DERZEE, KEITH; Canterbury HS; Sherman, CT; (Y); 8/85; Camera Clb; Church Yth Grp; Cmnty Wkr; Library Aide; Political Wkr; Service Clb; Var Stu Cncl; JV Bsbl; JV Capt Bsktbl; JV Socr; A Russell Ayre Schlrshp 86; Colgate U; Intl Rltns.

VAN DINE, HEATHER; East Catholic HS; Bolton, CT; (Y); 101/295; Cmnty Wkr; Hosp Aide; JV Trk; Instrctrs Handicapped Pres 85-86; Providence Coll; Math.

VAN DYKES, CYNTHIA; East Catholic HS; Manchester, CT; (Y); 50/350; French Clb; Hosp Aide; Office Aide; Mt Ida Schlrshp 86; Dr Geeter Schlrshp 86; Mt Ida Coll; Prlgl.

VAN NESS, HOLLY; Southington HS; Southington, CT; (Y); Latin Clb; Ski Clb; Concert Band; Mrchg Band; Nwsp Stf; Yrbk Ed-Chief; Ed Lit Mag; Hon Roll; Ctr Creative Yth Wesleyan U 84; Phillips Acad Andover 86; Southington Arts Cncl Rep 85-86.

VAN RAALTE, NANCY; Wilton HS; Wilton, CT; (Y); 21/352; Pres Temple Yth Grp; Madrigals; Swing Chorus; Rep Stu Cncl; Stat Ice Hcky; Var Capt Socr; High Hon Roll; Sec NHS; Ntl Merit Ltr; Invtn To Cnvctn Distngshd HS Stdnts 86.

VAN VALKENBURG, KAREN; Windsor Locks HS; Windsor Locks, CT; (Y); 26/164; Church Yth Grp; Concert Band; Mrchg Band; School Play; Trs Jr Cls; Sec Sr Cls; Stu Cncl; Var Capt Fld Hcky; Hon Roll; Nwsp Stf; Field Hcky All-Confrnc NCCC 85-86; Assumption Coll; Lib Arts.

VAN WILGEN, ELIZABETH; Branford HS; Branford, CT; (Y); 76/315; Latin Clb; SADD; Ed Yrbk Stf; Rep Frsh Cls; Chrmn Soph Cls; Rep Jr Cls; Var L Fld Hcky; Capt Lcrss; Var L Trk; Hon Roll; Lauren E Hayes Memrl Mst Imprvd Plyr Fld Hocky 85; Phsycl Thrpst.

VANASE, KIMBERLY J; Norwich Regional Vo Tech; Norwich, CT; (Y); Hosp Aide; VICA; Yrbk Stf; Mgr(s); Score Keeper; Hon Roll; VICA Lcl Clb Pres & ST Reporter 85-86; Micheal J Bohara Awd 82-83; Grphc Cmmnctns.

VANGHELE, NICK; Andrew Warde HS; Fairfield, CT; (Y); Church Yth Grp; Exploring; Key Clb; Var L Socr; Hon Roll; Cst Guard Acad.

VANOUREK, SCOTT; New Canaan HS; New Canaan, CT; (Y); NFL; Var Socr; Var Trk; Pomona Coll.

VARGA, GREGORY; Fairfield College Prep Schl; Easton, CT; (Y); Yrbk Ed-Chief; Rep Sr Cls; High Hon Roll; NHS; Spanish NHS; Spanish Clb; Church Choir; JV Bsbl; Bus Adm.

VARGAS, OMAYRA; Hartford Public HS; Hartford, CT; (Y); Science Clb; Sftbl; Vllybl.

VARGAS, SANDRA; Bassick HS; Bridgeport, CT; (Y); Computer Clb; Chorus; Rep Stu Cncl; JV Vllybl; Hon Roll; Schlstc Achvt Awd 84-85; Caduceus Clb 84-85; Southern CT ST U.

VARIEUR, CHRISTINE; Plainfield HS; Moosup, CT; (Y); 33/140; GAA; Pep Clb; Varsity Clb; Yrbk Phtg; Yrbk Stf; VP Soph Cls; Pres Stu Cncl; Im Powder Puff Ftbl; Var L Sftbl; Schlrshp Bk Nw Englnd, Schlrshp Girls Athltc Assn 86; Central CT ST U; Finc.

VATER, CRAIG J; Hartford Public HS; Hartford, CT; (Y); #2 In Class; Camera Clb; Debate Tm; Model UN; Political Wkr; Spanish Clb; Variety Show; Bsktbl; Crs Cntry; Socr; Tennis; 2nd Schlr Prize 84-86; US Hist Awd 86; Eng Lit Awd 85.

VECCHIO, CARA; Hamden HS; Hamden, CT; (Y); Ski Clb; VP Jr Cls; VP Sr Cls; Rep Stu Cncl; Var Trk; High Hon Roll; Hon Roll; U VT; Med.

VECCHITTO, LISA; Maloney HS; Meriden, CT; (Y); Key Clb; Hon Roll; Crescnt Clb; Fund Raisrs; Bus.

VEECH, MICHELLE; Nonnewaug HS; Woodbury, CT; (Y); Trs FBLA; School Play; Yrbk Stf; Trs Sr Cls; Var L Cheerleading; Coach Actv; JV Capt Fld Hcky; High Hon Roll; NHS; AFS; Exell In Hme Ecnmcs Swng; Exell In Acctg; Cert Nrs Aid; Fshn Merchandise.

VEGIARD, ROLAND LEE; East Catholic HS; E Hartford, CT; (Y); 52/298; CAP; Drama Clb; Red Cross Aide; Teachers Aide; Chorus; School Musical; Socr; High Hon Roll; Amelia Earhart Awd; Cadet Ldrshp Acadmy; Embry-Riddle Aerontcl U; Aerntl.

VELEZIS, MICHAEL; Holy Cross HS; Waterbury, CT; (Y); 41/403; Pres Church Yth Grp; VP Intnl Clb; Ski Clb; Teachers Aide; Crs Cntry; Score Keeper; Trk; High Hon Roll; NHS; Awd Socl Stds Hnr Soc; Italian Clb; Law.

VELKY, LISA A; Acad Of Our Lady Of Mercy; Milford, CT; (Y); Church Yth Grp; Sec Drama Clb; Model UN; Service Clb; School Play; Rep Frsh Cls; Pres Soph Cls; Sftbl; Swmmng; Rep NHS; Bus Admin.

VELLA, ANDREA; Bethel HS; Bethel, CT; (Y); 37/236; AFS; Church Yth Grp; Chorus; Church Choir; Socr; High Hon Roll; NHS; Pres Acdmc Fit Awd 86; Choral Awd 86; Becker Coll; Vet Tech.

VENDETTI, MARC; Farmington HS; Farmington, CT; (Y); Church Yth Grp; Cmnty Wkr; Varsity Clb; Off Frsh Cls; Off Soph Cls; Off Jr Cls; Stu Cncl; Bsbl; Bsktbl; Socr; Engl.

VENDITTO, JEREMY; East Granby HS; E Granby, CT; (Y); 18/62; Drama Clb; PAVAS; Thesps; Band; Chorus; School Musical; School Play; High Hon Roll; Hon Roll; Church Yth Grp; Cert Excellnc Drams 84-85; Grad YPI Drama 84-85; Pres Phys Ftns Awd 83-85; CA Inst Arts; Drama.

VENICE, ROBERT; Emmet O Brien Tech; Ansonia, CT; (Y); Boy Scts; Camera Clb; Debate Tm; Yrbk Stf; Stu Cncl; Crs Cntry; Trk; High Hon Roll; Trs NHS; U S Army; Telecmmnctns.

VERBITSKY, JOSEPH; Bristol Central HS; Bristol, CT; (Y); Boys Clb Am; JV Bsbl; Im Ftbl; Cit Awd; Hon Roll; Vet Sci.

VERCELLONE, DAVID; North Haven HS; N Haven, CT; (Y); Var JV Bsbl; Hon Roll.

VERENEAU, LYNNE; Southington HS; Southington, CT; (Y); 67/600; Pep Clb; Concert Band; Mrchg Band; Hon Roll; Pre Schl Ed.

VERNIK, AARON S; Trumbull HS; Trumbull, CT; (Y); 2/472; Computer Clb; Library Aide; JV Var Socr; JV Trk; Hon Roll; Ltr Soccer 85; George A Kelso Schlrshp 86; La Salle; Geolgy.

VERNO, CARMINE; Watertown HS; Watertown, CT; (Y); Boys Clb Am; Church Yth Grp; DECA; Variety Show; Yrbk Phtg; JV Ftbl; Bstn U; Cmrcl Art.

VERRILLI, DANIELLE; Joseph A Foran HS; Milford, CT; (Y); 29/240; Camera Clb; Drama Clb; JCL; Ski Clb; Spanish Clb; Band; Chorus; VP Soph Cls; Cheerleading; High Hon Roll; Sprntndnts Awd 86; U CT; Cmnctns.

VESSICHIO, LAURA; Lyman Hall HS; Wallingford, CT; (Y); 4/197; AFS; Yrbk Bus Mgr; Lit Mag; Powder Puff Ftbl; Cit Awd; High Hon Roll; NHS; Hon Roll; Wllngfrd Educ Assn Awd 86; Anna M Frdrcks Mem Schlrshp 86; Bryant Coll; Acctng.

VETRO, MARIA; Holy Cross HS; Cheshire, CT; (Y); 106/380; Church Yth Grp; Cmnty Wkr; Service Clb; Band; Church Choir; Color Guard; Concert Band; Mrchg Band; Pep Band; Stage Crew; Psych.

VIADELLA, CYNTHIA; Shelton HS; Shelton, CT; (Y); Art Clb; Cmnty Wkr; Drama Clb; Girl Scts; Hosp Aide; Pres JA; Library Aide; Political Wkr; Ski Clb; Sec SADD; Pres Of Yr In Naugatuck Vly JR Achvt 86; Schlrshp To Ctr For Creative Yth 84; Bus.

VIBERT, KELLY; New Britain HS; New Britain, CT; (Y); 24/340; Cmnty Wkr; JA; Key Clb; Political Wkr; JV Vllybl; Hon Roll; Bio.

VICENTE, SANTIAGO R; Conard HS; Hartford, CT; (Y); 30/360; Boy Scts; Cmnty Wkr; Drama Clb; Intnl Clb; JA; Math Clb; Math Tm; Rep Model UN; Science Clb; Service Clb; Math Tm Awd, Acting Awd CT Prama Assoc St Drama Fest 86; Pre-Med.

VIDETTO, CHRIS; Torrington HS; Torrington, CT; (Y); Band; Concert Band; Bsktbl; L Capt Ftbl; Swmmng; Wt Lftg; Physcl Thrpst.

VIEIRA, CATHERINE J; Holy Cross HS; Naugatuck, CT; (Y); Latin Clb; Service Clb; Spanish Clb; SADD; Variety Show; VP Frsh Cls; Var Capt Crs Cntry; Var Swmmng; Var Trk; Prfct Atten Awd; Perfect Attndnc 4 Yrs; Most Imprvd X-Cntry Rnr; Schl Turkey; NE U; Bus Mgmt.

VIEIRA, ROBERT; Ansonia HS; Stratford, CT; (Y); 18/145; Am Leg Boys St; Computer Clb; Latin Clb; Spanish Clb; Var L Bsktbl; Var L Ftbl; Cit Awd; Hon Roll; CT Schltc Achvt Schlrshp 86; Olderman Schlrshp 86; Hilltop PTO Prz 86; U Of CT; Elect Engrg.

VIERPS, PETER; Oliver Wolcott Tech Schl; Torrington, CT; (Y); 3/167; Ski Clb; Nwsp Phtg; Yrbk Phtg; JV Var Socr; High Hon Roll; Hon Roll; NHS; ASAF; Elec Tech.

VIETZKE, GAY; Branford HS; Branford, CT; (Y); 6/252; Sec Am Leg Aux Girls St; Band; Yrbk Stf; Lit Mag; Stu Cncl; Hon Roll; NHS; Pres Schlr; Stu Mnth 85; Stu Cncl Schrlshp 86; Top Ten Grad Awd 86; Middlebury Coll; Art.

VILLOTA, DORIS; Suffield HS; Suffield, CT; (Y); 8/141; SADD; Stage Crew; Nwsp Ed-Chief; Pres Jr Cls; Rep Stu Cncl; JV Cheerleading; Sftbl; High Hon Roll; NHS; Natl Hispanics Schlr Awds Pgm-Semifnlst 86; United Technologies Schlrshp Fnlst 86; Communctns.

VINICZAY, EVA; Joseph A Foran HS; Milford, CT; (Y); Hosp Aide; Hon Roll.

VIROSTEK, RACHEL; Marianapolis Prep; E Douglas, MA; (Y); 2/44; VP Soph Cls; Pres Stu Cncl; Capt Bsktbl; Capt Socr; Hon Roll; NHS; Ntl Merit Ltr; NEDT Awd; Cngrsnl Yth Ldrshp Cncl 85; Law.

VISHNETSKY, MARTHA; Brookfield HS; Brookfield, CT; (Y); 21/250; Girl Scts; JCL; Math Clb; Math Tm; Spanish Clb; Latn I & Spnsh II Awds 84; Latn II & Spnsh III 85; Acctg I, US Hstry, Trig Awd 86; U Of CT; Law.

VITALE, MARY LEE; St Marys HS; New Haven, CT; (Y); 2/100; School Musical; School Play; Variety Show; Nwsp Ed-Chief; Nwsp Rptr; Pres Jr Cls; Stu Cncl; High Hon Roll; NHS; Spanish NHS; Excllence In Engl 84; Excllence In Engl 85; Ldrshp Awd 86; Engl.

VITARELLI, RICHARD; Holy Cross HS; Middlebury, CT; (Y); 11/396; Variety Show; Sec Jr Cls; Trs Sr Cls; Lcrss; High Hon Roll; Pres NHS; Spanish NHS; Michael Jewelers Svc To Cmnty Awd 86; IGOR Rdr Shrt Essay-1st Pl Wnr 84.

VITOLO, ROBIN; West Haven HS; W Haven, CT; (Y); Dance Clb; Girl Scts; Jazz Band; Bsbl; Bsktbl; Gym; Sftbl; Swmmng; Vllybl; Hon Roll; Schlstc Excllnc Awd Alg 86; Bus.

VITTORIO, MICHELLE; Shelton HS; Shelton, CT; (Y); Drama Clb; School Musical; Gym; Sftbl; Secry.

VOGEL, ALBERT B; Immaculate HS; Danbury, CT; (Y); Yrbk Stf; Rep Stu Cncl; Mgr(s); Im Vllybl; High Hon Roll; NHS; Ntl Merit Ltr; Berklee Prof Music, J L Arjan Mem Schlrshps 86; Berklee Coll Music; Music Perf.

VOGT, JENNIFER; Staples HS; Westport, CT; (Y); French Clb; GAA; Capt L Crs Cntry; Mgr(s); L Var Trk; French Hon Soc; Hon Roll; Awd Exclnc Latin I 86; Hnr Ushr Grad 86; Chem.

VOLLONO, LAURA; Mark T Sheehan HS; Wallingford, CT; (Y); 35/236; Acpl Chr; Chorus; School Musical; Variety Show; Drama Clb; JA; Church Choir; School Play; Hon Roll; Delta Kappa Gamma Soc Of Tchr Schlrshp 86; Central CT ST U; Elem Ed.

VOLPE, MATT; Guilford HS; Guilford, CT; (Y); 33/340; Band; Concert Band; Jazz Band; Mrchg Band; Orch; School Musical; School Play; Lit Mag; Wt Lftg; Debate Tm; Natl Merit Schlr 85; Nassau COLL.

VORBACH, EMILY; St Bernard HS; Vienna, VA; (Y); 70/297; Off Stu Cncl; Var Swmmng; Trk; Hon Roll; Acad Ltr 85-86; Loyola Coll; Psych.

VOSE, HILARY; Valley Regional HS; Deep River, CT; (Y); Art Clb; Camera Clb; Drama Clb; Girl Scts; Library Aide; Ski Clb; Spanish Clb; SADD; Band; Chorus; Briarwood Coll; Fshn Merch.

VOSE, JESSE; Canton HS; Canton, CT; (Y); 3/84; Math Tm; Model UN; Quiz Bowl; Ski Clb; Band; Yrbk Ed-Chief; Var Crs Cntry; Bausch & Lomb Sci Awd; High Hon Roll; NHS; Rensselaer Polytech Inst; Engr.

VOYTEK, ALLAN; Shelton HS; Shelton, CT; (Y); Boys Clb Am; Cmnty Wkr; JA; Ski Clb; Spanish Clb; SADD; Rep Stu Cncl; Capt Bowling; High Hon Roll; Hon Roll; Southern CT ST U; Polit Sci.

VU, MYLINH; Windsor HS; Windsor, CT; (Y); Church Yth Grp; French Clb; VP Intnl Clb; Model UN; Yrbk Stf; Stu Cncl; Var Tennis; French Hon Soc; Hon Roll; Regl Hstry Day Awd 1st Pl 84; Wrld Affrs Semnr Publctn Papr S Arica 86; Intl Law.

WADDELL, JANE; Miss Porters Schl; Southington, CT; (Y); Latin Clb; Math Tm; Var Capt Bsktbl; JV Socr; Var Sftbl; High Hon Roll; Hon Roll; Ntl Merit Ltr; Cum Laude Natl Latinexam 84-85; 3rd Pl Tm CAML 84-85; Biochem.

WAGENMAN, KRISTIN; Stamford HS; Stamford, CT; (S); Church Yth Grp; Drama Clb; Sec JA; Ski Clb; School Musical; Stage Crew; Nwsp Bus Mgr; Jr NHS; NHS; Ntl Merit Ltr.

WAGER, JAY; Brien Mc Mahon HS; Norwalk, CT; (Y); 27/288; Key Clb; Pres Ski Clb; Jazz Band; Mrchg Band; Capt Crs Cntry; Capt Golf; Capt Swmmng; Hon Roll; NHS; Eagle Scout 86; Schlr Athlete 86; U Vermont; Bio.

WAGNER, ERIC; E Catholic HS; East Hartford, CT; (Y); 42/277; Boy Scts; Trs Chess Clb; Lit Mag; Ntl Merit Ltr; Elec Engr.

WAGNER, KATHERINE; Rockville HS; Vernon, CT; (Y); Church Yth Grp; Drama Clb; Ski Clb; Concert Band; Flag Corp; Mrchg Band; JV Var Sftbl; Var Trk; High Hon Roll; Hon Roll; Girl Scts; Bus Adm.

WAGNER, PAULINE; Holy Cross HS; Waterbury, CT; (Y); 140/342; Church Yth Grp; Stage Crew; Aerospc Engr.

WAGNER, SHELLY; Windsor HS; Windsor, CT; (Y); Aud/Vis; Cmnty Wkr; Computer Clb; Dance Clb; Exploring; FBLA; Intnl Clb; Science Clb; Spanish Clb; Nwsp Stf; Central CT Coll; Commnctns.

WAKEFIELD, TAMMY; Killingly HS; Dayville, CT; (Y); 24/275; Sec Girl Scts; SADD; Varsity Clb; Yrbk Stf; Crs Cntry; Trk; High Hon Roll; Hon Roll; NHS; Spanish NHS; Greg Typng Awds-52 WPM 85-86; Greg Shrthnd Awds-110 WPM 85-86; Outstndng Achvt Bus Awd 84 & 86; Bay Path JC; Mgmt.

WAKEM, MATTHEW; Kingswood-Oxford HS; Hartford, CT; (Y); Aud/Vis; Service Clb; Spanish Clb; SADD; Nwsp Phtg; Nwsp Stf; Lit Mag; Im Wt Lftg; Hon Roll; Stage Crew; Librl Arts.

WALCZAK, BARBARA; Plainville HS; Plainville, CT; (Y); Color Guard; Yrbk Stf; Hon Roll; NHS; Natl Yth Yr Essy Cntst 86; Chem.

WALDMAN, DAVID; St Lukes HS; Westport, CT; (Y); Cmnty Wkr; Model UN; JV Var Bsktbl; JV Bowling; JV Lcrss; Var L Socr; Var L Tennis; Bus.

WALDRON JR, DALE; St Bernard HS; Preston, CT; (Y); 20/289; Art Clb; Teachers Aide; JV Socr; High Hon Roll; Hon Roll; Pres Schlr; Art Cont Pen & Ink Drawing 1st Pl 86; Acad Hnrs 85; Magna Cum Laude 86; Belval Art Awd Vsl Arts 86; RISD; Arch.

WALKER, ERIN C; Enfield HS; Enfield, CT; (Y); Church Yth Grp; German Clb; Girl Scts; Hosp Aide; Office Aide; Trs Sr Cls; JV Var Vllybl; Hon Roll; Girl Scout Gold Awd Rcpnt 84; Beneficial Hodson Schlrshp 86-87; Hood Coll; Bio.

WALKER JR, JAMES L; Bassick HS; Bridgeport, CT; (Y); 10/200; Church Yth Grp; Pres Computer Clb; French Clb; Key Clb; Spanish Clb; Band; Church Choir; Concert Band; Mrchg Band; Pep Band; All Amer Music 84; Guardian Merit Achvt Awd 86; Howard U; Cmmnctns.

WALKER, JASON; Emmett O Brien Reg Tech; Oxford, CT; (Y); Ski Clb; CPI; Elec Tech.

WALKER, JESSICA J; E O Smith Schl; Mansfield Ctr, CT; (Y); 1/160; Computer Clb; Math Tm; Red Cross Aide; Ski Clb; SADD; Yrbk Stf; Var L Socr; Var L Trk; Williams Coll Bk Awd 86; Harvard-Radcliffe Bk Awd 86; U CT Hnrs Day Smnr 86; Brown; Engrng.

WALKER, MARGARET; Branford HS; Branford, CT; (Y); Am Leg Aux Girls St; Church Yth Grp; DECA; Latin Clb; Chorus; Var Crs Cntry; JV Fld Hcky; Var Trk; Hon Roll; DECA Confrnc Advertsng & Disply Awd 86; Hotel Adm.

WALKER, TIFFANY; Weaver HS; Hartford, CT; (Y); 14/317; Church Yth Grp; Drama Clb; JA; School Play; High Hon Roll; NHS; Delta Sigma Theta Schlrshp Intrcl Schlrshp 86; Wrld Dbl Dtch Trnmnt Schlrshp 84; U Of S CA; Psych.

WALKER, VANESSA; Norwalk HS; Norwalk, CT; (Y); 178/456; FBLA; JA; Office Aide; 1st Pl Grphc Art Layout & Dsgn 84-85; Trvl.

WALL, SUZANNE; The Taft HS; Rye, NY; (Y); Office Aide; Yrbk Sprt Ed; Yrbk Stf; Rep Jr Cls; JV Capt Bsktbl; Var Capt Crs Cntry; JV L Lcrss; Sftbl; Hon Roll; Pre-Med.

WALLACE, TYE; Farmington HS; Unionville, CT; (Y); 11/219; Am Leg Boys St; Var L Socr; Var L Trk; Bausch & Lomb Sci Awd; High Hon Roll; NHS; Math Tm; Yrbk Stf; Hly Crss Bk Awd 86; Outstndng Physcs Stu Awd 86; U Rchstr Schlrshp 86; US Naval Acad; Engrng.

WALLNER, ABBIE; Guilford HS; Guilford, CT; (Y); Model UN; Chorus; Church Choir; Off Sr Cls; Var Capt Socr; Var Trk; Hon Roll; All Am Soccer; All New England,ST 84-85; MVP Soccer 85; All ST Track 84; Boston Coll.

WALSH, ALYSON; Roger Ludlowe HS; Fairfield, CT; (Y); School Musical; School Play; Yrbk Sprt Ed; Rep Frsh Cls; Rep Stu Cncl; NHS; Spanish NHS; Chorus; Stage Crew; Variety Show; High Hnr Roll; Comptv Figure Sktng; CT Drama Awd For Custume Dsgn 85; Boston U; Intl Rltns.

WALSH, AMY; Southington HS; Southington, CT; (Y); 10/600; Art Clb; Sec German Clb; PAVAS; Nwsp Rptr; Stat Bsktbl; Elks Awd; High Hon Roll; NHS; Ntl Merit Schol; Rotary Awd; Art Stdnt Mnth 85; Elks Stdnt Mnth 85; Syracuse U; Visl Art.

WALSH, BRIAN; St Basil Prep HS; Stamford, CT; (Y); Computer Clb; Bsktbl; Socr; Construction Engnrng.

WALSH, KIM; The Taft Schl; Columbus, IN; (Y); Debate Tm; Speech Tm; Swing Chorus; Bsktbl; Socr; Swmmng; Trk; Ntl Merit SF.

WALSH, KRISTEN; Sacred Heart Acad; W Haven, CT; (Y); Art Clb; Camera Clb; Church Yth Grp; Cmnty Wkr; Hosp Aide; Pep Clb; Service Clb; Bowling; Im Vllybl; Hon Roll; Physcl Thrpy.

WALSH, LISSA EDEN; The Williams Schl; Killingworth, CT; (Y); Letterman Clb; Yrbk Phtg; Sr Cls; Var Capt Bsktbl; Stat Score Keeper; Var Capt Sftbl; Hon Roll; Ntl Merit Ltr; MVP Vrsty Bsktbl 86; Dept Hnrs Engl 85 & 86; Dept Hnrs Math Geom 85.

WALSH, NEIL; New Britain HS; New Britain, CT; (Y); 42/300; Aud/Vis; Church Yth Grp; JA; Var L Ftbl; Hon Roll; U Of CT; Mech Engnrng.

WALTO, JENNIFER; Torington HS; Torrington, CT; (Y); Pres French Clb; Ski Clb; Pres Thesps; Stage Crew; Nwsp Sprt Ed; Trk; Vllybl; High Hon Roll; NHS; U CT Math Achvt Awd 86; Bio Chem.

WALTON JR, LUTHER DEAN; Fairfield College Preparatory Schl; Bridgeport, CT; (Y); Pres Church Yth Grp; VP Drama Clb; Key Clb; Var JV Crs Cntry; Comm Ntl Achvt Schlrshp Pgm 85; Outstndng Negro Stu; Fairfield U; Theater Art.

WALTON, VALERIE; Southington HS; Plantsville, CT; (Y); 176/601; Church Yth Grp; Hosp Aide; SADD; Band; Chorus; Mrchg Band; Yrbk Stf; Rep Jr Cls; Stu Cncl; Trk; Nrsng.

WALTS, ALAN; Guilford HS; Guilford, CT; (Y); German Clb; Orch; JV Var Ftbl; High Hon Roll; Hon Roll; Ntl Merit Schol; Gen Excllnce Awd Lang Art 84-85; Guilford Ftbl MIP Awd 84-85; Tri-Cnty Orch 81-82; Wesleyan U; Psych.

WANAMAKER, LYNNE MARIE; Staples HS; Westport, CT; (Y); Lit Mag; Church Yth Grp; High Hon Roll; Hon Roll; Ntl Merit SF; Brwn Bk Awd 85; Hampshire Coll; Engl.

WANG, HSIU-HUI; New Britain HS; West Hartford, CT; (Y); 14/440; PAVAS; Madrigals; Orch; School Musical; Swing Chorus; High Hon Roll; Hon Roll; NHS; Wnnr Renee B Fisher Awd Outstndng Achvt Music 83; Day Pride Top 100 Stdnt Honrees CT 85; Hartt Schl Of Music; Cncrt Pian.

WANKERL, THOMAS; Newington HS; Newington, CT; (Y); 54/365; Am Leg Boys St; Church Yth Grp; Variety Show; Nwsp Ed-Chief; Yrbk Ed-Chief; Stu Cncl; Cit Awd; Dnfth Awd; High Hon Roll; NHS; Natl Hnr Soc Schlrshp 86; Herald Book Awd 86; Colgate U; Poltcl Sci.

WANOSKY, ROBIN; Lauralton Hall HS; Milford, CT; (Y); 5/111; Dance Clb; French Clb; PAVAS; Nwsp Ed-Chief; Nwsp Rptr; Nwsp Stf; Lit Mag; Hon Roll; NHS; NE Ltn Exm Cum Laude 84-85; Coll Of Willm & Mry; Educ.

WARD, ALVIC; James Hillhouse HS; New Haven, CT; (Y); Cmnty Wkr; Political Wkr; Service Clb; School Play; Lit Mag; Stu Cncl; Gov Hon Prg Awd; Ntl Merit Ltr; St Schlr; Yale Schaefer Family Schlrshp; Sci.

WARD, LINDA; Sacred Heart Acad; Seymour, CT; (Y); CT ST Coll.

WARDLOW, DEBRA; Stratford HS; Stratford, CT; (Y); 4/257; Nwsp Sprt Ed; Nwsp Stf; Lit Mag; Rep Frsh Cls; Rep Soph Cls; Trs Jr Cls; Trs Sr Cls; Stat Bsktbl; High Hon Roll; NHS; Schlrshp CT Bus Wk 85; Soc Of Women Engrs 86; Prelaw.

WARHOLIC, CRISTEN; Holy Cross HS; Ansonia, CT; (Y); Pres Church Yth Grp; Drama Clb; Hosp Aide; Spanish Clb; Im Sftbl; High Hon Roll; Hon Roll; NHS; Spanish NHS; Bsktbl 1st Plc Trphy 83-84; Bus Adm.

WARNER, CHARLENE; Cheshire HS; Cheshire, CT; (Y); GAA; Hosp Aide; Yrbk Stf; Bsktbl; Fld Hcky; Sftbl; Hon Roll; Rep Frsh Cls; Rep Frsh Cls; Rep Jr Cls; Hlth Sci.

WARNER, MARK; Holy Cross HS; Naugatuck, CT; (Y); 62/380; Ski Clb; Rep Stu Cncl; L Ftbl; JV Trk; Hon Roll; NHS; Ntl Merit SF; Mltry Ofcr.

WARNER, SHANNON; St Bernard HS; Oakdale, CT; (Y); 21/265; Drama Clb; French Clb; SADD; School Musical; School Play; Stage Crew; Lit Mag; Score Keeper; Hon Roll; Schl Nmbrs Vrsty Ftbl Statstitn 84; Vrsty Lttr Vrsty Ftbl Statstitn 85; Bio.

WASFEY, SHEILA; Trumbull HS; Trumbull, CT; (Y); VP JA; Pres Spanish Clb; JV Bsktbl; Coach Actv; Mgr(s); Co-Capt Sftbl; High Hon Roll; NHS; Prfct Atten Awd; All FCIAC 2nd Tm Sftbl 86; Outstndng Athletc Achvmt 83; TEA Ldrshp Schlrshp 86; UCONN; Ecnmcs.

WASKOM, TARA; Wilton HS; Wilton, CT; (Y); 59/360; Drama Clb; Chorus; School Play; Variety Show; JV Fld Hcky; Hon Roll; Secrtry Wilton Stu Smmr Plyshop 85; Publcst Wilton Stu Smmr Plyshop 86; Jrnlsm.

WATERHOUSE, HEGE LYNN; Torrington HS; Torrington, CT; (Y); 33/270; French Clb; Chorus; High Hon Roll; Hon Roll; Human Svcs.

WATERS, REGINA; Hartford Public HS; Elmwood, CT; (Y); Rep Soph Cls; Off Jr Cls; Var Crs Cntry; Var Trk; Hon Roll; Harold G Holcomb Prize Am Hist 85-86; Photo Jrnslsm.

WATKINS, EARL; Choate Rosemary Hall HS; Dhahran; (Y); Intnl Clb; JA; Math Tm; School Play; Pres Frsh Cls; Var Bowling; Var Lcrss; Var Vllybl; High Hon Roll; Ntl Merit Ltr; Ntl Hispnc Schlr Awd Semi Fnlst 86; MA Inst Of Tech; Chem Engr.

WATSON, CHRISTOPHER; Robert E Fitch SR HS; Groton, CT; (Y); Var Capt Bsbl; JV Im Bsktbl; Im Bowling; Im Ftbl; Im Tennis; High Hon Roll; Hon Roll; Stu Gvrnmnt Day 84; U Of AZ; Child Develp.

WATSON, DANA; Killingly HS; Dayville, CT; (Y); 3/275; Cmnty Wkr; JV Bsktbl; Var L Fld Hcky; High Hon Roll; NHS; Spanish NHS; Spnsh II,III Achvt Awds 84-86; Outstndng Achvt Math, Collg Prep, And Eng 86; Phys Thrpy.

WATSON, JOHN; Avon Old Farms Schl; Collinsville, CT; (Y); JV Bsbl; Var Ftbl; Var Swmmng; Latin & Engl Bk Prz.

WATSON, LAVONE A; Francis T Maloney HS; Meriden, CT; (S); Rep DECA; 4-H; Hosp Aide; JA; Rep Jr Cls; Rep Stu Cncl; JV Bsktbl; Var Capt Cheerleading; Powder Puff Ftbl; Hampton U; Mktg.

WATSON, MARTY; Watertown HS; Oakville, CT; (Y); Ed Yrbk Stf; Mgr(s); Var Capt Swmmng; Var Trk; Var Wrstlng; Cit Awd; DAR Awd; Hon Roll; Coaches Awd For Swmmng 85; Art.

WATSON, TONYA; Coventry HS; Coventry, CT; (Y); 33/112; Church Yth Grp; Hosp Aide; Office Aide; Concert Band; Hon Roll; Rnbw 2nd Term As Pres 86; Erly Chldhd Ed.

WATT, CHAD; Stratford HS; Stratford, CT; (Y); 33/265; Church Yth Grp; Drama Clb; Exploring; Trs Concert Band; Jazz Band; School Play; Rep Frsh Cls; Rep Soph Cls; Rep Jr Cls; Var L Trk; All Conf Track 86; Western Region Band 86; Aviation.

WAUGH, DIANA; Housatonic Valley Regional HS; Sharon, CT; (Y); Drama Clb; Science Clb; Ski Clb; School Play; Off Frsh Cls; Pres Soph Cls; Socr; Var Tennis; High Hon Roll; Hon Roll; Tennis Jacobsen Troph 85; Pre-Med.

WEAVER, MIKE; Killingly HS; Dayville, CT; (Y); 5/273; Latin Clb; JV Crs Cntry; High Hon Roll; Hon Roll; Lion Awd; NHS; Ntl Merit Ltr; Boy Scts; JV Trk; Engl Effrt Awd; Indstrl Arts Awd; JR Sci & Humnties Sympsm; Engrng.

WEBER, JENNIFER; Ridgefield HS; Ridgefield, CT; (Y); 17/370; Sec Temple Yth Grp; High Hon Roll; Hon Roll; NHS; Ridgefield Cvc Ballet 85-86; Vlnt R Actn Lvs Us Enrchd 84-86; Lbrl Arts Coll.

WEBSTER, CHRIS; Berlin HS; Berlin, CT; (Y); Am Leg Boys St; Boy Scts; Drama Clb; Radio Clb; Science Clb; Stage Crew; Nwsp Phtg; Nwsp Rptr; Stu Cncl; Socr; Newspr 85; Advncd Bio Rsrch Awd 86; Hist 86; Lndscp Arch.

WEDEMEYER, LAURA; Greenwich HS; Riverside, CT; (Y); Art Clb; Church Yth Grp; Cmnty Wkr; Service Clb; NHS; Colgate U; Phlsphy.

WEINBERG, SCOTT; Waterford HS; Waterford, CT; (Y); 3/224; Rep Sr Cls; Var Crs Cntry; Capt Var Trk; High Hon Roll; NHS; Rotary Awd; All ECC Indoor Track 85-86; CASS & CIAC Schlr Athl Awd 86; Boston U.

WEINER, JENNIFER; Simsbury HS; W Simsbury, CT; (Y); 47/410; Am Leg Aux Girls St; Teachers Aide; Chorus; Hon Roll; NHS; Ntl Merit SF; Vrsty Crew 85-86; Capt Crs Cntry Ski 87; Simsbury Summr Theater Yth 86.

WEINSTEIN, DARYL; Guilford HS; Guilford, CT; (Y); 33/350; Cmnty Wkr; Key Clb; Ski Clb; Temple Yth Grp; Band; Lib Orch; School Musical; Hon Roll; NHS; Sci.

WEISBLATT, JONATHAN; Danbury HS; Danbury, CT; (Y); Variety Show; Crs Cntry; Var Trk; DAR Awd; Hon Roll; NHS; Sprtsmnshp JV Indr Trck 83-84; Sprtsmnshp Vrsty X-Cntry 85; U Of CT; Bio.

WEISS, CATHERINE; Rham HS; Marlborough, CT; (Y); Art Clb; Church Yth Grp; Spanish Clb; Chorus; School Play; Mgr(s); Socr; Hon Roll; Drama Clb; FCA; Wslyn Cntr For Arts Smmr Pgm 84; LSU; Bus.

WEISS, DEIRDRE; Southington HS; Plantsville, CT; (Y); 43/600; Am Leg Aux Girls St; Key Clb; Latin Clb; School Play; Stage Crew; Nwsp Rptr; Nwsp Stf; Yrbk Stf; JV Sftbl; Hon Roll; Voluntrng 200 Hrs Awd 84-85; Bio.

WEISS, JEFFREY C; Holy Cross HS; Oakville, CT; (Y); 51/360; Art Clb; Computer Clb; Drama Clb; French Clb; Science Clb; Service Clb; School Play; Stage Crew; Lit Mag; French Hon Soc; Sci Achvt Awd 84; Worcester Polytech Inst; Comptr.

WEISS, MICHELLE; Watertown SR HS; Watertown, CT; (Y); 13/235; Hosp Aide; Library Aide; Spanish Clb; Chorus; Variety Show; Yrbk Stf; Var L Socr; Hon Roll; Sec NHS; Weslyan U CT Ctr For Creative Yth Schlrshp 84; Educ.

WELCH, JAMES; St Bernard HS; Lisbon, CT; (Y); 144/290; Am Leg Boys St; Boy Scts; Church Yth Grp; Exploring; VP Bsbl; JV Bsktbl; JV Coach Actv; VP Ftbl; Im Wt Lftg; Hon Roll; Pre-Law.

WELKES, DOROTA; Bullard-Havens Rvts; Bridgeport, CT; (S); Library Aide; Stu Cncl; Stat Cheerleading; Mgr(s); VP Sftbl; High Hon Roll; Hon Roll; Fashn Desgn.

WELLES, WARD; Kent Schl; Cold Spring Harbo, NY; (Y); 24/167; Cmnty Wkr; Library Aide; Nwsp Sprt Ed; Nwsp Stf; Ice Hcky; Lcrss; Hon Roll; Yth Hcky Tm Plyd Russia 82; Mst Imprvd Dfnsv Plyr Hcky 84-85; Capt Vrsty Hcky Tm 85-86; Princeton U; Bus.

WELLMAN, KATHRYN; Canterbury Schl; New Milford, CT; (Y); 3/88; Camera Clb; Cmnty Wkr; Nwsp Stf; Ed Yrbk Stf; JV Bsktbl; Var Mgr(s); JV Socr; Var Stat Vllybl; High Hon Roll; Hosp Aide; Hstry Thesis Awd 86; Harvard Alumni Bk Prize 86; Lib Arts.

WELLS, GARNET; Cooperative HS; Hamden, CT; (Y); Church Yth Grp; Ski Clb; SADD; Nwsp Stf; Lit Mag; Stu Cncl; Pres Acad Ftnss Awd Prog 85-86; Holy Cross Coll; Premed.

WELLS, JON; Cheshire HS; Cheshire, CT; (Y); Math Clb; Math Tm; Science Clb; High Hon Roll; Hon Roll; Jr NHS; Mu Alp Tht; Hnrs Banquet 86; Math Cntst 9th Pl Geo; MIT; Mech Engr.

WERKHEISER, LORA; Shelton HS; Shelton, CT; (Y); 59/315; Church Yth Grp; VP JA; Ski Clb; Spanish Clb; Yrbk Stf; Rep Jr Cls; Rep Sr Cls; Mgr(s); NHS; Wichita ST U; Bus.

WERTZ, INGRID M; William H Hall HS; W Hartford, CT; (Y); 9/300; Yrbk Sprt Ed; Stu Cncl; Var Capt Lcrss; Var Capt Swmmng; High Hon Roll; NHS; Ntl Merit SF; Pres Schlr; Spanish NHS; Pratt & Whitney Schlrshp 86; Northwestern U.

WESTBROOK, ROBERT; Cooperative HS; Rochester, NY; (Y); Trs Jr Cls; Hon Roll; Prfct Atten Awd; St Schlr; Harvard Clb Bk Awd 86; Rensselaer Polytech Inst Sci Awd 86.

WESTENHOFER, KIMBERLY; Brookfield HS; Brookfield, CT; (Y); 21/220; Chorus; Yrbk Stf; Stu Cncl; Var Capt Cheerleading; Mgr(s); High Hon Roll; NHS.

WESTMORELAND, STEPHEN; Canton HS; Collinsville, CT; (Y); 26/96; Church Yth Grp; Socr; Hon Roll; Hartford ST Tech Coll; Arch.

WESTON, SUSAN; Ridgefield HS; Ridgefield, CT; (Y); Church Yth Grp; Cmnty Wkr; Drama Clb; Girl Scts; Intnl Clb; Office Aide; Varsity Clb; Stage Crew; Stu Cncl; Sftbl; Scl Wrkr.

WHEELER JR, FREDERICK W; Jonathan Law HS; Milford, CT; (Y); 12/200; Am Leg Boys St; Computer Clb; Key Clb; Ski Clb; Var Tennis; Var Wrstlng; Hon Roll; Intnl Clb; Rep Soph Cls; Stu Cncl; Devon Rotary Scholar; Excllnce Comp Mth; Excllnce Calculus; Worcester Polytech; Elec Engr.

WHEELER, KRISTAN; Amity SR HS; Woodbridge, CT; (Y); Church Yth Grp; Cmnty Wkr; French Clb; SADD; Yrbk Stf; Cheerleading.

WHELAN, DANIEL J; St Bernard HS; Oakdale, CT; (Y); 14/265; Boy Scts; School Play; Stage Crew; NHS; Art Clb; Drama Clb; Lit Mag; Stu Cncl; Awd Acad Exc 85; Gen Exc Art 84.

WHISLER, ROBIN; Mark T Sheehan HS; Wallingford, CT; (Y); Pres AFS; Math Tm; Scholastic Bowl; Science Clb; Chorus; Flag Corp; Variety Show; Hon Roll; French Clb; Hosp Aide; Amer Legion Oratorical Cont 3rd Pl 85; CT Spcl Olympics Vlntr 83-86; CT Schlr At Choate Smmr 86; Genetics.

WHITE, BRID M; St Mary HS; Greenwich, CT; (Y); Art Clb; Drama Clb; French Clb; Intnl Clb; Math Tm; Pres Pep Clb; School Play; Yrbk Ed-Chief; Ed Yrbk Phtg; JV Cheerleading; Pres Acadmc Ftnss Awd 86; Carnegie Mellon U; Hstry.

WHITE, CAROLYN; Amity Regional SR HS; Orange, CT; (Y); 43/420; Art Clb; Church Yth Grp; Cmnty Wkr; French Clb; SADD; Var L Swmmng; JV Vllybl; Jr NHS; NHS; JV Trk; Ntl Art Hnr Soc; U Of CT; Pltcl Sci.

WHITE, CHRISTINE; Tolland HS; Tolland, CT; (Y); 4-H; Lit Mag; Var L Crs Cntry; Trk; 4-H Awd; Hon Roll; Mktg.

WHITE, CHRISTOPHER; Oliver Wolcott Regnl Voc Tech Schl; Winsted, CT; (Y); Teachers Aide; VICA; Cheerleading; Pom Pon; Hon Roll; Hugh O Brien Yth Fndtn 85; Tulane U; Hlth Occuptn.

WHITE, JENNIFER; Putnam HS; Putnam, CT; (Y); Chorus; Yrbk Ed-Chief; Rep Jr Cls; Sec Stu Cncl; Hon Roll; Prctcpt Spec Grp Prj Insight 84-85; Phrmcy.

WHITE, ROY; Enrico Fermi HS; Enfield, CT; (Y); Spanish Clb; Im Mgr Bsbl; JV Bsktbl; High Hon Roll; Hon Roll; U CT.

WHITE, TYRRELL; East Catholic HS; Hebron, CT; (Y); Church Yth Grp; Teachers Aide; Yrbk Stf; Capt Diving; Capt Sftbl; Capt Swmmng; Hon Roll; Physcl Educ.

WHITE, WILLIAM; Holy Cross HS; Waterbury, CT; (Y); 36/380; Cmnty Wkr; PAVAS; Sec Concert Band; Mrchg Band; Orch; Pep Band; School Musical; Stage Crew; Lit Mag; Hon Roll; Bro Leary Mem Schlrshp 83; Soc Stds Hnr Soc 85-86; Proj Sage 84; Bus.

WHITMORE, SUSAN; St Paul Catholic HS; Plantsville, CT; (Y); 22/246; Church Yth Grp; Cmnty Wkr; Drama Clb; Exploring; Teachers Aide; Band; Church Choir; School Play; Variety Show; Yrbk Stf; Frnch Merit Awd 82; Meml Schlrshp Awd 86; Boston U; Phys Thrpy.

WHITNEY, AUTUMN; Windham Tech; Andover, CT; (Y); 1/111; 4-H; Girl Scts; VICA; Yrbk Stf; Stu Cncl; Bsktbl; JV Trk; High Hon Roll; Hon Roll; Sec NHS; Bst Arch Drftsmn Awd 86; Drftsmn.

WHITNEY, CAROL E; Avon HS; Avon, CT; (Y); 10/170; Church Yth Grp; Band; Madrigals; Orch; Yrbk Stf; Rep Stu Cncl; JV Var Trk; NHS; Dance Clb; Chorus; All ST Band 84; Cert Merit Latin III, Amer Lit I & II, Lang Strucs 84 & 86; Avon Lg Scholar 86; U VT; Prof Nrsng.

WHITNEY, SARAH; Kingswood-Oxford HS; New Britain, CT; (Y); Church Yth Grp; Cmnty Wkr; Service Clb; Yrbk Phtg; Yrbk Stf; Var Capt Bsktbl; Var Socr; JV Capt Tennis; French Clb; GAA.

WHITTAKER, KELLEY; Foran HS; Milford, CT; (Y); Keywanettes; Service Clb; Spanish Clb; SADD; Sec Sr Cls; Rep Stu Cncl; JV Bsktbl; L Twrlr; Hon Roll; Teachers Aide; JR Awd Bst Tchrs Aide Engl Dept 86; Awd Btn Twrlr 83-86; Med.

WHITTAKER, KEVIN; Griswold HS; Lisbon, CT; (Y); #3 In Class; Varsity Clb; Rep Stu Cncl; Var JV Bsktbl; Var JV Ftbl; Var L Golf; High Hon Roll; NHS; Harvard Clb Southern CT Prize Bk 86; Engrng.

WHOLEY, ROBERT; Saint Mary HS; Pt Chester, NY; (Y); Boy Scts; Intnl Clb; JA; Stage Crew; Yrbk Bus Mgr; Stu Cncl; Var Ftbl; Lcrss; Hon Roll; Ntl Merit Ltr; Mth Awd 84; Engrng.

WHYTE, JEFFREY R; Southington HS; Plantsville, CT; (Y); 87/600; JA; Pres Frsh Cls; L Bsbl; Var L Bsktbl; L Socr; Hon Roll; Poly Sci.

WIEDERLIGHT, LISA M; Stamford HS; Stamford, CT; (Y); Political Wkr; Ski Clb; Rep Varsity Clb; Sec Frsh Cls; Sec Soph Cls; Rep Jr Cls; Rep Stu Cncl; Var Fld Hcky; JV Capt Sftbl; NHS; Lawyer.

WIEKRYKAS, CLEMENT; E Windsor HS; E Windsor, CT; (Y); 1/100; Political Wkr; Rptr Q&S; Jazz Band; Trs Frsh Cls; Trs Soph Cls; VP Pres Stu Cncl; Bsktbl; Var Capt Socr; Var Capt Trk; NHS; Hugh O Brien Yth Ldrshp Ambssdr 85; Mech Engrng.

WILCOX, CAROLINE; Torrington HS; Torrington, CT; (Y); 28/290; Trs French Clb; Band; School Play; Nwsp Rptr; Rep Sr Cls; Var L Cheerleading; Im Gym; Var L Trk; High Hon Roll; NHS; 4 X 400 Rcrd Hldg Tm 85.

WILCOX, LORI A; Southington HS; Southington, CT; (Y); 3/600; GAA; Key Clb; Math Tm; Stu Cncl; Bsktbl; Sftbl; Trk; Capt Vllybl; High Hon Roll; NHS; CIAC Schlr/Ath 86; Cls Essayst 3rd Of 600 86; Rotary Ctznshp Awd 86; U CT; Engrng.

WILCOX, PAUL; Kent Schl; S London, VT; (Y); Teachers Aide; Rep Frsh Cls; Rep Jr Cls; Stu Cncl; JV Pres Crs Cntry; Socr; JV Trk; Hon Roll; Top 10 86-87.

WILCOX, SHARON; Torrington HS; Torrington, CT; (Y); Cmnty Wkr; Thesps; School Musical; School Play; Nwsp Rptr; Yrbk Ed-Chief; High Hon Roll; Hon Roll; NHS; Prfct Atten Awd; Bus Mjr.

WILD, BRIAN; Windsor HS; Windsor, CT; (Y); 3/371; Pres VP Aud/Vis; Model UN; Scholastic Bowl; Spanish Clb; Stage Crew; Yrbk Stf; Hon Roll; Prfct Atten Awd; Spanish NHS; Trinity Book Awd 86; Future Prblm Slvng St Bowl 86; High Schlr Rcgntn 85; Engrng.

WILKOWSKI, MARCIA; Holy Cross HS; Waterbury, CT; (Y); 100/360; Church Yth Grp; Spanish Clb; Hon Roll; Spanish NHS; Bus Adm.

WILL, GABRIELLE; Ridgefield HS; Los Altos Hills, CA; (Y); Varsity Clb; Variety Show; Lit Mag; Socr; Var Vllybl; Bennington July Prog 86; Runnr-Up Gardens Comp Tate Gallery London 84; Lit.

WILLCOX JR, PETER; Kent Schl; Fairfield, CT; (Y); Church Yth Grp; Debate Tm; Key Clb; Ski Clb; Spanish Clb; Var Ftbl; Var JV Socr; Hon Roll; Mst Imprvd Plyr Sccr 84; Bus.

WILLIAMS, ANGELA; Sacred Heart Acad; New Haven, CT; (Y); Pres Church Yth Grp; Drama Clb; Hosp Aide; JA; JV Bsktbl; Cheerleading; French Hon Soc; NHS; High Hon Roll; United Ushers Schlrhsp, Debutante Christ Schlrshp 85; Immanuel Bapt Church Schlrshp 86; Pediatrician.

WILLIAMS, BRANDON; Rockville HS; Vernon, CT; (Y); Ski Clb; Ftbl; JV Var Wrstlng; Hon Roll; Aerontcl Engrng.

WILLIAMS, CHARLENE ANISSA; Northwest Catholic HS; Bloomfield, CT; (Y); 6/174; Church Yth Grp; Hosp Aide; Spanish Clb; Yrbk Stf; Capt Bsktbl; JV Trk; Cit Awd; High Hon Roll; Hon Roll; NHS; Top Mnrty Stu 85-86; Columbia U.

WILLIAMS, CLARENCE; Hartford Public HS; Hartford, CT; (Y); Aud/Vis; Computer Clb; Var Bsktbl; JV Crs Cntry; JV Trk; Embry-Riddle; Flight Aviantion.

WILLIAMS, DAVE; Simsbury HS; Simsbury, CT; (Y); 83/407; Boy Scts; JA; Bsbl; High Hon Roll; Hon Roll; Ntl Merit Ltr; Mc Ln Awd Math 84; All-Cnfrnc Tm Vrsty Bsbll 86; Bus Mgmt.

WILLIAMS, DAWN; William H Hall HS; W Hartford, CT; (Y); 11/346; Color Guard; Chorus; Madrigals; Swing Chorus; Yrbk Stf; Badmtn; Sftbl; Vllybl; Rodgers House Student Of The Month 86; Capitol Area Scholarship 86; Trinity Coll; The Humanities.

WILLIAMS, ERICA; Wethersfield HS; Wethersfield, CT; (Y); Am Leg Aux Girls St; Band; Var Capt Bsktbl; Var L Trk; Var Capt Vllybl; High Hon Roll; Hon Roll; NHS; Wethersfield Bsktbll Boosters Coaches Awd 86; ; All ST Team Track & Fld 85-86.

WILLIAMS, JANICE; Sacred Heart Acad; New Haven, CT; (Y); 32/122; Church Yth Grp; Dance Clb; FBLA; Hosp Aide; Chorus; Church Choir; School Musical; Im Vllybl; High Hon Roll; NHS; Cmmnded Schlr Of Ntl Achvt Pgm-Outstndng Negro Stu 85; CT ST Schlr 86; Wesleyan U; Accntng.

WILLIAMS, KAREN DANIELLE; R E Fitch SR HS; Mystic, CT; (Y); 12/321; Trs Girl Scts; Pres Key Clb; Varsity Clb; Ed Lit Mag; Pres Stu Cncl; Var Crs Cntry; Var Trk; NHS; Chorus; Nwsp Rptr; Amer H S Athl X-Cntry 84; Grl Sct Slvr Awd 84; Athl Traing.

WILLIAMS, MARC; Weaver HS; Hartford, CT; (Y); Boys Clb Am; Church Yth Grp; Exploring; Varsity Clb; Yrbk Stf; Rep Jr Cls; Var Im Bsktbl; Capt Var Ftbl; Var Trk; Hon Roll; Comp Sci.

WILLIAMS, PRESTON; Farmington HS; Farmington, CT; (Y); Ski Clb; Var Bsbl; Var Ice Hcky; Var Tennis; High Hon Roll; Hon Roll; Bus Admn.

WILLIAMS, RONALD; Cheshire HS; Cheshire, CT; (Y); 67/300; School Play; Rep Frsh Cls; Rep Soph Cls; Rep Jr Cls; Rep Sr Cls; Im Bsktbl; Bowling; High Hon Roll; Jr NHS; Chrmn Mag Dr 86; Chrmn JR Prm Cmte 85; Slvr Key Awd 86; U Of CT; Elec Egnrng.

WILLIAMS, STACEY M; Wilton HS; Wilton, CT; (Y); Key Clb; Nwsp Bus Mgr; Nwsp Rptr; Nwsp Stf; JV Var Tennis; High Hon Roll; Hon Roll; Jr NHS; Oberlin Coll Bk Engl Awd 85; Vlg Bnk Schlrshp Awd 86; Wilton PTSA Bk Rdng Awd 85.

WILLIS, KIM; Heritage Christian Acad; Naugatuck, CT; (S); Church Yth Grp; Band; School Play; Nwsp Rptr; Yrbk Ed-Chief; Sec Trs Stu Cncl; L Bsktbl; L Sftbl; Var Capt Vllybl; Hon Roll; 1st Rnr-Up CT Miss TEEN Pgnt 85; 1st Pl H S Woodwnd New Engld Chrstn Fine Art Fstvl 85; Spec Ed Tchr.

WILLS, KENNETH T; Conard HS; West Hartford, CT; (Y); PAVAS; Band; Concert Band; Drm & Bgl; Jazz Band; Mrchg Band; Orch; Pep Band; Symp Band; Var JV Socr; Schlrshp Berklee Schl Music 84; Hnrbl Mntn Arts Rcgntn & Tlnt Srch 85; Music Perf.

WILLS, NANCY; Masuk HS; Monroe, CT; (Y); 70/272; Church Yth Grp; Hon Roll; Stevenson Lumber Co Schlrshp 86; Masuk Parents Club Schlrshp 86; Cert Of Outstndng Achvt-Typng I 83; U Of CT; Elem Educ.

WILMOT, BRIAN; Norwalk HS; Norwalk, CT; (Y); 108/422; Letterman Clb; Capt Var Bsbl; Capt Var Crs Cntry; Var Capt Trk; Rotary Awd; All Dly Nws All Str Bsbl Tm 86; All FCIAC Blsbl Tm 86; All Cty MVP Bsbl Tm 86; U CT; Accntng.

WILOCK, ROB; Wilton HS; Wilton, CT; (Y); 37/353; Camera Clb; Cmnty Wkr; Yrbk Stf; Im Bsktbl; Im Sftbl; High Hon Roll; Hon Roll; Ntl Merit Ltr.

WILSON, BETHANY; Maloney HS; Meriden, CT; (Y); Church Yth Grp; Cmnty Wkr; Hosp Aide; Trs Key Clb; Spanish Clb; Var L Tennis; High Hon Roll; Hon Roll; NHS; Crescent Clb Sec 85-87; Pace U; Actuary.

WILSON, BILLI; Nathan Hale-Ray HS; Moodus, CT; (Y); 6/56; Sec Drama Clb; Girl Scts; Church Choir; School Musical; School Play; Ed Yrbk Ed-Chief; Var JV Vllybl; High Hon Roll; Sec NHS; Prfct Atten Awd; 1st Drwng Cngrssnl Arts 86; 5th Poster Wrld Peace 83; Excel Spnsh I, II, III 84-86; Fine Arts.

WILSON, CHARLES; Avon Old Farms Schl; Cleveland, OH; (Y); Nwsp Rptr; Nwsp Stf; Yrbk Rptr; Yrbk Stf; JV Var Lcrss; JV Var Swmmng; Cit Awd; Hon Roll; Mntr-Frshmn Drmtry 85-86; Head Mntr-Frshmn Drmtry 86-87; Eco.

WILSON, CHRISTOPHER A; Thomaston HS; Thomaston, CT; (Y); 1/67; Am Leg Boys St; Pres Soph Cls; Pres VP Stu Cncl; Var L Bsbl; Var L Socr; Bausch & Lomb Sci Awd; High Hon Roll; NHS; Ntl Merit Ltr; Spanish Clb; Rensselaer Math & Sci Awd 86; Polit Sci.

WILSON, CYNTHIA A; Hamden HS; Hamden, CT; (Y); Church Yth Grp; Concert Band; Jazz Band; Mrchg Band; Orch; School Musical; Swing Chorus; Hon Roll; Ntl Merit Ltr; Natl Arion Fndtn Awd Choral, Natl Precision Ice Sktng Champs 86.

WILSON, DONALD; Fairfield College Preparatory Schl; Shelton, CT; (Y); 23/231; Chess Clb; Pres VP Church Yth Grp; VP JA; Key Clb; JV Trk; High Hon Roll; NHS; Ntl Merit Ltr; Pres Schlr; Tufts U; Aerntcl Engrng.

WILSON, DOUGLAS; Bolton HS; W Willington, CT; (Y); Boy Scts; Spanish Clb; JV Socr; High Hon Roll; Hon Roll; NHS; Spanish NHS; Intrschl Awds Sci 9-84, Spnsh III-85 & Chem 86; Engnrng.

WILSON, JANELLE C; Lewis S Mills HS; Burlington, CT; (Y); Dance Clb; Hon Roll; Debate Tm; Drama Clb; Model UN; Color Guard; School Musical; School Play; Jr NHS; Civic Clb; Elctd CT Ynke Cncl Brd Drctrs 86; Chsn Atnd Ntl Cnfrnc MI 84; VP GS SR Plng Brd 85; U Of Ct; Med.

WILSON, KAREN; Jonathan Law HS; Milford, CT; (Y); 33/197; Pres Sec Keywanettes; Library Aide; Spanish Clb; Pres SADD; Color Guard; School Play; Rep Jr Cls; Rep Sr Cls; Rep Stu Cncl; Cit Awd; CT Assn Sec Schls Ldrshp Awd 86; S CT ST U; Sec Ed.

WILSON, MICHELE; Hartford Public HS; Bloomfield, CT; (S); AFS; Church Yth Grp; Cmnty Wkr; Sec DECA; JA; Model UN; Church Choir; Nwsp Rptr; Lit Mag; Prfct Atten Awd; U Of CT; Bus.

WILSON, NANCY; Conard HS; W Hartford, CT; (Y); 27/345; High Hon Roll; Hon Roll; Spanish NHS; Archlgy.

WILSON, PETER; St Bernard HS; Ledyard, CT; (Y); 69/265; Band; Concert Band; Mrchg Band; Stu Cncl; Diving; Swmmng; Trk.

WILSON, STEPHANIE; Richard C Lee HS; New Haven, CT; (Y).

WILTON, AMY A; Litchfield HS; Litchfield, CT; (Y); Sec AFS; Sec Art Clb; Camera Clb; Pres VP SADD; School Musical; Yrbk Phtg; Trs Jr Cls; Crs Cntry; Mgr JV Swmmng; George Washington U.

WINAKOR, DAVID; Nathan Hale-Ray HS; East Haddam, CT; (S); AFS; Model UN; Ski Clb; School Musical; Nwsp Rptr; Yrbk Sprt Ed; JV Bsktbl; JV Var Socr; Hon Roll; Pres NHS; Army ROTC 4 Yr Schlrshp; CT JR Intern; West Point; Mltry.

WIND, MARLENE; Nathan Hale Ray HS; Moodus, CT; (Y); Church Yth Grp; Stu Cncl; Bsktbl; Sftbl; High Hon Roll; Hon Roll; Briarwood Bk Awd 86; Outstndng Work Eng Awd 86; Exc Wrk Alg II Awd 85; Acctng.

WINES, JAMES; Fairfield College Prep HS; Stratford, CT; (Y); JV Bsbl; Var Bsktbl; Im Ftbl; JV Socr; Im Wt Lftg; High Hon Roll; NHS; Spanish NHS; Duke; Pre-Med.

WINKEL, ERIC R; Bunnell HS; Stratford, CT; (Y); Hon Roll; U Of RI; Bus Admin.

WINN, PAUL; Wilton HS; Wilton, CT; (Y); Boy Scts; Chess Clb; Letterman Clb; Ski Clb; Varsity Clb; Frsh Cls; Soph Cls; Swmmng; Tennis; Bus.

WINSLOW, ELIZABETH; Watertown HS; Oakville, CT; (Y); 28/235; Church Yth Grp; Hosp Aide; Church Choir; Rep Jr Cls; Rep Stu Cncl; Var Capt Twrlr; High Hon Roll; NHS; Nova Schlrshp To Talcott Mtn Sci Ctr 86; Sci.

WINTERS, LISA; Wamogo Regional HS; Morris, CT; (Y); Church Yth Grp; FBLA; Pep Clb; Yrbk Ed-Chief; Im Bsktbl; Hon Roll; NHS; Hghst Avg Data Proc 86; CT Bus Wk 86; Fnlst Wrd Proc FBLA 85-86; Htl Mgmt.

WISHARD, DIANA M; Westminster Schl; Reston, VA; (Y); 7/91; Drama Clb; French Clb; Hosp Aide; Service Clb; Chorus; Church Choir; School Play; Yrbk Phtg; Capt Swmmng; Jr NHS; Wellesley Bk Prz 85; Squibb Bowl Sportsmnshp Swmmng; William & Mary; Intl Rel.

WISNESKI, DANNY; Marianapolis Prep; Woodstock, CT; (Y); 4/46; Yrbk Bus Mgr; Yrbk Ed-Chief; Yrbk Phtg; VP Jr Cls; VP Bsbl; Capt JV Bsktbl; Capt Var Crs Cntry; High Hon Roll; Orch; Stu Cncl; Hugh O Brien Ldrshp Awd 85; Father Anthony Schrlshp; Awds Sports; Law.

WISNIESKI, JENNIFER A; St Mary HS; Cos Cob, CT; (Y); 2/64; Hosp Aide; Latin Clb; Spanish Clb; Yrbk Sprt Ed; Bsktbl; Var Sftbl; Vllybl; Cit Awd; High Hon Roll; NHS; Schlrshp Pitney Bowes 86; Schlrshp Pitsudski Soc 86; Awds Latn, Eng And Math 86; U Of CT; Bio.

WITCHER, LESLEE; West Haven HS; W Haven, CT; (Y); Stage Crew; Var Bsktbl; Var Sftbl; Var Vllybl; Commnctns.

WITT, PENNY; Naugatuck HS; Naugatuck, CT; (Y); 7/307; Sec Trs Library Aide; Orch; Rep Frsh Cls; Rep Soph Cls; Rep Jr Cls; Rep Sr Cls; Var L Trk; Hon Roll; NHS; Hugh O Brian Ldrshp Awd, Ambssdr 84; Cntrl CT ST U; Elem Ed.

WITTE, MARY K; Canterbury Schl; Annapolis, MD; (Y); 12/80; Drama Clb; Nwsp Stf; Ed Lit Mag; JV Capt Fld Hcky; Var L Lcrss; Var L Socr; Var L Swmmng; High Hon Roll; Hon Roll; Drmtory Prctr 85-86; Kenyon Coll Schlrshp 86; Kenyon Coll; Engl.

WLODARCZYK, MELISSA KAY; South Windsor HS; S Windsor, CT; (Y); 63/436; Rep Church Yth Grp; Cmnty Wkr; Dance Clb; Library Aide; Political Wkr; Ski Clb; Spanish Clb; SADD; JV Soph Cls; Hon Roll; CT Alchl & Drg Abuse Awd Outstndng Vol Svc 86; CT Assn Secndry Schls Cert 86; J Veiloux Schlrshp 86; U CT; Elem Ed.

WOFFORD, DAVID; Bullard Havens Tech Schl; Bridgeport, CT; (S); Boys Clb Am; Hosp Aide; Ski Clb; VICA; Co-Capt Crs Cntry; Co-Capt Trk; Chef.

WOJNAROWSKI, ADRIAN; Bristol Central HS; Bristol, CT; (Y); 89/287; Boys Clb Am; Church Yth Grp; Yrbk Sprt Ed; Lit Mag; Trs Jr Cls; JV Bsbl; Cit Awd; Hon Roll; Journalism.

WOJTOWICZ, LISA; Northwest Catholic HS; Hartford, CT; (Y); Pres Sec Church Yth Grp; Spanish Clb; Chorus; Yrbk Ed-Chief; Yrbk Stf; Hon Roll; NHS; New Britain Herald Jrnlsm Awd 86; Robert S Bagnall Mem Schlrshp 86; Eng Acadmc Cert 86; Wheelock Coll Boston; Elem Ed.

WOLFE, MARSHA; Staples HS; Westport, CT; (Y); VP Girl Scts; Acpl Chr; Band; Chorus; Church Choir; Concert Band; Orch; Symp Band; Var JV Fld Hcky; Hon Roll; Slvr Awd Grl Sctng 83; Gld Awd Grl Sctng 86; Htl & Rest Mngmnt.

WOLINSKI, ROBERT; Norwich Reg Voc Tech; Norwich, CT; (Y); 1/131; Am Leg Boys St; Pres VICA; High Hon Roll; Hon Roll; NHS; Prfct Atten Awd; Val; Conn Bus & Ind Awd 86; NE Utilities Awd 86; Outstndng Ldrshp & Svc 86; Thames Valley; Nclr Engr.

WOMACK, PAUL; Weaver HS; Hartford, CT; (Y); Var Trk; Wt Lftg; Capt Wrstlng; Hon Roll; MVP Wrstlng 86; 3rd In ST Open & 3rd In ST Trnmnt 85-86; Howard U; Elect Engrng.

WONG, LAI PING; Wethersfield HS; Wethersfield, CT; (Y); 80/298; Cmnty Wkr; Dance Clb; Office Aide; Orch; Variety Show; Lit Mag; Hon Roll; Prfct Atten Awd; Trophy Taps Dancing 83; Dean JC; Dance.

WOOD, AMANDA; Farmington HS; Avon, CT; (Y); Church Yth Grp; Cmnty Wkr; French Clb; Hosp Aide; Ski Clb; JV Fld Hcky; Wt Lftg; Hon Roll; Arch.

WOOD, ANGELA; East Catholic HS; East Hartford, CT; (Y); 92/294; Dance Clb; Latin Clb; Pep Clb; Nwsp Stf; Off Frsh Cls; Off Soph Cls; Stat Score Keeper; High Hon Roll; Bio.

WOOD, DAWN; Thomaston HS; Thomaston, CT; (Y); 16/68; Office Aide; Spanish Clb; Variety Show; Sec Frsh Cls; Off Soph Cls; Off Sr Cls; L Cheerleading; JV Var Sftbl; Bus Admin.

WOOD, KRISTEN; Shelton HS; Shelton, CT; (Y); VP Church Yth Grp; Political Wkr; Spanish Clb; JV Var Bsktbl; Var Trk; Hon Roll; Spanish NHS; High Avg Awd Spnsh 83; Most Imprvd Plyr Bsktbl 85; ST Cls LL Bsktbl 85; Marine Bio.

WOOD, LORI; Holy Cross HS; Southbury, CT; (Y); 160/380; Art Clb; Church Yth Grp; Cmnty Wkr; Pep Clb; Orch; Hon Roll; Bus.

WOODMAN, VALARIE; Southington HS; Southington, CT; (Y); Pep Clb; Varsity Clb; Concert Band; Pep Band; Var Cheerleading; Bus.

WOODS, KELLI; Stratford HS; Stratford, CT; (Y); Camera Clb; Nwsp Phtg; Nwsp Rptr; Nwsp Stf; Rep Jr Cls; Rep Stu Cncl; Hon Roll; Journslm.

WOODS, PATRICIA LEE; Cromwell HS; Cromwell, CT; (Y); 7/80; VP AFS; French Clb; Varsity Clb; Yrbk Stf; Stu Cncl; Var Cheerleading; Var Capt Crs Cntry; Trk; High Hon Roll; NHS; Cert Apprec Volnteer Handicap Swim Pgm 84-86; Pres Acad Fit Awd 84-85; Citation Excllnce Eng 85-86; Old Dominion U; Ed.

WOODS, SARA; Stratford HS; Stratford, CT; (Y); 43/242; VP FBLA; Nwsp Rptr; Nwsp Stf; Rep Jr Cls; Rep Stu Cncl; Hon Roll; Ushrs Gld Sec; Nws Pr Ftr Ed; U Of Brdgprt; Mass Cmmnctn.

WOODWARD, JASON; Oliver Wolcott Tech HS; Torrington, CT; (Y); Var L Crs Cntry; Hon Roll; CBIA Bus Week 85; Stu Congress Berkshire 86; Arch Bus Mgmt.

WOOTEN, CHERYL; Bassick HS; Bridgeport, CT; (Y); Sec DECA; Office Aide; VP Spanish Clb; Ed Yrbk Ed-Chief; Ed Yrbk Stf; Rep Jr Cls; Pres Sr Cls; Rep Stu Cncl; Hon Roll; Mayors Renssnc Career Internshp Awd 86-87; Howard U; Law.

WORDELL, MIKE; Southington HS; Plantsville, CT; (Y); 107/620; FCA; Key Clb; Latin Clb; Ski Clb; Spanish Clb; Stage Crew; Im Bowling; Im Golf; Var Socr; Hon Roll; Fnd-Rsng Awd 86; 1st Hnrs Yr 85; Vrsty Ltr 87.

WOROZILCAK, KRISTEN; Jonathan Law HS; Milford, CT; (Y); Camera Clb; Keywanettes; Library Aide; School Play; Nwsp Ed-Chief; Yrbk Ed-Chief; Var L Bsktbl; Var L Tennis; Hon Roll; Excllnc In Wrtg & Jrnlsm Awds 86; Syracuse U; Comm.

WORTH, T HUNTTING; Kent Schl; New York, NY; (Y); Off Frsh Cls; Off Soph Cls; Off Jr Cls; Off Sr Cls; Stu Cncl; Cls Pres 84-86; SR Prfct Kent Sch 86-87.

WOSKOW, LORRAINE B; Hamden HS; Hamden, CT; (Y); 1/419; Concert Band; Orch; Capt Crs Cntry; Trk; High Hon Roll; Ntl Merit SF; Harvard Book Awd.

WOZNIAK, JOHN; Hamden HS; Hamden, CT; (Y); JA; Pres Science Clb; JV Bsbl; JV Socr; Var Trk; Phrmclgy.

WRIGHT, RITA DANETTE; Stamford HS; Stamford, CT; (Y); Church Yth Grp; VP Sec Civic Clb; Cmnty Wkr; JA; Band; Church Choir; Stu Cncl; JV Var Bsktbl; Sftbl; Hon Roll; Cibs Inc Scholar 86; Girlfriends Inc Scholar 86; K Chevrolet Scholar 86; Boston Coll; Biochem.

WYDLER, JENNIFER; Robert E Fitch SR HS; Mystic, CT; (Y); Drama Clb; Acpl Chr; Band; Chorus; Jrnlsm.

WYLAND, LARRY; East Catholic HS; Tolland, CT; (Y); Boy Scts; Chess Clb; Hosp Aide; VP JA; Science Clb; Rep Jr Cls; Rep Sr Cls; Rep Stu Cncl; Var Trk; Var L Wrstlng; Air Force.

WYMES, TIMOTHY; Taft HS; Thomaston, CT; (Y); School Play; Bsktbl; JV Ftbl; JV Trk; Tour Gd Tour Of Schl For Prspctv Stu 85-86; Engnrng.

WYNN, PATRICK; Southington HS; Southington, CT; (Y); Concert Band; Jazz Band; Mrchg Band; Hon Roll; CT All-ST Band 86; CT Vly Yth Wnd Ensmbl 85-87.

WYSOCKI, CHRISTOPHER R; Brookfield HS; Brookfield Center, CT; (Y); 3/250; Math Tm; Scholastic Bowl; VP Capt Crs Cntry; Var Trk; High Hon Roll; NHS; Clss M All-ST X-Cntry 85; Achvmnt Awd Hnrs Algbra II-85 Earth Sci-84.

WYSOCKI, LINDA A; Wethersfield HS; Wethersfield, CT; (Y); 16/299; Church Yth Grp; 4-H; Science Clb; Nwsp Ed-Chief; Nwsp Rptr; Nwsp Sprt Ed; Rep Stu Cncl; Trk; Vllybl; High Hon Roll; WHS Prtcpnt Yale U 85-86; Attndnt Of Jrnlsm Smnr NY Vlntr Wthrfld Chptr Mls On Wheels 86.

WYSOWSKI, MICHELLE; Shelton HS; Shelton, CT; (Y); Drama Clb; Spanish Clb; Nrs.

XAVIER, ATANAZIA; Bassick HS; Bpt, CT; (Y); Camera Clb; Rep Stu Cncl; Wellsly Bk Awd, Soc Wmn Engnrs Awd 86; Schlstc Achvt Awd 85.

YACHTIS, DAVE; Holy Cross HS; Naugatuck, CT; (Y); 16/350; JV Bsktbl; JV Trk; High Hon Roll; Kiwanis Awd; NHS; Ntl Merit SF; Rensselaer Mdl Excllnce Mth & Sci 85; Exch Clb Scholar 86; CT ST Schlr 85; Northeastern U; Engrng.

YAEGER, ALLISON; Seymour HS; Seymour, CT; (Y); Variety Show; Yrbk Stf; Rep Frsh Cls; Rep Soph Cls; Rep Jr Cls; Rep Sr Cls; Var L Cheerleading; Var L Sftbl; All Vlly & Hnbl Mntn Lg Sftbl 86; Secry.

YAFFIE, JESSICA; Trumbull HS; Trumbull, CT; (Y); Church Yth Grp; Cmnty Wkr; Temple Yth Grp; Church Choir; Yrbk Stf; Off Jr Cls; Stu Cncl; Mgr Tennis; High Hon Roll; NHS; Focus Tufts Pre-Coll Pgm 86.

YANAGISAWA, RAY; Hopkins Grammar Day Prospect HS; Woodbridge, CT; (S); Nwsp Phtg; Yrbk Ed-Chief; Yrbk Phtg; Yrbk Stf; JV Bsbl; JV Bsktbl; Var Capt Socr; Var Trk; Engrng.

YANKE, DAWN; Farmington HS; Farmington, CT; (Y); 15/215; High Hon Roll; Hon Roll; NHS; U CT; Accntnt.

YANNUZZI, PAIGE; Greenwich HS; Greenwich, CT; (Y); Art Clb; Aud/Vis; Camera Clb; Girl Scts; Ski Clb; SADD; Chorus; School Musical; School Play; Stage Crew; Rdng Clb Awds 80-82; Sktng Mdls 80-83; Ithaca Coll.

YAW, HEATHER; Simsbury HS; Simsbury, CT; (Y); 84/406; Church Yth Grp; Ski Clb; Band; Badmtn; Im Powder Puff Ftbl; Hon Roll; Bus.

YI, JEFF CHAE HYOK; Manchester HS; Manchester, CT; (Y); German Clb; Math Tm; JV Var Bsbl; High Hon Roll; NHS; Stdnt Rsrch Fllwshp Amer Heart Assn, 8th CT Chemathon Comp, Outstndng Recog Outstndng Achvtmnt Sci; Pre Med.

YINDRA, JONATHAN; Lyme Old-Lyme HS; Old Lyme, CT; (Y); Church Yth Grp; Quiz Bowl; Chorus; School Play; Yrbk Stf; Im Bowling; JV Golf; Im Vllybl; Im Wt Lftg; Ntl Coll Stu Srch 86; Emerson Coll; Cmnctns.

YODER, JIM; Watertown HS; Oakville, CT; (Y); Church Yth Grp; Variety Show; Var Bsbl; Var L Ftbl; Hon Roll; Mst Comptv Plyr Babe Ruth Bsbl 85; Holy Cross; Mth.

YORK, MIKE; Wethersfield HS; Wethersfield, CT; (Y); 4/299; Cmnty Wkr; SADD; Yrbk Stf; Stu Cncl; Var Bsbl; Var Bsktbl; Var Ftbl; VP NHS; NEDT Awd; Pres Schlr; Drtmth Bk Awd For Acdmc Achvt 86; NPEA 82; Hnrb Mntn For Ntl Essay Cntst 85; Bus.

YORZINSKI, DEBBIE; Guilford HS; Guilford, CT; (Y); 71/317; Red Cross Aide; Sec Frsh Cls; Rep Stu Cncl; Powder Puff Ftbl; JV Tennis; Hon Roll; St Georges Knghts Of Clmbs-Schlrshp 86; Guilford Schlrshp Assn Schlrshp 86; U Of CT; Acctng.

YOUNG, AMY LEE; Woodstock Acad; S Woodstock, CT; (Y); 2/69; Am Leg Aux Girls St; Cmnty Wkr; Model UN; Chorus; Stat Bsktbl; Score Keeper; JV Sftbl; Im Vllybl; Pres NHS; Voice Dem Awd; Amer Lgn Amercnsm Awd 86; CT Clg; Edcu.

YOUNG, JEFFREY A; Francis T Maloney HS; Meriden, CT; (Y); Pres Computer Clb; Math Tm; Lit Mag; Hon Roll; Eagle Scout 85; CT Wtrs Sympsm Scdry Schl Stu; Compu Sci.

YOUNG, JENNIFER; Wilton HS; Wilton, CT; (Y); 63/352; Church Yth Grp; Cmnty Wkr; Drama Clb; French Clb; Pep Clb; Chorus; Church Choir; School Play; Yrbk Stf; Tennis; Hnrs Awd 84; Frnch Awd 84.

YOUNG, KIMBERLY; RHAM HS; Marlborough, CT; (Y); 20/250; High Hon Roll; Hon Roll; NHS; Cert Hnr Rll 84-86; Cert Achvt Art 84, 86; Cmmrcl Illus.

YU, MICHAEL; Taft Schl; Waterbury, CT; (Y); Chess Clb; Hosp Aide; Band; Concert Band; Jazz Band; Stat Var Bsktbl; JV Lcrss; Var JV Mgr(s); Var JV Score Keeper; Im Socr; Pre-Med.

YU, RONALD W; Fairfield College Prep; Trumbull, CT; (Y); Church Yth Grp; Key Clb; Ed Yrbk Stf; VP Jr Cls; VP Stu Cncl; VP Capt Swmmng; Tennis; High Hon Roll; Jr NHS; NHS; Tri-Pres Of Intr Rcl Yth Cncl.

YUHAS, TIMOTHY; Eat Lyme HS; E Lyme, CT; (Y); JV Var Bsbl; Capt Var Ice Hcky; Im Lcrss; Hon Roll; Civil Engr.

YUN, JAMES J; Hopkins Grammar Schl; Orange, CT; (Y); 4/108; Pres Chess Clb; Math Tm; Model UN; Radio Clb; SADD; Acpl Chr; Chorus; Orch; School Musical; Nwsp Ed-Chief; Harvard Bk Awd 85; Rensselaer Mdl Sci 85; Cm Laud Socty 85.

YURGAITIS, DEREK; Holy Cross HS; Wolcott, CT; (Y); 163/380; PAVAS; Bsbl; Var Ftbl; Var Wt Lftg; Var Wrstlng; Hon Roll; Avatr.

ZABLAN, GABRIELA; Wilbur Cross HS; New Haven, CT; (S); 10/250; French Clb; Hosp Aide; Ski Clb; Yrbk Stf; Lit Mag; Pom Pon; Socr; Hon Roll; Outstndng Achvt Geo 83, Frnch 83-84; Engrng.

ZACCHIA, ANGELO; Southington HS; Southington, CT; (Y); High Hon Roll; Hon Roll; NHS; Acctg.

ZACHARY, JOHN; Holy Cross HS; Waterbury, CT; (Y); 73/380; Church Yth Grp; FCA; Var Wrstlng; Hon Roll; Engineering.

ZADOROJNYI, NATASHA; Wilbur Cross HS; New Have, CT; (Y); Yrbk Stf; High Hon Roll; Hon Roll; NHS; John Steinbeck Awd 84-85; Excel Spnsh 84-85; Quinnipiac Coll; Phys Thrpy.

ZAGORA, LYNN MARIE; East Catholic HS; Tolland, CT; (Y); 68/293; Hon Roll; Bryant Coll; Ecnmcs.

ZAHN, HEIDI; Taft Preparatory Schl; Fairfield, CT; (Y); Pres Spanish Clb; Chorus; School Play; Variety Show; Yrbk Stf; Lit Mag; Pres Frsh Cls; Pres Stu Cncl; Capt Var Fld Hcky; Im Ice Hcky; U Of VT; Lang.

ZAK, EDWARD; Southington HS; Southington, CT; (Y); Church Yth Grp; Cmnty Wkr; Computer Clb; Key Clb; Hon Roll; Waterbury ST Tech Coll; Comp.

ZAK, REBECCA; Southingotn HS; Southington, CT; (Y); 19/600; Church Yth Grp; VP FTA; Hosp Aide; Key Clb; Latin Clb; High Hon Roll; Jr NHS; NHS; Cmnty Wkr; Teachers Aide; Southington Ed Assn Schlrshp 86; Philip Liquori Mem Schlrshp 86; Cntrl CT ST U; Elem Ed.

ZAK, VINCENT; Shelton HS; Shelton, CT; (Y); Yrbk Sprt Ed; Yrbk Stf; Var Trk; Hon Roll; Spanish NHS; Schlr Athlt Awd Trk 86; U Of CT; Engrng.

ZALINGER, KEITH; Branford HS; Branford, CT; (Y); Aud/Vis; Nwsp Stf; Hon Roll; Arista Awd Acad Achvt Soc Studies 85-86; Bio-Tech.

ZAMPAGLIONE, GLENNA; Torrington HS; Torrington, CT; (Y); 73/270; Civic Clb; Latin Clb; Ski Clb; Orch; School Play; Rep Frsh Cls; VP Cheerleading; Northwest Regionals Orchestra Violin 83-85; Scholarship To Laurel Music Camp 85; Marketing.

ZAMPARO, JOANN; Sacred Heart Academy; Hamden, CT; (Y); Drama Clb; Chorus; School Musical; Yrbk Bus Mgr; Yrbk Stf; Bausch & Lomb Sci Awd; High Hon Roll; NHS; Prfct Atten Awd; Spanish NHS; Pre-Med.

ZANARDI, LYNN; Valley Regional HS; Chester, CT; (Y); Hosp Aide; SADD; School Musical; Sec Stu Cncl; Var Cheerleading; JV Fld Hcky; Var Mgr(s); Var Trk; High Hon Roll; Hon Roll; Wesleyan Sci Sympsm 86; Med Tech.

ZANIEWSKI, JASON; New Britain HS; New Britain, CT; (Y); 87/370; Varsity Clb; Band; Bsbl; Bsktbl; Ftbl; Wt Lftg; Hon Roll; Vrsty Ltr Ftbl Bsktbl, Bsbl 84-86; 2nd Tm All Conf Bsktbl 85-86; JR Ldr YMCA 85-86; Cmmnctns.

ZAPPOLA, JANINE; East Catholic HS; Vernon Rockville, CT; (Y); French Clb; Capt Drill Tm; Tennis; Providence Coll; Cmmnctns.

ZAPPONE, RICHARD; Holy Cross HS; Waterbury, CT; (Y); High Hon Roll; Hon Roll; Bentley; CPA.

ZATULSKIS, PETER; Branford HS; Branford, CT; (Y); 52/312; Yrbk Stf; Off Frsh Cls; Rep Soph Cls; Rep Jr Cls; Rep Sr Cls; Rep Stu Cncl; JV Bsktbl; Var Trk; Hon Roll.

ZAVALIS, ALECK; Cheshire HS; Cheshire, CT; (Y); Church Yth Grp; Computer Clb; Math Tm; Ski Clb; JV Lcrss; High Hon Roll; Hon Roll; 2nd Pl New England Mth Lg Cont 86; 3.2 GPA 86; Arch.

ZAWACKI, KAREN MARIE; Danbury HS; Danbury, CT; (Y); Trs Key Clb; Acpl Chr; Capt Color Guard; School Musical; Variety Show; Yrbk Ed-Chief; Rep Stu Cncl; High Hon Roll; Jr NHS; Church Yth Grp; Miss CT Teen USA 86; Co-Hostess Chldrns TV Show 82-85; Mayor Prclmtn For Cmnty Svc 85 & 86; Syracuse U; Spch Cmmnctns.

ZDUN, PAMELA; Bristol Central HS; Bristol, CT; (Y); Pres Church Yth Grp; Hosp Aide; Trs JA; Church Choir; Capt Color Guard; Concert Band; Flag Corp; Mrchg Band; Symp Band; Hon Roll; Spch Thrpy.

ZELICK, FRED; Francis T Maloney HS; Meriden, CT; (Y); Trs Church Yth Grp; Computer Clb; Math Tm; Quiz Bowl; Scholastic Bowl; Trs Service Clb; High Hon Roll; Hon Roll; NHS; Ntl Merit Ltr; Yale U; Comps.

ZELLER, JAMES; Torrington HS; Harwinton, CT; (Y); 6/270; French Clb; Model UN; Varsity Clb; Stu Cncl; Bsktbl; Ftbl; NHS; Michael R Koury Achvt Awd Schlr Athlt 84; Torrington Brd Of Educ 86-87; Athlt Commp, Planning Comm 86; Economics.

ZELLNER, SCOTT; Foran HS; Milford, CT; (Y); Letterman Clb; JV Var Ftbl; Meteorlgy.

ZELMAN, DAVID; Kingswood-Oxford HS; W Hartford, CT; (Y); Computer Clb; Orch.

ZEOLLA, LISA; Shelton HS; Shelton, CT; (Y); Ski Clb; Stu Cncl; Elem Ed.

ZHANG, EUGENE; Ridgefield HS; Ridgefield, CT; (Y); AFS; Computer Clb; Math Tm; VP Radio Clb; Service Clb; Im Bsbl; Im Bsktbl; Im Tennis; High Hon Roll; Ntl Merit SF; Enrng.

ZICKWOLF, GRETCHEN; Norwich Free Acad; Bozrah, CT; (Y); Pres Church Yth Grp; VP 4-H; Im Sftbl; Im Vllybl; High Hon Roll; Hon Roll; 2nd Runner Up Norwich Rose Arts Pageant 86; U Of CT; Eng.

ZIELANSKI, GARY; Branford HS; Branford, CT; (Y); Var L Golf; Hon Roll; Typing Award; Computers.

ZIMMERLI, PATRICK J; William H Hall HS; W Hartford, CT; (Y); 11/324; Band; Church Choir; Concert Band; Jazz Band; Pep Band; School Musical; Symp Band; Variety Show; Lit Mag; High Hon Roll; Top Instrmntlst-Berklee Jazz Fstvl 85; Best Jazz Soloist-Downbeat Mag 85; Mc Donalds All-Amer Band 85.

ZIMMERMAN, PAMELA; Torrington HS; Torrington, CT; (Y); JA; Yrbk Stf; Cheerleading; Soc Wrkr.

ZIMMITTI, ANDREW; Cheshire HS; Cheshire, CT; (Y); Debate Tm; Band; Concert Band; Mrchg Band; Orch; Nwsp Bus Mgr; Nwsp Stf; Lit Mag; High Hon Roll; Hon Roll; Natl Piano Plyng Auditions-St Mbr, Photo Bd Ed 85; Neighborhood Mus Schl Merit Awd-Piano 86; Pol Sci.

ZINGO, GINA ANN; Masuk HS; Monroe, CT; (Y); AFS; Church Yth Grp; JA; Political Wkr; Trs Frsh Cls; Trs Stu Cncl; Hon Roll; W CT ST U; Law.

ZINGO, JAMES M; Masuk HS; Monroe, CT; (Y); 9/280; VP Exploring; Scholastic Bowl; Band; Stu Cncl; Var Crs Cntry; Var Swmmng; JV Var Trk; High Hon Roll; Ntl Merit Ltr; JCL; Ntl Latin Exam Mdlst Slvr, Gold, Slvr 83-86.

ZINSER, JANET; New Fairfield HS; New Fairfield, CT; (Y); 4/236; Church Yth Grp; Latin Clb; Science Clb; Lit Mag; Var Capt Sftbl; Var Capt Vllybl; High Hon Roll; Hon Roll; VP NHS; Sec Spanish NHS; Smith Coll Bk Awd 86; Exc llnce Soc Studies & Spn IV 86; Outstndng Perfrmnce Natl Latin Exam 85.

ZITO, ANTONY; East Granby HS; E Granby, CT; (Y); Drama Clb; PAVAS; Band; School Musical; Stage Crew; Variety Show; Lit Mag; Rep Stu Cncl; Trk; High Hon Roll; Awd For Artwork In Lit Mag 86; Presdntl Phys Fitness Awd 86; Fine Arts.

ZOLLA, PHILLIP; Notre Dame HS; Ansonia, CT; (Y); 27/269; Am Leg Boys St; Lit Mag; High Hon Roll; Jr NHS; NHS; Worcester Polytech Inst; Biotec.

ZSCHUNKE, GREG; Brookfield HS; Brookfield Center, CT; (Y); 44/239; Aud/Vis; Computer Clb; Math Tm; Spanish Clb; Stage Crew; Var Capt Ftbl; Var Capt Trk; Var L Wrstlng; High Hon Roll; Hon Roll; Spnsh Awd 85; Engr.

ZUBROWSKI, DIANA; Torrington HS; Torrington, CT; (Y); 42/278; Church Yth Grp; Girl Scts; Latin Clb; Spanish Clb; Stage Crew; Mgr Socr; Mgr Sftbl; High Hon Roll; Hon Roll; NHS; Bus Adm.

ZUCKER, AMY I; Hamden HS; Hamden, CT; (Y); 7/419; Cmnty Wkr; Political Wkr; Quiz Bowl; Temple Yth Grp; School Musical; School Play; Nwsp Stf; High Hon Roll; Ntl Merit SF; Engl, Chem, Psych Hnrs; Humanities.

ZUPA, MIKE; Holy Cross HS; Waterbury, CT; (Y); 59/380; Church Yth Grp; High Hon Roll; Hon Roll; NHS; Italian Hnr Scty 85; Itln Clb 85-87; Comp Sci.

ZUROLO, MARY; Sacred Heart Acad; Hamden, CT; (Y); 56/122; Red Cross Aide; Chorus; School Musical; Ed Nwsp Stf; High Hon Roll; Church Yth Grp; English Clb; French Clb; Mgr Bsktbl; Providence Coll; Jrnlsm.

ZUROWSKI, BRIAN H; Killingly HS; Dayville, CT; (Y); Ftbl; Hon Roll; Jr NHS; Spanish NHS; Recog At JSHS 86; Avtn.

ZUROWSKI, DEANA; Killingly HS; Dayville, CT; (Y); 79/275; Spanish Clb; Hon Roll; Spanish NHS; Steno Awds 50-100 Wam 85-86; Typg II Awds Spd Tsts 85-86; Phy Ed Awd 85-86; Bus Mgmt.

ZYGNERSKI, CHRISTINE; New Britain HS; New Britain, CT; (Y); Drill Tm; Mrchg Band; Orch; Cheerleading; Tennis; Hon Roll; Comm.

ZYMBA, PAUL F; Enfield HS; Enfield, CT; (Y); 11/340; JV Socr; Var High Hon Roll; Jr NHS; NHS; Pascal Awd, AARP, CSS Schlrshps 86; Northeastern U; Cmptr Sci.

MAINE

ABBIATI, JOE; Westbrook HS; Westbrook, ME; (Y); Key Clb; Band; Concert Band; Jazz Band; Mrchg Band; JV Bsbl; Var L Swmmng; All-St Band 86; Played In Band For Miss ME Pgnt 86.

ABBOTT, CHRISTINE; Gorham HS; Gorham, ME; (Y); Church Yth Grp; Girl Scts; JA; Latin Clb; Band; Concert Band; Drm Mjr(t); Jazz Band; Pep Band; Boy Scts; U Boston; Cmmnctn Law.

ABBOTT, LYNETTE; Mt Abram Regional HS; Phillips, ME; (Y); Am Leg Aux Girls St; Var JV Bsktbl; Var JV Sftbl; Var JV Trk; High Hon Roll; Hon Roll; NHS; Bio.

ABBOTT, SONJA M; Buckfield HS; Buckfield, ME; (Y); Am Leg Aux Girls St; Drama Clb; Sec Jr Cls; Mgr Bsktbl; Var Socr; Cit Awd; Hon Roll; NHS; Voice Dem Awd; ME Smr Arts Prog 86.

ABRAHAM, MICHAEL; Upper Kennebec Valley HS; West Forks, ME; (Y); Am Leg Boys St; Var Bsbl; Var Bsktbl; Capt Socr; Var Trk; Scholastic Bowl; Prfct Atten Awd.

ACETO, JONATHAN; Orono HS; Orono, ME; (S); 7/114; Sec Speech Tm; Orch; L Tennis; High Hon Roll; 2nd Bangor Symphny Yth Cmptn 86; ST Wnr Amer Strng Tchrs Assn Cmptn 86; 1st Pl Jr Div Bay Chmbr Cmptn; Profssnl Violnst.

ADAMS, KEVIN; Hodgdon HS; Houlton, ME; (Y); 10/72; Varsity Clb; L Var Bsktbl; Var L Crs Cntry; Im Socr; Im Vllybl; Hon Roll; US Army Cross Cntry Awd 85; Business.

ADELMAN, BETH; Bangor HS; Bangor, ME; (Y); 20/316; Variety Show; Yrbk Stf; Frsh Cls; Soph Cls; Jr Cls; Sr Cls; Trs Pres Stu Cncl; Cheerleading; Fld Hcky; Sftbl; Sch Serv Awd 86; WA U St Louis; Arch.

AIREY, MARK; Bangor HS; Bangor, ME; (Y); Swmmng; Hon Roll; U Of ME Augusta; Music Perfrmc.

AKERLEY, MELISSA; St Dominic Regional HS; Mechanic Falls, ME; (Y); 1/65; Drama Clb; Math Tm; SADD; School Musical; School Play; Stu Cncl; Cheerleading; High Hon Roll; Hon Roll; Val; Crtfct Rnkgn Tp 99% Frr NEDT Exm; Rnkd Tp 96% PSAT/NMSQT Exm; Crtfct Rnkng Tp 6% ST Natl Frnch Exm; INVSTMNTS.

ALBERT, MICHELLE; Fort Kent HS; Eagle Lake, ME; (Y); Church Yth Grp; Varsity Clb; Trk; Vllybl; Hon Roll; Lds Of St Anne Schlrshp 86-87; HS Schlrshp 86-87; Hgh Achvt Awd In Cvcs 82; U Of ME Ft Knt; Hmn Srvs.

ALDRICH, RICHARD; Marshwood HS; Eliot, ME; (Y); 23/121; Boy Scts; French Clb; Math Tm; Stage Crew; Yrbk Ed-Chief; Hon Roll; SAR Awd; Voice Dem Awd; Basic Oprtns Course Mc Donlds Mgmt 86; U Sthrn ME; Bus Adm.

ALEXANDER, HOLLY; Hodgdon HS; Houlton, ME; (Y); 2/76; Am Leg Aux Girls St; Varsity Clb; Band; School Musical; Yrbk Ed-Chief; Yrbk Stf; Mgr Bsktbl; High Hon Roll; VP NHS; St Schlr; Chem Awd; Accntng Awd; Gftd & Tlntd Prog.

ALEXANDER, LISA; Yarmouth HS; Yarmouth, ME; (Y); French Clb; Band; Sec Jr Cls; Var Tennis; French Hon Soc; NHS; Church Yth Grp; Yrbk Stf; Off Soph Cls; JV Sftbl; Williams Coll Bk Awd 86; Naturl Helpers Peer Cnslng Grp 85-86; Most Imprvd Tennis Plyr Awd 84-85; Psychlgy.

ALEXANDER, TRACY; Mount Desert Island HS; Southwest Harbor, ME; (Y); 5/125; Am Leg Aux Girls St; Church Yth Grp; Drama Clb; Girl Scts; Intnl Clb; Math Tm; Teachers Aide; Y-Teens; Band; Church Choir; Georgetown; Frgn Svc.

ALEXANDRE, MICHAEL S; Sanford HS; Sanford, ME; (Y); 4/224; Chess Clb; Cmnty Wkr; Key Clb; Math Tm; Var L Crs Cntry; High Hon Roll; Jr NHS; NHS; Church Yth Grp; Ping Pong 1st Pl Trophy 85; Yth Ftns Achvt Awd 86; CMUTI; Elect Mech.

ALLAIN, BARBARA; Cony HS; Augusta, ME; (Y); Church Yth Grp; Office Aide; VICA; Hon Roll; Nrsng.

ALLARD, NANCY ANNE; Noble HS; N Berwick, ME; (Y); 29/156; Rptr Am Leg Aux Girls St; Key Clb; Band; Jazz Band; School Musical; L Mgr Bsbl; Mgr Var Bsktbl; L Mgr Socr; L Var Sftbl; NHS; Presdntl Acad Fitness Awd 86; Svc Awd-Peer Cnslng 85; Pre-Med.

ALLEN, CHARLINE; Westbrook HS; Westbrook, ME; (Y); French Clb; Band; Concert Band; Mrchg Band; Pep Band; Rep Soph Cls; Rep Jr Cls; Var L Trk; All Star Select Trk, Coach Awd Trk 85; MIP, ST Champ, All Star Select 86; MVP Trk 84; Nrsg.

ALLEN, ELIZABETH; Rockland District HS; Rockland, ME; (Y); 4/110; Art Clb; JCL; Latin Clb; Capt Var Cheerleading; Trk; High Hon Roll; Hon Roll; Jr NHS; NHS; School Play; All Am Chrldr Fnlst 85; U New Hampshire; Theater.

ALLEN, KIMBERLY ANN; Lewiston HS; Lewiston, ME; (Y); Church Yth Grp; Cmnty Wkr; Pep Clb; Stu Cncl; Sftbl; Hon Roll; NHS; Westbrook Coll; Dntl Hygn.

ALLEY, KEVIN; Washington Acad; Jonesboro, ME; (Y); Computer Clb; Exploring; 4-H; Math Clb; Varsity Clb; Var Bsbl; JV Bsktbl; Var Crs Cntry; Var Trk; Hon Roll; Coaches Awd Bsbl 86; Perf Attndnc 85-86; Vrs Awd Bsbl & X-Cntry 85-86; U ME Machias; Accntg.

AMES, LIBBY; Edward Little HS; Auburn, ME; (Y); SADD; Off Band; Mrchg Band; Pres Soph Cls; Pres Jr Cls; Rep Sr Cls; High Hon Roll; Hon Roll; NHS; Prfct Atten Awd; Natl Hon Soc Init-Indctn Cerem 86; Cls Pres 84-87; Bnd Ofcr & Drum Major 84-87; U ME Orono.

ANASTASOFF, JENNIFER; Cape Elizabeth HS; Cape Elizabeth, ME; (Y); 1/115; Drama Clb; Hosp Aide; Sec SADD; Nwsp Rptr; Lit Mag; Sec Jr Cls; Sec Sr Cls; Bausch & Lomb Sci Awd; Ntl Merit Ltr; St Schlr; Harvrd Bk Awd; Ntl Hnr Soc; Grls ST.

ANCTIL, VICKY; Rumford HS; West Peru, ME; (Y); Am Leg Aux Girls St; JA; Letterman Clb; Office Aide; Teachers Aide; Capt Cheerleading; Trk; Hon Roll; Jr NHS; NHS; Mst Dedicated Chrldr Awd 85; Chrng Sqd Rep ME Natl 86; House Rep Dirigo Grls St 86.

ANDERSEN, KRISTINE; Skowhegan Area HS; Skowhegan, ME; (Y); Am Leg Aux Girls St; Church Yth Grp; Band; Nwsp Stf; Yrbk Bus Mgr; Cit Awd; Hon Roll; Stdnt Mnth 86; Kennebec Vly Voc Tech; Secy.

ANDERSON, RENEE; Brunswick HS; Brunswick, ME; (Y); 14/238; Drama Clb; Pep Clb; School Musical; Cheerleading; Gym; Hon Roll; Davis Awd; Brunswick Hnr Socy; Pearl H Baker Awd; Wellesley Coll; Psych.

ANDREWS, MARJORIE; Deering HS; Portland, ME; (Y); U Of VT; Asian Stud.

ANDREWS, MICHELLE; Traip Acad; Kittery, ME; (Y); Church Yth Grp; Chorus; Yrbk Stf; Var JV Bsktbl; Var Capt Crs Cntry; Var Sftbl; Var Trk; Wt Lftg; Hon Roll; Circle Of Excel Bonne Bell 85; Syssa Al-Str Grls Crs Cntry 84-85; Syssa Al-Leag Team Crs Cntry 83; Phys Educ.

ANNAL, MARIA; Van Buren District Secondary Schl; Lille, ME; (Y); 3/70; Am Leg Aux Girls St; Math Clb; Band; Nwsp Stf; Rep Stu Cncl; JV Var Cheerleading; Im Vllybl; Ntl Merit SF; St Schlr; Voice Dem Awd; U Of ME At Orono; Vet Sci.

ARBO, CINDY; Hodgdon HS; Houlton, ME; (Y); Am Leg Aux Girls St; French Clb; Yrbk Stf; High Hon Roll; Hon Roll; NHS; Nrsng.

ARMSTRONG, TIMMY; Washington Acad; Machias, ME; (Y); Var L Bsbl; Var Bsktbl; Var L Golf; Var L Socr; Hon Roll; Bsbl Tms Bst Dfnsv Plyr 84-85; U Of ME; Bus Admin.

ARNEAULT, STACY; Lewiston HS; Lewiston, ME; (Y); Church Yth Grp; Varsity Clb; Rep Frsh Cls; Rep Soph Cls; Rep Jr Cls; Sec Sr Cls; Capt Cheerleading; JV Fld Hcky; Capt Tennis; NHS; Coaches Awd-Tnns 86; SMAA Rnr Up-Tnns Dbls 85; U Of New England; Phys Thrpy.

ARSENAULT, WENDY L; Cape Elizabeth HS; Cape Elizabeth, ME; (Y); 68/141; Pres FBLA; Trs Intnl Clb; JA; Math Tm; Pep Clb; Chorus; Var Cheerleading; Hon Roll; Mst Outstndg Stu Acctg II 86; Pres Acad Fit Awd 86; Thomas Coll; Acctg.

ASKUE, DIANE ELISE; Camden-Rockport HS; Ashland, WI; (Y); 8/114; Am Leg Aux Girls St; French Clb; Latin Clb; Co-Capt Math Tm; SADD; Thesps; School Play; Lit Mag; NHS; Church Yth Grp; Gold Medl Ntl Latn Exm 86; Bryn Mawr Coll; Tch Latn.

ASSELIN, KAREN; Edward Little HS; Auburn, ME; (S); Sec Varsity Clb; VP Frsh Cls; Rep Jr Cls; Sec Stu Cncl; Var Cheerleading; Var Gym; Cit Awd; High Hon Roll; Tennis; Prfct Atten Awd; Miss Walton 83-84; Ldrshp Awd 83-84; Pres Fit Awd 83-85; Dartmouth; Pre-Law.

AUGER, MARIE ANN D; Edward Little HS; Auburn, ME; (S); Drama Clb; SADD; Pres Sr Cls; Off Stu Cncl; JV Var Fld Hcky; Var Gym; JV Var Sftbl; DAR Awd; NHS; Prfct Atten Awd; Gymnst Yr 85; Phys Thrpy.

AUSTIN, TARA; Nokomis Reg HS; Corinna, ME; (Y); 14/170; Am Leg Aux Girls St; Trs Church Yth Grp; Office Aide; SADD; Band; Mrchg Band; Pep Band; Symp Band; Rep Jr Cls; Var Socr; U Of ME Orono; Educ.

AVERY, MARK; Bucksport HS; Bucksport, ME; (Y); 25/144; Letterman Clb; Varsity Clb; Rep Stu Cncl; Var Bsbl; Var Ftbl; Var L Golf; Hon Roll; Med.

AYOTTE, SANDY; Wisdom HS; St Agatha, ME; (Y); 27/64; Var JV Bsktbl; Bus.

BACHELDER, CAROLYN; Leavitt Area HS; Leeds, ME; (Y); 3/124; Pres Church Yth Grp; Band; School Play; Ed Yrbk Ed-Chief; Pres Sr Cls; Var L Fld Hcky; DAR Awd; NHS; Math Clb; Math Tm; Fld Hcky Awd 85; Rotry Clb Schlrshp 86; William J Irish Awd 85.

BADGER, SHERI; Edward Little HS; Mechanic Falls, ME; (Y); 26/324; Pres AFS; VP Church Yth Grp; Debate Tm; Sec Speech Tm; School Play; JV Diving; U ME-ORONO; Attrny.

BAGLEY, JENNIFER; Deering HS; Portland, ME; (Y); 28/285; French Clb; Key Clb; Varsity Clb; Yrbk Stf; Fld Hcky; Swmmng; High Hon Roll; NHS; St All Acadmc Swim Tm 85-86; D Club Awd-Swmmng; U Of VT.

BAGLIVO, STEFANIE; Marshwood HS; Eliot, ME; (Y); 10/133; Art Clb; Sec Trs Church Yth Grp; Drama Clb; Sec French Clb; Latin Clb; Math Tm; Chorus; Church Choir; Stage Crew; Yrbk Stf; Elem Ed.

BAILEY, BILL; Portland HS; Portland, ME; (Y); Boys Clb Am; Var JV Ftbl; Capt Swmmng; Ftzptrck Awd Outstndng Undrclsmn Swmng 85; Marine Bio.

BAKER, SHELLEY; Cony HS; Augusta, ME; (Y); Church Yth Grp; Church Choir; Yrbk Stf; Stat Tennis; Vllybl; Hon Roll.

BARDEN, SARAH; Cony HS; Augusta, ME; (Y); 7/300; AFS; Drama Clb; JCL; Chorus; Madrigals; Symp Band; High Hon Roll; Church Yth Grp; French Clb; Latin Clb; Slvr Mdl ST Latin Exm; Schl Schlr; Elem Tchr.

BARLEY, DOUGLAS; Cony HS; Augusta, ME; (Y); 8/287; Drama Clb; French Clb; JCL; Math Tm; Science Clb; Spanish Clb; Pres Chorus; Madrigals; School Musical; School Play; 2nd Pl Essay Acad Deca 86; 4th Nation Ntl Frnch Ex 86; All ST Music Festvl 2nd Pl 86; Music.

BARNARD, AMY; Edward Little HS; Auburn, ME; (S); Pres Church Yth Grp; Drama Clb; Latin Clb; Spanish Clb; JV Fld Hcky; High Hon Roll; Hon Roll; NHS; Ntl Merit Ltr; Prfct Atten Awd.

BARNARD, ELIZABETH A; Woodland HS; Woodland, ME; (S); 13/51; Am Leg Aux Girls St; Church Yth Grp; Drama Clb; FBLA; Girl Scts; Hosp Aide; Letterman Clb; Red Cross Aide; SADD; Thesps; Hugh O Brien Yth Fndtn Sem For Outstndg Soph 84; DAC Alstar Bsktbl & Vlybl 85; Bus Adm.

BARNEY, JODY; Skowhegan Area HS; Skowhegan, ME; (Y); Varsity Clb; Bsbl.

BARRETT, RYAN; Lewiston HS; Lewiston, ME; (Y); High Hon Roll; Hon Roll; Engl.

BARTLETT, CHRISTINE; Lee Acad; Lee, ME; (Y); 3/61; AFS; Am Leg Aux Girls St; Letterman Clb; Math Tm; Stat Bsbl; Var Bsktbl; Socr; High Hon Roll; NHS; Husson; Nrsg.

BARTLETT, JOHN; Wells HS; Wells, ME; (Y); Spanish Clb; Rep Soph Cls; Sec Bsbl; Mgr(s); Hon Roll; Athltc Awd Vars Bsbl Mgr & Ltr 86; Excllnc In Sci Awd 86; JR Hnr Roll Awd 86; U Of Southern ME; Elec Cntrctr.

BARTLEY, ANGEL; Central Aroostook HS; Mars Hill, ME; (Y); Church Yth Grp; Sec French Clb; Math Tm; Band; Mgr Bsktbl; JV Sftbl; Cit Awd; High Hon Roll; Hon Roll; NHS; Hist Mdl 85; Frnch Mdl 86; Bst Sprt Awd Chrch Bsktbl Marathon 85; Elem Tchr.

BASTARACHE, DOLORES L; Biddeford HS; Biddeford, ME; (Y); 19/279; Bsktbl; Trk; Hon Roll; NHS; Dollars For Schlrs 85-86; Hnr Being In Top 10% Of Class 84-85 & 85-86; Amer Internatl Coll; Bus Manmnt.

BASTON, DAVID; Bonny Eagle HS; W Buxton, ME; (Y); JV Bsbl; Var Capt Bsktbl; Var Socr; Hon Roll; Jr NHS; NHS; Hlth Awd 84; Frst Tm All-Str Sccr 85; Hlth.

BATCHELDER, MICHAEL; Maine Central Inst; Pittsfield, ME; (Y); 20/110; Am Leg Boys St; Pres JCL; Pres Latin Clb; Spanish Clb; Lit Mag; High Hon Roll; Hon Roll; Commrcl Art.

BATCHELDER, TAMMY; Skouhegan Area HS; Skowhegan, ME; (Y); 9/199; Am Leg Aux Girls St; Math Tm; Trs Frsh Cls; Trs Soph Cls; Capt L Socr; Sftbl; High Hon Roll; Hon Roll; NHS; Mrchg Band; Hghst Rnkng Stu ATA Awd 84-85; Hghst Rnkng Stu Hist Awd 84-85; U Of ME; Teaching.

BATES, KEVIN S; Leavitt Area HS; Greene, ME; (Y); 5/162; French Clb; Math Tm; Quiz Bowl; School Play; Stage Crew; Variety Show; Nwsp Phtg; Yrbk Phtg; Stu Cncl; Bsbl; Olympics Of The Mind 84-86; New England Math Leag 85; French Natl Honor Soc 84-86; NY Inst Of Tech; Arch.

BEAL, HEIDI; Jonesport-Beals HS; Beals, ME; (Y); School Play; Yrbk Phtg; Var Bsktbl; JV Cheerleading; Var Sftbl; Var JV Vllybl; Acdmc All Amer Schlr Pgm 86; JR Prm Queen 86; Cmrcl Artst.

BEAUDETTE, ROLAND; St Dominic Regional HS; Lewiston, ME; (Y); 8/67; Church Yth Grp; VP Debate Tm; Key Clb; NFL; Hon Roll; NHS; Trophy Acadmc & Extra Curricular Achvt 86; 6th Pl Speaker, 3rd Pl Team ME ST Debate Finals 86.

BEAUDOIN, MARK; Rumford HS; Hanover, ME; (Y).

BEGIN, PAMELA; Brewer HS; Brewer, ME; (Y); English Clb; Key Clb; Letterman Clb; School Play; Yrbk Stf; Pres Frsh Cls; Pres Soph Cls; Rep Jr Cls; Var L Cheerleading; High Hon Roll; Hugh O Brien Ldrshp Awd 85; Crmnl Just.

BELL, JOHN C; Oxford Hills HS; Norway, ME; (Y); Am Leg Boys St; Math Tm; Pres Stu Cncl; Cit Awd; Trs Frsh Cls; Rep Soph Cls; Pres Jr Cls; Pres Sr Cls; JV Bsktbl; Advtsr Dem Schlrshp; Worcester Poly Inst; Engr.

BELLAVANCE, MARY; Thornton Acad; Saco, ME; (Y); 32/224; Am Leg Aux Girls St; Dance Clb; Co-Capt Color Guard; Yrbk Rptr; Sec Sr Cls; Stu Cncl; Var Capt Cheerleading; Twrlr; Hon Roll; NHS; U Of ME-FARMINGTON; Educ.

BELLEFLEUR, KEVIN; Edward Little HS; Auburn, ME; (S); AFS; FBLA; Spanish Clb; Hon Roll; NHS; ME Schlrs Day 85; Comm.

BELLFY, MICHELE; Edward Little HS; Auburn, ME; (S); Latin Clb; Varsity Clb; Variety Show; Capt Var Cheerleading; Sftbl; High Hon Roll; Hon Roll; Vetnrn.

BELLOMY, CHRISTOPHER; Hampden Acad; Winterport, ME; (Y); Am Leg Boys St; Drama Clb; Key Clb; Band; Chorus; School Play; Swing Chorus; Variety Show; High Hon Roll; Voice Dem Awd; Prof Spch.

BENNER, STACEY; Deering HS; Portland, ME; (Y); French Clb; Letterman Clb; Varsity Clb; Band; Mrchg Band; Stu Cncl; Capt JV Bsktbl; Var Fld Hcky; Sftbl; Hon Roll; Sftbl ST Champs 85 & 86; Marchng Band ST Champs 83-84.

BENNETT, AMBER; Fryeburg Acad; Lovell, ME; (S); Drama Clb; French Clb; SADD; School Musical; Sec Jr Cls; Bsktbl; Stat Fld Hcky; Sftbl; Hon Roll; Jr NHS; Fashion.

BENNETT, ELANIE; Buckfield HS; Buckfield, ME; (S); 2/42; Math Tm; Yrbk Stf; Pres Soph Cls; Rep Stu Cncl; Var Socr; Bausch & Lomb Sci Awd; Pres French Clb; Science Clb; Varsity Clb; Var Cheerleading; HOBY Ldrshp Sem 85; New England JR Sci & Humnities Sump 86.

BENNETT, KATHLEEN C; Lake Region HS; Naples, ME; (Y); AFS; Varsity Clb; Nwsp Stf; Yrbk Stf; Var Co-Capt Cheerleading; Coll; Pre-Med Dctr.

BENNETT, MELONIE; Gorham HS; Gorham, ME; (Y); Camera Clb; Exploring; Pres 4-H; Latin Clb; Nwsp Stf; Yrbk Phtg; 4-H Awd; Hon Roll; Natl 4-H Dairy Quiz Bwl Tm VA 83; Photogrphy 86; Art 85; Grphc Dsgn.

BENNETT, NOLA; Skowhegan Area HS; Skowhegan, ME; (Y); FCA; FBLA; Band; Nwsp Stf; Yrbk Stf; JV Fld Hcky; Med Secy.

BENTO, BARBARA; Portland HS; Portland, ME; (Y); 69/210; Church Yth Grp; Drama Clb; French Clb; JA; Mrchg Band; Nwsp Stf; Yrbk Stf; Frsh Cls; Soph Cls; Jr Cls; Kenneth Jordan Higgins 86; Bsktbl 86; U Of ME; Hist.

BERCE, WENDY; Foxcroft Acad; Dover, ME; (Y); Hon Roll; Fash Merch.

BERGERON, NICOLE; St Dominics Regional HS; Lewiston, ME; (Y); 8/70; Drama Clb; Tennis; Vllybl; High Hon Roll; Hon Roll; Jr NHS; NHS; Pres Schlr.

BERNARD, AMY M; Jay HS; Jay, ME; (Y); Math Tm; Science Clb; Var Cheerleading; Hon Roll; Coaches Awd Ftbl Chrldng 85; Med Tech.

BERNARD, DAVINE; Catherine Mcauley HS; So Portland, ME; (Y); 26/74; Pres Church Yth Grp; French Clb; Pres SADD; Math Awd 85; Awd For Engl III 86; Micro-Bio.

BERNIER, DEBBIE; Windham HS; Windham, ME; (Y); 1/185; French Clb; Math Tm; Rep Jr Cls; Rep Sr Cls; Rep Stu Cncl; French Hon Soc; NHS; Val; Chorus; Lit Mag; Art Insti Schls Inc; Wmns Ltry Union & Yth Cncl; Smith Coll; Sci.

BERRY, FRANK; Bucksport HS; Bucksport, ME; (Y); 20/130; Drama Clb; Political Wkr; School Play; Stage Crew; JV Ftbl; Var Trk; Hon Roll.

BERRY, GREGORY; Belfast Area HS; Belfast, ME; (Y); 24/119; Am Leg Boys St; Letterman Clb; Concert Band; Drm Mjr(t); Jazz Band; School Musical; School Play; Capt Socr; Hon Roll; Drm Mjr Awd-Bsktbl Pep Band 85-86; Delyd Entry Pgm US Army 85-86; ME Al-ST Band Music Fstvl 86; US Army; Army Band.

BERUBE, JOHN; Edward Little HS; Auburn, ME; (S); VP Drama Clb; French Clb; Thesps; School Musical; School Play; DAR Awd; High Hon Roll; NHS; All ST Cast Awd-Drama; Harvard Book Awd.

BERUBE, PATRICIA; Lewiston HS; Lewiston, ME; (Y); Am Leg Aux Girls St; Letterman Clb; SADD; Off Frsh Cls; Off Soph Cls; Rep Jr Cls; Rep Sr Cls; Stat Bsktbl; Stat Fld Hcky; NHS; Pre-Med.

BESS, STEPHANIE; Madison HS; Madison, ME; (Y); #16 In Class; Var Bsktbl; Var Cheerleading; Coach Actv; Var Sftbl; Hon Roll.

BICKFORD, SCOTT; Oxford Hills HS; S Paris, ME; (Y); 3/260; Key Clb; Math Tm; Stu Cncl; Bsktbl; U Of Maine; Civil Engineering.

BIGGIE, THERESE; Bucksport HS; Castine, ME; (Y); 2/117; Drama Clb; Varsity Clb; School Musical; Nwsp Stf; Capt Bsktbl; Hon Roll; VP NHS; Pres Schlr; Sal; Voice Dem Awd; Purdue Schlrshp 86; Chmpn Schlrshp 86; Mens Clb Schlrshp 86; Purdue U; Htl Mgmt.

BILLING, BETH; Cony HS; Augusta, ME; (Y); 54/300; Am Leg Aux Girls St; Church Yth Grp; French Clb; SADD; School Play; Variety Show; Yrbk Stf; Var Capt Crs Cntry; Var Gym; Var Capt Trk; Psychlgy.

BILLINGS, STACI; Brunswick HS; Brunswick, ME; (Y); Church Yth Grp; Drama Clb; Chorus; School Musical; Variety Show; Var Capt Cheerleading; Hon Roll; Richard Paradis Mem Schlrshp 86; Muriel Cross Mem Schlrshp 86; Booker/Mc Kenney Trust Fund 86; Mercyhurst Coll; Dance.

BILODEAU, JOHN; Lewiston HS; Lewiston, ME; (Y); Key Clb; Hon Roll; Bentley Coll; Bus Mgmt.

BILODEAU, ROBERT; Edward Little HS; Auburn, ME; (S); Computer Clb; Var Ftbl; Var Trk; Cit Awd; High Hon Roll; Coaches Awd 83-84; Comp Sci.

BISBEE, SUSAN W; Berwick Acad; Rochester, NH; (Y); Camera Clb; Drama Clb; German Clb; Chorus; School Musical; School Play; Yrbk Stf; Var L Socr; JV Var Tennis; High Hon Roll; Spnsh Hnr Awd 84-85; U CT; Ltn Amer Stds.

BLACK, WILLIAM; Nokomis Regional HS; Newport, ME; (Y); 21/171; French Clb; Ski Clb; Yrbk Phtg; Yrbk Stf; Stu Cncl; JV Bsktbl; High Hnrs; Arch.

BLACKMORE, REBECCAH; Presque Isle HS; Presque Isle, ME; (Y); 16/189; Am Leg Aux Girls St; Church Yth Grp; SADD; Drill Tm; Stage Crew; Ed Yrbk Stf; Rep Frsh Cls; Rep Soph Cls; Stu Cncl; Pom Pon; Top Of Cls 86; Bus Schlrshp 86; Chrch Schlrshp 86; Mark And Emily Turnr Found Schlrshp 86; Acadmc Achvt; Bryant Clg; Acctg.

BLAIS, RONALD; Lewiston HS; Lewiston, ME; (Y); 21/401; VP Computer Clb; High Hon Roll; Hon Roll; Jr NHS; NHS; Tchrs Scholar Awd 86; K Of C Scholar 86; Thomas Coll; Comp Info Sys.

BLEASE, AMY; Orono HS; Orono, ME; (S); 9/114; VP AFS; Pres 4-H; Yrbk Stf; Lit Mag; VP Soph Cls; Rep Stu Cncl; Var L Socr; 4-H Awd; Hon Roll; NHS; Acadmc Achvt Awd Frnch & Art 83-85; Psychtry.

BLIER, BEVERLY; Fort Kent Community HS; Ft Kent, ME; (Y); 32/142; Church Yth Grp; Pres DECA; Chorus; High Hon Roll; Hon Roll; Cert Of Hnr Adlt Lvng, Fds & Ntrtn & Encllnc Schlrshp 86; Scrtry.

BLOOD, KYLE T; Skowhegan Area HS; Skowhegan, ME; (Y); 1/189; Am Leg Boys St; Cmnty Wkr; Dance Clb; Drama Clb; French Clb; Math Tm; Pep Clb; Thesps; Varsity Clb; Band; Englsh Awd 82-85; Frnch Awd 83-86; Stu Of Mnth 85; Dartmouth Coll; Frgn Lng.

BOCCHINO, CHRIS; Mt Abram Regional HS; Stratton, ME; (Y); 1/93; Debate Tm; Concert Band; Pep Band; VP Jr Cls; Stu Cncl; L Trk; High Hon Roll; Ntl Merit SF; St Schlr; Am Leg Boys St; Olympics Of The Minds Wrld Fnlsts 86; French Examntn 85; U Of Miami; Bio Chem.

BOILEAU, DANIELLE; Livermore Falls HS; Livermore Falls, ME; (Y); Church Yth Grp; Drama Clb; 4-H; Math Tm; Band; Concert Band; Mrchg Band; Stu Cncl; 4-H Awd; High Hon Roll; Air Force Acad.

BOISSE, DEBRA J; Lewiston HS; Lewiston, ME; (Y); 65/395; Letterman Clb; School Play; Yrbk Stf; VP Soph Cls; Stat Bsktbl; Capt Cheerleading; Fld Hcky; Trk; Hon Roll; NHS; Johnson & Wales Acad Scholar 86; Johnson & Wales; Trvl.

BOISSONNEAULT, MARK; Sanford HS; Springvale, ME; (Y); SADD; Bsbl; Ftbl; Wt Lftg; Hon Roll.

BOLDUC, MARIE C; Waterville HS; Waterville, ME; (Y); 5/200; Math Clb; Trs Spanish Clb; High Hon Roll; NHS; Ntl Merit SF; Spanish NHS; St Schlr; Colby Bk Awd 85; U ME Farmington; Elem Ed.

BOLLES, THOMAS M; Gorham HS; Gorham, ME; (Y); 4/115; AFS; Boy Scts; Church Yth Grp; Math Tm; JV Bsktbl; Var Socr; Cit Awd; High Hon Roll; Hon Roll; NHS; Cumberland Cnty Med Soc Schlrshp 86; Natl Hnr Soc Schlrshp 86; Pres Acad Fitness Awd 86; Boston U; Bio.

BONARRIGO, ANGELA; Georges Valley HS; Thomaston, ME; (Y); 2/73; Am Leg Aux Girls St; 4-H; Intnl Clb; Pres Pep Clb; Red Cross Aide; Yrbk Sprt Ed; Rep Stu Cncl; Var Capt Crs Cntry; Var Trk; Sal; Prncpls Awd 85-86; NHS 85; Rotary Clb Scholar 86; Jackson Coll; Intl Rltns.

BONNER, LYN; Lewiston HS; Lewiston, ME; (Y); 57/384; JA; Letterman Clb; Crs Cntry; Trk; High Hon Roll; Hon Roll; NHS; Physcl Educ Awd 83; U Of ME; Elem Educ.

BOOKER, TIFFANY; Bonny Eagle HS; W Buxton, ME; (Y); Church Yth Grp; 4-H; Library Aide; Math Tm; Office Aide; Ski Clb; Nwsp Stf; Hon Roll; Jr NHS; Coll; Equine Studies.

BOPP, ANDREA; Waynflete Schl; Portland, ME; (Y); Church Yth Grp; Cmnty Wkr; VP Pres JA; SADD; Yrbk Phtg; Var Bsktbl; Var Capt Fld Hcky; Lcrss; Hon Roll; Camera Clb; Achvt Spch Wnnr 85-86; Most Imprvd 86; Bus.

BOUCHER, CHRISTINA; Lisbon HS; Lisbon, ME; (Y); 6/111; French Clb; JA; Band; Concert Band; Mrchg Band; Yrbk Stf; Hon Roll; 2nd Pl Schl Sci Fair Biol 85; 1st Pl Schl Sci Fair Chem 86; 2nd Pl ST Sci Fair Chem 86; U Miami; Pre-Med.

BOUCHER, KAREN; Livermore Falls HS; Livermore, ME; (Y); Am Leg Aux Girls St; French Clb; Ski Clb; Crs Cntry; Hon Roll; NHS; Prfct Atten Awd; PSAT Acad Achvt Awd 86; Soc Studys & Drvr Ed Awds 86; Helcptr Plt.

BOURGOIN, DEBBY; Lewiston HS; Lewiston, ME; (Y); Office Aide; Rep Stu Cncl; High Hon Roll; Hon Roll; NHS; Trphy Chld Car Aid-Tp Awd 86; Awd Hghst Achvt Engl 86; Bus.

BOWDEN, RICK; Central HS; Kenduskeag, ME; (Y); 8/75; Am Leg Boys St; Varsity Clb; Yrbk Ed-Chief; Yrbk Stf; Var L Bsbl; JV Bsktbl; Var L Golf; Hon Roll; U Of ME; Acctg.

BOYD, CYNTHIA B; Nokomis Regional HS; Newport, ME; (Y); 15/155; Drama Clb; Chorus; Drill Tm; Swing Chorus; Lit Mag; Rep Sr Cls; High Hon Roll; NHS; French Clb; School Musical; Mscnshp Awd 86; Dstrct V Hnrs Chorus 86; Typng I & Accntng I Awd 85; Cstltn ST Coll; Cmnctns.

BOYD, JULIET; Waynflete Schl; Yarmouth, ME; (Y); Cmnty Wkr; JA; SADD; VP Frsh Cls; Pres Soph Cls; Pres Jr Cls; Fld Hcky; Lcrss; Rotary Awd; Waynflt Schl Stu Of Yr 86; Cncl On Frgn Rltns Schlrshp 86.

BOYLES, AMANDA A; Greeley HS; Pownal, ME; (Y); 4/140; Drama Clb; Chorus; Madrigals; School Musical; Sec Stu Cncl; High Hon Roll; Hon Roll; Lion Awd; NHS; Church Yth Grp; Portland Ballet Reptry Co; Wellesley Bk Awd 85; U Of MI; Musicl Theatr.

BOYNTON, ANDREW; Leavitt Area HS; Turner, ME; (Y); School Play; Stage Crew; Socr; Hon Roll; NHS.

BRAGG, MARGARET S; Ellsworth HS; Ellsworth, ME; (Y); 12/110; Church Yth Grp; French Clb; Ed Yrbk Stf; Pres Frsh Cls; Stu Cncl; Var Capt Cheerleading; JV Capt Sftbl; Hon Roll; Pres NHS; Voice Dem Awd; Voic Of Democrcy Wnnr 86; Prncpls Awd 86; Grls ST Rep 85; Bus Mgmt.

BRANCELY, MELISSA LOUISE; Thornton Acad; Saco, ME; (Y); 9/197; Am Leg Aux Girls St; Church Yth Grp; Math Tm; Rep Soph Cls; Rep Sr Cls; Var L Bsktbl; Var L Trk; Hon Roll; NHS; Latin Clb; Lowell Innes Schlrshp 86-87; Coaches Awd In Track 86; U Of ME Orono.

BRANN, RONALD; Gardiner HS; Litchfield, ME; (Y); AFS; Boy Scts; French Clb; Model UN; SADD; Nwsp Rptr; Golf; Mgr Trk; Hon Roll; U Of ME; Bus Mgmt.

BRESHEARS, PATRICIA; Westbrook HS; Westbrook, ME; (Y); 4/220; Art Clb; French Clb; Band; Chorus; Hon Roll; Ntl Merit Ltr; Tellurd Assoc Smmr Prgrm U Of Chicago 86; Bangr Daily Nws Art Comp 86; UMO Trvlng Art Show 86.

BRETON, DAN; St Dominic Regional HS; Lewiston, ME; (Y); 20/65; Key Clb; School Play; Var L Bsbl; Im Bsktbl; Var L Ice Hcky; Im Var Socr; Im Sftbl; Im Tennis; Im Vllybl; Hon Roll; Mgmt.

BREZOVSKY, SCOTT; Calais HS; Robbinston, ME; (Y); Chess Clb; Hon Roll; U Of Rochester; Aerospace Engr.

BRIDGES, URSULA; Calais HS; Calais, ME; (Y); Am Leg Aux Girls St; Rep Chorus; Concert Band; Jazz Band; Yrbk Bus Mgr; Sec Frsh Cls; Off Soph Cls; Var Cheerleading; JV Var Vllybl; Hon Roll.

BRISKEY, HEATHER; Windham HS; Windham, ME; (Y); 12/195; AFS; Drama Clb; Spanish Clb; School Play; Stage Crew; Rep Stu Cncl; High Hon Roll; Hon Roll; NHS; Spanish NHS; Pres Acad Ftnss Awd 86; IFLS Awd Spnsh 83; Fnlst PA Govrs Schl Of Arts 83-84; Theatr.

BROCHU, TONYA; Valley HS; Bingham, ME; (Y); 2/29; Am Leg Aux Girls St; GAA; Chorus; Sec VP Stu Cncl; Var Capt Bsktbl; Var Crs Cntry; Var Socr; L Sftbl; High Hon Roll; Hon Roll; Hugh O Brien 85; U S Army Rsrv Natl Schlr/Athlt Awd 86; U Of ME Orono; Bus.

BROOKS, LAURA; Gardiner Area HS; Gardiner, ME; (Y); Office Aide; Drill Tm; Socr; Twrlr; High Hon Roll; Hon Roll; MSAD No 11 Sec Awd 86; ME ST Incntv Schlrshp 86; Briarwood Coll; Med Sec.

BROOKS, WENDY; R W Traip Acad; Kittery Pt, ME; (Y); 13/75; Church Yth Grp; Band; Jazz Band; Yrbk Bus Mgr; Yrbk Stf; Sec Trs Stu Cncl; JP Sousa Awd; NHS; Trustees Awd Schlrshp 86; Hnr Rll Pin 85-86; Endicott Coll; Intr Dsgn.

BROPHY II, RICHARD A; Livermore Falls HS; Livermore Falls, ME; (Y); Church Yth Grp; Letterman Clb; Varsity Clb; Band; Yrbk Stf; VP Jr Cls; Trs Sr Cls; Stu Cncl; Bsbl; Bsktbl; Bridgton Acad.

BROWN, KIRSTEN KELLEY; Mt Abram Regional HS; Kingfield, ME; (Y); 12/87; Radio Clb; Ski Clb; Band; Concert Band; Yrbk Bus Mgr; Yrbk Stf; Socr; Tennis; Trk; Hon Roll; Smmns Schlrshp Kngfld Fnd 86; Natl Hnr Scty Schlrshp 86; Ski Tm Mst Imprvd Skier 86; Mt Ida Coll; Grphc Dsgn.

BROWN, LORI; Belfast Area HS; Belfast, ME; (Y); 3/117; Am Leg Aux Girls St; Drama Clb; Math Tm; Band; VP Soph Cls; Sec Sr Cls; Var L Crs Cntry; Var L Swmmng; Var L Trk; High Hon Roll; Rensselaer Polytech Inst; Engr.

BROWN, MICHAEL; Lawrence HS; Clinton, ME; (Y); 4/215; Latin Clb; Var Bsbl; Var Capt Bsktbl; High Hon Roll; NHS; Prfct Atten Awd.

BROWN, PETER; Woodland HS; Princeton, ME; (S); 1/89; Chess Clb; Drama Clb; Thesps; School Play; Lit Mag; Crs Cntry; Mgr Sftbl; High Hon Roll; NHS; Law.

BROWN, RHONDA; Waterville HS; Waterville, ME; (Y); Chess Clb; Church Yth Grp; Drama Clb; French Clb; Chorus; Church Choir; JV Bsktbl; JV Vllybl; Hon Roll; All ST Chorus; Outstndng Achvt Tchr.

BROWN, STEVEN; Lee Acad; Lincoln Center, ME; (Y); AFS; Am Leg Boys St; Math Tm; Varsity Clb; Stu Cncl; Var Capt Bsktbl; Var Capt Socr; High Hon Roll; NHS; Comp Sci.

BROWNING, BRENDA; Fort Fairfield HS; Ft Fairfield, ME; (Y); Church Yth Grp; French Clb; School Play; Stage Crew; JV Bsktbl; Socr; Sftbl; Hon Roll; Prfct Atten Awd; Ch Awd Sccr 83; Pn For Sftbll & Shrthnd 86; Bus.

BRUNO, WENDY; Noble HS; Berwick, ME; (Y); Church Yth Grp; Yrbk Phtg; Yrbk Stf; Hon Roll; Prfct Atten Awd; Somersworth Women Clb 86; UMO; Biophyscs.

BRYAN, JAROD; Cony HS; Augusta, ME; (Y); 6/350; Chess Clb; Capt Math Tm; Science Clb; Bausch & Lomb Sci Awd; Elks Awd; High Hon Roll; Pres Schlr; St Schlr; Rensselaer Medal Math,Sci; KC Patriotic Awd; U ME-ORONO; Engrng.

BRYANT, CHRISTOPHER J; Jay HS; Jay, ME; (Y); 2/86; Am Leg Boys St; Math Tm; Band; Yrbk Sprt Ed; Pres Sr Cls; Rep Stu Cncl; Crs Cntry; Trk; Hon Roll; Ntl Merit SF; Mechncl Engrng.

BRYANT, DEBI; Windham HS; S Windham, ME; (Y); Church Yth Grp; Key Clb; Sec Soph Cls; Sec Jr Cls; Rep Sr Cls; Var JV Cheerleading; Var Mgr(s); Trk; Hon Roll; Jr NHS; Busnss.

BRYANT, JEFFREY; Edward Little HS; Auburn, ME; (S); Church Yth Grp; Cmnty Wkr; Debate Tm; French Clb; Speech Tm; Crs Cntry; Socr; Tennis; High Hon Roll; Hon Roll; Vet.

BRYANT, ROBERT; Edward Little HS; West Minot, ME; (S); AFS; Am Leg Boys St; Debate Tm; Trs Drama Clb; Pres 4-H; VP Latin Clb; Math Tm; VP Speech Tm; High Hon Roll; NHS; Holy Cross Bk Awd.

BRYANT, STEVE; Marshwood HS; Eliot, ME; (Y); 2/140; Drama Clb; Math Tm; Band; Var Socr; Var Trk; High Hon Roll; Trs NHS; Voice Dem Awd; Trs French Clb; Concert Band; Aimee Schram Book Awd 84 & 85 & 86; Otstndng Music Awd 85; Vet Med.

BRYER, VALERIE; Mattanawcook Acad; Lincoln, ME; (Y); 8/98; Pres French Clb; Letterman Clb; Band; School Musical; Var Capt Cheerleading; Pres NHS; Pres Schlr; Am Leg Aux Girls St; Pep Clb; Yrbk Stf; Colby Coll Bk Awd 85; Schl Spirit Awd 86; Mst Vlbl Cheerldr 85; Colby Coll; Socl Wrk.

BUBIER, KIMBERLY A; Leavitt Area HS; Greene, ME; (Y); 19/119; Yrbk Ed-Chief; Yrbk Stf; JV Bsktbl; Var JV Sftbl; Var Vllybl; High Hon Roll; Hon Roll; NHS; Chmstry Awd 85; Greene Grange Awd 86; Angelus Dedictn Serv Awd 86; Grace & Earl Hodgman Przs 86; Bernards Schl Of Hair Fshn; Csm.

BUCKLEY, MARCI A; Presque Isle HS; Presque Isle, ME; (Y); Am Leg Aux Girls St; Church Yth Grp; Letterman Clb; Pep Clb; SADD; Varsity Clb; Lit Mag; Trs Soph Cls; VP Jr Cls; VP Sr Cls; Founders Awd 86; Outstndng Ctzn Dirigo Girls ST 86; Law.

BUGBEE, ALVIN; Portland HS; Portland, ME; (Y); Latin Clb; Math Tm; Var Capt Bsbl; Var Capt Bsktbl; Var Capt Socr; Var Hon Roll; NHS.

BUKER, WENDY; Edward Little HS; Auburn, ME; (Y); Spanish Clb; High Hon Roll; Hon Roll; NHS; Prfct Atten Awd; Chldrns Thrpy.

BULGER, WENDY M; Temple Acad; Vassalboro, ME; (Y); 1/5; Church Yth Grp; Chorus; Sec Stu Cncl; L Capt Bsktbl; L Var Cheerleading; L Var Crs Cntry; Var Score Keeper; High Hon Roll; Val; School Play; MSSPA Prncpls Awd 86; J Swaggart Bible Coll; Tchng.

BURHOE, KAREN; Livermore Falls HS; Mt Vernon, ME; (Y); Art Clb; Church Yth Grp; Drama Clb; Varsity Clb; Band; Stage Crew; Var Cheerleading; L Trk; Hon Roll; NHS; Grmn Achvt Awd 86; Elem Educ.

BURKE, DIANNA; Woodland HS; Princeton, ME; (Y); Hon Roll; U Sthrn ME; Pol Sci.

BURLEIGH, PAMELA; Central HS; E Corinth, ME; (Y); 20/63; Church Yth Grp; Pres Key Clb; Band; Chorus; Ed Yrbk Phtg; Rep Stu Cncl; Var JV Mgr(s); Var Score Keeper; French Clb; Pres Girl Scts; JR Sci Hmnts Sympsm 86; Hugh O Brien Yth Ldrshp Smnr 85; U Of ME; Athltc Trng.

BURPEE, CAROLYN; St Dominics R HS; Lewiston, ME; (Y); Drama Clb; School Musical; School Play; Var Capt Tennis; High Hon Roll; Hon Roll; NHS; Cmmnctns Media.

BUSWELL, THERESA MARIE; Ellsworth HS; Ellsworth, ME; (Y); 15/110; AFS; French Clb; Orch; JV Socr; High Hon Roll; Hon Roll; Ntl Merit Ltr; Mt Holyoke Coll; Frnch.

BUTLER, LORI; Edward Little HS; Mechanic Falls, ME; (Y); 44/329; Church Yth Grp; French Clb; Rptr FBLA; JA; Pep Clb; Spanish Clb; Mgr(s); Hon Roll; Prfct Atten Awd; Becker JC; Trvl.

BUTTS, MARY ANN; Deering HS; Portland, ME; (Y); Drama Clb; Ski Clb; Hon Roll; U Of Southern ME; Educ.

BUZZELL, FELANCY; Skowhegun Area HS; Skowhegan, ME; (Y); 19/216; Band; Drill Tm; Mrchg Band.

BYAM, JENNIFER; Rumford JR SR HS; Rumford Point, ME; (Y); 19/117; Rep Drama Clb; VP French Clb; Sec SADD; Yrbk Rptr; Pres Sr Cls; Hon Roll; Prfct Atten Awd; Am Leg Aux Girls St; Church Choir; School Musical; Stdnt Mnth Awd 85; Actvty Peer Cnslg Advsry Brd 85-86; USM Smmr Inst Humnties & Tech 86; Psych.

BYRON, BETH; Hodgdon HS; Houlton, ME; (Y); Art Clb; Pres 4-H; Varsity Clb; Chorus; School Musical; Var Bsktbl; Var Crs Cntry; Var Socr; 4-H Awd; Art Nrthrn ME Fr Bst Shw 84; U Of ME; Rcrtnl Mngmnt.

BYRON, KEVEN L; Hodgdon HS; Houlton, ME; (Y); 1/50; Chess Clb; Church Yth Grp; French Clb; Math Clb; Quiz Bowl; Socr; Bausch & Lomb Sci Awd; Elks Awd; High Hon Roll; NHS; US Senat Yth, ST Altrnt 85; Ricker Schlrshp 86; Lodg Elks Schlrshp 86; U Of ME Orono; Hstry.

CAFFYN, KARENA; Skowhegan Area HS; Skowhegan, ME; (Y); 16/216; Am Leg Aux Girls St; French Clb; Yrbk Phtg; Yrbk Stf; Trs Sr Cls; Capt Socr; Var Tennis; NHS; Bio Awd 85.

CAGLEY, DAWN MARIE; Brunswick HS; Brunswick, ME; (Y); 9/243; Church Yth Grp; Latin Clb; Yrbk Stf; Sec Soph Cls; Var Cheerleading; Stat Trk; Lion Awd; Ntl Merit Ltr; Brunswick Hnr Soc 85-86; Middlebury Coll; Poli Sci.

CALDER, SARAH; Calais HS; Calais, ME; (Y); Drama Clb; Pep Clb; Band; Concert Band; Pep Band; Yrbk Phtg; Yrbk Stf; Sec Soph Cls; Sec Jr Cls; Sec Sr Cls; Pre-Med.

CALDWELL, CHRISTINE; Deering HS; Portland, ME; (Y); 24/326; Trs Latin Clb; Nwsp Stf; Yrbk Ed-Chief; Sec Frsh Cls; Rep Stu Cncl; French Hon Soc; Hon Roll; St Schlr; French Clb; Concert Band; Antmy Of Ldrshp Prgm Bk Awd 86; Mem Of Wmns Lit Unn Yth Cncl 85-86; Engl.

CALDWELL, DEIDRA; Leavitt Area HS; Turner, ME; (Y); 12/118; School Play; Yrbk Bus Mgr; Yrbk Phtg; Sec Frsh Cls; JV Fld Hcky; JV Var Sftbl; Vllybl; High Hon Roll; Hon Roll; Jr NHS; C L/H Eastman Schlrshp 86; U ME Orono.

CAMPBELL, CHERYL ANN; Edward Little HS; Auburn, ME; (Y); Am Leg Aux Girls St; Cmnty Wkr; French Clb; FBLA; Girl Scts; Pep Clb; Ski Clb; Nwsp Stf; Yrbk Stf; Hon Roll; Elem Educ.

CAMPBELL, KIM; Pendoscot Valley HS; Howland, ME; (Y); Pep Clb; Yrbk Stf; Sec Soph Cls; Sec Jr Cls; JV Var Cheerleading; Hon Roll; Prfct Atten Awd; Mst Outstndng JV Chrldr 84-85; Mst Imprvd In Trnscrptn 84-85; Best Persnlty 85-86; Husson Coll; Wrd Prcsng.

CAMPBELL, LAURIE; South Portland HS; S Portland, ME; (Y); 25/300; Key Clb; Hon Roll; Accntng.

CAMPBELL, ROBERT; Calais HS; Calais, ME; (Y); 6/80; Am Leg Boys St; Boy Scts; Chess Clb; Yrbk Phtg; Bsktbl; Ice Hcky; Socr; Tennis; Hon Roll.

CAMPBELL, ROBIN; Windham HS; Windham, ME; (Y); 21/200; Pres Chorus; VP Church Yth Grp; VP Jr Cls; VP Sr Cls; Rep Stu Cncl; Var L Bsktbl; Var Capt Socr; Var L Sftbl; Var L Trk; NHS; ME Med Ctr Schlrshp 86; Socl Stds Awd 86; U Of S ME; Pre-Med.

CAREY, MICHELLE; Skowhegan Area HS; Skowhegan, ME; (Y); FNA; GAA; JA; Latin Clb; Letterman Clb; Varsity Clb; Bsktbl; Socr; Sftbl; Hon Roll; Nrsng.

CARON, CATHY; Portland HS; Portland, ME; (Y); Math Tm; Nwsp Stf; Rep Frsh Cls; Var Tennis; High Hon Roll; NHS; Ntl Merit SF; 4 Brnz Mdls Lit,Sci,Ec,Intervw 86; Brown Bk Awd 86; Hgh Scorer AHME Schl 86; Rsrch Sci.

CARON, MICHELE LYNN; Washburn District HS; Washburn, ME; (Y); 4/50; Am Leg Aux Girls St; SADD; Band; Chorus; Jazz Band; Bsktbl; Socr; High Hon Roll; NHS; Acadmc Achvt Awd 83-85; Champ Bsktbl 84-85; Coaches Awd Soccr 85; Champs Sftbl 85; U Of ME; Phys Thrpy.

CARON, RONALD; Ft Kent Community HS; Ft Kent, ME; (Y); 6/161; Am Leg Boys St; Drama Clb; Pep Band; School Play; Nwsp Rptr; Cit Awd; NHS; Pres Schlr; St Schlr; Voice Dem Awd; ME Yth Ldrshp Smnr 84; St Anslm Coll; Psychlgy.

CARPENTER, CAROL; Greenville HS; Greenville, ME; (Y); 2/50; Am Leg Aux Girls St; JA; Band; Chorus; Jazz Band; School Musical; Variety Show; Yrbk Phtg; Yrbk Stf; Pres Frsh Cls; Outstndg Soph & JR 84-86; Johnson & Wales; Hrse Trnr.

CARPENTER, KAREN; Lewiston HS; Lewiston, ME; (Y); 26/350; Letterman Clb; Varsity Clb; Var Capt Bsktbl; Var Crs Cntry; Var Fld Hcky; Var Capt Sftbl; High Hon Roll; Hon Roll; Excllnc Math 84-85; U Of CT; Sprts Medcn.

CARPENTER, SARA; Fryeburg Acad; Hiram, ME; (S); Drama Clb; French Clb; SADD; Varsity Clb; School Musical; School Play; Pres Frsh Cls; Var Fld Hcky; Var Trk; Hon Roll; Natl Engl Mert Awd 85-86.

CARSON, TERI; Deering HS; Portland, ME; (Y); Pep Clb; Spanish Clb; Variety Show; Var Capt Cheerleading; Gym; X-Ray Tech.

CARTER, JENNIFER T; Ellsworth HS; Ellsworth, ME; (Y); 11/103; Sec AFS; Am Leg Aux Girls St; VP Sec French Clb; Ed Yrbk Stf; Trs Jr Cls; Hon Roll; NHS; Pres Classroom For Yng Amer 85; U Of ME; Pol Sci.

CARTER, MICHAEL; Bucksport HS; Castine, ME; (Y); Varsity Clb; Trs Soph Cls; Trs Jr Cls; Var Bsktbl; Hon Roll; American International; Pol Sci.

CARVER, CAROL; Medomak Valley HS; Warren, ME; (Y); Chorus; Variety Show; Golf; Prfct Atten Awd; Associated Schls Inc; Trvl Agnt.

CARVER, JEAN DENISE; Narraguagus HS; Addison, ME; (Y); 13/66; Am Leg Aux Girls St; Dance Clb; Drama Clb; Pres French Clb; Varsity Clb; Yrbk Stf; Rep Sr Cls; Var Cheerleading; Var Vllybl; High Hon Roll; Most Imprvd Stu Eng II 84; Highst Achvt Art Hist 85-86; High Achvt Clothing & Textls 85; U ME; Bus Admin.

CASALE, CHRIS; Derring HS; Portland, ME; (Y); 41/288; Drama Clb; French Clb; FTA; Key Clb; Political Wkr; Yrbk Ed-Chief; Golf; Vllybl; NHS; Hon Roll; George Poulos Memrl Trust Schlrshp 86; Kenneth Jordan Higgins Meml Trust Schlrshp 86; Key Club Bk Awd; U ME; Pre Med.

CASWELL, GINGER; Edward Little HS; Auburn, ME; (S); Am Leg Aux Girls St; VP Drama Clb; VP Pres French Clb; Math Tm; VP Pres Temple Yth Grp; Yrbk Ed-Chief; NHS; Pep Clb; School Musical; School Play; Hugh O Brian Yth Fndtn; Ldrshp Awd; Yrkbk Awd; Liberal Arts.

CHABOT, MAURICE; Lewiston HS; Lewiston, ME; (Y); Stu Cncl; Capt Bowling; Hon Roll; Upwrd Bnd Valentines Essay Cont 85; Law.

CHALMERS, JON; Portland HS; Portland, ME; (Y); Latin Clb; Crs Cntry; Trk; Hon Roll; Arch.

CHAMBERLAIN, DANNY; Erskine Acad; S China, ME; (Y); Am Leg Boys St; Church Yth Grp; French Clb; Math Tm; Speech Tm; Yrbk Stf; Frsh Cls; High Hon Roll; Hon Roll; Kennebec Sl Wtr Cnvsrvtn Essy Cont 84; U ME; Techn.

CHAMBERLAND, SHELLY; Widsom HS; St Agatha, ME; (Y); 3/48; Cmnty Wkr; SADD; Pres Sr Cls; Cheerleading; Vllybl; Cit Awd; High Hon Roll; Hon Roll; VP NHS; St Schlr; ME Scndry Schl Prncpls Awd 86; Paul E Chasse Awd 86; French & Math Awd 86; New England U; Physcl Thrpy.

CHAN, DAVID; Caribou HS; Caribou, ME; (S); Pres Chess Clb; Debate Tm; JV Bsbl; High Hon Roll.

CHANDLER, SUSAN; Fryeburg Acad; Fryeburg, ME; (S); Drama Clb; Sec Speech Tm; School Musical; School Play; Yrbk Bus Mgr; VP Pres Stu Cncl; Var Capt Cheerleading; DAR Awd; High Hon Roll; Pres NHS; Walter A Robinson Latin Awd 83-84; B W Tinker Schlstc Awd 83; Bowdoin Coll; Psych.

CHAPMAN, KRISTINA; Gardiner Area HS; Gardiner, ME; (Y); 4-H; Office Aide; Var Cheerleading; Capt Var Diving; Var Fld Hcky; Var Capt Swmmng; Var Trk; Hon Roll; Athltc Schlrshp Becker JC-FIELD Hockey 86; Becker JC; Rec Ldrshp.

CHAPMAN, SHELLY; Edward Little HS; Auburn, ME; (S); Church Yth Grp; Latin Clb; Pep Clb; High Hon Roll; Hon Roll; Nrsng.

CHARCZYNSKI, LYNNE; Jonesport-Beals HS; Beals, ME; (Y); French Clb; Yrbk Stf; VP Frsh Cls; Rep Soph Cls; Rep Jr Cls; Stu Cncl; Cheerleading; Hon Roll; NHS; Rotary Awd; U ME Machias; Bus.

CHAREST, DONNA; Lewiston HS; Lewiston, ME; (Y); 75/409; Hon Roll; NHS; Outstndng Unit Clrk; Med.

CHAREST, WENDY; Cony HS; Augusta, ME; (Y); 1/320; Trs AFS; Am Leg Aux Girls St; Debate Tm; Sec French Clb; Pres JCL; Yrbk Sprt Ed; Var Score Keeper; JV Sftbl; Im Vllybl; Val; Stu Mth 86; Blaine House Schlr 86; Outstndng Poli Sci Stu 86; Holy Cross Coll; Classcs.

CHARLES, STEVEN; Edward Little HS; Auburn, ME; (Y); Pres Computer Clb; Latin Clb; Band; Concert Band; Jazz Band; Mrchg Band; Hon Roll; Phrmcy.

CHASE, CHERI; Mt Abram HS; Carrabassett, ME; (Y); Cmnty Wkr; L Var Crs Cntry; L Var Socr; Var Tennis; L Var Trk; High Hon Roll; Hon Roll; NHS; Dale Carnegie Prsnl Devlopmtn Awd 84; Comp Progmmg Awd 86; Natl Hnr Soc Schlrshp 86; NH College; Bus Admn.

CHASE, DEBORAH RAE; Greenville HS; Greenville, ME; (Y); Am Leg Aux Girls St; Trs Drama Clb; Pres French Clb; Sec Key Clb; Math Tm; Band; Chorus; School Musical; Yrbk Ed-Chief; Trs VP Stu Cncl; Scotts Hi Q Quiz Tm 84-86.

CHASE, TINA; Fryeburg Acad; Fryeburg, ME; (Y); Church Yth Grp; High Hon Roll; Hon Roll; Accntng.

CHEEVER, KATIE; Noble HS; Lebanon, ME; (Y); Church Yth Grp; Key Clb; Band; Yrbk Stf; Capt Var Crs Cntry; Var Trk; Crss Cntry Mst Imprvd Plyr 83; Crss Cntry Coachs Awd 84-85; Phys Thrpst.

CHELIDONA, MICHAEL; Mt Abram HS; Stratton, ME; (Y); Am Leg Boys St; Intnl Clb; Ski Clb; Band; Jazz Band; Mrchg Band; Crs Cntry; Cmnty Wkr; Hon Roll; Comp Mgmt.

CHENEY, CHRISTOPHER; Yarmouth JR SR HS; Yarmouth, ME; (Y); 2/100; Am Leg Boys St; Scholastic Bowl; VP Stu Cncl; Var Bsbl; Var Capt Socr; Cmnty Wkr; Latin Clb; Math Tm; Model UN; Co-Capt Yrbk Ed-Chief; Dartmth Bk Awd; Trpl C Al-Star Crss Cntry Ski Tm; ME Smr Humants Giftd-Tlntd; Librl Arts.

CHESLEY, RANDALL; Buckfield JR SR HS; Buckfield, ME; (S); Am Leg Boys St; Letterman Clb; Math Clb; Math Tm; Varsity Clb; Trs Jr Cls; Var Bsbl; JV Bsktbl; Var Crs Cntry; Var Socr; Hist.

CHURCHILL, CAROLYN; Fort Fairfield HS; Ft Fairfield, ME; (Y); 5/70; Am Leg Aux Girls St; Trs Church Yth Grp; FBLA; SADD; Orch; Stu Cncl; High Hon Roll; Hon Roll; Schltc Achvt Awd 82-86; N ME Voc Tech; Acctg.

CHURCHILL, HEIDI A; Cony HS; Windsor, ME; (Y); Church Yth Grp; French Clb; Chorus; Concert Band; Jazz Band; Madrigals; High Hon Roll; Jr NHS; Ntl Merit SF; St Schlr; Bowdoin Coll; Pre-Law.

CIAMPI, JOANNA; Deering HS; Portland, ME; (Y); Latin Clb; Yrbk Ed-Chief; Lit Mag; Stu Cncl; Fld Hcky; High Hon Roll; VP NHS; Spanish NHS; St Schlr; Hosp Aide; Dartmouth Bk Awd 85-86.

CICCARELLI, MARIA; Portland HS; Portland, ME; (Y); Rep Frsh Cls; Rep Soph Cls; Rep Jr Cls; Var Cheerleading; Sftbl; Hon Roll; NHS; Med Field.

CICHOR, ROSEMARIE; Caribou HS; Caribou, ME; (Y); Am Leg Aux Girls St; Church Yth Grp; Debate Tm; Drama Clb; Key Clb; Library Aide; Office Aide; Speech Tm; SADD; Chorus; Pol Sci.

CLANCY, JON; Westbrook HS; Westbrook, ME; (Y); 4/190; French Clb; Latin Clb; Concert Band; Jazz Band; Mrchg Band; Pep Band; Nwsp Stf; Yrbk Stf; Crs Cntry; Hon Roll; ME Schlrs Days U ME 86; Williams Coll Bk Awd 86; Georgetown U; Frnch.

CLAPP, JOY; Skowhegan Area HS; Skowhegan, ME; (Y); 1/200; Am Leg Aux Girls St; Drama Clb; German Clb; Stage Crew; Nwsp Stf; Yrbk Stf; High Hon Roll; NHS; Maine Schlrs Days UMO 86.

CLARK, CARMEN; Fryeburg Acad; Waterville, ME; (Y); SADD; Stu Cncl; Var Trk; Hon Roll; U CO; Pre-Law.

CLARK, DONNA; Noble HS; North Berwick, ME; (Y); 89/250; Hosp Aide; Key Clb; Math Tm; Yrbk Phtg; Yrbk Stf; Var L Fld Hcky; Trk; Hon Roll; Prfct Atten Awd; Pre Med.

CLARK, JOEY; Calais HS; Calais, ME; (Y); 1/67; Computer Clb; English Clb; French Clb; Latin Clb; Varsity Clb; Var Bsbl; Var Bsktbl; Var Socr; High Hon Roll; JETS Awd; Bus Adm.

CLARK, RANAE; Mt Blue HS; Farmington, ME; (Y); Band; Concert Band; High Hon Roll; Prfct Atten Awd; Excllnc Schlrshp 84&85; Cazenovia Coll; Grphc Dsgn.

CLARK, SCOTT; Ft Fairfield HS; Ft Fairfield, ME; (Y); Art Clb; Church Yth Grp; Cmnty Wkr; FCA; Letterman Clb; Ski Clb; Varsity Clb; Var L Bsbl; Var L Golf; Hon Roll; Skiing Var Ltr 83-84; US Hist Hnr Soc, Hnr Book 85; Northern ME Vo-Tech; Acctg.

CLARK, SHARON; Hall-Dale HS; Farmingdale, ME; (Y); VP AFS; Rep Am Leg Aux Girls St; French Clb; Key Clb; Band; Chorus; Var Fld Hcky; Var Tennis; High Hon Roll; Hon Roll.

CLARK, TANIS; Penquis Valley HS; Milo, ME; (Y); 18/66; Am Leg Aux Girls St; Church Yth Grp; Drama Clb; Band; Concert Band; Jazz Band; Pep Band; School Musical; School Play; Stage Crew; Milo HS Alumni Schlrshp 86; Southern ME Vo Tech; Htl Mgmt.

CLAY, CARI; Gorham HS; Gorham, ME; (Y); Church Yth Grp; Spanish Clb; Teachers Aide; Varsity Clb; Concert Band; Nwsp Sprt Ed; Yrbk Stf; Var Fld Hcky; Var Trk; Spanish NHS; Spnsh Awd 85-86; Coll; Trnsltng.

CLAYMAN, PETER; Deering HS; Portland, ME; (Y); 92/326; Letterman Clb; JV Socr; Var L Trk; Bus.

CLEMENT, ANGELA; Bucksport HS; East Orland, ME; (Y); 21/117; FBLA; Varsity Clb; Band; Nwsp Stf; Trs Sr Cls; Var Capt Cheerleading; Hon Roll; All Star JV & Vrsty Cheerldr 83 & 86; Regnl Accntng Contst-3rd Pl 85; 1st Pl Cheerng Team 83-86; Busnss.

CLEMENT, JOEL; Bucksport SR HS; Orland, ME; (Y); Trk; Wrstlng; Hon Roll; LWYR.

CLEMENT, KEVIN; Bucksport HS; Bucksport, ME; (Y); 18/130; Pres 4-H; Varsity Clb; JV Crs Cntry; JV Var Ftbl; Var L Trk; Var L Wrstlng; 4-H Awd; Hon Roll; NHS; ME Schlrs Days 86; Natl 4-H Cngrss Chgo 86 & Washngton DC 87; Psychol.

CLIFFORD, KAREN L; Oxford Hills HS; Norway, ME; (Y); 8/217; Am Leg Aux Girls St; English Clb; Latin Clb; High Hon Roll; NHS; Ntl Merit SF; Pres Schlr; Publc TV Quiz Shw Statewide Wnnr 86; Bryn Mawr Coll; Pol Sci.

CLUFF, KELLY; Kennebunk Christian Acad; Kennebunk, ME; (Y); 1/4; Church Yth Grp; Drama Clb; Chorus; School Musical; Yrbk Ed-Chief; Pres Sr Cls; Co-Capt Bsktbl; Capt Cheerleading; High Hon Roll; Hon Roll; Hgst GPA Eng,Hist 85-86; Liberty U; Bus Adm.

COFFIN, BEVERLY; Bonny Eagle HS; Windham, ME; (Y); 7/235; Church Yth Grp; Latin Clb; Math Tm; Band; Church Choir; Stat Gym; High Hon Roll; Kiwanis Awd; NHS; Pres Schlr; U ME Orono; Pre-Med.

COGILL, SANDRA; Sacopee Valley HS; Limerick, ME; (Y); Band; Concert Band; Jazz Band; Mrchg Band; School Play; Stage Crew; JV Fld Hcky; Var Trk; VP Drama Clb; Vrsty Ltr In Trck; Western ME Band; Nmbrs In Fld Hcky; Plymouth ST NH; Prsnnl Mgr.

COHEN, STEPHEN; Lincoln Acad; Damariscotta, ME; (S); 5/150; French Clb; FBLA; JCL; Latin Clb; Math Clb; Math Tm; Variety Show; Bsktbl; Crs Cntry; Tennis.

COLE, KATHRINE A; Freeport HS; Freeport, ME; (Y); 4/70; Am Leg Aux Girls St; Drama Clb; School Musical; School Play; Yrbk Stf; Hon Roll; Sec NHS; JA; Math Tm; Band; Wellesley Bk Awd 85; Getting It Into Print-Writing Wrkshp Presenter 86; Breadloaf Yng Writers Conf 85; Colby Coll; Engl.

COLLINS, ANDREA; Mt Abram Regional HS; Strong, ME; (Y); 28/84; Drama Clb; Intnl Clb; Chorus; School Play; High Hon Roll; Hon Roll; Grls Dscssion Grp; Proj Grad, Prom Comm; Kennebec Vly Voc Tech; Nrsg.

COLLINS, LYNN; Westbrook HS; Westbrook, ME; (Y); Color Guard; U Of MA Farmington; Chld Ed.

COLLINS, MICHELLE; Deering HS; Portland, ME; (Y); 12/326; Spanish Clb; Band; Concert Band; Mrchg Band; High Hon Roll; Hon Roll; Spanish NHS; UMO ME Schlr 86; USM Frgn Lng Dy 2nd Pl 86; Intrprtr.

COLON, SILVIA; Fryeburg Acad; Chicato, IL; (Y); Cmnty Wkr; NFL; SADD; Varsity Clb; School Musical; School Play; Stu Cncl; Var Capt Cheerleading; Gym; Hon Roll; Schlrshp Fryeburg Acad 85-87; Corp Law.

COLUCCI, ANGELA; Westbrook HS; Westbrook, ME; (Y); Yrbk Stf; Pres Sr Cls; Bsktbl; Fld Hcky; Italn Heritg Schlrp 86; Mst Imprvd Defns Fld Hcky 86; U Southern ME; Bus Admin.

COMPTON, MARY; Mount Blue HS; East Wilton, ME; (Y); 3/196; Am Leg Aux Girls St; 4-H; Yrbk Stf; Capt L Cheerleading; 4-H Awd; High Hon Roll; NHS; Ntl Merit Ltr; Chorus; Jr NHS; Bowdoin Coll; Psych.

CONANT, KIMBERLY; Lewiston HS; Lewiston, ME; (Y); Intnl Clb; Yrbk Bus Mgr; Stat Bsktbl; Hon Roll.

CONARY, RICHARD; Bucksport HS; Ellsworth, ME; (Y); 12/135; French Clb; Varsity Clb; Stage Crew; Yrbk Bus Mgr; Yrbk Stf; Pres Sr Cls; Stu Cncl; JV Stat Crs Cntry; Stat Trk; Hon Roll; 2nd Pl Natnl Eclgy Postr Cont 83; Spencer Hartford Chem Awd 86; RI Schl Desgn; Arch.

CONDON, CHERIE; Freeport HS; Freeport, ME; (Y); Am Leg Aux Girls St; Pres French Clb; Band; Chorus; School Musical; Nwsp Stf; Stu Cncl; Var JV Fld Hcky; Internatl Order Rainbow For Girls Assembly Dist & Grand ST Offices Held; Humanities Clb-Sec.

CONLEY, KATHERINE; Deering HS; Portland, ME; (Y); 93/326; French Clb; Varsity Clb; Variety Show; Nwsp Rptr; Yrbk Stf; Pres Stu Cncl; Bsktbl; Capt Cheerleading; Tennis; Hon Roll; Mst Imprvd Chrldr 85; Bus.

CONNELL, ANGELA; Oxford Hills HS; So Paris, ME; (Y); 4-H; Office Aide; Yrbk Ed-Chief; Yrbk Sprt Ed; Yrbk Stf; JV Cheerleading; Hon Roll; Library Aide; Dance Marathon Key Clb 85; Spirit Awd Chrldng 85; Atheletic Schl Numerals & Cheering 85; Bus Mngmnt.

CONSALVO, MIA LYNN; Biddeford HS; Biddeford, ME; (Y); 6/300; Am Leg Aux Girls St; School Play; Stage Crew; Nwsp Ed-Chief; Nwsp Phtg; Nwsp Rptr; Nwsp Stf; Var Capt Crs Cntry; Var Trk; Pres NHS; Cousens Essay Fnlst 85-86; Pol Sci.

COOK, SHANA; Mt Blue HS; Farmington, ME; (Y); Ski Clb; Jazz Band; Yrbk Stf; JV Bsktbl; JV Fld Hcky; High Hon Roll; Hon Roll; Arch.

COOKSON, LYLA; Westbrook HS; Westbrook, ME; (Y); 10/192; French Clb; Band; Drm & Bgl; Mrchg Band; Yrbk Stf; Tennis; Hon Roll; NHS; Pres Schlr; Art Clb; Lions Clb Schlrshp 86; Bstn U; Engrng.

COOKSON, LYLE; Westbrook HS; Westbrook, ME; (Y); Boy Scts; Camp Fr Inc; Pep Clb; Spanish Clb; SADD; Acpl Chr; Band; Chorus; Concert Band; Drm & Bgl; Engrng.

COOPER, REBECCA SUZANNE; Saint Domincs Regional HS; Lewiston, ME; (Y); 1/70; Drama Clb; Hosp Aide; Key Clb; School Play; Trs Soph Cls; Hon Roll; Pres NHS; Chrgrphng St Doms Prod Cabret 85; Asstnt ME ST JR Miss Pgnt 83-85; Pre-Med.

COPP, DOREEN; Bucksport HS; Bucksport, ME; (Y); 21/125; Church Yth Grp; Drama Clb; 4-H; Girl Scts; Hosp Aide; Quiz Bowl; SADD; Thesps; Acpl Chr; Band; Northeastern U; Law.

COREAU, MICHELLE M; South Portland HS; South Portland, ME; (Y); 6/290; AFS; Am Leg Aux Girls St; Intnl Clb; Key Clb; Math Tm; Ed Yrbk Stf; Trk; High Hon Roll; Hon Roll; NHS; NSDAR Schlrshp 86; Colby Coll; Frnch.

COSSETTE, ANNETTE; Fryeburg Acad; Fryeburg, ME; (S); 6/150; Pres Church Yth Grp; Radio Clb; School Play; Yrbk Stf; Lit Mag; VP Frsh Cls; Mgr Socr; High Hon Roll; Hon Roll; NHS; Natl Engl Merit Awd 85-86; Intr Dsgn.

COTE, LAURIE; Old Town HS; Milford, ME; (Y); 15/250; Am Leg Aux Girls St; Ed Yrbk Stf; Rep Sr Cls; Trs Stu Cncl; JV Var Bsktbl; Mgr(s); Im Vllybl; Hon Roll; NHS; Art Clb; Typg II Awd 86; Husson College; Steno.

COULOMBE, TED; Oxford Hills HS; S Paris, ME; (Y); AFS; Boy Scts; French Clb; Latin Clb; Mgr Bsktbl; High Hon Roll; NHS.

COURANT, JAY; Leavitt Area HS; Greene, ME; (Y); 8/121; Band; High Hon Roll; Trs NHS; Capt Of X-Cntry & Alpine Ski Tms 85-86; Ntl Ski Patrl 86; Ntl Schlr/Athl Awd 86; U Of VT; Elec Engrng.

COURTEMANCHE, YVONNE; Skowhegan Area HS; Skowhegan, ME; (Y); Am Leg Aux Girls St; French Clb; High Hon Roll; Hon Roll; Pres NHS; St Schlr; Upwrd Bound 85-86; Wellesley.

COUSINEAU, KATHRYN; Westbrook HS; Raymond, ME; (Y); French Clb; Acpl Chr; Chorus; Mrchg Band; Swing Chorus; Symp Band; Nwsp Stf; Yrbk Stf; Rep Soph Cls; Pep Clb; ME All ST Music Fest 86; Lib Arts.

COUSINS, CALEB E; Narragnogus HS; Milbridge, ME; (Y); Am Leg Boys St; Chess Clb; Drama Clb; Math Clb; School Play; Stage Crew; High Hon Roll; Ntl Merit SF; Dartmouth; Engrg.

COUTURE, KIM; Gardiner Area HS; Gardiner, ME; (Y); Am Leg Aux Girls St; 4-H; French Clb; SADD; Varsity Clb; Band; Concert Band; Jazz Band; Mrchg Band; Yrbk Stf; U S ME; Acctnt.

CRABTREE, CHRIS; Morse HS; Bath, ME; (Y); Am Leg Boys St; Radio Clb; Temple Yth Grp; Im Vllybl; DAR Awd; Hon Roll; 1st Pl ME ST Sci Fair 85-86; Summr Inst Tech Course USM 85-86; Outstndng Achvt Econ 84-85; U PA; Law.

CRAGIN, CHRISTINE; Falmouth HS; Falmouth, ME; (Y); 3/103; French Clb; Leo Clb; Math Tm; Var Fld Hcky; Dnfth Awd; Hon Roll; Jr NHS; NHS; JA; Political Wkr; US Sen Page; Duke U; Biomed Engrng.

CRAIG, CHRIS; Telstar Regional HS; Bethel, ME; (Y); Boy Scts; Chess Clb; Church Yth Grp; Ski Clb; Spanish Clb; Bsbl; Castleton.

CRAIG, LORI; Ft Fairfield HS; Ft Fairfield, ME; (Y); Varsity Clb; Chorus; Sftbl; Trk; Hon Roll; Accntng.

CRAWFORD, DARREN; Deering HS; Portland, ME; (Y); French Clb; Latin Clb; Letterman Clb; Math Tm; Ski Clb; Ftbl; Hon Roll; U Of ME.

CRAWFORD, TARA; Morse HS; Woolwich, ME; (Y); Church Yth Grp; Radio Clb; Chorus; Variety Show; Var Swmmng; JV Tennis; Prfct Atten Awd; Exchng Stu Thrgh Nacel Mnth Of Aug 85; 2nd Pl Sci Fr Prjct 85; Cert Advcd Lfsvng & Wtr Sfty 86; Intl Stds.

CRONIN, JENNIFER; Cape Elizabeth HS; Cp Elizabeth, ME; (Y); Church Yth Grp; Drama Clb; Red Cross Aide; Spanish Clb; SADD; Varsity Clb; Yrbk Stf; Lit Mag; Capt Cheerleading; Capt Swmmng; Comm Art.

CRONKHITE, TRACY; Jay HS; Livermore Falls, ME; (Y); 5/86; Am Leg Aux Girls St; Office Aide; Ski Clb; Varsity Clb; Rep Soph Cls; Capt Crs Cntry; Capt Trk; High Hon Roll; Hon Roll; NHS; J Club Schlrshp 86; Coaches Trck Awd 86; Cmnty Schlrshp 86; U Of Southern ME; Nrsng.

CRONKRIGHT, DEWAYNE; Fort Fairfield HS; Ft Fairfield, ME; (Y); Chess Clb; Church Yth Grp; Band; Concert Band; Jazz Band; Mrchg Band; Pep Band; School Musical; Bsktbl; Hon Roll.

CROSBY, BONNIE; Lawrence HS; Waterville, ME; (Y); 34/225; Latin Clb; Sec Frsh Cls; L Trk; Hon Roll; Southern Maine Cov Tech; Arts.

CROWE, SHARON J; Mt Ararat Schl; Bailey Island, ME; (Y); 47/229; Chorus; Nwsp Rptr; Nwsp Stf; Sr Chorus Awd & Ltr Music 86; Secy, Clercl & Admin Awds 86; Prom Comm; Western ME Music Fest 86; Secy.

CRUZ, MARIO; Fryeburg Acad; Chicago, IL; (S); 9/126; Church Yth Grp; Political Wkr; Radio Clb; Science Clb; Spanish Clb; Orch; Ed Yrbk Stf; High Hon Roll; Hon Roll; NHS; DAR Molly Ockett Hstry Awd 85; Schl Fndtn Scholar 84-86; St Benedict Wrld Hstry & Geog Awd 3rd Pl 83.

CUNNINGHAM, ANGELA; Bangor HS; Bangor, ME; (Y); ROTC; Color Guard; Hon Roll; Map Rdng Awd ROTC 86; Gen D Mac Arthur Awd 86; Sup Cdt Awd ROTC 86; Nrsng.

CURRAN, RACHEL ANN; Caden-Rockport HS; Camden, ME; (Y); 15/143; Am Leg Aux Girls St; French Clb; Thesps; Chorus; Madrigals; School Musical; School Play; Stu Cncl; Hon Roll; Yrbk Stf; 1st Pl Clb Lvl Lions Clb Spk-Out, 2nd Pl Dist Lvl Lions Clb Spk-Out 86; Pltcl Sci.

CURTIS, NORMAN; Belfast Area HS; Belfast, ME; (Y); 5/121; Rep Am Leg Boys St; French Clb; Yrbk Ed-Chief; Yrbk Stf; Hon Roll; Jr NHS; NHS; Cmnty Wkr; Political Wkr; Nwsp Stf; Hugh O Brien Yth Semnr Delgt 84; Modl ST Legsltr 82 & 83; Excllnc Amercn Hstry Awd 86; Bates Coll; Poli Sci.

CUSHING, FRANK; Westbrook HS; Westbrook, ME; (Y); Latin Clb; Band; Concert Band; Jazz Band; Mrchg Band; Pep Band; Var L Ftbl; Var Trk; Wt Lftg; Var Capt Wrstlng; Acctng.

CUSHING, MICHELE; Washington Acad; Pembroke, ME; (Y); FHA; Yrbk Stf; Rep Jr Cls; JV Var Cheerleading; Prfct Attndnc; Secrtrl.

CUSHING, WEBBER; Bangor HS; Bangor, ME; (Y); Church Yth Grp; Y-Teens; Var Swmmng; Radio Comm.

CUSHMAN, DAPHNE; Hodgdon HS; Houlton, ME; (Y); 6/47; Am Leg Aux Girls St; Church Yth Grp; Pres SADD; School Musical; Yrbk Stf; Sec Sr Cls; Stu Cncl; Dnfth Awd; Drama Clb; Chorus; Blaine Hse Schlr 86; Sr Ctznshp Awd Miss ME Natl Tnagr Pgnt 86; U Of Sthrn ME; Elem Educ.

CUTTER, MARY; Edward Little HS; Auburn, ME; (S); AFS; Computer Clb; Off French Clb; Varsity Clb; Var L Cheerleading; JV Trk; Hon Roll; Coaches Awd Hockey Chrldr 85; Elem Educ.

CYR, ERIC; Van Buren District Secondary Schl; Van Buren, ME; (Y); 15/75; JV Bsktbl; Bowling; Var Tennis; High Hon Roll; Hon Roll; Sprtsmnshp JR Vrst Bsktbl 10th Grd 84; U Of Southern ME; Accntng.

CYR, KATHLEEN; Jay HS; Jay, ME; (Y); Var Sftbl; NHS; Bio.

CYR, LISA; Edward Little HS; Auburn, ME; (S); Church Yth Grp; Math Clb; Varsity Clb; Var L Cheerleading; Sftbl; Hon Roll; Chld Psych.

CYR, MARK; Fort Kent Community HS; Ft Kent, ME; (Y); 1/145; Am Leg Boys St; Quiz Bowl; Yrbk Phtg; Pres Frsh Cls; VP Stu Cncl; Im Vllybl; Cit Awd; Trs NHS; Val; Sci Stdy Schlrshp 86; NHS Schlrshp 86; ME Scndry Schl Prncpls Assn Awd 86; U Of VT; Bio.

D AUTEUIL JR, DANIEL; St Dominics Regional HS; Lewiston, ME; (Y); 22/80; French Clb; Variety Show; Var L Ice Hcky; Var L Socr; Im Vllybl; Im Wt Lftg; Hon Roll; NHS; Pres Acad Fitness Awd 86; Most Outstndg Defnsmn St Of ME 86; All Schlstc All St Hockey Allstar 86; St Anselms; Pre Law.

DAIGLE, GINGER; Community HS; Winterville, ME; (Y); 71/145; Church Yth Grp; Pres FHA; SADD; Varsity Clb; Var Mgr(s); JV Var Score Keeper; 4-H Awd; Upward Bound Stu 85 & 86; Upward Bound Smmr Exchg Stu To CO 86; History.

DAIGLE, GLENN; Ft Kent Community HS; Fort Kent, ME; (Y); Am Leg Boys St; Church Yth Grp; Band; Yrbk Phtg; Stu Cncl; L Var Socr; Var L Tennis; Cit Awd; Hon Roll; NHS; Engrng.

DAIGLE, MITZI; Fort Kent Community HS; Fort Kent, ME; (Y); 11/142; Am Leg Aux Girls St; SADD; Band; Church Choir; Concert Band; Mrchg Band; Rep Soph Cls; Rep Jr Cls; Var Bsktbl; Var Socr; Outstndng Undrcls Female Athlt 85; Ft Kents JR Miss 86; Westbrook Coll; Sys Anal.

DAIGLE, PAUL; Fort Kent Community HS; Ft Kent, ME; (Y); 9/151; Capt Ski Clb; SADD; Varsity Clb; Trs Frsh Cls; Trs Sr Cls; Var Socr; Var Tennis; High Hon Roll; St Schlr; Church Yth Grp; Pres Lcl Ntl Hon Soc Chptr 85-86; Treas Sec Rgnl Ntl Hon Soc 85-86; Ctznshp Awd 85; Syracuse U; Elec Engrng.

DAIGLE, ROBERT; Community HS; Fort Kent, ME; (Y); 2/145; Am Leg Boys St; Sec Church Yth Grp; Scholastic Bowl; Nwsp Rptr; Lit Mag; VP Jr Cls; Pres Sr Cls; Wrstlng; High Hon Roll; VP NHS; MSAD 27 Wrtng Cntst Wnnr 85; Keene ST Coll; Engl.

DAMERON, SHEILAGH; Lee Academy HS; Lee, ME; (Y); Am Leg Aux Girls St; Cmnty Wkr; Math Tm; Varsity Clb; Chorus; School Musical; School Play; Stu Cncl; Var Socr; Hon Roll; U Of ME; Psych.

DARBY, CONNIE; Edward Little HS; Auburn, ME; (S); Math Tm; Spanish Clb; High Hon Roll; Lang.

DARLING, DAVID; Cape Elizabeth HS; Cape Elizabeth, ME; (Y); Church Yth Grp; Cmnty Wkr; SADD; Varsity Clb; JV Ice Hcky; Var L Socr; Var L Tennis; Hon Roll; Math.

DAVENPORT, LISA; Ft Fairfield HS; Ft Fairfield, ME; (Y); 17/68; Rep French Clb; SADD; Varsity Clb; Chorus; Pres Soph Cls; Pres Jr Cls; Capt Bsktbl; L Socr; Capt Sftbl; Hon Roll; JR Exhbtn Awd; Prfct Attndnc; Cmmnctns.

DAVIS, GLENN; Lewiston HS; Lewiston, ME; (Y); Key Clb; Letterman Clb; Ski Clb; L Bsbl; Var Capt Socr; Hon Roll; Jr NHS; All SMAA Bsbl Leag & MVP Bsbl Sccr 86; Hstry.

DAVIS, MATTHEW; Edward Little HS; Auburn, ME; (Y); Drama Clb; 4-H; Latin Clb; Band; Concert Band; Jazz Band; Mrchg Band; Symp Band; Variety Show; High Hon Roll.

DAVIS III, RAY H; Bucksport HS; E Orland, ME; (Y); Am Leg Boys St; Crs Cntry; Hon Roll.

DAVIS, STUART; Nokomis Regional HS; Corinna, ME; (Y); 33/172; French Clb; Political Wkr; Varsity Clb; Band; Mrchg Band; Symp Band; Stu Cncl; JV Bsktbl; Var Capt Golf; Prfct Atten Awd; Hofstra U; Law.

DAY, ERIC; Deering HS; Portland, ME; (Y); 100/235; Debate Tm; Library Aide; Office Aide; ROTC; SADD; Yrbk Stf; Stu Cncl; Hon Roll; Pres Schlr; Voice Dem Awd; Asstg In Plnng & Opertns Of 1st ME Acdmc Decthln; Schlrshp Priv Pilots Licns; Data Proc.

DE GRINNEY, CAROLYN; St Dominics Regional HS; Livermore Falls, ME; (Y); Hosp Aide; Keywanettes; VP Sr Cls; Rep Stu Cncl; Var Capt Bsktbl; Var L Fld Hcky; Var L Sftbl; Capt Tennis; Dnfth Awd; Hon Roll; Soclgy.

DE LONG, DONNA L; Deering HS; Portland, ME; (Y); 2/285; Am Leg Aux Girls St; Drama Clb; Math Tm; Capt Pom Pon; Ntl Merit SF; Sal; St Schlr; ST Sci Fair 2nd Pl 85; Yale Bk Awd 85; Acadmc Decathln Tm 85-86; Chemcl Engrng.

DE LONG, TRUDY LYNN; Ashland Community HS; Ashland, ME; (Y); Am Leg Aux Girls St; Band; Pres Soph Cls; Pres Jr Cls; Stu Cncl; Var Capt Bsktbl; Var Capt Socr; High Hon Roll; Hon Roll; NHS; Mdl ST Leg 84-87; Coll Band 86; Aeronautical Engrng.

DEBLOIS, PAM; Lewiston HS; Lewiston, ME; (Y); Varsity Clb; Off Soph Cls; Fld Hcky; Sftbl; High Hon Roll; Jr NHS; NHS; Boston U; Med.

DECROW, TARA; Catherine Mc Auley HS; Windham, ME; (Y); 25/85; VP Soph Cls; Stu Cncl; Var Bsktbl; JV Cheerleading; JV Fld Hcky; Var Sftbl; Hon Roll; Art Hist.

DELAWARE, STACEY; Scarborough HS; Scarborough, ME; (Y); 9/110; Am Leg Aux Girls St; Sec French Clb; Key Clb; Science Clb; VP SADD; Pres Band; Pep Band; Yrbk Stf; Trs NHS; ME Sec Schl Prin Assoc Awd 86; Southern ME Mus Fest 85; Rgis Coll Weston MA; Pol Sci.

DEMERS, DAWN; Bonny Eagle HS; W Buxton, ME; (Y); 26/206; Drama Clb; Latin Clb; Ski Clb; Spanish Clb; Varsity Clb; Acpl Chr; Chorus; School Musical; School Play; Swing Chorus; Marymant Coll; Intl Bus.

DENIS, MICHAEL; Lawrence HS; Fairfield, ME; (Y); Math Tm; Spanish Clb; Hon Roll; WCSH TV Ch 6 Outstndg Knwldg Crrnt Evnts 83-84; Bus.

DENISON, DAVID; Telstar Regional HS; Bethel, ME; (Y); 19/62; Am Leg Boys St; Jazz Band; Variety Show; CC Awd; Cit Awd; Order Eagles Schlrshp 86; Balfour Music Awd 86; Drew U; Comp Sci.

DESCHENES, SUZANNE M; St Dominic Reg HS; Lewiston, ME; (Y); 1/67; Drama Clb; Pres French Clb; Co-Capt Math Clb; High Hon Roll; Pres NHS; Ntl Merit Ltr; Val; Qn Of Franco-Amer Fstvl 84; Holy Cross Bk Prz 85; Spcl Schltc/Co Crrclr Trphy 86; College Of The Holy Cross; Bio.

DESCOUTEAUX, ERNESTO; Cheverus HS; Cumberland, ME; (Y); Chess Clb; Church Yth Grp; Key Clb; Ski Clb; Stage Crew; Im Bsktbl; JV Crs Cntry; Im Ftbl; Im Vllybl; JV Wrstlng.

DESJARDINS, DONNA M; Fort Kent Community HS; Fort Kent, ME; (Y); Am Leg Aux Girls St; Teachers Aide; Varsity Clb; Yrbk Sprt Ed; Yrbk Stf; Trs Jr Cls; Var L Socr; Var L Sftbl; Vllybl; 1st N ME Wrtg Cntst Drama 84; Basc Resc And Advncd Lifesavg High Hnrs 84-85; Rehab Cnslng.

DESJARDINS, RACHEL; Fort Kent Community HS; Ft Kent, ME; (Y); Hon Roll; SAD Schlrshp 86; Schlrshp Cert Of Hnr 86; Cert Of Hnr Englsh 86; U Of ME Ft Kent; Behvrl Sci.

DEVOID, MARC A; Sanford HS; Sanford, ME; (Y); 85/217; Sec Chess Clb; Church Yth Grp; French Clb; Key Clb; Coach Actv; Score Keeper; Hon Roll; Schlrshps From Shaws Sprmrkt, Sanford Fire Dept Ladies Aux, S G Ricker & M Watson 86; St Anselm Coll; Lib Arts.

DIBIASE, SUZIE; South Portland HS; S Portland, ME; (Y); Am Leg Aux Girls St; Trs VP Key Clb; Service Clb; Ski Clb; Off Frsh Cls; Var Cheerleading; Tennis; Journalist.

DICKENS JR, JOHN D; Cony HS; Augusta, ME; (Y); 16/300; Chess Clb; Computer Clb; JCL; Crs Cntry; Hon Roll; 3rd Plc Awd HS ST Indvdl Chs Chmp 86; Magna Cum Laude Natl JCL Tst 84-86; Med.

DIFFIN, ANGELA; Woodland HS; Princeton, ME; (Y); Am Leg Aux Girls St; Church Yth Grp; Letterman Clb; Varsity Clb; Yrbk Stf; Stu Cncl; Var L Cheerleading; Var Mgr(s); Stat Socr; Var Timer; Bio Awd-Hghst Avg 84-85; Pierres Beauty Schl; Csmtlgy.

DILL, SHERRI; Lee Acad; Lee, ME; (Y); AFS; Rep Am Leg Aux Girls St; Pres Church Yth Grp; French Clb; Latin Clb; Yrbk Stf; Cheerleading; Score Keeper; High Hon Roll; Brigham Young U; Psych.

DILL, VALERIE; Lee Acad; Lee, ME; (Y); Am Leg Aux Girls St; Letterman Clb; Math Tm; Sec Soph Cls; VP Jr Cls; Var L Bsktbl; Var L Socr; Var L Sftbl; High Hon Roll; NHS.

DINSMORE JR, MEL; Georges Valley HS; Thomaston, ME; (Y); Science Clb; Ski Clb; Var Trk; Law Enfrcmnt.

DIRKMAN, JOHN; Skowhegan Area HS; Skowhegan, ME; (Y); 8/250; Drama Clb; Math Tm; Band; School Play; Lit Mag; Tennis; Trk; High Hon Roll; Ntl Merit SF; Latin I Awd 85; Engrg.

DIXON, DAVID; Mt Abram HS; Farmington, ME; (Y); 1/88; Am Leg Boys St; SADD; Jazz Band; VP Stu Cncl; Bsktbl; High Hon Roll; Debate Tm; Drama Clb; Pep Clb; Exchg Stu To Yugoslavia 86; Colby Coll Bk Awd 86; Hugh Obrien Yth Fndtn & ME Schlrs Day 85-86; US Naval Acad; Bio Sci.

DOBBIN, KATHRYN; Jonesport-Beals HS; Jonesport, ME; (Y); 5/35; Drama Clb; Sec French Clb; Yrbk Sprt Ed; Stu Cncl; Bsktbl; JV Cheerleading; Sftbl; Vllybl; Hon Roll; NHS; U Of Southern ME; Psych.

DOBENS, KRISTINA; Edward Little HS; Mechanic Falls, ME; (Y); 80/354; Hosp Aide; Latin Clb; Varsity Clb; Sftbl; Tennis; Andover; Accntng.

DODD, SHANNON; Bonny Eagle HS; Steep Fls, ME; (Y); JA; JV Bsktbl; JV Cheerleading; Capt JV Fld Hcky; Capt JV Sftbl; Hon Roll.

DOHERTY, COURTNEY; Catherine Mc Auley HS; Freeport, ME; (Y); 36/74; Cmnty Wkr; Drama Clb; Hosp Aide; Key Clb; School Play; Nwsp Stf; Rep Frsh Cls; Rep Soph Cls; Rep Jr Cls; Rep Sr Cls; Merit Awd Alg II 86; Merit Awd Stu Govt 86; UVM; Bio.

DOHERTY, ERIN; Wells HS; Wells, ME; (Y); JA; Rep Stu Cncl; Score Keeper; Hon Roll; Prfct Atten Awd; Prfct Hnr Roll Awd 84; Prfct Atten Awd 84-85; Ed.

DOIRON, PAMELA; Waynflete Schl; Scarborough, ME; (Y); Dance Clb; VP French Clb; VP JA; School Musical; Lit Mag; Pres Frsh Cls; Hon Roll; Cmnty Wkr; Drama Clb; School Play; Sch Rep Portland Exprs News 83-84; Wmns Lit Union 85-86; Jordan Marsh Jr Advsry Cncl 85-87; Advrtsg.

DOLAN, MARGARET ELIZABETH; Old Orchard Beach HS; Old Orchard Beach, ME; (Y); 12/90; Am Leg Aux Girls St; Drama Clb; English Clb; Ski Clb; Speech Tm; Stage Crew; JV Fld Hcky; L Capt Trk; High Hon Roll; Hon Roll; Track Captn Awd 85; Field Hockey Athletic Achvt Awd 85; Phrmclgy.

DONATELLI, LUANA; Catherine Mc Auley HS; Portland, ME; (Y); 32/76; Key Clb; Latin Clb; Nwsp Rptr; Lit Mag; Mgr Bsktbl; Crs Cntry; Mgr(s); Trk; Wrtg Awd Schl Newspr 83-85; Outstndng Awd Musc 84-85; St Anselms; Psychtry.

DONNELLY, MICHAEL W; Caribou HS; Caribou, ME; (S); Band; Concert Band; Mrchg Band; Var Crs Cntry; Var Trk; Hon Roll; U Of Southern ME; Bio.

DONOVAN, PAULINE; Deering HS; Portland, ME; (Y); 41/321; Church Yth Grp; French Clb; Latin Clb; Bsktbl; Sftbl; Hon Roll; NHS; Frnch Natl Tst Levl I-II 85-86; Rx Tech Traing Occptn 85-86; Pharm.

DOOLAN, LAWRENE AGNES; Belfast Area HS; Morrill, ME; (Y); Am Leg Aux Girls St; French Clb; Var Bsktbl; Var Trk; High Hon Roll; Farmington; Tchg.

DORION, TOM; Morse HS; Bath, ME; (Y); Am Leg Boys St; Church Yth Grp; Cmnty Wkr; Radio Clb; Var L Bsktbl; Var Capt Socr; Im Vllybl; Hon Roll.

DOUDEY, CRYSTAL; Calais HS; Calais, ME; (Y); Pres Church Yth Grp; Teachers Aide; Church Choir; Hon Roll; Psych.

DOUGHERTY, JOHN; Marshwood HS; Eliot, ME; (Y); 6/140; Church Yth Grp; Math Clb; Math Tm; Pres Spanish Clb; Rep Frsh Cls; Rep Soph Cls; Rep Jr Cls; JV Bsktbl; Var Capt Coach Actv; Var Trk; Cum Laude Natl Latn Exm 84; Regnl Jr Olympcs Crss Cntry 85; 1st SYSSA 2 Mile 86; Ecnmcs.

DOUGHTY, PATRICIA L; Woodland HS; Baileyville, ME; (Y); 3/48; FBLA; SADD; Chorus; Yrbk Ed-Chief; VP Sr Cls; Vllybl; High Hon Roll; NHS; Prfct Atten Awd; 1st Pl Regnl Typng I,Adv Typng Cntst 84-86; 3rd Pl Regnl Bus Math 86; U MEZ; Mgmt.

DOW, ERIN; Wells HS; Wells, ME; (Y); Yrbk Stf; Stu Cncl; Mgr Bsktbl; Sftbl; Hon Roll; Ntl Merit Ltr; Cert Of Achvt Rcgntn Prtcptn Mntgmry Cnty Flm Fstvl MD Sgn Lang Pres Ftnss Awd 80-84; Savannah Coll; Photo.

DOW, STEPHEN; Marshwood HS; Eliot, ME; (Y); Math Tm; Hon Roll; Pilot.

DOWNEY, LAURA; Orono HS; Orono, ME; (S); 2/115; Am Leg Aux Girls St; Drama Clb; French Clb; School Musical; School Play; Yrbk Bus Mgr; Yrbk Stf; Lit Mag; High Hon Roll; NHS; Awds For Achvmnt Engl & Soc Stds 83-85.

DOWNEY, PATRICK; Freeport HS; Freeport, ME; (Y); 1/69; Math Tm; Ed Yrbk Ed-Chief; VP Frsh Cls; Pres Jr Cls; Sec Sr Cls; Hon Roll; Val; U ME Orono; Pol Sci.

DOYLE, BRENDAN; Cony HS; Augusta, ME; (Y); AFS; Am Leg Boys St; JCL; Latin Clb; Ski Clb; Yrbk Bus Mgr; Hon Roll; Prfct Atten Awd; Holy Cross Bk Awd 85-86; JCL Ntl Latin Test 83-86; Congrsln Rep Am Leg Boys ST 86; Holy Cross; Law.

DREHER, RUSSELL; Georges Valley HS; Thomaston, ME; (Y); 3/70; Am Leg Boys St; Boy Scts; Pres Thesps; Band; Yrbk Ed-Chief; Stu Cncl; Hon Roll; NHS; Pres Drama Clb; Trs Intnl Clb; Thomaston Amblnc Svc Vol 86; Colby Coll Bk Awd 86; 1st Pl ST Sci Fair Physcs 86; Pre-Med.

DRISKO, ARTHUR A; Scarborough HS; Scarborough, ME; (Y); 1/120; Am Leg Boys St; JCL; Latin Clb; Math Tm; School Play; Nwsp Rptr; Var Capt Crs Cntry; Var Capt Trk; NHS; Ntl Merit SF; U S Acad Decthln Scholar; Century III Ldrs ST Fin; HOBY Fndtn ST Sem; Mth.

DUANE III, HERBERT TOBIAS; Fryeburg Acad; Braintree, MA; (Y); Ski Clb; SADD; Yrbk Stf; Socr; Dorm Proctor 86-87; Dorm Cncl 85-86 & 86-87; Business.

DUBE, EDWARD; Ashland Community HS; Portage Lake, ME; (Y); Am Leg Boys St; Band; Concert Band; Pep Band; Var Bsbl; Var Capt Socr; Dnfth Awd; High Hon Roll; Hon Roll; Schl Imprvmt Tm 86-87; Thomas Coll; Acctg.

DUBORD, GINA; Livermore Falls HS; East Livermore, ME; (Y); 13/82; Varsity Clb; Color Guard; Var Cheerleading; Hon Roll; NHS; Wilma Boyd Career Schl; Travel.

DUCHARME, DERRICK; Lewiston HS; Lewiston, ME; (Y); Hon Roll; Achvt Awd Enlg 83-84; U Southern CA; Flm.

DUCHETTE, MARC; St Dominic RHS HS; Lewiston, ME; (Y); 16/79; Pres Jr Cls; Pres Sr Cls; Var Capt Bsbl; Var Capt Ice Hcky; Var Capt Socr; Hon Roll; Trs NHS; Hugh O Brian Ldrshp; Colby Coll; Bio.

DUDLEY, JULI-ANN; Cony HS; Augusta, ME; (Y); 19/325; Am Leg Aux Girls St; French Clb; Spanish Clb; Trs Variety Show; JV Var Fld Hcky; Cit Awd; High Hon Roll; Hon Roll; Pres Schlr; St Schlr; Itaca Coll; Psychlgy.

DUDLEY, SHANNON; Woodland HS; Waite, ME; (Y); FBLA; Library Aide; Hon Roll; Beautcn.

DUEMLER, KRISTIN; Fryeburg Acad; Ctr Lovell, ME; (Y); Camera Clb; Church Yth Grp; Library Aide; SADD; Band; Chorus; Yrbk Phtg; Trk; Hon Roll; NHS; Chamberlayne JC; Fshn Mrchndsg.

DUGUAY, LAURA; Rumford HS; Rumford, ME; (Y); 7/126; Cmnty Wkr; Drama Clb; French Clb; FHA; Office Aide; SADD; Hon Roll; NHS; St Schlr; Voice Dem Awd; FHA Scholar 86; Le Paresseux Scholar 86; Top 10 Stu Awd 86; Palm Beach JC; Paralgl.

DUHL, KEVIN; Lawrence HS; Fairfield, ME; (Y); Church Yth Grp; Cmnty Wkr; Pres French Clb; FTA; Pep Clb; Teachers Aide; Nwsp Stf; Cheerleading; Hon Roll; Hghst Hnrs French; Excllnce Engl Awd; U Of ME Farmington; Elem Ed.

DUKES, TOM; Mount Blue HS; Temple, ME; (Y); Am Leg Boys St; Latin Clb; Math Tm; Science Clb; Spanish Clb; Variety Show; L Capt Wrstlng; High Hon Roll; NHS; Ntl Merit SF; Exobiolgst.

DUMOND, NATALIE; Van Buren District Secondary Schl; Lille, ME; (Y); 10/72; Am Leg Aux Girls St; Drm Mjr(t); Variety Show; Rep Stu Cncl; JV Capt Cheerleading; Twrlr; Pedtrc Nrs.

DUMONT, BRIAN; Sanford HS; Sanford, ME; (Y); 39/225; Am Leg Boys St; Boy Scts; Drama Clb; Ski Clb; Chorus; Church Choir; School Musical; Rep Stu Cncl; Hon Roll; NHS; St Anselm Coll.

DUNCAN III, LAWRENCE; Cheverus HS; Brunswick, ME; (Y); 10/90; Am Leg Boys St; Debate Tm; Drama Clb; VP Key Clb; Nwsp Ed-Chief; Yrbk Ed-Chief; Im Bsktbl; NHS; Ntl Merit Schol; Acad All Am 84-85; Georgetown U; Pol Sci.

DUNHAM, TERI; Gorham HS; Gorham, ME; (Y); Debate Tm; GAA; Ski Clb; Spanish Clb; Chorus; Im Bsktbl; Var Cheerleading; Var Tennis; Spanish NHS; U Southern ME; Bus.

DUNN, LORNA I; Buckfield JR SR HS; Buckfield, ME; (Y); 6/39; Art Clb; Drama Clb; German Clb; Stage Crew; Yrbk Stf; Var Capt Socr; Trs NHS; VP Church Yth Grp; Letterman Clb; Math Tm; Blaine Hse Schlr 86; Bucks Agnst Drunk Drvng BADD VP 86; Bst All Rnd Grmn Stu; Grmn Exch Stu; Emmanuel Coll; Art Ther.

DUNN, MARY; Houlton HS; Houlton, ME; (Y); 15/145; Camera Clb; Church Yth Grp; Math Clb; SADD; Bowling; Mgr(s); Socr; Tennis; Capt Vllybl; Hon Roll; 1st Single ST Ten 86; Vllybl Champs Schl Capt 84 & 86; 1st Bowler Schl 86; Springfield Coll; Rehab.

DUNTON III, WAYNE; Gorham HS; Gorham, ME; (Y); Computer Clb; High Hon Roll; Hon Roll; Chem Awd; Engl Awd; Sci & Hstry; Mltry.

DUPUIS, CINDY; Fryeburg Acad; Fryeburg, ME; (Y); FHA; Library Aide; SADD; School Play.

DURGIN, MARK; Edward Little HS; Auburn, ME; (Y); Cmnty Wkr; Debate Tm; Band; Concert Band; Jazz Band; Mrchg Band; Var Crs Cntry; Var L Trk; High Hon Roll; Hon Roll; Lyndon Coll Vermont; Meteorolgy.

DURGIN, WENDY; Windham HS; S Casco, ME; (Y); 4/175; Church Yth Grp; Math Tm; Rep Frsh Cls; Rep Soph Cls; Rep Jr Cls; Rep Sr Cls; JV Var Bsktbl; Var Fld Hcky; Jr NHS; NHS; Lylty Awd Vrsty Ldy Eagles Bsktbl Tm 85-86; Dlctrc Cmnctns Schlrshp 86; Gould/Pt Sebago Schlrshp 86; Bentley Coll; Acctg.

DUROST, ANTHONY TODD; Central Aroostook HS; Mars Hill, ME; (Y); 8/50; Church Yth Grp; Crs Cntry; High Hon Roll; Prfct Atten Awd; Achvt Awd HS Acadmcs 85-86; Apostolic Bible Inst St Paul.

DUROST, EDITH; Boothbay Region HS; Boothbay Harbor, ME; (Y); 8/59; Church Yth Grp; Science Clb; Varsity Clb; Jazz Band; Yrbk Stf; Var Capt Trk; Var Vllybl; High Hon Roll; Hon Roll; NHS; Cedarville Coll; Pre-Med.

DURRELL, ANGELA; Westbrook HS; Westbrook, ME; (Y); Drama Clb; English Clb; Office Aide; SADD; School Musical; Stage Crew; Nwsp Ed-Chief; Nwsp Rptr; Lit Mag; NHS; All-Star Cst Awd ME ST Drama Fstvl 86; Coll Clb Of Prtlnd Schlrshp 86; RSST Schlrshp 85; U Of ME Orono; Eng.

DYER, DALE; Portland HS; Portland, ME; (Y); Latin Clb; Spanish Clb; Rep Soph Cls; Var Trk; Im Vllybl; Im Wt Lftg; Hon Roll; ME Maritime Acad; Engrng.

DYER, VICKI; Catherine Mc Auley HS; Portland, ME; (Y); 29/59; Sec French Clb; Key Clb; Yrbk Stf; Trs Soph Cls; Trs Jr Cls; Trs Sr Cls; Var Capt Cheerleading; Var Trk; Hon Roll; Frnch, Typng Awds; All Amer; Katherine Gibbs; Sec.

EASTMAN, AMY; Central Aroostook HS; Mars Hill, ME; (Y); Church Yth Grp; Pres French Clb; Varsity Clb; Church Choir; Rep Stu Cncl; Var L Bsktbl; Var L Socr; Var L Sftbl; Hon Roll; Pres NHS; Frgn Lang.

EASTWOOD, SUSAN; Deering HS; Portland, ME; (Y); 73/327; Sec Letterman Clb; Varsity Clb; Var Capt Bsktbl; JV Fld Hcky; Var Trk.

EATON, CARRIE; Mt Blue HS; Farmington, ME; (Y); SADD; JV Bsktbl; Timer; Hon Roll; Prfct Atten Awd; U ME Farmington; Bus Mgt.

ECKENROAD, KIMBERLEY ANNE; Sumner Memorial HS; W Gouldsboro, ME; (Y); 24/87; Am Leg Aux Girls St; 4-H; Yrbk Bus Mgr; Pres Jr Cls; Sec Sr Cls; Rep Stu Cncl; Bsktbl; Socr; Sftbl; Cit Awd; I Dare You Awd 86; West Gouldsboro Vlg Imp Schlrshp 86; U ME Machias; Sec.

EDGECOMB, MARK; Bucksport HS; Bucksport, ME; (Y); Varsity Clb; Ftbl; Trk; Wt Lftg; Hon Roll.

EGERS, KEVIN; Gorham HS; Gorham, ME; (Y); Church Yth Grp; Drama Clb; Swmmng; Trk; Vllybl; Hon Roll; Vet.

EISENHART, JOHN A; Deering HS; Portland, ME; (Y); Boys Clb Am; Cmnty Wkr; Letterman Clb; Political Wkr; Var L Bsbl; JV Ftbl; Var L Swmmng; Ram Awd Swmg 86; ME Maritime; Dntstry.

ELA, DWAYNE; Fryeburg Acad; Fryeburg, ME; (Y); French Clb; Latin Clb; Science Clb; Ski Clb; SADD; Varsity Clb; Bsbl; Crs Cntry; Socr; Wt Lftg.

ELDRED, CHRISTINE; Bangor HS; Bangor, ME; (Y); Cmnty Wkr; Hosp Aide; Lit Mag; Hon Roll; Ntl Merit Ltr; Marine Summr Humnities Pgm Gftd & Talntd 86; Breadloaf New England Yng Wrtrs Conf 86; Eng.

ELDRED, GAIL; Bangor HS; Bangor, ME; (Y); Mrchg Band; High Hon Roll; NHS; Ntl Merit Ltr; Bowdian Hmnts Pgm 86; Marlboro; Intl Studies.

ELLSMORE, TRACY C; Machias Memorial HS; Machias, ME; (Y); 5/50; Cmnty Wkr; Math Tm; School Play; Pres Frsh Cls; Pres Soph Cls; Sec Jr Cls; VP Sr Cls; Cheerleading; Cit Awd; DAR Awd; Prncpls Awd 86; Chairmn Drug Free And Alchl Free Grad 86; Delia Hougton Awd 86; U Of ME Orono; Psych.

ELOWITCH, DAVID; Portland HS; Portland, ME; (Y); 8/256; Math Clb; Math Tm; Ski Clb; Temple Yth Grp; Off Jr Cls; Off Sr Cls; Capt Var Ftbl; Capt Var Wrstlng; Hon Roll; Bus.

ELWELL, ELIZABETH; Belfast Area HS; Belfast, ME; (Y); Church Yth Grp; Drama Clb; Chorus; Color Guard; Drill Tm; School Musical; School Play; Stage Crew; Variety Show; Cheerleading; Finlst Miss Maine Natl Tn Pagnt 84; Nursing.

ELY, CHRISTINE; Cape Elizabeth HS; Cp Elizabeth, ME; (Y); French Clb; Capt FBLA; Concert Band; JV Bsktbl; Hon Roll.

EMERSON, GREGORY; Jonesport-Beals HS; Jonesport, ME; (Y); Elec Engr.

EMERY, LARA E; Oxford Hills HS; W Paris, ME; (Y); Am Leg Aux Girls St; Debate Tm; Girl Scts; NFL; Sec Band; Chorus; Jazz Band; Orch; Hon Roll; Voice Dem Awd; Lib Arts.

ENRIGHT, SHAWN; Greenville HS; Greenville, ME; (Y); Band; Concert Band; Mrchg Band; School Musical; School Play; Yrbk Stf; Rep Stu Cncl; Var Crs Cntry; Var Socr; Var L Trk; Acdmc Achvmnt Awd 86; Embry Riddle; Aero Sci.

ERICKSON, STASIA W; Caribou HS; Caribou, ME; (Y); French Clb; Hosp Aide; VP Ski Clb; SADD; Yrbk Sprt Ed; Yrbk Stf; JV L Bsktbl; Var Socr; Var L Sftbl; Im Var Vllybl; U Sthrn ME; Bus Adm.

ESTABROOK, KEVIN; Yarmouth HS; Yarmouth, ME; (Y); Chess Clb; French Clb; JA; Science Clb; Ski Clb; Nwsp Ed-Chief; Nwsp Phtg; Nwsp Rptr; Yrbk Phtg; Yrbk Stf; Sociolgy.

EVANS, JILL; Fort Fairfield HS; Ft Fairfield, ME; (Y); 2/70; Am Leg Aux Girls St; French Clb; Ski Clb; SADD; Varsity Clb; Band; Jazz Band; Trs Soph Cls; Trs Jr Cls; Trs Sr Cls; Englsh, US Hstry, Antmy & Physlgy Awds; U Of ME Orono; Comm Dsrdrs.

EVANS, KATHI; Bonny Eagle HS; Sebago Lake, ME; (Y); Chorus; Real Est.

EVERETT, EARLA; Caribou HS; Caribou, ME; (Y); 83/185; Girl Scts; Stu Cncl; Var Capt Cheerleading; Hon Roll; Mansfield Beauty Schl; Beauticn.

EVERS, JOHN; Lawrence HS; Waterville, ME; (Y); VP Key Clb; Pres Jr Cls; Pres Sr Cls; Var Capt Bsktbl; Var L Ftbl; High Hon Roll; Hon Roll; NHS; Mltry Acad; Chmcl Engrng.

FAHY, THOMAS; Marshwood HS; S Berwick, ME; (Y); 5/125; Math Tm; Yrbk Ed-Chief; Yrbk Stf; Hon Roll; NHS; Ntl Merit Ltr; Biotech.

FALLAN, JOSEPH D; North Yarmouth Acad; Gardiner, ME; (Y); 4-H; Yrbk Phtg; Ice Hcky; Lcrss; Socr; Hon Roll; Arch.

FALLONA, CATHERINE; Cony HS; Augusta, ME; (Y); 27/300; Am Leg Aux Girls St; French Clb; Q&S; Yrbk Bus Mgr; Pres Frsh Cls; JV Capt Fld Hcky; L Trk; Hon Roll; Top 10% Of Class 84-85; Bus Mgt.

FALLONA, KAREN; Cony HS; Augusta, ME; (Y); 24/300; Am Leg Aux Girls St; JCL; Latin Clb; Yrbk Ed-Chief; Stu Cncl; Var L Fld Hcky; Trk; Hon Roll; Cony Schlr 84-85.

FARNSWORTH, KEVIN LEE; Narraguagus HS; Jefferson, OH; (Y); 6/66; Am Leg Boys St; Aud/Vis; Computer Clb; Drama Clb; Math Tm; Stage Crew; High Hon Roll; Chess Clb; Church Yth Grp; Mgr(s); ME Schlrs Dy 85; Ntl Hnr Soc Pres 85-86; Amrcn Lgn Axlry Schlrshp 86; OH ST U; Elec Engnrng.

FARR, JULIE; Catherine Mc Auley HS; Portland, ME; (Y); 6/74; Key Clb; Science Clb; SADD; Lit Mag; VP Jr Cls; Sec Sr Cls; Stat Var Bsktbl; Hon Roll; NHS; Church Yth Grp; Williams Coll Bk Awd 85-86; Marn Bio.

FARRAR, MARC; Edward Little HS; Poland Spgs, ME; (Y); Socr; Hon Roll; Latin Clb; Ski Clb; Varsity Clb; Crs Cntry; Prfct Atten Awd; Enviromental Design.

FELLIS, KIMBERLY J; Ellsworth SR HS; Ellsworth, ME; (Y); 5/129; AFS; Am Leg Aux Girls St; French Clb; Letterman Clb; Office Aide; Teachers Aide; Varsity Clb; Yrbk Stf; Rep Jr Cls; Rep Stu Cncl; Outstndng Fld Prfrmr 85; Advrtsng.

FERNALD, WENDY; Narraguagus HS; Cherryfield, ME; (Y); Am Leg Aux Girls St; Church Yth Grp; Drama Clb; Pres French Clb; Varsity Clb; Band; JV Cheerleading; Mgr(s); Var JV Vllybl; Hon Roll; Bus Admin.

FESTINO, PATRICIA; Catherine Mc Auley HS; Saco, ME; (Y); 37/74; Drama Clb; Chorus; JV Var Cheerleading; Simmons; Bio.

FICKETT, SUSAN; S Portland HS; S Portland, ME; (Y); 8/300; Yrbk Ed-Chief; Church Yth Grp; English Clb; 4-H; French Clb; Intnl Clb; SADD; Chorus; Swing Chorus; Nwsp Stf; Part Exprmnt In Intrntnl Lvng Smr Abrd Prgm 85; Slvr Poet Awd Frm Wrld Of Poetry 86; Engl.

FILES, WENDY; Deering HS; Portland, ME; (Y); Sec Church Yth Grp; VP Drama Clb; Chorus; Color Guard; VP Frsh Cls; VP Stu Cncl; Swmmng; Sec NHS; Am Leg Aux Girls St; French Clb; CSF 84-85; Cmmnctns.

FINDLAN, MEREDITH; Noble HS; North Berwick, ME; (Y); Pres Sec Key Clb; Acpl Chr; Chorus; Swing Chorus; Variety Show; Yrbk Stf; Rep Frsh Cls; Rep Stu Cncl; Var Diving; JV Var Socr; Trvl.

FINLEY, LYNN; Belfast Area HS; Belfast, ME; (Y); 27/115; Pres FBLA; Office Aide; Chorus; Hon Roll; Hussen; Bus Tchr.

FINN, HOPE C; Bangor HS; Bangor, ME; (Y); 21/316; Cmnty Wkr; Key Clb; Sec Temple Yth Grp; Band; Orch; Nwsp Stf; Ed Lit Mag; High Hon Roll; Hon Roll; Pres Acad Fit Awd 86; U MA Amherst.

FITZGIBBON, LISA; Windham HS; Windham, ME; (Y); Am Leg Aux Girls St; Drama Clb; Sec SADD; Chorus; School Musical; School Play; Stage Crew; Variety Show; Off Soph Cls; Off Jr Cls; Smith Coll Bk Awd; Pres Clsrm Yng Am; HOBY Ldrshp Sem.

FITZPATRICK, KELLEY; Houlton HS; Houlton, ME; (Y); 3/120; Pres Trs Church Yth Grp; Math Tm; SADD; Bowling; Vllybl; Hon Roll; NHS; St Schlr; 3rd Hnr Part-1st Hnr Essy; Math Awd; Thomas Coll; Accntng.

FLACKE, JULIA S; Belfast Area HS; Morrill, ME; (Y); Ski Clb; Bsktbl; Fld Hcky; Trk; Comm.

FLANDERS, BRETON; Cape Elizabeth HS; Cp Elizabeth, ME; (Y); Varsity Clb; Var L Bsbl; Var L Socr; Hon Roll; Engr.

FLANDERS, LORRI A; Piscataquis Community HS; Guilford, ME; (Y); 6/76; Am Leg Aux Girls St; Band; Jazz Band; Yrbk Rptr; Fld Hcky; Mgr Socr; Hon Roll; NHS; AFS; Church Yth Grp; Natl Eng Accdmc Awd 84-85; Stu Cncl Schlrshp 86; Natl Ldrshp Acad Awd 86; Westbrook Coll; Dntl Hygn.

FLEMING, MELANIE A; Mt Blue HS; New Sharon, ME; (Y); 6/211; Am Leg Aux Girls St; Debate Tm; NFL; Band; Chorus; Rep Soph Cls; Var Capt Crs Cntry; Var Capt Trk; Jr NHS; Pres NHS.

FLYNN, KELLY; Lee Acad; Carroll, ME; (Y); 4/45; Letterman Clb; Ski Clb; School Play; VP Frsh Cls; VP Soph Cls; Trs Jr Cls; VP Sr Cls; Im Vllybl; Hon Roll; NHS; Head Hunter II Sch; Csmtlgst.

FOLEY, JONATHAN; Nokomis Regional HS; Dixmont, ME; (Y); 6/158; Drama Clb; Sec Math Tm; Pres Science Clb; School Play; Stu Cncl; Bausch & Lomb Sci Awd; High Hon Roll; NHS; US Dept Of Enrgy Sprcmptng Hons Prgm Lvrmore 86; Cntrl Maine Power Engry Schlrshp 1st Pl 86; Rnslr Plytchnc Inst; Phy Astrph.

FOLSOM, KRISTEN; Bonny Eagle HS; Sebago Lake, ME; (Y); 26/260; Spanish Clb; Sec Frsh Cls; Sec Soph Cls; Sec Jr Cls; Sec Stu Cncl; Var Bsktbl; Var Capt Crs Cntry; Var Trk; Hon Roll; NHS; Army Schlr Athl; U NH; Htl Admn.

FORD, CNYTHIA; Edward Little HS; Mechanic Falls, ME; (S); Library Aide; Band; Chorus; School Play; Stat Bsktbl; Im Socr; High Hon Roll; Hon Roll; Trvl.

FORD, DAVE; Cheverus HS; Cumberland Ctr, ME; (Y); L Bsktbl; JV Socr; Hon Roll.

FORD, SHERRY; Edward Little HS; Auburn, ME; (S); FBLA; Spanish Clb; Drill Tm; Pom Pon; Hon Roll; Hnr Roll; Intl Bus.

FORS, CECILIA; Catherine Mc Auley HS; Portland, ME; (Y); 4/75; VP French Clb; Key Clb; Chorus; Lit Mag; Sec Jr Cls; Trk; High Hon Roll; Hon Roll; NEDT Awd; Bio.

FORST, CHRISTINE; Catherine Mc Auley HS; Cape Elizabeth, ME; (Y); 11/74; Hosp Aide; Sec Key Clb; Yrbk Phtg; Rep Frsh Cls; Sec Soph Cls; Rep Jr Cls; VP Stu Cncl; JV Var Fld Hcky; Var Capt Trk; NHS; Physcl Thrpy.

FORTIN, MICHELLE; Belfast Area HS; Lincolnville, ME; (Y); French Clb; Band; Concert Band; Mrchg Band; Fld Hcky; Var Capt Gym; Hon Roll; Amrcn HS Athlt 84-85; Floricltr.

FOSS, GLORIA E; Bonny Eagle HS; Hollis, ME; (Y); 6/260; Band; Chorus; SADD; Var Capt Cheerleading; Trs NHS; High Hon Roll; Church Yth Grp; 4-H; SADD; Concert Band; Wheaton Coll; Psych.

FOSS, JOHN; East Grand HS; Danforth, ME; (Y); 1/25; Am Leg Boys St; French Clb; Yrbk Stf; Trs Sr Cls; Stu Cncl; Bsbl; Bsktbl; Hon Roll; NHS; Val; U Of ME.

FOULKS, R ANDREW; Fort Fairfield HS; Ft Fairfield, ME; (Y); 8/64; Chess Clb; Computer Clb; Crs Cntry; High Hon Roll; Hnr Awd Geomtry Outstndg 84; Hnr Awd Frnch I 86; MVP Chss Tm 86; Aerontcl Engnr.

FOURNIER, DOREEN; Jay HS; Jay, ME; (Y); 8/86; Am Leg Aux Girls St; Band; Yrbk Ed-Chief; Trs Stu Cncl; Var Fld Hcky; Hon Roll; VP NHS; Pres Acmdc Ftns Awd, Outstndng Stu Awd Band, ME Sec Schl Prin Assoc Awd 86; U Southern ME; Elem Educ.

FOURNIER, GLEN; Lisbon HS; Lisbon Falls, ME; (Y); 3/119; Am Leg Boys St; VP Latin Clb; Math Clb; Band; Jazz Band; Mrchg Band; Var Capt Bsbl; Bausch & Lomb Sci Awd; High Hon Roll; NHS; Am Legion Schlrshp 86; Slovak Catholic Soc Schlrshp 86; U ME; Civil Engr.

FOURNIER, MELISSA; Edward Little HS; Auburn, ME; (S); Church Yth Grp; JCL; VP Latin Clb; Varsity Clb; Nwsp Phtg; Nwsp Rptr; Bsktbl; Sftbl; Swmmng; Phy Thrpy.

FOWLE, KATHLEEN; Westbrook HS; Westbrook, ME; (Y); 14/200; Church Yth Grp; Keywanettes; Latin Clb; Spanish Clb; Band; Chorus; Concert Band; Jazz Band; Madrigals; Orch; ME All-ST Orchstra 86; ST Jzz Band Chmpns 85; ST Mrchng Band Chmpns 86; Music Ed.

FOWLER, ANN; Belfast Area HS; Belfast, ME; (Y); French Clb; Girl Scts; Pep Clb; Ski Clb; Yrbk Phtg; Yrbk Sprt Ed; Yrbk Stf; JV Fld Hcky; JV Var Mgr(s); JV Score Keeper; Grl Sct Awd 82-85; West Brook; Cazenovia.

FOWLES, STEPHANIE; Gardiner Area HS; Randolph, ME; (Y); Spanish Clb; SADD; Var Cheerleading; Mgr(s); High Hon Roll; Hon Roll; ME Scholars Day Alt; Psych.

FOX, CHERYL; Lewiston HS; Lewiston, ME; (Y); Pep Clb; Teachers Aide; Yrbk Stf; Off Frsh Cls; Stat Socr; Hon Roll; NHS; Otstndng Chld Cr Aide Stu 85; U Of Me; Elem Educ.

FOX, RHYNE; Sumner Memorial HS; Gouldsboro, ME; (Y); Sec Church Yth Grp; 4-H; Chorus; Drm Mjr(t); Yrbk Stf; JV Cheerleading; Mgr(s); Hon Roll; Intr Dsgn.

FOX, WENDY; Fryeburg Acad; E Stoneham, ME; (Y); Exploring; Chorus; Church Choir; Sftbl; High Hon Roll; Hon Roll; JC Awd; Pine Tree Schlrp 86; St Josephs Coll Schlrp 86; St Josephs Coll; Nrsng.

FRANK, HEIDI; Hampden Acad; Hampden, ME; (Y); French Clb; Intnl Clb; Key Clb; Band; Concert Band; Jazz Band; Mrchg Band; VP Soph Cls; Stu Cncl; Crs Cntry; U Of ME; Optmtry.

FRECHETTE, SUSAN; Lewiston HS; Lewiston, ME; (Y); 69/400; Letterman Clb; Red Cross Aide; Ski Clb; Varsity Clb; Yrbk Stf; JV Var Fld Hcky; JV Var Tennis; NHS; Ntl Merit Ltr; Wheaton Coll MA; Med.

FRENCH, ANGELA; Belfast Area HS; Belfast, ME; (Y); Band; Chorus; Concert Band; Mrchg Band; Mgr(s); Husson Coll; Ofc Mgmt.

FRENCH, LAURA; Gorham HS; Gorham, ME; (Y); 5/114; Var L Bsktbl; Var Capt Crs Cntry; Var Capt Sftbl; High Hon Roll; NHS; Church Yth Grp; GAA; Science Clb; Spanish NHS; Gorhm Athltc Assoc 86; Leslie Kmbll Mem 86; Alpha Delta Kappa 86 Sorority; Wmns Ltry Union Schlrshp 86; Sprngfld Coll; Athltc Trng.

FREY, PHILIP J; Ellsworth HS; Ellsworth, ME; (Y); 8/108; Bsbl; Crs Cntry; Trk; High Hon Roll; NHS; Outstndng Art Awd 85; Partcpnt Maine Summr Arts Prog 85; Top 3 Bangor Art Shw 86; Columbus Clg; Illstrtn.

FRIEDMAN, TAMARA L; Scarborough HS; Scarborough, ME; (Y); Sec JCL; Sec Latin Clb; Nwsp Rptr; Sec Jr Cls; Rep Stu Cncl; Var Cheerleading; Var Tennis; Hon Roll; Psych.

FROST, LISA; Calais HS; Calais, ME; (Y); 14/80; Am Leg Aux Girls St; Church Yth Grp; Girl Scts; VP Chorus; Church Choir; School Musical; Variety Show; Yrbk Stf; Hon Roll; Trl Mngmt.

GAGNE, DAVID; St Dominic Regional HS; Lewiston, ME; (Y); 4/66; High Hon Roll; Hon Roll; NHS; NEDT Awd; SAT V 510 & M 620 86; PSAT V 52 & M 69 85; Harvard; Bus.

GAGNE, MICHELLE; Portland HS; Portland, ME; (Y); Latin Clb; Sec Frsh Cls; Sec Soph Cls; Rep Jr Cls; Rep Sr Cls; Sec Stu Cncl; JV Var Fld Hcky; JV Tennis; JV Trk; Hon Roll.

GAGNON, ANN; Lewiston HS; Lewiston, ME; (Y); Hosp Aide; SADD; Y-Teens; Socr; Sftbl; Hon Roll; Nrsng.

GAGNON, SARAH; Westbrook HS; Westbrook, ME; (Y); French Clb; Ski Clb; Swmmng; U Of ME; Law.

GALGOVITCH, DEANNA; Lisbon HS; Lisbon Falls, ME; (Y); Am Leg Aux Girls St; Exploring; Math Tm; Church Choir; School Musical; Yrbk Bus Mgr; Yrbk Ed-Chief; Fld Hcky; Cit Awd; NHS; N E U; Business Mgmt.

GALLAGHER, LINDA; Westbrook HS; Westbrook, ME; (Y); Church Yth Grp; Dance Clb; Drama Clb; GAA; Keywanettes; Letterman Clb; Varsity Clb; School Musical; School Play; Stage Crew; Mst Vlbl Indr Trck 85-86; Physcl Thrpy.

GAMACHE, LISA; Lewiston HS; Sabattys, ME; (Y); High Hon Roll; Med Asst.

GARCEAU, DAVID; Madison HS; Madison, ME; (Y); 5/79; Am Leg Boys St; Boy Scts; Drama Clb; French Clb; Math Tm; Ski Clb; Spanish Clb; SADD; Teachers Aide; School Musical; St Josephs; Dntstry.

GARDNER, BETSY; Edward Little HS; Auburn, ME; (S); Latin Clb; Math Tm; Pep Clb; Varsity Clb; Cheerleading; Var L Fld Hcky; JV Tennis; Cit Awd; High Hon Roll; Hon Roll; Schl Spirit Awd 83-84; Bates Coll; Law.

GARREPY, MARK C; Winthrop HS; Winthrop, ME; (Y); 3/100; Am Leg Boys St; Debate Tm; JCL; Latin Clb; Math Tm; SADD; Varsity Clb; Pres Soph Cls; Var Capt Bsbl; Var L Bsktbl; High O Brian Ldrshp Smnr; Clby Coll Bk Awd; Rnslr Poly Tech; Aero Spc Engr.

GARRIS, JOEL; Cony HS; Augusta, ME; (Y); 1/317; Chess Clb; Cmnty Wkr; Math Tm; Quiz Bowl; Bausch & Lomb Sci Awd; Ntl Merit Ltr; St Schlr; Church Yth Grp; JCL; Political Wkr; Rensselaer Polytech Inst Medl 86; Dartmouth Bk Awd 86; Engrng.

GARRITY, LYNNE; Yarmouth HS; Yarmouth, ME; (Y); Church Yth Grp; Math Tm; Trs Spanish Clb; Chorus; Yrbk Stf; Var Swmmng; Bausch & Lomb Sci Awd; High Hon Roll; Hon Roll; Spanish NHS; Ntnl Spnsh Exm 85-86; Cert Of Recog Maine Lgsltr 86; Biochmstry.

GARRITY, MARY; Deering HS; Portland, ME; (Y); 53/288; Drama Clb; JA; Key Clb; Hon Roll; Pres Acdmc Fit Awd 86; Boston U; Comp Sci.

GASPAR, DONNA E; Cape Elizabeth HS; Cape Elizabeth, ME; (Y); 14/142; Cmnty Wkr; Drama Clb; NFL; Speech Tm; Concert Band; VP Sr Cls; Var L Tennis; NHS; French Clb; Chorus; Arts Recgntn & Tlnt Srch Hnrb Mntn Awd 86; Amer Future Awd 85; ST Spch Champ Dramatic Interptn 86; U Of NH.

GASPAR, KENNETH C; Noble HS; North Berwick, ME; (Y); 1/150; Boy Scts; Capt Math Tm; Capt L Crs Cntry; Bausch & Lomb Sci Awd; Elks Awd; High Hon Roll; Pres NHS; Ntl Merit Ltr; Val; Am Leg Boys St; US Army Resrv Athlt Schlr Awd 86; Pres Acdmc Ftns Awd 86; Clarkson U; Chem Engnrng.

GAUDET, TERESA; Deering HS; Portland, ME; (Y); 46/286; Church Yth Grp; FTA; Key Clb; Political Wkr; Concert Band; Jazz Band; Mrchg Band; French Hon Soc; French Clb; Band; Forum Clb 84-86; Chns Lng Clb 84-86; Mt Hlyk Coll; Asian Stdys.

GAVIN III, MARTIN F; Windham HS; Windham, ME; (Y); Am Leg Boys St; Pres Sec Key Clb; Pres Latin Clb; Political Wkr; Nwsp Phtg; Nwsp Rptr; Rep Sr Cls; Kiwanis Awd; NHS; Amer Future Awd Outstndng Publc Svc 84-85; Colby Coll; Psych.

GEBHARDT, THOMAS; Skowhegan Area HS; Norridgewock, ME; (Y); Pres Latin Clb; Band; Jazz Band; Yrbk Phtg; JV Ftbl; Tennis; Trk; Latin Awd IV; U Rochester; Mech Engrng.

GEORGE, APRIL; Bangor HS; Bangor, ME; (Y); 24/316; Sec Key Clb; Rep Frsh Cls; Rep Soph Cls; Rep Jr Cls; Rep Sr Cls; Rep Stu Cncl; Elks Awd; NHS; Pres Schlr; Nwsp Rptr; Typg Awd; Kirstein Schlrshp Awd-Bangor Cty Cncl; Coachs Awd Sccr; Clark U.

GERRIOR, HILARY; Yarmouth HS; Freeport, ME; (Y); French Clb; Rep Frsh Cls; Var Capt Bsktbl; Var Fld Hcky; Var Sftbl; French Hon Soc; High Hon Roll; Hon Roll; Frnch Ntl Exm Awd 86.

GIBERSON, ERIC; Fort Fairfield HS; Ft Fair Field, ME; (Y); Chess Clb; FFA; Band; Jazz Band; Golf; High Hon Roll.

GIBSON, CYNTHIA; Van Buren District Secondary Schl; Van Buren, ME; (Y); 7/74; Hosp Aide; Yrbk Phtg; Yrbk Stf; High Hon Roll; NHS; Pres Acad Fit Awd 86; Hghst Achvt Accntg I & II 85-86; Hgh Achvt Engl 85; Central CT ST U; Elem Ed.

GIGUERE, STEVEN; Lewiston HS; Lewiston, ME; (Y); 10/369; Church Yth Grp; Letterman Clb; Lit Mag; Var L Diving; Var L Swmmng; High Hon Roll; NHS; Varsity Clb; Math Achvt Awd; Schlrshp Eng Awd; Norman Dionne Hnr Medal; U ME; Art.

GILLETTE, MATT; Fryeburg Acad; Brownfield, ME; (Y); French Clb; SADD; Varsity Clb; JV Bsbl; Var Ftbl; Var Wrstlng; High Hon Roll; Hon Roll; NHS; Engr.

GILLIAM, MELISSA; Deering HS; Portland, ME; (Y); Cmnty Wkr; Color Guard; Variety Show; USM; Data Prcssng.

GILPATRICK, JULIANA; Lawrence HS; Fairfield, ME; (Y); FCA; Spanish Clb; Yrbk Phtg; Yrbk Stf; Bsktbl; Crs Cntry; Fld Hcky; Trk; Hon Roll; EMVTI; Dntl Hyg.

GIORDANO, SHAWN; Piscataquis Community HS; Dexter, ME; (Y); 15/79; Am Leg Boys St; Boy Scts; Chess Clb; School Play; L Golf; Trk; Hon Roll; Comp Sci Stu Of Yr; U Of ME; Comp Sci.

GIROUX, GLEN; Lawrence HS; Fairfield, ME; (Y); 12/220; Am Leg Boys St; Nwsp Rptr; Var JV Bsbl; JV Bsktbl; Im Vllybl; High Hon Roll; Hon Roll; Prfct Atten Awd; Latn I Achvt Awd 85-86; Engrg.

GIVENS, NICOLE; Kents Hill Prep Schl; Central City, KY; (Y); Natl Beta Clb; Varsity Clb; Concert Band; Drm Mjr(t); Mrchg Band; School Play; Cheerleading; Fld Hcky; Tennis; High Hon Roll; Colby Bk Awd 86.

GLEESON, LAWRENCE; Belfast Area HS; Belfast, ME; (Y); 2/121; Drama Clb; Concert Band; Jazz Band; School Musical; Pres Sr Cls; Var L Socr; Var L Swmmng; JP Sousa Awd; NHS; French Clb; AF ROTC Schlrshp 86; Yale; Astrnt.

GLIDDEN, DEBORAH; Deering HS; Portland, ME; (Y); Church Yth Grp; Cmnty Wkr; JA; Math Tm; Science Clb; Church Choir; Orch; High Hon Roll; Hon Roll; Jr NHS; Math.

GOBEL, JOHN; Bucksport HS; Bucksport, ME; (Y); 25/130; Drama Clb; Varsity Clb; Stu Cncl; L Ftbl; Im Socr; L Trk; Im Wt Lftg; Capt Wrstlng; Hon Roll; Jr Exec Cncl; Bstr Clb; Comp Prog Awd; Comp Sci.

GODBOUT, MICHELLE; Edward Little HS; Auburn, ME; (S); 4-H; French Clb; Latin Clb; Math Tm; Varsity Clb; Var Bsktbl; Var Fld Hcky; JV Sftbl; High Hon Roll; Hon Roll; Archlgy.

GODIN, MICHAEL A; Lewiston HS; Lewiston, ME; (Y); Church Yth Grp; Letterman Clb; Varsity Clb; Var L Bsbl; Var Bsktbl; High Hon Roll; Hon Roll; Bus Mgmt.

GODING, JEFF; Lewiston HS; Lewiston, ME; (Y); Am Leg Boys St; Sec Key Clb; Letterman Clb; Var L Bsbl; Bsktbl; Var L Socr; High Hon Roll; NHS; All Conf 2nd Tm Sccr 85; Holycrss Bk Awd 86; Awd Excllnc Anlys Hnrs 86.

GOFF, MATT; Calais HS; Calais, ME; (Y); Band; Concert Band; Jazz Band; Mrchg Band; Pep Band; Yrbk Stf; All-ST Bnd 85 & 86; Full Schlrp To Jazz Cmp & Hlf Schlrp To ME Smmr Yth Cmp For Music 85; Music.

GOLDEN, KAREN; Woodland HS; Woodland, ME; (Y); 5/50; AFS; Church Yth Grp; Drama Clb; Girl Scts; Band; Jazz Band; School Play; Golf; Hon Roll; NHS; Englsh Awrd 86; St James Sodilty Schlrshp 86; Tammaro Oil Schlrshp 86; Knights Clmbs Schlrshp 86; Queens Coll; Child Psych.

GOLEC, MATTHEW; Waynflete Schl; Portland, ME; (Y); Yrbk Ed-Chief; Var L Crs Cntry; Socr; Hon Roll; NHS.

GOODMAN, LEAH K; Bangor HS; Bangor, ME; (Y); SADD; Temple Yth Grp; Stage Crew; Yrbk Stf; JV Fld Hcky; Var Trk; High Hon Roll; Hon Roll; NHS; Ntl Merit Ltr; Pres Schlr 85; Vet.

GOODRIDGE, SHERRI; Piscataquis Comm HS; Sangerville, ME; (Y); Church Yth Grp; Key Clb; Letterman Clb; Band; School Play; Yrbk Stf; Var Bsktbl; Var Capt Sftbl; Im Vllybl; Hon Roll; Eastern Maine Sftbl Champs Rnnr ST Champ 86; Bus Mgmt.

GOODWIN, JEFF; Marshwood HS; Eliot, ME; (Y); 20/117; Cmnty Wkr; Letterman Clb; Varsity Clb; JV Bsbl; JV Bsktbl; Im Coach Actv; Var L Ftbl; Var Trk; Wt Lftg; Var L Wrstlng; Elec Engrng.

GORAJ, KATHERINE J; Cony HS; Augusta, ME; (Y); 53/300; Am Leg Aux Girls St; Church Yth Grp; Computer Clb; German Clb; Nwsp Bus Mgr; Nwsp Rptr; Nwsp Stf; Hon Roll; Vet Mem Schlrshp 86; Thomas Coll Schlrshp Grnt 86; Suplmntl Ed Opportny Grnt 86; Thomas Coll; Comp Systms.

GORDON, NANCY; Greenville HS; Greenville Jct, ME; (Y); Var Trk; Farmington U; Elem Ed.

GORMLEY, FRANKLIN J; Rumford HS; Rumford, ME; (Y); Drama Clb; Band; Jazz Band; Variety Show; Bst Supporting Actr 85.

GORNEAU, MIKE; Gardiner Area HS; Gardiner, ME; (Y); Boy Scts; French Clb; Im Ftbl; Wt Lftg; JV Wrstlng; High Hon Roll; Hon Roll; St Schlr; Elec Engrng.

GORRIVAN, DEBORAH; Deering HS; Portland, ME; (Y); 50/325; Hosp Aide; JA; Letterman Clb; Ski Clb; Varsity Clb; Var Swmmng; Hon Roll; Gynclgy.

GOSSELIN, DENISE P; Lewiston HS; Lewiston, ME; (Y); 6/409; Lit Mag; Rep Jr Cls; VP Sr Cls; Twrlr; Cit Awd; DAR Awd; High Hon Roll; Kiwanis Awd; Rep NHS; Pres Schlr; Mst Vlbl Stu Awd 86; Hgh Achvt In Englsh, Math & Hstry 86; ST ME Miss Teen 85; Emrsn Coll MA; Cmnctns.

GOTT, KEVIN; Oxford Hills HS; Norway, ME; (Y); Math Tm; Ski Clb; Var Crs Cntry; JV Trk; Hon Roll; Comp.

GOULD, PAMELA; Belfast Area HS; Belfast, ME; (Y); FBLA; Sec Jr Cls; Var JV Bsktbl; JV Sftbl; Hon Roll; Acctg.

GOULD, WILLIAM T; Edward Little HS; Minot, ME; (Y); Capt Swmmng; Cit Awd; Hon Roll; Prfct Atten Awd; Chess Clb; Debate Tm; Drama Clb; Trk; ME Maritime Acad; Mrn Sci.

GOULDING, CHRISTINE; Edward Little HS; Danville, ME; (S); Latin Clb; Math Tm; Pep Clb; Rep Jr Cls; Rep Stu Cncl; Var L Fld Hcky; High Hon Roll; Prfct Atten Awd.

GOVE, MAURA; York HS; York, ME; (Y); 11/118; Church Yth Grp; German Clb; Math Tm; Church Choir; Yrbk Stf; L Var Bsktbl; JV Fld Hcky; Mgr(s); Var L Trk; High Hon Roll; Psych Soc Awd 85; German Awd 86; Yrk Teachers Assn Schlrshp 86; Houghton Coll; Elem Ed.

GRAHAM, BRENT; Cape Elizabeth HS; Cp Elizabeth, ME; (Y); Trs FBLA; Letterman Clb; Varsity Clb; Var Golf; Capt Var Ice Hcky; Advncd Acctng Awd; Bus Adm.

GRANNELL, GRETCHEN; Sanford HS; Sanford, ME; (Y); Math Tm; Varsity Clb; Sec Y-Teens; Trs Jr Cls; Var Cheerleading; JV Crs Cntry; Var Trk; Hon Roll; Bio.

GREATON, THOMAS; Leavitt Area HS; Buckfield, ME; (Y); Math Clb; Math Tm; Var Crs Cntry; Var Trk; Hghst Avg Chem Awd 86; Amer Chemcl Soc Awd-Chem Olympd 86; Electrncs Engrng.

GREEN, CHRISTI; Deering HS; Portland, ME; (Y); 84/323; Hst Church Yth Grp; Cmnty Wkr; FTA; Hosp Aide; JA; Key Clb; Crs Cntry; Capt L Trk; Hon Roll; Hnrd 1st ST Indoor Trk 86; Nrsng.

GREEN, CHRISTIE; Calvary Christian Acad; Island Falls, ME; (S); Church Yth Grp; FCA; FNA; Hosp Aide; Var Vllybl; High Hon Roll; Hon Roll; Fastest Readr Awd 85; Hghst Ovrll Avg 84-86; Zion Bible Inst; Bibl.

GREENLAW, JANEEN; Cony HS; Augusta, ME; (Y); 14/320; AFS; Computer Clb; Exploring; French Clb; Science Clb; Ed Nwsp Stf; High Hon Roll; Hon Roll; Prfct Atten Awd; Pres Schlr; Frshmn, Sphmor,JR & SR Schlrshp Awds; Hon Mntn, 2nd Pl Cony Sci Fair; U Of Southern Maine; Cmnctns.

GRENIER, MARCEL B J; Lewiston HS; Lewiston, ME; (Y); 128/367; Key Clb; Var Bsbl; JV Ice Hcky; Var Socr; Cert Of Merit Electrncs 86; Devry Inst Of Tech; Elec Engrng.

GRINDLE, CHRISTIE; Mt Abram Regional HS; Eustis, ME; (Y); Girl Scts; Band; Chorus; Mrchg Band; Pep Band; Var Mgr(s); Socr; Sftbl; Hon Roll; NHS; Hgh Hnrs In Rcrdkpng & Acctng 86-87; Bentley Coll; Acctnt.

GROH, AMY; Sumner Memorial HS; Franklin, ME; (Y); JA; Variety Show; JV Var Bsktbl; Var Socr; Var Sftbl; Church Yth Grp; Band; Concert Band; Yrbk Stf; Phrmcy.

GRONROS, ALAN; Georges Valley HS; Thomaston, ME; (Y); 8/85; Boy Scts; Drama Clb; Intnl Clb; Math Tm; Ski Clb; Band; Var Socr; Hon Roll; NHS; Prfct Atten Awd; Symphnc Band, Band Awd 83; Schlrshp Jazz 85 84; Amherst Coll; Bio.

GROVES, RACHEL; Livermore Falls HS; Livermore Falls, ME; (Y); Letterman Clb; Band; JV Bsktbl; JV Var Fld Hcky; JV Var Sftbl; High Hon Roll; NHS; Ger Achvt Awd 86; Math Achvt Awd 86; Engrng.

GURNEY, DONNA; Waterville SR HS; Waterville, ME; (Y); Latin Clb; Rep Frsh Cls; Var L Cheerleading; Var L Gym; Var Trk; Hon Roll.

GUTHRIE, LISA; Deering HS; Portland, ME; (Y); 23/300; Am Leg Aux Girls St; French Clb; JA; Varsity Clb; Concert Band; Mrchg Band; Var Fld Hcky; Var Capt Tennis; Hon Roll; NHS; Hon Ment AU Amer Tnns 85; Rep ME 17 Tourn CA 83-85.

HAINES, TAMMY; Fort Fairfield HS; Ft Fairfield, ME; (Y); 1/70; Am Leg Aux Girls St; Trs Church Yth Grp; Cmnty Wkr; Drama Clb; Sec French Clb; Red Cross Aide; Pres SADD; Varsity Clb; Band; Chorus; Pres Phy Ftnss Awd 86; Engl, Math, Physcs & Govt Awds 86; ME Sec Schl Prncpls Assn Awd 86; Bentley Coll; Bus Admin.

HALEY, SHANNON; Wells HS; N Berwick, ME; (Y); Letterman Clb; Pep Clb; PAVAS; Varsity Clb; Band; Concert Band; Jazz Band; Mrchg Band; Pep Band; Yrbk Stf; Arch.

HALL, MICHELLE LEE; Biddeford HS; Biddeford, ME; (Y); 14/300; Am Leg Aux Girls St; Church Yth Grp; VP Leo Clb; SADD; Teachers Aide; Capt Cheerleading; High Hon Roll; Hon Roll; Sec NHS; Miss Bddfrd/Miss ME Teen; ME Sum Arb Pgm For Dance; Talnt Am In NYC; Dance.

HALL, RICHARD; Wells HS; Springvale, ME; (Y); Hon Roll; U ME Orono; Data Prcsng.

HALLBAUER, DAMIAN; Noble HS; Berwick, ME; (Y); 2/200; Computer Clb; Key Clb; School Play; Stage Crew; Variety Show; Yrbk Phtg; Yrbk Stf; High Hon Roll; Jr NHS; Prfct Atten Awd; Comp Sci.

HALLOWELL, FRANI; Bucksport HS; Bucksport, ME; (Y); 16/121; Pres Drama Clb; Varsity Clb; Band; Chorus; School Musical; Yrbk Stf; Rep Sr Cls; Var Trk; Hon Roll; NHS; Jane Snow Kennedy Trst Schlrshp 86; U Of ME; Marine Bio.

HAM, HEATHER; Leavitt Area HS; Greene, ME; (Y); Church Yth Grp; 4-H; Intnl Clb; Band; Chorus; Church Choir; Variety Show; Nwsp Stf; 4-H Awd; Hon Roll; Mable J Deschon Schlrshp 86; U Southern ME; Socl Worker.

HAMELIN, MICHELLE; Gorham HS; Gorham, ME; (Y); Camp Fr Inc; 4-H; GAA; Spanish Clb; Varsity Clb; Yrbk Stf; Var Bsktbl; Var Fld Hcky; Var Sftbl; Hon Roll; Bus.

HAMLIN, LISA; Madison HS; Madison, ME; (Y); 28/104; Band; Concert Band; Mrchg Band; Var Capt Cheerleading; Coach Actv; Var Sftbl; Im Vllybl; Hon Roll; Prfct Atten Awd; Peer Cnslng 84-87; Usher Clss Nght, Grad 84-86; Psych.

HAMMOND, TRACY; Bangor HS; Bangor, ME; (Y); Am Leg Aux Girls St; Dance Clb; Speech Tm; School Musical; School Play; Rep Soph Cls; Rep Sr Cls; Hon Roll; VFW Awd; Voice Dem Awd; U ME Orono Spch Fstvl Supr 84 & 85; Brewer Herman & Bangor Hgh Spch Tourn 85; ME Smmr Art Pgm 1st Pl; Emerson Coll; Spch Comm.

HANCE, KATHLEEN; Gardiner Area HS; Gardiner, ME; (Y); Cmnty Wkr; SADD; Chorus; Hon Roll; QUEST Peer Cnclr; Cortez Petes Typng Awd; Chld Wlfr Lg Of Amrca; Trvl.

HANDY, DAWN; Narraguagus HS; Addison, ME; (Y); Trs Church Yth Grp; Drama Clb; Library Aide; Mgr Stage Crew; Hon Roll; Hist Awd 84.

HANEY, REBECCA; York HS; York, ME; (Y); 3/130; Drama Clb; French Clb; Math Tm; Band; Pep Band; School Musical; Yrbk Stf; Hon Roll; NHS; Pres Schlr; Grtr Prtsmth Cmmnty Fndtn Schlrshp 86; Wmns Ntl Frm & Gdn Assoc Schlrshp 86; Frnds St Chris Schlrshp; Smith Coll.

HANOSCOM, TRACI; MCI HS; Burnham, ME; (Y); Church Yth Grp; French Clb; Varsity Clb; Yrbk Rptr; Yrbk Stf; JV Var Cheerleading; JV Var Fld Hcky; Var Trk; High Hon Roll; Hon Roll; Manson Essays 86; Med.

HARGREAVES, ELIZABETH; Mt Abram HS; Strong, ME; (Y); Pres Church Yth Grp; Pres Girl Scts; Trs Intnl Clb; Red Cross Aide; Y-Teens; Capt Cheerleading; Mgr(s); Hon Roll; Alla Rnd Chrldr Awd 86; Frnch.

HARKINS, BETH; Lisbon HS; Lisbon Center, ME; (Y); Church Yth Grp; Drama Clb; Teachers Aide; Color Guard; School Musical; Hon Roll; Am Legion Oratrcl Spch Cntst 85-86; Child Psychlgst.

HARMON, LORI; Westbrook HS; Westbrook, ME; (Y); French Clb; Math Tm; Band; Chorus; Concert Band; Mrchg Band; Hon Roll; Natl Lang Arts Olympd Awd 83; ST Champs Marchg Band Awd 85; Barnard College; Eurp Hist.

HARRIMAN, JESSICA JEAN; Medomak Valley HS; Union, ME; (Y); Yrbk Sprt Ed; Yrbk Stf; Rep Soph Cls; Rep Jr Cls; VP Sr Cls; Stu Cncl; Var Bsktbl; Var Sftbl; DAR Awd; Prfct Atten Awd; B M Clark Fndtn Schlrshp 86; Toyotas Robt G Ahern Mem Schlrshp 86; Johnson & Wales Coll; Trvl Mgt.

HARRIMAN, JIM; Deering HS; Portland, ME; (Y); Babson; Bus.

HARRIMAN, TONI LYNN; John Bapst Memorial HS; Bangor, ME; (Y); 12/83; Dance Clb; Drama Clb; Hosp Aide; Key Clb; School Play; Yrbk Stf; JV Var Bsktbl; Var L Mgr(s); Var L Trk; High Hon Roll; Beta Sigma Phi, Annabel Duncan Schlrshp 86; John R Graham PTO Schlrshp 86; Algb III, Chem Awds 85-86; Kean Coll NJ; Occup Ther.

HARRIS, DAWN; Sumner Memorial HS; W Sullivan, ME; (Y); Rep Am Leg Aux Girls St; Yrbk Stf; Rep Frsh Cls; Rep Soph Cls; Rep Jr Cls; VP Stu Cncl; JV Var Bsktbl; Var Crs Cntry; JV Socr; JV Var Sftbl; JR Prom Queen 86; SR Class Marshl 86.

HARRIS, JULIANNE; Deering HS; Portland, ME; (Y); 88/330; Spanish Clb; Band; Color Guard; Mrchg Band; Rep Jr Cls; Pom Pon; Swmmng; Hon Roll; Bio.

HARRIS, KATIE; Catherine Mc Auley HS; Portland, ME; (Y); Church Yth Grp; French Clb; Key Clb; Letterman Clb; Science Clb; Chorus; Yrbk Ed-Chief; Yrbk Sprt Ed; Yrbk Stf; Stat Bsktbl; Mth Exclince 85-86; Sci Olympd ST & Regnl Level 85-86; Delg Natl CYO Conv 85; St Johns U; Ath Adm.

HARTLEY, JENNIFER A; Foxcroft Acad; Dover-Foxcroft, ME; (Y); School Musical; Nwsp Ed-Chief; Pres Frsh Cls; Pres Soph Cls; Pres Jr Cls; NHS; Ntl Merit SF; Math Tm; Office Aide; Political Wkr; Hoby Yth Ambssdr 84; Colby Coll Bk Prz 85; Intl Rltns.

HARTSGROVE, JANELLE; Skowhegan Area HS; Norridgewock, ME; (Y); German Clb; Nwsp Stf; Fld Hcky; Cit Awd; High Hon Roll; Hon Roll; Actvty Chrldng & Chorus 81-82; Scl Wrk.

HARVEY, BRENDAN; Bucksport HS; Bucksport, ME; (Y); Cmnty Wkr; Varsity Clb; Nwsp Stf; Sec Sr Cls; Ftbl; Hon Roll.

HARVEY, MICHELE; Belfast Area HS; Belfast, ME; (Y); Chorus; School Musical; Fld Hcky; Socr; Sftbl; Trk; Vllybl; Wt Lftg; Wrstlng; Prfct Atten Awd.

HASKELL, DAVID; Gardiner Area HS; Gardiner, ME; (Y); Band; Concert Band; Jazz Band; Mrchg Band; Pep Band; Bsbl; Hon Roll; U ME Orono; Comp Fld.

HASKELL, JENNIFER LYNN; Deer Isle-Stonington HS; Deer Isle, ME; (Y); 2/33; Am Leg Aux Girls St; Varsity Clb; Sec Frsh Cls; Trs Soph Cls; Sec Jr Cls; Sec Sr Cls; Var Capt Cheerleading; Var Sftbl; Cit Awd; High Hon Roll; Army Natl Res Hghst Schlr/Ath 86; ME Schlrs Day 85; Odd Fellows & Rebeccas Scholar 86; Husson Coll; Nrsng.

HASKELL, KERRI; Edward Little HS; Auburn, ME; (S); Letterman Clb; Ski Clb; Varsity Clb; Capt Fld Hcky; Hon Roll; 1st & 2nd SMAA Fld Hcky All Star Tm 84 & 85; Bates Coll; Med.

HASKELL, LISA; Edward Little HS; Auburn, ME; (S); VP Church Yth Grp; Trs Sec Spanish Clb; Band; Chorus; Church Choir; Color Guard; Concert Band; Mrchg Band; Pom Pon; Im Vllybl; Gld Mdl Lit Wrk 86; Eastern Nazarene Coll; Educ.

HATCH, ERIC; Nokomis Regional HS; Plymouth, ME; (Y); 20/171; High Hon Roll; Hon Roll.

HATCH, ROBIN; Georges Valley HS; Thomaston, ME; (Y); 4/75; Dance Clb; GAA; Math Tm; Pep Clb; Yrbk Stf; Soph Cls; Coach Actv; Fld Hcky; High Hon Roll; NHS; Band Outstndng Stu Awd; Alg Outstndng Stu Awd; Mth Tm Hgh Scorer; Psych.

HATT, JOAN; Westbrook HS; Westbrook, ME; (Y); 14/250; Church Yth Grp; French Clb; Hosp Aide; Math Tm; Teachers Aide; Concert Band; Nwsp Rptr; Yrbk Rptr; Yrbk Stf; Mgr(s); Var Letter Swmmng 85; Prtcpnt ST Swmmng Mt 85; Quinnipiac Coll; Physcl Thrpy.

HAVEY, WENDY; Sumner Memorial HS; W Sullivan, ME; (Y); SADD; Nwsp Ed-Chief; Nwsp Stf; Stu Cncl; Hon Roll; NHS; St Schlr; Yrbk Stf; Rep Frsh Cls; Sec Soph Cls; Hugh O Brien Outstndng Stu 85; ME Schlrs Day 86; Grls ST Altrnt 86; Cmnctns.

HAWKINS, PAMELA; Bonny Eagle HS; Saco, ME; (Y); Camp Fr Inc; 4-H; Trs Latin Clb; Math Tm; Ed Lit Mag; Stu Cncl; JV Crs Cntry; Frgn Lang.

HAWKSLEY, THOMAS W; Bangor HS; Bangor, ME; (Y); Pres Computer Clb; Pres Mathletes; Pres Math Clb; Pres Math Tm; Pres Sr Cls; Pres Stu Cncl; High Hon Roll; Cert Comp Prgrmr 84-86; Hghst Comp Prgrmmng Deg 84-86; Leslie G Dickerman Schlshrp 86; Husson Coll; Bus Mgmt.

HAYES, SAMANTHA; Cape Elizabeth HS; Cape Elizabeth, ME; (Y); 25/144; Spanish Clb; Varsity Clb; Variety Show; Yrbk Stf; JV Bsktbl; JV Var Fld Hcky; JV Sftbl; Var L Swmmng; Hon Roll; CPR Instr; Phineas Sprague Schlrshp Awd 86; Skidmore Coll; Bus.

HAYWARD, MARINA; Narraguagus HS; Columbia, ME; (Y); Church Yth Grp; Office Aide; Teachers Aide; Chorus; Stage Crew; Yrbk Phtg; Yrbk Stf; Rep Jr Cls; Stu Cncl; Hon Roll; Mnsfld Bty Acad; Btcn.

HAZARD, CARRIE; Yarmouth HS; Yarmouth, ME; (Y); 1/100; Am Leg Aux Girls St; Drama Clb; VP Pres French Clb; Latin Clb; Math Tm; Service Clb; SADD; Chorus; School Play; Yrbk Stf; Wellesley Book Awd; Natl Hist Day St Wnnr; Maine Smmr Humanities Prog.

HEBERT, SANDY; Leavitt Area HS; Turner, ME; (Y); 40/165; Speech Tm; Stage Crew; Variety Show; Trk; Vllybl; Hon Roll; VFW Awd; Wallace Viles Schlrshp For Med 86; Westbrook Coll; Nrsng.

HEIKKINEN, STEPHANIE; Livermore Falls HS; Livermore Falls, ME; (Y); Church Yth Grp; Pres 4-H; Math Tm; Stat Bsktbl; Var Cheerleading; 4-H Awd; High Hon Roll; Hon Roll; NHS; St Schlr; Vet Med.

HENDERSON, HEIDI; Yarmouth HS; Yarmouth, ME; (Y); Am Leg Aux Girls St; Thesps; Lit Mag; Pres Frsh Cls; Pres Soph Cls; Pres Jr Cls; Pres Stu Cncl; French Hon Soc; Pres NHS; Drama Clb; Smith Coll Bk Awd 86; Engl Awd 84 & 85; Hugh O Brian Yth Ldrshp Sem Ambsdr 85; Engl.

HENRIKSON, PER; Georges Valley HS; Thomaston, ME; (Y); Var L Bsktbl; Var L Socr; Var L Trk; High Hon Roll; Hon Roll; Aud/Vis; Science Clb; Springfield Coll MA; Phy Ed.

HERSOM, CATHERINE ANN; Sanford HS; Sanford, ME; (Y); 32/224; Am Leg Aux Girls St; Sec Church Yth Grp; Ski Clb; Varsity Clb; Lib Concert Band; Jazz Band; Var Capt Crs Cntry; Var JV Sftbl; Hon Roll; NHS; ME Schlrs Day 85; U Of NH; Biolgy.

HIGGINS, MICHAEL; Belfast Area HS; Belfast, ME; (Y); Am Leg Boys St; Church Yth Grp; Var Bsbl; JV Bsktbl; Var Ftbl; JV Wrstlng; Hon Roll; Vet.

HIGGINS, WENDY; Bucksport HS; Castine, ME; (Y); 3/120; SADD; Varsity Clb; Nwsp Stf; Rep Stu Cncl; Var L Crs Cntry; Trk; High Hon Roll; NHS; Engnrng.

HILBINGER, LINDA; Deering HS; Portland, ME; (Y); 26/321; FTA; Hosp Aide; Math Tm; Ed Yrbk Phtg; Lit Mag; Hon Roll; U Of Southern ME; Engrng.

HILDRETH, TIM; South Portland HS; S Portland, ME; (Y); 33/290; Pres Church Yth Grp; Band; Church Choir; Concert Band; Mrchg Band; Var L Crs Cntry; Var L Trk; JV Wrstlng; Hon Roll; Pres Schlrshp 86; Olivet Nazarene Coll; Sci.

HILL, LICIA; Oxford Hills HS; Norway, ME; (Y); FHA; Girl Scts; Office Aide; Chorus; Drill Tm; Slvr Awd Girl Sctng 84; ACCTG.

HILL, LYNNE; Edward Little HS; Auburn, ME; (Y); Chorus; Prfct Atten Awd.

HILL, ROBERT; Woodland HS; Woodland, ME; (S); 8/97; Thesps; Varsity Clb; School Play; Var Golf; Hon Roll; NHS.

HILTON, BETTY; Fryeburg Acad; Brownfield, ME; (Y); 11/140; Drama Clb; Library Aide; Teachers Aide; Yrbk Stf; High Hon Roll; Hon Roll; NH Tech; Bus.

HINCKLEY, JENNY; Buckfield JR SR HS; West Paris, ME; (S); 2/40; French Clb; SADD; Varsity Clb; Pres Jr Cls; Var Capt Bsktbl; Var Capt Socr; Var L Sftbl; NHS; Army Reserve Ntl Athletic; Schlstc Achvt Awd 85-86; Coachs Awd Bsktbl 84-85; Hgst Ranking Cls 85; Comm.

HIRSCH, JODI A; Deering HS; Portland, ME; (Y); 20/254; Rep Am Leg Aux Girls St; VP French Clb; Temple Yth Grp; Chorus; School Musical; School Play; Capt Pom Pon; French Hon Soc; Hon Roll; NHS; 3rd Pl AAFT Cntst 86; Awd Antmy Ldrshp 83-84; Brandeis U; Law.

HISCOCK, MICHAEL L; Leavitt Area HS; North Turner, ME; (Y); 60/129; Art Clb; Boy Scts; Drama Clb; French Clb; Chorus; Capt Bowling; JV Var Socr; Letterman Clb; Speech Tm; Varsity Clb; 1st Rspndr Amblnc Attndnt 85-86; Mr Awrns Grws Into Cncrn Schl Drg Tm 82-86; Mdl ST Lgsltr 85-86; Johnson & Wales Coll; Clnry Art.

HODGDON, TAMMY; Belfast Area HS; Belfast, ME; (Y); 4-H; FBLA; Cheerleading; Mgr(s); Score Keeper; Prfct Attndnc Awd; Typng Awd; Schlrshp; Machias U; Bus.

HODGKINS, ALLISON; Yarmouth HS; Yarmouth, ME; (Y); Am Leg Aux Girls St; Civic Clb; Off French Clb; Latin Clb; Ski Clb; SADD; Yrbk Stf; Lit Mag; Var Crs Cntry; Var Fld Hcky; Boston U; Anthroplgy.

HODGKINS, JOHN; Yarmouth SR HS; Yarmouth, ME; (Y); 24/82; Boy Scts; Church Yth Grp; Drama Clb; French Clb; Thesps; Band; Chorus; Jazz Band; Crs Cntry; Hon Roll; U ME Orono; Biochem.

HODGKINSON, DAVID; Jonesport-Beals HS; Jonesport, ME; (Y); Pres Latin Clb; VP Spanish Clb; School Play; Pres Soph Cls; VP Stu Cncl; Capt L Golf; Var L Socr; NHS; Am Leg Boys St; Boys Clb Am; All Amer Acad 85-86; Lang Awd 85-86; YMCA Mdl Yth Leg 85-86; Poli Sci.

HOEHLE, DEAN; Yarmouth JR SR HS; Yarmouth, ME; (Y); Aud/Vis; Cmnty Wkr; Latin Clb; Math Tm; Spanish Clb; Socr; Hon Roll; Continental Math Leag 1st In Grade 82-83; Project Encompass 80-84; Berkely Sch Of Music; Sound.

HOESCHEN, CHRISTINE; Morse HS; Georgetown, ME; (Y); 3/190; Capt Math Tm; Science Clb; Yrbk Stf; Elks Awd; High Hon Roll; NHS; Ntl Merit Ltr; Pres Schlr; Smmr Humanities Pgm Bowdoin Coll 85; 1st Chldrns Thtre ME Plywrtng Cntst 85; 1st/2nd Ntl Hstry 84-85; U Of CT; Mech Engrng.

HOFFMANN, GEORGE; Sumner Memorial HS; Winter Harbor, ME; (Y); Band; School Play; Variety Show; Nwsp Stf; Yrbk Stf; Trs Jr Cls; Bsktbl.

HOLINGER, CHRISTOPHER T; Lewiston HS; Lewiston, ME; (Y); 11/410; Am Leg Boys St; CAP; VP JA; Q&S; Ski Clb; Ed Nwsp Phtg; Ed Yrbk Phtg; Var L Crs Cntry; Trk; NHS; J A VP Prodctn Yr 85; Bus Adm.

HOLLEMAN, CINDY; Gorham HS; Gorham, ME; (Y); GAA; Var Bsktbl; Var Fld Hcky; Var Sftbl; Im Vllybl; NHS; Spanish NHS; Typng Awd 85; Physcl Ed Awd 85; U New England; Physcl Thrpy.

HOLMES, JEFF; Cony HS; Augusta, ME; (Y); 21/350; Debate Tm; Drama Clb; English Clb; Math Clb; Math Tm; Pep Clb; Political Wkr; Spanish Clb; Speech Tm; Yrbk Stf; ME Maritime; Engr.

HOLTENHOFF, MARC; South Portland HS; S Protland, ME; (Y); Am Leg Boys St; Boys Clb Am; Key Clb; Rep Soph Cls; Rep Jr Cls; Rep Sr Cls; Var Capt Bsktbl; Ftbl; L Trk; NHS; Hnrbl Mentn All ST Bsktbl ME 85-86; 1st Tm All Confrnc Bsktbl 85-86; Bus Admin.

HOPKINS, KRISTIN; Skowhegan HS; Norridgewock, ME; (Y); French Clb; Band; High Hon Roll; Hon Roll; Vet Sci.

HORTON, LAURIE; Fryeburg Acad; Fryeburg, ME; (S); 12/152; Trs SADD; Varsity Clb; Yrbk Sprt Ed; Rep Soph Cls; Rep Jr Cls; Rep Sr Cls; Sec Stu Cncl; Var Trk; High Hon Roll; NHS; Intl Frgn Lg Awd; Natl Engl Merit Awd; UNH; Educ.

HOTTE, KIRK A; Oxford Hills HS; Oxford, ME; (Y); 18/220; Debate Tm; Math Tm; NFL; Band; Concert Band; Mrchg Band; High Hon Roll; Hon Roll; NHS; U Of TX; Corp Law.

HOUGHTON, PAULA; Bangor HS; Bangor, ME; (Y); Pres Civic Clb; Pres Service Clb; Varsity Clb; Yrbk Stf; Off Frsh Cls; Cheerleading; Var Capt Socr; Vrsty Letter 85; Trvl.

HOVEY, SHANNON; Skowhegan Area HS; Skowhegan, ME; (Y); Drama Clb; French Clb; German Clb; Thesps; Band; Chorus; Concert Band; Mrchg Band; Nwsp Stf; Hon Roll; Pfrct Attndnc Awd 84-86; Girls State 86; Syracuse U; Foreign Reltns.

HOWE, RHONDA; Woodland HS; Woodland, ME; (Y); Am Leg Aux Girls St; Church Yth Grp; Computer Clb; FBLA; JV Cheerleading; Sftbl; Hon Roll; CO Typng Cntst 3rd Pl 85-86; ST Typng Cntst 4th Pl 85-86; Off Wrk.

HOY, NATHAN; Old Orchard Beach HS; Old Orchard Bch, ME; (Y); 10/80; High Hon Roll; Hon Roll; Pres Acdmc Fit Awd 86; U Of Southern ME; Compu.

HUBNER, KATHERINE; Deering HS; Portland, ME; (Y); 22/285; Key Clb; Varsity Clb; Rep Stu Cncl; Var Capt Bsktbl; JV Fld Hcky; Var Sftbl; Hon Roll; NHS; Ntl Merit Ltr; Randall & Mc Allister Athltc Of Yr 85-86; MI ST U; Frnsc Sci.

HUGHES, LINDA; Gorham HS; Gorham, ME; (Y); Spanish Clb; Mgr(s); Score Keeper; High Hon Roll; Hon Roll; Typng Awd 84; Cazenovia Jcfbus Mgmt.

HUJSAK, ELIZABETH; Bonny Eagle HS; W Buxton, ME; (Y); 7/260; Am Leg Aux Girls St; Ski Clb; Spanish Clb; Var Bsktbl; Var Mgr Fld Hcky; High Hon Roll; NHS; Cornell U; Cmnctn Arts.

HULSEY, DIANA J; Greely HS; Cumberland Center, ME; (Y); 11/141; Cmnty Wkr; Drama Clb; Science Clb; Mgr Stage Crew; Ed Nwsp Bus Mgr; Church Yth Grp; French Clb; JCL; Latin Clb; Math Tm; Maine Schlrs Day 85; Psych.

HUNTRESS, DIANE; Fryeburg Acad; Brownfield, ME; (Y); 24/137; Latin Clb; SADD; Varsity Clb; Yrbk Ed-Chief; Yrbk Stf; Sec Soph Cls; Var Fld Hcky; Mgr(s); Hon Roll; Jr NHS; Abby Page Schlrshp 86; Shaws Sprmkt Schlrshp 86; Oscar T Turner Awd 86; U Of ME Orono; Pre-Med.

HUOTARI, AARON; Livermore Falls HS; E Livermore, ME; (Y); Am Leg Boys St; Band; Mrchg Band; Frgn Exchng Stu-Finlnd 86; U Of ME Farmington; Engl.

HURLEY, GAIL; Lewiston HS; Lewiston, ME; (Y); 11/409; Letterman Clb; Varsity Clb; Lit Mag; JV Capt Fld Hcky; Trk; High Hon Roll; Jr NHS; NHS; Ntl Merit Ltr; IBEW Wrkrs Scholar 86; De Molay & Pintetree Yth Scholar 86; Androscoggin Vly Ins Wmn Scholar 86; Bentley Coll; Bus.

HURLEY, LYNN; Sacopee Valley HS; W Baldwin, ME; (Y); Drama Clb; Band; Jazz Band; Crs Cntry; JV Fld Hcky; Var Trk; Wstn ME Msc Fstvl; Rtl Mngmnt.

ILICK, LAURA; Georges Valley HS; Thomaston, ME; (Y); VP GAA; Intnl Clb; Pep Clb; School Musical; Trs Jr Cls; JV Var Bsktbl; Var Fld Hcky; Hon Roll; JV Sftbl; Var Trk; MVP-FIELD Hockey; Hrbl Mntn-Sci Fair-Bio; Courier-Gazette All Star.

INGERSON, SANDRA L; Libson HS; Lisbon Falls, ME; (Y); 9/120; Am Leg Aux Girls St; French Clb; Office Aide; Teachers Aide; Var Capt Bsktbl; Var Capt Socr; JV Var Sftbl; Hon Roll; NHS; Prfct Atten Awd; Sec Of Outing Clb; Top 10; Peer Cnslng; Outstdng Bus Stu Of Yr 86; Golden L Awd 86; Ct Sec.

IRISH, JENNIFER L; Bonny Eagle HS; Limington, ME; (Y); 1/260; VP Sec Church Yth Grp; Drama Clb; Thesps; Chorus; School Musical; School Play; NHS; Ntl Merit SF; Val; Mbr Rgnl All-Star Cast 85; Dartmouth Coll; Biochem.

JACQUES, ANDREW P; Upper Kenneboec Memorial HS; Bingham, ME; (Y); 5/34; Am Leg Boys St; Cmnty Wkr; Computer Clb; Debate Tm; Drama Clb; French Clb; FBLA; Red Cross Aide; Service Clb; Band; U ME Orono; Elec Engrng.

JACQUES, JENNIFER; St Dominics Regional HS; Auburn, ME; (Y); 12/60; Pep Clb; Ski Clb; Yrbk Stf; Bsktbl; Fld Hcky; Sftbl; High Hon Roll; Hon Roll; VP Jr Cls; Psych.

JACQUES, KATHY; Lewiston HS; Lewiston, ME; (Y); Pres Pep Clb; Stu Cncl; Hon Roll; NHS; Mr Richrds Hrstylng Acad; Barbr.

JALBERT, MICHELLE; Windham HS; North Windham, ME; (Y); Pep Clb; Nwsp Rptr; Nwsp Stf; Yrbk Stf; Cheerleading; Socr; Hon Roll; Johnson & Wales Schlrshp 86; Johnson & Wales Coll; Ct Rprtng.

JAMES, JILL; Presque Isle HS; Mapleton, ME; (Y); 3/184; Debate Tm; VP Drama Clb; Sec VP Spanish Clb; VP Speech Tm; Varsity Clb; Nwsp Phtg; Pres Soph Cls; Pres Jr Cls; Off Stu Cncl; NHS; MSSPA ST Prncpls Awd 86; Otstndng Frnscs 85; Rgnl Rnr Up Wstrn KY Dbte 85; Bowdoin Coll; Govt Admin.

JAMESON, LEA-ANNE; Yarmouth HS; Yarmouth, ME; (Y); 7/87; Am Leg Aux Girls St; French Clb; SADD; Yrbk Stf; Pres Frsh Cls; Pres Soph Cls; Pres Jr Cls; Pres Stu Cncl; Tennis; Cit Awd; Robert W Boyd Awd 86; Smith Coll.

JAMESON, MICHELLE; Medomak Valley HS; Friendship, ME; (Y); 14/120; Pres Art Clb; Drama Clb; PAVAS; Thesps; School Musical; School Play; Ed Yrbk Stf; Hon Roll; NHS; Prfct Atten Awd; Bst Actrs 84-86; Natl Hnr Soc 86; Bst Thespn 85-86; Hstry.

JAMESON, STEPHEN; Gardiner Area HS; Windsor, ME; (Y); Boy Scts; Cmnty Wkr; JCL; Latin Clb; JV Socr; Hon Roll; Licensed Basic Emrgncy Med Tech; U Of ME; Sci.

JAMIESON, JOHN; Louis Oak HS; Greenville, ME; (Y); Am Leg Boys St; Pres Drama Clb; Pres Key Clb; Letterman Clb; Trs Frsh Cls; Var L Bsktbl; Var L Crs Cntry; Var L Ftbl; Boy Scts; Cmnty Wkr; Pol Sci.

JAMISON, NATHALIE LYNN; Gardiner Area HS; Randolph, ME; (Y); 1/225; Am Leg Aux Girls St; Sec Church Yth Grp; Pres Latin Clb; Band; Chorus; DAR Awd; High Hon Roll; NHS; Val; U Of ME Orono; Spch Pathlgy.

JANDREAU, CONNIE; Fort Kent Community HS; Fort Kent, ME; (Y); 1/132; Am Leg Aux Girls St; VP SADD; Off Soph Cls; Pres Jr Cls; Off Sr Cls; Sec Stu Cncl; Cit Awd; High Hon Roll; NHS; St Schlr; Hghst Achvt In Mth & Chmstry 84 & 86; Bus.

JANDREAU, PAMELA; Fort Ken & Community HS; Fort Kent, ME; (Y); Hosp Aide; SADD; Hon Roll; Cert Hon Outstndng Achvt 86; Northern ME Voc Tech Inst; Nrs.

JANDREAU, RHONDA; Fort Kent Community HS; St Francis, ME; (Y); 15/140; SADD; Hon Roll; NHS; U Of ME; Med Lab Tech.

JANNENGA, STEPHANIE; Catherine Mc Auley HS; Cape Elizabeth, ME; (Y); 7/74; Drama Clb; Latin Clb; Lit Mag; High Hon Roll; Hon Roll; Acad Decath 86; Zool.

JAWORSKI, JULIE L; Cape Elizabeth HS; Cp Elizabeth, ME; (Y); Church Yth Grp; Band; Church Choir; Stage Crew; Socr; Sftbl; Swmmng; Hon Roll; Psych.

JELLISON, DAWN; Kennebunk HS; Kennebunkport, ME; (Y); 3/144; Math Tm; Pres Science Clb; Spanish Clb; Band; Gym; High Hon Roll; NHS; Ntl Merit Ltr; Smith Coll; Comp Sci.

JENKINS, ANDREA; Mount Desert Island HS; Bar Harbor, ME; (Y); 25/150; Am Leg Aux Girls St; Art Clb; Camera Clb; Drama Clb; PAVAS; School Play; Yrbk Phtg; Yrbk Stf; Lit Mag; Trk; Prtcptd In The Close VP Prgrm A Wk Lng Govt 86; Prtcpted In Olympcs Of The Mnd Wn Rgnls 86; Boston U; Media.

JERNIGAN, SHAWN; Nokomis Regional HS; Detroit, ME; (Y); 17/179; French Clb; Ski Clb; Varsity Clb; Yrbk Stf; Bsbl; Var Crs Cntry; JV Socr; JV Var Trk; High Hon Roll; NHS; Ancnt Hstry Awd; Modrn Hstry Awd; Hstry Techr.

JIPSON, MARY; Edward Little HS; Auburn, ME; (Y); Church Yth Grp; FCA; French Clb; Pep Clb; Spanish Clb; Band; Concert Band; Mrchg Band; Chldhd Educ.

JOHNSON, HARRISON; Morse HS; Bath, ME; (Y); Am Leg Boys St; Boy Scts; Church Yth Grp; Math Tm; Science Clb; Stage Crew; VP JV Socr; L VP Trk; Hon Roll; NHS; ME U; Engr.

JOHNSON, LOUISE; Piscakaquis Community HS; Guilford, ME; (Y); 18/85; AFS; Camera Clb; Church Yth Grp; FHA; Library Aide; SADD; Bsktbl; Trk; Hon Roll; JC Awd; Tchng.

JOHNSON, REBECCA; Houlton HS; Houlton, ME; (Y); 18/135; Church Yth Grp; Cmnty Wkr; Service Clb; Band; Chorus; Church Choir; Bowling; Vllybl; Hon Roll; U Of ME Orono; Elem Ed.

JOHNSTON, JANICE; Lisbon HS; Lisbon, ME; (Y); 25/130; Am Leg Aux Girls St; French Clb; Latin Clb; Red Cross Aide; SADD; VP Stu Cncl; JV Var Bsktbl; Var Socr; Var Sftbl; Cit Awd.

JONES, DAVID; Bangor HS; Bangor, ME; (Y); 93/302; Teachers Aide; Mgr(s); Hon Roll; U Of OR; Sci.

JONES, LESLIE; Bangor HS; Bangor, ME; (Y); Am Leg Aux Girls St; 4-H; Library Aide; Stage Crew; Var Socr; Var Trk; Hon Roll.

JONES, MELANIE; Bangor HS; Bangor, ME; (Y); 10/311; Hosp Aide; Key Clb; Library Aide; Band; Concert Band; Mrchg Band; Pep Band; School Play; Yrbk Rptr; Rep Soph Cls; Pres Acad Ftnss Awd 86; Engl Achvt Awd 84-86; Memrl Schlrshp Essay 86; U Maine; Bus Mgmt.

JONES, MELISSA; Woodland HS; Princeton, ME; (S); FBLA; Office Aide; Varsity Clb; Var Capt Cheerleading; Stat Vllybl; Hon Roll; Bio Awd 85; Gregg Jr Typng Awd-Accrcy 85; Century 21 Spd Typng Awd 85; Biolgst.

JONES, PATRICK B; Maranacook HS; Readfield, ME; (Y); Art Clb; German Clb; School Musical; Socr; Hon Roll; Art Cls-U ME Augusta 85-86; Yng Artst Drwng Cmptn Wnnr 86; Schl Of Art Chicago; Art.

JONES, SHELLY; Hogdon HS; Houlton, ME; (Y); 5/73; Pep Clb; Band; Chorus; Stu Cncl; Bsktbl; Mgr(s); Dnfth Awd; High Hon Roll; Hon Roll; NHS; Typing Awd.

JONES, STACEY; Deering HS; Portland, ME; (Y); 71/300; Hon Roll; Prfct Atten Awd; SR Leag All-Stars 83; Typng Cert 86; CPR Cert 85; MA; Pharm.

JONES, TAMMY; Skowhegan Area HS; Skowhegan, ME; (Y); German Clb; Chorus; School Play; Off Frsh Cls; Cheerleading; Fld Hcky; Co-Capt Gym; Tennis; Hon Roll; Boston U; Psych.

JORDAN, JAYNE; Lewiston HS; Lewiston, ME; (Y); Yrbk Stf; Stat JV Fld Hcky; Intrct Clb; JR SR Prm Committee; Cntrl ME Vctnl Tech Inst; Arts.

JORDAN, LISA; Telstar Regional HS; Locke Mills, ME; (Y); 13/60; Drama Clb; Teachers Aide; Chorus; Color Guard; Yrbk Ed-Chief; Yrbk Phtg; Cheerleading; Hon Roll; Otstndng Eng Awd 85; Otstndng SR Of Mnth 85; Greenwood Finlandia Schlrshp 86; Rhode Island Schl Phtgrphy.

JUTRAS, SANDRA; Lewiston HS; Lewiston, ME; (Y); 39/387; Ski Clb; Varsity Clb; L Capt Cheerleading; High Hon Roll; NHS; ME Schlrs Day 85; Husson Coll; Acctng.

KADEY, SCOTT; Woodland HS; Princeton, ME; (S); Camera Clb; Computer Clb; Drama Clb; FBLA; Varsity Clb; School Play; Lit Mag; High Hon Roll; NHS; Typng Awd 85; Algrba Awd 84; Englsh Awd 84 & 85; Engrng.

KANG, ROBERT Y; Cony HS; Togus, ME; (Y); 4/320; Am Leg Boys St; Pres Science Clb; Orch; Nwsp Ed-Chief; Pres Jr Cls; Pres Stu Cncl; Ntl Merit Schol; Chess Clb; Cmnty Wkr; Gold Mdl Ntl Latin Exam 85; Evertt Perkins Awd Most Outstndng Jr 85; 1st Degree Black Belt 85; Chem.

KANGAS, HOLLY; Buckfield JR SR HS; West Paris, ME; (S); 5/36; Am Leg Aux Girls St; Spanish Clb; Chorus; Yrbk Stf; High Hon Roll; Hon Roll; NHS; Commerc Awd 86; Mid ST Bus Coll; Adm Asst.

KARKOS, KERN; Mt Blue HS; Wilton, ME; (Y); 2/200; Am Leg Boys St; Intnl Clb; Ski Clb; Var Capt Crs Cntry; Var Capt Trk; High Hon Roll; Jr NHS; NHS; Ntl Merit SF; Sal; Emblm Clb Schlrshp 86; Bln Hs Schlrshp 86; Vncnt Lmx Mem Schlrshp 86; Bates Coll.

KASCHUB, ALAN; Skowhegan Area HS; Skowhegan, ME; (Y); Drama Clb; German Clb; Varsity Clb; Band; Concert Band; Jazz Band; Mrchg Band; Pep Band; School Musical; School Play; Shprd Prz Fnd 85; Louis Armstrng Jazz Awd 86; Msc Prfrmng.

KAZILIONIS, LEANNE; South Portland HS; S Portland, ME; (Y); 71/300; Drama Clb; Trs Intnl Clb; JCL; Key Clb; Latin Clb; Political Wkr; Ski Clb; SADD; Stage Crew; Nwsp Stf; Intl Law.

KELLEY, JANE A; Belfast Area HS; Belfast, ME; (Y); 6/118; Math Tm; Chorus; School Musical; Yrbk Sprt Ed; High Hon Roll; Hon Roll; NHS; Ntl Merit Ltr; Pres Schlr; Drama Clb; Caroln F Dntn Schlrshp 86; Upwrd Bound 84-86; U Of ME; Airln Plt.

KELLEY, MARSHA; Belfast Area HS; Belfast, ME; (Y); Teachers Aide; Im Coach Actv; JV Var Fld Hcky; L Var Gym; Hon Roll; Prfct Atten Awd; Mst Imprvd Plyr Awd Gymnstcs 84-85; Pyscl Educ.

KELLY, C TERRANCE; Ashland Community HS; Ashland, ME; (Y); Boy Scts; Pep Clb; SADD; Band; Concert Band; Pep Band; Var L Bsbl; Var Socr; High Hon Roll; Hon Roll; Bio.

KENNEDY, BETH; Edward Little HS; Auburn, ME; (Y); Spanish Clb; Chorus; Hon Roll; U Of ME Orono.

KENNEDY JR, FREDERICK L; Westbrook HS; Westbrook, ME; (Y); 35/200; Boy Scts; VP JA; Latin Clb; Nwsp Rptr; JV Trk; Hon Roll; Syracuse U; Ecnmcs.

KENNEY, MICHELLE L; Portland HS; Portland, ME; (Y); 8/200; Church Yth Grp; Yrbk Stf; Stu Cncl; Var Capt Cheerleading; Hon Roll; Kiwanis Awd; Pres NHS; French Clb; Latin Clb; Ski Clb; Brwn Mdl Top 5 Grls In Cls 86; Gld Key 86; Boston Coll; Bus.

KENNISTON, STEVEN N; Hall-Dale HS; Hallowell, ME; (Y); 17/93; Aud/Vis; Camera Clb; Key Clb; Latin Clb; Math Tm; Ed Yrbk Ed-Chief; Yrbk Phtg; Yrbk Rptr; Yrbk Sprt Ed; Yrbk Stf; U Of ME Orono; Engr.

KENT, MELISSA; Rumford HS; Rumford, ME; (Y); Am Leg Aux Girls St; French Clb; SADD; Teachers Aide; Chorus; School Musical; Hon Roll; Voice Dem Awd; Smith Coll Awd Outstndng Stu; UMO; Pblc Rltns.

KENT, STEVEN; Georges Valley HS; Thomaston, ME; (Y); 1/70; Math Tm; Pres Science Clb; Yrbk Stf; Var Bsktbl; Var Socr; High Hon Roll; VP NHS; Church Yth Grp; Intnl Clb; Math Clb; ST ME Ambl Atten; Prom Comm; Schl Imprvmnt Plan Comm; Pre Med.

KENYON, WANDA; Noble HS; Lebanon, ME; (Y); Key Clb; Math Tm; Teachers Aide; Crs Cntry; Trk; High Hon Roll; Sec NHS; Prfct Atten Awd; Debate Tm.

KETCHEN, KAREN; Woodland HS; Cooper, ME; (Y); 3/79; FBLA; SADD; Nwsp Phtg; Yrbk Stf; Lit Mag; High Hon Roll; Bus Adm.

KETOVER, JILL; Deering HS; Portland, ME; (Y); Cmnty Wkr; Pres FTA; Political Wkr; School Play; Stage Crew; Yrbk Stf; Hon Roll; Drama Clb; Hosp Aide; VP JA; FTA Schlrshp Awd 86; Co Chair Yng Dem Assoc 86; CT Coll; Pol Sci.

KILBORN, KAREN; Lake Region HS; Bridgton, ME; (Y); 41/133; AFS; Am Leg Aux Girls St; Pres Varsity Clb; Yrbk Ed-Chief; Trs Stu Cncl; Bsktbl; Fld Hcky; Trk; Hon Roll; NHS; U Of ME; Psych.

KIMBALL, SHARON; Westbrook HS; Westbrook, ME; (Y); Church Yth Grp; GAA; Varsity Clb; Bsktbl; Socr; Sftbl; Hon Roll; Capt Of Frsty Grls Socr Tm 86; Chld Care.

KING, STEVEN; Deering HS; Portland, ME; (Y); 58/318; Am Leg Boys St; Letterman Clb; Varsity Clb; Capt Var Bsktbl; Var Capt Socr; Hon Roll; Pol Sci.

KINNEY, VICKI; Central Aroostook HS; Blaine, ME; (Y); Am Leg Aux Girls St; Church Yth Grp; French Clb; FHA; Library Aide; Church Choir; JV Mgr(s); JV Score Keeper; Elem Educ.

KLAR, HANS; Bonny Eagle HS; Hollis, ME; (Y); Boy Scts; Cmnty Wkr; Bsbl; JV Bsktbl; Var Ice Hcky; Im Socr; Var Trk; Hon Roll; Eagle Sct BSA 85; Natl Fld Achers Assn Indoor Sec Champ 85; Marine ST Indr & Outdr Archry Chmp 83-85; Sec Schl Tchr.

KLUCK, KEVIN; Cony HS; Augusta, ME; (Y); Church Yth Grp; VP Computer Clb; German Clb; Science Clb; Im Vllybl; Hon Roll.

KNAPP, JENNIFER; Mt Abram HS; Kingfield, ME; (Y); Intnl Clb; Library Aide; Band; Concert Band; Jazz Band; Pep Band; Yrbk Stf; Var L Cheerleading; Stat Trk; Hon Roll; Chrldng Spirit Awd 85-86; ME Grls ST 86; Psych.

KNAPTON, JEFF; Westbrook HS; Westbrook, ME; (Y); 9/190; Am Leg Boys St; Church Yth Grp; Key Clb; VP Latin Clb; Pres Stu Cncl; Bsktbl; Capt Socr; Dnfth Awd; Elks Awd; NHS; Centry III Ldrshp Schlrshp; Hugh O Brien Yth Ldrshp Ambssdr; Schlr/Athlt Awd; Worcester Polytech; Chem Engrng.

KNIGHT, KATHRYN; Livermore Falls HS; Livermore Falls, ME; (Y); 1/90; Am Leg Aux Girls St; Hosp Aide; Math Tm; Var Capt Ski Clb; Mrchg Band; Trs Jr Cls; Var Sftbl; High Hon Roll; NHS; Band; Semi-Fnlst Cngrs/Bndstg Yth Exchng Prog 85-86; Colby Coll.

KNOWLTON, CAROLEE; Jonesport-Beals HS; Jonesport, ME; (Y); Am Leg Aux Girls St; Yrbk Stf; VP Jr Cls; Bsktbl; Var Sftbl; JV Vllybl; Hon Roll; SMVIT; Ckng.

KOKOSZKA, KENNETH; Fort Fairfield HS; Ft Fairfield, ME; (Y); 3/87; Am Leg Boys St; SADD; Concert Band; Jazz Band; Yrbk Stf; Var Bsbl; High Hon Roll; French Clb; Band; Mrchg Band; U S Hist Achvmnt Awd 85-86; Chem Achvmnt Awd 85-86; ME Schlrs Days 85-86; Pilot.

KOREN, SCOTT; Deering HS; Portland, ME; (Y); 27/321; Math Clb; Math Tm; Ski Clb; Varsity Clb; Var Bowling; Var L Golf; JV Tennis; Hon Roll; Acctng.

KORIS, TASHA; Rumford JR SR HS; Rumford, ME; (Y); 17/105; Am Leg Aux Girls St; Latin Clb; Yrbk Stf; Rep Trs Stu Cncl; Var Capt Bsktbl; Var L Fld Hcky; L Trk; NHS; SADD 85 & 86; Big Brthr, Bg Sistr 86; Acctng.

KOTSIMPULOS, KRISTA; Cape Elizabeth HS; Cape Elizabeth, ME; (Y); 23/115; Spanish Clb; SADD; Varsity Clb; Yrbk Stf; Var L Cheerleading; JV Fld Hcky; Hon Roll; Cert Achvmnt Modrn Miss 85; Pre-Law.

KOZA, MELANIE; Lisbon HS; Lisbon Falls, ME; (Y); 3/125; Am Leg Aux Girls St; Math Tm; Pres Frsh Cls; Rep Jr Cls; Rep Sr Cls; Sec Stu Cncl; L Bsktbl; Var L Socr; Var L Sftbl; NHS; Mst Outstndg Soph Girl 84-85; Pre-Med.

KROOK, BETH; R W Traip Acad; Kittery, ME; (Y); 6/70; Camera Clb; Nwsp Phtg; Nwsp Rptr; Nwsp Stf; Yrbk Phtg; Yrbk Stf; L Trk; High Hon Roll; Hon Roll; NHS; 1st Traip Acad Art Cntst 86; 1st Poetry Traid Acad Wtrs Fair 86; Portland Sch Of Art; Grphc Art.

KRUG, BRENT; Calais HS; Calais, ME; (Y); Am Leg Boys St; Concert Band; Jazz Band; Mrchg Band; Yrbk Ed-Chief; Pres Soph Cls; Pres Jr Cls; Rep Stu Cncl; Hon Roll; Mgr Crs Cntry; Stu Of Month 85; Compu Sci.

KRUPKE, DEBRA M; Bangor HS; Bangor, ME; (Y); 6/316; Sec SADD; Band; Chorus; Orch; School Musical; Yrbk Stf; Var L Sftbl; NHS; Ntl Merit SF; Bio Med Engrng.

KUHN, MARIE; Skowhegan Area HS; Hartland, ME; (Y); 6/208; Art Clb; German Clb; Band; Concert Band; Mrchg Band; Pep Band; Variety Show; High Hon Roll; NHS; Lisa Henderson Memrl Schlrshp Awd 86; ME Snwmbl Assoc Schlrshp Awd 86; Dora T Nye Music Awd 86; U Of VT; Bio.

KUPERMAN, MARINA; Portland HS; Portland, ME; (Y); 1/214; Am Leg Aux Girls St; Math Tm; Sec Soph Cls; Sec Jr Cls; Sec Sr Cls; Var Fld Hcky; Var Capt Trk; High Hon Roll; NHS; Val; Prix D Excllnc/French 85; Ntl Hnr Soc Essay Wnnr 86; Preti Awd Hghst Rnkng Schlr/Athlt 86; Brown U; Pre-Med.

LA COMBE, LORI; Lee Acad; Lee, ME; (Y); AFS; Am Leg Aux Girls St; Yrbk Stf; Sec Frsh Cls; Sec Jr Cls; Stu Cncl; High Hon Roll; NHS; Prfct Atten Awd; Guidnc Cnslr.

LA FOSSE, ALICIA; St Dominics Regional HS; Livermore Falls, ME; (Y); Debate Tm; Drama Clb; Keywanettes; NFL; School Play; Var Fld Hcky; L Score Keeper; JV Sftbl; Hon Roll; Psychbio.

LABERGE, CHRISTINA; Cape Elizabeth HS; Cape Elizabeth, ME; (Y); 14/130; Am Leg Aux Girls St; NFL; Speech Tm; Chorus; Church Choir; Pres Concert Band; Mgr Jazz Band; School Musical; Hon Roll; NHS; Gould Solst Music Awd 86; All ST Music Fstvl 84-86; Top Rtngs Solo & Ensmbl Fstvl 84-86; Boston U; Music Ed.

LACHANCE, DEBBIE; St Dominics R HS; Lewiston, ME; (Y); 25/70; Church Yth Grp; Drama Clb; JA; Keywanettes; Pep Clb; Church Choir; School Musical; School Play; Stage Crew; Variety Show; NEDT Scoring 83-84; Carnival Queen 86; Bentley Coll; Acctng.

LACHANCE, DOUGLAS; Biddeford HS; Biddeford, ME; (Y); 8/279; Am Leg Boys St; Art Clb; Yrbk Stf; Hon Roll; NHS; Pres Schlr; Dollars For Schlrs-Schlrshp 86; Excllnc Awds-Frnch, Eng, Art 86; U Of Hartford; Grphcs.

LACROIX, JOSEPH; Yarmouth HS; Yarmouth, ME; (Y); Church Yth Grp; Drama Clb; Key Clb; Latin Clb; SADD; Chorus; Yrbk Stf; Off Jr Cls; Bsbl; Ice Hcky; Air Force; Phys Thrpst.

LAGASSE, BERT; Lewiston HS; Sabattus, ME; (Y); Band; Concert Band; Jazz Band; Mrchg Band; Pep Band; JV Crs Cntry; Army; Pilot.

LAGASSE, NICHOLE; Westbrook HS; Westbrook, ME; (Y); 15/189; Am Leg Aux Girls St; English Clb; Spanish Clb; Stu Cncl; Mgr Wrstlng; Hon Roll; NHS; Pres Schlr; U Of Southern ME.

LAKEMAN, MICHELLE D; Jonesport-Beals HS; Jonesport, ME; (Y); Church Yth Grp; 4-H; FBLA; GAA; Varsity Clb; Band; Stage Crew; Bsktbl; Sftbl; Vllybl; Sftbl DAC Awd 86; Phy Ed Awd-Gymnstcs 85; U Sthrn ME; Bus Mgmt.

LAKIN, LYNN; Livermore Falls HS; Livermore Falls, ME; (Y); Drama Clb; French Clb; Varsity Clb; Band; Concert Band; Mrchg Band; Lit Mag; Var Trk; JR Prom Commtte 86; Jrnlsm.

LALONDE, LISA; Edward Little HS; Auburn, ME; (S); JCL; Latin Clb; Math Tm; Speech Tm; Color Guard; Trs Jr Cls; Stu Cncl; Twrlr; High Hon Roll; Acadmc Hnrs & Math Awds 84; Bus Mngmnt.

LAMMERT, PIET; Georges Valley HS; Thomaston, ME; (Y); 5/75; Am Leg Boys St; Church Yth Grp; Cmnty Wkr; Intnl Clb; Band; School Musical; School Play; Pres Jr Cls; Hon Roll; NHS; Englsh & Histry Awds 86; Comm.

LAMSON, LYNN; Deering HS; Portland, ME; (Y); 14/326; Drama Clb; Hon Roll.

LANDER, STUART A; Nokomis Regional HS; Newport, ME; (Y); 17/155; Band; Concert Band; Mrchg Band; Symp Band; Var Crs Cntry; Var Trk; Var L Wrstlng; High Hon Roll; Hon Roll; NHS; Outstndng Comptr Stu Of Yr 85; Outstndng Sci Awd 86; Engrg Schlrshp 86; U Of ME Orono; Engrg Physcs.

LANDRY, JAMES ROBERTSON; Yarmouth HS; Yarmouth, ME; (Y); Band; Chorus; Jazz Band; Orch; School Musical; Variety Show; Bsbl; Ice Hcky; Mgr(s); Socr.

LANDRY, JEFF; Lewiston HS; Lewiston, ME; (Y); 40/387; Boy Scts; Church Yth Grp; Exploring; JV Bsktbl; JV Mgr(s); High Hon Roll; Hon Roll; NHS; Prfct Atten Awd; Phys Ed Awd 82-83; 4th Pl Carpet Desgn Cont 85-86; Mpls Schl Art/Desgn; Indst Des.

LANDRY, JULIE C; Portland HS; Portland, ME; (Y); Latin Clb; Spanish Clb; Var L Tennis; Hon Roll; AMVETS Charles J Loving Post 25 86; Antmy Of Ldrshp 84; Most Improved Tennis 84; Bentley Coll; Finance.

LANE, REBECCA H; Edward Little HS; Auburn, ME; (Y); 12/324; Church Yth Grp; Spanish Clb; Church Choir; Lit Mag; High Hon Roll; Hon Roll; NHS; Spnsh Awd 85-86; Spnsh Schlrshp 86; U Of Southern ME; Englsh.

LANEY, SAMUEL; Skowhegan Area HS; Skowhegan, ME; (Y); 6/200; Am Leg Boys St; Boy Scts; Church Yth Grp; Latin Clb; Yrbk Phtg; Lit Mag; Var L Socr; High Hon Roll; NHS; Voice Dem Awd; Vigl Hnr Ordr Of Arrow BSA 85; Sci.

LANGILLE, JONATHAN; Orono HS; Orono, ME; (S); Church Yth Grp; English Clb; French Clb; Orch; Nwsp Stf; Yrbk Stf; Golf; Var L Swmmng; High Hon Roll; Hon Roll.

LANGIS, MICHELLE; Westbrook HS; Westbrook, ME; (Y); Church Yth Grp; French Clb; JA; Yrbk Stf; Lit Mag; Sec Jr Cls; JV Var Cheerleading; Trk; Hon Roll; U Of New England; Phys Thrpst.

LAPHAM, KEVIN; Freeport HS; Freeport, ME; (Y); 9/73; Pres Aud/Vis; Cmnty Wkr; JA; Library Aide; PAVAS; SADD; School Musical; Yrbk Ed-Chief; Cit Awd; DAR Awd; Amer Ftr Awd 84-85; Emerson Coll; Mass Comm.

LAPIERRE, KARA; Fryeburg Acad; Glen, NH; (Y); Chorus; Hon Roll; Ntl Merit Ltr; WA U; Psych.

LAPINSKY, ANDREW; Fryeburg Acad; Lovell, ME; (Y); French Clb; JV Bsktbl; Hon Roll; U NH; Acctng.

LAPOINTE, DANNY; Cony HS; Chelsea, ME; (Y); Cmnty Wkr; Hon Roll; Firefighter.

LAPPIN, DAVID; Cheverus HS; Portland, ME; (Y); 5/86; French Clb; Intnl Clb; JA; Key Clb; Latin Clb; Ski Clb; SADD; Teachers Aide; Nwsp Sprt Ed; Yrbk Stf; Knghts Of Clmbs $150 86; Holy Cross Coll.

LARGEY, LORINDA; Fryeburg Acad; Denmark, ME; (S); Am Leg Aux Girls St; Pres French Clb; SADD; Varsity Clb; Chorus; School Musical; Yrbk Ed-Chief; Var L Fld Hcky; Hon Roll; NHS; Ntl Engl Merit Awd 85-86; Intl Forgn Lang Awd 85-86; SYSSA Gd Citznshp Awd 86.

LARKIN, JOHN; Woodland HS; Waite, ME; (S); Chess Clb; Letterman Clb; Varsity Clb; Nwsp Phtg; VP Lit Mag; Var Bsbl; Im Bsktbl; Var Socr; Hon Roll; NHS.

LASH, SCOTT; Medomak Valley HS; Waldoboro, ME; (Y); 3/125; Am Leg Boys St; Church Yth Grp; Cmnty Wkr; 4-H; Stage Crew; Yrbk Stf; Stu Cncl; Mgr Bsktbl; Hon Roll; JCL; Waldoboro SR Ltjrns Schlrshp 86; 3rd Pl MVHS Sci Fair 86; U Of ME; Lbrl Arts.

LASTORIA, MARY KATHERINE; Catherine Mc Auley HS; Portland, ME; (Y); 2/74; Hosp Aide; Key Clb; VP Political Wkr; Ed Lit Mag; Trs Sr Cls; High Hon Roll; Hon Roll; Sal; Voice Dem Awd; Wellesley Bk Awd 86; Part In ME Smr Hmnts Prgm At Bowdoin Coll 86; Engl.

LATHROP, WM CORY; Gardiner Area HS; Gardiner, ME; (Y); Church Yth Grp; French Clb; JV Bsktbl; JV Var Ftbl; Trk; High Hon Roll; Hon Roll; Elec Engr.

LATULIPPE, ROGER; Lewiston HS; Lewiston, ME; (Y); 159/409; Boy Scts; Church Yth Grp; Computer Clb; VP Pres JA; Central ME Vo Tech; Elec Tech.

LAUCKNER, MICHELLE; Traip Acad; Kittery, ME; (Y); 34/68; Drama Clb; Thesps; Band; Concert Band; Jazz Band; Pep Band; School Musical; School Play; Stage Crew; Yrbk Stf; Bus.

LAUZE, LISA; Edward Little HS; Mechanic Falls, ME; (Y); 2/339; Drama Clb; Pres Latin Clb; School Play; Bausch & Lomb Sci Awd; High Hon Roll; Hon Roll; Sec NHS; Pres Schlr; Sal; St Schlr; Yale Bk Awd 85; Math, Sci Awds 86; Simmons Coll; Nrsg.

LAWLESS, VANCE; Woodland HS; Woodland, ME; (Y); Bsbl; U ME Machias; Bus Adm.

LAWRENCE, TARA; Deering HS; Portland, ME; (Y); 16/321; Exploring; French Clb; GAA; Latin Clb; Letterman Clb; Red Cross Aide; Ski Clb; Varsity Clb; Jazz Band; Fld Hcky; ST Champs Swimmng 85-86; SMAA 1st Tm All ST Goalie Fld Hcky 85-86; Mst Imprvd Swmmr Awd 85-86; Mt Allison U; Vet Med.

LAWSON, TARA; Bonny Eagle HS; W Windham, ME; (Y); Am Leg Aux Girls St; French Clb; VP Soph Cls; VP Pres Stu Cncl; JV Var Fld Hcky; Var Capt Trk; High Hon Roll; Hon Roll; Church Yth Grp; Girl Scts; Field Hockey ST Champs; Psych.

LAWSURE, SHAWN; Cape Elizabeth HS; Cape Elizabeth, ME; (Y); 28/126; Stat Bsktbl; Crs Cntry; Trk; Hon Roll; Astrnmy.

LE CLAIR, VICTORIA; Gardiner Area HS; Gardiner, ME; (Y); Am Leg Aux Girls St; Drama Clb; Hosp Aide; Pep Clb; Pres Spanish Clb; Sec Band; Pres Frsh Cls; Stu Cncl; Im JV Cheerleading; Concert Band; Natl Hnrs Scty 86; Solo & Ensbl Tnr Sax Solo 84; Math.

LE GALLEE, WILLIAM H; Biddeford HS; Arundel, ME; (Y); 2/292; Drama Clb; School Play; NHS; Ntl Merit SF; Sal; Hd Of Tutorg Prog 85-86; Georgetown U; Forgn Lang.

LEARNED, LINDA; Telstar Regional HS; Andover, ME; (Y); 11/77; Am Leg Aux Girls St; Church Yth Grp; Trs Frsh Cls; Pres Stu Cncl; Var JV Bsktbl; Crs Cntry; L Trk; Hon Roll.

LEARY, RHONDA; Lawrence HS; Fairfield, ME; (Y); French Clb; Ski Clb; Capt Cheerleading; Sftbl; High Hon Roll; Hon Roll; Westbrook Coll; Dntl Hygnest.

LEARY, STEPHANIE; Medomak Valley HS; Warren, ME; (Y); French Clb; Chorus; Var L Golf; JV Sftbl; Hon Roll; Natl Lang Arts Olympd 83-84; St Josephs Coll; Engl.

LEBEL, VICKIE; Oak Hill HS; Sabattus, ME; (Y); 21/85; Am Leg Aux Girls St; Office Aide; Capt JV Bsktbl; JV Var Fld Hcky; JV Var Sftbl; Hon Roll; SR Fince 85-86; Husson Coll.

LEBLANC, DANIEL; Presque Iole HS; Presque Isle, ME; (Y); Church Yth Grp; Drama Clb; Math Tm; Y-Teens; School Play; Stage Crew; JV Bsbl; Socr; Hon Roll; NHS; Coaches Awd-Soccer 84; Chemcl Engr.

LECOMPTE, CARRIE; St Dominic Regional HS; Lisbon, ME; (Y); 3/67; Nwsp Rptr; Var Capt Bsktbl; Var Capt Fld Hcky; Var Capt Sftbl; Hon Roll; VP NHS; Voice Dem Awd; ME H S Tchrs Assn Schlrshp 86; Blaine House Schlrs 86; Thomas Coll; Coll Prof.

LEDOUX II, WILLIAM R; St Dominic Regional HS; Greene, ME; (Y); 6/70; VP Drama Clb; Key Clb; Math Tm; School Musical; School Play; Stage Crew; Variety Show; Var Bsbl; Var Ice Hcky; Var Socr; NEDT Merit Achvt Awd; Minr Pt Trphy; Engrg Physcs.

LEE, LAURA; Calais HS; Calais, ME; (Y); Am Leg Aux Girls St; VP Drama Clb; School Musical; School Play; Stage Crew; Yrbk Bus Mgr; Hon Roll; Pres NHS; Bus Admn.

LEGENDRE, DIANE; Lewiston HS; Lewistin, ME; (Y); 4/380; Math Tm; Pep Clb; Q&S; Ski Clb; Lit Mag; High Hon Roll; NHS; Normand Dionne Awd; Worcester Poly Tech Inst; Bio.

LEGENDRE, THOMAS; Lewiston HS; Lewiston, ME; (Y); Am Leg Boys St; Key Clb; Lit Mag; Hon Roll; NHS; Modl ST Legs 84; U Of NH; Ecnmcs.

LEHAN, JEREMY; Skowhegan Area HS; Skowhegan, ME; (Y); 12/200; Drama Clb; Band; Nwsp Stf; Sec Sr Cls; Socr; Tennis; High Hon Roll; Jr NHS; NHS; Ntl Merit Ltr; Colby Coll Bk Awd 86; Englsh.

LEHANE, CHRISTOPHER; Kennebunk HS; Kennebunk, ME; (Y); 28/150; Boys Clb Am; Church Yth Grp; Drama Clb; Model UN; Spanish Clb; Yrbk Sprt Ed; Stu Cncl; Capt Var Bsktbl; High Hon Roll; NHS; Bob Butler Awd Mst Outstndg Bsktbll Plyr Cnty 85-86; Citi Bank Wrtng Fnlst 85-86; Natl Hist Wnnr 84; Amherst Coll; Pre Law.

LENFESTEY, SALLY; Jonesport-Beals HS; Beals, ME; (Y); 1/35; Yrbk Ed-Chief; VP Soph Cls; Pres Jr Cls; Pres Sr Cls; JV Cheerleading; Sftbl; Dnfth Awd; High Hon Roll; NHS; Frnch Awd 83-85; Amer Govt Awd 85-86; Home Ec Awd 85-86; U ME Machias; Pol Sci.

LENK, BRIAN; Nells HS; Ogunquit, ME; (Y); Camera Clb; Letterman Clb; Ski Clb; Varsity Clb; Nwsp Sprt Ed; Var L Ftbl; Var L Trk; Hon Roll; Jr NHS; NHS; ME Model ST Assmbly 86; Bus Adm.

LEPKOWSKI, MICHELE; Skowhegan Area HS; Skowhegan, ME; (Y); 3/199; Pres 4-H; Latin Clb; School Musical; Nwsp Rptr; Pres Frsh Cls; Rep Stu Cncl; JV Fld Hcky; L Tennis; High Hon Roll; NHS; Lat Awd 84-86; Sptsmnshp Awd 85; Girls ST Dely 86; Neurosrgn.

LETOURNEAU, DOREEN; Westbrook HS; Westbrook, ME; (Y); Keywanettes; Nwsp Ed-Chief; Nwsp Phtg; Nwsp Rptr; Lit Mag; Soph Cls; Jr Cls; L Var Tennis; L Var Trk; Dnfth Awd; Wmns Lit Un 85-86; Jrnlsm.

LEVASSEUR, PATTY; Fort Kent Community HS; Ft Kent, ME; (Y); 12/150; Am Leg Aux Girls St; Concert Band; Nwsp Stf; Ed Yrbk Ed-Chief; Pres Sr Cls; Stu Cncl; Cit Awd; Hon Roll; Pres NHS; MSAD 27 Scl Schlrshp 86; Actvty Ltr Awd 86; Pres Acdmc Fit Awd 86; U ME Orono; Lng.

LEVESQUE, JUAN; Bucksport HS; Bucksport, ME; (Y); 10/125; Cmnty Wkr; Ski Clb; Varsity Clb; Band; Concert Band; Jazz Band; Mrchg Band; Pep Band; School Musical; Variety Show; Schlrshp Outward Bound Trip 86; Stu Of Mnth 86; Top 10% Of Clss, Pres Ftnss Awd 86; U Of Miami; Maine Bio.

LEWIS, JONATHAN; Noble HS; North Berwick, ME; (Y); Church Yth Grp; Var Ftbl; Capt Trk; Var Wrstlng; Hon Roll; Jr NHS; Prfct Atten Awd; ME Maritime Acad; Navy.

LIBBEY, JANE; Edward Little HS; Auburn, ME; (S); JV Capt Bsktbl; High Hon Roll; Prfct Atten Awd; Sal; Eng Awd 84; U ME; Gentc Resrch.

LIBBY, JEFFREY; Edward Little HS; Poland, ME; (S); Key Clb; Varsity Clb; Var Bsbl; Var Bsktbl; Var Ftbl; High Hon Roll; Ldrshp Awd; Cls A All ST Pntr.

LIBBY, TRACEY; Cony HS; Augusta, ME; (Y); Yrbk Stf; Hon Roll; Lbrl Arts.

LIESE, ERIC; Cheverus HS; Windham, ME; (Y); Hosp Aide; High Hon Roll; Crs Cntry; Trk; Engl Achvt Awd 84-85; Aerontcl Engrng.

LIMOGES, BRADFORD; Edward Little HS; Auburn, ME; (S); Boy Scts; Church Yth Grp; Exploring; Key Clb; Socr; Hon Roll; Physcl Sci.

LINCOLN, LORI; Woodland HS; Woodland, ME; (Y); Hosp Aide; Letterman Clb; Pep Clb; SADD; Teachers Aide; Varsity Clb; VICA; Trs Sr Cls; Cheerleading; Tennis; JV Chrng Awd 83-84; Coaches Athlc Awd Chrldng 86; U ME; Childhood Educ.

LITCHFIELD, TIMOTHY W; Buckfield HS; West Sumner, ME; (S); 6/36; Am Leg Boys St; Church Yth Grp; Cmnty Wkr; 4-H; French Clb; Library Aide; Math Tm; SADD; Varsity Clb; Yrbk Stf; U Hatford Schlrshp 86; Sci Stu Mst Potntl, Bst Math Stu 86; US Army Schlr/Athlt 85 & 86; MVP Bsbl 85; U Of Hartford CT; Cvl Engrng.

LITTLE, DAVID; Fort Fairfield HS; Ft Fairfield, ME; (Y); 8/67; Chess Clb; French Clb; Trs SADD; Varsity Clb; Yrbk Stf; Var L Bsbl; Var L Bsktbl; Var Golf; High Hon Roll; Prfct Atten Awd; Top 10 Pct Cls Awds 84-86.

LIZOTTE, KIM; Wisdom HS; Madawaska, ME; (Y); French Clb; SADD; VICA; Var Stat Bsktbl; Score Keeper; Hon Roll; Nwsp Stf; JV Vllybl; Cert Nrsng Assistants 87; Reg Nrs.

LLOYD, MARGARET; Easton HS; Easton, ME; (Y); Am Leg Aux Girls St; Church Yth Grp; French Clb; Math Tm; Varsity Clb; Band; Chorus; Yrbk Stf; Sec Frsh Cls; Sec Soph Cls; Nrsng.

LOCKE, AMY; Caribou HS; Caribou, ME; (S); 12/240; Church Yth Grp; Debate Tm; Varsity Clb; Band; Concert Band; Mrchg Band; Trk; Hon Roll; NHS; St Schlr; Acad All Amer 86; Soc Distngshd Amer H S Stu 86; Psych.

LONDON, LISA; Hodgdon HS; New Limerick, ME; (Y); Mgr Bsktbl; Hon Roll; Dirigo Grls ST Altrnt 86; Bus.

LONGTIN, MICHAEL; St Dominics Regional HS; Greene, ME; (Y); 4/66; Computer Clb; Key Clb; Math Clb; Math Tm; Nwsp Rptr; Nwsp Stf; Lit Mag; Hon Roll; Kiwanis Awd; NHS; Key Clb Jacket 85; U Of ME Orono; Elec Engr.

LORD, LORI; Marshwood HS; S Berwick, ME; (Y); 11/150; Church Yth Grp; Math Tm; Band; Concert Band; Jazz Band; Mrchg Band; Yrbk Bus Mgr; Yrbk Stf; Stu Cncl; Fld Hcky; Educ.

LOVEJOY, STACEY; Buckfield JR SR HS; Buckfield, ME; (S); 1/4; Am Leg Aux Girls St; Pres 4-H; Varsity Clb; Yrbk Stf; JV Var Bsktbl; Var Socr; High Hon Roll; VP NHS; Sal; MSSPA Prncpls Awd-Acadmc Excllnc & Ctznshp 86; Presdntl Acadmc Ftns Awd 86; HOBY-OUTSTNDNG-LDRSHP Sm; Providence Coll; Psychlgy.

LOWANS, MICHELLE; Gardiner Area HS; Gardiner, ME; (Y); Office Aide; Spanish Clb; Yrbk Stf; Mgr(s); Score Keeper; Prfct Atten Awd; UMO; Psych.

LOWE, GRETA A; Sumner Memorial HS; Corea, ME; (Y); 1/80; Red Cross Aide; Rep Stu Cncl; JV Mgr(s); Var Capt Sftbl; High Hon Roll; NHS; St Schlr; Val; Math Dept Awd 85-86; NH U; Vet.

LUCE, GRAHAM; North Yarmouth Acad; Falmouth, ME; (Y); Computer Clb; Drama Clb; Math Tm; Model UN; Crs Cntry; JV Lcrss; JV Socr; JV Tennis; Hon Roll; Crtv Wrtng Awd 86.

LUCE, KATIE; Windham HS; Windham, ME; (Y); 20/195; Latin Clb; Varsity Clb; Yrbk Stf; Rep Frsh Cls; Rep Soph Cls; Rep Jr Cls; Rep Sr Cls; Rep Stu Cncl; Bsktbl; Socr; Democratie Prty Schlrshp 86; New Hampshire Coll; Accntng.

LUCE, STEPHANIE; North Yarmouth Acad; Cumberland, ME; (Y); Mrchg Band; Crs Cntry; Trk; Dance Clb; Band; Sftbl; Hon Roll; Effort Commendatn Lst 85-86; Peace Corps; Soclgy.

LUKE, LORRAINE; Oxford Hills HS; Oxford, ME; (Y); AFS; French Clb; Key Clb; Latin Clb; Sftbl; High Hon Roll; Hon Roll; NHS.

LUMPPIO, HEATHER; Orono HS; Orono, ME; (S); 4-H; Intnl Clb; VP Spanish Clb; SADD; Band; Concert Band; Jazz Band; Mrchg Band; Orch; Pep Band; Hugh O Brian Ldrshp Awd 84.

LUNT, KIM; Cony HS; Augusta, ME; (Y); Church Yth Grp; Library Aide; Office Aide; Chorus; School Musical; Variety Show; Hon Roll; SOC Svcs.

LYMAN, DANIEL; Skowhegan Area HS; Skowhegan, ME; (Y); Am Leg Boys St; Math Tm; Concert Band; Jazz Band; Mrchg Band; Pep Band; VP Sr Cls; Socr; High Hon Roll; Church Yth Grp; Annual H S Math Exam Awd 85.

LYMBURNER, ANDY; Bucksport SR HS; Orland, ME; (Y); 7/130; Var Bsbl; Var Trk; High Hon Roll; Hon Roll; Ntl Merit Ltr; St Schlr; U Of ME Smmr Prog Gftd Math & Sci Stu 86; Engrng.

LYMBURNER, JO DEE LYNN; George Stevens Acad; Penobscot, ME; (Y); Am Leg Aux Girls St; French Clb; Math Tm; Hon Roll; NHS.

LYNE, SEAN; Cheverus HS; Saco, ME; (Y); Letterman Clb; Office Aide; Ski Clb; Spanish Clb; Varsity Clb; Nwsp Rptr; Nwsp Stf; Yrbk Bus Mgr; Yrbk Stf; Hon Roll; Bio Awd 85; Spnsh Exchng 85-86; Dukane; Intl Bnkg.

MAC CONNELL, SHELLY A; Sanford HS; Springvale, ME; (Y); Math Tm; SADD; Y-Teens; Var L Cheerleading; NHS; Pres Frsh Cls; Pres Soph Cls; VP Jr Cls; Hugh O Brian Awd; Janap U S Senate Schlrshp.

MAC DONALD, MARY; Pine Tree Acad; Bowdoinham, ME; (Y); 3/24; Church Yth Grp; Ski Clb; Teachers Aide; Band; Chorus; Symp Band; High Hon Roll; School Play; Church Choir; Atlantic Union Coll Music Scholar 86; Atlantic Union Coll; Music.

MAC KINNON, KATHERINE; Rumford HS; West Peru, ME; (Y); 20/115; Am Leg Aux Girls St; Church Yth Grp; French Clb; Church Choir; Sec Stu Cncl; Capt Cheerleading; Hon Roll; NHS; Big Brothers Big Sisters 85-86; Nrsng.

MAC PHEE, LEONARD; Mt Blue HS; Farmington, ME; (Y); Am Leg Boys St; Church Yth Grp; School Musical; Var L Bsktbl; L Capt Socr; Hon Roll; NHS; Messiah Coll; Pol Sci.

MACLAUCHLAN, MARK; Deering HS; Portland, ME; (Y); 95/321; Cmnty Wkr; Radio Clb; SADD; Nwsp Bus Mgr; Bsktbl; Cit Awd; Hon Roll; Jr NHS; Prfct Atten Awd; Voice Dem Awd; U Of ME; Psych.

MADEAU, JOYE; Lewiston HS; Lewiston, ME; (Y); Cmnty Wkr; Intnl Clb; Sec Trs Ski Clb; Teachers Aide; Varsity Clb; Yrbk Stf; JV Trk; Hon Roll; Rotary Awd; Champlain Coll; Hmn Wlfr.

MADORE, KAREN; Van Buren District Secondry; Van Buren, ME; (Y); 10/69; SADD; Yrbk Bus Mgr; Yrbk Stf; Trs Frsh Cls; Trs Soph Cls; Trs Jr Cls; Trs Sr Cls; JV Var Cheerleading; Hon Roll; Legal Sec.

MAHER, SHANNON; Orono HS; Orono, ME; (S); 11/113; AFS; French Clb; VP Girl Scts; Hosp Aide; Math Tm; Chorus; School Musical; Yrbk Phtg; Stu Cncl; Hon Roll; Cadette SR Plng Brd With Grl Scts 85-86.

MAHEUX, JOLINE; Lewiston HS; Lewiston, ME; (Y); Sec Church Yth Grp; Girl Scts; Teachers Aide; Church Choir; Coach Actv; Socr; Vllybl; French Hon Soc; High Hon Roll; Hon Roll; Shrthnd Awd 86; Eng Dept Awd 86; Fr Awd 86; CMVTI; Sec.

MAILHOT, DARLENE; St Dominics Regional HS; Lewiston, ME; (Y); 5/60; VP Church Yth Grp; Rep Frsh Cls; Sec Jr Cls; Sec Sr Cls; Rep Stu Cncl; Hon Roll; VP Of St Petes Yth Grp 85-86; U Of ME Orono; Dntl Hygnst.

MAILHOT, DAWN; Fryeburg Acad; North Lovell, ME; (Y); Art Clb; Library Aide; Color Guard; Cheerleading; Gym; Sftbl; Hon Roll; Bently Coll; Acctng.

MAINS, CHARLENE; Windham HS; Windham, ME; (Y); 21/170; Band; Chorus; Jazz Band; Var JV Mgr(s); Hon Roll; Jr NHS; NHS; Acctg Awd 86; Band Awd 85; M S Hancock Inc Schlrshp 86; Thomas Coll; Acctg.

MAJOR, ELIZABETH; Catherine Mc Auley HS; Scarborough, ME; (Y); Key Clb; Radio Clb; Ski Clb; Yrbk Stf; Rep Frsh Cls; Rep Soph Cls; Var Cheerleading; Trk; Vllybl; Hon Roll; Pediatrician.

MALVESTA, JENNIFER; Bangor HS; Bangor, ME; (Y); Cmnty Wkr; Hosp Aide; SADD; Yrbk Phtg; Off Soph Cls; VP Stu Cncl; Fld Hcky; Trk; Hon Roll; Captn Firgure Sktng Drl Tm 85-86; Bus.

MANDARELLI, RHONDA MARIE; Catherine Mc Auley HS; S Windham, ME; (Y); 7/59; Am Leg Aux Girls St; Hosp Aide; Pres SADD; Lit Mag; Rep Jr Cls; VP Stu Cncl; Hon Roll; NHS; Voice Dem Awd; Fndr SADD Awd 86; Schl Cmmnctns Awd 86; Fordham U; Pre-Med.

MANGINO, SAMUEL; Falmouth HS; Falmouth, ME; (Y); 30/100; French Clb; Band; Var Capt Bsbl; Var JV Bsktbl; Var Capt Crs Cntry; Var Golf; JV Socr; Im Vllybl; Hon Roll; Bksbl Clss C ST Champs 85; Bsbl Cls Western ME Rnnr Up 86; Acctng.

MANK, HEATHER; Medomak Valley HS; Waldoboro, ME; (Y); Trs AFS; Church Yth Grp; VP Latin Clb; Yrbk Stf; Stu Cncl; JV Var Cheerleading; L Crs Cntry; L Trk; Hon Roll; Amer HS Athlt X-Cntry 84-85; Messiah Coll Grantham; Nrsng.

MANN, THOMAS; Bucksport HS; Bucksport, ME; (Y); Pres Church Yth Grp; Computer Clb; Pres Band; Jazz Band; Stu Cncl; Var Ftbl; Hon Roll; JP Sousa Awd; French Clb; Varsity Clb; Bucksport Allumni Schlrshp 86; John Forscyth Schlrshp 86; Plymouth ST Coll; Comp Info Sy.

MANNING, TOM; South Portland HS; S Portland, ME; (Y); 3/300; Boy Scts; SADD; Soph Cls; Jr Cls; JV Socr; Tennis; NHS; Yale Book Awd 86; Maine Schlrs 86; Dirigo Bys ST 86; Bus.

MANSUR, KENNETH; Edward Little HS; Auburn, ME; (S); Math Tm; Varsity Clb; Concert Band; Jazz Band; Mrchg Band; Nwsp Stf; Var L Trk; Hon Roll; Comp Pgmmr.

MARBLE, BECKY; Marshwood HS; Eliot, ME; (Y); 17/140; Latin Clb; Math Tm; Off Frsh Cls; Sec Soph Cls; Sec Jr Cls; Sec Sr Cls; Stu Cncl; Bsktbl; Fld Hcky; Trk; U Of ME; Comp Sci.

MARCOTTE, AMY L; Van Buren District Secondary Schl; Van Buren, ME; (Y); 6/74; Am Leg Aux Girls St; Church Yth Grp; Math Clb; Band; Concert Band; Jazz Band; Mrchg Band; Nwsp Stf; Yrbk Stf; Pres Sr Cls; Ricker Coll Schlrshp 86; Hgst Hnrs Hstry 86; MVP Sccr 86; St Josephs Coll; Pre-Law.

MARDIGIAN, ANISSA; South Portland HS; S Portland, ME; (Y); 34/301; Drama Clb; Intnl Clb; School Play; Yrbk Ed-Chief; Hon Roll; Cmnctns.

MARIN, JOSEPH P; Community HS; Fort Kent, ME; (Y); 12/160; Hon Roll; Ntl Merit SF; Pres Schlr; By Scts Frshmn Frnch Awd Cmstry Ad 84 & 85; ME Schlr Dy Cert Hnr Comp Pgm JR Yr; U Of ME; Engrng Physcs.

MARQUIS, PETER; Fort Kent Community HS; Ft Kent Mills, ME; (Y); SADD; Off Frsh Cls; Bsktbl; Golf; AMO; Mchncl Engnrng.

MARSTON, CHERYL; Bangor HS; Bangor, ME; (Y); Church Yth Grp; Cmnty Wkr; Band; Variety Show; Rep Frsh Cls; Var Capt Cheerleading; Hon Roll; Pres Phys Ftns Awd; Outstndng Achvt Phys Educ; EMVTI; Bus Mgmt.

MARTELL, HEIDI; Bonny Eagle HS; Limerick, ME; (Y); French Clb; Band; Stu Cncl; JV Fld Hcky; High Hon Roll; Hon Roll; Jr NHS; Arts.

MARTIN, CRYSTAL; Biddeford HS; Biddeford, ME; (Y); 69/280; Cheerleading; Westbrook Coll; Retlg.

MARTIN, GAIL; Caribou HS; Caribou, ME; (S); 4/200; Office Aide; Band; Mgr(s); High Hon Roll; Hon Roll; Ntl Merit Ltr; Psych.

MARTIN, LISA; Fort Kent Community HS; Fort Kent, ME; (Y); 12/135; Pep Clb; Ski Clb; Band; Concert Band; Pep Band; Vllybl; Hon Roll; Ski Tm Var Ltr 83; Mth & Civics Hnr Awd 83; Westbrook; Early Chldhd Ed.

MARTIN, TINA; Ft Kent Community HS; Eagle Lake, ME; (Y); 11/151; SADD; Varsity Clb; Chorus; Nwsp Rptr; JV Im Bsktbl; Var L Sftbl; Var L Tennis; Im Vllybl; Gov Hon Prg Awd; Hon Roll; Hghst Achvt In Sr Comp & In Creative Wrtng 86; Hghst Achvt In Psych Ii 85; U Of ME-FARMINGTON; Elem Ed.

MARTIN, TOMAS; Ft Kent Community HS; Fort Kent, ME; (Y); Chess Clb; Computer Clb; Math Clb; Political Wkr; Science Clb; Service Clb; SADD; Varsity Clb; Rep Frsh Cls; Rep Soph Cls; Hon HS SR Fully Enrlld Coll By HS 86; U FL Gainesville; Comp Engr.

MARTINDALE, SCOTT; South Hope Christian Schl; Waldoboro, ME; (S); 1/7; Church Yth Grp; Church Choir; Stage Crew; Yrbk Stf; Var Bsktbl; JV Socr; High Hon Roll; Lion Awd; Hghst Avg In H S 84-85; Awd For Acad Excllnc 83; Physcs.

MASON, PHILIP; Gorham HS; Gorham, ME; (Y); Pres Sec 4-H; JA; Math Tm; Band; Concert Band; Var Crs Cntry; JV Wrstlng; High Hon Roll; NHS; St Schlr; Sci.

MASSELLI, SHEILA; Lewiston HS; Lewiston, ME; (Y); Letterman Clb; Varsity Clb; L Var Bsktbl; L Var Fld Hcky; Hon Roll; Finance.

MASTERS, ERIC; Lincoln Acad; Medomak, ME; (S); 1/137; VP AFS; JCL; Pres Latin Clb; Math Tm; Speech Tm; Rep Jr Cls; Sec Stu Cncl; JV Bsbl; JV Capt Bsktbl; Var Socr; H S Schlr Pgm 86; Studnt Leadrshp Pgm-Bates Coll 86; Lawyer.

MATTHEWS, JEFF; St Domincs R HS; Lewiston, ME; (Y); 19/75; Chess Clb; Key Clb; Math Tm; Ed Nwsp Ed-Chief; Stu Cncl; Bsbl; Bsktbl; Hon Roll; NHS; Hugh O Brian Yth Fndtn Ldrshp Semnrs 85; UMO Pulp & Ppr Co Engrng Prog 86; Elctrnc Engr.

MATTSON, ERIK T; Bucksport HS; Bucksport, ME; (Y); 15/125; Varsity Clb; Nwsp Stf; Pres VP Stu Cncl; Capt Crs Cntry; Capt Trk; Cit Awd; Hon Roll; NHS; Prfct Atten Awd; Voice Dem Awd; Stu Yr 86; Hmcmng King 85; Exec Cncl 84-86; Bentley Coll; Bus Adm.

MATTSON, KIRSTEN; Bucksport HS; Bucksport, ME; (Y); 13/115; Church Yth Grp; Cmnty Wkr; Letterman Clb; Varsity Clb; Yrbk Bus Mgr; Capt Bsktbl; Var Socr; Hon Roll; Jr NHS; NHS; Hghst Awd ST Solo & Ensmbl Fest Piano 83; 3rd Regl Typg I Comptn 84; 1st Regl Shrthd I Comptn 86; Westbrook Coll; Dentl Hyg.

MAZEROLLE, LISA; Caribou HS; Caribou, ME; (S); 7/241; Am Leg Aux Girls St; Debate Tm; Drama Clb; Girl Scts; Varsity Clb; Chorus; School Play; Rep Frsh Cls; Rep Soph Cls; Var Bsktbl; Louisville U; Pblc Reltns.

MAZURKIEWICZ, STUART; Deerling HS; Portland, ME; (Y); 143/321; Boy Scts; JV Socr; Im Vllybl; Comp Sci.

MC ALLISTER, ALTHEA; Fryeburg Acad; Center Lovell, ME; (Y); Girl Scts; Latin Clb; Spanish Clb; SADD; School Play; Bsktbl; Mgr(s); Score Keeper; Sftbl; Hon Roll; Intl Frgn Lang Awd 85; Secndry Ed.

MC AULEY, CINNAMON; Cony HS; Augusta, ME; (Y); Church Yth Grp; Dance Clb; Pep Clb; Political Wkr; Spanish Clb; Variety Show; Hon Roll; Martin Luther King Schlrshp 86; 85 All 4 Yrs Awd 86; Holy Cross Coll; Psychlgy.

MC CANN, STACEY LYNN; Sanford HS; Sanford, ME; (Y); Science Clb; SADD; Varsity Clb; Bsktbl; Fld Hcky; Hon Roll; Elem Teacher.

MC CARTHY, COLLEEN; Catherine Mc Auley HS; Portland, ME; (Y); 1/75; Am Leg Aux Girls St; Cmnty Wkr; Hosp Aide; Pres Key Clb; Latin Clb; Scholastic Bowl; Nwsp Rptr; Nwsp Stf; Yrbk Stf; Sec Frsh Cls; Holy Cross Bk Awd 85-86; Bio.

MC CARTHY, LANE; Deering HS; C Elizabeth, ME; (Y); Ski Clb; Crs Cntry; Swmmng; Tennis; Dere Aglia Paraskevi; Phyl.

MC CATHY, PATRICIA; Westbrook HS; Westbrook, ME; (Y); 5/200; French Clb; Math Tm; Chorus; Color Guard; Mrchg Band; High Hon Roll; Hon Roll; NHS; St Schlr; Lib Arts Coll; Frnch.

MC CLEAVE, BONNIE; Orono HS; Orono, ME; (S); 18/114; SADD; Band; Nwsp Rptr; Nwsp Sprt Ed; Yrbk Stf; Var Stat Bsktbl; Var JV Score Keeper; Var Swmmng; High Hon Roll; Hon Roll.

MC COLLOR, BRUCE; Skowhegan Area HS; Skowhegan, ME; (Y); 15/175; Am Leg Boys St; Varsity Clb; Var Bsbl; JV Bsktbl; Var Socr; Var Trk; Hon Roll; NHS; U Of ME; Engrng.

MC COLLOUGH, KELLY SUSAN; Rumford JR SR HS; Rumford, ME; (Y); 1/126; Am Leg Aux Girls St; Math Tm; Pres Sr Cls; L Trk; Cit Awd; NHS; Pres Schlr; St Schlr; Val; Drama Clb; U Of New Englnd Pres Schlrshp 86; U Of New England; Phys Ther.

MC CONNELL, JEFFREY; Edward Little HS; Auburn, ME; (S); Computer Clb; Math Tm; JV Socr; Var Tennis; Vllybl; High Hon Roll; Hon Roll; ME Cnsrvtn Schl 85; Comp Sci.

MC CORMACK, TIM; Caribou HS; New Sweden, ME; (S); 1/250; Church Yth Grp; CAP; Debate Tm; 4-H; Varsity Clb; Band; Capt Drill Tm; Trs Stu Cncl; Cheerleading; JV Crs Cntry; Flgt Cmmdr-Natl Cadt Ofcr Schl-Cvl Air Patrl 85; Aerosp Engrng.

MC CORMICK, BOB; Orono HS; Orono, ME; (S); 16/115; Boy Scts; Chess Clb; Church Yth Grp; Math Tm; Spanish Clb; SADD; Nwsp Phtg; Yrbk Phtg; Yrbk Rptr; Yrbk Stf; Fredrick T Burpee Sportsmnshp Awd 85; All Conf, Acad Ftbl Tm 85; Mech Engrng.

MC CUE, AIMEE E; Fryeburg Acad; Bridgton, ME; (Y); Cmnty Wkr; Debate Tm; Drama Clb; French Clb; Radio Clb; Ski Clb; Varsity Clb; School Musical; Co-Capt Sftbl; Var L Tennis; Fshn Dsgnr.

MC DANIEL, JERRY M; Lake Region HS; Bridgton, ME; (Y); 2/127; Am Leg Boys St; Pres Science Clb; Off Band; Jazz Band; Pep Band; Nwsp Stf; High Hon Roll; Jr NHS; Pres NHS; Ntl Merit SF; U ME Orono; Cvl Engrg.

MC FADDEN, CARRIE C; Mt View HS; Liberty, ME; (Y); 9/98; Drama Clb; Hosp Aide; Service Clb; SADD; Color Guard; Lit Mag; JV Var Fld Hcky; Hon Roll; NHS; Pres Schlr; Trinity Coll; Pre-Med.

MC GLAUFLIN, DONNA; Edward Little HS; Mechanic Falls, ME; (Y); 18/329; Drama Clb; Pres Latin Clb; Math Tm; L Crs Cntry; Capt L Trk; Cit Awd; Hon Roll; Kiwanis Awd; NHS; Prfct Atten Awd; Clark U; Bio.

MC GLAUFLIN, WARREN; Edward Little HS; Mc Cannon Falls, ME; (S); Latin Clb; Math Tm; Band; Concert Band; Mrchg Band; Pep Band; Crs Cntry; Hon Roll; Vet.

MC GRATH, MICHAEL; Oxford Hills HS; Harrison, ME; (Y); Boy Scts; Church Yth Grp; Cmnty Wkr; Drama Clb; French Clb; Teachers Aide; Acpl Chr; Band; Concert Band; Drill Tm; Coaches Awd Sccr 85; Outstndng Musician 84-86; Frshmn ST Trck Champ 84; Juillard Schl Of Music; Music.

MC GREGOR II, RUSSELL C; Orono HS; Orono, ME; (S); Boy Scts; Exploring; Math Tm; Chorus; Yrbk Stf; Rep Stu Cncl; Stat Ice Hcky; Var L Socr; Hon Roll; NHS; Astrnmy.

MC GWIN, CHRISTINE; Catherine Mcauley HS; Portland, ME; (Y); 16/73; Sec French Clb; Lit Mag; NEDT Awd; Interview Natl Acad Decathln Awd 86; Excllnc In Understndng Frnch Lit 87; Englsh.

MC HALE, HEATHER; Wells HS; Wells, ME; (Y); Math Tm; VP Frsh Cls; Rep Trs Stu Cncl; High Hon Roll; VP NHS; Capt JV Bsktbl; JV Sftbl; Top Stu Alg,Pre Calculus 84-86; Top Stu Frnch IV 86; Top Stu Typng 86; Acctng.

MC HATTEN, MARCEY; Ashland Community HS; Ashland, ME; (Y); Am Leg Aux Girls St; Model UN; VP Band; VP Soph Cls; VP Jr Cls; Var L Bowling; Var L Socr; Im Vllybl; High Hon Roll; Pres NHS; Alg II Excllnce; Geom Excllnce; Colby Coll Book Prize; USAF Acad; Engrng.

MC INNIS, DEANA MARIE; Noble HS; West Lebanon, ME; (Y); Am Leg Aux Girls St; Debate Tm; French Clb; Sec Key Clb; Latin Clb; Math Tm; Nwsp Ed-Chief; Hon Roll; St Schlr; Peer Cnslr 85-87; Pltcl Sci.

MC INTIRE, AICHA; Hampden Acad; Hampden, ME; (Y); Cmnty Wkr; Pres Key Clb; Pep Clb; SADD; Y-Teens; Nwsp Stf; Yrbk Stf; Im Cheerleading; L Var Mgr(s); Im Capt Pom Pon; Prncpls Awd; Northeastern; Bus Mgmt.

MC INTIRE, CARROLL; Bonny Eagle HS; W Buxton, ME; (Y); 6/306; Boy Scts; Key Clb; Latin Clb; Math Tm; Teachers Aide; JV Crs Cntry; Var Trk; High Hon Roll; Jr NHS; NHS; Eagle Sct 85; Algbra I Awd 84; Albrga II & Trig Awd 86; Penn ST; Arch Engr.

MC KENNEY, RICK; Marshwood HS; Eliot, ME; (Y); 1/140; Math Tm; Yrbk Stf; Trs Frsh Cls; Trs Soph Cls; Trs Jr Cls; Trs Sr Cls; Trs Stu Cncl; Im Bsbl; L Bsktbl; Capt Ftbl; Hugh O Brian Yth Ldrshp Smnrs 85; Aimee Schram Bk Awd 84-86; Coll Course Gftd Stu UNH 86; MIT; Engrng.

MC KEOWN, TINA; Calais HS; Crawford, ME; (Y); Am Leg Aux Girls St; Band; Concert Band; Jazz Band; Mrchg Band; Pep Band; Yrbk Stf; JV Bsktbl; JV Cheerleading; JV Capt Vllybl; U Of Southern ME; Mrktng.

MC LEAN, PENNY; Calais HS; Calais, ME; (Y); Church Yth Grp; Dance Clb; Chorus; JV Bsktbl; Cert Awd Chorus 85; Athl Awd JV Bsktbl 84-85&85-86; Comp.

MC LELLAN, DARRIN; Calais HS; Calais, ME; (Y); French Clb; Band; Concert Band; Jazz Band; Mrchg Band; VP Soph Cls; VP Jr Cls; VP Sr Cls; Var Crs Cntry; Ski Clb; Schlrshp ME Smmr Yth Music Cmp 85; ME Jazz Fest Solo Awds 85; Southern ME U; Htl Mgmt.

MC LEOD, TROY; Lee Acad; Lee, ME; (Y); Am Leg Boys St; Math Tm; Var L Bsbl; Var L Bsktbl; Var Crs Cntry; Var Socr; Hon Roll; Mst Imp Bsktbl 85-86; Mst Imp Sccr 85-86; Bowdoin Coll Brunswick ME; Eng.

MC MANN, ANDREW; Skowhegan Area HS; Skowhegan, ME; (Y); 22/230; Church Yth Grp; Dance Clb; Debate Tm; Math Tm; Quiz Bowl; Ski Clb; Varsity Clb; Variety Show; Bsktbl; Golf; 3rd Pl AHSME Math Tst 84-85; Sctts Hgh-Q 84-86; Engnrng.

MC NABB, DENNIS; Deering HS; Portland, ME; (Y); 9/326; Am Leg Boys St; Math Tm; Varsity Clb; Band; Concert Band; Mrchg Band; Var Bsktbl; JV Tennis; Bausch & Lomb Sci Awd; High Hon Roll; Rensselaer Sci Awd 86; All ST Mth Tm 86; ME Schlrs Days Scholar 86.

MC WHINNIE, JOHN; Lewiston HS; Lewiston, ME; (Y); 12/403; Pres Trs Am Leg Boys St; Pres Key Clb; Pres Q&S; Yrbk Ed-Chief; Lit Mag; Co-Capt Tennis; High Hon Roll; JP Sousa Awd; Pres NHS; JA; Hnr Town Awd Boys ST 85; Gerold K Reed Schlrshp; Boston Coll; Engl.

MEAGHER, MAUREEN; Deering HS; Portland, ME; (Y); 56/326; Church Yth Grp; Drama Clb; FTA; Nwsp Stf; Trk; Hon Roll; Psych.

MEDD, DONALD; Oxford Hills HS; Paris, ME; (Y); Am Leg Boys St; Band; Concert Band; Mrchg Band; Rep Frsh Cls; Rep Jr Cls; Rep Sr Cls; Rep Stu Cncl; Var L Socr; Trk; Ski Tm, Vrsty, Lttr & Cptn; Wellesley Bk Awd; Hmnts.

MEGNA, SARAH J; Edward Little HS; Auburn, ME; (Y); 45/324; AFS; Trs FBLA; Swmmng; Hon Roll; Fernest M Shapiro Bus Awd 86; E Auburn Comm Unit Schlrsh P86; Pres Acad Ftns Awd 86; Bentley Coll; Bus Mgmt.

MENTAS, MICHELLE COLLEEN; Mt Ararat Schl; Bowdoinham, ME; (Y); 9/230; Pres Pep Clb; Pres SADD; Thesps; School Play; Chrmn Variety Show; Lit Mag; Rep Stu Cncl; High Hon Roll; Hon Roll; Jr NHS; Vntr Awd 86; Alg II & Trig Awd 85; Engl Awd 83; U Of Lowell; Rdlgcl Hlth Physcs.

MERRITHEW, TAMMY; Fort Fairfield HS; Ft Fairfield, ME; (Y); Church Yth Grp; French Clb; Red Cross Aide; SADD; Varsity Clb; Nwsp Stf; Yrbk Stf; Rep Stu Cncl; Capt Cheerleading; Hon Roll; U ME Orono; Fshn Merchandising.

MERWIN, CAROL; Wells HS; Wells, ME; (Y); Am Leg Aux Girls St; Band; Jazz Band; Rep Stu Cncl; Var L Fld Hcky; Var L Sftbl; NHS; Key Clb; Mrchg Band; Pep Band; Hugh O Brian Ldrshp Ambssdr 84-85; Yth & Govt Mdl Legsltr 85-86; US Acad Decthln 85-86; Bio Med.

MESERVE, MARY; Deering HS; Portland, ME; (Y); 31/326; Pres Drama Clb; VP Pres FTA; Chorus; School Musical; School Play; Stage Crew; Yrbk Phtg; NHS; Thesps; Yrbk Stf; Wellesley Bk Awd 86; Sci.

MESERVEY, JAMMIE; Bonny Eagle HS; Gorham, ME; (Y); 9/230; Pres Latin Clb; High Hon Roll; Jr NHS; NHS; Schlrshp Frm Groveville Grdn Clb Of ME 86; Pres Acad Ftnss Awd 86; U Of Southern ME; Bio.

MESSIER, PATRICIA; Wells HS; Wells, ME; (Y); Chorus; Nwsp Stf; Hon Roll; Pianist On Cmnty Adtns WBZ TV 85.

METCALF, ROBERT; Orono HS; Orono, ME; (S); 8/114; Aud/Vis; Boy Scts; Computer Clb; Nwsp Rptr; Nwsp Stf; Stu Cncl; High Hon Roll; NHS; Outstndng Sci Stu 85; Eagle Scout 86; Comp Sci.

METCALF, STEPHEN; Lincoln Acad; North Whitefield, ME; (Y); Aud/Vis; Drama Clb; SADD; Stage Crew; NCTE Awd; Weslyn U; Soc Sci.

MEYER, EMILY; Lewiston HS; Lewiston, ME; (Y); Q&S; Pres SADD; Nwsp Ed-Chief; Nwsp Rptr; Sec Frsh Cls; Stu Cncl; NHS; Letterman Clb; Yrbk Stf; Fld Hcky; Johnny M Robinson Mst Vlbl Nwspr Staffer Awd 86; Brown U Bk Awd 86; U S/Japan Snt Schlrshp Awd 86.

MICHAUD, MICHELLE L; Waterville SR HS; Waterville, ME; (Y); Am Leg Aux Girls St; Variety Show; JV Bsktbl; JV Var Fld Hcky; L Var Mgr(s); Var Capt Sftbl; Hon Roll; Prfct Atten Awd; Sr Athltc Awd 86; U Of ME.

MICHAUD JR, ROBERT P; Wisdom HS; St Agatha, ME; (Y); Am Leg Boys St; Church Yth Grp; Band; Mrchg Band; Pep Band; Rep Stu Cncl; Var L Mgr(s); Cit Awd; High Hon Roll; Hon Roll; MSAD No 33 Tchrs Assn Schlrshp 86; Stu Cncl Schlrshp 86; St Agatha Fdrl Crdt U Schlrshp 86; UMO; Engnrng.

MILLER, CHERYL; Upper Kennebec Valley HS; Bingham, ME; (Y); 1/31; Am Leg Aux Girls St; Church Yth Grp; Math Tm; Red Cross Aide; Sec Band; Pres Chorus; Church Choir; Concert Band; Mrchg Band; Pep Band.

MILLER, DARREN; Rumford JR SR HS; Rumford, ME; (Y); 21/114; Boy Scts; Drama Clb; Math Clb; Ski Clb; Varsity Clb; School Play; Yrbk Stf; Aerospc Engnrng.

MILLER, TABITHA C; Kennebunk HS; Kennebunkport, ME; (Y); PAVAS; SADD; Acpl Chr; Chorus; School Musical; School Play; Stage Crew; Variety Show; Hon Roll; Ballet.

MILLER, TYRA; Skowhegan Area HS; Norridgewock, ME; (Y); Am Leg Aux Girls St; GAA; Letterman Clb; Varsity Clb; Ed Yrbk Stf; Hon Roll; JV Bsktbl; Var L Sftbl; Hghst Bttng Avg Trphy Sftbl 85; Mst Dsr Bsktbl Cmp 84; ME Maritime Acad; Ntcl Engr.

MILLIGAN, DANIEL; Rumford HS; Bryant Pond, ME; (Y); 19/120; Latin Clb; Hon Roll; West Point; Comp Engr.

MILLIKEN, TERRI; Robert W Traip Acad; Kittery, ME; (Y); 16/78; Church Yth Grp; Letterman Clb; Spanish Clb; Varsity Clb; Yrbk Stf; Stat Bsbl; Var L Bsktbl; Var L Fld Hcky; JV Sftbl; Hon Roll; Hesser Coll; Accnt.

MILLS, CHRISTINE; Bucksport HS; Bucksport, ME; (Y); 14/125; Am Leg Aux Girls St; Drama Clb; 4-H; Chorus; School Musical; Stage Crew; Trk; 4-H Awd; Hon Roll; NHS; 4-H Equestrian Tm 85; Educ.

MINKOFF, NEIL; Lewiston HS; Lewiston, ME; (Y); VP Computer Clb; Hosp Aide; Capt Speech Tm; Ed Lit Mag; NHS; Pres Schlr; Church Yth Grp; Cmnty Wkr; Dance Clb; NFL; Ntl Hstry Day-Ntl Awd 84 & 83; HOBY Ldrshp Awd 85; Cntry III Ldrshp Awd 85; Bowdoin Coll; Hstry.

MITCHELL, CARRIE; Westbrook HS; Westbrook, ME; (Y); 13/192; Am Leg Aux Girls St; Sec English Clb; Keywanettes; Red Cross Aide; Variety Show; Yrbk Stf; Off Stu Cncl; Capt Cheerleading; Var Crs Cntry; Var Socr; Wrn Mem Nrsg Fndtn Schlrshp 86; Mary B Spear Nrsg Schlrshp 86; Marietta Coll; Sprts Med.

MONAHAN JR, JOHN M; Oxford Hills HS; Oxford, ME; (Y); 44/206; Church Yth Grp; FBLA; Library Aide; Yrbk Stf; Im Ftbl; Acctng.

MOON, HEATHER; Maine Central Inst; Burnham, ME; (Y); Am Leg Aux Girls St; Pres Spanish Clb; Sec Frsh Cls; Sec Soph Cls; Sec Jr Cls; Sec Sr Cls; High Hon Roll; NHS; Church Yth Grp; Drama Clb; Elem Ed.

MOORE, ALISON; Livermore Falls HS; Livermore Falls, ME; (Y); 3/81; Church Yth Grp; Math Tm; Varsity Clb; Band; Yrbk Ed-Chief; Rep Sr Cls; JV Bsktbl; Var Capt Sftbl; High Hon Roll; Trs NHS; Stu Of Mnth 85; Pres Acadmc Ftnss Awd 86; Schlrshp Awd 86; U Of ME Orono; Marine Bio.

MORAN, CALLIE J; Deer Isle-Stonington JR SR HS; Little Deerisle, ME; (Y); 10/33; Trs Church Yth Grp; Red Cross Aide; Band; Concert Band; Mrchg Band; Pep Band; Yrbk Stf; Trs Soph Cls; NHS; Betsy Bauter Richardson Schlrshp 86; Almni Assoc Schlrshp 86; Mst Imprvd Bnd 85; Mt Ida Coll; Vet Tech.

MOREAU, JULIE; Westbrook HS; Westbrook, ME; (Y); Art Clb; Church Yth Grp; FBLA; Christian Ldrshp Inst 86; Chldhd Ed.

MORIN, CELESTE; St Dominic Regional HS; Lewiston, ME; (Y); 2/67; School Musical; JV Var Bsktbl; JV Var Sftbl; Hon Roll; NHS.

MORIN, DANIEL D; Lewiston HS; Lewiston, ME; (Y); Key Clb; Letterman Clb; Varsity Clb; Var L Ftbl; Var L Trk; Wt Lftg; Hon Roll; PA ST U; Arch Engrng.

MORIN, DEBRA ANN; Lewiston HS; Lewiston, ME; (Y); Am Leg Aux Girls St; Letterman Clb; Rep Frsh Cls; Rep Soph Cls; Sec Jr Cls; Sec Sr Cls; Bsktbl; Capt Var Fld Hcky; Capt Var Trk; High Hon Roll; Excellnc Achvmnt Engl 84; Outstndng Physcl Educ Stu 84; Excellnc Achvmnt Eng 86; Engl.

MORIN, KRISTINA; Sanford HS; Sanford, ME; (Y); Church Yth Grp; Dance Clb; Math Tm; Varsity Clb; Variety Show; VP Frsh Cls; VP Soph Cls; Var L Cheerleading; Hon Roll; ME Schlrs Day Cnvntn 86; Ntl Chrldrs Assoc Awd Excllnc 85; Penn ST; Bus Admin.

MORIN, MARISA; Fryeburg Acad; Fryeburg, ME; (Y); Church Yth Grp; Drama Clb; Girl Scts; Latin Clb; Red Cross Aide; Chorus; Church Choir; Stage Crew; Lit Mag; Cit Awd; Lbrl Arts.

MORIN, PAMI; Yarmouth JR SR HS; Yarmouth, ME; (Y); French Clb; Math Tm; Var Crs Cntry; French Hon Soc; High Hon Roll; 1st Plp Regnl BEAM Bus Cntst 86; Accntng.

MORNEAULT, CONNIE; Ft Kent Community HS; Ft Kent, ME; (Y); 16/141; Mgr(s); Vllybl; High Hon Roll; Hon Roll; NHS; CHS Local Schlrp 86; Casco Bay Coll; Accntg.

MORRISON, JULIE; Fort Ketn Community HS; St Francis, ME; (Y); 8/132; Am Leg Aux Girls St; Church Yth Grp; SADD; Im Vllybl; Hon Roll; Lcl Wrtng Cntst Awds 85 & 86; Cert Hnr Hgh GPA 84; Jrnlsm.

MORRY, KRISTEN; Oxford Hills HS; Norway, ME; (Y); 6/218; Trs Spanish Clb; Teachers Aide; Color Guard; Nwsp Rptr; Var L Crs Cntry; High Hon Roll; Jr NHS; NHS; Amer Poetry Anthlgy 85-86; Tp Spnsh II Stdnt 83-84; Gen Lowe Mem Schlrshp 86; St Michaels Coll; Engl Lit.

MOSS, EMILY; Medomak Valley HS; Waldobor, ME; (Y); 6/114; Pres AFS; French Clb; Pep Clb; Yrbk Stf; Var Capt Gym; Var Socr; Var Trk; Hon Roll; NHS; Prfct Atten Awd; Wellesely Bk Awd 85; Ltr Jckt Recvd 86; MVP Gymnstcs 86; Macalester Clg; Libl Arts.

MOULTON, DAVID; Piscaraquis Community HS; Guilford, ME; (Y); Am Leg Boys St; Boy Scts; Letterman Clb; Band; Concert Band; Mrchg Band; Bsbl; Crs Cntry; Golf; Ice Hcky; Pilot.

MOWER, MELISSA; Leavitt Area HS; Greene, ME; (Y); 25/123; Pres Church Yth Grp; FHA; Math Tm; Nwsp Stf; Yrbk Stf; Var L Fld Hcky; Hon Roll; NHS; Vllybl; Hosp Aide; Ski Team; Lttr Bar; Crs Cntry Skng; JR Play; SR Play; SR Last Assemb; Bentley CollACCNTNG.

MOXCEY, MARSHA; Telstar Regional HS; Newry, ME; (Y); 2/67; Pres Trs Church Yth Grp; Drama Clb; Math Tm; Color Guard; Trs Sr Cls; Trk; Bausch & Lomb Sci Awd; Trs Jr NHS; Trs NHS; Sal.

MUDGETT, STACIE; Bangor HS; Glenurn, ME; (Y); Spanish Clb; Chorus; JV Bsktbl; Trk; Hon Roll; Business.

MULKERN, NICOLE; Deering HS; Portland, ME; (Y); Art Clb; French Clb; SADD; Chorus; Bsktbl; Sftbl; Tennis; Trk; Intl Order Of The Rainbow For Girls 82-86; U Of S ME; Elem Educ.

MULLANEY, KRISTEN; Georges Valley HS; Thomaston, ME; (Y); Am Leg Aux Girls St; Cmnty Wkr; Rep GAA; VP Pres Pep Clb; Teachers Aide; Band; Var JV Bsktbl; Var Fld Hcky; Var Trk; Hon Roll; Simmons Coll; Rtl Mgt.

MULLEN, BRIDGET; Vinalhaven HS; Vinalhaven, ME; (Y); Yrbk Ed-Chief; Lit Mag; Sec Soph Cls; Sec Jr Cls; Co-Capt Bsktbl; Hon Roll; Am Leg Aux Girls St; 4-H; French Clb; Hosp Aide; Art-Crft Soc Schlrshp 86.

MULLEN, MARCI; Belfast Area HS; Belfast, ME; (Y); 16/125; French Clb; Ski Clb; VP Soph Cls; Stat Bsktbl; JV Fld Hcky; Stat Swmmng; Hon Roll; VP Jr NHS; U Of CO Boulder.

MURPHY, MAURA; St Dominic Regional HS; Lewiston, ME; (Y); Cmnty Wkr; Debate Tm; Drama Clb; French Clb; Keywanettes; NFL; Rep Soph Cls; Hon Roll; Cngrs Exch Prgm Schlrshp 86.

MURPHY, SEAN E; Caribou HS; Caribou, ME; (Y); Rep Am Leg Boys St; Ski Clb; Rep Frsh Cls; Stu Cncl; Var Bsbl; Var Crs Cntry; Hon Roll; Thomas Coll; Bus Adm.

MURRAY, PETER; Gorham HS; Gorham, ME; (Y); Spanish Clb; Stage Crew; Aud/Vis; Boy Scts; Debate Tm; Trk; Hon Roll; Spanish NHS; Engr.

MYATT, MARYANN; Oak Hill HS; Litchfield, ME; (Y); 2/86; Am Leg Aux Girls St; Hosp Aide; Math Tm; Yrbk Ed-Chief; Pres Frsh Cls; Pres Soph Cls; Trs Jr Cls; Trs Sr Cls; NHS; Sal; 2nd Pl ST Typg Cntst 84; Natl Merit Ldrshp Awd 85; Thomas Coll; Acctg.

MYLER, MARLENE; Woodland HS; Princeton, ME; (Y); Drama Clb; Sec FBLA; Office Aide; Pep Clb; SADD; School Play; Yrbk Stf; JV Bsktbl; Var Cheerleading; Hon Roll; Jr Typist Awd 84-85; R Typist Awd 84-85; Bus Mgt.

MYNAHAN, PAULINE; St Dominics Regional HS; Lewiston, ME; (Y); 15/70; Sec French Clb; Sec Keywanettes; Church Choir; Nwsp Stf; French Hon Soc; Hon Roll; NHS; Mr & Mrs Jonas B Klein Mem Scholar 86; U ME; Elem Ed.

NADEAU, ANN MARIE; Lewiston HS; Lewiston, ME; (Y); Var JV Bsktbl; JV Fld Hcky; Hon Roll; NHS; Accntng.

NADEAU, KIMBERLY; Caribou HS; Caribou, ME; (Y); Church Yth Grp; Debate Tm; Pep Clb; SADD; Varsity Clb; Yrbk Stf; Rep Jr Cls; Var Capt Cheerleading; L Trk; Im Twrlr; U Of S ME; Psych.

NADEAU, SYLVIE; Fort Kent Community HS; Fort Kent, ME; (Y); Camera Clb; FHA; SADD; Yrbk Rptr; Yrbk Stf; Bsktbl; Var Socr; Trk; Vllybl; Parntng Mst Imprvd 85; AF CC Coll; Pilot.

NAOR, AYAL A; Waterville HS; Waterville, ME; (Y); 7/199; Jazz Band; Rep Frsh Cls; Rep Soph Cls; Rep Sr Cls; Var L Socr; High Hon Roll; Ntl Merit SF; Boy Scts; Key Clb; Band; ME Schlr Day 85; Hi Q Tm, Pulp-Paper Ftdn Pgm Gftd Tlntd 85; Engrng.

NAPOLITANO, MOLLY; Catherine Mc Auley HS; Portland, ME; (Y); 12/73; Am Leg Aux Girls St; Trs French Clb; Var Bsktbl; Capt Var Crs Cntry; Capt Var Trk; NHS; Accntng.

NAZZARO, AMY; Orono HS; Orono, ME; (S); AFS; Church Yth Grp; Debate Tm; Drama Clb; Pres French Clb; NFL; Speech Tm; School Musical; School Play; Stage Crew; 2nd Pl ST Natl Frnch Exm 85; Maxima Cum Laude Natl Ltn Exm 85; Lang Awd 85; Frnch.

NELSON, ERIC; Edward Little HS; Auburn, ME; (S); Pres Church Yth Grp; Drama Clb; Latin Clb; Mrchg Band; School Musical; Cit Awd; High Hon Roll; Hon Roll; Prfct Atten Awd; Schlrshp Awd 84.

NELSON, JEFFREY; Skowhegan Area HS; Norridgewock, ME; (Y); 17/180; Varsity Clb; Concert Band; Jazz Band; Yrbk Stf; Stu Cncl; Var Ftbl; Trk; High Hon Roll; Jr NHS; NHS; Worcester Plytchnc Inst; Comp.

NELSON, KERRI; Fort Kent Community HS; Fort Kent, ME; (Y); 3/137; Drama Clb; Hosp Aide; Office Aide; SADD; Chorus; School Musical; School Play; High Hon Roll; NHS; Voice Dem Awd; Maine Schlrs Days 86; Wrts Right Rgnl Wrtng Cntst 84; Vet.

NELSON, MATT; Bangor HS; Bangor, ME; (Y); Rep Am Leg Boys St; Church Yth Grp; Var L Bsbl; Var L Bsktbl; Var L Ftbl; Hon Roll; Var Wt Lftg; Commun.

NEWBEGIN, TROY; Caribou HS; Caribou, ME; (Y); JV Bsbl; Var Crs Cntry; Hon Roll; Pres Schlr; Fred Bell Meml Schlrshp 86; Pres Acadmc Ftnss Awd 86; Hesser Clg; Trvl.

NEWMAN, MICHELLE; Narraguagus HS; Harrington, ME; (Y); Cmnty Wkr; FHA; Variety Show; Hon Roll; Prfct Atten Awd; Dlgnce & Tncty Englsh II 85; Extrdnry Efft & Dedctn Imprv Art, Hghst Achvt Art Hstry 86; Northern ME Voc Inst; Nrsng.

NICHOLS, ANDREA JO; Ashland Comm HS; Ashland, ME; (Y); Church Yth Grp; Pep Clb; Am Leg Aux Girls St; French Clb; Band; Chorus; Concert Band; Pep Band; Variety Show; Yrbk Stf; All Aroostook Bnd 84-86; U Of ME Presque Isle Bnd 84-86; U Of Southern ME; Msc Educ.

NICHOLS, ELIZABETH; Edward Little HS; Auburn, ME; (S); Church Yth Grp; French Clb; Pep Clb; Sec Frsh Cls; Sec Soph Cls; Sec Jr Cls; Rep Stu Cncl; Hon Roll; Rcgntn Outstndng Acdmc Achvt 84; Psych.

NICHOLS, KRISTEN; Edward Little HS; Auburn, ME; (S); AFS; Trs Church Yth Grp; Latin Clb; Pep Clb; Yrbk Stf; High Hon Roll; Hon Roll; St Schlr; Magna Cum Laude Natl Latn Exm 83-84.

NICHOLSON, LISA; Portland HS; Portland, ME; (Y); FBLA; Latin Clb; Office Aide; Off Frsh Cls; Off Soph Cls; Off Jr Cls; Off Sr Cls; Crs Cntry; Trk; Hon Roll; U Of S ME; Ecnmcs.

NICKERSON, KELLY J; Presque Isle HS; Mapleton, ME; (Y); 62/189; 4-H; Office Aide; SADD; Varsity Clb; Rep Sec Stu Cncl; Var Capt Cheerleading; Im Vllybl; 4-H Awd; Hon Roll; ME Potato Grwrs Outstndg Stu 85; Outstndg Intrmdt Grl 4-H 84; Pny Clb D-2 Rlly Wnnr 84.

NILES, ANNETTE; Central HS; Bradford, ME; (Y); 5/70; French Clb; Library Aide; Teachers Aide; Band; Concert Band; Mrchg Band; Yrbk Bus Mgr; JV Fld Hcky; Hon Roll; NHS; Blaine House Schlrshp 86; E Corin Acad Trstees 86; U Of ME; Spec Ed.

NILES, MICHAEL P; South Portland HS; S Portland, ME; (Y); 10/290; Am Leg Boys St; Rptr Nwsp Rptr; Yrbk Ed-Chief; Capt L Swmmng; JV L Tennis; High Hon Roll; NHS; VP Exploring; Latin Clb; Math Tm; Yale Book Awd 85; ME ST Prncpls Awd Acad Excllnce & Ctznshp 86; Prncpls Mdl 86; MA Inst Tech; Elec Engrng.

NILSEN, VICTORIA; Skowhegan Area HS; Skowhegan, ME; (Y); 17/194; Church Yth Grp; Band; Church Choir; Concert Band; Mrchg Band; Pep Band; High Hon Roll; Sec NHS; Phy Sci Awd 83-84; Kings Coll; Hist.

NIXON, WILLIE; Calais HS; Calais, ME; (Y); Trs Soph Cls; Trs Jr Cls; Trs Sr Cls; Stat Bsbl; Armed Service.

NOBLE, SCOTT; Mt Abram Regional HS; Stratton, ME; (Y); Am Leg Boys St; Computer Clb; Sec Debate Tm; Intnl Clb; Ski Clb; Yrbk Stf; Var L Crs Cntry; Ski Tm V Ltrs & Mst Val 83-87; Amer H S Athl 85; Outstndg H S Athl 86.

NOEL, AMY KATHRYN; Temple Acad; Waterville, ME; (Y); 3/5; Church Yth Grp; Chorus; Church Choir; Var Bsktbl; Var Cheerleading; Var Crs Cntry; Stat Mgr(s); Score Keeper; Hon Roll; Amer Ldrshp Awd 86; The Ings Coll NY; Psych.

NORMAN, JULIE; Woodland HS; Woodland, ME; (S); 28/80; Trs FBLA; Trs Jr Cls; Var Mgr(s); Hon Roll; JR Typst Awd 85; St Petersburg JC; Fshn Merch.

NORRIS, LEE ANN; Rumford HS; Rumford, ME; (Y); Am Leg Aux Girls St; Cmnty Wkr; French Clb; Pres Latin Clb; SADD; School Play; Yrbk Ed-Chief; Yrbk Phtg; Stu Cncl; Voice Dem Awd; Ltn Clb Schlrshp 86; St An Selm; Nrsng.

NORTON, DAVID JAMES; Mt Abrom HS; Kingfield, ME; (Y); 20/90; Church Yth Grp; Computer Clb; Office Aide; Red Cross Aide; Var L Socr; Trk; Hon Roll; NHS; Bstr Clb 85; U Of Southern MI; Comp Sci.

NORTON, LISA; Buckfield JR SR HS; Buckfield, ME; (S); 2/40; French Clb; Sec SADD; Varsity Clb; Yrbk Stf; VP Soph Cls; Co-Capt Cheerleading; Mgr(s); Hon Roll; NHS; Sec.

NORTON, PAULA F; Washington Acad; Jonesboro, ME; (Y); Am Leg Aux Girls St; French Clb; Pres Sr Cls; Stu Cncl; Var Cheerleading; Var Mgr(s); Hon Roll; NHS; Prfct Atten Awd; JV Vllybl; WA DC Gov Stds Prgm 84; U Of ME Mchs; Elem Educ.

NORWOOD, KELLY SUE; Maranocook Community Schl; Readfield Depot, ME; (Y); 23/85; Cmnty Wkr; GAA; Girl Scts; JCL; VP Latin Clb; Teachers Aide; Band; Rep Stu Cncl; Var L Bsktbl; Var Fld Hcky; Ramsdell Schlrshp 86; UM At Orono; Speech Thrpy.

NUGENT, CHRISTOPHER; Cheverus HS; Yarmouth, ME; (Y); 1/100; Drama Clb; NFL; School Musical; School Play; Nwsp Ed-Chief; Nwsp Stf; Tennis; High Hon Roll; NHS; Ntl Merit SF; Ntl Lat Soc; 2nd & 3rd In Ntl Frnch Cntst; Pltcl Sci.

O BAR, MICHELLE; Central HS; E Corinth, ME; (Y); Yrbk Ed-Chief; Bsktbl; Hon Roll; 2 Acadmc Achvts-Spnsh 84-85; Sociolgy.

O BRYAN, BRIDGET ANN PATRICIA; Lincoln Acad; Damariscotta, ME; (Y); 9/112; Am Leg Aux Girls St; Latin Clb; Teachers Aide; Yrbk Sprt Ed; Pres Sr Cls; Capt Bsktbl; Capt Fld Hcky; Capt Sftbl; Hon Roll; NHS; Achvt Cup Babe Ruth Gd Sprtsmnshp 86; Newcastle Ext Schlrp Top 10 Cls 86; Bst Athl & Profcncy Acctg 85; St Josephs N Windham; Elem Ed.

O NEILL, LANCE; Woodland HS; Woodland, ME; (Y); Boys Clb Am; Boy Scts; Camera Clb; FBLA; Intnl Clb; Spanish Clb; SADD; School Play; Nwsp Stf; Lit Mag; USAF; Air Trffc Cntrllr.

OAKES, CONNIE; Easton HS; Eston, ME; (Y); Am Leg Aux Girls St; French Clb; Varsity Clb; Band; Chorus; Church Choir; Yrbk Phtg; Yrbk Stf; Trs Frsh Cls; Pres Jr Cls; U ME Presque Isle; Med Tech.

ODONAL, ELLEN; Gorham HS; Gorham, ME; (Y); 15/315; Church Yth Grp; Drama Clb; German Clb; Latin Clb; Science Clb; School Play; Stage Crew; Nwsp Stf; Yrbk Stf; Rep Stu Cncl; Frgn Exchng Stu Grmny 84-86; Wilma-Boyd Career Schl; Trvl Ag.

OLIVA, TRACEY; Calais Mem HS; Charlotte, ME; (Y); Dance Clb; Nwsp Phtg; JV Cheerleading; Hon Roll; Bus Math Awd 84-85; Typng II Awd 84-85; U ME Machais; Bus.

OLIVER, MELISSA; Catherine Mc Auley HS; Scarborough, ME; (Y); 3/60; Drama Clb; School Musical; School Play; Var Capt Cheerleading; Trs French Hon Soc; High Hon Roll; Hon Roll; NEDT Awd; Acad Excllnce Awd 86; Sr Mary Isabel Flanagan Scholar 86; Cazenovia Coll; Fshn Dsgn.

OLSEN, LISA; Mc Auley HS; Portland, ME; (Y); 25/75; Hosp Aide; Latin Clb; Varsity Clb; Trs Jr Cls; Rep Stu Cncl; Var L Bsktbl; Var L Fld Hcky; Capt L Sftbl; Elem Eductn.

ONEILL, COLENE; Gardiner Area HS; Gardiner, ME; (Y); AFS; FBLA; Girl Scts; Pep Clb; Q&S; Spanish Clb; SADD; Variety Show; Nwsp Stf; Yrbk Stf; Var Ltr 1st Yr Swmng 85; Strtng Grls Sccr Tm Clb Hon 84; SADD Clb Orgnzr 85; USM Coll; Acctnt.

OSGOOD, MARSHA; Belfast Area HS; Belfast, ME; (Y); 1/116; Band; Concert Band; Drm Mjr(t); Jazz Band; Mrchg Band; Pep Band; School Musical; L Bsktbl; Capt Fld Hcky; High Hon Roll; Hghst Gd Pt Avg Awd.

OUELLETTE, MICHAEL; Jay HS; Dryden, ME; (Y); JV Bsktbl; Im Coach Actv; Var L Ftbl; Im Score Keeper; Im Timer; Im Vllybl; High Hon Roll; Hon Roll; Arch.

OVELLETTE, KAREN; Jonesport-Beals HS; Jonesport, ME; (Y); French Clb; Yrbk Ed-Chief; Rep Frsh Cls; Pres Soph Cls; Var Cheerleading; Var Sftbl; JV Vllybl; Hon Roll; JR Prom Princess 86; Pierres Schl Of Beauty; Cosmetl.

OVERKAMP, JILL; Medomak Valley HS; W Boothbay Harbor, ME; (Y); 17/160; Church Yth Grp; Band; Chorus; Concert Band; Var Gym; JV Socr; High Hon Roll; Hon Roll; Schlrshp Gymnstcs Cmp 85; All-Str Gymnst Vrsty Gmnstcs Tm; Chld Psychlgy.

PAGE, NOEL; Upper Kennebec Valley Memorial HS; Bingham, ME; (Y); Am Leg Aux Girls St; Chorus; School Musical; School Play; JV L Cheerleading; L Socr; Var L Sftbl; Hon Roll; NHS; Church Yth Grp; Educ.

PAGE, SHELLY RAE; Limestone JR/SR HS; Limestone, ME; (Y); 7/78; Sec Trs Church Yth Grp; Trs SADD; Yrbk Ed-Chief; Rep Stu Cncl; L Trk; JP Sousa Awd; NHS; Pres Schlr; Drama Clb; French Clb; HOBY Ldrshp Schl Rep 84; Dirigo Grls ST 85; U ME; Bus Admin.

PAINE, SANDRA D; Carrabec HS; North Anson, ME; (Y); 10/63; Am Leg Aux Girls St; Church Yth Grp; Bsktbl; Sftbl; Trk; Hon Roll; NHS; Prfct Atten Awd; Bus Awd 86; Activities Awd 86; U Of ME Farmington; Elem Ed.

PALMER, CINDY; Portland HS; Portland, ME; (Y); 20/195; French Clb; Latin Clb; Off Frsh Cls; Stu Cncl; Co-Capt Cheerleading; Gym; Trk; Hon Roll; NHS; MVP Gym 82-83; U Of ME Orono; Pre-Med.

PANDORA, NEIL; Portland HS; Portland, ME; (Y); Math Tm; Nwsp Stf; Yrbk Sprt Ed; Stat Ftbl; Var Ice Hcky; Ec.

PARADIS, MARIE; Deering HS; Portland, ME; (Y); 49/321; French Clb; Letterman Clb; Varsity Clb; Cheerleading; Trk; Hon Roll; MV Chrldr 84; Most Spiritd Chrld 85.

PARADIS, SUZANNE LOUISE; Lewiston HS; Lewiston, ME; (Y); 16/409; Church Yth Grp; Hosp Aide; Yrbk Stf; Lit Mag; Crs Cntry; Trk; Hon Roll; Jr NHS; NHS; Engl Awd Outstndng Schlrshp 85; Frnch Awd Outstndng Wrk 84-85; Springfield Coll.

PARKER, JUDITH M; Deering HS; Portland, ME; (Y); 39/274; Church Yth Grp; French Clb; Key Clb; Service Clb; Ski Clb; Varsity Clb; Band; Concert Band; Jazz Band; Mrchg Band; Fclty Scholar Awd 86; Pres All Amer Fit Awd 86; Silver Dollar Cust Excllnce Awd 86; UNH; Polit Sci.

PARKER, KELLIE ANN; Lawrence HS; Clinton, ME; (Y); 62/196; Cmnty Wkr; Dance Clb; FCA; French Clb; Key Clb; Yrbk Stf; Fld Hcky; Trk; Hon Roll; Hussor Coll; Bus Admin.

PARLEE, DARCY; Nokomis Regional HS; Neport, ME; (Y); 15/155; French Clb; FBLA; Girl Scts; Pres Varsity Clb; Band; Concert Band; Mrchg Band; Pep Band; Symp Band; Pres Stu Cncl; Corinna Un Acad Schlrshp 86; Sportsmnshp Awd 86; Typing II Awd 86; Husson Coll; Bus Admn.

PATRIE, LAURA; Lewiston HS; Lewiston, ME; (Y); 54/387; Sec Letterman Clb; Office Aide; Bsktbl; Capt Crs Cntry; Capt Trk; Hon Roll; NHS; Var Lttrmns Club Schlrshp 86; Accntng I Hon Maintnng Grad 95 85; Bentley Coll; Accntng.

PATTERSON, JOHN; Central HS; Hudson, ME; (Y); 4/80; Am Leg Boys St; Band; Concert Band; Jazz Band; Stage Crew; Yrbk Sprt Ed; Yrbk Stf; Var Bsktbl; Var Capt Golf; Hon Roll; Engrng.

PAYNE, STEPHANIE; Fryeburg Acad; Denmark, ME; (Y); Church Yth Grp; Spanish Clb; SADD; Varsity Clb; Chorus; Var Mgr(s); Var JV Score Keeper.

PEASE, ROSEMARY; Livermore Falls HS; Leeds, ME; (Y); Exploring; SADD; Varsity Clb; Band; Concert Band; Mrchg Band; Lit Mag; L Crs Cntry; NHS; Pre Vet.

PELLETIER, ANNE-MARIE; St Dominic Regional HS; Lewiston, ME; (Y); 15/63; Drama Clb; Keywanettes; School Play; Var L Cheerleading; Hon Roll; Keyette Of Yr 84-85; Coachs Awd Chrldg 85-86; Sec Ed.

PELLETIER, JEFF; St Dominics R HS; Lewiston, ME; (Y); Drama Clb; Key Clb; Ski Clb; School Musical; School Play; Rep Stu Cncl; JV Ice Hcky; Var Socr; Hon Roll; NHS; Bio Chem.

PELLETIER, KENDRA D; Caribou HS; Caribou, ME; (Y); Church Yth Grp; Trs Key Clb; Office Aide; SADD; VP Varsity Clb; Band; Chorus; Concert Band; Mrchg Band; Pep Band; U Of ME; Psych.

PELLETIER, SANDRA; Caribou HS; Caribou, ME; (Y); Church Yth Grp; ROTC; VP SADD; Chorus; Rep Jr Cls; Rep Stu Cncl; Var Capt Cheerleading; JV L Fld Hcky; High Hon Roll; Hon Roll; U Of ME Orono; Cmnctn Brdcstng.

PELLETIER, SUSAN; Hodgdon HS; Houlton, ME; (Y); 4/50; Drama Clb; Trs Varsity Clb; Chorus; School Musical; School Play; Yrbk Stf; Rep Jr Cls; Sr Cls; Stu Cncl; Var L Bsktbl; U Of S ME; Bus.

PENDEXTER, PATRICIA; Easton HS; Easton, ME; (Y); Pres French Clb; Math Tm; Varsity Clb; Band; Yrbk Stf; Cheerleading; Sftbl; Vllybl; High Hon Roll; NHS; St Josephs Tfts U; Vet Med.

PEPIN, MICHELLE; Lewiston HS; Lewiston, ME; (Y); Var Bsktbl; Var Fld Hcky; Im Golf; Var Socr; Sftbl; Im Vllybl; Hon Roll; American Schl Switzerland; Vet.

PERKINS, JONATHAN; Rumford HS; Hanover, ME; (Y); Spanish Clb; JV Bsbl; Var L Bsktbl; Var L Ftbl; Var Tennis; Hon Roll; NHS.

PERKINS, JUDY; Wells HS; Wells, ME; (Y); 20/100; Church Yth Grp; Drama Clb; French Clb; Letterman Clb; Varsity Clb; Stu Cncl; Var Trk; Hon Roll; Jr NHS; NHS.

PERKINS, MARK; Bucksport HS; Pinellas Park, FL; (Y); VP Drama Clb; Thesps; School Play; Variety Show; Bst Actr 84-86.

PERREAULT, LYNN; Van Buren District Secondary Schl; Van Buren, ME; (Y); SADD; Teachers Aide; JV Cheerleading; Vllybl; Hon Roll; U Of ME; Bus Mgmt.

PETERS III, GEORGE; Caribou HS; Caribou, ME; (S); 3/200; Am Leg Boys St; Pres French Clb; Stat Bsktbl; Mgr Crs Cntry; Mgr(s); Trk; High Hon Roll; Hon Roll; NHS; Acad All Amer 84-86; U Of ME Orono; Chem Engrng.

PETERS, LAWRENCE; Bonny Eagle HS; W Buxton, ME; (Y); Im Bsbl; Var Ice Hcky; Im Vllybl; Rensselaer Polytech; Aerontcl.

PETERSON, DAVID; Westbrook HS; Westbrook, ME; (Y); 8/190; Latin Clb; Math Tm; Concert Band; Jazz Band; Mrchg Band; Pep Band; Hon Roll; NHS; Contntl Math Leag-Hghst Score Awd 85; U Of Hartfrd; Engrng.

PETERSON, DIANE; Marshwood HS; Eliot, ME; (Y); Library Aide; Yrbk Stf; Hon Roll.

PETTINELLI, JASON; Lewiston HS; Lewiston, ME; (Y); Am Leg Boys St; Key Clb; Varsity Clb; Yrbk Stf; JV Bsbl; L Socr; L Trk; Bus.

PHILBROOK, RACHEL; Belfast Area HS; Belfast, ME; (Y); Church Yth Grp; FBLA; JV Sftbl; Hon Roll; Chch Yth Grp Vllybl Sprtsmnshp Awd 85; Elem Ed.

PHILLBROOK, DENISE; Vinalhaven HS; Vinalhaven, ME; (Y); 4/14; Am Leg Aux Girls St; FBLA; Varsity Clb; Nwsp Stf; Yrbk Stf; Pres Sr Cls; Var Bsktbl; Var DAR Awd; Var Hon Roll; Pres Frsh Cls; Miss Vinalhaven 84; Gregg Shrthd Awd 86; Casco Bay; Legl Secy.

PHILLIPS, LORI; Caribou HS; Caribou, ME; (S); Chrmn Church Yth Grp; Hosp Aide; Band; Chorus; Tennis; High Hon Roll.

PHINNEY, ANGEL; Bangor Baptist Schls; Bangor, ME; (S); 2/15; Church Yth Grp; Pep Clb; Chorus; Church Choir; School Play; Stage Crew; Mgr(s); High Hon Roll; Hon Roll; NHS; Lbrty U; Piano Tchr.

PHINNEY, LOUIS; Skowhegon Area HS; Norridgewock, ME; (Y); 4/210; Bsbl; Wt Lftg; High Hon Roll; NHS; Blgy Awd 84-85; US Air Frc.

PICCININNI, DONNA; Gorham HS; Gorham, ME; (Y); Church Yth Grp; Spanish Clb; Sec Jr Cls; Sec Sr Cls; Pres Stu Cncl; Cheerleading; High Hon Roll; Hon Roll; Cmnty Wkr; Red Cross Aide; Sec Stu Council 86; All Am Chrldr 86; Southern ME U; Accntng.

PIERCE, CATHY; Sumner Memorial HS; Winter Harbor, ME; (Y); 15/75; Church Yth Grp; 4-H; Varsity Clb; Church Choir; JV Bsktbl; Mgr(s); Score Keeper; Socr; 4-H Awd; Hon Roll; Cnty Fair 4-H Awd 84; Hancock Cnty 4-H Fshn Revw Wnnr 84-85; ME ST 4-H Fshn Rvw Wnnr 85; Fshn Dsgn.

PIERCE, JOHN; Fryeburg Acad; Fryeburg, ME; (Y); SADD; Yrbk Ed-Chief; Off Frsh Cls; Off Soph Cls; Off Jr Cls; Stu Cncl; Bausch & Lomb Sci Awd; NHS; Engrng.

PIERCE, KATHY; Erskine Acad; Windsor, ME; (Y); 4/57; Am Leg Aux Girls St; Sec Latin Clb; Math Tm; Yrbk Sprt Ed; Yrbk Stf; JV Crs Cntry; Hon Roll; NHS; JCL; Math Clb; Bkkpng Awd 86; Stu Tutor 85; U ME Augusta; Lib Arts.

PIERCE, NICOLE; Central Aroostook HS; Mars Hill, ME; (Y); Drama Clb; Var Cheerleading; Var Socr; JV Sftbl; High Hon Roll; Guidnc.

PIERSON, BRONWEN; Caribou HS; Caribou, ME; (S); Debate Tm; Ski Clb; Varsity Clb; Rep Jr Cls; Gym; Socr; Tennis; Trk; High Hon Roll.

PIKE, HEATHER; Fryeburg Acad; Fryeburg, ME; (Y); Am Leg Aux Girls St; Ski Clb; SADD; Trs Varsity Clb; Yrbk Stf; Rep Frsh Cls; Rep Soph Cls; Rep Jr Cls; Rep Stu Cncl; Capt Fld Hcky.

PILGRIM, MELISSA; Telstar Regional HS; West Bethel, ME; (Y); 20/115; Key Clb; Office Aide; SADD; Hon Roll; Math Awd 85; Bio Awd 85; World Std Awd 83; Privt Sec.

PINKHAM, JULIE; Narraguagus HS; Harrington, ME; (Y); Drama Clb; French Clb; Teachers Aide; School Play; Nwsp Rptr; Yrbk Phtg; Yrbk Stf; Stu Cncl; Hon Roll; NHS; Mtnd Avrg Cllg Bnd Blgy 84-85; Fshn Mrcndsgn.

PIOTTER, LISA; Sumner Memorial HS; Winter Harbor, ME; (Y); Nwsp Rptr; Nwsp Stf; Yrbk Stf; Rep Stu Cncl; JV Bsktbl; Mgr(s); Score Keeper; Sftbl; Hon Roll; Nwsppr Prtcptn Awd 85 & 86; Hmtnts Prtcptn Awd 85 & 86.

PITCHER, DAWN A; Mt Abram Regional HS; Kingfield, ME; (Y); 3/89; Am Leg Aux Girls St; Var Capt Crs Cntry; Var Trk; Elks Awd; High Hon Roll; Hon Roll; NHS; Church Yth Grp; JV Bsktbl; Amer Assn Of U Wmn Schlrshp; Outstndng Amer Ctzn & Stud Awd; Mst Imprvd Crss Cntry Rnnr; Colby Coll; Bio.

PLATT, GINA; St Dominic Regional HS; Lewiston, ME; (Y); Church Yth Grp; Debate Tm; Drama Clb; Service Clb; Chorus; School Musical; School Play; Stage Crew; Nwsp Rptr; Nwsp Stf; Drma Awd/Lead, Supprtng Role 86; Marine Mammolgy.

PLOURDE, ALLEN; Fort Kent Community HS; Fort Kent, ME; (Y); Church Yth Grp; Band; Concert Band; Pep Band; Hon Roll; Certf Merit Frnch II 85; Bio.

PLOURDE, RONALD; Lewiston HS; Lewiston, ME; (Y); Key Clb; Var Bsbl; JV Bsktbl; Var Capt Socr; High Hon Roll; U Of ME.

POIRIER, BARBARA; Rumford JR SR HS; Rumford, ME; (Y); Am Leg Aux Girls St; French Clb; Ski Clb; Spanish Clb; Fld Hcky; Trk; Hon Roll; Spanish NHS.

POIRIER, NANCY J; Biddeford HS; Biddeford, ME; (Y); 14/292; Am Leg Aux Girls St; Trs Church Yth Grp; Cmnty Wkr; Dance Clb; Red Cross Aide; SADD; Church Choir; Hon Roll; Natl French Contest Awd 85-86; Hnrs Convocation 85-86; Psych.

POMELOW, TIM; Skowhegan Area HS; Skowhegan, ME; (S); 31/189; Library Aide; Ftbl; Hon Roll; Showkegan Voc Schlrshp 86; Johnsn & Wales DECA Schlrshp 86; Johnson & Wales Coll; Accntng.

POMEROY, BARBARA JEAN; Maine Central Inst; Pittsfield, ME; (Y); Am Leg Aux Girls St; Chess Clb; Library Aide; Capt Math Tm; Ed Nwsp Bus Mgr; High Hon Roll; NHS; Ntl Merit Ltr; Cmnty Wkr; French Clb; Geo M Parks Schlrshp Schlstc Achvt, ME Schlrs Day U ME Schlrshp 86.

POMEROY, PAULA; Noble HS; North Berwick, ME; (Y); Am Leg Aux Girls St; Church Yth Grp; Girl Scts; School Play; Stage Crew; Yrbk Stf; Fld Hcky; Trk; Hon Roll; Jr NHS; Grand Offcr Intl Order Rainbow Grls 86; Med.

POOLER, DENISE; Lawrence HS; Waterville, ME; (Y); CPA.

PORTER, PAMELA; Lee Acad; Lee, ME; (Y); Church Yth Grp; Chorus; School Play; Yrbk Stf; L Bsktbl; Mgr(s); Stat L Sftbl; High Hon Roll; Hon Roll; Blaine Clemons Schlrshp 86; Timothy Crosby Schlrshp 86; U Of ME Farmington; Elem Educ.

POSIK, CHARLIE; Leavitt Area HS; Leeds, ME; (Y); 13/117; Latin Clb; Math Tm; Ski Clb; Speech Tm; Varsity Clb; L Crs Cntry; Hon Roll; NHS; Bus Mgmt.

POTTER, BARRETT; Fort Fairfield HS; Fort Fairfield, ME; (Y); 5/63; Am Leg Boys St; Chess Clb; French Clb; Varsity Clb; Band; Concert Band; Mrchg Band; Nwsp Stf; Yrbk Stf; Bsbl; Olympcs Of Mnd Tm; Gift/Talntd Pgm; Top 10 Cls; Acctg.

POTTER, CHERYLE A; Madison HS; Madison, ME; (Y); 3/99; Math Tm; Yrbk Ed-Chief; Sec Soph Cls; VP Jr Cls; Var Capt Bsktbl; Var Capt Socr; Var Capt Sftbl; High Hon Roll; NHS; Prfct Atten Awd; Wentworth Inst Tech; Arch Engr.

POTTS, RUSSELL; Bangor HS; Bangor, ME; (Y); Church Yth Grp; Concert Band; Mrchg Band; Var L Ftbl; Hon Roll; Ntl Merit Ltr; Econ.

POTVIN, PETER; Edward Little HS; Auburn, ME; (S); JV Var Ice Hcky; JV Socr; High Hon Roll; Hon Roll; Sci.

POULIN, MICHELLE; Edward Little HS; Auburn, ME; (S); VP French Clb; Hosp Aide; Ski Clb; Varsity Clb; Band; Concert Band; Mrchg Band; Var Crs Cntry; Var Trk; Hon Roll; Courageous Rnnr Awd 84; Law.

POULIN, PHILIP; Cony HS; Augusta, ME; (Y); JCL; Latin Clb; Ftbl; High Hon Roll; Maine Schlrs Day 86; Pgm Giftd Math Sci Stu 86; Engrng.

POULOS, STEPHANIE; Deering HS; Portland, ME; (Y); 20/321; Sec French Clb; FTA; VP Jr Cls; Var L Tennis; French Hon Soc; Hon Roll; NHS; ST Champs Tenns 86; Bus.

POWERS, SHAWN; Deering HS; Portland, ME; (Y); 108/328; Socr; Vllybl; Us Army.

PRATT, GRETCHEN; Lawrence HS; Clinton, ME; (Y); 15/220; Am Leg Aux Girls St; Church Yth Grp; Dance Clb; Math Tm; Sec Trs Band; Church Choir; Sec Trs Concert Band; Sec Trs Mrchg Band; Pep Band; Hon Roll; Amer Musicl Ambssdrs Band 85; Kennebec Vly H S Band ME 84-86; Tchrs Aide 85; U Of ME Farmington; Elem Ed.

PRENDERGAST, SUZAN; Limestone HS; Loring, ME; (Y); 2/78; VP Letterman Clb; Trs Jr Cls; Capt L Bsktbl; L Trk; Mu Alp Tht; NHS; Rotary Awd; Pres Acad Ftnss Awd 85-86; U Of ME Orono; Phy Thrpst.

PRESBY, DANA L; Mt Abram HS; Phillips, ME; (Y); #12 In Class; Am Leg Aux Girls St; Drama Clb; Pres Intnl Clb; Yrbk Stf; Stu Cncl; Var Capt Cheerleading; Var L Sftbl; Im Vllybl; Hon Roll; NHS; Excllnce Ldrshp 85; U Maine Orono; Bus Mgmt.

PUMMILL, HOLLY; Freeport HS; Freeport, ME; (Y); Sec Church Yth Grp; Cmnty Wkr; French Clb; Band; Chorus; Church Choir; School Musical; School Play; Var Capt Cheerleading; JV Fld Hcky; Elem Educ.

PURI, RAJEEV; Orono HS; Orono, ME; (S); 3/130; Pres Frsh Cls; Pres Soph Cls; Rep Jr Cls; Rep Stu Cncl; Var Crs Cntry; Var Tennis; High Hon Roll; NHS; Ntl Merit SF; Engrng.

PUTNAM, MICHAEL; North Varmouth Acad; Bangor, ME; (Y); 3/26; Rptr Nwsp Rptr; Pres Frsh Cls; Rep Soph Cls; Rep Jr Cls; Sec Sr Cls; Sec Stu Cncl; Var Bsbl; Var Crs Cntry; Var Capt Ftbl; Var Ice Hcky; Denison U; Stock Brkr.

PYLES, DAVID; Orono HS; Orono, ME; (S); 1/110; Debate Tm; Math Tm; NFL; Mrchg Band; Orch; Yrbk Stf; Var Crs Cntry; Var L Swmmng; Var Trk; High Hon Roll; Summa Cum Laude Awd Natl Latn Exm 85; Acadmc Achvt Awds Math, Socl Sci, Engl 84-85; 6th ST Swmmg 85; Engrng.

QUIMBY, TROY; Washington Acad; E Machias, ME; (Y); 3/65; Am Leg Boys St; SADD; Band; Chorus; Yrbk Stf; Pres Sr Cls; Stat Bsktbl; Stat Vllybl; Hon Roll; NHS; Accntng.

QUINN, RYAN; Skowhegan Area HS; Skowhegan, ME; (Y); Am Leg Boys St; German Clb; Pep Band; Yrbk Stf; Stu Cncl; Hon Roll; ME Sclrs Day 86; UMO; Scndry Educ.

QURESHI, ROSHAN; Kents Hill HS; Togus, ME; (Y); 4-H; Yrbk Ed-Chief; Ftbl; Lcrss; Tennis; 4-H Awd; Hon Roll; Jr NHS; Engrng.

RACKLEY, SHAWN; Westbrook HS; Westbrook, ME; (Y); 6/200; French Clb; Math Tm; Concert Band; Jazz Band; Mrchg Band; Pep Band; Yrbk Stf; Var Hon Roll; NHS; Yale Bk Awd 86; Engrng.

RACKLIFF, HILARY; Georges Valley HS; Warren, ME; (Y); GAA; Intnl Clb; Math Tm; Science Clb; Thesps; School Musical; Sec Jr Cls; JV Var Fld Hcky; Hon Roll; NHS; Fld Hcky Coachs Awd 84; Psych.

RADZISZEWSKI, GREGORY; Edward Little HS; Poland Spring, ME; (S); French Clb; Ski Clb; SADD; Crs Cntry; JV Ftbl; Cit Awd; Hon Roll; NHS.

RADZISZEWSKI, MARY; Edward Little HS; Poland Spring, ME; (S); Church Yth Grp; Latin Clb; Pep Clb; Yrbk Stf; Mgr(s); Score Keeper; Swmmng; Cit Awd; Hon Roll.

RAITT, SHELLY; Marshwood HS; Eliot, ME; (Y); Latin Clb; VICA; Hon Roll; Strthm Vo Tech; Auto Mech.

RAND, ELIZABETH; Catherine Mc Auley HS; Portland, ME; (Y); 8/74; Church Yth Grp; Hosp Aide; Key Clb; Latin Clb; Chorus; Church Choir; Lit Mag; Hon Roll; Womens Literary Union Honor 86; History.

RANDALL, MICHAEL; Lewiston HS; Lewiston, ME; (Y); Church Yth Grp; Cmnty Wkr; Key Clb; JV Var Bsktbl; Var Socr; Hon Roll; Hgh Schlrshp-Engl 85-86; Excllnc-Geomtry 85-86; Bryant Coll RI; Bus Mngmt.

RANDOLPH, LESLIE; Caribou HS; Caribou, ME; (S); 15/180; Am Leg Aux Girls St; Ski Clb; SADD; Varsity Clb; Trs Soph Cls; Pres Jr Cls; Hon Roll; NHS; U Of New England; Phy Thrpy.

RANGER, ANN M; Westbrook HS; Westbrook, ME; (Y); 1/195; English Clb; French Clb; Hosp Aide; Keywanettes; Math Tm; Yrbk Stf; Trk; Bausch & Lomb Sci Awd; High Hon Roll; NCTE Awd; Natl Wmns Literary Union 85; Smith Bk Awd 85; Lab Tech.

RAWSTRON, MIRANDA; Portland HS; Portland, ME; (Y); 24/200; French Clb; JA; JV Fld Hcky; Hon Roll; Natl Sci Olympd Cert; U Of ME Orono; Bus Admin.

RAYMOND, KATHERINE; Cony HS; Augusta, ME; (Y); 8/320; AFS; FBLA; Political Wkr; Variety Show; Ed Yrbk Phtg; Rep Frsh Cls; Rep Soph Cls; Capt L Fld Hcky; Trk; High Hon Roll; 1st Pl-Wmn In Hstry Essay Cntst-Stwd 85; Amer Lgn Awd 86; ME St Emplyees Assn Schlrshp 86; Penn ST U; Arch.

RAYMOND, MICHAEL; Edward Little HS; E Poland, ME; (Y); Var Ftbl; Ice Hcky; Trk; Hon Roll; Lcrss; Wt Lftg; High Hon Roll; Prfct Atten Awd; WPI; Chem Engr.

RAYMOND, MONIQUE; Fort Kent Community HS; Fort Kent, ME; (Y); Drama Clb; Speech Tm; Trs SADD; School Play; Trs Stu Cncl; Hon Roll; NHS; Chorus; Yrbk Stf; Off Frsh Cls; Regnl Spear Spkng Cont 1st Pl Grls Div, 1st Overall 86; All Fest Cast Drama 86; Grls ST Delg 86.

RAYMOND, NANCY; Gardiner Area HS; W Gardiner, ME; (Y); Am Leg Aux Girls St; Cmnty Wkr; French Clb; SADD; Yrbk Stf; Rep Sec Stu Cncl; L Var Socr; Capt Var Swmmng; High Hon Roll; NHS; Tutr-Frnch & Hstry 84 & 85; Ocngrphy.

RAYMOND, STEVE; Fort Kent HS; Fort Kent, ME; (Y); 11/140; Am Leg Boys St; Chess Clb; Computer Clb; SADD; Varsity Clb; Bsbl; Var Bsktbl; High Hon Roll; OM Orono; Mech Engr.

READ, DEBORAH; Bangor HS; Bangor, ME; (Y); GAA; Key Clb; Letterman Clb; SADD; Varsity Clb; Yrbk Stf; Rep Frsh Cls; Rep Soph Cls; Rep Sr Cls; JV Fld Hcky; Psychology.

READ, SUSAN; Belfast Area HS; Belfast, ME; (Y); Am Leg Aux Girls St; Latin Clb; Ski Clb; Rep Soph Cls; Rep Jr Cls; Var Fld Hcky; Var Gym; High Hon Roll; Jr NHS; NHS; ST Chmps Fld Hcky 85; Bus.

REDDY, KATHLEEN MICHELE; Brunswick HS; Brunswick, ME; (Y); Am Leg Aux Girls St; Church Yth Grp; Hosp Aide; Pres Key Clb; SADD; Yrbk Bus Mgr; Yrbk Phtg; Hon Roll; Pr Tr & Cnslr 83-86.

REDMOND, MARY; Jay HS; Jay, ME; (Y); 24/86; Drama Clb; Teachers Aide; Y-Teens; School Play; Stage Crew; Variety Show; Yrbk Phtg; Vllybl; Cit Awd; Hon Roll; YMCA Tn Cncl Pres 85-86; Poland Sullivan Schlrshp 86; SR Edtr Yrbk 86; U Of ME Augusta; Photo.

REED, ERICH M; Lake Region HS; Raymond, ME; (Y); Varsity Clb; Nwsp Rptr; Capt Crs Cntry; Capt Trk; Hon Roll; Trs NHS; Ntl Merit SF; NEDT Awd; Colby; Pol Sci.

REED, MELANIE; Bangor Baptist Schl; Bangor, ME; (S); Church Yth Grp; School Play; Yrbk Stf; Sec Frsh Cls; Trs Soph Cls; Trs Jr Cls; Var Capt Cheerleading; Socr; Sftbl; Vllybl; Alg II, Bio, & Geogrphy Awds 85; Wrld Hstry, Wrld Lit, Alg I, & Phy Sci Awds 84; Liberty U.

REED, SHELLEY; Bangor Baptist Schl; Carmel, ME; (S); 2/15; Church Yth Grp; Pep Clb; Chorus; Stage Crew; Nwsp Rptr; Yrbk Stf; Trs Sr Cls; Var Capt Bsktbl; Var L Cheerleading; Var Capt Socr; U Of ME; Scndry Educ.

REMICK, CINDY; Westbrook HS; Westbrook, ME; (Y); Cmnty Wkr; GAA; Varsity Clb; Nwsp Stf; Yrbk Stf; Bsktbl; Capt Swmmng; Hon Roll; Coachs Awd Swmmng 85; Top Ten St 400 Free Relay & 200 Medley Relay Swmmng 86; Elem Educ.

REYNOLDS, JANICE; Bucksport HS; Penobscot, ME; (Y); Yrbk Stf; Tennis; Hon Roll; Phrmcy.

REYNOLDS, MICHELLE; Skowhegan Area HS; Skowhegan, ME; (Y); Church Yth Grp; Computer Clb; Mgr Drama Clb; VP German Clb; Letterman Clb; Red Cross Aide; Ski Clb; SADD; Varsity Clb; Yrbk Stf.

RHODA, ANGELA S; Penquis Valley HS; Milo, ME; (Y); 1/67; Am Leg Aux Girls St; Drama Clb; Jazz Band; Pep Band; Capt Crs Cntry; High Hon Roll; NHS; Ntl Merit Ltr; Pres Schlr; Val; ME Soc Of Pro Engnrs ST Awd 86; MA Inst Of Tech; Engnrng.

RHODES, TIMMY; Noble HS; North Berwick, ME; (Y); Drama Clb; Key Clb; Band; Chorus; Concert Band; Jazz Band; Mrchg Band; Pep Band; School Musical; School Play.

RI QUIER, MICHELLE; Washington Acad; Pembroke, ME; (Y); 8/67; Camera Clb; Drama Clb; Yrbk Phtg; Yrbk Stf; Var Bsktbl; JV Cheerleading; Var Mgr(s); Hon Roll; NHS; Husson Coll; Acctg.

RICE, NANCY; Stearns HS; Millinocket, ME; (Y); 5/113; Am Leg Aux Girls St; Chorus; VP Frsh Cls; JV Var Cheerleading; Hon Roll; NHS.

RICH, LARRY; Orono HS; Bangor, ME; (Y); 10/125; Boy Scts; Math Tm; Yrbk Stf; Var L Crs Cntry; Trk; High Hon Roll; NHS; Egl Sct Awd 84; Hgh O Brn Yth Ldrshp Cnfrnc 84; Plp R Paper Schlrshp 86; U Of ME Orono; Elec Engnrng.

RICHARD, CINDY; Woodland HS; Woodland, ME; (S); 7/81; Drama Clb; VP FBLA; Thesps; Yrbk Ed-Chief; Var Capt Cheerleading; Var Vllybl; High Hon Roll; Hon Roll; NHS; Church Yth Grp; U Of ME-ORONO; Bus Admin.

RICHARD, KIM; Deering HS; Portland, ME; (Y); Church Yth Grp; Cmnty Wkr; FCA; GAA; Model UN; Varsity Clb; Church Choir; Variety Show; Cheerleading; Coach Actv; Early Chldhd Ed.

RICHARDSON, JULIE; Yarmouth HS; Yarmouth, ME; (Y); Var High Hon Roll; Sci Awd 84; Frnch & Math Awds 86.

RICHARDSON, TAMMY; Morse HS; Bath, ME; (Y); 9/180; Radio Clb; Scholastic Bowl; Science Clb; Stage Crew; Variety Show; Ed Yrbk Stf; Rep Soph Cls; Rep Stu Cncl; Var L Tennis; Hon Roll; Morse Math Awd 84-85; Pres Acad Ftnss Awd 85-86; Tufts U.

RICHARDSON, TRICIA L; Hermon HS; Carmel, ME; (Y); Am Leg Aux Girls St; Pres Church Yth Grp; VP French Clb; Key Clb; Band; Chorus; Jazz Band; Cheerleading; Hon Roll; NHS; Paralegl.

RICHMOND, APRIL; Mexico HS; Mexico, ME; (Y); 25/52; Am Leg Aux Girls St; Computer Clb; Drama Clb; Pep Clb; Speech Tm; Chorus; Yrbk Stf; Pres Jr Cls; JV Bsktbl; Var Fld Hcky.

RICKER, GARNET; Piscataquis Community HS; Harmony, ME; (Y); Boy Scts; Chess Clb; JV Bsktbl; UM-ORONO; Forgn Lang Teachr.

RICKMAN, BRADLEY R; Yarmouth Jr-Sr HS; Yarmouth, ME; (Y); 2/80; Am Leg Boys St; Drama Clb; Latin Clb; Math Tm; Ski Clb; SADD; Chorus; School Musical; School Play; Yrbk Stf; Pres Drama Clb 85-86; Executive Coord Y-Care Orgnztn 85-86; All Star Rgnl Acting Cast 84-85; Law.

RILEY, DEBORAH; Windham HS; Raymond, ME; (Y); 15/181; Am Leg Aux Girls St; Drama Clb; Intnl Clb; VP Keywanettes; Political Wkr; VP SADD; Var Capt Fld Hcky; NHS; Pres Schlr; New England Yng Wrtrs Conf & Natl JA Conf 85; Beloit Coll; Intl Rel.

ROARKS, JAMES; Lee Acad; Winn, ME; (Y); Letterman Clb; School Play; Stage Crew; Stat Bsbl; Stat Bsktbl; Mgr(s); Score Keeper; Stat Socr; Timer; Marine Biolgst.

ROBBINS, BRUCE; Easton HS; Easton, ME; (Y); Am Leg Boys St; Church Yth Grp; French Clb; Yrbk Stf; Stu Cncl; JV Var Bsktbl; Var Socr; Hon Roll; NHS; Prfct Atten Awd; U ME; Engrng.

ROBBINS, KATHLEEN; Sacopee Valley JR SR HS; East Baldwin, ME; (Y); Church Yth Grp; Cmnty Wkr; FCA; French Hon Soc; Hon Roll; Jr NHS; NHS; French Clb; Pep Clb; Speech Tm; 1st Pl Poetry Forensics Tm 84; Mst Depndbl Vol Camp Civitan 85; Youth Cncls 85-86; U Of VA; Math.

ROBERTSON, ROBERT; Bucksport HS; Prospect, ME; (Y); 30/130; Drama Clb; Thesps; School Musical; School Play; Stage Crew; Variety Show; Var Mgr(s); Var Trk; Hon Roll; Dir Cup/Hlp Dir Preduction 85-86; U ME; Theatre.

ROBICHAUD, APRIL; Rumford JR SR HS; Rumford, ME; (Y); Am Leg Aux Girls St; French Clb; Math Tm; SADD; Church Choir; Yrbk Sprt Ed; Yrbk Stf; Trk; Hon Roll; Acctg.

ROBICHAUD, JULIE MARIE; Caribou HS; Caribou, ME; (S); 8/192; Church Yth Grp; Debate Tm; Drama Clb; Key Clb; SADD; Chorus; Church Choir; Jazz Band; School Musical; Variety Show.

ROBINSON, AMY; Lawrence HS; Albion, ME; (Y); 1/190; Math Tm; Spanish Clb; Church Choir; Yrbk Stf; Sftbl; Vllybl; Bausch & Lomb Sci Awd; High Hon Roll; NHS; Val; Colby Coll; Spnsh.

ROBINSON, JAY; Orono HS; Orono, ME; (S); Orch; Off Frsh Cls; Pres Soph Cls; Pres Jr Cls; Stu Cncl; Im Bsktbl; Var Golf; Var Swmmng; Var Tennis; Hon Roll; Engl.

ROBINSON, SUSAN; Oxford Hills HS; S Paris, ME; (Y); Key Clb; Band; Concert Band; Mrchg Band; Bowling; Sftbl; Hon Roll; Non-Athletic Awd Key Clb & Band 86; 3rd Pl Rgnl Accntng Cont 86; Thomas Coll; Accntng.

ROBITAILLE, JULIE; St Dominic R H S; Lewiston, ME; (Y); Trs VP Drama Clb; Pep Clb; School Play; Nwsp Rptr; Nwsp Stf; Hon Roll; NHS.

ROBITAILLE, LOUISE; Lewiston HS; Lewiston, ME; (Y); Office Aide; Stat Ice Hcky; Score Keeper; Sftbl; U Of ME Orono; Bus.

ROCHE, MAUREEN; Gorham HS; Gorham, ME; (Y); Drama Clb; Pres French Clb; Latin Clb; Leo Clb; Science Clb; School Play; Rep Stu Cncl; French Hon Soc; Hon Roll; NHS; Lang.

RODERICK, WILLIAM L; South Portland HS; S Portland, ME; (Y); 21/288; Drama Clb; Key Clb; VP Sr Cls; Bsbl; Bsktbl; Capt Ftbl; Trk; Jr NHS; NHS; Army Resrv Natl Schlr Athl; Randall & Mc Allister & H S Male Athl 86; Ftbl Schlrshp; Springfield Coll; Phy Thrpy.

RODRIGUE, RUSTY; Lewiston HS; Lewiston, ME; (Y); Letterman Clb; Ski Clb; Varsity Clb; Var L Bsktbl; Bsbl; Awds Excllnc Physcl Ed 84-85; JV Bsktbll Awd 84-85; Vrsty L Awd & Pin Hons Jr Yr 86; Optometry.

ROGAN, JAYNE; Deering HS; Portland, ME; (Y); 63/321; Yrbk Stf; Stu Cncl; Hon Roll; UMF; Hmn Srvcs.

ROGERS, KATY; Catherine Mc Auley HS; S Windham, ME; (Y); Computer Clb; French Clb; Key Clb; Ski Clb; Band; Mrchg Band; Nwsp Stf; Yrbk Stf; Sec Frsh Cls; Stu Cncl; Outstndng Awd Bio & Music 85; Child Psych.

ROLLINS, ANDREW; Cony HS; Augusta, ME; (Y); 29/345; FBLA; Spanish Clb; JV Bsktbl; Var Capt Golf; Hon Roll; Jon Crockett Mem Schlrhsp 86; Villanova U.

ROLLINS, HELEN; Mt Ararat Schl; Bowdoinham, ME; (Y); 14/228; Intnl Clb; Library Aide; Teachers Aide; Lit Mag; Elks Awd; High Hon Roll; Hon Roll; Lion Awd; NHS; Prfct Atten Awd; Most Outstndng Stu Awd 85-86; Hm Ec Exc Schlrshp Awds 86; Exc Intl Foods Awd 85; New Hampshire Coll; Culnry Arts.

ROLNICK, MATTHEW; Bangor HS; Bangor, ME; (Y); Am Leg Boys St; Pres Temple Yth Grp; Orch; Bus.

ROONEY, SHANNON; Edward Little HS; Auburn, ME; (Y); Debate Tm; Drama Clb; Spanish Clb; Speech Tm; Chorus; School Musical; Yrbk Stf; Hon Roll; Socl Stds Awd 84; Jrnlsm.

ROSE, WAYNE A; Fryeburg Acad; New York, NY; (Y); Art Clb; Aud/Vis; Cmnty Wkr; Drama Clb; Letterman Clb; Radio Clb; Spanish Clb; SADD; Varsity Clb; Variety Show; Dorm Proctor 86; Dorm Cncl 86; Boston U Syracuse; Pre-Law.

ROSS, LAURA; Orono HS; Bangor, ME; (S); 7/115; Am Leg Aux Girls St; SADD; School Play; Ed Yrbk Ed-Chief; Pres Jr Cls; Pres Sr Cls; Rep Stu Cncl; Crs Cntry; Capt Socr; Capt Trk; Trck Coaches Awd 85; Engl Awd 84; MIP Wntr Trck 83; Liberal Arts.

ROSS, SHARLARI; Georges Valley HS; Thomaston, ME; (Y); Church Yth Grp; FBLA; Chorus; Sftbl; Mansfield Beauty Acad; Beautcn.

ROSS, TINAMARIE; Catherine Mc Auley HS; Scarborough, ME; (Y); #49 In Class; Cmnty Wkr; French Clb; Key Clb; Pres Chorus; Rep Frsh Cls; U ME Farmington; Spec Ed.

ROSS, TROY; Mt Abram HS; Strong, ME; (Y); Ski Clb; Y-Teens; Rep Stu Cncl; Var L Bsbl; Var L Socr; Vllybl; Wt Lftg; Hon Roll; Prfct Atten Awd; Coaches Awd Bsbl 86; CMUTI; Carpntr.

ROSSIANOL, AMY; Van Buren District Secondary School; Van Buren, ME; (Y); Band; Nwsp Stf; Pres Rep Stu Cncl; High Hon Roll; NHS; Sal; Ed.

ROSSIGNOL, AMY A; Van Buren District Secondary Schl; Van Buren, ME; (Y); Band; Nwsp Rptr; Rep Stu Cncl; Socr; High Hon Roll; NHS; Sal; U Of ME; Edu.

ROSSIGNOL, LINDA; Edward Little HS; Auburn, ME; (S); Church Yth Grp; Latin Clb; Varsity Clb; Var Bsktbl; Var L Fld Hcky; JV Sftbl; High Hon Roll; Hon Roll; All ST Fld Hcky Hnrbl Ment 85; Edward Little Schl Rcrd 84; SMAA Fld Hcky Conf 84-85; Law.

ROSSIGNOL, VALERIE; Van Buren Dist Secondary Schl; Van Buren, ME; (Y); 1/72; Sec Frsh Cls; Sec Soph Cls; Pres Jr Cls; VP Sr Cls; Var Capt Cheerleading; Sftbl; Bausch & Lomb Sci Awd; High Hon Roll; NHS; Voice Dem Awd; Rivier Coll; Med.

ROULEAU, MICHAEL; Lewiston HS; Lewiston, ME; (Y); Am Leg Boys St; Boy Scts; Key Clb; Letterman Clb; Ski Clb; Varsity Clb; Yrbk Stf; Rep Sr Cls; Rep Stu Cncl; Var Ftbl; Class Awds 83-86; Tufts.

ROUNDY, BETH; Orono HS; Bangor, ME; (S); Key Clb; SADD; Chorus; Variety Show; Nwsp Rptr; Yrbk Stf; Rep Stu Cncl; Trk; Hon Roll; NHS; Jrnlsm.

ROUSE, LORIANN; Westbrook HS; Westbrook, ME; (Y); 12/200; Var L Cheerleading; High Hon Roll; Hon Roll; Bentley Coll; Comp Sci.

ROUX, DENIS; St Dominics Regional HS; Lewiston, ME; (Y); 30/70; Drama Clb; Key Clb; Ski Clb; School Play; Stage Crew; Bsbl; Golf; JV Ice Hcky; Var L Socr; NEDT Awd; Minor Trophy 87; Drama Clb Awd 87; Key Clb Jacket Awd 87; Arch.

ROWE, TRACY; Edward Little HS; Mechanic Falls, ME; (S); Varsity Clb; Ed Lit Mag; VP Bsktbl; JV VP Sftbl; Cit Awd; Hon Roll; Spch Pth.

ROWELL, WENDA; L H Blue HS; Wilton, ME; (Y); Am Leg Aux Girls St; German Clb; Hosp Aide; Color Guard; Mrchg Band; JV Bsktbl; JV Cheerleading; Var Trk; Wt Lftg; Hon Roll; Addie Jewel Stanley Schlrshp 86; Hazel M Chaney Schlrshp 86; Pres Acad Ftns Awd 86; Mr Bernards; Cosmtlgy.

ROY, ANNIE; Lewiston HS; Lewiston, ME; (Y); Hon Roll; Cert De Mrt 85-86; Econ.

ROY, FRANK; Lee Acad; Springfield, ME; (Y); Ski Clb; Bsbl; Capt Socr; Hon Roll; U Of ME; Archtctrl Engrng.

ROY, JENNIFER; Lewiston HS; Lewiston, ME; (Y); 7/387; Soph Cls; Jr Cls; Sr Cls; Cheerleading; Trk; High Hon Roll; Jr NHS; NHS; Normand Dionne Mdl 86; Sr Math Achvmnt Awd 86; Outstndng Schlrshp Sci 86; New Englnd U; Physcl Thrpy.

ROY, SHARON M; Fort Kent Community HS; Fort Kent, ME; (Y); 6/130; Am Leg Aux Girls St; Art Clb; Sec VP Hosp Aide; SADD; Yrbk Stf; Tennis; High Hon Roll; Hon Roll; NHS; ST & Rgnl BEAM Typ I 1st Pl 86; Cert Hnr Frnch I, Adv Engl II & Type I 84-86; Bangor CC; Med Rcd Tchnlgy.

RUBLEE, VIKKI; Penquis Valley HS; Milo, ME; (Y); 6/66; Church Yth Grp; Sec Sr Cls; Var L Socr; Var L Sftbl; High Hon Roll; Hon Roll; NHS; Sec Frsh Cls; Sec Jr Cls; JV Var Bsktbl; ME Ed Sec Assc Schlrshp 86; Knghts Clmbsfr Gabriel Druillette Assmbly Schlrshp 86; Unvrsty Coll; Bus.

RUDELITCH, JOANNA; Narraguagus HS; Harrington, ME; (Y); 4/63; Sec Am Leg Aux Girls St; Church Yth Grp; Drama Clb; Math Clb; Math Tm; Chorus; Church Choir; Jazz Band; School Play; Nwsp Rptr; Music Schlrshp 82; Prsdnts Schlrshp Cedarville Coll 85; Acadmc Schlrshp Cederville Coll 86; Cedarville Coll; Pre-Med.

RUDY, EDWINA K; South Portland HS; South Portland, ME; (Y); 79/300; Am Leg Aux Girls St; Cmnty Wkr; Debate Tm; Drama Clb; Key Clb; Pres SADD; School Play; Yrbk Stf; Sec Jr Cls; Off Stu Cncl; Am Future Awd 85; Intl Yth Yr Awd 85; Rose Meml Schlrshp 86; Drew U; Hist.

RUFF, SUSAN; Lewiston HS; Lewiston, ME; (Y); Drama Clb; Exploring; Sec Capt Math Tm; Trs Pres Thesps; School Musical; Stage Crew; VP JA; Letterman Clb; Quiz Bowl; Speech Tm; Rensselr Awd 86; Mbr ME Str Math Tm 84-86; LHS Odyssy Mnd Tm 85-86; Prtcpnt ME ST Chorus 86; Phys Sci.

RUOTOLO, JOANNA; Portland HS; Portland, ME; (Y); Church Yth Grp; Cmnty Wkr; Computer Clb; French Clb; Mathletes; Office Aide; Ski Clb; Teachers Aide; Pep Band; Rep Frsh Cls; U Of Sthrn ME; Trvl.

RUSSELL, MELISSA; Orono HS; Orono, ME; (S); 4/115; Key Clb; Math Tm; Yrbk Stf; Trs Frsh Cls; Trs Soph Cls; Trs Sr Cls; Stu Cncl; JV Bsktbl; JV Var Fld Hcky; Sftbl; UMO Schlrs Day 85; Accntnt.

RUTHERFORD, PATRICIA; South Portland HS; S Portland, ME; (Y); 5/320; Am Leg Aux Girls St; Pres Intnl Clb; Pres Stu Cncl; Capt Bsktbl; Var Cheerleading; Var Sftbl; VP NHS; St Schlr; Political Wkr; Smith Bk Awd 86; La.

RYAN, JOHN; Rumford JR SR HS; Rumford, ME; (Y); Varsity Clb; Chorus; School Musical; School Play; Bsbl; Bsktbl; Socr; Cit Awd; High Hon Roll; Hon Roll; Ptr Chmcl.

RYAN, TAMMI; North Yarmouth Acad; S Portland, ME; (Y); French Clb; German Clb; Pres Soph Cls; Pres Jr Cls; VP Sr Cls; VP Stu Cncl; Var L Fld Hcky; Var Lcrss; High Hon Roll; Hon Roll; Pyson-Brd Prze Excllence In Compstn 86; Smth Bk Awd 86; Crtive Wrtng Awd 86; Intl Rltns.

RYAN, TERRI; Westbrook HS; Westbrook, ME; (Y); Church Yth Grp; French Clb; Girl Scts; Band; Concert Band; Mrchg Band; Var Swmmng; JV Trk; Hon Roll; Spc Sci.

RYAN, THERESA; Mt Abram Reginal HS; Kingfield, ME; (Y); 25/88; Drama Clb; 4-H; FTA; Girl Scts; SADD; Teachers Aide; School Play; Yrbk Stf; Stat Mgr(s); Var L Socr; Norton Wuori Amer Lgn-Aux Schlrshp 86; C Rebekah Ldg Schlrshp 86; Natl Hnr Soc Schlrshp 86; U Of ME Farmingt; Elem Ed.

RYDER, DIANA; Edward Little HS; Auburn, ME; (S); Church Yth Grp; Drama Clb; FBLA; Latin Clb; Pep Clb; Band; Chorus; Color Guard; Yrbk Stf; Pom Pon; U ME Orono; Ed.

RYDER, LINDA; Belfast Area HS; Belfast, ME; (Y); 20/115; Hon Roll; Caroline F Duncton 86; EMVTI; Bus.

SABAN, KATHY; Erskine Acad; Palermo, ME; (Y); 2/57; French Clb; Letterman Clb; Trs Sr Cls; JV Var Bsktbl; Mgr(s); JV Sftbl; High Hon Roll; Hon Roll; NHS; Sal; Nebury Coll; Fash Mdsg.

SAMPRAKOS, EDWARD; Gorham HS; Scarbogo, ME; (Y); Ski Clb; Varsity Clb; Band; Concert Band; Jazz Band; Pep Band; Bsbl; Socr; Trk; Prfct Atten Awd; Berklee Coll; Music.

SAMPSON, KRIS; Wells HS; Wells, ME; (Y); Art Clb; French Clb; Ski Clb; Band; Yrbk Stf; Bsktbl; Cheerleading; Crs Cntry; Fld Hcky; Mgr(s); Art.

SAMSON, KIMBERLY; Lewiston HS; Lewiston, ME; (Y); Yrbk Stf; Bsktbl; Fld Hcky; Sftbl; Hon Roll.

SANBORN, DEBRA; Deering HS; Portland, ME; (Y); 13/326; Spanish Clb; High Hon Roll; Hon Roll; Spanish NHS; Westbrook Coll; Fash Merch.

SANDFORD, LORRAINE; Orono HS; Bangor, ME; (S); 5/115; Sec Trs AFS; Math Tm; Band; Nwsp Ed-Chief; Yrbk Stf; High Hon Roll; NHS; Ntl Merit SF.

SANDVOSS, DANA; Waynflete Schl; Kennebunkport, ME; (Y); Cmnty Wkr; Drama Clb; JCL; Library Aide; Band; JV Bsktbl; Im Swmmng; High Hon Roll; Hon Roll; Math.

SARGENT, JESSE; Waynflete HS; Portland, ME; (Y); Var L Ice Hcky; Var L Socr; Var L Tennis; Hon Roll; Faclty Citatn 86; Bus.

SAUCIER, GARY; Ft Fairfield HS; Ft Fairfield, ME; (Y); 4/70; Chess Clb; Yrbk Stf; High Hon Roll; Prfct Atten Awd; Schrlshp Alumni Assn; John Cyr Awd; Perf Atten; Soc Studies Awd; Northern ME Voc; Acctng.

SAUCIER, KIMBERLY; Lewiston HS; Lewiston, ME; (Y); Church Yth Grp; Hosp Aide; Red Cross Aide; Yrbk Stf; Paralgl.

SAUSCHUCK, TANIA; Mt Abram Reg HS; Phillips, ME; (Y); Computer Clb; Yrbk Stf; Sftbl; Hon Roll; Phy Thrpst.

SAVAGE, DAVID; Mount Abram HS; Phillips, ME; (Y); Boy Scts; Chess Clb; Church Yth Grp; Y-Teens; Var Socr; Var Tennis; L Var Trk; Assoc Schools Inc; Airlns.

SAVAGE, TODD; Rumford JR SR HS; Rumford, ME; (Y); Am Leg Boys St; School Play; Ed Yrbk Stf; Trs Frsh Cls; Pres Soph Cls; JV Bsktbl; Var L Socr; Var L Trk; Hon Roll; Accntng.

SAVAGE, TRACEY; Bonny Eagle HS; W Buxton, ME; (Y); Math Tm; Symp Band; JV Fld Hcky; Mgr(s); JV Tennis; High Hon Roll; Hon Roll; Kiwanis Awd.

SAVAGE, WILLIAM; Bonny Eagle HS; W Buxton, ME; (Y); Boy Scts; JA; Hon Roll; Jr NHS; NHS; Ntl Merit Ltr; Pres Schlr; St Schlr; NAJAC 85; Dirigo Schlr 86; Bares Coll; Ecnmcs.

SAWTELLE, DARCEY; Narraguagus HS; Cherryfield, ME; (Y); Girl Scts; Hosp Aide; ROTC; Teachers Aide; Chorus; School Musical; Crs Cntry; Sftbl; Sal; U Of ME; Engrg.

SAWYER, DAWN; Sacopee Valley HS; E Baldwin, ME; (Y); 5/80; Drama Clb; SADD; Band; Concert Band; Yrbk Ed-Chief; Sec Stu Cncl; JV Fld Hcky; Hon Roll; NHS; Voice Dem Awd; Hugh O Brian Yth Ldrshp Sem 84; NY U; Intl Business.

SCANLON, TERI; Fryeberg Acad; Fryeburg, ME; (Y); 75/150; Church Yth Grp; Drama Clb; Pres SADD; Varsity Clb; Chorus; School Musical; School Play; Ed Yrbk Stf; Lit Mag; Sec Trs Jr Cls; Fld Hcky All ST Tm Hnrbl Mntn 85; Fld Hcky All Star Tm 85; Fish & Game Schlrshp 86; U ME Orono; Rehab Cnslr.

SCHEELE, AMY; Marshwood HS; S Berwick, ME; (Y); 16/150; Drama Clb; VP French Clb; Math Tm; Stage Crew; VP Jr Cls; VP Sr Cls; JV Var Fld Hcky; Var Trk; Hon Roll; NHS.

SCHEIBA, MARLENA; Sanford HS; Sanford, ME; (Y); Am Leg Aux Girls St; Church Yth Grp; Math Clb; Math Tm; ROTC; Science Clb; SADD; Var Socr; High Hon Roll; Hon Roll; York U-PA; Med Tech.

SCHMIDT, JENNIFER; Fryeburg Acad; Denmark, ME; (Y); Church Yth Grp; French Clb; Latin Clb; Science Clb; SADD; School Musical; School Play; Stage Crew; Nwsp Phtg; Nwsp Stf.

SCHNEIT, ALISA; Deering HS; Portland, ME; (Y); 28/321; Cmnty Wkr; French Clb; JA; Pep Clb; Ski Clb; Temple Yth Grp; Church Choir; Yrbk Stf; Hon Roll; Maine Schlr 86; Jrdn Mrsh Advsry Cncl 86; Chld Psych.

SCHOENBROD, TANJA; Kennebunk HS; Kennebunkport, ME; (Y); 10/145; Spanish Clb; Yrbk Phtg; Yrbk Stf; Var Bsktbl; Var Vllybl; High Hon Roll; Hon Roll; NHS; Cmmrcl Phtogrphy.

SCHOLZ, RENATE; Oxford Hills HS; S Paris, ME; (Y); 11/206; Am Leg Aux Girls St; Church Yth Grp; Debate Tm; Latin Clb; Math Tm; Chorus; Orch; NHS; AFS; Hon Roll; Colby Bk Awd 85; Vkng A-D Englsh 86; Bowdoin Coll; Eng.

SCHROEDER, FRANCES F; Waynflete Schl; New Gloucester, ME; (Y); German Clb; PAVAS; Teachers Aide; Yrbk Ed-Chief; Var Bsktbl; Coach Actv; Var Fld Hcky; Var Lcrss; Var Socr; Hon Roll; Faclty Citatn 85; Art Rcgntn Awd 85; Sr Book Awd 85; Art Awd-Excllnc In Visual Arts 86; William Smith Coll.

SCHWINGLE, STACEY; Marshwood HS; S Berwick, ME; (Y); Girl Scts; VP Spanish Clb; Band; Church Choir; Concert Band; Jazz Band; Mrchg Band; Stage Crew; NHS; Church Yth Grp; Distngushd Svc Awd 84-86; Engl.

SCRIBNER, SHARON; Oxford Hills HS; South Paris, ME; (Y); 20/200; Church Yth Grp; Hosp Aide; Capt Color Guard; Im JV Bsktbl; Var L Socr; Hon Roll; NHS; U New Wnglnd; Physcl Thrpy.

SEABREASE, STACEY; Bongor HS; Bangor, ME; (Y); Hosp Aide; Band; Orch; Off Sr Cls; Stu Cncl; Var Fld Hcky; Capt Var Swmmng; 4-H Awd; U Maine; Phar.

SEELEY, RANDY; Woodland HS; Woodland, ME; (Y); Cmnty Wkr; Varsity Clb; JV Var Bsktbl; Var Socr; Var Tennis; Hon Roll; Prfct Atten Awd.

SEYMOUR, CELESTE; Deering HS; Portland, ME; (Y); Spanish Clb; Band; Concert Band; Flag Corp; Mrchg Band; Off Sr Cls; SW ST U; Physical Thrpy.

SEYMOUR, TANYA D; Marana Cook Community Schl; Mt Vernon, ME; (Y); Chorus; Variety Show; Crs Cntry; Trk; Excllnce Arts; USM; Art.

SHACKLEY, DEBORAH; Westbrook HS; Westbrook, ME; (Y); 19/190; Latin Clb; Stu Cncl; JV Bsktbl; Var Fld Hcky; Var Sftbl; Hon Roll; Prfct Atten Awd; Am Leg Aux Girls St; English Clb; Spanish Clb; Kenneth Jordan Higgins Mrl Schlrshp 86; Alpha Delta Kappa 86; Alia Richmond Schlrshp 86; Blaine Hs 86; U Of ME; Spec Educ.

SHAN, MARTHA; Orono HS; Orono, ME; (S); Nwsp Stf; JV Socr; High Hon Roll; Bstn U; Med.

SHAW, HEATHER; Lewiston HS; Lewiston, ME; (Y); VP Keywanettes; Varsity Clb; Y-Teens; Swmmng; U Southern ME; Elem Educ.

SHAW, MICHAEL; Easton HS; Easton, ME; (Y); Church Yth Grp; French Clb; School Play; Yrbk Ed-Chief; Rep Frsh Cls; Rep Soph Cls; Rep Jr Cls; Rep Stu Cncl; Hon Roll; 2-Dmnsnl Art.

SHAW, SUZANNE M; Scarborough HS; Scarborough, ME; (Y); 37/178; French Clb; Hosp Aide; Keywanettes; Trs Pep Clb; Chorus; School Musical; Ed Yrbk Stf; Var Cheerleading; Tennis; Hon Roll; Redskin Pride Awd 85.

SHEA, MATTHEW; Gardiner Area HS; Gardiner, ME; (Y); Band; Concert Band; Jazz Band; Mrchg Band; Pep Band; School Musical; School Play; Var L Bsbl; JV Socr; Math.

SHEA, RICHARD; Bangor HS; Bangor, ME; (Y); Latin Clb; Var L Swmmng; Timer; Var Trk; Hon Roll; Advrtsmt.

SIDDIQUI, JAVED; Caribou HS; Caribou, ME; (S); 4/250; Am Leg Boys St; Pres Church Yth Grp; Quiz Bowl; Capt Var Bsktbl; Var Trk; Im Vllybl; High Hon Roll; NHS; Ntl Merit Ltr; ME Schlrs Day 85; Summer Sci Semnr-USAF Acad, CO 85; MIT; Aerontcl Engrng.

SILVIUS, ROBERT; Lawrence HS; Clinton, ME; (Y); Var L Crs Cntry; Var L Trk; Hon Roll; Prfct Atten Awd; KVAC Al-Conf Crs Cntry Tm 85; Elec Engr.

SIMMONS, LYNN MARIE; Medomak Valley HS; Friendship, ME; (Y); Hst AFS; Am Leg Aux Girls St; Pres Trs Latin Clb; Ed Yrbk Stf; Trs Frsh Cls; Trs Jr Cls; Trs Sr Cls; JV Var Bsktbl; Var Trk; Trs NHS; Photo.

SIMOND, LORI; Lewiston HS; Lewiston, ME; (Y); DECA; Pep Clb; Hon Roll; Prfct Atten Awd; Rcvd Mktg & Awds 2nd & 3rd Pl 86; Bus Ed Assn ME Cert 85; DECA Chrmn Swtshrt Cmmttee 86; Dsgng.

SIMONTON, LISA J; Yarmouth HS; Yarmouth, ME; (Y); Cmnty Wkr; Band; Hon Roll; Writer.

SINGER, TINA; Ashland Community HS; Ashland, ME; (Y); Stage Crew; Yrbk Stf; Odd Flws & Rbkhs Nrsng Schlrshp, Elsie G Jns Mem Schlrshp 86; Pres Acdmc Ftns Awd 86; Husson Coll; Nrsng.

SIROIS, PHILLIP; Ashland Community HS; Ashland, ME; (Y); 9/100; Boy Scts; French Clb; Band; Pep Band; School Musical; Frsh Cls; Var Bsbl; Var Bsktbl; Var Vllybl; High Hon Roll; Rotary Schlrshp $200 86; J Paul Levesque & Fmly Schlrshp $500; U Of ME; Chem Engrng.

SITES, MELINDA; Lewiston HS; Greene, ME; (Y); 123/375; Church Yth Grp; Exploring; Letterman Clb; Service Clb; Pres SADD; Y-Teens; School Play; Bsktbl; Capt Swmmng; Hon Roll; St Joseph Coll; Med.

SKIDGEL, SANDRA; Caribou HS; Caribou, ME; (S); 14/185; Library Aide; SADD; Teachers Aide; Band; Chorus; Mrchg Band; Socr; Sftbl; Vllybl; High Hon Roll; Pres Schlrshp 86-87; Blaine House Schlrshp 86-87; SEOG Schlrshp 86-87; U ME; Elem Ed.

SKILLINGS, HILARY; Deering HS; Portland, ME; (Y); Math Tm; Orch; French Hon Soc; High Hon Roll; Jr NHS; NHS; Yth For Undrstndg Japan-U S Senate Scholar Japan 86; Piano Master Cls 85; Smith Coll Bk Awd 86; Chinese Lang.

SMALL, ANDREA; Skowhegan Area HS; Skowhegan, ME; (Y); 2/225; Pres 4-H; Sec French Clb; Math Tm; Chorus; Yrbk Ed-Chief; Sec Frsh Cls; Sec Soph Cls; Trs Jr Cls; Cheerleading; JV Fld Hcky; Delg 4-H Ctznshp WA Focus 85; Delg 4-H Natl Conf 87; Hugh O Brian Ldrshp Semnr Delg 85; USC Berkley; Lib Arts.

SMALL, DORIAN; Skowhegan Area HS; Skowhegan, ME; (Y); Hon Roll; NHS; St Schlr; Oscar T Turner Schlrshp Fund 86; Franklin Savngs Bnk Schlrshp Fnd 86-90; U Maine Orono; Soil Consrvtn Te.

SMITH, ANDREA; Fryeburg Acad; Lovell, ME; (Y); 15/152; Am Leg Aux Girls St; Latin Clb; SADD; Varsity Clb; Yrbk Rptr; Cheerleading; Socr; High Hon Roll; Hon Roll; NHS; Oxford Cnty Rtrd Tchrs Assoc Schlrshp 86; Fryeburg Acad Tchrs Assoc Schlrshp 86; Spkr At Grad 86; U Of S ME; Elem Educ.

SMITH, BETHANY; Buckfield JR SR HS; Buckfield, ME; (S); Art Clb; Pres Church Yth Grp; French Clb; SADD; Varsity Clb; Yrbk Stf; Var Bsktbl; Var Socr; Var Sftbl; Voice Dem Awd; CMVTI; Grphc Arts.

SMITH, BUFFY; Bucksport HS; Bucksport, ME; (Y); 4/117; Am Leg Aux Girls St; Sec FBLA; Varsity Clb; Band; Concert Band; Mrchg Band; Nwsp Stf; Capt Cheerleading; Sftbl; Hon Roll; ST Chmpns-Chrng Sqd 83-84; 1st Pl Chrng Comp 82-85; Chrng Comptn-11th Pl Natl 83-84; U Of ME Orono; Bus Adm.

SMITH, DANETTE; Lee Acad; Springfield, ME; (Y); Am Leg Aux Girls St; Church Yth Grp; Letterman Clb; Library Aide; Office Aide; Varsity Clb; Church Choir; Yrbk Stf; Var Bsktbl; JV Var Crs Cntry; Bus Mgt.

SMITH, JENNIFER JOY; Open Bible Baptist Christian Schl; Farmington, ME; (Y); Art Clb; Church Yth Grp; Chorus; Church Choir; Concert Band; Yrbk Stf; High Hon Roll; Jr NHS; Dance Clb; Political Wkr; Cultrl Achvt Awd 84-85; Cert Achvt Hnr Rll All 4 Qtrs 85-86; Rnr Up Stu Yr 84-85; Elem Ed.

SMITH, JULIE; Jonesport-Beals HS; Jonesport, ME; (Y); Cmnty Wkr; Drama Clb; Church Choir; Yrbk Stf; Pres Frsh Cls; VP Soph Cls; Trs Jr Cls; Hon Roll; NHS; Ntl Bus Hnr Scty 86; Travel.

SMITH, KATHRYN; Caribou HS; Caribou, ME; (S); Church Yth Grp; French Clb; Hosp Aide; Trs SADD; Varsity Clb; Band; Concert Band; Jazz Band; Mrchg Band; Yrbk Bus Mgr; U Of Southern ME; Socl Wrk.

SMITH, KATIE; Ashland Community HS; Ashland, ME; (Y); Am Leg Aux Girls St; Church Yth Grp; French Clb; Girl Scts; Model UN; Quiz Bowl; Band; Jazz Band; Mrchg Band; Pep Band; Hghst Avg Typing 86; Hghst Avg Amer Poli Sys 84; Rcvd Acdmc Letter 83; U Of ME.

SMITH, MELISSA; Lee Acad; Winn, ME; (Y); Am Leg Aux Girls St; Letterman Clb; Math Tm; Trs Frsh Cls; Rep Stu Cncl; Var L Cheerleading; Mgr(s); Var L Socr; Hon Roll; Bus Admin.

SMITH, NIKI L; Woodland HS; Meddybemps, ME; (S); Computer Clb; Drama Clb; FBLA; Varsity Clb; Color Guard; School Play; Ed Lit Mag; Rep Stu Cncl; Var Capt Cheerleading; Hon Roll.

SMITH, ROBERT; Westbrook HS; Westbrook, ME; (Y); 25/190; Church Yth Grp; Latin Clb; Band; Concert Band; Mrchg Band; Pep Band; Nwsp Rptr; Nwsp Sprt Ed; Bsbl; Bsktbl; Annapolis Summer Semnr 86; W Point Summee Semnr 86; U Maine Music Comp 86; Poltcl Sci.

SMITH, SANDRA; Catherine Mc Auley HS; Kennebunkport, ME; (Y); 18/73; French Clb; Chorus; School Play; Crs Cntry; Trk; Hon Roll; Hnr Rl 83-85; Prfct Attndnc Awd 85-86; U Of ME Farmington; Elem Educ.

SMITH, SUSAN; Gorham HS; Westbrook, ME; (Y); Cmnty Wkr; English Clb; Exploring; French Clb; Girl Scts; Hosp Aide; JA; Latin Clb; Science Clb; SADD; Geog Awd 84; Typg Awd 85; Ctznshp Awd 83; Med.

SMITH, TERRI; Central Aroostook HS; Mars Hill, ME; (Y); 4/72; Cmnty Wkr; French Clb; Hosp Aide; Math Tm; JV Bsktbl; Var Socr; Var Sftbl; Var Trk; High Hon Roll; NHS; Phy Thrpst.

SMITH, THERESA; Winslow HS; N Vassalboro, ME; (Y); AFS; Cmnty Wkr; Drama Clb; Red Cross Aide; Yrbk Stf; Rep Frsh Cls; Rep Soph Cls; L Capt Cheerleading; Hon Roll; Prfct Atten Awd; Elem Ed.

SMITH, TIM; Lewiston HS; Lewiston, ME; (Y); VP Key Clb; Letterman Clb; Rep Soph Cls; Trs Jr Cls; Stu Cncl; Coach Actv; Capt Ftbl; Capt Ice Hcky; Score Keeper; Wt Lftg; Jr Olympic Trning Ctr At N MI U 86; MEALL-STAR Mdgts 84-87; Bus Mgmt.

SNOW, SUSAN; Orono HS; Bangor, ME; (S); Math Tm; Trs Soph Cls; Rep Stu Cncl; Var L Socr; Var L Trk; High Hon Roll.

SOPER, HILLARY; Edward Little HS; Auburn, ME; (S); Sec AFS; Am Leg Aux Girls St; Cmnty Wkr; Trs Speech Tm; JV Mgr(s); Hon Roll; Hstry.

SOREL, DAVID; Fryeburg Acad; Seekonk, MA; (Y); Stu Cncl; Var Golf; Var Socr; Hon Roll; ME ST Slalom Champ 84-85; Sprng Series Giant Slalom & Slalom Champ 86; ME ST Overall Ski Champ 85; Bus.

SOUTHERN, JESSICA; Livermore Falls HS; Livermore Falls, ME; (Y); Am Leg Aux Girls St; Varsity Clb; Band; Lit Mag; Sec Jr Cls; Mgr(s); Score Keeper; Hon Roll; NHS; Hnrs Art Awd; Stu Of Mnth; Prtlnd Schl Of Art; Photo.

SPAULDING, ANNETTE; Woodland HS; Princeton, ME; (Y); Chess Clb; Computer Clb; FBLA; SADD; Varsity Clb; School Play; Yrbk Stf; Lit Mag; Var Cheerleading; Hon Roll; Educ.

SPECTRE, MAUREEN; Camden-Rockport HS; Camden, ME; (Y); 1/114; AFS; French Clb; Latin Clb; Band; Chorus; Madrigals; High Hon Roll; Hon Roll; NHS; Val; U Of ME Schlrs Day 85; CT Coll.

SPENCER, DEBORAH L; Mt Blue HS; Wilton, ME; (Y); Trs FBLA; High Hon Roll; NHS; Stu Of Mnth 86; Hghst Avg Acctg I & Typg II 86; Acctg.

SPINNEY, ROBERT; Shead HS; Eastport, ME; (S); Boy Scts; Church Yth Grp; Band; Mrchg Band; Pep Band; Trs Frsh Cls; Trs Soph Cls; Trs Jr Cls; Var Socr; High Hon Roll; U ME Orono.

SPOFFORD, MARIA; Westbrook HS; Westbrook, ME; (Y); DECA; Band; Color Guard; Mrchg Band; Nwsp Rptr; Prfct Atten Awd; Cosmtlgst.

SPRAGUE, FRANK; Ashland Community HS; Ashland, ME; (Y); Am Leg Boys St; Boy Scts; Church Yth Grp; Band; Concert Band; Mrchg Band; Pep Band; High Hon Roll; Hon Roll; Jr NHS; Bus.

SQUIERS, LISA; Penobscot Valley HS; Howland, ME; (Y); 13/69; Am Leg Aux Girls St; School Play; Variety Show; Yrbk Stf; Pres Stu Cncl; Var Capt Cheerleading; Var Socr; Hon Roll; Pres NHS; 4 Yr Dedctn Awd Vrsty Chrldng 86; Hmcmng Queen 85; U Of MA Orono; Bus Adm.

ST ONGE, LOUISE; St Dominic Regional HS; Lewiston, ME; (Y); 5/70; Drama Clb; French Clb; Hosp Aide; Trs Pres Keywanettes; Math Tm; Co-Capt L Tennis; Dnfth Awd; Hon Roll; Sec NHS; Frnch Ntl Ex 83-84; Schltsc Awd 84-86; Keyette Of Yr Awd 84; U ME-ORONO; Bus Adm.

ST PIERE, DEBBIE; Freeport HS; Freeport, ME; (Y); 14/68; JA; Library Aide; Chorus; Yrbk Stf; Var Capt Cheerleading; Var Fld Hcky; Im Gym; JV Sftbl; Im Vllybl; Hon Roll; L Carl Bean & Tchrs Assn & Lions Clb Schlrshps 86; U Of ME; Erly Chldhd Ed.

ST PIERRE, SUZANNE; Van Buren Dist Secondary Schl; Van Buren, ME; (Y); 3/69; Math Clb; VP Soph Cls; Rep Jr Cls; Rep Stu Cncl; JV Var Bsktbl; Var L Socr; High Hon Roll; Voice Dem Awd; St Josephs Coll; Med Tech.

STACK, SANDRA; Westbrook HS; Westbrook, ME; (Y); 2/190; Am Leg Aux Girls St; English Clb; VP French Clb; Math Tm; Chorus; Mrchg Band; Var L Tennis; High Hon Roll; VP NHS; Sal; Harvard Bk Awd 85; Georgetown U; Frnch.

STACKI, MATT; Cheverus HS; Portland, ME; (Y); 30/95; Boys Clb Am; Chess Clb; Church Yth Grp; Im Bsktbl; Im Ftbl; JV Var Tennis; Wt Lftg; High Hon Roll; Hon Roll; Excllnc In Latin 1st In Cls Latin II 84-85.

STAIRS, DARRIN B; Freeport HS; Freeport, ME; (Y); 2/90; Am Leg Boys St; Cmnty Wkr; French Clb; JA; Math Tm; Ski Clb; Yrbk Sprt Ed; Yrbk Stf; Trs Frsh Cls; VP Soph Cls; ME Conservtn Schl 85; Shearson Lehman Bros Scholar; U MA Amherst; Chem Engrng.

STANLEY, DEBORAH S; Temple Acad; Pittsfield, ME; (Y); 2/5; Church Yth Grp; Chorus; VP Stu Cncl; Capt L Bsktbl; L Cheerleading; Hon Roll; Sal; Prsdntl Acad Ftnss Awd, US Marine Cprs Dtngshed Ath Awd, Amer Leg Cert Ath Awd, Schl Awd 85-86; Cntrl ME Med Ctr; Nrsg.

STAPLES, JEANNE; Old Orchard Beach HS; Old Orchard Bch, ME; (Y); 16/78; Ski Clb; Band; Color Guard; Mrchg Band; Fld Hcky; Sftbl; Acctg Awd Acctg II 85-86; Comp Awd Comp Bscs 84-85; Rlph Prrlt Mem Schlrshp 85-86; CA CC Sierra; Acctg.

STAPLES, JENNIFER; Yarmouth JR SR HS; Yarmouth, ME; (Y); Church Yth Grp; Latin Clb; Ski Clb; Spanish Clb; SADD; Chorus; Yrbk Stf; Intl Rel.

STEDMAN, KATHLEEN; Catherine Mc Auley HS; Portland, ME; (Y); 19/75; Church Yth Grp; Cmnty Wkr; Key Clb; Latin Clb; VP Science Clb; Teachers Aide; Lit Mag; Stat Bsktbl; Hon Roll; Prfct Atten Awd; Sci Awd 84.

STEEVES, CARLA; Vonny Eagle HS; Saco, ME; (Y); 36/240; Dance Clb; Latin Clb; Teachers Aide; L Varsity Clb; JV Bsktbl; Var Sftbl; Hon Roll; Jr NHS; NHS; Blaine House Schlrshp 86; Saco Vly Cvc Assoc Schlrshp 86; Psych Awd 86; U Of ME Farmington; Chldhd Ed.

STEVENS, ELAINE GAIL; Mahanawcock Acad; Lincoln Center, ME; (Y); 4/103; Am Leg Aux Girls St; Drama Clb; Letterman Clb; Math Tm; Nwsp Rptr; Yrbk Rptr; L Trk; High Hon Roll; Sec NHS; Latin Clb; 2nd Hnr Essayist; Outstndng Achvt Latin; ME Schlr; U ME Orono; Elec Engrng.

STEVENS, KAREN ANN; Deering HS; Portland, ME; (Y); Am Leg Aux Girls St; Pres Varsity Clb; Var Socr; Var Capt Swmmng; French Hon Soc; NHS; French Clb; Key Clb; SADD; Variety Show; Colby Coll Bk Awd 86; X-Cntry Awd Super Dedctn & Courg 84; Slctd For The Anatomy Of Ldrshp Prog 85; Med.

STEVENS, TODD; Cony HS; Augusta, ME; (Y); JCL; Science Clb; Rep Frsh Cls; Var Capt Bsktbl; JV Crs Cntry; JV Trk; Hon Roll; Prfct Atten Awd; Ntl JCL Exam Gld Mdl 86.

STEWART, DONNA SARAH; Bangor HS; Bangor, ME; (Y); Am Leg Aux Girls St; NFL; Speech Tm; Yrbk Stf; Rep Jr Cls; Cheerleading; High Hon Roll; VFW Awd; Voice Dem Awd; Hon Roll; Cert Achvt Engl 84 & 86; Lewiston ST Spch Fest 3rd Orig Ortry 86; AZ ST U; Advrtsg.

STICHT, MICHELLE; Belfast Area HS; Belfast, ME; (Y); 19/121; Art Clb; Chorus; School Musical; Variety Show; JV Var Cheerleading; Var Mgr(s); Var Score Keeper; Hon Roll; Hghst Achvmnt Art; Endicott Coll; Cmmrcl Art.

STORER, RACHELLE; Mt Abram HS; Phillips, ME; (Y); Am Leg Aux Girls St; Debate Tm; Office Aide; Var L Bsktbl; L Crs Cntry; L Trk; Bsktbl 100% Awd 83-84; UMA; Assoc Dgree Sec Sci.

STOWELL, ALICIA; Yarmouth HS; Yarmouth, ME; (Y); Latin Clb; Spanish Clb; Band; Yrbk Stf; Sec Frsh Cls; Rep Soph Cls; Spanish NHS; Intntl Rltns.

STUBBS, MARK; Bucksport HS; Bucksport, ME; (Y); Varsity Clb; Nwsp Stf; JV Var Bsbl; JV Var Bsktbl; Hon Roll; NHS; Ntl Merit Ltr; Frd Frsyth Schlrshp 86; Thomas Coll; Comp Systms.

STUTZ, JOHN; Marshwood HS; S Berwick, ME; (Y); 4/150; Church Yth Grp; Math Tm; Yrbk Sprt Ed; Yrbk Stf; Off Sr Cls; Stu Cncl; Socr; Trk; Bausch & Lomb Sci Awd; High Hon Roll; Ntl Ltn Awd 84 & 85; Math.

SULLIVAN, ELIZABETH; Morse HS; Woolwich, ME; (Y); Am Leg Aux Girls St; Church Yth Grp; Variety Show; Rep Stu Cncl; Var Bsktbl; Var Fld Hcky; Var Sftbl; Hon Roll; NHS; MVP SR Yr Bsktbl 86; U Of ME; Physcl Educ.

SULT, TINA; Lisbon HS; Lisbon, ME; (Y); Cmnty Wkr; Office Aide; Pep Clb; Drm Mjr(t); Yrbk Stf; Cheerleading; Hon Roll; 4th Pl Bio Sci Fair 85; 3rd Pl Chem Sci Fair 86; Outstndng Acctg Awd 86; Concord Schl Nursing; Nrsng.

SUTHERLAND, CHERYL; Sumner Memorial HS; E Sullivan, ME; (Y); Yrbk Stf; Pres Frsh Cls; VP Jr Cls; Pres Sr Cls; Rep Stu Cncl; Hon Roll.

SWARZTRAUBER, HOLLY LYNN; George Stevens Acad; Castine, ME; (Y); 7/62; Am Leg Aux Girls St; Church Yth Grp; Spanish Clb; Nwsp Ed-Chief; Nwsp Phtg; Nwsp Rptr; Yrbk Phtg; Yrbk Stf; Cheerleading; Powder Puff Ftbl; Spnsh Awd 84; M Hincley Schlrshp 86; Smith Coll; Econ.

SWEET, KELLIE; Edward Little HS; Auburn, ME; (S); Acpl Chr; Chorus; School Musical; Var L Tennis; Vllybl; High Hon Roll; Hon Roll; Drama Clb; French Clb; Girl Scts; Physcl Thrpy.

SWEETSER, BECKY; Mt Abram HS; Phillips, ME; (Y); 28/80; Computer Clb; Yrbk Stf; Hon Roll; Westbrook Coll; Erly Chldhd Edu.

SWEETSIR, BETH; Yarmouth JR SR HS; Yarmouth, ME; (Y); Hon Roll; Prfct Atten Awd; Bus.

TABB, JAYME; Telstar HS; Andover, ME; (Y); Cmnty Wkr; Yrbk Stf; JV Fld Hcky; L Var Sftbl; Hon Roll; Nw Hmpshr Voc Tech Coll; Bus Mg.

TALARICO, LARA; Edward Little HS; Auburn, ME; (S); Pres Civic Clb; French Clb; Math Clb; Varsity Clb; Var L Fld Hcky; High Hon Roll; Lib Art.

TAPLEY, DAVE; Westbrook HS; Westbrook, ME; (Y); JA; Key Clb; SADD; Yrbk Stf; Hon Roll; Arch.

TARDIF, SCOTT; St Dominic Regional HS; Lewiston, ME; (Y); Drama Clb; Key Clb; School Play; Var Ice Hcky; Var Socr; Var Capt Tennis; St Schlr.

TARGETT, JILL ALMA; Gray-New Gloucester HS; Gray, ME; (Y); 9/115; Drama Clb; French Clb; Latin Clb; Math Tm; Yrbk Phtg; Yrbk Stf; L JV Fld Hcky; Im Vllybl; Hon Roll; Jr NHS; Frshmn Vldctrn 83; Top 10 Hnr Stu For Cls 86; St Jsphs Coll; Pre-Med.

TAYLOR, JON; Deering HS; Portland, ME; (Y); Library Aide; U S ME; Acctg.

TETENMAN, SCOTT; Eduward Little HS; Poland Springs, ME; (S); AFS; VP Church Yth Grp; French Clb; Math Tm; Ski Clb; SADD; Socr.

TETREAULT, MELISSA; Edward Little HS; Auburn, ME; (S); Pep Clb; Chorus; School Musical; School Play; U Of ME-FRMNGTN; Scndry Educ.

THEBARGE, JANELLE; Carrabec HS; Anson, ME; (Y); Art Clb; Church Yth Grp; FHA; German Clb; Ski Clb; Varsity Clb; Cheerleading; Socr; Tennis; Hon Roll; All-Star Chrng Awd; Hnr Cards; Cazenovia Coll; Fshn Dsgn.

THERIAULT, DENISE; Caribou HS; Caribou, ME; (S); 14/200; Cmnty Wkr; Office Aide; Rep Frsh Cls; Rep Jr Cls; Var Tennis; Stat Socr; High Hon Roll; Hon Roll; Ntl Merit Ltr; Cosmtlgy.

THERIAULT, VALERIE; Caribou HS; Caribou, ME; (Y); Church Yth Grp; FNA; Band; Concert Band; Mrchg Band; Var Cheerleading; Var Trk; Hon Roll; Nrs.

THERRIEN, KEVIN; Orono HS; Bangor, ME; (S); 3/114; Boy Scts; CAP; French Clb; Math Tm; Yrbk Phtg; Stu Cncl; Var L Socr; Var Trk; High Hon Roll; Sci Awd 84; Engrng.

THIBEAU, LAURA; Lawrence HS; Fairfield, ME; (Y); Art Clb; Color Guard; Cheerleading; Pom Pon; Swmmng; Hon Roll; Pres Schlr; Stella Thomas Meml Schlrshp 86; Hgh Achvt Engl Awd 86; Hgh Achvt Acctg Awd 86; Thomas Coll; Acctg.

THIBEAULT, DANIELLE; Fort Kent Community HS; Fort Kent, ME; (Y); FNA; Hosp Aide; SADD; Band; Concert Band; Yrbk Stf; Mgr(s); Score Keeper; Hon Roll; Trvl.

THIBEAULT, SHARI; Fort Kent Community HS; Fort Kent, ME; (Y); Pres Am Leg Aux Girls St; Pres Camera Clb; Varsity Clb; Band; Pep Band; Stage Crew; Nwsp Rptr; Yrbk Ed-Chief; Yrbk Phtg; Yrbk Stf; Pres Of Senate Dirigo Girls ST 86; U Of ME; Pblc Rltns.

THIBODEAU, BETTY; Lee Acad; Springfield, ME; (Y); 2/45; FBLA; Letterman Clb; Varsity Clb; Yrbk Ed-Chief; Sec Jr Cls; Trs Sr Cls; Var Capt Bsktbl; High Hon Roll; NHS; Sal; Rdrs Digest Schlrshp 86; U Of ME Machias; Comp Prog.

THIBODEAU, CARA; Caribou HS; Caribou, ME; (S); 16/250; Debate Tm; French Clb; Girl Scts; Hosp Aide; Letterman Clb; Pep Clb; Varsity Clb; Band; Concert Band; Mrchg Band; Dist Yng Ctzns Ldrshp 85-86; Sci Awds 85; Csmtlgy.

THIBODEAU, VICKI; Lawrence HS; Waterville, ME; (Y); 4-H; Ski Clb; Band; Concert Band; Mrchg Band; 4-H Awd; Hon Roll; Vet-Med.

THISSELL, TANYA; Medomak Valley HS; Friendship, ME; (Y); 14/120; AFS; VP Art Clb; Drama Clb; Pep Clb; School Play; Stage Crew; Yrbk Stf; High Hon Roll; Hon Roll; NHS; U Southern ME; Art.

THOMAS, HEIDI; Ellsworth HS; Ellsworth, ME; (Y); 19/110; AFS; French Clb; Band; Var Capt Cheerleading; Hon Roll; NHS; ME U Orono; Elem Ed.

THOMPSON, CHRIS; Deering HS; Portland, ME; (Y); 46/367; Computer Clb; Latin Clb; Math Clb; Math Tm; Ski Clb; Varsity Clb; Socr; Trk; Vllybl; Wt Lftg; Mst Imprvd Plyr Sccr 84-85; MVP Colby Sccr Camp 86; Comp Engrng.

THOMPSON, JERRY; Foxcroft Acad; Charleston, ME; (Y); Hon Roll; U Of ME; Frstry.

THOMPSON, KAREN; Catherine Mc Auley HS; South Portland, ME; (Y); 14/73; Am Leg Aux Girls St; Church Yth Grp; Girl Scts; SADD; Nwsp Stf; Lit Mag; VP Sr Cls; Rep Stu Cncl; Capt Vllybl; Hon Roll; Fshn Merch.

THOMPSON, ROBERT A; Brunswick HS; Brunswick, ME; (Y); 41/243; Boy Scts; JA; Letterman Clb; Math Tm; Scholastic Bowl; Bsbl; Ftbl; Sftbl; French Hon Soc; Hon Roll; U ME-ORONO; Chem Engr.

THOMS, WILLIAM; Fryeburg Acad; Eaton Center, NH; (S); Ski Clb; Varsity Clb; L Bsbl; L Ftbl; JV Tennis; High Hon Roll; Hon Roll; Jr NHS; NHS; Ntl Merit Ltr; Latn Schlr Awd 84.

THORESON, TAMI; Lewiston HS; Lewiston, ME; (Y); 33/389; Exploring; Pres Intnl Clb; Pep Clb; Pres Service Clb; SADD; Varsity Clb; Yrbk Stf; Rep Jr Cls; Coach Actv; JV Stat Fld Hcky; Grls ST 85; Gym Awd 85; Stu Mnth 86; ME Maritime; Engrng.

THORNE, JUDY; Edward Little HS; Auburn, ME; (S); Fld Hcky; Pep Clb; SADD; Varsity Clb; JV Crs Cntry; Stat Gym; Var L Tennis; Cit Awd; Hon Roll; Trs NHS; Spch Path.

THORNE, MICHELLE; Bonny Eagle HS; Windham, ME; (Y); Math Tm; Band; Var Bsktbl; JV Fld Hcky; Sftbl; High Hon Roll; Hon Roll; NHS; St Schlr; Engl Awd 86; Latin III Awd 86; ST ME Schlr 86; ST ME Humanities Bowdoin Coll Summr Pgm 86; Bowdoin Coll; Pol Sci.

THORNE, TAMMY; Edward Little HS; Mechanic Falls, ME; (Y); Church Yth Grp; 4-H; Library Aide; Office Aide; Teachers Aide; Hon Roll; Prfct Atten Awd; Sci.

THUOTTE, KRISTENE; Westbrook HS; Westbrook, ME; (Y); Trs Church Yth Grp; Cmnty Wkr; FBLA; Sec SADD; Yrbk Stf; Capt Var Mgr(s); Daniel Webster Coll; Travel.

TIMBERLAKE, JAMES; Lewiston HS; Lewiston, ME; (Y); 32/418; Q&S; Ed Lit Mag; High Hon Roll; Claire E Bldc Schlrshp Awd 86; ME Smr Hmnts Pgm 85; Boston Coll; Lbrl Arts.

TIMBERLAKE, SARAH; Livermore Falls HS; Turner, ME; (Y); Drama Clb; SADD; Hon Roll; NHS; Colby Book Awd 86; ME Smmr Humnts Pgm 86; Psych.

TIMPANY, CATHERINE; Edward Little HS; Auburn, ME; (S); Var Bsktbl; Var Sftbl; Hon Roll.

TODD, GAYLE; Belfast Area HS; Belfast, ME; (Y); 8/120; Pres Trs Church Yth Grp; Hon Roll; Prfct Atten Awd; Maintg 85 Thrght Spnsh 86; Pres Acadmc Ftnss Awd 86; Assoc Schools Inc; Trvl.

TODD, HEIDI; Caribou HS; Caribou, ME; (Y); Church Yth Grp; Band; Chorus; Church Choir; Mrchg Band; Pep Band; Hon Roll; Outstndng Concrt Band Mbr 86; Eastern Coll.

TODD, JENNIFER; Belfast Area HS; Belfast, ME; (Y); 12/120; Am Leg Aux Girls St; French Clb; Math Tm; Band; Chorus; Yrbk Stf; L Mgr Bsktbl; L Trk; Hon Roll; Girl Scts; Trinity Coll Of VT; Pre-Med.

TODD, JULIE; Cony HS; Augusta, ME; (Y); Library Aide; Political Wkr; Bsktbl; Coach Actv; Tennis; Hon Roll; MVP Tnns 86; Psych.

TOUSSAINT, JACQUES; Fort Kent Community HS; Fort Kent, ME; (Y); 5/138; Am Leg Boys St; Chess Clb; Teachers Aide; VP Sr Cls; Im Crs Cntry; NHS; Ntl Merit Ltr; Volunteer Tutor Awd 86; Outstndg Stu Math Awd Hghst Avg 84-86; U ME Orono; Ag Engrg.

TOWNSEND, KELLY; Kennebunk HS; Kennebunk, ME; (Y); 74/144; Sec Church Yth Grp; FBLA; Girl Scts; Letterman Clb; Pep Clb; Spanish Clb; Varsity Clb; VICA; Color Guard; Drm Mjr(t); Kennebunk Rotry Clb Schlrshp 86; Kennebunk Tchrs Schlrshp 86; De Molay Schlrshp 86; Endicott College; Fash Merch.

TRAISTER, MICHAEL; Edward Little HS; Auburn, ME; (S); AFS; Am Leg Boys St; French Clb; Trs Key Clb; Letterman Clb; Ski Clb; SADD; VP Temple Yth Grp; Varsity Clb; Variety Show; Bates Coll Stdnt 85; ME Schlrs Day 85; Pol Sci.

TRANBARGER, VICTORIA; Fort Fairfield HS; Ft Fairfield, ME; (Y); 2/70; Cmnty Wkr; Hosp Aide; Library Aide; SADD; Church Choir; Yrbk Bus Mgr; Yrbk Stf; Mgr(s); High Hon Roll; Typing I Awd 85; Shorthand I & Typing II Awds 86; Draughans; Exec Secry.

TRASK, DARLENE; Franklin Alternative HS; Mechanic, ME; (Y); Chorus; Twrlr; CMUTI; Nrsng.

TRASK, PETER; Edward Little HS; Auburn, ME; (S); AFS; Tennis; High Hon Roll; NHS; Church Yth Grp; Computer Clb; Drama Clb; Latin Clb; Spanish Clb; School Play; Yale Bk Awd; Psych.

TREBILCOCK, TEDDY; Oxford Hills HS; Oxford, ME; (Y); 24/225; Am Leg Boys St; Band; Concert Band; Jazz Band; Mrchg Band; Pep Band; School Musical; Var Crs Cntry; Var Ftbl; Var Trk; Vkng Awd-Music 86; Mst Vlubl Awd-Music 86; Coachs Awd-Trck 86; #1 All ST Trmbn 86; Armed Frcs Schl Of Music; Music.

TREIBER, JOHN; Morse HS; Honolulu, HI; (Y); Radio Clb; SADD; School Play; Variety Show; Yrbk Phtg; Var L Socr; Var L Tennis; Vrsty Ten-Coachs Awd 86; Loyola U NO; Cmmnctns.

TRUE, RENEE; Fryeburg Acad; Denmark, ME; (S); Church Yth Grp; French Clb; Girl Scts; SADD; Gym; Mgr(s); Socr; Sftbl; Hon Roll; Boston U; Lang.

TRUMBULL, MARY J; Fryeburg Acad; Fryeburg, ME; (S); Latin Clb; Girl Scts; Mgr(s); Score Keeper; Hon Roll; Rainbow; U ME; Dctr Vtrnry Med.

TSCHAMLER, TAFF; Cony HS; Augusta, ME; (Y); Variety Show; Sec Sr Cls; Stu Cncl; JV Ftbl; JV Var Socr; Colgate; Philosphy.

TUCKER, CYNTHIA; Edward Little HS; Mechanic Falls, ME; (S); Sec Trs French Clb; Chorus; Mgr(s); Var Sftbl; Cit Awd; Hon Roll; NHS; Frnch, Engl Awds 83; Elem Ed.

TUFTS, TIMOTHY; Fryburg Acad; Biddeford, ME; (S); Ski Clb; Bus Mgmt.

TURCOTTE, MICHELLE; Edward Little HS; Poland Spring, ME; (S); Drama Clb; French Clb; Pep Clb; School Musical; School Play; Stage Crew; Cit Awd; High Hon Roll; VFW Awd; Frgn Lang Awd 84; Tchr.

TURGEON, PAMELA; Westbrook HS; Westbrook, ME; (Y); Am Leg Aux Girls St; JA; Band; Chorus; Color Guard; Pep Band; Cheerleading; Hon Roll; Westbrook; Acctng.

TURNER, ERIC; Cony HS; Augusta, ME; (Y); 31/310; Am Leg Boys St; Exploring; SADD; Varsity Clb; Var Bsbl; Capt Ice Hcky; Socr; Im Sftbl; Im Vllybl; Im Wt Lftg; Maxima Cum Laude Natl Latin Exm 83-84; 2nd Alt Alexander Lafleur Schlrp 86; Psychol.

TURNER, JEFFREY; Edward Little HS; Auburn, ME; (S); Cmnty Wkr; FCA; Var Trk; Hnr Rll 84-85; Med.

TURNER, MAUREEN; Yarmouth HS; Yarmouth, ME; (Y); 14/86; Color Guard; Yrbk Ed-Chief; Yrbk Stf; Var Capt Fld Hcky; Var Capt Swmmng; French Hon Soc; Hon Roll; NHS; Keene ST Coll; Sprts Mngmnt.

TUTTLE, PAMELA LYNN; Portland HS; Portland, ME; (Y); 18/195; Cmnty Wkr; Latin Clb; Political Wkr; Nwsp Ed-Chief; Yrbk Bus Mgr; Off Frsh Cls; Off Soph Cls; Off Jr Cls; Off Sr Cls; Stu Cncl; Ithaca Coll; Bus.

VALLEAU, LAURA; Deering HS; Portland, ME; (Y); 48/340; Cmnty Wkr; Drama Clb; English Clb; French Clb; Hosp Aide; JA; Latin Clb; Pep Clb; Yrbk Stf; Hon Roll; 2nd Pl Wnnr-ST Wide Essy Cntst 85; Rep-HS-WMNS Lit Union 85.

VALLEE, CELESTE; Saint Dominics HS; Lewiston, ME; (Y); GAA; JA; Varsity Clb; Var Fld Hcky; Var Sftbl; St Michael; Acctng.

VALLIERE, CELESTE; Lewsiton HS; Lewiston, ME; (Y); Service Clb; Yrbk Sprt Ed; Stu Cncl; Hon Roll; Schl Ltr/Edtr Pin For Yrbk 85-86; Shorthn Awd 86.

VAMPATELLA, JOAN; Gary-New Gloucester HS; New Gloucester, ME; (Y); 11/115; Church Yth Grp; Drama Clb; French Clb; Hosp Aide; Band; Pres Church Yth Grp; Stu Cncl; Vllybl; Jr NHS; NHS; U Vermont; Pol Sci.

VAN HAM, MELISSA; Lewiston HS; Lewiston, ME; (Y); Am Leg Aux Girls St; GAA; Hosp Aide; VP L Bsktbl; VP Capt Fld Hcky; VP Trk; High Hon Roll; NHS; Sweet Briar Coll; Crtv Wrtng.

VARBEL, DELA; Deering HS; Portland, ME; (Y); Art Clb; JA; Teachers Aide; Variety Show; Lit Mag; Hon Roll; NHS; Cheeseborough Fmly Art Cntst 83-85; Proj Explortn 80-81; JR Great Bks 79-80; Art.

VARNEY, TROY; Leavitt Area HS; Turner, ME; (Y); Bsktbl; JV Trk; French Hon Soc; Hon Roll; Jr NHS; Wllm J Irish Awd 86; U Of ME; Math.

VARUGHESE, SHANTY; Catherine Mc Auley HS; Portland, ME; (Y); 15/74; Church Yth Grp; Cmnty Wkr; Drama Clb; French Clb; Red Cross Aide; Science Clb; School Play; Hon Roll; US Acad Dcthln 86; ME ST Sci Olympd 85-86; Rutgers U; Bio-Chem.

VERREAULT, SUZANNE; Lewiston HS; Lewiston, ME; (Y); 4-H; Teachers Aide; Y-Teens; Nwsp Rptr; JV Var Bsktbl; Var Socr; Vllybl; High Hon Roll; Hon Roll; Engl Awd; Pres Kids Animals; U ME Farmington; Socl Wrk.

VILLACCI, JENNIFER; Falmouth HS; Falmouth, ME; (Y); 20/90; French Clb; Band; Pep Band; Ed Yrbk Ed-Chief; Cheerleading; Fld Hcky; Sftbl; Swmmng; Vllybl; Hon Roll.

VINING, VALERIE; Lewiston HS; Lewiston, ME; (Y); Cmnty Wkr; Hosp Aide; Yrbk Stf; JV Stat Bsktbl; Hon Roll; Hgh Scholar Engl 86; Comp Sci.

VIOLETTE, SYLVIA; Skowhegan Area HS; Skowhegan, ME; (Y); Pres Church Yth Grp; Drama Clb; FCA; German Clb; Varsity Clb; Band; Chorus; Concert Band; Pep Band; School Play; Chrng Vrsty Mst Sprt 85; UM Orono; Elem Educ.

VIOLETTE, TERRI; Westbrook HS; Westbrook, ME; (Y); Latin Clb; Band; Chorus; Concert Band; Drm Mjr(t); Mrchg Band; Nwsp Stf; Stu Cncl; Var Capt Swmmng; Mst Imprvd Swmmng 85; Sci.

VITRANO, SHARON K; Mt Abram Regional HS; Phillips, ME; (Y); 6/89; Church Yth Grp; Drama Clb; Red Cross Aide; Church Choir; Hon Roll; NHS; Cmnty Wkr; Computer Clb; Library Aide; School Play; Rnnr Up TIME Mag Essay Cont 86; Casco Bay Coll; Paralegal.

VOISINE, LYNN; Van Buren Dist Secondary Schl; Vanburen, ME; (Y); 9/80; Band; Yrbk Stf; Sec Frsh Cls; Stu Cncl; Var Capt Cheerleading; Vllybl; High Hon Roll; Hon Roll; NHS; Pres Schlr; Rotary Clb, Dollars For Schlrs, Am Lg, Pres Acadmc Fitness Awd, Husson Coll Awd Schlrshps 86-87; Business Adm.

VOTER, TODD; Mt Abram HS; Strong, ME; (Y); AFS; Boys Clb Am; Cmnty Wkr; Computer Clb; DECA; English Clb; FBLA; FFA; Math Tm; Science Clb; Geology.

WAKEFIELD, ROGER P; Cape Elizabeth HS; Cape Elizabeth, ME; (Y); 1/137; Computer Clb; French Clb; Math Tm; Bausch & Lomb Sci Awd; High Hon Roll; JETS Awd; NHS; Ntl Merit Schol; St Schlr; Val; Rensselaer Polytech Inst; Elec.

WALCH, JENNIFER; Westbrook HS; Westbrook, ME; (Y); 5/198; Pres French Clb; Capt Math Tm; Quiz Bowl; Rep Sr Cls; Var Fld Hcky; Var L Trk; Pres NHS; Drama Clb; English Clb; Latin Clb; USM Summer Inst Giftd Talntd Stu 85; Williams Bk Awd 85; MVP Hockey 85; U PA; Bioengr.

WALKER, CLINT; Edward Little HS; Mechanics Falls, ME; (S); Church Yth Grp; Drama Clb; Latin Clb; Math Tm; School Musical; School Play; Yrbk Ed-Chief; Yrbk Stf; Lit Mag; Rep Soph Cls; Alumni Asscn Ldrshp Awd; Yrbk Awd.

WALKER, LORA; Bonny Eagle HS; Sebago Lk, ME; (Y); Cmnty Wkr; Drama Clb; Rep French Clb; Thesps; Chorus; Church Choir; Jazz Band; Variety Show; Rep Stu Cncl; NHS; Talent Wnnr Miss ME Natl Teen Pagnt 85; 3rd Rnr-Up Miss ME TEEN Pagnt 86; St Josephs Coll; Acctg.

WALKER, MICHELLE; Gorham HS; Gorham, ME; (Y); Art Clb; Church Yth Grp; Cmnty Wkr; Debate Tm; Drama Clb; GAA; Girl Scts; JA; Leo Clb; Pep Clb; Gorhams 250th Awd 86; Girls Varsty Bsktbl Triple C 86; V P Girls Athl Assn 86; FL ST U; Communications.

WALKER, TODD; Gorham HS; Gorham, ME; (Y); Spanish Clb; JV Var Bsbl; JV Var Bsktbl; JV Socr; Im Vllybl; Hon Roll; Spanish NHS; Business.

WALLACE, ANNETTE; Lisbon Falls Christian Acad; Lisbon Falls, ME; (Y); 1/5; Church Yth Grp; Chorus; School Play; Yrbk Stf; Capt Var Cheerleading; L Var Vllybl; High Hon Roll; Hghst Avg For 85-86; Chrstn Ldrshp Awd Of Hon 86; Schlrthp To Pensacola Chrstn Coll 86; Pensacola Chrstn Coll; Elem Edu.

WALLACE, KAREN; Lisbon Falls Christian Acad; Lisbon Falls, ME; (S); 1/4; Church Yth Grp; Chorus; School Play; Variety Show; Yrbk Ed-Chief; Yrbk Stf; Sec Sr Cls; Var Vllybl; High Hon Roll; Hon Roll; Natl Ace Convention 2nd & 3rd Hnrs Art 84; Natl Ace Convention 1st 2nd & 3rd Hnrs Art 85; Pensacola Chrstn Coll; Sec Sci.

WALLS, KAREN A; Machias HS; Machias, ME; (Y); 3/51; Church Yth Grp; Yrbk Ed-Chief; Yrbk Stf; Var Capt Bsktbl; Var L Sftbl; Var L Vllybl; High Hon Roll; Hon Roll; Trs NHS; Sci Awd 83-86; Athlt Awd 84-86; Hist Awd 85; U Of New England; Phys Thrpy.

WALSH, KATHLEEN; Fryeburg Acad; Denmark, ME; (S); French Clb; Spanish Clb; SADD; Varsity Clb; Yrbk Bus Mgr; Var L Cheerleading; Var L Fld Hcky; JV Trk; Ntl Engl Merit Awd 85 & 86.

WALTER, TASHA; Jay HS; Jay, ME; (Y); Church Yth Grp; Teachers Aide; Var Mgr(s); Hon Roll; Cmmnctns.

WARD, JILL; Catherine Mc Auley HS; Cape Elizabeth, ME; (Y); 3/66; Key Clb; Nwsp Rptr; Yrbk Ed-Chief; Lit Mag; Trs Frsh Cls; Soph Cls; Trs Stu Cncl; Var Capt Bsktbl; Var Sftbl; High Hon Roll; Smith Book Awd 86; Vrsty Sftbl Coaches Awd 84; Telegrm Lgue All Star 2nd Tm 86; Law.

WARD, RUSSELL; Fryeburg Acad; Wareham, MA; (Y); Radio Clb; Ski Clb; Band; Jazz Band; School Musical; Stage Crew; Variety Show; VP Sr Cls; Hon Roll; US Air Force.

WARDWELL II, DUANE B; Bucksport HS; Bucksport, ME; (Y); #16 In Class; Church Yth Grp; Cmnty Wkr; Varsity Clb; Var Bsbl; Im Bsktbl; Stat Ftbl; L Golf; Hon Roll; SR Lfsvng Cert Amer Red Cross 85; Archeology.

WARMAN, JOY S; Mt Ararat HS; Topsham, ME; (Y); 9/230; Church Yth Grp; Acpl Chr; Chorus; Madrigals; Chrmn Sr Cls; Var L Cheerleading; Mgr(s); High Hon Roll; Hon Roll; NHS; Word Of Life Schlrshp; Brunswick Stu Aid Fund; Cedarville Acad Schlrshp; Cedarville Coll.

WARREN, WENDY; Gardiner Area HS; Gardiner, ME; (Y); Church Yth Grp; Office Aide; Boys Clb Am; Drill Tm; Yrbk Stf; Pittston Parent Tchr Clb 86-87; Free Metho Schlrshp 86-87; Collins Mem Schlrshp Fund 86-87; Roberts Wesleyan Coll; Psychlgy.

WASSON, JERRY; Fort Fairfield HS; Ft Fairfield, ME; (Y); 9/65; Am Leg Boys St; SADD; Varsity Clb; Yrbk Ed-Chief; Var L Cheerleading; Var L Crs Cntry; Var Capt Socr; Var Capt Trk; High Hon Roll; NHS; Norwich U; Elec Engr.

WATSON, CLYDE W; Piscataquis Comnty HS; Cambridge, ME; (Y); 3/66; Chess Clb; Church Yth Grp; Computer Clb; Debate Tm; Band; Concert Band; Jazz Band; Mrchg Band; Pep Band; Stage Crew; Prsdntl Acdmc Fit Awd 86; Wentworth Inst Of Tech; Compu.

WATTS, CURT; Leavitt Area HS; Turner, ME; (Y); Band; Jazz Band; High Hon Roll; Hon Roll; Band Dir Awd 85; Soloist Awd 84; Music.

WEAVER, JAMES; Georges Valley HS; Thomaston, ME; (Y); Math Tm; Science Clb; Ski Clb; Rep Trs Stu Cncl; JV Var Socr; Trk; High Hon Roll; NHS; Ntl Merit Ltr; St Schlr; St Sci Fair 1st In Physics 86; Engrng.

WEBB, JENNIE; Pittston Area HS; Lee, ME; (Y); 11/348; Church Yth Grp; Nwsp Rptr; Hon Roll; NHS; Toccoa Falls Coll; Christian Ed.

WEBB, JON; Fryeburg Acad; Fryeburg, ME; (S); Debate Tm; French Clb; Nwsp Bus Mgr; Nwsp Stf; Pres Soph Cls; Pres Jr Cls; VP Stu Cncl; Var Capt Socr; Var Tennis; Hon Roll.

WEBBER, BILLY; Dexter Regional HS; Charleston, ME; (Y); 11/96; Math Tm; Band; Jazz Band; School Play; Var L Crs Cntry; Var Capt Trk; Var Capt Wrstlng; Hon Roll; Outstndng Physcs Stu Yr 86; Awd Memry E Theodore Nokes Dedctn Hnsty Intgrty & Acdmc Exclnc 86; U Of ME Oreno; Engr.

WEEKS, KRIS; Central Aroostook HS; Mars Hill, ME; (Y); 4/50; Church Yth Grp; French Clb; Math Tm.

WEEKS, STACY JO; Caribou HS; Caribou, ME; (S); 2/250; Debate Tm; Varsity Clb; Band; Concert Band; Mrchg Band; Var Bsktbl; Var L Crs Cntry; Var L Trk; High Hon Roll; Sal; Soc Distngshd Amercn H S Ctzns 85-86; Med.

WEINER, JOSEPH; Deering HS; Portland, ME; (Y); Church Yth Grp; Ski Clb; Tennis; High Hon Roll; Hon Roll; NHS; Med Rsrch.

WELCH, STACY LEE; Boothbay Region HS; W Boothbay Harbor, ME; (Y); Am Leg Aux Girls St; Band; Yrbk Stf; NHS; Dnr Bk Awd Bus 85; Am Legn Schlrshp 86; Thomas College; Offc Adm.

WELLS, KEVIN; Gardiner Area HS; Randolph, ME; (Y); SADD; Nwsp Stf; Socr; Trk; Hon Roll; Photographer.

WELLWOOD, CRYSTAL; Noble HS; North Berwick, ME; (Y); Chorus; Bus.

WELNER, KATHARINE; Morse HS; Bath, ME; (Y); 21/200; Am Leg Aux Girls St; Pres Church Yth Grp; VP Intnl Clb; Sec Science Clb; Yrbk Stf; Hon Roll; Blaine House Scholar 86; Word Of Life Scholar 83-86; Creatv Wrtng Natl Comptn 83-86; Cedarville Coll; Spec Ed.

WENTWORTH, DONNA; Fryeburg Acad; Fryeburg, ME; (S); French Clb; Science Clb; SADD; Lit Mag; JV Cheerleading; High Hon Roll; Hon Roll; Ntl Englsh Merit Awd 85-86; Writer.

WENTWORTH, DONNA; Woodland HS; Princeton, ME; (Y); FBLA; Hon Roll; Bus Adm.

WENTWORTH, ERIKA; Fryeburg Acad; Fryeburg, ME; (S); Church Yth Grp; Cmnty Wkr; French Clb; Science Clb; SADD; Church Choir; Nwsp Stf; Lit Mag; Capt JV Cheerleading; High Hon Roll; Natl Eng Merit Awd 85-86; Jrnlsm.

WESCOTT, RICK; Gorham HS; Gorham, ME; (Y); Aud/Vis; Boy Scts; Latin Clb; Leo Clb; Yrbk Bus Mgr; Yrbk Rptr; Yrbk Stf; Hon Roll; Yrbk Sectn Editor 85; Lyndon ST Coll; Meteorology.

WEST, TERISIA L; Mt Ararat Schl; Topsham, ME; (Y); 12/229; Drama Clb; Acpl Chr; Chorus; Madrigals; School Musical; School Play; Stage Crew; NHS; Mt Ararat Schlrs Progrm 85-86; All-St Chorus 86; Drew U; Theatre.

WESTLEIGH, LOUISA M; Oxford Hills HS; W Paris, ME; (Y); 37/206; Am Leg Aux Girls St; Drama Clb; Chorus; School Musical; Stage Crew; Hon Roll; NHS; TMH Tutor 83-86; Vike Hes 84-86; U ME Orono; Spec Ed.

WESTON, JULIE; Fryeburg Acad; Fryeburg, ME; (S); Drama Clb; 4-H; Latin Clb; Science Clb; Ski Clb; School Musical; School Play; Var L Socr; High Hon Roll; NHS; Latin Awd 84; Music Awd 84; Cornell U.

WHITE, ANGELA; Traip Academy HS; Mesa, AZ; (Y); Church Yth Grp; Drama Clb; French Clb; Thesps; Chorus; Church Choir; Nwsp Rptr; Yrbk Stf; Sec Stu Cncl; Var JV Cheerleading; KMBO Dee Bickmore Fndng Awd Schlrshpd 86; Cnstnl Aid Soc Schlrshp 86; Bst Thesbian 86; Grand Canyon Coll; Psych.

WHITE, CAROLYN; Fryeburg Acad; North Fryeburg, ME; (S); Pres Latin Clb; Science Clb; Varsity Clb; School Play; Stage Crew; Var L Bsktbl; Var L Fld Hcky; Var L Trk; High Hon Roll; Jr NHS.

WHITE, KRISTOPHER D; Bucksport HS; Stockton Spgs, ME; (Y); Boy Scts; Varsity Clb; Var L Bsktbl; Var L Trk; DAR Awd; Hon Roll; SAR Awd; Cmnty Wkr; Variety Show; Im Wt Lftg; Eagle Scout 86; Order Of Arrow Awd 84; ME ST Legsltr Proclmtn In Rcgntn Of Eagle Scout 86.

WHITE, MICHELLE; Sanford HS; Sanford, ME; (Y); 28/235; Science Clb; SADD; Yrbk Rptr; Yrbk Stf; JV Stat Bsktbl; JV Mgr(s); JV Capt Sftbl; Hon Roll; Elctrncs.

WHITE, PETER; Gorham HS; Scarborough, ME; (Y); 26/120; Church Yth Grp; Hon Roll; Jr-Sr Drafing Awd 86; U Of Southern ME; Cvl Engrng.

WHITE, ROSEMARY; Mt Abram HS; Strong, ME; (Y); Cmnty Wkr; Computer Clb; 4-H; Red Cross Aide; Ski Clb; Speech Tm; SADD; Varsity Clb; Y-Teens; Var Bsktbl; Pierpole-Hrs Clb-Grnd Chmpn 83; Sftbl Plyr Of Yr Awd 85; Spcl Friend Awd 81; Anml Sci.

WHITEHOUSE, BRIAN; Lee Acad; Topsfield, ME; (Y); 10/62; AFS; Church Yth Grp; Cmnty Wkr; Math Tm; Variety Show; Socr; Vllybl; High Hon Roll; Hon Roll; ME Schlrs Days 86; Acad All Amer 86; Marlboro Coll; Frgn Lang.

WHITNEY, ADAM; Seinar Memorial HS; Winter Harbor, ME; (Y); Pres Jr Cls; JV Bsktbl.

WHITTEN, SHANNON; Caribou HS; Caribou, ME; (S); 2/180; Band; Concert Band; Mrchg Band; Pep Band; School Musical; Sec Jr Cls; Sec Sr Cls; Cheerleading; High Hon Roll; Pres NHS; Sci Prjct Awd; Bowdoin; Pre Law.

WIGHT, DONALD; Westbrook HS; Westbrook, ME; (Y); Key Clb; Latin Clb; Nwsp Rptr; Nwsp Stf; Rep Jr Cls; Var Ftbl; JV Trk; Hon Roll.

WIGHT, JUDY; Bucksport HS; Bucksport, ME; (Y); 87/117; Cmnty Wkr; Varsity Clb; Church Choir; Variety Show; Rep Stu Cncl; JV Var Cheerleading; Hon Roll; Hmcmng Queen 86; SR Exec Cncl 86; Ntl Hnr Soc 86; U Of ME-FASRMINGTON; Elem Educ.

WILBURN II, EDWARD J; Yarmouth HS; Yarmouth, ME; (Y); SADD; VICA; Chorus; Wentworth Coll; Drftg.

WILCOX, TRINA; Caribou HS; Washburn, ME; (Y); 36/185; VP Key Clb; Yrbk Stf; Rep Jr Cls; Rep Sr Cls; Hon Roll; Pres Schlr; Bus Pro Womn Schlrshp 86; Key Clb Schlrshp 86; Westbrook College; Bus Adm.

WILEY, JENNIFER; Wiscasset HS; Dresden, ME; (Y); Pres 4-H; French Clb; SADD; Nwsp Rptr; Crs Cntry; Mgr(s); Socr; Trk; High Hon Roll; NHS; Wiscasset Amblnc Svc Schlrshp 86; Becker JC; Phys Ther Asstnt.

WILKINSON, JAN; Freeport HS; Freeport, ME; (Y); 7/70; Pres VP Aud/Vis; Math Tm; Chorus; Nwsp Stf; Yrbk Stf; Stu Cncl; Hon Roll; NHS; Cert Partcpnt Natl Hist Day 85; Smith Book Awd 86; Emerson Clg Boston; Edtr.

WILLETT, RICHARD; Skowhegan Area HS; Skowhegan, ME; (Y); 18/225; Varsity Clb; Band; Jazz Band; Mrchg Band; Variety Show; Var Bsbl; Var Socr; High Hon Roll; Hon Roll.

WILLIAMS, ELIZABETH; Orono HS; Bangor, ME; (S); Am Leg Aux Girls St; Nwsp Rptr; Yrbk Rptr; Pres Stu Cncl; Cheerleading; Socr; Tennis; Timer; High Hon Roll; VP NHS; All As Awd 85; U Of ME; Engl.

WILLIHNGANZ, HEATHER; Falmouth HS; Falmouth, ME; (Y); 32/99; Drama Clb; French Clb; SADD; School Musical; School Play; Im Vllybl; Hon Roll; NEDT Awd; Aaron Copeland Music Arts Pgm 83-84; Dramatic Arts.

WILLIS, ANDREW; Portland HS; Portland, ME; (Y); Math Tm; Model UN; Political Wkr; Ski Clb; Temple Yth Grp; Nwsp Stf; Yrbk Stf; Var Capt Golf; Im Vllybl; Hon Roll; Polit Sci.

WILSON, JENIFER; Gardiner Area HS; Gardiner, ME; (Y); Cmnty Wkr; French Clb; FNA; Spanish Clb; SADD; High Hon Roll; Hon Roll; Top 10 Hnr Awd; Top Rnk In Spnsh I & Bus; U Sthrn ME; Accntng.

WILSON, KATHRYN M; Portland HS; Portland, ME; (Y); Math Tm; Rptr Nwsp Stf; Ed Lit Mag; Rep Jr Cls; Hon Roll; NHS; Color Guard; 1st Pl In German Skit Cont During Frgn Lang Day 85; Chinese.

WILSON, MARK; Manmouth Acad; North Monmouth, ME; (Y); 8/43; Math Tm; Speech Tm; Band; Var Capt Socr; Bausch & Lomb Sci Awd; Hon Roll; Ntl Merit SF; 4 Yr AFROTC Schlrp 86; Embry-Riddle U; Aerontcl Engrg.

WILSON, MELISSA; Bonny Eagle HS; Steep Falls, ME; (Y); 22/260; Sec Church Yth Grp; Library Aide; Office Aide; Symp Band; High Hon Roll; Hon Roll; Jr NHS; NHS; Blaine House Schlr Awd; U Of ME Machias; Bus Tchr Educ.

WILSON, MICHELE; Lake Region HS; Raymond, ME; (Y); 12/133; AFS; Church Yth Grp; SADD; Yrbk Phtg; Yrbk Stf; JV Sftbl; DAR Awd; Hon Roll; NHS; Rochester Inst Tech; Med Tech.

WINCHENBACH, LYNETTE; Medomak Valley HS; Waldobor, ME; (Y); Cmnty Wkr; Latin Clb; Pep Clb; Band; Chorus; Yrbk Phtg; Yrbk Stf; JV Bsktbl; Trk; Hon Roll; Schlrshp 86; U Of ME Augusta; Med Lab Tech.

WING, IRENE E; Caribou HS; Caribou, ME; (Y); 39/162; Church Yth Grp; Hosp Aide; Key Clb; Yrbk Stf; High Hon Roll; Hon Roll; Pres Schlr; Roberts Wesleyan Coll; Nursing.

WINN, MIKE; Wells HS; Ogunquit, ME; (Y); 8/95; Rep Stu Cncl; Var Crs Cntry; Off Trk; Hon Roll; NHS; U Of ME; Pol Sci.

WINSLOW, SUSAN; Hampden Acad; Hampden, ME; (Y); 14/162; Drama Clb; French Clb; Hosp Aide; Intnl Clb; Key Clb; Band; Var Socr; Tennis; High Hon Roll; NHS; Stephen King Schlrsp 86; Rensselaer Polytech; Cvl Engr.

WITHAM, DENNIS; Oxford Hills HS; S Paris, ME; (Y); Church Yth Grp; 4-H; Im Socr; Im Sftbl; CMVTI; Comp Pgmng.

WOOD, REBECCA; Gorham HS; Gorham, ME; (Y); Aud/Vis; Camera Clb; Chess Clb; 4-H; French Clb; Spanish Clb; JV Fld Hcky; Bus Math Schlrshp 85; USM; Tchg.

WOODARD, COLIN; Mt Abram HS; Strong, ME; (Y); 8/87; Am Leg Boys St; Debate Tm; VP Intnl Clb; VP Stu Cncl; Capt Var Trk; Hon Roll; Computer Clb; Nwsp Stf; Indr Track 85-86; Olympcs Of The Mind Capt 85-86; Bio.

WOODARD, STEVE; Leavitt Area HS; Greene, ME; (Y); 1/100; School Play; Variety Show; Pres Frsh Cls; Stu Cncl; Var Ftbl; JV Trk; Im Wt Lftg; French Hon Soc; High Hon Roll; Hon Roll; Forestry Engrng.

WOODBURY, JAMES; Portland HS; Portland, ME; (Y); 9/197; Math Tm; Var L Bsktbl; VP NHS; Ntl Merit Ltr; Boys Clb Am; Exploring; French Clb; JA; Latin Clb; Im Vllybl; NROTC Scholr 86; Williams Coll Book Awd 85; Army Res Natl Schlr Ath Awd 86; Brown Mdl 86; Worcester Polytech; Mech Engr.

WOODMAN, JONATHAN; Lincoln Acad; Medomak, ME; (S); 7/114; JCL; VP Latin Clb; Var Capt Bsktbl; NCTE Awd; Excel Ltn Bk Awd 85; 3rd Pl Ovrl Acad Tstng ME JC Clsscl 85; Allegheny Coll; Pre Vet.

WOODWARD, KAREN S; Sumner Memorial HS; Gouldsboro, ME; (Y); 2/84; Am Leg Aux Girls St; Pres Sec Drama Clb; Band; Chorus; Church Choir; Jazz Band; School Musical; School Play; VP Stu Cncl; Cit Awd; Wellesley Coll.

WOODWARD, KELLEY; Nokomis Regional HS; Newport, ME; (Y); 17/171; Am Leg Aux Girls St; Office Aide; Jazz Band; Sec Symp Band; Yrbk Stf; Sec Jr Cls; Sec Sr Cls; Cheerleading; High Hon Roll; Hon Roll; Bus.

WORCESTER, DENISE; Mt Abram Regional HS; Strong, ME; (Y); 3/69; Am Leg Aux Girls St; Sec Jr Cls; Sec Stu Cncl; JV Bsktbl; JV Sftbl; L Trk; High Hon Roll; Hon Roll; NHS; Model Legsltr; ME Schlr; Williams Coll Book Awd; Pre-Med.

WORKMAN, DEANA; Sumner Memorial HS; Winter Harbor, ME; (Y); FHA; SADD; Mgr Bsbl; Var L Cheerleading; Mgr Crs Cntry; Mgr(s); U Of Machias; Sec Sci.

WORSTER, TRAVIS; Forest Hills HS; Jackman, ME; (Y); 2/16; Am Leg Boys St; Drama Clb; Math Tm; Var Capt Bsbl; Bausch & Lomb Sci Awd; Cit Awd; Hon Roll; NHS; Sal; Voice Dem Awd; Scotts Hi Q Team 86; Hist,Alg,Bio,Trig Awds 85-86; Merchant Amrine Acad; Engrng.

WORTHLEY, CAROL; Rumford HS; W Peru, ME; (Y); 10/129; Office Aide; Spanish Clb; Yrbk Stf; Crs Cntry; Sftbl; Hon Roll; Shrthnd 85; Top Ten 86; Schlrshp Boise Cascade Emply 86; U Southern ME; Acctng.

WRENN, PETER D; Hampden Acad; Winterport, ME; (Y); French Clb; Key Clb; Yrbk Stf; Rep Stu Cncl; Bsbl; Crs Cntry; Trk; Hon Roll; Cornell; Engrng.

WRIGHT, DEBORAH LOU; Searsport Districkt HS; Winterport, ME; (Y); 6/53; Pres French Clb; VP FBLA; Pres Pep Clb; SADD; Yrbk Ed-Chief; Pres Sr Cls; L Var Fld Hcky; Var L Sftbl; DAR Awd; NHS; U Of ME Orono; Educ.

WRIGHT, KENTON; Nokomis Regional HS; Newport, ME; (Y); 5/173; French Clb; Varsity Clb; Rep Frsh Cls; JV Var Bsktbl; Var JV Socr; Trk; High Hon Roll; Hon Roll; NHS; Outstndng Stu Awd 86; TX A & M; Ag.

WRIGHT, MELISSA; Penquis Valley HS; Milo, ME; (Y); 10/66; Camera Clb; Computer Clb; Teachers Aide; Stage Crew; Yrbk Phtg; Yrbk Stf; Hon Roll; Prfct Atten Awd; Regnl Bus Cntst Wnnr 1st Acctg, 1st Offc Proc, 2nd Shrthnd, 3rd Typg III; Sec.

YATES, JONATHAN A; Richmond JR SR HS; Richmond, ME; (Y); 1/34; Speech Tm; Trs Jr Cls; Pres Sr Cls; Bausch & Lomb Sci Awd; Cit Awd; DAR Awd; Hon Roll; NHS; Val; Ldrshp Awd SR Clss Pres & Pres Natl Hnr Socty & Pres Fit Awd 86; Boston U; Cmmnctns.

YORK, JODY; Houlton HS; Houlton, ME; (Y); Camera Clb; Sec Church Yth Grp; FHA; Stage Crew; Yrbk Stf; Hon Roll; Child Socl Wrkr.

YORK, KENNY; Medomak Valley HS; Waldoboro, ME; (Y); Church Yth Grp; Hon Roll.

YORK, VALERIE; Skowhegan Area HS; Skowhegan, ME; (Y); German Clb; Band; Concert Band; JV Capt Bsktbl; Sftbl; Hon Roll; Cchs Awd 84; Bus.

YOUNG, ANDREA; Gorham HS; S Windham, ME; (Y); Aud/Vis; Computer Clb; Drama Clb; French Clb; Library Aide; Yrbk Stf; Andover; Acctg.

YOUNG, CANDACE; Georges Valley HS; Port Clyde, ME; (Y); Drama Clb; Intnl Clb; Thesps; Chorus; School Play; Stage Crew; Yrbk Stf; Lit Mag; Sec Soph Cls; High Hon Roll; Excllnc Frnch III Hnrhigh Hist Avrg; Excllnc Frnch III Hnrs; U Of ME; Hist Prof.

YOUNG, NOREEN; Maranacook Community Schl; Manchester, ME; (Y); Art Clb; JCL; Trs Latin Clb; Stat Bsktbl; Lion Awd; Upwrd Bnd 84-86; Manchester Grange Schlrshp 86; Husson Coll; Nrsng.

ZIFFER, JENNIFER; Fryeburg Acad; Fryeburg, ME; (Y); Art Clb; Pep Band; Dance Clb; Radio Clb; Teachers Aide; Temple Yth Grp; Band; Variety Show; High Hon Roll; Hdmstrs Schlrshp Fryeburg Acad 86-87; Engrng.

ZIMMERMAN, KRISTINE; Lewiston HS; Lewiston, ME; (Y); Trs Sec Church Yth Grp; Teachers Aide; Yrbk Ed-Chief; Yrbk Stf; NHS; Librl Arts.

ZIPFEL, CATHY; Leavitt Area HS; Turner, ME; (Y); 4/129; Am Leg Aux Girls St; Yrbk Stf; Var L Fld Hcky; High Hon Roll; Sec NHS; St Schlr; FHA; Math Clb; Yrbk Ed-Chief; Var L Mgr(s); Acad Hnrs Schlrshp $1000 86; BEAM Schlrshp $2500 86; Husson Coll; Accntng.

MASSACHUSETTS

AARONSON, STEPHANIE R; Newton South HS; Newton, MA; (Y); Pres Drama Clb; Pres Model UN; Chorus; School Musical; School Play; Nwsp Stf; Stu Cncl; Ntl Merit Ltr; Faculty Awd; Cum Laude Soc; Columbia U.

ABANY, EDWARD; Boston Latin Schl; Boston, MA; (Y); 117/284; Boy Scts; Church Yth Grp; Cmnty Wkr; Latin Clb; Scholastic Bowl; Varsity Clb; Stage Crew; Var Bsbl; Var Capt Wrstlng; Hon Roll; Fdlty Awd 83-84.

ABARE, JULIANNE; Gardner HS; Gardner, MA; (Y); 29/141; GAA; Spanish Clb; JV Var Bsktbl; Var Fld Hcky; Var Sftbl; Hon Roll; NHS.

ABATE, DIANNE; Greater Lawrence Technical HS; Lawrence, MA; (Y); Nwsp Rptr; Sec Frsh Cls; Sec Soph Cls; Sec Jr Cls; Sec Sr Cls; Var Cheerleading; Var Pom Pon; JV Sftbl; Hon Roll; Stu Reportr For Locl Nwspr 86; Locl Design & Ad Contst-Cert Awd 85; Graphc Art.

ABELL, SHELLEY; Mounty Vo Tech; Sterling, MA; (Y); Hosp Aide; SADD; VICA; Yrbk Stf; Pres Soph Cls; Pres Jr Cls; Pres Sr Cls; Var Capt Cheerleading; Hon Roll; VP NHS; Mst Outstndg Stu Dntgl Asstng 86; Mst Improved Chrldr 84; Forsyth Schl; Dntl Hygnst.

ABESAMRA, ROBYN; Methuen HS; Methuen, MA; (Y); 59/353; Sec Church Yth Grp; Intnl Clb; SADD; Fld Hcky; Hon Roll; Bus Admn.

ABOUZEID, MIREILLE; Boston Latin Acad; W Roxbury, MA; (Y); Intnl Clb; Rep Frsh Cls; Rep Soph Cls; Rep Stu Cncl; JV Bsktbl; Hon Roll; NHS; Cty-Wd Spllng Bee Chmpn 83-86; Bk Awd 86; Natl Latin Exam Cum Laude & Magna Cum Laude 85-86; Harvard; Criminal Law.

ABRAHAM, LISA; Boston Technical HS; Jamaica Pl, MA; (Y); JA; Pep Clb; Var Cheerleading; Hon Roll; Bus Mgt.

ABRAMS, JOEL H; Brookline HS; Brookline, MA; (Y); Trs Computer Clb; Capt Math Tm; Temple Yth Grp; Nwsp Stf; Hon Roll; NHS; Ntl Merit SF; Drama Clb; Quiz Bowl; Concert Band; Dartmouth Alumni Bk Prz 85.

ABRUZZESE, MEREDITH; Braintree HS; Braintree, MA; (Y); 73/446; VP Spanish Clb; Hon Roll; VP Spanish NHS; Cmmnctns.

ACCOLLA, PAM; Medford HS; Medford, MA; (Y); Cmnty Wkr; Drama Clb; Hosp Aide; Chorus; School Play; Rep Sr Cls; Var Cheerleading; High Hon Roll; Hon Roll; NHS; Socl Wrk.

ACKERMAN, ROBERT; Marblehead HS; Marblehead, MA; (Y); 90/270; Var L Bsktbl; Var L Tennis; Coaches Awd Tns 85-86; Conf All-Str Tnns 84-86; Bus.

ADAMCZYK, CYNTHIA; Chicopee Comprehensive HS; Chicopee, MA; (Y); Cmnty Wkr; Girl Scts; Intnl Clb; Spanish Clb; Yrbk Stf; High Hon Roll; Hon Roll; NHS; Elem Educ.

ADAMIAK, NEAL F; St Johns HS; Worcester, MA; (Y); 88/280; Am Leg Boys St; Church Yth Grp; Cmnty Wkr; Ski Clb; Band; Nwsp Stf; Rep Soph Cls; Im Bsktbl; High Hon Roll; Hon Roll; Cthlc U; Archtctr.

ADAMOPOULOS, PATRICIA; Bartlett HS; Webster, MA; (Y); 5/152; Pres French Clb; Science Clb; Band; Crs Cntry; Trk; High Hon Roll; Lion Awd; VP NHS; Histry Achvt Mdl 86; Normandy Clb Frnch Awd 86; MFLA Brd Of Dir Awd 86; MA U Amherst; Elec Engr.

ADAMS, ANDREW; Arlington HS; Arlington, MA; (Y); Boys Clb Am; Boy Scts; Church Yth Grp; Spanish Clb; SADD; Im Bsktbl; Im Ice Hcky; Im Swmmng; Hon Roll.

ADAMS, APRIL; Duxbury HS; Duxbury, MA; (Y); 28/276; Drama Clb; School Musical; School Play; Stage Crew; Yrbk Stf; Lit Mag; High Hon Roll; Hon Roll; NHS; Ntl Merit Ltr; Wrote Novel 83; USSR Peace Mission 85; Designed Dragon Mascot For Gym Floor 86; Hampshire Coll; Psychology.

ADAMS, BRIAN; Attleboro HS; Attleboro, MA; (Y); Church Yth Grp; Ski Clb; Var Ftbl; Var L Golf; Var L Socr; Hon Roll; U MA; Cvl Engrng.

ADAMS, CHARLEEN; Marshfield HS; Coventry, RI; (Y); JA; Teachers Aide; SADD; Natl Jr Hnr Soc; Salve Regina; Bus Mgmt.

ADAMS, EDWARD A; Watertown HS; Watertown, MA; (Y); 8/250; Am Leg Boys St; Nwsp Rptr; Rep Frsh Cls; Off Soph Cls; Off Jr Cls; Off Sr Cls; Stat Bsbl; Var Trk; Hon Roll; NHS; Schltc Achvt Awd 84-86; Bus.

ADAMS, HILARY; Brockton HS; Brockton, MA; (Y); High Hon Roll; Hon Roll; NHS; Bay ST JC; Bus Adm.

ADAMS, JANICE; Bishop Feehan HS; Attleboro, MA; (Y); Drama Clb; School Musical; School Play; Stage Crew; Lit Mag; French Hon Soc; Hon Roll; Thtr Cert 86; Engl Lit 84; Math Achvt 86; Thtr.

ADAMS, JOHN S; Melrose HS; Melrose, MA; (Y); 38/437; Chess Clb; Computer Clb; Debate Tm; Chorus; Church Choir; School Musical.

ADAMS, JULIE; Haverhill HS; Haverhill, MA; (Y); Girl Scts; Spanish Clb; High Hon Roll; NHS; Sweet Bmar Coll; Comp Sci.

ADAMS, JULIE; Our Lady Of Nazareth Acad; Stoneham, MA; (Y); 32/74; Trs Cmnty Wkr; Sec Trs Drama Clb; Var Stage Crew; French Clb; Ski Clb; SADD; Chorus; NEDT Awd; Exec Sec.

ADAMS, TINA; South HS; Worcester, MA; (Y); 8/253; Dance Clb; Hon Roll; NHS; Commonwealth Schlr Grant 86; Tchng Abilty In Dance 86; Top Sci Stu 86; Holy Cross Coll; Bio.

ADEWOLE, BONIKE A; St Joseph Central HS; Williamstown, MA; (Y); 10/83; Art Clb; Drama Clb; JA; Nwsp Stf; Lit Mag; Trs Stu Cncl; Cheerleading; Capt Crs Cntry; NHS; Natl Merit Ltr Bio 83-84; Cornell U; Chem.

ADKINS, MELLISA; New Bedford HS; New Bedford, MA; (Y); 69/701; Drama Clb; Exploring; FHA; Hosp Aide; Stage Crew; Hon Roll; Vlntr Awd 85; SE MA U; Bus Mgmt.

ADLER, MARK; Monument Mt Reg HS; Stockbridge, MA; (Y); 11/150; Math Tm; Quiz Bowl; Band; School Musical; School Play; Nwsp Ed-Chief; High Hon Roll; Hon Roll; NHS; Ntl Merit Ltr; Math Leag Awd 86.

ADLER, OONA; Barnstable HS; Centerville, MA; (Y); Acpl Chr; Pres Chorus; Madrigals; School Musical; School Play; Variety Show; Hon Roll; Church Yth Grp; Drama Clb; Church Choir; Barnstable Comedy Clb Schlrshp 86; Cape Cod Chordaires Schlrshp 86; Cap Cod Cnsrvtry Schlrshp 85-86; Cap Cod CC; Musical Thtre.

ADOLPH, KEVIN; Burlington HS; Burlington, MA; (Y); 47/321; Boys Clb Am; Boy Scts; Rep Jr Cls; Rep Sr Cls; Var L Golf; Var L Lcrss; Var Swmmng; Hon Roll; BSA Explorer Future Engrs 83-85; U Of Lowell; Elec Engr.

ADRIANO, DARCI L; Grtr New Bedford Rgnl Vo-Tech HS; New Bedford, MA; (Y); FNA; Ski Clb; SADD; VICA; Cheerleading; Trk; NHS; Mst Poplr Cls 86; RN.

AFFANATO, STEPHEN P; Milton HS; Milton, MA; (Y); Am Leg Boys St; Church Yth Grp; SADD; Off Soph Cls; Off Sr Cls; Stu Cncl; JV Var Ftbl; Im Wt Lftg; Var Capt Wrstlng; Military Acad; Poli Sci.

AFFONSO, GEORGE D; Somerset HS; Somerset, MA; (Y); 45/310; Boy Scts; Church Yth Grp; School Play; Bsbl; Ice Hcky; Socr; High Hon Roll; Hon Roll; NHS; Riverside Art Schlrshp 86; Fall River Savings Schlrshp 86; James Noonan Mem Schlrshp 86; Fitchburg ST Coll; Comm.

AFIENKO, KRISTEN; Newton North HS; Newtonville, MA; (Y); Church Yth Grp; Dance Clb; Exploring; Teachers Aide; School Musical; Yrbk Stf; Jr Cls; Var L Cheerleading; Hon Roll; SOS Prog 86; Physcl Ed Ldrshp Ltr 85; Chryls Mdlng Prog 85; Pblic Rltns.

AGGANIS, MICHAEL; Dedham HS; Dedham, MA; (S); 1/250; SADD; Nwsp Stf; Stu Cncl; JV Tennis; Trk; High Hon Roll; NHS; Val.

AGOSTINI, PAULA; Bishop Feehan HS; Seekonk, MA; (Y); 4/232; Yrbk Stf; Var Trk; Im Library Aide; French Hon Soc; High Hon Roll; NHS; Pres Schlr; Outstndng Achvt In Engl 86; Cert Of Achvt In Chem 85; Excllnc In Mth Cert 84; Babson Coll; Acctng.

AGUIAR, CINDY; Somerset HS; Somerset, MA; (Y); 7/310; Chess Clb; Drama Clb; Ski Clb; Chorus; Madrigals; School Musical; School Play; Stage Crew; NHS; Ntl Merit SF; Honor Roll 82-85; Jazz Chorale 84-85; Tri-Cnty Music Fest 83-84; U Of RI; Pharmcy.

AGUILAR, MICHELLE; Nazareth Acad; Stoneham, MA; (Y); 8/78; Drama Clb; Intnl Clb; Model UN; Chorus; School Musical; Nwsp Rptr; Nwsp Stf; Lit Mag; High Hon Roll; Hon Roll; Journlsm.

AHEARN, JOHN; Milford HS; Milford, MA; (Y); 26/260; Capt Band; Concert Band; Jazz Band; Mrchg Band; Orch; Hon Roll; NHS; Soph Yr Band Awd; JR All Amer Hall Of Fm Band Hnrs; U Of NH; Mass Cmmnctns.

AHEARN, LORI; Natick HS; Natick, MA; (Y); 14/443; SADD; Rep Frsh Cls; Rep Soph Cls; Sec Jr Cls; Sec Sr Cls; Rep Stu Cncl; High Hon Roll; Hon Roll; NHS; St Schlr; Emly Shnnon Eng Awd; Boston Coll; Math.

AHERN, DEBORAH; Burlington HS; Burlington, MA; (Y); 40/327; Trs Church Yth Grp; Nwsp Sprt Ed; Yrbk Sprt Ed; Powder Puff Ftbl; Var Socr; Var Trk; Hon Roll; NHS; Schlr Ath Awd 86; MVP Middlesex Lg Trk 86; Silv Mdl NE Trk Mt 300 Low Hurdles 85; All Star Lg Trk; Smith Coll; Intl Studies.

AHERN, ELIZABETH; Notre Dame Acad; S Weymouth, MA; (Y); 34/109; Aud/Vis; Debate Tm; Hosp Aide; Political Wkr; Acpl Chr; School Musical; School Play; Nwsp Stf; Yrbk Stf; Hon Roll; Exc In Debatg 85; Cmmnctns.

AHERN, KELLY; Milford HS; Milford, MA; (Y); Office Aide; Var Gym; Var Trk; Rookie Of Yr Gymnstcs 83-84; Mst Dedctd Gymnstcs 84-85; Mst Dedctd & Sprtmnshp Awd Gymnstcs 85-86; Bus Adm.

AHERN, MICHAEL E; Dennis-Yarmouth Reg HS; W Yarmouth, MA; (Y); German Clb; Intnl Clb; Ski Clb; Yrbk Sprt Ed; Yrbk Stf; Im Badmtn; Im Bsktbl; JV Var Golf; Im Vllybl; Frdms Fndtn Yth Ldrshp Cnfrnc 85; Cmmnctns.

AHLQUIST, DAVID; Wakefield Memorial HS; Wakefield, MA; (Y); JA; Bsktbl; Tennis; Jr NHS; Pres Of 1st Educ Savings Branch 86-87.

AIELLO, MARLENE; Wakefield Memorial HS; Wakefield, MA; (Y); Chorus; School Play; Ice Hcky; Socr; 1st Girl Make Boys Ice Hockey Tm 84-86; Rcvd Citation Outstndg Plyng Girls Tourn Hockey 85; Northeastern; Lbrl Arts.

AIKEN, LISA; Westfield HS; Westfield, MA; (Y); Church Yth Grp; French Clb; Hosp Aide; Latin Clb; SADD; Nwsp Bus Mgr; JV Capt Cheerleading; Fash Merch.

AIKENS, GLENN; Gloucester HS; Gloucester, MA; (Y); 1/326; Math Tm; Capt L Bsktbl; Im Ftbl; Im Vllybl; Elks Awd; High Hon Roll; NHS; Ntl Merit Ltr; St Schlr; Sawyer Medl 83; Amer Lgn Schlrshp 86; Gnrl Mills Schlrshp 86; Clarkson U; Comp Sci.

AINSWORTH, KIM; Monson JR SR HS; Monson, MA; (Y); Church Yth Grp; French Clb; Hosp Aide; Civic Clb; Mathletes; Math Clb; Spanish Clb; Yrbk Stf; Hon Roll; Forgn Lang.

AIRASIAN, LYNN; Natick HS; Natick, MA; (Y); 8/400; Am Leg Aux Girls St; SADD; Yrbk Stf; Sec Frsh Cls; Sec Soph Cls; Sec Jr Cls; Sec Sr Cls; Stu Cncl; Var Bsktbl; Var JV Vllybl; Outstndng Bus Stu Awds Intro To DP, Pascal, Law; Olympic Vllybl.

AKINS, DANIEL; Old Rochester Regional HS; Rochester, MA; (Y); 14/141; JA.

ALAINE, TRISTAN; Peters HS; Southborough, MA; (Y); Church Yth Grp; FFA; Band; Church Choir; Mrchg Band; School Play; Tufts Schl Vet Med; Vet.

ALBERQUE, LISA; Marianhill CC HS; Spencer, MA; (Y); Art Clb; Church Yth Grp; School Musical; Yrbk Stf; Cheerleading; Sftbl; Sec Jr NHS; Sec Frsh Cls; VP Soph Cls; Trs Jr Cls.

ALBERTELLI, CHRISTINE; Melrose HS; Melrose, MA; (Y); Rep Stu Cncl; JV Var Bsktbl; JV Var Fld Hcky; JV Sftbl; High Hon Roll; Hon Roll; NHS; Rcgntn Math 86; Columbia U.

ALBERTELLI, JILL; Arlington Catholic HS; Arlington, MA; (Y); 13/139; Cmnty Wkr; Spanish Clb; Yrbk Stf; VP Jr Cls; Cheerleading; Hon Roll; NHS; Hosp Aide; Ski Clb; Boys Clb Am; Natl Latin Ex Silver Mdl 83-84; Darthmouth Bk Awd 85-86; Jordan Marsh Jr Cncl Fash Brd 86-87; Sci.

ALBERTELLI, SARA; Arlington Catholic HS; Arlington, MA; (Y); 5/148; Off JA; Ski Clb; Spanish Clb; SADD; School Play; Nwsp Phtg; Yrbk Phtg; Yrbk Stf; High Hon Roll; Pres NHS; 1st & 2nd Hnrs; Gld Mdls Natl Latin Exm; Schlrshp To MASP; Pres Natl Hnr Soc; Schlrshp U MA; Wellesley Coll; Pre-Med.

ALBERTI, CARMELA; Southwick HS; Southwick, MA; (Y); 4/126; Am Leg Aux Girls St; Drama Clb; 4-H; Acpl Chr; School Musical; School Play; Sec Frsh Cls; JV Sftbl; Hon Roll; Sec NHS; Bay Path; Exec Sec Sci.

ALBERTINI, PAUL; Bishop Fechan HS; E Mansfield, MA; (Y); JV Var Ftbl; Capt L Trk; Wt Lftg; Prfct Atten Awd; Bus.

ALBERTO, DONNA; Milford HS; Milford, MA; (Y); Hosp Aide; Office Aide; SADD; Yrbk Stf; Capt Diving; Capt Swmmng; Stu Of Wk-Prncpls List 83-84; Csmtlgy.

ALCALA, LISA; Doherty Memorial HS; Worcester, MA; (Y); Drama Clb; School Musical; School Play; Nwsp Rptr; High Hon Roll; NHS; Pres Schlr; Spanish NHS; Dance Clb; 4-H; Bst Feml Cast-St John Sprng Spctclr 85; Engl.

ALCONADA, TAMMY; Medway JR SR HS; Medway, MA; (Y); 2/140; VP Drama Clb; Lib Chorus; School Musical; School Play; Yrbk Stf; High Hon Roll; Sec NHS; Sal; Wellsley Bk Awd 86; Chancellors Talnt Awd 86; Spnsh.

ALDRICH, DANELLA; Medway JR SR HS; Medway, MA; (Y); #39 In Class; Chorus; Im Bsktbl; Hon Roll.

ALESSANDRO, STEPHANIE; Melrose HS; Boston, MA; (Y); 21/397; Camera Clb; SADD; Hon Roll; NHS; Itln Hnrb Mntn Awd 83-84; Bus.

ALEXANDRIDES, GREGORY; Belmont HS; Belmont, MA; (Y); 12/270; Church Yth Grp; JA; Spanish Clb; JV Ice Hcky; JV Wrstlng; High Hon Roll; Hon Roll; NHS; Sci Awd 85.

ALIBRANDI, PAULA; Bishop Freehan HS; Foxboro, MA; (Y); Girl Scts; JCL; JV Var Cheerleading; Mgr(s); Swmmng; French Hon Soc; Hon Roll; Engrng.

ALICEA, NORMA; High School Of Commerce; Springfield, MA; (S); 6/350; SADD; Hon Roll; Computer Clb; Office Aide; FL ST U; Comp Sci.

ALLARD, KIMBERLY; Cathedral HS; W Springfield, MA; (Y); Church Yth Grp; 4-H; Hosp Aide; Intnl Clb; Band; Church Choir; Drm Mjr(t); Hon Roll; Yth Undrstndng Peace Corps Schlrshp Overseas Study 86; Intl Studies.

ALLARD, RICHARD; Gardner HS; Gardner, MA; (Y); 42/153; Chess Clb; Mathletes; Teachers Aide; Varsity Clb; Score Keeper; Trk; Wrstlng; Comp Prog.

ALLAWAY, SHAWN; Lunenburg HS; Lunenburg, MA; (Y); 15/123; Am Leg Boys St; SADD; School Play; Stage Crew; Capt Ftbl; Capt Trk; Im Wt Lftg; Hon Roll; Im Coach Actv; Brian Mc Nally Meml Schlrshps 86; William Tapply Meml Trphy For Outstndg Lnmn 86; Bus Awd 86; Nichols Coll; Acctg.

ALLEGREZZA, AMY; Milford HS; Milford, MA; (Y); 3/265; Am Leg Aux Girls St; Church Yth Grp; Key Clb; Concert Band; Mrchg Band; Yrbk Stf; Stu Cncl; JV Fld Hcky; Var Tennis; High Hon Roll; Eng Awd 86; Commnwlth Schlr 86; Boston Clg; Intl Rel.

ALLEN, DANA; North Reading HS; N Reading, MA; (Y); 8/120; Math Clb; Math Tm; Varsity Clb; JV Bsktbl; JV Var Socr; Var Tennis; JV Var Trk; Hon Roll; Ntl Merit SF; Pilot.

ALLEN, DAWN MARIE; Reading Memorial HS; Reading, MA; (Y); 84/273; Hosp Aide; 4-H Awd; 4-H; SADD; Varsity Clb; Band; Concert Band; Mrchg Band; School Musical; Rep Frsh Cls; Vlnteer Of Yr-Wnchstr Hosp 86; Northeastern U; Phys Thrpy.

ALLEN, HOWARD; Boston Technical HS; Dorchester, MA; (Y); Var Socr; High Hon Roll; Hon Roll; Ntl Merit Ltr; Marion Davis Awd 84; U Of MA; Elctrcl Engrng.

ALLEN, JACQUELINE M; Randolph HS; Randolph, MA; (Y); 44/321; Church Yth Grp; Hon Roll; Stonehill Coll; Lbrl Arts.

ALLEN, JEFF; Blackstone Valley Regional HS; Upton, MA; (Y); Boy Scts; L Crs Cntry; L Trk; Elec Engr.

ALLEN, JULIA; Foxborough HS; Washington, DC; (Y); 9/254; English Clb; Intnl Clb; SADD; Varsity Clb; Off Jr Cls; Capt Gym; Tennis; VP NHS; St Schlr; Foxborough Hghr Ed Schrlp 86; Wrd Proc Lab Supv; Peer Tutor Bio, Frnch, Alg, Geo, Engl; Wrtng Flw Engl; The American U; Lgs.

ALLEN, LAURIE; Stoneleigh-Burnham Schl; Tampa, FL; (Y); Art Clb; French Clb; Nwsp Rptr; Nwsp Stf; Rep Frsh Cls; Pres Soph Cls; Stu Cncl; Tennis; Hon Roll.

ALLEN, LISA; Pentucket Reg SR HS; West Newbury, MA; (S); 57/168; OEA; SADD; Var Capt Cheerleading; Ski Clb; Teachers Aide; Variety Show; Yrbk Stf; Fld Hcky; Sftbl; High Hon Roll; Stu Govt Day Delegate 86; Yrbk Ad Editor 86; Presdntl Acad Fitness Awd 86; Bus.

ALLEN, MICHELLE; Whitinsville Christian Schl; Millbury, MA; (Y); 2/40; Church Yth Grp; Drama Clb; Hosp Aide; Sec Chorus; Co-Capt Cheerleading; 4-H Awd; High Hon Roll; NHS; Sal; Principals Awd 81-82; Gordon Coll; Med.

ALLEN, PAIGE; Westfield HS; Westfield, MA; (Y); 68/385; VP Church Yth Grp; Computer Clb; Pres French Clb; Band; Chorus; Concert Band; Mrchg Band; Pep Band; Natl Schl Chrl Awd 86; Lbrl Arts.

ALLEN, SETH; Milton Acad; Medford, MA; (Y); Art Clb; Cmnty Wkr; Letterman Clb; Nwsp Sprt Ed; Nwsp Stf; JV Bsktbl; Var Ftbl; Capt Lcrss; Im Wt Lftg; Varsity Clb; Sneath Fndtn Scholar 85; 2nd Pl Ralph Bradely Arts Comptn 86; Johns Hopkins; Bus.

ALLENDE, MARICZA; New Bedford HS; New Bedford, MA; (Y); Church Yth Grp; JA; ROTC; Hon Roll; JROTC Awds 83-86; K Gibbs Schl; Bus.

ALLEY, SUE; Brockton Christian Regional HS; N Easton, MA; (Y); 3/20; Church Yth Grp; Office Aide; Chorus; School Play; Stage Crew; Trs Jr Cls; Var L Cheerleading; Hon Roll; Prfct Atten Awd; Messiah Coll; Chldhd Educ.

ALLISON, MYLY E; Blackstone Millville Regional HS; Blackstone, MA; (Y); Band; Yrbk Stf; Trs Soph Cls; Trs Jr Cls; Var Crs Cntry; Var Chess Clb; High Hon Roll; Hon Roll; Hgh Hnr Roll; Sprts Awds; U Of MA; Mrn Bio.

ALLIX, DEBRA; S Buston Heights Acad; South Boston, MA; (Y); 1/45; Cmnty Wkr; High Hon Roll; Jr NHS; NHS; Val; Acadmc Excllnc Math, Frnch 86; Acadmc Excllnc Sci 84; U MA Boston; Frgn-Intl Mrktng.

ALLMAN, KRISTIN; Westwood HS; Westwood, MA; (Y); 12/205; AFS; Am Leg Aux Girls St; Key Clb; SADD; Orch; Yrbk Stf; Rep Stu Cncl; Capt Fld Hcky; Capt Tennis; NHS; Hnr Guard 85; Tri Vly Lg All Star Field Hcky & Ten 84-86; Westover Cmmnty Scholar 86; Georgetown U; Bus.

ALMEIDA, CRAIG A; Westport HS; N Dartmouth, MA; (Y); 11/144; Yrbk Ed-Chief; Pres Sr Cls; Stu Cncl; Elks Awd; Hon Roll; NHS; Pres Schlr; Amer Legn Cert Of Schl Awd 86; Elks Tngr Mnth Yr 86; Bristol CC; Sci Tchr.

ALMEIDA, DARREN; Westport HS; Westport, MA; (Y); Computer Clb; Nwsp Ed-Chief; Yrbk Stf; Hon Roll; Southeastern MA U; Elctrcl Eng.

ALMEIDA, DELIA; New Bedford HS; New Bedford, MA; (Y); Hon Roll; Oral Prfcncy In Frnch 85-86; Tchr.

ALMEIDA, EDWARD; Fairhaven HS; Fairhaven, MA; (Y); Band; Concert Band; Jazz Band; Mrchg Band; Orch; Music Prfrmnc.

ALMEIDA, KAREN; New Bedford HS; New Bedford, MA; (Y); 3/700; Drama Clb; JCL; Pres Science Clb; Orch; Stage Crew; Stu Cncl; Capt Var Fld Hcky; Var L Tennis; Rep NHS; Magna Cum Laude Natl Latin Exam 84; Hnrbl Ment 7th Annl Martin Luther King Jr Essy Cntst 85; Phrmcy.

ALMEIDA, KIMBERLY; New Bedford HS; New Bedford, MA; (Y); Church Yth Grp; Girl Scts; Office Aide; Flag Corp; Mrchg Band; Hon Roll; Nrsng.

ALOISI, ROBERT; Burlinton HS; Burlington, MA; (Y); 77/317; Band; Concert Band; Jazz Band; Mrchg Band; Orch; Swmmng; Trk; Hon Roll; BHS Clb Stud Of Wk 86; Outstndg Svc Burlington HS Band 85 & 86.

ALONG, ANTHONY; Dennis-Yarmouth Regional HS; Yarmouthport, MA; (Y); 4/300; Am Leg Boys St; Nwsp Stf; Lit Mag; Stu Cncl; NHS; Church Yth Grp; Debate Tm; Drama Clb; Band; Concert Band; Un Plgrmmge For Yth 86; S E Ma Music Fstvl & All St Rcmmndtn 86; Bst Spprtng Actor Schl Pay Comp 86; Jrnlsm.

ALPERT, CARYLL S; Framingham North HS; Framingham, MA; (Y); 10/341; Key Clb; Spanish Clb; Rep Stu Cncl; Cheerleading; Mgr(s); High Hon Roll; Hon Roll; NHS; Ntl Merit Ltr; Strng Committee; Georgetown U.

ALSAN, CIGDEM; Norwood SR HS; Norwood, MA; (Y); Band; Color Guard; Mrchg Band; Nwsp Stf; Rep Stu Cncl; Bsktbl; Hon Roll; Bus.

ALSTON, RICHARD; Boston Technical HS; Dorchester, MA; (Y); Hon Roll; JETS Awd; Mech Engrng.

ALTIERI, JOHN; Cardinal Spellman HS; Brockton, MA; (Y); 3/209; Trs Drama Clb; Thesps; Chorus; School Musical; Pres Jr Cls; Trs VP Stu Cncl; Pres NHS; Latin Clb; Stage Crew; Variety Show; Suffolk U Bk Awd Outstndng Sch Svc 86; Rep HOBY Ldrshp Sem 85; Natl Latin Exam Silver Medal 85; Architecture.

ALTMAN, ANNE; Swampscott HS; Swampscott, MA; (Y); 52/238; Camera Clb; Church Yth Grp; French Clb; Model UN; Ski Clb; SADD; Stage Crew; Variety Show; Nwsp Phtg; Nwsp Stf; Art Awd 86.

ALTMAN, WAYNE J; North Andover HS; North Andover, MA; (Y); 6/265; Cmnty Wkr; Math Tm; Political Wkr; Speech Tm; SADD; Pres Jr Cls; Pres Sr Cls; Stu Cncl; Tennis; NHS; Ntl Math Comptn 86; T Champ Radio Brdcstng 85-86; Brandeis U; Pre-Med.

ALTSHULER, EDWARD; Concord Carlisle HS; Concord, MA; (Y); Latin Clb; Ski Clb; Varsity Clb; School Musical; Stu Cncl; Crs Cntry; Var Trk; High Hon Roll; Hon Roll; Geomtry Dept Awd 84-85.

ALUKONIS, KAREN; Classical HS; Lynn, MA; (Y); 15/160; Aud/Vis; Dance Clb; Office Aide; Teachers Aide; Stage Crew; Variety Show; Yrbk Stf; High Hon Roll; Hon Roll; NHS; Lynn Tchrs Assn Schlrshp 86; Marion Ct JC Of Bus; Exec Sec.

ALUXEK, DAWN; Holyoke Catholic HS; Holyoke, MA; (Y); Camera Clb; French Clb; JV Bsktbl; JV Sftbl; Hon Roll; Cert Of Awd Frnch, Wrld Hstry, & Prfcncy In Typwrtng 84-85; U Of MA; Psych.

ALVAREZ, DIANE; Fontbonne Acad; Boston, MA; (Y); 38/133; Drama Clb; Library Aide; Pep Clb; Stu Cncl; Var Gym; Hon Roll; Prfct Atten Awd; Diploma De Merit Spn Awd 85; Hgh Hnrs Theol IV Religion Awd 86; Notre Dame; Bus Adm.

ALVES, ELIZABETH; New Bedford HS; New Bedford, MA; (Y); 9/614; Hosp Aide; Key Clb; Library Aide; SADD; Mrchg Band; Orch; Stu Cncl; Var Capt Crs Cntry; Var Capt Trk; High Hon Roll; Prnc Henry Soc Schlrshp 86; Alum Schlrshp 86; Mattapoisett Rd Race Schlrshp 86; Nrthestrn U; Psych.

ALVES, GRACIETE; Ludlow HS; Ludlow, MA; (Y); French Clb; Yrbk Stf; Pres Frsh Cls; Rep Soph Cls; Rep Jr Cls; Rep Sr Cls; Rep Stu Cncl; JV Capt Cheerleading; Assumption Coll; Intl Rltns.

ALVES, JOSE; New Bedford HS; New Bedford, MA; (Y); 150/701; JA; Library Aide; JV Trk; Hon Roll; Prfct Atten Awd; Boston Coll; Lawyer.

AMARAL, GREG; Westport HS; Westport, MA; (Y); Drama Clb; French Clb; Intnl Clb; Ski Clb; Stage Crew; Ed Nwsp Rptr; Nwsp Stf; Yrbk Stf; Hon Roll; Los Angeles Film Schl; Film Dir.

AMARAL, JASON; Attleboro HS; Attleboro, MA; (Y); #2 In Class; Am Leg Boys St; Church Yth Grp; Quiz Bowl; Rep Frsh Cls; Rep Soph Cls; Rep Jr Cls; Rep Sr Cls; Rep Stu Cncl; Crs Cntry; Capt Trk; Bk Awd Excel Engl; Dartmth Bk Awd; Wrld Aff Smnr Whtwtr WI Rtry; Engr.

AMARAL, MICHAEL; New Bedford HS; New Bedford, MA; (Y); Sec Chess Clb; French Clb; Im Bowling; Hon Roll; NHS; HS Alumni Schlrshp 86; Rgnts Merit Awd S E MA U 86; Southwestern MA U; Chem.

AMATO, PAUL; Blackstone Valley Reg Voc Tech HS; Sutton, MA; (Y); Library Aide; Trk; Trk Ltr 84 & 86; Attnd Quinigmnd Comm Coll 86; Green Peace; Elect Engnrg.

AMERO, CARRIE-ANN; Beverly HS; Beverly, MA; (Y); Yrbk Stf; Capt Cheerleading; L Ftbl; Powder Puff Ftbl; High Hon Roll; Peer Ed 86-87; Prom Cmmttee 87; Lbrl Arts.

AMES, ETHAN; Deerfield Acad; Woodstock, VT; (Y); Cmnty Wkr; FBLA; Model UN; Varsity Clb; Nwsp Ed-Chief; JV Lcrss; Var Hon Roll; Var Ski Jumping 85-86; Acad Tour Guidel 85-86; Georgetown; Intl Rltns.

AMES, RICHARD A; Quincy Vo Tech; Quincy, MA; (Y); Am Leg Boys St; Math Tm; JV Bsbl; Var Ice Hcky; Hon Roll; Electrical Engrng.

AMICANGELO, JAY C; Weymouth North HS; Weymouth, MA; (Y); 17/300; Boy Scts; Lcrss; High Hon Roll; Hon Roll; Stu Of Trm Indstrl Arts 85; Ma Inst Tech; Engr.

AMICANGIOLI, LINDA; Our Ladys Newton Catholic HS; Newton, MA; (Y); 6/59; Boy Scts; Church Yth Grp; Drama Clb; Exploring; Trs SADD; School Play; Lit Mag; VP Stu Cncl; Capt Cheerleading; NHS; Outstndng Yng Christn Womn Awd 86; David Mc Quinn Schlrshp 86; NY U; Jrnlsm.

AMIN, AISHA; Boston English HS; Boston, MA; (Y); Dance Clb; Library Aide; Office Aide; Chorus; Variety Show; Hon Roll; Prfct Atten Awd; Acad Achvt Awd 84; Cert Partic 84; Encrgmnt Awd 85; Music.

AMMERING, CAROL J; Medway HS; Medway, MA; (Y); 23/150; French Clb; Trs Chorus; Concert Band; Jazz Band; Mrchg Band; School Musical; Swing Chorus; High Hon Roll; Jr NHS; NHS; All ST Bnd 86; MA Cntrl Dstrct Bnd 85 & 86; Yeomans Mem Schlrhp 86; U MA Amhrst; Vtrnrn.

AMNOTTE, CAROLE; Chicopee Comprehensive HS; Chicopee, MA; (Y); 3/290; Trs French Clb; Office Aide; Tennis; DAR Awd; Trs NHS; St Schlr; Jr NHS; John L Fitzpatrick Scholar 86; Soc Studs Awd 86; Smith Coll Book Awd 85; Frnch Awd 85; U MA; Acctng.

AMRGARIDA, KELLY; BMC Durfee HS; Fall River, MA; (Y); Cmnty Wkr; VP JA; Hon Roll; Highest Sls Awd Jr Achvt 84; U MA; Psych.

AMSTEIN, JILL; Mohawk Trail Regional HS; Shelburne Falls, MA; (S); 1/117; Am Leg Aux Girls St; Varsity Clb; Yrbk Ed-Chief; Yrbk Stf; VP Sr Cls; Rep Stu Cncl; Var L Vllybl; High Hon Roll; Hon Roll; NHS; Supt Of Schls Awd 85; Frontiers In Sci & Math Apt WPI 85; Engrng.

ANAM, MAHBUB; Burlington HS; Burlington, MA; (Y); 14/321; Computer Clb; Math Tm; Science Clb; Im Bsbl; Im Bsktbl; Im Socr; Im JV Leo Clb; High Hon Roll; Hon Roll; Jr NHS; Acadmc Awd 83-84; Comp Lge Awd 85-86; Boston U; Elec Engr.

ANASTASI, MICHELLE; Lenox Memorial HS; Lenox, MA; (Y); 5/64; Pres Girl Scts; School Play; Yrbk Rptr; Yrbk Stf; Trs Soph Cls; Pres Jr Cls; Rep Stu Cncl; Var L Tennis; High Hon Roll; NHS; Drtmth Bk Awd 86.

ANDERLY, KRIS; New Bedford HS; New Bedford, MA; (Y); 247/701; Drama Clb; Exploring; Hosp Aide; School Musical; School Play; Yrbk Stf; Dncng Schl Awd 85 & 86.

ANDERSEN, KAREN; Wilmington HS; Wilmington, MA; (Y); GAA; Spanish Clb; Varsity Clb; Var Capt Bsktbl; Var Capt Fld Hcky; Var Sftbl; Hon Roll; Fld Hcky All Star 85; Bsktbl All Star All Conf MVT 3 Ldng Scorer 85-86; Middlebury Coll; Pre-Law.

ANDERSEN, ROBERT; Chicopee Comprehensive HS; Chicopee, MA; (Y); VICA; Hon Roll; Engrng.

ANDERSON, BETHANY; Medfield HS; Medfield, MA; (Y); 8/170; Teachers Aide; Mrchg Band; Sftbl; Vllybl; High Hon Roll; Hon Roll; NHS; Ntl Merit Ltr; Pres Schlr; Deans Scholar WA U 86; Deans Scholar U Sthrn CS 86; Pres Scholar U Sthrn CA 86; WA U; Engrng.

ANDERSON, CARRIEANN; Methuen HS; Methuen, MA; (Y); 18/350; Am Leg Aux Girls St; Intnl Clb; Model UN; Yrbk Stf; Powder Puff Ftbl; Sftbl; Swmmng; High Hon Roll; NHS; Spanish NHS; Tenney Schlrshp 86; Stephen Barker Schl PTO Schlrshp 86; Art Schlrshp 86; Southeastern MA U; Graph Dsgn.

ANDERSON, CHERI; New Bedford HS; New Bedfore, MA; (Y); Library Aide; Office Aide; Red Cross Aide; ROTC; Teachers Aide; Capt Drill Tm; Yrbk Phtg; Yrbk Stf; Trk; Nrthestrn U; Ansthlgst.

ANDERSON, DAVID; St Johns HS; Shrewsbury, MA; (Y); 50/290; Church Yth Grp; CAP; French Clb; Letterman Clb; Ski Clb; Trs Church Choir; Rep Sr Cls; High Hon Roll; St Johns Pioneer Awd 86; Rutgers Coll; Econ.

ANDERSON, GLENN S; St Johns HS; Sutton, MA; (Y); 82/252; Boy Scts; Capt Crs Cntry; L Trk; Hon Roll; Elec Engr.

ANDERSON, JIM; Barnstable HS; Centerville, MA; (Y); 30/392; Church Yth Grp; Hon Roll; Politics.

ANDERSON, JOSEPH; Braintree HS; Braintree, MA; (Y); 95/435; Church Yth Grp; Cmnty Wkr; FCA; SADD; Bsbl; JV Var DECA; JV Var Socr; Tennis.

ANDERSON, LISA D; St Berndards CCHS HS; Winchendon, MA; (Y); 2/168; Latin Clb; Model UN; Orch; School Musical; JV Trk; High Hon Roll; Hon Roll; NHS; Ntl Merit SF; All Dist Orchestra 85-86.

ANDERSON, MANUEL; Boston English 77 Louis Pastuer; Hyde Park, MA; (Y); Church Yth Grp; FBLA; Intnl Clb; JA; Math Tm; Chorus; Church Choir; School Play; Yrbk Stf; Rep Frsh Cls; MA Adv Studies Pgm 85; Eng Dept Awd 86; Outstndng Stu Awd 86; Boston Coll; Law.

ANDERSON, MATTHEW D; Marian HS; Framingham, MA; (Y); Drama Clb; Chorus; School Musical; School Play; Stage Crew; Yrbk Stf; Var Crs Cntry; Var Mgr(s); Im Tennis; Hon Roll; Musc Theatr Awd 86; Comm.

ANDERSON, RHONDA DENIECE; Boston Technical HS; Roxbury, MA; (Y); French Clb; SADD; Off Jr Cls; Off Stu Cncl; Sftbl; Hon Roll; Comp Tchnlgy.

ANDERSON, SCOTT D; David Prouty HS; Spencer, MA; (Y); 17/175; Am Leg Boys St; Boy Scts; Ski Clb; Stage Crew; Stat Bsktbl; Var Crs Cntry; JV Tennis; JV Trk; Hon Roll; NHS; Chemstry.

ANDIE, RONALD; Attleboro HS; Attleboro, MA; (Y); Church Yth Grp; Y-Teens; Socr; Hon Roll; NHS; RPI; Aero Engnr.

ANDON, STEVEN; Arlington HS; Arlington, MA; (Y); Office Aide; Concert Band; Symp Band; Yrbk Phtg; Rep Frsh Cls; Var JV Coach Actv; JV Ftbl; JV Trk; Hon Roll; NHS; Bus.

ANDRADE, CHRISTINE; Dartmouth HS; S Dartmouth, MA; (Y); 18/302; Band; Concert Band; Jazz Band; Mrchg Band; Orch; Sftbl; NHS; Cert Natl Educ Develp 84; Dartmouth Acad Encllc Awd 84 & 85 & 86; Poetry Contest Hnrble Mntn 85; U Of MA; Accntng.

ANDRADE, ELIZABETH; Woburn HS; Woburn, MA; (S); #11 In Class; JA; JCL; Latin Clb; Spanish Clb; SADD; Chorus; School Musical; Variety Show; Yrbk Rptr; Yrbk Stf; Latn Natl Hnr Soc 84; Athl Ftnss Awd 84; Boston U; Acctg.

ANDRADE, REBECCA; B M C Durfee HS; Fall River, MA; (Y); 84/600; Computer Clb; Science Clb; Spanish Clb; Camera Clb; Church Yth Grp; Cmnty Wkr; Hosp Aide; SADD; Teachers Aide; Yrbk Stf.

ANDREASSEN, CAROLYN; Groton Dunstable Regional HS; Groton, MA; (Y); 24/93; Sec Exploring; Diving; Swmmng; Hon Roll; Acctng Awd 86; NEBS Schrlshp 86; Proj Base Awd 85; Fitchburg ST Coll.

ANDRESS, WAYNE; Dennis-Yarmouth Regional HS; E Dennis, MA; (Y); 107/309; Ski Clb; Johnson & Peterson Schlrp 86; Ruth B Sears Mem Schlrp 86; Teamsters Union Lcl 59 Schlrp 86; Westfield St Coll; Bus Mgmt.

ANDREWS, CHRISTINA; Somerville HS; Somerville, MA; (Y); 47/500; Ski Clb; Spanish Clb; Hon Roll; Bently; Bus.

ANDREWS, CHRISTOPHER; Concord Carlisle HS; Concord, MA; (Y); 42/320; Latin Clb; JV Bsbl; Var Trk; Im Vllybl; NHS.

ANDREWS, JENNIFER; Westfield HS; Westfield, MA; (Y); Cmnty Wkr; Drama Clb; Library Aide; SADD; Chorus; Yrbk Stf; Cheerleading; Mat Maids; Swmmng; Trk; Cornell; Hotel-Rstrnt Mgnt.

ANELLO, ANGELO F; Norwood SR HS; Norwood, MA; (Y); Am Leg Boys St; School Play; Variety Show; Var Bsbl; Var Ftbl.

ANGELINI, DAVID G; Lynnfield HS; Lynnfield, MA; (Y); Intnl Clb; Spanish Clb; Band; Nwsp Rptr; Nwsp Sprt Ed; Nwsp Stf; Yrbk Stf; Bsbl; Bsktbl; High Hon Roll; Spnsh,Eng Awd; Pre-Law.

ANGELO, DENISE; Bartlett HS; Webster, MA; (Y); French Clb; Chorus; Yrbk Stf; VP Frsh Cls; VP Soph Cls; VP Jr Cls; Stu Cncl; Cheerleading; High Hon Roll; Hon Roll.

ANGLIN, KARIN; Cohasset HS; Cohasset, MA; (Y); 9/108; Drama Clb; School Musical; Yrbk Ed-Chief; JV Var Bsktbl; Im Powder Puff Ftbl; JV Var Socr; Var Tennis; High Hon Roll; Hon Roll; NHS; All-Str Cst MA HS Drama Fstvl 86; Stu Govt Day Rep 85-86; Prsdntl Physcl Ftnss Awd 86; Cmmnctns.

ANNAS, KAREN; Burlington HS; Burlington, MA; (Y); 42/314; Church Yth Grp; Chorus; Church Choir; Hon Roll; Grmn Awd For Good Wrk & Undrstndng Of The Lang 86; Chrs Awd For Outstndng Srvce 86; Music.

ANOOSHIAN, MARY; Wakefield Memorial HS; Wakefield, MA; (Y); 40/333; JA; Spanish Clb; Church Choir; School Musical; School Play; High Hon Roll; Jr NHS; NHS; Cmmnwlth Schlr 86; Suffolk U; Intl Econ.

ANTHONY, THOMAS H; Milton Acad; South Portland, ME; (Y); Cmnty Wkr; Debate Tm; 4-H; Math Tm; Model UN; Ski Clb; School Play; Stage Crew; Nwsp Rptr; Ntl Merit SF; Lawyer.

ANTIPPAS, FRANK; Wakefield Memorial HS; Wakefield, MA; (Y); Latin Clb; Yrbk Stf; Lit Mag; Var Bsktbl; Var L Crs Cntry; Var L Trk; Hon Roll; Hstry.

ANTONELLIS, MICHAEL; Watertown HS; Watertown, MA; (Y); 8/230; Am Leg Boys St; Drm Mjr(t); Jazz Band; Pres Sr Cls; JV Bsktbl; Hon Roll; NHS; Concert Band; Mrchg Band; Nwsp Stf; Hstry Essay Awd Phi Alpha Theta 86; Suffolk U Bk Awd 86; Bst Drum Major NESBA Band Comp 86; Upsilon; Art.

ANTONIO, JAMES P; Bishop Fenwick HS; Peabody, MA; (Y); 78/238; Church Yth Grp; Science Clb; Y-Teens; Capt Bsktbl; Var Socr; Var Trk; High Hon Roll; Hon Roll; Prfct Atten Awd; Merrimack Coll; Pol Sci.

ANTONUCCI, EVA; St Bernards Central Catholic HS; Leominster, MA; (S); 19/177; Drama Clb; Science Clb; Spanish Clb; Rep Frsh Cls; Rep Soph Cls; Rep Jr Cls; NHS; Lawyr.

ANTONUCCI, MARIA; St Bernards Central Catholic HS; Leominster, MA; (S); Drama Clb; Library Aide; Science Clb; Nwsp Stf; Yrbk Stf; Tennis; Hon Roll; Assumption Clg; Med.

ANUSZCZYK, SHERRI; New Bedford HS; New Bedford, MA; (Y); 24/701; SADD; Mrchg Band; Yrbk Stf; Stu Cncl; Var Crs Cntry; Var Trk; Var Twrlr; Hon Roll; NHS; AFS; Med.

ANYON, KELLEY; Auburn HS; Auburn, MA; (Y); Church Yth Grp; JA; Hon Roll; Accntng.

APHOLT, JOHN P; Newton North HS; Newton, MA; (Y); Am Leg Boys St; Boy Scts; Church Yth Grp; Cmnty Wkr; Y-Teens; Chorus; Off Jr Cls; Var L Bsktbl; Var L Ftbl; Eagle Scout Bronze Palm 85; Sandy Bartzak Awd Good Sportmshp 84; Unsung Hero Awd Vrsty Bsktbl 86; Pol Sci.

APKARIAN, DIANE; Presentation Of Mary Acad; Methuen, MA; (Y); 11/46; Sec French Clb; Hosp Aide; Yrbk Stf; Rep Frsh Cls; French Hon Soc; Hon Roll; NEDT Awd; Prfct Atten Awd; Awd Excllnc All Sbjcts 86; Merrimack Coll.

APONTE, MADELINE; Jamaica Plain HS; Roxbury, MA; (Y); Computer Clb; Hon Roll; Prfct Atten Awd; Acad Achvt Boston Area Hlth Ed Ctr 86; Applctn Awd Comp MASSPEP 86; Samuel Gross Davis Awd 86; Comp Sci.

APOVIAN III, JAMES; Central Catholic HS; Methuen, MA; (Y); Computer Clb; Im Bsktbl; Trk; Hon Roll; Comp Sci.

APPELL, JENNIFER; Triton Regional HS; Rowley, MA; (Y); AFS; Church Yth Grp; Band; Concert Band; Jazz Band; Mrchg Band; Orch; School Musical; Cheerleading; High Hon Roll; Engl Achvt Awd 85 & 86; Oustndng Music Stu 85; Music Schl Scholar 85; Bus.

APPLEGATE, DIANE; Melrose HS; Melrose, MA; (Y); 95/389; Pep Clb; SADD; Stu Cncl; Hon Roll; Hm Econ Awd; Polit Sci.

APPLIN, SUSAN; Reading Memorial HS; Reading, MA; (Y); Hosp Aide; Mathletes; French Hon Soc; High Hon Roll; NHS; Ntl Merit Ltr; Thrptc Wrk.

APRIL, KAREN; Bishop Feehan HS; Attleboro, MA; (Y); JCL; Chorus; French Hon Soc; Hon Roll; Vet.

APRUZZESE, THERESA; Everett HS; Everett, MA; (Y); 5/350; Church Yth Grp; Drama Clb; Office Aide; SADD; Varsity Clb; Cheerleading; JV Sftbl; Trk; High Hon Roll; NHS; Bus.

AQUIAR, JUDITH; Somerset HS; Somerset, MA; (Y); Ski Clb; Yrbk Stf; Bsktbl; Trk; Bausch & Lomb Sci Awd; High Hon Roll; NHS; Ntl Merit SF; Holy Crss Bk Awd 86; Chem Engrg.

ARANGIO, ALANA; Saugus HS; Saugus, MA; (Y); 1/276; Library Aide; Capt Bsktbl; Fld Hcky; Capt Sftbl; Bausch & Lomb Sci Awd; Cit Awd; Pres NHS; Pres Schlr; Val; Tufts U; Premed.

ARANGIO, CHRISTIAN; Boston Latin HS; E Boston, MA; (Y); 46/274; Rep Frsh Cls; Off Sr Cls; Rep Stu Cncl; Var L Ftbl; Mgr(s); Var Wt Lftg; NHS; Certfct Of Achvt In Math 85; Profesnl Club 84-86; Fidelity Prize 84; Corp Law.

ARANGIO, JENNIFER C; Saugus HS; Saugus, MA; (Y); 15/309; Hosp Aide; Yrbk Stf; Off Sr Cls; Stu Cncl; Cit Awd; Hon Roll; Jr NHS; NHS; Pres Schlr; Voice Dem Awd; Hugh O Brian Yth Fndtn Ldrshp Awd 84; Schl Srv Awd 85; Intl Hnr Soc Hstry Awd 85; Boston U; Phys Thrpy.

ARAUJO, SUSETE; BMC Durfee HS; Fall River, MA; (Y); 117/673; Church Yth Grp; Computer Clb; Hosp Aide; Teachers Aide; Color Guard; Yrbk Stf; Bus Clb 85-87; Pres Portugs Clb 85-86; Trvl Agnt.

ARBOUR, ROBERT; Monson JR SR HS; Monson, MA; (Y); School Musical; Var L Bsbl; Var Bsktbl; Var L Socr; Western MA Rnr-Ups-Soccer 84; Comp Sci.

ARCHAMBAULT, KAREN; Greater Lowell Reg Vo Tech; Lowell, MA; (Y); Hon Roll; Law.

ARCHAMBO, LYNNE; Holy Name C C HS; Shrewsbury, MA; (Y); Art Clb; 4-H; French Clb; Hon Roll; Readng & Rhetrc Awd 84; Relgn Awd 85; Pony Club D-3 Rtng Awd 85; Marketing.

ARCIDIACONO, LORI; Methuen HS; Methuen, MA; (Y); #19 In Class; Model UN; Yrbk Stf; JV Sftbl; Var Capt Swmmng; High Hon Roll; Hon Roll; NHS; Mst Imprvd Smwmr Awd 85.

ARCIERI, JOEL; Boston College HS; Milton, MA; (Y); SADD; Im Ftbl; Hon Roll; NHS; Natl Latn Exam Cert Of Hnrb Merit 85; B C High Cert Of Awd For Acad Exclnc In Algebra Ii 86.

ARENA, STEPHEN; St Dominic Savio HS; Wilmington, MA; (Y); 15/104; Camera Clb; Chess Clb; JA; Science Clb; Ski Clb; SADD; Variety Show; Yrbk Rptr; Yrbk Stf; Rep Frsh Cls; NEDT Awd Outstndng Achvt 84; Outstndng Fld Awd Relgn 85; Svrl Chss Awds Various Achvtmts 84-86; Suffolk U; Orthpdc Surgn.

ARENBURG, JASON; Attleboro HS; Attleboro, MA; (Y); Am Leg Boys St; Off Church Yth Grp; Scholastic Bowl; VP Acpl Chr; Chorus; Church Choir; Rep Frsh Cls; Rep Soph Cls; Trs Pres Stu Cncl; Var L Gym; J F Mc Govern Ldrshp Awd/Bridgewtr ST Coll Smr PCC Pgm 83; Ambassador Coll; Theolgy.

ARENT, SUSAN; Holyohe HS; Holyoke, MA; (Y); 14/360; French Clb; Latin Clb; Office Aide; Spanish Clb; JV Fld Hcky; High Hon Roll; NHS; Spanish NHS; Care Clb 86; Outstndndg Bus Stu Awd Svc & Ldrshp 86; Bay Path JC; Blngl Prlgl.

ARIAGNO, JAMES; Bourne HS; Buzzards Bay, MA; (Y); Im Bsbl; JV Var Ftbl; Ice Hcky; Wt Lftg; U Of MA.

ARLORO, JULIE; Reading Memorial HS; Reading, MA; (Y); 35/324; Camera Clb; Cmnty Wkr; French Clb; SADD; Band; Ed Yrbk Phtg; Pres Acad Fitness Awd 86; Schlstc Achvt Awd 85; Merrimac Coll; Acctng.

ARMANETTI, LISA; Middleborough HS; Middleboro, MA; (Y); 7/207; Drama Clb; Key Clb; Scholastic Bowl; Nwsp Stf; Rep Frsh Cls; Rep Soph Cls; Rep Sr Cls; Var L Bsktbl; Var L Fld Hcky; Powder Puff Ftbl; Wellesley Coll; Chem.

ARMANY, RONNIE; English HS; Roslindale, MA; (Y); Math Clb; Math Tm; Science Clb; Bsktbl; Ftbl; Gym; Trk; Wt Lftg; Hon Roll; Prfct Atten Awd; Sci Awd Bst Stu 86; Clss 1922 Schlrshp Awd 86; U Of MA; Med.

ARMATA, MATTHEW; Wilbraham & Manson Acad; Wilbraham, MA; (Y); 4/125; Aud/Vis; Mathletes; Q&S; Yrbk Ed-Chief; Stat Bsbl; Bausch & Lomb Sci Awd; Hon Roll; Trnty Coll Bk Awd 86; Evelyn Barber Deptmntl Prz AP Comp Sci 85; Comp Sci.

ARMENTO, CASSANDRA; Stoneleigh-Burnham HS; Brattleboro, VT; (Y); Debate Tm; Intnl Clb; SADD; Band; Chorus; School Musical; Nwsp Rptr; High Hon Roll; Hon Roll; NHS; Jr Essay Awd 85-86; Jr Engl Awd 85-86; Comm.

ARMIT, LYNN; Auburn HS; Auburn, MA; (Y); Camp Fr Inc; Computer Clb; Ski Clb; Sec SADD; Varsity Clb; Yrbk Stf; Tennis; High Hon Roll; NHS; Sec Church Yth Grp; Talnt Awd 86; Vlntr Sci Ctr 86; Worcester Polytech; Engrg.

ARMITAGE, MELISSA; Westford Acad; Westford, MA; (Y); AFS; Art Clb; Church Yth Grp; Sec Drama Clb; Spanish Clb; Mrchg Band; School Musical; School Play; Variety Show; Var Cheerleading; Chld Devlpmt Awd 86; Engl.

ARMSBY, MARGERY; Newton North HS; Newtonville, MA; (Y); Off Art Clb; Pres Drama Clb; Exploring; School Musical; School Play; Ed Lit Mag; Fine Art.

ARMSTRONG, CHRISTINE GAIL; Shepherd Hill Regional HS; Dudley, MA; (Y); 40/140; Church Yth Grp; Girl Scts; Hosp Aide; Spanish Clb; SADD; Band; Chorus; Color Guard; Flag Corp; Mrchg Band; Harrington Hosp Women Aux Schlrshp 86; Shepherd Hill Booster Clb Schlrshp 86; Prfrm Blue Bnnt Bwl 84; Hahnamman Hosp Schl Of Nrsng.

ARMSTRONG, DONALD; Lawrence Acad; Littleton, MA; (Y); 15/100; Boy Scts; Church Yth Grp; Teachers Aide; Varsity Clb; Band; School Musical; Rep Frsh Cls; Var L Bsktbl; JV Lcrss; JV Socr; NROTC Schlrshp; Holy Cross; Dmplmtc Lore.

ARMSTRONG, JAY; Newburyport HS; Newburypt, MA; (Y); 28/205; JCL; Political Wkr; Red Cross Aide; Scholastic Bowl; Yrbk Stf; VP Jr Cls; JV Bsktbl; Var Capt Tennis; Hon Roll; NHS; Coaches Awd Tennis 85; Bus.

ARMSTRONG, RICHARD; Melrose HS; Melrose, MA; (Y); 11/370; Cmnty Wkr; VP Drama Clb; School Musical; School Play; Stage Crew; High Hon Roll; NHS; Ntl Merit Ltr; Church Yth Grp; German Clb; Outstndg Perf-Mark Twain-MA HS Drama Guild Cmptn 85; Outstndg Perf-MHSDG Cmptn 86.

ARMSTRONG, TRACY; Agawam HS; Agawam, MA; (Y); 5/300; AFS; Chorus; Var Fld Hcky; JV Sftbl; Hon Roll; Spanish NHS; Brwn U Bk Awd, Smith Coll Bk Awd 86.

ARNOLD, MICHELLE; Hingham HS; Hingham, MA; (Y); 25/326; Cmnty Wkr; Debate Tm; Spanish Clb; Hon Roll; Ntl Merit Ltr; Hingham Hist Soc Awd 85; Pol Sci.

ARNOLD, TROY; Lee HS; Lee, MA; (Y); Pres Church Yth Grp; Drama Clb; French Clb; Spanish Clb; SADD; Chorus; School Musical; School Play; Stage Crew; Swing Chorus; Western MA Dist Chorus 84.

ARNOLD III, WILLIAM P; Longmeadow HS; Springfield, MA; (Y); 159/285; Aud/Vis; JA; Variety Show; Im JV Ftbl; Im Wt Lftg; JETS Awd; Mnrty Engrng Awd 83-85; U MA; Engrng.

ARNUM, MICHAEL; Lincoln Sudbury Regional HS; Sudbury, MA; (Y); Church Yth Grp; French Clb; Pres Key Clb; Church Choir; De Normandie Awd Outstndng Ctznshp 86; Metrolgy.

ARPANO, MATTHEW; Dennis Yarmouth Regional HS; Yarmouth Port, MA; (Y); 95/310; Church Yth Grp; Cmnty Wkr; Ski Clb; Bsbl; Coach Actv; Ftbl; Hon Roll; Cape & Islands All St Ftbl 85-86; Defensve Back Awd 85-86; Big Bro & Sister Orgzntn; U Of RI.

ARRINGTON, NERESSIA VEMA; Mission Church HS; Jamaica Plain, MA; (Y); Church Yth Grp; Cmnty Wkr; FHA; Hosp Aide; JA; Library Aide; Office Aide; Church Choir; Yrbk Stf; Sec Frsh Cls; U Mass-Boston; Nrsng.

ARROYO JR, EDDIE; North HS; Worcester, MA; (Y); Pres Church Yth Grp; Pres Jr Cls; Rep Stu Cncl; JV Var Bsbl; Citywd Tst Spnsh Awd 83-85; Our Lady Of Fatima Chrch Lectr 85; Engrng.

ARRUDA, CHERIE; New Bedford HS; New Bedford, MA; (Y); Church Yth Grp; Drama Clb; Key Clb; Rep Jr Cls; High Hon Roll; Hon Roll; NHS; St Lawrence U.

ARRUDA, CHRISTINE; Bishop Connolly HS; Fall River, MA; (Y); 69/170; Sec Church Yth Grp; Drama Clb; Girl Scts; Hosp Aide; Chorus; Church Choir; School Play; Variety Show; High Hon Roll; Hon Roll; Southeastrn MA U; Psych.

ARRUDA, ELISE M; Marlboro HS; Marlborough, MA; (Y); 43/263; Church Yth Grp; Ski Clb; Off Stu Cncl; Var Mgr(s); NHS; Social Work.

ARRUDA, KEITH J; Somerset HS; Somerset, MA; (Y); JA; VP Stu Cncl; Var L Tennis; High Hon Roll; NHS; Computer Clb; Dance Clb; Math Tm; Variety Show; Yrbk Stf; Unsng Hero Tnns; Lbrl Arts.

ARRUDA, MATTHEW; New Bedford HS; New Bedford, MA; (Y); 64/700; Church Yth Grp; Cmnty Wkr; High Hon Roll; Jr NHS; Prfct Atten Awd; 4th Rnnr Up Hnrbl Ment Essay Cntst 86; Crmnl Law.

ARSENAULT, CARI-ANN; B M C Durfee HS; Fall River, MA; (Y); 18/781; Boy Scts; Pres Computer Clb; Science Clb; Yrbk Stf; Bsktbl; Sftbl; Hon Roll; Kiwanis Awd; NHS; Comp Prog.

ARSENEAU, SANDRA; Gardner HS; Gardner, MA; (Y); 36/140; French Clb; Math Clb; Scholastic Bowl; Chorus; School Musical; Stage Crew; L Cheerleading; L Sftbl; Var Trk; New England Acad Decathalon 86; French.

ARTIOLI, MICHELLE; HS Of Commerce HS; Springfield, MA; (Y); 1/350; SADD; Pres Sr Cls; Capt Var Bsktbl; Cit Awd; High Hon Roll; Hon Roll; NHS; St Schlr; Val; Cmnty Wkr; JVFW Brthd Awd 86; Army Schlr Athlt Awd 86; Natl Hrn Roll; Johnson & Wales; Stngrphr.

ARUIN, RAYA; Peabody Veterans Memorial HS; Peabody, MA; (Y); 24/500; Computer Clb; Science Clb; High Hon Roll; Hon Roll; Lion Awd; NHS; Northeastern U; Elec Engrng.

ASGEIRSSON, JON; Greater Boston Acad; Reading, MA; (Y); Chess Clb; Church Yth Grp; Drama Clb; Math Tm; Concert Band; Orch; Nwsp Rptr; VP Frsh Cls; Im Socr; Hon Roll; Prfct Score Verbal Reasng PSAT 84-85; Atlantic Union Coll; Comp.

ASH, GEORGE; St Dominic Savio HS; Revere, MA; (Y); 13/104; Aud/Vis; Chess Clb; Cmnty Wkr; Computer Clb; Library Aide; Capt Science Clb; Nwsp Rptr; NHS; NEDT Awd; Outstndng Charctr Awd 86; Nrthestrn Hnrs Pgm 86; Nrthestrn U; Comp Sci.

ASHE, CHRISTOPHER; Marian HS; Holliston, MA; (Y); 29/130; Boy Scts; Church Yth Grp; Debate Tm; Office Aide; Political Wkr; Yrbk Bus Mgr; Yrbk Phtg; Rep Soph Cls; Sec Jr Cls; JV Crs Cntry; US Senate Page; Georgetown U; Politics.

ASHFORD, TAMARA WENDA; Buckingham Browne & Nichols Schl; Boston, MA; (Y); Office Aide; Rep Jr Cls; Rep Sr Cls; Rep Stu Cncl; Var L Fld Hcky; Var L Tennis; High Hon Roll; Wnr Aprl Teruel Prz 84; Ntl Schvt Schlrshp/Outstndng Negro Stu 84-85; Cltrl Awrns Grp 83-86; Doctor In Sprts Med.

ASHMAN, PAUL; East Boston HS; E Boston, MA; (Y); Cmnty Wkr; Nwsp Rptr; Civics Schlstc Achvt Awd 86; Med Tech.

ASHRAF, NAVEED; Hyde Park HS; Boston, MA; (S); Exploring; French Clb; JA; Math Clb; Political Wkr; Science Clb; Teachers Aide; Concert Band; Yrbk Rptr; Yrbk Stf; Cert Of Havg Excllnt Acadmc Yr 83; Natl Hnr Socty Inductn 84; Cert Comp Actvts 85; Physcs.

ASHWORTH, PETER; New Bedford HS; New Bedford, MA; (Y); 45/701; Boy Scts; Sec Drama Clb; JCL; Science Clb; Chorus; Orch; School Play; Stage Crew; Rep Jr Cls; Stu Cncl.

ASIKAINEN, JAY; Gardner HS; Gardner, MA; (Y); 7/150; Am Leg Boys St; Lit Mag; Capt Golf; High Hon Roll; Hon Roll; Pres NHS; Prfct Atten Awd; Cmmnctns.

ASKEW, ROBERT; Madison Park HS; Dorchester, MA; (Y); Boys Clb Am; Drm Mjr(t); Capt Ftbl; Prfct Atten Awd; Bus Admin.

ASKINS, BRAD; Marlborough HS; Marlboro, MA; (Y); Church Yth Grp; Ski Clb; SADD; Variety Show; Yrbk Stf; Rep Frsh Cls; Var L Ftbl; Var L Golf; Var L Wrstlng; Hon Roll; Marine Bio.

ASKLAND, MARK J; Burlington HS; Burlington, MA; (Y); 65/318; Rep Frsh Cls; Rep Soph Cls; Ftbl; Tennis; Wrstlng; Var Ltr Ten 85-86; JV Cert Ten 83-84; Cert Ftbl 83-84; Law.

ASSA, JENNIFER; Framingham South HS; Framingham, MA; (Y); 24/261; Drama Clb; Trs Key Clb; Rep Latin Clb; SADD; Diving; Gym; Lcrss; Swmmng; High Hon Roll; Hon Roll; Natl Hon Soc 84-85 & 85-86; Psychology.

ASSAD, SHARI; Westport HS; Westport, MA; (Y); Art Clb; Church Yth Grp; French Clb; Intnl Clb; Pep Clb; Yrbk Stf; Rep Soph Cls; Rep Jr Cls; Rep Sr Cls; Crs Cntry; Europe; Commrcl Dsgn.

ASSELIN, SUSAN; Chicopee Comprehensive HS; Chicopee, MA; (Y); 67/332; Camera Clb; Drama Clb; Pres Exploring; French Clb; Concert Band; Stage Crew; Ed Yrbk Phtg; Yrbk Stf; Stu Cncl; Var Tennis; Stu Cncl Ltr Pin 85-86; Band Pin 84-85; Schl Varty Show Cert 85-86; Telecommnctns.

ASTOR, TODD; Randolph HS; Randolph, MA; (Y); Temple Yth Grp; Var Bsbl; Var Crs Cntry; Hon Roll; Jr NHS; Pre-Med; Sprts Med.

ATEN, KIMBERLY E; Hingham HS; Hingham, MA; (Y); 90/360; AFS; Church Yth Grp; Pep Clb; Stage Crew; Yrbk Stf; Cheerleading; Sftbl; Penn ST; Mgmt Persnnl.

ATHANASATOS, CATHY; Haverhill HS; Haverhill, MA; (Y); 70/400; Church Yth Grp; Rep French Clb; Intnl Clb; Chorus; Church Choir; School Musical; Stage Crew; Tennis; Vllybl; Hon Roll; U Lowell; Psych.

ATHANASIA, CHRIS T; Wilmington HS; Wilmington, MA; (Y); 2/240; Church Yth Grp; Nwsp Stf; Off Stu Cncl; Var L Ftbl; Ice Hcky; Var L Trk; NHS; Ntl Merit SF; Sal; JR Rotrn 85; Awd Outstndng Achvt Math & Comp & Forgn Lang 85; Harvard; Med.

ATTARDO, JULIE; Braintree HS; Braintree, MA; (Y); 21/444; Pep Clb; Gym; Pom Pon; French Hon Soc; High Hon Roll; Merit Awd Frnch Ntl Exam 84; Aviation.

ATTEMANN, HUGO P; Dover Sherborn HS; Dover, MA; (Y); AFS; Am Leg Boys St; Boy Scts; SADD; Rep Frsh Cls; VP Soph Cls; Im Bsktbl; Var Capt Swmmng; Im Vllybl; Hon Roll.

ATTER, STEVEN; Gardner HS; Gardner, MA; (Y); 14/130; Am Leg Boys St; Chess Clb; L Var Bsbl; L Capt Ftbl; Wt Lftg; Hon Roll; Sec NHS.

ATWOOD, DEBORAH; Natick HS; Natick, MA; (Y); 1/400; JCL; Speech Tm; Chorus; Mrchg Band; School Play; Lit Mag; NHS; Ntl Merit Schol; Val; Harvard Bk Awd 85; Intl Ordr Of Foresters Schlrshp 86; Union Clg.

ATWOOD, PAULA; Somerville HS; Somerville, MA; (Y); 28/620; Cmnty Wkr; Dance Clb; Pep Clb; SADD; Varsity Clb; Stu Cncl; JV Capt Cheerleading; Pom Pon; Hon Roll; Physcl Thrpst.

AUDETTE, CHRISTINE; David Hale Fanning Trade HS; Leicester, MA; (Y); 31/124; SADD; Hon Roll; Teachers Aide; Variety Show; Cert In Bsc Lf Sprt Rscr 86; Cert In Mltimd Stndrd 1st Aid 86; Bckr JC; Early Chldhd Ed.

AUDETTE, RENEE; Somerset HS; Somerset, MA; (Y); 21/310; Church Yth Grp; Girl Scts; Math Tm; Band; Concert Band; Mrchg Band; High Hon Roll; Hon Roll; NHS; St Schlr; Music Awds 83-84; Southeastern MA U; Math.

AUREN, MICHELLE; Auburn HS; Auburn, MA; (Y); 15/158; Church Yth Grp; Band; Concert Band; Mrchg Band; Yrbk Stf; Rep Frsh Cls; Rep Soph Cls; High Hon Roll; NHS; Schlrshp Assoc Medcl Assist 86; Ntl Hnr Soc Schrlshp 86; Becker JC; Med Assist.

AUSTIN, JOHN; Central Catholic HS; Tewksbury, MA; (Y); 16/235; Boy Scts; Drama Clb; Ski Clb; School Musical; School Play; JV Trk; High Hon Roll; Hon Roll; Trs NHS; Ntl Merit Ltr; Princpls Schrlshp 85; Eagle Scout 85; Ntl Order Arrow Vigil Hnr 85; Mgmt.

AUSTIN, STEPHANIE; Weymouth North HS; Weymouth, MA; (Y); 13/328; Pep Clb; Ski Clb; Yrbk Ed-Chief; Var Bsktbl; High Hon Roll; Hon Roll; Stephen Rennie Mem Bsktbl Scholar 86; U Lowell; Nrsng.

AUSTIN, STEPHEN F; Taconia HS; Pittsfield, MA; (Y); 5/260; Am Leg Boys St; Boy Scts; Var L Bsktbl; High Hon Roll; VP NHS; Ntl Merit Ltr; UMASS Chncllrs Awd & Schlrshp 86; Rnsslr Polytchnc Inst Sci & Math Awd 86; Sci.

AVELLAR, ANN; Chatham HS; S Chatham, MA; (Y); 12/50; AFS; Church Yth Grp; Cmnty Wkr; Drama Clb; Girl Scts; Ski Clb; School Musical; School Play; Variety Show; Nwsp Rptr; Blfr Awd Mth 85; Prom Queen 85; Class Mrshl 85; Nrthestrn U Boston; Bus.

AVERY, CHRISTINE; Ashland HS; Ashland, MA; (Y); Key Clb; Fld Hcky; Trk; Hon Roll; Voice Dem Awd; Acad Awd Photo 85; 2nd Pl Intrschltc Athltc Assn E Div 2 Mile 85.

AVIS, MICHAEL; Agawam HS; Feeding Hls, MA; (Y); 100/370; Sec Sr Cls; Var Bsktbl; Rosry Alter Schlrshp 86; Bsketbll Schlrshp 86; North Adams ST; Bus Mang.

AVOGLIA, JENNIFER; Auburn HS; Auburn, MA; (Y); Yrbk Stf; Var Cheerleading.

AWARD, ELIZABETH; Quaboag Regional HS; Warren, MA; (Y); 7/85; Spanish Clb; SADD; Varsity Clb; Variety Show; Nwsp Stf; VP Stu Cncl; JV Bsktbl; Var JV Fld Hcky; High Hon Roll; NHS.

AXT JR, LOUIS; Drury SR HS; North Adams, MA; (S); 28/189; Trs Band; Concert Band; Jazz Band; Mrchg Band; Hon Roll; Ntl Merit Ltr; NEDT Awd; Rotary Awd; Var Golf; Boys St Alternate; Williams Coll; Economics.

AYENI, AKEEM; Doherty Memorial HS; Worcester, MA; (Y); 12/308; Boys Clb Am; Variety Show; Pres Frsh Cls; Pres Soph Cls; Im Bsktbl; Var Crs Cntry; Capt Trk; High Hon Roll; Jr NHS; NHS; Almni Of HOBY Ldrshp Fndtn 84; Dgtl Eqpmnt Corp Schlrshp 86; Cmmndtn-NASP-OUTSTNDNG Negro Stu 85; Harvard U.

AYLES, ROBERT J; St Bernards Central Catholic HS; Leominster, MA; (Y); Am Leg Boys St; Boy Scts; Sec Church Yth Grp; Nwsp Stf; Var Crs Cntry; Var Ice Hcky; Elks Awd.

AYOTTE, AUDRA; King Philip Regional HS; Norfolk, MA; (Y); 21/240; Ski Clb; Band; Concert Band; Sec Jr Cls; Sec Sr Cls; Var L Crs Cntry; JV Swmmng; L Capt Trk; Hon Roll; Hon Roll; Unsung Hero Wad Crss Cnty; US Model Senate; Lib Arts.

AZIZ, JASON; Methuen HS; Methuen, MA; (Y); Spanish Clb; JV Bsbl; Var Ftbl; Var Golf; Var Ice Hcky; Var Trk; Var Wrstlng; Hon Roll; Bus Adm.

AZZARITO, MARY; Newburyport HS; Newburyport, MA; (S); 30/192; JCL; Model UN; Band; Chorus; Concert Band; Jazz Band; School Musical; School Play; Nwsp Rptr; Yrbk Ed-Chief; US Cngrssnl Pge 85; Cum Laude Natl Ltn Exm; Intl Pltcs.

BABINEAU, ANGELA J; Fitchburg HS; Fitchburg, MA; (Y); 3/200; School Play; Stage Crew; Yrbk Stf; Pres Jr Cls; Pres Sr Cls; Stu Cncl; JV Trk; High Hon Roll; Ntl Merit SF; Rtry Clb Stu Mnth 85; Bnai Brith Amrcnsm Awd 85; Engr.

BABINSKI, HEIDI; Westfield HS; Westfield, MA; (Y); 24/350; Political Wkr; SADD; School Play; Yrbk Rptr; Sec Stu Cncl; Var Fld Hcky; Capt Var Trk; Jr NHS; Spanish Clb; Nwsp Rptr; Outstndg Soph By HOBY Fndtn 85; Awd Outstndg Ldrshp Ablts MASS Yth Ldrshp Fndtn 85; Chld Psychlgy.

BACON, AMY MAE; Palmer HS; Palmer, MA; (Y); 2/100; Pres VP French Clb; Pres VP JA; Math Tm; Band; School Play; Lit Mag; Stu Cncl; Bausch & Lomb Sci Awd; Pres Schlr; Sal; Rnnsslr Sci & Mth Awd 85; U Of MA Amhrst; Chem.

BACON, DAWN; Douglas Memorial HS; E Douglas, MA; (Y); 9/35; Band; Chorus; Concert Band; Jazz Band; Mrchg Band; Yrbk Stf; Hon Roll; Band Schlrshp 86; Greenfield CC; Erly Chldhd Ed.

BACZEWSKI, CHRISTINA; Gardner HS; Gardner, MA; (Y); 30/162; Spanish Clb; Band; Concert Band; Mrchg Band; Pep Band; JV Bsktbl; Var Crs Cntry; Hon Roll; Stone Find Schlrshp 86; MA ST Schlrshp 86; Howe Fund Schlrshp 86; Assumption Coll; Accntng.

BADAVAS, CHRISTOS; Algonguin Regional HS; Southboro, MA; (Y); 6/220; Band; Jazz Band; Orch; School Musical; Var L Socr; High Hon Roll; Hon Roll; NHS; Ntl Merit Ltr; Cntrl MA Dist Orch 84 & 86; Cntrl MA Jazz Ensmble & Concrt Band 85; MA All ST Orch 86; Econ.

BADDOUR, STEVEN; Methuen HS; Methuen, MA; (Y); Am Leg Boys St; Intnl Clb; Pep Clb; Yrbk Phtg; Jr Cls; Sr Cls; Tennis; Trk; High Hon Roll; Lawyer.

BADORINI, MICHAEL; Hoosac Valley HS; Adams, MA; (Y); 25/150; Cmnty Wkr; Var Ftbl; Im Socr; Var Trk; High Hon Roll; Hon Roll; NHS; Lowell U; Elec Engrng.

BAGHERPOUR, ATTESSA; Dedham HS; Dedham, MA; (Y); 72/242; Computer Clb; Rep Soph Cls; Rep Jr Cls; Hon Roll; Mst Imprvd Art Stu.

BAGOCIUS JR, JAMES J; Assabet Valley Tech HS; Westborough, MA; (Y); Wt Lftg; Northeastern U; Elec.

BAIER, MARGARET; Silver Lake Regional HS; Halifax, MA; (Y); Cmnty Wkr; Drama Clb; Girl Scts; Sec Latin Clb; Office Aide; Spanish Clb; Band; Stage Crew; Variety Show; JV Fld Hcky; Stu Of Mnth 85; Kthrn Gbbs Schl; Bus.

BAIKEWICZ, JOHN A; Newburyport HS; Newburyport, MA; (Y); 66/185; Am Leg Boys St; Political Wkr; Nwsp Rptr; Nwsp Stf; Var JV Bsbl; Var JV Ftbl; Im Score Keeper; Marshal 86-87; Mth 10 Achvt Awd 84-85; Off Procdrs Achvt Awd 85-86; Boston U; Jrnlsm.

BAILEN, RICHARD; St Johns Prep; Peabody, MA; (Y); Camera Clb; Temple Yth Grp; Jazz Band; Nwsp Rptr; JV Swmmng; Pre-Med.

BAILEY, CHRIS; North Middlesex Regional HS; Ashby, MA; (Y); Hosp Aide; Math Tm; Varsity Clb; Yrbk Sprt Ed; Rep Frsh Cls; Bsbl; Ftbl; Trk; Hon Roll; Jr NHS; Engrng.

BAILEY, CHRISTINE; Burncoat SR HS; Worcester, MA; (Y); Dance Clb; Church Choir; Swmmng; Elks Awd; VP Church Yth Grp; Hosp Aide; Rep JA; Library Aide; Office Aide; Teachers Aide; MA ST Plc Olympcs Awd 84; Dbthts Bll Awd 83-85; Prfsnl Dncr.

BAILEY, LEAH; Walpole HS; Walpole, MA; (Y); Camp Fr Inc; Chorus; Im Fld Hcky; Im Sftbl; High Hon Roll; Hon Roll; Stu Mnth Chem & Engl, Cert Prfrmnc US Hist Scl View, Cert Prfrmnc Chem 85-86.

BAIRD, LORI ANN; Clinton HS; Clinton, MA; (Y); 23/126; Church Yth Grp; Drama Clb; Intnl Clb; Spanish Clb; Yrbk Stf; Sec Frsh Cls; Sec Soph Cls; Sec Jr Cls; Sec Sr Cls; Rep Stu Cncl; Yuth Mnth, Chrmn Mrch Dimes 86; Framingham ST Coll; Pre Law.

BAIROS, DIANE; Taunton HS; Taunton, MA; (Y); Yrbk Stf; Southeastern MA U; Comp.

BAKAS, MICHAEL G T; Boston Latin HS; Westwood, MA; (Y); 53/300; Church Yth Grp; Computer Clb; Latin Clb; Political Wkr; Ski Clb; JV Var Ftbl; Wt Lftg; Hon Roll; NHS; Ftbl Awd Mr 100 Pct 86; UMBASS Amherstst; Mech Engrng.

BAKER, CHRISTINE; Stoughton HS; Stoughton, MA; (Y); 14/315; Church Yth Grp; Math Tm; Drill Tm; Yrbk Stf; Rep Frsh Cls; Rep Soph Cls; Stu Cncl; High Hon Roll; NHS; Pres Acad Ftns Awd 86; Shaws Sueprmrkt Schlrshp 86; Boston Coll Schlrshp 86; Boston Coll; Math.

BAKER, DIRK; Auburn HS; Auburn, MA; (Y); Nwsp Rptr; Nwsp Sprt Ed; Nwsp Stf; JV Var Bsbl; JV Var Socr; High Hon Roll; Hon Roll; NHS; Ace Carrier 85; Schlrshp Awd 86; Eng.

BAKER, GARY; Framingham South HS; Framingham, MA; (Y); Boy Scts; Computer Clb; Temple Yth Grp; JV Lcrss; Wt Lftg; Comp Sci.

BAKER, LAURA; St Columbkille HS; Allston, MA; (Y); Church Yth Grp; French Clb; Latin Clb; School Play; French Hon Soc; High Hon Roll; Hon Roll; Jr NHS; NHS.

BAKER, MELISSA; Winthrop SR HS; Winthrop, MA; (Y); 39/200; Drama Clb; School Musical; School Play; Stage Crew; Yrbk Bus Mgr; Hosp Aide; Library Aide; Spanish Clb; Nwsp Stf; Yrbk Stf; Drm Awds 84 & 85; Srgn.

BAKER, PAMELA; Walpole HS; E Walpole, MA; (Y); 11/286; Girl Scts; Hosp Aide; Leo Clb; Radio Clb; Lib Band; Chorus; Symp Band; Off Jr Cls; Hon Roll; NHS; Clssrm Prfrmnc Hnrs Geometry 84; Clssrm Prfrmnc Hnrs Spnsh III 85; Cert Of Merit Clsrm Achvt 84; Liberal Arts Coll; Spnsh Tchr.

BAKER, ROSEMARY; Cathedral HS; W Springfield, MA; (Y); 29/536; Political Wkr; SADD; VP Frsh Cls; Trk; Hon Roll; NHS; Acdmc Exclnc Algbra 84-86; Acdmc Exclnc Eurpn Hstry 84; Wstrn Mass Trck Awd 85-86; Bowdoin Coll; Med.

BAKSHI, VAISHALI; Buckingham Browne & Nichols HS; Waltham, MA; (Y); 2/101; Debate Tm; Pres Spanish Clb; Chorus; JV Bsktbl; JV Lcrss; JV Socr; Hon Roll; Ntl Merit SF; Pres Schlr; Harvard; Neurobio.

BALAS, CHRYSA; Lawrence Acad; Lowell, MA; (Y); Spanish Clb; Chorus; Yrbk Sprt Ed; Yrbk Stf; High Hon Roll; Hon Roll; JV Bsktbl; L Ice Hcky; L Lcrss; JV Socr; Prctrshp 85-86; Peer Cnslr 85-86; Vol Cnslr On Luk Htline 85-86; Georgetown; Psych.

BALDI, DIANE M; Bridgewater-Raynham Regional HS; Raynham, MA; (Y); 79/361; MA Coll Art; Comm.

BALDI, JAMES; Boston College HS; Quincy, MA; (Y); 115/300; Cmnty Wkr; Key Clb; SADD; Im Bsbl; Im Bsktbl; Im Ftbl; Im Vllybl; Hon Roll; Acadmc Excel Algebra I 83-84.

BALDO, KATIE; Foxboro HS; Foxboro, MA; (Y); Band; Concert Band; Jazz Band; Mrchg Band; Symp Band; Hon Roll; Music Ed.

BALDWIN, ELIZABETH; Milford HS; Milford, MA; (Y); 128/299; Htl Mgt.

BALDWIN, SUZANNE; Pittsfield HS; Pittsfield, MA; (Y); Exploring; French Clb; Var L Swmmng; Var L Trk; Hon Roll.

BALELO, GINA; Christopher Columbus HS; Boston, MA; (S); 9/22; Rep Soph Cls; Rep Stu Cncl; Mgr Ftbl; Cit Awd; Stu Cncl Rep Awd 85; Ftbl Mgr Var Ltr 83; Balboa Travel; Travel Agnt.

BALENTINE, ELLEN; Lynn Classical HS; Lynn, MA; (Y); 6/170; Church Yth Grp; Spanish Clb; SADD; Chorus; Yrbk Stf; Rep Jr Cls; High Hon Roll; NHS; Ntl Merit Ltr; Pep Clb; Cntmprary Affrs Clb 85-86; Mr & Mrs Pgnt 86; Wellesley; Comp Sci.

BALESTER, WENDY; Randolph HS; Randolph, MA; (Y); 52/351; Church Yth Grp; Civic Clb; Cmnty Wkr; Drama Clb; French Clb; Intnl Clb; Library Aide; SADD; Teachers Aide; Drm & Bgl; State Scholarship 86-87; Advisory Award 85-86; Northeastern U; Law.

BALEWICZ, JEFFREY D; Boston Coll HS; Hanover, MA; (Y); 67/300; Cmnty Wkr; French Clb; Key Clb; Ski Clb; SADD; Var Crs Cntry; Var Swmmng; Hon Roll; Arch.

BALLOU, ANNE; Saugus HS; Saugus, MA; (Y); Pep Clb; SADD; Yrbk Stf; Off Jr Cls; Off Sr Cls; High Hon Roll; Hon Roll; Jr NHS; Supr Acdmc Achvt Hon 84; Excllnce Spnsh 85; Sci Cert Mert Chem 85; Bus Mgt.

BALODIMAS, MARIA; Dracut HS; Dracut, MA; (Y); 1/250; Church Yth Grp; Cmnty Wkr; Math Clb; Math Tm; Office Aide; Science Clb; Pres SADD; Church Choir; Nwsp Ed-Chief; Yrbk Phtg; U Of MA Amherst Chancellors Schlrshp Awd 86; Acad Excllnc Awds; Phillips Ardover Acad Smmr Session 85.

BALUTIS, JOHN M; Cardinal Spellman HS; Bridgewater, MA; (Y); 32/208; Am Leg Boys St; Var Bsbl; Var Capt Bsktbl; Var Ftbl; Hon Roll; NHS; Bus.

BAMBAKIDOU, LISA; Cushins Acad; Torrington, CT; (Y); 10/108; Yrbk Phtg; VP Frsh Cls; Pres Soph Cls; Sec Stu Cncl; Var Capt Bsktbl; Var Capt Sftbl; Var Capt Vllybl; Schlr Athlt Grls 86-Cstng Acad 86; Omar Pollick Schlrshp 86; Merrimack Coll.

BAMFORD, TIM; Burlington HS; Burlington, MA; (Y); 160/317; Pres VP Aud/Vis; Church Yth Grp; SADD; Yrbk Stf; Lit Mag; Off Frsh Cls; Hon Roll; Comm.

BANASIESKI, MARK; Smith Acad; Hatfield, MA; (S); Var Golf; High Hon Roll; Hon Roll.

BANKS, BRYAN; Boston Latin Schl; Boston, MA; (Y); 20/274; Key Clb; Latin Clb; Ski Clb; Concert Band; Jazz Band; Mrchg Band; Yrbk Sprt Ed; Trs Sr Cls; Hon Roll; NHS; Clss Of 85 Awd; Ehren Urkunde Awd; Cert Hnrble Merit Ntl Latin Exam; Harvard U; Pre-Med.

BANKS, CHANDRA M; Cambridge Rindge & Latin HS; Cambridge, MA; (Y); Church Yth Grp; Church Choir; Yrbk Stf; Hon Roll; Cmmndtn Natl Achvt Pgm Outstndg Negro Stu 85; Lwyr.

BANKS, CHERYL; Fitchburg HS; Fitchburg, MA; (Y); 10/206; Library Aide; High Hon Roll; NHS; Red Cross Aide; SADD; Gold Ltr 3.6 GPA 86; Top 10 Pct Cls; Fitchburg ST Coll; Elem Educ.

BANNISTER, BRIAN; Taunton HS; Taunton, MA; (Y); DECA; Bus.

BANNISTER, JANE; Bartlett HS; Webster, MA; (Y); 3/166; Church Yth Grp; Spanish Clb; L Capt Crs Cntry; L Trk; High Hon Roll; VP NHS; Yth Ldrshp Slte 85-86; Med Crrs Clb 85-86; Med.

BANVILLE, DONNA; BMC Durfee HS; Fall River, MA; (Y); Church Yth Grp; Drama Clb; French Clb; Rep Soph Cls; Rep Jr Cls; Rep Sr Cls; JV Sftbl; JV Trk; JV Vllybl; NHS; Psych.

BARBER, TRACY; St Mary HS; Lynn, MA; (Y); 20/91; Pres Sr Cls; Var Capt Bsktbl; Var Powder Puff Ftbl; Hon Roll; NHS; Chld Psych.

BARBER, TRACY; Turners Falls HS; Montague, MA; (Y); AFS; Girl Scts; Hon Roll; Comp Pgm.

BARCA, AMY; Bishop Feehan HS; Foxboro, MA; (Y); 9/250; Church Yth Grp; Hosp Aide; School Play; Sec Frsh Cls; Sec Soph Cls; Rep Jr Cls; Sr Cls; Sec Stu Cncl; NHS; Ntl Merit Ltr; Boston Coll; Elem Educ.

BARCHARD, MICHAEL R; Woburn SR HS; Woburn, MA; (Y); 46/543; Boys Clb Am; Church Yth Grp; French Clb; Hon Roll; NHS; Merrimack Coll; Acctg.

BARCK, TIMOTHY J; Westbridge HS; Lowell, MA; (Y); 2/14; Service Clb; Stat Bsktbl; CC Awd; Hon Roll; Sec VP NHS; Ntl Merit Schol; Sal; Chrmn Chess Clb; Yrbk Stf; Rep Jr Cls; Comp Vision Schlrshp Awd 86; U Of WI; Mech Engrng.

BARCOMB, STEVEN; Hampshire Regional HS; Southampton, MA; (Y); 17/185; Rep Am Leg Boys St; Boy Scts; Sec 4-H; SADD; High Hon Roll; Eagle Scout 85; Mech Engr.

BARD, AIMEE; Lincoln-Sudbury Regional HS; Sudbury, MA; (Y); French Clb; Key Clb; Spanish Clb; Chorus; Yrbk Stf; Rep Stu Cncl.

BARDWELL, ROBERT; Frontier Regional HS; Whately, MA; (Y); Pres Trs 4-H; Office Aide; Lit Mag; Hst Frsh Cls; Hst Soph Cls; VP Jr Cls; Stu Cncl; Var Mgr(s); NHS; Prfct Atten Awd; Clss Rep For Mass Stu Govt Pay Rep 85-86; Sec & Mbr Of Mass Rgnl Stu Advsry Cncl 85-86; Adm.

BARKER, SOCTT; Silver Lake Regional HS; Kingston, MA; (Y); 29/300; Math Clb; Chorus; Var Tennis; Hon Roll; Commnctns.

BARKHOUSE, LEE-ANN; Franklin HS; Franklin, MA; (Y); Pres OEA; Ski Clb; Mgr Bsktbl; Cheerleading; Coach Actv; Gym; Score Keeper; 3rd Pl ST Typng Comptn 83; Fashn.

BARLETTA, BONNIE; Matignon HS; Medford, MA; (Y); Drama Clb; School Play; Rep Soph Cls; Rep Sr Cls; Off Stu Cncl; Capt Var Bsktbl; Var L Sftbl; Im Vllybl; Hon Roll; St Josephs Coll; Bus Adm.

BARLOW, AVLIN; Georgetown JR SR HS; Georgetown, MA; (Y); 1/85; Sec Band; Jazz Band; Mrchg Band; School Play; Yrbk Ed-Chief; Bausch & Lomb Sci Awd; Pres NHS; Val; Harvard Bk Awd, RPI Awd 84-85; MA Cmmnwlth Schlr 86; WPI; Bio-Tech.

BARNABO, SUSAN; Marian HS; Natick, MA; (Y); 15/177; Mgr Church Yth Grp; Mgr Girl Scts; Red Cross Aide; Mgr Yrbk Stf; Hon Roll; Mgr NHS; NEDT Awd; Cert Hnrbl Merit Cum Laude Ntl Latin Exm 83; Worcester Polytech Inst; Engnr.

BARNES, HEATHER; Walnut Hill Schl Of Performing Arts; Westfield, MA; (Y); Dance Clb; Intnl Clb; Off Soph Cls; Off Jr Cls; Off Sr Cls; Rep-USA Wrld Irish Dncno Chmpsnshps 84; Prfrmd-Schl Dance Gala 85 & 86; Chrstms Dnc Cncrt 84 &85; Prof Bllt Dncr.

BARNETT, BARRY; Sharon HS; Sharon, MA; (Y); 10/210; Chess Clb; Computer Clb; Math Tm; Spanish Clb; Nwsp Stf; Hon Roll; Ntl Merit SF; Amer Instnl Math Exam 86; Hnr Roll For Amer HS Math Exam 86; Cornell; Physics.

BARNEY, CHERYL; Blackstone Valley Reg Voc Tech HS; Whitinsville, MA; (Y); Library Aide; SADD; Hon Roll; Phtgrphy.

BARNEY, CHRISTINE; Boston Latin HS; Jamaica Plain, MA; (Y); 136/283; Sec VP Camera Clb; Hosp Aide; JA; High Hon Roll; Joseph P Kennedy Awd/Scholar 86; Northeastern U.

BARO, EDDIE; Nashoba Valley Technical HS; Townsend, MA; (Y); Boy Scts; Ski Clb; Ftbl; High Hon Roll; Hon Roll; Elctrncs.

BARON, ELIZABETH; Holyoke Catholic HS; Chicopee, MA; (Y); Art Clb; Cmnty Wkr; Spanish Clb; Stage Crew; High Hon Roll; Hon Roll; NHS; Arch.

BARONE, LISA; St Clare HS; Hyde Park, MA; (Y); Cmnty Wkr; JA; Sec Frsh Cls; Sec Jr Cls; Most Effrt Hist; High Avrg Spnsh; Boston Bus; Typg III.

BARR, LUKAS; Lincoln-Sudbury Regional HS; Sudbury, MA; (Y); German Clb; Math Tm; Orch; Nwsp Rptr; Trk; Bus Law.

BARR, PATRICIA; Whitman Hanson Reg HS; Hanson, MA; (Y); 12/298; Pres AFS; Camp Fr Inc; Church Yth Grp; Hosp Aide; Yrbk Bus Mgr; Yrbk Stf; Stu Cncl; Socr; Hon Roll; Jr NHS; Citzn Scholar Comm 82-86; Massasoit CC; Bus Adm.

BARREIRA, SHARON; Westport HS; Westport, MA; (Y); Dance Clb; JA; Ski Clb; Stage Crew; Variety Show; Yrbk Stf; Wt Lftg; High Hon Roll; Hon Roll; NHS; Bus Ed Awd 86; Ntl Hnr Soc 86; Secrtrl.

BARRETT, DANIEL; St Johns Prep; Lawrence, MA; (Y); Boys Clb Am; Church Yth Grp; Hon Roll; NHS; Cmmnctns.

BARRETT, PATRICIA; North Quincy HS; Quincy, MA; (Y); 89/366; Girl Scts; Hosp Aide; Spanish Clb; Yrbk Stf; Stu Cncl; Var Crs Cntry; Var Trk; Hon Roll; All Schlstc Grls X-Cntry Tm 84-85; JR Olympcs X-Cntry Ntchmpnshp Awd 84-85; Duke U; Sprts Med.

BARRINGER, SCOTT B; Belmont HS; Wellesley, MA; (Y); Am Leg Boys St; Varsity Clb; Chorus; Jr Cls; Sr Cls; Ice Hcky; Lcrss; Socr; Hon Roll; Certfd Scuba Diver PADI 85; Mass Midgt Hcky Tm 86.

BARRIONUEVO, CARLOS; Phillips Acad; Lincolnshire, IL; (Y); Band; Concert Band; Ftbl; Socr; Wrstlng; Hon Roll; Ntl Merit Ltr; Ntl Hispnc Schlrshp Awd 85-86; U Chicago; Hist.

BARRON, LAURA M; Norwell HS; Norwell, MA; (Y); 6/179; Church Yth Grp; Spanish Clb; Orch; Yrbk Stf; Rep Stu Cncl; Var Tennis; High Hon Roll; Arts Recog & Tlnt Srch Hnrbl Ment 85; Hghst Score Math Olympd Tst 85; Grtr Boston Yth Symphny Orchstra; Julliard Schl Of Msc; Msc Prfrm.

BARROS, EMANUEL M; Taunton HS; Taunton, MA; (Y); Boys Clb Am; Ski Clb; SADD; Nwsp Stf; Yrbk Stf; VP Frsh Cls; VP Soph Cls; VP Jr Cls; VP Sr Cls; Rep Stu Cncl; Hon Roll 86; Bus.

BARROWS, KATIE; Uxbridge HS; Uxbridge, MA; (Y); French Clb; Teachers Aide; High Hon Roll; Hon Roll; NHS; Cosmtlgy.

BARROWS, KEITH R; Murdock HS; Winchendon, MA; (Y); Am Leg Boys St; Var Ftbl; Var Trk; Hon Roll; Outstndng Running Back Awd 85; U Of MA; Sports Mgmnt.

BARROWS, KETARAH; Uxbridge HS; Uxbridge, MA; (Y); Library Aide; Teachers Aide; High Hon Roll; Hon Roll; Prfct Atten Awd; Cosmotology.

BARRY, CHRISTOPHER; Boston College HS; Wollaston, MA; (Y); Boy Scts; Church Yth Grp; Intnl Clb; JA; Off Key Clb; Political Wkr; Service Clb; Off SADD; Nwsp Bus Mgr; Lit Mag; Law.

BARRY, DEAN; Haverhill HS; Haverhill, MA; (Y); 173/416; Church Yth Grp; Varsity Clb; Var L Bsbl; Var L Ftbl; Var Trk; Var Wt Lftg; Var Wrstlng; Hon Roll; MIP Ftbl 86; 4-Time All Star Little Lge Bsbl 79-83; Fitchburg ST; Phys Ed.

BARRY, DIANE MARIE; Scituate HS; Scituate, MA; (Y); 104/277; Nwsp Stf; Sec Jr Cls; Sec Sr Cls; Var Capt Fld Hcky; Var Capt Powder Puff Ftbl; Var Capt Trk; Hon Roll; Church Yth Grp; Nwsp Rptr; Coach Actv; Prom Queen 85; S Shore League Hockey All Star 85; Hmcmng Queen 85; Bridgewater ST Coll; Physcl Ed.

BARRY, JOHN E; Everett HS; Everett, MA; (Y); 2/286; Boy Scts; Trs Letterman Clb; Pres Science Clb; Yrbk Phtg; Var Bsbl; Capt Socr; Sec NHS; Sal; NASSP Schlrshp Awd 86; Chancellors Tlnt Awd UMASS Amherst 86; RPI; Biomed Engrng.

BARRY, LYNNE M; Notre Pame Academy HS; Cohasset, MA; (Y); 24/111; Library Aide; Varsity Clb; Rep Soph Cls; Bsktbl; Sftbl; Trk; Vllybl; NHS; Law.

BARRY, VERONICA; Ware HS; Ware, MA; (Y); Art Clb; Drama Clb; 4-H; Library Aide; SADD; Color Guard; School Play; Hon Roll; Excllnc World Hstry & Sci 84; Psych.

BARRY, WILLIAM P; Watertown HS; Watertown, MA; (Y); 11/260; Am Leg Boys St; Nwsp Ed-Chief; Lit Mag; Rep Jr Cls; Var Capt Bsktbl; Var L Ftbl; NHS; Ntl Merit Ltr; Boys Clb Am; Cmnty Wkr; Amhrst Coll Bk Awd 86; HS Schlr Athlt 86; Superior Court Bys ST 86; Jrnlsm.

BARSAM, CHARLES; Belmont HS; Belmont, MA; (Y); 60/292; Church Yth Grp; PAVAS; SADD; JV Coach Actv; JV Var Swmmng; Tennis; Hon Roll; Grad Wth Hnrs-Hly Trnty Chrch Schl 86; Schlrshp Awd-St Nrsess Smnry 86; Med.

BARSHAK, JASON; Malden Catholic HS; Malden, MA; (Y); 1/180; Pres Intnl Clb; Trs VP Temple Yth Grp; VP Band; Yrbk Stf; Kiwanis Awd; NHS; Ntl Merit Ltr; Rotary Awd; St Schlr; Val; Eng Awd; Bst Cl TV & GM; Math Club High Scoring Fresh & Soph; Tufts U Medford MA.

BARSTOW, MATTHEW; Hopkins Acad; Hadley, MA; (Y); 6/46; Church Yth Grp; Spanish Clb; Band; Concert Band; Jazz Band; Mrchg Band; Pep Band; Trs Frsh Cls; Trs Soph Cls; High Hon Roll; Lane Prz Spkg Cont 84-86; Schl Match Wits Tm 84-86; Ntl Hon Soc VP 86-87; Psych.

BARSTOW, THOMAS J; Falmouth HS; Teaticket, MA; (Y); 2/350; Band; Jazz Band; Mrchg Band; NHS; Boy Scts; Natl Olympd Sci 83; Natl Socty Profssnl Engr Boston U Schlrshp 86; Boston U; Mech Engr.

BARSZEWSKI, TED; Ludlow HS; Ludlow, MA; (Y); 27/279; Drama Clb; Scholastic Bowl; School Play; Stage Crew; Variety Show; Bsktbl; High Hon Roll; Hon Roll; Ntl Merit Ltr; NEDT Awd; U MA; Fin.

BARTELL, WANDA; Jeremiah E Burke HS; Dorchester, MA; (Y); Church Yth Grp; Dance Clb; Drama Clb; 4-H; FBLA; Varsity Clb; Chorus; Church Choir; School Musical; School Play; Stdnt Ldrshp Cert 85-86; Bus Mgmt.

BARTFAY, ANNE; Northfield Mt Hermon HS; Fountain Vly, CA; (Y); Debate Tm; Orch; Yrbk Stf; Stu Cncl; JV Socr; Var Swmmng; Capt Trk; High Hon Roll; Hon Roll; Cum Laude Soc 86; Mc Burney Prz 86; Cornell U.

BARTKUS, PAULA; North HS; Worcester, MA; (Y); 17/208; Varsity Clb; Nwsp Rptr; Stu Cncl; Capt Bsktbl; Var Fld Hcky; Var Socr; Var Socr; Elks Awd; Hon Roll; NHS; Tlgrm & Gztt Bsktbll All-Star 86; Hugh O Briien Yth Ldrshp Smnr 84; Essy Cntst Wnnr Cr Dy Wrcster 85; Brandeis U; Educ.

BARTLETT, ABBE; Northfield Mount Herman Schl; Manheim, PA; (Y); Church Yth Grp; Pep Clb; Drill Tm; School Musical; Lit Mag; Var Trk; High Hon Roll; Hon Roll; Cum Laude Soc 86; Support Group Women Math,Sci 85-86; Peer Ed Role Playing 85; CT Coll.

BARTLETT, DIANE; Lawrence HS; Lawrence, MA; (Y); 1/400; Church Yth Grp; Hosp Aide; VP Frsh Cls; VP Soph Cls; Pres Jr Cls; Sec Sr Cls; Var Fld Hcky; Var Capt Trk; High Hon Roll; NHS; Harvard Bk Awd 86; MVP Indr Trk 86; MVP Otdr Trk 85.

BARTLEY, SUSAN; Holyoke Catholic HS; Holyoke, MA; (Y); VP Latin Clb; Spanish Clb; SADD; Nwsp Stf; Yrbk Stf; Sec Jr Cls; Sec Sr Cls; High Hon Roll; Hon Roll; NHS.

BARTOLOMEI, THOMAS; Shepherd Hill Regional HS; Dudley, MA; (Y); Am Leg Boys St; Church Yth Grp; School Play; Variety Show; Var Capt Bsbl; Var Capt Bsktbl; JV Socr; Hon Roll; NHS; Rotary Awd; USA Today All Bsktbl Team Of MA 85-86; Providence Coll; Engrng.

BARTON, AUDREY; Lenox Memorial HS; Lenox, MA; (Y); 2/63; Pres Church Yth Grp; Concert Band; Mgr Stage Crew; Crs Cntry; High Hon Roll; NHS; Ntl Merit Ltr; Polytech Inst Math And Sci Awd 86; Bates Clb Awd 86; Soclgy.

BARTON, DANI; Dand Hall HS; Canada; (Y); Cmnty Wkr; Chorus; School Musical; Swing Chorus; Yrbk Stf; Sftbl; Vllybl; Hon Roll; Frnch Exchange 85; Bennington Coll.

BARTOSCH, KRISTEN; Reading Memorial HS; Reading, MA; (Y); 40/350; Band; Concert Band; Drm Mjr(t); Jazz Band; Mrchg Band; Orch; School Musical; Bsktbl; High Hon Roll; Band Tres 84-86; CCD Tchr 85-86; Most Vlbl JR Band, Most Imprvd Plyr 86.

BARUNAS, KRISTINA M; Canton HS; Canton, MA; (Y); 23/240; Library Aide; Office Aide; Pep Clb; Varsity Clb; Chorus; Stage Crew; Cheerleading; Crs Cntry; Powder Puff Ftbl; Hon Roll; Pauls Dstrbtrs Inc, Ord Eastern Star Schlrshps 86; Century Clb 85-86; St Anselms Coll; Bus Mgmnt.

BASILE, DARIN; Waltham SR HS; Boston, MA; (Y); Aud/Vis; Library Aide; ROTC; Drill Tm; High Hon Roll; Hon Roll; NHS; Naval Acad; Aerosp Engrng.

BASILE, JENNIFER; Our Lady Of Nazareth Acad; Stoneham, MA; (Y); 10/87; Drama Clb; Science Clb; Ski Clb; Spanish Clb; SADD; Chorus; School Musical; VP Frsh Cls; Cheerleading; Trk; Chamber Singers 85-86; Music Awd 85-86; Berklee Coll Music; Music.

BASILE, MARGARET; West Roxbury HS; Roslindale, MA; (S); Hon Roll; NHS; Prfct Atten Awd.

BASKIN, HOSEA T; Northampton HS; Leeds, MA; (Y); Debate Tm; Science Clb; Speech Tm; Nwsp Rptr; Ntl Merit SF; Computer Clb; Lit Mag; Schlrshp 82-85; Math.

BASQUIAT, LOUIS; Marlboro HS; Marlboro, MA; (Y); Boys Clb Am; JV Bsktbl; Hon Roll; Bus Mgr.

BASS, DAVID R; Randolph HS; Randolph, MA; (Y); Am Leg Boys St; Boy Scts; Pres Church Yth Grp; Math Tm; Pres Trs Band; Concert Band; Jazz Band; Mrchg Band; NHS; Ntl Merit SF; Natl Hstry Day ST Wnr 86; Bus.

BASS, DENISE; Bellingham JR SR Mem HS; Bellingham, MA; (Y); DECA; Drill Tm; Nwsp Phtg; Yrbk Stf; Stu Cncl; Twrlr; Hon Roll; MA ST 3 Baton Grnd Champ 86; Engrng.

BASTARACHE, NANCY; Waltham SR HS; Boston, MA; (Y); Church Yth Grp; High Hon Roll.

BASTIAANS, SALLY; Easthampton HS; Easthampton, MA; (Y); 6/152; Am Leg Aux Girls St; French Clb; Hosp Aide; Teachers Aide; Chorus; Nwsp Ed-Chief; Nwsp Rptr; Yrbk Rptr; Yrbk Stf; High Hon Roll; Grls Al-ST Amer Lgn Alt 84-85; Natl Hnr Socty 84-86; Co-Edtr-Chf Nwspr 85-86; Law.

BASTIANELLI, LISA MARIE; St Clare HS; Roslindale, MA; (Y); 45/150; Hosp Aide; Variety Show; Yrbk Phtg; Yrbk Stf; Score Keeper; Elks Awd; High Hon Roll; Hon Roll; NHS.

BATEMAN, TIMOTHY CHARLES; Xaverian Brothers HS; Marshfield, MA; (Y); 7/213; Church Yth Grp; Drama Clb; Teachers Aide; School Musical; Yrbk Stf; Capt Var Socr; High Hon Roll; Sec NHS; Ntl Merit Ltr; Sfflk U Bk Awd 85; Gradtn Awds Engl, Frnch & Soc Stds 86; Prsh Yth Schlrshp 86; Columbia U; Law.

BATOR, BRIAN; Ludlow HS; Ludlow, MA; (Y); Art Clb; Boy Scts; Church Yth Grp; Civic Clb; Cmnty Wkr; French Clb; School Play; Nwsp Rptr; Nwsp Stf; Var Mgr(s); Adv Dsgn.

BATOR, MELISSA; Ludlow HS; Ludlow, MA; (S); 29/280; JCL; Nwsp Ed-Chief; Yrbk Sprt Ed; Rep Frsh Cls; Rep Sr Cls; Var Bsktbl; Var Capt Sftbl; Im Vllybl; Big Brthr-Sistr Pgm 84-85; Wstrn New Englnd Coll; Psychlgy.

BATTINELLI, ELISABETH M; Somerville HS; Somerville, MA; (Y); Intnl Clb; Sec Latin Clb; Sec Math Clb; Pres Science Clb; Rptr Nwsp Rptr; Rep Frsh Cls; Rep Soph Cls; Pres Stu Cncl; DAR Awd; High Hon Roll; 2nd Pl Intl Sci & Engrng Fair 86; Navy Resrch Scholar 86; 1st Pl MA ST Sci Fair 86; Bio.

BATTISTA, FRANK; Newton Catholic HS; Newton, MA; (Y); 2/50; Boys Clb Am; VP Church Yth Grp; Cmnty Wkr; Variety Show; Rep Frsh Cls; Rep Soph Cls; Rep Jr Cls; Rep Stu Cncl; Var Bsbl; Var Bsktbl; Sr Yth Awd 85; Mst Vlbl Plyr Bsbl 84-86; Bus Adm.

BATTISTA, LISA; Holy Name Central Catholic HS; Auburn, MA; (Y); 7/256; Dance Clb; Pep Clb; Teachers Aide; Varsity Clb; Cheerleading; Kiwanis Awd; NHS; WPI Schlrshp 86; WPI; Comp Sci.

BATTISTA, REBECCA; Shepherd Hill Regional HS; Dudley, MA; (Y); 4/129; Pres Church Yth Grp; School Musical; Trs Stu Cncl; High Hon Roll; Trs NHS; Ntl Merit Ltr; Pres Schlr; U PA; Bus Adm.

BAUCHMAN, LORI; Methuen HS; Methuen, MA; (Y); 4/300; Intnl Clb; Band; Concert Band; Drm Mjr(t); Jazz Band; Mrchg Band; NHS; Hosp Aide; Pep Band; School Musical; Outstndg Mrchr Awd 84-85; SOAR 84; Wellesley Coll Bk Awd 86; Child Cnsnlg.

BAUM, JEFF; Newton North HS; Newtonville, MA; (Y); Computer Clb; Math Tm; Political Wkr; Ski Clb; Band; JV Socr; JV Tennis; Hon Roll; Ntl Merit Ltr; MA Assn Of Math Leags-Cert Of Merit 85.

BAUMANN, ROBERTA; Lenox Memorial HS; Lenox, MA; (Y); 15/60; Church Yth Grp; Band; Yrbk Stf; Stu Cncl; Var Socr; Var Sftbl; Hon Roll; Bentley Coll; Mrktng.

BAXENDALE, GREG; Bishop Connally HS; Swansea, MA; (Y); Cmnty Wkr; Drama Clb; School Play; Stage Crew; Variety Show; Nwsp Stf; Capt Var Bsbl; Var Bsktbl; MVP Bsbl 85-86; Salt Erth Awd, Drama Awd 86; U NH; Pol Sci.

BAXTER, CHRIS; New Bedford HS; New Bedford, MA; (Y); 19/599; SADD; Yrbk Stf; Rep Stu Cncl; Crs Cntry; Trk; NHS; St Schlr; Drama Clb; Letterman Clb; Varsity Clb; Rgnl All Star Tm 85-86; Tufts U; Lawyer.

BAXTER, DONNA; Mohawk Trail Regional HS; Ashfield, MA; (Y); Trs AFS; Debate Tm; Political Wkr; Yrbk Sprt Ed; Stat Bsktbl; Var Fld Hcky; JV Tennis; Hon Roll; Hopwood Smmr Schlrshp Prgrm 85; U Of Lowell; Elec Engr.

BAXTER, IAN; New Bedford HS; New Bedford, MA; (Y); 74/700; Boys Clb Am; Cmnty Wkr; JCL; Varsity Clb; Var Capt Bsbl; Var JV Bsktbl; Var Coach Actv; Prfct Atten Awd; Bus.

BAZIN, STEVEN; Blackstone Valley Regional Vo Tech; Sutton, MA; (Y); Church Yth Grp; Computer Clb; SADD; Hon Roll; Compt Sci.

BEALL, KEVINA; Middlesex Schl; Palm Beach, FL; (Y); Scholastic Bowl; Varsity Clb; Yrbk Phtg; Lit Mag; Var Fld Hcky; Var Mgr(s); Var Socr; JV Tennis; Spnsh Awd 84; Bylss Cup Athltc & Acad Awd 84; Ntl Merit Sci Awd 84.

BEALS, SUSAN; Our Lady Of Nazareth Acad; Wilmington, MA; (Y); Ski Clb; Spanish Clb; SADD; Chorus; School Musical; School Play; Socr; Trk; Cert Of Educ Dvlpmnt Ntl 84; Outstndt Crft Stu 84 & 85; Sccr Awd, Concrt Chr 86; Psych.

BEAN, RITA; St Gregorys HS; Dorchester, MA; (Y); Church Yth Grp; Drama Clb; 4-H; Girl Scts; Hosp Aide; JA; Math Clb; Pep Clb; Spanish Clb; Varsity Clb; MVP-BSKTBL/Capt Of All-Star Team 85-86; 2dn An Shoot W/Stars Celbrty Bsktbll Game; Phys Thrpy.

BEANDO, CHERIE; Blackstone Valley Reg Vo Tech; Webster, MA; (Y); Library Aide; SADD; Yrbk Stf; Pres Schlr; Shp Schlrshp 86; Nichols Coll; Mngmnt Inf Sys.

BEANE, JENNIFER; Silver Lake Reg HS; Kingston, MA; (Y); Girl Scts; Hosp Aide; Yrbk Sprt Ed; Trs Frsh Cls; Sec Soph Cls; VP Jr Cls; VP Sr Cls; Stu Cncl; Socr; Cit Awd; Art Globe Shw Awd Gold Key; Natl Stu Cncl Awd; Slvr Awd Girl Scout; Westfield ST Coll; Comm Art.

BEARDSLEY, KATHRYN; Acton-Boxboro Regional HS; Acton, MA; (Y); 44/428; AFS; Church Yth Grp; Dance Clb; Drama Clb; Var Cheerleading; Powder Puff Ftbl; Hon Roll; NHS; Chem.

BEATO, RAFAEL; Madison Park HS; Boston, MA; (Y); Church Yth Grp; Hon Roll; Mgr NHS; Ntl Merit Ltr; Prfct Atten Awd; Schlrshp NE U 86; U MA Acdmc Achvt Awd 85; Achvt Hon Albgra II 84; Northeastern U; Elec Engrng.

BEATO, ROSA; English HS; Boston, MA; (Y); Hon Roll; Prfct Atten Awd; Alumni Schlrshp 86; Bay ST JC; Exec Secy.

BEATON, CAROLYN; Acad Of Notre Dame; Tewksbury, MA; (Y); 41/78; Cmnty Wkr; German Clb; Pep Clb; Bus Mgnt.

BEATTY, KAREN; Natick HS; Natick, MA; (Y); 22/400; Church Yth Grp; Nwsp Stf; Stu Cncl; JV Capt Bsktbl; Var Capt Vllybl; High Hon Roll; Hon Roll; Jr NHS; VP NHS; SADD; All Star Vlybl Leag 85-86; Engl.

BEAUCHESNE, P JONATHAN; Central Catholic HS; Methuen, MA; (Y); 8/259; Computer Clb; Var Bsbl; JV Crs Cntry; JV Trk; High Hon Roll; NHS; Prfct Atten Awd; Im Bsktbl; Im Vllybl; Pres Schlr; High Schltc Achvt Awd Relgn 84-85; Qrtrly Acadmc Schlrshp 84-85; Legn Of Hnr Awd 85-86; Holy Cross; Bio.

BEAUDET, CATHLEEN A; Auburn HS; Auburn, MA; (Y); 55/180; Church Yth Grp; Civic Clb; Cmnty Wkr; DECA; FHA; FTA; Pep Clb; Political Wkr; SADD; Varsity Clb; Jennifer Johnson Ed Schlrshp 86; Vrsty Chrldng Awd 83-86; Clss Srvc Awd 82-86; Elem Ed.

BEAUDOIN, ANDREW J; Arlington HS; Arlington, MA; (Y); Am Leg Boys St; Boys Clb Am; Pres French Clb; Math Tm; Model UN; Mrchg Band; Rep Jr Cls; L JV Bsktbl; Stat Crs Cntry; Mgr(s); 1st Pl-Wst Sbrbn Sci Leag Olympd 86; Rgnl Awd-Ntl Frnch Cntst 84.

BEAUDOIN, DANIELLE; Milford HS; Milford, MA; (Y); Church Yth Grp; Drama Clb; Key Clb; SADD; JV Bsktbl; Var Diving; JV Capt Sftbl; Hon Roll; Salve Regina; Bus Admin.

BEAUDOIN, STEVEN P; Bay Path Reg Vo-Tech HS; Charlton City, MA; (Y); Am Leg Boys St; VICA; Var Ftbl; Acad Achvt Awd Hstry 85-86; Army; Lit.

BEAUDRY, DAVID; Tantasqua Regional HS; Fiskdale, MA; (Y); Chess Clb; Im Ftbl; Hon Roll; NHS; Navy Nuclear Power Schl; Nuclr.

BEAULIEU, BECKY; Comprehensive HS; Chicopee, MA; (Y); 17/286; German Clb; VP JA; Hon Roll; Jr NHS; NHS; Nrsng.

BEAUMIER, SANDRA; Uxbridge HS; Uxbridge, MA; (Y); 10/87; Math Tm; Chorus; Yrbk Ed-Chief; Yrbk Rptr; Stu Cncl; L Cheerleading; Tennis; High Hon Roll; Hon Roll; NHS; Eleme D.

BEAUREGARD, TREVOR; Gardner HS; Gardner, MA; (Y); 33/166; Sec Chess Clb; VP DECA; Stage Crew; Var L Bsbl; Var L Bsktbl; Var Capt Ftbl; Cyrille P Landry Mem Schlrshp 86; Wildcat Gridiron Clb Schlrshp 86; Hector Lorion Unsung Plyr Awd Bsbl; Westfield ST Coll.

BEAUSOLEIL, MARK; Blackstone Millville Regional HS; Blackstone, MA; (Y); 4/100; Office Aide; Yrbk Stf; Elks Awd; High Hon Roll; Hon Roll; NHS; Phrmcy.

BEAVERSTOCK, JEFFREY U; Foxboro HS; Foxboro, MA; (Y); Am Leg Boys St; Boy Scts; Church Yth Grp; Debate Tm; Drama Clb; Chorus; Madrigals; School Musical; School Play; Hon Roll; Eagle Sct 85; Dewitt/Wallace Yth Ldrshp Amer Awd 85; Rnr-Up Am Leg Boy Sct Of Yr 86; Sclgy.

BECK, JULIE; Natick HS; Natick, MA; (Y); 21/443; Trs JA; Sec SADD; Nwsp Stf; Yrbk Stf; Sec Stu Cncl; Var Fld Hcky; Im Lcrss; JV Tennis; Hon Roll; NHS; Camp Sewataro Outstndng Cnslr Awd 85; Villanova U.

BECKER, DIANE; Uxbridge HS; N Uxbridge, MA; (Y); 7/81; Math Tm; Varsity Clb; School Play; Ed Yrbk Stf; Rep Pres Stu Cncl; Var L Bsktbl; Var L Fld Hcky; Var L Tennis; High Hon Roll; NHS; Hnrb Mntn All Star Tnns Tm 86; Med.

BECKETT, SALLY; Dennis Yarmouth HS; S Dennis, MA; (Y); Church Yth Grp; Dance Clb; Ski Clb; School Musical; School Play; Variety Show; Hon Roll; Cape Cod Coonsrvtry Music Schlrshp 79-86; 5 Natl Awd Natl Piano Plyng Adtns; Intl Awd Early Bach Slctn; Oberlin OH; Music.

BECKWITH, NADINE; Holy Name Central Catholic HS; Auburn, MA; (Y); Drama Clb; School Musical; School Play; High Hon Roll; Natl Sci Olympd 4th Pl; Forgn Lang Dept Awd French; Math Dept Awd Comp I.

BEDARD, AARON; New Bedford HS; Acushnet, MA; (Y); 5/700; Am Leg Boys St; Boys Clb Am; JCL; NFL; Stu Cncl; Capt L Bsktbl; JV Crs Cntry; L Trk; High Hon Roll; NHS; Stdnt Rep Schl Comm 86-87; Stdnt Congrss 86-87; MA Bay ST Games Bsktbl 86; Chem Engrng.

BEDARD, PETER J; Oakmont Regional HS; Westminster, MA; (Y); 16/120; Am Leg Boys St; Aud/Vis; Math Tm; Chorus; Var Bsktbl; Var Trk; Villanova PA; Engrng.

BEDARD, WENDY J; David Prouty HS; E Brookfield, MA; (Y); 7/168; SADD; Band; Color Guard; Flag Corp; Mrchg Band; Yrbk Stf; Hon Roll; Wht Swtr Awd Acdm Excllnc 85; SR Hon Soc 86; Worcester ST Coll; Finc.

BEEBE, KIRSTEN; Westfield HS; Westfield, MA; (Y); 38/357; Var Fld Hcky; JV Socr; Var L Swmmng; Var L Trk.

BEEMAN, CATHY; Tantasqua Regional HS; Sturbridge, MA; (Y); Band; Concert Band; Mrchg Band; Orch; Pep Band; School Musical; Symp Band; Yrbk Stf; Hon Roll; Principls Atten Awd 84-86; Culinary Inst; Culinary Arts.

BEGLEY, KRISTEN; Notre Dame Acad; Hanover, MA; (Y); Debate Tm; Library Aide; Ski Clb; Spanish Clb; Chorus; School Play; Nwsp Rptr; Yrbk Stf; Im Socr; Mrn Biol.

BELAND, BRIAN D; Wachusett Regional HS; Sterling, MA; (Y); 90/400; Am Leg Boys St; High Hon Roll; Hon Roll; NY Inst Of Tech Nnr & Chllng Schlrshp 86-87; NY Inst Of Tech; Arch.

BELAND, STEPHEN; Central Catholic HS; Lowell, MA; (Y); 13/215; Pres VP Church Yth Grp; Pres Science Clb; Pres Varsity Clb; Rep Stu Cncl; Capt Var Crs Cntry; Capt Var Trk; Hon Roll; Greg Alan Serio Mem Schlrshp 86; Cros Cnty Coaches Awd 86; Prncpls Schlrshp 85; Merrimack Coll; Elec Engr.

BELANGER, EMILY; Salem HS; Salem, MA; (Y); Church Yth Grp; Cheerleading; Fld Hcky; Hon Roll; Secy.

BELANGER, TIMOTHY; Leominster HS; Leominster, MA; (Y); 1/450; Am Leg Boys St; Off Church Yth Grp; School Musical; VP Soph Cls; VP Jr Cls; Rep Stu Cncl; Var L Crs Cntry; Var L Trk; High Hon Roll; NHS; Harvard Bk Clb Awd 86; Eng,Spnsh Awd 84-86; Engrng.

BELFER, RUSSELL H; Brookline HS; Brookline, MA; (Y); Science Clb; Ski Clb; Temple Yth Grp; Band; Chorus; Ntl Merit SF; Chess Clb; Math Tm; Variety Show; Cit Awd; Lngstcs.

BELISLE, GREG; South Hadley HS; S Hadley, MA; (Y); Ski Clb; Yrbk Stf; Vllybl; U MA; Bus Mngt.

BELIZAIRE, RENETTE; English HS; Boston, MA; (Y); Intnl Clb; JA; Office Aide; Teachers Aide; Stage Crew; Sec Sr Cls; Stu Cncl; Hon Roll; NHS; Prfct Atten Awd; MA Advncd Stds Prgrm 85; Commwlth MA Schlrshp 86; Myrs Schlrshp 86; Schl Almn Schlrshp 86; Emmanuel Coll; Med Lab Sci.

BELL, ANTOINETTE; Beverly HS; Beverly, MA; (Y); 25/374; Church Yth Grp; Cmnty Wkr; Stage Crew; Nwsp Rptr; Nwsp Stf; Lit Mag; Hon Roll; Prfct Atten Awd; DLD Coll London Englnd; Nrsng.

BELL, KRISTEN; Newburyport HS; Newburypt, MA; (Y); 22/186; Model UN; Trs Soph Cls; Trs Jr Cls; Stu Cncl; Capt Cheerleading; Hon Roll; NHS; Stu Cncl Delegate 83-84; Girls Ldr Club 84-86; Chrldng All-Star 85-86; Sci.

BELL, MARLENE; Dracut SR HS; Dracut, MA; (Y); Dance Clb; Sec Sr Cls; Cheerleading; Coach Actv; Cit Awd; Aud/Vis; Church Yth Grp; Office Aide; Variety Show; Nwsp Rptr; Pop Warner Schlrshp 86; Dracut Schlrshp Fndtn 86; Fitchburg ST Coll; Cmmnctns.

BELLINI, KRISTY; Agawam HS; Agawam, MA; (Y); 17/319; Dance Clb; Drama Clb; Ski Clb; Color Guard; Variety Show; Trk; High Hon Roll; Hon Roll; NHS; Natl Typg Awd 84; WNEC; Acctg.

BELLIVEAU, ROBERT; New Bedford HS; New Bedford, MA; (Y); 60/700; Var Bsbl; High Hon Roll; Prfct Atten Awd; Voice Dem Awd; Acted Play Frgn Lang Wk 86; Awds Exc Frgn Lang 85-86.

BELLIVEAU, TRACEY; Fairhaven HS; Fairhaven, MA; (Y); 43/178; Church Yth Grp; Cmnty Wkr; Capt Color Guard; Mrchg Band; Yrbk Stf; Capt Cheerleading; Coach Actv; Trk; Voice Dem Awd; Phys Ther.

BELMARSH, LISA; Weymouth North HS; Weymouth, MA; (Y); 12/323; Ski Clb; Yrbk Ed-Chief; Rep Sr Cls; Rep Stu Cncl; Var Bsktbl; Var Socr; High Hon Roll; Hon Roll; Cmnty Wkr; Office Aide; H S Bst Fml Schlr/Athlt 86; Cert Of Merit-Hgh Hnr-Sci & Math 86; Boston Coll; Lwyr.

BELONGIE, GLENN; Athol HS; Athol, MA; (Y); Civic Clb; Model UN; Science Clb; Var L Bsktbl; Var L Crs Cntry; Var L Trk; Im Vllybl; Elec Engr.

BEMIS, GREGORY H; David Prouty HS; Spencer, MA; (Y); 4/175; Am Leg Boys St; Church Yth Grp; Cmnty Wkr; Spanish Clb; Chorus; School Musical; School Play; High Hon Roll; NHS; Treas Chrs 86-87; Hstry.

BEN-MEIR, AVIV; Sharon HS; Sharon, MA; (Y); Hosp Aide; Math Tm; Model UN; Temple Yth Grp; Nwsp Bus Mgr; Var Socr; Hon Roll; NHS; Phi Alpha Theta Wrtg Awd 86; Lttl Leag Bsbl Coach 85-86; Pre-Med.

BENARD, JENNIFER; Holyoke Catholic HS; Chicopee, MA; (Y); Art Clb; Camera Clb; Cmnty Wkr; Speech Tm.

BENARD, ROBERT; Chicopee Comprehensive HS; Chicopee, MA; (Y); 32/332; Church Yth Grp; Cmnty Wkr; JV Bsbl; Var L Ftbl; Hon Roll; NHS; Chemical Engrng.

BENBENEK, MICHAEL S; Narragansett Regional HS; Templeton, MA; (Y); 10/100; Am Leg Boys St; Boy Scts; Church Yth Grp; Letterman Clb; L Var Bsktbl; Hon Roll; Mu Alp Tht; Sec NHS; Math.

BENDEL, TIM; Marian HS; Framingham, MA; (Y); CAP; JV Ftbl; U CO; Arntcl Engr.

BENEDETTI, MICHAEL; Natick HS; Natick, MA; (Y); 24/399; Math Tm; Band; Lit Mag; Var L Crs Cntry; Hon Roll; NHS; Earth Sci.

BENEDICT, AUGUSTA; Westford Acad; Westford, MA; (Y); 39/225; French Clb; Model UN; Ski Clb; VP Frsh Cls; VP Soph Cls; VP Jr Cls; VP Sr Cls; Fld Hcky; JV Tennis; Hon Roll; Hartwick Clg; Pltcl Sci.

BENEDICT, JOSEPH P; Plymouth-Carver HS; Plymouth, MA; (Y); #39 In Class; Am Leg Boys St; Red Cross Aide; Rep Jr Cls; Rep Sr Cls; JV Var Bsbl; JV Var Socr; Im Vllybl; Hon Roll; 6th Pl Sci Fair 83-84; 4th Pl Sci Fair 84-85; Engnrng.

BENEVIDES, DENISE M; Somerset HS; Somerset, MA; (Y); Church Yth Grp; Church Choir; High Hon Roll; Hon Roll; Miss Amer Coed Pag Awd 85; Boston U; Nrsng.

BENJAMIN, RICHARD; Greater Lawrence Vo Tech; Methuen, MA; (Y); 22/315; SADD; Yrbk Stf; Rep Frsh Cls; Rep Soph Cls; Rep Jr Cls; Var L Bsbl; Wrstlng; High Hon Roll; Hon Roll.

BENJAMIN, SCOTT; St Johns Prep; Peabody, MA; (Y); SADD; Temple Yth Grp; Nwsp Rptr; Nwsp Stf; Im Bsktbl; JV Var Crs Cntry; JV Var Trk; NHS; Im Golf; Im Tennis; JV Fencing 84; Bus.

BENNET, MICHAEL; Fitchburg HS; Fitchburg, MA; (Y); Spanish Clb; Varsity Clb; VP Frsh Cls; Var Capt Ftbl; Trk; Wt Lftg; Hon Roll; Natl, Intl St Hocky Trvlng Tm 81 & 85; Amiott Memrl Awd Phy Hlth 85; U Of MA; Real Estate.

BENNETT, BRENDA; Dedham HS; Dedham, MA; (S); 4/252; Church Yth Grp; Spanish Clb; Band; Jazz Band; Mrchg Band; School Musical; Variety Show; Hon Roll; JP Sousa Awd; Voice Dem Awd; Suffolk U Bk Awd 85; Bst Stu Math Awd 84; Fnlst Engl Essy Cntst 85.

BENNETT, DAWN M; Chicopee HS; Chicopee, MA; (Y); 22/255; Debate Tm; Hosp Aide; Spanish Clb; Sec Yrbk Stf; Rep Jr Cls; Rep Sr Cls; NHS; Pres Acdmc Ftns Awd 86; Chrls Clntn Abbey Schlrshp 86; Jhn F Ftzptrck Schlrshp 86; Smith Coll; Lbrl Arts.

BENNETT, KRISTEN; Reading Memorial HS; Reading, MA; (Y); Var Capt Bsktbl; Var Capt Socr; Var Capt Sftbl; Var Capt Vllybl; Hon Roll; Pres Schlr; Church Yth Grp; Office Aide; Chorus; Var Cheerleading; Bus Mngmnt.

BENNETT, LINDA; Auburn HS; Auburn, MA; (Y); Bsktbl; Crs Cntry; Sftbl; Hon Natl Scty Awd Outstndng Perfrmcn 86; MVP Crss Cnty Frshmn Yr 81-82; Brdr Confrcn Crss Cnty Sftbll; Chld Pshchlgy.

BENNETT, STEPHEN M; Norton HS; Norton, MA; (Y); 25/160; Am Leg Boys St; Boy Scts; JA; Math Tm; Yrbk Bus Mgr; Trk; Ntl Merit SF; Congress/Bundenstag Frgn Exchng Schlrshp 85.

BENNINGER, AMY; Northfield Mt Hermon HS; Lakeville, CT; (Y); French Clb; Library Aide; Varsity Clb; Nwsp Stf; Lit Mag; Sec Stu Cncl; Var L Fld Hcky; Trk; JV Vllybl; Hon Roll; MVP Offns Fld Hcky 84.

BENOIT, NICOLE A; Cathedral HS; Springfield, MA; (Y); 71/455; Prfct Atten Awd; Acad Excllnc & Alvin Com Acad Awd In Tech Drwng 86; Embry-Riddle Aeronautical U.

BENOIT, SUSAN; Somerville HS; Somerville, MA; (Y); 2/502; Church Yth Grp; Sec Math Tm; Ski Clb; Stu Cncl; JV Trk; Im Vllybl; Hon Roll; Trs NHS; Sal; Superintdnt Awd For Acadmc Exllnc 86; Presdentl Acadmc Fitness Awd 86; Boston Coll; Math.

BENSON, OLIVER H; Concord Acad; Newport, RI; (Y); Art Clb; German Clb; School Play; Nwsp Stf; Lit Mag; Crs Cntry; Socr; Theatr Dept Prmtnl Artst; Head Flm Clb; Edtr Art Mgzn.

BENSON, STEVE; Northfield Mount Hermon HS; E Walpole, MA; (Y); Church Yth Grp; Civic Clb; Cmnty Wkr; Leo Clb; Letterman Clb; Library Aide; Political Wkr; Ski Clb; Spanish Clb; SADD; Most Outstndng Athlete 84-85; Athlete Yr 85-86; Capt Hockey Teams 85-86; Brown U; Engrng.

BENT, CAROLIE; Apponquet Reginal Voc HS; Lakeville, MA; (Y); Church Yth Grp; SADD; Army Rsrv 86; Dctrs Asstnt.

BENTLEY, MICHELLE; David Hale Fanning Trade HS; Uxbridge, MA; (Y); 19/124; Drama Clb; Band; Chorus; Gym; Wt Lftg; Hon Roll; Csmtlgst.

BENTLEY, RHONDA; Boston Latin Acad; Jamaica Plain, MA; (Y); Intnl Clb; Band; Boston Coll; Pdtrcn.

BENTLEY, RHONDA MICHELLE; Berkshire Schl; New York, NY; (Y); Cmnty Wkr; Drama Clb; Hosp Aide; School Musical; Nwsp Rptr; VP Soph Cls; JV Capt Socr; JV Var Vllybl; Church Yth Grp; Band; Cum Laude Scty 85; William Coll Bk Awd Recipnt 85; Stephen Spaulding Schlrshp Recepnt 85; Medicine.

BERARDI, KAREN; Woburn SR HS; Woburn, MA; (S); 36/453; French Clb; Leo Clb; Ski Clb; SADD; Capt Flag Corp; Stu Cncl; Hon Roll; Jr NHS; NHS; Ntl Merit SF; Merrimack Coll; Bus Mgmt.

BERCIER, EARLE; Westport HS; Westport, MA; (Y); Boy Scts; Exploring; French Clb; Intnl Clb; Red Cross Aide; Ski Clb; JV Bsktbl; VP L Socr; Hon Roll; Embrey Riddle; Aviatn.

BERENGUER, JODIE; B M C Durfee HS; Fall River, MA; (Y); 47/600; French Clb; Yrbk Stf; NHS; Pres Schlr; Johnson & Wales Coll; Trvl.

BERENS, JODI; B M C Durfee HS; Fall River, MA; (Y); 20/683; Drama Clb; French Clb; Science Clb; Yrbk Stf; Hon Roll; NHS; USNLMA Merit Awd, Ldrshp Awd 86; Acad All Amer Awd 86; Marine Bio.

BERGER, MARK R; Plymouth-Carver HS; Plymouth, MA; (Y); Math Clb; Pres Debate Tm; French Clb; Model UN; Political Wkr; Science Clb; SADD; Temple Yth Grp; Nwsp Stf; Voice Dem Awd; Gooding Scholar Awd 86; Outstndng Delg Mdl Congress Awd 86; Schl Fin Voice Democracy Cont 86; Franklin Pierce Coll; Mktng.

BERGGREN, NATHAN; Walnut Hill Schl; Cleveland Hts, OH; (Y); Drama Clb; Jazz Band; Orch; School Play; Stage Crew; Crs Cntry; Trk; Hon Roll; Ntl Merit Ltr; Teachers Aide; Dorm Pres.

BERGIN, BRENDA; St Peter Marian HS; Worcester, MA; (Y); 6/180; Church Yth Grp; Cmnty Wkr; Political Wkr; SADD; Yrbk Stf; High Hon Roll; Hon Roll; NHS; Ed.

BERKOVITZ, ROBERT; Revere HS; Revere, MA; (Y); Am Leg Boys St; Aud/Vis; Boys Clb Am; Cmnty Wkr; Science Clb; Yrbk Stf; Rep Frsh Cls; Rep Stu Cncl; Brandeis; Psychology.

BERKOWITZ, JEREMY; Sharon HS; Sharon, MA; (Y); 4/230; JCL; Model UN; Temple Yth Grp; Nwsp Stf; Rep Stu Cncl; Bsktbl; Var Crs Cntry; High Hon Roll; Ntl Merit SF; Pres Schlr; CML; MAML; Lang.

BERMAN, MARISA; Cathedral HS; Holyoke, MA; (Y); 268/476; Ski Clb; Var Cheerleading; Var Trk; Excllnt Rbn & Sprt Awd 85; Framingham ST; Bus.

BERMANN, JOSEPH; Newton North HS; Newton, MA; (Y); Boy Scts; Church Yth Grp; Computer Clb; Pres Letterman Clb; Math Tm; SADD; School Play; Variety Show; Rep Soph Cls; Rep Jr Cls; MA Math Olympiad Fnlst 85-86; H L Grelck Math Awd 86; Dartmouth; Math.

BERMUDEZ, MICHAEL; Maynard HS; W Concord, MA; (Y); 33/112; Cmnty Wkr; Flag Corp; Bsbl; Bsktbl; Ftbl; Wt Lftg; Hon Roll; Chrstn A Heizter Mem Schlrshp 86; Northeastern; Law.

BERNARD, CHERYL; Uxbridge HS; Uxbridge, MA; (Y); 9/87; Yrbk Phtg; Yrbk Stf; Lit Mag; Stu Cncl; High Hon Roll; Hon Roll; NHS; Pblc Spkng 86; Piano Cert 85; Psych.

BERNARD, DIANE E; Reading Memorial HS; Reading, MA; (Y); 35/327; Hosp Aide; JA; SADD; Drill Tm; Nwsp Stf; Yrbk Sprt Ed; Var Capt Gym; Powder Puff Ftbl; Capt Twrlr; High Hon Roll; Batn Sqd Schlrshp 86; Stu Cncl Schlrshp 86; Providence College; Tchr.

BERNARD, MICHELLE; Bmc Durfee HS; Fall River, MA; (Y); 22/681; French Clb; Hosp Aide; Science Clb; Yrbk Stf; Rep Frsh Cls; JV Swmmng; High Hon Roll; Hon Roll; NHS; Ntl Merit Ltr; Delta In Stu Gvrnmnt 84; Med Tech.

BERNARD, PAMELA; Uxbridge HS; Uxbridge, MA; (Y); French Clb; Varsity Clb; Rep Soph Cls; Rep Jr Cls; JV Var Bsktbl; JV Capt Fld Hcky; Hon Roll; Nrsng.

BERNARD, STEPHEN J; Narranganasett Regional HS; Templeton, MA; (Y); 1/100; Am Leg Boys St; Letterman Clb; Math Clb; Yrbk Ed-Chief; JV Bsbl; Var Bsktbl; High Hon Roll; Mu Alp Tht; NHS; Val; Schlstc Lttr.

BERNAZANI, WENDY; Saugus HS; Saugus, MA; (Y); Art Clb; Concert Band; Mrchg Band; Hon Roll; Cmmrcl Dsgn.

BERNIER, ANNE MARIE; Bartlett HS; Webster, MA; (Y); 26/152; Trs Church Yth Grp; Spanish Clb; Church Choir; JV Var Bsktbl; Var Socr; Var Trk; High Hon Roll; Hon Roll; Sccr Ltr 84-86; Bsktbl Ltr 86; Regis Coll; Math.

BERNIER, JEANNE SIMONNE; Bishop Connolly HS; Fall River, MA; (Y); Cmnty Wkr; Drama Clb; French Clb; Hosp Aide; Nwsp Rptr; High Hon Roll; Hon Roll; Southeastern MA U; Nrsng.

BERNIER, MARC; Middleboro HS; Middleboro, MA; (Y); 13/200; Aud/Vis; Boy Scts; Computer Clb; JV Var Socr; JV Trk; Hon Roll; NHS; SMU; Engrng.

BERNSTEIN, BORIS; Doherty Memorial HS; Worcester, MA; (Y); 6/308; French Clb; Ski Clb; Band; Orch; Nwsp Rptr; French Hon Soc; High Hon Roll; Jr NHS; NHS; St Schlr; Ntnl Hnrs Orchestra 86; Harvard U; Bio.

BERNSTEIN, EMILY M; Phillips Acad; New York, NY; (Y); Model UN; NFL; Political Wkr; Ed Nwsp Stf; Var Ice Hcky; Hon Roll; Ntl Merit SF; Harvard Book Awd 85; Jrnlsm.

BERQUIST, JENNIFER; Westboro HS; Westboro, MA; (Y); 46/189; SADD; Acpl Chr; Chorus; JV Capt Fld Hcky; VP NHS; Church Yth Grp; German Clb; Mrchg Band; Variety Show; Yrbk Stf; Cntrl MA Distct Chorus 86; Rcmnd All-St Chorus 86; Rcvd Trphy Most Imprvd Field Hcky Player 86; Hlth Sci.

BERRY, SUZANNE C; Northfield Mount Hermon Schl; Mount Hermon, MA; (Y); Girl Scts; Math Tm; Church Choir; Stage Crew; Var L Crs Cntry; Var Trk; Hon Roll; Ntl Merit SF; Grl Scts Slvr Awd, Crss Cntry Skng Ltr 84.

BERRY, THOMAS M; Stoneham HS; Stoneham, MA; (Y); #4 In Class; Am Leg Boys St; Trs Drama Clb; Sec Spanish Clb; SADD; Mgr Chorus; School Play; Rep Stu Cncl; High Hon Roll; Jr NHS; NHS; Eagle Sct Awd 86; Bus.

BERRY, VICKIE; Milford HS; Milford, MA; (Y); 85/274; Church Yth Grp; Exploring; SADD; Color Guard; Yrbk Stf; Var Trk; Hon Roll; Amer Baptst Womn Schlrshp 86; MA Brd Regents Schlrshp 86; Fitchburg ST Coll; Nrsg.

BERRY, WILLIAM; Boston College HS; Canton, MA; (Y); 24/285; Capt Chess Clb; Math Tm; Im Bsktbl; JV Crs Cntry; Im Ftbl; High Hon Roll; NHS; Ntl Merit Ltr; Ltn Awd Acad Excel Ltn I 84; Bst Chess Plyr Awd 86.

BERRYMAN, SCOTT C; Leicester HS; Rochdale, MA; (Y); 25/102; Church Yth Grp; Drama Clb; Band; Chorus; Church Choir; School Play; Yrbk Stf; Wt Lftg; Hon Roll; Organ Perf.

BERTHIAUME, SCOTT; Quaboag Regional HS; Warren, MA; (Y); 15/80; Boy Scts; Pres Exploring; Latin Clb; Varsity Clb; School Play; Yrbk Stf; Trs Stu Cncl; JV Var Bsktbl; Var Golf; Hon Roll.

BERTOCCHI, WILLIAM; Everett HS; Everett, MA; (Y); Church Yth Grp; Ski Clb; Bsbl; Ftbl; Trk; U Lowell; Comp.

BERTOLINO, KIM; Gloucester HS; Gloucester, MA; (Y); 15/344; German Clb; Yrbk Stf; Rep Stu Cncl; Im Vllybl; Lib NHS; Rep Jr Cls; Rep Sr Cls; Hon Roll; Sawyer Medal 84; Hghst Avg & Achvmnt In German 86; Middlebury Coll.

BERTONE, SALVATORE; Franklin HS; Franklin, MA; (Y); JV Ftbl; Im Wt Lftg; JV Wrstlng; Hon Roll; Cvl Engrg.

BERTSEKAS, TELIS; Belmont HS; Belmont, MA; (Y); 5/292; Intnl Clb; Spanish Clb; JV Bsbl; Im Bsktbl; JV Trk; High Hon Roll; Hon Roll; NHS; Ntl Merit SF; Prfct Atten Awd; Ivy League Schl; Law.

BERUBE, MICHELLE M; Norwood HS; Norwood, MA; (Y); 9/320; Concert Band; Mrchg Band; Orch; Symp Band; Hon Roll; Jr NHS; Lion Awd; Pres Schlr; Princpls Awd 83; Contintl Mth Lg Comp 83; John C Lane Mem Awd 86; Holy Cross; Mth.

BERUBE, SANDRA; Leicester HS; Leicester, MA; (Y); Computer Clb; Spanish Clb; Chorus; Yrbk Stf; JV Bsktbl; Var L Crs Cntry; Capt L Sftbl; Hon Roll; MA Interschlstc Athletic Assn 85-86; Occuptnl Thrpst.

BERWALDT, KAREN; Chicopee Comprehensive HS; Chicopee, MA; (Y); 2/332; Church Yth Grp; German Clb; Church Choir; Yrbk Bus Mgr; Yrbk Stf; Tennis; High Hon Roll; Jr NHS; Schlstc Awds Grmn 84-86, Spnsh 85.

BETE, JOHN; Northfield Mount Hermon HS; Centerville, MA; (Y); Drama Clb; Swmmng; Hnrb Mntn In Schlstc Art Awds; RI Schl Of Dsgn; Dsgnr.

BETT, CHRISTOPHER J; Winchester HS; Winchester, MA; (Y); 2/284; Sec Am Leg Boys St; Boy Scts; VP Church Yth Grp; Nwsp Sprt Ed; Var L Trk; High Hon Roll; NHS; Ntl Merit Ltr; Stage Crew; JV Socr; Harvard Bk Awd 85; Cornell U Natl Schlr 86; Cornell U; Elec Engrng.

BETTENCOURT, MARK; Coyle-Cassidy HS; Raynham, MA; (Y); 2/169; Am Leg Boys St; Political Wkr; Rep Frsh Cls; VP Soph Cls; Pres Jr Cls; Pres Stu Cncl; Var JV Bsktbl; Ftbl; Var Trk; Cit Awd; Cngrsnl Yth Ldrshp Cncl 85; Hrvrd Bk Awd 86; Law.

BETTENCOURT, SHARON; Silver Lake Regional HS; Kingston, MA; (Y); 35/459; Pres Sec 4-H; French Clb; Latin Clb; Trs Math Clb; 4-H Awd; Hon Roll; NHS; Vet-Med.

BEWICK, JOHN W; Newton North HS; Newtonville, MA; (Y); Boy Scts; Concert Band; Jazz Band; Mrchg Band; Hon Roll; Ntl Merit Ltr; Eagle Sct 85.

BEYNOR, DEBORAH; Palmer HS; Brimfield, MA; (Y); Ski Clb; Band; Sec Frsh Cls; Sec Soph Cls; Sec Jr Cls; Sec Sr Cls; Var Cheerleading; Var Trk; Hon Roll; NHS; Bio.

BIALY, BETH; Bartlett HS; Webster, MA; (Y); 7/150; Church Yth Grp; Cmnty Wkr; French Clb; FBLA; Spanish Clb; Mrchg Band; Yrbk Bus Mgr; Yrbk Rptr; Tennis; NHS; 1st Pl Acctng II Div Cmptn 86; Rotary Schlrshp 86; Prfct Attndnc Awd 86; Nichols Coll; Acctng.

BIBEAULT, MAUREEN; Bishop Feehan HS; Attleboro, MA; (Y); 15/243; Church Yth Grp; Chorus; School Play; Yrbk Rptr; Capt L Crs Cntry; L Trk; Elks Awd; French Hon Soc; High Hon Roll; NHS; Pres Acdmc Fit Awd 86; Cert Achvt Math 86; Cert Achvt Hrvrd Proj Physcs 86; Northeastern U; Mech Engrng.

BICKFORD, MARK R; Winthrop HS; Winthrop, MA; (Y); 15/226; Trs Am Leg Boys St; Var L Bsbl; Var L Ftbl; Hon Roll; NHS.

BICKNELL, LAURA; Marshfield HS; Marshfield, MA; (Y); 58/380; Band; Mrchg Band; Var Bsktbl; Capt Fld Hcky; Var Tennis; Hon Roll; NHS; Bstn Glb All Schlstc Tnns 85-86; Bay St Tm For Fld Hcky 86; Brctn Enter All Schlstc Fld Hcky 85; Coll.

BIEL, MARGARET A; Lincoln-Sudbury Regional HS; Sudbury, MA; (Y); English Clb; Key Clb; Math Tm; Spanish Clb; Ed Yrbk Rptr; Ed Lit Mag; Hon Roll; Med.

BIELLO, GREG; Dighton-Rehoboth HS; Rehoboth, MA; (Y); Computer Clb; Science Clb; Hon Roll; NHS; Robtcs.

BIFANO, CHRISTINA; Boston Latin Acad; Boston, MA; (Y); Art Clb; Debate Tm; Drama Clb; French Clb; Library Aide; Office Aide; Ski Clb; Variety Show; Off Frsh Cls; Off Soph Cls; Advertsng.

BIGOS, CHERYL; Diman Reg Voc Tech HS; Fall River, MA; (Y); Dance Clb; Drama Clb; Key Clb; Church Choir; Stage Crew; Variety Show; Nwsp Stf; Sec Stu Cncl; Var Capt Cheerleading; Gym.

BILODEAU, NANCY; Boston Latin Acad; W Roxbury, MA; (Y); Church Yth Grp; Cmnty Wkr; Office Aide; Teachers Aide; Variety Show; Ed Lit Mag; Cheerleading; Hon Roll; Boston-Strasbourg Sister City Assoc Exch Partcpnt 86; Latin Achvt Coll Brd 86; Amer U DC; Brdcstng.

BILYEU, SCOTT; Lenox Memorial HS; Lenox, MA; (Y); 6/82; FCA; Quiz Bowl; Yrbk Sprt Ed; Bsbl; Crs Cntry; Socr; NHS; Church Yth Grp; Ski Clb; Yrbk Phtg; MA ST Ski Tm 86; Phi Alpha Theta Framingham ST Hstrl Conf 86; 2nd Tm Southern Berkshire Sccr 85; Dartmouth Coll; Engrng.

BINDER, DAWN; Belmont HS; Belmont, MA; (Y); 30/263; Civic Clb; Hosp Aide; Var Trk; Hon Roll; Globe Art Shw 83; Schlstc Art Shw 84, 86.

BINEAU, MICHAEL; Holyoke HS; Holyoke, MA; (Y); 170/400; Teachers Aide; Yrbk Stf; Sprtsmnshp Awd 79; Holyoke Cmnty Coll; Bus.

BING-ZAREMBA, ADRIAN CHARLES; St Marys HS; Southwick, MA; (Y); 9/60; Am Leg Boys St; Ski Clb; Spanish Clb; Nwsp Rptr; Yrbk Stf; Lit Mag; JV Socr; High Hon Roll; NHS; NEDT Awd; Sthwck Ctzns Schlrshp Awrd 86; GWV Trsts Schlrshp 86; Wstfld ST Coll HS Schlrs Prgm 85; George Washington U; Engr.

BIRCH, KRISTEN; West Ford Acad; Westford, MA; (Y); Band; Concert Band; Symp Band; Var Capt Cheerleading; JV Socr; Var Trk; Comp Sci.

BIRD, DEBORAH; Taunton HS; Taunton, MA; (Y); Hosp Aide; Pep Clb; Ski Clb; Varsity Clb; Flag Corp; Crs Cntry; Pom Pon; Swmmng; Bridgewater ST; Psychlgy.

BIRKBECK, CHRIS; King Philip HS; Plainville, MA; (Y); Im Bsktbl; Hon Roll.

BIRNBAUM, JOEL; Lincoln-Sudbury HS; Sudbury, MA; (Y); Political Wkr; Trs Temple Yth Grp; Nwsp Rptr; Rep Jr Cls; Var Bsktbl; Var Capt Tennis; Physcs.

BIRNSCHEIN, TIMOTHY A; Watertown SR HS; Watertown, MA; (Y); 6/252; Am Leg Boys St; Drama Clb; High Hon Roll; Jr NHS; NHS; Ntl Merit Ltr; Church Yth Grp; JA; PAVAS; Thesps; Bst Actr Wrtwn Hgh 86; Awd Acadm Excel 83-86; Trinity Coll.

BIRON, MELISSA; Shepherd Hill Regional HS; Southbridge, MA; (Y); 16/140; Church Yth Grp; Drama Clb; French Clb; Chorus; School Play; Variety Show; Yrbk Stf; VP Jr Cls; Pres Sr Cls; Stu Cncl; US Stu Council Awd Schlrshp 85; Quo Vardis Schrlshp 86; Amer Legn Schlrshp 86; Northeastern U; Physcl Ther.

BIRTWELL, KEVIN; Auburn HS; Auburn, MA; (Y); Drama Clb; Chorus; School Musical; School Play; Swing Chorus; Rep Frsh Cls; Rep Soph Cls; Rep Jr Cls; High Hon Roll; NHS; Prize Awd Moontwachusett CC Art Invit; Natl Hnr Soc Awd Outstndg Art Wrk 86; Art.

BISBEE, MARY E; Smith Voc-Agri HS; Chesterfield, MA; (Y); Am Leg Aux Girls St; 4-H; Ski Clb; Drill Tm; Yrbk Phtg; Yrbk Stf; Sec Jr Cls; Sec Stu Cncl; JV Var Cheerleading; 4-H Awd; Altrnt Grls ST; Hrsmnshp.

BISCEGLIA, SANDRA; Ursuline Acad; Hyde Park, MA; (Y); 2/81; Latin Clb; Service Clb; Spanish Clb; SADD; Pres Sr Cls; Var Sftbl; High Hon Roll; NHS; Schlrshp Ursuline 83-86; Bus Adm.

BISHOP, RACHEL; St Peter Marion HS; Worcester, MA; (Y); Orch; School Musical; Var Bsktbl; Var Sftbl; Sftbl Team Won St Title; Ptchd Prfct Game In St Semi-Fnl, Allowed One Run In 5 Trnmnt Games 86.

BISSAILLON, BRUCE; Hoosac Valley HS; Cheshire, MA; (Y); 49/149; Yrbk Stf; Im Socr; Im Vllybl; Hotel Mgmt.

BISSAILLON, GARY M; Hoosac Valley HS; Adams, MA; (Y); 32/160; Cmnty Wkr; Ski Clb; SADD; Nwsp Sprt Ed; Sec Jr Cls; Sec Sr Cls; Var L Crs Cntry; JV Ftbl; Var L Trk; Im Vllybl; Adams-Cheshire Ath Alumni Scholar 86; Teidemann Fmly Fnd Scholar 86; Henry Herbert Smythe Tst Fnd 86; Fitchburg ST.

BISSONNETTE, JILL; Cathedral HS; Springfield, MA; (Y); Dance Clb; Math Clb; Office Aide; Teachers Aide; Chorus; Stu Cncl; Cit Awd; Svc Awd 86; Off Procdrs Acad Awd 86; Springfield Tech CC; Bus Adm.

BITAR, JOHN; Foxboro HS; Foxboro, MA; (Y); 35/250; JA; Nwsp Stf; Yrbk Phtg; Yrbk Stf; NHS; NYC Schl Vsl Arts; Cnmatgrphy.

BIXBY, BARBARA; Westport HS; Westport, MA; (Y); 1/145; French Clb; Stu Cncl; Fld Hcky; Cit Awd; DAR Awd; Elks Awd; NHS; Pres Schlr; St Schlr; Val; Davidson Coll; Pol Sci.

BJELF, BILL; Marshfield HS; Marshfield, MA; (Y); 19/380; High Hon Roll; Hon Roll; NHS.

BJORSON, PAMELA; Gardner HS; Gardner, MA; (Y); 25/160; French Clb; Var L Cheerleading; JV Sftbl; Var Trk; Hon Roll; NHS; Ntl Sci Olympd Awd 86; U Of MA; Sec Educ.

BLACK, ANDREW; Lincoln-Sudbury Regional HS; Sudbury, MA; (Y); VP Key Clb; Chorus; Mgr Nwsp Stf; JV Trk; Ntl Merit Cmmndtn 86; Physcn.

BLACKBURN III, JAMES R; Scituate HS; Scituate, MA; (Y); 19/280; Am Leg Boys St; Trk; High Hon Roll; Hon Roll; NHS; Smmr Swmmg; Martial Arts Awds & Trphys; Sccr Yth Cmmnty; Nvl Aviator.

BLACKBURN, MARIA; Boston Latin Schl; Boston, MA; (Y); 76/284; Drama Clb; JA; Latin Clb; Concert Band; School Play; Stage Crew; Lit Mag; Var L Socr; JV Trk; NHS; Home & Schl Assn Schlrshp 85-86; Drby Mdl Orig Ply 85-86; Lvn Schlrshp 85-86; Trinity Coll; Engl.

BLACKINGTON, SUE; Haverhill HS; Haverhill, MA; (Y); 49/400; VP Pres Church Yth Grp; French Clb; Hosp Aide; Letterman Clb; Spanish Clb; Varsity Clb; Lib Chorus; Capt Trk; High Hon Roll; Hon Roll; Cert Awd For Sci Of HHS Chrs Lbrn 85; Dbl Vrsty Ltr Awds Indr Trck 85-86; R E Crstn Schlrshp Eglsh 86; Amer Intl Coll; Psychlgy.

BLACKSTONE, JON G; St Johns Preparatory Schl; Peabody, MA; (Y); 1/254; Capt Math Tm; School Play; Nwsp Bus Mgr; NHS; Ntl Merit Schol; St Schlr; Val; MA H S Drama Gld All ST Cast 86; New England Drama Cncls All New England Cast 86; Harvard U.

BLADES, LAURA L; Bellingham Memorial HS; Bellingham, MA; (Y); Mgr DECA; OEA; Ski Clb; SADD; Yrbk Stf; Stu Cncl; Golf; Hon Roll; DECA 1st Pl In Finance & Credit Written Event 86; Peer Cnclr.

BLAIR, RICHARD; Chelsea HS; Chelsea, MA; (Y); Aud/Vis; Y-Teens; Pep Band; Ice Hcky; Kiwanis Awd; Elctrcn.

BLAKE, AMY C; Reading Memorial HS; Reading, MA; (Y); Church Yth Grp; SADD; School Musical; Yrbk Phtg; Off Soph Cls; Off Jr Cls; JV Tennis; High Hon Roll; Hon Roll; Arch.

BLAKE, ROXANNE C; Roxanne C Blake HS; New Bedford, MA; (Y); 259/631; Cmnty Wkr; ROTC; Drill Tm; Rep Frsh Cls; DAR Awd; Hon Roll; ROTC Schlrshp 86; Post 1 New Bedford Amer Legn; Supr Cadt Awd 86; U Of MA; Cmmnctns.

BLAKE, SANDRA; Norwell HS; Norwell, MA; (Y); 5/180; French Clb; Band; Drill Tm; School Musical; Nwsp Stf; Yrbk Stf; JV Socr; High Hon Roll; VP NHS; NEDT Awd; U Of VT; Comm Sci.

BLAKE, SCOTT; Arlington HS; Arlington, MA; (Y); 62/381; Boys Clb Am; Pres Soph Cls; Radio Clb; SADD; JV Socr; Var Tennis; Hon Roll; NHS; Bus.

BLAKE, WILLIAM J; Cathedral HS; Springfield, MA; (Y); 133/516; Yrbk Ed-Chief; Var L Trk; Im Wt Lftg; Ntl Merit Ltr; Brian Sullivan Mem Schlrshp 86; James Z Naurison Schlrshp 86; Rochester Inst Tech; Photo.

BLANCHARD, CHERYL A; Bourne HS; Monument Beach, MA; (Y); 1/180; Math Tm; Band; Yrbk Ed-Chief; Powder Puff Ftbl; High Hon Roll; NHS; Ntl Merit Ltr; St Schlr; Val; Cert Of Acad Encllnc MA Spr Intndnts 86; Pres Acad Ftns Aws 86; Wellesley.

BLANCHARD, JAMES; Tantawqua Regional SR HS; Sturbridge, MA; (Y); Ski Clb; Concert Band; Jazz Band; Mrchg Band; School Musical; School Play; Rep Jr Cls; Rep Sr Cls; NHS; Ntl Merit Ltr; Mem Modern Music Mstrs Soc; Pol Sci.

BLANCHARD, MARC; Central Catholic HS; Methuen, MA; (Y); 63/231; Cmnty Wkr; JA; Ski Clb; Varsity Clb; Im Bsktbl; Capt Coach Actv; JV Ice Hcky; Capt Trk; Im Vllybl; Im Wt Lftg; Merrimack Valley Conf Div All Star 85-86; U NH; Engrng.

BLANCHARD, MICHAEL; New Bedford HS; New Bedford, MA; (Y); Chess Clb; Computer Clb; Exploring; JA; Hon Roll; Hnrbl Ment Art Show 85; Martial Arts 85-86; WPI; Comp Pgmr.

BLANCHARD, ROBIN; Cape Cod Regional Technical HS; South Yarmouth, MA; (Y); Hosp Aide; Nwsp Stf; Yrbk Stf; Hon Roll; CASE Project Member 84-86; Cape Cod Tech Tour Guide 85; Air Force; Security Police.

BLANCHARD, SAMANTHA JAYNE; Fitchburg HS; Fitchburg, MA; (Y); Church Yth Grp; Dance Clb; 4-H; French Clb; Latin Clb; SADD; Chorus; 4-H Awd; High Hon Roll; NHS; Frnch I Awd 83-84; Dance.

BLANEY, DARREN; Cathedral HS; Enfield, CT; (Y); 10/500; Office Aide; Band; Concert Band; Mrchg Band; School Musical; Hon Roll; Music.

BLASER, CHRISTOPHER J; Lunenburg HS; Lunenburg, MA; (Y); 11/123; Am Leg Boys St; SADD; School Play; Yrbk Ed-Chief; Rep Frsh Cls; Rep Soph Cls; Rep Jr Cls; Rep Sr Cls; High Hon Roll; NHS; Worcester Telegram & Gazette Achvr 86; Lunenburg Ctzns Schlrshp Fndtn Awd 86; Bentley Coll; Accntng.

BLATCHLEY, ELIZABETH; Hudson HS; Hudson, MA; (Y); 2/139; Church Yth Grp; Drama Clb; Pep Clb; Ski Clb; Chorus; School Musical; School Play; Yrbk Stf; Capt Tennis; Pres NHS; Wrcstr Tlgrm Gztt Stu Achv 86; Elizabeth Mcgorty Awd 86; Unsng Hro Grls Tns 85; Gordon Ccoll; Elmntry ED.

BLAUS, MARKUS M; Masconomet Regional HS; Middleton, MA; (Y); Am Leg Boys St; Thesps; School Musical; School Play; Bridgeport U; Advrtsng.

BLETSIS, PETRULA; Dracut SR HS; Dracut, MA; (Y); Sec Church Yth Grp; Drama Clb; Hosp Aide; Math Clb; Math Tm; SADD; Nwsp Bus Mgr; Nwsp Rptr; Nwsp Stf; Lit Mag; Flk Dnc Awd; Chrch Yth Serv Awd 84; Englsh, Hstry, Frnch & Geo Awds 85; Profsnl Fashn Mdl Hnrs 86; Clncl Phych.

BLITT, ALISA; Marblehead HS; Marblehead, MA; (Y); 90/250; Cmnty Wkr; French Clb; SADD; Temple Yth Grp; Yrbk Stf; Sftbl; Cit Awd; Ntl Piano Aud Awd 80-85; Lwyr.

BLOCK, ALISON; Bourne HS; Pocasset, MA; (Y); 19/187; French Clb; Model UN; Nwsp Stf; Yrbk Stf; JV Crs Cntry; Var Trk; Bus Mrchndsng.

BLOEMINK, KRISTINA; Franklin HS; Franklin, MA; (Y); Yrbk Stf; Stat Bsktbl; Stat Score Keeper; JV Socr; Cert Tutorng Frnch 86; Cert Sccr 84-85; Cet Bsktbl Mgr 84-85; Art.

BLOMQUIST, ROBERT D; Westwood HS; Westwood, MA; (Y); 41/212; Am Leg Boys St; Church Yth Grp; SADD; VP Frsh Cls; VP Jr Cls; VP Sr Cls; JV Var Ftbl; JV Var Ice Hcky; Hon Roll.

BLONIASZ, LISA; Douglas Memorial HS; E Douglas, MA; (Y); Church Yth Grp; Cmnty Wkr; Office Aide; Red Cross Aide; Band; Mrchg Band; Yrbk Stf; Stu Cncl; Bsktbl; Worcester St Coll; Cmmnctns.

BLOOD, REBECCA; Academy Of Notre Dame; Pepperell, MA; (Y); Hosp Aide; Pep Clb; School Musical; School Play; Stage Crew; Stu Cncl; Var Cheerleading; Var Sftbl; Var Swmmng; Hon Roll; Pre-Med.

BLOOM, STACEY; Braintree HS; Braintree, MA; (Y); 9/432; Pres JCL; Political Wkr; SADD; Yrbk Stf; Lit Mag; Rep Stu Cncl; Tennis; High Hon Roll; NHS; Pol Sci.

BLUMENTHAL, JEREMY; Sharon HS; Sharon, MA; (Y); Aud/Vis; VP Drama Clb; Pres Temple Yth Grp; Thesps; School Play; Stage Crew; Nwsp Stf; Lit Mag; JV Socr; Hon Roll; Harvard Prize Bk 86; Excllnct Actng 85-86; Law.

BOAN, SCOTT; Diman HS; Westport, MA; (Y); Aircrft Mech.

BOBACK, KERRI; Arlington Catholic HS; Reading, MA; (Y); Dance Clb; Drama Clb; Office Aide; School Musical; School Play; Cheerleading; Tennis; Emerson Coll; Mass Media.

BOBALA, LOUANNE; Hampshire Regional HS; Westhampton, MA; (Y); Sec Church Yth Grp; 4-H; Girl Scts; Ski Clb; Band; Chorus; Concert Band; Mrchg Band; Variety Show; Outstndg Musicnshp Awd 86; Dance Awd 84-86; Physcn Asst.

BOBALA, ROBERT; Chicopee HS; Chicopee, MA; (Y); 18/252; Nwsp Stf; Yrbk Stf; Sec Jr Cls; Sec Sr Cls; JV Socr; Hon Roll; NHS; Pres Schlr; John F Corridan Schlrshp 86; Pro Merito Socy 86; John L Fitzpatrick Schlrshp; U Of MA; Bus.

BOCK, KIMBERLY; Fontbonne Acad; Norwood, MA; (Y); Drama Clb; Yrbk Stf; Lit Mag; Jrnlsm.

BODEMER, SARAH L; King Phillip Regional HS; Wrentham, MA;'(Y); Church Yth Grp; Cmnty Wkr; Drama Clb; Girl Scts; Hosp Aide; SADD; Chorus; School Musical; Yrbk Stf; Powder Puff Ftbl; Advrtsng.

BODENRADER, FREDERICK; Central Catholic HS; Georgetown, MA; (Y); 47/237; Nwsp Sprt Ed; Nwsp Ed-Chief; Nwsp Rptr; L Bsbl; Var Trk; JV Wrstlng; Hon Roll; Yrbk Stf; Bst Overall Wrtng Prfrmnc 84-85; Bst Wrtng Style & Story Ideas HS Prfrmnc 84-85; Journlsm.

BODIE, MELINDA M; Leominster HS; Leominster, MA; (Y); Red Cross Aide; Var Capt Bsktbl; Coach Actv; Var Capt Sftbl; Elks Awd; High Hon Roll; Hon Roll; NHS; AF Of L CIO $1500 Union Schlrshp Wnnr 86; Full Athletic Schlrshp FL JC 86; FL JC; Bus Admin.

BODIO JR, ROBERT F; Milford HS; Milford, MA; (Y); 88/290; Am Leg Boys St; Boy Scts; Church Yth Grp; Band; Mrchg Band; JV Bsbl; JV Bsktbl; JV Var Ftbl; Var L Trk; Im Wt Lftg; Law.

BODZIN, STEVEN; Concord-Carlisle HS; Concord, MA; (Y); 107/328; Capt Debate Tm; Library Aide; Model UN; Radio Clb; Ed Lit Mag; Ntl Merit SF.

BOEY, LINDA; Boston Latin Acad; Boston, MA; (Y); Intnl Clb; JA; Hon Roll.

BOGWES, KELVIN; Boston Latin HS; Boston, MA; (Y); 80/274; Church Yth Grp; Band; Chorus; Church Choir; Variety Show; Stu Cncl; Var Capt Trk; NHS; All Lge Tm In Trck 85; Nat Meet 85; JR Olympcs 86; Brown Univ; Pre-Med.

BOHNE, LORIN; Westford Acad; Westford, MA; (Y); AFS; Swmmng; Trk; High Hon Roll; Hon Roll; Ntl Merit Ltr.

BOISSEAU, LINCOLN; Quaboag Regional HS; Warren, MA; (Y); Science Clb; Varsity Clb; Band; School Musical; Variety Show; Off Jr Cls; JV Bsbl; Var Crs Cntry; Im Vllybl; Hon Roll; Holy Cross; Sci.

BOISVERE, SALLY; Chicopee HS; Chicopee, MA; (Y); 52/265; Band; Color Guard; Concert Band; Drill Tm; Flag Corp; Madrigals; Mrchg Band; Pep Band; Ed Yrbk Stf; Hon Roll; Mst Imprvd Female Mus Band Bir Awd 86; Slvr Individuals Drill Tm 86; Cmmnty Schlrshp 86; Southeastern MA U; Comp Engrng.

BOISVERT, DAVID; Blackstone-Mullville Regional HS; Blackstone, MA; (Y); Band; Jazz Band; Mrchg Band; Orch; Stage Crew; Yrbk Stf; Hon Roll; Engrng.

BOKSANSKI, PETER; Haverhill HS; Bradford, MA; (Y); 1/400; Am Leg Boys St; German Clb; Latin Clb; Yrbk Stf; VP Jr Cls; VP Sr Cls; Capt L Crs Cntry; Capt L Trk; High Hon Roll; NHS; Dartmouth Bk Awd 86; U MA Chancllrs Tlnt Awd 86.

BOLAND, KELLY; Presentation Of Mary Acad; Lawrence, MA; (Y); 7/42; Math Clb; Ski Clb; Spanish Clb; SADD; Chorus; Yrbk Stf; Sec Soph Cls; Sec Sr Cls; Var Bsktbl; Var Vllybl; Natl Merit Frgn Lgs 85-86.

BOLANZ, LISA; Belmont HS; Belmont, MA; (Y); 6/85; Trs Church Yth Grp; Church Choir; Concert Band; Mrchg Band; Orch; NHS; Ntl Merit SF; Drama Clb; PAVAS; Band; Smith Coll Bk Awd 86; Ger Consulate Bk Awd & Goethe Inst Awd 84-86; Bundes Rep Deutschland Cert 86; Pre-Med.

BOLAS, JULIE A; Revere HS; Revere, MA; (Y); 16/350; Math Clb; Science Clb; Stu Cncl; Var L Trk; NHS; Math Tm; Office Aide; Yrbk Stf; Var L Crs Cntry; Wnr Mssprt Art Cntst; Prsdntl Acdmc Ftns Awd; Prtcptn Hndcppd Awrns; Hnrs Schlr; Rose Smith Schlrshp; Stonehill Coll; Lbrl Arts.

BOLDUC, C YVONNE; Matignon HS; Cambridge, MA; (S); 7/187; VP JA; Var Bsktbl; Co-Capt Var Crs Cntry; Var Trk; Hon Roll; NHS; Church Yth Grp; Church Choir; Score Keeper; 1st Pl Mtgnon Hstry Fair-2nd Dist-Hnrb Mntn ST Hstry Fair 83-84; 1st Pl Mtgnon Art Fair 84.

BOLDUC, JEANNE; Apponequer Regional HS; Assonet, MA; (Y); Drama Clb; Trs Pep Clb; SADD; School Musical; Nwsp Ed-Chief; Stu Cncl; Fld Hcky; Sftbl; Trk; NHS; Bus Wk Bentley Coll 85; St Johns U; Pharm.

BOLDUC, SHEILA; Chicopee Comprenhensive HS; Chicopee, MA; (Y); 20/332; German Clb; Yrbk Sprt Ed; Yrbk Stf; Mgr L Bsbl; Mgr L Bsktbl; Mgr(s); Score Keeper; Hon Roll; NHS; ST Senate Offcl Citatn Bsktbl 86.

BOLMAN, STEVEN H; The Pingree Schl; Beverly, MA; (Y); Drama Clb; Acpl Chr; Chorus; School Musical; School Play; Nwsp Ed-Chief; Yrbk Stf; Lit Mag; Stu Cncl; Hon Roll; Harvard Bk Prz 84-85; Hnrbl Mntn Engl 83-84 & Music Hist 83-84; Vassar Coll.

BOLTON, CHRISTINA; Wayland HS; Wayland, MA; (Y); Church Yth Grp; Drama Clb; French Clb; Ski Clb; Band; School Musical; School Play; Hon Roll.

BONACCORSI, MARY ALISE; Malden HS; Malden, MA; (Y); 33/500; Church Yth Grp; Key Clb; Office Aide; Pep Clb; Variety Show; Rep Frsh Cls; Hst Soph Cls; Hst Jr Cls; Stu Cncl; Pltcl Sci.

BONCZYK, LORI A; Holy Name CC HS; Worcester, MA; (Y); 27/262; Church Yth Grp; Stage Crew; Yrbk Stf; Bsktbl; Fld Hcky; Sftbl; High Hon Roll; Jr NHS; Acctng, Physcs, & Comp Awds 85-86; Sthestrn MA U; Bus Mgmt.

BOND IV, GEORGE W; Leominster HS; Leominster, MA; (Y); 62/350; Am Leg Boys St; Political Wkr; Sec Ski Clb; School Musical; School Play; Mgr Stage Crew; Yrbk Bus Mgr; Rep Stu Cncl; JV Socr; Hon Roll; U RI; Phrmcy.

BOND, GREGORY; Central Catholic HS; Haverhill, MA; (Y); Stage Crew; Im Bowling; Im Trk; High Hon Roll; Hon Roll; Merrimac; Math.

BOND, KIM; Framingham South HS; Framingham, MA; (S); 35/252; Dance Clb; Drama Clb; Acpl Chr; Chorus; Madrigals; School Musical; Variety Show; Var Cheerleading; Hon Roll; NHS; 5 Yr Danc Awd 84; Cheerng Outstndng Achvt Bay ST Leag 85; Bus Mgmt.

BONNAYER, JEANNINE M; Palmer HS; Three Rivers, MA; (Y); 35/100; Ski Clb; SADD; Varsity Clb; Band; Mrchg Band; Symp Band; Rep Stu Cncl; Bsktbl; Fld Hcky; Tennis; US Army Rsrv Athlt Schlr Awd 86; Plmr Little Grls Sftbl Schlrshp 86; Fld Hcky & Sftbl MVP 86; Brdgwtr ST Coll; Althtc Trnr.

BONNELL, CHRISTINE; Wachusett Regional HS; Sterling, MA; (Y); Model UN; Pep Clb; Ski Clb; SADD; Yrbk Stf; Bsktbl; Score Keeper; Hon Roll; Ntl Hnr Soc 82-83; Soc Wrk.

BONNER, CHRISTINE; Waltham HS; Wartham, MA; (Y); Aud/Vis; French Clb; SADD; Hon Roll; Kingsbury Temperance Essay Awd 1st Pl 86; Cmmnctns.

BONNETTE, DANIEL; South High Community Schl; Worcester, MA; (Y); 3/250; Am Leg Boys St; Scholastic Bowl; SADD; VP Jr Cls; VP Sr Cls; Pres Stu Cncl; Var Capt Bsbl; Var Capt Ftbl; Var Capt Trk; French Hon Soc; Holy Cross Clg; Ecnmcs.

BONOMO, CHRISTIAN; Nashoba Regional HS; Stow, MA; (Y); 2/165; Chess Clb; Trs Stu Cncl; Var L Socr; High Hon Roll; NHS; Ntl Merit SF; Pres Schlr; Sal; US Cngrs-Bundestag Awd-Exchng Stu W Grmny 85-86; Digtl Equpmnt Corp Schlrshp 86; BASF Corp Schlrshp; Dartmouth Coll; Bus.

BONVIN, JEANINE; Franklin HS; Franklin, MA; (Y); 19/225; Yrbk Stf; Rep Jr Cls; Hon Roll; NHS; Commnwlth Schlr 86; Cert Apprctn Peer Tutrg 85; Stonehill Coll; Engl.

BOOTH, BETHANY A; Bridgewater - Raynham Regional; Raynham, MA; (Y); 3/301; Math Tm; SADD; Stu Cncl; Var L Bsktbl; Elks Awd; High Hon Roll; Pres NHS; St Schlr; Science Clb; Yrbk Stf; Jostens Schlrshp Awd 86; Brdgwtr-Rynhm Awd For Schlstc Achvt 86; Providence Coll; Bio.

BOOTH, CAROL; Barnstable HS; Barnstable, MA; (Y); 17/376; Church Yth Grp; Drama Clb; Hosp Aide; Acpl Chr; Band; Church Choir; Madrigals; School Musical; Hon Roll; Slvr Acadmc Cert 84; Gordon Coll; Music Ed.

BORACCINI, PATRICIA; Auburn SR HS; Auburn, MA; (Y); Hosp Aide; Pep Clb; Varsity Clb; Sec Jr Cls; Rep Stu Cncl; Capt L Cheerleading; Var L Crs Cntry; Var L Trk; Hon Roll; Occuptnl Ed Awd Acctng 86; Acctng.

BORDIERI, PAULA; Reading Memorial HS; Reading, MA; (Y); 12/327; Hosp Aide; SADD; Nwsp Rptr; Rep Soph Cls; Rep Jr Cls; Rep Sr Cls; Sec Stu Cncl; Var Capt Tennis; Cit Awd; French Hon Soc; Mt Holyoke Book Awd 85; Grace & Robert Burns Mem Awd 86; Cls Awd 86; U NH; Bus Adm.

BORENSTEIN, DONALD F; Lexington Christian Acad; Winchester, MA; (Y); 12/60; Math Tm; Ski Clb; Variety Show; Nwsp Rptr; Sec Trs Soph Cls; VP Sr Cls; Stu Cncl; Var Bsbl; Bsktbl; Var Capt Socr; 1st Tm Bsbl All Strs Medford SR Leag 84; Marn Sci.

BORGAL, DAVID; Reading Memorial HS; Reading, MA; (Y); Boys Clb Am; Spanish Clb; SADD; Yrbk Stf; Rep Jr Cls; Rep Sr Cls; JV Bsbl; Var Bsktbl; Coach Actv.

BORGES, PAULA; Somerville HS; Somerville, MA; (Y); 35/550; FNA; Hosp Aide; Spanish Clb; Sprng Wrtng Fstvl 84-86; U MA; Nrs.

BORGIALLI, DANIELA SHELBY; Lawrence Acad; Nashua, NH; (Y); Dance Clb; School Musical; School Play; Swmmng; Camera Clb; French Clb; Spanish Clb; Stage Crew; Yrbk Bus Mgr; Rep Soph Cls; U Puget Sound; Lib Art.

BOROWKO, AMY; Hingham HS; Hingham, MA; (Y); Church Yth Grp; Cmnty Wkr; School Musical; School Play; Hon Roll; Elec Engrg.

BOROWSKI, MICHELLE; Shepherd Hill Reg HS; Dudley, MA; (Y); Hosp Aide; Math Tm; Chorus; High Hon Roll; NHS; NEDT Awd; Lnrd G Bdls Schlrshp Hghst Acdmc Avg 84; Fthr Anthny J Mcns MIC Schlrshp 84; Pre-Med.

BORRELLI, JOEL L; Methuen HS; Methuen, MA; (Y); 39/339; Band; Chorus; Concert Band; Jazz Band; Mrchg Band; School Musical; Swing Chorus; Gym; High Hon Roll; Stu Ovrall Achvt Awd 82; Mst Outstndng Trombone-Nrwd Clssc Cmptn 83; Appld Trombone.

BORTMAN, MARK; Winchester HS; Winchester, MA; (Y); 3/300; Model UN; VP Sr Cls; Rep Stu Cncl; Var L Lcrss; Var L Socr; Var L Wrstlng; High Hon Roll; Williams Coll Bk Awd 86; Jr Schlstc Awds Sci & Eng 86; Natl Latin Exam Magna Summa Maxima Cum Laud.

BORUKHOV, ROMAN; W Roxbury HS; W Roxbury, MA; (S); Hon Roll; NHS; Prfct Atten Awd; Hnr Rll Awd 83; Comp Sci.

BOSH, JOSEPH R; Norton HS; Norton, MA; (Y); Art Clb; Math Tm; Jazz Band; Tennis; Hon Roll; Boys ST 86; Engrng.

BOSLER, PAULA; Williston Northampton Schl; Forth Worth, TX; (Y); Ski Clb; Im Fld Hcky; Var Tennis; Hon Roll; MVP Ten 83-84; Ski Tm 85-86; Peer Ed; Law.

BOSMA, AMY; Douglas Memorial HS; Uxbridge, MA; (Y); Mrchg Band; Yrbk Stf; VP Soph Cls; VP Jr Cls; VP Sr Cls; Rep Stu Cncl; Golf; Twrlr; Cit Awd; Hon Roll; Bus.

BOTTOMLEY, CHRIS; Southwick HS; Sowick, MA; (Y); Church Yth Grp; Spanish Clb; Yrbk Stf; Hon Roll; Bus.

BOUCHARD, BETH; Easthampton HS; Easthampton, MA; (Y); 5/125; Math Clb; Math Tm; Yrbk Stf; Rep Frsh Cls; Rep Sr Cls; Rep Stu Cncl; JV Bsktbl; Var Diving; JV Sftbl; Var Swmmng; Rensselaer Mdl Excllnce Mth & Sci 86; Genetcs.

BOUCHARD, CLAUDINE; Agawam HS; Feeding Hills, MA; (Y); AFS; JCL; Capt Color Guard; Lit Mag; Var Swmmng; Hon Roll; Latin Clb; Mrchg Band; Coll; Math Mjr.

BOUCHARD, LOUISA MAY G; Minnechaug Regional HS; Wilbraham, MA; (Y); 15/314; VP PAVAS; Ski Clb; Rptr Yrbk Phtg; Crs Cntry; L Trk; Hon Roll; NHS; Ntl Merit SF; Camera Clb; Intnl Clb; Art 2 Awd Bst Art Stu; Wrld Wide Rnng Clb Peace Boston Peach Marathn 85; U MA Maherst Scholar; Archit.

BOUCHER, LYNNE; Methven HS; Methuen, MA; (Y); 21/340; Church Yth Grp; Intnl Clb; Model UN; Pep Clb; Sec Jr Cls; Sec Sr Cls; Var L Bsktbl; Var Capt Fld Hcky; French Hon Soc; Hon Roll; SOAR Awd 86; Edward Mulloy Scholar 86; Salem ST Coll; Elem Ed.

BOUCHER, MICHELLE; Apponequet Regional HS; Lakeville, MA; (Y); Church Yth Grp; Pep Clb; Variety Show; Sec Frsh Cls; Sec Soph Cls; Sec Jr Cls; Sec Sr Cls; Var L Cheerleading; Hon Roll; Paralgl.

BOUCIAS, BRANDON; Mohawk Trail Regional HS; Charlemont, MA; (Y); 6/142; Ski Clb; Spanish Clb; VP Jr Cls; JV Crs Cntry; JV Var Socr; Var Capt Trk; High Hon Roll; Pres Schlr; Vrsty Ski Team & Mst Vlbl Athlt Trphy 86; Pres Acdmc Ftns Awd 86; U MA Amhrst; Sci.

BOUDREAU, MICHAEL; Taunton HS; Taunton, MA; (Y); 7/300; Yrbk Stf; Lit Mag; Var Golf; Var Trk.

BOUDREAU, MONIQUE; Arlington Catholic HS; Waltham, MA; (Y); 49/143; Art Clb; Library Aide; Office Aide; Church Choir; School Musical; Variety Show; Yrbk Stf; Natl Latin Exam Cum Laude 82; Bridgewater ST Coll; Educ.

BOUDREAU, NEIL; Leominster HS; Leominster, MA; (S); Church Yth Grp; Political Wkr; School Play; Stage Crew; Rep Jr Cls; Rep Stu Cncl; High Hon Roll; Hon Roll; NHS; Arch.

BOUFFARD, RENEE; Georgetown HS; Georgetown, MA; (Y); Drama Clb; SADD; Powder Puff Ftbl; JV Var Sftbl; Hon Roll; Hghst Avrge In Algebra II 86; JR Vrsty Sftbl 84-85OUTSTNDNG Effrt In Physcl Ed 82; Acctg.

BOUGHTER, SUSAN; Malden HS; Malden, MA; (Y); 60/500; Pep Clb; Y-Teens; Rep Frsh Cls; Rep Soph Cls; Rep Jr Cls; Rep Sr Cls; Var Civic Clb; Var Swmmng; YMCA Ldr Of The Yr 85-86; US Swim Tm/Dvng Tm Rookie/Yr 83-84; Cpt Of MHS Swmg/Dvng Tm 86-87; U Of NH; Bus Admnstrtn.

BOULANGER, SHARON; New Bedford HS; New Bedford, MA; (Y); Mass St Schlrshp 86; Johnson; Fshn Mrchndnsng.

BOULAY, LAURA; Attleboro HS; Attleboro, MA; (Y).

BOULAY, MARC; Apponequet HS; Assonet, MA; (Y); Ski Clb; Yrbk Stf; JV Bsktbl; JV Trk.

BOULE, KAREN; Haverhill HS; Bradford, MA; (Y); Var Capt Bsktbl; Var Capt Sftbl; Hon Roll.

BOULETTE, DANIELLE; North HS; Worcester, MA; (Y); Library Aide; SADD; Yrbk Stf; Hon Roll; Nursing.

BOURAS, CHRISTINA; Damrers HS; Danvers, MA; (Y); 34/302; Spanish Clb; SADD; Sec Soph Cls; Sec Jr Cls; Cheerleading; High Hon Roll; Hon Roll; NHS; Spanish NHS; Lbty Tree Mall Mrchnts Schl 86; U Of New Hampshire; Crmnlgy.

BOURDEAU, GAYLE; Cathedral HS; Chicopee, MA; (Y); 97/536; Cmnty Wkr; Dance Clb; SADD; Var Cheerleading; Acad Excel Alg I Awd 84; U Of MA; Math.

BOURGEA, RENEE; Lawrence HS; Lawrence, MA; (Y); Church Yth Grp; SADD; Rep Frsh Cls; Rep Soph Cls; Rep Jr Cls; Rep Sr Cls; Var Capt Crs Cntry; Var Capt Trk; Hon Roll; Hibernians Shamrock Clssc Road Race 4th Pl 85; Hmcmng Parade 85; Bus.

BOURGEOIS, GAYNOR; Murdock HS; Winchendon, MA; (Y); 7/101; Art Clb; Model UN; Political Wkr; Nwsp Stf; Yrbk Ed-Chief; Pres Stu Cncl; Capt Fld Hcky; Hon Roll; Yrbk Stf; Sftbl; Mdl Cngrs Chairperson; Rgnl Stu Advsry Cnclr; Boston U.

BOURGET, TRACY; Bartlett HS; Webster, MA; (Y); French Clb; Band; Variety Show; Var Cheerleading; High Hon Roll; Hon Roll; Bst Gymnst 85; Bus.

BOURIE, JENNIFER; Auburn HS; Auburn, MA; (Y); Color Guard; Drill Tm; Swmmng; Hon Roll; Rl Estate Agnt.

BOURQUE, CANDI; Taunton HS; Berkley, MA; (Y); Ski Clb; Band; Chorus; Concert Band; Jazz Band; Mrchg Band; Yrbk Ed-Chief; Lit Mag; Stu Cncl; Trk; Typwrtg Awd 86; Wheaton College; Pre Med.

BOURQUE, TRACEY; Blackstone Valley Reg Vo Tech; Mendon, MA; (Y); Library Aide; VP SADD; Chorus; Color Guard; Drm & Bgl; School Musical; VP Soph Cls; Hon Roll; Bentley; Accntng.

BOUSQUET, AIMEE; Marianhill Central Catholic HS; Sturbridge, MA; (Y); Art Clb; Church Yth Grp; Dance Clb; Ski Clb; Chorus; Sec Frsh Cls; Stu Cncl; JV Cheerleading; Asst Dance Tchr 73-86; Outstndng Dance Stu Awd 85; John Robert Powers Modlng Schl Grad 85; Intr Desgn.

BOUSQUET, DAVID ANDRE; Methuen HS; Methuen, MA; (Y); 20/337; Nwsp Rptr; Model UN; Band; Concert Band; Mrchg Band; Rep Frsh Cls; Hon Roll; Prfct Atten Awd; Jrnlsm.

BOUSQUET, DEBORAH; Ware HS; Ware, MA; (Y); 14/112; Spanish Clb; Concert Band; Jazz Band; Mrchg Band; Yrbk Stf; Sec Frsh Cls; Var Bsktbl; Var Socr; Var Sftbl; Hon Roll; All League Sccr 85; Spec Educ.

BOUSQUET, PAULA; Seekonk HS; Seekonk, MA; (Y); 2/230; Drama Clb; Band; Concert Band; Mrchg Band; High Hon Roll; NHS; Spanish NHS; Acadmc Achvt Awd; Brown U Bk Awd; Jrnlsm.

BOUTIETTE, CHRISTIAN J; Bishop Stang HS; Wareham, MA; (Y); Am Leg Boys St; VP Church Yth Grp; Ski Clb; Stu Cncl; Ftbl; Trk; Wt Lftg; French Hon Soc; Hon Roll; NHS; Bus Admin.

BOUTIN, BERNADETTE; Bishop Connolly HS; Fall River, MA; (Y); 58/169; Drama Clb; Chorus; Church Choir; School Play; Variety Show; High Hon Roll; Hon Roll; SMU; Musc.

BOUTIN, DONALD; Central Catholic HS; Lowell, MA; (Y); Church Yth Grp; French Clb; Yrbk Stf; Rep Stu Cncl; Bsbl; JV Bsktbl; Coach Actv; Hon Roll; Cpa.

BOUTIN, TINA; Triton Regional HS; Salisbury, MA; (Y); AFS; Drama Clb; GAA; SADD; Varsity Clb; VP Band; Concert Band; Jazz Band; Mrchg Band; School Musical; Amer Muscl Fndtn Band Hnrs 84 & 86; Amer Muscl Ambssdrs Tour 84-85; Intl Rel.

BOUTOT, BRIAN; Chicopee Comprehensive HS; Chicopee, MA; (Y); 23/323; Church Yth Grp; CAP; French Clb; Teachers Aide; Crs Cntry; Var Tennis; NHS; Curry Achvt 86; U S Air Force Acad; Aerontcs.

BOUYEA, MICHAEL J; Ludlow HS; Ludlow, MA; (Y); Am Leg Boys St; Boys Clb Am; Church Yth Grp; Pres JA; School Musical; Bsbl; Var Ftbl; Var Trk; Hon Roll; Engrng.

BOVE, LISA; Mount St Joseph Academy; Newton, MA; (Y); 4/146; Church Yth Grp; Drama Clb; Exploring; GAA; Science Clb; Spanish Clb; SADD; Yrbk Stf; Soph Cls; Bowling; Colby Coll; Bio.

BOVELL, EDWINA; Boston English HS; Boston, MA; (Y); Church Yth Grp; JA; Teachers Aide; Church Choir; Hon Roll; NCTE Awd; Prfct Atten Awd; St Schlr; Pell Grnt; Newbury Coll; Fshn Dsgn.

BOVELL, W; Boston English HS; Boston, MA; (Y); Church Yth Grp; Computer Clb; Exploring; Teachers Aide; Church Choir; Hon Roll; NCTE Awd; NHS; Ntl Merit Schol; Prfct Atten Awd; Bay ST Coll; Word Procssng.

BOVIO, KELLY; Frontier Regional HS; Conway, MA; (Y); Ed Nwsp Ed-Chief; Nwsp Rptr; Nwsp Stf; French Clb; GAA; Office Aide; Ski Clb; Varsity Clb; JV Capt Bsktbl; JV Crs Cntry; All Franklin Co & Hnrbl Mentn Westrn MA Fld Hcky 85; Syracuse U; Jrnlsm.

BOWDITCH, KRISTINE; Bellingham HS; Bellingham, MA; (Y); Nwsp Stf; Yrbk Stf; Im Bsktbl; JV Tennis; Hon Roll; Church Yth Grp; U Of MA; Law.

BOWEN, JO-ANN CHRISTINE; Everett HS; Boston, MA; (Y); 18/300; Art Clb; Trs Church Yth Grp; Pres Key Clb; SADD; Yrbk Stf; Bsktbl; VP Capt Cheerleading; Var Capt Pom Pon; Hon Roll; New Englnd Rgnl Grand Chrldng Champs & Natl Fnlsts 85-86; Boston Coll; Attrny.

BOWEN JR, JOSEPH S; Melrose HS; Melrose, MA; (Y); 105/238; Boy Scts; Hosp Aide; Model UN; Ski Clb; SADD; Melrose Fireman Fund Assoc,Thomas E Johnson, Most Blessed Sacrament Memory 1981-82 Schlrshps; Lowell U; Ecectricial Engr.

BOWEN, LORI; Randolph HS; Randolph, MA; (Y); SADD; Drill Tm; Powder Puff Ftbl; Trk.

BOWER, PATRICK; Methuen HS; Methuen, MA; (Y); Cmnty Wkr; JV Crs Cntry; Var Wrstlng; Hon Roll; Rcgnzd Bon Secour Hosp Methuen 85; MA Cmmnty Srv Volunteer 86; Compu.

BOWERMAN, LAURA; Arlington HS; Arlington, MA; (Y); Hosp Aide; Library Aide; Stage Crew; Nwsp Rptr; Fld Hcky; Mgr(s); Trk; Cit Awd; Hon Roll; NHS; Bay Path JC Bk Awd 86.

BOWERS, JAMES; Winchester HS; Winchester, MA; (Y); 17/296; Cmnty Wkr; Letterman Clb; Varsity Clb; Rep Stu Cncl; Capt Swmmng; High Hon Roll; NHS; Sailng Clb Capt 83-87; World Champ 86; Swmmng All Schlstc 85.

BOWLES, STEVEN M; Rockland HS; Rockland, MA; (Y); 3/187; Am Leg Boys St; Var Capt Crs Cntry; Var L Trk; NHS; Church Yth Grp; Cmnty Wkr; Political Wkr; Scholastic Bowl; Band; Concert Band.

BOWMAN, STACY; BMC Durfee HS; Fall River, MA; (Y); 6/672; Boys Clb Am; Drama Clb; French Clb; Science Clb; Spanish Clb; Teachers Aide; Orch; Yrbk Stf; High Hon Roll; Hon Roll; Coll Math 85-86; Outstndng Excel Spnsh 86; Bridgewater; Sec Ed.

BOYD, DANIELLE; Concord-Carlisle HS; Concord, MA; (Y); GAA; Variety Show; Off Soph Cls; Off Jr Cls; Off Sr Cls; Var Lcrss; Score Keeper; Var Socr; High Hon Roll; Hon Roll.

BOYD, SUSAN; Bishop Feehan HS; Foxboro, MA; (Y); Political Wkr; Church Choir; French Hon Soc; High Hon Roll; Hon Roll; Schls Cert Mrt Psych; Schls Rcgntn 1 Hghst Avgs Brtsh Lit; Anna Maria Coll; Scl Wrk.

BOYD III, WILLIAM W; Medford HS; Medford, MA; (Y); 67/403; Trs Am Leg Boys St; Trs Band; Orch; Nwsp Stf; Pres Stu Cncl; Var Capt Crs Cntry; Var Capt Trk; NHS; Hon Roll; Rep Frsh Cls; Co-Chrmn Of Grtr Boston Stu Advsry Cncl 86; All-Star Grtr Boston League Cross-Cntry 85-86; Poltcl Sci.

BOYDACK, CHRISTA; Clinton HS; Clinton, MA; (Y); Church Yth Grp; French Clb; Intnl Clb; Library Aide; Spanish Clb; Varsity Clb; Yrbk Stf; Bsktbl; Coach Actv; Fld Hcky; Jr Hmcmng Queen 85-86; Jr Prom Court; Fashion Merchdsng.

BOYER, LAWRENCE; Smith Acad; Hatfield, MA; (Y); 2/32; Boy Scts; Hosp Aide; Key Clb; Quiz Bowl; Bowling; Bausch & Lomb Sci Awd; Hon Roll; Pres Schlr; Sal; St Schlr; 1st Pl MA ST Sci Fair; Cornell U; Physcs.

BOYKO, STEPHEN; Methuen HS; Methuen, MA; (Y); 21/349; Church Yth Grp; Cmnty Wkr; Exploring; Intnl Clb; Model UN; Band; Concert Band; Jazz Band; Mrchg Band; Hon Roll; Georgetown; Crmnlgy.

BOYLE, AMY; Marian HS; Framingham, MA; (Y); 27/187; Exploring; Girl Scts; School Musical; Rep Soph Cls; Rep Jr Cls; Var Bsktbl; Var Socr; Var Capt Trk; Hon Roll; Amer HS Athlete 84-85; Phys Thrpy.

BOYLE, JOHN; Pope John XXIII Central HS; Everett, MA; (Y); Chess Clb; Exploring; Hosp Aide; Key Clb; Salem ST Coll; Bus Mgmt.

BOYLE, KATHLEEN; Arlington Catholic HS; Arlington, MA; (Y); Cmnty Wkr; French Clb; Spanish Clb; Capt Var Socr; JV Trk; Phys Thrpy.

BOYLE, KELLY ANN; Taconic HS; Pittsfield, MA; (Y); 22/265; Cmnty Wkr; Political Wkr; SADD; JV Cheerleading; Capt Swmmng; High Hon Roll; Hon Roll; Pep Clb; Yrbk Stf; Spcl Olympcs Vlntr 83-86; Close-Up Wash 85; Promote Prof Bsbl - Mayoral Appntmnt 86.

BRACKEN, MARIANNE; Notre Dame Acad; Weymouth, MA; (Y); 60/111; Var Trk; Var Vllybl; Chorus; Variety Show; Nwsp Stf; JV Bsktbl; Hon Roll.

BRACKMAN, MATTHEW R; Stoughton HS; Stoughton, MA; (Y); Am Leg Boys St; Chess Clb; Intnl Clb; Math Tm; JV Bsbl; Var Ftbl; High Hon Roll; NHS; Ntl Merit SF; Church Yth Grp; Hnrb Mntn Sci Fair 86; 5th Pos Chess Tm 85; Harvard U; Pre-Med.

BRADANESE, MARC; Medford HS; Medford, MA; (Y); 17/426; Math Clb; Math Tm; Varsity Clb; VP Frsh Cls; VP Soph Cls; Rep Stu Cncl; Var Bsbl; Var Bsktbl; Mu Alp Tht; NHS; Biol 2nd Pl Sci Fair 84; Chem 85; Advncd Math Physcs 86; Engrng.

BRADFORD, LAUREN DEVRA; Reading Memorial HS; Reading, MA; (Y); 22/327; Church Yth Grp; Drama Clb; Hosp Aide; Nwsp Stf; Yrbk Bus Mgr; High Hon Roll; Pres Schlr; Pianist Amer Coll Of Musicians 82-86; Pres Ntl Ltn Hnr Soc 85-86; Vlntr Cnslr At Camp 81-84; Coll Of Holy Cross; Engl.

BRADLEY, BONNIE; Medway JR SR HS; Medway, MA; (Y); 21/140; Church Yth Grp; Drama Clb; Girl Scts; Hosp Aide; Stage Crew; Hon Roll; NHS; Soc Wrk.

BRADLEY, CYNTHIA; Walpole HS; E Walpole, MA; (Y); 13/286; French Clb; JCL; Latin Clb; Orch; Stu Cncl; JV Vllybl; Jr NHS.

BRADLEY, FRANK; Lawrence HS; Lawrence, MA; (Y); DECA; SADD; Yrbk Stf; JV Ftbl; Var Swmmng; DECA 85-86; Law Enfrcmnt.

BRADLEY, JILLIAN; Presentation Of Mary Acad; Methuen, MA; (S); 4/46; Trs Church Yth Grp; Hosp Aide; Spanish Clb; SADD; Church Choir; Yrbk Stf; Var Tennis; High Hon Roll; Hon Roll; Sec NHS; Pre Med.

BRADLEY, JOHN; Silver Lake Regional HS; Kingston, MA; (Y); Boy Scts; Debate Tm; Drama Clb; SADD; Stage Crew; Hon Roll; NHS; Voice Dem Awd; Eagle Scout 86; Engrng.

BRADLEY, KELLEY; Silver Lake Regional HS; Halifax, MA; (Y); 10/496; Camp Fr Inc; French Clb; Office Aide; Nwsp Ed-Chief; Nwsp Rptr; High Hon Roll; Hon Roll; NHS; VFW Awd; Acdmc All-Amer 85-86; US Jrnlsm Awd 85-86; Westfield ST Coll; Media.

BRADLEY, LAURA; Westfield HS; Westfield, MA; (Y); 76/350; Drama Clb; Art Clb; Nwsp Rptr; Yrbk Stf; Trk; U MA; Wrtg.

BRADLEY, LEE-ANN; Stoughton HS; Stoughton, MA; (Y); 48/314; Chorus; Drill Tm; Powder Puff Ftbl; High Hon Roll; Hon Roll; Rene Mandell Schlrshp 86; Fred & Sarah Lipsky Achvmnt Schlrshp 86; Southeastern MA U; Nrsng.

BRADY, KENNETH; Walpole Sr HS; S Walpole, MA; (Y); Ski Clb; Coach Actv; Var Golf; Var Ice Hcky; JV Socr; Hon Roll; Engrng.

BRADY, MICHAEL; Bishop Feehan HS; Attleboro, MA; (Y); 11/250; JCL; SADD; School Musical; JV Crs Cntry; French Hon Soc; High Hon Roll; Jr NHS; NHS; Chess Clb; Debate Tm.

BRAGA, JONATHAN; Bishop Feehan HS; Attleboro, MA; (Y); Am Leg Boys St; Computer Clb; Quiz Bowl; Scholastic Bowl; SADD; Rep Jr Cls; Stu Cncl; Im Bsktbl; JV Ftbl; Var L Ice Hcky; US Naval Acad; Engr.

BRAGA, ROBERT; Littleton HS; Littleton, MA; (Y); 10/84; Math Tm; JC Awd; NHS; U Of Lowell; Elect Engrg.

BRAGG, HANNAH; Bedford HS; Bedford, MA; (Y); 37/206; Aud/Vis; Girl Scts; Band; Concert Band; Mrchg Band; High Hon Roll; Hon Roll; Hon Rl; Ctzns Schlrshp; U Of MA Amherst.

BRAGG, SUSAN; Neuburyport HS; Newburyport, MA; (Y); JCL; Model UN; Political Wkr; Stu Cncl; Im JV Bsktbl; Fld Hcky; Im JV Sftbl; Trk; Hon Roll; Pres Physcl Ftns Awd 83-86; Law.

BRAIT, JEFFREY M; Catholic Memorial HS; Dedham, MA; (Y); 39/243; Am Leg Boys St; Computer Clb; Rep Jr Cls; Rep Sr Cls; Sec Stu Cncl; Var Bsbl; Var Capt Score Keeper; Var Capt Socr; Jr NHS; NHS; MA Boys ST 86; Cathlc Conf All-Stars Sccr 85.

BRANCA, ANGELA; Boston Latin Schl; Boslindale, MA; (Y); 26/274; Church Yth Grp; Band; Concert Band; Mrchg Band; Pep Band; Yrbk Stf; Hon Roll; Classical Prz-Latin 84-85; Fidelity Prz 86; Adv.

BRANCO, EVE MARIE; BMC Durfee HS; Fall River, MA; (Y); 68/700; Drama Clb; French Clb; Color Guard; Mrchg Band; Rep Soph Cls; Rep Jr Cls; Hon Roll; NHS; Psych.

BRANCO, JEFF; Bishop Connolly HS; Swansea, MA; (Y); L Swmmng; High Hon Roll; Grad With Dstnctn 86; Clarkson U; Engrng.

BRANDON, KERLA; Jeremiah & Burke HS; Dorchester, MA; (Y); Church Yth Grp; Computer Clb; Debate Tm; English Clb; JCL; Ski Clb; JV Bsktbl; Var Sftbl; Var Vllybl; Hon Roll; Physlgy.

BRANGIFORTE, MICHAEL; Reading Memorial HS; Reading, MA; (Y); JV Trk; High Hon Roll; Hon Roll; Spanish NHS; Peer Tutor Spnsh 85-86; Radio Brdcstng.

BRANN, JOHN; Milford HS; Milford, MA; (Y); Computer Clb; JV Bsktbl; Var Socr; Var Trk; Hon Roll; A Prz Comp Cntst 2nd 86; Engr.

BRASKIE, DANIEL; Monson JR SR HS; Wilbraham, MA; (Y); Cmnty Wkr; Computer Clb; English Clb; Var Socr; Church Yth Grp; Dance Clb; French Clb; SADD; Yrbk Stf; Trs Frsh Cls; All-Star Soccer 2 Yrs-5 Yr Starter 83-85; Bay-St Games-Soccer 86.

BRATHAS, CHRIS; Attleboro HS; Attleboro, MA; (Y); Am Leg Boys St; Church Yth Grp; Var Bsbl; JV Bsktbl; Score Keeper; Wt Lftg; High Hon Roll; NHS; Us Awd 84; Am Legion Boys ST Awd 86; Bus Adm.

BRATHWAITE, SONIA Y; Burlington HS; Burlington, MA; (Y); Church Yth Grp; Chorus; Swing Chorus; Variety Show; Yrbk Ed-Chief; Lit Mag; Powder Puff Ftbl; Hon Roll; NHS; Stu Gvt Elct Plc Chf 86; Outstndng Chrl Mem 82-86; Off Chrch Yth Grp; U MA Amhest; Pltcl Sci.

BRATSIS, KATHERINE; Holbrook JR SR HS; Holbrook, MA; (Y); 16/96; Library Aide; SADD; Off Jr Cls; Rep Stu Cncl; Hon Roll; NHS; Natl Spanish Exam-Hnrb Mntn Statewide 86; Mst Outstndng Stu Cncl MA 85-86.

BRAXTON, TANYA; Brookline HS; Brookline, MA; (Y); Dance Clb; Band; Symp Band; Im Mgr Bsktbl; Var Co-Capt Cheerleading; Im Mgr Sftbl; Hon Roll; Brookline HS Schlrshp 86; Blck Ctzns Brookline Awd 83 & 84; U Of MA; Chmcl Engrng.

BRAY, JONATHAN; Natick HS; Natick, MA; (Y); 53/400; Am Leg Boys St; Church Yth Grp; SADD; Trs Frsh Cls; Trs Soph Cls; Trs Jr Cls; Trs Sr Cls; JV Bsbl; JV Bsktbl; JV Ftbl.

BRAYTON, KELLI; Monson JR SR HS; Monson, MA; (Y); 12/68; French Clb; SADD; Stage Crew; Sec Stu Cncl; JV Bsktbl; Var Mgr(s); Capt L Socr; L Var Sftbl; Hon Roll; NHS; Girls Soccr 85 All Westn And Leag 85; Frgn Lang.

BRAZEAU, ELIZABETH; Pittsfirld HS; Pittsfield, MA; (Y); 44/450; VP JA; Chrmn Latin Clb; Y-Teens; Yrbk Stf; High Hon Roll; Hon Roll; NHS; French Clb; Wntr Crnvl Bttn Dsgn Grnd Prz 86; Natl Ltn Exm Gld Mdl 86; 3rd Plc ST Ltn Cnvtn Scrpbk 86; Grphc Desgn.

BRAZIL JR, DAVID M; Bridgewater-Raynham HS; Bridgewater, MA; (Y); 39/301; Am Leg Boys St; French Clb; Leo Clb; Red Cross Aide; Science Clb; Tennis; Cit Awd; Bridgewater Firfghtrs Assoc Schlrshp 86; Pres Acadmc Fitnss Awd 86; St Anseim Coll; Bio.

BREALEY, VICKI; Tahanto Regional HS; Berlin, MA; (Y); 20/57; Debate Tm; Pres 4-H; Hosp Aide; School Play; Yrbk Stf; Capt Cheerleading; 4h ST Lvl Prsntn 2nd Pl; Nsng.

BREAULT, DEBBIE; Attleboro HS; Attleboro, MA; (Y); 14/409; High Hon Roll; Hon Roll; NHS; NEDT Awd; Natl Lang Olympd Awd 84; Erly Chldhd Educ.

BREAULT, LISA; Dracut HS; Dracut, MA; (Y); SADD; Teachers Aide; Sftbl; Vllybl; Chamberlayne JC; Fshn Mrchndsg.

BREEN, DANIEL; Boston Latin Schl; Brighton, MA; (Y); 34/285; Am Leg Boys St; Pres Sr Cls; VP Rep Stu Cncl; Var L Trk; High Hon Roll; NHS; Am Leg Boys St; Rep Jr Cls; Im Mgr Bsktbl; Hon Roll; Gld Mdl Wnr Natl Latn Exm 86; Clsscl Awds Exclnc Latn 83-86; NSFC Acdmc All-Amer; Harvard; Latin.

BREEN, KATHLEEN; Bishop Feehan HS; Wrentham, MA; (Y); JV Var Bsktbl; Gym; Var L Sftbl; Tennis; High Hon Roll; Hon Roll; Spanish NHS; Bio.

BREGOLI, BRIAN; Southwick HS; Southwick, MA; (Y); 24/126; Church Yth Grp; Library Aide; Red Cross Aide; Ski Clb; Spanish Clb; SADD; Stage Crew; Hon Roll; U Of MA; Engrng.

BREIT, TRACY; Attleboro HS; Attleboro, MA; (Y); Drama Clb; Band; Mrchg Band; School Musical; Var Gym; Var Tennis; High Hon Roll; Hon Roll.

BRENNAN, ELIZABETH; Leominster HS; Leominster, MA; (Y); 32/350; School Musical; School Play; Stage Crew; Variety Show; Yrbk Stf; Elks Awd; Hon Roll; Leominster Ed Assn Scholar 86; Bridgewater ST Coll; Mktng.

BRENNAN, GREGORY; St Dominic Savio HS; Revere, MA; (Y); 3/95; Aud/Vis; Cmnty Wkr; Exploring; Key Clb; Math Clb; Ski Clb; Chorus; Var L Crs Cntry; Var L Trk; High Hon Roll; Chncllrs Talent Awd U MA Amherst 86; Physcs.

BRENNAN, JAMES; Pittsfield HS; Pittsfield, MA; (Y); #1 In Class; Exploring; JCL; Latin Clb; Quiz Bowl; High Hon Roll; NHS; Ntl Merit SF; Val; RPI Mth & Sci Awd 86; U MA Chancllrs Tlnt Awd Scholar 86; New England Mth Lg Awd 85; U MA.

BRENNAN, JOHN; Central Catholic HS; N Andover, MA; (Y); 68/231; Boy Scts; Ski Clb; Im Bsktbl; JV Trk; Im Vllybl; Hon Roll; Bus Mgmt.

BRENNAN III, JOSEPH J; Waltham HS; Waltham, MA; (Y); Cmnty Wkr; French Clb; Office Aide; School Play; Stage Crew; Elks Awd; Bentley Bus Wk 8l; Psychtry.

BRENNAN, KELLY; Cardinal Spellman HS; Whitman, MA; (Y); 15/226; Office Aide; Spanish Clb; SADD; Capt Socr; Sftbl; High Hon Roll; NHS; Church Yth Grp; Schl Sci Fair 2nd & 3rd Pl; Natl Latin Awd 2nd Pl; Physcl Therpst.

BRENNAN, PAULA; Lynn Classical HS; Lynn, MA; (Y); Office Aide; Capt Var Bsktbl; Hon Roll; Bus Adm.

BRENNAN, ROSE; Bishop Fenwick HS; Lynnfield, MA; (Y); 10/250; 4-H; Spanish Clb; SADD; Nwsp Stf; Rep Frsh Cls; Rep Soph Cls; Rep Jr Cls; Trk; NHS; Spanish NHS; Oxford U; Intl Fin.

BRENNAN, STEVEN; Randolph HS; Randolph, MA; (Y); Church Yth Grp; Rep Stu Cncl; L Ftbl; L Trk; Engrng.

BRENNEKE, JEFFREY; New Bedford HS; New Bedford, MA; (Y); 32/702; Exploring; Science Clb; Var Swmmng; Var L Tennis; High Hon Roll; Hon Roll; VP NHS.

BRENNEMAN, SUSAN; Bishop Feehan HS; Foxboro, MA; (Y); 28/256; Ski Clb; Spanish Clb; Trs Frsh Cls; Sec Stu Cncl; Tennis; High Hon Roll; Hon Roll; NHS; Spanish NHS.

BRENNER, CHARLENE; Marblehead HS; Marblehead, MA; (Y); 3/243; Trs Spanish Clb; Ed Yrbk Stf; Im Lcrss; Im Powder Puff Ftbl; High Hon Roll; Hon Roll; Jr NHS; NHS; Pres Schlr; Babson Coll; Bus.

BRENNER, STACEY; Randolph HS; Randolph, MA; (Y); 14/321; Drama Clb; Pres French Clb; Hosp Aide; Intnl Clb; SADD; Teachers Aide; School Musical; School Play; Stage Crew; Nwsp Rptr; Pres Acad Ftns Awd 86; Bryn Mawr Clg; Pre-Law.

BRENNICK, PAULA; St Clement HS; Somerville, MA; (Y); Yrbk Stf; High Hon Roll; NHS; Prfct Atten Awd; Art Clb; Camera Clb; Church Yth Grp; Cmnty Wkr; Dance Clb; Drama Clb; Hghst Avg Awds Yr In All Subjects 84-85; Emerson Coll; Actress.

BRENTON JR, JOHN J R; Silver Lake Regional HS; Halifax, MA; (Y); 66/492; Church Yth Grp; Math Clb; Varsity Clb; Var Bsbl; Var Bsktbl; Var Crs Cntry; Hon Roll; Voice Dem Awd; Halifax Athletic Assn Schlrshp 86; Syracuse U; Mngmnt.

BRESLIN, JENNIFER; Ursuline Acad; N Walpole, MA; (Y); Church Yth Grp; Service Clb; Ski Clb; Chorus; Nwsp Stf; Rep Soph Cls; JV Fld Hcky; Var Lcrss; L Tennis; Hon Roll; Bus.

BRESNAHAN, CHRISTINE; Bishop Fenwick HS; Peabody, MA; (Y); Church Yth Grp; Science Clb; Stage Crew; Yrbk Stf; Im Bsktbl; JV Var Cheerleading; Im Fld Hcky; JV Var Pom Pon; Var Powder Puff Ftbl; Im Socr; Pre-Med.

BRESNAHAN, PATRICK D M; Holyoke HS; Holyoke, MA; (Y); Cmnty Wkr; Latin Clb; Teachers Aide; Chorus; Yrbk Stf; Stu Cncl; Ice Hcky; Socr; Tennis; Cmnty Wkr; St Hyacinth Coll.

BRESSETTE, ANDREW R; Monson JR SR HS; Monson, MA; (Y); 6/80; Am Leg Boys St; Boy Scts; French Clb; SADD; Acpl Chr; School Musical; Sec Sr Cls; High Hon Roll; Hon Roll; NHS; Chrch Prsh Cncl 84-87; Doctor.

BREWER JR, JOHN D; Quabbin Regional HS; Southbarre, MA; (Y); Am Leg Boys St; Boy Scts; Pres Latin Clb; Letterman Clb; Ski Clb; Varsity Clb; School Play; Nwsp Rptr; Nwsp Stf; Yrbk Stf; Law.

BREWINGTON, JEFF C; Newton South HS; Dorchester, MA; (Y); Am Leg Boys St; Var L Bsktbl; Var L Ftbl; Var L Lcrss; Hon Roll; Faculty Ltr Commendatn 85-86.

BREYARE, KELLIE; Palmer HS; Palmer, MA; (Y); JA; Band; Concert Band; Jazz Band; Mrchg Band; Symp Band; Hon Roll; Thrpst.

BREZNAY, JENNIFER; Buckingham Browne & Nichols HS; Newton, MA; (Y); Chorus; Nwsp Ed-Chief; Var Lcrss; Var Capt Socr; Hon Roll; Ntl Merit Ltr; Harvard Book Prize 85; Nichols Prize 86; Yale Coll; Bio.

BRICE, SEAN J; Old Rochester Regional HS; Marion, MA; (Y); Am Leg Boys St; Im Golf; Capt Var Ice Hcky; Jr NHS; Rookie Yr Hcky 83-84; Bob Brwn Awd 84-85; MVP Hcky 85-86; Prjct Sptlght Sthestrn MA U 85; Arch.

BRICKNER, SHANNON; Middlesex Schl; Tulsa, OK; (Y); Teachers Aide; Nwsp Bus Mgr; Nwsp Phtg; Nwsp Rptr; Yrbk Bus Mgr; Yrbk Phtg; Yrbk Rptr; Stu Cncl; Var Ice Hcky; Hnrs With Crdts 83-85; Hd Peer Support Faciltr 86; Northwestern U; Comm.

BRIDEAU, MICHELLE; Fitchburg HS; Fitchburg, MA; (Y); 1/210; Dance Clb; Ski Clb; Band; Yrbk Stf; Stu Cncl; Fld Hcky; Sftbl; Trk; NHS; Val; MA Cmmwlth Schlr 86; Sprtndnts Awd Encllnc 86; Cls Spkr 86; Worcester Poly Inst; Engr.

BRIGGS, KARYN; Hoosac Valley HS; Savoy, MA; (Y); 24/158; French Clb; Pep Clb; Ski Clb; SADD; High Hon Roll; Hon Roll; NHS; Wm T Adams Schlrshp 86; Ftchbrg ST Coll; Bus Adm.

BRIGHT, CHARLOTTE; Canton HS; Canton, MA; (Y); 40/300; Dance Clb; Girl Scts; Spanish Clb; Drill Tm; School Musical; Yrbk Stf; Hon Roll; Girl Sct Gold Awd 84; Ed.

BRIGHT, KATHY; Madison Park HS; E Boston, MA; (Y); Drill Tm; Stage Crew; Nwsp Phtg; Prfct Atten Awd; Excell Theater Arts 85-86; Hnr Engl 85-86; MASP 85-86; Photogrphy.

BRIGHTMAN, ROSS; Newton North HS; Newton, MA; (Y); Boy Scts; Church Yth Grp; Stage Crew; Elks Awd; SAR Awd; Bus.

BRISSETTE, MICHELLE; Fitchburg HS; Fitchburg, MA; (Y); 19/210; Var Bsktbl; Var Capt Crs Cntry; Var Capt Sftbl; Var Trk; High Hon Roll; Hon Roll; CMC All Str Sftbl 84-86; MVP Defns Sftbl 85-86; Mt Ids Schlrshp 86; Mt Ida Coll; Vet Tech Pgm.

BRITTO, MICAILA; Taunton HS; Taunton, MA; (Y); Church Yth Grp; Intnl Clb; Office Aide; Political Wkr; Teachers Aide; Capt Color Guard; Yrbk Stf; Stat Bsktbl; Gym; Stat Sftbl; Arch.

BROADBENT, LYNNE; Middleboro HS; Middleboro, MA; (S); 15/200; DECA; Hon Roll; NHS; Bridgewater ST Coll; Acctnt.

BROCHI, JEAN; Medford HS; Medford, MA; (Y); Camp Fr Inc; Am Leg Aux Girls St; SADD; Chorus; Orch; Rep Jr Cls; Rep Stu Cncl; JV Gym; Sftbl; Wt Lftg; Katherine Gibbs; Bus Mgmt.

BRODERICK, DEBRA; Cardinal Spellman HS; Avon, MA; (Y); Drama Clb; Hosp Aide; Pep Clb; School Play; JV Vllybl; Hon Roll; Maxima Cum Laude Ntl Latin Exm 85.

BRODEUR, BRIAN; Athol HS; Athol, MA; (Y); Model UN; Ski Clb; Band; Concert Band; Jazz Band; Mrchg Band; Variety Show; Trs Frsh Cls; JV Socr; NHS; Lions All ST Band 86; Western MA Jazz Fest Outstndg Musicianship 86; Percussion.

BRODEUR, JULIE; Monson JR SR HS; Monson, MA; (Y); Library Aide; Spanish Clb; SADD; Yrbk Stf; Trs Sr Cls; Im Badmtn; Stat Bsktbl; JV Socr; High Hon Roll; NHS; Intl Bus.

BRODEUR, KARI; Smith Acad; Hatfield, MA; (Y); Intnl Clb; Key Clb; Variety Show; Yrbk Rptr; Yrbk Stf; JV Cheerleading; Hon Roll; Spch Thrpy.

BRODRICK, KATIE; St Peter-Marian C C HS; Sterling, MA; (Y); Church Yth Grp; Ski Clb; SADD; Yrbk Bus Mgr; Yrbk Stf; Hon Roll; Bus Mgmt.

BROGAN, JEFFREY; Wakefield Memorial HS; Wakefield, MA; (Y); Boy Scts; Exploring; VP JA; Key Clb; Science Clb; Spanish Clb; Band; Concert Band; Mrchg Band; Yrbk Stf; Eagl Sct Awd 85; Intnl Yth Exchng 86; Engrg.

BROGIE, MAUREEN; Marlborough HS; Marlborough, MA; (Y); 5/272; AFS; Math Tm; Ski Clb; Yrbk Stf; JV Trk; Var High Hon Roll; NHS; Pres Schlr; Mchl Fahey Schlrshp 86; Bstn Coll; Mrktng.

BROOKER, JAY; Sharon HS; Sharon, MA; (Y); Spanish Clb; Pres Trs Temple Yth Grp; Ed Nwsp Stf; Ed Yrbk Stf; Trs Sr Cls; High Hon Roll; VP NHS; 3rd Pl Framingham ST Coll Hstrcl Rsrch Conf 86; 3rd Pl Sharon MA Democ Twn Comm Essay Cont 86; Med.

BROOKS, CHRISTINE A; Ayer HS; Shirley, MA; (Y); 38/130; Aud/Vis; SADD; Acpl Chr; School Play; Rep Stu Cncl; Hon Roll; Ntl Schl Chrl Awd 86; Ayer Music Bstrs Schlrshp 86; Fitchburg Coll; Elem Ed.

BROOKS, JENNIFER; Southwick HS; Granville, MA; (Y); 2/133; Am Leg Aux Girls St; Drama Clb; Pres French Clb; Math Tm; Ski Clb; SADD; School Play; Stage Crew; Yrbk Phtg; Yrbk Rptr; Archlgy.

BROOKS, LISA; Academy Of Notre Dame; Westford, MA; (Y); 8/52; Church Yth Grp; VP French Clb; Hosp Aide; Pres Key Clb; Ski Clb; Hon Roll; Intl Frgn Lang Awd 84-85; Tulane U; Frgn Lang.

BROOKS, MARY; Burlington HS; Burlington, MA; (Y); 11/359; English Clb; Science Clb; SADD; Yrbk Ed-Chief; Lit Mag; NHS; Vetnry Tech.

BROOKS, SHEILA; Jamaica Plain HS; Dorchester, MA; (Y); Church Yth Grp; Hosp Aide; JA; Chorus; Church Choir; Score Keeper; Trk; Capt Vllybl; Hon Roll; Lincoln U; Music.

BROSNIHAN, EVEMARIE; Leicester HS; Leicester, MA; (S); Church Yth Grp; Spanish Clb; SADD; Sec Stu Cncl; Var Cheerleading; Hon Roll; Prm Committee 84-86; Fash Merch.

BROUILLETTE, MICHELLE; Cathedral HS; Chicopee, MA; (Y); Cmnty Wkr; Var Cheerleading; Acad Excll Engl II 85; Outstndng Srvce Gdnce Aide 86; Ski Team V Let 85-86; Indstrl Dsgn.

BROUSSEAU, ERIC; Southbridge HS; Southbridge, MA; (Y); 2/136; Am Leg Boys St; Church Yth Grp; Math Tm; Scholastic Bowl; Stat Mgr(s); Var L Trk; Cit Awd; Elks Awd; High Hon Roll; Hon Roll; Leonide J Lemire VFW Ctznshp Awd, Schlrshp 86; Sthbridge Educ Assn Schlrshp 86; Drew U; Poli Sci.

BROUSSEAU, RITA; Lawrence HS; Lawrence, MA; (S); 38/325; Trs Church Yth Grp; Band; Church Choir; Capt Color Guard; Concert Band; Drm & Bgl; Mrchg Band; High Hon Roll; Hon Roll; Castle JC; Exec Sec.

BROUWER, AMY; Northbridge JR SR HS; Whitinsville, MA; (Y); 3/150; Pep Clb; Spanish Clb; Yrbk Stf; Bsktbl; Fld Hcky; Sftbl; High Hon Roll; Hon Roll; NHS; Ntl Merit Ltr; Gold Mdl Acad Achvt 86; 10 Ltr Ath Achvt Awd 86; MVP Field Hockey 86; U CT; Acctng.

BROWN, ANDREW; Phillips Acad; Hanover, PA; (Y); Band; Concert Band; Orch; Pep Band; School Musical; School Play; Stage Crew; Yrbk Stf; VP Frsh Cls; High Hon Roll.

BROWN, BETH ANN; Silver Lake Regional HS; Kingston, MA; (Y); 11/458; Girl Scts; Hosp Aide; VP Math Clb; Spanish Clb; SADD; Socr; High Hon Roll; Hon Roll; NHS; Voice Dem Awd; Edna Maglathlin Schlrshp 86; Silver Lk Eng Dept Schlrshp 86; Ann White Washburn Schlrshp 86; Boston Coll; Comm.

BROWN, CHRISTOPHER; Medford HS; Medford, MA; (Y); 18/431; Am Leg Boys St; Debate Tm; Trs Drama Clb; School Musical; School Play; Var L Socr; Var L Trk; NHS; Voice Dem Awd; JCL; Amer Acdmc Achvmnt 86; Leag All Star Indr & Outdr Trck 86.

BROWN, COURTNEY; Northfield Mount Hermon HS; Abington, MA; (Y); Drill Tm; Flag Corp; Nwsp Stf; Yrbk Bus Mgr; Stu Cncl; Capt Crs Cntry; Fld Hcky; Stat Ice Hcky; Trk; St Michaels Coll.

BROWN, DAVID; Newburyport HS; Newburypt, MA; (Y); 7/208; Am Leg Boys St; Boy Scts; Church Yth Grp; Trs Intnl Clb; VP Model UN; Scholastic Bowl; Spanish Clb; School Musical; Hon Roll; NHS; Ldrshp Semnr 85; SR Mrshl 86; Scttsh Bagpipe Band 84-85; Dickinson; Secdry Schl Tchg.

BROWN, DEBORAH; Melrose HS; Melrose, MA; (Y); 23/368; Camera Clb; Spanish Clb; Sec SADD; Yrbk Phtg; Powder Puff Ftbl; Hon Roll; NHS; Ldrshp & Achvt Awd Yrbk 86; Presdntl Acadmc Fitns Awd 86; U NH; Animal Sci.

BROWN, DIANNE; King Philip Regional HS; Norfolk, MA; (Y); School Play; Yrbk Stf; Off Soph Cls; Cheerleading; Powder Puff Ftbl; Socr; Trk; Hon Roll; Natl Hstry Dy Cmptn 86; NHS 86; Law.

BROWN, DORIS; Hyde Park HS; Dorchester, MA; (S); 10/154; Boys Clb Am; Church Yth Grp; Cmnty Wkr; FCA; GAA; JA; School Musical; Swing Chorus; Yrbk Stf; Off Frsh Cls; Music Awd 84; Natl Hnr Soc 85; Simmons Coll; Comm.

BROWN, ELAINE ANDREA; Coyleland Cassidy HS; Raynham, MA; (Y); 52/140; Drama Clb; Ski Clb; Chorus; School Play; Variety Show; Yrbk Stf; Trs Sr Cls; Sftbl; Trk; Hon Roll; Vera Czanar Memrl Schlrshp 86; Taunton Wmns Clb Schlrshp 86; Syracuse U; Dsgn.

BROWN, ERIC; Saugus HS; Saugus, MA; (Y); Aud/Vis; Chess Clb; Computer Clb; Science Clb; Lit Mag; Var Crs Cntry; Hon Roll; NHS; Northeastern U Carl S Ell Pres Schlrshp 86; Northeastern U; Physcs.

BROWN, JEFFREY; Dedham HS; Dedham, MA; (Y); 20/250; Computer Clb; Lit Mag; JV Bsbl; Im Bsktbl; Im Sftbl; Im Vllybl; Hon Roll; Aeronutcl Engr.

BROWN, JENNIFER; Seekonk HS; Seekonk, MA; (Y); School Play; Sftbl; Swmmng; 6th Pl Grtstrk, 3rd Pl Mdly Rly Sth Sctnls 85; Sth Sctnl All Str Team 85 & 86; Hmn Svcs.

BROWN, JESSICA LARA; B M C Durfee HS; Fall River, MA; (Y); 33/791; Drama Clb; Pres 4-H; Band; Chorus; Flag Corp; School Musical; School Play; JV Twrlr; NHS; Natl 4-H Ldrshp Conf 85; Pblc Rel.

BROWN, JOANN; Marblehead HS; Marblehead, MA; (Y); 48/262; Drama Clb; SADD; Stage Crew; Yrbk Phtg; Yrbk Stf; Cheerleading; Gym; Powder Puff Ftbl; High Hon Roll; Hon Roll; Simmons Coll; Pre-Law.

BROWN, KAREN; Saugus HS; Saugus, MA; (Y); 17/297; Cmnty Wkr; Drama Clb; Library Aide; Office Aide; Spanish Clb; VP Chorus; Church Choir; School Musical; School Play; Yrbk Stf; U Of MA Amherst; Pre Med.

BROWN, KATHLEEN; Bartlett HS; Webster, MA; (Y); 20/150; French Clb; Pres Trs FBLA; Drm Mjr(t); Mgr Trk; NHS; Outstndng Bus Stu Awd; Bartlett Gold B Awd; Nichols; Comp.

BROWN, KRIS; Natick HS; Natick, MA; (Y); 32/399; DECA; JV Sftbl; High Hon Roll; Hon Roll; Bus Awd Typwrtg I & Acctg I & Distbtv Ed 84 & 86; Acctg.

BROWN, LAURIE; Natick HS; Natick, MA; (Y); 31/400; Speech Tm; School Musical; Yrbk Stf; Sec Stu Cncl; Var Fld Hcky; Hon Roll; Bus Ed Awd 83-84; Exec Bd Mem 83-86; Med.

BROWN, LIISA; St Bernards Central Catholic HS; W Townsend, MA; (S); 8/177; Church Yth Grp; Nwsp Rptr; Var Socr; Hon Roll; NHS; Pre Med.

BROWN, MARYLOU; East Longmeadow HS; E Longmeadow, MA; (Y); 10/197; Pres AFS; Debate Tm; VP Intnl Clb; Scholastic Bowl; School Play; Nwsp Rptr; Nwsp Stf; Trs Jr Cls; Socr; Var L Swmmng; Dartmth Coll Bk Awd 86; Mt Holyoke Sci Bk Awd 86fstu Rep Regnl Brd Ed 85-86; Intl Govrnmnt.

BROWN, MICHAEL; Cohasset JR/SR HS; Cohasset, MA; (Y); 47/107; Ski Clb; Spanish Clb; VICA; Band; Concert Band; Jazz Band; Orch; School Musical; Symp Band; Ice Hcky; Bus Admin.

BROWN, MONICA; Seekonk HS; Seekonk, MA; (Y); Church Yth Grp; SADD; Flag Corp; Hon Roll; Spanish NHS; Psych.

BROWN, PAMELA; Notre Dame Acad; Canton, MA; (Y); 25/111; Dance Clb; Spanish Clb; SADD; Chorus; Variety Show; Hon Roll; FAA Credit Union Schlrshp 86; Bridgewater ST Coll; Specl Ed.

BROWN, PHYLLIS; Jamaica Plain HS; Roxbury, MA; (Y); Church Yth Grp; Cmnty Wkr; FCA; FBLA; Library Aide; Office Aide; Chorus; Church Choir; Nwsp Rptr; Yrbk Stf; Received Awd For Being Faithful 84; Emerson; Comm.

BROWN, RAMONA; Mario Umana Technical HS; Dorchester, MA; (Y); 5/93; Pres JA; Church Choir; Yrbk Sprt Ed; Pres Jr Cls; Stu Cncl; Capt Var Trk; Co-Capt Var Vllybl; High Hon Roll; Hon Roll; Prfct Atten Awd; Sprtsmnshp Awd 85-86; Schlrshp Awds 82-83 & 85-86; PA ST U; Premed.

BROWN, SARAH; Doherty Memorial HS; Worcester, MA; (Y); Church Yth Grp; Spanish Clb; SADD; Stu Cncl; High Hon Roll; Hon Roll; NHS; Spanish NHS; Natl Spnsh Exam & Mexico Exam 84-86; Law.

BROWN, SCOTT CHARLES; Wachusett Regional HS; Holden, MA; (Y); 2/443; Boy Scts; Drama Clb; Model UN; Acpl Chr; School Musical; School Play; NHS; French Clb; Ski Clb; Chorus; Dartmouth Bk Awd 86; MA All ST Music Festvl 86.

BROWN, STEPHANIE; Northfield Mount Hermon Schl; Rumson, NJ; (Y); Library Aide; Yrbk Stf; JV Fld Hcky; Var L Sftbl; Hon Roll; CT Coll.

BROWN, STEVEN; Maynard HS; Maynard, MA; (Y); 15/96; Aud/Vis; Cmnty Wkr; Radio Clb; Teachers Aide; Band; Concert Band; Mrchg Band; JV Bsbl; Var L Ice Hcky; Var L Socr; Sprtsmnshp Awd 83-86; U S Army; Cnstrctn Engnr.

BROWN, SUSAN; Bellingham Memorial JRSR HS; Bellingham, MA; (Y); Pep Clb; Stu Cncl; Cit Awd; Hon Roll; Jr NHS; NHS.

BROWN, SUSAN; Milford HS; Milford, MA; (Y); 7/266; Bowling; High Hon Roll; NHS; Prfct Atten Awd; Schlrshp North Eastern U 86; Northeastern U; Phy Thrpy.

BROWN, SUSAN E; Haverhill HS; Bradford, MA; (Y); 9/450; Church Yth Grp; German Clb; Latin Clb; Nwsp Ed-Chief; Stu Cncl; Hon Roll; Jr NHS; NHS; Hgh O Brn Yth Ldrshp Fndtn Intl Ambssdr 85-86.

BROWN, THOMAS; Mario Umana Tech Of Sci & Technlgy; Dorchester, MA; (Y); Boys Clb Am; Boy Scts; Church Yth Grp; FCA; JA; Varsity Clb; Church Choir; Off Jr Cls; Stu Cncl; Bsktbl; Med.

BROYLES, JOEL; Chicopee Comprehensive HS; Chicopee, MA; (Y); 53/278; Spanish Clb; SADD; School Play; Variety Show; Trs Frsh Cls; Trs Soph Cls; Trs Jr Cls; Trs Sr Cls; Tennis; NHS.

BRUCE, JEFF; Westford Acad; Westford, MA; (Y); 42/225; Pres Ski Clb; Variety Show; Var Capt Golf; Hon Roll; Natl Acad Fit Awd 86; Advncd Comp Logic Awd 86; Alpha Data Assocs Scholar 86; Bentley Coll; Comp Sci.

BRUEN, LIAM; Boston Coll HS; Sherborn, MA; (Y); 15/300; Lit Mag; Var Ftbl; Var L Trk; High Hon Roll; NHS; Slvr Mdlst Natl Latin Exm.

BRULE, MATTHEW L; Blackstone Vly Regnl Vo Tech HS; E Douglas, MA; (Y); Mrchg Band; Hon Roll; Pres Schlr; Electrnc Engrng.

BRUNEAU, JOANNE; King Philip Regional HS; Wrentham, MA; (Y); Church Yth Grp; Hosp Aide; Intnl Clb; Band; Concert Band; Jazz Band; Mrchg Band; Lit Mag; Cheerleading; MIP Jazz Ens 86; Soc Svc.

BRUNO, DAVID; Revere HS; Revere, MA; (Y); 5/344; Math Tm; Quiz Bowl; VP Science Clb; Sec Stu Cncl; Var Socr; JV Trk; High Hon Roll; NHS; Ntl Merit Ltr; Pres Schlr; Star Wars Essay Cont Wnnr 85; Eric Carrozza Mem Scholar 86; Italian-Amer Chartbl Assn Scholar 86; PA ST; Meteorlgy.

BRUNO, PETER A; Mahar Regional HS; Orange, MA; (Y); 25/130; Am Leg Boys St; Key Clb; Model UN; Band; Chorus; Variety Show; Ftbl; Trk; Bus Adm.

BRUSH, CHERYL; Medway HS; Medway, MA; (Y); 11/135; Church Yth Grp; Drama Clb; Girl Scts; Stage Crew; High Hon Roll; NHS; Girl Sct Slvr & Gold Ldrshp Awd 84 & 85; Girl Sct Svc Awds; Girl Sct 10 Yr Awd.

BRYSON, JENNIFER; Medway HS; Medway, MA; (Y); 6/135; French Clb; JV Fld Hcky; Var Trk; Govt Intrnshp 85-86; Ntl Hnr Soc 85-86; Pre Law.

BUBA, SHELLEY; New Bedford HS; New Bedford, MA; (Y); 225/701; Band; Concert Band; Mrchg Band; Stu Cncl.

BUBAS, TRACEY; Milton HS; Milton, MA; (Y); Church Yth Grp; Cmnty Wkr; French Clb; SADD; Yrbk Stf; Rep Sr Cls; Rep Stu Cncl; Var L Cheerleading; Coach Actv; Var Capt Gym; Bus Adm.

BUBENCIK, ROBERT; Boston College HS; Quincy, MA; (Y); Im Bsktbl; JV Crs Cntry; Im Ftbl; Im Vllybl; Hon Roll; Recgntn Merit Frnch 85-86; Pilot.

BUCCHIERE, DIANE; Saugus HS; Saugus, MA; (Y); Cmnty Wkr; Pep Clb; VP Spanish Clb; JV Var Cheerleading; Jr NHS; NHS; VFW Awd; Phi Alpha Theta 13th Annl ST Hstry Conf Partcpnt 86; Boston U; Forgn Rel.

BUCCIERI, JOSEPH J; Dom Davio HS; East Boston, MA; (Y); 50/101; JA; SADD; Rep Frsh Cls; Capt JV Bsbl; Ftbl; Trk; Prfct Atten Awd; CPA.

BUCEY, ROB; Saugus HS; Saugus, MA; (Y); Concert Band; Mrchg Band; Pep Band; Hon Roll; NHS; Voice Dem Awd; Musicianshp Awd 84-85; Percussion Sectn Ldr Awd 85-86; Mechanical Engineering.

BUCHANAN, KARLA; Georgetown HS; Georgetown, MA; (Y); 17/80; Drama Clb; Spanish Clb; School Play; Yrbk Stf; VP Sr Cls; JV Var Fld Hcky; Hon Roll; Bus Mgmnt.

BUCK, KATHLEEN; Hyde Park Acad; Readville, MA; (S); Sec Jr Cls; Sec Sr Cls; High Hon Roll; Hon Roll.

BUCKEL, DENISE; Holyoke Catholic HS; Chicopee, MA; (Y); 10/129; Math Clb; Band; Jazz Band; Mrchg Band; Yrbk Stf; Hon Roll; NHS; Pres Schlr; Elms Coll; Scndry Ed.

BUCKLEY, CHRISTOPHER M; Waltham SR HS; Waltham, MA; (Y); Am Leg Boys St; Aud/Vis; Cmnty Wkr; Latin Clb; Pres Stu Cncl; L Golf; Hon Roll; Jr NHS; Sfflk U Bk Prz 86; Kngsbry Tmprnc Essy Awd 86; Bus Admin.

BUCKLEY, KEVIN; Reading HS; Reading, MA; (Y); SADD; Nwsp Ed-Chief; Nwsp Sprt Ed; Rep Soph Cls; Rep Jr Cls; Stu Cncl; Im Ftbl; Var Ice Hcky; Im Powder Puff Ftbl; Var Trk; Bio.

BUCKLEY, KEVIN; Woburn SR HS; Woburn, MA; (S); 25/453; Boys Clb Am; Drama Clb; French Clb; Leo Clb; Math Tm; Yrbk Sprt Ed; Stu Cncl; Capt Bsbl; Capt Bsktbl; NHS; All Star Ptchr Bsbl 85; Most Vlbl Pitcher 85; Rookie Of The Yr; Pre Med.

BUCKLEY, MARYANNE; Arlington HS; Arlington, MA; (Y); Church Yth Grp; Hosp Aide; Office Aide; Political Wkr; SADD; L Fld Hcky; L Sftbl; Hon Roll; NHS; Bentley Coll; Acctg.

BUCKMAN, TODD A; Oakmont Regional HS; Ashburnham, MA; (Y); 13/140; Am Leg Boys St; Radio Clb; Spanish Clb; Nwsp Stf; JV Var Bsktbl; Var Score Keeper; High Hon Roll; NHS; Jrnlsm.

BUDDE, JAMES; Hingham HS; Hingham, MA; (Y); 32/340; Church Yth Grp; Exploring; Math Tm; Stage Crew; Im Vllybl; High Hon Roll; Hon Roll; U Of MA; Mech Engrng.

BUDDEN, ELIZABETH; Reading Memorial HS; Reading, MA; (Y); Girl Scts; Hosp Aide; Library Aide; SADD; JV Fld Hcky; High Hon Roll; Hon Roll; Paralegal.

BUDDING, ANTHONY D; Lexington HS; Lexington, MA; (Y); Ski Clb; Spanish Clb; JV Lcrss; Var Socr; Var Trk; Hon Roll; Rgnl Sci Fair 84; Middlebury Col.

BUENAVENTURA, MARIA RUTH; Fontbonne Acad; Quincy, MA; (Y); Camera Clb; Drama Clb; Math Tm; Chorus; School Musical; School Play; Lit Mag; High Hon Roll; Hon Roll; VP NHS; Acad Exc Wlrd Hist, Theol, Span; Brnz Mdl Span Achvt Exm; Jordan March JR Cncl Comptn Wnr; Harvard; Bus Admin.

BUFALINO, CARA; Swampscott HS; Swampscott, MA; (Y); Church Yth Grp; Cmnty Wkr; French Clb; Variety Show; Nwsp Stf; Stu Cncl; Var Bsktbl; JV Cheerleading; Powder Puff Ftbl; Var Socr; Capt Vrsty Spring Trk 87; Capt Vrsty Bsktbl 87; Communctns.

BUI, TUNG; Ludlow HS; Ludlow, MA; (Y); French Clb; School Play; Variety Show; Rep Frsh Cls; Rep Soph Cls; Rep Jr Cls; Var Bsktbl; Var Capt Crs Cntry; Var Capt Trk; 3 Mdls In Wstrn MA Trck Chmpnshps 86; 1 Mdl In CT X-Cntry Race 86; Schl Rcrd In X-Cntry 86; U Of MA; Bus Mgmt.

BULARZIK-MUZAL, DANIEL P; Natick HS; Natick, MA; (Y); 18/444; Computer Clb; Exploring; German Clb; JA; Political Wkr; Science Clb; Speech Tm; SADD; Teachers Aide; School Musical; Awd Grp Discssn Spch Evnt 84; Liberty Bell Trphy Phila Spch Team 85; Theortcl Physcs.

BULDRINI, JANINA M; Southwick HS; Southwick, MA; (Y); 5/117; Dance Clb; Debate Tm; 4-H; French Clb; Library Aide; Teachers Aide; Chorus; Hon Roll; NHS; Rotary Awd; New Engl Deli/Dairy Assn Schlrshp 86; MA ST Schlrshp 86; Excllnc Acctg Awd 86; Excllnc Engl Awd 86; St Joseph Coll-Htfd Ct; Bus.

BULLARD, THOMAS; Leicester HS; Leicester, MA; (Y); Art Clb; Church Yth Grp; Prfct Atten Awd; Art.

BULLARD III, WILLIAM A; Bmc Durfee HS; Fall River, MA; (Y); 24/670; Boys Clb Am; Drama Clb; VP JA; Math Clb; School Musical; School Play; High Hon Roll; NHS; Computer Clb; Yrbk Stf; Navy ROTC Schlrshp 86; Worcester Polytech; Elec Engr.

BULLEN, HEIDI; Franklin HS; Franklin, MA; (Y); Latin Clb; Pep Clb; Ski Clb; VP Jr Cls; JV Var Cheerleading; JV Var Pom Pon; Hon Roll; Intr Desgn.

BULLENS, KAREN; Bartlett HS; Webster, MA; (Y); 22/164; Spanish Clb; Yrbk Stf; Var Crs Cntry; Var Tennis; High Hon Roll; Hon Roll; MVP Tnns; Nichols Coll; Psych.

BULLOCK, NANCY; Hudson HS; Hudson, MA; (Y); 6/160; Math Tm; Chorus; School Musical; Var Socr; JV Tennis; NHS; Ntl Merit SF; Drama Clb; Exploring; Math Clb; MA Youth Ldrshp Foundation Rep 85; All Eastern U S Chorus 86; MA All State Chorus 85 & 86; Med.

BUNNELL, LORI; St Mary Regional; Lynn, MA; (Y); 13/127; Computer Clb; Library Aide; Teachers Aide; School Play; Yrbk Stf; Cheerleading; Powder Puff Ftbl; High Hon Roll; Hon Roll; Stu Govt Day Data Prcsng Dir 85; Suffolk U; Comp Sci.

BUONCUORE, LISA; Arlington Catholic HS; Burlington, MA; (Y); 2/144; Drama Clb; Spanish Clb; Church Choir; Nwsp Stf; High Hon Roll; NHS; Sal; MA Adv Stds Pgm, Ntl Hnr Rll 85; MA Hnr Schlrshp 86-87; Smith Coll; Amer Stds.

BUONOPANE, JAMES; St Dom Savio HS; Winthrop, MA; (Y); Key Clb; Math Clb; Science Clb; Im Bsktbl.

BUONOPANE, STEPHEN; Westwood HS; Westwood, MA; (Y); 1/212; Math Tm; Lit Mag; Var L Crs Cntry; Var L Trk; Bausch & Lomb Sci Awd; French Hon Soc; Hon Roll; NHS; Ntl Merit Ltr; Engr.

BURBA, RANDALL; St Johns Prep; Salem, MA; (Y); Aud/Vis; Boy Scts; Camera Clb; Trk; Hon Roll; JR Schlr Awd 86; Orthodntst.

BURCHSTED JR, ROY; Brockton HS; Brockton, MA; (Y); 319/1000; Scholastic Bowl; Ski Clb; JV Bsbl; Hon Roll; Pre-Med.

BURDEN, LEANNE; Attleboro HS; Attleboro, MA; (Y); Church Yth Grp; Powder Puff Ftbl; L Trk; High Hon Roll; NHS.

BURDICK, ANDREW; Drury HS; North Adams, MA; (Y); Boy Scts; Church Yth Grp; Cmnty Wkr; School Musical; School Play; Trk.

BURDICK, MAX; Shepherd Hill Reg HS; Charlton, MA; (Y); Am Leg Boys St; Rep Jr Cls; JV Bsktbl; Capt Ftbl; Capt Trk; Im Wt Lftg; Hon Roll; Elect Engr.

BURDICK, THOMAS; Mc Cann Tech; Florida, MA; (Y); CAP; Cmnty Wkr; JV Bsktbl; Hon Roll; Electrncs.

BUREK, MATTHEW J; Tantasqua Regional HS; Brimfield, MA; (Y); 26/186; Church Yth Grp; Ski Clb; Varsity Clb; Var Socr; High Hon Roll; Hon Roll; NHS; H P Hood Scholar 86; Johnson & Wales; Culnry Art.

BURGESS, BRIAN; Quaboag Regional HS; W Brookfield, MA; (Y); Church Yth Grp; JA; Science Clb; Spanish Clb; SADD; Varsity Clb; Golf; Socr; Hon Roll; Mech Engrng.

BURGESS, BRUCE; Beverly HS; Beverly, MA; (Y); Boy Scts; Church Yth Grp; Cmnty Wkr; Var L Bsbl; Var L Ftbl; Var Wrstlng; Hon Roll; U Of NH; Pre-Law.

BURGESS, KEN D; Quaboag Regional HS; W Brookfield, MA; (Y); 19/77; Church Yth Grp; JA; Science Clb; Ski Clb; SADD; Varsity Clb; Var Golf; Var Socr; Jhn E Adms Mem Schlrshp, Moony Schlrshp 86; Syracuse U; Bus.

BURGOS, MARIBEL; Holyoke HS; Holyoke, MA; (Y); 42/360; Church Yth Grp; Latin Clb; Pep Clb; Spanish Clb; Church Choir; Yrbk Stf; Vllybl; Hon Roll; NHS; Ross Nrsng Schrlshp 86; Ldy Of Elms; Nrsng.

BURKE, BRIDGET; Lawrence Acad; Lawrence, MA; (Y); Cmnty Wkr; School Musical; Yrbk Stf; Lcrss; Vllybl; Hon Roll; Chorus; Stu Cncl; Bsktbl; Socr.

BURKE, ERIN; Billerica Memorial HS; Billerica, MA; (Y); 76/500; French Clb; Ski Clb; SADD; Badmtn; Powder Puff Ftbl; JV Sftbl; Var Capt Vllybl; Hon Roll.

BURKE, JOANNE; Mount St Joseph Acad; Brookline, MA; (Y); 50/167; Pres Church Yth Grp; Ski Clb; Spanish Clb; School Play; Hon Roll; Engrng.

BURKE, KAREN; Waltham SR HS; Waltham, MA; (Y); Church Yth Grp; Dance Clb; Drama Clb; School Musical; School Play; Nwsp Rptr; Hon Roll; French Clb; Stage Crew; Rep Frsh Cls; JR Cnslr-Anytwn/Natl Cncl Chrstns-Jews 85; MA Advncd Study Pgm 86; YMCA Yth, Govt Pgm 85-86; Nrthwstrn U; Drma.

BURKE, KELLY; B M C Durfee HS; Fall River, MA; (Y); 32/650; French Clb; Varsity Clb; Var Sftbl; Var L CC Awd; Var L Vllybl; Hon Roll; NHS.

BURKE, MICHELLE; South High Comm Schl; Worcester, MA; (S); Church Yth Grp; Office Aide; Science Clb; Rep Stu Cncl; Mgr(s); Co-Capt Tennis; Hon Roll; Jr NHS; NHS.

BURKE, MIKE; Boston College HS; S Boston, MA; (Y); Church Yth Grp; Cmnty Wkr; Key Clb; PAVAS; Spanish Clb; Variety Show; Nwsp Rptr; Jr Cls; Sr Cls; Stu Cncl.

BURKE, SEAN; Lawrence HS; Lawrence, MA; (Y); Model UN; Var Ftbl; Var Trk; Hon Roll.

BURKE, SUZY; Arlington HS; Arlington, MA; (Y); SADD; Capt Tennis; NHS; All Star Tnns Tm 84-86; MVP-TNNS-ARLNGTN Sprtsmn Clb 84-86; Rnkd 1 By NELTA-IGBS & 30-34 In A's 85.

BURLESON JR, ROGER; Frontier Regional HS; Sunderland, MA; (Y); 3/93; Yrbk Stf; VP Frsh Cls; VP Soph Cls; Pres Jr Cls; Rep Sr Cls; Rep Stu Cncl; Var L Bsbl; Var L Ftbl; Var Capt Wrstlng; Hon Roll; 3rd West MA Wrstlg 86; Worcester Polytech Inst; Engrng.

BURLINSON, AMY; Old Rochester Regional HS; Mattapoisett, MA; (Y); #13 In Class; AFS; Math Tm; Chorus; Crs Cntry; Trk; Hon Roll; NHS; Ntl Merit Ltr; Frnch 3 Awds 85, 4 Awds 86; Lib Arts.

BURNHAM, SHEILA; Chelmsford HS; Chelmsford, MA; (S); Art Clb; Pres Off DECA; Office Aide; High Hon Roll; Schlrshp Johnson & Wales Coll 1st Pl DECA ST Winner 86; Town Of Chelmsford Schlrshp 86; Johnson & Wales Coll; Fshn Merc.

BURNHAM, SUZANNE; Saugus HS; Saugus, MA; (Y); 3/300; Church Yth Grp; Hosp Aide; Library Aide; Spanish Clb; Yrbk Stf; Lit Mag; High Hon Roll; NHS; Ntl Merit Ltr; Voice Dem Awd; Chnclrs Tlnt Awd U MA Amhrst 86; Upsln Alpha Hnrb Mntn For Rsrch Paper In Hstry 86; Jrnlsm.

BURNS, JEFFREY S; Masconomet HS; Topsfield, MA; (Y); Civic Clb; German Clb; Math Tm; Model UN; Radio Clb; Science Clb; Speech Tm; Symp Band; Trk; High Hon Roll; Congrs Bundestag Schlrshp 84-85; Columbia U; Peace Corp.

BURNS, STEPHEN; Uxbridge HS; Uxbridge, MA; (Y); Am Leg Boys St; Trs Church Yth Grp; Varsity Clb; School Play; Yrbk Stf; Sec Sr Cls; Bsbl; Trs Ftbl; NCTE Awd; NHS; NCTE Wrtng Cntst 85-86; Sports Dir; Jrnlsm.

BURNS, STEVEN W; Palmer HS; Palmer, MA; (Y); Am Leg Boys St; Church Choir; Var L Bsbl; Var L Bsktbl; Var L Ftbl; Bausch & Lomb Sci Awd; High Hon Roll; NHS; Prfct Atten Awd; Church Yth Grp; MA Mth Lg Awd; Rensselaer Mdl Mth & Sci; All Lg & All Wstrn MA Ftbl, Bsbl, Bsktbl 85-86; Engrng.

BURRELL, ALEN; Holbrook HS; Holbrook, MA; (Y); 16/100; Boy Scts; Latin Clb; Band; Concert Band; Mrchg Band; Pep Band; Crs Cntry; Trk; Hon Roll; Engrng.

BURRILL, ELIZABETH; Quaboag Regoinal HS; West Brookfield, MA; (Y); 9/82; Red Cross Aide; Ski Clb; SADD; Varsity Clb; Var Capt Fld Hcky; Hon Roll; NHS; All-Star Fld Hockey; Hlth Scis.

BURSTEIN, JUDY; Longmeadow HS; Longmeadow, MA; (Y); 21/252; Pres Sec Boys Clb Am; Nwsp Bus Mgr; Nwsp Sprt Ed; Lit Mag; Stu Cncl; Capt Fld Hcky; Var Swmmng; High Hon Roll; NHS; Cum Laude Natl Lat Exam 85; Newspaper Svc Awd 86; Eng.

BURTON, CARLA A; Milton Acad; Chester, PA; (Y); GAA; Pres Spanish Clb; Church Choir; Yrbk Phtg; Yrbk Stf; Rep Frsh Cls; Rep Soph Cls; Rep Jr Cls; Var Capt Bsktbl; Var Trk; Bus.

BURTON, DIANA; Bedford HS; Bedford, MA; (Y); Pep Clb; Var Crs Cntry; Var Trk; High Hon Roll; Hon Roll; Schlrshp Awd Hm Econ 85; Ntl Yng Ldrs WA Dc 86; Intl Bus.

BURTON, HOPE; Georgetown JR-SR HS; Georgetown, MA; (Y); 22/83; AFS; Ed Lit Mag; Hon Roll; Mnstr.

BURY, LAURA J; North Attleboro HS; North Attleboro, MA; (Y); 4/258; Trs Art Clb; Math Clb; JV Bsktbl; Var L Fld Hcky; Im Powder Puff Ftbl; NHS; Ntl Merit Ltr; Boston Globe Schlstsc Art Awds 83 & 86; Commrcl Art Awd 85; Womens Clb Schlrshp 86; Carnegie-Mellon U; Wrtng.

BURZYNSKI, KATHY; Chicopee Comprehensive HS; Chicopee, MA; (Y); 14/332; German Clb; Yrbk Stf; Var L Socr; Var L Sftbl; High Hon Roll; Hon Roll; NHS; Coaches Awd Sftbl 86; U MA; Tchng.

BUSA, GINA; Tewksbury Memorial HS; Tewksbury, MA; (Y); 35/325; JA; Mrchg Band; Nwsp Ed-Chief; Nwsp Rptr; Rep Frsh Cls; Trs Soph Cls; Trs Jr Cls; Hon Roll; NHS; Ntl Merit Ltr; Schlrshps Prnt Advsry Cmmtee & Twksbry Tchrs Assoc; Northeastern U; Engl Educ.

BUSCEMI, SUSAN; Christopher Columbs Cntrl Cath HS; Boston, MA; (S); 1/126; Art Clb; Math Clb; Nwsp Stf; Yrbk Ed-Chief; Hon Roll; NHS; 2dn Pl Sci Fair 84; 1st Pl Phtgrphy Cntst 84; NEDT Cert 83-84; Boston Coll; Cmmnctns.

BUSCONE, ANDREA; Milford HS; Milford, MA; (Y); Am Leg Aux Girls St; Church Yth Grp; Cmnty Wkr; Office Aide; Ski Clb; Sec Frsh Cls; Sec Soph Cls; Sec Jr Cls; Var Fld Hcky; Var Score Keeper; Bst Sprtswmn-Fld Hockey 84; Employee Of Wk-Smmr Job 86; Babson Coll; Pub Rltns.

BUSH, BRETT M; Gardner HS; Gardner, MA; (Y); 2/168; Am Leg Boys St; Yrbk Stf; Pres Frsh Cls; Pres Jr Cls; Var Bsbl; Var Capt Bsktbl; Var Crs Cntry; Bausch & Lomb Sci Awd; NHS; Ntl Merit Ltr; Hrvrd Bk Awd 85; Hgh Obrn Smnr 84; Bst Athlt Dist 3 86; Boston Coll; Fínc.

BUSHEY, RACHEL; Gardner HS; Gardner, MA; (Y); 20/141; Spanish Clb; Im Swmmng; Hon Roll; Bus.

BUSKEY, TIMOTHY; Gardner HS; Gardner, MA; (Y); 3/150; Am Leg Boys St; Spanish Clb; Rep Frsh Cls; Rep Soph Cls; L Var Bsbl; L Var Bsktbl; High Hon Roll; NHS; Band; Mrchg Band; Hgh Obrn Yth Ldrshp Smnr 85; Amercn Dcthln 86; Harvord; Sci.

BUSTAMANTE, ALBERTO; Northfield Mount Hermon HS; Ecuador; (Y); Socr; Georgetown U; Intl Finance.

BUTCHER, EDWARD; Westfield HS; Westfield, MA; (Y); 35/430; Church Yth Grp; VP Sr Cls; JV Var Bsbl; JV Var Bsktbl; JV Var Ftbl; Govt.

BUTERA JR, ROBERT J; Bishop Feehan HS; Cumberland, RI; (Y); 1/232; Computer Clb; Math Tm; Chorus; Jazz Band; Mrchg Band; Dnfth Awd; DAR Awd; High Hon Roll; JETS Awd; NHS; New Englnd Schlrshp Hnrs Mrchng Bnd 85; GA Inst Of Tech; Elec Engrng.

BUTKUSS, KRISTYN; Fontbonne Acad; N Quincy, MA; (Y); Church Yth Grp; Drama Clb; Hosp Aide; Intnl Clb; Chorus; Stage Crew; Variety Show; NHS; Cum Laude Awd Spnsh Achvt 85; 2nd On Cert 86.

BUTLER, JENNIFER; Walpole HS; Walpole, MA; (Y); 30/260; Church Yth Grp; Cmnty Wkr; Drama Clb; Library Aide; Hon Roll; NHS; Clssrm Prfrmnc Awd French & Bus 84; Intl Bus.

BUTLER, JESSICA; Seekonk HS; Seekonk, MA; (Y); Spanish Clb; SADD; Nwsp Stf; Frsh Cls; Soph Cls; Jr Cls; Sr Cls; Stu Cncl; JV Crs Cntry; JV Tennis; Bus.

BUTLER, KIM; Reading Memorial HS; Reading, MA; (Y); Church Yth Grp; JA; Pep Clb; Chorus; Yrbk Phtg; Yrbk Stf; JV Socr; Var Trk; High Hon Roll; Ldrshp Training Conf Awd 85; Law.

BUTLER, SHARON; Medway HS; Medway, MA; (Y); 29/138; Church Yth Grp; Drama Clb; School Musical; School Play; Yrbk Stf; Missionette Yr Sthrn New England Dist 84-85; Ed.

BUTLER, SORAYA D; Boston Latin Schl; Boston, MA; (Y); 101/285; Debate Tm; Sec Drama Clb; Thesps; Band; School Play; Stage Crew; Yrbk Ed-Chief; Hon Roll; NHS; Rogers Prz-Pub Spkng 86; 2nd Pl-Boston Shakespeare Comptn 86; Lisch Schl Of Arts; Drama.

BUTLER, WILL; Brockton HS; Brockton, MA; (Y); FTA; Lit Mag; Hon Roll; Teacher.

BUTSON, KATE; Taunton HS; Taunton, MA; (Y); Sec Aud/Vis; Sec Camera Clb; French Clb; Intnl Clb; Library Aide; PAVAS; Concert Band; Mrchg Band; Lit Mag; Hon Roll; Southeastern MA U; Engl.

BUTTERWORTH, CHRISTINE; Masconomet Regional HS; Boxford, MA; (Y); Church Yth Grp; French Clb; Ski Clb; School Musical; Ed Yrbk Stf; Rep Frsh Cls; Stu Cncl; Var Capt Socr; Var Capt Sftbl; Hon Roll.

BYERS, DAVID; Rockland HS; Rockland, MA; (Y); Am Leg Boys St; Pres Debate Tm; Drama Clb; Quiz Bowl; Radio Clb; Scholastic Bowl; Speech Tm; Hon Roll; NHS; 4th MA Amer Legn Oratrcl Cntst 86; Socl Stds Acdmc Achvt Awd 86; MIT; Aerontcl Engrng.

BYERS, JAMES; Tewksbury Memorial HS; Tewksbury, MA; (Y); Church Yth Grp; DECA; Var Golf; JV Var Ice Hcky; DECA Dist Hnr Awd 86; DECA ST Competency Awd 86; Salem ST Coll.

BYRNE, MICHAEL; Bishop Connolly HS; Newport, RI; (Y); 50/172; Church Yth Grp; Quiz Bowl; Socr; Hon Roll; Christian Ldrshp Awds; Var Ltrs Soccr/Cyclng; Fish & Wldlife.

BYRNE, PAULINE A; Boston Latin Acad; Hyde Park, MA; (Y); Church Yth Grp; Cmnty Wkr; Drama Clb; Political Wkr; Variety Show; Ed Lit Mag; Rep Jr Cls; Var Sftbl; Hon Roll; Advertising.

BYRNES, CATHERINE; Auburn HS; Auburn, MA; (Y); VP Camp Fr Inc; Acpl Chr; Chorus; Color Guard; Drill Tm; Flag Corp; School Musical; School Play; JV Fld Hcky; Var Tennis; Stu Of 1986 Central Dist Choir 86; Tufts U; Vet.

BYRNES, CHERYL; Hudson HS; Hudson, MA; (Y); 2/140; Pep Clb; Yrbk Stf; Tennis; VP NHS; Sal; Cmnty Wkr; Ski Clb; High Hon Roll; MA Bd Regents Schlrshp; Hist,Eng,Frnch Awd 83-86; Smith Coll.

BYRON, JENNIFER; King Philip Regional HS; Norfolk, MA; (Y); 1/215; Sec Stu Cncl; Bsktbl; Socr; Sftbl; High Hon Roll; Hon Roll; Pres NHS; Emmanuel Coll Bk Awd 86.

CABECA, ANTHONY J; New Bedford HS; New Bedford, MA; (Y); 13/547; Am Leg Boys St; Church Yth Grp; Band; Concert Band; Jazz Band; Mrchg Band; Orch; School Musical; Hon Roll; NHS; Boston Coll; Psych.

CABELLO, DARWIN WILLY; North HS; Worcester, MA; (Y); Chess Clb; SADD; Yrbk Stf; Stu Cncl; Crs Cntry; Vllybl; Gntc Engrng.

CABRAL, CHARLENE; Bishop Connolly HS; Somerset, MA; (Y); 56/175; Cmnty Wkr; Chorus; Nwsp Bus Mgr; Nwsp Ed-Chief; Nwsp Stf; Rep Sr Cls; Trk; High Hon Roll; Hon Roll; Providence Coll; Bus Adm.

CABRAL, DANIEL; New Bedford HS; New Bedford, MA; (Y); 21/701; JCL; High Hon Roll; NHS; Ntl Merit Ltr; Aerontcl Engrng.

CABRAL III, R P; Middleboro HS; Middleboro, MA; (Y); 34/346; Am Leg Boys St; Church Yth Grp; Var Capt Bsbl; Var Capt Ftbl; Wrstlng; Ftbl Team MVP 85; Southshore Plyr Yr Ftbl 85; All League Ftbl 85; Boston Globe All ST Ftbl 85; Physcl Thrpst.

CABRINI, CARRIE; East Longmeadow HS; E Longmeadow, MA; (Y); 20/210; AFS; Dance Clb; Intnl Clb; Pep Clb; Chorus; School Play; Variety Show; Var L Cheerleading; Var Trk; Hon Roll; Psychol.

CABUCIO, RONALD; Diman Reg Voc Tech; Fall River, MA; (Y); Church Yth Grp; Debate Tm; Library Aide; Teachers Aide; Hon Roll; Pres Schlr; Southeastern MA U; Comp Sci.

CACCIAPUOTI, DEBRA; Reading Memorial HS; Reading, MA; (Y); Church Yth Grp; Cmnty Wkr; Drama Clb; Chorus; Stage Crew; Hon Roll; Dieosician Yth Rep Popes Yth Pilgrimage 85; Nrsng.

CACI, MELISSA; Winchester HS; Winchester, MA; (Y); Cmnty Wkr; French Clb; Latin Clb; Concert Band; Mrchg Band; Yrbk Phtg; Yrbk Stf; Var L Fld Hcky; High Hon Roll; Church Yth Grp; Natl Hstry Dy Hnrbl Mntn 85; Vlntr Roxbury Ttrng 85-86; Vlntr ST Hnr House Tr Gd 86; Mrchndsng.

CADDIGAN, SEAN; Westboro HS; Westboro, MA; (Y); 88/189; Church Yth Grp; Chorus; Yrbk Stf; JV Bsbl; JV Bsktbl; Var Ftbl; Var Trk; Hon Roll.

CAFFREY, PATRICIA A; Middleboro HS; Middleboro, MA; (Y); 30/207; Band; Chorus; Off Frsh Cls; Off Soph Cls; Off Jr Cls; Off Sr Cls; Stu Cncl; Bsktbl; Co-Capt Fld Hcky; NHS; Slvr M Socty VP 84-86; St Anselm Coll.

CAHILL, JAMES J; Boston College HS; Canton, MA; (Y); Am Leg Boys St; Trs Church Yth Grp; Im Bsktbl; Im Ftbl; JV Trk; Hon Roll; Prfct Atten Awd; Acad Awd Spn & Alg I 84; Acad Ad Alg II 86; BAYS Div 2 Lg Champs 86; Bus Adm.

CAHILL, JIM; Salem HS; Salem, MA; (Y); Church Yth Grp; Drama Clb; Pres German Clb; School Musical; School Play; Trs Stu Cncl; Var Crs Cntry; Var Lcrss; JV Var Socr; Hon Roll; Boston U; Advrtsng.

CAHILL, JOAN; Fontbonne Acad; Quincy, MA; (Y); Church Yth Grp; Cmnty Wkr; Computer Clb; Drama Clb; Hosp Aide; Intnl Clb; Red Cross Aide; Science Clb; SADD; Chorus; Prom Ct 86; Cum Laude Ntl Latin Ex 86; Top 10 Pct Olympiad Hist Ex 86; BC; Pediatrcn.

CAHILL, MAUREEN; Notre Dame Academy; Braintree, MA; (Y); Church Yth Grp; Chorus; Rep Stu Cncl; Hon Roll; Notre Dame Acad Alumnae Schlrshp 83-84; Mdrn Eurpn Hist Acadmc Awd 84-85.

CAIN, BRIAN M; Everett HS; Everett, MA; (Y); Church Yth Grp; Intnl Clb; Key Clb; Political Wkr; Science Clb; Var JV Bsbl; Im JV Bsktbl; Im Ftbl; Hon Roll; Jr NHS; Northeastern U.

CAINES, NADIA; Newton North HS; Dorchester, MA; (Y); Hon Roll; Child Psych.

CALDON, MAUREEN F; Cathedral HS; Hampden, MA; (Y); Dance Clb; Office Aide; Ski Clb; Lbrl Arts.

CALEF III, FRED J; Quincy HS; Quincy, MA; (Y); 43/276; Am Leg Boys St; Boy Scts; Exploring; Hosp Aide; ROTC; High Hon Roll; Hon Roll; Order Of The Arrow Natl Brotherhood Of Hnr Compers BSA 84-86; Won Distinction In Cntl Math Cnts 86; Geo.

CALL, JENNIFER; Beverly HS; Beverly, MA; (Y); Hosp Aide; Chorus; School Musical; Stage Crew; Nrsng.

CALLAGHAN, JAMES; Canton HS; Canton, MA; (Y); 19/249; Church Yth Grp; French Clb; Letterman Clb; Nwsp Stf; Lit Mag; Var Capt Crs Cntry; Var Capt Trk; High Hon Roll; Hon Roll; NHS.

CALLAHAN, JOHN; Revere HS; Revere, MA; (Y); 6/354; Am Leg Boys St; Math Tm; Quiz Bowl; Science Clb; Yrbk Stf; Mgr Bsktbl; Trk; Elks Awd; High Hon Roll; Pres NHS; Lowell U; Elec Engr.

CALLAHAN, JULIA; Northfield-Mt Hermon Schl; Old Mystic, CT; (Y); Library Aide; Radio Clb; Sec Stu Cncl; Cit Awd; Vrsty Crew 85-86; Barnard Coll:Russian Studies.

CALLAHAN, KERRY PATRICK; Leominster HS; Leominster, MA; (Y); 23/305; Am Leg Boys St; Ski Clb; Var Capt Bsbl; Var Capt Bsktbl; Var Capt Socr; NHS; Church Yth Grp; Letterman Clb; Varsity Clb; Hon Roll; Cntrl AM All Star Socr Bsktbl & Bsbl 85-86; MA ST Bsbl Champs 86; Coach Awd Outstndby Boy Ath 86; Tufts U; Econ.

CALLAHAN, MICHAEL; Austin Prep; Burlington, MA; (Y); 4/124; SADD; Rep Jr Cls; VP Sr Cls; Rep Stu Cncl; Var Ftbl; High Hon Roll; Jr NHS; Holy Crss Bnk Awd; Deans List; Holy Cross; Lib Arts.

CALLAHAN, TRACY; Mansfield HS; Mansfield, MA; (Y); 3/185; Am Leg Aux Girls St; French Clb; Key Clb; Var Crs Cntry; Var Trk; High Hon Roll; Hon Roll; NHS; Whittemore Excllnc Awd-Day Cmp Wk-From MA Audubon Soc 85.

CALLANAN, MARGARET MARY; Mt Greylock Regional HS; Williamstown, MA; (Y); 11/134; Mrchg Band; School Musical; Symp Band; Nwsp Bus Mgr; VP Sr Cls; L Socr; Cit Awd; DAR Awd; Elks Awd; Pres NHS; Most Wrthy Rep Of Cls Awd 84; Most Outstndng Hist Stu Awd 84; Hnrbl Mntn Papr Histconf 84; Williames College.

CALLENDER, MICHAEL; Bedford HS; Bedford, MA; (Y); 62/213; AFS; Boy Scts; Cmnty Wkr; PAVAS; ROTC; Science Clb; Chorus; School Play; Stage Crew; Variety Show; Jewish War Vet Brotherhood Awd 86; USAF Acad Vlley Forge; Engrng.

CALVILLO, AIDA; Fitchburg HS; Fitchburg, MA; (Y); Yrbk Stf; Stu Cncl; JV Cheerleading; Var Crs Cntry; JV Trk; High Hon Roll; Brandies; Family Physcn.

CAMAIONI, CAROL; New Bedford HS; New Bedford, MA; (Y); 1/547; Drama Clb; Key Clb; Chorus; Pres Stu Cncl; NHS; Pres Schlr; Val; SADD; School Musical; High Hon Roll; Acushnet Fndtn Scholar 86; Commonwlth MA Schlr 86; Stu Rep Stu Govt Day 86; SE MA U; Elec Engrng.

CAMARA, ROBERT; Somerset HS; Somerset, MA; (Y); Band; Chorus; Concert Band; Jazz Band; Mrchg Band; Orch; Symp Band; Nwsp Rptr; Nwsp Stf; Yrbk Stf; St John God Schlrshp 86; MA ST Schlrshp 86; Msc Ltr & Plq 85-86; Westfield ST Coll; Pblc Rltns.

CAMARA, VICTORIA; Apponequet Regional HS; Assonet, MA; (Y); Church Yth Grp; Pep Clb; Political Wkr; Rep Frsh Cls; Rep Soph Cls; Rep Jr Cls; Var L Bsktbl; Hon Roll; Educ.

CAMARATA, ANNA; Boston Latin HS; Boston, MA; (Y); French Clb; JA; Teachers Aide; Yrbk Stf; Hon Roll; Jr NHS; NHS; Mdrn Ms Merit Awd 85; Home-Schl Assn Schlrshp 86; Dsgnr Yrbk Cvr 86; Merit Art Awd 85; Wellesley Coll; Intl Bus.

CAMBRA, DAWN; Taunton HS; Taunton, MA; (Y); Bsktbl; Sftbl; High Hon Roll; Hon Roll; All Star Sftbl Tourn 86; MA Coll Pharm & Sci; Pharm.

CAMERON, CHRISTINE; Notre Dame Acad; South Weymouth, MA; (Y); Library Aide; Ski Clb; Chorus; School Play; Lit Mag; Rep Stu Cncl; French Hon Soc; High Hon Roll; Hon Roll; Hosp Aide; Salve Regina; Biol.

CAMIEL, MICHELLE; Randolph HS; Randolph, MA; (Y); Spanish Clb; SADD; Nwsp Stf; Swmmng; Comm.

CAMPANELLA, CHRISTINE; Everett HS; Everett, MA; (Y); 59/266; Church Yth Grp; Key Clb; Office Aide; Yrbk Stf; Salem ST Coll; Acctg.

CAMPBELL, BRENDA; North Quincy HS; Quincy, MA; (Y); 13/400; Latin Clb; Math Tm; Pep Clb; Yrbk Stf; Stu Cncl; Powder Puff Ftbl; Vllybl; High Hon Roll; Trs NHS; Prevent Dropouts Stu Comm 86.

CAMPBELL, CHRIS; Saint Johns Prep; Beverly, MA; (Y); Im Ftbl; Im Ice Hcky; Socr; Hon Roll; Bus.

CAMPBELL, CRAIG; Cambridge Rinoge And Catin HS; Cambridge, MA; (Y); Key Clb; Ski Clb; Var Bsbl; High Hon Roll; Hon Roll; NHS; Bus.

CAMPBELL, JOHN D; Hanover HS; Hanover, MA; (Y); Drama Clb; Math Tm; Band; Concert Band; Jazz Band; Mrchg Band; School Musical; School Play; Hon Roll.

CAMPBELL, KERRY; Taunton HS; Taunton, MA; (Y); 4/430; Church Yth Grp; JCL; Trs Ski Clb; Yrbk Stf; Lit Mag; Var Fld Hcky; Var Tennis; JV Trk; VP NHS; St Schlr; Arline Payson Pdlfrd Schlrsp 86; Taunton Educ Assoc Schlrshp 86; Helen H Turner Memrl Schlrsp 86; U Of MA; Elem Educ.

CAMPBELL, MATT; Billerica Memorial HS; Billerica, MA; (Y); 11/500; French Clb; Math Clb; Hon Roll; NHS; Ntl Merit Ltr; Outing Clb 85-86; Med.

CAMPBELL, MATTHEW; Brockton Christian Regnl HS; Raynham, MA; (Y); Drama Clb; School Play; Pres Soph Cls; Bsbl; Bsktbl; Var Capt Socr; High Hon Roll; Soccer MVP 84; Indoor Soccer MVOP 86.

CAMPBELL, ROBERTA M; Holy Name C C H S; Uxbridge, MA; (Y); Dance Clb; Math Clb; Pep Clb; Quiz Bowl; Orch; Hon Roll; Humanities II & III Awds 84 & 85; Steno I Awd 85; Typng I Awd 84; Quinsicamond CC; Bus Admin.

CAMPBELL, SARA; St Peter Marian HS; Worcester, MA; (Y); 19/170; Spanish Clb; SADD; Yrbk Stf; Stu Cncl; Crs Cntry; Sftbl; Hnrs In Englsh, Rlgn, Spnsh, Hstry & Latin 83-84; Hnrs In Wrld Hstry, Rlgn, Bio & Englsh 84-85; Physcl Thrpst.

CAMPO, ELIZABETH; Matignon HS; Somerville, MA; (S); 14/174; Drama Clb; SADD; School Musical; School Play; Yrbk Sprt Ed; Rep Soph Cls; Off Stu Cncl; Pres NHS; Spanish NHS; 1st Pl Hstry Fair 83; Bus Adm.

CANDELET, KEVIN; Attleboro HS; N Attleboro, MA; (Y); Rep Church Yth Grp; SADD; Teachers Aide; Varsity Clb; Y-Teens; Var L Bsbl; Var L Bsktbl; Var Capt Ftbl; Powder Puff Ftbl; Hon Roll.

CANDELORO, DENISE MARIE; Malden HS; Malden, MA; (Y); 84/500; Dance Clb; Spanish Clb; SADD; Teachers Aide; Yrbk Stf; High Hon Roll; Hon Roll; Spanish NHS; St Schlr; Bsktbl Unsung Hero Plaque 83-85; Jr Variety Show, Solo, Dance Trophy 86; Accntng.

CANDLER, DAVID; Frontier Regional Schl; Conway, MA; (Y); FCA; JA; Spanish Clb; Nwsp Rptr; Nwsp Sprt Ed; Var Bsktbl; JV Ftbl; Im Trk; L Wt Lftg; Hon Roll; Bus Mgmt.

CANELLOS, DIANE; North Quincy HS; N Quincy, MA; (Y); 52/350; Varsity Clb; Yrbk Stf; Rep Stu Cncl; L Tennis; High Hon Roll; Hon Roll; Science Clb; Teachers Aide; Outstndg Achvt In Vrsty Tennis 85; Outstndg Achvt Anthropology 86; Miss Am Co-Ed &gnt Cont; Northeastern U; Political Sci.

CANN, TONI; Cohasset JR SR HS; Cohasset, MA; (Y); Dance Clb; Temple Yth Grp; Band; Chorus; Mrchg Band; Crs Cntry; Powder Puff Ftbl; Socr; Sftbl; Swmmng; English & Math Hnrs Awds 84; Teaching.

CANNATELLI, CHARLENE M; Malden HS; Malden, MA; (Y); 115/470; Bsktbl; Fld Hcky; MVP JV Fld Hcky 83-84; Creat Wrtg Eng 83-84; MIP Bsktbl 84-85; NE U; Phys Ther.

CANNEY, CATHLEEN; Mount Saint Joseph Acad; Brookline, MA; (Y); 7/149; Church Yth Grp; Math Clb; High Hon Roll; Hon Roll; VP NHS; Socl Justice Clb; Holy Cross; Chem.

CANNEY, MICHAEL; Burlington HS; Burlington, MA; (Y); Yrbk Sprt Ed; Rep Jr Cls; Sr Cls; Var Ftbl; JV Lcrss; Powder Puff Ftbl; Hon Roll.

CANTWELL, AMY REGINA; Dennis Tarmouth Regional HS; Dennis, MA; (Y); 48/309; Church Yth Grp; Yrbk Sprt Ed; L Crs Cntry; JV Fld Hcky; Var L Trk; Wt Lftg; High Hon Roll; Stdnt Advsry Cncl 85-86; N Adams ST Coll; Psych.

CANTWELL JR, D PATRICK; Ware HS; Ware, MA; (Y); Bsbl; Bsktbl; Ftbl; Hon Roll; Engrng.

CANTY, ADRIA; Reading Memorial HS; Reading, MA; (Y); Band; Concert Band; Jazz Band; Mrchg Band; School Musical; JV Crs Cntry; JV Trk; High Hon Roll; Hon Roll; Concert Bnd Pres 86-87; Physcl Trpy.

CANTY, ANGELA; Newton Catholic HS; Newton Centre, MA; (Y); Church Yth Grp; Model UN; Orch; Vllybl; Hon Roll; Yrbk Stf; Bsktbl; Sftbl; Math.

CAPANO, STEPHEN; Austin Prep Schl; Burlington, MA; (Y); Computer Clb; Science Clb; Ski Clb; Socr; Hon Roll; Italian Clb 84-85; Worcester Poly Tech Inst; Engr.

CAPELLOS, KRISTEN; Presentation Of Mary Acad; Salem, NH; (Y); 10/40; French Clb; Math Clb; Pep Clb; SADD; Chorus; School Musical; Yrbk Sprt Ed; JV Bsktbl; Wt Lftg; Hon Roll; U Of NH; Intl Bus Mgmnt.

CAPLETTE, CYNTHIA; Shepherd Hill Regional HS; Charlton, MA; (Y); Am Leg Aux Girls St; Dance Clb; Latin Clb; Band; Jazz Band; Mrchg Band; School Musical; School Play; Variety Show; Stu Cncl; Yth Ldrshp Awd 86; Usherette At Gradtn 86; Excllnc Human Physlgy 86; Bio.

CAPOBIANCO, MICHAEL; St Dominic Savio HS; Revere, MA; (Y); 13/97; Math Clb; SADD; JV Bsbl; JV Bsktbl; Hon Roll; NEDT Awd; Boston U.

CAPOBIANCO, SARAH; Marian HS; Natick, MA; (Y); 27/187; Hosp Aide; Rep Soph Cls; JV Socr; Vllybl; High Hon Roll; Hon Roll; NHS; NEDT Awd.

CAPPARELLA, MARK; Walpole HS; Walpole, MA; (Y); 4/268; Am Leg Boys St; Math Tm; Var Capt Crs Cntry; Var Capt Trk; Elks Awd; High Hon Roll; Hon Roll; NHS; Ntl Merit SF; Leo Clb; Sci Dept Gld Mdl; 4th Plc E Mss Cls C Indr Trck 2 Ml; Brown U; Med.

CAPPELLO, GINA; Lawrence HS; Lawrence, MA; (Y); SADD; Rep Jr Cls; Im Bsktbl; Var JV Fld Hcky; Var JV Sftbl; High Hon Roll; Hon Roll; Spanish NHS; All Am Acadmc Awd 86; Natl Hist And Govt Awd 86.

CAPUTO, KARA ROGERS; Belmont HS; Belmont, MA; (Y); Church Yth Grp; Cmnty Wkr; GAA; Political Wkr; Service Clb; SADD; Varsity Clb; School Play; Sec Frsh Cls; Sec Soph Cls; PTA Rcgntn Awd Svcs 85; Blmnt Schl Cmmtee Awd Athltcs 84-85; Pg U S Hs Of Reps 86; Coll Of William & Mary; Govt.

CARABALLO, EFRAIN; Holyoke HS; Holyoke, MA; (Y); 54/360; Spanish Clb; Hon Roll; Prfct Atten Awd; Daniel J O Connell Awrd Memrl Schlrshp 86; Mary L Stiles Lang Awrd 86; Alice Meisel Schlrshp 86; U Mass-Amherst; Elec Engr.

CARABILLO, TERRI LEE; Concord-Carlisle HS; Concord, MA; (S); DECA; JA; Ski Clb; VP SADD; Yrbk Phtg; Var Fld Hcky; Trk; Hon Roll; U Of MA; Microbio.

CARACCIO, WILLIAM; Methuen HS; Methuen, MA; (Y); 10/380; Cmnty Wkr; Var Bsbl; JV Bsktbl; Var Socr; Hon Roll; Lion Awd; NHS; Spanish NHS; West Point; Engnrng.

CARAMANDO, ANDREA; St Clares HS; W Roxbury, MA; (Y); JA; Hon Roll; Hghst Avrg Spanish Ii 86; Hghst Avrg Engl 223-03 85; 2nd Hghst Avrg Bio 85; Hghst Avrg Lat Rvw 623 85; Hotel Mgmt.

CARBONE, CHRISTOPHER; Haverhill HS; Haverhill, MA; (Y); 12/400; VP Church Yth Grp; Latin Clb; Political Wkr; Ski Clb; Spanish Clb; SADD; Varsity Clb; Church Choir; Nwsp Rptr; VP Frsh Cls; Stud Of The Mnth 84-86; Wnnr Of Ltn Ptry Rdng 86; Magna Cum Laude Ntl Ltn Tst 86.

CARBONE, VALERIE; Auburn HS; Auburn, MA; (Y); Camp Fr Inc; Church Yth Grp; Math Tm; SADD; Concert Band; Yrbk Stf; JV Bsktbl; L Trk; VP NHS; Band.

CARBONE, WILLIAM; St Dominic Savio HS; Revere, MA; (Y); 9/95; JA; Nwsp Rptr; Nwsp Stf; Bsktbl; Bowling; Ftbl; Mgr(s); High Hon Roll; Hon Roll; NHS; Acadmc All Amrcn 86; Boston Coll; Law.

CARBONNEAU, MICHELLE; Southwick HS; Sowick, MA; (Y); Nwsp Stf; VP Frsh Cls; JV Bsktbl; JV Fld Hcky; Var Sftbl; Hon Roll; All Leag Sel Sftbl 86; Semi-Frml Comm 85; Guidnc Aide 86.

CARCHIA, MICHAEL; Austin Preparatory Schl; Windham, NH; (Y); Chess Clb; JV Crs Cntry; Socr; Im Sftbl; Var Tennis; Bus.

CARDARELLI, CHERYL; Malden HS; Malden, MA; (Y); 23/480; Church Yth Grp; French Clb; SADD; Flag Corp; Variety Show; Stu Cncl; Boston Coll; Nrsg.

CARDEIRO, ROBERT; St Johns HS; Westboro, MA; (Y); 100/278; Church Yth Grp; Trs Exploring; Spanish Clb; School Musical; Variety Show; Var L Crs Cntry; Var Capt Trk; High Hon Roll; Hon Roll; Natl Hnr Rll; CT Coll; Bio.

CARDOSO, MARIA; Attleboro HS; S Attleboro, MA; (Y); Church Yth Grp; SADD; Powder Puff Ftbl; High Hon Roll; NHS; Para Lgl.

CARDOSO, NANCY; B M C Durfee HS; Fall River, MA; (Y); Church Yth Grp; Variety Show; Hon Roll; St Schlr; Kngyn Cmpbl Schlrshp Awd 86; MA ST Schlrshp 86; PABA Schlrshp 86; Kinyon Campbell Bus; Acctg.

CARDOZA, KIMBERLY; Maynard HS; Maynard, MA; (Y); 18/100; Trs Church Yth Grp; Radio Clb; VP Frsh Cls; Sec Jr Cls; Var Fld Hcky; Var Capt Sftbl; Var Vllybl; SADD; Lit Mag; M H Duclos Schlrshp, Dst E Outstndng SR Fml Athl, MVP Fld Hcky, Sftbl 86; U MA Amherst; Zoolgy.

CARELLI, JOHN; St Peter-Marian HS; Worcester, MA; (Y); Off Frsh Cls; Off Soph Cls; Off Jr Cls; Stu Cncl; Capt L Bsbl; L Ice Hcky; Bus.

CAREY, DENISE; Bishop Feehan HS; Mansfield, MA; (Y); Powder Puff Ftbl; Trk; Hon Roll; Spanish NHS; Newberry Coll; Optmtry.

CARGILL, DONALD; Medford HS; Medford, MA; (Y); 27/267; SADD; Varsity Clb; JV Var Bsktbl; JV Crs Cntry; JV Trk; Masonic Awd; Anna Marie; Draftng.

CARIGLIA, TAMMY; Wachusett Regional HS; Holden, MA; (Y); 128/436; Church Yth Grp; Cmnty Wkr; Computer Clb; Drama Clb; French Clb; Hosp Aide; Library Aide; Model UN; Ski Clb; SADD; Psych.

CARINI, MICHAEL C; Wachusett Regional HS; Holden, MA; (Y); 3/396; Church Yth Grp; Sec Trs Model UN; Science Clb; French Hon Soc; High Hon Roll; NHS; Pres Schlr; Stage Crew; Ashland Schlr 86; Amer HS Math Awd 84; U MA Chncllrs Tlnt Awd 85; Tufts U; Math.

CARINO, CHRISANNE M; Pope John XXIII HS; Medford, MA; (Y); 22/208; Key Clb; Nwsp Stf; Sec Jr Cls; Sec Sr Cls; Trs Stu Cncl; Hon Roll; NHS; Son Of Italy Schlrshp Awd 86; Rlgous Educ Tchr 86; Jordan Marsh Cncl 85-86; Boston Clg; Psych.

CARLOS, NANCY; Chicopee Comprehensive HS; Chicopee, MA; (Y); 18/278; Political Wkr; Yrbk Stf; Stu Cncl; Socr; Hon Roll; NHS; Spn Awds 84-86.

CARLOW, KAREN; King Philip Regional HS; Norfolk, MA; (Y); 51/228; Hosp Aide; Yrbk Stf; Stu Cncl; Var L Cheerleading; JV Sftbl; Hon Roll; Natl Hstry Day Comptitn Regnl Fnlst 86; Comm.

CARLSON, ROSS; Wellesley SR HS; Wellesley, MA; (Y); Pres Church Yth Grp; German Clb; Sec Band; Sec Concert Band; Sec Jazz Band; Mrchg Band; Yrbk Stf; Var Capt Swmmng; Hon Roll; Employee Of Mnth-HYATT Reg 86; Emory U Atlanta; Bus Admin.

CARMEL, MICHAEL; Wahconah Regional HS; Dalton, MA; (Y); 45/350; JCL; Latin Clb; Varsity Clb; Var L Bsbl; Im Bsktbl; Var L Socr; Clemson U; Psych.

CARMELL, JENNIFER; Pittsfield HS; Pittsfield, MA; (Y); Dance Clb; French Clb; Math Clb; Pep Clb; Gym; High Hon Roll; Hon Roll; NHS.

CARNEIRO, SUZANNE; Milford HS; Milford, MA; (Y); 5/275; Hosp Aide; Key Clb; SADD; High Hon Roll; Hon Roll; NHS; Stu Of Natl Hnr Soc 86.

CARNELL, JOHN; Arlington HS; Arlington, MA; (Y); Trk; Hon Roll; Law.

CARNES, GRETCHEN; Shawsheen Valley Vo-Tech; Tewksbury, MA; (Y); 13/392; Exploring; Hosp Aide; VICA; School Play; Var JV Sftbl; Var Swmmng; Elks Awd; Hon Roll; Poli Offcr.

CARNEY, DEBRA; Danvers HS; Danvers, MA; (Y); 6/307; Capt Drm Mjr(t); Yrbk Stf; Rep Soph Cls; Rep Jr Cls; Var L Cheerleading; L Twrlr; French Hon Soc; High Hon Roll; NHS; JR Marshall 86.

CAROLINE, GLEN; Canton HS; Canton, MA; (Y); 51/250; Political Wkr; Pres Soph Cls; Stu Cncl; Ice Hcky; Hon Roll.

CARON, CYNTHIA; St Bernards Central Catholic HS; Fitchburg, MA; (S); 18/159; Girl Scts; Model UN; Political Wkr; Sec Jr Cls; Sec Sr Cls; L Capt Cheerleading; Var L Socr; Hon Roll; NHS; Girl Sct Slvr Ldrshp Awd 83; Girl Sct 10 Yrs Svc Awd 86; Poltcl Sci.

CARON, JAMES; New Bedford HS; New Bedford, MA; (Y); 59/650; Science Clb; SADD; Teachers Aide; Crs Cntry; Ice Hcky; Trk; Mrtn Lthr Kng Essy Awd-1st Pl 85; Engrng.

CARON, JANE; Lynnfield HS; Lynnfield, MA; (Y); 5/173; VP AFS; Church Yth Grp; Cmnty Wkr; Dance Clb; VP Debate Tm; Drama Clb; Intnl Clb; JA; Math Tm; Political Wkr; Cmmndtn Excllnce Eng 84 & 86; Cmmndtn Excllnce Modern European Hist 85; Engrng.

CARON, LISA; Agawam HS; Feeding Hls, MA; (Y); 59/350; Drama Clb; Sec Latin Clb; School Play; Nwsp Sprt Ed; Sec Stu Cncl; Var L Bsktbl; Var L Fld Hcky; Var L Sftbl; Var L Trk; NHS; MV SR MIP Vrsty Bsktbll 85-86; 3rd Pl Brnz Mdl Prsnl Intervw Ctgry ST Fnls Acad Decthln 86; U MA; Pre-Med.

CARON, MELISSA; New Bedford HS; New Bedford, MA; (Y); 63/550; Church Yth Grp; Drama Clb; Hosp Aide; Stage Crew; Off Stu Cncl; Var L Trk; Hon Roll; NHS; Brdgwtr ST Coll; Scl Wrk.

CARON, MICHELLE; Foxboro HS; Foxboro, MA; (Y); 9/200; Sec Church Yth Grp; Varsity Clb; Rep Stu Cncl; JV Bsktbl; JV Socr; Capt Var Trk; Hon Roll.

CARON, PAUL; Central Catholic HS; N Andover, MA; (Y); Boys Clb Am; Library Aide; Service Clb; Nwsp Rptr; Rep Frsh Cls; Rep Jr Cls; Stu Cncl; Var Bsktbl; JV Crs Cntry; Cit Awd; Lgn Hnr Awd 84; Comm.

CARON, ROSEMARY; Billerica Memorial HS; Billerica, MA; (Y); 4/450; Camera Clb; Math Clb; Science Clb; High Hon Roll; Hon Roll; NHS; French Clb; Intnl Clb; Math Tm; Yrbk Stf; Miss Teen Schlrshp And Recog Pgnt 85; Top 20 Prog Regis Clg 86; Elks Stu Of Mnth 86; Regis College; Bio.

CARPENTER, AMY; Ware HS; Ware, MA; (Y); 12/112; Am Leg Aux Girls St; Key Clb; Model UN; Yrbk Ed-Chief; Hst Jr Cls; Var Socr; Var Sftbl; Hon Roll; Prfct Atten Awd; Oprtn Frndshp Of Amer 84-86.

CARPENTER, LAUREL; Hingham HS; Hingham, MA; (Y); L Debate Tm; Drama Clb; Thesps; Band; School Play; Stage Crew; Nwsp Phtg; Chrmn Stu Cncl; NCTE Awd; NHS; Stu Advsry Cncl Schl Cmmt; Manhattonville Bk Awd; AFS Excng Stu Ntherlands 84; Tufts U; Law.

CARPENTER, LYNN H; Lynn English HS; Lynn, MA; (Y); Trs Church Yth Grp; Drama Clb; Hosp Aide; Chorus; Church Choir; School Play; Yrbk Ed-Chief; Trs Soph Cls; Jr Cls; Sr Cls; Concrt Chr 85-86; Music Educ.

CARPENTER, MARYANN; Ayer SR HS; Ayer, MA; (Y); 13/130; Church Yth Grp; Drama Clb; Pep Clb; VP Spanish Clb; High Hon Roll; NHS; Rotary Awd; Nshta Bus & Prfsnl Wmns Schlrshp 86; Assumption Coll; Acctg.

CARPENTER, WILLIAM; Silver Lake Regional HS; Pembroke, MA; (Y); 62/502; Boy Scts; Church Yth Grp; Cmnty Wkr; Drama Clb; Political Wkr; Ski Clb; Ftbl; Sptlght Prog 85; Hanson Pembroke Womns Clb Schlrshp 86; Franklin Pierce Clg; Rec Mgmt.

CARR, CHRIS; Salem HS; Salem, MA; (Y); Hon Roll; Phys Fitness.

CARR, MELISSA; Concord-Carlisle Regional HS; Concord, MA; (Y); 12/328; Orch; School Musical; Rep Soph Cls; Trs Jr Cls; JV Var Fld Hcky; Var Trk; High Hon Roll; NHS; Ntl Merit Ltr; Trck-Vrsty Leag Al-Star; Ntl Affrs.

CARR, SCOTT; Salem HS; Salem, MA; (Y); Var L Socr; Hon Roll; Perfct Attndnc Awd; Outstndng Athlt Awd 83; US Military; Law Enforcmnt.

CARR, STEPHANIE C; Framingham North HS; Framingham, MA; (Y); 4/365; Rep Am Leg Aux Girls St; Drama Clb; French Clb; Mrchg Band; School Musical; School Play; High Hon Roll; NHS; Ntl Merit SF; Colby Coll Bk Awd 85; Natl Latn Exm Summa Cum Laude Awd 85.

CARRATU, JOHN SCOTT; Beverly HS; Beverly, MA; (Y); Am Leg Boys St; Nwsp Stf; JV Ftbl; Var Ice Hcky; JV Lcrss; Hcky-Nrthestrn Conf All Star-Slm Evning News 85-86; All Star-HS Tms All Star 85-86; Crmnl Jstc.

CARREIRO, LUCY; B M C Durfee HS; Fall River, MA; (Y); Hosp Aide; Office Aide; Teachers Aide; Principles List 85-86; Cert Achvt Presch Lang 84-85; Cert Achvt Mdrn Miss & A Child Wish Come True; URI; Work With Abused Children.

CARREIRO, STEVEN H; New Bedford HS; New Bedford, MA; (Y); 160/600; Political Wkr; Band; Concert Band; Mrchg Band; Variety Show; Rep Stu Cncl; Badmtn; Trk; Hon Roll; C L Yaeger Music Schlrshp 86; P J Antunes Music Schlrshp 86; Berklee Coll; Prof Drummer.

CARRIGG, LISA; Governor Dummer Acad; N Hampton, NH; (Y); Art Clb; PAVAS; Thesps; School Musical; School Play; Pres Soph Cls; Pres Jr Cls; Pres Sr Cls; JV Capt Socr; Hnr Socty 85-87; Murphy Mercer Shrt Stry Cntst 86; Chrprsn Big Sistr Prog; Engl.

CARRINGTON, HEATHER; Westfield SR HS; Westfield, MA; (Y); Church Yth Grp; Sftbl; Law.

CARRIS, EUGENIA; Boston Latin Schl; Boston, MA; (Y); 31/285; Trs Key Clb; Pres Speech Tm; Chorus; Lit Mag; L Swmmng; VP NHS; French Clb; Swing Chorus; Rep Stu Cncl; Mgr(s); 1st Pl Prz Declmtn 86; Girls HS Assn Schlrshp 86; Ward Fllwshp 86; Harvard U.

CARROLL, ERIN; Montachusett Regional Vo-Tech; Royalston, MA; (Y); Office Aide; SADD; VICA; Yrbk Stf; Rep Frsh Cls; Crs Cntry; Hon Roll; Trs NHS; Compu Info Systms.

CARROLL, JAMIE; Hingham HS; Hingham, MA; (Y); Cmnty Wkr; Varsity Clb; JV Ftbl; Var L Tennis; Hon Roll; Bus.

CARROLL, JULIE; Smith Acad; Hatfield, MA; (S); Hst Key Clb; Yrbk Stf; VP Frsh Cls; Trs Soph Cls; Trs Jr Cls; Bsktbl; Fld Hcky; Sftbl; Cit Awd; High Hon Roll; Math.

CARROLL, MARGARET; Malden HS; Malden, MA; (Y); 19/450; Key Clb; Office Aide; Chrmn Variety Show; Trs Soph Cls; Trs Jr Cls; Trs Sr Cls; JV Var Fld Hcky; Hon Roll; NHS; JV Tennis; Harvard Book Prize 86.

CARROLL, PAUL; Woburn HS; Woburn, MA; (S); JA; Leo Clb; Spanish Clb; SADD; Yrbk Sprt Ed; Yrbk Stf; Stu Cncl; Wrstlng; Hon Roll; North Adams ST; Elem Educ.

CARROLL, SUELLEN; Bishop Feehan HS; Cumberland, RI; (Y); 11/240; FFA; Yrbk Rptr; Stu Cncl; Capt L Crs Cntry; Capt L Trk; Trs French Hon Soc; High Hon Roll; NHS; Pres Schlr; St Schlr; Cert Of Achvt-Excllnc In Engl 85-86; Catholic U Of America; Pol Sci.

CARSON, ANITA; King Philip HS; Norfolk, MA; (Y); 1/177; Am Leg Aux Girls St; Church Yth Grp; Yrbk Stf; Var Capt Socr; Var Capt Sftbl; Bausch & Lomb Sci Awd; Cit Awd; DAR Awd; High Hon Roll; Hon Roll; Superintendents Awd For Acadmc Excllnc; U Of MA Amhearst; Engrng.

CARTER, BETH; Presentation Of Mary HS; Methuen, MA; (Y); Cmnty Wkr; Debate Tm; French Clb; Hosp Aide; SADD; Bio.

CARTER, CYNTHIA E; Norwood SR HS; Norwood, MA; (Y); 110/370; Art Clb; Hosp Aide; PAVAS; Cheerleading; JV Fld Hcky; Sftbl; Hon Roll; Pres-Natl Art Hnr Soc; Arts Recgntn & Tlnt Srch; Globe Schltc Art Awds; Art.

CARTER, DANIEL; Haverhill HS; Haverhill, MA; (Y); Boy Scts; Ftbl; Swmmng; Cit Awd; God Cntry Awd; High Hon Roll.

CARTER, MONIQUE; Boston Technical HS; Dorchester, MA; (Y); Church Yth Grp; Cmnty Wkr; Debate Tm; Ski Clb; SADD; Teachers Aide; Nwsp Ed-Chief; Nwsp Rptr; Nwsp Stf; Stu Cncl; Most Outstndng Eng Stu 84; Most Outstnndg Wrtng Stu 86; NC A&T; Pre-Law.

CARTER, NICHOLAS; The Pingree Schl; Peabody, MA; (Y); Computer Clb; Math Tm; Quiz Bowl; Science Clb; Chorus; Nwsp Rptr; Lcrss; Socr; Wrstlng; High Hon Roll; Cum Laude Soc 85; Elec Engrng.

CARTIER, CHARLENE; Bishop Feehan HS; Attleboro, MA; (Y); 99/254; Cmnty Wkr; SADD; Band; Concert Band; Drm & Bgl; Mrchg Band; Hon Roll; Prfct Atten Awd; Spanish NHS; Psychlgy.

CARTY, DERRICK; Boston Latin Schl; Boston, MA; (Y); 30/274; Church Yth Grp; Cmnty Wkr; Pep Clb; Science Clb; Hon Roll; NHS; Ntl Merit Ltr; Math Cert/Schl Comm Of Boston 86; Hnrbl Mntn Cert Ntn Latin Exam 86; Math Comptn 86; Comp.

CARUSO, JODIE; Woburn HS; Woburn, MA; (Y); FTA; Leo Clb; SADD; Cheerleading; Sftbl; High Hon Roll; Specl Eductn.

CARVALHO, JOSEPH; Bishop Feehan HS; Pawtucket, RI; (Y); JCL; Band; Chorus; Jazz Band; Orch; Nwsp Ed-Chief; Nwsp Rptr; Gov Hon Prg Awd; High Hon Roll; Cum Laude Ntl Ltn Exm 85-86; Rhode Island Coll; Bio.

CARVALHO, SUSAN; Attleboro HS; Attleboro, MA; (Y); Powder Puff Ftbl; High Hon Roll; Pres NHS; Latin Natl Hnr Society 85-86; RI Coll; Nrsng.

CARVELLI, ROSEMARY; Newton North HS; W Newton, MA; (Y); Exploring; Office Aide; Sec Frsh Cls; Cheerleading; Cit Awd; High Hon Roll; Clinton S Schovell Schlrshp 86; Regis Coll; Bus Adm.

CASALETTO, ROBERT A; Malden Catholic HS; Revere, MA; (Y); L Var Ice Hcky; Hon Roll; Engrng.

CASCIATO, LEONARDO; Boston Latin Acad; E Boston, MA; (Y); Math Clb; Math Tm; Political Wkr; Var Ice Hcky; Hon Roll; Bus Adming.

CASE, DAVID; Reading Memorial HS; Reading, MA; (Y); Church Yth Grp; Drama Clb; School Play; High Hon Roll; Hon Roll; Rep Frsh Cls; Rep Sr Cls; Bsktbl; Var L Socr; JV Tennis.

CASEY, DIANE; Mount Saint Joseph Acad; Brighton, MA; (Y); 42/162; Math Clb; Hon Roll; NHS; St Anselm Coll; Nrsng.

CASEY, JOANNA; Waltham HS; Waltham, MA; (Y); French Clb; SADD; JV Var Bsktbl; JV Capt Sftbl; 3rd Temprnce Fund Essay 86; MVP JV Sftbl 85-86; Bus.

CASEY, KELLY; Turners Fall HS; Turners Fls, MA; (Y); 7/100; GAA; Varsity Clb; Rep Stu Cncl; JV Bsktbl; Var Capt Crs Cntry; Var L Fld Hcky; Var L Trk; High Hon Roll; Jr NHS; NHS; All Lg Crs Cntry 84; Springfield Coll; Physcl Thrpy.

CASEY, KERRY; Walpole HS; Walpole, MA; (Y); 48/261; French Clb; Var Capt Gym; Var L Trk; Hon Roll; Pres Phy Ftnss Awd 84; Gymnstcs Mst Imprvd 86; Frnch Exchng Prog 86; Nrsng.

CASEY, KEVIN; East Longmeadow HS; E Longmeadow, MA; (Y); Jazz Band; School Play; Variety Show; Nwsp Stf; Yrbk Stf; Rep Soph Cls; Pres Jr Cls; Rep Sr Cls; Rep Stu Cncl; Var Socr; Clncl Psych.

CASEY, MAUREEN; Reading Memorial HS; Reading, MA; (Y); 7/327; Dance Clb; Pep Clb; Varsity Clb; Variety Show; Yrbk Stf; Var Cheerleading; Im Powder Puff Ftbl; JV Trk; High Hon Roll; Pres Schlr; UNH; Nrsng.

CASEY, PATRICIA; Natick HS; Natick, MA; (Y); 71/423; SADD; Var Cheerleading; JV Trk; JV Vllybl; Elks Awd; High Hon Roll; Hon Roll; Prfct Atten Awd; Redmen Scholar 86; Excllnce Acctng Awd 86; Word Proc Excllnce Awd 86; U MA Amherst; Acctng.

CASEY, THOMAS; North Quincy HS; Quincy, MA; (Y); 19/388; Am Leg Boys St; Boy Scts; JA; Scholastic Bowl; School Play; Var L Bsbl; Var L Ftbl; Powder Puff Ftbl; Var Capt Wrstlng; Sci Fair Hnrb Mntn 84-85; Elec Engrng.

CASEY, THOMAS F; Boston College HS; Hanover, MA; (Y); Intnl Clb; Key Clb; Ski Clb; Spanish Clb; SADD; Band; Crs Cntry; Swmmng; Hon Roll; NHS; Natl Hnr Socty 86; Bus.

CASH, LARRY; St Marys HS; Lynn, MA; (Y); #27 In Class; Art Clb; Var Bsbl; Var Ice Hcky; Hon Roll; Engrng.

CASHIN, MAUREEN; Tahanto Regional Schl; Berlin, MA; (Y); Aud/Vis; Camera Clb; Church Yth Grp; Drama Clb; English Clb; 4-H; Girl Scts; Intnl Clb; JA; Key Clb; Fashion Merch.

CASHMON, ROB; Maynard HS; Maynard, MA; (Y); 9/92; Band; Concert Band; Jazz Band; Mrchg Band; School Musical; L Socr; Hon Roll; JP Sousa Awd; NHS; Ntl Merit Schol; Marine Corps ROTC Schlrshp 86; Norwich U; Comp Sci.

CASON, SHANDOLYN; Boston Tech HS; Mattapan, MA; (Y); Cmnty Wkr; Rep Soph Cls; Var L Trk; Cert Awd Prtcptn Law Day 84; Prog Cet Awd Outdr Trck 86; Sclgy.

CASPEROWTTZ, STACY; Marian HS; Framingham, MA; (Y); Girl Scts; Ski Clb; Church Choir; Yrbk Stf; JV Var Socr; Var L Trk; Rookie Yr Wintr Indr Trck Ltr Vrsty 85-86; CCL Leag Mt 2nd Pl Sht Put 86.

CASSERY, KAREN; Foxborough HS; Foxboro, MA; (Y); 4/240; Church Yth Grp; Drama Clb; Intnl Clb; Mathletes; Math Tm; Stage Crew; Var JV Fld Hcky; Hon Roll; NHS; Ntl Merit Ltr; Engrng.

CASSIDY, BRIAN; St Dominic Savio HS; Revere, MA; (Y); 6/94; Computer Clb; JA; SADD; Rep Jr Cls; Rep Stu Cncl; Im Bsktbl; Im Fld Hcky; High Hon Roll; Hon Roll; Air Frc Acad CO; Medcl.

CASSIDY, KATHLEEN; Arlington Catholic HS; Ft Lauderdale, FL; (Y); 13/143; Dance Clb; Hosp Aide; Spanish Clb; Teachers Aide; Nwsp Rptr; Crs Cntry; Sftbl; Hon Roll; NHS; Presdential Merit; Boston Hunger Walk 85-86; Barry U.

CASSIDY, LAURA JEAN; Mansfield HS; Mansfield, MA; (Y); 2/200; Key Clb; Ski Clb; Spanish Clb; SADD; Color Guard; Drill Tm; Yrbk Stf; High Hon Roll; NHS; Sal; Cmmnwlth MA Schlr 86; U Of Mass; Bio-Chem.

CASSIDY, SHARON; Medway JR SR HS; Medway, MA; (Y); 1/140; Am Leg Aux Girls St; Drama Clb; SADD; Sec Stu Cncl; Var Cheerleading; High Hon Roll; NHS; Hugh O Brien Yth Found Ldrshp Semnr 85; Asst Prodcr Cabl Tv Newswtch 86; Excllnc Math, Eng 86.

CASSIE, JONATHAN; Rockland HS; Rockland, MA; (Y); 16/253; Debate Tm; Drama Clb; Quiz Bowl; Scholastic Bowl; School Musical; School Play; Stage Crew; Hon Roll; Ntl Merit Ltr; NEDT Awd; Commnwlth Schrlshp 86-90; U MA.

CASSO, DEBORAH; Falmouth HS; Falmouth, MA; (Y); 1/370; AFS; French Clb; Var Capt Crs Cntry; Var Capt Tennis; Var Trk; Jr NHS; NHS; Emory U.

CASTANO, CORINNE; Hudson HS; Hudson, MA; (Y); 1/140; Pep Clb; Yrbk Stf; Rep Stu Cncl; Elks Awd; NHS; St Schlr; Val; Math Tm; Band; High Hon Roll; Gen Rad Sci Schlrshp 86; Stu Cncl Schlrshp 86; John E Delaney Math Awd 86; Boston Coll.

CASTANO, JIM; Hudson HS; Hudson, MA; (Y); Var JV Bsbl; JV Bsktbl; Hon Roll; NHS; Prfct Atten Awd; Natl Hist Day 2nd & 3rd Pl 83 & 84; Architectual Engr.

CASTELLI, JOE; Reading Memorial HS; Reading, MA; (Y); Var Capt Gym; Var L Trk; Hon Roll; Pres Schlr; Engrng.

CASTELLON, LINDA; Marian HS; Framingham, MA; (Y); Church Yth Grp; Latin Clb; SADD; Band; School Musical; Yrbk Stf; Rep Frsh Cls; Hon Roll; Phi Alpha Theta Hist Hon Merit Awd 85-86; Law.

CASTELLUCCI, SUE; Groton/Dunstable Regional HS; Groton, MA; (Y); Dance Clb; Var Cheerleading; JV Mgr(s); JV Trk; Bus.

CASTELLUZZI, CHRISTOPHER; Brockton HS; Brockton, MA; (Y); 212/1000; Trs Aud/Vis; Boy Scts; Key Clb; Trs Radio Clb; Teachers Aide; Stage Crew; Hon Roll; New Eng Yng Wrtrs Conf 86; Ad Altore Dei & Pipe Pius Xii Awds BSA 84-85; Emerson Coll; T V Prod.

CASTNER, CHRISTINE; Westforo Acad; Westford, MA; (Y); Pres AFS; Drama Clb; Sec French Clb; Pres German Clb; Model UN; Ski Clb; VP Frsh Cls; Pres Soph Cls; Rep Stu Cncl; Var Crs Cntry; Intl Bus.

CASTRO, JAMES; Bishop Feehan HS; Attleboro, MA; (Y); 85/250; Letterman Clb; Ftbl; Trk; High Hon Roll; Hon Roll; Bus Mgt.

CATALDO, JOANNA; Boston Latin HS; E Boston, MA; (Y); 36/274; Drama Clb; JA; Ski Clb; School Play; Yrbk Stf; Powder Puff Ftbl; Hon Roll; NHS; Hnrbl Mntn Globe Schlstc Art Cmptn 86.

CATALDO, PAUL; King Philip HS; Wrentham, MA; (Y); 104/220; JV Bsktbl; Var Ftbl; Bryant COLL; Bus Adm.

CATANESE, ANTHONY; Boston College HS; Braintree, MA; (Y); 90/325; Key Clb; Spanish Clb; SADD; JV Var Bsbl; JV Socr; Bus.

CATELLIER, DIANE; Cathedral HS; Springfield, MA; (Y); 78/533; Church Yth Grp; Cmnty Wkr; Service Clb; Sec SADD; Yrbk Stf; Trs Sr Cls; Gym; Hon Roll; Cls Prom Chrprsn 86; 2nd Rnnr Up Miss MA Teen Pagnt 86; Model Senate 86-87; Bus.

CAVALLARO, RICHARD; Central Catholic HS; Andover, MA; (Y); 106/231; Church Yth Grp; JA; Bowling; Engrng.

CAVANAUGH, LISA; Foxboro HS; Foxboro, MA; (Y); Band; Concert Band; Drm Mjr(t); Jazz Band; Mrchg Band; Hon Roll; Ntl Merit Ltr; Computer Clb; Teachers Aide; Southeastern MA Dist Jazz Ensem 86; MA All ST Jazz Ensem 86; All Eastrn Jazz Ensem 86; Music Educ.

CAVANAUGH, NANCY A; Malden HS; Malden, MA; (Y); Church Yth Grp; School Play; Yrbk Sprt Ed; Lit Mag; Rep Frsh Cls; Var Capt Crs Cntry; Var Capt Trk; Pres Schlr; Lions Clb Schlrshp 86; Alumni Schlrshp 86; Lrd Fmly Schlrshp 86; U MA Amberst.

CAVANAUGH, SUSAN; Girls Catholic HS; Malden, MA; (Y); French Clb; SADD; Var Sftbl; Var Vllybl; Hon Roll.

CELONA, STEPHEN; Fitchburg HS; Fitchburg, MA; (Y); Band; Chorus; Concert Band; Mrchg Band; Yrbk Stf; High Hon Roll; Hon Roll; Band Pres 86-87; Fitchburg ST Coll.

CENAFILS, EVENS; West Roxbury HS; Mattapan, MA; (S); Church Yth Grp; FCA; Acpl Chr; Capt Socr; Hon Roll; NHS; Prfct Atten Awd; Samuel Davis Gross Awd 81-82; Comp Engrng.

CENTRELLA, SUZANNE; Billerica Memorial HS; Billerica, MA; (Y); 18/480; French Clb; SADD; Powder Puff Ftbl; NHS; Psychlgy.

CEPACHIONE, JOHN; East Bridgewater HS; E Bridgewater, MA; (Y); 54/165; Drama Clb; Key Clb; School Musical; School Play; Var Capt Ftbl; Score Keeper; L Trk; Wt Lftg; Brockton Entrpse All Schltc Ftbl 85; South Shore All League Ftbl 85; Plyr Week WACD Ftbl 85; U MA; Bus Mgt.

CEPPETELLI, KAREN; Marianhill Central Catholic HS; Webster, MA; (Y); 4/40; Computer Clb; Chorus; Nwsp Rptr; Yrbk Bus Mgr; Sec Soph Cls; Hon Roll; Jr NHS; Trs NHS; Excllnc-Scl Stds; Effrt-Alg I; Hnr Cert-Psychlgy.

CERASUOLO, JOELLE M; Maynard HS; Maynard, MA; (Y); 6/87; Aud/Vis; Varsity Clb; Chorus; Concert Band; Mrchg Band; Sec Frsh Cls; VP Soph Cls; Var L Cheerleading; French Clb; School Play; Frgn Lang Outstndg SR; Digital Equipmnt Corp Scholar; DAR Revolution Scholar; U MA; Opthlmglst.

CERNAK, PAUL; Northampton HS; Northampton, MA; (Y); German Clb; Hon Roll.

CERVASSI, ANTHONY; Blackstone Valley Tech; Upton, MA; (Y); Var Bsbl; JV Bsktbl; Var Socr; Hon Roll.

CESARINI, PAUL; Shepherd Hill Regional HS; Dudley, MA; (Y); Debate Tm; Political Wkr; Stage Crew; Nwsp Stf; Yrbk Stf; Crs Cntry; Boy Scts; VP Stu Cncl; Art.

CESTRONE, ALBERT; Central Catholic HS; Lawrence, MA; (Y); School Musical; Var Ftbl; JV Trk; Bus Mgmnt.

CHABOT, KIMBERLY; Somerset HS; Somerset, MA; (Y); 1/310; Drama Clb; Hosp Aide; Nwsp Ed-Chief; VP Trs Stu Cncl; L Trk; Bausch & Lomb Sci Awd; VP NHS; Ntl Merit Schol; Pres Schlr; Val; Harvard U; Engl Prof.

CHADOROWSKY, LEISA BETH; Malden HS; Malden, MA; (Y); 47/475; Key Clb; Sec Temple Yth Grp; Chorus; Bowling; Sftbl; Hon Roll; Prfct Atten Awd; Nrtheastrn U; Physcl Thrpy.

CHADWELL, JAMES; Chicopee Comprehensive HS; Chicopee, MA; (Y); 3/300; Am Leg Boys St; Boys Clb Am; Quiz Bowl; Bsbl; JV Bsktbl; Mgr Tennis; High Hon Roll; Jr NHS; Spnsh Acdmc Awds 84-86; UMASS Chncllrs Tlnt Awd Prgrm 86; 3rd Hghst PSAT In Schl 86.

CHADWICK, LAURIE; Haverhill HS; Haverhill, MA; (Y); High Hon Roll; Hon Roll; Ecology Clb; Photo.

CHADWICK JR, NEIL E; Rockport HS; Rockport, MA; (Y); 6/74; Am Leg Boys St; Church Yth Grp; Ski Clb; Acpl Chr; Band; Chorus; Sec Sr Cls; High Hon Roll; NHS; Boys Nation 86 Gen Accntng Ofc 86; Chairman Stu Advsry Comm 86-87; Stu Rep Schl Comm 86-87; Physics.

CHAGNON, STEVE; Greater Lowell Reg Vo-Tech Schl; Lowell, MA; (Y); Elec.

CHAKRAVARTY, ANANDA; Georgetown JR SR HS; Georgetown, MA; (Y); Boy Scts; Cmnty Wkr; VP Computer Clb; Exploring; Quiz Bowl; Teachers Aide; Orch; Lit Mag; Rep Jr Cls; Im Tennis; Eagle Scout Bank 85-86; 1st Pl Comp Sci 84-85; Engrng.

CHALUPA, KLAUS; Pittsfield HS; Pittsfield, MA; (Y); 40/379; German Clb; Math Clb; JV Socr; Var Trk; Hon Roll; NHS; Archit.

CHAMBERLAIN, ELIZABETH; Fontbonnie Acad; Milton, MA; (Y); 10/180; Office Aide; JV Fld Hcky; High Hon Roll; Hon Roll; NHS; Awd Achvt Geom 85; 2nd Pl Fontbonne Sci Fair 84; Awds Achvt Bio II & Hnrs Theolgy III 86; Med.

CHAMBERLAIN, ROBERT V; Woburn HS; Woburn, MA; (Y); 13/476; Boys Clb Am; Church Yth Grp; German Clb; Math Tm; Golf; Tennis; High Hon Roll; NHS; Pres Acad Ftnss Awd; Keystone Club; CT Coll New London; Economics.

CHAMBERLIN, STACEY; Revere HS; Revere, MA; (Y); 10/346; Math Tm; Political Wkr; Yrbk Stf; Rep Stu Cncl; Var Capt Crs Cntry; Var Capt Trk; CC Awd; Elks Awd; High Hon Roll; Hon Roll; PTA Scholar 86; Boston Coll.

CHAMBERS, JEAN; Lynnfield HS; Lynnfield, MA; (Y); JA; Spanish Clb; JV Var Bsktbl; Powder Puff Ftbl; VP Capt Vllybl; High Hon Roll; Hon Roll; NHS; Spanish NHS; Church Yth Grp; JR Olympcs Vllybll 84-86; Bay ST Gms Vllybll 86; Vllybll All-Str 85; Pre-Med.

CHAMPOUX, NOELLE; Rever HS; Revere, MA; (Y); 17/344; Math Tm; Yrbk Stf; VP Jr Cls; Var L Cheerleading; Var L Fld Hcky; Powder Puff Ftbl; Var Capt Trk; High Hon Roll; NHS; Prncpls JR Aid Schrlshp 86; Prsdntl Acdmc Ftnss Awd 86; Soph Clss Rep 83-84; Boston Coll.

CHAN, EVA; Boston Latin Schl; Boston, MA; (Y); 98/284; French Clb; Key Clb; SADD; Nwsp Stf; Lit Mag; NHS; Open Gate Schrlshp Awd 86; Pres Ftns Awd 86; MA ST Schrlshp; Boston U; Engrng.

CHAN, HAN FONG; Boston Technical HS; Boston, MA; (Y); Varsity Clb; Hon Roll; Prfct Atten Awd; Bstn Intl Yth Exchng Awd 86.

CHAN, KEITH; Boston Latin Acad; W Roxbury, MA; (Y); Cmnty Wkr; Hon Roll; NHS; Bus.

CHANG, DORIS; Reading Memorial HS; Reading, MA; (Y); Hosp Aide; PAVAS; Teachers Aide; Band; Chorus; Orch; School Play; French Hon Soc; AFS; Church Yth Grp; Dist Music Fstvl-Nrthestrn MA-VIOLNST 84-86; Peer-Tutrng Awd 86; Crtv Arts For Kids Awd 85; Bus Adm.

CHANG, PAUL; Wachusett Regional HS; Holden, MA; (Y); 9/443; Aud/Vis; Boys Clb Am; Var Bsbl; Var Bsktbl; JV Ftbl; French Hon Soc; High Hon Roll; NHS; Boston Globe Art Awd 85; Arch.

CHANG, TZU; Newton North HS; W Newton, MA; (Y); Math Tm; Off Jr Cls; JV Lcrss; Mgr(s); Hon Roll; Sci.

CHAO, YVONNE Y; Lexington HS; Lexington, MA; (Y); Trs French Clb; Math Tm; Pres Orch; School Musical; Yrbk Stf; Var Crs Cntry; Var Trk; Hon Roll; Hnrb Mntn Crs Cntry 83; Frnch Achvt Awd 85; U Rochester.

CHAPAS, PETER; Dracut SR HS; Dracut, MA; (Y); Chess Clb; Computer Clb; Math Clb; Hon Roll; NHS; Final Hnrs 85; U Of Lowell; Bus.

CHAPATES, DIANE; Wachusett Regional HS; Holden, MA; (Y); SADD; Rep Stu Cncl; JV Var Cheerleading; Trk; Hon Roll; Boston Coll; Psych.

CHAPMAN, MARC; Don Bosco Tech HS; Readville, MA; (Y); 11/187; Cmnty Wkr; Lit Mag; Hon Roll; NHS; Hyde Pk Rotary Clb Schlrshp 86-87; Sprts Awds; Art Awds; U Of MA Amherst.

CHAPMAN, MIKE; Wakefield HS; Wakefield, MA; (Y); School Play; Yrbk Sprt Ed; Yrbk Stf; Pres Frsh Cls; Pres Soph Cls; Pres Jr Cls; Pres Sr Cls; Var L Bsbl; Var Capt Ice Hcky; Var Capt Socr; Outstndg Plyr Awd Vrsty Sccr 85-86; Mddlsx Lg All-Lg Dfnsmn Hcky Tm 85-86; Elk Chrstmn Hcky Trnmnt 85; Sprts Med.

CHAPUT, AMY; Haverhill HS; Haverhill, MA; (Y); 168/600; Teachers Aide; High Hon Roll; Hon Roll; Bus.

CHARETTE, ROBERT; Taunton HS; Taunton, MA; (Y); Boys Clb Am; Var Bsbl; Var Bsktbl; Wt Lftg; Hon Roll; Physcl Thrpy.

CHARLTON, KEVIN; Lee HS; Lee, MA; (Y); 8/80; Drama Clb; Quiz Bowl; Spanish Clb; Chorus; School Musical; School Play; Rep Jr Cls; Rep Stu Cncl; Hon Roll; Math Clb; Recgntn Prodctn Mgr Drama Clb 85-86; Acadmc Decathln Certfctn 85-86; Stu Advsry Cncl 85-86; Berkshire CC; Bus Adm.

CHARON, JOSEPH; Hoosac Valley HS; Adams, MA; (Y); 32/149; CAP; Var Capt Socr; Rep Frsh Cls; Sec Soph Cls; Ring Committee Awd 85; Martial Arts Awd 84; Two Time Var Letter Wnnr Sccr 84-85; US Naval Acad; Compu Sci.

CHARPENTIER, SUZANNE; Attleboro HS; S Attleboro, MA; (Y); High Hon Roll; NHS; Sports Mgmt.

CHARSKY, DOUGLAS; Frontier Regional HS; Sunderland, MA; (Y); 39/93; Var Ftbl; JV Wt Lftg; U Mass.

CHARTIER, MERRIDETH; Norton HS; Norton, MA; (S); Debate Tm; Drama Clb; Pres French Clb; Tennis; High Hon Roll; Hon Roll; NHS; Psych.

CHARTIER, MICHAEL; Attleboro HS; Attleboro, MA; (Y); L Var Bsbl; JV Bsktbl; Var L Ftbl; High Hon Roll; Acctng I Schlrshp Achvt 85; Acctng II Schlrshp Achvt 86; Bentley Coll; Acctng.

CHARTOFF, MICHAEL; Doherty Memorial HS; Worcester, MA; (Y); JA; Ski Clb; Spanish Clb; Socr; Med.

CHASSE, DEANNE MARIE; Lawrence HS; Lawrence, MA; (Y); Science Clb; Teachers Aide; School Play; Yrbk Stf; Hon Roll; St Schlr; Andrew B Reusch Mem Awd 86; Simmons; Pre-Med.

CHECHILE, CHRISTINE; Monson JR SR HS; Monson, MA; (Y); 4/72; Drama Clb; Spanish Clb; SADD; Varsity Clb; Band; Concert Band; School Musical; Trs Jr Cls; Capt Var Cheerleading; NHS; Intl Bus.

CHECKOWAY, ROBERT; Winthrop HS; Winthrop, MA; (Y); 1/200; Am Leg Boys St; Math Tm; School Play; Yrbk Bus Mgr; Yrbk Ed-Chief; Off Sr Cls; Co-Capt Tennis; High Hon Roll; NHS; Drama Clb; Harvard Bk Clb Awd; Jrnlsm.

CHEN, IVY Y; Newton North HS; West Newton, MA; (Y); Orch; Yrbk Stf; Hon Roll; Hnrb Mntn Brookline Chamber Music Comptn 84-85.

CHEN, JOHN; Newton North HS; Newton, MA; (Y); French Clb; Math Tm; Ski Clb; Varsity Clb; Jazz Band; Nwsp Stf; Yrbk Stf; Rep Stu Cncl; Var L Trk; Im Vllybl; Astrphyscs.

CHEN, KEVIN; Quincy Voc Tech Schl; Quincy, MA; (Y); 2/24; Am Leg Boys St; Camera Clb; English Clb; FBLA; FHA; Math Tm; Science Clb; VICA; Yrbk Phtg; Yrbk Stf; Thames Vly Tech Coll; Elec Engr.

CHENARD, BOB; Medway HS; Medway, MA; (Y); Church Yth Grp; SADD; Pres Jr Cls; Sec Sr Cls; Rep Stu Cncl; Var Capt Bsbl; Var Capt Ice Hcky; Var Capt Socr; Hon Roll; VFW Awd; VFW Ladies Aux Schlrshp 86; U S Marn Corps Distngshd Athl Awd 86; Russell Shaw Memrl Athl Awd 86; SM U; Bus Adm.

CHENEY, HEATHER; Reading HS; Reading, MA; (Y); Church Yth Grp; French Clb; Hosp Aide; SADD; Rep Soph Cls; JV Fld Hcky; Var JV Gym; JV Trk; Hon Roll; Psych.

CHEONG, LILY; Boston Technical HS; Boston, MA; (Y); French Clb; Vllybl; High Hon Roll; Hon Roll; Vllybll Awd 84-85; Bus.

CHERIES, KEITH; St Bernards HS; Fitchburg, MA; (S); 11/185; Var Crs Cntry; Var Capt Golf; Var Ice Hcky; Hon Roll; NHS; Fld Engrng.

CHERNEY, ALISA; Marlboro HS; Marlboro, MA; (Y); 27/350; AFS; Ski Clb; High Hon Roll; Hon Roll; NHS; Bus.

CHERUBINI, PAUL A; Clinton HS; Clinton, MA; (Y); Am Leg Boys St; Boy Scts; Church Yth Grp; JA; Spanish Clb; JV Bsktbl; L Ftbl; Swmmng; L Trk; Wt Lftg.

CHERY, CARLINE; English HS; Cambridge, MA; (Y); Dance Clb; French Clb; Math Clb; Math Tm; School Play; Gym; Tennis; Vllybl; Hon Roll; NCTE Awd; Boston Bus Schl; Bus.

CHESBRO, BRIAN H; Mc Cann Vocational Technical HS; Clarksburg, MA; (Y); VICA; Stu Cncl; JV Bsbl; JV Bsktbl; High Hon Roll; NHS; Hugh Obrien Awd 85; Elec.

CHESNICKA, DANIEL J; Westfield HS; Westfield, MA; (Y); 78/335; Sec Am Leg Boys St; Drama Clb; School Play; Nwsp Stf; Capt Diving; Capt Swmmng; Trk; Rotary Awd; Bst Actr Awd; Wstn MA Chmpn Dvr; MVP In Swmng; Pres Clsrm; U MA.

CHESTER, JOHN; Uxbridge HS; Uxbridge, MA; (Y); Church Yth Grp; Drama Clb; Yrbk Phtg; Yrbk Stf; Hon Roll; Tuitn Schlrshp La Salle Inst 83-84; Yrbk Stff Awd.

CHEVERIE, JUSTIN; N Reading HS; N Reading, MA; (Y); Church Yth Grp; Band; Nwsp Rptr; Nwsp Stf; Yrbk Stf; Hon Roll; Mensa; Ntl Yuth Evnt 83; Camp Anytwn 84; Peace Tour Russa 86; Mgmnt.

CHIAMPA, LAURA; North Uincy HS; Quincy, MA; (Y); 43/400; Pep Clb; Ski Clb; SADD; Sec Frsh Cls; Sec Soph Cls; Sec Jr Cls; Sec Sr Cls; Cheerleading; High Hon Roll; Hon Roll.

CHIANGO, LAURIANNE; North Reading HS; N Reading, MA; (Y); Concert Band; Jazz Band; Mrchg Band; School Musical; School Play; Stage Crew; Nwsp Ed-Chief; Bausch & Lomb Sci Awd; High Hon Roll; NHS; Chncllrs Tlnt Awd-U Of MA-AMHRST 86; Bus Adm.

CHIARELLA, TANYA; Barnstable HS; Hyannis, MA; (Y); AFS; Stat Bsbl; JV Trk; Marine Biolgst.

CHIASSON, DANIELLE; Maynard HS; Maynard, MA; (Y); 5/88; Aud/Vis; Radio Clb; Chorus; Concert Band; Mrchg Band; Lit Mag; JV Var Fld Hcky; Hon Roll; NHS; Digital Equip Corp Scholar 86; Soc Wmn Engrs Hnr Sci & Mth 86; Amer Lg Cert Schl Awd 86; U MA; Psych.

CHIASSON, PATRICIA; Waltham HS; Waltham, MA; (Y); French Clb; Office Aide; SADD; JV Vllybl; 2nd Pl Tmprnc Essay 86; Scl Wrk.

CHICCA, KARIE; Dimon Regional Vocational Tech HS; Fall River, MA; (Y); 9/228; JA; VICA; Yrbk Stf; Cit Awd; High Hon Roll; Hon Roll; Providence Coll; Elem Ed.

CHICKERING, TROY; Northampton HS; Northampton, MA; (Y); Golf; Bio.

CHICOINE, STEPHANIE C; Attleboro HS; Attleboro, MA; (Y); Drama Clb; Acpl Chr; Rep Band; Rep Mrchg Band; Rep Jr Cls; Stu Cncl; JV Tennis; High Hon Roll; Hon Roll; NHS; Bus Mgnt.

CHIEN, JENVA; Boston Latin Acad; Allston, MA; (Y); Mth Clb Pres; Mth Tm; Chinese Clb; Chinese Yth Christ; Church Choir; NHS 86; 3rd Awd Sci Fair 86; Engrng.

CHILDS, STEPHANIE; Newburyport HS; Byfield, MA; (Y); 18/184; Intnl Clb; Math Tm; Model UN; Science Clb; SADD; Nwsp Rptr; Var Fld Hcky; Var Tennis; NHS; Maxima Cum Laude Natl Latin Exm 83-84; Alg II Awd Exc 84-85; John Calvin Noyes Schlrp 85-86; Bates Coll.

CHIN, CRAIG; Norwood SR HS; Norwood, MA; (Y); 6/360; Civic Clb; Varsity Clb; Socr; Trk; High Hon Roll; Hon Roll; Jr NHS; Trs NHS.

CHIN, EDWARD J; Medford HS; Malden, MA; (Y); 110/450; Am Leg Boys St; Math Tm; Science Clb; Tennis; Im Vllybl; Ntl Merit Ltr; NEDT Awd; Chess Clb; Computer Clb; Mathletes; Ntl Essy Cntst US Army Rsrv 84; Ntl Ltn Exm Cum Laude 85; U Of CA-BERKELEY; Lbrl Arts.

CHIN, SYLVIA; Girls Catholic HS; Saugus, MA; (Y); Art Clb; Hon Roll; No Demerits Awd 84-85 & 85-86; Prfct Atndnc Awd 85-86; U Lowell; Math.

CHIN, VICTOR F; Randolph HS; Randolph, MA; (Y); 11/321; VP Computer Clb; Math Tm; School Play; Nwsp Stf; Rep Soph Cls; Rep Jr Cls; Rep Sr Cls; Trk; High Hon Roll; Rotary Awd; Tufts U; Engrng.

CHING, FANNY; Medford HS; Medford, MA; (Y); 5/435; Hosp Aide; Math Tm; Science Clb; SADD; Yrbk Stf; Rep Stu Cncl; Im Vllybl; High Hon Roll; Mu Alp Tht; NHS; Eng,Physics,Harvard Bk Awd 83-86; Engrng.

CHIPMAN, SCOTT; Holyoke HS; Holyoke, MA; (Y); Computer Clb; JA; Office Aide; Teachers Aide; Cit Awd; Hon Roll; Stu Cncl HS Awd 86; Wstrn NEW Englnd Coll; Mngt.

CHIRICOTTI, JENNIFER; Westwood HS; Westwood, MA; (Y); 78/212; Key Clb; Pep Clb; Ski Clb; Spanish Clb; Band; Concert Band; Mrchg Band; Pep Band; Capt Var Cheerleading; Hon Roll; Ntl Ldrshp & Svc Awd 85; Villanova U; Bus.

CHISHOLM, HEATHER; Danvers HS; Danvers, MA; (Y); 11/280; Varsity Clb; Yrbk Stf; Var Coach Actv; Var Gym; Var Mgr(s); Var Tennis; High Hon Roll; NHS; Spanish NHS; Med.

CHISHOLM, PATRICIA; Haverhill HS; Haverhill, MA; (Y); JA; Band; Concert Band; Drm Mjr(t); Jazz Band; Mrchg Band; Swing Chorus; Symp Band; High Hon Roll; Hon Roll; Natl Dir Awd Achvmnt In Music 84; Music.

CHIU, CATHERINE; Boston Latin HS; Allston, MA; (Y); 51/274; Church Yth Grp; German Clb; Science Clb; Chorus; Nwsp Bus Mgr; Nwsp Rptr; Nwsp Stf; Hon Roll; NHS; Cnty Chmpns Mock Trl Trnmnt 86; Cert Of Merit Stu Ldrshp 85-86.

CHIU, SO FAN; Boston Latin Acad; N Quincy, MA; (Y); Hon Roll; Ntl Merit Ltr; Comp.

CHMIELEWSKI, STEVEN; Somerset HS; Somerset, MA; (Y); 10/315; Ski Clb; Rep Sr Cls; Var L Ftbl; Var L Ice Hcky; High Hon Roll; Hon Roll; NHS; Williams Coll Bk Awd; Top 10 Stu; Commwlth Of MA Schlr; Colby Coll; Crmnl Justice.

CHOATE, JENNIFER; Medford HS; Medford, MA; (Y); Dance Clb; Drama Clb; Ski Clb; SADD; Acpl Chr; Pres Chorus; Madrigals; School Musical; Nwsp Stf; Gftd & Tlntd Prog 83-87.

CHOQUETTE, SCOTT; Hoosac Valley HS; Adams, MA; (Y); 40/180; Aud/Vis; Ski Clb; School Musical; School Play; Stage Crew; Hon Roll; Bus Mngmnt.

CHORNEY, MICHELLE; Sharon HS; Sharon, MA; (Y); 34/210; English Clb; Red Cross Aide; Temple Yth Grp; Y-Teens; Yrbk Phtg; Yrbk Stf; Timer; Hon Roll; Queens Crt Jr Prom 86.

CHOUINARD, KIMBERLY; Bishop Connolly HS; Fall River, MA; (Y); 19/167; Cmnty Wkr; Rep Sr Cls; Var L Cheerleading; Cit Awd; High Hon Roll; NHS; Pres Schlr; SADD; Hon Roll; Retreat Team 85-86; Tutoring Pgm 83-86; Pst Prom Committee Agnst Drnkg 85-86; Providence Coll.

CHOW, HERBERT; Somerville HS; Somerville, MA; (Y); Boys Clb Am; Chess Clb; Math Clb; Diving; High Hon Roll; St Schlr; 2nd Annl Compt Cntst 2nd Pl 84-85; Outstndng Achvt Physcs 85-86; 1st Pl CML Calculus Leag 85-86; NE U; Engrng.

CHRISTIAN, DANIEL G; Mohawk Trail Regional HS; Shelburne Falls, MA; (Y); Am Leg Boys St; Rep Jr Cls; Rep Sr Cls; Var Crs Cntry; JV Var Socr; Var Tennis; Hon Roll; NHS; Eclgst.

CHRISTIAN, LEE; Plymouth Carver HS; Plymouth, MA; (Y); Key Clb; Model UN; Pep Clb; Quiz Bowl; Speech Tm; SADD; Cheerleading; Trk; Hon Roll; Bus Mgmt.

CHRISTO, PAULA SANTO; Westport HS; Westport, MA; (Y); 5/180; Sec French Clb; Rep Frsh Cls; Rep Soph Cls; Rep Jr Cls; Sec Sr Cls; VP Stu Cncl; Capt Vllybl; Betsy Tabor Schlrshp 86; Pres Acad Achmnt 86; Stu Cncl Schlrshp & Our Lady Of Grace Schlrshp 86; Southeastern MA U; Med Tech.

CHRISTOFERSON, LAUREL; Hampshire Regional HS; Southampton, MA; (Y); 2/137; Church Yth Grp; Hosp Aide; Drm & Bgl; Nwsp Sprt Ed; Nwsp Stf; Yrbk Stf; Var Bsktbl; Socr; Trk; NHS; Drtmth & Ynkee Mgzne Book Awd 86.

CHRISTOPOULOS, LISA; Hanover HS; West Palm Beach, FL; (Y); Drama Clb; School Play; Stage Crew; Palm Beach JC; Chld Psychlgy.

CHU, BENSON; Boston Latin Schl; Jamaica Plain, MA; (Y); 12/274; Chess Clb; Pres Science Clb; Ed Nwsp Ed-Chief; Var L Crs Cntry; Var L Trk; Hon Roll; NHS; Stu Of Dual Cnty Lg X-Cntry Chmpns 84; 1st Pl JHA Rd Race 84; Chem Engrng.

CHU, MAY SUM; Boston Technical HS; Boston, MA; (Y); French Clb; Pep Clb; Vllybl; NHS; Boston Coll; Bus Mngmnt.

CHU, RUTH; Boston Latin Schl; Boston, MA; (Y); 72/285; Camera Clb; Church Yth Grp; Exploring; French Clb; Yrbk Bus Mgr; Yrbk Stf; JV L Vllybl; NHS; Pres Schlr; St Schlr; Cls 1929 Schlrshp 86; Boston U; Fncng.

CHU, WINNE; Randolph HS; Randolph, MA; (Y); 3/317; Sec Intnl Clb; Capt Color Guard; Nwsp Stf; Sec Stu Cncl; High Hon Roll; NHS; Pres Schlr; Dartmouth Clb Bk Awd 85; 2nd Annl Outstndg Randolph Yth Awd 85; Cert Mrt Sci & Math Soc Wmn Engrs 86; Dartmouth Coll; Engrg.

CHUNG, CHARLES; Northfield Mt Hermon HS; Whitinsville, MA; (Y); Ski Clb; Band; Jazz Band; School Play; Yrbk Phtg; Yrbk Stf; Stu Cncl; JV Lcrss; JV Socr; Var Trk.

CHUNG, PIERRE; Hingham HS; Hingham, MA; (Y); 150/347; AFS; Band; Orch; Variety Show; Im Badmtn; Im Bsktbl; JV Ftbl; JV Tennis; Im Vllybl; Im Wt Lftg; Ntnl Hstry Day 86; Coll; Pre-Med.

CHUNG, STEVEN; Charlestown HS; Boston, MA; (Y); Rep Soph Cls; Rep Stu Cncl; Capt Coach Actv; Hnrbl Ment Prmgmnng 84-85; VP Asian Stdnt Clb 84-85; Hugh O Brian Yuth Fdtn, MA Ldrshp Smnr 85-86; Engrng.

CHUNG, TERESA Y; Phillips Acad; Tallmadge, OH; (Y); Band; Concert Band; Mrchg Band; Orch; Lit Mag; JV Fld Hcky; JV Lcrss; Im Swmmng; Im Tennis; Cit Awd; Philosophys Physcn.

CHURCH, BONNIE; King Philip Regional HS; Norfolk, MA; (Y); #28 In Class; Church Yth Grp; Cmnty Wkr; Intnl Clb; Ed Lit Mag; Hon Roll; NHS; Cosmtlgy.

CIACCIARELLI, MICHAEL; Everett HS; Everett, MA; (Y); Key Clb; SADD; Rep Frsh Cls; Rep Soph Cls; Rep Jr Cls; Rep Sr Cls; Stu Cncl; Crs Cntry; Hon Roll; NHS; Hugh O Brian Leadrshp Awd 84-85.

CIAMPA, TOM; Boston College HS; Arlington, MA; (Y); 40/293; Church Yth Grp; SADD; Teachers Aide; JV Socr; Hon Roll; NHS; Ntl Merit Ltr; Boys Clb Am; Latin Clb; Partial Schlrshp 83-87; Awd Acdmc Excllnc Chem & Trignmtry 85-86; Dartmouth; Pre Law.

CIANCIOLO, NANCY; Methuen HS; Methuen, MA; (Y); 3/348; Rep Am Leg Aux Girls St; Intnl Clb; Model UN; Concert Band; Mrchg Band; High Hon Roll; Pres NHS; Ntl Merit Ltr; Hrvrd Book Awd 86; Phi Alpha Thta Hstrcl Conf Prtcpnt 85-86; Biomdcl Engnrng.

CIAVOLA, GINA; South High Community Schl; Worcester, MA; (S); Sec Church Yth Grp; SADD; Pres Jr Cls; Sec Stu Cncl; Capt Fld Hcky; Var Sftbl; Capt Trk; Hon Roll; NHS; Spanish NHS; Hugh O Brian Ldrshp Fndtn Rep 85; Acad Olympcs 85; Stu Govt Day Rep 85-86; Bus.

CIBELLI, PHIL; St Johns Prep; Peabody, MA; (Y); Cmnty Wkr; Im Bowling; Im Ftbl; Im Golf; Im Tennis; Hon Roll; Bus.

CICCIA, LARRY; Medford HS; Medford, MA; (Y); Ski Clb; SADD; Varsity Clb; Rep Frsh Cls; JV Bsbl; Var JV Ice Hcky; Sci Awd; U MA Amherst; Acctng.

CICCOLINI, CHRISTOPHER; Fitchburg HS; Fitchburg, MA; (Y); 3/208; Stu Cncl; Im Bsktbl; Var L Ftbl; Var L Trk; High Hon Roll; Trck-Schl Javln Rcrd 86; DCMC Conf, Dist E Javln Chmpn 86; Mltry Pilot.

CICCONE, JONATHAN; Medway JR/Sr HS; Medway, MA; (Y); 18/130; Boy Scts; Drama Clb; SADD; Band; Jazz Band; School Musical; Trs Pres Stu Cncl; Var Trk; High Hon Roll; Pres NHS; Set Designer Statewide Drama Fnls 85; 1 Of 300 Chosen Annapolis Summer Seminar 86; Annapolis; Marine Sci.

CICCONE JR, RONALD W; Bishop Feehan HS; Attleboro, MA; (Y); Boy Scts; Debate Tm; Ski Clb; Yrbk Stf; Im Mgr Bsktbl; JV Trk; Elks Awd; High Hon Roll; Eagle Scout & Elk Youth Achvt 84; Northeastern U; Mech Engrng.

CIEPLIK, TODD; Ludlow HS; Ludlow, MA; (Y); Am Leg Boys St; Church Yth Grp; Cmnty Wkr; Varsity Clb; School Play; Capt Bsbl; Capt Bsktbl; Im Vllybl; Accntng.

CIEPLINSKI, CARL; Cathedral HS; Springfield, MA; (Y); 130/500; Red Cross Aide; JV Bsktbl; JV Ftbl; Var L Golf; Prfct Atten Awd; Bus.

CIESLA, TAMMY; Frontier Regional Schl; S Deerfield, MA; (Y); Church Yth Grp; Drama Clb; French Clb; GAA; Pep Clb; Political Wkr; Ski Clb; SADD; Varsity Clb; School Play; Crs Cntry & Trk 84-85; Girls Athltc Assn Awd 84; Zool.

CINCOTTO, JEFFREY; Austin Prep Schl; N Andover, MA; (Y); 63/130; French Clb.

CIOSEK, RICHARD F; Bishop Connolly HS; Swansea, MA; (Y); Computer Clb; Church Choir; School Musical; Variety Show; High Hon Roll; Hon Roll; SMU; Elec Engrng.

CIPOLLA, LISA; Cathedral HS; Springfield, MA; (Y); 15/570; Spanish Clb; NHS; Intnl Clb; Red Cross Aide; JV Socr; Swmmng; High Hon Roll; Awd Excllnc Spnsh, Albgra II 86; Mdl OAS Stu 83; Bio.

CIULLA, JULIE; Everett HS; Everett, MA; (Y); Church Yth Grp; Hosp Aide; Intnl Clb; Key Clb; Office Aide; SADD; Nwsp Rptr; Nwsp Stf; Yrbk Stf; High Hon Roll; Stu Advsry Brd 85-86; Church Yth Grp Chrldr 84-85; Bus Adm.

CIULLA, ROSE ANNE; Bishop Fenwick HS; Gloucester, MA; (S); 14/238; Art Clb; Cmnty Wkr; English Clb; Math Clb; Science Clb; Teachers Aide; Nwsp Stf; Yrbk Stf; High Hon Roll; NHS; Chem.

CIULLA, TRACY; Notre Dame Acad; Hull, MA; (Y); 50/120; French Clb; Chorus; Nwsp Stf; Yrbk Stf; Frnch II Awd Excll In Frnch II 85; Excll In Rlgn 86; Cmnctns.

CLANCY, MARY; Ursuline Acad; Canton, MA; (Y); Cmnty Wkr; Hosp Aide; Political Wkr; Spanish Clb; Swmmng; Hon Roll; Patriot Leader All Scholastic Awd 85; Swimming Rookie Of Year; Phys Therapy.

CLANCY, SUSAN A; Bedford HS; Bedford, MA; (Y); AFS; Church Yth Grp; Ski Clb; SADD; Stage Crew; Nwsp Ed-Chief; Var L Crs Cntry; Trk; Hon Roll; U Of PA; Soclgy.

CLARK, BILLY; St Dominic Savio HS; Revere, MA; (Y); 19/101; Boys Clb Am; Church Yth Grp; Cmnty Wkr; Computer Clb; Key Clb; Math Clb; Math Tm; Ski Clb; SADD; Varsity Clb; St Anslems NH; Engrng.

CLARK, BOBBY; Salem HS; Salem, MA; (Y); Church Yth Grp; SADD; Varsity Clb; Stu Cncl; Var Capt Golf; Var Trk; Hon Roll; Bus Adm.

CLARK, ERIC; Newburyport HS; Newburypt, MA; (Y); 33/200; Church Yth Grp; Political Wkr; Varsity Clb; Pres Soph Cls; Var L Bsbl; JV Bsktbl; Var L Socr; Hon Roll; Ldrshp Cls 85-86; Mrshl For Sci Cls 86-87.

CLARK, GORDON; Athol HS; Athol, MA; (Y); #5 In Class; Church Yth Grp; Model UN; SADD; Var Bsktbl; Var Crs Cntry; Var Trk; Var L Vllybl; High Hon Roll; Hon Roll; NHS; ARCH.

CLARK, JAMES E; Oakmont Regional HS; Ashburnham, MA; (Y); 17/120; Am Leg Boys St; Concert Band; Mrchg Band; Yrbk Sprt Ed; Bsbl; Mgr(s); High Hon Roll; NHS; Pres Schlr; Rotary Awd; Ashburnham Historical Soc Awd 86; U MA; Journalism.

CLARK, JENNIFER; Presentation Of Mary Acad; Methuen, MA; (Y); 17/43; Math Clb; Rep SADD; School Musical; Variety Show; Yrbk Stf; VP Soph Cls; Rep Stu Cncl; JV Bsktbl; Var Cheerleading; Hon Roll; Ocngrphy.

CLARK, JONATHAN; Maynard HS; Maynard, MA; (Y); Boy Scts; SADD; Ftbl; Trk; Hon Roll; Aerontc Tech.

CLARK, KARA; Our Lady Of Nazareth Acad; Wilmington, MA; (Y); 29/76; Church Yth Grp; Ski Clb; Spanish Clb; SADD; School Musical; School Play; Var Cheerleading; Im Crs Cntry; Var Pom Pon; Chrldng Awd 86; Soc Services.

CLARK, KERRY; Shepherd Hill Regional HS; Dudley, MA; (Y); Socr; Tennis; Phys Thrpy.

CLARK, KIMBERLY A; Archbishop Williams HS; Braintree, MA; (Y); 23/189; Yrbk Ed-Chief; Trs Sr Cls; Rep Stu Cncl; JV Var DECA; Pres Schlr; Grossman Svc, Ldrshp Awd 86; Tufts U; Engrng.

CLARK, MIKE; Barnstable HS; Centerville, MA; (Y); 129/395; Church Yth Grp; Civic Clb; Cmnty Wkr; Political Wkr; Bsbl; Bsktbl; Coach Actv; Hon Roll; Frsh Cls; Soph Cls; Fin Law Day Essay Cont 86; Capt JV Bsktbl 85-86; U MA; Crimnl Justc.

CLARK, RICHARD; Maynard HS; Maynard, MA; (Y); 8/100; Am Leg Boys St; Mrchg Band; Var L Ftbl; Capt L Trk; Wt Lftg; Hon Roll; NHS; Cmpltd Mass Adv Stds Pgm 85; Appt US Mltry Acad 86; West Point; Aerospc Engrng.

CLARK, STEPHANIE; Chatham JR SR HS; South Chatham, MA; (Y); 15/49; AFS; Church Yth Grp; Cmnty Wkr; GAA; Girl Scts; Math Tm; Political Wkr; Ski Clb; Spanish Clb; School Musical; Gallaudet Coll; Lbrl Arts.

CLARK, STEPHANIE; Norwell HS; Norwell, MA; (Y); 24/175; VP Pres AFS; Am Leg Aux Girls St; Drama Clb; 4-H; Ed Nwsp Stf; Capt Fld Hcky; 4-H Awd; Sec NHS; Speech Tm; Chorus; Trip To Ntl 4-H Cngrss In Chicago 85; E Marston Awd Schlrshp Excllnce In Dramatics 86; St Mock Trl 86; Cornell U; Anml Sci.

CLARK, THERESA; Holyoke Catholic HS; S Hadley, MA; (Y); Exploring; Spanish Clb; Speech Tm; Nwsp Rptr; Yrbk Rptr; Lit Mag; Socr; Law.

CLARK, THOMAS; Hopkins Acad; Hadley, MA; (Y); Church Yth Grp; 4-H; Spanish Clb; Band; Concert Band; Jazz Band; Mrchg Band; Pep Band; Yrbk Stf; Dnfth Awd; 1st Natl JR Hort Assn MA 85:22nd Natl JR Hort Assn 85; Outstndng Wrk Spnsh Awd 86; Hort.

CLARK, THOMAS; West Springfield HS; W Springfield, MA; (Y); Church Yth Grp; Nwsp Phtg; Hon Roll; NHS; Boston U; Aero Engrng.

CLARKE, BRIAN; Medfield HS; Medfield, MA; (Y); 44/180; Am Leg Boys St; Church Yth Grp; Ski Clb; Crs Cntry; Trk; Hon Roll; Jr NHS; Babson Coll; Mgt.

CLARKE, ESTHER; South Lancaster Acad; S Lancaster, MA; (S); Teachers Aide; Church Choir; School Musical; Nwsp Ed-Chief; Yrbk Phtg; Yrbk Rptr; Rep Stu Cncl; High Hon Roll; NHS; Tuitn Schlrshp Acdmc Exclnc 83-84.

CLARKE, FRED; Newton North HS; Newton, MA; (Y); Drama Clb; VP Mrchg Band; Orch; Stage Crew; Rep Jr Cls; Rep Sr Cls; L Trk; High Hon Roll; Ntl Merit Ltr; Church Yth Grp; GBYSO 85-87; Yth Chamber Orch 85-87; Music.

CLARKE, JODI; Melrose HS; Melrose, MA; (Y); Im Sftbl; Im Vllybl; Phys Ed Awd 84; Phys Thrpy.

CLARKE, KEVIN; Swampscott HS; Swampscott, MA; (Y); 30/238; Church Yth Grp; Drama Clb; Math Tm; Science Clb; Band; Chorus; Concert Band; Drm Mjr(t); Jazz Band; Mrchg Band; Liberal Arts Coll; Professor.

CLARKE, LISA; Commerce HS; Springfield, MA; (S); Off Soph Cls; Hon Roll; Bus Mgmt.

CLARKE, MARILYN; Marlboro HS; Marlborough, MA; (Y); 6/245; Pres Church Yth Grp; Var Fld Hcky; NHS; Pres Schlr; MIP Fld Hcky 84; Fld Hcky Unsung Hero Awd 85; Providence Coll; Law.

CLARKE, SUSAN; Acton-Boxboro Regional HS; Acton, MA; (Y); 152/428; Art Clb; Radio Clb; SADD; Nwsp Rptr; Nwsp Stf; JV Capt Cheerleading; JV Lcrss; Powder Puff Ftbl; Hon Roll; Design.

CLARKSON, DAVID C; Newburyport HS; Newburyport, MA; (Y); 135/200; Am Leg Boys St; Church Yth Grp; Computer Clb; Intnl Clb; Library Aide; Model UN; Science Clb; Rotary Awd; Elliot M Gordon Mem Schlrshp 86; Willmont Roby Evans Schlrshp 86; Franklin Pierce Coll; Psych.

CLASBY, ERIN; Silver Lake Regional HS; Plympton, MA; (Y); 1/480; Am Leg Aux Girls St; Church Yth Grp; French Clb; Chorus; Rep Frsh Cls; Pres Jr Cls; Var Capt Cheerleading; Tennis; High Hon Roll; Pres NHS; Dartmouth Bk Awd 85-86; Jrnlsm.

CLAUS, JENNIFER; Natick HS; Natick, MA; (Y); 19/399; Girl Scts; Speech Tm; Chorus; School Musical; School Play; Nwsp Stf; Lit Mag; High Hon Roll; Hon Roll; NHS; Indctn Natl Hnr Socty 86; Actng.

CLAVEAU, JEANNINE L; Bishop Fenwick HS; Salem, MA; (Y); Hon Roll; Salem ST Coll; Nrsng.

CLEARY, ELIZABETH; Attleboro HS; Attleboro, MA; (Y); Cmnty Wkr; High Hon Roll; Outstdng Shrthnd I Awd 86; 2 Filing Awds 86; Dean JC; Dance.

CLEARY, JENNIFER; Haverhill HS; Haverhill, MA; (Y); Hosp Aide; Spanish Clb; Powder Puff Ftbl; High Hon Roll; NHS.

CLEARY, NANCY C; Westford Acad; Westford, MA; (Y); 7/225; Pres Art Clb; Pep Clb; Spanish Clb; SADD; Nwsp Ed-Chief; Yrbk Ed-Chief; Var Capt Bsktbl; Var Capt Socr; Trk; High Hon Roll; Boston Globe Schltc Art Awd 83; Acton Arts Lg Scholar 86; Stu Mnth; RI Schl Desgn; Comm Art.

CLEMENT, JENNIFER; B M C Durfee HS; Fall River, MA; (Y); 25/661; VP French Clb; Yrbk Stf; High Hon Roll; Hon Roll; NHS; Christa Mc Auliff Schlrshp 86; Stonehill Hnr Shclrshp 86; Citizen Schlrshp Foundation Awd 86; Stonehill Coll; Elem Edu.

CLEMENT, MARK; Barnstable HS; W Barnstable, MA; (Y); 49/376; Trs Stu Cncl; Var L Crs Cntry; Var L Trk; Elks Awd; Hon Roll; NHS; Rotary Awd; Upr Cape Womns Republcn Clb 86; Kiwanis Clb 86; St Michaels Coll; Englsh.

CLEMENT, TRICIA; St Bernards C C HS; Winchendon, MA; (S); 25/177; Am Leg Aux Girls St; Church Yth Grp; Drama Clb; Spanish Clb; School Play; Var Socr; Var Trk; Hon Roll; NHS; Girls All-Star Soccer Tm 85; Bentley; Accntng.

CLIFFORD, CHERYL; Randolph HS; Randolph, MA; (Y); 101/327; Art Clb; Walter Nicholson Schlrshp 86; Sthestrn MA U; Art.

CLIFFORD, JOSEPH P; Dedham HS; Dedham, MA; (S); 6/252; Am Leg Boys St; Nwsp Rptr; Nwsp Sprt Ed; Capt Bsbl; Capt Bsktbl; Elks Awd; High Hon Roll; Pres NHS; Ntl Merit SF; Clby Coll Bk Prz; Bst In Sci.

CLOHERTY, JANET; Waltham HS; Waltham, MA; (Y); Cmnty Wkr; Latin Clb; Rep Stu Cncl; Var L Bsktbl; Var L Sftbl; DAR Awd; High Hon Roll; Pres NHS; Lawyer.

CLOUTIER, LISA; Attleboro HS; Attleboro, MA; (Y); Chorus; Yrbk Stf; Var Trk; High Hon Roll; Hon Roll; Med.

CLOUTIER II, RONALD; Bishop Feehan HS; N Attleboro, MA; (Y); Ski Clb; Ice Hcky; Johnson & Wales; Culnary Arts.

CLOWES, MELISSA; Ludlow HS; Ludlow, MA; (Y); 51/270; SADD; Band; Concert Band; Symp Band; Variety Show; Cheerleading; Hon Roll; Dance Clb; JA; Library Aide; Berklee Coll; Singer.

CO-WALLIS, GWEN MARIE; Silver Lake Regional HS; Halifax, MA; (Y); 14/500; Dance Clb; Spanish Clb; Yrbk Stf; Pres Soph Cls; Var JV Cheerleading; Hon Roll; Hst NHS; Northeastern U; Acctng.

COADY, MAUREEN E; Weymouth North HS; N Weymouth, MA; (Y); 4/360; Church Yth Grp; Dance Clb; Key Clb; Pep Clb; High Hon Roll; Hon Roll; Jr NHS; NHS; Suffolk U Bk Awd 86.

COAKLEY, ERIN; Wachusett Regional HS; Sterling Jct, MA; (Y); 120/400; Art Clb; Pres Church Yth Grp; Dance Clb; Chorus; Yrbk Stf; Stu Cncl; PAVAS; Bsktbl; Gym; Worcester Ballet Socy Schlrshp 84; 2nd Run-Up Jr Miss Dnce Of Amer 84; Gold Mdl-Rgnl Showstpr Comp 86; Prof Dancer.

COAKLEY, ROBERT PAUL; Blackstone Vly Rgnl Vo Tech HS; Northbridge, MA; (Y); 10/186; Computer Clb; Drm & Bgl; Trk; Hon Roll; Pres Schlr; Tchrs Assn Acad Scholar Awd 86; MA ST Scholar 86; SE MA U; Comp Sci.

COATES, JENNIFER; Boston Latin Schl; Boston, MA; (Y); 100/289; Church Yth Grp; Key Clb; Church Choir; Lit Mag; Rep Jr Cls; Rep Sr Cls; Rep Stu Cncl; Hon Roll; Bstn Ltn Schl Home & Schl Assn Ad 86; Bstn Ltn Schl Aprbtn Lst 85-86; Brdgwtr ST Coll; Elem Ed.

COBB, MELISSA; Bishop Feehan HS; Seekonk, MA; (Y); JCL; Color Guard; Rep Frsh Cls; JV Cheerleading; Trk; High Hon Roll; Hon Roll; St Anselm Coll.

COCCA, ROBERT; Winthrop HS; Winthrop, MA; (Y); 1/212; Am Leg Boys St; Drama Clb; Math Tm; Pres Science Clb; Acpl Chr; School Musical; Yrbk Stf; Var L Socr; JV Trk; Val; Hi-Scrng Sr 86 Math Tm 86; Harvard; Bio.

COCO, JANIS; Presentation Of Mary Acad; Methuen, MA; (S); 2/46; Nwsp Ed-Chief; Yrbk Stf; Pres Soph Cls; Pres Jr Cls; Pres Sr Cls; Stat Sftbl; High Hon Roll; NHS; Church Yth Grp; Computer Clb; HOBY Ldrshp Ambssdr; Stu Govt Rep; 1st Pl Sci Fair Local; Regnl Wnnr Sci Fair; Advrtsng.

CODRINGTON, VERONICA; Boiston Lahn Schl; Dorchester, MA; (Y); 160/274; Church Yth Grp; Hosp Aide; JCL; Orch; School Musical; Ed Nwsp Rptr; Trk; Hon Roll; Cmnty Wkr; Variety Show; Classdicl Leag Awd 86; Law.

COE, KATHLEEN; Stoughton HS; Stoughton, MA; (Y); Pres Church Yth Grp; Cmnty Wkr; Office Aide; Sec SADD; Drm Mjr(t); Mrchg Band; Tennis; Twrlr; Scholar Fund Awd 86; Massasoit CC; Early Chldhd Ed.

COELLN, ROBERT; Agawam HS; Feeding Hills, MA; (Y); 51/350; French Clb; Band; Concert Band; Jazz Band; Var L Ice Hcky; Var L Tennis; Hon Roll; Lion Awd; NHS; A Avg Century 21 Accntng 86; Pierce Schl Schlrshp 86; Prov MA Farms Schrlshp 86; Westfield ST Coll; Accntng.

COEN, MARK J; Manchester JR-SR HS; Manchester, MA; (Y); Am Leg Boys St; Boy Scts; Lib Debate Tm; Math Tm; NFL; Capt Quiz Bowl; Capt Scholastic Bowl; Sec Frsh Cls; VP Soph Cls; Pres Stu Cncl; Grad Marshal 86.

COFFEY, BILL; Braintree HS; Braintree, MA; (Y); 17/441; JV Bsbl; Var Capt Bsktbl; Hon Roll; NHS; Ntl Merit Ltr; Stu Agnst Drunk Drvng 86.

COFFEY, JULIA; Bishop Connolly HS; Portsmouth, RI; (Y); 31/175; Dance Clb; Trk; Vllybl; High Hon Roll; Hon Roll.

COGLIANO, JIM; Westford Acad; Westford, MA; (Y); Var L Ftbl; Var L Ice Hcky; Hon Roll.

COHAN, CAROLYN; Holbrook HS; Holbrook, MA; (Y); 3/102; Sec Latin Clb; Rep Frsh Cls; Rep Soph Cls; Rep Jr Cls; Rep Sr Cls; Bsktbl; Socr; Sftbl; NHS; Sal; Cmmnwlth MA Schlr 86; Stonehill Hnr Schlr 86; Stonehill Coll; Mgmt.

COHAN, JOHN C; St Patricks HS; Brighton, MA; (Y); 14/44; Boys Clb Am; Boy Scts; Ftbl; Wt Lftg; Hon Roll; Psych.

COHAN, KERRYN; Marshfield HS; Marshfield, MA; (Y); 139/380; Key Clb; SADD; Yrbk Stf; Hon Roll; Stu Gov Day 86; Psych.

COHEN, ADAM R; Buckingham Browne & Nichols HS; Cambridge, MA; (Y); Ed Nwsp Stf; Ed Yrbk Stf; Lit Mag; Hon Roll; Ntl Merit SF; Schltc Writing Awds 85; Natl Latin Exam Silver Medal 84; Harvard; Financial Wrld.

COHEN, DANIEL J; Brockton HS; Brockton, MA; (Y); 23/1000; Am Leg Boys St; SADD; Band; Concert Band; Mrchg Band; Lit Mag; Tennis; High Hon Roll; Hon Roll; NHS; Engr.

COHEN, DEIRDRE; Newton North HS; Newton, MA; (Y); French Clb; Pres Ski Clb; Teachers Aide; Temple Yth Grp; Rep Jr Cls; Sec Stu Cncl; Hon Roll; Poli Sci.

COHEN, JAY; Randoph HS; Randolph, MA; (Y); 40/321; Boy Scts; Computer Clb; Drama Clb; Temple Yth Grp; Stage Crew; Crs Cntry; Trk; Hon Roll; Jr NHS; NHS; U Of VT.

COHEN, JENNIFER; Brookline HS; Brookline, MA; (Y); Dance Clb; Drama Clb; Office Aide; Ski Clb; Spanish Clb; Off Soph Cls; Off Jr Cls; Off Sr Cls; Off Stu Cncl; Crs Cntry; Barnard Coll; Hist.

COHEN, JULIE; Natick HS; Natick, MA; (Y); 200/450; Dance Clb; Ski Clb; SADD; Nwsp Stf; Off Jr Cls; Off Sr Cls; Off Stu Cncl; JV Sftbl; Hon Roll; Prfct Atten Awd; Bus Awd Typng 86; U MA; Hotel Mgmt.

COHEN, MELISSA; Framingham South HS; Natick, MA; (Y); 85/248; French Clb; SADD; Temple Yth Grp; Variety Show; JV Tennis; Hon Roll; SMARC Party 85-86; U WI Madison.

COHEN, RANDY; Stoughton HS; Stoughton, MA; (Y); Soroptimist; Temple Yth Grp; Im Bsbl; Var JV Ice Hcky; Hon Roll; Bus.

COHEN, STEPHEN N; Lincoln-Sudbury Regional HS; Sudbury, MA; (Y); Computer Clb; Math Tm; Model UN; Science Clb; Ed Lit Mag; Ntl Merit SF; Outstndng Sci Stdnt Awd Boston Musicn Sci 85; Astrnmy.

COKER, MARCIA; Burncoat SR HS; Dudley, MA; (Y); Dance Clb; Intnl Clb; Science Clb; Cheerleading; Equestrian Highpoint Champion Worcester Foundation 83; Law.

COKERDEM, SHAYNE; Salem HS; Salem, MA; (Y); 2/280; Am Leg Boys St; Math Tm; Science Clb; Stu Cncl; Var Golf; Var Tennis; Pres NHS; Sal; Pres Spanish NHS; Chess Clb; Renslr Mdl/Best Math & Sci Stu 86; Chancellors Tlnt Awd Wnnr 86; Hago Mem Golf Trophy 85; Sci.

COLBATH, ELISABETH ANN; Bedford HS; Bedford, MA; (Y); 40/200; AFS; Camera Clb; Church Yth Grp; SADD; Jazz Band; Mrchg Band; Orch; Pep Band; Yrbk Stf; Var JV Tennis; Psych.

COLBERT, CATHY L; Mascoromet Regional HS; Topsfield, MA; (Y); Camera Clb; Spanish Clb; Stage Crew; Variety Show; Yrbk Phtg; 4 Yr $30,000 Schlrshp To Pratt Inst 86; A P Exam Score Of 5 For Studio Art 86; Pratt Inst; Art & Dsgn.

COLBERT, JAMES; St Johns Prep; Lynn, MA; (Y); 22/241; Cmnty Wkr; Political Wkr; Science Clb; Im Bsktbl; JV Swmmng; JV Var Trk; High Hon Roll; Hon Roll; West Point; Law.

COLBERT, PATRICIA; Norwell HS; Norwell, MA; (Y); GAA; Hosp Aide; Stage Crew; Variety Show; Nwsp Rptr; Yrbk Stf; Mgr Socr; Hon Roll; Fnlst N E Yng Wrtrs Conf Middleburg COLL 86; W New England COLL Engl.

COLBY, PAULA M; Billerica Mem HS; N Billerica, MA; (Y); Girl Scts; Hosp Aide; Political Wkr; Yrbk Stf; Rep Stu Cncl; Capt Crs Cntry; Capt Powder Puff Ftbl; Var Trk; Var Vllybl; Mstr Sprts Awd 86; Shffln Shoes Schlrshp 86; U Lowell; Bus Mgt.

COLDWELL, LAURA; Assabet Valley Reg Voc HS; Southborough, MA; (Y); #3 In Class; Church Yth Grp; Computer Clb; Drama Clb; Math Clb; Math Tm; SADD; Chorus; School Musical; School Play; Frsh Cls; Acadmc Achvt Awd Acadmc Ltr 85; Comp Sci.

COLE, JANET; Silver Lake Regional HS; Halifax, MA; (Y); 44/500; Cmnty Wkr; French Clb; Latin Clb; Library Aide; Nwsp Stf; Yrbk Stf; NHS; Office Aide; Cert Of Excllnc For Paper Wrtn For MA ST Hstry Day 86.

COLE, LISA; Marlboro HS; Marlboro, MA; (Y); 7/355; Yrbk Stf; Var Mgr(s); Hon Roll; Bus.

COLE, PAULA D; Rockport HS; Rockport, MA; (Y); 3/72; Drama Clb; Spanish Clb; VP Chorus; School Musical; Sec Frsh Cls; Pres Soph Cls; Pres Jr Cls; Pres Sr Cls; Var Cheerleading; High Hon Roll; Colby Coll Bk Prz 85; Best Actrss 85; NE Dist Chr 85 & 86; Music Perfmnc.

COLEMAN, CHRISTOPHER; Braintree HS; Braintree, MA; (Y); Church Yth Grp; Im Bsktbl; JV Crs Cntry; Im Socr; Hon Roll.

COLEMAN, JACQUELINE; Walnut Hill HS; Wellesley, MA; (Y); Drama Clb; PAVAS; School Play; Yrbk Stf; Pres Frsh Cls; Rep Stu Cncl; Hon Roll; Debate Tm; French Clb; PAVAS; Ldrshp Forum; Stu Dir Play; Drama Fest Excllnce Awd; U CT; Theatre.

COLENA, MICHAEL; Assabet Valley Regional Voc HS; Marlboro, MA; (Y); 9/800; Boy Scts; Church Yth Grp; Computer Clb; Math Tm; SADD; Chorus; Church Choir; School Play; God Cntry Awd; NHS; Data Prcssng.

COLLAMORE, BETH; Holyoke Catholic HS; Holyoke, MA; (Y); 2/132; Computer Clb; Math Clb; Stat Bsbl; Stat Bsktbl; Stat Socr; High Hon Roll; NHS; School Musical; Lit Mag; CAP; Holy Cross Bk Prz 86; Awds Engl,Algebra,Geo,Spanish,Rlgn,Sci,Bio,Chem & Econ; Med.

COLLER, JOSEPH; Gardner HS; Gardner, MA; (Y); 26/137; Spanish Clb; Stage Crew; Hon Roll; Embry-Riddle Aero UAERO Engnr.

COLLETTA, NORMA; Melrose HS; Melrose, MA; (Y); 9/400; German Clb; Quiz Bowl; SADD; Stu Cncl; High Hon Roll; Hon Roll; NHS; Bio.

COLLETTA, VALERIE; Melrose HS; Melrose, MA; (Y); 25/400; German Clb; SADD; Stu Cncl; Tennis; Hon Roll; NHS; U MA Boston; Bio.

COLLIGAN, SHARON; Lincoln-Sudbury Reg HS; Sudbury, MA; (Y); Pres Church Yth Grp; French Clb; Pres Intnl Clb; Bausch & Lomb Sci Awd; Cum Laude Soc 85-86; Esprnto Leag Of N Amer Thompson Fund 84-85.

COLLINS, APRIL; Brockton HS; Brockton, MA; (Y); Church Yth Grp; Hosp Aide; Key Clb; Office Aide; Band; Concert Band; Mrchg Band; Var Crs Cntry; Var Trk; Hon Roll; Engrng.

COLLINS, CHRISTIN; Winchester HS; Winchester, MA; (Y); Church Yth Grp; Drama Clb; French Clb; Bsktbl; French Hon Soc; Hon Roll; Hon Mntn Ntl Frnch Exm 84; Frnch.

COLLINS, DARYL; Acton-Boxborough HS; Acton, MA; (Y); 46/428; Yrbk Stf; Capt Cheerleading; Powder Puff Ftbl; Hon Roll; Bio.

COLLINS, DONALD; Saugus HS; Saugus, MA; (Y); Variety Show; Yrbk Sprt Ed; Rep Jr Cls; Rep Sr Cls; Bsbl; Coach Actv; Var Capt Ice Hcky; Var Capt Socr; Hon Roll; NHS; Accntnt.

COLLINS, JEFF; Westport HS; Westport, MA; (Y); 10/150; French Clb; Intnl Clb; Bsktbl; Crs Cntry; Golf; Trk; High Hon Roll; Hon Roll; Jr NHS; NHS; Betsy Tabor Schlrshp 86; Sthestrn MA U; Poli Sci.

COLLINS, KELLY; New Bedford HS; New Bedford, MA; (Y); 114/701; Hon Roll; Spch Therpy.

COLLINS, NEAL O; Stoneham HS; Stoneham, MA; (Y); 20/285; Am Leg Boys St; Boy Scts; VP Debate Tm; Exploring; Sec French Clb; Math Tm; Ski Clb; Band; Concert Band; Yrbk Ed-Chief; Boston U; Engrng.

COLLINS, ROBERT; Faith Christian Acad; Centerville, MA; (S); 1/22; School Play; Yrbk Stf; Pres Stu Cncl; Ice Hcky; L Socr; High Hon Roll; Ntl Merit Ltr; Church Yth Grp; DECA; Hghst Pace Avg 84-85; Merit Mdl 84-85; Supv Awd 85; Harvard U; Bus Mngmnt.

COLLINS, ROSLINDE M; Westford Acad; Westford, MA; (Y); 15/225; SADD; Pres Frsh Cls; Var Capt Cheerleading; Var Trk; High Hon Roll; Kiwanis Awd; NHS; Pres Schlr; French Clb; 1st Rnnr Up Miss MA Amer Coed Pag 85; Boston Coll; Pre-Med.

COLLINS, SHAWN M; Abington HS; Abington, MA; (Y); Am Leg Boys St; French Clb; Political Wkr; SADD; Rep Jr Cls; Rep Sr Cls; Im Crs Cntry; Var L Golf; Var L Ice Hcky; Hon Roll; Bus.

COLLINS, STEVEN J; Abington HS; Abington, MA; (Y); Am Leg Boys St; Math Clb; Rep Sr Cls; Stu Cncl; Im Crs Cntry; L Golf; Wt Lftg; Hon Roll; Voice Dem Awd; Math Tm; Outstndng Achvmnt US Hstry Awd 85-86; Bus Law.

COLOMBO, MICHAEL; Marian HS; Framingham, MA; (Y); 16/175; Yrbk Stf; Rep Jr Cls; Rep Stu Cncl; Hon Roll; NHS; Awd Exc Spnsh,Bio,Chem 85-86; Corp Law.

COLOMBO, PATRICIA; Attleboro HS; Attleboro, MA; (Y); Acpl Chr; Chorus; Yrbk Stf; Trs Frsh Cls; Rep Jr Cls; Rep Sr Cls; Stu Cncl; Var L Fld Hcky; Hon Roll; Ntl Lang Arts Olympd 1st Pl Gld Mdl; Ltn Hon Soc; Med.

COLOMEY, KEVIN G; Catholic Memorial HS; Dedham, MA; (Y); 62/247; Am Leg Boys St; VP Key Clb; Ski Clb; School Musical; Yrbk Stf; VP Sr Cls; VP Stu Cncl; Swmmng; Hon Roll; Kiwanis Awd; U Lowell; Acctg.

COLON-FRANCIA, SHIRLITTA A; Groton Schl; Washington, DC; (Y); Church Yth Grp; Dance Clb; Teachers Aide; VP Sr Cls; VP Stu Cncl; Var Capt Bsktbl; Var Socr; Hon Roll; Pres Of Alliance For Stu Hrmny Mnrty Org 85-86; Mgr Of Groton Schl Bkstore 85-86; Brown U; Bus.

COLPACK, THOS; Holyoke Catholic HS; Easthampton, MA; (Y); 40/126; JV Bsbl; JV Bsktbl; Golf; JV Socr; Myles Barrett Awd 86; Bus Adm.

COLPITTS, TODD; Westwood HS; Westwood, MA; (Y); 147/212; Ski Clb; Var Ftbl; U MA-AMHERST; Acctng.

COLSIA, CHRISTOPHER; Central Catholic HS; Andover, MA; (Y); SADD; Var Bsbl; Hon Roll; Engrng.

COLUCCI, DAN; Marian HS; Natick, MA; (Y); 42/200; Varsity Clb; Var L Bsbl; JV Bsktbl; Framington ST Coll Hstrcl Fair 86; Babson Coll MA; Bus Mktg.

COLUMBO, JULIA; Dedham HS; Dedham, MA; (S); 5/252; Church Yth Grp; Intnl Clb; Spanish Clb; SADD; Concert Band; L Mrchg Band; Orch; High Hon Roll; Hon Roll; Ntl Merit Ltr.

COMEAU, LISA J; Methuen HS; Methuen, MA; (Y); SADD; Teachers Aide; Cheerleading; Coach Actv; Powder Puff Ftbl; Mthvn Yth Ftbl Schlrshp 86; Mthvn Frfghtrs Rlf Schlrshp 86; U Lowell; Comp Sci.

COMEAU III, WILLIAM J; Foxboro HS; Foxboro, MA; (Y); 7/240; Letterman Clb; Varsity Clb; JV Var Bsbl; JV Bsktbl; Var L Golf; Hon Roll; U Of CO; Archttr.

COMMITO, AMY; Our Lady Of Nazareth Acad; Medford, MA; (Y); 2/76; SADD; Nwsp Ed-Chief; Ed Lit Mag; Sec Frsh Cls; High Hon Roll; VP NHS; Ntl Merit Ltr; NEDT Awd; Hghst Avrg Awd In Englsh I, Frnch I, Wstrn Cvl, Hlth & Msc I 83-84; Law.

COMO, KRISTIN; Frontier Regional HS; S Deerfield, MA; (Y); Church Yth Grp; Cmnty Wkr; VP French Clb; GAA; SADD; Nwsp Stf; Ed Yrbk Stf; Cheerleading; High Hon Roll; Hon Roll; 4 Vrsty Lttrs, 3 Chrldg, & U Bsbl Mgr 83-85; Corporate Law.

CONANT, CHRIS; Cohasset HS; Cohasset, MA; (Y); 33/120; FTA; Acpl Chr; Yrbk Ed-Chief; Trs Jr Cls; Var L Bowling; Var L Ftbl; Btty Crckr Awd; High Hon Roll; Dickenson; Interdscplnry Stds.

CONANT, HEATHER; Hudson HS; Hudson, MA; (Y); #8 In Class; Boy Scts; Math Tm; Ski Clb; Band; School Play; Yrbk Stf; Co-Capt Socr; Tennis; High Hon Roll; NHS; Natl Latin Exam Maxima Cum Laude 86; Natl Hstry Day Natl Comptn 85; Pre-Med.

CONATY, CATHLEEN; King Philip Reg HS; Wrentham, MA; (Y); 6/167; Math Tm; Concert Band; Jazz Band; Mrchg Band; Sec Jr Cls; Var L Bsktbl; Var Trk; Sec NHS; Ntl Merit Ltr; Pres Schlr; Excllnce Biol 83; Excllnce Chem 84; NESBA Hnr Bnd 83 & 84; UNH; Elec Engr.

CONCANNON, KATERI; Revere HS; Revere, MA; (Y); Chorus; Bus Admin.

CONCEICAO, ALCINA; B M C Durfee HS; Fall River, MA; (Y); Hon Roll; Southeastern MA U.

CONCEMI, ROSEANN; Methuen HS; Methuen, MA; (Y); Model UN; U Lowell; Phys Thrpy.

CONDON, DAVID M; Ludlow HS; Ludlow, MA; (Y); 5/279; Am Leg Boys St; Chess Clb; Math Tm; Political Wkr; Quiz Bowl; Variety Show; Nwsp Stf; Yrbk Stf; High Hon Roll; NHS; Ludlow Educ Assoc Schlrp 86; Achvt Awds US Hist & Engl 86; Harvard U; Econ.

CONDON, MARK; Bishp Connolly HS; Westport, MA; (Y); 6/167; Art Clb; Debate Tm; Math Tm; JV Crs Cntry; Bausch & Lomb Sci Awd; Elks Awd; High Hon Roll; Pres NHS; Ntl Merit Ltr; Capt Of Var Cycling; Melville Schlrshp; MA Inst Tech; Chem.

CONDON, MARYLEE K; Silver Lake Reegional HS; Kingston, MA; (Y); 25/450; Art Clb; Drama Clb; Red Cross Aide; Ski Clb; School Musical; Yrbk Stf; Var Cheerleading; JV Socr; Hon Roll; Miss America Co-Ed MA Fnlst; Acad All-American & Natl Awd Wnnr-Math 85-86; Med Tech.

CONDRON, CHRISTOPHER; Southwick HS; Southwick, MA; (Y); 18/128; Drama Clb; Math Tm; School Musical; School Play; Var L Crs Cntry; Var L Trk; Hon Roll; Ntl Merit SF; Ylw Blt In Karate 86; Boys ST 86; Engrng.

CONGER, AMY; Northfield Mount Hermon Schl; Turners Falls, MA; (Y); Exploring; Library Aide; Concert Band; Yrbk Stf; VP Frsh Cls; Var Mgr(s); Var L Swmmng; Hon Roll; Boy Scts; Church Yth Grp; Peterson Memrl Prz Advncd Chem 86; U Of MA; Mdcl Illstratn.

CONLAN, RICHARD; Reading Memorial HS; Reading, MA; (Y); 22/327; Pres Church Yth Grp; Pres Exploring; Yrbk Stf; Ice Hcky; Socr; Trk; NHS; Boy Scts; Drama Clb; Army, Air Force, Navy Rotc Schlrshp Rcpnt 86; Eagle Scout Awd 86; Brown Engl Prz Hghst GPA 86; U Of NH; Bus Admin.

CONLEY, CAREY ANN; Northampton HS; Florence, MA; (Y); 31/222; 4-H; Nwsp Rptr; Bsktbl; Coach Actv; Socr; High Hon Roll; Mst Imprvd Plyr Chmpnshp Sccr Tm 84; 60th Annvrsry Fnd Prz Ozebekah Assmbly Schlrshp 86; Wheaton Coll.

CONLEY, ELIZABETH; Westford Acad; Westford, MA; (Y); Trs AFS; VP Art Clb; Drama Clb; French Clb; Model UN; SADD; Var L Gym; High Hon Roll; Hon Roll; NHS; Charactr Awd Ntl Hnr Soc 86; Med.

CONLIN, RICHARD F; King Philip Reg HS; Norfolk, MA; (Y); 15/189; Am Leg Boys St; Stat Ftbl; L Socr; Hon Roll; NHS; Excllnc In Comp Sci 86; Pres Acad Ftns 86; Vrsty Sccr Unsng Hero 86; Wrcstr Polytech Inst; Comp Engr.

CONLON, TRACEY; Bishop Feehan HS; Rumford, RI; (Y); 79/254; Church Yth Grp; Cmnty Wkr; Hosp Aide; Ski Clb; SADD; Yrbk Stf; Hon Roll; Spanish NHS; Summer Exchnge Abroad Rotary 85; Bus.

CONNALLY, MEGHAN; Chicopee Comprehensive HS; Chicopee, MA; (Y); 59/281; German Clb; Office Aide; Spanish Clb; SADD; Stage Crew; Variety Show; Nwsp Stf; Yrbk Stf; Rep Soph Cls; Rep Jr Cls; Htl Mgmt.

CONNELL, JENNIFER; Bishop Stang HS; Fall River, MA; (S); Church Yth Grp; SADD; Yrbk Stf; Var Bsktbl; Capt Var Fld Hcky; JV Sftbl; Var Trk; John C O Brien Mem Awd 86; Brenda Stetson Awd 85; Mst Ath 83-86; Elizabeth Taber Scholar 86; SMU; Elem Ed.

CONNELL, MAUREEN; Westfield HS; Westfield, MA; (Y); Am Leg Aux Girls St; Latin Clb; Rep Stu Cncl; Var L Diving; Var Socr; Var L Sftbl; Var L Swmmng; Jr NHS; 2nd Tm Western MA Sccr 85; 1st Tm Western MA Sftbl 86; MA ST Stu Advsry Cncl 86-87; Phy Thrpy.

CONNELL, PAULA; North Quincy HS; Quincy, MA; (Y); SADD; Yrbk Stf; JV Cheerleading; JV Var Powder Puff Ftbl; JV Socr; Photo Awd 85; Cazenovia Coll; Psych.

CONNELL, THOMAS; Arlington Catholic HS; Burlington, MA; (Y); 10/170; Church Yth Grp; Spanish Clb; Varsity Clb; Capt Crs Cntry; Trk; High Hon Roll; Hon Roll; NHS; NEDT Awd; Qulfd Jr Olympc TAC Rgnl Crss Cntry 85; MA Advnd Stdy Prog MASP Coll Courses 86; US Air Force Acad; Aero Engr.

CONNELLY, CHRIS; Danvers HS; Danvers, MA; (Y); 11/305; Church Yth Grp; Pres Sr Cls; Stu Cncl; JV Bsbl; Var L Bsktbl; Im Ftbl; Mgr(s); Hon Roll; NHS; Spanish NHS; Thorpe Schrlsh P86; Marshal 85; Phi Lambda Shiba 86; Colby Coll; Pre-Med.

CONNERTY, PATRICK; Arlington Cathalic HS; Billerica, MA; (Y); 25/160; Boys Clb Am; Church Yth Grp; Spanish Clb; JV Bsktbl; Var L Ftbl; Ntl Merit Schol; Lowell U; Engr.

CONNERY, JULIE; Leicester HS; Leicester, MA; (Y); 20/105; Church Yth Grp; French Clb; Latin Clb; Math Tm; Political Wkr; Badmtn; Vllybl; Hon Roll; Mthrs Clb Schlrshp 86; MA ST Schlrshp 86; Uestfield ST; Acctg.

CONNOLLY, BRENDA; Malden HS; Malden, MA; (Y); Pres Key Clb; Spanish Clb; SADD; Band; Concert Band; Mrchg Band; Chrmn Variety Show; Sftbl; Cit Awd; Kiwanis Awd; U MA; Comp Sci.

CONNOLLY, EMILY; Fontbonne Acad; Dorchester, MA; (Y); Church Yth Grp; Computer Clb; Drama Clb; Girl Scts; Sec Library Aide; Hon Roll; U Maine Orono.

CONNOLLY, KATHERINE; Natick HS; Natick, MA; (Y); 106/400; Church Yth Grp; Trs SADD; Chorus; Off Stu Cncl; JV Var Mgr(s); JV Var Score Keeper; Socr; Hon Roll; Plyr Awd JV Sccr 84; Acadia U.

CONNOLLY, SCOTT; Clinton HS; Clinton, MA; (Y); 1/150; Am Leg Boys St; Church Yth Grp; Intnl Clb; Political Wkr; Yrbk Ed-Chief; Var L Bsktbl; Var Capt Ftbl; Var Capt Trk; Im Vllybl; Im Wt Lftg; Harvard Radcliffe Prz Bk Awd 86; U S Air Force Acad; Aerosp Engr.

CONNOLLY, STEVEN C; North Awdover HS; North Andover, MA; (Y); 31/260; Am Leg Boys St; Ftbl; Trk; High Hon Roll; Hon Roll; US Coast Grd Acad; Crmnl Jstc.

CONNOLLY, TERESA; Marblehead HS; Marblehead, MA; (Y); Var Capt Cheerleading; Var L Sftbl.

CONNOR, JEANNE D; Tewisbury Memorial HS; Tewksbury, MA; (Y); 11/322; Hosp Aide; Mathletes; Red Cross Aide; Rep Frsh Cls; VP Soph Cls; Rep Jr Cls; Rep Sr Cls; Stu Cncl; Twrlr; High Hon Roll; Stu Of Month 86; Dgtl Schlrshp 86; Natl Hon Soc Schlrshp 86; Rensselaer Polytech; Engrng.

CONNOR, WENDY; Tantasqua Regional HS; Brimfield, MA; (Y); 22/150; Math Tm; Varsity Clb; Var L Bsktbl; Var Socr; Var L Sftbl; High Hon Roll; Hon Roll; Bus Adm.

CONNORS, SCOTT; Melrfose HS; Boston, MA; (Y); 95/400; Spanish Clb; Off Sr Cls; JV Bsbl; JV Ice Hcky; High Hon Roll; Hon Roll; Westfield ST; Crmnl Jstc.

CONNORS, WENDY; Bourne HS; Monument Bch, MA; (Y); Chorus; Yrbk Stf; Stat Ice Hcky; Sftbl; UNH; Acctg.

CONRAD, JENNIFER; Westfield HS; Westfield, MA; (Y); 11/357; Cmnty Wkr; Debate Tm; Trs French Clb; School Play; Ed Nwsp Stf; Var Fld Hcky; Var Swmmng; DAR Awd; NHS; Ltr-Fld Hcky 85; Presdntl Ftns Awd 86; Pltcl Sci.

CONRAD, PAUL; South Hadley HS; S Hadley, MA; (Y); Latin Clb; Var Capt Swmmng; Hon Roll; MVP Swm Tm 86; Bus.

CONROY, AMY; North Quincy HS; Quincy, MA; (Y); Pres Church Yth Grp; Cmnty Wkr; FBLA; JA; SADD; Teachers Aide; Yrbk Phtg; Socr; Vllybl; Hon Roll.

CONSALVI III, ANTHONY J; St Dominic Savio HS; Revere, MA; (Y); 3/94; Ski Clb; SADD; Sec Sr Cls; Bowling; Ice Hcky; Trk; Hon Roll; Prfct Atten Awd; Acad All-Amer 86; Acad All-Amer Large Div 86; Pre-Med.

CONSOLATTI, SCOTT M; Lawrence Acad; Sharon, NH; (Y); Spanish Clb; Yrbk Phtg; Rep Sr Cls; Var Bsbl; Var Bsktbl; High Hon Roll; Jr NHS; Rep Frsh Cls; Rep Soph Cls; Rep Jr Cls; Cum Laude Soc 85-87; Holmes Comp Sci Pez 86; Prctrshp 86-87.

CONSTANTINE, JENNIFER; New Bedford HS; New Bedford, MA; (Y); 25/701; AFS; Church Yth Grp; VP Pres Drama Clb; JCL; Latin Clb; Political Wkr; Science Clb; SADD; Church Choir; School Musical; Awd Stdnt Advsry Commte 85-86; Oustndng Stu Awd Latin 85-86; Awd Merit Excptnl Frnch 85-86; Harvard; Law.

CONSTANTINE, KAREN; Chicopee Comprehensive HS; Chicopee, MA; (Y); 24/322; German Clb; Office Aide; Yrbk Stf; Rep Soph Cls; Rep Jr Cls; L Cheerleading; Powder Puff Ftbl; Trk; Sec NHS; Sprngfld Tech; Physcl Thrpy.

CONSTANTINE, ROB; King Philip Reg HS; Norfolk, MA; (Y); 22/213; NHS; Prfct Atten Awd.

CONTABILE, ANTONIO; Chicopee Comprehensive HS; Chicopee, MA; (Y); #4 In Class; Boys Clb Am; German Clb; Rep Frsh Cls; JV Socr; High Hon Roll; Hon Roll; Jr NHS; Intl Finc.

CONTE, SAM J; North Andover HS; North Andover, MA; (Y); Am Leg Boys St; Letterman Clb; Varsity Clb; Sec Stu Cncl; Capt Bsbl; Bsktbl; Capt Ftbl; Hon Roll; ST Adtr ST Wide Boys ST 86; Rookie Yr 85; Bus.

CONTRERAS, ROSSANNA; Classical HS; Lynn, MA; (Y); 11/205; Chorus; Hon Roll; NHS.

CONUI, CARL; Ludlow HS; Ludlow, MA; (Y); Am Leg Boys St; Varsity Clb; Variety Show; Rep Jr Cls; Var Capt Bsbl; Var Bsktbl; Im Sftbl; Im Vllybl; Hon Roll; Prfct Atten Awd; Boston Coll; Pre-Med.

CONWAY, DIANE; Melrose HS; Melrose, MA; (Y); 52/350; French Clb; Library Aide; Political Wkr; SADD; Nwsp Stf; Yrbk Stf; High Hon Roll; Hon Roll; Im Bsktbl; Im Vllybl; Kappa Delta Psi Schlrshp 86; U NH; Cmnctns.

CONWAY, NANCY; Holbrook JR SR HS; Holbrook, MA; (Y); 17/95; Latin Clb; Library Aide; Chorus; Variety Show; Nwsp Bus Mgr; Nwsp Stf; Stu Cncl; Bsktbl; Var Capt Socr; Var Capt Sftbl; Sftbl Unsung Hero Awd On Varsity Tm; Bsktbl Mvp Awd On Varsity Tm.

CONWAY, STEVEN; St Johns Prep; Danvers, MA; (Y); Boy Scts; Civic Clb; Cmnty Wkr; Drama Clb; Varsity Clb; Stage Crew; Ftbl; Trk; Wt Lftg; Wrstlng; Prep Ldrshp Inst 86; Physclgy.

CONWAY, TERESA; Westford Acad; Westford, MA; (Y); 2/255; Sec Math Tm; Teachers Aide; Stu Cncl; Socr; Trk; High Hon Roll; NHS; Art Clb; Exploring; Library Aide; Chncllrs Tlnt Awd Schlrshp-U Of MA 86; Hstry Hnr Awd 85 & 86; Vet Med.

COOK, AMY; Shrewsbury HS; Shrewsbury, MA; (Y); 33/262; JA; Trk; Wt Lftg; Hon Roll; Ntl Merit Ltr; Westfield; Crmnl Jstc.

COOK, CHRIS; Bedford HS; Bedford, MA; (Y); 56/198; Var Socr; Var L Tennis; Illstrtr.

COOK JR, HARLAND L; Walpole HS; Walpole, MA; (Y); 25/270; Am Leg Boys St; Boy Scts; Church Yth Grp; Latin Clb; Bsbl; Crs Cntry; Trk; Wrstlng; Elks Awd; Hon Roll; Outstndng Svc Awd; Ad Altare Dei Awd; Pres Physcl Ftns Awd; RI U; Phrmcy.

COOK, JOY MARLENE; Haverhill HS; Haverhill, MA; (Y); Art Clb; German Clb; Intnl Clb; Church Choir; School Musical; Variety Show; Hon Roll; Music Awd NJ Acclrtd Chrstn Schl Comp 83; Art Awd 1st Pl 83; Bob Jones Comptn Art & Piano 85; Middlebury Coll; Lingstcs.

COOK, KEVIN; New Bedford HS; New Bedford, MA; (Y); 85/631; Aud/Vis; Drama Clb; SADD; Stage Crew; Variety Show; Yrbk Stf; Rep Sr Cls; Rep Stu Cncl; Var L Crs Cntry; Var L Trk; Betsy Taber Schlrshp Awd 86; New Bedford HS Alumni Comm Awd 86; Southeastern MA U; Psych.

COOK, LISA; Sharon HS; Sharon, MA; (Y); Computer Clb; Drama Clb; Spanish Clb; Temple Yth Grp; Chorus; School Musical; Nwsp Stf; Vllybl; Hon Roll; NHS; Framingham ST Coll Annl ST Hstrcl Conf Awd 86; Cornell U; Engrng.

COOKE, FRANCIS; Boston Latin Schl; Boston, MA; (Y); 75/283; Computer Clb; JA; Latin Clb; Yrbk Bus Mgr; Im Bsktbl; Hon Roll; NHS; Ntl Merit Ltr; Pres Schlr; Lafayette; Engr.

COOKE, SUZANNE; Mt Greylock Regional HS; Brooklyn, NY; (Y); 26/138; Cmnty Wkr; Drama Clb; JCL; School Play; Yrbk Stf; Mgr(s); Hon Roll; NHS; JR Arista 83; Arthur Ceely Awd Greylock ABC Chaptr 86; ABC Stu; Vassar Coll; Liberal Arts.

COOMBS, DAVID L; Whitman-Hanson Regional HS; Whitman, MA; (Y); 1/281; Am Leg Boys St; Jazz Band; Var Capt Socr; Bausch & Lomb Sci Awd; High Hon Roll; NHS; Ntl Merit Ltr; Political Wkr; Band; Concert Band; Rnsslr Math Awd 85-86; 1st Pl Dist Lvl ST Hstry Day 85-86; Suma Cum Laude Ntl Ltn Exm 85-86; Engrng.

COONEY, CAROLYN; Acad Of Notre Dame; Lowell, MA; (Y); 7/78; Church Yth Grp; Hosp Aide; Key Clb; Nwsp Rptr; Nwsp Stf; Swmmng; High Hon Roll; NHS; Trs Frsh Cls; Schlstc Schlrshp Notre Dame Awd; GATE Stu 83-84; Intl Rel.

COONROD, LAURA; Lynnfield HS; Lynnfield, MA; (Y); 2/170; Church Yth Grp; Drama Clb; French Clb; Acpl Chr; Chorus; Church Choir; School Musical; French Hon Soc; NHS; Ntl Merit SF; Awds Frnch And Eng 84; Awds Frnch And Chrs 86; Engrg.

COOPER, AMY; Hopedale JR SR HS; Hopedale, MA; (Y); SADD; Yrbk Stf; JV Bsktbl; Mgr(s); Score Keeper; Socr; Stat Sftbl; High Hon Roll.

COOPER, DAVID A; Rockport HS; Rockport, MA; (Y); 1/65; Am Leg Boys St; Political Wkr; Pres Frsh Cls; Pres Soph Cls; Pres Jr Cls; Pres Sr Cls; Stu Cncl; Capt Tennis; High Hon Roll; NHS; Hugh O Brien Yth Ldrshp 85; Excllnc In Chem 84-85; Excllnc In Physcs & Frnch 85-86; Intl Pol Sci.

COOPER, ELIZABETH; Southwick HS; Southwick, MA; (Y); Office Aide; Pep Clb; Ski Clb; Spanish Clb; SADD; School Play; Rep Stu Cncl; Var Cheerleading; Fld Hcky; Mgr(s); Drtmth Club Spngfld Bk Awd 86; Bst Sprtng Actrs 85; Studnt Adv Cncl Rep 85-86; Boston Coll; Psych.

COOTEY, STEPHEN; Central Catholic HS; Salem, NH; (Y); 20/231; Math Clb; Ski Clb; Yrbk Stf; L Bsbl; Im Bsktbl; L Ftbl; High Hon Roll; NHS; SR Lgue Bsbl Rookie Of The Yr 83; SR Lgue Bsbl Mst Vlbl Plyr 84; Derry-Salem Elus Ldg Teen Mnth 83; Cornell; Engrng.

COPPETA, GREG; Central Catholic HS; Methuen, MA; (Y); 90/231; Var Bsbl; JV Bsktbl; Hon Roll; Acctg.

COPPINGER, HOPE; Beaver Country Day HS; Chestnut Hill, MA; (Y); Drama Clb; Trs Spanish Clb; Rep Stu Cncl; Dance Clb; Model UN; Acpl Chr; Chorus; Madrigals; School Play; Stage Crew; Jrnlsm.

COPPINGER, TIMOTHY L; Northfield Mount Hermon Schl; Montague, MA; (Y); JV Ice Hcky; Var Lcrss; Hampshire Coll; Bio.

COPPOLA, PATRICIA; Methven HS; Methuen, MA; (Y); 6/385; Intnl Clb; Political Wkr; SADD; High Hon Roll; NHS; Spanish NHS; Boston Coll; Med.

COPPOLA, REBECCA C; Holy Name Central Catholic HS; Douglas, MA; (Y); Drama Clb; Ski Clb; Concert Band; Mrchg Band; School Play; Nwsp Rptr; Yrbk Stf; JV Fld Hcky; Mgr Vllybl; Hon Roll; Boston U.

COPPOLA, STEVEN; Franklin HS; Franklin, MA; (Y); Chess Clb; Cmnty Wkr; Drama Clb; Political Wkr; SADD; School Play; Trk; Hon Roll; Bsbl; Distgshd Cmnty Awd Franklin Histcl Soc 86; U Of Lowell; Physcl Thrpy.

CORBETT, ANN E; Briegewater-Raynham Regional HS; Bridgewater, MA; (Y); 5/316; Drama Clb; Model UN; SADD; Chorus; Nwsp Rptr; NHS; Ntl Merit Ltr; French Clb; School Play; High Hon Roll; Balfour Schlr Wheaton Coll 86; Acushnet Fndtn Scholar 86; Pres Acad Fit Awd 86; Wheaton Coll; Writer.

CORBETT, KELLEY; Attleboro HS; Attleboro, MA; (Y); Church Yth Grp; Girl Scts; Spanish Clb; Acpl Chr; Concert Band; Drm Mjr(t); Mrchg Band; Elks Awd; Hon Roll; Cmnty Wkr; Girl Scout Gold Awd 85; Hairdressing.

CORBETT, KELLY; Monument Mountain Regional HS; Gt Barrington, MA; (Y); Ski Clb; Yrbk Stf; Lit Mag; JV Socr; JV Trk; Hon Roll; Young Writers In Berkshires 86; English.

CORBITT, JEFF; Methuen HS; Methuen, MA; (Y); 97/300; Church Yth Grp; Model UN; Stu Govt Day 86; Engrng.

CORBOSIERO, JILL; Hudson Catholic HS; S Lancaster, MA; (Y); 16/66; Cmnty Wkr; Yrbk Stf; Bsktbl; Fld Hcky; Sftbl; Elks Awd; NHS; Merit Awd Bio 83-84; Excllnc Awd Hstry 84-85; CHASE 84-85; Assumption Coll; Elem Ed.

CORBOSIERO, MICHAEL J; Cushing Acad; Winchendon, MA; (Y); 33/110; Chess Clb; Dance Clb; Spanish Clb; Varsity Clb; JV Bsktbl; JV Ice Hcky; Var Capt Socr; Hon Roll; Finest Contrbtn Sprt Ovr Career Sccr 85; Bst Offnsv Plyr Sccr 85; Wrkd At Four Str Catrg; Northeastern; Bus.

CORBY, STEPHANIE; Oakmont Regional HS; Ashburnham, MA; (Y); 20/120; Am Leg Aux Girls St; Church Yth Grp; Girl Scts; Latin Clb; Red Cross Aide; SADD; Chorus; School Musical; School Play; Yrbk Stf; Outstndng Achvt Awd In Jazz & Sel Choirs 85; Natl Chorale Awd & MA All-State Choir 86; U Of MA; Med.

CORCORAN, LOUISE; Burlington HS; Burlington, MA; (Y); Church Yth Grp; JA; Nwsp Stf; Yrbk Stf; Bsktbl; JV Socr; Hon Roll; NHS; Ntl Merit Ltr; Englsh Awd 84 & 86.

CORCORAN, MARY; Arlington Catholic HS; Arlington, MA; (Y); 7/143; Latin Clb; Service Clb; Trs SADD; Var Rep Jr Cls; Rep Sr Cls; Var Trk; Hon Roll; NHS; Pres Schlr; St Schlr; Hnrs Schlr Stonehill Coll 86; Silv Mdl Natl Latin Exam 86; Magna Cum Laude Natl Latin Exam 85; Stonehill Coll; Bus Adm.

CORDELL, DON J J; Lexington HS; Lexington, MA; (Y); Church Yth Grp; Cmnty Wkr; Political Wkr; Nwsp Rptr; Var Bsbl; JV Coach Actv; JV Ftbl; Hon Roll; Jr NHS; Ntl Merit Ltr; Fren Commendation 84; Boston Coll.

CORDES, VAUGHN MICHAEL H; Groton Schl; Bronx, NY; (Y); Computer Clb; Yrbk Stf; Var L Jr Cls; Var L Ftbl; Schlrp To Groton Schl 82; Undeftd Crew Seasn & Wnr Of Quinsigamond Regatta 85; Undeftd Ftbl Tm 85; Comp Sci.

COREY, WILLIAM; B M C Furfee HS; Fall River, MA; (Y); 48/650; Library Aide; Math Clb; Science Clb; JV Var Bsbl; Bsktbl; Hon Roll; NHS; Hnrble Mntn In Sci Fair 3 Yrs; Engrng.

CORMIER, JENNIFER; New Bedford HS; Acushnet, MA; (Y); Camera Clb; Exploring; Ed Yrbk Stf; Var L Diving; Var L Sftbl; Var Swmmng; Hon Roll; NHS; FL ST U; Chem Engr.

CORMIER, JULIENNE; Taunton HS; Taunton, MA; (Y); Drama Clb; Office Aide; Sec Service Clb; Teachers Aide; Chorus; High Hon Roll; Hon Roll; Med.

CORMIER, REBECCA; Montachusett Regional Vo-Tech HS; Ashby, MA; (Y); VICA; Capt Sftbl; Tennis; Hon Roll; NHS; Most Outstndng Stu Awds Phys Educ Pgm 85 & 86, Sci Pgm Bio 86, & Engl Pgm 86; Sci.

CORMIER, STACEY; Douglas Memorial HS; Douglas, MA; (Y); FHA; Varsity Clb; Yrbk Stf; Trs Stu Cncl; Sftbl; Psych.

CORMIER, TRACEY; Douglas Memorial HS; E Douglas, MA; (Y); FHA; Yrbk Stf; Rep Stu Cncl; Sftbl; Hon Roll; Engl.

CORRIERI, ALFRED; Wilmington HS; Wilmington, MA; (Y); French Clb; Math Clb; Ski Clb; Varsity Clb; Yrbk Stf; Rep Stu Cncl; Var L Trk; High Hon Roll; NHS; Ntl Merit Ltr.

CORRIGAN, LISA; Bellingham Memorial HS; Bellingham, MA; (Y); Hosp Aide; Ski Clb; Color Guard; Hon Roll; Peer Cnslr 86.

CORRIVEAU, MELISSA; Bourne HS; Pocasset, MA; (Y); Library Aide; Office Aide; VP Jr NHS; Bridgewater ST Coll; Engl.

CORSHIA, CYNTHIA; Old Colony Regional Vo Tech HS; Carver, MA; (Y); Hosp Aide; Hon Roll; Geriatrc Care.

CORSI, MARIA; Drury SR HS; North Adams, MA; (Y).

CORVINO, JENNIFER; Melrose HS; Melrose, MA; (Y); 43/391; Art Clb; Intnl Clb; Pep Clb; SADD; Yrbk Stf; Tennis; Hon Roll; RI Schl Dsgn; Fshn Ill.

COSBY, LINDA; Agawam HS; Feeding Hills, MA; (Y); 43/400; JCL; Latin Clb; Library Aide; SADD; Band; Var L Cheerleading; Socr; Var L Trk; Hon Roll; Fshn Mdse.

COSGROVE, KATHLEEN; Holyoke Catholic HS; Holyoke, MA; (Y); 11/132; Drama Clb; Spanish Clb; SADD; School Musical; School Play; Yrbk Ed-Chief; Yrbk Rptr; Yrbk Stf; Rep Jr Cls; Rep Sr Cls; MA Girls ST 86; Congressional Schlr Ntl Young Ldrs Conf 86; Early Childhood Educ.

COSSITT, CHRISTINE; Jamaica Plain HS; Jamaica Plain, MA; (Y); NHS; Vtrnrn.

COSTA, ANA; Our Lady Of Nazareth Acad; Peabody, MA; (Y); Cmnty Wkr; Red Cross Aide; Science Clb; Spanish Clb; VP SADD; Acpl Chr; Chorus; School Musical; Yrbk Stf; Rep Stu Cncl; Schlrshp Spnsh 83-85; Hnrbl Ment Ntl Spnsh Cntst 85-86; Dartmouth Clb Bk Awd 85-86; Psychlgst.

COSTA, DONNA M; Ursuline Acad; Medfield, MA; (Y); 25/71; Church Yth Grp; Drama Clb; Service Clb; Spanish Clb; SADD; Stage Crew; Yrbk Stf; Pres Stu Cncl; Hon Roll; Mktg.

COSTA, KENT; Norwood SR HS; Norwood, MA; (Y); 26/323; Hon Roll; Engrng.

COSTA, LAURA; Oakmont Reg HS; Westminster, MA; (Y); Art Clb; FHA; Spanish Clb; Hon Roll; Psych.

COSTA, MARY; King Philip Reginal HS; Wrentham, MA; (Y); Church Yth Grp; DECA; Vllybl; Hon Roll.

COSTA, RACHEL; Revere HS; Revere, MA; (Y); 10/475; Cmnty Wkr; Math Clb; Pep Clb; Yrbk Stf; Capt Var Cheerleading; Capt Var Gym; Coaches Awd Gymnstcs 86; City Cncl Recgntn Chrldng 85; Schl Comm Recgntn Chrldng 85-86; Bus.

COSTA, SUSAN; Natick HS; Natick, MA; (Y); SADD; Teachers Aide; Rep Frsh Cls; Rep Soph Cls; Rep Jr Cls; Rep Sr Cls; Rep Stu Cncl; Cheerleading; Hon Roll; Miss Natick Beauty Pgnt 86; Regis Coll; Law.

COSTA, SUSAN; Tawnton HS; East Taunton, MA; (Y); JV Fld Hcky; Hon Roll; Fshn Dsgn.

COSTA, VICTOR; Diman Reg Voc Tech HS; Fall River, MA; (Y); Boys Clb Am; Key Clb; Soph Cls; Bsktbl; Bsktbll Ltr 85-86.

COSTANZA, MICHELLE; Our Layd Of Nazareth Acad; Wilmington, MA; (Y); Drama Clb; Spanish Clb; SADD; Yrbk Stf; Cheerleading; Trk; Hon Roll; Achvt Awd 84; Hnr Roll 84-85.

COSTELLO, JILL; Bedford HS; Bedford, MA; (Y); AFS; SADD; Chorus; School Musical; School Play; Yrbk Stf; Var Socr; Bausch & Lomb Sci Awd; High Hon Roll; Pres NHS; Renesselaer Medal 86; Lib Arts.

COSTELLO, JULIE; Fontbonne Acad; Milton, MA; (Y); 60/163; Off Sec Drama Clb; School Play; Yrbk Stf; Var L Tennis; Hon Roll; Cum Laude On Ntl Ltn Exm 84; Excll In Frnch I 85; Bst Actrss Awd 83 Drama Fstvl 83; Boston Coll; Drama.

COSTIGAN, JAMES; Holyoke HS; Holyoke, MA; (Y); Boys Clb Am; Boy Scts; Letterman Clb; Red Cross Aide; Nwsp Rptr; VP Frsh Cls; Pres Soph Cls; L Bsktbl; High Hon Roll; Hon Roll; Springfield Tech; Cmptr.

COSTIGAN, WILLIAM; Saint Dominic Savio HS; E Boston, MA; (Y); 39/104; SADD; Capt VP Bsbl; VP Bsktbl; Capt VP Ftbl; MVP Savio Ftbll 85-86; Outstndg Ftbll Athlete E B Athlete Brd Zito Mem Awd 85-86; Northeastern U; Elec Engrng.

COTE, BRENDA; Easthampton HS; Easthampton, MA; (Y); 32/140; Church Yth Grp; Drama Clb; School Play; Nwsp Stf; Yrbk Stf; Stu Cncl; Hon Roll; Joyce Ann Le Beau Memrl Awd 86; Elms Coll; Nrsng.

COTE, CHRISTINA; Chelmsford HS; Chelmsford, MA; (Y); DECA; Political Wkr; Hon Roll; Ms Amercn Co-Ed ST Fnlst 86; Poli Sci.

COTER, PATTY; North Reading HS; N Reading, MA; (Y); Girl Scts; Varsity Clb; Var L Bsktbl; Var Capt Sftbl; Var Capt Vllybl; Coaches Awd Mem Awds Mvp Unsung Heroine 84-86; Phys Thrpy.

COTTON, COLEEN; Marlboro HS; Marlboro, MA; (Y); Babson Coll.

COTTON, SHERRIE; Southbridge HS; Southbridge, MA; (Y); 4/164; 4-H; JA; Math Clb; Math Tm; High Hon Roll; Hon Roll; NHS; Wheaton Coll; Lbrl Arts.

COTTON, STACEY; Norton HS; Norton, MA; (S); 8/148; Key Clb; Pep Clb; Ski Clb; Teachers Aide; Varsity Clb; Yrbk Sprt Ed; Sec Soph Cls; Sec Jr Cls; Sec Sr Cls; Rep Stu Cncl; Var Bsktbl, Vlybl & Sftbl Awds; Engr.

COUGHLAN, ANNE; St Gregory HS; Dorchester, MA; (Y); Church Yth Grp; Office Aide; Nwsp Stf; Yrbk Stf; Rep Frsh Cls; Stu Cncl; Mgr(s); Score Keeper; High Hon Roll; Hon Roll; Sadie Croix Scholar 83; Interclrl Awd 85; Publc Spkng Awd 85.

COULL, STEPHANIE; Barnstable HS; Cotuit, MA; (Y); Camera Clb; SADD; Nwsp Ed-Chief; Nwsp Rptr; Nwsp Stf; Yrbk Stf; Lit Mag; Hon Roll; Voice Dem Awd; Jrnlsm.

COULOMBE, DONALD; Chicopee Comprehensvie HS; Chicopee, MA; (Y); Band; Concert Band; Mrchg Band; Orch; Pep Band; FNA; Standex Schlrshp 86; Western New England; Sci.

COULON, MICHELLE; Presentation Of Mary Acad; Methuen, MA; (S); 17/46; Church Yth Grp; Math Clb; Spanish Clb; Yrbk Stf; Jr NHS; NHS.

COUMOUNDUROS, PETER; St Johns Prep Schl; Stoneham, MA; (Y); Cmnty Wkr; VP Spanish Clb; JV Swmmng; JV Trk; Im Vllybl; Hon Roll; Jr NHS; Spanish NHS; Bus Explrtn Pgm-Babsn Coll 85; Babson Coll; Bus Mngmt.

COURNOYER, DONNA; Fitchburg HS; Fitchburg, MA; (Y); Pep Clb; Band; Concert Band; Mrchg Band; Crs Cntry; Typg I And II Awd 85-86; Bus.

COURNOYER, JEFF; Lawrence Acad; Acton, MA; (Y); Camera Clb; Yrbk Sprt Ed; Lit Mag; Rep Jr Cls; Coach Actv; JV Lcrss; Var L Wrstlng; Hon Roll; Cmnty Wkr; Library Aide; Peer Cnslr; Writng Lit Prize; Reading Prize.

COURTNEY, JASON; Bedford HS; Bedford, MA; (Y); Boy Scts; SADD; Var Capt Bsktbl; U TX; Bus Mgmnt.

COURTNEY, MARY; Lynnfield HS; Lynnfield, MA; (Y); Camp Fr Inc; Church Yth Grp; 4-H; JA; Spanish Clb; SADD; Yrbk Stf; JV Bsktbl; Var Fld Hcky; JV Mgr(s); Spanish 3 Award 85-86; Art Award 85-86; U Of MA-AMHERST.

COUSINEAU, GUY; Bishop Connolly HS; Fall River, MA; (Y); 75/200; JV Var Bsbl; Var L Ice Hcky.

COUTO, MANUELA; BMC Dufree HS; Fall River, MA; (Y); 63/670; NHS; Southeastern MA U; Med.

COUTU, GREGORY; St Joseph Regional HS; Lowell, MA; (Y); Ski Clb; Soph Cls; Jr Cls; Stu Cncl; Bsktbl; FIT; Aviatn.

COUTU, LINDA; Holyoke Catholic HS; Chicopee, MA; (Y); 1/129; Math Clb; Spanish Clb; Var Yrbk Stf; High Hon Roll; Ntl Merit Ltr; Val; Amrcn Intl Coll Acdmc Schlrshp 86; Big Y Schlrshp 86; Nw Englnd Deli & Dairy Schlrshp 86; Amrcn Intl Coll; Acctg.

COVE, JENNIFER; Cathedral HS; Ludlow, MA; (Y); 95/570; Church Yth Grp; Hosp Aide; Library Aide; Model UN; Church Choir; Hon Roll; Hosp Volunteer Awd 84; Bus.

COVENEY, EDWARD; Marlbobo HS; Marlboro, MA; (Y); 27/304; Frsh Cls; Soph Cls; Jr Cls; Sr Cls; Stu Cncl; Bsbl; Ice Hcky; Socr; NHS; Acad All Amer 86; Bus.

COWLES, KAREN; Algonquin Regional HS; Southborough, MA; (Y); 7/212; JA; Yrbk Bus Mgr; Rep Jr Cls; JV Bsktbl; Capt L Tennis; High Hon Roll; NHS; Supt Cmmttee On Excllnc/Educ 85-86; Bus Wk 85.

COX, DAVID S; Phillips Acad; Andover, MA; (Y); Cmnty Wkr; Radio Clb; Rep Sr Cls; Rep Stu Cncl; Hon Roll; Ntl Merit SF; Nwsp Rptr; Brnze Mdl Russian Olympd 85; Webster Hist Prz 84; Kates Hist Prz 85; Pol Sci.

COX, ELIZABETH; Millbury Memorial HS; Auburn, MA; (Y); Church Yth Grp; Drama Clb; Girl Scts; Hosp Aide; Intnl Clb; Library Aide; PAVAS; School Musical; School Play; Stage Crew; Hotel Mngt.

COX, JEFF; Barnstable HS; Marstons Mills, MA; (Y); Boy Scts; Church Yth Grp; Debate Tm; Speech Tm; JV Bsbl; Elks Awd; God Cntry Awd; Hon Roll; Gold Cert; Eagle Scout; Annapolis.

COX, JENNIFER; Saugus HS; Saugus, MA; (Y); Church Yth Grp; Hosp Aide; Spanish Clb; Church Choir; Ed Lit Mag; Hon Roll; Jr NHS; NHS; Office Aide; Chorus; Exc Spnsh,Chem 85.

COX, MICHAEL; Phillips Acad; Andover, MA; (Y); Boy Scts; Computer Clb; Hosp Aide; Science Clb; Concert Band; Im Bsktbl; Hon Roll; Troop Sct Of Yr Boy Scts 84; Sci.

COZZENS, BARBARA; Hanover HS; Hanover, MA; (Y); 3/200; Drama Clb; Math Tm; Band; School Play; Gym; High Hon Roll; Hon Roll; NHS; 1st Pl H S Sci Fair 86; 2nd Pl Dist Sci Fair 86; 3rd Pl Math Tm Comptn-Museum Of Sci 86; Bio.

CRAFT, SAMANTHA; Dighbora-Rehobath Regional HS; Rehoboth, MA; (Y); Church Yth Grp; Girl Scts; Concert Band; Mrchg Band; Trk; Proj Contmpry Comptvnss 84; Spotlgt-Proj For Hghr Lrng SMU 85.

CRAIG, JENNIFER W; Northampton HS; Northampton, MA; (Y); 5/228; Am Leg Aux Girls St; Science Clb; School Musical; Lit Mag; Rep Frsh Cls; Rep Soph Cls; Rep Jr Cls; Rep Stu Cncl; JV Var Fld Hcky; JV Socr; 2nd Pl Wstrn MA Chptr Ntl Spnsh Exm Spnsh I, Spnsh II 85 & 86.

CRAIG, SHEILA; Dedham HS; Dedham, MA; (Y); 17/271; Am Leg Aux Girls St; Hosp Aide; Pres Spanish Clb; Rep Frsh Cls; Rep Soph Cls; Rep Jr Cls; Rep Sr Cls; Stu Cncl; Var Fld Hcky; Var Trk; Hugh O Brien Smnr 85; Grl ST, MASP 86.

CRAMSTORFF, CHRIS; Shepherd Hill Regional HS; Dudley, MA; (Y); Ski Clb; Spanish Clb; Varsity Clb; Var Bsbl; JV Bsktbl; Im Diving; Im Ftbl; Var Trk; Wake Forest U; Liberal Arts.

CRANE, WENDY; Fairhaven HS; South Dartmouth, MA; (Y); 14/175; French Clb; Math Tm; VP Chorus; Jazz Band; Orch; School Musical; High Hon Roll; Hon Roll; Jr NHS; NHS; S E MA U; Elect Engineering.

CRAW, BARBARA; Attleboro HS; Attleboro, MA; (Y); JA; JV Sftbl; High Hon Roll; Hon Roll; Trs NHS; Hmrm Capt; U Of MA; Veternrn.

CRAWFORD, JANET; Winchester HS; Winchester, MA; (Y); Church Yth Grp; Hosp Aide; Spanish Clb; SADD; Yrbk Ed-Chief; Yrbk Stf; Cit Awd; Phys Ther.

CRAWFORD, MARVA; Everett HS; Everett, MA; (Y); Church Yth Grp; Chorus; Church Choir; Bus Adm.

CRAWFORD, RICK; Attleboro HS; Attleboro, MA; (Y); Cmnty Wkr; Computer Clb; Capt L Crs Cntry; Capt L Trk; High Hon Roll; Jr NHS; NHS; Ntl Merit Ltr; NEDT Awd; Lang Arts Olympiad Awd 83-84; Chem.

CREAN JR, WILLIAM J; Saint Marys HS; Westfield, MA; (Y); 3/49; Am Leg Boys St; Pres Jr Cls; Pres Sr Cls; Rep Stu Cncl; Capt Var Bsbl; Var Bsktbl; Var Socr; High Hon Roll; Hon Roll; NHS; Boys ST Chrmn Politicl Party 86; Pol Sci.

CREED, LISA; Marshfield HS; Green Harbor, MA; (Y); Capt Dance Clb; Mgr DECA; Drama Clb; Chorus; School Musical; School Play; Var Gym; Hon Roll; Ltrs Gymnstcs Music 85; Semsba Music Fest Bay ST Shw Choir 85-86; Grad Comm Schlrshp Fest 86; Cape Cod CC; Actrss.

CREEDEN, YOLANDA E; Plymouth Carver HS; Plymouth, MA; (Y); 64/459; Cmnty Wkr; Hosp Aide; Latin Clb; Science Clb; Concert Band; Drm Mjr(t); Mrchg Band; Variety Show; Hon Roll; Prfct Atten Awd; MA ST Schlrshp; Ansto Clb Awd; Leontina Ferrari Schlrshp; Simmons Clg; Chem.

CRESCENZI, GREG; Bedford HS; Bedford, MA; (Y); 24/206; Am Leg Boys St; Church Yth Grp; Science Clb; Chrmn SADD; Nwsp Rptr; Rep Frsh Cls; Rep Jr Cls; Pres Sr Cls; JV Bsbl; JV L Bsktbl; Bay ST Games Sccr Tm 86; Engrng.

CRESSEY, WENDY C; Masconomet Regional HS; Topfield, MA; (Y); Art Clb; Camera Clb; Church Yth Grp; 4-H; Girl Scts; Stage Crew; Yrbk Phtg; Var Powder Puff Ftbl; Var Sftbl; Var Vllybl; Pratt Ntl Tlnt Srch Archtctr Schlrshp 86; Pratt Inst; Archtctr Dsgn.

CRESSOTTI, DEANNA; Hampshire Regional HS; Southampton, MA; (Y); 15/130; Teachers Aide; Band; Chorus; Variety Show; Variety Show; Var Stat Bsktbl; Var Socr; Var Sftbl; Hon Roll; Trs NHS; Outstndng Mscnshp Awd 86; Trsr Natl Hnr Scty 86-87.

CRESTWELL, ROBIN S; Phillips Acad; Washington, DC; (Y); Church Choir; Var Capt Bsktbl; Im Sftbl; Var Co-Capt Trk; Var Capt Vllybl; 1st Pl Span Oratrcl Cntst 85; Engrg.

CREWE, LISA; Arlington HS; Arlington, MA; (Y); 66/381; Office Aide; SADD; Chorus; Yrbk Stf; Var L Bsktbl; L Capt Socr; Var L Trk; Hon Roll; NHS; MVP Vrsty Girls Sccr Tm 86.

CRIDGE, PATTI; Westford Acad; Reston, VA; (Y); 41/225; Church Yth Grp; Hosp Aide; Model UN; SADD; Concert Band; Jazz Band; Mrchg Band; Orch; School Musical; Nwsp Stf; Emerson Coll; Mass Comm.

CRINO, CYNTHIA A; Wellesley HS; Wellesley, MA; (Y); Church Yth Grp; German Clb; Spanish Clb; Hon Roll; NHS; Ntl Merit SF; Art Hstry.

CRISAFULLI, AMY; Medway JR SR HS; Medway, MA; (Y); Chorus; School Musical; Ipec Ldr CPR First Aid Ropes Etc 85-86; Schlstc Awd 84-85; Nrsng.

CRISTINA, FARA; Shepherd Hill Regional HS; Dudley, MA; (Y); 16/134; Chorus; Crs Cntry; Tennis; NHS; Excllnc In Alg I, Spnsh I 83; Excllnc In Alg II, Spnsh II 84; Comp Geom Excllnc Awd 85; Bryant Coll; Bus Adm.

CROCCO, MIKE; Central Catholic HS; Salem, NH; (Y); 77/231; Computer Clb; Ski Clb; Im Bsktbl; Im Golf; Hon Roll; U Of NH; Law.

CROCKER, AMY; St Josephs Regional HS; Lowell, MA; (Y); Nwsp Rptr; Nwsp Stf; Rep Stu Cncl; Var Bsktbl; Var Sftbl; Hon Roll; Algbr II Awd 86; Svc Awd 85-86; Elem Ed.

CROFT, ALISA; West Roxbury HS; Dorchester, MA; (S); ROTC; Nwsp Rptr; Nwsp Stf; Rep Frsh Cls; Vllybl; Hon Roll; NHS; Prfct Atten Awd; Northeastern U; Psychlgy.

CRONIN, DAVID P; Braintee HS; Braintree, MA; (Y); 39/450; French Clb; SADD; JV Bsktbl; Var L Ftbl; Var L Golf; Var L Trk; Hon Roll; Indr Trk Dvsn A Ml Rly 6th ST 85-86; Outdr Trk 10th In ST At 200 Yd Rn 3rd Emass Spnnt Rly 86; Bus Mgmt.

CRONIN, ELISABETH; Westwood HS; Westwood, MA; (Y); 56/212; AFS; Church Yth Grp; Cmnty Wkr; Hosp Aide; Off Key Clb; Political Wkr; SADD; Yrbk Stf; Fld Hcky; Powder Puff Ftbl; Wenaumet Blfs Yacht Clb Racng Awd 85; Librl Arts.

CRONIN, KATHLEEN; Westwood HS; Westwood, MA; (Y); 26/212; AFS; Church Yth Grp; Key Clb; SADD; School Musical; Hon Roll; NHS; Spanish NHS; Frgn Lang.

CRONIS, MIKE; Methuen HS; Methuen, MA; (Y); Model UN; Nrtheastern U; Robotics Engr.

CROOK, SHARA; New Bedford HS; New Bedford, MA; (Y); 36/702; Drama Clb; VP JA; JCL; Stage Crew; Swmmng; Hon Roll; NHS; Tufts U; Vet Med.

CROWE, CHRISTINE; Waltham HS; Boston, MA; (Y); Church Yth Grp; Drama Clb; Hosp Aide; Ski Clb; SADD; Thesps; Orch; School Play; Swmmng; Kingsburry Temperance Essay Awd 86; Waltham Hosp Cndystrpg Awd 86; Swm & Ski Tm Awds 84-86; Advrtsg.

CROWELL, JERELYN J; Woburn SR HS; Woburn, MA; (Y); 151/453; French Clb; Intnl Clb; Key Clb; Ski Clb; SADD; Chorus; Drill Tm; School Musical; Yrbk Stf; Hon Roll; Wrthy Advsr Intl Ord Rnbw Grls 85; Grl Sct Schlrshp Awd $100 86; Mddlsx Comm Coll; Rdlgy.

CROWELL, TIMOTHY A; Somerset HS; Somerset, MA; (Y); 80/230; Ski Clb; JV Socr; Var L Tennis; Hon Roll; SHS Class Of 56 86; James Le Comte Mem 86; U Of MA; Bus.

CROWLEY, DENNIS; Melrose HS; Melrose, MA; (Y); 1/394; Var L Bsbl; Var L Ftbl; Var L Ice Hcky; High Hon Roll; NHS; Ntl Merit SF; Harvard Prize Bk Awd 86; Harvard; Libl Arts.

CROWLEY, MARGARET; St Peter-Marian HS; Worcestr, MA; (Y); Cmnty Wkr; Hosp Aide; SADD; Yrbk Stf; Hon Roll; NHS; Law.

CROWLEY, MAUREEN; Franklin HS; Franklin, MA; (Y); 13/224; Am Leg Aux Girls St; Trs Church Yth Grp; Math Tm; Lit Mag; Capt Cheerleading; Socr; Hon Roll; Sec NHS; Mc Donalds Schlrshp 86; Syracuse U; Arch.

CROWLEY, STEPHANIE; Dedham HS; Dedham, MA; (S); 10/255; Church Yth Grp; Drama Clb; Church Choir; Variety Show; Nwsp Rptr; Nwsp Stf; Hon Roll; 3rd Pl In MA For Clssc Assn Of New Engld Annl Essay Cont 85; 1st Pl In Dedham Hgh Essay Cont 84-85; Theatrcs.

CRYAN, KERRY; Westford Acad; Westford, MA; (Y); Ski Clb; Yrbk Ed-Chief; Var Socr; JV Trk; Trvl.

CULLEN, ELIZABETH; Bishop Feehan HS; Foxboro, MA; (Y); Debate Tm; 4-H; JCL; Band; Chorus; Concert Band; Drill Tm; Mrchg Band; Yrbk Stf; Hon Roll; Debate Awd 86; Math Awd 86; Engl.

CULLEN, KELLIE; Christopher Columbus HS; Charlestown, MA; (S); Political Wkr; Ski Clb; Yrbk Stf; Cheerleading; Sftbl.

CULLEN, TIMOTHY M; Hamilton-Wenham Regional HS; S Hamilton, MA; (Y); 50/183; Am Leg Boys St; Church Yth Grp; Chorus; Var Bsbl; Var Socr; Var Trk; Hon Roll; Ntl Merit SF; Boys ST 85; Chouinard Schlrshp 86; Villanova U; Cmmrc.

CULLINANE, CAREY; Marian HS; Sudbury, MA; (Y); 59/177; Church Yth Grp; Rep Stu Cncl; Var Bsktbl; Im Vllybl; Hon Roll; MA ST Sci & Engrng Fair Wnr 84; Worcester Rgnl Engrng Fair Wnr 84; NEDT Awd Wnr 84; CCD Tchr 85-86; Mt Holyoke Coll; Bio.

CULVERHOUSE, BRYAN; Lawrence Acad; Groton, MA; (Y); Band; Chorus; Nwsp Stf; Rep Stu Cncl; Var Co-Capt Cheerleading; Var Fld Hcky; Var Sftbl; JV Vllybl; Jr NHS.

CUMMINGS, EFFIE; Chatham JR SR HS; West Chatham, MA; (Y); 3/40; Trs Drama Clb; Chorus; Madrigals; School Musical; School Play; Variety Show; NHS; Math Tm; Lit Mag; Pres Frsh Cls; Wellesley Clb Cape Cod Bk Awd; Wnnr Poetry Rectatn Cont; Coll Willaim & Mary; Theater.

CUMMINGS, JULIE; Ware HS; Ware, MA; (Y); Math Tm; SADD; Lit Mag; Rep Stu Cncl; Var L Cheerleading; Var L Pom Pon; Var L Sftbl; High Hon Roll; Hon Roll; Pro Merito 85-86; Bus.

CUMMINGS, SUSAN; Sharon HS; Sharon, MA; (Y); Am Leg Aux Girls St; Church Yth Grp; VP Varsity Clb; Chorus; Pres Sr Cls; Var Capt Bsktbl; Var Capt Fld Hcky; Powder Puff Ftbl; Var Capt Trk; Cit Awd; Phy Ed Stu Of Mnth 86; Mst Imprvd Bsktbll 86; Colye Cssdy All-Str Tm Bsktbll 86; Mrktg.

CUNEO, PAULA; The Bromfield Schl; Harvard, MA; (Y); 9/85; Off Church Yth Grp; VP Spanish Clb; Teachers Aide; Chorus; Pres Sr Cls; Var Capt Cheerleading; Var Capt Fld Hcky; Sftbl; DAR Awd; Hon Roll; Rlgs Ed Tchr 85-86; Art Tchr 85-86; Pro Musica Awd & Hrvrd Tchrs Assn Schlrshp Awd 85-6; U Of Sthrn CA; Fine Arts.

CUNHA, GARY; Malden HS; Malden, MA; (Y); 25/500; Am Leg Boys St; SADD; Pres Band; Concert Band; Jazz Band; Madrigals; Mrchg Band; Pep Band; Variety Show; L Swmmng; Prsdntl Acdmc Ftns Awd 85-86; Dstrct Chrs 85-86; Lions All-ST Bnd 85-86; Northeastern U; Cmptr Sci.

CUNHA, TAMMI LYNN; New Bedford HS; Acushnet, MA; (Y); 29/631; Drama Clb; Color Guard; Mrchg Band; Yrbk Stf; Soph Cls; Stu Cncl; High Hon Roll; NHS; Ntl Merit SF; Pres Schlr; Sthestrn MA U; Cmnctns.

CUNNIFF, SUSAN; St Joseph Regional HS; Lowell, MA; (Y); Church Yth Grp; Office Aide; Radio Clb; Church Choir; Yrbk Stf; Sec Soph Cls; Pres VP Stu Cncl; Var Cheerleading; Var Crs Cntry; Var Sftbl; Northern Essex CC; Bus Mgmt.

CUNNINGHAM, CAROLINE; Miss Halls Schl; Lagrangeville, NY; (Y); Sr Cls; Var Vllybl; Meus Hnr Stat Key Awd 86; Margaret Witherspoon Awd 86; Nancy L Coleman Awd 86; Simmons Coll; Mgmt.

CURCIO, LYN; Girls Catholic HS; E Boston, MA; (Y); SADD; Yrbk Phtg; Yrbk Stf; Hon Roll; Suffolk U; Sociology.

CURCURU, STEPHANIE E; Beverly HS; Beverly, MA; (Y); 5/374; Am Leg Aux Girls St; Math Tm; Red Cross Aide; Yrbk Stf; Var Bsktbl; Var Socr; Var Trk; Bausch & Lomb Sci Awd; NHS; Ntl Merit Ltr; Beverly Coll Clb Schlrshp 86; Princeton U; Aerosp Engrng.

CURDO, MARK; St Johns Prep; Lynn, MA; (Y); Boy Scts; Math Tm; Science Clb; Im Bsktbl; High Hon Roll; Hon Roll; Pre-Vet.

CURLEY, AUSTIN; Revere HS; Revere, MA; (Y); Rep VP Stu Cncl; Runway Model Awd; Csmtlgy.

CURLEY, DAVID; Westwood HS; Westwood, MA; (Y); 7/212; Am Leg Boys St; Debate Tm; SADD; Pres Sr Cls; Stu Cncl; Var Capt Ftbl; L Trk; High Hon Roll; VP NHS; Spanish NHS; Daily Transcript Ftbl All-Star Lnbckr 86; 9th In Sci Fair 86; Good Mornings Americas Prom Fash Shw 86; Sci.

CURRAN, DENISE; Medford HS; Medford, MA; (Y); 8/435; Math Clb; Math Tm; Science Clb; SADD; Varsity Clb; Nwsp Stf; Yrbk Stf; Stu Cncl; Var Pom Pon; Mu Alp Tht; Dist Sci Fair 86; 2nd & 3rd Przs Sci Fair 84&86; Achvmnt Awds Engl, Math, Sci & Hstry 84-86; Tufts; Math.

CURRAN, SUSAN; Melrose HS; Boston, MA; (Y); Camera Clb; Drama Clb; Legal Sec.

CURRAN, THERESA; Walpole SR HS; S Walpole, MA; (Y); 29/268; Church Yth Grp; Drama Clb; Spanish Clb; Pres Chorus; School Musical; Swing Chorus; VP Frsh Cls; VP Soph Cls; VP Jr Cls; VP Sr Cls; Svc Awd 85-86; Natl Hnr Soc 85-86; Hnr Roll 83-86; Frgn Lang.

CURRIE, JENNIFER A; Fontbonne Acad; Plymouth, MA; (Y); 6/133; Drama Clb; Science Clb; Stage Crew; Lit Mag; High Hon Roll; Hon Roll; Jr NHS; NHS; St Schlr; Excllnc In Shkspeare/Outstndng Achvt In Amer Hstry 85; Cmmnwlth Schlr/Outstndng Achvt In Arts 86; Coll Of The Holy Cross.

CURRIE, PETER; Newton Catholic HS; Waltham, MA; (Y); 3/50; Model UN; Nwsp Ed-Chief; Rep Jr Cls; Pres Rep Stu Cncl; Hon Roll; Law.

CURRIER, GREG; Nauset Regional HS; N Truro, MA; (Y); 3/140; Chorus; Var Bsktbl; Var Trk; High Hon Roll; NHS; Pres Schlr; H H Snow Fmly Schlrshp; Hghst GPA; VA Polytech Inst; Mech Engrng.

CURRIER, HEIDI; Commerce HS; Springfield, MA; (Y); Church Yth Grp; 4-H; JA; Library Aide; Red Cross Aide; SADD; Trk; Cit Awd; Computer Clb; Hon Roll; Admin Spec US Army.

CURRIER, JIM; Reading HS; Reading, MA; (Y); JV Capt Ice Hcky; French Hon Soc; High Hon Roll; NHS.

CURRIER, PAUL; Haverhill HS; Haverhill, MA; (Y); Nwsp Stf; Yrbk Stf; Cartooning.

CURRY, CATHERINE; Westfield HS; Westfield, MA; (Y); Flag Corp; Bay Pth JC Alumn Assoc Awd Excllnc Bus Stds & Schl Ctznshp 86; Acctg.

CURRY, TIMOTHY; New Bedford HS; New Bedford, MA; (Y); 200/700; Civic Clb; Cmnty Wkr; Exploring; Key Clb; Letterman Clb; Office Aide; Political Wkr; Ski Clb; SADD; Varsity Clb; All Schlstc Stndrd Tms Glf 86; Sprts Med.

CURTI, SABINA B; Berkshire Schl; Hollowville, NY; (Y); PAVAS; Varsity Clb; Yrbk Stf; Var L Socr; Var L Sftbl; Var L Tennis; Var L Trk; Var L Vllybl; Var High Hon Roll; Var Hon Roll; Cum Laude 86; Regnl Schlrshp NY St; MA Inst Tech; Bio.

CURTIN, DEIRDRE; Westwood HS; Westwood, MA; (Y); Church Yth Grp; Cmnty Wkr; Hosp Aide; SADD; Hon Roll; Accntng.

CURTIS, DONNA; Norfolk County Agricultural HS; Hanover, MA; (S); Pres FFA; Pres Sr Cls; Pres Stu Cncl; Var Capt Bsktbl; Var Capt Vllybl; Nwsp Rptr; Yrbk Ed-Chief; JV Crs Cntry; JV Socr; Westfield ST; Phy Ed.

CURTIS, KELLEY; Shawsheen Val Tech; Tewksbury, MA; (Y); 78/400; Phrmclgy.

CURTIS, ROSEMARY; Stoughton SR HS; Stoughton, MA; (Y); Fld Hcky; Timer; High Hon Roll; NHS; Johnson & Wales Coll; Chef.

CUSACK, MARY ELLEN; Dedham HS; Dedham, MA; (S); 9/252; Aud/Vis; Computer Clb; Chrmn SADD; Yrbk Stf; Pres Stu Cncl; L Trk; Hon Roll; NHS; Ntl Hnr Soc; Magna Cum Laude Cert Ntl Latin Exam-Ntl Classical League; Nr Roll 4 Erms All Yrs; Ecnmcs.

CUSSON, AMY; Auburn HS; Auburn, MA; (Y); Church Yth Grp; Library Aide; High Hon Roll; Hon Roll; Prfct Atten Awd; Nichol Coll; Acctng.

CUSSON, RENE; Westfield HS; Granville, MA; (Y); Church Yth Grp; French Clb; Nwsp Phtg; Nwsp Rptr; Yrbk Stf; Rep Frsh Cls; Trs Soph Cls; Score Keeper; English, Writing.

CUSSON, THERESA B; Milford HS; Milford, MA; (Y); 16/266; Drama Clb; Hosp Aide; Yrbk Stf; High Hon Roll; NHS; Pres Schlr; Richard J Tavano Jrnlsm Schrlshp 86; Harold M Moran Mem Schlrshp 86; Salem ST Coll; Eng.

CUSTER, JENNIFER; Marthas Vineyard Regional HS; Vineyard Haven, MA; (Y); 9/104; SADD; Band; Chorus; Church Choir; Concert Band; Madrigals; Nwsp Rptr; Lit Mag; Frsh Cls; Jr Cls; Lang.

CUTLER, MICHELLE; Hoosac Valley HS; Adams, MA; (Y); 22/149; Hon Roll; Awd Entry Acknwldgmnt Boston Globe Cntst 86; Graphic Dsgn.

CUTRONI, DANIELLE; North HS; Worcester, MA; (Y); 10/208; Elks Awd; NHS; East Side Schlrshp 86; John Bonofiglio Meml Schlrshp 86; Worcester ST Clg; Acctnt.

CYBULSKI, SUE; Chicopee HS; Chicopee, MA; (Y); 40/200; Var L Bsktbl; Var L Sftbl.

CYR, PAMELA LEE; Bartlett HS; Webster, MA; (Y); 3/152; Math Tm; Ski Clb; School Play; Var Capt Bsktbl; Var Capt Socr; Var L Sftbl; High Hon Roll; NHS; NEDT Awd; St Schlr; Cmmnwlth Schlr Schlrshp 86-87; Lucy T Phllps Wight Math Awd 86; Prncpls Athltc Awd & Schlrshp 86; U Of MA; Elctrcl Engr.

CYRULIK, LYNDA; King Philip Regnl HS; Plainvlle, MA; (Y); 66/230; Rep Frsh Cls; Rep Soph Cls; Rep Jr Cls; Rep Sr Cls; JV Bsktbl; JV Capt Fld Hcky; Var Capt Tennis; Hon Roll; COMM Art.

CZAPOROWSKI, LYNN; Chicopee Comp HS; Chicopee, MA; (Y); German Clb; NHS; Purler & Chester Inst; Comp Ins.

CZARNICK, KEITH; Brockton HS; Brockton, MA; (Y); Boy Scts; Key Clb; Band; Lit Mag; Eng.

CZEDIK, CRISTIN; Marlboro HS; Marlboro, MA; (Y); Church Yth Grp; Sec OEA; SADD; Varsity Clb; Nwsp Rptr; Var Trk; Var Vllybl; Exec Sec.

CZEPIEL, EDWARD; Cathedral HS; Chicopee, MA; (Y); Trs Math Clb; NHS; Ntl Merit Ltr; Prfct Atten Awd; Church Yth Grp; Political Wkr; Hon Roll; U MA Amherst Chancellors Tlnt Awd 86; Civil Engnrng.

D ALESSANDRO, JEFFREY; St Johns Prep School; Lynnfield, MA; (Y); Aud/Vis; Radio Clb; Jazz Band; Im Bsktbl; Im Ftbl; Im Vllybl; High Hon Roll; Hon Roll; Ntl Hon Soc Stu 86; Bus.

D ALESSANDRO, MARIA; Christopher Columbus HS; East Boston, MA; (S); Hon Roll; Ntl Merit Ltr; Suffolk U; Bus.

D AMICO, ANTHONY; Waltham SR HS; Waltham, MA; (Y); Boys Clb Am; Bsktbl; Var Socr; Hon Roll; Engrng.

D AMORE, CONNIE; Christopher Columbus HS; Boston, MA; (S); 3/111; JA; Math Clb; High Hon Roll; Hon Roll; Jr NHS; NHS; Ntl Merit Ltr; Italn & Bio Awds 84-85; Top 90 Pctl NEDT 84-85; Boston Coll; Bus.

D AMORE, DINA; Foxboro HS; Foxboro, MA; (Y); 51/220; Aud/Vis; JA; Ski Clb; Nwsp Rptr; Yrbk Ed-Chief; Yrbk Rptr; Sec Frsh Cls; Rep Sr Cls; Cit Awd; Hon Roll; JR Achvt Co Mst Sls Awd; Awd Stu Cncl; Comm.

D ANGELO, ANDREW M; Westwood HS; Westwood, MA; (Y); 32/209; Am Leg Boys St; Jazz Band; Yrbk Ed-Chief; Pres Stu Cncl; Var L Bsbl; Var L Ftbl; Capt Trk; Lion Awd; NHS; Boy Scts; Edwarrd Huber Mem Awd 86; Coll Of Holy Cross; Poli Sci.

D ENTREMONT III, EARL; Canton HS; Canton, MA; (Y); 26/260; Rep Jr Cls; Rep Sr Cls; JV Bsbl; Var L Bsktbl; Var L Socr; Var L Trk; Im Vllybl; Hon Roll; St Schlr; Pres Phy Fit Awd 85-86; Assumpton Coll; Pltcl Sci.

D ESPINOSA, JOHN V; Tri-County Reg Voc Tech Schl; Walpole, MA; (Y); 16/202; Rep Sr Cls; Hon Roll; Bud Allen Schlrshp 85-86; Walpole Epiphany Prsh Schlrshp 85-86; Top Stu Awd In Auto Body 85-86; Wentworth Inst; Aerontcs.

D ITRIA, DAYNA; Our Lady Of Nazareth Acad; Revere, MA; (Y); 12/74; Dance Clb; Drama Clb; Science Clb; Ski Clb; Spanish Clb; SADD; School Musical; School Play; Lit Mag; Hon Roll; Dlgnc Sci & Algbr 84; US Achvt Acad Nat Awd Sci 85.

D ONOFRIO, MICHAEL D; St Johns HS; Upton, MA; (Y); 96/291; Am Leg Boys St; Boys Clb Am; Boy Scts; Church Yth Grp; English Clb; Library Aide; Model UN; Political Wkr; Im Bsktbl; Im Sftbl; Boston Coll; Poli Sci.

DA COSTA, ZOLA F; Umana HS; Dorchester, MA; (Y); Bsbl; Socr; MIT Boston; Physics.

DA CRUZ, JOHN; Ludlow HS; Ludlow, MA; (Y); Yrbk Stf; Rep Sr Cls; Hon Roll; NEDT Awd; Bentley Coll; Bus Adm.

DABOROWSKI, KAREN; Agawam HS; Agawam, MA; (Y); #27 In Class; Drama Clb; Latin Clb; Band; Var Cheerleading; Var Trk; Hon Roll; 2nd Pl Vally Wheel Trk Mt 85; 3rd Pl Western MA Div Trk Mt 85; 1st Pl NCA Chrldng Tourn Cmp 85.

DACEY, RICHARD; Bedford HS; Bedford, MA; (Y); Am Leg Boys St; Pres Church Yth Grp; Capt ROTC; Chorus; Drm Mjr(t); Mrchg Band; School Musical; Nwsp Stf; Aud/Vis; Acpl Chr; Prncpls Awd 86; K L Phnny Outstndg Music Stu Awd 85&86; N E Dist Chorus 85&86; Gordon Coll; Mnstry.

DACOSTA, MARIA; New Bedford HS; New Bedford, MA; (Y); 19/701; Church Yth Grp; Intnl Clb; Science Clb; High Hon Roll; Hon Roll; Jr NHS; NHS; 1st Pl & 2nd Pl Portuguese Cntst Awds 84 & 85; Com Sci.

DACRUZ, ANTONIO; Ludlow HS; Ludlow, MA; (Y); 36/280; Church Yth Grp; Library Aide; Acpl Chr; Bowling; Socr; Vllybl; Porter & Chester Inst; Drftg.

DACRUZ, GINA; Milford HS; Milford, MA; (Y); 53/290; Hosp Aide; Band; Concert Band; Mrchg Band; School Musical; Providence Coll; Psych.

DACRUZ, SUSANNE; New Bedford HS; New Bedford, MA; (Y); Cmnty Wkr; Color Guard; Mrchg Band; Rep Jr Cls; Rep Stu Cncl; Twrlr; Hon Roll; Jr NHS; Ntl Merit SF; Grad With Hnrs 86; Wstrn New Engld Coll; Phrmcy.

DACUNHA, LISA; B M C Durfee HS; Fall River, MA; (Y); Spanish Clb; Band; Concert Band; Mrchg Band; Twrlr; Hon Roll; NHS; Diploma Of Merit/Spnsh 85-86.

DAEE, JACOB; English HS; Sepulveda, CA; (Y); Art Clb; AFS; Intnl Clb; Math Tm; Pep Clb; Nwsp Rptr; Yrbk Rptr; Off Sr Cls; Stu Cncl; Badmtn; Awd Frm Clss 86; Schlrshp WA 86; Dfrnt Awds Thrw HS 84-86; Med Engr.

DAGILUS, LINDA; Turners Falls HS; Montague, MA; (Y); 9/91; Yrbk Stf; Var Capt Swmmng; NHS; Excllnt Eng,Chem,Spnsh; Swmmng Divng Champ 85; Swm Champ 2nd Pl 85.

DAHL, ERIC; Matignon HS; Cambridge, MA; (S); Computer Clb; Math Clb; Hon Roll.

DAIGLE, JAMES; Chicopee Comprehensive HS; Chicopee, MA; (Y); 39/300; Am Leg Boys St; German Clb; JV Bsbl; JV Bsktbl; L Trk; NHS.

DAIGLE, WILLIAM; Central Catholic HS; Lowell, MA; (Y); 41/231; Boy Scts; Church Yth Grp; Ski Clb; Variety Show; Nwsp Rptr; Im Trk; Hon Roll; St Michaels Grmr Schl Schlrshp 83; Eagle Scout 84; Gen Hoyt S Vandenberg Awd-Eagle Scout Of Yr 86; U Lowell.

DAIGNAULT, STEVEN; Auburn HS; Auburn, MA; (Y); Am Leg Boys St; Math Tm; Concert Band; Jazz Band; Mrchg Band; Off Sr Cls; Var L Bsktbl; Var L Trk; Ed Trs Jr NHS; NHS.

DAIGNEAU, JULIE; Southwick HS; Granville, MA; (Y); 3/152; Church Yth Grp; Cmnty Wkr; French Clb; Library Aide; Office Aide; Yrbk Stf; Sec Soph Cls; Cheerleading; Coach Actv; Mgr(s); Wstrn New England; Bus Admin.

DAILEY, JONATHAN C; Mount Greylock Regional HS; Williamstown, MA; (Y); 12/127; Am Leg Boys St; Boy Scts; Model UN; Political Wkr; Pres Sr Cls; Var L Ftbl; High Hon Roll; NHS; Voice Dem Awd; JCL; Bcntnnl Yngr Schlr Grant 86.

DAILEY, STACEY; Attleboro HS; Attleboro, MA; (Y); Band; Mrchg Band; Rep Sr Cls; NHS; Schlrshp Awd In Acctng 86; Engl Attndnc Awd 86; Acctng.

DAKERS, DARCEY; Silver Lake Regional HS; Kingston, MA; (Y); 11/450; French Clb; Math Clb; Var Capt Cheerleading; Hon Roll; NHS.

DAKIN, STEPHANIE; Saugus HS; Saugus, MA; (Y); 37/300; Camp Fr Inc; Yrbk Ed-Chief; Off Sr Cls; JV Bsktbl; Hon Roll; Jr NHS; Johnson & Wales; Bus Mngmnt.

DALE, ANN; Mount St Joseph Acad; Roslindale, MA; (Y); 30/169; Church Yth Grp; Service Clb; Hon Roll; Ntl Bus Hnr Soc 85-86; Engrng.

DALEY, BILL; Wesfield HS; Westfield, MA; (Y); 50/387; Var Capt Bsbl; Var Capt Bsktbl; Var Capt Socr; Hon Roll.

DALEY, SIMONE; Mount Saint Joseph Acad; Boston, MA; (Y); 43/167; GAA; JA; Crs Cntry; Trk; Hon Roll; All Schltcs 85; Golden Sneaker Awd 84; West Point Mil Schl; Law.

DALEY, TRACEY L; Boston Latin Schl; Dorchester, MA; (Y); 54/285; Exploring; French Clb; Off JA; Hon Roll; NHS; Ntl Merit Ltr; Prfct Atten Awd; Stu Of Yr Awd For Piano 82; Stu Schlrshp In Piano 83; Bio.

DALLAMORA, JEANINE; Framingham South HS; Framingham, MA; (S); 50/240; School Musical; Bsktbl; Cheerleading; Capt Fld Hcky; Gym; Hon Roll; Prom Coord Chrprsn Decoratn Comm 85; Media Cmmnctns.

DALTERIO, JOHN; St Johns HS; Hyannisport, MA; (Y); Am Leg Boys St; Science Clb; Ski Clb; Varsity Clb; JV Bsbl; Var L Ftbl; U RI; Pre-Med.

DALTON, JOSEPH W; Arlington HS; Arlington, MA; (Y); Am Leg Boys St; Drama Clb; School Musical; School Play; Yrbk Stf; Rep Jr Cls; Var JV Bsbl; JV Trk; High Hon Roll; NHS; Harvard U Prz Bk Awd 86; Arlington Friend Drama Awd 86; Law.

DALY, DONNA; Taconic HS; Pittsfield, MA; (Y); FBLA; Girl Scts; Office Aide; Chorus.

DALY, ELIZABETH; Notre Dame Acad; Minot, MA; (Y); Im Bsktbl; Hon Roll; Prfct Atten Awd; Spanish NHS; Bus Admn.

DALY, MICHAEL T; Boston Latin Acad; West Roxbury, MA; (Y); Drama Clb; PAVAS; Band; Church Choir; School Musical; School Play; Stage Crew; Variety Show; Ftbl; Outstndng Actr Awd 84; Moffat Awd 85-86; MA HS Drama Guld Awd For Excelnce 86; Ithaca Coll; Theatre.

DAMATO, NICOLE; King Philip Regional HS; Wrentham, MA; (Y); Sec Pres Church Yth Grp; Sec Pres 4-H; Intnl Clb; Trs Stu Cncl; Var Capt Crs Cntry; Var Capt Trk; Sec NHS; Radio Clb; Hon Roll; Hckmck Mdl Sntr 86; ST Cntst Natl Hstry Dy 86; Hckmck Lge All-Str Crs Cntry 84-85; Lbrl Arts.

DAMON, ALAN; Gardner HS; Gardner, MA; (Y); 23/180; Pres Trs Church Yth Grp; Yrbk Phtg; Yrbk Stf; Rptr Lit Mag; JV Crs Cntry; Mgr(s); JV Trk; Ski Clb; Stat Bsktbl; Score Keeper; U Of MA; Engl.

DAMOUR, A MARYLINE; St Clare HS; Brockton, MA; (Y); 19/139; Church Yth Grp; French Clb; Lib Library Aide; Church Choir; Nwsp Ed-Chief; Nwsp Rptr; NHS; Ntl Merit Ltr; Nwsp Stf; Suffolk U Awd Outstndg Schl Svc 85; Silvr Medl Wnr Natl Lat Exam 84; Polit Sci.

DANAHAR, DEIDRE MODESTA; Doherty Memorial HS; Worcester, MA; (Y); Church Yth Grp; Spanish Clb; SADD; Variety Show; Nwsp Stf; JV Fld Hcky; Var Trk; Hon Roll; MADS U Amherst; Psychlgy.

DANAS, CHRISTINE; St Joseph Regional HS; Lowell, MA; (Y); Church Yth Grp; Tennis; Hon Roll; Jr NHS; NHS; Church Choir; Bsbl; Bsktbl; Socr; Sftbl; U Of Lowell; Elem Ed.

DANDINI, MICHAEL P; St Bernards CC HS; Fitchburg, MA; (Y); Trs Am Leg Boys St; Variety Show; Stu Cncl; Bsktbl; Var JV Ftbl; JV Trk; Ftbl Council; Law.

DANEHY, ELIZABETH; Matignon HS; Cambridge, MA; (S); Church Yth Grp; Spanish Clb; Off Soph Cls; Off Jr Cls; Bsktbl; JV Sftbl; Var JV Vllybl; NHS; Natl Ldrshp & Svc Awd 84; Acdmc All Am 85; Natl Hnr Rl 84.

DANEHY, MARYLOU; Woburn HS; Woburn, MA; (S); 17/453; Church Yth Grp; JCL; Key Clb; Latin Clb; Spanish Clb; SADD; Varsity Clb; Stu Cncl; Bsktbl; Hon Roll; Natl Latn Hnr Soc 85-86; St Michaels Coll; Pilot.

DANFORTH, DARYL; West Springfield SR HS; W Springfield, MA; (Y); Computer Clb; Yrbk Phtg; Yrbk Rptr; Yrbk Stf; Rep Frsh Cls; Rep Soph Cls; High Hon Roll; Hon Roll; Mrktng.

DANGELO, LAURA; Medford HS; Medford, MA; (Y); 76/426; SADD; Nwsp Stf; Yrbk Stf; Bsbl; Vllybl; Merit Rl 83; Fund Raisg Asst Awd Bsbl 84; Lang.

DANGELO, LISA; Everett HS; Everett, MA; (Y); Church Yth Grp; Intnl Clb; Key Clb; Office Aide; SADD; Teachers Aide; Nwsp Stf; Yrbk Stf; Hon Roll; Merrimack Coll; Bus Admin.

DANGREDO, MELISSA; David Hale Fanning Trade HS; Worcester, MA; (Y); SADD; Fash Design.

DANIEL, KELLY; Madison Park HS; Boston, MA; (Y); Art Clb; Math Tm; Band; Concert Band; Nwsp Sprt Ed; Off Sr Cls; Bsbl; Bsktbl; Ftbl; Trk; NE U; Arch.

DANIEL, LESLIE; Our Lady Of Nazareth Acad; Peabody, MA; (Y); 5/70; Art Clb; English Clb; French Clb; Science Clb; Cit Awd; High Hon Roll; Trs NHS; Awds Biol, Alg II & Trig 85; Engl Awd 86; Holy Cross Bk Awd 86; Elec Engrg.

DANIEL, SAUDONYA; Madison Park HS; Dorchester, MA; (Y); Hosp Aide; SADD; Concert Band; Jazz Band; Stu Cncl; Bsktbl; Mgr(s); Swmmng; High Hon Roll; Outstndg Stu Awd Music 86; Mst Dedictd Stu Vet Admin Hosp 83; Mth Achvt 83; Springfield Coll; Crim Just.

DANIELL, ADRIENNE; Bedford HS; Bedford, MA; (Y); 86/201; Church Yth Grp; Hosp Aide; Teachers Aide; Mgr(s); Tennis; Hon Roll; Bentley Coll.

DANIELS, KEVIN; Austin Prep; Stoneham, MA; (Y); 16/124; French Clb; Var JV Bsktbl; High Hon Roll; Hon Roll; Engrng.

DANIELS, TROY; Chatham JR SR HS; Chatham, MA; (Y); 6/39; Hon Roll; NHS; SAR Awd.

DANIELSON, ELAINE; Gardner HS; Gardner, MA; (Y); 35/149; French Clb; Lit Mag; Var Capt Crs Cntry; Var L Trk; Hon Roll; Perfect Attndnc Awd; U Of CT; Corp Ftns.

DANO, LAURA; Auburn HS; Auburn, MA; (Y); Exploring; Band; Concert Band; Mrchg Band; Law Enfrcmnt.

DAPPER, DIANE; Holyname C C HS; Worcester, MA; (Y); 88/270; Church Yth Grp; Var Socr; JV Sftbl; Hon Roll; Prfct Atten Awd; Math Awd 84; Typng Awd 85; Worcester ST; Acctg.

DARSCH, GREGG; Silver Lake Regional HS; Kingston, MA; (Y); French Clb; Math Clb; School Play; Variety Show; JV Bsktbl; Capt L Tennis; Hon Roll.

DATTERO, JANET F; Girls Catholic HS; Malden, MA; (Y); 9/36; Church Yth Grp; SADD; School Play; Stage Crew; Yrbk Stf; Pres Sr Cls; Stu Cncl; Sftbl; Vllybl; Hon Roll; Regis Coll; Cmnctns.

DAUNAIS, MICHELLE; Hoosac Valley HS; Adams, MA; (Y); 2/153; Debate Tm; Quiz Bowl; Nwsp Ed-Chief; Nwsp Rptr; Lit Mag; Crs Cntry; High Hon Roll; NHS; Sal; MA Advncd Studies Prog 85; MA Assoc HS Supr Awd 86; MA Grls ST Altnt 85; Coll Of The Holy Cross; Bio.

DAUPHINAIS, KEVIN; Braintree HS; Abington, MA; (Y); 63/416; Am Leg Boys St; Church Yth Grp; Cmnty Wkr; Ski Clb; SADD; Varsity Clb; Lit Mag; Rep Sr Cls; JV Var Bsbl; JV Bsktbl; Natl Athletic Plcmnt 85; Schester Daily Family Schlrshp 86; Sci Fair Recgntn 85-86; U Of MA; Elec Engrng.

DAUPHINAIS, STEVEN; Woburn HS; Woburn, MA; (S); 17/453; Church Yth Grp; Cmnty Wkr; French Clb; JCL; Latin Clb; Leo Clb; Science Clb; Capt Tennis; High Hon Roll; Pres NHS; Ntl Latin Exam-Cum Laude 83-4; Ntl Sci Awd 82-3; Tufts U.

DAVID, JENNIFER; Nipmuc Regional HS; Upton, MA; (Y); 15/95; Art Clb; Ski Clb; JV Bsktbl; Mgr Socr; Hon Roll; Spnsh Awd 84; Johnson & Wales; Htl/Rest Mgmt.

DAVIDSON, BRIDGETTE; Our Lady Of Nazareth Acad; Lynnfield, MA; (Y); 4-H; Science Clb; Rep Stu Cncl; Bsktbl; Bausch & Lomb Sci Awd; High Hon Roll; Church Yth Grp; Exploring; Ski Clb; Mntrshp Awd By Musm Of Sci Bstn 85; TX A&M Schlrshp 86-87; OLN Rlgn Dept Awd Acdmc Resp 86; TX A&M; Mrn Bio.

DAVIDSON, LAURA; Brockton HS; Brockton, MA; (Y); 253/867; Dance Clb; Drama Clb; Office Aide; School Musical; School Play; Var Cheerleading; Hon Roll; Teen Miss MA Charm 86; MA Teen Miss 85; Greater Brockton JR Miss 87; Cmnctns.

DAVIES, CARRIE; Concord-Carlisle Regional HS; Concord, MA; (Y); 5/328; Math Tm; Concert Band; Mrchg Band; Symp Band; Yrbk Stf; Lit Mag; Var Mgr(s); High Hon Roll; NHS; Ntl Merit Ltr; Englsh Dept Awd 85-86; Dept Awd Math, Hstry 84-86.

DAVIES, TREVOR H; Chatham HS; N Chatham, MA; (Y); 12/45; Am Leg Boys St; Cmnty Wkr; Drama Clb; Key Clb; Ski Clb; SADD; Teachers Aide; Stage Crew; Rep Soph Cls; JV Bsktbl; Bus.

DAVIGNON, SCOTT; Fairhaven HS; Fairhaven, MA; (Y); AFS; Aud/Vis; French Clb; Key Clb; Yrbk Bus Mgr; Yrbk Stf; Off Frsh Cls; Off Soph Cls; Stu Cncl; Bsktbl; Tchr.

DAVIS, ANDREA; Ayer JR-SR HS; Ayer, MA; (S); Cmnty Wkr; DECA; Concert Band; School Musical; School Play; Yrbk Bus Mgr; Rep Sec Stu Cncl; NHS; Spelman Coll; Music.

DAVIS, ANDREW J; N Middlesex Regional HS; E Pepperell, MA; (Y); 14/210; NHS; Schlstc Art Awds Blue Rbn 85-86; Mass Marn Edctrs 1st Pl 85.

DAVIS, ANN; Notre Dame Acad; Milton, MA; (Y); 26/109; Church Yth Grp; Chorus; Var Vllybl; High Hon Roll; Bio Med Engrng.

DAVIS, CHRISTOPHER; Barnstable HS; W Barnstable, MA; (Y); 50/380; Cmnty Wkr; SADD; Rep Soph Cls; Rep Jr Cls; Rep Sr Cls; JV Bsbl; Var Socr; Wt Lftg; High Hon Roll; Hon Roll; Silver,Gold Acad Awd 82-83; U MA-AMHERST; Lib Arts.

DAVIS, CONSTANCE I; Burlington HS; Burlington, MA; (Y); 33/321; JV Bsktbl; Capt Var Cheerleading; Im Powder Puff Ftbl; Capt Sftbl; High Hon Roll; Hon Roll; NHS; VFW Awd; Voice Dem Awd; Hlth Acad Achvt Awds 85; Grphc Dsgn & German Acad Achvt Awds 86; Comm Art.

DAVIS, DONNA; Groton-Dunstable Rgnl Secondry Schl; Dunstable, MA; (Y); 6/92; Office Aide; Acpl Chr; Chorus; High Hon Roll; Hon Roll; Pres Jr NHS; Pres NHS; Natl Schl Chrl Awd 86; Tyngsborough Dunstble Rtry Clb Schlrshp 86; Tyngsborough Dunstbl Chrl Scty 86; New Hampshire Voc Tech; Bus Mgt.

DAVIS, ERIC JAMES; Phillips Acad; Sharon, MA; (Y); Aud/Vis; Cmnty Wkr; Exploring; German Clb; Stage Crew; Ntl Merit Ltr; Math Clb; Hon Roll; Stevenson Prize German 86; Pamelo Weidenman Prz Architecture 86; Cum Laude Soc 86; Cornell U.

DAVIS, ERIKA; Newburyport HS; Newburypt, MA; (Y); 8/192; Model UN; Yrbk Sprt Ed; Rep Stu Cncl; Capt Cheerleading; Hon Roll; NHS; Political Wkr; Elem Ed.

DAVIS, HELEN; Blackstone Valley Regnl Vocatl HS; Whitinsville, MA; (Y); Library Aide; SADD; Chorus; Var Bsktbl; Bus Adm.

DAVIS, JACQUELINE; Silver Lake Regional HS; Kingston, MA; (Y); Cmnty Wkr; Sec French Clb; Chorus; Yrbk Stf; Pres Frsh Cls; VP Soph Cls; VP Sr Cls; Var Cheerleading; Hon Roll; NHS.

DAVIS, JAYNE; North Reading HS; N Reading, MA; (Y); Drama Clb; Band; Chorus; Concert Band; Jazz Band; Mrchg Band; Stage Crew; Nwsp Stf; Yrbk Stf; JV Bsktbl; Mst Coachbl Plyr Sccr 85; Outstndg Muscn 84; Bus.

DAVIS, JOEL; Wakefield HS; Jonesboro, GA; (Y); 85/333; JA; Natl Achvt Conference 85; Outstndng Young Bus Man Eastern Ma 86; Vp Personnel Eastern MA 85; GA Inst Tech; Engrng.

DAVIS, MICHAEL; Apponequet Regional HS; Lakeville, MA; (Y); Cit Awd; Hon Roll; Comp.

DAVIS, PALMER; Deerfield Acad; Erie, PA; (Y); Pres Computer Clb; Debate Tm; Model UN; Pres Political Wkr; Coach Actv; Hon Roll; Jr NHS; Ntl Merit SF; Boy Scts; Church Yth Grp; PHEAA Cert Merit 85; Sailng Tm Capt 85; Pre-Med.

DAVIS, PETER; Taunton HS; Berkley, MA; (Y); Art Clb; JCL; Teachers Aide; Yrbk Stf; Lit Mag; Var Crs Cntry; Var Trk; Hon Roll; Art.

DAVIS, STEVE; Old Rochester Regional HS; Marion, MA; (Y); Church Yth Grp; Cmnty Wkr; Exploring; Spanish Clb; Lit Mag; Var Bsbl; JV Bsktbl; High Hon Roll; Jr NHS; NHS; Pres Acadmc Ftnss Awd 86; Tri ST Fr Art Cntst Wnnr HS Div 85; Brigham Young U.

DAVIS, TODD; North Brookfield HS; N Brookfield, MA; (Y); 4/38; Computer Clb; Math Tm; SADD; Varsity Clb; School Play; JV Bsktbl; JV Var Socr; Hon Roll; NHS; WPT; Elect Engr.

DAVIS, WENDY; Methuen HS; Methuen, MA; (Y); Dance Clb; Chorus; School Musical; Hon Roll; Colby-Sawyer Coll; Music.

DAWAY, LORETTA A; Newton Cntry Day/Sacred Heart HS; Roxbury, MA; (Y); Church Yth Grp; Yrbk Rptr; Yrbk Stf; Pres Sr Cls; Var Bsktbl; Hon Roll; Jr NHS; NHS; Schlrshp Pres Clsrm Wash DC 85; Natl Merit Schl Negro Stu 85; Natl Hnr Soc; Harvard; Polit Sci.

DAWSON, KARI; Norton HS; Norton, MA; (Y); 55/125; Pep Clb; Ski Clb; Varsity Clb; Chorus; Variety Show; Yrbk Stf; Trs Stu Cncl; Var Capt Cheerleading; Var Capt Pom Pon; Var Sftbl; U Of MA-AMHERST; Bus.

DAWSON, KIM; Barnstable HS; Cotuit, MA; (Y); 172/384; Church Yth Grp; Drama Clb; Varsity Clb; Band; Color Guard; Concert Band; Drill Tm; Drm & Bgl; Flag Corp; Mrchg Band; Bridgewater ST Coll; Chldhd Ed.

DAWSON, MICHAEL; New Bedford HS; New Bedford, MA; (Y); JA; Stu Cncl; Hon Roll; Aud/Vis; Camera Clb; Computer Clb; Off Frsh Cls; Jr NHS; Grad With Hnrs 86; SE MA U; Engrg.

DAY, NEVA; Miss Halls Schl; Miami, FL; (Y); 3/62; Rep GAA; School Play; VP Soph Cls; Pres Jr Cls; Rep Stu Cncl; Var Capt Lcrss; Var Capt Socr; Hon Roll; Ski Clb; Spanish Clb; Soc Clb; Ski Tm; Stu Assembly.

DAY, REBECCA; Marblehead SR HS; Marblehead, MA; (Y); Drama Clb; French Clb; Band; Chorus; Church Choir; Concert Band; Jazz Band; Mrchg Band; Orch; School Musical; Sr Dist Chrs 83-86; Outstndng Musc Awd 86; Andrew J Trembly Meml Schlrshp 86; Becklee Clg Musc; Commrcl Arng.

DAY, ROBERT; Westford Acad; Westford, MA; (Y); German Clb; Im Bsbl; Im Bsktbl; Hon Roll; Arctctrl.

DE ANDRADE, ALCIRA; Gardner HS; Gardner, MA; (Y); 42/150; Girl Scts; Trk; Hon Roll; Bus.

DE BAUN, ROBERT; Groton Schl; South Harwich, MA; (Y); 11/81; Debate Tm; Drama Clb; Chorus; Church Choir; Madrigals; Yrbk Ed-Chief; Yrbk Stf; Stu Cncl; Var Bsbl; JV Capt Socr; Lower Schl Math Awd 83; Frgn Svc.

DE BLOIS, ALEXANDER A; Mt Greylock Regional HS; Williamstown, MA; (Y); 29/133; Boy Scts; JCL; Key Clb; School Musical; School Play; Nwsp Phtg; Nwsp Rptr; Var Golf; Lion Awd; NHS; Coll William & Mary; Comp Sci.

DE BLOIS, WILLIAM; Hoosac Valley HS; Adams, MA; (Y); 57/143; Boy Scts; Church Yth Grp; Ski Clb; Band; Concert Band; Jazz Band; Mrchg Band; School Musical; Variety Show; Grion Awd 86; Berklee Coll Music 86; Music.

DE CESARE, CHRISTINA; Methuen HS; Methuen, MA; (Y); 57/333; Model UN; Bsktbl; JV Var Fld Hcky; Im Powder Puff Ftbl; JV Sftbl; Hon Roll; Marine Bio.

DE COSTE, DENNIS M; Quincy HS; Quincy, MA; (Y); 39/1000; Am Leg Aux Girls St; English Clb; FCA; FNA; FTA; Hosp Aide; JA; Pep Clb; SADD; Varsity Clb; High Hnr Roll 84-85; Natl Hnr Soc 85-86; Prfct Atten Awd 85-86; Phys Ther.

DE COURCY, CHERYL; Wakefield HS; Wakefield, MA; (Y); 61/333; Church Yth Grp; Variety Show; Yrbk Stf; Bsktbl; Fld Hcky; Hon Roll; Fitchburg ST Coll; Nrsng.

DE FILLIPPO, TERESA J; Hull HS; Hull, MA; (Y); 33/139; SADD; Yrbk Stf; Rep Sr Cls; JV Bsktbl; Var Fld Hcky; Var JV Powder Puff Ftbl; JV Sftbl; Homeroom Rep 86; Engl & Typng II Achvt Awds 82-86; U Of MA Amherst; Engl Comm.

DE FREITAS, ZORAIDA R; Taunton HS; Taunton, MA; (Y); Drama Clb; Office Aide; Spanish Clb; Teachers Aide; Yrbk Stf; Stu Cncl; Fld Hcky; Frgn Lang.

DE FUSCO, ANDREA; Presentation Of Mary Acad; Methuen, MA; (S); 1/46; Church Yth Grp; VP Spanish Clb; Yrbk Stf; Sec Jr Cls; Cit Awd; DAR Awd; High Hon Roll; Pres NHS; NEDT Awd; Voice Dem Awd; Sci Fair Rgnl Wnr 85; Natl Sci Olympd 82; Bio.

DE GREGORIO, ROBERT; Cambridge Rindge & Latin HS; Cambridge, MA; (Y); Key Clb; NHS; David Barry Mem Schlrshp 86; Hpkns Awd 86; Soc Stds Achvmnt Awd 86; Boston U.

DE HETRE, MICHELLE; Triton Regional HS; Byfield, MA; (Y); Hosp Aide; Trs Frsh Cls; Trs Soph Cls; Trs Jr Cls; Bsktbl; Mgr(s); Sftbl; Hon Roll; Leaders Club 85-86; Nrsng.

DE LARIA JR, ALLAN P; Arlington Catholic HS; Medford, MA; (Y); 35/150; French Clb; JV Bsktbl; Var Crs Cntry; Hon Roll; NHS; Acad Schlrshp-Merrimack Coll 86; MA St Schlrshp 86; Merrimack Coll.

DE LENA, ROBERT C; Governor Dummer Acad; Revere, MA; (Y); 20/90; Varsity Clb; Pres Stu Cncl; Var Capt Bsbl; Var Crs Cntry; Var Ftbl; Hon Roll; Cmnty Wkr; Spanish Clb; JV Bsktbl; High Hon Roll; Stdnt Bdy Pres; All Indpndt Schl Leag Bsbl; MVP Gov Dmmr Bsbl & Discpln Comm.

DE LOCHE, JEANNINE; Dana Hall Schl; Ocean, NJ; (Y); Dance Clb; Pres Key Clb; Political Wkr; Q&S; Nwsp Ed-Chief; High Hon Roll; Ntl Merit Ltr; Church Yth Grp; Cmnty Wkr; Drama Clb; Cum Laude Soc 86; Bronze Congrsnl Awd 85; Brown Bk Prz 86; Columbia U; Pre-Law.

DE LORENZO, JENNIFER K; Weymouth South HS; S Weymouth, MA; (Y); 98/348; Hosp Aide; Pep Clb; Rep Sr Cls; Cheerleading; Sftbl; Trk; Hon Roll; Prfct Atten Awd; St Michaels Coll; Psych.

DE LUCA, KELEY ANN; Wilmington HS; Wilmington, MA; (Y); 11/250; SADD; Varsity Clb; Nwsp Stf; Yrbk Stf; Stu Cncl; Var Crs Cntry; Var Gym; JV Sftbl; Hon Roll; Kiwanis Awd; Excllnce Frgn Lang 85; Outstndng Achvt Hstry 84; U MA Amherst; Engrng.

DE MARTINO, ANDREA D; Pittsfield HS; Pittsfield, MA; (Y); 7/280; JCL; Latin Clb; SADD; Yrbk Stf; Trs Soph Cls; Trs Jr Cls; Trs Sr Cls; Im Vllybl; High Hon Roll; NHS; Grand Lodge Order Sons Italy Am Schl; Gold Medals Ntl Latin Ex; Citzns Schlrshp Awd; Skidmore Coll; Bus Adm.

DE MASI, DIANE; North Quincy HS; N Quincy, MA; (Y); Cmnty Wkr; Band; Concert Band; Jazz Band; Mrchg Band; High Hon Roll; Hon Roll; NHS; Outstndg Musicn 84-86; Diane Jsph Awd Bio 86; Vet Med.

DE MATOS, DANIEL; Agawam HS; Feeding Hills, MA; (Y); Bsbl; Ftbl; Wt Lftg; High Hon Roll; Hon Roll; Arch Engr.

DE MELO, NANCY; New Bedford HS; New Bedford, MA; (Y); French Clb; French Hon Soc; Hon Roll; Law.

DE NARDO, TOM; Agawam HS; Agawam, MA; (Y); 2/350; Am Leg Boys St; Debate Tm; Im Socr; Hon Roll; NHS; Spanish NHS; Spnsh.

DE NINO, ROGER; Cathedral HS; Springfield, MA; (Y); Church Yth Grp; JA; Westfeild ST; Law Enfrcmnt.

DE PALMA II, ANTHONY V; Burlington HS; Burlington, MA; (Y); 36/319; JA; Rep Soph Cls; Rep Jr Cls; VP Sr Cls; Var Gym; JV Ice Hcky; Capt Var Socr; Im Wt Lftg; High Hon Roll; Hon Roll; Hlth Awd; Phy Ed Awd; Comm.

DE QUATTRO, NICOLE; Quaboag Regional HS; W Brookfield, MA; (Y); 1/77; Am Leg Aux Girls St; Latin Clb; Pres Soph Cls; Capt Bsktbl; Capt Fld Hcky; High Hon Roll; Pres NHS; Pres Schlr; St Schlr; Val; Supt Acadmc Excllnc Awd 86; MA All ST Acadmc Bsktbl Tm 86; Hnrbl Mntn All Am Bsktbl 86; Holy Cross College; Bio.

DE ROSA, TRACY; Maiden HS; Malden, MA; (Y); Church Yth Grp; Girl Scts; Key Clb; Chorus; School Musical; Variety Show; Hon Roll; NHS; Vet.

DE ROSSI, SCOTT S; New Bedford HS; Acushnet, MA; (Y); 12/701; Am Leg Boys St; Church Yth Grp; Science Clb; Stu Cncl; JV Bsktbl; Var Trk; Var Vllybl; Jr NHS; NHS; Pre-Med.

DE RUBEIS, POMPEO; Newton Catholic HS; Newton, MA; (Y); 1/57; Pres Church Yth Grp; Model UN; SADD; Yrbk Ed-Chief; Yrbk Phtg; Yrbk Rptr; Yrbk Sprt Ed; Yrbk Stf; Pres Sec Stu Cncl; High Hon Roll; Chapdelaine Schlrshp 86; Boston Coll.

DE SANTIS, DIANA; Leominster HS; Leominster, MA; (S); 70/320; French Clb; Political Wkr; School Musical; VP Frsh Cls; VP Soph Cls; VP Jr Cls; VP Sr Cls; VP Stu Cncl; Var Bsktbl; Var Sftbl; Bus Adm.

DE SOUZA, REBECCA A; Fairhaven HS; Fairhaven, MA; (Y); 2/166; VP AFS; French Clb; Yrbk Ed-Chief; High Hon Roll; NHS; Ntl Merit Ltr; Pres Schlr; Sal; St Schlr; Math Tm; Bentley Coll Merit Schrlshp 86-87; Brown U Bk Awd 85; Frnch Oral Spkng Cntst 85-86; Bentley Coll; Mgmt.

DE TESO, LORI-ANN; Winchester HS; Winchester, MA; (Y); 111/296; Church Yth Grp; Var Cheerleading; Var Trk; High Hon Roll; Legal.

DE VEAUX, DARRELL E; Arlington HS; Arlington, MA; (Y); Exploring; French Clb; Rep Sr Cls; Im Bsktbl; Im Socr; Im Trk; Lowell U; Law.

DE VITO, ALYSSA; Stoneleigh-Burnham Schl; Greenfield, MA; (Y); GAA; Spanish Clb; Chorus; School Musical; Nwsp Rptr; Ed Lit Mag; Socr; Sftbl; Vllybl; Hon Roll; Wellesley Coll Bk Awd; U Of NH; Comm.

DE VRIES, JEFF; Whitinsville Christian HS; Uxbridge, MA; (Y); Pres Church Yth Grp; Drama Clb; Band; Chorus; School Play; Rep Jr Cls; Rep Stu Cncl; JV Var Bsktbl; Hon Roll; JV Basketball MVP 84; Calvin Coll; Acctng.

DE YOUNG, KELLIE JEANNE; Wilmington HS; Wilmington, MA; (Y); Church Yth Grp; Dance Clb; Drama Clb; French Clb; Ski Clb; SADD; School Play; Stage Crew; JV Socr; Var Swmmng; Nrsng.

DEACON, WILLIAM C; Gardner HS; Gardiner, MA; (Y); 15/144; Boy Scts; Church Yth Grp; Spanish Clb; SADD; Rep Frsh Cls; Rep Soph Cls; Pres Jr Cls; Off Sr Cls; Rep Stu Cncl; Var L Bsktbl; MA Stu Advsry Cncl & Bys ST 85; Stu Repr VP Srch Cmt 85; Jrnlsm.

DEAN, MATTHEW; Central Catholic HS; Lowell, MA; (Y); 80/215; Ski Clb; Im Bsktbl; Hon Roll; U Of Lowell; Bus Manag.

DEAN, MELANIE; Mc Cann Tech; Adams, MA; (Y); SADD; Stu Cncl; JV Var Bsktbl; JV Var Socr; Hon Roll; NHS.

DEANE, SHARON; Northfield Mount Hermon HS; Northfield, MA; (Y); Pres 4-H; Capt Quiz Bowl; Teachers Aide; Varsity Clb; 4-H Awd; Hon Roll; Intnatl 4-H Yth Exchng Ambssdr Swtzrlnd 85; MA Horse Bwl Tm 85; JOAD 85; Agibus.

DEANGELS, TINAMARIE; St Gregorys HS; Hyde Park, MA; (Y); Drama Clb; Nwsp Stf; Yrbk Stf; High Hon Roll; Hon Roll; NHS; Schlrshp Hgh Rnk Cls 83-84; Lesley Coll; Physcl Thrpy.

DEARNESS, ANISSA; Ludlow HS; Ludlow, MA; (Y); Dance Clb; Exploring; French Clb; Hosp Aide; Band; Concert Band; Mrchg Band; Symp Band; Variety Show; Lit Mag; Comm.

DEARY, KIM; Bartlett HS; Webster, MA; (Y); 2/169; Mgr Capt Math Tm; Spanish Clb; Yrbk Stf; Sec Frsh Cls; JV Var High Hon Roll; NHS; Acdmc All-Amrcn 86; Yth Ldrshp Salute 86; Optmtry.

DEBIASI, LORI; Foxborough HS; Foxborough, MA; (Y); 30/235; Ski Clb; Var Cheerleading; Var Gym; Var Mgr(s); Im Socr; JV Var Sftbl; High Hon Roll; Hon Roll; NHS; Mvp JV Sftbll 85.

DECHENE, LAURIE; Bourne HS; Buzzards Bay, MA; (Y); 70/190; Hosp Aide; SADD; Mrchg Band; Nwsp Rptr; Yrbk Stf; L Var Bsktbl; L Var Sftbl; Capt L Vllybl; Model UN; Concert Band; Vlybl Sprtsmnshp Awd 84-85; Bsktbl MVP 85-86; Plymth ST Coll NH; Phy Ed.

DECIE, AL; Newburyport HS; Newburyport, MA; (S); 18/185; VP JA; Trs JCL; Model UN; Band; Jazz Band; Crs Cntry; Hon Roll; NHS; Latin Achvt Awd 84; Band Awds 84; Lawyer.

DECKER, LISA; Burncoat SR HS; Worcester, MA; (Y); 5/238; Pres Church Yth Grp; Dance Clb; VP JA; Pres SADD; Pres Stu Cncl; Elks Awd; Hon Roll; Jr NHS; Trs NHS; Spanish NHS; Williams Coll Bk Awd 85; Holy Cross Coll; Vet.

DECKER, PAMELA; Shepherd Hill Regional HS; Charlton, MA; (Y); Drama Clb; Acpl Chr; Chorus; Madrigals; School Musical; School Play; Variety Show; Yrbk Rptr; Var Socr; High Hon Roll; Charlton All Star MVP Lassie Lgue Sftbl 83-85; Dual Cnty Music Fest Part 83-85; Dist Show Choir 83-84; Emerson Coll; Cnslng.

DECKER, ROBERT; Lenox Memorial HS; Lenoxdale, MA; (Y); Yrbk Stf; Var Bsbl; Var Bsktbl; Socr; Law Enfrcmnt.

DECKER, STEPHEN; Pittsfield HS; Pittsfield, MA; (Y); 40/400; Church Yth Grp; Exploring; Latin Clb; Rep Stu Cncl; Var Trk; High Hon Roll; NHS.

DECKER, TIM; Bartlett HS; Webster, MA; (Y); JA; Math Tm; Scholastic Bowl; Science Clb; Spanish Clb; Chorus; School Play; JV Bsbl; JV Bsktbl; JV Var Ftbl; 1st Pl Spllng Bee 84; Mth Awd 84-85; U MA Amherst; Civil Engrng.

DECUBELLIS, BRIAN; Bishop Feehan HS; Pawtucket, RI; (Y); Band; Chorus; Concert Band; Jazz Band; Mrchg Band; School Musical; School Play; Pres Soph Cls; Hon Roll; Cinematography.

DEE, JOHN; Holyoke Catholic HS; Easthampton, MA; (Y); Debate Tm; Q&S; Ski Clb; SADD; Crs Cntry; Golf; Trk; Hon Roll; Accntng.

DEERING, SHERYL; Blackstone Valley Reg Voc Tech; Upton, MA; (Y); Computer Clb; SADD; Hon Roll; Bus Mgmt.

DEGNAN, SCOTT P; Monson JR SR HS; Monson, MA; (Y); 4/66; Church Yth Grp; Trs French Clb; Mathletes; Yrbk Bus Mgr; Yrbk Rptr; Trs Sec Jr Cls; VP Sr Cls; High Hon Roll; Hon Roll; Trs NHS; Bentley Coll; Bus Admin.

DEGON, JOHN; Holy Name C C HS; Worcester, MA; (Y); Church Yth Grp; SADD; Varsity Clb; Stage Crew; Yrbk Stf; Var Bsbl; Im Bsktbl; Ftbl; Im Wt Lftg; Hon Roll; Bus.

DEGRE, CRAIG; Blackstone Vly Regionl Vo-Tech HS; Bellingham, MA; (Y); VICA; VICA Auto Bdy 3rd Pl Divsnl Cntst, 6th Pl ST Fnls 86; Auto Bdy Repair Tech.

DEGREGORY, CHRISTOPHER; Ludlow HS; Ludlow, MA; (Y); Am Leg Boys St; Pres VP Church Yth Grp; JCL; Band; Variety Show; Stf; Var L Bsbl; Var L Ftbl; High Hon Roll; Hon Roll; Cert Of Hnrb Merit Cum Laude Natl Latn Exam 86; Cert Superior Perfrmnce On NEDT 85; U S Military Acad; Engrng.

DEL GRECO, ADRIANA; Our Lady Of Nazareth Acad; Revere, MA; (Y); #6 In Class; Intnl Clb; Ski Clb; SADD; School Musical; Lit Mag; High Hon Roll; NHS; NEDT Awd; Sec Ntl Hon Soc 86; Sec Impct Clb 85; Chldhd Educ.

DEL TUFO, ROSE T; Dedham HS; Dedham, MA; (S); 8/252; Church Yth Grp; Drama Clb; Pres Service Clb; SADD; Stage Crew; Rep Soph Cls; High Hon Roll; Cmnty Wkr; School Play; Hon Roll; Cum Laude Awd In Latin 85; Ms Teen Pgnt 84; Rlgn Tchr 84-85; Phycsl Thrpst.

DELAMERE, SUZANNE; Mt St Josephs Acad; Boston, MA; (Y); 44/169; Boys Clb Am; Church Yth Grp; JA; Hon Roll; NHS; Boston Coll; Accntng.

DELANDE, CATHY; Danvers HS; Danvers, MA; (Y); 62/300; Church Yth Grp; Science Clb; NHS; Spanish NHS; Awd Churchs Ssr Bsktbll Tm 84; Fshn Merch.

DELANEY, LAURA; Notre Dame Acad; W Boylston, MA; (Y); Capt Crs Cntry; Var Tennis; MA Cmmnwlth Schlrp 86; Centrl MA Conf Tnns All-Star 83-86; Dist E Div Ii Tnns Tm 84-86; U Connecticut; Biol.

DELANO, BRIAN; Walpole SR HS; Walpole, MA; (Y); Computer Clb; Mathletes; Ski Clb; Varsity Clb; Var Stat Golf; Var Stat Ice Hcky; Acctg.

DELAY, TIM; Hingham HS; Hingham, MA; (Y); 65/320; Drama Clb; Band; Concert Band; Mrchg Band; Symp Band; Rep Frsh Cls; Bsbl; Ice Hcky; Socr; Boston Coll Athltc Awd 86; C Croosley Memrl Awd 86; Lincoln Trst Co Hcky Schlrshp 86; Boston Coll; Librl Arts.

DELCORE, HENRY D; Catholic Memorial HS; Dedham, MA; (Y); 2/225; Am Leg Boys St; Church Yth Grp; Computer Clb; JA; Math Clb; Scholastic Bowl; Science Clb; VP Spanish Clb; Nwsp Ed-Chief; Socr; Gen Excllnce; Salutatrn; Georgetown U; Frgn-Svc.

DELEHANTY, THOMAS P; Newbury Prot HS; Newburyport, MA; (Y); Am Leg Boys St; Model UN; Red Cross Aide; ROTC; JV Var Bsbl; JV Bsktbl; Coach Actv; Swmmng; Hon Roll; Phy Ed Awd 86; Close-Up Prog 86; Pys Ftnss Awd; Sci.

DELEIRE, THOMAS C; Phillips Acad; Andover, MA; (Y); Church Yth Grp; Math Clb; JV Bsbl; Bsktbl; Var Golf; JV Socr; Ntl Merit SF.

DELGRECO, MARK; Medford HS; Medford, MA; (Y); 27/452; Red Cross Aide; SADD; Im Bsbl; Im Ftbl; Im Sftbl; Im Vllybl; Hon Roll; NHS; Alg Awd 84; Hnrs Bio Awd 85.

DELL ANNO, CHERIE; Somerville HS; Somerville, MA; (Y); 71/650; Sec Jr Cls; Var Bsktbl; Var Capt Sftbl; Grtr Bstn Leag Div I 1st Strng All Str Ctchr 85; GBL All Str Ctchr MVP GBL 86; Glbe Estrn Ms Div 86; Elem Tchr.

DELLAGATTA, SANDY; Malden HS; Malden, MA; (Y); 3/500; Math Tm; Sec Band; Mrchg Band; Variety Show; Var Fld Hcky; Var Capt Trk; NHS; Zonta Awd Ctznshp & Scholar 86; Natl Engl Merit Awd 86; Lit Soc 85-87; Secndry Ed.

DELLAVALLE, CHRISTINE; Weymouth South HS; S Weymouth, MA; (Y); Drama Clb; School Play; Yrbk Phtg; Yrbk Stf; Rep Sr Cls; Capt Cheerleading; Stu Govt Day Rep 86; U Of MA-AMHERST; Pltcl Sci.

DELLOVO, VICTOR; St Peter Marian HS; Worcester, MA; (Y); 21/180; Church Yth Grp; Computer Clb; SADD; Stage Crew; JV Bsbl; JV Bsktbl; Var Ftbl; Hon Roll; Worcester Poly Tech Inst; Engr.

DELOREY, KELLY; Burlington HS; Burlington, MA; (Y); 20/328; Church Yth Grp; Science Clb; SADD; Yrbk Stf; Bsktbl; Mgr(s); Powder Puff Ftbl; High Hon Roll; Hon Roll; NHS; MA Adv Studies Pgm 86; Med.

DELORIE JR, RALPH C; Malden Catholic HS; Melrose, MA; (Y); 2/185; Computer Clb; Math Tm; Var Capt Swmmng; Im Vllybl; NHS; Ntl Merit Ltr; Sal; Stu Athlt 86; Swmng MVP 85-86; Frnch, Math Awds 86; Stanford U; Pre-Med.

DELVECCHIO, MARIA; Burlington HS; Burlington, MA; (Y); 7/318; Sec Church Yth Grp; Math Tm; Yrbk Stf; Im Bsktbl; Hon Roll; NHS; Blgy.

DEMASTRIE, TINA; Pittsfield HS; Pittsfield, MA; (Y); 5/386; VP JA; Latin Clb; Math Clb; Yrbk Stf; High Hon Roll; NHS; Slvr Mdl Natl Lat Exam 85-86; Hgh Scr Mth Olympd Test Awd 85; Hgh Scr New England Mth Lg Tests 85-86.

DEMBLING, JON; Haverhill HS; Bradford, MA; (Y); 22/416; Political Wkr; School Play; Variety Show; Rptr Nwsp Rptr; Ed Yrbk Ed-Chief; NHS; Ntl Merit Ltr; Hampshire Coll; Writer.

DEMELLO IV, ANTONE C; New Bedford HS; Middleboro, MA; (Y); Art Clb; Drama Clb; Political Wkr; School Musical; School Play; Yrbk Stf; Vllybl; French Hon Soc; Hon Roll; Acdmc Achvt Awd 84; Frnch Hgh Hon Awd 85; Bus Admn.

DEMELO, LINDA; B M C Durfee HS; Fall River, MA; (Y); Hon Roll; NHS; Comp Sci.

DEMEO, JEAN; Waltham HS; Boston, MA; (Y); Church Yth Grp; Concert Band; Mrchg Band; Socr; Trk; Twrlr; Hon Roll; NHS; Music Awd 84; Italian Clb 85-86; Physcl Thrpy.

DEMERSKI, TINA L; Cathedral HS; W Springfield, MA; (Y); 89/557; Socr; Timer; Trk; Hon Roll; Comp Tchnlgy.

DEMOGENES, STEPHANIE; Concord Carlisle HS; Carlisle, MA; (Y); DECA; 4-H; Varsity Clb; Variety Show; Capt Var Sftbl; Hon Roll; Phy Ed Awd 84-85; Law.

DEMOS, DEAN; Natick HS; Natick, MA; (Y); 85/425; Sec Church Yth Grp; JA; Church Choir; Lit Mag; Hon Roll; Prfct Atten Awd; Bus Awd For Exceptional Grades Notetaking 85; Bus Awd Straight As Acctng I 86; Business Mgr.

DEMPSEY, APRIL; North Quincy HS; N Quincy, MA; (Y); Church Yth Grp; Dance Clb.

DEN BOGGENDE, JERRY; Marlboro HS; Marlboro, MA; (Y); Boys Clb Am; Civic Clb; SADD; Varsity Clb; L Bsktbl; Var Ftbl; L Var Trk; Hon Roll; Bus Admin.

DENAPOLI, JAN; Algonquin R HS; Southboro, MA; (Y); 30/200; Church Yth Grp; Chorus; School Musical; Co-Capt Cheerleading; Co-Capt Swmmng; Cit Awd; Hon Roll; Dickinson Coll.

DENARDO, GINA; B M C Durfee HS; Fall River, MA; (Y); Bus.

DENEEN, J MICHAEL; Arlington HS; Waltham, MA; (Y); 10/150; SADD; JV Bsbl; Im Capt Bsktbl; Var Trk; Hon Roll; NHS; Bus Mgmt.

DENHAM, MARK; Leicester HS; Leicester, MA; (S); 10/102; Ski Clb; Trk; Hnr Rll; Leicester Athl Ltr Awd Vrsty Trck; Nichols Coll MA; Bus Adm.

DENIS, BRUCE; Leominster HS; Leominster, MA; (Y); 3/305; Am Leg Boys St; Pres Chess Clb; Trs Church Yth Grp; Math Tm; Stu Cncl; High Hon Roll; NHS; St Schlr; Gen Rad Fndtn Schlrshp 86; Excllence In Math At LHA 84-86; Worcester Polytch Inst; Chem En.

DENNEN, DONNA; Taunton HS; Taunton, MA; (Y); Church Yth Grp; Cmnty Wkr; Drama Clb; FBLA; Latin Clb; Ski Clb; Teachers Aide; Varsity Clb; Var Crs Cntry; Trk; Cert/Cntry 21 Typwrtng Credit 84; Peer Alchl Ed Cert 84; Reed-N-Barton Schlrshp 86; Brfgwtr ST Coll; Cmnctns Dsrdr.

DENNER, ALEXANDER; St John Prep; Lynn, MA; (Y); 15/260; Math Clb; Math Tm; Science Clb; Hon Roll; Ntl Merit Ltr; Spanish NHS; Camera Clb; Church Yth Grp; Computer Clb; JA; Engrng.

DENNEY, SHARON; Gardner HS; Gardner, MA; (Y); 18/162; GAA; Spanish Clb; Teachers Aide; JV Var Bsktbl; Var Swmmng; Var Trk; Lib Arts.

DENSMORE, WILLIAM E; Triton Regional HS; Rowley, MA; (Y); 22/191; Band; Chorus; Concert Band; Jazz Band; Mrchg Band; Pep Band; School Musical; School Play; Variety Show; Var Capt Trk; N TX ST U; Jazz.

DEPINA, MARIA; Maria A HS; Boston, MA; (Y); 2/315; Office Aide; School Play; Yrbk Ed-Chief; Yrbk Rptr; Yrbk Stf; Stu Cncl; Hon Roll; Pres NHS; Prfct Atten Awd; Commnwlth Schlrshp 86; Outstndng Achvt Math 86; Sci & Engr Freedom House Awd 86; Wellesley Coll; Sci.

DEPLEDGE, JANE; Concord Carlisle HS; Concord, MA; (Y); Chess Clb; Lit Mag; High Hon Roll; Brown U Bk Awd 86.

DEPPERT, JODI; Milford HS; Milford, MA; (Y); Church Yth Grp; Cmnty Wkr; FNA; Hosp Aide; SADD; Band; Capt Color Guard; Flag Corp; Yrbk Ed-Chief; Var Trk; Margret T Omalley Schlrshp, Claire Winkler Stone Schlrshp 86; Rhode Island Coll; Nrsng.

DEPUTAT, DANIELLE; Saugus HS; Saugus, MA; (Y); 63/292; Cmnty Wkr; Pres VP JA; SADD; Orch; Lit Mag; JR Achvrs Assn Eastern MA 84-86; Abraham Pincisss Mem Schlrshp 86; ROJAC NAJAC Regnl Natl Conf 85; Salem ST Coll; Bus Mgmt.

DERGARABEDIAN, SANDRA; Gr Lowell Regional Voc-Tech Schl; Lowell, MA; (Y); Stu Cncl; Hon Roll; NCTE Awd; Emerson Coll; Theater.

DEROCHE, DEANNA; Haverhill HS; Haverhill, MA; (Y); 27/417; Latin Clb; SADD; Sec Jr Cls; Sec Sr Cls; Im Bsktbl; Powder Puff Ftbl; Var Capt Swmmng; Var Capt Tennis; High Hon Roll; Hon Roll; Eclgy Clb Offcr; Cum Laude Ntl Latin Exam Hnr 86; Sprtsmnshp Awd; Coaches Awd; Psych.

DEROIAN, DEBBIE; Haverhill HS; Haverhill, MA; (Y); 13/423; Church Yth Grp; Key Clb; Latin Clb; Scholastic Bowl; Spanish Clb; SADD; School Play; Nwsp Rptr; Yrbk Rptr; Hon Roll.

DERR, KATHLEEN A; Dighton-Rehoboth Regional HS; Rehoboth, MA; (Y); 15/235; Art Clb; Church Yth Grp; Pres French Clb; Band; Chorus; Concert Band; Mrchg Band; Fld Hcky; Hon Roll; NHS; USAF; Illust Art.

DES MARAIS, CHRISTOPHER P; Haverhill HS; Haverhill, MA; (Y); 40/425; Art Clb; Ski Clb; Yrbk Stf; Hon Roll; Boston Glob Art Awd Gold Key Wnnr 86; NY Schl Visual Arts; Comm Art.

DESFORGE, JOHN C; Wilmington HS; Wilmington, MA; (Y); Am Leg Boys St; School Play; Yrbk Stf; VP Frsh Cls; VP Soph Cls; VP Jr Cls; VP Sr Cls; Var L Ftbl; Capt Var Trk; Hon Roll; Paul Revere Bowl Wnnr 86; Rcvd Cnvrs Schlrshp 86; MVP In Winter Trck 85; Westfield ST Coll; Pre-Law.

DESHAIES, LORI; Lawrence HS; Lawrence, MA; (Y); SADD; Pres Band; Chorus; Capt Color Guard; Concert Band; Drm & Bgl; Mrchg Band; Hon Roll; Amer Mscl Fndtn Bnd Awd 83; Robert E Sault Memrl Schlrshp 86; Robert E Sault Bnd Awd 86; Middlesex CC; Dntl Hygn.

DESILETS, CHRISTINE; Agawam SR HS; Feeding Hills, MA; (Y); AFS; Band; Concert Band; Mrchg Band; Orch; Pep Band; School Musical; Var Fld Hcky; JV Sftbl; Var Capt Swmmng; Bio.

DESILETS, TERESA; King Philip Regional HS; Holliston, MA; (Y); 73/200; Art Clb; Band; Concert Band; Mrchg Band; Vllybl; Hon Roll; Mst Indstrious Math Stu 83; Mass Bay CC; Med.

DESINCE, MAGALIE; St Gregory HS; Providence, RI; (Y); 4/99; Church Yth Grp; Drama Clb; Temple Yth Grp; Chorus; Pres Church Choir; Nwsp Ed-Chief; Rep Stu Cncl; Hon Roll; NHS; Pres Schlr; Boston U; Psych.

DESJARDINS-CANADA, PAMELA; N Brookfield HS; N Brookfield, MA; (Y); 10/40; Church Yth Grp; Cmnty Wkr; Drama Clb; Hosp Aide; Math Clb; Math Tm; Office Aide; Pres Spanish Clb; Pres SADD; Band; Greater Worcester Communty Found Schlrshp 86; Anna Maria Coll; Lib Arts.

DESMARAIS, ANNE NICOLE; Somerset HS; Somerset, MA; (Y); 80/320; Cmnty Wkr; Teachers Aide; School Musical; Nwsp Rptr; Rep Stu Cncl; Wt Lftg; Elks Awd; High Hon Roll; SADD; Nwsp Stf; Edythe Merle Cook Schlrshp 86; Bridgewtr ST Coll; Math Educ.

DESMARAIS, DARREN; Northampton HS; Leeds, MA; (Y); 73/253; Var L Bsbl; Var L Bsktbl; Var L Socr; Hon Roll; Bridgewater ST; Sprts Med.

DESMARAIS, MICHAEL; Bishop Feehen HS; Rumford, RI; (Y); VP Church Yth Grp; Political Wkr; Ski Clb; Rep Jr Cls; VP Sr Cls; JV Crs Cntry; Var Capt Tennis.

DESMARAIS, ROBERT; Haverhill HS; Haverhill, MA; (Y); 17/400; French Clb; Yrbk Phtg; Im Crs Cntry; Var L Swmmng; Var Trk; Im Wt Lftg; High Hon Roll; NHS; Ntl Merit Schol.

DESMOND JR, EDWARD A; St Johns Prep Schl; Beverly, MA; (Y); Red Cross Aide; Sr Schlr 86; Beverly Hosp Med Schlrshp 86; U Of VT; Bio Sci.

DESMOND, JENNIFER; Lowell HS; Lowell, MA; (Y); 75/526; Church Yth Grp; Hosp Aide; JCL; Science Clb; Spanish Clb; Variety Show; Var Capt Cheerleading; Hon Roll; Miss MA Am Coed ST Semi-Finslst 85; Pub Svc Teenager Of Yr Finslt 86; Lowell HS JR Clss Hmcmng Qn; Medical.

DESORCY, DONNA; New Bedford HS; New Bedford, MA; (Y); Drama Clb; Exploring; Science Clb; Chorus; Tennis; Vllybl; U Mass Amhrst; Vet Med.

DESOURDY, SANDRA; Worcester North HS; Worcester, MA; (Y); 23/208; Cmnty Wkr; Library Aide; Pep Clb; Varsity Clb; Stu Cncl; Var Bsktbl; Var Capt Socr; Im Swmmng; Var Tennis; 1st Pl J W Vets 85; Clark U; Frgn Lang.

DESOUSA, ESTHER; Gardner HS; Gardner, MA; (Y); Spanish Clb; SADD; Chorus; School Play; Stage Crew; Variety Show; Nwsp Stf; Lit Mag; Trs Sr Cls; Var Fld Hcky; Stu Govt Dy Dlgt 86; Stu Govt Schlrshp 86; Stone Fnd Schlrshp 86; PA ST U; Intl Rltns.

DESPER, HELEN; King Philip Regional HS; Plainville, MA; (Y); Cmnty Wkr; Office Aide; SADD; Yrbk Stf; Hon Roll; NHS; Excllnce Typg Awd 86.

DESROCHERS, CHRISTINE; North Middlesex Regional HS; Pepperell, MA; (Y); JV Tennis; High Hon Roll; Hon Roll; Elem Tchr.

DESROCHERS, LISA; Chicopee Comprehensive HS; Chicopee, MA; (Y); 11/260; Spanish Clb; Var Capt Bsktbl; Powder Puff Ftbl; Var L Socr; Var L Sftbl; Hon Roll; NHS; Coachs Awd Vrsty Sccr 85; MVP Awd JV Bsktbl 84-85; MVP JV Sftbl 84; Nrsg.

DESROSIERS, ROBIN; B M C Durfee HS; Fall River, MA; (Y); 16/680; Church Yth Grp; Girl Scts; Bsktbl; Sftbl; Swmmng; Vllybl; High Hon Roll; Hon Roll; NHS; Yrbk Stf; Bus.

DESROSIERS, SIMONE; Taunton HS; East Taunton, MA; (Y); Political Wkr; Ski Clb; Temple Yth Grp; Band; Concert Band; Mrchg Band; Wrld Affairs Clb-Pres 86; Intl Order Rnbw Grls Ofc 85-86; Prjct Cntmprry Comp Advncd Studies Pgm 84; Malprctc Lawyer.

DESTREMPES, CHARLES; Northbridge JR SR HS; Whitinsville, MA; (Y); 2/143; Am Leg Boys St; Chess Clb; Latin Clb; School Play; Nwsp Stf; Rep Frsh Cls; Rep Soph Cls; JV Socr; High Hon Roll; JETS Awd; Comp Sci Dept Awd 86; Blckstn Vly Educ Fndtn 86-89; Worcester Polytech; Elec Engr.

DESY, MARGARET; Holy Name CC HS; Worcester, MA; (Y); 19/257; Art Clb; JA; Stage Crew; Nwsp Stf; Rohde Island Schl Of Dsgn Bk Awd 86; Parsons Schl Of Design.

DETORA, DANIEL; Central Catholic HS; N Andover, MA; (Y); 105/253; Rep Frsh Cls; Var L Bsbl; Var L Ftbl; Var Capt Wrstlng; Hon Roll; Bus.

DEVEAU, SEAN; Deerfield Acad; Branford, CT; (Y); Computer Clb; French Clb; German Clb; Model UN; Radio Clb; Spanish Clb; School Play; Lit Mag; VP Capt Swmmng; Hon Roll; All Amer Swmr 85 & 86; Pdgn Awd 86; Bucknell U.

DEVEAUX, JENNIFER; Waltham HS; Waltham, MA; (Y); Aud/Vis; Church Yth Grp; 4-H; French Clb; JCL; Science Clb; JV Bsktbl; JV Socr; Hon Roll; Jr NHS; Smith Coll Bk Awd 86; Wheelock Coll; Elem Ed.

DEVEREAUX, LISA; Burlington HS; Burlington, MA; (Y); 63/314; Sec OEA; Science Clb; Yrbk Stf; Im Cheerleading; Var JV Mgr(s); Var Capt Socr; Hon Roll; Sec.

DEVINE, AMY; Hopkins Acad; Hadley, MA; (Y); French Clb; Yrbk Stf; Stu Cncl; Socr; Hon Roll; NHS; Harvard Bk Prz 86; Excel Frnch 84-86; Intl Bus.

DEVINE JR, JOSEPH M; Arlington SR HS; Arlington, MA; (Y); 29/397; Pres Debate Tm; Latin Clb; Quiz Bowl; Scholastic Bowl; Orch; Nwsp Rptr; Nwsp Stf; Rep Stu Cncl; Var L Socr; Ntl Merit SF; Econ.

DEVINE, KEVIN; Seekonk HS; Seekonk, MA; (Y); Church Yth Grp; Jazz Band; Yrbk Stf; Var L Swmmng; Hon Roll; NHS; Spanish NHS; Georgetown U; Psych.

DEVINE, ROBERT IAN; North HS; Worcester, MA; (Y); 1/208; Boys Clb Am; Stu Cncl; High Hon Roll; NHS; Ntl Merit Schol; Hiatt Schlrshp, Worc Telegrams/Gazette Stu Achvr 86; Harvard.

DEVLIN, KELLY; Ware HS; Ware, MA; (Y); 10/115; Cmnty Wkr; French Clb; Hosp Aide; Yrbk Stf; Lit Mag; High Hon Roll; Hon Roll; Pres Schlr; Mry Ln Hosp Axlry Schlrshp 86; American Intl Coll; Optmtry.

DEWALD, NICOLE M; Cardinal Spellman HS; Rockland, MA; (Y); 1/208; Sec SADD; School Musical; Lit Mag; NHS; Ntl Merit Ltr; Val; Voice Dem Awd; Library Aide; 1st Pl Schl Sci Fair 85-86; Hon Ment Regnl Sci Fair 86; Exhbtd MA ST Sci Fair 86.

DHIMITRI, KRISTINA; Lynn Classical HS; Lynn, MA; (Y); 18/180; Chess Clb; French Clb; Var Capt Cheerleading; Hon Roll; NHS.

DI BARTOLO, JOHN; Westbridge HS; Medford, MA; (S); 1/14; Art Clb; Church Choir; School Play; Nwsp Rptr; Yrbk Stf; JV Bsbl; Var Crs Cntry; Var Tennis; High Hon Roll; NHS; Math, Sci & Hmnts Awds 84-85; Schlstc Awd 84.

DI BARTOLOMEO, ISABELLA; St Patrick HS; Watertown, MA; (S); 1/47; Cmnty Wkr; Yrbk Stf; Rep Jr Cls; Rep Stu Cncl; Mgr(s); High Hon Roll; NHS; Prfct Atten Awd; Acad All Amer 83-86; Spnsh Awd 83 & 85; Soclgy Awd 84; Simmons Coll; Phys Ther.

DI BENEDETTO, MARY; B M C Durfee HS; Fall River, MA; (Y); French Clb; Hon Roll; NHS; Southeastern MA U.

DI BLASI, JAMES; North Reading HS; N Reading, MA; (Y); Rep Frsh Cls; Sec VP Stu Cncl; Im JV Bsbl; Im JV Bsktbl; Im Wt Lftg; High Hon Roll; Boston U; Lib Arts.

DI CECCA, LOUIS V; Medford HS; Medford, MA; (Y); 67/409; Hon Roll; Life Sci Awd 84; Bus Mgmt.

DI CICCO, RENE; Boston Latin HS; E Boston, MA; (Y); French Clb; JA; Library Aide; Pep Clb; SADD; School Play; Class Lang.

DI DONATO, PAMELA; Shepherd Hill Regional HS; Dudley, MA; (Y); Red Cross Aide; Band; Rep Sec Stu Cncl; VP Gym; Elks Awd; High Hon Roll; NHS; Rotary Awd; Acad All Amer 86; Acad Excllnce Cert 83-86; NE Regnl Gym Champnshps Comptr 84; Psych.

DI FIORE, ERNEST; Methuen HS; Methuen, MA; (Y); SADD; Teachers Aide; Var L Ftbl; Var L Trk; Var L Wrstlng; Norwich U; Phys Ed.

DI GIACOMO, JULIE; Medford HS; Medford, MA; (Y); 6/448; Church Yth Grp; Drama Clb; Math Tm; Ski Clb; SADD; Yrbk Ed-Chief; Stu Cncl; Cheerleading; High Hon Roll; Mu Alp Tht; Lions Clb Awd; Grls ST; Tufts U; Med.

DI GIORGIO, CARLA; Our Lady Of Nazareth Acad; Reading, MA; (Y); Pres Art Clb; Dance Clb; English Clb; Intnl Clb; VP Science Clb; School Musical; Crs Cntry; Exc In Spnsh III,Lrn Spada Schl Of Dance 5 Yr Awd & Cert For Ntl Spnsh Exam 86; Fash Inst Of Tech; Fash Merch.

DI LULLO, DONNA; Agawam HS; Agawam, MA; (Y); 3/320; Yrbk Stf; Stat Ftbl; Cit Awd; NHS; Spanish NHS; St Schlr; Frgn Lang Clb; Brwn Bk Awd; Coll Of Holy Cross; Chem.

DI MARCO, DIANE; Malden HS; Malden, MA; (Y); 28/477; Drama Clb; Key Clb; Trs SADD; Variety Show; Trs Soph Cls; Trs Jr Cls; Trs Sr Cls; Var L Bsktbl; Var Fld Hcky; Capt JV Sftbl; Havard Book Awd 85; Attnnd Ldrshp Seminar 84; Bridgewater ST; Theatre.

DI MARE, STEPHEN; Hudson HS; Hudson, MA; (Y); 5/139; Drama Clb; Math Clb; Math Tm; Chorus; Yrbk Stf; Golf; Var Ice Hcky; Bausch & Lomb Sci Awd; NHS; 2nd Pl ST Math Team 86; Acad All Am 86; Stu Yr Elks Awd 86; Rensselaer Poly Tech Inst; Sci.

DI MASCIO, KRISTEN; Duxbury HS; Duxbury, MA; (Y); 110/276; AFS; Drama Clb; Hosp Aide; PAVAS; Spanish Clb; Thesps; School Play; Stage Crew; Swing Chorus; Nwsp Stf; Actng Awd Spring Fest Plays 85; Eben Briggs Am Leg Scholar 86; Korean/Vietnam War Mem Designr 85-86; Emerson Coll; Cmmnctns.

DI NAPOLI, LEAH; Braintree HS; Braintree, MA; (Y); 13/442; Am Leg Aux Girls St; Nwsp Rptr; Nwsp Stf; Yrbk Stf; High Hon Roll; NHS; Prfct Atten Awd; Spanish NHS; Cmmnctns.

DI PALERMO, JOSEPH; Arlington HS; Arlington, MA; (Y); Church Yth Grp; Intnl Clb; Church Choir; High Hon Roll; NHS.

DI PAOLO, LISA; Woburn HS; Woburn, MA; (S); 144/454; French Clb; Leo Clb; SADD; Off Stu Cncl; Cheerleading; Hon Roll; Stu Cncl Awd 86; Hnr Rll; Mktg.

DI PERNA, LAUREN; Somerville HS; Somerville, MA; (Y); 8/500; Hosp Aide; Ski Clb; Var Trk; NHS; Somerville Ladies Lodge 1424 Order Sons Italy 86; Pres Awd Acad Achvt 86; Tufts U; Pre-Med.

DI PIETRANTONIO, EMILIA; Somerville HS; Somerville, MA; (Y); 79/600; Hon Roll; Trphy Spellng Bee 81; Plaque Typng Achvt 83; Accptnc Mdrn Mss Tn Schlrshp Prgm 85; Burdett Bus Schl; Lgl Secr.

DI RUSSO, ANTHONY S; Leominster HS; Leominster, MA; (Y); Am Leg Boys St; Art Clb; SADD; School Play; Stage Crew; Yrbk Stf; Hon Roll; U MA.

DI SANO, DANIEL; Malden HS; Malden, MA; (Y); 2/470; Key Clb; Capt Math Tm; Quiz Bowl; Rep Soph Cls; Rep Jr Cls; VP Sr Cls; Capt Tennis; Kiwanis Awd; NHS; Sal; Brown U Bk Awd 85; Rotary Citizens Schlr 86; GBL All Star Tennis Tm 85; Clark U; Bus Mngmnt.

DI TOMASSO, JOHN C; Northampton HS; Northampton, MA; (Y); 22/223; Am Leg Boys St; Crs Cntry; Swmmng; Trk; High Hon Roll; NHS; Nwspr Boy Carrier Mnth 84; MIT; Mech Engrng.

DIALESSI, GINA; Agawam HS; Agawam, MA; (Y); 13/350; French Clb; Trs JCL; Church Choir; Yrbk Ed-Chief; Var Capt Cheerleading; Im Socr; High Hon Roll; NHS; Chrldng Acadmc Awd 85; Acadmc All Am Awd 85; U Of CT; Phrmcy.

DIATCHENKO, DIMITRI; Newton North HS; Newtonville, MA; (Y); Am Leg Boys St; FFA; Natl Beta Clb; Ftbl; Gym; Trk; Wt Lftg; Art Clb; Variety Show; All Lge Lnbckr-All Div I Offnsv Lineman 85-86; U PA; Aerosp.

DIAZ, VILMA; North HS; Worcester, MA; (Y); Church Yth Grp; Cmnty Wkr; Chorus; Church Choir; Rep Stu Cncl; JV Bsktbl; Hon Roll; Achvt Awd; Boston U; Bus Mgt.

DIBONA, ANNEMARIE; Brockton HS; Brockton, MA; (Y); 42/882; Spanish Clb; Band; Concert Band; Mrchg Band; Symp Band; High Hon Roll; Hon Roll; Pres Schlr; Silv Mdl Latin Achvt 83-84; Goddard Hosp Schl; Radlgc Tech.

DIBRINDISI, ERIC; Northampton HS; Florence, MA; (Y); 85/253; Boy Scts; Church Yth Grp; JV Swmmng; God Cntry Awd; U Of MA.

DICHIAPPARI, MARIA; Winchester HS; Winchester, MA; (Y); French Clb; Hosp Aide; Band; Mrchg Band; Yrbk Stf; High Hon Roll; Hon Roll; Vlntr Svc Awd; Bllt Dncng Awd; Band Awd.

DICKERSON, SONYA; Melroge SR HS; Boston, MA; (Y); Drama Clb; Hosp Aide; Spanish Clb; SADD; Varsity Clb; Nwsp Rptr; Var JV Bsktbl; Var JV Fld Hcky; Var L Trk; Spanish NHS; UNH; Lbrl Arts.

DICKINSON, KELLY; Frontier Regional HS; Sunderland, MA; (Y); 20/100; GAA; Latin Clb; Nwsp Rptr; Trk; Hon Roll; NHS; Jrnlsm.

DICOLOGERO, ANTHONY; Saugus HS; Saugus, MA; (Y); Church Yth Grp; Cmnty Wkr; Ed Lit Mag; Stu Cncl; JV Ftbl; Var Wrstlng; High Hon Roll; Hon Roll; NHS; Voice Dem Awd.

DICORCIA, KATHLEEN; Old Rochester Regional HS; Rochester, MA; (Y); Cmnty Wkr; Office Aide; Ski Clb; Yrbk Stf; Rep Soph Cls; Rep Jr Cls; Var Cheerleading; Var Sftbl; Hon Roll; Voice Dem Awd; Otstandng Spratan 84; Pres Ftnss Awd 86; Tri-Town Dllrs Schrls Schlrshp 86; Rutgers U; Bio-Chem.

DIDIERJEAN, SHERRY; Chicopee Comprehensive HS; Chicopee, MA; (Y); 11/245; Girl Scts; Hosp Aide; Spanish Clb; Yrbk Stf; Hon Roll; Jr NHS; NHS; U Of MA; Nrsng.

DIEDRICH, FREDERICK J; Lincoln-Sudbury Regional HS; Sudbury, MA; (Y); Key Clb; Chorus; Concert Band; Jazz Band; JV Trk; Director Prize Music 86; Hamilton Coll.

DIETCH, DANIEL; Ipswich HS; Ipswich, MA; (Y); Cmnty Wkr; French Clb; Ski Clb; SADD; Temple Yth Grp; Variety Show; Yrbk Stf; Off Frsh Cls; Off Soph Cls; Off Jr Cls; Schl Hnr Awd For Schlrshp & Actng 84-86; Marine Engrng.

DIETERLE, SUSAN; Bishop Feehan HS; Attleboro, MA; (Y); 105/250; JV Im Bsktbl; JV Crs Cntry; JV Var Sftbl; JV Var Vllybl; Hon Roll; Engl,Am Hist Awd 83-85.

DIGAN, STACEY ANN; Dennis-Yarmouth Regional HS; S Yarmouth, MA; (Y); 11/288; VP German Clb; Intnl Clb; Math Tm; Sec Soph Cls; Stu Cncl; JV Bsktbl; JV Sftbl; Sec NHS; Pres Schlr; Outstndg Prfrmnce Awd Ger 86; Outstndg Prfrmnce Awd Phys Ed 86; Mt Holyoke Coll; Ger.

DIGGIN, JENNIFER; Braintree HS; Braintree, MA; (Y); 26/440; Var Trk; Hon Roll; Soc Stu Awd Braintree Hist Soc 85.

DIGOVANNI, AMY; Melrose HS; Boston, MA; (Y); Pep Clb; Spanish Clb; Yrbk Ed-Chief; Var L Trk; U ; Nh; Vtrnrn.

DIGREGORIO, CARLA; Milford HS; Milford, MA; (Y); Church Yth Grp; Pep Clb; Teachers Aide; JV Vllybl; Bus Mgmt.

DILISIO, DANA; Swampscott HS; Swampscott, MA; (Y); 47/216; Church Yth Grp; Band; Chorus; Church Choir; Concert Band; Drm Mjr(t); Jazz Band; Mrchg Band; Orch; Swing Chorus; NCC Indvdl Glf Chmp 84-86; NEC Tm Chmpns 83-86; Cls 1950 Schlrshp 85-86; Providence Coll; Finance.

DILLINGHAM, STEVEN G; Burlington HS; Burlington, MA; (Y); 155/316; VP JA; Math Tm; Var L Ftbl; JV Lcrss; Var L Wrstlng; Wrcstr Polytech Inst; Engrng.

DILLON, DAWN; Billerica Memorial HS; Billerica, MA; (Y); 15/430; Spanish Clb; Yrbk Stf; Rep Frsh Cls; Rep Soph Cls; Rep Jr Cls; Rep Sr Cls; Powder Puff Ftbl; High Hon Roll; Hon Roll; Jr NHS; Teen Of Mnth Bill Elks Clb 86; Pres Awd 86; Frgn Lang Awd 86; Emmanuel Coll; Bus Mgmt.

DILLON, MAUREEN; Cardinal Spellman HS; Brockton, MA; (Y); 8/209; SADD; High Hon Roll; NHS; Fren II Awd 85-86; Law.

DILLON, TRACE; Concord-Carlisle Regional HS; Carlisle, MA; (Y); Radio Clb; Rep Stu Cncl; Ice Hcky; JV Tennis; Hon Roll; Bus Dept Awd Accntng Awd 86.

DILORENZO, RENATO; Lawrence Acad; Westford, MA; (Y); VP Chess Clb; Cmnty Wkr; Ski Clb; Nwsp Stf; Harvard Model Congress 86; Rochester Inst Tech; Mech Engr.

DIMIDJIAN, LISA; Mount St Joseph Acad; Waltham, MA; (Y); 12/169; Art Clb; Church Yth Grp; Drama Clb; French Clb; Spanish Clb; School Musical; Hon Roll; Jr NHS; NHS; Ntl Sco Studies Olympiad World Hist Cntst 84.

DIMUZIO, ANGELA; Rockland HS; Rockland, MA; (Y); 52/252; Nwsp Ed-Chief; Yrbk Sprt Ed; Bsktbl; Im Coach Actv; Var L Trk; Cit Awd; Hon Roll; Bsktbl Coaching Schlrshp 86; ST Acadmc Schlrshp 86; Nichols Coll; Accntnt.

DINDY, JESSICA; North Quincy HS; Quincy, MA; (Y); Church Yth Grp; Dance Clb; Hosp Aide; JA; Trs Latin Clb; Band; Concert Band; Mrchg Band; High Hon Roll; NHS; Natl Frgn Lang Hnr Soc Latn 86; Holy Cross Clg.

DINEEN, MAUREEN; Lynn Classical HS; Lynn, MA; (Y); 38/174; Capt Math Tm; Science Clb; Yrbk Ed-Chief; Stu Cncl; Bausch & Lomb Sci Awd; Hon Roll; Jr NHS; Prfct Atten Awd; Var Capt Powder Puff Ftbl; Var Socr; Sci Hnr Leag; Advsr Frshmn Cls; Suffolk; Law.

DINGWELL, SUZETTE B; South Lancaster Acad; Clinton, MA; (S); Church Yth Grp; Cmnty Wkr; Church Choir; VP Jr Cls; Sec Sr Cls; High Hon Roll; Hon Roll; NHS; Southern Coll TN.

DINITTO, JENNIFER; Melrose HS; Melrose, MA; (Y); Hosp Aide; Pep Clb; Spanish Clb; SADD; Trk.

DIOGO, LISA; Bishop Feehan HS; Attlebro, MA; (Y); Chorus; Trk; High Hon Roll; Hon Roll; Bio L-I Awd; Engl L-I Awd; Bus Manag.

DIOHEP, TRACEY; Bishop Feehan HS; Cumberland, RI; (Y); JCL; Latin Clb; Sec Library Aide; Chorus; Rep Frsh Cls; Rep Soph Cls; Rep Stu Cncl; Trk; Elem Educ.

DION, JOELLE; Agawam HS; Feeding Hls, MA; (Y); 80/345; AFS; Cmnty Wkr; GAA; Chorus; Capt Bsktbl; Tennis; Bd Of Rltrs Schlrshp 86; Rsry Altr Soc Schlrshp 86; Edtr Layout Staff Yrbk 86; Western New England Coll.

DION, KRISTEN M; Burlington HS; Burlington, MA; (Y); 18/314; Math Tm; Sec SADD; Chorus; Mrchg Band; Yrbk Stf; Rep Stu Cncl; Sftbl; Capt Twrlr; Hon Roll; NHS; Hstry Awd 84; Psych.

DION, MICHELLE; St Peter-Marian C C HS; Sterling Junction, MA; (Y); 1/175; Camera Clb; Drama Clb; School Musical; School Play; Yrbk Phtg; High Hon Roll; NHS; Ntl Merit Ltr; Val; Carl S Ell Schlrshp 86; Hghst Acadmc Awd Math 86; Nrthestrn U; Chem Engr.

DIONNE, MICHELE M; Needham HS; Needham, MA; (Y); 40/342; Spanish Clb; SADD; Hon Roll; Cert Of Merit Math Olympd 85; SE MA U; Engrg.

DIPACE, TRICIA; Belmont HS; Belmont, MA; (Y); 24/330; Church Yth Grp; Chorus; Nwsp Stf; Bsktbl; Socr; Var JV Sftbl; Hon Roll; NHS; Peer Ldrshp 83-86.

DIPASQUALE, ANNE; Phillips Acad; Dothan, AL; (Y); Sec Debate Tm; French Clb; Math Tm; Chorus; Nwsp Rptr; JV Ice Hcky; Hon Roll; Jr NHS; NHS; Means Essay Prise 86; Supr Awd Frnch 85; Hustler Awd Chem 85; Sci.

DIPIERO, SUZANNE; Braintree HS; Btaintree, MA; (Y); 58/442; Church Yth Grp; SADD; Pres Band; Jazz Band; Orch; Nwsp Rptr; Rep Frsh Cls; Rep Soph Cls; Rep Jr Cls; Rep Sr Cls; Yth Of Amer Eur Concrt Tour 86; Intl Rltns.

DISQUE, ERIC J; Belchertown HS; Belchertown, MA; (Y); Am Leg Boys St; Church Yth Grp; Rep Jr Cls; Rep Sr Cls; JV Bsbl; Hon Roll; Oriole Scholar 86; Pol Sci.

DISTLER, ALICIA; Lincoln-Sudbury RHS; Sudbury, MA; (Y); Orch; Nwsp Bus Mgr; Ed Lit Mag; Rep Soph Cls; Rep Stu Cncl; Var L Fld Hcky; Var Trk.

DITTRICH, JEAN; Plymouth-Carver HS; Plymouth, MA; (S); 108/600; Church Yth Grp; Band; Concert Band; Jazz Band; Mrchg Band; Condctrs Awd 80-81; Outstndng Muscn Awd 81-82; Band Hnrs 82-83 & 83-84; Music Ed.

DIXON, KRISTI; Northfield Mt Hermon HS; Chatham, MA; (Y); Pep Clb; Radio Clb; Chorus; Nwsp Phtg; Nwsp Rptr; Nwsp Sprt Ed; Yrbk Stf; Capt L Bsktbl; Trk; Hon Roll; Stu Ldrshp 86; Mrqtt U; Jrnlsm.

DIXON, MICHAEL; Austin Prep; Melrose, MA; (Y); 26/124; Boy Scts; Exploring; Latin Clb; Political Wkr; Bsktbl; Trk; Hon Roll; Lwyr.

DOANE, KAREN; Classical HS; Lynn, MA; (Y); 67/280; Chess Clb; French Clb; Office Aide; Varsity Clb; Cheerleading; Powder Puff Ftbl; Hon Roll.

DOANE, TIM; Medway HS; Medway, MA; (Y); 26/140; Church Yth Grp; Var Capt Ftbl; Var Capt Tennis; Im Vllybl; Im Wt Lftg; Bus.

DOBBYN, DEBRA; E Bridgewater HS; E Bridgewater, MA; (Y); 3/147; Art Clb; Girl Scts; Variety Show; Var Cheerleading; Var Fld Hcky; Var Capt Sftbl; High Hon Roll; Hon Roll; NHS; Pres Schlr; Shea Mem Schlrshp, Calc, Art, Physic Awds, Babe Ruth Awd 86; Schlstc Art Awd, Hmcmng Queen 85; Bridgewater ST Coll; Math.

DOBOSZ, GERALD; Turners Falls HS; Turners Fls, MA; (Y); Letterman Clb; Var Bsktbl; Capt Crs Cntry; Capt Trk; X-Cntry All-Str 83-85; Trck All-Str 84&85; X-Cntyr All-Wstrn Mass 85.

DOCKERY, MIKE; Boston Technical HS; Dorchester, MA; (Y); Ftbl; Socr; Trk; Wt Lftg; 2 Awds-Brkng Rcrd-Pwrlftng 500 Deadlft & 550 Squat 86; Comp Engrng.

DODSON, DONNA; Algonquin Regional HS; Northboro, MA; (Y); 2/186; Church Yth Grp; Chorus; Church Choir; Var Capt Crs Cntry; Var Capt Trk; High Hon Roll; NHS; Sal; Outstndng Achvt Awd Acad 84-86; Army Resrve Ntl Schlr Athlete 85-86; Commnwlth Schlr 85-86; Wellesley Coll; Psychlbio.

DOHERTY, DANIEL; Leicester HS; Leicester, MA; (S); 9/106; Band; High Hon Roll; Hon Roll; Ntl Merit Ltr; Prfct Atten Awd; STATE Police Ofcr.

DOHERTY, DAVID R; Wakefield HS; Wakefield, MA; (Y); Church Yth Grp; Key Clb; JV Ftbl; Var Ice Hcky; Var Socr; Var Tennis; Hon Roll; Engrg.

DOHERTY, GREG; Winchester HS; Winchester, MA; (Y); Church Yth Grp; Cmnty Wkr; Nwsp Rptr; Rep Jr Cls; Rep Sr Cls; Var Capt Wrstlng; Ntl Merit SF; Boys Clb Am; English Clb; French Clb; Exp Int Living Homestay/Travl Trip Japan 86; Wrstlng Middlesex Lg All Star & Sectnl Champ 84-86; Georgetown U; Intl Bus.

DOHERTY, JANET; Natick HS; Natick, MA; (Y); Trs Speech Tm; School Musical; Ed Nwsp Rptr; Hon Roll; NHS; Edith M Nutt Mem Schlrshp 86; 3rd Pl Extemporanous Spkng ST Tourn 84; MA Rep To Natl Spch Tourn; Wheaton Coll.

DOHERTY, JOSEPH; Arlington Catholic HS; Billerica, MA; (Y); Church Yth Grp; Drama Clb; Spanish Clb; School Play; Ftbl; Hon Roll; Engrg.

DOHERTY, LISA A; Rockport HS; Rockport, MA; (Y); 7/70; Am Leg Aux Girls St; SADD; VP Frsh Cls; VP Soph Cls; VP Jr Cls; VP Sr Cls; Var JV Fld Hcky; Hon Roll; 4-H; French Clb; Mst Imprvd Field Hockey 84; Comm.

DOHERTY, PAUL; Methuen HS; Methuen, MA; (Y); 82/333; Church Yth Grp; Hosp Aide; Crs Cntry; Golf; Socr; Hon Roll.

DOHERTY, PHIL; St Johns Prep; Billerica, MA; (Y); JV Bsbl; Im Ftbl; Im Golf; Im Vllybl; Hon Roll; NHS; U Of Lowell; Sci.

DOHERTY, WAYNE; Boston Lafin HS; Boston, MA; (Y); JA; Latin Clb; Nwsp Stf; Yrbk Stf; Rep Jr Cls; Rep Sr Cls; Rep Stu Cncl; JV Bsbl; Im Bsktbl; High Hon Roll; Boston Ltn Schl Alumni Pnvn Awd 86; U Of VT; Ecnmcs.

DOLAN, ERINN; Chicopee Comprehensive HS; Chicopee, MA; (Y); 38/307; Hosp Aide; Office Aide; Nwsp Rptr; Nwsp Stf; Var Capt Sftbl; Hon Roll; NHS; Am Intl Coll Acdmc Schlrshp 86; Pinned Sftbl; Charles Abbey Schlrshp 86; American Intl Coll; Nrsng.

DOLAN, FRANCI; Winthrop HS; Winthrop, MA; (Y); 20/209; French Clb; GAA; Capt Var Bsktbl; Capt Var Crs Cntry; Var Powder Puff Ftbl; Capt Var Trk; Var Vllybl; Elks Awd; High Hon Roll; Hon Roll; Wallace B Mc Lean Athletc Awd 86; MVP Crss Cntry 85; All Star X-Cntry, Bsktbll, Trck & Field 84-86; Emmanuel Coll; Bus Mngmnt.

DOLAN, JULIE; Marlboro HS; Marlboro, MA; (Y); AFS; Church Yth Grp; Exploring; Hosp Aide; Im Bsktbl; Hon Roll; Nrsg.

DOLAN, TOM; Bishop Feehan HS; N Attleboro, MA; (Y); Cmnty Wkr; SADD; Flagler Coll; Bus Adm.

DOLAN, TOM; N Quincy HS; Quincy, MA; (Y); Ski Clb; Capt Ftbl; Trk; Wt Lftg; Law Enforcement.

DOMBROWSKI, VANESSA; Somerville HS; Somerville, MA; (Y); VP French Clb; Intnl Clb; Latin Clb; Yrbk Stf; High Hon Roll; Hon Roll; Gold Medal Womens Midle Weight Div 86; Bus.

DOMINIE, ANITA; Ware HS; Ware, MA; (Y); 2/105; Math Tm; Spanish Clb; Band; JV Socr; Bausch & Lomb Sci Awd; High Hon Roll; Pres Schlr; Concert Band; Jazz Band; Mrchg Band; Schlrshp To Cntrl New Englnd Coll 86; Rnsslr Awd Excllnc In Mth & Sci 85; Spnsh Awds Excllnc 83 & 86; Cntrl New Englnd Coll; Bio-Med.

DONAHER, PETE; Ipswich HS; Ipswich, MA; (Y); Boy Scts; Drama Clb; Science Clb; School Play; Stage Crew; Variety Show; Var L Lcrss; JV Socr; Var L Wrstlng; Hon Roll; Schl Hnr Awd 84.

DONAHUE, KAREN; Barnstable HS; Centerville, MA; (Y); Church Yth Grp; SADD; Lit Mag; Trk; High Hon Roll; Hon Roll; NHS; Slvr Acdmc Cert Awd 84; Gld Acdmc Cert 85; Acdmc Ltr 86.

DONAHUE, LISA; Greater Lawrence Technical Schl; Lawrence, MA; (Y); 5/385; SADD; High Hon Roll; Hon Roll; NHS; Data Mgmt Shop Awds 84-86; Acctnt.

DONAHUE, MAUREEN; St Clement HS; Somerville, MA; (Y); Am Leg Aux Girls St; Cmnty Wkr; Teachers Aide; Variety Show; Yrbk Stf; High Hon Roll; Hon Roll; Hghst Avg Alg II 86; Hghst Avg Latin III 86; Hghst Avg Chem 86; Bus.

DONAHUE, MICHELLE; Belmont HS; Belmont, MA; (Y); 70/262; Aud/Vis; Dance Clb; GAA; Letterman Clb; Service Clb; Y-Teens; Var Capt Gym; Hon Roll; 7 Gymnstcs Plqs 85; Cmmnctns.

DONAHUE, NANCY; Matignon HS; Cambridge, MA; (Y); 39/181; Var Cheerleading; Hon Roll; Spanish NHS; U Of MA; Erly Chldhd Ed.

DONAVAN, WILLIAM; Bridgewater-Raynham Regional HS; Bridgewater, MA; (Y); Am Leg Boys St; Math Clb; VP Frsh Cls; Trs Soph Cls; Trs Jr Cls; Capt Bsbl; Var Ftbl; Var Trk; Hon Roll; NHS; Ubsiness Finance.

DONNELLY, JENNIFER; Notre Dame Acad; Weymouth, MA; (Y); 21/111; Spanish Clb; Acpl Chr; Band; Chorus; Church Choir; Concert Band; Madrigals; School Musical; School Play; Stage Crew; Sthestrn MA Dist Chrs 85; U NH; Occptnl Thrpy.

DONNELLY, MICHELE; Bishop Feehan HS; Foxboro, MA; (Y); Cmnty Wkr; Var Bsktbl; Var Trk; Hon Roll; Bridgewater State.

DONNELLY, SARAH; Natick HS; Natick, MA; (Y); 60/450; Aud/Vis; Drama Clb; NFL; Pres VP Speech Tm; Chorus; School Musical; School Play; Variety Show; Nwsp Stf; Yrbk Stf; Ortrcl Intrprtn Chmpn-Villager Trnmnt PA 84; Cmmnctns.

DONNELLY, STACEY; Braintree HS; Braintree, MA; (Y); Nwsp Rptr; Nwsp Stf; Rep Jr Cls; High Hon Roll; Hon Roll; Typng Awd 84-85; Law.

DONOFRIO, MICHAEL W; Saint Bernards HS; Winchendon, MA; (Y); Am Leg Boys St; Art Clb; Ski Clb; Golf; Socr; Wrstlng; Hon Roll; NHS; Headmasters Hnrs 83; Math.

DONOGHUE, CHRISTINE ANN; Wachusett Regional HS; Rutland, MA; (Y); 21/400; Church Yth Grp; Science Clb; Yrbk Bus Mgr; Powder Puff Ftbl; High Hon Roll; NHS; Pres Schlr; Spanish NHS; Library Aide; Teachers Aide; Beta Sigma Phi Sorty Schlrshp 86; Henry S Miles Schlrshp 86; Worcester Polytechnic Inst; Eng.

DONOVAN, BETH; Westford Acad; Westford, MA; (Y); AFS; JCL; Trs Spanish Clb; Nwsp Rptr; Var L Swmmng; Hon Roll; Ntl Merit Ltr; Cmnty Wkr; Var Timer; JV Trk; Hs Swin Team Mvp 84; MA N Sectional Champ 84-85; Bus Mgmt.

DONOVAN, KRISTIN; Attleboro HS; Attleboro, MA; (Y); JV Bsktbl; Powder Puff Ftbl; JV Sftbl; High Hon Roll; Hon Roll; Latn Hon Soc; U Of VT; Vet Sci.

DONOVAN, MAUREEN; North Quincy HS; Quincy, MA; (Y); 23/400; VP Church Yth Grp; Hosp Aide; Math Tm; Pep Clb; Sec Political Wkr; Ski Clb; Varsity Clb; Yrbk Stf; Off Jr Cls; Trs Stu Cncl.

DOOLEY, JOHN T; Arlington Catholic HS; Lexington, MA; (Y); 1/149; French Clb; JA; JCL; Latin Clb; Var Trk; Hon Roll; NHS; Val; Rensselaery Poly Inst Math Sci Awd 85-86; Gold Medals Ntl Latin Ex 83-86; Cary Mem Schrshp 86; Holy Cross Coll; Pre-Med.

DOOLEY, KEVIN P; Wakefield Memorial HS; Wakefield, MA; (Y); 58/332; Aud/Vis; Boy Scts; Cmnty Wkr; Debate Tm; JA; ROTC; Lit Mag; Swmmng; Wt Lftg; Hon Roll; Rcvd Prncpl NROTC Schlrshp 86; Hon Roll 86; Boston U Boston.

DORAIN, KEVIN; Northfield Mount Hermon HS; Morrisville, VT; (Y); Var JV Bsktbl; Var Golf; JV Socr; High Hon Roll; Hon Roll; John E Baldwin Glf Awd 85; Mc Burney Awd Outstndng Contrbtn To Schl Life 86; Frosh Alg Awd 83; Purdue U; Engrg.

DORAN, DAVID J; Norwood HS; Norwood, MA; (Y); Am Leg Boys St; Band; Jazz Band; Mrchg Band; Orch; Symp Band; Rep Stu Cncl; JV Ftbl; JC Awd; MA Lions Clb Intl Band 86; Wentworth Inst; Arch.

DORGAN, DANIEL; Lynn Classical HS; Lynn, MA; (Y); #6 In Class; Political Wkr; Pres Rep Frsh Cls; Rep Soph Cls; Rep Jr Cls; Var Bsbl; CC Awd; High Hon Roll; Hon Roll; Jr NHS; NHS; Frntrs Sci & Math Prog Wrcstr Polytech Inst 86.

DORGAN, KEVIN; Malden Catholic HS; Everett, MA; (Y); Church Yth Grp; Computer Clb; Nwsp Rptr; Nwsp Stf; Var Ftbl; Hon Roll; Ntl Merit SF; Pres Schlr; Letterman Clb; Rptr Jr Cls; Johns Hopkins U; Med.

DORMAN, CAROLYN; Wachusett Regional HS; Holden, MA; (Y); 20/443; Church Yth Grp; French Clb; Model UN; Acpl Chr; Orch; School Musical; Stu Cncl; Var Socr; Var Trk; Hon Roll; Ntl Merit SF.

DORR, WENDY; Franklin HS; Franklin, MA; (Y); Church Yth Grp; Drama Clb; Ski Clb; Stage Crew; Variety Show; Sec Sr Cls; Var Fld Hcky; Mgr(s); Hon Roll; Philadelphia Coll; Fshn Merch.

DOS SANTOS, CARL P; Pentucket Regional HS; Merrimac, MA; (Y); Off Am Leg Boys St; Pres Computer Clb; German Clb; JV Crs Cntry; Hon Roll; 2nd Pl-Bentley Coll Comp Comptn 86; 5th Out Of 440-Law Exam Boys St 86; Comp Sci.

DOSTOU, CHRISTINE; Bishop Connolly HS; Fall River, MA; (Y); 10/169; Cmnty Wkr; Hosp Aide; Math Tm; Off Spanish Clb; Elks Awd; High Hon Roll; NHS; Ntl Merit Ltr; Chnclrs Tlnt Awd Acad Excllnce 86; Prsdntl Acad Ftns Awd 86; Rensselaer Plytch Inst; Com Eng.

DOUCET, LINDA; Gardner HS; Gardner, MA; (Y); 47/150; French Clb; SADD; Var Cheerleading; Bsktbl; Fld Hcky; JV Trk; Swmmng; Cit Awd; Hon Roll; Mt Wachusett; Sec.

DOUCETTE, CHRISTINE; North Shore Regional Vctnl; Beverly, MA; (Y); 11/88; Ski Clb; Sr Cls; High Hon Roll; Hon Roll; Bst All Around Stu Awd 86; Engl, Sci, Phys Ed, Comp Awds 86; Northeastern; Comp Tech.

DOUCETTE, DARLENE L; Newburyport HS; Newburyport, MA; (Y); 21/185; JA; Office Aide; SADD; Nwsp Stf; Yrbk Stf; JV Sftbl; High Hon Roll; Hon Roll; NHS; NHS Achvt Awd-Steno I 84, Steno II 85; NHS Achvt Awd-Acctg I, Bus Adm, Wrd Proc 86; Salem ST Coll; Bus Adm.

DOUCETTE, HEATHER; Fairhaven HS; Fairhaven, MA; (Y); Art Clb; Nwsp Stf; Yrbk Stf; Var Bsktbl; Trk; Vllybl; Hon Roll; NHS; Pre-Med.

DOUCETTE, JOHN; Whitman-Hanson Reg HS; Whitman, MA; (Y); 11/291; Bsbl; L Ftbl; Im Vllybl; Im Wt Lftg; Hon Roll; Jr NHS; NHS; Bentley; Acctng.

DOUGHERTY, MAUREEN; Medford HS; Medford, MA; (Y); 42/540; Church Yth Grp; SADD; Rep Stu Cncl; JV Sftbl; Hon Roll; NHS; Gftd-Tlntd Pgm; Sci Fair; Natl Lang Arts Olympd Awd; Boston U; Phy Thrpy.

DOUILLETTE, BRIDGET; Swampscott HS; Nahant, MA; (Y); 70/236; Aud/Vis; Church Yth Grp; Drama Clb; Chorus; Stage Crew; Yrbk Stf; Sftbl.

DOW, KELLEY; Westfield HS; Westfield, MA; (Y); 77/357; Yrbk Bus Mgr; Yrbk Ed-Chief; Yrbk Stf; Off Soph Cls; Sec Jr Cls; Sec Sr Cls; Var Fld Hcky; Jr NHS; Bus.

DOWD, DONNA M; Marshfield HS; Marshfield, MA; (Y); 118/342; AFS; Key Clb; SADD; Gym; Mgr(s); Elks Awd; Hon Roll; Ntl Merit SF; VFW Awd; Commonwlth MA Brd Regnts Of Hghr Ed Schlrshp 86; Evelyn Hughes Memrl Schlrshp 86; Southeastern MA U; Bus Adm.

DOWNE, LYNNE F; Burncoat HS; Worcester, MA; (Y); Trs Church Yth Grp; Girl Scts; Church Choir; Johnson & Wales; Chef.

DOWNES, MELISSA M; Milford HS; Milford, MA; (Y); Pres Chorus; Stage Crew; Var Trk; Chrls J Tasker Mem Schlrshp 86; Ntl Schl Orchstra Assn Awd 86; U MA Amherst; Engrng.

DOWNEY, CHRISTEL; Taunton HS; Taunton, MA; (Y); Church Yth Grp; JCL; Latin Clb; Band; Church Choir; Concert Band; Mrchg Band; Crs Cntry; Polit Sci.

DOWNEY, CHRISTINA; Maynard HS; Maynard, MA; (Y); 21/106; Ski Clb; School Musical; JV Bsktbl; JV Crs Cntry; Var Sftbl; Var Vllybl; Hon Roll; Chem.

DOWNEY, KRISTIE; Taunton HS; Taunton, MA; (Y); Church Yth Grp; Drama Clb; JCL; Latin Clb; Band; Concert Band; Mrchg Band; Hon Roll; NHS; Jr Clsscl Lge Natl Latn Awd Cum Laude 84-85; Bently Coll; Mrchndsng.

DOWNEY, PATRICK; St Johns Prep; Peabody, MA; (Y); Drama Clb; School Play; Stage Crew; Lit Mag; Hon Roll; Ntl Merit Ltr; Schrlshp St Johns Prep 82-85; Drama Festvl 85; Gen ST Schrlshp 86; Boston Coll; Visual Art.

DOWNIE, CHANDRA; Our Lady Of Nazareth Acad; Malden, MA; (Y); Pres Girl Scts; Red Cross Aide; Science Clb; Swmmng; Christian Virture Awd 84.

DOWNING, KIMBERLY; Agawam HS; South Royalton, VT; (Y); 10/380; AFS; Cmnty Wkr; Pres VP JA; Spanish Clb; Orch; Tennis; High Hon Roll; NHS; Spanish NHS; U MA; Math.

DOWNING, MARGARET; Chicopee Comprehensive HS; Chicopee, MA; (Y); German Clb; SADD; Stage Crew; Nwsp Stf; Yrbk Rptr; Yrbk Stf; Pres Jr Cls; Stu Cncl; Powder Puff Ftbl; Trk; Stu Cncl Ltr 85, Pin 86; U MA; Htl/Rest Mgmt.

DOWNS, DAVID; Swampscott HS; Swampscott, MA; (Y); #1 In Class; Boy Scts; Math Tm; Concert Band; Mrchg Band; Bausch & Lomb Sci Awd; Hon Roll; Pres NHS; Library Aide; Orch; Brown Bk Awd 86; Marin Blgy Clb Trsr 85-86; Lbrl Arts.

DOWNS, NICOLE Y; Tantasqua Regional HS; Sturbridge, MA; (Y); 48/174; Church Yth Grp; Drama Clb; Pep Clb; Chorus; School Musical; School Play; Stage Crew; JV Cheerleading; Stat Coach Actv; Gym; Eastrn Coll St Davids; Yth Mnst.

DOYLE, CATHERINE M; Cathedral HS; Wilbraham, MA; (Y); Civic Clb; Office Aide; SADD; Varsity Clb; School Musical; Swmmng; Timer; NHS; Math Awd Alg I 83-84; Librl Arts.

DOYLE, CRAIG M; Waltham HS; Waltham, MA; (Y); Am Leg Boys St; Boy Scts; Church Yth Grp; Library Aide; Bsktbl; Socr; Tennis; Timer; Trk; Vllybl; CT Coll.

DOYLE, DANNA; The Waring Schl; Marblehead, MA; (Y); Art Clb; Drama Clb; Girl Scts; Hosp Aide; Chorus; School Musical; School Play; Stage Crew; Lit Mag; Var L Bsktbl; French.

DOYLE, MICHELLE P; Newton North HS; Newtonville, MA; (Y); French Clb; SADD; Acpl Chr; Band; Orch; High Hon Roll; Ntl Merit Ltr; Model UN; Ski Clb; Chorus; Downhill Ski Tm V 84; Princpl Clarinet Symp Orch 84-86; All Easten Music Festvl Band 85; U MI; Music.

DOYLE, RYAN; Antral Catholic HS; Andover, MA; (Y); 18/231; Computer Clb; Math Clb; JV Crs Cntry; JV Trk; Hon Roll; Engrng.

DOYLE, SARAH; King Philip Regional HS; Norfolk, MA; (Y); 58/203; Trs DECA; VP Frsh Cls; Pres Soph Cls; Pres Jr Cls; Pres Sr Cls; Rep Stu Cncl; Capt Var Cheerleading; NHS; MVP Chrldng 84-86; Accntng.

DRADRANSKY, DAVID; Austin Preparatory Schl; Billerica, MA; (Y); 29/124; Pep Clb; SADD; Nwsp Rptr; High Hon Roll; Hon Roll; Arch.

DRAIN, AMY; North Quincy HS; Quincy, MA; (Y); 15/323; Math Tm; Office Aide; Pep Clb; Band; Chorus; Concert Band; Drill Tm; Drm & Bgl; Mrchg Band; Geometry League 84; Excellnce In Bio II 86; Pres Acad Fitness Awd 86; Stonehill Coll; Bio.

DRAKE, ERIK P; Lexington HS; Lexington, MA; (Y); Church Yth Grp; Var Trk; Hon Roll; Vrsty Indoor Track Awd 85-86; Archtctr.

DRAKE, MICHELLE; Holyoke Catholic HS; Holyoke, MA; (Y); 15/100; Computer Clb; Pres DECA; Latin Clb; Library Aide; Math Clb; Office Aide; Rep Spanish Clb; Lit Mag; High Hon Roll; NHS; Bio.

DRAKES, RICHARD; Hyde Park HS; Mattapan, MA; (Y); Off JA; Rep Jr Cls; Bsktbl; Var L Ftbl; Trk; Vllybl; Hon Roll; NHS; MIT; Mechncl Engr.

DRESCHER, SANDRA LYNN; Ayer SR HS; Ayer, MA; (Y); 38/130; Pep Clb; Spanish Clb; SADD; School Play; Nwsp Stf; Yrbk Stf; Stu Cncl; Powder Puff Ftbl; Hon Roll; JP Sullivan Schlrshp 86; Fitchburg ST; Law.

DRESSER, STEPHANIE; Walnut Hill Schl Of Performing Arts; Durham, NH; (Y); Intnl Clb; Director.

DREW, DEBBIE; South HS Comm; Worcester, MA; (Y); Church Yth Grp; Girl Scts; Mst Imprvd Stu Piano 86; Worcester ST; Bus Adm.

DREW, MICHELE; Lynn Classical HS; Lynn, MA; (Y); Church Yth Grp; Drama Clb; Hosp Aide; Office Aide; Pep Clb; SADD; Powder Puff Ftbl; Hon Roll; VP NHS; USAA Frnch,Ldrshp Awd 84-85; Framingham ST Coll.

DREWNIAK, KRIS; Somerset HS; Somerset, MA; (Y); Nwsp Rptr; Hon Roll; Nrs.

DREYFUS, JEFF; Marlboro HS; Marlboro, MA; (Y); 86/351; Computer Clb; Ski Clb; Lit Mag; JV Socr; High Hon Roll; Hon Roll.

DRISCOLL, ANNMARIE; Belmont HS; Belmont, MA; (Y); Church Yth Grp; Hosp Aide; JA; Service Clb; Spanish Clb; School Play; JV Socr; Var Trk; Hon Roll; Bsktbl; Irish Step Dncg Trphs & Mdls 73-85; Bus.

DRISCOLL, BRENDAN; Arlington Catholic HS; Medford, MA; (Y); Church Yth Grp; French Clb; Office Aide; Spanish Clb; Hon Roll; NEDT Awd; Prfct Atten Awd; U Of Lowell; Elec Engnrng.

DRISCOLL, BRIAN; Arlington Catholic HS; Arlington, MA; (Y); Var L Bsbl; Var L Bsktbl; Var Capt Ftbl; Im Swmmng; Im Wt Lftg; Cit Awd; Hon Roll; Boys Clb Am; Boy Scts; Red Cross Aide; Fr Manning Schlrshp Outstdng Svc To Yth Of Fidelity House 83; Natl Latin Exam-Summa Cum Laude 83-84.

DRISCOLL, DEBBIE; Lawrence HS; Lawrence, MA; (Y); #21 In Class; VP DECA; SADD; Rep Frsh Cls; Rep Soph Cls; Rep Jr Cls; Var Cheerleading; High Hon Roll; NHS; U S Chrldng Achvt Awd 86.

DRISCOLL, KRISTINE; Methuen HS; Methuen, MA; (Y); 20/340; Girl Scts; Intnl Clb; Model UN; Pep Clb; Pres Stu Cncl; Var Capt Fld Hcky; Powder Puff Ftbl; DAR Awd; Sec NHS; Pres Schlr; SOAR Awd 86; Bentley Coll; Acctg.

DRISCOLL, MARK M; Saint Patricks HS; Watertown, MA; (Y); 7/45; Am Leg Boys St; Boys Clb Am; Church Yth Grp; Trs Soph Cls; Stu Cncl; Capt Var Bsbl; Var Bsktbl; Var Ftbl; Hon Roll; NHS; Rep Stu Advsry Cncl 85; Acdmc All Amer 86; Holy Corss; Bus.

DROBNIS, BRIAN; Brockton HS; Brockton, MA; (Y); 120/1000; Temple Yth Grp; Concert Band; Bsktbl; Co-Capt Golf; Hon Roll; NHS; Boston College; Dntstry.

DRUMMY, PATTI; Fontbonne Acad; Dorchester, MA; (Y); 23/133; Church Yth Grp; Dance Clb; Drama Clb; Girl Scts; Intnl Clb; Key Clb; Political Wkr; Red Cross Aide; SADD; Stage Crew; Natl Labor Exm Schlrshp 86; U Of CT; Math.

DRURY, STEVEN J; Canton HS; Canton, MA; (Y); 30/265; Ed Am Leg Boys St; Church Yth Grp; Rep Frsh Cls; Rep Soph Cls; Pres Sec Stu Cncl; Golf; Cit Awd; DAR Awd; Hon Roll; Natl Assoc Of Stu Cncl Awd 85; Boston Coll; Educ.

DU BOIS, DOUGLAS; Newton North HS; W Newton, MA; (Y); Boy Scts; Trk; Wt Lftg; Hon Roll; Norwich; Mech Engrng.

DU LONG, SUZANNE; Billerica Memorial HS; Billerica, MA; (Y); 32/460; Drama Clb; Pres French Clb; Ski Clb; Yrbk Stf; Im Badmtn; Var Capt Socr; Var Trk; Emerson Coll; Mass Comm.

DU MONT, JOSEPH; Westfield HS; Westfield, MA; (Y); 190/360; Golf; 1st Prz Wst Pblctns 1st Anl Cmptr Cntst Kds 85; Lndscpng.

DUANE, BRIAN; West Springfield SR HS; W Springfield, MA; (Y); Chess Clb; Pres Drama Clb; Band; Chorus; Concert Band; Jazz Band; Pep Band; School Musical; West MA Dist Chrs 84-86; Music.

DUARTE, LAURA; New Bedford HS; New Bedford, MA; (Y); 55/701; Office Aide; Var L Sftbl; Var Trk; Hon Roll.

DUBREUIL, DONNA L; Somerset HS; Somerset, MA; (Y); 5/310; Hosp Aide; Office Aide; Varsity Clb; Bsktbl; Crs Cntry; Score Keeper; Trk; High Hon Roll; NHS; Pres Schlr; Bridgewater ST Coll; Elem.

DUBREVIL, DONNA; Somerset HS; Somerset, MA; (Y); 5/310; Hosp Aide; Office Aide; Varsity Clb; Bsktbl; Crs Cntry; Trk; High Hon Roll; NHS; Pres Schlr; Bridgewater ST Coll; Elem Tchr.

DUCEY, KATHLEEN; Our Lady Of Nazareth Acad; Wilmington, MA; (Y); 10/75; Girl Scts; Red Cross Aide; SADD; Chorus; Church Choir; School Musical; Hon Roll; NEDT Awd; Excllnc In Bio 85; Elem Ed.

DUCHARME, DOUGLAS RAOUL; Coyle-Cassidy Mem HS; Taunton, MA; (Y); 10/140; Sec Frsh Cls; Rep Sr Cls; Var Capt Bsbl; Var Capt Ftbl; VP NHS; Rotary Awd; Spanish NHS; Coyle-Cassidy Man Yr Awd 85-86; Blck Granit Outstndng Linemn Awd-Fnlst 85; Worcester Polytech Inst; Engrng.

DUCHARME, JESSICA; Dracut SR HS; Dracut, MA; (Y); Office Aide; Yrbk Stf; Var L Cheerleading; Var Capt Gym; L Trk; Hon Roll; NHS; Lowell Sun All Star Gymnstc 84; Lowell Sun All Star Tm Gymnst Of Yr 85-86.

DUCHESNEAU, AMY B; West Springfield HS; W Springfield, MA; (Y); 9/210; Library Aide; Office Aide; Ski Clb; Flag Corp; Tennis; Lion Awd; NHS; Spanish NHS; James Z Naurison Schlrshp 86; Barcomb Trowbridge Post 6714 VFW & Aux Schlrshp 86; Bay Path JC; Bus Admin.

DUDEK, MARTIN J; Pathfinder Regional Tech Vo; Belchertown, MA; (Y); Am Leg Boys St; Church Choir; Yrbk Stf; Stu Cncl; Bsbl; Bsktbl; JV Socr; Hon Roll; Excllnc In Culinary Arts Awd 84; Culinary Inst Of Am; Chef.

DUDLEY, ELIZABETH; Old Rochester Regional HS; Marion, MA; (Y); 16/147; AFS; Girl Scts; Rep Frsh Cls; Var L Crs Cntry; Var L Trk; Im Vllybl; Hon Roll; Voice Dem Awd; Hghst GPA Sci 83; Hghst GPA Soclgy 86; Pres Phys Ftns Awds 83-86; U Of Lavell; Phys Ther.

DUDLEY, JENNIFER; Maynard HS; Maynard, MA; (Y); Art Clb; Library Aide; Spanish Clb; Hon Roll; Bio.

DUERDEN, RACHAEL; Plymouth-Carver HS; Plymouth, MA; (Y); 7/500; Am Leg Aux Girls St; Yrbk Phtg; Yrbk Stf; Hon Roll; Jr NHS; NHS; Ntl Merit Ltr; Pres Schlr; St Schlr; Boston U; Occptnl Thrpy.

DUFAULT, TIMOTHY M; Holy Name C C H S; Worcester, MA; (Y); Var Trk; High Hon Roll; Hon Roll; Am Lit Awd 86; Wentworth Inst Of Tech; Archite.

DUFF, LISA; Marian HS; Framingham, MA; (Y); 1/204; Spanish Clb; Yrbk Ed-Chief; Trs Soph Cls; Capt Var Tennis; High Hon Roll; Pres NHS; Spanish NHS; Stu Cncl; Cmnty Wkr; Teachers Aide; 3rd MIT St Sci Fair; 3rd Rgnl Sci Fair; Wellesley Coll Book Awd; Awd MA Assn Sci Tchrs; Law.

DUFFETT, KENNETH; Matignon HS; Arlington, MA; (S); 19/186; Boys Clb Am; Church Yth Grp; French Clb; Science Clb; JV Bsbl; Var Bsktbl; Im Vllybl; NHS; Ntl Merit Ltr.

DUFFY, AMY; Fontbonne Acad; Milton, MA; (Y); Drama Clb; Intnl Clb; School Musical; School Play; Yrbk Stf; Rep Soph Cls; Rep Jr Cls; Rep Stu Cncl; Hon Roll; Drama Awd.

DUFFY, KIM; Bristol Plymouth Regional Tech; E Taunton, MA; (Y); Library Aide; Nwsp Stf; Hon Roll.

DUFFY, MARY KATE; Marian HS; Natick, MA; (Y); 51/179; Hosp Aide; Ski Clb; Mgr Socr; High Hon Roll; NHS; John Gilhouly Schlrshp 86; Excllnc Trignmtry Cert 86; Stonehill Coll; Elem Ed.

DUFFY, PAUL; Woburn SR HS; Woburn, MA; (Y); Church Yth Grp; Ski Clb; Var L Ftbl; FL ST; Engrng.

DUFFY JR, THOMAS J; Norwood SR HS; Norwood, MA; (Y); Am Leg Boys St; Drama Clb; JA; Key Clb; SADD; School Play; Variety Show; Off Frsh Cls; VP Soph Cls; VP Jr Cls; Prsctt Grad Awd 86; Boston Coll; Physcs.

DUFRESNE, JAMES; New Bedford HS; New Bedford, MA; (Y); 78/790; Boy Scts; Chess Clb; Computer Clb; Science Clb; SADD; Rep Stu Cncl; Worcester Polytech; Chem Engr.

DUGGAN, PATRICIA; Marlboro HS; Marlboro, MA; (Y); Dance Clb; Ski Clb; Chorus; Variety Show; Yrbk Bus Mgr; Yrbk Stf; Rep Jr Cls; Rep Sr Cls; Sec Stu Cncl; Cheerleading; Prom Qn Ct 86; Ofc Cltrl Affrs Prfrs 84-85; Acctg.

DUGUETTE, KEITH D; Northbridge JR/SR HS; Whitinsville, MA; (Y); 44/139; Am Leg Boys St; Cmnty Wkr; Latin Clb; Spanish Clb; Var L Bsktbl; Var L Trk; Bus.

DULCHINAS, SUE; Chicopee HS; Chicopee, MA; (Y); 32/267; Cmnty Wkr; Dance Clb; FCA; Girl Scts; Hosp Aide; Red Cross Aide; SADD; Cheerleading; Mgr(s); Score Keeper; Westfield ST Coll; Tchng.

DULTZ, TINA MARIE K; West Springfield SR HS; West Springfield, MA; (Y); 17/215; Drama Clb; Q&S; Nwsp Stf; JV Socr; Swmmng; Trk; French Hon Soc; Hon Roll; Sec NHS; Itln Natl Hnr Soc 84-85; Awd Excllnc In Titln 86; MA Frgn Lang Assoc Awd Germ 86; St Josephs U; Intl Rel.

DUMARESG, STEVEN; Central Catholic HS; Dracut, MA; (Y); 33/231; Math Clb; Ski Clb; Trk; Hon Roll.

DUMAS, MIRIAM BERNADETTE; King Philip Rgnl HS; Norfolk, MA; (Y); #10 In Class; Church Yth Grp; Cmnty Wkr; French Clb; Math Tm; Lit Mag; Var Crs Cntry; Trk; Hon Roll; NHS; Dance Clb; Natl PTA Schol 86; Unsung Hero Awd X-Cntry 83; 10th Sr Cls 86; Bridgewater ST Coll; Elem Educ.

DUMAS, PAUL; Northbridge JR SR HS; Whitinsville, MA; (Y); 1/153; Am Leg Boys St; Drama Clb; Latin Clb; Ski Clb; SADD; Stu Cncl; Bausch & Lomb Sci Awd; High Hon Roll; VP NHS; Val; Bausch & Lomb Schlrshp 86; U Of Rochester; Optcl Engrng.

DUMONT, MICHELLE; Presentation Of Mary Acad; Methuen, MA; (Y); Trs French Clb; Math Clb; Rep Frsh Cls; Var Sftbl; Capt JV Vllybl; Hon Roll; NHS; Int Dsgn.

DUMONT, RANDY; Douglas Memorial HS; Douglas, MA; (Y); Varsity Clb; Yrbk Sprt Ed; Stu Cncl; Var Bsbl; JV Var Bsktbl; Hon Roll; Natl Math Awds 84-85; Bryant Coll; Bus.

DUMONT, STACIE; Attleboro HS; Attleboro, MA; (Y); Church Yth Grp; Varsity Clb; Acpl Chr; Var Diving; Var Capt Gym; Var Swmmng; Hon Roll; NHS; Var Trk; Typg Awd 86; Aquinas Typg Cont-Hnrbl Mntn 86.

DUMOUCHEL, DAVID; Bishop Feeham HS; Cumberland, RI; (Y); Capt L Crs Cntry; Var Swmmng; Var Capt Trk; Hon Roll; Bus Adm.

DUMOULIN, TRICIA; Cathedral HS; Enfield, CT; (Y); Intnl Clb; JA; Band; Church Choir; Concert Band; Mrchg Band; Hon Roll; Burton Henry Schlrshp Fund 85; Music Therpst.

DUNHAM JR, WILLIAM H; Apponequet Regional HS; Middleboro, MA; (Y); 7/250; Var Capt Ftbl; Var Trk; Hon Roll; NHS; Cmnwlth Schlr Awd 86; ST Schlrshp 86; Elzbth Cshmn Schlrshp 86; MA Maritm Acad; Engrng.

DUNIGAN, KATHLEEN; Lowell HS; Lowell, MA; (Y); 4/500; VP Intnl Clb; VP JA; JCL; Spanish Clb; Nwsp Ed-Chief; NHS; St Schlr; Church Yth Grp; Latin Clb; Science Clb; Cum Laude Natl Latin Exam 83 & 84; Middlesex Cnty Womens Coll Clb Schlrhp 86; Lowell Coll Schlrshp 86; U Of PA; Law.

DUNLAP, JOSEPH C; Southwick HS; Southwick, MA; (Y); 2/137; Am Leg Boys St; Debate Tm; French Clb; JA; Math Clb; SADD; Stu Cncl; Presdnt Natl Hnr Socty 86; Western Nw Englnd; Engnrg.

DUNLOP, SCOTT; East Longmeadow HS; E Longmeadow, MA; (Y); 25/180; Church Yth Grp; Computer Clb; Spanish Clb; Variety Show; Yrbk Stf; Var Capt Bsbl; Im Bsktbl; Var Capt Socr; Hon Roll; Comp Sci.

DUNLOP, THOMAS; Medford HS; Medford, MA; (Y); Boy Scts; Math Tm; L Var Swmmng.

DUNN, ANNEMARIE; Burlington HS; Burlington, MA; (Y); 19/322; Drama Clb; Chorus; Yrbk Stf; NHS; U MA; Biochem.

DUNN, DARLENE; Shawsheen Valley HS; Bedford, MA; (Y); 4/400; SADD; VP VICA; Yrbk Stf; Stu Cncl; Cit Awd; Elks Awd; High Hon Roll; Rotary Awd; St Schlr; Amer Lge Schlrshp 86; Vica Otstndng Ldrshp Awd 85; SE MA U; Bus Admin.

DUNN, DIANE; St Bernards C C HS; Fitchburg, MA; (S); 16/159; Ski Clb; Capt Socr; Hon Roll; NHS; MVP-SOCCER 85; Most Imprvd Player-Soccer 84; Leag All Stars-Soccer 83; Fitchburg ST Coll.

DUNN, JOE; St Clements HS; Somerville, MA; (Y); JV Bsktbl; Var Ftbl; Hon Roll; NHS; Mary & John J Healy Schlrp St Clements 86-87; Banking.

DUNN, KELLY; Taunton HS; Taunton, MA; (Y); Cmnty Wkr; Drama Clb; French Clb; Office Aide; Ski Clb; Spanish Clb; SADD; Yrbk Stf; Rep Frsh Cls; Rep Soph Cls; Commnctns.

DUNN, KRISTIN; Quincy HS; Quincy, MA; (Y); 33/300; JA; SADD; Im Vllybl; High Hon Roll; Prfct Atten Awd; Sci Awd Gen Sci & Chem 84 & 86.

DUNN, LISA; Marlboro HS; Marlboro, MA; (Y); 49/300; Church Yth Grp; Ski Clb; Variety Show; Stu Cncl; Var Mgr(s); Capt Socr; Var Trk; Hon Roll; Unsung Hero Awd-Soccr 85; Fshn Merchndsng.

DUNN, TOM; Marlboro HS; Marlboro, MA; (Y); 20/300; Boys Clb Am; Church Yth Grp; Ski Clb; Varsity Clb; Crs Cntry; Golf; Trk; Elks Awd; High Hon Roll; NHS; Faclty Awd Outstndng Achvt Art 83-84; Elec Engrng.

DUNNE, CHARLES M; Waltham HS; Waltham, MA; (Y); 113/576; Am Leg Boys St; Boys Clb Am; Ftbl; JV Im Ice Hcky; Capt Lcrss; JV Socr; Var Wrstlng; Hon Roll; 110 Pct Awd Wrstlng 86; St Mary Chrch Schlrshp 86; Citadel; Physcl Ed.

DUNNE, SUSAN M; E Bridgewater HS; E Bridgewater, MA; (Y); 6/139; Debate Tm; Drama Clb; Math Tm; SADD; Chorus; Church Choir; Yrbk Bus Mgr; Yrbk Ed-Chief; Yrbk Stf; Rep Frsh Cls; Ntl Hstry Day-Rgnl & ST Grp Chmpn 83; Suffolk U; Law.

DUPILL, ANN; North Quincy HS; Quincy, MA; (Y); 30/396; Church Yth Grp; Cmnty Wkr; Hosp Aide; Band; Mrchg Band; Yrbk Stf; Var Swmmng; Var L Trk; Prfct Atten Awd; Bus Acctng.

DUPRE, ANGELA; Nipmuc Regional HS; Upton, MA; (Y); 14/95; Church Yth Grp; French Clb; Teachers Aide; Yrbk Stf; High Hon Roll; Hon Roll; NHS; Acctng.

DUPREY, CHERYL; Groton-Dunstable Regnl Secndry Schl; W Groton, MA; (Y); 6/93; 4-H; Girl Scts; Band; Yrbk Stf; Wt Lftg; High Hon Roll; Hon Roll; Frank Waters Voctnl Schrlshp 86; Cert, Medl Hnr Outstndng Achvt Svc 86; Blaine Hair Schl; Cosmetology.

DUPREZ, MICHELLE; Waltham HS; Waltham, MA; (Y); Dance Clb; Hosp Aide; Intnl Clb; School Musical; Var Trk.

DUPUIS, LISA; Lawrence HS; Pepperell, MA; (S); Hosp Aide; SADD; Capt Color Guard; Mrchg Band; School Play; Stage Crew; Yrbk Stf; High Hon Roll; NHS; Spanish NHS; Fitchburg ST Coll; Nrs.

DUQUETTE, MARIE L; Chicopee HS; Chicopee, MA; (Y); 13/250; Aud/Vis; Library Aide; Nwsp Rptr; Nwsp Stf; High Hon Roll; Hon Roll; NHS; Ntl Merit SF; Pres Schlr; St Schlr; U Massachusetts.

DURAND, KEVIN; Holyoke Cthollc HS; S Hadley, MA; (Y); Chess Clb; Math Clb; Office Aide; Ski Clb; Spanish Clb; School Musical; School Play; Stage Crew; Yrbk Stf; Var L Tennis; Assumption Coll; Frgn Lang.

DURGA, REGINA; Blackstone-Millville Regional HS; Millville, MA; (Y); 7/95; Hosp Aide; SADD; Band; Concert Band; Mrchg Band; Yrbk Stf; Hst Jr Cls; Var Cheerleading; Hon Roll; Trs NHS; Sci.

DURGIN, BRIAN; North Quincy HS; N Quincy, MA; (Y); 20/500; JA; Math Clb; Yrbk Stf; Bsbl; Ftbl; Wt Lftg; High Hon Roll; Hon Roll; NHS; Ntl Merit Schol.

DURKIN, JULIANNE; Bedford HS; Bedford, MA; (Y); 66/198; Rep Church Yth Grp; Drama Clb; SADD; Band; Concert Band; Mrchg Band; Orch; Pep Band; School Musical; Stage Crew.

DURKIN, ROBERT; Cohasset HS; Cohasset, MA; (Y); 7/110; Math Tm; Varsity Clb; Nwsp Stf; Yrbk Sprt Ed; Yrbk Stf; Pres Frsh Cls; Pres Soph Cls; Pres Jr Cls; VP Stu Cncl; Var Capt Ftbl; Holy Cross Bk Awd 86; Ftbl SSSL All Str JR; Engrng.

DURONIO, SHARON; Franklin HS; Franklin, MA; (Y); 1/224; Church Yth Grp; Math Tm; OEA; Trs Frsh Cls; Trs Soph Cls; Trs Jr Cls; Trs Sr Cls; Stu Cncl; High Hon Roll; Hon Roll; Excllnc Math & Engl Awd 86; Rensselear Poly Tech Inst Math & Sci Awd 85; Holycross Coll; Sci.

DURSO, CATHERINE; Milton HS; Milton, MA; (Y); Pres Art Clb; Drama Clb; VP French Clb; School Play; Variety Show; Yrbk Phtg; Yrbk Stf; Socr; Tennis; Hon Roll; Adv Exec.

DUSO, LUANN; Easthampton HS; Easthampton, MA; (Y); French Clb; GAA; Yrbk Stf; Hon Roll; Bus.

DUSTIN, CRAIG; St Dominic Savio HS; Everett, MA; (Y); 3/110; Cmnty Wkr; Math Clb; SADD; Nwsp Stf; Rep Stu Cncl; JV Ice Hcky; High Hon Roll; Hon Roll; Prfct Atten Awd; Religion Awd Hgh Avg 84; Geom Awd Hgh Avg 85; CPA.

DUTEAU, NATALIE; Bartlett HS; Webster, MA; (Y); 16/160; Math Tm; Spanish Clb; Nwsp Stf; Var L Socr; Var L Trk; High Hon Roll; Hon Roll; NHS; Prfct Atten Awd; MVP Awd Trck 86; Border Conf All Star Trck 86; 1st Pl Awds Trck 86; Computerized Math.

DUTRA, SERGIO; Bristol-Plymouth Vocational HS; Taunton, MA; (S); 2/140; Computer Clb; Rep Soph Cls; High Hon Roll; NHS; Rotary Awd; S MA U; Elec Engrng.

DUVAL, MARK; Haverhill HS; Haverhill, MA; (Y); 84/416; Ski Clb; Hon Roll; Med Tech.

DUVAL, RICHARD; Murdock HS; Winchendon, MA; (Y); #26 In Class; Am Leg Boys St; JV Bsbl; JV Var Bsktbl; Var Crs Cntry; Var Ftbl; Hon Roll; State Plc Ofcr.

DUVAL, STEPHEN; Leominster HS; Leominster, MA; (Y); 10/305; Am Leg Boys St; Rep Stu Cncl; Bsktbl; High Hon Roll; Hon Roll; Pres NHS; Enclle In Bio 85; Awd Prof In Sci 86; Emblem Clb Schlrshp & Billy Lefebure Mem Schlrshp 86; MA Coll; Pharm.

DUVELSON, MARIE PAULA; St Gregory HS; Mattapan, MA; (Y); Dance Clb; Office Aide; School Musical; Ice Hcky; Swmmng; High Hon Roll; Hon Roll; Pres Schlr; U MA; Gyn.

DWYER, COLLEEN; Doherty Memorial HS; Worcester, MA; (Y); Church Yth Grp; Spanish Clb; Variety Show; Yrbk Stf; Ntl Merit Ltr; Psych.

DWYER, DERYN; Saugus HS; Boxford, MA; (Y); Art Clb; Civic Clb; Hosp Aide; Library Aide; Office Aide; Voice Dem Awd; Grand Cross Of Color 85; Commrcl Art.

DYE, MICHAEL; Brockton HS; Brockton, MA; (Y); 30/822; German Clb; Ski Clb; Stage Crew; Nwsp Stf; Trs Jr Cls; JV Socr; Var Wrstlng; High Hon Roll; Pres Acad Fit Awd 86; Boston U; Intl Rltns.

DYER, GEORGE M; Cambridge Rindge & Latin Schl; Cambridge, MA; (Y); 5/550; Boy Scts; Pres Debate Tm; Model UN; NFL; Speech Tm; Lit Mag; Bsktbl; Socr; Trk; High Hon Roll; Ntl Achvt Schlrshp Semi-Fnlst 85; Bio.

DYER, KAREN; Braintree HS; Braintree, MA; (Y); 144/370; Church Yth Grp; Pep Clb; Spanish Clb; SADD; Yrbk Stf; Cheerleading; Pom Pon; Spanish NHS; Dr Archie Kegan Schlrshp 86; Braingree Grange Schlrshp; Our Lady Of Elms Coll; Nrsng.

DYER, MELISSA; Governor Dummer Acad; Georgetown, MA; (Y); 1/86; Church Yth Grp; Dance Clb; Ski Clb; Church Choir; School Play; Yrbk Bus Mgr; Var L Crs Cntry; Capt JV Socr; High Hon Roll; Val; Cum Laude Soc 85-86; Coll Of William & Mary.

DYGON, BRIAN; Ludlow HS; Ludlow, MA; (S); Chorus; Nwsp Rptr; Mgr Nwsp Stf; Rep Frsh Cls; Rep Soph Cls; Rep Jr Cls; Hon Roll; Cmnty Wkr; Ambass HOBY Fndtn Sem 85; Bst Feat Article Awd Holyoke CC Jrnlsm Conf 84; W MA Dist Chrs 86; Jrnlsm.

DYMENT, LAWRENCE; North Reading HS; N Reading, MA; (Y); Cmnty Wkr; JV Bsbl; Ftbl; Trk; Schlrs & Artsts 86; Engrng.

DZIALO, EDWARD; B M C Durfee HS; Fall River, MA; (Y); Church Yth Grp; Cmnty Wkr; French Clb; German Clb; JA; Science Clb; Spanish Clb; Church Choir; Yrbk Stf; High Hon Roll.

EARLES, TRINA; Concord-Carlisle HS; Concord, MA; (Y); 6/328; Church Yth Grp; Math Tm; Science Clb; Color Guard; Yrbk Stf; High Hon Roll; NHS; Ntl Merit SF; Acadmc Excell Awds Frnch/Chem/Soc Stud 85/Engl Calcls Soc Stu 86.

EASLER, ERIK C; Blackstone Vly Regional Vo-Tech; Milford, MA; (Y); Lit Mag; Hon Roll; Ntl Merit SF; JC Awd; Central New England; Comp Sci.

EAST, KRISTEN; Christopher Columbus HS; Boston, MA; (Y); 25/126; Cmnty Wkr; Hosp Aide; JA; Spanish Clb; Rep Stu Cncl; Swmmng; Hon Roll; Hghst Avg Span 84; St Anselm Coll; Psych.

EATON, SERITA; Lynn Classical HS; Lynn, MA; (Y); Dance Clb; JA; Pep Clb; Church Choir; Drm & Bgl; School Musical; Var Capt Bsktbl; Bus Admin.

EBBESON, AMY; Wachusett Regional HS; Holden, MA; (Y); Drama Clb; Model UN; Chorus; School Musical; School Play; Rep Jr Cls; Stu Cncl; Exprsn Theatre Bst Actrs 86; Drmtc Arts.

EBY, DAVID; Marshfield HS; Marshfield, MA; (Y); 100/400; Yrbk Sprt Ed; Yrbk Stf; Var Bsktbl; Var Crs Cntry; Var Trk; William J Conaghan Mem Awd 80.

ECKER, AMY BETH; Salem HS; Salem, MA; (Y); Drama Clb; Temple Yth Grp; School Play; Yrbk Stf; Stu Cncl; Cheerleading; Hon Roll; P T Kennedy Schlrshp 86; Interfor Clb Schlrshp 86; MA U; Jrnlsm.

ECKER, DAWN; Chicopee Comprehensive HS; Chicopee, MA; (Y); 18/386; Girl Scts; Office Aide; Quiz Bowl; Red Cross Aide; SADD; Pep Band; Yrbk Phtg; VP Stu Cncl; High Hon Roll; Jr NHS; Grl Sct Gld Awd 85; Hugh O Brien Yth Ldrshp Awd 85; Stu Cncl Ltr 86; Mdcl Tech.

EDDLESTON, KRISTINE; Fairhaven HS; Fairhaven, MA; (Y); Art Clb; Psychlgy.

EDDY, ERIC; Salem HS; Salem, MA; (Y); Ski Clb; Spanish Clb; Band; Concert Band; Jazz Band; Mrchg Band; Orch; School Musical; School Play; Symp Band.

EDDY, HEATHER; Natick HS; Natick, MA; (Y); 12/400; Pres Service Clb; Speech Tm; Acpl Chr; School Musical; Trs Jr Cls; High Hon Roll; NHS; Hon Roll; Prfct Atten Awd; Chorus; Bus Wk Bentley Coll 85; Spotlght Bentley Coll 85-86; Bus Awds; Engrng.

EDDY, MARK; Wilmington HS; Wilmington, MA; (Y); Cmnty Wkr; DECA; L Var Bsbl; L Var Bsktbl; L Var Crs Cntry; Var Trk; Hon Roll; Prfct Atten Awd; Leag Bsbl All Str 86; 3rd Pl Awd DECA Rgnls; Bus.

EDELMANN, LISA; Northfield Mount Hermon HS; Nantucket, MA; (Y); AFS; Hosp Aide; Radio Clb; Stu Cncl; JV Bsktbl; Var JV Fld Hcky; US Hstry Awd 86; Vrsty Dwnhl Sking 85 & 86; U Of MA; Pre-Med.

EDGERLY, CYNTHIA; Wilmington HS; Wilmington, MA; (Y); Exploring; Model UN; Spanish Clb; Varsity Clb; Yrbk Phtg; Yrbk Stf; Cheerleading; Tennis; High Hon Roll; Hon Roll; Psychlgy.

EDWARDS, ANNIE R; Madison Park HS; Dorchester, MA; (Y); Hosp Aide; Science Clb; Concert Band; Drm Mjr(t); High Hon Roll; Hon Roll; Prfct Atten Awd; Fredm Hs Inst 2nd Anl Schlrshp Awd 86; Ctywd Sci Fair, 3rd Pl Awd 86; Northeastern U; Engrng.

EDWARDS, DAVID; Westfield HS; Westfield, MA; (Y); Cmnty Wkr; French Clb; Ski Clb; Concert Band; Jazz Band; Mrchg Band; Pep Band; Jr NHS; Civl Engr.

EDWARDS, DIANA; Beverly HS; Beverly, MA; (Y); 47/374; Church Yth Grp; Hosp Aide; Quiz Bowl; Scholastic Bowl; Nwsp Stf; Trk; Hon Roll; 2nd Sci Fair 84; Sclrshps Lothrop Clb, Beverly Womens Coll Clb, & Kevin Mc Niff 86; Albertus Magnus Coll; Foreign.

EDWARDS, JOHN J; Scituate HS; Scituate, MA; (Y); Am Leg Boys St; Computer Clb; SADD; Rep Soph Cls; Rep Jr Cls; Rep Sr Cls; Rep Stu Cncl; Crs Cntry; Ftbl; Trk.

EDWARDS, ROSE A; Stoughton HS; Stoughton, MA; (Y); Church Yth Grp; Dance Clb; PAVAS; Acpl Chr; Chorus; Church Choir; Swing Chorus; Variety Show; Hon Roll; Psychlgy.

EGAN, JOANNA LEIGH; Dennis-Yarmouth Regional HS; W Yarmouth, MA; (Y); 52/310; Am Leg Aux Girls St; Camera Clb; Church Yth Grp; Ski Clb; Drill Tm; Drm Mjr(t); Yrbk Sprt Ed; JV Crs Cntry; JV Trk; Var Twrlr; Coors Colonial Whlsl Bevrg Corp Scholar 86; Ctzns Scholar Comm 86; Sthestrn MA U; Acctng.

EGAN, TIMOTHY; Boston College HS; Braintree, MA; (Y); Pres Drama Clb; Key Clb; Ski Clb; SADD; School Musical; School Play; Im Bsktbl; Im Vllybl; Prfct Atten Awd; Nwsp Rptr; Sectry Dramatics Society 84-85.

EGIZIO, MICHAEL; Bishop Feehan HS; Mansfield, MA; (Y); 16/256; Am Leg Boys St; Im Bsktbl; Var Ice Hcky; High Hon Roll; Hon Roll; NHS; Spanish NHS.

EHLEN, JON; Holyoke Catholic HS; S Hadley, MA; (Y); Art Clb; Church Yth Grp; Drama Clb; English Clb; French Clb; Speech Tm; Stage Crew; Nwsp Stf; Yrbk Stf; Lit Mag; AMA Modlng Comptn 84; Spch Grp 1st 85; Trnscrpt And Telegrm 1st Art Awd 86; Springfield Tech CC; Mech Engr.

EIBEN, DAGMAR; Hudson HS; Hudson, MA; (Y); 29/158; Cmnty Wkr; Pep Clb; Band; School Play; Yrbk Stf; MA Indstrl Hstry Awd 83; Physcs.

EIRES, ANTONIO; New Bedford HS; New Bedford, MA; (Y); 124/700; JV Bsbl.

EISENHAUR, AMY; Marblehead HS; Marblehead, MA; (Y); 41/259; Cmnty Wkr; Drama Clb; Political Wkr; Thesps; School Musical; School Play; Stage Crew; Hst Frsh Cls; Hst Soph Cls; Hst Jr Cls.

EKBORG, KELLY; Gloucester HS; Gloucester, MA; (Y); VP German Clb; Variety Show; Rep Frsh Cls; Var Soph Cls; Var Jr Cls; Var Sr Cls; Rep Stu Cncl; JV Sftbl; Var L Tennis; Var L Trk; Outstndng Chrch Stu 84; Med.

EKSTROM, KELLY A; Nauset Regional HS; Orleans, MA; (Y); Var Cheerleading; Var Socr; Achvt Awd-Hm Ec 86; Tufts; Arts.

EKTERMANIS, ELIZABETH; Lenox Memorial HS; Lenox, MA; (Y); CAP; Cmnty Wkr; Hosp Aide; Color Guard; School Play; Stage Crew; Var L Tennis; All Am Perfrmnc Tm 85; Wellesleyan Clg Bk Awd 86; Drmtc Arts.

ELDRIDGE, BARBARA; Marian HS; Framingham, MA; (Y); Church Yth Grp; Cmnty Wkr; Library Aide; School Musical; Stage Crew; Variety Show; Nwsp Stf; Rep Frsh Cls; Var Cheerleading; Intnl Clb.

ELLERIN, TODD; Lynnfield HS; Lynnfield, MA; (Y); 20/170; Drama Clb; Intnl Clb; JA; Var Capt Tennis; Kiwanis Awd; Ntl Merit Ltr; Spanish NHS; Latin Clb; Math Clb; School Play; Intl Sci & Engrng Fair 1st Prz 86; MIT ST Sci Fair 1st Prz 85-86; New Englnd Lwn Tnns Assn 83-85.

ELLERY, SARAH; Danvers HS; Danvers, MA; (Y); Band; Camp Fr Inc; Drm Mjr(t); Mrchg Band; Yrbk Stf; Var L Sftbl; Var L Swmmng; Hon Roll.

ELLIOT, LYNN; Westwood HS; Westwood, MA; (Y); 67/212; Church Yth Grp; Key Clb; Varsity Clb; Rep Frsh Cls; Rep Soph Cls; Rep Jr Cls; Rep Sr Cls; Pres Stu Cncl; L Var Bsktbl; Var Socr; Tri Vly Leag Track All Star 86; Daily Transcprt Track 86.

ELLIOT, LYNNE; Marlborough HS; Marlboro, MA; (Y); 16/300; Girl Scts; Var L Socr; High Hon Roll; NHS.

ELLIOTT, CAROLE-ANNE; Marian HS; Sudbury, MA; (Y); 48/200; Off French Clb; Sec Intnl Clb; SADD; JV Crs Cntry; Hon Roll; Outstndg Achvt Advncd Alg I & Advncd Frnch I; Langs.

ELLIOTT, KATHLEEN; Quaboag Regiona HS; Warren, MA; (Y); 1/87; Math Tm; SADD; Variety Show; Yrbk Stf; Sec Soph Cls; Sec Jr Cls; Sec Sr Cls; Hon Roll; NHS; Prfct Atten Awd; Class Marshall 86.

ELLIOTT, KIMBERLY; Holyoke HS; Holyoke, MA; (Y); Art Clb; Dance Clb; Girl Scts; JA; Office Aide; Teachers Aide; Gym; Hlyk Leag Arts & Crfts Awd 86; Wm Peck JR Hi Art Awd 83; Holyoke CC; Art.

ELLIOTT, STEVEN; Bristol-Plymouth Voc Reg Tech HS; Bridgewater, MA; (Y); Lion Awd; Auto Rpr Shop Awd; Auto Mchncs.

ELLIS, ERIK; Reading Mem HS; Reading, MA; (Y); Magna Cum Laude Ntl Latin 86; Cinematgrphy.

ELLIS, JILL; Marshfield HS; Marshfield, MA; (Y); 38/363; Key Clb; SADD; Capt Cheerleading; Swmmng; Trk; High Hon Roll; Kiwanis Awd; NHS; Boston Coll.

ELLIS, KENNETH J; Plymount-Carver HS; Plymouth, MA; (Y); 26/452; Drama Clb; Ed Lit Mag; Elks Awd; Hon Roll; Ntl Merit Ltr; Rockland Trst Schlrshp & Anchor Rlty Sc Hlrshp 86; 1st Pl Schl Sci Fair 84; Ithaca Coll; TV-RADIO.

ELLIS, KRISTA; Wakefield HS; Wakefield, MA; (Y); Key Clb; Latin Clb; Yrbk Stf; Var L Bsktbl; Coach Actv; Socr; Sftbl; Hon Roll; MVP & MIP Bsktbl; Cnstncy Adv Math; Med.

ELLIS, MAUREEN; Saint Clements HS; Somerville, MA; (Y); 5/69; Church Yth Grp; Cmnty Wkr; OEA; Y-Teens; School Play; Yrbk Phtg; Yrbk Stf; Hon Roll; VP NHS; Acvt Awds; Regis Coll; Bio.

ELLIS, TANIA; Boston Technical HS; Boston, MA; (Y); 15/120; Dance Clb; GAA; JCL; Latin Clb; Teachers Aide; Orch; Lit Mag; Trk; Hon Roll; Prfct Atten Awd; U Of MA; Peace Corp.

ELLISON, TERRY; Easthampton HS; Easthampton, MA; (Y); Church Yth Grp; Office Aide; Stu Cncl; JV Cheerleading; Hon Roll; Ntl Soc Stds Olympd Hstry 86.

ELLSWORTH, SUSAN; North Quincy HS; N Quincy, MA; (Y); 60/400; French Clb; Teachers Aide; French Hon Soc; Hon Roll; Frnch.

ELWOOD, DAWN; North Quincy HS; Quincy, MA; (Y); 23/380; Drama Clb; Hosp Aide; VP JA; VP Latin Clb; Chorus; School Play; Yrbk Stf; High Hon Roll; NHS; Brett Hall Awd Bio Sci Fair; Intl Rel.

EMENS, NANCY; Hingham HS; Hingham, MA; (Y); 145/335; Church Yth Grp; Cmnty Wkr; Orch; School Play; Rep Stu Cncl; Var Mgr(s); Var Socr; Var Capt Tennis; Offcr Chrch Yth Grp 85-86; Yth Rep Chrch Cncl 86-87; Chld Dev Awd 86; Alld Hlth.

EMERY, ANNE; The Waring Schl; Manchester, MA; (Y); Orch; Var Capt Bsktbl; JV Var Lcrss; JV Var Socr; Ntl Merit Ltr; Schl Frnch Prz; Frnch Tchr-Begining Stus 85-86; Exchng Stu France 84; Rice U; Math.

EMERY, MICHAEL S; Oakmont Regional HS; Westminster, MA; (Y); 16/140; Am Leg Boys St; Red Cross Aide; Ski Clb; Var JV Bsbl; Im Bsktbl.

EMMA, KAREN; North Reading HS; N Reading, MA; (Y); Church Yth Grp; Dance Clb; Variety Show; Yrbk Stf; Sec Frsh Cls; Pres Jr Cls; JV Cheerleading; Hon Roll; U MA Amherst; Bus Admin.

ENDRIS, STEPHANIE; Cohasset HS; Cohasset, MA; (Y); Church Yth Grp; Ski Clb; Yrbk Stf; Bsktbl; Capt Crs Cntry; Lcrss; Powder Puff Ftbl; Trk; Hon Roll.

ENG, ANGELA K; Ashland HS; Ashland, MA; (Y); Am Leg Aux Girls St; Church Yth Grp; Hosp Aide; Library Aide; SADD; Jazz Band; Variety Show; Yrbk Stf; Sec Jr Cls; Score Keeper; Intl Rel.

ENG, DAVID; Haverhill HS; Haverhill, MA; (Y); 4/416; VP German Clb; SADD; Nwsp Rptr; Sec Stu Cncl; Var Capt Swmmng; High Hon Roll; NHS; Boys Swim Tm-Awd 84; Stu Of Mnth 85; Boys Swim Tm-Most Dedicated 86; Engrng.

ENGLISH, PATRICIA; Mt St Joseph Acad; Dorchester, MA; (Y); 5/167; Church Yth Grp; Trs French Clb; GAA; JA; Rep Soph Cls; Rep Jr Cls; Trs Sr Cls; Stu Cncl; Socr; Swmmng; Moira Dyer Meml Schlrshp 83; Stu Govt Day Delg 86.

ENNEGUESS, JEANNE; Maynard HS; Maynard, MA; (Y); 1/100; Hosp Aide; Band; Jazz Band; Nwsp Sprt Ed; Rep Frsh Cls; VP Soph Cls; VP Jr Cls; Pres Stu Cncl; Fld Hcky; Golf; Bausch & Lomb Sci Awd 86; Williams Coll Bk Awd 86; Natl Hnr Soc Pres 86; Med.

ENNIS, SHAUN; Haverhill HS; Haverhill, MA; (Y); 50/250; German Clb; JV Im Bsktbl; JV Golf; Var L Tennis; High Hon Roll; Church Yth Grp; Im Vllybl; Comp Tech.

ENOS, ERIC SCOTT; Taunton HS; Taunton, MA; (Y); 30/371; Trs Church Yth Grp; Library Aide; Yrbk Stf; Var L Swmmng; Ntl Merit Ltr; Magna Cum Laude Cert Natl Lat Exm 83; 4 Yr Coll Scholar Navy ROTC & Army ROTC 86; Cum Laude Grad 86; West Point USMA; Humnties.

ENOS, KIM; Taunton HS; Taunton, MA; (Y); Drama Clb; Ski Clb; Rep Frsh Cls; Rep Soph Cls; Rep Jr Cls; Rep Sr Cls; Rep Stu Cncl; Var Crs Cntry; Var Gym; JV Sftbl; Drama.

ENRIGHT, MICHELE; Silver Lake Regional HS; Plympton, MA; (Y); Yrbk Bus Mgr; Stonehill; Lngs.

ENRIQUEZ, DAVID; Silver Lake HS; Kingston, MA; (Y); Boy Scts; Drama Clb; Spanish Clb; SADD; School Play; Variety Show; Sr Cls; Crs Cntry; Socr; Voice Dem Awd; Arch.

ENZIAN, THOMAS; Central Catholic HS; Dracut, MA; (Y); 89/231; Church Yth Grp; Im Bowling; JV Trk; Var Wrstlng; Tufts U; Psych.

EPPS, SHAUN; Winchester HS; St Paul, MN; (Y); Church Yth Grp; Cmnty Wkr; Varsity Clb; Variety Show; Rep Stu Cncl; Var Bsbl; Var Bsktbl; Var Ftbl; Hon Roll; Natl TV Commrcl W/Tide 82; Comp Pgmr.

ERBES, JOHN W; Westford Acad; Westford, MA; (Y); AFS; Art Clb; German Clb; Nwsp Stf; Hon Roll; Fin NY Schl Visl Arts Scholar Comptn 86; Stu At Calendr 84; Art Clb Calendr 85; Cooper Union; Fine Art.

ERICKSON, CHRISTINA; Phillips Acad; Durham, NC; (Y); AFS; Church Yth Grp; Drama Clb; French Clb; Hosp Aide; Model UN; School Play; Cheerleading; Hon Roll; Schlrshp Genoea Switzerland 85-86; Tlnt Idntfctn Prgm Eng Awd Duke U 82; Schlrshp To Phllps Acad 85-87; Intl Studies.

ERICKSON, HARLEY A; Harwich HS; N Harwich, MA; (Y); 5/96; Drama Clb; Pres 4-H; Spanish Clb; School Play; 4-H Awd; High Hon Roll; NHS; Hrvrd Bk Prize 85; Jhnsn ULM Schlrshp Mntng Abv 90 Aver; Boston U; Bio.

ERINGI, KRISTINE; Fitchburg HS; Fitchburg, MA; (Y); Cmnty Wkr; Yrbk Stf; JV Var Bsktbl; JV Crs Cntry; Var Sftbl; High Hon Roll; Cmplmntry Jr Ftchbrgs Wmns Clb 86-87; Physcl Ther.

ERLICH, ADAM E; Bedford HS; Bedford, MA; (Y); 3/200; Am Leg Boys St; Capt Debate Tm; ROTC; Jazz Band; Nwsp Ed-Chief; Var Bsktbl; JV Tennis; High Hon Roll; NHS; Voice Dem Awd; Harvard Prz Bk Awd 86; Amer Legion Schlstc Mdl 86; Scl Stds Awd 85-86; MIT; Engrng.

ERMINI, MICHAEL; Wareham HS; East Wareham, MA; (Y); 3/150; Am Leg Boys St; DECA; SADD; Varsity Clb; Yrbk Bus Mgr; VP Sr Cls; Rep Stu Cncl; Var L Tennis; High Hon Roll; NHS; Bentley Coll; Bus.

ERNEST, JASON A; Framingham South HS; Framingham, MA; (Y); 7/275; Am Leg Boys St; Drama Clb; Trs Exploring; Mgr JA; VP Key Clb; Latin Clb; Spanish Clb; Madrigals; School Musical; Stage Crew; Summa Cum Laude Natl Latn Exm Gld Medl 85-86; Argus Postr Wrtg Cntst Awd 85-86; Dntstry.

ERNST, MARIANNE; Pittsfield HS; Pittsfield, MA; (Y); Church Yth Grp; Cmnty Wkr; French Clb; Var Trk; Hon Roll; Elem Educ.

ERREDE, LAURA LEE; Auburn HS; Auburn, MA; (Y); Camp Fr Inc; Girl Scts; Spanish Clb; SADD; Yrbk Stf; Trk; High Hon Roll; Hon Roll; Intl Order Of Rainbow For Girls; Pharmcst.

ESPANOLA, DIANA; Phillips Acad; Natick, MA; (Y); Var L Bsktbl; Var Crs Cntry; JV Fld Hcky; JV Var Sftbl; High Hon Roll; Ntl Merit Ltr; Cum Laude Soc 86; Warren Prize 86; Amherst Coll.

ESPOSITO, KRISTIN; Wakefield HS; Wakefield, MA; (Y); Hnrbl Mntn 85-86; Consumer Math Awd 86; Bus.

ESTACIO, BEVERLY; Diman Regional Voc Tech HS; Fall River, MA; (Y); Key Clb; Library Aide; Yrbk Stf; Voc Ed Wk Bmpr Stckr Dsgn Cntst Pstr Cntst Essy Cntst 85; Cmmrcl Art.

EUSTACE, DANIEL; North Reading HS; N Reading, MA; (Y); Church Yth Grp; Math Tm; Nwsp Stf; High Hon Roll; Hon Roll; Bio.

EVANS, BETSY; Walnut Hill Schl; Needham, MA; (Y); Camera Clb; Drama Clb; Intnl Clb; Nwsp Stf; Yrbk Stf; VP Soph Cls; VP Jr Cls; VP Sr Cls; Var Gym; Church Yth Grp; Peer Tutor 84-86; Phys Thrpy.

EVANS, DENNIS P; West Roxbury HS; Roslindale, MA; (S); Church Yth Grp; Variety Show; Bsktbl; Hon Roll; NHS; Prfct Attndnc; Accntng.

EVANS, HEATHER; North Midlesex Regional HS; Pepperell, MA; (Y); Dance Clb; Sec Debate Tm; Drama Clb; Hosp Aide; Intnl Clb; Ski Clb; Chorus; Gym; Tennis; Trk; Recog Vlntrg Hosp Cir 85; Awd Outstndng Accmplshmts Debt 85; U Of MA; Psych.

EVANS, LYNN; Ludlow HS; Ludlow, MA; (Y); 2/250; Hosp Aide; Band; Yrbk Ed-Chief; Rep Soph Cls; Rep Jr Cls; Sec Sr Cls; Rep Stu Cncl; Var Capt Cheerleading; Var Sftbl; Sec NHS; Rensselaer Medl Top Rnkg Math & Sci 86; Co Prom Coord 86; Regl Stdnt Advsry Cncl Rep 85-86; Bio.

EVANS, MARK; Old Rochester Regional HS; Mattapoisett, MA; (Y); Cmnty Wkr; Teachers Aide; Golf; Socr; Hon Roll; Jr NHS; NHS; Hnrs Awd Excllnc Natl Sci 86; Bus.

EVANS, MEGAN; Concord-Carlisle HS; Concord, MA; (Y); 130/328; Church Yth Grp; Dance Clb; Stu Cncl; Var Lcrss; JV Socr; Dept Awd Engl 85.

EVANS, NOREEN; Fontbonne Acad; Quincy, MA; (Y); 9/134; Drama Clb; Hosp Aide; Intnl Clb; Chorus; Mrchg Band; Mgr(s); High Hon Roll; Hon Roll; Trs NHS; Prfct Atten Awd; Boston Coll; Nrsng.

EVANS, SAMUEL J; Sharon HS; Sharon, MA; (Y); 3/190; Chorus; Pres Concert Band; School Musical; Ed Nwsp Stf; VP Jr Cls; High Hon Roll; Pres NHS; Ntl Merit SF; Pres Schlr; Nancy Lohmiller Mem Awd Excllnc Wrtng 85; Yale U; Econ.

EVERSOLL, RHONDA; Murdock HS; Winchendon, MA; (Y); Art Clb; Camera Clb; Dance Clb; Math Clb; Spanish Clb; JV Capt Cheerleading; Powder Puff Ftbl; Sftbl; Swmmng; Hon Roll; Cazenovia Coll; Arch.

EVITTS, SUSAN; Saugus HS; Saugus, MA; (Y); 7/266; Yrbk Stf; Tennis; High Hon Roll; Jr NHS; NHS; L H Martin Schlrshp, Stonehl Coll Hnrs Schrl 86; Hnrbl Ment Sci 85; Stonehill Coll; Bio.

EVON, PAUL; Chicopee Comprehensive HS; Chicopee, MA; (Y); Capt Ice Hcky; NHS; Natl Hon Soc 84-85 & 85-86; Westfield ST Coll.

EWALD, ERIC; Winchester HS; Winchester, MA; (Y); Spanish Clb; Ftbl; Wt Lftg; Wrstlng; High Hon Roll; Hon Roll; Lafayette; Bus.

EWALD, JOHN C; Amherst Regional HS; Amherst, MA; (Y); Am Leg Boys St; FBLA; Ski Clb; Nwsp Rptr; Nwsp Stf; Im Bsktbl; JV Var Socr; Hon Roll; Bus.

EYLES, HEATHER; Tantasqua Regional HS; Sturbridge, MA; (Y); 10/189; Yrbk Stf; NHS; Pres Schlr; MA Forgn Lang Assn Awd Span 86; Tantasgua Teachrs Assn Schlrshp 86; Anna Maria Coll; Spanis Teacher.

FABERMAN, STEPHEN; Leominster HS; Leominster, MA; (S); Debate Tm; Spanish Clb; VP Temple Yth Grp; School Play; Nwsp Sprt Ed; Rep Soph Cls; Rep Stu Cncl; High Hon Roll; NHS; Outstndng Achvt In Civics Awd 83; Brandeis; Lawyer.

FABIANO, TINA; Boston Latin HS; Charlestown, MA; (Y); Boys Clb Am; Church Yth Grp; Var Capt Bsktbl; Powder Puff Ftbl; Var Socr; Var Capt Sftbl; Girl Of Yr Boys & Girls Clb 84; MVP Sftbl 86; Unsung Hero Bsktbl 86.

FABRI, RICH A; Saugus HS; Saugus, MA; (Y); 36/300; Bsbl; Bsktbl; Hon Roll; Jr NHS; NHS; VFW Awd; Bsktbl Coaches Awd 85 & 86; CYO Sportsmnshp Awd 85; U Hartford; Engrng.

FACE, KYLE; Georgetown JR SR HS; Georgetown, MA; (Y); 11/100; Church Yth Grp; Spanish Clb; JV Bsktbl; Hon Roll; NHS; Electrncs.

FACTOR, TRACY; Randolph HS; Randolph, MA; (Y); French Clb; Off Jr Cls; Nrsng.

FAFORD, DAWN; Shepherd Hill Regional HS; S Bridge, MA; (Y); Church Yth Grp; Cmnty Wkr; Computer Clb; Dance Clb; Debate Tm; 4-H; Math Tm; Spanish Clb; Variety Show; Ftbl; Alge I Awd 85; Hon Roll 85-86; Law.

FAGAN, HEIDI; Mount Alvernia HS; West Roxbury, MA; (Y); 16/41; Church Yth Grp; Girl Scts; Sec Soph Cls; Pres Jr Cls; Off Stu Cncl; 2nd Pl Awd Archdioc Art Fair 83; Ldrshp Awd Excllnc Archbshp Boston Cardnl Bernard Law 86; Merrimack Coll; Bus Mgmt.

FAGAN, SEBASTIAN J; Narragansett Regional HS; Templeton, MA; (Y); 12/76; Am Leg Boys St; Boy Scts; Letterman Clb; L Band; JV Trk; Hon Roll; Mu Alp Tht; NHS; Acadmc Ltr Scholtc Achvt; Liberal Arts.

FAHEY, ERIN; Hudson HS; Hudson, MA; (Y); 26/140; Church Yth Grp; Pep Clb; Trs Ski Clb; SADD; School Musical; Powder Puff Ftbl; Hon Roll; Regis Coll; Mngmnt.

FAHEY, KERRY; Tahanto Regional HS; Boylston, MA; (Y); VP Sec JA; Chorus; Variety Show; Pres Frsh Cls; Pres Soph Cls; Pres Jr Cls; Drugs/Alchl Spkr 84; Outstndng Ldr; HOBY Ldrshp Sem 85; U New Orleans; Htl/Rest Mngmnt.

FAILLACE, JOEL; East Longmeadow HS; E Longmeadow, MA; (Y); Chess Clb; Debate Tm; Intnl Clb; Math Tm; Band; School Play; Trs Stu Cncl; Crs Cntry; Score Keeper; Trk; Ecnmcs.

FAJARDO, SUZANNE; North Quincy HS; Quincy, MA; (Y); Church Yth Grp; Teachers Aide; High Hon Roll; Hon Roll; Erly Chldhd.

FALAISE, JEAN BALACUER; C R L S HS; Cambridge, MA; (Y); Debate Tm; French Clb; School Musical; L Badmtn; L CAP; L Swmmng; L Trk; L Wt Lftg; Hon Roll; Antoine Happoljle Schlrshp Fund 86; Bunker Hill CC; Elec Tech.

FALANDEAU, CLAIRE; Holyoke HS; Holyoke, MA; (Y); Dance Clb; Girl Scts; Hosp Aide; Library Aide.

FALCHLIK, LESLIE; Newton North HS; Newton, MA; (Y); Hosp Aide; Ski Clb; Spanish Clb; Temple Yth Grp; Varsity Clb; Nwsp Stf; Yrbk Stf; Cheerleading; Tennis; Hon Roll.

FALCONE, GINA M; Leominster HS; Leominster, MA; (Y); Yrbk Stf; Pres Frsh Cls; Pres Soph Cls; Pres Jr Cls; Pres Sr Cls; Var Bsktbl; Var Sftbl; Var Capt Swmmng; High Hon Roll; NHS; Ruth Piermarini Awd 85; Math.

FALCONE, MICHAEL A; Catholic Memorial HS; Readville, MA; (Y); 1/240; Am Leg Boys St; Dance Clb; Drama Clb; Math Clb; School Play; Variety Show; High Hon Roll; Jr NHS; NHS; Acad Achvt Awds 84-86; Sci Prjct Awd 86.

FALER, SETH; Wakefield HS; Wakefield, MA; (Y); 1/303; VP JA; VP JCL; Pres Key Clb; Capt Math Tm; Nwsp Ed-Chief; Yrbk Stf; Var Socr; Ntl Merit Schol; Val; Var L Trk; Brown U Book Awd 85; Harvard U; Ecnmcs.

FALKENGREN, WENDY; Auburn SR HS; Auburn, MA; (Y); 4-H; Ski Clb; SADD; Fld Hcky; Score Keeper; High Hon Roll; Hon Roll; Marine Bio.

FALLER, BERNARD; Medford HS; Medford, MA; (Y); Art Clb; SADD; Yrbk Stf; JV Tennis; Im Vllybl; Excel Engl Awd 86; Med.

FALLON, TRACEY; Westford Acad; Westford, MA; (Y); 17/225; Sec German Clb; Model UN; Pres SADD; Nwsp Rptr; Yrbk Stf; Var Fld Hcky; Capt Gym; Var Tennis; High Hon Roll; NHS; NHS Ldrshp Awd 85; Century III Ldrs Rnnr-Up 86; Excllnc In Germn 86; Worcester Polytec Inst; Biomed.

FALVEY, JOAN; Randolph HS; Randolph, MA; (Y); 38/323; Chrmn SADD; Pres Soph Cls; Pres Jr Cls; Pres Sr Cls; JC Awd; Sec NHS; Am Leg Aux Girls St; Cmnty Wkr; Political Wkr; Rep Frsh Cls; Chrprsn Stu Cmmtee; Stu Cncl; Boston Coll; Poli Sci.

FALVEY, KERRY; Frontier Regional HS; S Deerfield, MA; (Y); 2/91; Nwsp Rptr; Yrbk Stf; Ed Lit Mag; High Hon Roll; Hon Roll; Sec NHS; Engl.

FALVEY, SUSAN; Dedham HS; Dedham, MA; (Y); Pres Church Yth Grp; Rep Stu Cncl; Var Capt Bsktbl; Var Fld Hcky; Var Trk; Hon Roll; NHS; Cmnty Wkr; Computer Clb; French Clb; St Marys Catholic Yth Ministry Mst Active 85-86; Phys Thrpy.

FAMA, PAUL; C Columbus Central Cath HS; Medford, MA; (S); 9/111; Computer Clb; Stage Crew; Variety Show; Nwsp Stf; Hon Roll; Comp Prog.

FANDREYER, CARL; Fitchburg HS; Ashby, MA; (Y); Am Leg Boys St; Church Yth Grp; CAP; German Clb; Red Cross Aide; Church Choir; Stage Crew; High Hon Roll; Hon Roll; U Of MA; Pre-Med.

FANTASIA, STEVEN; Bishop Feehan HS; Norton, MA; (Y); Math Tm; School Play; Stage Crew; Nwsp Stf; Yrbk Stf; Im Bsbl; JV Var Bsktbl; JV Ftbl; JV Score Keeper; Im Wt Lftg; Comp Progrmmng.

FANTONI, STEPHANIE; Medway JR SR HS; Medway, MA; (Y); 9/140; Church Yth Grp; French Clb; Yrbk Stf; JV Bsktbl; Var Fld Hcky; Capt Trk; High Hon Roll; Hon Roll; NHS; Prfct Atten Awd; Bus.

FARBEROV, INNA; Marblehead HS; Marblehead, MA; (Y); Chess Clb; Im Badmtn; Im Swmmng; Im Vllybl; Hon Roll; Aeronautical Engr.

FARESE, KARLA; Waltham HS; Waltham, MA; (Y); Cmnty Wkr; Dance Clb; Political Wkr; SADD; Chorus; School Play; Variety Show; High Hon Roll; Gold Musc Awd, Outstndng Chrl Membr 85-86; Kingsbury Tempernc Post Essy Cntst 86; Eng.

FARIA, SUSANA; Newbedford HS; Newbedford, MA; (Y); JCL; Office Aide; Rptr Yrbk Stf; Crs Cntry; Trk; High Hon Roll; Jr NHS; NHS; Prfct Atten Awd; Alumni Schlrshp 86; Newbedford Ladies Schlrshp 86; Lesle Coll; Cnslng Psych.

FARIAS, ROBERT A; New Bedford HS; New Bedford, MA; (Y); 141/701; Exploring; Political Wkr; SADD; JV Var Ftbl; JV Var Trk; Im Wt Lftg; PSYCHLGY.

FARINHA JR, PAUL W; Taunton HS; E Taunton, MA; (Y); High Hon Roll; NHS; Ntl Math Awd 83; Hon Mntn Cum Laude Ntl Ltn Exm Awd 84; Slvr Awd Magna Cum Lau De Ntl Ltn Exm Awd 85.

FARIVAR-SADRI, KAMRAN; Milford HS; Milford, MA; (Y); Boy Scts; Var Socr; Var Trk; JV Var Wrstlng; High Hon Roll; Jr NHS; NHS; Town Soccer League Tm Captn 83-84; Worcester Poly Inst Awd 86; Worcester Poly Tech Inst; Engr.

FARLEY, LISA; Beverly HS; Beverly, MA; (Y); Ski Clb; Yrbk Stf; JV Var Bsktbl; Var L Socr; Var Sftbl; Bay St Games-Sccr 83-84; No 1 Goalkpr-Boston Globe 84-85; All Conf-Sccr Tm-To Playy In Europe 85-86.

FARLEY, SEAN M; Noble & Greenough HS; Charlestown, MA; (Y); Am Leg Boys St; Boys Clb Am; Church Yth Grp; Cmnty Wkr; Political Wkr; Bsbl; Ftbl; Ice Hcky; Hon Roll; Prfct Atten Awd; Schlrshp Noble & Greenough 84-87; JR Olympcs Ice Hcky CO 85; Bus.

FARMER, KELLY; Haverhill HS; Bradford, MA; (Y); 45/416; Church Yth Grp; German Clb; Yrbk Stf; Cheerleading; Swmmng; Tennis; Bates; Psych.

FARO, GINA; Presentation Of Mary Acad; Atkinson, NH; (S); 1/50; Math Clb; Spanish Clb; SADD; Yrbk Stf; Sec Frsh Cls; Sec Soph Cls; Pres Stu Cncl; High Hon Roll; NHS; NEDT Awd; Pre-Med.

FARO, GINA; Winthrop HS; Winthrop, MA; (Y); 15/220; Math Tm; Nwsp Sprt Ed; Yrbk Sprt Ed; Var Fld Hcky; Hon Roll; NHS; Rep Alfred Saggese Awd 86; Awd Merit 84; Suffolk U; Acctng.

FARO, JOSEPH; Central Catholic HS; Atkinson, NH; (Y); 41/231; Ski Clb; Im Bsktbl; JV Trk; Im Wt Lftg; High Hon Roll; Hon Roll; Arch.

FARQUHAR, BRIAN; BMC Durfee HS; Fall River, MA; (Y); 70/650; Varsity Clb; Yrbk Stf; Var Ftbl; Var Ice Hcky; Trk; Herald News All Schltc Hcky Tm 1st Tm 85; Engrng.

FARR, KELLY ANN; Sacred Heart HS; Hanover, MA; (Y); 25/90; Cmnty Wkr; Drama Clb; Sec Key Clb; Ski Clb; School Play; Nwsp Ed-Chief; Nwsp Rptr; Stu Cncl; Capt Vllybl; Hon Roll; Outstndng Excllnc Edtr And Reprtr Awd 85-86; Stonehill Clg; Bus.

FARRAND, KAREN; Southbridge HS; Southbridge, MA; (Y); 1/144; Art Clb; Math Tm; Soph Cls; High Hon Roll; NHS; Ntl Merit Ltr; Chrch Yth Grp Sec 85-86.

FARRAR, DAVE; St Marys HS; Lynn, MA; (Y); 8/97; Var Crs Cntry; Var Trk; High Hon Roll; Hon Roll; Acdmc Excllnc Chem, US Hstry & Alg II 86; Northeastern MIT; Chem Engnrng.

FARRELL, LINDA; Holbrook JR SR HS; Holbrook, MA; (Y); Church Yth Grp; Cmnty Wkr; Capt Color Guard; Bsktbl; Sftbl; Princpl Awd U S Hist 86; Princess Prom 86; Int Design.

FARRELL, MARK; Xaverian Brothers HS; Stoughton, MA; (Y); 33/208; Aud/Vis; Drama Clb; School Musical; School Play; Stage Crew; Ntl Merit Ltr; Scl Cmt; Tech Crea Awd; Lylty & Srv Awd; Rnslr Poly Tech Inst; Engr.

FARRELL, STEPHEN J; Holy Name C C HS; North Grafton, MA; (Y); 87/259; Chrmn School Musical; Var L Ftbl; L Capt Trk; Hon Roll; Church Yth Grp; 4-H; Chem Awd Oustndng Achvt 84-85; 20th Cen Hist Awd Outstndng Achvt 85-86; Supervisor Stu Workers 85-86; Norwich U; Elec Engrng.

FARRELL, WILLIAM B; Holliston HS; Holliston, MA; (Y); VP Pres AFS; Am Leg Boys St; Boy Scts; Drama Clb; Trs Frsh Cls; Trs Soph Cls; Pres Jr Cls; Pres Sr Cls; Var L Trk; Hon Roll.

FARREN, LISA; Plymouth-Carver HS; Plymouth, MA; (Y); Am Leg Aux Girls St; Dance Clb; Girl Scts; Model UN; Yrbk Stf; VP Jr Cls; Hon Roll; Alt Stu Govt Day Prog 86; Northeastern U; Phys Ther.

FARWELL, TERRY; Acton-Boxboro HS; Acton, MA; (Y); 141/428; Church Yth Grp; Cmnty Wkr; Dance Clb; Hosp Aide; Teachers Aide; Variety Show; Yrbk Stf; Var Capt Swmmng; Hon Roll.

FASANO, LINDA A; Braintree HS; Braintree, MA; (Y); 22/416; Church Yth Grp; Cmnty Wkr; Spanish Clb; Lit Mag; High Hon Roll; NHS; Spanish NHS; Sci Fair Hnrbl Mntn 82; Volntr Love-Dedctn Awd 83; Typewrtng Awd 84-85; U Of MA Boston; Engl.

FASSELL, KATE; Hoosac Valley HS; Adams, MA; (Y); 10/140; Ski Clb; Var L Crs Cntry; Var L Trk; Hon Roll; NHS; Girls ST 86; NEMA Awd 86; Sprts Med.

FASY, ELIZABETH; Bishop Connolly HS; Portsmouth, RI; (Y); 2/167; Cmnty Wkr; French Clb; Math Clb; Math Tm; Ski Clb; SADD; Var Capt Crs Cntry; Var Trk; Elks Awd; High Hon Roll; Crss Cntry Coachs Awd 86; Acad Mdlln In Engl & Sci 86:Hly Crss Book Awd 85; Coll Of The Hly Crss; Pre-Med.

FATYOL, JUDITH; Georgetown JR SR HS; Georgetown, MA; (Y); 8/100; AFS; OEA; Lit Mag; Hon Roll; NHS; Engrng.

FAULKNER, MICHAEL; Assabet Valley Reg Voc HS; Northboro, MA; (Y); #9 In Class; Ski Clb; High Hon Roll; Elec Engrng.

FAUST, LISA; Stoughton HS; Stoughton, MA; (Y); Church Yth Grp; Yrbk Stf; Fld Hcky; Powder Puff Ftbl; Sftbl; NHS; Bus.

FAVAZZA, MARY; Gloucester HS; Gloucester, MA; (Y); 3/342; Pres Frsh Cls; Var Capt Bsktbl; Var Capt Sftbl; High Hon Roll; Pres NHS; Ntl Merit Ltr; Pres JR Rtrns 86; Outstndng Athlete Of Yr 86; Smith Coll; Med.

FAY, HEIDI; Nipmuc Regional HS; Mendon, MA; (Y); 33/90; Art Clb; Church Yth Grp; Dance Clb; Drama Clb; Hosp Aide; SADD; Yrbk Rptr; Sec Jr Cls; Sec Sr Cls; JV Crs Cntry; JC Hnr Englsh Class 85-86; Spnsh Hnr Class 86-87; Art Exibit Awd 84-86; LAW Enfrcmnt.

FAZEKAS, KAREN; Newton Country Day Schl; Needham, MA; (Y); Church Yth Grp; Model UN; Speech Tm; School Play; High Hon Roll; Hon Roll; Jr NHS; NHS; MA Adv Studys Prog Schlrshp 86; Pres Clsrm Frnch Exch; Arch.

FAZIO, GIOVANNA; Waltham HS; Waltham, MA; (Y); Sec Church Yth Grp; Intnl Clb; Cmpltng Stps Gds Ryl Kngdm 85; Bentley Coll; Bus Mngmt.

FAZZINA, KIMBERLY; B M C Durfee HS; Fall River, MA; (Y); Hosp Aide; Office Aide; Spanish Clb; Varsity Clb; Capt Flag Corp; Yrbk Stf; Var L Gym; Im Powder Puff Ftbl; Capt Twrlr; Hon Roll; Unsung Hero Awd 85; Sci.

FECTEAU, SHARI; Salem HS; Salem, MA; (Y); 27/240; Church Yth Grp; Yrbk Stf; JV Var Cheerleading; JV Var Tennis; High Hon Roll; Hon Roll; NHS; Spanish NHS; Fash Merch.

FEDELIA, TAMMY; Attleboro HS; Attleboro, MA; (Y); Sec Church Yth Grp; Girl Scts; JV L Hosp Aide; Color Guard; Drill Tm; Elks Awd; Med.

FEDERICO, LISA; Christopher Columbus HS; Boston, MA; (S); 3/127; Cmnty Wkr; Library Aide; Math Tm; Science Clb; Yrbk Rptr; Hon Roll; NHS; NEDT Awd; U Of MA Boston; Bus Mgmt.

FEDERICO, MARGHERITA; Christopher Columbus HS; Malden, MA; (S); 14/111; Computer Clb; Office Aide; Rep Stu Cncl; Hon Roll; Ntl Merit Ltr; Italian Lang.

FEDOR, CHRISTOPHER; St Johns HS; Sterling, MA; (Y); 150/272; Church Yth Grp; Debate Tm; Drama Clb; English Clb; French Clb; Ski Clb; SADD; Varsity Clb; Rep Sr Cls; Var Capt Bsktbl; Cntrl MA Div 1 Sprbwl Chmp Ftbll 85-86; Cntrl MA All Str Bsktbll 85-86; Loyola Coll; Bus Mngmnt.

FEELEY, DANIEL; Franklin HS; Franklin, MA; (Y); Concert Band; School Musical; Stage Crew; Variety Show; JV Bsbl; JV Ice Hcky; Hon Roll; Lib Arts.

FEENER, SUZANNE; Acton-Boxboro Regional HS; Acton, MA; (Y); 108/410; VP AFS; Band; Concert Band; Mrchg Band; Powder Puff Ftbl; JV Socr; NHS; Engrng.

FEENEY, DENICE; Marshfield HS; Marshfield, MA; (Y); #185 In Class; Yrbk Stf; JV Powder Puff Ftbl; Child Psychlgst.

FEERICK, MAURA; North Quincy HS; Quincy, MA; (Y); 70/366; Yrbk Stf; Hon Roll; Ntl Merit Ltr; Bus.

FEINBERG, DONNA; Lincoln-Sudbury Regional HS; Sudbury, MA; (Y); Hon Roll; Ithaca Coll; Psych.

FELDER JR, RONALD E; Milton Acad; Cincinnati, OH; (Y); Aud/Vis; Pres Church Yth Grp; Computer Clb; Debate Tm; Math Tm; Model UN; Church Choir; Stage Crew; Im Socr; Var Trk; ABC Mnrty Recruit 83; LEAD Pgm-Bus Orntd Minorities 86; West Point; Engrng.

FELIX, CATHY; Mc Cann Tech; North Adams, MA; (Y); SADD; High Hon Roll; Hon Roll; Berkshire CC; Comp.

FELTCH, STACIE; Everett HS; Everett, MA; (Y); 5/286; Church Yth Grp; Intnl Clb; Trs Key Clb; Varsity Clb; Chorus; Yrbk Stf; Var L Trk; High Hon Roll; Lion Awd; NHS; Lions Clb Serv To Blnd Awd 85; Vrsty Trck Ltrs 83-85; U Of RI; Phrmcy.

FENICK, DEIRDRE A; Braintree HS; Braintree, MA; (Y); 42/372; Church Yth Grp; Off Frsh Cls; Rep Soph Cls; Off Jr Cls; Off Sr Cls; Coach Actv; JV Fld Hcky; JV Sftbl; High Hon Roll; Hon Roll; Mary Loo Walsh Mem Schlrshp 86; Boston U; Bus.

FENTON, DAWN; Medford HS; Medford, MA; (Y); 7/434; Dance Clb; Math Tm; Science Clb; SADD; Chorus; Nwsp Stf; High Hon Roll; Hon Roll; Mu Alp Tht; NHS; Top Intrmdt Math Stu 85; Hnrs Chmstry Awd 85; Gftd & Tlntd Prgm 84-87; Comp Engrng.

FERBER, MICHAEL; Brockton HS; Brockton, MA; (Y); 120/1000; Cmnty Wkr; Computer Clb; Key Clb; Temple Yth Grp; High Hon Roll; Hon Roll; Anshe Sphard Schlrshp 86.

FERGUSON, MARTHA L; Dover Shergorn HS; Sherborn, MA; (Y); Church Yth Grp; Intnl Clb; JCL; Trs Latin Clb; Ski Clb; Varsity Clb; Orch; Yrbk Phtg; Bsktbl; Var Crs Cntry; Skidmore Coll; Lib Arts.

FERGUSON, PAULA M; Shrewsbury HS; Shrewsbury, MA; (Y); 1/225; Math Tm; NFL; School Play; Yrbk Phtg; Yrbk Rptr; NHS; Ntl Merit SF; Val; Harvard Bk Awd; Suprtndt Awd Acad Excl; MA Advncd Stds Prgrm; MA Inst Of Tech; Elec Engr.

FERIOLI, JULIE; Cathedral HS; Feeding Hls, MA; (Y); 7/455; Dance Clb; Intnl Clb; Office Aide; Chorus; Nwsp Rptr; Nwsp Sprt Ed; Nwsp Stf; Var JV Cheerleading; High Hon Roll; NHS; UNICO Schlrshp 86; Italian Wmns Clb Schlrshp 86; Bst Physcs Awd 86; Rensselaer Polytech Inst; Engrn.

FERNANDES, LISA M; Medfield HS; Medfield, MA; (Y); 8/163; AFS; Am Leg Aux Girls St; Quiz Bowl; Teachers Aide; Nwsp Rptr; High Hon Roll; Hon Roll; Jr NHS; NCTE Awd; NHS; Bd Of Regnts Schlrshp 86; Tuffs; Sci.

FERNANDEZ, ALEX; Greater Lawrence Tech Schl; Lawrence, MA; (Y); 1/335; Computer Clb; SADD; Rep Frsh Cls; High Hon Roll; NHS; Elctd Vc Pres Natl Hnr Scty 86-87; Lowell U; Elctrncs Engr.

FERNANDEZ, JEANNE; Bishop Stang HS; N Dartmouth, MA; (Y); Drama Clb; Hosp Aide; Ski Clb; Chorus; School Musical; School Play; JV Sftbl; High Hon Roll; Hon Roll; NHS; Stonehill; Crimnl Lawyer.

FERNNDES, MARIA; Jeremiah E Burke HS; Dorechester, MA; (Y); Key Clb; Rep Soph Cls; Cit Awd; French Hon Soc; Hon Roll; Jr NHS; Prfct Atten Awd; The Most Outstndng JR 86; Stu Ldrshp Awd 86; Hnr Rl Awd 86; Comp Prgrmr.

FERRANDI, NICOLE; Pope John XXIII Central HS; Revere, MA; (Y); Office Aide; Hon Roll; Psych.

FERRANTINO, DAVID; Ware HS; Ware, MA; (Y); Am Leg Boys St; French Clb; Key Clb; Band; Mgr Stage Crew; Yrbk Sprt Ed; Rep Stu Cncl; Golf; Hon Roll; All Westrn MA Glf Tm 86; W MA HS Indvdl Trnmnt 86; Pr Mrt 86; Mech Engrng.

FERRARA, BILL; North Quincy HS; Quincy, MA; (Y); Ice Hcky; Wrstlng; High Hon Roll; Hon Roll; 3rd Pl Cty Art Pcture Awd 84; Hnrb Mntn ST Art Pcture 85; Awd Agnst Prjdc; Comp Sci.

FERRARI, DONNA; Norwood HS; Norwood, MA; (Y); 20/331; Hosp Aide; JA; SADD; Band; Concert Band; Symp Band; Stu Cncl; Hon Roll; Jr NHS; Jr All-Amer Hl Fm 85; Alc Plimptn Memrl Schlrshp 86; Pres Acdmc Ftns Awd 86; UMASS Amherst; Accntng.

FERRARI, KRISTINA; Marian HS; Framingham, MA; (Y); Church Yth Grp; Cmnty Wkr; Rep Jr Cls; Var Cheerleading; JV Crs Cntry; Var Sftbl; High Hon Roll; Hon Roll; NHS; :Advrstng.

FERRARI, LISA A; Medway JR SR HS; Medway, MA; (Y); Pres Drama Clb; Teachers Aide; Sec Chorus; Church Choir; School Musical; School Play; Nwsp Rptr; Hon Roll; MA Drama Festvls All Star Cast Awd 84-86; Music Ed Ctrl Dist Chorus 83-86; All ST Chorus 86; Boston U; Music.

FERREIRA, CARLA; New Bedford HS; New Bedford, MA; (Y); 178/701; Hosp Aide; Stage Crew; Teachers Aide; Prfct Atten Awd; French I Awd 85; Hnr Stu Tutor 84; Phys Thrpy.

FERREIRA, ELIZABETH; New Bedford HS; New Bedford, MA; (Y); French Clb; Ski Clb; Chorus; School Musical; Stage Crew; JV Var Bsktbl; Hon Roll; Stonehill Coll; Lbrl Arts.

FERREIRA, JOSEPH; Boston Latin Schl; E Boston, MA; (Y); 48/274; Computer Clb; Latin Clb; Ski Clb; Var Ice Hcky; Wt Lftg; Hon Roll; Mst Outstndng Plyr In Vrsty Hcky 86; Bus Admin.

FERREIRA, MARK; Bishop Connolly HS; Westport, MA; (Y); 50/180; Boys Clb Am; Church Yth Grp; JA; Ski Clb; Yrbk Stf; Im Mgr Bsktbl; Im JV Socr; High Hon Roll; Hon Roll; Prfct Atten Awd; Trsr Ski Clb 85-87; Bus Adm.

FERREIRA, MICHAEL; Taunton HS; Taunton, MA; (Y); JCL; Latin Clb; Math Tm; Yrbk Stf; Bsktbl; L Golf; NHS; UMASS Amherst Chancellors Awd 86; Comp Engrng.

FERREIRA, SHERYL; B M C Durfee HS; Fall River, MA; (Y); 80/763; French Clb; Sec Trs Soph Cls; Accntn.

FERRI, JENNIFER; East Longmeadow HS; E Longmeadow, MA; (Y); 20/201; Sec Frsh Cls; Sec Soph Cls; VP Jr Cls; Mgr Capt Bsktbl; Var Socr; Var L Socr; Cit Awd; Hon Roll; Lbry Aide Awd; Amer Lgn Merit; Bryant Coll; Mthmtcs.

FERRI, TERESA; Norwood HS; Norwood, MA; (Y); 4/323; Library Aide; SADD; Band; Hon Roll; Jr NHS; Eng,Spnsh Awd 84-85; Awd Exc Eng Compstn 86; Bus.

FERRO, ROSANNA; Methuen HS; Methuen, MA; (Y); 99/366; Drama Clb; Acpl Chr; Chorus; Variety Show; Musc Schlrshp Outstndng Musc Ablty 86; Sons Of Itly Schlrshp 86; Castle Fund Schlrshp 86; Berkley Clg; Musc.

FESMIRE, SUZANNE; Westford Acad; Westford, MA; (Y); JA; SADD; Teachers Aide; Hon Roll; Psychol.

FESSLER, SHAWN; Hudson HS; Hudson, MA; (Y); 9/158; Band; Var L Bsktbl; Var L Crs Cntry; Var L Trk; High Hon Roll; NHS; Boys Clb Am; Boy Scts; Church Yth Grp; Mrchg Band; Harvard Bk Awd 86; 1st Pl Local Dist & St Natl Hist Cmpttn 84-85; Unsung Hero Awd Boys Crss Cntry 85; Genetics.

FIALKY, JEFFREY; Wilbraham Monson Acad; Longmeadow, MA; (Y); Key Clb; Model UN; Q&S; SADD; Nwsp Ed-Chief; Lit Mag; Im Bsktbl; Im Ftbl; Im Socr; Var L Tennis; Jrnlsm.

FIELD, JODIE A; Pentucket Regional SR HS; North Hampton, NH; (Y); 8/153; Drama Clb; Girl Scts; Spanish Clb; Trs SADD; Band; School Play; Yrbk Stf; High Hon Roll; Hon Roll; NHS; U Of NH; Anml Sci.

FIELD, TIFFANY; Miss Halls HS; Minnetonka, MN; (Y); Cmnty Wkr; French Clb; Hosp Aide; Chorus; JV Var Crs Cntry; Hon Roll; U Of VA; Bus Mgmt.

FIELDS, LORE; Bedford HS; Bedford, MA; (Y); Church Yth Grp; Intnl Clb; Pep Clb; Chorus; Church Choir; School Musical; Capt Var Cheerleading; Im Powder Puff Ftbl; Intrntl Reltns.

FIERIMONTE, STEVEN; Malden HS; Malden, MA; (Y); 13/500; Math Clb; Science Clb; Hon Roll; NHS; Lowell Tech; Nclr Engr.

FIGENBAUM, KIM; Burlington HS; Burlington, MA; (Y); 49/314; VP JA; OEA; Science Clb; Stu Cncl; Im Bsktbl; VP Capt Cheerleading; Powder Puff Ftbl; Var Swmmng; Hon Roll; Jr Achvmnt Co Yr Estrn MA 86; Elctd Rgnl& ST Rep Stu Advsry Cncl 85-87; Bus Commnctns.

FIGUERIDO, ANTHONY; Hopedale HS; Hopedale, MA; (Y); 5/60; Am Leg Boys St; SADD; School Play; Yrbk Stf; VP Soph Cls; VP Jr Cls; VP Sr Cls; Stat Bsktbl; Capt Golf; NHS; Tri-Vlly Lge Glf All-STR 86; Manhattanville Coll; Econ.

FILETTI, SAL; Austin Prep Schl; Methuen, MA; (Y); 46/128; Church Yth Grp; Cmnty Wkr; Math Clb; Science Clb; SADD; JV Bsbl; Var Crs Cntry; Var Ice Hcky; Var Trk; Hon Roll; Austin Prep Sci Fair 84; Rep MA ST Sci Fair 84; Bus Mgmt.

FILIPPI, MATT; Malden HS; Malden, MA; (Y); 41/470; Church Yth Grp; SADD; Band; Chorus; Church Choir; Concert Band; Drm & Bgl; Jazz Band; Mrchg Band; Pep Band; $1000 Acadmc/Ldrshp & $750 Music Schlrshps 86-87; 200 Music Schlrshp 86; Plymouth ST Coll; Music Educ.

FILOMIA, GAYLE; Presentation Of Mary Acad; Methuen, MA; (Y); Pep Clb; Spanish Clb; Chorus; School Musical; Yrbk Stf; Rep Jr Cls; Rep Stu Cncl; Acctg.

FINEBERG, DONNA G; Dartmouth HS; Fairhaven, MA; (Y); 34/223; Church Yth Grp; Cmnty Wkr; Office Aide; Teachers Aide; Im Badmtn; Hon Roll; NCTE Awd; Ntl Merit Ltr; Pres Schlr; Acdmc Exc In Englsh 86; Acdmc Exc In Amer Govt 84; Brstl CC; Nrng.

FINEMAN, DEBORAH; Newton North HS; Newton Centre, MA; (Y); Camera Clb; Ski Clb; Pres Temple Yth Grp; Var Fld Hcky; Var Capt Gym; High Hon Roll; Ntl Merit Schol; Kennedy Bk Prz US Hist Essay 85; U PA.

FINER, HOWARD; Randolph HS; Randolph, MA; (Y); 16/321; Am Leg Boys St; Drama Clb; Pres Temple Yth Grp; Yrbk Bus Mgr; Rep Soph Cls; Socr; Hon Roll; JC Awd; NHS; Pres Schlr; Mc Donalds Schlrshp 86; Llyod Young Mem Awd 83-85; Syracuse U; Comp Engrng.

FINI, MARIA; St Bernards C C HS; Lunenburg, MA; (Y); 20/159; Am Leg Aux Girls St; Office Aide; School Play; Nwsp Stf; Yrbk Stf; Sec Stu Cncl; Var Cheerleading; Var Socr; Var Trk; Hon Roll; Coll Wrtg Awd 86; Spnsh III-IV Awds 84-85; Anna Manion Awd 85; Boston Coll; Cmmnctns.

FINN, CHRISTOPHER; Malden HS; Malden, MA; (Y); 20/480; Am Leg Boys St; Key Clb; Variety Show; Im Bsktbl; Capt Ftbl; Trk; NHS; Rotary Awd; Cornell U; Engrng.

FINN, MEGAN; Burncoat SR HS; Worcester, MA; (Y); Intnl Clb; JA; Crs Cntry; JV Fld Hcky; 4-H Awd; Hotel/Restrnt Mgmt.

FINN, ROB; Burlington HS; Burlington, MA; (Y); 37/315; Yrbk Stf; JV Capt Socr; Phys Educ Awd-Tchrs Choice; Art Awd; Illustration.

FINN, STACY; Randolph HS; Randolph, MA; (Y); 56/321; Intnl Clb; SADD; High Hon Roll; Hon Roll; JC Awd; Jr NHS; NHS; Stu Gov Awd 84; U MA Amherst; Bus.

FINNEGAN, KELLY; Holbrook HS; Holbrook, MA; (Y); 4/96; Latin Clb; SADD; Rep Frsh Cls; Rep Soph Cls; Trs Jr Cls; Rep Stu Cncl; Hon Roll; NHS; Stu Cncl Merit Awd 84-85; Stu Cncl Pres Awd 85-86; Sec Of MA Assn Of Stu Cncls 86-87; Bus.

FINNERAN, ELLEN; Marshfield HS; Marshfield, MA; (Y); 100/350; Pres AFS; Dance Clb; Drama Clb; Sec 4-H; Hosp Aide; Key Clb; School Play; Yrbk Stf; Bsktbl; 4-H Awd; Marshfld Tchrs & Amer Legn & Kiwannis Schlrshps 86; U Of MA Amherst; Psych.

FINNERAN, JOHN P; Xaverian Brothers HS; Marshfield, MA; (Y); 7/220; Art Clb; Church Yth Grp; Trs 4-H; Im Bsktbl; High Hon Roll; Hon Roll; JETS Awd; NHS; Ntl Merit Ltr; Boston Fire Fighters Local No 718 Schlrshp 83.

FINNESSEY JR, SAMUEL; Frontier Reg HS; S Deerfield, MA; (Y); 20/100; Debate Tm; Drama Clb; Latin Clb; Yrbk Bus Mgr; Pres Sr Cls; Var Ftbl; L Var Trk; Hon Roll; Mdl Cngrss Dlgt 86; Stu Govt Day Rep 86.

FIORE, LISA MARIE; Fontbonne Acad; Hyde Park, MA; (Y); 20/133; Drama Clb; School Musical; Stage Crew; Variety Show; Hon Roll; NHS; Church Yth Grp; Hosp Aide; Sec Intnl Clb; Teachers Aide; Outstndng Excllnc In Drama 86; Chrgrphr For Schl Mscl 86; Wrld Snshn Gldn Grl 86; Nrthestrn U; Acctng.

FIORE, MICHELLE; South Boston Heights Acad; S Boston, MA; (Y); 13/45; French Clb; Chorus; Variety Show; Vllybl; Wt Lftg; Hon Roll; U Of MA Boston; Bus.

FIORE, ROBIN; Mount St Joseph Acad; Readville, MA; (Y); 11/169; Art Clb; Drama Clb; School Play; Stage Crew; Bowling; Coach Actv; High Hon Roll; NHS; Yrbk Bus Mgr; Ed Yrbk Ed-Chief.

FIORENTINO, MICHAEL; Boston Latin HS; Boston, MA; (Y); 60/294; Key Clb; NHS; Presdntl Acad Fitness Awd 86; Open Gate Schlrshp 86; U Of MA; CPA.

FIORINO, DEAN; South Hadley HS; S Hadley, MA; (Y); Yrbk Stf; Var L Swmmng; Art Achvmnt Awd 86; Var Letter Fencing 85; Springfield Coll; Art.

FIRICANO, CAROL; Medford HS; Medford, MA; (Y); 19/396; Church Yth Grp; Cmnty Wkr; Office Aide; Ski Clb; SADD; Yrbk Stf; Pom Pon; Hon Roll; Jr NHS; NHS; Amer Legn Post 45 Schlrshp 86; Acdmc Excllnc Engl 86; MA JR Miss Schlrshp Prog Medfords JR Miss 86; Boston Coll; Cmmnctns.

FIRICANO, MISSY; St Clement HS; Medford, MA; (Y); Hosp Aide; Teachers Aide; Merit Awd Accntng 86; Endicott Coll; Accntng.

FIRMIN, SCOTT M; Bridgewater Rayham Regional HS; Raynham, MA; (Y); Am Leg Boys St; French Clb; VP Soph Cls; VP Stu Cncl; Var L Crs Cntry; JV Socr; Im Wt Lftg; Var L Wrstlng; High Hon Roll; Hon Roll; Bio.

FISCHLER, MELISSA SUE; Westwood HS; Westwood, MA; (Y); 10/217; School Musical; Yrbk Ed-Chief; Capt L Trk; Hon Roll; NHS; Pres Spanish NHS; Trs AFS; Camera Clb; Drama Clb; Key Clb; Kevin Harnett Mem Trphy Scholar Svc Athltcs & Char 86; Bruce Gaynor Awd Outstndg Trk 86; U Miami.

FISET, ANDREA; Barnstable HS; Barnstable, MA; (Y); AFS; Church Yth Grp; Yrbk Stf; Sec Frsh Cls; Sec Soph Cls; Sec Jr Cls; Sec Sr Cls; Rep Stu Cncl; Var L Fld Hcky; Co-Capt Trk; U S Dept Of Ed Peer Ldrshp Prgm 84-85; Athlt Of Wk 85; Acdmc Achvt Awd 84; Lbrl Arts.

FISH III, JOHN C; Newburyport HS; Newburyport, MA; (Y); Ski Clb; Y-Teens; Wt Lftg; Amrcn Inst Awd 86; Prsdntl Physcl Ftnss Awd 84.

FISHER, DANIEL; Haverhill HS; Haverhill, MA; (Y); Boy Scts; German Clb; Band; JV Var Ftbl; Hon Roll; Philmont Sct Rnch Cmmrn New Mexico 84; Coll.

FISHER, ERIC; Leominster HS; Leominster, MA; (Y); 4/305; Am Leg Boys St; Ski Clb; Var L Tennis; High Hon Roll; NHS; Ntl Merit Stdnt 85; Cornell U; Econ.

FISHER, MELANIE; Holbrook HS; Holbrook, MA; (Y); Library Aide; Variety Show; Hon Roll; Jr NHS; NHS.

FISHER, TERRANCE; Boston Latin Schl; Boston, MA; (Y); Art Clb; Dance Clb; JA; School Musical; Im Bsktbl; Im Crs Cntry; Im Trk; Mech Engrng.

FISKE, LORI; Burncoat SR HS; Worcester, MA; (Y); Drama Clb; Intnl Clb; Band; School Play; Nwsp Stf; Yrbk Stf; Stu Cncl; Crs Cntry; Trk; Hon Roll; Emerson; Comm.

FISKE, TRACY; Monument Mt Rgnl HS; W Stockbridge, MA; (Y); 8/142; Drama Clb; Intnl Clb; School Musical; School Play; Lit Mag; High Hon Roll; Hon Roll; Debate Tm; Chorus; Color Guard; Wheeler & Taylor Ins Agncy Schlrshp 86; Wellesley Coll Book Awd 86; VT Coll; Modern Lang.

FISZMAN, LISA; Cushing Acad; Ashburnham, MA; (Y); Intnl Clb; Vllybl; Wt Lftg; French Hon Soc; High Hon Roll; Hon Roll; Emory U.

FITCHETT, GABRIELLE; Chatham HS; North Chatham, MA; (Y); 1/38; Math Tm; Band; Chorus; High Hon Roll; Jr NHS; NHS; Val; Church Yth Grp; Girl Scts; Mrchg Band; Brown U Bk Awd 86; Balfour Awds Chem, Hstry, Eng, Mth, Comp 86; Chmpnshp Comp Fig Sktr New Engld Mdlst; Intl Corp Law.

FITZGERALD, CARYN; Medway JR SR HS; Medway, MA; (Y); Var Sftbl; Hon Roll; MVP Girls Varsity Sftbl 85-86; Tri-Vly All-Star Slctn 85-86; Excllnc In Art-Schl Boosters Awd 85-86.

FITZGERALD, KATHLEEN; Bishop Fenwick HS; North Reading, MA; (Y); Cmnty Wkr; Math Clb; School Musical; Nwsp Bus Mgr; Nwsp Ed-Chief; High Hon Roll; NHS; Drama Clb; School Play; Nwsp Rptr; Holy Crss Bk Prz 86; Bishop Fenwick Relgn Awd 86; Bshp Fenwick Frnch II Hnrs Awd 85; Poli Sci.

FITZGERALD, KELLY; Leicester HS; Cherry Valley, MA; (S); 6/102; Art Clb; Church Yth Grp; French Clb; Latin Clb; School Play; Nwsp Rptr; Yrbk Stf; VP Stu Cncl; Capt Cheerleading; U Of MA; Psychbio.

FITZGERALD, KRISTIE; Cathedral HS; Ludlow, MA; (Y); 136/536; Cmnty Wkr; Dance Clb; SADD; Yrbk Stf; Var Capt Cheerleading; Comm.

FITZGERALD, LEEANNE; North Quincy HS; Quincy, MA; (Y); 52/344; Var Crs Cntry; Im Gym; Var Trk; St Joseph Coll VT; Acctng.

FITZGERALD, LISA; North Middlesex Regional HS; Townsend, MA; (Y); Var Cheerleading; Var Crs Cntry; Hon Roll; Talntd Giftd 85-86; Law.

FITZGERALD, PAT; Cambridge Rindge & Latin Schl; Cambridge, MA; (Y); Pres Key Clb; Radio Clb; Nwsp Sprt Ed; Var L Ftbl; Capt L Trk; Capt L Wrstlng; Cit Awd; French Clb; Rep Jr Cls; Rep Sr Cls; Acad Decthln Gld Mdlst 85-86; MLK Schlrshp 86; Schlr/Athltc 85; Boston U; Lbrl Arts.

FITZGERALD, PATRICK J; Stoneham HS; Stoneham, MA; (Y); 9/235; Drama Clb; Band; Chorus; Concert Band; Mrchg Band; School Musical; School Play; High Hon Roll; NHS; Am Leg Boys St; Pres Spanish Club 86-87; Band Ofcr 84-87; Vrsty Schlr 84-87; Engr Mech.

FITZGERALD, PAULA; Everett HS; Everett, MA; (Y); Art Clb; Hosp Aide; Key Clb; Office Aide; SADD; Nwsp Ed-Chief; Nwsp Stf; Yrbk Stf; Stu Cncl; U Of LA CA; Phys Thrpy.

FITZGERALD, SCOTT; Saugus HS; Saugus, MA; (Y); 10/300; Aud/Vis; Ski Clb; Spanish Clb; Lit Mag; Im Crs Cntry; Im Trk; NHS; Ntl Merit Schol; VFW Awd; Voice Dem Awd; USAFA Sci Smmr Smnr 86; Stu Govt Day 85-86; USAF Acad; Aerospace Engrng.

FITZGERALD, SEAN; Medford HS; Medford, MA; (Y); Varsity Clb; Pres Frsh Cls; Var Socr; Var Trk; Hon Roll.

FITZHENRY, BOB; Foxborough HS; Foxboro, MA; (Y); 22/230; Var JV Bsbl; Im JV Bsktbl; Capt JV Ftbl; Im Wt Lftg; Hon Roll; Ftbl Unsung Linemn Awd 83; Mech Engr.

FITZMAURICE, MICHELE; Notre Dame Acad; Holbrook, MA; (Y); Church Yth Grp; Drama Clb; Acpl Chr; Chorus; School Musical; School Play; Nwsp Rptr; Nwsp Stf; Yrbk Stf; Rep Trs Stu Cncl.

FITZPATRICK, DAWN; Fontbonne Acad; Quincy, MA; (Y); Computer Clb; Math Tm; Ed Lit Mag; Hon Roll; Sec NHS; Ntl Merit Ltr; Prfct Atten Awd; Monsgnr Hawko Schlrshp; Magnu Cum Laude Nalt Latn Exm; Natl Socl Studies Olympd US Hstry Awd.

FITZPATRICK, ROBERT; Taunton HS; East Taunton, MA; (Y); 34/396; Office Aide; Bsktbl; Trk; Hon Roll; Glenn Maloney Mem Schlrshp 86; MA Sst Genrl Schlrshp 86; MA Maritime Acad; Nclr Engrng.

FITZPATRICK, WILLIAM; Austin Preparatory Schl; Billerica, MA; (Y); 20/124; French Clb; Yrbk Stf; Var Capt Bsbl; Var Capt Ice Hcky; High Hon Roll; Hon Roll; Cthlc Cntrl Hcky League All Str 85-86.

FITZSIMMONS, MAURA; Matignon HS; Melrose, MA; (S); 20/189; Church Yth Grp; Hosp Aide; Y-Teens; Rep Frsh Cls; Rep Soph Cls; Im Swmmng; French Hon Soc; Hon Roll; NHS; YMCA Ldr Of Yr 83-84; Boston U; Bio Med Engrng.

FITZWILLIAM, KERRY; Ursuline Acad; Canton, MA; (Y); 35/83; Dance Clb; Drama Clb; Latin Clb; Library Aide; Spanish Clb; Color Guard; School Musical; Yrbk Stf; JV Vllybl; Hon Roll; Bus.

FLACHBART, KAREN; Marblehead HS; Marblehead, MA; (Y); 124/259; Ski Clb; SADD; Var Capt Bsktbl; Var Powder Puff Ftbl; Var Socr; Var Capt Sftbl; Boostrs Schlrshp 86; MVP Sftbl Tm 86; Coach Awd-Bsktbl 85-86; U Of RI.

FLAGG, BEVERLY; Brackton Christian Regional HS; Wareham, MA; (Y); 4/20; Camera Clb; School Play; Bsktbl; Cheerleading; Hon Roll; VP Frsh Cls; VP Soph Cls; Sec Jr Cls; Gordon Coll; Acctng.

FLAHERTY, DEIRDRE; Marian HS; Hopkinton, MA; (Y); 50/200; Church Yth Grp; Cmnty Wkr; Chorus; Church Choir; Concert Band; Jazz Band; Mrchg Band; School Musical; Hon Roll; NEDT Awd; Acctg.

FLAHERTY, KATHLEEN; Medway JR SR HS; Medway, MA; (Y); Church Yth Grp; Hosp Aide; SADD; Yrbk Stf; 1 Yr Schlstc Awd 86; Clark U; Engl.

FLAHERTY, MAUREEN ELIZABETH; Notre Dame Acad; N Quincy, MA; (Y); 50/114; Trs Church Yth Grp; Hosp Aide; Political Wkr; Chorus; School Musical; School Play; Variety Show; Nwsp Stf; Mgr Bsktbl; Hon Roll; Schlstc Excllnc Awd Algbra I, Geo & Spnsh II 83-84; Knights Columbus Schlrshp Awd 86; St Michaels Coll; Bio.

FLAHERTY, NORA; Marblehead HS; Marblehead, MA; (Y); 16/250; Drama Clb; Intnl Clb; Sec Thesps; Yrbk Stf; Lit Mag; Lcrss; Powder Puff Ftbl; NHS; Ntl Merit SF; St Schlr; Presdnl Schlr Semi Fnlst 86; Natl Hipsanic Schlr 86; Yale U; Med.

FLAMAND, CHARLENE; Ware HS; Ware, MA; (Y); 13/112; Art Clb; Church Yth Grp; Key Clb; Drm Mjr(t); Sec Soph Cls; JV Cheerleading; Var Twrlr; High Hon Roll; Hon Roll; Algebra Awd 86; Art Awd 86; Springfield Coll; Psych.

FLANAGAN, TIM; Methuen HS; Methuen, MA; (Y); 34/375; Am Leg Boys St; Model UN; JV Bsbl; JV Bsktbl; JV Ftbl; Var Golf; Var Trk; High Hon Roll; Hon Roll; Cvnl Engr.

FLANDERS, PAUL N; Beverly HS; Beverly, MA; (Y); Am Leg Boys St; Band; Concert Band; Jazz Band; Mrchg Band; Nwsp Sprt Ed; Nwsp Stf; Var Tennis; High Hon Roll; NHS; Frnch Awd 84-85.

FLANNAGAN, LIAM; Gloucester HS; Gloucester, MA; (Y); Political Wkr; Jazz Band; Pep Band; Ftbl; Vllybl; Wt Lftg; Stop & Shop Prdc Clrk 85-86; 5 Yr Gtrst & Bsst 81-86; UMASS Amherst; Tchng.

FLANNAGAN, THOMAS J; Gloucester HS; Gloucester, MA; (Y); 18/320; Am Leg Boys St; Political Wkr; Yrbk Rptr; Yrbk Stf; Ed Lit Mag; Crs Cntry; Var JV Tennis; Im Vllybl; Elks Awd; Hon Roll; Stu Govt Day; Coll Fair Day; Army ROTC Schlrshp Wnr; Ithaca Coll; Intl Rel.

FLANNERY, CHRISTINE; Auburn HS; Auburn, MA; (Y); VP Church Yth Grp; Ski Clb; SADD; Band; Mrchg Band; Nwsp Ed-Chief; Yrbk Stf; Var Fld Hcky; High Hon Roll; NHS; Law.

FLAVIN, LEO; Austin Prep; Billerica, MA; (Y); Cmnty Wkr; Political Wkr; Var L Bsbl; Var L Ice Hcky; Im Lcrss; JV Socr; Im Sftbl; Var Hon Roll; Dvsn ST Hcky Chmpshp Tm 86; Austin Prep Dscplnry 85; Mrktng.

FLEMING, JONATHAN; St Bernards Central Catholic HS; Lunenburg, MA; (S); 1/175; Science Clb; Ski Clb; Im Bsktbl; Trk; High Hon Roll; NHS; Engrng.

FLEMING, KELLIE; Nipmuc Regional HS; Upton, MA; (Y); 22/92; Political Wkr; VP SADD; Off Frsh Cls; Off Jr Cls; Trs Stu Cncl; Im Bsktbl; JV Var Socr; JV Var Sftbl; High Hon Roll; NHS.

FLEMING, LINDA; Billerica Memorial HS; Billerica, MA; (Y); 49/489; Church Yth Grp; French Clb; Color Guard; Flag Corp; Mrchg Band; Yrbk Stf; Stu Cncl; Hon Roll; Good Sprt Awd 84; Merrimack Coll; Bio.

FLEMING, MARY; Billerica Memorial HS; Billerica, MA; (Y); 48/489; Church Yth Grp; French Clb; Color Guard; Flag Corp; Mrchg Band; Yrbk Stf; Stu Cncl; Hon Roll; Mst Imprvd Rfl 84; Merrimack Coll; Bio.

FLEMING, STEVEN; St Bernards Central Catholic HS; Lunenburg, MA; (S); 4/159; Ski Clb; Nwsp Rptr; JV Bsbl; Im Bsktbl; High Hon Roll; NHS; Mech Engrng.

FLETCHER, JENNIFER; Marblehead HS; Marblehead, MA; (Y); 3/270; Drama Clb; French Clb; Thesps; School Play; Yrbk Stf; Pres Sec Stu Cncl; High Hon Roll; Hon Roll; NHS; AFS; U-Penn Bk Awd 86.

FLEURY, LINDA; Bellingham Memorial JR/SR HS; Bellingham, MA; (Y); Hosp Aide; Library Aide; Nwsp Stf; High Hon Roll; NHS; Acadmc All Am Awd 84; Outstndg Stud 86; Phys Therapy.

FLEWELLING, CHRIS; Haverhill HS; Haverhill, MA; (Y); 49/400; Debate Tm; Latin Clb; Spanish Clb; School Play; JV Bsktbl; Var Powder Puff Ftbl; Im Vllybl; Hon Roll; Socl Sci.

FLOOD, JANETTE; Saugus HS; Saugus, MA; (Y); Cmnty Wkr; GAA; Hosp Aide; Stu Cncl; Voice Dem Awd; Hon Men Upsilon Alpha 86; Sprts Rprtng.

FLORES, REBECCA; Acad Of Notre Dame; Concord, NH; (Y); Art Clb; Stage Crew; Yrbk Phtg; Yrbk Stf; Hon Roll; NHS; Rivier Coll Chllng Pgm 85; Yrbk Co-Edtr 86; Emmanuel Coll; Engl Cmnctn.

FLORIO, MICHAEL; Austin Prep; Tewksbury, MA; (Y); 8/137; Latin Clb; Letterman Clb; JV Bsktbl; Var Ftbl; Im Sftbl; JV Trk; High Hon Roll; Hon Roll; Aerospc.

FLORO, GRACE; MT ST Joseph Acad; Brighton, MA; (Y); 4/169; VP Chess Clb; SADD; Variety Show; Yrbk Stf; Var Trk; Hon Roll; VP NHS.

FLOROS, CONSTANTINE; Lunenburg HS; Lunenburg, MA; (Y); Am Leg Boys St; Debate Tm; Math Clb; Political Wkr; Rep Soph Cls; Trs Jr Cls; Trs Sr Cls; Capt L Bsbl; Capt L Ftbl; Capt L Socr; Physics Schlrshp Harvard U 85-86; Harvard; Acctng.

FLYNN, CARA; Christopher Columbus HS; E Boston, MA; (S); 2/127; Church Yth Grp; JA; Hon Roll; NHS; NEDT Awd; Suffolk U.

FLYNN, CHRISTINA; Braintree HS; Braintree, MA; (Y); 42/442; JCL; SADD; Nwsp Rptr; Yrbk Rptr; Fld Hcky; Holy Cross; Bus.

FLYNN, COLLEEN; Arlington Catholic HS; Medford, MA; (Y); Church Yth Grp; Dance Clb; Office Aide; Spanish Clb; Stu Cncl; JV Socr; Hon Roll; NHS; Nrth Amer 1st Plc Solo Irsh Stpdncng Chmpn 85; Dncr Bstn Tms 83-84; NE 1st Plc Solo Irsh Stpdncng Chm; Lbrl Arts.

FLYNN, JENNIFER; Dedham HS; Dedham, MA; (Y); 17/271; Pres Sec Drama Clb; Spanish Clb; School Play; Variety Show; Nwsp Rptr; Yrbk Ed-Chief; Lit Mag; Sec Stu Cncl; Hon Roll; Fnlst Essy Cntst 85; 1st Essy Cntst 86; Wnnr Best Actrss Trphy 86; Jrnlsm.

FLYNN, KEVIN; Marlborough HS; Marlboro, MA; (Y); Boys Clb Am; JV Bsbl; JV Bsktbl; JV Socr; Hon Roll; Assumption Coll; Bus.

FLYNN, PATRICIA; Cathedral HS; Springfield, MA; (Y); 46/510; Cmnty Wkr; Office Aide; Ed Yrbk Stf; Var Capt Crs Cntry; Var Capt Trk; Hon Roll; NHS; Parsh Cncl 85-86; All League Coachs Tm CC & Trck 85-86; Spec Ed.

FLYNN, SEAN P; Saint Johns HS; Worcester, MA; (Y); 33/252; Sec Am Leg Boys St; Pres JA; Spanish Clb; Variety Show; Im Bsktbl; Im Sftbl; High Hon Roll; Hon Roll; NHS; Tutor Spn & Alg Private Schl 85-86; Yale U; Psych.

FLYNN, SHAWN; Brockton Christian Regional HS; Raynham, MA; (Y); Drama Clb; VP Rep Jr Cls; Pres Stu Cncl; Var L Bsbl; Var Bsktbl; Var Capt Socr; Hon Roll; 2nd Pl ACSI Sci Fair Life Sci 86; Princpls Awd 86; Messiah Coll; Phys Thrpy.

FOGARTY, MARY; Holyoke Catholic HS; Holyoke, MA; (Y); Dance Clb; Drama Clb; Latin Clb; School Musical; School Play; Var Trk; High Hon Roll; NHS; Church Choir; Hnrs Engl Awd 85; Latn Awd 85; Spnsh Awd 86.

FOHL, PETER; Concord-Carlisle Regional HS; Carlisle, MA; (Y); Ski Clb; Hon Roll; Ntl Merit SF; Deptmntl Hnrs-Physics 84-85; US San Diego; Physics.

FOLEY, CAROLYN; Braintree HS; Braintree, MA; (Y); 57/413; Rep Soph Cls; Var Cheerleading; Hon Roll; Buckley Assocs Inc Scholr; Bridgewater ST Coll; Elem Ed.

FOLEY, CATHY; Girls Catholic HS; Melrose, MA; (Y); Pres French Clb; SADD; Yrbk Stf; Rep Frsh Cls; Trs Soph Cls; Rep Jr Cls; High Hon Roll; NHS; NEDT Awd; Art Clb; Zonta Clb Schlrshp/Ctznshp Awd 86; Boston Coll; Bus Mgmt.

FOLEY, DAN; Burncoat SR HS; Worcester, MA; (Y); Ski Clb; Varsity Clb; Band; Stage Crew; Var L Bsbl; JV Bsktbl; Var Ice Hcky; Var Capt Socr; High Hon Roll; Hon Roll; Capt Sccr Tm Vrsty 86; Bates; Lbrl Arts.

FOLEY, DONNA; St Clare HS; Boston, MA; (Y); 8/124; Drama Clb; JCL; Ski Clb; SADD; School Musical; Nwsp Stf; Trs Soph Cls; Pres Jr Cls; Stu Cncl; Magna Cum Laude Cert 83-84; Yuth Mnstry Tm Awd; Hghst Ovrll Aver Rlgn; Pre Med.

FOLEY III, FRANKLIN J; Malden Catholic HS; Everett, MA; (Y); JV Socr; Hon Roll; U Of Lowell; Elec Engrng.

FOLEY, KELLY; Quaboag Regional HS; West Brookfield, MA; (Y); 15/85; Pres Science Clb; SADD; Varsity Clb; Rep Stu Cncl; Capt French Clb; Tennis; Hon Roll; NHS; Stu Govt Rep 85-86; Assumption Clg; Poltc Sci.

FOLEY, KERRI; Woburn HS; Woburn, MA; (Y); Color Guard; Cheerleading; Gym.

FOLEY, LORI; Bishop Feehan HS; Seekonk, MA; (Y); Cmnty Wkr; French Hon Soc; Hon Roll; Schlrshp Awd For Hghst Avgs In Frsh Sntn & Cmnctn 83; RI Coll; Rdlgy.

FOLEY, MICHAEL; English HS; Lynn, MA; (Y); Science Clb; Yrbk Stf; Off Stu Cncl; Golf; Hon Roll; U Of MA.

FOLEY, SEAN; Chicopee Comprehensive HS; Chicopee, MA; (Y); Political Wkr; Ski Clb; Stage Crew; Rep Frsh Cls; Rep Soph Cls; Rep Jr Cls; Stu Cncl; Ftbl; Trk; Hon Roll.

FOLEY, SIOBHAN; St Peter Marion Cc HS; Worcester, MA; (Y); 7/200; Drama Clb; School Musical; School Play; Yrbk Stf; High Hon Roll; Hon Roll; NHS; Church Yth Grp; Dance Clb; Spanish Clb; Flow Prog 86; Teachng.

FOLLANSBEE, CAROLINE J; Ipswich HS; Ipswich, MA; (Y); 3/120; Leo Clb; Variety Show; Yrbk Stf; Var Capt Bsktbl; Var Capt Socr; Var Capt Sftbl; High Hon Roll; NHS; Pres Schlr; Channel 7 Superstar Awd 86; Athlete Awd 86; Salem ST Coll; Ftns.

FONG, KATHY; Algonquin Regional HS; Southboro, MA; (Y); 1/230; VP JA; Yrbk Stf; Lit Mag; Trs Frsh Cls; Trs Soph Cls; JV Bsktbl; Var L Crs Cntry; Var L Trk; High Hon Roll; NHS; Holy Cross Bk Awd 86; Outstndg Achvt Awd 84-86; Elec Engrng.

FONNER, SUZANNE; Cathedral HS; Springfield, MA; (Y); 47/530; VP JA; Model UN; Office Aide; Political Wkr; Ski Clb; Nwsp Stf; Var Trk; Hon Roll; NHS; Bryant Coll; Fin.

FONTAINE, DANIEL; Lynn Classical HS; Lynn, MA; (Y); French Clb; Science Clb; Church Choir; Golf; Tennis; Cls Schrlshp 86; Stu Gov Day 86; Divine Word Coll; Relgion.

FONTAINE, FAHY; Bellingham JR SR Memorial HS; Bellingham, MA; (Y); Trs DECA; Sec 4-H; Pep Clb; Color Guard; Yrbk Stf; Sec Jr Cls; Stu Cncl; 4-H Awd; Hon Roll; Peer Cnslr; Stu Advsry Cncl; Bridgewater St; Early Chldhd Ed.

FONTES, JILL; Dracut SR HS; Dracut, MA; (Y); Key Clb; Sftbl; High Hon Roll; Hon Roll; Acdmc Excllnc Soph Engl 84-85; U Lowell; Nrsng.

FOOTE, EDWARD; Bridgewater-Raynham Reg HS; Bridgewater, MA; (Y); Am Leg Boys St; Ski Clb; Bsktbl; Crs Cntry; Trk; High Hon Roll; Hon Roll; NHS; U Of MA Amherst; Bus Adm.

FORBES, ERIKA E; Bishop Fenwick HS; Salem, MA; (S); Sec Drama Clb; Math Clb; Science Clb; Chorus; School Musical; Stu Cncl; High Hon Roll; Chrmn-Cltrl Comm 85-86; Hnrs Chem Awd 84-85; Hnrs Spnsh I & Spnsh II Awds 83-85; Intl Technlgy.

FORBES, MICHAEL; Wahconah Regional HS; Windsor, MA; (Y); Rep Frsh Cls; JV Bsbl; Im Bsktbl; Var Ftbl; High Hon Roll; Hon Roll; NHS; Acctg.

FORBES, RAYMOND; Marblehead HS; Marblehead, MA; (Y); 42/289; Drama Clb; FCA; French Clb; Ski Clb; School Play; Capt Ftbl; Capt JV Ice Hcky; Capt Tennis; High Hon Roll; Frnch Drama Clb 86; U Of Denver; Real Estate Dvlpr.

FORD, AMY; Presentation Of Mary HS; Boxford, MA; (Y); Camera Clb; French Clb; Yrbk Stf; Trs Sr Cls; Swmmng; YMCA Swmmg Champnshps Natl, Dist & New Engld 84-86; Framingham ST; Nutrtn.

FORD, DAVID; Winchester HS; Winchester, MA; (Y); VP Church Yth Grp; Rep Stu Cncl; Var Bsbl; Var Ftbl; Hon Roll; Magna Cum Laude Ntl Latn 85.

FORD, DEBORAH; Saugus HS; Saugus, MA; (Y); 44/297; GAA; Yrbk Stf; Var Capt Bsktbl; Var JV Socr; Var Trk; Var Wt Lftg; Hon Roll; Jr NHS; Bsktbl Coaches Awd 84-85; Track Coaches Awd 85; Bsktbl Jr Olympc Tm 86.

FORD JR, JOHN K; St Peter-Marian CC HS; Worcester, MA; (S); 16/167; Pres VP Church Yth Grp; Political Wkr; Stage Crew; Variety Show; Yrbk Stf; Pres Stu Cncl; Var L Ftbl; Hon Roll; NHS; Ambssdr MA Ldrshp Sem 84; Cvl Engrng.

FORD, KATHRYN; Lexington HS; Lexington, MA; (Y); Church Yth Grp; 4-H; Chorus; Orch; School Musical; School Play; Variety Show; 4-H Awd; Hon Roll.

FORD, SUZANNE; Nipmuc Regional HS; Mendon, MA; (Y); 6/98; Band; Concert Band; Jazz Band; Stu Cncl; High Hon Roll; Hon Roll; NHS; Pol Sci.

FOREST, JENNIFER; South Hadley HS; S Hadley, MA; (Y); 19/172; Yrbk Stf; Sec Soph Cls; Sec Jr Cls; Sec Sr Cls; Var Fld Hcky; Hon Roll; NHS.

FORGIT, JO ANN; Fontbonne Academy HS; Norwood, MA; (Y); 19/169; Sec Computer Clb; Dance Clb; Math Clb; Math Tm; School Musical; Lit Mag; Hon Roll; NHS; Prfct Atten Awd; Bst In Ballet 85; 3rd Pl DEA Rgnls In Ballet 85; 1st Pl Pyric Grp 86; Cnmtgrphy.

FORGUES, TINA; Agawam HS; Feeding Hills, MA; (Y); Dance Clb; GAA; JCL; Chorus; Jazz Band; Swing Chorus; Variety Show; Yrbk Stf; Var Socr; Hon Roll; PSYCH.

FORMISANO, PAUL; Joseph Case HS; Swansea, MA; (Y); Am Leg Boys St; Camera Clb; Bausch & Lomb Sci Awd; High Hon Roll; NHS; 2nd Pl Awd MA ST Sci Fair MIT 86; 2nd Pl Awd Prvdnc Coll Comp Pgmg Cntst 86; Math & Sci Achvmnt Mdl; Worcester Polytech; Mech Engnr.

FORNARA, CYNTHIA; Georgetown HS; Georgetwon, MA; (Y); 2/88; AFS; Drama Clb; Yrbk Stf; Trs Sr Cls; High Hon Roll; NHS; Pres Schlr; Sal; Cmnwlth Of MA Schlrshp 86; Drtmth Clb Awd 85; Bntly Coll; Accntng.

FORRESTER, KOLBY; Southbridge HS; Sbridge, MA; (Y); 7/136; Var Math Tm; Concert Band; Mrchg Band; School Musical; Rep Soph Cls; Rep Jr Cls; Rep Sr Cls; Var Trk; High Hon Roll; Hon Roll; Outstndng JR Band 85; Rotry Clb Cert Outstndng Acdmc Achvt 86; New Hampshire Coll; Bus.

FORTIER, CHERYL; Tantasqua Regional HS; Wales, MA; (Y); 10/250; Am Leg Aux Girls St; Church Yth Grp; Ski Clb; Capt Var Bsktbl; Var Sftbl; High Hon Roll; Hon Roll; NHS; Stu Advsry Council; Pre Vet.

FORTIER, GARY; King Philip Regional HS; Plainville, MA; (Y); Am Leg Boys St; Capt Tennis; Hon Roll; NHS; Actng.

FORTIER, JACQUELINE; Chicopee Comprehensive HS; Chicopee, MA; (Y); 48/320; Church Choir; Yrbk Stf; VP Sr Cls; CC Awd; DAR Awd; Trs Soph Cls; VP Jr Cls; Mss Chicopee Ct 85; Bay Path JC; Intr Dsgn.

FORTIER, LYNNE; Bishop Feehan HS; Attleboro, MA; (Y); French Clb; French Hon Soc; Hon Roll; Hnrb Mntn Natl Frnch Exam; Psych.

FORTIN, ANNETTE; Cardinal Spellman HS; Bridgewater, MA; (Y); Pep Clb; School Musical; Pres Frsh Cls; Rep Jr Cls; Rep Stu Cncl; Bsktbl; JV Tennis; NHS; 3rd Pl Sci Fair Awd 86.

FORTNER, FRANK; Bellingham JR SR Memorial HS; Bellingham, MA; (Y); Drama Clb; Stu Cncl; JV Var Ftbl; Var Trk; Im Wt Lftg; Hon Roll; Outstndng Stdnt 3rd Qrtr 85-86; ROTC; Comp Sci.

FORTUNA, KAREN; Zuaboag Regional HS; Warren, MA; (Y); JA; SADD; Varsity Clb; Chorus; Nwsp Ed-Chief; Yrbk Stf; Stu Cncl; Tennis; Ldrshp Sem 85; Bus Wk 86; Bus Adm.

FORZIATI, GINA; Easthampton HS; Easthampton, MA; (Y); 1/130; Am Leg Aux Girls St; Spanish Clb; Pres Band; Off Stu Cncl; Cheerleading; Diving; Gym; Socr; NHS; Dartmouth Bk Clb Awd 86; Fash Dsgn.

FOSSELLA, ROBERT M; Stoughton HS; Stoughton, MA; (Y); 27/313; High Hon Roll; Pioneering/Bethel Svc; Steel Wk.

FOSTER, CATHY; New Bedford HS; New Bedford, MA; (Y); 79/701; Church Yth Grp; Capt Var Swmmng; Hon Roll; Fall Rvr YMCA Swm Team Ntls 86; Phys Ed.

FOSTER, CHIQUITA; West Roxbury HS; Dorchester, MA; (Y); Aud/Vis; Church Yth Grp; Dance Clb; Office Aide; Teachers Aide; Chorus; Church Choir; Drill Tm; Mrchg Band; JV Bsktbl; NYU Emersn; Dance.

FOSTER, DEBBIE; Hampshire Regional HS; Southampton, MA; (Y); 15/132; Church Yth Grp; Band; Chorus; Concert Band; Jazz Band; Mrchg Band; Variety Show; Sec Frsh Cls; Hon Roll; Sec NHS.

FOSTER, DERITH; Bishop Feehan HS; Plainville, MA; (Y); Cmnty Wkr; Hosp Aide; Ski Clb; Var JV Sftbl; Hon Roll.

FOSTER, JON; Bishop Feehan HS; Attleboro, MA; (Y); AFS; Pres Exploring; Spanish Clb; SADD; JV Crs Cntry; Ftbl; JV Trk; High Hon Roll; Hon Roll; Spanish NHS.

FOSTER, KIM; Canton HS; Canton, MA; (Y); 49/250; Cmnty Wkr; SADD; Yrbk Bus Mgr; Rep Frsh Cls; JV Bsktbl; Im Tennis; JV Trk; Im Vllybl; Hon Roll; Jr NHS; Boston U; Bus Mgmt.

FOSTER, LAUREN; Brookline HS; Brookline, MA; (Y); Cmnty Wkr; Drama Clb; French Clb; Ski Clb; Crs Cntry; Lcrss; Tennis; Hon Roll; NHS; Ntl Merit Ltr; AATF Hnrb Mntn 83; Haverford Coll; Natrl Sci.

FOSTER, LESLIE; Cahrles H Mc Cann Tech; North Adams, MA; (Y); SADD; Rep Stu Cncl; High Hon Roll; Hon Roll; Jr NHS; NHS; Fitchburg; Mech Engrng.

FOSTER, LYNN; Shepherd Hill Regional HS; Dudley, MA; (Y); 5/170; Am Leg Aux Girls St; Rep Stu Cncl; Var Socr; JV Var Sftbl; High Hon Roll; NHS; Prfct Atten Awd; Church Yth Grp; Math Tm; School Play; Yth Salute Awd Wnnr 86; Harvard Bk Prz 86; Hnr Ment Regnl ST Sci Fair 86; Physcis.

FOSTER, TOM; Stoughton HS; Stoughton, MA; (Y); Math Tm; Band; Concert Band; Jazz Band; Mrchg Band; Ind Design.

FOTIADES, DENISE; Fanning Trade HS; Worcester, MA; (Y); 11/131; SADD; High Hon Roll; Hon Roll; NHS; Prfct Atten Awd; Jr Prm Cmmtee 86; Advncd Prep Grp 83-87; Northeastern U; Bus Mgmt.

FOUNTAIN, ANDREA; Danvers HS; Danvers, MA; (Y); 33/306; Girl Scts; Pep Clb; Spanish Clb; Band; Var L Cheerleading; Hon Roll; NHS; Spanish NHS; Rep Frsh Cls; Occptnl Thrpy.

FOURNIER, LISA M; Chicopee HS; Chicopee, MA; (Y); 75/250; Dance Clb; JA; Yrbk Stf; Var L Cheerleading; Hon Roll; Bay Path JC; Bus Mgmt.

FOURNIER, MICHELLE; Somerville HS; Somerville, MA; (Y); Camp Fr Inc; French Clb; Ski Clb; VP Spanish Clb; Vllybl; Hon Roll; Hnrbl Mntn Sprng Wrtng Fstvl 85; Boston Coll; Socl Wrkr.

FOURNIER, STEVEN; Central Catholic HS; Lowell, MA; (Y); 64/235; Church Yth Grp; Im Bsktbl; Var L Tennis; Hon Roll; MVP In Tennis 86; All Star Tns Team 86; U Lowell; Chmstry.

FOURNIER, VICTOR P; Amesbury HS; Amesbury, MA; (Y); 13/215; Am Leg Boys St; Band; Nwsp Ed-Chief; Hon Roll; VP NHS; Big Bros/Big Sister 85-86; Merrimac Coll; Bio.

FOWLIE, ELISABETH J; Algonquin Regional HS; Northboro, MA; (Y); 4/230; Acpl Chr; Church Choir; Concert Band; Drm Mjr(t); Orch; JV Var Bsktbl; Coach Actv; L Capt Trk; NHS; AFS; Hugh O Brien Yth Ldrshp Smnr Dlgt 85; Med.

FOX, DINA; Comprehensive HS; Chicopee, MA; (Y); 28/300; German Clb; Yrbk Stf; Rep Jr Cls; Var Mgr(s); High Hon Roll; Hon Roll; NHS; Elec Engrng.

FOX, RICHARD; Weymouth South HS; S Weymouth, MA; (Y); Church Yth Grp; Yrbk Stf; VP Jr Cls; VP Sr Cls; Var L Socr; Var L Trk; High Hon Roll; Art Clb; Trs Frsh Cls; Trs Soph Cls; Chancelors Schlrsp 86; Schlr Athlete Awd 86; All Schltc Pole Vaulter 86; U MA Amherst; Art.

FOX, STEVEN; Malden HS; Malden, MA; (Y); 16/480; VP SADD; Sec Temple Yth Grp; Var Capt Crs Cntry; Var L Trk; Letterman Clb; Quiz Bowl; Band; Concert Band; Mrchg Band; VP Stu Cncl; Ntl Hon Soc Qrtly Awd 85; Rgnl Sec Bnai Brith Yth Org; U Miami; Cmnctn.

FOX TREE, ERICH; Concord-Carlisle HS; Concord, MA; (Y); 3/330; Debate Tm; Spanish Clb; Chorus; Stage Crew; Nwsp Stf; Ed Lit Mag; High Hon Roll; Ntl Merit SF; Librl Arts.

FRABOTTA, JULIE; Walnut HS; Shrewsbury, MA; (Y); Church Yth Grp; Intnl Clb; PAVAS; Ballet.

FRABOTTA, MIA; Nipmuc Regional HS; Mendon, MA; (Y); 4/100; Church Yth Grp; Yrbk Stf; Pres Sr Cls; Var L Fld Hcky; High Hon Roll; NHS; Am Leg Aux Girls St; Ski Clb; SADD; Soph Cls; Hnrs Eng 84-85; Spnsh Achvt Awd 85; Poltcl Sci.

FRAIDIN, MICHELLE; Kentshill Schl; Boston, MA; (Y); Camera Clb; Dance Clb; Drama Clb; JA; Teachers Aide; Varsity Clb; Band; Var Socr; Var Tennis; Hon Roll; Acctng.

FRANCE III, THADDEUS J; Palmer HS; Palmer, MA; (Y); Am Leg Boys St; VP Church Yth Grp; Cmnty Wkr; Letterman Clb; Ski Clb; Pres Spanish Clb; Varsity Clb; Variety Show; Yrbk Rptr; Yrbk Stf; All Westrn MA 1st Tm Ftbl 85; All Inter County 1st Tm Ftbl 85; Communications.

FRANCHI, LISA; St Clement HS; Medford, MA; (Y); Pres Jr Cls; JV Vllybl; Hon Roll; NHS; Suffolk U Book Awd; Pedtrcn.

FRANCIS, DEBBIE; Concord-Carlisle HS; Concord, MA; (Y); 1/255; Spanish Clb; Mrchg Band; Symp Band; High Hon Roll; NHS; Val; Concert Band; Jr NHS; Ntl Merit Ltr; Super Schls Acdmc Achvt Awd 86; 3 Local Slrshps 86; Dept Awds All Subjects 82-86; Wesleyan U CT.

FRANCIS, DEBORAH; Dartmouth HS; N Dartmouth, MA; (Y); Aud/Vis; Nwsp Rptr; Schl Art Show 2nd Pl Crfts 3rd Pl Drwng 84; Acad Let Portugvese Cert 85; Schl Art Show 1st Pl 86; Fshn Inst Of Tech; Advrtsng.

FRANCIS, KIMBERLY; New Bedford HS; New Bedford, MA; (Y); 150/400; 4-H; Yrbk Stf; High Hon Roll; Hon Roll; Outstndng Achvt Frnch 85-86; Phys Thrpy.

FRANCIS, STEPHANIE; North Quincy HS; Quincy, MA; (S); 5/325; Sec Church Yth Grp; Cmnty Wkr; Math Tm; SADD; Nwsp Rptr; Yrbk Ed-Chief; Var L Swmmng; High Hon Roll; NHS; Spanish NHS; Drtmth Bk Awd 85; Schlrshp To Emmnl Coll Acad 86; Emmanuel Coll; Biomed Engnrng.

FRANCO, DICKSON E; Westfield HS; Westfield, MA; (Y); Church Yth Grp; FBLA; Political Wkr; SADD; Bsbl; Ftbl; Trk; Wt Lftg; Var Wrstlng; High Hon Roll; Syracuse U; Elctrnc Engr.

FRANCO, MICHAEL; Taunton HS; Taunton, MA; (Y); 2/425; Cmnty Wkr; VP Library Aide; Political Wkr; Nwsp Rptr; High Hon Roll; NHS; Hly Crss Bk Awd Outstndng Schlrshp 86; Nwspr Typgrphr & Lyout Edtr 85-86; JR Mrshl 86; Pre Law.

FRANKLIN, JASON; Chicopee Comprehensive HS; Chicopee, MA; (Y); 28/322; Am Leg Boys St; JA; JV Bsbl; L Bsktbl; Hon Roll; Jr NHS; Spanish NHS; Sprts Psychlgy.

FRANKS, CAROLINE; Hopedale JR SR HS; Hopedale, MA; (Y); 35/73; Drama Clb; Office Aide; SADD; Chorus; Yrbk Stf; Var Bsktbl; Var Crs Cntry; JV Socr; Var Sftbl; Hon Roll; Resp Thrpy.

FRANSON, STEPHEN; Austin Prep Schl; Woburn, MA; (Y); 8/130; Boy Scts; English Clb; VP French Clb; Ski Clb; SADD; Nwsp Stf; Pres Frsh Cls; Pres Soph Cls; Pres Jr Cls; Stu Cncl; Amreo Petoselli Mem Schlrshp 85; Alice Gill Mem Schlrshp 86; Dartmouth Book Awd 86; Pre-Med.

FRARY, AMY; Hampshire Regional HS; Southampton, MA; (S); 1/100; 4-H; High Hon Roll; Sec NHS; Ntl Merit SF; Natl Hist Day SF 85; Bio.

FRARY, ANNE; Hampshire Regional HS; Southampton, MA; (S); 2/100; 4-H; High Hon Roll; NHS; Ntl Merit SF; Ntl Histry Day Semfnlst 85; Biolgy.

FRASER, JOAN; Fanning Trade HS; Worcester, MA; (Y); 9/124; Library Aide; High Hon Roll; Hon Roll; Jr NHS; Cosmetlgy.

FRASER, LAURA; Lee HS; Lee, MA; (Y); 21/85; French Clb; Math Clb; School Play; Variety Show; Yrbk Ed-Chief; Sec Soph Cls; Sec Jr Cls; Sec Sr Cls; Stat Ftbl; Stat Socr.

FRASSICA, LYNN; King Philip HS; Wrentham, MA; (Y); Art Clb; Cheerleading; Gym; High Hon Roll; Hon Roll; Eqstrn Study.

FRAUWIRTH, STACY B; Dartmouth HS; N Dartmouth, MA; (Y); 4/236; Debate Tm; Hosp Aide; Math Tm; Pres Temple Yth Grp; Chorus; School Play; NHS; Ntl Merit SF; Acadmc Excllnc Awd 83-85; St Lukes Hosp Vlntr Svc Awd 85; Math Tm Ltr 85; Occptnl Thrpy.

FRAWLEY, MATTHEW J; Dedham SR HS; Dedham, MA; (Y); 31/260; Am Leg Boys St; Church Yth Grp; SADD; Var Capt Ice Hcky; Var Capt Socr; Var Capt Tennis; Hon Roll; Outstndng Stu Phy Ed & Hlth 84 & 86; HS Rcrd Of Erng 12 Var Ltrs Whl Mntng Hon Grds 86-87; Intl Bnkng.

FREDERICK, JONATHAN; Arlington HS; Arlington, MA; (Y); Boy Scts; Yrbk Stf; Lit Mag; Art Clb; Radio Clb; Ski Clb; SADD; Egle Sct 86; Rhode Islnd Sch Desgn; Art.

FREDERICKS, JENA; Acton-Boxboro HS; Boxborough, MA; (Y); 200/400; Church Yth Grp; Cmnty Wkr; Ski Clb; SADD; Var Pom Pon; Var Powder Puff Ftbl; Hon Roll; Gordon Cromwell Coll.

FREDETTE, CHRISTINA; Holyoke Catholic HS; Chicopee, MA; (Y); 52/129; Computer Clb; Spanish Clb; Chorus; School Musical; Var Capt Sftbl; Judy Morgan Mem Schlrhsp 86; Fitzpatrick Schlrshp 86; MA ST Schlrshp 86; Holyoke CC; Elem Tchr.

FREDETTE, KRISTIE; Chicopee Comprehensive HS; Chicopee, MA; (Y); 9/332; Debate Tm; 4-H; Quiz Bowl; Spanish Clb; Teachers Aide; Yrbk Stf; Rep Frsh Cls; Hon Roll; NHS; Achvt Spnsh Awd 84 & 86; Tchr Spcl Ed.

FREDRICKSON, KIMBERLY; Nauset Regional HS; N Eastham, MA; (Y); Pres Ski Clb; Spanish Clb; SADD; Nwsp Stf; Yrbk Phtg; Lit Mag; High Hon Roll; NHS; Hon Roll; Underclsmn Awd Frgn Lang Spn 86; Linguist.

FREEDMAN, MATTHEW; Marblehead HS; Marblehead, MA; (Y); Pres Drama Clb; Political Wkr; Thesps; School Musical; School Play; Nwsp Rptr; High Hon Roll; Fndr/Pres Yng Dmcrts 85-86; Edtr Chldrns Exprss 80-85; Harvard U; Pol Sci.

FREEDMAN, MICHELLE; Sharon HS; Sharon, MA; (Y); 65/220; Spanish Clb; SADD; Temple Yth Grp; Nwsp Sprt Ed; Yrbk Stf; Trs Frsh Cls; Trs Soph Cls; Trs Jr Cls; Trs Sr Cls; JV Score Keeper; Hugh Obrian Youth Leadership Convention 85.

FREELEY, ELIZABETH; Milford HS; Milford, MA; (Y); Church Yth Grp; Office Aide; Teachers Aide; JV Bsktbl; High Hon Roll; Hon Roll; Busd.

FREELEY, KATHLEEN A; Milford HS; Milford, MA; (Y); 10/290; Church Yth Grp; SADD; Teachers Aide; JV Tennis; JV Vllybl; High Hon Roll; Hon Roll; NHS; Manahan Fmly Schlrshp 86; NH U; Vet Med.

FREEMAN, AUDRA; Burlington HS; Burlington, MA; (Y); 32/314; Drama Clb; School Musical; School Play; Stage Crew; Yrbk Phtg; Lit Mag; Trk; Hon Roll; Ntl Merit Ltr; Math Tm; Engl Awd Acadmc Achvt 86; Cineamtgrphy.

FREEMAN, JANET; Taunton HS; Taunton, MA; (Y); Drama Clb; Hosp Aide; Ski Clb; Yrbk Stf; Rep Stu Cncl; High Hon Roll; Hon Roll; Johnson I Wales; Fshn Retail.

FREEMAN, RANDY R; Auburn HS; Auburn, MA; (Y); Am Leg Boys St; Church Yth Grp; Computer Clb; Drama Clb; Math Tm; Teachers Aide; Stu Cncl; Var Socr; Var Trk; NHS; Mech Engrng.

FREITAS, CHRISTINA MARIE A; Westport High School HS; Westport, MA; (Y); Drama Clb; French Clb; Intnl Clb; Ski Clb; Chorus; School Play; Nwsp Stf; Yrbk Stf; Lit Mag; High Hon Roll; Psych.

FREITAS, CHRISTINE; Bishop Connolly HS; Fall River, MA; (Y); High Hon Roll; Hon Roll.

FREITAS, RENEE; Silver Lake Regional HS; Kingston, MA; (Y); 34/496; Cmnty Wkr; Library Aide; Office Aide; SADD; Yrbk Stf; Hon Roll; Indstrl Psych.

FRENCH, HEATHER; Bourne HS; Monument Beach, MA; (Y); Yrbk Stf; Fld Hcky; Jr NHS; Nrthestrn U; Arch.

FRENCH, RICHARD; Beverly HS; Beverly, MA; (Y); JV Lcrss; JV Socr; High Hon Roll; Hon Roll; Sci Fair Awd 3rd Pl 85; Bio-Engrng.

FRENETTE, GLENN R; Athol HS; Athol, MA; (Y); Boy Scts; Church Yth Grp; Cmnty Wkr; Varsity Clb; Nwsp Rptr; Nwsp Sprt Ed; Var JV Bsbl; JV Bsktbl; Elks Awd; St Schlr; Athol Alumni Assn Athol Boosters Assn 86; Athol Little Lg Scholar 86; Sunday Morn Sftbl Lg Scholar 86; Becher JC; Spts Adm.

FRIEDMAN, LAURIE; Attleboro HS; Attleboro, MA; (Y); 6/385; Church Yth Grp; Fld Hcky; Gym; Trk; High Hon Roll; Hon Roll; NHS; Outstndng Physcs Awd 86; Attlboro Brnch Amer Assoc U Wmn Schlrshp 86; Prsdntl Ftns Awd 86; GA Inst Of Tech; Engr.

FRIEL, MICHELE; Melrose HS; Boston, MA; (Y); 15/400; Hosp Aide; Pep Clb; Spanish Clb; SADD; Var L Gym; Var L Trk; High Hon Roll; NHS; Ski Clb; Smmr Yth Gym Pgm 85-86; Free Lance Wrtr Sports 86-87.

FRIGO, MARIA; Wilbraham & Monson Acad; Enfield, CT; (Y); Key Clb; Nwsp Stf; VP Frsh Cls; Var Bsktbl; Var Socr; Var Sftbl; Hon Roll; Natl Sci Merit Awd 84; Eveline Barber Dept Prz Frnch II 84; Eveline Barber Dept Prz-Englsh & U S Hsty.

FRITCHY, LORRE; Methuen HS; Methuen, MA; (Y); 22/375; Model UN; SADD; School Play; Stu Cncl; Powder Puff Ftbl; Vllybl; High Hon Roll; Hon Roll; UCLA; Drama.

FRONGILLO, KRISTINE; Medford HS; Medford, MA; (Y); 24/460; Ski Clb; SADD; Y-Teens; High Hon Roll; Englsh Awd; Geo: Algbra II & Englsh.

FROSTHOLM, JILL; Barnstable HS; Hyannis, MA; (Y); 40/392; Speech Tm; VP Rep Frsh Cls; Rep Trs Stu Cncl; Var JV Fld Hcky; Var L Trk; Hon Roll; NHS; Speech Tm; Rep Soph Cls; Rep Jr Cls; Acctng.

FUCHS, JULIUS A; St Joseph Central HS; Pittsfield, MA; (Y); 3/83; Am Leg Boys St; Boy Scts; Math Tm; Nwsp Rptr; VP Stu Cncl; Var Capt Crs Cntry; Var Capt Wrstlng; High Hon Roll; NHS; Spanish NHS; MA Adv Stds Prog 85; Eagl Sct 82; USA Wrstlg ST All Str Tm MA 86; U S Naval Acad; Nuclr Engr.

FUCILE, JEANINE MARIE; Holbrook JR SR HS; Holbrook, MA; (Y); Band; Concert Band; Mrchg Band; School Musical; Variety Show; Var Capt Fld Hcky; Hon Roll; NHS; Ntl Merit Ltr; Engrng.

FUHS, KIMBERLY; St Bernards C C HS; Fitchburg, MA; (S); 33/187; Church Choir; Yrbk Stf; JV Bsktbl; Var Socr; Hon Roll; NHS; Ntl Merit Ltr; Christian Herter Schlrshp 85; Outing Clb Adv 84-86; Northeastern U; Phrmcy.

FULGINITI, JOANNE; Burlington HS; Burlington, MA; (Y); 55/315; Am Leg Aux Girls St; Yrbk Ed-Chief; Rep Soph Cls; Trs Jr Cls; Trs Sr Cls; JV Var Fld Hcky; JV Var Gym; Hon Roll; NHS; Stu Cncl Awd.

FULLER, BRUCE E; East Bridgewate HS; East Bridgewater, MA; (Y); Am Leg Boys St; Aud/Vis; Drama Clb; Band; Concert Band; Jazz Band; Mrchg Band; Hon Roll; NHS; Computer Clb; Chncllrs Tlnt Awd Schlrshp 86; MAML Math Olympd 85 & 86; Chem Olympd 86; Engrng.

FULLER, ELIZABETH; Reading Memorial HS; Reading, MA; (Y); 18/327; Yrbk Stf; Rep Stu Cncl; Var Capt Trk; High Hon Roll; NHS; Pres Acdmc Ftns Awd 86; Mdlsx League All Star Wntr Trck 82-86; Sprng Track 83-86; Hmltn Coll.

FULLER, JODI; Presentation Of Mary Acad; Bradford, MA; (Y); 4/42; Church Yth Grp; French Clb; Math Clb; Pep Clb; SADD; Chorus; School Musical; Nwsp Stf; Yrbk Stf; Sftbl; Engl Gold Achvt Awd 86; Frnch Silv Achvt Awd 86.

FULLER, KAREN; St Mary Regional HS; Lynn, MA; (Y); 5/99; Dance Clb; Hosp Aide; School Musical; Im JV Cheerleading; High Hon Roll; Jr NHS; Pres NHS; NEDT Awd; Pre-Med.

FULLERTON, ELIZABETH; Dana Hall Schl; Wellesley, MA; (Y); Drama Clb; Key Clb; Pres Political Wkr; Acpl Chr; Chorus; Madrigals; School Musical; School Play; Swing Chorus; Nwsp Bus Mgr; Hobart William Smith Coll; Law.

FURBER, JEFF; Haverhill HS; Haverhill, MA; (Y); 58/367; Aud/Vis; Band; Chorus; Concert Band; Jazz Band; Mrchg Band; School Musical; High Hon Roll; Tri M Music Hnr Soc 84-86; Band Schlrshp 86; Band Prnts Assoc 86; Fitchburg ST Coll; Acctg.

FURBUSH, MICHAEL; Marlboro HS; Marlboro, MA; (Y); Ski Clb; Varsity Clb; Trs Soph Cls; Sec Jr Cls; VP Stu Cncl; Var Ftbl; Var Trk; High Hon Roll; High Hon Roll; NHS; Engl Awd.

FUREY, MARY; St Marys Regional HS; Lynn, MA; (S); 40/127; Sec Drama Clb; Church Choir; School Musical; Stage Crew; Nwsp Stf; Yrbk Stf; Hon Roll; Bus Admin.

FURLONG, DIANNA; Braintree HS; Braintree, MA; (Y); 67/420; Church Yth Grp; Girl Scts; Latin Clb; Var L Gym; Var L Trk; High Hon Roll; Hon Roll; Natl Art Awd 4th Pl Q-Tip 82; GATE Pgm 80; E MA Assn Chmp Javelin Schl Recd Hldr 86; Comp.

FURLONG, MICHAEL; Watertown HS; Watertown, MA; (Y); 10/253; Church Yth Grp; 4-H; VP Intnl Clb; VP JA; Sec SADD; Yrbk Bus Mgr; Rep Sr Cls; Var Ftbl; Hon Roll; VP NHS; Sons Of Itly Schlrshp Awd Lcl & ST Brnch 86; Outstndng Sci Achvt Awd 82; Babson Coll; Finance.

FURNESS, TRACY; B M C Durfee HS; Fall River, MA; (Y); 21/620; French Clb; Drill Tm; Capt Drm Mjr(t); Flag Corp; Mrchg Band; Yrbk Stf; Powder Puff Ftbl; Capt Twrlr; Hon Roll; NHS; Asst Capt JR Vrsty Mjrtts 85-86; Hnr Grd 84-85.

FURTAD, CARLA; Plymouth-Carver HS; Carver, MA; (Y); Church Yth Grp; Dance Clb; Hon Roll; Jr NHS; Northeastern U; Bus Adm.

FUSCO, KATHLEEN; Presentation Of Mary Acad; Methuen, MA; (Y); Spanish Clb; SADD; Chorus; School Musical; School Play; Variety Show; Yrbk Stf; Pres Frsh Cls; Pres Soph Cls; Pres Sr Cls; Nrsng.

FYRBERG, DENISE M; David Prouty HS; Spencer, MA; (Y); 6/184; Church Yth Grp; SADD; Drm Mjr(t); Mrchg Band; School Musical; Crs Cntry; JP Sousa Awd; NHS; St Schlr; Church Yth Grp; White Sweater Awd 86; Stu Govt Day Rep 86; Coll Of The Holy Cross; Pre Med.

GABORIAULT, DENNIS; Blackstone Valley Regional HS; Millbury, MA; (Y); Church Yth Grp; Cmnty Wkr; JV Var Bsbl; Var L Socr; Outstndng Jr 85-86; Millbury Sr Bsbll All-Star 84 & 85; Air Condtnng.

GADBOIS, MICHELLE; Assabet Vly Technical Vocation HS; Marlboro, MA; (Y); Church Yth Grp; Computer Clb; SADD; Yrbk Stf; VP Frsh Cls; Var Bsktbl; Var Fld Hcky; Capt Trk; Mst Imprvd Trck Awd 84; Cchs Awd-Trch 85; 9th Pl Cntrl MA Pnthln Chmpns 84; Comp Sci.

GAGNE, AMY; Athol HS; Athol, MA; (Y); 37/146; Am Leg Aux Girls St; Church Yth Grp; Model UN; Ski Clb; SADD; Band; Mrchg Band; Yrbk Stf; JV Bsktbl; Hon Roll; Ntl Hnr Soc Acad Excllnc 84-85; Bridgewater ST Coll; Phys Ed.

GAGNE, MELISSA; Monson JR SR HS; Monson, MA; (Y); 4/72; Am Leg Aux Girls St; Church Yth Grp; Pres VP 4-H; French Clb; School Musical; School Play; Yrbk Stf; Rep Frsh Cls; Stu Cncl; High Hon Roll; Drama.

GAGNON, ANNE; Arlington HS; Arlington, MA; (Y); 26/381; Art Clb; Computer Clb; Hosp Aide; Library Aide; Science Clb; Nwsp Rptr; Nwsp Stf; High Hon Roll; NHS; Ntl Merit Ltr; Med.

GAGNON, DEBRA; Mount Saint Joseph Acad; Boston, MA; (Y); 45/169; SADD; Art Awd 83-84; Mass Bay CC; Legl Sec.

GAGNON, DOMINIC; Cathedral HS; Springfield, MA; (Y); Computer Clb; JA; Red Cross Aide; Hon Roll; Johnson ST Coll; Hotl Mgmt.

GAGNON, GREG; Cathedral HS; Springfield, MA; (Y); 69/535; Am Leg Boys St; Church Yth Grp; Civic Clb; Debate Tm; Intnl Clb; VP JA; Political Wkr; Nwsp Stf; VP Jr Cls; Hon Roll; Bronze Mdlst Ntl Social Studies Olympiad 84; Amer Intl Coll Model Congress 86; Close Up Fndtn Prog 85; Social Studies.

GAGNON, JOEL; Central Catholic HS; N Andover, MA; (Y); 2/231; Art Clb; VP JA; Math Clb; Science Clb; Ed Yrbk Stf; High Hon Roll; NHS; Computer Clb; Im Vllybl; 7 Acad Awds 83-86; 11 Schlrshps For Acad Achvt 83-86; Offcr Of The Yr 86; Catholic U Of Amer; Arch.

GAGNON, MARY BETH; Bishop Connolly HS; Fall River, MA; (Y); 80/164; Cmnty Wkr; Hosp Aide; JV Vllybl; Hon Roll; Fr Wolf Mem Schlrshp 86; Salve Regina; Bio.

GAGNON, MICHELLE; B M C Durfee HS; Fall River, MA; (Y); 161/662; Trs Church Yth Grp; French Clb; Girl Scts; School Musical; Yrbk Stf; High Hon Roll; Hon Roll; MA ST Schlrshp 86; Becker JC; Travl & Trsm.

GAGNON, MICHELLE A; Weymouth North HS; Weymouth, MA; (Y); 23/358; Band; Concert Band; Jazz Band; Mrchg Band; Pep Band; School Musical; High Hon Roll; Hon Roll; Music.

GAGNON, PAUL; Bishop Feehan HS; Wapole, MA; (Y); Band; Chorus; Concert Band; Jazz Band; Mrchg Band; School Musical; School Play; Rhode Island Schl Dsgn; Arts.

GAGNON, WILLIAM; Easthampton HS; Easthampton, MA; (Y); 24/300; Computer Clb; French Clb; Capt Swmmng; Bus Mgt.

GAHAGAN, PAULA; Our Lady Of Nazareth Acad; Peabody, MA; (Y); Art Clb; Church Yth Grp; Pres SADD; Acpl Chr; Chorus; School Musical; Variety Show; Lit Mag; VP Jr Cls; Rep Stu Cncl; Fndr & Pres SADD Chptr At Schl 85-86; Hugh O Brian Yth Ldrshp Fndtn Schl Wnnr 84-85; Bus Mgmt.

GAHAN, PATRICIA ANN; Holy Name C C HS; Worcester, MA; (Y); 78/252; Ski Clb; Nwsp Stf; Hon Roll; Jr NHS; Stu Cncl Schlrshp 86; Wrcstr ST Coll; Cmnctns Dsrdrs.

GAI, ALISA NINA; Marian HS; Holliston, MA; (Y); 19/189; Spanish Clb; Nwsp Sprt Ed; Mgr(s); JV Socr; Hon Roll; Pres Spanish NHS; Ntl Rtng Supr Clscl Piano Comptn 84-86; Miss Tn MA Fnlst 84; Interntl Bankng.

GAINES, MICHAEL T; Copley Sq HS; Boston, MA; (Y); Boys Clb Am; Cmnty Wkr; Computer Clb; FCA; French Clb; Intnl Clb; Letterman Clb; Bsktbl; French Hon Soc; Hon Roll; Freedom House Awd 86; Boston Coll.

GALARNEAU, KRISTEN; Attleboro HS; Attleboro, MA; (Y); Trs Church Yth Grp; Drama Clb; JA; Pep Clb; Band; Mrchg Band; School Musical; School Play; NHS; Latin Natl Hnr Soc 86; Sec Ed.

GALAS JR, RAYMOND E; Dartmouth HS; N Dartmouth, MA; (Y); 17/250; AFS; Chorus; Trk; Wt Lftg; NHS; DECA; JR Dstc Chrs 83; Providence Coll; Pltcl Sci.

GALE, DANIEL; Athol HS; Athol, MA; (Y); 3/148; Var JV Ftbl; Var Trk; High Hon Roll; Sec NHS; Church Yth Grp; JA; Ski Clb; SADD; Yrbk Stf; Hugh O Brian Tyh Ldrshp 85; Hrvrd U Physcs Schlrshp 86; Air Force Acad Smr Sci Smnr 86; Air Force Acad; Arntcl Engrng.

GALEGO, DEBBIE; New Bedford HS; New Bedford, MA; (Y); 96/681; Computer Clb; Intnl Clb; Key Clb; Hon Roll; Voice Dem Awd; I L G W U Schlrshp 86; SMU; Math.

GALLAGHER, JON; King Philip Regional HS; Norfolk, MA; (Y); 8/270; Ski Clb; Var Capt Golf; Hon Roll; NHS; Ntl Merit Schol; Chancellors Tlnt Awd Scholar U MA Amherst 86; MVP Var Golf 85; Outstndng Racer Old Colony Ski 86; Bus.

GALLAGHER, MATTHEW; Waltham HS; Boston, MA; (Y); Am Leg Boys St; Church Yth Grp; Cmnty Wkr; School Play; VP Stu Cncl; Var Capt Bsktbl; Var JV Socr; Hon Roll; Jr NHS; NHS; Soc Presrvtn Antiquities 86; Hist.

GALLAGHER, SHANNON; Taconic HS; Pittsfield, MA; (Y); 14/261; Hosp Aide; Pep Clb; SADD; Band; Concert Band; Nwsp Stf; Capt Cheerleading; High Hon Roll; Hon Roll; Physcl Thrpy.

GALLAGHER, TAMMY; Mc Cann Tech HS; N Adams, MA; (Y); High Hon Roll; Hon Roll; NHS; Comp Prgmr.

GALLAGHER, TERESA; King Philip Regional HS; Norfolk, MA; (Y); 3/203; Off Frsh Cls; Off Soph Cls; Off Jr Cls; Stu Cncl; Var L Socr; JV Var Sftbl; High Hon Roll; Hon Roll; VP NHS; Natl Histry Day 3rd Pl Dist Lvl 86; Excellence In Chem 85; Eng.

GALLAGHER, THERESA; King Philip Regional HS; Plainville, MA; (Y); JV Var Sftbl; Engl.

GALLANT, CHRIS; Haverhill HS; Haverhill, MA; (Y); 33/400; German Clb; High Hon Roll; NHS; Pres Foreign Exchange Club; Stu Of Eclgy Club; Foreign Lang Tutor; Foreign Lang.

GALLANT, SHARON M; Littleton HS; Littleton, MA; (Y); 4/84; 4-H; Band; School Play; Nwsp Stf; Yrbk Stf; Var Capt Socr; Var Trk; Hon Roll; NHS; St Schlr; Mst Dedctd Band Awd 85-86; 4-H Ambssdr-Pblc Spkng 84-85; Boston U; Jrnlsm.

GALLANT, STEVEN L; Pentucket Regional HS; Merrimac, MA; (Y); 5/174; Am Leg Boys St; Cmnty Wkr; French Clb; Scholastic Bowl; Service Clb; High Hon Roll; NHS; Hnr Schlrs Awd 86; St Johns U.

GALLI, KEVIN; Burlington HS; Burlington, MA; (Y); 4/321; JV Var Socr; Var L Trk; High Hon Roll; Hon Roll; NHS; Ntl Merit Ltr; Boy Scts; Church Yth Grp; JV Ice Hcky; Chancllrs Tlnt Awd U MA Amherst 86; US Military Acad Invtnl Acad Wrkshp 86; Acad Excllnce Awds 85-86; Engrng.

GALLIVAN, BRIAN; Dedham HS; Dedham, MA; (S); 7/257; Cmnty Wkr; Nwsp Rptr; Nwsp Sprt Ed; Var Crs Cntry; Var Trk; Hon Roll; NHS; Communctns.

GALLIVAN, LEIGH; Easthampton HS; Easthampton, MA; (Y); 19/130; Drama Clb; Hosp Aide; Spanish Clb; Yrbk Bus Mgr; Stu Cncl; JV Bsktbl; Capt Cheerleading; Mgr(s); Score Keeper; Olympd Test Hist Natl Recog 84-86; Chrldrs Achvt Awd 84-86; Poltcl Sci.

GALLIVAN, TIMOTHY G; Foxboro HS; Foxboro, MA; (Y); 24/243; Am Leg Boys St; Letterman Clb; Ski Clb; SADD; Varsity Clb; Stu Cncl; Var Bsktbl; Var Capt Socr; Var Capt Tennis; Hon Roll; Coll Of The Holy Cross; Law.

GALLO, CHRISTINA; Reading Memorial HS; Reading, MA; (Y); SADD; Rep Frsh Cls; Rep Soph Cls; Rep Jr Cls; French Hon Soc; High Hon Roll; NHS; Mount Holyoke Awd 86; La Pierre Stu Dance Co 86; Miss Teen Ager Of MA 84; Pre Law.

GALO, MICHAEL; Deerfield Acad; Laredo, TX; (Y); Debate Tm; 4-H; Spanish Clb; Rep Stu Cncl; 4-H Awd; NHS.

GALVIN, DIANE; Braintree HS; Braintree, MA; (Y); 25/381; Church Yth Grp; Spanish Clb; NHS; Spanish NHS; Anne Horne Little Fllwshp 86; Belmont Abbey Coll; Pre-Law.

GALVIN, PAULA; Woburn HS; Woburn, MA; (S); 43/453; Church Yth Grp; SADD; Leo Clb; Varsity Clb; Capt Color Guard; Capt Trk; Capt Twrlr; Hon Roll; Jr NHS; NHS; Phys Ftns Awd And Recd Hldr 83-86; High Jmp,Meter Hrdls,Rely 85-86; MVP Awd Grls Trk 86; Northeastern U; Phys Thrpy.

GAMELLI, DEBORAH; Westfield HS; Westfield, MA; (Y); Cmnty Wkr; Girl Scts; Spanish Clb; Chorus; Gym; Hon Roll; Jr NHS; Holyoke CC; Secy.

GAMELLI, WILLIAM; W Springfield HS; W Springfield, MA; (Y); Ski Clb; Rep Frsh Cls; Rep Soph Cls; Rep Jr Cls; Pres Sr Cls; Pres Stu Cncl; Var JV Socr; JV Trk; Hon Roll; NHS; Pol Sci.

GAMST, NICOLE C; Cohasset HS; Cohasset, MA; (Y); 15/106; Yrbk Stf; High Hon Roll; Hon Roll; NHS; U MA Amherst.

GANCARSKI, STEVEN G; Bishop Stang HS; Fall River, MA; (Y); Pres Art Clb; VP Drama Clb; School Play; Stage Crew; Ed Lit Mag; Hon Roll; Scholar Schl Musuem Fine Art Boston 85; Hnrs Awd Bst Shw Arts Fstvl 85; 1st Pl Hnr Awd Bst Shw 85; Schl Musuem Fine Art; Fine Art.

GANCARZ, ROBERT M; Cathedral HS; Chicopee, MA; (Y); Boy Scts; Prfct Atten Awd; Western New England Coll; Elec.

GANDHI, HEMANGEENI SARITA V; The Cambridge Schl Of Weston; Malden, MA; (Y); Pres Chess Clb; School Play; Variety Show; Nwsp Ed-Chief; Yrbk Ed-Chief; Off Jr Cls; Off Sr Cls; Kiwanis Awd; Ntl Merit SF; Trs Girl Scts.

GANGEMI, DAWN; Braintree HS; Braintree, MA; (Y); 186/460; Sftbl; Hon Roll; Psych.

GANGI, SUSAN; Methuen HS; Methuen, MA; (Y); Spanish Clb; SADD; Rep Stu Cncl; Northern Essex CC; Bus Mgmt.

GANNON, BRIAN; Marian HS; Natick, MA; (Y); Church Yth Grp; Band; Concert Band; JV Ftbl; JV Im Ice Hcky; Im Wt Lftg; High Hon Roll; Hon Roll; Spanish NHS; Spanish Clb.

GANONG, TAMMY; Gorton-Dunstable Regional Secd Schl; Groton, MA; (Y); 11/92; Church Yth Grp; Rptr Sec 4-H; SADD; Yrbk Stf; Stu Cncl; High Hon Roll; Ntl Merit Ltr; Art Clb; Drama Clb; MA Yth Ldrshp Alumni, Hugh O Brien Yth Ldrshp Semnr 84-86; Womns Clb Schlrshp 86; U Of NH; Orthdntstry.

GARABEDIAN JR, LEONARD M; Hopedale JR/SR HS; Hopedale, MA; (Y); 15/73; Am Leg Boys St; Church Yth Grp; SADD; Band; Jazz Band; Yrbk Stf; Var Bsbl; Var Bsktbl; Var Socr; NHS; Bus.

GARANT, PAMELA; Foxboro HS; Foxboro, MA; (Y); Aud/Vis; Cmnty Wkr; Hosp Aide; Library Aide; Varsity Clb; JV Bsktbl; Var Fld Hcky; Im Tennis; Im Vllybl; Im Wt Lftg; WJCC Comm Salute Awd 85; Foxboro Cable Access HS Rprtr 84-87; Foxboro JR Firefighter 86; Massasoit; Fire Sci.

GARBARINO, NICOLE; Marian HS; Framingham, MA; (Y); Computer Clb; Drama Clb; Pep Clb; Variety Show; Cheerleading; Sftbl; Trk; Hon Roll; TV Fld.

GARCIA, PATRICIA; Malden HS; Malden, MA; (Y); 33/470; SADD; Hon Roll; Trustees Malden HS Schlrshp Inc 86; Malden HS Fclty Awd 86; Wentworth Inst Tech; Elec Engr.

GARD, ROBERT; Shepherd Hill Regional HS; Charlton Depot, MA; (Y); Am Leg Boys St; Teachers Aide; Var Trk; High Hon Roll; NHS; WDI; Engrng.

GARDINER, EDWARD J; Dedham HS; Dedham, MA; (S); 8/250; Church Yth Grp; Computer Clb; Spanish Clb; Variety Show; Var JV Socr; JV Trk; Hon Roll; United Nations Pilgrmg Yth Essay Cont Fnlst 85.

GARDINER, SARA; Lincoln-Sudbury Regional HS; Sudbury, MA; (Y); Church Yth Grp; French Clb; Trs Ed Key Clb; SADD; School Musical; Rep Soph Cls; Rep Jr Cls; Var Trk; Law.

GARDNER, ALBERT; Mccann Technical Voc Regional HS; North Adams, MA; (Y); Band; Chorus; Church Choir; Concert Band; Jazz Band; Hon Roll; Elec Engrng.

GARDNER, AMIE L; Macduffie HS; Springfield, MA; (Y); Camera Clb; Sec JA; Yrbk Phtg; Jr NHS; Ntl Merit Schol; Natl Merit Achvt Outstndng Negro Stu 85; Bio.

GARDNER, ROBERT; Reading Memorial HS; Reading, MA; (Y); Church Yth Grp; French Clb; JA; Red Cross Aide; SADD; Nwsp Rptr; Bsktbl; Socr; Tennis; Computer Clb; Peer Tutor Awd 86; Good Ctzn Awd 84; Bus.

GAREY, KELLEY; Holliston HS; Crosby, TX; (Y); FHA; Office Aide; VICA; Drill Tm; Hon Roll; MA ST Schlrshp 86; A-Bnqt Awd 83-84; Engl Awd 83-84; U Of Houston; Bus Admin.

GARIEPY, DAVID; Ludlow HS; Ludlow, MA; (Y); 53/279; Aud/Vis; Chess Clb; Church Yth Grp; JCL; Latin Clb; Political Wkr; Stage Crew; Hon Roll; Stu Of St John The Bptst Prsh 85; Cncl Ldr Of Yth Grp; Spgfld Tech Coll; Telecomm.

GARIPAY, MICHAEL; Melrose HS; Melrose, MA; (Y); 28/379; Boy Scts; Computer Clb; Red Cross Aide; Spanish Clb; Varsity Clb; Bsbl; Var Crs Cntry; Var L Swmmng; Var Trk; Hon Roll; Crtfd Red Cross Lfgrd; Life Scout; Crtfd Scuba Diver; Elec Engrng.

GARLAND, AMY K; Brockton HS; Brockton, MA; (Y); 58/900; JA; Band; Concert Band; Mrchg Band; School Musical; Symp Band; High Hon Roll; Hon Roll; SE Dist Concert Bnd 86; Pres Acadmc Ftns Awd 86; Bridgewater ST Coll; Bus.

GARNETT, RACHAEL; Westport HS; Westport, MA; (Y); Church Yth Grp; Debate Tm; Drama Clb; French Clb; Intnl Clb; Yrbk Stf; Hon Roll; Sec NHS; Stonehill Coll; Pblc Rltns.

GARRAWAY, GAYLORD; Milford HS; Milford, MA; (Y); Var L Trk; Hon Roll; Arch.

GARRETT, MELISSA; Our Lady Of Nazareth Acad; Revere, MA; (Y); 1/74; French Clb; Ski Clb; Lit Mag; Crs Cntry; High Hon Roll; Prfct Atten Awd; Exc Alg,Geo,Chem 84-86; Acctng.

GARRITY, SCOTT; Hopkins Acad; Hadley, MA; (Y); 6/48; Am Leg Boys St; French Clb; Political Wkr; Ski Clb; Band; Concert Band; Mrchg Band; Pep Band; School Play; Stu Cncl.

GARRON, JOHN; Everett HS; Everett, MA; (Y); Key Clb; Letterman Clb; SADD; Rep Frsh Cls; Rep Soph Cls; Rep Jr Cls; Rep Sr Cls; JV Bsbl; Var Capt Crs Cntry; Var Capt Ice Hcky; GBL Hcky All-Str 85-86; Mldn Evng Nws All-Schlstc Hcky 85-86; Bus Mgmt.

GARTH, LYNN VIRGINIA; Lincoln-Sudbury Regional HS; Lincoln, MA; (Y); Orch; School Musical; School Play; Lit Mag; Stu Cncl; Ntl Merit Ltr; Church Yth Grp; Drama Clb; French Clb; Acpl Chr; Cum Laude Scty; Hrvd Book Prize; Brown U Book Awd 85; Fcty Plq Drma Awd Bowl; Frnch Mrt Awd 86; Princeton U; Russian Stds.

GARVEY, CHERYL; Westfield HS; Westfield, MA; (Y); 8/357; Cmnty Wkr; Debate Tm; French Clb; Nwsp Ed-Chief; VP NHS; Jrnslm Awd 86; Girl Scout Troop Appreciatn Cert 85; Engr.

GASCO, BRIAN KEITH; Blackstone Valley Tech; Millbury, MA; (Y); Boy Scts; High Hon Roll; Hon Roll.

GASCO, WAYNE M; Blackstone Valley Tech; Millbury, MA; (Y); 2/11; Boy Scts; VICA; Elec Engr.

GASQUE, DEIRDRE; Westborough HS; Westborough, MA; (Y); Church Yth Grp; Chorus; Church Choir; Color Guard; Yrbk Stf; Tennis; Mst Imprvd Grls Tennis Awd 86.

GASS, WILLIAM; Hyde Park HS; Boston, MA; (Y); Franklin Inst; Automtv Mchncs.

GASTALL, JOHN RYAN; B M C Durfee HS; Fall River, MA; (Y); Boy Scts; Church Yth Grp; Cmnty Wkr; JV Golf; Hon Roll; Bus.

GASTONGUAY, DOUGLAS J; Fitchburg HS; Fitchburg, MA; (Y); 35/208; Am Leg Boys St; Letterman Clb; Political Wkr; Ski Clb; Varsity Clb; Var L Crs Cntry; Var L Trk; 2nd Pl Fnsh Dist Cls Meet Outdr Trk 86; Ran Fsts 880, 1 Mile, 2 Mile Trk 86; Top 10 Fres, Soph, Jr; U MA; Sprts Mgnt.

GATES, KATRINA; Haverhill HS; Haverhill, MA; (Y); 96/400; Church Yth Grp; Exploring; Intnl Clb; High Hon Roll; Hon Roll; Cmmnctns.

GATES, LISA; Newburyport HS; Newburpt, MA; (Y); Math Tm; SADD; Pres Frsh Cls; Var Socr; Var Trk; Hon Roll; NHS; Med.

GATHERUM, KAREN; Dracut HS; Dracut, MA; (Y); Computer Clb; FHA; Office Aide; School Play, High Hon Roll; Hon Roll; Jr NHS; NHS; Prfct Atten Awd; U Lowell; Accntng.

GATTUSO, MARC; Drury SR HS; North Adams, MA; (S); Church Yth Grp; Spanish Clb; Trs Band; Drm Mjr(t); Jazz Band; Rep Jr Cls; Var JV Golf; High Hon Roll; NHS; Mrchg Band.

GATZKE, JENNIFER; Bartlett HS; Webster, MA; (Y); #8 In Class; Trs VP Science Clb; Chorus; Yrbk Stf; Socr; High Hon Roll; NHS; NEDT Awd; Church Yth Grp; Spanish Clb; Nwsp Stf; Outstndng Soph Grl Awd 85; Brown U Bk Awd 86; Rotry Clb Yth Ldrshp Salute 86; Marine Bio.

GATZKE, ROBIN; Lexington HS; Lexington, MA; (Y); Orch; Cncrtmstr New Englnd Cnsvtry YCO 86; New Englnd Cnsvtry Hnrs Qurtet 85; Estmn Schlrshp Hwltt Pckd 86; Estmn Schl Of Music.

GAUCHER, ROBERT; Pittsfield HS; Pittsfield, MA; (Y); 3/380; Church Yth Grp; VP German Clb; Latin Clb; Capt Quiz Bowl; Scholastic Bowl; Rep Frsh Cls; Rep Soph Cls; Rep Jr Cls; Var L Ftbl; Im Ice Hcky; Dartmouth Coll Bk Awd 86; Gld Mdl Natl Lat Exam 86; Mth Lg Wnr 83-86.

GAUDET, HEIDI; HS Of Commerce; Springfield, MA; (S); 4/350; Hosp Aide; Band; Yrbk Stf; Sftbl; High Hon Roll; NHS; Bus.

GAUDETTE, LISA; Tantasqua Reg SR HS; Holland, MA; (Y); Cmnty Wkr; Drama Clb; School Musical; Hon Roll; CO ST; Law.

GAUDETTE, PAMELA; Plymouth Carver HS; Plymouth, MA; (Y); 70/517; Sec Drama Clb; Girl Scts; Varsity Clb; Chorus; School Musical; School Play; Stage Crew; Var Gym; Hon Roll; Girl Scout Silver Award; Spc Ed.

GAUDRAULT, THOMAS; Masconomet Regional HS; Topsfield, MA; (Y); French Clb; Teachers Aide; Yrbk Phtg; Var Capt Crs Cntry; Var Trk; Hon Roll; NHS; Paul Revere Bowl For 9 Vrsty Lttrs 86; Indr Trck-3 Vrsty Lttrs-Capt 84-86; Holy Cross.

GAUDREAU, THERESA; Ludlow HS; Ludlow, MA; (Y); Church Yth Grp; GAA; Concert Band; Mrchg Band; Yrbk Stf; Capt Socr; Hon Roll; Prfct Atten Awd; Pres Schlr; Wstrn New Englnd; Acctng.

GAUGHAN, NANCY; Clintin HS; Clinton, MA; (Y); 9/121; Church Yth Grp; JA; Spanish Clb; Varsity Clb; Yrbk Stf; Frsh Cls; Soph Cls; Jr Cls; Bsktbl; Fld Hcky; Marketing.

GAUGLER, DARLEEN; Ware HS; Ware, MA; (Y); Church Yth Grp; French Clb; Model UN; Spanish Clb; SADD; Yrbk Rptr; Yrbk Stf; JV Cheerleading; Im Vllybl; Hon Roll; Jrnlsm Hnr 84-85; Htl Mgmt.

GAULIN, MICHELLE; Southbridge HS; Southbridge, MA; (Y); Concert Band; Mrchg Band; Var Cheerleading; Hon Roll; Gregg Typng Awd 86; Concert Band Awd 84-86; Awd Ftbl,Bsktbl 84-86.

GAUMOND, LEON; Cathedral HS; Springfield, MA; (Y); 111/536; Boy Scts; Church Yth Grp; Model UN; Var L Swmmng; Hon Roll; Prfct Atten Awd; Le Fstvl French Comp Poetry Wnnr 85; St Joseph Schlrshp Awd 83; Aerospace Engr.

GAUNT, KELLY; S Hadley HS; S Hadly, MA; (Y); 54/170; Camera Clb; SADD; Nwsp Phtg; Nwsp Stf; Yrbk Phtg; Yrbk Stf; Rep Sr Cls; Cheerleading; High Hon Roll; Yrbk Photo Edtr Hghst Achvt 86; Holyoke CC; Mgmt.

GAUTHIER, CYNTHIA; Gardner HS; Gardner, MA; (Y); Spanish Clb; Sec Frsh Cls; Rep Soph Cls; Var L Bsktbl; Var L Fld Hcky; Var L Trk; Hon Roll; Mst Imprvd Fld Hcky Awd 85; Poly Sci.

GAUTHIER, FAY; Blackstone-Millville-Rgnl HS; Blackstone, MA; (Y); 2/96; Cmnty Wkr; Band; Mrchg Band; Yrbk Stf; Off Stu Cncl; Bsktbl; Fld Hcky; Trk; High Hon Roll; Ntl Hon Soc 86; Blckstn Vly Bnd Fstvl; Mtls Prtcptn Dist Trck & Fld 84-86.

GAUTHIER, JEFFREY; Silver Lake Regional HS; Kingston, MA; (Y); 3/519; Am Leg Boys St; Latin Clb; Math Clb; SADD; Var L Bsbl; Bsktbl; Var L Crs Cntry; JV Capt Ice Hcky; High Hon Roll; Hon Roll; Rensselaer Polytechnic Inst 86; Natl Ledrshp Awd 86; Engrng.

GAUTHIER, MARYBETH; Holy Name Central Catholic HS; Millbury, MA; (Y); 10/252; Nwsp Ed-Chief; Nwsp Rptr; Yrbk Sprt Ed; Yrbk Stf; Rep Stu Cncl; JV Cheerleading; NHS; Nwsp Stf; Cit Awd; Elks Awd; Most Outstndng Stu Awd 86; Yth Of Mnth Awd, Yth Of Yr Awd 86; Mdls Cretv Wrtg, Ad Eng, Psych, Relgn, N; Clg Of Holy Cross; Eng.

GAUTHIER, TAMMI; Chelmsford HS; Chelmsford, MA; (Y); AFS; Sec Trs Drama Clb; Girl Scts; Chorus; School Musical; School Play; Nwsp Rptr; High Hon Roll; NHS; Spanish NHS; Modern Ms ST Finals 86; Frgn Reltns.

GAUTHIER, TINA; Grafton HS; S Grafton, MA; (Y); Church Yth Grp; Hosp Aide; SADD; Band; School Play; Stat Bsktbl; L Var Crs Cntry; L Var Trk; Hon Roll; Lion Awd; Athltcs Prsdntl Awd 83-84; 3rd Yr Athltc Awd Trck 86; Amherst U Mass; Nrs.

GAUTREAU, KEITH; Austin Prep; Rowley, MA; (Y); Am Leg Boys St; Ski Clb; SADD; VP Soph Cls; Off Jr Cls; Pres Stu Cncl; Var Bsbl; Var Capt Socr; Hon Roll.

GAUVREAU, TAMI; Melrose HS; Melrose, MA; (Y); 20/401; Art Clb; Church Yth Grp; Pep Clb; Spanish Clb; SADD; Yrbk Stf; Hon Roll; NHS; Art.

GAVIN, HEIDI; Whitman-Hanson Regional HS; Whitman, MA; (Y); Trk; Hon Roll; NHS; Upsilon Alpha Hist Conf 86; Trvl.

GAYNOR, ANN; Randolph HS; Randolph, MA; (Y); 72/321; Cmnty Wkr; SADD; Yrbk Stf; Rep Stu Cncl; Var Capt Cheerleading; Coach Actv; Powder Puff Ftbl; JV Sftbl; Var Hockey Booster Assoc, Thos Pirrera Schlrshp PTO, Cyril T Powderly Schlrshp 86; S Eastern MA U; Bus.

GAYOSKI, MICHELLE; Old Rochester Regional HS; Mattapoisett, MA; (Y); 19/130; Drama Clb; Ski Clb; Chorus; School Musical; Sec Jr Cls; Sec Sr Cls; Rep Stu Cncl; Capt Var Cheerleading; VP NHS; ACT Drama Awd 86; Hghst Acad Avg Alg I 84.

GAYTON, CYNTHIA; Natick HS; Natick, MA; (Y); 33/423; High Hon Roll; NHS; Acctng Awd 86; Data Prcssng Awd 86; Coll Of The Holy Crss; Acctng.

GAZDA, PETER; Chicopee HS; Chicopee, MA; (Y); 16/206; Debate Tm; Ed Yrbk Ed-Chief; Stu Cncl; Hon Roll; NHS; Cert Achvt Natl Hnr Soc 86; Dartmouth Coll; Ind Psych.

GAZIANO, KRISTEN; Belmont HS; Belmont, MA; (Y); Church Yth Grp; Civic Clb; Pep Clb; Bsktbl; Coach Actv; Socr; High Hon Roll; Hon Roll; Natl Latin Awd Maxima Cum Laude 86; Coaches Awd JV Bsktbl 85.

GEDDES, ERIN; Attleboro HS; S Attleboro, MA; (Y); Ski Clb; SADD; Yrbk Bus Mgr; Yrbk Ed-Chief; Yrbk Stf; Capt Cheerleading; Fld Hcky; Powder Puff Ftbl; Trk; CC Awd; Katheryn Gibby; Bus.

GEIB, ANDREW; Cathedral HS; Enfield, CT; (Y); 40/557; Intnl Clb; Math Clb; Office Aide; Varsity Clb; Var L Trk; Hon Roll; NHS.

GEIB, MICHELLE; Canton HS; Canton, MA; (Y); Pres VP Church Yth Grp; Drama Clb; German Clb; Band; Concert Band; Jazz Band; Mrchg Band; School Musical; Stage Crew; Best Musicl Perf, Trio 84-86; Plymouth ST Coll; Mktg.

GEISLER, HEATHER; Hoosac Valley HS; Adams, MA; (Y); 15/150; Sec Jr Cls; Sec Sr Cls; High Hon Roll; Hon Roll; Bus Admn.

GELB, LAURIE I; Lexington HS; Lexington, MA; (Y); AFS; Cmnty Wkr; Computer Clb; French Clb; Teachers Aide; Temple Yth Grp; Yrbk Ed-Chief; Stu Cncl; L Crs Cntry; Hon Roll; Margret Kinley Jrnslsm Awd 86; Spcl Needs Tchrs Aide Awd 85; U Of PA.

GELINEAU, LISA; Blackstone-Millville Regional Schl; Blackstone, MA; (Y); Sec Church Yth Grp; SADD; Teachers Aide; Band; Mrchg Band; Ed Yrbk Ed-Chief; Off Soph Cls; Chrmn Jr Cls; Stu Cncl; Hon Roll; Exclnt Achvmnt Msc Awds 84-86; Sci Fr Hnrbl Mntn 86; Mbr Of Peers Eductng Peers & 86; Elem Educ.

GEMME, MICHELLE; Cathedral HS; Chicopee, MA; (Y); 74/536; Art Clb; Red Cross Aide; Stage Crew; Nwsp Stf; Yrbk Stf; Hon Roll; E Layne Art Awd 86; Grphc Artst.

GENNELL, ERIC; Central Catholic HS; Dracut, MA; (Y); Var JV Ftbl; High Hon Roll; Hon Roll; UN MA; Bus Adm.

GENTRY, ALFRED; Mario Umana Tech HS; Boston, MA; (Y); Cmnty Wkr; Alcoa Lab Cert Cmpltn-Sci Pgm 85-86; Comp Engr.

GENZALE, JULIE; Malden HS; Malden, MA; (Y); Office Aide; Hon Roll; Burdett Schl Boston; Bus.

GEORGE, DONNA; St Mary Regional HS; Lynn, MA; (Y); 28/94; Art Clb; Church Choir; Hon Roll; Acctng.

GEORGE, JENNIFER; Wachusett Regional HS; Holden, MA; (Y); 27/381; Cmnty Wkr; Library Aide; Office Aide; Teachers Aide; Hon Roll; NHS; Pres Schlr; Chld Study Cert 86; Worcester ST Coll; Elem Educ.

GEORGE, MARIANNE; Weymouth North HS; N Weymouth, MA; (Y); 32/329; Church Yth Grp; JA; Band; Mrchg Band; JV Bsktbl; Var JV Vllybl; Hon Roll; Jr NHS; Concert Band; Rep Jr Cls; Century III Ldrshp Awd 86; AFL Labor Union Lcl 444 Schlrshp Awd 86; Acad Decthln Tm 86; Wstrn New England Coll; Pre Law.

GEORGE, STEPHANIE L; Newburyport HS; Newburyport, MA; (Y); 52/188; Yrbk Stf; Rep Soph Cls; Rep Jr Cls; Secy Grls Ldrs Phys Ed 85-87; Ldrshp Semnr 85-86; Comp Sci.

GEORGE, SUZANNE; Brockton HS; Brockton, MA; (Y); 1/871; Drama Clb; Ski Clb; Band; Mrchg Band; VP Pres Sr Cls; Pres Stu Cncl; NCTE Awd; Am Leg Aux Girls St; SADD; School Musical; Suprtndts Awd; Nrmn B Nasn Chem Awd; Harvard.

GEORGIADIS, PAMELA; Presentation Of Mary Acad; Haverhill, MA; (Y); Church Yth Grp; French Clb; Nwsp Stf; Yrbk Ed-Chief; Drama Clb; Hosp Aide; Pep Clb; SADD; Chorus; School Musical; Mrktng.

GERAGHTY, DEBRA A; Notre Dame Acad; Canton, MA; (Y); 25/109; Art Clb; Church Yth Grp; Civic Clb; Cmnty Wkr; Dance Clb; Debate Tm; English Clb; 4-H; French Clb; FBLA; Awd Ntl Rcgntn For Being Undftd X-Ctry Tm 85; Awd Exclnt Tchng Ablts CCD Chldrn 85; Bus.

GERALD, PATRICIA; Madison Park HS; Brighton, MA; (Y); Church Yth Grp; Dance Clb; Drama Clb; Church Choir; School Musical; School Play; Hon Roll.

GERARD, LORI; Monument Mountain Regional HS; Housatonic, MA; (Y); 6/132; French Clb; Varsity Clb; Yrbk Stf; JV Bsktbl; Var L Socr; Var L Sftbl; Bausch & Lomb Sci Awd; High Hon Roll; NHS; Monumnt Mntn Educ Assn Schlrshp 86; MIAA Div II Chmpnshp Sccr Tm 84-85; MIAA ST Rnnr-Up Sccr Tm 84; Intl Stud.

GERARDI, JOYCE; North Reading HS; N Reading, MA; (Y); Band; Chorus; Concert Band; Mrchg Band; Nwsp Rptr; VP Soph Cls; Stu Cncl; Var L Bsktbl; Var L Fld Hcky; Var L Trk; Baystate Games Trck 85; Baystate Games Fld Hcky 85; MVP Fld Hcky; Cal Chmpn Trck 85-86.

GERKEN, HEATHER K; Nashoba Regional HS; Bolton, MA; (Y); 1/205; Cmnty Wkr; SADD; Nwsp Ed-Chief; Yrbk Stf; Socr; Bausch & Lomb Sci Awd; High Hon Roll; NHS; Ntl Merit Ltr; RPI Medl Math, Sci 86; Harvard Bk Worcester Cnty 86; Bst Stu Awd 86; Pre-Law.

GEROMINI, LAURIE; Hanover HS; Hanover, MA; (Y); Aud/Vis; SADD; JV Var Bsktbl; Var Capt Fld Hcky; Sftbl; Tennis; Trk; Hon Roll; NHS; Stu Of The Month-Engl 85; Stu Of The Month-Socl Studies 84; Comm.

GERRISH, SCOTT; Canton HS; Canton, MA; (Y); 15/250; Am Leg Boys St; Church Yth Grp; Varsity Clb; Nwsp Stf; JV Ice Hcky; Var Trk; Hon Roll; Cntry Clb 86; Boys ST 86; Engrng.

GERROIR, STEVEN; Central Catholic HS; Andover, MA; (Y); 50/231; Im Bowling; JV Trk; JV Wrstlng; High Hon Roll; Hon Roll; Northeastern; Engrng.

GERSON, ILANA B; Marblehead HS; Marblehead, MA; (Y); SADD; Yrbk Bus Mgr; Capt Cheerleading; Var Powder Puff Ftbl; HS Ldrshp Corps 86-87; Hebrew HS Hons 85; Intl Fiance.

GERVASI, DAVID; Weymouth North HS; Weymouth, MA; (Y); 44/328; Var Ice Hcky; High Hon Roll; Hon Roll; Rennie Cup Schlrshp 86; Bentley Coll; Bus Mgmt.

GESNER, DAVID; Watertown HS; Allston, MA; (Y); 16/283; Am Leg Boys St; Boys Clb Am; JV Bsbl; Var Ftbl; Var Wrstlng; Hon Roll; Magna Cum Laude Natl Jr Clsscl Lge Ltn Exam 86; Med.

GETSON, DEBBIE; Framingham South HS; Framingham, MA; (S); 13/260; Drama Clb; VP Latin Clb; Political Wkr; School Musical; School Play; Yrbk Stf; VP Cheerleading; VP Capt Cheerleading; Mgr(s); High Hon Roll; Prom Coordntr 85; Stu Govt Day 85; Citation-Govr Of MA 86.

GETSON, JULIE; Framingham South HS; Framingham, MA; (S); Drama Clb; Spanish Clb; SADD; School Musical; Variety Show; Jr Cls; Trs Stu Cncl; Var Cheerleading; Var Trk.

GHAZIL, LEE ANN; Bishop Feehan HS; Attleboro, MA; (Y); 17/265; Math Tm; Chorus; Concert Band; Jazz Band; Mrchg Band; Orch; High Hon Roll; NHS; Ntl Merit Ltr; Spanish NHS; Engrng.

GIAKOUMIS, TINA; Bartlett HS; Webster, MA; (Y); 12/150; Pres Spanish Clb; Capt Flag Corp; Nwsp Ed-Chief; High Hon Roll; Hon Roll; NHS; Rsc & Amblnc Squad Schlrshp 86; Dsbld Amer Vtrns Schlrshp 86; Vtrn Of Frgn Ward Schlrshp 86; Siena Coll; Psychlgy.

GIAMMARCO, DOREEN; Mount St Joseph Acad; Boston, MA; (Y); 15/169; JA; VP Trs Spanish Clb; SADD; Nwsp Stf; Yrbk Stf; Hon Roll; NHS; Math Fair 3rd 83; Corp Law.

GIAMMARCO, GREGORIO; Christopher Columbus HS; Boston, MA; (S); JA; Math Clb; Science Clb; Hon Roll; NEDT Awd; Prfct Atten Awd; Floor Hockey IM; Italian Schl; Socy Of Dstngshd Amer HS Stu; Northeastern U; Bus.

GIANELLY, ROBERT C; Longmeadow HS; Longmeadow, MA; (Y); 62/280; Am Leg Boys St; Key Clb; Stu Cncl; Var Bsktbl; Capt Ftbl; Hon Roll; NHS; Dagenais Awd 85; UNICO Awd 86; All Western MS Ftbl 85; Middlebury Coll.

GIANGRANDE, SCOTT; Boston Coll HS; Woburn, MA; (Y); 85/300; Aud/Vis; Cmnty Wkr; VP Drama Clb; German Clb; Key Clb; PAVAS; Band; School Musical; School Play; Nwsp Rptr; Awd Excllnc Chem I & Grmn II Hnrs 84-85; Chem.

GIANNANDREA, ITALIA; Archbishop Williams HS; Quincy, MA; (Y); Yrbk Stf; Socr; Spnsh Merit Awd 83-86; Framingham ST U; Cmnctns.

GIANSANTI, LISA; Clinton HS; Clinton, MA; (Y); 2/122; JA; Spanish Clb; VP Band; Concert Band; Mrchg Band; Yrbk Stf; High Hon Roll; NHS; Harvard Bk Awd 86; Elem Ed.

GIARGIARI, ROBERT P; Natick HS; Natick, MA; (Y); 9/416; SADD; Jazz Band; School Musical; VP Jr Cls; Var L Ftbl; Var L Trk; High Hon Roll; NHS; Ntl Merit Ltr; Rotary Awd; Harvard U; Lib Arts.

GIASI, MARY THERESA; Wachusett Regional HS; Holden, MA; (Y); 27/443; Hon Roll; NHS; Hnrbl Mntn Sci Fair 84.

GIBBER, JESSICA; Hampshire Regional HS; Northampton, MA; (Y); 18/135; 4-H; SADD; Teachers Aide; Chorus; Swing Chorus; Variety Show; 4-H Awd; Hon Roll; Art.

GIBBONS, DEBORAH; Westwood HS; Westwood, MA; (Y); 96/214; SADD; Var L Mrchg Band; Var L Cheerleading; Color Guard; Stage Crew; Im Powder Puff Ftbl; Hon Roll; Amdin.

GIBBONS, KEITH; Newburyport HS; Newburypt, MA; (Y); 12/185; Am Leg Boys St; JA; Var Capt Bsktbl; Var L Ftbl; Var Capt Trk; High Hon Roll; Hon Roll; NHS; Bsktbl MVP 85-86; Trck MVP 84-86; Physcl Thrpy.

GIBBS, CHRISTINE; Milton HS; Milton, MA; (Y); Art Clb; JV Capt Fld Hcky; Var L Trk; Hon Roll; NHS; Layout & Dsgn Edtr Of Yrbk 86-87.

GIGUERE-STELLMACK, DONNA; Blackstone-Millvl Rgnl JR SR HS; Virginia Bch, VA; (Y); 22/100; Church Yth Grp; Nwsp Ed-Chief; Pres Frsh Cls; Pres Soph Cls; Pres Sr Cls; Stu Cncl; Cheerleading; Trk; Hon Roll; NHS; Eductrs Assoc Awd Schlrshp 86; Worcester Polytchncl Inst Sci Fair Awd 85; Tide Water Coll; Bus Admin.

GILARDI, STEPHANIE; North Cambridge Catholic HS; Cambridge, MA; (Y); Rep Stu Cncl; New Englnd Schl Accntng; Accntn.

GILBERT, JOHN; Burlington HS; Burlington, MA; (Y); 2/314; JA; Var Capt Golf; High Hon Roll; NHS; Glf Hon Mntn 85; Sci Olympd 86; Chmstry Awd 85; Engrng.

GILBERT, LISA; Drury HS; N Adams, MA; (S); Pep Clb; Band; Concert Band; Mrchg Band; JV Var Cheerleading; Hon Roll.

GILBERT, ROBERT J; Burlington HS; Burlington, MA; (Y); 22/321; Var Capt Bsktbl; Var Capt Golf; Hon Roll; NHS; Hon Mntn Golf 84; Cchs Awd Bsktbl 86; Worcester Polytech; Elec Engr.

GILCHRIST, MILES; Fitchburg HS; Fitchburg, MA; (Y); Am Leg Boys St; Latin Clb; Nwsp Rptr; High Hon Roll; NHS; Latin Prz 84; Spec Stu 84-86; Lib Arts.

GILEFSKY, SCOTT; St Johns Prep Schl; Marblehead, MA; (Y); 40/270; Art Clb; SADD; Nwsp Sprt Ed; Im Bsktbl; Im Ftbl; Im Tennis; Im Vllybl; Hon Roll; Ntl Merit SF; Jewish Cmnty Ctr Yth Grp Exec Pres 85-86.

GILLEN, DANIELLE; Mac Duffie Schl; Magnolia, MA; (Y); 1/36; Debate Tm; Key Clb; Rep Frsh Cls; Rep Jr Cls; Rep Stu Cncl; Var Fld Hcky; Hon Roll; Var Sftbl; Var Tennis; Dartmouth Bk Awd 85-86; HOBY Ldrshp Awd 84-85; Pres Stu Body 86-87.

GILLESPIE, KELLY; South High Community HS; Worcester, MA; (Y); 4/220; Rep Stu Cncl; High Hon Roll; Hon Roll; NHS; Hugh O Brien Yth Foundtn; Schls Adm Yth Mnth; Georgiana Newton Awd Grad; Assumption Coll; Poltcs.

GILLESPIE, KEVIN M; Plymouth-Carver HS; Carver, MA; (Y); 15/550; Am Leg Boys St; High Hon Roll; Hon Roll; Comp Engrng.

GILLESPIE, KRISTINE; Randolph HS; Randolph, MA; (Y); 49/321; Church Yth Grp; Cmnty Wkr; FNA; Intnl Clb; Spanish Clb; SADD; Variety Show; High Hon Roll; Hon Roll; JC Awd; Stud Gvrnmnt Awd 85; Bridgewater ST Coll; Chldhd Ed.

GILLETT, ERIN B; Monument Mt Regional HS; Stockbridge, MA; (Y); 4/150; Nwsp Ed-Chief; Ed Lit Mag; VP Stu Cncl; Var Tennis; High Hon Roll; NHS; Band; Nwsp Stf; Var Crs Cntry; Var Gym; Stu Cncl Awd & Schlrshp 86; Socl Stds Achvt Awd 86; Dartmouth Book Awd 86; Lit Magzn Awd 86; Lbrl Arts.

GILLETTE, DANIEL; Malden HS; Malden, MA; (Y); 55/500; Church Yth Grp; JA; Nwsp Bus Mgr; Nwsp Stf; Var Tennis; Hon Roll; Tennis Tourn Champ 83-84; VP St Josephs CYO & Capt Bsktbl Tm 85-86; BC; Jrnlsm.

GILLINGHAM, JAMES; Medway HS; Medway, MA; (Y); French Clb; Yrbk Bus Mgr; Ftbl; Golf; High Hon Roll; Hon Roll; Century 21 Acctng Awd 85; Century 21 Advncd Acctng Awd 86; Bus Week Awd Bentley Coll 85; Bentley Coll; Acctng.

GILLIS, KRISTIN; Marian HS; Framingham, MA; (Y); 31/180; Am Leg Aux Girls St; Band; Yrbk Stf; Var Socr; Sec Frsh Cls; Rep Soph Cls; Rep Jr Cls; Off Sr Cls; Var Tennis.

GILLOOLY, VANESSA; Drury SR HS; N Adams, MA; (S); 29/180; Dance Clb; Pep Clb; Spanish Clb; Trs VP Concert Band; Mrchg Band; Pep Band; School Musical; Yrbk Stf; Hon Roll; NHS; Smr Music Schlrshps 84 & 85; Rotry Tlnt Awd 83; MA Wstrn Dist 86; Brenall Wmns Coll; Pre-Law.

GILMAN, PIPPIN; Georgetown HS; Georgetown, MA; (Y); AFS; Boy Scts; Band; Color Guard; Jazz Band; Bsbl; Wrstlng; High Hon Roll; NHS; Lawyer.

GILMER, JEWEL; Mario Umana HS; Dorchester, MA; (Y); Church Yth Grp; Hosp Aide; Sec Jr Cls; Pres Sr Cls; Rep Stu Cncl; JV Var Sftbl; Var Trk; Hon Roll; Prfct Atten Awd; 2nd Pl In Cty Sci Fair 84-85; Ulmass Med Hlth Pln Awd 85-86; Outstndng - Most Imprvd Sftbl Plyr 85-86.

GILMORE, BRIAN; Central Catholic HS; Atkinson, NH; (Y); 6/231; Computer Clb; Math Tm; Science Clb; Stage Crew; Nwsp Rptr; Yrbk Stf; Trk; High Hon Roll; Hon Roll; 1st Pl Awd Sci, Hist And Spnsh 86; Engrg.

GILMORE, GREGORY; Uxbridge HS; Uxbridge, MA; (Y); Library Aide; Im Ftbl; Var L Tennis; Hon Roll; Athl Awd 84-86; Eng.

GINES, AGNES; Southbridge HS; Southbridge, MA; (Y); Church Yth Grp; Science Clb; Church Choir; Yrbk Stf; Hon Roll; Mktg Mgmt.

GINSBURG, JESSICA L; Northfield Mount Hermon Schl; Shelburne, VT; (Y); Teachers Aide; Yrbk Sprt Ed; Rep Jr Cls; Rep Sr Cls; Var JV Crs Cntry; Var JV Trk; Hon Roll; Kenyon Coll; Psych.

GIOIOSO, JENNIFER; Danvers HS; Danvers, MA; (Y); 3/300; French Clb; Hosp Aide; Capt Color Guard; Capt Flag Corp; Yrbk Rptr; Yrbk Stf; French Hon Soc; High Hon Roll; NHS; Spanish NHS; Outstndng Ldrshp Awd 84-86; Clr Grd Outstnding Mbr Awd 83-84; Boston Coll; Mrktng.

GIONFRIDDO, TINA; Holyoke Catholic HS; Holyoke, MA; (Y); 34/134; Drama Clb; English Clb; Spanish Clb; School Musical; School Play; Lit Mag; Var L Cheerleading; Hon Roll; Frgn Lang.

GIONFRIDDO, TOM; Agawam HS; Feeding Hills, MA; (Y); 24/350; Pres Band; Pres Concert Band; Jazz Band; Pres Mrchg Band; Ed Lit Mag; JP Sousa Awd; NHS; Drama Clb; French Clb; Variety Show; 1st Plc Mass Assoc Jazz Edctrs Compstn Cntst 84-86; Mass All ST Jazz Band 86; Lions Clb All ST Band; U Hartford; Acoustical Engr.

GIOVINO, CHRIS; Lunenburg HS; Lunenburg, MA; (Y); Am Leg Boys St; Math Tm; School Musical; Trs Stu Cncl; Var JV Bsktbl; Var Tennis; Im Vllybl; High Hon Roll; Trs NHS; Bus.

GIRACE, SETH; Southwick HS; Southwick, MA; (Y); 4/120; Am Leg Boys St; Church Yth Grp; CAP; Mathletes; Math Clb; Math Tm; SADD; Varsity Clb; Im Bsbl; Var Capt Bsktbl; Chrch Vstry & Stu Cncl 85; Embry-Rdl U; Aerontcl Engrng.

GIRARD, BONNIE; Haverhill HS; Bradford, MA; (Y); 63/400; Political Wkr; Yrbk Stf; Off Stu Cncl; Var Capt Fld Hcky; High Hon Roll; 1st JV Fld Hcky Plyr Sprtsmn Awd 84; Comp Pgmr.

GIRARD, LISA; Burncoat SR HS; Worcester, MA; (Y); French Clb; Intnl Clb; French Hon Soc; High Hon Roll; Hon Roll; Jr NHS; NHS; Plcd 1st In City-Wide Ntl French Exam 84; 7th In St 84; 1st In City 86.

GIRARD, PAUL J; Swampscott HS; Nahant, MA; (Y); 46/238; Am Leg Boys St; Science Clb; Variety Show; Capt Var Ftbl; Var Trk; Wt Lftg.

GIRDIS, JAIME S; Hampshire Regional HS; Goshen, MA; (Y); SADD; Nwsp Rptr; Nwsp Stf; Hon Roll; Chorus; Harrogate Coll N Yorkshire Great Brit 85; Yale; Lit.

GIRELLI, TAMMIE; Norton HS; Norton, MA; (S); 18/174; Cmnty Wkr; Pres JA; Letterman Clb; Varsity Clb; Chorus; Variety Show; Trk; Hon Roll; NHS; Mst Outstndg Frsh Lg Meet 84; Mst Imprvd Ath Trk 85; Silvr Mdls Trk 85.

GIROUARD, CAROLINE; Holyoke Catholic HS; Chicopee, MA; (Y); #12 In Class; Spanish Clb; SADD; Varsity Clb; Church Choir; Rep Soph Cls; Rep Jr Cls; Rep Stu Cncl; Var Capt Bsktbl; Sftbl; High Hon Roll; Sprtsmnshp Awd Vrsty Bsktbl 86; Bus.

GIROUARD, JACK; Brockton HS; Brockton, MA; (Y); 96/1100; Boy Scts; Var Ftbl; Wt Lftg; High Hon Roll; Hon Roll; NHS; Engrng.

GIROUARD, PAULA; Reading Memorial HS; Reading, MA; (Y); School Musical; Rep Frsh Cls; Rep Soph Cls; Rep Jr Cls; Gym; Twrlr.

GIULIANO JR, ANTHONY; Hopedale JR SR HS; Hopedale, MA; (S); 3/70; SADD; Pres Soph Cls; JV Bsktbl; Var Socr; High Hon Roll.

GLASGOW, CYNTHIA M; St Bernards C C HS; Fitchburg, MA; (Y); 3/177; Spanish Clb; Variety Show; Var Cheerleading; Var Lcrss; JV Vllybl; Hon Roll; NHS; Phrmcy.

GLASTONE, DEBRA; Sharon HS; Sharon, MA; (Y); Drama Clb; Spanish Clb; Temple Yth Grp; Chorus; School Musical; Yrbk Stf; Lit Mag; Vllybl; Hon Roll; ST Schlrshp Ballet Arts Of Sharon 84-85; Psych.

GLAVICKAS, CATHERINE; Easthampton HS; Easthampton, MA; (Y); Rep Jr Cls; VP Sr Cls; Rep Stu Cncl; 1st Runnr-Up Jr Miss Pgnt 86; Sr Travel Club 86; Bentley Coll; Accntng.

GLEASON, JONATHAN P; Newton South HS; Newton, MA; (Y); Am Leg Boys St; Capt Chess Clb; JA; Nwsp Stf; Rep Stu Cncl; Im Badmtn; Var Capt Lcrss; Boston Globe Gld Key Awd 85.

GLENN, TONYA; Natick HS; Natick, MA; (Y); 3/399; German Clb; SADD; High Hon Roll; Hon Roll; Ntl Merit Ltr; Chancellors Awd Schlrshp 87-91; Wellesley Coll Bk Awd 86; Hnrbl Ment AATF Ex 86; Psychiatry.

GLENN, TRACEY; Acton Boxboro Regional HS; Acton, MA; (Y); 89/428; Hon Roll; NHS; Bus.

GLENNON, DAVID; Everett HS; Everett, MA; (Y); Northeastern U; Elec Engr.

GLIDDEN, CHRISTOPHER; St Bernards HS; Lancaster, MA; (S); 16/176; French Clb; Ftbl; Golf; Hon Roll; NHS.

GLINIECKI, COREY; Shepherd Hill Regional HS; Dudley, MA; (Y); Computer Clb; Nwsp Bus Mgr; Nwsp Rptr; Rep Stu Cncl; Hon Roll; Dance Clb; Variety Show; Var Ftbl; Dgtl Cmptr Camp; Yrbk Stf 86-87; Debate Team 86-87; Nchls Coll; Bus Mngmnt.

GLIST, ADAM O; Lincoln/Sudbury Regional HS; Sudbury, MA; (Y); Political Wkr; Nwsp Ed-Chief; Nwsp Rptr; Nwsp Stf; Lit Mag; Ntl Merit SF; Cm Laud; Harvard Prz Bk; Jrnlsm.

GLOSE, KIMBERLY; Blackstone-Millville Reg HS; Blackstone, MA; (Y); Band; Mrchg Band; Pep Band; Yrbk Stf; JV Cheerleading; Im Socr; High Hon Roll; Hon Roll; Hon Mntn B/M Reg Sci Fr 85-86; Exclnt Achvt Bnd Awd 85-86; Prfct Atten 84-85; ROTC Air Frc; Med.

GLOWIK, ANDY; Lynn Classical HS; Lynn, MA; (Y); 10/168; Chess Clb; Spanish Clb; Yrbk Stf; VP Jr Cls; Rep Stu Cncl; Socr; Trk; High Hon Roll; Jr NHS; NHS; Engrng.

GLOWIK, JOAN; Lynn Classical HS; Lynn, MA; (Y); 8/168; Church Yth Grp; Dance Clb; Service Clb; Spanish Clb; Chorus; School Musical; Variety Show; Yrbk Stf; Var JV Cheerleading; Var Swmmng; Advrtsng.

GLOWIK, TIMOTHY J; St Mary Regional HS; Lynn, MA; (Y); 2/130; Pres Sr Cls; Var Capt Bsbl; Var Capt Bsktbl; Var Capt Socr; NHS; Sal; St Schlr; Acad All-ST Bsktbll Tm 86; Lg All-ST Bsbl Bsktbl Sccr 85-86; Tufts U; Dntl.

GLUSHIK, JOHN; Westfield HS; Westfield, MA; (Y); 1/340; Scholastic Bowl; Band; Jazz Band; Stu Cncl; Co-Capt Bsktbl; Socr; Tennis; Elks Awd; Kiwanis Awd; NHS; Raymond Fitzgerald Schlr Athlt Awd 86; Vrsty Bsktbl Coachs Awd 86; Louis Armstrong Jazz Bnd Awd 86; Duke U; Engr.

GLYNN, DENISE; Cardinal Spellman HS; Whitman, MA; (Y); 17/203; Dance Clb; School Musical; Variety Show; JV Var Cheerleading; Hon Roll; Choreogrphy Cntst 86; Cmnty Theatr Prdctns 85 & 86; Dance.

GLYNN, DIANNE; Plymouth-Carver HS; Plymouth, MA; (Y); 22/600; Pres Sec Drama Clb; Chorus; School Musical; School Play; Variety Show; Hon Roll; NHS; MA Drama Comptn Fest 3rd ST 86; SEMSBA Vocal Concert 83-86; Vocal Ensem Pres,VP 85-86; Arts.

GNIADEK, STEVE; Pittsfield HS; Pittsfield, MA; (Y); Cmnty Wkr; Var L Bsbl; High Hon Roll; Hon Roll; NHS; Prfct Atten Awd; Colin A Keegan Awd Outstndng Sprtsmnshp & Cndct 84.

GOBEILLE, STEPHEN; Cathedral HS; Springfield, MA; (Y); JV Ice Hcky; Engrng.

GODA, JOHN; Cathedral HS; Springfield, MA; (Y); Math Clb; Office Aide; L Crs Cntry; L Trk; NHS; Math Awd, Attndnce Awd 83-85.

GODBOUT, KEVIN; Chicopee Comprehensive HS; Chicopee, MA; (Y); Am Leg Boys St; CAP; Debate Tm; 4-H; Drill Tm; Rep Frsh Cls; 4-H Awd; Pres ST Senate Bys ST 86; Cert Apprctn USAF Rcrtng Svc 86; Awds Cvl Air Ptrl 86; Cadet Cmmndr 86; HCC; Avation.

GODDARD, LANCE; Natick HS; Natick, MA; (Y); CAP; German Clb; Intnl Clb; Hon Roll; Grmn Club Schlrshp 86; Bus Awd Data Proc 84; Boston U; Aerontcl Engrng.

GODEK, KIRSTEN; Chicopee Comprehensive HS; Chicopee, MA; (Y); 50/300; German Clb; Office Aide; Ski Clb; Rep Sr Cls; Stu Cncl; Socr; Tennis; Jr NHS; Rep Frsh Cls; Rep Soph Cls; Prm Cmmtte 85-86; Mdrn Frgn Lang Clb 85; Bus Adm.

GODINHO, STEVEN; Pittsfield HS; Pittsfield, MA; (Y); 70/400; JA; Latin Clb; VP Soph Cls; VP Jr Cls; VP Sr Cls; Var L Ftbl; Var Capt Ice Hcky; Var L Trk; Hon Roll; Ntl Merit Ltr.

GOEDECKE, ERIC; Hudson HS; Hudson, MA; (Y); 13/160; Exploring; Math Tm; Yrbk Stf; Off Stu Cncl; Stat JV Bsktbl; Var Ftbl; NHS; Ntl Merit SF; Tufts U; Bio.

GOETZ, TOM; Attleboro HS; Attleboro, MA; (Y); JA; Crs Cntry; Trk; High Hon Roll; Hon Roll; NHS; Engrng.

GOFF, KARL; Acton Boxboro Regional HS; Acton, MA; (Y); 37/428; Church Yth Grp; Computer Clb; Radio Clb; Nwsp Rptr; Nwsp Stf; Hon Roll; Jr NHS; NHS; Engrng.

GOGAS, MICHELE; Haverhill HS; Haverhill, MA; (Y); Hon Roll; NY; Art.

GOGUEN, CRAIG; Gardner HS; Gardner, MA; (Y); 2/135; Am Leg Boys St; Chess Clb; Quiz Bowl; Scholastic Bowl; Pres Frsh Cls; Var Bsbl; Var JV Ftbl; High Hon Roll; NHS; Math.

GOGUEN, FRANK; Clinton JR SR HS; Clinton, MA; (Y); 22/123; Am Leg Boys St; Yrbk Stf; Hon Roll; Aud/Vis; Library Aide; Var L Bsbl; Stat L Bsktbl; Var JV Mgr(s); Var JV Score Keeper; JV Socr; Cmnctns.

GOLD, LORIN; Wachusett Regional HS; Princeton, MA; (Y); 51/443; Art Clb; Drama Clb; Model UN; Science Clb; School Musical; School Play; Nwsp Stf; Im Socr; Hon Roll; NHS; Zoolgy.

GOLDBERG, CARLA; Newton North HS; Chestnut Hill, MA; (Y); Sec Spanish Clb; Temple Yth Grp; Acpl Chr; Chorus; Mrchg Band; School Musical; Nwsp Stf; Stu Cncl; Var Trk; Hon Roll; Suffolk U Bk Ad 86; Mem Schlrshp 86; Bus.

GOLDBERG, HEIDI; Beaver Country Day Schl; Sharon, MA; (Y); Dance Clb; VP Drama Clb; Pres Spanish Clb; Chorus; Madrigals; School Musical; School Play; Stage Crew; Swing Chorus; Lit Mag.

GOLDBERG, JOEL; Buckingham Brown & Nichols HS; Cambridge, MA; (S); Nwsp Rptr; Nwsp Sprt Ed; Rep Frsh Cls; Rep Soph Cls; Rep Jr Cls; Rep Sr Cls; Pres Stu Cncl; Var Bsktbl; Hon Roll; Ntl Merit SF; All Star Debater & All Star Debate Wnnr 85; Poetry Readoff Cls Rep 86; Schl Pres 86-87.

GOLDBERG, MATTHEW J; Newton South HS; Newton, MA; (Y); Pep Clb; Spanish Clb; Temple Yth Grp; Variety Show; JV Im Bsktbl; JV Var Lcrss; Im Wt Lftg; Hon Roll; Bus Mgmt.

GOLDEN, DAVID; Natick HS; Natick, MA; (Y); 8/404; Computer Clb; German Clb; SADD; Temple Yth Grp; High Hon Roll; Ntl Merit SF.

GOLDFARB, DEBRA; Westwood HS; Westwood, MA; (Y); 54/210; Dance Clb; VP Intnl Clb; Key Clb; Political Wkr; SADD; VP Temple Yth Grp; Yrbk Stf; Var Capt Cheerleading; Var Swmmng; Var Trk; Mel Goldman Memrl Awd Yth Grp 86; Abraham Joshua Heschel Hnr Socty 85-86; Skidmore Coll; Pltcl Sci.

GOLDMAN, LAUREN; Norton HS; Norton, MA; (S); 6/174; French Clb; Temple Yth Grp; High Hon Roll; NEDT Awd.

GOLDMAN, RITA; Randolph HS; Randolph, MA; (Y); Sec Church Yth Grp; Dance Clb; SADD; Chorus; School Musical; Swing Chorus; Mgr Crs Cntry; Hon Roll; NHS; Psych.

GOLDSTEIN, AMY; Wakefield Memorial HS; Wakefield, MA; (Y); 33/333; Key Clb; Spanish Clb; Yrbk Stf; High Hon Roll; Hon Roll; Jr NHS; NHS; JR Writing Awd 85; Endicott Coll; Inter Desgn.

GOLDSTEIN, DAMON; Medford HS; Medford, MA; (Y); 12/375; Pres Drama Clb; Var Math Tm; VP Chorus; Stu Cncl; Capt Swmmng; VP Tennis; Mu Alp Tht; NHS; Navy ROTC 4yr Schlrshp 86; MVP Var Swm Team 85; Tufts U.

GOLDSTEIN, JAMES B; Burlington HS; Burlington, MA; (Y); 11/321; Trs Debate Tm; Math Tm; Im Bsbl; Im Bsktbl; High Hon Roll; Hon Roll; NHS; Dartmouth Clb Bk Awd 84-85; Acad Exc Soc Stds 85-86; Cornell U; Econ.

GOLEMBEWSKI, MELISSA BETH; North Attleboro HS; N Attleboro, MA; (Y); 10/258; Sec Art Clb; Church Yth Grp; Thesps; Chorus; Yrbk Stf; Lit Mag; Capt Var Gym; Trk; High Hon Roll; NHS; Frnch Excel Awd 86; Unsng Trck Hero 86; Cmmnwlth Schlr 86; U Of MA; Lbrl Arts.

GOLON, SARA; Holyoke Catholic HS; Holyoke, MA; (Y); Drama Clb; Hosp Aide; Spanish Clb; Church Choir; School Musical; Hon Roll; U Of MA; Chld Psych.

GOMES, ANTOINETTE; New Bedford HS; New Bedford, MA; (Y); 58/701; Drama Clb; Sec Science Clb; Stage Crew; Ed Yrbk Phtg; Rep Stu Cncl; JV Bsktbl; Capt Fld Hcky; Hon Roll; Brown U; Chld Psych.

GOMES, RON; Bishop Feehan HS; Mansfield, MA; (Y); Im Bsktbl; JV Ftbl; Hon Roll.

GONCALVES, ANA; New Bedford HS; New Bedford, MA; (Y); 13/700; Intnl Clb; High Hon Roll; Prfct Atten Awd; Acctng.

GONCALVES, MANUEL; Christopher Columbus HS; Boston, MA; (S); 2/111; JA; Math Clb; Varsity Clb; Rep Jr Cls; Stu Cncl; Ftbl; Wt Lftg; High Hon Roll; Hon Roll; NHS; Interculturel Clb Awd 85; Sci Merit Awd 84-85; Ldrshp Awd 84-85; BC; Engr.

GONSALVES, TYRONE; Taunton HS; Taunton, MA; (Y); Psych.

GONYA, JENNIFER; Bellingham HS; Bellingham, MA; (Y); Church Yth Grp; Quiz Bowl; Band; Concert Band; Mrchg Band; Nwsp Stf; JV Bsktbl; Hon Roll; NHS; Nrsg.

GONZALEZ, JULIO; Bay Pathe RVT HS; Southbridge, MA; (Y); Am Leg Boys St; Trs Church Yth Grp; VICA; High Hon Roll; Hon Roll; NHS; Prfct Atten Awd; Mst Athl Phys Ed 85; MIT; Data Prcssng.

GOODE JR, ROBERT; Bishop Feehan HS; Norton, MA; (Y); JCL; JV Ice Hcky; High Hon Roll; Hon Roll; Mgnm Cum Laude Intl Ltn Exams 85; SE MA U; Bus.

GOODMAN, ERIC MICHAEL; North Quincy HS; Quincy, MA; (Y); Am Leg Boys St; SADD; Yrbk Stf; High Hon Roll; Hon Roll; VP Temple Yth Grp; Var Bsbl; Capt Wrstlng; Honrbl Mention Sci Fair 86; 3 Yr Colunteer At Camp For People With Specl Needs 84; Am Lifesaving 86; Physician.

GOODWIN, CAROL; Malden HS; Malden, MA; (Y); 21/460; Camp Fr Inc; Church Yth Grp; Key Clb; Office Aide; SADD; Teachers Aide; Color Guard; School Musical; Variety Show; Rep Jr Cls; Zunta Interntl Ctznshp Schlrshp Awd 85; Beston U; Advertising.

GOODWIN, JEFFREY; Central Catholic HS; Bradford, MA; (Y); 28/231; Boys Clb Am; Ski Clb; Im Bsktbl; L JV Crs Cntry; JV L Trk; Bio.

GOODWIN, SANDRA; Wakefield HS; Wakefield, MA; (Y); Drama Clb; Chorus; Madrigals; School Play; Stage Crew.

GOON, GEORGE; Boston Latin Schl; Boston, MA; (Y); 32/274; Trs Chess Clb; Computer Clb; JA; Pres Science Clb; NHS; Ntl Merit SF; Ntl Sci Cert 86; Hsptl Vlntr Awd 86; Chess Trny Trphy 86; Engr.

GOONAN, PATRICK; Boston Latin Schl; Dorchester, MA; (Y); 118/278; Boys Clb Am; Church Yth Grp; Latin Clb; Stage Crew; Var L Bsktbl; Wt Lftg; Cit Awd; Law.

GORDON, ANDREW; Methuen HS; Methuen, MA; (Y); Intnl Clb; Model UN; Band; Concert Band; Pep Band; Stanford U; Mech Engr.

GORDON, CARLA; Old Rochester Regional HS; Mattapoisett, MA; (Y); AFS; Ski Clb; Var L Sftbl; JV Vllybl; High Hon Roll; Hon Roll; Sftbl JV Coaches Awd 85; Bllybl JV MVP85; Colby-Sawyer.

GORDON III, DONALD; Milford HS; Milford, MA; (Y); 13/270; Boy Scts; SADD; Socr; Trk; High Hon Roll; Ware Polytechnic Inst; Engrng.

GORDON, MICHAEL; Greater Lowell Vo Tech; Tygnsboro, MA; (Y); Boy Scts; SADD; Teachers Aide; Weldng.

GORDON, MICHAEL A; Murdock HS; Winchendon, MA; (Y); 4/100; Am Leg Boys St; Aud/Vis; Model UN; School Musical; School Play; Nwsp Stf; Yrbk Phtg; Hon Roll; NHS; Pres Schlr; Clar U Alumni Schlrshp 86; Murdock Alumni Schlrshp 86; Hattie M Tucker Schlrshp 86; Clark U; Cinematogrphy.

GORDON, MICHAEL A; North Andover HS; North Andover, MA; (Y); 80/240; Am Leg Boys St; Pres Stu Cncl; Var L Bsktbl; Var L Ftbl; Var L Trk; Plc Sci.

GORDON, MICHELLE; Framingham South HS; Framingham, MA; (Y); 80/230; Drama Clb; Sec VP French Clb; Sec JA; Sec Trs SADD; Capt Color Guard; Variety Show; Yrbk Stf; Sec Soph Cls; Sec Jr Cls; Sec Sr Cls; Ldrshp & Svc Schl 86; Svc Drama Clb 86; Ithaca Coll; Advrtsg.

GORDON, ROBERT P; Mansfield HS; Mansfield, MA; (Y); 34/182; Am Leg Boys St; Church Yth Grp; SADD; Nwsp Stf; Var Bsbl; Var Golf; Hon Roll; U Of Miami; Jrnlsm.

GORDON, SHAWN J; David Prouty HS; Spencer, MA; (Y); 1/200; Am Leg Boys St; Teachers Aide; Yrbk Ed-Chief; JV Socr; High Hon Roll; Boys ST Bentley Coll 86; Arntcl Engrng.

GORDON, STEPHANIE; Sharon HS; Sharon, MA; (Y); Drama Clb; Hosp Aide; Intnl Clb; Spanish Clb; Teachers Aide; Stage Crew; Nwsp Stf; Yrbk Stf; Intl Exchng Stu Yr Spain 84-85; George Washington U.

GORDON, STEVE; Medway JR & SR HS; Medway, MA; (Y); 7/140; Var L Bsbl; Var Capt Crs Cntry; High Hon Roll; Hon Roll; NHS; MVP X-Cntry 85; Tri-Vlly Lg All-Str X-Cntry 85; Mlfrd Dly Nws All-Str Bsbll 86; Finance.

GOREN, BARRY; Newton North HS; Newton, MA; (Y); 2/800; Ski Clb; Nwsp Phtg; JV Var Tennis; Hon Roll; U Of FL; Bus.

GORMAN, DEBORAH; King Philip Regional HS; Plainville, MA; (Y); 43/217; Church Yth Grp; Powder Puff Ftbl; Sftbl; Vllybl; Hon Roll; NHS; Psychlgy.

GORMAN, JENNIFER E; Hamilton-Wenham Regional HS; South Hamilton, MA; (Y); 34/185; SADD; JV Fld Hcky; JV Trk; CC Awd; Cit Awd; NHS; Pres Schlr; Church Yth Grp; Cmnty Wkr; Hosp Aide; Jwsh War Vtrns Awd 1st Pl St Wnnr In Rdng Qlfd 3 Yrs For New England Hrsmn Cncl Fnls MA Miss Teen; Duke U; Public Plcy Studies.

GORMAN, LAUREEN; Norwood HS; Norwood, MA; (Y); 59/350; French Clb; L Trk; Hon Roll; Princpls Awd 84; Frnch.

GORMAN, MARCIA; Arlington Catholic HS; Somerville, MA; (Y); Dance Clb; SADD; Yrbk Ed-Chief; Tennis; Hon Roll; Teens Srvng Elderly 85-86.

GORMLEY, NANCI; King Philip Regional HS; Plainville, MA; (Y); 55/260; Capt Bsktbl; Im Powder Puff Ftbl; Capt Score Keeper; Hon Roll; Jr NHS; Psych.

GOSS, JILL; Agawam HS; Agawam, MA; (Y); 74/324; AFS; Ski Clb; Trk; High Hon Roll; Hon Roll; Var Ski Tm 85; Lwyr.

GOSSELIN, CHERYL; Presentation Of Mary Acad; Lawrence, MA; (Y); 5/43; Trs Sec Church Yth Grp; Ski Clb; Spanish Clb; SADD; Yrbk Stf; Bsktbl; Hon Roll; NHS; Tennis; Financl Mgmt.

GOSSELIN, JOHN T; Winchester HS; Winchester, MA; (Y); 40/320; Am Leg Boys St; Boy Scts; Church Yth Grp; French Clb; Hosp Aide; JCL; Latin Clb; Model UN; Political Wkr; Radio Clb; MA St Stu Advsry Cncl 83-86; Gov Block Grnt Advsry Cncl 84-86; Wnnr Ntl Hstry Day Paper Cont 85; Political Econ.

GOSSELIN, RAYMOND; Holyoke HS; Holyoke, MA; (Y); French Clb; Nwsp Phtg; Var Ftbl; Var Trk; Hon Roll; William H Mc Garry Mem Schlrshp 86; Plyr Awd Ftbl 85; Holyoke CC; Mech Engr.

GOUDEY, DOUG; Monument Mountain Regional HS; Stockbridge, MA; (Y); Bsbl; Socr; High Hon Roll; Hon Roll; Spec Awd Bus Bkkpng; Bus.

GOUDREAU, JOHN; Central Catholic HS; Salem, NH; (Y); 42/231; Boys Clb Am; Church Yth Grp; Im Bsktbl; JV Trk; Hon Roll; Worcester Polytechnic; Chem Eng.

GOULART, MAUREEN; Bristol Plymouth Reg Tech Voc Schl; Taunton, MA; (S); VP SADD; Variety Show; Lit Mag; Pres Frsh Cls; Pres Church Yth Grp; Pres Jr Cls; Pres Sr Cls; Pres Stu Cncl; Hon Roll; NHS; Mngmnt.

GOULD, LISA; Dedham HS; Dedham, MA; (S); 2/255; French Clb; SADD; Capt Varsity Clb; Nwsp Rptr; Nwsp Stf; Stu Cncl; Var Capt Socr; High Hon Roll; Hon Roll; NHS; Best Frgn Lang Stu Awd 84-85; Intl Bus.

GOULET, DARLENE; Taunton HS; Taunton, MA; (Y); Stu Cncl; Var Trk; Hon Roll; NHS; Nrsng.

GOULET, LYDIA; Concord-Carlisle Regional HS; Carlisle, MA; (Y); Girl Scts; Science Clb; Acpl Chr; Chorus; Church Choir; School Musical; School Play; Stage Crew; Lit Mag; Hon Roll; N E Annl Dist & All-ST Cncrt Chorus 85-86; Awds Exclnc Engl, Frnch & Chem 85; Tchr Aide Phlppn Schl; Vcl Music.

GOULLAUD, ELIZABETH; Malden HS; Malden, MA; (Y); Church Yth Grp; Hosp Aide; Science Clb; SADD; Chorus; Madrigals; Variety Show; Lit Mag; Var L Crs Cntry; Var L Trk; Bst Vcl Awd JR Vrts Shw; Rookie Of Yr Indr Trk; Unsng Hero Awd Crs Cntry; Psych.

GOULSTON, KENNETH; Newton North HS; Newtonville, MA; (Y); OEA; Science Clb; Ski Clb; SADD; Yrbk Stf; Var Capt Swmmng; High Hon Roll; Am Swmng Rcrd Brst Strk 85; Won Dr Thompson Schlrshp Awd 86; CA ST U.

GOUTHRO, NANCY; King Philip Regional HS; Wrentham, MA; (Y); Sec Church Yth Grp; Radio Clb; Bsktbl; Crs Cntry; Socr; Capt Trk; NHS; Ntl Hnr Soc 86; MVP Trck 84; Hgh Pt Screr Trck 84-86; Southern CT ST U; Phys Educ.

GOUVEIA, SUZANNE; Arlington HS; Arlington, MA; (Y); Church Yth Grp; Cmnty Wkr; Drama Clb; Hosp Aide; PAVAS; SADD; Chorus; School Musical; Rptr Yrbk Stf; Rep Frsh Cls; Law.

GOVONI, MARK; Sandwich HS; Sandwich, MA; (Y); 8/172; Am Leg Boys St; Math Tm; Var Lcrss; Hon Roll; NHS; Ntl Merit SF; Outstndng Achvt Awd Latn 84; Outstndng Achvt Awd Amercn Hstry 86.

GOWING, JAMIE; Tantasqua Regional HS; Sturbridge, MA; (Y); Varsity Clb; Acpl Chr; Chorus; Church Choir; Madrigals; School Musical; School Play; Variety Show; Tennis; Hon Roll; Mdrn Msc Mstrs Scty 86; Med.

GOYETTE, KEVIN S; Central Catholic HS; Lowell, MA; (Y); 33/233; Boy Scts; Im Bsktbl; Im Bowling; JV Ftbl; JV Trk; High Hon Roll; Hon Roll; U Of Lowell, Lowell MA; Engrng.

GOYETTE, SUSANNE; Westfield HS; Westfield, MA; (Y); Pres AFS1; Drama Clb; French Clb; Office Aide; Political Wkr; Stage Crew; Nwsp Stf; Yrbk Stf; Mgr Bsktbl; Political Science.

GRABIEC, TINA; Hopkins Acad; Hadley, MA; (Y); 12/50; 4-H; Spanish Clb; Band; Chorus; Yrbk Stf; Sftbl; Twrlr; 4-H Awd; Hon Roll; NHS; Elem Educ.

GRACE JR, JOHN J; Belchertown HS; Belchertown, MA; (Y); Am Leg Boys St; Model UN; Ski Clb; Jazz Band; Mrchg Band; Symp Band; Yrbk Stf; JV Bsbl; Var Socr; Hon Roll; Iaasc Hdgn Mst Imprvd Bnd Awd 85-86; Math.

GRACIA, KAREN; Old Rochester Regnl HS; Mattapoisett, MA; (Y); Am Leg Aux Girls St; Pres Church Yth Grp; Pres Trs Drama Clb; Trs Ski Clb; Band; School Musical; School Play; Trs Frsh Cls; JV Bsktbl; VP Trk; Delta Kappa Gamma Soc Poetry Cont Wnnr 86; Harvard; Med.

GRACIA, MICHAEL J; New Bedford HS; New Bedford, MA; (Y); Am Leg Boys St; Drama Clb; VP Pres JA; Key Clb; SADD; Stage Crew; Rep Jr Cls; Rep Sr Cls; Stu Cncl; Ftbl; Law.

GRADY, PATRICIA; Mount Saint Joseph Acad; E Boston, MA; (Y); 11/168; VP Church Yth Grp; VP Dance Clb; VP Drama Clb; VP JA; VP Teachers Aide; School Musical; School Play; VP High Hon Roll; VP NHS; Ntl Merit SF; Boston Coll; Acctng.

GRAHAM, CHARLES; Doherty Memorial HS; Worcester, MA; (Y); JA; Spanish Clb; JV Var Bsbl; Bowling; Var Trk; Career Day Essay Wnnr 86; SITE Wrk Prg 86; Libral Arts.

GRANDE, CYNTHIA; Marthas Vineyard Regional HS; Oak Bluffs, MA; (Y); 11/93; Church Yth Grp; Drama Clb; French Clb; School Musical; Stage Crew; Lit Mag; Golf; Var L Socr; Hon Roll; NHS; Adv Bio Hnrs Awd 86; Citznshp Awd 86; US Coast Guard Acad; Sci.

GRANDE, GINA; Attleboro HS; Attleboro, MA; (Y); Church Yth Grp; Pep Clb; Color Guard; High Hon Roll; Hon Roll; Nrsg.

GRANGER, RICHARD; Leicester HS; Leicester, MA; (Y); Math Tm; Capt Crs Cntry; Capt Trk; Hon Roll; NHS.

GRANN, ERIC; Westford Acad; Westford, MA; (Y); AFS; German Clb; Ski Clb; Teachers Aide; Varsity Clb; Band; Jazz Band; Variety Show; Var Crs Cntry; Ftbl; Mst Imprvd Sking 86; Lowell Sn All-Str Tennis 86; U Of MA; Elec Engrng.

GRANT, EDWARD; Taunton HS; Taunton, MA; (Y); Hon Roll; Acctng.

GRANT, HOLLY A; Saint Clare HS; Roslindale, MA; (Y); Art Clb; Church Yth Grp; Hosp Aide; Pep Clb; Church Choir; School Play; Variety Show; Pres Soph Cls; Pres Jr Cls; Var Golf; Fshn Dsgn.

GRANT, LORINE; North Attleboro HS; Attleboro Falls, MA; (Y); Art Clb; JCL; Latin Clb; Var L Bsktbl; Var L Fld Hcky; Var L Sftbl; Hon Roll; NHS; Vet.

GRANT, PATRICIA M; North Quincy HS; N Quincy, MA; (Y); 68/348; Drama Clb; JA; SADD; Chorus; Church Choir; Stage Crew; Yrbk Phtg; Yrbk Stf; Var Socr; JV Var Sftbl; Bridgewater ST; Phy Ed.

GRANT, SARAH; Canton HS; Canton, MA; (Y); 72/263; German Clb; GAA; SADD; Varsity Clb; Nwsp Stf; Yrbk Sprt Ed; Rep Jr Cls; Rep Sr Cls; Var Capt Fld Hcky; Var Gym; Ntl Stu Cncl Awd 85; All Am Fld Hockey Plyr 85-86; U NH; Sports Med.

GRANT, SHERYL ANN; North Middlesex Regional HS; Townsend, MA; (Y); 44/210; Church Yth Grp; Debate Tm; Band; Concert Band; Orch; Nwsp Rptr; Yrbk Rptr; Yrbk Stf; VP Stu Cncl; Hon Roll; Evangel Coll; Acctng.

GRANT, STEVE; King Philip Regional HS; Plainville, MA; (Y); Var JV Bsktbl; Var JV Trk.

GRAVEL, CHRISTINE; Bishop Feehan HS; S Attleboro, MA; (Y); 85/200; French Clb; Lit Mag; French Hon Soc; High Hon Roll; 3rd Hghst Aver In Essntl Skills Englsh 85-86; Rhode Island Schl; Art.

GRAVEL, MARK; Bishop Frehan HS; S Attleboro, MA; (Y); Bus.

GRAVEL, MICHELE; Attleboro HS; Attleboro, MA; (Y); Ski Clb; Varsity Clb; Y-Teens; Yrbk Stf; Capt Bsktbl; Powder Puff Ftbl; Var Trk; Var L Vllybl; Hon Roll; NHS; Bio.

GRAVELINE, NANCY; Barnstable HS; Hyannis, MA; (Y); Church Yth Grp; Drama Clb; SADD; Concert Band; Mrchg Band; Hon Roll; Bus Adm.

GRAVES, KELLY; Turners Falls HS; Erving, MA; (Y); 15/98; Spanish Clb; Chorus; Variety Show; Yrbk Stf; Rep Jr Cls; Stu Cncl; JV Bsktbl; Tennis; Vllybl; Tchng.

GRAY, BETH; Douglas HS; E Douglas, MA; (Y); 5/36; Varsity Clb; Mrchg Band; Yrbk Ed-Chief; Trs Soph Cls; Trs Jr Cls; Trs Sr Cls; Rep Stu Cncl; Cheerleading; Sftbl; Hon Roll; Jrnlsm Awd 86; Clark U; Psychlgy.

GRAY, EMILY P; Mohawk Trail Regional HS; Ashfield, MA; (Y); 5/116; Chorus; School Musical; Hon Roll; NHS; Cmmnwlth Schlrs MA 86; Pres Acdmc Ftns Awd 86; Am Heart Assn Part Awd 86; U MA Amherst; Anthropology.

GRAY, JENNIFER; Franklin HS; Franklin, MA; (Y); 10/226; Church Yth Grp; Church Choir; Hon Roll; NHS; USAA-FRNCH 86; Schltc Awd-Frnch 86; U Of RI; Phrmcy.

GRAY, JULIE; Newburyport HS; Newburyport, MA; (Y); 33/185; Lit Mag; Sec Stu Cncl; Fld Hcky; JV Sftbl; Var Trk; Hon Roll; NHS 122 Eng Achvmnt Mdl 85; NHS Eng Ach Vmnt 133 86; All Am Acad Achvmnt Awd 86; U Of MA; Scndry Eng Educ.

GRAY, SHERI; Malden HS; Malden, MA; (Y); 28/456; Office Aide; Lit Mag; Hon Roll; NEMA 84-85; Northeastern U; Comp Sci.

GRAY, WENDY; Methuen HS; Methuen, MA; (Y); 60/333; Intnl Clb; Color Guard; Hon Roll; Bus Adm.

GRAYDEN, DIANNE; Marianhill Central Catholic HS; Webster, MA; (Y); Drama Clb; Spanish Clb; Chorus; Stage Crew; Yrbk Stf; Var Cheerleading; Var Tennis; Art.

GRAZIANI, LAURA; Brockton HS; Brockton, MA; (Y); 49/850; Exploring; Hosp Aide; High Hon Roll; Hon Roll; Prfct Atten Awd; Pres Schlr; Outstndng Stu In Latin Awd 86; Cum Laude-Natl Latin Exam 86; U Of MA Amherst; Surgeon.

GRAZIANO, ANNEMARIE; Waltham HS; Boston, MA; (Y); Cmnty Wkr; Hosp Aide; SADD; Band; Color Guard; Jr Vlntr Awd 86; Early Ed.

GRAZIANO, MARIA; East Longmeadow HS; E Longmeadow, MA; (Y); Intnl Clb; Teachers Aide; Hon Roll; Outstndg Typg Stu Awd 85; Outstndg Steno Stu Awd 86; Bay Path JR Coll Awd 86; Bay Path JC; Exec Sec.

GREB, CHRISTINA; Wahconah Regional HS; Hinsdale, MA; (Y); Church Yth Grp; Office Aide; Teachers Aide; Band; Nwsp Rptr; Nwsp Stf; Hon Roll; N Adams ST Coll; Comp Sci.

GREELEY, ALYSSA; Sharon HS; Sharon, MA; (Y); Church Yth Grp; Teachers Aide; Band; Concert Band; Stu Of Mnth Art Dept 86; Elem Ed.

GREEN, CAROLYN; Bishop Feehan HS; Plainville, MA; (Y); Drama Clb; JCL; Color Guard; Mrchg Band; School Musical; Stage Crew; Yrbk Stf; Trk; 3 Yr Colorgrd Pin 86; Cert Of Appreciatn-Play Productn 84; Primry Eductn.

GREEN, CLIFF; Cathedral HS; Enfield, CT; (Y); 20/476; Boy Scts; Computer Clb; Math Clb; Tennis; High Hon Roll; NHS; Pres Schlr; Air Frc ROTC 4-Yr Schlrshp 86; Rensselaer Polytech; Elec Engr.

GREEN, DENNIS; Natick HS; Natick, MA; (Y); Am Leg Boys St; Church Yth Grp; Cmnty Wkr; SADD; Rep Jr Cls; JV Bsbl; Var Capt Bsktbl; Var Capt Ftbl; Im Sftbl; Im Wt Lftg; Nasiatka Boys St 86; Rep Stu Gvrnmnt Day 86.

GREEN, JOSEPH; Malden HS; Malden, MA; (Y); 50/550; Cmnty Wkr; Hosp Aide; Chrmn Key Clb; Political Wkr; SADD; Rep Frsh Cls; Rep Soph Cls; Rep Jr Cls; Rep Sr Cls; JV Ftbl.

GREEN, LAUREL; Melrose HS; Melrose, MA; (Y); 30/391; French Clb; Latin Clb; Yrbk Rptr; Yrbk Stf; JV Im Bsktbl; Mgr Sftbl; Var Capt Vllybl; Hon Roll; NHS; Lawyer.

GREEN, STEPHEN R; Northfield-Moutn Herman HS; Goshen, NY; (Y); Boy Scts; Cmnty Wkr; Chinese Lang Dept Stu Yr 85-86; Scholar Fudon U 85; Chinese Lang Nwsp Edtr 85-86; Chinese Lang.

GREENBERG, DEBORAH; Academy Of Notre Dame; Dracut, MA; (Y); Key Clb; Library Aide; Ski Clb; SADD; Band; Chorus; School Musical; Trs Jr Cls; JV Sftbl; JV Vllybl; Bnkng.

GREENBERG, JONATHAN; Newton North HS; Newton, MA; (Y); 1/598; Letterman Clb; Lit Mag; L Socr; L Trk; High Hon Roll; Ntl Merit Schol; Ntl Ltn Exm Gld Mdl & Schlrshp 86; Phi Beta Kappa Awd 86; MA Cmmnwlth Schlr 86; Harvard U.

GREENE, BETH; Methuen HS; Methuen, MA; (Y); Intnl Clb; JV Bsktbl; Var Cheerleading.

GREENE, GARY; Quincy HS; Quincy, MA; (Y); Yrbk Stf; Hon Roll; Sci Rcgntn Awd 86; 2 Clnry Arts Awds 85-86; Johnson & Wales; Clnry Arts.

GREENE, ROBERT A; Westfield HS; Westfield, MA; (Y); 30/350; Am Leg Boys St; Debate Tm; Drama Clb; French Clb; Political Wkr; SADD; Trs Soph Cls; Trs Sr Cls; Var Trk; Pres NHS; Ctzns Schlrshp Awd Of Westfield 86; Rep To Pres Clsrm WA D C 86; U Of MA; Chem Engrng.

GREENE, SHARYN; North Middlesex Regional HS; Pepperell, MA; (Y); 30/260; Church Yth Grp; Drama Clb; Ski Clb; SADD; Pres Chorus; Pep Band; School Musical; School Play; Nwsp Phtg; Nwsp Rptr; Emerson U; Comm.

GREENE, SHERRY L; Wachusett Regional HS; Princeton, MA; (Y); 143/433; Intnl Clb; Ski Clb; Yrbk Phtg; Var Fld Hcky; Var Lcrss; Var Trk; Hon Roll; Art Awd 84.

GREENIDGE, ANDREA; Sharon HS; Sharon, MA; (Y); 43/250; Am Leg Aux Girls St; Civic Clb; Cmnty Wkr; SADD; Sec Varsity Clb; Stu Cncl; Var L Bsktbl; Var Capt Fld Hcky; Var L Trk; Hon Roll; Mip Hockey 86; High Scorer Hockey 85; Mem Of Class Plng Brd 83-86; Howard U; Math.

GREENLAW, PAULA; Nipmuc Regional HS; Mendon, MA; (Y); 15/80; Church Yth Grp; JA; SADD; Church Choir; Crs Cntry; L Trk; High Hon Roll; NHS; Stockwell Schlrshp Mendon Upton Tchrs Assoc 86; Womens Literary Lg Southern ME 84; S W Bapt U.

GREENWOOD, DONALD GARRETT; North Quincy HS; Quincy, MA; (Y); 25/325; JV Ftbl; L Trk; Var Capt Wrstlng; Hon Roll; Cls Of 1958 Scholar 86; Div I Coaces TMB Wrstlng 86; Ithaca Coll Acad Scholar 86; Ithaca Coll.

GREENWOOD, GREGG; Blackstone Valley Reg Vo-Tech; Millbury, MA; (Y); Boy Scts; Church Yth Grp; Var Bsktbl; Var Crs Cntry; Var Trk; Comp.

GREENWOOD, JEAN; Westfield HS; Westfield, MA; (Y); 50/259; JA; Spanish Clb; Band; Concert Band; Mrchg Band; Stage Crew; Var Trk.

GREGORY, MICHAEL; Doherty Memorial HS; Worcester, MA; (Y); Boy Scts; Trs Church Yth Grp; French Clb; JA; Yrbk Stf; Cit Awd; Elks Awd; High Hon Roll; Albn Amer Natl Orgnztn Schlrshp 86; SITE 85-86; Intrmrl Vllybl 86; Syracuse U; Pltcl Sci.

GREGORY, SHANNON; Marthas Vineyard Regional HS; Vineyard Haven, MA; (Y); Art Clb; 4-H; Pep Clb; Service Clb; Spanish Clb; Chorus; Madrigals; School Musical; Yrbk Stf; JV Fld Hcky; Atnd Cnly Schl Of Holy Chld 85-86.

GREGORY, TRACY; C H Mc Cann Technical HS; N Adams, MA; (Y); 5/20; High Hon Roll; Hon Roll; NHS; Comp Pgmng.

GRENIER, KRISTINE; David Prouty HS; Spencer, MA; (Y); 7/184; Am Leg Aux Girls St; Church Yth Grp; Spanish Clb; SADD; Var Fld Hcky; Mgr(s); Sftbl; Var Trk; High Hon Roll; NHS; SR Hnr Soc 86; White Sweater Awd 85; Grtr Media Cabel Stu Athl Awd 86; U MA; Chem Engrng.

GRENIER, MELISSA; St Peter-Marian C C HS; Worcester, MA; (Y); 13/190; Church Yth Grp; SADD; School Musical; Yrbk Stf; High Hon Roll; Hon Roll; Sec NHS; Hstry.

GRENNAN, ALEEL; South Hadley HS; S Hadley, MA; (Y); Var Trk; Hon Roll; Gvnrs Rcgntn Awd 85; U MA.

GRENTZENBERG, MARK; Lincoln-Sudbury R HS; Sudbury, MA; (Y); Church Yth Grp; JV Bsbl; JV Socr; JV Wrstlng; Ntl Merit Ltr; Biolgcl Sci.

GREW, LAURIE; Matignon HS; Somerville, MA; (Y); 47/190; Camera Clb; Cmnty Wkr; Spanish Clb; SADD; Hon Roll; NEDT Awd; Spanish NHS; VFW Awd; Suffolk U; Law.

GRICUS, LAURA; Everett HS; Everett, MA; (Y); Church Yth Grp; GAA; Hosp Aide; SADD; Bus Adm.

GRIFFIN, AMY CHRISTINE; Middlesex Schl; Melrose, MA; (Y); #9 In Class; Chorus; Madrigals; School Musical; School Play; Lit Mag; High Hon Roll; Ntl Merit Ltr; Dance Clb; Drama Clb; Best Per Supprt Role 83; Thoreau Mdl Drama 84; Brolon U Book Awd 85; Northwestern U.

GRIFFIN, CHERYLNN; St Peter-Marian CC HS; Worcester, MA; (Y); 2/210; Church Yth Grp; Cmnty Wkr; SADD; Yrbk Rptr; Ed Yrbk Stf; Rep Frsh Cls; High Hon Roll; NHS; Prfct Atten Awd; Med.

GRIFFIN, HELEN; St Clare HS; Roslindale, MA; (Y); 29/149; SADD; School Musical; Trk; High Hon Roll; Hon Roll; St Schlr; Soffolk U; Sclgy.

GRIFFIN, MARK; Somerset HS; Somerset, MA; (Y); L Bsbl; L Ftbl; High Hon Roll; Hon Roll; NHS; Navy ROTC Schlrshp; Worcester Polytech; Chem Engrg.

GRIFFIN, SARAH; Lunenburg HS; Lunenburg, MA; (Y); Cmnty Wkr; SADD; Teachers Aide; Var JV Bsktbl; Var Socr; Var Sftbl; High Hon Roll; Hon Roll; JR Cls Court Homecmg 85; Fr Awd 85; Athltc Trnr.

GRIFFIN, SHEILA; St Patrick HS; Watertown, MA; (S); 6/47; Boys Clb Am; Church Yth Grp; Yrbk Stf; Var Capt Bsktbl; Var Sftbl; Swmmng; Var Vllybl; High Hon Roll; NHS; Prfct Atten Awd; Suffolk U; Bus.

GRIFFITH, JEFF; Lexington HS; Lexington, MA; (Y); L Bsbl; L Bsktbl; Var L Ice Hcky; Var L Lcrss; Hon Roll; All Star Rm 86; Hockey Tm 85-86; MVP Hockey 85-86; Avon Old Farms Schl; Bus.

GRIFFITH, REBECCA A; Shrewsbury HS; Shrewsbury, MA; (Y); 1/265; Math Tm; Pres Science Clb; Lib Mrchg Band; Var Trk; High Hon Roll; NHS; Ntl Merit Ltr; Church Yth Grp; JA; NFL; Brwn Bk Awd 86; Hugh O Brian Yth Ldrshp Conf Rep 85; MA Adv Studys Prog 86; Biomdcl Engrng.

GRIGELEVICH III, JOSEPH M; Bishop Feehan HS; N Attleboro, MA; (Y); Art Clb; Church Yth Grp; Drama Clb; Library Aide; School Musical; School Play; Stage Crew; Hon Roll; Comm Desgn.

GRIMES, CRAIG A; Hamilton Wenham Regional HS; South Hamilton, MA; (Y); 1/201; Am Leg Boys St; Science Clb; VP Soph Cls; Var Capt Socr; High Hon Roll; NHS; Dartmouth Bowl 86; State Sci Fair 86; Salem Evening News All Star Soccer Team 85; Latin Awd 86; Med.

GRIMLEY, KAREN; Maynard HS; Maynard, MA; (Y); Red Cross Aide; Rep Frsh Cls; Pres Soph Cls; Pres Jr Cls; Stu Cncl; Var Trk; Hon Roll; Stu Advisory Board 85-86.

GRINNELL, TODD; Foxborough HS; Foxborough, MA; (Y); 1/250; Capt Math Tm; Var L Bsktbl; High Hon Roll; NCTE Awd; Pres NHS; Chancellrs Talnt Awd Schrlshp 86; Yale U; Chem Bio.

GRINSHPAN, MARINA; Doherty Memorial HS; Worcester, MA; (Y); High Hon Roll; Hon Roll.

GRISSO, HEATHER; Bishop Stang HS; New Bedford, MA; (Y); Camera Clb; Dance Clb; Math Clb; Ski Clb; Yrbk Stf; Trk; High Hon Roll; Hon Roll; NHS; Bus Admin.

GROGAN, DANIEL; Holyoke Catholic HS; Easthampton, MA; (Y); Chess Clb; Computer Clb; French Clb; JA; Math Clb; Ski Clb; SADD; Tennis.

GROLEAU, JEREMY; Westfield HS; Westfield, MA; (Y); Aud/Vis; Boy Scts; Jazz Band; JV Ftbl; Trk; Holy Cross; Bus.

GROLEAU, LYNN; Oxford HS; Oxford, MA; (Y); 2/135; Am Leg Aux Girls St; Dance Clb; Chorus; Color Guard; Drill Tm; School Musical; Yrbk Stf; Cheerleading; High Hon Roll; Nichols Coll; Bus Admin.

GRONBLOM, LISA; Plymouth Carver HS; Manomet, MA; (Y); 55/500; Debate Tm; Drama Clb; Northeastern U; Med Tech.

GRONDIN, WENDY MARIE; Westport HS; Westport, MA; (Y); Exploring; French Clb; Intnl Clb; Library Aide; Office Aide; Ski Clb; SADD; School Play; Stage Crew; Nwsp Rptr; BCC; Nurse.

GROSSMAN, MARC; Malden Catholic HS; Malden, MA; (Y); 13/175; Computer Clb; Latin Clb; Teachers Aide; Nwsp Rptr; Frsh Cls; Soph Cls; High Hon Roll; Hon Roll; NHS; Soc Stud Awd 86; MA ST Scholar 86; Trinity Coll; Polit Sci.

GRUBB, ANDREA; Danvers HS; Danvers, MA; (Y); 57/303; Hosp Aide; High Hon Roll; NHS; Ntl Hnr Soc; North Shore CC; RN.

GRUBER, JULIE; Dana Hall Schl; Lexington, MA; (Y); Yrbk Phtg; Yrbk Stf; Lit Mag; Hon Roll; Putnam Purchase Awd 86; George Washington U.

GRUMBACHER, M AARON; Deerfield Acad; York, PA; (Y); Var Crs Cntry; Im Ice Hcky; Var Wt Lftg; Hon Roll; MVP JV Crs Cntry 84; Edmond J Saunders JV Crs Cntry Trophy 84; Liberal Arts.

GRZEMBSKI, EDW; Bartlett HS; Webster, MA; (Y); 43/148; Am Leg Boys St; Boys Clb Am; Ski Clb; Stu Cncl; Var Bsbl; Capt Var Bsktbl; Coach Actv; Prfct Atten Awd; MVP Bsktbl; MVP Bsbl; All Star; Busnss.

GUARINO, DANIEL P; St Dominic Savio HS; Revere, MA; (Y); 4/104; Pres Church Yth Grp; Math Clb; Science Clb; SADD; Yrbk Ed-Chief; JV Ftbl; Var Trs Wt Lftg; NHS; Pres Schlr; NE U; Elec Engrng.

GUARINO, HONORIA; Haverhill HS; Bradford, MA; (Y); 1/365; Pres French Clb; Jr NHS; Kiwanis Awd; NHS; Ntl Merit Ltr; Val; VFW Awd; Exploring; Latin Clb; Nwsp Stf; Wellsly Coll Almni Assoc Bk Awd 85; US Acdmc Dcthln Slvr Mdl Wnr Fine Arts 85; Acdmc Exclnc Awd 86; NY U; Lbrl Arts.

GUARNERA, MICHAEL S; Winthrop HS; Winthrop, MA; (Y); 12/223; Art Clb; Drama Clb; Hosp Aide; Model UN; Band; Chorus; Color Guard; Concert Band; Drm & Bgl; Jazz Band; Steven M Coler Awd/Al-Arnd By 83; Mr Dnc USA 85; Bst Actr MA ST Drma Fstvl 83; Danc.

GUARNIERI, MICHELLE; Mount Alvernia HS; Wellesley, MA; (Y); 5/55; Cmnty Wkr; Exploring; Hosp Aide; Latin Clb; Church Choir; Nwsp Stf; Yrbk Stf; Hon Roll; Jr NHS; NHS; Spnsh 85-86; Engl Lit 85-86; US Govt 85-86; Wheaton Col6; Intl Rltns.

GUEN, JOHNNY; Boston Technical HS; Boston, MA; (Y); 10/205; Math Tm; Yrbk Stf; Im Bsbl; Im Bsktbl; Vllybl; Hon Roll; NHS; St Schlr; Schl Sprt Awd 86; VP Asian Clrs Clb 85-86; Mass Pre-Engr Prgm; Boston U; Mngmt.

GUENTHER, CHRISTINE; Reading Memorial HS; Reading, MA; (Y); Church Yth Grp; VP 4-H; Sec JA; Pep Clb; Lit Mag; Rep Frsh Cls; Rep Soph Cls; Rep Sr Cls; Var Cheerleading; JV Fld Hcky; Bus Mgmnt.

GUERCIO, MARY; Everett HS; Everett, MA; (Y); Chorus; Hon Roll; NHS; Bus Mngmnt.

GUERIN, DONNA; Greater Lowell Regionarl Vo Tech; Lowell, MA; (Y); FBLA; JA; SADD; Yrbk Stf; VP Jr Cls; Pres Stu Cncl; Hon Roll; Typng Achvt Awd 82-86; US Stu Cncl Awd 85; Stu Cncl Acht Awd 86; Nwbry JC; Bus Mgmt.

GUERRA, SALVATORE F; Abington HS; Abington, MA; (Y); 6/180; Am Leg Boys St; Yrbk Stf; VP Frsh Cls; Stu Cncl; Capt Socr; Tennis; Hon Roll; Chrmn NHS; Rep Schl Comm 85-86; Plymouth Hm Ntl Bk Schlrshp 86; Soccer All Star; Coaches Awd 84-85; Brandeis U.

GUERRIERO, WILLIAM; Holbrook HS; Holbrook, MA; (Y); 9/95; Latin Clb; Letterman Clb; Variety Show; Rep Frsh Cls; Rep Soph Cls; Rep Jr Cls; Rep Stu Cncl; Capt Var Socr; L Var Trk; VP NHS; Outstndg Prfrmnc Ecnmcs 86; JR Prm Cmmtee 86; Syracuse U; Lbrl Arts.

GUERRINI, JODI; Saugus HS; Saugus, MA; (Y); 64/276; Church Yth Grp; Cmnty Wkr; Hosp Aide; Library Aide; Office Aide; SADD; Yrbk Stf; Ed Lit Mag; Stu Cncl; Hon Roll; Saugus Rotry Schlrshp 86; ST Schlrshp 86; North Shore CC; Med Sec.

GUERTIN, DOTTIE; Auburn HS; Auburn, MA; (Y); Church Yth Grp; Sec JA; Ski Clb; Yrbk Stf; Rep Frsh Cls; Var L Cheerleading; JV Fld Hcky; Im Sftbl; High Hon Roll; NHS; Math.

GUERTIN, LISA; St Bernards HS; Winchendon, MA; (S); 22/154; Church Yth Grp; Drama Clb; 4-H; Library Aide; Pep Clb; Science Clb; Varsity Clb; Var Trk; Hon Roll; NHS; Fitchburg ST Coll; Microbio.

GUERTIN, MICHELLE; Arlington Catholic HS; Billerica, MA; (Y); 11/148; Cmnty Wkr; Drama Clb; Ski Clb; Spanish Clb; Yrbk Stf; Trk; Vllybl; High Hon Roll; Hon Roll; NHS; Attnry.

GUGLIELMI, ANN MARIE; Westwood HS; Westwood, MA; (Y); 16/210; Spanish Clb; SADD; Powder Puff Ftbl; Var Swmmng; Hon Roll; NHS; Spanish NHS; Capt All Star Swim Tm 84; 7 Of 10 Rec Var Girls Swim Tm 82-85; Globe All Star Tm Swim 83-85; Lake Forest Coll; Psych.

GUIFFRE, CHRISTOPHER DAMIEN; Wellesley HS; Wellesley, MA; (Y); 63/289; Pres German Clb; Latin Clb; SADD; Yrbk Stf; Hon Roll; NHS; Ntl Merit SF; Pres Schlr; Im Bsktbl; Im Golf; Babson College.

GUILBEAULT, SCOTT; Central Catholic HS; Lowell, MA; (Y); 46/231; Church Yth Grp; VP JA; Stage Crew; Bsktbl; JV Trk; Acctng.

GUILLEMETTE, MICHELLE; Blackstone-Millville Regional HS; Blackstone, MA; (Y); Office Aide; Teachers Aide; Yrbk Stf; High Hon Roll; Hon Roll; NHS; Bryant Coll; Bus.

GUILLOTTE, KELLY A; Fairhaven HS; Fairhaven, MA; (Y); 5/188; Drama Clb; Sec French Clb; Spanish Clb; School Musical; Stu Cncl; Capt Var Cheerleading; High Hon Roll; NHS; NEDT Awd; Church Yth Grp; 1st Pl Wnnr Grtr New Bedford JR Miss Pgnt-Schlrshop 86; 1st Pl Wnnr Spnsh Oral Cont 85; U Of MA Amherst; Frgn Lang.

GUILLOTTE, RONNIE; Fairhaven HS; Fairhaven, MA; (Y); Boys Clb Am; Boy Scts; Chess Clb; Church Yth Grp; Ski Clb; Chorus; Church Choir; Im Stu Cncl; JV Bsbl; Im Bsktbl; U MA Amherst; Bus.

GUIN, MICHAEL; Bellingham Memorial JR HS; Bellingham, MA; (Y); VP Drama Clb; 4-H; Service Clb; Concert Band; School Play; Nwsp Ed-Chief; Ice Hcky; Tennis; Trk; Hon Roll; King Phlp Chptr Dmly Mstr Cnclr 86; Arch.

GUINEE, JEFF; Leicester HS; Rochdale, MA; (Y); L Bsbl; L Bsktbl; Crs Cntry; L Trk; U MA; Bus.

GUISTINA, DAVID; Holyoke Catholic HS; Easthampton, MA; (Y); Church Yth Grp; Band; Jazz Band; Mrchg Band; Golf; Socr; Hon Roll; Syracuse U; Media.

GUNDAL, CHRISTINE; Barnstable HS; Centerville, MA; (Y); 1/360; Math Tm; Var Capt Gym; Var L Tennis; Bausch & Lomb Sci Awd; Elks Awd; High Hon Roll; NHS; Ntl Merit Ltr; Rotary Awd; Val; Brwn Bk Awd 85; Cmmnwlth Schlr 86; Cert Acadmc Exclnc 85; MIT; Chem.

GUNN, KATY; Frontier Regional HS; Sunderand, MA; (Y); 1/98; Spanish Clb; Yrbk Stf; Var Cheerleading; High Hon Roll; VP NHS; Wellesley & Dartmouth Bk Awds 86; No 1 Clb Max Hnrs 85; Comp Engrg.

GUPTA, HIMANSHU; Norwood SR HS; Norwood, MA; (Y); 3/323; Aud/Vis; Computer Clb; Yrbk Bus Mgr; JV Bsbl; JV Tennis; High Hon Roll; NHS; Rensselaer Poly Tech Inst Awd Math Sci; Math Physcis Awd; Med.

GUREVICH, TANYA; Framingham South HS; Framingham, MA; (Y); 7/256; School Play; Variety Show; Nwsp Stf; Yrbk Stf; Tennis; Vllybl; High Hon Roll; NHS; Ntl Merit Ltr; Rotary Awd; Brandeis U; Ecnmcs.

GURLEY, MARGRETTA; Bedford HS; Bedford, MA; (Y); 28/198; Pres AFS; SADD; Band; Chorus; Off Jr Cls; Off Sr Cls; JV Socr; JV Var Trk; Hon Roll; NHS.

GURRY, RENEE; North Quincy HS; Quincy, MA; (S); 20/333; Church Yth Grp; FBLA; JA; SADD; Nwsp Rptr; Yrbk Ed-Chief; Swmmng; High Hon Roll; NHS; Spanish NHS; Lttr Recgntn Fshr Scintfc Co; Accntng.

GUSTOWSKI, DIANNE H; St Marys HS; Worcester, MA; (Y); 2/49; Pres Church Yth Grp; Drama Clb; Pres JA; School Musical; Nwsp Rptr; Yrbk Ed-Chief; High Hon Roll; Sal; U Of Lowell; Nrsng.

GUTHRO, JAMES; Austin Prep Schl; Saugus, MA; (Y); 62/138; Computer Clb; French Clb; Spanish Clb; SADD; Pres Soph Cls; High Hon Roll; Pres & Fndr Para-Lgl Soc 84-86; WV Wesleyan Coll; Pre-Law.

GUTIERREZ, CARMEN; Classical HS; Lynn, MA; (Y); Dance Clb; French Clb; JA; Library Aide; Office Aide; Spanish Clb; Chorus; JV Var Cheerleading; Vllybl; Hon Roll; Bus Mgmt.

GUTKOSKI, JOHN; Burncoat SR HS; Worcester, MA; (Y); Boy Scts; Drama Clb; Math Tm; School Play; Intnl Clb; Math Clb; Chorus; School Musical; Rep Stu Cncl; Jr NHS; Eglr Sct BSA 85; Chf Pachachaug Ldg 525 Ordr Arrow BSA 86; Acad Olympcs Tm 85; Bus.

GUZMAN, EVELYN JANETTE; Gr Lawrence Technical HS; Lawrence, MA; (Y); 6/480; Mgr Pep Clb; Var L Bsktbl; Crs Cntry; Var L Sftbl; Var L Vllybl; High Hon Roll; NHS; Prtcpnt Boy ST Games 86; Stu Natl Hon Soc 86-87; MIP Bsktbll 86; Unsung Hero Awd 86; MIP Sftbll 85; U Of Lowell; Elec Engrng.

GUZOWSKI, KIMBERLY ANN; Phillips Acad; Andover, MA; (Y); Church Yth Grp; Debate Tm; Drama Clb; PAVAS; Political Wkr; Thesps; Acpl Chr; Band; Chorus; Stage Crew; Hd Of Drama Dept-Phillips Acad 86; Silvr Mdl-New Engl Russn Olympiad 85; Mc Cardle Awd Excl Perf Arts; Intl Relat.

GYLES, TREVOR; Masconomet Regional HS; Boxford, MA; (Y); Cmnty Wkr; Var Ski Clb; Var Opt Clb Awd; Hon Roll; Pre-Med.

HA, DUNG X; St Johns HS; Worcester, MA; (Y); 27/252; Art Clb; Chess Clb; Math Clb; Math Tm; JV Crs Cntry; High Hon Roll; Hon Roll; NHS; Slctd 1 Of 12 Prtcpnts Dynmy Ftr Ldrs Wrcstr Prgm 86; Engrng.

HAALAND, JOHN; Fairhaven HS; Fairhaven, MA; (Y); 9/178; Intnl Clb; Yrbk Bus Mgr; Trs Jr Cls; Cit Awd; High Hon Roll; Pres Jr NHS; Trs NHS; Aud/Vis; French Clb; Math Tm; NROTC Schlrshp 86; Bsbl All Star Hnrb Mntn 86; MVP In Bsbl 86; Wrcstr Poly Tech; Cvl Engrng.

HACKETT, ANGELIQUE; Drury SR HS; North Adams, MA; (Y); Boy Scts; Office Aide; Teachers Aide; Band; Chorus; Concert Band; Mrchg Band; Pep Band; High Hon Roll; Hon Roll; R C Lussier Jr Mem Schlrshp 86; MA St Sclrshp 86; Berkshire CC; Exec Sec.

HADDAD, MICHAEL; Triton Regional HS; Byfield, MA; (Y); 3/188; Varsity Clb; JV Bsbl; Var Bsktbl; Socr; Hon Roll; NHS; Wm Coll Bk Awd 85; Cmnwlth Of MA Schlrshp Awd 86; Top Male Stu Ldrshp Awd 86; U Of Lowell; Mtrlgy.

HADLOCK, CHARLES J; Lincoln Sudbury Regional HS; Lincoln, MA; (Y); 1/320; Boy Scts; Exploring; Key Clb; Math Tm; Model UN; Political Wkr; Science Clb; Nwsp Stf; Ntl Merit SF; Mathletes; Eagle Scout 83; Renssalaer Medallion For Excllnc In Math & Sci 85; Harvard; Econ.

HADMACK, KIM; Gardner HS; Gardner, MA; (Y); French Clb; Capt Color Guard; Capt Drm & Bgl; JV Capt Cheerleading; JV Sftbl; JV Trk; Chrng 85; Eng 84; MT Wachuse Cmnty Coll; Wrd Prc.

HAEHNEL, LEDA; King Philip Regional HS; Norfolk, MA; (Y); #17 In Class; Pres VP 4-H; Pres VP Service Clb; Lit Mag; 4-H Awd; Hon Roll; NHS; MA ST Visnl Presntn Wnnr 84; 4-H Hrse Bowl Wnnr 85; Natl 4-H Congrss Delgt 86; UMASS Amherst; Micrbio.

HAFEY, RICHARD; East Longmeadow HS; E Longmeadow, MA; (Y); Intnl Clb; Pep Clb; Band; School Musical; Variety Show; Yrbk Stf; Crs Cntry; Swmmng; Trk; Hon Roll.

HAGERTY, STEPHEN; Attleboro HS; Attleboro, MA; (Y); Church Yth Grp; Pres 4-H; Variety Show; JV Crs Cntry; Var Ftbl; Capt Swmmng; Capt Trk; 4-H Awd; Hon Roll; Prfct Atten Awd; MA 4-H Dele To Natl Prfls For Tommrrw Prog 85; MA ST Teen Cncl Rep 85-87; MA Ldrshp 4-H Natl 86; Comm.

HAGGIS, APRIL; Fairhaven HS; Fairhaven, MA; (Y); Girl Scts; JA; Yrbk Stf; Var Trk; High Hon Roll; Hon Roll; Jr NHS; Rep Jr Cls; Stu Mth 84; Acadmc Ltr 85; Sthestrn U Of MA; Bus Mgmt.

HAGGLUND, JOHN; St Johns HS; Sutton, MA; (Y); 43/264; Am Leg Boys St; Church Yth Grp; 4-H; French Clb; Office Aide; Rep Frsh Cls; Hon Roll; Jr NHS; NHS; Francis Ouimet Caddie Schlrshp 86; 1st Pl Frnch Lang Wrtng Cntst 86; Bentley Coll; Quantitative Anly.

HAGOPIAN, JASON R; Lexington HS; Lexington, MA; (Y); Pres Church Yth Grp; French Clb; Ski Clb; Lit Mag; Hon Roll; Rensselaer Polytech Inst; Arch.

HAGUE, MARC; Northbridge JR SR HS; Whitinsville, MA; (Y); 22/143; Band; Concert Band; Jazz Band; Yrbk Ed-Chief; Stu Cncl; Coach Actv; Capt Var Ftbl; Powder Puff Ftbl; Capt Var Trk; U Of MA; Envrnmntl Sci.

HAHN, MARCI; New Bedford HS; New Bedford, MA; (Y); Drama Clb; SADD; Chorus; School Musical; School Play; Nwsp Rptr; Nwsp Stf; Lit Mag; Rep Soph Cls; Fld Hcky; Boston U; Governess.

HAIRSTON, ERIC; Boston Latin HS; Boston, MA; (Y); Chess Clb; Math Tm; Science Clb; High Hon Roll; Hon Roll; NHS; Pres Schlr; Natl Merit Commndtn Outstng Stu 84-85; Austin Jones Schlrshp 85-86; MA ST Hnr Schlrshp Awd 85-86; Renssalaer Polytech; Compr Sci.

HAKKARAINEN, ADAM; Wachusett Regional HS; Holden, MA; (Y); Model UN; Science Clb; Ski Clb; Pres SADD; JV Crs Cntry; Var Trk; Wt Lftg.

HALE, CAROLYN; Wilmington HS; Wilmington, MA; (Y); French Clb; Office Aide; Spanish Clb; Stu Cncl; JV Tennis; Hon Roll; Masonic Awd; Stu Schl Cmmnttee 86-87; JR Prm Plnng Cmmttee 86.

HALE, SUZANNE; Reading Memorial HS; Reading, MA; (Y); VP French Clb; PAVAS; Lit Mag; French Hon Soc; High Hon Roll; NHS; Boston Globe Schlstc Art Awds 84&86; Schlrshp Pro-Arts Smmr Pgm 84.

HALE, TIMOTHY K; Thayer Academy; Plymouth, MA; (Y); 24/100; Boy Scts; Varsity Clb; Variety Show; JV Bsbl; Var Ftbl; Var Capt Ice Hcky; Var Capt Lcrss; God Cntry Awd; Hon Roll; Thomas J Berry Scholar 85-87; Sci.

HALEY, CHRISTOPHER R; Narragansett Regional HS; Templeton, MA; (Y); 9/98; Am Leg Boys St; Aud/Vis; Letterman Clb; Ski Clb; Varsity Clb; School Musical; School Play; Stage Crew; Yrbk Stf; VP Sr Cls; Bus Mgmt.

HALEY, KAREN; Matignon HS; Arlington, MA; (S); 13/181; Cmnty Wkr; Drama Clb; Spanish Clb; SADD; School Musical; Nwsp Ed-Chief; Var Sftbl; Var Vllybl; NHS; Spanish NHS; Ntl Merit Ltr 85; Acadmc All Amercn 85; Soc Distngshd Amercn H S Stu 85; Law.

HALEY, MARYKATE; Notre Dame Acad; Weymouth, MA; (Y); 40/111; Art Clb; Varsity Clb; Capt L Crs Cntry; L Gym; Capt L Trk; Hon Roll; Prfct Atten Awd; 1st Pl Boston Globe Art Cont 84; Capt MA All ST Crs Cntry Champ Teams 83-85; 25th Pl MA ST Crs Cnt; U Of MA; Graphc Art.

HALIO, MICHELLE; Sharon HS; Sharon, MA; (Y); Drama Clb; Spanish Clb; SADD; Sec Temple Yth Grp; Nwsp Rptr; Nwsp Stf; Hon Roll; Hebrew H S-Deans List 84-86; Bus.

HALL, ELISABETH; Northfield Mt Hermon HS; Portsmouth, NH; (Y); Cmnty Wkr; SADD; Varsity Clb; Nwsp Bus Mgr; Nwsp Phtg; Nwsp Sprt Ed; Trs Jr Cls; Var L Tennis; Var L Trk; Hon Roll; MIP Varsity Tennis Tm 84; Psychology.

HALL, JASON M; Worcester Vocational Tech; Spencer, MA; (Y); 23/181; Am Leg Boys St; Boy Scts; Chorus; Nwsp Sprt Ed; Bsktbl; Ftbl; High Hon Roll; Comp Desgn.

HALL, JOYCE; Gardner HS; Gardner, MA; (Y); 33/160; Chess Clb; Office Aide; Band; JV Sftbl; Hon Roll; NHS; Mt Wachusetts Tlnt Schlrshp 86; Covenant Lthrn Chrch Schlrshp 86; Mt Wachusetts CC; Bus Adm.

HALL, KIMBERLY; Nipmuc Regional HS; Mendon, MA; (Y); Pres Drama Clb; SADD; Drill Tm; Flag Corp; Rep Stu Cncl; NHS; Framingham ST; Psych.

HALL, MIKE; Winchester HS; Winchester, MA; (Y); Art Clb; Boy Scts; Church Yth Grp; English Clb; Letterman Clb; Varsity Clb; Variety Show; Ed Nwsp Stf; Rep Soph Cls; Rep Jr Cls; Eagle Scout SR Patrol Ldr BSA 85-86; St Boston Globe Show 84-86; Life Guard BSA 85; Writer.

HALL, SHEILA; Sharon HS; Sharon, MA; (Y); #51 In Class; Drama Clb; Spanish Clb; Ed Nwsp Stf; Ed Yrbk Stf; Hon Roll; Spnsh Stu Mth 84; Edward Koskella Memrl Schlrshp 86; Bryant Coll; Mrktng.

HALLIDAY, ISHMAEL; Reading Memorial HS; Reading, MA; (Y); Computer Clb; Latin Clb; JV Socr; JV Tennis; High Hon Roll; Hon Roll; Ntl Merit Ltr; Elec Engrng.

HALLINAN, KRISTEN; Notre Dame Acad; Hanover, MA; (Y); 30/109; Art Clb; Latin Clb; Library Aide; Nwsp Rptr; Nwsp Stf; Yrbk Stf; Lit Mag; High Hon Roll; Girl Scts; Math Achvmnt Awd 84-85; Bstn Glb Art Awd 85-86; Bus.

HALLISEY, MARTHA; Fontbonne Acad; Avon, MA; (Y); 2/132; Drama Clb; Intnl Clb; Math Clb; School Play; Lit Mag; Crs Cntry; Trk; High Hon Roll; NHS; Ntl Merit Ltr; Shaws Schrlshp 86; Salutatorian Cls 86; Eng,Theolgy Awds 86; Holy Cross.

HALLOCK, KEVIN; Hopkins Acad; Hadley, MA; (S); 2/48; Band; Concert Band; Jazz Band; Mrchg Band; Stu Cncl; Var L Bsbl; Var L Socr; Hon Roll; Sal; Spgfld Rgnl Stu Adv Cncl 84-85 & 85-86; Stu Advsry Comm 84-85 & 85-86.

HALLORAN, PATRICIA; Methuen HS; Methuen, MA; (Y); Church Yth Grp; Chorus; Church Choir; School Musical; School Play; Var Tennis; Hon Roll; Nrsng.

HAMBURG, LOUISE; Northfield Mount Hermon HS; Forest Hills, NY; (Y); Cmnty Wkr; Spanish Clb; Yrbk Bus Mgr; Yrbk Rptr; Yrbk Stf; Var Mgr Mgr(s); Hon Roll; Jr NHS; Willow Bend Ests Rdng Show 1st,3rd Pl Ribbons 84; Yale U Summr Schl 86; Pltcl Sci.

HAMBY, HENRY; Bedford HS; Bedford, MA; (Y); 48/205; Church Yth Grp; FBLA; Latin Clb; Var Capt Crs Cntry; Var Trk; Hon Roll; USAFA Prep Schl; Engr.

HAMEL, JANELLE; Tahanto Regional HS; Boylston, MA; (Y); 17/57; Science Clb; Yrbk Stf; Rep Stu Cncl; Var Cheerleading; Capt Fld Hcky; Hon Roll; Sec NHS; Bay Path JC Alumna Assn Awd 86; Spch Thrpy.

HAMEL, KEVIN; Chicopee Comprehensive HS; Chicopee, MA; (Y); 141/310; Var L Tennis; Fr Donohoe Mem Schlrshp 86; Fr Shannon Mem Schlrshp 86; Wstfld ST Coll; Cmptr Sci.

HAMEL, PAUL; St Dominic Savio HS; Revere, MA; (Y); Chess Clb; Computer Clb; JA; Key Clb; Ski Clb; Nwsp Phtg; Yrbk Phtg; Yrbk Stf; JV Rep Stu Cncl; Im Bsktbl; Acad All Amer 85-86; Math Awd 85-86; Stu Cncl Awd 85-86; Boston Coll; Biol.

HAMELBURG, STACEY; Braintree HS; Braintree, MA; (Y); 28/442; Girl Scts; Off Frsh Cls; Off Soph Cls; Off Jr Cls; Off Sr Cls; Bsktbl; Sftbl; Tennis; NHS; Trs Spanish NHS; Jrnlsm.

HAMILTON, ALISON B; Bridgewater-Raynham Regional HS; Bridgewater, MA; (Y); 14/301; FTA; Model UN; SADD; Chorus; Orch; Nwsp Stf; Yrbk Stf; Im Tennis; Im Vllybl; Hon Roll; MA Arts Lottery Grnt 84; Brockton Symph Orch Scholar 84 & 86; Rita Dziergowski Civic Awd 86; Vassar Coll; Russn.

HAMILTON, BRONWYN; South Lancaster Acad; Lancaster, MA; (S); FCA; Church Choir; Nwsp Rptr; Yrbk Rptr; Rep Soph Cls; Pres Jr Cls; Gym; High Hon Roll; Hon Roll; NHS; Sci.

HAMILTON, CHRIS; Belmont HS; Belmont, MA; (Y); 31/262; JA; Band; Concert Band; Mrchg Band; School Play; Yrbk Stf; JV Capt Bsbl; Var Swmmng; Hon Roll; Governors Alliance Against Drugs Smnr 86; Psych.

HAMILTON, ERIKA; St Bernards Regional HS; Templeton, MA; (S); 2/177; Trs Drama Clb; French Clb; Science Clb; Nwsp Stf; CC Awd; Elks Awd; Hon Roll; NHS; Horseback Rdng Shows 83; Tutor Geo,Trigo And Chem 84-85; Work JR SR Recptn 85-86; Biochem.

HAMILTON, MICHAEL P; Braintree HS; Braintree, MA; (Y); 69/438; Am Leg Boys St; Math Tm; Ski Clb; Rep Frsh Cls; Soph Cls; Jr Cls; JV Socr; JV Trk; Cit Awd; High Hon Roll; Engnrng.

HAMILTON, REBECCA; Medford HS; Medford, MA; (Y); 23/500; French Clb; Letterman Clb; Math Tm; SADD; Yrbk Stf; Capt Var Cheerleading; Capt Var Gym; Hon Roll; NHS; Ntl Merit SF; Eng Olympiad Awd; Top Alg,Eng Stu; Unsung Hero Gym; Tufts.

HAMILTON, SANDY; Newton Catholic HS; Auburndale, MA; (Y); Church Yth Grp; Cmnty Wkr; Hon Roll; Burdett; Merch Mgt.

HAMLING, HOLLY; Monument Mountain HS; Flowery Branch, GA; (Y); Cmnty Wkr; Teachers Aide; Color Guard; Stage Crew; Erly Chldhd Dvlpmt.

HAMMOND, ADAM; Austin Preparatory Schl; Burlington, MA; (Y); 14/124; Ed Lit Mag; High Hon Roll; Deans List; Brown U Bk Awd; Engl.

HAMMOND, ALYSA D; Lincoln-Sudbury Reg HS; Sudbury, MA; (Y); Art Clb; Sec Church Yth Grp; French Clb; Chorus; Church Choir; School Musical; Stu Cncl; Var L Trk; Var Vllybl; Ithacca Col; Acctng.

HAMPSON, TRACI; Hudson HS; Hudson, MA; (Y); 41/149; Pep Clb; Ski Clb; Chorus; Stage Crew; Sec Frsh Cls; VP Sr Cls; Capt L Cheerleading; Powder Puff Ftbl; Elks Awd; Hon Roll; Schlrshps-Emblm Clb, MA ST & James Jnkns Memrl 86; Newbury JC; Intr Dsgn.

HAMPTON, JAMES J; Middleboro HS; Middleboro, MA; (Y); Am Leg Boys St; Art Clb; Drama Clb; School Play; Stage Crew; Variety Show; Nwsp Rptr.

HAMRE, JOHN T; Cathedral HS; W Springfield, MA; (Y); 119/474; Rep Frsh Cls; Rep Jr Cls; Rep Sr Cls; Var L Bsktbl; Var L Socr; William Sullivan Schlrhsp 86; 2nd Tm All-Wstrn MA Sccr Awd 84-85; Stonehill.

HANC, BETZI-LYNN; Hampshire Regional HS; Southampton, MA; (S); 1/129; Concert Band; Variety Show; Yrbk Stf; Trs Soph Cls; High Hon Roll; Jazz Band; Mrchg Band; Nwsp Stf; Trs Frsh Cls; Rep Jr Cls; Actvty Peer Ed.

HAND, ALEX; The Mac Duffie Schl; Springfield, MA; (Y); Aud/Vis; Church Yth Grp; Cmnty Wkr; Debate Tm; Drama Clb; Hosp Aide; Thesps; Band; Mrchg Band; School Musical; Vrsty Let 84-86; Best Actress 86; Drama.

HAND, CATHY; Sharon HS; Sharon, MA; (Y); 22/210; Church Yth Grp; Spanish Clb; SADD; Yrbk Stf; Lit Mag; Sec Sr Cls; Rep Stu Cncl; Vllybl; High Hon Roll; Hon Roll; Hon Mntn Frm Framingham ST Coll For Term Ppr 86; Stu Of Mnth Art 86; Cmmrcl Artst.

HAND, KATHRYN E; Barnstable HS; W Hyannisport, MA; (Y); 6/392; Capt NFL; Capt Speech Tm; Nwsp Ed-Chief; Var Powder Puff Ftbl; L Capt Trk; High Hon Roll; NHS; Voice Dem Awd; Cmnty Wkr; Nwsp Rptr; Wellesley Book Awd For Schlrshp & Ldrshp 86; Jrnlsm.

HANDLER, CINDY M; Sharon HS; Sharon, MA; (Y); 4/190; Drama Clb; Ski Clb; Spanish Clb; SADD; Temple Yth Grp; Stage Crew; Yrbk Stf; High Hon Roll; Hon Roll; NHS; Pres Acad Fit Awd 86; Fortnightly Clb Awd Acad Achvt 86; Engl Excllnce Awd 86; Brandeis U; Pre-Med.

HANDREN, MARK; Coyle & Cassidy HS; Taunton, MA; (Y); 6/140; Am Leg Boys St; Boy Scts; Varsity Clb; Var L Ftbl; Var L Trk; Im Wt Lftg; Hon Roll; Kiwanis Awd; Lion Awd; NHS; Egl Sct 86; Purdue; Cnslng.

HANKINSON, DENISE; Foxboro HS; Foxboro, MA; (Y); Church Yth Grp; Dance Clb; Hon Roll.

HANLON, KERRY; Pope John Xxiii HS; Chelsea, MA; (Y); Aud/Vis; Dance Clb; French Clb; Chorus; Variety Show; Im Bsktbl; Im Cheerleading; Hon Roll; Ma St Schlrshp 86; U Lowell; Crmnl Jstc.

HANLON, MICHELLE; Plymouth-Carver HS; Plymouth, MA; (Y); Debate Tm; Drama Clb; Hosp Aide; Intnl Clb; Model UN; Hon Roll; Psych.

HANLON, SHAWN; Canton HS; Canton, MA; (Y); 32/250; Church Yth Grp; Cmnty Wkr; German Clb; Hon Roll; Jr NHS; Prfct Atten Awd; Stonehill Coll; Bus Admn.

HANNABURY, JOHN; Malden Catholic HS; Malden, MA; (Y); 15/173; Band; Var L Trk; Im Vllybl; High Hon Roll; NHS; Ntl Merit Ltr; Outdr Trck MVP 85-86; John A Saragosa Awd Exc Schlrp & Athltcs 86; Boston U; Phys Ther.

HANNAN, BRUCE; St Dom Savio HS; Revere, MA; (Y); 40/100; Art Clb; JA; Yrbk Stf; JV Bsbl; JV Bsktbl; Suffolk U; Crimnl Just.

HANNAWAY, HOLLY; Marblehead HS; Marblehead, MA; (Y); Ski Clb; Spanish Clb; SADD; Var Fld Hcky; JV Lcrss; Var Powder Puff Ftbl; JV Sftbl; Var Swmmng; High Hon Roll; Hon Roll; Comm.

HANNON, COLLEEN; North Quincy HS; Quincy, MA; (Y); 15/402; Cmnty Wkr; Drama Clb; SADD; School Play; Rep Frsh Cls; Capt Powder Puff Ftbl; Capt Sftbl; High Hon Roll; NHS; Spanish NHS; Sprngfld Coll; Sprts Sci.

HANSBERRY, KENNETH M; Norwood HS; Norwood, MA; (Y); 2/324; School Play; Variety Show; Trs Frsh Cls; Trs Soph Cls; Var L Golf; Var L Tennis; High Hon Roll; JC Awd; Ntl Merit Ltr; Sal; Dartmouth Clg; Law.

HANSEN, GAYLE; Wayland HS; Wayland, MA; (Y); 89/233; Church Yth Grp; Hosp Aide; SADD; Yrbk Bus Mgr; VP Frsh Cls; Rep Soph Cls; Mgr(s); JV Var Socr; Var Sftbl; JV Tennis; Stu Awareness Pgm Cmmndtn 85-86; U MA; Tchg.

HANSON, DARRELL; Bedford HS; Bedford, MA; (Y); 7/200; AFS; SADD; Stage Crew; JV Bsbl; Var Socr; Var Trk; French Hon Soc; Hon Roll; NHS; Chem Engrng.

HANSON, JIM; Agawam HS; Feeding Hls, MA; (Y); 10/300; Var Capt Bsktbl; Hon Roll.

HANSON, MARTHA; Apponequet Regional HS; Lakeville, MA; (Y); Church Yth Grp; Cmnty Wkr; Office Aide; Psych.

HANSON, WENDY; Bristol Plymouth Regional Voc Tech HS; Bridgewater, MA; (Y); Pres Sec 4-H; SADD; Ntl Merit Ltr; Church Yth Grp; VICA; Church Choir; Yrbk Stf; JV Score Keeper; Elks Awd; 4-H Awd; Schlrshp; Top Female Studnt 86; Johnson & Whales Coll; Culnary.

HANSSEN, KAREN; King Philip HS; Norfolk, MA; (Y); 6/280; Church Yth Grp; Dance Clb; Ski Clb; Varsity Clb; Rep Frsh Cls; L Socr; Trk; NHS.

HAPPE, KARL; Cambridge Rindge & Latin Schl; Cambridge, MA; (S); 1/600; Church Yth Grp; Key Clb; Service Clb; Ski Clb; Trs Jr Cls; Var L Ftbl; Var L Trk; Var L Wrstlng; High Hon Roll; Prfct Atten Awd; Alg II Prize Ex Awd 85; 1st Hnrs 83-85; Comp Sci Awd 85; Geomtry Awd 84; Brown; Engrng.

HAQUE, MOFIZ; North Quincy HS; Quincy, MA; (Y); 36/400; Pres Computer Clb; Scholastic Bowl; Science Clb; Yrbk Rptr; Capt Socr; Var Trk; High Hon Roll; MYSA All Star Soccer Lgu 83 & 83.

HARAN, REGINA; Burncoat HS; Worcester, MA; (Y); 11/240; Cmnty Wkr; Hosp Aide; Office Aide; Socr; Elks Awd; Hon Roll; Jr NHS; NHS; Froshin Clb Awd; U MA Amherst; Art.

HARCOVITZ, KATHERINE; King Philip Regional HS; Norfolk, MA; (Y); Church Yth Grp; French Clb; Girl Scts; Concert Band; Jazz Band; Sec Mrchg Band; Hon Roll; NHS; U Lowell; Med Lab Tech.

HARDIN, MELISSA; Phillips Acad; New York, NY; (Y); Nwsp Bus Mgr; Pres Stu Cncl; Ntl Merit SF; Smmr Intrnshp Mtrpltn Msmn NYC 86.

HARDING II, JOHN J; Arlington Catholic HS; Wilmington, MA; (Y); 65/146; Church Yth Grp; Spanish Clb; Nwsp Ed-Chief; Capt JV Bsktbl; Var Ftbl; Var Trk; Wt Lftg; Tns Srvng Eldrly Clb 86; Bstn U; Aviation.

HARDMAN, MICHELLE; Madison Park HS; Boston, MA; (Y); Church Yth Grp; Church Choir; Hampton U; Archtrl Dsgn.

HARDY III, HUDSON E; Old Rochester Regional HS; Mattapoisett, MA; (Y); 13/160; Am Leg Boys St; Computer Clb; French Clb; JA; Var L Bsbl; Var L Trk; Im Vllybl; Hon Roll; Southeastern MA U; Accntng.

HARDY, JENNIFER; Wakefield HS; Wakefield, MA; (Y); AFS; Aud/Vis; Church Yth Grp; Key Clb; School Play; Yrbk Stf; Var Fld Hcky; JV Var Tennis.

HARDY, STEPHANIE; Chatham JR SR HS; South Chatham, MA; (Y); 4/40; Drama Clb; 4-H; FBLA; Chorus; Stage Crew; Ed Lit Mag; Off Stu Cncl; Mat Maids; High Hon Roll; Hon Roll; Physcl Thrpy.

HARGRAVES, GAYLIN; Marian HS; Framingham, MA; (Y); Art Clb; Church Yth Grp; Cmnty Wkr; SADD; School Musical; Lit Mag; Var Cheerleading; JV Socr; Hon Roll; Latin Clb; Sci Fair Awd 85.

HARKARINEN, ADAM; Wachusett Regional HS; Holden, MA; (Y); Model UN; Science Clb; Ski Clb; Pres SADD; Var Crs Cntry; Var Trk; Hon Roll; U Of CA; Anthrplgy.

HARKIN, MICHAEL J; North Cambridge Catholic HS; Cambridge, MA; (Y); Boy Scts; Red Cross Aide; Church Choir; Bsbl; Score Keeper; Northeastern U; Elec Engr.

HARLOW, LYNNE; Norton HS; Norton, MA; (Y); 19/140; Pres Art Clb; Key Clb; Stage Crew; Yrbk Stf; Stu Cncl; Capt L Fld Hcky; NEDT Awd; Rep Frsh Cls; Rep Soph Cls; High Hon Roll; MA Govt Day Del 85; Hugh O Brian Ldrshp Fndtn Rnnr Up 83; Norton Arts Lottery Schlrshp 86; Emmanuel Coll; Art Hist.

HARLOW, MICHAELA; Mohawk Trail Regional HS; Plainfield, MA; (Y); Lit Mag; Jr Cls; Trs Sr Cls; Var Vllybl; Hon Roll; NHS; Art Clb; Chorus; School Musical; School Play; Soc Stds Awd 86; Eric Allan March Ldrshp & Svc Awd 86; John Pollard Svc Awd 86; Greenfield CC; Bus Mgmt.

HARNEY, MICHAEL; Walpole HS; Walpole, MA; (Y); 5/268; JCL; Math Tm; Ski Clb; Spanish Clb; Concert Band; Drm & Bgl; Mrchg Band; Stu Cncl; Hon Roll; NHS; Ntl Latn Exm Silvr Mdl 84; Silvr Mdl Awd Frgn Lang 84-86; Stu Advsry Cncl 84-86; Physcs.

HAROLD III, JOSEPH R; Thayer Acad; Hingham, MA; (Y); Am Leg Boys St; Church Yth Grp; Office Aide; SADD; Varsity Clb; Var Ice Hcky; Var Lcrss; Im Tennis; Plmbng Cntrctng.

HAROOTIAN, PETER; Reading Memorial HS; Reading, MA; (Y); 41/327; SADD; Yrbk Phtg; Stu Cncl; Crs Cntry; Socr; Var Capt Trk; High Hon Roll; JC Awd; Utlty Cntrctrs Assn New England Schlrshp Inc 86; Readg Tchrs Assn Schlrshp 86; U Of NH; Mech Engrng.

HARPER, DAVID M; Northbridge JR SR HS; Whitinsville, MA; (Y); Am Leg Boys St; Boy Scts; French Clb; Ski Clb; Band; Stu Cncl; Var JV Ftbl; JV Socr; Trk; Im Wt Lftg; Veterinary Medicine.

HARPER, MITCH; Boston Latin Schl; Roslindale, MA; (Y); 142/289; German Clb; Latin Clb; Band; Concert Band; Var Capt Ftbl; Trk; Wt Lftg; Wrstlng; All Leag & All Div III Tm Ftbl 85; Harry Agganis All Star Ftbl Gm 86; Middlebury Coll; Engl.

HARPLEY, BARBARA; Westford Acad; Westford, MA; (Y); AFS; German Clb; Model UN; Pep Clb; SADD; Rep Pres Stu Cncl; Chef.

HARRELL, AARON G; Newton North HS; Mattapan, MA; (Y); Chess Clb; Var Ftbl; Var Wrstlng; Hon Roll; Syracuse; Advtsng.

HARRIGAN, MICHAEL; East Longmeadow HS; E Longmeadow, MA; (Y); 28/210; Intnl Clb; Political Wkr; Radio Clb; School Play; Nwsp Sprt Ed; JV Bsbl; JV Bsktbl; Var Crs Cntry; Hon Roll; NHS; Bentley; Bus Comm.

HARRINGTON, BETH; Notre Dame Acad; Hanover, MA; (Y); 32/118; Drama Clb; Hosp Aide; Science Clb; Chorus; School Musical; School Play; Bsktbl; Socr; Vllybl; Hon Roll; Outstndng Hstry 84; Best Actress Awd 85; 1st Pl Craft Exhib 85; Stonehill; Criminal Justice.

HARRINGTON, BRIAN; Cathedral HS; Springfield, MA; (Y); 41/455; Cmnty Wkr; Office Aide; Political Wkr; Quiz Bowl; DAR Awd; NHS; Ntl Merit Ltr; Pres Schlr; DAR Hstry Awd 86; Mod Senate 84-86; Bowling Tm 82-86; Hstry.

HARRINGTON, GLENN; Manchester JR SR HS; Manchester, MA; (Y); 20/83; Science Clb; SADD; L Stu Cncl; Var L Ftbl; Im Vllybl; Maine Maritime; Marin Trans.

HARRINGTON, KELLI; Durfee HS; Fall River, MA; (Y); 74/804; Teachers Aide; Fld Hcky; Spanish Clb; Pharmclgy.

HARRINGTON, MARK; Old Colony Vo-Tech; Carver, MA; (Y); Church Yth Grp; JV Bsbl; Var L Bsktbl; Hon Roll; Rochester Inst Of Tech; Arts Mg.

HARRINGTON, MICHAEL; Cathedral HS; Somers, CT; (Y); 32/530; Am Leg Boys St; Drama Clb; Red Cross Aide; SADD; Stu Cncl; Hon Roll; NHS; Rotary Awd; Egl Sct 84; Frshmn Advsr 86; Bus.

HARRIS, LYNN C; The Winsor Schl; Lexington, MA; (Y); Cmnty Wkr; Chorus; School Musical; School Play; Ed Nwsp Stf; Lit Mag; Sec Trs Jr Cls; Ntl Merit SF; Rep Drama Clb; French Clb; Frances Cabot Putnam Frnch Prz 85; Ruth Sabine Prz For Excllnc In Wrtng 85; Smpl Wrtng Englsn Txtbks; Humnts.

HARRIS, PHILIP F; Cambridge Rindge & Latin HS; Cambridge, MA; (Y); Camera Clb; Scholastic Bowl; Ski Clb; Jazz Band; Orch; Sr Cls; L Trk; Hon Roll; Ntl Merit Ltr.

HARRIS, PHILLIP L; Jamaica Plain HS; Roxbury, MA; (Y); Am Leg Boys St; Church Yth Grp; VP JA; Church Choir; Cit Awd; Boy Scts; Cmnty Wkr; Computer Clb; Political Wkr; Tuskogee U; Electric Engrng.

HARRIS, RICHARD; Marblehead HS; Marblehead, MA; (Y); 52/260; Lib Band; Lib Concert Band; Lib Mrchg Band; Orch; School Musical; Symp Band; Trk; Hon Roll; Micro Elec Engrng.

HARRIS, ROBERT E; Malden HS; Malden, MA; (Y); Drama Clb; Spanish Clb; Temple Yth Grp; Band; Concert Band; Mrchg Band; School Play; Rotary Awd; HS Band Prnts Assoc Schlrshp 86; HS Almni Schlrshp 86; Prsdnts Acdmc Ftnss Awd 86; Suffolk U; Cmmnctns.

HARRIS, RONALD; Waltham HS; Waltham, MA; (Y); Boys Clb Am; Church Yth Grp; Drama Clb; ROTC; Drill Tm; High Hon Roll; Hon Roll; Jr NHS; NHS; Mltry Ordr Wrld Wars 85; Flm.

HARRIS, SARAH; Framingham North HS; Framingham, MA; (Y); 52/350; Trs Spanish Clb; Teachers Aide; Chorus; Trs Soph Cls; Trs Jr Cls; Trs Sr Cls; Var Capt Cheerleading; Stat Lcrss; High Hon Roll; Hon Roll; Ldrshp Schlrshp 86; Miami U Oxford OH.

HARRISON, BETH; Beverly HS; Beverly, MA; (Y); Church Yth Grp; Pep Clb; Varsity Clb; Rep Frsh Cls; Rep Sr Cls; Var L Cheerleading; JV Coach Actv; Wt Lftg; Hon Roll; Frnch Awd 83-85; Mktg.

HARRISON, JACQUELINE A; Duxbury HS; Duxbury, MA; (Y); 25/276; Dance Clb; Teachers Aide; School Musical; Hon Roll; NHS; U Of MA-AMHERST; Hotel Mgmt.

HARRISON, LYNNE ANNE; Saugus HS; Saugus, MA; (Y); Church Yth Grp; Library Aide; Office Aide; Church Choir; Masonic Awd; Prfct Atten Awd; Outstndng Schl Librarian 83-84; Order Rainbow Awd Perf Atten; Tchng.

HART, CHRISTOPHER S; Westwood HS; Westwood, MA; (Y); Am Leg Boys St; Nwsp Rptr; Pres Sec Stu Cncl; Var L Crs Cntry; Var L Swmmng; Hon Roll; Spanish NHS; New England JR Olympc Boxing Champ 83-85; New England Golden Gloves Champ 86.

HART JR, GERALD J; Westwood HS; Westwood, MA; (Y); Am Leg Boys St; SADD; Varsity Clb; Stu Cncl; Var L Crs Cntry; Var L Swmmng; Hon Roll; Boxing New England JR Olympc Champ 83-85; E Coast & Natl JR Olympc Champ Boxing 84; Military.

HART, JOSEPH; West Roxbury HS; Boston, MA; (Y); Am Leg Boys St; Boys Clb Am; Boy Scts; Church Yth Grp; Spanish Clb; Varsity Clb; Band; Chorus; Church Choir; Concert Band; Babson Coll Minority Wk 85; Cmmnwlth Of MA Schlrshp 86; FL ST Coll; Bus Mgmt.

HART, MAUREEN; Presentation Of Mary Acad; Lawrence, MA; (Y); Church Yth Grp; Math Clb; Pep Clb; Spanish Clb; SADD; Stage Crew; Yrbk Phtg; Capt Bsktbl; High Hon Roll; Hon Roll; Pre Med.

HART, PATRICIA M; Notre Dame Acad; Hingham, MA; (Y); 36/109; French Clb; Latin Clb; Ski Clb; Concert Band; Trs Sr Cls; Var L Crs Cntry; Var Trk; Sec French Hon Soc; High Hon Roll; Hon Roll; Acad Excllnce Bio I.

HARTEL, JENNIFER KATE; Presentation Of Mary Acad; Andover, MA; (Y); 7/44; Spanish Clb; SADD; School Play; Nwsp Rptr; Yrbk Stf; VP Frsh Cls; VP Sr Cls; Var Sftbl; Var Vllybl; High Hon Roll; MA ST Sci Fair; Hugh O Brien Ldrshp Semnr Rep 85; Regnl Sci Fair Hnrbl Mntn 85; Tufts U.

HARTFORD, DAVID; Somerville HS; Somerville, MA; (Y); #4 In Class; High Hon Roll; Hon Roll; Hnrbl Mntn Schl Sci Fair 84; Elec Engnrng.

HARTMANN, WILLIAM C; Milton Acad; Weston, MA; (Y); Aud/Vis; Cmnty Wkr; Math Tm; Jazz Band; Rep Soph Cls; JV Socr; JV Trk; High Hon Roll; Hon Roll; Ntl Merit SF; Harvard; Frgn Svc.

HARTNETT, JOHN; Leicester HS; Leicester, MA; (Y); Am Leg Boys St; Church Yth Grp; Math Clb; Math Tm; Pres Frsh Cls; Pres Soph Cls; L Bsbl; L Bsktbl; L Ftbl; Hon Roll; Bay ST Bsktbl Tm Boston 86; Pre-Law.

HARTNETT, LAUREEN; Cambridge Rindge & Latin HS; Cambridge, MA; (Y); Dance Clb; French Clb; Hosp Aide; Key Clb; Band; Deta Kappa Gamma Scty Schlrshp 86; William E Gurry Mem Schlrshp 86; Elms Coll; Chem.

HARTWELL, JEFFREY S; Cohasset JR SR HS; Cohasset, MA; (Y); 12/105; Yrbk Sprt Ed; Yrbk Stf; High Hon Roll; Hon Roll; NHS; Cmnty Wkr; Rep Jr Cls; Rep Sr Cls; Var L Ftbl; Capt Golf; ST Stu Govt Day 85-86; Essy Wnr ST Stu Govt Pgm 85-86; Bobby Orr Sprtsmnshp Hockey Awd 84.

HARTWELL, SCOTT; Brockton HS; Brockton, MA; (Y); 138/1249; VP Church Yth Grp; Var Ice Hcky; High Hon Roll; Aud/Vis; Varsity Clb; Hon Roll; New England Chmpn Bantam Div, Yth Hockey 84; Bass & Keybrd Plyr In Essence Of Steel Rock Band 84; Music.

HARUBIN, BETH; Smith Acad; North Hatfield, MA; (Y); Cmnty Wkr; Key Clb; Variety Show; Yrbk Rptr; Yrbk Stf; JV Cheerleading; Var Mgr(s); Var Score Keeper; Hon Roll; Amer Heart Assoc Awd 85; Med Tech.

HARVEY, KATHERINE ELIZABETH; Littleton HS; Littleton, MA; (Y); 8/84; Drama Clb; Math Clb; Math Tm; Band; Church Choir; Concert Band; Jazz Band; Mrchg Band; School Musical; Yrbk Stf; 3rd Pl In SS Olympd; Tufts U; Hist.

HASAN, SHAMIM; Wakefield HS; Wakefield, MA; (Y); French Clb; Orch; High Hon Roll; Hon Roll; Engrng.

HASCHE, TINA; Lincoln-Sudbury Regional HS; Sudbury, MA; (Y); Drama Clb; Pep Clb; Band; Chorus; Concert Band; Pep Band; School Musical; Rep Stu Cncl; Bentley Coll Bus Wk Schlrshp 86; Hmcmng Queen 85; Miss MA American Co-Ed 86-87; Bentley Coll; Real Est Entrprnr.

HASKINS, ERIC; Bishop Feehan HS; Attleboro Falls, MA; (Y); 2/252; Math Clb; Math Tm; Crs Cntry; Trk; French Hon Soc; High Hon Roll; NHS; Ntl Merit Ltr; Ntl Olympd Math Tst Wnnr 85-86; Chem Engnrng.

HASTIE, ELIZABETH; Boston Latin HS; Boston, MA; (Y); 54/274; Drama Clb; German Clb; Ski Clb; Band; Concert Band; Stage Crew; JV Socr; Church Yth Grp; Latin Clb; Science Clb; Stu Mst Imprvd John K Richardson Prz 85; Cert Hnrbl Merit Natl Latn Exam 86; Cert Merit Nat Grk Ex 86.

HASTINGS, KEVIN; David Prouty HS; Spencer, MA; (Y); 33/200; Varsity Clb; Stage Crew; Var Ftbl; Var Tennis; High Hon Roll; Hon Roll; NHS; Bus Mgmt.

HASTINGS, LEIGH; Wilmington HS; Wilmington, MA; (Y); Spanish Clb; Varsity Clb; Yrbk Stf; Var L Bsktbl; Var L Sftbl; Var L Vllybl; Hon Roll; NHS; Prfct Atten Awd; MVP Awd Vllybll 85-86; Co-Capt Vllybll 86-87; Cert Of Hnr Pre-Calc 86; UNH; Phys Educ.

HATCH, CAROLYN; Monument Mountain Rgnl HS; W Stockbridge, MA; (Y); 24/132; Church Yth Grp; Drama Clb; Pres 4-H; Intnl Clb; School Musical; Nwsp Rptr; Yrbk Stf; Lit Mag; 4-H Awd; High Hon Roll; Lbrl Arts.

HATEM, NEIL M; Newton North HS; Newton, MA; (Y); Am Leg Boys St; Church Yth Grp; French Clb; Model UN; Varsity Clb; Jr Cls; Sr Cls; Stu Cncl; High Hon Roll; Hon Roll.

HATFIELD, ERIK; Swampscott HS; Nahant, MA; (Y); 60/238; Aud/Vis; JV Bsbl; Bsktbl; Ftbl; Hon Roll; U NH; Lndscp Dsgn.

HATHAWAY, TRACY; New Bedford HS; New Bedford, MA; (Y); 90/701; AFS; Hon Roll; Bus.

HAUR, MANITA; Greater Lowell Rgnl Voc Tech Schl; Lowell, MA; (Y); VICA; Trk; Hon Roll; Typng Awd 86; Middlesex Comm; Acctnt.

HAUSEN, FRANCOISE; Bishop Connolly HS; Middletown, RI; (Y); 13/167; Drama Clb; Var JA; Var Ski Clb; Var Band; Var Trk; High Hon Roll; NHS; Vllybl; 1st Prz Schlrshp Lassn Frnco Phone De Fall Rvr 86; Grmn Hnr Socty 84; Ben Franklin Schlrshp 86; Schiller Intl U; Intl Bus.

HAUSER, JONI; Oliver Ames HS; North Easton, MA; (Y); 6/270; Debate Tm; SADD; Nwsp Ed-Chief; Off Sr Cls; Stu Cncl; Im Trk; High Hon Roll; NHS; Pres Schlr; Mst Indvdl Grl 86; ST Fnlst Miss Co-Ed Pgnt 86; Syracuse U; Cmmnctns.

HAVENER, KAREN; Natick HS; Natick, MA; (Y); Drama Clb; Ski Clb; Speech Tm; SADD; Chorus; Color Guard; Mrchg Band; School Musical; School Play; Nwsp Stf; Amer Poetry Antholgy 85; Best New Poets Of Yr 86; Media.

HAWCO, KAREN; Holbrook JR SR HS; Boston, MA; (Y); GAA; Library Aide; Timer; Hon Roll.

HAWKE, CHRISTOPHER M; Swampscott HS; Swampscott, MA; (Y); 1/225; Church Yth Grp; Sec Stu Cncl; Var Bsktbl; Capt Socr; Var Trk; Trs NHS; Ntl Merit SF; Rotary Awd; Math Tm; Prfct Atten Awd; Dartmouth Bowl 85; Rensselaer Medal 85.

HAWKINS, JESSICA; Tantasqua HS; Wales, MA; (Y); 26/250; Band; Concert Band; Lit Mag; Var Socr; Hon Roll; Fitnss Advsr.

HAY, HEATHER; Ware HS; Ware, MA; (Y); 10/106; Art Clb; French Clb; Hosp Aide; Key Clb; Variety Show; JV Bsktbl; Stat Socr; High Hon Roll; Hon Roll; Pres Schlr; Polish Amer Ctzn Schlrshp 86; Cadet Corps Schlrshp 86; Smith Coll.

HAYDEN, KIMBERLEY; Marblehead HS; Marblehead, MA; (Y); 17/250; Intnl Clb; Spanish Clb; Yrbk Stf; High Hon Roll; Jr NHS; Brwn U Bk Awd 86.

HAYES, BRIAN; Melrose HS; Melrose, MA; (Y); 5/371; Boy Scts; German Clb; SADD; Band; Nwsp Rptr; Stat Bsbl; Stat Bsktbl; Hon Roll; NHS; Ntl Merit Ltr; Rtrd Ofcrs Amer Schlrshp 86; Dghtrs Amer Rvltn Hstry Awd 86; Lang Arts Awd 86; Dartmouth Coll.

HAYES, BRYON; Nauset Regional HS; N Eastham, MA; (Y); 12/157; Drama Clb; School Musical; School Play; Stage Crew; Variety Show; Hon Roll; NHS; Pres Acdmc Ftns Awd 85-86; Bridgewater ST Coll; Eng Tchr.

HAYES, CARRIE; Fontbonne Acad; Milton, MA; (Y); Art Clb; Church Yth Grp; Drama Clb; Hosp Aide; SADD; Stage Crew; Yrbk Stf; Fnces.

HAYES, JESSICA; Hopedale JR SR HS; Hopedale, MA; (S); 7/59; Church Yth Grp; Chorus; Yrbk Stf; Mgr(s); High Hon Roll; NHS; Pres Acad Fit Awd 86; Clss Of 1935 Alumni Awd 86; Clss Of 1983 Awd 86; Soc Stds Awd 86; Blaine Hair Schl; Hair Drssng.

HAYES, MAUREEN; Brockton Christian Regional HS; E Bridgewater, MA; (Y); 3/20; Camera Clb; Drama Clb; Chorus; School Play; Nwsp Stf; Pres Frsh Cls; Sec Soph Cls; VP Jr Cls; Rep Stu Cncl; Capt Cheerleading.

HAYES, MICHAEL E; Canton HS; Canton, MA; (Y); 9/265; Church Yth Grp; Math Tm; Science Clb; Rep Sr Cls; Rep Stu Cncl; Var L Crs Cntry; Var L Ice Hcky; Var L Socr; Var L Trk; Im Vllybl; Cornell U; Engrng.

HAYES, PATRICK; Arlington Catholic HS; Arlington, MA; (Y); JA; Rep Frsh Cls; Rep Soph Cls; Rep Jr Cls; Rep Sr Cls; Rep Stu Cncl; Var L Bsktbl; Coach Actv; Score Keeper; Var L Trk.

HAYNE, SUZANNE; Miss Halls Schl; Lenox, MA; (Y); 4-H; Variety Show; Im Golf; JV Socr; Im Tennis; Hon Roll; Psychlgy.

HAYNES, CATHERINE; Danvers HS; Danvers, MA; (Y); 26/300; Church Yth Grp; Math Tm; Yrbk Stf; Rep Frsh Cls; JV Bsktbl; Var Coach Actv; JV Fld Hcky; Im Sftbl; High Hon Roll; Hon Roll; Psych.

HAYNES, MARGARET M; Hudson HS; Hudson, MA; (Y); Pep Clb; Ski Clb; SADD; Concert Band; Yrbk Stf; Var Capt Cheerleading; Powder Puff Ftbl; JV Sftbl; Debra Smith Memrl Schlrshp 86; Becker JC; Bus.

HAYWARD, DENISE; North Middlesex HS; Pepperell, MA; (Y); Library Aide; Pep Clb; SADD; Varsity Clb; Yrbk Stf; Frsh Cls; Cheerleading; Coach Actv; Mgr(s); Powder Puff Ftbl; U CT; Med.

HAYWARD, MARK S; Falmouth HS; Falmouth, MA; (Y); Boy Scts; Chess Clb; French Clb; Science Clb; JV Crs Cntry; NHS; Ntl Merit SF; Voice Dem Awd; High Hon Roll; Hon Roll; Hnrb Mntn Interlochn Natl Youth Wrtng Comp 83-84; 1st Pl Paffords Essay Comptn 84-85; Eagle Sct 85-86; Hstry.

HEAFITZ, ANDREW; Newton South HS; Newton, MA; (Y); Stage Crew; Cit Awd; Hon Roll; Ntl Merit Ltr; 1st Pl MA ST Sci Fair 86; 13th Pl Nvl Ntl Sci Awds Comptn 86; US Dept Of Engry Hnrs Prog 86; Engrng.

HEALEY, CHRISTINE; Randolph HS; Randolph, MA; (Y); Am Leg Aux Girls St; Drama Clb; Mgr Chorus; School Musical; School Play; Swing Chorus; Variety Show; U MA Amherst.

HEALEY, DAVID; Wakefield HS; Wakefield, MA; (Y); Varsity Clb; Var Capt Ftbl; Trk; Wt Lftg; Bus.

HEALEY, DENISE E; Franklin County Christian Acad; Greenfield, MA; (Y); 1/2; Church Yth Grp; French Clb; GAA; Church Choir; Yrbk Ed-Chief; Rep Stu Cncl; Sftbl; Val; Hghst Acad Awd 86; Greenfield CC; Early Chldhd Ed.

HEALY, COLEEN; Wakefield Memorial HS; Wakefield, MA; (S); Church Yth Grp; DECA; Ski Clb; SADD; Flag Corp; Pom Pon; Cit Awd; High Hon Roll; Hon Roll; 1ST Pl Mrktng Mgnt DECA Locals 86; 2dn Pl Mrktng Mgnt DECA ST 86; Endicott COLL; Hotel Mgnt.

HEALY, JAY; Malden HS; Malden, MA; (Y); Church Yth Grp; Y-Teens; Wrstlng; Schlrshp 86; Phy Ed.

HEALY, MARY BETH; Bishop Feehan HS; Attleboro, MA; (Y); 26/250; Exploring; School Musical; High Hon Roll; NHS; Spanish NHS; Scps At Clrksn U 86; Psych Cert Of Merit 86; Psych.

HEANUE, JOSEPH; Boston College HS; Randolph, MA; (Y); 2/270; Math Tm; Nwsp Rptr; Im Bsktbl; Im Vllybl; NHS; Aerosp Engrng.

HEASLEY, D CRESSLER; Governor Dummer Acad; Kensington, NH; (Y); 1/90; Band; Jazz Band; School Play; Yrbk Stf; Stat Bsktbl; Var Crs Cntry; Var Lcrss; Var Trk; Bausch & Lomb Sci Awd; High Hon Roll; Harvard Book Prz 85; Ntl Cum Laude Soc 85.

HEATON, ANDREW P; Central Catholic HS; Groveland, MA; (Y); 65/260; Church Yth Grp; JV Bsbl; JV Ftbl.

HEATON, MICHAEL; Medway JR SR HS; Medway, MA; (Y); 43/150; Am Leg Boys St; SADD; Band; Jazz Band; Mrchg Band; Yrbk Stf; Sec Soph Cls; Stu Cncl; Var Ftbl; Var Golf; U MA; Lbrl Arts.

HEBERT, JEFFREY M; Grafton Memorial SR HS; S Grafton, MA; (Y); 1/106; Am Leg Boys St; Church Yth Grp; Quiz Bowl; Nwsp Ed-Chief; Rep Stu Cncl; Bausch & Lomb Sci Awd; Hon Roll; Air Force ROTC 4 Yr Schlrshp 86; Worcester Polytech; Elec Engrng.

HEBERT, LINDA; Smith Acad; Hatfield, MA; (Y); Art Clb; Drama Clb; French Clb; Spanish Clb; Thesps; School Musical; School Play; Stage Crew; Variety Show; Yrbk Bus Mgr; MA Forgn Lang Assn 86; Army; Chrptology.

HEBERT, PATRICE; Gr Lawrence Technical HS; Lawrence, MA; (Y); SADD; Trs Soph Cls; Trs Jr Cls; Trs Sr Cls; Cheerleading; 3rd Mst Outstndng Stu 85-86; Hstolgy.

HEBERT, PAUL; Blackstone-Millville Regional HS; Blackstone, MA; (Y); Var Bsbl; JV Bsktbl; Comp Tech.

HEFFERNAN, BRENDA; Southwick HS; Southwick, MA; (Y); Am Leg Aux Girls St; Ski Clb; SADD; Concert Band; VP Soph Cls; VP Jr Cls; VP Sr Cls; Var Fld Hcky; Var Capt Trk; Hon Roll.

HEFFERNAN, KRISTEN; Methuen HS; Methuen, MA; (Y); 48/349; Church Yth Grp; Intnl Clb; Spanish Clb; SADD; Band; Concert Band; Mrchg Band; High Hon Roll; Hon Roll; Spanish NHS; U Lowell; Bus Mgmnt.

HEFFERNAN, MELISSA; Medford HS; Medford, MA; (Y); Dance Clb; Ski Clb; SADD; Yrbk Stf; Sec Soph Cls; Sec Jr Cls; Sec Sr Cls; JV Capt Sftbl; JV Trk; Cmnctns.

HEGARTY, MARGARET; Blemont HS; Belmont, MA; (Y); 40/270; Church Yth Grp; PAVAS; Political Wkr; Service Clb; SADD; Orch; Var Capt Fld Hcky; Var Capt Trk; Mbr Natl Stu Advsry Cncl-Washingtn Wrk Shps 86; St House Summer Intershp Prog 86; Pltcl Sci.

HEGARTY, MARY-EDNA; Medford HS; Medford, MA; (Y); #42 In Class; Color Guard; Orch; School Musical; Hon Roll; NHS; Greater Boston Yth Symphy Orch 85-86; New England Consrvtrs Yth Orch 85-86; Music.

HEGNER, JEANNE M; Sacred Heart HS; Plymouth, MA; (Y); 4/90; NFL; School Musical; Yrbk Ed-Chief; High Hon Roll; Kiwanis Awd; VP NHS; Dance Clb; Debate Tm; Drama Clb; Intnl Clb; Gld Mdl Acdmc Excllnc & Achvt Drama & Frnscs 86; Achvt Clcls Awd 86; 6th Pl MA Stu Cngrs 86; Boston Coll.

HEIMBERG, MARY D; Maynard HS; Maynard, MA; (Y); 1/100; Band; Chorus; Concert Band; Mrchg Band; Var L Cheerleading; Var L Trk; Hst DAR Awd; Hon Roll; NHS; Val; U Of MA Chncllrs Tlnt Schlrshp; Sprintndnts Awd; Dgtl Equip Corp Schlrshp; U MA Amherst; Ophthlmlgst.

HELD, ROBERT MICHAEL; Nashoba Regional HS; Bolton, MA; (Y); 5/150; AFS; Ski Clb; SADD; Pres Stu Cncl; Var Socr; DAR Awd; Hon Roll; NHS; Ntl Merit Ltr; Prsdntl Acadmc Ftns Awd 86; Exchng Clb Yth Of Mnth 86; Stu Advsry Brd & Outstndng Contrbtn Awd 85-86; Stanford.

HELDENBERGH, PAMELA; Holy Name Central Catholic HS; E Douglas, MA; (Y); 43/285; Varsity Clb; Chorus; Church Choir; School Musical; Capt Var Socr; Cit Awd; High Hon Roll; Hon Roll; JV Bsktbl; Var JV Sftbl; Alumni & Friends Schlrshp Clark U; 86; Mss Natl Tngr Pgnt Ctznshp Schlrshp 86; Clark U; Psych.

HELIE, KENNETH; Auburn HS; Auburn, MA; (Y); Aud/Vis; Yrbk Phtg; Yrbk Rptr; Yrbk Stf; Trs Stu Cncl; Var Socr; High Hon Roll; Hon Roll; Englsh.

HELLSTEDT, KRISTIN; Westford Acad; Westford, MA; (Y); Art Clb; French Clb; Nwsp Stf; Lit Mag; Stu Cncl; JV Var Socr; Var L Tennis; Hon Roll; Jr Ntl Freestyle Skiing Team 85-87; Eastern Freestyle Team 83-87; Intr Dsgn.

HENNESSEY, ARTHUR; Austin Preparatory Schl; Billerica, MA; (Y); 9/124; SADD; Var Ftbl; Var Trk; Hon Roll; Off Spanish Clb; Deans Lst; Engrng.

HENNESSEY, JOAN P; Arlington Catholic HS; Arlington, MA; (Y); 17/143; Intnl Clb; Spanish Clb; Yrbk Stf; Cheerleading; High Hon Roll; Hon Roll; Sec NHS; Pres Schlr; Catholic Daugh Am Schrlshp 86; Svc Awd Arlington 86; Stonehill Coll; Lib Arts.

HENNESSEY, PATRICK M; Fitchburg HS; Fitchburg, MA; (Y); Am Leg Boys St; Pep Clb; Ski Clb; Var Bsbl; Var Crs Cntry; Var L Golf; Hon Roll; Prfct Atten Awd; Law.

HENNESSY, MELISSA; Marian HS; Framingham, MA; (Y); School Musical; Variety Show; Nwsp Rptr; Yrbk Stf; Cheerleading; High Hon Roll; NCTE Awd; NHS; Church Yth Grp; Dance Clb; Excllnc-Antmy & Physlgy Awd & Creatv Wrtng/Jrnlsm Awd 86; Excllnc-Geomtry Awd 84; Boston Coll; Wrtr.

HENNIGAN, EDW; Westwood HS; Westwood, MA; (Y); Church Yth Grp; Cmnty Wkr; Golf; Ice Hcky; Hon Roll; Eastern MA Div III Champs Hockey Tm 85-86; Comp Sci.

HENRIKSEN, DINA; Braintree HS; Braintree, MA; (Y); 30/442; High Hon Roll; Hon Roll; Med Tech.

HENRY, AUDREY; Malden HS; Malden, MA; (Y); 42/500; Debate Tm; Key Clb; Pep Clb; Quiz Bowl; SADD; Variety Show; Yrbk Phtg; Rep Frsh Cls; Rep Soph Cls; Rep Jr Cls.

HENRY, MAUREEN; Methuen HS; Methuen, MA; (Y); Dance Clb; Model UN; Trs Jr Cls; Trs Sr Cls; Var Cheerleading; Intnl Clb; SADD; Stu Cncl; Gym; Ldrshp Cnfrnce 86; Health Care.

HENRY, SUZANNE; Franklin HS; Franklin, MA; (Y); Church Yth Grp; Cmnty Wkr; Office Aide; JV Bsktbl; Var Socr; Capt Var Tennis; USTA & NELTA 85-87; No 1 Sngls Tnns Plyr 83-86.

HENSHAW, JEANETTE FRANCES; North Middlesex Regional HS; W Townsend, MA; (Y); 12/210; Church Yth Grp; Computer Clb; Drama Clb; SADD; Teachers Aide; Band; Concert Band; Pep Band; School Musical; Stage Crew; Wheelock Coll Grnt & 2 Locl Scholar Awds 86; Wheelock Coll; Elem Ed.

HERBERT, CLESTINE; Milton HS; Randolph, MA; (Y); Exploring; FHA; Library Aide; Spanish Clb; Acpl Chr; Church Choir; Variety Show; Bus.

HERK, DONNA; Athol HS; Athol, MA; (Y); 32/160; Model UN; SADD; Var Bsktbl; Var Sftbl; Var Trk; Var Capt Vllybl; Acctng.

HERMAN, DEBRA; Old Rochester Regional HS; Rochester, MA; (Y); 11/154; Math Tm; Nwsp Rptr; Rep Jr Cls; Var L Bsktbl; Var L Sftbl; High Hon Roll; Hon Roll; Jr NHS; NHS; U Of MA; Bus.

HERMAN, KARA; Westfield HS; Westfield, MA; (Y); 75/359; Cmnty Wkr; Political Wkr; Spanish Clb; Band; Church Choir; Concert Band; Mrchg Band; Pep Band; Stat Bsbl; Stat Bsktbl; Math.

HERMAN, LISA; Haverhill HS; Haverhill, MA; (Y); 6/450; Church Yth Grp; Key Clb; Latin Clb; SADD; Stu Cncl; High Hon Roll; NHS; Stu Cncl Awd Outstndg Achvt Hstry 84; Natl Amer Clsscl Lg Natl Lat Exam Cum Laude 86.

HERMANS, SANDY; Westford Acad; Westford, MA; (Y); 4/225; Rep Drama Clb; Chorus; School Musical; School Play; Variety Show; JV Crs Cntry; High Hon Roll; NHS; AFS; Church Yth Grp; Exclnce Eng Awd 85; Exclnce Mus Chorus/Theory 83, 85 & 86; Exclnce Span 83; Pinecrest Bib Trng Ctr; Mus Min.

HERNANDEZ, LETITA; Greater Lowell Regional Vo-Tec HS; Lowell, MA; (Y); Church Yth Grp; Cmnty Wkr; DECA; Library Aide; Office Aide; Chorus; Church Choir; Jr NHS; Comp Tech Engr.

HERNANDEZ, MARIA; Greater Lawrence Tech; Lawrence, MA; (Y); 47/385; SADD; Hon Roll; Shop Awd Data Mgmt 84.

HERNON, JOSEPH; Braintree HS; Braintree, MA; (Y); Computer Clb; Latin Clb; Math Clb; Math Tm; Teachers Aide; Hon Roll; High Scorer Schl Math Olympd 85-86; Engr.

HERRICK, PAM; Fitchburg HS; Fitchburg, MA; (Y); Pep Clb; Political Wkr; Ski Clb; SADD; Varsity Clb; School Play; Yrbk Phtg; Yrbk Stf; JV Crs Cntry; Capt Tennis; Bus.

HERSEY, MYRA; King Philip Regional HS; Plainville, MA; (Y); Church Yth Grp; 4-H; Girl Scts; VICA; Church Choir; 4-H Awd; Mechncl Eng.

HERSEY, STEPHEN; Westford Acad; Westford, MA; (Y); 43/225; AFS; French Clb; Intnl Clb; Ski Clb; VP Spanish Clb; Var L Golf; Var L Socr; High Hon Roll; George Washington U; Mktg.

HERSON, NANCI SUE; Natick HS; Natick, MA; (Y); 60/423; NFL; Speech Tm; SADD; Teachers Aide; School Musical; School Play; Stage Crew; Yrbk Bus Mgr; Yrbk Ed-Chief; Voice Dem Awd; Educ Assn Natick; Natick Arts Cncl; Ithaca Coll; Sec Educ.

HERZBERG, BECKY; Hingham HS; Hingham, MA; (Y); Drama Clb; Thesps; Chorus; Jazz Band; School Musical; School Play; Stage Crew; Madrigals; Swing Chorus; Variety Show; Globe Fstvl Ply All Str Adtng Awds 85 & 86; Mst Prmsng JR Thespian Soc 86; Actrs.

HESKESTAD, KRISTA; Dover-Sherborn Regional HS; Dover, MA; (Y); 20/153; Church Yth Grp; Capt Ski Clb; Pres Band; Orch; Trs Frsh Cls; Trs Soph Cls; VP Jr Cls; VP Sr Cls; JV Capt Socr; Hon Roll; Amer Musicl Fndtn Band Hnrs 84-86; MA Bay E Leag Chmpns-Ski Tm 86; New Eng Cnsrvtry Yth Reprtry Orch; Pblc Policy.

HESLAM, WILLIAM; North Middlesex Reg HS; Ashby, MA; (Y); Library Aide; Varsity Clb; VP Soph Cls; Trs Stu Cncl; Var Bsbl; JV Var Bsktbl; Var Crs Cntry; High Hon Roll; NHS; Math Clb; Mrshl For Grads 86; Engrng.

HESS, HEIDI E; Dover-Sherborn HS; Sherborn, MA; (Y); 1/157; AFS; Camp Fr Inc; Trs Exploring; Band; Pep Band; Stage Crew; Variety Show; Nwsp Stf; Var Bsktbl; Swmmng; Am Musicl Found Band Hnr 86; Dover Sherborn Hnr Soc Merit Cum Laude 85; Holy Cross Bk Prz Awd 85; Yale U.

HESSE, ALICIA C; Noble & Greznovott Schl; Weston, MA; (Y); Cmnty Wkr; PAVAS; Teachers Aide; Chorus; Madrigals; School Musical; School Play; Variety Show; Fld Hcky; Ice Hcky; Cmmndtn Outstndng Invlvmnt Cmmnty Svc 84-85; CT Coll; Govmnt Cmmnty Svc.

HESSION, ANN MARIE; Dedham SR HS; Dedham, MA; (S); 2/252; Mrchg Band; Orch; Bsktbl; Swmmng; Trk; NHS; Ntl Merit Ltr; Sal; Rnsllr Mdl 85; Chncllrs Tlnt Awd 85; Chem Engrng.

HEWITT JR, RICHARD; Arlington Catholic HS; Arlington, MA; (Y); Spanish Clb; SADD; Bsbl; Bsktbl; Ftbl; U Of NH; Busnss.

HEWITT, WILLIAM; Reading Memorial HS; Reading, MA; (Y); JV Socr; High Hon Roll; Hon Roll; Boston U; Bus Mgmt.

HEYWOOD, KENDRA; Attleboro HS; Attleboro, MA; (Y); Art Clb; Church Yth Grp; Acpl Chr; Chorus; Church Choir; Powder Puff Ftbl; High Hon Roll; Jr NHS; NHS; NEDT Awd; Psych.

HIBBERT, CHRISTINE ANN; New Bedford HS; New Bedford, MA; (Y); 170/670; Frsh Cls; Soph Cls; Jr Cls; Stu Cncl; High Hon Roll; Hon Roll; St Schlr; Prprfssnl Schlrshp 86; SE MA U; Accntnt.

HICKS, SHERRY; Haverhill HS; Haverhill, MA; (Y); 10/364; Band; Chorus; Concert Band; Orch; School Musical; Symp Band; High Hon Roll; NHS; Prfct Atten Awd; Boston U Schl Of Music; Music.

HIGBY, SHARON; Cathedral HS; Longmeadow, MA; (Y); 64/458; Church Yth Grp; Spanish Clb; School Musical; School Play; Stu Cncl; Trk; Vllybl; Variety Show; Pres Frsh Cls; Model Sent 86; Art Awd; Pro-Life Clb; Christendom Coll.

HIGGINS, CHARMANE; Boston Latin Schl; Boston, MA; (Y); 24/274; Church Yth Grp; Debate Tm; JCL; Key Clb; Church Choir; Nwsp Rptr; Yrbk Ed-Chief; Sr Cls; ACL/NJCL Ntl Grk Exam Merit; Awd Hnr Prz Rdng; Harvard-Rdclff U; Clsscl Cvlztn.

HIGGINS, MARIA; Medford HS; Medford, MA; (Y); 107/435; Church Yth Grp; SADD; Engl Awd; Biol Awd; U MA; Sci.

HIGGINS, MICHAEL; Medway JR SR HS; Medway, MA; (Y); 27/140; JV Var Bsbl; JV Var Ftbl; Hon Roll; Schltc Awd; Atten Awd; Elec Engr.

HIGGINS, PAUL; Bellingham Memorial JR SR HS; Bellingham, MA; (Y); Var Golf; JV Tennis; Hon Roll.

HIGGINS, RANDY; Monument Mountain Regional HS; Great Barrington, MA; (Y); Am Leg Boys St; Aud/Vis; Church Yth Grp; High Hon Roll; Hon Roll; Elec & Engl Sustained Effort Awds 85-86; Berkshire CC; Elec Engrng.

HIGGINS, ROBERT; Boston Coll HS; W Quincy, MA; (Y); Key Clb; Latin Clb; Spanish Clb; SADD; Var L Bsbl; Im Bsktbl; Im Ftbl; Im Vllybl; Hghst Grade Spn II 84-85; Pre-Law.

HIGH, ELIZABETH; Clinton HS; Clinton, MA; (Y); Drama Clb; Intnl Clb; Chorus; School Play; Stage Crew; Ed Yrbk Stf; Elks Awd; Hon Roll; VFW Awd; Acvt Awd Pointe Dncng 85; Achvt Awd Tap Dncng 86; U Of NH; Lbrl Arts.

HIGH, RON; St Johns Prep; Danvers, MA; (Y); Var Ice Hcky; JV Lcrss; JV Socr; High Hon Roll; Hon Roll; Ntl Merit SF; Hnrbl Mntn Hcky 86; Hcky Nght Boston 86; Engrng.

HILDESHEIM, RAPHAEL; Haverhill HS; Haverhill, MA; (Y); 20/430; Aud/Vis; VP JA; Pres Temple Yth Grp; JV Bsktbl; High Hon Roll; NHS; 3rd Pl Comp Prog Cntst 84; Comp Sci.

HILDITCH, PAMELA; Hepedale HS; Hopedale, MA; (Y); SADD; Pres Sec Band; Yrbk Stf; JV Bsktbl; L Var Crs Cntry; Var Mgr(s); Hon Roll; Boston Coll; Psychllgy.

HILL, CAROL; Doherty Memorial HS; Worcester, MA; (Y); 48/308; Spanish Clb; SADD; School Play; Yrbk Stf; Hon Roll; Jr NHS; Bryant Coll; Bus Mgmt.

HILL, HEIDI JO; N Attleboro HS; N Attleboro, MA; (Y); 14/250; VP Drama Clb; Thesps; Ed Yrbk Stf; Sec Jr Cls; Sec Sr Cls; Var L Fld Hcky; Var L Trk; High Hon Roll; Hon Roll; NHS; Merle B Crocket Awd; U Of NH; Lbrl Arts.

HILL, JEANETTE; Boston English HS; Roslindale, MA; (Y); Cmnty Wkr; Drama Clb; Office Aide; School Play; Lit Mag; Rep Jr Cls; Rep Stu Cncl; High Hon Roll; Hon Roll; Teachers Aide; Dept Awd Eng 85-86.

HILL, KAREN; Bedford HS; Bedford, MA; (Y); Hosp Aide; SADD; Yrbk Stf; JV Bsktbl; JV Sftbl; Capt L Swmmng; Hon Roll; NHS; Freestyle 3rd,5th Pl ST Champ 83-84; Tufts; Occuptnl Thrpy.

HILL, LAUREN; Bishop Stang HS; Fall River, MA; (Y); 25/250; Art Clb; Church Choir; Hon Roll; NHS; Awd For High Religion Grades 85; Southeastern MA U; Tchr.

HILL, MALCOLM S; Natick HS; Natick, MA; (Y); 65/442; Am Leg Boys St; Church Yth Grp; JCL; SADD; Off Jr Cls; VP Sr Cls; Var Capt Crs Cntry; Var Capt Trk; Hon Roll; Kiwanis Awd; Evng Div Schlrshp 86; Colby Coll; Med.

HILL, MARCIA; B M C Durfee HS; Fall River, MA; (Y); 88/687; Sec Church Yth Grp; VP JA; Office Aide; Yrbk Stf; Hon Roll; Prfct Atten Awd; Sec Of Bus Clb 85-86; Offcr Of The Yr Fnlst, JR Achvt 85-86; Sales Clb JR Achvt 84-85; Asst VP Fin; Exec Sec.

HILL, MICHAEL; Chicopee HS; Chicopee, MA; (Y); 29/253; Boy Scts; Nwsp Stf; Var Capt Crs Cntry; Var Capt Trk; NHS; Pres Schlr; Knghts Of Clmbs Schrlshp 86; U Of Hrtfrd; Engrng.

HILL, MICHAEL; Old Colony Regional Vo Tech; Carver, MA; (Y); Ski Clb; VICA; Off Jr Cls; Trs Stu Cncl; Var Bsbl; Var Capt Ftbl; Lg Bsbl All Star Soph Yr; Lg Ftbl All Star Jr-Sr Yr; Boston Gobe All Lg All Star Tackle, All Lg Str.

HILL, SCOTT C; Uxbridge HS; Uxbridge, MA; (Y); 10/100; Var Capt Bsktbl; Var Ftbl; Hon Roll; Pre-Law.

HILL, SHARON; Doherty Memorial HS; Worcester, MA; (Y); Church Yth Grp; Spanish Clb; SADD; Chorus; Hon Roll; Im Bsktbl; Im Sftbl; Im Vllybl; Psych.

HILL, TAMMY; Bristol Plymouth HS; Taunton, MA; (Y); Drama Clb; JV Var Cheerleading; Im Gym; Hon Roll; Bridgewater ST.

HILL, TIFFANY; Bishop Stang HS; Wareham, MA; (Y); Drama Clb; Intnl Clb; Church Choir; Color Guard; Mrchg Band; School Musical; School Play; Stage Crew; Hon Roll; Pst Wrthy Advsr Of Wrhm Assmbly 84; Pst Grnd Hp Of Grnd Assmbly Of MA 85-86; Grnd Wrty Advsr 86-87; Brdcstng.

HILL, TIMOTHY; Norton HS; Norton, MA; (S); 13/143; Am Leg Boys St; Varsity Clb; Yrbk Stf; Rep Stu Cncl; JV Bsktbl; Var Ftbl; JV Trk; Hon Roll; NHS; All Star Chrch Bsktbl Tm 84; U Lowel.

HILL, TRACIE; Easthampton HS; Easthampton, MA; (Y); 3/130; French Clb; Office Aide; Rep Stu Cncl; Hon Roll; Ntl Merit SF; Smith Coll.

HILLIARD, CATHERINE; Hopedale JR SR HS; Hopedale, MA; (Y); 5/58; Sec Aud/Vis; Yrbk Stf; Bausch & Lomb Sci Awd; High Hon Roll; NHS; Cmnty Wkr; Library Aide; SADD; School Play; Stage Crew; Pres Acdmc Fit Awd 86; Almn Assn Awd 86; Hopedale Polc Assn Awd 86; U Of VT; Vet.

HINCHEY, MANIK T; Boston Latin Schl; Boston, MA; (Y); 2/285; Pres Debate Tm; Model UN; Pres Speech Tm; Chorus; NCTE Awd; NHS; Ntl Merit Schol; Sal; Voice Dem Awd; ST Sci Fair 3rd Pl 83-84; Brown Bk Awd 85; MA Inst Of Tech; Elec Engrng.

HINES, DAVID; Lynn English HS; Lynn, MA; (Y); AFS; Drama Clb; Ski Clb; Chorus; School Musical; Variety Show; Yrbk Stf; Rep Sr Cls; Ftbl; Trk; Suffolk U Boston; Law.

HINES, DOUGLAS; Boston Latin Schl; Boston, MA; (Y); 90/285; Political Wkr; Band; Stage Crew; Rep Frsh Cls; Rep Jr Cls; Var Ftbl; Var Trk; Var Wt Lftg; Drby Mdl For Engl Ortn 86; Nchls Mdl For Mst Imprvd Acad 86; Music Mdl 86; Hamilton Coll; Law.

HINES, THERESA E; Weymouth South HS; South Weymouth, MA; (Y); Hosp Aide; Varsity Clb; Orch; Socr; Trk; High Hon Roll; Hon Roll; NHS; Mst Imprvd Sccr 85.

HINGSTON, JAMES; Christopher Columbus HS; Charlestown, MA; (S); 27/137; Boys Clb Am; Cmnty Wkr; SADD; Varsity Clb; Var JV Bsbl; JV Bsktbl; JV Ftbl; Var Capt Ice Hcky; Hon Roll; NHS; Rookie Of Yr & MVP-JV Basebl 82; Stonehill Coll; Busnss.

HINNERS, DAVID; Barnstable HS; Osterville, MA; (Y); Aud/Vis; NFL; Speech Tm; Hon Roll; Boston U; Aerspc Engr.

HIRSHSON, MELISSA; Newton Cntry Dy Schl Of Sacred Heart; Cambridge, MA; (Y); Drama Clb; Chorus; Madrigals; School Musical; Mgr(s); Camera Clb; Church Yth Grp; Cmnty Wkr; French Clb; Model UN; All-Schl Msc Awd 86; Crtfd Braille Transcrbr 86; Hstry.

HITCHCOCK, LYNN; Palmer HS; Palmer, MA; (Y); Spanish Clb; Sec Band; Sec Concert Band; Sec Jazz Band; Sec Mrchg Band; Sec Symp Band; Yrbk Phtg; Hon Roll; Prfct Atten Awd; Quabbin Vly Music Eductrs Assn; Hnrary Band Membr 85-86; Local Lions Clb Spch Contst Fnlst 86; Elms Coll; Elem Ed.

HITCHCOCK, TIMOTHY S; Brookline HS; Brookline, MA; (Y); Church Yth Grp; Ski Clb; Acpl Chr; Church Choir; Madrigals; Aud/Vis; Red Cross Aide; Science Clb; Band; School Musical; Courage & Persistence Awd 86; Oberlin Coll; Hist.

HO, TAILEE; Medford HS; Medford, MA; (Y); 117/400; JV Crs Cntry; Engl Awd 84; Cert Of Apprctn-Crss Cntry 84; Tufts U; Engrng.

HO, WAI-YING; Boston Technical HS; Boston, MA; (Y); Fshn Merch.

HOANG, KIEU NGAN; Boston Technical HS; North Quincy, MA; (S); 2/205; Library Aide; Pep Clb; Temple Yth Grp; Yrbk Stf; High Hon Roll; Hon Roll; NHS; Prfct Atten Awd; Harvards Awd Outstndng Stu 85; Math Awd 82; Comp Sci.

HOANG, NGUYEN; Boston Technical HS; E Boston, MA; (Y); Boys Clb Am; Library Aide; Pep Clb; Teachers Aide; Nwsp Rptr; Stu Cncl; High Hon Roll; Hon Roll; Outstndng Math Stu 83; Stu Exchng 85.

HOBBS, ED; Ipswich HS; Ipswich, MA; (Y); Quiz Bowl; Yrbk Stf; Bsbl; Bsktbl; Ftbl; Hon Roll; Bus Adm.

HOBBY, SHERI; Leicester HS; Cherry Valley, MA; (Y); French Clb; Pep Clb; SADD; Varsity Clb; Yrbk Stf; Hon Roll; VP Frsh Cls; VP Soph Cls; VP Soph Cls; VP Sr Cls; Vrsty Bsktbl Finls MIAA Awd 85-86; Elem Educ.

HOCKER, KRISTEN; Bedford HS; Bedford, MA; (Y); 3/200; AFS; Bsktbl; Var Mgr(s); Capt Powder Puff Ftbl; Var Capt Socr; High Hon Roll; Hon Roll; NHS; Ntl Merit Ltr; Hall Fame 86; Hanscom AFB Ofcrs Wives Clb Scholar; Georgetown U; Japanese.

HODAPP, JAIME; Fontbonne Acad; Milton, MA; (Y); 91/170; JV Var Fld Hcky; Var Tennis; Nrsng.

HODGDON, KATHRYN; Medway JR SR HS; Medway, MA; (Y); 57/147; Church Yth Grp; Varsity Clb; Yrbk Phtg; Coach Actv; Var Crs Cntry; Var Mgr(s); Powder Puff Ftbl; Score Keeper; Var Sftbl; Var Trk; Tri Vly Lgu All Star Awd Crss Cnty 82-83; Sociolgy.

HODGES, GREG; Whitman-Hanson Regional HS; Whitman, MA; (Y); Boy Scts; Computer Clb; Radio Clb; Hon Roll; Elec Engr.

HODOS, EMILY; Stoneleigh Burnham HS; Greenfield, MA; (Y); DECA; Nwsp Stf; Var Fld Hcky; Var Lcrss; Hon Roll; NHS; Boston Glb Schlstc Art Awds, Gld Key, Ble Rbbn ST Fnlsh 86; Math Awd; Arch.

HOFFER, DAVID P; Brookline HS; Brookline, MA; (Y); Temple Yth Grp; Band; Orch; School Musical; Symp Band; Var L Tennis; Hon Roll; NHS; Ntl Merit SF; Wm H Lncln Mdl, Rnslr Mdl & Hrvrd Prz Bk 85; Book Awd 85; Amer Assoc Of Tchrs Frnch Awd 84 & 85; Hrvrd Coll; Comp Sci.

HOFFMAN, JENNIFER; Presentation Of Mary Acad; Methuen, MA; (Y); 9/43; French Clb; Service Clb; SADD; Chorus; School Musical; School Play; Hon Roll; NHS; Engrng.

HOFFMEISTER, MITCHELL; Franklin HS; Franklin, MA; (Y); 36/221; Boy Scts; DECA; Ski Clb; Variety Show; VP Sr Cls; Var L Socr; Var L Wrstlng; High Hon Roll; Hon Roll; NHS; Exclnce Bus Awd 86; Frances Eddy King Mdl 86; NHS Scholar 86; U MA; Bus Mgmt.

HOGAN, CHRIS; Foxborough HS; Foxboro, MA; (Y); 48/240; Church Yth Grp; JCL; Ski Clb; Varsity Clb; Stu Cncl; JV Var Socr; Var Capt Trk; Boys ST; Poly Sci.

HOGAN, DANIEL J; Weymouth Vocational Tech HS; Weymouth, MA; (Y); 1/90; Am Leg Boys St; Church Yth Grp; Math Tm; VP Sr Cls; Cit Awd; High Hon Roll; NHS; Rotary Awd; Val; Nwsp Ed-Chief; Founded Schl Bible Stdy 84-85; Lbrty U; Yth Pstr.

HOGAN, JENNIFER; Ursuline Acad; Needham, MA; (Y); 16/89; Political Wkr; Service Clb; Pres Sr Cls; Rep Stu Cncl; Var L Sftbl; Hon Roll; Pltcl Sci.

HOGAN III, JOHN J; Arlington HS; Arlington, MA; (Y); 101/390; Church Yth Grp; Cmnty Wkr; SADD.

HOGAN, LORI; Christopher Columbus HS; S Boston, MA; (S); 15/127; Yrbk Stf; High Hon Roll; Hon Roll; Ntl Merit Ltr; Fitchburg ST; Nrsng.

HOGAN, MAUREEN; Westwood HS; Westwood, MA; (Y); 11/218; Am Leg Aux Girls St; Church Yth Grp; Debate Tm; Girl Scts; Key Clb; SADD; Acpl Chr; Chorus; Jazz Band; Mrchg Band; Pre-Med.

HOGARTH, HELEN; Douglas Memorial HS; E Douglas, MA; (Y); 4-H; FHA; Teachers Aide; Bsktbl; Sftbl; Vllybl; God Cntry Awd; Hon Roll; Lion Awd; NV ST Champn Demo; Natl Mth Awd; US Coast Guard; Engrng.

HOHMANN, PRISCILLA; Marian HS; Framingham, MA; (Y); French Clb; Intnl Clb; Yrbk Phtg; Rep Frsh Cls; Rep Soph Cls; Stu Cncl; Mgr Bsktbl; JV Socr; Tennis; Hon Roll; 2nd-Schl Sci Fair 85; Indstrl Awd-Rgnl Sci Fair 85.

HOHOS, ERICA; St Barnards Central Catholic HS; Fitchburg, MA; (S); 16/177; Church Yth Grp; Spanish Clb; Capt Bsktbl; JV Var Trk; NHS; Comm.

HOIKALA, ANDREA; Billerica Memorial HS; Billerica, MA; (Y); French Clb; Ski Clb; Chorus; Yrbk Stf; Badmtn; Powder Puff Ftbl; Trk; Hon Roll; Ntl Merit Ltr; U Of MA; Bio Chmstry.

HOLBROOK, HEATHER; Reding Memorial HS; Reading, MA; (Y); 14/373; Service Clb; Spanish Clb; SADD; Swmmng; High Hon Roll; NHS; Sports Psychology.

HOLDEN, JULIE; Old Rochester Regional HS; Mattapoisett, MA; (Y); Math Tm; Band; Orch; Symp Band; Var L Crs Cntry; Var L Trk; Elks Awd; Hon Roll; NHS; Ntl Merit SF; Altrnt Exch Stdnt Finland Yth Undrstndg 86; Biomed Engrng.

HOLDING, KELLY; Uxbridge HS; Uxbridge, MA; (Y); Varsity Clb; Band; Chorus; Church Choir; Concert Band; Mrchg Band; Fld Hcky; Sftbl; Church Yth Grp; Cmnty Wkr; MVP Awd Sftbl 86; Musc Thtr.

HOLLAND, BRENDA; Dennis-Yarmouth Regional HS; E Dennis, MA; (Y); Am Leg Aux Girls St; Church Yth Grp; Sftbl; Vllybl; Hon Roll; Interact Clb 85-86; Big Brother Big Sister Soc 85-86; Tufts Med Inst; Med.

HOLLAND, DEBBIE; Methuen HS; Methuen, MA; (Y); 70/359; Camp Fr Inc; Dance Clb; Hosp Aide; Intnl Clb; Model UN; Spanish Clb; Yrbk Stf; Hon Roll; Pi Mu Epsilon Awd Delta Chptr 86; Psych.

HOLLAND, DIANE; Walpole SR HS; Walpole, MA; (Y); 33/258; Church Yth Grp; Cmnty Wkr; Hosp Aide; Office Aide; Orch; High Hon Roll; Hon Roll; Jr NHS; NHS.

HOLLAND, MARY; Bishop Connolly HS; Tiverton, RI; (Y); 3/170; Math Tm; Yrbk Rptr; Yrbk Stf; Sr Cls; Crs Cntry; Trk; French Hon Soc; High Hon Roll; NHS; Dr Omer Boivin French Schlrshp 86; U Of Notre Dame; Pre-Med.

HOLLAND, MARY; Our Ladys Newton Catholic HS; Waltham, MA; (Y); Model UN; Yrbk Phtg; Var Bsktbl; Var Sftbl; Var Vllybl; Hon Roll; NEDT Awd.

HOLLORAN, PATTI A; Winchester HS; Winchester, MA; (Y); 32/280; Church Yth Grp; French Clb; Band; Concert Band; Mrchg Band; Nwsp Stf; High Hon Roll; Hon Roll; Horsebck Riding Awd 83; Coll Holy Cross; Bus.

HOLMAN, KYVA; Reading Memorial HS; Boston, MA; (Y); Nwsp Rptr; Lit Mag; METCO Prfct Attndc & Schlstc Imprvmnt 85-86; Upward Bound Schlstc Achvt; Jrnlsm.

HOLMES, AMY; Wilmington HS; Wilmington, MA; (Y); Intnl Clb; JA; SADD; Band; Chorus; Gov Hon Prg Awd; Hon Roll; Child Psych.

HOLMES, CHRISTOPHER; Newburyport HS; Newburyport, MA; (S); 20/192; Hosp Aide; Pres JCL; Science Clb; Band; Concert Band; Jazz Band; JV Crs Cntry; Var JV Trk; Hon Roll; NHS; Pre-Med.

HOLMES, JENNIFER LOUISE; Dennis-Yarmouth R HS; Dennis, MA; (Y); 58/327; Am Leg Aux Girls St; Church Yth Grp; Model UN; Ski Clb; Drill Tm; Yrbk Stf; Var Crs Cntry; Var Trk; Var JV Twrlr; Hon Roll; Grfn Pblshng Co Schlrshp For Essay 86; Emmanuel Coll Acdmc Schlrshp 86; Emmanuel Coll; Pltcl Sci.

HOLMES, KERRI; Joseph Case HS; Swansea, MA; (Y); 7/220; French Clb; SADD; Var L Cheerleading; Var L Fld Hcky; Var Capt Tennis; French Hon Soc; High Hon Roll; Hon Roll; NHS; Ntl Merit Ltr; Intl Frgn Lng Awd 85; Boston Coll; Nrsng.

HOLMES, KIMBERLY; Brockton Christian Regional HS; Brockton, MA; (Y); Drama Clb; Cheerleading; Sftbl; Hon Roll; Bus Admin.

HOLMES, KIRSTEN ERICA; Holy Name C C HS; Auburn, MA; (Y); 1/253; Am Leg Aux Girls St; Dance Clb; Mgr Drama Clb; School Musical; School Play; High Hon Roll; NHS; Val; Yrbk Rptr; Jr NHS; Hrvrd Bk Prz 85; Sns Itly Amer Schlrshp, Amer Lgn Axlry Schlrshp; Georgetown U; Bus Mgt.

HOLMES, KRISTEN; Norton HS; Norton, MA; (S); 8/150; Pep Clb; Ski Clb; Varsity Clb; Chorus; School Play; Var L Cheerleading; Im Gym; Var Capt Tennis; Hon Roll; NHS; Comms.

HOLMES, LAURIE; Barnstable HS; Hyannis, MA; (Y); Church Yth Grp; Civic Clb; Rep Stu Cncl; NHS; Lit Mag; Trs Frsh Cls; Var JV Fld Hcky; Var Powder Puff Ftbl; Var Trk; Bio Math.

HOLOHAN, SHEILA; Northmiddlesex Regional HS; Townsend, MA; (Y); SADD; Hon Roll; JV Var Mgr(s); Var Powder Puff Ftbl; JV Var Score Keeper; Child Psych.

HOLT, CAROLYN; Wachusett Regional HS; Holden, MA; (Y); Cmnty Wkr; Office Aide; Hon Roll.

HOLT, DEREK; North Quincy HS; Quincy, MA; (Y); Pres Frsh Cls; Pres Soph Cls; Stu Cncl; Var Golf; JV Hon Roll; New England CYO Golf Champ 84; ST Champ Insurance Yth Classic 85; Boston Globe All Schltc Golf 86; Bus.

HOLT, KELLY; Melrose HS; Melrose, MA; (S); 4/380; Art Clb; Sec French Clb; Yrbk Stf; Var Capt Cheerleading; High Hon Roll; Hon Roll; NHS; Intl Concours Frnch Awd 10th Pl 84; Brown U Bk Awd Achvt Engl 86; Acad Awd Vrsty Chrldg 85 & 86; Engl.

HOLWAY III, LOWELL H; Natick HS; S Natick, MA; (Y); 30/414; CAP; Trk; Dartmouth Coll.

HOMAN, MARK D; Longmeadow HS; Longmeadow, MA; (Y); 37/286; Stu Cncl; JV Var Bsbl; Var Ftbl; High Hon Roll; NHS; Jewish Wmns Cncl 86; Jets Inc Cert Of Outstndng Perf 86; Cornell U; Mech Engr.

HOMER JR, MICHAEL R; Brockton HS; Brockton, MA; (Y); 220/1100; Church Yth Grp; Cmnty Wkr; Drama Clb; Political Wkr; School Musical; School Play; Stage Crew; Tchncl Theatre.

HOOBEN, ERIC; West Springfield SR HS; W Springfield, MA; (Y); Drama Clb; Jazz Band; JV Bsktbl; Var Socr; Var Tennis; Hon Roll; Frgn Reltns.

HOOPER, PETER; South Hadley HS; South Hadley, MA; (Y); 35/125; Am Leg Boys St; Art Clb; Bsbl; Ftbl; Socr; Swmmng; Wrstlng; U MA; Aerospace.

HOOVER, ANDREA; E Longmeadow HS; E Longmeadow, MA; (Y); #1 In Class; Intnl Clb; Latin Clb; Service Clb; Chorus; Nwsp Rptr; Off Frsh Cls; Off Soph Cls; Sec Jr Cls; Off Sr Cls; Ntl Merit Ltr; Brown Bk Awd 86; Rensselaer Mdl 86; Ltn Awd 86; Brown U.

HORAN, CATHIE; Reading Memorial HS; Reading, MA; (Y); 63/327; Hosp Aide; Band; Chorus; Concert Band; Jazz Band; Mrchg Band; School Musical; Rep Frsh Cls; Rep Soph Cls; Rep Jr Cls; Bank Schlrshp 85-86; Rdng Choral Soc Schlrshp 86; Emmanuel Coll; Music Thrpy.

HORAN, KIMBERLY; Greater Lawrence Tech; Andover, MA; (Y); Yrbk Stf; High Hon Roll; Hon Roll.

HORGAN, BETH; Arlington HS; Arlington, MA; (Y); 50/370; Sec Church Yth Grp; Girl Scts; Hosp Aide; Band; Concert Band; Symp Band; Yrbk Stf; Var JV Trk; God Cntry Awd; High Hon Roll; John L Asinari Mem Scholar 86; Francis E Thompson Scholar 86; AZ ST U; Nrsng.

HORKAN, MICHELLE; Malden HS; Malden, MA; (Y); 53/500; Key Clb; Office Aide; SADD; Variety Show; Rep Frsh Cls; Rep Soph Cls; Rep Jr Cls; Rep Sr Cls; JV Var Fld Hcky; Hon Roll.

HORN, RACHEL; Notre Dame Acad; Plymouth, MA; (Y); 7/109; Church Yth Grp; Political Wkr; Acpl Chr; Madrigals; School Musical; Im Bsktbl; Var Sftbl; High Hon Roll; Ntl Merit Ltr; Hnrbl Ment Schl Sci Fair 85; Aweds Exc Eng,Sci 84-86; Georgetown U; Intl Rel.

HORN, STEVEN; Taconic HS; Lenox, MA; (Y); 11/289; Science Clb; SADD; Temple Yth Grp; Nwsp Bus Mgr; Yrbk Stf; Tennis; Hon Roll; NHS; U Of MA Chncllrs Schlrshp Awd 86; Pre-Med.

HOSKER, MICHAEL; Newburyport HS; Newburyport, MA; (Y); 30/185; Am Leg Boys St; Chorus; School Musical; Yrbk Stf; Hon Roll; Science.

HOSLEY, CHERYL; Hoosac Valley HS; Cheshire, MA; (Y); 10/149; Ski Clb; SADD; School Play; Yrbk Stf; Rep Frsh Cls; Rep Soph Cls; Sec Stu Cncl; High Hon Roll; Hon Roll; NHS.

HOSTETTER, BRECK; Marblehead HS; Marblehead, MA; (Y); 40/260; Pres Intnl Clb; SADD; Band; Concert Band; Hon Roll; Commrcl Desgn.

HOTTENROTT, DANIELLE; Southeastern Regional Vocation HS; Norton, MA; (S); 1/315; DECA; Yrbk Stf; VP Sr Cls; High Hon Roll; Chrstn A Hrtr Mem Schlrshp 86; SE Reg Shp Achvt Awd 84-86; Dstrbtv Educ Clbs Amer Dst & ST Achvt Awd; Mktg.

HOULE, DENISE M; Chicopee Comprehensive HS; Chicopee, MA; (Y); 31/306; German Clb; Library Aide; Chorus; Church Choir; Yrbk Stf; Sec Frsh Cls; Sec Soph Cls; Var Swmmng; NHS; MA ST Gutr Chmpn 85; Acdmc All Amer, All Nw Englnd Music Fstvl 86; U Tampa; Music.

HOULE, KAREN; Chicopee Comprehensive HS; Chicopee, MA; (Y); 42/255; Dance Clb; Spanish Clb; Yrbk Stf; Powder Puff Ftbl; Var Capt Socr; Var JV Sftbl; Var Swmmng; Jr NHS; Guidence Dept Aide 83-84&84-85; MVP Awd 84-85; Advrt Sng Comm Yrbk 85-86.

HOULE, LAURIE; Bartlett HS; Webster, MA; (Y); Girl Scts; Spanish Clb; Church Choir; Cheerleading; High Hon Roll; Hon Roll.

HOULE, TINA M; Cathedral HS; Chicopee, MA; (Y); Pres Camera Clb; Library Aide; Color Guard; Nwsp Phtg; Nwsp Stf; Yrbk Phtg; Yrbk Stf; Twrlr; Hon Roll; 4-H.

HOUSE, BRYAN E; Longmeadow HS; Longmeadow, MA; (Y); 38/280; Am Leg Boys St; Key Clb; Stage Crew; JV Bsbl; JV Socr; Im Vllybl; High Hon Roll; Hon Roll; Bus.

HOVEY, CHERYL; Franklin HS; Franklin, MA; (Y); Cmnty Wkr; Exploring; French Clb; Office Aide; OEA; Teachers Aide; Yrbk Phtg; Yrbk Stf; Hon Roll; Alt OEA Natl Comp 83 & 86; Chapter I Aide-Child Dvlpmnt 86; Prom Princess 86; Early Childhood Educ.

HOWARD, INA; Lynn English HS; Lynn, MA; (Y); 87/356; French Clb; JA; Office Aide; Spanish Clb; Varsity Clb; Chorus; Off Frsh Cls; Rep Soph Cls; Rep Jr Cls; VP Sr Cls; Schlrshp Lynn Yth Fndtn 86 & Brotherhdd Of Lynn 86; Boston Coll; Poltcl Sci.

HOWARD, LAURIE; Hampshire Regional HS; Southampton, MA; (Y); 4-H; JA; Drill Tm; 4-H Awd; U Of MA; Equine.

HOWARD IV, THOMAS J; Cathedral HS; W Springfield, MA; (Y); Church Yth Grp; Cmnty Wkr; SADD; Stu Cncl; Capt Var Socr; Engrng.

HOWARTH, JENNIFER; Nipmus Regional HS; Upton, MA; (Y); 6/78; Art Clb; SADD; School Play; Yrbk Stf; Sec Jr Cls; Sec Sr Cls; Bausch & Lomb Sci Awd; High Hon Roll; NHS; VFW Awd; Ltn Awd 86; Johnna Gould Bradley Memrl Scshp 86; Yendon/Upton Tchrs Assoc 86; SE MA U; Commrcl Edctn.

HOWE, REGINA M; Wareham HS; W Wareham, MA; (Y); 6/150; Nwsp Rptr; Nwsp Stf; Yrbk Phtg; High Hon Roll; NHS; Pres Schlr; Acdmc Exclnc Awd 86; Schlstc Achvmnt For Ecnmcs & Colll Prep Engl 86; Cape Cod CC; Real Est.

HOWES, KAROL; Triton Regional HS; Salisbury, MA; (Y); Service Clb; Stu Cncl; Mgr(s); CC Awd; Hon Roll; NHS; Finance.

HOWLAND, KAREN; Wachusett Regional HS; Holden, MA; (Y); 4-H; Science Clb; Lit Mag; JV Bsktbl; 4-H Awd; Prfct Atten Awd; 3rd Tm Natl Hortcltr Cont 85; Hnrbl Mntn Sci Fair 85; Pre-Med.

HOWLEY, KARA; Waltham HS; Waltham, MA; (Y); 107/525; French Clb; JA; Chorus; Capt Cheerleading; Trk; Med Asst.

HOYT, BONNIE; Dennis-Yarmouth HS; Dennis, MA; (Y); Church Yth Grp; Cmnty Wkr; Service Clb; Ski Clb; School Play; Stage Crew; Var Cheerleading; Var Sftbl; Var Vllybl; Hon Roll; Child Psych.

HROSZOWY, PATRICIA; Blkstne-Millvle Reg JR SR HS; Blackstone, MA; (Y); Church Yth Grp; Concert Band; Jazz Band; Nwsp Sprt Ed; Off Soph Cls; Stat Bsktbl; Var Sftbl; High Hon Roll; Hon Roll.

HRYZAN, MICHELE; Marian Hill Central Catholic HS; N Grosvenordale, CT; (Y); Drama Clb; Girl Scts; Chorus; School Play; Stage Crew; Yrbk Stf; Var Sftbl; Trvl.

HSU, MICHAEL; Natick HS; Natick, MA; (Y); VP Art Clb; Radio Clb; SADD; Stu Cncl; Socr; Trk; Hon Roll; Natl Art Honor Society 82-86; Francis W Cronan Art Award 86; N Adams ST; Communications.

HUANG, CHRISTINE L; Belmont HS; Belmont, MA; (Y); 38/281; Orch; Trk; High Hon Roll; Hon Roll; NHS; Physcs Awd Outstndng Prfrmnce 85; Boston U; Med.

HUANG, KELLY; Dennis-Yarmouth Regional HS; Yarmouth Port, MA; (Y); 2/330; Am Leg Boys St; Var L Ftbl; Var Trk; High Hon Roll; Hon Roll; Jr NHS; NHS; Sal; Cape Cod Times & Hughs Nwspr Ftbl All Star Team 86; Yale Bk Awd 86; U Of MA Chncllrs Awd 86; Chem Engrng.

HUBBARD, MICHELLE; Hudson HS; Hudson, MA; (Y); 13/141; Math Tm; Pep Clb; Yrbk Stf; Elks Awd; Trs NHS; Hdsn Bys Clb Inc Schlrshp 86; Hdsn Rtry Clb Schlrshp 86; Math Leag Awd 9th Pl 83; Bryant Coll; Acctg.

HUBER, CHRISTINE; Georgetown HS; Georgetown, MA; (Y); 10/85; AFS; Drama Clb; Yrbk Stf; JV Bsktbl; JV Var Fld Hcky; Var L Sftbl; Hon Roll; Otstndng Achvt Chmstry; Otstndng Effrt Acad Avrg Englsh; Pres Physcl Ftns Awd; Babson; Bus Mngmnt.

HUBLER, JONATHAN; Stoughton HS; Stoughton, MA; (Y); Rep Stu Cncl; Bsbl; Bsktbl; Swmmng; Tennis; Vllybl; Wt Lftg; High Hon Roll; NHS; 6th Man Awd Bsktbll 86; Bus.

HUDAK, KATIE; Acton Boxborough Regional HS; Ridgefield, CT; (Y); 188/428; SADD; School Musical; Variety Show; Yrbk Stf; JV Capt Fld Hcky; JV Lcrss; JV Mgr(s); Hon Roll; Hnr Rll 83-86; Syracuse U; Bus.

HUDSON, MATT; Boston Latin HS; Boston, MA; (Y); 73/274; Boys Clb Am; Boy Scts; Church Yth Grp; Cmnty Wkr; JV Var Bsktbl; JV Var Ftbl; Var Vllybl; Wt Lftg; High Hon Roll; Hon Roll; Clscl Awd Latin 85; Bus.

HUETTNER, LAURA J; Acton-Boxboro Regional HS; Acton, MA; (Y); 24/380; Church Yth Grp; Sec SADD; Yrbk Stf; Var Lcrss; Im Powder Puff Ftbl; JV Socr; Hon Roll; NHS; Ntl Merit SF; Law.

HUGHES, KEVIN; C Columbus HS; Dorchester, MA; (Y); 2/129; Math Clb; SADD; Bsktbl; Hon Roll; NHS; IL Inst Of Tech; Archt.

HUGHES, KRISTIN; Swampscott HS; Swampscott, MA; (Y); 22/380; Church Yth Grp; Capt FCA; Capt GAA; JA; Letterman Clb; SADD; Varsity Clb; Nwsp Stf; Var Capt Bsktbl; Coach Actv; Hrld Mrtn Schlr Athlt Awd 85; Cchs Awd Vrsty Sprng Trck 86; NE Bay ST Team Rep 86.

HUGHES, MICHAEL D; Plymouth-Carver Regional HS; Plymouth, MA; (Y); Am Leg Boys St; Varsity Clb; Var Bsbl; Coach Actv; Crs Cntry; Var Socr; Var Capt Wrstlng; Sports Psych.

HUGHES, SHARON; Medway HS; Medway, MA; (Y); 5/148; French Clb; Hosp Aide; Yrbk Stf; Hon Roll; NHS; Ntl Merit Ltr; Worcester Polytechnic Inst; Bio.

HULTIN, STEPHEN O; Rockport HS; Rockport, MA; (Y); 9/70; Am Leg Boys St; Math Tm; Trs Soph Cls; Capt Var Bsktbl; Var Socr; Hon Roll; NHS; St Schlr; Michael D Eaton Sprtsmnshp Memrl Awd 85-86; Boston Coll; Bus Finc.

HUME, SHANNON; St Marys Regional HS; Lynn, MA; (Y); 20/89; SADD; Chorus; School Musical; School Play; Yrbk Stf; DAR Awd; Hon Roll; Camp Fr Inc; Hosp Aide; Nwsp Stf; Engl.

HUMLIN, RACHEL; Marblehead HS; Marblehead, MA; (Y); 39/300; French Clb; Sec SADD; School Musical; Nwsp Stf; Ed Yrbk Bus Mgr; Yrbk Stf; Ed Lit Mag; Hon Roll; Mst Imprvd Rprtr Of Hdlt 86; 2nd Pl ST Wd Nwspr Cntst Edtrl Spcshttl 86; Mst Prlfc Wrtr Of Hdlt 86; Anchr Wmn.

HUMPHRIES, EVAN; Agawam HS; Agawam, MA; (Y); Var Bsbl; Var Ftbl; Var Wrstlng; American Intl Coll; Bus.

HUNICKE, ELIZABETH K; Needham HS; Needham, MA; (Y); 109/372; Church Yth Grp; Acpl Chr; Chorus; Madrigals; School Musical; Hon Roll; Ntl Merit SF; Linguistcs.

HUNNEWELL, LAUREN; Foxboro HS; Foxboro, MA; (Y); Yrbk Stf; Trs Frsh Cls; Trs Soph Cls; Trs Jr Cls; Var Cheerleading; Hon Roll; NHS; Homecmng Princess 83; 2nd Prom Princss JR Prm 86; SADD 85-87.

HUNSAKER, LEE; Walnut Hill HS; Roanoke, VA; (Y); Drama Clb; Key Clb; PAVAS; School Musical; School Play; Stage Crew; Variety Show; Yrbk Stf; Rep Stu Cncl; Ntl Merit Ltr; Pres Of Stud Actvties 86-87; Theater.

HUNT, CHRISTOPHER; Westfield HS; Westfield, MA; (Y); Nwsp Stf; Film Mkng.

HUNT, DEBORAH; Holbrook HS; Holbrook, MA; (Y); 24/102; DECA; Office Aide; OEA; Yrbk Stf; Capt Cheerleading; Hon Roll; Top Dog Scholar 86; Newbury Coll; Htl/Rest Mngmnt.

HUNT, JENNIFER; Bishop Feehan HS; Pawtucket, RI; (Y); Drama Clb; JCL; Stage Crew; Im Bsktbl; Var Trk; Hon Roll; Chemistry Awd 85; Magna Cum Laude Natl Latin Exam 86; Emmanuel Coll; Lbrl Arts.

HUNT, JOANNE J; Sharon HS; Sharon, MA; (Y); 5/199; Drama Clb; VP Spanish Clb; SADD; Temple Yth Grp; Nwsp Stf; Yrbk Stf; Hon Roll; NHS; Pres Acad Fit Awd 86; Cornell U; Advrtsr.

HUNT, JODIE; Triton Regional HS; Salisbury, MA; (S); 96/192; Church Yth Grp; OEA; Yrbk Stf; Elks Awd; Hon Roll; MA Ofc Educ Assn ST Pres 85-86; MA Outstndg Svc Awd 86; Katharine Gibbs Schl; Lgl Sec.

HUNT, KIM; Cohasset JR SR HS; Cohasset, MA; (Y); 18/104; AFS; Nwsp Stf; Yrbk Stf; Hon Roll.

HUNT, ROBERT; Central Catholic HS; Tewksbury, MA; (Y); Cmnty Wkr; JA; Math Clb; Ski Clb; Stage Crew; Yrbk Stf; Im Bsktbl; Im Bowling; JV Ftbl; Im Ice Hcky; Cmmnctns.

HUNT, STEVEN; Ipswich HS; Ipswich, MA; (Y); 5/120; Am Leg Boys St; Math Tm; Science Clb; Socr; Trk; Bausch & Lomb Sci Awd; High Hon Roll; NHS; Rensselaer Polytech Inst; Engrg.

HUNTER, ELIZABETH; Marblehead HS; Marbleahead, MA; (Y); 13/250; High Hon Roll; Hon Roll; Jr NHS; NHS; Ntl Merit Ltr; Rep Frsh Cls; Rep Soph Cls; JV Fld Hcky; JV Swmmng; MA Advncd Stds Prg 86; Lbrl Arts.

HUNTLEY JR, CHARLES EDWARD; Melrose HS; Melrose, MA; (Y); 100/400; Boy Scts; Church Yth Grp; German Clb; Ski Clb; SADD; Band; Trk; Hon Roll; German Amer Prtnshp Prgm Exchng Stu Prgm 85-86; MA Clg; Dentistry.

HURD, STACEY; Holbrook JR-SR HS; Holbrook, MA; (Y); 4/104; Church Yth Grp; SADD; School Musical; Yrbk Bus Mgr; Pres Sec Stu Cncl; Capt Socr; Trk; DAR Awd; NHS; Ntl Merit Ltr; William M Ryan Mem Schlrshp 86; Clssmts Today Neighbors Tomorrow 86; Century II Ldrs ST Fin 86; Wheaton Coll; Econ.

HURLEY, BRIAN C; Doherty Memorial HS; Worcester, MA; (Y); 8/308; Boy Scts; Church Yth Grp; Stage Crew; Variety Show; Yrbk Bus Mgr; Var L Golf; Var L Trk; High Hon Roll; Trs NHS; Spanish NHS; 3 Acadmc Ltrs 82-85; Worcester Wmns Clb Schlrshp 86; Clark U; Bio.

HURLEY, JOHN; Shepherd Hill Reg HS; Dudley, MA; (Y); Law.

HURLEY, MARILYN; North Cambridge Catholic HS; Cambridge, MA; (Y); Office Aide; Hon Roll; Acad Awd In Accntng & Svc Awd/Offce Asstnce 86; Bentley Coll; Accntnt.

HURLEY, MICHELLE; Archbishop Williams HS; Braintree, MA; (Y); Camera Clb; Key Clb; SADD; Chorus; School Play; Yrbk Stf; High Hon Roll; Hon Roll; NEDT Awd; Fire Fighters Local 718 82; Castleton ST; Communication.

HURLEY, REBECCA; Walnut Hill Schl; Center Harbor, NH; (Y); Dance Clb; Drama Clb; Chorus; Madrigals; School Musical; Variety Show; Gym; Swmmng; High Hon Roll; NHS.

HURLEY, THOMAS M; Coyle & Cassidy HS; South Easton, MA; (Y); Cmnty Wkr; Pres Latin Clb; Co-Capt Ski Clb; Stu Cncl; Tennis; Northeastern U; Engrng.

HURWITZ, JOANNE; Natick HS; Natick, MA; (Y); 48/400; Am Leg Aux Girls St; Cmnty Wkr; Spanish Clb; VP SADD; Rep Stu Cncl; Var L Bsktbl; Var L Socr; JV Sftbl; JV L Trk; Hon Roll; Soc Sci.

HUSSEY, STEPHEN; Braintree HS; Braintree, MA; (Y); Cmnty Wkr; High Hon Roll; Ntl Merit Ltr; Maxmum Hnrs All A's 85-86; MA Coll; Poltcl Sci.

HUTCHINS, DEIRDRE; Littleton HS; Littleton, MA; (Y); 24/84; Church Yth Grp; Hosp Aide; Math Tm; Stage Crew; Yrbk Bus Mgr; Yrbk Stf; Var Socr; NHS; Ntl & Intl Fgure Sktng 84-86; Mdls; Slvr Mdlst Estrn Presn Chmpnshps 85; Wheaton Coll; Physcl Thrpst.

HUTCHINSON, CHERIE; Dracut SR HS; Dracut, MA; (Y); Latin Clb; Varsity Clb; Pres Frsh Cls; Pres Soph Cls; Pres Jr Cls; Pres Sr Cls; Var L Fld Hcky; JV Sftbl; High Hon Roll; Hon Roll; Prncpl Aide 83-86; Jnr Prom Co-Ordntr 85; Fitchburg; Elem Educ.

HUTCHINSON, JENNIFER; Westford Acad; Westford, MA; (Y); 29/227; AFS; Art Clb; Church Yth Grp; French Clb; Pep Clb; SADD; Stat Bsbl; Capt Var Cheerleading; Trk; High Hon Roll; Boston Globe Show Art Awd; Acad All-Am Awd; U NH.

HUTNAK, STEPHANIE; Douglas Memorial HS; Douglas, MA; (Y); 2/38; Quiz Bowl; Mrchg Band; Capt Sftbl; Cit Awd; High Hon Roll; NHS; Pres Schlr; Sal; St Schlr; Ntl Ldrshp & Serv Awd 84-85; Framingham ST Coll.

HUYNH, HOANG; South Boston HS; Dorchester, MA; (S); 3/150; Library Aide; Socr; Wt Lftg; Hon Roll; Mech Engr.

HUYNH, NHUT; South Boston HS; Dorchester, MA; (S); Band; Mrchg Band; Socr; Hon Roll; NHS; Wrk Awd; Cert For Excllnc In Art; Bus Mgr.

HUYNH, PHILIP; Boston Technical HS; Boston, MA; (Y); Aud/Vis; French Clb; Library Aide; Office Aide; SADD; Yrbk Stf; Rep Frsh Cls; Rep Soph Cls; Im Bsktbl; Im Bsktbl; BPS Math Comptn Trig Hnrs 85-86; Natl Hon Soc Of Sec Schls 86; Tufts U; Elec Engr.

HUYNH, TRI; S Boston HS; Dorchester, MA; (S); 2/155; Cmnty Wkr; Intnl Clb; Nwsp Rptr; Nwsp Stf; Badmtn; Bsktbl; Socr; Vllybl; Hon Roll; NHS; Cert Wrld Of Wrk 85; Prfct Atten 85; Elec Engrng.

HWANG, CHRISTINE S; Phillips Acad; Carthage, MO; (Y); Pres Church Yth Grp; JV Capt Bsktbl; JV Var Tennis; High Hon Roll; Band; Concert Band; School Play; Rep Frsh Cls; Jr NHS; Russian Lang Essay Cls Hnr 85; Russn Lang.

HWANG, JANG-WOOK; Cambridge Rindge & Latin HS; Cambridge, MA; (S); Key Clb; Math Tm; Lit Mag; Vllybl; Sci Fctn Essay Awd 84; Mech Engrng.

HYATT, MATTHEW D; Oliver Ames HS; South Easton, MA; (Y); 9/240; Am Leg Boys St; Pres Church Yth Grp; Pres Latin Clb; Lit Mag; VP Jr Cls; Rep Stu Cncl; Socr; Tennis; NHS; Pres Schlr; MA Technel Drwng Exam-1st Pl 86; Cornell U; Arch.

HYLTON JR, DONALD C; Hopkins Acad; Hadley, MA; (Y); Cmnty Wkr; Spanish Clb; Yrbk Phtg; Yrbk Stf; Jr Cls; Bsbl; Socr; Wrstlng; High Hon Roll; Hon Roll.

HYMANSON, SHELLY; Marblehead HS; Marblehead, MA; (Y); SADD; Temple Yth Grp; Yrbk Phtg; Yrbk Stf; Powder Puff Ftbl; Var Tennis.

HYNES, KELLY; Georgetown JR SR HS; Georgetown, MA; (Y); 13/88; AFS; Drama Clb; Hon Roll; NHS; Suffolk U; Intl Ecnmcs.

HYPPOLITE, JOANNE; Boston Latin Schl; Boston, MA; (Y); Pres French Clb; Acpl Chr; Chorus; Variety Show; Nwsp Rptr; Yrbk Stf; Var L Trk; Hon Roll; Church Yth Grp; Drama Clb; Cls Awd Top 10 84; Mock Trial Awd Cty Fnlst 86; Freedom Hse Awd Outstndng Minorty 86; Writing.

IACOPUCCI, WILLIAM J; Medford HS; Medford, MA; (Y); 50/425; Am Leg Boys St; Math Clb; Math Tm; Varsity Clb; Ftbl; Var Lcrss; Var Trk; Im Vllybl; Hon Roll; Bys ST-BNTLY Coll 85; Fnkng Pgm-H S 85-86; Math Awd 84; Salem ST Coll; CPA.

IACOVELLI, LISA; Abington HS; Abington, MA; (Y); 14/171; VP French Clb; Yrbk Stf; JV Fld Hcky; Var Tennis; High Hon Roll; Hon Roll; NHS; Pres Schlr; Sons Of Itly Schlrshp 86; U Of NH; Bus Admin.

IANNACO, JULIANE; Woburn SR HS; Woburn, MA; (Y); 119/453; Girl Scts; Hosp Aide; Var Sftbl; Hon Roll; NHS; Stu Govmt Day Dir Of Conservation & Enviroment 85; U Of Lowell; Accounting.

IANNALFO, MARINA; Presentation Of Mary Acad; Methuen, MA; (S); Math Clb; Spanish Clb; Nwsp Stf; Yrbk Stf; JV Var Bsktbl; Var Tennis; High Hon Roll; Hon Roll; NHS; Prfct Atten Awd; Cert Of Ntl Eductnl Devlpmntl Tsts 83; Psych.

IBBOTSON, SHEILA; Granby HS; Chicopee, MA; (Y); Acctng.

IBRAHEEM, SULE; Methuen HS; Methuen, MA; (Y); Var Crs Cntry; Var Tennis; Var Trk; MA Inst Of Tech; Elec Engr.

IDZAL, THOMAS P; Wellesley HS; Wellesley, MA; (Y); 97/300; Am Leg Boys St; Varsity Clb; Yrbk Stf; VP Jr Cls; Pres Sr Cls; Stat Bsbl; L Capt Gym; JV Var Socr; Var Trk; Kiwanis Awd.

IELLAMO, PAUL; Cathedral HS; Springfield, MA; (Y); Church Yth Grp; JA; SADD; Bsbl; Var Capt Ftbl; Im Wt Lftg.

IEVINS, LYDIA H; Walnut Hill School Of Performg Arts; Binghamton, NY; (Y); 2/39; Girl Scts; Mathletes; Church Choir; Concert Band; Orch; High Hon Roll; NHS; Ntl Merit SF; Sal; Scholar String Quartet 85-86; Mth.

IMBARO, GREGORY; Dedham HS; Dedham, MA; (S); 4/270; Drama Clb; Spanish Clb; SADD; School Play; Stu Cncl; High Hon Roll; Hon Roll; NHS; Bst Sci Stu 84, Mth 85; Engr.

IMBRESCIA, PHILIP; Everett HS; Everett, MA; (Y); 26/250; Letterman Clb; Yrbk Stf; VP Frsh Cls; VP Soph Cls; Stu Cncl; JV Bsbl; Var Ice Hcky; Var Tennis; Hon Roll; Lowell U; Elec Engr.

IMBRIANO, GREG; Lynn Classical HS; Lynn, MA; (Y); 15/176; Exploring; Science Clb; SADD; Stage Crew; Var Golf; Capt Tennis; Hon Roll; Prfct Atten Awd; Taggert Meml Awd Sprtsmnshp 83; Meml Awd W Lynn Am Littl Leag 86; U Of Lowell; Indtl Engrg.

INDECK, ALEXANDER M; Wakefield HS; Wakefield, MA; (Y); 21/350; Temple Yth Grp; Coach Actv; Socr; Trk; Wrstlng; Hon Roll; Jr NHS; Worcester Polytechnic Inst.

INFANTINO, SANDRA; Dartmouth HS; N Dartmouth, MA; (Y); 40/240; Pres Jr Cls; Stu Cncl; JV Bsktbl; Var Cheerleading; JV Var Fld Hcky; Var Capt Trk; Cit Awd; Pres Schlr; Prvdnce Coll; Accntng.

INGALLS, KAREN; Norton HS; Norton, MA; (S); 43/148; Hosp Aide; Key Clb; Concert Band; Mgr Mrchg Band; Hon Roll; Burdett Coll; Accntng.

INNELLO, JOSEPH M; Quincy HS; Quincy, MA; (Y); 37/323; Am Leg Boys St; SADD; Var Capt Bsbl; Var Bsktbl; Var Coach Actv; Capt Var Ftbl; Var Capt Trk; Var Wrstlng; High Hon Roll; VFW Awd; Law.

INSLEY, LEE; Dennis-Yarmouth Regional HS; West Yarmouth, MA; (Y); Am Leg Boys St; Trs Key Clb; Teachers Aide; Im Bsbl; Im Bsktbl; High Hon Roll; Hon Roll; Comp Engr.

IOAKIMIDIS, ELIZABETH; West Roxbury HS; West Roxbury, MA; (S); 2/250; Library Aide; Hon Roll; NHS.

IPPOLITO, SCOTT; Newburyport HS; Newburyport, MA; (Y); 39/190; Am Leg Boys St; Sec Model UN; Scholastic Bowl; School Musical; Yrbk Ed-Chief; Lit Mag; Var Socr; JV Tennis; Hon Roll; Firemens Ldrshp Awd 86.

IRELAND, CHRISTOPHER J; Ayer HS; Ft Devens, MA; (Y); 7/175; Am Leg Boys St; Church Yth Grp; Ski Clb; Concert Band; Mrchg Band; Rep Jr Cls; Rep Stu Cncl; Var L Tennis; Hon Roll; Mu Alp Tht; MA Adv Stds Pgm 86; Purdue U; Aerntcl Engrng.

ISHERWOOD, JEFFREY C; Plymouth-Carver Regional HS; Plymouth, MA; (Y); AFS; Church Yth Grp; Drama Clb; Exploring; Mrchg Band; School Musical; Stage Crew; Variety Show; Yrbk Phtg; Yrbk Rptr; Jrnlsm.

IULIANO, STEPHEN; Watertown HS; Watertown, MA; (Y); 6/236; SADD; Band; Concert Band; Drm Mjr(t); Jazz Band; Mrchg Band; Stu Cncl; L Trk; NHS; Ntl Merit Ltr; Sci Awd Acdmc Exclnc 84-86; Cum Laude Scty Trsr 85-86; NE Schlstc Bnd Assoc 85-86; Sci.

IVANOUSKAS, VIDA; St Gregory HS; Boston, MA; (Y); Church Yth Grp; Dance Clb; Hosp Aide; Political Wkr; 1st Pl Amvets National Essay Contest 84.

IVES, DEBORAH; Concord Carlisle HS; Carlisle, MA; (Y); Yrbk Stf; JV Var Sftbl; High Hon Roll; Hon Roll; Math.

IVRY, SARA; Newton North HS; W Newton, MA; (Y); French Clb; Nwsp Rptr; Ed Lit Mag; Hon Roll; Ntl Merit Ltr; Gold Medal Natl Latin Exam 85; Commndtn Natl Latin Exam 86.

JACKMAN, ANDREW; Turners Falls HS; Turners Fls, MA; (Y); Band; Concert Band; Jazz Band; Mrchg Band; JV Bsktbl; Var Ftbl; Var Golf; Hon Roll; Berklee; Music.

JACKMAN, CHRISTOPHER M; Newburyport HS; Newburyport, MA; (Y); 26/196; Am Leg Boys St; Key Clb; Spanish Clb; Hon Roll; NHS; Christian A Herter Mem Scholar 86; Engl Awd 86; Marshall 85-86; Bowdoin Coll; Econ.

JACKSON, CHRISTINA; Copley Square HS; Boston, MA; (Y); 19/120; School Play; Yrbk Phtg; Yrbk Rptr; Yrbk Stf; Rep Sr Cls; Hon Roll; Prfct Atten Awd; Smmns Coll Schlrshp 86; Simmons Coll; Commnctns.

JACKSON, ELLIOT; Copley Square HS; Boston, MA; (Y); French Clb; Intnl Clb; Bsbl; Tufts ULAW.

JACKSON, GEORGE; Haverhill HS; Haverhill, MA; (Y); Key Clb; Band; Concert Band; Jazz Band; Var Bsbl; Im Wt Lftg; High Hon Roll; Hon Roll; Instrmntlst Mag Awd 86; Lieut Governor Of NE Dist Key Clbs 86; VP HS Key Clb 86; Berklee Coll Of Music; Music.

JACKSON, JANET; Fellowship Bible Schl; Lowell, MA; (Y); Church Yth Grp; Drama Clb; Spanish Clb; Chorus; School Play; Sec Soph Cls; Var Sftbl; Var Vllybl; High Hon Roll; Hon Roll; Housewf.

JACKSON, RANDALL J; Greater Lawrence Tech; Lawrence, MA; (Y); Ice Hcky; Cert Of Lawrence Eagle Trbn Crtv Ad 85; Dsgn 86; Prfsnl Hvy Mtl Drmmr.

JACOBSON, SARAH G; Lexington HS; Lexington, MA; (Y); AFS; Cmnty Wkr; SADD; Teachers Aide; School Musical; School Play; Var L Trk; French Hon Soc; Hon Roll; NHS; Hnrbl Mntn All-Amer 4x100 M Rly Tm 85; Dartmouth Coll; Frnch.

JACOBSON, SCOTT; Saint Johns Preparatory Schl; Peabody, MA; (Y); Camera Clb; Red Cross Aide; Science Clb; Ski Clb; VP Temple Yth Grp; Im Bsktbl; Hon Roll; NHS; Chem.

JACQUES, BOB; Cathedral HS; Springfield, MA; (Y); Intnl Clb; Political Wkr; Var Swmmng; Var Tennis; NHS; Pltcl Sci.

JACQUES, ERIC; Gardner HS; Gardner, MA; (Y); 32/168; Am Leg Boys St; Church Yth Grp; Pres VP Debate Tm; Model UN; NFL; Political Wkr; Speech Tm; SADD; School Play; Yrbk Stf; Am Intrnl Coll 2nd Pl Sprkr Awd 86; Ntnl Mdl Untd Ntns Otstndng Spkr Awd 86; Fnlst Exchng Clb Yth Yr; Am Intrntl Coll; Radio.

JACQUES, MARC; David Hale Fanning Trade HS; Worcester, MA; (Y); 16/200; Sec Jr Cls; VP Sr Cls; High Hon Roll; Hon Roll; NHS; Bio.

JAHNCKE, HERB; Bridgewater-Raynham Regional HS; Bridgewater, MA; (Y); 9/300; Am Leg Boys St; Pres Art Clb; Camera Clb; Math Tm; Political Wkr; Sec Science Clb; Ski Clb; Tennis; 4-H Awd; NHS; Rollins Coll.

JAILLET, MICHAEL S; Newton North HS; Newtonville, MA; (Y); Am Leg Boys St; Boy Scts; Church Yth Grp; Red Cross Aide; Chorus; Mrchg Band; School Musical; Variety Show; Nwsp Stf; Elks Awd.

JAILLET, TINA; Gardner HS; Gardner, MA; (Y); 57/191; Dance Clb; Exploring; Library Aide; Office Aide; Yrbk Stf; Rep Stu Cncl; Mt Wchstt Cmnty Coll; Bus Admin.

JAKIMCZYK, JOHN; Arlington Catholic HS; Medford, MA; (Y); 1/139; Frsh Cls; Soph Cls; Pres Jr Cls; Var L Bsbl; Capt Var Bsktbl; Bausch & Lomb Sci Awd; NHS; Ntl Merit Ltr; John Cronin Outstndng Bsktbl Plyr Awd 86; Cathlc Centrl Leag All Str Bsktbl 85-86.

JAMES, ARLENE T; Hingham HS; Hingham, MA; (Y); Church Yth Grp; Cmnty Wkr; GAA; Office Aide; Off Band; Off Concert Band; Off Mrchg Band; Off Symp Band; Yrbk Stf; Rep Frsh Cls; Psych.

JAMES, CHRISTINE; B M C Durfee HS; Fall River, MA; (Y); 10/718; French Clb; Science Clb; Yrbk Stf; High Hon Roll; NHS; Fall River Schls Recog Prog; Natl Sci Merit Awd; Natl Ldrshp Awd.

JAMES, DAVID G; Milton HS; Milton, MA; (Y); 1/270; AFS; Debate Tm; Pres Math Clb; Math Tm; Nwsp Stf; Var L Socr; Var Capt Trk; NHS; Ntl Merit Ltr; Val; MA Assn Schl Supts Cert Acadmc Excllnc 86; Sailng-Crew Bill Rghts 84; Princeton U; Engrng.

JAMES, DEBRA; New Bedford HS; New Bedford, MA; (Y); Church Yth Grp; Dance Clb; Drama Clb; JA; Math Clb; SADD; Chorus; Nwsp Stf; Elks Awd; NAACP Act/Prog 3rd Pl Dance 86; Pikes Peak CC; Lawyer.

JAMES, JOLENA O; Phillips Andover Acad; Los Angeles, CA; (Y); Cmnty Wkr; Red Cross Aide; Science Clb; Service Clb; Spanish Clb; Church Choir; Pres Orch; School Play; Stage Crew; Variety Show; Cluster Pres 85-86; ; Bio.

JAMES, KATHRYN; Silver Lake Regional HS; Kingston, MA; (Y); 92/450; Camp Fr Inc; French Clb; Girl Scts; Library Aide; Color Guard; Drill Tm; Mrchg Band; Stage Crew; Variety Show; Nwsp Rptr; Lakes Yr 86; Best Flag Color Guard 86; Cert Drum Major 86; Notre Dame; Pol Sci.

JAMES, KIMBERLY L; Natick HS; Natick, MA; (Y); 44/422; SADD; Nwsp Rptr; Yrbk Stf; Lit Mag; Off Jr Cls; Off Sr Cls; Stu Cncl; Cheerleading; NHS; Tufts U; Pol Sci.

JAMES, MARIANNE; N Middlesex Regional HS; Townsend, MA; (Y); SADD; Yrbk Stf; Bsbl; Powder Puff Ftbl; Trk; Hon Roll; NHS; Amer Heart Assc 85-86; Fitchburg ST; Sci.

JAMIESON, JENNIFER; Uxbridge HS; Uxbridge, MA; (Y); 6/81; Co-Capt Math Tm; Band; Concert Band; Mrchg Band; Stu Cncl; Var L Fld Hcky; Hon Roll; NHS; Ntl Merit Ltr; Grand Mrshl-Clss Of 86-86; Math.

JANDA, MARCY; Clinton HS; Clinton, MA; (Y); Spanish Clb; School Play; Nwsp Stf; Yrbk Stf; Rep Jr Cls; Stu Cncl; Hon Roll; JV Bsktbl; Var Cheerleading; JV Var Sftbl; Socl Wrkr.

JANIK, CHRISTOPHER; Blackstone Valley Reg Voc Tech HS; Uxbridge, MA; (Y); Ski Clb; SADD; Hon Roll; Lowell U; Mech Engrng.

JANSEN, ANNALISE; Mansfield HS; Mansfield, MA; (Y); 14/184; French Clb; Key Clb; Math Clb; Model UN; JV Var Fld Hcky; Var Capt Tennis; Trk; Hon Roll; NHS; Bay St Games Fld Hcky Tm-Bronze 86; Mech Engrng.

JANSEN, LISA KAREN; Silver Lake HS; Bryantville, MA; (Y); Pres Church Yth Grp; French Clb; Office Aide; Nwsp Stf; Yrbk Ed-Chief; Hon Roll; Pre-Med.

JARVIS, JANINE; Masconomet Regional HS; Boxford, MA; (Y); 2/239; Co-Capt Math Tm; Var Cheerleading; Var Vllybl; NHS; Ntl Merit Ltr; St Schlr; Office Aide; Science Clb; Color Guard; Powder Puff Ftbl; Rodman Schlr U VA 86; 2nd Hghst Hnrs Grad 86; Miss MA Teen USA Pag 85; 2nd Rnnr Up Bst Costume; U VA; Engrng.

JARVIS, KIMBERLY; Burncoat SR HS; Worcester, MA; (Y); Church Yth Grp; Intnl Clb; School Play; Stu Cncl; Cheerleading; Var Sftbl; Trinity Luthrn Pastrs Awd Partcptn Chrch Actvts 86; Nrsng.

JARZOBSKI, CHRISTINE ANN; Holy Name C C HS; Worcester, MA; (Y); 3/250; Church Yth Grp; VP JA; Chorus; Sftbl; Trk; High Hon Roll; NHS; Bishop Bernard J Flanagan Schrlshp 86; Norton Schlrshp Awd 85; Sci Achvt Awd 86; Worc Poly Inst; Bio.

JASPERSON, AMY; Wachusett Regional HS; Holden, MA; (Y); 13/435; Church Yth Grp; Sec Trs Model UN; School Play; Stu Cncl; JV Var Fld Hcky; Gym; Hon Roll; NHS.

JEAN, CHRIS; Marshfield HS; Marshfield, MA; (Y); 95/380; Key Clb; SADD; High Hon Roll; Hon Roll; Ec Stockbroker.

JEAN, ELIZABETH; BMC Durfee HS; Fall River, MA; (Y); 29/670; Capt GAA; Varsity Clb; Flag Corp; Variety Show; Yrbk Stf; Capt Var Fld Hcky; Trk; Twrlr; Hon Roll; Jr NHS; Mrn Bio.

JEAN, JENNIFER; Jamaica Plain HS; Dorchester, MA; (Y); Boys Clb Am; Church Yth Grp; Dance Clb; Drama Clb; Church Choir; School Play; Hon Roll; Exec Secty.

JEAN-MARY, MARIE ROSE; North Cambridge Catholic HS; Cambridge, MA; (Y); 11/90; Hosp Aide; High Hon Roll; Hon Roll; NHS; Prfct Atten Awd; French Awd 83-84; Eng Awd 84; U MA Boston; Surg Nrsng.

JEDRASZEK, PAULA; Beverly HS; Beverly, MA; (Y); 126/373; Trs Frsh Cls; VP Soph Cls; Pres Jr Cls; JV Cheerleading; Sftbl; Hon Roll; Hnr Roll 84 & 85; Hnr Sci Fair 84; Salem ST Coll; Bus.

JEKANOWSKI, JACLYNN; Hopkins Acad; Hadley, MA; (S); 1/45; Band; Sec Frsh Cls; Sec Soph Cls; Sec Jr Cls; Rep Stu Cncl; Var Cheerleading; JV Sftbl; High Hon Roll; Hon Roll.

JEMIOLO, KATHY; Agawam HS; Agawam, MA; (Y); Chorus; Var Cheerleading; Var Tennis; Hon Roll; U Of Ma Amherst; Ed.

JENKINS, ELIZABETH; Westford Acad; Westford, MA; (Y); 45/227; AFS; Exploring; French Clb; Model UN; SADD; Concert Band; Drm & Bgl; Stat Crs Cntry; Stat Fld Hcky; Var Swmmng; Framnghm Esy Cntst Hon Mntn 85; VFW Pst Schlrshp 86; Trusts Awd 86; Fairfield U; Bus Adm.

JENNINGS, PAUL; Bristol Plymouth Tech HS; Taunton, MA; (Y); VICA; Lit Mag; Church Yth Grp; Nwsp Rptr; Nwsp Stf; Tennis; Hon Roll; Eqstrn Shw Rdng 85-86; Engrng.

JENSEN, STACEY; South Lancaster Acad; Hudson, MA; (S); 3/15; Church Yth Grp; Trs Ski Clb; Chorus; Rep Soph Cls; Off Jr Cls; Pres Stu Cncl; Im Bsktbl; NHS; Atlantic Union Coll Schlrshp 86; Sthrn Coll Schlrshp 86; Southern Coll; Accntng.

JESERSKI, SHERI; Southwick HS; Southwick, MA; (Y); 37/140; French Clb; Library Aide; Pep Clb; Variety Show; Yrbk Stf; Mgr(s); Score Keeper; Hon Roll; Elms Coll; Bus.

JESSIMAN, PETER C; Reading Memorial HS; Rlading, MA; (Y); Band; Ice Hcky; Law.

JESUDAS, RACHEL; Lincoln Sudbury HS; Auburn, MA; (Y); Church Yth Grp; Key Clb; Red Cross Aide; Chorus; Church Choir; School Musical; School Play; Variety Show; Frsh Cls; Soph Cls; SAA Stu Against Apartheid 86; In India 84; In S Am Suriname 85; Physician.

JETTE, STEVE; Holy Name CC HS; Millbury, MA; (Y); 99/300; Church Yth Grp; Ski Clb; Var Capt Bsbl; JV Bsktbl; Hon Roll; Centrl MA Conf All Star 86.

JHAVERI, MONA M; Apponequet Reg HS; Lakeville, MA; (Y); 2/211; Pres French Clb; Nwsp Rptr; Yrbk Bus Mgr; Trs Sr Cls; Stu Cncl; Golf; Pres NHS; Ntl Merit Ltr; Young Writers Conf 86; MA Adv Studies Pgm 86; Bio.

JILIAN, ZOVIG; Watertown HS; Watertown, MA; (Y); 29/250; Dance Clb; Girl Scts; School Play; Trk; High Hon Roll; Hon Roll; NHS; Armenian Clb Treas 86; Tri Hi Y Clb 86; Hay Guin Awd 84; MA Coll; Phrmcst.

JILLETT, MAUREEN; Medford HS; Medford, MA; (Y); Cmnty Wkr; Ski Clb; SADD; Yrbk Rptr; Off Jr Cls; Rep Sr Cls; High Hon Roll; Hon Roll; NHS; Church Yth Grp; Achvt & Natl Olymiad Awd Engl 84-86; Home Ec Awd Explrng Early Chldhd 86.

JOASSAINTE, MAGALIE; Fontbonne Acad; Mattapon, MA; (Y); Church Yth Grp; Drama Clb; Intnl Clb; Church Choir; Achvmnt Geom Alg II 85-86; Outstndg Prgrss Piano 85; Outstndg Tm Wrk & Prgrss Piano Ensmbl 85; Intl Rltns.

JOCHIM, CAROLYN; Agawam HS; Feeding Hills, MA; (Y); GAA; Chorus; Capt Var Bsktbl; JV Capt Socr; JV Var Sftbl; Hon Roll.

JOHNSON, ALISA; Natick HS; Mattapan, MA; (Y); Hosp Aide; Spanish Clb; Stu Cncl; Var Trk; JV Vllybl; Hon Roll; Mecto Span 85; Mecto Eng 85; Trk Ltr 84; Peds.

JOHNSON, BETH; Acton-Boxboro Regional HS; Acton, MA; (Y); 188/410; Var L Cheerleading; Var Capt Gym; Var L Mgr(s); Im Powder Puff Ftbl; Hon Roll; Homerm Rep Stu Cncl 85; Prom Ct 86; Bentley; Bus Mgmt.

JOHNSON, BRENDA; South High Community Schl; Worcester, MA; (Y); 5/250; Sec Jr Cls; Sec Sr Cls; Var Capt Bsktbl; Var Capt Socr; Var Capt Sftbl; DAR Awd; Sec NHS; Church Yth Grp; Elks Awd; High Hon Roll; Outstndng Bus Stu 86; US Army Rsrv Ntl Schlr & Athlt Awd Michael J Kustigian Mem Awd; Nichols 4 Yr Bus Coll; Acctg.

JOHNSON, BRIAN; Shepherd Hill Regional HS; Dudley, MA; (Y); Boy Scts; Band; Jazz Band; Mrchg Band; Off Stu Cncl; Golf; Capt Socr; Hon Roll; Biolgcl Sci.

JOHNSON, CAROLINE; Arlington Catholic HS; Arlington, MA; (Y); Church Yth Grp; Drama Clb; School Play; Nwsp Stf; Rep Jr Cls; JV Bsktbl; Var L Sftbl; Arlington Pop Wnnr Assoc Chrldr Coach 85-86; Bio.

JOHNSON, CHRISTOPHER E; Norwood HS; Norwood, MA; (Y); Am Leg Boys St; SADD; Yrbk Stf; Pres Frsh Cls; Pres Soph Cls; Pres Jr Cls; Pres Sr Cls; Ftbl; Elks Awd; Pres Schlr; Stu Of Mnth 86; Stu Cncl; Bus.

JOHNSON, COURTNEY; Burncoat SR HS; Worcester, MA; (Y); 10/242; GAA; Math Tm; Sec Stu Cncl; Var L Bsktbl; JV Capt Fld Hcky; Var Socr; Elks Awd; Hon Roll; Kiwanis Awd; VP NHS; Phys Educ Ldrs Clb Schlrshp 86; U Of MA; Lawyer.

JOHNSON, DAVID; Hampshire Regional HS; Southampton, MA; (Y); 18/135; Boy Scts; SADD; Var Crs Cntry; Var Score Keeper; Var Swmmng; Hon Roll; NHS; New England YMCA Swmmng & Dvng Champ 86; Boy ST Games 86.

JOHNSON, JAMES V; Greater Lowell Regionl Voca HS; Lowell, MA; (Y); Varsity Clb; Var Bsktbl; Var Ftbl; Var Trk.

JOHNSON, JAMIE; Boston Technical HS; Roxbury, MA; (Y); Drama Clb; Library Aide; Office Aide; Thesps; Nwsp Stf; Rep Stu Cncl; Hon Roll.

JOHNSON, JEANNE; West Springfield HS; W Springfield, MA; (Y); French Clb; Hosp Aide; Library Aide; Spanish Clb; French Hon Soc; High Hon Roll; Hon Roll; NHS; Spanish NHS; Daisy Chain 86; Med.

JOHNSON, KATHY; Milton HS; Milton, MA; (Y); 6/250; Church Yth Grp; French Clb; Letterman Clb; SADD; Varsity Clb; Yrbk Sprt Ed; Var L Cheerleading; Var L Gym; Var L Trk; Hon Roll; Odd Flws Untd Ntns Plgrmg For Yth 85; Intl Bus.

JOHNSON, KRISTIN; Westwood HS; Westwood, MA; (Y); 19/210; Church Yth Grp; SADD; JV Var Socr; JV Sftbl; Var Hon Roll; NHS.

JOHNSON, LAURA J; Leominster HS; Leominster, MA; (Y); 21/350; School Musical; School Play; Yrbk Rptr; High Hon Roll; NHS; Best Actress Awd 85-86; Merit Schlrshp Bradford Coll 86; Bradford Coll; Prfrmng Arts.

JOHNSON, LISA; West Springfield SR HS; W Springfield, MA; (Y); Camera Clb; Church Yth Grp; Drama Clb; Intnl Clb; Church Choir; Nwsp Stf; French Hon Soc; Hon Roll; Library Aide; Hnrbl Mntn Phtgrphy Schl Nwspapr Cntst 86; 1st Plc Phtgrphy Jr Div Camera Clb 85; Englsh.

JOHNSON, MARC; Cathedral HS; Southampton, MA; (Y); 104/600; Boy Scts; Chess Clb; Cmnty Wkr; Latin Clb; Stage Crew; Rep Stu Cncl; Hon Roll; Outstndng Schl Svc 86; Cathedral Story; Phrmcst.

JOHNSON, MATTHEW; Austin Prep; Billerica, MA; (Y); 27/124; Boys Clb Am; French Clb; SADD; Lit Mag; Im Bsktbl; Var Crs Cntry; Im Sftbl; Var Trk; High Hon Roll; Hon Roll.

JOHNSON, MATTHEW D; Bromfield Schl; Harvard, MA; (Y); 3/86; Church Yth Grp; Computer Clb; Drama Clb; Latin Clb; Model UN; Spanish Clb; School Musical; School Play; Nwsp Stf; Ed Yrbk Ed-Chief; Amer Comp Sci Leag Tp Scor Awds 85; PTA Shrt Fctn Awds 84 & 85; MA HS Drma Fstvl Actng Awd 85; Engrng.

JOHNSON, MAUREEN FRANCES; Girls Catholic HS; Melrose, MA; (Y); Church Yth Grp; Dance Clb; Teachers Aide; School Play; Variety Show; Yrbk Stf; Rep Stu Cncl; Capt VP Cheerleading; Var Coach Actv; Frshmn Yr 83; Capt Vrsty Chrldrs 85-86; Salem ST Coll MA; Bus Ed.

JOHNSON, MICHAEL; B M C Durfee HS; Fall River, MA; (Y); Computer Clb; Band; Mrchg Band; Hon Roll; NHS; Outstndg Sci Stu 84; Elec Engnrng.

JOHNSON, MICHELLE RENEE; Auburn SR HS; Auburn, MA; (Y); 2/160; Acpl Chr; Socr; High Hon Roll; Sec NHS; Sal; Am Leg Aux Girls St; Church Yth Grp; JA; Chorus; NAJE Mst Valuable Musician Awd 84; Outstndng Jazz Voclst 86; Co-Composer Cls Song 86; Georgetown U; French.

JOHNSON, NICOLE; Stoughton HS; Stoughton, MA; (Y); 74/345; Church Yth Grp; Drill Tm; Nwsp Rptr; Yrbk Stf; Powder Puff Ftbl; Sftbl; Vllybl; Outstndg Wtnss For Chrst 85; Rprtr For Day 85; Outstndg Teen Jck & Jll Clb 86; Boston U; Cmmnctns.

JOHNSON, PETER; Old Rochester Regional HS; Marion, MA; (Y); 9/149; Ski Clb; Socr; Trk; Hon Roll; Jr NHS; Pres Acdmc Ftns Awd, MA Citn Acdmc Excllcne 86; Providence Coll; Pltcl Sci.

JOHNSON, STEPHANIE BECKY; Silver Lake Regional HS; Plympton, MA; (Y); Am Leg Aux Girls St; Church Yth Grp; SADD; Band; Concert Band; Mgr(s); Trk; Hon Roll; Lion Awd; NHS; Northeastrn U; Bus Admn.

JOHNSON, STEVE; Leicester HS; Rochdale, MA; (S); #3 In Class; Latin Clb; Math Tm; Nwsp Sprt Ed; Stu Cncl; Var Bsbl; Var Bsktbl; NHS.

JOHNSON, SUZANNE; Lawrence HS; Lawrence, MA; (Y); 2/300; Church Yth Grp; SADD; School Play; Cheerleading; Sftbl; Vllybl; NHS; Sal; Exchange Clb Stu Of Yr 86; Worcester Polytechnic; Engrng.

JOHNSON, TIMOTHY A; Burlington HS; Acton, MA; (Y); 59/324; Church Yth Grp; Yrbk Phtg; Yrbk Stf; Var L Swmmng; NHS; Middlesex All Star Swim Tm 84, 85&86lowel Sun All Str Swm Tm Hnbl Mntn 84, 85&86; Trinity Coll Hartford CT; Econ.

JOHNSTON, LESLIE; Arlington HS; Arlington, MA; (Y); Drama Clb; Band; Chorus; Jazz Band; Madrigals; Mrchg Band; Orch; School Musical; School Play; Stage Crew; Boston U; Libl Arts.

JOINSON, TRACY; Gmc Durfee HS Of Fall River; Fall River, MA; (Y); Sec JA; Office Aide; Spanish Clb; Yrbk Stf; U Of MA; Visul Art.

JONAH, PAMELA; Quincy HS; Quincy, MA; (Y); 6/285; Girl Scts; Office Aide; Yrbk Stf; Powder Puff Ftbl; High Hon Roll; NHS; Outstndng Gen Sci Awd 83-84; Hghst Avg Bio Awd 84-85; Made Distnctn 83-86; Jrnlsm.

JONCAS, DAVID W; Bishop Connolly HS; Fall River, MA; (Y); Am Leg Boys St; Church Yth Grp; Civic Clb; Cmnty Wkr; JA; Political Wkr; Quiz Bowl; Ski Clb; Stage Crew; Nwsp Stf; (AJAC 86; Milton Acad Ldrshp Conf 85; U RI; Oceangrphy.

JONCAS, JAMES M; Grafton Memorial HS; Grafton, MA; (Y); Am Leg Boys St; Church Yth Grp; Pres Frsh Cls; Rep Soph Cls; Capt Ftbl; Capt Trk; Vllybl; FL ST; Bus Mgmt.

JONES, ALLAN P; Austin Preparatory Schl; Burlington, MA; (Y); 22/124; Camera Clb; Intnl Clb; Latin Clb; Ski Clb; Hon Roll; Apprntcshp 8 Wks Air Force Geophyscs Lab 86; Aerontcl Engnr.

JONES, ANDREA; Smith Acad; W Hatfield, MA; (S); Key Clb; Chorus; Rep Stu Cncl; Score Keeper; High Hon Roll; Hon Roll; Pro-Merito; Engrng.

JONES, BRADLEY; Plymouth-Carver HS; Plymouth, MA; (Y); 26/541; Boy Scts; Model UN; Lit Mag; JV Socr; JV Wrstlng; Hon Roll; NHS; Engrng.

JONES, DARIN R; Wachusett Regional HS; Rutland, MA; (Y); 51/446; Am Leg Boys St; Drama Clb; Model UN; Madrigals; School Musical; Var Crs Cntry; NHS; Ntl Merit Ltr; Church Yth Grp; 4-H; Lions Clb Dist Spch Comptn Wnnr 86; Cntrl MA Music Fest 86; Wachusett Hnrs Choir & Hnrs Band 85-86; Perfrmng Arts.

JONES, DEBORAH; Whitman-Hanson Regional HS; Hanson, MA; (Y); 10/325; AFS; Teachers Aide; Chorus; School Musical; Nwsp Rptr; Stu Cncl; Swmmng; High Hon Roll; Kiwanis Awd; NHS; Abington Hstrcl Soc 85; Cls 1934 Hstry Prize 86; Natl Hstry Day Hstrcl Paper Fin 84 & 85; American U; Intl Rltns.

JONES, DENISE; Jamaica Plain HS; Roxbury, MA; (Y); Band; Chorus; Rep Jr Cls; Rep Stu Cncl; JV Var Sftbl; Var Vllybl; Exec Secy.

JONES JR, E WESLEY; Middlesex Schl; Concord, MA; (Y); Art Clb; Ski Clb; Yrbk Phtg; Yrbk Stf; Im Bsktbl; JV Var Ftbl; JV Lcrss; Im Sftbl; Im Tennis; Im Vllybl; JR & SR Yr Hons; Yale U.

JONES, GRETCHEN; King Philip Regional HS; Wrentham, MA; (Y); 66/213; Var Cheerleading; Var Fld Hcky; Powder Puff Ftbl; Tennis; Hon Roll; SMU; Merch.

JONES, JONATHAN; Pittsfield HS; Pittsfield, MA; (Y); French Clb; Math Clb; Yrbk Stf; High Hon Roll; NHS; AHSME Hnr Rll 86; Comp Sci.

JONES, JOSH; Arlilngton HS; Arlington, MA; (Y); Spanish Clb; Band; Jazz Band; Mrchg Band; Yrbk Stf; Jr Cls; Socr; Hon Roll; NHS; Ntl Merit Ltr.

JONES, KAREN; Malden HS; Malden, MA; (Y); Ski Clb; Hon Roll; Administrative-Wrkd For Vice Prncpl 3 Yrs; Bunker Hill CC; Nuclear Med.

JONES, KAREN A; Burlington HS; Burlington, MA; (Y); 34/321; Nwsp Phtg; Yrbk Phtg; Powder Puff Ftbl; Hon Roll; NHS; Secty Ntl Hon Soc 85-86; Rcvd Thms & Jean Price Schlrshp; North Adams ST Coll; Envrnmntl.

JONES, KIMBERLY; Boston Latin Acad; Boston, MA; (Y); Dance Clb; Drama Clb; MASP Smmr Prog At Milton Acad 86; Comm.

JONES, LAURIE; Bishop Feehan HS; Seekonk, MA; (Y); SADD; Stu Cncl; Var L Cheerleading; Var JV Trk; Perf Attndnc 84-86; Spec Ed.

JONES, MARK K; Peabody Vets HS; Peabody, MA; (Y); 44/466; Am Leg Boys St; Math Tm; Pres Jr Cls; Pres Sr Cls; Rep Stu Cncl; Var Ftbl; Var Lcrss; JV Wrstlng; Hon Roll; Pres-Nrth Estrn MA Assn Of Stu Cncl 86-87; NROTC Schlrshp Fnlsts 87; Yale/Norwich U; Pltcl Sci.

JONES, MEREDITH; Wakefield HS; Wakefield, MA; (Y); Church Yth Grp; French Clb; Girl Scts; JV Bsktbl; Var Diving; Var Socr; JV Sftbl; Var Swmmng; Var Capt Trk; MVP Bsktbll, Unsung Hero Sftbll & Mst Potential Sccr 83-84; Capt Awd, MVP Sccr & MVP Trck 84-85; Engrng.

JONES, MICHAEL; Westford Acad; Westford, MA; (Y); Art Clb; Church Yth Grp; Ski Clb; Capt L Bsbl; L Bsktbl; Nrowich U; Militry.

JONES, MICHELLE; Hanover HS; Rockland, MA; (Y); 45/180; Yrbk Stf; Var Capt Cheerleading; High Hon Roll; Hon Roll; Fisher JC; Lgl Sec.

JONES, NICOLE; Reading Memorial HS; Reading, MA; (Y); JV Var Fld Hcky; High Hon Roll; Hon Roll; Bus.

JONES, REGINA; Technical HS; Springfield, MA; (Y); Cmnty Wkr; Girl Scts; JA; ROTC; Color Guard; Drill Tm; VP Soph Cls; Stu Cncl; Bsktbl; Sftbl; AF Ofcr.

JONES, SHARON ALANE; Greater Lowell Regnl Vo Tech Schl Dis; Dunstable, MA; (Y); 4-H; Cheerleading; Future Sec Assoc 84-86; JR Fisher Coll; Bus Mgt.

JONES, SUZANNE; Notre Dame Acad; Milton, MA; (Y); 17/109; Pres Church Yth Grp; Library Aide; Spanish Clb; Nwsp Rptr; Nwsp Sprt Ed; Var L Crs Cntry; Var L Trk; Hon Roll; Patriot Ledger All Schltc Cross Cntry 85; League All Star Cross Cntry 85; Editor Schl Newspaper 85-86; Pre-Law.

JONES JR, WILLIAM F; Boston College HS; Braintree, MA; (Y); 67/273; Boy Scts; Church Yth Grp; Im Bsktbl; Im Ftbl; Hon Roll; NHS; Eagle Scout 85; Babson Coll; Infrmtn Systms.

JORDAN, CAROLYN; Norton HS; Norton, MA; (S); Exploring; French Clb; Varsity Clb; Band; Yrbk Stf; Rep Stu Cncl; Var L Bsktbl; Var Tennis; Voice Dem Awd; Church Yth Grp; MA Stu Govt Day Alt 85; Bio.

JORDAN, JENNIFER; New Bedford HS; New Bedford, MA; (Y); 93/701; Pres SADD; Stage Crew; L Crs Cntry; Var Trk; Hon Roll; Stu Tutor Awd/Latin 86; Med.

JORDAN, MARC; Waltham HS; Boston, MA; (Y); SADD; Bsbl; JV Var Bsktbl; Hon Roll; No Hitter Bsbl Pitch Awd 84; Bsktbl Champ Awd 85; Meteor.

JORDAN, PAMELA R; Boston Latin Schl; Boston, MA; (Y); 93/288; Church Yth Grp; Cmnty Wkr; JA; Key Clb; Spanish Clb; Church Choir; Rep Jr Cls; Rep Stu Cncl; High Hon Roll; Hon Roll; Merit Tuition Schlrshp, Open Gate Awd 86; U MA Amherst; Nrsg.

JORGE, CHRISTINE; New Bedford HS; New Bedford, MA; (Y); 42/549; Drama Clb; Trs Intnl Clb; Key Clb; Library Aide; Stu Cncl; Hon Roll; NHS; Marion Art Ctr Schrlshp 86; Intl Frgn Lang Clb Schrlshp 86; Swain Schl Schrlshp 86; Swain Schl Design; Graphic Desg.

JORGE, LINDA E; Bishop Stang HS; Assonet, MA; (Y); Civic Clb; Cmnty Wkr; Intnl Clb; SADD; Chorus; Yrbk Bus Mgr; Yrbk Stf; High Hon Roll; Hon Roll; NHS; Clark U; Bus.

JORGENSEN, LUKE R; Brockton HS; Brockton, MA; (Y); Am Leg Boys St; Drama Clb; VP Pres Key Clb; Office Aide; Political Wkr; SADD; Nwsp Rptr; Pres Stu Cncl; NCTE Awd; Teachers Aide; Hugh O Brian Intl Youth Leadership ST Rep; 1st In ST Leadership Awd; ST Level Acting Awds.

JOSEPHSON, PATRICIA; Dracut HS; Dracut, MA; (Y); Civic Clb; Chorus; Yrbk Stf; JV Bsktbl; Var Capt Vllybl; Hon Roll; NHS; Rivier Coll; Elem Ed.

JOSHI, SANJIV; The Lawrence Acad; Westford, MA; (Y); Cmnty Wkr; Ski Clb; Rep Jr Cls; Rep Sr Cls; Im Bsbl; Im Bsktbl; Im Ice Hcky; Im Socr; JV Tennis; Hon Roll; Pre Med.

JOSLIN, ROBIN; Fitchburg HS; Fitchburg, MA; (Y); SADD; School Play; Yrbk Stf; High Hon Roll; Hon Roll; Gmtry Prz Exm 86; Nichols Coll; Mrktng.

JOVENICH, BRENDA; Marian HS; Framingham, MA; (Y); Camp Fr Inc; Church Yth Grp; Sec Exploring; Latin Clb; Spanish Clb; SADD; School Musical; Cheerleading; Crs Cntry; Trk; Mst Sprtd Awd 85-86; Psych.

JOVORSKI, JENNIFER; Leicester HS; Leicester, MA; (Y); Math Clb; Math Tm; SADD; Teachers Aide; Bsktbl; Sftbl; High Hon Roll; Hon Roll; Jr NHS; Hist Ntl Hnr Scty 86.

JOY, CHRISTINE; Murdock HS; Winchendon, MA; (Y); 11/110; Model UN; School Play; Trs Frsh Cls; Pres Sr Cls; Cheerleading; High Hon Roll; Hon Roll; NHS; Framingham ST Clg; Psych.

JOY, MEAGHAN; Hopkins Acad; Hadley, MA; (Y); English Clb; French Clb; Girl Scts; Chorus; Color Guard; School Play; Yrbk Stf; VP Soph Cls; VP Jr Cls; VP Sr Cls.

JOYCE, CHRISTOPHER; Braintree HS; Braintree, MA; (Y); 58/413; Ski Clb; SADD; JV Var Bsbl; Var JV Socr; Hon Roll; Brdgwtr ST Coll; Phys Ed.

JOYCE, JOHN; Don Bosco Tech; Dorchester, MA; (Y); 44/176; Chess Clb; Church Yth Grp; Ski Clb; SADD; Rep Stu Cncl; Capt Trk; Hon Roll; Mst Athltc 83 & 84; Mst Vlbl Crs Cntry Rnnr 85; Comp Sci.

JOYCE, MERALEE; Wilbraham & Monson Acad; Springfield, MA; (Y); Cmnty Wkr; Dance Clb; GAA; Pep Clb; Ski Clb; Ice Hcky; Lcrss; Mgr(s); Socr; Trk; Lbrl Arts.

JOYNER, JENNIFER; Hampshire Regional HS; Goshen, MA; (Y); 3/129; High Hon Roll; Pres NHS; Ntl Merit Ltr; Natl Hstry Day Dist 84.

JOYNT III, ERNEST H; Bishop Stang HS; East Wareham, MA; (Y); 9/200; Am Leg Boys St; Boy Scts; Chess Clb; VP Pres JA; Quiz Bowl; Service Clb; High Hon Roll; Hon Roll; NHS; Astrnmy.

JUAN, DARREN; Technical HS; Springfield, MA; (Y); ROTC; Color Guard; Drill Tm; Drm & Bgl; Pilot.

JULIAN, DEEDEE; Northfield Mount Hermon HS; Westport, CT; (Y); Yrbk Phtg; Yrbk Stf; Ice Hcky; Powder Puff Ftbl; High Hon Roll; Hon Roll; Sci.

JULIAN, GIULIANO P; Cambridge Rindge & Latin HS; Cambridge, MA; (Y); Trs Church Yth Grp; High Hon Roll; Hon Roll; Jr NHS; NHS; Natl Achvt Schlrshp-Commended Stdnt 85; MA Pre Engrng Pgm Awd 84; Engrng.

JULIANO, MELISSA; Waltham SR HS; Waltham, MA; (Y); Church Yth Grp; JA; Band; Color Guard; Concert Band; Jazz Band; Mrchg Band; Orch; Most Impvd Band Stu 84-85; Outstndg Band Stu Hon 85-86; Phys Ther.

JULIANO, NICOLE; Melrose HS; Melrose, MA; (Y); Camera Clb; Yrbk Ed-Chief; Off Stu Cncl; Var L Vllybl; High Hon Roll; Hon Roll; NHS; Jr NHS; JV Trk; Pep Clb; Dartmouth Bk Awd 86; Harvard Secndry Schl Prog 86; Law.

JULIEN, HEATHER J; Swampscott HS; Swampscott, MA; (Y); 63/232; Cmnty Wkr; Model UN; SADD; Stu Cncl; Var L Crs Cntry; Powder Puff Ftbl; Capt Var Trk; Cit Awd; Hon Roll; Excel Technel Drwng/Drftng 85-86; Apprectnshp Awd 85; Stu Cncl Schlrshp 86; Worcester Polytech; Mech Engrng.

JULIEN, MARYANNE; Salem HS; Salem, MA; (Y); Chorus; School Play; Hon Roll; Harvard; Crmnl Justc.

JUMP, KERRI-LYNN; Academy Of Notre Dame; Lowell, MA; (Y); 14/52; Hosp Aide; Key Clb; Office Aide; Sec SADD; Chorus; Hon Roll; Prfct Atten Awd; 3rd Pl Hnrs Physcs 86; 1st Pl Comptr Progrmng 85; Finlst Teenager Yr Cont 86; U Lowell; Comp Sci.

JUNAS, ANDREW; Arlington HS; Arlington, MA; (Y); 55/369; Library Aide; Radio Clb; JV Bsbl; Var Capt Crs Cntry; Var Capt Trk; Bill Squires Awd-Bst Dstnc Runner 86; MVP Cross Cntry 85; GBL All Star Crss Cntry, Trck 85-86; Brandeis; Bus.

JURGELEWICZ, STACY L; Middleboro HS; Wareham, MA; (Y); 14/207; Cmnty Wkr; Drama Clb; School Play; Variety Show; Rep Stu Cncl; JV Bsktbl; Socr; Sftbl; Hon Roll; NHS; Greater Middleboros Jr Miss 86; Silver M Scsty Sec; Middleboro Rtry Clb Schlrshp 86-87; Syracuse U; Chem Engr.

KADLEC, KENNETH M; Nashoba Regional HS; Lancaster, MA; (Y); 4/161; Chess Clb; Drama Clb; Library Aide; SADD; School Musical; Stage Crew; Nwsp Rptr; Ed Nwsp Stf; Yrbk Stf; Elks Awd; Intl Law.

KAISER, MICHELLE R; Frontier Regional Schl; Whately, MA; (Y); Church Yth Grp; French Clb; GAA; Library Aide; Office Aide; Church Choir; Capt Cheerleading; Pom Pon; Trk; Hon Roll.

KALAITZIDIS, DENNIS; West Roxbury HS; Roslindale, MA; (S); Aud/Vis; Chess Clb; Socr; Hon Roll; NHS; Prfct Atten Awd.

KALIKOW, JOANNA M; Natich HS; Natick, MA; (Y); 10/440; Cmnty Wkr; French Clb; NFL; Speech Tm; School Musical; School Play; High Hon Roll; NHS; Ntl Merit SF; Natl Lvl Compt-Spch Tm 85; Brown U; Frnch.

KALMAN, HEIDI; Malden HS; Malden, MA; (Y); 101/480; Math Tm; Office Aide; SADD; Variety Show; Var Fld Hcky; JV Sftbl; Timer; Boston Coll; Nrsng.

KALNS, ANDREW; Boston Coll HS; Pembroke, MA; (Y); 32/350; Church Yth Grp; Cmnty Wkr; French Clb; Im Ftbl; High Hon Roll; Hon Roll; NHS; Outstndng Stu Bio I & Undrstndng Faith 83-84; Outstndng Stu Frnch 85-86; Dentistry.

KALOSHIS, EVA; Silver Lake Regional HS; Halifax, MA; (Y); Church Yth Grp; Dance Clb; Latin Clb; Office Aide; Capt Cheerleading; Socr; Trk; NHS; Ntl Merit Ltr; Early Matriculation From HS 85-86; Spotlight Prgm For Gftd & Talented HS Stu 85; U Of New England; Phys Thrpy.

KALSEY, GREGORY; New Bedford HS; New Bedford, MA; (Y); 94/701; Boy Scts; Chess Clb; Computer Clb; Wt Lftg; Hon Roll; Prfct Atten Awd; Yng Clmbs XXVIIII Awd 85; Cvl Engrng.

KAM, PAUL VANG; Burlington HS; Burlington, MA; (Y); 8/321; Am Leg Boys St; Debate Tm; Math Tm; Stat Bsbl; Stat Bsktbl; VP NHS; Acad Excllnce Engl 83-86, US Hstry, Soc Studs 85-86, Hlth, Latin 84; Tufts U; Pre-Med.

KAMINSKI, MIKE; Wachusett Regional HS; Holden, MA; (Y); 101/428; Computer Clb; Exploring; Mathletes; Ski Clb; Im Socr; Hon Roll; Meteorlgy.

KAMINSKI, ROBERT; St Peter-Marian HS; Worcester, MA; (Y); Ec.

KAMINSKY, DANIEL; Methuen HS; Methuen, MA; (Y); Model UN; Band; Concert Band; Jazz Band; Mrchg Band; School Musical; JV Trk; SOAR Awd; MA NE Dist Band; MA All ST Band.

KAMMERER, G SCOTT; King Philip Regional HS; Wrentham, MA; (Y); 7/240; Aud/Vis; Church Yth Grp; Drama Clb; Mathletes; School Play; Stage Crew; High Hon Roll; NHS; Chrstn Brdcstg.

KANAGY, LEIGH ANNE; Medway JR SR HS; Medway, MA; (Y); 10/136; Church Yth Grp; Drama Clb; SADD; Teachers Aide; VP Band; Yrbk Stf; JV Vllybl; High Hon Roll; Hon Roll; NHS; Schlstc Awd 85 Avg Fll Yr 84-86; Exclnc Math 83-84; Denison U; Pltcl Sci.

KANE, CHRISTOPHER; Newton Catholic HS; Brookline, MA; (Y); Debate Tm; Letterman Clb; Office Aide; Political Wkr; ROTC; Varsity Clb; Nwsp Bus Mgr; Nwsp Ed-Chief; Nwsp Rptr; Nwsp Sprt Ed; Law.

KANE, KELLY; Christopher Columbus HS; South Boston, MA; (S); 1/111; Hosp Aide; VP JA; Math Clb; Stu Cncl; High Hon Roll; NHS; Ntl Merit Ltr; NEDT Awd; Proj Summa Emmanuel Coll 84-85; Med.

KANE, SEAN; Marian HS; Natick, MA; (Y); Var Bsbl; Var Bsktbl; Var Ftbl; High Hon Roll; Hon Roll; Ntl Merit SF; NEDT Awd; Boston U; Biomedical Engrng.

KANELLIAS, VASILIKI; West Roxbury HS; Roslindale, MA; (S); Library Aide; Hon Roll; VP NHS; Prfct Atten Awd; Pre Med.

KANN, ROBERTA; Auburn HS; Auburn, MA; (Y); Sec Church Yth Grp; Acpl Chr; Chorus; Capt Drill Tm; Capt Nwsp Ed-Chief; Rep Jr Cls; High Hon Roll; Hon Roll; NHS; Prfct Atten Awd; Socl Wrk.

KANTORSKI, LINDA; Southbridge HS; Southbridge, MA; (Y); 12/185; Sec VP Stu Cncl; JV Var Bsktbl; Var Capt Fld Hcky; Capt Var Sftbl; Hon Roll; NHS; Opt Clb Awd; CCD 83-86; Engr.

KANTROWITZ, TRACY; Natick HS; Natick, MA; (Y); 59/423; Drama Clb; NFL; SADD; Chorus; School Musical; School Play; Nwsp Ed-Chief; Yrbk Stf; High Hon Roll; NHS; Dlvrd Grad Spch 86; Natick Arts Cncl Dance Schlrshp 86; Comp Natl Speech Baltimore 84-86; Syracuse U; Broadcast Jrnlsm.

KAO, SHIN C; Newburyport HS; Newburyport, MA; (Y); 15/200; Math Tm; Model UN; Science Clb; Nwsp Rptr; Nwsp Stf; Yrbk Stf; Ed Lit Mag; Hon Roll; NHS; Ntl Merit Ltr; U Of CA Berkeley.

KAPLAN, RHONDA; Newton South HS; Newton, MA; (Y); Pres Spanish Clb; Sec Temple Yth Grp; Nwsp Stf; Yrbk Stf; Pres Stu Cncl; High Hon Roll; Hon Roll; Bus Delivering Fruits & Vegs 86; Vice Pres Chinese Clb Russian Clb 86.

KAPSALIS, KATHY; Belmont HS; Belmont, MA; (Y); 49/263; Spanish Clb; Hon Roll; Sci Awd 85; Arch.

KARAJOHN, LANA; New Bedford HS; New Bedford, MA; (Y); Office Aide; Im Swmmng; Cert Nrs Aide Cert 85-86; RN.

KARALEKAS, CHRISTOPHER; New Bedford HS; New Bedford, MA; (Y); 22/550; Art Clb; Pres Church Yth Grp; Pres Key Clb; SADD; Yrbk Stf; VP Soph Cls; Rep Jr Cls; Stu Cncl; Crs Cntry; Trk; Centry III Ldrs Awd Schl Wnr 86; Providence Coll; Bio.

KARAM, THOMAS; B M C Durfee HS; Fall River, MA; (Y); 47/665; Boys Clb Am; Varsity Clb; Nwsp Rptr; Nwsp Stf; Bsktbl; Ftbl; Hon Roll; NHS; Ftbl Gridiron Clb Schlrshp Awd 86; Fall Rvr Eductrs Assn Schlrshp Awd 86; Boston U; Fin Mgmt.

KARASOULOS, STACEY; Medford HS; Medford, MA; (Y); Church Yth Grp; Hosp Aide; SADD; Church Choir; Yrbk Stf; Vllybl; Hon Roll; NHS; Prfrmng Arts Piano Plyng 86; Cert For Tchng Sun Schl 86.

KARAVETSOS, MARIA; Haverhill HS; Haverhill, MA; (Y); Aud/Vis; German Clb; SADD; Mgr Band; Mgr Concert Band; Mgr Mrchg Band; School Play; Yrbk Stf; UNH; Anml Sci.

KARAYIANES, DORA M; Haverhill HS; Haverhill, MA; (Y); 104/450; Spanish Clb; Nwsp Ed-Chief; Var Powder Puff Ftbl; High Hon Roll; Hon Roll; NECCO; Bus Mngmnt.

KARKUTT, KAREN; St Bernards C C HS; Fitchburg, MA; (S); 8/154; Camera Clb; Church Yth Grp; Cmnty Wkr; Hosp Aide; Latin Clb; Teachers Aide; Variety Show; Yrbk Stf; Rep Stu Cncl; Im Bsktbl; Ntl Conf Christians & Jews 84; Stonehill Coll; Elem Ed.

KARL, LEIGHA; Dennis-Yarmouth Reg HS; Cummaquid, MA; (Y); 32/316; Art Clb; 4-H; Trs Key Clb; Chorus; Madrigals; School Musical; School Play; 4-H Awd; Hon Roll; Jr NHS; Coon Dog Scholar 85-86; Dennis/Harwich Rotary Clb Scholar 85-86; Gdn Clb Yarmouth 85-86; Early Grad 86; ST U NY Pittsburgh; Biol.

KARRAS, MARLO L; Dennis-Yarmouth Regional HS; W Yarmouth, MA; (Y); 44/309; Art Clb; Intnl Clb; Ski Clb; Band; Concert Band; Jazz Band; Mrchg Band; Orch; Vllybl; Art Awds; Southeastern Acad; Travel Indst.

KARTONO, CHRISTINA LYNN; Wachusett Regional HS; Holden, MA; (Y); 11/400; Dance Clb; Teachers Aide; Concert Band; Symp Band; French Hon Soc; High Hon Roll; NHS; Pres Schlr; Natl Hnrs Cncrt Bnd 86; MA Cntrl Dist Bnd 86; Schlrps Ashland Oil, Holden Wmns Clb, Frohsinn 86; Rutgers U; Frnch.

KASABULA, STEPHEN; St Johns HS; N Grafton, MA; (Y); 3/265; Church Yth Grp; Crs Cntry; Trk; High Hon Roll; NHS; Ntl Merit Ltr; Stu Cncl Awd 85; Brother Carl Awd Excllnc In Spnsh 86; U Of PA; Bio.

KASELIS, JOANNA; Dedham HS; Dedham, MA; (Y); 10/357; Church Yth Grp; Stage Crew; Variety Show; Nwsp Bus Mgr; Nwsp Rptr; High Hon Roll; NHS; Hnrbl Mntn Ntl Essay Cntst 85; Englsh Essay Cntst Awd Achvt Wrtng 84; Excllnc Outstndng Achvt Greek Lg; Jrnlsm.

KASPER, JOHN D; Palmer HS; Palmer, MA; (Y); Am Leg Boys St; Church Yth Grp; Math Clb; Spanish Clb; Band; Concert Band; Jazz Band; Mrchg Band; Pep Band; Symp Band; Pro Merito Honor Scty 85-86; Western Dist Music Awd 85-86; Med.

KASPER, S ANDREW; Waltham HS; Waltham, MA; (Y); 35/580; Am Leg Boys St; Aud/Vis; Church Yth Grp; JA; Pres Sr Cls; Golf; Hon Roll; Jr NHS; Cmnty Wkr; Computer Clb; Supr Court Justice Boys ST Bentley Coll 86; Volunteer St Nicholas Chapl MA Mntl Hlth 82-286; Harvard; Med.

KATES, LINDA J V; Natick HS; Millis, MA; (Y); 7/443; Pres Church Yth Grp; Service Clb; Sec Chorus; Church Choir; School Musical; Swing Chorus; NHS; High Hon Roll; Hon Roll; St Schlr; H S Wmns Clb-Schlrshp 86; Intrntn Ordr Of Rnbw For Grls-Schlrshp 86; Ntl Schl Chrl Awd 86; Syracuse U; Musical Thtre.

KATIN, TANYA; Bishop Fenwick HS; Lynn, MA; (S); Girl Scts; Science Clb; Band; Fld Hcky; Socr; High Hon Roll; Hist Awds 84-85; Chrstn Stds Awd 85; Intl Frgn Lng Awd Spnch 86; Frgn Svc.

KATINAS, DANA JOSEPH; St Johns HS; Millbury, MA; (Y); 40/265; Boy Scts; Church Yth Grp; French Clb; Jazz Band; Bsktbl; High Hon Roll; NHS; Eagle Scout W/Gld Palm 83; Wrcstr Poly Tech; Mech Engrng.

KATSOS, GEORGE E; Arlington HS; Arlington, MA; (Y); Church Yth Grp; Political Wkr; Band; Church Choir; Concert Band; Madrigals; School Musical; Off Frsh Cls; Off Soph Cls; Off Jr Cls; Stdnt Cncl Ofcr 86; Northeastern U; Poltcl Sci.

KATZ, DANIEL; Sharon HS; Sharon, MA; (Y); Am Leg Boys St; Pres Drama Clb; Thesps; Chorus; Madrigals; School Musical; School Play; Nwsp Stf; Ed Lit Mag; NHS; Lohmiller Awd Exclnc Wrtng 86; Phi-Alpha-Theta Top 10 Hstrcl Rsrch Papr 86; All-Str Cst MA Drma Fest; Crtv Wrtng.

KATZ, ROBERT L; New Bedford HS; New Bedford, MA; (Y); 63/550; Band; Chorus; Concert Band; Jazz Band; Mrchg Band; School Musical; Hon Roll; NHS; New Englnd Schlstc Band Assn Chmpns 84-86; U Of MA; Schl Mgmt.

KATZEFF, TAMMY; Beaver County Day HS; Framingham, MA; (Y); Cmnty Wkr; Dance Clb; Spanish Clb; Temple Yth Grp; Band; Concert Band; Mrchg Band; Orch; Variety Show; Hon Roll; Psychol.

KATZOFF, IDA; Stoughton HS; Stoughton, MA; (Y); Dance Clb; Hosp Aide; Temple Yth Grp; Hon Roll; U Of MA; Merch.

KAUFMAN, ADAM; Concord Carlilse HS; Concord, MA; (Y); 7/323; Church Yth Grp; Letterman Clb; Varsity Clb; Var Lcrss; Var Socr; High Hon Roll; Hon Roll; NHS; Ntl Merit Schol; Cert Awd Excllnc Math, Physcs Phy Ed 85- 86; Princton; Intl Finc.

KAUFMAN, MARC; Sharon HS; Sharon, MA; (Y); Am Leg Boys St; Math Tm; Pres Spanish Clb; Rptr Nwsp Rptr; Rptr Yrbk Rptr; Rep Sr Cls; Stu Cncl; High Hon Roll; Pres NHS; JCL; Framingham ST Coll Hstrcl Rsrch Awd 86; Engrng.

KAWACHI, NICOLE; Natick HS; Natick, MA; (Y); 5/399; German Clb; SADD; Orch; High Hon Roll; Hon Roll; Ntl Merit SF.

KAYDEN, AMY; Madison Park HS; Jamaica Plain, MA; (Y); Art Clb; Cmnty Wkr; Dance Clb; Hosp Aide; JA; Rep Frsh Cls; Var Cheerleading; Advncd Plcmnt Vsl Arts Clss 84-85; Merit Awd 85-86; Boston U Coll SVAT 84-85; Arch Dsgn.

KAYE, LUCINDA; Boston Latin Schl; Boston, MA; (Y); Computer Clb; Hon Roll; Ntl Merit SF; Natl Sci Olympd Biol Cert Awd.

KAYSER, RICHARD; Southbridge HS; Southbridge, MA; (Y); Hon Roll; Frnch I Awd 84; Bryant Coll RI; Bus Admin.

KAZANJIAN, JILL; Newton Catholic HS; Waltham, MA; (Y); Church Yth Grp; Hosp Aide; Letterman Clb; Model UN; SADD; Varsity Clb; Yrbk Rptr; Yrbk Stf; Lit Mag; Rep Stu Cncl; Psychtry.

KEALY, SEAN; Cathedral HS; Hampden, MA; (Y); Am Leg Boys St; Political Wkr; Quiz Bowl; School Musical; School Play; Swmmng; Voice Dem Awd; Boy Scts; Chess Clb; Chorus; Eagl Sct 83; Pres Close Up Govt Clb 85; Modl Sent 85; Law.

KEAMY, MATTHEW; Methuen HS; Methuen, MA; (Y); 15/349; Am Leg Boys St; Church Yth Grp; Intnl Clb; Math Tm; School Play; Yrbk Ed-Chief; Trs Frsh Cls; Trs Stu Cncl; Ftbl; NHS; Presdntl Acd Ftnss Awds Prog 85-86; Castl Mem Schlrsp ALAA Schlrshp Awd 86; Ortrcl Essy Cntst 1st 86; Worcester Polytech Inst; Engr.

KEANE, BRIAN P; Sandwich JR SR HS; Sagamore Beach, MA; (Y); 4/171; Model UN; Rep Stu Cncl; Var Lcrss; Var Swmmng; High Hon Roll; NHS; Ntl Merit Ltr; Am Leg Boys St; Math Tm; Ski Clb; Local, Regnl, ST Stu Advsry Cncl 85-87; MA Stu Govt Day Rep 85-86; Outstndng Svc Stu Govt 85-86; Astront.

KEANE, ELIZABETH; Concord-Carlisle HS; Concord, MA; (Y); Church Yth Grp; GAA; Rep Soph Cls; Rep Jr Cls; Var Crs Cntry; JV Socr; Var Tennis; Hon Roll; NHS; 3 Time ST Champ Tennis Team Mem 84-86; New Englnd Girls 18's Tennis Top 10 85-86.

KEANE, MARY FRANCES; Wakefield Memorial HS; Wakefield, MA; (Y); Church Yth Grp; Political Wkr; Science Clb; Crs Cntry; Gym; Trk; Jordan Marsh JR Cncl 86-87; Pre-Med.

KEANE, ROBERT; Hanover HS; Hanover, MA; (Y); Aud/Vis; Church Yth Grp; Spanish Clb; Nwsp Rptr; Nwsp Stf; Yrbk Bus Mgr; Yrbk Stf; Hon Roll; Emerson; Wrtr.

KEANEY, SEAN; North Quincy HS; Milton, MA; (Y); ROTC; Sclstc Awd Ribbon 85; Fit Awd 85; Top Flight Awd 85; U Of MA; Archtctr.

KEANEY, TIMOTHY J; Methuen HS; Methuen, MA; (Y); 9/350; JV Bsktbl; Var Ftbl; Var Trk; High Hon Roll; NHS; Upsilon Alph 86; Bio.

KEARNAN, SALLY; Blackstone-Millville Regional HS; Blackstone, MA; (Y); Cmnty Wkr; Office Aide; Red Cross Aide; SADD; Band; Yrbk Stf; Fld Hcky; Score Keeper; High Hon Roll; Hon Roll; Fash Mdsg.

KEARNEY, JOHN J; Milton HS; Milton, MA; (Y); 5/250; Am Leg Boys St; Pres Math Clb; Nwsp Sprt Ed; Ed Lit Mag; Var Capt Crs Cntry; Capt Var Trk; NHS; Ntl Merit Ltr; Art Clb; Church Yth Grp; Outstndng Soph Awd 85; Brown U Book Awd 86.

KEARNEY, VINCENT; Marian HS; Framingham, MA; (Y); JV Bsbl; High Hon Roll; Spanish NHS; Geom 85; Chem Lab 86.

KEARNS, SHARON; Marlboro HS; Marlboro, MA; (Y); Church Yth Grp; Exploring; Pep Clb; SADD; Varsity Clb; Yrbk Stf; Rep Frsh Cls; Rep Soph Cls; Rep Jr Cls; Var Cheerleading; Fac Awd Outstndng Achvt; Bus.

KEATING, KRISTIN; Cardinal Cushing HS; S Boston, MA; (Y); SADD; School Musical; Yrbk Stf; VP Sr Cls; NHS; Inner Schl Schlrshp; St Anthony Fund 84-85; Northeastern U; Crmnl Just.

KEATING, LYNNE; Reading Memorial HS; Reading, MA; (Y); Pep Clb; SADD; Yrbk Phtg; Yrbk Stf; VP Jr Cls; Sec Sr Cls; Stu Cncl; JV Trk; Hon Roll; Schlstc Awd 86; Communications.

KEATING, MICHELLE; Reading Memorial HS; Reading, MA; (Y); SADD; Yrbk Phtg; Yrbk Stf; Lit Mag; Stu Cncl; JV Var Trk; French Hon Soc; High Hon Roll; NHS; Science Clb; Comm.

KEDDIE, ROBERT; Christopher Columbus HS; Roslindale, MA; (S); 44/127; Boy Scts; CAP; JA; Math Clb; Science Clb; Color Guard; Drill Tm; Yrbk Ed-Chief; Rep Jr Cls; Rep Sr Cls; JA Schlrshp; Embry-Riddle; Pilot.

KEEFE, KRISTEN; Waltham HS; Boston, MA; (Y); French Clb; Schlrshp Skidmore Coll 86; Skidmore; Hist.

KEEGAN, DAVID; Hanover HS; Hanover, MA; (Y); SADD; Rep Jr Cls; Trs Sr Cls; Var L Ftbl; L Golf; JV Ice Hcky; Im Socr; Hon Roll; Jr NHS; NHS; Engrng.

KEEGAN, JAMES; Milton HS; Milton, MA; (Y); Am Leg Boys St; French Clb; Math Clb; Math Tm; SADD; Nwsp Ed-Chief; Nwsp Rptr; Nwsp Sprt Ed; Nwsp Stf; Stu Cncl; Bus.

KEELEY, MATTHEW J; Tabor Acad; Tampa, FL; (Y); 17/141; Debate Tm; Intnl Clb; NFL; Speech Tm; Nwsp Stf; Hon Roll; Ntl Merit SF; Radio Clb; Rowing Vrsty 83-86; Squash JV 85; People To People Stu Ambassador Nrthrn Europe 85; Georgetown U; Intl Rel.

KEENAN, KATHLEEN A; New Bedford HS; New Bedford, MA; (Y); 133/650; SADD; School Play; Stage Crew; Yrbk Stf; Stu Cncl; Hon Roll; Nchls B Ottwy Schlrshp 86; Alumni Schlrshp 86; Framingham ST Coll; Econ.

KEENE, BARBARA; Saugus HS; Saugus, MA; (Y); Church Yth Grp; Civic Clb; Dance Clb; Library Aide; Office Aide; SADD; Swmmng; Hon Roll; Jr NHS; Bentley Coll; Econ.

KEENE, DEBRA; Girls Catholic HS; Malden, MA; (Y); Spanish Clb; Pres Frsh Cls; High Hon Roll; Hon Roll; NEDT Awd; Acctg.

KEENE, REBECCA; Bishop Fenwick HS; Marblehead, MA; (Y); 9/239; Math Clb; School Musical; Var Capt Bsktbl; Var Capt Fld Hcky; CC Awd; High Hon Roll; NHS; St Julie Billiart Awd 86; Salem News Stu Athlt Awd 86; Gld Mdl Team In Field Hockey 85; St Michaels; Engrng.

KEHOE, DEAN; Revere HS; Revere, MA; (Y); 1/344; Drama Clb; Math Tm; Capt Scholastic Bowl; Pres Science Clb; Stage Crew; Elks Awd; NHS; Ntl Merit SF; Pres Schlr; Art Clb; Cmmnwealth Schlr 86; NCSM Math Awd 86; Rensselaer; Aerospc Engrng.

KEIGWIN, TODD; Marlboro HS; Marlborough, MA; (Y); 19/320; Boys Clb Am; Church Yth Grp; Math Tm; SADD; Varsity Clb; JV Bsktbl; Capt Crs Cntry; Var Trk; High Hon Roll; NHS; Bus Mgmt.

KEILTY, CHRISSY; Natick HS; Natick, MA; (Y); 67/400; High Hon Roll; Hon Roll; Early Chldhd Educ.

KEITH, DENISE; East Bridgewater HS; E Bridgewater, MA; (Y); Church Yth Grp; SADD; Hon Roll; Legal Sec.

KELL, ROBERT; St Johns HS; S Grafton, MA; (Y); 41/270; Spanish Clb; NHS; Assumptn Coll Scholar 86-87; Assumption Coll.

KELLEHER, CATHERINE; St Clements HS; Medford, MA; (Y); 1/85; Art Clb; Church Yth Grp; Rep Stu Cncl; Var Cheerleading; Var Capt Vllybl; Hon Roll; Pres NHS; Srvc Schlrshp Invlmnt Schl; Hghst Rnkng Jr Clss Schlrshp; Bus.

KELLEHER, DAVID; Tewksbury Memorial HS; Tewksbury, MA; (Y); 122/330; JV Bsbl; JV Bsktbl; Var JV Crs Cntry; Stat Score Keeper; Var Trk; Hon Roll; Coachs Awd Wntr Trck 85-86; X-Cntry Rookie & Rnnr Of Yr Awds 83-85; Bio.

KELLEHER, JENNIFER; Westford Acad; Westford, MA; (Y); SADD; Yrbk Stf; Var Bsktbl; Var Socr; Hon Roll; Bsktbl, Sccr Capt 86; Cmnctns.

KELLEN, HEIDI; Marshfield HS; Marshfield, MA; (Y); 86/346; Church Yth Grp; Cmnty Wkr; Key Clb; Ski Clb; Band; Chorus; Church Choir; Concert Band; Mrchg Band; Pep Band; MIP Band Awd 82-83; Band & Chorus Lttr 85; 1 & 2nd Pl Art Awds Hnr Mntn 86; FL ST U; Interior Design.

KELLER, FREDERICK; Lenox Memorial HS; Lenox, MA; (Y); Yrbk Stf; Golf; Socr; High Hon Roll; Hon Roll; NHS; Fash Inst Tech; Fash Prodctn.

KELLER, REBECCA; Lawrence Acad; Leominster, MA; (Y); Camera Clb; French Clb; School Musical; School Play; Yrbk Phtg; Rep Stu Cncl; Var L Ice Hcky; Im Swmmng; Hon Roll; Tufts U.

KELLEY, COLLEEN; St Peter-Marion HS; Worcester, MA; (Y); 50/200; Drama Clb; Office Aide; Pres SADD; School Musical; School Play; Rep Frsh Cls; Rep Soph Cls; Rep Jr Cls; Sec Stu Cncl; Var Tennis; Dance Scholar 84; Frnch I, Humanities, Relgion Hnrs 83-84; Religion 2 Hnrs 84-85; Htl Mgmt.

KELLEY, ERIN; Lawrence Acad; Ayer, MA; (Y); Chorus; Ed Yrbk Stf; Bsktbl; Fld Hcky; Ice Hcky; Lcrss; Mgr(s); High Hon Roll; Hon Roll; Art Awd 84.

KELLEY, JENNIFER; Arlington Catholic HS; Arlington, MA; (Y); #5 In Class; Church Yth Grp; French Clb; Stu Cncl; Var Bsktbl; Var Sftbl; Hon Roll; NHS; Prfct Atten Awd; Service Clb; Suffolk U Bk Awd Schl Svc 86; All Star Bsktbl Sftbl 86.

KELLEY, JENNIFER; Nauset Regional HS; Eastham, MA; (Y); Math Tm; High Hon Roll; Hon Roll; NHS; Ntl Merit Ltr; Natrl Sci.

KELLEY, KIMBERLY A; Scituate HS; Scituate, MA; (Y); 42/300; Ski Clb; Nwsp Rptr; Nwsp Stf; Stu Cncl; Var Fld Hcky; Var Tennis; Var Trk; U New Hampshire; Liberal Arts.

KELLEY, LAWRENCE; Milton HS; Milton, MA; (Y); Boy Scts; Chess Clb; Computer Clb; French Clb; Math Clb; Chorus; School Musical; Nwsp Stf; Lit Mag; Capt L Trk; Systms Anlyss.

KELLEY, MAUREEN A; Westwood HS; Westwood, MA; (Y); 74/212; Key Clb; SADD; Yrbk Stf; Stu Cncl; JV Bsktbl; JV Socr; Hon Roll; Bus.

KELLEY, ROBERT; Arlington HS; Arlington, MA; (Y); 100/388; Yrbk Sprt Ed; Yrbk Stf; Rep Frsh Cls; Rep Jr Cls; Rep Sr Cls; Var L Bsbl; Var L Ftbl; Var L Ice Hcky; Wt Lftg; Hon Roll; Bys Ice Hcky Lge Chmpns 85-86.

KELLEY, THERESE; Coyle Cassidy HS; Taunton, MA; (Y); Keywanettes; Spanish Clb; Rep Jr Cls; VP Sr Cls; Var Bsktbl; Var Capt Crs Cntry; Var Capt Trk; Hon Roll; NHS; Spanish NHS; Cross Cnty All Cnfrnc Tm 85; Cross Cnty All Cnfrnc Tm 86; Bryant Coll; Intrntl Mrktng.

KELLEY, WILLIAM; Milford HS; Milford, MA; (Y); 90/320; Am Leg Boys St; Boy Scts; Chess Clb; Church Yth Grp; Ski Clb; SADD; JV Bsbl; JV Bsktbl; Var L Ftbl; Trk; U Of Rhode Island; Engrng.

KELLIHER, JESSICA; Blackstone Valley Reg Vo Tech; Uxbridge, MA; (Y); Red Cross Aide; SADD; Sec Jr Cls; Hon Roll; Prfct Atten Awd; Bus Adm.

KELLN, REBECCA; South Lancaster Acad; Layton, UT; (S); Church Yth Grp; Chorus; Orch; Pres Frsh Cls; Stu Cncl; Bsktbl; Cit Awd; Hon Roll.

KELLS, ASHLEY; New Bedford HS; Acushnet, MA; (Y); 126/701; ROTC; Lyndon ST Coll; Meteorlgy.

KELLY, AMANDA; Andover HS; Andover, MA; (Y); Church Yth Grp; Q&S; SADD; Nwsp Ed-Chief; Rptr Nwsp Rptr; Yrbk Stf; Lit Mag; Stu Cncl; Hon Roll; Ntl Merit SF; Pres Arts Scholar Creatv Wrtng 86; Town Nwsp Publctn 85-86; Salem ST Coll; Creatv Wrtng.

KELLY, BILLY; Boston College HS; Arlington, MA; (Y); Church Yth Grp; Key Clb; Latin Clb; Spanish Clb; SADD; Im Capt Bsktbl; Im Capt Ftbl; JV Ice Hcky; Var Trk; Im Vllybl; Natl Latin Exam Magna Cum Laude 84; Math.

KELLY, ERIN; King Philip Regional HS; Norfolk, MA; (Y); 42/213; Am Leg Aux Girls St; Sec Frsh Cls; Sec Soph Cls; Var L Cheerleading; L Var Gym; JV Sftbl; High Hon Roll; NHS; Unsung Hero Awd Chrldg 86; 4th Pl Gymnstcs Balnc Tm 86; Cmmnctns.

KELLY, HEATHER; Ipswich HS; Ipswich, MA; (Y); Church Yth Grp; Drama Clb; Office Aide; Science Clb; Spanish Clb; SADD; Teachers Aide; Sftbl; High Hon Roll; NHS; Engrng.

KELLY, KERRY; Norwood SR HS; Norwood, MA; (Y); 126/359; Church Yth Grp; Civic Clb; Cmnty Wkr; Computer Clb; 4-H; French Clb; Girl Scts; Hosp Aide; Office Aide; Pep Clb; Anna Maria Coll; Comm.

KELLY, KIM; Old Rochester Regional HS; Mattapoisett, MA; (Y); Church Yth Grp; Rep Soph Cls; Var Fld Hcky; Trk; Hon Roll; Bus Mrktng.

KELLY, LISA; Bishop Feehan HS; Pawtucket, RI; (Y); 71/256; Drill Tm; Nwsp Stf; Tennis; Twrlr; High Hon Roll; St Anselm; Lbrl Arts.

KELLY, MARY; Wakefield Memorial HS; Wakefield, MA; (Y); AFS; JCL; Latin Clb; Yrbk Stf; JV Fld Hcky; Sftbl; Hon Roll; Nrsng.

KELLY, MARY TERESA; Walpole HS; E Walpole, MA; (Y); 42/268; Cmnty Wkr; Library Aide; SADD; Chorus; School Musical; School Play; Stage Crew; Hon Roll; NHS; Prfct Atten Awd; Clsrm Prfmnce Awd Math, Engl, Wrd Proc, US Hstry 85-86; Electrncs.

KELLY, MICHAEL; Boston Latin School; Boston, MA; (Y); 68/297; Aud/Vis; Chess Clb; Debate Tm; Drama Clb; French Clb; Latin Clb; NFL; Ski Clb; Speech Tm; Thesps; Cmmnctns.

KELLY, PAUL; Marian HS; Natick, MA; (Y); 30/180; French Clb; Lit Mag; Crs Cntry; Hon Roll; NEDT Awd; Phi Alpha Theta Hon Mntn Hstrcl Cnfrnc; Awd Sci Fair 84-85; Excllnc Erth Sci; Syracuse U; Engrng.

KELLY, PAULETTE; Boston Latin Acad; Mattapan, MA; (Y); JA; Library Aide; Math Clb; Math Tm; JV Bsktbl; Trk; Var Vllybl; Hon Roll; Hly Crs Coll Bk Awds 86; Drtmth; Bus.

KELLY, SHARRON; Billerica Memorial HS; Billerica, MA; (Y); 19/450; French Clb; Yrbk Stf; Crs Cntry; Var Capt Trk; High Hon Roll; NHS; Athlete Schrlshp 86; Bus Reltd Schlrshp 86; SF Good Citzn Awd 86; Bentley Coll; Acctng.

KELLY, SUSAN; Stoneham HS; Stoneham, MA; (Y); Church Yth Grp; Dance Clb; Debate Tm; Drama Clb; French Clb; Model UN; Science Clb; Ski Clb; School Musical; School Play; Model UN Awd 86; Tufts U; Engrng.

KELLY, TRACY; Bishop Feehan HS; Pawtucket, RI; (Y); 37/245; Drama Clb; Chorus; Church Choir; School Musical; School Play; Stage Crew; High Hon Roll; Hon Roll; NHS; St Schlr; Assumption Coll; Pltcl Sci.

KEMP, ARNOLD J; Boston Latin Schl; Boston, MA; (Y); Trs Drama Clb; JA; School Play; Stage Crew; Ed Lit Mag; NHS; Martin Luther King Jr Awd 86; Arthur Gattling Awd 86; Boston Schl Committee Art Scholar 86; Tufts U; Fine Arts.

KEMP, KIMBERLY; Lunenburg JR SR HS; Lunenburg, MA; (Y); 26/123; Aud/Vis; Intnl Clb; SADD; Nwsp Rptr; Yrbk Stf; Sftbl; Trk; Hon Roll; Intership Pgm; Mt Wachusett CC; Comm Adm.

KEMPTON, KIMBERLY; Blackstone Vly Rgnl Voc Tech HS; Upton, MA; (Y); 1/200; Library Aide; Teachers Aide; Nwsp Ed-Chief; Sftbl; DAR Awd; High Hon Roll; Prfct Atten Awd; Pres Schlr; Val; Northeastrn U Carl S Ell Prs Schlrshp 86-91; Natl Merit Corp Spec Schlrshp 86-90; Northeastern U; Lwyr.

KENCH, HEATHER; St Marys Regional HS; Lynn, MA; (Y); 6/89; SADD; Chorus; Church Choir; Stage Crew; Variety Show; Yrbk Stf; Capt Bsktbl; Capt Socr; VP NHS; Hugh O Brien 85; Bus.

KENN, ROBERT; E Bridgewater HS; E Bridgewater, MA; (Y); Boy Scts; Church Yth Grp; Drama Clb; Key Clb; Spanish Clb; SADD; Pres Soph Cls; VP Jr Cls; VP Sr Cls; Var Bsbl; MA Div 4 South Shore League Team 85; Phy Educ.

KENNARD, DONNA M; Phillips Acad; St Albans, NY; (Y); Cmnty Wkr; Trk; Key Clb; Yrbk Phtg; Yrbk Stf; Cmrcl Airln Pilt.

KENNEALY, RICHARD; Natick HS; Natick, MA; (Y); 26/414; Var L Ice Hcky; High Hon Roll; Hon Roll; NHS; Prfct Atten Awd; Dgtl Equip Corp Schlrshp 86; Lt Wllm J Cavngh Mem Schlrshp 86; Rensselaer Plytchnc Inst; Engr.

KENNEDY, ELIZABETH; Medford HS; Medford, MA; (Y); 69/434; Jr NHS; Acctg.

KENNEDY, MAUREEN; Fontbonne Acad; Quincy, MA; (Y); 11/134; Dance Clb; Debate Tm; Drama Clb; Intnl Clb; Variety Show; Yrbk Stf; Hon Roll; NHS; Hon Mntn Fontbonne Acad Sci Fair 84; Northeastern U; Biol.

KENNEDY, MICHELLE; Melrose HS; Melrose, MA; (Y); 17/390; Pep Clb; Political Wkr; Spanish Clb; SADD; Yrbk Stf; Var L Trk; JV Var Vllybl; High Hon Roll; Hon Roll; NHS.

KENNEDY, MIKE; Tahanto Regional HS; Boylston, MA; (Y); Church Yth Grp; Variety Show; JV Var Bsbl; JV Var Bsktbl; Var Crs Cntry; Var Socr; Var Tennis; Hon Roll; Wentworth Inst Tech; Bldg Tech.

KENNESON, KATHERINE; Acton-Boxborough Regional HS; Acton, MA; (Y); Cmnty Wkr; Office Aide; Teachers Aide; School Musical; Variety Show; Yrbk Stf; Var L Fld Hcky; Var L Lcrss; Im Powder Puff Ftbl; Hon Roll.

KENNEY, MARY KATE; Weymouth North HS; Weymouth, MA; (Y); Dance Clb; Math Tm; Lit Mag; High Hon Roll; NHS; Ntl Merit Ltr; Pres Schlr; French Clb; Yrbk Stf; Hon Roll; MA Advanced Studies Pgm 85; Hon Soc Pres; Gen Mills Schlrshp; Marist Coll; Bus.

KENNISTON, BETH; Attleboro HS; Attleboro, MA; (Y); Varsity Clb; Yrbk Bus Mgr; Yrbk Ed-Chief; Capt Fld Hcky; Sftbl; Hon Roll; Latn Hnr Soc; Physcl Thrpy.

KENNY, ERIN MARIE; Thayer Acad; Milton, MA; (Y); 4/106; Chorus; School Musical; School Play; Ed Nwsp Stf; Ed Yrbk Stf; High Hon Roll; Spanish NHS; Church Yth Grp; PAVAS; Q&S; Cum Laude Soc 86; Schls Spnsh Level I,II,III,IV 82-86; Ntl Spnsh Ex 4th 85-86; Middlebury Coll; Spnsh.

KENT, ANNE MARIE; Woodward HS; Scituate, MA; (Y); 1/18; Aud/Vis; Camera Clb; Cmnty Wkr; Drama Clb; Library Aide; School Play; Nwsp Ed-Chief; Nwsp Phtg; Yrbk Phtg; Yrbk Rptr; Quincy Histrcl Soc Awd 86; Commnwlth Schlrshp 86; Cls Engl Awd 86; Boston Coll; Hist.

KENT, SUSAN; Holbrook HS; Holbrook, MA; (Y); 7/96; Library Aide; Spanish Clb; NHS; Bentley; Bus Mgmt.

KENYON, BRIAN; East Longmeadow HS; E Longmeadow, MA; (Y); Church Yth Grp; Intnl Clb; JA; Church Choir; Stage Crew; Var L Crs Cntry; JV Golf; Var Capt Swmmng; Engnrng.

KEO, CHINTANA; BMC Durfee HS; Fall River, MA; (Y); 76/661; Hon Roll; Schlstc Awds 82-83; Bristol CC; Engr.

KEOGH, JUDITH A; Mt St Joseph Acad; Boston, MA; (Y); 54/145; Church Yth Grp; Drama Clb; French Clb; Math Clb; School Musical; School Play; Variety Show; Yrbk Stf; Rep Stu Cncl; Stonehill Coll; Bus.

KEOGH, SHEILA; Fontbonne Acad; Milton, MA; (Y); Drama Clb; Girl Scts; School Play; Hon Roll; Pre-Law.

KEOHANE, DAN; Dedham HS; Dedham, MA; (Y); 11/280; Church Yth Grp; Latin Clb; Var Capt Crs Cntry; Var L Trk; High Hon Roll; Hon Roll; X-Cntry 7VP Awd 84 & 85; Squire Yr Awd Jhn J Smith Cir 230 86.

KEOHANE, MARY JEAN; Arlington HS; Arlington, MA; (Y); SADD; Var Sftbl; Hon Roll; NHS; All Str Awd Tennis 86; 2 Vrsty Ltrs 85-86; Legl Stds.

KEOPRASEUTH, BOUNSANA; English HS; Dorchester, MA; (Y); Camp Fr Inc; JA; PAVAS; Teachers Aide; Varsity Clb; School Play; Stage Crew; Rep Soph Cls; Var Ice Hcky; Var Socr; Northeastern U; Mech Power Engr.

KEOUGH, KAREN; Notre Dame Acad; Weymouth, MA; (Y); 16/109; Dance Clb; Nwsp Stf; Crs Cntry; Trk; Hon Roll; Jr NHS; Capt Crs Cntry; Past Cmmndr Chester Ovesen Mem Scholar Amvets 86; Vet.

KERMAN, KEITH; Methuen HS; Methuen, MA; (Y); #1 In Class; Am Leg Boys St; Math Tm; Model UN; Bsbl; Var L Trk; Wt Lftg; High Hon Roll; NHS; Math Clb; Spanish Clb; Cert Of Awd Boys ST 86; Harvard Clg Bk Awd 86.

KERNEY, JOHN; Arlington Catholic HS; Arlington, MA; (Y); 4/168; JCL; Latin Clb; Im Bsbl; JV Ice Hcky; Var Socr; Var L Trk; High Hon Roll; NHS; Exploring; Nwsp Rptr; MA Adv Stds Prog 86; Slvr Medlst Natl Latn Exm 84-86; Engrng.

KERR, DONALD; Arlington HS; Arlington, MA; (Y); Boys Clb Am; Church Yth Grp; SADD; L Capt Bsktbl; JV Coach Actv; JV Trk; High Hon Roll; NHS; Engrng.

KERR, LARK; Milford HS; Milford, MA; (Y); 62/290; Church Yth Grp; Office Aide; Color Guard; Trk; High Hon Roll; Hon Roll; Comp Pgm.

KERR, STEVEN; Beverly HS; Beverly, MA; (Y); Bsbl; Var Capt Bsktbl; Var L Lcrss; Comp Sci.

KERRIGAN, KIRSTEN; Attleboro HS; Attleboro, MA; (Y); Am Leg Aux Girls St; Sec Jr Cls; Sec Sr Cls; Var Capt Swmmng; High Hon Roll; NHS; NEDT Awd; Dance Clb; Chorus; Rep Frsh Cls; Harvard Bk Awd 86; Upsilon Alpha Awd 85; Stu Cncl Svc Awd 85-86.

KERRIGAN, SHANNON; Haverhill HS; Haverhill, MA; (Y); Cheerleading; Hon Roll; Intr Decrtr.

KEYWORTH, JODI; Mansfield HS; Mansfield, MA; (Y); 5/186; Church Yth Grp; Key Clb; Band; Concert Band; Mrchg Band; Frsh Cls; Soph Cls; Stu Cncl; Bsktbl; Sftbl; Cmmnwlth Massachustts Schlrshp 86; Northeastern U; Blgy.

KHAMBATY, MURRIAM JEAN; Gloucester HS; Gloucester, MA; (Y); 11/297; German Clb; Political Wkr; Red Cross Aide; SADD; Yrbk Ed-Chief; Off Sr Cls; Stu Cncl; High Hon Roll; NHS; Off Soph Cls; Acad Achvt 84-85; Tufts 1; Med.

KHAN, MIRIAM; Marlboro HS; Marlboro, MA; (Y); 22/250; Sec AFS; Sec Church Yth Grp; Computer Clb; Drama Clb; Hosp Aide; JA; Pep Clb; Science Clb; Lit Mag; Im Trk; Northwestern U; Phys Ther.

KHAN, REHANA; Newton North HS; Newton, MA; (Y); Chess Clb; Latin Clb; Pres Pep Clb; High Hon Roll; Hon Roll; Rep Jr Cls; Rep Stu Cncl; Im Vllybl; Jazz Dance Cert Of Hnr 85; Natl Latn Exam Awd 86; Bio.

KHATAK, NABEELA; Mac Duffie Schl; S Hadley, MA; (Y); Rptr Nwsp Rptr; Trk; Hon Roll; Debate Tm; Intnl Clb; Sec Jr Cls; Off Sr Cls; Var Capt Bsktbl; JV Capt Fld Hcky; Var Lcrss; 2nd In Western MA Home Bldg Cont 85; 2nd In Sci Fair 85; Elected Head Day Of The Schl 86; Journalist.

KHUC, TAN H; Somerville HS; Somerville, MA; (Y); High Hon Roll; Sci Proj Awd 86; New England Math Clb Awd 86; Biochem.

KICKHAM, JAMES; Boston College HS; Milton, MA; (Y); Cmnty Wkr; Debate Tm; French Clb; JA; Key Clb; SADD; Nwsp Rptr; JV Swmmng; Var Tennis; Hon Roll; Poli Sci.

KIELBANIA, DONNA; Cathedral HS; Chicopee, MA; (Y); 101/557; Trs Girl Scts; Chorus; Church Choir; School Musical; School Play; Variety Show; Chrs-Vrsty Lttr Awd 86; Johnson & Wales; Clnry Arts.

KIERNAN, KERRY; Sharon HS; Sharon, MA; (Y); Pres Church Yth Grp; Spanish Clb; SADD; Nwsp Stf; Yrbk Stf; Rep Frsh Cls; Sec Soph Cls; Sec Jr Cls; Rep Sr Cls; Jrnlsm.

KIJAK, MICHAEL S; Chicopee Comprehensive HS; Chicopee, MA; (Y); 2/306; Am Leg Boys St; Yrbk Stf; Var L Bsbl; Var Capt Bsktbl; Var Capt Socr; Bausch & Lomb Sci Awd; Elks Awd; High Hon Roll; NHS; Sal; RPI Mth Awd 86; Union Coll; Engrng.

KILARU, ERIN; Northfield Mount Hermon Schl; Cold Spring, NY; (Y); AFS; Ski Clb; Acpl Chr; Chorus; Lit Mag; Rep Stu Cncl; Var Tennis; Var Trk; Var Bsktbl; JV Vllybl; Area All ST Chorus; Dbls Chmpn Bi-Valley Lg; Bio.

KILDUFF, CHRISTINE; Bishop Feehan HS; E Walpole, MA; (Y); 12/247; Dance Clb; Hosp Aide; JCL; SADD; Yrbk Ed-Chief; Yrbk Stf; French Hon Soc; High Hon Roll; NHS; Magna Cum Laude Honors On National Latin Exam 86; Bus.

KILEY, ANDREW D; Westbridge HS; Woburn, MA; (Y); 1/15; Chess Clb; Ski Clb; Stat Bsktbl; Golf; Score Keeper; Timer; High Hon Roll; Pres NHS; Ntl Merit SF.

KILEY, MEGAN P; Andover HS; Andover, MA; (Y); 47/400; Dance Clb; Pep Clb; Chorus; Yrbk Stf; Fld Hcky; Trk; High Hon Roll; Hon Roll; Prfct Atten Awd; Skidmore Coll.

KILLION, JENNIFER; Governor Dummer Acad; Peoria, AZ; (Y); 10/92; Dance Clb; FCA; French Clb; Library Aide; Service Clb; Thesps; Chorus; School Musical; School Play; Stage Crew; Brown Bk Prize Mst Outstndng Engl 86; SR Dorm Proctor 86-87; Head Tour Guide 86-87; Comm.

KILLIZLI, MARY; Boston Technical HS; Roslindale, MA; (S); 6/205; Church Yth Grp; Sec French Clb; SADD; Yrbk Stf; Off Jr Cls; Off Stu Cncl; Sftbl; Hon Roll; Boston Coll; Bus Mngmnt.

KILMER, CHARLIE; Bourne HS; Pocasset, MA; (Y); Med.

KIM, ANDREW D; Malden Catholic HS; Medford, MA; (Y); 5/184; Drama Clb; VP Sec Intnl Clb; Math Tm; SADD; Nwsp Stf; Yrbk Ed-Chief; Stu Cncl; NHS; Art Clb; Church Yth Grp; Arts Recgntn & Talnt 85-86; Hnr Cert Acad Decthln 85-86; Med.

KIM, CHEANG; Boston Technical HS; Allston, MA; (Y); Socr; Trk; Hon Roll; Ntl Jr Hnrs Scty 83; Cert Of Achvmnt 84; Elec Engr.

KIM, EUNE; Algonquin Regional HS; Northboro, MA; (Y); 3/250; Hosp Aide; JA; Orch; School Musical; Yrbk Stf; Var L Crs Cntry; High Hon Roll; NHS; Ntl Merit Ltr; Outstndng Achvt Awd For ARHS Stu 84-86; MA Cntrl Dist Orch 85-86; Harvard Bk Awd 86; Med.

KIMBALL, JERRY; Hingham HS; Hingham, MA; (Y); 15/341; Math Tm; Concert Band; Jazz Band; Mrchg Band; JV Bsbl; Hon Roll; NHS; U Of MA Amherst; Elec Engr.

KIMBALL, KELLY; Holbrook JR SR HS; Holbrook, MA; (Y); Princpls Awd Stngrphy I 85-86; Catherine Gibbs Schl; Bus.

KIMBALL, THOS; St Josephs Regional HS; Westford, MA; (Y); Art Clb; Boy Scts; Computer Clb; Var Bsbl; Var Capt Crs Cntry; Natl Sci Olympiad 86; Graphics.

KIMBROUGH, KARIN JANEL; Northfield Mt Herman HS; Cambridge, MA; (Y); French Clb; Hosp Aide; Service Clb; Chorus; School Musical; School Play; Pres Soph Cls; Var L Lcrss; Nwsp Stf; Natl Merit Rcgntn 85.

KIMBROUGH, M SCOTT; St Bernards Central Catholic HS; Ft Devens, MA; (Y); 20/176; Am Leg Boys St; Band; Mrchg Band; Variety Show; Yrbk Stf; Ftbl; Socr; Tennis; Hon Roll; NHS; Algbra II & Trig Awd 85-86; Bus.

KING, BRENDA; Shepherd Hill Regional HS; Dudley, MA; (Y); Mrchg Band; Stat Crs Cntry; JV Gym; The American Classical League & The National Junior League Certificate Of Maxima Cum Laude 86; Bus.

KING, BRIAN; St Johns Preparatory Schl; Peabody, MA; (Y); Boy Scts; Church Yth Grp; Cmnty Wkr; Computer Clb; Drama Clb; Library Aide; Radio Clb; Stage Crew; Im Bsktbl; High Hon Roll.

KING, DANIEL; Chicopee Comprehensive HS; Chicopee, MA; (Y); 35/325; Cmnty Wkr; Pep Clb; Spanish Clb; SADD; Stage Crew; Variety Show; Yrbk Rptr; Yrbk Stf; Jr NHS; NHS; Stu Cncl Ltr 85; Cert Awd For Prtcptn In Frolics 86; Stu Cncl Pin 86; U Of MA; Bus.

KING, DARREN; Central Catholic HS; Lawrence, MA; (Y); 53/250; Red Cross Aide; Ski Clb; Bsbl; Bsktbl; Ftbl; Hon Roll; Boston U; Engrng.

KING, DEBORAH; Gerogetown JR SR HS; Georgetown, MA; (Y); AFS; Church Yth Grp; Drama Clb; Chorus; School Play; JV Fld Hcky; JV Socr; Brdcstg.

KING, DENNIS; Diaman Reginal Voc Tech HS; Fall River, MA; (Y); 50/224; Sec JA; VICA; Rep Soph Cls; JV Bsbl; JV Socr.

KING, EDWARD A; Leominster HS; Leominster, MA; (Y); Am Leg Boys St; Im Bsbl; Var Ftbl; Im Capt Socr; Swmmng; High Hon Roll; Hon Roll; Sectnl Champs Swmmg 85-86; U Of MA; Engineering.

KING, ELIZABETH E; Swampscott HS; Swampscott, MA; (Y); 31/232; Church Yth Grp; Cmnty Wkr; Model UN; Sec Trs Spanish Clb; Sec Trs Band; Lit Mag; Stu Cncl; Capt Cheerleading; Cit Awd; Hon Roll; Pres Acad Fit Awd 86; Prnt/Tchrs Assn Scholar 86; Clssmates Today/Neighbrs Tomorrow Awd 86; Syracuse U; Cmmnctns.

KING, JOSEPH; Boston Latin Sch; Boston, MA; (Y); 95/274; Boys Clb Am; Church Yth Grp; Latin Clb; Varsity Clb; JV Var Bsktbl; JV Crs Cntry; Wt Lftg; High Hon Roll; Classical Awd 84.

KING, JOSEPH; Hingham HS; Hingham, MA; (Y); 6/350; Rep AFS; Nwsp Stf; Yrbk Stf; Var Crs Cntry; Var L Trk; Im Vllybl; Hon Roll; Humanitarian Stu Awd; Engrng.

KING, KIM; Frontier Regional HS; S Deerfield, MA; (Y); French Clb; VP GAA; JV Bsktbl; Var Fld Hcky; Var Sftbl; High Hon Roll; Hon Roll; US Natl Math Awd 85; Acad All Am Schlr Prgm 85.

KING, LISA; Reading Memorial HS; Reading, MA; (Y); Dance Clb; SADD; Band; School Musical; Yrbk Stf; Mgr(s); Var Trk; High Hon Roll; Hon Roll; Sci Fld.

KING, LISA A; Maynard HS; Maynard, MA; (Y); 4/100; Am Leg Aux Girls St; Sec Sr Cls; Pres Sec Stu Cncl; Var Capt Bsktbl; Var Capt Fld Hcky; Var Capt Trk; Hon Roll; Radio Clb; Red Cross Aide; Pres Band; Anne Duclos Schlrshp 86; Wmns Sprts Fndnt HS All Star Awd 86; HS Sprtsmnshp Awd 86; Wrcstr Poly Tech; Engr Mngmnt.

KING, MICHELLE; Medway JR SR HS; Medway, MA; (Y); Dance Clb; Drama Clb; SADD; School Play; Stage Crew; Yrbk Stf; IPEC Ldr 85-86; Intl Ord Rainbow Girls 82-86; MA Coll Art; Cmmrcl Art.

KING, NICOLE; Latin Acad; Roxbury, MA; (Y); Drama Clb; English Clb; Spanish Clb; Drill Tm; Nwsp Rptr; Nwsp Stf; Rep Sftbl; Rep Trk; Pres Vllybl; Spanish NHS.

KING, ROBIN; Nasheba Regional HS; Bolton, MA; (Y); Church Yth Grp; 4-H; Band; Concert Band; Mrchg Band; Yrbk Stf; Var Cheerleading; JV Fld Hcky; JV Sftbl; Hon Roll; Math Awd 84-85; Bus.

KING, SEAN; Burncoat SR HS; Worcester, MA; (Y); Church Yth Grp; Computer Clb; Intnl Clb; Variety Show; Hon Roll; NHS; Spanish NHS; Anthropology.

KING, THOMAS; Agawam HS; Agawam, MA; (Y); 13/373; Yrbk Bus Mgr; Bsbl; Ftbl; Capt Wrstlng; Hon Roll; NHS; Boy Scts; Spanish Clb; 6 Awds Lttrng Sprts Hnr Rl 85-87; Cls Marshall 87; Military.

KING, TRACY; Bellingham Memorial JR SR HS; Bellingham, MA; (Y); VP DECA; Drm Mjr(t); Yrbk Stf; Stu Cncl; Var Capt Fld Hcky; Hon Roll.

KINGMAN, EAMON R; East Bridgewater HS; East Bridgwater, MA; (Y); 7/149; Am Leg Boys St; Pres Key Clb; SADD; VP Stu Cncl; Var Capt Bsbl; Var Capt Bsktbl; Var Capt Socr; Cit Awd; Kiwanis Awd; NHS; Jewis Wr Vets USA Brtherhd Awd 86; Bsbll Sccr Brcktn Entrpc All Schlstc Tms 85-86; U Of NE; Cvl Engr.

KINGMAN, LORI; Attelboro HS; Attleboro, MA; (Y); Yrbk Stf; Var L Bsktbl; Var Capt Sftbl; Capt L Vllybl; NHS; Bus Mgmt.

KINNALY, PAUL; Saugus HS; Saugus, MA; (Y); 30/290; SADD; School Play; Yrbk Stf; Stu Cncl; Bsbl; Crs Cntry; Ice Hcky; NHS; VFW Awd; Voice Dem Awd; Hcky Nght In Bstn N Tm 85 & 86; Nrthestrn Conf All Str Hcky Tm 85.

KINNEY, SUSAN; Copley Square HS; Boston, MA; (Y); Stu Cncl; Sftbl; Hon Roll; Sftbl; Stu Cncl; Spenea Proj; FL Sthrn Coll; Child Psych.

KINSBOVRNE, DAN; Winchester HS; Winchester, MA; (Y); Crs Cntry; Socr; Trk; Rep Soph Cls; Rep Jr Cls.

KINSELLA, DANIEL; Salem HS; Salem, MA; (Y); Ski Clb; Golf; Socr; Marine Bio.

KINSLEY, MARY; Sacred Heart HS; Plymouth, MA; (Y); 22/91; Art Clb; Intnl Clb; Key Clb; Speech Tm; Chorus; School Musical; Hon Roll; VFW Awd; 4th Pl St Fnlst MA Forensic League 86; St Fnls Poetry Rdng; Boston U; Law.

KINSLEY, WILLIAM; Burlington HS; Burlington, MA; (Y); 40/321; German Clb; JA; Concert Band; Bsbl; Var Gym; Socr; Hon Roll; NHS; Gym Awd 86.

KIRBY, TRACEY; Westfield HS; Westfield, MA; (Y); 16/359; French Clb; High Hon Roll; Hon Roll; Jr NHS; Frnch 3 Bk Awd; Gilead Schl NY; Missnry Wrk.

KIRKITELOS, PAUL C; Ludlow HS; Ludlow, MA; (Y); 3/280; Am Leg Boys St; Mathletes; Speech Tm; Yrbk Stf; Rep Soph Cls; Crs Cntry; Golf; Capt Wrstlng; High Hon Roll; NHS; Air Frc ROTC Schlrshp 86; Elks Ntl Schlrshp 86; U S Army Schlr/Athlt Mdl 86; Wrcstr Poly Tech; Elec Engrng.

KIRWAN, JOHN M; Masconomet Regional HS; Middleton, MA; (Y); 13/252; Am Leg Boys St; JV Ftbl; JV Trk; Var L Wrstlng; Hon Roll; Jr NHS; NHS; German Clb; Advanced Plcmnt Exam Bio 86; German Exchng Pgm 86; Natl Hnr Soc Tutor 85-86; MIT; Biomed.

KIRWIN JR, JAMES P; Wellesley SR HS; Wellesley, MA; (Y); 153/311; Am Leg Boys St; Trs Varsity Clb; Chorus; Pres Soph Cls; Pres Jr Cls; Var Capt Bsbl; Var Capt Crs Cntry; Var L Trk; Hon Roll; Phys Ed.

KIRWIN, LAURA ANN; Brainbree HS; Braintree, MA; (Y); 60/435; Cmnty Wkr; Library Aide; Yrbk Bus Mgr; Yrbk Ed-Chief; Sec Lit Mag; Var L Bsktbl; High Hon Roll; Hon Roll; Jr NHS; NHS; Ind Arts Awd 86; Yrbk Awd 86; Wheaton Coll; Physcl Thrpy.

KISER, DOUGLAS; Ayer HS; Ft Devens, MA; (Y); 33/135; Varsity Clb; Ftbl; Trk.

KISHBACH, RAYELLEN; Taunton HS; Taunton, MA; (Y); Science Clb; Spanish Clb; Band; Concert Band; Mrchg Band; Yrbk Stf; Lit Mag; Cheerleading; Trk; Hon Roll; Biochem.

KITTREDGE, REBECCA; Longmeadow HS; Longmeadow, MA; (Y); 3/263; Latin Clb; Yrbk Ed-Chief; Yrbk Stf; Diving; Capt Gym; Powder Puff Ftbl; Trk; High Hon Roll; NHS; Ntl Merit Ltr; Welsley Bk Awd Engl 86; French Awd Achvmnt 86; All Wstrn Mass Gymnstcs 83-85; Psych.

KIVIMAKI, KEVIN; Acton Boxboro Regional HS; Acton, MA; (Y); 121/428; Church Yth Grp; Orch; Nwsp Rptr; Nwsp Sprt Ed; Nwsp Stf; JV Trk; NHS; Poli Sci.

KLAHRE, MICHELE; North Middlesex Regional HS; Townsend, MA; (Y); Trs Sec Exploring; Pep Clb; SADD; Varsity Clb; Yrbk Stf; Rep Frsh Cls; Rep Soph Cls; Var Mgr(s); Powder Puff Ftbl; Score Keeper; Pedtrcn.

KLAIN, DANIEL A; Lowell HS; Lowell, MA; (Y); 1/700; Capt Chess Clb; JCL; Science Clb; High Hon Roll; NHS; Ntl Merit SF; U MA Chancellors Tlnt Awd 85; Harvard Bk Awd 85; Slvr Mdl Natl Latin Exam 84; Cosmo Rsrch.

KLATTE, CINDY; Chicopee HS; Chicopee, MA; (Y); Exploring; Band; Concert Band; Mrchg Band; High Hon Roll; Hon Roll; NHS.

KLEIN, KRISTEN; Milford HS; Milford, MA; (Y); 4/320; Am Leg Aux Girls St; SADD; Band; Chorus; Rep Stu Cncl; JV Capt Fld Hcky; NHS; Ntl Merit Ltr; Church Yth Grp; Hosp Aide; Rgnl-Natl Danc Awds 84-86; Corprt Law.

KLIMA, ELIZABETH; Hingham HS; Hingham, MA; (Y); 12/342; Sec Pres AFS; Off Band; Concert Band; School Musical; Var L Lcrss; Hon Roll; NHS; Church Yth Grp; Drama Clb; French Clb; Colby Coll Bk Awd 86; Outstndng Contrbtn To Band 86; MI-BAND 85-86; Lbrl Arts.

KLINE, TRAVIS; Berkshire Schl; Hudson, NY; (Y); 25/145; Cmnty Wkr; 4-H; Key Clb; Nwsp Rptr; Yrbk Stf; Off Stu Cncl; Bsbl; High Hon Roll; Rotary Awd; Ski Tm 84-86; Rtry Clb Exchng Stu Eng 85 & 84; Gms Clb Fly Fhsng Clb; Vet Med.

KLING, SUZANNE; Sharon HS; Stoughton, MA; (Y); Cmnty Wkr; Math Tm; Spanish Clb; Pres Temple Yth Grp; Nwsp Stf; Yrbk Stf; High Hon Roll; Hon Roll; Sec NHS; Ntl Merit Ltr; Spnsh Stu Mnth 86.

KMETZ, CHRISTAL; Norton HS; Norton, MA; (S); 1/148; Drm Mjr(t); Mrchg Band; Pres Frsh Cls; Pres Soph Cls; Pres Jr Cls; Pres Sr Cls; Var Bsktbl; DAR Awd; Pres NHS; Ntl Merit Ltr; Most Outstndng Drum Major Awd; Amherst Coll; Eng.

KNAPTON, RYAN; Bishop Feehan HS; Attleboro, MA; (Y); Cmnty Wkr; Y-Teens; Stat Bsktbl; JV Var Mgr(s); Phy Ed.

KNIGHT, MATTHEW; Old Rochester Regional HS; Mattapoisett, MA; (Y); Am Leg Boys St; Drama Clb; School Play; Ftbl; Trk; Wt Lftg; High Hon Roll; Hon Roll; NHS; Am Heart Assoc 86; Engrg.

KNOSPINS, ROBERT J; Boston Tech HS; Jamaica Plain, MA; (Y); Boy Scts; Church Choir; Boys Clb Am; L Swmmng; Var L Trk; God Cntry Awd; Samuel Gross Davis Awd 86; Wentworth Inst Tech; Mech Engr.

KNOWLES, GEORGE; Boston Latin HS; W Roxbury, MA; (Y); 126/275; Boys Clb Am; Chess Clb; Church Yth Grp; Latin Clb; Y-Teens; Im Tennis; Schl Sci Fair 84; Natl Greek Exmntn Awd 86; Marines; Law.

KNOWLTON, JULIE-KIRSTEN; Acton-Baxboro Reg HS; Acton, MA; (Y); 285/428; Pres Church Yth Grp; Chorus; School Musical; School Play; Variety Show; Var L Pom Pon; Drama Clb; Girl Scts; Band; Church Choir; Ranbw Grls Advsr 85-86; Rainbw Grls Grnd Offcr ST 86-87; Grl Scts Gld Ldrshp Awd 86; Early Ed.

KNUFF, KETRINA M; Lawrence Acad; Groton, MA; (Y); Dance Clb; Office Aide; Spanish Clb; Chorus; Rep Frsh Cls; Rep Soph Cls; Rep Jr Cls; Sec Sr Cls; Rep Stu Cncl; Var Capt Fld Hcky; Intl Bus.

KOBEL, KAREN; Leicester HS; Cherry Valley, MA; (S); Im Church Yth Grp; Im French Clb; Im Latin Clb; Stat Crs Cntry; Var Fld Hcky; Var Mgr(s); Im Sftbl; Stat Timer; Stat Trk; Im Hon Roll; Becker JC; Vet Med.

KOBELSKI, BRIAN; Central Catholic HS; Tewksbury, MA; (Y); 9/231; Boys Clb Am; Church Yth Grp; Var Bsktbl; Var Ftbl; Var Trk; Im Vllybl; High Hon Roll; NHS.

KOCH, DEBI; Milford HS; Milford, MA; (Y); Key Clb; SADD; Var Bsktbl; Var Fld Hcky; JV Cheerleading; Var Sftbl; Hon Roll; Jr NHS; NHS; Boys Clb Am; Mst Vlbl Plyr Fld Hcky 83-84; Rookie Yr Fld Hcky Bsktbl & Sftbl 84-85.

KOCIUR, JOANNE; Ware HS; Ware, MA; (Y); Spanish Clb; Ed Lit Mag; JV Cheerleading; Var Socr; High Hon Roll; Rep Frsh Cls; VP Soph Cls; VP Jr Cls; VP Sr Cls; Rep Stu Cncl; Bus Mgmt.

KOFTON, BRANDT; Brockton HS; Brockton, MA; (Y); CAP; Computer Clb; Latin Clb; Scholastic Bowl; Lit Mag; High Hon Roll; Hon Roll; NHS; Prfct Atten Awd; Wrkd Cty Hall Adtrs Off 84; Sys Op Cmptr Blltn Bd 80-85; Cstmr Rltns Kmart Corp 85-86; Boston U; Law.

KOH, BERNARD; Phillips Acad; Andover, MA; (Y); Chess Clb; Cmnty Wkr; JV Trk; JV Wrstlng.

KOHRI, SHINICHIRO; St Johns Prep Schl; Marblehead, MA; (Y); Ski Clb; Var Socr; Var Trk; Engr.

KOLEK, CRAIG; Austin Prep Schl; Tewksbury, MA; (Y); 34/140; French Clb; Latin Clb; Pep Clb; Ski Clb; SADD; Im Bsbl; Im JV Bsktbl; Im Ice Hcky; Var Mgr(s); Im Sftbl.

KOLESAR, KIMBERELY; Academy Of Notre Dame; Tewksbury, MA; (Y); 11/80; Drama Clb; Nwsp Ed-Chief; Nwsp Rptr; Ed Nwsp Stf; Hon Roll; NHS.

KOLOKITHAS, DEMETRIOS; St Marys HS; Lynn, MA; (Y); 10/90; Am Leg Boys St; French Clb; CC Awd; High Hon Roll; Hon Roll; Jr NHS; Prfct Atten Awd; Candt Joe Nashak Awd Hghst Awd Boys ST 86; Schl Awd 84-86; MIT; Comp Engr.

KOLOSKI, JAMES M; Sandwich JR SR HS; E Sandwich, MA; (Y); Am Leg Boys St; Church Yth Grp; Cmnty Wkr; Political Wkr; SADD; Yrbk Stf; Pres Jr Cls; Stu Cncl; L Var Lcrss; Sndwch Lcrss Clb All Str Dfns 85&86; Bus.

KONOWITZ, JEFFREY CHIP; Northfield Mt Hermon HS; Dover, DE; (Y); Boy Scts; Varsity Clb; Chorus; JV Lcrss; Socr; SAR Awd; Library Aide; Office Aide; Nwsp Stf; Yrbk Stf; Cls Orator 86; Peer Ed Cnslr 83-86; Tulane U; Optmtry.

KONTOS, NICHOLAS; Waltham HS; Waltham, MA; (Y); Aud/Vis; Jazz Band; Yrbk Stf; High Hon Roll; Hon Roll; Jr NHS; NHS; Kingsbury Temperance Essay Awd 86; Bio.

KOOPMAN, DENISE; Whitinsville Christian HS; Whitinsville, MA; (Y); 2/20; Church Yth Grp; Drama Clb; Band; Chorus; Pres Stu Cncl; JV Var Bsktbl; JV Var Vllybl; Hon Roll; JP Sousa Awd; NHS; Bus.

KOPEC, BOZENA; Commerce HS; Springfield, MA; (Y); Math Clb; NFL; SADD; Off Jr Cls; Bsbl; Gym; Socr; Sftbl; STTC; Math.

KOPELMAN, DAN; Lincoln-Sudbury Regional HS; Sudbury, MA; (Y); SADD; Temple Yth Grp; Nwsp Rptr; Nwsp Stf; Rep Jr Cls; Var L Bsbl; Var Golf; Var Gym; JV Im Lcrss; Ntl Merit Ltr.

KOPPY, BRIAN; Mansfield HS; Mansfield, MA; (Y); Church Yth Grp; Stage Crew; Stu Cncl; JV Var Bsbl; JV Var Ftbl; Capt Vllybl; High Hon Roll; Hon Roll; Jr NHS; NHS; Corp Fincr.

KORBUT, ANNEMARIE; Cathedral HS; W Springfield, MA; (Y); 128/520; Church Yth Grp; JA; Political Wkr; SADD; Band; School Play; Rep Stu Cncl; Crs Cntry; JV Socr; Trk; Hstry.

KORHONEN, ELLEN; Gardner HS; Gardner, MA; (Y); 23/146; Band; Chorus; Yrbk Ed-Chief; Yrbk Stf; Pres Soph Cls; Fld Hcky; Mgr(s); Sftbl; Hon Roll.

KORITSAS, LISA; Winthrop HS; Winthrop, MA; (Y); VP Church Yth Grp; 4-H; Office Aide; Variety Show; Im Bsktbl; High Hon Roll; Bus.

KORITSAS, TAMMY; Winthrop HS; Winthrop, MA; (Y); Sec Church Yth Grp; 4-H; Office Aide; Variety Show; Trs Soph Cls; Im Bsktbl; High Hon Roll; Bus.

KORN, REBECCA; Newton North HS; Newton, MA; (Y); Cmnty Wkr; Exploring; French Clb; Ski Clb; Temple Yth Grp; Nwsp Rptr; Nwsp Stf; Yrbk Phtg; Yrbk Stf; Lit Mag; Creative Wrtng.

KORTEKAMP, TODD; Monson JR SR HS; Monson, MA; (Y); 5/86; Am Leg Boys St; Church Yth Grp; French Clb; JV Var Bsktbl; JV Var Socr; Hon Roll; NHS; Pres Schlr; VFW Awd; Navy ROTC Schlrshp 87; Natl Assoc Powr Engr Schlrshp 86; Rochester Inst Of Tech; Microel.

KOSINSKI, KATHY; Stoughton HS; Stoughton, MA; (Y); Trs Church Yth Grp; Concert Band; Mrchg Band; Nwsp Stf; Trs Frsh Cls; JV Bsktbl; JV Fld Hcky; JV Var Sftbl; Grad-Yth Ldrshp Core Assn 85-86; 5th & 6th Grd Vlntr Cnslr-Grtn Wood Cmp 86; Grad-Sun Schl Tchr Aprntc.

KOSLOWSKI, CHRISTINE; Quaboag Regional HS; Warren, MA; (Y); 12/87; Church Yth Grp; JA; Math Tm; Spanish Clb; SADD; Varsity Clb; Variety Show; Rep Stu Cncl; Sftbl; Hon Roll; Lib Art.

KOTLARSKI, CHRISTINE; Dartmouth HS; Dartmouth, MA; (Y); Cmnty Wkr; Dance Clb; Hosp Aide; Pres JA; Rep Jr Cls; Rep Stu Cncl; JV Bsktbl; Cit Awd; Hon Roll; Jr Achvt-Outstndng Yng Busnss Woman 84-85; Jr Achvt-Sales Clb Awd 85-86; Jr Achvt-Prfct Attndc 83-86; Busnss.

KOTSIRAS, STEVEN; Watertown HS; Watertown, MA; (Y); 21/250; Boys Clb Am; Church Yth Grp; Nwsp Rptr; Nwsp Stf; Bsktbl; Hon Roll; NHS; Top 20 Awd; Librl Arts.

KOVALSKI, KEVIN C; Smith Vocational Agricultural HS; Hatfield, MA; (Y); Am Leg Boys St; Stu Cncl; Bsbl; Bsktbl; Hon Roll; All Leag Bsktbl 85-86; Dr Lawrence P Chase Ctznshp Awd 86; Engrg.

KOWAL, JENNIFER; Hopkins Acad; Northampton, MA; (S); 5/48; Church Yth Grp; French Clb; Hosp Aide; Library Aide; Chorus; Nwsp Ed-Chief; Nwsp Stf; Yrbk Stf; JV Bsktbl; JV Capt Sftbl; Frnch Awd Hghst Achvr 85; 100 Hour Pin Candy Strpng 83; Nrsg.

KOWAL, WILLIAM J; Northampton HS; Northampton, MA; (Y); 3/272; Am Leg Boys St; Quiz Bowl; Scholastic Bowl; Science Clb; Var L Bsbl; Var L Crs Cntry; High Hon Roll; Trs NHS; Ntl Merit Ltr; Math.

KOWALSKI, ROSEMARIE; Arlington HS; Arlington, MA; (Y); 4/370; Art Clb; French Clb; Mrchg Band; School Play; Symp Band; Nwsp Stf; Trk; Vllybl; High Hon Roll; NHS; Cornell U; Arch.

KOZIAK, AMELIA; Leicester HS; Cherry Valley, MA; (Y); Drama Clb; Math Tm; Band; Chorus; Jazz Band; School Play; Variety Show; JV Var Socr; Var Tennis; 1st, 2nd & 4th Pl Ntl Hstry Dstrct & ST 85 86; Pre-Law.

KOZIMOR, DANA; Westford Acad; Westford, MA; (Y); AFS; Spanish Clb; Capt Var Diving; Capt Var Swmmng; NHS; VP Gym; Im Tennis; VP Trk; ST Diving Champ & Rcrd Hldr 84-85; All Amer HS Dvng 85; Cum Laude Ntl Latin Exam 85.

KOZIOL, JEFFREY J; St Marys HS; Westfield, MA; (Y); 3/51; Am Leg Boys St; Sr Cls; Bsbl; Bsktbl; Socr; High Hon Roll; Jr NHS; NHS; Coaches Awd-Bsbll 86; Engrng.

KOZLOWSKI, DEBRA; Bartlett HS; Webster, MA; (Y); 21/150; Church Yth Grp; Trs Spanish Clb; Variety Show; Yrbk Ed-Chief; Off Stu Cncl; Capt Cheerleading; Sftbl; High Hon Roll; Hon Roll; NHS; Fnlst All Amer Chrldr 85; Perf Attndnc Awd 83; Mt Ida Coll; Fshn Mrch.

KOZLOWSKI, KARA; Ware HS; Ware, MA; (Y); 3/108; Am Leg Aux Girls St; Art Clb; 4-H; Spanish Clb; Jazz Band; Variety Show; Lit Mag; Var L Bsktbl; Var L Sftbl; High Hon Roll; Boston Glb Schlstc Art Hon Mntn Awd 85; W MA All Star Bsktbl Tm 86; Pioneer Vly Intrschlstc Athltc Tm; Educ.

KOZUB, LYNN; Wilbraham Monson Acad; Wilbraham, MA; (Y); SADD; Nwsp Stf; Lit Mag; Frsh Cls; Soph Cls; Var Capt Bsktbl; Var Socr; Var Capt Sftbl; Hon Roll; Sprts Med.

KOZUCH, KARIE; Fairhaven HS; Worcester, MA; (Y); 11/180; Cmnty Wkr; Political Wkr; Nwsp Ed-Chief; Yrbk Stf; VP Jr Cls; Capt Tennis; High Hon Roll; Hon Roll; Jr NHS; NHS; Acadmc Schlrshp Assmptn Coll-$4000 86; Acadmc Ltr Of Achvt 90 & Abv 84-86; Ctatn For 85 Avg 86; Assumption Coll; Pltcl Sci.

KRATZ, DAWN; Presentation Of Mary Acad; N Andover, MA; (Y); Trs Church Yth Grp; Debate Tm; Exploring; GAA; Girl Scts; SADD; Chorus; Trs Frsh Cls; Trs Soph Cls; Trs Jr Cls; Merrimack Coll; Lwyr.

KRAUNELIS, MATTHEW; Methuen HS; Methuen, MA; (Y); Hosp Aide; Model UN; SADD; Ftbl; Trk; Poet Laureate, Antchn Orthodox Chrstn Assn N Amer 85-86; Merit Awd & Pblshd Poet-Wrld Poetry 86; Boston Coll; Polit Sci.

KRAUSE, SARA; So Hadley HS; S Hadley, MA; (Y); Church Yth Grp; Exploring; Trs Band; Concert Band; Mrchg Band; Hon Roll; NHS; Semi-Finlst Congrss Bundestag Progrm 85-86; Mt Holyoke Smr Thtre 85; Mt Holyoke Coll; Bio Chem.

KRAUSS, WENDY A; Milford HS; Milford, MA; (Y); Yrbk Stf; Assumption Coll; Bus.

KRAUT, DAVID T; Beaver Country Day HS; Chestnut Hill, MA; (Y); Var Bsbl; JV Bsktbl; Capt Var Crs Cntry; Var Tennis; Hon Roll; Elctd Capt Beaver Crss Cnty Tm 86; Estrn Leag Champs & New England Champs Crss Cntry 85; Lib Arts.

KRAVITZ, ALLYSON; Medway JR SR HS; Medway, MA; (Y); Drama Clb; French Clb; Library Aide; Trs Temple Yth Grp; Band; Mrchg Band; School Musical; School Play; Ed.

KRAWCHUK, KEVIN; Montachusett Reg HS; Fitchburg, MA; (Y); Ski Clb; Hon Roll.

KRAWCZYK, KAREN; Westfield HS; Westfield, MA; (Y); 27/327; Yrbk Sprt Ed; JV Capt Bsktbl; Var Capt Fld Hcky; JV Capt Sftbl; NHS; FL Southern Coll; Cmmnctns.

KRCMARIK, AMY; Coyle And Cassidy HS; N Dighton, MA; (Y); 20/130; Cmnty Wkr; French Clb; Band; Yrbk Stf; Trk; French Hon Soc; NHS; Bridgewater ST Coll.

KREIDER, JAMES; Newton North HS; Newton, MA; (Y); Church Yth Grp; Rep Sr Cls; Rep Stu Cncl; Var L Crs Cntry; Var L Trk; Cit Awd; Hon Roll; 2 Orange Crds Awd Svc To Schl 85; Awds Outstndng Acdmc Achvmnt 83&86; Air Force, Navy & Army ROTC Sch; U Of PA; Elec Engr.

KREILKAMP, IVAN; Commonwealth HS; Cambridge, MA; (Y); FCA; Hosp Aide; Drm & Bgl; Pep Band; Pom Pon; Powder Puff Ftbl; Btty Crckr Awd; Ntl Merit SF; Opt Clb Awd; Yale; Intr Dcrtr.

KRESS, WALTER P; Easthampton HS; Easthampton, MA; (Y); 4/134; Trs Am Leg Boys St; Church Yth Grp; VP Chorus; Swing Chorus; Stu Cncl; JV Bsbl; High Hon Roll; Sec NHS; St Schlr; HOBY Fndtn MA Ldrshp Sem 84; Easthampton Ed Assn Scholar 86; MA Commonwlth Schlrs Grant 86; Gordon Coll; Episcpl Priesthood.

KRIEGER, CRAIG; Agawam SR HS; Agawam, MA; (Y); Acctnt.

KRINSKY, DANIELLE; Randolph HS; Randolph, MA; (Y); Drama Clb; French Clb; SADD; Teachers Aide; School Play; Mgr(s); Score Keeper; Timer; Hon Roll; Intl Bus Adm.

KRISHNASWAMY, SARATH; Hudson HS; Hudson, MA; (Y); 1/135; VP Exploring; Mathletes; Math Clb; Math Tm; Band; Concert Band; Rep Jr Cls; Bausch & Lomb Sci Awd; Ntl Merit SF; Boy Scts; Kodak Intl Schlstc Newspaper Awd; MIT; Engrng.

KRITIKOS, EVELYN; Salem HS; Salem, MA; (Y); 3/290; Church Choir; High Hon Roll; NHS; Sci Proj Awd 84-85; Choir Awd 86; Tchng.

KRITIKOS, GEORGIA; Salem HS; Salem, MA; (Y); 6/280; Church Choir; High Hon Roll; NHS; Awd Sci Fair 84-86; Awd Choir 86; Bus.

KRUCKEMEYER, KATHERINE; Boston Latin Schl; Boston, MA; (Y); 1/281; Capt Math Tm; NHS; Ntl Merit Schol; Val; AM Acad Achvmnt; Franklin Mdl; Brown U.

KRUGER, MICHAEL; Brockton HS; Brockton, MA; (Y); Camera Clb; Exploring; Science Clb; Ski Clb; Stage Crew; Nwsp Phtg; Astrophyscs.

KRUZEWSKI, TANYA; Quaboag Regional HS; W Brookfield, MA; (Y); Church Yth Grp; JA; Math Tm; Spanish Clb; SADD; Teachers Aide; Varsity Clb; Off Frsh Cls; Off Soph Cls; Off Jr Cls; MVP Bsktbl Camp 84-85.

KRYGOWSKI, TOM; Marlborough HS; Marlboro, MA; (Y); Variety Show; Northeastern U; Bus Mgt.

KRZYNOWEK, KERRY A; East Longmeadow HS; E Longmeadow, MA; (Y); 8/210; Rep AFS; Church Yth Grp; Intnl Clb; Pep Clb; JV Bsktbl; Capt Fld Hcky; Trk; High Hon Roll; Hon Roll; Grad Marshall Cls 86; Engrg.

KSEN, DENISE; Quaboag Regional HS; W Warren, MA; (Y); 10/87; Hosp Aide; Pres Math Tm; Office Aide; Church Choir; Variety Show; High Hon Roll; Hon Roll; NHS; Stu Advsry Cncl Rep 84-86; 1st Prize Lions Club Spllng Bee 85; 2nd Prize 86; Lib Arts.

KSIAZYK, LORI ANN; Medford HS; Medford, MA; (Y); 26/407; Capt Color Guard; High Hon Roll; Hon Roll; NHS; Band & Color Grd Parents Schlrshp 86; John Hancock Awd 86; Chamberlayne JC; Advertsng.

KSIENIEWICZ, AMY; Hopkins Acad; Hadley, MA; (Y); 16/44; French Clb; Chorus; Color Guard; Nwsp Stf; Yrbk Stf; Var L Cheerleading; Var L Sftbl; Hon Roll; NHS; MVP JV Sftbl 85; Mst Imprvd Plyr Vrsty Sftbl 86; Law.

KUENSTER, TIMOTHY N; Somerset HS; Diamond Springs, CA; (Y); 4-H; Ski Clb; School Musical; School Play; Stage Crew; JV Crs Cntry; Var Capt Socr; JV Wrstlng; High Hon Roll; Hon Roll; U Of CA Santa Cruz; Comp Engrg.

KUKLA, BRIAN P; Murdock HS; Winchendon, MA; (Y); 6/100; Am Leg Boys St; Band; Stage Crew; Nwsp Stf; Yrbk Stf; Var JV Bsbl; Var JV Bsktbl; Var JV Ftbl; Hon Roll; NHS; Comp.

KUKLINSKI, EDWARD; Medway JR-SR HS; Medway, MA; (Y); 13/150; Var L Golf; Hon Roll; NHS; Ntl Merit Ltr; Govt Intrshp Cable TV 84-86; Prom Comm 84-85; Clark U.

KUKLINSKI, SUSAN; Northfield Mount Hermon HS; Wellesley, MA; (Y); Varsity Clb; Yrbk Stf; Crs Cntry; Socr; Swmmng; Trk; Hon Roll; Vrsty X Cntry Skng Awd 85; Lfsvng Awd 86; Comptv Hrsbck Rdng A Circuit; Ec.

KUKUCKA, PAULA; Smith Acad; Hatfield, MA; (Y); Cmnty Wkr; Key Clb; Variety Show; Yrbk Rptr; Cheerleading; Hon Roll; Yrbk Stf; High Hon Roll; USNMA Awd 86; Otstndng Frnch Stu 86; Prm Queen 86; Engr.

KULAS, ELIZABETH D; Berkshire Schl; Sheffield, MA; (Y); 8/110; VP Drama Clb; Intnl Clb; Key Clb; Stage Crew; Ed Nwsp Phtg; Nwsp Stf; JV Var Socr; Hon Roll; Ntl Merit SF; Ski Clb; Prefect 85-86; Schlrshp Awd 85-86; Economics.

KULKKULA, JANE E; Fitchburg HS; Fitchburg, MA; (Y); Church Yth Grp; Cmnty Wkr; Political Wkr; School Play; Var Capt Crs Cntry; Im Trk; High Hon Roll; Prfct Atten Awd; Drama Clb; Girl Scts; 5k Burbank Hosp Rd Race, 3rd Female JR Awd 84; Bst Sprtsmnshp Awd, Fth United Parish, Chrh Bsktbl 85; Fitchburg ST Coll; Hstry.

KULSICK, ROSEANN; Acton-Boxboro Regional HS; Acton, MA; (Y); 24/428; Church Yth Grp; Science Clb; Lit Mag; Off Jr Cls; Lcrss; JV Capt Socr; High Hon Roll; Hon Roll; VP NHS; Jr Cls Englsh Awd 86; Mst Dedctd JV Scr Tm 86; Educ.

KUO, BENJAMIN; Phillips Acad; Starkville, MS; (Y); Band; Jazz Band; Orch; School Musical; JV Lcrss; JV Socr; Ntl Merit Ltr; Inst Of Nclr Pwrs Orgnztn 86-87; Carnegie-Mellon U; Chem Engrng.

KUPA JR, EDWARD J; Phillips Acad; Andover, MA; (Y); Church Yth Grp; Ski Clb; Capt Bsktbl; Vrsty Crew Hd Charles Race 85-86; Blue Key 85-86; U S JR Mens Rowg Tm 86; Trinity Coll; Arch Engrng.

KURCHIAN, JOEL; Methuen HS; Methuen, MA; (Y); Bsktbl; Ftbl; Trk; U Lowell; Engrng.

KUSEK, MICHAEL; Holyoke HS; Holyoke, MA; (Y); 71/360; Am Leg Boys St; Capt Debate Tm; Drama Clb; Latin Clb; Capt NFL; Band; Concert Band; School Play; Stage Crew; Nwsp Phtg; Valley Press Clb Schlrshp; Frnsc & Debate Awds; Ithaca Coll; Pol Sci.

KUSEK, STACEY; Ware HS; Ware, MA; (Y); 1/120; Cmnty Wkr; Computer Clb; Debate Tm; Drama Clb; Model UN; Political Wkr; Spanish Clb; Teachers Aide; Chorus; School Musical; Hghst Avg Coll Bio & Geo 84-85; Acad Ftnss Asst Schlrshp 86; Western NE Coll.

KUTA, LISA; King Philip HS; Wrentham, MA; (Y); 31/217; Am Leg Aux Girls St; Trs Church Yth Grp; School Play; Yrbk Stf; Trs Frsh Cls; VP Soph Cls; VP Jr Cls; VP Sr Cls; Var L Crs Cntry; Var L Sftbl; Unsung Hero Awd Crss Cntry 85-86; Bio.

KUTZ, DALE; Lincoln-Sudbury Regional HS; Sudbury, MA; (Y); Church Yth Grp; Hosp Aide; Chorus; The Cum Laude Soc; Gordon Coll; Math.

KUTZ, DAVID; St Johns Prep; Ipswich, MA; (Y); 11/255; Spanish Clb; Im Mgr Bsktbl; Im Mgr Ftbl; Im Mgr Tennis; Im Mgr Vllybl; Hon Roll; NHS; Ntl Merit Ltr; Spanish NHS; G E Star Schlrshp 86; North Shore Hon Schlr 86; Cornell U; Engrng.

KUZA, KATHY; King Phillip Regional HS; Plainville, MA; (Y); 15/215; Sec Stu Cncl; VP Capt Bsktbl; Mgr(s); JV Socr; Hon Roll; NHS; 1st Rnnr-Up GRLS ST 86; Prom Prncss 86; Sprts Med.

KUZIA, MELISSA M; Monument Mountain Regional HS; Gt Barrington, MA; (Y); #30 In Class; German Clb; Red Cross Aide; Ski Clb; Varsity Clb; Chorus; Orch; School Musical; School Play; Trk; Hon Roll; Engl.

KWAN, HUBERT SHUMAN; Brookline HS; Brookline, MA; (Y); Pres Intnl Clb; Lit Mag; Rep Jr Cls; Rep Sr Cls; Var L Trk; Var L Vllybl; Hon Roll; NHS; Prfct Atten Awd; St Schlr; 2nd Pl Awd Joseph M Smith Mem 10k Rd Race 84; Boston U Scholar 86-90; Akers House Awd Acad Excllnce 86; Harvard Bus Schl; Mngmnt.

KWAN, JOHNNY; Boston Latin Schl; Boston, MA; (Y); Sec Chess Clb; L Science Clb; Hon Roll; NHS; Schlrshp Art Crs At Museum Of Fine Arts 83-87.

KWAPIEN, MARY; Westfield HS; Westfield, MA; (Y); Drama Clb; French Clb; Orch; School Play; Stage Crew; Jr NHS; Typng Awd 85; Comp Sci.

KWONG, JOEL; Boston Latin Schl; Jamaica Plain, MA; (Y); 21/275; Pres Chess Clb; Computer Clb; Key Clb; Chorus; Swing Chorus; Nwsp Rptr; Lit Mag; High Hon Roll; NHS; Ntl Merit Ltr; Harvard U/MIT Careers Med Cert Wnr 86; Tnager Hosp Vlntr Awd 85; Bio Olympd Awd Wnr 84; Pre Med.

KYRANIS, ALEXANDRA; Braintree HS; E Braintree, MA; (Y); 29/442; Spanish Clb; Nwsp Rptr; Nwsp Stf; Hon Roll; NHS; Sec Spanish NHS; Exchng Pgm Madrid Spn Cardnl Herrera Oria HS 86; Intl Rltns.

L HEUREUX, DAVID; Bishop Connolly HS; Fall River, MA; (Y); 30/167; Cmnty Wkr; Drama Clb; Acpl Chr; Chorus; Church Choir; School Musical; High Hon Roll; Hon Roll; Southeastern MA U; Ed.

LA BAIRE, WILLIAM; Bartlett HS; Webster, MA; (Y); Boy Scts; Camera Clb; Cmnty Wkr; French Clb; Library Aide; Political Wkr; Variety Show; Yrbk Phtg; Trk; Bus.

LA BASTIE, CURT; Blackstone Valley Tech; Mendon, MA; (Y); Boy Scts; Church Yth Grp; SADD; Trk; Hon Roll; Pres Schlr.

LA BRUNERIE, REBECCA; Dana Hall HS; Columbia, MO; (Y); Pres Intnl Clb; JCL; Key Clb; Latin Clb; Political Wkr; Pres Science Clb; Nwsp Rptr; Mgr(s); Var Tennis; Hon Roll; Intl Politcl Awrns Awd 86; U Of IN Bloomington.

LA FLAMME, JEFFREY R; Bristol Plymouth Reg HS; Taunton, MA; (Y); 21/185; Boy Scts; Church Yth Grp; Bsktbl; Ftbl; Wt Lftg; Elks Awd; Hon Roll; St Schlr; Wllm Meunier Schlrshp 86; Paul Couture Schlrshp 86; Brstl-Plymth Prnts Clb Schlrshp 86; Southeastern MA U; Bus.

LA FLAND, TRACEY; Our Lady Of Nazareth Acad; Methuen, MA; (Y); 19/56; Spanish Clb; School Musical; Nwsp Stf; Ed Yrbk Phtg; Pres Trs Stu Cncl; Mgr(s); Score Keeper; Hon Roll; Prfct Atten Awd; U Of NH; Pre-Med.

LA FLEUR, CHERYL L; Chicopee Comprehensive HS; Chicopee, MA; (Y); French Clb; Yrbk Stf; Rep Jr Cls; Rep Sr Cls; Var Powder Puff Ftbl; Var Socr; Var Trk; Scr All Str Tm 84-85; Johnson ST VT; Hlth Sci.

LA FLEUR, SCOTT; Hudson HS; Hudson, MA; (Y); Church Yth Grp; Exploring; Pep Clb; Ski Clb; Varsity Clb; School Musical; Yrbk Stf; Var Ftbl; Hon Roll; Mrktng.

LA FONTAINE, MICHELE; Holy Name CCHS; Worcester, MA; (Y); 88/290; School Musical; Lit Mag; Hon Roll; Algbra I Awd; Art II Awd; Lit, Art III Awd; Fshn Dsgn.

LA FOSSE, JULIE; Hampshire Regional HS; Southampton, MA; (Y); 4-H; Political Wkr; SADD; Band; Chorus; Mrchg Band; Variety Show; Stu Cncl; Bsktbl; Hon Roll; Outstndng Vocalist 84-85; Bus Admin.

LA POINTE, BRIAN M; Grafton HS; Grafton, MA; (Y); Am Leg Boys St; Church Yth Grp; Band; School Musical; Stu Cncl; Var L Ftbl; Var L Tennis; Engrng.

LA PORT, BRENNA; Hoosac Valley HS; Adams, MA; (Y); 36/150; Cmnty Wkr; Pep Clb; Ski Clb; School Play; Yrbk Stf; JV Cheerleading; L Crs Cntry; Exec Sec.

LA PORTE, RENEE; Seekonk HS; Seekonk, MA; (Y); 80/233; Church Yth Grp; Hosp Aide; SADD; Nwsp Rptr; Yrbk Rptr; L Swmmng; Hon Roll; FBI.

LA ROCHELLE, CHRISTOPHER; Sandwich HS; E Sandwich, MA; (Y); 30/183; Am Leg Boys St; Ski Clb; SADD; Yrbk Stf; Stu Cncl; Var Capt Ice Hcky; Var Capt Socr; Hon Roll; NHS.

LA ROCHELLE, STEVEN; Chicopee Comp HS; Chicopee, MA; (Y); 81/310; Var L Ice Hcky; Latin Awd 83-84; American Intl Coll; Comp.

LA ROSA, CHRISTINE; Boston Latin Schl; Hyde Park, MA; (Y); 14/274; Church Yth Grp; Cmnty Wkr; Band; Concert Band; Nwsp Ed-Chief; Lit Mag; Hon Roll; NHS; Holy Cross Bk Awd 86; Jordan Marsh JR Cncl,Yth Advsry Concil 85-86; MA Advnc D Studies Prgm 86.

LA ROSA, MARY BETH; Boston Latin Schl; Hyde Park, MA; (Y); 27/284; Church Yth Grp; Cmnty Wkr; Computer Clb; VP JA; Varsity Clb; Cheerleading; Var L Tennis; NHS; Pres Schlr; Boston U.

LA VALLEE JR, EDWIN J; Plymouth Carver HS; Plymouth, MA; (Y); 31/545; Boys Clb Am; Boy Scts; Church Yth Grp; Var L Bsbl; Var L Bsktbl; Var L Ftbl; Im Lcrss; Im Vllybl; Hon Roll; NHS; Math.

LA VALLEY, KRISTEN; East Longmeadow HS; E Longmeadow, MA; (Y); 18/200; AFS; Church Yth Grp; Hosp Aide; Intnl Clb; VP Frsh Cls; Pres Stu Cncl; JV Bsktbl; JV Var Sftbl; Var Swmmng; Hon Roll; Bio.

LA VERDA, DAVID; Pittsfield HS; Pittsfield, MA; (Y); 25/400; Computer Clb; Exploring; JA; Latin Clb; High Hon Roll; Hon Roll; NHS; JA Achvr Awd 84-86; Silvr Mdl Natl JR Clsscl Leag Latn Exm 84-86; Magna Cum Laude Cert Natl 85; Pre Med.

LA VIOLETTE, LISA; Holyoke HS; Holyoke, MA; (Y); 82/400; Art Clb; Pres Church Yth Grp; Cmnty Wkr; Teachers Aide; High Hon Roll; Hon Roll; Trd Stus 84-85; Chrg Of Trtng Pgm 85-86; BYU; Accntng.

LABBEE, MICHELE; Smith Acad; Hatfield, MA; (Y); Hst Drama Clb; Sec Key Clb; School Play; Nwsp Rptr; Nwsp Stf; Score Keeper; L Sftbl; Hon Roll; 1st Declamations Smith Acad, 2nd St Am Leg Oratorical Cntst 86; Brdcst Jrnlsm.

LABERGE, AMY; St Bernards HS; Lunenburg, MA; (Y); Sec Drama Clb; Hosp Aide; VP Spanish Clb; School Musical; Off Soph Cls; Off Stu Cncl; JV Fld Hcky; Bay ST JC; Travel/Trsm.

LABOSSIERE, ROBERT; Wilmington HS; Wilmington, MA; (Y); Camera Clb; JA; Ski Clb; Spanish Clb; Band; Concert Band; Mrchg Band; Nwsp Stf; Yrbk Phtg; Yrbk Sprt Ed; GA Tech; Engrng.

LACASSE, JENNIFER; New Bedford HS; New Bedford, MA; (Y); #46 In Class; Drama Clb; VP JA; JCL; Science Clb; SADD; School Musical; Stage Crew; Stu Cncl; Hon Roll; Southeastern MA U; CPA.

LACAVA, MICHAEL; Wilmington HS; Wilmington, MA; (Y); Pres JA; Science Clb; SADD; Band; Jazz Band; Mrchg Band; School Play; Nwsp Rptr; Hon Roll; NHS; Music.

LACET, YONETTE; Boston Tech HS; Boston, MA; (Y); Bsktbl; Sftbl; Wt Lftg; Hon Roll; Prfct Atten Awd; Schl Spirit Awd 83-84; Mech Engr.

LACEY, ANNETTE; St Gregorys HS; Dorchester, MA; (Y); French Clb; Mission Clb 85-86.

LACHANCE, KEVIN; Athol HS; Athol, MA; (Y); 10/150; Nwsp Sprt Ed; Var Bsktbl; Var Ftbl; Var Trk; Hon Roll; NHS; Comp Prog.

LACHAPELLE, JULI E; Southbridge HS; Southbridge, MA; (Y); 35/123; Art Clb; Dance Clb; Band; Concert Band; Mrchg Band; Nwsp Ed-Chief; Nwsp Stf; Hon Roll; Band Awd 85; Hunter Coll; Theater.

LACIVITA, CHRISTOPHER; Silver Lake Regional HS; Halifax, MA; (Y); 69/450; Boy Scts; Chess Clb; SADD; Band; Chorus; Concert Band; Drm Mjr(t); Jazz Band; Mrchg Band; Orch; Aerospc Engrng.

LACROIX, MARIE; Chicopee Comprehensive HS; Chicopee, MA; (Y); 6/332; German Clb; Variety Show; Yrbk Stf; Var Cheerleading; High Hon Roll; VP NHS; Prfct Atten Awd.

LACROSSE, MEREDITH; Old Rochester Regional HS; Marion, MA; (Y); 35/147; Cmnty Wkr; Drama Clb; Hosp Aide; Office Aide; Ski Clb; Rep Stu Cncl; Fld Hcky; Trk; Top 10 Engl 84; UCLA; Bus Adm.

LADGE, JODI; Randolph HS; Randolph, MA; (Y); Cmnty Wkr; SADD; Drill Tm; Yrbk Stf; Var Capt Cheerleading; Powder Puff Ftbl; Hon Roll; NHS; Bus Admn.

LADURANTAVE, LISA; Taunton HS; Taunton, MA; (Y); Hosp Aide; Library Aide; Office Aide; Ski Clb; JV Crs Cntry; Pom Pon; Hon Roll; Brdcst Jrnlsm.

LAFLEUR, JENNIFER; Walpole HS; E Walpole, MA; (Y); 55/287; Drama Clb; Leo Clb; Stage Crew; Socr; Hon Roll; Fash Dsgn.

LAFONTAINE, KIMBERLY A; Drury SR HS; Clarksburg, MA; (Y); 5/189; Nwsp Ed-Chief; Yrbk Stf; Stu Cncl; High Hon Roll; Hon Roll; NHS; Elk Stu Mnth 85; Amer Lg Essay Cont Wnnr 85; Drury Faclty Assn Scholar 86; Anna Maria Coll; Med Tech.

LAFRENAIS, KERRY; Southbridge HS; Southbridge, MA; (Y); 11/136; Yrbk Ed-Chief; Yrbk Stf; Frsh Cls; Soph Cls; Jr Cls; Sr Cls; High Hon Roll; Hon Roll; Jr NHS; NHS; Southeastern MA U; Med Tech.

LAGRANT, ANNETTE; Pathfinder Regional V T HS; Ware, MA; (Y); SADD; Nwsp Rptr; Nwsp Stf; Yrbk Stf; Sec Frsh Cls; Sec Stu Cncl; Math Awd 84; Englsh Awd 85; UMASS; Comp.

LAGUE, LORI; New Bedford HS; New Bedford, MA; (Y); 47/701; Drama Clb; Exploring; Stage Crew; Stu Cncl; High Hon Roll; Hon Roll; Jr NHS; Bus Adm.

LAHAM, BRUCE; Boston Technical HS; Boston, MA; (Y); Off Church Yth Grp; Office Aide; Teachers Aide; Variety Show; Hon Roll; Prfct Atten Awd; Amer Yth Fndtn I Dare You Awd 86; Digital Eqpmnt AYF Scholar 86; Comp Elec Engrng.

LAIDLAW, ANNEMARIE; Norton HS; Norton, MA; (S); 15/160; SADD; Varsity Clb; Yrbk Bus Mgr; Yrbk Stf; VP Stu Cncl; Var L Cheerleading; Trk; Hon Roll; NEDT Awd.

LAJOIE, ROBERT; Leicester HS; Cherry Valley, MA; (Y); Latin Clb; Clark U; Comptrs.

LAK, CAROL; Cathedral HS; Indian Orchard, MA; (Y); 164/508; Chorus; School Musical; Variety Show; Educ.

LALAKIDIS, MELINA; W Roxbury HS; Roslindale, MA; (S); 6/250; Political Wkr; Yrbk Bus Mgr; Yrbk Stf; Hon Roll; Ntl Merit Ltr; Secry Natl Hnr Soc 85-86; Bus Admin.

LALLIER, JOANNE; Bishop Feehan HS; N Attleboro, MA; (Y); Cmnty Wkr; Band; Drill Tm; Mrchg Band; Swmmng; Twrlr; Vrsty Ltr, Pin Majrtts 85 & 86; Advrtsng.

LALLY, DONNA; Dracut HS; Dracut, MA; (Y); High Hon Roll; Hon Roll; Hnr Awds All A Spnsh & Typg 84-85; Exec Secy.

LAM, KING; Cambridge Rindge And Latin HS; Cambridge, MA; (S); Church Yth Grp; Cmnty Wkr; Intnl Clb; Key Clb; Math Clb; Science Clb; Ski Clb; Off Jr Cls; Badmtn; Coach Actv; Math & Sci Hghst Achvt-Upward Bound 85; Engl Hghst Achvt-Upward Bound 85; Hghst Acad Awd-Upwrd Bnd 85.

LAM, MICHAEL; Doherty Memorial HS; Worcester, MA; (Y); JA; Spanish Clb; Variety Show; Ed Yrbk Phtg; Var Bowling; Var L Trk; Hon Roll.

LAM, THANH; Burncoat SR HS; Worcester, MA; (Y); Intnl Clb; Band; Variety Show; Var Capt Socr; Var Tennis; Hon Roll; NHS; Prfct Atten Awd; Ntl French Test Awd 85; Worcester Poly Tech Inst; Engr.

LAM, VINH; Boston Technical HS; Dorchester, MA; (Y); Boys Clb Am; Intnl Clb; High Hon Roll; Hon Roll; Ntl Merit Ltr; Prfct Atten Awd; Cert Of Recog & Awds 84-85 & 85-86; Hnr Roll Awd Prft Attend 82-83; Elec Engr.

LAMALFA, CHRISTINA; Swampscott HS; Nahant, MA; (Y); 15/238; Church Yth Grp; French Clb; Frnch Awd 86; Nrsg.

LAMARRE, DENISE; Mansfield HS; Mansfield, MA; (Y); 22/203; SADD; Stage Crew; VP Stu Cncl; Capt Fld Hcky; Capt Trk; Hon Roll; J J Kelly Rlys 1st Pl 85; Psychlgy.

LAMBERT, CATHY; Tahanto Regional HS; Berlin, MA; (Y); 4/57; JA; Ski Clb; Band; Nwsp Stf; Bausch & Lomb Sci Awd; High Hon Roll; Jr NHS; Lion Awd; NHS; Ntl Merit Ltr; Arch.

LAMBERT, CHRISTINE; Phillips Acad; Andover, MA; (Y); Letterman Clb; Speech Tm; Hon Roll; Ntl Merit SF; L Bsktbl; Med.

LAMBERT, DAVID; Westport HS; N Westport, MA; (Y); Exploring; Paper Boy Of Mnth 85; SMU; Engr.

LAMBERT, DONNA; Bishop Connolly HS; Somerset, MA; (Y); Cmnty Wkr; High Hon Roll; St Schlr; Church Yth Grp; Drama Clb; Yrbk Stf; Hon Roll; MA ST Schlrshp 86; Ctzns Schlrshp Fndtn Somerset 86; Highest Achvt Law 86; Framingham ST; Mgnt.

LAMBERT, KATHLEEN; St Marys HS; Westfield, MA; (Y); 6/59; Camera Clb; Teachers Aide; Chorus; Nwsp Rptr; Yrbk Stf; Lit Mag; Var Capt Socr; Hon Roll; NHS; Hofstra U; Jrnlsm.

LAMBERT, KIMBERLY A; Saint Bernards HS; Leominster, MA; (Y); 41/152; Art Clb; Office Aide; Chorus; Nwsp Stf; Hon Roll; Anna Maria Coll Grnt 86; Anna Maria Coll; Lgl Asstnt.

LAMBERT, LISA; Newburyport HS; Newburyport, MA; (Y); Hosp Aide; VP Soph Cls; JV Capt Bsktbl; Var L Cheerleading; Var L Crs Cntry; Var L Trk; Hon Roll; Span Awd; Pyschology.

LAMBERT, MICHELLE; Turners Falls HS; Turners Fls, MA; (Y); 5/85; Cmnty Wkr; Sec Jr Cls; Sec Sr Cls; Rep Stu Cncl; JV Bsktbl; JV Cheerleading; Var Trk; Hon Roll; NHS; Excllnc Spnsh III & IV 84-86; Cnstnt Hgh Aver In Typg I 84-85.

LAMKIN, JONATHAN; Randolph HS; Randolph, MA; (Y); Trs SADD; School Play; Variety Show; Yrbk Stf; Rep Soph Cls; Rep Jr Cls; Rep Sr Cls; JV Var Bsktbl; JV Var Socr; Var Trk; KIDS Awd Hgh Achvt US Hstry 84; Bus.

LAMOTHE, BARRETT; Concord/Carlisle HS; Lincoln, MA; (Y); 45/321; Rep Soph Cls; Rep Jr Cls; Rep Sr Cls; Var Fld Hcky; Var Capt Lcrss; NHS.

LAMOTHE, RONALD M; Lunenburg HS; Lunenburg, MA; (Y); 17/123; School Play; Yrbk Stf; VP Frsh Cls; VP Soph Cls; VP Jr Cls; VP Sr Cls; Capt Bsbl; Capt Bsktbl; Capt Ftbl; NHS; HS Cmnty Schlrshp-Hnrb Mntn Amercn Leg Schl Awd 86; HS Toko Cmnty Snr Awd-Athltc Dirctrs Awd 86; Tufts U; Lbrl Arts.

LAMPHIER, JOHN; Wakefield HS; Wakefield, MA; (Y); Am Leg Boys St; Church Yth Grp; Trs Key Clb; JV Ice Hcky; JV Socr; Var L Tennis; High Hon Roll; Stu Adv Cncl 86; Treas Ntl Hnr Soc 83; U PA; Bus.

LAMPROS, ELENA M; Lynn English HS; Lynn, MA; (Y); 1/338; Am Leg Aux Girls St; Cmnty Wkr; Drama Clb; Pres Science Clb; Spanish Clb; School Play; Bausch & Lomb Sci Awd; Elks Awd; High Hon Roll; NHS; Hrvrd Prz Book Awd 85; Stu Govrnmnt Day 86; Fnlst MA JR Miss Pgnt 86; Hrvard U; Vtrnry Med.

LAMSON, BRIAN; South High Community Schl; Worcester, MA; (Y); 9/225; SADD; Capt Bowling; Hon Roll; NHS; Georgiana Newton Awd 86; Assumption Coll; Acctng.

LANCKTON, BENJAMIN E; Newton South HS; Newton, MA; (Y); 4/273; Drama Clb; French Clb; Temple Yth Grp; School Musical; School Play; Lit Mag; French Hon Soc; High Hon Roll; Ntl Merit Schol; Zeiderman Awd Otstndng Hebrew HS 83; Fclty Awd Newton S HS 86; Thtr Arts Awd Newton S HS 86; Yale Coll; Mlclr Blgy.

LANDO, DIANA; Watertown HS; Watertown, MA; (Y); Aud/Vis; Cmnty Wkr; SADD; Teachers Aide; Yrbk Phtg; Hon Roll; Photo Awd 85; Dance Awd 84-86; Dean JC; Dance.

LANDRY, KEITH D; Waltham HS; Waltham, MA; (Y); 11/575; Am Leg Boys St; VP Church Yth Grp; Drama Clb; French Clb; Latin Clb; School Musical; School Play; Nwsp Ed-Chief; Trk; NHS; Emerson Coll; Brdcst Jrnlsm.

LANDRY, RICHARD F; Maynard HS; Maynard, MA; (Y); 25/100; Am Leg Boys St; Var L Bsbl; JV Bsktbl; Var L Ftbl; JV Var Score Keeper; JV Var Timer; Hon Roll; Prfct Atten Awd; Hly Cross; Pltcl Sci.

LANE, JOANNE; Braintree HS; Braintree, MA; (Y); 99/416; Cmnty Wkr; Ski Clb; Hon Roll; Englsh Olympd Awd 83; Bridgewater ST Coll; Chld Educ.

LANE, STEVEN; Taunton HS; Taunton, MA; (Y); #3 In Class; Am Leg Boys St; Boy Scts; Math Tm; Ski Clb; Var Tennis; JV Trk; High Hon Roll; NHS; :Arch.

LANE, TIMOTHY; Westfield HS; Westfield, MA; (Y); 4/350; Am Leg Boys St; Latin Clb; School Musical; Rep Frsh Cls; JV Socr; Var L Swmmng; Var L Trk; Pres NHS; Excllnce Frnch I 85; Excllnce Latin I 84; Excllnce Latin II 86; Govt.

LANFRANCHI, CHRIS; Saint Dominic Savio HS; E Boston, MA; (Y); 3/110; Pres Key Clb; Math Clb; SADD; School Play; Nwsp Ed-Chief; VP Stu Cncl; Var Bsbl; High Hon Roll; Pres Schlr; Science Clb; Semi Schlrshp Boston Coll 86; Boston Coll; Law.

LANG, PATRICIA; King Philip Regional HS; Norfolk, MA; (Y); 58/213; Church Yth Grp; Office Aide; School Play; Im Powder Puff Ftbl; JV Sftbl; Hon Roll; NHS.

LANGADINOS, NICHOLAS; Arlington HS; Arlington, MA; (Y); Church Yth Grp; SADD; Church Choir; Concert Band; Var Ftbl; Hon Roll; Pres Awdd Phys Ed 82; Comp Awd 82; Wentworth Coll; Drftng.

LANGENHAGEN, RODD; Hingham HS; Hingham, MA; (Y); 1/340; Boy Scts; Chrmn Red Cross Aide; Off Jazz Band; Capt Stu Cncl; L Socr; Var L Trk; Bausch & Lomb Sci Awd; Drama Clb; Off Band; Off Concert Band; Superior Rnkg Ntl Hstry Dy Wash DC 86; Hrvd Bk Awd 86; Old Clny Lg Trpl Jmp Chmp 86; OCL Chmp Rly 86.

LANGER JR, ALAN K; Greater Lawrence Technical HS; Lawrence, MA; (Y); 3/400; Model UN; SADD; High Hon Roll; NHS; Electronic Technician.

LANGGUTH, CHRISTEN; Marlboro HS; Marlboro, MA; (Y); Church Yth Grp; JA; Teachers Aide; Band; Concert Band; Mrchg Band; Trk; Hon Roll; Bus.

LANGHILL, TODD; St Johns HS; Westboro, MA; (Y); Aud/Vis; Boy Scts; Exploring; Ski Clb; Im Bsbl; Im Bsktbl; Im Ftbl; Im Socr; Im Sftbl; Scandinavian Athltc Clb 86; U S ME; Crmnlgy.

LANGILLE, KRISTEN; Twin City Christian Schl; Leominster, MA; (Y); 1/8; Church Yth Grp; Chorus; School Play; Stage Crew; Yrbk Bus Mgr; Yrbk Ed-Chief; Yrbk Phtg; Yrbk Sprt Ed; Yrbk Stf; Var Bsktbl; Adavanced Algebra Ii & Trig Awd 85-86; Liberty U; Acctnt.

LANGILLE, STEPHEN; Taunton HS; Taunton, MA; (Y); Band; Concert Band; Mrchg Band; Crs Cntry; Trk; Hon Roll; Most Imprvd Spring Trk Tm 86; Bio.

LANGLAN, ERIC E; Silver Lake Regional HS; Kingston, MA; (Y); #21 In Class; Am Leg Boys St; JV Bsktbl; Var Socr; Var Tennis; Hon Roll; NHS; Voice Dem Awd; OB.

LANGLEY, KEVIN; Bishop Feehan HS; Attleboro, MA; (Y); Computer Clb; Ski Clb; Y-Teens; Var Crs Cntry; Var Trk; Hon Roll; Prfct Atten Awd; Spanish NHS; Outstndng In Bio 84 & 85; Sprts Med.

LANIER, TINA; Quaboag Regional HS; Warren, MA; (Y); 19/85; JA; Varsity Clb; Hst Sr Cls; JV Bsktbl; JV Fld Hcky; Var Sftbl; High Hon Roll; Hon Roll; NHS; Bus Admin.

LANKARGE, KIMBERLY; Hopkins Acad; Hadley, MA; (S); #2 In Class; Spanish Clb; Band; Chorus; Concert Band; Mrchg Band; High Hon Roll; Hon Roll; NHS; Pres Jr Cls.

LANNI, KEITH ADAM; North Attleboro HS; North Attleboro, MA; (Y); 49/249; JCL; Latin Clb; Capt Varsity Clb; Capt L Bsbl; JV Bsktbl; Im Vllybl; Hon Roll; Fisher-Kelly Schlrshp 86; Harry W & Beatrice H Fisher Mem Schlrshp Fund 86; Syracuse U; Jrnlsm.

LANNI, PASQUALE; Lunenburg HS; Lunenburg, MA; (Y); 29/124; Intnl Clb; School Play; Stage Crew; Im Stat Bsktbl; Var L Ftbl; Var Mgr(s); Im Wt Lftg; High Hon Roll; Hon Roll; Laurel Garden Clb Awd 86; Lundenburg Citzns Schlrhsp 86; Lunenburg Grange Schlrshp 86; Cornell U; Agronomy.

LANUCHA, SUSAN; Easthampton HS; Easthampton, MA; (Y); 14/142; Yrbk Stf; JV Socr; High Hon Roll; Hon Roll; Jr NHS; NHS; Esthmptn Rtry Clb Awd Schlrshp 86; Sprngfld Coll; Rehab Srvs.

LANZETTA, LISA; Attleboro HS; Attleboro, MA; (Y); Band; Concert Band; Mrchg Band; High Hon Roll; NHS; Grnd Concour Frnch Awd 86; Typng Schlrshp 86; Exc Atndnc 86; Physcl Thrpy.

LAPERRIERE, CHRISTINE; Malden HS; Malden, MA; (Y); #29 In Class; Key Clb; SADD; Hst Band; Concert Band; Mrchg Band; Variety Show.

LAPINSKI, ALLISON; Foxboro HS; Foxboro, MA; (Y); 95/230; SADD; Yrbk Sprt Ed; Yrbk Stf; Hon Roll; Psych.

LAPLANTE, LISA; Foxboro HS; Foxboro, MA; (Y); 13/216; Dance Clb; French Clb; JA; Ski Clb; Nwsp Rptr; Yrbk Stf; Rep Frsh Cls; Rep Soph Cls; Rep Jr Cls; Rep Sr Cls.

LAPRAD, JAMES; Medway HS; Medway, MA; (Y); 43/140; Pres Drama Clb; Band; Concert Band; Jazz Band; Mrchg Band; Pep Band; School Play; Golf; Hon Roll; Psychlgy.

LAPRADE, MELISSA; North HS; Worcester, MA; (Y); Hon Roll; Worc ST Coll; Bus.

LAQUE, LORI; New Bedford HS; New Bedford, MA; (Y); 47/701; Drama Clb; Exploring; Stu Cncl; High Hon Roll; Hon Roll.

LAQUIDARA, MICHAEL; North Reading HS; N Reading, MA; (Y); Computer Clb; Math Clb; Math Tm; Elec Engr.

LARA, AL; Central Catholic HS; Lawrence, MA; (Y); Political Wkr; Nwsp Rptr; Nwsp Stf; Trk; Art Clb; Church Yth Grp; Cmnty Wkr; Teachers Aide; Church Choir; High Hon Roll; Perkins Prz Wrtng 82.

LARDEN, DEBORAH; Concord/Carlisle HS; Concord, MA; (S); DECA; Cheerleading; Wittenberg U; Bus.

LAREAU, ANN A; Concord Acad; Englewood, CO; (Y); Drama Clb; Chorus; School Musical; School Play; Stage Crew; Rep Soph Cls; Pres Jr Cls; VP Stu Cncl; JV Fld Hcky; JV Lcrss; Syracuse U; Theatre.

LAREAU, CRAIG; Fitchburg HS; Fitchburg, MA; (Y); 4/214; Am Leg Boys St; Yrbk Stf; Capt Bsbl; Var Ftbl; Capt Trk; NHS; Cntrl MA Cnfrnc Ftbll Offcls Schlrshp Awd 85; Nat Ftbll Fndtn Hll Fm Schlr Athlt Awd 85; Yale U; Med.

LAREAU, JOHANE; Douglas Memorial HS; Douglas, MA; (Y); 4-H; Hosp Aide; Yrbk Phtg; Yrbk Stf; Rep Frsh Cls; Rep Soph Cls; Pres Jr Cls; Pres Sr Cls; Badmtn; Vllybl; Bio.

LARIVIERE, CRISTIE; Gardners HS; Gardner, MA; (Y); 25/150; Church Yth Grp; French Clb; Chorus; Madrigals; School Musical; Nwsp Stf; Rep Jr Cls; Var Crs Cntry; Var Trk; Hon Roll; Pre Med.

LARIVIERE, KRIS; Barnstable HS; Hyannis, MA; (Y); 20/392; Drama Clb; Band; Concert Band; Drm Mjr(t); Flag Corp; Mrchg Band; Orch; School Play; Hon Roll.

LARIVIERE, LYNN; Douglas Memorial HS; E Douglas, MA; (Y); 3/39; Church Yth Grp; Varsity Clb; Ed Yrbk Ed-Chief; VP Soph Cls; VP Jr Cls; VP Sr Cls; Capt Bsktbl; Sftbl; DAR Awd; Hon Roll; 3rd Clss Schlstc Achvt 86; MA ST Schlr 86; Poltcl Sci Awd 86; Northeastern U; Phy Thrpy.

LARKIN, BILL; Bedford HS; Bedford, MA; (Y); 105/210; Aud/Vis; Church Yth Grp; Drama Clb; Math Tm; Political Wkr; Thesps; Chorus; Madrigals; School Musical; School Play; Dram Fest 86; Part Of Bet Ensmbl 86; Part Of Best Ply 85; Communications.

LARKIN, DEBRA; Tahanto Regional HS; Boylston, MA; (Y); 25/60; Church Yth Grp; Drama Clb; JA; Band; Chorus; Nwsp Stf; Yrbk Stf; Sftbl; Vllybl; Hon Roll; Fitchburg ST Coll; Educ.

LARKIN, PETER; Bishop Feehan HS; Attleboro, MA; (Y); Hosp Aide; SADD; Yrbk Stf; Rep Jr Cls; Stu Cncl; Var L Bsbl; Var L Bsktbl; Var L Ftbl; Powder Puff Ftbl; Prfct Atten 85-86.

LARSON, CECILIA; Douglas Memorial HS; E Douglas, MA; (Y); Color Guard; Mrchg Band; NHS; Bus.

LARSON, JANINE; Dana Hall School; Woodbury Heights, NJ; (Y); Hosp Aide; Library Aide; Political Wkr; Lit Mag; Stu Cncl; Var Capt Fld Hcky; JV Lcrss; L Var Sftbl; L Var Swmmng; Var Vllybl; Modern Lang Awd-Frnch 85-86; The Band Coll Prz For Critical Wrtng 86; Bryn Mawr Coll.

LARSON, JILEE; Nauset Regional HS; S Orleans, MA; (Y); 4-H; German Clb; Band; Yrbk Stf; Hon Roll; Lbrl Arts.

LARSON, KRISTINA B; North HS; Worcester, MA; (Y); 3/208; Pep Clb; Varsity Clb; Nwsp Rptr; Hst Sr Cls; Var L Cheerleading; Var Socr; Bausch & Lomb Sci Awd; Elks Awd; High Hon Roll; NHS; Frances Hiatt Schlrhsp 86-90; Comm Wealth Schlr Grnt 85; MA U Amhearst; Med Engr.

LARSON, SHERRI; Apponequet Regional HS; Assonet, MA; (Y); Office Aide; Teachers Aide; Stage Crew; Hon Roll; NHS; Engrng.

LASHWAY, DEBORAH M; Hampshire Regional HS; Goshen, MA; (Y); 6/135; Sec Jr Cls; Sec Sr Cls; Sec Stu Cncl; High Hon Roll; Hon Roll; NHS; 3rd Pl Ntl Math Exm 85.

LASSIGE, JENNIFER; Silver Lake Regional HS; Kingston, MA; (Y); 60/450; Am Leg Aux Girls St; Hosp Aide; Library Aide; Nwsp Stf; Yrbk Stf; Sec Jr Cls; Sec Sr Cls; JV Var Cheerleading; JV Var Socr; Hon Roll; Fash Dsgn.

LATAILLE, MICHAEL; Tantasqua Regional HS; Sturbridge, MA; (Y); Varsity Clb; Ftbl; Trk; High Hon Roll; Hon Roll; NHS; Bus Mgmt.

LATCH, SCOTT; Westford Acad; Westford, MA; (Y); AFS; French Clb; Swmmng; High Hon Roll; Hon Roll; Athlete Rep To New England Swmmng 85-87; Architecture.

LATESSA, ROBYN; B M C Durfee HS; Fall River, MA; (Y); 2/691; Sec Varsity Clb; Concert Band; Mrchg Band; Trs Stu Cncl; Var Capt Cheerleading; Pres NHS; Sal; Intnl Clb; Math Clb; Math Tm; Elks Teen Of Yr 86; Karen A Jarabek Mem Awd Top Schlr/Ath 86; Durfee Hilltop Hall Fame Bst All Arnd 86; Holy Cross Coll; Pre-Med.

LATHAM, EDWARD A; Sandwich HS; Sandwich, MA; (Y); 1/157; Am Leg Boys St; Cmnty Wkr; Math Tm; Ski Clb; Var Capt Bsktbl; High Hon Roll; Hon Roll; Pres NHS; Ntl Merit SF; Val; Tp Math Awd 86; Physcs Awd 86; Sndwch JR Wmns Clb Awd 86; Prsdntl Acdmc Ftnss Awd 86; Hrvrd Bk Awd 85; Worcester Polytech Inst; Engnrn.

LATHAM, STEVEN; Hopkins Acad; Hadley, MA; (Y); 5/48; Latin Clb; Spanish Clb; Band; Mrchg Band; Stu Cncl; Var Bsbl; Var Bsktbl; Var Socr; Hon Roll; Trs NHS.

LATHAM, WILLIAM; Sandwich HS; Sandwich, MA; (Y); 27/180; Am Leg Boys St; Ski Clb; Rep Soph Cls; Rep Jr Cls; JV Bsktbl; Var Lcrss; Hon Roll.

LATHAN, CHRISTOPHER S; Classical HS; Springfield, MA; (Y); 135/389; Church Yth Grp; Service Clb; Spanish Clb; Church Choir; Trs Frsh Cls; Var Wrstlng; Ntl Merit SF; Prfct Atten Awd; Commdtn Outstndng Negro Stdnt, Negro Schlr 85; UMASS; Chem Engr.

LATOUR, DEBRA; Gardner HS; Gardner, MA; (Y); 14/164; GAA; Spanish Clb; Chorus; Rep Sr Cls; Bsktbl; Fld Hcky; Tennis; Hon Roll; Fairfield; Bio.

LATTI, CAROLYN; Concord-Carlisle HS; Concord, MA; (Y); Varsity Clb; Off Soph Cls; Off Soph Cls; Off Jr Cls; JV Var Fld Hcky; JV Lcrss; Hon Roll.

LAUB, CHARLES; Longmeadow HS; Longmeadow, MA; (Y); 48/265; Church Yth Grp; Acpl Chr; Chorus; School Play; Variety Show; Yrbk Stf; Capt Trk; High Hon Roll; MA Inst Of Tech; Polymer Sci.

LAUCKS, MELINDA; Dana Hall Schl; Needham, MA; (Y); Cmnty Wkr; Key Clb; Q&S; School Play; Nwsp Phtg; Nwsp Rptr; Nwsp Sprt Ed; Nwsp Stf; Var L Fld Hcky; Hon Roll; Marguerite Aldridge Putnum Prchse Prze Art 85; Pltcl Clb; Barnard Coll.

LAULETTA, ANTHONY; Boston Latin Schl; Boston, MA; (Y); Boy Scts; Camera Clb; Political Wkr; VP Ski Clb; Yrbk Stf; Hon Roll; Vice President CYO 83-85; Aeronautical Engrng.

LAURENZA, LYNDA; Matignon HS; Cambridge, MA; (S); 17/179; Drama Clb; JA; Library Aide; Math Clb; Spanish Clb; SADD; Teachers Aide; Yrbk Ed-Chief; Hon Roll; NHS; Bentley Coll; Accntng.

LAVALLEE, DAWN; Southbridge HS; Sbridge, MA; (Y); 18/136; Concert Band; Mrchg Band; JV Fld Hcky; Hon Roll; Rotary Awd; Pratt Inst; Illstrtn.

LAVALLEE, JILL; Ware HS; Ware, MA; (Y); Am Leg Aux Girls St; French Clb; SADD; Yrbk Ed-Chief; Yrbk Phtg; Rep Stu Cncl; L Var Bsktbl; L Var Socr; L Var Sftbl; Hon Roll.

LAVALLEE, ROD; East Longmeadow HS; E Longmeadow, MA; (Y); AFS; Aud/Vis; Intnl Clb; Radio Clb; Teachers Aide; Golf; Hon Roll; MA U; Tel Comm.

LAVALLEY, MICHELLE; King Philip R HS; Norfolk, MA; (Y); Office Aide; School Play; High Hon Roll; Hon Roll; Peabody; Csmtlgy.

LAVAN, DEREK; Lynnfield HS; Lynnfield, MA; (Y); 7/160; Boy Scts; Debate Tm; Math Tm; Band; Jazz Band; Mrchg Band; High Hon Roll; Hon Roll; NHS; Spanish NHS; Wrtng Cntst Schl Rep 86; Arch & MAML Awd 85; Spnsh III & US Hist Awds 86; Engr.

LAVELLE, LISA; Holyoke Catholic HS; Holyoke, MA; (Y); Hosp Aide; Office Aide; Political Wkr; Ski Clb; Spanish Clb; SADD; VP Soph Cls; VP Jr Cls; Pres Sr Cls; Socr; Bus.

LAVELLE, MICHAEL; Arlington Catholic HS; Arlington, MA; (Y); Drama Clb; Bsktbl; Score Keeper; Hon Roll; Sports Mgmt.

LAVELLE, TIMOTHY J; Holyoke HS; Holyoke, MA; (Y); 35/373; Trs German Clb; VP Latin Clb; Science Clb; Yrbk Phtg; Off Sr Cls; Rep Stu Cncl; Var Ftbl; High Hon Roll; Hon Roll; NHS; Amer Clscl Leagues Cert Of Merit Cum Laude; Fairfield U; Bio.

LAVERNE, MICHELLE; Bellingham J S Memorial HS; Bellingham, MA; (Y); Pep Clb; Color Guard; Stu Cncl; Pre-Med.

LAVERTY, KATHIE; Attleboro HS; Attleboro, MA; (Y); Trs VICA; Hon Roll; Hnrb Mntn Boston Globe Schltc Art Awd 85; 1st Pl MA Elec Poster Cont 85; Dist Comptn VICA 86; Clothing Desgn.

LAVOIE, LINDA; Presentation Of Mary Acad; Salem, NH; (S); 11/46; Church Yth Grp; French Clb; Pep Clb; Church Choir; Nwsp Stf; Yrbk Stf; Rep Soph Cls; VP Sr Cls; VP Stu Cncl; Hon Roll; Castle JC NH; Exec Secy.

LAVOIE, LORIE; BMC Durfee HS; Fall River, MA; (Y); Teachers Aide; High Hon Roll; Hon Roll; Nrsng.

LAVOIE JR, ROBERT; Central Catholic HS; Lawrence, MA; (Y); 134/231; Boys Clb Am; Boy Scts; Exploring; JA; Bsktbl; Wt Lftg; Schlrshp Lady Nights Of Columbus 86; Air Force Acad; Aviation.

LAW, AMY; S Hadley HS; S Hadley, MA; (Y); Trs Church Yth Grp; Cmnty Wkr; Hosp Aide; Yrbk Stf; Pres Soph Cls; Pres Jr Cls; Pres Sr Cls; Stu Cncl; Capt Var Fld Hcky; Var Tennis; Sunday Schl Tchr; Missnry Wrk Mexico; Vactn Bibl Schl Tchr; Early Chldhd Develpmnt.

LAWLER, CHRISTINE; Westfield HS; Westfield, MA; (Y); Drama Clb; JA; School Play; Nwsp Stf; Var Crs Cntry; Var L Swmmng; JV Tennis; Var L Trk; Hon Roll; Psych.

LAWLESS, CHRISTOPHER J; Newton North HS; Newton, MA; (Y); Stu Cncl; JV Var Ftbl; MA Boys ST 86; Nvl Offcr.

LAWLOR, BONNIE; Coyle & Cassidy HS; Berkley, MA; (Y); 6/130; Drama Clb; Latin Clb; Spanish Clb; Chorus; Yrbk Stf; Hon Roll; Lion Awd; NHS; Acadmc Ltr 85; NHS Schlrshp 86; Outstndng Serv 86; MA Clg Of Pharmacy; Pharmclgy.

LAWRENCE, DONNA; Fairhaven HS; Fairhaven, MA; (Y); AFS; Girl Scts; JA; Spanish Clb; Band; Concert Band; Mrchg Band; Orch; Fld Hcky; Hon Roll; Rotry Yth Exch Brasil 86-87; SMU; Forgn Affrs.

LAWRENCE, JACQUELINE; Mansfield HS; Mansfield, MA; (Y); Trk; Hon Roll; Jhnsn & Wls Acad Schlrshp 86-87; Jhnsn & Wls Coll; Acctng.

LAWRENCE, JOSEPH; St Dominic Savio HS; E Boston, MA; (Y); 7/95; Computer Clb; Math Clb; Hon Roll; Prfct Atten Awd; Engrng.

LAWRENCE, LARA J; Danvers HS; Danvers, MA; (Y); Cmnty Wkr; Girl Scts; Band; Capt Mrchg Band; Hon Roll; NHS; Slvr Awd In Grl Scouts 82 & 83; Ldrshp Awd In Baton 84 & 85; Dstngshd Srv Awd 82.

LAWSON, ELIZABETH; Drawt HS; Dracut, MA; (Y); Rep Frsh Cls; Rep Soph Cls; Coach Actv; JV Var Score Keeper; Hon Roll; U Of MA; Socl Wkr.

LAWSON, HEATHER; Cardinal Spellman HS; Pembroke, MA; (Y); Dance Clb; JV Capt Cheerleading; Diving; Gym; Swmmng; Tennis; L Trk; MVP Hanover Swm & Tns Clb & Outstndng Sprntr Awd 85; Cathlc Cntrl League Meet 3rd Pl In 220 86; Bus Admin.

LAWSON, PATRICIA; Braintree HS; Braintree, MA; (Y); Orch; French Hon Soc; Hon Roll; Merch.

LAWTON, KRISTEN; Ipswich HS; Ipswich, MA; (Y); SADD; JV Var Fld Hcky; Hon Roll; Church Yth Grp; Drama Clb; Ski Clb; Chorus; Stu Cncl; Bsktbl; Trk; Brnz Hon Pin Awd 83-84.

LAY, GREGORY; Newburyport HS; Newburypt, MA; (Y); 17/198; Church Yth Grp; JCL; Model UN; Bsktbl; Crs Cntry; Trk; Hon Roll; NHS; 1st Pl Sci Fair 85; Honrbl Mention Sci Fair 86; Bronze Key 86; Pre-Med.

LE, JANE; Burlington HS; Burlington, MA; (Y); 116/314; Church Yth Grp; Dance Clb; VP JA; JCL; Latin Clb; SADD; Church Choir; Orch; Yrbk Stf; Powder Puff Ftbl; Ldrshp Awd Tanglewood 85; Chrch Recog Awd 85; Sci.

LE BEAU, DAVID; New Bedford HS; Acushnet, MA; (Y); Drama Clb; VP Exploring; JA; SADD; School Musical; School Play; Stage Crew; Yrbk Stf; Stu Cncl; Jr NHS.

LE BEL, KELLY; Salem HS; Salem, MA; (Y); Variety Show; Yrbk Stf; Rep Frsh Cls; Rep Soph Cls; Rep Jr Cls; Rep Sr Cls; Sec Stu Cncl; Var Cheerleading; JV Swmmng; JV Var Tennis; Bus Educ Tchr.

LE BLANC, CELESTE; Gardner HS; Gardner, MA; (Y); #6 In Class; Am Leg Aux Girls St; French Clb; School Play; Stage Crew; JV Bsktbl; Var Tennis; High Hon Roll; Hon Roll; NHS; Aerntcl Engrng.

LE BLANC, JACQUELINE B; Grtr New Bedford Regnl Vo Tech HS; New Bedford, MA; (Y); Radio Clb; VICA; Var Cheerleading; Var Trk; Sec NHS; Hgst Achvmnt Data Prcssng, Shop & Rltd Sbjcts 84; Comp Prog.

LE BLANC, LISA; New Bedford HS; Acushnet, MA; (Y); 71/700; Dance Clb; Ski Clb; Yrbk Stf; Var L Cheerleading; Var Swmmng; Hon Roll; Jr NHS; Bio-Med.

LE BLANC III, RAYMOND G; Salem HS; Salem, MA; (Y); 11/277; Am Leg Boys St; Boy Scts; Church Yth Grp; Bsbl; Ice Hcky; High Hon Roll; NHS; Norwich U; Pilot.

LE CAIN, CHRISTINE A; St Mary HS; Lawrence, MA; (Y); 15/83; Art Clb; Church Yth Grp; Red Cross Aide; School Musical; School Play; Stage Crew; Yrbk Stf; Lit Mag; High Hon Roll; Hon Roll; Bio, Spnsh & Geo Awds 84; Englsh & Alg Awds 85; Relgn, Math & Art Awds 86; Louis Giarusso Schlrshp; Northeastern U; Mntl Psych.

LE CLAIR, JULIE; Cathedral HS; Springfield, MA; (Y); Intnl Clb; Pres Library Aide; Red Cross Aide; SADD; Prfct Atten Awd; Physclgy.

LE FAVE, SUZANNE; Matignon HS; Medford, MA; (S); 4/178; Hosp Aide; Trs JA; Sec Library Aide; SADD; Yrbk Stf; Capt Crs Cntry; Capt Trk; NHS; Ntl Merit Ltr; Poltcl Sci.

LE FLEUR, MICHELLE; Newburyport HS; Newburyport, MA; (Y); 17/185; Girl Scts; Intnl Clb; JA; Band; Concert Band; Jazz Band; Mrchg Band; JV Bsktbl; Var Trk; Hon Roll; Mrktng.

LE MAY, STEVEN; Methuen HS; Methuen, MA; (Y); 29/360; Intnl Clb; Capt Ski Clb; Yrbk Stf; Tennis; French Hon Soc; Ashford PTO Schlrshp 86; RI Schl Dsgn; Arch.

LE NOIR, DAVID A; Reading Memorial HS; Reading, MA; (Y); French Clb; JA; Spanish Clb; SADD; Teachers Aide; Band; Concert Band; Mrchg Band; Crs Cntry; Trk; Frnch Hnr Schlrshp 86; Peer Tutrng & Band Awd 86; U Of MA-BOSTON; Intntl Law.

LE PAGE, DAVE; South Hadley HS; S Hadley, MA; (Y); 15/180; Yrbk Rptr; Var Bsktbl; Var Capt Ftbl; Var Capt Trk; NHS; Ntl Merit Ltr; Natl Secndry Educ Cncl Acad All-Amer 86; Bus Admin.

LE RAY, MELISSA; Malden HS; Malden, MA; (Y); 21/500; Drama Clb; Pres Girl Scts; SADD; Variety Show; Lit Mag; Hon Roll; Socl Stds Tchr.

LE ROY, ELIZABETH; Miss Halls Schl; Laconia, NH; (Y); GAA; Political Wkr; Sec Frsh Cls; Rep Soph Cls; Pres Jr Cls; Pres Stu Cncl; Var Capt Fld Hcky; Capt Var Lcrss; Var Swmmng; Var Tennis; Colby Coll; Pltcl Sci.

LEACH, ARTHUR; Bridgewater-Raynham Regional HS; Bridgewater, MA; (Y); 25/301; Am Leg Boys St; Boy Scts; Spanish Clb; Yrbk Phtg; Yrbk Stf; JV Ftbl; JV Trk; High Hon Roll; Hon Roll; Hnrs Schlr Awd 86; Stonehill Clg; Mech Engr.

LEAL, MONICA; Oliver Ames HS; South Easton, MA; (Y); 120/300; Church Yth Grp; Cmnty Wkr; Drama Clb; Model UN; Orch; School Musical; Symp Band; Mgr Jr Cls; Pres Sr Cls; Hon Roll; Awd SEMSBA Orch 82-86; Awd SE Dist Orch 82-86; Awd Exect Bd 84-86; Boston U; Hist Tchr.

LEANUES, PAULA; Mansfield HS; Mansfield, MA; (Y); Key Clb; Hon Roll; Schltc Achvt Social Studies,Frgn Lang & Bus 83-86; Engl Freelance Wrtr.

LEAPER, HEIDI; Chicopee Comprehensive HS; Chicopee, MA; (Y); Church Yth Grp; Library Aide; Office Aide; Yrbk Stf; Stu Cncl; Bus Adm.

LEARNED, JONATHAN; Monson JR SR HS; Palmer, MA; (Y); 8/88; 4-H; Mathletes; Symp Band; High Hon Roll; Hon Roll.

LEARY, MAUREEN; St Bernards C C HS; Fitchburg, MA; (S); 14/175; French Clb; Ski Clb; Hon Roll; NHS; Cmmnctns.

LEARY, PATRICK; Boston College HS; Quincy, MA; (Y); Ski Clb; SADD; Im Bsktbl; Var Crs Cntry; Im Ftbl; Var Trk; Im Vllybl; Ntl Merit Ltr; Acctg.

LEASURE, DAN; St Johns Prep Schl; Newburyport; MA; (Y); Cmnty Wkr; Ski Clb; JV Var Ftbl; Wt Lftg; Elec Engrng.

LEBEAU, KATHRYN; Pittsfield HS; Pittsfield, MA; (Y); Hosp Aide; Latin Clb; Yrbk Stf; Swmmng; Trk; Hon Roll; Phys Thrpy.

LEBEAU, LISA; Chicopee Comprehensive HS; Chicopee, MA; (Y); German Clb; Hosp Aide; JV Capt Cheerleading; High Hon Roll; Hon Roll; Socl Svc.

LEBLANC, CHRISTINE; St Columbkille HS; Allston, MA; (Y); Church Yth Grp; Yrbk Stf; High Hon Roll; Law.

LEBLANC, JOANNE; Gardner HS; Gardner, MA; (Y); French Clb; Spanish Clb; Cheerleading; Trk; Hon Roll.

LEBLANC, LOUISE; New Bedford HS; New Bedford, MA; (Y); 96/400; Cmnty Wkr; Dance Clb; Exploring; Chorus; School Musical; School Play; Hon Roll; Excllnt Chrgrphy Awd 85; Mdlg.

LEBOEUF, MELISSA; Tantasqua HS; Southbridge, MA; (Y); 75/350; Drama Clb; FHA; Pep Clb; Ski Clb; Acpl Chr; Chorus; Color Guard; Drm Mjr(t); Swing Chorus; Coach Actv; Quinsigmond Coll; Fshn Merch.

LECLERC, SCOTT; St Peter-Marion CCHS; Worcester, MA; (Y); 5/170; Church Yth Grp; Exploring; Band; School Musical; Nwsp Rptr; Hon Roll; NHS; Ntl Merit SF; Hayatt Scholar; Rennselaer Polytech Inst; Engrn.

LEDERMAN, CRAIG; Beverly HS; Beverly, MA; (Y); Cmnty Wkr; JA; Math Clb; OEA; Nwsp Stf; Yrbk Stf; JV Var Lcrss; JV Var Trk; High Hon Roll; Hon Roll; Bus.

LEDGER, EDWARD M; Mohawk Trl Regional HS; Shelburne Falls, MA; (Y); 6/115; Am Leg Boys St; Trs Frsh Cls; Rep Jr Cls; Rep Sr Cls; Sec Stu Cncl; Var Crs Cntry; Var Golf; Hon Roll; NHS; Aeronatcl Engrng.

LEDGISTER, FLOYD; Randolph HS; Randolph, MA; (Y); 80/321; Am Leg Boys St; CAP; Capt L Crs Cntry; Capt L Trk; Hon Roll; 1 Yr Schlrshp-Lowell U 86; Awd-Excllnc & Achvt-Cmnty Sci-Govt Dukaks 86; 1st Cngrsnl Chrch Schlrshp 86; Naval Acad Prep Schl; Elec Engr.

LEDOUX, DAVID; Westport HS; Westport, MA; (Y); Art Clb; Nwsp Rptr; Yrbk Stf; High Hon Roll; NHS; Bio Chem.

LEDOUX, LINDA; David Hale Fanning Trade HS; Worcester, MA; (Y); 42/130; Score Keeper; Swmmng; Vllybl; Hon Roll; Prfct Atten Awd.

LEDUC, PAMELA; Southbridge HS; Southbridge, MA; (Y); Capt Twrlr; Hon Roll; Bkkpng Medal 86; Bd Of Dirs Awd-Frgn Lang Ldrshp 86; $1000 Trustees Spec Grnt 86-87; Nichols Coll; CPA.

LEDUC, RACHELLE L; Broackton HS; Brockton, MA; (Y); 50/850; Church Yth Grp; Dance Clb; Ski Clb; SADD; Rep Soph Cls; VP Jr Cls; Pres Sr Cls; Score Keeper; High Hon Roll; Crtv Wrtng Awd 84; Northeastern U; Jrnlsm.

LEE, BRENDA; Easthampton HS; Easthampton, MA; (Y); Girl Scts; Office Aide; Teachers Aide; Chorus; Chess Clb; Bsktbl; Socr; Hon Roll; Westfield ST Coll; Telemktg.

LEE, CALVIN; Boston Technical HS; Boston, MA; (Y); 23/375; Chess Clb; Ice Hcky; Swmmng; Vllybl; Hon Roll; NHS; Hnr Rl 80-86; MA Inst Of Tech; Aerspc Tech.

LEE, CONNIE HON; North Quincy HS; N Quincy, MA; (Y); Church Yth Grp; OEA; Teachers Aide; U Of MA-BOSTON; Ec.

LEE, DES; Boston Technical HS; Allston, MA; (Y); Boys Clb Am; Cmnty Wkr; High Hon Roll; Hon Roll; Prfct Atten Awd; Elec Engrng.

LEE, DONALD; Arlington Catholic HS; Arlington, MA; (Y); 65/170; Spanish Clb; Varsity Clb; Yrbk Stf; Sec Sr Cls; Var Bsbl; Var Ice Hcky; Trk; Hon Roll; Prfct Atten Awd; Bus.

LEE, HELEN; Boston Latin Acad; Boston, MA; (Y); Drama Clb; Hosp Aide; Var Trk; Lab Inst; Fshn Mrchndsng.

LEE, JENNIFER; Tantasqua Regional SR HS; Brimfield, MA; (Y); 19/176; Lit Mag; Var Hon Roll; U Of CT; Creatv Wrtg.

LEE, JOHN; Middlesex Schl; Carlisle, MA; (Y); Scholastic Bowl; Chorus; Concert Band; Pep Band; JV Bsbl; High Hon Roll; Hon Roll; Ntl Merit Ltr; Debate Tm; JV Bsktbl; Dorothy Melcher Sneath Schlrshp 86; Interschltc Bowl-1st Pl 84; Bus.

LEE, JONATHAN; Austin Prep; N Billerica, MA; (Y); 5/124; French Clb; Math Clb; Math Tm; Stage Crew; Nwsp Rptr; Im Sftbl; Hon Roll; NHS; Ntl Merit Ltr; Sct J Hsltn Mem Schlrshp 85; Mchl Drwn Mem Schlrshp 86.

LEE, KATHERINE; Auburn HS; Auburn, MA; (Y); Am Leg Aux Girls St; VP SADD; Sec Band; Sec Soph Cls; Var L Tennis; NHS; Math Tm; Jazz Band; Mrchg Band; Harvard Bk Awd 86; Music Camp Hnr Musician Awd 85; Worcester Cty Math League 84-85.

LEE, LINDA T; Brookline HS; Cupertino, CA; (Y); Key Clb; Sec Science Clb; Flag Corp; Ed Yrbk Stf; Rep Jr Cls; Rep Sr Cls; Var Gym; NHS; NEDT Awd; St Schlr; Soc Women Engr Awd 86; Galileo Pgm Sci 83; 2ndpl Tm Sci League 86; Cornell U; Bio.

LEE, SHARON; Boston Latin Acad; Boston, MA; (Y); Hosp Aide; Hon Roll; NHS; Natl Latin Exam Slvr Mdl 84-85; Med.

LEE, THOMAS; Milton Acad; Randolph, MA; (Y); Art Clb; JV Bsbl; JV Im Bsktbl; JV Var Socr; Arch Engr.

LEGAULT, KEVIN; Bishop Connolly HS; Swansea, MA; (Y); 17/170; Chess Clb; Capt Golf; Worcstr Plytchnc Inst; Elec Eng.

LEGER, CHRIS; Swampscott HS; Swampscott, MA; (Y); 21/240; Church Yth Grp; Ski Clb; SADD; Variety Show; Debate Tm; JV Bsktbl; Capt Tennis; Hon Roll; MVP Ten 85 & 86; Conf All Star Ten 85 & 86; Grad Usher 86; Bowdoin Coll; Sci.

LEGERE, DENISE; Montachusett Reg Vo Tech; Gardner, MA; (Y); Exploring; SADD; VICA; Church Choir; Yrbk Stf; Var Crs Cntry; Hon Roll; NHS; U Bridgeport; Mgmt Infrmtn Syst.

LEHRER, PHILIPP; Amherst Regional HS; Amherst, MA; (Y); Drama Clb; Yrbk Phtg.

LEHRICH, M JONATHAN; Roxbury Latin Schl; Chestnut Hill, MA; (Y); Co-Capt Debate Tm; Acpl Chr; Ed Lit Mag; Trs Sr Cls; Mgr(s); Ntl Merit SF; Chess Clb; Drama Clb; JCL; Math Tm; Math Prize 82-84; Engl Detur 83; Latin Detur 85; Math.

LEIGHTON, BRADFORD E; Brockton HS; Brockton, MA; (Y); Am Leg Boys St; Drama Clb; Key Clb; Varsity Clb; Chorus; School Play; Var Socr; High Hon Roll; Boy Scts; SADD; Variety Show; Coached Yth Sccr For Cmnty; Brockton All-Star Sccr Tm; Accptd Into Tms USA Sccr; Psych.

LEIJON, YLVA; Westfield HS; Sweden; (Y); Church Yth Grp; Ski Clb; Y-Teens; Chorus; Church Choir; Cmptr Sci.

LEINOMEN, CHARLENE M; David Prouty HS; Spencer, MA; (Y); 33/181; DECA; Office Aide; Concert Band; Jazz Band; Trs Mrchg Band; School Musical; Trk; High Hon Roll; Hon Roll; JP Sousa Awd; Dvd Plante JR Mem Schlrshp, Dvd Prouty Bnd Prnt Schlrshp & SR Hnrs Scty 86; Bentley; Accntng.

LEISTRITZ, MICHAEL; Holy Name Central Catholic HS; Worcester, MA; (Y); 35/260; Boys Clb Am; Church Yth Grp; JA; Y-Teens; Var Bsbl; Im Bsktbl; Hon Roll; St Schlr; Tom Ash Babe Ruth Lg All Str 83-84; SR Recogntn Bsbl 86; Chem & Cmmnctn Skls Awd 85-84; Nrthestrn U; Bus Adm.

LEITH, MICHELE; Commerce HS; Springfield, MA; (Y); Church Yth Grp; Cmnty Wkr; JA; SADD; Chorus; Church Choir; Madrigals; Prfct Atten Awd; Cert Appreciation Freedom Choir 85; Cert Acdmc Achvt MA 86.

LELAND, DAVID A; Wellesley HS; Wellesley, MA; (Y); Acpl Chr; Band; Chorus; Concert Band; Jazz Band; Mrchg Band; Orch; School Musical; School Play; Stage Crew; Woodsman Awd For Forestry 84.

LELAND, DIANE; Concord*carlisle HS; Concord, MA; (Y); Cmnty Wkr; Teachers Aide; Lib Band; Color Guard; Concert Band; Mrchg Band; Hon Roll; Psych.

LELE, ARUNA; Burlington HS; Burlington, MA; (Y); 30/321; Ski Clb; Nwsp Rptr; Nwsp Stf; Yrbk Sprt Ed; Lit Mag; Var Crs Cntry; Var Trk; Hon Roll; NHS; Ntl Merit Ltr; Comm.

LEMAIRE, LAURIE; Mc Cann Tech Voc; Clarksburg, MA; (Y); Church Yth Grp; Yrbk Stf; Hvy Eqpmnt Oprtr.

LEMAR, JODY; Westport HS; Westport, MA; (Y); Ski Clb; Cheerleading; Ldrshp Awd Futr Sec 86; Katharine Gibbs; Sec.

LEMAY, MICHELLE; Diman Regional Vo Tech; Fall River, MA; (Y); High Hon Roll.

LEMAY, ROBIN; Greater-Lowell Voke HS; Dracut, MA; (Y); Hosp Aide; SADD; VICA; Yrbk Stf; Hon Roll; Rcvd Cert For Nurses Aide 85-86; Nurse.

LEMERISE, ANDREA; David Prouty HS; Spencer, MA; (Y); 3/165; Church Yth Grp; Chorus; Color Guard; Mrchg Band; School Musical; Var Tennis; High Hon Roll; JP Sousa Awd; NHS; Commonwealth Schlrs Schlrshp 86; Hrn Socty 86; Hnrd Spkr-Grad 86; Clark U; Bio.

LEMIEUX, CHRISTEN; Bishop Connolly HS; Portsmouth, RI; (Y); 49/180; Cmnty Wkr; Hosp Aide; High Hon Roll; VFW Awd; Providence Coll; Jrnlsm.

LEMIEUX, JON; Cardinal Spellman HS; Brockton, MA; (Y); 2/206; Computer Clb; VP Drama Clb; VP Thesps; School Musical; School Play; Stage Crew; Rep Jr Cls; High Hon Roll; NHS; Chancellors Awd U MA Amherst Scholar 86; Civil Engrng.

LEMIRE, SHELBEY; Southwick HS; Sowick, MA; (Y); 28/126; Library Aide; Pres Office Aide; Pep Clb; Spanish Clb; SADD; Rep Stu Cncl; Capt Cheerleading; Capt Fld Hcky; JV Mgr(s); Sftbl.

LEMON, CHRISTIE; Hopedale JR SR HS; Hopedale, MA; (S); 12/59; SADD; Chorus; School Play; Yrbk Stf; Var Capt Bsktbl; Var L Fld Hcky; Var Capt Sftbl; Hon Roll; NHS; Clrk U MA; Psychlgy.

LENAHAN, DEBORAH; Monsignor Ryan Memorial HS; Dorchester, MA; (Y); 1/89; Pres Church Yth Grp; Hosp Aide; Library Aide; Spanish Clb; Variety Show; Pres Soph Cls; Trs Sr Cls; Bowling; High Hon Roll; NHS; Northeastern U; Phys Thrpy.

LENBURG, MARC E; Amherst Regional; Amherst, MA; (Y); 17/270.

LENIHAN, KELLY; South High Community School; Worcester, MA; (S); Church Yth Grp; SADD; Trs Jr Cls; Stu Cncl; Cheerleading; Pom Pon; Sftbl; Supt Advsry Cncl; Stu Adjustmnt Cnslr.

LENS, JOHN; Auburn HS; Auburn, MA; (Y); Church Yth Grp; Computer Clb; Ski Clb; Band; Jazz Band; Mrchg Band; Variety Show; Im Bsbl; Im Vllybl; High Hon Roll; U MA Amherst; Cmptrs.

LEONARD, DONNA R; Lowell HS; Lowell, MA; (Y); 6/525; Intnl Clb; Scholastic Bowl; Science Clb; Concert Band; Jazz Band; Mrchg Band; Ed Nwsp Stf; Capt Tennis; VP NHS; Ntl Soc Prfsnl Engrs Schlrshp 86; Wang Schlrshp/Comp 86; MVP Awd Ten 86; U Of Lowell; Elec Engrng.

LEONARD, KERRY; Woburn SR HS; Woburn, MA; (S); 200/454; Church Yth Grp; French Clb; Key Clb; Ski Clb; Hon Roll; Math.

LEONARD, MICHAEL R; North Quincy HS; Quinc, MA; (Y); 70/345; Boy Scts; Quiz Bowl; Spanish Clb; Var Ice Hcky; Var Tennis; High Hon Roll; Hon Roll; Peter Bouchie Mrl Schlrshp 86; John P Mckeon Pst Schlrshp 86; Crtfct Of Exclnc Prd Cmmtee 86; Wentworth Inst Of Tech; Elc Eng.

LEONARD, PAUL W; Northbridge JR SR HS; Whitinsville, MA; (Y); Am Leg Boys St; Latin Clb; JV Var Bsktbl; JV Var Crs Cntry; JV Var Trk.

LEONARD, PETER; New Bedford HS; Acushnet, MA; (Y); Band; Bsbl; Score Keeper.

LEONARD, STEPHANIE; Matignon HS; Somerville, MA; (S); 1/200; Church Yth Grp; Dance Clb; Latin Clb; Rep Soph Cls; Trk; Vllybl; Elks Awd; High Hon Roll; NHS; Md.

LEONE, LARRY; Saint Dominic Savio HS; Rever, MA; (Y); 45/112; Nwsp Rptr; Nwsp Stf; Bsbl; Bsktbl; Ftbl; Engnrng.

LEONE, SUZANNE; Natick HS; Natick, MA; (Y); 100/400; Am Leg Aux Girls St; Church Yth Grp; Cmnty Wkr; SADD; Off Soph Cls; Off Jr Cls; Off Sr Cls; Rep Stu Cncl; Coach Actv; Score Keeper; Pres Physcl Ftns Awd 83; All Str, All Trnmnt Awd Vllybl 85; Chsn Bay ST Vllybl Team 85; Law.

LEPKOWSKI, KATHRYN; Gardner HS; Gardner, MA; (Y); 17/140; Am Leg Aux Girls St; Church Yth Grp; Spanish Clb; Band; Var Crs Cntry; Var L Tennis; NHS; Goodsprtsmnshp Awd JR Tm Tnns 85.

LEPORE, ALEXANDRA; Newburyport HS; Newburyport, MA; (Y); 63/184; Dance Clb; Var Cheerleading; Var Pom Pon.

LEPPER, MARK; Agawam HS; Ágawam, MA; (Y); AFS; Boy Scts; Church Yth Grp; French Clb; Math Clb; Hon Roll; Pres NHS; Tchng.

LEROUX, DAVID; Attleboro HS; Attleboro, MA; (Y); 5/409; Am Leg Boys St; Church Yth Grp; Bsbl; JV Var Bsktbl; JV Var Ftbl; High Hon Roll; NHS; Part Time Job 85-86; USMA.

LEROY, EMMLYNN L; North Cambridge Catholic HS; Somerville, MA; (Y); 5/93; Camera Clb; Computer Clb; French Clb; Intnl Clb; Math Clb; Red Cross Aide; Church Choir; School Play; Yrbk Ed-Chief; Yrbk Phtg; Miss Mass Teen USA 85; Awd Schlrshp Commonwlth Schlr 86; Recog Womn Engrng 86; Northwestern U; Bus.

LESCANO, YVETTE; Matignon HS; Cambridge, MA; (S); 17/189; Computer Clb; Drama Clb; Spanish Clb; Chorus; JV Bsktbl; JV Var Vllybl; Hon Roll; NHS; Spanish NHS; Comp.

LESLIE, CHERYL; Northbridge JR SR HS; Whitinsville, MA; (Y); 7/152; Am Leg Aux Girls St; Girl Scts; Band; Yrbk Phtg; Stu Cncl; Score Keeper; High Hon Roll; NHS; Ntl Merit Ltr; Sec Latin Clb; Worcester Polytechnic; Elec Eng.

LESLIE, DAVID; West Boylston JR SR HS; W Boylston, MA; (Y); 2/87; Mathletes; Varsity Clb; Chorus; Concert Band; Jazz Band; Mrchg Band; Var Tennis; Trs NHS; Ntl Merit SF; Sal; U Of Lowell; Advrtsng.

LESPASIO, JAY T; Quincy HS; Quincy, MA; (Y); 50/300; Am Leg Boys St; Var Bsbl; Var Trk; JV Var Wrstlng; Hon Roll; Prfct Atten Awd.

LESPERANCE, JENNIFER; Gardner HS; Gardner, MA; (Y); 17/170; Chess Clb; Trs Debate Tm; Pres VP French Clb; Model UN; Chorus; School Musical; Var Capt Crs Cntry; Var Swmmng; Var Capt Trk; Hon Roll; Bst Spkr Awd Mdl UN 85-86; Grls Ath Booster Clb Scholar 86; Gardner Coll Clb Scholar 86; U MA; Art.

LESSARD, PETER; Brockton HS; Brockton, MA; (Y); 27/850; JCL; Key Clb; Red Cross Aide; Nwsp Rptr; Lit Mag; High Hon Roll; NHS; Pres Schlr; Voice Dem Awd; Two-Ten Schlrshp 86-87; DW RA Fields 86-87; U Of RI; Chem Engr.

LESSARD, SUSY; Presentation Of Mary Acad; Dracut, MA; (Y); 4/34; 4-H; French Clb; Library Aide; Science Clb; Ski Clb; Nwsp Stf; Yrbk Stf; Trs Frsh Cls; Sec Soph Cls; Rep Jr Cls; Gold Cord For Keeping 88 Or Higher Grd 86; Middlesex CC; Med Asstng.

LETCHFORD, EMMA E; Franklin HS; Franklin, MA; (Y); 25/224; Band; Chorus; Concert Band; Drm Mjr(t); Jazz Band; Mrchg Band; Orch; Pep Band; School Musical; School Play; Arion Awd Music Exclinc 85; All ST Chorus 85-86; Cntrl Dist Chorus 85-86; Miami U; Music.

LEUTHOLD, MARINA; King Philip Regional HS; Norfolk, MA; (Y); Trs VICA; Var Sftbl; Hon Roll; Rcvd Bronze Mdl Rgnl Cmpttn Accntng 86; Bus Mgmt.

LEVEE, MINETTE; Bishop Fenwick HS; W Medford, MA; (S); 6/230; Cmnty Wkr; Hosp Aide; Library Aide; Nwsp Ed-Chief; JV Cheerleading; High Hon Roll; NHS; Ntl Merit SF; School Play; JV Trk; Englsh,Hstry & Sci Hnrs Awds 83; Bio Hnrs Awd 84; Biotechnlgy.

LEVERONE, PAUL; Bristol Plymouth Regional Tech; Taunton, MA; (Y); Boys Clb Am; JV Bsbl; JV Ftbl.

LEVIN, KIMBERLY S; Mt Greylock Regional HS; Williamstown, MA; (Y); 3/140; Am Leg Aux Girls St; Varsity Clb; Orch; School Musical; Nwsp Phtg; Lit Mag; Var Fld Hcky; Var Socr; Elks Awd; High Hon Roll; Harvard.

LEVINE, ALEX G; Newton South HS; Brookline, MA; (Y); Am Leg Boys St; French Clb; School Musical; Var Bsktbl; Var Lcrss; Var Socr; Boston Globe Div 2 Plyr Of The Yr In Lacrosse 86; Div 2 St Champs In Lacrosse 84-85; All-League 84-86; Skidmore Clg.

LEVINE, JEFFREY; Newton North HS; Newton, MA; (Y); Drama Clb; Socl Sci.

LEVINE, JEFFREY S; Brockton HS; Brockton, MA; (Y); 60/900; Am Leg Boys St; Ski Clb; SADD; Concert Band; Jazz Band; Madrigals; Off Jr Cls; Var Ftbl; Wt Lftg; Hon Roll; Brandeis U; Econ.

LEVINE, JOSHUA A; Brookline HS; Brookline, MA; (Y); Am Leg Boys St; Nwsp Rptr; JV Lcrss; Var Tennis; Hon Roll; Awd-Mrs Mchl Dkaks-Acadmc Exclinc 86.

LEVINE, STEPHANIE; Randolph HS; Randolph, MA; (Y); SADD; Rep Frsh Cls; Rep Soph Cls; Rep Jr Cls; Rep Sr Cls; Stu Cncl; Var Cheerleading; Powder Puff Ftbl; Var Sftbl; JC Awd; Stdnt Govt Awd; Advsrs, Athl Awds; Westfield ST Coll; Spec Ed.

LEVY, ERICA J; Belmont HS; Belmont, MA; (Y); 17/261; Am Leg Aux Girls St; Temple Yth Grp; Band; Mrchg Band; Yrbk Ed-Chief; Bsktbl; Cit Awd; Hon Roll; Jr NHS; NHS; Schl Comm Awd 84-86; Schlumberger Scholar 86; Carnegie-Mellon U; Mth.

LEWANDOWSKI, LIZ; Holyoke HS; Holyoke, MA; (Y); Art Clb; German Clb; MA Coll Of Art; Fine Art.

LEWIS, AYN; David Hale Fanning Trade HS; Worcester, MA; (Y); 13/124; Dance Clb; Drama Clb; SADD; Teachers Aide; Nwsp Stf; JV Cheerleading; High Hon Roll; Hon Roll; NHS; Erly Chldhd Tchr.

LEWIS, DEBORAH; Haverhill HS; Pittsburgh, PA; (Y); 46/380; Church Yth Grp; French Clb; Acpl Chr; Pres Chorus; School Musical; School Play; Swing Chorus; Variety Show; Gov Hon Prg Awd; Hon Roll; Natl Hon Soc Music 84-85; Natl Choral Awd 86; Most Improved Frnch Stu 83; The Boyd Schl; Trvl Indstry.

LEWIS, DONALD; Melrose HS; Melrose, MA; (Y); 12/400; Spanish Clb; JV Var Bsbl; JV Ice Hcky; Bus Mgmt.

LEWIS, IAN; Newton North HS; W Newton, MA; (Y); Am Leg Boys St; Var Capt Gym; Ntl Merit Schol; Hnr Roll 84-86; MA Coll Of Art; Blow Glss Prof.

LEWIS, JASON; South Lancaster Acad; Angwin, CA; (Y); Boy Scts; Church Yth Grp; Ski Clb; Var L Bsktbl; Var L Ftbl; Hon Roll; Schlstc Schlrshp 83; UCLA; Bus.

LEWIS, MICHAEL R; Burlington HS; Burlington, MA; (Y); VP Chess Clb; Computer Clb; Math Clb; Science Clb; Spanish Clb; Tennis; Trk; Schl Lttr 85; Chess Trphy 85; 2 Chess Mdls 86-85; Northeastern U; Elec Engr.

LEWIS, SONIA; Boston Latin Schl; Boston, MA; (Y); 64/276; Sec French Clb; JA; Library Aide; SADD; Nwsp Stf; Yrbk Stf; Trk; Vllybl; High Hon Roll; Med.

LEWIS, SUSAN; Saugus HS; Saugus, MA; (Y); Pres Church Yth Grp; Library Aide; Hon Roll; NHS; Voice Dem Awd; CCD Tchr 85; Echrstc Mnstr 85; Math.

LEWIS, TONYA T; Boston Latin Acad; Dorchester, MA; (Y); 23/137; Sec Church Yth Grp; Sec Church Choir; Capt Drill Tm; Variety Show; Sec Soph Cls; Rep Stu Cncl; L Cheerleading; Vllybl; Hon Roll; Ntl Merit Ltr; Syracuse U; Clin Psych.

LEZON, PAUL; Marian HS; Hudson, MA; (Y); 29/178; Var Capt Ftbl; Var L Trk; Var Vllybl; High Hon Roll; Hon Roll; NHS.

LI, CHI-WEN; Newton North HS; Newton, MA; (Y); Intnl Clb; Capt Math Tm; Service Clb; Orch; High Hon Roll; Jr NHS; Prfct Atten Awd; Teachers Aide; School Musical; Nwsp Stf; Natl Spn Exam 6th Pl MA Lvl 3 86; Essay Cont Mth & Sci Orgnztn Chin Amer Wmn Hon Men 85; Dstng Schlr; Med.

LI, YUEN; B M C Durfee HS; Fall River, MA; (Y); 44/600; Computer Clb; Drama Clb; Hosp Aide; Hon Roll; NHS; Comp.

LIBBY, ANDREA; Malden HS; Malden, MA; (Y); Sec Key Clb; Math Tm; Science Clb; Band; Concert Band; Drill Tm; Mrchg Band; Nwsp Rptr; Rep Frsh Cls; Rep Soph Cls.

LIBERTY JR, ROBERT E; Southwick HS; Southwick, MA; (Y); Rep Am Leg Boys St; VP Church Yth Grp; Math Tm; Church Choir; Concert Band; Orch; Var L Trk; VP NHS; Hon Roll; Sectnl, Dist & Rgnl Teen Tlnt Wnnr Vocal Ensmbl 86; Music.

LICCIARDI, TERRY; Metheun HS; Methuen, MA; (Y); 29/349; Aud/Vis; Cmnty Wkr; Bsbl; JV Bsktbl; Var L Ftbl; Var L Trk; Cit Awd; Hon Roll; Colby; Pre-Med.

LICHOULAS, THEODORE; Reading Memorial HS; Reading, MA; (Y); Cmnty Wkr; Computer Clb; Math Tm; Science Clb; Stage Crew; Nwsp Stf; High Hon Roll; Ntl Merit Ltr; 1st Natl Hstry Day Dist Comptn 86; 1st Wentworth Inst Tech Comp Cont 86; Harvard Extension 84-86.

LICHT, JENNIFER; Wellesley SR HS; Wellesley, MA; (Y); 1/315; French Clb; VP JA; JCL; Sec Latin Clb; Nwsp Rptr; Var Mgr(s); High Hon Roll; Hon Roll; NHS; Ntl Merit Ltr; Acad Awds Englsh, Hstry, Math, Mod Eur. & Chem; Natl Latin Tst Gld Medal; Wheaton Coll Bk Awd.

LIEN, DAVE; Beverly HS; Beverly, MA; (Y); Var Bsbl; Var L Bsktbl; Var L Ftbl; Var L Golf; Hon Roll; Bus Admn.

LIEU, TINA; Newton North HS; W Newton, MA; (Y); Math Tm; Orch; Cit Awd; Hon Roll; Ntl Merit Ltr; Williams Coll; Frnch.

LIFRAK, JOSEPH; Bishop Connolly HS; Fall River, MA; (Y); 30/174; Cmnty Wkr; Ski Clb; Var Bsktbl; Var Crs Cntry; Var Capt Golf; High Hon Roll; NHS; Pres Schlr; Stu Athlt Whl Schl; Pre Med.

LIGHT, TRACI; Everett HS; Everett, MA; (Y); Office Aide; SADD; Yrbk Stf; Pres Frsh Cls; Sec Soph Cls; Off Jr Cls; Off Sr Cls; Stu Cncl; Cheerleading; Pom Pon; Little Schlrs Awd 83-84.

LILJEGREN, ERIK K; Shawsheen Valley Voc Tech HS; Tewksbury, MA; (Y); 20/359; Capt CAP; Dance Clb; Color Guard; Drill Tm; JV Socr; Hon Roll; Amelia Earhart Awd Cvl Air Patrl 86; Genrl Billy Mitchell Awd Cvl Air Patrl 85; U Of MA Amherst; Astrnmy.

LILJEGREN, KRISTEN; Foxboro HS; Foxboro, MA; (Y); 23/230; Church Yth Grp; Cmnty Wkr; French Clb; Intnl Clb; Varsity Clb; Concert Band; Drm Mjr(t); Jazz Band; Mrchg Band; Yrbk Stf; Mngmnt.

LIM, MAY; Marlborough HS; Marlboro, MA; (Y); 13/350; Math Clb; Math Tm; Science Clb; Var Tennis; JV Trk; High Hon Roll; Hon Roll; NHS; Fclty Awd Engl, Math,Sci,Art,Frnch 84; Fclty Awd Math, Sci 85; Fclty Awd Sci Hstry 86; Med.

LIN, EDSEL YEH-SHENG; Newton North HS; Framingham, MA; (Y); Am Leg Boys St; JV Capt Ftbl; Var Lcrss; Var Capt Wrstlng; UCLA; Bus.

LINBERG, GREGORY; Fairhaven HS; Fairhaven, MA; (Y); Varsity Clb; School Musical; JV Ftbl; Var Ice Hcky.

LINCOLN, DEKE; Wilbraham And Monson Acad; Ware, MA; (Y); 3/120; Band; Var Bsbl; Var Ftbl; JV Ice Hcky; Cit Awd; High Hon Roll; Hon Roll; Dartmouth Book Awd 86; Precalculus Awd Outstndng Achvt 86.

LINCOLN, NANCY; Cohasset JR SR HS; Cohasset, MA; (Y); Band; Stat Bsktbl; Var Mgr(s); Powder Puff Ftbl; Var Score Keeper; Stat Socr; Hon Roll; Ntl Merit Ltr; Psych.

LINDBERG, KRISTEN; Sharon HS; Sharon, MA; (Y); Library Aide; Math Clb; Stage Crew; High Hon Roll; Hon Roll; Chnclrs Tlnt Awd Acdmc Exclinc 86; Grls Hgh Avg Bwlng Lg 86; Stu Of Mnth Mech Drwg Frnch Math 83-85; Math.

LINDE, LAURA; Hanover HS; Hanover, MA; (Y); Church Yth Grp; Cmnty Wkr; Chorus; Concert Band; Mrchg Band; School Musical; Stage Crew; Var L Bsktbl; JV Tennis; Hon Roll; Msc Stu Mnth Oct 86; 4th Plc Hist Olympd 86; Dirctrs Awd Schl Band 86-87; Comm.

LINDENFELD, RALPH C; Tantasqua Regional HS; Sturbridge, MA; (Y); 6/180; Am Leg Boys St; Ski Clb; Varsity Clb; Acpl Chr; Chorus; Var Tennis; Hon Roll; NHS; Engnrng.

LINDQUIST, TRICIA; Burncoat SR HS; Worcester, MA; (Y); Church Yth Grp; Science Clb; Chorus; Variety Show; Var Socr; Var JV Sftbl; Hon Roll; Occptnl Thrpy.

LINDSAY JR, ROBERT; Tantasqua Regional SR HS; Sturbridge, MA; (Y); Exploring; Lit Mag; Hon Roll; Ma Frgn Lang Awd German 86; Vermont Tech Coll; Comp Tech.

LINGERMAN, ERIC; Newburyport HS; Newburyport, MA; (Y); Church Yth Grp; Band; Mrchg Band; Trk; Hon Roll; Marshall Staff Ldrshp Grp 85-87.

LINKER, DEBORAH; Athol HS; Athol, MA; (Y); 16/120; Am Leg Aux Girls St; Church Yth Grp; Model UN; Ski Clb; Nwsp Stf; Yrbk Stf; JV Bsktbl; JV Fld Hcky; Hon Roll.

LINNELL, AMY; Nanset Regional HS; Brewstr, MA; (Y); 7/157; Ski Clb; Fld Hcky; Hon Roll; NHS; Pres Acad Ftns Awd 86; Scrtry NHS 86; U Of Rhode Island; Forgn Lng.

LINSCOTT, JULIE; Newburyport HS; Newburyport, MA; (Y); 64/186; GAA; Library Aide; Trs Frsh Cls; Rep Soph Cls; Im Bsktbl; L Capt Cheerleading; Hon Roll; Wilmot Roby Evans Corp Schlrhsp 86; Swasey Orphn Fnd Schlrshp 86; Thomas Coll; Accntng.

LINTON, CHARLES; Northfield Mount Herman Schl; Wilton, CT; (Y); 68/342; Boy Scts; JV Socr; Hon Roll; Rnnr Up-Riflery 83.

LINZ, CHRISTINE; Bedford HS; Bedford, MA; (Y); 7/201; Church Yth Grp; SADD; Chorus; Yrbk Stf; Rep Soph Cls; Var Capt Fld Hcky; Powder Puff Ftbl; Hon Roll; NHS; Knghts Columbus Schlrshp 86; St Michaels Michaelmas Awd 86; Stouffers Schlrshp 86; Holy Cross Coll; Psych.

LINZ, LISA; Bedford HS; Bedford, MA; (Y); 26/198; AFS; Capt Ski Clb; Nwsp Stf; Yrbk Stf; Rep Frsh Cls; Chrmn Jr Cls; Chrmn Sr Cls; Var Capt Fld Hcky; JV Sftbl; Hon Roll; Advtsg.

LIPMAN, CHUCK; Randolph HS; Randolph, MA; (Y); Drama Clb; Library Aide; Temple Yth Grp; School Play; Variety Show; JV Var Ftbl; Bus Law.

LIPSON, REBECCA; Seekonk HS; Seekonk, MA; (Y); 10/223; Yrbk Stf; Fld Hcky; Tennis; High Hon Roll; Trs NHS; Spanish NHS.

LIS, JENNIFER; Ware HS; Ware, MA; (Y); 4/120; Math Clb; Spanish Clb; Nwsp Stf; High Hon Roll.

LISIEN, CHRIS; Westford Acad; Westford, MA; (Y); French Clb; Spanish Clb; SADD; Concert Band; Symp Band; Var Capt Bsktbl; Var Fld Hcky; JV Socr; Var Sftbl; Hon Roll; Pre Law.

LISOWSKI, DUANE; Chicopee HS; Chicopee, MA; (Y); 17/253; Nwsp Ed-Chief; Yrbk Stf; Trs Stu Cncl; JV Socr; High Hon Roll; Jr NHS; Pres NHS; Pres Schlr; Stat Bsktbl; Var Score Keeper; Stu Advsry Cncl; Rep Stu Govt Day; Lake Forest Coll; Intl Finance.

LITCHFIELD, BRENDA; Burncoat SR HS; Worcester, MA; (Y); 13/238; Church Yth Grp; Intnl Clb; JV Bsktbl; Var Capt Sftbl; Elks Awd; Hon Roll; Jr NHS; NHS; Assumption Clg; Psych.

LITCHFIELD, KERRY; Bedford HS; Bedford, MA; (Y); Swmmng; Hon Roll; U Lowell.

LITHERLAND, SHANNON; Monument Mountain Regional HS; Housatonic, MA; (Y); 44/144; Yrbk Stf; Hon & High Hon Cert 85-86; Berkshire CC; Bus.

LITTLE, SCOTT; Algonquin Regional HS; Southboro, MA; (Y); 25/240; Computer Clb; Yrbk Phtg; Yrbk Stf; Hon Roll; NHS; Ntl Merit SF; DECS Proj, Comptr Camp 83-85; Med.

LIU, CHESTER; Winchester HS; Winchester, MA; (Y); Church Yth Grp; French Clb; Library Aide; Math Tm; Science Clb; Orch; Nwsp Stf; French Hon Soc; Harvard Book Awd; Continental Acalculus Lg Awd.

LIVINGSTON, LOREE; Lynn Classical HS; Lynn, MA; (Y); Office Aide; SADD; Powder Puff Ftbl; Phys Fit Achvt Cert 83; Cert Greater Lynn Mntl Hlth & Retardtn Assn 85; Mayor Di Virgili Ltr Grad 86; Marion Ct JC; Travel/Trsm.

LIZANO, GRETHEL; St Peter-Marian HS; Worcestr, MA; (Y); Church Yth Grp; Drama Clb; JA; Spanish Clb; SADD; School Musical; Yrbk Stf; High Hon Roll; Hon Roll; NHS.

LIZOTTE, AMY; Montachusett Regional VTS; Sterling, MA; (Y); Dance Clb; VICA; Yrbk Stf; Socr; Tennis; Bus.

LIZOTTE, CHRIS; Holy Name Central Catholic HS; Oxford, MA; (Y); 104/306; French Clb; Girl Scts; Leo Clb; Radio Clb; Ski Clb; Spanish Clb; School Musical; Wt Lftg; Hon Roll; U Of MA; Tchg.

LLEWELYN, FREDERICK G; Pioneer Valley Regional HS; Northfield, MA; (Y); Am Leg Boys St; Drama Clb; Varsity Clb; School Play; Var L Bsbl; JV Bsktbl; Var L Socr; High Hon Roll; Hon Roll; Engnrng.

LLOYD, CHRISTINE; Burlington HS; Burlington, MA; (Y); 31/314; Debate Tm; Yrbk Sprt Ed; Var Capt Crs Cntry; Powder Puff Ftbl; Var L Trk; Hon Roll; NHS; Cross Cntry Plyrs Awd.

LLOYD, GLYNN T; Sharon HS; Sharon, MA; (Y); 40/207; SADD; Nwsp Stf; Yrbk Bus Mgr; Pres Frsh Cls; Pres Jr Cls; Var Capt Tennis; Hon Roll; Ntl Merit Schol; Boston U; Bus.

LOANDO, HEIDI-ANN; Milford HS; Milford, MA; (Y); 24/266; Am Leg Aux Girls St; Dance Clb; Drama Clb; Hosp Aide; Teachers Aide; Stage Crew; NHS; Clark U; Psych.

LOBO, JOSE; South Boston HS; Dorchester, MA; (S); Letterman Clb; Yrbk Sprt Ed; Capt Ftbl; Socr; Trk; Hon Roll; Embry-Riddle U; Pilot.

LOBO, PAULA; Shepherd Hill Regional HS; Dudley, MA; (Y); Church Yth Grp; Hosp Aide; Pep Clb; Band; Church Choir; Color Guard; Flag Corp; Mrchg Band; Stage Crew; High Hon Roll; Phys Therapy.

LOCKERBY, KELLY; Hoosac Valley HS; Adams, MA; (Y); Vllybl; Hon Roll; Law.

LOCKHART, ELAINE; Malden HS; Malden, MA; (Y); 5/500; Math Tm; Band; Concert Band; Drm Mjr(t); Mrchg Band; Hon Roll; Jr NHS; Kiwanis Awd; NHS; Pep Clb; Mbr Of Lit Socy 85-86; Psych.

LOCKHART, TARA E; Bourne HS; Otis ANGB, MA; (Y); Church Yth Grp; SADD; Church Choir; Yrbk Stf; Var Cheerleading; High Hon Roll; Hon Roll; NHS; French Clb; Latin Clb; Pres 100 Clb; Miss Pace; Hgst Pace Avg.

LOCKHEAD, TINA M; Classical HS; Lynn, MA; (Y); Aud/Vis; Dance Clb; French Clb; Office Aide; Spanish Clb; Chorus; School Musical; Rep Frsh Cls; Stu Cncl; Girl Scts; Frgn Lang Tchr.

LODGE, SHERRA; Hyde Park HS; Dorchester, MA; (S); Teachers Aide; Church Choir; Yrbk Stf; Pres Sr Cls; Capt Vllybl; Hon Roll; NHS; Prfct Atten Awd; Cmnty Wkr; JA; Brandeis U; Bus Mgmt.

LOEFFLER, KATHE; Marshfield HS; Marshfield, MA; (Y); AFS; Drama Clb; Acpl Chr; Chorus; Concert Band; Mrchg Band; Trk; Key Clb; Office Aide; Stage Crew; SEMSBA 85 & 86; Nw Englnd Music Fstvl 86; Law.

LOGAN, BARRY; Newton North HS; Newton, MA; (Y); Am Leg Boys St; Sr Cls; Crs Cntry; Swmmng; Trk; Hon Roll; Jewish War Vets Brotherhood; Richard Meechem Awd; Cornell; Pre-Med.

LOGAN, KERI; Bishop Feehan HS; Attleboro, MA; (Y); SADD; Var Cheerleading; Im Trk; Hon Roll; Early Chldhd Dev.

LOHR, HEIDI; Hampshire Regional HS; Southampton, MA; (Y); Church Yth Grp; Drama Clb; Girl Scts; Spanish Clb; Acpl Chr; Chorus; Church Choir; Color Guard; Concert Band; Mrchg Band; U MA.

LOHREY, JENNIFER; Academy Of Notre Dame; Tewksbury, MA; (Y); 6/62; Church Yth Grp; Dance Clb; Hosp Aide; Ski Clb; SADD; Trs Sr Cls; NHS; Assumption Coll; Bio.

LOHRI, PETER; Georgetown HS; Georgetown, MA; (Y); 12/90; Math Tm; Political Wkr; ROTC; SADD; Var Capt Ftbl; Wt Lftg; High Hon Roll; Hon Roll; Ntl Merit Ltr; Boston U; Engrng.

LOISELLE, KELLY; Chicopee Comprehensive HS; Chicopee, MA; (Y); 43/320; Art Clb; Spanish Clb; Yrbk Stf; Rep Frsh Cls; Rep Soph Cls; Rep Jr Cls; Rep Sr Cls; Pres Stu Cncl; Var L Cheerleading; Var Trk; Coachs Awd Chrldg 85; Art Apprctn Awd 85; Soclgy.

LOMANO, KRISTINA; Archbishop Williams HS; Marshfield, MA; (Y); Church Yth Grp; Hosp Aide; Teachers Aide; Chorus; School Musical; Yrbk Stf; Hon Roll; NHS; Quincy Catholic Clb Scholar 86; Spn Achvt Awds 84 & 85; Salve Regina Coll; Nrsng.

LOMBARA, JOHN; St Johns Preparatory Schl; Lynn, MA; (Y); AFS; Political Wkr; SADD; Var Bsbl; Im Mgr Bsktbl; Im Mgr Ftbl; Capt Ice Hcky; Hon Roll; NHS; Hubart Coll.

LOMBARA, MELISSA; Lynn Classical HS; Lynn, MA; (Y); Chess Clb; French Clb; SADD; Cheerleading; Powder Puff Ftbl; Swmmng; Fash Desgnr.

LOMBARD, THERESA; Norton HS; Norton, MA; (S); 5/148; Cmnty Wkr; Pep Clb; Varsity Clb; Concert Band; Pres Mrchg Band; Rep Stu Cncl; Bsktbl; VP NHS; Ntl Merit Ltr; Most Imprvd Band Stu.

LOMBARDO, BRENDA; Marian HS; Framingham, MA; (Y); Church Yth Grp; Computer Clb; Drama Clb; Chorus; School Musical; Nwsp Stf; JV Var Cheerleading; Hon Roll; Elem Educ.

LOMBARDO, SHERRI; North Middlesex Regional HS; Townsend, MA; (Y); Latin Clb; SADD; Teachers Aide; Varsity Clb; Rep Soph Cls; Rep Jr Cls; Var Cheerleading; Hon Roll; NHS; Psych.

LOMBERTO, TIMOTHY; Bellingham HS; Bellingham, MA; (Y); Boy Scts; Cmnty Wkr; SADD; Varsity Clb; Var Ftbl; Stat Score Keeper; Var Trk; Wt Lftg; Cnstrctn.

LONERGAN, LORI; Woburn HS; Woburn, MA; (Y); Sec Frsh Cls; Stu Cncl; Var Cheerleading; Var Capt Gym; Merrimack.

LONG, ANDREA; Notre Dame Acad; Hanover, MA; (Y); Debate Tm; Drama Clb; Intnl Clb; Spanish Clb; Varsity Clb; Chorus; Nwsp Rptr; Nwsp Stf; Im Bsktbl; Im Socr; Excllnc Alg Awd; All Star Vllybl Tm; Edtr Sch Newspapr; Comm.

LONG, DAVID P; Bourne HS; Monument Beach, MA; (Y); Chess Clb; Church Yth Grp; Cmnty Wkr; Model UN; Political Wkr; SADD; Nwsp Rptr; Yrbk Rptr; Bsbl; Bsktbl; JR Yr 6th Man Awd; Prom Committe Chrmn; St Michaels Coll; Hmn Srv.

LONG, DEBORAH; Bourne HS; Buzzards Bay, MA; (Y); 9/180; Church Yth Grp; Spanish Clb; Trk; Hon Roll; Jr NHS; NHS; Prfct Atten Awd; Mst Imprvd Trck 85&86; Bst All-Arnd Grl JR Clss 86; Math.

LONG, ELAINE; Bishop Feehan HS; S Attleboro, MA; (Y); Yrbk Stf; Prfct Atten Awd; Svc Awd From The Fued Raising Office 86; SMU.

LONG, KEVIN M; Agawam HS; Westfield, MA; (Y); 130/350; Boy Scts; Church Yth Grp; Ski Clb; Bsbl; Var Ftbl; Var Capt Trk; Wt Lftg; Ftbl Gridiron Moms Schlrshp 85; Trck Gussen Yck Tn Awd 86; Grngr Pto Schlrshp 86; Westfield ST Coll; Comp Sci.

LONG, LUCINDA; Hopedale JR SR HS; Hopedale, MA; (Y); 2/58; Chorus; School Play; Yrbk Ed-Chief; Stu Cncl; High Hon Roll; Jr NHS; NHS; Pres Schlr; Sal; Cmnwlth Schlr Awd 86; MA ST Hon Schlrshp 86; Boston U; Engrng.

LONGE, KIM; Holyoke HS; Holyoke, MA; (Y); Spanish Clb; Band; Concert Band; Drm Mjr(t); Mrchg Band; Symp Band; Bsktbl; Hon Roll; NHS; UMASS; Bus.

LONGLEY, ANDREW; Reading Memorial HS; Reading, MA; (Y); 1/327; Church Yth Grp; Latin Clb; Math Tm; Science Clb; Church Choir; Lit Mag; Trk; High Hon Roll; NHS; Val; Brwn Bk Awd 85; Armd Frces Cmmnctns & Elctrncs Assoc Fllwshp Awd 86; Full Schlrhsp Phllps Andovr 85; Brown U; Engr.

LONGO, ROB; Agawam HS; Agawam, MA; (Y); Ski Clb; SADD; Bsbl; Ftbl; Hon Roll.

LONNBERG, KRISTIN; Medford HS; Medford, MA; (Y); Letterman Clb; Ski Clb; SADD; Var Socr; Var L Tennis; Merrimack Coll; Bus Admn.

LONSKE, BENJAMIN; Lincoln-Sudbury Regional HS; Sudbury, MA; (Y); Boy Scts; Math Tm; Band; Chorus; Concert Band; Orch; MA Yth Wind Ensmbl 84-87; SR NE Dist Music Fest 86; JR NE Dist Music Fest 84; Engr.

LOONEY, KIMBERLY; Lynn English HS; Lynn, MA; (Y); Dance Clb; Drama Clb; JCL; Latin Clb; Chorus; School Musical; School Play; Variety Show; Hon Roll; St Josephs Coll; Accntnt.

LOPEZ, MIRIAN; St Gregorys HS; Boston, MA; (Y); Church Yth Grp; Prfct Atten Awd; Outward Bound ME Awd 85; Frnch, Geom, Engl, Art Awds 85-86; Wentworth Inst Tech; Arch.

LOPEZ, NILDA; Northfield Mount Hermon HS; Brooklyn, NY; (Y); Aud/Vis; Library Aide; Mgr(s); JV Trk; VP Church Yth Grp; Rep Jr Cls; Rep Stu Cncl; JV Socr; NYU; Lib Arts.

LOPEZ, NOEMI; Technical HS; Springfield, MA; (Y); 3/219; Yrbk Stf; Bsktbl; Sftbl; Stu Cncl; Charles A Warner Achvt 86; Acad Achvt & Accmplshmnts 86; Marshall At Grad 86; Air Force; Zoologist.

LORD, LORI; Mc Cann Technical Voc Schl; Adams, MA; (Y); Sec Frsh Cls; Stu Cncl; Mgr(s); High Hon Roll; NHS; Brkshr Cmmnty Coll; Acctg.

LORDEN, DIANA; Groton Dunstable Regional Schl; Groton, MA; (Y); Band; Yrbk Stf; Rep Frsh Cls; Rep Soph Cls; Rep Jr Cls; Rep Sr Cls; Hon Roll; Jr NHS; VFW Awd; Voice Dem Awd; Providence Coll; Fin.

LORENTE, RAFAEL; Phillips Acad; Miami, FL; (Y); Jazz Band; Pep Band; Nwsp Stf; JV Bsbl; JV Ftbl; JV Wrstlng; Hon Roll; 1st Pl MA Natl Spn Exam 85; U Miami; Pol Sci.

LORING, JAMES; Altleboro HS; Attleboro, MA; (Y); Varsity Clb; Stage Crew; Var L Socr; High Hon Roll; Hon Roll; NHS; Capt Of JV Sccr Tm 83-84; 12th Plyr Awd Sccr 84; Mst Imprvd Plyr Awd Var Sccr 85; Norheastern U; Comp Engrng.

LORION, KRISTIN; Cathedral HS; Springfield, MA; (Y); Teachers Aide; Chorus; School Musical; School Play; Swing Chorus; Variety Show; Spfld Tech CC; Paralegal.

LOSEE, DAVID; Taconic HS; Pittsfield, MA; (Y); 33/250; Art Clb; Nwsp Stf; JV Crs Cntry; JV Trk; Hon Roll; Berkshire Eagle Carrier Scholar 87; Bus Cmmnctns.

LOUGHLIN, RAYMOND K; Leo T Doherty HS; Worcester, MA; (S); Computer Clb; Drama Clb; Intnl Clb; Spanish Clb; School Play; Stage Crew; Worcester Polytechnic Ins; Comp.

LOUIE, DEREK; Norwood SR HS; Norwood, MA; (Y); Boy Scts; CAP; Computer Clb; Service Clb; Band; Orch; Var Ftbl; Im Socr; Capt Tennis; Hon Roll; Cert Of Awd/Soc Stud 83; PA ST U; Arch Engrng.

LOUIS, SAMUEL; English HS; Hyde Park, MA; (Y); Church Yth Grp; Intnl Clb; Math Tm; Chorus; Church Choir; Yrbk Stf; Stu Cncl; High Hon Roll; NHS; Prfct Atten Awd; Tm Wnr Blk Hstry Olympc 86; Lawrence Awds SR Dept Hnrs Bilngl 86; Tm Wnr Mth Olympc Alg II 86; Boston Coll; Pre-Med.

LOURIE, MICHAEL; Natick HS; Natick, MA; (Y); 23/440; Aud/Vis; Nwsp Sprt Ed; Trs Stu Cncl; JV Var Bsbl; JV Bsktbl; Ftbl; Score Keeper; High Hon Roll; Hon Roll; NHS; Prsnl Typng Achvt; Liberal Arts.

LOUTRARIS, MICHAEL; Meford HS; Medford, MA; (Y); Am Leg Boys St; Math Tm; Science Clb; Hon Roll; Mu Alp Tht; NHS; Engrng.

LOVE, AMY; Mohawk Trail Reg HS; Shelburne Fls, MA; (Y); 22/116; Yrbk Phtg; Yrbk Stf; Sec Frsh Cls; Sec Soph Cls; Sec Jr Cls; Sec Sr Cls; Stu Cncl; Score Keeper; Hon Roll; Maude Francis Chldrns Schlrshp Fund 86; Excllnc Spnsh 84-86; Recog Clss Dedctn 86; Greenfield CC.

LOVE, WILLIAM; Billencia Memorial HS; Billerica, MA; (Y); 30/500; SADD; Var Ftbl; Var Trk; Ntl Merit Ltr; West Point; Aero Sp Engr.

LOVELL, REBECCA; Medford HS; Medford, MA; (Y); 85/406; Church Yth Grp; Dance Clb; Hosp Aide; SADD; Eng Schlrshp Awd 83-84; Achvt Awd-Math 84-85; Occptnl Thrpst.

LOVELLETTE, SHELLI; Taconic HS; Pittsfield, MA; (Y); Cmnty Wkr; Drama Clb; German Clb; Girl Scts; Pres SADD; School Play; Nwsp Rptr; Capt Socr; Var Sftbl; Gov Hon Prg Awd; Boston U; Crmnl Just.

LOVELY, WILLIAM; St Peter Marian HS; Worcester, MA; (Y); Boy Scts; JA; SADD; JV Ftbl; JV Swmmng; Engrng.

LOVINGER, JOANNA; Hingham HS; Hingham, MA; (Y); 38/340; AFS; Drama Clb; French Clb; Thesps; Trs Chorus; Trs Orch; School Musical; School Play; Lcrss; Slvr Medl Natl Latin Ex 1st Yr Latin 85; 2nd Plc 2nd Parish Chrch Art Shw 84; Commnctns.

LOWDER, AMY JO; Lexington HS; Lexington, MA; (Y); French Clb; Service Clb; Chorus; Var Tennis; Ntl Merit Ltr; Boston Coll.

LOWE, KERIN; Hanover HS; Hanover, MA; (Y); Church Yth Grp; Church Choir; Variety Show; Yrbk Stf; Capt Socr; Hon Roll; NHS; Stu Of Mnth Spnsh 85; Natl Spnsh Exms 85-86.

LOWENHAGEN, TRACY; Cohasset SR HS; Cohasset, MA; (Y); 31/130; AFS; Art Clb; Concert Band; Yrbk Stf; Hon Roll; Art.

LOWENSTEIN, DOUGLAS; Bishop Connolly HS; Newport, RI; (Y); 8/167; Latin Clb; Math Tm; Band; Nwsp Stf; L Bsktbl; L Tennis; High Hon Roll; NHS; Harvard Bk Awd 85-86; Brown U; Engrg.

LOWERY, MICHELE; Cathedral HS; Springfield, MA; (Y); Am Leg Aux Girls St; Intnl Clb; SADD; Nwsp Rptr; Rptr Nwsp Stf; Hon Roll; VFW Awd; Jrnlsm.

LOWEY, MELISSA; Lynnfield HS; Lynnfield, MA; (Y); 21/166; JA; Library Aide; Political Wkr; Crs Cntry; JV Tennis; Trk; French Hon Soc; Hon Roll; NHS.

LOWRY, ELAINE; Somerville HS; Somerville, MA; (Y); Am Leg Aux Girls St; Girl Scts; Yrbk Stf; Stu Cncl; Crs Cntry; Trk; Vllybl; Sci Fair 84-85 & 85-86; ESSEX Ag & Tech Inst; Vet Tech.

LOWTHERS, DENNIS; Medford HS; Medford, MA; (Y); Lowell; Bus Mgmt.

LUBOLD, MARK; Holyoke HS; Holyoke, MA; (Y); Boys Clb Am; Church Yth Grp; Spanish Clb; School Play; JV Bsbl; Var L Ftbl; Var L Trk; Wstrn MA Javln Champ Gld Mdl 85 & Slvr Mdl 86; Baystate Gms Brnz Mdl Jvln 86; Bus.

LUCAS, BEVERLY A; Rockland HS; Rockland, MA; (Y); 18/200; Art Clb; Drama Clb; Letterman Clb; PAVAS; Ski Clb; School Musical; School Play; Stage Crew; Hugh O Brian Yth Ldrshp 85; Awds For Artwrk Boston Glb Rck Art Assoc; Elmntry.

LUCAS, KATHY; Marlboro HS; Marlboro, MA; (Y); 12/270; Ski Clb; Varsity Clb; Nwsp Rptr; Var Capt Socr; Var Trk; High Hon Roll; NHS.

LUCCHESE, KERRY; Waltham HS; Boston, MA; (Y); Dance Clb; French Clb; Teachers Aide; Chorus; Trk; Hon Roll; Liberal Arts.

LUCE, BETHANIE; Hanover HS; Hanover, MA; (Y); Church Yth Grp; Drama Clb; Math Tm; High Hon Roll; Hon Roll; Ntl Merit Ltr; Stu Mnth Frgn Lang; Hnrb Mntn Hanover Sci Fair; 4th Pl Hanover Sci Fair; Chem.

LUCHINI, RICHARD; Milford HS; Milford, MA; (Y); Yrbk Stf; JV Bsktbl; Var L Socr; Var Capt Trk; Hon Roll; NHS; Prfct Atten Awd; Mst Decdtd Bys Trk & Fld 86; MHS Bstrs Clb Schlrshp 86; Bryant Coll; Accntng.

LUCIA, RICHARD; Holyoke HS; Holyoke, MA; (Y); 129/380; Math Clb; Teachers Aide; Varsity Clb; Var Crs Cntry; Var Trk; Hon Roll; Mtrlgy.

LUCIANO, ROBERT; Dedham HS; Dedham, MA; (Y); 34/250; Church Yth Grp; Ski Clb; SADD; Yrbk Stf; Ftbl; Capt Wrstlng; N Eastern U; Bus Adm.

LUCIER, DAWN; Hopedale JR SR HS; Hopedale, MA; (Y); 4/60; SADD; Chorus; Yrbk Stf; Pres Stu Cncl; Capt Var Sftbl; High Hon Roll; NHS; Church Yth Grp; School Play; Stage Crew; Prsdntl Acad Fitness Awd; Hopedale Hgh Alumni Awd; Stu Cncl Awd; Boston U; Phys Thrpy.

LUCIER, SCOTT; Franklin HS; Franklin, MA; (Y); 15/200; Am Leg Boys St; OEA; Yrbk Stf; Stu Cncl; Harvard Book Awd 86; MA Advanced Stds Prgm 86; Comp Sci.

LUCIER, SCOTT; St Peter-Marian HS; Millbury, MA; (Y); 20/170; Art Clb; Boy Scts; Camera Clb; French Clb; ROTC; Ski Clb; Varsity Clb; Im Bsbl; Var Ice Hcky; High Hon Roll; Elect Engr.

LUCY, MARTHA; Lenox Memorial SR HS; Lenox, MA; (Y); 3/60; Quiz Bowl; Yrbk Stf; Lit Mag; Stu Cncl; Var Bsktbl; Var Socr; Var Sftbl; Var Tennis; Var Trk; High Hon Roll; Williams Clg Bk Awd 86; Framingham Hstry Papr Cntst Hnbl Mntn 86; All Southern Berkshire Bstkbl Tm 86; Williams Coll; Pedtrcs.

LUCZKOW, CHRISTOPHER; Nipmuc Regional HS; Mendon, MA; (Y); 7/100; Am Leg Boys St; Computer Clb; SADD; Stat Bsktbl; Var Crs Cntry; High Hon Roll; Hon Roll; NHS; Comp Sci.

LUKEN, MATTHEW; Wakefield Memorial HS; Wakefield, MA; (Y); AFS; Church Yth Grp; German Clb; Chorus; Madrigals; Orch; School Play; Yrbk Rptr; Eagle Sct Awd 86; Stdnt Advsry Comm 86-87; Aerontcl Sci.

LUKINS, JEFF; No Middlesex Reg HS; Pepperell, MA; (Y); Boy Scts; Church Yth Grp; Ski Clb; Ed Yrbk Stf; JV Capt Socr; Vllybl; High Hon Roll; NHS; Computer Clb; Math Tm; Sccr MVP 85-86; Army Awd 86; 2 Regnl HS Comp Comptitns 1st Pl 86; USAF Acad; Aerospc Engr.

LUMPKIN, DEBORAH; Sandwich JR SR HS; East Sandwich, MA; (Y); 8/158; Church Yth Grp; Band; Concert Band; Mrchg Band; Variety Show; Sec Lit Mag; Hon Roll; NHS; VA Intrmnt Coll Pres Schlrshp $1000 86; Mary Crocker Bkr Schlrshp $1500 86; Wellesley Bk Awd; VA Intermont Coll; Bio.

LUNARDINI, MATTHEW; Chicopee Comprehensive HS; Chicopee, MA; (Y); 52/300; German Clb; Rep Stu Cncl; JV Bsktbl; Var L Ftbl; Var L Trk; High Hon Roll; Hon Roll; Frsh Cls; Soph Cls; Jr Cls; Ofcl Citatn MA ST Snt Ftbl 85; Big Oly Game Awd WREB Radio Ftbl 84-85; US Coast Guard Acad; Bus Mgt.

LUND, SHARON; Taconic HS; Pittsfield, MA; (Y); Band; Concert Band; Mrchg Band; Pep Band; Sftbl; Elem Ed.

LUNDBERG JR, ROBERT S; Shepherd Hill Regional HS; Brookfield, MA; (Y); 41/131; Am Leg Boys St; Debate Tm; School Musical; Stu Cncl; Var L Socr; Trk; Hon Roll; U MA-AMHERST; Elect Engr.

LUPI, ANDREA; Matignon HS; Somerville, MA; (S); 3/178; Camera Clb; Church Yth Grp; Drama Clb; School Musical; JV Trk; Mgr Vllybl; French Hon Soc; Hon Roll; NHS; NEDT Awd; Bentley; Bus Adm.

LUZ, TROY; Diaman Voch HS; Fall River, MA; (Y); Boys Clb Am; Boy Scts; Cmnty Wkr; Socr; Hon Roll; Navy.

LYDON, AMY; Marion HS; Framingham, MA; (Y); School Play; Nwsp Stf; Yrbk Ed-Chief; Lit Mag; Crs Cntry; Vllybl; Hon Roll; NEDT Awd; Outstndng Perfrmnc In Creative Wrtng/Jrnlsm Awd 86; Commnctns.

LYDON JR, JAMES F; St Dominic Savio HS; Chelsea, MA; (Y); 24/104; SADD; Variety Show; Nwsp Stf; Yrbk Stf; Lit Mag; Trk; Hon Roll; Prfct Atten Awd; U MA Amherst; Htl/Rest Mgt.

LYLE, ANN; Hampshire Regional HS; Southampton, MA; (Y); 22/132; Pres Band; Concert Band; Jazz Band; Mrchg Band; Variety Show; Nwsp Stf; Yrbk Ed-Chief; Yrbk Sprt Ed; Yrbk Stf; Hon Roll; Yng Peoples Symphony 86; Western Dist Bnd 86.

LYLE, ROBERT P; Georgetown JR SR HS; Georgetown, MA; (Y); 3/83; Pres AFS; Letterman Clb; Model UN; Rep Stu Cncl; Crs Cntry; Var Socr; Tennis; High Hon Roll; Jr NHS; NHS; Stu Govt Day 86; Engrng.

LYNCH, ALLISON; Melrose HS; Melrose, MA; (Y); 10/370; French Clb; Hosp Aide; SADD; Chorus; Flag Corp; School Musical; Yrbk Bus Mgr; Hon Roll; NHS; Church Yth Grp; French Exm La Concorde Recgntn; Tufts U; Lang.

LYNCH, CLOVE; Buxton Schl; Petersburg, NY; (Y); Chess Clb; Science Clb; Orch; Rep Stu Cncl; Var Socr; High Hon Roll; Prfct Atten Awd; Natl Lang Arts Olympd 84; Answers Please 85; Envrnmntl Engrg.

LYNCH, DIANE; Greater Lawrence Tech; Lawrence, MA; (Y); 12/385; SADD; High Hon Roll; Hon Roll; NHS; Data Mgmt Shop Awds 83-86; Nrthrn Essex; Bus Mgmt.

LYNCH, SUSAN; Norwood HS; Norwood, MA; (Y); 40/366; VP SADD; Concert Band; Yrbk Bus Mgr; Stu Cncl; JV Var Fld Hcky; Var Co-Capt Sftbl; Hon Roll; Princpls Awd 84; Stu Yr Bay ST Lg Sftbl 85; Bay ST Lg All Star Sftbl 86; Advrtsng.

LYNDON, DIANE; Braintree HS; Braintree, MA; (Y); 1/442; JCL; Math Tm; Orch; Lit Mag; Rep Jr Cls; JV Var Socr; JV Trk; High Hon Roll; NHS; Harvard Bk Awd 86; Braun Bk Awd 86; Rensselaer Medl 86.

LYNE, SANDRA; B M C Durfee HS; Fall River, MA; (Y); Rep Church Yth Grp; Hon Roll; Bus Clb.

LYON, MARGARET; Hanover HS; Hanover, MA; (Y); Church Yth Grp; Math Tm; Acpl Chr; Concert Band; Drm Mjr(t); Mrchg Band; School Musical; Rep Jr Cls; Hon Roll; NHS; Music Scholar Smmr Stdy 86; Hnrb Mntn Sci Fair 85; 5th Pl Schl Sci Fair 86; Music Ed.

LYON, RUTH A; West Boylston JR SR HS; W Boylston, MA; (Y); Camp Fr Inc; Church Yth Grp; Drama Clb; Band; Concert Band; Mrchg Band; School Musical; School Play; Yrbk Stf; Hon Roll; Excllnce Drama & Art; Bus.

LYONNAIS, NICOLE; Old Rochester Regional HS; Mattapoisett, MA; (Y); 23/162; Office Aide; Nwsp Rptr; Yrbk Stf; Var L Bsktbl; Capt L Trk; L Var Vllybl; Sec NHS; Hghst Schltc Avg Wrld Hstry 86; Natl Chem Olympiad Top 10 85; Natl Physcs Olympd Top 10 86; Secndry Ed.

LYONNAIS, ROBERT; Bishop Stang HS; Fairhaven, MA; (S); 6/250; Math Tm; Ski Clb; JV Bsbl; Var L Trk; High Hon Roll; NHS; Cngrssnl Schlr 85; West Point; Engr.

LYONS, DENISE; Our Lady Of Nazareth Academy HS; Woburn, MA; (Y); Pep Clb; SADD; Thesps; Stage Crew; Rep Stu Cncl; Hon Roll; Consistnt Effort Christn Svc Awd 85; Outstndng Achvt Alg II Awd 85; Dilignc Bus Studies Awd 86; Providence Coll; Civil Engr.

LYONS, ELLEN; Chelmsford HS; Chelmsford, MA; (Y); 120/517; Camera Clb; Church Yth Grp; Exploring; High Hon Roll; Hon Roll; NHS; Bus Ed Awd Typng; U Lowell.

LYONS, JOHN; Boston Latin HS; Boston, MA; (Y); 68/274; Boys Clb Am; Church Yth Grp; Cmnty Wkr; Ski Clb; Bsbl; Var Ice Hcky; Hon Roll; NHS; Histrl Scty Essay Awd 1st Pl 83; Ice Hcky Hat Trick Awd 84; Pre Law.

LYONS, MARIANNE; Natick HS; Natick, MA; (Y); 24/399; Church Yth Grp; NFL; L Speech Tm; School Musical; School Play; Stu Cncl; High Hon Roll; Hon Roll; Jr NHS; NHS; Psych.

LYONS, MICHAEL; Central Catholic HS; Lowell, MA; (Y); 1/231; VP Church Yth Grp; Computer Clb; Math Clb; Church Choir; Rep Soph Cls; Rep Stu Cncl; Im Bsktbl; High Hon Roll; Pres NHS; Ntl Merit Ltr; Harvard Book Awd 86; Rensselaer Mdl Math & Sci 86; 1st Pl Gen Excllnc 86; Pre Med.

LYONS, MICHAEL; St Johns Preparatory Schl; Peabody, MA; (Y); Science Clb; Sec Spanish Clb; Var Bsbl; Hon Roll; NHS; Spanish NHS; Cmnty Wkr; Im Ftbl; Im Vllybl; 6th ST Ntl Spnsh Test 85; 1st Eastern MA Ntl Spnsh Test 86; Bio.

LYONS, SHARI; Sharon HS; Sharon, MA; (Y); 43/211; Drama Clb; Model UN; Political Wkr; Red Cross Aide; Trs Temple Yth Grp; Chorus; Nwsp Stf; Yrbk Stf; Rep Stu Cncl; Hon Roll; Cable TV-TEEN Magzn 85-87; Comm.

LYONS, SHARYN L; Sharon HS; Sharon, MA; (Y); 20/209; Computer Clb; Spanish Clb; Nwsp Stf; Bryant Coll; Acctg.

MAC BRIDE, SUE; Walpale HS; Walpole, MA; (Y); 6/268; Art Clb; Sec Church Yth Grp; Cmnty Wkr; French Clb; Sec Girl Scts; Band; Church Choir; Concert Band; Drm Mjr(t); Mrchg Band; Slvr & Gold Awds Girl Scts 85-86; Intl Rel.

MAC CALLUM, TIMOTHY G; East Longmeadow HS; E Longmeadow, MA; (Y); 4/201; VP Church Yth Grp; Var Debate Tm; Sec Drama Clb; Sec Intnl Clb; Jazz Band; Variety Show; Nwsp Stf; Var Tennis; High Hon Roll; Sec NHS; Pres Acad Fit Awd 86; Rotary Clb Schlrshp 86; Hofstra U; Cmmnctns.

MAC CORMACK, DENISE; Saint Clare HS; Boston, MA; (Y); 2/150; Church Yth Grp; JCL; Political Wkr; Nwsp Stf; Pres Stu Cncl; High Hon Roll; NHS; Pres Schlr; Sal; St Schlr; Sherman H Starr Human Rel Yth Awd 86; Cum Laude Cert Natl Lat Exam 83-86; Magna Cum Laude Cert 84; Boston Coll; Bnkg.

MAC DONALD, CHRISTINA; Wilmington HS; Wilmington, MA; (Y); Church Yth Grp; Hosp Aide; Intnl Clb; Office Aide; Science Clb; Spanish Clb; SADD; Hon Roll; Psych.

MAC DONALD, CHRISTOPHER; Revere HS; Revere, MA; (Y); Boy Scts; VP Church Yth Grp; Drama Clb; Math Clb; SADD; School Play; Nwsp Stf; Yrbk Stf; Rep Jr Cls; Stu Cncl; Star Wars Essy-Hon Mntn 85; Pol Sci.

MAC DONALD, DEBORAH LYNN; Braintree HS; Braintree, MA; (Y); 8/415; Church Yth Grp; Spanish Clb; Capt Var Gym; Var L Trk; High Hon Roll; JC Awd; NHS; Pres Schlr; Spanish NHS; Boy Scts; Tp Female Athlt Awd 86; Acdmc Exclnc Spnsh 86; Grnd Crss Clr Intl Ordr Rnbw Fr Grls 86; Bridgewater ST Coll; Elem Educ.

MAC DONALD, MATTHEW F; Burlington HS; Burlington, MA; (Y); 5/325; Pres Debate Tm; Concert Band; Mrchg Band; Symp Band; Var Socr; JV Trk; High Hon Roll; Hon Roll; NHS; Ntl Merit Ltr; Awd Acadmc Excllnc Engl 84-85; Awd Acadmc Excllnc Math 85; Awd Acadmc Excllnc Hstry 84-86; Bus.

MAC DONALD, ROBIN; Bridgewater-Raynham Regional HS; Raynham, MA; (Y); 58/370; Pres Church Yth Grp; SADD; Band; Concert Band; Drm Mjr(t); Jazz Band; Mrchg Band; Hon Roll; JP Sousa Awd; L Armstrong Jazz Awd 86; Taunton Mscl Art Clb Schlrshp 86; Francis R Hill Music & W Green Schlrshps 86; Boston U; Marine Sci.

MAC DONALD, STEPHEN J; St Patricks HS; Waltham, MA; (Y); 21/48; Am Leg Boys St; Boys Clb Am; VP Frsh Cls; VP Jr Cls; VP Sr Cls; Capt Bsktbl; Capt Ftbl; NEDT Awd; MA ST Schlrshp 86; Ftbl All Star 85; Boston U; Phy Ed.

MAC DONALD, TRACY; Walnut Hill Schl /Performing Arts; North Kingstown, RI; (Y); Drama Clb; School Play; Nwsp Ed-Chief; Yrbk Ed-Chief; Lit Mag; Sr Cls; DAR Awd; Hon Roll; Intnl Clb; Pep Clb; Walnut Hill Schl Wrtg Cont 86; Natl Lang Art Olympd 84; Theatr.

MAC DOUGALL, KELLEY; Marshfield HS; Marshfield, MA; (Y); 6/363; Key Clb; SADD; Nwsp Rptr; Yrbk Stf; Stu Cncl; Bsktbl; Tennis; French Hon Soc; Jr NHS; NHS; Chnclrs Tlnt Awd 85; Cmnwlth Schlr 86; Georgetown U; Intrntl Mngmnt.

MAC GILLIVRAY, MARY JO; Silver Lake Regional HS; Halifax, MA; (Y); Church Yth Grp; French Clb; Band; Symp Band; Var Tennis; Hon Roll; Fshn Mdse.

MAC GREGOR, DAWN; Medway JR SR HS; Medway, MA; (Y); 35/137; Am Leg Aux Girls St; Church Yth Grp; Trs Exploring; Office Aide; SADD; VP Jr Cls; VP Sr Cls; Var Socr; Var Tennis; Hnrb Mntn; Law.

MAC INNIS, MARGARET; Holy Name CC HS; Douglas, MA; (Y); #22 In Class; Church Yth Grp; Drama Clb; School Play; Stage Crew; Yrbk Stf; Lit Mag; Var Fld Hcky; High Hon Roll; Hon Roll; NHS; 20th Century Hstry Awd; Humanities Awds; Religion Awds; Emmanuel Coll; Art Hstry.

MAC KAY, ROBERT D; Hopkins Acad; Hadley, MA; (Y); 36/50; Letterman Clb; Varsity Clb; Chorus; Pres Stu Cncl; VP Capt Bsbl; VP Capt Bsktbl; VP Capt Socr; Hon Roll; Spanish Clb; MVP Bsbl 85; Stu Princpls Adv Cncl 85-86; All Western MA Bsbl; Worcester Acad.

MAC LEOD, KRISTEN; Holyoke Catholic HS; Easthampton, MA; (Y); 13/130; Drama Clb; Spanish Clb; SADD; Yrbk Rptr; Ed Yrbk Stf; High Hon Roll; NHS; Physcl Sci Awd; Bio Awd; Bio.

MAC MILLAN, HEATHER; St Joseph Regional HS; Chelmsford, MA; (Y); SADD; Ntl Merit Ltr; Pres Frsh Cls; Trs Soph Cls; Trs VP Stu Cncl; Hon Roll; Acadmc All Am 85-86; Outstndng Serv Mnstry 85-86.

MAC MURRAY, JENNIFER; King Philip Regional HS; Plainville, MA; (Y); Drama Clb; Hosp Aide; School Play; Hon Roll; NHS.

MAC NEILL, PAUL; Concord Carlisle HS; Concord, MA; (Y); Cmnty Wkr; Im Bsktbl; Var Lcrss; Im Sftbl; Im Vllybl; Hon Roll; NHS; Deptmntl Awds Math-84 & Phy Ed-86.

MACADAMS, KIRSTEN; Medford HS; Medford, MA; (Y); Church Yth Grp; Intnl Clb; Ski Clb; SADD; Varsity Clb; L Cheerleading; Tufts U; Bus Mgmt.

MACDONALD, DOUG; Walpole HS; Walpole, MA; (Y); Rep Frsh Cls; Rep Soph Cls; JV Capt Socr; Hon Roll; Indstrl Arts Prfrmnc Awd 85; Aerontcl Engr.

MACDONALD, MELINDA; Wakefield HS; Wakefield, MA; (Y); 42/322; Pres VP AFS; Spanish Clb; Yrbk Stf; Hon Roll; Sec NHS; Ctzn Schlrshp Fndtn Schlrshp 86-87; Cosmos Clb Awd 86; Pol Sci Awd Excel 85-86; Springfield Coll; Phys Thrpy.

MACE, NICHOLE; Ware HS; Ware, MA; (Y); 5/125; Pep Clb; Spanish Clb; Cheerleading; Pom Pon; High Hon Roll; Hon Roll; Dplma Of Merit Excllnc In Spnsh III 86; Spnsh.

MACEACHERN, JUNE; Mt St Joseph Acad; Boston, MA; (Y); 81/169; JA; SADD; Capt Cheerleading; Sftbl; Hon Roll; Ntl Bus Hon Soc 85-86; Bus Clb 85-86; Sec PSTA 86-87.

MACERO, JEAN MARIE; St Clement HS; W Somerville, MA; (Y); Church Yth Grp; Cmnty Wkr; Latin Clb; Library Aide; Office Aide; Teachers Aide; Chorus; Church Choir; School Play; Stage Crew; Achvmnt Awds 83-86; Schlrshp Excllnc Stds 83-84; Lesley Coll; Elem Educ.

MACGREGOR, ANNA; Boston Latin HS; Boston, MA; (Y); 55/284; Church Yth Grp; Cmnty Wkr; Debate Tm; Drama Clb; Latin Clb; Church Choir; School Play; Stage Crew; Nwsp Rptr; Lit Mag; Natl Clsscl Leag Cert Merit 86; 5 Awds Mass Drama Fstvl For Ex In Actng 85-86; Harvard Cmmcmnt Ushr 86; Harvard; Teacher.

MACHADO JR, PAUL; B M C Durfee HS; Fall River, MA; (Y); 224/673; Boy Scts; Church Yth Grp; Band; Concert Band; Mrchg Band; Symp Band; JV Bsbl; Var Swmmng; Ocngrphy.

MACHNIK, MICHELE; Presentation Of Mary Acad; Salem, NH; (Y); Church Yth Grp; French Clb; Math Clb; Var Tennis; High Hon Roll; Hon Roll; VP NHS; NEDT Awd; Engl Slvr Mdl, Frnch Gold Mdl 86; Psych.

MACK, AMY; Governor Dummer Acad; Byfield, MA; (Y); Ski Clb; Varsity Clb; Yrbk Sprt Ed; Var Capt Fld Hcky; Var Capt Ice Hcky; Var Capt Trk; Hon Roll; All Lgu Awd Fld Hcky 85; Gvnr Dummer Hnr Soc 85; Bay ST Games Fld Hcky 86; Englsh.

MACKEEN, DAVID; Archbishop Williams HS; Canton, MA; (Y); Church Yth Grp; Library Aide; Ice Hcky; Trk; High Hon Roll; NHS; Pres Schlr; U Of MA; Elec Engrng.

MACKIE, SEAN; Milford HS; Milford, MA; (Y); Aud/Vis; Boy Scts; Ski Clb; Band; Concert Band; Jazz Band; Mrchg Band; Orch; Yrbk Stf; Var Golf; Cmmnctns.

MACKIERNAN, HAROLD; Plymouth-Carver HS; Plymouth, MA; (Y); Church Yth Grp; Drama Clb; School Play; Stage Crew; Lit Mag; NHS; Carnegie-Mellon U; Physics.

MACKINNON, LORI; Bishop Feehan HS; Walpole, MA; (Y); 78/268; Church Yth Grp; Cmnty Wkr; Dance Clb; Girl Scts; Ski Clb; SADD; Capt Drill Tm; Trk; High Hon Roll; Hon Roll; Providence Coll.

MACKLIN, ANN; Bedford HS; Bedford, MA; (Y); 67/220; Temple Yth Grp; Orch; ROTC; Off Soph Cls; JV Bsktbl; JV Var Tennis; Tp Girl Shooter Of HS 85-86; Grphc Art.

MACKLOW, MELANIE; Milford HS; Milford, MA; (Y); 29/290; Am Leg Aux Girls St; Key Clb; JV Sftbl; JV Vllybl; Hon Roll; NHS; Lawyer.

MACLELLAND, PAUL; Dennis-Yarmouth Reg HS; Yarmouth, MA; (Y); Var Letterman Clb; Ski Clb; Varsity Clb; JV Bsktbl; JV Golf; Im Lcrss; Var JV Socr; Im Vllybl; Hon Roll; Bus Arch.

MACLSAAC, BRENDA; St Gregorys HS; Boston, MA; (Y); 5/99; Drama Clb; Chorus; School Musical; School Play; Stage Crew; Nwsp Ed-Chief; Elks Awd; Hon Roll; NHS; Umass Amherst; Eng.

MACPHAIL, SARAH; Westford Acad; Westford, MA; (Y); AFS; Drama Clb; French Clb; Girl Scts; Hosp Aide; Model UN; Teachers Aide; Hon Roll; Gold Awd Girl Scout 86; Bd Dir Cncl 86-87.

MACRINA, RICHARD C; Oliver Ames HS; S Easton, MA; (Y); 7/243; Church Yth Grp; FBLA; Var Bsbl; Bsktbl; Var Capt Golf; Hon Roll; Masonic Awd; NHS; Pres Schlr; Cert Of Acdmc Excllnc 86; Mary A Stone Schlrshp Brwnng Clb Schlrshp 86; Easton Lttl League Schlrshp 86; U Of Notre Dame; Bus.

MADDALONI, MARIA E; East Longmeadow HS; E Longmeadow, MA; (Y); 22/195; Trs Church Yth Grp; Intnl Clb; Math Tm; Nwsp Sprt Ed; Rep Stu Cncl; Stat Bsktbl; Hon Roll; 1st Pl Ntl Mthmtcs Cntst 86; Stu Rep To E Lngmdw Schl Cmty 86; Stu As Schls Mtch Wits Team 83-87.

MADDEN JR, JOHN F; Boston College HS; N Weymouth, MA; (Y); Church Yth Grp; Key Clb; Red Cross Aide; SADD; Teachers Aide; Im Bsktbl; JV Socr; JV Trk; Im Vllybl; NHS; Jrnlsm.

MADDEN, NORA C; Milford HS; Milford, MA; (Y); 131/300; FTA; Girl Scts; Office Aide; Political Wkr; Yrbk Stf; JV Fld Hcky; Bridgewater ST; Hstry.

MADDOCK, THOMAS MORE; Berkshire Schl; Camillus, NY; (Y); Church Yth Grp; Cmnty Wkr; Dance Clb; Intnl Clb; Letterman Clb; Radio Clb; Red Cross Aide; Ski Clb; Spanish Clb; Varsity Clb; Readers Digest Schlrshp 86; Bus.

MADIGAN, ERIN; Dover-Sherborn Regional; Sherborn, MA; (Y); 60/152; AFS; Camp Fr Inc; Church Yth Grp; Drama Clb; Library Aide; PAVAS; Spanish Clb; Teachers Aide; Chorus; Variety Show; Ruth L Bean Svc Awd Nat Camp Fire 85; Boston Cncl 85; Brd Dir Camp Fire; Mktg.

MADORE, SHERRIE; South High Community Schl; Worcester, MA; (Y); Tennis; Hon Roll; Bus.

MAFFEI, PETER; Natick HS; Natick, MA; (Y); 27/400; JV Tennis; L Wrstlng; Hon Roll; Elec Engrng.

MAFFEO, ANTHONY; East Boston HS; E Boston, MA; (Y); Art Clb; Boys Clb Am; Cmnty Wkr; JA; SADD; Socr; Trk; U MA Amherst; Soclgy.

MAGALDI, DIANA; Coyle & Cassidy Mem HS; S Easton, MA; (Y); 10/156; Library Aide; VP Pres Band; Hon Roll; Jr NHS; NHS; Spanish NHS; 4 Yr Plaque For Band 86; Hghst Hnrs-Govt, Acctng & 2nd Religion Iv 86; Bryant Coll; Bus Mgmt.

MAGGIO, CARA; Cambridge Rindge & Latin HS; Cambridge, MA; (Y); Library Aide; Political Wkr; Yrbk Stf; Rep Frsh Cls; JV Sftbl; JV Swmmng; High Hon Roll; Prfct Atten Awd; Nrsg.

MAGGIONI, CARA; Ursuline Acad; Dedham, MA; (Y); Latin Clb; Math Tm; Nwsp Rptr; Rep Stu Cncl; JV Vllybl; High Hon Roll; Hon Roll; NHS; Ntl Merit SF; Hgh Obrn Yth Ldrshp Ambsdr 85.

MAGGIORE, LAURIE; Bishop Fenwick HS; Saugus, MA; (Y); Math Clb; Nwsp Stf; Sftbl; High Hon Roll; Accntng.

MAGLIOZZI, JAMES; Wilmington HS; Wilmington, MA; (Y); Nwsp Rptr; Yrbk Stf; Bsbl; JV Bsktbl; Var Capt Socr; Wt Lftg; JV Wrstlng; High Hon Roll; Hon Roll; Worcester Polytech; Engrng.

MAGNANI, DIANNA; Boston Latin HS; Boston, MA; (Y); Art Clb; Swing Chorus; Yrbk Ed-Chief; L Trk; NHS; Ntl Merit Ltr; St Schlr; High Hon Roll; Chorus; Acdmc All-Amer 86; Wrd Fllwshp 86; Bstn Glb Gld Ky Art Awd 85; Harvard.

MAGNER, ROBIN; Billerica HS; Billerica, MA; (Y); 70/500; Church Yth Grp; Cmnty Wkr; Ski Clb; Teachers Aide; Rep Frsh Cls; Rep Jr Cls; Rep Sr Cls; Var Capt Cheerleading; Powder Puff Ftbl; High Hon Roll; Bentley Coll; Bus Mngmnt.

MAGNUS-GEORGE, CHARITY; Marlboro HS; Marlboro, MA; (Y); Drama Clb; Chorus; Badmtn; Bsbl; Bowling; Fld Hcky; Ftbl; Sftbl; Vllybl; Hon Roll; MA Bay CC; Medcl Rcds Tech.

MAGUIRE JR, DENNIS F; Bishop Fenwick HS; Lynn, MA; (Y); 20/238; Church Yth Grp; Math Tm; Variety Show; Var L Bsktbl; High Hon Roll; Hon Roll; NHS; Ntl Merit Ltr; Achvt Overall Math Awd 86; Hgst Achvt Math Olympiad 85-86; Alg Hnrs Awd 85; Yale; Math.

MAGUIRE, INGRID; Hyde Park HS; Hyde Park, MA; (S); 9/152; Sftbl; Vllybl; NHS; Natl Hnr Socty 84-85; VP Natl Hnr Socty 85-86; Boston U; Bus Mgmt.

MAGUIRE, KEVIN; Bishop Feehan HS; N Attleboro, MA; (Y); Boy Scts; Drama Clb; Chorus; School Musical; School Play; Stage Crew; Yrbk Stf; Slctd Eurpn Cncrt Tour/Yth Of AM Choir 86; Slctd Stheastrn Dstrct Chorus 85; Awd In Theatre Ltr 86; Psych.

MAGUIRE, MARY; Bishop Fenwick HS; Lynn, MA; (Y); JV Tennis; 2nd Hnrs 84-86; Dentstry.

MAHAN, ERIN; Marblehead HS; Marblehead, MA; (Y); 52/259; JV Var Bsktbl; JV Var Socr; Sftbl; Tennis; Awd For Engl Crtcl Thnkng Lit 85; MVP For Jv Bsktbll; Ldng Scorer Soccer.

MAHEU, DAWN; Milford HS; Milford, MA; (Y); 45/319; Key Clb; Office Aide; Pep Clb; SADD; Teachers Aide; Band; Yrbk Stf; Rep Stu Cncl; Vllybl; Hon Roll.

MAHON, LISA; St Marys HS; Lynn, MA; (Y); Art Clb; JA; French Hon Soc; Hnr Rll JR; Hnrs Algbr Blgn 84; Hnrs Algbr 2 Rlgn Hnrs Engl Relgn Hstry; UCLA; BC Soc Srv.

MAHON, ROBERTA; Attleboro HS; Attleboro, MA; (Y); Chorus; Powder Puff Ftbl; High Hon Roll; NHS; Church Yth Grp; Hosp Aide; Gym; Hnrb Mntn For Crtv Wrtng; Exc In Attitude.

MAHONEY, ANN; Lynn Classical HS; Lynn, MA; (Y); 4-H; JA; Pep Clb; Spanish Clb; SADD; Bowling; Burdett Schl; CPA.

MAHONEY, GERALD J; Cardinal Spellman HS; Brockton, MA; (Y); 11/208; Am Leg Boys St; Boy Scts; Church Yth Grp; ROTC; Spanish Clb; SADD; Var Crs Cntry; Var Trk; Kiwanis Awd; Pres Schlr; Veterans Frgn Wars Post 1046 Schlrshp 86; CUA Cardinal Gibbans Hnr Schlrshp 86-87; Cath U Hnr Prog 86; Catholic U Of Am; Internatl Pol.

MAHONEY, IAN P; Boston College HS; South Weymouth, MA; (Y); Am Leg Boys St; Church Yth Grp; Cmnty Wkr; Drama Clb; Off Key Clb; Ski Clb; Spanish Clb; SADD; School Play; VP Key Clb 87; Norwich U; Military Lawyer.

MAHONEY, JAMES; South High Communty Schl; Worcester, MA; (S); #11 In Class; Aud/Vis; Science Clb; Ski Clb; Variety Show; Nwsp Ed-Chief; Yrbk Stf; Hon Roll; Milestones Of Freedm Awd 85; Eng.

MAHONEY, JOANNE; Uxbridge HS; Uxbridge, MA; (Y); 4/81; Trs Church Yth Grp; Math Tm; Varsity Clb; Trs Rep Stu Cncl; JV Bsktbl; Var Fld Hcky; Var Tennis; High Hon Roll; VP NHS; Alt/Good Govt Day 85-86; Bryant Coll; Actuary Sci.

MAHONEY, KRISTEN; Arlington HS; Arlington, MA; (Y); 17/381; Office Aide; SADD; Mrchg Band; Orch; School Musical; Ed Yrbk Stf; Sec Stu Cncl; Var JV Fld Hcky; Hon Roll; NHS; Bio.

MAHONEY, LINDSEY; Arlington HS; Arlington, MA; (Y); 14/400; Math Tm; SADD; Ed Yrbk Stf; Off Soph Cls; JV Capt Socr; Var Capt Trk; High Hon Roll; VP NHS; Off Jr Cls; Off Sr Cls; MVP Soccer; Bus.

MAHONEY, MARY; Maynard HS; Maynard, MA; (Y); 2/100; Am Leg Aux Girls St; French Clb; Chorus; Mrchg Band; Orch; School Musical; Off Stu Cncl; High Hon Roll; NHS; Sal; Williams Coll Book Awd 85; Soc Wmn Engrs Awd 86; MA Commonwealth Schlr 86; Brandeis U.

MAHONEY, PHILIP W; St Bernards Regional Catholic HS; Fitchburg, MA; (Y); 30/158; Am Leg Boys St; Model UN; Ski Clb; Church Choir; School Play; Nwsp Ed-Chief; NHS; Ntl Merit Ltr; Rep Jr Cls; Var Crs Cntry; Middlebury Coll; Tchr.

MAHONEY, SHEILA; N Reading HS; N Reading, MA; (Y); Political Wkr; Nwsp Stf; JV Bsktbl; JV Fld Hcky; JV Sftbl; Art Awd 84; Bus.

MAHONEY, TERENCE; Marian HS; Framingham, MA; (Y); 19/187; Cmnty Wkr; Rep Frsh Cls; Rep Soph Cls; Var L Bsktbl; Im Vllybl; Hon Roll; NHS; Bus Law.

MAHONEY, TOMMY; Natick HS; Natick, MA; (Y); 155/486; Boy Scts; Pres Church Yth Grp; Band; Concert Band; Mrchg Band; Nwsp Stf; Coach Actv; Score Keeper; Socr; Swmmng; MI ST; Lib Arts.

MAHONY, MEGAN; Norwell HS; Norwell, MA; (Y); 6/166; AFS; Am Leg Aux Girls St; Church Yth Grp; French Clb; Nwsp Rptr; Yrbk Stf; Fld Hcky; High Hon Roll; Hon Roll; NHS; Sci Fair Hnrbl Ment 85; Regnl Sci Fair 2nd Pl 86; Hugh O Brien Yth Ldrshp Amb 85; Ed.

MAHONY, SUSAN; Lynnfield HS; Lynnfield, MA; (Y); 16/170; Yrbk Sprt Ed; Var L Bsktbl; Powder Puff Ftbl; Var L Socr; Var L Sftbl; Rep NHS; CAL All Lg Goalie 84-85.

MAILLET, LAURIE; Auburn HS; Auburn, MA; (Y); Church Yth Grp; Drill Tm; Variety Show; Yrbk Stf; Cheerleading; Hon Roll; Excllnc Bus Ed 86; Excllnc Shrthnd 86; Quinsigamond CC; Sec.

MAILLET, THERESA A; Belmont HS; Belmont, MA; (Y); 26/263; Band; Mrchg Band; Hon Roll; NHS; Awd For Band 86; Lions Clb Richard Price Mem Schlrshp 86; NH U; Lib Arts.

MAISONET, JENNIFER; Holyoke HS; Holyoke, MA; (Y); Church Yth Grp; JA; Vllybl; Cit Awd; Hon Roll.

MAJESKI, KRISTINA; Wakefield HS; Wakefield, MA; (Y); 40/333; Church Yth Grp; Cmnty Wkr; French Clb; GAA; Hosp Aide; Key Clb; Teachers Aide; Varsity Clb; Chorus; Church Choir; Jr Districts Chorus 86; U MA AmherstMGMT.

MAJKUT, KIMBERLY; Taunton HS; East Taunton, MA; (Y); 6/400; Office Aide; Ski Clb; Spanish Clb; Yrbk Stf; Lit Mag; Sec Stu Cncl; Var Capt Fld Hcky; Sftbl; High Hon Roll; NHS; Hnr Mntn Schlstc Fld Hcky Tm 85; Hnr Mntn All Schlstc Sftbl Tm 86; Padelford Schlrshp 86; Simmons Coll; Psychlgy.

MAKAREWICZ, DIANE; Longmeadow HS; Longmeadow, MA; (Y); 46/265; AFS; Art Clb; Keywanettes; School Play; Nwsp Rptr; Ed Yrbk Stf; Stu Cncl; Trk; High Hon Roll; Hon Roll; Natl Art Hnr Socty 86; Yrbk Art Edtr Ads Layout Edtr 85-86.

MAKI, ERIC; Cohasset HS; Cohasset, MA; (Y); 6/104; Band; Jazz Band; Yrbk Stf; Pres Sr Cls; High Hon Roll; Hon Roll; NHS; Williams Coll Book Awd 86.

MAKOWSKI, LISA; Greater Lawrence Technical HS; N Andover, MA; (Y); 138/412; Church Yth Grp; Teachers Aide; Im Bsktbl; Hon Roll; CIT Prgm Cmp Evrgrn Andvr MA 83; Stu Rep Snt Schls Rcrt New Stu 85; Pol Sci.

MALDONADO, JOHN; Greater Lawrence Technical Schl; Lawrence, MA; (Y); 2/350; Boy Scts; Church Yth Grp; Political Wkr; Radio Clb; SADD; Teachers Aide; Rep Frsh Cls; Rep Soph Cls; Rep Jr Cls; Rep Stu Cncl; U Of Lowell; Elctrncs Engrng.

MALE, LAUREN L; Lunenburg HS; Lunenburg, MA; (Y); 5/123; VP Church Yth Grp; Ski Clb; Teachers Aide; Acpl Chr; NHS; Pres Schlr; Intnl Clb; SADD; Chorus; Outstndng Snr Comp Stu 86; Jnr Engl Awd 85; Ntl Merit Cmmnded Schlr 86; Middlebury Coll; Frgn Lang.

MALIK, TAHIRA; Gardner HS; Gardner, MA; (Y); 30/150; Spanish Clb; School Musical; Var Crs Cntry; Rad Brdcstr.

MALIN, GWYNNETH C; Phillips Academy Andover; Arlington, MA; (Y); Dance Clb; Drama Clb; Chorus; School Musical; School Play; Variety Show; Hon Roll; Schl Schlrshp Andover 83-86; Hnr Roll; Dance Awd; NYU; Dance.

MALIONEK, MARY; Salem HS; Salem, MA; (Y); Stu Cncl; Bsktbl; High Hon Roll; Hon Roll; Marian Court-N Shore; Secy.

MALLORY, MICHAEL; Quaboag Regional HS; Warren, MA; (Y); 4/90; Drama Clb; School Play; Nwsp Rptr; Yrbk Bus Mgr; Yrbk Rptr; Yrbk Stf; High Hon Roll; Hon Roll; NHS; MA Advncd Studies Pgm At Milton Acad 86; Duke U; Genetics.

MALLOY, SHEILA; Walpole HS; E Walpole, MA; (Y); 12/268; French Clb; JCL; Latin Clb; Math Tm; JV Bsktbl; JV Fld Hcky; Hon Roll; NHS; Ntl Ltn Exm Slvr Mdl 86; Hon Mntn 13th Annl ST Hstry Conf 86; Psych.

MALNATI, SCOTT; Weymouth North HS; Weymouth, MA; (Y); SADD; Bsbl; Bsktbl; Ftbl; High Hon Roll; Hon Roll; JC Awd.

MALONE, DAVID A; Gardner HS; Gardner, MA; (Y); 18/145; Am Leg Boys St; Yrbk Bus Mgr; Lit Mag; JV DECA; Var Capt Tennis; Hon Roll; NHS; Sprts Jrnlsm.

MALONE, EILEEN; Notre Dame Acad; Scituate, MA; (Y); Ski Clb; Sec Trs Band; School Play; Stage Crew; Nwsp Rptr; Var Crs Cntry; Var Trk; Hon Roll; Prfct Atten Awd; Bus.

MALONE, JIM; Plymouth Carver Regional HS; Plymouth, MA; (Y); VP AFS; Drama Clb; Chorus; School Musical; Lit Mag; Var Tennis; Hon Roll; AFS Exchng Stu Campinas Brzl 86; Modl Cngrs 85; Select Vocl Ensmbl 85; Engl.

MALONE, MAUREEN; Reading Memorial HS; Reading, MA; (Y); Church Yth Grp; Band; Concert Band; Mrchg Band; Orch; Var Crs Cntry; Var Trk; High Hon Roll; Hon Roll; Ntl Merit Ltr; Presdntl Acadmc Ftns Awd 86; U Of New Hampshire; Lbrl Arts.

MALONE, SHAWN P; Chicopee Comprehensive HS; Chicopee, MA; (Y); 13/297; Yrbk Sprt Ed; Stu Cncl; Var L Bsktbl; Capt Var Ftbl; L Trk; Hon Roll; NHS; US Naval Acad.

MALONEY, DEBORAH; Ursuline Acad; Dedham, MA; (Y); Spanish Clb; SADD; Prfct Atten Awd; Schl Clbs-Hnrshs, SOS & PAN 86; Bus.

MALONEY, MICHELLE; Our Lady Of Nazareth Acad; Wakefield, MA; (Y); 24/74; Art Clb; Drama Clb; Spanish Clb; SADD; School Musical; Stage Crew; Sec Sr Cls; Var Socr; Var Tennis; JV Vllybl; Mktg.

MALONEY, WILLIAM; Burncoat SR HS; Worcester, MA; (Y); Intnl Clb; School Musical; Nwsp Rptr; Crs Cntry; Trk; Hon Roll; Jr NHS; NHS; Brown U; Engrng.

MANEVICH, ALEJANDRO; Newton North HS; Newton, MA; (Y); Drama Clb; School Play; High Hon Roll; Hon Roll; Russn Olympd-Gld Medl 85; Amer Amth Exm-Hnrbl Mntn 86.

MANI, CHARU; Bedford HS; Bedford, MA; (Y); 12/198; SADD; Englsh Awd 83; Bus Adm.

MANKODI, SONAL; Peabody Veterans Memorial HS; Peabody, MA; (Y); 1/513; French Clb; Math Tm; Science Clb; Rep Sr Cls; Capt Tennis; Bausch & Lomb Sci Awd; CC Awd; NHS; Ntl Merit Ltr; Val; Harvard Clb Bk Awd 85; Mdl Outstndng Math And Sci 85; George Peabody Mdl 86; Brandeis U; Pre Med.

MANLEY, MICHELLE; St Clare HS; Roslindale, MA; (Y); French Clb; SADD; School Play; Stage Crew; Nwsp Rptr; Pres Frsh Cls; Ntl Merit Ltr; Voice Dem Awd.

MANN, JOANNA; Walpole HS; Walpole, MA; (Y); 40/263; Church Yth Grp; Drama Clb; French Clb; Hosp Aide; Ski Clb; Chorus; Trk; Ntl Merit Ltr; Wrtng.

MANN, KIM MARIE; Oxford HS; Oxford, MA; (Y); 23/142; Cmnty Wkr; Pep Clb; Chorus; School Musical; Yrbk Stf; Hon Roll; NHS; Womens Aux Amer Lgn Schlrshp 86; Outstndg Achvmnt Offc Prcdrs Clssrm Awd 86; Typng 71 WPM Awd 86; Becker JC; Exec Sec.

MANNA, ANN-MARIE; Natick HS; Natick, MA; (Y); 100/400; Capt Pep Clb; SADD; Stu Cncl; Var Capt Cheerleading; Capt Pom Pon; Var L Trk; Hon Roll; Comp Desgnr.

MANNING, HILLARY; Douglas Memorial HS; E Douglas, MA; (Y); Varsity Clb; Chorus; Color Guard; Flag Corp; Yrbk Ed-Chief; Trs Frsh Cls; Trs Soph Cls; Trs Jr Cls; Trs Sr Cls; Stu Cncl; Hugh O Brien Ldrshp Conf 85; Comm.

MANNING, KEVIN; Braintree HS; Braintree, MA; (Y); 18/422; JCL; Math Tm; Socr; Hon Roll; NHS; Engrng.

MANNING, MARK; Walpole HS; Walpole, MA; (Y); 3/268; Am Leg Boys St; Church Yth Grp; Ski Clb; Bsbl; Ftbl; Wt Lftg; High Hon Roll; NHS; Gld Mdl Ad US Hstry A P I & II; Engr.

MANNING, SUSAN; Hingham HS; Hingham, MA; (Y); 13/347; Church Yth Grp; Drama Clb; School Musical; School Play; Yrbk Ed-Chief; Rep Frsh Cls; Rep Soph Cls; Rep Stu Cncl; Capt Var Cheerleading; Var L Gym; Hmnts Awd 84; 4th Pl Ntl Frnch Cntst 84; 1st Pl Ntl Hstry Day 84.

MANNION, MICHAEL; Lynn Classical HS; Lynn, MA; (Y); 27/170; Boy Scts; VP Chess Clb; Church Yth Grp; Debate Tm; French Clb; JA; Math Tm; Red Cross Aide; SADD; Stage Crew; Bus Mgmt.

MANOOGIAN, MYRA; Saugus HS; Saugus, MA; (Y); Church Yth Grp; Office Aide; Political Wkr; Spanish Clb; SADD; Rep Frsh Cls; Rep Soph Cls; Rep Jr Cls; Rep Sr Cls; Stu Cncl.

MANSFIELD, DEBRA; Northampton HS; Florence, MA; (Y); 8/218; Drama Clb; Thesps; School Musical; School Play; VP Capt Fld Hcky; Hon Roll; NHS; MVP Dfns 2 Yrs Fld Hcky 84-85; MA Cmmnwlth Schlr 86; 3rd Prz Natl Spnsh Exm 85; Tufts U; Blgy.

MANSFIELD, HOLLY; Walnut Hill Schl; Portland, ME; (Y); Cmnty Wkr; Intnl Clb; Nwsp Stf; Hon Roll; Ntl Merit SF; Engl.

MANSTREAM, KATHLEEN; Nipmuc Regional HS; Upton, MA; (Y); 5/92; SADD; Chorus; Church Choir; Yrbk Ed-Chief; Stu Cncl; Var Sftbl; High Hon Roll; NHS; Psych.

MANSUR, SHARON; Natick HS; Natick, MA; (Y); 18/399; Sec Art Clb; Church Yth Grp; Hosp Aide; SADD; School Musical; Rep Frsh Cls; Rep Soph Cls; Rep Jr Cls; Rep Stu Cncl; Vllybl; Essy Cntst; Hnrbl Mntn 86.

MANTEGANI, CATHY; Milford HS; Milford, MA; (Y); 83/268; Hosp Aide; Pep Clb; SADD; Score Keeper; Trk; Hon Roll; Pres Schlr; Framingham ST Coll; Chldhd Ed.

MANTEGNA, JOSEPH; Northampton HS; Florence, MA; (Y); 57/359; Var Capt Bsktbl; Socr; All Leag Bsktbl 86; Comm.

MANTEL, KEITH; Medford HS; Medford, MA; (Y); 73/360; Cmnty Wkr; Exploring; Ski Clb; SADD; Varsity Clb; Capt Lcrss; Capt Socr; Swmmng; Wt Lftg; Hon Roll; Outstndng Prog Engl 85-86; Engrng.

MANTELLI, LYNN; Shepherd Hill Regional HS; Dudley, MA; (Y); 35/133; Yrbk Stf; Hon Roll; Webster Womans Club Schlrshp, Shepherd Hill Booster Club Schlrshp, Estelle Ziemski Mem Schlrshp 86; Worcester ST Coll; Bus Admin.

MANTIA, ELAINE; Reading Memorial HS; Reading, MA; (Y); 30/327; Spanish Clb; SADD; Band; Concert Band; Mrchg Band; Bsktbl; JV Fld Hcky; Var Socr; High Hon Roll; Hon Roll; Dr J Kelly Awd 86; St Anselm Coll.

MAO, MICHAEL; Westwood HS; Westwood, MA; (Y); 46/212; Orch; Ftbl; Trk; Engrng.

MARAMO, SCOTT; Marianhill Central Catholic HS; Sturbridge, MA; (Y); Computer Clb; Math Tm; School Musical; Socr; Var Tennis; High Hon Roll; NHS; Pres Schlr; Chess Clb; Church Yth Grp; New England Math Leag Awd 86; Accptnc Frontiers Sci & Math Prog WPI 86; Math.

MARBLE, DAVID W; Oakmont Regional HS; Westminster, MA; (Y); Am Leg Boys St; Church Yth Grp; JV Bsbl; Var L Bsktbl; Hon Roll; Prfct Atten Awd; Jrnlsm.

MARCHAND, LEIGH; Arlington Catholic HS; W Medford, MA; (Y); Spanish Clb; SADD; School Play; Yrbk Stf; Lit Mag; Coach Actv; Var Socr; Var Sftbl; Cit Awd; New England Rgnl Schlr Chrldr 84; Sprtsmnshp Awd 85; Coaching Awd Chrldng 85; Emerson; Cmmnctns.

MARCHESE, MICHAEL; Arlington Catholic HS; Burlington, MA; (Y); 30/160; Var Bsbl; Var Capt Ice Hcky; Hon Roll; Leading Hockey Scorer 85-86; Catholic Conf All-Star Team 86; Leading Pitcher Catholic Conf 86; Law.

MARCHESE, MICHELLE; Medford HS; Medford, MA; (Y); 10/375; SADD; Band; Drm Mjr(t); Trs Orch; Ed Yrbk Ed-Chief; Stu Cncl; Var L Tennis; Im Vllybl; Hon Roll; NHS; Acdmc Excllnc Engl 83-86; 1st Annl Pres Awd Outstndng Svc 86; Outstndng Perf In Band & Orch 86; Tufts U; Bio.

MARCHESSAULT, SCOTT; New Bedford HS; New Bedford, MA; (Y); Band; Concert Band; Drm & Bgl; Mrchg Band; Stu Cngrs 85-86.

MARCHESSAULT, SHERRY; Ware HS; Ware, MA; (Y); French Clb; Band; Concert Band; Mrchg Band; Var Bsktbl; Capt Var Socr; Capt Var Sftbl; Hon Roll; Wstrn MA All Star Team In Soccer 85 & 86; Wstrn MA All Star Team Sftbl 85 & 86; MVP Soccer 86; Physcl Ed Tchr.

MARCHETERRE, LISA; Triton Regional HS; Salisbury, MA; (Y); AFS; Computer Clb; Math Tm; SADD; Teachers Aide; Chorus; Yrbk Stf; Hon Roll; Superior Achvt Awd New England Math League 86; Educ.

MARCIANO, JAMES; Westfield HS; Westfield, MA; (Y); Drama Clb; Political Wkr; School Play; Pres Sr Cls; Var Coach Actv; Var Ftbl; Var Lcrss; JV Socr; JV Wrstlng; Rep To Myrl Yth Cncl 85.

MARCOS, LISA; Beverly HS; Beverly, MA; (Y); Yrbk Stf; Bsktbl; Var L Tennis; JV Trk; Hon Roll; BHS Sci Fair Hnrbl Mentn; Librl Arts.

MARCOTTE, DANIEL; New Bedford HS; New Bedford, MA; (Y); 35/615; JCL; Key Clb; SADD; Yrbk Stf; Rep Frsh Cls; Rep Soph Cls; Rep Jr Cls; Rep Sr Cls; Stu Cncl; Elks Awd; Boston U; Acctng.

MARCOTTE, JODI; Masconomet HS; Boxford, MA; (Y); French Clb; Teachers Aide; JV Var Fld Hcky; Var Score Keeper; JV Sftbl; JV Timer; French Hon Soc; Hon Roll; Engl.

MARCOUX, SUZY; Cathedral HS; Springfield, MA; (Y); 42/518; Accntng I & Ii, Germn I & Ii 86; Grad 2nd Hnrs 86; Northeastern U; Phys Therpy.

MARCUS, AMY GAIL; Milford HS; Milford, MA; (Y); 30/350; Drama Clb; High Hon Roll; Hon Roll; NHS; Johnson-Wales Culnry Arts Explrtn 85; Johnson-Wales Pastry Arts Explrtn 86; Johnson & Wales; Pastry Arts.

MARCUS, GRETA; Randolph HS; Randolph, MA; (Y); 63/365; Ski Clb; Yrbk Bus Mgr; Stu Cncl; Var Capt Cheerleading; Var Swmmng; Hon Roll; NHS; Black Belt Karate 84; Hugh O Rian MA Yth Ldrshp Soc; Randolph Outstndng Yth 83&84; U ME Orono; Pre-Med.

MARENGO, JOSEPH; Leicester HS; Leicester, MA; (Y); Boy Scts; Var Socr; Im Vllybl; Prfct Atten Awd.

MARENGO, PAULA; Bartlett HS; Webster, MA; (Y); Am Leg Aux Girls St; French Clb; Spanish Clb; Yrbk Stf; Hon Roll; NHS; Nrsng.

MARESCALCHI, CINDI; Beverly HS; Beverly, MA; (Y); Aud/Vis; Church Yth Grp; Cmnty Wkr; Drama Clb; Hosp Aide; Trs Jr Cls; Peom Publshd Am Assoc Poetry Bk 86; Poem Publ In Wexford Ireland; 100 Hrs Candy Striping Awd; Radio Broadcasting.

MARGGRAF, JEFFREY P; Central Catholic HS; Methuen, MA; (Y); 115/231; Var L Ftbl; Var Capt Ice Hcky; Im Wt Lftg; Hon Roll; Sports Med.

MARGOLIS, GARY J; Sharon HS; Sharon, MA; (Y); Am Leg Boys St; Computer Clb; Science Clb; Concert Band; Nwsp Stf; Socr; Trk; Hon Roll; Hon Mntn Frmnghm ST Intl Hstrcl Hon Soc 85; Med.

MARIANO, NANETTE; Weymouth North HS; Weymouth, MA; (Y); 22/300; Drama Clb; French Clb; Hosp Aide; Math Tm; School Play; Yrbk Stf; Sftbl; Vllybl; Elks Awd; High Hon Roll; Englsh, Languages, Home Ec Awds; Salem ST Coll; Scl Wrk.

MARINELLI, BRIAN; Malden Catholic HS; Malden, MA; (Y); 18/180; French Clb; Nwsp Stf; Im Vllybl; High Hon Roll; Hon Roll; NHS; Rotary Awd; Bentley Coll; Bus.

MARINI, JENNIFER; Foxboro HS; Foxboro, MA; (Y); 33/230; Dance Clb; Ski Clb; SADD; Chorus; Jazz Band; School Musical; Swing Chorus; Stu Cncl; Hon Roll; Foxboro Music Assc Schlrshp 85; Advrtsng.

MARINO, LIZ; Nauset Regional HS; Orleans, MA; (Y); Teachers Aide; Nwsp Rptr; Nwsp Stf; Jr Cls; Sec Stu Cncl; Cheerleading; Fld Hcky; Hon Roll; Anthrplgy.

MARINO, MICHAEL; Lynn Classcal HS; Lynn, MA; (Y); 2/178; Debate Tm; French Clb; Math Tm; Spanish Clb; Stage Crew; Rep Frsh Cls; CC Awd; High Hon Roll; Jr NHS; NHS; Boys ST Pgm 86; Frontiers Math,Sci 86; Corp Law.

MARION, THERESA; Holyoke Catholic HS; Holyoke, MA; (Y); Sec 4-H; French Clb; 4-H Awd; STCC; Laser Elctro Optc Tech.

MARIZOLI, RACHEL; Haverhill HS; Haverhill, MA; (Y); 34/380; Sec Spanish Clb; Bsktbl; Hon Roll; NHS; Prfct Atten Awd; John T Sullivan Mem Awd 86; Rivier Coll; Early Chldhd Educ.

MARK, BRYAN G; Dover-Sherborn Reg HS; Dover, MA; (Y); 6/160; AFS; Am Leg Boys St; Boy Scts; Church Yth Grp; Debate Tm; VP Exploring; Nwsp Rptr; Var L Socr; Co-Capt Swmmng; High Hon Roll.

MARKEY, GLEN G; Rockland HS; Rockland, MA; (Y); 27/190; Church Yth Grp; Letterman Clb; Varsity Clb; JV Bsktbl; Im Golf; Var Socr; Im Trk; Hon Roll; 4th Pl Mth Tst 85-86; Capt JV Socr Tm 84-85; Div II H S ST Chmps Socr 85-86; Elec Engrng.

MARKIEWICZ, KAREN ANN; Cathedral HS; Springfield, MA; (Y); 23/475; Dance Clb; Library Aide; Math Clb; Ski Clb; Teachers Aide; Variety Show; Off Sr Cls; Var Capt Cheerleading; Var Mgr(s); Var L Sftbl; Sullivan Schlrshp 86; Arthur T Talmadge Awd Schlrshp 86; MA ST Schlrshp 86; U Of VT; Chem.

MARKOWSKI, CHRISTOPHER J; Turners Falls HS; Turners Falls, MA; (Y); Trs Frsh Cls; Rep Soph Cls; Trs Jr Cls; Trs Sr Cls; Rep Stu Cncl; Var L Bsbl; JV Bsktbl; Capt Ftbl; Lib Arts.

MARMER, MARK; Andover HS; Andover, MA; (Y); 2/412; Pep Clb; SADD; School Musical; Nwsp Stf; Sec Sr Cls; Trk; NHS; Ntl Merit SF; High Hon Roll; Chncllrs Talnt Awd U MA 85; Brown U Bk Awd.

MARONEY, KATIE; Reading Memorial HS; Reading, MA; (Y); Hosp Aide; VP Frsh Cls; Rep Stu Cncl; Capt Cheerleading; JV Fld Hcky; Var Gym; Trk; High Hon Roll; Hon Roll; Schlstc Achvt Cert 86; Dartmouth; Chem Engnrng.

MAROTZ, LISA; Lincoln-Sudbury Regional HS; Sudbury, MA; (Y); FCA; French Clb; SADD; Varsity Clb; Rep Soph Cls; Rep Jr Cls; Rep Stu Cncl; Var Tennis; JV Trk; Hon Roll; Creative Writing.

MAROUN, JEFFREY; Boston Latin HS; Boston, MA; (Y); 146/270; Drama Clb; Key Clb; Ski Clb; School Play; Lit Mag; Socr; Wrstlng.

MARQUARDT, CHARLES J; Winchester HS; Winchester, MA; (Y); Church Yth Grp; French Clb; Latin Clb; Varsity Clb; Var L Golf; Ntl Merit Fnlst 86; Ntl Sci Sprvsrs Assoc Sci Awd 86; Wms Coll.

MARQUARDT, DANIEL; Arlington Catholic HS; Winchester, MA; (Y); Church Yth Grp; Cmnty Wkr; Spanish Clb; Nwsp Rptr; Yrbk Stf; Hon Roll; Bus.

MARQUIS, MELISSA W; Andover HS; Andover, MA; (Y); 23/389; VP AFS; Co-Capt Church Yth Grp; Concert Band; Mrchg Band; JV Trk; High Hon Roll; NHS; Shawsheen Vlg Womns Assn & William H Trow Schlrshps 86; CT Coll; Chld Psych.

MARRAH, TIMOTHY; Bishop Feehan HS; Attleboro, MA; (Y); 8/260; Boy Scts; JV Crs Cntry; Var Trk; Bausch & Lomb Sci Awd; High Hon Roll; Jr NHS; NHS; Spanish NHS; BSA Eagl Sct 83; Govr MA Citatn Rcgntn 84; MA House Rep Offcl Citatn 84; Engrng.

MARROCHELLO, ANDREW; Arlington HS; Arlington, MA; (Y); Latin Clb; SADD; Rep Stu Cncl; Var L Bsbl; Bsktbl; Var L Ftbl; Var L Trk; Hon Roll; NHS; Arlngtn Yth Bsbl MVP 84; Lge Chmpnshp Awd 86; Law.

MARRONE, PHILIP; Malden Catholic HS; Everett, MA; (Y); 3/185; Church Yth Grp; Pres Computer Clb; Science Clb; Rep Stu Cncl; Im Bsktbl; Im Fld Hcky; Im Vllybl; High Hon Roll; Hon Roll; Trs NHS; Natl Merit Scholar Commended Stu 85; Columbia U; Engrng.

MARRYAT, GLENN H; Sandwich JR SR HS; Sandwich, MA; (Y); 20/150; Am Leg Boys St; Math Tm; Var L Crs Cntry; Var L Tennis; Hon Roll; NHS; U Of MD Coll Pk; Bus.

MARSCHKE, EDWARD; Walpole HS; Walpole, MA; (Y); 22/260; Band; Church Choir; Concert Band; Jazz Band; Mrchg Band; Orch; Hon Roll; NHS; Music Hnr Awd 84; Engl,Geo Perf Awd 84-85; Bus.

MARSH, SHARON; Chicopee HS; Chicopee, MA; (Y); 51/200; FTA; German Clb; GAA; Pep Clb; SADD; Varsity Clb; Rep Frsh Cls; Rep Soph Cls; Rep Jr Cls; Rep Sr Cls; N Adams ST; Elem Ed.

MARSHALL, DAVE; Newburyport HS; Newburyport, MA; (Y); 2/185; Rep Am Leg Boys St; Var L Crs Cntry; Var L Trk; CC Awd; High Hon Roll; Hon Roll; NHS; Ldrshp Smnr 84-85; Close Up 86; Jr Sr Marshall 86-87; Mech Engr.

MARTEL, AMY; Boston Latin Schl; Boston, MA; (Y); 102/285; Drama Clb; JA; School Play; Stage Crew; Lit Mag; JV Socr; High Hon Roll; Hon Roll; NHS; Gold Medal Natl Latin Exam 86; Boston Coll; Lib Arts.

MARTEL, KRISTA; Hudson HS; Hudson, MA; (Y); 38/156; Pep Clb; Ski Clb; SADD; Mgr(s); Powder Puff Ftbl; Hon Roll; Med.

MARTELL, CHRISTINE R; Bedford HS; Bedford, MA; (Y); 23/206; AFS; Am Leg Aux Girls St; Church Yth Grp; Girl Scts; SADD; Chorus; Rep Sr Cls; Var Capt Gym; JV Var Socr; High Hon Roll; U MA Amherst; Math.

MARTELL, JO; David Hale Fanning Trade Schl; Worcester, MA; (Y); 12/133; Office Aide; SADD; High Hon Roll; Hon Roll; NHS; Salter Schl; Bus.

MARTIN, DARLENE; New Bedford HS; New Bedford, MA; (Y); Exploring; Bowling; Hon Roll; Bus Admin.

MARTIN, DOUGLAS R; Belmont HS; Belmont, MA; (Y); 18/262; Am Leg Boys St; SADD; Concert Band; Mrchg Band; Var Capt Trk; Hon Roll; Jr NHS; NHS; Actry.

MARTIN, JAY; Attleboro HS; Attleboro, MA; (Y); Var Capt Crs Cntry; Var Capt Trk; High Hon Roll; NHS; Prfct Atten Awd.

MARTIN, KEVIN; Milford HS; Milford, MA; (Y); School Play; Stage Crew; Bsktbl; Tennis; Hon Roll; Bus Adm.

MARTIN, LEANN; Wilmington HS; Wilmington, MA; (Y); VP Trs French Clb; Office Aide; VP Trs Spanish Clb; SADD; Rep Frsh Cls; Rep Soph Cls; Rep Jr Cls; Stu Cncl; High Hon Roll; NHS; Pre Med.

MARTIN, LESLIE; Notre Dame Acad; Lowell, MA; (Y); 18/78; Church Yth Grp; Cmnty Wkr; Drama Clb; Political Wkr; Chorus; School Musical; Variety Show; Yrbk Phtg; Pres Soph Cls; VP Jr Cls; Mktg/Publ Rel.

MARTIN, LORI; Gardner HS; Gardner, MA; (Y); French Clb; Sec Soph Cls; Rep Jr Cls; Rep Stu Cncl; Var L Bsktbl; Var Capt Fld Hcky; Var L Sftbl; Hon Roll; Biol.

MARTIN, LYNN; Durfee HS; Fall River, MA; (Y); 113/673; Boys Clb Am; French Clb; Hosp Aide; Office Aide; Variety Show; Yrbk Stf; Hon Roll; NHS; JR-SR Prm Comm 85-87; Bus Clb 86-87; Boston Coll; Pre Law.

MARTIN, MARK; New Bedford HS; Acushnet, MA; (Y); 10/701; Am Leg Boys St; VP Computer Clb; JA; VP Science Clb; Jr NHS; NHS.

MARTIN, MARYANNE C; Foxboro HS; Foxboro, MA; (Y); 49/255; Church Yth Grp; Varsity Clb; Mrchg Band; Nwsp Stf; JV Var Bsktbl; Var Capt Crs Cntry; Var Trk; Hon Roll; U Of MA; Comm.

MARTIN, MERIDETH; Lunenburg HS; Lunenberg, MA; (Y); Intnl Clb; SADD; Teachers Aide; High Hon Roll; NHS.

MARTIN, PAMELA; Chicopee Comprehensive HS; Chicopee, MA; (Y); 109/250; Dance Clb; French Clb; Girl Scts; Sec Soph Cls; Sec Jr Cls; Stu Cncl; Cheerleading; Diving; Pom Pon; Powder Puff Ftbl; Dance Comp Awds 79-83; U MA; Dance.

MARTIN, PAUL; Taunton HS; Taunton, MA; (Y); Aud/Vis; Ski Clb; VP L Ftbl; VP L Trk; Im Wt Lftg; Northeastern; Comp Sci.

MARTIN, PAULA; Methven HS; Methuen, MA; (Y); 10/450; Am Leg Aux Girls St; Cmnty Wkr; Dance Clb; Hosp Aide; Intnl Clb; Model UN; Spanish Clb; SADD; Color Guard; NHS; Psychlgy.

MARTIN, SCOTT; Holyoke Catholic HS; Easthampton, MA; (Y); Art Clb; Dance Clb; Nwsp Bus Mgr; Yrbk Bus Mgr; Yrbk Stf; VP Sr Cls; Var Golf; Bus Adm.

MARTIN, SCOTT; Tantasqua Regional HS; Wales, MA; (Y); 22/180; Varsity Clb; VP Jr Cls; Var Capt Bsktbl; Var Capt Socr; Var Capt Trk; Hon Roll; Art.

MARTIN, SCOTT; Wahconah Regional HS; Cummington, MA; (Y); Church Yth Grp; Ski Clb; Varsity Clb; Var Crs Cntry; Var Capt Golf; High Hon Roll; Hon Roll; NHS.

MARTIN, SUSAN; Nazareth Acad; Reading, MA; (Y); 13/74; Camp Fr Inc; Drama Clb; French Clb; SADD; School Musical; School Play; Stage Crew; Sftbl; Hon Roll; Outstndng Efft And Achvt Frnch III; Excllnc Geo; Christn Serv; Med.

MARTINAGE, ROBERT; Reading Memorial HS; Reading, MA; (Y); Boy Scts; Math Tm; SADD; Madrigals; High Hon Roll; NHS; Ntl Merit SF; Peer Tutrng 83-87; Ftr Prbl Slvrs Am 85-86; Brnls Grts Swm Clb; Elec Engr.

MARTINDELL, MICHELE; Northampton HS; Florence, MA; (Y); 33/223; Debate Tm; 4-H; Hosp Aide; Nwsp Rptr; Crs Cntry; Trk; Hon Roll; Bio.

MARTINEAU, GLORIA; Salem HS; Salem, MA; (Y); 74/260; Church Yth Grp; Key Clb; Office Aide; Chorus; School Musical; School Play; Yrbk Stf; Rep Stu Cncl; Hon Roll; Drama Awd 85-86.

MARTINEZ, ELIZABETH O; St Gregory HS; Dorchester, MA; (Y); School Play; Nwsp Phtg; Stu Cncl; Hon Roll; Prfct Atten Awd; Pres Schlr; Art Acad Awd 82-83; Erpn Hsty, Bio, & US Hstry Acad Awds 83-85; Hstry Clb Awd 83-85; Harvard U; Lbrl Arts.

MARTINEZ, FELIX; Phillips Acad; New York, NY; (Y); Latin Clb; Varsity Clb; Var Ftbl; JV Lcrss; Spanish NHS; Boston U; Econ.

MARTINEZ, JOHN; Middlesex Schl; Westford, MA; (Y); Pres Church Yth Grp; Computer Clb; Dance Clb; Math Tm; Stage Crew; JV Bsbl; JV Ice Hcky; Var JV Socr; Ntl Merit Ltr; Hatl Hspnc Schlr Awds Pgm Fnlst 85; Elec Engrng.

MARTINEZ, SONIA; Braintree HS; Spain; (Y); Socr; Tennis; Trk; Hon Roll; Ntl Merit Ltr; U Madrid; Econ.

MARTINO, TRACY; Haverhill HS; Haverhill, MA; (Y); #32 In Class; CAP; Varsity Clb; Coach Actv; Var JV Fld Hcky; Var Sftbl; Im Vllybl; Hon Roll.

MARTINOLI II, BILL; Haverhill HS; Methuen, MA; (Y); Letterman Clb; Varsity Clb; JV Var Ftbl; Wt Lftg; JV Var Wrstlng; Hon Roll; Regnl Sec Wrstlg Tourn Trphy 2nd Pl; JV Rstlg Trphy Outstndg Ath; Wentworth Inst; Arch Engrng.

MARTINS, ELIZABETH; Bishop Connolly HS; Fall River, MA; (Y); Church Yth Grp; Cmnty Wkr; Teachers Aide; High Hon Roll; Hon Roll; Salem ST Coll; Nrsng.

MARTINS, ELIZABETH; Ludlow HS; Ludlow, MA; (Y); Church Yth Grp; Cmnty Wkr; French Clb; Hosp Aide; Teachers Aide; School Play; Yrbk Stf; Jr Cls; Sr Cls; Hon Roll; Grad Of Ldlws Prtgs Schl 85; U Of MA; Ed.

MARTINS, LUIZA; Ludlow HS; Ludlow, MA; (Y); 16/279; JCL; Band; Chorus; Variety Show; Yrbk Stf; VP Jr Cls; VP Sr Cls; Pres Stu Cncl; JV Var Cheerleading; DAR Awd; Civitn Awd; W D Mullins Stu Govt Awd; Amer Lgn Awd; Emmanuel Coll; Medcl Technlgy.

MARTINS, SANDRA; B M C Dufee HS; Fall River, MA; (Y); Sec Church Yth Grp; High Hon Roll; Hon Roll; Achvt Awd In Chem 86; SMU; Med Tech.

MARTULA, AMY; Hopkins Acad; Hadley, MA; (Y); 10/49; Spanish Clb; Chorus; School Play; Yrbk Stf; VP Stu Cncl; Var Socr; Var Sftbl; Hon Roll; All Amer Stu 86; All ST Sccr 85; All Hmpshr Lg Sftbl 86; Clark U; Phys Ed.

MARVELLI, CHRISTOPHER A; Northampton HS; Northampton, MA; (Y); 23/263; Am Leg Boys St; Church Yth Grp; Hosp Aide; Ski Clb; Var Lcrss; Var Socr; JV Tennis; High Hon Roll; NHS.

MARVIN, MELISSA; North HS; Worcester, MA; (Y); Yrbk Stf; Tennis; NHS; Dental Hygiene.

MASCARENHAS, MELISSA; Randolph HS; Randolph, MA; (Y); Art Clb; SADD; Teachers Aide; Yrbk Stf; Powder Puff Ftbl; Hon Roll; Nrtheastn U; Law.

MASCART, DIANE; Cohasset HS; Cohasset, MA; (Y); French Clb; Rep Stu Cncl; Var Tennis; Hon Roll; U TX Austin; Bio.

MASCIANGIOLI, TINA; Nauset Region HS; Phillipines #4701; (Y); 10/196; Nwsp Ed-Chief; Var Sftbl; NHS; Scholastic Bowl; Band; Yrbk Phtg; Yrbk Stf; Stu Cncl; JV Socr; Hon Roll; Rotary Stu Exc Pgm 86-87; Italian Clb 83-84; Yth Conservtn Corps 85; U MI-ANN Arbor; African Studie.

MASCIARELLI, LISA; Medford HS; Medford, MA; (Y); Cmnty Wkr; Hosp Aide; SADD; Yrbk Stf; Rep Frsh Cls; Rep Soph Cls; Rep Jr Cls; Rep Sr Cls; Pres Stu Cncl; Var Vllybl; Intrdctry Phys Sci-Bio 84-85; JR Mrshll 85-86; Gftd & Tlntd 84-87; U Of Bstn MA; Chld Psych.

MASHIA, LINDA; Chicopee Comprehensive HS; Chicopee, MA; (Y); 8/332; Pres Church Yth Grp; Band; Church Choir; Variety Show; Yrbk Ed-Chief; Rep Stu Cncl; Mgr(s); Trk; NHS; French Clb; Smith Bk Awd 86; Gerontology.

MASKELL, MERRI; Melrose HS; Boston, MA; (Y); 69/391; Church Yth Grp; Chorus; Church Choir; Hon Roll; Gordon Coll; Elem Educ.

MASON, CHRISTOPHER WHITTIER; Deerfield Acad; Hinsdale, IL; (Y); Spanish Clb; Radio Clb; Spanish Clb; Yrbk Phtg; Bsbl; Im Ice Hcky; Socr; Im Sftbl; Ntl Merit Ltr; St Schlr; U MI; Ecnmcs & Hstry.

MASON, DIANA; Westwood HS; Westwood, MA; (Y); 52/208; AFS; Church Yth Grp; Key Clb; SADD; Frsh Cls; Stu Cncl; VP Swmmng; JV Tennis; Hon Roll; Cert Of Hnr From Govnr Dukakis 86; Phy Thrpy.

MASON, KAREN A; Winthrop SR HS; Winthrop, MA; (Y); 8/216; Drama Clb; Stage Crew; Nwsp Stf; Yrbk Phtg; Capt Fld Hcky; High Hon Roll; Sec NHS; Rotary Club Schlrshp & Bstn Tchrs Union Schlrshp 86; St Michaels Coll; Journalism.

MASON, KIMBERLY; Hampshire Regional HS; Southampton, MA; (Y); #8 In Class; Concert Band; Mrchg Band; Variety Show; Var JV Bsktbl; Var JV Mgr(s); Var JV Socr; Var JV Sftbl; Stat Trk; High Hon Roll; NHS; Coaches All Lg Girls Sccr Tm 85.

MASON, LELANA; Natick HS; Natick, MA; (Y); 6/399; Church Yth Grp; Concert Band; Mrchg Band; Symp Band; Rep Soph Cls; Rep Jr Cls; Var Cheerleading; High Hon Roll; Hon Roll; Pres NHS.

MASON, MICHAEL; St Dominic Savio HS; Revere, MA; (Y); 50/120; Art Clb; Chess Clb; Computer Clb; Key Clb; Science Clb; Ski Clb; SADD; Nwsp Stf; Trk; ITT Tech Inst; Auto Mchncs.

MASON, MIKE; Foxborough HS; Foxborough, MA; (Y); 10/225; Am Leg Boys St; Church Yth Grp; Drama Clb; JA; School Play; Nwsp Rptr; Im Bsktbl; Golf; Var Tennis; Hon Roll; Duke U; Bus.

MASOW, ALAN H; Westford Acad; Westford, MA; (Y); French Clb; JCL; Latin Clb; Model UN; Office Aide; Ski Clb; SADD; Teachers Aide; Nwsp Stf; Golf; Bus Mgmt.

MASSA, NEIL; Winthrop HS; Winthrop, MA; (Y); 33/203; Drama Clb; Math Tm; School Musical; School Play; Stage Crew; JV Crs Cntry; Var Trk; Drama Bnqt Rookie Of Yr 83; Boston U; Engl.

MASSANO, JENNIFER; Woburn SR HS; Woburn, MA; (S); 93/490; Art Clb; Leo Clb; SADD; Capt Flag Corp; Stu Cncl; Tennis; Hon Roll; Jr NHS; NHS; Graphc Desgn.

MASSE, THOMAS; Dracut SR HS; Dracut, MA; (Y); Concert Band; Jazz Band; Mrchg Band; L Var Trk; Hon Roll; JP Sousa Awd; NHS; Pres Schlr; Exploring; JV Bsktbl; Army Rsrv Schlr Athl Awd 86; 4 Yr Perf Attndnc Awd 86; Tufts U; Comp Sci.

MASSICOTTE, MARK; Shepherd Hill Regional HS; Dudley, MA; (Y); Band; Var Crs Cntry; Hon Roll; Chiroprctr.

MASSON, LAURIE; Marian HS; Holliston, MA; (Y); 4-H; Girl Scts; Hosp Aide; Variety Show; Yrbk Stf; Var Cheerleading; Crs Cntry; Johnson & Wales; Clnry Arts.

MASTIN, JOSEPH; Bristol Plymouth Regional HS; East Taunton, MA; (S); 6/175; SADD; Varsity Clb; VICA; Rep Jr Cls; Rep Sr Cls; JV Bsktbl; Var Ftbl; Var Capt Trk; Hon Roll; NHS; Wentworth; Tool Tech.

MASTIN IV, THEODORE H; Dennis-Yarmouth Regional HS; East Dennis, MA; (Y); 24/321; Am Leg Boys St; Church Yth Grp; Cmnty Wkr; Ski Clb; Lit Mag; Rep Stu Cncl; Var Im Socr; Var L Tennis; Im Capt Vllybl; Hon Roll; Big Brother Pgm 85-87; Intl Bus.

MASTRANGELO, MARIA; Pittsfield HS; Pittsfield, MA; (Y); Hosp Aide; JA; JV Sftbl; NHS; Bentley Coll; Acctng.

MASTROIANNI, CLAUDIA; Milford HS; Milford, MA; (Y); 3/300; Drama Clb; Acpl Chr; Chorus; Concert Band; Mrchg Band; Orch; Pres School Musical; High Hon Roll; NHS; Political Wkr; Chancellors Talnt Awd Acad Exc 86; Math.

MASTROIANNI, FRAN; Buckingham Browne & Nichols Schl; Watertown, MA; (S); 15/107; Boy Scts; JCL; Nwsp Stf; Rep Frsh Cls; Rep Soph Cls; Rep Jr Cls; Rep Sr Cls; Rep Stu Cncl; JV Var Bsbl; Hon Roll.

MATACHUN, GEORGE; Central Catholic HS; Lawrence, MA; (Y); 69/231; Boys Clb Am; Off Church Yth Grp; Ski Clb; Im Bsktbl; JV Ftbl; Engineering.

MATARAZZO, MICHELLE; Winthrop HS; Winthrop, MA; (Y); 17/216; Hosp Aide; Color Guard; Flag Corp; Im Bsktbl; Powder Puff Ftbl; High Hon Roll; Hon Roll; NHS; Hosp Jnr Vlnteer Of Yr 86; Ldg Of Elks Epsln Awd 86; Bnjmn Grmn Post #104 Awd 86; Boston Coll; Nrsng.

MATARESE, JOSEPH; St Dominic Savio HS; Revere, MA; (Y); 18/104; Boy Scts; SADD; Yrbk Sprt Ed; Rep Frsh Cls; Im Bsktbl; Var Crs Cntry; Var Stat Ice Hcky; Var Mgr(s); High Hon Roll; Hon Roll; Natl Mth Awd; Boston Coll; Bus Finance.

MATHENY, SERGE A; Barnstable HS; Hyannis, MA; (Y); 25/376; Camera Clb; Exploring; Library Aide; Science Clb; Lit Mag; High Hon Roll; Hon Roll; Kiwanis Awd; Lion Awd; Slvr Acdmc Crtfct Achvmnt 84; Acdmc All-Amer Awd 86; Home Bldrs Assoc Schlrshp Awd 86; U Of VT; Biolgst.

MATOS, MILENA; New Bedford HS; New Bedford, MA; (Y); 26/701; Intnl Clb; JA; High Hon Roll; Jr NHS; NHS.

MATRA, LINCOLN; Boston Latin HS; Boston, MA; (Y); 137/284; Pep Clb; Nwsp Stf; Lit Mag; Hon Roll; NHS; Latin Schl Hm & Schl Assoc Awd 86; Mass Pep Cert Of Achvmnt 85; S CA U; Elec Engrng.

MATRANGA, MICHELLE; Newbury Port HS; Newburypt, MA; (Y); 4/190; Am Leg Aux Girls St; Sec Frsh Cls; Sec Soph Cls; Pres Jr Cls; Pres Sr Cls; Stu Cncl; Var Capt Crs Cntry; Cit Awd; NHS; Intnl Clb; Hugh O Brien Ldrshp Prog; Wellesley Bk Awd; Hnrs Schlr Nght; Poli Sci.

MATRISHON, JOHN; Northampton HS; Florence, MA; (Y); 63/265; VP Boy Scts; Exploring; Im Trk; Cit Awd; Hon Roll; Grahm Crckr Clssc Triathln Rnr-Up 84; Wstrn MA Hm Shw-Bst Bluprnt 2nd Pl 86; US Air Frc; Precsn Measrng Eqp.

MATRONI, LISA; Cathedral HS; Springfield, MA; (Y); 76/450; Library Aide; Office Aide; Ski Clb; SADD; Var Mgr(s); Var Score Keeper; Hon Roll; 1st, 2nd & 3rd Mdl Awds Ice Fig Sktng 82-86; Catholic U; Pol Sci.

MATRUNDOLA, JENNIFER; Winchester HS; Winchester, MA; (Y); Sec French Clb; Ski Clb; Band; Mrchg Band; Yrbk Stf; Sec Jr Cls; Off Stu Cncl; Var Fld Hcky; Tennis; Trk.

MATSON, CAROLINE; North Middlesex Regional HS; Townsend, MA; (Y); French Clb; Spanish Clb; Powder Puff Ftbl; Hon Roll.

MATTE, JONATHAN D; Chicopee HS; Chicopee, MA; (Y); 1/206; Debate Tm; Math Tm; Quiz Bowl; Art Clb; Church Yth Grp; Mathletes; Math Clb; Scholastic Bowl; Spanish Clb; Yrbk Stf; Dartmouth; Hstry.

MATTHEWS III, GERARD J; Uxbridge HS; Uxbridge, MA; (Y); Am Leg Boys St; Pres Church Yth Grp; Math Tm; Varsity Clb; Chorus; Stu Cncl; Capt Ftbl; NHS; Ntl Merit Ltr; U Miami; Law.

MATYS, MARK JOHN; Holy Name Central Catholic HS; Worcester, MA; (Y); 66/252; Computer Clb; Math Clb; Im Bsktbl; L Socr; L Tennis; Var Trk; Hon Roll; Schlrshps Bshp Flanagan, Betsy Pinkerton; Sr Rcgntn Awd; Hnrbl Mntn Annl St Hstrclconf; Humants III; U Of MA; Eng.

MAUCERI, DAVID; North Reading HS; N Reading, MA; (Y); Church Yth Grp; Math Clb; Math Tm; Science Clb; School Musical; Stage Crew; Bsktbl; Socr; Tennis; Trk; Mech Engrng.

MAUGER, DAVID J; Wayland HS; Wayland, MA; (Y); 105/234; Art Clb; Hon Roll; Ntl Fndtn Advncmnt Of Arts 86; Boston Globe Schlstc Art Awd 86; Vis Art.

MAUK, AMY; Westport HS; Westport, MA; (Y); Debate Tm; Exploring; Intnl Clb; Crs Cntry; U Of MA Amherst; Economics.

MAVRO, MARIA; Natick HS; Wayland, MA; (Y); 52/420; Pep Clb; Spanish Clb; Rep Jr Cls; Fld Hcky; Hon Roll; Prfct Atten Awd; Intr Dsgn.

MAXON, JENNIFER; Bedford HS; Bedford, MA; (Y); 9/201; Nwsp Rptr; Yrbk Rptr; Var Bsktbl; Var Swmmng; Cit Awd; High Hon Roll; NHS; St Schlr; Church Yth Grp; All Star Swmmr 82-83; Dartmouth Bk Awd 85; Holy Cross Clg.

MAXWELL, KIMBERLY A; Natick HS; Natick, MA; (Y); 14/399; Dance Clb; Pep Clb; SADD; Chorus; School Musical; High Hon Roll; Hon Roll; Worthy Advsr Natick Assmbly 28 86; Frgn Lang.

MAY, KEVIN; Hudson HS; Hudson, MA; (Y); 21/158; JV Bsbl; JV Bsktbl; Hon Roll; NHS; Spnsh Awd; Sci.

MAYER, ANDREA; Hingham HS; Hingham, MA; (Y); 128/375; Church Yth Grp; Drama Clb; Hosp Aide; Variety Show; Im Badmtn; Im Bsktbl; Var Capt Lcrss; Var Socr; Im Vllybl; High Hon Roll; Sprngfield; Art.

MAYNARD, DEBORAH; Somerville HS; Somerville, MA; (Y); 3/510; Pres Spanish Clb; Rep Stu Cncl; Kiwanis Awd; NHS; Pres Schlr; St Schlr; Sprtndnt Awd For Acad Excllence 86; MIT; Aero Engrng.

MAYNARD, EDWIN; Pittsfield HS; Pittsfield, MA; (Y); Computer Clb; Debate Tm; Drama Clb; Latin Clb; Math Tm; Quiz Bowl; Var L Trk; High Hon Roll; Ntl Merit Ltr; Boy Scts; Egl Sct Awd 85; U Of PA; Bus.

MAYNARD, JAMES M; Brockton HS; Brockton, MA; (Y); 20/822; Am Leg Boys St; Church Yth Grp; Computer Clb; Trk; High Hon Roll; Hon Roll; NHS; MA Advncd Stds Pgm 85; YMCA Chrch Lg Bsktbl Capt Tm MVP 83-85; Eclgy & Canoe Clb Treas 85-86; Wrcstr Plytch Inst; Eltrl Engr.

MAZIARZ, CHRISTINE; Holyoke HS; Holyoke, MA; (Y); German Clb; Color Guard; VP Frsh Cls; Var Cheerleading; High Hon Roll; Hon Roll; NHS; Med Clb 85; Pre-Med.

MAZIARZ, CHRISTINE; Ludlow HS; Ludlow, MA; (Y); French Clb; Library Aide; School Play; Sftbl; High Hon Roll; Hon Roll; NHS; Acctg.

MAZZEI, JOSEPH; Cambridge Ridge & Latin HS; Cambridge, MA; (Y); Debate Tm; FBLA; Key Clb; Yrbk Stf; Capt Ftbl; Wrstlng; High Hon Roll; Curry Coll; Pltcl.

MAZZEI, MICHAEL; Cambridge Rindge & Latin HS; Cambridge, MA; (Y); Church Yth Grp; Key Clb; Wt Lftg; Wrstlng; Ftbl; Hon Roll; SADD; Yrbk Rptr; Yrbk Stf; Rep Frsh Cls.

MAZZU, JOHN; Holyoke HS; Holyoke, MA; (Y); Boy Scts; Computer Clb; French Clb; Quiz Bowl; Scholastic Bowl; Var L Trk; Var Wrstlng; Hon Roll; 6th Pl Wstrn Mass Awd 86.

MC ADAMS, JAMES; Boston College HS; N Quincy, MA; (Y); Art Clb; Church Yth Grp; FCA; Ski Clb; Varsity Clb; Rep Frsh Cls; Rep Soph Cls; Rep Jr Cls; Rep Stu Cncl; Im Bsktbl; Fordham U.

MC ALLISTER, PATRICK; Bedford HS; Bedford, MA; (Y); 98/199; Boy Scts; Church Yth Grp; Cmnty Wkr; Nwsp Stf; JV Var Lcrss; JV Var Socr; Ski Tm JT 84-85; Stu Athltc Trnr Vrsty 83-84; Altr By 80-86.

MC AULEY JR, DANIEL; Medford HS; Medford, MA; (Y); 38/400; SADD; Off Jr Cls; Var Ftbl; Var Trk; Hon Roll; NHS; Letterman Clb; Mathletes; Math Clb; Red Cross Aide; Tom Mc Cann Awd & Schlrshp Athltc & Acadmc Excllnce 86; Athltc & Acadmc Excllne Awd 86.

MC BRIDE, BARBARA E; Burlington HS; Burlington, MA; (Y); 15/323; Drama Clb; Math Tm; Flag Corp; School Musical; School Play; Stage Crew; Yrbk Stf; Hon Roll; NHS; U Of Lowell; Plstcs Engrg.

MC BRINE, CHRISTINE; Medford HS; Medford, MA; (Y); Chorus; Hon Roll; U Lowell; Psych.

MC CABE, COLLEEN; Ursuline Acad; Dedham, MA; (Y); 3/81; Cmnty Wkr; French Clb; Math Tm; Rep Service Clb; Nwsp Rptr; Mgr Bsktbl; Var Sftbl; JV Vllybl; High Hon Roll; VP NHS; Acdmc Schlrshp 84 & 85; Cornell U; Htl Mgt.

MC CABE, KIM; Marlboro HS; Marlboro, MA; (Y); Ski Clb; Varsity Clb; Rep Stu Cncl; Fld Hcky; Sftbl; Hon Roll; Vrsty Sftbll MIP 86; Elctd Cptn Vrsty Fld Hcky Tm 86; Bus.

MC CABE, SCOTT; Marlborough HS; Marlboro, MA; (Y); 11/280; Boys Clb Am; Ski Clb; Varsity Clb; Var Bsbl; Var Capt Bsktbl; Var Capt Crs Cntry; High Hon Roll; VP NHS; Faculty Awd Oustndng Achvt Soc Studies,Engl 85-86.

MC CAFFREY, KATHRYN; Plymouth-Carver Regional HS; Plymouth, MA; (Y); Trs Church Yth Grp; Girl Scts; Chorus; Hon Roll; Occ Therapy.

MC CAIN, LAURA; West Springfield HS; W Springfield, MA; (Y); Cmnty Wkr; Hosp Aide; Spanish Clb; High Hon Roll; NHS; Spanish NHS; Tchg.

MC CALL, KATHY M; Maynard HS; Maynard, MA; (Y); 31/100; Bsktbl; Hon Roll; SR Excutv Brd 85-86; 3rd Pl Splng Bee Awd 84; Htl Rest.

MC CANN, MAUREEN; Plymouth-Carver HS; Plymouth, MA; (Y); Office Aide; Variety Show; Yrbk Stf; Pres Soph Cls; Off Jr Cls; Off Sr Cls; Stu Cncl; Cheerleading; Gym; Hon Roll; Capt Hcky & Sccr Chlrldng Squd 86-87; VP SE MA Assn Stu Cncl 86-87; Soph Cls Pres 84-85; Cmnctns.

MC CANN, MICHAEL; Holy Name Central Catholic HS; North Grafton, MA; (Y); Church Yth Grp; JA; School Musical; School Play; Stage Crew; JV Socr; Var Tennis; Framingham St Hstrcl Conf-Hrbl Mntn Awd 86; Framingham ST Coll; Chem.

MC CANN, NEAL; Norwood HS; Norwood, MA; (Y); 9/370; Band; Jazz Band; Mrchg Band; Orch; Symp Band; Var Trk; NHS; Chess Clb; Concert Band; Drm & Bgl; Amrcn Legn Awd 84; All Amrcn Hall Fame Band Hons 86; Outstndng Muscn UNH Jazz Fest 86; Elec Engr.

MC CARRON, HEATHER; Bishop Feehan HS; Pawtucket, RI; (Y); 67/250; Dance Clb; Exploring; Hosp Aide; Yrbk Bus Mgr; Yrbk Stf; Stu Cncl; Cheerleading; Trk; Hon Roll; Englsh Olympiad Awd; Fash Merch.

MC CARTHY, ANN MARIE; Danvers HS; Danvers, MA; (Y); 50/300; Church Yth Grp; Girl Scts; Teachers Aide; Chorus; Yrbk Stf; Var L Cheerleading; L Var Gym; Var Trk; Hon Roll; NHS; Grnt Johnson & Wales Clg 86; Slvr Awd Grl Scts 82; Art Natl Hnr Socty Awd 86; Johnson & Wales Coll; Fshn Mrch.

MC CARTHY, CLAIRE; Boston Latin Acad; W Roxbury, MA; (Y); Church Yth Grp; Sec Ski Clb; Spanish Clb; Variety Show; Rep Frsh Cls; Rep Soph Cls; JV Sftbl; Bsktbl; Cheerleading; Summa Cum Laude Natl Latin Exam 86; Mary C Mc Laughlin Awd Read/Lang Arts Cert 86; Providence Coll; Spec Ed.

MC CARTHY, JIM; Marlboro HS; Marlboro, MA; (Y); 91/310; Ice Hcky; Trk; Vrsty Awd Hcky 84-86; Bus Prncpls.

MC CARTHY, JOHN; North Quincy HS; Quincy, MA; (Y); JV Swmmng; JV Trk; High Hon Roll; Arch.

MC CARTHY, JOHN D; Boston College HS; Scituate, MA; (Y); Cmnty Wkr; Key Clb; Library Aide; SADD; Teachers Aide; Nwsp Rptr; Diving; JV Ftbl; Swmmng; Tennis; Patriot Ledger 86; All Schltc/Cathlc Conf All Star 84-86; 1st Pl Cath Conf Diving Champnshp 85 & 86; Northeastern; Jrnlsm.

MC CARTHY, KIM; Stoughton HS; Stoughton, MA; (Y); Church Yth Grp; Hosp Aide; Chorus; Hon Roll; Occ Ther.

MC CARTHY, KIMBERLY A; Holyoke Catholic HS; Holyeke, MA; (Y); 6/129; Computer Clb; VP Latin Clb; Spanish Clb; SADD; Nwsp Rptr; Yrbk Stf; High Hon Roll; Hon Roll; Trs NHS; St Schlr; MA Cmmnwlth Schlr; Mrgrt J Hghlnd Schlrshp Awd; U Of MA; Law.

MC CARTHY, KRISTEN; Duxbury HS; Duxbury, MA; (Y); 91/276; SADD; Band; Mrchg Band; School Play; Rep Stu Cncl; Var Capt Cheerleading; Stat Ice Hcky; JV Socr; Var Capt Trk; Hon Roll; Annie Drew Dunham Schlrshp 86; Duxbury PTA Schlrshp 86; MA ST Schlrshp 86; Springfield Coll; Hlth Ftns.

MC CARTHY, LINDA; Arlington Catholic HS; Waltham, MA; (Y); 9/148; Church Yth Grp; Sec Drama Clb; School Musical; School Play; Nwsp Rptr; Yrbk Stf; Rep Frsh Cls; Rep Soph Cls; Capt Crs Cntry; NHS; US Natl Engl Merit Awd 84-86; US Natl Ldrshp & Svc Awd 84-86; US Natl Jrnlsm Awd 85-86; Holy Cross; Engl.

MC CARTHY, MAURA; Ursuline Acad; Jamaica Plain, MA; (Y); Spanish Clb; SADD; Pres Frsh Cls; Socr; VP Stu Offr Svc 85-86; Providence Coll.

MC CARTHY, MICHAEL W; Taunton HS; Taunton, MA; (Y); 14/430; Latin Clb; Yrbk Sprt Ed; Rep Stu Cncl; Var Capt Bsktbl; Var L Ftbl; Var L Trk; Elks Awd; Im Wt Lftg; High Hon Roll; Rotary Awd; Rec Taunton Cathlc Yth Organ Josph Kusek Mem Trphy 83; Taunton HS Vrsty Bsktbl Unsung Hero Trphy 86; MA Maritime Acad; Engrng.

MC CARTHY, NEIL; Arlington Catholic HS; North Billerica, MA; (Y); Off Soph Cls; Off Jr Cls; Off Sr Cls; L Var Ftbl; L Var Ice Hcky; Hon Roll; Lbrl Arts.

MC CARTHY, PAMELA J; Marshfield HS; Green Harbor, MA; (Y); Key Clb; Band; Var Cheerleading; JV Fld Hcky; Hon Roll.

MC CARTHY, ROBERT; Everett HS; Everett, MA; (Y); 10/300; Key Clb; Letterman Clb; Var L Ftbl; Hon Roll; NHS; Pres Schlr; Delia R O Donnel Scholar Awd 86; Louis Ramboli Mem Scholar Awd 86; Tufts U; Elec Engrng.

MC CARTHY, SHEILA; Marblehead HS; Marblehead, MA; (Y); 44/257; Cheerleading; Swmmng; Martha E Pecker Schlrshp 86; Harbor Wmns Clb Clb Schlrshp 86; VFW Schlrshp 86; U Of NH; Chem.

MC CLURE, HEATHER; Newton North HS; Newton, MA; (Y); Var Score Keeper; Ed.

MC CLUSKEY, MICHAEL; Marlborough HS; Marlboro, MA; (Y); 6/420; Boys Clb Am; Ski Clb; VP SADD; Varsity Clb; JV Socr; Var L Tennis; High Hon Roll; NHS; Ntl Merit Ltr; Faclty Awd Outstndng Achvt Forgn Lang 84.

MC COOK, NOEL; Wilbraham & Monson Acad; Springfield, MA; (Y); Drama Clb; Nwsp Ed-Chief; VP Sr Cls; Var Capt Lcrss; Var Socr; Rotary Awd; Chess Clb; Library Aide; Q&S; Ski Clb; Cum Laude Soc 86; Bates Coll; Hosp Admin.

MC COOL, JOHN; North Middlesex Regional HS; Townsend, MA; (Y); Church Yth Grp; Dance Clb; Trk; Vllybl; Bio.

MC CORMACK, SHANNON; Holbrook HS; Holbrook, MA; (Y); 8/95; Latin Clb; Hon Roll; NHS.

MC COY, TODD; Northampton HS; Florence, MA; (Y); 137/253; Var Capt Ftbl; Trk; Wrstlng.

MC CRACKEN, JAMES; Bishop Feehan HS; Attleboro, MA; (Y); Ftbl; Trk; Wt Lftg; Avtn Air Trffc Cntrl.

MC CREADY, CINDY; Gateway Regional HS; Huntington, MA; (Y); 14/78; Band; Mrchg Band; Yrbk Ed-Chief; Mgr(s); Score Keeper; Stat Sftbl; Cit Awd; DAR Awd; High Hon Roll; Voice Dem Awd; Western New England Coll; Bus.

MC CREDIE, EMILY; Lincoln-Sudbury Regional HS; Sudbury, MA; (Y); Pres Mgr Church Yth Grp; Hosp Aide; Acpl Chr; School Play; Stage Crew; Yrbk Phtg; Var Capt Ftbl; JV Var Lcrss; JV Tennis; Ntl Merit Ltr; Cum Laude 86; Bio Chmstry.

MC CULLOM, PATRICK; Governor Dummer Acad; N Andover, MA; (Y); Camera Clb; Key Clb; Service Clb; Varsity Clb; JV Bsktbl; Var Socr; Var Tennis; Capt Trk; Bates; Poli Sci.

MC DERMOTT, KELLY; Academy Of Notre Dame; Dracut, MA; (Y); Sec Soph Cls; Trs Stu Cncl; Capt Swmmng; Var Tennis; Hon Roll; Trs NHS; Pres Schlr; Franklin & Marshall Coll.

MC DEVITT, MICHAEL; Boston College HS; Medford, MA; (Y); 80/315; SADD; Hon Roll; Boston Coll; Acctng.

MC DONAGH, ERIN; Foxboro HS; Foxboro, MA; (Y); 25/225; Ski Clb; Rep Sr Cls; Cheerleading; Hon Roll; Dance Clb; Exploring; SADD; School Musical; Yrbk Stf; Mgmt.

MC DONALD, DAVID; Arlington Catholic HS; Arlington, MA; (Y); 3/145; Latin Clb; JV Bsbl; Var L Bsktbl; Var L Ftbl; L Trk; Hon Roll; NHS; Prfct Atten Awd; Maxima Cum Laude Slvr Medl Awd-NJCL Latn Exm 84 & 86; Thomas H Duffy Awd-Outstndg Trck 86; Engrng.

MC DONALD, DAWN D; East Longmeadow HS; E Longmeadow, MA; (Y); 16/197; Chrmn Intnl Clb; VP JA; Library Aide; Teachers Aide; School Play; Variety Show; Var Nwsp Stf; Var JV Bsktbl; Hon Roll; U Of MA; Busnss Admin.

MC DONALD, GREGORY; Northfield Mt Herman Schl; Boston, MA; (Y); Var Bsbl; Var Ice Hcky; Hon Roll; Cum Laude Sco At Thayer Acad; Tufts U; Business.

MC DONALD, KERRIE; Douglas Memorial HS; E Douglas, MA; (Y); Church Yth Grp; Girl Scts; Band; Color Guard; Drm Mjr(t); Mrchg Band; Hon Roll; Csmtlgy.

MC DONALD, LYNNE; Christopher Columbus HS; East Boston, MA; (S); 14/137; Math Tm; Yrbk Stf; High Hon Roll; Hon Roll; Jr NHS; NHS; Canada Schl Of Trvl; Trvl.

MC DONALD, MARGARET; Miss Halls Schl; Houston, TX; (Y); 2/65; Church Yth Grp; French Clb; Pep Clb; Orch; Nwsp Ed-Chief; Nwsp Stf; Lit Mag; Var Bsktbl; Golf; Mgr(s); Psych.

MC DONOUGH, JUNE; Billerica Memorial HS; Billerica, MA; (Y); 30/430; French Clb; SADD; Band; Concert Band; Mrchg Band; Hon Roll; NHS; John Di Glorian Awd 85; 3 Lttr Awd Music 86; Hmrm Rep 84-86; Babsom; Accntng.

MC DONOUGH, SEAN; Boston College HS; Hanover, MA; (Y); 77/296; Cmnty Wkr; Key Clb; SADD; Nwsp Rptr; Lit Mag; Im Bsktbl; Im Ftbl; Im Vllybl; Hon Roll; Ntl Latin Exam Cum Laude 85-86; Marquette U; Journalist.

MC ELENEY, PATRICK; Arlington Catholic HS; Arlington, MA; (Y); 20/142; Am Leg Boys St; Var Trk; Hon Roll; NHS; Prfct Atten Awd; Slvr Mdl Maxima Cum Laude-Natl Latin Exam 86; Arlington Cathlc Schlrshp 86; Boston Coll.

MC ELLIGOTT, STEVEN; Arlington Catholic HS; Arlington, MA; (Y); Art Clb; SADD; Yrbk Stf; Bsbl; Capt Var Bsktbl; JV Ftbl; Hon Roll; Acad All Amer 85-86; MVP Bsebll 84; Arch.

MC FADDEN, KAREN; Medford HS; Medford, MA; (Y); Church Yth Grp; Dance Clb; Office Aide; SADD; Chorus; Yrbk Stf; Cheerleading; Hon Roll; Camp Fr Inc; Library Aide; Victoria & Roland Dnc Studos 75-86; MA Awd Ms Chrm Pgnt 86; Nrthestrn U; Biochem.

MC GAFFIGAN, KEVIN; Medford HS; Medford, MA; (Y); 91/476; JV Var Crs Cntry; Var Trk; Hon Roll; A B Crowley Awd Outstndng Hist Stu 85-86; Math Awd 84-85; UMA Boston; Accntng.

MC GANN, SHEILA; Waltham HS; Boston, MA; (Y); Church Yth Grp; Spanish Clb; SADD; Color Guard; Concert Band; Symp Band; Capt Twrlr; Hon Roll; Jr NHS; Prfct Atten Awd; Music Rep 85-86; Stu Santa 84-86; Bentley Coll Spotlight Pgm 85-86; Phys Thrpy.

MC GATHEY, JAMES; Hingham HS; Hingham, MA; (Y); Band; Jazz Band; Stu Cncl; Hon Roll; Mrchg Band; Orch; Symp Band; Lcrss; Pre Law.

MC GEEHAN, JANICE; Weymouth North HS; N Weymouth, MA; (Y); #26 In Class; Hosp Aide; School Play; Yrbk Phtg; Yrbk Stf; Trk; High Hon Roll; Hon Roll; Jr NHS; Pres Ntl Acad Ftnss Awd, Soc Stds Stdnt Yr, A Lambert, Frt Ord Eagls Lad Aux Schlrshps 86; Boston Coll; Law.

MC GEORGE, JENNIFER; Winthrop HS; Winthrop, MA; (Y); 32/203; Art Clb; Math Tm; Ed Yrbk Stf; Sec Soph Cls; Off Sr Cls; Stat Bsbl; Im Bsktbl; Stat Fld Hcky; Mgr(s); Score Keeper; Art.

MC GILL, SIOBHAN; Ursuline Acad; Westwood, MA; (Y); 12/72; Church Yth Grp; Drama Clb; VP French Clb; Girl Scts; Library Aide; SADD; School Musical; School Play; Socr; Hon Roll; Cathlc Leag Sccr All Star 85; Trnscrpt Pgm All Star 85; Pltcl Sci.

MC GILLICUDDY, JANET; St Clare HS; Milton, MA; (Y); 33/120; Church Yth Grp; Im Bsktbl; Im Sftbl; Im Trk; Hon Roll; Yth Mnstry 84-87; Spec Ed.

MC GINLEY, BARBARA; Tewksbury Memorial HS; Tewksbury, MA; (Y); 90/263; Church Yth Grp; Hosp Aide; Color Guard; Mgr(s); Hon Roll; Prfct Attnd Awd; Anatomy & Physlgy Awd 86; Fitchburg ST Coll; Elem Educ.

MC GONAGLE, MICHAEL D; Sandwich JR SR HS; Sandwich, MA; (Y); 17/153; Am Leg Boys St; Boy Scts; Band; Lcrss; Hon Roll; NHS; Pres Acadmc Fitnss Awd 86; Rose Hulman Hnrs Schlrshp 86; Order Of The Arrow 84; R Hulman Inst Tech; Mech Engrng.

MC GOUGH, JILL; Auburn SR HS; Auburn, MA; (Y); Var Crs Cntry; JV Var Trk; High Hon Roll; Hon Roll; Psych.

MC GOUGH, KAREN; Arlington Catholic HS; Arlington, MA; (Y); 24/143; Cmnty Wkr; Drama Clb; French Clb; Office Aide; Service Clb; School Musical; School Play; Var Cheerleading; Hon Roll; NHS; Candinal Cushing Schlrshp Regis Coll 86; Regis; Chld Psych.

MC GOVERN, KATHI; Bedford HS; Bedford, MA; (Y); 16/220; Aud/Vis; GAA; SADD; Rep Frsh Cls; Rep Soph Cls; Rep Jr Cls; Rep Sr Cls; Var Capt Bsktbl; Var Capt Fld Hcky; Var Capt Sftbl; Acad Achvt Awd Bus Ed & Phys Ed; Bus.

MC GOVERN, KELLY; Hopedale JR SR HS; Hopedale, MA; (Y); 14/70; Yrbk Stf; Sec Frsh Cls; JV Bsktbl; JV Socr; Var L Sftbl; High Hon Roll; Hon Roll; NHS; Boston U; Pre-Med.

MC GOWAN, MARY; Bishop Stang HS; Mattapoisett, MA; (S); 4/268; Math Tm; Nwsp Ed-Chief; Stu Cncl; Fld Hcky; Trk; High Hon Roll; Jr NHS; NHS; TX Instrmnts Awd 85; Tom Cahil Awd 85; Wellesley Coll.

MC GOWAN, MARY; Medwauy JRSR HS; Medway, MA; (Y); 30/150; Church Yth Grp; SADD; Stu Cncl; Coach Actv; Socr; High Hon Roll; NHS; Bsktbl; Powder Puff Ftbl; Vllybl; Ntl Schlr Athlete 86; Schlstc Awd 86; Exc Acctng Awd 86; Endicott Coll; Travel.

MC GRAIL, CHRISTINE; Leicester HS; Rochdale, MA; (S); 7/102; Church Yth Grp; French Clb; Latin Clb; SADD; Nwsp Stf; Yrbk Stf; Rep Stu Cncl; Var L Fld Hcky; Var L Trk; Hon Roll; Pres Phys Ftns Awd; Educ.

MC GRAIL, SUZANNE; Clinton HS; Clinton, MA; (Y); 8/125; French Clb; Pres Intnl Clb; Nwsp Rptr; Yrbk Bus Mgr; Cheerleading; Capt Fld Hcky; Sftbl; Hon Roll; NHS; Voice Dem Awd; Rev Gerald Dupond Schlstc Hnr Awd, Acht Incoming Mbr Frshman Cls SMC 86; St Michaels Coll; Eng.

MC GRATH, MICHAEL; Agawam HS; Feeding Hls, MA; (Y); 65/370; Library Aide; Lit Mag; JV Bsktbl; Var L Ftbl; Im Wt Lftg; Lion Awd; Cert Of Achvt-Adelphi Group 85; Providence Coll; Stk Brkr.

MC GRATH, RICHARD; Milford HS; Milford, MA; (Y); 1/263; Band; Yrbk Bus Mgr; Pres Soph Cls; Rep Stu Cncl; Var Capt Swmmng; Var Tennis; Bausch & Lomb Sci Awd; Elks Awd; NHS; Val; Harvard Clb Of Worchester Awd 85; 4 Yr NRTOC Schlrshp 86; MIT; Engrg.

MC GREEVY, ERIN; Metheun HS; Methuen, MA; (Y); Intnl Clb; SADD; Rep Stu Cncl; Im Bsktbl; Var L Crs Cntry; Im L Fld Hcky; Stat Ftbl; Var L Sftbl.

MC GUIRE, AIMEE; Clinton HS; Clinton, MA; (Y); Church Yth Grp; Dance Clb; French Clb; Intnl Clb; Yrbk Stf; Bsbl; Bsktbl; Fld Hcky; Sftbl; Swmmng; Cmmnctns.

MC GUIRE, GLENN S; Algonquin Regional HS; Southboro, MA; (Y); 16/225; Band; Jazz Band; School Musical; Concert Band; Orch; High Hon Roll; Hon Roll; Ntl Merit SF; Invit Acad Wrkshp USMA West Point 85; Worcester Polytech; Elec Engrng.

MC GUIRE, NANCY; Melrose HS; Melrose, MA; (Y); 12/375; Dance Clb; Hosp Aide; Ski Clb; Spanish Clb; SADD; Yrbk Stf; Hon Roll; NHS; Pres Acdmc Ftns Awd 86; Schlstc Awd Math 83; U NH; Med Tech.

MC GUIRE, RACHEL; Matingnon HS; Somerville, MA; (S); 8/179; Art Clb; Drama Clb; Math Clb; SADD; School Musical; School Play; Stage Crew; Nwsp Stf; Yrbk Stf; VP NHS; Century III Ldrs Scholar 85; NEDT Awd 83; Soc Distngshd Amer H S Stu 83-85; Arch.

MC GUIRK, ELIZABETH; St Bernards HS; Fitchburg, MA; (S); 11/177; Drama Clb; NHS; Sci.

MC GUIRK, LYNDA; Leominster HS; Leominster, MA; (Y); Pep Clb; School Musical; School Play; Yrbk Stf; Cheerleading; Fitchbrg ST Coll; Communctns.

MC HUGH, MICHAEL; Hopedale JR SR HS; Hopedale, MA; (Y); 1/80; Trs Aud/Vis; Boy Scts; Exploring; Office Aide; School Play; Yrbk Stf; Var L Golf; JV Socr; High Hon Roll; Pres NHS; Colby Coll; Bio.

MC INNIS, KELLI ANN; South High Community Schl; Worcester, MA; (Y); 45/250; Church Yth Grp; Cmnty Wkr; Dance Clb; Political Wkr; Ski Clb; Teachers Aide; Band; Jazz Band; Mrchg Band; Sec Frsh Cls; Worcester ST; Elem Ed.

MC INTOSH, ARTHUR P; Hingham HS; Hingham, MA; (Y); 137/325; AFS; Model UN; Spanish Clb; Nwsp Phtg; Nwsp Stf; Hon Roll; Frank, Ellen Cobb Schlrshp 86; Hingham HS Math Awd 86; Fitchburg ST Coll; Medcl Fld.

MC INTOSH, BRIAN J; Leominster HS; Leominster, MA; (Y); Am Leg Boys St; Cmnty Wkr; Red Cross Aide; High Hon Roll; Hon Roll; Bus Mang.

MC INTOSH, LINDA; Ursuline Acad; Dedham, MA; (Y); 30/82; Cmnty Wkr; Service Clb; Spanish Clb; SADD; Capt Varsity Clb; Pres Stu Cncl; Capt Sftbl; Hon Roll; Hnrbl Ment 84; Comp Sci.

MC INTYCE, DREW; Stoughton SR HS; Stoughton, MA; (Y); Bsbl; Ftbl; Sftbl; Trk; Vllybl; Astrnmyt.

MC INTYRE, JOHN D; Fitchburg HS; Fitchburg, MA; (Y); Am Leg Boys St; Pep Clb; Ski Clb; Var Ftbl; Var Trk; High Hon Roll; Hon Roll; Geo Prize Awd; Sci Merit Awd; Engrg.

MC INTYRE, JULIE; Plymouth-Caver HS; Plymouth, MA; (Y); High Hon Roll; Hon Roll; Accntng.

MC ISAAC, HEATHER; Our Ladys Newton Catholic HS; Newton, MA; (Y); 5/52; Church Yth Grp; Drama Clb; Var Cheerleading; Pom Pon; JV Vllybl; Cmmnctns.

MC ISSAAC, SCOTT; Milford HS; Milford, MA; (Y); 22/300; Yrbk Stf; Var L Crs Cntry; Var L Trk; Hon Roll; NHS; Bst Sprtsmn Trck Tm; Acctng.

MC KAY, SCOTT; Wilbraham & Monson Acad; Shutesbury, MA; (Y); 19/42; Boy Scts; Chess Clb; Im Bowling; Im Socr; Boy Scout Eagle 85; Ithaca Coll; Lawyer.

MC KENNA, JOHN; Boston College HS; Quincy, MA; (Y); Cmnty Wkr; Debate Tm; Varsity Clb; Im Bsktbl; Im Ftbl; Var Swmmng; Im Vllybl; Hon Roll; NHS; Elect Engr.

MC KENNA, JULIE; Braintree HS; Braintree, MA; (Y); 31/447; SADD; Nwsp Bus Mgr; Nwsp Ed-Chief; Sec Frsh Cls; Sec Soph Cls; Sec Jr Cls; Sec Sr Cls; Var Fld Hcky; Hon Roll; NHS; Hugh O Brien Yth Foundtn MA Ldrshp Semnr 85; Colby Clg Bk Awd 86; Cmmnctns.

MC KENNA, PATRICIA; Sacred Heart HS; N Quincy, MA; (Y); 5/60; Church Yth Grp; French Clb; Math Clb; Variety Show; Yrbk Stf; Capt Var Bsktbl; Capt Var Sftbl; Capt Var Vllybl; NHS; Prfct Atten Awd; Mgr Beatty Awd 86; Bridgewater ST; Physcl Educ.

MC KENNEY, BRIAN; Marshfield HS; Marshfield, MA; (Y); 18/380; Letterman Clb; Varsity Clb; Var Bsktbl; Var Capt Tennis; Hon Roll; Jr NHS; NHS; Worcester Poly Tech; Engrng.

MC KENNEY, JOHN; Lynn Tech; Lynn, MA; (Y); Var Crs Cntry; Var Trk; Comptr Pgmmg.

MC KENNITT, CAMERON; Concord-Carlisle HS; Concord, MA; (Y); 17/328; Nwsp Rptr; Var Capt Bsbl; Var Capt Golf; Var Capt Ice Hcky; High Hon Roll; Hon Roll; NHS; Nwsp Sprt Ed; Yrbk Rptr; Ntl Merit Ltr; Cnty Lg Hockey Leadng Scorer 85-86; DCL All Star Tms Hockey 84-86, Bsbl 84-86.

MC KENZIE, DEXTER; Classical HS; Lynn, MA; (Y); Boys Clb Am; Spanish Clb; Bsktbl; Ftbl; Trk; Hon Roll; Boston Coll; Bus.

MC KEON, BRYAN P; Don Bosco Technical HS; Dorchester, MA; (Y); 106/202; Swmmng; Spelling Comptn 4th Pl 84-85; Engrng.

MC KINNEY, KAREN; Pittsfield HS; Pittsfield, MA; (Y); 19/280; Math Clb; Office Aide; Pep Clb; SADD; VP Jr Cls; VP Sr Cls; High Hon Roll; Hon Roll; NHS; Pres Schlr; Pittsfield Wntr Carnival Queen 86; Tutor Aide 86; Berkshire CC; Bus Adm.

MC KINNON, MONICA M; Stoughton HS; Stoughton, MA; (Y); 10/314; Chorus; Off Frsh Cls; Off Soph Cls; Off Jr Cls; Off Sr Cls; Rep Stu Cncl; Var L Diving; Var Capt Trk; High Hon Roll; Schlrshp 86; Switzer Schlrshp 86; Champion ST Class B Hurdles Trk 86; Tufts U; Bio.

MC KINNON, TIMOTHY; Belchertown HS; Belchertown, MA; (Y); Am Leg Boys St; Var JV Bsbl; Var JV Bsktbl; Var Socr; High Hon Roll; Hon Roll; Excllnc Alge I 83-84; Bus.

MC KINSTRY, MARLENE; North Middlesex R HS; Townsend, MA; (Y); Exploring; Hosp Aide; SADD; Yrbk Stf; Var Trk; Hon Roll; Elem Educ.

MC LAUGHLIN, CHRISTINE; Tridon Regional HS; Salisbury, MA; (Y); 13/192; Rep Stu Cncl; Mgr(s); Trk; Hon Roll; NHS; Holy Cross Coll; Pre-Med.

MC LAUGHLIN, DAWNA; Dracut SR HS; Dracut, MA; (Y); Color Guard; Yrbk Stf; Sec Jr Cls; Sec Sr Cls; JV Bsktbl; JV Var Fld Hcky; Hon Roll; Jr NHS; NHS; SC St Coll; Elect Engineering.

MC LAUGHLIN, JANET; St Clement HS; Medford, MA; (Y); 2/100; Dance Clb; Drama Clb; French Clb; Teachers Aide; Yrbk Stf; Var Cheerleading; Var Capt Vllybl; High Hon Roll; Hon Roll; NHS; Good Grades-Schl Actvties Partcptn Schlrshp 84-86; Med.

MC LAUGHLIN, MARGARET; Revere HS; Revere, MA; (Y); 1/350; Math Tm; Band; Concert Band; Yrbk Stf; Sec Stu Cncl; Harvard Bk Awd 86; Ed.

MC LAUGHLIN, PATRICIA; Marian HS; Framingham, MA; (Y); Church Yth Grp; Cmnty Wkr; Teachers Aide; Variety Show; Yrbk Stf; Rep Frsh Cls; Rep Soph Cls; Rep Jr Cls; Var Stu Cncl; JV Cheerleading; Psych.

MC LAUGHLIN, TRACY; Clinton HS; Clinton, MA; (Y); Cmnty Wkr; Intnl Clb; School Play; Yrbk Ed-Chief; Rep Frsh Cls; Rep Soph Cls; Rep Stu Cncl; Var L Bsktbl; JV Fld Hcky; Pre-Law.

MC LEAN, ANDREA; Westfield HS; Westfield, MA; (Y); 21/400; Church Yth Grp; Spanish Clb; Im Gym; Hon Roll; Jr NHS; Engrng.

MC LEAN, SCOTT; Chicopee Comprehensive HS; Chicopee, MA; (Y); 10/278; Am Leg Boys St; Cmnty Wkr; German Clb; Varsity Clb; Yrbk Phtg; Rep Jr Cls; Rep Stu Cncl; Var JV Bsktbl; Capt L Ftbl; Var Trk; Def Plyr Yr Ftbl; Worcester Polytech; Engrng.

MC LEMAN, HEATHER; Winchester HS; Winchester, MA; (Y); Church Yth Grp; Drama Clb; French Clb; Girl Scts; JCL; Latin Clb; Chorus; Church Choir; School Musical; Off Stu Cncl; Slvr Mdl Ntl Latin Exam 85; Forgn Lang.

MC LOUGHLIN, CAROL; Mount Saint Joseph Acad; Boston, MA; (Y); Drama Clb; JA; Pep Clb; SADD; School Play; Yrbk Stf; Lit Mag; Hon Roll; Bus Clb; Ntl Bus Hnr Soc; Bus.

MC LOUGHLIN II, JOSEPH R; Attleboro HS; S Attleboro, MA; (Y); Am Leg Boys St; Boy Scts; Church Yth Grp; High Hon Roll; NHS; NEDT Awd; Worcester Poly Tech Inst; Engr.

MC LOUGHLIN, LISA; Northampton HS; Northampton, MA; (Y); Ski Clb; Band; High Hon Roll; Jr NHS; Ind Bus.

MC MAHON, DEIRDRE; Winthrop HS; Winthrop, MA; (Y); Camp Fr Inc; Drama Clb; French Clb; Math Clb; Scholastic Bowl; Science Clb; Nwsp Ed-Chief; Yrbk Ed-Chief; High Hon Roll; NHS; Mst Lkly To Sccd 83-86; JR Ofcr Natl Hon Soc 85-86; Brown U Bk Awd 86.

MC MAHON, JOHN; Foxboro HS; Foxboro, MA; (Y); 39/250; Am Leg Boys St; Co-Capt Debate Tm; Latin Clb; NFL; Varsity Clb; Var Bsbl; Var Golf; Hon Roll; Debate Div ST Champ 86; Lawyer.

MC MAHON, MICHAEL G; B M C Dur Fee HS; Fall River, MA; (Y); 117/676; Var Capt Ftbl; Var L Trk; Var Capt Wrstlng; Gridiron Clb Totl Effrt Awd 85-86; Sth Estrn MA Coaches Defnsive All-Star 85-86; Wrstlng Awd 85-86.

MC MAINS, SARA; Concord Carlisle Regional HS; Concord, MA; (Y); 1/327; French Clb; Capt Math Tm; Stage Crew; Ed Lit Mag; High Hon Roll; NHS; Ntl Merit Ltr; Harvard Bk Awd, Estrn MA All Star Math Tm 86; Dpt Hnrs Engl, Frnch, Math, Hist, Sci, Art 84-86.

MC MANUS, MARY M; Dover-Sherborn HS; Sherborn, MA; (Y); 4/157; AFS; Camp Fr Inc; Church Yth Grp; Library Aide; Nwsp Ed-Chief; Ed Lit Mag; Stat Trk; Hon Roll; Ntl Merit Schol; Drama Clb; Schmalenberger Art Awd 85-86; Dover Arts-Crfts Shw 1st Pl Hnrbl Mntn 83-84 & 85-86; Hnr Soc Mert 84-86; U Of PA.

MC MILLAN, GREG; Maynard HS; Maynard, MA; (Y); 11/106; Camera Clb; CAP; ROTC; Science Clb; Swmmng; Hon Roll; Opt Clb Awd; Am Leg Boys St; Art Clb; Aud/Vis; Embry Riddle Aeron U; Comm Airl.

MC MILLAN, LAURIE; Reading Memorial HS; Reading, MA; (Y); Ed Lit Mag; Mgr Wrstlng; Church Yth Grp; Drama Clb; School Play; Nwsp Rptr; Yrbk Stf; High Hon Roll; NHS; Psych.

MC MILLAN, WEDNESDAY; Mansfield HS; Mansfield, MA; (Y); 2/181; Trs French Clb; Church Choir; Mgr(s); High Hon Roll; Hon Roll; NHS; JV L Fld Hcky; Var L Tennis; Brown U Bk Awd 86.

MC MULLEN, YVETTE; Sharon HS; Sharon, MA; (Y); 71/215; Trs Varsity Clb; Nwsp Sprt Ed; VP Frsh Cls; VP Soph Cls; VP Jr Cls; Off Sr Cls; Stu Cncl; Coach Actv; Capt Gym; Capt Trk; Lg All Schlstc Gym Tm 83-84 & 85-86; ST Champ Gym Competitor 85-86; Howard U; Physical Therapist.

MC NALL, HEATHER L; Leominster HS; Leominster, MA; (Y); Ski Clb; Church Choir; Mrchg Band; School Musical; Var Crs Cntry; Var Trk; High Hon Roll; Trs NHS; Church Yth Grp; Rep Frsh Cls; Intl Order Rainbow Grls 86; US Hstry Survey Awd Hghst Hstry Avg 86; Prom Comm 86; Engrng.

MC NALLY, DAN; Southbridge HS; Southbridge, MA; (Y); 32/142; Ski Clb; JV Lcrss; VP L Socr; Im Vllybl; Hon Roll; U Of MA-AMHERST; Arch.

MC NALLY, MATTHEW B; Saint Johns HS; Clinton, MA; (Y); Am Leg Boys St; Drama Clb; Nwsp Stf; Lit Mag; Cmmnctns.

MC NALLY, RACHAEL M; Matignon HS; Cambridge, MA; (Y); 27/187; Camera Clb; Trs Sec Drama Clb; Political Wkr; School Musical; School Play; Stage Crew; Variety Show; Nwsp Ed-Chief; Yrbk Ed-Chief; Rep Frsh Cls; Outstndg Schl Svc; Middlesex Cty Bar Assn Awd; NYU.

MC NAMARA, BRIDGET; Plymouth-Carver HS; Plymouth, MA; (Y); Soph Cls; Jr Cls; Var Trk; High Hon Roll; Hon Roll; Chrprsn Stu Stndpnt 86; Physcl Thrpy.

MC NAMARA, KARYN; Leicester HS; Leicester, MA; (S); #13 In Class; Church Yth Grp; Drama Clb; Hosp Aide; School Play; Yrbk Phtg; Yrbk Stf; Coach Actv; Gym; Gov Hon Prg Awd; Hon Roll; U FL; Psych.

MC NEELY, DAWN; Plymouth-Carver HS; Plymouth, MA; (Y); Church Yth Grp; JV Fld Hcky; JV Ice Hcky; Hon Roll; 1st Girl On Boys Ice Hcky Tm 85-86; Acctg.

MC NEELY, SHANNON; Randolph HS; Randolph, MA; (Y); Art Clb; Church Yth Grp; Library Aide; Service Clb; Teachers Aide; Color Guard; Drm & Bgl; Elks Awd; Hon Roll; Powder Puff Ftbl; Solar Energy Awd 84; U Of New Hampshire; Vet Med.

MC NEIL, CRISTON; Malden HS; Malden, MA; (Y); 32/465; Girl Scts; Key Clb; Latin Clb; Acpl Chr; Chorus; Madrigals; Variety Show; Hon Roll; Zonta & Malden H S & Daniells Fmly Schlrshps 86; Suffolk U; Soclgy.

MC NEIL, KARYN; Fontbonne Acad; Readville, MA; (Y); 13/133; Drama Clb; Intnl Clb; Ed Lit Mag; Rep Frsh Cls; Rep Soph Cls; Hon Roll; NHS; Rotary Awd; Providence Coll; Bio.

MC NIFF, KELLY; Brockton HS; Brockton, MA; (Y); 126/894; Lit Mag; Var L Diving; JV Mgr(s); Var Trk; Hon Roll; NHS; Nrsng.

MC PARTLAN, MICHELLE; Randolph HS; Randolph, MA; (Y); Church Yth Grp; Cmnty Wkr; Pep Clb; SADD; Varsity Clb; Rep Jr Cls; Capt Cheerleading; Powder Puff Ftbl; Sftbl; Jr NHS; Coached Chrldng Team 83-86; 3rd Pl Chrng Comptn At Bstn Coll 86; Crmnl Law.

MC PARTLIN, EDWARD; Austin Prep; Reading, MA; (Y); 17/124; Boy Scts; Chess Clb; Am Leg Boys St; French Clb; Math Tm; Pep Clb; Trs Stu Cncl; Tuitn Merit Schlrshp; Cornell; Bio.

MC QUOID, SAMUEL J; Wachusett Regional HS; Sterling, MA; (Y); 28/396; JA; Mathletes; Hon Roll; Ntl Merit SF; Psych.

MC SHANE, JAMES J; Duxbury HS; Duxbury, MA; (Y); Cmnty Wkr; Nwsp Rptr; Yrbk Rptr; Im Bsktbl; JV Ftbl; Capt Var Socr; Var L Trk; Im Vllybl; Im Wt Lftg.

MC SORLEY, LISA; Brockton HS; Bridgewater, MA; (Y); 55/1000; Dance Clb; French Clb; Hosp Aide; School Play; Rep Jr Cls; Trk; Hon Roll; NHS; U MA Amherst; Cmptr Pgrmr.

MC WALTER, CHRISTINA; Concord-Carlisle HS; Concord, MA; (Y); 54/329; French Clb; Hosp Aide; Sec Band; Sec Concert Band; Sec Mrchg Band; Sec Symp Band; Rep Frsh Cls; Rep Soph Cls; NHS; Socl Wrk.

MEAD, CAROL; Bartlett HS; Webster, MA; (Y); 27/150; French Clb; FNA; Math Tm; Hon Roll; JETS Awd; Libry Aide 83-86; Nrsg.

MEADE, TOM; Monument Mountain HS; W Stockbridge, MA; (Y); 14/132; Band; Mrchg Band; JV Golf; JV Socr; High Hon Roll; Hon Roll.

MEADOR III, THOMAS D; Montachusett Regional Vo Tech Schl; Gardner, MA; (Y); 4-H; VICA; Hon Roll; Prfct Atten Awd; Mst Outstndng Stu Awd-Auto Body 84-86; Perfect Discplnry Record 85-86; Mt Wachusett CC; Auto Tech.

MEAUSKY, DAVID; Athol HS; Athol, MA; (Y); 14/147; Band; Concert Band; Jazz Band; Mrchg Band; School Musical; Variety Show; Wrstlng; Hon Roll; NHS; Outstndng Muscnshp Awd 86.

MECCA, KRISTEN; Tahanto Regional HS; Boylston, MA; (Y); 25/59; JA; Science Clb; Chorus; School Play; Nwsp Stf; Yrbk Stf; Rep Soph Cls; Rep Jr Cls; Var Bsktbl; Frsh Cls.

MECIAK, DAVID; Shepherd Hill Regional HS; Dudley, MA; (Y); Pres Church Yth Grp; Ski Clb; Yrbk Phtg; Rep Jr Cls; VP Capt Socr; VP Capt Trk; High Hon Roll; Hon Roll; Telegrm & Gztte Plyr Of The Wk For Trck & Fld; Ecnmcs.

MEDAILLEU, KAREN; Walpole HS; Walpole, MA; (Y); 9/268; Cmnty Wkr; Drama Clb; Hosp Aide; SADD; Chorus; Color Guard; Rep Frsh Cls; Rep Soph Cls; Rep Jr Cls; Im Fld Hcky; Gold Mdl Awd/Englsh 85; Geomntry & Hstry Perfm Awd 85-86; Stu Of Mnth Awd 85; Wesleyan; Jrnlsm.

MEDEIROS, CHARLENE; Diman Reg Voc Tec HS; Fall River, MA; (Y); Cmnty Wkr; Var Cheerleading; Hon Roll; Reg Dietcn.

MEDEIROS, DEBORAH LYNN; B M C Durfee HS; Fall River, MA; (Y); Camera Clb; Teachers Aide; Yrbk Rptr; Yrbk Stf; Fld Hcky; Trk; Hon Roll; Fash Merch.

MEDEIROS, JOANNE MARIE; B M C Durfee HS; Fall River, MA; (Y); #103 In Class; Art Clb; French Clb; Hosp Aide; VP Letterman Clb; Office Aide; VP Varsity Clb; Band; Capt Color Guard; Concert Band; Flag Corp; U Of MA.

MEDEIROS, RAQUEL; B M C Durfee HS; Fall River, MA; (Y); Church Yth Grp; French Clb; Chorus; Hon Roll; NHS; Awd In Portuguese Lang 85 & 86; Medicine.

MEDEIROS, STEPHENIE; Fairhaven HS; Acushnet, MA; (Y); Cmnty Wkr; FBLA; Hosp Aide; Office Aide; Teachers Aide; Hon Roll; Ntl Merit Ltr; Hnrb Mntn-Katherine Gibbs Schl Typing Cntst 84 & 85; Acctng.

MEDINA, WILLIAM; Chicopee Comprehensive HS; Chicopee, MA; (Y); 30/350; Cmnty Wkr; Yrbk Stf; Rep Jr Cls; Rep Sr Cls; Stu Cncl; JV Var Bsbl; Var L Bsktbl; Var L Socr; Hon Roll; Jr NHS.

MEDUGNO, JEANETTE; Girls Catholic HS; Malden, MA; (Y); Art Clb; Church Yth Grp; Service Clb; Spanish Clb; SADD; Stu Cncl; Stage Crew; Yrbk Stf; Pres Frsh Cls; Rep Soph Cls; Merit Awd 85-86; Scholar Awd NHS 85-86; Chrprsn Prom Comm 86-87; Phys Thrpy.

MEE, EILEEN C; Mount St Joseph Acad; Brighton, MA; (Y); 29/145; Church Yth Grp; Office Aide; Hon Roll; NHS; Bus Ntl Hon Soc; Providence Coll; Bus.

MEECH, MARIANNE; Waltham HS; Boston, MA; (Y); Boys Clb Am; Spanish Clb; Speech Tm; SADD; Varsity Clb; Coach Actv; Swmmng; Trk; Fshn Retl-Mrchndsng.

MEEGAN, JOANNE; Boston Latin Acad; Roslindale, MA; (Y); Church Yth Grp; Debate Tm; German Clb; Color Guard; Yrbk Ed-Chief; Yrbk Stf; Hon Roll; NHS; Wesleyan Coll Acad Achvt Awd 86; Goethe-Instint Awd; Boston Mucnhen For German Achvt 85.

MEEGAN, THOMAS F; Bishop Feehan HS; Mansfield, MA; (Y); 10/260; Am Leg Boys St; Nwsp Stf; Yrbk Stf; Lit Mag; Rep Sr Cls; Stu Cncl; JV Crs Cntry; JV Ftbl; Var Trk; NHS; Spcl Olympc Coach 86; Librl Arts.

MEEHEN, KELLY; Belmont HS; Belmont, MA; (Y); Church Yth Grp; Service Clb; Orch; Var Swmmng; JV Tennis; Orchestra Awd 85-86; Librl Arts.

MEEKER, ANN MARIE; Wilmington HS; Wilmington, MA; (Y); French Clb; Spanish Clb; SADD; Pres Rep Stu Cncl; Var L Trk; High Hon Roll; NHS; Church Yth Grp; JA; Office Aide; Coachs Awd-Wntr Trck 86; Outstndng Acad Achvt 84-85; Cert Of Awd-Outstndg Accmplshmnt Mdl Cngrss 86.

MEGAN, JOSEPH F; Bishop Feehan HS; Attleboro, MA; (Y); 8/232; Rep Am Leg Boys St; Math Clb; VP Stu Cncl; L Crs Cntry; L Trk; High Hon Roll; NHS; Spanish NHS; Commonwlth Schlr 86; Joseph C Megan Jr Schlrshp 86; Pres Acad Fitness Awd 86; U Of MA; Engrng.

MEGIAS, MARIA; North Quincy HS; N Quincy, MA; (Y); 1/372; Church Yth Grp; VP Drama Clb; Madrigals; School Play; Yrbk Ed-Chief; Var Socr; NHS; Pres Spanish NHS; Val; JA; Harvard Bk Prz 86.

MEHLIN, CHRISTOPHER; Hamilton-Wenham Regional HS; S Hamilton, MA; (Y); 20/180; Chess Clb; Math Tm; Pres Science Clb; Band; Concert Band; Jazz Band; Mrchg Band; Hon Roll; Ntl Merit SF.

MEISSNER, EDWARD P; The Roxbury Latin Schl; Canton, MA; (Y); Am Leg Boys St; Church Yth Grp; Cmnty Wkr; Chorus; Nwsp Sprt Ed; Yrbk Stf; Coach Actv; Socr; Cit Awd; Ntl Merit Ltr; Otstndng Yng Ctzn Ctn Hmtwn 85; U Of Notre Dame; Cpa.

MEISSNER, JOAN; Ursuline Acad; Canton, MA; (Y); 1/81; Am Leg Aux Girls St; Trs Latin Clb; Nwsp Rptr; Yrbk Bus Mgr; VP Stu Cncl; Var Stat Bsktbl; JV Var Vllybl; NHS; Church Yth Grp; Dance Clb; MA Senator Girls Natn 86; U MA Chncllrs Talent Awd 86; Humnities Clb Ofcr 86.

MELAHN, LUCIE M; St Mary HS; Andover, MA; (Y); 2/84; Cmnty Wkr; Library Aide; Office Aide; Political Wkr; Church Choir; Nwsp Rptr; Lit Mag; High Hon Roll; Hon Roll; NHS; Knghts Of Clmbs Schlrshp 84; Archdcn Yth Cncl 840-86; Med Rsrch.

MELANSON, MARK; Burlington HS; Burlington, MA; (Y); 43/318; Bsktbl; NHS.

MELCHIN, PAUL; Braintree HS; Braintree, MA; (Y); Boy Scts; Church Yth Grp; Chorus; Madrigals; Lit Mag; Ftbl; Trk; Wt Lftg; Sr Patrol Ldr Natl BSA Jamboree 85; Hnbl Mntn Chem HS Sci Fair 86.

MELCHIOR, SEANNA; Brookline HS; Brookline, MA; (Y); Drama Clb; Thesps; School Play; Variety Show; JV Bsktbl; JV Socr; NHS; Morris Rand Schlrshp 86; Outstndng Drama Socty 86; Cert Merit Hnbl Mntn Natl De Francais 84; Bryn Mawr Coll.

MELCHOIR, CORLIS; Jamaica Plain HS; Roxbury, MA; (Y); Library Aide; Office Aide; Jr Cls; Stu Cncl; Sftbl; Hon Roll; Sci Fair Awd 84; Yth Awareness 83; Fisher JC; Comp Sci.

MELITO, STEPHEN V; Drury SR HS; North Adams, MA; (Y); Am Leg Boys St; French Clb; Political Wkr; Nwsp Rptr; JV Crs Cntry; Var Trk; Cit Awd; Hon Roll; Ntl Merit SF; Nu Sigma Hob Soc 85-86; Phillips Exeter Smmr Prog Schlrshp Wnnr 85; MA Advncd Stds Prog 86; Poltcl Sci.

MELLO, CARL; B M C Durfee HS; Fall River, MA; (Y); 27/673; Boys Clb Am; Church Yth Grp; Letterman Clb; Varsity Clb; Yrbk Stf; Var L Bsbl; Bsktbl; Hon Roll; NHS; Bus.

MELLO, DIANE; Bishop Stang HS; S Dartmouth, MA; (Y); 3/223; Math Clb; Ski Clb; Yrbk Stf; Var Bsktbl; Var Capt Sftbl; High Hon Roll; Sec NHS; St Schlr; Commonwealth Of MA Schlrshp 86; All-Star Sftbl Tm 85; Boston Coll; Psych.

MELLO, JANIS; Greater New Bedford Regional Vo-Tech; New Bedford, MA; (Y); Dance Clb; Hosp Aide; Red Cross Aide; VICA; Variety Show; Capt Cheerleading; Newbury JC; Physcl Thrpst Asst.

MELLO, JOCELYN; Apponequet Regional HS; Assonet, MA; (Y); 9/220; Dance Clb; Pep Clb; Rep Soph Cls; JV Fld Hcky; Hon Roll; NHS; Bntly Coll Bus Wk 86; Bus Admin.

MELLO, RENA; Methuen HS; Methuen, MA; (Y); Off Intnl Clb; Rep SADD; Chorus; School Play; Sec Jr Cls; Sec Sr Cls; JV Bsktbl; Var Tennis; U Of MA; Art.

MELVIN, SUZANNE; Notre Dame Acad; S Weymouth, MA; (Y); Church Yth Grp; Latin Clb; Spanish Clb; School Musical; Stage Crew; Variety Show; Yrbk Stf; Bsktbl; Socr; Sftbl; Communications.

MEMMOLO, DANNY; Randolph HS; Randolph, MA; (Y); Variety Show; Nwsp Stf; Var Bsktbl; Var Trk; Hon Roll; 10th Plyr Awd Babe Ruth Bsbl Rndlph 83; Hournlstc Stud.

MENARD, HOPE; Bellingham Memorial HS; Bellingham, MA; (Y); 1/200; Dance Clb; Nwsp Stf; Yrbk Stf; Stu Cncl; Bausch & Lomb Sci Awd; High Hon Roll; Pres NHS; Milton Adv Studies Pgm Hnrs 86; Margaret Rogers Tap Scholar 85; Grand Lodge Stu Yr Awd 86; Bates Coll; Sci.

MENARD, JOHN; B M C Durfee HS; Fall River, MA; (Y); 30/673; Boys Clb Am; Boy Scts; Computer Clb; Varsity Clb; Var Bsbl; Var Trk; High Hon Roll; Hon Roll; NHS; Engrng.

MENARD, LISA; Bristol Plymouth Reg Tech; Taunton, MA; (Y); Hosp Aide; JV Var Bsktbl; Var Cheerleading; JV Var Sftbl; Hon Roll; Nursing.

MENARD, LORI; Southbridge HS; Southridge, MA; (Y); Mrchg Band; Hon Roll; Gregg Typng Test 85-86; Jrnlsm.

MENCHIN, MICHELLE; Cardinal Spellman HS; Whitman, MA; (Y); 72/205; Cmnty Wkr; Lit Mag; Rep Soph Cls; Rep Jr Cls; Rep Stu Cncl; Var Cheerleading; Var Socr; French Hon Soc; JC Awd; Sci Fair 3rd Prize Wnnr 85; Exec Brd Stu; Emmerson; Journlsm.

MENDEL, ROBERT; Hoosac Valley HS; Adams, MA; (Y); 25/186; Ski Clb; SADD; Band; Concert Band; Jazz Band; Mrchg Band; Pep Band; School Play; Yrbk Stf; Hon Roll; Bkpng Awd 86; Northeastern U; Bus Adm.

MENDELSOHN, DAVID; Dennis Yarmouth Regional HS; Dennisport, MA; (Y); Socr; FL Atlntc U; Mrn Bio.

MENDELSON, KIM G; Brookline HS; Brookline, MA; (Y); Hosp Aide; Sec Model UN; Science Clb; Spanish Clb; Acpl Chr; Chorus; School Musical; Pres Lit Mag; High Hon Roll; NHS; U PA; Bio-Chem.

MENDES, STEPHANIE; Somerset HS; Somerset, MA; (Y); 13/310; Ski Clb; Variety Show; Yrbk Stf; Rep Jr Cls; VP Sr Cls; Rep Stu Cncl; Var L Cheerleading; JV Fld Hcky; High Hon Roll; Hon Roll; Boston U; Bus.

MENDONCA, EDWARD; St Josephs Regional HS; Lowell, MA; (Y); Nwsp Stf; JV Bsktbl; JV Tennis; Hon Roll; Acad All Amer Awd 86; U Of Lowell; Comp Sci.

MENDRALA, MICHAEL; West Springfield SR HS; W Springfield, MA; (Y); Cmnty Wkr; JV Tennis; French Hon Soc; Western New England Coll; Engr.

MENDRALA, NANCY; Westfield HS; Westfield, MA; (Y); 57/359; French Clb; Yrbk Stf; Swmmng; Intl Rltns.

MENGONI, MARK; Phillips Acad; N Hollywood, CA; (Y); Art Clb; JA; Varsity Clb; Band; Orch; Var Bsbl; Var Ftbl.

MENZ, KAREN L; Weymouth North HS; E Weymouth, MA; (Y); 3/329; Pres Key Clb; Band; Yrbk Ed-Chief; Elks Awd; High Hon Roll; Kiwanis Awd; NHS; Pres Schlr; Helen Tonroy Scholar 86; Richard B Dywer Scholar 86; Home Ec Stu Yr 86; CA Poly Tech; Dietics.

MERCADO, ANTHONY; Winchester HS; Bronx, NY; (Y); 90/283; Boys Clb Am; Church Yth Grp; Office Aide; VP Spanish Clb; JV Socr; Capt Wrstlng; Hon Roll; YMCA Awd 85-86; Better Chance Pgm House Ldr 82-86; Liv; Bus Admin & Mgt.

MERCIER, MICHELLE; Marthas Vineyard Regional HS; Edgartown, MA; (Y); 5/98; Church Yth Grp; French Clb; Varsity Clb; Var Capt Socr; Var L Tennis; Hon Roll; Lion Awd; NHS; Pres Schlr; Coll Holy Cross; Bio.

MERCURE, LORI; Blackstone-Millville Regional HS; Millville, MA; (Y); Leo Clb; SADD; Band; Concert Band; Jazz Band; Mrchg Band; Yrbk Stf; Rep Frsh Cls; VP Jr Cls; Rep Stu Cncl; CC Of RI; Exec Sec.

MEREDITH, DEIRDRE; Bishop Stang HS; New Bedford, MA; (Y); 13/221; Church Yth Grp; Cmnty Wkr; SADD; Chorus; Stu Cncl; Cheerleading; High Hon Roll; NHS; Bishop Stand Acdmc Awds 83-85; Pres Merit Schlrshp Colby Sawyer Coll 86; Colby-Sawyer Coll; Chld Study.

MEREDITH, JOSEPH H; Phillips Acad; Cincinnati, OH; (Y); JV Ftbl; JV Trk; Var L Wrstlng; Math, Physcs, Comp & Engl Awds 85-86; Math.

MERRICK, CARRIE; Walpole HS; E Walpole, MA; (Y); 1/270; Dance Clb; Latin Clb; Math Tm; Orch; Stu Cncl; Var Cheerleading; Var L Gym; JV Sftbl; NHS; Var Val; Most Outstndng Fresh & Soph Awd 83-85; Natl Latin Exam-Magna Cum Laude Gold & Slvr Mdl 83-85; Intl Reltns.

MERRIGAN, MARIBETH; Notre Dame Academy; Milton, MA; (Y); Church Yth Grp; Dance Clb; Debate Tm; Math Tm; Y-Teens; Lit Mag; Var L Crs Cntry; Var L Trk; Hon Roll; Prfct Atten Awd; Spnsrshp Close-Up Prgrm WA DC 86.

MERRILL, DWIGHT W; Austin Prepatory Schl; Stoneham, MA; (Y); VP Computer Clb; Exploring; SADD; Var Crs Cntry; Hon Roll; Chess Clb; Church Yth Grp; Library Aide; Spanish Clb; JV Trk; Brown Belt-Shotokan Karate 84; Pres-Austin Paralgl Soc 86-87; Englsh.

MERRILL, HEATHER; Acton-Boxborough Regional HS; Acton, MA; (Y); 36/390; AFS; Hon Roll; Supervisor At Clothes Corner 86; Early Grad 87; Law.

MERRILL, MIKE; Marshfield HS; Marshfield, MA; (Y); 151/382; Key Clb; Varsity Clb; Var Bsbl; Im Bsktbl; JV Ice Hcky; Im Vllybl; Im Wt Lftg.

MERRILLES, ANTHONY; Randolph HS; Randolph, MA; (Y); Church Yth Grp; Drama Clb; Library Aide; JV Bsbl; Im Bsktbl; Ftbl; Im Tennis; Im Vllybl; Hon Roll; Pres Yth Commtte 85; Pub Rel.

MERSELIS III, JOHN G; Mt Greylock Regional HS; Williamstown, MA; (Y); 18/135; Am Leg Boys St; Boy Scts; Drama Clb; Ski Clb; Band; School Musical; Nwsp Phtg; Nwsp Rptr; Yrbk Phtg; Trs Jr Cls; Hamilton Coll.

MERSHA, FANA; Lynn Classical HS; Lynn, MA; (Y); 1/200; French Clb; Hosp Aide; JA; Math Tm; Pep Clb; SADD; Swmmng; Bausch & Lomb Sci Awd; High Hon Roll; NHS; Harvard Bk Awd 86; Lyon Area Mr&mrs Pagent 86; Engrng.

MERULLO, BERNADETTE; Mt St Joseph Acad; Boston, MA; (Y); JA; Stage Crew; Lit Mag; Cheerleading; Swmmng; Prfct Atten Awd.

MESS, ROBERT; St Johns HS; Worcester, MA; (Y); Boy Scts; Drama Clb; Thesps; School Play; Stage Crew; Variety Show; Frsh Cls; Bsbl; Pres Of Drama Club; Regligous Retreat Team; U CT; Drama.

MESSALINE, LINDA; Martha Vineyard Regional HS; Vineyard Haven, MA; (Y); 2/93; AFS; Chorus; Lit Mag; High Hon Roll; NHS; Ntl Merit Ltr; Pres Schlr; Sal; Full Tuition Hnr Schlrshp-Gwu 86; Awd Excellence Calculus Frnch Engl 86; George Washington U; Elec Engrn.

MESSAM, CONRAD; Hyde Park HS; Mattapan, MA; (S); 1/152; Boy Scts; VP JA; Drill Tm; Yrbk Bus Mgr; Var Socr; Var Trk; Hon Roll; NHS; Voice Dem Awd; 3rd Prz City Boston Sci Fair 85; 2nd Pl Act Sci Fair 85; Med.

MESSIER, KATHLEEN; Arlington Catholic HS; Bedford, MA; (Y); Ski Clb; Spanish Clb; Church Choir; Yrbk Stf; 1st Prize Arlngtn Art Fair Sculptr 86; Northeastern U.

METCALF, LARA; Dedham HS; Dedham, MA; (S); 7/252; Aud/Vis; Computer Clb; Drama Clb; Ski Clb; SADD; Band; Concert Band; Drm & Bgl; Drm Mjr(t); Mrchg Band; Lgsltv Inrn To ST Rep 85; Frgn Exc Prgm To Nthrlnds 85; Sctn Ldr Cncrt Bnd Flute Sctn 85-86; Bus/Fnc.

METCALF, ROBERT; Salem HS; Salem, MA; (Y); 32/260; Church Yth Grp; Civic Clb; German Clb; ROTC; JV Im Socr; JV Swmmng; High Hon Roll; Hon Roll; Certfd Open Water Dvr SCUBA; NROTC; Aerntcl Engrng.

METCALFE, MARK; Haverhill HS; Haverhill, MA; (Y); 56/423; German Clb; Var Bsktbl; JV Crs Cntry; Var Ftbl; JV Trk; High Hon Roll; Astrnmy.

METRO, WESLEY; Newton North HS; Newton, MA; (Y); 6/618; Dance Clb; PAVAS; Cit Awd; Hon Roll; Ellen Silk Awd 86; Comm Clb Schrlshp 86; K C Awd 84; U MA; Engl.

METZGER, ANNE; Westborough HS; Westborough, MA; (Y); 105/190; Dance Clb; Drama Clb; Teachers Aide; Band; Chorus; Church Choir; Madrigals; Var Gym; 4-H Awd; Charlotte Klein Dancer Ctrs Mst Imprvd Awd 86; Brnz Mdl Dance Cmpttn 86; Awd Hghst Grd Chld Dev I 86; Elem Ed.

METZGER, TRACI; Westfield HS; Westfield, MA; (Y); 45/329; Ed Nwsp Sprt Ed; Var Capt Bsktbl; Var Sftbl; Jrnlsm Excllnce 86; MVP Bsktbl 86; All Wstrn MA Bsktbl 86; All Lg Sftbl 85 & 86; St Anselm Coll; Psych.

MEUNIER, DANIELLE M; HS Of Commerce; Springfield, MA; (Y); 43/400; GAA; SADD; Rep Soph Cls; Rep Jr Cls; Rep Stu Cncl; Var Trk; Cit Awd; Hon Roll; NHS; Proj Lead 84-86; Rep On Schl Comm 84-86; Ldrshp Pgm At Wstrn New Engld Coll 85; Spch Pathlgst.

MEYER, ANDREA; Sacred Heart HS; Halifax, MA; (Y); 5/90; Art Clb; Church Yth Grp; Cmnty Wkr; GAA; Intnl Clb; Letterman Clb; Political Wkr; Ski Clb; Varsity Clb; Yrbk Sprt Ed; Outstndng JR Stdnt; Martin J Kelley Achvt Schlrshp; Bay ST Gms Fld Hcky 85; Assumption Coll; Pol Sci.

MEYER, DEBRA; High School Of Commerce; Springfield, MA; (Y); 15/325; Hosp Aide; JA; Nwsp Ed-Chief; Yrbk Stf; Rep Frsh Cls; Rep Jr Cls; Rep Sr Cls; Elks Awd; High Hon Roll; Hon Roll; Hampden Dstrct Med Scty Schlrshp Awd 86; Spfld Tech CC; Nrsng.

MEYER, DONNA; High School Of Commerce; Springfield, MA; (Y); Hosp Aide; JA; Office Aide; SADD; Church Choir; Nwsp Rptr; Nwsp Stf; Yrbk Stf; Hon Roll; Bus Adm.

MEYETTE, LOUISE; Palmer HS; Palmer, MA; (Y); High Hon Roll; Hon Roll; Prfct Atten Awd; Rotary Awd; Pro-Merito Hnr Soc 84-86; Pres Acad Fit Awd 86; Springfield Coll; Pediat Rehab.

MIARECKI, PAUL; Palmer HS; Palmer, MA; (Y); Chess Clb; Drama Clb; JA; Spanish Clb; Stage Crew; Lit Mag; L Tennis; Hon Roll; NHS; Prfct Atten Awd.

MICHALAK, MICHELE; Holy Name Cchs HS; Millbury, MA; (Y); 29/259; French Clb; Service Clb; School Musical; Lit Mag; Millbury Ctzns Schlrshp Fndtn 86; Holy Nm Boostr Clb Schlrshp 86; Awds Comp, Rev Grmmr & Hnr Rll 86; U Of Lowell; Chem.

MICHALEWICH, RICHARD; Bishop Connolly HS; Somerset, MA; (Y); 22/250; Cmnty Wkr; Computer Clb; Math Clb; Math Tm; Yrbk Stf; Var Capt Tennis; High Hon Roll; St Schlr; Cmmnwlth Schlr 86; New Bedford Stndrd Tm All Str Tnns Tm 85-86; MVP Tnns 86; Worcester Polytech Inst; Mch.

MICHALSKI, ANN MARIE; Arlington Catholic HS; Billerica, MA; (Y); Dance Clb; Hosp Aide; SADD; Var Trk; Hon Roll; NHS.

MICHNA, JODI; Hopedale JR SR HS; Hopedale, MA; (Y); SADD; Jazz Band; Var L Bsktbl; Var L Fld Hcky; Var L Sftbl; Hon Roll; Band; All Star Fld Hockey & Sftbl; Brdgwter ST Coll; Phy Ed.

MICK, ERIC; King Phillip Regional HS; Wrentham, MA; (Y); Am Leg Boys St; JV Bsktbl; JV Trk; Hon Roll; NHS; Ntl Merit Schol; Med.

MIDDLEN, MARK H; Murdock HS; Winchendon, MA; (Y); 2/88; Am Leg Boys St; Model UN; Trs Science Clb; Yrbk Rptr; Yrbk Stf; L Var Crs Cntry; L Var Trk; Hon Roll; NHS; Mdl Cngrss 86; Engl.

MIDDLETON, CHRISTINE; Lee HS; Otis, MA; (Y); Teachers Aide; Dog Grooming Schl CT; Dog Grmn.

MIDDLETON, JANE; Marian HS; Holliston, MA; (Y); Church Yth Grp; Bus.

MIELE, ERIC; Marlborough HS; Marlboro, MA; (Y); 81/289; Camera Clb; Letterman Clb; Varsity Clb; Variety Show; Yrbk Phtg; Ftbl; Socr; Trk; Wt Lftg; Hon Roll; Northeastern U; Sports Med.

MIELE, MONICA; Cathedral HS; Hampden, MA; (Y); 2/455; Intnl Clb; Pres Math Clb; Office Aide; Red Cross Aide; High Hon Roll; NHS; Sal; Mu Alp Tht; Holy Cross Coll.

MIGNACCA, LYNN; Bishop Feehan HS; Seekonk, MA; (Y); 87/264; Pep Clb; Lit Mag; Rep Soph Cls; Var L Cheerleading; Var L Trk; High Hon Roll; Hon Roll; Providence Coll; Spcl Ed.

MIGNAULT, LISA; Methuen HS; Methuen, MA; (Y); 7/375; Model UN; JV Bsktbl; Var Fld Hcky; Var Sftbl; High Hon Roll; Hon Roll; NHS.

MIKULE, KEITH; Austin Prep HS; Tewksbury, MA; (Y); 35/150; French Clb; Ski Clb; SADD; Lit Mag; Im Lcrss; Im Sftbl; Im Vllybl; Im Wt Lftg; Var Skiing 85-86; Med.

MILASZEWSKI, CARYN; Marian HS; Milford, MA; (Y); Ski Clb; Rep Frsh Cls; Var JV Cheerleading; Im Vllybl; High Hon Roll; Hon Roll; NHS; Latin I Cmptv Exm Cum Laude 85; Cert Awd Chem 85; Mrktng.

MILCH, HEIDI; Fontbonne Acad; Milton, MA; (Y); 37/136; Drama Clb; Girl Scts; Intnl Clb; SADD; Stage Crew; Badmtn; Hon Roll; Excln Music Lit 84; Exclnc Spnsh III 85; Typwrtng Profcncy Cert 84; U MA Boston; Communctn Disordr.

MILES, KIM; Medford HS; Medford, MA; (Y); 43/450; Church Yth Grp; Dance Clb; Exploring; Girl Scts; Ski Clb; Church Choir; Hon Roll; Pre-Prmry Educ.

MILES, SHANNON MEGAN; Holyoke HS; Holyoke, MA; (Y); 10/400; Drama Clb; French Clb; Latin Clb; Office Aide; Speech Tm; Nwsp Rptr; Nwsp Stf; Yrbk Stf; High Hon Roll; Jr NHS; Wellesley Acad Excllnce Awd; Franco-Amer Frnch Awd; Frnch Awd; Engl Awd; NOPA Scholar; Pres Acad Fit Awd; Mt Holyoke Coll; Psych.

MILITELLO, FRANK S; Gloucester HS; Gloucester, MA; (Y); 37/333; Am Leg Boys St; Pres Thesps; School Musical; School Play; Stage Crew; Yrbk Stf; Hon Roll; NHS; Pdtrcn.

MILLAR, CARRIE; Auburn HS; Auburn, MA; (Y); Church Yth Grp; Teachers Aide; Acpl Chr; Chorus; Swing Chorus; Hon Roll; Worcester Ind Tech; Comp Sci.

MILLARD, STEVEN; Newburyport HS; Newburyport, MA; (Y); Boy Scts; Nwsp Rptr; Coach Actv; Var Socr; Var Trk; Crtfct Mrt Art 83-84; Wentwroth Inst Of Tech; Archtrl.

MILLER, BRAD; Stoughton HS; Stoughton, MA; (Y); Nwsp Sprt Ed; Am Leg Boys St; Cmnty Wkr; Red Cross Aide; Varsity Clb; Rep Jr Cls; Rep Sr Cls; Var Bsbl; Var Bsktbl; Var Ftbl; Syracuse.

MILLER, BRIAN; Hanover HS; Hanover, MA; (Y); Boys Clb Am; SADD; Capt Var Socr; Var L Tennis; Im Vllybl; Hon Roll; Stu Of Mnth 84; Bus.

MILLER, CATHIE; King Philip Regional HS; Plainville, MA; (Y); 66/250; JV Fld Hcky; Hon Roll; Ldrshp Awd Bus 2nd Pl 86; Fashn Merchndsr.

MILLER, DAVID; New Bedford HS; New Bedford, MA; (Y); 207/701; JV Ftbl; JV Ice Hcky; Hon Roll; Lowell U; Bus Mgmt.

MILLER, DAVID; Stoughton HS; Stoughton, MA; (Y); 42/336; Cmnty Wkr; Office Aide; Political Wkr; Science Clb; Service Clb; SADD; Teachers Aide; School Play; Stu Cncl; JV Bsbl; Paul Goulston Mem Scholar 86; Moses Mendelsohn Free Sons Israel 86; Syracuse U; Arts.

MILLER, EDWARD; Hanover HS; Hanover, MA; (Y); Church Yth Grp; Pres Trs Drama Clb; Acpl Chr; School Musical; School Play; Stage Crew; NHS; Ntl Merit Ltr; Semi-Fnl All-Star Cst MA HS Dram Fest 86; Gradtd MA Advncd Stds Pgm 86; Music.

MILLER, GRETCHEN; Dana Hall Schl; St Andrews, TN; (Y); Church Yth Grp; Dance Clb; Key Clb; School Play; Rep Frsh Cls; VP Jr Cls; VP Stu Cncl; Var Swmmng; High Hon Roll; Hon Roll; U PA Book Prize 85; Camp Alleghany Hnr Girl 84; Congden Schrshp Fnlst 83; Haverford Coll; Law.

MILLER, SCOTT; Chatham HS; Chatham, MA; (Y); 10/40; French Clb; Band; Concert Band; Jazz Band; School Play; Variety Show; JV Var Bsktbl; JV Var Socr; Var Tennis; Hon Roll; Cape Islands Tennis Dbls Champs 86; 101 Pct On Sccr Tm 85-86; Bronze Mdl Boy ST Games Sccr 86; Musician.

MILLER, SCOTT MICHAEL; Lexington HS; Lexington, MA; (Y); Nwsp Rptr; Rep Soph Cls; Trs Sr Cls; Rep Stu Cncl; JV Im Bsktbl; Trk; Hon Roll; Jr NHS; NHS; Ntl Merit Ltr; AATF Ntl Frnch Cntst; Dartmouth Coll.

MILLER, SETH; Sharon HS; Sharon, MA; (Y); 1/194; Math Tm; Nwsp Bus Mgr; Nwsp Rptr; Yrbk Stf; Im Bsktbl; JV Socr; High Hon Roll; NHS; Ntl Merit SF; Chess Clb; Renssalaer Awd Math, Sci 85.

MILLER, TARA; Presentation Of Mary Acad; Haverhill, MA; (Y); Pep Clb; Political Wkr; SADD; School Play; Nwsp Rptr; Lit Mag; Pres Jr Cls; JV Sftbl; High Hon Roll; NHS; Stu Govnmt Rep MA 86; UCLA; Cmmnctns.

MILLER, TINA; High School Of Commerce; Springfield, MA; (Y); Chorus; Church Choir; VP Soph Cls; Rep Jr Cls; Off Sr Cls; Stu Cncl; JV Var Bsktbl; Trk; Hon Roll; NHS; Lowell U Acdmc Achvmnt Awd 85; U MA Chllng Prg Awd 84-86; Howard U; Orthdntst.

MILLER, TRACEY; Boston Latin Schl; Jamaica Plain, MA; (Y); 127/300; Office Aide; Chorus; Rdng, Lang Arts Cert 86; Bryant Coll RI; Accntng.

MILLETT, MARTHA; Academy Of Notre Dame; Tewksbury, MA; (Y); 9/73; Cmnty Wkr; Drama Clb; Hosp Aide; SADD; Chorus; School Musical; Stage Crew; Hon Roll; NHS; Religion & Comp Lit Awds 85; Engl, Hstry, Religion Awds 86; Acctng.

MILLETTE, PAUL; St Josephs Regional HS; Lowell, MA; (Y); Math Tm; Concert Band; Rep Soph Cls; Rep Jr Cls; Stu Cncl; Bsbl; Var JV Bsktbl; Ftbl; JV Tennis; Wt Lftg; U Lowell; Engr.

MILLETTE, RICHARD; Leominster HS; Leominsten, MA; (S); Am Leg Boys St; Drama Clb; Political Wkr; Ski Clb; School Musical; School Play; Stage Crew; Rep Frsh Cls; Rep Soph Cls; Rep Jr Cls; Bus.

MILLS, BRYAN; Burlington HS; Burlington, MA; (Y); 29/314; Church Yth Grp; Math Tm; JV Bsktbl; JV Trk; Hon Roll; NHS; Elec Engnrng.

MILLS, CINTOWAY; Hyde Park HS; Dorchester, MA; (Y); Aud/Vis; Cmnty Wkr; Exploring; Office Aide; Political Wkr; Prfct Atten Awd; Price Olsen Schlrshp 85-86; Outstndng Keybrdng Awd 85-86; Trans-Africa Schlrshp 85-86; Bay ST JC; Acctnt.

MILLS, MICHELLE; Haverhill HS; Haverhill, MA; (Y); 75/430; Church Yth Grp; Spanish Clb; Trs Y-Teens; Yrbk Stf; Var L Fld Hcky; JV Var Sftbl; Hon Roll; Bio.

MILLSTONE, JAY E; Revere HS; Revere, MA; (Y); Math Tm; Trs Quiz Bowl; Yrbk Stf; Off Frsh Cls; Off Soph Cls; Off Jr Cls; Stu Cncl; Hon Roll; Chancellars Schlrshp Awd Prog 86; Bus Admin.

MILNER, JULIE; Plymouth Carver HS; Plymouth, MA; (Y); 21/528; French Clb; SADD; Yrbk Phtg; Var Capt Cheerleading; Var Trk; Im Vllybl; VP NHS; Marshfield Swm Tm Mst Dedctd Swmmr 83 & Capt 85-87.

MINASIAN, LYNN; St Mary HS; Haverhill, MA; (Y); 4/82; Church Yth Grp; Pep Clb; Ski Clb; Teachers Aide; Var Cheerleading; JV Trk; Hon Roll; NHS; Diocesan Yth Cncl 85-86.

MINEAR, JENAI; Plymouth-Carver HS; Plymouth, MA; (Y); Drama Clb; SADD; Jr Cls; Rep Stu Cncl; Cape Cod CC; Drmtc Arts.

MINER, MICHELLE; Fitchburd HS; Fitchburg, MA; (Y); 27/209; Pres Church Yth Grp; Pres Pep Clb; School Play; Stage Crew; Yrbk Stf; Sr Cls; Bsktbl; Mgr(s); JV Sftbl; 3 Yrs Chrch Spnsrd Bskbl; 4 Yrs Volunteer Bible Schl Tchr; Endicott Coll; Int Design.

MINISTERI, DENISE; Tewksbury Memorial HS; Tewksbury, MA; (Y); Dance Clb; SADD; Cheerleading; Hon Roll; X-Ray Tech.

MIRABILE, CARMEN; Ware HS; Ware, MA; (Y); 18/112; Cmnty Wkr; Model UN; Red Cross Aide; SADD; Yrbk Rptr; Yrbk Sprt Ed; Yrbk Stf; Lit Mag; Rep Stu Cncl; JV Var Bsktbl; Awd Excllnc Jrnslm 85; Citn Hse Of Rep 86; Avtn.

MIRANDA, FELIPE; S Boston HS; Boston, MA; (S); Church Yth Grp; French Clb; Letterman Clb; Varsity Clb; Var Co-Capt Socr; Hon Roll; NHS.

MIRANDA, MICHAEL; Westport HS; Westport, MA; (Y); 2/125; JA; School Play; Var L Golf; Mgr(s); High Hon Roll; Hon Roll; NHS; MA ST Hnr Scholar 86-87; Mth Awd 85-86; Sci Awd 85-86; Sthestrn MA U; Elec Engrng.

MIRARCHI, SHEPHEN; Marshfield HS; Marshfield, MA; (Y); 102/390; Sec Key Clb; SADD; Stu Cncl; Trk; U NH; Bus Admn.

MIRRA, ELAINE; St Clare HS; Roslindale, MA; (Y); 8/150; French Clb; JA; Political Wkr; Nwsp Rptr; Yrbk Stf; Trs Frsh Cls; High Hon Roll; Trs NHS; NEDT Awd; Magna Cum Laude Natl Latin Exam 83-84; Northeastern U; Jrnlsm.

MIRSKY, DAVID; Newton North HS; Newton, MA; (Y); Variety Show; Pres Sr Cls; High Hon Roll; Hon Roll; Val; Riley House Awd Schlrshp 86; Latin Awd 83; Acdmc Awd & Social Svc Awd 86; Harvard U; Flm Mkr.

MISURACA, CHRISTOPHER; St Dominic Savio HS; Everett, MA; (Y); 42/94; Boys Clb Am; Letterman Clb; VP Ski Clb; Spanish Clb; SADD; Yrbk Stf; Rep Stu Cncl; Bsktbl; Ftbl; Wt Lftg.

MITCHEL, STEPHANIE; Reading Memorial HS; Reading, MA; (Y); Drama Clb; Chorus; Church Choir; School Play; Stage Crew; French Hon Soc; High Hon Roll; Ntl Merit Ltr; Pres Schlr; Bst Supprtng Actress 1 Act Play 85; MA Frgn Lang Assn Excllnce 86; Bst Grp Perfrmnc Natl Hstry Day 84; Wellesley Coll; Intl Rltns.

MITCHELL, DAVID; Lawrence Acad; Calais, ME; (Y); Latin Clb; Rep Frsh Cls; Rep Jr Cls; Rep Sr Cls; Rep Stu Cncl; Var L Bsbl; Var L Ice Hcky; Var L Socr; Hon Roll; NHS; Pre-Med.

MITCHELL, DINA; Tantasqua Regional HS; Sturbridge, MA; (Y); Church Yth Grp; Dance Clb; Ski Clb; Chorus; School Musical; School Play; Bus Adm.

MITCHELL, JOHN J; Archbishop Williams HS; Quincy, MA; (Y); Church Yth Grp; Cmnty Wkr; School Musical; Rep Frsh Cls; Rep Soph Cls; Trs Jr Cls; Rep Sr Cls; Rep Stu Cncl; St Johns Schlrshp Awd 85; Stdnt Cncl 4 Yrs; Bus.

MITCHELL, LISA MARIE; Mohawk Trail Regional HS; Shattuckville, MA; (Y); 20/116; Bentley Coll; Bus Mgmt.

MITCHELL, ROSEMARIE; Newburyport HS; Newburyport, MA; (Y); 83/183; Cmnty Wkr; Political Wkr; Band; Concert Band; Mrchg Band; JV Bsktbl; Var JV Fld Hcky; Var JV Sftbl; Prfct Atten Awd; Outstdng Awd Chem 85-86; Arch Of Roses 85-86; Bus.

MITCHELL, STEPHANIE; Boston Latin HS; Dorchester, MA; (Y); JA; Church Choir; Amer Cncr Soc Wm B Price Unit Achvt Awd 86; Mrt Awd Natl Grk Exm 86; Outstndg Achvt Roxbury Multi-Svc; Hampton Inst; Pre-Med.

MOES, ERICA; North HS; Worcester, MA; (Y); 4/208; Varsity Clb; Stu Cncl; Var Socr; Capt Var Trk; Hon Roll; NHS; Pres Schlr; Wmns Tchrs Assn Scholar 86; Forsyth Schl; Dentl Hyg.

MOGRASS, LUCILLE; Falmouth HS; Mashpee, MA; (Y); Church Yth Grp; Computer Clb; French Clb; PAVAS; Varsity Clb; Var Fld Hcky; Var JV Sftbl; Hon Roll; Pom Pon; Powder Puff Ftbl; Acctg.

MOHAN, BRIAN; Milford HS; Milford, MA; (Y); 2/283; Am Leg Boys St; Trs Frsh Cls; Trs Soph Cls; Trs Jr Cls; Trs Sr Cls; Capt Var Tennis; Capt Var Wrstlng; NHS; Ntl Merit Ltr; Eagle Sct; Harvard; Econ.

MOISAN, JOHN; Bartlett HS; Webster, MA; (Y); 1/151; Math Tm; Science Clb; Yrbk Rptr; Yrbk Stf; High Hon Roll; JETS Awd; NHS; NEDT Awd; The Harvrd Bk 86; Cert Of Profcncy Acctg 86; Elec Engrng.

MOKRZYCKI, KERRY J; West Springfield SR HS; W Springfield, MA; (Y); Art Clb; Camera Clb; Chess Clb; Church Yth Grp; Drama Clb; Pep Clb; Q&S; Ski Clb; Color Guard; Yrbk Phtg; Var Ltr 84-85; Bay Path JC; Fshn Dsgnr.

MOLL, ALEX; Tahanto Regional HS; Boylston, MA; (Y); 7/57; Debate Tm; JA; School Play; Nwsp Ed-Chief; Yrbk Stf; JV Mgr(s); High Hon Roll; NHS.

MOLTENBREY, AMBER; Hampshire Regional HS; Southampton, MA; (Y); 43/150; 4-H; Pep Clb; Ski Clb; Yrbk Stf; Stu Cncl; Cheerleading; Capt Trk; Hon Roll; Johnson & Wales; Htl Mgmnt.

MOMPHO, BO; Wilbraham-Monson Acad; Wilbraham, MA; (Y); Chess Clb; Church Yth Grp; Girl Scts; Mathletes; Church Choir; Pres Frsh Cls; VP Soph Cls; Var L Lcrss; Capt L Socr; Var L Trk; Sci Awd 84; Med.

MONAGHAN, CAROL; Cathedral HS; Springfield, MA; (Y); Church Yth Grp; Dance Clb; German Clb; Math Clb; Office Aide; Yrbk Rptr; Yrbk Stf; High Hon Roll; NHS; Prfct Atten Awd; Religion Awd 84; Perfect Attndnc 82-85; St Michaels Coll; Chem.

MONAGHAN, KELLY; Holyoke HS; S Hadley, MA; (Y); GAA; Girl Scts; Chorus; Church Choir; Fld Hcky; Sftbl; Poetry Awd Clss Poet 86; Holyoke CC; Bus Mgmt.

MONAHAN JR, JOSEPH M; Cathedral HS; Longmeadow, MA; (Y); Church Yth Grp; Cmnty Wkr; Model UN; Political Wkr; Teachers Aide; Yrbk Stf; Im Bsbl; JV Im Bsktbl; Im Wt Lftg; Pre-Law.

MONAHAN, LAURA B; Foxboro HS; Foxboro, MA; (Y); 38/215; French Clb; Girl Scts; Latin Clb; JV Bsktbl; JV Socr; JV Trk; Frgn Lang.

MONAHAN, MICHELE; Mount St Joeseph Acad; Boston, MA; (Y); 49/160; Church Yth Grp; Drama Clb; PAVAS; Church Choir; School Musical; Yrbk Stf; Lit Mag; Gym; Comm.

MONAHAN, SEAN; Wakefield HS; Wakefield, MA; (Y); Var Capt Bsbl; Var L Bsktbl; Var Capt Socr; Soccer Hnrbl Ment All Star Stu 84; Bsbl All League MVP 86; Med.

MONDAZZI, ANGELA; Dracut SR HS; Dracut, MA; (Y); Cmnty Wkr; Dance Clb; Girl Scts; Letterman Clb; Office Aide; Pep Clb; Political Wkr; Teachers Aide; Varsity Clb; Band; Dartmouth; Law.

MONEY, PAM; Chelmsford HS; Chelmsford, MA; (Y); 37/560; Ski Clb; Spanish Clb; Socr; Swmmng; Trk; High Hon Roll; Hon Roll; NHS; Pres Schlr; Spanish NHS; Twn Of Chlmsfrd Schlrshp 86; MA ST Schlrshp 86; Fordham U; Pre-Law.

MONGE, MARLYN; Boston Latin Schl; E Boston, MA; (Y); 73/274; Camera Clb; Trs French Clb; SADD; Orch; Nwsp Stf; Var L Crs Cntry; Var Powder Puff Ftbl; Hon Roll; Prfct Atten Awd; Outstndng Stud Awd 86; Mbr Of Mock Trl Sfflk Cnty Champs 86; Clb Stud Ldrshp Co-Chrprsn 82-86; U Of Syracuse; Psych.

MONIAK, JULIE; Billerica Memorial HS; Billerica, MA; (Y); 19/430; Camera Clb; Cmnty Wkr; Dance Clb; French Clb; Nwsp Rptr; Nwsp Stf; Yrbk Stf; Badmtn; Powder Puff Ftbl; High Hon Roll; Woburn Five Cents Svngs Bnk Schlrshp 86; Western WA U; Cmmnctns.

MONIZ, MARC; New Bedford HS; New Bedford, MA; (Y); 25/599; JCL; Concert Band; Mrchg Band; Orch; School Musical; Stu Cncl; Var L Tennis; High Hon Roll; NHS; 4-X New Englnd Schltc Band Assn Chmpns-HS Whlng Mrchng Band 82-86; Mgna Cum Laude-Ntl Latin Exm 82; Brandeis U; Plnthrplgst.

MONIZ, ROBERT; B M C Durfee HS; Fall River, MA; (Y); Hon Roll; Stdnt Drftsmn Mnth 86; Schlrshp Hall Inst RI 86; ST Schlrshp 86; Hall Inst Pawtucket RI; Arch.

MONKS, STACY; Nauset Regional HS; Brewster, MA; (Y); Church Yth Grp; Drama Clb; Girl Scts; Variety Show; Cheerleading; Hon Roll; Lit.

MONTANARI, MICHAEL A; Wellesley SR HS; Wellesley, MA; (Y); 180/289; Off Exploring; Band; Concert Band; Jazz Band; Mrchg Band; Orch; School Musical; Im Badmtn; Mgr(s); Samuel M Graves 86; Bridgewater ST; Math.

MONTEIRO, CATARINA; Boston Latin Acad; Roxbury, MA; (Y); Church Yth Grp; Cmnty Wkr; Excell In German Awd 85.

MONTEIRO, ETELVINA; St Gregory HS; Hyde Park, MA; (Y); Cmnty Wkr; DECA; Hosp Aide; Red Cross Aide; Science Clb; VICA; Swmmng; Vllybl; NHS; Achvt Awds 84-86; Hnr Awds Acadmc Excllnc 85; Mildred Fitzgerald Schlrshp Awd 86; Bio.

MONTESI, MICHELLE; Agawam HS; Feeding Hills, MA; (Y); 11/83; JCL; Ski Clb; Chorus; Yrbk Stf; Sec Soph Cls; Sec Jr Cls; Var Capt Cheerleading; Hon Roll; Sec NHS; Spanish NHS; Prncpls Awd Outstndg Stdnt 84.

MONTGOMERY, CARA; Marlboro HS; Marlboro, MA; (Y); Pres AFS; VP Church Yth Grp; JA; OEA; Pep Clb; SADD; Variety Show; Hon Roll; Int Dsgn.

MONTGOMERY, THOS; Winthrop HS; Winthrop, MA; (Y); 21/210; Am Leg Boys St; Math Tm; Nwsp Stf; Var Bsbl; Var Bsktbl; Elks Awd; Hon Roll; Jr NHS; NHS; Prfct Atten Awd; Bus Admn.

MONTY, DIANE; Greater Lowell Vote HS; Lowell, MA; (Y); Church Yth Grp; French Clb; SADD; Cheerleading; Secy.

MONTY, JOSEE P; Leominster HS; Leominster, MA; (Y); 6/350; Ski Clb; SADD; School Play; Yrbk Ed-Chief; Cit Awd; High Hon Roll; NHS; Ntl Merit Ltr; Soc Plstcs Engnrs Schlrshp 86; Awd Excllnc Engl 86; 1st Pl Awd Lcl Hstry Wrtg & Rsrch Cntst 85; U Of MA Amherst; Pre-Med.

MOODY, KAREN L; Madison Park HS; Boston, MA; (Y); Teachers Aide; Jazz Band; Orch; School Play; Lit Mag; Sr Cls; Hon Roll; NHS; Prfct Atten Awd; Gld Medl Natl NAACP ACT-SO Tlnt Comptn Dallas TX; Citatn MA ST Senate Acadmc Achvt; Microbio.

MOODY, PEGGY ANN; Quaboag Regional HS; Warren, MA; (Y); 12/89; Church Yth Grp; JA; Math Tm; Spanish Clb; SADD; Varsity Clb; Variety Show; Yrbk Stf; Hst Sr Cls; Hon Roll; Bus.

MOODY, RHETT; Winchester HS; Winchester, MA; (Y); Church Yth Grp; Spanish Clb; SADD; Rep Frsh Cls; VP Soph Cls; Pres Jr Cls; Var JV Ftbl; Var Trk; Var Wt Lftg; Jr NHS; HOBY Fndtn; Arch.

MOONEY, BARBARA; Shepherd Hill Regional HS; Dudley, MA; (Y); 10/180; VP Debate Tm; Chorus; Church Choir; Madrigals; Mrchg Band; School Musical; Variety Show; Stu Cncl; Hon Roll; NHS; Prtcpnt Miss Tn Amer 85; Plg Good Wrk Stu Cncl 86; Performnc.

MOORE, CAROLYN; South Lancaster Acad; Feeding Hills, MA; (S); Church Yth Grp; JA; Math Clb; Chorus; Yrbk Stf; Rep Sr Cls; Var Bsktbl; Im Sftbl; Hon Roll; NHS; Southern College; Nrsg.

MOORE, DAVID E; Rockport HS; Rockport, MA; (Y); 14/70; Am Leg Boys St; Drama Clb; French Clb; Chorus; School Play; Nwsp Ed-Chief; Nwsp Rptr; Thesps; Ntl Merit SF; Jrnlsm.

MOORE, ELIZABETH; Bishop Feehan HS; N Attleboro, MA; (Y); 59/232; Rep Frsh Cls; Rep Soph Cls; Rep Jr Cls; Rep Sr Cls; Rep Stu Cncl; Var L Cheerleading; Var Tennis; Var L Trk; Elks Awd; High Hon Roll; Svc Awd Stu Cncl; Southeastern MA U; Engrng.

MOORE, SCOTT B; Nauset Regional HS; East Dennis, MA; (Y); VP SADD; VP Sr Cls; Rep Stu Cncl; Var Capt Bsktbl; JV Capt Socr; Var L Trk; Hon Roll; Ski Clb; JV Bsbl; Cit Awd; Brhmmr Cup 85-86; MA Bay ST Games-Bsktbl 85-86; MA Bys ST 85-86.

MOORE, THOMAS; Hudson HS; Hudson, MA; (Y); Math Tm; Ski Clb; Stu Cncl; JV Bsktbl; Var JV Ftbl; High Hon Roll; NHS.

MOORE, THOMAS C; Tantasqua Regional HS; Fiskdale, MA; (Y); Church Yth Grp; Letterman Clb; Ski Clb; Varsity Clb; School Play; JV Bsktbl; Var L Ftbl; Var L Trk; Hon Roll; NHS; Brdr Conf Leag Trck Meet-1st Pl Pole Vlt 86; H S Wrriors Boostrs-Un-Sung Athlt Awd 86; Engl.

MOORE, VALERIE; Pittsfield HS; Pittsfield, MA; (Y); VP Church Yth Grp; Drama Clb; Pep Clb; SADD; Chorus; Church Choir; Madrigals; School Musical; School Play; Nwsp Phtg; Theatre.

MOOREHOUSE, JOHN; Lynn Classical HS; Lynn, MA; (Y); 20/171; Am Leg Boys St; Stu Cncl; Hon Roll; Ntl Merit Ltr; Chess Clb; Political Wkr; Var Ftbl; Wt Lftg; Acad All Am 86; ST Stu Adv Cncl 86.

MOORER, MARIAH; Taconic HS; Pittsfield, MA; (Y); Hon Roll.

MOOTAFIAN, STEPHEN H; Peabody Veterans Memorial HS; Peabody, MA; (Y); 113/494; Boy Scts; Church Yth Grp; Trs Drama Clb; Thesps; Band; School Musical; School Play; Stage Crew; Variety Show; Hon Roll; Intl Thespian Soc 86; U Ma-Amherst; Bus Mgmt.

MORAD, STEPHEN S; Don Bosco Tech; Quincy, MA; (Y); 14/202; Rep Frsh Cls; Sec VP Stu Cncl; High Hon Roll; Hon Roll; Jr NHS; Pat Logan Scholar 85-86; Elec.

MORAN, AMY; Burlington HS; Burlington, MA; (Y); 65/323; Church Yth Grp; Capt Pep Clb; VP SADD; VP Soph Cls; Var Capt Cheerleading; Powder Puff Ftbl; Hon Roll; Outstndng Achvt Stu Govt 84; Stu Govt Day 85-86; Burlington Mall Scholar 86; Merrimack Coll; Mktng.

MORAN, AMY LADD; Amherst Regional HS; Pelham, MA; (Y); Acpl Chr; Band; Orch; School Musical; L Socr; Ntl Merit SF.

MORAN, KAREN; Nipmuc Regional HS; Upton, MA; (Y); 4/90; Spanish Clb; Rep Stu Cncl; High Hon Roll; NHS; Ntl Merit SF; Bio.

MORAN, STEPHEN W; Canton HS; Canton, MA; (Y); 25/250; Var Bsbl; Var Capt Golf; Var Ice Hcky; Hon Roll; All Str In Hcky & Glf 85-86; Cntry Clb 84-86; Engrng.

MORDO, LISA; Marlboro HS; Marlboro, MA; (Y); 68/272; Cmnty Wkr; GAA; Varsity Clb; Var Capt Socr; CC Awd; High Hon Roll; ST Scr Champs 85; ST Selct Scr Team Plyr & Centrl Mass Dist All Star 85-86; Regn I Scr Rep 85; Keene ST Coll; Bio.

MOREAU, JAYNE; Norton HS; Norton, MA; (S); 3/173; Church Yth Grp; French Clb; Math Tm; Church Choir; High Hon Roll; NHS; NEDT Awd; Toccoa Falls Coll; Tchr.

MORECROFT, TRACY; Saugus HS; Saugus, MA; (Y); 52/268; Church Yth Grp; Library Aide; Office Aide; Spanish Clb; Yrbk Stf; St Hstrcl Conf Awd 86; Nrsng.

MOREL, DAVID; Central Catholic HS; Tewksbury, MA; (Y); 7/231; Boy Scts; Computer Clb; French Clb; Chrmn JA; Math Tm; Ski Clb; School Play; High Hon Roll; NHS; Ad Altare Dei Medal 83; Cmmnctns.

MORELAND, SUSAN; Salem HS; Salem, MA; (Y); 4/225; Orch; School Musical; Bsktbl; Socr; High Hon Roll; Trs NHS; Spanish NHS.

MORENCY, DAVID; St Dominic Savio HS; Chelsea, MA; (Y); 12/92; Chess Clb; Church Yth Grp; Exploring; SADD; Nwsp Sprt Ed; Nwsp Stf; Yrbk Stf; JV Ice Hcky; Hon Roll; Prfct Atten Awd; Engrng.

MORETON, JOAN; Melrose HS; Melrose, MA; (Y); 8/398; French Clb; Color Guard; Ed Yrbk Phtg; JV Trk; High Hon Roll; Hon Roll; NHS; Regntn French.

MOREY, KAREN; Longmeadow HS; Longmeadow, MA; (Y); 34/256; Sec Pres AFS; Keywanettes; Library Aide; Teachers Aide; Nwsp Bus Mgr; Nwsp Stf; Stat Bsktbl; Vllybl; High Hon Roll; Hon Roll; Merit UPENN Bk Awd, Cert Hnr Career Educ Internshp Pgm, Cert Hnr Ldrshp & Svc AFS Stu Clb Awd 86; Educ.

MORGAN, BETHANY; Old Rochester Regional HS; Mattapoisett, MA; (Y); 36/138; Art Clb; Church Yth Grp; Drama Clb; Ski Clb; SADD; School Musical; School Play; Yrbk Stf; Crs Cntry; Fine Arts.

MORGAN, DORI; North HS; Worcester, MA; (Y); Dance Clb; Debate Tm; Model UN; Ski Clb; SADD; Yrbk Stf; Hon Roll; Early Chldhd.

MORGAN, STEPHEN; Salem HS; Salem, MA; (Y); 18/269; Boy Scts; Drama Clb; Orch; School Musical; School Play; Symp Band; JV Var Ftbl; High Hon Roll; Trs NHS; Church Yth Grp; Dir Awd 86; Biotech.

MORGESE, RON; Andover HS; Andover, MA; (S); Church Yth Grp; DECA; Political Wkr; SADD; Nwsp Rptr; Outstndng Achvt Mrktg 86; 1st Pl Reg DECA Comp, 3rd Pl St Natl Finalist 86; Mrktg Bus Mgmt.

MORHY, PAUL; Diman Regional Voc Tech HS; Fall River, MA; (Y); 2/200; Bsktbl; Ftbl; Tennis; High Hon Roll; Recrdng Engr.

MORIARTY, DANIEL; Monson JR SR HS; Monson, MA; (Y); 6/84; Am Leg Boys St; SADD; Varsity Clb; Stage Crew; Var L Bsbl; Var L Bsktbl; Var L Socr; High Hon Roll; Hon Roll; NHS; MVP Vrsty Baseball 86; Accntng.

MORIARTY, JENNIFER; Westfield HS; Westfield, MA; (Y); Hosp Aide; Chorus; Orch; School Play; Off Soph Cls; Off Jr Cls; Off Sr Cls; Cheerleading; Trk; U Of MA; Music.

MORIARTY, KARA; Westfield HS; Westfield, MA; (Y); 33/370; Cmnty Wkr; Hosp Aide; Latin Clb; Political Wkr; Spanish Clb; SADD; Hst Frsh Cls; Hst Soph Cls; Hst Jr Cls; Hst Sr Cls.

MORIARTY, KATHLEEN; Mount Saint Joseph Acad; Brookline, MA; (Y); 15/145; Church Yth Grp; Yrbk Stf; Var Trk; NHS; Wellesley Coll; Education.

MORIARTY, MATTHEW; Southbridge HS; Southbridge, MA; (Y); U Of MA; Elec Engrng.

MORIARTY JR, MICHAEL J; Ware HS; Ware, MA; (Y); Band; Concert Band; Jazz Band; Mrchg Band; High Hon Roll.

MORIARTY, PATRICIA; Tewksbury Memorial HS; Tewksbury, MA; (Y); 10/350; Intnl Clb; Service Clb; School Musical; School Play; Rep Stu Cncl; JV Socr; JV Sftbl; JV Vllybl; High Hon Roll; NHS; Chem Matters Blimp Cont 86; Comp Bay St Games Sccr 86; AFS Host Stu 86; Phys Therapist.

MORIARTY, THOMAS M; Quabbin Regional JRSR HS; Gilbertville, MA; (Y); 1/134; Am Leg Boys St; ROTC; Spanish Clb; Golf; High Hon Roll; NHS; Ntl Merit Ltr; Val; Pres Acad Fit Awd 86; US Naval Acad; Engrng.

MORICZ, EDITH; Cardinal Spellman HS; Holbrook, MA; (Y); 3/275; Drama Clb; Hosp Aide; Pres Latin Clb; Library Aide; Rep Stu Cncl; High Hon Roll; Hon Roll; NHS; Natl Latin Awd 85; Edu.

MORIN, DENISE; Assabet Valley Rgnl Vo Tech HS; Hudson, MA; (Y); 11/287; Computer Clb; Drama Clb; Math Clb; SADD; Chorus; Capt Fld Hcky; High Hon Roll; NHS; Prfct Atten Awd; Acadmc Ltr 85-86; Data Proc.

MORIN, PAUL A; Westfield HS; Westfield, MA; (Y); 12/327; NHS; Grad 1/2 Yr Early 86; Carl S Ell Full Tguition Schlrshp; Northeastern U; Psysphy.

MORISSETTE, AMY; Mansfield HS; Mansfield, MA; (Y); 6/200; Am Leg Aux Girls St; Key Clb; Trs Spanish Clb; SADD; Yrbk Stf; JV Capt Fld Hcky; Var Tennis; Hon Roll; NHS; Hugh O Brien Ldrshp Semnr 85; Pre-Law.

MORLEY, BRENDA; Mt St Joseph Acad; Brookline, MA; (Y); 21/146; Church Yth Grp; GAA; Ski Clb; Yrbk Stf; Trk; Hon Roll; Natl Bus Hnr Soc; Suffolk U; Accntng.

MORNEAU, KIMBERLY; Burlington HS; Burlington, MA; (Y); Church Yth Grp; Yrbk Stf; Bsktbl; Powder Puff Ftbl; JV Var Sftbl; Grphc Dsgn.

MORNEAU, MICHELLE; Easthampton HS; Easthampton, MA; (Y); 5/137; Intnl Clb; JA; Office Aide; Spanish Clb; Yrbk Bus Mgr; Var L Swmmng; High Hon Roll; Hon Roll; NHS; Cmnty Wkr; Pres Acdmc Fit Awd 86; Syracuse U; Intl Bus.

MORONEY, PETER; Acton Bocborough Regional HS; Acton, MA; (Y); 175/428; SADD; Var Capt Crs Cntry; Var Capt Trk; Hon Roll; Law.

MORRIS, ANTHONY; Concord Acad; Concord, MA; (Y); Church Yth Grp; German Clb; Teachers Aide; Jazz Band; Lit Mag; Var Bsktbl; Var Lcrss; Hon Roll; Ntl Merit SF; Chorus; Amer Assn Tchrs Ger Inc Awd 85; MIP Vrsty La Crosse 84.

MORRIS, ERIK G; Old Rochester Regional HS; Rochester, MA; (Y); 1/160; Am Leg Boys St; Boy Scts; Computer Clb; Math Tm; Service Clb; Teachers Aide; Rep Jr Cls; Rep Sr Cls; Pres VP Stu Cncl; Var Bsbl; Rensselaer Polytchnc Inst Mth Sci Awd 86; Harvard Bk Awd 86; Amrcn Invtatnl Mathmtcs Exam 86; MIT; Engr.

MORRIS, JENNIFER; Dennis-Yarmouth Regional HS; W Yarmouth, MA; (Y); 59/305; Ski Clb; Chorus; Orch; School Play; Stu Cncl; Var L Crs Cntry; Var L Trk; JV Vllybl; Hon Roll; St Schlr; SR Excllnc Soc Stds Awd 86; Bst Sprtng Actrss Schl Drama Cmptn 86; Crss Cnty Plyr Awd 85; Wheaton Coll; Lawyer.

MORRIS, KELLY; Arlington Catholic HS; Arlington, MA; (Y); 11/148; Dance Clb; Hosp Aide; Ski Clb; SADD; Varsity Clb; Trs Jr Cls; Crs Cntry; Trk; High Hon Roll; Hon Roll; Pres Acad Ftns Awd; A Or Bttr 4 Yrs; Nat Englsh Merit Awd Wnnr; St Michaels Coll.

MORRIS, KENNETH J; Oakmont Regional HS; Westminster, MA; (Y); 1/137; Am Leg Boys St; Aud/Vis; Camera Clb; Chess Clb; Radio Clb; Band; Concert Band; Mrchg Band; Nwsp Stf; JV Bsbl; Cazenovia; Cmmrcl Artst.

MORRIS, PHILIP; St Dominic Savio HS; Everett, MA; (Y); Chess Clb; JA; Math Clb; Stage Crew; Nwsp Phtg; Rep Soph Cls; NHS; Voice Dem Awd; Eagle Scout 85; Mech Engr.

MORRIS, TRISHA; New Bedford HS; New Bedford, MA; (Y); 11/701; AFS; Exploring; Yrbk Stf; Stu Cncl; High Hon Roll; Jr NHS; NHS; Ntl Merit Ltr; Chnclrs Schlrshp U MA 86; 3rd Pl New Bedfrd Holocaust Essay 86; Cert Of Merit For Achvt In Frnch 86; Intl Law.

MORRISON, COLLEEN M; Billerica Memorial HS; Billerica, MA; (Y); 28/430; Spanish Clb; Yrbk Stf; Coach Actv; Hon Roll; NHS; NEN Dupnt Schlrshp 86-87; Bstn U Schlrshp & Grnt; Boston U; Nrsng.

MORRISON, ELIZABETH ANN; Miss Hallis Schl; Reading, PA; (Y); Art Clb; Drama Clb; Spanish Clb; Speech Tm; Stage Crew; Pres Frsh Cls; Rep Soph Cls; VP Jr Cls; Stu Cncl; Cheerleading; Skidmore Coll; Law.

MORRISON, JAMES M; Weymouth North HS; Weymouth, MA; (Y); Aud/Vis; Church Yth Grp; Stage Crew; High Hon Roll; Hon Roll; Voice Dem Awd; Tv Prod High Achvt Awd 84; Tech Drwg Recog Awd 84; Grad With 4 Yrs Hnrs 86; U MA Boston; Tv Prod.

MORRISON, JOY C M; Hyde Park HS; Dorchester, MA; (S); JV Sftbl; Var Trk; Hon Roll; NHS; JV Bsktbl; Christian A Herter Memrl Schlrshp 86; Wellesly Coll; Pre-Med.

MORRISON, SEAN; Triton Regional HS; Salisbury, MA; (Y); Math Tm; JV Capt Bsbl; Var Socr; NHS; Tritn Ldrs Clb 86; Math Exam Sch Wnnr 86; Bowdoin; Comm.

MORRISON, TAMMY; Waltham HS; Waltham, MA; (Y); French Clb; JCL; Latin Clb; SADD; Hon Roll; Bentley Coll Sptlght Pgrm 85-86; Bus.

MORRISSETTE, CAROLYN; Uxbridge HS; Uxbridge, MA; (Y); 12/81; Sec Church Yth Grp; Hosp Aide; Library Aide; Stat Sftbl; Hon Roll; NHS; Pre-Law.

MORRISSETTE, JACLYN; Southbridge HS; Southbridge, MA; (Y); 18/145; Church Yth Grp; Intnl Clb; Yrbk Stf; Off Frsh Cls; Off Soph Cls; Off Jr Cls; Cheerleading; Fld Hcky; 4-H Awd; Hon Roll; Barry U; Med.

MORRISSETTE, LAURA; Bishop Feehan HS; Wrentham, MA; (Y); VP Church Yth Grp; Drama Clb; Spanish Clb; Chorus; School Musical; Lit Mag; NHS; Spanish NHS; Cert Achvt Syntax/Cmnctns 85; Theatre Arts.

MORRISSEY, KEITH; Taunton HS; Taunton, MA; (Y); 44/420; Aud/Vis; Church Yth Grp; Hosp Aide; JCL; Latin Clb; Office Aide; Var Bsbl; Capt Var Bsktbl; Hon Roll; Quinnipiac Scholar 86; All Schltc Bsktbl 86; All Schltc Bsbl 86; Quinnipiac Coll; Phys Thrpy.

MORRISSEY, NANCY; Silver Lake Regional HS; Pembroke, MA; (Y); 11/480; Pep Clb; Varsity Clb; Rep Frsh Cls; Rep Soph Cls; Rep Jr Cls; Cheerleading; Sftbl; Vllybl; High Hon Roll; Hon Roll; Stonehill Coll Acdmc Achvt 86; Stonehill Coll; Intl Rel.

MORSE, KERRI; Academy Of Notre Dame; Westford, MA; (Y); Art Clb; Cmnty Wkr; Hosp Aide; Office Aide; Nwsp Stf; Cit Awd; NHS; Japanese Clb 84-85; Jrnlsm Clb 85-86; Mod Miss Teen Pag MA 2nd Rnnr Up 85; Engl.

MORSE, PATRICK; Blackstone Valley Regional Tech; Sutton, MA; (Y); Church Yth Grp; Red Cross Aide; SADD; Trs Frsh Cls; Pres Jr Cls; Trs Soph Cls; Stu Cncl; Trk; Hon Roll; Stu Govt Rep, Chrmn Jr Cls Comm; Worcester Tech Inst; Engrng.

MORTENSEN, MALANA; Old Colony Reg Voc Tech; Acushnet, MA; (Y); VICA; Yrbk Stf; Var L Bsktbl; Var L Sftbl; Hon Roll; Jr NHS; Pres Schlr; Standard Times All Str Sftbl 85; Mayflower All Str Bsktbl 85; Elctrcl Engr.

MORTON, KEN; St Johns Prep Schl; Topsfield, MA; (Y); Boy Scts; Band; Jazz Band; Var Crs Cntry; Im Ftbl; Im Socr; Var Trk; Hon Roll; Ntl Merit SF; VA U; Arch.

MORTON, SARAH; Amherst Regional HS; Amherst, MA; (Y); Drama Clb; Chorus; School Musical; School Play; Capt Var Cheerleading; Hon Roll; Presdntl Acadmc Ftns Awd 86; Graphc Arts Awd 86; U Of MA Amherst; Engrng.

MOSCARITDLO, REMI; Swampscott HS; Swampscott, MA; (Y); 76/236; Variety Show; Yrbk Stf; Capt Cheerleading; Powder Puff Ftbl; Hon Roll; Varsty Ltr 84-87.

MOSCARITO, JOSEPH; Georgetown JR SR HS; Georgetown, MA; (Y); Ski Clb; Capt Bsbl; Capt L Ftbl; Capt L Ice Hcky; Hon Roll; Northeastern; Bus Admin.

MOSCARITOLO, KARA; Melrose HS; Melrose, MA; (Y); Cmnty Wkr; Hosp Aide; Band; Concert Band; Jazz Band; Mrchg Band; High Hon Roll; Hon Roll; NHS; Recog Awd Outstndga Chvt Itln 84; Natl Guild Piano Plyg Audtns 84; Biol.

MOSCHELLA, FELICIA; Newton North HS; Newton, MA; (Y); SADD; VP Temple Yth Grp; VP Stu Cncl; Im Coach Actv; Var Capt Fld Hcky; Var Sftbl; Var Trk; Phys Ed.

MOSCHELLA, MICHAEL; Newton North HS; Newton, MA; (Y); Am Leg Boys St; Var Ftbl; JV Lcrss; Var Trk; Var Wrstlng; Hon Roll; Pres Photo Clb 85.

MOSES, VIKKI-LYNN; West Roxbury HS; W Roxbury, MA; (S); 11/240; Library Aide; Nwsp Rptr; Yrbk Stf; Pres Sr Cls; Swmmng; High Hon Roll; Hon Roll; NHS; Nwsp Stf; Rep Soph Cls; Bently Coll; Bus Mgmt.

MOSHER, PETER; Dartmouth HS; Dartmouth, MA; (Y); 16/235; Key Clb; Political Wkr; Radio Clb; Nwsp Rptr; Yrbk Stf; JV Crs Cntry; JV Trk; Hon Roll; NHS; St Schlr; Betsy Tabor Schlrshp 86; U MA Amherst; Jrnlsm.

MOSMAN, DEBORAH; Holy Name Central Catholic HS; Grafton, MA; (Y); Church Yth Grp; Ski Clb; SADD; Nwsp Rptr; Nwsp Stf; Ed Yrbk Bus Mgr; Yrbk Rptr; Yrbk Stf; Lit Mag; Crs Cntry; Hnr Roll Awd; Achvmnt Engl; Achvmnt Relign; Colby Sawyer Coll; Chld Psychlg.

MOSS, ERIC; Concord-Carlisle HS; Concord, MA; (Y); VP SADD; JV Lcrss; High Hon Roll; Hon Roll; Chem & Engl & Geom Dept Awds; Elctrcl Engrng.

MOTA, ROBERT S; New Bedford HS; New Bedford, MA; (Y); 20/614; Am Leg Boys St; JA; JCL; Key Clb; SADD; VP Soph Cls; Trk; High Hon Roll; Hon Roll; Jr NHS; Presidents Schlrshp Of UNE 86; ILGWU Schlrshp 86; Silver Medal In NJCL 83; U Of New England; Physical Thpy.

MOTT, ROBERT K; Brakton Christian Regional HS; Carver, MA; (Y); Church Yth Grp; 4-H; Yrbk Phtg; Yrbk Stf; Pres Jr Cls; L Var Bsktbl; Var L Var L Trk; Hon Roll; ST Sci Fair Awd Wnnr 85; Chrstn Serv Brgd 3 Str Rnd 85; Yth Mnstr.

MOTTOLO, DAVID; Tewksbury Memorial HS; Tewksbury, MA; (Y); JCL; SADD; Im Ftbl; Var L Ice Hcky; Bus.

MOURADIAN, HOLLY; Winchester HS; Winchester, MA; (Y); Church Yth Grp; French Clb; Hosp Aide; Yrbk Stf.

MOUSSA, ABRAHAM; Northfield Mt Herman HS; Mount Hermon, MA; (Y); Ftbl; Trk; Wt Lftg; High Hon Roll; Hon Roll; Columbia U; Med.

MOUSSETTE, SALLY; Uxbridge HS; Uxbridge, MA; (Y); 14/84; Office Aide; Yrbk Phtg; Ed Yrbk Stf; Ed Lit Mag; Trs Frsh Cls; Off Sr Cls; Stu Cncl; Hon Roll; Sec NHS; Ntl Merit Ltr; Cmnctns.

MOW, KELVIN; Northfield Mount Hermon Schl; Briarcliff Manor, NY; (Y); Capt SADD; Band; Mrchg Band; Pep Band; Yrbk Phtg; JV Var Socr; Var Tennis; High Hon Roll; Foundr Indpndnt Study Snwboardng 85-86; Bst Drbblr Sccr/Rcrd Hldr; U Of CO; Math.

MOZDZIERZ, TREVOR; Quaboag Regional HS; West Brookfield, MA; (Y); Aud/Vis; JA; Library Aide; Pilot.

MUCCIARONE, GARY; Franklin HS; Franklin, MA; (Y); 82/225; Letterman Clb; Varsity Clb; JV Bsbl; Var Bsktbl; Im Socr; Var Tennis; Hon Roll; U MA; Elec Engrng.

MUCKENSTROM, ANN MARIE; Wachusett Regional HS; Sterling, MA; (Y); Camera Clb; Chess Clb; Church Yth Grp; Library Aide; Ski Clb; Yrbk Stf; Cheerleading; Crs Cntry; Socr; Sftbl; Interior Desgn.

MUELLER, GREGORY J; Concord-Carlisle HS; Concord, MA; (Y); 65/328; Church Yth Grp; Spanish Clb; Var Ftbl; Var Lcrss; NHS; Hist.

MUISE, DAWN; Gloucester HS; Gloucester, MA; (Y); 50/385; Am Leg Aux Girls St; Var Capt Cheerleading; Var Capt Pom Pon; Hon Roll; Prfct Atten Awd; Bay ST JC; Travl.

MUKHERJEE, LOPAMUDRA; Hamilton Country Day Schl; Attleboro, MA; (Y); 1/3; Library Aide; Math Clb; Math Tm; Chorus; Orch; Symp Band; High Hon Roll; Ntl Merit SF; Pres Schlr; MA ST Sci Fairs 3rd 83, 2nd 84; Prsdntl Cmmndtn Envir Issues 83, Scintfc Achvtmnet 83-84; Columbia U; Bio Med Engrng.

MUKSURIS, STELYIO; Father Matignon HS; Cambridge, MA; (S); 6/178; Drama Clb; Rep Soph Cls; Mgr Bsktbl; Im Mgr Vllybl; French Hon Soc; High Hon Roll; Hon Roll; NHS; Natl Sci Mrt Awd 84; Hellenic Coll; Prsthd.

MULARELLA, GLEN; Gardner HS; Gardner, MA; (Y); 5/160; Am Leg Boys St; JV Bsktbl; Var Tennis; Var Trk; High Hon Roll; NHS; Lmp Lrng Awd 85; Acdmc Dcthln 86; Insrnce.

MULL, KIM; Old Colony Reg Vo Tech HS; Rochester, MA; (Y); Dance Clb; Pep Clb; VICA; Yrbk Stf; Cheerleading; Pom Pon; Hon Roll; Spot Light Pgms Of Prjcts For High Lrng 85-86; Potential VICA Regnl Bronze Mdlst 86; Cosmetologist.

MULLANEY, ELIZABETH; Reading Memorial HS; Reading, MA; (Y); Church Yth Grp; Hosp Aide; Pep Clb; SADD; Variety Show; Yrbk Stf; Lit Mag; Mgr(s); Powder Puff Ftbl; Var Tennis; Accmplshmnts Publshd Reading Chronicle Nwsppr 86; U Of MA; Lbrl Arts & Sci.

MULLANEY, KAREN; Melrose HS; Melrose, MA; (Y); Cmnty Wkr; French Clb; Hosp Aide; School Musical; Yrbk Stf; Powder Puff Ftbl; Hon Roll; Excllnc Latin Awd 83; Smith Coll.

MULLANEY, MICHELLE; Hoosac Valley HS; Cheshire, MA; (Y); 42/149; Girl Scts; Pep Clb; School Play; Yrbk Stf; Cheerleading; Hon Roll; JR Prz Spkg 86; Med.

MULLANEY, STEPHEN; St Bernards Central Catholic HS; Leominster, MA; (S); 1/154; Am Leg Boys St; Pres Drama Clb; Nwsp Rptr; Stu Cncl; Ntl Merit Ltr; Voice Dem Awd; Boy Scts; Pres Latin Clb; Quiz Bowl; Ski Clb; U Of MA Amhrst Chnclrs Tlnt Awd-4 Yr Tuitn Schlrshp; Nrthestrn U Carl S Ell Presdntl Schlrshp; Cvl Engrng.

MULLEN, MARY; North Middlesex Regional HS; Townsend, MA; (Y); Yrbk Stf; Powder Puff Ftbl; Hon Roll; Elem Ed Tchr.

MULLIGAN, KATHLEEN; Kathleen New Bedford HS; New Bedford, MA; (Y); 110/547; Office Aide; Crs Cntry; Trk; Hon Roll; Vrsty Ltr Crss Cntry 85; Vrsty Ltr Wntr Track 85; Vrsty Ltr Sprg Trck 85; Southeastern MA U; Illustr.

MULLIGAN, KRISTEN; Fontbonne Acad; Hyde Park, MA; (Y); 20/179; Church Yth Grp; Hosp Aide; Math Tm; SADD; Trk; Hon Roll; NHS; Prfct Atten Awd; Cum Laude Natl Latin Exam 84; Acad Excllnc Music Lit 85; Hnrb Mntn Sci Fair 84; Peerldrshp Inst 86; Boston Coll; Pre Med.

MULLIGAN, RICHARD; Westwood HS; Westwood, MA; (Y); 56/212; SADD; Hon Roll; Prfct Atten Awd; Lwyr.

MULLIN, CAITLIN; Winchester HS; Winchester, MA; (Y); Church Yth Grp; Drama Clb; French Clb; Latin Clb; Rptr Nwsp Rptr; Rptr Nwsp Stf; French Hon Soc; May Milliken Bk Awd Soc Studies 86.

MULLOY, ROBERT A; East Bridgewater HS; E Bridgewater, MA; (Y); Am Leg Boys St; Boy Scts; Bsbl; Ftbl; Trk; Wt Lftg; Hon Roll; Crmnl Jstc.

MULROONEY, JONATHAN; Methuen HS; Methuen, MA; (Y); 2/335; Am Leg Boys St; Pres Church Yth Grp; VP Drama Clb; Model UN; SADD; Acpl Chr; Chorus; School Musical; School Play; Stage Crew; British Exchn Clb 83-84; Historical Conf 85-86; Chosen Opera 83-84.

MUMFORD, DAVID D; Duxbury HS; Duxbury, MA; (Y); Am Leg Boys St; Debate Tm; Nwsp Rptr; Im Bsktbl; Var L Crs Cntry; Var L Trk; Var DECA; Cit Awd; Hon Roll; NHS; Econmcs.

MUNRO JR, JOHN C; Gloucester HS; Gloucester, MA; (Y); ROTC; Band; Concert Band; Jazz Band; Mrchg Band; Pep Band; Yrbk Stf; Var Trk; Hon Roll; NHS; St Josephs Coll; Bio.

MURAD, ELAINE; St Clare HS; Roslindale, MA; (Y); 1/150; JA; Library Aide; Quiz Bowl; Nwsp Ed-Chief; Nwsp Stf; High Hon Roll; Hon Roll; NHS; Prfct Atten Awd; Val; Natl Lat Exam Slvr Mdl, Maxima Cum Laude Cert 83 & 85; Natl Lat Exam Magna Cum Laude Cert 86; Suffolk U; Soclgy.

MURCHIE, MARY BETH; St Bernards HS; Fitchburg, MA; (Y); Ski Clb; Spanish Clb; School Musical; Yrbk Ed-Chief; Var L Cheerleading; Hon Roll; NHS; Bentley Coll; Accntg.

MURDZIA, MICHAEL A; West Springfield HS; West Springfield, MA; (Y); Am Leg Boys St; Band; Rep Jr Cls; Rep Sr Cls; JV Bsktbl; JV Socr; Var Tennis; High Hon Roll; VP NHS; Spanish NHS; Engrng.

MURLEY, CHARLES A; Saugus HS; Saugus, MA; (Y); 6/260; Boys Clb Am; Chess Clb; Ed Lit Mag; Ntl Merit Ltr; Voice Dem Awd; Rnsslr Math & Sci Awd 85; Hon Ment MAML Math Olympd 85-86; U Of Lowell; Math.

MURPHY, BRIAN; Hingham HS; Hingham, MA; (Y); 17/348; Church Yth Grp; French Clb; Var Lcrss; Im Vllybl; Hon Roll.

MURPHY, CAROLYN; Holyoke HS; Holyoke, MA; (Y); 52/430; Latin Clb; Office Aide; Ski Clb; Spanish Clb; School Play; Nwsp Ed-Chief; Var Capt Fld Hcky; JV Var Sftbl; High Hon Roll; Hon Roll; Minn Radner Schlrshp 86; Wheaton Coll.

MURPHY, CHRISTOPHER; Bishop Connolly HS; Tiverton, RI; (Y); Computer Clb; Hon Roll; Coroner.

MURPHY, DANIEL; Danvers HS; Danvers, MA; (Y); 12/307; School Musical; School Play; High Hon Roll; Hon Roll; NHS; Spanish NHS; Spnsh Merit Diploma Exc Cert 84-86; Acad Theatre Role 85-86; Hist Conf Awd Cert 86; U Lowell; Comp Sci.

MURPHY, DANIEL; Matignon HS; Cambridge, MA; (Y); Rep Stu Cncl; VP Ftbl; Var Capt Golf; Var Socr; French Hon Soc; NHS; Ntl Merit Ltr; Harvard U; Bus.

MURPHY, DAVID P; Walpole HS; Walpole, MA; (Y); 28/270; Var Capt Bsbl; Var Capt Ftbl; Var Trk; Hon Roll; NHS; Natl Ftbl Fndtn & Hall Of Fame Schlr/Ath 86; Holy Cross Coll Ftbl Schlrshp 86; Holy Cross; Econ.

MURPHY, DENNIS J; Noble & Greenough Schl; Canton, MA; (Y); SADD; School Play; Yrbk Bus Mgr; Yrbk Stf; Ntl Merit SF.

MURPHY, EDWARD; Quincy HS; Quincy, MA; (Y); JA; SADD; Bsbl; Tennis; Hon Roll; Northeastern; Acctng.

MURPHY, IRENE; Braintree HS; Braintree, MA; (Y); 38/442; Church Yth Grp; Sec SADD; Off Frsh Cls; Off Soph Cls; Off Jr Cls; Stu Cncl; Var L Bsktbl; Var L Socr; Var L Sftbl; High Hon Roll; Physcl Thrpy.

MURPHY, JONATHAN; Saint Johns HS; Worcester, MA; (Y); 84/273; Aud/Vis; French Clb; Model UN; PAVAS; Concert Band; Orch; Symp Band; Nwsp Stf; Yrbk Stf; Lit Mag; Syracuse U; Comm.

MURPHY, JOSEPH; Boston College HS; Milton, MA; (Y); 148/295; Cmnty Wkr; Debate Tm; Key Clb; Political Wkr; ROTC; Ski Clb; SADD; Im Bsktbl; Im JV Ftbl; Im JV Swmmng; Ftbl Var Ltr; Bsktbl Announcer; US Naval Acad; Engrng.

MURPHY, KATHLEEN; Auburn HS; Auburn, MA; (Y); Trs Church Yth Grp; Cmnty Wkr; Band; Var Bsktbl; Var JV Fld Hcky; JV Sftbl; High Hon Roll; NHS; SADD; Concert Band; Captn Chrch Vlybl Leag 85-86; Co Captn All Star Sftbl 84; Ed.

MURPHY, KELI-JO; Braintree HS; Braintree, MA; (Y); Sftbl; Vllybl; Spanish NHS; Frgn Lang.

MURPHY, KELLY; Bishop Feehan HS; Wrentham, MA; (Y); Sec Pres 4-H; Sec Service Clb; Band; Concert Band; Mrchg Band; Cit Awd; French Hon Soc; 4-H Awd; High Hon Roll; NHS; Math Awd 85.

MURPHY, KERRY; Athol HS; Athol, MA; (Y); Model UN; Im Trk; Hesser Coll; Bus Adm.

MURPHY, KEVIN; Lynnfield HS; Lynnfield, MA; (Y); Church Yth Grp; JA; Band; Yrbk Stf; JV Bsbl; JV Bsktbl; Var Ftbl; Hon Roll; U Of VT; Electrical Engineerin.

MURPHY, KIMBERLY; Bedford HS; Billerica, MA; (Y); Aud/Vis; Church Yth Grp; Cmnty Wkr; Girl Scts; Band; Chorus; Yrbk Stf; Lit Mag; Bsbl; Bowling; Dllrs Schlrs 86; Vrsty Ltr Stu Athltc Trng 86; Salem ST Coll; Bio.

MURPHY, MARY; Arlington HS; Arlington, MA; (Y); DECA; Hosp Aide; Office Aide; Teachers Aide; Drm Mjr(t); Yrbk Stf; Twrlr; Distrbtv Educ Awd Dist Comptn 3rd Plc Finc & Crdt 86; Northeastern; Med Adm.

MURPHY, MAURA; Cathedral HS; Springfield, MA; (Y); Hosp Aide; Intnl Clb; Model UN; Political Wkr; Chorus; Nwsp Sprt Ed; Var Crs Cntry; Var Trk; Hstry.

MURPHY, MAUREEN; Silver Lake Regional HS; Plympton, MA; (Y); 54/520; Drama Clb; 4-H; Key Clb; Office Aide; VP Spanish Clb; Mrchg Band; School Play; Yrbk Sprt Ed; Rep Frsh Cls; Actng Awd Regnl MA Drama Fstvl 86; Stonehill Coll; Lbrl Arts.

MURPHY, MELISSA; North Quincy HS; Quincy, MA; (Y); 16/400; Hosp Aide; Spanish Clb; Yrbk Stf; Lit Mag; Jr NHS; NHS; Spanish NHS; Distnctn 83-85.

MURPHY, MIKE; Holyoke Catholic HS; Holyoke, MA; (Y); 10/142; Am Leg Boys St; Drama Clb; Quiz Bowl; Band; School Musical; Trs Jr Cls; Rep Stu Cncl; High Hon Roll; Trs NHS; Ntl Merit Ltr; Phys Sci Awd 83-84.

MURPHY, PATRICIA A; Belmont HS; Belmont, MA; (Y); 35/261; Church Yth Grp; Debate Tm; VP JA; Latin Clb; Nwsp Rptr; Ed Lit Mag; Socr; Trk; Hon Roll; NHS; Belmont PTA Scholar 86; MA Girls ST Socr Tm 85; Boston Coll; Pre-Law.

MURPHY, PAUL J; Marian HS; Framingham, MA; (Y); Boy Scts; Crs Cntry; Trk; High Hon Roll; Hon Roll; NHS; NEDT Awd; Sci Fair Fnlst Schl/Sec/St; Bus.

MURPHY, ROBERT A; Austin Preparatory Schl; Medford, MA; (Y); 60/140; Political Wkr; Ski Clb; Hon Roll; Ftbl; U Lowell; Mech Engr.

MURPHY, SARAH; Burlington HS; Burlington, MA; (Y); 53/314; GAA; Hosp Aide; Red Cross Aide; Varsity Clb; Rep Soph Cls; Var L Cheerleading; Im Powder Puff Ftbl; Var L Tennis; Hon Roll; Vrsty Ltr Ftbl & Bsktbl Cheerg & Tennis; Certf Red Crss CPR & JR Lfsvr; Alcohol Ed Prog; Nrsg.

MURPHY, SEAN; Concord-Carlisle HS; Carlisle, MA; (Y); AFS; Boy Scts; Rep Soph Cls; JV Tennis; Hon Roll; 2nd Degree Black Belt In Karate 83.

MURPHY, STEPHANIE A; Silver Lake Regional HS; Halifax, MA; (Y); 99/458; Cmnty Wkr; French Clb; Spanish Clb; SADD; Nwsp Rptr; Yrbk Bus Mgr; Rep Soph Cls; Var Capt Crs Cntry; Var Capt Trk; Hon Roll; Halifax Prnt Tchr Assn Scholar 86; Halifax Grls Sprts Lg Scholar 86; Halifax Kiwanis Clb Scholar 86; Boston U; TV Cmmnctns.

MURRAY, AMY; Westford Acad; Westford, MA; (Y); Dance Clb; Pres Drama Clb; Chorus; School Musical; School Play; Symp Band; Hon Roll; Ntl Merit Ltr; Church Yth Grp; French Clb; H O Brien Ldrshp Awd 84-85; Frshmn & JR English Awd 83-86; Stdnt Of Mnth 83-84; Thtr.

MURRAY, BETH; Arlington Catholic HS; Waltham, MA; (Y); Spanish Clb; Var Cheerleading; JV Crs Cntry; JV Sftbl; Var Trk; Hon Roll; Chld Psych.

MURRAY, BETH; Franklin HS; Franklin, MA; (Y); Cmnty Wkr; Latin Clb; Varsity Clb; Bsktbl; Socr; Sftbl; Hon Roll; Achvt Acad 85; Med.

MURRAY, CAROLYN; Fairhaven HS; Fairhaven, MA; (Y); 1/167; AFS; French Clb; Key Clb; Varsity Clb; Val; VFW Awd; Voice Dem Awd; Math Tm; Office Aide; Service Clb; Commwlth Schlr 85-86; Walter D Wood Mem Awd Hist 86; Bristol Cty Ed Assoc Recgntn Awd 86; Smith Coll; Gov.

MURRAY, DANIEL EVAN; Lawrence Acad; Groton, MA; (Y); JCL; Church Choir; Bsbl; Bsktbl; Socr; High Hon Roll; Hon Roll; Amnesty Intl; Cum Laude Soc 85-86.

MURRAY, GEORGE; St Marys Regional HS; Lynn, MA; (Y); Boy Scts; Var L Ftbl; Var L Socr; Var L Trk; Bus.

MURRAY, GRANT A; Framingham North HS; Framington, MA; (Y); 19/400; Pres Chess Clb; Band; Hon Roll; NHS; Ntl Merit SF; Slvr Mdl-Ntl Latin; AHSME Awd; CA Inst Of Tech; Thrtcl Pyscs.

MURRAY, JEFF; Melrose HS; Boston, MA; (Y); 124/395; Orch; Rep Jr Cls; Pres Sr Cls; Var L Bsbl; Var L Golf; Hon Roll.

MURRAY, MARLENE; Hingham HS; Hingham, MA; (Y); 60/400; Drama Clb; French Clb; Yrbk Stf; JV Var Cheerleading; AFS; Church Yth Grp; Cmnty Wkr; Girl Scts; Library Aide; Thesps; Psych.

MURRAY, MICHAEL; Boston College HS; Milton, MA; (Y); 95/310; Boy Scts; French Clb; Pres JA; Key Clb; Math Tm; Trs Ski Clb; Var Crs Cntry; JV Swmmng; Var Tennis; Hon Roll.

MURRAY, SUSAN; Holyoke Catholic HS; Holyoke, MA; (Y); Cmnty Wkr; Drama Clb; Latin Clb; Math Clb; Spanish Clb; SADD; Pres Latin Club; Georgetown U; Psych.

MURRAY, SUSAN; Swampscott HS; Swampscott, MA; (Y); 43/238; Church Yth Grp; French Clb; Hosp Aide; Hon Roll; Intl Foods Achvt Awd 86; Intl Hnr Soc Hist 86; U Of MA Amherst; Bus.

MUSCI, TODD; Marian Hill C C HS; Charlton City, MA; (Y); School Musical; Nwsp Rptr; Nwsp Stf; JV Bsktbl; Var Socr; Hon Roll; NHS; Excllnc Spnsh I 84; Engrng.

MUSI, DIANE M; Winthrop HS; Winthrop, MA; (Y); 2/216; Math Tm; Powder Puff Ftbl; Co-Capt Sftbl; Co-Capt Tennis; DAR Awd; Elks Awd; High Hon Roll; Pres NHS; Sal; Bst All Arnd Grl 85-86; Coaches Awds Tnns & Sftbl; Dartmouth Coll.

MUSINSKI, KEITH; Aqawam HS; Agawam, MA; (Y); AFS; Chorus; School Musical; Variety Show; Hon Roll; Arch.

MUTHER, CHRISTOPHER; Athol HS; Athol, MA; (Y); Church Yth Grp; Trs Debate Tm; Radio Clb; Ski Clb; Band; Jazz Band; School Musical; Nwsp Stf; Stu Cncl; Trk; Hnrb Mntn Sci Fair 84; Law.

MYEROW, DEAN; Swampscott HS; Swampscott, MA; (Y); 17/232; Model UN; Im Political Wkr; Ski Clb; Nwsp Stf; JV Bsktbl; Var Socr; Hon Roll; NHS; Delg Arab-Israeli Conflict Series 86; Young Poltcn Commonwlth JFK Libr 86; VP Meteorlgy Clb 86; U MA Amherst; Bus Mktng.

MYERS, LISA; Bellingham Memorial HS; Bellingham, MA; (Y); Art Clb; Church Yth Grp; Hosp Aide; SADD; School Play; Stage Crew; Hon Roll; Pres Phys Ftns Awd 84; Framingham ST Coll; Lab.

MYERS, MICHAEL; Fairhaven HS; Fairhaven, MA; (Y); Ski Clb; Spanish Clb; VP Jr Cls; JV Var Bsbl; JV Bsktbl; Var Capt Ftbl; Var Trk; NHS; Bridgewater ST Coll; Phys Ed.

MYERS, ROBIN; Hoosac Valley HS; Adams, MA; (Y); 33/149; SADD; Yrbk Rptr; Yrbk Stf; Trs Jr Cls; Trs Sr Cls; Var L Sftbl; JV Capt Vllybl; Cit Awd; Hon Roll; Prfct Atten Awd; OK U; Intl Pub Rtlns.

MYERS, WILLIAM; Revere HS; Revere, MA; (Y); Church Yth Grp; Cmnty Wkr; Key Clb; Math Clb; Math Tm; SADD; Var Bsktbl; Coach Actv; Im Ftbl; Score Keeper; Hnbl Mntn Peace Comm Essy Cntst 86; Mst Unslfsh Plyr Brookln Invitl Bsktbl Tourn 84; Boston Coll; Pltcl Sci.

MYERSON, LORY; Natick HS; Natick, MA; (Y); 13/443; French Clb; SADD; Rep Frsh Cls; Rep Soph Cls; Rep Jr Cls; Rep Sr Cls; Rep Stu Cncl; JV Vllybl; High Hon Roll; Hon Roll; Middlebury Coll.

MYERSON, PETER; Marblehead HS; Marblehead, MA; (Y); Capt Var Bsbl; Capt Var Bsktbl; Capt Var Socr; Hon Roll; MVP Bsbl 86; Salem News & Lynn Item Nwsp All Star Bsbl 86; Stu Ldrshp Cncl; Bus.

NABI, ROBIN L; Sharon HS; Sharon, MA; (Y); 1/199; VP Drama Clb; Library Aide; Varsity Clb; Nwsp Sprt Ed; Nwsp Stf; Cmnty Wkr; Var Crs Cntry; Val; French Clb; Red Cross Aide; 1st Pl Framingham ST Hist Conf; U Of Penn Bk Awd; All Star Awd Drama Fstvl; Harvard; Corp Law.

NADEAU, DAVID; Westfield HS; Westfield, MA; (Y); 10/360; Church Yth Grp; Y-Teens; Var L Bsktbl; Var L Ftbl; Var L Trk; Wt Lftg; Hon Roll; Jr NHS; NHS; Bsktbl Coach YMCA 84-86.

NADEAU, SUZANNE; Methuen High HS; Methuen, MA; (Y); Trs Church Yth Grp; Dance Clb; Model UN; Variety Show; Hon Roll.

NADER, KIM; Our Lady Of Nazareth Acad; Andover, MA; (Y); French Clb; Hosp Aide; Teachers Aide; Stage Crew; Var Cheerleading; Var Socr; Hon Roll; Engrng.

NAFFAH, MICHAEL; Methuen HS; Methuen, MA; (Y); 72/333; Intnl Clb; SADD; Pres Soph Cls; Rep Trs Stu Cncl; Pol Sci.

NAFTOLY, ROBERT A; Dartmouth HS; N Dartmouth, MA; (Y); 32/265; Key Clb; Temple Yth Grp; Varsity Clb; Var L Tennis; U MA Engrng Schl; Civl Engrng.

NAGAI, BUNSAKU; Berkshire Schl; Agana, GU; (Y); 4/127; Intnl Clb; Math Tm; Band; Chorus; Concert Band; Mrchg Band; Orch; Socr; Trk.

NAGLE, DAVID A; Malden HS; Malden, MA; (Y); 4/410; Am Leg Boys St; Political Wkr; Band; Ed Nwsp Stf; Pres Jr Cls; Pres Sr Cls; Mgr JV Ice Hcky; NHS; Voice Dem Awd; MA Yth Ldrshp Semnr 85; Hist Tchr.

NAGLE, REBECCA; Notre Dame Acad; Hanover, MA; (Y); 50/100; Debate Tm; Ski Clb; Stage Crew; Off Stu Cncl; Cheerleading; Capt Socr; Trk; French Hon Soc; Hon Roll; Nrsng.

NAGLE, TRICIA; Haerhill HS; Haverhill, MA; (Y); 39/400; Latin Clb; Yrbk Stf; Cheerleading; Trk; High Hon Roll; Hon Roll; NHS.

NAGY, KIMBERLY F; Ludlow HS; Belchertown, MA; (Y); 22/279; Band; Concert Band; Jazz Band; Mrchg Band; Orch; Pep Band; Yrbk Stf; Hon Roll; Jr NHS; U Of MA; Psych.

NAHIL, KAITLIN; Our Lady Of Nazareth Acad; North Andover, MA; (Y); 29/74; Drama Clb; Intnl Clb; Science Clb; Ski Clb; Spanish Clb; SADD; Chorus; School Musical; School Play; Stage Crew; Bus.

NAIDUCCI, JOSEPH; Franklin HS; Franklin, MA; (Y); Wrstlng; Hon Roll; Woodwrkng 83-86; Bus Mgmt.

NAJARIAM, HOLLY; Salem HS; Salem, MA; (Y); Science Clb; SADD; Concert Band; Mrchg Band; Orch; Rep Stu Cncl; Var Bsktbl; JV Trk; Hon Roll; YMCA Yth Gov Stu 84.

NAJJAR, DEBORAH M; Westwood HS; Westwood, MA; (Y); 21/212; Pres Debate Tm; Chorus; School Musical; Yrbk Stf; Lit Mag; Var L Swmmng; Hon Roll; NHS; Church Yth Grp; School Play; Dbl Quartet 86-87; Outstndng Awd In Music 86; Mgmt.

NALE, JOHN; Tanatasqua HS; Brookfield, MA; (Y); JV Bsktbl; JV Ftbl; Social Sci.

NALI, LEIGH; Silver Lake Regional HS; Kingston, MA; (Y); 74/500; Ski Clb; Im Bsktbl; Var Ftbl; Var Tennis; Im Vllybl; Hon Roll; MA ST Bwlg Champ 16 & Under 85, 13 & Under 82 & 83; Acctg.

NANIS, SOPHIA; Salem HS; Salem, MA; (Y); Church Yth Grp; Church Choir; Var Cheerleading; Var Trk; Hon Roll; Spanish NHS; Endicott; Trvl.

NAPIER, CHARLES J; Old Colony Regional Vocational Tech; Carver, MA; (Y); Church Yth Grp; VICA; Var L Bsbl; Var Capt Bsktbl; Var L Socr; Hon Roll; Comp Sci.

NARDI, KIM; Agawam HS; Feeding Hills, MA; (Y); 1/300; Cmnty Wkr; Intnl Clb; Library Aide; Spanish Clb; Teachers Aide; Chorus; High Hon Roll; NHS; Spanish NHS; Gnrl Crghtn Abrhms Schlrshp 85-86; Bus.

NARDONE, MARK A; Lynn English HS; Lynn, MA; (Y); 13/336; Ski Clb; Yrbk Sprt Ed; High Hon Roll; Hon Roll; NHS; Outstndng Acdmc Achvmnt Awd 86; U Of MA; Engr.

NASH, JENNIFER; Concord Carlisle HS; Concord, MA; (Y); 77/327; Cmnty Wkr; Office Aide; Political Wkr; Trs Science Clb; Lit Mag; Hon Roll; Co-Fndr Tres Sci Fctn Fntsy Clb 84-86; Dprtmntl Awd Cmmnty Srv 85; Blgy.

NASIOS, PENNY; Cardinal Spellman HS; Holbrook, MA; (Y); Church Yth Grp; School Musical; Lit Mag; Var Cheerleading; Var Trk; Ed.

NASON, DANIEL F; St Bernards Central Catholic HS; Westminster, MA; (Y); Am Leg Boys St; Camera Clb; Drama Clb; Ski Clb; Chorus; Nwsp Stf; Yrbk Stf; Wntwrth Inst Tech; Engrng.

NASON, SHERYL; Sharon HS; Sharon, MA; (Y); Spanish Clb; Sec Frsh Cls; Cheerleading; Var Tennis; US JR Ntl Frstyl Ski Team 85-86; US ST Ntl Wmns Arlst Chmpn 86; US Wrld Cup Frstyl Ski Team 86-87.

NASSER, DAVID; Methuen HS; Methuen, MA; (Y); Intnl Clb; Model UN; SADD; School Musical; JV Bsktbl; Var Ftbl; Var Tennis; Var Trk; Hon Roll; Pre-Law.

NATALE, DANIELLE; West Roxbury HS; Roslindale, MA; (S); 1/250; Hon Roll; Pres NHS; Church Yth Grp; Hnrs Pgm 80-86; Boston U; Pre-Med.

NATALE, WILLIAM; Somerville HS; Somerville, MA; (Y); #25 In Class; Ski Clb; Chorus; Diving; Ice Hcky; Tennis; Wt Lftg; Hon Roll; U MA Amherst; Bus Admn.

NATHAN, RUSSELL; Northfield Mt Hermon HS; S Orange, NJ; (Y); Latin Clb; Rep Jr Cls; Var Mgr(s); Mgr Trk; DNA For A Clb; Arch.

NATOLA, LAURIE; Saugus HS; Saugus, MA; (Y); 4/246; Cmnty Wkr; Spanish Clb; Stu Cncl; Bsktbl; Socr; High Hon Roll; Jr NHS; NHS; Pres Schlr; Physcs Awd 85; Calculus Awd 86; Babson Coll; Fin.

NAUGHTON, TRISHA; Marian HS; Ashland, MA; (Y); 49/187; Church Yth Grp; Cmnty Wkr; Hosp Aide; Spanish Clb; SADD; Yrbk Stf; Lit Mag; Cheerleading; Crs Cntry; Hon Roll; Nrsng.

NAUMANN, DAWN; Bartlett HS; Orchad Park, NY; (Y); 32/167; Ski Clb; Spanish Clb; Crs Cntry; Trk; Hon Roll; FNA; Town Spring Sccr Leag 85; Psych.

NAVAROLI JR, THOMAS J; Leicester HS; Cherry Valley, MA; (Y); Math Tm; School Play; Yrbk Ed-Chief; Yrbk Phtg; Bsbl; Socr; Tennis; Ldrshp Svc Awd 86; Contrbutng Most Cls 86; Most Spirited 86; Nichols Coll; Acctng.

NAWN, CHRISTOPHER D; Arlinton HS; Arlington, MA; (Y); Aud/Vis; Boys Clb Am; Church Yth Grp; Cmnty Wkr; Library Aide; Radio Clb; SADD; Ice Hcky; Suffol U; Law.

NAZARIO, CARLA; High Schl Of Commerce; Indian Orchard, MA; (S); French Clb; GAA; Library Aide; Yrbk Stf; Socr; French Hon Soc; Hon Roll; Eng,Sci; STCC Coll.

NEARY, LORI; Reading Memorial HS; Reading, MA; (Y); 57/325; Dance Clb; Rep Frsh Cls; Var Trk; High Hon Roll; Hon Roll; Rdng Coll Clb Schlrshp 86; Unsng Athlt Awd 86; Schlrshp Achvt Awd 85 & 86; Bentley Coll; Mktg.

NEARY, PATRICIA; Dighton-Rehoboth HS; Rehoboth, MA; (Y); 56/227; Church Yth Grp; Cmnty Wkr; Dance Clb; DECA; 4-H; FBLA; Hosp Aide; JA; Library Aide; Office Aide; Burdett Schl; Mrktg.

NEELY, MAURA; Bishop Feehan HS; N Attleboro, MA; (Y); 6/240; Hosp Aide; Drill Tm; Mrchg Band; Trk; Var Capt Twrlr; High Hon Roll; Hon Roll; NHS; Pres Schlr; Spanish NHS; Spnsh Natl Hnr Soc Gold Mdl 86; Schlrshp NEMA 86; Sociology Awd 86; Wellesley Coll; Lang.

NEGRON, MARVIN; Gardner HS; Gardner, MA; (Y); 43/150; Chess Clb; Var L Bsktbl; Var Crs Cntry; Var L Ftbl; Var L Trk; Prshmn Achvt Awd 84; Sphmr Athltc Achvt Awd 85; Wachosett Lg All Strs Trk 86; Psych.

NEIDICH, PAUL I; Leominster HS; Leominster, MA; (Y); 19/305; Am Leg Boys St; Temple Yth Grp; Stage Crew; Nwsp Rptr; Rptr Frsh Cls; Var Capt Swmmng; Hon Roll; NHS; Ntl Merit Ltr; Colby Coll.

NELSON, BRIAN; Bishop Feehan HS; Plainville, MA; (Y); Yrbk Stf; Hon Roll; Var L Bsbl; Var L Bsktbl; SMC II 1st Tm All Star Sun Chrncl 1st Bsbl 86, SMC I Bsktbl 86; Bus Adm.

NELSON, BRIAN D; East Bridgewater HS; East Bridgewater, MA; (Y); Am Leg Boys St; Boy Scts; Church Yth Grp; Rep Jr Cls; Var Crs Cntry; Hon Roll; NHS; Cert Acad Achvt Biol, Anc Hstry 84; Cert Acad Achvt Chem 85; Ocnogrphy.

NELSON, CHRISTINE; Dover/Sherborn Regional HS; Dover, MA; (Y); AFS; Church Yth Grp; Debate Tm; Exploring; Concert Band; Pep Band; School Musical; JV Var Fld Hcky; L Trk; Hon Roll; AFS Exchng Stu Fnlnd 86; ME Islnd Ecolgy Pgm 85; Ptry Pblshd Runes 84; Arch.

NELSON, CHRISTOPHER; Natick HS; Natick, MA; (Y); Boys Clb Am; Boy Scts; Church Yth Grp; JA; Letterman Clb; Ski Clb; Varsity Clb; Coach Actv; Ftbl; Trk; Vrsty Ftbl Vrsty Wrstlng 85; U Of MA; Architectal Landscpng.

NELSON, CRAIG JOSEPH; Cathedral HS; Chicopee, MA; (Y); 53/455; Boy Scts; VP Camera Clb; VP JA; Model UN; Nwsp Phtg; Yrbk Phtg; Off Frsh Cls; Rep Sr Cls; Var L Trk; Hon Roll; Pres Acdmc Fit Awd 86; 3 Yr Nvy ROTC Schlrshp 86; MA Schlrshp 86; U MA; Chem Engrng.

NELSON, DEBORAH LEE; Holy Name C C HS; Worcester, MA; (Y); Office Aide; Bus.

NELSON, DIANE C; Watertown HS; Watertown, MA; (Y); 7/236; VP Drama Clb; Thesps; School Play; Variety Show; Hon Roll; NCTE Awd; NHS; Ntl Merit Ltr; Voice Dem Awd; Exchng Stu Australia 84; Cum Laud 85-86; Columbia Coll NY; Intl Rltns.

NELSON, KAREN; King Philip HS; Plainville, MA; (Y); 41/187; Church Yth Grp; Girl Scts; Intnl Clb; Church Choir; Stu Cncl; High Hon Roll; Hon Roll; JC Awd; NHS; Hugh O Brien Foundtn 84; Bristol CC; Flrl Dsgn.

NELSON, KARIN; Marlborough HS; Marlboro, MA; (Y); 4/272; Pep Clb; Ski Clb; Yrbk Stf; Mgr(s); Trk; Elks Awd; High Hon Roll; NHS; Pres Schlr; Rotary Awd; Faculty Awds Exc Sci Frgn Lang 83; Exc Sec,Eng 84-85; Providence Coll; Math.

NELSON, LAURIE; St Mary Regional HS; Lynn, MA; (Y); #4 In Class; Hosp Aide; Teachers Aide; Nwsp Rptr; High Hon Roll; Hon Roll; NHS; 3rd, 4th & 5th Schlrshp Rnks 83-86; Nrthestrn U; Arntcl Engr.

NELSON, LORI; Melrose HS; Melrose, MA; (Y); 116/400; Drama Clb; Pep Clb; Chorus; Color Guard; School Musical; School Play; Socr; Swmmng; Best M&M Rifle 85; Superior All Star Perfrmr M/A 86; Blue Bonnet Bowl TX 86; U Lowell; Liberal Arts.

NELSON, MARGARET C; Northfield Mount Hermon HS; Middlebury, VT; (Y); Church Yth Grp; Chorus; Church Choir; Orch; Var Swmmng; Var Trk; Hon Roll; Wlsly Coll; Math.

NELSON, MISTI; Hyde Park HS; Roxbury, MA; (S); Church Yth Grp; Cmnty Wkr; Drama Clb; Hosp Aide; JA; Spanish Clb; Chorus; Church Choir; Variety Show; Sftbl; Ed Excl Awd 85; Wellesley Coll; Arch.

NEMECZKY, DORIS; Natick HS; Natick, MA; (Y); 43/399; Church Yth Grp; Yrbk Stf; Var Crs Cntry; JV Capt Socr; Var Capt Trk; Engrng.

NESBITT, CAITLIN; Classical HS; Springfield, MA; (Y); 45/389; JA; Key Clb; Hon Roll; Jr NHS; MA Bd Of Regnts Schlrshp 86; ACE 86; U Of MA; Zllgy.

NEUBER, SUSAN; Walpole HS; Walpole, MA; (Y); 4/273; JCL; Latin Clb; Spanish Clb; SADD; Var L Bsktbl; Var L Fld Hcky; Hon Roll; NHS; Ntl Merit Ltr; Pres Schlr; All Star Fld Hcky Goalie & All Schltc Goalie 84-86; Odd Fllws Schlr 86; Dollars Schlrs Scholar 86; Mc Gill U; Pre-Med.

NEUSCHATZ, STEPHANIE; Lunenburg HS; Lunenberg, MA; (Y); Civic Clb; Ski Clb; Sec SADD; Variety Show; Yrbk Phtg; Fld Hcky; Trk; High Hon Roll.

NEVALA, TOM; Maynard HS; Maynard, MA; (Y); 3/100; Am Leg Boys St; Band; Var L Ftbl; Var L Golf; Bausch & Lomb Sci Awd; Hon Roll; JP Sousa Awd; NHS; Church Yth Grp; Chorus; Schlr Boy Athlt 86; Hrvrd Bk Awd 85; Frncs Qunt Cadde Schlrshp 86; U Of Notre Dame; Aero Engr.

NEVES, DONNA; East Longmeadow HS; E Longmeadow, MA; (Y); 5/200; Intnl Clb; School Play; Variety Show; Yrbk Phtg; Pres Sr Cls; Off Stu Cncl; Var Socr; Powder Puff Ftbl; Wt Lftg; High Hon Roll; Hugh O Brien Ldrsyp Awd 85; Stu Advsry Comm 85; E L Comm Theater Grp 80-86; Med.

NEVES, MARIA; Madison Park HS; Boston, MA; (Y); Teachers Aide; School Play; Rep Stu Cncl; JV Socr; Hon Roll; Prfct Atten Awd; Cert Merit Engl 82; Hnr Roll 83 & 84; Prfct Attndnc Awd 83-85; U MA Boston; Psych.

NEVEU, MANDA; Holyoke Catholic HS; Granby, MA; (Y); 4/150; English Clb; French Clb; Math Clb; Service Clb; Speech Tm; Teachers Aide; Band; Lit Mag; High Hon Roll; NHS; Exclinc Physcl Sci Frnch I 83-84; Exclinc Frnch II Relgn Awd 84-85; Engl Lit Awd Chem Awd 85-86.

NEVILLE, SHEILA M; Wayland HS; Roxbury, MA; (Y); Church Yth Grp; Dance Clb; Drama Clb; Spanish Clb; CAPA Art Awd; Dorothy Hamill Awd; Arts Inst Of Boston; Fshn Dsgn.

NEVINS, MARC; Northfield Mount Herman Schl; Swampscott, MA; (Y); Ski Clb; Temple Yth Grp; Lit Mag; JV Bsbl; JV Socr; Hon Roll.

NEVUE, PAT; Quaboag Regional HS; Warren, MA; (Y); Boy Scts; Church Yth Grp; Stat Bsktbl; JV Crs Cntry; Var JV Score Keeper; High Hon Roll; Hon Roll; Mech Engrng.

NEWBEGIN, TRACEY; Dracut HS; Dracut, MA; (Y); Hosp Aide; Office Aide; Acpl Chr; Nwsp Stf; Yrbk Stf; Soph Cls; Sr Cls; Bsbl; Bsktbl; JV Mgr(s); Lukemia Typthn 85; Boston Coll; Bus.

NEWBERN, ANNA; North Reading HS; N Reading, MA; (Y); Church Yth Grp; Math Tm; Yrbk Ed-Chief; Trs Stu Cncl; Var Capt Tennis; Var Vllybl; High Hon Roll; NHS; Bus.

NEWBERRY, JOHN; Pope John XXIII; Chelsea, MA; (Y); 27/214; Bentley Coll; Bus.

NEWCOMER, MARY; Leicester HS; Leicester, MA; (S); 2/115; Trs Church Yth Grp; Drama Clb; Latin Clb; Math Tm; Ski Clb; School Play; Stat Bsktbl; JV Var Cheerleading; JV Fld Hcky; Var Score Keeper; Coll Of William/Mary; Psychtry.

NEWCOMER, PATRICIA; Leicester HS; Leicester, MA; (S); 1/102; Sec Church Yth Grp; Co-Capt Math Tm; Band; Yrbk Stf; Var Bsktbl; Var Fld Hcky; Capt Tennis; Pres NHS; Century III Ldrshp Schl Wnr 85; Hugh O Brien Yth Fndtn Semnr 83; Natl Conf Of Christns & Jews 84; Engrng.

NEWHALL, BRIAN; Whitinsville Christian HS; Uxbridge, MA; (Y); 6/23; Band; Chorus; Church Choir; School Play; JV Bsktbl; Hon Roll; NHS; Moody Bible Inst; Chrstn Educ.

NEWHALL, ROBERT; Hopedale JR SR HS; Hopedale, MA; (Y); Church Yth Grp; Debate Tm; Drama Clb; Pep Clb; Science Clb; SADD; Teachers Aide; Chorus; School Play; Yrbk Stf; Ntl Hnr Scty Awd 82; U MA; Wldlf Mngr.

NEWMAN, CHERYL; Athol HS; S Royalston, MA; (Y); Library Aide; Model UN; Hon Roll; NHS; U Of MA; Acctng.

NEWMAN, DAVID A; Oakmont Regional HS; Ashburnham, MA; (Y); 6/137; Am Leg Boys St; Boy Scts; Pres Church Yth Grp; School Play; Yrbk Stf; High Hon Roll; Math Tm; Im Socr; Eagle Sct Awd 86; Biochem.

NEWMAN, ERIC; Sharon HS; Sharon, MA; (Y); Computer Clb; JCL; Math Tm; Spanish Clb; Ftbl; High Hon Roll; NHS; Rensselaer Polytechnc Inst Awd Exclinc Math & Sci; Spnsh & Latn Stdnt Mnth; Engrng.

NEWMAN, VANESSA; Haverhill HS; Bradford, MA; (Y); 35/400; Cmnty Wkr; Hosp Aide; High Hon Roll; NHS; Italn Clb Awds; Cls Of 1942 Awd; Prsnl Achvt Awd; Indpndnt Stud For Psych; Clark U; Psych.

NEWTON, JAMES; Burlington HS; Burlington, MA; (Y); 46/320; Church Yth Grp; JA; Ed Yrbk Stf; Rep Sr Cls; Rep Stu Cncl; PTSO Schlrshp 86; Merrimack College.

NEWTON, LANI; Belligham Memorial JR SR HS; Bellingham, MA; (Y); DECA; Drama Clb; School Play; Yrbk Ed-Chief; Yrbk Stf; Pres Frsh Cls; Pres Soph Cls; Stu Cncl; Hon Roll; NHS.

NEWTON, SHERYL; Cardinal Spellman HS; Hanson, MA; (Y); Library Aide; High Hon Roll; Hon Roll; Comm.

NEYLON, JOSEPH; Saint Clement HS; Somerville, MA; (Y); Art Clb; Boy Scts; Church Yth Grp; School Play; Yrbk Stf; Pres Stu Cncl; Ftbl; Capt Ice Hcky; Im Trk; Hon Roll; Cathlc Sch Wk Essy Cntst Wnnr; Partl Schlrshp 83-86; All Leag Hcky Tm; Comm.

NG, EILEEN; Boston Technical HS; Boston, MA; (Y); Church Yth Grp; French Clb; Hosp Aide; Office Aide; Spanish Clb; Teachers Aide; Varsity Clb; Stu Cncl; Vllybl; Hon Roll; Spn Natl Exam Awd 85; New England Med Ctr Volunteers Awd 84; NHS 86; Bus Adm.

NG, MING; Boston Latin Schl; Boston, MA; (Y); Cmnty Wkr; JA; Science Clb; Hon Roll; Boston U; Chem.

NG, SUI M; Boston Technical HS; Boston, MA; (Y); 33/208; Hosp Aide; Yrbk Stf; Rep Sr Cls; Rep Stu Cncl; Vllybl; Hon Roll; NHS; Mc Carthy Frnch Schlrshp 86; Jewsh War Vetrns Canton Schlrshp 86; Schl Spirt Schlrshps Awd 86; Lesley Coll; Cnslng.

NGUYEN, JOHN; Burncoat SR HS; Worcester, MA; (Y); Var Tennis; Hon Roll; NHS; Proj 50 50 Comp Camp 83-85; Engr.

NGUYEN, KIMBERLY; Dracut SR HS; Dracut, MA; (Y); Church Yth Grp; Math Clb; Ski Clb; Nwsp Stf; Yrbk Stf; JV Capt Socr; Cit Awd; Hon Roll; Dracut Schlrshp Foundtn 86; Lowell U; Engrng.

NGUYEN, KIMBERLY NHUNG; Brooline HS; Brookline, MA; (Y); Computer Clb; Dance Clb; Intnl Clb; Math Clb; Science Clb; Teachers Aide; School Musical; Badmtn; Bsktbl; Socr; French Cntst Awd 83-84; Northern U; Compu Sci Engrng.

NGUYEN, LONG; Salem HS; Lynn, MA; (Y); 11/275; Am Leg Boys St; Math Clb; Socr; High Hon Roll; NHS; Boston U; Mth.

NGUYEN, QUOC; Mario Umana HS; Brighton, MA; (Y); 1/32; Church Yth Grp; French Clb; Math Clb; Math Tm; ROTC; Yrbk Stf; Bausch & Lomb Sci Awd; High Hon Roll; Hon Roll; NHS; Med.

NGUYEN, THANG D; Brighton HS; Allston, MA; (Y); Church Yth Grp; Library Aide; Varsity Clb; Lit Mag; Sec Stu Cncl; Hon Roll; NHS; Model UN; Off Soph Cls; Math Awd; Recog Outstndng Ldrshp Awd 85; Fresh Tuitn Grnt 86; Northeastern U; Elec Engrg.

NICE, RICHARD; Wakefield HS; Wakefield, MA; (Y); Art Clb; Var Capt Bsbl; Wentworth Inst Tech; Electrcn.

NICHOLS, DONNA L; Whitinsville Christian HS; Mendon, MA; (Y); 2/40; Church Yth Grp; Drama Clb; Chorus; School Play; VP Frsh Cls; Pres Sr Cls; Bsktbl; Socr; High Hon Roll; Hon Roll; Syracuse U; Bus.

NICHOLS, HOWARD; Tewksbury Memorial HS; Tewksbury, MA; (Y); 64/328; Var Bsktbl; Hon Roll; Im Golf; Var Score Keeper; Rookie Of Yr Amer Power Boat & Racng Assn Regn 1 78; S Methodist U.

NICHOLS, SANDY; Governor Summer Acad; Manchester, MA; (Y); Camera Clb; French Clb; Hosp Aide; Nwsp Rptr; Yrbk Stf; Ed Lit Mag; JV Fld Hcky; Var Ice Hcky; Var Lcrss; Hon Roll; U Of NH; Vet Med.

NICKERSON, MATTHEW; Millis HS; Millis, MA; (Y); 1/86; Stage Crew; Variety Show; Var Capt Crs Cntry; Var Socr; Var Trk; Hon Roll; Jr NHS; NHS; Ntl Merit SF; Harvard Bk Awds 86; Engrng.

NICOLAKAKIS, LOUISE; Dracut SR HS; Dracut, MA; (Y); Sec Church Yth Grp; Math Clb; Math Tm; SADD; Nwsp Rptr; Nwsp Stf; Lit Mag; High Hon Roll; Hon Roll; NHS; Phy Sci Hnrs 83-84; Acad Cert Europn Hist, Hnrs Engl, Frnch 84-85; Sci.

NIEBRZYDOWSKI, SUSAN L; Peabody Vets Mem HS; Peabody, MA; (Y); 3/550; VP Key Clb; Science Clb; Spanish Clb; Chorus; Sec Stu Cncl; Powder Puff Ftbl; High Hon Roll; NHS; Ntl Merit SF; Chncllrs Talent Awd U MA 85; MASS Awd Acad Excllnce 86; Engrng.

NIELSEN, CARL DANIEL; Tantasqua Regional HS; Brookfield, MA; (Y); 16/180; Math Tm; Ski Clb; Yrbk Stf; Trs Sr Cls; Var Swmmng; Hon Roll; Lion Awd; NHS; Pres Schlr; Colgate U; Med.

NIELSEN, NATALEE A; Burlington HS; Burlington, MA; (Y); 20/350; Boys Clb Am; Boy Scts; Church Yth Grp; VP Debate Tm; OEA; Yrbk Stf; Var L Swmmng; High Hon Roll; NHS; Hewlett Packard Merit Schlrshp 86; Memrl Schl Parnt-Tchr Org Schlrshp; U Of NH; Comp Sci.

NIELSEN, TROY; Burlington HS; Burlington, MA; (Y); 21/314; Church Yth Grp; Pres Debate Tm; Exploring; Band; School Musical; Lit Mag; Trk; Hon Roll; NHS; Acadmc Awd US Hstry 86; Mechncl Engr.

NIERINTZ, ROBERT; Hudson HS; Hudson, MA; (Y); 20/150; Acpl Chr; Band; Chorus; Church Choir; Concert Band; Mrchg Band; School Musical; School Play; Yrbk Stf; Statlr Fndtn Schlrshp 86; Abry Prtr Msnc Schlrshp 86; Vets Frgn War Schlrsh& 86; Boston U; Htl Admin.

NIESSEN, PETER; Concord-Carlisle Regional HS; Carlisle, MA; (Y); 84/356; Cmnty Wkr; French Clb; Model UN; Radio Clb; Ski Clb; SADD; Nwsp Stf; Hon Roll; Ntl Merit SF; Pltcs.

NIESTEPSKI, CHRIS; Barnstable HS; Centerville, MA; (Y); 8/376; Jazz Band; Symp Band; Yrbk Stf; Off Jr Cls; Hon Roll; NHS; Church Yth Grp; SADD; Band; Concert Band; Slvr & Gld Acad Certs; Acad Ltr; Acad Mdl; U Of Sthrn CA; Aerosp Engrng.

NIEUWENHOFF, CINDY; Trantasqua Regional HS; Brookfield, MA; (Y); 50/176; Girl Scts; Office Aide; Chorus; Hon Roll; Lion Awd; Hnr For Outstndng Prfrmnc In Phy Ed 83; Brkfld Rtry Clb Schlrshp 86; Alfred De Angelis Schlrshp 86; Bob Jones U; Tchr.

NIGLOSCHY, KAREN; Marian HS; Framingham, MA; (Y); Church Yth Grp; Cmnty Wkr; Yrbk Stf; Hon Roll; Bus.

NIHAN, CHRISTOPHER; St Marys Regional HS; Lynn, MA; (Y); Pres Soph Cls; Ftbl; Law.

NIKOLOPOULOS, CHRIS; Boston Latin Acad; Roslindale, MA; (Y); Church Yth Grp; JA; Soph Cls; Jr Cls; Bsbl; Socr; Hon Roll; Rookie Yr Vrsty Bsbl.

NILSSON, DONALD; Austin Prep Schl; Woburn, MA; (Y); 3/127; French Clb; SADD; Varsity Clb; Trs Frsh Cls; Trs Jr Cls; Var Crs Cntry; Hon Roll; Jr NHS; NHS; Anne Couture Acadmc Schlrshp 86; Suffolk U Bk Awd 86; Villanoua; Law.

NIRO, CHRIS; Milford HS; Milford, MA; (Y); Boy Scts; Cmnty Wkr; Ski Clb; JV Var Ftbl; JV Var Wrstlng; High Hon Roll; Hon Roll; Franklin Inst; Arch Engr.

NIRO, LATICIA; Milford HS; Milford, MA; (Y); 8/296; Am Leg Aux Girls St; VP Soph Cls; Rep Stu Cncl; Fld Hcky; VP NHS; Key Clb; SADD; Yrbk Stf; High Hon Roll; MA Brd Regnts ST Schlr Schlrshp 86; Boston Coll; Finc.

NOEL, DEBORAH; Medford HS; Medford, MA; (Y); 50/435; Church Yth Grp; Drama Clb; PAVAS; Orch; School Musical; Hon Roll; NHS; Debate Tm; PAVAS; Acpl Chr; Sci Achvmnt Awd; Natl Lang Olympd Achvmnt; Achvmnt Excllnc Wrtng Awd; Bio Achvmnt Awd; Music.

NOGA, CHRISTINE S; Chicopee HS; Chicopee, MA; (Y); 13/256; Church Yth Grp; Library Aide; Church Choir; Capt Color Guard; Madrigals; Yrbk Ed-Chief; Mgr(s); CC Awd; Trs NHS; Pres Schlr; Pro Meriot Soc 85; Coll Hnr Schlrshp 86; Colorguard Liason 85; Stonehill Coll; Bio.

NOGUEIRA, DAVID; Bristol Plymouth Reg Tech; Taunton, MA; (Y); Hon Roll; Trade Schl; Auto Rpr.

NOLAN, ELIZABETH; Bourne HS; Pocasset, MA; (Y); 2/171; Model UN; Var L Bsktbl; Var Capt Crs Cntry; Var Tennis; Var L Trk; Dnfth Awd; Hon Roll; Jr NHS; NHS; Ntl Merit Ltr; Wellesley Book Awd 86; Sprtsmnshp Awd Track 84; Engrng.

NOLAN, JAMES; Boston College HS; Dedham, MA; (Y); 40/300; Am Leg Boys St; Pres VP Church Yth Grp; Cmnty Wkr; French Clb; Key Clb; SADD; Var JV Swmmng; Var Tennis; High Hon Roll; NHS.

NOLAN, KATHLEEN; Whitman-Hanson Regional HS; Hanson, MA; (Y); 1/284; Band; Var Socr; Var Sftbl; High Hon Roll; JP Sousa Awd; Kiwanis Awd; Trs NHS; Val; Rensselaer Mdl 85; Cum Laude Natl Latn Exm 85; Rensselaer Polytech Inst; Engrg.

NOLAN, LISA; Attleboro HS; Attleboro, MA; (Y); Powder Puff Ftbl; Hon Roll; Nrsng.

NOLET, JULIE; Haverhill HS; Haverhill, MA; (Y); 55/400; Sec Church Yth Grp; Hosp Aide; Pres Spanish Clb; Church Choir; School Play; Nwsp Ed-Chief; Ed Yrbk Rptr; Rep Stu Cncl; High Hon Roll; Hon Roll; Prsnl Achvtmnt Awd, R E Croston, E Richardson Schlrshps 86; Emmanuel Coll; Engl.

NOONAN, LAURA; East Longmeadow HS; E Longmeadow, MA; (Y); 13/197; Camp Fr Inc; Exploring; Girl Scts; Intnl Clb; Key Clb; Library Aide; Red Cross Aide; Spanish Clb; Teachers Aide; Nwsp Rptr; Law.

NOOONAN, TODD M; N Andover HS; N Andover, MA; (Y); 2/265; Math Tm; Var L Socr; Var L Trk; High Hon Roll; NHS; Prfct Atten Awd; Dartmouth Bk Awd 85; N Andover Exch Clb Yth Of Mnth 85; Dartmouth; Bus.

NORDIN, AMY; Monson JR SR HS; Monson, MA; (Y); 1/76; SADD; Stage Crew; Yrbk Stf; Sec Frsh Cls; Rep Stu Cncl; Var L Bsktbl; Var L Socr; High Hon Roll; NHS; Rensselaer Polytechnc Inst Awd Math & Sci 86.

NORMANDIN, MELODY; Bishop Connolly HS; Somerset, MA; (Y); 57/174; Church Yth Grp; Cmnty Wkr; Drama Clb; Intnl Clb; Teachers Aide; Var Cheerleading; High Hon Roll; Hon Roll.

NORRIS, PAM; Melrose HS; Melrose, MA; (S); German Clb; Ski Clb; SADD; Off Stu Cncl; Cheerleading; Hon Roll; Acad All Amer 85-86; Dntst.

NORTHGRAVES, PETER; Holliston HS; Holliston, MA; (Y); Am Leg Boys St; Church Yth Grp; Yrbk Stf; Pres Soph Cls; Trs Jr Cls; Trs Sr Cls; Var L Bsbl; Capt Ftbl; Hon Roll; NHS.

NORTHROP, BETH; Monument Mountain HS; Gt Barrington, MA; (Y); Church Yth Grp; Dance Clb; French Clb; Girl Scts; Hosp Aide; Band; Church Choir; Concert Band; Mrchg Band; Yrbk Stf; Outstndng Achvt Music 84-85; Futr Lifegrd Awd 84-85; Barbizon; Fshn Mdlng.

NORTON, AMY; Boston Latin Acad; W Roxbury, MA; (Y); Church Yth Grp; VP German Clb; School Play; Yrbk Bus Mgr; Yrbk Stf; Hon Roll; NHS; Ntl Ltn Exm Cum Laude 84-85; Bk Awds Hon Roll 84-86; Grmn Awd Goethe Inst Bstn 84-85; Psych.

NORTON, DANIELLE; Bartlett HS; Webster, MA; (Y); 22/165; Sec Science Clb; JV Cheerleading; Var Capt Socr; Var Capt Sftbl; High Hon Roll; Pres NHS; NEDT Awd; Church Yth Grp; Cmnty Wkr; Spanish Clb; Citatn Sec ST Achvt Sci 86; Sftbl MVP 86; Ctrl MA All Star Soccer 86; West Point; Frgn Rel.

NORTON, DAPHNE A; Stoughton HS; Stoughton, MA; (Y); 1/314; Math Tm; Concert Band; Mrchg Band; Nwsp Ed-Chief; Nwsp Rptr; NHS; Ntl Merit SF; Val; Band; Jazz Band; MA Adv Stds Prg Grad 85; Phi Alpha Theta Hstrcl Conf Hnrb Mntn 85; Sprntndnt Cert Acad Achvt 85.

NORTON, JO ANN; Fitchburg HS; Fitchburg, MA; (Y); 10/206; High Hon Roll; Hon Roll; Denah Fine Awd Acctng II 86; JR Stu Of Ftchbrg Wmns Clb 85; Hnrs Mdl 86; Ftchbrg ST Coll; Comp Sci.

NORTON, KRISTINE; Apponequet Regional HS; Assonet, MA; (Y); Hosp Aide; Pep Clb; Acpl Chr; Chorus; Mrchg Band; School Musical; Variety Show; L Var Twrlr; Hon Roll; NHS; Southeastern MA U; Advrtsng.

NOSEWORTHY, MARY; Gloucester HS; Gloucester, MA; (Y); 38/298; Church Yth Grp; Thesps; School Musical; Stage Crew; Hon Roll; NHS; Acad Hnrd In 82-86; Essex Ag & Tech Inst; Cosm.

NOVAK, PAMELA; Presentation Of Mary Acad; Methuen, MA; (Y); 4/43; French Clb; Math Clb; Service Clb; Chorus; Var Vllybl; High Hon Roll; Hon Roll; NHS; NEDT Awd.

NOVIO, EDWARD; Braintree HS; Braintree, MA; (Y); 112/442; Am Leg Boys St; Var Capt Bsbl; Var Capt Ftbl; Var Trk; Hon Roll; Pre Law.

NOWACKI, MARK; Cathedral HS; Feeding Hls, MA; (Y); Chess Clb; Computer Clb; Mathletes; Chorus; School Musical; School Play; Nwsp Rptr; Bausch & Lomb Sci Awd; High Hon Roll; NHS; Chem Awd 85; Comp Engr.

NOWAK, JULIE; Natick HS; Natick, MA; (Y); 10/410; Latin Clb; Concert Band; School Musical; Symp Band; English Clb; Girl Scts; JCL; Office Aide; Mrchg Band; Crs Cntry; Brwn Bk Awd 85; Trstee Schlrshp Boston U 4 Yrs Tuitn & Fees 1 Of 35 Grntd Ech Yr Wrld Wide 86; Boston U; Wrtng.

NOYES, DOUGLAS EVAN; Tewksbury Memorial HS; Tewksbury, MA; (Y); Ski Clb; Band; Jazz Band; Trs Score Keeper; JV Socr; VP Trk; Hon Roll; Tewisbury Gdn Clb Schlrshp 86; Springfield Coll; Phy Ed.

NUGENT, MARY; Westborough HS; Westborough, MA; (Y); 73/189; Band; Concert Band; Mrchg Band; JV Fld Hcky; JV Cmnty Wkr.

NUNES, ANDREA; Attleboro HS; Attleboro, MA; (Y); Office Aide; School Play; Rep Jr Cls; Trs Sr Cls; Rep Stu Cncl; Powder Puff Ftbl; Hon Roll; NHS; Yrbk Stf; Rep Frsh Cls; Boston Globe Schlstc Art Awd 84-86; Art.

NUNEZ, JIMMY; South Boston HS; Boston, MA; (S); Rep Church Yth Grp; French Clb; JV Bsbl; JV Bsktbl; JV Var Trk; Hon Roll; Trs NHS; Engrng.

NUTT, KIRSTEN M; Brookline HS; Brookline, MA; (Y); JCL; Pres Latin Clb; Orch; School Musical; JV Swmmng; Ntl Merit SF; Drama Clb; Political Wkr; Varsity Clb; J Murray Kaye Awd Citznshp 85; Art.

NUTTALL-VAZQUEZ, KIM HELLAINE; Newton North HS; Newton, MA; (Y); SADD; School Play; Var L Swmmng; Var L Vllybl; SAR Awd; Spanish NHS; U MA; Writer.

NYHAN, NICHOLAS W; Noble & Greenough Schl; N Scituate, MA; (Y); Drama Clb; Var Ski Clb; Variety Show; Nwsp Ed-Chief; Var Lcrss; Pres Schlr; Natl Fndtn Adv Arts 86; Wisewell Engl Prz 86; Wiggins Essy Prz 85; Scotland.

NYSTROM, THOMAS M; Medfield HS; Medfield, MA; (Y); Am Leg Boys St; Boy Scts; Church Yth Grp; Debate Tm; Drama Clb; School Musical; School Play; Bsbl; Ftbl; Hon Roll; Bd Of Dir/Chm Of Fnds Yth Nightspot 85-86; Intl Bus.

O BLENES, TARA; Notre Dame Acad; Hingham, MA; (Y); Drama Clb; French Clb; Acpl Chr; School Musical; Variety Show; Nwsp Stf; Yrbk Stf; San Diego ST U; Telecomm.

O BOY, KRISTEN; Bishop Feehan HS; Taunton, MA; (Y); 4-H; Library Aide; Chorus; Var Cheerleading; Early Chldhd Ed.

O BRIEN, BERNADETTE; Mount Saint Joseph Acad; Brighton, MA; (Y); Art Clb; AFS; Dance Clb; Pep Clb; SADD; Variety Show; Yrbk Stf; Bsktbl; Var L Trk; Hon Roll; St Anselm Coll; Nrsng.

O BRIEN, CHRISTINE; Holy Name CCHS; Worcester, MA; (Y); 42/275; Church Yth Grp; FNA; Hosp Aide; School Play; Capt Sftbl; Trk; High Hon Roll; Hstrcl Awd Framingham ST Coll-Hon Mntn 86; Trig, Hstry, Hmnties, & Bio Awds; Athl Awd Sftbl & Trck; Southeastern MA U; Nrsg.

O BRIEN, CHRISTOPHER P; Reading Memorial HS; Reading, MA; (Y); Sales.

O BRIEN, DANIEL G; Hudson Catholic HS; Hudson, MA; (Y); 11/65; Am Leg Boys St; Math Tm; Stage Crew; Variety Show; Nwsp Stf; Yrbk Sprt Ed; Capt Bsktbl; Capt Crs Cntry; Capt Trk; Hon Roll; Francis Gurl Mem Schlrshp 86; Elks Schlrshp 86; John P O Connor Mem Stu Athlete Awd 86; Manhattanville Coll; Math.

O BRIEN, DAVID L; Winthrop HS; Winthrop, MA; (Y); 35/202; Am Leg Boys St; Math Tm; Stage Crew; Var Tennis; Comptr Engr.

O BRIEN, ERIN; Melrose HS; Melrose, MA; (Y); 63/391; French Clb; Pres SADD; Yrbk Stf; Off Sr Cls; Off Stu Cncl; JV Var Sftbl; JV Var Vllybl; Sftbll Awds 84-86; Vllybll Awds 85-86; St Anslems; Acctg.

O BRIEN, JENNIFER; Ursuline Acad; Norwood, MA; (Y); 43/90; Spanish Clb; SADD; Var Bsktbl; Var Capt Tennis; All Str Awd Bsktbl & Tennis 86; Jordan Marsh JR Cncl 86; Fshn Merch.

O BRIEN, JUDYANE M; King Philip Regional HS; Norfolk, MA; (Y); Art Clb; Hosp Aide; OEA; Teachers Aide; Sftbl; Tutr Math & Spnsh Frshmn Lvl 85-86; RI Schl Design; Art.

O BRIEN, MICHAEL C; Hudson Catholic HS; Hudson, MA; (Y); 5/58; Am Leg Boys St; Boys Clb Am; SADD; School Musical; Stu Cncl; Var L Bsbl; Var L Bsktbl; Var L Ftbl; High Hon Roll; VP NHS.

O BRIEN, MICHELLE A; Boston Latin HS; West Roxbury, MA; (Y); 29/285; Church Yth Grp; German Clb; Key Clb; VP Science Clb; Teachers Aide; Hon Roll; NHS; H S Schlr 86; Natl Sci Olympiad Chem 85 & 86; City Sci Fair 2nd 86; Boston U; Chem.

O BRIEN, ROBERT; Braintree HS; Braintree, MA; (Y); 54/442; Am Leg Boys St; SADD; Var Ice Hcky; Var Capt Socr; NHS; Wldlf Mgmt.

O BRIEN, SEAN M; Wellesley HS; Wellesley, MA; (Y); 64/284; Band; Concert Band; Jazz Band; Mrchg Band; Orch; School Musical; Yrbk Phtg; Lit Mag; Ntl Merit SF; Wellesly Arts & Crfts Guild JR Yr Art Awd; Eng.

O BRIEN, THOMAS M; Boston College HS; Braintree, MA; (Y); 128/258; Boy Scts; Church Yth Grp; French Clb; JA; Key Clb; Political Wkr; Ski Clb; SADD; Swmmng; Bys Sct Egl Awd 86; Pltcl Sci.

O BRYON, LESLIE; Newburyport HS; Newburyport, MA; (Y); 9/200; Cmnty Wkr; English Clb; Political Wkr; Science Clb; Spanish Clb; School Play; Yrbk Stf; Fld Hcky; Hon Roll; Pres NHS; Hnrs Lev Amer Inst Awd; A P Bio Lev Awd; Corp Law.

O CALLAGHAN, EILEEN; Boston Latin Acad; Hyde Park, MA; (Y); 2/129; Math Clb; VP Math Tm; Band; Hon Roll; Jr NHS; NHS; Pres Schlr; Sal; Rotary Awd; Hly Crs Bk Awd 85; Franklin Awd Mdl 86; Boston Ltn Acad Kimball Ingalls Math Awd 86; Rensselaer Poly Inst; Engrng.

O CONNELL, BRYAN; Reading Memorial HS; Reading, MA; (Y); Boy Scts; Rep SADD; Co-Capt Yrbk Bus Mgr; Rep Stu Cncl; JV Ftbl; JV Trk; Var Wrstlng; High Hon Roll; 3rd Pl-Middlesex Leag Wrestlng Trnmnt & Div I North Sectnl Wrestlng Trnmnt 86; Bay ST Games-Brnz 86; Aerospc Engrng.

O CONNELL, DEBRA; Natick HS; Natick, MA; (Y); 13/400; SADD; Rep Soph Cls; JV Lcrss; JV Socr; Im Sftbl; High Hon Roll; NHS; Bus Typng Awd 85; Bus Law Awd 86; Psych.

O CONNELL, DEIRDRE; Lynnfield HS; Lynnfield, MA; (Y); Cmnty Wkr; SADD; Yrbk Stf; Var L Bsktbl; Var L Fld Hcky; Im Powder Puff Ftbl; JV Sftbl; Var L Trk; Hon Roll; NHS; Biol.

O CONNELL, DIANE; Billerica Memorial HS; Billerica, MA; (Y); 57/400; Aud/Vis; Camp Fr Inc; Ski Clb; Powder Puff Ftbl; JV Capt Sftbl; Hon Roll; Boston Globe Schltc Art Awd Hnrbl Mntn 86; Visual Arts Prdctn.

O CONNELL, ELLEN M; Seekonk HS; Seekonk, MA; (Y); 1/174; Sec Computer Clb; Nwsp Stf; Yrbk Stf; Var L Swmmng; Sec Trs French Hon Soc; High Hon Roll; NHS; Ntl Merit SF; Brown U Bk Awd 85; Outstndg Undrgrad Awd 85; Supt Cert Acad Excllnc 85; Math.

O CONNELL, KEVIN D; South High Community Schl; Worcester, MA; (Y); Am Leg Boys St; Stu Cncl; JV Bsbl; Var Bsktbl; Var Ftbl; Var Tennis; Hon Roll; Acdmc Olympic Team 84-85; In Schl Tutor 85-86.

O CONNELL, KRISTIN; Notre Dame Acad; Norwell, MA; (Y); 26/114; Church Yth Grp; Debate Tm; Yrbk Stf; JV Cheerleading; Var Gym; Var Trk; High Hon Roll; Hon Roll; Spanish NHS; Recgntn Pgnt Miss Teen Of Amer 86.

O CONNELL, MAUREEN; Arlington Catholic HS; Billerica, MA; (Y); 19/146; French Clb; Service Clb; SADD; Yrbk Stf; Hon Roll; NHS; NEDT Awd; U Of Lowell; Nrsng.

O CONNELL, PETER; Bishop Connolly HS; Tiverton, RI; (Y); Trs Latin Clb; SADD; JV Socr; High Hon Roll; NHS; Ntl Merit Ltr; Union Coll; Mech Engrng.

O CONNOR, DENNIS; Cathedral HS; W Springfield, MA; (Y); Boys Clb Am; JA; Quiz Bowl; Ski Clb; SADD; JV Bsbl; Cathdrl HS Awd Acadmc Excllnc World Cultures 83-84; U MA; Soc Sci.

O CONNOR, SUSAN; Whitman-Hanson RHS; Whitman, MA; (Y); 4/292; Color Guard; Yrbk Stf; Bsktbl; Sftbl; Vllybl; High Hon Roll; Hon Roll; Kiwanis Awd; Lion Awd; NHS; Cum Laude Natl Latin Exam 85 & 86; Boston Coll; Pre-Med.

O DEA, TINA; Murdock HS; Winchendon, MA; (Y); 26/105; Office Aide; Trs Sr Cls; Bsktbl; Fld Hcky; Sftbl; Wt Lftg; Hon Roll; Lion Awd; Wrcstr Tlgrm & Gzt Fld Hcky All-Str 86; Fld Hcky & Sftbl Wchstt Lge All-Str 86; Becker JC; Phys Educ.

O DONNELL, CYNTHIA; Fontbonne Acad; W Roxbury, MA; (Y); Camera Clb; VP Church Yth Grp; Cmnty Wkr; Computer Clb; Dance Clb; Debate Tm; Drama Clb; Hosp Aide; VP Library Aide; Science Clb; Boston Globe Art Awd 83; Framingham ST Coll; Pltcs.

O DONNELL, DANIEL; Wilmington HS; Wilmington, MA; (Y); Boy Scts; OEA; Spanish Clb; Yrbk Stf; Stu Cncl; Ftbl; Trk; High Hon Roll; Ntl Eagle Scout Assn 86; Eng & Law Cert Of Hnr 85-86; Math Hnr Scty 86; Tufts; Mech Engr.

O DONNELL, JULIE; Msgr Ryan Memorial HS; Dorchester, MA; (Y); 19/80; Art Clb; Pres Church Yth Grp; Variety Show; Ed Yrbk Stf; Trs Frsh Cls; Sec Soph Cls; Pres Jr Cls; Pres Sr Cls; Var Co-Capt Bsktbl; Hon Roll; Suffolk U Bk Awd Outstndg Schl Svc 84-85; 2nd Rnr-Up Outstndg Cath Yth 85.

O DONNELL, KELLIE; Agawam HS; Feeding Hills, MA; (Y); Church Yth Grp; JCL; Pep Clb; Ski Clb; SADD; Chorus; Sec Jr Cls; Var Cheerleading; Var Pom Pon; Hon Roll; Boston U; Cmnctns.

O DONNELL, MEGAN; Shrews SR HS; Shrewsbury, MA; (Y); 27/250; Drama Clb; Letterman Clb; Acpl Chr; Band; Sec Chorus; Concert Band; Mrchg Band; School Musical; School Play; Hnrs 84-86.

O DONNELL, PATRICK; Attleboro HS; Attleboro, MA; (Y); Cmnty Wkr; Letterman Clb; Varsity Clb; Stat Score Keeper; Var Capt Swmmng; Stat Timer; Hon Roll; Ltn Ntl Hon Soc 86-87.

O DONNELL, PAUL; Milton HS; Milton, MA; (Y); 74/245; Church Yth Grp; SADD; Variety Show; Var L Bsbl; Var L Ftbl; Im Wt Lftg; Var Capt Wrstlng; Vlntns Offcr Soph Yr Milton Hgh 84; Bay ST Gms Fnlst Wrstlng Boston MA 86; Amer Legn Bsbll Mltn MA; Bus Adm.

O DONNELL, REBECCA; Bedford HS; Bedford, MA; (Y); 43/198; Cmnty Wkr; SADD; Orch; Trs Sr Cls; JV Fld Hcky; Var Mgr(s); Var Powder Puff Ftbl; JV Var Sftbl; Hon Roll; Prfct Atten Awd; Med.

O GARA, DONNA; Braintree HS; Braintree, MA; (Y); 37/442; Church Yth Grp; SADD; Nwsp Rptr; Lit Mag; Off Frsh Cls; Off Soph Cls; Off Jr Cls; Off Sr Cls; Off Stu Cncl; Capt Fld Hcky; Schlrshp Bus Wk Bentley Coll 86; Intl Baccalaureate Prog 85-87; Hnbl Mntn Sci Fair Bio 84; Intl Bus.

O GRADY, LAURIE; Tantasqua Reg HS; Sturbridge, MA; (Y); Ski Clb; Varsity Clb; Yrbk Stf; JV Crs Cntry; JV Fld Hcky; JV Var Score Keeper; Var Capt Socr.

O KEEFFE, JONATHAN; Barnstable HS; Marstons Mills, MA; (Y); 11/392; Debate Tm; NFL; Speech Tm; NHS; Nwsp Rptr; Nwsp Stf; High Hon Roll; Hon Roll; Voice Dem Awd; Harvard Bk Awd 86; Renssealer Mdl 86; Acdmc Lttr 12 Consec Trms On Hon Roll 82-86; MA Inst Of Tech; Engineering.

O LEARY, BILL; St Johns Prep; Boxford, MA; (Y); Art Clb; Cmnty Wkr; Model UN; Nwsp Rptr; Yrbk Ed-Chief; JV Trk; Natl Hnr Roll 86; 1st Pl Schl Art Shw 86; Comm.

O LEARY, BRIAN F; Catholic Memorial HS; Foxboro, MA; (Y); 9/235; Math Clb; Science Clb; Spanish Clb; Varsity Clb; Trs Sr Cls; Im Bsktbl; Im Ftbl; Var Capt Golf; High Hon Roll; Hon Roll; Rnld Perry Schlr Athlt Awd 86; Boston Coll; Finc.

O LEARY, JOHN A; Doherty Memorial HS; Worcester, MA; (Y); Pres Church Yth Grp; Cmnty Wkr; JA; Latin Clb; Political Wkr; Spanish Clb; SADD; Stage Crew; Nwsp Stf; Var L Golf; Bus.

O LEARY, KATHLEEN; Arlington HS; Medford, MA; (Y); 53/143; Church Yth Grp; Hosp Aide; SADD; School Musical; Var L Cheerleading; Hon Roll; NHS; St Anselm Coll Manchester; Bus.

O LEARY, KEVIN; Bishop Feehan HS; Foxboro, MA; (Y); 20/240; VP Ski Clb; Var L Bsbl; Var L Bsktbl; Im Vllybl; High Hon Roll; Hon Roll; NHS; Prfct Atten Awd; Exc Econ; Exc Wrld Hstry; Exc Engl 4 Yrs; Syracuse; Pblc Cmnctns.

O NEAL, ELIZABETH; Marshfield HS; Marshfield, MA; (Y); 88/380; Key Clb; SADD; Band; Concert Band; Var Cheerleading; JV Fld Hcky; Hon Roll; John Hacking Mem Dance Scholar 86; Bus Mgmt.

O NEALL-WAITE, HOLLY; Notre Dame Acad; Worcester, MA; (Y); Cmnty Wkr; Drama Clb; Chorus; School Musical; School Play; Nwsp Stf; DAR Awd; Boston Globe Acting Awd 85; Co-Chrmn Notre Dame Theatre Arts Clb 86-87; Boston U; Drama.

O NEIL, CHRISTINE E; Rockland HS; Rockland, MA; (Y); 3/214; Drama Clb; Church Choir; Jazz Band; School Musical; Variety Show; Rep Soph Cls; Rep Stu Cncl; Hon Roll; NHS; NEDT Awd; Acad Achvt Awds Math & Lang 84-85; Fnlst In MS MA TEEN Pgnt 84; MA JS Drama Fstvl All-Star Mbr 85; Brown U.

O NEIL, CHRISTOPHER W; Bishop Feehan HS; Mansfield, MA; (Y); 83/285; Am Leg Boys St; Boy Scts; Red Cross Aide; SADD; School Play; Stu Cncl; Im Ftbl; JV Trk; Hon Roll; Notre Dame; Pre-Med.

O NEIL, JENNIFER; Marian HS; Framingham, MA; (Y); 60/200; Drama Clb; Pres French Clb; Pres Intnl Clb; Latin Clb; Chorus; School Musical; School Play; Yrbk Stf.

O NEIL, KELLY; Auburn HS; Auburn, MA; (Y); Chess Clb; Dance Clb; Drama Clb; FHA; Ski Clb; JV Crs Cntry; JV Trk; JV Hon Roll; Var Bowling; 4th July Running Race Awd 83; Awd Outstndng Achvt Span Child Devlpt 84; Law.

O NEIL, SHEILA A; Charles H Mc Conn Technical HS; N Adams, MA; (Y); High Hon Roll; Hon Roll; NHS; Lgl Secty.

O REGAN, TIMOTHY; Melrose HS; Melrose, MA; (Y); 20/600; Computer Clb; Library Aide; Spanish Clb; Teachers Aide; Band; Concert Band; Mrchg Band; Orch; School Musical; Yrbk Stf; Enrgy Cnsrvtn Awd 83; Mrchng Band Awd 85; Pjct Smm 85 & 86; Intl Law.

O REILLY, DEIRDRE; Newton North HS; Chestnut Hill, MA; (Y); Church Yth Grp; French Clb; Teachers Aide; Nwsp Phtg; Yrbk Phtg; Yrbk Stf; Pres Stu Cncl; Capt Var Crs Cntry; Var Trk; Hon Roll; 1st Pl Sbrbn Lgue Chmpnshps Rly 86; Clrfctn Of #114 Co-Pres One Of 4 Hse Cncls 86-87; Lang.

O ROURKE, CARRIE A; Acton-Boxboro Regional HS; Avton, MA; (Y); 106/428; Chorus; Madrigals; School Musical; Variety Show; Var Cheerleading; Powder Puff Ftbl; Hon Roll; NHS; Church Yth Grp; Drama Clb; Miss Amer Coed Pagnt ST Fnlst 85; Engrng.

O ROURKE, KATRINA; Burncoat SR HS; Worcester, MA; (Y); 32/242; Drama Clb; Chorus; School Play; Stage Crew; Yrbk Stf; Hon Roll; Fitchburg ST Coll; Nrsg.

O SHAUGHNESSY, JOHN P; Minnechauy HS; Wilbraham, MA; (Y); 44/311; Am Leg Boys St; Nwsp Rptr; Yrbk Rptr; Pres Frsh Cls; Pres Soph Cls; Pres Jr Cls; Pres Sr Cls; Rep Stu Cncl; Var Capt Ice Hcky; Var L Socr; Boston Coll; Englsh.

O SHAUGHNESSY, MICHAEL F; Lexington HS; Lexington, MA; (Y); Am Leg Boys St; Church Yth Grp; Intnl Clb; Jazz Band; Rep Soph Cls; VP Jr Cls; VP Sr Cls; Rep Stu Cncl; Bsktbl; Ftbl; American U.

O SHEA, CHRISTINE; Fontbonne Acad; Roslindale, MA; (Y); 130/200; Church Yth Grp; Drama Clb; PAVAS; Service Clb; Chorus; Pep Band; School Play; Mgr(s); Trk; Vllybl; Ntl Ltn Exm-Cum Laude 84; Schltc Art Awds-1st, 2nd & 2 3rds 84; Emerson U MA; Theatr.

O SHEA, ERIN; Norton HS; Norton, MA; (S); 19/170; Hosp Aide; VP JA; Rep VP Pep Clb; Spanish Clb; Teachers Aide; Varsity Clb; Nwsp Stf; Trk; Vllybl; Hon Roll; Track Medal Leag Meet; Acctg.

O SHEA, KELLY; Norton HS; Norton, MA; (S); 9/170; French Clb; Hosp Aide; Varsity Clb; Yrbk Stf; Trk; High Hon Roll; Hon Roll; NHS; JR Theme Wrtrs Awd; Phys Ther.

O SHEA, MARGARET; Cathedral HS; Springfield, MA; (Y); 14/560; Cmnty Wkr; Hosp Aide; Intnl Clb; SADD; Rep Frsh Cls; High Hon Roll; Hon Roll; NHS; Awd Excllnce Alg II & Spn III 85-86; Biol.

O SULLIVAN, PATRICIA; Foxboro HS; Foxboro, MA; (Y); 6/225; Church Yth Grp; VP JA; SADD; Sec Stu Cncl; JV Bsktbl; Var Capt Tennis; Hon Roll; NHS; Ntl Merit SF; All Hockomock Leag All Star Tennis; Patriot Ledger; MVP Tennis; Bus.

O TOOLE, ANDREA; Uxbridge HS; Uxbridge, MA; (Y); 8/81; Math Tm; SADD; Varsity Clb; Nwsp Stf; Yrbk Phtg; Yrbk Rptr; Yrbk Stf; Stu Cncl; Var JV Bsktbl; Var JV Fld Hcky; 2nd Pl & 1st Pl Schl Art Shw 84-85; Chrprsn Lcl Stu Advsry Commtte, Stu Cncl Actvts Comm 86-87.

O TOOLE, ROSEMARY; Somerset HS; Somerset, MA; (Y); Boston U; Lib Arts.

OBER, CHERYL E; Franklin HS; Franklin, MA; (Y); 20/224; OEA; Yrbk Ed-Chief; Yrbk Stf; Lit Mag; Rep Soph Cls; Rep Stu Cncl; Hon Roll; Sthestrn MA U; Psych.

OBRIEN, EDWARD; Revere HS; Revere, MA; (Y); Math Clb; Band; Hon Roll; Schlrshp To Berklee Coll Of Music-Smmr Pgm 85; Music Cmpstn.

OBRIEN, JAMES; Ware HS; Ware, MA; (Y); 1/120; Am Leg Boys St; Art Clb; French Clb; Bausch & Lomb Sci Awd; High Hon Roll; VFW Awd; Rensselaer Medl 86; UMASS Wrtg 85; Comp Sci.

OBRIEN, LISA; St Clares HS; Hyde Park, MA; (Y); 20/120; Political Wkr; Powder Puff Ftbl; Sftbl; High Hon Roll; Hon Roll; Cmnty Wkr; Hosp Aide; Latin Clb; Psych.

OCONNELL, PAMELA; Haverhill HS; Haverhill, MA; (Y); Latin Clb; Spanish Clb; Yrbk Stf; Capt Cheerleading; Hon Roll; Psychlgy.

OCONNOR, JOHN; North Attleboro HS; N Attleboro, MA; (Y); Spanish Clb; Rep Jr Cls; Trs Sr Cls; JV Bsktbl; L Ftbl; Powder Puff Ftbl; Im Vllybl; Hon Roll; Accntng.

ODIERNA, LORI; Longmeadow HS; Longmeadow, MA; (Y); 28/275; AFS; Sec Keywanettes; Nwsp Bus Mgr; Nwsp Stf; Var Capt Gym; JV Trk; Law.

OHANIAN, TRACY; Methuen HS; Methuen, MA; (Y); 35/385; Intnl Clb; Model UN; Spanish Clb; High Hon Roll; Spanish NHS; Law.

OHEAR, KEVIN J; Sandwich HS; E Sandwich, MA; (Y); 15/175; Am Leg Boys St; Ski Clb; SADD; Pres Stu Cncl; Var L Ice Hcky; Var Capt Socr; Var Capt Tennis; NHS; Elks Club Tnagr Of The Yr 86; Babson Coll; Bus Mgmt.

OKEEFE, LEAH; Salem HS; Salem, MA; (Y); 180/262; Church Yth Grp; Girl Scts; Mgr(s); Score Keeper; JV Var Socr; Var Sftbl; Hon Roll; Sftbl Coaches Awd 86; Accntng.

OLANDER, LORI; East Longmeadow HS; E Longmeadow, MA; (Y); AFS; Intnl Clb; Library Aide; Natl Beta Clb; School Play; Stage Crew; Rep Sr Cls; Var Fld Hcky; Var Mgr(s); U Of RI; Psych.

OLEARY, BRIAN; Boston Latin Schl; Boston, MA; (Y); 74/285; Church Yth Grp; Cmnty Wkr; Mathletes; Bsktbl; Var Crs Cntry; High Hon Roll; Hon Roll; Ntl Merit Ltr; Pres Schlr; Lttl Leag Coach 82-86; Boston U; Engrng.

OLIVA, TRACY; Malden HS; Malden, MA; (Y); Office Aide; Variety Show; Burdett Schl Bus; Lgl Secy.

OLIVEIRA, PAUL; Matignon HS; Somerville, MA; (S); 10/190; French Hon Soc; Hon Roll; NHS; Ntl Merit Ltr; U MT; Wld Life Mngmnt.

OLIVERIA, DAVID; Saugus HS; Saugus, MA; (Y); SADD; Yrbk Stf; Socr; Law Enfrcmnt.

OLIVIERI, MARK; Matignon HS; Somerville, MA; (Y); 49/179; Cmnty Wkr; Library Aide; SADD; Ed Lit Mag; Var L Bsktbl; Im Vllybl; Hon Roll; VP Hist Clb; Merrimack Clg; Mktg.

OLSEN, MICHELLE; Braintree Mass HS; Braintree, MA; (Y); 198/423; Sftbl; High Hon Roll; Hon Roll; Prfct Atten Awd; U MA Boston; Psych.

OLSON, JAMES J; Randolph HS; Randolph, MA; (Y); Boy Scts; French Clb; Band; Church Choir; Drm Mjr(t); Jazz Band; Mrchg Band; Nwsp Ed-Chief; NHS; Am Leg Boys St; Eagle Sct BSA 84; ME Maritime Acad; Deck Ofcr.

OLSON, KENNETH; Somerville HS; Somerville, MA; (Y); 56/450; Boys Clb Am; Bsbl; Bsktbl; Crs Cntry; Hon Roll; All Star MA Amer Lgn Bsebl Tm 86; FL ST; Bus.

OMALLEY, MARY; Mt St Joseph Acad; Boston, MA; (Y); Drama Clb; Spanish Clb; Chorus; School Musical; Yrbk Stf; Mgr(s); Close Up Schrslhp 85; Princpls Awd 86; U Steubenville.

ONEILL, JAMES; St Dominic Savio HS; Dorchester, MA; (Y); Computer Clb; Ski Clb; SADD; Rep Frsh Cls; Rep Soph Cls; Rep Stu Cncl; Im Ftbl; JV Ice Hcky; Im Wt Lftg; Wentworth Inst Tech; Elctrncs.

ONEILL, MARY; Holyoke HS; Holyoke, MA; (Y); Art Clb; Dance Clb; Hosp Aide; Var Trk; Hon Roll; Art Dept 86; Margaret J Hyland Schlrshp Fund Awd 86; U MA.

ONOYAN, CATHY; North Atleboro HS; N Attleboro, MA; (Y); Hosp Aide; JCL; Trs Latin Clb; SADD; Yrbk Ed-Chief; Yrbk Stf; JV Var Fld Hcky; Var Trk; High Hon Roll; NHS; Ofcr In Stu Advsry Committee 85-87; SAC Rgnl 85-86; Nrsg.

ONTSO, CHRISTOPHER; Algonquin Regional HS; Northboro, MA; (Y); Acpl Chr; Concert Band; Jazz Band; Mrchg Band; Orch; School Play; Dist Jazz Band 86; Elec Engrng.

OPERACH, CHARLOTTE; King Philip HS; Norfolk, MA; (Y); Dance Clb; Drama Clb; Hosp Aide; Science Clb; SADD; Color Guard; Yrbk Bus Mgr; Rep Frsh Cls; Stu Cncl; Fld Hcky; N Adams ST; Bio.

ORFAO, JANET; Woburn SR HS; Hull, MA; (Y); 153/451; Sec Leo Clb; Office Aide; Ski Clb; Spanish Clb; School Play; Yrbk Stf; Stu Cncl; JV Var Fld Hcky; JV Sftbl; Hon Roll; SE MA U; Civl Engrng.

ORLANDO, ANGELA; Waltham HS; Waltham, MA; (Y); 20/575; VP Drama Clb; Key Clb; Varsity Clb; Chorus; School Musical; Socr; Sftbl; Hon Roll; Jr NHS; NHS; Outstndng Chrl Stu 84 & 86; 4 Yr Schlarshp Bstn Coll 86; Boston Coll; Engl.

ORLANDO, EMILY; Reading Memorial HS; Reading, MA; (Y); French Clb; Pep Clb; Crs Cntry; JV Trk; Peer Tutoring, Schlstc Achvt Awd, Jr Class Comm 85-86.

ORMSBEE, KIMBERLY; Easthampton HS; Easthampton, MA; (Y); Hosp Aide; Spanish Clb; SADD; Teachers Aide; Chorus; High Hon Roll; Hon Roll; Fshn Merch.

ORMSBY, KAREN; West Springfield HS; West Springfield, MA; (S); 3/219; Am Leg Aux Girls St; Ski Clb; Band; Drm Mjr(t); Var L Crs Cntry; Var L Tennis; DAR Awd; High Hon Roll; Lion Awd; NHS; Commonwlth ST Schlrshp Wnnr 86; Benjamen H Wood Musc Schlrshp 86; Hofstra U; Bio.

ORRALL, NORMAN; Appohequet Regional HS; Lakeville, MA; (Y); 23/225; Church Yth Grp; Band; Jazz Band; Mrchg Band; Symp Band; Hon Roll; NHS; Louis Armstrong Jazz Awd 86; Middlboro Rtry Clb Schlrshp 86; Dena Ballou Schlrshp 86; U Of MA; Elec Engr.

ORWAT, MARK E; West Springfield HS; West Springfield, MA; (Y); Am Leg Boys St; Boy Scts; Computer Clb; Band; Stu Cncl; Var Bsbl; Var Bsktbl; Pres NHS; Pres Spanish NHS; Rensselaer Medl Recpnt 86; MA Adv Stds Prog Desgnee 86; Stdnt Rep Chrmn 86; Cvl Engrng.

ORZULAK, DANIEL M; Ware HS; Ware, MA; (Y); Am Leg Boys St; Math Tm; Spanish Clb; Yrbk Stf; Bsktbl; Golf; Vllybl; Big Y Plyr Of Yr Bsktbl 85-86; Ware Rvr Nerwspapr Plyr Of Wk 85; Western New Englnd; Math.

OSETEK, ALAN; Marlboro HS; Marlboro, MA; (Y); 23/320; Boys Clb Am; Dance Clb; Service Clb; Ski Clb; Varsity Clb; Var Bsbl; Var Bsktbl; Crs Cntry; High Hon Roll; NHS; MVP Ptchr Vrsty Bsebl 86.

OSGOOD, JAY; Archbishop Williams HS; Quincy, MA; (Y); 48/196; Nwsp Sprt Ed; Var Capt Bsktbl; Var L Ftbl; Var L Trk; Hon Roll; Brn F Cullinan Mem Schlrshp Awd 86; Astro Trnmnt MVP, Shrn Trnmnt All Str 86; Excllnc Rlgs Stds 83; Maine Central Inst.

OSHAUGHNESSY, TORI; Marblehead HS; Marblehead, MA; (Y); 67/250; Dance Clb; Ski Clb; Yrbk Phtg; Im Powder Puff Ftbl; Var L Socr; Capt L Trk; Olympc Trang Ctr Rifle Shtng 86; Coaches Awd & JR Awd Trk 86; Bus Awd Excllnt 85; Bus.

OSLEY, BRIAN; Smith Acad; Hatfield, MA; (Y); Pres Trs Key Clb; Bsbl; Bsktbl; Socr; Cit Awd.

OSTLER, KAREN LYNNE; Bishop Stang HS; New Bedford, MA; (Y); 40/250; Cmnty Wkr; Political Wkr; Chorus; Stu Cncl; Cit Awd; Hon Roll; NHS; Spotlight Pgm Sthestrn MA U 84-85; Soclgy & Relgn Cls Hghst Hnr 85-86; Cmmnty Svc Spec Awd 85-86; Sthestrn MA U; Bus Adm.

OSTRO, ALLA; Classical HS; Springfield, MA; (Y); Dance Clb; GAA; Hosp Aide; SADD; Teachers Aide; Chorus; Gym; Swmmng; High Hon Roll; Hon Roll; Cert Achvt Awd U Lowell & U MA Amherst 85; Cert Achvt Ache/Reach Pgm 84; Cert Part 83; Comp Sci.

OSTROSKEY, KAREN; Uxbridge HS; Uxbridge, MA; (Y); Pres Church Yth Grp; Library Aide; Church Choir; Concert Band; Jazz Band; Mrchg Band; Score Keeper; Var Sftbl; NHS; Pres Phys Ftnss Awd 81-83.

OSTRUM, JEFF; Hanover HS; Hanover, MA; (Y); Boys Clb Am; Rep Sr Cls; Rep Stu Cncl; Bsktbl; Ftbl; Wt Lftg; Hon Roll.

OTTAVIANO, ELLEN; Winthrop HS; Winthrop, MA; (Y); 34/205; Cmnty Wkr; Red Cross Aide; SADD; Teachers Aide; Off Soph Cls; Off Jr Cls; Off Sr Cls; Off Stu Cncl; Cheerleading; Hon Roll.

OUELLETTE, ERIC G; Wilmington HS; Wilmington, MA; (Y); 12/240; Cmnty Wkr; Varsity Clb; JV Var Ftbl; Im JV Ice Hcky; Hon Roll; NHS; Ntl Merit SF; St Schlr; Spanish Clb; Stu Mnth Awd Engl 85; Outstndng Achvt Engl Awd 85; Elec Engrng.

OUELLETTE, JULIE; Marblehead HS; Marblehead, MA; (Y); French Clb; SADD; Thesps; Sec Concert Band; Orch; Rep Stu Cncl; Var Swmmng; Church Yth Grp; Drama Clb; Latin Clb; NE Msc Fest Blue Mdl Awd 85-86; Natl Schl Orch Awd 86; Bates Coll; Psych.

OUELLETTE, KAREN A; Wilmington HS; Wilmington, MA; (Y); Church Yth Grp; JA; Rep Stu Cncl; JV Bsktbl; Var Fld Hcky; Trk; Hon Roll; NHS; Awd For Excllnc Scl Sci 84; Assumption Coll; Psychlgy.

OUELLETTE, ROBERT; Bishop Connolly HS; Westport, MA; (Y); 16/169; Drama Clb; Latin Clb; Nwsp Ed-Chief; Elks Awd; High Hon Roll; NHS; Ntl Merit Ltr; St Schlr; Voice Dem Awd; Holy Cross Coll; Pre-Med.

OUELLETTE, STEVEN; Central Catholic HS; Methuen, MA; (Y); 46/231; Boy Scts; Hon Roll; Wentworth Inst; Arch Engrng.

OVERTON, THOMAS; Medway JR SR HS; Medway, MA; (Y); 4/140; Yrbk Phtg; Yrbk Stf; Var L Cheerleading; Bausch & Lomb Sci Awd; High Hon Roll; Hon Roll; NHS; Sci.

OWCZARSKI, CHRISTINA; Mac Duffie Schl For Girls; Agawam, MA; (Y); Drill Tm; Yrbk Ed-Chief; Hon Roll; Most Valuble Plyr Horsebck Rdng 83-85; Wellesey Bk Awd 86; 1st Pl Macduffie Sci Fair 85; Vet Sci.

OWEN, JEN; ABR HS; Acton, MA; (Y); 136/428; Drama Clb; Radio Clb; School Musical; School Play; Stage Crew; Hon Roll; Drama Hnrs Soc; Comm.

OWENS, MARTHA; Jeremiah E Burke HS; Dorchester, MA; (Y); Church Yth Grp; Cmnty Wkr; Dance Clb; JA; Band; Chorus; Bsktbl; Sftbl; Hon Roll; Jr Achvmnt Initial Time $100 Sls 85; Northeastern; Comp Sci.

PACCIONE, LISA; Bishop Feehan HS; Plainville, MA; (Y); 32/267; Ski Clb; JV Bsktbl; Crs Cntry; Var Ice Hcky; Var Sftbl; French Hon Soc; High Hon Roll; NHS; 2-Tm Al-Conf 3rd Bsmn 84-86; 3-Tm Al-Leag Wmns Hcky Leag 83-86.

PACECCA, MICHELLE; Everett HS; Everett, MA; (Y); Church Yth Grp; Cmnty Wkr; Intnl Clb; Key Clb; VP Pres Chorus; School Musical; JV Var Tennis; Outstndng Vocalist 84-85&85-86; Pol Sci.

PACEWICZ, HEIDI; Cardinal Spellman HS; Brockton, MA; (Y); 28/208; Drama Clb; Office Aide; Thesps; Chorus; School Musical; School Play; Stu Cncl; Hon Roll; Intl Thespian Soc Awd 85-86.

PACHECO, FRANK D; New Bedford HS; New Bedford, MA; (Y); 41/631; NHS; Prfct Atten Awd; Pres Acadmc Fit Awd 86; Faclty Hnr Rll 3rd Mrkg Qrtr 86; Southeastern MA U; Bus Adm.

PACHECO, LISA A; Fairhaven HS; Fairhaven, MA; (Y); 2/184; Math Tm; School Musical; L Cheerleading; High Hon Roll; Jr NHS; NHS; NEDT Awd; Voice Dem Awd; Church Yth Grp; Drama Clb; Proj Excell Sthestrn MA U 85; Ltr Excllnct All Acad 85; Stu Mnth 84; Intl Law.

PACHECO, MICHAEL; Arlington HS; Arlington, MA; (Y); Latin Clb; Rep Stu Cncl; Var Capt Crs Cntry; Var L Trk; Mst Improved Spring Track 84-85; Superintendant Of Recreation 86; Redevelopmnt Brd Stu Govt Day 86.

PACHECO, THOMAS; New Bedford HS; New Bedford, MA; (Y); 44/650; Office Aide; SADD; Sec Stu Cncl; Bsbl; Coach Actv; Crs Cntry; Twrlr; God Cntry Awd; NHS; Pres Schlr; Providence Coll; Bus Admin.

PACIFIC, LAUREN; Wakefield HS; Wakefield, MA; (Y); JA; Key Clb; Latin Clb; Pep Clb; Spanish Clb; SADD; Yrbk Stf; JV Socr; Hon Roll; Magna Cum Laude Lat Awd; Phys Ther.

PACINO, JOHN; North Quincy HS; N Quincy, MA; (Y); 10/400; Am Leg Boys St; Computer Clb; JA; Bsbl; Ftbl; Ice Hcky; Wt Lftg; High Hon Roll; NHS; Pride Committee; Distinction; Babson; Bus Adm.

PADUCK, EDWARD C; Barnstable HS; Hyannis, MA; (Y); Drama Clb; Band; Chorus; Concert Band; Jazz Band; Mrchg Band; School Musical; School Play; Stage Crew; Variety Show; Outstndg Frosh Bnd 83; Berklee Schl Msc; Rcrdg Tech.

PAGAN, HILDA MARIA; Hayoke HS; Holyoke, MA; (Y); #18 In Class; Boys Clb Am; Hosp Aide; ROTC; Chorus; Church Choir; Variety Show; Frsh Cls; High Hon Roll; Herbert Goldberg Fam Schrlshp Awd 86; Holyoke Hm Ec Awd 86; Joseph B Weis Prz 86; Springfield Coll; Physcl Thrpst.

PAGAN, YOLANDA; S Boston HS; Dorchester, MA; (S); Church Yth Grp; Office Aide; Spanish Clb; Teachers Aide; Yrbk Stf; Hon Roll; Pres NHS; Two-Way-Toutoring-Elem Chldrn 84; Intl Bus.

PAGANO, DEBBIE; Attleboro HS; S Attleboro, MA; (Y); Latin Clb; Yrbk Stf; Var Capt Cheerleading; Powder Puff Ftbl; NHS; Katherine Gibbs JR Leadership Awd For Future Secretaries Winner 86; Katherine Gibbs; Bus.

PAGE, ADAM; St Johns Prep; Topsfield, MA; (Y); JA; Im Ftbl; JV Lcrss; Im Vllybl; Hon Roll; NHS; Scuba Diving; Karate; Travel-Sailing; U Of VT; Poli Sci.

PAGE, GUY; St Johns Prep; Peabody, MA; (Y); Hon Roll; Ntl Merit Ltr; MIT; Comp Prog.

PAGE, STEPHANIE; Fitchburg HS; Fitchburg, MA; (Y); Drama Clb; Band; Chorus; Concert Band; Jazz Band; Mrchg Band; School Play; Var Fld Hcky; High Hon Roll; Russn Lang, Hist Inst Schlrshp 86; Frgn Lang.

PAGLIUCA, DAVID; Taunton HS; Taunton, MA; (Y); Yrbk Stf; Var Bsbl; Var Ftbl; Bus Mgmt.

PAGNOTTA, PAULA; Brockton Christian Reginal HS; Brockton, MA; (Y); 1/20; Drama Clb; Chorus; Yrbk Stf; Pres Sr Cls; Bsktbl; Vllybl; Val; School Play; High Hon Roll; Kiwanis Awd; Prncpls Awd 84-86; Aquns JC Typg Awd 86; Bible Awd 83-86; Eastern Nazerene Coll; Pre-Med.

PAIGE, KELLIE; Bedford HS; Bedford, MA; (Y); AFS; Art Clb; Girl Scts; Rep Frsh Cls; Hon Roll; Horseback Riding Awds NEDA 76-86; Tufts; Vet.

PAILES, ANN MARIE; Triton Regional HS; Rowley, MA; (Y); 16/192; Var Service Clb; Sec Frsh Cls; Sec Soph Cls; Sec Jr Cls; Sec Sr Cls; Var Capt Fld Hcky; Var Capt Trk; DAR Awd; NHS; Yrbk Stf; Ldrshp Sprtsmnshp Awd Fld Hcky; All-Str Fld Hcky; Mst Vlbl Rnnr Trck; U Of MA; Bus.

PAIS, ANA; B M C Durfee HS; Fall River, MA; (Y); 151/650; Church Yth Grp; Cmnty Wkr; Office Aide; Spanish Clb; Hon Roll; Rep Church At Bishops Ball 86; Spnsh Clb Tres & Press 85-87; Excllnc In Spnsh Awd 85-86; Psych.

PALADINO, NANCY; Doherty Memorial HS; Worcester, MA; (Y); Ski Clb; Spanish Clb; SADD; Ed Yrbk Bus Mgr; Var L Bsktbl; Var L Socr; JV Sftbl; Var Trk; Hon Roll; Spanish NHS; High Achvmnt Ntl Span Exam 86; Biol Sci.

PALERMO, RICHARD; Central Catholic HS; Plaistow, NH; (Y); 24/215; JV Bsbl.

PALLATRONI, HENRY F; Old Rochester Regional HS; Mattapoisett, MA; (Y); 27/150; Am Leg Boys St; Boy Scts; Ski Clb; Rep Frsh Cls; Rep Soph Cls; Rep Jr Cls; Rep Sr Cls; Sec Stu Cncl; Ftbl; Trk.

PALLEIKO, JEFFREY J; Walpole HS; Walpole, MA; (Y); 75/270; Church Yth Grp; Q&S; Ski Clb; Nwsp Stf; Yrbk Stf; Lit Mag; JV Bsktbl; Var Capt Golf; Var Trk; RI Schl Of Design; Fine Art.

PALMER, DANIELLE; Braintree HS; Braintree, MA; (Y); 4/442; SADD; Trs Band; Concert Band; Orch; Nwsp Rptr; Rep Stu Cncl; Var Fld Hcky; High Hon Roll; Hon Roll; NHS; Spanish NHS; MA Msc Edctrs Assoc SE Dstrct Bnd; SE MA Bndmstrs Assoc Bnd & Orchstra; Phlsphy.

PALMER, DAVID; Auburn HS; Auburn, MA; (Y); Church Yth Grp; Ski Clb; Varsity Clb; Var Bsktbl; Var Capt Crs Cntry; Var Capt Trk; High Hon Roll; Border Conf All Star Cross Cty,Track 84-86.

PALMER, JIM; East Longmeadow HS; East Longmeadow, MA; (Y); Socr; Hon Roll.

PALMERI, ANDREA; Marshfield HS; Marshfield, MA; (Y); Dance Clb; Key Clb; SADD; Nwsp Stf; Yrbk Stf; Crs Cntry; Capt Gym; Powder Puff Ftbl; Jr NHS; Music Awds Piano 84; Commun.

PALOUKOS, APHRODITE; Boston English HS; Boston, MA; (Y); Office Aide; Teachers Aide; School Play; Stage Crew; Lit Mag; Var Stu Cncl; Mary C Mc Laughlin Readg Lang Arts 86; Engl Hgh Engl Dept Awd 86; Phy Thrpy.

PANACOPOULOS, ROSS; St Marys Regional HS; Lynn, MA; (Y); 45/105; Boy Scts; Political Wkr; Variety Show; Rep Frsh Cls; VP Sr Cls; JV Bsbl; JV Bsktbl; JV Ftbl; Hon Roll; Monsigneur O Brien Awd 85; Bus Mgmt.

PANICO, SUZANNE F; Boston Latin Schl; South Boston, MA; (Y); 30/284; Church Yth Grp; Dance Clb; Hosp Aide; JA; Library Aide; Sec Science Clb; Nwsp Stf; Rptr Yrbk Stf; High Hon Roll; NHS; Stride Rite & Grls High Schlrshp 85-86; Dvdsn Prz 85-86; Harvard; Sci.

PANITSIDIS, CHARLIE; Arlington HS; Arlington, MA; (Y); Boys Clb Am; Socr; Letterman, Allstar & MVP 85; U Lowell; Cvl Engr.

PANKO, JESSICA; Waring Schl; S Hamilton, MA; (Y); GAA; Library Aide; Model UN; Scholastic Bowl; Varsity Clb; Chorus; Orch; School Play; Swing Chorus; Var L Bsktbl.

PANSEWICZ, ERIC; Christopher Columus HS; Boston, MA; (Y); 13/126; Church Yth Grp; Political Wkr; Hon Roll; Student Trainer 84; Northeastern U; Criminal Law.

PAONE, LINDA; Matignon HS; Lexington, MA; (S); English Clb; French Clb; Library Aide; Lit Mag; Hon Roll; NHS; Ntl Merit Ltr; Law.

PAPAGIANNIS, DINO; Belmont HS; Belmont, MA; (Y); Boy Scts; Church Yth Grp; Band; Concert Band; Mrchg Band; Im Bsktbl.

PAPANGELIS, JOANNE; Boston Latin Schl; Boston, MA; (Y); Church Yth Grp; French Clb; Latin Clb; Hon Roll; Jr NHS; NHS; Fidelty Awd 84-85; Psychol.

PAPANTONIOU, HERCULES; Everett HS; Everett, MA; (Y); Key Clb; SADD; Pres Soph Cls; Pres Jr Cls; Rep Stu Cncl; Var Socr; Northeastern Boston U.

PAPAPIETRO, DAVID; Don Bosco Tech HS; East Boston, MA; (Y); 26/202; Radio Clb; School Play; Lit Mag; Off Soph Cls; Off Jr Cls; JV Var Crs Cntry; Hon Roll; NHS; Prfct Atten Awd; Reading & Hstry Awd 83-84; Scholar Awd 86-87.

PAPAVIZAS, HELLEN; Boston Latin Schl; Boston, MA; (Y); Key Clb; Science Clb; Teachers Aide; JV Tennis; High Hon Roll; Hon Roll; NHS; Wesleyan U.

PAPAYASILIOU, ACHILLES; Holliston HS; Holliston, MA; (Y); Am Leg Boys St; Chess Clb; Church Yth Grp; Capt Var Wrstlng; High Hon Roll; NCTE Awd; NHS; Boy Scts; Trk; Hon Roll; Hugh O Brian Yth Ldrshp Smnr 85; Eagle Scout 85; Acdmc Awds In Spnsh & Scl Stdys 86; Pre-Med.

PAPLEACOS, MARIA; Notre Dame Acad; Tewksbury, MA; (Y); Art Clb; Teachers Aide; Stage Crew; Yrbk Stf; JV Var Bsktbl; Var L Socr; JV L Sftbl.

PAPPALARDO, DAVID A; Central Catholic HS; Methuen, MA; (Y); 3/215; Nwsp Stf; Ed Yrbk Stf; Im Bsktbl; Im Bowling; Im Vllybl; High Hon Roll; NHS; Ntl Merit SF; Harvard Book Awd 85; Lawyer.

PAPPALARDO, MARC; Central Catholic HS; N Andover, MA; (Y); 28/235; JA; Ski Clb; Im Bsktbl; Im Ice Hcky; JV Var Trk; Im Vllybl; High Hon Roll; Hon Roll; Bus.

PAPPAS, PENELOPE; Mario Umana Tech; Boston, MA; (Y); 18/86; Capt ROTC; SADD; DAR Awd; VFW Awd; Mass Port 86; Retired Offcrs Assn TROA ROTC Mdl 86; Paul Revere Chptr Scholar Awd 86; N Adams ST Coll; Med Tech.

PAPPATHANASI, KYM; Swampscott HS; Swampscott, MA; (Y); 53/220; Church Yth Grp; Model UN; SADD; Church Choir; Var Capt Cheerleading; Var Powder Puff Ftbl; Var Tennis; Var Trk; Hon Roll; Ski Clb; Tradition In Tennis Awd 85; Outstndng Achvt In Ind Arts Awd 86; Conf All Star Salem News All Star 85; U Of VT; Mech Engr.

PAQUET, VICTOR L; Marshfield HS; Green Harbor, MA; (Y); 16/390; Am Leg Boys St; Var Capt Ftbl; NHS; Red Cross Aide; High Hon Roll; Taddy Corp Forgn Exchange Schlrshp 86; Engr.

PAQUETTE, DANIELLE; Marblehead HS; Marblehead, MA; (Y); Band; Mrchg Band; Var L Cheerleading; Var Capt Gym; Var Capt Socr; Var Capt Trk; MVP In Soccer 84; Physcl Ed.

PAQUETTE, KATHLEEN M; Quaboag Regional HS; W Brookfield, MA; (Y); 10/75; Am Leg Aux Girls St; Math Tm; VP Science Clb; SADD; School Play; Yrbk Stf; Sr Cls; Var Capt Fld Hcky; Mgr(s); Hon Roll; Ntl Assn Of Wmn-Cnstrctn Schlrshp 86; U Of MA-AMHERST; Elec Engrng.

PAQUETTE, R ERIC; Marblehead HS; Marblehead, MA; (Y); 14/240; Am Leg Boys St; Math Tm; Pres Soph Cls; Pres Jr Cls; Pres Sr Cls; Var L Bsbl; Var L Socr; Var L Trk; NHS; Ski Clb; Drtmth Bowl 85; Cntry III Ldrs Schlrshp ST Rnr-Up 86; Middlebury Coll.

PAQUETTE, VALARIE; Dracut SR HS; Dracut, MA; (Y); 3/250; Art Clb; Math Clb; Math Tm; VP Service Clb; Nwsp Bus Mgr; Nwsp Rptr; Im JV Bsktbl; Im Sftbl; Im Vllybl; High Hon Roll; Bio & Geometry Hnrs Certs 85; Frnch Hnr Cert 83-86; Rsrch Bio Chmst.

PAQUIN, ANGELA; New Bedford HS; New Bedford, MA; (Y); 110/701; Church Yth Grp; VP Drama Clb; Key Clb; Chorus; Church Choir; School Musical; School Play; Stage Crew; Variety Show; Rep Jr Cls; Sthstr MA Dstrct Chorus 85-86; Ntl Ltn Schlr Awd.

PAQUIN, CHRISTOPHER; Uxbridge HS; Uxbridge, MA; (Y); 15/400; Rep Am Leg Boys St; Computer Clb; Library Aide; Var Crs Cntry; High Hon Roll; Hon Roll; NHS; MIT; Comp Sci.

PARADIS, CHRIS; N Attleboro HS; N Attleboro, MA; (Y); Art Clb; SADD; Nwsp Stf; Yrbk Stf; Rep Stu Cncl; JV Var Ftbl; Var Capt Trk; Hon Roll; Sun Chronicle Spg Trck-All Star 86; Hockomock Leag All Star Tm 86; Grntlgy.

PARADIS, JOHN; Arlington HS; Arlington, MA; (Y); Church Yth Grp; Drama Clb; SADD; Acpl Chr; Madrigals; School Musical; School Play; Stage Crew; Lit Mag; Pres Stu Cncl; U MA Amherst; Theater.

PARADIS, LISA; Methuen HS; Methuen, MA; (Y); 120/360; GAA; Intnl Clb; JV Bsktbl; Capt Fld Hcky; Var Sftbl; Hon Roll.

PARANDELIS, CHERYL; BMC Durfee HS; Fall River, MA; (Y); 81/600; Drama Clb; Library Aide; Nwsp Rptr; Nwsp Stf; Rptr Sr Cls; Hon Roll; Delta Stu Gvt 86; Entrtnmt Edtr 85-86; Johnson & Wales; Fshn Merch.

PAREDES, MARIBEL; David Hale Fanning Trade High; Worcester, MA; (Y); 3/124; Dance Clb; Pep Clb; Variety Show; Yrbk Stf; Rep Soph Cls; VP Jr Cls; Pres Sr Cls; JV Bsktbl; Cit Awd; High Hon Roll; Dance.

PARENT, ALBERT; New Bedford HS; New Bedford, MA; (Y); 98/547; Capt Chess Clb; Capt Bowling; Hon Roll; JR Chess Lg 85; Concorus De Francais Des Cooperants 84; 2nd Pl Bowling Lg, 2nd Pl Chess Clb 86; Northeastern U; Physics.

PARENT, CHRISTOPHER; Lynnfield HS; Lynnfield, MA; (Y); 20/163; Church Yth Grp; Cmnty Wkr; SADD; Sec Stu Cncl; Capt Var Crs Cntry; L Var Trk; Hon Roll; NHS; Cape Ann MA League Track All Star 86; Aeronautical Engr.

PARENT, ELIZABETH; Cathedral HS; Palmer, MA; (Y); Drama Clb; Scholastic Bowl; Chorus; Church Choir; School Musical; Variety Show; Ed Nwsp Stf; Sec Soph Cls; Wstrn MA Dist Fstvl 85-86; U Of Hartford Schl Msc Yth Smr Cmp 86; Bio.

PARENT, VICKI; Waltham SR HS; Waltham, MA; (Y); Church Yth Grp; Drama Clb; French Clb; JCL; Latin Clb; Stage Crew; High Hon Roll; Hon Roll; NHS; Regis; Frgn.

PARIS, DEBORAH A; Fitchburg HS; Fitchburg, MA; (Y); 13/208; Office Aide; Yrbk Phtg; High Hon Roll; Burdett Coll; Bus Mgmt.

PARISE, ROBERT; Hyde Park Acad; Boston, MA; (S); Off Jr Cls; High Hon Roll; Prfct Atten Awd; Lamp Knwldg Awd Bio 85; Hghst Ovral Grd Avg Awd 85; Bus.

PARK, ROBERT D; Westboro HS; Westboro, MA; (Y); 13/170; Am Leg Boys St; Varsity Clb; Concert Band; Drm & Bgl; Stu Cncl; JV Var Bsktbl; JV Var Golf; Im Vllybl; Hon Roll; NHS; Rensselaer Poly Inst; Comp Engr.

PARKER, ALYSSA BETH; Winchester HS; Winchester, MA; (Y); JA; Var Capt Bsktbl; Var JV Socr; Var Capt Sftbl; High Hon Roll; Church Yth Grp; GAA; Letterman Clb; Varsity Clb; Nwsp Rptr; Hist Dept Schlrshp Awd 86.

PARKER, ANDREW; Taunton HS; Berkley, MA; (Y); 7/450; Computer Clb; Drama Clb; Math Tm; Science Clb; Ski Clb; Yrbk Stf; Lit Mag; Tennis; High Hon Roll; Band; Natl Latin Exam Awd 84; Comp Instruc 84-86; US Air Force Acad; Mission Sp.

PARKER, BOB; Old Colony Regional Vo-Tech; Acushnet, MA; (Y); Church Yth Grp; VICA; Hon Roll; VICA ST Fnlst Prcsn Machng 86; Tool & Die Mkr.

PARKER, CHERYL; Hopkias Acad; Hadley, MA; (S); 6/49; Am Leg Aux Girls St; Church Yth Grp; 4-H; Band; Chorus; Yrbk Stf; Stat Bsktbl; JV Score Keeper; Trs NHS; Wstrn MA Dist Chorus 82-86; MA ST 4-H Tn Cncl 84-86; Locl 4-H Swng Clb Ldr 85-86; Bus Mgmt.

PARKER, CHRISTINE; Bishop Feehan HS; Attleboro, MA; (Y); Church Yth Grp; Hosp Aide; Pep Clb; SADD; Yrbk Stf; Hon Roll; Bridgewater ST Coll; Med.

PARKER, GILES; Braintree HS; Braintree, MA; (Y); 27/480; Cmnty Wkr; VP SADD; Nwsp Rptr; Rep Soph Cls; Rep Jr Cls; Rep Sr Cls; Var JV Bsktbl; Var JV Socr; Var Trk; High Hon Roll; Archtctr.

PARKER, JOE; Methuen HS; Methuen, MA; (Y); Model UN; School Play; Var L Ftbl; Var L Trk; Hon Roll; Stu Govt Day 86; Bus.

PARKER, MICHAEL E; North Andover HS; N Andover, MA; (Y); Am Leg Boys St; Pep Clb; Rep Soph Cls; Rep Stu Cncl; Capt Bsbl; Capt Ftbl; Capt Ice Hcky; Hon Roll; West Point; Engr.

PARKER, MONICA; Norwood SR HS; Norwood, MA; (Y); 40/352; Cmnty Wkr; Girl Scts; Key Clb; Pep Clb; Yrbk Bus Mgr; Pres Frsh Cls; JV Sftbl; Hon Roll; JC Awd; Ten Outstndng Norwood Yths TONY Awd 86; GSA Gold Awd 85; Boston U; Jrnlsm.

PARKER, TODD; Silver Lake Regional HS; Kingston, MA; (Y); 2/458; Sec Debate Tm; French Clb; Math Tm; Band; Im Wrstlng; Bausch & Lomb Sci Awd; High Hon Roll; NHS; Sal; NFL; Worcester Poly Tech Inst; Engr.

PARKHURST, JILL; Methuen HS; Methuen, MA; (Y); 7/330; Hosp Aide; Intnl Clb; Model UN; VP Stu Cncl; High Hon Roll; NHS; HOBY Ldrshp Rep 84-85; Rep Stu Adv Cncl 83-84.

PAROLISI, CHERYL ANNE; Presentation Of Mary Academy; Lawrence, MA; (Y); Math Clb; Spanish Clb; Yrbk Stf; JV Sftbl; High Hon Roll; NHS; NEDT Awd; Computer Clb; Pep Clb; Nwsp Stf; Archdiocs Of Bostons Ldrshp Conf 85-86; Genl Exc Awd 85-86; Span Awd 85-86; Law.

PAROYON, GREG; Arlington HS; Arlington, MA; (Y); Aud/Vis; Boys Clb Am; Chess Clb; Church Yth Grp; Computer Clb; FCA; Radio Clb; Spanish Clb; JV Bsktbl; Hon Roll.

PARRINELLO, MICHAEL; Natrich HS; Natick, MA; (Y); 69/375; Im Bsktbl; Var Tennis; JV Trk.

PARRISH, KATHY; Quincy HS; Quincy, MA; (Y); Dance Clb; SADD; Yrbk Stf; Sec Jr Cls; Sec Stu Cncl; Var Powder Puff Ftbl; Ntl Merit Schol; Bus.

PARSONS, CONNIE; Westfield HS; Westfield, MA; (Y); 28/329; Sec Trs Church Yth Grp; JA; Spanish Clb; Hon Roll; Jr NHS; NHS; U Of MA; Math.

PARTENHEIMER, ANN M; Leicester HS; Leicester, MA; (Y); French Clb; Ski Clb; School Play; Yrbk Stf; Cheerleading; Trk; Schlrshp U MA 86; Hist, Govt Awds 85; U Of MA; Dance.

PARTYKA, MELANIE; Williston Northampton Schl; Chicopee, MA; (Y); Spanish Clb; Yrbk Phtg; Yrbk Stf; Sec Frsh Cls; JV Bsktbl; Var Lcrss; Var Mgr(s); Var Socr; Var Trk; Busnss Mgmt.

PARZYCH, MARIA; Easthampton HS; Easthampton, MA; (Y); 36/140; Nwsp Stf; Yrbk Phtg; Yrbk Stf; Sec Jr Cls; Pres Sr Cls; Var Capt Cheerleading; Var Socr; Hon Roll; Early Chldhd Educ.

PASCIUTO, PAUL; Winchester HS; Winchester, MA; (Y); Spanish Clb; Stu Cncl; Bsktbl; Hon Roll.

PASCIUTO, SUSAN; Auburn HS; Auburn, MA; (Y); Varsity Clb; Band; Concert Band; Drm Mjr(t); Mrchg Band; School Play; Var Fld Hcky; Music Band Dir Awd; Worcester ST Coll; Media.

PASIC, PATRICIA; North HS; Worcester, MA; (Y); Pep Clb; Varsity Clb; Nwsp Rptr; Rep Soph Cls; Off Stu Cncl; Co-Capt Cheerleading; Co-Capt Pom Pon; Hon Roll; Jr NHS; Cty Wide Essy Cntst 86; Alt Rep-Stu Govt Day 86; Jrnlsm.

PASQUALE, LISA M; Coyle & Cassidy HS; S Easton, MA; (Y); 16/131; Art Clb; Church Yth Grp; Latin Clb; Ski Clb; Variety Show; Yrbk Stf; 4-H Awd; Hon Roll; Tutr-H S Stu 85-86; U Of Lowell; Accntng.

PASSACANTILLI, NICOLE; Pope John XXIII HS; Medford, MA; (Y); Church Yth Grp; French Clb; Hosp Aide; SADD; Cheerleading; Trk; Prfct Atten Awd; Dntstry.

PASSETTO, CHRISTINA; Monument Mountain HS; Lee, MA; (Y); 11/125; Church Yth Grp; French Clb; Girl Scts; Hosp Aide; Red Cross Aide; SADD; Teachers Aide; Color Guard; Flag Corp; School Play; Educ Assist Schlrshp 86; Jr Early Schlrshp 85; 7 Local Schlrshps 86; Green Mountain Coll; Spec Educ.

PASTORE, ERIC; Burlington HS; Burlington, MA; (Y); 66/321; Aud/Vis; Im Bsktbl; Var L Ftbl; Im Socr; Im Wt Lftg; Boston Coll; Med.

PASTORELLO, THERESA; Our Lady Of Nazareth HS; Saugus, MA; (Y); Pres Drama Clb; Intnl Clb; SADD; Band; Chorus; School Musical; School Play; Trs Jr Cls; NEDT Awd; Cmnty Wkr; SR Christian Ldrshp; Boston Shakespeare Comptn; Music Awds; Musical Theatre.

PATALANO, CARLA; North Quincy HS; Quincy, MA; (Y); Church Yth Grp; Cmnty Wkr; JA; Pep Clb; Spanish Clb; Acpl Chr; Chorus; School Musical; School Play; Variety Show; Fine Arts Chorale-Semi Prof Chorus 84-86.

PATCH, STEPHANIE; Hingham HS; Hingham, MA; (Y); 147/300; AFS; Im Bsktbl; JV Var Sftbl; Hon Roll; Yth Art Awd 86; Engrng.

PATEL, ERIC; St Johns Pre; Peabody, MA; (Y); Boy Scts; Camera Clb; Church Yth Grp; Yrbk Stf; Hon Roll; Piano; Pre-Law.

PATEL, PRATIKSHA; Wachusett Regional HS; Holden, MA; (Y); 10/443; Hosp Aide; Science Clb; Nwsp Rptr; French Hon Soc; Hon Roll; Sec NHS; Raytheon Co Awd 86; Wrcstr Dntl Scty Awd 85; Dartmouth; Med.

PATEL, PRITI; Woburn SR HS; Woburn, MA; (Y); Chorus; Stu Cncl; High Hon Roll; Hon Roll; NHS; Hosp Aide Schlrshp 86; U Of MA Boston; Bio.

PATEL, VIBHA; Braintree HS; Braintree, MA; (Y); 74/443; Chorus; Swing Chorus; Nwsp Rptr; Co-Capt Twrlr; High Hon Roll; Hon Roll; Ntl Merit SF; Most Dedicated Majorette Twirling; Law.

PATOULIDIS, STACEY; Saugus HS; Saugus, MA; (Y); Dance Clb; Intnl Clb; Library Aide; Office Aide; SADD; Teachers Aide; Yrbk Rptr; Yrbk Stf; Rep Stu Cncl; Mth.

PATTERSON, BETH; Wilmington HS; Wilmington, MA; (Y); Church Yth Grp; Cmnty Wkr; Pres French Clb; Pres Spanish Clb; Rep Frsh Cls; Rep Soph Cls; Rep Jr Cls; Rep Sr Cls; Rep Stu Cncl; JV Capt Tennis; Grnd Cross Of Clr-Rnbw Grls 86; Citation Of Merit; Mltpl Sclrosis Soc 86; Worthy Advsr-Rnbw Assmbly 85.

PATTERSON, LEE ANN; Sacred Heart HS; S Weymouth, MA; (Y); 2/60; Math Clb; Spanish Clb; Variety Show; Yrbk Stf; High Hon Roll; Hon Roll; NHS; Prfct Atten Awd; St Schlr; Weymouth Cthlc Wmns Clb Schrlshp 86; Stonehill; Math.

PATTERSON, NANCY; Fairhaven HS; Acushnet, MA; (Y); Chorus; School Musical; Yrbk Stf; Hon Roll; Jr NHS; VFW Awd; Engl Awd 84; Bus Math Awd 84; Achvmnt ATA Awd 84; SMU; Bus Ed.

PATTERSON, NATALIE; Phillips Acad; Chicago, IL; (Y); Cmnty Wkr; Office Aide; Teachers Aide; Chorus; School Musical; Mgr JV Swmmng; Hon Roll; Pre-Med.

PATTERSON, SCOTT; Randolph HS; Randolph, MA; (Y); French Clb; Temple Yth Grp; Nwsp Rptr; Rep Stu Cncl; Bsbl; Ftbl; High Hon Roll; Hon Roll; Jr NHS.

PATTON, CLARENCE; Middlesex Schl; Ithaca, NY; (Y); Yrbk Rptr; Ntl Merit SF; Schlrshp 82-86; Cornell Schl Of Arch; Arch.

PATWARI, PURVI; Arlington HS; Arlington, MA; (Y); Art Clb; Camera Clb; Nwsp Phtg; Nwsp Stf; Rep Stu Cncl; Crs Cntry; Mgr(s); Trk; Hon Roll; NHS; Bus.

PAUL, DAVE; Plymouth Carver HS; Plymouth, MA; (Y); JV Bsktbl; Var JV Socr; Hon Roll.

PAUL, RICK; Taconic HS; Richmond, MA; (Y); Bus.

PAULHUS, WILLIAM J; Blackstone Valley Reg Voc Tech HS; Linwood, MA; (Y); Am Leg Boys St; Boy Scts; Church Yth Grp; VICA; High Hon Roll; Prfct Atten Awd; Stu Adlt Advsry Cmt 86-87; Elec Engrng.

PAULL, DAVISON C; Bishop Stang HS; Westport Point, MA; (Y); Drama Clb; Radio Clb; School Play; Rep Stu Cncl; JV Ftbl; Var L Trk; High Hon Roll; NHS; Ntl Merit SF; Actor.

PAVAO, JOSEPH; Winchester HS; Winchester, MA; (Y); Im Bsktbl; Hon Roll; NHS; Engrng.

PAVAO, PAULA; BMC Durfee HS; Fall River, MA; (Y); 130/700; Cmnty Wkr; Hosp Aide; Chorus; School Musical; School Play; Variety Show; Nwsp Rptr; Lit Mag; Hon Roll; Cert Of Merit Excel Portgs 86; Bridgewater ST Coll; Educ.

PAWLIK, PATRICIA; Presentation Of Mary Acad; No Andover, MA; (S); 12/50; Var Capt Bsktbl; Spanish Clb; Nwsp Rptr; Var Sftbl; Var Vllybl; Hon Roll; NHS; Mst Outstndng Underclssmn Christmas Bsktbl Tourn 84; Ed.

PAYETTE, ALISON; Auburn HS; Auburn, MA; (Y); Chorus; Math Awd 82-83; Vet.

PAYSON, WENDY; Easthampton HS; Easthampton, MA; (Y); Sec Church Yth Grp; French Clb; JA; Library Aide; Spanish Clb; Chorus; Church Choir; Cit Awd; High Hon Roll; Prfct Atten Awd; Robert Joseph Wallace Prz Stengrphy 86; W L Lovell Prz 86; Katharine Gibbs Schl; Sectrl.

PEABODY, DEBRA; Haverhill HS; Haverhill, MA; (Y); Spanish Clb; Hon Roll; Chem Engrng.

PEACH, ANDREW; Marblehead HS; Marblehead, MA; (Y); 7/250; Boy Scts; French Clb; Intnl Clb; Political Wkr; Band; Jazz Band; Yrbk Stf; High Hon Roll; NHS; Colby Coll Book Awd 85; Bus.

PEACHEY, JOHN; Westbridge HS; Littleton, MA; (S); 3/14; Art Clb; Yrbk Ed-Chief; Gov Hon Prg Awd; High Hon Roll; NHS; 3rd Pl MA ST Sci Fair 84-85; 1st Pl Westbrdg Sci Fair 84-85; Boston Coll.

PEARSON, CHERYL; Westfield HS; Westfield, MA; (Y); 5/330; Am Leg Aux Girls St; Dance Clb; Intnl Clb; Spanish Clb; Nwsp Rptr; Yrbk Rptr; Jr NHS; NHS; Drama Clb; Model UN; James R Shea Mem Awd Excllnce Spn 84-86; Worcester Polytech; Chem Engrng.

PEARSON, DANIEL; Bishop Feehan HS; Norton, MA; (Y); 29/241; Debate Tm; JCL; Yrbk Phtg; Yrbk Rptr; Yrbk Stf; Lit Mag; Hon Roll; NHS; Prfct Atten Awd; Maxima Cum Laude Natl Latin Exam 84-85; MA Debate Lg Trophy 85; Cum Laude Natl Latin Exam 86; Classics.

PEARSON, ELIZABETH; Weymouth South HS; S Weymouth, MA; (Y); 50/338; Church Yth Grp; Key Clb; JV Sftbl; High Hon Roll; Hon Roll; NHS; Pres Schlr; JV Crs Cntry; JV Trk; Fnlst In Dennis F Ryan Essay Cntst 85; Achvt Awd In Soc Studies 85; Ctzns Schrlshp Awd 86; U Of Lowell; Elec Engrng.

PEARSON, SARAH LUCK; Cambridge School Of Weston; San Francisco, CA; (Y); CAP; FBLA; Mat Maids; Timer; Twrlr; Opt Clb Awd; Clnst Desk Awd.

PEATFIELD, GREGORY; Georgetown HS; Georgetown, MA; (Y); 9/86; Boy Scts; Computer Clb; Drama Clb; Math Tm; Teachers Aide; Band; Concert Band; Mrchg Band; Stage Crew; Nwsp Ed-Chief; Top Scr Annl HS Math Exm 86; Ntl Hnr Soc 86; Comptr Instctr For JH 82-86; U Of Lowell; Elec Engrng.

PECCI, MATTHEW; Waltham HS; Waltham, MA; (Y); 1/600; Am Leg Boys St; Band; Mrchg Band; Stu Cncl; Trk; High Hon Roll; NHS; Sci & Math Mdl Rnsselaer Polytech Inst 86; Cty-Spnsrd Bsbll & Bsktbll Lgs 83-86; Sci Mdl 86; Med.

PECK, DAVID; Medway SR JR HS; Medway, MA; (Y); 20/150; Teachers Aide; High Hon Roll; Hon Roll; Ntl Merit Ltr; Schltc Awds 83-85; Aero Engr.

PECK JR, RUSSELL K; Bourne HS; Buzzards Bay, MA; (Y); Am Leg Boys St; Computer Clb; Math Tm; Ski Clb; Teachers Aide; Stat Bsbl; Stat Bsktbl; Pres NHS; Prfct Atten Awd; Data Prcssng Mgmt.

PECK, STEPHEN; Norton HS; Norton, MA; (Y); #11 In Class; Key Clb; Pep Clb; Pres Stu Cncl; Capt Bsbl; Capt Ftbl; High Hon Roll; Natl Schlr/Athlt Awd 86; Alumni Awd 86; All Schltc Bsbl Boston Globe-Herald 86; T Bch Perry Schlrshp 86; Coll Of Holy Cross.

PECKHAM, CHRISTOPHER; Medford HS; Medford, MA; (Y); 3/417; Math Tm; Science Clb; Rep Frsh Cls; Rep Soph Cls; Rep Jr Cls; Rep Sr Cls; Ice Hcky; Capt Var Socr; Mu Alp Tht; Trs NHS; Top Geomtry Stu 83-84; Top Alg II Stu 85-86; Top Comp Math Stu 84-85; Comp Sci.

PECKHAM, TINA; Sharon HS; Sharon, MA; (Y); 13/210; Cmnty Wkr; Dance Clb; Capt Var Gym; Var Trk; High Hon Roll; Hon Roll; NHS; U PA Book Awd 86; MVP Gym Globe All Schltc 84-86; Phys Thrpy.

PEDRINI, RICK; Boston College HS; Arlington, MA; (Y); Boys Clb Am; Church Yth Grp; SADD; Varsity Clb; Bsbl; L Ftbl; Im Capt Vllybl; Im Wt Lftg; Norwich U.

PEDRO, CARLOS; Cathedral HS; Springfield, MA; (Y); JA; Prfct Atten Awd; STCC; Comp Prgmng.

PEGNATO, MICHAEL; St Dominic Savio HS; Chelsea, MA; (Y); 13/95; SADD; Nwsp Rptr; Nwsp Stf; Lit Mag; Rep Frsh Cls; Rep Soph Cls; Ftbl; Ice Hcky; Hon Roll; Law.

PEKARSKI, BRIAN; Methuen HS; Methuen, MA; (Y); 47/350; Church Yth Grp; Art Clb; JV Ice Hcky; High Hon Roll; Hon Roll; Hnrbl Mntn St Hist Conf 85; Engr.

PELCZAR, KELLY; Fairhaven HS; Fairhaven, MA; (Y); Band; Chorus; Color Guard; Mrchg Band; Orch; Sci.

PELIS, NANCY; Smith Acad; Hatfield, MA; (S); Drama Clb; School Play; Stage Crew; Trs Frsh Cls; Trs Jr Cls; High Hon Roll.

PELLAND, RACHEL; Dracut SR HS; Dracut, MA; (Y); Var Cheerleading; Var Gym; Var Trk; Hon Roll; Outstndng Typing 85-86; Katharine Gibbs Schlrshp 85-86; Dracut Tchrs Assoc Schlrshp 85-86; Katherine Gibbs Schl; Secy.

PELLEGRINO, JOANNE; Arlington HS; Arlington, MA; (Y); Color Guard; Hon Roll; Suffolk U; Bus Adm.

PELLEGRINO, LINDA; Medford HS; Medford, MA; (Y); Cheerleading; High Hon Roll; Hon Roll; NHS; Math, Engl Awds 84-85; Bus.

PELLERIN, SHARON; Classical HS; Lynn, MA; (Y); French Clb; Hosp Aide; JA; Math Tm; Chorus; Rep Frsh Cls; Capt Swmmng; High Hon Roll; Jr NHS; NHS.

PELLETIER, JESSICA; Presentation Of Mary Acad; Bradford, MA; (Y); French Clb; SADD; Chorus; Yrbk Stf; Trs Soph Cls; Var Bsktbl; Var Sftbl; Vllybl; Hon Roll.

PELLETIER, JILL E; Salem HS; Salem, MA; (Y); 5/265; Church Yth Grp; Pres Key Clb; Math Clb; Science Clb; High Hon Roll; NHS; Prsdntl Acdmc Ftns Awd 86; Scty Wmn Engrs Hgh Hnrs 86; Margaret M Postles Fnd Schlrshp 86; U Of NH; Elctrcl Engr.

PELLETIER, ROBIN; Bishop Fenwick HS; Beverly, MA; (Y); 5/238; AFS; Hosp Aide; SADD; Rep Stu Cncl; NHS; Intl Frgn Lang Awd-Frnch 86; Mt Holyoke Coll; Spnsh.

PELOQUIN, JILL; Easthampton HS; Easthampton, MA; (Y); 28/132; Pep Clb; Spanish Clb; Yrbk Stf; Stu Cncl; Cheerleading; Mgr(s); Hon Roll; Citzn Schlrshp 86; Leslie Zive Memrl Awd 86; Holyoke CC; Radiolgcl Tchnlgy.

PELOQUIN, ROBERT; Chicopee Comprehensive HS; Chicopee, MA; (Y); 33/332; Church Yth Grp; French Clb; Bsbl; Hon Roll; Bus.

PELOQUIN, TINA MARIE; Easthampton HS; Easthampton, MA; (Y); 4-H; Ed Nwsp Ed-Chief; Nwsp Stf; Yrbk Phtg; Yrbk Stf; Stu Cncl; 4-H Awd; High Hon Roll; Achvt Awd, Ctzn Schlrshp Awd & Hampshire Cnty Awd 86; Boston U; Ob/Gyn.

PELTIER, SANDRA; Agawam HS; Agawam, MA; (Y); 32/320; Dance Clb; GAA; Color Guard; Yrbk Stf; Var Tennis; Hon Roll; Margaret H Gloster Meml Schlrshp 86; U Of MA; Htl.

PENDEGRAST, MICHAEL; Bellingham HS; Bellingham, MA; (Y); Var L Bsktbl; Var L Socr; Hon Roll; Prfct Atten Awd; Tri Valley Lg All Star Soccr Awd 85; Bsktbl Capt 86-87; Soccr Capt 86-87; U Miami; Brdcstng.

PENNA, CLAUDIA; Westfield HS; Westfield, MA; (Y); 29/338; Church Yth Grp; Spanish Clb; Yrbk Ed-Chief; Yrbk Stf; Var Capt Socr; Var Sftbl; NHS; Vtd-Bst Personality; U Of MA; Acctng.

PENNIMAN, ALAN J; Waltham SR HS; Waltham, MA; (Y); Am Leg Boys St; Aud/Vis; Exploring; Stage Crew; Var Crs Cntry; Var Trk; Hon Roll; Bentley Coll-Comp Pgmng Cntst 3rd Pl 86; Wrcstr Polytech Inst; Comp Engr.

PENNINGTON, GREG; Augtin Preparatory HS; Billerica, MA; (Y); Drama Clb; Pep Clb; School Play; Stage Crew; Hon Roll; Bronze Mdl Olympda Of Spkn Rssn 84.

PENTA, PASQUALE; Medford HS; Medford, MA; (Y); 13/372; VP Church Yth Grp; Cmnty Wkr; Math Tm; Red Cross Aide; VP Ski Clb; VP SADD; Yrbk Stf; Stu Cncl; Vllybl; High Hon Roll; Hedford Womens Clb Schlrshp 86; Sainta Maria Sommervle Ct Schlrshp 86; Holy Cross Coll; Pre-Dentl.

PENTA, SUSAN; Mategnon HS; Somerville, MA; (S); 2/178; Library Aide; SADD; Bsktbl; Var Trk; Var Vllybl; High Hon Roll; NHS; Spanish NHS; Natl Sci Merit; Natl Ldrshp Merit; Acadmc Al-Amer; Bus.

PENTO, LAURA; Holbrook HS; Holbrook, MA; (Y); 6/100; OEA; Var Bsktbl; JV Var Sftbl; Hon Roll; NHS; MVP In Bsktbl 86; U MA Bstn; Accntnt.

PEPKA, DAVID; Bartlett HS; Webster, MA; (Y); 10/160; Jazz Band; Mrchg Band; Variety Show; Pres Soph Cls; Pres Jr Cls; NHS; Rotary Awd; Science Clb; Concert Band; Stu Adv Cncl Rep 85-87; Schl Atten Dance Bd 86-87; Ntl Assoc Jazz Ed 86; Comp.

PERCIVAL, PENNY; Frontier Regional HS; S Deerfield, MA; (Y); 6/96; French Clb; Library Aide; Ski Clb; Yrbk Phtg; Var Tennis; Var Vllybl; Hon Roll; U MA; Sci.

PERCIVAL, RACHEL; St Bernards HS; Fitchburg, MA; (S); 28/177; Aud/Vis; Library Aide; Cheerleading; Hon Roll; NHS; Schlrshp Twrds Tuition 83; Prfct Attdnce; Psych.

PEREA, JOSE; Madison Park HS; Boston, MA; (Y); Mst Imprv Jnr Awd 86; Comp Tech.

PEREIRA, PATRICIA JANE F M; Bishop Connolly HS; Fall River, MA; (Y); 50/167; Cmnty Wkr; Drama Clb; Exploring; Hosp Aide; Teachers Aide; Chorus; School Play; Stage Crew; High Hon Roll; Pep Clb; Fall Rvr Ctzns Schlrshp Fndtn Awd 86; St Marys Coll; Educ.

PERGAKIS, NICOLE; Westford Acad; Westford, MA; (Y); Office Aide; Ski Clb; Spanish Clb; SADD; Yrbk Stf; JV Var Fld Hcky; JV Sftbl; High Hon Roll; Hon Roll; Alg I Awd 84; U Lowell; Math.

PERILLO, PAUL; Everett HS; Everett, MA; (Y); 29/365; Church Yth Grp; Intnl Clb; Nwsp Rptr; Yrbk Sprt Ed; Bsbl; Ftbl; Elks Awd; Hon Roll; Bstn U; Jrnlsm.

PERILLO, RANDALL; Methuen HS; Methuen, MA; (Y); 52/333; Chess Clb; Model UN; JV Stat Bsbl; Var L Ftbl; Score Keeper; Stat Sftbl; Var L Trk; Merrimack Vly Conf Ftbl All Star 85; MVP Ftbl Game Vctry 85.

PERKINS, LYNNE; Quaboag Regional HS; Warren, MA; (Y); Church Yth Grp; Exploring; Girl Scts; Ski Clb; Spanish Clb; SADD; Varsity Clb; Variety Show; Nwsp Stf; Yrbk Stf; Bridgewater ST Clg; Comm.

PERKS, SHARON; Westborough HS; Westboro, MA; (Y); 28/189; Spanish Clb; Band; Mrchg Band; Yrbk Phtg; Tennis; Hon Roll; NHS; MA Music Eductrs Centrl Dist Band 86.

PERLMAN, JULIA; Newton North HS; Newton, MA; (Y); 2/611; Drama Clb; French Clb; Ski Clb; Temple Yth Grp; School Musical; Ed Yrbk Rptr; Lit Mag; JV Crs Cntry; JV Tennis; Hon Roll; Engl.

PERRAULT, CAROLINE; Taunton HS; East Taunton, MA; (Y); 65/400; Dance Clb; Sec French Clb; Hosp Aide; Sec Ski Clb; Yrbk Stf; Lit Mag; Vicki Daub Friedman Meml Schlrshp 86; St Elizabeths Schl/Nrsg; Nrsg.

PERRIN, MICHELLE; Quaboag Regional HS; Warren, MA; (Y); SADD; Varsity Clb; Var JV Bsktbl; Var JV Fld Hcky; Hon Roll; NHS.

PERRINGTON, DENISE; West Roxbury HS; Mattapan, MA; (S); Intnl Clb; JV Var Bsktbl; NHS; Brown U.

PERRON, SCOTT G; Austin Preparatory Schl; Billerica, MA; (Y); Debate Tm; Latin Clb; Im Sftbl; Im Wt Lftg; Hon Roll; U MA Amherst; Engrng.

PERRONE, MARIO R; Arlington HS; Arlington, MA; (Y); Model UN; Radio Clb; Band; Concert Band; Mrchg Band; Pep Band; Symp Band; Sec Stu Cncl; Bsktbl; Trk; Harvard U; Pre Med.

PERROTTA, GWEN; Silver Lake Regional HS; Pembroke, MA; (Y); Latin Clb; Ski Clb; Chorus; School Musical; Stage Crew; Yrbk Stf; Hon Roll; Bentley Coll; Fin.

PERROTTO, LOUANN; Attleboro HS; Attleboro, MA; (Y); Powder Puff Ftbl; Hon Roll; Bus.

PERRY VI, JAMES DE W; The Roxbury Latin Schl; Newton, MA; (Y); Boy Scts; Pres Chess Clb; Pres Church Yth Grp; Debate Tm; Model UN; Nwsp Rptr; Yrbk Phtg; L Var Crs Cntry; Ntl Merit SF; French Clb; Brown U Bk Awd 85; Harvard; Physcs.

PERRY, JENNIFER; Dartmouth HS; S Dartmouth, MA; (Y); Var Capt Bsktbl; Var Capt Sftbl; Lion Awd; Acad Lttr 85-86; Lwyr.

PERRY, KAREN; Matignon HS; Somerville, MA; (S); 16/174; Dance Clb; Drama Clb; Spanish Clb; SADD; Sec Ed Yrbk Stf; Ed Lit Mag; Trk; NHS; Spanish NHS; Natl Hnr Rl 83; Mktg.

PERRY, KEVIN A; Bridgewater Rayham Regional HS; Bridgewater, MA; (Y); Am Leg Boys St; Boy Scts; Cmnty Wkr; Trs Pres Leo Clb; Var Ftbl; Var JV Wrstlng; Hon Roll; Sci.

PERRY, KRISTINE; Haverhill HS; Bradford, MA; (Y); 3/400; Church Yth Grp; Sec Trs Latin Clb; Ski Clb; Spanish Clb; Yrbk Stf; High Hon Roll; Kiwanis Awd; NHS; St Schlr; Brd Dir NE Conf Tchg Frgn Lang Awd Excllnce Lang Stdy 86; Achvt Awd Lat 86; Carleton Przе Scholar 86; Coll Of Holy Cross; Biol.

PERRY, LESLIE; Phillips Acad; Danville, PA; (Y); JV Var Lcrss; Var JV Swmmng; Var Vllybl.

PERRY, MELISSA; North Quincy HS; Quincy, MA; (Y); 35/380; Church Yth Grp; JA; Band; Concert Band; Mrchg Band; High Hon Roll; Hon Roll; Spanish NHS; Speech/Hrng Pathlgst.

PERRY, MICHELLE; Bishop Feehan HS; Attleboro, MA; (Y); Fshn Merch.

PERRY, MONICA; Cushing Acad; Costa Mesa, CA; (Y); Sec Key Clb; Red Cross Aide; Yrbk Stf; L Var Crs Cntry; JV Fld Hcky; L Var Lcrss; L Var Swmmng; L Var Trk; Hon Roll; Bus Admn.

PERRY, ROBERT; Newton North HS; Newton Centre, MA; (Y); Chess Clb; Church Yth Grp; Computer Clb; Exploring; Bsbl; Bsktbl; Socr; Hon Roll; Comp Sci.

PERRY, ROBYN; Bishop Feehan HS; Attleboro, MA; (Y); Hosp Aide; Swmmng; Hon Roll; Bus.

PERRY, TAMATHA; Shepherd Hill Regional HS; Dudley, MA; (Y); Am Leg Aux Girls St; Church Yth Grp; Pep Clb; School Musical; School Play; Variety Show; Pres Frsh Cls; Pres Soph Cls; Pres Jr Cls; Pres Sr Cls; Stu Gvrnmnt Day Dlgt 86; Yth Ldrshp Salute Nmnee 86; Aero.

PERRYMAN, RICHARD; Swampscott HS; Boston, MA; (Y); Boy Scts; Political Wkr; Var Capt Bsktbl; Var Ftbl; Hon Roll; Mrktng.

PERSUITTE, KAREN; Montachusett Regional Vo-Tech HS; Fitchburg, MA; (Y); Pep Clb; SADD; VICA; Sec Frsh Cls; Rep Stu Cncl; Var Cheerleading; Sftbl; Hon Roll; Data Prcssng.

PESSOLANO, MARK; Wilbraham & Monson Acad; Wilbraham, MA; (Y); Varsity Clb; Band; Mrchg Band; JV Bsbl; Var Ice Hcky; Hon Roll; Bus.

PETERS, ERIC; Central Catholic HS; Andover, MA; (Y); 35/215; Math Clb; Red Cross Aide; Varsity Clb; Var Capt Bsbl; Im Capt Bsktbl; L Ftbl; Hon Roll; Im Coach Actv; Im Socr; Im Vllybl; Bentley Coll.

PETERS, KIMBERLY; Greater Lawrence Vo Tech HS; Methuen, MA; (Y); Hosp Aide; Am Red Cross First Aid 85; MA Ed Nrs Aide Trng Course 86; Dietian.

PETERS, MARIE; Tantasqua Regional SR HS; Brimfield, MA; (Y); 1/200; Drama Clb; Intnl Clb; Math Tm; Band; Concert Band; Mrchg Band; Pep Band; School Play; Symp Band; Yrbk Stf; Harvard Bk Awd 86; Dirtrs Awd For Concert Band 84; SCI.

PETERSEN, WILLIAM; Winchester HS; Winchester, MA; (Y); Band; Concert Band; Mrchg Band; Ftbl; Music Awd 84-86; Sftbl Coach 86.

PETERSON, KEVIN O; Natick HS; Hyde Park, MA; (Y); Church Yth Grp; FBLA; SADD; Band; Church Choir; Im Badmtn; Var L Ftbl; Var Capt Trk; Im Wt Lftg; Hon Roll; Dean JC; Wrd Proc.

PETERSON, KIM; Notre Dame Acad; Duxbury, MA; (Y); French Clb; Latin Clb; High Hon Roll; Hon Roll; Law.

PETERSON, LARA; Marblehead HS; Marblehead, MA; (Y); French Clb; Stage Crew; Nwsp Ed-Chief; Stu Cncl; Var Crs Cntry; JV Fld Hcky; Var Lcrss; Hon Roll; Schlrshp Career Discvry Pgm Arth; Lang.

PETERSON, THOMAS; Barnstable HS; Centerville, MA; (Y); 27/392; Church Yth Grp; SADD; Hon Roll; NHS; Comp Pgmng.

PETERSON, THOMAS A; Shrewsbury SR HS; Shrewsbury, MA; (Y); 36/225; Am Leg Boys St; Letterman Clb; Band; School Musical; Yrbk Sprt Ed; Jr Cls; Crs Cntry; Trk; NHS; U MA Amherst; Comp Sci.

PETITPAS, KAREN; Mount Saint Joseph Acad; Boston, MA; (Y); 51/155; Drama Clb; French Clb; Political Wkr; Teachers Aide; School Musical; School Play; Drama Awd 86; Emerson Coll; Theatr Arts.

PETO, JEFFREY; Clinton HS; Clinton, MA; (Y); 4/126; Pres JA; School Play; Yrbk Stf; Pres Jr Cls; Rep Stu Cncl; JV Bsktbl; L Pres Ftbl; L Trk; High Hon Roll; NHS; Bst Supprtg Actor Schl Play 85; Worcester Polytech Inst; Engrng.

PETRILLI, PATRICIA; Archbishop Williams HS; Quincy, MA; (Y); Drama Clb; Key Clb; VP Ski Clb; SADD; Chorus; School Musical; School Play; Variety Show; VP Soph Cls; VP Sr Cls; $500 Schlrshp-Women Aux Plmbng, Htng, & Cooling Cntrctrs Of MA 86; Framingham ST Coll; Clothing.

PETRILLO, ANTHONY J; Dedham HS; Dedham, MA; (S); 10/252; Computer Clb; French Clb; School Play; Rep Frsh Cls; Rep Sr Cls; Var L Ftbl; Im Wt Lftg; High Hon Roll; Hon Roll; VFW Awd; Awd Cert Outstndng Sic Mntrshp Pgm 85; Awd Trphy, Cert ST Wnner Liberty Amer 85; Tufts U; Pre Med.

PETRIN, JAMIE; Quaboag Regional HS; West Brookfield, MA; (Y); Spanish Clb; SADD; Varsity Clb; VP Frsh Cls; VP Soph Cls; VP Jr Cls; Pres Sr Cls; Var Bsktbl; High Hon Roll; Hon Roll.

PETROULAS, STAVROULA; West Roxbury HS; Roslindale, MA; (S); Library Aide; Teachers Aide; Chorus; Swmmng; Hon Roll; NHS; Boston U; Sargent.

PETRUCCELLI, RICHARD; St Dominics Savio HS; E Boston, MA; (Y); 11/94; Im Bsktbl; Hon Roll; Prfct Atten Awd; Acad All-Am 85-86; Boston U; Cmptr Sci.

PETRUZZIELLO, IVA; Saint Clare HS; Dedham, MA; (Y); 2/120; JCL; Nwsp Rptr; Stu Cncl; Crs Cntry; Trk; NHS; NEDT Awd; Vllybl; High Hon Roll; Prfct Atten Awd.

PETTINE, MATT; Braintree HS; Braintree, MA; (Y); 19/443; Computer Clb; Math Tm; Spanish Clb; Yrbk Bus Mgr; Yrbk Ed-Chief; Yrbk Phtg; Yrbk Rptr; NHS; Spanish NHS; Comp Sci.

PETTINELLI, GAIL; Billerica Memorial HS; Billerica, MA; (Y); 112/500; Church Yth Grp; French Clb; Girl Scts; School Musical; Stage Crew; Variety Show; Hon Roll; Bus Mgmt.

PETTIS, VINCENT; Haverhill HS; Haverhill, MA; (Y); 89/414; Capt Ftbl; Var Trk; Var L Wrstlng; Hon Roll; Econ.

PEURA, SCOTT; Wachusett Regional HS; Princeton, MA; (Y); 15/443; Church Yth Grp; Mathletes; Var L Ftbl; Var L Trk; French Hon Soc; NHS; Hon Roll.

PHAM, SON; Dedham HS; Dedham, MA; (Y); Boy Scts; Computer Clb; Diving; Swmmng; High Hon Roll; MA Adv Stds Prog 86; Engrng.

PHAM, THANH; Pittsfield HS; Pittsfield, MA; (Y); French Clb; German Clb; Mathletes; Yrbk Stf; High Hon Roll; NHS; Pre Med.

PHAN, HUNG; South Boston HS; Dorchester, MA; (S); 3/20; Computer Clb; Band; Socr; Vllybl; Hon Roll; NHS; Comp Engr.

PHANEUF, ROBIN; Fitchburg HS; Fitchburg, MA; (Y); Pep Clb; Ski Clb; School Play; Yrbk Stf; VP Soph Cls; VP Jr Cls; VP Sr Cls; Stu Cncl; Crs Cntry; Trk; French II Awd:JR Engl Awd; JR Hnry Fitchburg Womans Clb; Educ.

PHAT, BROS; South Boston HS; Brighton, MA; (S); Hon Roll; NHS; Spllng Bee Awd; Yr Bk Awd; Wrld Wrk Awd; Bus.

PHELAN, JACQUELYN; Mount Alvernia HS; Roslindale, MA; (Y); Hosp Aide; School Musical; Trs Soph Cls; VP Jr Cls; Pres Sr Cls; Hon Roll; Coop & Schl Spirit Awd; Med.

PHELAN, JAMES; North Quincy HS; Quincy, MA; (Y); 11/375; Sec Am Leg Boys St; Drama Clb; Political Wkr; Red Cross Aide; VP Frsh Cls; Trs Jr Cls; Trs Sr Cls; Var Capt Bsktbl; High Hon Roll; Var NHS; Foreign Lang Hon Soc Treas 86-87.

PHELAN, JESSICA; Beverly HS; Beverly, MA; (Y); Church Yth Grp; Cmnty Wkr; SADD; Yrbk Stf; Hon Roll; Humanities.

PHELPS, AIMEE; Falmouth HS; Falmouth, MA; (Y); Church Yth Grp; Dance Clb; Drama Clb; French Clb; Key Clb; Thesps; Acpl Chr; Chorus; Church Choir; Madrigals; Yale Book Awd 85; Rotary Clb Awd 86; Miami U OH; Intl Pol.

PHETTEPLACE, JUDITH; Stoughton HS; Stoughton, MA; (Y); Church Yth Grp; Cmnty Wkr; Intnl Clb; Library Aide; Church Choir; Camp Fr Inc; Yrbk Stf; Soph Cls; Jr Cls; Im Swmmng; Spec Achvt Awd Tnns 85; Spch Thrpst.

PHETTEPLACE, LAURA; Westfield HS; Westfield, MA; (Y); Western New England; Finc.

PHILBIN, SARAH E; Wachusett Regional HS; Sterling, MA; (Y); 9/396; Am Leg Aux Girls St; Hosp Aide; Science Clb; Band; Nwsp Rptr; Hon Roll; Lion Awd; NHS; Pres Schlr; Socty Womn Engrs Awd 84; Century 3 Ldrshp 85; Holy Cross; Pre-Law.

PHILLIPS, ANDREW; Stjohns Prep HS; Lynnfield, MA; (Y); Spanish Clb; Nwsp Rptr; Bsktbl; Golf; Ice Hcky; Hon Roll; Varsity Clb; Spanish NHS.

PHILLIPS, JOHN; Tantosgua HS; Sturbridge, MA; (Y); #3 In Class; Boy Scts; Chorus; Yrbk Stf; Pres Soph Cls; Pres Jr Cls; Pres Sr Cls; JV Bsbl; Var Bsktbl; Var Crs Cntry; High Hon Roll; Oceangrphy.

PHILLIPS, JOSEPH P; Mansfield HS; Mansfield, MA; (Y); 12/201; Chorus; Drm Mjr(t); Jazz Band; School Musical; Lion Awd; NHS; Pres Schlr; Drama Clb; SADD; Acpl Chr; Semper Fideles Awd-Excllnc In Music 86; Excllnc In Humnties 86; Excllnc In Band 86; Berklee Coll Of Music; Music.

PHILLIPS, PAM; Braintree HS; Braintree, MA; (Y); 15/440; JCL; Latin Clb; Nwsp Stf; Ed Yrbk Stf; Lit Mag; Fld Hcky; Hon Roll; NHS; Spanish NHS; Engrng.

PHILLIPS, STEPHANIE; Norton HS; Norton, MA; (Y); 15/135; Pep Clb; Concert Band; Mrchg Band; School Play; Yrbk Stf; Stu Cncl; High Hon Roll; Prfct Atten Awd; Henri A Yelle Ed Career Schlrshp 86; Bridgewater ST Coll; Chldhd Ed.

PHIPPS, KATHIE; North Attleboro HS; N Attleboro, MA; (Y); Cmnty Wkr; JCL; Latin Clb; Rep Stu Cncl; Powder Puff Ftbl; JV Sftbl; High Hon Roll; Hon Roll; Ltn Ntl Hon Soc 85-86; Bus.

PIAZZA, JOANNE; Methuen HS; Methuen, MA; (Y); 49/337; Hosp Aide; Intnl Clb; Var Capt Tennis; Stat Vllybl; Spanish NHS; MVP Tennis 86; NH Coll; Accntng.

PICARD, CRAIG; Blackstone Valley Reg Voc Tech HS; Upton, MA; (Y); Pres SADD; Yrbk Stf; Pres Frsh Cls; Pres Soph Cls; Var L Bsbl; Var Capt Bsktbl; Var L Crs Cntry; Var L Socr; Var L Trk; Superntntnts Commdtn List 84-86; Dual Vly 1st Tm Allstar Bsktbl 86; Albert Moultan Mem Awd 86; NE Univ; Electrcl Engrng.

PICARD, PATRICIA; Bishop Stang HS; Acushnet, MA; (S); 2/221; JA; Speech Tm; Chorus; Yrbk Stf; L Vllybl; NHS; Pres Physcl Ftns Awd; SE MA U; Nrsg.

PICARD, PATTI; Leicester HS; Leicester, MA; (Y); Crs Cntry; Fld Hcky; Hon Roll; Quinsiaamond Coll; Bus.

PICARD, STEVEN; Ludlow HS; Ludlow, MA; (Y); JCL; Latin Clb; Pep Clb; School Play; Variety Show; Nwsp Phtg; Nwsp Stf; JV Bsbl; Var Ice Hcky; Robt Costa Schlrshp 86; Salem ST Coll; Englsh.

PICARDI, JENNIFER; Marshfield HS; Marshfield, MA; (Y); 128/530; Key Clb; Office Aide; OEA; SADD; Trk; Bus Mgmt.

PICKARD, LAUREN; Andover HS; Andover, MA; (Y); 25/408; French Clb; Quiz Bowl; Scholastic Bowl; Ski Clb; Var Swmmng; Hon Roll; NHS; Ntl Merit Ltr; Punchard Trustees Fllwshp Schlrshp 86; Cornell U; Intl Bus.

PICKETT, KAREN; Matignan HS; Somerville, MA; (S); 1/178; Cmnty Wkr; Science Clb; Spanish Clb; School Musical; High Hon Roll; NHS; Ntl Merit Ltr; Spanish NHS.

PIEPIORA, DEAN; St Bernard CC HS; Shirley, MA; (S); French Clb; Hon Roll; NHS.

PIERANTOZZI, CRAIG; Nauset Regional HS; North Eastham, MA; (Y); #12 In Class; Am Leg Boys St; Varsity Clb; Var Capt Bsbl; Var Bsktbl; Hon Roll; NHS; Cmstry.

PIERCE, DARREN; Amherst Regional HS; Amherst, MA; (Y); Boy Scts; Church Yth Grp; Im Bsbl; Im Bsktbl; Var Capt Ftbl; Var L Lcrss; Var Wt Lftg; Hon Roll; HS Chem Achvt Awd 86; Fairfield U; Psych.

PIERCE, KIMBERLY; Dover-Sherborn Reg HS; Sherborn, MA; (Y); 23/157; Var Trk; JV Vllybl; Hon Roll; Engl I Cert Awd 84; Wrld Lit Cert Awd 85; Alg II Lev II Cert Awd 86; Bus.

PIERCE, MARK A; Fitchburg HS; Fitchburg, MA; (Y); 8/250; Am Leg Boys St; Cmnty Wkr; Varsity Clb; Bsbl; Bsktbl; Ftbl; High Hon Roll; Amer Lgn Bsbl 85 & 86; Bsktbl Bst Dfns 86; Bsbl Bst Offns & CMC Allstar 86.

PIERCE, RONALD; Clinton HS; Clinton, MA; (Y); 4/150; High Hon Roll; Lion Awd; NHS; Fitchburg ST Coll; Cmptr Sci.

PIERI, ANDREA; Agawan HS; Feeding Hls, MA; (Y); French Clb; Hon Roll; Genl C Abrams 85; Holyoke CC; Bus Adm.

PIERRE, MICHAEL; St Johns Prep Schl; Prides Crossing, MA; (Y); Church Yth Grp; Sec Frsh Cls; Sec Soph Cls; Rep Jr Cls; Im Bsktbl; JV Golf; NHS; Spanish NHS; Spanish Clb; SADD; Golf Coaches Awd 85; Plaque Exc Ntl Spnsh Ex 86; Law.

PIERRO, TODD; Foxboro HS; Foxboro, MA; (Y); 27/225; Chess Clb; Church Yth Grp; Ski Clb; Nwsp Stf; Ftbl; Wrstlng; Hon Roll; VP NHS; Bus.

PIERSON, NIKKI; Chatham JR SR HS; North Chatham, MA; (Y); 13/35; Art Clb; Drama Clb; Trs SADD; Sec Chorus; Madrigals; School Play; Ed Yrbk Stf; Var Fld Hcky; Im Vllybl; Hon Roll; Balfour Key Art 86; Intr Dsgn.

PIETROPOLO, MICHAEL; St Dominic Savio HS; Revere, MA; (Y); 11/95; JA; Math Clb; Ski Clb; Yrbk Stf; Im Bsktbl; Im Bowling; Ital II Awd 84-85; Lib Arts.

PIGNATARE, JUDITH N; Agawam HS; Agawam, MA; (Y); GAA; JA; Concert Band; Cheerleading; Capt Fld Hcky; Sftbl; Capt Swmmng; Trk; Hon Roll; Lion Awd; Western MA Trk & Swmmng Chmps 84-85; Qlfd Bay ST Games 5th 800 Mtr Run 85; Spts Med.

PIGNATIELLO, LISA; Bedford HS; Bedford, MA; (Y); 64/198; Yrbk Stf; Powder Puff Ftbl; Swmmng.

PIKE, JENNIFER M; Douglas Memorial HS; E Douglas, MA; (Y); Quiz Bowl; Cmmrcl Art.

PIKE, JONATHAN; Brockton HS; Brockton, MA; (Y); 201/1200; Church Yth Grp; Computer Clb; JA; Lit Mag; Hon Roll; JA Bus Basics 86; Pony & Colt Lg 84-86; Thom Mc An Wrkr 85-86; UMASS Bus Schl; Bus.

PIKE, RENA; Attleboro HS; North Attleboro, MA; (Y); Crs Cntry; Trk; Acctg.

PIKORA, DEBRA; Shepherd Hill Regional HS; Dudley, MA; (Y); 1/170; Trs Church Yth Grp; French Clb; Math Tm; School Musical; Stu Cncl; Bausch & Lomb Sci Awd; High Hon Roll; NHS; Mbrshp In MENSA 86; Vrious Acad Awds Math Sci Engl 84-86; MIT; Comp Sci.

PILIBOSIAN, JULIE; Arlington HS; Arlington, MA; (Y); Church Yth Grp; Office Aide; SADD; Church Choir; Orch; Rep Soph Cls; JV Socr; Hon Roll; NHS.

PIMENTAL, MICHAEL; New Bedford HS; New Bedford, MA; (Y); 30/631; Church Yth Grp; Cmnty Wkr; Intnl Clb; Key Clb; Office Aide; Yrbk Stf; Rep Jr Cls; Rep Sr Cls; Rep Stu Cncl; High Hon Roll; Boston Coll; Bus Admin.

PIMENTEL, DINIS; Assabet Valley Reg Voc HS; Hudson, MA; (Y); 14/278; Math Clb; Math Tm; Yrbk Stf; NHS; Outstndng Soph Mach Shop 84-85; Outstndng Junior Mach Shop 85-86; Acad Ltr 85-86; Engrng.

PIMENTEL, KELLY; New Bedford HS; New Bedford, MA; (Y); 4/700; Dance Clb; Drama Clb; JCL; Stage Crew; High Hon Roll; Jr NHS; NEDT Awd; Church Yth Grp; Science Clb; Church Choir; Wnnr Spllng Bee 83; 3rd Pl Essy Cntst Super Hero 82; MA Coll Pharmacy; Reg Phrmcst.

PIMENTEL, LOUIS; Diman Reg Voc Tech HS; Fall River, MA; (Y); Boys Clb Am; Church Yth Grp; Yrbk Stf; Hon Roll; Trades Fair 1st Pl Wnnr; Arch Drftng.

PINE, DANIEL R; Matignon HS; Somerville, MA; (Y); 70/179; Teachers Aide; Bowling; Hon Roll; Spanish NHS; Suffolk U.

PINET, LILLIAN; Madison Park HS; Boston, MA; (Y); Camera Clb; Church Yth Grp; Hon Roll; NHS; Tufts U; Erly Chldhd Ed.

PINGLEY, MARYBETH; Bishop Connolly HS; Fall River, MA; (Y); 50/176; Cmnty Wkr; Trk; High Hon Roll; Hon Roll; :Riha Equtn Mdl 84; SE MA U; Bio.

PINO, LORI J; Barnstable HS; Centerville, MA; (Y); 53/376; Church Yth Grp; Cmnty Wkr; Drama Clb; School Play; Variety Show; Nwsp Rptr; Pres Nwsp Stf; Wheelock Coll Bk Awd 85; Chld Dvlpmnt Prgm Schlrshp & Cntrvl-Ostrvl Vlntrs Schlrshp 86; Wheelock Col6; Erly Chldhd.

PINTO, ANGELA; Ludlow HS; Ludlow, MA; (Y); 37/280; GAA; Nwsp Rptr; Nwsp Stf; Socr; Portuguese Lang Awd 86; U MA; Psych.

PIOTTE, KRISTIN; Maynard HS; Maynard, MA; (Y); 64/106; Band; Chorus; Church Choir; Concert Band; Mrchg Band; Var Crs Cntry; JV Sftbl; Timer; Twrlr; Trvl Agnt.

PIPCZYNSKI, JILL; Hopkins Acad; Hadley, MA; (Y); 9/50; Spanish Clb; Chorus; Var Capt Bsktbl; Var Socr; Hon Roll; NHS; Med Tech.

PIRES, LUBELIA; Durfee HS; Fall River, MA; (Y); 35/600; Church Yth Grp; Teachers Aide; Yrbk Stf; Hon Roll; Pres Schlr; Bridgewater ST Coll; Phys Ed.

PISANO JR, ROBERT; Franklin HS; Franklin, MA; (Y); 77/221; Variety Show; Bsbl; Hon Roll; Global Schlstc Awds Art 84-85; MVP Awds Bsbl 85-86; Garelicks Bennys Oil Schlrshp 86; U CT; Graphic Arts.

PISARCZYK, DANIEL; Holyoke Catholic HS; Easthampton, MA; (Y); 30/129; Chess Clb; Computer Clb; Spanish Clb; Sec Stu Cncl; Var Tennis; UMASS; Psych.

PISCOPO, EDWARD; Tewksbury Memorial HS; Tewksbury, MA; (S); 108/340; Boy Scts; Church Yth Grp; DECA; Drama Clb; Chorus; School Play; Variety Show; Bsbl; Crs Cntry; Ftbl; DECA Dedctn Awd 86; Trck All Conf All Star 86; Crss Cntry Coaches Awd 86; Westfield ST Coll; Bus.

PISIEWSKI, KARIN; Hudson HS; Hudson, MA; (Y); 7/163; Math Tm; Band; Concert Band; Jazz Band; Mrchg Band; Orch; Pep Band; Symp Band; Yrbk Stf; JV Bsktbl; 2nd Pl Natl Hstry Day ST 85; Engl Awd & Frnch Awd 85; Atty.

PISSIMISSIS, HARIKLEIA; Barnstable HS; Hyannis, MA; (Y); 3/376; Pres Church Yth Grp; Drama Clb; Math Tm; NFL; Speech Tm; SADD; Lit Mag; Elks Awd; NCTE Awd; NHS; Brnstble JR Miss 86; Boston Coll.

PITEO, MARCY ANN; East Longmeadow HS; E Longmeadow, MA; (Y); Church Yth Grp; Office Aide; Ski Clb; School Play; Var Capt Bsktbl; Var L Socr; Springfield Coll; Phys Thrpy.

PITT, MIKE; King Philip Regional HS; Norfolk, MA; (Y); Var L Crs Cntry; Var Capt Trk; Hon Roll; NHS; U Of MA; Elec Engrng.

PIZZELLO, CHRIS; Salem HS; Salem, MA; (Y); Spanish Clb; Lit Mag; Stu Cncl; Bsbl; Golf; Tennis; High Hon Roll; NHS; Spanish NHS; Cmnctns.

PIZZICONI, MELISSA; Leominster HS; Leominster, MA; (S); Ed Nwsp Stf; Rep Stu Cncl; High Hon Roll; Hon Roll; Bentley Coll; Acctg.

PIZZUTI, TINA; Lynnfield HS; Lynnfield, MA; (Y); Debate Tm; Intnl Clb; Spanish Clb; Band; Mrchg Band; Var Capt Socr; Var JV Trk; Hon Roll; Boston Globe Schlstc Art Awd Gold Key 84; Lynnfield Comptnc Awd Accntng 86; News Phot Cntst 86; Bus.

PLAGGE, PAUL J; Arlington HS; Arlington, MA; (Y); 80/381; Boys Clb Am; SADD; Var Socr; High Hon Roll; Hon Roll.

PLANSKY, MICHAEL; Wakefield Memorial HS; Wakefield, MA; (Y); Church Yth Grp; Key Clb; Math Clb; Yrbk Stf; Capt Var Bsbl; Capt Var Bsktbl; Hon Roll; Fairfield; Mth.

PLANT, GREGORY B; Ayer HS; Ft Devens, MA; (Y); 24/123; Var Ftbl; Var Trk; Hon Roll; Mst Outstdng Wrk In Wrld Rgns 83; Achvt Awd Bkpng I 86; Nichols Coll; Accntng.

PLANTE, CHRISTINE; North HS; Worcester, MA; (Y); 10/208; Church Yth Grp; Ski Clb; Nwsp Stf; Sec Jr Cls; Stu Cncl; Capt Var Socr; Capt Sftbl; Capt Var Trk; Hon Roll; NHS; Clsscl H S Scholar 86; Stonehill Coll; Math.

PLANTE, MARC; Marlborough HS; Marlborough, MA; (Y); 33/269; Church Yth Grp; Computer Clb; Science Clb; Crs Cntry; Hon Roll; NHS; Chem Engrng.

PLASSE, CHRIS; Billerica Memorial HS; Billerica, MA; (Y); 84/500; 4-H; French Clb; Girl Scts; Math Clb; Math Tm; Varsity Clb; Diving; Hon Roll; Biomed Engrng.

PLATT, CHRISTINE; Saugus HS; Lynn, MA; (Y); Coll Of New Rochelle; Elem Educ.

PLATTS, MIKE; Haverhill HS; Haverhill, MA; (Y); Bsktbl; Trk; Lttr In Trck 86; Gld Mdl In MA JR Olympics 82-84; Engineering.

PLEASANT, ANGELINA; Lynn Classical HS; Lynn, MA; (Y); Dance Clb; JA; Chorus; School Musical; Hon Roll; Burdett; Accntg.

PLOTCZYK, MIKE; Shepherd Hill Reg HS; Dudley, MA; (Y); Boy Scts; JV Bsbl; Im Bsktbl; Im Bowling; JV Ftbl; JV Var Socr; Im Sftbl; Var Trk; Im Vllybl; Hon Roll; BSA Eagle Scout Awd 84; Pope Pius XII Religous Awd 85; Archtctr.

PLOURDE, TERI; Cathedral HS; E Longmeadow, MA; (Y); 23/500; Camera Clb; Drama Clb; Intnl Clb; Service Clb; Color Guard; Nwsp Ed-Chief; High Hon Roll; NHS; Hosp Aide; Red Cross Aide; Acdmc Exclnce Bio 85; Acdmc Exclnce World Cultures 84; Med.

PLUNKETT, BETH; Wellesley HS; Wellesley, MA; (Y); 9/330; AFS; Dance Clb; French Clb; Red Cross Aide; Sec Sr Cls; Var Gym; Capt Twrlr; Hon Roll; NHS; Harvard Bk Awd 86; Earth Sci.

PLUNKETT, MARY; Wellesley HS; Wellesley, MA; (Y); Sec AFS; German Clb; Red Cross Aide; Hon Roll; AFS Awd; Simmons Coll; Retail.

PLUNKETT JR, ROBERT W; Belmont HS; Belmont, MA; (Y); 10/270; Am Leg Boys St; Church Yth Grp; Cmnty Wkr; Key Clb; Letterman Clb; Red Cross Aide; Band; Yrbk Stf; Trs Jr Cls; Trs Sr Cls; ST Top 10 Swmmng Awd 86; Hstry Dept Awd 86; Hly X Bk Awd 86.

PLUTNICKI, PAUL; Marlboro HS; Marlboro, MA; (Y); 3/315; Pres VP SADD; Rep Frsh Cls; Rep Soph Cls; Rep Jr Cls; Var L Crs Cntry; JV Socr; Var L Trk; High Hon Roll; NHS; Faclty Awd-Acctng, Spnsh 85-86; U Of PA; Acctng.

PODOLSKI, JUDITH; Tahanto Regional HS; Boylston, MA; (Y); 10/60; Church Yth Grp; Debate Tm; Drama Clb; Exploring; Band; Nwsp Bus Mgr; Nwsp Stf; Yrbk Phtg; High Hon Roll; NHS; Bryant Coll; Mktng.

PODOSEK, PAULA JEAN; Cathedral HS; Ludlow, MA; (Y); 66/455; Sec Trs Intnl Clb; Red Cross Aide; SADD; Hon Roll; Exc Frnch 83-84; Distngushd Svc Interntl Clb 85-86; U MA-AMHERST; Frnch.

POHL, BETH; Randolph HS; Randolph, MA; (Y); Church Yth Grp; Drill Tm; Rep Frsh Cls; Rep Soph Cls; Rep Jr Cls; JV Var Cheerleading; Hon Roll; Bus Mgmt.

POIRIER, LAURIE; Leicester HS; Rochdale, MA; (Y); Spanish Clb; Yrbk Stf; Var Capt Cheerleading; Im Vllybl; High Hon Roll; Hon Roll; NHS.

POLAGRUTO, JOHN; Natick HS; Natick, MA; (Y); 2/502; Am Leg Boys St; Boys Clb Am; Chess Clb; English Clb; JA; Math Clb; Varsity Clb; Yrbk Sprt Ed; Capt Bsktbl; Capt Ftbl; Natl Hnr Soc; IBM Comp Elec Schlrshp; Harvard Bk; MA U; Nuclr Engrng.

POLEY, CHERYL; Haverhill HS; Haverhill, MA; (Y); 19/392; Latin Clb; Ski Clb; Spanish Clb; Varsity Clb; JV Var Sftbl; Im Vllybl; High Hon Roll; NHS; Distinction 83-86.

POLITZER, DANIEL JACARD; Brookline HS; Brookline, MA; (Y); Drama Clb; Ski Clb; School Play; Nwsp Stf; Lit Mag; Socr; Hon Roll; Pres NHS; Ntl Merit SF; Jr NHS; Amer Assn Tchrs Frnch Tst Hnrbl Mntn 82-83; Amer Assn Tchrs Frnch Tst 6th ST MA 84; Intnatl Reltns.

POLLOCK, JODI; Salem HS; Salem, MA; (Y); 9/270; Spanish Clb; VP Jr Cls; Sftbl; CC Awd; Elks Awd; High Hon Roll; Hon Roll; NHS; Spanish NHS; Marion Court JC; Paralegal.

POLOM, MARGARET; Tantasqua Regional HS; Fiskdale, MA; (Y); 16/178; Chorus; Yrbk Stf; Trk; Hon Roll; NHS; Boston U; Psych.

POMARE, MONICA M; Boston Latin Acad; Dorchester, MA; (Y); Drama Clb; JA; JV Sftbl; Var L Vllybl; Hon Roll; Spnsh Ed.

POMERLEAU, KRISTIN; Presentation Of Mary HS; Methuen, MA; (Y); French Clb; SADD; Chorus; Coach Actv; Hon Roll; Sci Fair Prsntn Mary 2nd Pl 85; Sci Fair Boston Hnrb Mntn 85; Suffolk U; Pre-Law.

POMEROY, ROBERT D; Manchester JR SR HS; Manchester, MA; (Y); 15/85; Am Leg Boys St; Boy Scts; Math Tm; Scholastic Bowl; Science Clb; Stage Crew; Stat Bsktbl; Im Vllybl; High Hon Roll; Ntl Merit SF; Elec Engrng.

POMFRET, HEIDI; Wellesley SR HS; Wellesley, MA; (Y); 53/300; Church Yth Grp; Yrbk Stf; Trs Sr Cls; Sec Trs Stu Cncl; Var Capt Lcrss; Var Capt Socr; Hon Roll; NHS; Hnrbl Mntn Sccr 84; All-Str 85; Skng X-Cntry Chmp 81-86; Skng Dwnhll Chmp 85-86.

POMICTER, BENJAMIN; Boston Latin Schl; Boston, MA; (Y); 6/285; FCA; FHA; Math Clb; Math Tm; School Play; High Hon Roll; Hon Roll; NHS; Ntl Merit Ltr; Harvard Coll; Math.

POMPHRET, JENNIFER; Methuen HS; Methuen, MA; (Y); 23/339; Pep Clb; JV Bsktbl; Powder Puff Ftbl; High Hon Roll; Hon Roll.

POND, JULIANNE; Milford HS; Milford, MA; (Y); Sec Church Yth Grp; Hosp Aide; Key Clb; SADD; Hon Roll; Phys Thrpy.

POOLE, EMILY R; The Cambridge Schl; Watertown, MA; (Y); Drama Clb; Exploring; Chorus; School Play; Lit Mag; Chrmn MIT Edctnl Stds Pgm; Guild Mstr Cmptr; Arch Engrng.

POPA, JENICA; Boston Technical HS; Boston, MA; (Y); 17/205; Church Yth Grp; Ski Clb; Frsh Cls; Soph Cls; Hon Roll; Jr NHS; NHS; Ntl Merit Schol; Prfct Atten Awd; Edwards Scholar 86; Two/Ten Scholar 86; Samuel Gross Davis Awd 86; Boston U; Intl Rltns.

POPAT, ALKA; Norton HS; Norton, MA; (S); 8/179; Church Yth Grp; Varsity Clb; Yrbk Stf; JV Tennis; Hon Roll; NHS; Med.

POPE, STEPHANIE; Doherty Memorial HS; Worcester, MA; (Y); Church Yth Grp; French Clb; Band; Pres Chorus; Church Choir; Orch; French Hon Soc; Hon Roll; NHS; Ntl Merit Ltr; Greatr Boston Yth Symphny Orch 84-87; All-ST Band & Orchstrs 83-86; Clarinet Perf.

POPP, ALFRED; South Hadley HS; S Hadley, MA; (Y); 9/172; Church Yth Grp; Mathletes; Rep Jr Cls; Ntl Merit SF; Naval Acad Smmr Semnr 86; Aerntcl Engr.

POPSON, DREW; Westford Acad; Westford, MA; (Y); 30/250; Art Clb; Church Yth Grp; Trs Soph Cls; Pres Jr Cls; Pres Sr Cls; Var Capt Socr; Hon Roll; NHS; West Point; Frgn Lang.

PORCARO, DENISE; Everett HS; Everett, MA; (Y); Burdett Schl; Exec Sec.

PORCARO, PAULA J; Medford HS; Medford, MA; (Y); 50/435; Hosp Aide; SADD; Varsity Clb; Yrbk Stf; Stu Cncl; Capt Swmmng; Tennis; Hon Roll; Acadmc Excllnc Awd Bio, Physlgy, Engl 86; Outstndng Achvt Swmmg 86; U MA Boston; Mgmt.

PORCARO, PETER; Everett HS; Everett, MA; (Y); 25/266; Drama Clb; Exploring; Key Clb; Science Clb; SADD; Varsity Clb; School Musical; School Play; Stage Crew; Yrbk Stf; U Of Lowell; Chem Engrng.

PORTE, ANDREW; Marshfield HS; Marshfield, MA; (Y); Boy Scts; Key Clb; Ski Clb; SADD; Im Lcrss; Im Swmmng; Im Wt Lftg; Hon Roll; Bus.

POSER, NICK; Maynard HS; Maynard, MA; (Y); 40/100; Aud/Vis; Boy Scts; French Clb; Band; Jazz Band; Mrchg Band; VP Sr Cls; Ftbl; Ice Hcky; Trk; Htl & Rest Mgmt.

POSHKUS, MICHAEL T; Stoughton HS; Stoughton, MA; (Y); Am Leg Boys St; Church Yth Grp; Drama Clb; Math Tm; School Musical; School Play; Stage Crew; Rptr Lit Mag; Crs Cntry; Ice Hcky; Bio Chem.

POTENZA, PETER; St Dominic Savio HS; Saugus, MA; (Y); 6/95; Math Clb; Ski Clb; Yrbk Stf; Trs Stu Cncl; Var Golf; JV Ice Hcky; JV Trk; Im Wt Lftg; High Hon Roll; Hon Roll; Acdmc All Amer 85; U S Ldrshp Awd 85-86; Elctrcl Engr.

POTHIER, MATTHEW; Pittsfield HS; Pittsfield, MA; (Y); JA; Letterman Clb; Yrbk Stf; Socr; Capt Trk; Hon Roll; Arch.

POTTLE, JENNIFER LYNN; Blackstone Valley Reg Vo Tech; Milford, MA; (Y); Var Capt Bsktbl; High Hon Roll; Schlrshp To Johnson & Wales 86; Schlrshp Frm Tchrs Assoc From Buruths 86; $100 Valley Tech; Johnson & Wales Coll; Clnry Art.

POTVIN, ALAN; Central Catholic HS; Lawrence, MA; (Y); 74/263; Church Yth Grp; JV Bsktbl; Var Trk; High Hon Roll; Hon Roll; Bio.

POTVIN, ANDREW F; Drury SR HS; North Adams, MA; (Y); 1/189; Computer Clb; Var Crs Cntry; Capt Wrstlng; DAR Awd; Elks Awd; High Hon Roll; Ntl Merit SF; NEDT Awd; Val; IAM & AW Schlrshp 86; MIT; El Engrng.

POTYRALA, MARTHA; Chicopee Comprehensive HS; Chicopee, MA; (Y); 46/280; Latin Clb; Library Aide; School Musical; Stage Crew; Rep Soph Cls; Rep Jr Cls; Stu Cncl; Powder Puff Ftbl; Trk; NHS; Engl.

POULIN, CELESTE; Haverhill HS; Haverhill, MA; (Y); 3/412; Church Yth Grp; French Clb; Spanish Clb; SADD; Yrbk Stf; Stu Cncl; Var L Crs Cntry; Var Capt Trk; High Hon Roll; NHS.

POULIOT, DEANNA; Blackstone-Millville Regional HS; Blackstone, MA; (Y); Concert Band; Mrchg Band; Yrbk Stf; Rep Stu Cncl; Var Capt Bsktbl; Var Capt Fld Hcky; High Hon Roll; NHS; Band; Trk; Bay ST Games Fld Hcky 86; All Str Hnrs Both Fld Hcky & Bsktbl 86; Sprts Med.

POWELL, DAVID; Holyoke HS; Holyoke, MA; (Y); 78/380; Am Leg Boys St; Boys Clb Am; Debate Tm; Drama Clb; English Clb; German Clb; Latin Clb; Spanish Clb; Speech Tm; School Play; Springfield Coll; Psych.

POWELL, ERIC; Wakefield Memorial HS; Wakefield, MA; (Y); Church Yth Grp; JA; School Play; JV Socr; Wt Lftg; JV Wrstlng; Hon Roll; Bus.

POWELL, MICHAEL; Monument Mountain Regional HS; Gt Barrington, MA; (Y); 3/121; Teachers Aide; Variety Show; VP Sr Cls; Var Bsktbl; Var Socr; Capt Tennis; High Hon Roll; NHS; Yrbk Stf; Stu Cncl; MVP JR & SR Tnns 84-86; Wm Sdny Fndtn Schlrshp 85; MVP Bsktbl 85-86; Hartwick Coll.

POWELL, SARAH; Notre Dame Acad; Duxbury, MA; (Y); 25/109; Cmnty Wkr; Key Clb; Ski Clb; Stage Crew; Yrbk Stf; VP Jr Cls; VP Sr Cls; Capt Var Tennis; Hon Roll; VP Of Cls 85-87; Var Tnns 84-87; Hnr Rll 84-87; Intl Bus.

POWELL, STEVEN; Georgetown JR SR HS; Georgetown, MA; (Y); Boy Scts; SADD; Hon Roll; NHS; Church Yth Grp; Political Wkr; Spanish Clb; Im JV Bsktbl; JV Ftbl; A Team-Acadmc 86; Brwnsea Trning 80; Spnsh Achvt Awd 85; Cbnt Mkng.

POWER, DAVID; Waltham HS; Boston, MA; (Y); Exploring; Stage Crew; Socr; Trk; Vllybl; Hon Roll; Comp Sci.

POWER, RICHARD M; Boston College HS; Norwood, MA; (Y); Am Leg Boys St; Key Clb; Spanish Clb; SADD; Var Ftbl; Hon Roll; JC Awd; NHS; Im Bsktbl; Mst Dedctd Athlete 86; Awd Acdmc Excllnc Alge II 86; CYO Of Month 86.

POWER, SANDRA; Salem HS; Salem, MA; (Y); Chorus; Bggst Contrbtn Pop/Rock Chorus 84-85; Mst Likely Succeed 85-86; Educ.

POWERS, BRIAN; Taunton HS; Taunton, MA; (Y); 4/400; Am Leg Boys St; Math Clb; Math Tm; Political Wkr; Var L Bsbl; Var L Bsktbl; High Hon Roll; Hon Roll; NHS; Church Yth Grp; Lcl Nwsppr All Schlstc Baseball Team 86; Engr.

POWERS, CRAIG R; North Brookfield HS; N Brookfield, MA; (Y); 7/38; Mathletes; Pep Clb; Band; Var L Bsbl; Var Capt Bsktbl; JV Socr; NHS; Pres Schlr; Coach Actv; Hon Roll; MA Bsktbl All ST Acdmc Team 86; Geo R Wrin Mem Schlrshp & Slvrbrg Mem Schlrshp 86; Babson Coll; Bus Mngmnt.

POWERS, DAWN E; Malden HS; Malden, MA; (Y); 9/470; Hosp Aide; Nwsp Rptr; Nwsp Stf; Bowling; Var Sftbl; Hon Roll; Varsity Clb; Ntl Merit SF; Pres Acad Fit Awd 86; Northeastern U; Nrsng.

POWERS JR, GERALD; Canton HS; Canton, MA; (Y); 16/255; Pres Church Yth Grp; German Clb; JV Crs Cntry; Var Trk; Hon Roll; Century Club; Sci.

POWERS, JENNIFER; Marblehead HS; Marblehead, MA; (Y); 79/259; Dance Clb; Band; Concert Band; Mrchg Band; Hon Roll; Exc Acctng 86; The Young Dance Co Of Am 82-86; Finance.

POWERS, KAREN; Matignon HS; Somerville, MA; (S); 5/190; JA; Math Clb; Science Clb; Spanish Clb; SADD; Hon Roll; NHS; NEDT Awd; Engr.

POWERS, KELLY; Beverly HS; Beverly, MA; (Y); 41/375; Band; Concert Band; Mrchg Band; JV Bsktbl; Powder Puff Ftbl; JV Socr; JV Sftbl; JV Trk; High Hon Roll; Hon Roll; Annl Schlrs Bnqt 86; Frnch Awd 82-84; Salem ST.

POWERS, KELLY; Salem HS; Salem, MA; (Y); 38/242; Church Yth Grp; Trs Key Clb; Spanish Clb; SADD; Jazz Band; Mrchg Band; Nwsp Rptr; Var L Sftbl; NHS; Spanish NHS; Psych.

POWERS, MAURA; Southbridge HS; Sbridge, MA; (Y); 29/138; Band; Yrbk Phtg; Yrbk Stf; Sec Soph Cls; Sec Jr Cls; Sec Sr Cls; Var Bsktbl; Var Fld Hcky; L Trk; Sthbrdg Ed Assn Schlrshp 86; Frnch Hnrs Awd 84; Brdgwtr ST Coll; Phy Ed.

POWERS, STEPHANIE; Presentation Of Mary Acad; Salem, NH; (Y); 5/45; Sec Cmnty Wkr; Math Clb; Spanish Clb; VP SADD; Stage Crew; Variety Show; Nwsp Stf; Var Tennis; High Hon Roll; NHS; Coaches Awd Atnns 85; Acdmc Achvt Amer Hstry 86.

POWILATIS, BRIAN R; Boston College HS; Holbrook, MA; (Y); 21/300; Church Yth Grp; SADD; Sec VP Stu Cncl; Var L Ftbl; High Hon Roll; NHS; Ntl Merit SF; Am Leg Boys St; German Clb; Political Wkr; Nasiatka Awd 86; Coll Of Hly Crs Bk Awd 86; Ntl Ltn Awd 86; Ivy League; Scl Sci.

POZNIAK, BARBARA; Jamaica Plain HS; Roslindale, MA; (Y); Dance Clb; Hon Roll; Wrd Prcssng.

PRAJZNER, CHRIS E; Holyoke HS; Holyoke, MA; (Y); 20/360; Latin Clb; Spanish Clb; Nwsp Stf; Golf; High Hon Roll; Trs NHS; Holyoke Yth Bsbl League Schlrshp 86; J A Schielbel Awd In Engrng 86; U MA; Engrng.

PRALINSKY, SCOTT D; Athol HS; Athol, MA; (Y); Church Yth Grp; Drama Clb; Intnl Clb; Model UN; Chorus; School Musical; Yrbk Stf; Off Stu Cncl; Jr NHS; Nwspr Stff Ad Edtr; Schlrp MA Bus Week; Swng Mgr Of Mnth Awd Mcdonalds; Bus Adm.

PRANSKIEWICZ, ANDREA; North HS; Worcester, MA; (Y); Art Clb; Church Yth Grp; Drama Clb; English Clb; FBLA; Letterman Clb; Pep Clb; Ski Clb; Spanish Clb; SADD; Worcester ST; Retail Mgmt.

PRATT, GAYLE; Natick HS; Natick, MA; (Y); 83/399; Am Leg Aux Girls St; Church Yth Grp; Speech Tm; Stu Cncl; Im Socr; Var Capt Swmmng; Hon Roll; MVP Grls Swmng 85-86; Psych.

PRATT, GREG; Northfield Mount Hermon HS; Bernardston, MA; (Y); JV Var Socr; Howard & Margaret Jones Awd 85; U Of MA.

PRATT, PAULINE; B M C Durfee HS; Fall River, MA; (Y); Drama Clb; Trs Library Aide; Varsity Clb; Mrchg Band; Yrbk Stf; Cheerleading; Gym; Powder Puff Ftbl; Vllybl; Hon Roll; ICF Chrldng Camp 3rd Pl 85; Grnd Champ ICF Chrldng Camp 86; Tchr.

PRATT, TAMMY; Wachusett Reginal HS; Sterling, MA; (Y); 4-H; Hosp Aide; Band; Concert Band; Symp Band; Hon Roll; Msc Awd 85-86; U MA Amhrst; Eqstn Sci.

PRAYZNER, PAULA; Bmc Durfee HS; Fall River, MA; (Y); 18/735; Cmnty Wkr; French Clb; Red Cross Aide; Science Clb; Yrbk Stf; High Hon Roll; Hon Roll; NHS; Chem.

PREMO, LESA; Saint Peter-Marian CC HS; Worcester, MA; (Y); Pep Clb; Yrbk Phtg; Yrbk Stf; JV Cheerleading; Hon Roll; High Hons Art I & Hon Hmnts 100 & Latin I, II, Bio I, Rlgn II, III, Engl II, & Chem I 84-86; Dntl Hygnst.

PRESCOTT, ELIZABETH; Franklin HS; Franklin, MA; (Y); 14/230; Dance Clb; French Clb; Math Tm; OEA; Stage Crew; JV Trk; Var Hon Roll; Voice Dem Awd; Church Yth Grp; Awd Exclnc 86; Ordr Eastrn Str Schlrshp 86; Sr Cls Schlrshp 86; U Of CT; Bus.

PRESH, LEE; Cathedral HS; Wst Springfield, MA; (Y); 258/537; Church Yth Grp; GAA; Ski Clb; JV Socr; Hon Roll; Western NE Coll; Bus Mgmt.

PRESS, SUE; Hudson HS; Hudson, MA; (Y); 2/150; Math Tm; Band; Concert Band; Mrchg Band; School Musical; Var L Gym; JV Tennis; High Hon Roll; NHS; Sci.

PRESTON, DAVID J; Belchertown HS; Belchertown, MA; (Y); 11/79; Am Leg Boys St; Boy Scts; Yrbk Stf; Stu Cncl; Var Capt Bsbl; Var Socr; Hon Roll; NHS; Eagle Scout 85; All Westn MA 1st Team Bsbl 86; Norwich U; Criml Justce.

PRESTON, TOD; Barnstable HS; Centerville, MA; (Y); Church Yth Grp; Band; Concert Band; Mrchg Band; Orch; Golf; Tennis; High Hon Roll; Hon Roll; NHS; Slvr Achvt Awd 84; Gld Achvt Awd 85; T C Clark Law Day Essay Cntst 86; Politics.

PREVETT, TIMOTHY; St Josephs Regional HS; Westford, MA; (Y); AFS; Boy Scts; Church Yth Grp; German Clb; Spanish Clb; Rep Frsh Cls; Rep Soph Cls; Rep Jr Cls; Rep Sr Cls; Ftbl; Spcl Ldrshp Awd Cardinal Law 86; Daniel Webster; Aviatn.

PREVITE, GAIL KRISTINA; Matignon HS; Lexington, MA; (Y); GAA; Library Aide; Spanish Clb; Chorus; Hon Roll; Lexington Yth Comm Awd Drug/Alcohol Awareness Wk 86; CPR Cert; Assumption Coll.

PREWITT, ROBYN; Fontbonne Acad; Quincy, MA; (Y); 28/180; Cmnty Wkr; Dance Clb; Drama Clb; Intnl Clb; Math Clb; Chorus; Ed Yrbk Ed-Chief; Lit Mag; Hon Roll; Prfct Atten Awd; Sci Fair Honrbl Mention 83-84; Acadmc Schlrshp 83-87; Pre-Law.

PREZEAU, CHERCHE; Dana Hall Schl; Whitefish, MT; (Y); Intnl Clb; Key Clb; Ski Clb; VP Chorus; Nwsp Sprt Ed; Pres Sr Cls; Var Fld Hcky; Var Lcrss; High Hon Roll; Hon Roll; Boston U; Law.

PRICE, HEATHER; Winchester HS; Winchester, MA; (Y); 78/296; Church Yth Grp; Spanish Clb; Concert Band; Mrchg Band; High Hon Roll; Hon Roll.

PRIEST, SANDRA; Academy Of Notre Dame; Groton, MA; (Y); 28/73; Hosp Aide; Key Clb; SADD; Acpl Chr; Chorus; School Musical; Nwsp Stf; Yrbk Stf; Hon Roll; Prfct Attndnce 83-84&84-85; Bus.

PRIEST, SONJA; North Reading HS; N Reading, MA; (Y); 3/130; Hosp Aide; Nwsp Stf; Yrbk Stf; Trs Soph Cls; Trs Jr Cls; Stu Cncl; Var Capt Bsktbl; Var Capt Trk; High Hon Roll; Church Yth Grp; H O Brien Ldrshp Semnr Recpnt 85; Cape Ann Leag MVP Grls Sprng Trck, Mst Vlbl Team 85; Duke; Intl Bus.

PRIETO, NANCY; South Boston HS; Roxbury, MA; (S); Church Yth Grp; French Clb; Chorus; School Musical; High Hon Roll; Hon Roll; NHS.

PRINCE, GEORGE; Monson JR-SR HS; Monson, MA; (Y); Boy Scts; Mech Engr.

PROAKIS, ADRIA; Macduffie School For Girls; Chicopee, MA; (Y); Church Yth Grp; Dance Clb; Nwsp Stf; Yrbk Stf; Lit Mag; Prfct Day Stdnts 87; Mss Chicpee Cntstnt 86; Mss MA AM Co-Ed Fntlst 86; Intrprtr.

PROCOPIO, JENNIFER; Pittsfield HS; Pittsfield, MA; (Y); VP JA; Latin Clb; Nwsp Stf; Var L Diving; Var Capt Gym; Var Trk; Hon Roll; Mzaima Cum Laude & Slvr Mdl Natl JR Classcl League 86; Mgnt Info Syst.

PROFIS, DEAN; Arlington HS; Arlington, MA; (Y); 49/381; JV Ftbl; JV Socr; JV Trk; Ntl Merit Ltr; Engnrng.

PROIA, MARK M; Attleboro HS; Attleboro, MA; (Y); Am Leg Boys St; Yrbk Stf; Sr Cls; Stu Cncl; Socr; Debate Tm; Tennis; High Hon Roll; NHS; Soccr ST All Stars 85; Villanova; Engrng.

PROIA, TOM; Belmont HS; Balmont, MA; (Y); 54/259; Camera Clb; Church Yth Grp; Cmnty Wkr; Computer Clb; Latin Clb; Nwsp Stf; Coach Actv; Ftbl; Ice Hcky; Hon Roll; US Air Force Acad; Plt.

PROU, DARATH; Boston Tech HS; Brighton, MA; (Y); Boys Clb Am; French Clb; French Hon Soc; High Hon Roll; Hon Roll; Electrnc Engrng.

PROULX, CHRISTOPHER; Southbridge HS; Southbridge, MA; (Y); 3/163; Am Leg Boys St; Church Yth Grp; Math Tm; VP Pres Band; School Musical; Nwsp Rptr; Trs Frsh Cls; Trs Soph Cls; High Hon Roll; NHS; Metrlgy.

PROULX, JEANETTE; Somerville HS; Somerville, MA; (Y); 27/540; Camera Clb; Intnl Clb; Yrbk Stf; High Hon Roll; Hon Roll.

PROULX, KAREN; BMC Durfee HS; Fall River, MA; (Y); Cmnty Wkr; Hosp Aide; Spanish Clb; High Hon Roll; Hon Roll; Mthmtcs.

PROUT, JOANNE; Archbishop Williams HS; Braintree, MA; (Y); 36/200; High Hon Roll; Hon Roll; Jr NHS; Kiwanis Awd; NHS; Spanish NHS; Hist Gold Mdl Awd 86; Brauntree Kiwanis Schlrshp 86; Pres Acadmc Ftnss Awd 86; Suffolk U; Social Wrk.

PROUTY, CHRISTOPHER; Monson JR SR HS; Monson, MA; (Y); Art Clb; Church Yth Grp; French Clb; Mathletes; Math Clb; Math Tm; SADD; Band; Concert Band; Variety Show; Westrn New Englnd Coll; Arch.

PROUTY, ILASAHAI; Waring Schl; Gloucester, MA; (Y); Chorus; Stage Crew; Nwsp Stf; Var L DECA; Var L Lcrss; Var L Socr; Hon Roll; Sch Art Awd 86.

PROUTY, JANE; Auburn HS; Auburn, MA; (Y); SADD; Pres Frsh Cls; Pres Soph Cls; Stu Cncl; Var Crs Cntry; Var Trk; Hon Roll; Hugh O Brien Outstndng Soph Awd 84-85; YFU Summr Exchng Stu.

PRUCNAL, KELLY; Hopkins Acad; Hadley, MA; (S); 1/47; French Clb; Library Aide; Yrbk Ed-Chief; French Hon Soc; Hon Roll; Japan/US Senat Schlrshp 85; Rensselaer Sci-Math Awd 85; Wellesley Bk Awd 85; Engl.

PRUETT, ROBIN ELIZABETH; Minnechug Regional HS; Wilbraham, MA; (Y); 2/309; Debate Tm; Mathletes; Trs PAVAS; Jazz Band; Madrigals; Lit Mag; High Hon Roll; NHS; Rotary Awd; Sal; 5th Rnnrup To Miss Teen Of MA 84; Dartmouth Bk Awd 85; Pres Of JR Extnsn 85-86; Colgate U; Bio.

PRUITT, BETH; Nipmuc Regional HS; Mendon, MA; (Y); 1/92; Am Leg Aux Girls St; Church Yth Grp; SADD; Varsity Clb; Yrbk Ed-Chief; Rep Stu Cncl; JV Var Bsktbl; Var Sftbl; High Hon Roll; Pres NHS; Engl, Physics & Psychology Awd; Engrng.

PRZECHOCKI, JOSEPH MICHAEL; Agawam HS; Feeding Hills, MA; (Y); Trs Math Clb; Math Tm; High Hon Roll; Math Clb Prblm Slvng Awd; U MA; Physcst.

PSATTIS, GEORGE; Longmeadow HS; Longmeadow, MA; (Y); 75/356; Church Yth Grp; Intnl Clb; Chrmn Key Clb; ROTC; Ski Clb; Church Choir; Nwsp Rptr; Socr; Trk; High Hon Roll; St Geo Yth Schlrshp 86; Law.

PUCILLO, MICHELLE; Saugas HS; Saugus, MA; (Y); 10/300; Cmnty Wkr; Spanish Clb; Band; Concert Band; Flag Corp; Mrchg Band; Pep Band; School Musical; Variety Show; Twrlr; Excllnce Spn Cert Awd; Cert Awd Marchng Band; Cert Awd Trig Hnrs; Bio.

PUESCHEL, GREGORY; South Hadley HS; S Hadley, MA; (Y); 10/270; Cmnty Wkr; Drama Clb; School Musical; School Play; Tennis; Most Imprvd Eng Stu Awd 85.

PUGLIELLI, LISA; Waltham HS; Waltham, MA; (Y); Church Yth Grp; JCL; Latin Clb; SADD; Mrchg Band; Capt Cheerleading; High Hon Roll; Hon Roll; Jr NHS; NHS; Italian Lng & Cltur Awd 84-86; Italian Clb.

PUHALA, JIM; Agawam HS; Feeding Hills, MA; (Y); French Clb; Quiz Bowl; Scholastic Bowl; Tennis; French Hon Soc; Hon Roll; NHS.

PULICHINO, CHRIS; Wellesley SR HS; Wellesley, MA; (Y); 71/305; Cmnty Wkr; Yrbk Stf; VP Stu Cncl; Var Golf; JV Trk; Hon Roll; Church Yth Grp; Ski Clb; Im Badmtn; Stu Adv Comtte 83-86; Dir Guidance 86; Jrnlsm.

PULVER, CHRISTINE; Natick HS; Natick, MA; (Y); 82/423; Sec Trs Art Clb; Cmnty Wkr; Mgr JA; High Hon Roll; Hon Roll; NHS; Wrthy Advsr Of Rnbw 85-86; Chmstry Sci Aid; Frncs Cronan Art Awwd; RI Schl Of Dsgn; Archtctr.

PUPEK, DIANE; South Hadley HS; S Hadley, MA; (Y); #39 In Class; Band; Concert Band; Mrchg Band; U Of Miami; Bio.

PURCELL, GLENN; Marianhill HS; Southbridge, MA; (Y); Math Tm; Nwsp Stf; Yrbk Stf; Pres Soph Cls; L Bsbl; JV Capt Bsktbl; Capt L Socr; Hon Roll; Jr NHS.

PURCELL, KAREN; Burlington HS; Burlington, MA; (Y); 103/321; Church Yth Grp; JA; Science Clb; Var Socr; Hon Roll; JV Bsktbl; Var Sftbl; B M Ganley Mem Schlrshp 86; U MA; Htl Mgmnt.

PURNELL, KIM; Hopkins Acad; Hadley, MA; (Y); Art Clb; Hosp Aide; Political Wkr; Spanish Clb; Yrbk Stf; Hon Roll; Awd-Cermcs 84; Hnrb Mntn-Hlyk CC Art Show-Stnd Gls 85; Awd-Stnd Gls 86.

PUTNAM, PAUL; Hopkins Acad; Hadley, MA; (S); 4/48; Am Leg Boys St; Church Yth Grp; Library Aide; Acpl Chr; Band; Chorus; Church Choir; Concert Band; Jazz Band; Mrchg Band; U Of MA; Hotel/Rstrnt Mgmnt.

PUTNAM, SUSAN; St Bernards Central Catholic; Fitchburg, MA; (S); 31/177; Church Yth Grp; Socr; High Hon Roll; NHS; Psych.

PUZYN, LORI; Matignon HS; Cambridge, MA; (Y); Cmnty Wkr; Drama Clb; Spanish Clb; SADD; School Musical; School Play; Variety Show; Var JV Sftbl; Var L Vllybl; Spanish NHS; Hnrbl Mntn Sci Fair 84; Hnrbl Mntn Hstry Fair 85; U Of ME Orono; Bio.

PYNE, JOHN F; Boston College HS; Scituate, MA; (Y); Am Leg Boys St; Boy Scts; Cmnty Wkr; Key Clb; Spanish Clb; SADD; JV Bsktbl; Var L Ftbl; Var Trk; Im Vllybl.

PYSCZYNSKI, LINDA; Bedford HS; Bedford, MA; (Y); 90/201; Church Yth Grp; Concert Band; Mrchg Band; Yrbk Stf; Bowling; Mgr(s); Powder Puff Ftbl; Hon Roll; Rep Jr Cls; Rep Sr Cls; Townline Ten Pne Bowlng Schlrshp 86; GBJBA Schlrshp 86; Salem St Coll; Bio.

QUAIL, AMY; New Bedford HS; Rochester, MA; (Y); 14/701; Drama Clb; Library Aide; Science Clb; Var Gym; Var Trk; Jr NHS; Sec NHS; Frnch Excllnc Awd 85; Bus Exec.

QUAN, QUA; Millbury HS; Millbury, MA; (Y); Trk; Engrng.

QUARANTO, CHRISTINE; Natick HS; Natick, MA; (Y); Hon Roll; Mansfield Beauty Acad; Hrdrssng.

QUIDLEY, CHRISTOPHER; Chatham JR-SR HS; South Chatham, MA; (Y); 6/40; Am Leg Boys St; SADD; Chorus; Nwsp Phtg; Nwsp Rptr; Yrbk Phtg; Yrbk Stf; Sec Frsh Cls; VP Soph Cls; Hon Roll; Harvard Bk Prize Awd 86.

QUIGLEY, DENISE; Westwood HS; Westwood, MA; (Y); 58/212; AFS; SADD; Varsity Clb; School Play; Var L Cheerleading; Powder Puff Ftbl; Hon Roll; Law.

QUIGLEY, LISA; BMC Durfee HS; Fall River, MA; (Y); 9/734; French Clb; Science Clb; Band; Concert Band; Mrchg Band; Orch; Var Swmmng; High Hon Roll; NHS; Mdrn Music Mstrs 86; Envrnmntl Cntrl Comm 85-86; Psychol.

QUILLIA, BRIAN R; Holy Name Central Catholic HS; Oxford, MA; (Y); 30/300; Boy Scts; Stu Cncl; Var L Crs Cntry; Var L Tennis; Var L Trk; High Hon Roll; NHS; Stat Bsktbl; Var Mgr(s); Var Timer; Futr Ldrs Worcester Pgm Fnlst 86; Tp Stu Chem, Alg, Relgn 86; Cvl Engrng.

QUINK, CASEY; Belmont HS; Belmont, MA; (Y); Church Yth Grp; Cmnty Wkr; Letterman Clb; Spanish Clb; SADD; Nwsp Rptr; Diving; Socr; Swmmng; Tennis.

QUINLAN, COLLEEN; Matignon HS; Somerville, MA; (Y); Church Yth Grp; Drama Clb; SADD; School Musical; School Play; Variety Show; Ed Nwsp Rptr; Yrbk Stf; Cheerleading; U Lowell; Nrsng.

QUINLAN, FRED; Milton HS; Milton, MA; (Y); Letterman Clb; Var L Bsbl; Boston U; Jrnlsm.

QUINN, JAMES A; Milton HS; Milton, MA; (Y); 60/250; Nwsp Stf; Im Bsbl; JV Im Bsktbl; L Ftbl; Im Wt Lftg; Hon Roll; Plymouth St; Bus Adm.

QUINN, JOSEPH; Taconic HS; Pittsfield, MA; (Y); Art Clb; Computer Clb; Intnl Clb; JA; SADD; Yrbk Stf; Off Frsh Cls; Off Soph Cls; Off Jr Cls; Off Sr Cls; UCLA; Bus Mgmt.

QUINN, TOM; St Johns Prep; Nahant, MA; (Y); Aud/Vis; Boy Scts; Church Yth Grp; Pep Clb; Var Ski Clb; SADD; Nwsp Phtg; Nwsp Stf; Yrbk Phtg; Yrbk Stf; Htl Rest Mgmt.

QUINN, WILLIAM; Natick HS; Natick, MA; (Y); Varsity Clb; Socr; Hon Roll; 4 Yr Vrsty Lttrmn Sccr 84-87; Sccr Capt 87; Lbrl Arts.

QUINTAL, MICHELLE; Dedham HS; Dedham, MA; (Y); 47/245; Teachers Aide; Band; Concert Band; Mrchg Band; Hon Roll; Simmons Coll; Intl Reltns.

QUINTILIANI, DAWN; Matignon HS; Watertown, MA; (S); 3/182; Drama Clb; School Play; Rep Stu Cncl; Var Cheerleading; High Hon Roll; NHS; Cmnty Wkr; Office Aide; Hugh O Brian Ldrshp Conf Rep As Mst Outstndg Soph 85; Boston Chldrns Thtr Female Ld 84; Acad All-Amer.

QUIRK, DANIEL; Sharon HS; Sharon, MA; (Y); 51/250; Boys Clb Am; Cmnty Wkr; Debate Tm; Varsity Clb; Nwsp Stf; Yrbk Stf; VP Soph Cls; Rep Stu Cncl; Var L Bsktbl; Var L Ftbl; Colby College; Bus.

QUIRK, JENIFER; Lunenburg HS; Lunenburg, MA; (Y); Art Clb; PAVAS; SADD; Teachers Aide; Varsity Clb; JV Var Bsktbl; JV Var Sftbl; Church Yth Grp; Intnl Clb; Office Aide; Ntl Art Hon Soc 84-87; Sec Ntl Art Hon Soc 86-87; 1st Pl FGE Art Mntg Cntst 86; Art.

QUIRK, KRISTIN A; Belmont HS; Belmont, MA; (Y); 24/260; Church Yth Grp; Service Clb; Band; Concert Band; School Play; Nwsp Stf; Pres Stu Cncl; Var Bsktbl; Var Socr; Var Trk; Boston Coll; Law.

QUIRK, PATRICK J; Boston College HS; Brockton, MA; (Y); 8/290; Am Leg Boys St; Cmnty Wkr; Ed Lit Mag; Im Ftbl; NHS; Ntl Merit SF; Sal; Nwsp Stf; Yrbk Stf; Im Bsktbl; Por Cristo Mdcl Tm Ecuador 86; HS Hgh Entrnc Exm, J J Dunn Schlrshps 82-86; Holy Crss Bk Awd 85; U Of Chicago; Dr.

RABATTINI, CHRISTINA; Fontbonne Acad; Stoughton, MA; (Y); 60/135; Intnl Clb; Pres Chorus; Yrbk Stf; Hon Roll; Jr NHS; Outstndng Wrk In Span 85; Outstndng Ldrshp In Chorus 86; MA Bd Of Rgnts Schlrshp 86; Bridgewater ST Coll; Span.

RABIDEAU, JEANNIE; Clinton HS; Clinton, MA; (Y); 16/122; Church Yth Grp; Sec Trs Intnl Clb; Yrbk Stf; Off Soph Cls; Var JV Fld Hcky; Hon Roll; NHS; Prfct Atten Awd.

RABOIN, APRIL; Woburn HS; Woburn, MA; (Y); Church Yth Grp; French Clb; Stu Cncl; Cheerleading; Hon Roll; Plcd Sci Fair 84; Physcl Ftns Awd 84 & 85; Dntl Hygn.

RACICOT, MARK; Bartlett HS; Webster, MA; (Y); 5/160; Science Clb; Yrbk Stf; JV Bsktbl; Var L Crs Cntry; Var L Trk; Hon Roll; NHS; Civil Engr.

RACKLEY, KELLY; Bishop Connolly HS; Westport, MA; (Y); Cmnty Wkr; Ski Clb; Chorus; Church Choir; Trk; Bridgewater ST; Spcl Ed.

RACZKOWSKI, AMY; Tantasqua Regional HS; Sturbridge, MA; (Y); 4/180; Am Leg Aux Girls St; Math Tm; Ski Clb; Varsity Clb; Acpl Chr; Chorus; Madrigals; School Musical; School Play; Variety Show; Ntl Music Hon Soc 84; Wnnr Chncllrs Tlnt Awd 86; Sci.

RADSKEN, JILL; Pittsfield HS; Pittsfield, MA; (Y); 16/400; Sec Exploring; JCL; Latin Clb; Pep Clb; Trs Temple Yth Grp; Yrbk Stf; Trs Frsh Cls; Trs Soph Cls; Trs Jr Cls; Trs Sr Cls; Hebrew Awd 85 & 86; Magna Cum Laude & Cu M Laude Awds Natl Latin Exam 85 & 86; Pol Sci.

RADULA, SANDRA J; South High Community Schl; Worcester, MA; (S); Hosp Aide; SADD; Tennis; Trk; High Hon Roll; Hon Roll; NHS; Spanish NHS; Boston Coll; Intl Rltns.

RAFFAELE, FELICIA; Reading Memorial HS; Reading, MA; (Y); Dance Clb; Spanish Clb; SADD; Pep Band; Variety Show; Rep Frsh Cls; Rep Stu Cncl; Powder Puff Ftbl; JV Capt Socr; High Hon Roll; Health.

RAFFERTY, KAREN; Haverhill HS; Haverhill, MA; (Y); Art Clb; Cmnty Wkr; Teachers Aide; Bsktbl; Sftbl; Wt Lftg; High Hon Roll; Hon Roll; Nrthrn Essex CC; Socl Wrkr.

RAFFONI, CYNTHIA; St Clare HS; Roslindale, MA; (Y); 5/149; Church Yth Grp; JCL; Nwsp Rptr; Nwsp Stf; Yrbk Stf; High Hon Roll; Hon Roll; NHS; NEDT Awd; Prfct Atten Awd; Magna Cum Laude Cert Of Hnrbl Meirt Nalt Latn Exm 82-83; High Acadmc Avrg Eng 83-84; High Acadmc Relgn; U Of MA Boston; Bio.

RAFTERY, ELLEN; Lynn English HS; Lynn, MA; (Y); AFS; Church Yth Grp; Drama Clb; Sec JCL; Office Aide; Nwsp Ed-Chief; Yrbk Ed-Chief; Jake Finkle Jrnlsm Schlrshp 86; LFHS Drama Clb Schlrshp 86; St Josephs Coll; Brdcstng.

RAFTERY, JENNIFER; North Quincy HS; Quincy, MA; (Y); 18/390; Cmnty Wkr; Chorus; Yrbk Stf; Var Gym; Capt Swmmng; Capt Trk; High Hon Roll; NHS; Secndry Educ.

RAFTERY, KIM; Monument Mountain Regional HS; Lee, MA; (Y); 16/116; Church Yth Grp; 4-H; Concert Band; Mrchg Band; Nwsp Rptr; Var JV Bsktbl; Band; Wards Nursery Env Studies Schlrshp 86; Outstndng Young Christn Women 85; Southern Sem JC; Equine Studie.

RAFTERY, MICHAEL; Holyoke Catholic HS; Holyoke, MA; (Y); Math Clb; Bsktbl; Socr; Trk; Wt Lftg; Northeastern U; Law.

RAGO, CAROLYNN; Arlington Catholic HS; Somerville, MA; (Y); 30/167; Var Crs Cntry; Var L Trk; Hon Roll; Prfct Atten Awd; Outstndng Athlt Awd Trck 86; Magna Cum Lauda Awd Ltn Ntl Ltn Exm 86; Cum Lauda Awd Ntl Ltn Exm 84; Bus Manag.

RAGUIN, JOHN; Medford HS; Medford, MA; (Y); 9/450; Am Leg Boys St; Pres Math Clb; Science Clb; Nwsp Rptr; Trk; Vllybl; Pres Mu Alp Tht; Pres NHS; Ntl Merit Ltr; Rensslr Mdl Math & Sci 86; Top Stu Advnce Math 86; Physics Awd; Stanford; Math.

RAIMONDI, MARIA; Matignon HS; Somerville, MA; (S); 19/178; Science Clb; Spanish Clb; SADD; Church Choir; High Hon Roll; NHS; Spanish NHS; Emmanuel Coll; Psych.

RAINEY, DONNA; Attleboro HS; Attleboro, MA; (Y); Pres Acpl Chr; VP Band; VP Concert Band; VP Mrchg Band; Hon Roll; NHS; Music.

RAINVILLE, CRYSTAL; Attleboro HS; Attleboro, MA; (Y); Am Leg Aux Girls St; Math Tm; Chorus; Sec Frsh Cls; Sec Soph Cls; VP Jr Cls; VP Sr Cls; Rep Stu Cncl; JV Cheerleading; Gym; Brwn U Bk Awd 86; HS Essy Drnk Drvng 1st Pl 85; Schlstc Achvmnt Engl Bk Awd 86.

RAISS, THOURAYA; Braintree HS; Braintree, MA; (Y); 5/442; JCL; Latin Clb; Orch; Lit Mag; Fld Hcky; French Hon Soc; High Hon Roll; NHS; Prfct Atten Awd; Lat Awd 85; Hon Men Sci Fair 85; SEMSBA Prfmnce 84-86; Intl Bus.

RAJANIEMI, SHERRY LYNN; Murdock HS; Winchendon, MA; (Y); 4/110; Art Clb; Band; Chorus; Mrchg Band; School Musical; School Play; High Hon Roll; Hon Roll; NHS; Pres Schlr; Schlstc Ltr 83; Keene ST Coll; Pre-Med.

RAKAUSKAS, DAVID; Silver Lake Regional HS; Kingston, MA; (Y); 16/430; Cmnty Wkr; Latin Clb; Math Clb; Trs Stu Cncl; Im Bsktbl; JV Crs Cntry; Var L Ice Hcky; Var Capt Tennis; Hon Roll; NHS; Engrng.

RALSTON, AMY; Concord-Carlisle HS; Glen Mills, PA; (Y); 28/328; Band; Concert Band; Mrchg Band; JV Lcrss; JV Socr; High Hon Roll; Hon Roll; NHS; Ntl Merit Ltr; Elec Engrng.

RAMOS, MONICA; BMC Durfee HS; Fall River, MA; (Y); Church Yth Grp; Variety Show; Gordon Coll; Soc Wrkr.

RAMPULLA, MARK; Haverhill HS; Haverhill, MA; (Y); JV Bsktbl; Var JV Ftbl; Im Wt Lftg; High Hon Roll; Hon Roll; MVP Bsktbl 82-83; Stu Cncl Awd Achvt 82-83; Bys Clb Awd MVP Bsktbl 84-85; Plymouth ST.

RAMSDEN, LISA; North Quincy HS; Wollaston, MA; (Y); 4/400; VP JA; Pres Latin Clb; Math Tm; Band; Swmmng; High Hon Roll; NHS; Ltn Ntl Hon Soc 86; Bio.

RAMSTROM, WILLIAM D; St Marks HS; Grafton, MA; (Y); 1/95; Math Tm; JV Crs Cntry; Im Tennis; Im Vllybl; High Hon Roll; Hon Roll; Ntl Merit SF; Im Bsktbl; Cum Laude Soc 85; St Marks Schlrshp 85; Meteorology.

RANESE, MICHELE; Taunton HS; Berkley/Assonet, MA; (Y); 74/400; Am Leg Aux Girls St; Church Yth Grp; Office Aide; Ski Clb; Drm Mjr(t); Hon Roll; Amer Lg Scup Rose Mem Scholar 86; Bridgewater ST Coll; Psych.

RANIERI, CHRISTINA; Braintree HS; Braintree, MA; (Y); 168/442; Church Yth Grp; SADD; Y-Teens; Band; Orch; Pep Band; Lit Mag; Rep Frsh Cls; Rep Soph Cls; Sftbl; Hnrbl Mntn School Sci Fair 85; South Shore Ymca Girl Of The Year 84; Springfield ST; Fitness.

RANTANEN, DAVID J; Lunenburg HS; Lunenburg, MA; (Y); Chess Clb; High Hon Roll; Hon Roll; Astrnmy.

RAO, VARSHA; Framingham South HS; Framingham, MA; (S); 1/300; Cmnty Wkr; Key Clb; Model UN; Radio Clb; Yrbk Stf; Bsktbl; Cheerleading; Lcrss; High Hon Roll; NHS; Bus.

RAPHEL, BRUCE S; Brockton HS; Brockton, MA; (Y); 48/1000; Am Leg Boys St; French Clb; SADD; Capt Temple Yth Grp; Wt Lftg; Hon Roll; Syracuse U; Lawyr.

RAPPAPORT, LEE; Natick HS; Natick, MA; (Y); Ski Clb; Spanish Clb; SADD; Temple Yth Grp; Lit Mag; Stu Cncl; Var Swmmng; Bay St League Swmmng Champs 86; Lttrmn Swmmng 85-86.

RASMUSSEN, CHRISTINE A; Westford Acad; Westford, MA; (Y); 24/224; AFS; Art Clb; French Clb; German Clb; Office Aide; SADD; High Hon Roll; Hon Roll; Westford Acad Trustee Scholar 86; Excllnce Ger Lang 85 & 86; Pres Acad Fit Awd 86; UNH; Intl Bus.

RATH, JOHN; Boston College HS; Boston, MA; (Y); French Clb; Var Swmmng; Lbrl Arts.

RAU, LINDA; Foxboro HS; Foxboro, MA; (Y); 7/229; Church Yth Grp; Hosp Aide; SADD; JV Stat Bsktbl; High Hon Roll; Hon Roll; NHS; U Of NH; Occ Thrpst.

RAU, TRACY; Macduffie Schl; Springfield, MA; (Y); Art Clb; Camera Clb; Debate Tm; Exploring; 4-H; Girl Scts; Ski Clb; Nwsp Rptr; Nwsp Stf; Lit Mag; Hampshire Coll; Amer Lit.

RAUCH, HENRY J; St Johns HS; Westboro, MA; (Y); 85/250; Am Leg Boys St; Boy Scts; Drama Clb; Exploring; Math Tm; Ski Clb; Stage Crew; Hon Roll; Egl Sct 85; Ordr Arrw Hnr Cmprs Sctg 83; Physcs.

RAUCH, JACQUELINE; Natick HS; Natick, MA; (Y); 116/443; Church Yth Grp; Latin Clb; Band; Nwsp Sprt Ed; Capt Fld Hcky; Swmmng; Capt Trk; Mst Outstndng Female Athlt 86; Unsng Hero Trck 86; MVP Fld Hcky 86; Framingham ST Coll; Cmnctns.

RAUSCHER, HEIDI; Monument Mountain Regional HS; Glendale, MA; (Y); 51/155; French Clb; Band; Mrchg Band; Yrbk Stf; Cheerleading; Trk; PSYCH.

RAUSCHER, SARA; Tohanto Regional HS; Berlin, MA; (Y); 1/56; Math Clb; School Musical; School Play; Trs Frsh Cls; Trs Soph Cls; Rep Jr Cls; NHS; Ntl Merit Ltr; Val; Nwsp Stf; Chnclrs Tlnt Awd UMASS 86; Intl Rltns.

RAVANIS, TINA; Winchester HS; Winchester, MA; (Y); Church Yth Grp; Drama Clb; French Clb; German Clb; Hosp Aide; Mrchg Band; School Musical; French Hon Soc; High Hon Roll; Hon Roll; Lib Arts.

RAWDING, BRIDGET; Haverhill HS; Ward Hill, MA; (Y); 2/370; NHS; Sal; St Schlr; Key Clb; Latin Clb; Spanish Clb; Nwsp Stf; DAR Awd; High Hon Roll; Ntl Merit Ltr; Rbrt D Ftzgrld Mem Schlrshp 86; MA Assoc Schl Sprntndnts Cert Acdmc Excllnc 86; 1st Prz Fair Hsg Essy; Boston Coll.

RAWLINGS, CHARLES; Williston Northampton Schl; Wilton, CT; (Y); Chess Clb; Var Capt Lcrss; Var Capt Socr.

RAY, NICOLE; Burlington HS; Burlington, MA; (Y); 84/318; Church Yth Grp; Dance Clb; Hosp Aide; OEA; Varsity Clb; Rep Frsh Cls; Rep Soph Cls; Off Jr Cls; Off Sr Cls; Var Cheerleading; SF Miss MA Teen USA Pag 84; Word Proc Awd 86; Bentley; Bus.

RAYMENT, SEAN A; Dennis-Yarmouth Regional HS; Hyannis, MA; (Y); 6/400; Am Leg Boys St; Boy Scts; Model UN; Varsity Clb; JV Bsbl; Ftbl; Hon Roll; NHS; Ntl Merit Schol; UN Pilgrimage Yth; Holy Cross; Engrng.

RAYMOND, DARLENE; Greater Lowell Rgnl Voc Tech Schl; Lowell, MA; (Y); Cmnty Wkr; FCA; Hosp Aide; JA; Office Aide; Red Cross Aide; SADD; VICA; Vllybl; Prfct Atten Awd; Northern Essex; Sec.

RAYMOND, JILL; King Philip Regional HS; Wrentham, MA; (Y); Church Yth Grp; OEA; SADD; Church Choir; Rep Frsh Cls; Rep Soph Cls; Rep Jr Cls; Rep Sr Cls; Sec Pres Stu Cncl; Powder Puff Ftbl; Paralgl Stds.

RAYMOND, PAUL; North Attleboro HS; N Attleboro, MA; (Y); JA; JV Trk; Hon Roll; Comp Pgmr.

RAYNARD, YVONNE; Eastbridgewater HS; E Bridgewater, MA; (Y); Dance Clb; Trs SADD; Yrbk Ed-Chief; Stu Cncl; Trk; Hon Roll; NHS; Church Yth Grp; Yrbk Stf; Sec Soph Cls; Capeway JR Miss 86; Prom Queen 85; Pres Acad Fit Awd 86; Salem ST Coll; Geogrphy.

RAYNER, STEVEN; Medford HS; W Medford, MA; (Y); Bsbl; Score Keeper; Hon Roll; Bus.

RAZZABONI, LORI; North Middlesex RHS; Hollis, NH; (Y); 13/210; SADD; Varsity Clb; Rep Frsh Cls; Rep Soph Cls; Trs Jr Cls; Rep Sr Cls; Rep Stu Cncl; JV Var Fld Hcky; Hon Roll; NHS.

READE, JANET; Beverly HS; Beverly, MA; (Y); Hosp Aide; Chorus; Color Guard; Drill Tm; School Musical; Lit Mag; VP Jr Cls; VP Sr Cls; JV Var Cheerleading; JV Tennis; Chrldng Awd 110 Pct 86; Bus.

REAGAN, MARK; Salem HS; Salem, MA; (Y); 8/287; Am Leg Boys St; Math Clb; Math Tm; Science Clb; Spanish Clb; Tennis; High Hon Roll; NHS; Sec Spanish NHS; Outstndng Mathlt Salem 85-86; Secy Spnsh Hnr Socty 86-87; Worcester Polytechnic Inst.

REAGAN, PETER; Belmont HS; Belmont, MA; (Y); Band; Concert Band; Mrchg Band; Var Ice Hcky; Var Trk; Amigos Pblc Hlth Vlntr 86; Schl Cmmttee Awd Band 86; Law.

REAGAN, SIOBHAN; Northfield Mt Hermon Schl; Albany, NY; (Y); Cmnty Wkr; Dance Clb; Drama Clb; Political Wkr; Chorus; School Musical; School Play; Nwsp Stf; Yrbk Stf; Pres Soph Cls; Stdnt Ldr Northfield Mt Hermon 86-87; Archlgy.

REAGAN, THOMAS E; Norwell HS; Norwell, MA; (Y); 20/169; Am Leg Boys St; Spanish Clb; Nwsp Sprt Ed; Nwsp Stf; Ftbl; Var Trk; Hon Roll; Boston U; Archtrl Engrng.

REARDON, AMY; Old Rochester Regional HS; Marion, MA; (Y); 8/138; AFS; Church Yth Grp; Math Clb; Math Tm; Ski Clb; Var Crs Cntry; Var Trk; High Hon Roll; NHS; Prfct Atten Awd; Hnrs Ancient Hstry Awd 84; Hnrs Frnch Awd 85; Vrsty Lttr Trck; Princeton U; Chem Engrng.

REARDON, ERIC; Acton-Boxboro Regional HS; Acton, MA; (Y); 144/428; Varsity Clb; Var L Socr; Hon Roll; NHS; Bus Adm.

REARDON, JOHN C; Walpole HS; Walpole, MA; (Y); Church Yth Grp; English Clb; Latin Clb; Science Clb; Spanish Clb; SADD; Rep Soph Cls; Rep Jr Cls; Rep Sr Cls; Stu Cncl; Amer Hstry AP Hnrs 86; Commodore-W Dennis Yth Clb 86; Hstry.

REARDON, JOSEPH M; Boston Coll HS; Milton, MA; (Y); Am Leg Boys St; Church Yth Grp; Cmnty Wkr; Key Clb; SADD; Rep Soph Cls; Rep Jr Cls; Rep Sr Cls; Rep Stu Cncl; Im Bsktbl; Hugh O Brian Yth Fndtn MA Yth Ldrshp Smnr 85.

REARDON, KELLIE; Pittsfield HS; Pittsfield, MA; (Y); Church Yth Grp; Exploring; 4-H; Latin Clb; Pep Clb; Yrbk Stf; Sec Frsh Cls; Sec Soph Cls; Sec Jr Cls; Sec Sr Cls.

REBELLO, KIMBERLY; Taunton HS; Taunton, MA; (Y); Yrbk Stf; Becker JC; Fshn Mrchndsng.

REBHAN, MARIA; Franklin HS; Franklin, MA; (Y); Hon Roll; St Schlr; Knighs Of Columbus; Suffolk U; Pre Law.

REDDY, COLLEEN; Georgetown JR SR HS; Georgetown, MA; (Y); Church Yth Grp; Drama Clb; Spanish Clb; Yrbk Phtg; Yrbk Stf; JV Var Fld Hcky; Powder Puff Ftbl; JV Var Sftbl; Hon Roll; Prfct Atten Awd; Cape Ann Leag All-STRS In Fld Hcky 85; 3 Pres Physcl Ftnss Awds 84-86; Engl Ptry Awd 86; Arch.

REECE, CHARLOTTE; Winchester HS; Winchester, MA; (Y); Church Yth Grp; Drama Clb; JCL; Latin Clb; Spanish Clb; Band; Concert Band; Jazz Band; Mrchg Band; School Musical; Natl Latin Exam Cum Laude 84-86; Natl Hstry Dy Bstn Mtrplt 85; WHS Mrch Bnd; Pch Bwl 86.

REED, KATIE-SUE; Tantasqua Regional HS; Brookfield, MA; (Y); 17/174; Church Yth Grp; 4-H; Acpl Chr; Chorus; Church Choir; Madrigals; Swing Chorus; Variety Show; High Hon Roll; Hon Roll; Modern Music Masters Tri-M Hist; Best All Around Bus Stu Awd; Outstndg Bus Stu Awd & Cross Pen ST Mut.

REEJHSINGHANI, ALOK; Minnechaug Regional HS; Wilbraham, MA; (Y); 7/314; JV Bsbl; Bsktbl; JV Ftbl; Var Trk; Hon Roll; NHS; Ntl Merit SF; Williams Bk Awd; 1st Pl ATAM-SNARE Drum Solo 83.

REENTS, GRETCHEN E; Westborough HS; Westborough, MA; (Y); 2/163; Band; Yrbk Bus Mgr; Capt Bsktbl; Fld Hcky; Capt Tennis; CC Awd; NHS; Pres Schlr; Sal; AFS; Dist E Athlc Awd 86; Marlborough Hosp Aux Awd 86; Res Ofcrs Assoc Awd 86; U Of VA; Bio.

REGAN III, RICHARD P; Old Rochester Regional HS; Mattapoisett, MA; (Y); 7/147; Am Leg Boys St; Rep Frsh Cls; VP Soph Cls; VP Jr Cls; VP Sr Cls; Rep Stu Cncl; Var Bsktbl; Var Capt Crs Cntry; Var Capt Tennis; Hon Roll; ORR Tnns Awd 86; Brdcstng.

REGAN, SHEILA F; Natick HS; Natick, MA; (Y); 97/411; Art Clb; Speech Tm; Chorus; School Musical; School Play; Nwsp Stf; Yrbk Stf; Lit Mag; Trk; Hnrb Mntn-Bstn Glb Schltc Art Awds 86; 1st Pl Ntck Arts Cncl Stu Awds 86; RI Schl Of Design; Illstrtr.

REGAN, TINA M; Fontbonne Acad; Milton, MA; (Y); 20/134; Cmnty Wkr; Hosp Aide; Intnl Clb; Teachers Aide; Variety Show; Var L Bsktbl; Var L Fld Hcky; High Hon Roll; Hon Roll; NHS; Achtv In Triognometry; Excllnc In Chem & Hstry; High Achvt In Bio; Georgetown U; Nrsng.

REGGIO, JEANNE R; Silver Lake Regional HS; Pembroke, MA; (Y); 5/494; Debate Tm; 4-H; Intnl Clb; Library Aide; Math Tm; Color Guard; High Hon Roll; Pres Schlr; Voice Dem Awd; Mrchg Band; Commnwlth MA Schlrshp 86; READ Magzn Wrtg Cntst Hnbl Mntn 84; Stonehill Coll; Lib Arts.

REGINA, SUSAN; King Philip Regional HS; Norfolk, MA; (Y); Church Yth Grp; DECA; Hon Roll; DECA Dist,ST Conf 4th,3rd Pl 84-85; DECA Dist Gold,Silver Level; Henry O Peabody; Cosmotlgy.

REGIS, MARK; Assabet Vally RV HS; Hudson, MA; (Y); #8 In Class; NHS; Lowell; Electnc Engr.

REGO, DEBBIE; BMC Durfee HS; Fall River, MA; (Y); 2/700; Pres JA; Pres Math Clb; Pres Science Clb; Varsity Clb; Chorus; VP Orch; Rep Stu Cncl; Gym; Trk; Capt Vllybl; Rensselaer Sci & Math Awd 86; RPI; Engrng.

REGO, JAMES R; New Bedford HS; New Bedford, MA; (Y); 71/631; Boy Scts; Political Wkr; Ski Clb; VP Frsh Cls; Trs Jr Cls; Rep Stu Cncl; Hon Roll; NHS; Southeastern MA U.

REGO, MICHAEL; Taunton HS; Taunton, MA; (Y); Latin Clb; Diving; Swmmng; Trk; Rochester Inst Of Tech; Art.

REI, JOHN N; Masconomet Regional HS; Boxford, MA; (Y); 24/247; Am Leg Boys St; Cmnty Wkr; Capt L Crs Cntry; Var Trk; Hon Roll; USAF; Aerospace Engrng.

REID, MICHELLE; King Philip Regional HS; Norfolk, MA; (Y); 2/224; Sec Soph Cls; VP Jr Cls; VP Sr Cls; VP Capt Tennis; Hon Roll; NHS; Sal; Excllnc In Frnch 86; Excllnc In Hist 86; Outstndng SR Mdl 86; Stonehill Coll.

REID, ROMEO; Boston Latin HS; Mattapan, MA; (Y); Boy Scts; JA; Latin Clb; ROTC; VP Jr Cls; Rep Stu Cncl; Bsbl; Bsktbl; Capt Wrstlng; Hon Roll; Embry-Riddle U; Aero Engr.

REIDY, KEVIN; Boston College HS; Norwell, MA; (Y); Am Leg Boys St; Cmnty Wkr; Key Clb; Ski Clb; Spanish Clb; SADD; High Hon Roll; NHS; Intnl Clb; Hon Roll; Intl Exchng Stu-Spain 86; Out Of Schl Tutor; Georgetown; Intl Affairs.

REIDY, SUSAN E; Notre Dame Acad; Shrewsbury, MA; (Y); 18/75; Cmnty Wkr; Drama Clb; Hosp Aide; Spanish Clb; Chorus; School Musical; Stage Crew; Yrbk Stf; St Schlr; Shrewsbury Wmns Clb Schlrshp 86; MA ST Schlrshp 86; Froshinn Clb Schlrshp 86; Providence Coll; Bio.

REIL, PEGGY L; Shepherd Hill Regional HS; Charlton Depot, MA; (Y); Church Yth Grp; French Clb; Chorus; Church Choir; School Play; High Hon Roll; NHS; Prfct Atten Awd; Dudley Hall Schrlshp 85-86; Emma Hammond Bus Awd 86; Dudley Hall Career Inst; Bus.

REILEY, DEBORAH; Bishop Feehan HS; Attleboro, MA; (Y); Sec Church Yth Grp; Chorus; Church Choir; School Musical; School Play; Stage Crew; Elks Awd; Dance Clb; Drama Clb; Girl Scts; Sthestrn Dist Chorus 86; All ST Chorus 86; Freedoms Fndtn 85; Wheelock Coll; Ed.

REILLY, JOSEPH; Dighton-Rehoboth Reg HS; Rehoboth, MA; (Y); Math Clb; Math Tm; High Hon Roll; Hon Roll; NHS; SMU; Elec Engr.

REILLY, KRISTEN; Ursuline Acad; Dedham, MA; (Y); 25/82; Dance Clb; Service Clb; Spanish Clb; SADD; Band; School Musical; School Play; Stage Crew; Ed Nwsp Stf; Capt Var Socr; Natl Sci Olympd 83; Vrsty Lttrs 84-86; Unsung Hero 85-86; Hlth Care Adm.

REILLY, MATTHEW; Marian HS; Ashland, MA; (S); Letterman Clb; Band; Concert Band; Jazz Band; Pep Band; School Musical; School Play; Stage Crew; Variety Show; Var L Bsbl; U Of MA.

REILLY, REBECCA; Cathedral HS; Ludlow, MA; (Y); 90/500; Cmnty Wkr; Hon Roll; Htl Sales.

REINBERGS, INDRA ANNIJA; Attleboro HS; Attleboro, MA; (Y); 1/438; Am Leg Aux Girls St; Church Yth Grp; Trs Drama Clb; Pres Acpl Chr; School Musical; NHS; Ntl Merit Ltr; Val; Chorus; School Play; U MA Chncllrs Acad Tlnt Awd 84; Awd Exc German 85; Dist Music Fest 84; Wellesley Coll; Intl Rltns.

REINER, CHRIS; Boston Latin Schl; Boston, MA; (Y); 26/274; Drama Clb; Trs Ski Clb; School Play; Capt Socr; NCTE Awd; NHS; JA; Key Clb; Red Cross Aide; SADD; AFS Intl Exch Pgm Italy 85; Boston Pub Schl Intl Exch Schlrshp 85; Dartmouth Coll; Lang.

REINERMAN, MARGARET; Newton County Day Schl; Newton Center, MA; (Y); 4/40; Camera Clb; Cmnty Wkr; Model UN; Chorus; Madrigals; Socr; Hon Roll; NHS; Ntl Merit SF; SADD; Bus.

REINKE, RUSSELL E; Northampton HS; Northampton, MA; (Y); 86/214; Cmnty Wkr; Drama Clb; Thesps; Flag Corp; School Musical; School Play; Stage Crew; Flag Corps Ltr 85; Hnr Thespn Awd 85; Excllnc Actg Awds 86; U Of MA; Theatr.

REINO, KAREN; Frontier Regional HS; S Deerfield, MA; (Y); Ski Clb; Spanish Clb; Yrbk Bus Mgr; Cheerleading; Crs Cntry; Fld Hcky; Mgr(s); Sftbl; High Hon Roll; Usherette Gradtn & Cls Nght 86; Peer Educ 87; U MA; Bus Admin.

REIS, ROSE; B M C Durfee HS; Fall River, MA; (Y); Hon Roll; Kinyon Campbell Schrlsh P86; Kinyon Campbell Bus; Acctng.

REITSHAMER, STEFAN; Marian HS; Framingham, MA; (Y); Im Vllybl; Hgst Achvt Physcs II,Trignmtry,Geo; Top Score Math Comptn; Hgst NEDT Score; Elect Engr.

REKULA, VENKAT; Marlboro HS; Marlboro, MA; (Y); Cmnty Wkr; Computer Clb; Science Clb; Nwsp Stf; High Hon Roll; NHS; Ntl Merit Ltr; Prfct Atten Awd; Carnegie-Mellon U; Elec Engrng.

REMIGIO, NATALIE; Somerville HS; Somerville, MA; (Y); 1/600; Spanish Clb; Chorus; High Hon Roll; Hon Roll; VP NHS; Pres Schlr; Val; Harvard Bk Awd 85; Cert Acdmc Excllnc 86; Chem Awd 86; Tufts U; Sci.

RENIHAN, LAUREN M; Shrewsbury HS; Shrewsbury, MA; (Y); 40/200; Aud/Vis; Debate Tm; NFL; PAVAS; Political Wkr; Orch; School Play; Variety Show; Yrbk Phtg; Yrbk Stf; MA Commonwealth Schlrshp 86; Stu Mnth 85; Yth Mnth Tri-Toun Exch Clb 86; Northeastern U; Spch Cmmnctns.

RENZI, KRISTEN; Marian HS; Framingham, MA; (Y); 29/186; Church Yth Grp; JV Crs Cntry; JV Sftbl; Advrtsng.

REPASKY, LISA; Tantasqua Regional HS; Sturbridge, MA; (Y); French Clb; Band; Concert Band; Drm Mjr(t); Jazz Band; Yrbk Sprt Ed; Lit Mag; Sec Jr Cls; Sec Sr Cls; Trk; Modern Music Mstrs 84-86; Priv Art Classes 80-86; 2nd Place Oils 85; Advrtsng.

REPPAS, PETER A; Cushing Acad; Orange, MA; (Y); 10/108; Var Capt Bsbl; Var Capt Bsktbl; Var Capt Socr; Hon Roll; Jr NHS; NHS; Bettie Davis Awd Jr Athl Of Yr Cshng Acad 84-86; Wstrn New Engl Prep Schl All Star Soccer 85-86; Ithaca Coll; Bus Mgmt.

RESENDES, LUISA; BMC Durfee HS; Fall River, MA; (Y); 84/700; Teachers Aide; Hon Roll; Church Yth Grp; JA; Salve Regina; Sci.

RESPASS, MARC; Tahanto Regional HS; Boylston, MA; (Y); French Clb; German Clb; Ski Clb; Spanish Clb; Jazz Band; Stage Crew; Nwsp Stf; Yrbk Stf; Rep Jr Cls; Socr; Frgn Lang.

REUL, ROBIN; Bishop Stang HS; New Bedford, MA; (Y); SADD; Chorus; Mrchg Band; Var L Trk; Var Twrlr; High Hon Roll; Hon Roll; Spch Thrpy.

REUSCH, MARTHA J; Lawrence HS; Lawrence, MA; (Y); 9/330; Red Cross Aide; Pres SADD; School Play; Pres VP Stu Cncl; Capt Fld Hcky; Capt Sftbl; High Hon Roll; NHS; Teen Of Yr 86; Boston Mlobe All Schltc 2nd Tm Fld Hcky 85-86; Bentley Coll; Bus Mgmt.

REYES, ZULEMA; Boston Technical HS; Dorchester, MA; (Y); Sftbl; Tufts U; Pre-Med.

REYNOLDS, CARYL; Holbrook JR SR HS; Holbrook, MA; (Y); 1/99; Library Aide; Yrbk Stf; Off Soph Cls; Off Jr Cls; Off Sr Cls; High Hon Roll; Hon Roll; NHS; VFW Awd.

REYNOLDS, GEOFFREY; Bridgewater-Raynham Regional HS; Bridgewater, MA; (Y); Am Leg Boys St; Chess Clb; Trs Church Yth Grp; Pres Computer Clb; Math Tm; Model UN; Quiz Bowl; Science Clb; Church Choir; Hon Roll; Worcester Polytech Inst; Math.

REYNOLDS, JONATHAN; Doherty Memorial HS; Worcester, MA; (Y); 78/308; Chess Clb; Drama Clb; Pres JA; Latin Clb; Bowling; Brandeis U; Pew-Law.

REYNOLDS, MARYELLEN; Leicester HS; Rochdale, MA; (S); 6/102; French Clb; SADD; Stu Cncl; Mgr Bsbl; Capt Cheerleading; Var Fld Hcky; Var Tennis; High Hon Roll; NHS; Ntl Merit Ltr; Nichols Coll; Acctng.

REYNOLDS, MICHAEL; Marlboro HS; Marlboro, MA; (Y); 23/269; Boys Clb Am; Office Aide; Varsity Clb; Nwsp Ed-Chief; Bsbl; Bsktbl; Socr; High Hon Roll; NHS; Fclty Awds Hstry Physcl Educ 85; MVP Bsbll Marlboro HS 86; Cntrl MA All Str Tm 86.

REYNOLDS, TARA M; Milford HS; Milford, MA; (Y); 32/315; Am Leg Aux Girls St; Church Yth Grp; Intnl Clb; Key Clb; SADD; Nwsp Stf; Rep Stu Cncl; Var Bsktbl; Var Sftbl; Var Swmmng; Mst Dedctd Vrsty Bsktbl 85-86; Bst Sprtswmn Vrsty Sftbl 85-86; Stdnt Govt Day Delg 85-86; Lib Arts Coll; Med Lwyr.

REYNOLDS, TRACY A; Mt Saint Joseph Acad; Brighton, MA; (Y); 35/163; Church Yth Grp; French Clb; Hosp Aide; JA; Teachers Aide; Im Bsktbl; NHS; Boston U Scholar 86-87; MA ST Scholar 86-87; Boston U; Ed.

REZENDES, CHRIS; BMC Durfee HS; Fall River, MA; (Y); 11/678; Cmnty Wkr; Pres Frsh Cls; Pres Soph Cls; Pres Jr Cls; Pres Sr Cls; L Ftbl; L Trk; High Hon Roll; NHS; Bsktbl; Won Holy Crss Bk Awd For Acad Excllnc & Comm Svc 86; Acad All Amer 84; MVP Wtr Track; JR 50 Yd Dsh Rd.

REZENDES, DAVID; Silver Lake Regional HS; Kingston, MA; (Y); 28/420; Rep Am Leg Boys St; Math Clb; Office Aide; Varsity Clb; Hst Frsh Cls; JV Bsktbl; Capt Var Socr; Hon Roll; NHS; Bus.

RIBEIRO, DAVID; New Bedford HS; New Bedford, MA; (Y); 189/530; Bridgewater ST Coll; Aviatn.

RIBEIRO, HELENA; Ludlow HS; Ludlow, MA; (Y); Church Yth Grp; French Clb; Capt Teachers Aide; Chorus; Church Choir; Sec Jr Cls; Off Sr Cls; High Hon Roll; Hon Roll; Stu Cncl; MA Frgn Lang Assoc Awd 86; Lawyer.

RIBEIRO, JURACI; New Bedford HS; New Bedford, MA; (Y); Intnl Clb; JA; Pep Clb; SADD; Stu Cncl; Hon Roll; U Southeast MA.

RICARD, BETH; Uxbridge HS; Uxbridge, MA; (Y); Office Aide; Spanish Clb; Yrbk Stf; Hon Roll; Psychlgy.

RICCI, JEANNE; Reading Memorial HS; Reading, MA; (Y); JV Bsktbl; JV Fld Hcky; Var Powder Puff Ftbl; Im Sftbl; High Hon Roll; Hon Roll; Readng Art Assoc Awd 86; Field Hcky MVP Awd 85; Field Hcky Bst Dfnse Awd 83; Vet.

RICCIOLI, KENNETH; St Dominic Savio HS; Revere, MA; (Y); 15/105; Math Clb; Crs Cntry; Capt Ice Hcky; Hon Roll; Sec NHS; Boston Herald All Schltc Hockey Tm 86; Acad All Amer 85; TAFT.

RICCIOTI, MICHAEL; Matignon HS; Arlington, MA; (S); 12/178; Trs Camera Clb; Math Clb; Crs Cntry; Trk; Hon Roll; NHS; Ntl Merit Ltr; NEDT Awd; Red Cross Cert Extraordnry Prsnl Actn 85; Marksmn 1st Clss 85; Mech Engrng.

RICE, DAVID; Randlolph HS; Randolph, MA; (Y); Band; Concert Band; Mrchg Band; Pep Band; High Hon Roll; Hon Roll; Jr NHS.

RICE, LETITIA; Boston Latin Acad; Mattapan, MA; (Y); Church Yth Grp; Pep Clb; Church Choir; Drill Tm; Cheerleading; Hon Roll; Magna Cm Laud-Natl Latn Exm 86; Cert Merit Natl Frnch Exm 84; U Of PA; Acctng.

RICE, ROBERT; Revere HS; Revere, MA; (Y); 15/350; Church Yth Grp; Math Clb; Science Clb; SADD; L Bsktbl; Hon Roll; U Of Lowell; Cvl Engr.

RICE, TRACY; Belmont HS; Belmont, MA; (Y); Church Yth Grp; Cmnty Wkr; Pep Clb; SADD; Stage Crew; Yrbk Stf; Hon Roll; Psych.

RICH, JOEL; Marblehead HS; Marblehead, MA; (Y); 19/257; Temple Yth Grp; Varsity Clb; Capt L Crs Cntry; Capt Var Trk; High Hon Roll; Hon Roll; Jr NHS; NHS; Mst Vlbl Rnnr X-Cntry 85; Mst Imprvd Rnnr Indr Trck Team 85; 10,000 Mtr JR Div Wnnr Bay ST Gms 85; Med.

RICH, KENNETH; Dominic Savio HS; Revere, MA; (Y); 57/98; Cmnty Wkr; Computer Clb; Dance Clb; Ski Clb; SADD; Varsity Clb; Off Jr Cls; Im Bowling; Var Ftbl; JV Var Ice Hcky; Engnrng.

RICHARD, BRIAN; Wakefield HS; Wakefield, MA; (Y); Church Yth Grp; Key Clb; Yrbk Stf; JV Ice Hcky; JV Tennis.

RICHARD, JAMES; Eardner HS; Gardner, MA; (Y); Am Leg Boys St; Chess Clb; French Clb; Crs Cntry; Trk; Hon Roll; NHS; Ntl Merit SF.

RICHARD, KAREN; Gardner HS; Gardner, MA; (Y); 1/137; Am Leg Aux Girls St; French Clb; Band; Var Score Keeper; High Hon Roll; NHS; Harvard Bk Prize 86; US Air Force Acad; Aero Sci.

RICHARD, MICHELLE; Acad Of Notre Dame; Groton, MA; (Y); 6/52; Art Clb; 4-H; German Clb; 4-H Awd; High Hon Roll; Hon Roll; Jr NHS; NHS; Pres Schlr; Hghst Avg Awds Accntng, Englsh, Chmstry, Frnch, Rlgn & Cmptr 83-86; Bentley Coll; Bus.

RICHARD, MONIQUE; Bishop Feenan HS; Plainville, MA; (Y); Church Yth Grp; Cheerleading; Powder Puff Ftbl; 1st Rnnr Up Miss Black Teen 86; Most Photo; Best Talent; Caznovia; Fash Desgn.

RICHARDS, DEBBIE; Charles H Mc Cann Tech; Clarksburg, MA; (Y); Am Leg Aux Girls St; Sec SADD; Rep Frsh Cls; VP Soph Cls; VP Jr Cls; VP Sr Cls; JV Socr; Var Sftbl; Hon Roll; Jr NHS; Wmn Athl Yr 86; Trnscrpt Awd Sftbl 85; Endicott Coll; Sectrl Wrk.

RICHARDS, KEVIN M; St Johns HS; Clinton, MA; (Y); 60/251; Am Leg Boys St; Model UN; Political Wkr; Nwsp Stf; High Hon Roll; Hon Roll; J F Kennedy Lrbry Wrkshp For Yng Pltcns 86; Pltcl Sci.

RICHARDS, LINDA MARIE; Reading Memorial HS; Reading, MA; (Y); 9/328; Nwsp Rptr; Yrbk Ed-Chief; Ed Lit Mag; Elks Awd; High Hon Roll; NHS; Ntl Merit Ltr; Rep Stu Cncl; Latin NHS; Stu Advsry Cncl; Frgn Lang Latin Awd; Boston Coll; Cmmnctns.

RICHARDS, WENDY; David Hale Fanning Trade HS; Worcester, MA; (Y); 41/124; Church Yth Grp; SADD; Yrbk Stf; Off Soph Cls; Trs Jr Cls; Sec Sr Cls; Var Cheerleading; Sftbl; Bckr JR Coll; Physcl Thrpst.

RICHARDSON, AMI; Fontbonne Acad; Hyde Park, MA; (Y); Cmnty Wkr; Hosp Aide; Math Tm; Nwsp Stf; Rep Frsh Cls; Rep Stu Cncl; Trk; High Hon Roll; Pres NHS; Prfct Atten Awd; Med.

RICHARDSON, DEBBIE; Methven HS; Methuen, MA; (Y); 122/336; Intnl Clb; Yrbk Stf; Bsktbl; Powder Puff Ftbl; Trk; Bsktbl St Champs MIP 85-86; Bsktbl MIP 83-84; Rainbow Girls Worth Advsr Pres 85-86; Salem ST Coll; Crmnl Just.

RICHARDSON, NEHEMIAH E; Ayer HS; Shirley, MA; (Y); 1/129; Math Clb; Orch; Cit Awd; High Hon Roll; Mu Alp Tht; NHS; Ntl Merit Ltr; Pres Schlr; St Schlr; Val; MIT; Elctrcl Engrng.

RICHARDSON, STEPHEN KYE; Ayer HS; Shirley, MA; (Y); 5/135; Am Leg Boys St; Math Clb; Orch; Hon Roll; Mu Alp Tht; NHS; Boston Symphy Orch Yth Cncrts Comp 86; Worcester Music Assn Comp 86; Salem Philharmonic Comp 86.

RICHARDSON, STEVEN; Hull HS; Hull, MA; (Y); 7/137; Jazz Band; Mrchg Band; Yrbk Bus Mgr; Pres Jr Cls; Pres Stu Cncl; JP Sousa Awd; Bentley Coll; Bus Mngmnt.

RICHMOND, ANN; Salem HS; Salem, MA; (Y); Church Yth Grp; Hosp Aide; Office Aide; Science Clb; Spanish Clb; Varsity Clb; Nwsp Ed-Chief; Rep Frsh Cls; Rep Soph Cls; Bsktbl; Salem ST Coll; Psych.

RICHMOND, SHEILA; Matignon HS; Medford, MA; (S); 5/180; VP Art Clb; Camera Clb; Church Yth Grp; Letterman Clb; VP Library Aide; Math Clb; SADD; Nwsp Stf; Yrbk Bus Mgr; Yrbk Stf; Century III Ldrshp Awd 85; Schlrshp Women Engrng Prog Stevens Tech 85; Bio Engrng.

RICK, BRIAN; Northfield Mt Hermon HS; Reading, PA; (Y); Wrstlng; High Hon Roll; Hon Roll; Ntl Merit Ltr; Cum Laude.

RIDEOUT, SANDRA; Reading Memorial HS; Reading, MA; (Y); Church Yth Grp; Hon Roll; Prfct Atten Awd; Bus Admin.

RIDOLFI, TARA; Milford HS; Milford, MA; (Y); 35/300; Am Leg Aux Girls St; Trs Key Clb; SADD; Yrbk Rptr; JV Capt Sftbl; JV Capt Vllybl; Hon Roll; NHS; Nrsng.

RIEDL, SUZANNE; Wachusett Rgnl HS; Holden, MA; (Y); 96/430; GAA; SADD; Concert Band; Mrchg Band; Symp Band; Lit Mag; L Var Crs Cntry; Var Socr; Capt L Trk; Cntrl MA All Star Track Relay 84-85&85-86; Capt Winter Track 85-86; MVP Awd 85-86; Vet.

RIEGER, ALIZA; Marblehead HS; Marblehead, MA; (Y); 45/245; Debate Tm; Drama Clb; SADD; Temple Yth Grp; Off Nwsp Bus Mgr; Off Nwsp Rptr; Off Yrbk Bus Mgr; Swmmng; High Hon Roll; Hon Roll; Advisors Awd Schl Nwsppr; Intl Rltns.

RIEKE, NEIL; Lee HS; Lee, MA; (Y); 16/80; Nwsp Stf; Yrbk Stf; JV Bsbl; Hon Roll; U Of MA; Frstry.

RIEL, MATTHEW; Hampshire Regional HS; Southampton, MA; (Y); 17/137; Am Leg Boys St; SADD; VP Jr Cls; VP Sr Cls; VP Stu Cncl; Var L Bsktbl; Var L Crs Cntry; Var L Trk; Hon Roll; NHS; W MA Div II Trck 6th Pl Mile Rly-85 2nd Pl Mile Rly-86 6th Pl 300 Lw Hrdls 85-86.

RIGANO, CHARISSA M; Belmont HS; Belmont, MA; (Y); 13/260; Hosp Aide; Band; Concert Band; Mrchg Band; Orch; Stage Crew; Symp Band; Yrbk Stf; Stat Bsktbl; JV Var Score Keeper; Belmont Schl Cmmtee Awd Msc 83-86; Slctd Mbr Of All-ST Bnd 86; Tufts U; Biomed Engr.

RIGNEY, RACHEL; Fanning Trade HS; Worcester, MA; (Y); SADD; Variety Show; Yrbk Stf; Cheerleading; Hon Roll; Becker JC; Bus.

RIGO, MICHAEL; Boston Latin HS; Jamaica Plain, MA; (Y); 41/278; Am Leg Boys St; Church Choir; Concert Band; Jazz Band; Mrchg Band; Swing Chorus; Lit Mag; NHS; Church Yth Grp; Ski Clb; Comm Theatre Musicals; Engrng.

RIHM, NOEL N; Minnecdhaug Regional HS; Wilbraham, MA; (Y); 23/314; Key Clb; Madrigals; Sec Soph Cls; Sec Stu Cncl; Capt Cheerleading; Swmmng; NCTE Awd; NHS; Church Yth Grp; JCL; Mdl Congrss Bst Dlgate 86; Jr Wrtng Awd 85; Northwestern U; Pol Sci.

RILEY, DARON; Medford HS; Medford, MA; (Y); 12/438; Math Tm; Science Clb; Rep Stu Cncl; JV Capt Bsbl; High Hon Roll; Mu Alp Tht; NHS; Natl Lang Arts Olympd 84; Engl Awd 84; Physics Awd 86; Pre-Med.

RILEY, JORDANA; Westwood HS; Westwood, MA; (Y); Debate Tm; Drama Clb; SADD; School Musical; Lit Mag; Hon Roll; Ntl Merit Ltr; Wnnr HS Poetry 86; Yuth Co Ord 85-86.

RILEY, KAREN; Saugus HS; Saugus, MA; (Y); Library Aide; SADD; Yrbk Stf; Trs Pres Stu Cncl; Socr; Var Tennis; Hon Roll; Jr NHS; NHS; Itln Clb VP; ST Hstrcl Cnfrnc Prtcpnt.

RILEY, KAREN A; Gr Lawrence Technical Schl; Lawrence, MA; (Y); 12/350; Girl Scts; SADD; High Hon Roll; NHS; Hghst Data Mngmnt Awds For Achvt & Attitude 84-85 & 85-86; Grls Scout Slvr Awd 85; Nrthrn Essex CC; Comp Tech.

RILEY, PATRICIA E; Woburn HS; Woburn, MA; (Y); Camp Fr Inc; Cmnty Wkr; Math Tm; Office Aide; Yrbk Stf; Swmmng; High Hon Roll; Jr NHS; Spanish NHS; Mbr Brd Dir Grtr Bostn Cncl Cmp Fire 84-86; Germn Exchng 86; Engrng.

RILEY, SANDRA; Winchester HS; Winchester, MA; (Y); 54/296; Dance Clb; JCL; VP Latin Clb; Sec Stu Cncl; Var L Crs Cntry; Var L Trk; Hon Roll; Ntl Merit Ltr; NJCL Natl Lat Exam Magna Cum Laude 85 & 86; Stu Union Svc Awd 86.

RIMMER, DAVID; Medford HS; Medford, MA; (Y); 66/430; Church Yth Grp; Ski Clb; SADD; Varsity Clb; Var Bsbl; Var Socr; Var Trk; Hon Roll; Cert Hnbl Merit Cum Laude Latn 86; Outstndng Prog Awd Engl 85; Sci Awd Outstndng Achvt 84; Pre-Med.

RIMOVITZ, CHRISTINA; Quincy Vocational Technical HS; Quincy, MA; (Y); 5/20; Church Yth Grp; FNA; Girl Scts; Hosp Aide; Office Aide; SADD; Band; School Play; Yrbk Stf; Bsktbl; Day Care Ctr Aid; Nrsng.

RINALDO, KRISTINA; Fanning Trade HS; Worcester, MA; (Y); 24/124; SADD; Cheerleading; Hon Roll; Bus.

RING, MARK; Westfield HS; Westfield, MA; (Y); Church Yth Grp; Exploring; Band; Concert Band; Mrchg Band; Pep Band; JV Socr; High Hon Roll; Hon Roll; Jr NHS; WPI; Engrng.

RING, SALLY; Wachusett Regional HS; Sterling, MA; (Y); 77/443; Church Yth Grp; Intnl Clb; Yrbk Stf; Rep Stu Cncl; Hon Roll; Grnd Asmbly Of MA Intl Order Of Th Rnbw Grls 86; Bus.

RINOLDO, SUE; Framingham South HS; Framingham, MA; (S); 84/240; Drama Clb; Spanish Clb; SADD; School Musical; Variety Show; Yrbk Sprt Ed; Capt Cheerleading; Gym; Lcrss; Hon Roll; Emerson; Mass Comm.

RIPLEY, RALPH E; Wareham HS; Wareham, MA; (Y); Am Leg Boys St; Boy Scts; Church Yth Grp; Exploring; Var Bsbl; JV Var Ftbl; Sftbl; Var Trk; Wt Lftg; Hon Roll; Comp Sci.

RIPLEY, REBECCA; Hanover HS; Hanover, MA; (Y); 20/180; Church Yth Grp; Concert Band; Mrchg Band; School Musical; Hon Roll; Hanover Vstng Nrs Schlrshp 86; Typiing I Awd 84; Fitchburg ST Coll; Nrsng.

RISCHITELLI, MARC D; Shrewsbury SR HS; Shrewsbury, MA; (Y); 64/263; Am Leg Boys St; Drama Clb; NFL; Trs Pres Speech Tm; VP Chorus; School Musical; School Play; Yrbk Rptr; Rep Stu Cncl; Trk; Stu Mnth Awd 85; Oratrcl Declmtn Natl Cath Forn Lg Grand Trnmnt 85; Duo Actng Natl Cath Forn Lg 86; Rest Mgmt.

RISING, KATHLEEN; Westfield HS; Westfield, MA; (Y); Church Yth Grp; Cmnty Wkr; Library Aide; Orch; Stage Crew; Jr NHS; NHS; Ntl Merit Ltr; Chncllr Tlnt Awd Full Schlrshp U MA 86; Dartmouth Bk Awd 86; Natrl Sci.

RITCHIE, MATTHEW; Boston Latin Schl; W Roxbury, MA; (Y); 41/279; Am Leg Boys St; Church Yth Grp; German Clb; Teachers Aide; Band; Concert Band; Orch; Pep Band; Lit Mag; NHS; Clscl Prz 84; Ntl Ltn & Grk Exm 86; Music.

RITTENBERG, SHERI R; Burlington HS; Burlington, MA; (Y); 54/325; Cheerleading; Var Capt Gym; Powder Puff Ftbl; Hon Roll; NHS; Jewish War Vet Awd 86; Agnes Mc Leod Schlrshp 86; U Of Hatford; Accntng.

RITTGERS, KARLA; Pentucket HS; West Newbury, MA; (Y); 7/174; Sec Computer Clb; Pep Clb; Spanish Clb; Im Bsktbl; Var Cheerleading; Im Sftbl; High Hon Roll; Hon Roll; Comp Sci.

RITZINGER, HOLLY; Bishop Frehan HS; Walpole, MA; (Y); Exploring; Ski Clb; Trk; Bus Law.

RIUTANKOSKI, MAUREEN S; Fitchburg HS; Fitchburg, MA; (Y); 16/204; Cmnty Wkr; French Clb; Ski Clb; Cheerleading; High Hon Roll; Hon Roll; JR Membr Ftchbrg Wmns Clb 86; Ftchbrg HS Alumni Schlrshp 86; Nina Pierce Mem Schrlshp 86; Booster Clb; Bentley Coll; Bus.

RIVELA, STEVE; Woburn SR HS; Woburn, MA; (S); SADD; Teachers Aide; Stu Cncl; Var Co-Capt Bsbl; Var L Bsktbl; Var L Ftbl; Rotary Awd; Presdntl Physcl Ftnss Awd 83; Gldn Glv Awd-Bsbl 85; Mitchell Coll; Physcl Ed.

RIVERA, KATHLEEN; Boston Technical HS; Dorchester, MA; (Y); Church Yth Grp; Cmnty Wkr; Spanish Clb; Church Choir; High Hon Roll; Hon Roll; Prfct Atten Awd; Scrtry Dghtrs Of Vrgn Mry Chrch 84-86; Catechism Tchrs Awd 83-86; Tufts U; Vtrnrn.

RIVERA, LOUIS; Burncoat SR HS; Worcester, MA; (Y); Intnl Clb; JA; Pep Clb; SADD; Yrbk Stf; Stu Cncl; Capt Bsktbl; Crs Cntry; Mgr(s); Score Keeper; Law.

RIVERA, LUIS; Haverhill HS; Haverhill, MA; (Y); 128/316; Boys Clb Am; JA; Red Cross Aide; Spanish Clb; Teachers Aide; Chorus; Yrbk Stf; JV Socr; Im Vllybl; MA ST Schlrshp 86-87; Spplmnt Ed Opp Grant 86-87; Pell Grant 86-87; Northern Essex CC; Elec Tech.

RIVERS, DONNA; Amherst Regional HS; Amherst, MA; (Y); Drama Clb; Hosp Aide; Latin Clb; School Play; Stage Crew; Tennis; Hon Roll; Jr NHS; NHS; Art.

RIZZOTTO, KERRI; Randolph HS; Randolph, MA; (Y); 99/350; Church Yth Grp; Cmnty Wkr; Spanish Clb; Yrbk Sprt Ed; Yrbk Stf; Rep Frsh Cls; Rep Soph Cls; Rep Jr Cls; Rep Sr Cls; Rep Stu Cncl; H O Briens Outstndng Soph Awd; SADD Capt; All-Star Bsktbl Tm; Lowell U; Bus.

ROBAK, KRISTEN; Billerica Memorial HS; Billerica, MA; (Y); French Clb; Hosp Aide; Color Guard; High Hon Roll; Hon Roll; Jr NHS; NHS; Emply Mnth K-Mart Mary 85; Northeastern U; Chem Engr.

ROBBINS, SCOTT; Ludlow HS; Ludlow, MA; (Y); 6/250; Am Leg Boys St; Church Yth Grp; JCL; VP Soph Cls; VP Jr Cls; JV Ftbl; Ice Hcky; Tennis; High Hon Roll; NHS; Navy ROTC; Engrng.

ROBBINS, STEVEN; Doherty Memorial HS; Worcester, MA; (Y); Art Clb; French Clb; JA; Boston Glb Art Awds 83-86; Fn Arts Schlrshp; Worcester Art Msm; Wlrd Crft Ct 85-86; Your Gtta Hv Arts 86; Grphc Arts.

ROBENS, NANCY; Taunton HS; Taunton, MA; (Y); Church Choir; Yrbk Stf; Fld Hcky; Swmmng; Trk; Hon Roll; Ntl Latine Exam Cum Laude 85; Cert Of Credit Speed Typng 85; Comp Prgmng.

ROBERGE, RAELENE; Wellesley SR HS; Wellesley, MA; (Y); 63/310; Off Church Yth Grp; Computer Clb; Trs Drama Clb; French Clb; Church Choir; Madrigals; Mrchg Band; School Musical; School Play; Mgr Stage Crew; Worthy Advsr Wellsly Assmbly Intl Ordr Rainbw Grls 85-86; Bus.

ROBERT, MARTIN; Arlington Catholic HS; Lexington, MA; (Y); Church Yth Grp; French Clb; SADD; Nwsp Stf; Rep Frsh Cls; Rep Jr Cls; Hon Roll; Jr NHS; NHS; Prfct Atten Awd; Law.

ROBERTS, AMY; Westford Acad; Westford, MA; (Y); SADD; Concert Band; Jazz Band; Yrbk Bus Mgr; Capt Cheerleading; Im Powder Puff Ftbl; Hon Roll; Watchusett Lg Band 83-84; Exrcse Sci.

ROBERTS, BRIAN; Haverhill HS; Haverhill, MA; (Y); 48/500; Boys Clb Am; Church Yth Grp; French Clb; Letterman Clb; Bsbl; Ftbl; Ice Hcky; Wt Lftg; High Hon Roll; Hon Roll; Math.

ROBERTS, GLENN; Austin Prep; Reading, MA; (Y); 28/136; French Clb; SADD; Im Sftbl; David Nelson Mem Schlrshp 86; Emerson; Cmmnctns.

ROBERTS, KIMBERLY; C H Mc Cann Technical HS; Clarksburg, MA; (Y); Church Yth Grp; Cmnty Wkr; SADD; Nwsp Rptr; Trs Sr Cls; Var Bsktbl; JV Var Sftbl; High Hon Roll; Hon Roll; NHS; Stud Advsr To The Schl Cmmttee 86-87; Bnkng.

ROBERTS, LAURA; Bellingham Memorial HS; Bellingham, MA; (Y); 3/191; Nwsp Ed-Chief; Off Stu Cncl; JV Var Fld Hcky; Var Tennis; NHS; NEDT Awd; Yrbk Stf; Hon Roll; Hon Mntn Phi Alpha ST Hstrcl Conf 86; FL Inst Of Tech; Sci.

ROBERTS, LAUREN; Braintree HS; Braintree, MA; (Y); 84/400; JV Gym; Var Capt Socr; JV Sftbl; JV Trk; Hon Roll; Hon Men Girls Socr BSL 85; Bridgewater ST; Ed.

ROBERTS, LISA M; Boston Latin Schl; Brighton, MA; (Y); 53/300; Chorus; Hon Roll; Ntl Merit Ltr; 4 Yr Schlrshp-Museum Of Fine Arts 82-86; Natl Achvt Semifnlst 85-86; Art.

ROBERTS, MARK; Catherdral HS; Springfield, MA; (Y); Political Wkr; JV Socr; Presdntl Phys Fitns Awd; Westrn-New Englnd Coll; Elect.

ROBERTS, SUSAN; Masconomet Regional HS; Topsfield, MA; (Y); 47/246; French Clb; Office Aide; Radio Clb; Sec Stu Cncl; Var Gym; Capt Powder Puff Ftbl; Hon Roll; Phys Ther.

ROBERTS, WILLIAM M; Acton-Boxborough Regional HS; Acton, MA; (Y); 3/346; Math Clb; Math Tm; Science Clb; JV Crs Cntry; JV Tennis; High Hon Roll; Hon Roll; NHS; Ntl Merit SF; Pres Schlr; Rensselaer Medal 85; Math & Chem Achvt Awds 82-85; Estrn MA Atlntc Rgn Math Leag A Tm 84-85; Princeton U; Math.

ROBERTSON JR, JOHN; Bishop Feehan HS; Attleboro, MA; (Y); 83/256; Boy Scts; Elks Awd; French Hon Soc; High Hon Roll; Hon Roll; Prfct Atten Awd; Lit Mag; Ftbl; Prfct Atten Awd 83-85; Eagle Sct 85; JR Yeoman 85; Bus.

ROBERTSON, LYNN; Hampshire Regional HS; Westhampton, MA; (Y); 6/130; Church Yth Grp; Girl Scts; Hosp Aide; Spanish Clb; Nwsp Rptr; Trk; High Hon Roll; Hon Roll; Jr NHS; NHS; Hmn Rltns.

ROBIDOUX, NEIL; Leicester HS; Rochdale, MA; (Y); French Clb; Science Clb; High Hon Roll; Hon Roll; Environmental Sci.

ROBIE, STEPHEN I; Brockton HS; Brockton, MA; (Y); 3/880; Am Leg Boys St; Key Clb; Temple Yth Grp; Var Bsktbl; High Hon Roll; NHS; Pres Schlr; St Schlr; Williams Coll Bk Awd 85; Sherman H Starr Hmn Rltns Yth Awd 86; Kiwanis Hnrs For Acads Awd 86; Tufts U; Med.

ROBINSON, KENNETH; Marshfield HS; Marshfield, MA; (Y); 23/380; Am Leg Boys St; Chrmn Church Yth Grp; Pres Key Clb; SADD; Pres Frsh Cls; Pres Soph Cls; Pres Jr Cls; Pres Sr Cls; Capt Tennis; Rep Stu Cncl; Otstndng Ldrshp MA ST Snt 86; Gvrnmnt.

ROBINSON, LAURIE; Hoosac Valley HS; Adams, MA; (Y); 13/153; Pep Clb; Ski Clb; Band; Concert Band; Mrchg Band; Yrbk Stf; Crs Cntry; Hon Roll; NHS; Pres Schlr; Pres Acad Ftnss Awd 86; Mass Coll; Phar.

ROBINSON JR, LEONARD B; Oakmont Regional HS; Ashburnham, MA; (Y); 50/150; Am Leg Boys St; Camera Clb; Var Bsbl; JV Bsktbl; Im Vllybl; Hon Roll.

ROBINSON, MARK; Greater Boston Acad; Milton, MA; (Y); Hosp Aide; Band; Chorus; Drm Mjr(t); Orch; Off Frsh Cls; Off Soph Cls; Pres Stu Cncl; Swmmng; Hon Roll; High Scoring TAP & Highest In Schl PSAT, SAT, & ACT 85-86; Bus Adm.

ROBINSON, THOMAS; St Dominic Savio HS; E Boston, MA; (Y); 1/105; Chess Clb; Ski Clb; Yrbk Ed-Chief; High Hon Roll; VP NHS; Ntl Merit SF; Val; Presdlnt Acadmc Fitns Awd 86; Navy ROTC Schlrshp 86; Holy Cross Coll; Physics.

ROCHE, CHRISTOPHER; North Attleboro HS; N Attleboro, MA; (Y); Latin Clb; Letterman Clb; Math Clb; Var Capt Bsbl; JV Bsktbl; JV Var Ftbl; L Var Trk; Im Vllybl; High Hon Roll; Hon Roll.

ROCHE, JIM; Hudson HS; Hudson, MA; (Y); 3/125; Exploring; Math Tm; Yrbk Stf; Rep Sr Cls; High Hon Roll; Ntl Merit SF.

ROCHE, KERRY; Westwood HS; Westwood, MA; (Y); 17/212; SADD; Trs Jr Cls; Trs Sr Cls; Stu Cncl; Socr; Var Capt Sftbl; Jr NHS; NHS; Hon Roll; CYO Bsktbl MVP & Mst Dedctd Plyr 84; Tri Vly Lgu All Star Game 86; Daily Trnscp Sftbl All Star 86.

ROCHE, NEIL; Maynard HS; Maynard, MA; (Y); 18/106; Am Leg Boys St; Color Guard; Yrbk Stf; Ftbl; Trk; Hon Roll; Worcete Poly Tech; Engrng.

ROCHELEAU, BILLY; Shrewsbury HS; Shrewsbury, MA; (Y); Cmnty Wkr; JA; Letterman Clb; Pep Clb; SADD; Varsity Clb; Band; Mrchg Band; School Musical; Var L Bsbl; Tchr.

ROCHELEAU, DENISE; Gardner HS; Gardner, MA; (Y); 26/166; Church Yth Grp; Trs DECA; Ed Lit Mag; Trk; Stone Fund Schlrshp 86; Nchls Coll Schlrshp 86; HOWC Fnd Schlrshp 86; Nichols Coll; Accntng.

ROCHELEAU, MICHELLE; Taconic HS; Pittsfield, MA; (Y); Cmnty Wkr; Hon Roll; Comp.

ROCHON, GLEN; Eastampton HS; East Hampton, MA; (Y); Am Leg Boys St; VP JA; Band; Sec Frsh Cls; Rep Stu Cncl; VP Golf; High Hon Roll; Hon Roll; NHS; Engrng.

ROCKWAL, MICHAEL T; St Marys HS; Westfield, MA; (Y); 10/60; Am Leg Boys St; Chess Clb; Church Yth Grp; Yrbk Sprt Ed; JV Bsbl; JV Socr; Var Tennis; Hon Roll; NHS; Westfield ST Coll; Bus.

ROCKWELL, STEVEN; Tewksbury Memorial HS; Tewksbury, MA; (S); Pres DECA; Pres SADD; Rep Jr Cls; VP Sr Cls; Pres Stu Cncl; HS Schlrshp 86; Rotary Clb Hats Off Awd Stu Of Month 86; DECA 4th Pl Natl Fnlst 86; Newbury Coll; Bus Mgmt.

ROCQUE, DANNIELLE; Pittsfield HS; Pittsfield, MA; (Y); Sec Church Yth Grp; VP Pres JA; Chrmn Latin Clb; Pep Clb; SADD; Stat Bsktbl; High Hon Roll; NHS; Mass Advncd Studies Prog 86; Smi-Fnlst For Finland U S Senate Yth Exch Prog; Bus.

RODERICKS, RON; Brockton HS; Brockton, MA; (Y); 37/800; Am Leg Boys St; JCL; Key Clb; SADD; Yrbk Sprt Ed; Off Frsh Cls; Off Jr Cls; Off Sr Cls; Off Stu Cncl; L Var Ftbl; Wayne Mitchell Hi-Y Awd; Justice Superior Ct-MA Boys St; Cum Laude Natl Latin Exam 85; Dickinson Coll; Dentstry.

RODERIQUES, KIMBERLY; New Bedford HS; New Bedford, MA; (Y); 63/700; Band; Acctg.

RODGERS, DAVID J; Hingham HS; Hingham, MA; (Y); 71/340; Church Yth Grp; Ski Clb; Yrbk Stf; VP Frsh Cls; Var Ice Hcky; JV Var Socr; Hon Roll.

RODNEY, NADINE; North Cambridge Catholic HS; Cambridge, MA; (Y); Cmnty Wkr; Intnl Clb; Spanish Clb; JV Bsktbl; Tennis; Hon Roll; NHS; Algebra I 83-84; Chem 85-86; Spanish III 85-86; Law.

RODOPHELE JR, JOHN L; North Quincy HS; Quincy, MA; (Y); 45/340; JA; Ftbl; Trk; Wrstlng; U MA Amhrst; Mngmnt & Finance.

RODRIGUES, BEVERLY; Bmc Durfee HS; Fall River, MA; (Y); 58/673; Hon Roll; Jr NHS; SMU; Cmptr Engr.

RODRIGUES, KRISTEN; Norton HS; Norton, MA; (S); French Clb; Math Clb; Tennis; Hon Roll; NEDT Awd.

RODRIGUEZ, CINDY; Lawrence HS; Lawrence, MA; (Y); 30/266; Library Aide; Science Clb; SADD; School Play; Nwsp Ed-Chief; Var Crs Cntry; Var Tennis; Capt Trk; High Hon Roll; Hon Roll; Amer Lgn Cert 85-86; Clark U; Pre-Med.

RODRIGUEZ, DAVID; Amherst Regional HS; Hadley, MA; (Y); 4-H; Hosp Aide; Band; Concert Band; Jazz Band; Mrchg Band; Nwsp Stf; JV Socr; Hon Roll; Ntl Merit Ltr; Ntl Hispnc Schlr Semi Fnlst 85-86.

RODRIGUEZ, EILEEN; South Lancaster Acad; Worcester, MA; (S); 3/20; Drill Tm; Nwsp Rptr; Yrbk Rptr; Pres VP Stu Cncl; Cheerleading; Hon Roll; NHS; Nwsp Stf; Yrbk Stf; Gym; Alumni Schlrshp 85; Bus Ed Awd 86; Spnsh Awd 86; Atlantic Union Coll; Bus.

RODRIQUE, JACQUELINE; Leicester HS; Cherry Valley, MA; (Y); 17/104; Pres Church Yth Grp; Latin Clb; Math Tm; SADD; School Play; Yrbk Bus Mgr; Yrbk Ed-Chief; Pres Sr Cls; Ntl Merit Ltr; Chrmn Prm & Dnnr Dnc Cmmte; Hrc Mann Chptr Natl Hnr Soc Schlrshp; Leicstr Mthrs Clb Shclrshp; St Josephs Coll; Bio.

RODRIQUES, ANGELA; St Clement HS; Somerville, MA; (Y); Church Yth Grp; Hosp Aide; Office Aide; Church Choir; School Play; High Hon Roll; Hon Roll; Prfct Atten Awd; Secy.

RODSKI, PETER; Gardner HS; Gardner, MA; (Y); 3/164; Am Leg Boys St; Chess Clb; Computer Clb; Trs Frsh Cls; Trs Jr Cls; Var Bsbl; Var Trk; All Star Bsbl 85-86; Awd For Excllnc In Comptrs 86; Worcester Polytech; Math.

ROGALSKI, APRIL DAWNE; Saugus HS; Saugus, MA; (Y); 15/300; Art Clb; Spanish Clb; Band; Concert Band; Drm Mjr(t); Flag Corp; Sec Sr Cls; Pom Pon; High Hon Roll; Rotary Clb Schlrshp 86; Mac Kenzie-Price Wanapaunaquins Twrlng Schlrshp 86; Boston Glb Schltc Art 86; Boston U; Comm.

ROGERS, BETSY A; Shepherd Hill Regional HS; Charlton, MA; (Y); 8/132; Drama Clb; Math Tm; SADD; Yrbk Bus Mgr; Rep Sr Cls; High Hon Roll; NHS; Ntl Merit Ltr; Prfct Atten Awd; Pres Schlr; Assmptn Coll; Engl Law.

ROGERS, HEIDI; New Bedford HS; New Bedford, MA; (Y); 81/630; Church Yth Grp; Dance Clb; Drama Clb; Library Aide; Stu Cncl; High Hon Roll; Hon Roll; Jr NHS; Southeastern MA U; Psych.

ROGERS, J PETER; Bishop Feehan HS; Attleboro, MA; (Y); Var Ftbl; Var Ice Hcky; Var Trk; Hon Roll; Bryant Coll; Bus Mgmt.

ROGERS, JEFFREY W; Walpole HS; E Walpole, MA; (Y); 64/270; Ski Clb; Capt Golf; Capt Wrstlng; Clinton Schlrshp; U Of NH; Chrpctc.

ROGERS, JENNIFER; Easthampton HS; Easthampton, MA; (Y); 17/135; French Clb; Spanish Clb; JV Bsktbl; Var Socr; JV Var Sftbl; High Hon Roll; Hon Roll; Psych.

ROGERS, LISA; Hull HS; Hull, MA; (Y); 7/125; Aud/Vis; Yrbk Bus Mgr; Lit Mag; Pres Frsh Cls; Trs Stu Cncl; Var Bsktbl; Powder Puff Ftbl; Var Sftbl; Hon Roll; NHS; US Stu Cncl Awd 86; All-Star Bsktbl 86; All-Star Sftbl 86; Cmnctns.

ROGERS, TONY; Jeremiah E Burke HS; Dorchester, MA; (Y); Cmnty Wkr; Computer Clb; DECA; Key Clb; Office Aide; Teachers Aide; Yrbk Stf; Pres Sr Cls; Rep Stu Cncl; NHS; Pres Acad Ftns Awd 86; John Hancock Hnrs Awd 86; ST Achvt Awd 86; Newbury Coll; Bus Mgmt.

ROHDE, LAURA; Wellesley SR HS; Wellesley, MA; (Y); 129/296; Church Yth Grp; Cmnty Wkr; Hosp Aide; Office Aide; Chorus; Stage Crew; Im Gym; JV Socr; JV Sftbl; Hon Roll; Physcl Thrpy.

ROHDE, PETER F; North Andover HS; North Andover, MA; (Y); 20/289; Am Leg Boys St; Yrbk Phtg; Stu Cncl; Bsktbl; Trk; Vllybl; Hon Roll.

ROHRS, SUSANNAH; Frontier Regional HS; S Deerfield, MA; (Y); 3/98; Ski Clb; Rep Frsh Cls; Rep Soph Cls; Rep Stu Cncl; JV Cheerleading; Bausch & Lomb Sci Awd; High Hon Roll; Hon Roll; Pres NHS; Smith Coll Bk Awd 85; Ptrlm Engrng.

ROJAS, ELVITA; Greater Lawrence Tech; Lawrence, MA; (Y); Computer Clb; Exploring; FHA; FNA; Hosp Aide; Office Aide; Spanish Clb; SADD; Yrbk Stf; Pres VP Jr Cls; Northen Essex; Rgstr Nrs.

ROJAS, LISA; Hopedale JR SR HS; Hopedale, MA; (Y); 17/70; Sec Church Yth Grp; Office Aide; SADD; Yrbk Stf; Var L Cheerleading; Socr; Var L Sftbl; JV Vllybl; High Hon Roll; Hon Roll; HOBY Fndtn Delg 85.

ROLANTI, DAVID; Dennis-Yarmouth Regional HS; Dennisport, MA; (Y); Boy Scts; German Clb; Lcrss; Trk; Boston Coll; Avionics.

ROLLEND, MICHELLE; Cathedral HS; Springfield, MA; (Y); NHS; Prfct Atten Awd.

ROLLINS, ANDREA; Wachusett Regional HS; Holden, MA; (Y); 21/463; Cmnty Wkr; 4-H; Hosp Aide; SADD; Teachers Aide; School Musical; Hon Roll; NHS; Lbrl Arts.

ROMANI JR, DANIEL A; Framingham South HS; Framingham, MA; (Y); 10/245; Jazz Band; Pres Soph Cls; Pres Jr Cls; Pres Sr Cls; Var Capt Ftbl; High Hon Roll; NHS; Rotary Awd; Band; Mrchg Band; Mdlbry Coll; Lawyer.

ROMANI, JEFFREY R; St Marys HS; Russell, MA; (Y); 7/50; Am Leg Boys St; Nwsp Stf; Yrbk Sprt Ed; Yrbk Stf; Var Bsbl; JV Socr; Hon Roll; NHS; Outstndg Prfrmnc Alge 84-85; Excllnc Bio 85-86; Turtoring Alge & Geo 84-86; Engrng.

ROMANO, LISA; Medford HS; Medford, MA; (Y); 7/375; Math Tm; Ski Clb; Varsity Clb; Yrbk Stf; Stu Cncl; Var L Cheerleading; Var L Pom Pon; Cit Awd; High Hon Roll; NHS; Mu Alpha Theta-Math Ntl Hnr Soc 85; Schlrshp 4 Yrs-Stop & Shop Co 86; Engl Awd-Outstndg Achvt 86; Tufts U; Cvl Engrng.

ROMANOWSKI, LINDA; Wilmington HS; Wilmington, MA; (Y); Church Yth Grp; Sec French Clb; Science Clb; Nwsp Ed-Chief; Nwsp Phtg; Yrbk Phtg; Yrbk Stf; High Hon Roll; NHS.

ROME, AARON; Beverly HS; Beverly, MA; (Y); Yrbk Stf; Crs Cntry; JV Var Socr; Var JV Tennis; Hon Roll; Boys St-Bentley 86; Arch.

ROMEO, JENNIFER; Bishop Connolly HS; Fall River, MA; (Y); 31/167; Cmnty Wkr; Girl Scts; Chorus; Church Choir; High Hon Roll; Hon Roll; Johnson & Wales Coll; Htl Mgmt.

ROMEUS, FRITZ; Boston English HS; Mattapan, MA; (Y); 1/300; Boy Scts; Church Yth Grp; Intnl Clb; Varsity Clb; Yrbk Stf; Socr; Swmmng; High Hon Roll; Hon Roll; NHS; Pres Schl Bilingual Clb 86; Schl Star Grp 86; Cabinet Rep; Boston Coll; Pre-Med.

RONCKA, JEFFREY J; New Bedford HS; New Bedford, MA; (Y); 6/701; Am Leg Boys St; Drama Clb; JCL; Orch; Rep Jr Cls; JV Bsktbl; Var Vllybl; Cit Awd; Pres NHS; Ntl Merit SF; Mech Engrng.

RONCKA, SCOTT; Marian HS; Westboro, MA; (Y); JV Bsbl; Var Hon Roll; NHS; Bus Princpls, Mgmt Awd 86; Phys Educ Awd 85; Business.

RONEY, STEPHEN; Bishop Fenwick HS; Lynn, MA; (Y); Var Bsbl; Var Hon Roll; Babe Ruth US All Str Tm 83; Engr.

RONIS, JOHN; Acton Boxboro Regional HS; Acton, MA; (Y); JV Bsktbl; Var L Golf; Outstndg Ath Golf 86; Bus Adm.

ROOD, JEFFREY; Barnstable HS; Hyannis, MA; (Y); Boy Scts; Cmnty Wkr; Political Wkr; Ski Clb; VICA; Ftbl; Bus.

ROODE, CHARLES; Wahconah HS; Becket, MA; (Y); Exploring; Hosp Aide; Math Clb; Office Aide; Science Clb; Ski Clb; Teachers Aide; School Play; Im Socr; Boy Scts; Ski 83-86; Work With Spec Ed 83-86; Ordrly Mapleview Nrsg Home 83-86; U MA; BSN.

ROONEY, CHRISTINE; Cathedral HS; Springfield, MA; (Y); 59/569; Church Yth Grp; Cmnty Wkr; SADD; Nwsp Stf; JV Var Bsktbl; JV Var Bsktbl; JV Var Socr; JV Var Sftbl; High Hon Roll; Hon Roll; Bus.

ROONEY, JANE; Cardinal Spellman HS; W Bridgewater, MA; (Y); 16/209; Cmnty Wkr; Pep Clb; School Musical; School Play; Variety Show; Off Jr Cls; Var Cheerleading; High Hon Roll; NHS; 2nd Pl Sci Fair 86; Cert Regnl Sci Fair 86; Bus Adm.

ROOS, TIM; Burlington HS; Burlington, MA; (Y); 32/339; JA; Math Tm; Var Lcrss; High Hon Roll; Hon Roll; Basic Mech Draw 83-84; Mech Engr.

ROOVER, MELISSA; Natick HS; Natick, MA; (Y); 28/399; JA; SADD; Temple Yth Grp; Mrchg Band; Symp Band; Yrbk Stf; Stu Cncl; Hon Roll.

ROSATI, DEBRA; Matignon HS; Watertown, MA; (S); 2/180; Hosp Aide; JA; SADD; High Hon Roll; Jr NHS; NHS; Spanish NHS; Voice Dem Awd; Camera Clb; Med.

ROSATO, BARBARA; Arlington Catholic HS; Medford, MA; (Y); 23/144; Church Yth Grp; Office Aide; Spanish Clb; SADD; Yrbk Stf; Socr; Hon Roll; NHS; Nrsng.

ROSCIGNO, LAURA; Saint Mary HS; Lawrence, MA; (Y); 1/82; Office Aide; School Play; Yrbk Stf; Capt Tennis; Bausch & Lomb Sci Awd; High Hon Roll; Trs NHS; Pres Schlr; St Schlr; Val; U MA.

ROSE, VALERIE; Pittsfield HS; Pittsfield, MA; (Y); Latin Clb; Lit Mag; Trk.

ROSEBERRY, DEANNA; Montachusett Reg Voc Tech; Sterling, MA; (Y); 8/150; Yrbk Stf; Hon Roll; VP NHS; Pres Acadmc Ftnss Awd 86; Mst Outstndng Stu-Physics 86; Mst Outstndng Stu-Grphc Arts 84-86; Mt Wachusett CC; Brdcstng.

ROSEN, ALISA; Lincoln-Sudbury Regional HS; Sudbury, MA; (Y); Chorus; School Musical; School Play; Stage Crew; Rep Frsh Cls; Rep Soph Cls; Var Socr; Var Trk; Ski Clb; Concert Band.

ROSENBERG, ADAM; Randolph HS; Randolph, MA; (Y); Capt SADD; Temple Yth Grp; Trs Jr Cls; Trs Sr Cls; Stu Cncl; JV Var Bsktbl; JV Var Socr; Var Trk; High Hon Roll; NHS; Ntl Merit Achvt Ltr; Bus.

ROSENBERG, LAURA A; Canton HS; Canton, MA; (Y); 2/265; Math Tm; VP Science Clb; Yrbk Stf; Var Socr; NHS; Ntl Merit SF; Sal; German Clb; Hosp Aide; Office Aide; ARML Comptr Eastern Mass; SF YFU Exc Finland; Bays Soccer; U PA; Elect Engr.

ROSENBERG, LISA; Winthrop HS; Winthrop, MA; (Y); 7/205; Dance Clb; Chorus; Nwsp Stf; Powder Puff Ftbl; High Hon Roll; Hon Roll; Jr NHS; NHS; Prfct Atten Awd; 4-H; SR Clss Day Committee 86-87; American U; Languages.

ROSENBERGER, SCOTT A; Framingham South HS; Framingham, MA; (Y); Church Yth Grp; German Clb; Jazz Band; Mrchg Band; Orch; Variety Show; L Ftbl; L Trk; Tchrs Assn Schlrshp 86; Stvns Inst Schlrshp 86; Stvns Inst Of Tech; Mecn Engrng.

ROSENBLUM, WILLIAM; The Lawrence Acad; S Hadley, MA; (Y); Chorus; School Play; Yrbk Stf; Rep Jr Cls; Rep Sr Cls; Rep Stu Cncl; Coach Actv; Var Capt Golf; Var L Ice Hcky; Var L Socr; Hon Roll; Duke U; Law.

ROSENFIELD, SETH; North HS; Worcester, MA; (Y); CAP; Drama Clb; Ski Clb; Nwsp Stf; Jr Cls; Bsbl; Ftbl; Ice Hcky; Wt Lftg; U MA Amherst; Bus.

ROSENTHAL, JOHN; Walpole HS; Walpole, MA; (Y); 53/185; Church Yth Grp; JCL; Latin Clb; Socr; Cert De Merit Natl Span Exam 86.

ROSENTHAL, MARJORY; Randolph HS; Randolph, MA; (Y); 69/325; Drama Clb; SADD; Yrbk Stf; Capt Cheerleading; Capt Gym; Capt Powder Puff Ftbl; Hon Roll; Ftbl Scholar 86; Randolph Mariner Nwsp Scholar 86; Hockey Scholar 86; Ithica; Cmmnctns.

ROSNER, CINDY; Agawam HS; Agawam, MA; (Y); #10 In Class; Drama Clb; Library Aide; PAVAS; Chorus; School Musical; School Play; Variety Show; Hon Roll; NHS; Spanish NHS.

ROSS, DOUGLAS; Hingham HS; Hingham, MA; (Y); Band; Jazz Band; School Musical; Variety Show; Nwsp Stf; Bandmasters Awd 84; Boston Globe Schlstc Art Awds 84; Hingham High Jr Cls Outstndng Art Achvt 86; Art Illustration.

ROSS, JOHN; Milford HS; Milford, MA; (Y); 27/300; Var JV Bsbl; JV Bsktbl; JV Ftbl; High Hon Roll; Hon Roll; NHS; Most Dedctd Bsbl 86; Worcester Poly Tech; Elect Engr.

ROSS, LORI; Bishop Feehan HS; Walpole, MA; (Y); Elem Ed.

ROSS, MICHAEL G; Grafton HS; Grafton, MA; (Y); Am Leg Boys St; Church Yth Grp; Var Bsktbl; Var Capt Ftbl; Swmmng; Wt Lftg; Soc Wrkr.

ROSS, PAUL; St Johns Prep Schl; Lynnfield, MA; (Y); Boy Scts; Church Yth Grp; Drama Clb; JA; Office Aide; Hon Roll; NHS; Eagle Scout 85; Worcester Poly Tech; Civil Engr.

ROSSI, THOMAS; Revere HS; Revere, MA; (Y); 15/350; Debate Tm; Political Wkr; Quiz Bowl; Yrbk Stf; Capt Bsktbl; Im Coach Actv; Im Ftbl; Im Score Keeper; High Hon Roll; Acctg.

ROSSITER, RENEE; Easthampton HS; Easthampton, MA; (Y); Dance Clb; Drama Clb; Spanish Clb; School Play; Yrbk Stf; Hon Roll; Helena C Evans Art Prz 86; 3rd Rnr-Up Esthmptns JR Miss Pgnt 86; Yrbk Art Edtr 86; Holyoke Cmnty Coll; Prfrmg Arts.

ROSSOL, JOSH; Brookline HS; Brookline, MA; (Y); Am Leg Boys St; DECA; Orch; JV Tennis; Hon Roll; NHS; Ntl Merit SF; Harvard U Book Prz 86; U Penn Awd 86; Bus.

ROTHERA, MATTHEW; Westford Acad; Westford, MA; (Y); AFS; German Clb; Capt Var Bsktbl; Capt Var Socr; High Hon Roll; NHS; Lowell Sun Newspaper Sccr All-Str 85; Sci.

ROTONDO, ANDREA; Reading Memorial HS; Reading, MA; (Y); Church Yth Grp; Band; Concert Band; Nwsp Rptr; Ed Lit Mag; Rep Frsh Cls; Rep Soph Cls; Rep Jr Cls; Hon Roll; Yrbk Phtg; USFSA Figure Sktng Badge 84; EDCO Pathways 85-86; Audio Engrng.

ROUNDS, KENNY; King Philip HS; Plainvlle, MA; (Y); 96/200; Camera Clb; Yrbk Ed-Chief; Yrbk Phtg; Yrbk Rptr; Yrbk Stf; Hon Roll; MA Tech Drwng Tchrs Assco 86; King Philip Rgnl Voc Awd 85; Emply Of Mt Papa Ginos 85-86; Worchester Poly-Tech; Indust En.

ROURKE, LINDA; Lynnfield HS; Lynnfield, MA; (Y); JA; Band; Bsktbl; Fld Hcky; Mgr(s); Powder Puff Ftbl; Sftbl; High Hon Roll; NHS; Spanish NHS; Commdentn Eng Hnrs 85; Lynnfield Schlrshp Foundtn 86; Bucnkell U; Bus Mgt.

ROUTHIER, KENNETH P; Easthampton HS; East Hampton, MA; (Y); 7/130; Am Leg Boys St; Pres JA; VP Frsh Cls; Trs Soph Cls; Trs Jr Cls; Trs Sr Cls; Var Bsktbl; Var Golf; Var Socr; NHS; Acctg.

ROUZAUT, TRACEY; Millis HS; Millis, MA; (Y); 7/80; Am Leg Aux Girls St; Trs Band; School Play; Ed Yrbk Ed-Chief; Rep Stu Cncl; Var Fld Hcky; Var Capt Tennis; Hon Roll; NHS; Prfct Atten Awd; GAF Schlrshp 86; U MA; Zoology.

ROWE, CYNTHIA; Salem HS; Salem, MA; (Y); 2/262; Sec Key Clb; Trs SADD; Orch; Yrbk Stf; NHS; Sal; Spanish NHS; St Schlr; Church Yth Grp; Civic Clb; Dartmouth Bwl Awd 85; Rgnl Sci Fair, Clsmts Today, Nghbrs Tmmrw Awd 86; Providence Coll.

ROWE, DANIELLE; Georgetown JR SR HS; Georgetown, MA; (Y); 7/85; Trs AFS; Church Yth Grp; VP Drama Clb; Hosp Aide; Lit Mag; Var Capt Socr; High Hon Roll; Hon Roll; Pres NHS; U Of IA Smr Sci Prog 85; Bio.

ROWE, GARY; Salem HS; Salem, MA; (Y); 89/280; JV Bsbl; JV Bsktbl; Var Ftbl.

ROWE, JILL; Acton-Boxboro Regional HS; Boxboro, MA; (Y); Stu Cncl; Var L Cheerleading; Var L Fld Hcky; Var Capt Sftbl; High Hon Roll; Hon Roll; Elem Ed.

ROY, JEFFREY; Charles H Mc Cann Tech; North Adams, MA; (Y); Am Leg Boys St; VICA; Var Bsbl; JV Ftbl; High Hon Roll; NHS; TCI; Elect.

ROY, JOHN A; Brockton HS; Brockton, MA; (Y); Am Leg Boys St; Boy Scts; Church Yth Grp; Key Clb; Ski Clb; SADD; Trk; Hon Roll; Stonehill Coll; Lib Arts.

ROY, LISA; Greater Boston Acad; Reading, MA; (Y); Church Yth Grp; Drama Clb; Hosp Aide; Office Aide; Teachers Aide; Acpl Chr; Band; Chorus; Drm & Bgl; School Play; Frnch Hon Soc 86; Hon Roll 84-86; Ntl Hon Soc 86; Loma Linda U; Dntl Hygn.

ROY, PAUL; New Bedford HS; New Bedford, MA; (Y); 59/701; JA; JCL; Hon Roll; Frgn Lang Clb; Sthestrn MA U; Engrng.

ROYAL, MICHELLE; Malden HS; Malden, MA; (Y); MA Gnrl ST Schlrshp 86-87; U Of MA Boston; Frgn Lang.

ROZMAN, JILL; Haverhill HS; Haverhill, MA; (Y); 88/417; Hosp Aide; VP Spanish Clb; SADD; Temple Yth Grp; Yrbk Stf; Stu Cncl; Powder Puff Ftbl; Var L Tennis; High Hon Roll; Hon Roll; Bst Tm Wrk Tnns 85; Bst Tm Plyr Tnns 86; Ed.

RUBIN, LISA; Bridgewater-Raynham Regional HS; Raynham, MA; (Y); 10/316; Am Leg Aux Girls St; Model UN; Pres Temple Yth Grp; Nwsp Rptr; Var Bsktbl; High Hon Roll; NHS; NEDT Awd; Voice Dem Awd; Vrsty Bsktbl Unsng Hero Awd 86; Shrmn H Starr Hmn Rltns Yth Awd 86; Colgate U; Sclgy.

RUBIN, LORI; Lynnfield HS; Lynnfield, MA; (Y); Intnl Clb; Spanish Clb; Chorus; Rep Frsh Cls; Sec Soph Cls; Sec Jr Cls; Sec Sr Cls; Var Capt Cheerleading; Powder Puff Ftbl; Sftbl.

RUBIN, MARK E; Framingham North HS; Framingham, MA; (Y); 6/380; Boy Scts; Chess Clb; Computer Clb; Exploring; JCL; High Hon Roll; Hon Roll; NHS; Ntl Merit SF; Natl Latin Exam-Magna Cum Laude 84; MA Inst Of Tech; Physics.

RUFFIN, ADA; Boston Technical HS; Dorchester, MA; (Y); 6/200; Church Yth Grp; Cmnty Wkr; Office Aide; Teachers Aide; Chorus; Church Choir; Yrbk Stf; Rep Stu Cncl; Badmtn; Sftbl; Close Up Fndtn WA DC 86; Alpha Kappa Alpha Schlrshp 86; Tchrs Aide Citation Vlntr 85; Wheelock Coll; Elem Educ.

RUGOLETTI, CHRISTINA; St Marys Regional HS; E Boston, MA; (Y); High Hon Roll; Hon Roll; Gym 82-86; Salem ST Coll; Acctg.

RULNICK, DEBORAH; Pittsfield HS; Pittsfield, MA; (Y); JCL; Latin Clb; Trs Pres Temple Yth Grp; Chorus; High Hon Roll; NHS.

RUMMO, PAUL; Marian HS; Milford, MA; (Y); 14/179; Church Yth Grp; Var JV Ice Hcky; Var Socr; Var Capt Trk; High Hon Roll; Hon Roll; NHS; Marian Schlr Athlete Awd 86; MVP Track 86; Coachs Awd 86; James G Nadeau Mem Most Sportsmnlke Awd; St Anslem Coll; Bio.

RUMSEY, SUZANNE; Braintree HS; Braintree, MA; (Y); Church Yth Grp; Drm & Bgl; Yrbk Stf; Bowling; Sftbl; High Hon Roll; Hon Roll; Curry Coll; Psychlgy.

RUOKIS, PHIL; Brockton HS; Brockton, MA; (Y); Pres Computer Clb; SADD; Band; Concert Band; Mrchg Band; School Musical; Symp Band; Pres Schlr; Boston Consrvtry Outstndng Prfrmnc Merit Schlrshp 86; Boston Consrvtry Music; Compstn.

RUOTOLO, ANDREA; Saugus HS; Saugus, MA; (Y); Cmnty Wkr; GAA; JV Socr; Var Trk; Flght Attdnt.

RUSELL, FREDERICK; Somerville HS; Somerville, MA; (Y); 24/502; Am Leg Boys St; Ski Clb; Stu Cncl; JV Bsktbl; Var L Ftbl; High Hon Roll; Hon Roll; NHS; St Schlr; Elmer Bumpus Hnry Schlrsp 86; Philip Trabucco Schlrshp 86; Somerville Dist Trial Ct Schlrshp 86; Boston Coll; Comp Sci.

RUSIN, KIMBERLY A; Williston Northampton Schl; Easthampton, MA; (Y); 14/142; Drama Clb; School Play; Stage Crew; Stu Cncl; High Hon Roll; Ntl Merit SF; Ferguson Schlrshp 84-85; Williston Theatre Price 84-85; TEAM 84-86.

RUSSELL, ANN; Miss Halls Schl; St Charles, IL; (Y); Debate Tm; French Clb; Nwsp Stf; Yrbk Stf; Var Socr; Hon Roll; SR Yr Proctor 86-87; Law.

RUSSELL, CHRISTINE; Milford HS; Burlington, MA; (Y); Dance Clb; Model UN; Color Guard; Stage Crew; Hon Roll; NH Voc Tech Coll; Acctng.

RUSSELL, DAVID; Methuen HS; Lawrence, MA; (Y); 4/356; Am Leg Boys St; Math Tm; JV Socr; Var Trk; High Hon Roll; Ntl Merit SF; Engr.

RUSSELL, FREDERICK J; Somerville HS; Somerville, MA; (Y); 24/502; Am Leg Boys St; Ski Clb; Stu Cncl; JV Im Bsktbl; Var L Ftbl; High Hon Roll; Hon Roll; NHS; St Schlr; Smrvl Dstrct Trl Ct Schlrshp 86; Philip Trabucco Mem Shclrshp 86f Hon Elmr Dympusschlrshp 86; Boston Coll; Cmptr Sci.

RUSSELL, JEANNETTE; Easthampton HS; Easthampton, MA; (Y); VP Church Yth Grp; Drama Clb; French Clb; Chorus; Church Choir; School Play; Stage Crew; Cit Awd; Hon Roll; Acad Awd, Ntl Flt Schlrshp 86; Fitchberg ST Coll; Nrsg.

RUSSELL, LEANNE; Malden HS; Malden, MA; (Y); Key Clb; SADD; Concert Band; Mrchg Band; Variety Show; Yrbk Phtg; Yrbk Rptr; Var L Tennis; Hon Roll; Spirit & Dctn Awd Bsktbl 83-84; Mktg.

RUSSELL, LEIGH; Tantasqua Regional HS; Sturbridge, MA; (Y); 2/180; Church Yth Grp; Drama Clb; Math Tm; Chorus; Madrigals; School Musical; Yrbk Ed-Chief; Yrbk Stf; VP Stu Cncl; High Hon Roll; Stu Tri-M Music Hon Soc 84.

RUSSO, DOMENIC MICHAEL; Hudson HS; Hudson, MA; (Y); 4/158; Exploring; Yrbk Rptr; Pres Sr Cls; Var Bsbl; JV Bsktbl; Var Ftbl; Elks Awd; High Hon Roll; NHS; Ntl Merit Ltr; Teenager Am 86; MVP Ftbl 85; Bio Sci.

RUSSO, REBECCA; Girls Catholic HS; Revere, MA; (Y); Art Clb; Intnl Clb; Science Clb; SADD; Capt Var Cheerleading; Hon Roll; Math.

RUTKA, TIMOTHY F; Pittsfield HS; Pittsfield, MA; (Y); 5/275; Pres Church Yth Grp; Drama Clb; VP Latin Clb; Math Clb; School Play; High Hon Roll; NHS; St Schlr; Chess Clb; Red Cross Aide; Boston U.

RYAN, CHERYL; Monument Mountain Regional HS; Gr Barrington, MA; (Y); Art Clb; Church Yth Grp; Spanish Clb; SADD; Hon Roll; Kathleen Mc Dermott Schlrshp 86; Gt Brrngtn Plc Assoc Schlrshp 86; FL Inst Of Tech; Marine Biolgy.

RYAN, DAWN; Blackstone Valley Reg Voc Tech HS; Bellingham, MA; (Y); Drama Clb; Library Aide; Ed Lit Mag; Stu Cncl; Var Socr; High Hon Roll; NHS; Church Yth Grp; Cmnty Wkr; Scholastic Bowl; Pres Acad Ftns Awd 86; Stu Advsry Cncl; Voc Acad Awd; U Lowell; Comp Sci.

RYAN, DIANE; North Quincy HS; Wollaston, MA; (Y); 16/430; French Clb; JA; Latin Clb; Var Swmmng; Hon Roll; NHS; Latin Natl Foreign Lang Hon Soc Sec; Volunteer Museum Of Sci; Med.

RYAN, JAMES; Winthrop HS; Winthrop, MA; (Y); 2/205; Am Leg Boys St; Church Yth Grp; Computer Clb; Drama Clb; Math Tm; Stage Crew; Rep Frsh Cls; Var L Crs Cntry; JV Ice Hcky; Var L Tennis; Engrng.

RYAN, JOHN C; Plymouth Carver HS; Carver, MA; (Y); 98/523; Am Leg Boys St; Var Trk; Bridgewater ST Col6; Hlth Ftns.

RYAN, LISA; Taunton HS; Taunton, MA; (Y); Church Yth Grp; Cmnty Wkr; Pep Clb; Spanish Clb; SADD; Yrbk Stf; Stu Cncl; JV Pom Pon; Hon Roll; SMU; Rn.

RYAN, MAURA; Holy Name C C HS; Worcester, MA; (Y); Girl Scts; Ski Clb; Chorus; Church Choir; School Musical; Gym; Var Trk; Grl Sct Marian Medae 83; Amer Yth Ftns Awd 85; Cntrl Mass Conf Trk Awds 85; News Reprtr.

RYAN, MICHAEL H; Boston College HS; Weymouth, MA; (Y); Am Leg Boys St; Church Yth Grp; JA; Latin Clb; Ski Clb; Rep Soph Cls; Rep Stu Cncl; Var Socr; JV Swmmng; Var Trk.

RYAN, MICHELLE A; Blue Hills Regional Vo-Tech HS; Holbrook, MA; (Y); 2/262; Church Yth Grp; Hosp Aide; VICA; Variety Show; JV Bsktbl; Var Cheerleading; Var Sftbl; Hon Roll; Pres Schlr; St Schlr; Varty Clb Awd, Tech Prfcncy Awd 86; Supt Cert Acad Excel 85-86; Salem ST; Nrsg.

RYAN, PETER; Boston College HS; Braintree, MA; (Y); Drama Clb; Latin Clb; School Musical; School Play; Nwsp Stf; Trk; Var Hon Roll; Magna Cum Laude Natl Latn Exm 84; Cum Laude Natl Exm 82-83.

RYAN, SUSAN; Taunton HS; Taunton, MA; (Y); 5/430; JCL; Latin Clb; Office Aide; Yrbk Stf; Lit Mag; Trs Frsh Cls; Trs Soph Cls; Trs Jr Cls; Trs Sr Cls; Rep Stu Cncl; Victoria A Gallego Meml Schlrshp 86; Joseph Mac Donald Meml Schlrshp 86; Arlene Padelford Meml Schlrsh; Northeastern U; Physc Thrpy.

RYAN, TRACY; Girls Catholic HS; Malden, MA; (Y); French Clb; SADD; JV Sftbl; Im Tennis; High Hon Roll; Hon Roll; Cmmnctns.

RYAN, WILLIAM; Quincy Vo-Tech; Quincy, MA; (Y); 2/141; Am Leg Boys St; Boy Scts; JA; Political Wkr; VICA; Variety Show; Yrbk Sprt Ed; JV Bsbl; JV Bsktbl; JV Ftbl; Distinction; Elect Engr.

RYDER, LEE; Westford Acad; Westford, MA; (Y); Art Clb; Church Yth Grp; 4-H; French Clb; Intnl Clb; Var Gym; 4-H Awd; Hon Roll; Natl Ftns Chmpn Awd 86; Bus Mgmt.

SAAB, GREG; Greater Lawrence Tech; Methuen, MA; (Y); Jr Cls; Var Ftbl; Var Wt Lftg; Hon Roll.

SAAD, BARBARA J; Marian Hill C C HS; Oxford, MA; (Y); Chorus; School Musical; Nwsp Rptr; Nwsp Sprt Ed; Pres Jr Cls; Var Capt Cheerleading; Hon Roll; Comm.

SAAD, RICHARD J; Boston College HS; Avon, MA; (Y); 6/299; Rep Am Leg Boys St; Boy Scts; Church Yth Grp; Key Clb; JV Crs Cntry; Var L Swmmng; JV Trk; High Hon Roll; NHS; Natl Latin & Greek Tests Awds86.

SAART, DAVID; Hudson HS; Hudson, MA; (Y); 15/150; Rep Church Yth Grp; Red Cross Aide; Variety Show; VP Jr Cls; VP Sr Cls; JV Bsktbl; Var Crs Cntry; High Hon Roll; Hon Roll; NHS; Ntl Hstry Day ST Champ-Grp Prjct 84; Arch.

SAART, MICHELLE; Hudson HS; Hudson, MA; (Y); 10/152; Church Yth Grp; Pep Clb; Ski Clb; Stu Cncl; Cheerleading; Sftbl; Trk; High Hon Roll; Hon Roll; NHS; Health.

SABAJ, SHARON; Bartlett HS; Webster, MA; (Y); Spanish Clb; Yrbk Stf; Cheerleading; High Hon Roll; Acctnt.

SABATINI, JENNIFER; Walpole HS; Walpole, MA; (Y); 8/268; Church Yth Grp; Girl Scts; Chorus; Color Guard; Madrigals; Rep Jr Cls; Im Gym; NHS; Drama Clb; Stage Crew; Girl Sct Gld, Slvr Awds; Clsrm Prfrmnc Awd Physcs Hon; Engrng.

SABEAN, MELISSA; Natick HS; Natick, MA; (Y); 46/423; Ski Clb; SADD; Capt Cheerleading; Coach Actv; Gym; Trk; Hon Roll; NHS; French Clb; Swmmng; Allc Onf Chrldng Awd 85; Gennie Rich Schlrshp 86; RI U; Ed.

SABELLA, MARIANNE; Our Lady Of Nazareth HS; Revere, MA; (Y); 3/74; Cmnty Wkr; Intnl Clb; Ski Clb; School Play; Lit Mag; High Hon Roll; NHS; Prfct Atten Awd; Essy Wnnr Christophers Essy Cntst 86; Chmstry Excel 86; SR Chrstn Ldrsrhp 86.

SABEN, JOHN; Athol HS; Athol, MA; (Y); Model UN; JV Bsbl; Var Bsktbl; Var Ftbl; Var Trk; Elec Engrng.

SABETTA, TONI; Marshfield HS; Marshfield, MA; (Y); 136/380; Hosp Aide; Key Clb; Mat Maids; Hon Roll; Prfct Atten Awd; Nrsng.

SABIN, PAUL; Newton North HS; Waban, MA; (Y); Computer Clb; Mathletes; Math Tm; Nwsp Rptr; Nwsp Stf; Ntl Merit SF.

SABOURIN, ANN; Holyoke Catholic HS; Holyoke, MA; (Y); French Clb; Hosp Aide; Sec OEA; School Musical; Diving.

SABRA, ADAM A; Lexington HS; Lexinton, MA; (Y); Ntl Merit SF; Harvard U; Pol Sci.

SACCAMANDO, CHELSEY; Cathedral HS; Spfld, MA; (Y); Cmnty Wkr; FBLA; GAA; Girl Scts; Hosp Aide; Intnl Clb; Latin Clb; Library Aide; Office Aide; Spanish Clb; MVP Field Hockey Trophy 83; Cert Activty Prtcptn & Excllnc 85-86; Acad Excllnc Ribbons 82-83; Bay Path JC; Para-Lgl.

SACCHETTI, TRICIA L; Hoosac Valley HS; Cheshire, MA; (Y); 12/150; Drama Clb; Red Cross Aide; SADD; Sec Stu Cncl; Var JV Sftbl; Hon Roll; Vrsty Ltr Ftbl 86.

SACK, DARREN; Silver Lake Regional HS; Plympton, MA; (Y); 24/450; Am Leg Boys St; Church Yth Grp; French Clb; Latin Clb; Math Clb; Symp Band; Yrbk Stf; JV Tennis; High Hon Roll; Hon Roll; Radlgic.

SADLOWSKI, KRISTIN; Hopkins Acad; Hadley, MA; (Y); Spanish Clb; JV Bsktbl; Hon Roll; Excllnc Algbra II Awd 86; Art Awds 84.

SADOWSKI, JILL; Westfield HS; Westfield, MA; (Y); 39/357; Church Yth Grp; French Clb; Hosp Aide; Latin Clb; Fld Hcky; Trk; Hon Roll; Jr NHS; Shw Of Shws Tlnt Shw-1st Pl Lipsync Grp Of Girls 85; Med.

SAHADY JR, JAMES; BMC Durfee HS; Fall River, MA; (Y); Cmnty Wkr; Office Aide; Red Cross Aide; Spanish Clb; Sec Stu Cncl; JV Bsbl; JV Crs Cntry; JV Trk; Hon Roll; Bridgewater; Sci.

SAIA JR, JOHN J; Billerica Memorial HS; Billerica, MA; (Y); 11/430; Computer Clb; SADD; Var L Bsktbl; Coach Actv; Var L Tennis; NHS; Digtl Equpmt Corp Schlrshp, RPI Schlrshp 86; Coch-Capt Awd/Tnns 86; S Hutanagle Memrl Awd Bsktbl 86; Rensselear Polytech; Chem Engr.

SAINT LEGER, MARIE C; St Gregory HS; Dorchester, MA; (Y); Church Yth Grp; Rep Frsh Cls; Rep Soph Cls; Rep Jr Cls; Rep Sr Cls; Hon Roll; NHS; Prfct Atten Awd; Lawyer.

SALAMEH, FAIDA; Everett HS; Everett, MA; (Y); Intnl Clb; Key Clb; Library Aide; Teachers Aide; Chorus; Hon Roll; Crdt Rll 85, 86; Boston Coll; Pltcl Sci.

SALAMIPOUR, ROYA; Dracut HS; Dracut, MA; (Y); Library Aide; Chorus; Hon Roll; Prfct Atten Awd; ACADFMIC Excllnc 84-86; Bus.

SALAMONE, PAMELA; Medford HS; Medford, MA; (Y); Math Tm; Hon Roll; NHS; Engl Awd 83.

SALEK, LAURA; Leicester HS; Leicester, MA; (S); Church Yth Grp; Math Tm; Spanish Clb; JV L Cheerleading; High Hon Roll; Rotary Awd; Law.

SALETNIK, MICHAEL J; Ludlow HS; Ludlow, MA; (Y); 1/240; Am Leg Boys St; Scholastic Bowl; VP Band; Drm Mjr(t); Yrbk Stf; Tennis; NHS; Ntl Merit SF; Aud/Vis; Church Yth Grp; Outstndng Achvt In JETS Engrng Tst 85-86; Wstrn MA Dstrct Orchstra 85-86; Peer Ed Ltr Cmndtn 85-86; Med.

SALIBA, MAUREEN; Methuen HS; Methuen, MA; (Y); 38/325; Girl Scts; Intnl Clb; Pep Clb; Stu Cncl; Im Bsktbl; Powder Puff Ftbl; Im Sftbl; Hon Roll; Grad With Hnrs 86; Bridgewater ST Coll; Mgmt Sci.

SALIBY, WAFAA; Lawrence HS; Lawrence, MA; (Y); Art Clb; Church Yth Grp; French Clb; Intnl Clb; Math Clb; SADD; Varsity Clb; Score Keeper; Tennis; Timer; Am Lebanese Awareness Assn Inc 86; Nrthrn Essex CC; Comm Art.

SALINES, KRISTEN; Saugus HS; Saugus, MA; (Y); 25/276; Cmnty Wkr; Stu Cncl; Capt Socr; Elks Awd; High Hon Roll; Jr NHS; NHS; Cnfrnc Sccr All Str 86; Acad Schlrshp Merrimack Coll 86; Merrimack Coll; Psych.

SALING, HARRY; Dennis-Yarmouth Regional HS; Yarmouthport, MA; (Y); Im Bsktbl.

SALLS, MADELEINE; Marian HS; Ashland, MA; (Y); Church Yth Grp; Yrbk Rptr; Bsktbl; Sftbl; Tufes U; Vet.

SALLS, TIMOTHY; Tahanto Regional HS; Berlin, MA; (Y); 11/58; Am Leg Boys St; Boy Scts; Math Tm; Nwsp Stf; Yrbk Stf; Var Bsbl; Capt Crs Cntry; Hon Roll; NHS; Science Clb; Eagle Scout Rank 84; West Point; Physics.

SALM, SUSAN; Archbishop Williams HS; Holbrook, MA; (Y); 6/203; Math Clb; Math Tm; Spanish Clb; Chorus; High Hon Roll; NHS; St Schlr; Acad Excel & Achvt Awds 84-85; Stonehill Coll; Elec Engrng.

SALMONSEN, JULIE; Danvers HS; Danvers, MA; (Y); 15/300; Church Yth Grp; GAA; Spanish Clb; Band; Concert Band; Bsktbl; Var JV Fld Hcky; Hon Roll; NHS; Spanish NHS; Elem Educ.

SALON, JON; Sharon HS; Sharon, MA; (Y); Model UN; Spanish Clb; Nwsp Rptr; Bsktbl; JV Ftbl; JV Var Tennis; Var L Trk; High Hon Roll; Hon Roll; NHS; Stu Of Mnth Engl Soc Stds 85-86; ACA Chem Tst 85; Law.

SALUSTRO, KEITH W; Rivers Country Day HS; Natick, MA; (Y); Cmnty Wkr; Nwsp Rptr; L Crs Cntry; Im Golf; JV Lcrss; Im Tennis; High Hon Roll; Hghst Schlr Uppr Schl 86; Mst Imprvd Crss Cntry 84; Engnrng.

SALVATORE, LARA E; Norwood SR HS; Norwood, MA; (Y); 7/326; Red Cross Aide; Variety Show; Yrbk Stf; Rep Stu Cncl; Var Capt Cheerleading; Var L Gym; Var L Trk; Pres NHS; Pres Schlr; 1st Pl Comp Math 86; TONY Awd 83; Grk Arthdx Yth Assoc 83-86; Tufts U; Bus.

SAMELA, GARY; Burncoat SR HS; Worcester, MA; (Y); Church Yth Grp; Hosp Aide; Intnl Clb; Hon Roll; Creer Essy Cntst 86; Spnsh Cntst 85; Cls 3 All Arnd Gymnst 86; Holy Cross.

SAMPSON, MICHAEL; St Johns Preparatory Schl; Lynn, MA; (Y); FCA; Letterman Clb; Science Clb; Varsity Clb; Im Var Bsktbl; Ftbl; Var Trk; Boy Scts; Church Yth Grp; Church Choir.

SAMSON, MELISSA; Chicopee HS; Chicopee, MA; (Y); 34/202; Rep Soph Cls; Sec Rep Jr Cls; Var Cheerleading; Hon Roll; NHS; Educ.

SAMUEL, DENISE; Boston Latin Schl; Dorchester, MA; (Y); 156/273; Cmnty Wkr; JA; Chorus; Boston U; Bus Mgmt.

SAN CLEMENTE, ANDREW E; Shrewsbury HS; Shrewsbury, MA; (Y); 45/275; Am Leg Boys St; Letterman Clb; Band; Concert Band; Jazz Band; Mrchg Band; Var L Golf; Var L Ice Hcky; Mgr(s); High Hon Roll; Schlstc Achvt Awd 86; All Dist Orch/Percsn 85; US Military Acad; Engr.

SANABIA, JULIO; Salem HS; Salem, MA; (Y); Camera Clb; Spanish Clb; Var Ftbl; Capt Wrstlng; Accntng.

SANCHEZ JR, FRANK J; Swampscott HS; Swampscott, MA; (Y); 51/238; Church Yth Grp; Var JV Bsbl; Co-Capt Var Bsktbl; Var Ftbl; Bio.

SANDAHL, LYNN E; Walpole HS; Walpole, MA; (Y); 31/263; Church Yth Grp; Band; Chorus; Church Choir; Mrchg Band; Swing Chorus; Arthur E Willey Schlrshp 86; Mary F Hoey Memrl Schlrshp 86; Silvr Awd Excllnc Band 83; Bentley Coll; Comp Inf Sys.

SANDAHL, PAM; Weymouth North HS; Weymouth, MA; (Y); 27/343; Am Leg Aux Girls St; Pres Stu Cncl; Coach Actv; Var Socr; Var Capt Trk; Elks Awd; Hon Roll; Sec NHS; Female Ath Of Yr 86; Pilgrim Sktg Arena Schlrshp 86; Patriot Ledgr All-Schlstc Indr Trck Team 85-86; Boston Coll; Elem Edi.

SANDBERG, PETER; King Philp HS; Plainville, MA; (Y); Aud/Vis; Boy Scts.

SANDERS, DAWN; Turners Falls HS; Turners Fls, MA; (Y); 8/91; Concert Band; Jazz Band; Hst Soph Cls; Hst Jr Cls; Hst Sr Cls; Stu Cncl; High Hon Roll; NHS; Excllnc Spnsh I And Hist 85; Bio Semnr 85; Law.

SANDERS, ERIC; Marshfield HS; Marshfield, MA; (Y); 118/380; Key Clb; SADD; Var Capt Crs Cntry; Var Trk; Rcvd All ST Awd Crss Cntry 85-86; Rcvd Letters Trck & Crss Cntry 84-85; Sprts Med.

SANDERS, JEANNE F; Lincoln-Sudbury Regional HS; Sudbury, MA; (Y); Cmnty Wkr; French Clb; Trs Key Clb; Service Clb; Spanish Clb; Teachers Aide; Lit Mag; Var L Sftbl; Hon Roll; Lbrl Arts.

SANDSTEAD, WILLIAM H; Brookline HS; Galveston, TX; (Y); Thesps; Chorus; Madrigals; School Musical; School Play; Variety Show; Hon Roll; Rep Soph Cls; Yrbk Rptr; Yrbk Stf; Helen S Slosberg Memrl Awd Music 86; Oberlin Coll; Phlsphy.

SANFORD, ERIC D; Walpole HS; Walpole, MA; (Y); 1/265; Lit Mag; JV Crs Cntry; Var Trk; High Hon Roll; NHS; Ntl Merit SF; Val; Outstndng Soph Awd 83; Outstndng Jr Awd 84; Biomed Engrng.

SANGER, JONATHAN; Georgetown HS; Georgetown, MA; (Y); Drama Clb; JA; Scholastic Bowl; Spanish Clb; SADD; School Play; Yrbk Stf; Lit Mag; JV Var Bsbl; JV Var Bsktbl; Acdmc Decathln 85&86; Math.

SANNELLA, SUSAN; Arlington Catholic HS; Medford, MA; (Y); 2/166; Cmnty Wkr; Spanish Clb; Teachers Aide; Nwsp Bus Mgr; Nwsp Rptr; Nwsp Stf; High Hon Roll; NHS; St Anthnys Schlrshp 85; Nrthestrn U; Physcl Thrpy.

SANON, JOSEPH PIERRE; English HS; Mattapan, MA; (Y); Cmnty Wkr; Socr; Vllybl; Mgmt.

SANTANA, CARMEN VIVIANA; South High Community Schl; Worcester, MA; (S); Band; School Musical; Variety Show; Stu Cncl; High Hon Roll; Prfct Atten Awd; Doc.

SANTANGELO, KATHLEEN; Appnequet HS; E Freetown, MA; (Y); Church Yth Grp; VP Drama Clb; Trs Band; Chorus; Concert Band; Mrchg Band; School Musical; School Play; Mgr Stage Crew; Symp Band; Lions Clb All ST Bnd 85.

SANTAPAOLA, CHRISTINE M; Arlington Catholic HS; Medford, MA; (Y); 16/143; Church Yth Grp; French Clb; Hon Roll; Pres Schlr; JV Bsktbl; Highest GPA French Awd.

SANTARELLI, JENNIFER; Triton Regional HS; Rowley, MA; (Y); 35/200; AFS; Cmnty Wkr; Color Guard; Drill Tm; Mrchg Band; Hon Roll; Prfct Atten Awd; Clr Gd Awd 85; URI; Cmmnctns.

SANTIAGO, CARMEN; Greater Lowell Regional Vo-Tech; Lowell, MA; (Y); DECA; SADD; Off Jr Cls; Var Cheerleading; Hon Roll; 1st Fd Mktg Awd 86; Middlesex CC; Mrktg.

SANTIAGO, ROBIN; New Bedford HS; New Bedford, MA; (Y); VP JA; VP JCL; SADD; Chorus; Pres Frsh Cls; Pres Soph Cls; VP Jr Cls; Off Stu Cncl; CC Awd; Cit Awd; Outstndng Choral Awd 83; Natl Fndtn Excptnl Chldrn 85; Fisher.

SANTIAGO, WANDA; Madison Park HS; Dorchester, MA; (Y); Church Yth Grp; Office Aide; ROTC; Yrbk Stf; Hon Roll; Prfct Atten Awd; Spec Awd Schl Spirit 86; Psych.

SANTO, JULIE; Doherty Memoril HS; Worcester, MA; (Y); Church Yth Grp; Latin Clb; Ski Clb; SADD; Stu Cncl; Fld Hcky; Sftbl; Hon Roll; Girls Sftbl Leag Capt 84; Bus.

SANTORO, ANGELA; East Boston HS; E Boston, MA; (Y); 1/200; Teachers Aide; High Hon Roll; Hon Roll; NHS; Prfct Atten Awd; Val; 2nd Pl Cty Wide Type Off 84-85; Harvard Prz Bk 84-85; H S Scholar 85-86; Boston U; Acctg.

SANTOS, CHRISTOPHER; Seekonk HS; Seekonk, MA; (Y); 64/234; Letterman Clb; Var Crs Cntry; Var L Trk; Engrng.

SANTOS JR, LEONARD A; New Bedford HS; New Bedford, MA; (Y); 39/631; Church Yth Grp; Band; Concert Band; Mrchg Band; High Hon Roll; Hon Roll; Jr NHS; NHS; Pres Schlr; Elwyn G Cmpbl Schlrshp 86; Crista Mc Aulliffe Mem Schlrshp 86; Bnd Booster Schlrshp 86; S E MA U; Chmstry.

SANTOS, LOUIS MELO; Diman Regional Vo-Tech HS; Fall River, MA; (Y); Boy Scts; Exploring; Hon Roll; SMU Sptlght II Prog 85-86; Eagle Scout 85; Army Rsrve 85; SMU; Elec Engr.

SANTOS, MICHAEL; New Bedford HS; New Bedford, MA; (Y); 23/700; Church Yth Grp; Exploring; High Hon Roll; NHS; Southeastern MA U; Math.

SANTOS, PATRICIA; Plymouth-Carver HS; Plymouth, MA; (Y); 117/495; DECA; Intnl Clb; Im Cheerleading; Johnson & Wales DECA Schlrshp 86-87; Cmnwlth Of MA ST Schlrshp 86-87; Johnson & Wales Coll; Fshn.

SANTOS, RIC P; Apponequet Reg HS; Assonet, MA; (Y); 40/268; Chess Clb; French Clb; Letterman Clb; Math Clb; Band; Chorus; Variety Show; Nwsp Rptr; High Hon Roll; NHS; Bus.

SANTRY, JOHN C; Boston College HS; Weymouth, MA; (Y); 8/286; Cmnty Wkr; JCL; Latin Clb; Ed Lit Mag; Trk; High Hon Roll; Ntl Merit SF; Chess Clb; Math Clb; Ftbl; Bstn Pstl Dist Schlrshp Wnnr 86; High Hnr Natl Greek Exm 86; Clscl Assn MA Ptry Sgnt Trnsltn Chmp 86; Harvard Coll; Engl.

SANUITA, CHERYL; Holyoke Catholic HS; Chicopee, MA; (Y); Art Clb; Cmnty Wkr; English Clb; French Clb; Hosp Aide; Math Clb; Red Cross Aide; Lit Mag; High Hon Roll; Hon Roll.

SAPORITO, LAURA; Ipswich HS; Ipswich, MA; (Y); SADD; Yrbk Stf; JV Bsktbl; High Hon Roll; Hon Roll; Stu Adbsry Brd; Edtr Sctn Of Yrbk; Strng Comm; Pre Med.

SARACENO, SCOTT; Central Catholic HS; N Andover, MA; (Y); 22/215; Art Clb; Camera Clb; Drama Clb; School Musical; Yrbk Phtg; Hon Roll; Lawrence Eagel Trib Carrier Schlshp Awd; French & Sci Excllnc Awd 2nd Pl; Boston U; Comm.

SARGENT, DAVID; Norton HS; Norton, MA; (S); 12/130; Church Yth Grp; Yrbk Stf; High Hon Roll; Hon Roll; Wentworth Inst; Arch Engr & Des.

SARKIS, ANTHONY M; Drury SR HS; North Adams, MA; (Y); Am Leg Boys St; Boy Scts; Computer Clb; W MA Acad Decath 85; Josh Billings Runaground 3rd Pl 85; Berkshire CC Bike Marathon 3rd Pl 84; NE U; Comp Sci.

SARKIS, SUSAN; Lawrence HS; Lawrence, MA; (Y); 8/200; Pres VP Church Yth Grp; Church Choir; School Play; Nwsp Rptr; Yrbk Stf; JV Swmmng; JV Vllybl; 4-H Awd; High Hon Roll; Hon Roll; NEDT Awd 86; L-Pin 86; Hmn Food.

SARKISIAN, DIANNE E; Dracut HS; Dracut, MA; (Y); Computer Clb; Office Aide; Nwsp Sprt Ed; Sec Stu Cncl; High Hon Roll; Hon Roll; NHS; Prfct Atten Awd; Pres Schlr; Supt Acad Achvt Awd 85; Merrimack Vly Schl Comm Awd 86; G W Murphy Awd Draftng 86; Worcester Polytech; Elec Engr.

SARKISIAN, ROBERT; Natick HS; Natick, MA; (Y); Camera Clb; Church Yth Grp; Cmnty Wkr; SADD; Yrbk Phtg; Rep Stu Cncl; Capt Var Crs Cntry; Trk; High Hon Roll; Hon Roll; Vrsty Ltr In X-Cntry 83-86; Pilot.

SARNSETHSIRI, NARIPUN; Mac Dufie HS; Bloomfield Hills, MI; (Y); Intnl Clb; Yrbk Rptr; Yrbk Stf; High Hon Roll; Hon Roll; Mt Holyoke Coll Awd 86; Intl Bus.

SARO, CHERYL; Malden HS; Malden, MA; (Y); 16/480; Sec Science Clb; SADD; Band; Concert Band; Mrchg Band; Variety Show; Hon Roll; NHS; Bus.

SASSO, LORI ANN; Our Lady Of Nazareth Acad; Revere, MA; (Y); 14/74; Dance Clb; Spanish Clb; School Musical; Lit Mag; Hon Roll; NEDT Awd; Impact Clb; Psychlgy.

SATKOWSKI, CHRIS; Palmer HS; Bondsville, MA; (Y); Boy Scts; Chess Clb; Band; Ftbl; Hon Roll; Arch Dsgn.

SATYASAI, SERENA; Buckingham Browne & Nichols HS; Watertown, MA; (S); Cmnty Wkr; Lit Mag; Rep Frsh Cls; Rep Soph Cls; Rep Jr Cls; Capt Bsktbl; Var Fld Hcky; Var Lcrss; Hon Roll; GAA.

SAUCIER, EDWARD T; Holy Name CCHS HS; Worcester, MA; (Y); 31/310; Am Leg Boys St; Ski Clb; SADD; Bsbl; Var Capt Ftbl; Wt Lftg; Hon Roll; Business Law.

SAURIOL, ROBIN; Holy Name C C HS; Worcester, MA; (Y); 5/250; Church Yth Grp; SADD; School Musical; High Hon Roll; NHS; Acad Schrlshp Am Intl Dept Awd 86-90; Am Intl Coll; Elem Ed.

SAVAGE, MICHAEL; Doherty Memorial HS; Worcester, MA; (Y); JA; Latin Clb; Ski Clb; SADD; Sec Temple Yth Grp; Stage Crew; Nwsp Stf; Stu Cncl; RI School Design; Arch.

SAVAGEAUX, MICHAEL K; Grafton Memorial SR HS; Grafton, MA; (Y); 3/130; Am Leg Boys St; Boy Scts; School Play; Yrbk Bus Mgr; Yrbk Ed-Chief; High Hon Roll; NHS; Ntl Merit SF; Elec Engr.

SAVARIA, LAURA; Gardner HS; Gardner, MA; (Y); 9/140; Am Leg Aux Girls St; Spanish Clb; Drm Mjr(t); Rep Jr Cls; Var L Cheerleading; Var L Pom Pon; Var L Twrlr; Hon Roll; NHS; Chem Engrg.

SAVICKI, MICHAEL; Franklin HS; Franklin, MA; (Y); 4/225; Boy Scts; Math Tm; Lit Mag; VP Stu Cncl; Capt Bsktbl; Golf; Var L Socr; Trk; Hon Roll; NHS; Tufts U.

SAVJE, KIM; Plymouth-Carver HS; Plymouth, MA; (Y); Church Yth Grp; Hosp Aide; Office Aide; Pep Clb; SADD; Yrbk Stf; JV VP Cheerleading; Crs Cntry; Usher At Grad 86; Travel.

SAVOY, SUZANNE; Maynard HS; Mayanrd, MA; (Y); Office Aide; SADD; Chorus; Drm Mjr(t); Var Crs Cntry; JV Sftbl; Var Trk; Var Twrlr; Grphc Arts.

SAWAN, CHARBEL; English HS; W Roxbury, MA; (Y); Compu Engr.

SAWYER, TISHA LEE; Doherty Memorial HS; Worcester, MA; (Y); Drama Clb; Spanish Clb; Band; Chorus; Variety Show; Hon Roll; Career Day Wnnr, Frgn Lang Fair Awd, Cntrl Dist & All St Chorus 86; Co-Host & Guest TV Pgms 85; U MA Amherst; Music.

SAY, OLAY; English HS; Boston, MA; (Y); English Clb; Mathletes; Science Clb; Variety Show; Rep Jr Cls; Prfct Atten Awd.

SBUTTONI, ANN; Medford HS; Medford, MA; (Y); 55/400; Hosp Aide; Ski Clb; SADD; Yrbk Stf; Hon Roll; Math Awd 84; Engl Awd 86.

SCALISI, DEBRA LYNN; Greater Lawrence Technical Schl; Methuen, MA; (Y); Church Yth Grp; SADD; Sftbl; Hon Roll; Reg Nrse.

SCAMPOLI, DAVID; Dedham HS; Dedham, MA; (Y); 18/269; Computer Clb; Nwsp Stf; Lit Mag; Var L Golf; Im Ice Hcky; Var Trk; Hon Roll; Odd Fllws/U N Pilgrimage Yth Essay Cont Fnlst 85; Engrng.

SCANGAS, LARRY; Salem HS; Salem, MA; (Y); 20/262; JV Bsbl; CC Awd; High Hon Roll; Hon Roll; Pres Schlr; U Lowell; Mech Engrng.

SCANLON, JULIE A; Hudson HS; Hudson, MA; (Y); 16/158; SADD; Var Mgr Bsktbl; Var Mgr Crs Cntry; Mgr(s); High Hon Roll; Hon Roll; NHS; Bus Mngmnt.

SCANNELL, ANDREA; Sacred Heart HS; Bourne, MA; (Y); Church Yth Grp; Intnl Clb; Key Clb; Ski Clb; Yrbk Stf; Bsktbl; Sftbl; Pblshd Artcl Lcl Nwsppr-Lit Awd 84; Syracuse U; Arch.

SCANNELL, HEATHER COLLEEN S; High School Of Commerce; Springfield, MA; (S); SADD; Chorus; Rep Frsh Cls; Rep Soph Cls; Rep Jr Cls; Sec Stu Cncl; Cit Awd; Hon Roll; NHS; Jr Ldrshp Inst 85; Drug Abuse Educ 85; Fshn Dsgn.

SCARAFONI, NATALIE; Taconic HS; Pittsfield, MA; (Y).

SCARCELLA, LISA; Dedham HS; Dedham, MA; (Y); 14/292; Computer Clb; Lit Mag; Hon Roll; Bst JR Comp Dept 84-85; U Of MA Boston; Bio.

SCARFO, ELAINE; Burlington HS; Burlington, MA; (Y); 45/314; Church Yth Grp; Exploring; JA; Hon Roll; Ntl Hnr Soc 85-86; Boston Coll; Nrs.

SCENNA, MICHELE; Northbridge HS; Northbridge, MA; (Y); 13/143; Girl Scts; VP Pep Clb; Yrbk Stf; Pres Stu Cncl; Capt Bsktbl; Capt Fld Hcky; Im Powder Puff Ftbl; Capt Trk; Hon Roll; NHS; Hugh O Brien Awd 84; U Of NH; Pltcl Sci.

SCESNY, JAMES F; Saint Bernards Central Catholi HS; Westminster, MA; (Y); Am Leg Boys St; Boy Scts; Church Yth Grp; Latin Clb; Office Aide; Soroptimist; Varsity Clb; Variety Show; Frsh Cls; Soph Cls; Betnley Stetson U; Real Estate.

SCHAEFER, MICHELLE; Cardinal Spellman HS; Avon, MA; (Y); 40/207; Church Yth Grp; Girl Scts; Pep Clb; School Musical; Var Capt Cheerleading; Trk; High Hon Roll; Hon Roll; Acdmc Schlrshp 86; Merrimack Coll; Elem Educ.

SCHAEFFER, JOSEPH; Cathedral HS; Feeding Hills, MA; (Y); Model UN; Schl Svc Awd 85-86; Model Cong 85-86; Bus.

SCHAFER, SCOTT; Framingham South HS; Framingham, MA; (Y); 4/256; Church Yth Grp; Pres French Clb; Key Clb; Latin Clb; SADD; Stu Cncl; Trk; High Hon Roll; NHS; Ntl Merit Ltr; Wesleyan U; Intl Rltns.

SCHAFFNER, MOLLYE; Marblehead HS; Marblehead, MA; (Y); 20/240; Yrbk Ed-Chief; Var Crs Cntry; Var Trk; High Hon Roll; Hon Roll; NHS; Pres Schlr; Rotary Awd; D Cashman Mem Schlrshp 86; Howard Wordie Williams Schlrshp 86; ANPA Fndtn Schltc Jrnlstc Awd 86; Bowdoin Clg; Pltcl Sci.

SCHATZEL, KRISTEN; Old Rochester Regional HS; Stanton, NJ; (Y); 15/180; AFS; Sec 4-H; Yrbk Stf; Rep Jr Cls; Var Capt Crs Cntry; Var Capt Trk; NHS; Capt Quiz Bowl; Nwsp Stf; Rep Soph Cls; Hgh Achvmnt Awd Ntl Wrld Hstry Olympd 86; Ntl Latin Exm Cum Laude 85; Div III ST 800 Chmpn 86; Bus.

SCHEFFLER, HEIDI; Bridgewater-Raynham Regional HS; Bridgewater, MA; (Y); 1/316; Church Yth Grp; Cmnty Wkr; VP French Clb; Hosp Aide; Intnl Clb; Math Tm; VP Model UN; Science Clb; Ski Clb; VP Spanish Clb; Pres Awd Acad Ftns 86; Alternate Japan Schrlshp 85; SF Finland ST Schlrshp 85; Wellesley Coll; Lang.

SCHEIDLE, PETER; Agawam HS; Agawam, MA; (Y); 4/325; Church Yth Grp; Cmnty Wkr; French Clb; NHS; Rnsslr Mdl 86; Chmcl Engrng.

SCHETZEL, JULIE; Monson JR-SR HS; Monson, MA; (Y); 3/68; Church Yth Grp; French Clb; Spanish Clb; Band; Church Choir; Yrbk Ed-Chief; Yrbk Stf; High Hon Roll; Hon Roll; Sec NHS; Elizabeth Elliot Awd Monson Womens Clb 86; Bivier Coll 86; Commonwlth Hnr Schl 86; Rivier Coll; Spnsh.

SCHEUFELE, MATTHEW; Silver Lake Regional HS; Pembroke, MA; (Y); 48/494; Camera Clb; Cmnty Wkr; Debate Tm; 4-H; Pres Intnl Clb; Political Wkr; Band; Concert Band; Orch; School Musical; Photo Svc Rep; Ntl Photo Exh 85; U MA; Hist.

SCHIAPPA, SUSAN; Notre Dame Acad; Hull, MA; (Y); 11/125; French Clb; 4-H; Library Aide; School Musical; Nwsp Stf; Socr; Tennis; French Hon Soc; High Hon Roll; Hnrs Bio Awd 85; Alg II & Trig Awd 86; Frnch III Awd 86; Med.

SCHLICKE, KEVIN S; Narragansett Regional HS; Phillipston, MA; (Y); 8/100; Am Leg Boys St; Pres Letterman Clb; School Play; Ed Yrbk Stf; Var Capt Bsbl; Var Capt Bsktbl; Var Capt Ftbl; Mu Alp Tht; Pres NHS; Pres Schlr; Centry III Ldrs Awd; Assumption Coll; Engrng.

SCHLOSSER, DAVID; Lincoln-Sudbury Regional HS; Sudbury, MA; (Y); L Golf; JV Lcrss; Ski Tm Co-Capt.

SCHMERGEL, GREG E; Roxbury Latin HS; Wellesley, MA; (Y); Chess Clb; Debate Tm; French Clb; Var Crs Cntry; Socr; Var Tennis; Ntl Merit SF.

SCHMIDT, LUCILLE; Cathedral HS; Chicopee, MA; (Y); 16/536; Intnl Clb; Math Clb; School Musical; Sec Jr Cls; Sec Sr Cls; JV Cheerleading; NHS; Ntl Merit Ltr; Wllsly Bk Awd 86; Ntl Mth Hnr Roll 86; Pltcl Sci.

SCHMITH, TAMMY J; Northampton HS; Florence, MA; (Y); 40/222; Hosp Aide; Yrbk Phtg; Yrbk Stf; Var L Fld Hcky; Mgr(s); Score Keeper; High Hon Roll; Emmanuel Coll; Med.

SCHMITT, DAVID; Austin Prep; Wilmington, MA; (Y); 20/124; Ski Clb; Yrbk Stf; Im Bsktbl; Var Ftbl; Im Sftbl; Hon Roll; Deans List.

SCHNOPP, KEVIN M; Wahconah Regional HS; Dalton, MA; (Y); Band; Bsbl; Socr; Hon Roll; NHS; Natl Hnr Soc 86; Berk CC; Engrng.

SCHOFIELD, KAREN; Nauset Regional HS; E Orleans, MA; (Y); Church Yth Grp; Drama Clb; Pres SADD; Temple Yth Grp; Acpl Chr; Band; Chorus; Concert Band; Orch; School Musical; Cape & Ilsnds Music Fstvl Orch 84-86; MA SE Dist Music Fstvl Bnd 84-86; MA AllST Music Fstvl 86; Music.

SCHOLTZ, TABITHA; Triton Regional JR/SR HS; Salisbury, MA; (Y); Nwsp Stf; JV Capt Sftbl; Hon Roll; Photo Jrnlsm.

SCHONBACK, KIM; Monson JR SR HS; Monson, MA; (Y); 19/80; Church Yth Grp; Library Aide; Stu Cncl; Im JV Socr; Var L Sftbl; Hon Roll; Sci.

SCHONBERG, AMY; Tahanto Regional HS; Boylston, MA; (Y); 2/57; Math Tm; Band; Yrbk Ed-Chief; Sec Soph Cls; Sec Jr Cls; Stu Cncl; Im Vllybl; NHS; Ntl Merit Ltr; Science Clb; Top 10 Framingham ST Coll Essay Cont 84; MA Lions All Star Intl Band 86; Acad All Amer Schlr Pgm 86; Mth Ed.

SCHREIBER, MICHAEL S; Oliver Ames HS; N Easton, MA; (Y); 2/280; Am Leg Boys St; Pres Drama Clb; School Musical; Ed Lit Mag; Var Tennis; Var High Hon Roll; NHS; Ntl Merit Ltr; Sal; Model UN; Hckmck Mdl Senate 85&86; Venezuela Exchng Pgm 85; Close-Up Pgm 86.

SCHROCK, JAMES C; Hamilton-Wenham Regional HS; Hamilton, MA; (Y); Am Leg Boys St; Chorus; Capt Bsbl; Capt Bsktbl; Ftbl; Wt Lftg; Set Pass Intrcptn Recrd 85-86; Yth Awd 86; Hamilton-Wenham Regnl HS Schlrshp 86; Baldwin-Wallace Coll; Bus Adm.

SCHULTZ, NANCY; Pittsfield HS; Pittsfield, MA; (Y); Boy Scts; Trs Church Yth Grp; Exploring; Trs Band; Trs Concert Band; Jazz Band; Trs Mrchg Band; Orch; Stage Crew; JV Sftbl; Gen Engr.

SCHUMACHER, MATTHEW C; Quincy HS; Quincy, MA; (Y); 64/380; Am Leg Boys St; Boy Scts; Computer Clb; French Clb; FFA; ROTC; SADD; Color Guard; Drill Tm; Flag Corp; Hgh Hnrs Boys ST Bentley Coll 86; Hnr Roll 85-86; Natl Sojournors Awd USAF JROTC 85; MIT; Aero Engrng.

SCHUMAKER, JOHN; Melrose HS; Melrose, MA; (Y); 73/376; Boy Scts; ROTC; Ski Clb; Pres Schlr; VFW Awd; 4 Yr Alt NROTC Schlrshp Pgm 86; Norwich U; Crmnl Just.

SCHUMAKER, KRISTEN; Malden HS; Malden, MA; (Y); 89/450; Swmmng; Mktg.

SCHWAB, KRISTEN; Marian HS; Framingham, MA; (Y); Boy Scts; Latin Clb; Lit Mag; Trs Soph Cls; Var Trk; Hon Roll; Ski Clb; Hnrbl Mntn Sci Fair 83-84; Schlrshp Quinnipiac Cll 86; Quinnipiac Coll; Physcl Thrpy.

SCHWABE, LARA; Northfield Mt Herman Schl; Petersburg, NY; (Y); GAA; Quiz Bowl; Chorus; JV Vllybl; Hon Roll; Prfct Atten Awd; Answrs Please Trphy 85-86; Martha & Howard Jones Awd 86; Vet Med.

SCHWALM, MARK; Reading Memorial HS; Reading, MA; (Y); Art Clb; Mathletes; SADD; Nwsp Stf; Lit Mag; Rep Soph Cls; Rep Jr Cls; Rep Sr Cls; JV Bsbl; JV Ftbl; Dartmouth Bk Awd 86; Engrng.

SCHWAMB, JOHN; Matignon HS; Lexington, MA; (S); 4/180; Church Yth Grp; Pres Science Clb; Rep Soph Cls; Rep Jr Cls; Rep Stu Cncl; Im Bsktbl; L Ftbl; Var Trk; Hon Roll; NHS; Military Acad; Engrng.

SCHWARTZ, BETHANY; Brimmer & May Schl; Newton, MA; (S); Hosp Aide; Model UN; Teachers Aide; Chorus; School Musical; Nwsp Bus Mgr; Yrbk Stf; Var Lcrss; Hon Roll; Kenyon Coll.

SCHWARTZ, ERIC; Algonquin Regional HS; Northboro, MA; (Y); 2/250; Am Leg Boys St; Concert Band; Jazz Band; Orch; Var Capt Crs Cntry; High Hon Roll; NHS; Ntl Merit Ltr; Trs Temple Yth Grp; Band; Williams Coll Bk Awd 86; Superintndnts Awd Acad Music 84-86.

SCHWARTZ, JONATHAN; Georgetown SR HS; Georgetown, MA; (Y); Nwsp Rptr; Bsbl; Ftbl; Ice Hcky.

SCHWARTZ, NEIL D; Newton South HS; Newton, MA; (Y); Am Leg Boys St; School Play; Yrbk Ed-Chief; VP Stu Cncl; Var Socr; Cit Awd; Hon Roll; Drama Clb; Political Wkr; Spanish Clb; Fclty Awd-For Chrctr, Intgrty & Maturity 83-86; MA Lacrosse Champs Tm 85; Frgn Lang Awd-Spnsh 85; Tufts U; Bus.

SCIOLA, KIRK M; Saugus HS; Saugus, MA; (Y); 2/266; Chess Clb; Library Aide; Stu Cncl; NHS; Ntl Merit SF; Pres Schlr; Sal; St Schlr; U Lowell; Elec Engrng.

SCIRETTO, SAL; Melrose HS; Melrose, MA; (Y); 33/434; FCA; Ski Clb; Spanish Clb; SADD; Varsity Clb; Variety Show; JV Bsktbl; Var L Ftbl; Var L Trk; Im Wt Lftg; Hotel Mngt.

SCIVOLETTO, JOHN C; Salem HS; Salem, MA; (Y); 13/400; Drama Clb; Spanish Clb; Jazz Band; School Play; Variety Show; Var Capt Socr; High Hon Roll; VP NHS; VP Spanish NHS; 12th Plyr Awd Socr 85; Conf Socr All Starr 85; Williams Coll Bk Awd 86; UCSD; Music.

SCLAR JR, BARRY; Blackstone Valley Reg Voc Tech HS; Millbury, MA; (Y); Library Aide; SADD; Sec Frsh Cls; Sec Soph Cls; Var L Bsbl; Var L Bsktbl; Var L Socr; Hon Roll; Worcester Polytechnic Inst, Frontiers In Sci & Math Prog 86; Worcester Polytech Inst; Engr.

SCOLAMIERO, SAMANTHA; Swampscott HS; Swampscott, MA; (Y); 4/250; Science Clb; Orch; Lit Mag; Var Mgr Fld Hcky; Var Ftbl; NHS; Ntl Merit Ltr; Church Yth Grp; Intnl Clb; Model UN; The Dartmouth Bowl 86; Outstndng Latin Stu Awd 86; Awd For Excllnce In US Gov 84.

SCOLNICK, ADAM; Randolph HS; Randolph, MA; (Y); Computer Clb.

SCOTT, BILL; Deerfield Acad; Duxbury, MA; (Y); Cmnty Wkr; French Clb; Model UN; Varsity Clb; Concert Band; Jazz Band; Var L Bsbl; Var L Ftbl; Im Ice Hcky; Hon Roll; Ecnmcs.

SCOTT, ELAINE; Boston Technical HS; Dorchester, MA; (Y); French Clb; Church Choir; JV Score Keeper; JV Sftbl; Var Vllybl; Hon Roll; Prfct Atten Awd; Burdett School; Scrtrl.

SCOTT, JULIE H; Middlesex Schl; Concord, MA; (S); 1/76; Acpl Chr; Chorus; School Musical; Variety Show; Lit Mag; Socr; High Hon Roll; Library Aide; Teachers Aide; Nwsp Rptr; Williams Coll Bk Prz 85; Prz For Excell In Chem 84; W H Howe Bio Awd 83; Harvard U; Biochem.

SCOTT, MARCIE A; English HS; Roxbury, MA; (Y); Dance Clb; Variety Show; Rep Stu Cncl; Var Cheerleading; Hon Roll; Awd Dance 85-86; North CA; Comp.

SCOTT, MICHAEL; Scitvate HS; Scituate, MA; (Y); 22/277; Im Bsktbl; Var L Golf; JV Ice Hcky; Var L Socr; Hon Roll; Jr NHS; NHS; Church Yth Grp; Ski Clb; Stu, Tchrs Assn Schlrshp 86; Div 2 ST Glf Chmpns 85 & 86; Furman U.

SCOTT, ROBYN; Wachusett Regional HS; Jefferson, MA; (Y); 36/443; Church Yth Grp; Drama Clb; SADD; School Musical; JV Cheerleading; Trk; Hon Roll; NHS; Schlrshp To MA Advanced Stds Prog 86; Schlrshp To New England Bapt Yth-Share Our Joy Crss-Cntry Bus; Bio.

SCOTT, VALERIA; Newton North HS; Newton, MA; (Y); Church Yth Grp; Cmnty Wkr; French Clb; Political Wkr; Ski Clb; Varsity Clb; Soph Cls; Jr Cls; Sr Cls; Stu Cncl; Intl Rltns.

SCOVILLE, KATHERINE; Walnut Hill Schl Of Performing Arts; Chelmsford, MA; (Y); 1/40; Intnl Clb; School Musical; Nwsp Stf; Yrbk Stf; French Hon Soc; High Hon Roll; Jr NHS; Cum Laude Soc 86; Smith Coll Book Awd 86; Dance.

SCRIBNER, KELLY; Walnut Hill Schl For The Prfmg Arts; Upton, MA; (Y); Art Clb; Dance Clb; Hon Roll; Prfct Atten Awd; Some Tuitn Towrds HS 83-86; Musem Schl Fine Arts 1 Yrs Befr HS Grad 86; Museum Schl Fine Arts; Visl Art.

SEARS, ANN; Holyoke Catholic HS; Holyoke, MA; (Y); Drama Clb; VP Spanish Clb; SADD; Yrbk Phtg; Lit Mag; Sec Stu Cncl; JV Crs Cntry; JV Socr; Var Tennis; Cert Awd Exclnc Chem 86; MIAA Trnmnt Sc Tnl Tm Rnr-Up Tnns 86; Stonehill; Psych.

SEARS, STACEY; Georgetown JR SR HS; Georgetown, MA; (Y); 3/88; Var Fld Hcky; High Hon Roll; NHS; Gould Corp Schlrshp, Georgetown Educ Assn Schlrshp & Superintendant Schls Acdmc Awd 85 & 86; U NH; Mech Engrng.

SECRIST, PHYLLIS; Matignon HS; Somerville, MA; (Y); 17/179; Science Clb; Varsity Clb; Var Trk; Hon Roll; NHS; Harvard; Law.

SEDARES, ROBERT; South High Community HS; Worcester, MA; (S); Boys Clb Am; Church Yth Grp; SADD; Var Bsktbl; Var Golf; Hon Roll; NHS; Acad Olympc Tm 84-85; NHS Tutor Pgm 84-86; Sportsmnshp Awd Bsktbl Lg 84.

SEDIVEC, LISA; Presentation Of Mary Acad; Lawrence, MA; (Y); 9/44; Math Clb; Spanish Clb; Chorus; Nwsp Rptr; Nwsp Stf; Hon Roll; NHS; Regional Sci Fair; Engrng.

SEEG, RICHARD J L; Marshfield HS; Marshfield, MA; (Y); 20/363; Boy Scts; Church Yth Grp; Key Clb; Math Clb; ROTC; SADD; Chorus; High Hon Roll; Hon Roll; Jr NHS; Eagle Scout 86; ROTC & NROTC Schlrshps 86; Bio.

SEGARRA, EDWIN; Greater Lowell Regional Vo Tech; Lowell, MA; (Y); Varsity Clb; JV Var Bsktbl; JV Var Socr; Hon Roll; Commendbl Perf Alg 86; Exc Engl 2nd Lang & Devlpmntl Readg 86; Toolg & Machng.

SEIDEL, KEITH; Attleboro HS; Attleboro, MA; (Y); Concert Band; Var Capt Tennis; High Hon Roll; Hon Roll; NHS; Prfct Atten Awd; Art Illstrtn.

SEILE, SHANNON; Westboro HS; Westboro, MA; (Y); 57/189; Band; Concert Band; Mrchg Band; Pep Band; Powder Puff Ftbl; Socr; Hon Roll; 2nd Pl Art Cont 85; Rochester Inst Tech; Int Dcrtr.

SEILE, SHON M; Westborough HS; Westborough, MA; (Y); 35/189; Am Leg Boys St; Boy Scts; Debate Tm; Chorus; Im Bsktbl; Im Wt Lftg; Hon Roll; Boston U; Poltcl Sci.

SELFE, SUSAN; Masconomet HS; Lock Haven, PA; (Y); 33/260; Church Yth Grp; Hosp Aide; Spanish Clb; Chorus; Stage Crew; Variety Show; Wt Lftg; High Hon Roll; Hon Roll; Fnlst Mss Co-Ed Pgnt 86; Lock Haven U; Math.

SELIBER, JAY; Stoughton HS; Stoughton, MA; (Y); 1/314; Pres Chess Clb; Math Tm; Nwsp Stf; JV Ice Hcky; Var L Tennis; High Hon Roll; NHS; Ntl Merit Ltr; Pres Schlr; Val; ST Olympd Tst Math Fnlst 80th In ST 85; Olympd Tst Fnlst 19th In ST 86; U Of PA; Accntng.

SELINGA, KATHLEEN A; Middlesex Schl; Fitchburg, MA; (Y); Camera Clb; Cmnty Wkr; Dance Clb; Chorus; School Play; Yrbk Ed-Chief; JV Socr; High Hon Roll; Susan J Winthrop Eng Awd Applewild Schl Fitchburg 84; Wm Laverack Awd Highest Overall Acdmc Record 84.

SELLS, GEORGE; Attleboro HS; S Attleboro, MA; (Y); SADD; Var Capt Bsbl; JV Bsktbl; Im Socr; Im Swmmng; Bus.

SELOVER, ELIZABETH B; Greenfield HS; Greenfield, MA; (Y); 27/153; Spanish Clb; Band; Concert Band; Capt Flag Corp; Mrchg Band; Ed Yrbk Stf; Var Golf; Hon Roll; Fld Hcky; Silver G Awd 86; U Of MA; Microbio.

SELWYN, MARK D; Brookline HS; Chestnut Hill, MA; (Y); Latin Clb; Scholastic Bowl; Nwsp Bus Mgr; Var Crs Cntry; Var Trk; High Hon Roll; NHS; Ntl Merit SF; Latin IV Ntl Exm Magna Cum Laude, Presdntl Schlr 85.

SENA, SUZANNE; Southwick HS; Southwick, MA; (Y); 27/134; Sec Church Yth Grp; Concert Band; Jazz Band; Mrchg Band; JV Var Bsktbl; Var Capt Crs Cntry; Var Trk; Hon Roll; Voice Dem Awd; JV Fld Hcky; Mrn Blgy.

SENIER, LAURA; Our Lady Of Nazareth Acad; Reading, MA; (Y); 5/56; Church Yth Grp; Drama Clb; Chorus; School Play; Nwsp Ed-Chief; High Hon Roll; NHS; NEDT Awd; Teachers Aide; Church Choir; Dartmouth Bk Awd 85; HS Drama Guild 84-86; Colby Coll; Englsh.

SENNA, JOYCE; Old Rochester Regional HS; Mattapoisett, MA; (Y); 10/150; Am Leg Aux Girls St; Band; Sec Frsh Cls; Sec Soph Cls; Pres Jr Cls; Pres Sr Cls; Pres Stu Cncl; Cit Awd; Elks Awd; NHS; Hghst Acad Avg Frnch III 85; Cum Laude Natl Latin Exam 86; Outstndng Soph Of The Yr 85; Pol Sci.

SEPUKA, LISA; Holy Name HS; Auburn, MA; (Y); 52/256; Ski Clb; Spanish Clb; Stu Cncl; Cheerleading; Coach Actv; Fld Hcky; Gym; Capt Sftbl; Elks Awd; Hon Roll; Auburn Emblen No 344 Schlrshp 86; Mass Elks Assoc Schlrshp 86; Westfield ST Coll; Crmnl Just.

SEPULVEDA, JOSE; Milford HS; Milford, MA; (Y); FTA; SADD; Band; Orch; School Play; Var L Bsktbl; Swmmng; JV Trk; Cit Awd; NHS; Educ.

SEQUEIRA, ANTHONY; Tahanto Regional HS; Boylston, MA; (Y); 5/56; School Play; Nwsp Stf; Yrbk Stf; Var Bsbl; JV Bsktbl; High Hon Roll; Pres NHS; Lions Clb Spch Cont Wnr 86; American U; Law.

SERA, LAURIE; Newton North HS; Newton, MA; (Y); 5/618; Aud/Vis; Cmnty Wkr; JA; Political Wkr; Stu Cncl; Cheerleading; Score Keeper; Cit Awd; High Hon Roll; Hon Roll; Karste Awds 78-86; Boston Coll; Bus Mgmt.

SERA, SUSAN; Ware HS; Ware, MA; (Y); 14/110; Am Leg Aux Girls St; Church Yth Grp; French Clb; Hosp Aide; Library Aide; Model UN; Yrbk Stf; Chrmn Lit Mag; VP Jr Cls; Hon Roll; Estrn Star Schlrshp; NEA Schlrshp; Grnwch Fndtn Schlrshp; U RI; Phrmcy.

SERGEL, THERESA C; Bartlett HS; Webster, MA; (Y); 6/152; Cmnty Wkr; Hosp Aide; Pres Intnl Clb; VP Pres Science Clb; Drm Mjr(t); JETS Awd; NHS; NEDT Awd; Drama Clb; Exploring; Ind Awd Regnl Sci & Engrng Fair 86; 3rd Pl MA ST Sci Fair 85 & 86; Pres Schlrshp 86; Our Lady Of The Elms; Bio.

SERGI, MAUREEN E; North Andover HS; N Andover, MA; (Y); 74/260; AFS; Chorus; Color Guard; Variety Show; Yrbk Stf; Hon Roll; Ntl Merit Ltr; Bstn U; Intl Rltns.

SERGI, PAUL; Canton HS; Canton, MA; (Y); 16/255; Trk; Chess Clb; Cmnty Wkr; Office Aide; SADD; Socr; Hon Roll; Dartmouth Coll.

SERVIDIO, MARIA; Minnechaug HS; Wilbraham, MA; (Y); 87/315; Dance Clb; Yrbk Bus Mgr; Yrbk Stf; JV Var Cheerleading; Outstndng Stu Frm Bus Dep 85; Rest Mgmt.

SERWATKA, CHERYL; Dracut SR HS; Dracut, MA; (Y); Office Aide; SADD; Rep Stu Cncl; Hon Roll; NHS; Pres Schlr; Dracut Schlrshp Fndtn; U Of Lowell; Nrsg.

SEVIOUR, SCOTT; Barnstable HS; Hyannis, MA; (Y); Camera Clb; Drama Clb; Ski Clb; Hon Roll; Stu Spksmn-Stu Asst Pgm 85-86; Peer Ldrshp Pgm 84-85; Partic Awd-Voice Of Dmcrcy Cntst 85; Pre Med.

SEYLER, JEFF; East Longmeadow HS; E Longmeadow, MA; (Y); 17/211; Am Leg Boys St; Church Yth Grp; Intnl Clb; Office Aide; Band; Crs Cntry; Trk; Hon Roll.

SEYMOUR, KENNETH; Chicpee Comprehensive HS; Chicopee, MA; (Y); #52 In Class; Var L Bsbl; Hon Roll; NHS; Westfield ST Coll; Bus Mgmt.

SEYMOUR, NANCY; Southwick HS; Sowick, MA; (Y); 19/175; Trs Drama Clb; Band; Chorus; Church Choir; Concert Band; Jazz Band; Mrchg Band; School Musical; School Play; Trk; Wstrn MA Dist Choir 83-86; All ST Choir Rcmndtn 85-86; Our Lady Of Elms; Ped Nrs Prac.

SEYMOUR, STEPHANIE; Mohawk Trail Regional HS; Ashfield, MA; (Y); 14/142; School Musical; School Play; Nwsp Stf; Yrbk Bus Mgr; Rep Soph Cls; Rep Jr Cls; Tennis; Score Keeper; Mgr Socr; Hon Roll; Friendlst Stu 86; Overall Exc Spnsh 84-85; Most Talkative Stu; U MA; Pol Sci.

SHAFF, HEATHER; Lawrence Acad; Amherst, NH; (Y); Band; Concert Band; Mrchg Band; School Musical; Rep Soph Cls; JV Fld Hcky; Var L Lcrss; JV Mgr(s); Var L Vllybl; High Hon Roll; Cum Laude Soc 85-87; Law.

SHAFFER, DARREN GLENN; West Springfield HS; W Springfield, MA; (Y); 11/219; German Clb; Intnl Clb; Ski Clb; Im Coach Actv; Im Golf; Var Capt Swmmng; Hon Roll; MVP Swmng 86; Massachusetts U; Engr.

SHAFNER, CHRISTINE M; Lynnfield HS; Lynnfield, MA; (Y); 31/179; Church Yth Grp; School Play; Yrbk Stf; High Hon Roll; U MI Ann Arbor; Zoology.

SHAHEEN, JENNIFER; Lawrence HS; Lawrence, MA; (Y); DECA; Hosp Aide; Rep Soph Cls; Rep Jr Cls; Stu Cncl; Var Crs Cntry; Var Trk; High Hon Roll; Hon Roll; NHS; Bus.

SHAKER, KELLY; Westfield HS; Westfield, MA; (Y); Pep Clb; Nwsp Phtg; Nwsp Rptr; Var JV Cheerleading; Hon Roll; Jr NHS; U Of MA; Bus Mgmt.

SHALNO, STEVEN; Christopher Columbus HS; Dorchester, MA; (S); JA; Stu Cncl; Bsktbl; Var Ftbl; Wt Lftg; NHS; Ftbl; Stud Cncl; U Of MA Amherst; Mgmt.

SHAMON, LYNN; Walpole HS; Walpole, MA; (Y); JCL; Latin Clb; Spanish Clb; Rep Soph Cls; Rep Jr Cls; Score Keeper; JV Capt Vllybl; Hon Roll; Cert Prfrmnc Spnsh IV & JR Engl 86; Cert Merit Natl Enrgy Ed 85; Lngstcs.

SHANE, DAVID; Hingham HS; Hingham, MA; (Y); 2/347; Nwsp Rptr; Var Capt Wrstlng; High Hon Roll; NCTE Awd; Pres NHS; Ntl Merit SF; JV Socr; Renssalaer Mdl NEML Hgh Scrng JR 86; U Mass Chncllrs Schlrshp 86; Ntl Latin Exm Magna Cum Laude 85; Princtn; Elec Engnrng.

SHANKS, ROBIN LISA; Apponequet Regional HS; Lakeville, MA; (Y); Pep Clb; Hon Roll; Educ.

SHANNON, JOHN H; Swampscott HS; Nahant, MA; (Y); 39/239; Cmnty Wkr; Var Bsbl; Var Ice Hcky; Hon Roll; SR Babe Ruth League All Star 86; Succssfl Cand Prof Bsbl Major; League Tryout Camp 86; Engr.

SHAPIRO, SANDRA; Sahron HS; Sharon, MA; (Y); Cmnty Wkr; French Clb; Hosp Aide; SADD; Varsity Clb; Nwsp Stf; Off Frsh Cls; Off Soph Cls; Off Jr Cls; Off Sr Cls; Mgmt.

SHAPLEIGH, STEVEN S; North Reading HS; North Reading, MA; (Y); Band; Jazz Band; Mrchg Band; Stage Crew; Bsktbl; JV Socr.

SHARP, GARY; Bishop Stang HS; N Dartmouth, MA; (Y); Aud/Vis; JA; Science Clb; Service Clb; Stage Crew; Var L Bsbl; Hon Roll; Comp Techn.

SHARTRAND, ANGELA; Drury SR HS; N Adams, MA; (S); Band; Concert Band; Mrchg Band; Trk; High Hon Roll; NEDT Awd.

SHATZER, SUSAN E; Ludlow HS; Ludlow, MA; (Y); 53/279; JA; JCL; PAVAS; Variety Show; Sr Cls; Cheerleading; Chrldr 4 Yrs; CPR; Schl Store Empl 84-85; Awd Phys Ftnss 83-84; Jr Achvmnt Vp 84; Grad 84-85; Jazz; U Of MA; FBI.

SHAUGHNESSY, TODD; Greater Boston Acad; Osterville, MA; (Y); 5/26; Aud/Vis; Church Yth Grp; French Clb; Hosp Aide; Chorus; School Play; Stage Crew; Var Bsktbl; Im Ftbl; Im Sftbl; Engrng.

SHAW, JEAN; Southbridge HS; Sbridge, MA; (Y); 1/134; Pres Church Yth Grp; Math Tm; Band; Bausch & Lomb Sci Awd; NHS; Ntl Merit Ltr; Val; Voice Dem Awd; Hugh O Brian Yth Foundtn HOBY & MA Yth Ldrshp Foundtn 84; MA Assoc Schl Suprntndt Awd Acadmc 85; U Of MA Amherst; Psych.

SHAW, JOHN; Norton HS; Norton, MA; (S); 1/148; Am Leg Aux Girls St; Debate Tm; Pres Math Tm; Mrchg Band; Yrbk Bus Mgr; Var Crs Cntry; Capt Trk; Trs NHS; Ntl Merit SF; NEDT Awd; Engrng.

SHAW, JOSEPH; Apponequet Reg HS; E Freetown, MA; (Y); Church Yth Grp; Cmnty Wkr; Letterman Clb; Varsity Clb; VP L Ftbl; Mat Maids; Sftbl; Var Trk; Im Wt Lftg; NE U; Cvl Engrng.

SHAW, MARY; Frontier Regional Schl; S Deerfield, MA; (Y); 8/100; VP French Clb; Yrbk Bus Mgr; Var Capt Cheerleading; Var Trk; Hon Roll; Trvl Trsm.

SHAW, STACY; New Bedford HS; New Bedford, MA; (Y); 126/701; Cmnty Wkr; Drama Clb; JA; Stage Crew; Var Trk; Hon Roll; Jr NHS; SMU; Med.

SHEA III, JAMES A; Concord-Carlisle Reg HS; Carlisle, MA; (S); 130/350; DECA; Drama Clb; JA; School Play; Rep Frsh Cls; Rep Soph Cls; Rep Jr Cls; Stu Cncl; Socr; Hon Roll; Deca 1st Pl Regnl Comp 86; Lib Arts.

SHEA, JENNIFER; Westwood SR HS; Westwood, MA; (Y); 90/208; AFS; Key Clb; SADD; Yrbk Stf; Stat Bsktbl; L Mgr(s); Powder Puff Ftbl; Var L Socr; Hon Roll; Chrstn A Herter Mem Schlrshp 84; Bryant Coll; Mktg.

SHEA, KATHLEEN; Holy Name CC HS; Rochdale, MA; (Y); 49/305; Dance Clb; SADD; Teachers Aide; Off Frsh Cls; Cheerleading; Coach Actv; Gym; Hon Roll; 6th Pl ST Finls Gym 84; USGF & NEAAAU Gymnst 77-86; 2nd Pl Chrldng Trnmnt 86; U MA.

SHEA, KELLY; Boston Latin HS; Hyde Pk, MA; (Y); 114/286; Church Yth Grp; JA; Key Clb; Latin Clb; Ski Clb; Chorus; Stat Ice Hcky; Mgr(s); Powder Puff Ftbl; JV Socr; Apprbtn With Dstnctn; Babson Coll; Bus Admin.

SHEA, KEVIN; Acton-Boxboro HS; Acton, MA; (Y); 130/420; Var L Ftbl; Var Capt Lcrss; Var L Trk; Hon Roll; Lacrosse Scott Kennaugh Ldrshp Awd 85; Bus Adm.

SHEA, KIMBERLY; Lynn Classical HS; Lynn, MA; (Y); 29/265; Hosp Aide; JA; SADD; Band; Concert Band; Mrchg Band; Pre Med.

SHEA, MARK; Concord-Carlisle HS; Concord, MA; (Y); Pilot.

SHEA, MATTHEW; Cathedral HS; Springfield, MA; (Y); 15/450; Mathletes; VP Math Clb; Office Aide; Tennis; NHS; Ntl Merit Ltr; Prfct Atten Awd; Best Senator Awd & Model Snt 86; Boston Coll; Ecnmcs.

SHEA, MAUREEN; Acad Of Notre Dame; Lowell, MA; (Y); Chorus; Yrbk Stf; Hon Roll.

SHEA, MELISSA; Cohasset JR SR HS; Cohasset, MA; (Y); 15/104; Cmnty Wkr; Drama Clb; JV Var Bsktbl; Powder Puff Ftbl; JV Var Socr; Soccer & Bsktbl Vrty Ltr 85; Sptlgh Prog 85.

SHEA, STEPHEN; Central Catholic HS; Pelham, NH; (Y); 76/278; U Of MA Lowell.

SHEA, TERRENCE; Marian HS; Framingham, MA; (Y); Am Leg Boys St; Political Wkr; Rep Soph Cls; JV Ice Hcky; Var Trk; Hon Roll; NHS; Rep MA Stu Govt Day 86; Boston Coll; Corp Law.

SHEARER, IAN GARY; Hamilton Wenham Regional HS; S Hamilton, MA; (Y); 9/200; Am Leg Boys St; Church Yth Grp; Band; Chorus; Concert Band; Mrchg Band; School Musical; School Play; Nwsp Rptr; VP Pres Stu Cncl; Harvard Bk Awd 86; Histry.

SHEDD, SUSAN; Notre Dame Acad; Weymouth, MA; (Y); 15/111; French Clb; Hosp Aide; Orch; French Hon Soc; High Hon Roll; NHS; Prfct Atten Awd; 2dn Pl Schl Sci Fair 86; Acad All Am 8.

SHEEDY, CHRISTINE; Barnstable HS; Cotuit, MA; (Y); 10/392; Drama Clb; Hosp Aide; Math Tm; SADD; School Musical; Nwsp Ed-Chief; Yrbk Stf; Lit Mag; Hon Roll; NHS; Harvard College; Eng.

SHEEHAN, ANN; Girls Catholic HS; Malden, MA; (Y); French Clb; SADD; Var Bsktbl; Var Sftbl; Var Vllybl; Hon Roll; Kiwanis Awd; Lion Awd; Mud Vllybl 86; 6th Plyr Awd Bsktbl 86; Coaches Awd Sftbl 86.

SHEEHAN, COLLEEN; Brockton HS; Brockton, MA; (Y); Drama Clb; Hosp Aide; JCL; Key Clb; Ski Clb; School Musical; School Play; Stage Crew; Yrbk Stf; Southeastern MA U; Accntng.

SHEEHAN, EDWARD; St Dominic Savio Prep HS For Boys; Revere, MA; (Y); 17/93; Ski Clb; Yrbk Stf; Bowling; Crs Cntry; Trk; Hon Roll; Prfct Atten Awd; Mass Coll Of Pharmacy; Pharm.

SHEEHAN, LISA; St Columbkille HS; Watertown, MA; (Y); 1/52; Yrbk Stf; Lit Mag; High Hon Roll; NHS; Natl Sci Awd 86; Med.

SHEEHAN, MONICA; Lynnfield HS; Lynnfield, MA; (Y); 49/162; Church Yth Grp; SADD; Chorus; Capt Cheerleading; Powder Puff Ftbl; Sftbl; French Hon Soc; High Hon Roll; Hon Roll; VP Frsh Cls; Nrsng.

SHEEHY, SUZANNE; Archbishop Williams HS; Quincy, MA; (Y); Church Yth Grp; Girl Scts; Ski Clb; Variety Show; JC Awd; NHS; Merrimack Coll Acad Scholar 86; Merrimack Coll; Elec Engrng.

SHELDON, SERENA; Drury SR HS; N Adams, MA; (S); 12/189; Dance Clb; Pep Clb; Sec Band; Sec Concert Band; Sec Mrchg Band; School Musical; Var Cheerleading; High Hon Roll; Hon Roll; Nu Sigma Hnr Soc 84-85; Pro Merito Hnr Soc 85-86; Berkshire JR Miss Fnlst & Schlrshp Wnnr 85.

SHELLITO, MICHAEL; Pioneer Valley Regional Schl; Northfield, MA; (Y); Am Leg Boys St; Aud/Vis; Boy Scts; Drama Clb; Ski Clb; Varsity Clb; Yrbk Stf; Socr; Hon Roll; Band; 3rd Pl Comp Pgmng Comptn 86; U VT; Comp Sci.

SHENK, MARTIN P; Bishop Stang HS; North Dartmouth, MA; (Y); 7/225; Am Leg Boys St; Latin Clb; JV Var Bsktbl; JV Ftbl; JV Golf; JV Tennis; Hon Roll; NHS; NEDT Awd; Natl Latn Awd 84; Engrg.

SHEPARD, DONNA; Gardner HS; Gardner, MA; (Y); 20/140; Ski Clb; Spanish Clb; Rep Jr Cls; Var Cheerleading; Hon Roll; Bus Mrktng.

SHEPARD, STEVEN; Methuen HS; Methuen, MA; (Y); 4/340; Am Leg Boys St; Intnl Clb; Math Tm; Model UN; L Socr; L Trk; High Hon Roll; NHS; Spanish NHS; St Schlr; Cls Math Awd 86; Christopher Quake Mem Schlrshp 86; James Inaalls Awd 86; Bentley Coll; Acctnt.

SHEPARD, SUSAN; Marblehead HS; Marblehead, MA; (Y); 30/249; Church Yth Grp; French Clb; Ski Clb; Yrbk Phtg; JV Lcrss; Powder Puff Ftbl; JV Var Socr; JV Var Swmmng; High Hon Roll; Hon Roll; U Of FL Gainsville; Vet.

SHEPPARD, MARGARET; Fitchburg HS; Fitchburg, MA; (Y); Drama Clb; GAA; SADD; School Play; Rep Stu Cncl; Var Cheerleading; Var Trk; High Hon Roll; NHS; Civic Days Awd 85; Special Hnr Stu 83; US Hstry Contest For Fitchburg St Clg 85; Holy Cross; Pre-Law.

SHERIDAN, MELISSA; Clinton HS; Clinton, MA; (Y); Yrbk Stf; JV Bsktbl; Hon Roll; NHS; Food Svc Mgmt.

SHERMAN, COLLEEN; C H Mc Cann Vo Tech HS; Savoy, MA; (Y); Am Leg Aux Girls St; SADD; Yrbk Stf; Rep Frsh Cls; Sec Soph Cls; Sec Jr Cls; Sec Sr Cls; Rep Stu Cncl; Var Bsktbl; Mgr(s); Physcl Thrpst.

SHERMAN, MATTHEW; Melrose HS; Boston, MA; (Y); 5/390; Drama Clb; School Musical; School Play; Stage Crew; L Capt Crs Cntry; Var Trk; High Hon Roll; NHS; Ntl Merit SF; VFW Awd; Stu Rep To H S Permanent Schlrp Fnd 84-87; Mech Engrg.

SHERRIFF, MISSY; Bishop Fenwick HS; Peabody, MA; (Y); Church Yth Grp; ROTC; Teachers Aide; Yrbk Stf; Rep Stu Cncl; Var Capt Socr; Var Capt Trk; High Hon Roll; Hon Roll; Holy Cross Coll; Engnrng.

SHERRY, JENNIFER; Hampshire Regional HS; Williamsburg, MA; (Y); FBLA; Ski Clb; Variety Show; Sec Soph Cls; Diving; Gym; Socr; Sftbl; Hon Roll; Bus.

SHERYS, JOANNE; Saugus HS; Saugus, MA; (Y); Cmnty Wkr; Library Aide; Office Aide; Spanish Clb; Elem Educ.

SHIELDS, MATTHEW JON; Hudson HS; Hudson, MA; (Y); Camera Clb; Cmnty Wkr; Var Capt Bsktbl; Var L Socr; Var L Trk; Am Leg Boys St; MA Hstry Day Cont 85; Local Up To ST Comp Cert Achvt; MIAA Trk & Fld Champ 86.

SHIMKUS, KIMBERLY; Greater Lawrence Technical HS; Methuen, MA; (Y); Church Yth Grp; Girl Scts; Teachers Aide; Chorus; Church Choir; School Play; Yrbk Stf; Rep Jr Cls; Rep Stu Cncl; Cheerleading; Grtst Achvt & Imprvmnt Awd 84-85; Hgst Attitude Awd 85-86; Bus Mgnt.

SHIMOMURA, SACHI; Falmouth HS; Falmouth, MA; (Y); Chess Clb; Math Tm; Science Clb; High Hon Roll; Hon Roll; NHS; Ntl Merit SF; Supr Awd Acdmc Excllnc 85; Amer Chem Scty Awd 85; Harvard Bk Awd 85.

SHIRE, KIMBERLY; Westford Acad; Westford, MA; (Y); Sec Drama Clb; French Clb; SADD; Var L Swmmng; Hon Roll; NHS; All Star Swmmng 83-86; New Engl Athl Swmmng 84-86; NC Chapel Hill; Phy Thrpy.

SHLYAM, ROSE; Algonquin Regional HS; Northboro, MA; (Y); 5/200; French Clb; Latin Clb; Teachers Aide; Temple Yth Grp; Chorus; School Musical; Variety Show; High Hon Roll; Jr NHS; Frank Edward & Martha Brunner Orne Awd-Chamber Music Excllnc 85; Eastern Music Fest Awd 83; Oberlin Conservatory; Music.

SHOPE, BONNIE; Northfield Mount Hermon Schl; Branford, CT; (Y); Yrbk Stf; Rep Stu Cncl; JV Fld Hcky; JV Ice Hcky; JV Vllybl; High Hon Roll; Hon Roll; Excllnc Views Amercn Lit Awd 86; NMH Sailng Awd Varsty Sailng 86.

SHORES, JENNIFER; North Quincy HS; Quincy, MA; (Y); 5/395; Pres Drama Clb; JA; Spanish Clb; School Play; Stage Crew; Yrbk Stf; Var L Tennis; Pres NHS; Spanish NHS; Cmnty Wkr; Hnr Roll Dstnctn 83-86.

SHORT, CAROL; Old Rochester Regional HS; Mattapoisett, MA; (Y); Dance Clb; Drama Clb; Ski Clb; School Play; Var Capt Fld Hcky; Trk; Prfct Atten Awd; Trphy Awd Trk 85; Vrsty Lttr Fld Hcky 86; Dntstry.

SHRIBER, TODD D; Worcester Acad; Worcester, MA; (Y); Math Tm; Spanish Clb; Temple Yth Grp; Nwsp Stf; JV Tennis; Top Schlr 85-86; Bio Achvt Awd 85; Law.

SHULER, STEPHEN; Tahanto Regional HS; Boylston, MA; (Y); JA; Math Tm; Science Clb; High Hon Roll; Hon Roll; Essay Om Wmn 84; NE U; Bus.

SHULMAN, RICHARD; Boston Latin Acad; Boston, MA; (Y); Chess Clb; Yrbk Phtg; Hnrbl Ment Schl Sci Fair 86.

SHUMWAY, DAVID C; Duxbury HS; Duxbury, MA; (Y); Am Leg Boys St; Aud/Vis; Boy Scts; Library Aide; Church Choir; Stage Crew; Hon Roll; Pre-Law.

SHUMWAY, KARY R; Amherst Regional HS; Pelham, MA; (Y); Am Leg Boys St; Cmnty Wkr; 4-H; FBLA; Nwsp Rptr; Nwsp Sprt Ed; Nwsp Stf; Yrbk Rptr; Yrbk Stf; Lit Mag; Am Lgn Bys ST Rep 86; Thomas Coll; Bus Mgmt.

SHUMWAY, SUZANNE; Hampshire Regional HS; Williamsburg, MA; (Y); 30/132; Rep Frsh Cls; Var Gym; Mgr(s); Hon Roll; U MA.

SIBLEY, GLENRAY; Holyoke HS; Holyoke, MA; (Y); 69/503; Pres Computer Clb; Teachers Aide; Stu Cncl; Var Capt Ftbl; Gym; Var Capt Trk; Western New England Ftbl Schlrshp 86; Cls Soldier 86; Boy ST Gymnastic Finalist 86; Western New England Coll; Comp.

SICA, SCOTT; Saugus HS; Saugus, MA; (Y); Art Clb; Band; Concert Band; Drill Tm; Jazz Band; Mrchg Band; Orch; School Musical; School Play; Symp Band; Bus Admin.

SIDUR, CYNTHIA; Ware HS; Ware, MA; (Y); 7/110; Am Leg Aux Girls St; Church Yth Grp; 4-H; French Clb; Hosp Aide; Math Tm; Model UN; Yrbk Ed-Chief; Yrbk Phtg; Yrbk Stf; Bk Awd 85; High Avrg Hist 85; Worcester Polytech; Mech Engrg.

SIDWELL, KRISTIN; Northfield Mount Herman HS; Northfield, MA; (Y); Teachers Aide; Yrbk Stf; JV Ice Hcky; Stat Mgr(s); High Hon Roll; Hon Roll; Ntl Merit SF; Awd Excllnc Engl 84; Advncd Placement Engl 85-86; Judicial Committee 85-86; Engl.

SIEMER, SHIRLEY ANNE; Navset Regional HS; Wellfleet, MA; (Y); German Clb; SADD; Chorus; Concert Band; Orch; School Musical; Stat Bsbl; Stat Bsktbl; Socr; Hon Roll; Northeastern U; Intrprtr.

SIENKIEWICZ, MAUREEN; Ursuline Acad; Dedham, MA; (Y); 23/82; French Clb; Service Clb; Rep SADD; Hon Roll; NHS; Sci Fair 1st 84; Humanities Club 86-84, 84-85&85-86; Aerobics 84-85; Pol Sci.

SIGDA, MARK; Chicopee Comprehensive HS; Chicopee, MA; (Y); Hon Roll; Electronics.

SIKORSKI, MATTHEW; Holyoke HS; Holyoke, MA; (Y); Drama Clb; French Clb; Latin Clb; Office Aide; Stage Crew; Trs Frsh Cls; Trs Jr Cls; High Hon Roll; Hon Roll; Jr NHS; Comp Sci.

SILLIKER, KAREN; Malden HS; Malden, MA; (Y); 15/480; Cmnty Wkr; Key Clb; Math Tm; Office Aide; SADD; Yrbk Stf; Sec Sr Cls; NHS; Pres Schlr; Stonehill Coll Frshmn Schlr 86; Acad Ftns Awd 86; Stonehill Coll; Bio.

SILTANEN, LORI; Hanover HS; Hanover, MA; (Y); Fld Hcky; Hon Roll; Lbrl Arts.

SILVA, CHERYL L; Dighton-Rehoboth Regional HS; Rehoboth, MA; (Y); 2/235; Math Tm; Trs SADD; VP Frsh Cls; Trs Stu Cncl; Score Keeper; Var L Tennis; VP NHS; Ntl Merit Ltr; NEDT Awd; Prfct Atten Awd; Citizens Schlrshp Fndtn Of Amer Awd 86; Noranda Grp Schlrshp 86; James Frates Mdl 86; Bowdoin Coll; Math.

SILVA, DOMINGO; Southeastern Vo-Tech; East Bridgewater, MA; (Y).

SILVA, KIMBERLY; New Bedford HS; New Bedford, MA; (Y); 77/702; Dance Clb; Pep Clb; Mrchg Band; Nwsp Rptr; Rep Soph Cls; Var Cheerleading; Trk; Hon Roll; Brdcst Jrnlsm.

SILVA, LUCIANA; New Bedford HS; New Bedford, MA; (Y); Drama Clb; VP SADD; Stage Crew; High Hon Roll; Psychtrst.

SILVA, MARK; Mansfield HS; Mansfield, MA; (Y); 16/208; Trs Am Leg Boys St; Chrmn Debate Tm; Ski Clb; School Play; Stage Crew; Rep Frsh Cls; Rep Soph Cls; Rep Jr Cls; Stu Cncl; JV Bsbl; Real Estate.

SILVEIRA, STEVEN; Bristol Plymouth Regional HS; Taunton, MA; (Y); 2/189; Am Leg Boys St; Political Wkr; VP Frsh Cls; High Hon Roll; Hon Roll; Acad All Amer Awd 86; Stu Advsry Board 84; Archtctr.

SILVEIRA, THOMAS J; Bishop Stang HS; Mattapoisett, MA; (Y); 77/254; Am Leg Boys St; Church Yth Grp; VP PAVAS; Thesps; School Play; Lit Mag; Mgr(s); Trk; High Hon Roll; MA Stu Govt Day 85-86; Skidmore Coll; Us Frgn Svc.

SILVEIRA, VICTOR; New Bedford HS; New Bedford, MA; (Y); Sec Drama Clb; Office Aide; Chorus; School Musical; School Play; NHS; Hghst Hnrs Grad 86; Boston U; Geolgy.

SILVERSTEIN, SAM; Lincoln-Sudbury R H S; Lincoln, MA; (Y); Boy Scts; Exploring; Nwsp Rptr; Nwsp Sprt Ed; Lit Mag; Stu Cncl; JV Stat Bsbl; Stat Bsktbl; Score Keeper; JV Socr.

SILVESTER, DENISE; Clinton HS; Clinton, MA; (Y); Dance Clb; Intnl Clb; Rep Frsh Cls; Rep Soph Cls; Rep Jr Cls; Rep Sr Cls; JV Bsktbl; Var L Fld Hcky; Var L Sftbl; NHS; X-Ray Tech.

SILVI, SCOTT R; Walpole HS; Walpole, MA; (Y); 7/268; Am Leg Boys St; Boy Scts; JV Crs Cntry; JV Trk; Var Wrstlng; Hon Roll; NHS; Acad Decthln Tm 85-86; Gold Awd Engl 86; Silv Awd Soc Studs 85 & 86; Mech Engrng.

SIMEONE, DEBORAH; Acton Boxboro Regional HS; Acton, MA; (Y); 228/428; Dance Clb; Bus.

SIMM, PETER; Westfield HS; Westfield, MA; (Y); 6/350; Drama Clb; French Clb; School Play; Variety Show; Nwsp Rptr; Pres Jr Cls; French Hon Soc; High Hon Roll; NHS; Bst Sprtng Actor 85; Marseille France W/AISE 86; Rep Govt Day Boston 86; Rep Model Cngrs Am Intl Coll; Econ.

SIMMER, ROBERT; King Philip Regional HS; Plainville, MA; (Y); 23/240; Ski Clb; Varsity Clb; Var L Ftbl; JV Trk; Im Wt Lftg; Hon Roll; Jr NHS; NHS; Rep Stu Govt Day 86; Unsung Hero Awd Ftbl 86; Plainville Beagle Clb Scholar 86; U VT; Natrl Rsrcs.

SIMMONS, MICHAEL; Nipmuc Regional HS; Upton, MA; (Y); 16/90; Church Yth Grp; Drama Clb; French Clb; Chorus; Church Choir; School Musical; School Play; Stage Crew; Yrbk Stf; Stu Cncl; Cllnry Arts.

SIMMONS, STEPHANIE; Cathedral HS; Springfield, MA; (Y); 3/455; Hosp Aide; Math Clb; Office Aide; Service Clb; Rep Stu Cncl; Var Capt Swmmng; High Hon Roll; NHS; Ntl Merit Ltr; St Schlr; U Of MA; Chem Engrg.

SIMONE, BOBBI JEAN; Arlington Catholic HS; Arlington, MA; (Y); #7 In Class; French Clb; Yrbk Stf; Hon Roll; NHS; NEDT Awd; William J Manning Schlrshp 84; Suffolk U; Law.

SIMONE, DIANE; North HS; Worcester, MA; (Y); Church Yth Grp; Dance Clb; Pep Clb; Yrbk Stf; Framingham ST Coll; Bus Mgmt.

SIMONIS, BRENDA; Brockton HS; Brockton, MA; (Y); Church Yth Grp; 4-H; Church Choir; Concert Band; Mrchg Band; Bsktbl; 4-H Awd; Hon Roll; ST 4-H Ldrshp Prjct Wnnr Chgo 85; Elem Ed.

SIMPSON, ELLEN; Academy Of Notre Dame; Chelmsford, MA; (Y); 4/52; Cmnty Wkr; Hosp Aide; Math Clb; Band; Ed Yrbk Stf; Rep Stu Cncl; JV Bsktbl; High Hon Roll; NHS; Ntl Merit Ltr; Pres Acad Ftnss Awd 85-86; Tufts U.

SINGH, REENA; Burlington HS; Burlington, MA; (Y); 42/321; Am Leg Aux Girls St; JA; SADD; Yrbk Bus Mgr; Off Soph Cls; VP Stu Cncl; Fld Hcky; Trk; Hon Roll; NHS; Phys Educ Awd 86; Med.

SINKIEWICH, LYNDA M; Pittsfield HS; Pittsfield, MA; (Y); Trs Church Yth Grp; Drama Clb; Political Wkr; SADD; School Musical; School Play; Nwsp Rptr; Nwsp Stf; Lit Mag; Cit Awd; First Baptst Chrch Schlrshp 86; N Adams ST Coll; Engl.

SIPLEY, CHRISTINA; Attleboro HS; Attleboro, MA; (Y); SADD; Color Guard; Powder Puff Ftbl; JV Sftbl; Hon Roll; NHS.

SISTERSON, JAMES K; Lexington HS; Lexington, MA; (Y); Orch; Var Ice Hcky; JV Lcrss; Sci.

SKARENI, GLENN; Southbridge HS; Southbridge, MA; (Y); Band; Concert Band; Jazz Band; Mrchg Band; Orch; Pep Band; School Musical; Symp Band; JV Ftbl; Var Golf; Band Awd 84-86; MA U; Engr.

SKARP, SARA; Monson HS; Monson, MA; (Y); 14/68; Am Leg Aux Girls St; French Clb; SADD; Varsity Clb; Band; School Musical; Stu Cncl; Bsktbl; Socr; Hon Roll; Monson Athletic Boosters Clb Schlrshp 86; Deans Schlrshp 86; Dept Schlrshp 86; Daemen Coll; Physcl Thrpy.

SKEHAN, MELISSA; Winchester HS; Winchester, MA; (Y); Church Yth Grp; Model UN; Spanish Clb; Rep Soph Cls; Rep Jr Cls; Rep Stu Cncl; JV Var Socr; Var Capt Trk; U VT; Phys Thrpy.

SKELTON, SARAH; Sharon HS; Sharon, MA; (Y); Church Yth Grp; Cmnty Wkr; Drama Clb; French Clb; PAVAS; Political Wkr; Thesps; Chorus; Church Choir; School Musical; Cmmnctns.

SKILTON, DEBORAH; Manchester JR SR HS; Manchester, MA; (Y); 1/60; Debate Tm; Math Tm; Band; Concert Band; Trs Jr Cls; Trs Sr Cls; NHS; Val; NFL; Science Clb; SR Schlr/Commonwlth Schlr 86; Herbert Hahn Bk Awd 85; Sci Awd 85; Cornell U; Engrng.

SKINDER, JENNIFER; Beaver Country Day HS; Auburndale, MA; (Y); Drama Clb; Model UN; Spanish Clb; Chorus; School Musical; School Play; Stage Crew; Swing Chorus; Lit Mag; Rep Stu Cncl; Bio.

SKINNER, CHRISTOPHER; Lenox Memorial HS; Lenox, MA; (Y); Boy Scts; Computer Clb; Debate Tm; Band; Concert Band; Jazz Band; Mrchg Band; School Play; Yrbk Bus Mgr; Sec Sr Cls; Jv Cross Cntry Skiing; Comp Sci.

SKINNION, MARY; Marian HS; Sudbury, MA; (Y); 21/187; Rep Frsh Cls; Var L Bsktbl; Var L Socr; Var Capt Sftbl; Im Vllybl; Hon Roll; NHS; Cnty Dist Select Sccr Tm 85; MA ST Slct Sccr Tm 86; Cntrl Cath Grls All Str Sftbl Tm 86; Phys Ed.

SKOCZYLAS, ELIZABETH; Ludlow HS; Ludlow, MA; (Y); Church Yth Grp; Dance Clb; French Clb; School Play; Stage Crew; Yrbk Stf; Stu Cncl; High Hon Roll; Hon Roll; Prfct Atten Awd; Pedtrcs.

SKOG, RICHARD; Medway JR SR HS; Medway, MA; (Y); 13/136; Boy Scts; Drama Clb; French Clb; VP Chorus; School Musical; Yrbk Stf; Hon Roll; NHS; Vet.

SKOLNICK, DANIEL; Beverly HS; Beverly, MA; (Y); 33/375; Exploring; Math Tm; Temple Yth Grp; Nwsp Stf; Lit Mag; VP Stu Cncl; Var Crs Cntry; JV Wrstlng; Clark U; Psychol.

SKRZYNIARZ, LISA; Holyoke Catholic HS; S Hadley, MA; (Y); 22/128; Church Yth Grp; Computer Clb; French Clb; Color Guard; Hon Roll; Prfct Atten Awd.

SLACK, STEVE; Bourne HS; Monument Beach, MA; (Y); 4-H; Ski Clb; Ice Hcky; Trk; Hon Roll; Engrng.

SLADDIN, TANIA; Tantasqua Regional HS; Sturbridge, MA; (Y); 24/148; Ski Clb; Varsity Clb; Var Stat Bsktbl; Var L Fld Hcky; JV Capt Sftbl; Trk; Hon Roll; S Dennint Awd Outstndng Cntribtn Athl 86; Bus Mgmnt.

SLATER, PETER; Boston College HS; Chelsea, MA; (Y); 45/200; Art Clb; Ed Nwsp Stf; Yrbk Stf; Lit Mag; High Hon Roll; Latin Clb; SADD; Gold Mdl Art 84-85; 2 Gld Mdls Art 85-86; Boston Coll; Lib Art.

SLATTERY, ANN; Boston Latin Schl; Roslindale, MA; (Y); Church Yth Grp; FBLA; JA; Key Clb; Ski Clb; Yrbk Stf; Var L Tennis; Hon Roll; NHS; Fclty Schlrshp 86; Mdrn Prz 84; Providence Coll; Econ.

SLEEPER, RACHEL; Shepherd Hill Regional HS; Charlton City, MA; (Y); 3/130; Drama Clb; Math Tm; SADD; Chorus; Color Guard; Drill Tm; Flag Corp; School Play; Swing Chorus; Yrbk Stf; AFROTC Scholar 86-90; Raymond Fiske Awd 86; Outstndng Aux Awd 86; USAF Acad; Aerospc Engr.

SLEPECKI, DIANE M; Ludlow HS; Ludlow, MA; (Y); 72/289; Hosp Aide; JCL; Pres Band; Chorus; Mrchg Band; Sec Frsh Cls; Sec Soph Cls; Sec Stu Cncl; Var Cheerleading; Stat Wrstlng; Toys For Tots Chrpsn; Scrtry Wstrn MA Dist Of Stu Cncls; U Of MA Amherst; Educ.

SLOCUMB, DAMON; Classical HS; Springfield, MA; (Y); 91/357; Church Yth Grp; Computer Clb; Westfield ST Coll; Comp Sci.

SLOMBA, ELIZABETH; Marion HS; Milford, MA; (Y); 3/183; Am Leg Aux Girls St; Hosp Aide; Lit Mag; Hon Roll; NHS; Hnrbv Mntn For Paper Sbmttd To Annual St Hstrcl Conf 86; Schl Wnnr Of Natl Army Rsrv Essay Cntst 85.

SLOWEY, KATHLEEN; Burlington HS; Burlington, MA; (Y); 105/321; Graphic Desgnr.

SLOWICK, RENEE; Cathedral HS; W Springfield, MA; (Y); 38/520; Pres 4-H; VP JA; Office Aide; SADD; Hon Roll; NHS; Goethe Inst Of Bostons Awd For Excllnce In German 86; Vet Med.

SLYSZ, LISA; Smith Acad; Hatfield, MA; (Y); 5/32; Sec Trs Drama Clb; Ski Clb; Yrbk Ed-Chief; Yrbk Sprt Ed; Sftbl; Hon Roll; Lion Awd; Dstngshd Yng Ldrshp Awd 84-86; U Of MA; Elec Engnrng.

SMARZ JR, GEORGE; Smith Acad; Hatfield, MA; (Y); Drama Clb; 4-H; Key Clb; Yrbk Stf; JV Bsktbl; Var Golf; JV Socr; Hon Roll; 2nd Pl Wnnr Priz Spkng.

SMIGLIANO, JONATHAN; Salem HS; Salem, MA; (Y); High Hon Roll; Hon Roll; NHS; Spanish NHS; Pro Music.

SMITH, ALAN L; Boston Latin Acad; Boston, MA; (Y); 53/135; Yrbk Stf; Pres Sr Cls; Var Bsbl; Var Bsktbl; Cit Awd; High Hon Roll; Ntl Merit SF; Rep Soph Cls; Rep Jr Cls; Rep Stu Cncl; Omega Psi Phi Achvt Awd 85; Orthopedic.

SMITH, AUSTIN; Tri-County Voc Tech HS; Medfield, MA; (Y); Boy Scts; Church Yth Grp; Socr; 3rd Pl Rgnl Speed Sktng , Sr Four Man Team Relay Race Qulfd Ntls 86; Qlfd 2 Man Team Ntls 85; Graphic Arts.

SMITH, BENJAMIN P; Triton Regioniall HS; Rowley, MA; (Y); 20/186; Am Leg Boys St; Science Clb; Yrbk Stf; Rep Stu Cncl; Hon Roll; NHS.

SMITH, BRAD; B Uxbridge HS; Whitinsville, MA; (Y); 14/86; Art Clb; Stu Cncl; Var Ftbl; Wt Lftg; Hon Roll; Gldn Ky Wnnr Bstn Globe Schlstc Art Awds 84.

SMITH, BRUCE C; Belchertown JR SR HS; Belchertown, MA; (Y); Am Leg Boys St; Boy Scts; Church Yth Grp; Ski Clb; Band; Concert Band; Jazz Band; Mrchg Band; Orch; Symp Band; Music US Achvt Acad 85; Boys ST 86; Dist Band & All ST Auditions 85; Engrng.

SMITH, CARLA; Monument Mountain HS; Gt Barrington, MA; (Y); Pep Clb; Yrbk Stf; Stu Cncl; Bsktbl; Socr; Sftbl; Trk; Hon Roll; Athlt Of Yr 85; Sprtsmnshp Of Yr Awd 85; Emmanuel Coll; Psychlgy.

SMITH, CHARLES R; Athol-Royalston Regional HS; Athol, MA; (Y); Am Leg Boys St; Boy Scts; Exploring; Model UN; SADD; Bsbl; Bsktbl; Ftbl; Sftbl; Trk; Wentworth Inst; Elec Engrng.

SMITH, CHRISTINA N; Concord-Carlisle HS; Concord, MA; (Y); 20/293; Dance Clb; French Clb; Hosp Aide; Math Clb; Science Clb; Nwsp Stf; Ed Yrbk Stf; Rep Frsh Cls; Trs Soph Cls; Pres Jr Cls; U Of PABOOK Awd 85; Flag Awd & Poltcl Sci Awd 86; Harvard U; Bio.

SMITH, CHRISTOPHER E; Bedford HS; Bedford, MA; (Y); 10/240; Boy Scts; Church Yth Grp; Debate Tm; Concert Band; Lcrss; High Hon Roll; NHS; Ntl Merit Ltr; Commnded Stdnt Ntl Achvt Schlrshp, Rsrch Apprentice Smmr Pgm 85; Brown; Med.

SMITH, CLAIRE; King Philip Regional HS; Norfolk, MA; (Y); 21/203; Fld Hcky; Hon Roll; NHS.

SMITH, CYNTHIA; Foxboro HS; Foxboro, MA; (Y); Varsity Clb; Capt Fld Hcky; NHS; Church Yth Grp; Concert Band; Mrchg Band; Yrbk Stf; Gym; Trk; Hon Roll; Pediatrics.

SMITH, DANA; Braintree HS; Braintree, MA; (Y); #128 In Class; Lit Mag; Northeastern U; Law Enfrcmnt.

SMITH, DANNY; Franklin HS; Franklin, MA; (Y); 31/225; Varsity Clb; Var Bsbl; Var Capt Ftbl; Var Capt Ice Hcky; Knights Of Columbus Schlrshp 86; Leag All Star Ftbl 86; Leag All Star Bsbl 85; Stonehill; Fin.

SMITH, DARYL; Mario Umana Tech; Boston, MA; (Y); 3/100; Computer Clb; Intnl Clb; JA; ROTC; Color Guard; Drill Tm; Yrbk Rptr; Rep Sr Cls; Capt Bowling; Hon Roll; Bus.

SMITH, DAVE; Billerica Memorial HS; Billerica, MA; (Y); French Clb; Ski Clb; JV Bsktbl; JV Lcrss; JV Tennis; Hon Roll; Ntl Merit Ltr; Pre-Med.

SMITH, DEAN; Bridgewater-Raynham Regional HS; Raynham, MA; (Y); 88/301; SADD; Band; Concert Band; Jazz Band; Mrchg Band; Pep Band; Stage Crew; Badmtn; Lion Awd; Stu Govt Day Super-Raynham Schls 86; Bridgewater St Coll; Aviatn.

SMITH, ERIC C; Notre Dame Prep; Fitchburg, MA; (Y); 14/25; Am Leg Boys St; Yrbk Bus Mgr; Rep Sr Cls; Bsbl; Ftbl; Lcrss; Var Capt Socr; JC Awd; Prfct Atten Awd; Most Improved Person Boston Architectural Center 86; Arch.

SMITH, GARRISON; Beverly HS; Beverly, MA; (Y); JA; JV Ftbl; Var L Ice Hcky; Pebnzi Sci Awd; Sci Fair 2nd Pl; Peer Educ.

SMITH, JOHN; Notre Dame HS; Shirley, MA; (Y); 8/20; Yrbk Stf; Pres Sr Cls; Var Capt Bsbl; Var Capt Bsktbl; Var Capt Ftbl; Hon Roll; NHS; Ray Delorne 85; US Marines Schlr/Athlete Awd Ldrshp 85; US Army Acdmc/Athletic Awd 86; Syracuse U; Poli Sci.

SMITH, JULIE A; Billerica Memorial HS; Billerica, MA; (Y); 24/430; Art Clb; Ski Clb; Stage Crew; Yrbk Stf; Powder Puff Ftbl; Sftbl; Vllybl; High Hon Roll; Hon Roll; NHS; Rotary Clb Scholar 86; St Theresa Parish Scholar 86; Boston U; Comm Arts.

SMITH, KERRI; Bishop Feehan HS; Attleboro, MA; (Y); Dance Clb; Hosp Aide; JCL; Rep Soph Cls; Rep Jr Cls; Stu Cncl; Var L Trk; High Hon Roll; NHS; Excllnc Frnch II; Excllnc Amer Hstry; Abv Natl Avg 2 Yrs Latn Exm; Chld Psych.

SMITH, KERRY; Greater Lawrence Techical HS; Methuen, MA; (Y); Church Yth Grp; Hon Roll.

SMITH, KIMBERLEY; Reading Memorial HS; Reading, MA; (Y); VP Exploring; 4-H; French Clb; Science Clb; Band; Mrchg Band; Rep Frsh Cls; Rep Soph Cls; Rep Jr Cls; L Mgr(s); Boston Museum Sci Vlntr Recog 85; Holy Cross; Bus Adm.

SMITH, KIMBERLY; Taunton HS; Taunton, MA; (Y); 2/400; Am Leg Aux Girls St; Hosp Aide; Trs JCL; Ski Clb; Yrbk Ed-Chief; Lit Mag; Var Cheerleading; NHS; Sal; St Schlr; Boston Coll; Biochmstry.

SMITH, LAURA; Westwood HS; Westwood, MA; (Y); 22/208; SADD; Yrbk Ed-Chief; Sec Soph Cls; Rep Stu Cncl; Var Capt Bsktbl; Powder Puff Ftbl; Var Socr; Var Sftbl; Hon Roll; NHS; Bus Admn.

SMITH, LEANNE; Bishop Feehan HS; S Attleboro, MA; (Y); Hosp Aide; JCL; Latin Clb; Var Cheerleading; Powder Puff Ftbl; Trk; French Hon Soc; Hon Roll; Pepperdine; Pre-Law.

SMITH, LINDA; Arlington Catholic HS; Woburn, MA; (Y); Church Yth Grp; French Clb; JA; Office Aide; SADD; Yrbk Stf; Hon Roll; Prfct Atten Awd; Bentley Coll; Bus.

SMITH, MAURA K; Chicopee Comprehensive HS; Chicopee, MA; (Y); 15/310; Variety Show; Yrbk Stf; Rep Jr Cls; Rep Sr Cls; VP Stu Cncl; Im Powder Puff Ftbl; JV Capt Sftbl; Im Vllybl; NHS; Pro Merit Soc 85-86; U MA; Med.

SMITH, MAUREEN; Holy Name CC HS; Atlantic Bch, FL; (Y); 24/252; Church Yth Grp; Drama Clb; Church Choir; School Play; Hon Roll; Tm Ministry 83-85; Music Ministry At HNCCHS 85-86; Stockbroker.

SMITH, MAX; Amherst Reg HS; Amherst, MA; (Y); Nwsp Phtg; Yrbk Phtg; JV Ftbl; Var Golf; Hon Roll; Pol Sci.

SMITH, MICHAEL G; The Broomfield Schl; Harvard, MA; (Y); 2/86; Drama Clb; School Play; Nwsp Stf; Ed Lit Mag; Sal; Latin Clb; Model UN; Science Clb; JV Crs Cntry; Hon Roll; MA Drama Gld Plywrtg Comp 1st Pl 85; Fitchburg Coll Poetry Cont Wnr 84; PTA Poetry Awds; MIT; Astrnmy.

SMITH, NERISSA; Boston Latin Schl; Brighton, MA; (Y); 125/274; Church Yth Grp; VP JA; Chorus; Sec Church Choir; Swing Chorus; Nwsp Ed-Chief; Hosp Aide; Hon Roll; Howard U; Nrsng.

SMITH, PARRISH; Boston Technical HS; Boston, MA; (Y); 68/205; Drama Clb; ROTC; Crtv Wrtng.

SMITH, PETER C; Norton HS; Norton, MA; (Y); Letterman Clb; Pep Clb; Church Choir; Pres Stu Cncl; Bsktbl; Trk; Hon Roll; Boys ST 86; Springfield Coll; Sports Med.

SMITH, ROBIN; Bishop Connolly HS; Westport, MA; (Y); 60/168; Ski Clb; Yrbk Stf; Var Fld Hcky; Gym; High Hon Roll; Hon Roll; Latin Clb; Rep Stu Cncl; Trk; Salt Earth Awd, Hnr Grad 86; U NH; Lib Arts.

SMITH, SANDRA; Foxborough HS; Foxboro, MA; (Y); Church Yth Grp; JA; SADD; Nwsp Stf; Ed Yrbk Stf; Rep Stu Cncl; Var Mgr Socr; Hon Roll; Frgn Exchnge Prog France 87; Comm.

SMITH, SARA; Norton HS; Norton, MA; (S); 3/148; Math Tm; Chorus; Church Choir; Variety Show; Yrbk Stf; High Hon Roll; NHS; Ntl Merit Ltr; NEDT Awd; Dist Chours 83, 85-86; All ST Chorus 85.

SMITH, SCOTT; Old Rochester Regional HS; Marion, MA; (Y); 17/135; Sec Jr Cls; JV Bsbl; VP Crs Cntry; VP L Ftbl; High Hon Roll; Hon Roll; Jr NHS; 1st Pl Schlrshp Marion Art Cntr 86; Sippican Wmns Clb Schlrshp 86; Old Rchstr Rgnl Schl Schlrshp 86; RI Schl Dsgn; Cmrcl Art.

SMITH, SHANNON M; Cardinal Spellman HS; Whitman, MA; (Y); 11/220; Drama Clb; Girl Scts; Hosp Aide; School Play; Hon Roll; NHS; Pres Schlr; Whitman Police Assn Schlrshp 86; Citzns Schlrshp Fund 86; Bridgewater ST Coll; Bus Comm.

SMITH, STACEY; Our Lady Of Nazareth Acad; Salem, NH; (Y); Art Clb; Drama Clb; Science Clb; Chorus; Stage Crew; Nwsp Rptr; Nwsp Stf; Yrbk Stf; Lit Mag; Tennis; Frshmn Essay Cntst Awd 84; Hstry Awd 84; Piano Achvt Awd 85.

SMITH, STEPHANIE; Bellingham JR SR HS; Bellingham, MA; (Y); Nwsp Stf; Yrbk Stf; Hon Roll; Ring Dance Cmmtte 85.

SMITH, TOM; Shepherd Hill Regional HS; Dudley, MA; (Y); Off Stu Cncl; Capt Bsbl; Var Socr; Hon Roll; NHS; Ntl Merit Ltr; Nuc Engrng.

SMITH, TOM; Westwood HS; Westwood, MA; (Y); 29/204; Cmnty Wkr; SADD; Varsity Clb; Trs Stu Cncl; Var Bsbl; Var Trk; Hon Roll; Trs NHS; ST Sci Fair 86; Bus.

SMOLA, ANNE; Hopkins Acad; Hadley, MA; (Y); 11/45; 4-H; Hosp Aide; Spanish Clb; Chorus; Yrbk Stf; Hon Roll; NHS; Grls St Altnt Rep 86; Lane Prz Speaking Cntst 84-86; Spcl Educ.

SMTIH, COLIN; Boston Technical HS; Boston, MA; (Y); Boy Scts; Math Clb; Math Tm; Off Frsh Cls; Off Soph Cls; Off Jr Cls; Off Sr Cls; Off Stu Cncl; Bsbl; Bsktbl; Med.

SMYTH, JENNIFER; Burlington HS; Burlington, MA; (Y); 45/318; Math Clb; Math Tm; Yrbk Stf; Pratt; Grphc Dsgn.

SNEIDER, BETH; Stoughton HS; Stoughton, MA; (Y); Mathletes; VP Temple Yth Grp; Var Trk; High Hon Roll; Hon Roll; National Span Exam 4th Pl 86; Bus Mgmt.

SNEIRSON, STACEY; Framingham South HS; Framingham, MA; (Y); 11/252; French Clb; Hosp Aide; Key Clb; SADD; Chorus; School Play; Lit Mag; High Hon Roll; Hon Roll; NHS; U Rochester.

SNOW, LISA; Sharon HS; Sharon, MA; (Y); 4-H; SADD; Varsity Clb; Lit Mag; Rep Frsh Cls; Capt Var Cheerleading; Pom Pon; Stu Of Month Spnsh 86; Semi Fnlst Miss MA Teen USA Pgnt 85.

SNYDER, RICHARD; Stoughton HS; Stoughton, MA; (Y); Civic Clb; Red Cross Aide; Temple Yth Grp; JV Trk; Hon Roll; Northeastern U; Marktng.

SNYER, KRISTYN; Academy Of Notre Dame; Tyngsboro, MA; (Y); Girl Scts; Key Clb; Chorus; School Musical; Sec Stu Cncl; Hon Roll; NHS; Tyngsboro-Dunstable Rtry Schlrshp 86; Tyngsboro Schlrshp Cmtte Schlrshp 86; Pres Acad Ftns Awd 86; Coll Of Holy Cross; Englsh Atty.

SOARES, JEFFREY M; B M C Durfee HS; Fall River, MA; (Y); 15/650; French Clb; JA; Band; Mrchg Band; Soph Cls; Sec Jr Cls; Sec Sr Cls; JV Socr; Hon Roll; NHS; ROTC; Aviation.

SOBOCIENSKI III, THEODORE A; Ashland HS; Ashland, MA; (Y); Boy Scts; Var JV Trk; Hon Roll; Comp Sci.

SOBOCZINSKI, JULIE; Salem HS; Salem, MA; (Y); 31/262; Church Yth Grp; Stu Cncl; Capt Cheerleading; Var Fld Hcky; Hon Roll; Fitchburg ST Coll.

SOBOLEWSKI, ANN; Concord-Carlisle HS; Concord, MA; (Y); Dance Clb; Drama Clb; Acpl Chr; Chorus; Capt Color Guard; School Musical; School Play; Cmmnctns.

SOHMER, BRADLEY; Brockton HS; Brockton, MA; (Y); Temple Yth Grp; Varsity Clb; Band; VP Frsh Cls; Var Wrstlng; Hon Roll; Bus Mgmt.

SOKOL, MICHAEL; Wilbraham & Monson Acad; Sturbridge, MA; (Y); 13/170; Chess Clb; Ski Clb; Yrbk Phtg; Yrbk Stf; Im Ftbl; Im Lcrss; Im Socr; Im Sftbl; Im Swmmng; Im Vllybl; MA ST Schlrshp Awd 86; Ithaca Coll; Pol Sci.

SOLITRO, LAURA; North HS; Worcester, MA; (Y); Nwsp Stf; Yrbk Stf; Stu Cncl; Var Tennis; Hon Roll; Jr NHS; NHS; Holy Cross Coll; Corp Law.

SOLIZ, GINA; Tantasqua Regional HS; Sturbridge, MA; (Y); 17/200; Drama Clb; Acpl Chr; Pres Chorus; Madrigals; School Musical; Swing Chorus; Variety Show; Yrbk Ed-Chief; Rep Stu Cncl; Sec NHS; Tri-M Music Hnr Soc 84; Librl Arts.

SOLOVIEFF, TRACY; Fanning Trade HS; Worcester, MA; (Y); 6/124; Church Yth Grp; SADD; Var Capt Bowling; High Hon Roll; Hon Roll; NHS; Prfct Atten Awd; Cty Mgrs Yth Cncl 83; Bus.

SOLTESZ, JEFFREY; Cohasset HS; Cohasset, MA; (Y); 36/106; VP Jr Cls; Var L Bsbl; Var L Ftbl; Im Mgr Wt Lftg; Var Wrstlng; Hon Roll; Leag All Schltc Ftbl 85; Leag All Star Ftbll 85; Blue Chip Awd Ftbll 86; Bus.

SOMERS, MICHAEL; East Boston HS; E Boston, MA; (Y); 16/200; Boys Clb Am; Computer Clb; High Hon Roll; Hon Roll; NHS; 4 Yr Schlrshp UMASS Boston 86; UMASS; Cmptr Sci.

SOMERS, MICHELE; South Hadley HS; S Hadley, MA; (Y); SADD; Nwsp Rptr; Yrbk Stf; Rep Stu Cncl; Cheerleading; Trk; Hon Roll; NHS; Mt Holyoke Coll Bk Awd 86.

SOMPPI JR, JAMES L; Westfield HS; Westfield, MA; (Y); 23/327; Camera Clb; Computer Clb; Office Aide; Yrbk Phtg; Trk; Vllybl; Hon Roll; US Nvl Acad; Nvl Engr.

SONIER, JULIE J; Notre Dame Acad; Rutland, MA; (Y); French Clb; Hosp Aide; Math Clb; Chorus; Jazz Band; Yrbk Stf; Ntl Merit SF; NEDT Awd; Smith Coll Bk Awd 85; Pre-Med.

SOPCZAK, JOANNE; Holy Name C C HS; Worcester, MA; (Y); 75/301; Ski Clb; Var Socr; High Hon Roll; Hon Roll; Lit Awd 86; Religion Awd 86; Cert Of MUAA-DIV I Rnr Up Sccr Tm 86.

SOREL, JOHN; Norton HS; Norton, MA; (S); 12/148; Am Leg Boys St; Boy Scts; Math Tm; Varsity Clb; Crs Cntry; Trk; NEDT Awd; Commended Stu PSAT 84-85; Comp Engr.

SORGI, ANDREA; Notre Dame Acad; Abington, MA; (Y); Cmnty Wkr; Drama Clb; Acpl Chr; Chorus; Im Bsktbl; Capt Socr; Hon Roll; Bus.

SOUCIE, CHRIS; Dennis-Yarmouth Regional HS; W Dennis, MA; (Y); 40/317; Math Tm; JV Bsbl; Im Bsktbl; Var Ftbl; Var L Ice Hcky; JV Socr; Im Vllybl; Elctcl Engrng.

SOUCIE, NORMAN; Leicester HS; Leicester, MA; (S); 4/102; Am Leg Boys St; Boy Scts; VP Frsh Cls; VP Soph Cls; VP Sr Cls; Var Bsktbl; Var Ftbl; Dnfth Awd; NHS; Worcester Poly Inst; Aero Engr.

SOUCY, ROBERT; North HS; Worcester, MA; (Y); Boy Scts; Church Yth Grp; Red Cross Aide; Teachers Aide; Var L Bsbl; Var L Bsktbl; Var L Ftbl; Hon Roll; U S Army Rsrv Schlrshp/Athlt Awd 86; Ftbl All Str For Tackle 85; Wrcstr Ind Tech Inst.

SOULOR, JANA; Douglas Memorial HS; E Douglas, MA; (Y); Trs Pres FHA; Yrbk Bus Mgr; Yrbk Stf; Cit Awd; High Hon Roll; Hon Roll; Csmtlgy.

SOURDIFFE, RAY; South Hadley HS; S Hadley, MA; (Y); Nwsp Rptr; Holyoke Cmnty Coll; Tv.

SOUSA, KASANDRA; Reading Memorial HS; Reading, MA; (Y); Lit Mag; High Hon Roll; Hon Roll; Ntl Merit Ltr; Ntl Latin Hnr Soc 86; 2nd Pl Annual Poetry Cntst 84; 1st Pl Annual Schl Typng Cntst 84; Simmons Coll; Bus Mgmt.

SOUSA, KIMBERLY; Academy Of Notre Dame; Westford, MA; (Y); 16/52; Girl Scts; Hosp Aide; Key Clb; Library Aide; SADD; Chorus; School Musical; Yrbk Stf; Hon Roll; Ntl Merit Ltr; YFU Stu Exchng To Japan 85; U Of MA Amherst; Speech Path.

SOUSA, LAWRENCE W; Brockton HS; Brockton, MA; (Y); 118/850; Am Leg Boys St; Drama Clb; Q&S; School Musical; School Play; Stage Crew; Nwsp Ed-Chief; Caputo Awd Outstndng Cntrbutn HS Thtr 85-86; Hawtrn Grant Excll Crtv Arts Flds 85-86; ITHACA Coll; Design.

SOUSA, MARIA; New Bedford HS; New Bedford, MA; (Y); 4/547; Key Clb; Office Aide; Yrbk Stf; Sec Stu Cncl; Var Capt Gym; DAR Awd; High Hon Roll; Pres NHS; Pres Schlr; Top Hnrs For The Stdy Of Frnch; SE Mass U; Med Tech.

SOUSA, SHELLI; Bishop Connolly HS; Fall River, MA; (Y); Ski Clb; Spanish Clb; Capt Vllybl; Big Sister; Life Grd; U MA Amherst; Cmmnctn.

SOUTHERN, MICHAEL; Tantasqua Regional HS; Alpharetta, GA; (Y); 15/174; Church Yth Grp; Intnl Clb; Varsity Clb; Yrbk Stf; Lit Mag; Var L Bsbl; Var L Socr; Hon Roll; NHS; MVP-GLDN Glv-Stwrt Awd-Ldrshp-Bsbl 86; Artst Of Yr 82, 86; Unsung Hero-Sccr; Hampshire Coll; Lbrl Arts.

SOUTHWICK JR, THOMAS E; Leicester HS; Leicester, MA; (Y); Latin Clb; Math Tm; JV Socr; JV Tennis; JV Trk; High Hon Roll; Hon Roll; NHS; Prfct Atten Awd; Sal; Worcester ST Coll.

SOUZA, BARBARA; Bellingham Memorial HS; Franklin, MA; (Y); 23/191; Yrbk Stf; Stu Cncl; High Hon Roll; Hon Roll; Jr NHS; Lion Awd; Pres NHS; Pres Acdmc Ftns Awd, Peer Cnslng, Robt M Purich Mem Schlrhsp 86; Framingham ST; Chldhood Dev.

SOUZA, DIANE; Westport HS; East Providence, RI; (Y); 19/150; Drama Clb; VP French Clb; School Play; Variety Show; JV Sftbl; Rhode Island Coll; Thtr.

SOUZA, DONNA; Old Colony Reg Vo Tech; Acushnet, MA; (Y); Ski Clb; Capt Cheerleading; Capt Pom Pon; Score Keeper; Bristol CC; Nrsng.

SOUZA, HEIDI ALCOBIA; Westport HS; Westport, MA; (Y); Pres 4-H; Ski Clb; Yrbk Stf; Var Bsktbl; 4-H Awd; Hon Roll; MA Gold Mdl Vis Presentatn 85; 6th Natl Comp Vis Presentatn 85; Burdett Coll; Acctnt.

SOUZA, ROGER; B M C Durfee HS; Fall River, MA; (Y); Spanish Clb; Varsity Clb; Var L Ftbl; Var L Ice Hcky; Var L Trk; Hon Roll; NHS; Rookie Yr Awd Ice Hcky; Boston Coll; Pre-Med.

SOUZA, VICTORIA; BMC Durfee HS; Fall River, MA; (Y); #40 In Class; French Clb; Var Trk; NHS; Accntng.

SOUZA, WADE; Partmouth HS; N Dartmouth, MA; (Y); Capt Ftbl; Trk; Wt Lftg; Springfield Coll; Phys Ed.

SOWALSKY, FRANK; Taconic HS; Pittsfield, MA; (Y); Boys Clb Am; Var Socr; Trk; Hon Roll.

SPADAFORA, LISA; Girls Catholic HS; Malden, MA; (Y); Cmnty Wkr; French Clb; Hosp Aide; Latin Clb; SADD; Pres Frsh Cls; Rep Soph Cls; Pres Jr Cls; Cit Awd; High Hon Roll; All Str Chrldr Awd 83-84; CYO Bwlng Trphs 83-84; Holycross Regis; Law.

SPADAFORA, MELISSA; Malden HS; Malden, MA; (Y); 12/450; Math Tm; Color Guard; Yrbk Stf; Hon Roll; NHS; Literary Soc 85-86; Tufts U; Child Psych.

SPADONI, CHRISTIANE; Bishop Feehan HS; Plainville, MA; (Y); Trs JCL; Chorus; Concert Band; Drm Mjr(t); Jazz Band; Mrchg Band; Swmmng; Trk; NHS; Spanish NHS; Natl Lang Arts Olympiad 84; Natl Latin Exam Maxima Cum Laude 86; New England Schlstc Hons Band 86; Political Science.

SPAGNUOLO, CHRIS; Beaver Country Day Schl; Dorchester, MA; (Y); Varsity Clb; Chorus; Nwsp Phtg; Yrbk Phtg; Yrbk Stf; Sec Jr Cls; Var L Bsbl; Var L Bsktbl; Var L Socr; Hon Roll; Biomed Engrng.

SPAGONE, MICHELLE; East Bridgewater HS; E Bridgewater, MA; (Y); Church Yth Grp; Dance Clb; GAA; Key Clb; Pep Clb; SADD; Yrbk Phtg; Yrbk Rptr; Yrbk Stf; Sec Frsh Cls; Rcgntn Awd EB Schl Cmmnty 86; Admin Awd 86; NH Coll; Bus.

SPAMPINATO, CHRIS; Natick HS; Watertown, MA; (Y); German Clb; Hon Roll; Prfct Atten Awd; Sci Aide 84-86; Military.

SPANNAGEL, CAROLE; Hingham HS; Hingham, MA; (Y); 115/346; Drama Clb; Thesps; Church Choir; Color Guard; School Musical; School Play; Stage Crew; Hon Roll; 2 Thespian Awds 85 & 86; Hon Thespian 86; S E MA U; Physical Chem.

SPARKS, DAVID; Hopedale HS; Hopedale, MA; (Y); 6/70; Church Yth Grp; SADD; Band; Chorus; Mrchg Band; Yrbk Ed-Chief; Bsktbl; Socr; High Hon Roll; NHS.

SPEIGHT, MONIQUE; B M C Durfee HS; Fall River, MA; (Y); Church Yth Grp; Drama Clb; French Clb; Chorus; Church Choir; Yrbk Stf; Durfee Vocalaires-Sec & Treas 84-86; Hmcmng Queen-Nom 86; Bristol CC; Bus Admin.

SPEILBERG, KAREN; Bourne HS; Otis Afb, MA; (Y); 4-H; Color Guard; Hon Roll; Pre Med.

SPELIOTES, ELIZABETH K; Newton North HS; W Newton, MA; (Y); Pres Intnl Clb; Capt Math Tm; Yrbk Stf; Var Capt Bsktbl; Var Capt Socr; Var Sftbl; Hon Roll; Ntl Merit Ltr; Exploring; Bk Awd Outstndng Citznshp Acad 85; Jim Short Awd Exc Math 86; Ntl Spnsh Ex 5th Pl 86; Yale U; Bio.

SPELLMAN, JOSEPH J; Shrewsbury HS; Shrewsbury, MA; (Y); 26/247; Am Leg Boys St; Letterman Clb; NFL; Stage Crew; Pres Jr Cls; Pres Sr Cls; Var L Ftbl; Var Trk; Im Wt Lftg; NHS; Schl Comm Stu Mbr-Schl Impr Comm 87; MA Bus Wk Bentley Coll 86; Acctg.

SPELMAN, JENNIFER; Marianhill C C HS; Southbridge, MA; (Y); Girl Scts; Hosp Aide; Ski Clb; School Musical; School Play; Stage Crew; Cheerleading; Sftbl; Tennis; Prsdntl Acdmc Ftnss Awd 84-85; Coaches Awd Tnns 85-86; Outstndg Achvmnt Comp 84; Elem Educ.

SPENCER, CHERYL L; The Winsor Schl; Jamaica Plain, MA; (Y); Cmnty Wkr; Drama Clb; Office Aide; SADD; Concert Band; Stage Crew; Variety Show; Yrbk Ed-Chief; JV Bsktbl; Natl Merit Schlrshp Cmmndbl Stu 85; Engl Ed.

SPENCER, KELLEY; Southwick HS; Granville, MA; (Y); 1/127; Am Leg Aux Girls St; Church Yth Grp; Drama Clb; 4-H; Hosp Aide; Quiz Bowl; Teachers Aide; Thesps; School Musical; School Play; Smith Coll Bk Awd 86; Amer Chmcl Scty Cmptv Tm 85.

SPENCER, LISA; Winchester HS; Winchester, MA; (Y); AFS; Aud/Vis; Intnl Clb; Concert Band; Mrchg Band; JV Fld Hcky; High Hon Roll; Hon Roll; 96% On Grmn Lvl 2 AATG Tst 86; Frgn Lng.

SPENCER, SHAUN; Arlington Catholic HS; Arlington, MA; (Y); 10/160; Drama Clb; JA; School Musical; School Play; Yrbk Stf; JV Ftbl; Hon Roll; NHS; Gold Mdl Natl Latin Exam 84-85; Chancellors Tltn Awd 86; Bus Adm.

SPIEWAK, BRIAN; Pittsfield HS; Pittsfield, MA; (Y); Boy Scts; Church Yth Grp; Exploring; Latin Clb; Var Golf; Gym; Engr.

SPINDLER, BRIAN; Somerville HS; Somerville, MA; (Y); 61/576; Boys Clb Am; Computer Clb; High Hon Roll; Hon Roll; 1st Pl Annl Comp Cont 85; 2nd Pl Annl Comp Cont 84; Comp Sci Awd Of Excllnc 86; Comp Engrng.

SPIRO, MICHAEL D; Norwood SR HS; Norwood, MA; (Y); 67/210; Am Leg Boys St; Aud/Vis; Boy Scts; Camera Clb; CAP; English Clb; Math Tm; Temple Yth Grp; Band; Nwsp Rptr; Bike Ride Multiple Sclrs 84; Sci Achvt Awd 84; Physics Extension Course 86; Mc Gill U; Physics.

SPRINGER, JULIE CHRISTINE; Shepherd Hill Regional HS; Dudley, MA; (Y); 4/133; Drama Clb; Math Tm; Mrchg Band; Yrbk Ed-Chief; Yrbk Stf; Twrlr; High Hon Roll; NHS; Webster Dudley Amer Legion Schl Awd 86; Boston U; Biomed.

SQUILLANTE, SHERI; Mount Alvernia HS; West Roxbury, MA; (Y); Church Yth Grp; Girl Scts; Teachers Aide; Color Guard; Variety Show; JV Bsktbl; Var Swmmng; JV Vllybl; Best Effort Awd 84; Salve Regina; Ed.

SQUIRE, AMY; Nauset Regional HS; Brewster, MA; (Y); 5/120; Trs Am Leg Aux Girls St; Varsity Clb; Off Soph Cls; Sec Jr Cls; Sec Sr Cls; Trs Stu Cncl; Var Capt Fld Hcky; Trk; Hon Roll; NHS; All Star Plyr Fld Hcky 85 & 86, Trk 86; Boston Coll.

SQUIRES, DEBRA A; Plymouth-Carver HS; Plymouth, MA; (Y); Church Yth Grp; Drama Clb; GAA; SADD; School Play; Yrbk Stf; Var L Bsktbl; Var L Sftbl; Var L Trk; High Hon Roll.

SROCZINSKI, AMI; Shepherd Hill HS; Dudley, MA; (Y); Chorus; Yrbk Bus Mgr; Yrbk Stf; Var Socr; Co-Capt Trk; All ST Awds Trck 86; Soc Wrker.

SROCZYNSKI, MICHAEL; Taunton HS; Taunton, MA; (Y); 18/400; Ski Clb; SADD; Varsity Clb; Yrbk Bus Mgr; Yrbk Stf; Rep Stu Cncl; Var Bsbl; JV Bsktbl; Var Golf; Var Trk; Bus.

ST AMOUR, ANTHONY; Bedford HS; Bedford, MA; (Y); 18/198; Church Yth Grp; Cmnty Wkr; Im Lcrss; Im Socr; JV Trk; High Hon Roll; Hon Roll; NHS; Ntl Merit SF; Engrg.

ST AMOUR, PAUL; Bedford HS; Bedford, MA; (Y); 36/201; Am Leg Boys St; Boy Scts; Church Yth Grp; Exploring; Var Lcrss; Var Socr; Hon Roll; Army ROTC 3 Yr Schlrshp; Rutgers U; Engr.

ST DENIS, CHRISTIE; Hoosac Valley HS; Adams, MA; (Y); 29/150; Camera Clb; Pep Clb; School Play; Yrbk Stf; Var Capt Cheerleading; Trk; Hon Roll; NHS.

ST HILAIRE, ELIZABETH J; Westfield HS; Westfield, MA; (Y); 31/327; Art Clb; CAP; Drama Clb; GAA; PAVAS; Orch; School Play; Stage Crew; Cit Awd; NHS; MA Commonwealth Schlrshp 86; Wakefield HS Cls 63 86; Westfield Womens Clb Excllnce Art 86; Syracuse U; Advrtsng.

ST JOHN, LAURA; Marianhill CCHS HS; Spencer, MA; (Y); Church Yth Grp; Drama Clb; Hosp Aide; Chorus; School Musical; Ed Nwsp Stf; Ed Yrbk Stf; Var Cheerleading; Crs Cntry.

ST LAURENT, HENRY; Tantasqua Regional HS; Sturbridge, MA; (Y); 15/149; Am Leg Boys St; School Musical; School Play; Trs Soph Cls; Off Stu Cncl; Var L Crs Cntry; Var L Tennis; Hon Roll; NHS; Ntl Merit Ltr; Religion.

ST LOUIS, DONNA; St Bernards Central Catholic HS; Fitchburg, MA; (S); 7/159; Cmnty Wkr; Sec Latin Clb; Library Aide; School Musical; Nwsp Stf; Fld Hcky; Mgr(s); High Hon Roll; NHS; MVP Trck & Fild Var Ltrs; Class I ST And Regnl Gym; CMC All Conf Tm Trk And Fld; U Of Lowell; Phys Thrpy.

ST ONGE, KIM; Apponequet Regional HS; E Freetown, MA; (Y); 14/220; Cmnty Wkr; Office Aide; Hon Roll; NHS; Schltc Awd 84; Lakeville Eagles Schlrshp 86; Pocksha Canine Clb Schlrshp 86; Mount Ida Coll; Vet Tech.

ST PIERRE, JAMES F; Attleboro HS; South Attleboro, MA; (Y); 20/402; Am Leg Boys St; Cmnty Wkr; Rep Jr Cls; Pres Stu Cncl; Var Socr; Var Trk; DAR Awd; High Hon Roll; Hon Roll; NHS; Century III Ldrshp Awd Runner-Up 86; 2nd Statewide Wrtng Cntst 85; Vanderbilt U; Bio.

ST PIERRE, KALA; Weymouth North HS; Weymouth, MA; (Y); Dance Clb; GAA; JA; PAVAS; Stage Crew; Variety Show; Yrbk Stf; Cheerleading; High Hon Roll; Hon Roll; 2 Cert Rcgntn Hlth 85; Cert Rcgntn Soc Stds 86; U NC; Lbrl Arts.

ST PIERRE, LORI; Chicopee Comprehensive HS; Chicopee, MA; (Y); #27 In Class; Church Yth Grp; German Clb; Ski Clb; VP Frsh Cls; Rep Soph Cls; Rep Jr Cls; JV Socr; JV Sftbl; 4-H Awd; Hon Roll.

ST PIERRE, MICHELLE; Somerville HS; Somerville, MA; (Y); 49/550; Dance Clb; Trs French Clb; SADD; Yrbk Ed-Chief; Yrbk Stf; Rep Soph Cls; Rep Jr Cls.

ST PIERRE, PATRICIA ANN; Salem HS; Salem, MA; (Y); 25/265; Drama Clb; Chorus; School Musical; School Play; CC Awd; High Hon Roll; Hon Roll; NHS; Pop Rock Chorus Awd 86; Drama Awd 86.

ST PIERRE, THOMAS R; Fitchburg HS; Fitchburg, MA; (Y); 14/230; Am Leg Boys St; Golf; Trk; High Hon Roll; Aeronautical Engrng.

STACEY, AMY ELIZABETH; Hampshire Regional HS; Westhampton, MA; (Y); SADD; Yrbk Stf; Rep Stu Cncl; VP Cheerleading; Var Mgr(s); Var Sftbl; Office Aide; Ski Clb; Rep Frsh Cls; Stu Advsry Comm 85-87; ST Stu Advsry Cncl Rep Alt To Boston & Western MA 86-87; Early Chldhd.

STACHOWICZ, LINDA; Ware HS; Ware, MA; (Y); 8/112; Color Guard; Lit Mag; Stu Cncl; Var Capt Socr; Hon Roll; Excllnce Awd Spn 2 85, Spn 3 86; Cmmnctns.

STACHOWSKI, KIM; Woburn HS; Woburn, MA; (S); 43/453; Church Yth Grp; Drama Clb; Leo Clb; Ski Clb; Spanish Clb; School Play; Yrbk Stf; High Hon Roll; Hon Roll; NHS; St Michaels Coll; Mrktng.

STACK, ROSEMARIE; Agawam HS; Agawam, MA; (Y); Hosp Aide; Spanish Clb; Nwsp Stf; Lit Mag; JV Cheerleading; Var Trk; High Hon Roll; Hon Roll; Amer Lgn Oratrcl Cont Lcl & ST 85; Forgn Lang Wk Poetry Wrtng Cont 86; Westfield ST Coll; Elem Ed.

STAFFORD, ANDREA; Turners Falls HS; Millers Fls, MA; (Y); 4/91; Trs Spanish Clb; Varsity Clb; Yrbk Sprt Ed; Var Bsktbl; Var Trk; Var Vllybl; High Hon Roll; Hon Roll; Jr NHS; NHS; Smith Coll Bk Awd 86; Acad Excllnc Comp Sci 86; Excllnc Advncd Chem 86; Comp.

STALEY, VICTORIA A; Nashoba Regional HS; Easton, PA; (Y); 9/178; Church Yth Grp; Drama Clb; Ski Clb; SADD; Thesps; Band; School Musical; Stage Crew; High Hon Roll; NHS; Comptv Figure Sktng 9 Yrs; Lafayette Coll; Econmcs.

STANCO, MICHAEL C; Ralph C Mahar Regional HS; Orange, MA; (Y); 57/126; Am Leg Boys St; Key Clb; Model UN; Var Ftbl; Var Trk; Boy Scts; Cmnty Wkr; Exploring; Library Aide; JV Bsktbl; ST Rep Boys ST 86; Bus.

STANEK, LYNN; Holyoke Catholic HS; Holyoke, MA; (Y); Art Clb; Computer Clb; Drama Clb; Spanish Clb; SADD; Lit Mag; Trs Stu Cncl; Var Cheerleading.

STANFA, CHRIS; Bishop Feehan HS; Mansfield, MA; (Y); Debate Tm; Drama Clb; School Musical; School Play; Stage Crew; High Hon Roll; Hon Roll; U Of Hartford; Music.

STANIUL, MARK; Austin Preparatory Sahl; Reading, MA; (Y); Cmnty Wkr; Red Cross Aide; Spanish Clb; Varsity Clb; Yrbk Stf; Off Jr Cls; Off Sr Cls; Stu Cncl; Ftbl; Sftbl; Spnsh Clb Pres 85-86; Stu Cncl Awd 86; Holy Cross.

STANLEY, MAUREEN; Notre Dame Acad; Hanover, MA; (Y); 40/120; Church Yth Grp; Debate Tm; French Clb; Ski Clb; Varsity Clb; Stage Crew; Var Capt Crs Cntry; Var Trk; Hon Roll; Bonne Bell Cert Excllnce Crs Cntry 86; Tufts U; Phys Thrpy.

STANLEY, SCOTT; Danvers HS; Danvers, MA; (Y); 56/286; Im JV Bsktbl; Im Ftbl; Hon Roll; NHS; Prfct Atten Awd; Bio.

STANNARD, SHAUN; Taconic HS; Pittsfield, MA; (Y); Varsity Clb; Im Badmtn; Var Bsbl; Var Bsktbl; Im Ftbl; VP Capt Socr; Im Vllybl; All Sthrn Brkshr 1st Team 85; Physcl Ed.

STAPLES, CHRISTOPHER S D; Haverhill HS; Haverhill, MA; (Y); FTA; Ski Clb; Stu Cncl Awd Outstndng Skier 83-84; Var Ltr Skiing 84-86; Var Capt Skiing 86-87; Parks Mgmt.

STARBLE, MARY ELLEN; St Clement HS; Somerville, MA; (Y); Art Clb; Cmnty Wkr; School Play; Yrbk Stf; Cheerleading; Pom Pon; NHS; Prfct Atten Awd; Hghst Avg Religion; Vet Sci.

STARR, ERICK; Assabet Valley Vo; Hudson, MA; (Y); 3/400; Ski Clb; Var Capt Ftbl; Var Trk; Im Wt Lftg; Im Wrstlng; Hon Roll; NHS; Prfct Atten Awd.

STARR, JONATHAN; Marblehead HS; Marblehead, MA; (Y); 17/259; Drama Clb; Thesps; Chorus; Concert Band; Mrchg Band; School Play; Ed Yrbk Phtg; High Hon Roll; Hon Roll; NHS; Med.

STARVASKI, AMY; St Peter-Marian HS; Worcester, MA; (Y); 24/180; Church Yth Grp; Hosp Aide; Spanish Clb; School Musical; Stage Crew; Yrbk Stf; Hon Roll.

STATHIS, ANDREW W; Brockton HS; Brockton, MA; (Y); Nwsp Stf; High Hon Roll; Pres Schlr; Genrl Cnslt Fedrl Rpblc Germany Excnc Study Grmn Awd; Emerson Coll; Mass Comm.

STAUB, LARA; Lawrence Acad; Groton, MA; (Y); Teachers Aide; Chorus; School Musical; Stu Cncl; Var Fld Hcky; Vllybl; High Hon Roll; Engl Awd 84; Brown U Engl Awd 86; Cum Laud 86; Engl Awd-Wrtng 86; Ntl Rltns.

STAWASZ, DAVID; S Hadley HS; S Hadley, MA; (Y); 4/171; Church Yth Grp; Quiz Bowl; Nwsp Rptr; Nwsp Stf; Yrbk Rptr; Yrbk Stf; Frsh Cls; Soph Cls; Jr Cls; Bsktbl; Holy Cross Bk Awd 86; Comm.

STEARNS, CARL; Cathedral HS; Longmeadow, MA; (Y); Boy Scts; Political Wkr; Var L Wrstlng; Hon Roll; Elec Engnrng.

STEARNS, LORI; Hudson Catholic HS; Marlboro, MA; (Y); 3/67; Spanish Clb; Lit Mag; Cheerleading; Mgr Trk; High Hon Roll; NHS; Spanish NHS; Pres Acdmc Ftns Awd 86; MA Cmnwlth Schlrshp 86; Bstn Coll; Pltcl Sci.

STEBBINS, KRISTEN; Notre Dame Acad; Scituate, MA; (Y); Camp Fr Inc; Dance Clb; Debate Tm; Ski Clb; Spanish Clb; Chorus; JV Cheerleading; Diving; Var Gym; Swmmng; Mc Donough Cup Awd-Outstndg Merit, Sprtsmnshp 85; Vrsty Lttrs-Gym & Trck 85; 3rd Fastst Rec 330 Hrdls; Sclgy.

STEELE, ANDY; Acton-Boxborough Reg HS; Boxboro, MA; (Y); 60/406; Ski Clb; Varsity Clb; Stage Crew; Variety Show; Yrbk Phtg; Capt Crs Cntry; Capt Socr; Trk; Hon Roll; Sec NHS; Coch Litl Leag Bsbl 86; Bus.

STEELE, MARK; Concord-Carlisle HS; Concord, MA; (Y); 40/330; Radio Clb; SADD; Jazz Band; Variety Show; Nwsp Rptr; Rep Jr Cls; Pres Stu Cncl; Var Socr; NHS; Model UN; Clrk U Mdl UN Outstndng Dlgt 86.

STEEN, SANDRA; Bancroft Schl; Southbridge, MA; (Y); Pres Art Clb; Camera Clb; Church Yth Grp; Science Clb; Yrbk Phtg; Yrbk Stf; High Hon Roll; Hon Roll; Ntl Merit Ltr; Cum Laud Socty 86; Harvard Bk Prz 86; Creatv Wrtng Awd 85 & 86.

STEENBRUGGEN, JOHN; Marlboro HS; Marlboro, MA; (Y); AFS; Computer Clb; JA; Science Clb; High Hon Roll; Hon Roll; Worcester Polytech Inst; Comp.

STEFANIK, AUDRA; Westfield HS; Westfield, MA; (Y); 40/357; Boys Clb Am; Church Yth Grp; GAA; JA; Spanish Clb; Varsity Clb; Yrbk Bus Mgr; Rep Frsh Cls; Rep Soph Cls; Rep Jr Cls; Mst Vlbl Swmr 84-85; Syracuse U; Educ.

STEFANIK, STEPHEN; Chicopee Comprehensive HS; Chicopee, MA; (Y); 7/285; German Clb; Orch; Hon Roll; Jr NHS; Germn Lang Awd 84; Engrng.

STEIN, JONATHAN; North Quincy HS; Quincy, MA; (Y); #2 In Class; Boy Scts; Computer Clb; Exploring; Quiz Bowl; Science Clb; Sec Spanish Clb; Temple Yth Grp; Band; Concert Band; Mrchg Band; Suffolk Coll Bk Awd 86; Hnrb Mntn Sci Fair 85; Awd In Math Thru Sci Fair 86; FL Inst Of Tech; Elec Engrng.

STEINBERG, SARAJANE; Swampscott HS; Swampscott, MA; (Y); 7/230; Cmnty Wkr; Model UN; Nwsp Stf; Lit Mag.

STELLER, LAURIE; Malden HS; Malden, MA; (Y); 26/500; Dance Clb; Hosp Aide; Trs Science Clb; Pres Temple Yth Grp; Variety Show; Yrbk Rptr; Hon Roll.

STEPHEN, ROBERT J; Melrose HS; Melrose, MA; (Y); 21/300; Aud/Vis; Computer Clb; Hon Roll; Comp Sci.

STEPHENS, CHRISTOPHER J; Groton Schl; New York, NY; (Y); Off Debate Tm; Drama Clb; VP Church Choir; Madrigals; School Musical; School Play; Ed Lit Mag; Rep Stu Cncl; VP Mgr Socr; Ntl Merit SF; Law.

STEPHENS, TRACY; Danvers HS; Danvers, MA; (Y); Rep Jr Cls; Rep Sr Cls; Hon Roll; NHS; MA ST Schlrshp 86; N Adams ST Coll.

STEPHENSON, TENELY; Milton Acad; Westwood, MA; (Y); GAA; Latin Clb; Political Wkr; School Play; Yrbk Phtg; Var Bsktbl; Var Lcrss; Var Capt Socr; Mod Lang.

STERCZALA, BETH; Bartlett HS; Webster, MA; (Y); 1/152; Science Clb; Spanish Clb; Nwsp Rptr; Ed Yrbk Stf; Capt Tennis; Bausch & Lomb Sci Awd; Elks Awd; Pres NHS; St Schlr; Val; 1st Pl St Sci Fair 86; Frances Burns Schlrshp 86; Worcester Telegram/Gazette Stu Ach Awd 86; Worcesterh Poly Tech; Pre-Med.

STERLING, IAN WAYNE; Noble & Greenough Schl; Hopkinton, MA; (Y); Civic Clb; Acpl Chr; Chorus; School Musical; Variety Show; Nwsp Bus Mgr; Nwsp Stf; JV Socr; High Hon Roll; NHS; New England Tel Minority Mgmt Schlrshp 86; The Girl Frnds Schlrshp Awd 86; Russel B Sterns Awd 86; Harvard Coll; Business.

STERN, DONNA; Hopkins Acad; Hadley, MA; (Y); French Clb; Chorus; Concert Band; Mrchg Band; Pep Band; Yrbk Phtg; Yrbk Stf; Off Sr Cls; Stu Cncl; Var Stat Bsktbl; Bates Coll.

STERNICK, JEFFREY R; Needham HS; Needham, MA; (Y); AFS; Am Leg Boys St; German Clb; Temple Yth Grp; Band; Jazz Band; Bus.

STETSON, MELISSA; Frontier Regional HS; S Deerfield, MA; (Y); French Clb; FBLA; GAA; Var Capt Sftbl; High Hon Roll; Hon Roll; Rnr-Up Hmcmng Qn 85; Rnr-Up Prm Qn 86; Bentley Coll; Mrktng.

STEVENS, KAREN; Waltham HS; Waltham, MA; (Y); Yrbk Rptr; Var Cheerleading; Hon Roll; 2nd Pl Kingsbury Temprnc Soc Essay Cntst 85-86; Smmr Sessn Boston Coll 85-86; Boston Coll; Ecnmst.

STEVENS, LISA; Foxboro HS; Foxboro, MA; (Y); 18/236; Church Yth Grp; French Clb; JA; Key Clb; Ski Clb; SADD; Varsity Clb; Yrbk Ed-Chief; Rep Frsh Cls; VP Soph Cls; Simmons; Physcl Thrpy.

STEVENS, SHANON; Marlboro HS; Marlboro, MA; (Y); 52/250; Church Yth Grp; Radio Clb; Science Clb; SADD; Yrbk Stf; High Hon Roll; Hon Roll; Fclty Achvt Awd In Amer Govt 84; Wheaton Coll; Ed.

STEVENSON, ROBERT A G; Concord-Carlisle R HS; Carlisle, MA; (Y); 28/328; Boy Scts; Jazz Band; Trs Mrchg Band; VP Symp Band; Ftbl; JV Lcrss; Var L Wrstlng; High Hon Roll; NHS; NE MA SR Dist Music Fest 85-86.

STEWART, JILL L; Lunenburg HS; Lunenburg, MA; (Y); 14/123; SADD; Sec Chorus; Rep Frsh Cls; Rep Soph Cls; Sec Jr Cls; Sec Sr Cls; Var Capt Bsktbl; High Hon Roll; NHS; Pres Schlr; Grvr C Brny Sr Stu Athlt Mem Awd 86; Army Rsrv Awd Ntl Schlr Athlt 86; All Trnmnt Team MVP 85; Ftchburg ST Coll; Chldhd Educ.

STGEORGE, SHERYL; Attleboro HS; S Attleboro, MA; (Y); Varsity Clb; Chorus; Var Capt Gym; High Hon Roll; Hon Roll; Engl Awd 86; Costins; Hrdrssr Csmtlgst.

STIFFLER, KIM; Taconic HS; Pittsfield, MA; (Y); Church Yth Grp; Hosp Aide; Pep Clb; SADD; Chorus; Rep Soph Cls; Var Cheerleading; Im Gym; JV Socr; Var Sftbl.

STILLWELL, TITIA; Mario Umaria Tech; Roxbury, MA; (Y); Church Yth Grp; JA; Church Choir; Rep Stu Cncl; JV Trk; Hon Roll; Jr NHS; NHS; Prfct Atten Awd; Pre-Med.

STIRES, CHRISTINE; Acton-Boxborough Regional HS; Acton, MA; (Y); 34/347; Church Yth Grp; Spanish Clb; High Hon Roll; Hon Roll; NHS; Spanish NHS; Yng Wmhd Rcgntn 86; Fll Titn Schrlshp BYU 86; Ldrshp Frgn Lng Actvts Awd 86; BYU; Spnsh.

STJEAN, LAURIE; Methuen HS; Methuen, MA; (Y); FBLA; Intnl Clb; SADD; Yrbk Stf; Fld Hcky; Sftbl; U Of Lowell; Crmnl Jstc.

STOCHAJ, KATIE; Shepherd Hill Regional HS; Dudley, MA; (Y); Band; Trs Frsh Cls; Trs Soph Cls; Trs Jr Cls; Trs Sr Cls; Stu Cncl; Var L Bsktbl; Var L Fld Hcky; Var L Trk; Hon Roll; Outstndng Def Plyr 86; Bay ST Games Tm 86; Cntrl MA JR Olympc Bsktbll 86; Sec Educ.

STOCKBRIDGE, LORI; Wilmington HS; Wilmington, MA; (Y); French Clb; JV Trk; Hon Roll; Psychlgy.

STOCKWELL, JASON; King Philips Regnl HS; Plinville, MA; (Y); 11/227; School Play; Trs Sr Cls; Var L Bsktbl; Coach Actv; JV Golf; Im Wt Lftg; High Hon Roll; NHS; Fish-Wldlf Mgmt.

STOEHR, MARNA; Dennis-Yarmouth Regional HS; S Dennis, MA; (Y); 14/309; FCA; Girl Scts; Sec Stu Cncl; Elks Awd; Kiwanis Awd; NHS; Political Wkr; Church Choir; Orch; Cngrssnl Pg U S Hs Of Reps 84-85; Gld Awd 86; Ottwy Nwspaper Schlrshp 86; Mt Holyoke Coll; Lbrl Arts.

STOKLAS, BARBARA; St Marys HS; Lynn, MA; (Y); 6/92; School Musical; Stage Crew; Capt Vllybl; Hon Roll; NHS; Pre-Law.

STOMSKI, DAVID BRUCE; Lenox Memorial HS; Lenox, MA; (Y); 5/55; Nwsp Ed-Chief; Yrbk Bus Mgr; Pres Stu Cncl; High Hon Roll; Pres Schlr; Boy Scts; Drama Clb; Exploring; Political Wkr; School Play; Cornell Natl Schlr Awd 86; Cornell U; Govt.

STONE, CARRIE; Westfield HS; Westfield, MA; (Y); Acctng.

STONE, DANIEL; Malden HS; Malden, MA; (Y); 44/450; Drama Clb; 4-H; French Clb; Key Clb; PAVAS; Scholastic Bowl; Spanish Clb; SADD; Teachers Aide; Temple Yth Grp; Tufts U Mgc Cir Theatre 81-83; Emerson Coll Yth Theatre 84-86; Nrthwstrn; Theater.

STONE, LORI; Natick HS; Natick, MA; (Y); Hosp Aide; Pep Clb; Spanish Clb; SADD; JV Tennis; Wellesley Coll; Nrsng.

STONE, VICTORIA; Belmont HS; Belmont, MA; (Y); Church Yth Grp; Civic Clb; JA; Acpl Chr; Chorus; Var JV Fld Hcky; Var JV Trk; Geothe Inst Awd Germn 84 & 86; Lib Arts.

STOREY, JOHN; North Reading HS; N Reading, MA; (Y); Nwsp Ed-Chief; Nwsp Rptr; Comp Sci.

STORM, AMY; Gardner HS; Gardner, MA; (Y); Spanish Clb; Score Keeper; Trk; Hon Roll; U Of RI; Anml Sci.

STRACCIA, PASQUALE; Boston College HS; Roslindale, MA; (Y); SADD; Rep Jr Cls; Rep Stu Cncl; JV Swmmng; Im Vllybl; Hon Roll; JR Sons Itly Amer Pres 85; Law.

STRACHOTA, DAN; Greenfield HS; Greenfield, MA; (Y); 4/153; Var Capt Bsktbl; JV Socr; Var L Tennis; Var L Trk; High Hon Roll; NHS; Pres Schlr; Natl Schlr Atht Awd; All-Wstrn MA Bsktbl Tm; Colby Bk Awd; Wooster Coll.

STRAND, KRISTIN; Burncoat SR HS; Scarborough, ME; (Y); Cmnty Wkr; Office Aide; SADD; Hon Roll.

STRASSEL, DAVID; Plymouth-Carver HS; Plymouth, MA; (Y); 165/528; Boy Scts; Church Yth Grp; Cmnty Wkr; Band; Concert Band; Mrchg Band; Im Badmtn; Cit Awd; God Cntry Awd; VIP For Twn Of Plymouth 85; MA St Senate Citation 85; MA Hse Of Rep Citation 85; FL Inst Of Tech; Marine Bio.

STRAZZULLO, LESLIE; Winchester HS; Winchester, MA; (Y); Church Yth Grp; Cmnty Wkr; Spanish Clb; SADD; Sec Sr Cls; Stu Cncl; Capt Var Socr; Trk; High Hon Roll; Hon Roll; Bus.

STRIMLING, JONATHAN M; Weston HS; Weston, MA; (Y); SADD; Temple Yth Grp; Chorus; Orch; JV Socr; L Swmmng; L Trk; High Hon Roll; NHS; Ntl Merit SF; Rensslr Mdl 85; Strtgc Plnnr.

STROHL, HEATHER; King Philip HS; Norfolk, MA; (Y); Chrmn Church Yth Grp; Band; Church Choir; Concert Band; Mrchg Band; JV Tennis; Hon Roll; NHS; Pre-Med.

STROM, CHERYLANN; Fanning Trade HS; Wrocester, MA; (Y); 47/124; SADD; Jr NHS; Csmtlgst.

STROM, SHANNON; Agawam HS; Feeding Hills, MA; (Y); 4-H; OEA; Ski Clb; SADD; Chorus; Hon Roll; Typng Awd 86; Gregg Shrthnd Thry Tst Awd 86; Bus.

STROUT, CYNTHIA; South High Comm; Worcester, MA; (Y); 6/200; Church Yth Grp; Tennis; Hon Roll; Kiwanis Awd; NHS; Spanish NHS; Charles F Daly Awd 86; Outstndng Excllnce In Engl & Spn 86; Pres Acdmc Ftnss Awd 86; U MA Amherst; Lib Arts.

STROUT, MATTHEW; Auburn HS; Auburn, MA; (Y); Am Leg Boys St; Var Ice Hcky; High Hon Roll; Hon Roll; Jr NHS; NHS; Mrn Bio.

STUFFLEBEAM, JULIE; Marshfield HS; Marshfield, MA; (Y); 36/365; Drama Clb; SADD; Teachers Aide; Band; Mrchg Band; Symp Band; Yrbk Stf; Hon Roll; NHS; Prfct Atten Awd; New Hampshire U; Bus Adm.

STUGER, NICOLA; Boston Technical HS; Roxbury, MA; (Y); Church Yth Grp; Chorus; Church Choir; Yrbk Stf; Var Bsktbl; Bsktbl Awd 86; Bus Mngmt.

STUKULS, DEREK; Concord Carlisle Regional HS; Concord, MA; (Y); 73/328; Boy Scts; Lit Mag; Var Crs Cntry; Im Tennis; Trk; Art.

SUJDAK, ANDREW J; Athol HS; Athol, MA; (Y); Am Leg Boys St; Model UN; Band; Chorus; Concert Band; Jazz Band; School Musical; Stage Crew; Variety Show; Cntrl Dist Chorus; Mus.

SUJDAK, ANDY; Athol HS; Athol, MA; (Y); Am Leg Boys St; Drama Clb; PAVAS; SADD; Band; Chorus; Jazz Band; School Musical; School Play; Variety Show; Berklee Coll Music; Music.

SULFARO JR, DOMENIC; St Dominic Savio HS; S Boston, MA; (Y); 16/92; Ski Clb; Lit Mag; High Hon Roll; Hon Roll; NHS; Church Yth Grp; Pres Jr Cls; Rep Stu Cncl; Var Bsbl; Var Trk; Northeastern U; Bus.

SULLIVAN, BETH; Arlington Catholic HS; Waltham, MA; (Y); Church Yth Grp; Cmnty Wkr; JA; Office Aide; Spanish Clb; Nwsp Rptr; Yrbk Stf; Crs Cntry; Trk; Ntl Merit Schol; Acdmc Schlrshp 86; Merrimack Coll; Cmnctns.

SULLIVAN, BRADFORD; Apponequet Regional HS; Lakeville, MA; (Y); Pres Band; Pres Concert Band; Pres Jazz Band; Mrchg Band; Pres Symp Band; Yrbk Rptr; Ed Yrbk Stf; JV Bsbl; Var Swmmng; Hon Roll; Outstndg Musicnshp Awd Natl Assn Jazz Educ 86; Bryant Coll; CPA.

SULLIVAN, CHRISTINE; Matignon HS; Malden, MA; (S); 26/178; Church Yth Grp; Drama Clb; SADD; Chorus; School Musical; Yrbk Ed-Chief; Var L Swmmng; NHS; Spanish NHS; Providence Coll; Forgn Lang.

SULLIVAN, COLLEEN; Bishop Connolly HS; Westport, MA; (Y); 60/160; Sec Latin Clb; Trs Ski Clb; Var Capt Crs Cntry; High Hon Roll; Hon Roll; Lbrl Arts.

SULLIVAN, COLLEEN; Seekonk HS; Seekonk, MA; (Y); 22/240; School Play; Stage Crew; Yrbk Stf; Pres Frsh Cls; Pres Soph Cls; Rep Jr Cls; Rep Sr Cls; Stu Cncl; High Hon Roll; Hon Roll; Schrlshp Millikin U 83; Comm.

SULLIVAN, ELIZABETH; Bishop Freehan HS; Foxboro, MA; (Y); Drama Clb; Girl Scts; Spanish Clb; SADD; Nwsp Stf; Yrbk Stf; Lit Mag; Stu Cncl; Bsktbl; Swmmng; NEI Engl Awd 86.

SULLIVAN, ERIN; Notre Dame Acad; Dedham, MA; (Y); Debate Tm; Office Aide; Stage Crew; Trk; St Michaels; Pre Med.

SULLIVAN, EVAN; Burlington HS; Burlington, MA; (Y); 27/314; Computer Clb; VP JA; Math Tm; SADD; JV Lcrss; High Hon Roll; NHS; Acdmc Excllnce In Math 85-86.

SULLIVAN, JAMES; Westwood HS; Westwood, MA; (Y); 16/216; CAP; Off Exploring; Math Tm; Hon Roll; NHS; Drftng Awd; Elec Engr.

SULLIVAN, JOANNE; Holy Name CC HS; N Grafton, MA; (Y); 25/250; Ski Clb; Sec Church Yth Grp; VP Jr Cls; Rep Sr Cls; Stu Cncl; High Hon Roll; Hon Roll; NHS; Amer Lit Achvt Awd; Comp Pgmng Achvt Awd; Bus Princpls/Mgmt Awd; Bryant Coll; Acctg.

SULLIVAN, KAREN; Medfield HS; Medfield, MA; (Y); Church Yth Grp; VP Intnl Clb; Natl Beta Clb; VP Spanish Clb; VP Frsh Cls; Rep Stu Cncl; Capt Cheerleading; High Hon Roll; Jr NHS; NHS; Coaches Awd Chrldng; Outstndg Frshmn Awd.

SULLIVAN, KATHLEEN; Arlington Catholic HS; Medford, MA; (Y); 26/149; Hosp Aide; Spanish Clb; Variety Show; Nwsp Rptr; Nwsp Stf; Var L Bsktbl; Var L Trk; Hon Roll; NHS; Nrsng.

SULLIVAN, KELLY; Lenox Memorial HS; Lenox, MA; (Y); Church Yth Grp; Drama Clb; Library Aide; School Play; Stage Crew; Yrbk Stf; Hon Roll; Kiwanis Awd; NHS; MA ST Scholar 86; N Adams ST Coll Merit Waiver 86; Berkshire Cnty Chptr Ins Wmn Scholar 86; N Adams ST Coll; Acctng.

SULLIVAN, KERRI; Doherty Memorial HS; Worcester, MA; (Y); Pres Drama Clb; Hosp Aide; Ski Clb; SADD; School Musical; Variety Show; Tennis; High Hon Roll; Hon Roll; NHS; Career Day Worcester Essy Cont 86; Highest Scorer In City Wide Standardized Span Exam 85; Business.

SULLIVAN, KEVIN; Bishop Feehan HS; Foxboro, MA; (Y); Golf; Ice Hcky; Wt Lftg; High Hon Roll; Hon Roll; IUEC Lcl 4 Soc Actn Comm Awd 86; Merrimach Coll; News Brdcstng.

SULLIVAN, KEVIN; Marion HS; Natick, MA; (Y); Var Capt Ftbl; Var Capt Trk; Hon Roll; Natl AP Trm Paper Part Awd 87; Cmp Cnslr 87; Scholar Catholic Archdiocese 87; Holy Cross U; Lib Art.

SULLIVAN, LAURA; Danvers HS; Danvers, MA; (Y); 2/268; Church Yth Grp; Chorus; Yrbk Stf; Var Capt Fld Hcky; Var L Sftbl; Var L Trk; NHS; Sal; Var Capt Bsktbl; Stu Ldr; Ntl Hon Soc Tutr; Brown U.

SULLIVAN, MARIE; Malden HS; Malden, MA; (Y); 47/500; Key Clb; Pep Clb; Band; Variety Show; Rep Frsh Cls; Rep Soph Cls; Rep Jr Cls; Rep Sr Cls; Cheerleading; Hon Roll; U NH; Htl Mgmt.

SULLIVAN, MARIE; Monument Mountain Regional HS; Gt Barrington, MA; (Y); Cmnty Wkr; Stage Crew; Hon Roll; Cert Achvmnt Vlntr Nrsng Hm 86; Treas Cmmnty Yth Grp 86; Edtr Yth Nwslttr 86; Psych.

SULLIVAN, MARK; Cathedral HS; W Springfld, MA; (Y); SADD; Var L Crs Cntry; Var L Trk; Hon Roll; Rotary Awd; Worcester Poly Tech; Chem Engrg.

SULLIVAN, MAURA; Newburyport HS; Newburyport, MA; (S); 22/191; JCL; Math Tm; Model UN; Q&S; Chorus; Nwsp Ed-Chief; Lit Mag; Hon Roll; NCTE Awd; NHS; Brnz Key Awd 85; Natl Jrnlsm Awd 85.

SULLIVAN, MICHAEL; Westfield HS; Westfield, MA; (Y); Band; Jazz Band; Mrchg Band; Nwsp Phtg; JV Var Lcrss; JV Var Socr; Im Vllybl; Pan MA Challnge Jimmy Fnd-Dana Farber Cancer Inst 86.

SULLIVAN, NANCY; Marshfield HS; Marshfield, MA; (Y); 30/380; Am Leg Aux Girls St; Key Clb; Rep Stu Cncl; Var Capt Bsktbl; Var Capt Crs Cntry; Var Capt Trk; Hon Roll; NHS; Jr NHS; All Schlstc Cross Cty 83-85; All Schlstc Track 85; All Star Bsktbl 86.

SULLIVAN, PATRICIA; Cathedral HS; Springfield, MA; (Y); 105/535; Church Yth Grp; Cmnty Wkr; Intnl Clb; Office Aide; Stat Bsktbl; Mgr(s); Im Socr; Im Sftbl; Physcl Thrpy.

SULLIVAN, PATRICIA; Marian HS; Southboro, MA; (Y); 46/183; Drama Clb; School Musical; Lit Mag; JV Socr; Hon Roll; NEDT Awd; Psychlgy.

SULLIVAN, RACHEL; Plymouth-Carver HS; Carver, MA; (Y); Art Clb; Church Yth Grp; French Clb; Variety Show; Lit Mag; Cheerleading; Swmmng; Tennis; French Hon Soc; Hon Roll; Fnlst In 17 Mag Cover Modl Cont 85; Nutcracker With The Boston Ballet 80 & 84; Teach CCD At Parish; Medical.

SULLIVAN, REGAN E; Hull HS; Hull, MA; (Y); Church Yth Grp; 4-H; Girl Scts; SADD; Band; Yrbk Rptr; Yrbk Stf; Socr; Hon Roll; NHS; Sptlght Pgm 85-86; Frnd-Frnd Pgm 83-84; Engrng.

SULLIVAN, ROBERT; Ludlow HS; Ludlow, MA; (Y); 34/260; Drama Clb; JCL; Mgr School Play; Variety Show; Rep Jr Cls; Drama Schlrshp $100 86; Holyoke CC; Retail Mgmnt.

SULLIVAN, SEAN P; Sandwich HS; E Sandwich, MA; (Y); 18/179; Am Leg Boys St; Cmnty Wkr; Red Cross Aide; Nwsp Rptr; Nwsp Stf; Yrbk Rptr; Yrbk Stf; Lit Mag; Var Capt Crs Cntry; Var L Trk; Jrnlsm.

SULLIVAN, SHERRI; Easthampton HS; Northampton, MA; (Y); 8/126; AFS; Dance Clb; French Clb; Hosp Aide; JA; School Play; Bausch & Lomb Sci Awd; NHS; Hugh O Brien Yth Ldrshp 85; Med Resrch.

SULLIVAN, THERESA; Dracut HS; Dracut, MA; (Y); Office Aide; Trs Service Clb; Yrbk Stf; Rep Jr Cls; Pres Stu Cncl; JV Bsktbl; Var Fld Hcky; Var Capt Trk; High Hon Roll; NHS; High O Brian Ldrshp Semnr Rep 85; All Star Fld Hcky 85; MVP Dracut High Var Trk 86; Med.

SULLIVAN, TIM; Bishop Feehan HS; Foxboro, MA; (Y); 12/250; Nwsp Sprt Ed; Nwsp Stf; Yrbk Sprt Ed; Trs Stu Cncl; Golf; Cit Awd; French Hon Soc; NHS; Ntl Merit Ltr; Cmnty Wkr; Holy Cross Clb Of Bristol Cnty Bk Prize; Hugh Obrien Yth Ldrshp Semnr Rep; Law.

SULLIVAN, TIMOTHY; Billerica Memorial HS; Billerica, MA; (Y); 7/430; French Clb; Concert Band; Mrchg Band; School Musical; High Hon Roll; NHS; Ntl Merit Ltr; Semper Fidelis Awd 86; Billerica Elks Tngr Of The Mnth 85; U Of Rochester; Physcs.

SULSKI, JOHN L; Doherty Memorial HS; Worcester, MA; (Y); 7/290; Debate Tm; Exploring; Latin Clb; PAVAS; Political Wkr; Jazz Band; Variety Show; L Wt Lftg; High Hon Roll; NHS; Dartmouth Col6; Portugese.

SULSKI, MIKE; Doherty Memorial HS; Worcester, MA; (Y); Church Yth Grp; JA; Latin Clb; Library Aide; Math Clb; Var Bowling; Hon Roll; Cornell; Archlgy.

SUMMERFORD, CANDACE; Leominster HS; Leominster, MA; (Y); Church Yth Grp; Cmnty Wkr; Band; Church Choir; Yrbk Stf; Swmmng; High Hon Roll; NHS; Prof Sci Awd Cls Of 1937 86; Fitchburg ST Coll; Bio.

SUND, SARAH; Wachusett Regional HS; Sterling, MA; (Y); 136/425; 4-H; VP Library Aide; 4-H Awd; 2nd Pl Cnty Prsntn 4-H 84; U Of AK Fairbanks; Mrn Bio.

SUNDERLAND, LESLEY; Westfield HS; Westfield, MA; (Y); Band; Concert Band; Drill Tm; Mrchg Band; Stu Cncl; Var Fld Hcky; Mgr(s); Hon Roll; Jr NHS; Nrs.

SUPERNOR, MARK E; West Boylston JR SR HS; W Boylston, MA; (Y); Am Leg Boys St; Boy Scts; Math Clb; School Play; Stage Crew; Var Socr; Im Vllybl; Southern MA U; Cvl Engr.

SURETTE, KAREN; Malden HS; Malden, MA; (Y); 6/470; Am Leg Aux Girls St; Key Clb; Capt Math Tm; Ski Clb; Rep Stu Cncl; Bowling; Swmmng; Trs NHS; Pres Schlr; St Schlr; Merrimack Coll; Acctng.

SUROWIEC, DOROTHY; Easthampton HS; Easthampton, MA; (Y); Spanish Clb; SADD; Yrbk Rptr; Yrbk Stf; Stu Cncl; Sftbl; High Hon Roll; Hon Roll; NHS; Prfct Atten Awd; Bus Adm.

SUSZEK, SCOTT; Central Catholic HS; Salem, NH; (Y); Church Yth Grp; Ski Clb; Drm & Bgl; Im Bsktbl; JV Crs Cntry; Var Trk; Im Vllybl; Hon Roll; NHS; Prfct Atten Awd.

SUTCLIFFE, ERIK; King Philip Regional HS; Sheldonville, MA; (Y); Am Leg Boys St; Var L Socr; Var L Tennis; Hon Roll; NHS; Ntl Hist Day Cntst 1st Pl Dist Lvl 3rd Pl ST Lvl 85; Daniel Webster Coll; Avtnl.

SUTERA, GINA; Gloucester HS; Gloucester, MA; (Y); Band; Var Capt Cheerleading; Hon Roll; Endicott JC; Toursm.

SUTSON, GLENN; Lynn Classical HS; Lynn, MA; (Y); Boys Clb Am; Cmnty Wkr; Dance Clb; Stage Crew; Bsktbl; Ftbl; Hon Roll; Acctg.

SUTTON, JENNIFER; Newton North HS; Newtonville, MA; (Y); Church Yth Grp; SADD; Stage Crew; Rep Stu Cncl; Hon Roll; Advrtsng Dsgn.

SUTTON, LINDA; B M C Dur Fee HS; Fall River, MA; (Y); Hosp Aide; Teachers Aide; Cmndtn Wrkng Hndcpd Chldrn 84-85; Cmndtn Compltn Wrk Exprnce Pgm 85-86; Salve Regina Newport; Nrsng.

SUTTON, SHERRI; North Middlesex Regional HS; Townsend, MA; (Y); 2/210; Drama Clb; Capt Color Guard; School Musical; Stage Crew; VP Sec Jr NHS; NHS; Sal; St Schlr; Acad Recgtn Microcomp 84; Outstndng Acvht Spn 86; U MA Amherst; Spn.

SVEC, THOMAS J; W Springfield HS; W Springfield, MA; (Y); Art Clb; Church Yth Grp; Var L Bsbl; JV Var Ftbl; Var Capt Wrstlng; Springfield Coll; Law Enfrcmtn.

SVENDSEN, KRISTEN; North Attleboro HS; N Attleboro, MA; (Y); 4-H; JCL; Quiz Bowl; Drill Tm; Nwsp Phtg; Yrbk Stf; 4-H Awd; High Hon Roll; NHS; Natl Latin Hnr Scty 86; Vet Med.

SVENSON, KERRY; Foxboro HS; Foxboro, MA; (Y); 52/225; Ski Clb; Varsity Clb; Bsktbl; Coach Actv; Mgr(s); Socr; Hon Roll; Bus.

SWAHN, PATRICIA; Simons Rock College; Delaware, NJ; (Y); Office Aide; Pep Clb; Yrbk Phtg; JV Bsktbl; JV Sftbl; Mst Imprvd Plyr Bsktbl 85-86; Pltcl Sci.

SWAN, EILEEN; Our Ladys Newton Catholic HS; Newton, MA; (Y); Church Yth Grp; Drama Clb; GAA; Model UN; Chorus; Church Choir; School Play; Yrbk Stf; Rep Frsh Cls; Rep Soph Cls; Suffolk U Bk Awd 86; Cmmnctns.

SWANK, TOM; Lincoln-Sudbury Regional HS; Sudbury, MA; (Y); Ski Clb; Nwsp Stf; Var Bsktbl; JV Ftbl; Var Lcrss; Hon Roll; Ntl Merit Ltr; U Of VA; Ecnmcs.

SWANSON, JENNIFER; Cathedral HS; Springfield, MA; (Y); Dance Clb; Intnl Clb; School Musical; School Play; Variety Show; Hon Roll; Prfct Atten Awd.

SWANSON, JILL; Nipmuc Regional HS; Mendon, MA; (Y); 9/91; Am Leg Aux Girls St; Ski Clb; Stat Bsktbl; Var Cheerleading; JV Capt Fld Hcky; Score Keeper; JV Sftbl; High Hon Roll; Hon Roll; NHS; Psychlgy.

SWARTZ, STEPHEN; Lincoln Subbury Regional HS; Sudbury, MA; (Y); Cmnty Wkr; Office Aide; Red Cross Aide; Pres Temple Yth Grp; JV Bsbl; Crs Cntry; JV Socr; Pol Sci.

SWEENEY, ANN; Fontbonne Acad; Milton, MA; (Y); Math Tm; Bsktbl; Fld Hcky; Tennis; Hon Roll; Letter Tennis; Sci Fair 3rd Pl.

SWEENEY, BRIAN; Attleboro HS; Attleboro, MA; (Y); ROTC; Ski Clb; VICA; JV Bsbl; JV Var Powder Puff Ftbl; Wt Lftg; Marine Corps.

SWEENEY, CHERYL; Matignon HS; Somerville, MA; (Y); Drama Clb; Hosp Aide; SADD; Chorus; Church Choir; School Musical; School Play; Stage Crew; Variety Show; Lit Mag; Stonehill Coll; Pre-Med.

SWEENEY, JAMES; Austin Prep; Reading, MA; (Y); High Hon Roll; Hon Roll; US Olym Sprts Fest Swimming 86; Jr Olym Mdlst 84-86; Top 16 US Swmmng & New Eng Top Perf 84-86; Law.

SWEENEY, MARGARET; Whitman Hanson Regional HS; Whitman, MA; (Y); 60/291; Church Yth Grp; Yrbk Stf; Rep Jr Cls; Rep Sr Cls; Rep Stu Cncl; Sftbl; Whitman Democrtc Twn Cmmttee Schlrshp 86; Plymouth ST Coll; Acctg.

SWEENEY, MARY BETH; Franklin HS; Franklin, MA; (Y); 9/231; Math Clb; Math Tm; OEA; Varsity Clb; Variety Show; Yrbk Ed-Chief; Yrbk Phtg; Var Capt Cheerleading; High Hon Roll; Hon Roll; Boston Coll; Mktg.

SWEENEY, MELISSA; Bishop Connolly HS; Fall River, MA; (Y); 23/175; Boys Clb Am; Church Yth Grp; Var L Bsktbl; JV Crs Cntry; L Var Sftbl; High Hon Roll; MVP Bsktbl Tm 85-86; Co Captn Bsktbl Tm 85-86; Bus.

SWEENEY, PAMELA; Keith Catholic HS; Lowell, MA; (Y); 3/40; Drama Clb; Exploring; Ski Clb; Spanish Clb; Acpl Chr; Chorus; Church Choir; School Musical; Variety Show; Nwsp Rptr; Grade Based Scholar; U Lowell; Biol Sci.

SWEENEY, SONIA; Beverly HS; Beverly, MA; (Y); Church Yth Grp; Science Clb; Nwsp Phtg; Rep Stu Cncl; Fld Hcky; Swmmng; Hon Roll; Powder Puff Ftbl; Rep Frsh Cls; Rep Soph Cls; 1st Pl Sci Fair Wnnr 86; Lab Aide 85-86; Simons Rock; Sci Resrch.

SWEET, MIKE; Arlington HS; Arlington, MA; (Y); Computer Clb; Model UN; Spanish Clb.

SWENSON, DANIEL F; Waltham HS; Waltham, MA; (Y); 51/697; Am Leg Boys St; Stu Cncl; Co-Capt Bsktbl; Trk; NHS; Nobel Prize For Athltcs 83; Bentley Coll; Acctg.

SWENSON, DEBORAH R; Danvers HS; Danvers, MA; (Y); 4/307; Cmnty Wkr; Hosp Aide; Service Clb; Yrbk Stf; Trs Frsh Cls; Trs Soph Cls; Trs Jr Cls; Trs Sr Cls; Cheerleading; Var Fld Hcky; Jr Clss Mrshll 86; N E Conf Hnrble Mntn Fldhcky 85; Chem.

SWENSON, LAURA; Salem HS; Salem, MA; (Y); 27/270; Church Yth Grp; Concert Band; Mrchg Band; Orch; School Musical; Cheerleading; Tennis; NHS; Fine Applied & Perf Arts Awd 86; Outstndng Ldrshp Awd 85; Jr Dist Band 83; Engrng.

SWETT, JEFFREY; Newton North HS; W Newton, MA; (Y); Am Leg Boys St; Concert Band; Jazz Band; Symp Band; Var Capt Bsktbl; Lcrss; Var L Socr; Im Wt Lftg; Hon Roll.

SWIECANSKI, MARCIA M; Cathedral HS; Indian Orchard, MA; (Y); 67/455; Intnl Clb; Chorus; School Musical; School Play; Sprngfld Kiwanis Clbs Dear Mr Pres Cntst 86; Cthdrl HS Outstndg Svc Awd 85; Prjct Bus Cert 84; Wstrn Nw Englnd Coll; Bus Mgmt.

SWIFT, DAVID; Milford HS; Milford, MA; (Y); 14/300; Am Leg Boys St; JV Bsktbl; Var Socr; JV Trk; High Hon Roll; NHS; Bst Sprtsman In Soccer 84 & 85.

SWIFT, JENNIFER A; Weymouth South HS; South Weymouth, MA; (Y); Church Yth Grp; Math Tm; Orch; High Hon Roll; NHS.

SYLVIA, BARRY B; Medfield HS; Medfield, MA; (Y); Pres AFS; Sec Am Leg Boys St; Rep Soph Cls; Trs Jr Cls; Rep Stu Cncl; Var L Bsktbl; Var L Socr; Hon Roll; Church Yth Grp; SADD; Bd Of Dir Stu Rstrnt 86; Cert BAYS GBYS Sccr Rfree 84-88; Engrng.

SYLVIA, BOBBI; New Bedford HS; New Bedford, MA; (Y); 214/706; Exploring; JA; SADD; Color Guard; Stage Crew; Var L Swmmng; JV Trk; Prfct Atten Awd; Arch.

SYLVIA, EDWARD; Middleborough HS; Middleboro, MA; (Y); 3/200; VP Drama Clb; Acpl Chr; Mrchg Band; School Musical; School Play; Symp Band; Var Trk; Elks Awd; High Hon Roll; NHS; Yth Am European Concert Tour Chorus 84-86; Dist Chorus 84-86; SEMSBA Chorus 84-86; All ST Chorus; Brandeis U; Theatre Arts.

SYLVIA, KEVIN; Old Colony Vocational Tech; Acushnet, MA; (Y); Art Clb; Computer Clb; JA; Radio Clb; VICA; Stage Crew; Variety Show; Trs Soph Cls; Socr; Hon Roll; AVAA Gradute Awd 81; RSROA Awd 79 & 80; Pres Ftns Awd 80; Art.

SYMANSKI, AMY; Smith Acad; Hatfield, MA; (S); Key Clb; Spanish Clb; Varsity Clb; Chorus; Yrbk Stf; Pres Frsh Cls; VP Jr Cls; Var Bsktbl; Var Fld Hcky; High Hon Roll; Natl Sci Merit Awd 86; Mgmt.

SYMISTER, RICHARD A; Holbrook JR SR HS; Holbrook, MA; (Y); Band; Bsktbl; Ftbl; Cmnty Wkr; Latin Clb; Concert Band; Pep Band; School Musical; Socr; Uosung Hero/Bsktbl 86; Southeastern MA U; Bus Mgmt.

SYMONAICK, JANET L; North HS; Worcester, MA; (Y); Pep Clb; Spanish Clb; Varsity Clb; Nwsp Rptr; Nwsp Stf; Yrbk Stf; Rep Stu Cncl; Co-Capt Cheerleading; Co-Capt Pom Pon; Mst Dedctd Chrldr 85-86; Quinsigamond CC; Bus.

SYMONDS, JENNIFER; Bishop Fenwick HS; Essex, MA; (Y); 8/350; Math Clb; Math Tm; Science Clb; High Hon Roll; NHS; C Nelson Hardy Schlrshp 86; Essex Elem ETA Acdmc Acknwldgmt Awd 86; Colby Coll; Intl Bus.

SYMONDS, STEPHANIE; Marlboro HS; Marlboro, MA; (Y); Church Yth Grp; OEA; Varsity Clb; Chorus; Crs Cntry; Trk; Hon Roll; Elem Ed.

SYNGAY, SUSAN; Franklin HS; Franklin, MA; (Y); 26/224; Church Yth Grp; Dance Clb; Math Tm; Sec SADD; Teachers Aide; Ed Yrbk Stf; Mgr(s); Sftbl; Hon Roll; Lion Awd; Snr Cls Schlrshp 86; Frncs Eddy King Schlrshp 86; Frnkln Jnr Miss Pgm 85; Southeastern MA U; Bus.

SYRIGOS, TAMMY; Girls Catholic HS; Malden, MA; (Y); Art Clb; Church Yth Grp; Hosp Aide; Spanish Clb; High Hon Roll; Sec NHS; Pre-Vet.

SZAX, MARIA; Dracut HS; Dracut, MA; (Y); Art Clb; Key Clb; Teachers Aide; Nwsp Stf; Yrbk Stf; Hon Roll; Jr NHS; NHS; Art Awd 83-86; Engl & Bio Awd 84; Tchr Aide Awd, Hon Rl Awd, Crmnlgy Awd 86; Rivier COLL; Cmmrcl Art.

SZCZEPANIK, HEIDI; Dracut SR HS; Dracut, MA; (Y); Pres Church Yth Grp; Math Clb; SADD; Nwsp Stf; Yrbk Stf; Rep Sr Cls; Var L Trk; High Hon Roll; Hon Roll; NHS.

SZUKALA, JENNIFER; Hoosac Valley HS; Adams, MA; (Y); 6/149; Am Leg Aux Girls St; Pep Clb; School Play; Yrbk Stf; Rep Frsh Cls; Rep Soph Cls; Pres Jr Cls; Rep Sr Cls; High Hon Roll; NCTE Awd; Comp Sci.

SZULKIN, DANIEL; Newton South HS; Newton Centre, MA; (Y); Concert Band; Orch; School Musical; Symp Band; Ed Nwsp Stf; High Hon Roll; Hon Roll; Band; 3rd, 7th, & 8th Pl In NE Ntl Frnch Cntst 84-86; Englsh.

SZWARC, LEANNE; Tantasqua Regional HS; Sturbridge, MA; (Y); 14/179; Math Tm; Chorus; Fld Hcky; Capt Tennis; Hon Roll; Sec NHS; Pres Schlr; Kodak Mdln Of Excllnc Photo 86; Hitchcock Free Acad Schlrshp 86; Sturbridge Grdn Clb Schlrshp 86; Rochester Inst Of Tech; Photo.

TACCINI, AMY; Weymouth North HS; Weymouth, MA; (Y); 51/328; Cmmndtn Math Alge II; Forsyth Schl; Dntl Hygn.

TAFE, JOHN; Newton North HS; Newton Ctr, MA; (Y); Am Leg Boys St; Church Yth Grp; Model UN; Office Aide; Jr Cls; JV Bsbl; Var Crs Cntry; Var Trk; Hon Roll; Art.

TAFT, JUSTIN; Uxbridge HS; Uxbridge, MA; (Y); 19/81; Library Aide; Ftbl; Tennis; Hon Roll; Engrng.

TAFT, THOMAS; Phillips Acad; Zionsville, IN; (Y); Pres Model UN; Thesps; School Play; VP Frsh Cls; Var JV Bsbl; Var JV Ftbl; Var Swmmng; High Hon Roll; Rockwell Proctor; Cluster Blue Key Head.

TAGLIERI, MARK; Taconic HS; Pittsfield, MA; (Y); Boys Clb Am; JA; SADD; VP Soph Cls; VP Jr Cls; Var Bsbl; Var Bsktbl; Var Ftbl; Im Vllybl; Hon Roll.

TAKESUE, KIMI L; Amherst Regional HS; Leverett, MA; (Y); Dance Clb; Drama Clb; Thesps; School Play; Stage Crew; Variety Show; Fld Hcky; Jr NHS; NFAA Awd 86; Oberlin Coll.

TALBOT, LYNNE; Billerica Memorial HS; Billerica, MA; (Y); 9/430; Boys Clb Am; French Clb; Yrbk Stf; Jr Cls; Sr Cls; Crs Cntry; Powder Puff Ftbl; Trk; High Hon Roll; Commonwlth Schlrs Grant 86; Chuck Lampson Acad/Athltc Schlrshp 86; Gond Ctzn Awd-Dghtrs Of Amer Rev 86; U Of MA; Zoolgy.

TALBOT, MONICA; Ludlow HS; Ludlow, MA; (Y); Church Yth Grp; JCL; Latin Clb; Hon Roll; Comp Engr.

TALBOT, ROBERT; Austin Prep; Pelham, NH; (Y); French Clb; Var Golf; Var Ice Hcky; Im Lcrss; Jrnlsm.

TALBOTT, DEREK; Dennis-Yarmouth Regional HS; Dennis, MA; (Y); 12/300; Am Leg Boys St; Civic Clb; Cmnty Wkr; Im Coach Actv; Im Lcrss; L Socr; L Tennis; Im Vllybl; Im Wt Lftg; High Hon Roll; Pres Ntl Hnrs Soc, Pres Bk Awd, Northside Bus Assn Schlrshp 86; Middleburg Coll.

TALLMAN, KRISTIN; Bishop Stang HS; Fall River, MA; (Y); 127/269; Boys Clb Am; Church Yth Grp; SADD; Chorus; Yrbk Stf; Sec Soph Cls; Sec Jr Cls; Off Stu Cncl; JV Bsktbl; JV Var Fld Hcky; Stu Ldrshp 85; SE MA U; Bus Mgt.

TALLMAN, TODD M; Narragansett Regional HS; Phillipston, MA; (Y); 2/100; Am Leg Boys St; Letterman Clb; Yrbk Stf; Pres Frsh Cls; JV Bsbl; Var L Crs Cntry; Var Trk; High Hon Roll; Hon Roll; NHS.

TAMBASCIO, JOHN; Mario Umana Technical HS; Brighton, MA; (Y); 26/98; Boys Clb Am; Boy Scts; JA; ROTC; SADD; Stage Crew; Variety Show; Var Bsbl; JV Var Ftbl; Hon Roll; Massport Authrty Schlrshp 86; Daniel Webster Coll Schlrshp 86; Daniel Webster Coll; Aviatn Mgt.

TAMBOLLEO, NIKKI; Sheperd Hill Regional HS; Charlton, MA; (Y); Church Yth Grp; French Clb; Chorus; Var Trk; Hon Roll; Bio.

TAMBURRINO, GINA; Barnstable HS; Hyannis, MA; (Y); Ski Clb; Hon Roll; Slvr Acdmc Achvt Awd 86; Whlck Coll Almni Bk Awd 85; Cert Merit Spnsh 83-85; Southeastern MA U; Bus Admn.

TAMM, ROBERT; Quaboag Regional HS; West Brookfield, MA; (Y); 34/73; Boy Scts; JA; Q&S; Ski Clb; Varsity Clb; Nwsp Rptr; Yrbk Rptr; Var Golf; Hon Roll; Bentley Coll Bus Wk; Engrng.

TAMMARO, JOHN; Stoughton HS; Stoughton, MA; (Y); 100/314; Boy Scts; Church Yth Grp; Varsity Clb; Band; Mrchg Band; JV Bsbl; Var Ftbl; Var Capt Ice Hcky; Wt Lftg; Charles C Tucker Mem Schlrshp 86; Nichols Coll; Accntng.

TANANBAUM, KENNETH L; Framingham North HS; Framingham, MA; (Y); 5/370; JCL; Im Bsktbl; Var Capt Crs Cntry; Var Trk; High Hon Roll; NHS; Ntl Merit SF; Maxima Cum Laude, Cum Laude.

TANGUAY, RONDA; Bristol-Plymouth RVT HS; Middleboro, MA; (S); #3 In Class; Church Yth Grp; Drama Clb; SADD; Pres VICA; School Musical; Variety Show; Rep Soph Cls; Rep Jr Cls; Rep Sr Cls; High Hon Roll; VICA Brnz Mdl 84; VICA Gld Mdl 85; Intr Dcrtr.

TANONA, SCOTT; Marlboro HS; Marlboro, MA; (Y); 1/300; VP Computer Clb; Pres JA; Pres Science Clb; Mgr Nwsp Stf; Bausch & Lomb Sci Awd; NHS; Ntl Merit Ltr; Val; Math Clb; Hrvrd Book Awd 86; Chem.

TARBELL, MAUREEN; Walpole HS; Walpole, MA; (Y); 52/260; Church Yth Grp; Sec Frsh Cls; Sec Soph Cls; Sec Jr Cls; Stu Cncl; Var L Cheerleading; Var Gym; Var L Socr; Var Capt Tennis; Spnsh Awd 86.

TARDIE, NICOLE A; Walpole SR HS; Walpole, MA; (Y); 21/261; Church Yth Grp; Cmnty Wkr; Spanish Clb; SADD; Temple Yth Grp; Varsity Clb; Crs Cntry; Trk; High Hon Roll; Prfct Atten Awd; Jean Thackaberry Mem Awd Track 84; Ltr Cross Cty 84-86; Simmons; Nrs.

TARTARINI, KIM; Natick HS; Natick, MA; (Y); 22/423; Teachers Aide; Var L Bsktbl; Var L Trk; Var Capt Vllybl; High Hon Roll; Hon Roll; NHS; St Schlr; Schlrshp To Framingham ST Coll 85; 4 Yr Schlrshp To Coll Of My Choice From GTE 86; Clark U; Bio.

TARULLI, SABRINA; Quincy HS; Quincy, MA; (Y); Drama Clb; ROTC; Acpl Chr; Band; Chorus; Concert Band; Mrchg Band; School Play; Yrbk Stf; Swmmng; Mem Scholar 86; Sci Achvt 86; U MA; Engl.

TASCA, ANGELA; Methuen HS; Methuen, MA; (Y); 50/332; Drama Clb; School Play; Stage Crew; Var L Vllybl; High Hon Roll; Hon Roll; Edwn J Cstl Fund & MA Gnrl ST Schlrshps 86-87; Coaches Awd-Vllybl 85-86; Salem ST Coll; Bio.

TASHO, KENNETH; Bishop Feehan HS; Norton, MA; (Y); Nwsp Rptr; Nwsp Stf; High Hon Roll; Hon Roll; Spanish NHS.

TASSINARI, CAROLYN; Westwood SR HS; Westwood, MA; (Y); 109/212; AFS; Hosp Aide; SADD; JV Capt Fld Hcky; Tennis; Intrntnl Bus.

TASSINARI, JANEEN; Palmer HS; Palmer, MA; (Y); Ski Clb; Spanish Clb; Varsity Clb; Var Bsktbl; JV Fld Hcky; Stat Ftbl; Var Sftbl; Hon Roll; Prfct Atten Awd; Pres Physical Fitness Awd 84-85; Bsktbl All Star Tm Lcl Paper 85-86; Physical Education.

TASTE, NICHOLAS; Boston Technical HS; Brighton, MA; (Y); Art Clb; Boys Clb Am; Church Yth Grp; Church Choir; School Play; Yrbk Bus Mgr; Rep Stu Cncl; JV Var Bsktbl; JV Var Score Keeper; Arch.

TATA, CRAIG; Southbridge HS; Southbridge, MA; (Y); Church Yth Grp; Band; Chorus; Church Choir; Concert Band; Mrchg Band; Pep Band; School Musical; Swing Chorus; Hon Roll; MA Lions Clb All ST Bnd 86; Music.

TATEM, ELIZABETH; Bishop Connolly HS; Portsmouth, RI; (Y); 29/179; Latin Clb; Math Clb; Sec SADD; High Hon Roll; Pres Schlr; Lehigh U; Elec Engnr.

TATLOCK, DANA; Lincoln Sudbury Regional HS; Lincoln, MA; (Y); Yrbk Stf; Rep Jr Cls; JV Bsktbl; Var Lcrss; Var Capt Socr; Intl Rel.

TATREAU, MELISSA; Braintree HS; Braintree, MA; (Y); 83/424; Madrigals; School Musical; School Play; Variety Show; Hon Roll; Quincy JC Psych, Fantasy Lit 84; U Amherst; Zoolgy.

TATTRIE, CHRISTOPHER; Franklin HS; Franklin, MA; (Y); Trs Sr Cls; Var L Bsbl; Var L Crs Cntry; Var L Ice Hcky; Im Socr; Hon Roll; NHS; FHS Rep Stu Govt Day 86.

TATTRIE, KEVIN; Franklin HS; Franklin, MA; (Y); 18/221; Am Leg Boys St; Math Tm; OEA; Capt Bsbl; Capt Ftbl; Var L Ice Hcky; Hon Roll; Ntl Merit Ltr; Franklin HS Male Schlr Athlte Of The Yr 86; Stonehill Coll; Comp Sci.

TAURO, TAMMY; Greater Boston Acad; Stoneham, MA; (Y); 1/20; Church Yth Grp; French Clb; Hosp Aide; Teachers Aide; Band; Chorus; Church Choir; Concert Band; Orch; Variety Show; Engl Awds; Awd Acad Excllnce; Frnch Awds; Atlantic Union Coll; Phys Thrpy.

TAUSEK, JENNIFER; Bishop Feehan HS; Attleboro, MA; (Y); Pep Clb; Ski Clb; Spanish Clb; SADD; Concert Band; Nwsp Stf; Yrbk Stf; Stu Cncl; Cheerleading; NHS; Big Sistr Orgnztn; Fairfield U; Psychlgy.

TAVANO, LYNN M; Milford HS; Milford, MA; (Y); Church Yth Grp; Dance Clb; Hosp Aide; Yrbk Stf; High Hon Roll; NHS; Prfct Atten Awd; Mlfrd Tchrs Assn Schlrshp 86; Brd Of Rgnts Schlrshp 86; Frgn Lang Schlrshp 86; Ftchbrg ST Coll; Nrs.

TAVARES, DEBORAH; Dartmouth HS; S Dartmouth, MA; (Y); 50/226; Office Aide; Typewrtng & Wrd Prcssng Speed Awd; Acdmc Excllnc Awd; Camoe Club Schlrshp; Southeastern MA U; Bus Admin.

TAVARES, FILOMENA; BMC Durfee HS; Fall River, MA; (Y); FNA; Girl Scts; SADD; Cit Awd; NHS; Prfct Atten Awd; St Schlr; Hosp Aide; Hon Roll; Nrsng.

TAVARES, NANCY; B M C Durfee HS; Fall River, MA; (Y); Church Yth Grp; Nwsp Stf; Yrbk Stf; Lit Mag; High Hon Roll; Hon Roll; Bus Clb Awd 86; Psychlgy.

TAVARES, REBECCA; Somerset HS; Somerset, MA; (Y); Trs Church Yth Grp; Band; Chorus; Concert Band; Mrchg Band; Orch; School Play; Symp Band; Hon Roll; NHS; Brdgwtr ST Coll; Elem Ed.

TAYLOR, CATHERINE; Milford HS; Milford, MA; (Y); 100/300; VP Trs Church Yth Grp; Dance Clb; Drama Clb; Science Clb; Band; Chorus; Concert Band; Drill Tm; Mrchg Band; Orch; Pre Med.

TAYLOR, JOHANNA; Concord-Carlisle HS; Concord, MA; (Y); Church Yth Grp; Band; Concert Band; Mrchg Band; High Hon Roll; Hon Roll; NHS; Spnsh, Hstry & Spnsh 85-86.

TAYLOR, SUNDAY; Needham HS; Boston, MA; (Y); Cmnty Wkr; Hosp Aide; Spanish Clb; Speech Tm; Rep Jr Cls; Rep Sr Cls; Drama Clb; Political Wkr; Stage Crew; Ntl Merit Ltr; Cmmndtn Prom Ntl Achvt Schlrshp Pgm For Outstndng Negro Stus 85-86; Med.

TEAGUE, ANDREA; Beverly HS; Beverly, MA; (Y); 13/374; Mgr Chorus; School Musical; School Play; Mgr Stage Crew; Nwsp Stf; Lit Mag; Hon Roll; NHS; Engl Awd 86; Boston U; Comm.

TEDROW, COREY; Acton-Boxbon Regional HS; Acton, MA; (Y); 66/410; Chorus; Pres Stu Cncl; Var Bsktbl; Capt Powder Puff Ftbl; JV Sftbl; Capt Trk; High Hon Roll; Hon Roll; NHS; Exclnc Frnch Awd 86; Drmtc Arts.

TEEHAN, SUSAN; Dedham HS; Dedham, MA; (S); 9/300; Computer Clb; Spanish Clb; Capt Bsktbl; Var Capt Socr; Var Trk; Hon Roll; Boy ST Lgu All Star Soccer & Bsktbl 85-86; Schl Rcrd 800-M Trck 84; Physcl Thrpy.

TEFTS, VALERIE A; Holyoke Catholic HS; Easthampton, MA; (Y); Church Yth Grp; Computer Clb; 4-H; Library Aide; Math Clb; Office Aide; Spanish Clb; Teachers Aide; Hon Roll; Outstndng Comp Pgmmg Awd 86; Italian Progrssv Soc Scholar 86; James F Naurison Scholar 86; Westfield ST Coll; Mth.

TEIXEIRA, ROBERT; Bishop Feehan HS; Attleboro, MA; (Y); 36/241; Boy Scts; JV Bsktbl; JV Crs Cntry; Trk; NHS; Hse Of Rep Offcl Citn 84; Citn Gvrnr Michael S Dukakis 84; Acctg.

TELFORD, MANDY; Bedford HS; Bedford, MA; (Y); 7/240; Church Yth Grp; Band; Jazz Band; Madrigals; Mrchg Band; Orch; Pep Band; School Musical; Var Capt Gym; NHS; Bus.

TENAGLIA, DAVID; St Dominic Savio HS; Revere, MA; (Y); 21/95; Chess Clb; Computer Clb; French Clb; Ski Clb; SADD; Rep Soph Cls; Rep Stu Cncl; Socr; Hon Roll; Stu Govt Day 85-86; Stu Convtn Days 85-86; Babson College; Bus Law.

TENNEY, BOBBY; Miklford HS; Milford, MA; (Y); 27/310; Cmnty Wkr; Teachers Aide; Band; Concert Band; Yrbk Stf; Stu Cncl; JV Bsbl; Var Bsktbl; Var Socr; High Hon Roll; Wittorf Noferi Noferi & Rosen Law Schlrshp 86; Boston Coll; Lawyer.

TENNIHAN, LISA; Pope John XXIII HS; Everett, MA; (Y); Key Clb; Science Clb; Color Guard; Drill Tm; Drm & Bgl; Mrchg Band.

TEPEROW, JULIE; Boston Latin Schl; W Roxbury, MA; (Y); 45/274; French Clb; Ski Clb; JV Bsktbl; Cheerleading; Powder Puff Ftbl; JV Tennis; JV Trk; High Hon Roll; Hon Roll; Clscl Prz 85; Bus.

TEPLITZ, JEFFREY; Stoughton HS; Stoughton, MA; (Y); Yrbk Stf; Var Bsbl; JV Bsktbl; Var Ftbl; JV Ice Hcky; Sphmr Ftbll Plyr Of Yr 84-85.

TERCANLI, DILEK; Walpole HS; E Walpole, MA; (Y); 29/270; Model UN; Rep Frsh Cls; Rep Soph Cls; Rep Jr Cls; Rep Sr Cls; Trk; Vllybl; Hon Roll; Awd Of Merit Natl Frnch Exm 83-84; Awd Of Merit Natl Spnsh Exm 85-86; Pres Acadmc Ftns Awd 86; Northeastern U; Intl Bus.

TERRY, MELISSA; Arlington Catholic HS; Arlington, MA; (Y); Church Yth Grp; Hosp Aide; JA; Spanish Clb; Hon Roll; Awd Merit Outstndng Accmplshmnt Teens Srvng The Eldrly 86; Quinnipiac Coll.

TESO, ANTONIO; Natick HS; Natick, MA; (Y); Church Yth Grp; Cmnty Wkr; JCL; SADD; Band; Pres Stu Cncl; Hon Roll; Antonio J Teso; Acctg.

TESO, JOYCE; Natick HS; Natick, MA; (Y); SADD; Band; Off Stu Cncl; Var Capt Bsktbl; L Var Trk; Hon Roll; MVP Bsktbl 86; Middlesx Nws Bsktbl Plyr Wk 86; Al-Star Bsktbl Boy ST Leag 86; Emplye Mth 86; Phy Thrpy.

TESSI, ANN-MARGARET; St Bernards Central Catholic HS; Fitchburg, MA; (S); 15/178; Hosp Aide; Spanish Clb; School Play; Sec Soph Cls; Sec Jr Cls; Hon Roll; NHS; Still Life Art Awd-Fitchburg Art Museum 84; Coll Of Holy Cross; Bio.

TESSIER, JODI; Durfee HS; Fall River, MA; (Y); Mrchg Band; Yrbk Stf; Powder Puff Ftbl; Twrlr; Hon Roll; Hnr Grd 84-85; Comptn Majrtt 83-87.

TESTAGROSSA, JOSEPH; Montachusetts Reg Voc Tech HS; Ashburnham, MA; (Y); SADD; JV Bsbl; JV Var Bsktbl; Var Crs Cntry; Socr; Hon Roll; NHS; Dist Athltc Drctrs Awd 86; Coachs Awd Sccr Tm Trophy 85-86; Mst Outstndng Stu Electrncs 84-85; Fitchburg ST Coll; Bus Adm.

TESTASECCA, BRENDA; Drury SR HS; N Adams, MA; (S); 17/189; Church Yth Grp; Drama Clb; Spanish Clb; Sec Band; Chorus; Church Choir; Concert Band; Jazz Band; Mrchg Band; Pep Band; JR Miss Berkshire Cty Wnnr 85-86; JR Miss MA 1st Rnnr Up 86; Oral Roberts U; Psychlgy.

TETI, PATRICIA; Dedham HS; Dedham, MA; (S); 1/252; Drama Clb; Pres French Clb; Band; Stu Cncl; High Hon Roll; NHS; Ntl Merit Ltr; Church Yth Grp; Concert Band; Jazz Band; Rotary Essex Pgm Frnce 85; Odd Fllws Plgrmage NY City, UN 84; Arion Awd Music; Intl Awd.

TETRAULT, RICHARD; Dartmouth HS; N Dartmouth, MA; (Y); 26/226; Key Clb; Band; Nwsp Rptr; Ftbl; NHS; Southeastern MA U; Mrktng.

TETREAU, TERESE; Douglas Memorial HS; E Douglas, MA; (Y); 7/37; Varsity Clb; Drm Mjr(t); Pres Soph Cls; Pres Jr Cls; Pres Sr Cls; Var Capt Cheerleading; Var Capt Fld Hcky; Var Capt Sftbl; Hon Roll; NHS; Century III Ldrshp Awd 86; Stu Ath 86; Douglas Ath Dirctrs Awd 86; Fitchburg ST Coll; Nrsng.

TETREAULT, SCOTT; Hampshire Regional HS; Southampton, MA; (Y); #7 In Class; Trk; High Hon Roll; Hon Roll; Aero Engr.

TEUTEN, PAM; Marshfield HS; Marshfield, MA; (Y); Church Yth Grp; 4-H; Girl Scts; Key Clb; SADD; Acpl Chr; Chorus; Yrbk Stf; Var Fld Hcky; Powder Puff Ftbl; Hnr Rl 86; 4h Awd 82; Bus.

TEWS, TRACY; Wachusett Regional HS; Holden, MA; (Y); 4/444; Madrigals; Stage Crew; Hon Roll; VP NHS; Church Yth Grp; Mathletes; New England Music Fes 86-87.

TEXEIRA, JEAN; Silver Lake Regional HS; Kingston, MA; (Y); 20/435; Church Yth Grp; Office Aide; Teachers Aide; Band; Concert Band; Jazz Band; School Musical; Hon Roll; NHS; SE MA Band Assoc 84-86; SE Dist Concerl 84-86; MA Music Ed All ST Concert 85-86.

THACKERAY, KARY; Old Rochester Regional HS; Marion, MA; (Y); 59/135; Church Yth Grp; Hosp Aide; Church Choir; JV Score Keeper; JV Trk; JV Vllybl; Nrthestrn U; Nrg.

THAI, PHUONG; Brockton HS; Brockton, MA; (Y); High Hon Roll; Hon Roll; Mstr Mrnrs Awd 83; Cert Of Prfncy In Typwrtng 84; Bst Cls Artst Awd 85; U MA Amhrst; Rdlgy.

THAYER, CHRIS; Hingham HS; Hingham, MA; (Y); 21/325; Church Yth Grp; Ski Clb; Bsktbl; NHS; Frank & Ellen Cobb Schlrshp 86; Middlebury Coll.

THEBODO, LISA; Shepherd Hill Regional HS; Charlton, MA; (Y); French Clb; Variety Show; Hon Roll; Accntg.

THEO, PAULA; Danvers HS; Danvers, MA; (Y); Aud/Vis; Teachers Aide; Capt Varsity Clb; Rep Stu Cncl; JV Cheerleading; Capt Tennis; Mst Imprvd Plyr In Tennis 83-84; Pres Awd/Physcl Ftns Awd 81-86; Cmnctns.

THEODORE, STEFAN E; Westwood HS; Westwood, MA; (Y); Aud/Vis; Chess Clb; Exploring; Ski Clb; Spanish Clb; Lit Mag; Tennis; Wt Lftg; Westwood Polc Explrs Sergnt 84-86; MA Ski Clb 82-85; Grk Orthdx Yth Amerc 83-86; Finc.

THERIAULT, BRENDA; Gr Lowell Vo-Tech; Lowell, MA; (Y); Hosp Aide; Sftbl; Nrs.

THEROUX, CHERYL; Chicopee Comprehensive HS; Chicopee, MA; (Y); 1/310; French Clb; Rep Stu Cncl; Var Capt Crs Cntry; Var L Trk; Pres Schlr; Val; Church Yth Grp; Exploring; Teachers Aide; Supt Schls Awd Sci & Mth 86; MA Commonwlth Scholar 86; Soc Wmn Engrs Hghst Hnr 85; Bentley Coll; Bus.

THERRIEN, CHRISTOPHER; St Bernards C C HS; Fitchburg, MA; (S); 6/170; Aud/Vis; Church Yth Grp; Library Aide; Political Wkr; School Play; Nwsp Rptr; Crs Cntry; High Hon Roll; Hon Roll; NHS; Spnsh Awd 85; Sr Altar Svr Awd 84; YMCA Yth & Gov Prog; Elctd Chpln 86; Northeastern U; Hist Teach.

THERRIEN, DONNA; Methuen HS; Methuen, MA; (Y); Drm Mjr(t); Variety Show; Tchr.

THIBAULT, JEFFREY W; Mansfield HS; Mansfield, MA; (Y); 26/185; Am Leg Boys St; Var L Crs Cntry; Var L Trk; Hon Roll; Schltc Recgntn Engl 84, Mth 85.

THIBEAULT, ROBIN; Concord-Carlisle HS; Concord, MA; (Y); DECA; Yrbk Stf; Stu Cncl; Im Fld Hcky; Im Lcrss; Fencg JV 84-86; Russn Clb 84-86; Bus.

THIBODEAU, KELLY; Lyn Classical HS; Lynn, MA; (Y); #50 In Class; Church Yth Grp; Cmnty Wkr; French Clb; Girl Scts; Intnl Clb; JA; Library Aide; Pep Clb; SADD; Powder Puff Ftbl; Slvr Ldrshp Awd Girl Scout 83; Outstndng Vlntr 84; Spcl Rcgntn Awd 83; Accntng.

THIBOUDEAU, JOE; Montachusett Reg Voc Tech; Ashby, MA; (Y); Boys Clb Am; Boy Scts; Church Yth Grp; Pres VICA; Bsbl; Crs Cntry; Socr; Wt Lftg; Hon Roll; NHS; Mst Outstndng Stu Awd Elec 86; 1st Pl VICA Comptn Elec 85; Elec Engr.

THIMAS, JOHN U; Silver Lake Regional HS; Kingston, MA; (Y); 51/500; Am Leg Boys St; French Clb; Latin Clb; Stu Cncl; Var Bsbl; Var Ftbl; Hon Roll; NHS; Bus Admn.

THIRUMALAISAMY, PILLAN K; Newton South HS; Newton, MA; (Y); Am Leg Boys St; Var Capt Bsbl; Var Capt Bsktbl; Var Capt Socr; Hon Roll; Fclty Ltr Recog 83 & 85-86; Colby Coll Bk Prize Ltr Recog Achvt Russn 85; Sr Cup 86; MA Inst.

THOIDIS, GEORGIA; West Roxbury HS; Boston, MA; (S); Library Aide; Vllybl; High Hon Roll; NHS; Prfct Atten Awd; All Star Vllybl Tm-City Of Bstn 85-86; Bio.

THOMA, ELIZABETH; Methven HS; Methuen, MA; (Y); 7/330; Am Leg Aux Girls St; Intnl Clb; Library Aide; Model UN; Var L Tennis; High Hon Roll; Sec NHS; Ntl Merit SF; Pre-Law.

THOMAS, GISEL; Boston Technical HS; Dorchester, MA; (Y); Cmnty Wkr; Computer Clb; Dance Clb; French Clb; FBLA; JA; Library Aide; Gym; Hon Roll; Bus Cmmnctn.

THOMAS, MYLA; Navset Regional HS; Wellfleet, MA; (Y); Yrbk Stf; High Hon Roll; Hon Roll; NHS; Wheaton Coll Bk Awd 86.

THOMAS, REBEKAH; Winthrop HS; Winthrop, MA; (Y); 6/206; Drama Clb; Math Tm; Science Clb; Temple Yth Grp; School Musical; Nwsp Stf; Yrbk Bus Mgr; NHS; MA Commnwlth Schlr 86; Jewish War Vtrns Brothrhd Awd 85-86; Bradeis U.

THOMAS, TODD; Williston-Northampton Schl; Springfield, MA; (Y); 28/125; Church Yth Grp; JA; Mathletes; Office Aide; Science Clb; Var Capt Bsktbl; Var Trk; Hon Roll; Ntl Merit Ltr; Mst Outstndng Geom 83; Mst Outstndng Afro-Amer Hstry 83; Roger L Clapp Awd 85; Econ.

THOMAS, YVONNE; Madison Park HS; Boston, MA; (Y); Dance Clb; Prfct Atten Awd; Outstndng Awd Dance 86; Proj Perf Attdnc 86; Physcl Ed Awd 86; Bunker Hill Coll; Photo.

THOMEN, REBECCA; Monument Mountain HS; Gt Barrington, MA; (Y); 16/100; FFA; Red Cross Aide; Trk; High Hon Roll; Hon Roll; NHS; Presdntl Awd For Vctnl Ag 86; Army.

THOMPSON, CHRIS; Westwood HS; Westwood, MA; (Y); Political Wkr; Ski Clb; Var L Socr; Hon Roll; Ski Team; Unsung Hero; St Michaels Coll; Bus.

THOMPSON, ERIN; Reading Memorfial HS; Reading, MA; (Y); Ski Clb; Band; Concert Band; Mrchg Band; Yrbk Phtg; Lit Mag; High Hon Roll; Hon Roll; Pep Clb; Mgr(s).

THOMPSON, KATHLEEN MARIE; Hudson Catholic HS; Hudson, MA; (Y); School Musical; Trs Sr Cls; Stu Cncl; Var L Bsktbl; JV Capt Cheerleading; Var L Crs Cntry; Var L Sftbl; Var L Trk; High Hon Roll; NHS; Acctng.

THOMPSON, LISA; Cathedral HS; Springfield, MA; (Y); Hon Roll; Law.

THOMPSON, RICHARD E; Wilbram & Honson Acad; Westfield, MA; (Y); 39/150; Bsbl; Bsktbl; Stetson U.

THOMPSON, SHAUNA; Groton-Dunstable Reg Secondary HS; Groton, MA; (Y); Crs Cntry; Hon Roll; Hnr Roll 84-86; Frank Waters Schlrshp 86; Hesser Coll; Trvl & Trsm.

THOMPSON, SUSAN; Georgetown HS; Georgetown, MA; (Y); 43/86; Church Yth Grp; Trs Drama Clb; Pres Concert Band; Jazz Band; Mrchg Band; School Play; Nwsp Stf; Hon Roll; JC Awd; JP Sousa Awd; Perley Free Schlr Schlrshp, Drama Club Schlrshp, Phys Ftns Awd Trophy 86; Salem ST U; Chldhd Educ.

THOMSON, RONALD; Reading Memorial HS; Reading, MA; (Y); Cmnty Wkr; Library Aide; Hon Roll; Ntl Merit Ltr; North Shore CC; Cmnctns.

THOMSON, SCOTT; Marlboro HS; Marlboro, MA; (Y); 37/321; Boy Scts; Church Yth Grp; JA; Math Clb; Science Clb; Ski Clb; SADD; JV Socr; High Hon Roll; NHS; Eagl Sct Boys Sct Amer 84.

THONG, YOEUN; South Boston HS; Jamaica Plain, MA; (S); DECA; Hon Roll; NHS; U Of MA-BOSTON; Accntng.

THORNBLADE, SARAH; Newton North HS; Auburndale, MA; (Y); French Clb; German Clb; Chorus; Orch; Rep Jr Cls; JV Tennis; Newton Symphny Comcerto Comptn 85; Hon Dabbs Awd 85; NE Cmptn 3rd Plc 85-86; Conservatory; Music Perf.

THORNTON, BETH; Bellingham HS; Bellingham, MA; (Y); Sec DECA; Nwsp Sprt Ed; Sec Frsh Cls; Var Bsktbl; Var Fld Hcky; Var Sftbl; Jr NHS; NHS; Vrsty Bsktbl MVP 84-85.

THORNTON, THOMAS; Wilmington HS; Wilmington, MA; (Y); JV Socr; Boston Globe Schlstc Art Awd-Gold Key 83; Engrng.

THORPE, ELLEN; Cathedral HS; Springfield, MA; (Y); 25/500; Dance Clb; JA; Nwsp Stf; Hon Roll; NHS; Engl.

THRASHER, MARY; North Middlesex Regional HS; W Townsend, MA; (Y); 31/210; Ski Clb; Nwsp Stf; Yrbk Stf; JV Var Crs Cntry; NHS; Assumption Coll; Biol.

THURBER, ANDREA; Assabet Valley Regional Voc HS; Marlboro, MA; (Y); 1/356; School Play; Stage Crew; Var JV Bsktbl; Var Socr; High Hon Roll; NHS; Draftng Awd 84-85; Acad Awd 84-86.

THURBER, NEIL D; Westborough HS; Westborough, MA; (Y); 11/189; Am Leg Boys St; Trs Exploring; Red Cross Aide; Band; Chorus; Stu Cncl; Im Gym; Var Socr; NHS; Natl Hnr Roll 86; Comp Sci.

TIBBETTS, CHRISTOPHER; Burncoat SR HS; Worcester, MA; (Y); 40/225; Church Yth Grp; Cmnty Wkr; JV Bsktbl; Hon Roll; Hstry.

TIBBETTS, JOHN; Wakefield Memorial HS; Wakefield, MA; (Y); Boy Scts; Church Yth Grp; FCA; Key Clb; Letterman Clb; SADD; Teachers Aide; Varsity Clb; Yrbk Stf; Bsbl; Loaches Awd 86; Christian Yth Ldrshp Schlrshp PBAC 86; Palm Bch Atlantic Clg; Bus Mngm.

TIBBETTS, ROBIN; Tantasqua Regional HS; Brookfield, MA; (Y); Varsity Clb; Band; Concert Band; Mrchg Band; Variety Show; Yrbk Stf; VP Frsh Cls; Var Capt Bsktbl; Var Capt Fld Hcky; Var Capt Sftbl; Lgl Scrtry.

TIBERT, KAREN; Franklin HS; Franklin, MA; (Y); Church Yth Grp; Girl Scts; Church Choir; Yrbk Stf; Sftbl; Hon Roll; NHS; Sci.

TIERNAN, JIM; Boston Latin Schl; Boston, MA; (Y); 155/273; Boy Scts; Chess Clb; Computer Clb; JA; JV Capt Ice Hcky; Var Mgr(s); Var Swmmng; Var Trk; JV Socr; Eagle Sct Awd 87; CPR Instrctr 86; Adelphi U; Law.

TIERNEY, CHRISTINE M; Marian HS; Framingham, MA; (Y); Hosp Aide; Political Wkr; Chorus; School Musical; Yrbk Stf; Crs Cntry; Trk; Hon Roll; NHS; Church Choir; Candy Dr; Legn Of Mary Sec; Dncg; Boston College.

TILLOTSON, LISA E; Grafton HS; Grafton, MA; (Y); 49/111; SADD; School Play; Nwsp Phtg; Nwsp Rptr; Nwsp Stf; Yrbk Stf; Stu Cncl; Stat Bsbl; Var JV Bsktbl; Var Cheerleading; Lloyd Pat Padgent Scholar 86; Mason Mem Scholar 86; Johnson ST Coll; Hotl Hosptlty.

TILLOTSON, MARY; Chicopee Comnprehensive HS; Chicopee, MA; (Y); 6/293; Am Leg Aux Girls St; Yrbk Stf; Sec Soph Cls; Sec Jr Cls; Sec CAP; Stu Cncl; Var Capt Socr; Trk; NHS; Lt Brnslw Stpzyk Mem Awd 85; MA Bus Wk Chllng Schlrshp 84; Pro-Merito 85; Villanova U; Bus.

TILLSON, ROBERT; Dracut HS; Dracut, MA; (Y); Boy Scts; JA; Math Clb; SADD; Bsktbl; Capt Crs Cntry; Trk; Hon Roll; NHS; Prfct Atten Awd; Elec Engrng.

TILMAN, TERESSA; Bedford HS; Boston, MA; (Y); 59/213; Church Yth Grp; Office Aide; Ski Clb; Church Choir; Variety Show; Var Trk; Hon Roll; Hmcmng Awd 83; Cncrnd Blk Ctzns Schlrshp 86; Nrthestrn U; Bus.

TIMCNEY, SUSAN; North Reading HS; N Reading, MA; (Y); Nwsp Stf; Yrbk Stf; Stu Cncl; Bsktbl; Hon Roll; NHS; Rgnl Stu Advsry Cncl 85-86; Dancing Stu Lorraine Spada Schl Dance; Bus Admin.

TIMMERMEISTER, KARIN; Stoneleigh-Burnham Schl; Lima, OH; (Y); French Clb; School Musical; School Play; Tennis; High Hon Roll; Hon Roll; NHS; Jr Hstry Paper Awd 86; Proctor 86; Librl Arts.

TIMONEY, SUSAN; N Reading HS; N Reading, MA; (Y); Dance Clb; Nwsp Stf; Yrbk Stf; Stu Cncl; Bsktbl; Hon Roll; NHS; Rgnl Stu Advsry Cncl Mbr 85-87; Lorainne Spada Schl Of Dance 82-86; Bus Adm.

TINGER, JOHN P; St Joseph Central HS; Pittsfield, MA; (Y); 3/110; Am Leg Boys St; Cmnty Wkr; Math Clb; Capt Var Crs Cntry; Var Trk; Var Wrstlng; Bausch & Lomb Sci Awd; High Hon Roll; NHS; Spanish NHS; Archtctr.

TINGLEY, VINCENT J; Natick HS; Natick, MA; (Y); Church Yth Grp; Teachers Aide; Stu Cncl; Engl Achvt Awd 86; Electrcn.

TIPPER, GEOFFREY; Algonquin Regional HS; Northboro, MA; (Y); 13/256; Nwsp Rptr; Yrbk Stf; Lit Mag; High Hon Roll; NHS; Awd For Acad Excllnc 84; Oxford U OK; Philosophy.

TIRONE, PAUL; Waltham HS; Waltham, MA; (Y); Church Yth Grp; Drama Clb; JA; Ski Clb; Thesps; School Musical; School Play; Variety Show; Socr; Trk; Annual Temperance Essay Cont Awd 86; Acting.

TIVNAN, KATHLEEN; Holy Name Central Catholic HS; Boylston, MA; (Y); 80/297; Church Yth Grp; Girl Scts; Bsktbl; Trk; Lawyr.

TIVNAN, STEPHANIE; Barnstable HS; Hyannis, MA; (Y); Church Yth Grp; Drama Clb; SADD; Chorus; Stage Crew; Hon Roll; Yarmouth Assmbly Intl Ordr Of Rainbow Girls Wrthy Advsr 85; Grnd Rep VT MA Grnd Assmbly MA 86-87; Pre-Vet.

TOABE, STACY; New Bedford HS; New Bedford, MA; (Y); JA; Office Aide; Tennis; Hon Roll; U MA.

TOBIASON, JENNIFER L; Winchester HS; Winchester, MA; (Y); 6/281; Church Yth Grp; French Clb; Latin Clb; Flag Corp; French Hon Soc; High Hon Roll; Hon Roll; Ntl Latn Exam Silver Mdl 86; Awd Excellnc Lang Study Frnch 86; Cert Mrt Histry 85; Bowdoin Coll.

TOBIN, MARK J; Weymouth North HS; Weymouth, MA; (Y); 2/450; Library Aide; Math Tm; Capt Quiz Bowl; Ed Yrbk Stf; Bausch & Lomb Sci Awd; High Hon Roll; NHS; Ntl Merit Schol; Sal; St Schlr; MA Assn Of Schl Supt Awd 86; Physic Stu Of Yr 85; UMASS Amherst Chancellors Schlrshp Awd 85; Worcester Polytechnic Inst.

TOBIN, THERESA; St Columbkilles HS; Brighton, MA; (Y); 2/60; Spanish Clb; Rep Jr Cls; Trs Sr Cls; Sftbl; High Hon Roll; Jr NHS; NHS; Suffolk U Bk Awd 85-86; Hghst Aver In Frgn Lang & Thlgy Schlrshps 85-86; Vet-Med.

TOCCHIO, JAMES; Boston College HS; Weymouth, MA; (Y); Chess Clb; Church Yth Grp; Computer Clb; JA; Lit Mag; Hnr Rll 86; Boston Coll; Comp.

TODIS, ELENI; Milton HS; Milton, MA; (Y); Art Clb; Church Yth Grp; Sec French Clb; Yrbk Stf; Hon Roll; Prfct Atten Awd; Med.

TODISCO, TAMMY; Medford HS; Meford, MA; (Y); Am Leg Aux Girls St; Dance Clb; Var JV Math Tm; SADD; Yrbk Stf; Pres Jr Cls; Pres Sr Cls; Var JV Sftbl; High Hon Roll; NHS; Frank Call Civics Awd 84; Hugh O Brien Ldrshp Sem 85; Bk Awd 86.

TODRES, JONATHAN; Dennis-Yarmouth Regional HS; South Yarmouth, MA; (Y); 9/309; Am Leg Boys St; Nwsp Rptr; Yrbk Sprt Ed; Im Capt Bsktbl; L Crs Cntry; L Trk; High Hon Roll; Hon Roll; NHS; Pres Schlr; US Army Rerseve Natl Scholar Athl Awd 86; Grad Of Mass Advanced Studies Pgm 85; William Coll Book Awd; Clark U; Psychology.

TOKARCZYK, GRETCHEN; Natick HS; Natick, MA; (Y); Girl Scts; JA; Office Aide; Spanish Clb; Speech Tm; VP SADD; Yrbk Stf; Rep Sec Stu Cncl; Capt Cheerleading; Var Gym; Nrthestrn U; Bus.

TOLAND, BRIAN P; Brockton HS; Brockton, MA; (Y); Am Leg Boys St; Aud/Vis; Church Yth Grp; Key Clb; Political Wkr; Radio Clb; Scholastic Bowl; Stage Crew; Trk; Hon Roll; Politics.

TOLI, KRISTIN; Dedham HS; Dedham, MA; (Y); 36/256; Exploring; Ski Clb; Spanish Clb; Varsity Clb; Nwsp Stf; Bsktbl; Socr; Tennis; Hon Roll; VFW Awd; Pilgrmg To UN Essy Cont Fnlst 85; Law.

TOMASELLO, LOUIS; Reading Memorial HS; Reading, MA; (Y); Jazz Band; JV Var Ice Hcky; Wt Lftg; Hon Roll; Pre Law.

TOMASKO, MARK ANDREW; Shepherd Hill Regional HS; Southbridge, MA; (Y); 10/130; Boy Scts; Stu Cncl; Var Trk; Hon Roll; NHS; Dudley Lions Clb Schlrshp Awd 86; Stu Cncl Schlrshp 86; Bstr Clb Schlrshp 86; U Of MA; Engrng.

TOMKINSON, TODD; King Philip Regional HS; Norfolk, MA; (Y); 3/240; Am Leg Boys St; Drama Clb; French Clb; Math Tm; Var Crs Cntry; Var Trk; Bausch & Lomb Sci Awd; High Hon Roll; NHS; Intnl Clb; Hgh Scrng JR Mth Lg 86; Engrng.

TOMSHO, KATHY; Salem HS; Salem, MA; (Y); 5/300; VP Church Yth Grp; Church Choir; School Musical; School Play; Lit Mag; Var JV Socr; High Hon Roll; NHS; Ntl Merit Ltr; Spanish NHS; Ed.

TOMSU, DANIELLE; Holy Name CCHS; Sulton, MA; (Y); 27/259; English Clb; 4-H; Quiz Bowl; Science Clb; Ski Clb; 4-H Awd; High Hon Roll; Hon Roll; Church Yth Grp; Cmnty Wkr; Pony Clbs Of USA 82-86; Hrs Shows & Clncs 82-86; Assumption Coll; Bus Fin.

TONDEL, TIMOTHY; Lenox Memorial HS; Lenox, MA; (Y); Band; Concert Band; School Play; Yrbk Stf; Var L Bsbl; Var L Bsktbl; Var L Socr; NHS; Boys Clb Am; Boy Scts; All Berkshire Soccr 2nd Tm 84; Sthrn Div Soccr Berkshire Cnty 84-85; Engrng.

TONER, BETTINA; Mansfield HS; Mansfield, MA; (Y); 48/180; French Clb; Hosp Aide; Band; Concert Band; Mrchg Band; Var L Tennis; Hon Roll.

TONRY, TAMMY; Montochusett Regional HS; Fitchburg, MA; (Y); VICA; Yrbk Ed-Chief; Yrbk Phtg; VP Soph Cls; VP Jr Cls; VP Sr Cls; Stu Cncl; Capt Var Crs Cntry; Hon Roll; Pres NHS; Mst Outstndg Stu Vctnl Area Med Asst 85-86; Rep Fitchburg Outstndg Young Amer 86; X-Cnty Unsng Hero 86; Physcl Thrpy.

TOOMEY, LISA; Melrose HS; Melrose, MA; (Y); Girl Scts; Hosp Aide; Pep Clb; Spanish Clb; SADD; JV Fld Hcky; JV Trk; High Hon Roll; Hon Roll; NHS.

TOOMEY, PATRICIA M; Danvers HS; Danvers, MA; (Y); 7/307; Hosp Aide; Var Fld Hcky; Bausch & Lomb Sci Awd; French Hon Soc; NHS; 4-H; Yrbk Stf; JV Bsktbl; JV Sftbl; High Hon Roll; Thrope Schlrshp 86; Russell Sage Founders Schlrshp 86; Beverly Hosp Aid Assn Schlrshp 86; Russell Sage Coll; Phys Thrpy.

TOONE, JENNIFER A; Marlborough HS; Marlboro, MA; (Y); Pres Drama Clb; Chorus; School Play; Stage Crew; Variety Show; Hon Roll; VFW Awd; All Star Cast Awd-MA Drama Gld 85; Muscl Theatr.

TOPJIAN, STACY; Westford Acad; Westford, MA; (Y); Art Clb; Spanish Clb; SADD; Mrchg Band; Stage Crew; High Hon Roll; Hon Roll; Recog Cert Vlntr Wrk 84; Commrcl Art.

TOPPI, DIONNE; Arlington HS; Arlington, MA; (Y); 19/390; SADD; Yrbk Stf; JV Var Vllybl; NHS; Church Yth Grp; French Clb; Hosp Aide; Chorus; Stage Crew; Lit Mag; Concours Natl De Francais Cert Merit 84.

TOPPING, GLENN; King Philip Regional HS; Wrentham, MA; (Y); L Bsktbl; JV Socr; L Trk.

TORREY, LINCOLN; Mansfield HS; Mansfield, MA; (Y); #28 In Class; Im Vllybl; Hon Roll; Literatr.

TORTORA, DEBBIE; Medford HS; Medford, MA; (Y); 69/400; Letterman Clb; Pep Clb; Ski Clb; SADD; Cheerleading; Pom Pon; Engl Awds 83-85; U Of Lowell; Bus Adm.

TOSI, LISA; Arlington HS; Arlington, MA; (Y); Sec Art Clb; Camera Clb; Church Yth Grp; Ed Cmnty Wkr; Dance Clb; SADD; Capt Color Guard; Yrbk Phtg; Var Sftbl; NHS; Young Ambssdr In Spain 86; Miss MA Teen USA Pgnt Contsnt 85; Tchr Training Clb Of Boston For Dncng; Bus Mgmt.

TOSSAVAINEN, THOMAS J; Monument Mountain Regional HS; Great Barrington, MA; (Y); 12/130; Am Leg Boys St; JCL; Yrbk Stf; Pres Frsh Cls; JV Bsbl; JV Sftbl; Var Trk; High Hon Roll; Hon Roll; NHS; L Eden Day Mem JR Schlrshp 86; Bently Coll; Mrktng.

TOTH, MICHELLE; Weymouth South HS; S Weymouth, MA; (Y); 28/338; Am Leg Aux Girls St; Drama Clb; SADD; School Play; Nwsp Rptr; Pres Frsh Cls; Off Soph Cls; Pres Jr Cls; Pres Sr Cls; Stu Cncl; MS JR Ms Prgm 86; Ntl Hnr Scty; Bus.

TOUPIN, TERRI; Westford Acad; Westford, MA; (Y); AFS; Exploring; Hosp Aide; Spanish Clb; SADD; VP Stu Cncl; Hon Roll; Chld Dvlpmnt Awd 86; Lesley Coll; Chld Psychlgy.

TOUPONCE, DAWN; Lee HS; Lee, MA; (Y); 14/85; French Clb; GAA; Math Clb; JV Socr; JV Sftbl; Vet.

TOURIGNY, MARTIN R; Shrewsbury HS; Shrewsbury, MA; (Y); 5/250; Am Leg Boys St; Boy Scts; Mgr JA; Letterman Clb; Math Tm; Speech Tm; Rep Stu Cncl; Var Bsktbl; Capt Tennis; High Hon Roll; Bus Wk Chllng Bentley 85.

TOURTELOTTE, JOHN H; Cathedral HS; Springfield, MA; (Y); 30/550; Intnl Clb; Math Clb; Model UN; Var Bsbl; JV Ftbl; JV Socr; High Hon Roll; NHS; Prfct Atten Awd; Mst Outstndng Stdnt Hnrs Hstry & Engl 86; 2nd Pl Frnch Poetry Comptn 85.

TOWLE, LARRY; Shepherd Hill Regional HS; Dudley, MA; (Y); Rep Stu Cncl; Var Bsktbl; Var Ftbl; Var Golf; Score Keeper; High Hon Roll; Jr NHS; NHS; Prfct Atten Awd; Acad Awd Excllnc Basic Pgmng 86; Comp Pgmng.

TOWLE, LORINDA; Shepherd Hill Regional HS; Charlton, MA; (Y); Sec Pres Church Yth Grp; Drama Clb; Library Aide; Band; Chorus; Mrchg Band; School Musical; Variety Show; High Hon Roll; Hon Roll; Music Educ.

TOWLER, MATTHEW; North HS; Worcester, MA; (Y); #8 In Class; Varsity Clb; Nwsp Rptr; Nwsp Stf; Var L Crs Cntry; Var L Socr; Var L Trk; NHS; Outstndng Achvt Art 86; MA Coll Art; Cmmrcl Art.

TOWNE, ERIC A; N Shore Regional Voc Tech; So Hamilton, MA; (Y); 1/185; Band; Concert Band; Jazz Band; Mrchg Band; CC Awd; High Hon Roll; Val; Schl Committe Schlrshp 86; Math, English Awd 86; Pres Acad Fitness Awd 86; Wentworth InstCIVIL Engrng.

TRACHTMAN, JONATHAN; Natick HS; Natick, MA; (Y); 11/399; Cmnty Wkr; SADD; Temple Yth Grp; Nwsp Stf; Symp Band; JV Var Socr; High Hon Roll; Hon Roll; Trs NHS; Law.

TRACY, JOANNA; Westboro HS; Westboro, MA; (Y); Sec AFS; Pres Church Yth Grp; Girl Scts; Yrbk Stf; Bsktbl; Powder Puff Ftbl; Score Keeper; Vllybl; Sftbl; Madrigals; All ST Chrs 85-86; All Eastern Chrs 85-87; All Eastern Hnrs Choir 84-85; U Of ME Orono; Bio Sci.

TRACY, SUSANNAH; Hampshire Regional HS; Westhampton, MA; (S); 9/132; Band; Nwsp Rptr; Yrbk Stf; Var L Bsktbl; Var L Crs Cntry; Var Capt Trk; High Hon Roll; Hon Roll; Sec Church Yth Grp; Concert Band; Hugh O Brien Yth Fndtn MA Ldrshp Semnr Rep 85; MA Hstry Day Comptn 3rd Pl 83-84; Bio.

TRAHANT, MATTHEW J; Lynn English HS; Lynn, MA; (Y); 35/380; Am Leg Boys St; Boy Scts; Drama Clb; Ski Clb; VP Soph Cls; VP Jr Cls; Pres Sr Cls; Rep Stu Cncl; Var Capt Swmmng; Hon Roll.

TRAN, HIEP; Newton North HS; Newton, MA; (Y); 5/15; Intnl Clb; Hon Roll; Prfct Atten Awd; Exc Alg I 83; Hnr Cert 86; Palmer House Cert 86; U MA-AMHERST; Engrng.

TRAN, KHIEM T; Clinton HS; Fitchburg, MA; (Y); 3/130; Am Leg Boys St; Aud/Vis; Boy Scts; Cmnty Wkr; Intnl Clb; JA; Library Aide; Math Tm; Nwsp Rptr; Yrbk Stf; Yth Mth 86; MA Schlr Schlrshp 86; Presdntl Acadmc Awd 86; U Of NH; Medcn.

TRANFAGLIA, MARIA; Medford HS; Medford, MA; (Y); SADD; Vllybl; Bio Awd 85; Med.

TRATT, NOAH; Barnstable HS; Centerville, MA; (Y); Camera Clb; Debate Tm; Political Wkr; Temple Yth Grp; Yrbk Phtg; VP Soph Cls; Pres Jr Cls; AFS; Drama Clb; Key Clb; US Senate Pase 86; US Hrs Rprsntvs 85-86; Soc Sci Exclnc Awd; U Of Penn; Bus.

TRAUB, STEPHEN J; Xaverian Brothers HS; Sharon, MA; (Y); 1/209; Capt Math Tm; JV Bsbl; Var L Ftbl; High Hon Roll; NHS; Ntl Merit SF; St Schlr; Val; Wt Lftg; Elks Awd; Smmr Abrd Schlrshp France 84; Harvard Bk Awd 85; Harvard U; Chem.

TRAUBER, ROBERT S; Dover-Sherborn HS; Brookline, MA; (Y); AFS; Am Leg Boys St; Church Yth Grp; Cmnty Wkr; Exploring; Political Wkr; Radio Clb; SADD; Varsity Clb; School Play; Either Emory U; Bus.

TRAUPE, ERIC H; Ashland HS; Ashland, MA; (Y); Am Leg Boys St; Church Yth Grp; SADD; Varsity Clb; Stu Cncl; L Bsbl; Var Capt Ftbl; Var Capt Trk; Hon Roll; Voice Dem Awd; All Lg Lnbckr 85; All Lg Trk 86; Top Prep Ftbl Plyr Cntry 86; Bus.

TRAVAGLINI, DAVID M; Burlington HS; Burlington, MA; (Y); 32/320; Am Leg Boys St; VP Frsh Cls; Pres Soph Cls; Pres Jr Cls; Pres Sr Cls; Var L Ftbl; Var L Wrstlng; Cit Awd; Hon Roll; NHS; Suffolk Bk Awd 86; Bus.

TRAVASSOS, CHRISTINE; B M C Durfee HS; Fall River, MA; (Y); 5/673; French Clb; Concert Band; Mrchg Band; Pep Band; Lit Mag; Hon Roll; NHS; Band; All A Lst 85-86; Awd Ecllnc Frnch 85; Ushrntl Hnr Soc 85; Law.

TRAVERS, AMY M; Hopedale JR SR HS; Hopedale, MA; (Y); 1/59; Yrbk Rptr; Rep Trs Stu Cncl; Var L Tennis; Pres NHS; Ntl Merit Ltr; Val; Am Leg Aux Girls St; Chorus; Concert Band; High Hon Roll; MA Commonwealth Schlrshp 86; Math Awd Outstdng Achvt Math 86; Pres Phy Ftnss Awd 86; Wellesley Coll; Econ.

TRAVERS, DEBBIE; Marlboro HS; Marlboro, MA; (Y); 7/304; VP OEA; High Hon Roll; NHS; Ofc Ed Assn ST Conf 1st Pl Acctg & Reltd II & 1st Pl Bus Proofrdg 86; Acctg.

TRAVERS, JEFF; East Longmeadow HS; E Longmeadow, MA; (Y); 2/200; Debate Tm; Drama Clb; Math Tm; Nwsp Bus Mgr; Nwsp Ed-Chief; Off Soph Cls; VP Sr Cls; High Hon Roll; NHS; Ntl Merit Ltr; Bus.

TRAVERS, MARIE; Notre Dame Acad; N Marshfield, MA; (Y); 20/114; Church Yth Grp; Drama Clb; JCL; Acpl Chr; School Musical; School Play; Sec Soph Cls; Pres Jr Cls; Pres Sr Cls; JV Trk; Awd Achvt Religion,Eng,Choir 85-86; Elem Ed.

TRAVIS, MARK W; Norwell HS; Norwell, MA; (Y); Boy Scts; Church Yth Grp; Teachers Aide; Varsity Clb; School Play; Rep Stu Cncl; Var Ftbl; Var Capt Trk; Hope Coll; Thlgy.

TRAVNICEK, JULIE; Southbridge HS; Southbridge, MA; (Y); 6/135; Sec Church Yth Grp; Math Tm; Sec Concert Band; Sec Mrchg Band; Var Trk; Hon Roll; JP Sousa Awd; VP NHS; Ntl Merit Ltr; U VT; Math.

TRAWICK, GEOFFREY A; Boston College HS; Braintree, MA; (Y); Church Yth Grp; Cmnty Wkr; Ski Clb; SADD; Im Bsktbl; Im Ice Hcky; Im Vllybl; Hon Roll.

TRAYERS III, FREDERICK; Saint Johns Preparatory School; Peabody, MA; (Y); Aud/Vis; Boy Scts; Church Yth Grp; Cmnty Wkr; Political Wkr; Im Vllybl; Hon Roll; Eagl Sct Ordr Arrw Compltd MICE Swm 85; JR Olmpc Sectnl Traing Cmp 84-85; Bay ST Gms Fencg 85; Aerosp Engrng.

TREEN, ERIN; Bishop Feehan HS; Attleboro, MA; (Y); 39/234; Church Yth Grp; Hosp Aide; Ski Clb; Lit Mag; French Hon Soc; NHS; Elks Awd; High Hon Roll; Rensselaer Polytech Inst; Archt.

TREMBA, STEPHANIE; Holyn Name CCHS; Shrewsbury, MA; (Y); Pep Clb; School Play; Yrbk Ed-Chief; Yrbk Stf; High Hon Roll; Hon Roll; St Marys Wmn Guild Schlrshp 86; Holy Name Schlrshp 86; Northeastern U; Bus.

TREMBLAY, JILL M; Cathedral HS; Springfield, MA; (Y); 99/476; Pres Intnl Clb; VP Jr Cls; Jr NHS; Spfld Colleen & Ct 85; 1st Pl Frnch Ptry Cntst 85; Mdl Snt 86; Bentley Coll; Finance.

TREMBLAY, JOYCE; Melrose HS; Melrose, MA; (Y); 46/350; Pep Clb; Varsity Clb; Orch; Yrbk Stf; Rep Soph Cls; Rep Jr Cls; Rep Sr Cls; Stu Cncl; Var L Swmmng; Var Trk; NE Regl YMCA Hnr Bwl 84; U Of Lowell; Phy Thrpy.

TREMBLAY, PATRICIA; Billerica Memorial HS; N Billerica, MA; (Y); 112/480; Office Aide; SADD; Boys Clb Am; French Clb; Intnl Clb; Yrbk Stf; Hon Roll; Psychlgy.

TREMBLE, MATTHEW; Medway JR SR HS; Medway, MA; (Y); 16/145; Drama Clb; Pres Band; Jazz Band; School Musical; Yrbk Stf; Rep Stu Cncl; Hon Roll; Trs NHS; Ntl Merit SF; Outstndng Jr Boy 85-86; Bentley; Mngmnt.

TREMBLEY, DAVID; Chicopee Comprehensive HS; Chicopee, MA; (Y); 22/305; Stu Cncl; Trk; High Hon Roll; Hon Roll; NHS; Pro Merito 86; Merrimack Coll; Elec Engr.

TREMBLEY, THERESA; Chicopee Comprehensive HS; Chicopee, MA; (Y); 5/306; Girl Scts; Library Aide; Ed Sec Yrbk Stf; Stu Cncl; Im Powder Puff Ftbl; Elks Awd; NHS; St Schlr; Worcester Polytech Inst; Biomed.

TRETHEWEY, SCOTT; Walpole HS; Walpole, MA; (Y); 39/266; Ski Clb; Rep Stu Cncl; JV Bsbl; Var Capt Golf; Var Tennis; JV Trk; Hon Roll; Stu Of Mo Econ 86; Business.

TRIANT, DEBORAH; Everett HS; Everett, MA; (Y); 7/300; Intnl Clb; Sec Key Clb; Letterman Clb; Science Clb; Teachers Aide; Yrbk Stf; Var L Trk; Hon Roll; Trs NHS; E Clb Of Everett Schlshp Awd 85-86; Thomas Mem Schlrshp 85-86; S B Milonas Shepa Awd 85-86; Boston Coll; Lib Arts.

TRICCA, MARK; Medford HS; Medford, MA; (Y); Boy Scts; Letterman Clb; Ski Clb; Crs Cntry; Trk; Hon Roll; Sci Achvt Awd 86; Eng Achvt Awd 84; U MA Amherst; Engrng.

TRICK, JULI; Montachusett Regional Vo Tech; Lunenburg, MA; (Y); Yrbk Stf; High Hon Roll; Hon Roll; NHS; Outstndng Stu Awd Graphc Arts, Sci & Geom; Graphic Arts.

TRICKETT, SEAN; Malden HS; Malden, MA; (Y); 86/485; Band; Hon Mntn Cert Boston Globe Schltc Art Awd 84-85; Chamberlayne JC; Jwlry Dsgn.

TRIONFI, ANGELA; Revere HS; Revere, MA; (Y); 95/400; Office Aide; SADD; Yrbk Stf; Rep Soph Cls; Sec Jr Cls; Rep Stu Cncl; Fld Hcky; Score Keeper; High Hon Roll; Hon Roll; Nwbry JR Schlrshp 86; Nwbry JC; Clnry Arts.

TRIPLETT, CARLA; High School Of Commerce; Springfield, MA; (S); Drama Clb; JA; Office Aide; SADD; Church Choir; School Play; Nwsp Rptr; Rep Frsh Cls; VP Jr Cls; Rep Stu Cncl; Acad Achvt Awd 85; Mnrty Acad Achvt Awd 86; Adelphi U; Bus Adm.

TRIPODI, MARK; Acton Boxborough Regional HS; Acton, MA; (Y); 102/405; Boy Scts; Radio Clb; Ski Clb; Hon Roll; Art Postr Cntst 1st Pl 85.

TRIPP, CARY; Old Rochester Regional HS; Mattapoisett, MA; (Y); 2/147; Sec AFS; Am Leg Aux Girls St; Ski Clb; Pres Sr Cls; Rep Stu Cncl; Cit Awd; Sec NHS; Pres Schlr; Commonwlth Schlrshp Awd 86; Stonehill Coll; Law.

TRIPP, CHRISTOPHER; New Bedford HS; Acushnet, MA; (Y); 14/599; JA; JCL; Key Clb; ROTC; Yrbk Stf; Stu Cncl; High Hon Roll; NHS; Ntl Merit Ltr; Natl Latin Exm Slvr Mdl 84-86; Acushnet Tchtrs Assn Schlrshp 86; Yth Ldrshp Conf Frdms Fond 85; Rnsslr Polytechnic Inst; Physcs.

TRIPP, DORIS; Marlboro HS; Marlboro, MA; (Y); 28/269; Church Yth Grp; Sec Varsity Clb; Band; Church Choir; Concert Band; Mrchg Band; Var Capt Crs Cntry; Trk; NHS; Awd Outstndng Achvmnt Soc Studs 86; Phy Ther.

TRIPP, RUSSELL; Amherst Regional HS; Amherst, MA; (Y); Boy Scts; Cmnty Wkr; Science Clb; School Play; Stage Crew; Yrbk Stf; Var L Ftbl; Wt Lftg; Hon Roll; Rutgers U; Elec Engr.

TROIANO, TIMOTHY; Newton North HS; Newton, MA; (Y); Am Leg Boys St; Red Cross Aide; Rep Stu Cncl; Var Crs Cntry; Var Lcrss; Var Capt Swmmng; Church Schlrshp 86; Northeastern; Physcl Thrpy.

TROIANO, TRICIA; King Philip Reg HS; Norfolk, MA; (Y); Ed Yrbk Stf; Trs VP Stu Cncl; Var Gym; Im Powder Puff Ftbl; JV Socr; JV Sftbl; 2 Vrsty Ltrs Gymnstcs 85-86; Grphc Dsgnr.

TROMBLY, PATRICK; Central Catholic HS; N Andover, MA; (Y); 17/231; Hosp Aide; Political Wkr; NHS; Boy Scts; JV Var Crs Cntry; JV Var Trk; High Hon Roll; Hon Roll; Poltc Sci.

TROUP, KENNETH; Silver Lake Regional HS; Halifax, MA; (Y); 43/450; L Bsbl; L Bsktbl; Comp Engrng.

TROWBRIDGE, CHERYL; Attleboro HS; Attleboro, MA; (Y); Church Yth Grp; PAVAS; Spanish Clb; Band; Concert Band; Pep Band; Nwsp Rptr; Nwsp Stf; Fld Hcky; Tennis; Bio.

TROWBRIDGE, ELIZABETH; Newton Country Day Schl; Burlington, MA; (Y); Cmnty Wkr; Drama Clb; Model UN; SADD; Chorus; School Musical; School Play; Stage Crew; Nwsp Stf; Lit Mag; Poli Sci.

TRUMBULL, JOHNATHAN G; Falmouth HS; Woods Hole, MA; (Y); Boy Scts; Pres French Clb; Pres Science Clb; Nwsp Ed-Chief; NHS; Ntl Merit SF; SAR Awd; AFS; JV Crs Cntry; JV Trk; Fnlnd US Snt Yth Exch Prgm 85; Sci Awds 85; Sprntndnt Awd Of Exc 85.

TRUONG, TRUNG; Classical HS; Lynn, MA; (Y); Boys Clb Am; Off Sr Cls; Hon Roll; NE U; Elec Tech.

TRUONG, TUONG; West Roxbury HS; Dorchester, MA; (S); Ski Clb; Stu Cncl; Hon Roll; NHS; Arson Watch Reward Prog Awd Wng Poster 83; Holiday Grtng Card Cntst Awd Wng Dsgn 84; Hnr Rl 85; Natl Tech Inst For Deaf; Archtc.

TSANG, ADRIENNE; Bedford HS; Bedford, MA; (Y); 27/198; Am Leg Aux Girls St; SADD; Yrbk Bus Mgr; Yrbk Ed-Chief; Var Crs Cntry; Var Mgr(s); Var Capt Tennis; High Hon Roll; Hon Roll; Trs NHS; MA Bus Wk 86.

TSAPARLIS II, NICHOLAS MICHAEL; Lynn Classical HS; Lynn, MA; (Y); 10/180; Am Leg Boys St; Hosp Aide; Yrbk Stf; VP Soph Cls; VP Sr Cls; Stu Cncl; JV Bsktbl; Coach Actv; Hon Roll; NHS; Med.

TSITOS, ANDREAS; Malden Catholic HS; Malden, MA; (Y); 54/184; MA ST Schlrshp 86; Boston U; Elec Engrng.

TSONGALIS, EUDOXIA; Southbridge HS; Southbridge, MA; (Y); 18/163; Math Tm; Rep Frsh Cls; Pres Soph Cls; Pres Jr Cls; Pres Sr Cls; Rep Stu Cncl; Hon Roll; U MA Amherst; Optmtrst.

TU, PAUL; Boston Technical HS; East Boston, MA; (Y); SADD; Varsity Clb; Sec Soph Cls; Rep Jr Cls; Rep Stu Cncl; JV Bsktbl; Socr; Swmmng; High Hon Roll; Hon Roll; Amer Rgn Cert Of Schl Awd 83; Boston Coll; Bus Mngmnt.

TUBEROSA, MICHAEL; Silver Lake Regional HS; Kingston, MA; (Y); 52/460; Nwsp Sprt Ed; Var Bsktbl; Hon Roll; NHS; Edna Mglthln Schlrshp Twn Kngston MA 86; Syracuse U; Brdcst Jrnlsm.

TUCK, ELIZABETH; Sharon HS; Sharon, MA; (Y); Off Band; Chorus; Off Concert Band; L Pep Band; School Musical; Nwsp Rptr; Nwsp Stf; Yrbk Stf; Ntl Merit Ltr; Church Yth Grp; SE Bandmstrs Assoc Fstvl 86; Framingham ST Hstrcl Rsrch Cnvtn Hnr Mntn 85; Law.

TUCKER, DAVID; St Johns Prep; Lynn, MA; (Y); Var L Ice Hcky; Hon Roll; Cathlc Conf All Str 85-86; Lynn Dly Evng Item All Str 85-86; Princeton; Bus.

TUCKER, DEBRA ANNE; Needham HS; Needham, MA; (Y); 17/348; Pres Church Yth Grp; German Clb; Chorus; School Musical; Stage Crew; Ed Lit Mag; Hon Roll; NHS; Ntl Merit Ltr; NEDT Awd; Rice U.

TUCKER, KERRY L; Hamilton-Wenham Regional HS; South Hamilton, MA; (Y); 3/190; Capt Math Tm; VP Science Clb; JV Trk; High Hon Roll; Ntl Merit SF; Outstndg Stu Wmns Aux S Essex Med Soc 85; MIT; Gentc Engr.

TUCKER, MARJORIE; Burlington HS; Burlington, MA; (Y); 79/314; VP Church Yth Grp; Political Wkr; Trs SADD; Yrbk Stf; Var Cheerleading; Var Trk; Hon Roll; Piano Student; Hampton U; Comp Graphics.

TUCKER, PAULA; Girls Catholic HS; Malden, MA; (Y); Church Yth Grp; Girl Scts; Spanish Clb; SADD; Var JV Cheerleading; BUS Admin.

TUCKER, TANYA M; Boston Latin Acad; Mattapan, MA; (Y); 22/133; Camera Clb; Debate Tm; German Clb; Intnl Clb; Political Wkr; Church Choir; Sec Sr Cls; Hon Roll; Ntl Merit Ltr; Goethe Inst Book Awd 85; Math Awd; Politicn.

TUDOR, PAULA; Plymouth-Carver HS; Plymouth, MA; (Y); AFS; Drama Clb; Sec French Clb; Math Tm; Nwsp Rptr; Yrbk Bus Mgr; Hon Roll; USFSA 85-86; Bentley Clg; Ecnmcs.

TUDRYN, REBECCA; Hopkins Acad; Hadley, MA; (Y); Am Leg Aux Girls St; Band; Chorus; Drm Mjr(t); Pres Frsh Cls; Pres Soph Cls; Pres Jr Cls; Rep Stu Cncl; NHS.

TULLI, STEPHEN M; Franklin HS; Franklin, MA; (Y); Political Wkr; Concert Band; Mrchg Band; Yrbk Stf; Rep Stu Cncl; Var Tennis; Hon Roll; Holy Cross Book Prz 86; Hockomock Mdl Snt 85-87; Law Day 85; Comp Sci.

TULLY, ALISON; Woburn SR HS; Woburn, MA; (S); 25/453; Boys Clb Am; Camp Fr Inc; Church Yth Grp; JA; Leo Clb; SADD; Yrbk Stf; Capt Cheerleading; High Hon Roll; Hon Roll; 3rd Pl Sci Fair 84; 3rd Pl MA Sci Fair MIT 83; Histrcl Essay Wnnr 84; Nrs.

TUMAS, SHARON; Shrewsbury HS; Shrewsbury, MA; (Y); Letterman Clb; Math Clb; Math Tm; Var Mgr(s); Sftbl; Hon Roll; Fshn Merch.

TUMILTY, SHEILA M; Mount Saint Joseph Acad; Boston, MA; (Y); 18/146; Church Yth Grp; VP JA; Science Clb; AFS; Band; Concert Band; Drm & Bgl; Mrchg Band; Stage Crew; Nwsp Rptr; Georgetown U; Nrsng.

TUPPER, WALTER; Groton-Dunstable Regional HS; Dunstable, MA; (Y); 15/112; Capt Var Ice Hcky; Hon Roll; Jr NHS; NHS; Lwll Sun All Str Hcky Tm, 1st Tm All Str Hcky, Mst Vlbl Ply Hcky 86; NH All Str Ice Hcky Tm 83; Bus.

TURA, LINDA M; Silver Lake Regional, HS; Kingston, MA; (Y); 9/494; Am Leg Aux Girls St; Church Yth Grp; Spanish Clb; Fld Hcky; High Hon Roll; NHS; French Clb; Library Aide; Math Clb; Natl Ldrshp Svc Awd 84 & 86; Acadmc All Amer 84; Brockton Enterprise All Schlstc Fld Hcky 85; Stonehill; Law.

TURBA, FRANK; Assabet Valley Regional Vo-Tech; Hudson, MA; (Y); 30/310; Computer Clb; Band; Chorus; Stu Cncl; Ftbl; Wt Lftg; Hon Roll; Rgnl Stu Advsry Cncl Rep 84, 85 & 86; Comp.

TURCHETTE, QUENTIN; Dedham HS; Dedham, MA; (S); 6/256; Computer Clb; Ed Nwsp Rptr; Lit Mag; JV Bsbl; High Hon Roll; NHS; Wnnr Odd Fllws & Rebeba Untd Natns Essy & Spch Cntst 85; Bst Frshmn Math Dept & Bst Soph Sci 84 & 85; Sci.

TURICK, JEFF S; St Johns HS; Shrewsbury, MA; (Y); 72/286; Church Yth Grp; Lit Mag; Cmnty Wkr; English Clb; Model UN; Spanish Clb; Var Trk; High Hon Roll; Hon Roll; PA ST U; Arch.

TURLEY, KELLY; Attleboro HS; Attleboro, MA; (Y); Band; Concert Band; Mrchg Band; JV Bsktbl; Powder Puff Ftbl; JV Vllybl; High Hon Roll; NEDT Awd; Psychlgy.

TURNER, DE ANNE; Reading Memorial HS; Reading, MA; (Y); French Clb; SADD; Var Bsktbl; Var Capt Fld Hcky; Var Sftbl; High Hon Roll; Hon Roll; Bus.

TURNER, JEAN; Marlboro HS; Marlboro, MA; (Y); VP Boys Clb Am; Varsity Clb; Var L Bsktbl; JV Sftbl; Var L Vllybl; Hon Roll; Fclty Awd Outstndg Achvmnt Art 86; Engnrng.

TURNER, STEPHANIE; Waltham HS; Waltham, MA; (Y); Art Clb; French Clb; Library Aide; Office Aide; Pep Clb; Yrbk Ed-Chief; Yrbk Stf; Cheerleading; Pom Pon; Tennis; Moore Coll; Fshn Dsgnr.

TURNER, WES; Billerica Memorial HS; Billerica, MA; (Y); 62/450; Ski Clb; SADD; Nwsp Rptr; Nwsp Sprt Ed; Nwsp Stf; JV Ftbl; JV Ice Hcky; JV Var Lcrss; Hon Roll; Bus.

TURNQUIST, RODD F; Walpole HS; E Walpole, MA; (Y); 40/256; Radio Clb; Concert Band; Jazz Band; Mrchg Band; Orch; Pres Schlr; U MA Amherst; Mech Engr.

TUTTLE, ANNE; Norwell HS; Norwell, MA; (Y); 3/177; Drama Clb; Concert Band; Yrbk Ed-Chief; Rep Stu Cncl; Trk; Bausch & Lomb Sci Awd; Cit Awd; High Hon Roll; Pres NHS; St Schlr; Drtmth Bk Awd; Lcl Harry Merritt Awd; Wmns Clb Awd; MA Inst Of Tech; Bio-Med Engr.

TUTTLE, JAMES; Millbury Memorial HS; Millbury, MA; (Y); 1/135; Church Yth Grp; Computer Clb; ROTC; Pres SADD; JV Var Socr; Var L Trk; High Hon Roll; VP NHS; Val; Harvrd Book Awd 86; MA Inst Of Tech; Cmptr Sci.

TUTTLE, SCOTT S; Whitman-Hanson HS; Whitman, MA; (Y); 16/281; Computer Clb; JV Socr; Im Tennis; Trk; Hon Roll; NHS; Bus.

TUTTLE, SHANNON; Norton HS; Norton, MA; (S); 8/174; Hosp Aide; Trk; Hon Roll; VFW 85; Nrs.

TWADDLE, THERESA C; Bishop Connolly HS; Newport, RI; (Y); 12/175; Off Church Yth Grp; French Clb; Rep Frsh Cls; Var Bsktbl; Var Sftbl; Im Vllybl; High Hon Roll; Ntl Merit Ltr; Vrsty Lttr Cyclng 85-86; 2nd Grnt Metrns Awds Bichmstry Expo Sci Fr 84; 2nd Tm All-ST Bsktbll Tm 84.

TWOHIG, MARY; Silver Lake HS; Kingston, MA; (Y); French Clb; Sec Soph Cls; JV Socr; Var Capt Tennis; Hon Roll.

TWORIG, MICHELLE; Drury SR HS; N Adams, MA; (Y); 4/190; Am Leg Aux Girls St; French Clb; SADD; Sec Frsh Cls; VP Soph Cls; Trs Sr Cls; JV Sftbl; Capt L Tennis; High Hon Roll; VFW Awd; Mst Outstndng Feml Swmr YMCA 86; Intl Brthrhd Polc Ofcr Schlrshp 86; Clark U; Pre-Med.

TY, CHHORYY; South Boston HS; Allston, MA; (S); Nwsp Stf; High Hon Roll; NHS; Quincy JC; Offc Educ.

TYBURSKI, MARC; Ludlow HS; Ludlow, MA; (Y); JCL; Bsbl; JV Bsktbl; Hon Roll.

TYLER, CARRIE; Commerce HS; Springfield, MA; (Y); JA; Library Aide; Office Aide; Ski Clb; Band; Yrbk Ed-Chief; Yrbk Phtg; Yrbk Stf; Cheerleading; High Hon Roll; U Of MA; Comp.

TYLER, TRACY; Maynard HS; Maynard, MA; (Y); Library Aide; Sec Soph Cls; JV Var Fld Hcky; JV Var Sftbl; Hgh O Brn Yth Ldrshp Awd 84-85; Mrktg.

TYMANN, NATHAN J; Triton Regional HS; Byfield, MA; (Y); Am Leg Boys St; Church Yth Grp; Cmnty Wkr; Letterman Clb; Teachers Aide; JV Var Bsbl; Var L Bsktbl; Var L Trk; NHS; Hon Roll; Nwbryprt Chmbr Commrc Hnrs Awd 86; MIP Bsktbl 86; Engr.

TYRIE, SANDRA; Georgetown JR SR HS; Georgetown, MA; (Y); 20/85; Church Yth Grp; Drama Clb; Spanish Clb; School Play; Sec Sr Cls; Var Capt Bsktbl; JV Fld Hcky; JV Sftbl; Hon Roll; Sci.

TZORTZIS, SOPHIE; Salem HS; Salem, MA; (Y); Church Yth Grp; Variety Show; High Hon Roll; Hon Roll; NHS; Hnrbl Mntn Sci Fair 86; Geog.

ULM, GARRETT C; Bridgewater-Raynham Regional HS; Raynham, MA; (Y); Am Leg Boys St; Art Clb; Camera Clb; Church Yth Grp; Model UN; Ski Clb; Yrbk Stf; Var Trk; Pro Arts Consortium At Boston Arch Ctr 86; AZ ST U; Architecture.

UMSCHEID, CAROL; Westwood HS; Westwood, MA; (Y); 77/215; AFS; Church Yth Grp; SADD; Stage Crew; Var Diving; Powder Puff Ftbl; Swmmng; Hon Roll; Bus.

UNDERWOOD, ERIN; Northfield Mount Hermon Schl; Gill, MA; (Y); Church Yth Grp; Cmnty Wkr; Lcrss; JV Socr; Hon Roll; Comp Sci.

UNDERWOOD, PAMELA; Chicoee HS; Chicopee, MA; (Y); 40/243; Church Yth Grp; Church Choir; Yrbk Stf; Rep Jr Cls; Var L Crs Cntry; Var Capt Swmmng; Var L Trk; Hon Roll; NHS; Accntnt.

UNDERWOOD, SHARON; Uxbridge HS; N Uxbridge, MA; (Y); 11/87; French Clb; Trs Soph Cls; Trs Jr Cls; Stu Cncl; Var Capt Cheerleading; Var Capt Fld Hcky; Var Sftbl; Hon Roll; Sec NHS.

URBAN, RACHEL; Drury SR HS; North Adams, MA; (Y); Church Yth Grp; Cmnty Wkr; Spanish Clb; Stat Bsktbl; JV Var Socr; Trk; Hon Roll; Art Stu Of Mnth 85; Art.

URBONAS, STACEY A; Peabody Vets Memorial HS; Peabody, MA; (Y); 7/500; VP Drama Clb; Thesps; Chorus; School Musical; School Play; Stage Crew; Variety Show; Ed Nwsp Ed-Chief; Lit Mag; Sec NHS; Drama.

URCH, CRAIG E; Hopkins Acad; Hadley, MA; (Y); Am Leg Boys St; Church Yth Grp; Scholastic Bowl; Band; Nwsp Ed-Chief; Pres Stu Cncl; Mgr(s); Var Socr; Hon Roll; NHS; 1st Pl Lane Prz Spkng Cntst 86; Soc Sci.

URDA, JULIANNE; Acton-Boxborough Regional HS; Acton, MA; (Y); 3/347; Church Yth Grp; Cmnty Wkr; Red Cross Aide; Church Choir; Orch; Var L Lcrss; Var L Swmmng; French Hon Soc; Hon Roll; NHS; Natl Hnr Socty & Fred L Robbins Trust Schlrshps 86; Dartmouth Coll; Lib Arts.

USALIS, INGA; Thayer Acad; Hanover, MA; (Y); 7/106; Church Yth Grp; GAA; Q&S; Yrbk Stf; JV Fld Hcky; Var Lcrss; High Hon Roll; Hon Roll; NHS; Spanish NHS; Span II Awd Excllnce; Boston Coll; Bus.

USALIS, KARLA; Thayer Acad; Hanover, MA; (Y); 1/106; School Musical; Pep Band; Ed Yrbk Stf; Lit Mag; L Bsktbl; L Fld Hcky; L Lcrss; Ntl Merit Ltr; Harvard Bk Prize 85; Renssalaer Mdl 85; Princeton U.

USHAKOFF, NICOLE; Beverly HS; Beverly, MA; (Y); 8/374; Am Leg Aux Girls St; German Clb; Science Clb; Concert Band; Jazz Band; Nwsp Bus Mgr; High Hon Roll; NHS; Band; Mrchg Band; Dartmouth Band Awd 85; Beverly Coll Clb Schrlshp 86; Tufts U; Biochem.

UYEMUKI, SHARON; Amherst Regional HS; Amherst, MA; (Y); 4-H; Girl Scts; Yrbk Stf; Rep Stu Cncl; JV Bsktbl; Hon Roll; Holyoke CC; Acctg.

UYENOYAMA, CATHARINE; Barnstable HS; Cotuit, MA; (Y); NFL; Speech Tm; Cheerleading; Powder Puff Ftbl; Trk; Hon Roll; Cert Of Awd/Orgnl Ortry 85; Ntl Frnsc Lgu85; Bamstable Pbl Schls Spch Ortry 85; Crmnl Prosecutor.

UZDAVINIS, LORI; Presentation Of Mary Acad; Salem, NH; (Y); Dance Clb; Spanish Clb; SADD; Chorus; Hon Roll; UNH; Psych.

VACCARELLA, VINCENT; Marlboro HS; Marlboro, MA; (Y); 17/368; Ski Clb; Stu Cncl; JV Var Bsbl; JV Var Ftbl; NHS; Ntl Merit Ltr; Law.

VACHER, LISA; Attleboro HS; S Attleboro, MA; (Y); Trs Frsh Cls; Bsktbl; Var Crs Cntry; Var Gym; High Hon Roll; Hon Roll; NHS; Exec Secy.

VACHON, RONALD J; Newton South HS; Newton, MA; (Y); Var Bsbl; Var Capt Wrstlng; Hon Roll; Schl Faclty Ltr Of Recog 85-86.

VADALA, MARIE THERESA; Gloucester HS; Gloucester, MA; (Y); Math Tm; Off Band; Off Concert Band; Off Mrchg Band; Rep Soph Cls; Hon Roll; Rotary Awd; NESBA Hnrs Band 84 & 85; Semper Fidelis Music Awd 86; Acad All-Amer Schlr Pgm 84-85.

VADNAIS, JOHN PAUL; Ware HS; Ware, MA; (Y); 6/111; Math Clb; Spanish Clb; School Play; VP Frsh Cls; Rep Stu Cncl; L Bsbl; L Ftbl; L Golf; High Hon Roll; Hon Roll; Hugh Obrien Yth Ldrs Rep 85; Good Govt Day Rep 86; Congrssnl Uth Ldrshp Cncl 86; Naval Acad; Naval Arch.

VAGIANOS, EGUENICA; Melrose HS; Melrose, MA; (Y); 73/450; Church Yth Grp; Hosp Aide; SADD; Chorus; Orch; School Musical; JV Fld Hcky; JV Sftbl; Wheaton; Hstry.

VAGOS, MICHAEL; Gloucester HS; Gloucester, MA; (Y); Church Yth Grp; Yrbk Stf; Kiwanis Awd; NHS; B C Grant 86-87; Gilbert Grant 86-87; Awd Acad Exclnc 83-86; Boston Coll; Bus.

VALANTE, JAMES; Boston College HS; Quincy, MA; (Y); Aud/Vis; Church Yth Grp; Sec Drama Clb; JA; Key Clb; Math Clb; Ski Clb; SADD; Concert Band; School Musical; Chem Engr.

VALATKA III, JOSEPH A; Wilmington HS; Wilmington, MA; (Y); 40/244; Boy Scts; Math Clb; Science Clb; SADD; Chorus; School Play; High Hon Roll; Hon Roll; Ntl Merit SF; Comp Pgmmng.

VALCOURT, LYNN; Presentation Of Mary Acad; Lawrence, MA; (Y); Debate Tm; Political Wkr; Nwsp Stf; Yrbk Stf; Hon Roll; Church Yth Grp; French Clb; SADD; Chorus; School Musical; Thelgy Awd 86; Polit Sci.

VALDES, JONNI; Gardner HS; Gardner, MA; (Y); 27/149; Girl Scts; Sec SADD; Chorus; Church Choir; School Musical; Lit Mag; 4-H; School Play; Stage Crew; Score Keeper; National Sci Olympiad In Chem 86; Industrial Arts Club 85-86; Civil Engrng.

VALENCOURT, MICHELLE; North Brookfield HS; N Brookfield, MA; (Y); 6/40; Red Cross Aide; School Play; Yrbk Ed-Chief; Sec Jr Cls; Sec Sr Cls; Off Stu Cncl; Capt Var Cheerleading; Hon Roll; Sec NHS; Pres Schlr; Englsh Awd 86; Lioness Clb Schlrshp 86; Police Assoc Schlrshp 86; Quinnipiac Coll; Occup Thrpy.

VALENTE, CHRISTINE; BMC Durke HS; Fall River, MA; (Y); 4/681; AFS; Science Clb; Varsity Clb; Var L Swmmng; Var L Tennis; High Hon Roll; NHS; Hon Roll; Williams Coll Bk Awd 86; Boston Globe All Schltc Swmmg 83-85; Engrng.

VALERIO, NANCY; Melrose HS; Melrose, MA; (Y); 48/402; Church Yth Grp; Drama Clb; Hosp Aide; Political Wkr; SADD; Band; Chorus; Ed Nwsp Rptr; NHS; Pep Clb; Colgate U; Polit Sci.

VALKANAS, MICHAEL A; Xaverian Brothers HS; Dedham, MA; (Y); 46/207; Stage Crew; Nwsp Rptr; Yrbk Phtg; Trk; Elks Awd; Hon Roll; Edward H Hinds Schlrshps 86; Abepa Dist 8 Harris J Booras Awd 86; Boston Coll; Lbrl Arts.

VALOIS, KATHERINE; Gardner HS; Gardner, MA; (Y); 8/162; Church Yth Grp; French Clb; Chorus; Lit Mag; Var L Trk; NHS; Lttr Of Cmmndtn 85; Clark U; Engl.

VAN PROOYEN, PETER; Lexington HS; Lexington, MA; (Y); Boy Scts; Sec Church Yth Grp; Computer Clb; Sec 4-H; German Clb; Varsity Clb; Rep Stu Cncl; Var Socr; JV Wrstlng; Hon Roll; Hermiston HS Hnr Pgs Cert Achvt 84-85; West Point; Engrng.

VANASSE, CATHERINE; Notre Dame Acad; Weymouth, MA; (Y); Drama Clb; French Clb; Latin Clb; Office Aide; Ski Clb; Spanish Clb; Im Bsktbl; Stat Var Gym; Hon Roll; Prfct Atten Awd; Cert Merit French Exam 85; U Lowell; Bus.

VANASSE, DAN; Reading Memorial HS; Reading, MA; (Y); Band; High Hon Roll; Hon Roll.

VANASSE, KAREN; Holyoke Catholic HS; Northampton, MA; (Y); Camera Clb; Church Yth Grp; Cmnty Wkr; Computer Clb; French Clb; Political Wkr; Ski Clb; SADD; Varsity Clb; School Play; Helping Hands Awd 85; U MA Comp II Camp Outstndng Awd 84; Yale Med Schl; Med Resrch.

VANCE, FELICIA; Fanning Trade HS; Worcester, MA; (Y); Church Yth Grp; Girl Scts; Chorus; Church Choir; Off Jr Cls; Gym; Trk; Prfct Atten Awd; Bus Adm.

VANDAL, PAULA; Chicopee HS; Chicopee, MA; (Y); 61/253; Cmnty Wkr; Nwsp Ed-Chief; Nwsp Rptr; Var L Bsktbl; JV Sftbl; Westfield ST Coll; Engl.

VANDERGRIFT, ROB; Agawam HS; Agawam, MA; (Y); Boy Scts; Var Capt Bsktbl; Im Golf; Im Ice Hcky; Im Vllybl; Im Wt Lftg.

VANGA, JORGE E; Winchester HS; Boston, MA; (Y); Church Yth Grp; Spanish Clb; Church Choir; Im Var Bsktbl; Var Ftbl; Var Trk; JV Wt Lftg; Lion Awd; Outstndng Achvt Acadmc High Hnr Rll 81; Outstndng Achvt Eng 86; Northeastern U; Engr.

VANT, LAUREL; Reading Memorial HS; Reading, MA; (Y); 53/325; VP AFS; Sec Church Yth Grp; German Clb; VP Girl Scts; Church Choir; JV Bsktbl; Var L Socr; Var L Trk; Hon Roll; Rdng Schrshp 86; Rdng Rnbws Alice Moody Schlrshp 86; Untd Mthdst Chrch Schlrshp 86; Merrimack Coll; Accntng.

VANWOERT, NANCY; Stoneleigh-Burnham HS; Oneonta, NY; (Y); 4-H; JV Bowling; Hon Roll; Typng Awd 85; Gen Chem 85; Cazenovia Coll.

VARANOSKE, JOSEPH; Central Catholic HS; Dracut, MA; (Y); 12/231; Ski Clb; High Hon Roll; NHS; 1st Pl Fr Awds 85; 2nd Pl Relig Awd 86.

VARDIS, MARIA T; Apponequet Regional HS; Lakeville, MA; (Y); Church Yth Grp; Trs French Clb; Yrbk Stf; Sec Pres Stu Cncl; Var L Fld Hcky; Var L Tennis; High Hon Roll; VP NHS; Delg Hugh O Brian Yth Ldrshp Semnr 85; Secy Hugh O Brian Almn Assn 86-87; Stdnt Govt Day Rep 86; Poltcl Sci.

VARESCHI, KIRSTIN; Haverhill HS; Haverhill, MA; (Y); Cmnty Wkr; Political Wkr; Var Cheerleading; High Hon Roll; Hon Roll.

VARGO, MIKE; New Bedford HS; New Bedford, MA; (Y); 100/609; Drama Clb; SADD; Band; Chorus; Concert Band; Mrchg Band; Orch; School Musical; School Play; Stu Of ST & New Englnd Mrchng Band Chmpnshp 84-86; Soloist In Band 86-87; Comp Sci.

VARGOS, NANCY; Bishop Stang HS; Tiverton, RI; (Y); Girl Scts; Hosp Aide; SADD; Band; Concert Band; Orch; Pep Band; Symp Band; Variety Show; Nwsp Stf; Music Awds 80-85; Nursing.

VARITIMOS, NINA; Presentation Of Mary Acad; Methuen, MA; (Y); Political Wkr; Yrbk Stf; Trs Frsh Cls; Sec Jr Cls; JV Var Sftbl; JV Var Vllybl; Hon Roll; Church Yth Grp; Office Aide; Spanish Clb; Lgn Of Hnr 86; Sci Fair 3rd Pl 84; Coachs Awd Sftbl & Vllybl 85; Gvrnmnt Srv.

VARNEY, KIM; Bishop Fenwick HS; Peabody, MA; (Y); Art Clb; Church Yth Grp; Band; Chorus; Concert Band; Mrchg Band; Nwsp Rptr; Yrbk Rptr; High Hon Roll; NHS; Envrnmntl Analysis.

VARRAS, NICK; Haverhill HS; Haverhill, MA; (Y); 59/289; Church Yth Grp; Latin Clb; Letterman Clb; Varsity Clb; Var L Socr; High Hon Roll; Hon Roll; Accntnt.

VARRIEUR, TRACY; Attleboro HS; Attleboro, MA; (Y); Yrbk Stf; Stat Bsktbl; Var Fld Hcky; Var Tennis; High Hon Roll; Hon Roll; NHS; Ntl Merit SF; U MA; Nrsng.

VARTABEDIAN, ARA; Haverhill HS; Haverhill, MA; (Y); 8/420; Boys Clb Am; Boy Scts; Nwsp Phtg; Yrbk Stf; Stu Cncl; Var Capt Crs Cntry; Var L Ice Hcky; Var L Trk; High Hon Roll; NHS; Mst Imprvd Rnr Sprng Trk 86; Maksudian Awd Top Armnian Schl Stu 86; Engrng.

VASALLO, SUSANA; Christopher Columbus HS; Jamaica Plain, MA; (S); 20/127; Art Clb; Yrbk Stf; High Hon Roll; Ntl Merit Ltr; Boston Coll; Graphc Desgn.

VASILE, ANGELINA; Beverly HS; Beverly, MA; (Y); 123/377; Girl Scts; Varsity Clb; Rep Frsh Cls; Rep Soph Cls; Trs Sr Cls; Var Cheerleading; Hon Roll; Chamberlayne JC; Rtl Mrchndsng.

VASQUES, ROY; Lawrence HS; Lawrence, MA; (S); 77/266; Pres DECA; FBLA; Letterman Clb; Yrbk Stf; Ftbl; Capt Var Ice Hcky; CC Awd; Hon Roll; Distributive Educ Mktg Natl Wnnr & St Champ 86; Distr Ed Mktg Merrimack Vly Wnnr 85-86; Merrimack Coll; Bus Mktg.

VASQUEZI, JAMES; Hudson HS; Hudson, MA; (Y); 12/158; Boys Clb Am; Yrbk Stf; Bsktbl; High Hon Roll; NHS; Boston Coll; Mrktng.

VAUGHN, JANAN; Reading Memorial HS; Reading, MA; (Y); Church Yth Grp; Drama Clb; SADD; Nwsp Rptr; Lit Mag; Rep Soph Cls; Stat Bsktbl; High Hon Roll; Hon Roll; Ntl Hstry Day 1st Reg, 2nd Dist, 3rd ST 83; Nw Englnd Snshn Mdl 82; Advrtsng.

VAUTOUR, KELLIANN; Saugus HS; Saugus, MA; (Y); 10/280; Spanish Clb; Yrbk Stf; High Hon Roll; Hon Roll; Jr NHS; NHS; Voice Dem Awd; Hnrbl Mntn Phi Alpha Theta Hstrcl Conf Framingham ST Coll 86.

VAYLE, ADAM N; Newton South HS; Newton Center, MA; (Y); Spanish Clb; Temple Yth Grp; Nwsp Rptr; Var Bsktbl; JV Ftbl; Var JV Tennis; Hon Roll; MA Boys ST 86; Recmmndtn Spn Dept 85-86.

VAZ, MARIA; Ludlow HS; Ludlow, MA; (Y); High Hon Roll; Accntng.

VECCHIONE, CHRIS; St Dominic Savio HS; E Boston, MA; (Y); 6/109; Computer Clb; JA; Math Clb; Rep Stu Cncl; Im Bsktbl; JV Crs Cntry; Im Golf; Var L Trk; High Hon Roll; NHS; Boston U; Data Base Mgmt.

VEGA, ELIZABETH; Phillips Acad; Los Angeles, CA; (Y); Cmnty Wkr; Service Clb; Pres Spanish Clb; Stage Crew; Nwsp Ed-Chief; Lit Mag; Hon Roll; Ntl Merit Ltr; Prfct Atten Awd; Socl Sci Stu Of Yr Awd 84; Full Schlrshp 84; Pltcl Sci.

VEGUILLA, RAYMOND; St Marys Regional HS; Lynn, MA; (Y); 2/100; Am Leg Boys St; Var Capt Bsbl; JV Bsktbl; High Hon Roll; Hon Roll; NHS; Williams Bk Awd 86; Nipper Clancy Sprtsmnshp Awd 86; St Marys Schlrshp 86.

VEILLEUX, CHARLES; Central Catholic HS; Methuen, MA; (Y); 35/231; Art Clb; Exploring; JA; Nwsp Rptr; Bowling; Crs Cntry; Hon Roll; Chem.

VELAZQUEZ, TERESA L; Classical HS; Springfield, MA; (Y); JA; Madrigals; Ntl Merit SF; Acpl Chr; Chorus; School Musical; School Play; Crs Cntry; Trk; Ntl Achvt Schlrshp Pgm-Cmmded Stu.

VELELLA, ALBERT; Waltham HS; Boston, MA; (Y); Orch; Hon Roll; Comp Sci.

VELYVIS, KRISTEN; Drury SR HS; N Adams, MA; (Y); 2/189; Church Yth Grp; Pres 4-H; SADD; Stage Crew; Var L Socr; Var Capt Trk; Cit Awd; Pres NHS; Sal; Drama Clb; Commonwealth Schlrshp MA 86; Harvard U; Missionary.

VENA, EMANUEL A; Blue Hills Reg Voc Tech Schl; Braintree, MA; (Y); Aud/Vis; Boy Scts; VICA; Im Bsktbl; Im Fld Hcky; Im Vllybl; Northeastern; Comp Engr.

VENEMAN, STEVEN C; Milford HS; Milford, MA; (Y); 40/296; Boy Scts; Church Yth Grp; Band; Concert Band; Jazz Band; Madrigals; School Musical; Yrbk Stf; Swmmng; NHS; Electd Boy Sct Hon Camper Soc 86; Rcvd Accptnc Jr Band Hall Fame 85; Elec Engr.

VENETO, MICHELE; Hingham HS; Hingham, MA; (Y); 3/345; Band; VP Stu Cncl; Var Capt Gym; Var L Socr; NCTE Awd; VP NHS; Ntl Merit SF; Brown U, Mt Holyoke Bk Awd 86; Chanclrs Schlrshp 86.

VENETOS, MILTON; Westfield HS; Westfield, MA; (Y); 7/360; CAP; French Clb; Im Vllybl; Aerontcl Engr.

VENETSANAKOS, KATHY; Salem HS; Salem, MA; (Y); 18/405; Rep Frsh Cls; Sec Rep Soph Cls; Sec Rep Jr Cls; Sec Sr Cls; Sec Stu Cncl; Var JV Bsktbl; Capt Fld Hcky; Var L Trk; High Hon Roll; NHS; Dartsmouth; Mltry Ldrshp.

VENTOLA, CHERYL; East Bridgewater HS; E Bridgewater, MA; (Y); 12/150; Church Yth Grp; Key Clb; Science Clb; Yrbk Stf; Bausch & Lomb Sci Awd; Hon Roll; PCC 82-85; Womens Clb Schlrshp 86; Foxboro Co Schlrshp 86; Marquette U; Elect Engr.

VENTRY, DONNA MARIE; Bartlett HS; Webster, MA; (Y); 30/150; Church Yth Grp; DECA; FNA; Spanish Clb; Teachers Aide; School Play; Nwsp Stf; Sec Soph Cls; Var L Socr; JV Sftbl; Mdrn Miss Schlrhsp 83; Typng Crtfcts 83-84; 3 Edctnl Schlrshp Awds 86; Fitchburg ST Coll; Spcl Educ.

VENTURA, EDYTHANN; Cushing Acad; Lynnfield, MA; (Y); Hosp Aide; Sec Soph Cls; Socr; Var Capt Trk; Hon Roll; Cum Laude 86; Headmaster Awd 86; Comp Sci Awd 84; Wheaton Coll; Psych.

VENTURA, JAMES S; Malden HS; Medford, MA; (Y); 30/485; Co-Capt Socr; Hon Roll; NHS; Mrdn H Alumni Schlrshp 85-86; U MA Amhrst; Doctor.

VENTURELLI, PETER; Arlington Catholic HS; Arlington, MA; (Y); Spanish Clb; Varsity Clb; Bsbl; Bsktbl; Var L Ftbl; Swmmng; Tennis; Hon Roll; Tufts; Bus.

VENUTI, JOSEPH; Reading Memorial HS; Reading, MA; (Y); 20/375; Rep Frsh Cls; Sec Soph Cls; Rep Jr Cls; Var L Ftbl; Im Socr; JV Trk; High Hon Roll; NHS; Spanish NHS; USAF Acad; Aerosp Eng.

VERBICKY, ANNIE; Presentation Of Mary Acad; Lawrence, MA; (Y); Church Yth Grp; Cmnty Wkr; Political Wkr; Spanish Clb; SADD; Chorus; School Musical; School Play; Nwsp Rptr; Nwsp Stf; Lawrence Eagle Tribn Stdnt Rprtr Go Gttr Awd 86; Var Cert Nws Wrtg 86; Jrnlsm.

VERDERICO, PATRICK; St Dominic Savio HS; Saugus, MA; (Y); 34/104; JA; Bsktbl; Ftbl; Score Keeper; Wt Lftg; Merrimack Coll.

VERGA, JOE; Plymouth Carver HS; Plymouth, MA; (Y); AFS; Church Yth Grp; Model UN; Band; Jazz Band; Var Ftbl; Im Capt Vllybl; Hon Roll; Thomas A Edison Awd Sci 85; Citation By Sec Of St Of MA 3rd Pl In St Sci Fair 85; U TX At Austin; Robotics.

VERGOTH, LARA; Dartmouth HS; S Dartmouth, MA; (Y); 15/237; AFS; Math Tm; Yrbk Stf; Var Capt Crs Cntry; Var Capt Trk; Sec NHS; Smith Coll; Bio.

VERNA, CHRISTINE; King Philip Regional HS; Wrentham, MA; (Y); Yrbk Ed-Chief; Cheerleading; Powder Puff Ftbl; NHS; Hosp Aide; Variety Show; Yrbk Rptr; Yrbk Stf; Hon Roll; Jr NHS; Var Awds & Mdls Dancing; Arch.

VERNON, DANICA; King Philip Regional HS; Norfolk, MA; (Y); 33/250; Church Yth Grp; Concert Band; Jazz Band; Mrchg Band; JV Crs Cntry; JV Socr; JV Trk; Hon Roll; NHS; Natl Piano Gld Adutn Awd 86; Med Rsrch.

VERREE, MICHAEL; Malden HS; Malden, MA; (Y); Bsktbl; Northeastern Clg; Rdo Brdcstg.

VICINO, JOHN; Bishop Stang HS; Wareham, MA; (Y); Church Yth Grp; Cmnty Wkr; SADD; Teachers Aide; Varsity Clb; Band; Mrchg Band; Var Trk; Cit Awd; Hon Roll; Cert Of Hon US Hist 86; Cert Of Merite French I 84; Business Management.

VIDAL, ZULEIKA; New Bedford HS; New Bedford, MA; (Y); Art Clb; Church Yth Grp; Dance Clb; French Clb; French Hon Soc; Hon Roll; Prfct Atten Awd; Portuguese Hnr Soc 83-85; La Barons Schl; Csmtlgst.

VIEIRA, CECILIA MARGARET; Dartmouth HS; S Dartmouth, MA; (Y); Pres AFS; Math Tm; Lib Chorus; Church Choir; Mrchg Band; Rep Frsh Cls; Rep Soph Cls; Rep Jr Cls; Rep Sr Cls; Brown U; Med.

VIEIRA, DELIA; B M C Durfee HS; Fall River, MA; (Y); 99/673; Varsity Clb; JV Var Bsktbl; JV Var Sftbl; JV Var Vllybl; Sprts Med.

VIEIRA, KATHY; B M C Durfee HS; Fall River, MA; (Y); Science Clb; Spanish Clb; Varsity Clb; Concert Band; Mrchg Band; Orch; Pep Band; Var Trk; Hon Roll; Music Hon Soc 85; Envrnmntl Cntrl Cmmte Secty 85; Med.

VIEIRA, LUBELIA; New Bedford HS; New Bedford, MA; (Y); 51/701; High Hon Roll; Prfct Atten Awd; Mrktng.

VIEITES III, ROLANDO R; Matignon HS; Cambridge, MA; (S); 11/178; Cmnty Wkr; Science Clb; Spanish Clb; SADD; Rep Frsh Cls; Im Bsktbl; Hon Roll; NHS; Spanish NHS; Bentley Coll; Bus Mgmt.

VIERA, STEPHEN; Bristol-Plymouth Technical HS; Taunton, MA; (Y); 16/200; Ski Clb; Varsity Clb; VICA; Yrbk Stf; JV Bsktbl; Capt Crs Cntry; Co-Capt Trk; Hon Roll; Kiwanis Awd; NHS; Shop Awd Best Electrncs Stu; Elect Engr.

VIGLIETTI, TINA; Everett HS; Everett, MA; (Y); 48/285; Intnl Clb; Key Clb; Varsity Clb; Yrbk Stf; JV Var Bsktbl; Var Tennis; Hon Roll; Suffolk U; Hist.

VIGNALI, AMY; Seekonk HS; Seekonk, MA; (Y); 19/231; SADD; Rep Frsh Cls; Rep Soph Cls; Sec Jr Cls; Trs Sr Cls; Var Tennis; Var Trk; Var Capt Vllybl; High Hon Roll; NHS; Acdmc Excllnc Awd; Int Dsgn.

VILLECCO, SUSAN; Burlington HS; Burlington, MA; (Y); Math Tm; Yrbk Stf; Hon Roll; Law.

VILLELA, MICHAEL; Old Rochester Regional HS; Mattapoisett, MA; (Y); JV Bsktbl; JV Socr; Var Tennis; High Hon Roll; Pres NHS; MA Acdmc Dcthln 86; Engr.

VILLIOTTE, RICHARD; St Dominic Savio HS; Revere, MA; (Y); 10/110; Math Tm; Ski Clb; SADD; Im Bsktbl; Capt Var Golf; Im Ice Hcky; Tennis; Hon Roll; NHS; Pres Acadmc Ftnss Awd 85-86; Clark U; Bus.

VILOT, HEATHER; Lee HS; Lee, MA; (Y); Cmnty Wkr; Drama Clb; French Clb; Girl Scts; SADD; Band; Chorus; Church Choir; Mrchg Band; School Musical; Miss MA Teen USA Pgnt, 10th Natl Outdoor Speed Sktng 85; Optometry.

VINCENT, DENISE; Groton/Dunstable Regional Sec Schl; Dunstable, MA; (Y); Yrbk Ed-Chief; Yrbk Phtg; Yrbk Rptr; Yrbk Sprt Ed; Yrbk Stf; JV Socr; Hon Roll; Jr NHS; NHS; Prom Comm Stf 85-86; Wrkd At Purity Supreme 85; Elem Schl Asst 85-86; U Of Lowell; Psych.

VINCENT, LORI; Pittsfield HS; Pittsfield, MA; (Y); Boys Clb Am; Trs German Clb; Hosp Aide; Pres JA; Pep Clb; Yrbk Stf; Capt Diving; Capt Swmmng; Hon Roll; Sir Thomas Lipton Awd Boys Clb 86; Top Sales Prsn Yr JA 86.

VINCENT, LUKE; Bishop Connolly HS; Fall River, MA; (Y); Computer Clb; Drama Clb; Office Aide; Teachers Aide; School Play; Nwsp Rptr; High Hon Roll; NHS; Presdntl Acad Fitness Awd 86.

VINCENT, MARK; North Reading HS; N Reading, MA; (Y); Church Yth Grp; Computer Clb; Math Tm; Science Clb; Nwsp Stf; High Hon Roll; NHS; Comp Engrng.

VINCENT, MARK; Taconic HS; Pittsfield, MA; (Y); Cmnty Wkr; SADD; Rep Stu Cncl; Bowling; Coach Actv; Socr; Trk; Engrng.

VINCEQUERE, THOMAS ANTHONY; Holy Name Catholic HS; Worcester, MA; (Y); 111/294; Readg & Rhetrc 84; Cmmnctn Sklls 85; Relig Studs II 85; Boston Coll.

VISCONTI, GERRY; St Dominic Savio HS; E Boston, MA; (Y); 30/100; Ski Clb; Varsity Clb; Bowling; Ftbl; Northeastern U; Bus.

VISCONTI JR, JOHN A; Medford HS; Medford, MA; (Y); 5/400; Am Leg Boys St; Cmnty Wkr; Math Clb; Math Tm; Science Clb; SADD; Var Capt Tennis; Pres NHS; Library Aide; Mathletes; Grand Sci Awd 86; Somerville Dist Ct Schlrshp $1000 86; Achvt Awd-Eng-4 Yrs Of A Avg 86; Engrng.

VITKUS, RICHARD A; Minnechaug Regional HS; Wilbraham, MA; (Y); 18/288; Boys Clb Am; Teachers Aide; Var L Crs Cntry; Var L Swmmng; Var L Trk; Hon Roll; NHS; Intnl Clb; Im Vllybl; Tp 10 Pct JETS Ntl Engrng Apt 85; MA Swm Tm Chmps, 1st W MA Cmptr Cntst 86; Cmptr Sci.

VITO, RANDY; Franlin HS; Franklin, MA; (Y); Church Yth Grp; DECA; Library Aide; Office Aide; Chorus; Yrbk Phtg; Yrbk Stf; Stu Cncl; Bus.

VITTERS, SUSAN; Arlington HS; Arlington, MA; (Y); Aud/Vis; Camera Clb; Stage Crew; Nwsp Stf; Crs Cntry; Trk; Hon Roll; NHS; Art Cntst 1st Pl Pntng 85; Hnrb Mntn Art Cntst Pntng 86.

VITUKEVICH, VICKI L; Melrose HS; Wakefield, MA; (S); Pep Clb; Spanish Clb; SADD; Trs Soph Cls; Sec Jr Cls; Stu Cncl; Cheerleading; Powder Puff Ftbl; High Hon Roll; Hon Roll; U MA; Fashion Merchandise.

VIVEIROS, JOHN; Old Rochester Regional HS; Rochester, MA; (Y); 7/150; Trs AFS; Am Leg Boys St; Ski Clb; Rep Sr Cls; Var Capt Socr; Pres Schlr; St Schlr; Math Tm; Bsbl; Trk; Outstandng Engl Stu AP Engl 85; MMR Dollrs Schlrs Schlrshp 86; New Befrd Ed Assc Schlrshp 86; Prvdnc Coll; Bio.

VIVEIROS, SUZANNA; Bishop Connolly HS; Fall River, MA; (Y); 61/182; Bristol CC; Bus Admn.

VIVIER, JAMES; Mohawk Trail Reg HS; Rowe, MA; (Y); 23/116; Pres Church Yth Grp; Letterman Clb; Ski Clb; SADD; Varsity Clb; School Musical; School Play; Stu Cncl; Var Capt Bsbl; JV Bsktbl; Schl Peer Educ Prgrm 84-86; AZ ST U; Mech Engr.

VO, THONG H; S Boston HS; S Boston, MA; (S); Boy Scts; Math Tm; Socr; Hon Roll; NHS; 1st Awds-Cmmnty Svc Boy Scouts 82; Northeastern U; Chem Engrng.

VOGEL, FRED; Northfield Mt Hermon HS; Lake George, NY; (Y); Var Capt Bsbl; Var Ftbl; Var Ice Hcky; Hon Roll; Trs Jr NHS; Union Coll; Law.

VOGEL, KATHY; North Middlesex HS; Pepperell, MA; (Y); 10/200; Math Tm; SADD; Off Jr Cls; Off Sr Cls; Var Mgr(s); Trk; Dnfth Awd; Elizabeth Haskins Mth Cont Spcl Hnrs 86; NE Mth Lg Hnrs 86; Vet.

VOGEL, LAUREN; Braintree HS; Braintree, MA; (Y); 24/442; Yrbk Stf; Lit Mag; Var Fld Hcky; Hon Roll; NHS; Spanish NHS; Peer Cnslr Trng 86; Bus Wk Bentley Coll 86; Intl Bus.

VOISINE, KRISTEN; Presentation Of Mary Acad; North Andover, MA; (Y); 9/45; Girl Scts; Spanish Clb; Chorus; JV Sftbl; Hon Roll; NHS; 4th Dgr Knights Of Columbus Schlrshp 83,85; Awd For Asst Lawrence Pop Warner 86; Med.

VOLKER, CHRIS; Ludlow HS; Ludlow, MA; (Y); Art Clb; Church Yth Grp; Drama Clb; Ntl Jnr Clsscl Leag Cert Of Hnrb Merit 86; Cmmrcl Art.

VOLPE, ROBERT; Boston College HS; Quincy, MA; (Y); 52/295; Pres JA; SADD; Capt Bsktbl; Capt Ftbl; Tennis; Wt Lftg; High Hon Roll; Hon Roll; NHS; Ntl Merit Ltr; Natl Latin Exm Awd Otstndng Prfrmc 84-86; Bio Med.

VON DER HEYDEN, ERIC; Berkshire Schl; Pittsburgh, PA; (Y); Cmnty Wkr; Ski Clb; Nwsp Rptr; Lit Mag; JV Lcrss; Var Capt Socr; JV Tennis; High Hon Roll; Hon Roll; Vrsty Sqush Cptn.

VREELAND, SANDY; Monument Mountain Regional HS; Lenox, MA; (Y); 1/110; Math Tm; Quiz Bowl; Cit Awd; High Hon Roll; NHS; Church Yth Grp; JCL; Church Choir; Orch; School Play; Rensselaer Medl-Math & Sci 86; Math, Sci Schlrshp Awds 84-86; Soc Sci, Lang & Engl Awds 85 & 86; Elem Ed.

VYRAVANATHAN, INDRA; Somerville HS; Somerville, MA; (Y); #5 In Class; Intnl Clb; Spanish Clb; Stu Cncl; High Hon Roll; Hon Roll; NHS; Bus.

WADE, MATT; Silver Lake Regional HS; Kingston, MA; (Y); 99/400; Cmnty Wkr; Var JV Bsktbl; Var L Golf; Var L Tennis; Hon Roll; U Miami; Attrny.

WADE, RICHARD E; Bristol Plymouth HS; Raynham, MA; (S); 1/180; Computer Clb; VICA; Nwsp Rptr; Im Bsktbl; High Hon Roll; Hon Roll; Pres NHS; Ntl Merit Ltr; Rotary Awd; Stu Govt Day In Boston; Elec Engrng.

WADLEGGER, KELLY C; Classical HS; Springfield, MA; (Y); 23/389; Church Yth Grp; Dance Clb; Pep Clb; PAVAS; Variety Show; High Hon Roll; Maxmum Hnrs 83-84; Arts & Schltcs Awds 85-86; Semi Profsnl Sprngfld Dance Co 82-86; MA Coll Of Art; Graphic Arts.

WAGNER, BETH A; Norton HS; Norton, MA; (Y); Pep Clb; Spanish Clb; Color Guard; School Play; High Hon Roll; Hon Roll; Prfct Atten Awd; Chorus; Variety Show; Yrbk Stf; Drm Mgr Awd; Johnson & Wales Acad Schlrshp; Norton SH Prnt Advsry Brd Schlrshp; Johnson & Wales Coll; Rcrtn.

WAHLSTROM, ERIK; Shepherd Hill Regional HS; Charlton, MA; (Y); Am Leg Boys St; Rep Soph Cls; Rep Stu Cncl; Var JV Bsbl; High Hon Roll; NHS; Hugh O Brian Ldrshp Smnr 85; Srvd On Self-Evaltn Cmmttee 84; Bus.

WAHNON, CARLA; Seekonk HS; Seekonk, MA; (Y); 4/230; Yrbk Stf; High Hon Roll; NHS; Spanish NHS; Acadm Excllnc Awd Recepient; Veterinarian.

WAILGUM, ANDREW G; Westfield HS; Westfield, MA; (Y); 45/370; Church Yth Grp; Cmnty Wkr; Band; Concert Band; Mrchg Band; Pep Band; Yrbk Stf; Var L Ice Hcky; Var L Socr; Var L Tennis; Pre-Law.

WAINIO, HEATHER; Milford HS; Milford, MA; (Y); 69/290; Drama Clb; Chorus; School Play; Var Swmmng; High Hon Roll; Hon Roll.

WAITE, JENNIFER; Westport HS; Westport, MA; (Y); French Clb; Intnl Clb; Yrbk Stf; Hon Roll; NHS; Law.

WALDMAN, ROBIN L; Framingham South HS; Framingham, MA; (Y); 26/250; French Clb; Latin Clb; SADD; Temple Yth Grp; School Play; Variety Show; Nwsp Rptr; Yrbk Stf; Swmmng; Cit Awd; FTA Schlrshp 86; Mcrblgy Awd Stu Of Mnth 86; Ldrshp & Svc; E Cohen Awd 86; Barnard Coll; French.

WALDRON, JOE; Boston Coll HS; N Quincy, MA; (Y); Aud/Vis; Chess Clb; SADD; Nwsp Rptr; Lit Mag; JV Swmmng; Hon Roll; Englsh Tchr.

WALENTY, MARGARET; Uxbridge HS; Uxbridge, MA; (Y); 2/87; Church Yth Grp; Computer Clb; Hosp Aide; Math Tm; Red Cross Aide; Speech Tm; Concert Band; Jazz Band; Mrchg Band; Nwsp Rptr; Baker Mem Scholar 86; Band Achvt Awd 86; Cntrl District Band 81-86; Hgh Hnrs Grad 86; Worcester Polytech Inst; Engrng.

WALGREEN, ALBERT; Bishop Feehan HS; Mansfield, MA; (Y); 2/238; Boy Scts; Chess Clb; Math Tm; Spanish Clb; Var Trk; High Hon Roll; NHS; Ntl Merit Schol; Pres Schlr; Sal; Henry J Reilly Mem Schlrshp Res Off Assn 86; Eugene Dupont Mem Schlrshp 86; U Of DE; Intl Rltns.

WALKER, DAVID; Somerset HS; Somerset, MA; (Y); 24/320; Band; Concert Band; Jazz Band; Mrchg Band; Symp Band; NHS; ST Hnr, M Raposa Schlrshps, P Petrillo Awd 86; U MA Amherst; Pre Med.

WALKER, JANET; Malden HS; Malden, MA; (Y); Pres Church Yth Grp; VP PAVAS; Chorus; Madrigals; Variety Show; Salem ST Coll; Bus Adm.

WALKER, JENNIFER L; Plymouth-Carver HS; Plymouth, MA; (Y); 20/455; Hosp Aide; SADD; Nwsp Stf; Sec Stu Cncl; Var L Socr; Var L Trk; Im Vllybl; Hon Roll; Top 5 Pct Cls Awd 86; Beta Sigma Phi Plymouth Schlrp 86; Plymouth Yth Sccr Assoc Schlrp 86; Stonehill Coll; Crim Jstc.

WALKER, LISA; Wakefield HS; Wakefield, MA; (Y); Church Yth Grp; SADD; Yrbk Stf; Rep Jr Cls; Capt Pom Pon; Hon Roll; Law.

WALKER, MELISSA; Reading Memorial HS; Reading, MA; (Y); 45/327; Pres French Clb; Band; Concert Band; Jazz Band; Nwsp Rptr; Ed Yrbk Sprt Ed; Rep Stu Cncl; High Hon Roll; Pres Schlr; Rdng Wmns Bus Clb Schlrshp 86; Mrrmck Acadmc Schlrshp 86; Merrimack Coll; Bus.

WALKER, NANCY; Cardinal Spellman HS; Brockton, MA; (Y); 18/209; Drama Clb; Political Wkr; Trs SADD; School Musical; Lit Mag; High Hon Roll; NHS; Voice Dem Awd; Cmnty Wkr; 4-H; Bridgewater Area Nuclear Disarmament Band 85 & 86; Monsignor J S Richard Schlrshp Awd 83-86; Creative Writing.

WALKER, NORALEE; Medford HS; Medford, MA; (Y); #6 In Class; SADD; Color Guard; Orch; Rep Frsh Cls; Rep Soph Cls; Rep Jr Cls; Hon Roll; NHS; Excllnc Wrtng Awd 86; JR Marshall 86; Gifted/Tlntd Pgm 83-86; Viola Perfrmnce.

WALKER, STEPHANIE M; Randolph HS; Randolph, MA; (Y); Church Yth Grp; French Clb; Band; Concert Band; Jazz Band; Mrchg Band; Swing Chorus; Yrbk Ed-Chief; NHS; Drama Clb; Natl Piano Plyng Audtns Dist 84-85; Natl Hstry Day 86; U MA Amherst; Comp Engrng.

WALKER, WESLEY R; Hanover HS; Hanover, MA; (Y); Am Leg Boys St; Ski Clb; SADD; Var L Bsktbl; Coach Actv; L Var Golf; Im Vllybl; Hon Roll; Ecnmcs.

WALL, DAWN; Longmeadow HS; Longmeadow, MA; (Y); 45/290; Hosp Aide; Keywanettes; School Play; Yrbk Sprt Ed; Stu Cncl; Var Cheerleading; Powder Puff Ftbl; DAR Awd; High Hon Roll; Jr NHS; Boston Coll; Nrsng.

WALL, JAMES; Newburyport HS; Newburyport, MA; (Y); 97/185; Boy Scts; Library Aide; Model UN; Political Wkr; Q&S; Nwsp Stf; Ftbl; Med.

WALL, PHILIP N; Mansfield HS; Mansfield, MA; (Y); 44/198; Letterman Clb; Varsity Clb; Stage Crew; Var Bsktbl; Var Ftbl; Wentwrth Inst Of Tech; Elec Eng.

WALLAT, JEFFREY; Wachusett Regional HS; Holden, MA; (Y); 157/443; Boys Clb Am; Church Yth Grp; Letterman Clb; Varsity Clb; Variety Show; Var L Bsbl; Im JV Bsktbl; Coach Actv; Var Capt Ftbl; Sports Admin.

WALLEN, ROBERT; Nipmuc Regional HS; West Upton, MA; (Y); #1 In Class; Nwsp Stf; Rep Frsh Cls; Rep Soph Cls; Capt Bowling; Capt Vllybl; Elks Awd; High Hon Roll; Pres Schlr; Chistian A Herter Schlrshp 84-85; Rensselaer Polytech Inst; Gentc.

WALSH, BARRY J; Norton HS; Norton, MA; (Y); Am Leg Boys St; Quiz Bowl; Varsity Clb; Band; Concert Band; Mrchg Band; Golf; Tennis; Hon Roll; Vp Of Art Hnr Scty 86-87; The Citadel; Pol Sci.

WALSH, CAROLINE; Milton Acad; Milton, MA; (Y); Cmnty Wkr; Dance Clb; Chorus; School Musical; School Play; Stage Crew; Im Swmmng; Ntl Merit Ltr; Grad W/ Dstnctn 86; Elected To Cum Laude Scty 85; Harvard U; Econ.

WALSH, CHRISTINA; Agawam HS; Agawam, MA; (Y); Church Yth Grp; Library Aide; Socr; Trk; Hon Roll; U Of MA; Biochem.

WALSH, KATHLEEN; Cohasset HS; Cohasset, MA; (Y); 19/104; AFS; Aud/Vis; Nwsp Stf; Yrbk Stf; NHS; Acad Awd 83-84; Bancroft Trophy 83; Bus.

WALSH, KERRY; Medway JR SR HS; Medway, MA; (Y); 27/150; Church Yth Grp; Var Socr; High Hon Roll; Hon Roll; Dr Jacob Sheinkopf Mem Schlrshp 86; New England U; Physcl Thrpy.

WALSH, MARK; Dennis-Yarmouth Regional HS; S Yarmouth, MA; (Y); Var L Bsbl; Var L Bsktbl.

WALSH, MAURA C; St Bernards HS; Fitchburg, MA; (S); 5/177; Drama Clb; Pres French Clb; Ski Clb; School Play; Rep Frsh Cls; Rep Soph Cls; Rep Stu Cncl; Hon Roll; NHS; Algbr Awd 83-84; Hist Awd 84-85; Bentley; Accntng.

WALSH III, MICHAEL J; Randolph HS; Randolph, MA; (Y); 18/321; Am Leg Boys St; VP Church Yth Grp; Sec Band; Mrchg Band; Nwsp Sprt Ed; Capt Crs Cntry; Capt Trk; Kiwanis Awd; NHS; Pres Schlr; Tommy Pirrera Mem Scholar 86; Jean Noblin Scholar 86; Randolph Rotary Scholar; Stonehill Coll; Hstry.

WALSH, SUSAN; Boston Latin Acad; Dorchester, MA; (Y); Debate Tm; German Clb; Political Wkr; Nwsp Rptr; Swmmng; Hon Roll; Otwrd Bnd 85; Tufts Harvard; Intrntnl Rltns.

WALSH, SUSAN; Canton HS; Canton, MA; (Y); 45/245; Church Yth Grp; Dance Clb; Office Aide; Drill Tm; Rep Frsh Cls; Powder Puff Ftbl; Hon Roll.

WALSH, THOMAS; Hudson HS; Hudson, MA; (Y); SADD; Yrbk Stf; Stu Cncl; Bsktbl; Tennis; Vllybl; High Hon Roll; NHS; Worcester Poly Tech; Engrng.

WALTER, KIMBERLY; Chicopee Comprehensive HS; Chicopee, MA; (Y); 4-H; Powder Puff Ftbl; Sftbl; Vllybl; 4-H Awd; Hon Roll; Bnkng.

WALTER, PATRICIA; Grafton Memorial HS; Brooklyn, NY; (Y); 5/115; Drama Clb; Science Clb; Chorus; School Play; Mgr Stage Crew; Rep Stu Cncl; Co-Capt Cheerleading; High Hon Roll; Hon Roll; NHS; Span Fair 2nd Pl 85; Pres Schlrp St Jospehs Pre-Med Prog 86; Mst Lkly To Sccd 86; U Scranton; Pre-Med.

WALTERS JR, MELVIN; Peter Fanueil Acc; Dorchester, MA; (Y); Boys Clb Am; Teachers Aide; Band; Off Jr Cls; Var Bsbl; Var Bsktbl; Var Ftbl; Var Trk; Hon Roll; Engrng Tech.

WALTON, DEBRA; Academy Of Notre Dame; Tewksbury, MA; (Y); 5/80; Art Clb; SADD; Chorus; School Musical; Nwsp Rptr; VP Soph Cls; Rep Jr Cls; High Hon Roll; Hon Roll; NHS; 1st Pl Art Shw 85 & 86; Communctns.

WAMBACH, ANN; Fanning Trade HS; Worcester, MA; (Y); 4/124; FHA; SADD; Sftbl; High Hon Roll; Hon Roll; NHS; Med.

WANDELOSKI, MARY E; Greenfield HS; Greenfield, MA; (Y); 35/157; DECA; Spanish Clb; SADD; JV Stat Bsktbl; Mgr(s); Score Keeper; High Hon Roll; Dstributve Educ Clubs Of Amer Bk Awd 86; GBI Marktng Schlrshp DECA 86; Peer Educ Awd 85 & 86; Worcester ST Coll; Educ.

WANDREI, KELLY; Hoosac Vly HS; Adams, MA; (Y); Pep Clb; Ski Clb; School Play; Yrbk Stf; NHS.

WANG, YIN-HUEI; Amherst Regional HS; Amherst, MA; (Y); Computer Clb; Pres Sec Intnl Clb; Math Clb; Math Tm; Ski Clb; Teachers Aide; Hon Roll; Elec Engrng.

WARD, JOHN JERRY; Lexington HS; Lexington, MA; (Y); Church Yth Grp; Var Capt Lcrss; Var Socr; Var Capt Swmmng; Hon Roll; Dr Rudolph J Forbert Mem Awd 86; Mst Valuable Swmmr Soph 85; Boston Herld All Schltc Lacrosse 86.

WARD, KAREN; Saugus HS; Saugus, MA; (Y); 2/250; Church Yth Grp; Hosp Aide; Yrbk Stf; Stu Cncl; High Hon Roll; NHS; Voice Dem Awd; MA Yth Ldrshp Smnr; Attndnc Aide; Chrch Lctr; Pre-Med.

WARD, THERESSA; Boston Technical HS; Mattapan, MA; (Y); Dance Clb; FBLA; GAA; JA; Pep Clb; Spanish Clb; SADD; Variety Show; Yrbk Stf; JV Bsktbl; Centenary Coll; Bus Admn.

WARGO, CHRIS; W Springfield SR HS; W Springfield, MA; (Y); Mrktng.

WARNER JR, CRAIG S; Athol HS; Athol, MA; (Y); #13 In Class; Am Leg Boys St; Drama Clb; Spanish Clb; SADD; Band; Concert Band; Mrchg Band; School Musical; Trk; Hon Roll; U Of MA; Pre-Med.

WARNER, DANIEL T; Grafton HS; Grafton, MA; (Y); Am Leg Boys St; Pres Church Yth Grp; L Bsktbl; L Ftbl; NHS.

WARNER, DENNIS; E Longmeadow HS; E Longmeadow, MA; (Y); 50/230; Intnl Clb; Spanish Clb; Speech Tm; Varsity Clb; Bsktbl; Crs Cntry; Trk; Bus.

WARREN, LISA; Foxborough HS; Foxborough, MA; (Y); 3/223; VP Pres Church Yth Grp; Ski Clb; SADD; Ed Yrbk Stf; Rep VP Stu Cncl; Var L Socr; Var L Trk; NHS; Math Tm; Varsity Clb; MA Assn Stu Cncl Convtn 85; Contntl Math Leag Rgnl Wnnr 83-84; N E Young Wrtrs Cnvtn 86; Vet Med.

WARREN, MARY; Natick HS; Natick, MA; (Y); 78/400; Spanish Clb; Hon Roll.

WARREN, MICHELLE; Marlboro HS; Marlboro, MA; (Y); Key Clb; Cheerleading; High Hon Roll; Hon Roll; Cert Of Awd JV Chrldng 83; U Of Santa Barbara; Bus.

WARREN, PETER; Bishop Stang HS; New Bedford, MA; (Y); 101/245; JA; Var Bsktbl; Var Crs Cntry; JV Trk; Im Wt Lftg; Bus.

WARREN, RONALD; Reading Memorial HS; Reading, MA; (Y); Var Ftbl; High Hon Roll; NHS; Engrng.

WARSOFSKY, REBECCA; Canton HS; Canton, MA; (Y); 10/245; French Clb; Office Aide; Temple Yth Grp; Stage Crew; Nwsp Stf; Yrbk Stf; Vllybl; Hon Roll; NHS; Century Clb; Math.

WASHER, SHARAN L; King Philip Regional HS; Wrentham, MA; (Y); 113/240; Dance Clb; Spanish Clb; SADD; Varsity Clb; Band; Color Guard; Drill Tm; Nwsp Stf; Fld Hcky; Powder Puff Ftbl; Roger Williams Coll; Bus Mgmt.

WASLASKE, KATHLEEN; Wachusett Regional HS; Rutland, MA; (Y); 31/447; Yrbk Stf; High Hon Roll; Hon Roll; Phys Sci.

WASNER, JESSICA; Belmont HS; Belmont, MA; (Y); 75/260; Aud/Vis; Drama Clb; PAVAS; School Musical; School Play; Stage Crew; Yrbk Stf; Blmnt Dramatc Clb Yth Hnrary Membrshp 86; Drama Fstvl 86; Fstvl Stg Mgr 86; Thtr Arts.

WASSON, LAURA J; Walpole HS; Walpole, MA; (Y); 20/261; Hosp Aide; Radio Clb; Spanish Clb; Chorus; Hon Roll; NHS; Gld Mdl Art 86; 1st Prz Walpole Mall Art Shw 86; 1st Prz Liberty Vlg Mall Art Cntst 85; Art.

WATERMAN, BRAD; Dighton-Rehaboth Regional HS; Rehoboth, MA; (Y); 59/230; Church Yth Grp; Hon Roll; U Of MA; Econ.

WATERS, DOLORES; East Boston HS; E Boston, MA; (Y); 45/205; Pep Clb; Varsity Clb; Yrbk Stf; Off Soph Cls; Off Jr Cls; Stu Cncl; Var Capt Sftbl; Hon Roll; Kiwanis Awd; Kearns Schlrshp 86; Access Schlrshp 86; James H Satori Schlrshp 86; Nrtheastrn U; Crmnl Jstice.

WATERS, KATHLEEN; Whitman-Hanson Regional HS; Whitman, MA; (Y); 2/288; Am Leg Aux Girls St; Church Yth Grp; Hosp Aide; Office Aide; Flag Corp; Elks Awd; High Hon Roll; Kiwanis Awd; NHS; Sal; Englsh Prz 86; Eln Cnwy Splmn Esy Wnr 85-86; Cmnwlth MA Schlrshp 86; Tufts U; Pthlgst.

WATKINS, KELLIE; Melrose HS; Boston, MA; (Y); German Clb; JV Bsktbl; JV Sftbl; Hon Roll; NHS; Acad All Amer 86; Bio.

WATSON, ANNE-MARIE; Chicopee Comprehensive HS; Chicopee, MA; (Y); Drama Clb; Girl Scts; Chorus; School Play; Variety Show; Nwsp Rptr; Mgr(s); Powder Puff Ftbl; Trk; Air Force; Law Enforcement.

WATSON, JARED A; Rockport HS; Rockport, MA; (Y); 11/65; Am Leg Boys St; Drama Clb; French Clb; Hosp Aide; Chorus; School Play; Trs Frsh Cls; Trs Soph Cls; Tennis; NHS.

WATTERS, GIRARD; Barnstable HS; Hyannis, MA; (Y); JV Im Bsbl; JV Ice Hcky; JV Var Socr; Hon Roll; Rollins Coll.

WATTU, LAURA J; Marlborough HS; Marlborough, MA; (Y); 14/274; Trs Church Yth Grp; Varsity Clb; Yrbk Stf; Capt Crs Cntry; Capt Trk; High Hon Roll; NHS; Pres Schlr; Fclty Awd Bus 84; Fclty Awd Phtgrphy Cmmnctns 86; Bertley Coll; Acctg.

WAYMAN, PAULA J; Bartlett HS; Webster, MA; (Y); 8/152; School Play; Ed Yrbk Rptr; Trs Soph Cls; Trs Jr Cls; Trs Sr Cls; Stu Cncl; Twrlr; Cit Awd; DAR Awd; NHS; Most Depndbl Cls 86; Am Legion Schl Awd 86; Stu Cncl Schlrshp 86; Westfield ST Coll; Bus.

WEAGLE, AARON D; Shrewsbury HS; Shrewsbury, MA; (Y); Am Leg Boys St; Church Yth Grp; Science Clb; Orch; Hon Roll; Pre-Med.

WEATHERWAX, JOHN M; Westfield HS; Westfield, MA; (Y); Boy Scts; JA; Ed Lit Mag; Springfield Tech CC; Arch Engr.

WEBB, JENNIFER; Malden HS; Malden, MA; (Y); 32/540; Pep Clb; Rep Frsh Cls; Rep Soph Cls; Rep Jr Cls; Var Cheerleading; JR Varieties; Natl Lit Soc; Psych.

WEBB, KENNETH M; Saugus HS; Saugus, MA; (Y); Band; Concert Band; Drm Mjr(t); Jazz Band; Mrchg Band; JV Bsktbl; JV Var Socr; Comp Sci.

WEBBER, KIM; Foxborough HS; Foxboro, MA; (Y); 7/226; Ski Clb; Yrbk Stf; Socr; Swmmng; Trk; Hon Roll; NHS; Bio.

WEBER, MICHELLE; Walpole HS; Walpole, MA; (Y); 2/265; Math Tm; Band; Trs Jr Cls; Trs Sr Cls; Rep Stu Cncl; Var Socr; JV Trk; Hon Roll; NHS; Outstndng JR Awd 86; Engrng.

WEBSTER, BRIAN; Haverhill HS; Haverhill, MA; (Y); 69/400; Church Yth Grp; Latin Clb; SADD; Nwsp Rptr; High Hon Roll; Outstndng Acad Achvt Italn Awd 83-84; 100 Pct Avr Pblc Spkng 85-86; Prof Brdcstng Schl; Brdcstng.

WEDGE, JAMES; Pope John XXIII HS; Revere, MA; (Y); 50/215; Var L Bsbl; Var L DECA; Var Capt Socr; Bst Schlstc/Athltc Awd 86; Hghst Alg I Awd 82; Coachs Sccr Awd 86; N Adams ST; Bus Admin.

WEDGE, JASON; Methuen HS; Methuen, MA; (Y); 200/312; Boys Clb Am; Boy Scts; Library Aide; Office Aide; SADD; Chorus; School Play; Variety Show; Stu Cncl; Ice Hcky; Mnchstr Schl Of Auto; Auto Tech.

WEED, GEOFFREY; Northfield Mt Hermon Schl; Mt Hermon, MA; (Y); SADD; Var Golf; JV Socr; Hon Roll; Prfct Atten Awd; Stu Ldrshp 86-87; Trm Abrd To France 85-86; Frgn Srv.

WEENE, DANIEL S; Brockton HS; Brockton, MA; (Y); 10/1000; Am Leg Boys St; Drama Clb; School Musical; School Play; Nwsp Ed-Chief; Nwsp Rptr; Nwsp Stf; VP Jr Cls; VP Sr Cls; Var JV Socr; All-Star Actng Awd MHS DG Drama Fstvl 86; Wnr Crsby Book Awd Otstndng Extra Crrclrs 86.

WEGMAN, SARAH; Malden HS; Malden, MA; (Y); 60/500; Office Aide; Variety Show; Hon Roll; Natl Engl Merit Awd 86; Engl.

WEHTJE, JAMES; South Lancaster Acad; S Lancaster, MA; (S); Church Yth Grp; FCA; Nwsp Rptr; Nwsp Stf; Yrbk Rptr; Yrbk Stf; Pres Frsh Cls; Jr Cls; Var Capt Bsktbl; Var Ftbl.

WEHTJE, THOMAS J; South Lancaster Acad; S Lancaster, MA; (Y); 1/17; Yrbk Ed-Chief; VP Soph Cls; Pres Sr Cls; Trs Stu Cncl; Capt Var Bsktbl; Capt Var Ftbl; NHS; Ntl Merit SF; Val; Church Yth Grp; 8 Deptmntl Outstndng Stu Awd In 3 Yrs; Atlantic Union Coll; Archlgy.

WEICKER, NATHALIE; Bedford HS; Bedford, MA; (Y); 5/198; AFS; Church Yth Grp; Math Tm; Science Clb; Chorus; Orch; School Musical; Var Capt Socr; High Hon Roll; NHS.

WEINBERG, LISA; Somerset HS; Somerset, MA; (Y); 42/310; Drama Clb; School Play; Variety Show; Nwsp Stf; Var Capt Stu Cncl; Capt L Trk; L Var Vllybl; High Hon Roll; Hon Roll; NHS; SE Coast All Star Tm Trk 86; Stephen Prefontaine Awd 86; Coach Awd Vllybl 85-86; Ath Of Yr 85-86; Westfield ST Coll; Comm.

WEINER, ELIZABETH; Randolph HS; Randolph, MA; (Y); Cmnty Wkr; French Clb; Pre-Law.

WEINER, STUART; Malden HS; Malden, MA; (Y); 82/415; Boy Scts; Political Wkr; Temple Yth Grp; JV Bsbl; JV Bsktbl; Mgr(s); JV Var Socr; Hon Roll; Ntl Merit Ltr; Rotary Awd; Bus Mngmnt.

WEINGARTAN, LISA; Andover HS; Andover, MA; (Y); 11/387; Hosp Aide; SADD; Temple Yth Grp; Nwsp Rptr; Var Capt Tennis; High Hon Roll; Jr NHS; Cmnty Wkr; Drama Clb; Intnl Clb; Pre-Med.

WEINMANN, CHRISTOPHER; Westfield HS; Westfield, MA; (Y); 20/357; NHS; Ntl Merit Ltr; Lib Art.

WEINSTEIN, STEPHANIE; Newton North HS; Newton, MA; (Y); French Clb; Pres Service Clb; Ski Clb; VP Temple Yth Grp; Yrbk Stf; JV Bsktbl; JV Lcrss; Hon Roll; Ec.

WEISENSEE, SCOTT; Tewksbury Memorial HS; Tewksbury, MA; (Y); 28/330; Var Ftbl; Var Trk; Var Wrstlng; Hon Roll; NHS; Merrimack Coll; Bus.

WEISS, CATHERINE; Bishop Feehan HS; Foxboro, MA; (Y); 90/240; Pres Trs SADD; Yrbk Stf; Pres Stu Cncl; Var Tennis; Dnfth Awd; Elks Awd; High Hon Roll; Hon Roll; Feehanite Of Yr 86; St Michls VT; Pltcl Sci.

WEISS, DOUGLAS S; Commonwealth Schl; Brookline, MA; (Y); Chess Clb; Latin Clb; Jazz Band; Nwsp Rptr; JV Trk; Hon Roll; Ntl Merit SF; Bus.

WEISSE, LAURIE; Cathedral HS; Springfield, MA; (Y); Socr; Hon Roll; Work Open Antry Fd Pgm 86; Business.

WEISSMAN, BRIAN; BMC Durfee HS; Fall River, MA; (Y); 5/691; Computer Clb; VP JA; Math Clb; Band; Chorus; Mrchg Band; Yrbk Sprt Ed; Bausch & Lomb Sci Awd; NHS; St Schlr; Clby Coll Bk Awd; U S Achvmnt Acad; Wrcstr Plytech Inst; Comp Sci.

WELCH, GREGORY; Marian HS; Framingham, MA; (Y); JA; Ski Clb; Spanish Clb; Yrbk Stf; NEDT Awd.

WELCH, LAURENCE J; Methuen HS; Methuen, MA; (Y); Chess Clb; Computer Clb; Intnl Clb; Library Aide; Hon Roll; MA ST Hnrs Scholar 86-90; U Lowell; Chem Engrng.

WELCH, MEREDITH; Whitman-Hanson Reg HS; Whitman, MA; (Y); Cmnty Wkr; Office Aide; Cheerleading; Bus Adm.

WELCH, THOMAS J; Bedford HS; Bedford, MA; (Y); 1/198; Am Leg Boys St; Church Yth Grp; Debate Tm; Madrigals; School Musical; Ed Nwsp Stf; Var Crs Cntry; Var Swmmng; Var Tennis; NHS; Brown U Bk Awd 86.

WELCOME, ANGELA; Lee HS; Lee, MA; (Y); 8/84; Spanish Clb; Church Choir; Trs Soph Cls; Trs Jr Cls; JV Bsktbl; Var L Socr; Var L Sftbl; Stu Cncl; Wntr Crnvl; Rng Cmmttee Prm Cmmttee.

WELLES, STEPHEN; Dennis Yarmouth Regional HS; West Dennis, MA; (S); 5/310; Am Leg Boys St; Concert Band; Jazz Band; Mrchg Band; Orch; VP Soph Cls; Hon Roll; NHS; Ntl Merit Ltr; Md Donalds All Amer Mrchng Bnd 85.

WELLS, CYNTHIA; Saint Gregory HS; Dorchester, MA; (Y); 1/99; Church Yth Grp; Drama Clb; Chorus; School Musical; School Play; Stage Crew; Variety Show; NHS; Pres Schlr; Val; Achvt Sci, Stu Svc Awds, Accptnc Salem ST Hnrs Pgm; Salem ST Coll; Bio.

WELLS, JENNIFER; Walnut Hill Schl; Cranston, RI; (Y); Computer Clb; Drama Clb; German Clb; Latin Clb; SADD; Acpl Chr; Chorus; Orch; Stage Crew; Lit Mag; Cum Laude Natl Latin Exam Lvl 2 & 3 84-85; Music.

WELLS, LISA; Easthampton HS; Easthampton, MA; (Y); Church Yth Grp; Dance Clb; Drama Clb; JA; Spanish Clb; SADD; School Play; Bst Actrss Awd 86; Bay Path JR Coll; Fshn Mrchnd.

WELLS, LISA; Winthrop HS; Winthrop, MA; (Y); 36/202; Civic Clb; Nwsp Rptr; Im Bsktbl; Var L Fld Hcky; Var Mgr(s); Var Socr; Im Sftbl; JV Var Trk; Indstrl Arts Awd 84; Helen & Sidney Bloomfield Awd 84; Crmnl Justc.

WELLS, RUSSELL; Lenox Memorial HS; Lenox, MA; (Y); Office Aide; Ski Clb; Bsbl; Socr; Hon Roll; Prfct Atten Awd; Ltr Sccr & Bsbl 85&86; N Adams ST; Bus Acctg.

WELLS, SUZANNE; Natick HS; Natick, MA; (Y); 66/416; Am Leg Aux Girls St; Spanish Clb; SADD; Bsbl; Co-Capt Sftbl; Co-Capt Swmmng; Hon Roll; NHS; Ed Assctn Natick Schlrshp 86; Sns Itly Natick Schlrshp 86; Bates; Poli Sci.

WELSH, KENNETH; S Hadley HS; S Hadley, MA; (Y); Latin Clb; Rnk Ikkyo In Shito-Ryu Karate 86; Ntl Karate Union; Bus.

WENTWORTH, WENDY; Winchester HS; Winchester, MA; (Y); 77/296; Exploring; Spanish Clb; Capt Drill Tm; Mrchg Band; High Hon Roll; Hon Roll; Elem Ed.

WENTZ, LISA; Newton North HS; W Newton, MA; (Y); Church Yth Grp; Exploring; Teachers Aide; Acpl Chr; Chorus; Variety Show; Sons & Daughters Of Pilgrims 86; Psychlgy.

WENTZELL, STEVE; Tahanto Regional HS; Boylston, MA; (Y); Am Leg Boys St; JA; Yrbk Stf; Var Bsktbl; Var Golf; Var Socr; Hon Roll; NHS; Quist Mem Schlrshp 86; Jeffrey Navin Mem Schlrshp 86; U Of Lowell.

WENZ, CRAIG; Monument Mountain Regional HS; W Stockbridge, MA; (Y); 10/142; Am Leg Boys St; Church Yth Grp; Soph Cls; Jr Cls; Socr; Wrstlng; High Hon Roll; Hon Roll; NHS; Jr Early Schlrshp Awd-Local Bus 86; Aerospace.

WERETA, RICHARD; Dedham HS; Dedham, MA; (S); 3/300; Computer Clb; Spanish Clb; SADD; Stu Cncl; High Hon Roll; Embry Riddle Aerontcl U; Pilot.

WERGLAND, JENNIFER LYNNE; Pittsfield HS; Pittsfield, MA; (Y); 29/300; Rep Frsh Cls; Hon Roll; NHS; Ntl Merit Ltr; Pres Schlr; Prsdntl Schlrshp 86; Schlrshp Sierra Coll; Bentley Coll; Acctng.

WESLEY, PETER; Salem HS; Salem, MA; (Y); Var Wrstlng; High Hon Roll; Hon Roll.

WESLEY, RICHARD; Medford HS; Medford, MA; (Y); 70/453; Boy Scts; SADD; Trs Soph Cls; Trs Jr Cls; Trs Stu Cncl; JV Bsktbl; Hon Roll; NHS; Math Awd Geom 85; Engl Awd 84-85; Bus Mgmt.

WEST, JENNY; Stoneleigh-Burnham Schl; Grosse Pointe Pk, MI; (Y); Acpl Chr; Chorus; Madrigals; Ed Lit Mag; Tennis; Hon Roll; Nancy Hodermarsky Poetry Awd 86; Elem Ed.

WEST, KENNETH; Chicopee Comprehensive HS; Chicopee, MA; (Y); German Clb; Variety Show; Stu Cncl.

WEST, ROBIN L; Fitchburg HS; Fitchburg, MA; (Y); Cmnty Wkr; Office Aide; Off Frsh Cls; Bsktbl; Hon Roll; Retail Mngt.

WEST, STEPHEN; Austin Prep HS; Billerica, MA; (Y); 5/154; JV Ice Hcky; Wt Lftg; Hon Roll; Elec Engrng.

WESTGATE, RICHARD; Old Colony R Voc Tech; Rochester, MA; (Y); Ski Clb; VICA; Ftbl; Robotics.

WESTPHALEN, AMY; Acton-Boxboro Regional HS; Acton, MA; (Y); 101/428; Hosp Aide; SADD; Yrbk Stf; Powder Puff Ftbl; Hon Roll.

WETZEL, TODD B; Westborough HS; Westborough, MA; (Y); 15/189; Spanish Clb; Nwsp Stf; Yrbk Stf; Rep Frsh Cls; Var L Bsktbl; JV L Ftbl; Var L Golf; Var L Socr; High Hon Roll; Boys ST MA 86.

WEYE, PATRICIA; Cathedral HS; Springfield, MA; (Y); 138/526; Hosp Aide; Var Gym; Physcl Thrpy.

WHALEN, KEVIN; Beverly HS; Beverly, MA; (Y); Am Leg Boys St; Boy Scts; Pres Frsh Cls; Pres Soph Cls; Pres Jr Cls; Pres Sr Cls; Var Capt Bsktbl; Var Capt Ftbl; Var Capt Trk; Hon Roll; Hnrbl Ment All Star Bkstbl Track 85-86; Recgntn Awd Handicapped Stu 86; Colby Coll; Teacher.

WHEATON, SANDRA; Wakefield Memorial HS; Wakefield, MA; (Y); 24/333; AFS; Church Yth Grp; Key Clb; Spanish Clb; Teachers Aide; School Play; Yrbk Stf; Bsktbl; Fld Hcky; Mgr(s); JR Wmns Clb Schlrshp 86; Stonehill Coll; Elem Educ.

WHEELER III, GERALD; New Bedford HS; New Bedford, MA; (Y); 17/700; Boy Scts; Church Yth Grp; High Hon Roll; Hon Roll; NHS; Southeastern 7A U; Mech Engr.

WHEELER, LINNEA; Quaboag Regional HS; W Warren, MA; (Y); Cmnty Wkr; Hosp Aide; Teachers Aide; Chorus; Church Choir; Nwsp Rptr; Hon Roll; Worcester ST Coll; Elem Ed.

WHEELER, MICHAEL; Waltham HS; Waltham, MA; (Y); High Hon Roll; Hon Roll; 2nd Pl Kngsbury Temprnc Fnd Annl Essay Cntst 86; Bentley Coll; Mgmt.

WHEELER, ROGER J; Medfield HS; Medfield, MA; (Y); 25/174; Am Leg Boys St; Church Yth Grp; Political Wkr; Trs Sr Cls; Stu Cncl; Var L Bsbl; Var L Ftbl; DAR Awd; Hon Roll; NHS; Boostrs Awd 85-86; Military Acad; Ofcr.

WHEELER, VIRGINIA; Tahanto Regional HS; Berlin, MA; (Y); 7/56; Pres 4-H; Math Tm; Quiz Bowl; Band; Concert Band; Yrbk Phtg; Yrbk Stf; Im Bsktbl; Im Vllybl; 4-H Awd; Vet Sci.

WHEELOCK, CHRISTOPHER B; Westboro HS; Westborough, MA; (Y); 3/189; Rep Am Leg Boys St; VP Computer Clb; Debate Tm; Drama Clb; Exploring; Hosp Aide; School Musical; Capt Var Socr; Var Trk; Ntl Merit Ltr; Cmdtn Mdl In AP Amrcn Hstry 86; Hon Rl 83-87; Chmpnshp Vlybl Tm Boys ST 86; U Chicago; Bio.

WHELAN, MICHAEL; Greater Lowell Voc Tech; Lowell, MA; (Y); Boys Clb Am; Bsbl; Bowling; Wt Lftg; Hon Roll; Prfct Atten Awd.

WHITAKER, DONNA; Sacred Heart HS; Duxbury, MA; (Y); Hosp Aide; Intnl Clb; Key Clb; Var Capt Bsktbl; Capt Bowling; Var Capt Fld Hcky; Var Capt Sftbl; Im Vllybl; Hon Roll; NHS; Spnsh Awd 84; MA ST Champ Bwlng 82-84; NE Candlepin Champ Bwlng 83-85; U Of VT.

WHITE, ALICIA; Milford HS; Milford, MA; (Y); 19/326; Drama Clb; School Musical; School Play; Stage Crew; High Hon Roll; Hon Roll; NHS; Ntl Merit SF; Frnch.

WHITE, CAMI; Athol HS; Athol, MA; (Y); 1/147; Am Leg Aux Girls St; Trs SADD; VP Frsh Cls; VP Soph Cls; VP Jr Cls; Var Capt Bsktbl; Var Fld Hcky; Var Trk; High Hon Roll; VP NHS; Westrn MA All Stars Bsktbl 83-86; Westn MA All Stars Fld Hcky 84-85; Hnry Membr Womns Clb 86.

WHITE, CHRISTOPHER; Westfield HS; Westfield, MA; (Y); 59/359; Sec Am Leg Boys St; Stage Crew; Nwsp Rptr; JV Lcrss; Capt Var Swmmng; Trk; Champnshp Wstrn MA Medley Relay Anchormn 84; ST Swmmng Champnshp Tm 83; Bay ST Games Swmmng 86; Bus.

WHITE, CHRISTOPHER A; Bladstone Vly Regional Voc Tec HS; Millbury, MA; (Y); Pres Church Yth Grp; Stu Cncl; Hon Roll; Clnry Arts.

WHITE, COLLEEN; Haverhill HS; Haverhill, MA; (Y); Church Yth Grp; Ski Clb; Powder Puff Ftbl; High Hon Roll; Merrimack Coll; Bus.

WHITE, DAVID; Hampshire Regional HS; Southampton, MA; (Y); Boy Scts; Cmnty Wkr; Service Clb; Ski Clb; Spanish Clb; Variety Show; Crs Cntry; Mgr(s); Trk; Hon Roll; Life Sct 85; 50 Miler Awd 85; Aviatn Sci.

WHITE, ELLEN P; Frontier Regional HS; Whately, MA; (Y); 13/73; Sec French Clb; Ed Yrbk Stf; Rep Jr Cls; Stu Cncl; Var L Trk; Var L Vllybl; High Hon Roll; Hon Roll; Lion Awd; NHS; S Deerfield Womens Club Awd Schlrshp 86; John Hopkins U; Civil Engrng.

WHITE, GAYLE; Randolph HS; Randolph, MA; (Y); Drama Clb; Temple Yth Grp; Chorus; School Musical; School Play; Frsh Cls; Gym; Jr NHS; Business Management.

WHITE, GREGORY S; Newton North HS; Newtonville, MA; (Y); Off Ski Clb; Teachers Aide; Varsity Clb; Im Bsktbl; Var L Socr; Swmmng; Var L Trk; Bus.

WHITE, JAMES; Algonquin Regional HS; Northboro, MA; (Y); 17/260; Drama Clb; Acpl Chr; VP Chorus; School Musical; School Play; Lit Mag; Hon Roll; Pres NHS; Brennan Awd 86; Physcs.

WHITE, JAMES; East Longmeadow HS; E Longmeadow, MA; (Y); Am Leg Boys St; Church Yth Grp; Intnl Clb; Band; Concert Band; Jazz Band; Yrbk Rptr; Var Capt Crs Cntry; Var Capt Swmmng; Var Trk; MA Lions Clb Al-ST Band 86; MA Boys ST 86; Bus.

WHITE, JEANINE; Notre Dame Acad; Hingham, MA; (Y); Drama Clb; Acpl Chr; Band; Concert Band; School Play; Hon Roll.

WHITE, JEFF; Melrose HS; Boston, MA; (Y); SADD; Im Sftbl; Achvmnt Awd Indstrl Arts; Arch.

WHITE, KRISTEN; Faith Christian Acad; W Dennis, MA; (Y); Church Yth Grp; Girl Scts; Office Aide; Chorus; Church Choir; Yrbk Stf; Stu Cncl; JV Bsktbl; High Hon Roll; Hon Roll; Hghst Class Avg 84; Mst Wrk Achvd Above Grde Lvl 84; Katherine Gubbs; Lgl Sec.

WHITE, LEONARD; St Johns Prep; Lynn, MA; (Y); Camera Clb; Spanish Clb; Hon Roll; NHS; Spanish NHS; Boston Coll; Bus Mgmt.

WHITE, LISA; Matignon HS; Revere, MA; (S); 14/183; Church Yth Grp; Spanish Clb; SADD; Hon Roll; NHS; Med.

WHITE, MARSHA; Boston Technical HS; Dorchester, MA; (Y); ROTC; Hon Roll; Smmy Grss Dvs Awd 83; Bus Adm.

WHITE, MARY; Brockton HS; Brockton, MA; (Y); 282/908; Cmnty Wkr; Office Aide; High Hon Roll; Hon Roll.

WHITE, MELISSA; Palmer HS; Palmer, MA; (Y); Cmnty Wkr; Pres Exploring; Hosp Aide; Math Tm; Spanish Clb; Hon Roll; Prfct Atten Awd; Smith Coll Bk Awd Outstndg Achvt Acadmcs & Cmmnty Wrk 86; Rgstrd Phys Ther.

WHITE, MICHELE; Salem HS; Salem, MA; (Y); Camp Fr Inc; Variety Show; Yrbk Stf; Var Powder Puff Ftbl; Var Score Keeper; Var Socr; Var Trk; High Hon Roll; Hon Roll; Plaq Vars Bsktbl Tm Mgr 84-85; Plaq Sccr U-16 Div I Champs 84; Biol.

WHITE, ROBERTA; Uxbridge HS; Uxbridge, MA; (Y); 20/84; French Clb; Yrbk Stf; Hon Roll; Intl Bus.

WHITE, SHARYL; Tantasqua Regional HS; Sturbridge, MA; (Y); 11/146; Ski Clb; Varsity Clb; Pres Band; Concert Band; Mrchg Band; Pep Band; School Play; Symp Band; Variety Show; Yrbk Stf; All-Stars Bordr Conf 86; Modrn Music Mstrs 84.

WHITE, TERI; Franklin HS; Franklin, MA; (Y); Var Capt Cheerleading; Hon Roll; NHS; Med.

WHITE, VERONICA LESLIE; Nipmoc Regional HS; Mendon, MA; (Y); 23/90; Camera Clb; DECA; Ski Clb; Yrbk Phtg; Cheerleading; Fld Hcky; Score Keeper; Sftbl; NHS; JV Fld Hcky Cptn 85; Bus Cnsltnt.

WHITEHEAD, JANICE; Wakefield HS; Wakefield, MA; (Y); 99/333; AFS; Rep Church Yth Grp; Sec French Clb; Hosp Aide; JA; Church Choir; School Play; JV Fld Hcky; Var Trk; Key Clb; JR Achvt Sls Awds 84; Simmons Coll; Comm.

WHITEHEAD, RICHARD; St Bernards HS; Rindge, NH; (S); 21/170; Boy Scts; Ski Clb; Var Ftbl; JV Trk; Var Wt Lftg; Hon Roll; NHS; JV Ftbl Coaches Awd 85-86; Boys ST Amer Lg Pgm 85-86; Aerontcl Engrng.

WHITEHOUSE, MARK; Haverhill HS; Haverhill, MA; (Y); Boys Clb Am; Boy Scts; Church Yth Grp; German Clb; NHS.

WHITING, ELLEN; Foxboro HS; Foxboro, MA; (Y); Church Yth Grp; Hosp Aide; Nwsp Rptr; JV Var Fld Hcky; Psych.

WHITMAN, TRICIA; Barnstable HS; Cummawuid, MA; (Y); 26/392; Drama Clb; Ski Clb; Sec Trs Color Guard; Yrbk Bus Mgr; Yrbk Phtg; High Hon Roll; Hon Roll; NHS; Drctrs Awd-Clr Grd 85; Awd Cnstnt Hrn Rll 84-86; Coll; Accntng Cpa.

WHITNEY, JENNIFER; Natick HS; Natick, MA; (Y); 51/380; SADD; Nwsp Rptr; Rep Stu Cncl; JV Bsktbl; Capt Cheerleading; JV Fld Hcky; Hon Roll; Jrnlsm.

WHITNEY, KARL; Arlington HS; Arlington, MA; (Y); Boy Scts; Camera Clb; Church Yth Grp; Math Tm; NHS; Brown Coll; Psych.

WHITNEY, KEVIN B; Oakmont Regional HS; Ashburnham, MA; (Y); 13/120; Am Leg Boys St; Band; Chorus; Yrbk Bus Mgr; High Hon Roll; Hon Roll; NHS; Instrmntl Awd Amer Fdrtn Of Musicials 86; MA Lions All ST Band 84; UMASS All SR Hnr Band 86; Fitchburg ST; Med Tech.

WHITON, KRISTINA; Fontbonne Acad; W Roxbury, MA; (Y); Church Yth Grp; Drama Clb; Intnl Clb; Library Aide; Chorus; School Musical; School Play; Hon Roll; Ntl Latin Ex Cum Laude Awd 84; Drama Festvl Awd 84-85; Bio.

WHITTAKER, ALDEN; Miss Halls Schl; Waban, MA; (Y); 1/56; French Clb; Acpl Chr; Stage Crew; Nwsp Rptr; Nwsp Stf; High Hon Roll; Hon Roll; Wellsley Coll Bk Awd 86; Cum Laude Soc 86; Stu Faculty Advsry Comm 86; Ecolgy.

WHITTEMORE, REBECCA; Quaboag Regional HS; Warren, MA; (Y); 4/87; Aud/Vis; Science Clb; Ski Clb; Varsity Clb; Variety Show; Bsktbl; Fld Hcky; Sftbl; High Hon Roll; NHS; All Stars Field Hockey 85; ST Champ Bsktbl 84-86; Cornell; Sci.

WHITTIER, NANCY; Blackstone Valley Reg Voc Tech HS; W Sutton, MA; (Y); Trs 4-H; Quiz Bowl; 4-H Awd; Hon Roll; Assbt Vlly Fgr Sktg Clb Gld Mdl-85 & Brnz Mdl-86; Ovrll Chmpn Fttg & Shwmnshp Hlstn Div 85; Htl Mgmt.

WHITTY, WILLIAM; B M C Durfee HS; Fall River, MA; (Y); 119/600; Capt L Wrstlng; Hon Roll; Engr.

WHOOLERY, PRISCILLA; Lincoln-Sudbury Regional HS; Sudbury, MA; (Y); Church Yth Grp; Dance Clb; French Clb; Chorus; School Musical; School Play; Nwsp Stf; Lit Mag; Rep Soph Cls; Trk; Brown Bk Awd 86; Harbard Bk Awd 86; Stu Ambssdr Schlrshp-France 86.

WHOOLEY, JOANNE; Ipswich HS; Ipswich, MA; (Y); 16/118; Leo Clb; Ski Clb; Band; Variety Show; Yrbk Sprt Ed; Stu Cncl; Var Capt Fld Hcky; Var Capt Trk; Hon Roll; Lion Awd; Fld Hcky All Star & MVP 85; Tck Coachs Awd & MVP 84-86; U Of MA-AMHERST; Bus Mngmnt.

WHORISKEY, MICHAEL; Central Catholic HS; Plaistow, NH; (Y); 9/231; Computer Clb; Math Clb; Science Clb; Im Bowling; Hon Roll.

WICKS, PATRICIA S; Haverhill HS; Haverhill, MA; (Y); 60/356; SADD; Nwsp Rptr; Nwsp Stf; High Hon Roll; Slvr Medl Intl Piano Cmptn 85; Leonard Johnson Awd 86; Itln Clb, Ecolgy Clb; U Of NH; Cmnctns.

WIDEMAN, THOMAS; Deerfield Acad; South Deerfield, MA; (Y); Cmnty Wkr; Lcrss; JV Socr; Var Wrstlng; Nutritnl Biochem.

WIEDL, CRAIG J; Middleborough HS; Middleboro, MA; (Y); 4/181; Am Leg Boys St; Band; Jazz Band; Orch; Var Co-Capt Crs Cntry; Var Capt Trk; Var Co-Capt Wrstlng; High Hon Roll; NHS; Prfct Atten Awd; All ST & Dstrct Bands & MVP Crs Cntry.

WIERBOWICZ, PAULA; Everett HS; Everett, MA; (Y); 8/280; Key Clb; Library Aide; SADD; High Hon Roll; Hon Roll; NHS; Pres Acad Fit Awd 86.

WIEZBICKI, JOY; East Longmeadow HS; E Longmeadow, MA; (Y); AFS; 4-H; Library Aide; Nwsp Rptr; Yrbk Stf; Stu Cncl; Socr; JV Swmmng; Var L Tennis; 4-H Awd; B Rtd US Pony Clb 84; Tutr-Math & Frnch 85-86; Projct Lfwrk; Engrng.

WIGGIN, CINDY; South Hadley HS; S Hadley, MA; (Y); 81/180; Art Clb; Church Yth Grp; Latin Clb; Band; Concert Band; Mrchg Band; Artwrk Apprctn 84; 1st Poetry BYF 1st Craft BYF 2nd Art BYF 86; Artst.

WIGHTMAN, HEATHER; Haverhill HS; Haverhill, MA; (Y); 40/420; Church Yth Grp; Office Aide; Political Wkr; Temple Yth Grp; Vllybl; High Hon Roll; Hon Roll; Prfct Atten Awd.

WILCOX, JAMES; Durfee HS; Fall River, MA; (Y); 16/690; Varsity Clb; JV Var Crs Cntry; JV Var Trk; High Hon Roll; Hon Roll; NHS; LTX Corp Schlrshp 86; Citzns Schlrshp Fndtn Awd 86; Alumni Schlrshp Awd 86; SE MA U; Cvl Engrg.

WILCOX, RACHAEL; Ipswich HS; Ipswich, MA; (Y); Church Yth Grp; Cmnty Wkr; Drama Clb; French Clb; Ski Clb; Spanish Clb; SADD; Varsity Clb; Band; Mrchg Band; Ring & Pin Awd Acad Excllnce 86; Bowdoin; Pre-Law.

WILCOX, SARAH; B M C Durfee HS; Fall River, MA; (Y); 1/600; French Clb; Nwsp Rptr; Rep Soph Cls; Rep Jr Cls; Rep Sr Cls; Capt Crs Cntry; Capt Trk; High Hon Roll; NHS; Ntl Merit Schol; Harvard Bk Awd 86; MA U Chancellors Tlnt Awd 86; Jrnlsm.

WILDER, LANCE W; Chelmsford HS; Chelmsford, MA; (Y); 151/540; Art Clb; Boy Scts; Church Yth Grp; Nwsp Stf; Lit Mag; Bsktbl; Hon Roll; Bstn Globe Schlstc Art Awds-Gold Medls & Blue Rbbn 85-86; 5th Dist Congrsnl HSART Comptn-Fnlst 85-86; MD Inst Coll Of Art; Fine Arts.

WILDES, STEVEN; North Quincy HS; Wollaston, MA; (Y); 17/400; Quiz Bowl; Yrbk Stf; Bsbl; Var Capt Socr; High Hon Roll; Jr NHS; Sci Awd Annl Sci Fair 86; Bus.

WILHELMSEN, HEATHER; North Middlesex Regional HS; Townsend, MA; (Y); Church Yth Grp; Library Aide; Math Clb; SADD; Color Guard; Yrbk Ed-Chief; JV Sftbl; Hon Roll; Voice Dem Awd; Elizabeth Haskins Math Cntst Hnry Mntn 85; Bus Adm.

WILKER, WENDY E; St Joseph Central HS; Dalton, MA; (Y); 10/80; Cmnty Wkr; Hosp Aide; Sec JA; Model UN; Red Cross Aide; Nwsp Rptr; Yrbk Stf; VP Stu Cncl; JV Bsktbl; Var L Socr; U Of MA; Hotel.

WILKINS, NANCY; Hudson HS; Hudson, MA; (Y); 25/140; Aud/Vis; Teachers Aide; Band; Concert Band; Mrchg Band; Orch; Pep Band; School Musical; Stage Crew; Nwsp Rptr; Natl Hstry Day Cnty Lvl 82-83; Unsung Hero Awd Vllybll 85; Coaches Awd 83; Keene ST Coll.

WILKINS, STEVEN; Randolph HS; Randolph, MA; (Y); Band; Concert Band; Drm & Bgl; Camera Clb; Mrchg Band; Orch; Variety Show; Stu Cncl; Crs Cntry; Socr; U MA; Bus.

WILKINSON II, DENNIS J; New Bedford HS; New Bedford, MA; (Y); 162/701; Boy Scts; Chess Clb; Sec Computer Clb; Political Wkr; Jr NHS; Ntl Merit Ltr; Rfl Team 84-85; Ntl Judo Fedrtn 83-85; Won 1st Pl-Holocst Essy Cntst 86; Sys Anlysis.

WILLARD, ELIZABETH A; Westford Acad; Westford, MA; (Y); 1/225; Art Clb; Chess Clb; Ski Clb; Chrmn Spanish Clb; Band; Rep Stu Cncl; Tennis; High Hon Roll; NHS; Val; Digtl Equip Corp Schlrshp Greatr Lowell Womns Clb Schlrshp 86; Lowell Sun All Str Awd Tennis 85; U Of CA San Diego; Bio Engrng.

WILLETT, RENEE; Barnstable HS; Hyannis, MA; (Y); 129/392; Church Yth Grp; GAA; Stu Cncl; Cheerleading; Fld Hcky; Lcrss; Trk; Hon Roll; Bus Mgmt.

WILLETTE, LAURA; Malden HS; Malden, MA; (Y); Pres Band; Chorus; Concert Band; Mrchg Band; Variety Show; Office Aide.

WILLIAMS, CAROL; North Quincy HS; Quincy, MA; (Y); 16/325; Church Yth Grp; JA; Science Clb; School Play; High Hon Roll; Hon Roll; NHS; Pres Schlr; Spanish NHS; Alumni Assoc Schlrshp 86-87; Robert Charles Billings Schlrshp 86-87; Distinction Hnrs 82-86; Salem ST Coll; Psych.

WILLIAMS, DARNYL; Farihaven HS; Acushnet, MA; (Y); Church Yth Grp; Teachers Aide; Band; Mrchg Band; L Trk; High Hon Roll; Hon Roll; Jr NHS; Instructors Awd French 83; Acamdc Lttr 84; Acdmc Pin Awd 86; S E MA U; Nursing.

WILLIAMS, DE AVEN; Commerce HS; Springfield, MA; (Y); VP Church Yth Grp; Drama Clb; Band; Church Choir; Rep Frsh Cls; Rep Stu Cncl; Var JV Bsktbl; Outstndng Prfrmc Awd Stu Cncl 84; Bus Admn.

WILLIAMS, GREGORY R; Athol HS; Athol, MA; (Y); 2/118; Am Leg Boys St; Model UN; Chrmn Radio Clb; Band; Nwsp Rptr; Yrbk Stf; Pres Stu Cncl; Mgr Bsktbl; Mgr Socr; Mgr Trk; Exchng Club Std Of Yr 86; Salutatorian Awd 86; Gold Plaque 86; Ithaca Coll; Mgnt.

WILLIAMS, JENNIFER; Northfield Mt Hermon Schl; Lunenburg, MA; (Y); Dance Clb; Drama Clb; Pres Math Clb; SADD; Varsity Clb; Acpl Chr; Orch; School Musical; School Play; Hon Roll.

WILLIAMS, JENNIFER; Northfield-Mt Hermon Schl; Crosswicks, NJ; (Y); Radio Clb; JV Fld Hcky; JV Lcrss; Var Swmmng; Hon Roll; E Asian.

WILLIAMS, JULIE; Methuen HS; Methuen, MA; (Y); Intnl Clb; Model UN; SADD; Color Guard; Yrbk Stf; Sftbl; Westbrook Coll; Secretarial.

WILLIAMS, KATHLEEN; Notre Dame Acad; Milton, MA; (Y); 21/109; Cmnty Wkr; Rep Stu Cncl; Var L Crs Cntry; Var L Trk; High Hon Roll; Hon Roll; Excllnc-Latin 85; Hnrb Mntn-Sci Fair 85; Bus Wk Schlrshp 86; Intl Bus.

WILLIAMS, LINDA; Frontier Regional HS; Sunderland, MA; (Y); 6/95; GAA; Hosp Aide; Latin Clb; Var Crs Cntry; Var Trk; High Hon Roll; Hon Roll; U MA; Engrng.

WILLIAMS, LISA; Medway JR SR HS; Medway, MA; (Y); 28/136; French Clb; Band; Yrbk Stf; Trs Frsh Cls; Trs Soph Cls; Trs Jr Cls; Trs Sr Cls; Var Socr; Var Sftbl; Trk; Medway Boosters Clb Outstndng JR Girl 85-86; Bio Med.

WILLIAMS, NAOMI; Bay Path Reg Vo Tech; Webster, MA; (Y); 50/236; DECA; SADD; VP Soph Cls; Top Engl Wrtr 85; Top Soph 85; Stu Advsry Cncl 86-87; Worcester ST Coll; Sctrl.

WILLIAMS, NEIL; Boston Latin Acad; Boston, MA; (Y); Var Capt Ftbl; Var Trk; Var Wt Lftg; Hon Roll; US Air Frc Acad; Aerospc Stds.

WILLIAMS, PAUL; Central Catholic HS; Hampstead, NH; (Y); 56/231; Art Clb; Cmnty Wkr; Science Clb; Im Score Keeper; Hon Roll; Weapns Engr.

WILLIAMS, RANA; Lenox Memorial HS; Lenox, MA; (Y); Girl Scts; Concert Band; Mrchg Band; JV Crs Cntry; Var JA; Acctg.

WILLIAMS, TONYA; Mario Umana Tech; Hyde Park, MA; (Y); Church Yth Grp; Drama Clb; French Clb; ROTC; Church Choir; Yrbk Stf; Hon Roll; Brown U; Psychlgy.

WILLIAMSON, BRIAN; Holyoke HS; Holyoke, MA; (Y); French Clb; Latin Clb; Yrbk Stf; Var Bsbl; Hon Roll.

WILLIAMSON, DEBRA; Hoosac Valley HS; Adams, MA; (Y); 12/158; Intnl Clb; JA; Pep Clb; Ski Clb; School Play; Trs Sr Cls; Rep Stu Cncl; Capt Socr; Sftbl; Hon Roll; Hon Mntn Jr Prize Spkng 84; Peer Ed Certf 85-86; Skidmore Coll NY.

WILLIS, LAUREN E; Acton-Boxboro Regional HS; Acton, MA; (Y); 2/354; Church Yth Grp; Drama Clb; School Musical; School Play; Stage Crew; Hon Roll; NHS; Ntl Merit SF; Sal; Frnch Natl Hnr Soc; Slavic Antl Hnr Soc; Intl Rltns.

WILSON, AMANDA LYNN; Ayer HS; Ayer, MA; (Y); 30/134; Pres Church Yth Grp; 4-H; Hosp Aide; Ski Clb; Ed Yrbk Stf; 4-H Awd; Hon Roll; HS Schlrshp 86; Estrn Star & Burdett Schl Schlrshp 86; Burdett Schl; Accntng.

WILSON, CATHARINE L; Hamilton Wenham Regional HS; S Hamilton, MA; (Y); 5/180; Church Yth Grp; Exploring; Concert Band; Mrchg Band; School Musical; Trk; High Hon Roll; NHS; Ntl Merit SF; Drama Clb; 1st Prize Schl Sci Fair 83; Dartmouth; Botany.

WILSON, CHRISTY L; Sacred Heart HS; Duxbury, MA; (S); 12/85; Key Clb; Chorus; School Musical; Stu Cncl; Var Cheerleading; JV Sftbl; Hon Roll; NHS; Voice Dem Awd; Outstndng Stu 85; MA Yth Ldrshp Semnr Rep; Outstndng Amer Govt Stu; Theatr.

WILSON, ELIZABETH; Cathedral HS; Springfield, MA; (Y); Civic Clb; Cmnty Wkr; Pres Red Cross Aide; Church Choir; Color Guard; School Musical; Yrbk Phtg; Yrbk Rptr; Yrbk Stf; Red Crss Reach-Out Clb Scv Awd 85-86; Panthrpx Yrbk Awd 86; Pre-Law.

WILSON, JEAN; Lincoln Sudbury Regional HS; Sudbury, MA; (Y); Key Clb; Spanish Clb; Ed Nwsp Stf; JV Ice Hcky; JV Var Vllybl; Hon Roll; Hamilton Coll; Med.

WILSON, JENNIFER; Saugus HS; Saugus, MA; (Y); French Clb; SADD; Socr; Trk; Hon Roll; Jr NHS; Superior Academic Achievment; Psych.

WILSON, JIM; Doherty Memorial HS; Worcester, MA; (Y); JV Var Bsbl; JV Var Ftbl; Hon Roll; Bus Adm.

WILSON, MARGUERITE; Mac Duffie Schl For Girls; Norfolk, VA; (Y); Dance Clb; School Musical; School Play; Library Aide; Variety Show; Hon Roll; Tlnt Teen VA 83; 1st Rnnr-Up Intl Pgnt 83; Fin All Amer Teen 85; Wnnr Of Music Video Cont For Elec 86; Duke U; Jrnlsm.

WILSON, MARK C; Boston HS; Roxbury, MA; (Y); Model UN; Nwsp Stf; Pres Sr Cls; Sal; Cert Of Excllnc Secdry Schl Math 85; Natl Achvt SF 85; Harvard Coll; Ec.

WILSON, MARY ELLEN; Holy Name Central Catholic HS; Northbridge, MA; (Y); 11/252; Drama Clb; French Clb; Pep Clb; Science Clb; Chorus; School Musical; Stage Crew; Trk; High Hon Roll; NHS; Mst Outstndng Studnt Frnch I 82; Mst Outstndng Studnt Awd Grmn I 85; NHS Schlrshp 86; Smith Coll; Frgn Lang.

WILSON, NATALIE; Boston Technical HS; Dorchester, MA; (Y); Drama Clb; VP Sec Church Choir; Yrbk Stf; Rep Soph Cls; Stu Cncl; Vllybl; Hon Roll; Hnrb Mntn 84 & 86; Emerson Coll; Communications.

WILSON, RONALD; Holyoke Catholic HS; Chicopee, MA; (Y); 45/138; Boys Clb Am; Computer Clb; JA; Spanish Clb; Varsity Clb; Y-Teens; School Musical; School Play; Stage Crew; Sec Jr Cls; Robert H Dempsey Bsktbl Schlshp 86; Syracuse; Crmnl Jstc.

WILSON, ROSS A; Mansfield HS; Mansfield, MA; (Y); Am Leg Boys St; Varsity Clb; Band; Var L Ftbl; Var L Trk; Hon Roll; Schlstc Recog Sci 84 & 85; 1st Pl J J Kelly Trck Relays 85.

WILSON, SHANNON; Walnut Hill Schl; Los Alamos, NM; (Y); Dance Clb; Variety Show; Var L Gym; Ldrshp Conf 86-87; Audio Engrng.

WILUSZ, NIKOLE; Holyoke Catholic HS; Holyoke, MA; (Y); Art Clb; Drama Clb; Spanish Clb; School Musical; School Play; Yrbk Stf; Intr Dsgn.

WINCHESTER, JOAN; Milton HS; Milton, MA; (Y); AFS; Church Yth Grp; Pres French Clb; Math Clb; Var L Ski Clb; Rep Stu Cncl; Var L Fld Hcky; Var Capt Sftbl; NHS; Outstndng Stu 85; Harvard Book Awd 86; MA Meth Olympd Fin 86; Mth Cont Awd 86; Engrng.

WING, CHERI LYNN; Hampshire Regional HS; Southampton, MA; (Y); 43/105; Church Yth Grp; Dance Clb; Variety Show; Gym; Hon Roll; Gymnastics Team Dedication Awards 85 & 86; Prom Queen; Westfield ST Coll.

WING, LORRIE; Braintree HS; Braintree, MA; (Y); VP Church Yth Grp; Various Offcs Intl Order Of Rainbow For Girls 81-86; Bridgewater ST Coll; Elem Educ.

WINIG, ANDY; Buckingham Browne & Nichols HS; Brookline, MA; (S); Drama Clb; School Musical; School Play; Stage Crew; Nwsp Ed-Chief; Rep Soph Cls; Rep Jr Cls; Var L Bsbl; Var L Wrstlng; High Hon Roll.

WINKLER, RICHARD A; Sharon HS; Sharon, MA; (Y); 11/200; Cmnty Wkr; Letterman Clb; Math Tm; Spanish Clb; Temple Yth Grp; Nwsp Rptr; Yrbk Rptr; Rep Sr Cls; Trs Stu Cncl; Im Bsktbl; U MI.

WINNING, KELLY; Whitman-Hanson Rgnl HS; Hanson, MA; (Y); 14/291; Cmnty Wkr; Dance Clb; Rep Frsh Cls; JV Bsktbl; JV Crs Cntry; JV Trk; Hon Roll; NHS; VFW Awd; Ctzn Shclrshp Fndtn Awds 86; U MA Amherst; Intl Bus.

WINOKUR, REBECCA; Hingham HS; Hingham, MA; (Y); Ski Clb; School Musical; Cheerleading; JV Var Socr; Var L Trk; Hon Roll.

WINSLOW, ELAINE P; Walpole HS; Walpole, MA; (Y); 53/270; Church Yth Grp; Dance Clb; Hon Roll; Jazz,Tap And Ballt 72-81; Boston Ballt 78-86; Drama 79-81; Nutcrckr 79-85; Mdlng 80-82; Dance Prog 82; Umass Amherst; Muscl Thtre.

WINSLOW, REBECCA; Pittsfield HS; Chesapeake, VA; (Y); Drama Clb; Pep Clb; School Play; Nwsp Stf; Cheerleading; Offc Wrk Awd 81; Comp Sci.

WINSTON, PADRAIC; Lenox Memorial HS; Lenox, MA; (Y); 1/62; Church Yth Grp; Quiz Bowl; VP Band; Church Choir; Yrbk Bus Mgr; Var L Bsbl; Var L Bsktbl; Bausch & Lomb Sci Awd; High Hon Roll; NHS; Hugh O Brian Yth Fndtn MA Ldrshp Smnr 85; Berkshire Bates Clb Awd Outstndng Male JR In Cnty 86; Biomed Enrng.

WINTERLE, GAIL; Brockton HS; Brockton, MA; (Y); 227/897; Band; Concert Band; Mrchg Band; Symp Band; High Hon Roll; Hon Roll; Comm.

WIRONEN, JOHN F; Oakmont Reg HS; Westminster, MA; (Y); Am Leg Boys St; Yrbk Phtg; Astrnmy.

WIRTZ, LILA KATHERINE B; Auburn HS; Auburn, MA; (Y); Church Yth Grp; Cmnty Wkr; Girl Scts; Hosp Aide; JA; Band; Chorus; Mrchg Band; School Musical; School Play; Epscpl Dics Western MA Yth Comm; Crop Wk; March Of Dimes Wkth 78-86; Girl St Counslr 86; Dietician.

WISCARVA, THERESE; Groton-Dunstable Rgnl Scndry Schl; Dunstable, MA; (Y); 13/100; Office Aide; Teachers Aide; Hon Roll; Jr NHS; NHS; Voice Dem Awd; Excllncy US Hstry 86; Gld Key Boston Globe Schlrtc Art Cmptn 84; U Of Lowell; Bus.

WISE, KHALID; Boston Latin Acad; Boston, MA; (Y); Camera Clb; Teachers Aide; Varsity Clb; Var L Ftbl; Hon Roll; Magna Cm Laud Natl Latn Exm 83; GA Inst Tech; Biochem.

WISE, SARA; Marthas Vineyard Regional HS; Chilmark, MA; (Y); 4/114; Pres 4-H; Nwsp Stf; Lit Mag; 4-H Awd; High Hon Roll; Hon Roll; NHS; Smith Coll Book Awd 86; Hnr Roll Status Awd 85-86; Hnr Achvmnt Awds In Spanish, US Hist, Engl 86.

WISNASKAS, WILLIAM; Whitman-Hanson Regional HS; Whitman, MA; (Y); 8/287; Boy Scts; Var Crs Cntry; Var Capt Trk; Hon Roll; NHS; Prfct Atten Awd; Carl S Ell Schlr Awd-Northeastern U 86; Earnest A Moore Schlrshp 86; Donald F Flaherty Meml Awd 86; Northeastern U; Comp Sci.

WITEK, DAVID C; Gloucester HS; Magnolia, MA; (Y); Am Leg Boys St; JCL; Latin Clb; Varsity Clb; JV Socr; JV Swmmng; Var Trk; Hon Roll; Jr NHS; Otstndng JR Awd Accntng 86; Bus.

WITHBROE, NANCY; Arlington HS; Arlington, MA; (Y); 4/372; Church Choir; Madrigals; School Musical; Swing Chorus; High Hon Roll; NHS; Church Yth Grp; Sec French Clb; Chorus; Rep Stu Cncl; Francis E Thompson Schlrshp 86; Dr Arthur Awd-Outstndng Ach-Hstry 86; CFA Town Of Arlngtn Schlrshp 86; Carleton Coll; Music.

WITHINGTON, WENDY; St Bernards Central Catholic HS; Fitchburg, MA; (S); 19/159; Drama Clb; French Clb; Nwsp Rptr; Yrbk Stf; Var Fld Hcky; Var Sftbl; Hon Roll; Trs NHS; Frnch III Awd 85; Boston U; Physlgy.

WITKOSKI, DANIEL; Dennis-Yarmouth Regional HS; Dennis, MA; (Y); Am Leg Boys St; Church Yth Grp; FCA; Key Clb; Model UN; Service Clb; Ski Clb; Varsity Clb; Band; Concert Band.

WITTMAN, JENNIFER; Sharon HS; Sharon, MA; (Y); 33/210; Drama Clb; Pep Clb; Spanish Clb; Nwsp Stf; Yrbk Stf; Hon Roll; Bus Admin.

WIZWER, HEIDI; Greenfield HS; Greenfield, MA; (Y); 19/159; Spanish Clb; Temple Yth Grp; Var L Tennis; Var L Vllybl; High Hon Roll; Hon Roll; GAA; Bay St Games-Vllybl 85; U Of Hartford.

WOELFLEIN, MICHAEL; St Johns Prep; Hampstead, NH; (Y); Church Yth Grp; Ski Clb; Nwsp Rptr; JV Capt Ice Hcky; Ntl Merit Ltr; Sprts Jrnlsm.

WOHLER, JAMES; Marian HS; Framingham, MA; (Y); Church Yth Grp; CAP; JA; School Play; Var L Bsbl; Var L Ftbl; Zone Champ Punt, Pass & Kick 77; JR Achvts 80-81; Legn Bsbl 86; Aero Engrg.

WOJCIK, GARY; Hoosac Valley HS; Adams, MA; (Y); 3/149; Am Leg Boys St; Pres Band; Concert Band; Mrchg Band; Pep Band; School Musical; Im Vllybl; Cit Awd; High Hon Roll; Hon Roll; Dir Awd Band 84.

WOJCIK, JOHN; Cathedral HS; Springfield, MA; (Y); 114/570; SADD; Nwsp Rptr; Var Bsbl; Bsktbl; Hon Roll; NHS; U MA; Bus Mgt.

WOJCIK, MARLENE; Holyoke HS; Holyoke, MA; (Y); Art Clb; Latin Clb; Nwsp Rptr; Yrbk Rptr; Off Soph Cls; Off Jr Cls; Off Sr Cls; Rep Stu Cncl; Var Tennis; NHS; Lib Arts.

WOLF, SCOTT I; Canton HS; Canton, MA; (Y); 25/255; Am Leg Boys St; Drama Clb; French Clb; Teachers Aide; Temple Yth Grp; Band; Concert Band; Pep Band; School Musical; School Play; Word Proc Typesetting Edtr Schl Newspr; Co Chrmn Natl Hons Soc Am Heart Fun Telethon; Economics.

WOLFE, DEREK; Monument Mountain Reg HS; Lee, MA; (Y); 12/120; Math Tm; Ski Clb; Yrbk Ed-Chief; Var Bsbl; Bausch & Lomb Sci Awd; High Hon Roll; NHS; Pres Schlr; Computer Clb; Varsity Clb; Rensselaer Medl 85; Charles Owen Schlrshp 86; Mass Electric Grant 86; Rensselaer Polytech; Nuclr Phys.

WOLFE, RANDY; Hudson HS; Hudson, MA; (Y); 18/150; Church Yth Grp; Yrbk Stf; Var Bsktbl; JV Var Ftbl; High Hon Roll; NHS; Vrsty Ltrs 84-85; Engrng.

WOLFF, PATRICK G; Belmont HS; Belmont, MA; (Y); 15/280; Chess Clb; Latin Clb; Math Clb; Hon Roll; Ntl Merit SF; Ntl HS Chess Champ 83; New Engl Jr Chesschamp Under 21 83-84; Psych.

WOLFSON, LISA; Medford HS; Medford, MA; (Y); Hosp Aide; SADD; Nwsp Bus Mgr; Yrbk Stf; Awd Of Achvt 86-87; Early Childhd Eductn.

WOLK, AMY; Natick HS; Natick, MA; (Y); Drama Clb; Intnl Clb; Ski Clb; Temple Yth Grp; School Play; Rep Frsh Cls; Rep Soph Cls; Rep Jr Cls; Rep Sr Cls; Rep Stu Cncl; Bus Awd Prsnl Law Clss 86; U Of VT.

WOLLEY, DEBORAH; Milford HS; Milford, MA; (Y); 85/290; Hosp Aide; Band; Concert Band; Mrchg Band; Orch; Pep Band; School Musical; School Play; Symp Band; Variety Show.

WOLOSZ, BARBARA; St Marys HS; Worcester, MA; (Y); 8/50; Drama Clb; Spanish Clb; School Musical; Nwsp Sprt Ed; Yrbk Sprt Ed; Var Capt Bsktbl; Var Capt Sftbl; Var Capt Vllybl; Hon Roll; Jr NHS; Msgr Baronowski Schlrshp; Bst Ath Awd; Bishops Fnd Slgn Cont; U Lowell.

WOLSKI, KATHY; Attleboro HS; Attleboro, MA; (Y); 65/495; SADD; Varsity Clb; Color Guard; Gym; Powder Puff Ftbl; High Hon Roll; Hon Roll; Med.

WOMBWELL, ELIZABETH; St Bernards Central Catholic HS; Winchendon, MA; (S); 4/177; Drama Clb; Teachers Aide; School Play; Stage Crew; Fld Hcky; Swmmng; Vllybl; High Hon Roll; Hon Roll; NHS; Acctg.

WONG, BOBBY; Boston Latin HS; Randolph, MA; (Y); 25/284; JA; Varsity Clb; Lit Mag; Var L Crs Cntry; Var L Trk; High Hon Roll; Hon Roll; NHS; Ntl Merit Ltr; Pres Schlr; 1st Ntl Sci Olympd Bio 86; Brandeis U; Pre Med.

WONG, CHRISTINA; Boston Tech HS; Boston, MA; (Y); French Clb; Spanish Clb; SADD; Yrbk Stf; Hon Roll; Act Chinese Club 86-87; Busi Admnstrtn.

WONG, FUNGWAH; Cambridge Ridge & Latin Schl; Cambridge, MA; (Y); Art Clb; FBLA; Intnl Clb; Key Clb; Office Aide; OEA; PAVAS; Nwsp Bus Mgr; Badmtn; Bowling; Acctng.

WONG, HENRY; Saugus HS; Saugus, MA; (Y); Im Bsktbl; Coach Actv; Score Keeper; Prfct Atten Awd; Voice Dem Awd; Hon Ment Engl Dept Wrtng Cntst 84-85; Elect Engr.

WONG, HUBERT S; Drury SR HS; N Adams, MA; (Y); 47/189; Church Yth Grp; JV Crs Cntry; Var Capt Golf; Hon Roll; Bentley College; Acctg.

WONG, ROSA; Boston Tech; Boston, MA; (Y); French Clb; Bus Mngmnt.

WONG, WAYNE; Brookline HS; Brookline, MA; (Y); Key Clb; Library Aide; Service Clb; Rep Jr Cls; Rep Sr Cls; Im Bsktbl; Cit Awd; Hon Roll; Cavendish Clb Boston Schlrshp 86; Syracuse U; Comp Sci.

WOO, JUDY; Randolph HS; Randolph, MA; (Y); Dance Clb; French Clb; Hon Roll; NHS; Comm Art.

WOOD, CAROLINE; Nipmuc Regional HS; Upton, MA; (Y); 8/95; Am Leg Aux Girls St; Church Yth Grp; SADD; Band; Church Choir; Spanish Clb; Yrbk Stf; Pres Trs Stu Cncl; High Hon Roll; Trs NHS.

WOOD, LAURA; Brockton Christian Regional HS; N Easton, MA; (Y); 1/18; Church Yth Grp; Chorus; Church Choir; Yrbk Stf; Var L Vllybl; Hon Roll; Wnnr-Sci Fair 86; Bentley; Bus.

WOOD, SUSAN; North Reading HS; N Reading, MA; (Y); Church Yth Grp; Band; Chorus; Church Choir; Concert Band; Drill Tm; Mrchg Band; Yrbk Stf; Stu Cncl; God Cntry Awd; Most Improved Woodwind Awd Marching Band 85; Salem ST Coll; Child Care.

WOOD, TERRI; Commerce HS; Springfield, MA; (Y); JA; Library Aide; SADD; Bsktbl; Spnsh Awd 84; Westfld CC Stu 85.

WOOD, TINA; Lincoln-Sudbury Regional HS; Sudbury, MA; (Y); Trs French Clb; Ski Clb; SADD; Yrbk Stf; Rep Frsh Cls; Rep Soph Cls; Rep Jr Cls; Rep Sr Cls; Stu Cncl; Var Cheerleading; Ltr Ski Tm,Chrldng 86; Lehigh U; Frgn Careers.

WOODRUFF, MARY ELIZABETH; Plymouth-Carver HS; Plymouth, MA; (Y); 59/578; AFS; Am Leg Aux Girls St; Drama Clb; Model UN; Acpl Chr; School Musical; Ed Yrbk Stf; Rep Stu Cncl; Var Fld Hcky; Hon Roll; YFU Semstr Exch Prog 86; Lang.

WOODS, THOMAS E; St Johns HS; Worcester, MA; (Y); 17/286; Church Yth Grp; Sec Model UN; Church Choir; School Musical; Variety Show; Hon Roll; NHS; Ntl Merit SF; French Clb; HS Crew Tm-Vrsty-1T Boat Head Of Charles Regatta 84-86; Model UN-CLARK U-Dstngshd Delegate 85; Ecnmcs.

WOODSIDE, AMY; Seekonk HS; Seekonk, MA; (Y); Rep Band; Chorus; Concert Band; Jazz Band; Mrchg Band; Hon Roll; Johnson & Wales; Cooking.

WOODWORTH, DAVID A; Peabody Veterans Memorial HS; Peabody, MA; (Y); 28/501; Church Yth Grp; Nwsp Bus Mgr; Nwsp Ed-Chief; Nwsp Phtg; Nwsp Rptr; Nwsp Sprt Ed; Yrbk Ed-Chief; Yrbk Phtg; Yrbk Stf; Lit Mag; Philip E Searle Schlrshp 86; Gnsbr Std Schrlshp 86; Messiah Coll; Bus.

WOOLFE, ANDREA E; Canton HS; Canton, MA; (Y); 1/265; Math Tm; Spanish Clb; Temple Yth Grp; Stage Crew; High Hon Roll; NHS; Ntl Merit SF; Val; Aero Sp Engr.

WOOLLEY, ELIZABETH; Lincoln-Sudbury Regional HS; Sudbury, MA; (Y); Key Clb; SADD; Yrbk Sprt Ed; Var L Swmmng; Athl Wk, Domestc Exch Stdnt 86; Psych.

WOOLNER, GENA; Acton-Boxborough Regional HS; Acton, MA; (Y); 70/428; Aud/Vis; Model UN; Capt Flag Corp; Stage Crew; Var Cheerleading; Powder Puff Ftbl; NHS; US Hstry & Govt Cert Awd Achvt 85; Amer Clsscl Lg & Natl JR Clsscl Lg Cert Hnrb Mntn 84; Govt Svc.

WORCESTER, SHARON L; Andover HS; Andover, MA; (Y); 40/412; Church Yth Grp; DECA; Socr; NHS; AFS; Quiz Bowl; Yrbk Stf; Trk; High Hon Roll; Hon Roll; Edward Erickson Schlrshp Ctznshp 86; Excllnc Mktg 86; Mt Holyoke Coll.

WORDELL, STACY; BMC Durfee HS; Fall River, MA; (Y); 11/600; Spanish Clb; Varsity Clb; VP Frsh Cls; VP Soph Cls; VP Jr Cls; VP Sr Cls; Fld Hcky; Powder Puff Ftbl; Trk; Twrlr.

WORDEN, PAUL S; Dartmouth HS; N Dartmouth, MA; (Y); 60/240; Key Clb; Bsbl; Ftbl; St Julie Billiart Ladies Guild Schlrshp 86; Bryant Coll; Finance.

WORENKA, ANDREW; Central Catholic HS; Methuen, MA; (Y); 99/231; Ski Clb; Sr Cls; Bsbl; Socr; Wt Lftg.

WORNHAM, MICHELE; North Middlesez Regional HS; Townsend, MA; (Y); Pres Boy Scts; Girl Scts; Var Cheerleading; Powder Puff Ftbl; Hon Roll; NHS; Pres Exploring; Vtrnrn.

WORONZOFF DASHKOFF, HILARION; Northampton HS; Leeds, MA; (Y); 18/225; Rptr Nwsp Rptr; Capt Bsktbl; Capt Ftbl; Var Lcrss; Im Wt Lftg; High Hon Roll; Jr NHS; NHS; Ntl Merit Ltr; MVP Ftbl 81; Plyr Wk All Lg Bsktbl; Schlr Ath All Lg; Leage Referees Scholar; Top Ath Scholar; Amherst Coll; Bus.

WORRELL, A BABETTE; Tantasqua Regional SR HS; Brimfield, MA; (Y); 25/183; Pres Church Yth Grp; Drama Clb; Varsity Clb; Chorus; School Musical; School Play; Variety Show; Var Fld Hcky; Var Sftbl; Prfct Atten Awd; Ntl Hnr Soc Schlrshp 86; Htchcck Acad Schlrshp 86; Allghny Coll; Cmmnctns.

WRIGHT, CHRISTINE; Doherty Memorial HS; Worchester, MA; (Y); Hosp Aide; Sec JA; SADD; Variety Show; Nwsp Rptr; Yrbk Rptr; High Hon Roll; NHS; Spanish NHS; Church Yth Grp; 2nd Pl Spanish IV Natl Spanish Exm 85; U Of MA; Commnctns.

WRIGHT, DAVE; Berkshire Schl; Skaneateles, NY; (Y); Nwsp Ed-Chief; Yrbk Rptr; Lit Mag; Var Bsbl; Var Bsktbl; Var Crs Cntry; Var Capt Trk; NHS; High Hon Roll; Hon Roll; Head Prefect 86-87; Readers Digst Schlrshp 86-87; Bus.

WRIGHT JR, DONALD WILLIAM; Hoosac Valley HS; Adams, MA; (Y); Varsity Clb; Bsbl; Bsktbl; Ftbl; Trk; Wt Lftg; Ath Scholar Amer Intl Coll 86; Hnrb Mntn All Wstrn MA Ftbl 86; All Cls A Ftbl 85 & 86; American Intl Coll; Crimnl Just.

WRIGHT, HELEN; Lexington HS; Lexington, MA; (Y); Computer Clb; Dance Clb; Drama Clb; Math Clb; Spanish Clb; Madrigals; School Musical; School Play; Gym; Trk; Vermont U; Histry.

WRIGHT, JAIMYE; Turners Falls HS; Turners Fls, MA; (Y); 5/91; Varsity Clb; Band; Yrbk Stf; VP Soph Cls; Off Stu Cncl; Stat Var Bsktbl; Var Capt Fld Hcky; Mgr(s); Hon Roll; NHS; Book Awd 86; Svc To Schl Awd 86; Bentley; Bus Adm.

WRIGHT, MONIQUE; Marlboro HS; Marlboro, MA; (Y); 47/250; AFS; Church Yth Grp; Ski Clb; Varsity Clb; Var Crs Cntry; JV Trk; High Hon Roll; Hon Roll; Mktg.

WRIGHT, STEPHNIE; Miss Halls HS; Pittsfield, MA; (Y); VP Camera Clb; Pres Church Yth Grp; VP Hosp Aide; Spanish Clb; Band; Pres Church Choir; Yrbk Bus Mgr; Stu Cncl; Var Bsktbl; JV Socr; Mst Outstndng Awd From Hosp 85; Oral Roberts U; Med.

WRIGHTINGTON, TAMMY; B M C Durfee HS; Fall River, MA; (Y); 92/687; Church Yth Grp; Drama Clb; Hosp Aide; Spanish Clb; School Musical; Miss Columbus 85; Regis Coll; Sociology.

WROBEL, GARY; Westfield HS; Westfield, MA; (Y); School Musical; School Play; Stage Crew; Yrbk Stf; Var Trk.

WRONA, MARGUERITE; Ludlow HS; Ludlow, MA; (Y); 1/279; Am Leg Aux Girls St; Band; Chorus; Rep Stu Cncl; Bausch & Lomb Sci Awd; High Hon Roll; VP Sec NHS; Val; Church Yth Grp; Hosp Aide; Rennsselaer Poly Tech Medal Hnr 85; Wellesley Coll Bk Awd 85; Smith Coll Bk Awd 85; U MA; Engrng.

WRUBEL, TINA; North HS; Worcester, MA; (Y); 21/208; Church Yth Grp; Office Aide; Varsity Clb; Off Stu Cncl; Var Socr; Hon Roll; Bank Schlrshp $1000 86; Assumption Coll Schlrshp $1000 86; Assumption Coll; Acctng.

WU, CECILIA; Boston Latin Schl; Brighton, MA; (Y); 44/274; Hosp Aide; Library Aide; Office Aide; Nwsp Rptr; Yrbk Sprt Ed; Lit Mag; NHS; Schlrshp Art Classes 83-87; Latin Exam Cum Laude Certificate 86.

WU, CURTIS Q; Agawam HS; Agawam, MA; (Y); 1/319; Sec AFS; Capt Quiz Bowl; Scholastic Bowl; Band; Lit Mag; Var Tennis; VP NHS; Ntl Merit SF; Val; French Clb; Cvtn Awd; Rnsslr Awd; Drtmth Bk Awd; MA Inst Of Tech; Engrng.

WU, LILY; Boston Technical HS; Boston, MA; (Y); Trs French Clb; Hosp Aide; Library Aide; Office Aide; SADD; Rep Stu Cncl; Score Keeper; Vllybl; Hon Roll; Prfct Atten Awd; Vllybl Trphy 85-86; Pre Med.

WU, MICHAEL; Boston Technical HS; Boston, MA; (Y); 3/205; Boys Clb Am; Chess Clb; Cmnty Wkr; Computer Clb; Intnl Clb; Library Aide; Bsktbl; Socr; Vllybl; Hon Roll; Boston U Schlrshp 86; MA Gen Schlrshp 86; Boston U.

WU, STEVEN S; Phillips Acad; Andover, MA; (Y); FHA; Math Tm; Yrbk Phtg; Im Socr; Im Tennis; High Hon Roll; Hon Roll; Ntl Merit SF; Art Awd Drft Awd 83; 2nd Yr Fr Awd 1st Pl 84; 3rd Yr Fr Awd 2nd Pl Calc Awd 2nd Pl 85; Harvard; Biol.

WUNCH, DAVID; Cathedral HS; Springfield, MA; (Y); JV Trk; High Hon Roll.

WUORINEN, ANNA; North Reading HS; N Reading, MA; (Y); Church Yth Grp; Chorus; Church Choir; Nwsp Stf; Rep Stu Cncl; Diving; Swmmng; High Hon Roll; NHS; Most Dedicated Swmmr Trophy-Thomson Cntry Clb 85; Missinettes Star-Girls Church Clb Pgm 84.

WYCHORSKI, HENRY; Marian HS; Framingham, MA; (Y); Elec Engr.

WYMAN, THOMAS; Northfield Mount Hermon HS; Leominster, MA; (Y); JV Bsktbl; Var Ftbl; Var Lcrss; JV Socr; Hon Roll; Russian II Lang Awd 86.

WYSZYNSKI, JANINE; Cathedral HS; Springfield, MA; (Y); VP JA; Red Cross Aide; Service Clb; Flag Corp; School Play; Trk; Awd Svc Red Corss,Cafeteria 84-86; Bus.

YACINO, JUDY; Bourne HS; Buzzards Bay, MA; (Y); 22/187; Office Aide; Band; Concert Band; Drm Mjr(t); Jazz Band; Mrchg Band; Orch; Yrbk Stf; Hon Roll; Bus.

YACOVONE, FRANCES; Cathedral HS; Springfield, MA; (Y); 28/536; Aud/Vis; Hosp Aide; Office Aide; Hon Roll; NHS; Voice Dem Awd; Med.

YAEGER JR, ROBERT; Holy Name Central Catholic HS; Worcester, MA; (Y); Stage Crew; Im Bsktbl; Var Crs Cntry; Var Trk; Hon Roll; Engrng.

YAFFE, ALAN; St Marys Regional HS; Lynn, MA; (Y); #15 In Class; Yrbk Stf; Rep Sr Cls; Var Capt Socr; Jr NHS; NHS; JV Bsbl; JV Ftbl; Hon Roll; Spnsh II, Eng I, Gen Sci, Gmtry, & Art I Awds 84; Acc Bio, Typg I, Eng II, & Alg II Awds 85; Engrng.

YAMPOLSKY, SASHA; Newton North HS; Newton, MA; (Y); Ski Clb; Trk; French Clb; Intnl Clb; Math Tm; Temple Yth Grp; Nwsp Stf; Socr; Hon Roll; NEDT Awd; JV Ltrs Ski Team & Trck & Fld 84 & 86; Gldn Ptry Awd, Pblshd 85 & 86; Tufts; Elec Engrng.

YAN, ALBERT W; Boston HS; Somerville, MA; (Y); 18/284; Chess Clb; JA; Science Clb; Stage Crew; High Hon Roll; Hon Roll; NHS; Ntl Merit Ltr; Prfct Atten Awd; Open Gate Schlrshp 86; Crnl U; Mech Engrng.

YAN, JENNY; Boston Latin Schl; Boston, MA; (Y); 7/276; French Clb; Trs Science Clb; SADD; Stage Crew; Nwsp Stf; Yrbk Stf; Lit Mag; High Hon Roll; Trs NHS; Museum Of Fine Arts Schlrshp Clsses 83-87; Lib Arts.

YANOVER, MICHAEL; Natick HS; Natick, MA; (Y); 23/406; Jazz Band; School Musical; School Play; Nwsp Bus Mgr; High Hon Roll; Hon Roll; JETS Awd; NHS; All ST Band 1st Chair 85-86; Dist Band 1st Chair 86; Museum Fine Arts Hnrs Pgm 85; U MA-AMHERST; Engr.

YANTOSCA, ROBERT; Boston College HS; E Boston, MA; (Y); 5/300; Chess Clb; Church Yth Grp; Cmnty Wkr; Latin Clb; Science Clb; High Hon Roll; NHS; Classics Assn MA Latin Transltn Cont 1st Prz 86; Natl Latin Exam Summa Cum Laude 85; Latin III Hnrs; Astrnmy.

YARKEY, JODI; Catherdral HS; Springfield, MA; (Y); Dance Clb; Prfct Atten Awd; Framingham; Tchng.

YARUSSI, LISA; Fitchburg HS; Fitchburg, MA; (Y); Ski Clb; Var Crs Cntry; Var Trk; High Hon Roll; Hon Roll; MVP Crs Cntry 85; Outdoor Trk Schl Recrd Mile 86, Indoor Rcrd 2 Mile 84; Bus Adm.

YATSUHASHI, CHRISTINA; King Philip Regional HS; Norfolk, MA; (Y); 5/213; Var Cheerleading; Var Mgr(s); High Hon Roll; Hon Roll; NHS; Wrld JR Figure Sktng Bronze Mdlst 83; Wrld JR Figure Sktng Slvr Mdlst 84; US JR Dance Champ 84.

YAVANIAN, ELIZABETH; Burlington HS; Burlington, MA; (Y); 13/321; Math Tm; Science Clb; Yrbk Stf; Hon Roll; NHS; Pre-Med.

YEE, ANDREW; Boston Latin Acad; Allston, MA; (Y); Math Clb; Boston U; Electrnc.

YEE, EUGENE; North Quincy HS; Quincy, MA; (Y); 7/408; French Clb; Trs FBLA; VP JA; Teachers Aide; Nwsp Rptr; Yrbk Stf; French Hon Soc; High Hon Roll; Schl Imprvmt Cncl 86; MA ST Sci Fair Hnrbl Mntn Awd 86.

YEE, JEANNE N; Northfield Mount Hermon Schl; Malden, MA; (Y); Cmnty Wkr; Debate Tm; Library Aide; Rptr Yrbk Stf; Rep Stu Cncl; High Hon Roll; Ntl Merit Ltr; Cum Laude Soc 86; Harvard U.

YEE, JULIE; Boston Latin Acad; Brighton, MA; (Y); Intnl Clb; Boston U; Bus.

YEE, MARY; Salem HS; Salem, MA; (Y); #10 In Class; German Clb; Math Tm; Science Clb; Orch; School Musical; Rep Frsh Cls; JV Fld Hcky; High Hon Roll; NHS; Polytechnic U; Engnrng.

YEE, STEPHEN; Boston Technical HS; Brighton, MA; (Y); Hon Roll; NHS; Prfct Atten Awd.

YELLE, TAREN; Norton HS; Norton, MA; (S); 7/148; Math Tm; Concert Band; Drm & Bgl; Jazz Band; Mrchg Band; Yrbk Bus Mgr; Swmmng; NHS; Debate Tm; French Clb; S Eastern Dist Orch Music 85-86; All ST Recmndtn Music 85-86; Rensselaer; Aero Sp Engr.

YEOMANS, NANCY; Cohasset HS; Cohasset, MA; (Y); 35/110; Chorus; JV Fld Hcky; Hon Roll; Hnrs Awd 84-85; Anthrplgy.

YEOMANS, PETER D; Concord Acad; Concord, MA; (Y); Chorus; School Play; Stage Crew; Pres Soph Cls; Pres Stu Cncl; Var Socr; Tchr Eng.

YERAGOTELIS, JOHN D; Braintree HS; Braintree, MA; (Y); 12/450; Am Leg Boys St; SADD; Var Bsbl; High Hon Roll; NHS; Engrg.

YESKEVICZ, DAWN; St Peter Marian C C HS; Worcester, MA; (Y); 50/205; Church Yth Grp; SADD; Trs Frsh Cls; Trs Soph Cls; Trs Jr Cls; Trs Sr Cls; Capt Bsktbl; JV Sftbl; Hon Roll; Hnrs Latin, Religion 84; Hnrs Bio, Religion 85; Hnrs Religion, Chem, Typing 86; St Vincents Nrsng Schl; Nrsng.

YESKEWICZ, JAMES J; Middleboro HS; Middleboro, MA; (Y); Am Leg Boys St; Computer Clb; Band; Concert Band; Jazz Band; Mrchg Band; Orch; School Musical; School Play; Symp Band; VP Natl Soc 86; Semsba Band Awd 84-86; Boston Globe South Shore All Star Swim Tm 86; Private Bus.

YFANTOPULOS, DORA; Bishop Fenwick HS; Salem, NH; (Y); Hosp Aide; Chorus; Yrbk Stf; Score Keeper; Var Vllybl; High Hon Roll; Hon Roll; Spnsh Awd-Spnsh II Lvl II 84; Wlk For Hngr 85.

YOCCO, STEPHEN; Milton HS; Milton, MA; (Y); Var JV Bsbl; Var JV Crs Cntry; Hon Roll; Comm.

YORK, SUSAN; Medway JR SR HS; Medway, MA; (Y); 31/145; Hosp Aide; Band; Concert Band; Mrchg Band; Var L Socr; Hon Roll; U Of AK Fairbanks; Marine Bio.

YORK, SUSANNA; Hopedale JR SR HS; Hopedale, MA; (Y); 12/80; Art Clb; Church Yth Grp; Yrbk Stf; High Hon Roll; Hon Roll; Bentley; Acctnt.

YOUNG, ELIZABETH; Scitvate HS; Scituate, MA; (Y); 17/280; Pres Church Yth Grp; Yrbk Stf; Stu Cncl; JV Bsktbl; JV Socr; Hon Roll; NHS; Sr Bstr Clb Awd 86; Hnvr Mall Ornmnt Cntst Wnr 83; Fairfield U; Biolgy.

YOUNG, JASON D; Scituate HS; N Scituate, MA; (Y); 1/277; Cmnty Wkr; Computer Clb; Pres Church Yth Grp; Math Tm; Political Wkr; Rep Stu Cncl; Bausch & Lomb Sci Awd; French Hon Soc; High Hon Roll; NHS; Assoc Tchrs Math Mass Achvt Awd 86; Rnsslr Math & Sci Mdl 85; Assoc Sprntdnts Mass Awd Acad Excel 86; Harvard U.

YOUNG, JULIA; Hingham HS; Hingham, MA; (Y); 60/350; French Clb; Varsity Clb; Var Gym; Var Trk; Hon Roll; Boston Coll Var Rcrd Pentathln 84; Estrn Regnl Invtatnl Trk 85; Harvard Diving 85; Arch Engrng.

YOUNG, JULIE; West Springfield HS; W Springfield, MA; (Y); Am Leg Aux Girls St; Church Yth Grp; Q&S; Yrbk Stf; Pres Jr Cls; VP Stu Cncl; Var Capt Gym; High Hon Roll; NHS; Spanish NHS; Ltn Natl Hnr Scty; Natl Ltn Exm Awd Magna Cum Laude.

YOUNG, MEG; Tahanto Regional HS; Morningdale, MA; (Y); 19/57; 4-H; Hosp Aide; Varsity Clb; Trs Stu Cncl; Capt Cheerleading; JV Fld Hcky; Awd Acadmc Excllnc 84; Air Force.

YOUNG, PAMELA J; Braintree HS; Braintree, MA; (Y); Nwsp Rptr; Ed Yrbk Sprt Ed; Rep Stu Cncl; Var L Gym; Pom Pon; Im Trk; Hon Roll; Armenian Church Yth Orgnztn Treas 85-86; Co-Chrmn Electns Comm Stu Govt 86; Intl Order Rainbow Grls 82; Govt.

YOUNG, SHARON; Pittsfield HS; Pittsfield, MA; (Y); 4/419; Exploring; Girl Scts; JCL; Latin Clb; Math Clb; Band; Mrchg Band; Yrbk Stf; High Hon Roll; NHS; Chem Engr.

YOUNG, SUSAN; W Springfield HS; W Springfield, MA; (Y); Cmnty Wkr; French Clb; Pep Clb; Ski Clb; JV Bsktbl; JV Var Cheerleading; French Hon Soc; Ntl Merit Ltr.

YU, TA CHIEN; Waltham HS; Waltham, MA; (Y); French Clb; Math Clb; Math Tm; Science Clb; Hon Roll; Jr NHS.

YUEN, HARVEY; Boston Latin Acad; Boston, MA; (Y); Exploring; Math Clb; Math Tm; Hon Roll; Natl Latin Exam Cum Laude Cert Merit 85; Outstndng Achvt Awd Germn 85; IBM Hnr Rl Ltr Recgntn 86; Johns Hopkins U; Mech Engrng.

YUNG, ALAN; Brookline HS; Brookline, MA; (Y); Computer Clb; Teachers Aide; Cit Awd; French Hon Soc; Hon Roll; Prfct Atten Awd; Milton Silverman Awd 86; Excllnc Compu Rltd Bus 86; Northeastern U; Compu Sci.

ZACCHEO, JOSEPH; Boston College HS; Quincy, MA; (Y); 26/290; JA; Science Clb; Spanish Clb; Im Bsbl; Im Bsktbl; Im Ftbl; JV Trk; High Hon Roll; Jr NHS; NHS; Acad Awd Alg II 84; Acad Awd Chem I 84; Acad Awd Spn III 85; Boston Coll; Acctng.

ZACCHERA, MICHAEL; Southwick HS; Southwick, MA; (Y); 19/137; Am Leg Boys St; Chess Clb; Drama Clb; VP French Clb; Pep Clb; SADD; Band; Chorus; School Musical; Pres Frsh Cls; Delg Intl Stu Ldrshp Pgm 85; Delg Natl Ldrshp Training Ctr 84; Tutor; Biochem.

ZACHARA, KATHY; Bartlett HS; Webster, MA; (Y); Spanish Clb; Yrbk Stf; Var Cheerleading; High Hon Roll; Anna Maria Coll; Med Lab Tech.

ZAFFINO, BRIAN; Dennis Yarmouth Regional HS; Dennis, MA; (Y); 17/310; Am Leg Boys St; Church Yth Grp; FCA; Math Tm; Ski Clb; Spanish Clb; Yrbk Stf; JV L Trk; Im Vllybl; Hon Roll; U N Plgrmg For Yth 85; Bates Coll; Corp Law.

ZAGARELLA, KRISTEN; Pope John XXIII Central Cath HS; Malden, MA; (S); 33/214; Church Yth Grp; Drama Clb; Hosp Aide; Key Clb; NFL; SADD; Yrbk Stf; Rep Stu Cncl; Hon Roll; VP NHS; Awd Scrng 92 Prcttl NEDT Stndrdzd Tst 83; Awds Bst Cls Avg-Spnsh III & Engl Comp 84; Law.

ZAHKA, CYNTHIA L; Belmont HS; Belmont, MA; (Y); 32/263; Church Yth Grp; Variety Show; NHS; Orch; School Play; Yrbk Stf; Socr; JV Trk; High Hon Roll; Hon Roll; Smmr Mentorship Pgm Bstn Museum Sci; Tufts U; Chem Engrng.

ZAJAC, LISA; Cathedral HS; Chicopee, MA; (Y); Quiz Bowl; Chorus; Color Guard; Stage Crew; Variety Show; Prfct Atten Awd; Frnch Pstr Awd Le Festival 85; 3rd Hghst Seller Candy Drive 85; Elec Engrng.

ZALESKI, KRISTEN; Westford Acad; Westford, MA; (Y); French Clb; Sec Frsh Cls; Sec Soph Cls; Sec Jr Cls; Sec Sr Cls; Var Capt Fld Hcky; VP Sftbl; Hon Roll; NHS; Ntl Merit Ltr; Achvt Awd Advncd Foods Cls 84-85; Most Imprvd Plyr Fld Hcky 85-86; Pre Med.

ZALL, SUSAN J; Canton HS; Canton, MA; (Y); 7/265; Church Yth Grp; Math Tm; Nwsp Ed-Chief; French Clb; Science Clb; School Play; Hon Roll; NHS; Northeastern Scholar 86-87; Schlr Dollar Merit Awd 86; Northeastern U; Engrng.

ZALVAN, CRAIG; Randolph HS; Randolph, MA; (Y); Drama Clb; Ski Clb; SADD; Pres Temple Yth Grp; School Play; Stage Crew; Yrbk Stf; Swmmng; Hon Roll; Jr NHS; Stu Advsr 86-87; Med.

ZAMAGNI, ANDY; Malden HS; Malden, MA; (Y); 86/480; Key Clb; Rep Soph Cls; Mgr VP Golf; Capt L Swmmng; A Garden Club Ldr At Chrch 3 Yrs & Mbr For 4 Yrs 79-86; YMCA Bwlng Team 78-81; UMASS Boston; Bus Htl Mgmt.

ZAMMITTI, MARIA; Pope John XXIII Central HS; Medford, MA; (S); 36/247; Church Yth Grp; Cmnty Wkr; French Clb; Hosp Aide; JA; Key Clb; Science Clb; Hon Roll; Hosp Vlntr 60 Hr Ptch Awd 86; Geom Achvmnt Awd 85; Boston U; Bio.

ZANAUSKAS, KRISTINE; Auburn HS; Auburn, MA; (Y); Ski Clb; Occptnl Ed Awd Typng 86; Sec.

ZANGARI, REBECCA; Haverhill HS; Haverhill, MA; (Y); Spanish Clb; Yrbk Stf; Off Soph Cls; Off Jr Cls; Rep Stu Cncl; Capt Cheerleading; Hon Roll; Nrthestrn U; Accntng.

ZANNOTTI, LISA; Auburn HS; Auburn, MA; (Y); Church Yth Grp; Varsity Clb; Yrbk Stf; Var Capt Cheerleading; Var Trk; Conf All Star/Trck 86.

ZANZOT, EMILY; Lincoln-Sudbury Regional HS; Sudbury, MA; (Y); Church Yth Grp; Pres French Clb; VP Key Clb; Chorus; School Musical; Ed Yrbk Stf; Lit Mag; Cum Laude Soc 86.

ZAPATKA, ANDREA; Tahanto Regional HS; Boylston, MA; (Y); 3/64; Pres Church Yth Grp; Hosp Aide; Math Tm; Ski Clb; School Play; Variety Show; Nwsp Ed-Chief; JV Cheerleading; High Hon Roll; NHS; Econ.

ZAPATKA, ANDREA; Tahonto Regional HS; Morningdale, MA; (Y); 3/64; Pres Church Yth Grp; Hosp Aide; Math Tm; Ski Clb; School Play; Nwsp Ed-Chief; Cheerleading; High Hon Roll; Jr NHS; NHS; Finance.

ZAPERT, LISA; Westfield HS; Westfield, MA; (Y); Art Clb; Varsity Clb; JV Capt Socr; Jr NHS; NHS; Art.

ZAPPULA, MIKE; Hoosac Valley HS; Cheshire, MA; (Y); 9/149; Pep Clb; Ski Clb; Varsity Clb; Ftbl; Ice Hcky; Trk; High Hon Roll; NHS; Trnscrpt Rcgntn Awd 85 & 86; Mst Vlbl Dfnsv Plyr Ftbl 85; Engr.

ZARLENGO, AMY; East Longmeadow HS; E Longmeadow, MA; (Y); 19/201; Hon Roll; Danc.

ZAROZINSKI, CHRISTOPHER; Gardner HS; Gardner, MA; (Y); 3/137; Am Leg Boys St; Spanish Clb; Stage Crew; Yrbk Phtg; Yrbk Stf; High Hon Roll; Hon Roll; NHS; Bio.

ZASKEY, CHRISTINE; Cathedral HS; Chicopee, MA; (Y); 10/455; School Musical; Yrbk Stf; Stu Cncl; Trk; Hon Roll; VP NHS; Pres Schlr; Commonwealth Scholar; Boston Coll; Pol Sci.

ZASKEY, DIANE; Cathedral HS; Chicopee, MA; (Y); 60/500; Church Yth Grp; Dance Clb; Hosp Aide; Intnl Clb; Model UN; SADD; School Musical; Intl Studies.

ZASTREA, LEE; Newton North HS; Auburndale, MA; (Y); Fash.

ZAYAS, GERARDO; Madison Park HS; Boston, MA; (Y); JA; Acpl Chr; Band; Chorus; School Play; Swing Chorus; Nwsp Stf; VP Jr Cls; Stu Cncl; Swmmng; Outstndng Excllnc World Culture 83-84; Stu Achvt Stu Cncl & Music 84-85; Outstndg Stu, Oustndg In Music; Boston Coll; Political Govt.

ZECHA, ANNE THERESE; Chelsea HS; Chelsea, MA; (Y); 2/207; Church Yth Grp; Cmnty Wkr; JCL; Latin Clb; SADD; Variety Show; Yrbk Stf; Rep Frsh Cls; Pres Soph Cls; Rep Jr Cls; Grad Dance Tchrs Trnng Tchrs Clb Boston 85; MA All Am Tn Grl 84; MA JR Ms 86; Hly Crss; Cmmnctns.

ZEIDMAN, HEATHER; Acad Of Notre Dame; Lowell, MA; (Y); SADD; Chorus; Yrbk Stf; Cmmnctns.

ZELNICK, MICHAEL; Algonquin Regional HS; Northboro, MA; (Y); Band; Concert Band; Jazz Band; Mrchg Band; Orch; Bsbl; Mgr(s); Hon Roll; NHS; Engrng.

ZENISKY, KIMBERLY; Southwick HS; Southwick, MA; (Y); 15/126; Am Leg Aux Girls St; GAA; Pep Clb; Ski Clb; Band; Var L Bsktbl; Var L Fld Hcky; Var L Sftbl; Hon Roll; Most Vlbl Plyr Sftbl 83-86; Most Vlbl Plyr Fld Hcky 85; Most Vlbl Plyr Bsktbl 85-86.

ZENOFSKY, AMY; Foxborough HS; Foxboro, MA; (Y); 2/243; Pres Math Tm; Nwsp Ed-Chief; Pres Jr NHS; Pres NHS; Sal; VP JA; Scholastic Bowl; Pres Spanish Clb; SADD; Nwsp Stf; MASS U Chancllrs Full Schlrshp 85-86; Model Congrs 84-86; Hnry Stu Womens Lgu 85-86; Tufts Jackson Coll; Pre-Med.

ZENTMEYER, JULIE; The Williston-Northampton Schl; Westfield, MA; (Y); 68/118; Key Clb; Library Aide; Office Aide; Spanish Clb; Stage Crew; Yrbk Phtg; Yrbk Stf; Var L Ice Hcky; Var Trk; Hon Roll; Intrepreting.

ZERN, JOANNE; Bishop Feehan HS; Attleboro, MA; (Y); JCL; Yrbk Stf; JV Bsktbl; Var Capt Trk; Var L Vllybl; High Hon Roll; NHS; Spanish NHS; Vlybl All Star Tm 85; Spg Track All Star Tm 86.

ZERRIEN, SPENCER; King Philip Regional HS; Norfolk, MA; (Y); VICA; High Hon Roll; Hon Roll; Dist II Sklls Olympcs Archtctrl Drftg Fnlst; VICA Awd Apprctn; Northeastern U; Archtctrl Dsgn.

ZGRODNIK, ANN; Smith Acad; Hatfield, MA; (Y); Dance Clb; Drama Clb; 4-H; Girl Scts; Key Clb; Ski Clb; SADD; Band; Church Choir; Yrbk Stf; Prize Speaking 86; Green Thumb Awd 84-87; NJHA 1st Pl In State 86; Educ.

ZICHELLE, KATHRYN; St Bernards Central Catholic HS; Leominster, MA; (Y); Church Yth Grp; Latin Clb; Model UN; Ski Clb; Church Choir; Fld Hcky; Lcrss; Trk; NHS; Ntl Merit Ltr; U VT; Pol Sci.

ZIELINSKI, DAN; Cathedral HS; Springfield, MA; (Y); Drama Clb; Mathletes; Math Clb; Math Tm; PAVAS; Acpl Chr; Chorus; Madrigals; School Musical; School Play; Westrn Dist Chrs MMEA 84-86; MA Musc Eductrs Assoc All ST Chrs 85-86; Math Awds 85-86; Westfield ST Clg; Math.

ZIEMBA, JOHN S; Ludlow HS; Ludlow, MA; (Y); 11/275; Am Leg Boys St; JCL; Nwsp Rptr; Yrbk Ed-Chief; Rep Jr Cls; Rep Sr Cls; Bsbl; Crs Cntry; NEDT Awd; Voice Dem Awd; MA Cmmnwlth Schlrshp 86; Coll Of Hly Crss; Engl.

ZIMMERMAN, RHONDA; Randolph HS; Brockton, MA; (Y); Capt Hosp Aide; SADD; Temple Yth Grp; Band; Concert Band; JR Volunteer 500 HR Pin 86; American Heart Assn Cert Of Appreciation 86; Labouree; Med.

ZION, ANN MARIE; Medford HS; Medford, MA; (Y); 53/406; Ski Clb; SADD; Hon Roll; Engl Awd Outstndng Progrss 83-84; Engl Awd Acad Excllnce 85-86; Salem ST; Law.

ZIRPOLO, JOHN; Christopher Columbus HS; East Boston, MA; (S); JA; Stu Cncl; Ftbl; Ice Hcky.

ZOHN, MARJORIE E; Newton North HS; W Newton, MA; (Y); Drama Clb; German Clb; Speech Tm; School Play; JV Socr; Hon Roll; Ntl Merit SF; Band; Chorus; Concert Band; Slvr Mdl Natl Latin Exam 85; Fnlst Boston Shakespeare Co Monolg Comp 85; Dir Entry MA Drama Fest 86.

ZOKOWSKI, MARGARET; Smith Acad; Hatfield, MA; (Y); 1/32; Am Leg Aux Girls St; Sec Trs Church Yth Grp; Nwsp Ed-Chief; Sec Soph Cls; VP Jr Cls; Pres Sr Cls; VP Bsktbl; Capt Var Sftbl; DAR Awd; Hon Roll; Amb Robt J Ryan Intl Rel Awd 86; Match Wits Team 82-86; 1st Pl Declmtn Spkng Cntst 85; Smith Coll; Intl Rel.

ZOMMER, LORA; Norton HS; Norton, MA; (S); 5/170; Concert Band; Mrchg Band; Orch; High Hon Roll; NHS; NEDT Awd; Voice Dem Awd; Sthestrn MA Dist Band 84, 86; Hnrb Mntn Phi Alpha Trm Papr Comptn 85; Flute-Yngh Pepls Symphny RI.

ZORFASS, DEBORAH; Natick HS; Natick, MA; (Y); 1/399; SADD; Rep Temple Yth Grp; Orch; School Musical; Nwsp Ed-Chief; Nwsp Stf; Off Frsh Cls; Off Soph Cls; Sec Stu Cncl; High Hon Roll; Harvard Bk Awd 86; Brown Book Awd 86.

ZUKOWSKY, KATHRYN; Tantasqua Regional SR HS; Fiskdale, MA; (Y); 51/186; Letterman Clb; Ski Clb; Varsity Clb; School Play; Variety Show; Yrbk Stf; Stat Bsktbl; Var JV Fld Hcky; Var Score Keeper; Var JV Sftbl; Major John F Reagan Mem Schlrshp 86; Hitchock Free Acad Schlrshp 86; Am Lg Womens Aux Schlrshp 86; Roanoke Coll; Intl Relations.

ZULETA, BILLY; Somerville HS; Somerville, MA; (Y); 2/23.

ZULON, KAREN; Fontbonne Acad; Dorchester, MA; (Y); Pres Dance Clb; Drama Clb; Capt Color Guard; School Play; Hon Roll; Magna Cum Laude Natl Latin Exam 83-84.

ZUMPFE, CHRISTOPHER; Shepherd Hill Regional JR SR HS; Dudley, MA; (Y); 20/173; Math Tm; Band; Mrchg Band; Trk; High Hon Roll; JETS Awd; NHS; Prfct Atten Awd; Am Class Leag Cert Of Hnrbl Merit Cum Laude 85; Worcester Polytech; Engrg.

ZUNIGA, STEPHANIE; Hingham HS; Hingham, MA; (Y); 75/347; AFS; Art Clb; Spanish Clb; High Hon Roll; Hon Roll; Church Yth Grp; Drama Clb; Boston Globe Schlstc Arts Awd Gold Key 85-86; Vet-Med.

ZWICKER, STEPHEN; Burlington HS; Burlington, MA; (Y); 8/321; Math Tm; Science Clb; Bsktbl; Hon Roll; NHS; Ntl Merit Ltr; Acadmc Excellnc Awd-Math 86; Med.

ZYGOURAS, HELEN; Milton HS; Milton, MA; (Y); Art Clb; French Clb; Yrbk Stf; Bio.

ZYMROZ, WENDI; Agawam HS; Feeding Hls, MA; (Y); 30/350; Latin Clb; Nwsp Stf; Capt Gym; Trk; Wt Lftg; Hon Roll; NHS; Polish Amer Club Of Agawam Schlrshp 86; Brehend Schlrshp 86; Agawam Police Schlrshp 86; U Of MA; Nrsng.

ZYWNA, KIMBERLY; Turners Falls HS; Turners Fls, MA; (Y); Girl Scts; Concert Band; Mrchg Band; Yrbk Stf; Bsktbl; Sftbl; Trk.

NEW HAMPSHIRE

ABBADESSA, MARY E; St Thomas Aquinas HS; Dover, NH; (Y); Cmnty Wkr; French Clb; Sec Frsh Cls; High Hon Roll; Acad Achvt Awd Engl,Math,French & Span 85-86; Bus.

ABBERTON, MICHAEL; Alvirne HS; Hudson, NH; (Y); 3/375; Math Tm; Ski Clb; Teachers Aide; Trs Soph Cls; Bausch & Lomb Sci Awd; High Hon Roll; Hon Roll; NHS; Physics.

ABBOTT, DAVID; St Thomas Aguinas HS; Gonic, NH; (Y); 30/85; Key Clb; Latin Clb; Rep Frsh Cls; VP Jr Cls; VP Sr Cls; Var Capt Bsbl; Var Capt Ftbl; Var Capt Ice Hcky; Hon Roll.

ABELE, APRIL; Alvirne HS; Hudson, NH; (Y); 30/333; Ski Clb; Var L Sftbl; Hon Roll; Prom Comm & Trea 85; NH U; Bus.

ACKERSON, MATTHEW S; Franklin JR SR HS; Franklin, NH; (Y); 1/91; Computer Clb; French Clb; Math Tm; Golf; Trk; High Hon Roll; NHS; Prfct Atten Awd; Voice Dem Awd; Mth Tm Hghst Tm Scorer; Hugh O Brian Ldrshp Conf; Mth.

ADAMS, AMY; Hopkinton HS; Hopkinton, NH; (Y); 7/65; Pres Drama Clb; French Clb; Hosp Aide; Model UN; SADD; Chorus; School Play; Stage Crew; NHS; Honor Rl; Bus Adm.

ADAMS, DEBERAH; Alton Central HS; Alton, NH; (S); VP French Clb; Girl Scts; School Musical; School Play; Stage Crew; Cheerleading; Crs Cntry; Trk; Hon Roll; UNH.

ADAMS, HEATHER; Hillsboro-Deering HS; Hillsboro, NH; (S); 7/69; Teachers Aide; Hon Roll; Military.

ADAMS, TIFFANY; Spaulding HS; Rochester, NH; (S); 3/400; Church Yth Grp; Math Clb; Math Tm; Church Choir; Color Guard; Concert Band; Jazz Band; Mrchg Band; High Hon Roll; NHS; Neurolgst.

ADRIGNOLA, TOM; Laconia HS; Lakeport, NH; (Y); 10/180; Cmnty Wkr; Computer Clb; Drama Clb; Key Clb; School Play; Stage Crew; Yrbk Stf; High Hon Roll; Hon Roll; Elec Engr.

AHLGREN, KIM; Memorial HS; Manchester, NH; (Y); 8/341; Sec Exploring; Intnl Clb; SADD; Teachers Aide; Lit Mag; Var Mgr(s); Var Twrlr; High Hon Roll; Sec NHS; UNH; Psychlgy.

ALBAHARY, RONALD; Nashua SR HS; Aberdeen, NJ; (Y); 23/900; Debate Tm; Drama Clb; Model UN; Yrbk Bus Mgr; Im Bsktbl; Gov Hon Prg Awd; High Hon Roll; NHS; Ntl Merit Ltr; Rotary Awd.

ALCOTT, KRISTINE; Hopkinton HS; Hopkinton, NH; (Y); DECA; Drama Clb; Chorus; School Musical; School Play; Cheerleading; Lion Awd; DECA Schlrshp 86; Store Mgr Stu Run Store 86; Johnson Wales Coll; Fash Merch.

ALLARD, BARBARA; Manchester Central HS; Manchester, NH; (Y); 11/430; High Hon Roll; NHS; Tchr.

ALLBEE, TRACY; Woodsville HS; N Haverhill, NH; (Y); 7/75; FBLA; Office Aide; Pep Clb; Yrbk Bus Mgr; Yrbk Stf; Dnfth Awd; Hon Roll; Sec Mgr Jr NHS; Sec Mgr NHS; Prfct Atten Awd; J Hesser Mem Schlrshp Rebekahs Ldg Schlrshp 86; Bus Stu Of Yr 84-86; Natl Hnr Soc Schlrshp 86; Hesser Coll; Acctng.

ALLEN, BONNIE LYNN; Newport HS; Newport, NH; (Y); 8/85; Dance Clb; Math Tm; Pep Clb; Spanish Clb; Band; Concert Band; Jazz Band; Mrchg Band; Pep Band; Nwsp Stf; Judith Johnson Bus Memrl Awd 86; Travel.

ALLEN, KAI-UWE; Hopkinton HS; Cantoocook, NH; (Y); German Clb; Model UN; Ski Clb; Varsity Clb; Stage Crew; Yrbk Stf; Hon Roll; Prfct Atten Awd; US Hstry Profcncy Awd 87; Hstry Awd 85; Landscape Arch.

ALLEN, LEE; Fall Mtn Regional HS; Charlestown, NH; (Y); Math Tm; Band; Mrchg Band; Pep Band; Var JV Bsbl; Bsktbl; Var JV Socr; Hon Roll; NHS; Geo Awd 85; Alg II Awd 86.

ALLEN, MARY E; Spaulding HS; Rochester, NH; (S); Chorus; Hon Roll.

ALLEN, VICKI; Concord HS; Concord, NH; (Y); 54/345; Cmnty Wkr; Computer Clb; Chorus; High Hon Roll; Kiwanis Awd; NHS; Wmns Clb Scholar 86; JR Wmns Clb Scholar 86; Clark U; Law.

ALLISON, DEBBIE; Alvirne HS; Hudson, NH; (Y); 7/338; Yrbk Ed-Chief; High Hon Roll; Hon Roll; NHS; Ntl Merit Schol; Rivier Coll Challenge Pgm 85; Boston U; Psych.

ALTY, JOE; Dover HS; Dover, NH; (Y); 89/289; Var L Bsbl; Hon Roll; Coachs Awd Bsbll 86; Acctg.

AMEDEN, JOSIE; High Mowing Schl; Londonderry, VT; (Y); French Clb; Science Clb; Chorus; School Musical; Variety Show; Lit Mag; Rep Stu Cncl; Var Bsktbl.

AMMON, KIMBERLY JEAN; Salem HS; Salem, NH; (S); 3/350; Model UN; Spanish Clb; SADD; Teachers Aide; Concert Band; Mrchg Band; Elks Awd; High Hon Roll; NHS; Spanish NHS; Tngr Of Mnth 85; Cntry III Ldrs Schlrshp 2nd Pl 85; Spnsh Awd 84 & 85; Med.

ANAYA, DOMINIC; St Thomas Aquinas HS; Welk, ME; (Y); Art Clb; Hon Roll; Brown Belt 2nd Degree 86.

ANDREWS, SCOTT; Milford Area SR HS; Amherst, NH; (Y); Am Leg Boys St; Cmnty Wkr; Letterman Clb; Varsity Clb; Var Capt Socr; Var Capt Trk; Hon Roll; Bsktbl; Bus.

ANZALONE, KARA; Portsmouth HS; Portsmouth, NH; (Y); 91/379; Art Clb; SADD; Yrbk Stf; Sr Cls; Var L Swmmng; JV Trk; Var Capt Vllybl; High Hon Roll; Hon Roll; JR World Cncl Pblcty Dir 87; Mdl Congress; Psychlgy.

APPLETON, PAUL; Hanover HS; Hanover, NH; (Y); 30/177; Concert Band; Yrbk Ed-Chief; Yrbk Phtg; Trs Frsh Cls; Pres Soph Cls; Pres Jr Cls; Pres Sr Cls; Trs Stu Cncl; Var Bsktbl; Var Capt Lcrss; Bsktbl Total Tm Commitmnt Awd 86; La Crosse Mst Imprvd Awd 86.

APTE, ARIEL; Kennett HS; N Conway, NH; (Y); 12/180; French Clb; Yrbk Phtg; Yrbk Sprt Ed; Rep Jr Cls; JV Var Fld Hcky; French Hon Soc; Hon Roll; NHS; Lib Arts.

ARBO, RICKY; Pembroke Acad; Pembroke, NH; (Y); 60/188; French Clb; FBLA; Ski Clb; JV Var Bsbl; Crmnl Jstc.

AREVALO, CARLOS; The Phillips Exeter Acad; Mesquite, TX; (Y); Aud/Vis; Spanish Clb; Band; Mrchg Band; School Play; Stage Crew; Im Ice Hcky; Hon Roll; Jr NHS; Ntl Merit Ltr; Hispanic Schlr Awds Prgm 86; Arts.

ARGUE, MAUREEN; Bishop Brady HS; Pittsfield, NH; (Y); 6/74; Church Yth Grp; 4-H; Sec Jr Cls; Sec Sr Cls; JV Var Bsktbl; Var JV Sftbl; 4-H Awd; Hon Roll; NHS; 4h Ctznshp WA Fcs WA DC 85.

ARSENAULT, ANTHONY JAMES; Gilford Middle HS; Lanconia, NH; (Y); Drama Clb; Thesps; School Musical; School Play; Pres Stu Cncl; Hon Roll; NH All ST Drama Cst 85; Utstndng Bus Stu 85-86; Schlrshp Awd Lks Rgn Schlrshp Found 86; Bentley Coll; Accntng.

ARTHUR, JONATHAN B; Keene HS; Alstead, NH; (Y); CAP; Debate Tm; JV Crs Cntry; High Hon Roll; Hon Roll; City Brd 86-87; Private Pilots License 87.

ASHOUR, FUAD T; Milford Area SR HS; Amherst, NH; (Y); 160/311; Pres Chess Clb; 4-H; JV Socr; Im Vllybl; 4-H Awd; Im Sftbl; Hon Roll; U Of Lowell; Indstrl Mgmt.

ASHTON, KEN; Kearsarge Regional HS; Bradford, NH; (S); Pres DECA; Drama Clb; Model UN; Ski Clb; JV Socr; Cit Awd; Political Wkr; School Play; Doris Sargent Schlrshp, Most Imprvd Sr Awd 86; Mktg/Distributive Educ Awds 85&86; New England Coll Henniker NH.

ASPINALL, LORIANN; Salem HS; Salem, NH; (Y); Model UN; Ski Clb; Teachers Aide; Hon Roll; Lwyr.

ASTRACHAN, ZOEE; Kennett HS; Intervale, NH; (Y); 1/191; Pres 4-H; Trs French Clb; Key Clb; Crs Cntry; Bausch & Lomb Sci Awd; French Hon Soc; Pres NHS; Val; Govs Schlr Schlrshp; U PA; Vet Med.

ATHANAS, JULIE; Newfound HS; New Hampton, NH; (Y); 10/65; Nwsp Rptr; Yrbk Stf; Sec Stu Cncl; Capt Bsktbl; Fld Hcky; Sftbl; Hon Roll; Crnvl Queen Stu 84 & 86; Bio Sci.

ATHERTON, DAVE; Londonderry HS; Londonderry, NH; (Y); Church Yth Grp; Ski Clb; SADD; Lcrss; French Hon Soc; High Hon Roll; Ntl Merit Ltr; Math Clb; Math Tm; Science Clb; Phllps Extr Acad Smmr Pgm 85; U S Vl Acad Invtnl Acdmc Wrkshp 86; St Pauls Advncd Studies Pgm 86; Math.

AUBE, JONATHAN; Berlin HS; Berlin, NH; (Y); 11/240; Am Leg Boys St; SADD; Band; Jazz Band; Pep Band; School Play; Var Socr; Hon Roll; NHS; Drama Clb; UMO Pulp & Paper Fndtn Schlrshp 86; Engrng Career Orntatn Prog 86; Engrng.

AUCLAIR, TIMOTHY; Spaulding HS; Rochester, NH; (S); 14/356; Key Clb; Hon Roll; 2nd Pl Advncd Accntg Cntst 85; Bentley Coll; Accntg.

AUCOIN, LORRAINE; Bishop Brady HS; Henniker, NH; (Y); Intnl Clb; Ski Clb; Chorus; Yrbk Stf; Bausch & Lomb Sci Awd; High Hon Roll; Hon Roll; NHS; NEDT Awd; Rensselaer Polytech Inst-Sci & Math Awds 85-86; Analysis & Chem Awd 85-86; Tchr.

AUCOIN, RICHARD; Henniker HS; Henniker, NH; (Y); Computer Clb; Math Tm; Office Aide; SADD; Nwsp Stf; Trs Soph Cls; Bsbl; Crs Cntry; Hon Roll; Dartmouth Coll; Arch Engr.

AUDLEY, SHANNON; Manchester HS West; Manchester, NH; (Y); Pres FBLA; Ski Clb; Band; Color Guard; Concert Band; Mrchg Band; School Play; Hon Roll; Emerson Coll; Brdcstng.

AUER, KEVIN; Bishop Guertin HS; Hollis, NH; (Y); 4/120; FCA; French Clb; Key Clb; Ski Clb; SADD; Im Bsktbl; Im Var Socr; Im Vllybl; High Hon Roll; Hon Roll; Natl Hnr Socty Rep 86.

AUGER, MICHAEL R; Pinkerton Acad; Hampstead, NH; (Y); Am Leg Boys St; Aud/Vis; Ice Hcky; Lcrss; Socr; Hon Roll; MA Coll Of Pharmacy; Pharmacst.

AVALLON, SUZANNE; Pinkerton Acad; Hampstead, NH; (Y); Hosp Aide; Real Est Agt.

AYERS, CHRISTINA; Pembroke Acad; Pembroke, NH; (Y); Am Leg Aux Girls St; Cmnty Wkr; French Clb; Sec Key Clb; SADD; Yrbk Stf; Stu Cncl; JV Capt Fld Hcky; Sftbl; Hon Roll; Benlty; Acctnt.

AYOTTE, LYNNE ANN; Keene HS; Keene, NH; (Y); 34/362; Am Leg Aux Girls St; French Clb; Latin Clb; Service Clb; Chorus; Sec Soph Cls; Sec Jr Cls; Sec Sr Cls; Bsktbl; Fld Hcky; Coaches Awd Tnns; Proj Excel; Nrsng.

BACHELDER, BRAD; Pembroke Acad; Suncook, NH; (Y); Cmnty Wkr; FFA; Key Clb; Band; Jazz Band; Pep Band; Var JV Socr; Var Trk; Hon Roll; Ag Awd 86; Technical Inst.

BAILEY, ABIGAIL L; Kearsarge Regional HS; New London, NH; (Y); 19/115; Drama Clb; Chorus; Church Choir; School Musical; School Play; Pres Sr Cls; NHS; Ntl Merit Ltr; Model UN; Rep Stu Cncl; Wellsley Coll Bk Awd 85; St Pauls Schl Advncd Stds Prog 85; Prg Poltcs 84; Musical Theatr.

BAKANEC, BRADLEY S; Londonderry HS; Londonderry, NH; (Y); Ski Clb; Var L Lcrss; Var L Socr; Hon Roll; Sci Olympd Physcs 86; U Of NH; Bus Adm.

BAKER, KIMBERLY; Mascoma Valley Regional HS; Canaan, NH; (Y); 2/101; Drama Clb; French Clb; Math Tm; Quiz Bowl; Band; Jazz Band; School Musical; School Play; Yrbk Ed-Chief; Yrbk Stf; Wmns Engr Awd 86; Stu Cncl Awd 85; Eng Awd 85; Hstry Awd 86; Bucknell U; Intl Rltns.

BALDWIN JR, SCOTT K; Londonderry HS; Londonderry, NH; (Y); 10/290; German Clb; Math Tm; Ski Clb; Teachers Aide; Band; Mrchg Band; Var Crs Cntry; Mgr(s); Var Trk; High Hon Roll; Germn Ntl Hon Soc; Northeastern U; Mech Engrng.

BALL, LANCE; Profile HS; Franconia, NH; (Y); Church Yth Grp; Math Tm; Var Bsbl; Var Bsktbl; Var Ice Hcky; Var Capt Socr; Hon Roll; U Of NH; Cvl Engrng.

BALLARD, BRIAN; Concord HS; Bow, NH; (Y); Math Tm; Nwsp Ed-Chief; Nwsp Rptr; JV Bsbl; Var L Golf; High Hon Roll; Pres NHS; Rensselaer Medal Math/Sci, Top Math Stu Awd; MIT; Comp Engrng.

BAMFORD, LUCEEN; Central HS; Manchester, NH; (S); 129/424; Hon Roll.

BANKS, ANNA; St Pauls Schl; San Francisco, CA; (Y); Debate Tm; French Clb; Radio Clb; School Play; JV Fld Hcky; Var Capt Trk; Im Vllybl; High Hon Roll; Schl Rcrd Trck 300 M Hurdles 85-86; Schl Repo Natl Essay 86; Activities Comm Wrtng Cntst Fnlst 85-86.

BANKS, LAURA; Nute HS; Milton, NH; (S); 5/89; Sec FBLA; Math Tm; VP Band; VP Chorus; Yrbk Stf; VP Soph Cls; Trs Sr Cls; Hon Roll; NHS; Baufeur Awd Accntng 85; Hesser Coll; Accntng.

BARCLAY, SEAN; St Thomas Aquinas HS; Dover, NH; (Y); Key Clb; Yrbk Phtg; Yrbk Stf; Sec Stu Cncl; Var Bsktbl; Var Socr; Tennis; Outstndg Photography For Yrbk; Business.

BARLOW, GREGORY; Bishop Brady HS; Suncook, NH; (Y); 1/57; Boy Scts; Hosp Aide; Band; Yrbk Phtg; Pres Frsh Cls; Pres Soph Cls; Trs Sr Cls; Var Crs Cntry; Pres NHS; Val; U Of Notre Dame.

BARNES, DOREEN; Alvirne HS; Hudson, NH; (Y); 16/350; Teachers Aide; JV Bsktbl; Var Crs Cntry; JV Socr; JV Sftbl; Var Trk; High Hon Roll; Hon Roll; Trs NHS; Dartmouth Bk Awd 85-86; Athletic Schlr; Most Imprvd Plyr Sftbl 85; Boston Coll; Fash Merch.

BARNEY, SHERRY; Spaulding HS; Rochester, NH; (S); 16/397; Hosp Aide; Sec Band; Color Guard; Concert Band; Jazz Band; Mrchg Band; Variety Show; Hon Roll; NHS; Cert Merit Holiday Wrtg & Art Cont 84.

BARON, JONATHAN E; Manchester High Schl Cntrl; Manchester, NH; (Y); 54/393; Am Leg Boys St; Pres VP SADD; Temple Yth Grp; Nwsp Bus Mgr; Rep Stu Cncl; High Hon Roll; Hon Roll; Pres Acad Ftnss Awd 86; Soc Stds Dprtmnt Awd 86; U Of NH; Bus Admn.

BARON, PAUL; Bishop Brady HS; Laconia, NH; (Y); 4/58; Ski Clb; VP Frsh Cls; Sec Jr Cls; Var Bsbl; Var Ftbl; Var Wt Lftg; Hon Roll; Schlr Athlt 86; Ftbl Coaches Awd 85; Boston Coll; Financ.

BARRY, JENNIFER; Hanover HS; E Thetford, VT; (Y); Sec AFS; Church Yth Grp; Cmnty Wkr; 4-H; French Clb; German Clb; Girl Scts; Intnl Clb; Service Clb; Hon Roll; Germn Honorary Schlstc Achvt Awd 86; Eng Teachr.

BARSALOU, LAURIE; Concord HS; Concord, NH; (Y); 69/395; Varsity Clb; Sec Sr Cls; Rep Stu Cncl; L Capt Cheerleading; High Hon Roll; Hon Roll; NHS.

BARSALOU, SHERRIE; Pelham HS; Pelham, NH; (Y); Church Yth Grp; Pres French Clb; Yrbk Stf; High Hon Roll; Hon Roll; NHS; Bryant Coll; Htl Adm.

BART, MELISSA; Concord HS; Concord, NH; (Y); 11/350; GAA; Varsity Clb; Bsktbl; Var Capt Crs Cntry; Var Trk; High Hon Roll; NHS; Excllnc In Engl & Spnsh 86.

BARTLETT, JEFFREY; Alton Central HS; Alton Bay, NH; (S); 5/35; Boy Scts; French Clb; Math Clb; Quiz Bowl; Ski Clb; Trs Frsh Cls; VP Jr Cls; Var Socr; Hon Roll; Perf Atten 84-85; Comptr Mgmnt.

BARTZ, MARGO; Franklin JR SR HS; Franklin, NH; (Y); Teachers Aide; Yrbk Phtg; Yrbk Stf; Hon Roll; Franklin-Tilton Northfield Schlrshp 86; Frank & Laura Tessier Schlrshp 86; Arwood Corp Schlrshp 86; Concord Tech Inst; Bus Admin.

BASSETT, APRIL; Alton Central HS; Alton, NH; (S); 10/37; Drama Clb; OEA; Band; Mrchg Band; School Play; Nwsp Stf; Yrbk Stf; 4-H Awd; Hon Roll; Jr NHS; Word Proc Mgr.

BATES, CHRISTOPHER; Keene HS; Keene, NH; (Y); 100/315; CAP; Trk; Hon Roll; Air Force; Aviatn.

BAUM, AARON; Portsmouth HS; Portsmouth, NH; (S); 1/450; Pres Latin Clb; Math Tm; High Hon Roll; NHS.

BAXTER, CARA; Memorial HS; Manchester, NH; (Y); 19/344; Sec Church Yth Grp; Dance Clb; Q&S; Teachers Aide; Variety Show; Nwsp Ed-Chief; High Hon Roll; Hosp Aide; Nwsp Rptr; Nwsp Stf; Crusader Awd 86; Faculty Scholar 86; Edtr Chief 1st Pl Nwsp Cnty 86; Emerson Coll; Brdcst Jrnlsm.

BEAN, SAMANTHA; Stevens HS; Claremont, NH; (Y); High Hon Roll; Hon Roll; St Pauls Schl Advncd Stds Prgrm 86; Boston U; Bus.

BEAUCHESNE, RICHARD; Newmarket HS; Newmarket, NH; (Y); 3/63; Am Leg Boys St; Art Clb; Boy Scts; Camera Clb; Ski Clb; Band; Concert Band; Jazz Band; Pep Band; Nwsp Phtg; Hgh O Brn Awd Soph; Harvard U; Law.

BEAUDET, SELENE; Central HS; Manchester, NH; (Y); 232/430; Church Yth Grp; DECA; Girl Scts; ST DECA Tres 86-87; Grl Sct Slvr Awd 84; Bus Sci.

BEAUDET, TAMI; Memorial HS; Manchester, NH; (Y); 38/355; Stu Cncl; Socr; Trk; High Hon Roll; Hon Roll; Johnson & Wales Schlrshp 86; Parent-Tchr Booster Clb Schlrshp 86; Johnson & Wales Coll; Retailing.

BEAULIEU, LISA; Berlin SR HS; Berlin, NH; (Y); Church Yth Grp; Dance Clb; FNA; Red Cross Aide; Church Choir; Im Bsktbl; Im Vllybl; Hon Roll; Pharm Assist; Nrsng Hm Aide; Concord Vo-Tech; X-Ray Tech.

BEAUREGARD, RENEE; Alvirne HS; Hudson, NH; (Y); Church Yth Grp; SADD; Sec Stu Cncl; Coach Actv; Mgr(s); JV Var Socr; Hon Roll; Yth In Govt; Grad Ushrt 86; Rivier Coll Pgm.

BECHARD, DEBORAH; Mount Saint Mary Seminary; Nashua, NH; (Y); Camera Clb; Intnl Clb; Ski Clb; SADD; School Musical; Ed Yrbk Stf; JV Capt Cheerleading; Hon Roll; Hons In Debate; St Michaels Coll; Cmmnctns.

BECHARD, KATHI; Londonderry HS; Londonderry, NH; (Y); Math Tm; Teachers Aide; Rep Sr Cls; Rep Stu Cncl; Mgr(s); Var Socr; French Hon Soc; High Hon Roll; NHS; Pres Schlr; Ntl German Hnr Soc 85-86; Whittamore Schl Bus; Bus Adm.

BECKER, MARK; Hillsboro-Deering HS; Hillsboro, NH; (Y); Chess Clb; Debate Tm; French Clb; Math Tm; Teachers Aide; Comp Prog.

BEDARD, LORRICE; Mt St Mary Seminary; Nashua, NH; (Y); 4/74; Pres French Clb; Ed Yrbk Phtg; Sec Sr Cls; High Hon Roll; Rep NHS; Ntl Merit Ltr; Prfct Atten Awd; Am Leg Aux Girls St; Pres Debate Tm; Drama Clb; NH Sentr Grls Ntn 85; Cathlc Fornsc Leag Natl Debate Fnlst 85; Presdntl Acadmc Ftns Awd 86; St Anselm Coll.

BEECHER, TIAUNA; Merrimack HS; Merrimak, NH; (Y); 5/215; Church Yth Grp; Cmnty Wkr; Dance Clb; Drama Clb; 4-H; FBLA; Hosp Aide; Library Aide; Office Aide; Pep Clb; Ricks Coll Schlrshp 86; Dan Moffit Mem Schlrshp 86; Reeds Ferry Womens Club Schlrshp 86; Ricks Coll; Chld Psych.

BEELER, EMILY; Phillips Exeter Acad; Hampton Falls, NH; (S); Model UN; Im Bsktbl; Im Lcrss; JV Mgr(s); JV Score Keeper; Im Tennis; JV Timer; High Hon Roll; Math.

BEIGHLEY, MICHAEL; Salem HS; Salem, NH; (Y); Model UN; Band; Concert Band; Jazz Band; Hon Roll.

BELAND, DAVID; Stevens HS; Claremont, NH; (Y); Camera Clb; Church Yth Grp; Computer Clb; Exploring; French Clb; Political Wkr; Ski Clb; Crs Cntry; Ftbl; Trk; USHGA Rcrd Out & Return Flight NE Ctr 85; USHGA Youngest Pilot Launch Mt Ascutney VT 85; US Military Acad; Mth.

BELDEN, MARK; Stevens HS; Claremont, NH; (Y); Am Leg Boys St; Math Tm; Var Capt Ski Clb; SADD; Pres Frsh Cls; Pres Soph Cls; Var Capt Socr; Var Trk; High Hon Roll; Hon Roll; Soccer Bruce Dumont Awd 84; MVP Awd 85.

BELISLE, DENISE; Stevens HS; Claremont, NH; (Y); Political Wkr; Trs SADD; Varsity Clb; Band; Concert Band; Mrchg Band; School Play; Yrbk Sprt Ed; Bowling; Var Capt Crs Cntry; Bus Mgmt.

BELL, WENDY; Newport HS; Newport, NH; (Y); French Clb; Letterman Clb; Math Tm; Yrbk Ed-Chief; Rep Stu Cncl; Var L Bsktbl; Coach Actv; JV Sftbl; Trk; NHS; Pre Med.

BELLAVANCE, JAMES; Lebanon HS; Lebanon, NH; (Y); Trs VP AFS; Cmnty Wkr; French Clb; Intnl Clb; Ski Clb; Band; Concert Band; Mrchg Band; School Play; Yrbk Stf; Tour Europe Prfrmng Group 85; Intl Rltns.

BELLETETE, NANCY; Conant HS; Jaffrey, NH; (Y); Am Leg Aux Girls St; Yrbk Stf; Sec Sr Cls; Var Capt Cheerleading; Hon Roll; Yrbk Rptr; VP Frsh Cls; VP Soph Cls; Sec Bsbl; DAR Awd; Early Chldhd Ed.

BENNETT, CYNTHIA; Manchester Central HS; Manchester, NH; (Y); 157/430; JV Bsktbl; Var Capt Crs Cntry; Var Capt Trk; High Hon Roll; Hon Roll; Hnrb Mntn 300 Mtr Dash Wntr Trk 85-86; Hnrb Merit Magna Cum Laude Natl Latin Exam 85-86.

BENNETT, MARCIA; Memorial HS; Manchester, NH; (Y); 25/341; Nwsp Rptr; Rptr Nwsp Stf; Stu Cncl; Hon Roll; Powder Puff Ftbl; Law.

BENO, BRETT; Newfound Mem HS; Bristol, NH; (Y); 2/53; Nwsp Rptr; Pres Frsh Cls; JV Bsktbl; Var L Crs Cntry; Var Trk; Bausch & Lomb Sci Awd; Hon Roll; NHS; Physcs.

BENOIT, TINA; Groveton HS; Groveton, NH; (Y); Drama Clb; French Clb; Variety Show; Nwsp Stf; Yrbk Stf; VP Frsh Cls; Pres Soph Cls; Pres Jr Cls; Stu Cncl; Hon Roll; Hugh Obrian Yth Ldrshp Fndtn Ambssdr 85; Journlsm.

BENSON, LYA; St Thomas Quinas HS; Barrington, NH; (Y); Cmnty Wkr; Hosp Aide; Key Clb; Chorus; Pres Stu Cncl; Var Cheerleading; French Clb; Latin Clb; Nwsp Stf; Yrbk Stf; Catholic U; Nrsng.

BENTAS, JOHN; Manchester Memorial HS; Manchester, NH; (Y); 3/341; Latin Clb; Math Clb; Math Tm; High Hon Roll; NHS; Beatley Coll; Bus Mgmt.

BERG, PHILLIP; Newport HS; Newport, NH; (Y); Am Leg Boys St; French Clb; Math Tm; Science Clb; Nwsp Stf; Yrbk Stf; Pres Frsh Cls; Rep Stu Cncl; Var Bsbl; Var Bsktbl; YMCA Yth & Govt Prog 86; U Of VA; Accntng.

BERGER, ALEX; Hanover HS; Hanover, NH; (Y); 71/159; VP AFS; French Clb; Quiz Bowl; Ed Nwsp Sprt Ed; Yrbk Phtg; JV Tennis; JV Trk; JV Wrstlng; U NH; Cmmnctns.

BERGER, JONATHAN; Manchester HS West; Bedford, NH; (Y); 11/430; Computer Clb; Drama Clb; NEDT Awd; School Play; Stage Crew; High Hon Roll; Hon Roll; Ntl Merit SF; Thtre Knghts Cert Of Awd & Prtcptn 85-86; Comp Sci.

BERGERON, RICHARD; Keene HS; Keene, NH; (Y); 85/365; Church Yth Grp; Bsbl; Var JV Bsktbl; Stu Of STOPP 86; Elec Engr.

BERGERON, TAMMY; Memorial HS; Manchester, NH; (Y); 28/430; French Clb; Drm Mjr(t); Crs Cntry; Trk; Twrlr; High Hon Roll; Hon Roll; Student Council Schlrshp 86; Natl PTA Art Awd 2nd Pl 75; New Hampshire U; Med Tech.

BERGERON, WARREN C; Salem HS; Salem, NH; (S); Math Clb; Math Tm; Accntnt.

BERNARDUCCI, MARC; Bishop Guertin HS; Hudson, NH; (Y); 13/151; Church Yth Grp; FCA; ROTC; Trs SADD; Nwsp Stf; Var Socr; Var Wrstlng; NHS; Prfct Atten Awd; U Of RI; Phrmcy.

BERNHARD, CARMEN; Hopkinton HS; Hopkinton, NH; (Y); Chorus; Bsktbl; Coach Actv; Crs Cntry; Mgr(s); Trk; Soc Wrk.

BERNIER, STEVEN P; Nashua HS; Nashua, NH; (Y); Am Leg Boys St; Var L Socr; High Hon Roll; NHS; German Clb; Math Clb; Ski Clb; Hon Roll; Jr NHS; Rotary Awd; Engrng.

BERNIER, TIM; Gorham HS; Gorham, NH; (Y); Art Clb; Stage Crew; Var Bsktbl; Im Vllybl; High Hon Roll; Hon Roll; Prfct Atten Awd; Archtctr.

BESSETTE, DAN; Dover HS; Dover, NH; (Y); 85/283; Key Clb; Pres Jr Cls; JV Var Ftbl; Var Capt Trk; High Hon Roll; Bio.

BICKFORD, JOANNA; Inter-Lakes HS; Center Harbor, NH; (Y); Quiz Bowl; SADD; Band; VP Chorus; School Musical; Variety Show; Var L Bsktbl; Sftbl; Vllybl; High Hon Roll; Outstndng Svc Awd 86; Harvard Radcliffe Bk Awd 86; Med Tech.

BIELLO, STEPHANY; Merrimack HS; Merrimack, NH; (Y); 7/218; Sec Church Yth Grp; Nwsp Ed-Chief; Yrbk Bus Mgr; Sec Soph Cls; Sec Stu Cncl; Hon Roll; Century Ldr Schlrshp 86; Ntl Yth Sci Awd 85; Hugh O Brian Ldr 84; Georgetown U; Social Sci.

BILODEAU, DANNY; Berlin HS; Berlin, NH; (Y); Chrmn Pres FBLA; Nwsp Phtg; Nwsp Rptr; Yrbk Phtg; Devotion Hardwork & Faithful Svc Guardian Angel Parish 86; Androscoggin Vly Hosp Poster Cont Awd 80; Plymouth ST Coll; Bus Mgmnt.

BILODEAU, PAULA; Manchester West HS; Manchester, NH; (Y); 25/338; Cmnty Wkr; Pep Clb; Ski Clb; Chorus; Trs Frsh Cls; Trs Soph Cls; Trs Jr Cls; Trs Sr Cls; Cheerleading; Tennis; Mnchstr JR Wmns Clb Schlrshp 86; Dllrs Schlrs Schlrshp 86; Bryant Coll; Mgmt.

BIRD, SARAH S; Tilton Schl; Meredith, NH; (S); 2/70; Cmnty Wkr; Drama Clb; School Musical; Rep Frsh Cls; Pres Jr Cls; Lcrss; Capt Socr; Cit Awd; High Hon Roll; NEDT Awd; Jrnlsm.

BIRON, KATY; Colebrook Acad; Colebrook, NH; (Y); 3/60; Church Yth Grp; Drama Clb; Varsity Clb; Band; Chorus; School Musical; School Play; Yrbk Stf; Capt L Cheerleading; NHS; Mst Sprtd Chrldr 86; 2nd VP Statewide For NH YMCA Older Grls Conf 86; YMCA Cmp Counselor.

BISAILLON, STEVEN; Spaulding HS; Rochester, NH; (S); 6/397; Key Clb; Math Tm; Trs Soph Cls; Trs Jr Cls; L Var Ice Hcky; Var Socr; L Var Tennis; High Hon Roll; NHS; ROTC; Outstndng Aerospc Cadet ROTC 84 & 85; Squadron Commndr ROTC 86; USAF Acad; Aerospc Engrng.

BISSON, CAROL; Berlin HS; Berlin, NH; (Y); Library Aide; Yrbk Stf; Hon Roll; Am Leg Schlrshp 86; Plymouth ST Coll; Elem Ed.

BLACK, JOSH; Spaulding HS; Strafford, NH; (S); 13/400; Jazz Band; JV Var Bsktbl; High Hon Roll; Hon Roll; NHS; U NH.

BLACKWOOD, TOM; Weare HS; Weare, NH; (S); 2/48; Trs Drama Clb; French Clb; School Musical; School Play; Nwsp Ed-Chief; High Hon Roll; NHS; Ntl Merit Ltr; YFU Intl Exchng Schlrshp 86; Spac Sci.

BLAIR, AMY; Belmont HS; Laconia, NH; (Y); 20/80; VP 4-H; French Clb; Office Aide; Teachers Aide; Varsity Clb; Yrbk Sprt Ed; Yrbk Stf; Sec Frsh Cls; Sec Soph Cls; Sec Jr Cls; MVP Offnsv Plyr Vrsty Bsktbll 85-86; Prm Qn 86.

BLAIS, AARON; Memorial HS; Manchester, NH; (Y); 15/398; French Clb; High Hon Roll; Hon Roll; AZ ST U; Bus.

BLAIS, SHANE; Berlin HS; Berlin, NH; (Y); Band; Concert Band; Jazz Band; Mrchg Band; Pep Band; Im Bsktbl; Var Crs Cntry; Var Trk; Im Vllybl; JP Sousa Awd; All ST Bnd 86; Jazz All ST 86; U NH; Mech Engrng.

BLAISDELL, DONALD; Spaulding HS; Rochester, NH; (S); 59/397; Hon Roll; Navy; Hvy Equpmnt Oprtn.

BLAKE, DIANE ELIZABETH; Salem HS; Salem, NH; (S); 24/385; Church Yth Grp; Hosp Aide; Latin Clb; Model UN; SADD; High Hon Roll; Hon Roll; Cmnty Wkr; Rockingham Hospice Grad-Wrk Aids/Cancr Ptnts 85; Awd Ovr 200 Hrs Svc 85; BU; Nrsng.

BLAKE, EDWARD; Concord HS; Bow, NH; (Y); 13/369; Quiz Bowl; Chrmn Varsity Clb; Coach Actv; Var L Socr; Capt Trk; High Hon Roll; NHS; JV Bsktbl; Im Vllybl; Bow Mns Clb Schlrshp 86; Trck & Fld Mvp 86; U Of PA; Law.

BLAKELEY, DOUGLAS; Newfound Memorial HS; Bristol, NH; (Y); 3/57; Quiz Bowl; Band; School Play; Nwsp Rptr; Pres VP Stu Cncl; Bsbl; Bsktbl; Socr; High Hon Roll; NHS; Hugh O Brian Yth Fndtn Intl Semnr NH Rep 85; Acdmc Decthln Tm 86; Blu Rbbn Comm Twn Yth 86; Sci Engrng.

BLANC, MATHEW E; Fall Mountain Regional HS; Charlestown, NH; (Y); Am Leg Boys St; Boy Scts; L Var Ftbl; L Var Ice Hcky; Wt Lftg; Hon Roll; Prom Commitee 85-86.

BLANCHETTE, AMY; Pelham HS; Pelham, NH; (Y); Church Yth Grp; Cmnty Wkr; Spanish Clb; Chorus; Nwsp Rptr; Yrbk Stf; Hon Roll; Voice Dem Awd; Rivier Coll; Scl Wrk.

BLASTOS, STEPHANNIE; Keene HS; Keene, NH; (Y); 50/368; Am Leg Aux Girls St; Drama Clb; Acpl Chr; Concert Band; Jazz Band; Rep Frsh Cls; Rep Soph Cls; Rep Jr Cls; Rep Sr Cls; Pres Stu Cncl; Distinguished Svc HS & Stu Cncl 86; Sherman Coll; Chiropracting.

BLECHARCZYK, PAMELA; Pelham HS; Pelham, NH; (Y); 15/130; Drama Clb; Pep Clb; Church Choir; Stage Crew; Capt JV Cheerleading; L Var Fld Hcky; Hon Roll; NHS; Voice Dem Awd; Vol At NH Winter & Summer Spcl 84-86.

BLENKINSOP, KATHRYN; St Pauls Schl; Bedford, NH; (Y); Debate Tm; Latin Clb; Pres Math Tm; Political Wkr; JV Lcrss; Im Tennis; Im Vllybl; Cum Laude Soc; Fergusn Schlr 86; Presdntl Clsrm 86; Economics.

BLONDIN, DANIEL ARCHIE; Nashua SR HS; Nashua, NH; (Y); Boy Scts; Church Yth Grp; Hon Roll; NHS; Compu Sci.

BLOOM, BECKY; Alvirne HS; Litchfield, NH; (Y); 58/338; Science Clb; Varsity Clb; Var Capt Bsktbl; Var L Socr; Var L Sftbl; Var L Trk; Hon Roll; Physcl Thrpy.

BLOOM, KAREN A; New Market HS; Newmarket, NH; (Y); 1/45; SADD; Concert Band; Pep Band; Yrbk Bus Mgr; Yrbk Stf; Fld Hcky; NHS; Val; Am Leg Aux Girls St; Girl Scts; Govnrs Schlrs Schlrshp Awd 86; David Blair Schlrshp Awd 86; Lamprey River Schlrshp 86; American Intl Clg; Pre Med.

BLOUIN, KATHLEEN A; Pinkerton Acad; Derry, NH; (Y); 52/435; Ski Clb; Crs Cntry; Hon Roll; Acctng II Awd 86; Ntl Hnr Soc Schlrshp 86; 1st Pl Typng Cntst 85; New Hampshrie Coll; Acctng.

BLOUIN, MONIQUE; Manchester Memorial HS; Manchester, NH; (Y); 118/350; Church Yth Grp; French Clb; Pres FBLA; VP Pres SADD; Teachers Aide; Chorus; Nwsp Rptr; Swmmng; Hon Roll; Crusader Awd 84-86; Stu Svc Awd 86; Johnson & Wales; Bus Adm.

BLY, PATRICIA A; Kingswood Regional HS; Wolfeboro Falls, NH; (Y); 2/123; Church Yth Grp; Debate Tm; 4-H; JCL; Math Tm; Model UN; Quiz Bowl; Band; Chorus; Church Choir; Govt Awd 85; 4 Yr Sci Awd 86; Bowdoin Coll; Music.

BOARDMAN, KAREN; Stevens HS; Claremont, NH; (S); DECA; Hon Roll; 2nd Pl Deca ST Finc-Credt 86; NH Vocatnl Schl; Acctnt.

BOCICHIE, LYNETTE; Epping HS; Epping, NH; (S); 1/60; Pres French Clb; Math Clb; Scholastic Bowl; Varsity Clb; Band; Trs Stu Cncl; JV Bsktbl; High Hon Roll; NHS.

BODNAR, SANDRA; Manchester Memorial HS; Manchester, NH; (Y); 55/349; Hosp Aide; Intnl Clb; Variety Show; JV Var Trk; JV Vllybl; Hon Roll; Miss NH Teen USA Pgnt Miss Phtgnc, 1st Rnr-Up Bst Cstm & Smi-Fnlst 86; Jr Prm Crt 86; Med.

BOEHLE, KATHY; Laconia HS; Laconia, NH; (Y); Church Yth Grp; GAA; Im Bsktbl; JV Var Fld Hcky; Hon Roll.

BOIVIN, LISA; Groveton HS; Stark, NH; (Y); FHA; Band; Concert Band; Mrchg Band; Hon Roll; CT K-9 Educ Ctr; Pet Grmng.

BOLDUC, DAVID R; Bishop Brady HS; Laconia, NH; (Y); French Clb; Rep Frsh Cls; Rep Jr Cls; Rep Sr Cls; Stu Cncl; Swmmng; Trk; Hon Roll; Cadet Rangers Am 2nd Lt; Hstry Club Highst Achvt; Capt Swim Team; ROTC Schlrshp; US Miltry Acad; Hist.

BOLSTRIDGE, MARK; Belmont HS; Belmont, NH; (Y); School Play; Stage Crew; Yrbk Stf; Rep Frsh Cls; Rep VP Soph Cls; Rep Stu Cncl; Var Mgr(s); Outstndng Achvt Indpndt Study Wood 86.

BOND, DANIELLE; Spaulding HS; Rochester, NH; (Y); 52/354; Key Clb; Yrbk Bus Mgr; Yrbk Stf; Rep Jr Cls; Rep Sr Cls; Rep Stu Cncl; U Of NH.

BOOKER, LAURIE; Manchester Central HS; Manchester, NH; (S); DECA; Band; Hon Roll; Sctn Ldr Band 86; Bus.

BOOTHBY, MICHELLE; Kennett HS; W Ossipee, NH; (Y); 35/200; Key Clb; Math Tm; Yrbk Stf; Im JV Bsktbl; JV Var Trk; Latin Awd.

BOPPEL, MELISSA; Salem HS; Salem, NH; (S); Key Clb; Hosp Aide; Ski Clb; Spanish Clb; SADD; Teachers Aide; JV Bsktbl; Var Mgr(s); JV Sftbl; Hon Roll; Bus.

BOROS, ALEXANDER J; Nashua SR HS; Nashua, NH; (Y); 60/700; Am Leg Boys St; Ski Clb; Hon Roll; Jr NHS; Vars Skiing 84-85 & Co-Capt 85-86; U NH; Frnch.

BOSSI, AMY; Bishop Brady HS; Contoocook, NH; (Y); Girl Scts; Hosp Aide; Intnl Clb; Service Clb; Band; Chorus; Church Choir; Concert Band; Nwsp Stf; Yrbk Stf; NH Rhythmc Gymnstc Champ 79-86; Rgnl Rhythmc Gymnstc Champ 83-85; Outstndng Rhythmc Gymnst Yr Rgnl 82; Phythmic Gymnstc Instr.

BOUCHER, CARL; Berlin SR HS; Berlin, NH; (Y); 26/230; Church Yth Grp; Yrbk Phtg; Yrbk Rptr; Yrbk Stf; Ftbl; Ice Hcky; Mgr(s); Hon Roll; Jr NHS; URI; Pharm.

BOUCHER, JAMES; Berlin HS; Berlin, NH; (Y); Comp.

BOUCHER, MICHAEL C; Trinity HS; Manchester, NH; (Y); 1/165; Boy Scts; Math Tm; Pres Stu Cncl; Im Bsktbl; Var Capt Crs Cntry; Var Capt Trk; Bausch & Lomb Sci Awd; Elks Awd; High Hon Roll; NHS; Eagle Scout Awd BSA 86; Fairfield U.

BOUCHIE, JAMES; Epping HS; Epping, NH; (S); 1/60; French Clb; Math Clb; Scholastic Bowl; Varsity Clb; Rep Stu Cncl; High Hon Roll; Rep NHS; Im Wt Lftg; Amer Lgn Ortrl Cntst 84; Granite ST Chllng 85; U Of NH; Bus Mgmt.

BOUDREAU, TAMMY; Spaulding HS; Rochester, NH; (Y); 89/380; FBLA; Office Aide; Band; Color Guard; Concert Band; Mrchg Band; Yrbk Bus Mgr; Yrbk Stf; Rep Frsh Cls; Stu Cncl; Bus Mgmt.

BOUDRIAS, KECIA; Groveton HS; Groveton, NH; (Y); Church Yth Grp; French Clb; Hosp Aide; Band; Yrbk Stf; VP Stu Cncl; JV Var Cheerleading; Hon Roll; Nrsng.

BOURASSA, LISA; Berlin HS; Berlin, NH; (Y); 36/214; Am Leg Aux Girls St; Church Yth Grp; FNA; SADD; Yrbk Stf; Mgr(s); Score Keeper; Stat Socr; Speech Pathlgy.

BOURBEAU, MICHELE; Berlin HS; Milan, NH; (Y); 21/220; SADD; Band; Concert Band; Jazz Band; Mrchg Band; Pep Band; Var Gym; Hon Roll; Church Yth Grp; Drama Clb; Natl Lang Arts Olympd 83-84; Seacoast Fstvl Band Awd 84.

BOURGEOIS, HEATHER; Plymouth Area HS; Plymouth, NH; (Y); 8/135; Church Yth Grp; French Clb; School Musical; Rep Stu Cncl; Var Crs Cntry; Var Fld Hcky; Var Trk; Hon Roll; NHS; Eligble For Japanese-Amer Youth Exchng 85; Comm.

BOUTIN, MICHELLE ANNETTE; Spaulding HS; Dover, NH; (Y); 16/365; Am Leg Aux Girls St; French Clb; VP FBLA; Hosp Aide; Red Cross Aide; VP Stu Cncl; Hon Roll; NHS; HOBY ST Ldrhsp Sem 84; Grls Natl Alt 85; U NH; Med Tech.

BOWEN, CHRISTOPHER J; Salem HS; Salem, NH; (S); 18/340; Model UN; Teachers Aide; Var Crs Cntry; Var Trk; High Hon Roll; Hon Roll; Trs NHS; Pre-Law.

BOYLE, PAULA; Lin-Wood HS; N Woodotock, NH; (S); 6/24; Pres Rptr FBLA; Office Aide; Teachers Aide; Chorus; Nwsp Stf; Yrbk Stf; Capt Cheerleading; NHS; Sec Trs Frsh Cls; Sec Trs Soph Cls; Plymouth ST Col; Erly Chdhd Ed.

BOZAK, JEN; St Thomas Aguinas HS; Rochester, NH; (Y); 143/376; Dance Clb; Hon Roll; U Of NH; Peac Crps.

BRACKETT, BECCA; Hanover HS; Hanover, NH; (Y); Church Yth Grp; Latin Clb; Orch; Var L Lcrss; Var L Socr; High Hon Roll; Hon Roll; All-ST Violin & Viola 84-86.

BRADLEY, KAREN; Newport JR & SR HS; Newport, NH; (Y); Sec French Clb; Nwsp Stf; Yrbk Stf; Sec Frsh Cls; Rep Stu Cncl; Hon Roll; NHS; VFW Awd; Voice Dem Awd; Yng Wrtrs Cnfrnc 86; Psychlgy.

BRADLEY, LYNN P; Lin-Wood HS; Campton, NH; (Y); Hst FBLA; Math Tm; Model UN; Band; Chorus; Nwsp Rptr; Var Bsktbl; Var L Vllybl; Bausch & Lomb Sci Awd; Sec NHS; FL Inst Of Tech; Biophy.

BRASSARD, DAWN; Central HS; Manchester, NH; (S); DECA; Rep Soph Cls; Rep Jr Cls; Rep Sr Cls; Rep Stu Cncl; Hon Roll; UCF; Fash Mktg.

BRAUNSTEIN, ALEXANDRA; Concord HS; Concord, NH; (Y); 37/390; Drama Clb; Color Guard; Mrchg Band; Stage Crew; Symp Band; Nwsp Stf; High Hon Roll; Hon Roll; NHS; Prfct Atten Awd; Outstndng Musicianshp Awd 84; Nutritn.

BRAWN, JAMES; Portsmouth HS; Newington, NH; (S); 9/387; Latin Clb; Model UN; Political Wkr; Var Socr; Capt Var Swmmng; High Hon Roll; Hon Roll; NHS; Ntl Merit Ltr; St Pauls Advncd Stu Prog 85; Schlr Athl Awd 82-86; JR Wrld Cncl; Pre-Law.

BRAZELIS, GITA; Salem HS; Salem, NH; (S); German Clb; Key Clb; Ski Clb; Teachers Aide; School Play; Stage Crew; Yrbk Stf; Var Cheerleading; Var Mgr(s); High Hon Roll; Mst Imprvd Chrldr Awd 85; Cert Of Apprctn 84; Goethe Awd Germn 84-85; Bus Adm.

BRAZINSKY, PETER; Bishop Guertin HS; Nashua, NH; (Y); Chess Clb; Computer Clb; Im Bsktbl; Swmmng; Var Tennis; Hon Roll.

BREEN, THERESA; Spaulding HS; Rochester, NH; (S); 9/397; Key Clb; Math Clb; Math Tm; Yrbk Stf; Rep Frsh Cls; Sftbl; Var Capt Vllybl; High Hon Roll; NHS; Hon Roll; Vllybl Tm Coachs Awd; Holy Cross; Medicine.

BRETON, SANDRA L; Spaulding HS; Rochester, NH; (Y); 110/348; Sec Trs Church Yth Grp; FBLA; Key Clb; Off Frsh Cls; Sec Stu Cncl; JV Var Bsktbl; Var L Socr; JV Stat Sftbl; U Of NH; Poly Sci.

BRIGGS, JENNIFER; Belmont HS; Belmont, NH; (Y); 5/73; Drama Clb; French Clb; Math Tm; Yrbk Stf; Sec Soph Cls; Sec Jr Cls; Sec Sr Cls; Var Capt Crs Cntry; Var Co-Capt Trk; High Hon Roll; MVP Awd Crss-Cntry 82-85; U S Army Rsrv-Schlr/Athlt Awd 86; Pres Acad Ftnss Awd 86; U Of NH; Intl Rel.

BRINDLE, ANDREA; Portsmouth HS; Portsmouth, NH; (S); 12/405; Church Yth Grp; Math Tm; Model UN; Band; Church Choir; Concert Band; Mrchg Band; High Hon Roll; NHS; Georgetown Coll; Math.

BROADY, JOEL; Manchester HS; Bedford, NH; (Y); 80/338; Ski Clb; Var L Bsbl; Hon Roll; Plymth ST Coll; Bus Mngmnt.

BROMLEY, SUZI; Stevens HS; Claremont, NH; (Y); AFS; Church Yth Grp; Letterman Clb; Spanish Clb; Varsity Clb; Yrbk Stf; Var Crs Cntry; Var L Trk; Hon Roll; Trvl & Trsm.

BRONSON, ANDREW C; White Mountain Regional HS; Lancaster, NH; (Y); 10/108; Math Tm; Teachers Aide; Stu Cncl; Socr; Trk; Wrstlng; Hon Roll; Ntl Merit Ltr; West Point; Engrng.

BROOKFIELD, ANDREA; Hopkinton HS; Cantoocook, NH; (Y); German Clb; Band; Chorus; Orch; Nwsp Stf; Hon Roll; Band Awd; All ST; Boston U; Music.

BROOKS, DARLENE; Conant HS; Jaffrey, NH; (Y); 5/94; Church Yth Grp; Pres JCL; Pres Latin Clb; Band; Jazz Band; Mrchg Band; Nwsp Ed-Chief; High Hon Roll; Hon Roll; NHS; Wheaton CollIL; Bio Arch.

BROOKS, DAVID; Portsmouth HS; Greenland, NH; (S); 1/359; CAP; Math Tm; DAR Awd; High Hon Roll; NHS; Hrvrd Bk Awd; Clse Up Pgm Prtcpnt; NH Cntry III Tchrs Smi-Fnlst 85-86; US Air Frc Acad; Pilot.

BROOKS, ETHEL; Spaulding HS; Rochester, NH; (S); 2/467; Church Yth Grp; Civic Clb; Cmnty Wkr; Key Clb; Math Clb; Math Tm; Political Wkr; Church Choir; Yrbk Stf; Rep Frsh Cls; Century III Schlr 85-86; Rainbow Grls Offcr & Advrs 80-86; Poltcl Sci.

BROOKS JR, RAY; Stevens HS; Claremont, NH; (Y); Am Leg Boys St; Varsity Clb; School Play; Yrbk Stf; Pres Sr Cls; Var Bsktbl; Var Ftbl; Var Socr; Var Trk; Hon Roll.

BROWN, CHERYL; Nute HS; Milton, NH; (S); Trs FBLA; Trs JCL; VP Latin Clb; Teachers Aide; Yrbk Stf; Cheerleading; Cit Awd; Hon Roll; NHS; Amer Legion Awd 84; Bus Adm.

BROWN, CHRISTINE A; Kearsarge Regional HS; Wilmot Flat, NH; (Y); 34/106; Model UN; Spanish Clb; Nwsp Rptr; Nwsp Stf; JV Bsktbl; JV Sftbl; Var Capt Tennis; Hon Roll; Bay ST JC Schlrshp 86; Baystate JC; Fshn Merch.

BROWN, DAN; Alvirne HS; Hudson, NH; (Y); 25/338; Bsbl; Wrstlng; Hon Roll; Gnsmthng.

BROWN, HEATHER; Belmont HS; Canterbury, NH; (Y); 12/70; Band; Concert Band; Mrchg Band; Pep Band; Yrbk Stf; Hon Roll; NHS; Church Yth Grp; French Clb; Girl Scts; Lodge Elks & Amer Legn Schlrshps 86; Lakes Regn Schlrshp Fndtn Schlrshps 86; U Of NH; Anml Sci.

BROWN, JAY; Pembroke Acad; Suncook, NH; (Y); Trs Spanish Clb; Hon Roll; Prfct Atten Awd; Law.

BROWN, KEITH; Berlin HS; Stratford, CT; (Y); 12/216; Church Yth Grp; Yrbk Phtg; VP Frsh Cls; VP Soph Cls; Var Bsktbl; Var Crs Cntry; Var Trk; Im Vllybl; Pres Jr NHS; NHS; VPI; Elec Engr.

BROWN, KEITH; Coe-Brown Acad; Ctr Strafford, NH; (Y); 6/56; FFA; Math Tm; Pres SADD; Nwsp Rptr; Yrbk Stf; Bsktbl; Socr; NHS; Northeastern U; Engnrng.

BROWN, MARTIN; Milford Area SR HS; Amherst, NH; (Y); Boy Scts; Exploring; Stage Crew; Lit Mag; Grphc Arts.

BROWN, MAUREEN D; Phillips Exeter Acad; Cleveland, OH; (Y); FBLA; Political Wkr; Varsity Clb; Church Choir; School Play; Lit Mag; Stu Cncl; Im Bsktbl; Im Sftbl; Im Tennis; U Of Penn; Bus.

BROWN, ROBIN; Newport HS; Newport, NH; (Y); Am Leg Aux Girls St; Acpl Chr; Band; Chorus; Concert Band; Jazz Band; Trs Frsh Cls; Trs Soph Cls; Var L Fld Hcky; NHS; NH All ST Music Fest 84-86; Pre-Med.

BROWN, STEPHEN; Belmont HS; Canterbury, NH; (Y); 30/80; Boy Scts; Varsity Clb; Band; Jazz Band; Pep Band; Socr; Hon Roll; Phys Educ.

BRUCE, THERESA; Lebanon HS; Lebanon, NH; (Y); AFS; Church Yth Grp; Sec Latin Clb; Letterman Clb; Sec Soph Cls; Sec Jr Cls; Sec Sr Cls; Hon Roll; Ski Clb; Varsity Clb; Ntl Soc Studies Olympiad 86; Cls Outstndng Perf Latin 84; Acctng.

BRUNNHOELZL, CHERYL; Henniker HS; Henniker, NH; (Y); DECA; Ski Clb; Yrbk Stf; Pres Frsh Cls; VP Jr Cls; Rep Stu Cncl; Mgr Bsbl; Mgr Bsktbl; Var Cheerleading; Im Var Vllybl; 1st Pl Gen Mktg ST Career Dev Conf 86; Trvl.

BRUSSEAU, WILLIAM; Littleton HS; Littleton, NH; (Y); 5/98; Boy Scts; VP Soph Cls; VP Jr Cls; Var Capt Bsbl; Var Bsktbl; Var Capt Ftbl; Elks Awd; NHS; Boy Scts; Im Wt Lftg; Edward R Cole, Tom Walker & David Newton Mem Awds 84-86; St Joseph Coll; Psych.

BUCHANAN, AILEEN; Spaulding HS; E Rochester, NH; (S); 16/397; French Clb; Key Clb; Math Clb; Pep Clb; Yrbk Stf; L Socr; L Trk; Hon Roll; Jr NHS; NHS; Pedtrcn.

BUCHANAN, HOMER G; St Pauls Schl; New York, NY; (Y); Chess Clb; Computer Clb; Intnl Clb; Spanish Clb; JV Ftbl; Var Trk; Var Wrstlng; ABC Scholar 82; Engrng.

BUCHANNAN, AILEEN; Spaulding HS; E Rochester, NH; (Y); 16/387; French Clb; Key Clb; Math Clb; Math Tm; Pep Clb; Varsity Clb; Yrbk Stf; Var L Socr; Var L Tennis; Var L Trk; Med.

BULLOCK, SARAH; Brewster Acad; Hilton Hd Islnd, SC; (Y); 5/60; Drama Clb; Latin Clb; Stage Crew; Bsktbl; JV Socr; JV Tennis; Var Vllybl; Jr NHS; Bst Physcs Stu Awd HS 86; 2nd Pl Ovrall HS Sci Fair 85; Spcl Rcgntn ST Sci Fair 85; Lbrl Arts.

BUONOPANE, SHARON C; Spaulding HS; Center Strafford, NH; (S); 3/356; Rep Jr Cls; High Hon Roll; VP NHS; Ntl Merit Ltr; St Pauls Schl Advncd Studs Pgm 85; UNH Srch Pgm 84-86; U Of NH.

BURBANK, BARBARA; Spaulding HS; Rochester, NH; (Y); 101/358; Hosp Aide; Office Aide; Red Cross Aide; Cheerleading; Hon Roll; HOSA 84-86; Prom Suite 85; NH ST Chrldng Champs 86; Plymouth ST Coll; Early Chldhd.

BURCHYNS, AMY; Nashua SR HS; Nashua, NH; (Y); 31/998; SADD; Cheerleading; High Hon Roll; NHS; Spanish NHS; Church Yth Grp; Service Clb; Spanish Clb; Spch Thrpy.

BURGESS, CLINTON T; Contoocook Valley Regional HS; Peterborough, NH; (Y); Nwsp Rptr; Var L Bsbl; Var L Bsktbl; Var L Socr; Bus Mgt.

BURKE, CHRIS; Memorial HS; Manchester, NH; (Y); Pres Church Yth Grp; Sec Pres FFA; Hosp Aide; Crs Cntry; Trk; Hon Roll; M H Thompson Schl Appld Sci.

BURKE, DARIN M; Alton Central HS; Alton, NH; (Y); Am Leg Boys St; Boy Scts; Band; School Play; Nwsp Stf; Yrbk Stf; Bsktbl; Crs Cntry; Trk; NHS.

BURNHAM, VICTORIA J; Plymouth Area HS; Plymouth, NH; (Y); 19/138; French Clb; FBLA; Math Tm; Office Aide; Nwsp Stf; Yrbk Stf; Stu Cncl; Hon Roll; Pres Schlr; George C Zoulias Mem Scholar 86; U NH; Vet.

BURTT, SALLY; Manchester Memorial HS; Auburn, NH; (Y); 27/369; Nwsp Stf; Var Trk; High Hon Roll; Hon Roll; Aerontcl Engr.

BUSH, THEODORE J; Nashua HS; Nashua, NH; (Y); 47/850; Am Leg Boys St; JV Bsbl; Var Capt Ftbl; Var L Trk; Hon Roll; Jr NHS; NHS; Spanish NHS; Pre-Law.

BUTLER, MICHELLE; Coe-Brown Northwood Acad; Deerfield, NH; (Y); Hosp Aide; Yrbk Ed-Chief; Yrbk Stf; Stu Cncl; High Hon Roll; Hon Roll; NHS; Typng 1 Awd 84-85; Cert Of Certfctn 85; Concord Schl Of Nrsng; RN.

BUTTRICK, MELANIE LEE; Concord HS; Bow, NH; (Y); Church Yth Grp; Cmnty Wkr; Science Clb; Ski Clb; SADD; Chorus; Cheerleading; Sftbl; Hon Roll; NHS; Bio Awd For Outstndng Achvt 83-84; Wrd Of Life Schlrshp To Bible Camp 83-85; Merrimack Cnty Rep 85; U Of NH; Zlgy.

BYRNES, JOHN LAWRENCE; Fall Mtn Regional HS; Walpole, NH; (Y); 54/130; Pep Clb; Varsity Clb; Band; Concert Band; Mrchg Band; Pep Band; JV Bsktbl; Var Golf; Var Trk; Hon Roll; MVP Var Trk 85-86; IAC Chem Awd 86; Nuc Physcs.

CADORETTE, ANDREW J; Hollis Area HS; Brookline, NH; (Y); Spanish Clb; Yrbk Stf; Hon Roll; Art Portfoloio Cert Hnr 86; Souheban Ntl Bk Annual Schlrshp 86; Nancy Archambault Rata Mem Schlrshp; Keene ST Coll.

CADWALLADER, KARI; Manchester H S West; Bedford, NH; (Y); 44/420; Cmnty Wkr; Ski Clb; Stage Crew; Variety Show; Nwsp Rptr; Stu Cncl; Capt Sftbl; High Hon Roll; Hon Roll.

CAFORIO, CHRIS; St Thomas Aquinas HS; Barrington, NH; (Y); Am Leg Boys St; Debate Tm; Drama Clb; NFL; Speech Tm; Church Choir; Orch; Rep Stu Cncl; Var L Crs Cntry; Ntl Merit Ltr.

CALLAHAN, VIGDIS; Concord HS; Concord, NH; (Y); Drama Clb; French Clb; School Play; Stage Crew; Yrbk Stf; Hon Roll; Northeastern U Boston; Psych.

CALLUM, RHONDA; Stevens HS; Newport, NH; (Y); Church Yth Grp; FHA; Library Aide; Ski Clb; Im Fld Hcky; Im Socr; High Hon Roll; Paran Schlr 84; Fashion Dsgn.

CAMPAGNA, DAWN; Spaulding HS; Rochester, NH; (S); 40/397; Key Clb; Chorus; School Musical; Hon Roll; Marine Bio.

CAMPBELL, ROBERT; Belmont HS; Canterbury, NH; (Y); Drama Clb; Pres French Clb; Ski Clb; Speech Tm; School Play; Yrbk Sprt Ed; Hon Roll; Paul Smiths Coll; Culinary Arts.

CANNATA, JODI ANMARIE; Nashua HS; Nashua, NH; (Y); 132/783; Computer Clb; Rep Frsh Cls; Stu Cncl; Cheerleading; Hon Roll; NHS; Boston U; Comp Engrng.

CAOUETTE, CHRIS; Nashua SR HS; Nashua, NH; (Y); Boy Scts; CAP; Library Aide; Ski Clb; Drm & Bgl; Socr; Cit Awd; Embry Riddle; Aerontcl Engrng.

CARBONNEAU, RENEE; Pelham HS; Pelham, NH; (Y); Church Yth Grp; Girl Scts; Spanish Clb; Chorus; Yrbk Stf; Trvl Agnt.

CAREY, MALIALOU; Alvirne HS; Hudson, NH; (Y); Color Guard; Drm & Bgl; Hon Roll.

CARIGNAN, ALLEN; St Thomas Aquinas HS; Somersworth, NH; (Y); 1/80; Latin Clb; Math Clb; Yrbk Stf; High Hon Roll; NHS; Prfct Atten Awd; Med.

CARIGNAN, NICOLE; Manchester Memorial HS; Manchester, NH; (Y); 18/341; Cmnty Wkr; Varsity Clb; Variety Show; Lit Mag; Crs Cntry; Trk; Hon Roll; Prfct Atten Awd; MVP-SPNG Trck 85; Rookie Of Yr-Sprng Trck 84; Htl Mngmt.

CARLTON, TREVOR W; Nashua SR HS; Nashua, NH; (Y); 1/950; Am Leg Boys St; Trs Church Yth Grp; Computer Clb; Latin Clb; Math Clb; Math Tm; Ski Clb; Spanish Clb; SADD; Var Golf; Tm Plcd 2nd In Odessey Of The Mind Wrld Fnls 86; Air Force Acad Smmr Scientific Sem 86; Pre-Medicine.

CARLUCCIO, MARIO K; Trinity HS; Bedford, NH; (Y); Am Leg Boys St; Model UN; Jazz Band; Pres Frsh Cls; VP Jr Cls; Pres Sr Cls; Var L Crs Cntry; Var L Golf; Var L Tennis; Hon Roll; Bus.

CARNEY, KATIE; Inter Lakes HS; North Sandwich, NH; (Y); Camera Clb; Pres Church Yth Grp; Chorus; School Musical; Sec Stu Cncl; Var Cheerleading; Var Trk; Cit Awd; High Hon Roll; NHS; Typng I Awd 86; Comm.

CARON, CRAIG; Newport JR SR HS; Goshen, NH; (Y); Letterman Clb; Math Tm; ROTC; Science Clb; Nwsp Sprt Ed; Yrbk Sprt Ed; Rep Stu Cncl; Var L Bsbl; Var L Bsktbl; Var L Ftbl; NH Consrvtn Commission Schlrshp 84; Mst Valuable Plyr Bsktbl 86; Outstndng Achvt Hstry 86; Engrng.

CARON, SUZANNE; Manchester West HS; Manchester, NH; (Y); FBLA; Hon Roll; Acctng.

CARR, TROY D; Newmarket Central Schl; Newmarket, NH; (Y); 1/45; Am Leg Boys St; Pres Frsh Cls; Trs Jr Cls; VP Sr Cls; Var JV Bsktbl; Var JV Socr; Bausch & Lomb Sci Awd; High Hon Roll; NHS; Val; Achvt Calculas & Engsh 86; Bruce Dziedzic Sprtsmnshp Awrd 86; Amer Lgn Pst & Lamprey Rvr Schlrshp 86; U Of NH; Bus Admin.

CARRIER, SCOTT; Bennett HS; Conway, NH; (Y); JV Var Ftbl; Im Wt Lftg; Im Wrstlng; Hon Roll; Tool & Die.

CARROLL, TENLEY; Concord HS; Concord, NH; (Y); Varsity Clb; Var L Cheerleading; Var Capt Crs Cntry; Var L Trk; Hon Roll; NHS.

CARTER, BRIAN; Concord HS; Bow, NH; (Y); Church Yth Grp; Science Clb; JV Mgr(s); Swmmng; Mgr Trk; High Hon Roll; Hon Roll; NHS; Achvt Awd Drftng, Cert Advncd Open Water PADI Scuba Diver, Marin Bio/Scuba Pgm 86; Marine Bio.

CARUSO, MICHELLE; Nashua SR HS; Nashua, NH; (Y); Model UN; Variety Show; Nwsp Ed-Chief; Yrbk Ed-Chief; High Hon Roll; Pres Jr NHS; NHS; Voice Dem Awd; Church Yth Grp; Spanish Clb; 4th ST Am Leg Oratorical Cont 84-85; Harvard Bk Recip 86; Natl Army Essay Cont Schl Wnr 85; Jrnlsm.

CASELLINI, PETER J; Tilton Schl; Newburyport, MA; (S); Stage Crew; Pres Frsh Cls; Pres Soph Cls; Rep Stu Cncl; Var Lcrss; Var Socr; Hon Roll; Alg I Awd 84; Capt, Vrsty Alpine Ski Tm 86; CPA.

CASEY, KIMBERLY ANN; Manchester Hs West; Bedford, NH; (Y); 76/420; Cmnty Wkr; Ski Clb; Variety Show; Nwsp Stf; Yrbk Stf; Trs Stu Cncl; High Hon Roll; Hon Roll; Capt Var Sftbl; Psychlgy.

CASEY, LORI; Dover HS; Dover, NH; (Y); 32/300; Yrbk Stf; JV Bsktbl; Im Mgr Powder Puff Ftbl; Hon Roll; Sci.

CASS, SCOTT; Belmont HS; Belmont, NH; (S); 9/70; Church Yth Grp; Pres Frsh Cls; Pres Jr Cls; Pres Sr Cls; Var Score Keeper; Hon Roll; NHS.

CASSELBERRY, RICHARD; Spaulding HS; Rochester, NH; (S); 39/390; Computer Clb; Hon Roll; NHS; Electrncs Engr.

CASWELL III, H TAYLOR; Littleton HS; Littleton, NH; (Y); Am Leg Boys St; Drama Clb; Stage Crew; Variety Show; Nwsp Stf; Bsktbl; Capt Capt Golf; Hon Roll; YMCA Uth & Gvrnmnt Comm Chrmn 86; Hstry.

CATALANO, MARC; Bishop Guertin HS; Nashua, NH; (Y); Var L Bsbl; Im JV Bsktbl; Hon Roll; Jr NHS; Communications.

CAVOLI, STEPHEN; Bishop Brady HS; Bow, NH; (Y); 13/82; Am Leg Boys St; Boy Scts; Ski Clb; Chorus; Rep Frsh Cls; Pres Soph Cls; VP Stu Cncl; Var Ftbl; Var Capt Trk; NHS; IFLA Spnsh Awd; H S Stu Athlt Awd; U S Army; Offcr.

CEA, STEPHEN; Salem HS; Salem, NH; (S); 20/353; Math Tm; Var Ftbl; Var Trk; High Hon Roll; Hon Roll; NEDT Awd; U Of Lowell; Elctrcl Engrng.

CEGELSKI JR, KENNETH F; Winnisquam Regional HS; Sanbornton, NH; (Y); 3/100; Cmnty Wkr; Drama Clb; Pres 4-H; French Clb; Chorus; School Play; Pres Jr Cls; Pres Sr Cls; Crs Cntry; Bausch & Lomb Sci Awd; Youngest Pilot Awd-Alton Bay Fly In 85; Airline Pilot.

CENTER, LESLIE; Keene HS; Keene, NH; (Y); 26/350; Church Yth Grp; French Clb; Var JV Bsktbl; JV Mgr(s); JV Socr; JV Trk; High Hon Roll; Hon Roll; Fashn Merch.

CHAISSON, LEE; Concord HS; Bow, NH; (Y); 81/390; JV Bsbl; JV Socr; High Hon Roll; Hon Roll; Bio Achvt Awd 85; New Hampshire Coll; Bus Mgt.

CHAMPAGNE, LISA; Alvirne HS; Hudson, NH; (Y); 1/300; Am Leg Aux Girls St; Key Clb; Teachers Aide; Yrbk Ed-Chief; Stu Cncl; High Hon Roll; Hon Roll; NHS; Val.

CHAMPAGNE, LISA; Manchester Memorial HS; Manchester, NH; (Y); 81/341; Church Yth Grp; Capt Varsity Clb; Trs VICA; Var Capt Trk; Var Capt Vllybl; Hon Roll; Graphic Arts Exprnce 86; Rochester Inst Tech; Graphic.

CHAMPNEY, SCOTT; Concord HS; Concord, NH; (Y); Bus.

CHAPDELAINE, MARIA L; Tilton Schl; Laconia, NH; (S); Drama Clb; French Clb; Key Clb; Teachers Aide; Chorus; School Musical; Var Lcrss; JV Socr; Var Tennis; High Hon Roll; Law.

CHAPMAN, MARTHA; Weare HS; Weare, NH; (S); 4/37; Pres 4-H; Yrbk Sprt Ed; Trs Jr Cls; Trs Sr Cls; Var Capt Bsktbl; Var Vllybl; Hon Roll; NHS; Acdmc All Amer 84-85; Math All Amer.

CHARLEBOIS, NICOLE; Newport JR/SR HS; Newport, NH; (Y); 6/89; Letterman Clb; Math Tm; Acpl Chr; Nwsp Stf; Var L Cheerleading; Var L Fld Hcky; DAR Awd; NHS; Rotary Awd; Keene ST Coll; Lbrl Arts.

CHARRON, DAVID REGINALD; Manchester HS West; Manchester, NH; (Y); 38/338; Cmnty Wkr; Ski Clb; L Wrstlng; High Hon Roll; Yth Of Yr YMCA 82; Pres Mancheter YMCA Ldr Corps 84-85 & 85-86; Rochester Inst Of Tech; Elect.

CHARRON, JOHN; Bishop Guertin HS; Nashua, NH; (Y); Church Yth Grp; Nwsp Rptr; Nwsp Sprt Ed; Stat Bsktbl; Im Score Keeper; Im Wt Lftg; JRNLSM.

CHARRON, KRISTEN; Memorial HS; Manchester, NH; (Y); 4/340; Chorus; Lit Mag; Crs Cntry; Trk; High Hon Roll; Pres Schlr; Ger Awd 86; Interpreter For Deaf.

CHASSE, VALERIE S; Nashua SR HS; Nashua, NH; (Y); 107/900; Am Leg Aux Girls St; SADD; Nwsp Sprt Ed; Stu Cncl; Var Cheerleading; Coach Actv; Im Vllybl; Pres Jr NHS; Sec Spanish NHS; Plymouth ST Coll; Engl.

CHATMAN, SUSAN; Alton Central HS; Alton, NH; (S); 1/37; Cmnty Wkr; Library Aide; Scholastic Bowl; Chorus; Nwsp Rptr; Yrbk Bus Mgr; Yrbk Stf; Lit Mag; High Hon Roll; Amer H S Mater Exm 2nd Pl Schl 85; Concrs Natl De Francais Cert Merit 85.

CHESTER, JEN; Pelham HS; Pelham, NH; (Y); Church Yth Grp; French Clb; Teachers Aide; Var Fld Hcky; Hon Roll; NHS; Voice Dem Awd; Granite St Challenge Tm 86-87; Chrmn NHS Stu Tutrng Pgm 86-87.

CHILD, C JEFFREY; Fall Mountain Regional HS; Charlestown, NH; (Y); Computer Clb; Drama Clb; PAVAS; Radio Clb; Red Cross Aide; Band; Mrchg Band; Stage Crew; Variety Show; Bsktbl; Electrncs.

CHINCHAR, CHRIS ANN; Portsmouth HS; Rye, NH; (Y); 22/359; CAP; Model UN; Ski Clb; Rep Jr Cls; Bsktbl; JV Sftbl; High Hon Roll; Hon Roll; NHS; Rye Lions Clb Scholar 86; Bertha I Norton Scholar 86; UNH Hnrs Pgm 86; UNH; Hotl Adm.

CHOATE, JO-ELLEN; Alvirne HS; Hudson, NH; (Y); Dance Clb; Office Aide; SADD; Variety Show; L Var Crs Cntry; JV Socr; L Var Trk; 1st Pl N E Dance Wrkshp 85; St Marshall STOPP 84; Tchr Of Dance & Gymnstcs 84-86; Comm.

CHOW, KEYE S; St Pauls Schl; Wellesley, MA; (Y); Chess Clb; English Clb; FCA; Intnl Clb; Library Aide; Math Tm; Radio Clb; JV Bsktbl; Var Tennis; Cit Awd; Cum Laude Soc 84; Corp Mgr.

CHRETIEN, BROOKS; Bishop Guertin HS; Nashua, NH; (Y); FCA; Ski Clb; SADD; Var L Ice Hcky; Var L Socr; Var L Tennis; Hon Roll; Athlt Of Wk Hcky; Goaltndrs Cmp CO Spgs Olympc Ctr 84; Hcky Cmp Mrqtt MI Olympc Ctr 86; Arch.

CHRISTINE, GAGNON; Manchester Central HS; Hooksett, NH; (Y); 188/430; Var JV Trk; Hon Roll; Cooprtv Educ Cert 86; Hlth Occup Stus Of Amer Cert Partcptn 86; Med Lab Tech.

CHUM, RONG; White Mtns Regional HS; Laconia, NH; (Y); Teachers Aide; JV Bsktbl; JV Socr; French Hon Soc; High Hon Roll; Hon Roll; NHS; Acctg.

CIBOTTI, DEAN; Nashua SR HS; Nashua, NH; (Y); 50/980; Am Leg Boys St; Latin Clb; SADD; Pres Frsh Cls; Pres Sr Cls; VP Stu Cncl; Bsktbl; Var Capt Ftbl; Hon Roll; MVP Frosh Ftbl 84; Outstndng Bckfld 84.

CLAIR, DAN; Bishop Guertin HS; Merrimack, NH; (Y); Ski Clb; Im Bsktbl; JV Ftbl; Var Trk; Im Wt Lftg.

CLAIRMONT, MICHELLE; Belmont HS; Belmont, NH; (S); 1/68; French Clb; Math Tm; Varsity Clb; Trs Frsh Cls; Trs Soph Cls; JV Var Bsktbl; Var Crs Cntry; Var Trk; Bausch & Lomb Sci Awd; High Hon Roll.

CLAIRMONT, PETER; Belmont HS; Belmont, NH; (Y); 10/76; Math Tm; Varsity Clb; Nwsp Bus Mgr; Socr; High Hon Roll; NHS; 1st Pl Sci Fair 85; MVP Var Soccer 86; Outstndng Achvt Indstrl Art Awd 86; U NH; Comp Sci.

CLARK, CELIA; Fall Mt Regional HS; Charlestown, NH; (Y); 13/130; Am Leg Aux Girls St; Church Yth Grp; 4-H; Var Capt Socr; Var L Trk; 4-H Awd; Hon Roll; NHS; Cmnty Wkr; Schlr/Athl Awd Top Sr Girl 86; Springfield Coll; Envrnmntl.

CLARK, ERIC; Fall Mountain Regional HS; Charlestown, NH; (Y); Chess Clb; Computer Clb; 4-H; Trk; 4-H Awd; Hon Roll; Arch.

CLARK, JOSEPH D; Alvirne HS; Hudson, NH; (Y); Ski Clb; JV Bsbl; Hon Roll; U Lowell; Drafting.

CLARK, MATT; Stevens HS; Claremont, NH; (Y); Am Leg Boys St; Drama Clb; Ski Clb; Varsity Clb; Variety Show; Bsbl; Ftbl; Wt Lftg; Cit Awd; Hon Roll; Plymouth ST Coll; Bus Mgmt.

CLARK, REBECCA; Alvirne HS; Hudson, NH; (Y); 98/331; Cmnty Wkr; GAA; SADD; Varsity Clb; Socr; Trk; Hon Roll; 1st Speech, 2nd Formal, 2 ST Titles Miss TEEN NH Pgnt $600 Schlrshp & Trophies 85; Cmmnctn.

CLAY, HEIDI; Keene HS; Keene, NH; (Y); 81/362; Art Clb; Camera Clb; Cmnty Wkr; Hosp Aide; JA; Yrbk Stf; Hon Roll; 25 Hrs Vlntr Wrk Schl Yr 86; Art Therapy.

CLEM, TAMMY; Hinsdale HS; Hinsdale, NH; (Y); 3/50; Drama Clb; 4-H; Yrbk Stf; Var Bsktbl; Var JV Cheerleading; Var JV Fld Hcky; Var Mgr(s); 4-H Awd; High Hon Roll; Hon Roll; Comp Sci.

CLEMONS, MICHAEL; Kennett HS; Jackson, NH; (Y); 29/182; Nwsp Rptr; JV Var Bsbl; JV Var Bsktbl.

CLOGSTON III, WILLIAM H; Tilton Schl; Tilton, NH; (S); Church Yth Grp; Computer Clb; Drama Clb; Science Clb; Varsity Clb; Bsktbl; Lcrss; Socr; Hon Roll; NHS; Mth.

CLOOS, KIM; Alvirne HS; Hudson, NH; (Y); Cmnty Wkr; SADD; Teachers Aide; Capt Var Bsktbl; Var Crs Cntry; JV Socr; JV Sftbl; Var Capt Tennis; Hon Roll; Nutrition.

CLOUGH, SAMANTHA; Newport JR SR HS; Goshen, NH; (Y); Spanish Clb; Nwsp Stf; NHS; Astrnmy.

CLOUGH, VALERIE; Concord HS; Concord, NH; (Y); Dance Clb; Office Aide; Pep Clb; Variety Show; Stu Cncl; Cheerleading; Score Keeper; Hon Roll; Prfct Atten Awd.

CLOUGHERTY, TIM; Manchester Memorial HS; Manchester, NH; (Y); 41/341; Var Capt Ice Hcky; JV Socr; Hon Roll; Cmptr.

CLOUTIER, JACQUELINE; Manchester H S West; Manchester, NH; (Y); Church Yth Grp; FBLA; Band; Concert Band; Mrchg Band; Yrbk Stf; Notre Dame; Legal Sec.

COATE, THOMAS; Bishop Guertin HS; Windham, NH; (Y); Var L Bsbl; Var L Bsktbl; Var L Socr; Im Wt Lftg; Hon Roll; Awd Hnr Rl; Capt Vrsty Bsbl & Sccr Tm; Cvl Engrng.

COCCHIARO, LISA M; Salem HS; Salem, NH; (Y); 10/312; Church Yth Grp; French Clb; FBLA; Model UN; Color Guard; School Play; Stage Crew; High Hon Roll; NHS; Dollars For Schlrs 86; Contintl Acad Hair Dsgn; Csmtlg.

COCCHIARO, LYNNE; Salem HS; Salem, NH; (S); 2/340; Pres French Clb; High Hon Roll; NHS; Miss Salem JR Teen 85.

COCHRANE, DONALD P; Pinkerton Acad; Windham, NH; (Y); Am Leg Boys St; Ski Clb; JV Socr; Var Tennis; Med.

COE, GRAIG ROBERT; Phillips Exeter Acad; Avon, CO; (Y); Varsity Clb; Off Frsh Cls; Off Soph Cls; Stu Cncl; Ice Hcky; Socr; Swmmng; Tennis; High Hon Roll; Dartmouth; Med Rsrch.

COMER, JOHN; Memorial HS; Manchester, NH; (Y); 13/341; Boy Scts; Teachers Aide; Yrbk Phtg; Ntl Merit Ltr; Engrng.

CONDON, TAMARA; St Thomas Aquinas HS; Barrington, NH; (Y); Art Clb; French Clb; Pres Key Clb; Sec VP Stu Cncl; High Hon Roll; NHS; Holy Corss Bk Awd 86; Hugh O Brian Yth Ldrshp Sem 85; Intl Bus.

CONGER, JOHN; Bishop Guertin HS; Nashua, NH; (Y); 2/145; Pres Chess Clb; French Clb; Math Clb; Nwsp Rptr; Yrbk Stf; Stat Bsbl; Im Bsktbl; High Hon Roll; NHS; Renssalaer Mth & Sci Awd 86.

CONKLIN, HEATHER; Oyster River HS; Madbury, NH; (Y); 17/150; Am Leg Aux Girls St; 4-H; Pres French Clb; Math Clb; Math Tm; Dnfth Awd; JETS Awd; Mu Alp Tht; NHS; Ntl Merit Ltr; NH Rep Natl 4-H Club Congress 83; Honor Scty 85; Natl Merit Commnd Stu 85; NE; Elec Engr.

CONNER, DOUG; Memorial HS; Litchfield, NH; (Y); 7/349; Art Clb; Church Yth Grp; Exploring; Yrbk Stf; Rep Frsh Cls; Powder Puff Ftbl; Var L Swmmng; High Hon Roll; Pres NHS; John Hopkins; Medcn.

COOK, JOHN; Concord HS; Concord, NH; (Y); Drama Clb; Math Tm; Band; Chorus; School Musical; School Play; Nwsp Rptr; Lit Mag; High Hon Roll; NHS; Choral Dir Awd Music 84.

COOPER, CHERYL; Spaulding HS; Rochester, NH; (S); Drama Clb; Pres FBLA; Political Wkr; Hon Roll; Gldn Poet Awd 85; U Of NH; Hotl Mgr.

COOPER, GREGORY; Bishop Guertin HS; Merrimack, NH; (Y); Cmnty Wkr; Spanish Clb; JV Bsktbl; Im Vllybl; Hon Roll; Spanish NHS; Gen Bus.

COPP, LAURA; Berlin SR HS; Errol, NH; (Y); 7/212; Drama Clb; VP FBLA; Yrbk Stf; Var Crs Cntry; Var Trk; High Hon Roll; NHS; 1st Pl Wrtng Cont 84; Golden Poet Awd Wrld Poetry 85; 3rd Rnnr Up Miss Amer Co-Ed Pag 85; New Rochelle; Cmmnctns.

CORMACK, JANINE; Kennett HS; Conway, NH; (Y); 15/213; Pres Church Yth Grp; Red Cross Aide; SADD; Teachers Aide; Varsity Clb; Mrchg Band; School Musical; Swing Chorus; Nwsp Ed-Chief; Nwsp Stf; Med.

CORRENTE, DANA; Salem HS; Salem, NH; (Y); 84/383; Cmnty Wkr; French Clb; Model UN; Ski Clb; Concert Band; Mrchg Band; Stage Crew; Hon Roll.

CORRIGON, MIKE; Berlin HS; Berlin, NH; (Y); 30/215; Am Leg Boys St; Drama Clb; FBLA; Ski Clb; Band; Pep Band; School Play; Nwsp Rptr; Nwsp Stf; Yrbk Rptr; Rookie Yr Awd Upwrd Bnd 85 & 86; Upwrd Bnd Rep WA DC-LOBBYST 85; Cmnctns.

CORRIVEAU, CAMILLE; West HS; Manchester, NH; (Y); 100/420; Ski Clb; Contntl Acad Hair Dsgn; Cosmotl.

COSTANZO, GLENN A; Farmington HS; Farmington, NH; (Y); 4/75; Am Leg Boys St; JV Stat Bsktbl; NHS; Odyssey Mind Tm 3rd ST 84; Bus Mgmt.

COTA, LESLIE; Hillsboro-Deering HS; Hillsboro, NH; (S); 6/72; Church Yth Grp; SADD; Band; Mrchg Band; Symp Band; Yrbk Stf; Rep Stu Cncl; Var JV Mgr(s); Var JV Score Keeper; Hon Roll; Comm.

COTE, ANDREA; West HS; Manchester, NH; (Y); 66/420; Pres Church Yth Grp; Ski Clb; Variety Show; Yrbk Sprt Ed; Capt Socr; High Hon Roll; Hon Roll; Ntl Art Hnr Soc 86-87; Strng Cmmttee 84-86; Bus.

COTE, DAVE; Belmont HS; Canterbury, NH; (Y); 20/74; Art Clb; French Clb; Ski Clb; Speech Tm; Varsity Clb; Variety Show; Ed Yrbk Stf; VP Pres Stu Cncl; Hon Roll; Prfct Atten Awd; Rochester Inst Of Tech; Grphcs.

COTE, DAVID; Manchester Central HS; Manchester, NH; (Y); 150/450; Boys Clb Am; Cmnty Wkr; Yrbk Stf; Lit Mag; Trs Frsh Cls; Trk; High Hon Roll; Physician.

COTE, KRISTIE; Londonderry HS; Londonderry, NH; (Y); Ski Clb; Stu Cncl; Socr; High Hon Roll; NHS; Prfct Atten Awd; Pres Schlr; Frnch Awd Exc 82-83; Rotary Club Schlrshp 86; Acad Exc Awd 86; U NH; Bus Adm.

COULOMBE, TAMMY; Berlin HS; Berlin, NH; (Y); FBLA; SADD; Fashion Merchandising.

COUNCIL, WILLIAM A; Phillips Exeter Acad; Brooklyn, NY; (Y); Aud/Vis; Church Yth Grp; Computer Clb; Chorus; Church Choir; School Play; Im Bsbl; Im Bsktbl; Im Socr; JV Trk; Comp Sci.

COUNTER, CATHY; Memorial HS; Manchester, NH; (Y); 51/389; French Clb; Political Wkr; Variety Show; Hon Roll; Bus Adm.

COUTURE, GISELLE; Spaulding HS; Rochester, NH; (S); Chess Clb; Drama Clb; Key Clb; ROTC; School Play; Yrbk Stf; Bsktbl; Hon Roll; NHS.

COUTURE, KIM; Berliin HS; Berlin, NH; (Y); SADD; Jr NHS.

COUTURE, LISA; Berlin SR HS; Berlin, NH; (Y); SADD; Pres Frsh Cls; Pres Soph Cls; JV Var Bsktbl; JV Var Fld Hcky; JV Var Sftbl; Hon Roll; Csmtlgy.

COUTURE-WHITE, ANN; Concord HS; Concord, NH; (Y); Church Yth Grp; Cmnty Wkr; French Clb; Band; Chorus; Off Concert Band; Drm Mjr(t); Jazz Band; Mrchg Band; Pep Band; Semper Fidelis Awd Musicl Excllnc 86; Amer Musicl Fndtn Band Hnr 86; U Of NH; Music Ed.

COX, DOUGLAS M; Manchester West HS; Bedford, NH; (Y); 54/420; Boys Clb Am; Ski Clb; Chorus; Stage Crew; Nwsp Rptr; Im Bsbl; Im Bsktbl; Var Golf; Im Lcrss; High Hon Roll.

COX, PHILIP; Alvirne HS; Manchester, NH; (Y); 17/333; Boy Scts; SADD.

COYNE, JONATHAN; Moultonborough Acad; Center Harbor, NH; (Y); 14/41; Boy Scts; Spanish Clb; Nwsp Ed-Chief; JV Var Bsbl; JV Bsktbl; Im Golf; Im Tennis; Im Vllybl; High Hon Roll; Hon Roll; Pres Physcl Ftnss Awd 84-85; Excllnc Jrnlsm 86; Mrktng.

CRABTREE, PATRICIA; Hanover HS; Hanover, NH; (Y); 50/159; French Clb; German Clb; JV Fld Hcky; JV Lcrss; Hon Roll; Delta Epsilon Phi 85-86; Oceanogrphy.

CRAM, STEPHANIE; Alvirne HS; Litchfield, NH; (Y); 106/136; Church Yth Grp; Church Choir; Pres Frsh Cls; Pres Soph Cls; Pres Sr Cls; Stu Cncl; JV Socr; Swmmng; Trk; Drama Clb; Ltr Trk, Crss Cntry, Chrldng Sccr 82-86; Regan Mem Schlrshp, Scrpbk Awd 82; Mst Sprtd Chrldr 85; U Steubenville; Psych.

CRANDALL, MELISSA; Alvirne HS; Hudson, NH; (Y); 48/338; Am Leg Aux Girls St; SADD; Teachers Aide; Varsity Clb; VP Sr Cls; Trs Stu Cncl; Var Bsktbl; Var Crs Cntry; Var Sftbl; Hon Roll; Foren Sci.

CRAVEN, ERIC V; Conant HS; Jaffrey, NH; (Y); Am Leg Boys St; Computer Clb; Chorus; School Musical; School Play; Nwsp Rptr; Pres Frsh Cls; Var JV Bsktbl; Var Socr; Hon Roll; Bus Manag.

CRISP, STEPHEN; Bishop Gurtin HS; Hollis, NH; (Y); FCA; Bsbl; Plymouth ST Coll; Bus.

CRISS, JENNIFER; Newmarket HS; Newmarket, NH; (Y); 5/60; Off Band; VP Jr Cls; Bsktbl; Fld Hcky; Sftbl; Hon Roll; Hon Roll; Band Serv Awd 85-86; Bus Admin.

CRONIN, SUSAN M; Salem HS; Salem, NH; (S); 16/353; Exploring; Key Clb; Trs Latin Clb; Math Tm; Model UN; Ski Clb; Yrbk Ed-Chief; JV Trk; High Hon Roll; NHS; Medcn.

CRONSHAW, SCOTT; Spaulding HS; Rochester, NH; (S); 36/400; Drama Clb; School Musical; School Play; Socr; High Hon Roll; Hon Roll; Gld Mdl-50 Ft Smllbr Rfle- JR Olympcs 84; Arch.

CROOKER, ROBERTA; Pembroke Acad; Suncook, NH; (Y); Church Yth Grp; Cmnty Wkr; Spanish Clb; SADD; Church Bd 84-86; New Hampshire Coll; Lgl Secy.

CROSS, KAREN; Concord HS; Concord, NH; (Y); 36/393; High Hon Roll; Hon Roll; Achievement In Psych 86; Achievement In Anthro 84; Psych.

CROSSMAN, SHELLEY; Fall Mountain Regional HS; Langdon, NH; (Y); #7 In Class; Am Leg Aux Girls St; Spanish Clb; Band; Color Guard; Concert Band; Yrbk Stf; Trs Pres Stu Cncl; Socr; High Hon Roll; NHS; Awd Excllnc Chem 86; Bus Admin.

CROTEAU, DIANE; Berlin HS; Berlin, NH; (Y); 4/200; SADD; Stat Bsktbl; Stat Socr; JV Trk; Hon Roll; NHS; Girls ST 86; Acctng.

CROWLEY, LISA; Newport HS; Newport, NH; (Y); Am Leg Aux Girls St; Letterman Clb; SADD; Chorus; School Musical; Nwsp Rptr; Yrbk Rptr; Fld Hcky; Hon Roll; NHS; Vrsty Skiing 85; U MA; Marktng.

CUNNINGHAM, JULIE; Groveton HS; Groveton, NH; (Y); Dance Clb; French Clb; School Play; Var L Bsktbl; Im Gym; Pres Frsh Cls; Stu Cncl Awds Dedctn & Outstndng Mbr 84.

CUNNINGHAM, KERI; Keene HS; Keene, NH; (Y); 4/362; Chrmn Am Leg Aux Girls St; French Clb; Hosp Aide; Service Clb; Acpl Chr; Variety Show; Rep Jr Cls; Stu Cncl; High Hon Roll; NHS.

CUNNINGHAM, LYNN; Salem HS; Salem, NH; (Y); #44 In Class; Boys Clb Am; Yrbk Phtg; VP Capt Bsktbl; Var Crs Cntry; JV Sftbl; JV Trk; High Hon Roll; Hon Roll; St Schlr; Chllnge Gftd Tlntd Stdnts 85; Faclty, W Ackerman Mem Schlrshps 86; Wheelock Coll; Erly Chldhd Ed.

CUNNINGHAM, MARY ANN; Pinkerton Acad; Windham, NH; (Y); 22/525; Hosp Aide; Band; Chorus; Church Choir; Concert Band; Mrchg Band; Stage Crew; JV Socr; Hon Roll; Schlrshp Acdmc Achvmnt 85; U Of NH; Ocptnl Thpry.

CURDIE, STACEY; Newfound Memorial HS; Bristol, NH; (Y); 7/68; Cmnty Wkr; School Play; Nwsp Ed-Chief; Pres Jr Cls; Stu Cncl; Hon Roll; NHS; Emerson Coll; Writing.

CURRIER, KELLY; Central HS; Manchester, NH; (Y); 57/430; Drama Clb; Intnl Clb; Math Clb; SADD; Ed Lit Mag; Hon Roll; Peer Cnslng; Frgn Lang.

CUSANELLI, MICHAEL; Stevens HS; Claremont, NH; (Y); Am Leg Boys St; Boy Scts; Dance Clb; Teachers Aide; Yrbk Stf; Bsbl; Trk; High Hon Roll; Hon Roll; Prfct Atten Awd; TV.

CUSHING, KRISSY; Plymouth Area HS; Plymouth, NH; (Y); 32/127; Trk; Hon Roll; Trvl.

CUSSON, CARMELA; Pembroke Acad; Suncook, NH; (Y); 12/180; Drama Clb; Sec Exploring; Pep Clb; Band; Church Choir; Pep Band; Symp Band; Hon Roll; Comm.

CUTTER, VALERIE ANN; Hinsdale HS; Newport, NH; (Y); Hon Roll; Rsrvtnist.

CYNN, CHRISTINE J; Phillips Exeter Acad; Old Lyme, CT; (Y); Chorus; Orch; VP Frsh Cls; Rep Stu Cncl; Var Capt Crs Cntry; Var Lcrss; High Hon Roll; Ntl Merit SF; Dual Cnty League Crs Cntry Mdl 82; Ntl Frnch Cntst 82; New Englnd Intrschlstc Crs Cntry Mdl 85.

CYR, MICHELLE MARIE; Memorial HS; Auburn, NH; (Y); 57/341; DECA; Tennis; Hon Roll; Advrtsg.

CZARNEC, STACIA ARIANNA; Pinkerton Acad; Chester, NH; (Y); 30/496; Hosp Aide; JCL; Latin Clb; Library Aide; SADD; Mgr(s); High Hon Roll; Hon Roll; NHS; St Josephs Coll.

DAIGLE, FRANCES; Goffstown HS; Goffstown, NH; (Y); 1/215; Church Yth Grp; Exploring; FNA; Red Cross Aide; Ski Clb; Sec Stu Cncl; Cheerleading; High Hon Roll; Sec NHS; Val; Gov Schlrshp 86; Thos J Leone Schlrshp 86; U VT; Phys Ther.

DAISY, JESSICA; Kingswood Regional HS; Barnstead, NH; (Y); Band; Church Choir; Capt Var Bsktbl; Capt Var Socr; Sftbl; High Hon Roll; Hon Roll; NHS; MVP In Sccr 85 & 86; Embry Riddle; Pilot.

DAMI, STEVEN; Belmont HS; Laconia, NH; (Y); 12/70; Ski Clb; VP Jr Cls; VP Sr Cls; Stu Cncl; High Hon Roll; Hon Roll; NHS; Outstndng Achvmnt In Indus Arts Wdwrkng & Indpndnt Study Wdwrkng 86; NH Tech Inst; Engr.

DANAIS, MIKE; Berlin HS; Berlin, NH; (Y); 30/208; Var L Bsbl; Var L Ice Hcky; Var L Socr.

DANIELS, LAUREL A; St Pauls Schl; Concord, NH; (Y); Capt Dance Clb; Pep Clb; Service Clb; School Play; Variety Show; Yrbk Stf; Cit Awd; Dickey Prz Dance 83; 2nd Testmnl Acad Achvt 84; 1st Tstmnl & Valpey Prz Acad Achvt 85; Dancer.

DANIELS, MICHELLE; Winnisquam Regional HS; Tilton, NH; (Y); 13/97; Church Yth Grp; French Clb; Math Tm; Ski Clb; Yrbk Stf; Trs Frsh Cls; Pres Soph Cls; VP Stu Cncl; Trk; Hon Roll; Rbt H & Grtrd E Sedgley Chrtbl Fndn Awd 86; Schl Almn Assn Schlrshp 86; John T Dodge Mem Schlrshp 86; U NH; Bio.

DAVIIS, CHRIS; Bishop Guertin HS; Nashua, NH; (Y); Im Tennis; Hon Roll.

DAVIS, JENNIFER SARA; Nashua HS; Nashua, NH; (Y); Am Leg Aux Girls St; Letterman Clb; SADD; Rep Frsh Cls; JV Bsktbl; Var L Socr; Var L Swmmng; Hon Roll; NHS; Church Yth Grp; Med Tech.

DAVIS, LEE-ANNE; Timberlane Regional HS; Plaistow, NH; (Y); Library Aide; Model UN; Teachers Aide; Yrbk Stf; Hon Roll; Pres Schlr; Plaistow Fish & Gm Clb Schlrshp 86; Northland Coll; Wldlf Mgmt.

DAY, SUSAN; Inter Lakes HS; Moultonboro, NH; (Y); Art Clb; Spanish Clb; Yrbk Stf; Zoology.

DE GRANDPRE, BETSY J; Conant HS; Jaffrey, NH; (Y); 1/91; Teachers Aide; Concert Band; Mrchg Band; Orch; Gov Hon Prg Awd; High Hon Roll; JP Sousa Awd; NHS; NEDT Awd; Val; Wmns Clb Scholar 86; Ellen Bean Scholar 86; Sci Achvt Awd 86; Colby Coll.

DEAN, JULIE A; Salem HS; Salem, NH; (Y); 100/385; French Clb; Model UN; VP SADD; L Sec Chorus; Madrigals; School Musical; Nwsp Rptr; Pres Stu Cncl; Var Crs Cntry; Hon Roll; U Of Lowell; Music Educ.

DEARBORN, LEIGH ANN; Franklin JR SR HS; Hill, NH; (Y); Yrbk Stf; High Hon Roll; Hon Roll; Frank & Laura Tssler Schlrshp Fnd 86; Rtry Bus Awd 86; New Hampshire Coll; Accntng.

DEBLOIS, CAROLYN; Crosby Kennett HS; Conway, NH; (Y); 23/213; SADD; Band; Sftbl; High Hon Roll; Hon Roll; 4-H; Girl Scts; Chorus; Concert Band; Mrchg Band; Cncr Frnch Awd 83-84; Csmtlgst.

DEBUTTS, PATRICIA; Coe Brown Northwood Acad; W Nottingham, NH; (Y); 1/56; Sec FHA; Yrbk Ed-Chief; Stu Cncl; High Hon Roll; Hon Roll; VP NHS; Exc Geo,Comp Pgmr,US Hist 85-86; U NH; Bus Mgmt.

DECAREAU, MARIA F; Milford Area SR HS; Amherst, NH; (Y); French Clb; Color Guard; Drm & Bgl; Flag Corp; Mrchg Band; Yrbk Stf; JV Powder Puff Ftbl; Im Vllybl; DAR Awd; Hon Roll; Schl Ltr & Jckt For Mrchng Bnd 85 & 86; Bates Coll; Chld Psychlgy.

DEERY, SUZANNE; Alvirne HS; Hudson, NH; (Y); Teachers Aide; Variety Show; JV Bsktbl; Var Crs Cntry; Mgr(s); Score Keeper; Capt Var Trk; Hon Roll; HS Track All Am Honrbl Mention 84-85; NH All Star Winter Trck Awd 85-86ALL Star Awd Trck 84-85.

DEIS, STACEY; Conant HS; Jaffrey, NH; (Y); Dance Clb; Hosp Aide; Office Aide; Cheerleading; Crmnl Law.

DELAY, KATHLEEN; Contoocook Valley Regional HS; Bennington, NH; (Y); 6/162; Drama Clb; French Clb; Service Clb; Soph Cls; Jr Cls; Stu Cncl; Fld Hcky; Elks Awd; High Hon Roll; NHS; Yth Gov Clb Pres; Ithaca Coll.

DELISLE, CHRISTINE; Manchester West HS; Manchester, NH; (Y); Ski Clb; Lit Mag; NH Coll; Accntng.

DELISLE, JENNIFER; Berlin SR HS; Berlin, NH; (Y); Yrbk Stf; Var Bsktbl; Im Coach Actv; Var Sftbl; Hon Roll; 4 Engl Achvt Awds 82; U Of NH; Nrsng.

DEMARS, ALYSSA J; Salem HS; Salem, NH; (S); German Clb; GAA; Key Clb; Ski Clb; Band; Mrchg Band; School Musical; Stage Crew; High Hon Roll; Hon Roll; Silver Mdl Schlrshp 82-83; MVP Fld Hcky 83; Hgh Hnr Roll; Hnr Roll; Culinary Arts.

DEMERITT, EDWARD; Coe-Brown Northwood Acad; Barrington, NH; (Y); 1/49; Church Yth Grp; Capt Math Tm; Trs SADD; Church Choir; Dnfth Awd; Gov Hon Prg Awd; NHS; Val; Boy Scts; St Puals Schl Adv Studies Pgm Adv Frnch 85; Granite Challenge Tm 85; Bentley Coll; Bus Adm.

DEMERS, ABIGAIL; Spaulding HS; Rochester, NH; (S); 56/400; Church Yth Grp; Drama Clb; Pep Clb; Chorus; Church Choir; Swing Chorus; Rep Frsh Cls; Rep Jr Cls; Cheerleading; Pom Pon; Jrnlsm.

DEMERS, KATIE; Manchester Central HS; Manchester, NH; (S); 116/454; DECA.

DEMERS, LISA; Stevens HS; Claremont, NH; (Y); Jazz Band; Madrigals; Orch; Yrbk Bus Mgr; High Hon Roll; Hon Roll; NHS; Church Yth Grp; Cmnty Wkr; Computer Clb; All ST Band 84-86; Yth Orch 84-86; New England Fest Band 85-86; Wellesley; Bio.

DEMERS, MATTHEW J; Memorial HS; Manchester, NH; (Y); #9 In Class; Math Tm; Nwsp Ed-Chief; Nwsp Stf; Yrbk Bus Mgr; Yrbk Stf; Trs Stu Cncl; Var JV Ftbl; High Hon Roll; Hon Roll; VP NHS; Bus Adm.

DEMERS, SUZANNE; Pembroke Acad; Suncook, NH; (S); Church Yth Grp; DECA; French Clb; Nwsp Stf; Yrbk Stf; Off Frsh Cls; Entrepreneurshp DECA 1st Pl In NH 86; Hesser Coll; Bus.

DEMORE, KATIE; Portsmouth SR HS; Portsmouth, NH; (Y); High Hon Roll; Hon Roll; Awd Supr Work French 85-86; Awd Outstndng Achvt Engl 85-86; Literature.

DENIS, DEBBIE; Nashua HS; Nashua, NH; (Y); Church Yth Grp; Political Wkr; School Play; VP Frsh Cls; Var JV Cheerleading; CYO Yth Of Yr 82; Physcl Thrpy.

DEPALO, JENNIFER; Lebanon HS; Lebanon, NH; (Y); 20/200; Church Yth Grp; Spanish Clb; Varsity Clb; Band; Concert Band; Mrchg Band; VP Jr Cls; VP Sr Cls; Hon Roll; Spch Pathlgy.

DEPEW, GLENN C; Monadnock Regional HS; Fitzwilliam, NH; (Y); 3/150; Church Yth Grp; Pres Jr Cls; NHS; Ntl Merit SF; Camper Yr 85; Baptist Bible Coll E; Pastor.

DES MEULES, KATHERINE A; Memorial HS; Manchester, NH; (Y); 5/341; Computer Clb; French Clb; Math Tm; Lit Mag; High Hon Roll; Trs NHS.

DESMOND, KEVIN D; Hopkinton HS; Contoocook, NH; (Y); 18/65; French Clb; German Clb; SADD; Pres Band; Pres Chorus; Yrbk Stf; Pres Stu Cncl; Var Bsktbl; Var Golf; Var Trk; Psychtry.

DESROCHERS, COLETTE R; Presentation Of Mary Acad; Lowell, MA; (Y); 3/34; Church Yth Grp; Sec Drama Clb; Hosp Aide; Pres Science Clb; VP Service Clb; Ski Clb; Yrbk Stf; Pres Soph Cls; Stu Cncl; High Hon Roll; St Pauls Schl Advncd Stys Prgm 85; Hugh O Brian Yth Fndtn 84; Johns Hpkns U; Med.

DESROCHERS, LISA; Trinity HS; Manchester, NH; (Y); 6/160; Trs Church Yth Grp; Capt Math Tm; Color Guard; Yrbk Stf; High Hon Roll; NHS; Ntl Merit Ltr; NEDT Awd; Pres Acad Ftns Awd 86; Worcester Polytech Inst; Cmptr.

DESRUISSEAUX, MICHAEL; Manchester HS West; Manchester, NH; (Y); 31/338; Trs Exploring; 2nd Drftg,Indtl Arts Comptn 84-85; Pres Acadmc Awd, Ftnss Awd Prgm 85-86; RI Sch Of Dsgn; Arch.

DEWEY, BRIT; Phillips Exeter Acad; Greenwich, CT; (S); Key Clb; Acpl Chr; Chorus; Jazz Band; Rep Jr Cls; VP Sr Cls; Var Capt Fld Hcky; Var Capt Lcrss; High Hon Roll; Ntl Merit Ltr; J L Gavit Memrl Cup 85-86; Princeton U; Hstry.

DICKERMAN, KIMBERLEY; Profile Jr SR HS; Littleton, NH; (Y); Pres Church Yth Grp; Band; Chorus; School Musical; Sftbl; Vllybl; High Hon Roll; Hon Roll; NHS; Hnrs Grad; Spring Arbor Coll; Yth Ministry.

DICKOWSKI, WENDY; Profile HS; Bethlehem, NH; (Y); Church Yth Grp; Cmnty Wkr; Drama Clb; French Clb; Girl Scts; Hosp Aide; Chorus; Church Choir; School Musical; School Play; Breadloaf Writers Conf 85; Cert Merit Ntl Frnch Ex 84-85; Med.

DIHARCE, ROBERT; Dover HS; Dover, NH; (Y); Spanish Clb; Var Capt Bsbl; Var Capt Ftbl; Var Trk; Hon Roll; MVP Ftbl 84; Spec Tms Plyr Ftbl 85; All ST Hnrb Mntn Ftbl 85; Bus.

DILLON, JAMES P; Nashua HS; Nashua, NH; (Y); Am Leg Boys St; VICA; Chess Clb; Revernc Lf Awd 85; Wrtr.

DIMASCOLA, MIKE; Lebanon HS; Lebanon, NH; (Y); Church Yth Grp; Latin Clb; Letterman Clb; Spanish Clb; Varsity Clb; Chorus; Nwsp Stf; Rep Jr Cls; Bsktbl; Var Ftbl; Physcl Educ.

DION, LORI A; Pelham HS; Pelham, NH; (Y); 3/128; French Clb; Model UN; Teachers Aide; Yrbk Stf; Var Capt Cheerleading; Coach Actv; JV Var Sftbl; High Hon Roll; Trs NHS; Voice Dem Awd; Phy Ed Awd, Mst Enthustc Chrldng 83; Outstndnt, MVP Chrldr 86; :MIP Sftbll 85; Elem Ed.

DION, THOMAS; Keene HS; Keene, NH; (Y); Am Leg Boys St; Hosp Aide; Var L Bsbl; JV Bsktbl; Coach Actv; Var L Socr; Accntng.

DIONNE, PAUL; Concord HS; Penacook, NH; (Y); 11/390; JV Bsbl; JV Ice Hcky; Im Wt Lftg; High Hon Roll; NHS; Frgn Lang Frnch 84; Outstndng Achvt Alg 84; Frgn Lang 86; Arch Eng.

DOBE, CYNTHIA L; Manchester High Schl West; Manchester, NH; (Y); 6/352; Church Yth Grp; Political Wkr; Yrbk Ed-Chief; Lit Mag; Coach Actv; High Hon Roll; NHS; Ntl Merit SF; Wellsley Book Awd 85; Natl Merit Fndtns Natl Hnr Roll 85; Nthrn N E Jr Sci & Humanities Symposium 85; Engl.

DOBSON, TERESA; Spaulding HS; Barrington, NH; (S); 9/350; Am Leg Aux Girls St; Math Clb; Math Tm; Office Aide; High Hon Roll; Hon Roll; NHS; SEARCH-SMNRS At UNH; Bus Admin.

DODD, BARBRA; Inter-Lakes JR & SR HS; Ctr Sandwich, NH; (Y); Am Leg Aux Girls St; SADD; Band; Chorus; Mrchg Band; School Musical; Yrbk Stf; JV Var Bsktbl; Var Trk; Cit Awd; U Of RI; Poly Sci.

DODDS, ZACHARY; Phillips Exeter Acad; Pittsburgh, PA; (S); Nwsp Stf; Var Crs Cntry; JV Trk; Yale.

DOHERTY, STEPHEN; Keene HS; Westmoreland, NH; (Y); 48/357; Am Leg Boys St; Im Socr; Hon Roll; Ntl Merit Ltr; Pre-Law.

DONAH, CRAIG; Alvirne HS; Hudson, NH; (Y); 54/338; Church Yth Grp; SADD; JV Var Bsbl; JV L Socr; Timer; Hon Roll; U Of Miami; Comp Sci.

DONAVAN, HANNAH; Holderness Schl; Bennington, VT; (Y); 41/77; Camera Clb; Service Clb; Spanish Clb; School Play; Crs Cntry; Lcrss; Socr; Hon Roll; U Of Vermont.

DONESKI, JAMES S; Plymouth Area HS; Plymouth, NH; (Y); Am Leg Boys St; Church Yth Grp; Ski Clb; Variety Show; Var L Bsbl; L Capt Crs Cntry; JV L Ftbl; Hon Roll; St X-Cntry Skiing Champnshps Brnz Mdl 85 & Slvr Mdl 86; Rnr-Up St Champ Bsbl Tm 86; Biol.

DONNELLY, KEVIN; Mascoma Valley Regional HS; Grafton, NH; (Y); 27/108; Boy Scts; Library Aide; Ski Clb; Crs Cntry; Hofstra U; Elec Engr.

DONNELLY, KRISTEN A; Raymond JR SR HS; Raymond, NH; (Y); 4-H; Teachers Aide; VICA; Band; Color Guard; Bsktbl; Cheerleading; Hesser Coll; Bus Mngmnt.

DONOVAN, HEATHER LYNN; Londonderry HS; Londonderry, NH; (Y); Model UN; Pres Frsh Cls; Rep Soph Cls; Pres Sr Cls; Stu Cncl; Var Cheerleading; Stat Lcrss; SADD; Lit Mag; Ntl Ldrshp Trng Ctr; NH Acad Of Dnc Jzz Awd; Stu Cncl Schlrshp; U Of NH; Psychlgy.

DONOVAN, KATHY; Dover HS; Dover, NH; (Y); High Hon Roll; Hon Roll; Jr NHS; Picture Of Christa Mcauliffe Pblshd 86; Dsgnd Cvr For The Swain Schl Of Dsgn Advrtsng Guide 85; Artist.

DOPP, CHERYL; Spaulding HS; E Rochester, NH; (Y); 100/400; Dance Clb; Drama Clb; Key Clb; Ski Clb; Hon Roll; UNH; Chld Psych.

DORR, BRENDA; Stevens HS; Claremont, NH; (Y); Church Yth Grp; Drm & Bgl; Yrbk Stf; Var Stu Cncl; High Hon Roll; Hon Roll; Phrmcy.

DORSCH, ANNA; Pembroke Acad; Allenstown, NH; (Y); 20/200; Latin Clb; Var Pres Spanish Clb; Var L Bsktbl; Hon Roll; Secndry Educ.

DOUBEK, GREG J; Winnacunnet HS; Hampton, NH; (Y); 7/300; Cmnty Wkr; Quiz Bowl; Lit Mag; Var Socr; JV Var Trk; High Hon Roll; NHS; Ntl Merit Ltr; Proj Srch Sem Adv Stu; Cretv Wrtng Wrkshp.

DOWNS, NANCY JO; Nute HS; Milton, NH; (S); 6/35; French Clb; Var Bsktbl; JV Sftbl; JV Var Vllybl; Hon Roll; Prfct Atten Awd; US Natl Math Awd; US Natl Merit Awd.

DRESCHER, LISA; Mt St Mary Seminary; Nashua, NH; (Y); 14/77; Am Leg Aux Girls St; Spanish Clb; SADD; Lit Mag; Var Socr; Hon Roll; De Paul Schlrshp 85-86.

DRUKE, JENNIFER; Bishop Brady HS; Concord, NH; (Y); JV Bsktbl; JV Fld Hcky; High Hon Roll; Hon Roll; Sci.

DU BOIS, CAROLINE ANNE; Trinity HS; Bedford, NH; (Y); 8/185; Am Leg Aux Girls St; Model UN; Ski Clb; Pres Stu Cncl; Capt JV Socr; Trk; High Hon Roll; Hon Roll; Jr NHS; NHS; Frnch Awd 83; Stu Cncnl Awd 86; Hgh Obrn 85; Med.

DU BOIS, SARA; Laconia HS; Laconia, NH; (Y); Band; Concert Band; Mrchg Band; Pep Band; Swmmng; Hon Roll; Bus.

DU MONT, SUSAN; Salem HS; Salem, NH; (Y); Teachers Aide; Band; Lit Mag; JV Var Fld Hcky; Stat Ftbl; Mgr(s); JV Sftbl; JV Trk; Hon Roll; Keene ST Coll; Physcl Ed.

DUBE, MICHAEL D; Kearsarge Regional HS; Contoocook, NH; (Y); 12/120; Am Leg Boys St; Chess Clb; Model UN; Hon Roll; NHS; Ntl Merit SF; Pres Schlr; NH Acad Decthln; U Of ME Farmington; Wrtg.

DUBE, STEPHEN; Berlin HS; Berlin, NH; (Y); 32/201; SADD; Var Socr; Var Trk; Jr NHS; Engrng.

DUBOIS, JOHN A; Spaulding HS; Rochester, NH; (S); 66/385; Var Ftbl; Engrng.

DUBREUIL, JAMES L; Somersworth HS; Somersworth, NH; (Y); 22/190; Am Leg Boys St; Cmnty Wkr; DECA; JCL; Keywanettes; Ski Clb; Crs Cntry; Trk; Hon Roll; Ranatra Fusca Creativity Awd-OM Assoc 86; 2nd Pl Awd OM 85-86; UNH; Bus Adm.

DUCHARME, JIM; Dover HS; Dover, NH; (Y); Aud/Vis; Computer Clb; Hon Roll; Contntl Math Lge 86; Rochester Inst Of Tech; Comp Pr.

DUCHARME, LORI; Newport HS; Newport, NH; (Y); French Clb; Math Tm; School Musical; Sec Soph Cls; Stu Cncl; Bsktbl; Fld Hcky; Sftbl; Hon Roll; Fds & Nutrtn.

DUFF, PAULA; Concord HS; Concord, NH; (Y); 36/345; Drama Clb; Sec Chorus; Yrbk Bus Mgr; High Hon Roll; Hon Roll; Chrmn NHS; Pres Schlr; French Clb; School Musical; School Play; Antrim Schlrshp P86; TNT 86; Challenge Schlrshp 86; Keene ST Coll; Dietetics.

DUFFY, MAURA; Alvirne HS; Litchfield, NH; (Y); 60/338; Var Crs Cntry; Var Trk; Hon Roll; MVP Crss Cntry; Bus Mgmnt.

DUFORD, SHERYL; Winnisquam Regional HS; Sanbornton, NH; (Y); 4/90; Sec French Clb; Math Clb; Pres Jr Cls; Pres Sr Cls; Rep Stu Cncl; Hon Roll; Dennis R Huckins Mem Schlrp; Frnch Clb Awd; Robert H & Gertrude E Sedgley Charitbl Fndtn Awd; U NH; Comp Sci.

DUFOUR, NICOLE; Milford Area SR HS; Amherst, NH; (Y); 33/311; Yrbk Phtg; Mgr Trk; Hon Roll; NHS; Exclince Spn 86; Challange Pgm 84-85; Simons Rock Bard Coll Summr Study Scholar; Rutgers Coll; Spn.

DUFOUR, PETER R; Nashua HS; Nashua, NH; (Y); 80/900; Am Leg Boys St; Band; Var L Bsbl; JV L Bsktbl; Hon Roll; Jr NHS; Naval Acad Annapolis; Aviation.

DUHAIME, GARY; Memorial HS; Manchester, NH; (Y); Rep Stu Cncl; Var Socr; Crsdr Awd Otstndng 85; Prnt Tchr Bstr Clbschlrshp 86; Wentworth Inst Tech; Cmptr Engr.

DUMAS, REBECCA LEE; Mt St Mary Seminary HS; Hudson, NH; (Y); 1/74; Ed Lit Mag; Var Bsktbl; Var Socr; Var Sftbl; Bausch & Lomb Sci Awd; CC Awd; High Hon Roll; Lion Awd; NHS; Val; Rensselaer Mdl 85; Sci Fair Wnnr 84; Gov Schlr 86; MA Inst Tech; Chem Engrng.

DUNBAR, WENDY; Milford Area SR HS; Amherst, NH; (Y); 60/311; FBLA; SADD; Rep Jr Cls; Im Powder Puff Ftbl; Im Vllybl; Hon Roll; ST Ofcr Intl Ordr Rnbw For Grls 86-87; Dir Of Chrch JR Bell Choir 82-83; Bentley Coll; Bus Mngmnt.

DUNHAM, KATHY; Berlin SR HS; Berlin, NH; (Y); Church Yth Grp; 4-H; Band; Concert Band; Pep Band; Stage Crew; Im Vllybl; 4-H Awd; Hon Roll; Physcl Thrpy.

DUNLAP, JULIE; Pembroke Acad; Chichester, NH; (Y); 6/180; Church Yth Grp; SADD; High Hon Roll; Hon Roll; Prfct Atten Awd; Mngmnt.

DUNLOP, SCOTT; Winnisquam Regional HS; Tilton, NH; (Y); Church Yth Grp; Capt Var Bsbl; Var Bsktbl; Im Ftbl; Mgr(s); Var Score Keeper; Capt Var Socr; Im Tennis; Im Vllybl; Im Wt Lftg.

DUNNE, JOHN; Pittsfield HS; Pittsfield, NH; (Y); 2/76; Drama Clb; French Clb; Capt Quiz Bowl; Pres Varsity Clb; Var L Bsbl; Var L Bsktbl; Var L Socr; DAR Awd; High Hon Roll; NHS; 4 Yr NROTC Schlrshp 85-86; U S Armys Dstngshd Schlr Athlt 86; St Pauls Advncd Stds Pgm-Bio 85; Rnsslr Poly Inst; Arntcl Engrng.

DUPUIS, MARC; Berlin HS; Berlin, NH; (Y); 6/225; Band; Concert Band; Jazz Band; Mrchg Band; Pep Band; School Musical; Yrbk Phtg; Hon Roll; Jr NHS; NHS; Phrmcy.

DUPUIS, PAMELA; Spaulding HS; Rochester, NH; (S); 18/356; FBLA; Band; Chorus; Concert Band; Mrchg Band; Rep Jr Cls; Rep Sr Cls; Hon Roll; Drm & Bgl; Jazz Band; HOBY Fndtn Ambass 84; NH All ST Bnd 84.

DURAND, COLLEEN; Winnisquam Regional HS; Tilton, NH; (Y); French Clb; Hosp Aide; Math Clb; High Hon Roll; Hon Roll; Concord Hosp Schl Nrsng; RN.

DUSSAULT, ALFRED; Alvirne HS; Hudson, NH; (Y); Chess Clb; Science Clb; SADD; Yrbk Phtg; Hon Roll; Culinary Inst Amer; Master Chef.

DUTTON, AMY S; Alvirne HS; Hudson, NH; (Y); SADD; JV Var Bsktbl; Var Crs Cntry; Im Ftbl; JV Var Socr; JV Var Sftbl; Im Tennis; Im Vllybl; Im Wt Lftg; Hon Roll; Phy Ed.

DWYER, DAVID; Memorial HS; Manchester, NH; (Y); 122/350; VICA; Nwsp Rptr; Trk; Hon Roll; Plcmns Wives Schlrshp 86; UNH.

DYER, CYNTHIA; Keene HS; Keene, NH; (Y); 26/354; Pres VP Church Yth Grp; Drama Clb; JA; Hon Roll; NHS; Accntng.

EAMES, ELIZABETH; Berlin SR HS; Errol, NH; (Y); 13/220; Am Leg Aux Girls St; Cmnty Wkr; French Clb; PAVAS; Chorus; JV Capt Bsktbl; Score Keeper; Tennis; NHS.

EASTMAN, TIM; Berlin HS; Berlin, NH; (Y); 80/191; Boy Scts; SADD; Im Bsbl; Var Tennis; NHS; BVCES Proj Engr 85-86; Drftg.

EATON, PERRY; Concord Christian HS; Pittsfield, NH; (S); Boy Scts; Chess Clb; Computer Clb; Chorus; School Play; Capt Jr Cls; Bsktbl; Crs Cntry; Socr; Outstndg Chrstn Char Awd 86; Mighty In Spirit Awd 86.

EDMOND, LAURIE; Pembroke Acad; Concord, NH; (Y); 5/180; Rep Stu Cncl; Var Cheerleading; Var Crs Cntry; Co-Capt Trk; Im Vllybl; High Hon Roll; Hon Roll; Rotary Awd; Advrtsng.

EDWARDS, ANTHONY DOUGLAS; Londonderry HS; Londonderry, NH; (Y); Boy Scts; CAP; Debate Tm; Math Tm; Band; Socr; Hon Roll; Ntl Merit Ltr; Carl C Conway Schlrp 86-90; Century III Ldrs Prog Schl Wnr 86; U NH; Math.

EDWARDS, MARK J; Merrimack Valley HS; Andover, NH; (Y); Am Leg Boys St; Ski Clb; Var L Bsbl; High Hon Roll; Hon Roll; Mdcl.

EGLINTON, KENNETH; Milford Area SR HS; Amherst, NH; (Y); 17/309; Am Leg Boys St; Church Yth Grp; Pres Band; Concert Band; Jazz Band; Mrchg Band; School Musical; JP Sousa Awd; NHS; Pres Acad Fit Awd 85-86; Colby Coll.

EGNER, PENNY; Mascoma Valley Regional HS; Enfield, NH; (Y); French Clb; SADD; Hon Roll; Hm Econ Awd 85; Bus Ed Awd 86; Real Estate Schl; Real Est.

EHRENS, J SCOTT; Phillips Exeter Acad; Wilmington, DE; (Y); Art Clb; Aud/Vis; Drama Clb; English Clb; PAVAS; Radio Clb; School Play; Lit Mag; Im Bsbl; Im Tennis; Stu Dir Schl Ply 85; 1st Pl Acclrtd Fr 84; Harvard; Film Dir.

ELLIOT, SCOTT; High Mowing Schl; Gt Barrington, MA; (Y); Drama Clb; Acpl Chr; Chorus; Orch; School Musical; Swing Chorus; Yrbk Stf; Pres Jr Cls; Pres Sr Cls; Capt Cheerleading; Hgh Acad & Extra Crcclr Hons 85-86; Bard Coll; Drama.

ELLIOTT, DANIEL; Littleton HS; Littleton, NH; (S); 40/100; Trs Sec DECA; Drama Clb; School Play; JV Var Bsbl; JV Var Bsktbl; Var Score Keeper; Hon Roll; 3rd Pl ST DECA Conf 84; 2nd Pl ST DECA Conf 86; Natl DECA Conv Atlanta 86; Plymouth ST Coll; Acctg.

ELLIS, BRIAN; Spaulding HS; Rochester, NH; (S); 56/398; Cmnty Wkr; Ftbl; Socr; High Hon Roll; Hon Roll; NHS.

ELMAN, MARK; Hanover HS; Hanover, NH; (Y); French Clb; Latin Clb; Yrbk Phtg; JV Ice Hcky; JV Socr; Var Capt Tennis; High Hon Roll; Hon Roll; Econ.

EMOND, DAWN MARIE; Alvirne HS; Hudson, NH; (Y); 2/334; Cmnty Wkr; Lit Mag; Stu Cncl; High Hon Roll; NHS; Ntl Merit Ltr; Sal; St Joseph Aux Schlrshp 86; Mrch Dimes Schlrshp 86; Gvrnr Schlr 86; Tufts U; Bio.

ENMAN, DOREEN; Spaulding HS; Rochester, NH; (Y); 153/400; Church Yth Grp; Yrbk Ed-Chief; Yrbk Stf; Trs Frsh Cls; Coach Actv; Wilfred Acad; Cosmotology.

ENNIS, CHRIS; Belmont HS; Canterbury, NH; (Y); 15/67; Boy Scts; Teachers Aide; Varsity Clb; Camp Fr Inc; Yrbk Phtg; Rep Stu Cncl; JV Var Bsktbl; Capt Var Socr; Hon Roll; NHS; Bus.

ENO III, PAUL; Saint Thomas Aquinas HS; Exeter, NH; (Y); Key Clb; Latin Clb; Spanish Clb; Yrbk Phtg; Yrbk Stf; Frsh Cls; Soph Cls; Stu Cncl; Ftbl; Ice Hcky.

ENRIGHT, JOHN; Saint Thomas Aquinas HS; Rochester, NH; (Y); Am Leg Boys St; Debate Tm; Drama Clb; Key Clb; Quiz Bowl; Speech Tm; Stu Cncl; JV Bsktbl; Var Crs Cntry.

ERICSON, SUSAN K; New Hampton Schl; Laconia, NH; (Y); 1/115; French Clb; Math Tm; Yrbk Stf; Sec Jr Cls; Fld Hcky; Tennis; Vllybl; High Hon Roll; NHS; Ntl Merit SF; Charles E Merill Publ Awd Worcester Regl Sci Fair 83; Indstrl Awd Worcester Regnl Sci Fair 84.

ERLANSON, AMANDA; Stevens HS; Claremont, NH; (Y); Key Clb; Pres SADD; Acpl Chr; Chorus; Nwsp Stf; Yrbk Stf; High Hon Roll; NHS; St Pauls Schl Adv Studies Pgm 86.

ESPELIN, CHRIS; Bishop Guertin HS; Nashua, NH; (Y); 20/150; Chess Clb; Off French Clb; Im Bsktbl; JV L Socr; High Hon Roll; NHS; Ntl Ed Dev Test Awd 84; Hnr Rl Awds 84-86; Ntl Hnr Soc Svc Awd 86; Pre-Med.

ESTES, KIM; Dover HS; Dover, NH; (Y); 4-H; 4-H Awd; High Hon Roll; Hon Roll; U Of NH; Marine Bio.

ESTES, SALLY; Pembroke Acad; Suncook, NH; (Y); 35/188; Cmnty Wkr; French Clb; FBLA; FHA; Office Aide; Ski Clb; Yrbk Ed-Chief; Yrbk Phtg; Yrbk Sprt Ed; Yrbk Stf; 50 Hrs Vlntr Wrk Concord Hosp 84; Brdcstng.

ESTEY, MICHELE; Mascoma Valley Regional HS; Enfield, NH; (Y); Art Clb; Lit Mag; Undrgrd HS Art Awd 85; Undrgrd HS Art Awd 86; Fine Arts.

EVANS, MICHAEL; Manchester Central HS; Manchester, NH; (Y); 10/460; Nwsp Sprt Ed; Pres Frsh Cls; Var Capt Bsktbl; Socr; Trk; High Hon Roll; NHS; Exploring; Rep Stu Cncl; Ntl Merit Ltr; Concours De Francais Des Cooperants 84; Amer HS Math Exam Schl Wnr & ST Hnr Rl; All-ST Sccr Slctn.

FAIRMAN, HELEN A; St Pauls Schl; Locust Valley, NY; (Y); Pres French Clb; Hosp Aide; Chorus; School Musical; Im Fld Hcky; JV Tennis; Hon Roll; Ntl Merit SF; Engl.

FALK, TATIANA P; Phillips Exeter Acad; Okemos, MI; (Y); Art Clb; Cmnty Wkr; Drama Clb; Chorus; School Musical; Stage Crew; Var JV Mgr(s); Ntl Merit SF; Pres Schlr; School Play; Hnrs Calculus Crs 84-86; Hns Frnch Crs 83-85; 3rd Prz 1st Yr Frnch 83; Englsh.

FARR, ROCHELLE; Woodsville HS; Monroe, NH; (Y); 14/75; Church Yth Grp; Cmnty Wkr; 4-H; Church Choir; Yrbk Stf; Sec Sr Cls; Capt Var Bsktbl; Dnfth Awd; Hon Roll; NHS; Frshmn Crnvl Qn 82; Alg Awd 82; Typg Awd 83; MVP Bsktbll Awd 84-86; Bentley Coll; Comp Info Systms.

FARRINGTON, DAVID; David Farrington HS; Berlin, NH; (Y); SADD; Band; Bsktbl; Socr; Comp Drftng.

FAULHABER, SHERRY; Spaulding HS; Rochester, NH; (Y); 54/385; Church Yth Grp; FNA; Red Cross Aide; JV Bsktbl; JV Trk; Hon Roll; Shana Bennett Mem Schlrp 86; U NH; Nrsng.

FAVREAU, PETER; Memorial HS; Manchester, NH; (Y); 48/341; French Clb; Stage Crew; Variety Show; Yrbk Stf; Var Ftbl; Var Ice Hcky; Var Capt Socr; Var Trk; Wt Lftg; Hon Roll.

FECTEAU, RICHARD J; Franklin JR SR HS; Franklin, NH; (Y); 5/90; Boy Scts; Church Yth Grp; Var Trk; Hon Roll; NHS; Pres Schlr; Tessier Schlrshp 86; Dllrs For Schlrs 86; NH Tech Inst; Elctrnc Engr.

FELCH, LEISA; Manchester Central HS; Hooksett, NH; (Y); 106/430; Church Yth Grp; FBLA; GAA; High Hon Roll; Hon Roll; Bus.

FELGATE, ALAN; Profile JR SR HS; Littleton, NH; (Y); 2/42; Church Yth Grp; French Clb; Math Tm; Quiz Bowl; Chorus; Stage Crew; Yrbk Phtg; VP Stu Cncl; Socr; Pres NHS.

FELTON, DAVID; Kimball Union Acad; Killington, VT; (Y); Cmnty Wkr; Ski Clb; Yrbk Phtg; Var L Lcrss; Var L Socr; Hon Roll; Alpine Skiing Vrsty Ltr 84-86; Engrng.

FENTON, CHRISTINE; St Thomas Aquinas HS; Dover, NH; (Y); Church Yth Grp; Cmnty Wkr; Girl Scts; Key Clb; Latin Clb; Church Choir; Yrbk Phtg; Rep Jr Cls; Stu Cncl; Hon Roll; Pres Girl Scout Troop 1109 3 Yrs 84-86; ; Rlgs Awdd & Flk Grp Awd 85; Engl, Latin, Rlgs Awds 86; U Of NH; Engl.

FERLAND, KEVIN K; Plymouth Area HS; Plymouth, NH; (Y); 3/150; Am Leg Boys St; Math Tm; JV Bsbl; Var Crs Cntry; Var Tennis; High Hon Roll; NHS; Prfct Atten Awd; Outstndg Achvt Awds Adv Math, Chem, Frnch, Alg II, Bio, Geom & Erth Sci 84-86; Math.

FERNS, TERRENCE; Concord HS; Concord, NH; (Y); 17/379; Math Tm; Varsity Clb; Crs Cntry; Socr; Trk; High Hon Roll; NHS; Ntl Merit Ltr; MIT; Aeronaut Engrng.

FICKETT, ANDREW R; Kennett HS; Conway, NH; (Y); 27/200; Band; JV Bsbl; Var Bsktbl; JV Ftbl; Hon Roll; U NH; Engrng.

FIELD, KEN A; Pinkerton Academy; Windham, NH; (Y); 81/500; Latin Clb; Ski Clb; JV Crs Cntry; JV Trk; Hon Roll; NHS; Latin Club Schlrshp 86; Med Schl.

FILIPPINI, ANGELA; Nashua HS; Portsmouth, RI; (Y); 140/765; Am Leg Aux Girls St; Flag Corp; Orch; Hon Roll; Riflery 84-85; Northeastern U; Elec Engr.

FILLIO, CHRISTOPHER P; Exeter Area HS; East Kingston, NH; (Y); 3/300; Am Leg Boys St; Ed Ski Clb; Ed Band; Ed Chorus; Ed Concert Band; Ed Mrchg Band; Ed Nwsp Stf; Ed Yrbk Stf; Sec Jr Cls; Rep Stu Cncl; Governrs Schlr 86; Frnch Awd 84; 1920 Cp 86; Notre Dame; Comp Sci.

FILLION, JOE; Franklin HS; Franklin, NH; (Y); 30/90; Band; Jazz Band; Mrchg Band; Pep Band; Yrbk Sprt Ed; Rep Sr Cls; Var JV Bsbl; Im Golf; Im Ice Hcky; Hon Roll; Vocational Educ Awd 86; Elks Yth Govt Awd 86; De Vry Inst Columbus; Electrncs.

FINAN, KATHLEEN M; Portsmouth HS; Portsmouth, NH; (Y); 80/459; Drama Clb; School Musical; School Play; Stage Crew; Yrbk Stf; JV Sftbl; Hon Roll; U Of NH; Comp Sci.

FISHER, MICHAEL; Kingswood Regional HS; Ossipee, NH; (Y); 29/136; Boy Scts; Church Yth Grp; Yrbk Stf; JV Ftbl; Var Capt Trk; JV Var Wt Lftg; Hon Roll; Awd Eagl Sct Rnk 83; Natl Eagl Sct Assoc 84; Engrg.

FLANDERS, CHARLES; Inter Lakes HS; Hollis, NH; (Y); 17/58; Art Clb; Boy Scts; Church Yth Grp; Library Aide; Varsity Clb; Im Bsbl; Im Bsktbl; Var Socr; Var Trk; Hon Roll; UNH; Hist.

FLANIGAN, DANIEL; Pinkerton Acad; Derry, NH; (Y); Variety Show; Var Crs Cntry; Var Trk; High Hon Roll; Hon Roll; Varsity Clb; New Englnd Cncl Yth Rep 86-87; Diocesan Yth Ofcr 85-87; MIT; Chem Engr.

FLEMING, ELIZABETH ANNE; Phillips Exeter Acad; Spartanburg, SC; (S); Ski Clb; Pres Frsh Cls; Pres Sr Cls; L Crs Cntry; L Trk; High Hon Roll; NHS; Harvard.

FLEMING, ELLEN; Timberlane Regional HS; Atkinson, NH; (Y); Spanish Clb; Yrbk Stf; Sec Jr Cls; Off Sr Cls; Fld Hcky; Trk; Vllybl; Hon Roll; Spanish NHS; Bus Mgmt.

FLYNN, ROBERT; Spaulding HS; Barrington, NH; (S); 5/340; Aud/Vis; Sec Drama Clb; Key Clb; ROTC; School Musical; Yrbk Stf; High Hon Roll; NHS; Church Yth Grp; School Play; St Pauls Adv Stds Prog 85; Flmmkr.

FOISIE, ELLEN; Pelham HS; Pelham, NH; (Y); 4/120; Yrbk Stf; Rep Frsh Cls; Rep Stu Cncl; Var Bsktbl; Var Fld Hcky; JV Sftbl; High Hon Roll; Hon Roll; Pres NHS; Voice Dem Awd; Dartmth Bk Clb Awd; Gd Sprt Essy Cntst; Physcl Therpy.

FOLEY, PATRICK E; Keene HS; Keene, NH; (Y); Am Leg Boys St; Church Yth Grp; Latin Clb; Political Wkr; Pres Soph Cls; JV Socr; Trk; Hon Roll; Ntl Merit SF; Attnd Natl Stu Cncl Cnvntn 84; Sccr Co-Capt 83.

FOLEY, PATRICK R; Mascana Valley Regional HS; Enfield, NH; (Y); 1/101; Boys Clb Am; Church Yth Grp; French Clb; Math Clb; Band; Stu Cncl; Mgr Var Socr; Gov Hon Prg Awd; NHS; Val; Math Tm Partcpnt 85; Outstnding Math 85; Drew U.

FOLLUM, ELIZABETH; Spaulding HS; Rochester, NH; (S); #16 In Class; Pres Church Yth Grp; Cmnty Wkr; Key Clb; Latin Clb; Office Aide; Speech Tm; Thesps; Chorus; Church Choir; School Musical; Comm.

FORD, KATHARINE S; Phllips Exeter Acad; Durham, NH; (Y); English Clb; Library Aide; Nwsp Stf; Lit Mag; High Hon Roll; Ntl Merit SF; Schl Hstry Przs 83-85; Seventeen Fctn Cntst Hnrb Mntn 85; Schl Engl Awd 84; Hstry.

FORDE, MARK; Dover HS; Dover, NH; (Y); Pres FFA; L Crs Cntry; L Ftbl; L Trk; Hon Roll; Star ST Agribusnsmn Awd 86; Friends Of Ag Schlrshp 86; Cobleskill Ag; Anml Hsbndry.

FORSYTHE, DAVID; Phillips Exeter Acad; Charleston, SC; (Y); Off Sr Cls; Var Crs Cntry; JV Var Trk; Hon Roll; Schl High Jump Rcd 84; Hall Of Fame Times High Jmp, Hurdles & High Hurdles 86; MVP Trck 85-86; Georgetown U; Pre Med.

FORTE, RACHELLE; Salem HS; Salem, NH; (Y); 19/300; French Clb; Key Clb; Latin Clb; Cheerleading; Coach Actv; Mgr Ftbl; Mgr(s); Sftbl; High Hon Roll; Hon Roll; Hnrs Awds Frnch I, II, III; Awd Latin I; Mss Cngnalty; U NH; Htl Admn.

FORTIER, CHRIS; Nashua SR HS; Nashua, NH; (Y); AFS; Aud/Vis; Drama Clb; Thesps; Church Choir; School Play; Hon Roll; Jr NHS; Spanish NHS; Berklee Schl Of Music.

FORTIER, DEIRDRE A; Alton Central HS; Laconia, NH; (S); VP Trs Leo Clb; Band; School Musical; School Play; Stage Crew; Nwsp Rptr; Yrbk Stf; Trs Rep Stu Cncl; JV Bsktbl; Hon Roll; Med.

FORTIER, JACKIE; Berlin HS; Berlin, NH; (Y); Girl Scts; VICA; Cnstnl Quiz Awd 83; Mdcl Termnlgy Awd 86; NHVTC Claremont; Phy Thrpy.

FORTIN, JANINE; Berlin HS; Berlin, NH; (Y); 3/225; SADD; Band; Concert Band; Mrchg Band; Pep Band; Hon Roll; Jr NHS; NHS; Coll; Nrsng.

FORTIN, JENNIFER; Belmont HS; Belmont, NH; (S); 7/67; Drama Clb; Sec Speech Tm; Varsity Clb; Yrbk Ed-Chief; Trs Rep Stu Cncl; Stat Bsktbl; Stat Vllybl; Sec NHS; Sec Debate Tm; School Musical; Hugh O Brien Yth Ambssdr 85; Astra Clb 85-86; Educ.

FORTIN, LISA; Berlin HS; Berlin, NH; (Y); 15/212; Cmnty Wkr; Computer Clb; FBLA; FHA; GAA; Hosp Aide; OEA; Red Cross Aide; SADD; VICA; Berlin Vo-Tech Schl; Secy.

FORTUNE, SARAH M; Phillips Exeter Acad; Lexington, KY; (Y); Orch; School Play; High Hon Roll.

FORWARD, DEBBIE; Hanover HS; Hanover, NH; (S); 106/159; Sec DECA; Chorus; Var Stat Fld Hcky; Mgr(s); Score Keeper; Var Stat Sftbl; Timer; High Hon Roll; Hon Roll; 3rd Pl & 1st Pl Awds Finc & Credt VT ST DECA Conv 85-86; HAVC Outstndng Stdnt Awd 85-86; Johnson & Wales Coll; Mktg.

FOSTER, KELLY J; A Crosby Kennett HS; Fryeburg, ME; (Y); 2/200; VP Pres Church Yth Grp; Pres French Clb; Rep Jr Cls; French Hon Soc; Gov Hon Prg Awd; High Hon Roll; NHS; Pres Schlr; Sal; Frnch Awd 84-86; Middlebury Coll; Frnch.

FOURNIER, NICOLE; Spaulding HS; Barrington, NH; (Y); 17/388; Drama Clb; PAVAS; Acpl Chr; Chorus; Church Choir; Madrigals; School Play; Variety Show; High Hon Roll; Hon Roll; Rchstr Amrcn Rvltn Bicntnl Schlrshp 86; Arts Rchstr Schlrshp Music 86; UNH; Music.

FOX, KATHERINE W; Phillips Exeter Acad; Greenwich, CT; (Y); Debate Tm; School Musical; School Play; Stu Cncl; Var Fld Hcky; Var Lcrss; High Hon Roll; Ntl Merit SF; Awd Excllnc In Chinese/Japanese Hist; Awd Excllnc In Russian Hist; Polit Sci.

FRAIN, TAMMY LYNN; Trinity HS; Bedford, NH; (Y); Am Leg Aux Girls St; Model UN; Rep Stu Cncl; Var L Bsktbl; Var Capt Socr; Var L Sftbl; High Hon Roll; Hon Roll; NHS; Bus Adm.

FRANCOIS, ANDRE A; Phillips Exeter Acad; Brooklyn, NY; (Y); Acpl Chr; Var Ftbl; JV Trk; High Hon Roll; Hon Roll; Ntl Merit SF; Elec Engrng.

FRANK, KARL THOMAS; The Tilton Schl; Laconia, NH; (S); 15/69; SADD; Stage Crew; Rep Frsh Cls; Rep Soph Cls; JV Lcrss; JV Socr; Wt Lftg; High Hon Roll; Hon Roll; NEDT Awd; Acadmc Commtt; Gold Key Club; Ski Tm-JV & Vrsty; Marine Bio.

FRANK, MAXWELL; Hanover HS; Stafford, VT; (Y); German Clb; Chorus; School Play; Pres Yrbk Phtg; Im Bsktbl; Im Crs Cntry; JV Trk; Hon Roll.

FRECHETTE, ANN; Merrimack HS; Merrimack, NH; (Y); 2/218; Band; School Musical; Nwsp Rptr; Yrbk Ed-Chief; Var L Bsktbl; Var Capt Fld Hcky; Var L Trk; Rptr NHS; Sal; Office Aide; St Pauls Advncd Stud Prgm; Prgm Comm; Invstgtv Jrnlsm.

FREDE, MICHAEL A; Contoocook Valley Regional HS; Peterborough, NH; (Y); Am Leg Boys St; Drama Clb; Chorus; Socr; Hon Roll; Prfct Atten Awd.

FREDERICK, AARON; Alvine HS; Hudson, NH; (Y); 5/340; Am Leg Boys St; Boy Scts; Concert Band; Jazz Band; Pep Band; Trs Sr Cls; High Hon Roll; Hon Roll; Pres NHS; SAR Awd; Rivier Coll Challenge Pgm 84-85; Pre-Med.

FREESE, CHRIS; Manchester Memorial HS; Manchester, NH; (Y); 38/341; Teachers Aide; Powder Puff Ftbl; Hon Roll; Rensselaer Plythch; Elec Engr.

FREYENHOGEN, LORI; Thoyer HS; Winchester, NH; (Y); 2/33; VP Sr Cls; Var Capt Fld Hcky; Hon Roll; NHS; Sal; Church Yth Grp; Temple Yth Grp; Sec Frsh Cls; VP Jr Cls; Capt Var Bsktbl; Accntng Awd 86; Keene ST Coll; Erly Chldhd Ed.

FRIEDMAN, RENEE; Pelham HS; Pelham, NH; (Y); 10/130; AFS; Drama Clb; French Clb; Chorus; School Musical; Stage Crew; Rep Soph Cls; JV Fld Hcky; Hon Roll; NHS; Frnch II Awd 83-84; Frnch III Awd 84-85; Cmnctns.

FRITSCH, CHRISTINE; Salem HS; Salem, NH; (S); Model UN; High Hon Roll; German Clb; Ski Clb; School Play; Hon Roll; Germn Awd 83 & 84; Roger Williams Coll; Refuge Mgr.

FRIZZELL, DEBBIE; Fall Mt Regional HS; Charlestown, NH; (Y); 9/120; Spanish Clb; Band; Mrchg Band; Trs Jr Cls; VP Sr Cls; Capt Cheerleading; Trk; Elks Awd; High Hon Roll; Hon Roll; Jr Clss Awd Certfct 86; Amrcn Lit Awd Certfct 86; Chem Awd Certfct 86; Elem Ed.

FROST, KELLEY; Spaulding HS; Rochester, NH; (S); 6/392; Am Leg Aux Girls St; Key Clb; Rep Jr Cls; Rep Sr Cls; High Hon Roll; Hon Roll; NHS; 1st Pl ST Chmpn Mass II Gymnstcs 84 & 85; Gymnstcs Coachng Assist; Physcl Thrpst.

FROST, MICHEAL; Memorial HS; Manchester, NH; (Y); 5/344; Boy Scts; Ice Hcky; Bausch & Lomb Sci Awd; High Hon Roll; NHS; Clinton Scovell Awd 86; St Michaels Coll; Chem.

FRYER, JO ANN L; Pembroke Acad; Concord, NH; (Y); 5/165; Church Yth Grp; Drama Clb; French Clb; Sec FBLA; School Play; Var Fld Hcky; High Hon Roll; NHS; Balfour Awd 86; Arch.

FRYER, VIRGINIA; Pembroke Acad; Concord, NH; (Y); 6/165; Church Yth Grp; Drama Clb; Pres FBLA; JV Var Fld Hcky; High Hon Roll; NHS; Bus Admn.

FUCHSLOCHER, ANITA; Fall Mountain Regional HS; Charlestown, NH; (Y); 4/150; Am Leg Aux Girls St; Hosp Aide; Spanish Clb; Band; Chorus; Madrigals; Rep Stu Cncl; Var Capt Cheerleading; High Hon Roll; NHS; SF Congress Bundestag Yth Exch 85-86; Proj Excel 84-85; Wellsleys Book Awd Lit 86; Pre-Med.

FULLER, AMEY JORDAN; Oyster River HS; Durham, NH; (Y); 16/150; Drama Clb; Band; Chorus; School Musical; High Hon Roll; JP Sousa Awd; Ntl Merit Ltr; SADD; Orch; Pep Band; All ST Chrs; Schltc Hnr Soc; ORHS Chambr Sngrs; Plymouth ST Clg; Musc Mgmt.

FULLER, THARA M; Phillips Exeter Acad; Aurora, IL; (Y); English Clb; Sec Latin Clb; Chorus; School Musical; School Play; High Hon Roll; Ntl Merit Ltr; IL ST Schlr 86; Prfrmr, Chrgrphr Danc Cncrt 84-86; Haig-Ramage Clsscs Awd Wnnr 86; Engl.

FURLONG, SIGNE; Tilton Prep Schl; Brookline, MA; (Y); 6/70; Art Clb; Cmnty Wkr; School Play; Nwsp Rptr; Yrbk Stf; Lit Mag; Var Bsktbl; JV Socr; Hon Roll; Drama Clb; Proctor Dormitory 86; Pre-Med.

GAFFNEY, BRENDA; Weare HS; Weare, NH; (S); 1/48; VP Drama Clb; School Musical; School Play; Ed Nwsp Ed-Chief; Pres Stu Cncl; Bsktbl; Trk; Vllybl; High Hon Roll; VP NHS.

GAGNE, CHRISTINE; Salem HS; Salem, NH; (S); Cmnty Wkr; French Clb; VP FBLA; Model UN; Ski Clb; Capt Color Guard; School Play; Yrbk Stf; JV Trk; Hon Roll; U NH; Bus Adm.

GAGNE, LISA; Spaulding HS; Rochester, NH; (S); 61/397; Vllybl; Hon Roll; Med.

GAGNE, SYLVIE JEANNETTE; Littleton HS; Littleton, NH; (Y); 3/78; Am Leg Aux Girls St; Y-Teens; Band; Yrbk Stf; Sec Frsh Cls; Sec Soph Cls; Bsktbl; Coach Actv; Fld Hcky; High Hon Roll; HOBY Ldrshp 85; 2nd Pl Local Rotary Clb LFP Cntst 86; Social Sci.

GAGNER, DAEL; Kingswood Regional HS; Wolfeboro Falls, NH; (Y); 3/123; Debate Tm; Yrbk Ed-Chief; Rep Frsh Cls; Trs Stu Cncl; Var L Socr; Var L Tennis; Elks Awd; High Hon Roll; NHS; Prfct Atten Awd; Ranling Schlr In German At St Pauls 85; Latin Schlrshp 83; Brown U; Russian.

GAGNON, SHELLY; Londonderry HS; Londonderry, NH; (Y); GAA; Teachers Aide; Varsity Clb; Var Capt Bsktbl; Var Capt Socr; Var Capt Sftbl; Hon Roll; Londonderry Expss Sccr Schlrshp; Sccr NH Lions Cup All Star NHSCA All Star Div II Tm All Str 85-86; Keene ST Coll; Sprts Med.

GAGNON, TRACEY; Concord HS; Concord, NH; (Y); Church Yth Grp; VICA.

GALATI, ROD A; Trinity HS; Bedford, NH; (Y); 20/180; Am Leg Boys St; CAP; Model UN; Pres Soph Cls; Pres Jr Cls; Var Capt Trk; NHS; NEDT Awd; Im Bsktbl; Capt Var Crs Cntry; Latn Awd 84; Socl Stds Awd 84; Lib Art.

GANNON, DAVID; Concord HS; Concord, NH; (Y); Pres Spanish Clb; SADD; Varsity Clb; Var L Tennis; Hon Roll; NHS; Prfct Atten Awd; U NH; Bus.

GARASKY, DONALD; Bishop Guertin HS; Nashua, NH; (Y); Cmnty Wkr; FCA; Ski Clb; SADD; Stu Cncl; Im JV Socr; JV Var Trk; Hon Roll; Prfct Atten Awd; U Of Brdgprt; Engrng.

GARDEN, CHRISTINA L; Milford Area SR HS; Amherst, NH; (Y); 14/310; Computer Clb; Math Tm; Q&S; Nwsp Rptr; Hon Roll; NHS; Ntl Merit Schol; Pres Schlr; Exploring; Im Powder Puff Ftbl; Ltr Alpine Sking 84-86; Cpt Granite ST Chllng Tm 85-86; CA Inst Tech; Physc.

GARLAND, ED; Kenneth HS; Bartlett, NH; (Y); Bsbl; Bsktbl; Ftbl; Golf; Lcrss; Socr; Sftbl; Swmmng; Tennis; Trk; Bus Mgmt.

GARLAND, HEATHER; Keene HS; Keene, NH; (Y); 31/357; Art Clb; Drama Clb; Band; Concert Band; Mrchg Band; Yrbk Stf; High Hon Roll; Hon Roll; JV Tennis; Var Trk; Fine Arts.

GARVEY, BRIAN; Bishop Guertin HS; Dracut, MA; (Y); Church Yth Grp; Cmnty Wkr; Key Clb; Ski Clb; Var Bsbl; Im Bsktbl; High Hon Roll; NHS; NEDT Awd.

GARVEY, MICHELLE; Alvirne HS; Hudson, NH; (Y); Concert Band; JV Bsktbl; Var Tennis; Hon Roll; Rivier Coll Chllng Pgm; Smmr Bsktbl Lg.

GAUCHER, DANIEL; Trinity HS; Manchester, NH; (Y); Am Leg Boys St; Sec Trs Art Clb; Yrbk Phtg; JV Var Ftbl; High Hon Roll; Hon Roll; NEDT Awd; U Of NH; Visual Studies.

GAUDREAULT, DARREN; Nashua SR HS; Nashua, NH; (Y); Am Leg Boys St; Boy Scts; Ski Clb; Lcrss; Trk; Hon Roll; Jr NHS; U Of NH; Bus Admin.

GAUVIN, LISA; Mascenic Regional HS; New Ipswich, NH; (Y); Chorus; Trs Soph Cls; Trs Jr Cls; Var Capt Bsktbl; Var Sftbl; Var Capt Vllybl; Hon Roll; Pres NHS; Hugh O Brian Yth Fndtn Ldrshp Sem-Rep 84; Schlrs/Athlete Awd-Army 86; Wellesley Bk Awd 86; Hlth Field.

GEAR, CHRISTINE M; Salem HS; Salem, NH; (S); Church Yth Grp; Hosp Aide; SADD; JV Var Crs Cntry; JV Trk.

GENDREN, LISA; Pembroke Acad; Suncook, NH; (Y); 2/176; Sec French Clb; Office Aide; Sec Pres Stu Cncl; Bausch & Lomb Sci Awd; DAR Awd; High Hon Roll; NHS; Sal; Hghst Hnrs In Frnch I, II, & III; Outstndng Srv To Stu Cncl Awd; Bausch & Lomb Saci Awd; Bio.

GENDRON, JEFFREY; Alvirne HS; Hudson, NH; (Y); 64/338; Pres Frsh Cls; JV Crs Cntry; JV Var Trk; Hon Roll; New England; Music.

GENEST, JOHN; Pittsfield HS; Pittsfield, NH; (Y); 5/76; Am Leg Boys St; English Clb; SADD; VP Varsity Clb; School Play; Nwsp Stf; Yrbk Bus Mgr; Pres Frsh Cls; Rep Soph Cls; VP Jr Cls; Tilton Acad; Engrng.

GENGRAS, JENNIFER M; Tilton Schl; Tilton, NH; (S); Drama Clb; School Musical; School Play; Stage Crew; Variety Show; Lit Mag; Ice Hcky; Var Lcrss; Var Socr; Hon Roll.

GENUALDO, PAUL R; Timberlane Regional HS; Sandown, NH; (Y); 33/227; Model UN; Cheerleading; Ftbl; High Hon Roll; Hon Roll; Spanish NHS; U Of NH; Pol Sci.

GERACE, TINA; Pelham HS; Pelham, NH; (Y); 22/128; Church Yth Grp; FHA; Yrbk Stf; Pres Frsh Cls; Pres Soph Cls; Pres Stu Cncl; JV Cheerleading; Hon Roll; NHS; Voice Dem Awd; Accntng Awd 86; U Of NH; Lbrl Arts.

GERARD, ANDREW; Lebanon HS; Lebanon, NH; (Y); 1/142; Math Tm; Band; Yrbk Bus Mgr; Crs Cntry; Trk; Bausch & Lomb Sci Awd; Pres NHS; Pres Schlr; Val; Govrnrs Awd 86; Colgate U; Marn Bio.

GERMAIN, SUZANNE; Alvirne HS; Hudson, NH; (Y); 64/335; Church Yth Grp; Pep Clb; Quiz Bowl; Band; Chorus; Church Choir; Concert Band; Jazz Band; Pep Band; Variety Show; NH All ST Chorus 86; VP STOPP 85-86; Msc Prfrmnc.

GERTZ, ELISABETH; Pembroke Acad; Pembroke, NH; (S); Art Clb; French Clb; German Clb; Band; Orch; Im Swmmng; Hon Roll; Dstngshd Music 84; London Yth Symp Orch 81-84; Greatr Boston Yth Symp Orch 85; Juilliard Schl Music; Music.

GFROERER, JILL; Concord HS; Concord, NH; (Y); Church Yth Grp; German Clb; Ski Clb; Orch; Rep Stu Cncl; Bsktbl; JV Capt Fld Hcky; JV Sftbl; Var Trk; NHS; Pres ST Natl Hnr Soc 86-87; Treas HS Natl Hnr Soc 86-87; Mst Impvd Ski Jmpr 86.

GILBERT, DANIELLE; Spaulding HS; Strafford, NH; (S); 4-H; FBLA; Band; Concert Band; Jazz Band; Mrchg Band; NHS; Hon Roll; Distngshd Perfrmnc Awd Organ Fest 85; Bentley; Acctg.

GILBERT, DEBBIE; Central HS; Manchester, NH; (S); Sec DECA; Rep Soph Cls; Off Jr Cls; Hon Roll; Fshn Mrchndsng.

GILBERT, JENNIFER LEIGH; White Mountains Regional HS; Twin Mountain, NH; (Y); 9/110; Ski Clb; Spanish Clb; Chorus; Yrbk Stf; Rep Stu Cncl; Hon Roll; NHS; Twin Mountain Wmns Discussion Grp 86; Mitchell Coll; Computer.

GILBRIDE, SEAN; Nashua SR HS; Nashua, NH; (S); DECA; Trk; DECA ST Comp, 2nd & 3rd Pl Mdl, 3rd P L Trphy 86; DECA Natl Conf 86.

GILETT, BETH; Hillsboro Deering HS; Hillsboro, NH; (Y); 2/70; Am Leg Aux Girls St; Drama Clb; Math Tm; Yrbk Stf; Rep Frsh Cls; JV Cheerleading; Hon Roll; Sec NHS; Sal; U Of NH; Poli Sci.

GILLETT, BETH; Hillsboro-Deering HS; Hillsboro, NH; (S); 2/69; Am Leg Aux Girls St; Debate Tm; Drama Clb; Math Tm; Yrbk Stf; Rep Frsh Cls; Sec Stu Cncl; JV Cheerleading; Hon Roll; Sec NHS; Typing Awd 84; Hugh Obrian Yth Ledrshp Rep 84; Intl Rel.

GINGRAS, DAVID R; Nashua HS; Nashua, NH; (Y); 180/900; Am Leg Boys St; Teachers Aide; Yrbk Sprt Ed; Rep Frsh Cls; Trs Soph Cls; Trs Jr Cls; Var L Bsbl; Bsktbl; L Var Ftbl; Hon Roll; Aerontcl Engrng.

GIORDANO, MONIQUE; Salem HS; Salem, NH; (S); Church Yth Grp; Model UN; Teachers Aide; High Hon Roll; Hon Roll; Chllnge Pgm Rivier Coll; Jrny Ldr Mary Qn Of Pce Chrch; Ed.

GIRARD, LAUREN; Hanover HS; Norwich, VT; (Y); Church Yth Grp; Cmnty Wkr; Latin Clb; Yrbk Phtg; Yrbk Stf; Frsh Cls; Jr Cls; Bsktbl; Ice Hcky; Score Keeper; Spec Ed.

GIUST, GARY K; Pinkerton Academy; Hampstead, NH; (Y); Civic Clb; Spanish Clb; Band; Lit Mag; Bsktbl; Socr; Hon Roll; Prfct Atten Awd; UNH; Elctrcl Engrng.

GLADU, NICOLE; Tilton Schl; Lakeville, CT; (S); 4/75; French Clb; Math Tm; School Musical; School Play; Stage Crew; Yrbk Stf; Rep Soph Cls; Capt Var Lcrss; L Var Socr; High Hon Roll; Outstndg In Math 84.

GLIDDEN, DONNA J; White Mountains Regional HS; Whitefield, NH; (Y); 12/112; Spanish Clb; Var JV Bsktbl; Var JV Fld Hcky; JV Sftbl; Hon Roll; NHS; Pthlgy.

GLIDDEN, JANET; Spaulding HS; E Wakefield, NH; (Y); 107/360; Color Guard; School Play; Hon Roll; Rchstr Grng Schlrshp 86; NH Coll; Clnry Arts.

GLOVER, REGINA; Berlin HS; Milan, NH; (Y); 56/230; Pres Church Yth Grp; Drama Clb; Church Choir; Hon Roll.

GLOW, SARAH; Milford Area SR HS; Milford, NH; (Y); Am Leg Aux Girls St; Computer Clb; French Clb; SADD; Off Band; Swmmng; Trk; Bausch & Lomb Sci Awd; High Hon Roll; VP NHS; Wellesley Bk Awd 86; Swmng Sprtsmnshp Awd 85; Chem.

GODZYK, MELANIE; Colebrook Acad; Colebrook, NH; (Y); 5/48; Band; Chorus; Mrchg Band; Yrbk Stf; Hon Roll; Kiwanis Awd; NHS; 1st Colebrook Bnk Awd 86; Champlain Clg; Offc Mgmt.

GOELZER, BETH P; Timberlane Regional HS; Atkinson, NH; (Y); 2/208; Am Leg Aux Girls St; 4-H; Band; Flag Corp; Yrbk Ed-Chief; Bausch & Lomb Sci Awd; High Hon Roll; NHS; Spanish NHS; Yrbk Rptr; NH All ST Band 86; Acdmc Decthln 86; Wellesley Bk Awd 86; UNH; Vet.

GOLD, ERIC; Portsmouth HS; Portsmouth, NH; (Y); Art Clb; Aud/Vis; Latin Clb; Letterman Clb; Model UN; PAVAS; Varsity Clb; Yrbk Phtg; Yrbk Stf; Var Crs Cntry; Mst Imprvd Plyr Awd Var Hcky 86; 1st Pl Bttle Of The Bands 86; Emerson; Prodctn.

GOLINSKI, GREG; Saint Thomas Aquinas HS; Hampton, NH; (Y); Latin Clb; Varsity Clb; JV Bsktbl; Var Ftbl; Var Golf; Var Tennis; Hon Roll; Electrical Engr.

GONDEK, WENDY; Nashua SR HS; Nashua, NH; (Y); Ski Clb; Var Tennis; Mgr Vllybl; Hon Roll; Marine Sci.

GOODEN, MICHELE; White Mt Regional HS; Whitefield, NH; (Y); Art Clb; Debate Tm; Girl Scts; Cheerleading; French Hon Soc; Hon Roll; Jo Anne Gleason Schlrshp 86; Berlin Vo-Tech; Nrsng.

GOODSON JR, BILLY; Pembroke Acad; Bastrop, TX; (Y); Concert Band; Variety Show; U TX; Pre-Law.

GORDON, JUDY; Alvirne HS; Hudson, NH; (Y); 64/351; Var JV Socr; Var Capt Trk; Lion Awd; Fmle Athlt Yr 86; Mst Vlbl Plyr Trck 85-86; Springfield Coll; Hlth Ftns.

GORDON, MICHELLE; Spaulding HS; Rochester, NH; (Y); 44/396; Yrbk Stf; Rep Frsh Cls; Var Bsktbl; Hon Roll; U Of NH; Fshn Merch.

GOSS, APRIL; Pelham HS; Pelham, NH; (Y); Church Yth Grp; Drama Clb; Thesps; Band; Church Choir; Mgr Stage Crew; Ed Lit Mag; Hon Roll; NHS; Silver Awd Girl Scouts 85.

GOSSELIN, LAUREN; Manchester HS West; Bedford, NH; (Y); Church Yth Grp; Chorus; Church Choir; Nwsp Rptr; Nwsp Stf; Capt Cheerleading; JV Sftbl; Hon Roll; Variety Show; New England Youth Cncl Rep 84-85; NFCYM Regnl Yth Rep 85-87; Publc Rltns.

GOULD, LAURIE; Alvirne HS; Hudson, NH; (Y); 12/190; Ski Clb; Im Socr; JV Sftbl; Hon Roll; NHS; U Of New Englnd; Phys Thrpy.

GOULET, KELLY ANN; Nashua SR HS; Nashua, NH; (Y); 131/1000; Office Aide; Ski Clb; SADD; Stu Cncl; Var Capt Cheerleading; Hon Roll; Jr NHS; Advrtsng.

GOWING, DEBORAH; Alvirne HS; Hudson, NH; (Y); 10/338; Sec Sr Cls; Rep Stu Cncl; JV Bsktbl; Var Socr; JV Sftbl; Var Trk; High Hon Roll; Hon Roll; NHS; U NH; Bus.

GOZINSKI, GREG; St Thomas Aquinas HS; Hampton, NH; (Y); French Clb; Latin Clb; Varsity Clb; JV Bsktbl; Var Ftbl; Var Golf; Hon Roll; Engrng.

GRANT, CHARLENE; Concord HS; Concord, NH; (Y); 5/356; Math Tm; Capt Band; Color Guard; Capt Concert Band; Jazz Band; Mrchg Band; High Hon Roll; NHS; Pres Schlr; Geraldine Dodge Fndtn 86; Kiwanis Clb Schlrshp 86; MA Inst Tech; Astrphscs.

GRAY, MERIDITH; Concord HS; Concord, NH; (Y); Cmnty Wkr; French Clb; Intnl Clb; Fld Hcky; Var L Socr; Hon Roll; NHS; Prfct Atten Awd; Cross Cntry Ski Tm; Christa Mcaullif Commndtn Awd 86; Film Prod.

GRAY, SUSAN; Portsmouth SR HS; Rye, NH; (S); 29/405; Church Yth Grp; Model UN; Ski Clb; SADD; Teachers Aide; JV Cheerleading; Coach Actv; Co-Capt Fld Hcky; Var Tennis; High Hon Roll; French Awd 84.

GREEN, J; Hanover HS; Norwich, VT; (Y); 40/176; School Musical; Variety Show; Nwsp Stf; Yrbk Bus Mgr; Frsh Cls; Soph Cls; Trs Jr Cls; Sr Cls; Var Socr; Hon Roll.

GREEN, MICHELLE; Keene HS; Keene, NH; (Y); 27/357; Church Yth Grp; Cmnty Wkr; French Clb; Hosp Aide; Teachers Aide; Yrbk Stf; Hon Roll.

GREENLAF, PATTI; Pembroke Acad; Suncook, NH; (Y); 13/160; Off Jr Cls; Fld Hcky; Hon Roll; Intr Dsgn.

GREGOIRE, JAMES; Central HS; Manchester, NH; (Y); 198/430; Art Clb; Motion Pictures.

GREGOIRE, MICHELLE; Dover HS; Dover, NH; (Y); JA; SADD; JC Awd; JR Achvt Rlctd To Represent At Cnvntn 83-84; March Of Dimes Special Hnr For Help 85-86; Bus Mngmnt.

GRIBBEL, DOUG; A Crosby Kennett HS; N Conway, NH; (Y); 2/200; Var L Bsktbl; Var L Ftbl; Var L Trk; Bausch & Lomb Sci Awd; French Hon Soc; JETS Awd; Pres NHS; ST Decthln Fran Tate Trphy, Mark Butler Mem Trk Awd 85; Trk Awd 86; U PA; Engrng.

GRIDLEY, HEATHER; Kingswood Regional HS; Ossipee, NH; (Y); Art Clb; Church Yth Grp; Church Choir; Pep Band; Symp Band; Yrbk Ed-Chief; Tennis; Hon Roll.

GRIFFIN, GLENNA; Presentation 3 Mary Acad; Nahsua, NH; (Y); Hosp Aide; Science Clb; Pres Service Clb; Church Choir; Ed Nwsp Ed-Chief; Yrbk Stf; Sec Jr Cls; Sec Stu Cncl; Cheerleading; Drama Clb; Rivier Coll Chall Prog Cert Achvt 85; Amer Inst Frgn Stdy Cert Achvt 85; St Anselm Coll; Psych.

GRIMBILAS, THOMAS C; Portsmouth SR HS; Portsmouth, NH; (Y); 17/376; Church Yth Grp; Latin Clb; Model UN; SADD; JV Bsktbl; Var Tennis; High Hon Roll; NHS; Mstr Cnslr Prtsmth Chptr De Molay 86; Jr Wrld Cncl 84-86; Mdl Cngrss; Engr.

GRIMSHAW, MARK; Bishop Guertin HS; Nashua, NH; (Y); 59/138; Im Capt Bsktbl; JV Crs Cntry; Var Ftbl; Var Trk; Hon Roll; NEDT Awd; Embry-Riddle Aerontcl U; Engrng.

GRISWOLD, HANNAH EUGENIA; Saint Pauls Schl; Chicago, IL; (Y); Church Yth Grp; Dance Clb; French Clb; Service Clb; VP Soph Cls; Stu Cncl; Cit Awd; Kenyon Coll.

GROAT, RICHARD; Spaulding HS; Rochester, NH; (S); High Hon Roll; Hon Roll; NHS; U NH; Mech Engrng.

GROGAN, KIMBERLY; The Derryfield Schl; Suncook, NH; (Y); Art Clb; Sec Model UN; Concert Band; JV Var Cheerleading; Sftbl; Art Recog Wrk Area Batikg 83; Advrtsg.

GROVE, ERIK; Timberlane Regional HS; Sandown, NH; (Y); Cmnty Wkr; Pres 4-H; Dnfth Awd; 4-H Awd; Hon Roll; Schlrshp Ntl Ldrshp Amer Yth Fndtn 86; NH Ntl Frstry Invtnl 85; NH Ntl 4h Cngrs 86; Frstry.

GRUCA, ROBERT; Bishop Guertin HS; Lowell, MA; (Y); Spanish Clb; Hon Roll; Spanish NHS; U Of Lowell; Sound Tech.

GUANGA, MARIE; Sanborn Regional HS; Fremont, NH; (Y); 54/127; 4-H; FBLA; Girl Scts; Stage Crew; Cit Awd; 4-H Awd; Hon Roll; 4-H Cnsmr Educ 85; Anmls.

GUERIN, PAULA; Berlin HS; Berlin, NH; (Y); Letterman Clb; Varsity Clb; Rep Soph Cls; Rep Jr Cls; Stu Cncl; Var Bsktbl; Var Sftbl; Athltc Awd Bsktbl 86; NH Votech Coll; Bus Mgmt.

GUERTIN, LYNNE; Manchester Central HS; Hooksett, NH; (Y); Church Yth Grp; VP FBLA; High Hon Roll; Hon Roll; 2nd Pl Future Bus Ldrs Amer Acctg I 86; Acctnt.

GUILMETT, BRENDA C; Laconia HS; Laconia, NH; (Y); 7/157; French Clb; GAA; Varsity Clb; JV Capt Bsktbl; Var Capt Sftbl; Hon Roll; NHS; Eleanor Parker Awd 86; Amer Legn & Knghts Of Columbus Schlrshps 86; Keene ST Coll; Bus Mgmt.

GUIMOND, ALISON; Pinkerton Acad; Auburn, NH; (S); 123/466; DECA; Library Aide; Quiz Bowl; SADD; Lit Mag; Rep Soph Cls; Rep Jr Cls; Rep Sr Cls; Voice Dem Awd; Voice Of Demo 85; DECA 1st Pl Trphy-Avtg 86; DECA Ntl Top 10 Medlst-Avtg 86; Johnson & Wales Coll; Avtg.

GULLEY, KATHLEEN M; Lin-Wood HS; Lincoln, NH; (S); Var Ski Clb; Band; Chorus; Pres Soph Cls; Pres Jr Cls; Capt Vllybl; Dnfth Awd; Hon Roll; NHS; All ST Chorus Stu 85-86; Engr.

GUSTAFSON, KRIS; Alvirne HS; Hudson, NH; (Y); Science Clb; JV Socr; Hon Roll; UNH; Hist.

HACKETT, DANIEL; Portsmouth HS; Rye Beach, NH; (S); 8/405; Intnl Clb; Math Clb; Math Tm; Var L Bsktbl; Var L Crs Cntry; Var L Trk; High Hon Roll; Hon Roll; NHS; Frnch Awd NFTA 85; Swathmore U; Jrnlsm.

HADDIX, ERIC; Con Val HS; Temple, NH; (Y); Church Yth Grp; Cmnty Wkr; 4-H; Latin Clb; Pep Clb; Band; Concert Band; Jazz Band; Mrchg Band; Pep Band; Elon Coll; Hstry.

HAFFER, GRETCHEN; Concord HS; Concord, NH; (Y); 15/390; Dance Clb; Ski Clb; Ed Yrbk Stf; Var Crs Cntry; Mgr Socr; High Hon Roll; Ntl Merit Ltr; Prfct Atten Awd; Sal; Outstndg Achvmnt Engl Awd 85; Lttr Grls Sccr Mgr 84; Lylty Awd Sue Srtorelli Dnc Studio 86.

HAHN, CAROL L; Timberlane Regional HS; Atkinson, NH; (Y); Church Yth Grp; Debate Tm; French Clb; Math Clb; Science Clb; SADD; Im Vllybl; High Hon Roll; Hon Roll; Prfct Atten Awd; Ntl Sci Olympd Bio 85; Mth.

HAIGIS, MARK; Alvirne HS; Hudson, NH; (Y); Am Leg Boys St; Church Yth Grp; Ski Clb; SADD; VP Jr Cls; Var Crs Cntry; Var Trk; Hon Roll; U S Naval Acad; Nvl Offcr.

HALE, PATRICIA; Spaulding HS; Rochester, NH; (S); 12/387; Key Clb; JV Cheerleading; High Hon Roll; Hon Roll; NHS; Frgn Lang.

HALEY, ANDREW; St Thomas Aquinas HS; Dover, NH; (Y); 7/90; Am Leg Boys St; VP Church Yth Grp; Capt Debate Tm; Drama Clb; NFL; Speech Tm; Church Choir; Nwsp Stf; NHS; Ntl Merit SF; US/Japan Sen Exchg Schlrshp Semi-Fnlst 85-86; Hstry.

HALL, HEATHER; Bishop Brady HS; Concord, NH; (Y); 26/85; Drama Clb; Intnl Clb; Ski Clb; SADD; Acpl Chr; Yrbk Stf; Trk; Hon Roll; NEDT Awd; Prof Wrtng.

HALLECK, COLLEEN; Newport HS; Newport, NH; (Y); Math Tm; VP Frsh Cls; VP Soph Cls; Stu Cncl; Var L Bsktbl; Var L Crs Cntry; Var L Trk; High Hon Roll; Hon Roll; NHS; Am Leg Aux Essay-Natl Freedom Under Stars/Stripes 86.

HAMEL, GARY J; Goffstown Area HS; New Boston, NH; (Y); 65/210; Var Capt Bsbl; JV Bsktbl; Var Capt Socr; Var Trk; Hon Roll; Lion Awd; Lions Clb Twn ST Soccer Team 85-86; Babe Rth Sprtsmnshp Awd 86; Gftstwn Ed Assn Schlrshp 86; Sprngfld Coll; Phy Ed.

HAMEL, LISA P; Manchester West HS; Manchester, NH; (Y); 16/336; Am Leg Boys St; Ski Clb; Church Choir; Swing Chorus; Variety Show; Lit Mag; Rep Stu Cncl; Cheerleading; High Hon Roll; NHS; U Of NH; Art.

HAMEL, SHARON D; Salem HS; Salem, NH; (S); 7/353; Sec French Clb; Model UN; SADD; High Hon Roll; Hon Roll; Fr Schltc Awd; Nrsg.

HAMILTON, GAYLE; Spaulding HS; Rochester, NH; (S); 47/397; Drama Clb; Key Clb; Concert Band; Jazz Band; Mrchg Band; Vllybl; Hon Roll; Jrnlsm.

HAMILTON, JULIA E; Salem HS; Salem, NH; (S); 49/383; Model UN; Ski Clb; SADD; Band; Concert Band; Mrchg Band; Hon Roll; Arts.

HAMILTON, TAMARA; Spaulding HS; Rochester, NH; (S); Church Yth Grp; VP Drama Clb; School Play; Rep Frsh Cls; Mgr(s); Var L Socr; Hon Roll; NHS; Dramtc Arts.

HAMLIN, LESLEY; Pelham HS; Pelham, NH; (Y); Drama Clb; French Clb; Chorus; Rep Frsh Cls; Rep Soph Cls; Pres Jr Cls; Stu Cncl; Dnfth Awd; High Hon Roll; NHS.

HANCOCK, THOMAS; Fall Mountain Regional HS; Alstead, NH; (Y); 29/135; Am Leg Boys St; Church Yth Grp; Cmnty Wkr; Band; Mrchg Band; Bsbl; Ftbl; Prfct Atten Awd.

HANKS, NANCY; Nashua HS; Nashua, NH; (Y); 224/783; Dance Clb; Ski Clb; Hon Roll; Dance Trphy 85; Mount Ida Coll; Int Dsgn.

HANSEN VI, OTTO E; Wilton-Lyndeborough Coop; Wilton, NH; (Y); Am Leg Boys St; Camera Clb; Pres VP Computer Clb; Drama Clb; FBLA; Math Tm; Ski Clb; School Musical; School Play; Stage Crew; Bus.

HARDING, DARRYL E; St Pauls Schl; Cambridge, MA; (Y); Drama Clb; Model UN; Radio Clb; Chorus; School Play; Off Stu Cncl; Bsktbl; Ftbl; Lcrss; Engrng.

HARMACINSKI, JAMES; Salem HS; Salem, NH; (S); 23/340; Model UN; Ski Clb; Var JV Bsktbl; JV Crs Cntry; JV Socr; JV Trk; High Hon Roll; Hon Roll; Bus Adm.

HARMON, TAMMY; Concord HS; Manchester, NH; (Y); 10/323; Drama Clb; Model UN; Sec SADD; Chorus; Yrbk Stf; High Hon Roll; NHS; Pres Schlr; Rotary Awd; Peer Counseling Chrprsn; U Of VT; Bio.

HARNEY, MELISSA; Raymond JR SR HS; Raymond, NH; (S); DECA; Yrbk Stf; Sec Frsh Cls; Rep Soph Cls; Rep Jr Cls; VP Stu Cncl; Cheerleading; Stat Mgr(s); Hon Roll; ST DECA Pres 86-87; Jonson Wale COLL; Htl Rstnt.

HARRIS, ROBYN; Laconia HS; Laconia, NH; (Y); 4/204; Ski Clb; Drm Mjr(t); Sec Jr Cls; Hon Roll; NHS; Civic Clb; 3rd Div I St Ski Chmpnshps 86; U MA; Lib Arts.

HARTMAN, KIMBERLY S; West HS; Bedford, NH; (Y); Am Leg Aux Girls St; Ski Clb; Nwsp Bus Mgr; Pres Frsh Cls; Pres Soph Cls; Pres Jr Cls; Pres Sr Cls; DAR Awd; Mayors Awd, Svc Awd, Pres Awd 86; WSBE UNH; Bus Admin.

HARTWELL, DANA; Manchester HS West; Chadds Ford, PA; (Y); 88/338; Ski Clb; Nwsp Stf; JV Ftbl; Capt Swmmng; JV Wrstlng; U NH; Hotel Adm.

HARVEY, BARBARA; Salem HS; Salem, NH; (S); Dance Clb; Model UN; School Play; Var Cheerleading; Var Mgr(s); High Hon Roll; Hon Roll; Spanish NHS; Dance Tchr Clb Boston 85; Phy Thrpy.

HASKELL, CHRIS; Epping HS; Epping, NH; (S); 5/53; Am Leg Boys St; CAP; Quiz Bowl; Scholastic Bowl; Pres SADD; Trs Frsh Cls; Sec Soph Cls; Sec Jr Cls; High Hon Roll; NHS; 4th Pl Trphy-Natl Fr Cont 83; Plymouth ST Coll; Hstry Tchr.

HASTINGS, DARLENE; Newport JR SR HS; Newport, NH; (Y); Sec Church Yth Grp; Pres 4-H; Girl Scts; Library Aide; Spanish Clb; DAR Awd; 4-H Awd; High Hon Roll; Hon Roll; Daemen U; Spec Educ.

HATFIELD, STEVEN; Hillsboro-Deering HS; Hillsboro, NH; (S); 3/70; Church Yth Grp; Cmnty Wkr; Band; Concert Band; Pep Band; Yrbk Stf; JV Var Bsbl; JV Var Bsktbl; JV Var Socr; Hon Roll; St Pauls Advncd Studs Pgm 85.

HATTAN, EILEEN; Bishop Brady HS; Salisbury, NH; (Y); 1/81; Church Yth Grp; Math Tm; VP Frsh Cls; Sec Soph Cls; Pres Jr Cls; Pres Sr Cls; Fld Hcky; Tennis; High Hon Roll; NHS; Drtmth Coll Book Awd 86; Wlsly Coll Book Awd 86; Frnch I & 222 Awds 84 & 86.

HATTORI, DAVID A; Salem HS; Salem, NH; (S); Trs Math Tm; Model UN; Spanish Clb; School Play; Yrbk Stf; Rep Jr Cls; Stu Cncl; High Hon Roll; Hon Roll; Ntl Merit SF; Rep To Challng Prog 84-85; Comp Sci.

HAUBRICH, JULIE; Stevens HS; Claremont, NH; (Y); Rep Soph Cls; JV Bsktbl; JV Tennis; DAR Awd; Hon Roll; St Pauls Sch; Prom Comm.

HAYDEN, WENDY; Hopkinton HS; Contoocook, NH; (S); DECA; German Clb; Var Cheerleading; ST DECA Reportr NH 85-86; Johnson & Whales Clg; Entrpnrsp.

HAYES, JEFFREY R; Kennett HS; Bartlett, NH; (Y); Pres Soph Cls; JV Bsktbl; Var Ftbl; Hon Roll; Alice Barrows Schlrshp 86; UNH; Lib Arts.

HAYES JR, JOHN R; Bishop Guertin HS; Pelham, NH; (Y); 8/142; Church Yth Grp; Nwsp Stf; Yrbk Rptr; Yrbk Stf; Im Bsktbl; Var Crs Cntry; JV Trk; High Hon Roll; Hon Roll; NHS; Colby Coll Bk Awd 85-86.

HAYES, SCOT; Concord HS; Concord, NH; (Y); Boys Clb Am; Hon Roll; NH Tech; Police Ofcr.

HAZELTON III, ROBERT G; Londonderry HS; Manchester, NH; (Y); Boys Clb Am; Church Yth Grp; Letterman Clb; Varsity Clb; Variety Show; JV Bsbl; Var L Bsktbl; JV Ftbl; Var L Trk; Hon Roll; Hnred In Rsng $1700 For Famine Strckn People In Africa 85; Hnred In Rsng $1500 In Schl-Hnds Acrss Ame; Northern U; Mktg.

HEALEY, KELLY; Manchester Central HS; Deerfield, NH; (Y); 116/393; Am Leg Aux Girls St; Var Bsktbl; Var Capt Socr; Var Capt Trk; High Hon Roll; NH Lions Cup All-Star Sccr Team 86; Springfield Coll; Physcl Educ.

HEBERT, JAMES; Salem HS; Salem, NH; (Y); Boys Clb Am; Model UN; Ski Clb; JV Bsktbl; Var L Crs Cntry; Var L Trk; Hon Roll; Plymouth ST Coll; Real Est.

HEBERT, PAUL; Bishop Guertin HS; Nashua, NH; (Y); 32/140; Yrbk Sprt Ed; Pres Stu Cncl; L Stu Cncl; Im Bsktbl; Coach Actv; Im Vllybl; Dnfth Awd; Hon Roll; NHS; Physcl Thrpy.

HEDSTROM, CHRIS; Winnisquam Regnl HS; Northfield, NH; (Y); Church Yth Grp; French Clb; Library Aide; Math Clb; Math Tm; Chorus; High Hon Roll; Hon Roll; Pres Acad Ftnss Awd 86; Plymouth ST; Modern Lang.

HEFFERNAN, PATRICK; Bishop Guertin HS; Nashua, NH; (Y); VP Drama Clb; Ski Clb; Spanish Clb; School Musical; School Play; Ed Nwsp Stf; Im Bsktbl; JV Var Ftbl; NHS; Spanish NHS; USMA; Engrng.

HEINO, HEATHER; Weare HS; Weare, NH; (S); 3/50; Sec Trs 4-H; French Clb; FHA; SADD; Nwsp Stf; Rptr Yrbk Stf; Var JV Bsktbl; Var JV Vllybl; Hon Roll; NHS; Carnival Ball 81-86; Arch Dsgn.

HELMSTADTER, JOHN; Newport HS; Newport, NH; (Y); PAVAS; Spanish Clb; Band; Concert Band; Jazz Band; Mrchg Band; Pep Band; Var Bsktbl; ME Summr Yth Music Scholar 85; Berklee Schl Music; Music.

HEMMERLING, ANDREW; Moscoma Valley Reg HS; Enfield, NH; (Y); French Clb; Off Stu Cncl; JV Capt Bsktbl; JV Var Socr; Hon Roll; Coaches Awd JV Bsktbl 83-84.

HENAULT, MARK; Manchester West HS; Bedford, NH; (Y); 3/340; Computer Clb; Math Clb; Nwsp Bus Mgr; Yrbk Bus Mgr; Lit Mag; High Hon Roll; NHS; NEDT Awd; Pres Schlr; Digital Equip Corp Schlrshp 86; NH Top Achievers Schlrshp 86; Additon Schlrshp 86; MA Inst Of Tech; Engrng.

HENDEE, SUSAN; Pembroke Acad; Concord, NH; (Y); 1/180; Pres 4-H; Sec JCL; Key Clb; Latin Clb; Stu Cncl; Capt Cheerleading; Var Sftbl; High Hon Roll; NHS; Ntl Merit Ltr; Rensselgen Mdl For Excllnc In Math & Sci 86; Military Acad; Engnrng.

HENNESSEY, ELLEN M; White Mountains Regional HS; Whitefield, NH; (Y); 4/107; Band; Yrbk Sprt Ed; Yrbk Stf; Var L Bsktbl; Var Capt Fld Hcky; Var L Sftbl; Kiwanis Awd; NHS; Letterman Clb; Teachers Aide; Ferguson Schlrshp 86; Natl Schlr-Athlt Awd 86; U Of NH; Exercise Speclst.

HENRIKSON, SCOTT A; Conant HS; Rindge, NH; (Y); Am Leg Boys St; Boy Scts; Exploring; JCL; Science Clb; Band; Madrigals; School Musical; Nwsp Bus Mgr; Hon Roll; Medical.

HERR, TINA A; Kennett HS; Conway, NH; (Y); 50/190; SADD; Teachers Aide; Cheerleading; Hon Roll; Bus.

HERTZLER, TIMOTHY; Keene SR HS; Spofford, NH; (Y); 54/350; Church Yth Grp; Var Bsktbl; Var Ftbl; Var Trk; Hon Roll; Sprts Med.

HICKS, SHAWNA; Hopkinton HS; Contoocook, NH; (S); 4-H; German Clb; Yrbk Stf; Rep Stu Cncl; Mgr(s); Cmnty Wkr; Office Aide; 4-H Awd; Hon Roll; Masonic Awd; DECA ST Histrn 85-86; RMANH Schlrshp 86; Prom Commtte; Art-Fashion Inst; Fshn Merch.

HIGGINS, STEPHEN; Coe-Brown Northwood Acad; Barrington, NH; (Y); 15/49; Church Yth Grp; Nwsp Bus Mgr; Var Bsktbl; NHS; Prfct Atten Awd; US Achvt Acad 84; US Achvt Acad 85; Brkshr Chrstn Coll; Bus Adm.

HIGMAN, ANITA; Pembroke Acad; Epsom, NH; (Y); 7/180; Church Yth Grp; Latin Clb; JV Bsktbl; JV Fld Hcky; JV Trk; High Hon Roll; Hon Roll; Pre Med.

HILLSGROVE JR, JAMES A; Milford Area SR HS; Amherst, NH; (Y); Am Leg Boys St; Wt Lftg; High Hon Roll; Hon Roll; St Pauls Advncd Stds Prgrm 86; Ntl Hnr Soc 86; Bus Mgt.

HILTUNEN, BECKY; Stevens HS; Claremont, NH; (Y); 3/255; Quiz Bowl; Ski Clb; Sec Varsity Clb; Yrbk Ed-Chief; VP Capt Tennis; High Hon Roll; NHS; Rotary Awd; Wellesley Clb Awd 86; Schlrshp Awd 86; Stanford; Bus Mgmt.

HINTON, DONNA; Salem HS; Salem, NH; (Y); German Clb; Model UN; Band; Concert Band; Drm & Bgl; Jazz Band; Mrchg Band; Pep Band; Sftbl; Hon Roll; Music Lang.

HJULSTROM, KATRINA; Stevens HS; Claremont, NH; (Y); Church Yth Grp; Political Wkr; Varsity Clb; Chorus; School Musical; Yrbk Ed-Chief; Yrbk Stf; VP Soph Cls; Pres Jr Cls; Stu Cncl; Fld Hcky Coachs Awd 110% 85; Jr Cls Mrshl Grad 86; Crt Jr Prom 85; Comm.

HOAG, DANIEL; Bishop Guertin HS; Chelmsford, MA; (Y); 30/156; FCA; Math Clb; Yrbk Stf; Im Bsktbl; Var Crs Cntry; L Tennis; Hon Roll; Spanish NHS; Tnns Seasn MVP 85-86; Hnr Roll; Providence Coll; Pre-Med.

HOAG, HEIDI-JANE; Inter-Lakes HS; Center Sandwich, NH; (Y); Drama Clb; Pep Clb; Rep SADD; Chorus; School Musical; Rep Soph Cls; Rep Jr Cls; Pres Stu Cncl; L Cheerleading; Score Keeper; Natl Stu Councl Convntn 86; UNH; Poltcl Sci.

HODDESON, ALAN; Newmarket Central HS; Newmarket, NH; (Y); Ski Clb; Var Crs Cntry; JV Var High Hon Roll; JV Hon Roll; USMC.

HODGKINS JR, DAVID; Concord HS; Bow, NH; (S); Boy Scts; DECA; Nwsp Stf; Socr; Trk; ST Offcr Deca 86-87; Cus.

HOEING, SEAN; St Thomas Aquinas HS; Dover, NH; (Y); Key Clb; Latin Clb; Pres Sr Cls; Rep Stu Cncl; Bsktbl; Ftbl; Tennis; Pre-Law.

HOFFMAN, JASON; Concord Christian Schl; Laconia, NH; (S); Am Leg Boys St; CAP; Math Tm; Science Clb; Ski Clb; School Play; Pres Stu Cncl; Var L Crs Cntry; Var Socr; Hon Roll; Chrmn Cadet Advsry Cncl 86; American Legion Certif Award; 85-86 Teachers Award In Ldrshp,Citznship.

HOFFMAN, JON ERIC; Pembroke Acad; Suncook, NH; (Y); De Vry; Engrng.

HOKANSON, KELLY; Manchester Memorial HS; Manchester, NH; (Y); 19/341; Church Yth Grp; Debate Tm; Drama Clb; French Clb; Girl Scts; Latin Clb; Bsktbl; Hon Roll; 1st Pl Frnch Cmptn 85; N E Chrst JC; Govt.

HOLBROOK, TODD; Bishop Guertin HS; Nashua, NH; (Y); Spanish Clb; Var Bsbl; Hon Roll; Ntl Merit Ltr; Spanish NHS; Acdmc All-Amrcn 85-86; Bus.

HOLDEN, HEATHER; Nashua SR HS; Nashua, NH; (Y); 16/838; Church Yth Grp; Model UN; Spanish Clb; SADD; Yrbk Stf; Cheerleading; Hon Roll; Jr NHS; NHS; U Of NH.

HOLLORAN, GARY; Bishop Quertin HS; Lowell, MA; (Y); Spanish Clb; JV Stat Bsktbl; JV Var Socr; Var Trk; Hon Roll; Spanish NHS; Finc.

HOLLOWAY, HILLARY; Concord HS; Concord, NH; (Y); 7/398; VP Drama Clb; German Clb; Intnl Clb; Math Tm; Sec Soph Cls; Sec Stu Cncl; Var Crs Cntry; NHS; Band; School Musical; Mt Holyoke Bk Awd 86; Hghst Mth Achvt & Avg 84-85; Outstndng Engl Achvt 85-86; Mth.

HOLMES, JEANNIE; Pinkerton Acad; Chester, NH; (Y); 114/606; Church Yth Grp; Pres 4-H; SADD; Band; Concert Band; Mrchg Band; Pep Band; Swmmng; 4-H Awd; Hon Roll; Plymouth ST Coll; Educ.

HOLMES, KAREN; Hanover HS; Lyme Ctr, NH; (Y); Drama Clb; French Clb; Chorus; Orch; School Play; Nwsp Stf; JV Capt Bsktbl; High Hon Roll.

HOLMES, PATTI; Salem HS; Salem, NH; (Y); Boys Clb Am; French Clb; Pep Clb; Spanish Clb; Teachers Aide; JV Cheerleading; Stat Fld Hcky; JV Sftbl; Var Trk; Plymouth ST Coll; Bus Mgmt.

HOLT, KEITH; Portsmouth HS; Portsmouth, NH; (Y); Band; Chorus; Concert Band; Jazz Band; Mrchg Band; Orch; Pep Band; School Musical; Hon Roll; New England Schlstc Band Assn Hnrs Band 85-86; Parents Music Clb Schlrshp Syms Mucis Schl 84; Music.

HOLT, TIMOTHY; Mancheste Central HS; Manchester, NH; (Y); DECA; UNH.

HOOK, KATHLEEN; Keene HS; Keene, NH; (Y); 70/356; French Clb; Hosp Aide; VP Soph Cls; Pres Jr Cls; VP Sr Cls; L Stu Cncl; L Swmmng; Trk; Hon Roll; Hugh O Brien Outstndg Soph 85; U MN; Biol.

HOOKER, JULIE; Bishop Brady HS; Henniker, NH; (Y); Church Yth Grp; Cmnty Wkr; Drama Clb; Girl Scts; Chorus; School Musical; School Play; Stage Crew; Nwsp Rptr; Nwsp Stf; Child Psychlgy.

HOPKINS, JO; Profile JR SR HS; Franconia, NH; (Y); Sftbl; Hon Roll; Spirit Awd 84-85; Crimnlgy.

HOPKINS, PENNY; Fall Mountain Regional HS; Claremont, NH; (Y); 4/130; French Clb; Elks Awd; High Hon Roll; Hon Roll; NHS; Joel Hesser Mem Schlrshp 86-87; Bixby Schlrshp 86-87; Dollars Schlrs Schlrshp 86-87; Hesser Bus Coll; Mgmt.

HOPKINS II, WIGHTMAN B; Moultonborough Acad; Center Harbor, NH; (Y); 2/41; Math Tm; Variety Show; Pres Sr Cls; Var Capt Bsbl; Var Capt Bsktbl; Var Capt Socr; Im Tennis; Im Vllybl; High Hon Roll; NHS; Rnkd 1st In Class 85; Prncpls Awd 85; MVP Sccr & Bsbl Coaches Awd 86; ROTC; Engrng.

HOUDE, LESLIE; Dover HS; Dover, NH; (Y); 31/289; Church Yth Grp; Spanish Clb; Jazz Band; Var Bsktbl; Hon Roll; Phrmcy.

HOULDSWORTH, CHRIS; Portsmouth HS; Portsmouth, NH; (Y); Yrbk Stf; De Vry Inst Of Tech; Tech Engr.

HOWARD, CLINT; Spaulding HS; Rochester, NH; (S); 12/359; 4-H; Key Clb; High Hon Roll; Bryant Coll; Acctng.

HOWARD, JOSHUA; Keene HS; Keene, NH; (Y); 51/386; Am Leg Boys St; Boy Scts; Church Yth Grp; Political Wkr; Ski Clb; Acpl Chr; Stu Cncl; Trk; God Cntry Awd; Hon Roll; Mayors Advsry Bd 85-87; Drug & Alcohol Abuse Pgm 85-86; NH Teen Inst Drug & Alcohol Pgm 85; Law.

HOWARD, TIMOTHY; Plymouth Area HS; Plymouth, NH; (Y); Am Leg Boys St; Band; Jazz Band; Mrchg Band; Pep Band; School Musical; School Play; Pres Sr Cls; Var Ftbl; NHS; Bsktbl Sprtsmnshp, Effrt Awd; Fdrlst Prty Whip Boys ST; Band Pres; Emerson Coll; Perf Thtre Arts.

HOWORTH, JOANNA K; Mount St Marys HS; Nashua, NH; (Y); 2/75; Ski Clb; Speech Tm; SADD; School Play; Ed Lit Mag; L Tennis; Ntl Merit SF; Latin Clb; Yrbk Stf; High Hon Roll; Schlrshp 4 Yr 82; St Pauls Adv Studies Pgm 825; Schl Spirit Awd 85; Eng.

HUFF, MELISSA LEIGH; Somersworth HS; Somersworth, NH; (Y); 8/165; Am Leg Aux Girls St; Capt Math Tm; Yrbk Stf; Trs Sr Cls; Trs Stu Cncl; Hon Roll; NHS; U Of NH; Econ.

HUGHES, CRAIG; Portsmouth HS; Rye, NH; (Y); Model UN; Ftbl; Trk; Wt Lftg; Hon Roll; Ntl Merit Ltr; Syracuse U; Cmnctns.

HUGHES, HEATHER; Hanover HS; Hanover, NH; (Y); 40/177; Church Yth Grp; French Clb; German Clb; Hosp Aide; Latin Clb; Quiz Bowl; Var Socr; Var Tennis; High Hon Roll; Hon Roll; Sccr Def Awd 84; Sccr Awd Most Improved 85; Nutritionist.

HUGHES, MARK; Salem HS; Salem, NH; (S); High Hon Roll; Hon Roll; Challenge Pgm Rivier Coll 85-86; Accelrtd Sci Studs 82-83; U Lowell; Elec Engrng.

HULSE, SHARON; Plymouth Area HS; Sanbornton, NH; (Y); 47/138; FBLA; Drm & Bgl; Yrbk Stf; Var Cheerleading; Mgr(s); Capt Trk; Hon Roll; Geo Z Zoulious Schlrshp Awd 86; U Of NH; Spch Pthlgy.

HUNEKE, LORI; St Pauls Schl; Menlo Park, CA; (Y); French Clb; Var L Crs Cntry; JV Socr; Var L Tennis; Hon Roll; Pres Of Chinese Clb 86-87.

HUNTER, SCOTT; Fall Mtn Rgional HS; N Walpole, NH; (Y); 40/120; Am Leg Boys St; Spanish Clb; Yrbk Stf; Var Bsbl; JV Bsktbl; Var Capt Ftbl; Var Ice Hcky; Im Wt Lftg; Finc.

HUNTINGTON, NEAL; Milford Area SR HS; Amherst, NH; (Y); Am Leg Boys St; 4-H; Var Capt Bsbl; Var Capt Bsktbl; Coach Actv; Cit Awd; 4-H Awd; Hon Roll; Powder Puff Ftbl; Ath Mnth Bsbl 86; All Area Bsbl Plyr 85-86; Bus.

HUTCHINS, WILLIAM K; Raymon JR/Sr HS; Candia, NH; (Y); Pres 4-H; Var Capt Crs Cntry; Var Capt Trk; Dnfth Awd; 4-H Awd; Hon Roll; Lion Awd; Ski Clb; Sec VICA; 4-H Wildlf & Fisheries Awd 85; 4-H Consrvtn Awd 85; NRA 22 Cal Rfl Trgt Shootng Exprt 85; Wldlf & Fish Consrvtn.

HYBSCH, MARY BETH; Bishop Brady HS; Hooksett, NH; (Y); Church Yth Grp; Drama Clb; School Play; Cheerleading; Hon Roll.

INGERSOLL, ANN; Plymouth Area HS; Plymouth, NH; (Y); Capt Ski Clb; Rep Frsh Cls; Hst Soph Cls; Hst Jr Cls; Rep Stu Cncl; JV Bsktbl; Var Fld Hcky; Var Trk; Hon Roll; Sec 4-H; Chief Justice Yth Gov 85-86; Lawyer.

INGLIS, MELISSA; Spaulding HS; Ctr Strafford, NH; (S); VP Church Yth Grp; Key Clb; Pep Clb; Yrbk Stf; Bsktbl; Hon Roll; Sci.

INGRAFFIA, CELESTE; Phillips Exeter Acad; Pearl River, LA; (Y); School Musical; Nwsp Bus Mgr; Yrbk Ed-Chief; Yrbk Stf; Stu Cncl.

IOANNOU, STEVEN; Keene HS; Keene, NH; (Y); 98/362; Art.

JABLONSKI, SUSAN LYNNE; Pinkerton Acad; Derry, NH; (Y); 90/496; Pres VP 4-H; Office Aide; Quiz Bowl; Ski Clb; Spanish Clb; Chorus; Stage Crew; Nwsp Rptr; JV Socr; 4-H Awd; UNH Calculus Cls I-B 85; 96 Per-Cent UNH Calculus II 85; Rochestern Inst Tech; Micr Engr.

JACKMAN, GREG; Bishop Guertin HS; Amherst, NH; (Y); Red Cross Aide; Yrbk Stf; JV Bsbl; Im Bsktbl; Var Tennis; High Hon Roll; NEDT Awd; Bus.

JACOBS, KARL; Memorial HS; Manchester, NH; (Y); Yrbk Stf; Bowling; Im Wt Lftg; Hon Roll; Bus Adm.

JAMES, LORA; Oyster River HS; Madbury, NH; (Y); Church Yth Grp; Drama Clb; 4-H; French Clb; Math Tm; Stage Crew; Yrbk Stf; 4-H Awd; Hon Roll; HOBY Ldrshp Conf Dely 84; Natl 4-H Cmmdty Mktg Symp 85; Natl 4-H Clb Congrss 85; Chld Psych.

JANELLE, LISA; Spaulding HS; Rochester, NH; (S); 6/397; Girl Scts; Rep Jr Cls; Stu Cncl; JV Var Vllybl; High Hon Roll; Hon Roll; NHS; Bst Fair Awd 85; Commrcl Art.

JANKOWSKY, DEBBIE; Fall Mountain Regional HS; Walpole, NH; (Y); 10/148; French Clb; Band; Mrchg Band; Stu Cncl; Bsktbl; Sftbl; Swmmng; Twrlr; Hon Roll; U NH; Hotel Mgmt.

JANO, LONNIE; Portsmouth HS; Portsmouth, NH; (Y); Church Yth Grp; Computer Clb; Math Clb; Ftbl; Wt Lftg; High Hon Roll; Hon Roll; Marines; Comp Scientst.

JANOS, CHRISTOPHER MICHAEL; Salem HS; Salem, NH; (S); 61/356; French Clb; Model UN; Ski Clb; SADD; Nwsp Sprt Ed; Bsktbl; High Hon Roll; Hon Roll; Math.

JAROSZ, RENEE; Newmarket HS; Newmarket, NH; (Y); 7/60; Girl Scts; Band; Concert Band; Mrchg Band; Pep Band; Yrbk Stf; JV Fld Hcky; High Hon Roll; Bus.

JEFFREY, MARLA L; Milford Area SR HS; Amherst, NH; (Y); Cmnty Wkr; GAA; School Musical; School Play; Var Fld Hcky; Var Mgr(s); Var Score Keeper; Im Vllybl; Hon Roll; Ntl Merit Ltr; NH Mock Trl Cmptn 2nd Plc 86; NH Mdl Brdg Bldng Awd 86; Dartmouth; Psych.

JENKINS, ADAM; Monadnock Regional HS; W Swanzey, NH; (Y); Lit Mag; Hon Roll; Aeronutcl Engr.

JENKINS, JANIE; Fall Mountain Regional HS; Charlestown, NH; (Y); 27/159; Drama Clb; 4-H; French Clb; Sec Girl Scts; Math Tm; Sec SADD; Chorus; Madrigals; School Musical; Stage Crew; Upward Bound 84-86; Plymouth ST Coll; Econ.

JENKINS, JENNIFER; Concord HS; Concord, NH; (Y); 44/392; Art Clb; Pres Intnl Clb; Band; Lit Mag; Var L Crs Cntry; High Hon Roll; NHS; Ntl Merit SF; Church Yth Grp; Mrchg Band; Achvt Awd Art, Engl 84-86; Christa Mc Aucliffe Cmndtn Awd Wrld Hstry 85-86; Wrtng.

JENKINS, STEVE; Timberlane Regional HS; Plaistow, NH; (Y); FBLA; German Clb; Socr; Trk; Hon Roll; Bus.

JENNINGS, TIMOTHY; Bishop Guertin HS; Merrimack, NH; (Y); Camera Clb; Stu Cncl; Crs Cntry; Trk; Wt Lftg; Hon Roll; Nclr Med.

JENSEN, IRENE; Nashura SR HS; Nashua, NH; (Y); 215/786; Church Yth Grp; Drama Clb; Science Clb; Pres Church Yth Grp; Hon Roll; Exchng Stu In Frnc 82-83; Chllng Pgm Rvr Coll 84-85; Evng Cls At Dnl Wbstr Coll 85-86; Gntc Engrng.

JIMENEZ, JULIE; Pelham HS; Pelham, NH; (Y); 49/120; Church Yth Grp; French Clb; Ski Clb; VP Spanish Clb; Sec Frsh Cls; Sec Soph Cls; Var Bsktbl; Coach Actv; Var Sftbl; JV Vllybl; U DELAWARE; Htl Mgt.

JOHNSON, BRIAN; Pembroke Acad; Suncook, NH; (Y); 36/160; French Clb; Ski Clb; L Bsbl; JV Bsktbl; JV Socr; Hon Roll; Sci.

JOHNSON, ELAINE; Wilton-Lydeborough Coop HS; Wilton, NH; (Y); Math Tm; SADD; Mrchg Band; Sec Soph Cls; Sec Jr Cls; JV Var Bsktbl; Var Crs Cntry; Var Capt Tennis; Trk; Hon Roll; Schl Fair Outstndg Achvt Awd 86; Frnch.

JOHNSON, KRISTIN; Pinkerton Acad; Derry, NH; (Y); 65/490; L Am Leg Aux Girls St; Cmnty Wkr; Ski Clb; Drill Tm; Rep Soph Cls; Rep Jr Cls; Rep Sr Cls; JV Socr; JV Trk; Hon Roll; U NH; Child Psych.

JOHNSON, LAURIE ANN; Sunapee JR SR HS; Sunapee, NH; (Y); 1/28; Trs 4-H; Teachers Aide; Stu Cncl; Var Bsktbl; Var Sftbl; Vllybl; Gov Hon Prg Awd; High Hon Roll; NHS; Val; Athletic Awd 86; John M Della V Emerson Schlrshp 86; Bentley Coll; Acctng.

JOHNSON, RHONDA M; The New Hampton Schl; Bellerose, NY; (Y); Cmnty Wkr; Math Tm; Sec Stu Cncl; Var Lcrss; Var Vllybl; Cit Awd; Hon Roll; Ntl Merit SF; Art Clb; French Clb; Airsta; Trustees Plnng Brd; Amherst; Advertsng.

JOHNSON, SUE; Keene HS; Keene, NH; (Y); 63/354; French Clb; JA; Color Guard; Drm & Bgl; Mrchg Band; Yrbk Stf; JV Var Sftbl; Hon Roll; Bus Mgt.

JOHNSON, TAMMI L; White Mountains Regional HS; Whitefield, NH; (Y); Church Yth Grp; Math Tm; Scrd Top 10% JETS NEAS 85-86; Engr.

JONES, DAVID; Newmarket HS; Newmarket, NH; (Y); Church Yth Grp; Drama Clb; French Clb; Trs SADD; Sec Frsh Cls; Sec Soph Cls; Sec Jr Cls; Sec Sr Cls; High Hon Roll; Hon Roll; Outstndng Achvmnt Awd Art Hist 85-86; UNH; Hist.

JONES, KIM; Inter-Lakes HS; Meredith, NH; (Y); 1/80; Dance Clb; SADD; Pres Jr Cls; Pres Sr Cls; Rep Stu Cncl; Cheerleading; High Hon Roll; NHS; Church Yth Grp; French Clb; US Hstry Awd 85; Schlstc Schlrshp St Pls 86; Typng Awd 86; Amrcn U; Pltcl Sci.

JOZITIS, JOE; Nashuen HS; Nashua, NH; (Y); 57/810; Computer Clb; German Clb; Hon Roll; NHS; Ntl Merit Ltr; U Of VT; Physcs.

JUDGE, WILLIAM; Moultonborough Acad; Ctr Harbor, NH; (Y); 1/41; Math Clb; Math Tm; Spanish Clb; Band; Concert Band; Mrchg Band; Pep Band; VP Soph Cls; Rep Stu Cncl; Bsbl; Achvt Span, Crtv Wrtg, Biol & Alg; Pres Phys Fit Awd; Schl Top Screr NE Math Lg; MVP Vars Bsbl; Bus.

KACZMAREK, THOMAS D; Phillips Exeter Acad; Inverness, IL; (Y); Cmnty Wkr; FBLA; Nwsp Rptr; Yrbk Stf; Rep Stu Cncl; JV Ftbl; Im Lcrss; Var L Swmmng; Var L Tennis; High Hon Roll; Wtrpl-Vrty Ltr 83-85; Assoc Collgt Entrprnrs 85-86; Gradtng In-Depth Coll Lvl Engl & Math 86; Law.

KAISER, JEFF; Keene HS; Westmoreland, NH; (Y); VICA; Golf; Trk; Arch.

KANAVOS, STEPHANIE; Alvirne HS; Hudson, NH; (Y); 32/338; Ski Clb; Var Bsktbl; Var Crs Cntry; Var Socr; Var Trk; Johnson & Wales Coll; Acctng.

KANE, ROSELIE; Portsmouth HS; Portsmouth, NH; (S); 7/359; Yrbk Stf; Cit Awd; High Hon Roll; Jr NHS; Katharine Gibbs Boston; Lgl Sec.

KARAVASILIS, TAKI; Bishop Guertin HS; Nashua, NH; (Y); Pep Clb; SADD; Stu Cncl; Trk; Wt Lftg; High Hon Roll; NHS; Spanish NHS; Frgn Lang Clb Pres; Pre-Med.

KARCZ, KEVIN JOHN; Salem HS; Salem, NH; (S); German Clb; Math Tm; Ski Clb; Spanish Clb; Trs Soph Cls; Trs Jr Cls; Socr; Trk; High Hon Roll; Ntl Merit Ltr; Rensselaer Polytech; Elec Engr.

KARLIK, CHRISTINE; Spaulding HS; Rochester, NH; (S); Band; Mrchg Band; Bsktbl; Sftbl; Phtgrphy.

KARNACEWICZ, MARTIN; Portsmouth HS; Greenland, NH; (S); 9/359; Latin Clb; Ski Clb; Concert Band; Jazz Band; Mrchg Band; Pep Band; Var L Trk; NHS; JV Bsbl; JV Bsktbl; New Englnd Schltc Band Assoc-Hnrs Band 85 & 86; New Hmpshr All ST Music Fstvl-Percssn 86; U Of NH; Elec Engrng.

KASE, DINA; Manchester Central HS; Manchester, NH; (S); DECA; Var JV Sftbl; Var JV Vllybl; High Hon Roll; Hon Roll; NH Tech Inst; Banking.

KATZ, SHARON; Milford Area SR HS; Amherst, NH; (Y); Drama Clb; School Musical; School Play; Stage Crew; Nwsp Stf; Yrbk Stf; Ed Lit Mag; Hon Roll; Jr NHS; Yng Vlntrs Actns Vlntr Of Yr 85.

KEALEY, JOLEEN M; Salem HS; Salem, NH; (Y); 35/341; Debate Tm; Girl Scts; Key Clb; Model UN; Spanish Clb; Speech Tm; SADD; Band; Chorus; Spanish NHS; UNH; Elec Engrng.

KEARNS, JEFFREY W; Nashua HS; Nashua, NH; (Y); 96/800; Drama Clb; Ski Clb; Spanish Clb; School Musical; School Play; Stage Crew; Hon Roll; Jr NHS; NHS; Woccester Poly-Tech; Chem Engr.

KEARNS, KRISTIN; Phillips Exeter Acad; Exeter, NH; (S); Cmnty Wkr; Church Choir; School Musical; JV Fld Hcky; Var Ice Hcky; High Hon Roll; 1st Pl 2nd Yr Frnch 84-85; 2nd Pl 1st Yr Frnch 83-84; Bus.

KEENAN, KAREN; Interlakes HS; Meredith, NH; (Y); Quiz Bowl; Cheerleading; High Hon Roll; Hon Roll; NHS; Helen Penn US Hstry Awd 85; Pres Astra 86-87; YMCA Yth & Govt Rep 85-87; Pre-Law.

KEISKI, LISA K; Londonderry HS; Londonderry, NH; (Y); Trs Intnl Clb; French Hon Soc; VP NHS; Ntl Merit SF; Quiz Bowl; Teachers Aide; Band; Orch; High Hon Roll; Acadmic Achvt Awd 83-85; Frgn Lang Awd 85; Chem Awd 84; Grinnell Coll; Bio.

KELLEHER, THOMAS; St Thomas Aquinas HS; Dover, NH; (Y); 4/85; French Clb; Key Clb; Letterman Clb; Math Tm; Ski Clb; JV Var Bsktbl; Var Capt Crs Cntry; Hon Roll; NHS; Acad Excel Math & Sci 86; Dover Prfssnl Firefghtrs Schlrshp 86; Boston Coll; Math.

KELLEY, JOHN; Milford Area SR HS; Amherst, NH; (Y); 24/311; Am Leg Boys St; Q&S; Quiz Bowl; Nwsp Sprt Ed; Yrbk Rptr; Rep Stu Cncl; Bsktbl; Capt Golf; Powder Puff Ftbl; Im Vllybl; Outstndng Chem Stdnt 85; Mst Vlbl Stffr Schl Nwsppr 86; Stdnt Cncl Schlrshp 86; U Of NH; Math.

KELLEY, KRISTIN; Hanover HS; Hanover, NH; (Y); 4/170; Church Yth Grp; Band; Ed Yrbk Ed-Chief; Sec Stu Cncl; Var JV Socr; Var JV Sftbl; High Hon Roll; Church Yth Grp; Concert Band; Yrbk Stf; Soccr Coaches Awd 85; Dartmouth Coll Book Awd 86; Cmmnctns.

KELSEY II, DONALD; Spaulding HS; Rochester, NH; (S); 36/397; Boys Clb Am; Boy Scts; French Clb; JV Var Ftbl; Trk; Hon Roll; NHS.

KENDALL, JULIA; Spaulding HS; Rochester, NH; (S); 23/394; Drama Clb; Math Tm; Model UN; Band; Chorus; Concert Band; Jazz Band; Mrchg Band; Pep Band; School Musical; Emerson; Jrnlsm.

KENNEDY, ERIN; White Mnts Reg HS; Whitefield, NH; (Y); 5/100; Art Clb; Pres Drama Clb; Ski Clb; Thesps; School Play; Mgr(s); Pres NHS; NH ST Drma Fstvl Perfm Awd 86; UNH; Psych.

KENNEY, JAMES; Central Catholic HS; Salem, NH; (Y); 60/266; Computer Clb; Ski Clb; Crs Cntry; Trk; Prfct Atten Awd; U Of NH; Lbrl Arts.

KENNEY, PETER; Portsmouth HS; Rye, NH; (S); Church Yth Grp; Bsbl; JV Bsktbl; High Hon Roll; Hon Roll; NHS.

KHAN, SALIM; Portsmouth HS; Portsmouth, NH; (S); 13/450; Church Yth Grp; French Clb; Math Tm; Ski Clb; JV Socr; Var L Tennis; High Hon Roll; NHS.

KIAH, RICHARD G; Inter-Lakes HS; Meredith, NH; (Y); Dance Clb; Debate Tm; Math Clb; Math Tm; Quiz Bowl; Spanish Clb; SADD; Band; Yrbk Phtg; Pres Frsh Cls; Pre Med.

KIBBY, SCOTT; Concord HS; Concord, NH; (Y); 94/390; Boy Scts; Yrbk Ed-Chief; Yrbk Phtg; JV Socr; Var Swmmng; JV Trk; Bow Ed Assoc Schlrshp 84; Citznshp Awd 84; Aernutcl Engr.

KIDDER, HEATHER; Central HS; Hooksett, NH; (Y); 94/430; Boys Clb Am; Rep Stu Cncl; JV Bsktbl; Var L Vllybl; High Hon Roll; Hon Roll; Vet.

KILUK, STEPHANIE; Berlin HS; Berlin, NH; (Y); 30/212; French Clb; Color Guard; Nwsp Rptr; Var L Tennis; Im Vllybl; Hon Roll; 2nd Plc Frshmn Clss Wrtng Cntst 83-84; 2nd Plc Prvntn Of Drg & Alchl Abs Of Berlin Wrtng Awd 84-85; Jrnlsm.

KING, ANDREW; Dover HS; Dover, NH; (Y); 60/330; Band; Chorus; Concert Band; Jazz Band; Mrchg Band; Pep Band; Stage Crew; Symp Band; Variety Show; JV Ice Hcky; NH All ST Festival 84-86; SYMS At U Of NH 84-86; Mcdonalds All Am HS Marching Bnd 86; Music Performer.

KING, KAREN J; Somersworth HS; Somersworth, NH; (Y); 35/165; Nwsp Rptr; Nwsp Stf; Yrbk Ed-Chief; Yrbk Stf; Rep Frsh Cls; Rep Stu Cncl; Var L Bsktbl; Var L Fld Hcky; Var L Sftbl; Hon Roll; Bsktbl Coachs Awd 85; Mbr St Bsktbl & Sftbl Champ Team 85-86; Lyndon ST Coll; Phys Ed.

KING, LARA D; Somersworth HS; Rollinsford, NH; (Y); Latin Clb; Math Tm; Ski Clb; Yrbk Stf; Capt Var Bsktbl; Capt Var Crs Cntry; Var L Fld Hcky; Capt Var Sftbl; Hon Roll; VFW Awd; A Wentworth Baer Schlrshp 86; Beccaris Mem Schlrshp Fnd 86; Brandeis U; Engrng.

KING, SHERRI; Mascoma Valley HS; Enfield, NH; (Y); Church Yth Grp; French Clb; Office Aide; Spanish Clb; Trs Soph Cls; Var L Cheerleading; JV Sftbl; Twrlr; Hon Roll; Guidnc Aid Awd 86; Vrsty Chrldg Sprtsmnshp Awd 86; Intrprtr.

KINGBURY, LYNNE; Kenne HS; Keene, NH; (Y); 17/368; French Clb; Latin Clb; Ski Clb; Var Fld Hcky; JV Sftbl; Hon Roll.

KINNE, BRION; Nashua SR HS; Nashua, NH; (Y); Science Clb; Ski Clb; JV Trk.

KINSON, ELIZABETH; Fall Mountain Regional HS; Drewsville, NH; (Y); 10/147; Am Leg Aux Girls St; Spanish Clb; Yrbk Phtg; Pres Jr Cls; Pres Sr Cls; Socr; Sftbl; Hon Roll; NHS; Science Clb.

KLAMKA, PETER; Bishop Guertin HS; Nashua, NH; (Y); Pres Debate Tm; Ed Nwsp Rptr; Off Sr Cls; Stu Cncl; NHS; NFL; Speech Tm; Bates Coll; Law.

KLECK, JENNIFER; Hanover HS; Hanover, NH; (Y); French Clb; Ski Clb; JV Lcrss; High Hon Roll; Hon Roll; Essay Dsplyd Concord NH 84; Magna Cum Laude Awd Natl Latin Exam 86.

KLEINSCHMIDT, MARIA; Hanover HS; Hanover, NH; (Y); 14/149; Latin Clb; Band; Jazz Band; Nwsp Stf; French Hon Soc; High Hon Roll; Hon Roll; Ntl Merit Ltr; Latin Awd; German Hnr Soc; Soc Studies.

KLOTZ, EMILY; Portsmouth HS; New Castle, NH; (S); 2/359; Church Yth Grp; Pres French Clb; Math Tm; Model UN; Quiz Bowl; Red Cross Aide; Var L Swmmng; High Hon Roll; NHS; Smith Bk Awd 85; SEARCH 84-86; Frnch Awd 84; Biol.

KNIFFIN, DAVID W; Hanover HS; Norwich, VT; (Y); Yrbk Phtg; Yrbk Stf; Jr Cls; Sr Cls; Stu Cncl; JV Bsktbl; Capt Socr; Hon Roll; Ntl Merit Ltr; Schl Comm Investigating Open Campus Policy 86; Bus.

KNOWLES, ERIC; Nashua HS; Nashua, NH; (Y); Ski Clb; Var Socr; Hon Roll; MVP & Coaches Awd In Soccer 84; NH ST Select Soccer Team 85; Bus.

KNOX, CAROLYN; Coe-Brown Acad; Northwood, NH; (Y); 5/60; French Clb; SADD; Pres Frsh Cls; Pres Soph Cls; Pres Jr Cls; Pres Sr Cls; Sec Stu Cncl; JV Var Bsktbl; Var Sftbl; Capt Vllybl; Concord Tech Inst; Dntl Hygn.

KOCH, THOMAS; Bishop Guertin HS; Nashua, NH; (Y); Computer Clb; French Clb; Off Intnl Clb; Im Bsktbl; High Hon Roll; Hon Roll; NHS; Prfct Atten Awd; Sci.

KOPKA, PETER; Bishop Buertin HS; Nashua, NH; (Y); Ski Clb; Stage Crew; Off Frsh Cls; Off Soph Cls; Var Ftbl; Im Wt Lftg; Var Wrstlng; Bus Mgmt.

KOSKI, RONNIE; Keene HS; Keene, NH; (Y); Varsity Clb; Var Ice Hcky; Var Capt Socr; Var Trk; Hon Roll; JV Socr MVP/Capt; Hockey ST Champs MVP 82; Socr ST Champs 85.

KOSMO, AUDREY; Keene HS; Westmoreland, NH; (Y); 43/362; Spanish Clb; Var Fld Hcky; Var Trk; Hon Roll.

KOUNAS, KRISANNE; Central HS; Candia, NH; (Y); 39/438; Latin Clb; SADD; High Hon Roll; Hon Roll; Amer Lg 83; Natl Latin Exam 85; Lib Arts.

KRASKO, MELISSA; Portsmouth SR HS; Portsmouth, NH; (S); 7/450; Latin Clb; JV Fld Hcky; JV Mgr(s); JV Score Keeper; JV Sftbl; High Hon Roll; NHS; Strep Trning Pgm 85-86; Boston U; Physcns Asst.

KRECKLOW, KARRYE; Dover HS; Dover, NH; (Y); Drama Clb; Key Clb; SADD; Chorus; School Musical; Variety Show; Hon Roll; Dvr Prnts Music Clb Schrlshp 86; Grrsn Plyrs Awd & Schrshp 86; U NH; Music.

KUCER, ANTON; Hanover HS; Norwich, VT; (Y); Exploring; German Clb; Ski Clb; Orch; JV Socr; High Hon Roll; Hon Roll; Lit Mag; Exc Music 86; NH All ST Orch 84-85; Awd Partcptn With Distnctn Natl Soc Stds Olymp 85; Engrg.

KUEHN, KATHY; Salem HS; Salem, NH; (S); 3/383; French Clb; Model UN; SADD; Im Bsktbl; Var Capt Crs Cntry; JV Trk; High Hon Roll; NHS; Mst Imprvd Rnnr Crss Cntry 84.

KUNZ, SHARON; Alton HS; Alton, NH; (S); French Clb; German Clb; VP Leo Clb; High Hon Roll; Hon Roll; Alton High Sci Fair 4th Pl 85.

KWIATKOWSKI, KARI; Pinkerton Acad; Windham, NH; (Y); 7/600; Am Leg Aux Girls St; Latin Clb; Math Tm; Yrbk Rptr; Yrbk Sprt Ed; Yrbk Stf; JV Bsktbl; Var Fld Hcky; Var L Tennis; High Hon Roll; Cornell U; Bio Sci.

KYRIAZIS, JOHN; Manchester Central HS; Manchester, NH; (Y); Rep Am Leg Boys St; Church Yth Grp; Nwsp Bus Mgr; Lit Mag; Rep Frsh Cls; Rep Soph Cls; Rep Jr Cls; Trs Stu Cncl; Hon Roll; Boy Scts; Law.

LA BARGE, NICOLE; Newfound Memorial HS; Bristol, NH; (Y); 5/55; Math Tm; Chorus; School Play; Nwsp Rptr; Pres Sr Cls; Rep Stu Cncl; Bsktbl; Vllybl; Hon Roll; NHS; St Pauls Schl Adv Studs Pgm 86; Teen Cncl 84-86; Lib Arts.

LA FOND, HOLLY; Nashua SR HS; Nashua, NH; (Y); Nwsp Stf; High Hon Roll; NHS; Gftd Tlntd Stds; Natl JR Hnr Scty 82-83; U Of NH; Sci.

LA MONTAGUE, LYNN; Central HS; Manchester, NH; (Y); Church Yth Grp; Cmnty Wkr; Drama Clb; 4-H; Girl Scts; Hosp Aide; Math Clb; Math Tm; Red Cross Aide; Varsity Clb; Cystic Fibrosis Found Vol Yr 85-86; Jacksonvill U; Bus Mgmt.

LA PLANTE, TROY; Franklin JR SR HS; Franklin, NH; (Y); 6/87; Am Leg Boys St; Computer Clb; Exploring; French Clb; Nwsp Stf; Ftbl; Elks Awd; High Hon Roll; Hon Roll; Pres Schlr; NH Vo Tech Laconia; Fire Prtct.

LA POINTE, ALAN; Oyster River HS; Claremont, NH; (Y); 4-H; FFA; SADD; VICA; Lit Mag; Var Ftbl; 4-H Awd; High Hon Roll; Hon Roll; Auto Tech.

LA ROCCA, DENISE; Manchester HS West; Bedford, NH; (Y); 39/434; Cmnty Wkr; Hosp Aide; Library Aide; Var L Crs Cntry; Var L Trk; Hon Roll; Phy Thrpy.

LA ROCHE, ERIC; Merrimack Valley HS; Penacook, NH; (Y); 20/110; Am Leg Boys St; Boy Scts; Var L Bsbl; Var L Bsktbl; JV Capt Ftbl; Var L Socr; CT Vlly All Lg Tm 1st Bs 84; U Of NH; Med Tech.

LA ROCHE, MARIE B; Manchester Memorial HS; Manchester, NH; (Y); 19/344; Var Capt Bsktbl; Var Capt Socr; Var Sftbl; High Hon Roll; Athlete Of Month 83-84; Athlete Of Yr 85; David Campano & Richard Laberge Schlrshp 86; U Of NH; Sci.

LABRANCH, SUSAN; Pelham HS; Pelham, NH; (Y); 19/130; French Clb; FHA; Yrbk Stf; Rep Stu Cncl; Var Capt Cheerleading; JV Fld Hcky; Var Tennis; Hon Roll; NHS; Voice Dem Awd; Bus Adm.

LABRECQUE, MICHAEL; Spaulding HS; Barrington, NH; (S); 24/397; Church Yth Grp; Pep Clb; Bsbl; Hon Roll; NHS; Recmmnded St Pauls Schl Advncd Stud 85; Vet Med.

LABRECQUE, SONIA; Goffstown HS; Goffstown, NH; (Y); 10/200; Church Yth Grp; Dance Clb; Pres FNA; Red Cross Aide; Ski Clb; Sec Soph Cls; JV Cheerleading; High Hon Roll; Hon Roll; NHS; Frnch IV Awd 85; Adv Bio & Soc Sci Awds 85-86; Ftr Mdcs & Wendy Morrissey Scanell Mem Schlrshps 86; St Michaels Coll; Librl Arts.

LAFERRIERE, MARGUERITE; Presentation Of Mary Acad; Tewksbury, MA; (Y); Drama Clb; Science Clb; Service Clb; Ski Clb; Concert Band; Orch; Symp Band; Nwsp Phtg; Yrbk Sprt Ed; Capt Bsktbl; Gldn Grffn Awd Bsktbl 85-86; Myrs Cup Sailng 82-83; CPI; Wrd Proc.

LAFERTE, DENISE; Spaulding HS; Barrington, NH; (S); 4/350; Am Leg Aux Girls St; Yrbk Stf; High Hon Roll; Hon Roll; Sec NHS; Srch-UNH Pgm Gftd Tlntd Stu 84-86.

LAFLEUR, ROGER; Bishop Brady HS; Pembroke, NH; (Y); JV Bsbl; Var L Ftbl; Var L Ice Hcky; Amercn Lgn Bsbl-Al-Stars 86; Engrng.

LAKIN, MARGO; Spaulding HS; Rochester, NH; (S); 18/397; Key Clb; Hon Roll; NHS; Biolgcl Oceanogrphr.

LALOPOULOS, JIM; Memorial HS; Manchester, NH; (Y); 2/341; Cmnty Wkr; Math Tm; High Hon Roll; NHS; Dartmouth Bk Awd 85-86; Math.

LAMARRE, JACQUES; Milford Area SR HS; Amherst, NH; (Y); 20/311; Am Leg Boys St; FBLA; Acpl Chr; Band; Yrbk Bus Mgr; Lit Mag; Sec Soph Cls; Sec Jr Cls; Hon Roll; Rotary Awd; Hugh O Brian Yuth Ldrshp; P Andover Acad; 1st FBLA Bus Grphcs; Providence Coll; Pol Sci.

LAMB, BETH-ANNE; Milford Area SR HS; Milford, NH; (Y); 33/300; Computer Clb; Chorus; Flag Corp; Trs Frsh Cls; Trs Soph Cls; Trs Jr Cls; Rep Stu Cncl; Masonic Awd; NHS; Math Tm; Dlrs Schlrs Schlrshp 86; WA & Lee U.

LAMBERT, KRISTINE; Concord HS; Bow, NH; (Y); Church Yth Grp; Sec Chorus; High Hon Roll; NHS; NH Hosa ST Sec 86-87; Chrsta Mcalffe Schlrshp-Super Cmp 86.

LAMMERS, STEVE; Portsmouth SR HS; Portsmouth, NH; (Y); 40/376; Band; Jazz Band; Mrchg Band; JV Bsbl; JV Bsktbl; Var L Socr; Var L Tennis; Var L Trk; Hon Roll; Pep Band; JR Wrld Cncl Treas Modl Congrss; New Englnd Hnrs Bnd; Semnrs Adv Stdnts; Olympcs Mind 3rd ST 86; Service Acad; Engrng.

LAMONTAGNE, ANNE-LOUISE; St Thomas Aquinas HS; Rochester, NH; (Y); Church Yth Grp; Drama Clb; VP Pres French Clb; Key Clb; Stu Cncl; High Hon Roll; Hon Roll; Kiwanis Awd; NHS; Pres Schlr; Attnded St Pauls Schl Advnced Stdies Pgm 85; Dover Kwns Clb Schlrshp 86; Rchstr Kwns Clb Schlrshp 86; Colby Coll; Bio.

LAMONTAGNE, COLETTE; Saint Thopmas Aquinas HS; Rochester, NH; (Y); 2/80; Church Yth Grp; Pres French Clb; Key Clb; Yrbk Stf; Bsktbl; High Hon Roll; Hon Roll; NHS; St Pauls Schl Adv Stds Prog 86; Biochem.

LAMSON, JAMES; Weare HS; Weare, NH; (Y); 3/38; Stu Cncl; Crs Cntry; Socr; Trk; Hon Roll; Prfct Atten Awd; Rotary Awd; SR Physcl Ed Hghst Hons Awd 86; Indstrl Arts Hghst Hons Awd 86; Joseph Perrigo Mem Schlrshp; NH Tech Inst; Mech Engrng.

LAMY, ROLAND; Concord HS; Concord, NH; (Y); 38/356; Var L Bsktbl; Var Capt Tennis; High Hon Roll; NHS; Ruel W Colby Awd Sprtsmnshp, Ldrshp & Dctn 86; Prince All Amer Hnrb Mntn Tnns 86; William & Mary Coll; Engrng.

LANDRY, DAVID; Hopkinton HS; Contoocook, NH; (Y); 19/72; Intnl Clb; Quiz Bowl; Stage Crew; Nwsp Rptr; VP Soph Cls; Dollars For Schlrs Scholar 85-86; NH Acad Decthln ST Champs 85-86; Gold Mdl Hstry Div Acad Dechhln; UNM; Pol Sci.

LANGLEY, AMY JO; Keene HS; Marlborough, NH; (Y); Drama Clb; French Clb; Girl Scts; Library Aide; Acpl Chr; Chorus; Church Choir; Stage Crew; Variety Show; JV Cheerleading; Ntl French Examination 84; Law.

LANGLOIS, TYHISE; Dover HS; Barrington, NH; (Y); 54/264; Am Leg Aux Girls St; VICA; Nwsp Rptr; VP Jr Cls; Bsktbl; Crs Cntry; Powder Puff Ftbl; Hon Roll; Plymouth U; Bus Mgmt.

LARLEE, MELINDA BETH; Alvirne HS; Hudson, NH; (Y); 15/300; Lit Mag; Hon Roll; Rvr Coll Chllng Pgm 85-86; Comm.

LARSON, JENNIFER; Conant HS; Rindge, NH; (Y); French Clb; GAA; Pep Clb; Science Clb; Varsity Clb; Var Bsktbl; Var Fld Hcky; Sftbl; High Hon Roll; Hon Roll; Amiott Awd 83-84; Tm Awd Sftbll 84; Can-Am Strt Hcky Chmpnshp Awd 84-85; Springfield Coll; Physcl Thrpy.

LASSONDE, STEVEN; Concord HS; Concord, NH; (Y); 38/350; Chess Clb; Var Ftbl; Trk; Wt Lftg; High Hon Roll; Hon Roll; Lttrd Ftbl 85-86; Mchncl Engrng.

LATAILLE, MICHAEL R; Alvirne HS; Hudson, NH; (Y); 22/338; French Clb; Math Tm; Band; Concert Band; Mrchg Band; Pep Band; Yrbk Bus Mgr; High Hon Roll; Hon Roll; NHS; Hudsons Lions Clb Schlrshp 86; Awd Of Recongtn Music 86; Concours Natl De Francais 84; ST U Of NY Albany; Math.

LAUGHY, JENNIFER; Winnisquam Regional HS; Franklin, NH; (Y); French Clb; Math Clb; Math Tm; Quiz Bowl; Variety Show; Hon Roll.

LAUNDERVILLE, THADDIUS; Kimball Union Acad; Cabot, VT; (Y); Computer Clb; Math Tm; Concert Band; Nwsp Rptr; JV Bsbl; Var Swmmng; High Hon Roll; Cum Laude Soc 86.

LAVALLEE, CHRISTINE; Manchester Memorial HS; Manchester, NH; (Y); 12/390; Lit Mag; High Hon Roll; NHS; Pol Sci.

LAVALLEE, DAVID; Bishop Guertin HS; Lowell, MA; (Y); 38/146; FCA; SADD; VP Soph Cls; Trs Jr Cls; Capt Bsbl; Capt Bsktbl; L Socr; Hon Roll; Spanish NHS; Acad All Am Schlr Pgm 86.

LAVENTURE, KEVIN; Winnisquam Regional HS; Tilton, NH; (Y); 19/91; Computer Clb; Spanish Clb; Stu Cncl; Var Capt Bsktbl; Var Trk; Hon Roll; Prfct Atten Awd; MIP-JV Bsktbl 83; MVP-JV Bsktbl 84; MVP Vrsty Bsktbl 86; Plymouth ST Coll; Comp Sci.

LAVERTU, ANN; Berlin HS; Berlin, NH; (Y); 91/191; Band; JV Bsktbl; Business.

LAVERTUE, MARVIN; Berlin HS; Berlin, NH; (Y); Hon Roll; Air Frc Pilot.

LAVIGNE, KEVIN; Gorham HS; Gorham, NH; (Y); Boy Scts; Drama Clb; Varsity Clb; School Play; Yrbk Sprt Ed; Yrbk Stf; Var Bsbl; Var Bsktbl; Coach Actv; Var Socr; Above 90 Pct SRA Testng Awd; Engl Awd; Optmtrst.

LAVIGNE, MICHELLE; Nashua HS; Nashua, NH; (Y); 150/972; Cmnty Wkr; French Clb; Office Aide; Ski Clb; Variety Show; Rep Frsh Cls; Rep Stu Cncl; Var JV Cheerleading; JV Fld Hcky; Hon Roll; Outreach Accptnc-Drug & Alcohol Abuse Prog 84-86; Piano Awds Lvls I-V 80-86; Camp JR Life Savng 82-84; U Of NH; Psych.

LAVOIE, SUSAN; Plymouth Area SR HS; Plymouth, NH; (Y); 27/137; DECA; Hosp Aide; Office Aide; Science Clb; SADD; School Musical; School Play; JV Bsktbl; Powder Puff Ftbl; Dstrbt Ed Clubs Amer Schlrshp 86; Plymth Bus & Profssnl Wmns Clb Schlrshp 86; M J Dunigan Schlrshp 86; NH Tech Isnt; Nrsng.

LAVOIE, WILLIAM; Bishop Guertin HS; Hudson, NH; (Y); Cmnty Wkr; JV Ftbl; Asst Coach Boys Hcky Team 84-86.

LAWN, MELODY S; Conant HS; Jaffrey, NH; (Y); 2/91; Yrbk Stf; Trs Frsh Cls; Trs Soph Cls; Bsktbl; Fld Hcky; Sftbl; High Hon Roll; NHS; Sal; US Army Rsrv Ntl Schlr/Athl Awd 86; Amer Lgn Schlrshp 86; Hofstra U; Accntng.

LAWRENCE, AMY; Keene HS; Keene, NH; (Y); 30/362; Office Aide; Band; Concert Band; Mrchg Band; Yrbk Stf; Trk; Hon Roll; Nrnsng.

LAY, MARNIE; Colebrook Acad; Canaan, VT; (Y); FBLA; Yrbk Stf; Hon Roll; VT Stu Assistance Grant 86; Champlain Coll; Retailing.

LAZOS, SPIROS; Manchester Central HS; Manchester, NH; (Y); 1/438; Church Yth Grp; Rep Stu Cncl; Var Capt Bsbl; JV Bsktbl; Var L Ftbl; High Hon Roll; NHS; Boys Clb Am; JA; Math Clb; Dartmouth Bk Awd 86; ST Qulfr Math Tst 86; Natl Greek Exm-Hgh Hnrs 86; Harvard; Pre-Med.

LAZOTT, JOHN; Manchester HS West; Bedford, NH; (Y); Ski Clb; Stage Crew; Yrbk Phtg; Yrbk Rptr; Mgr(s); Var L Socr; JV Wrstlng; High Hon Roll; Hon Roll; NH Coll; Mktg.

LE BLANC, JEFF; Manchester Memorial HS; Manchester, NH; (Y); 37/341; Am Leg Boys St; Sec Drama Clb; Teachers Aide; School Play; Yrbk Rptr; Yrbk Stf; Rep Stu Cncl; Bowling; JV Ice Hcky; L Var Tennis; Bobby Orr Sprtsmnshp Awd 84; Otstndgn Awd Hcky Rfrncs AHAUS 84; Cmmnctns.

LE CLAIR, MICHELLE; Pinkerton Acad; Chester, NH; (Y); 5/450; Latin Clb; SADD; Soph Cls; Jr Cls; Sr Cls; High Hon Roll; Hon Roll; NHS; Rollins Olonzo Scholar 86; Govnrs Schlr Awd 86; N Chester Ladies Aid Awd 86; Rollins Coll; Mth.

LE DUC, TODD; Bishop Guertin HS; Lowell, MA; (Y); 40/155; Church Yth Grp; Var Debate Tm; French Clb; NFL; Nwsp Rptr; Pres Frsh Cls; Rep Stu Cncl; Hon Roll; Hugh O Brien Ldrshp Awd H N Altrnt; Stu Gldr Plt Solo Status; MA EMT Trnd; Pltcl Sci.

LEA, SUSAN; Concord HS; Concord, NH; (Y); 22/350; Sec Varsity Clb; Nwsp Sprt Ed; Var L Bsktbl; Mgr Ftbl; Var L Tennis; Swmmng; Hon Roll; NHS; Keith Danie Awd; Best Feml Athlt 84; AAU All Star Bsktbl Tm 86; U Of VT; Sprts Med.

LEARNARD, REBECCA A; Newport JR SR HS; Newport, NH; (Y); Am Leg Aux Girls St; French Clb; Letterman Clb; Red Cross Aide; Yrbk Bus Mgr; Yrbk Stf; Rep Stu Cncl; Var Bsktbl; JV Capt Fld Hcky; Var Sftbl; Phys Thrpy.

LEAVITT, SHARI; Monadnock Regional HS; Keene, NH; (Y); Phys Thrpy.

LEBLOND, PAUL; Manchester Central HS; Manchester, NH; (Y); 60/430; French Clb; Rep Frsh Cls; Rep Soph Cls; Rep Jr Cls; Var L Bsbl; Var L Ftbl; Wt Lftg; High Hon Roll; Acad All-Amer 86; Bus Econ.

LEE, BRIAN P; Trinity HS; Merrimack, NH; (Y); Am Leg Boys St; Cmnty Wkr; Model UN; Spanish Clb; JV Socr; Hon Roll; NEDT Awd; Hnr Mntn Model UN 86; Poltcl Sci.

LEE, CARRIE; Alvirne HS; Hudson, NH; (Y); Key Clb; Pep Clb; Yrbk Stf; Im Bsktbl; Im Socr; Var Trk; Im Vllybl; Hon Roll.

LEE, DAVID HYUN C; Phillips Exeter Acad; Chicago, IL; (Y); Church Yth Grp; Intnl Clb; Chorus; Yrbk Stf; Socr; Tennis; Trk; Vllybl; Hon Roll; St Schlr; Wrkng At Law Firm 1-86 To 9-86; U Of Chicago; Law.

LEE, MELISSA J; Phillips Exeter Acad; Norman, OK; (Y); Off English Clb; French Clb; JCL; Latin Clb; Math Clb; School Play; Ed Lit Mag; High Hon Roll; Jr NHS; Ntl Merit SF; Cum Laude Soc 85; Lewis Sibley Poetry Prz 85; Abbey Manton Polleys Mem Prz 84; Engl.

LEE, SUZANNE A; Con Val Regional HS; Wilton, NH; (Y); Am Leg Aux Girls St; Drama Clb; Sec JCL; Band; School Play; JV Fld Hcky; High Hon Roll; VP NHS; JV Tennis; Edith Bird Bass Essay 1st Prz 86.

LEE, WON K; Phillips Exeter Acad; Lexington, KY; (Y); Church Yth Grp; French Clb; Natl Beta Clb; Orch; High Hon Roll; Ntl Merit SF; News Ed 82-83; Soclgy.

LEGARA, SHERRY; St Thomas Aquinas HS; New Castle, NH; (Y); 13/85; Am Leg Aux Girls St; Drama Clb; Speech Tm; School Musical; School Play; Var Crs Cntry; High Hon Roll; Hon Roll; Spanish NHS; Cert US Hstry & Wrld Relgns Avg Hnrs 86-87; Drm Clb Cert 87; Thrtr Arts.

LEGARE, GINA; St Thomas Aquinas HS; New Castle, NH; (Y); French Clb; ROTC; Bsktbl; Crs Cntry; High Hon Roll; Debate Tm; Drama Clb; Sftbl; Swmmng; Coast Guard Acad; Vet.

LEGARE, SHERRY; Saint Thomas Aquiras HS; New Castle, NH; (Y); 13/65; Am Leg Aux Girls St; Drama Clb; School Musical; School Play; Crs Cntry; Spanish NHS; Cert A Avg Hnrs Hist 86; Drama Cert 86; Theater.

LEHMAN, KIMBERLEY S; Hopkinton HS; Contoocook, NH; (Y); Yrbk Stf; Bsktbl; VP Capt Sftbl; Bsktbl/MIP, MVP, Capt; Sftbl ST Chmpns 86; Keene ST Coll NH; Lbrl Arts.

LEHMANN, SCOTT; Kennett HS; Ctr Conway, NH; (Y); 5/200; French Clb; Var Socr; French Hon Soc; High Hon Roll; Hon Roll; NHS; Ntl Merit Ltr; Poltcl Sci.

LEIGHTON, TRACY L; Concord HS; Concord, NH; (Y); 36/400; Varsity Clb; Capt L Cheerleading; High Hon Roll; NHS; Prfct Atten Awd; Outstndng Perfmnc In Eng 85-86.

LELAND, DAVID; Portsmouth SR HS; Rye, NH; (S); 7/420; Ski Clb; JV Bsbl; Capt Socr; Var Swmmng; Var Trk; High Hon Roll; NHS; Church Yth Grp; Im Bsktbl; Schlr Athl Awd 84; JR Wrld Cncl 85-86.

LELAND, WENDY; Pinkerton Acad; East Hampstead, NH; (Y); 10/496; 4-H; Hosp Aide; Band; Concert Band; Mrchg Band; School Musical; Yrbk Stf; Dnfth Awd; 4-H Awd; NHS; U NH; Brdcst Jrnlsm.

LEMAY, SHANE; Kingswood Regional HS; Ctr Ossipee, NH; (Y); Yrbk Stf; JV Bsbl; Ftbl; Var Ice Hcky; Hon Roll; Boston Coll; Law.

LEMAY, SHELLY; Salem HS; Salem, NH; (Y); FBLA; JA; Office Aide; Ski Clb; School Play; Yrbk Rptr; Yrbk Stf; Coach Actv; Var JV Gym; Cit Awd.

LEMIEUX, KRISTIN; Stevens HS; Claremont, NH; (Y); VP Church Yth Grp; VP SADD; Chorus; Church Choir; Drm Mjr(t); Mrchg Band; School Musical; Capt Twrlr; Hon Roll; All New Englnd Chrl Fstvl 86; Acctng.

LEMPNER, MICHAEL S; Milford Area SR HS; Amherst, NH; (Y); Am Leg Boys St; Church Yth Grp; French Clb; Ski Clb; Band; Concert Band; Mrchg Band; Orch; Trs Sr Cls; Rep Stu Cncl; Finance.

LENNERTON, BRETT ALAN; Salem HS; Salem, NH; (Y); 51/352; Computer Clb; Math Tm; Model UN; Spanish Clb; Concert Band; Mrchg Band; Var Capt Bsbl; Im Ice Hcky; JV Var Trk; Hon Roll; Digital Schlrshp 86; Bsbl Coach Awd 86; U Of Lowell; Comp Sci.

LEPAGE, RICHARD; Kingswood Regional HS; Wolfeboro Falls, NH; (Y); Sec Am Leg Boys St; Boy Scts; VP Church Yth Grp; 4-H; Spanish Clb; Chrmn SADD; Var Crs Cntry; Var Swmmng; Im Wt Lftg; High Hon Roll; US Naval Sea Cadet Corps Drill Instrctr Meritorious Unit Commendotion 84; W Point Grinell Norwich; Rltns.

LEPISTO, CHRISTY; Keene HS; Keene, NH; (Y); 57/362; Service Clb; Ski Clb; Spanish Clb; Concert Band; Stu Cncl; Var Crs Cntry; Var Trk; Hon Roll.

LEVEILLE, LISA M; Berlin HS; Berlin, NH; (Y); 1/225; Art Clb; Church Yth Grp; Computer Clb; Drama Clb; English Clb; French Clb; Math Clb; Pep Clb; Ski Clb; SADD; Aeronutc Engr.

LEWIS, KIMBALL A; Exetes Area HS; Exeter, NH; (Y); Am Leg Boys St; Bausch & Lomb Sci Awd; High Hon Roll; NHS; Ntl Merit Ltr; Var L Crs Cntry; Var L Golf; Var L Tennis; Brown U Book Awd 85-86.

LEWIS, RAQUEL; Phillips Exeter Acad; Cleveland, OH; (Y); Camera Clb; Church Yth Grp; Nwsp Rptr; Bsktbl; Im Socr; Im Tennis; Var Trk; Im Vllybl; Cit Awd; DAR Awd; KSU Whitney Young Schlrshp Awd 83; CABSE Pursuit Excllnc Essy Cntst 83; Begnng Germn Stdnt Awd 84; Stanford U; Intl Rel.

LEYTHAM, MISSI; Hanover HS; Cheslea, VT; (Y); AFS; 4-H; German Clb; Latin Clb; Lit Mag; 4-H Awd; Jrnlsm Day Part Awd 86; Lngst Trnsltr.

LINDSAY, CHRISTINE; Oyster River HS; Durham, NH; (Y); Am Leg Aux Girls St; Cmnty Wkr; Drama Clb; Office Aide; Var Capt Cheerleading; Swmmng; High Hon Roll; Hon Roll; $5000 Acadmc Schlrshp-Belmont Coll Nashville TN 86; MVP-CHRLDR 85-86; MIP-CHRLDR 83; Belmont Coll; Music Bus.

LINNEY, SARAH; Keene HS; Keene, NH; (Y); 45/360; Church Yth Grp; Drama Clb; 4-H; French Clb; Hosp Aide; Pep Clb; Chorus; Var Crs Cntry; Var Trk; Ntl Merit SF; Accntng.

LIOLIS, LAURA; Concord HS; Concord, NH; (Y); 25/390; Varsity Clb; Cheerleading; Var L Tennis; High Hon Roll; Hon Roll; NHS; Prfct Atten Awd; Hghst Achvmnt Spnsh II 84; Hghst Achvmnt Latn I Awd 85; NH ST Chmpn Tm & Dbls Cmptn 85.

LIPNICK, MICHAEL; Bishop Guertin HS; Nashua, NH; (Y); Church Yth Grp; Cmnty Wkr; Dance Clb; Key Clb; JV Bsbl; JV Bsktbl; Var L Golf; Hon Roll; MVP Awd Golf 85; Pre-Law.

LITMAN, JOSEPH; Bishop Guertin HS; Hudson, NH; (Y); Spanish Clb; L Var Crs Cntry; Trk; High Hon Roll; Trs NHS; Spanish NHS; Gate City Strider Awd 85; Outstndng Svc Natl Hnr Soc 86.

LIZIE, MARY; Manchester HS Central; Manchester, NH; (Y); 16/430; Math Clb; Math Tm; Concert Band; Orch; High Hon Roll; NHS; NH All-ST Orch 84; Queen Cty Music Fstvl 84-85; Ntl Ltn Exam Smma Cum Laude 86.

LOCKE, KELLY M; Kennett HS; Tamworth, NH; (Y); Church Yth Grp; Cmnty Wkr; Dance Clb; Office Aide; Color Guard; Drill Tm; Drm & Bgl; Flag Corp; Mrchg Band; School Play; U NH; Ocengrphy.

LOCKE, LISA; Kennett HS; Center Conway, NH; (Y); 80/213; Church Yth Grp; Girl Scts; Hosp Aide; Office Aide; Teachers Aide; Band; Chorus; Concert Band; Madrigals; Hon Roll; Chrl Arts Awds 86; Chorus Awd 84, Chorus Soprano 86; Berlin Vo Tech; Nrsg.

LOCKE, LISA M; Lisbon Regional HS; Lisbon, NH; (Y); 4/29; Church Yth Grp; Office Aide; Band; Church Choir; Yrbk Stf; Cheerleading; Score Keeper; Sftbl; High Hon Roll; NHS; I O F Concordia Awd 86; Lisbon Citzns Schlrshp Fndtn 86; U Of CT; Phrmclgy.

LOESCHORN, KENNETH; Kennett HS; Glen, NH; (Y); 87/184; Church Yth Grp; Hst FBLA; Trs Key Clb; Yrbk Bus Mgr; Hon Roll; Outstndng Achvt Sci 83-84; New Hampshire Coll; Bus Adm.

LOGUE JR, DENNIS E; Hanover HS; Hanover, NH; (Y); Church Yth Grp; Cmnty Wkr; Debate Tm; Political Wkr; Quiz Bowl; Scholastic Bowl; Yrbk Bus Mgr; Var Stu Cncl; Im Bsktbl; JV Var Crs Cntry; Latin Awd For Trnsltn 86; ST Michaus Clg Schlrs Awd 86; U Of VA; Engl.

LOMBARDI, VINCE; Milford Area SR HS; Amherst, NH; (Y); 62/309; Pres VP FBLA; Trs Band; Band; VP Stu Cncl; Hon Roll; Debate Tm; Ski Clb; Chorus; Concert Band; Drm & Bgl; Stu Mnth 84-85; Solist All ST Music Conf 85-86; 3rd ST Palimntry Proc 85-86; U NH; Bus Adm.

LOPES, WARD; Concord HS; Concord, NH; (Y); 16/390; Boy Scts; Church Yth Grp; German Clb; Math Tm; Lit Mag; High Hon Roll; Hon Roll; NHS; Ntl Merit SF; Chess Clb; Outstndng Achvt German-W German Counsul Genl 86; Lang.

LORD, AMY ELIZABETH; Newport JR/Sr HS; Newport, NH; (Y); Am Leg Aux Girls St; Pres French Clb; Concert Band; Jazz Band; School Musical; Yrbk Stf; Capt JV Bsktbl; NHS; Pep Clb; Band; Tri-M Music Hnr Soc 85; Geraldinne Rudenfeldt Schlrshp 85; Art.

LORD, KELLY D; Hopkinton HS; Contoocook, NH; (Y); 11/62; Am Leg Aux Girls St; French Clb; Cmnty Wkr; Yrbk Stf; Var Stu Cncl; Var Capt Cheerleading; JV Var Fld Hcky; Hon Roll; NHS; U S Air Force Acad Smmr Sci Semnr 86; Oldr Grls Conf 86; Intl Mgmt.

LORD, MATTHEW; Central HS; Manchester, NH; (Y); Boys Clb Am; Boy Scts; Church Yth Grp; 4-H; Leo Clb; Library Aide; Band; Chorus; 4-H Awd; God Cntry Awd; Egl Sct Awd 83; God & Fmly Awd 82; Eastern Baptist Coll; Law.

LORD, SUSAN; Manchester Memorial HS; Auburn, NH; (Y); 10/350; Art Clb; French Clb; Nwsp Stf; High Hon Roll; NHS; Clntn E Scvl Schlrshp 86; Pres Acad Ftns Awd 86; Acad Frshmn Schlrshp Fr Bntly Coll 86; Bentley Coll; Bus Mgmt.

LOTO, KATHY; Inter-Lakes HS; Meredith, NH; (Y); 16/83; Church Yth Grp; SADD; Concert Band; Mrchg Band; Yrbk Stf; Var Cheerleading; Mgr Trk; Hon Roll; Engrng.

LOVE, GARRETT R; Tilton Schl; Tilton, NH; (S); 1/69; 4-H; Chorus; School Play; Var Lcrss; JV Socr; 4-H Awd; High Hon Roll; NEDT Awd; NH Al-ST Choir 86.

LOVELAND, ANDREW; Keene HS; Keene, NH; (Y); 14/363; Boy Scts; Church Yth Grp; Library Aide; Band; Mrchg Band; Var L Wrstlng; Hon Roll; Lion Awd; Ntl Merit Ltr; Rotary Awd; Mst Imprvd Undrclss Wrstlng, USAFA Scntfc Smnr, Adv Stds Pgm 86; Sci.

LOVELL, LINDA; Inter Lakes HS; Meredith, NH; (Y); Girl Scts; Office Aide; Yrbk Stf; High Hon Roll; Hon Roll; Acctg.

LOVELL, MICHELE; Keene HS; Keene, NH; (Y); 38/330; Camp Fr Inc; Church Yth Grp; Computer Clb; Dance Clb; English Clb; FBLA; Sec JA; Math Clb; Red Cross Aide; Science Clb; Plymouth Schlr Awd 86; Plymouth ST Coll; Accntng.

LOVELY JR, PETER R; Newport HS; Newport, NH; (Y); Am Leg Boys St; French Clb; School Play; Stu Cncl; Capt Bsktbl; L Ftbl; L Trk; Phy Ed.

LOW, JODY B; Coe-Brown Acad; Dover, NH; (Y); Boy Scts; Cmnty Wkr; Computer Clb; FCA; FFA; Ski Clb; SADD; School Play; JV Capt Bsktbl; Socr.

LOZEAU, ANNEMARIE; Bishop Brady HS; Concord, NH; (Y); 18/74; Trs Church Yth Grp; Ski Clb; Var L Fld Hcky; Im Ice Hcky; Var L Sftbl; Hon Roll; Skiing Nastar 3rd 85; Most Imprvd Sftbl 86; Math.

LOZEAU, CHRISTINE; Alvirne HS; Litchfield, NH; (Y); 20/338; FBLA; Hon Roll; Jr NHS.

LOZIER, MELISSA; Berlin HS; Berlin, NH; (Y); 31/219; Drama Clb; SADD; School Play; Yrbk Stf; JV Bsktbl; JV Fld Hcky; Var JV Tennis; Hon Roll; Physcl Thrpst.

LUCIA, TAMMY; Stevens HS; Claremont, NH; (Y); Trs Key Clb; Capt Math Tm; SADD; Rep Stu Cncl; High Hon Roll; Hon Roll; NHS; Math.

LUCK, CHRISTINE LYNN; Newport HS; Newport, NH; (Y); Capt Am Leg Aux Girls St; Cmnty Wkr; English Clb; French Clb; VP Letterman Clb; Math Clb; Math Tm; Model UN; Pep Clb; Science Clb; Twin ST Mth Lg Awd Top 10 86; U S Hstry Awd 86; Miss Teen NH 84; NH Miss TEEN 85; Princeton U; Pre-Law.

LYNCH, HELEN; Colebrook Acad; Colebrook, NH; (Y); 1/49; Pres Church Yth Grp; CAP; Drama Clb; Pres Sec French Clb; Sec Science Clb; Chorus; School Musical; Bausch & Lomb Sci Awd; NHS; Val; Gov Schl 86; Hghst Avg Sci & Mth 82-86; Bst Actress 86; Boston U; Bio.

LYNCH, KARA; Phillips Exeter Acad; Manhattan Beach, CA; (Y); Radio Clb; Chorus; School Musical; School Play; Yrbk Ed-Chief; Var Capt Ice Hcky; Var JV Lcrss; JV Socr; Hon Roll; Engl.

LYNCH, TERRI; Concord HS; Bow, NH; (Y); 3/390; Varsity Clb; Var L Tennis; High Hon Roll; VP NHS; Arthur R Virgin Music Cmptn 84-86; St Tennis Chmpns Var Tm 85; Accptd St Pauls Schl 84.

LYNDES, CHRISTIAN; Portsmouth HS; Greenland, NH; (Y); Boy Scts; Ski Clb; Bsktbl; Ftbl; VP Swmmng; JV Trk; Im Wt Lftg; Hon Roll; Socl Studies Awd 86; Engrng.

LYON, JASON; Newfound Memorial HS; Bristol, NH; (Y); 10/57; French Clb; Chorus; School Musical; Nwsp Bus Mgr; Yrbk Bus Mgr; VP Stu Cncl; Mgr(s); Hon Roll; Yrbk Edtr 86-87; Johnson Coll; Bus Mgmt.

MAC DONALD, BRUCE; Colebrook Acad; Colebrook, NH; (Y); Art Clb; Varsity Clb; JV Var Bsktbl; Score Keeper; L Capt Socr; Vllybl; Hon Roll; Woodbury Art Awd 85-86; Boys JV & Var Awd 86; Boys Var Lttr & Pin 86; Bus.

MAC GREGOR, MARC; Merrimack Valley HS; Webster, NH; (Y); Boy Scts; Chess Clb; Math Tm; SADD; Band; Jazz Band; Mrchg Band; Var Crs Cntry; Var Trk; Hon Roll; Math.

MAC ILVANE, RUTH M; Groveton HS; Guildhall, VT; (S); 2/47; French Clb; FBLA; Hosp Aide; Yrbk Stf; Stu Cncl; Capt Cheerleading; Fld Hcky; High Hon Roll; Hon Roll; Sec NHS; Med.

MAC KAY, KEITH J; Newfound Memorial HS; Danbury, NH; (Y); 1/60; Church Yth Grp; School Musical; Yrbk Stf; Pres Soph Cls; Pres Jr Cls; Var Trk; Bausch & Lomb Sci Awd; DAR Awd; Pres Schlr; Val; Mr B Comm Svc Awd 86; MA Inst Of Tech; Comp Sci.

MAC SWEENEY, DARLENE M; Alvirne HS; Hudson, NH; (Y); 16/338; Am Leg Aux Girls St; School Play; Sec Jr Cls; Stu Cncl; Var Capt Cheerleading; Sec NHS; Hon Roll; Intnl Clb; Teachers Aide; Alvirne Cent III Ldrshp Awd 85-86; Stu Of Yr Awd 85-86; Mst Valbl Chrldr Awd 85-86; Skidmore Coll; Elem Ed.

MACDONALD, WENDY; Kennett HS; Madison, NH; (Y); 28/180; Am Leg Aux Girls St; 4-H; French Clb; Teachers Aide; Nwsp Rptr; Nwsp Stf; French Hon Soc; High Hon Roll; Hon Roll; French II Awd 85; French Hnr Socy 85-86; Amer Lgn Aux Girls St 86.

MACEY, SHAWN; Bishop Brady HS; Bow, NH; (Y); Camera Clb; FCA; Intnl Clb; Math Tm; Yrbk Stf; Stu Cncl; High Hon Roll; NHS; Prfct Atten Awd; Val; Arch.

MACFARQUHAR, LARISSA; Phillips Exeter Acad; Cambridge, MA; (Y); Cmnty Wkr; Chorus; Madrigals; Orch; School Musical; Ed Lit Mag; Im Tennis; Im Trk; Ntl Merit SF; Vllybl; Cum Laude Socty 86.

MACKENZIE, DIANA; Concord HS; Concord, NH; (Y); Office Aide; Y-Teens; Orch; Off Jr Cls; Rep Stu Cncl; Stat Mgr(s); Score Keeper; Trk; Hon Roll.

MACKEY, BRIAN D; Dover HS; Dover, NH; (Y); 34/281; Am Leg Boys St; Boy Scts; Exploring; High Hon Roll; Hon Roll; Egl Sct 83; U Of NH; Elec Engr.

MACRI, LISA; Alvirne HS; Hudson, NH; (Y); 199/338; Cmnty Wkr; Drama Clb; French Clb; Intnl Clb; Letterman Clb; Pep Clb; SADD; Varsity Clb; Chorus; School Play; Plymouth ST Coll; Law.

MAGAN, ROBERT; Pembroke Acad; Epsom, NH; (Y); Pres Church Yth Grp; JA; OEA; SADD; Var Capt Socr; High Hon Roll; Hon Roll; Pres Of NHS 85-86; Bus Adm.

MAHEU, MARY; Mascorna Valley Regional HS; Enfield Ctr, NH; (Y); 25/98; Var Cheerleading; Var Mgr(s); Hon Roll; Plymth ST Coll.

MAHLER, TIMOTHY W; Dublin Christian Acad; Gorham, ME; (Y); Church Yth Grp; Chorus; Church Choir; VP Sr Cls; Rep Stu Cncl; Var Capt Bsktbl; Var Crs Cntry; Var Capt Socr; High Hon Roll; Pres Schlr; Otstndng Ble Stu Awd; Christian Chrctr Awd 82; Awna LIT Seaman & Cmpng Awds; Achvt Awds 84-85; Bob Jones U; Pstrl.

MAHONEY, JACKI; Concord HS; Concord, NH; (Y); Church Yth Grp; VP FHA; Girl Scts; Hosp Aide; Yrbk Stf; High Hon Roll; NHS; HOSA Hstrn 85-86; Srgn.

MAJOROS, CHRISTOPHER P; Newport HS; Guild, NH; (Y); 1/90; Chorus; Concert Band; Ed Yrbk Ed-Chief; Bausch & Lomb Sci Awd; Cit Awd; NHS; Ntl Merit SF; Val; Math Tm; Ski Clb; Pres Tri-M Music Hon Soc; Hgh Achvt Awds; Granite ST Challenge Tm; Physics.

MALM, KAREN; Mascona Valley Regional HS; Enfield, NH; (Y); 4/101; Pres Spanish Clb; Teachers Aide; Concert Band; Var Capt Cheerleading; High Hon Roll; Hon Roll; VP NHS; Pres Acadmc Ftnss Awd 86; Outstndng H S SR 86; Home Ec Awd 86; Cazenovia Clg; Fash Merch.

MALONE, SEAN P; Bishop Guertin HS; Amherst, NH; (Y); Trs Church Yth Grp; Cmnty Wkr; VP FCA; Key Clb; Q&S; Varsity Clb; Nwsp Rptr; Nwsp Stf; Yrbk Stf; Drama Clb; Marquette,Law.

MALSBURY, WILLIAM; Dover HS; Dover, NH; (Y); Boy Scts; Exploring; Vllybl; Hon Roll; Natl Yth Ldrshp Awd 85; Law Enfrcmt.

MANDERACH, FRANK; Salem HS; Salem, NH; (Y); 125/383; Boys Clb Am; Model UN; Var Ftbl; L Trk; Hon Roll; Kiwanis Awd; 1st Trple Jmp, 3rd Lng Jmp New England, 4th Lng Jmp JR Olympcs Regn 86; Arch.

MANLEY, WILLIAM; Nashua SR HS; Nashua, NH; (Y); 200/890; SADD; Band; Concert Band; Mrchg Band; Orch; Variety Show; Hon Roll; Jr NHS; Sec Band 83-84; MCEE Talnt Show 84.

MANN, JULIE; Pinkerton Acad; Windham, NH; (Y); 45/400; Church Yth Grp; Ski Clb; Band; Mrchg Band; Pep Band; School Musical; Yrbk Stf; NHS; Natl Hnr Soc Schlrshp 86; Prsdntl Acadmc Ftns Awd 86; Stetson U; Bio.

MANNING, SHAWN; Manchester HS West; Bedford, NH; (Y); 9/420; Drama Clb; SADD; School Play; Rep Soph Cls; High Hon Roll; Jr NHS; Acctnt.

MANSEAU, CAROLYN C; West HS; Bedford, NH; (Y); 143/420; Cmnty Wkr; Ski Clb; Nwsp Rptr; Socr; Trk; Vllybl; High Hon Roll; Hon Roll; NEDT Awd; UNH; Bus.

MANTER, DAN; Central HS; Manchester, NH; (Y); 17/430; Am Leg Boys St; Math Tm; Yrbk Stf; Rep Stu Cncl; Crs Cntry; JV Socr; Var Trk; High Hon Roll; Jr NHS; Ski Tm Capt.

MANTZOUFAS, OLGA; Central HS; Manchester, NH; (Y); Sec Church Yth Grp; Computer Clb; Nwsp Rptr; Yrbk Stf; Rep Frsh Cls; Rep Soph Cls; Rep Jr Cls; Rep Stu Cncl; Co-Capt Cheerleading; High Hon Roll.

MARCHI, LISA; Alvirne HS; Hudson, NH; (Y); 4/338; Church Yth Grp; Cmnty Wkr; Ed Lit Mag; Stu Cncl; Hon Roll; Sec NHS; Ed Yrbk Stf; Govnrs Schlr 86; Hudson Kiwanis Clb Schlrshp 86; Hudson Furtnightly Schlrshp 86; U Of New Hampshire; Zoology.

MARCOTTE, TAMMY; Concord HS; Penacook, NH; (Y); Dance Clb; Band; High Hon Roll; Hon Roll; Dance Awd 84-86; Keene ST Coll; Psych.

MARCOUX, PAULA L; St Thomas Aquinas HS; Kittery, ME; (Y); 12/78; Debate Tm; Drama Clb; French Clb; Math Tm; Teachers Aide; Model UN; Church Choir; Orch; School Play; Mgr Stage Crew; Educ.

MARDER, WENDY; Kennett HS; N Conway, NH; (Y); 37/182; French Clb; Nwsp Rptr; Yrbk Stf; JV Bsktbl; Var L Crs Cntry; Var Trk; French Hon Soc; Hon Roll; Tufts U; Psych.

MARINELLI, TINA; Salem HS; Salem, NH; (Y); 6/360; Model UN; Teachers Aide; VP Frsh Cls; Rep Stu Cncl; Var Fld Hcky; Var Capt Sftbl; High Hon Roll; Hon Roll; Julio Camba Hnrary Soc Spnsh Lang 86; Holly Corss; Ecnmcs.

MARKSON, SCOTT; Coe-Brown Northwood Acad; Deerfield, NH; (Y); Church Yth Grp; Exploring; Cit Awd; Prfct Atten Awd; Bus.

MAROIS, JEANNE; Berlin HS; Berlin, NH; (Y); Pep Clb; SADD; Yrbk Stf; JV Fld Hcky; JV Sftbl; Spcl Ed Tchr.

MARSDEN, JULIE; Kennett HS; N Conway, NH; (Y); 9/180; Sec French Clb; Yrbk Stf; Fld Hcky; VP Jr Cls; Stu Cncl; Sec NHS; Wellesley Bk Awd 85-86; Art.

MARSH, SHAWN; Spaulding HS; Rochester, NH; (Y); 60/365; Boy Scts; Rep Sr Cls; Var L Ftbl; Hon Roll; Eagle Scout Awd 86; Lorette Savary Unsung Hero Awd Ftbl 86; Boys ST 85; U NH; Elec Engrng.

MARSHALL, KIM; Kennett HS; Conway, NH; (Y); 2/182; VP French Clb; Yrbk Stf; Trs Jr Cls; Rep Stu Cncl; Var Fld Hcky; Var Tennis; French Hon Soc; Hon Roll; Nwsp Sprt Ed; Rep Frsh Cls; Heldman Awd Tennis 85; MCRC Tennis Schlr Awd 86; Math.

MARSHALL, STEPHANIE D; Oyster River HS; Durham, NH; (Y); Drama Clb; Acpl Chr; Chorus; Concert Band; School Musical; Trs Soph Cls; Trs Jr Cls; VP Sr Cls; Band; Color Guard; Girls St 86; Mst Imprvd Chorale Singer Awd 86; Music.

MARSTON, DARLENE; Coe Brown Northwood Acad; Northwood, NH; (Y); 2/50; Am Leg Aux Girls St; Sec Frsh Cls; Sec Soph Cls; Sec Jr Cls; Sec Sr Cls; JV Bsktbl; Var Sftbl; JV Var Vllybl; Hon Roll; Sec NHS; Algebra Awd 86; French Awd 84-85; Cosmtlgy.

MARTEL, KAREN; Pembroke Acad; Allenstown, NH; (Y); 8/185; Rep Soph Cls; Rep Jr Cls; Rep Sr Cls; Var L Bsktbl; Var L Fld Hcky; JV Sftbl; Var L Trk; High Hon Roll; Hon Roll; Sec Trs NHS; Med.

MARTIN, JOHN; Inter-Lakes HS; Meredith, NH; (Y); 14/87; Camera Clb; Church Yth Grp; CAP; Exploring; French Clb; Quiz Bowl; Varsity Clb; Var L Crs Cntry; Var L Trk; High Hon Roll; Aerontcl Engrng.

MARTIN, MONICA; Keene HS; Keene, NH; (Y); 12/395; Church Yth Grp; Acpl Chr; Band; Color Guard; Concert Band; Mrchg Band; Yrbk Stf; Hon Roll; Flight Atten.

MARTINEAU, MICHELLE; Memorial HS; Manchester, NH; (Y); Hosp Aide; Gym; Trk; Wt Lftg; NH Voc Tech Coll; Nrsng.

MARZLOFF, KAREN; Memorial HS; Auburn, NH; (Y); 19/341; Art Clb; Church Yth Grp; Cmnty Wkr; Pres Rptr 4-H; Capt Ski Clb; Teachers Aide; Var Crs Cntry; Var Tennis; 4-H Awd; High Hon Roll; Crusader Fall Ath Awd 85.

MASON, DEBORAH; Littleton HS; Littleton, NH; (Y); 20/97; VP Sec FBLA; Yrbk Stf; JV Var Bsktbl; JV Var Fld Hcky; JV Mgr(s); JV Var Sftbl; High Hon Roll; Hon Roll; Lion Awd; NHS; MVP Fld Hcky And Sftbl 85-86; Emblm Schlrshp 86; Plymouth ST Clg; Bus Mgmt.

MASON, KRISTIN; Kennett HS; N Conway, NH; (Y); 29/201; Hosp Aide; Key Clb; Fld Hcky; Hon Roll; Pres Schlrshp To Colby Sawyer 87; Colby Sawyer; Nrsng.

MASON, MATTHEW C; Winnisquam Regional HS; Tilton, NH; (Y); 1/92; Ski Clb; VP Jr Cls; VP Sr Cls; Stu Cncl; Bausch & Lomb Sci Awd; DAR Awd; Gov Hon Prg Awd; NHS; Pres Schlr; U Of NH; Bus Admin.

MASTEN, TAMMY; Portsmouth HS; Portsmouth, NH; (Y); Band; Concert Band; Mrchg Band; Orch; Pep Band; Symp Band; JV Var Mgr(s); JV Var Score Keeper; High Hon Roll; Hon Roll; UNH; Bus Mgmt.

MATA, HUMBERTO; Phillips Exeter Acad; Ecuador; (S); Pres Intnl Clb; Model UN; Spanish Clb; Pres Stu Cncl; Im Tennis; Econ.

MATHEWS, KIMBERLY; Henniker HS; Henniker, NH; (Y); 3/16; SADD; Chorus; School Musical; Nwsp Rptr; Nwsp Stf; Yrbk Stf; Drama Clb; French Clb; Math Tm; Hon Roll; Ntl Hstry Day 2nd Pl In Media 85; Ntl Hstry Day Mdl For Outstndng ST Engry 85; Cornell Coll; Crmnlgy.

MATOS, MICHAEL; Portsmouth SR HS; Portsmouth, NH; (S); 4/403; Drama Clb; Math Tm; Band; Drm Mjr(t); Jazz Band; School Musical; Im Socr; Var L Trk; High Hon Roll; VP NHS; Stu Mnth Awds Math,Music,Sci 83-84; Engrng.

MATSON, CHARLOTTE; St Thomas Aquinas HS; Eliot, ME; (Y); Drama Clb; Latin Clb; Chorus; School Play; Stage Crew; Nwsp Phtg; Eckers Coll; Oceangrphy.

MATTE, PETER J; Nashua SR HS; Nadshue, NH; (S); Cmnty Wkr; DECA; Hosp Aide; Office Aide; JV Ftbl; JV Trk; 1st Pl Deca Rest Mrktgn 86; Deca Stu 86; Awd Track 83; Johnson & Wales.

MATTHEWS, HEATHER; Stevens HS; Claremont, NH; (Y); German Clb; Key Clb; Ski Clb; Var Crs Cntry; JV Socr; High Hon Roll; NHS; St Pauls Advncd Stu 86; 3 Yr Avrg Of 90 Abvd 86; Bio.

MATUSOW, JEFFREY M; Phillips Exeter Acad; Durham, NH; (Y); Pres Frsh Cls; JV Capt Swmmng; Var L Tennis; Ntl Merit SF; Math Tm; Orch; Yrbk Stf; Adv Russian Prz; Silver Russian Olympiade; Lang.

MAXWELL, CHRISTINA; Hollis Area HS; Hollis, NH; (Y); Church Yth Grp; Color Guard; Concert Band; Capt Flag Corp; High Hon Roll; Hon Roll; NHS; Math.

MAYHEW, BRUCE; Concord HS; Concord, NH; (Y); 22/394; Var L Debate Tm; DECA; L Var FBLA; High Hon Roll; Hon Roll; NHS; Danie Awd 84; Hon Mntn All ST 86; Outstndng Bck Ftbll Tm 86.

MAYHEW, KAREN; Milford Area SR HS; Amherst, NH; (Y); 13/311; Church Yth Grp; Hon Roll; NHS; Pres Ftns Awd 86; U NH-MANCHESTER; Bus Adm.

MAYNARD, KELLY; Mascoma Valley Regional HS; Canaan, NH; (Y); Spanish Clb; Swmmng; High Hon Roll; Spnsh Underclsmn Awd 86; Liberal Arts Coll; Engl.

MAZIARZ, JEFFREY J; Salem HS; Salem, NH; (Y); Latin Clb; Model UN; Teachers Aide; High Hon Roll; Hon Roll; Latin Awd; U Lowell; Comp Sci.

MC ALARY, PATRICK; Goffstown HS; Goffstown, NH; (Y); 4/225; Exploring; Math Tm; Varsity Clb; Nwsp Rptr; Var Capt Bsktbl; JV Socr; High Hon Roll; NHS; Ntl Merit Ltr; Variety Show; Bio, Hstry, Geom, Engl, Chem, Analysis I & Physics Awds; Tufts U; Biochem Engrng.

MC CABE JR, EDMUND JAMES; St Thomas Aquinas HS; Dover, NH; (Y); Pres Am Leg Boys St; Church Yth Grp; Cmnty Wkr; Political Wkr; Hon Roll; Kiwanis Awd; Prfct Atten Awd; Boys Clb Am; French Clb; Republcn Pres Task Force 85; US Capital Hstrcl Soc 85; U NH; Hstry.

MC CABE, KIMBERLY; Profile JR SR HS; Littleton, NH; (Y); Camera Clb; French Clb; Var L Crs Cntry; Var L Sftbl; High Hon Roll; Hon Roll; Hgh Acdmc Hnrs Awd 84; Outstndng Art Stu Awd 86; Outstndng Indstrl Arts Stu Awd 86; Art.

MC CALLISTER, SHARON; Nute HS; Milton, NH; (S); 4/41; Art Clb; FBLA; Math Clb; VP Chorus; Jazz Band; Variety Show; Yrbk Stf; Hon Roll; NHS; Jhnsn & Whls Acadmc Schlrshp 86; Cert Musicnshp-Brkle Coll 85; Acadmc All Amercn 86; Johnson & Whales; Accntng.

MC CANN, MARTIN; Bishop Guertin HS; Lowell, MA; (Y); Boy Scts; Exploring; Var Ftbl; L Wrstlng; Hon Roll; NEDT Awd; Comp Sci.

MC CLEARY, ELENA; Portsmouth SR HS; Portsmouth, NH; (Y); 170/368; Model UN; Band; Concert Band; Mrchg Band; School Play; Stage Crew; Swmmng; Ntl Merit Ltr; Bus Mngmnt.

MC COOLE, KAREN; Dover HS; Dover, NH; (Y); 20/281; Capt Var Bsktbl; Powder Puff Ftbl; Var L Sftbl; High Hon Roll; Capt JV Bsktbl Tm 85; U Of CT; Phrmcy.

MC CORGRAY, PATRICIA; Concord HS; Concord, NH; (Y); Drama Clb; Band; Concert Band; Mrchg Band; School Musical; School Play; Stage Crew; Int Span Recitatn 1st Pl 86.

MC CORMACK, BRIAN; Pembroke Acad; Epsom, NH; (Y); Boys Clb Am; FHA; Teachers Aide; Masonry.

MC CORMICK, MARY; Bishop Brady HS; Concord, NH; (Y); 16/82; Nwsp Stf; L Var Cheerleading; Var Capt Fld Hcky; Hon Roll; Outstndng Awd Accntng I 86; Outstndng Awd Typng I 86; Marymount Coll Tarrytown; CPA.

MC CRACKEN, KRISTEN; Kennett HS; Freedom, NH; (Y); 19/216; Church Yth Grp; Drama Clb; Key Clb; Math Tm; Thesps; Chorus; Nwsp Bus Mgr; Stu Cncl; Tennis; Spnsh I,II,III Drama 84-86; Mt Holyoke Coll; Math.

MC DONALD, PAM; Winnisquam Regional HS; Tilton, NH; (Y); FHA; Chorus; Hon Roll; Robet H & Gertrude E Seddey Chrtbl Fndtn Awd 86; Irving C & Katherine M Johnson Awd 86; Plymouth ST Coll; Gen Stds.

MC DONALD, SHEILA; Laconia HS; Laconia, NH; (Y); Drama Clb; GAA; Ski Clb; Chorus; Yrbk Stf; JV Bsktbl; Var Sftbl; Var Trk; Hon Roll; Letterman Clb; JR Prom Queen 8l; Cmnctns.

MC GAUNN, JON; Central HS; Manchester, NH; (Y); 196/450; Boys Clb Am; Spanish Clb; SADD; Nwsp Stf; Off Stu Cncl; Capt Bsktbl; Coach Actv; L Ftbl; L Golf; L Tennis; Criminlgy.

MC GEE, KIM; Spaulding HS; Rochester, NH; (Y); FBLA; Band; Chorus; Color Guard; Concert Band; Mrchg Band; Pep Band; Rep Frsh Cls; Rep Stu Cncl; Var Cheerleading; FL ST U; Bus Adm.

MC KENNEY, JENNIFER; Milford Area SR HS; Amherst, NH; (Y); 9/311; Computer Clb; Math Tm; Hon Roll; Hon Roll; NHS; Ntl Merit SF; Pres Schlr; MA Inst Tech.

MC KENNEY, TINA; Mascoma Valley Regional HS; Enfield, NH; (Y); Church Yth Grp; DECA; Band; Concert Band; Mrchg Band; Bsktbl; Fld Hcky; High Hon Roll; Hon Roll; Mgr Sftbl; VT ST DECA Pblc Spkng, Apparel-Accssries 2nd Pl 86; Acctng.

MC KINNEY, MELISSA; Alvirne HS; Litchfield, NH; (Y); 39/338; Var Crs Cntry; Var Mgr(s); Var Trk; Hon Roll; Stus To Offset Peer Prssr 84-85; Valparaiso U; Crim Jstc.

MC LAUGHLIN, MARK W; Exeter Area HS; E Kingston, NH; (Y); Am Leg Boys St; Chess Clb; Rep Jr Cls; Var L Bsktbl; Var L Sftbl; Var Capt Ftbl; High Hon Roll; NHS; Ntl Merit Ltr; Excllnc In Eng Awd 85-86; Best Defensive Plyr Ftbl 85-86; Co MVP JV Bsbl 85-86; Oceanography.

MC LAUGHLIN, MATTHEW P; Laconia HS; Laconia, NH; (Y); Am Leg Boys St; Key Clb; Yrbk Stf; VP Sr Cls; Rep Stu Cncl; Var Capt Bsbl; JV Ftbl; Var Swmmng; Attend St Pauls Advncd Studies Pgm 86; Sprtsmnshp Awd Bsbl 86; Most Imprvd Swmmr Awd 86; Boston Coll; Polyscience.

MC LAUGHLIN, ROBERT; Salem HS; Salem, NH; (Y); 40/370; Cmnty Wkr; German Clb; Model UN; JV Var Bsbl; Var Capt Bsktbl; JV Crs Cntry; Var Socr; Hon Roll; German Awd 86; Math.

MC LENNAND, ROBERT; Kearsarge Regard HS; Grantham, NH; (S); Aud/Vis; DECA; Model UN; Var Crs Cntry; JV Socr; Var Trk; Im Vllybl; Im Wt Lftg; Hon Roll; DECA Chptr Trsr 85-86; Bus Admin.

MC NAMARA, ERIN; Newport HS; Newport, NH; (Y); Cmnty Wkr; Computer Clb; French Clb; Hosp Aide; Red Cross Aide; JV Bsktbl; Powder Puff Ftbl; Trk; Boston Coll.

MC NAMARA, MELISSA; Pelham HS; Pelham, NH; (Y); Yrbk Stf; Var Bsktbl; Socr; Var Sftbl; Hon Roll; NHS; U Of NH; Bus Adm.

MC NAMARA, SUSAN; Saint Thomas Aquinas HS; Rye, NH; (Y); Am Leg Aux Girls St; Church Yth Grp; French Clb; Latin Clb; Variety Show; Yrbk Phtg; Trk; Hon Roll; Girls ST NH 86; Stu Of JR Prom Cart 86; Johnson & Wales; Mngmnt.

MC NULTY, NANCY JEAN; Nashua HS; Nashua, NH; (Y); Church Yth Grp; Rep Stu Cncl; JV Cheerleading; Var Trk; High Hon Roll; Hon Roll; Jr NHS; NHS; Spanish NHS; St Pauls Advncd Stud Pgm-Bio 86; Bio.

MC SHANE, ELIZABETH C; Salem HS; Salem, NH; (S); 1/340; Trs Church Yth Grp; French Clb; Girl Scts; Latin Clb; Model UN; SADD; Chorus; High Hon Roll; Pres NHS; Hghst Acadmc Avg 83-85; Frnch Cert Merit & Latn Cert Merit 84-85; Bio.

MC VEIGH, CHERYL; Manchester Central HS; Manchester, NH; (Y); 139/438; Stu Cncl; Var Cheerleading; Var Trk; Hon Roll; U Of NH; Commnctns.

MEIGHAN, JOANNA; Manchester HS West; Bedford, NH; (Y); 23/420; Ski Clb; Spanish Clb; Lit Mag; High Hon Roll; NHS; Nat Art Hnr Soc 85; Advrtsng Art.

MEJIA, MICAELA; Concord HS; Concord, NH; (Y); 69/398; Intnl Clb; Nwsp Stf; Pres Stu Cncl; Co-Capt Swmmng; Hon Roll; Sec NHS; Prfct Atten Awd; Wellsley Bk Awd 86; World Affars Sem 86; Hugh O Brian Yth Ldrshp Sem 86; Comm.

MELANDER, HEATHER; Hopkinton HS; Contoocook, NH; (Y); Art Clb; Sec Pres French Clb; Office Aide; SADD; Teachers Aide; School Play; Yrbk Stf; French Hon Soc; Art Achvt Awd 84-86; Concours De Francois Des Cooperarts 84; Art Educ.

MELLETT, JENNIFER; Lin-Wood HS; N Woodstock, NH; (S); 3/27; Church Yth Grp; FBLA; Band; Chorus; School Musical; School Play; Yrbk Stf; Rep Soph Cls; Sec Trs Stu Cncl; NHS; Hugh O Brian Yth Fndtn 84; Awds In Spkng 82 & 84; Yth & Gvmnt House Chpln 85; Lbrl Arts Psychlgy.

MELTON, JEFF; Laconia HS; Laconia, NH; (Y); 7/200; Math Tm; Quiz Bowl; Variety Show; L Trk; Hon Roll; NHS; Ntl Merit Ltr; Harry F Wiley Sci Awd 83; Bucknell; Mech Engrng.

MENDOLUSKY, JOEL; Bishop Guertin HS; Amherst, NH; (Y); Chess Clb; Debate Tm; NFL; Speech Tm; NHS; Ntl Merit Ltr.

MENTZ II, JOHN; Portsmouth HS; Portsmouth, NH; (S); 13/400; Ski Clb; Var Capt Socr; Var Capt Trk; Hon Roll; NHS.

MERCIER, CARL; Berlin HS; Berlin, NH; (Y); 47/191; Ice Hcky; Hon Roll; NH Voc Tech Coll; Paper Tech.

MERRIHEW, MICHAEL; Spaulding HS; Rochester, NH; (S); 11/350; Var L Tennis; High Hon Roll; Hon Roll; NHS; Plymouth ST Coll; Accntg.

MESSER, CYNTHIA; Keene HS; Keene, NH; (Y); 23/357; Church Yth Grp; Dance Clb; Hosp Aide; Band; Color Guard; Concert Band; Mrchg Band; Yrbk Stf; Trk; Cit Awd; Cmmnctns.

MESSINA, DONNA JEAN; Salem HS; Salem, NH; (S); 20/383; Dance Clb; VP German Clb; Hosp Aide; SADD; Color Guard; Bsktbl; Var Capt Trk; High Hon Roll; Hon Roll; Church Yth Grp; Germn Cert Acad Achvt 83-85; Peer Cnslr-Drg & Alchl Rltd Prblms 85-86; Acad Achvt Awd Miss Natl Teen; Psych.

MICHAELS, LYNDA JOAN; Londonderry HS; Londonderry, NH; (Y); Spanish Clb; JV Sftbl; High Hon Roll; Hon Roll; Spanish NHS; Keene ST Frosh Challenge, Tuiten Schlrshps 86; Presdntl Schltc Achvt Awd 86; Keene ST Coll; Bio.

MICHAUD, JENNIFER; Portsmouth SR HS; Portsmouth, NH; (Y); Color Guard; Flag Corp; School Musical; High Hon Roll; Hon Roll.

MICHAUD, PETER A; Hollis HS; Hollis, NH; (Y); 15/120; Am Leg Boys St; Church Yth Grp; Spanish Clb; Band; Concert Band; Jazz Band; Pep Band; Pres Frsh Cls; Pres Stu Cncl; Var Bsbl; Dartmouth Bk Awd 85-86; Sports Med.

MICHAUD, SUZANNE; Memorial HS; Manchester, NH; (Y); 7/350; Church Yth Grp; Math Tm; Stu Cncl; Powder Puff Ftbl; High Hon Roll; NHS; Clinton H Scovell Awd 86; Acad Awd 86; Neal A Batchelder Accntg Schlrp Trust 86; U NH; Admin.

MIERINS, SUSANNE; Hillsboro-Deering HS; Hillsboro, NH; (S); 13/70; Church Yth Grp; Sec DECA; SADD; Teachers Aide; Mgr(s); 3rd Pl Advrtsng Svcs NHDECA Career Dev Conf 86, Top 20 Natl DECA Career Dev 86, Top 8 86; Endicott Coll; Advrtsng.

MIHALKO, REID S; Pinkerton Acad; Pelham, NH; (Y); 18/496; Am Leg Boys St; Variety Show; Lit Mag; Var Bsktbl; Var Capt Ftbl; Var Capt Trk; Cit Awd; Elks Awd; Hon Roll; Pres NHS; Mike Mortensen Never Quit Awd 86; Mackenzie Mem Prz 86; Brown U; Art.

MIKULIS, ELIZAETH A; Mt St Mary Seminary; Nashua, NH; (Y); 3/74; Debate Tm; NFL; Yrbk Phtg; Ed Yrbk Stf; Var L Trk; ST Sci Fair 83-84; Natl Frnsc Leag Hnr & Excllnc 85-86; Natl Yth Sci 86; Pres Acadmc Ftnss Awd 86; U Of NH; Envrnmntl Engrg.

MILLER, GARY; Central HS; Manchester, NH; (Y); 28/430; Am Leg Boys St; Computer Clb; Temple Yth Grp; Nwsp Rptr; VP Lit Mag; High Hon Roll; NHS; Wrld Affairs Sem UW Whitewater Scholar 86; Engrng.

MILLET, MARK; Bishop Guertin HS; Salem, NH; (Y); Red Cross Aide; SADD; Yrbk Sprt Ed; Var L Mgr(s); JV Var Score Keeper; Var L Wrstlng; Sports Med.

MILLS, KYLIE K; Oyster River HS; Durham, NH; (Y); 2/140; Trs Drama Clb; Math Tm; Spanish Clb; School Play; Var L Socr; High Hon Roll; Ntl Merit SF; Sal; Spanish NHS; Am Leg Aux Girls St; Wellesley Bk Awd 85.

MILLS, MIKE; Groveton HS; Groveton, NH; (Y); Hon Roll; NH Tech Inst; Elctrnc Engnrng.

MILLS, POLLY; Belmont HS; Canterbury, NH; (Y); 8/75; French Clb; Band; Yrbk Ed-Chief; Var Capt Trk; Var Vllybl; Cit Awd; DAR Awd; Hon Roll; NHS; U CO Boulder; Intl Affrs.

MINER, JONATHAN; Hopkinton HS; Hopkinton, NH; (Y); 6/63; Pres Computer Clb; Math Tm; Ski Clb; Yrbk Stf; JV Var Socr; Hon Roll; NHS; French Clb; Quiz Bowl; Prfct Atten Awd; Hgst Pre Calculus,Alg II,Geo Avg 83-85; AF Acad; Comp Sci.

MINGIONE, SCOTT; Bishop Guertin HS; Nashua, NH; (Y); Bsbl; Im Bsktbl; Ftbl; Im Gym; Im Vllybl; Im Wt Lftg; Hon Roll; Spanish NHS; UNC; Acctg.

MINICHIELLO, MICHELE; Henniker HS; Henniker, NH; (Y); 3/26; Math Tm; Chorus; School Musical; Nwsp Stf; Rep Stu Cncl; Var Vllybl; Hon Roll; NHS; Voice Dem Awd.

MINICKIELLO, SCOTT; Keene HS; Keene, NH; (Y); Pres Sr Cls; Var Ftbl; Var JV Socr; Var Wrstlng; Hon Roll; Var Wrstlng ST Pl Wnnr NE Champn 85; ST Champn Socr Team Var 83; JR Lion & Rotarian 86; Math Educ.

MITCHELL, PAULA K; Hopkinton HS; Contoocook, NH; (Y); 16/63; Sec Am Leg Aux Girls St; Cmnty Wkr; Drama Clb; VP Chorus; School Play; Variety Show; Yrbk Stf; Cit Awd; Hon Roll; Church Yth Grp; Bst Actrss 86; Elem Ed.

MITCHELL, SHARON; Londonderry HS; Londonderry, NH; (Y); Band; Mrchg Band; High Hon Roll; Hon Roll; NHS; Spanish NHS; Lib Arts.

MLOCEK, JONATHN; Salem HS; Salem, NH; (S); 7/350; Church Yth Grp; Cmnty Wkr; French Clb; Model UN; JV Trk; High Hon Roll; NHS; Outstndg Achvt Frnch 84-85; Doctor.

MOCK, LAURIE; Hopkinton HS; Contoocook, NH; (Y); 3/65; Church Yth Grp; JV Var Bsktbl; JV Var Fld Hcky; Var Sftbl; High Hon Roll; NHS; Yrbk Stf; Hon Roll; Prfcncy Awd Advncd Ec & US Hstry; Mst Vlbl Plyr Vrty Bsktbl & Sftbl; Prfcncy Awd Hstry Of Cvlztn; Athlt Trng.

MOLLICA, MARISA; Concord HS; Concord, NH; (Y); Exploring; Hosp Aide; Concert Band; Ed Yrbk Stf; Var Trk; High Hon Roll; NHS; Pres Acdmc Fit Awd 86; Achvt Fine Metls 86; U Of ME.

MONAHAN, THOMAS; Pembroke Acad; Concord, NH; (Y); Boys Clb Am; Var L Bsbl; Var L Bsktbl; Hon Roll; Communicatns.

MONE, LISA MARIE; Dover HS; Dover, NH; (Y); 17/277; Am Leg Aux Girls St; Sec French Clb; Yrbk Stf; Trs Sr Cls; Var Capt Bsktbl; Var Capt Fld Hcky; Im Powder Puff Ftbl; JV Capt Sftbl; DAR Awd; High Hon Roll; Stnhl Acad Schlrshp 86; Outstndng SR 86; ABC Schlrshp 86; Stonhill Coll; Acctng.

MONIGLE, DEBBIE; Milford Ared SR HS; Amherst, NH; (Y); 18/311; Church Yth Grp; Drama Clb; Acpl Chr; Chorus; School Musical; Variety Show; High Hon Roll; Hon Roll; NHS; Ntl Merit Schol; U NH; Ed Cnslng.

MOODY, KIM; Weare HS; Weare, NH; (S); Math Tm; Nwsp Stf; Yrbk Stf; VP Frsh Cls; Trs Soph Cls; Sec Sr Cls; High Hon Roll; NHS.

MORAN, PATRICIA; Mont Saint Marys Seminary; Hudson, NH; (Y); Am Leg Aux Girls St; Church Yth Grp; Model UN; SADD; Teachers Aide; VP Jr Cls; Rep Stu Cncl; Capt Var Bsktbl; Hon Roll; JR Wmns Clb Schlrshp 86; Lesley COLL; Spcl Ed.

MOREL, ELAINE; Berlin HS; Berlin, NH; (Y); VICA; Nwsp Ed-Chief; Hon Roll; Dsgn.

MORGAN, MAUREEN MOLLY; Spaulding SR HS; Rochester, NH; (Y); Church Yth Grp; Cmnty Wkr; Political Wkr; High Hon Roll; Hon Roll; Kiwanis Awd; Sprngfield Hon Awd 85-86; Art Shwng Lilac Mall Rchstr NH 86; Art Shwng Rchstr Lbrry 86; Leslie Coll Cmbrdg MA; Art Thr.

MORGANTI, CAROLYN; Berlin HS; Rochester, NH; (Y); 5/200; Drama Clb; Lit Mag; Hon Roll; NHS.

MORIARTY, JOE; Portsmouth HS; Rye, NH; (Y); Ski Clb; Var L Bsbl; Cit Awd; High Hon Roll; Hon Roll; Schlr Athl 86; UNH; Mech Engrng.

MORIN, BRYAN; Berlin SR HS; Berlin, NH; (Y); 10/220; Church Yth Grp; JV Score Keeper; Hon Roll; NHS; Frnch Awd Hgh Lvl Acclrtd Frnch I 84-85.

MORIN, SHELLY; White Mtn Regional HS; Lancaster, NH; (Y); 10/104; Band; Concert Band; Yrbk Stf; Trs Soph Cls; Pres Jr Cls; Var Capt Bsktbl; Var L Sftbl; Hon Roll; NHS; Pres Schlr; Carroll Stoughton Schrshp 86; Plymouth ST Coll Schlrshp 86; Mst Dstngshd Sftbl Plyr 86; Plymouth ST Coll; Bus Mngmnt.

MORRISON, BETTINA; Laconia HS; Laconia, NH; (Y); Concert Band; Mrchg Band; Yrbk Phtg; Yrbk Stf; Mgr(s); Hon Roll; Vet.

MORRISON, LOU; Lebanon HS; Lebanon, NH; (S); Boy Scts; DECA; DECA 1st Pl St Comptns Credt & Fin 86; Bus Adm.

MORRISON, MICHAEL; Lebanon HS; Lebanon, NH; (Y); Boy Scts; Band; Im Bsbl; Hon Roll; NHS; Plymouth St; Pre Med.

MORTON, CHRISTINE; Timberlane Regional HS; Atkinson, NH; (Y); Church Yth Grp; German Clb; Teachers Aide; Band; Concert Band; Jazz Band; Mrchg Band; Pep Band; Var Bsktbl; Hon Roll; Russell Sage Coll; Med Tech.

MOSKOWITZ, KURT M; Londonderry HS; Londonderry, NH; (Y); Am Leg Boys St; Ski Clb; Band; Concert Band; Drm & Bgl; Jazz Band; Orch; Rep Soph Cls; Rep Jr Cls; Rep Stu Cncl; Prsdntl Ingrl Ceremonies 84; Pilot.

MOULTON, CHRISTINE; Laconia HS; Lakeport, NH; (Y); French Clb; Band; Concert Band; Mrchg Band; Pep Band; Comp Sci.

MOULTON, ROBERT; Nashua SR HS; Nashua, NH; (Y); 235/900; Am Leg Boys St; JV Bsbl; JV Ftbl; Capt Ice Hcky; NH All Star Tm Hcky 86; U Of NH; Elec Engrng.

MOYER, JENNIFER; Pinkerton Acad; Hampstead, NH; (Y); 4-H; VP FFA; Hosp Aide; Latin Clb; Band; School Musical; 4-H Awd; ST 4-H Shp Wnr-Trp To Natl Cngrs 84; ST FFA ST Star Grnhnd & SOEP Wnr ST Rprtr 82-86; Med.

MUDGE, KRISTINE P; Memorial HS; Manchester, NH; (Y); 146/350; Church Yth Grp; Cmnty Wkr; French Clb; FTA; Teachers Aide; Nwsp Stf; Powder Puff Ftbl; Keene ST Coll; Elem Ed.

MUELLER, SCOTT; Salem HS; Salem, NH; (S); 51/340; German Clb; Math Tm; Model UN; Concert Band; Jazz Band; Mrchg Band; Pep Band; Yrbk Bus Mgr; High Hon Roll; Hon Roll; Seige Perilous Awd 83; Century III Ldrs Cmptn Wnnr, ST Fnlst 85; Bentley; Fin.

MULLANE, SHERYL ANN; Mount St Mary Seminary; Nashua, NH; (Y); Am Leg Aux Girls St; French Clb; Model UN; PAVAS; SADD; School Play; Yrbk Stf; Ed Yrbk Sprt Ed; Rep Frsh Cls; Hon Roll; 3rd Pl NH ST Solar Enrgy Sci Fair 84; Hnrb Mntn Nashua Art Assn Outside Exhib 85; Keene ST Chllng; Keene ST Coll; Jrnlsm.

MULLEAVEY, SCOTT; Lin-Wood Public Schl; Lincoln, NH; (Y); Am Leg Boys St; Varsity Clb; Bsbl; Bsktbl; Crs Cntry; Socr; MVP Bsbl 86; Most Imprvd Stu Verbal Awd 85-86.

MULLIN, TERESA; Phillips Exeter Acad; Allentown, PA; (S); Dance Clb; School Musical; Ed Nwsp Stf; Ntl Merit Ltr; Co-Pres Exeters Comm Nuclr Awarenss 85-86; Asst Dir Dance Concrt 84-86; Engl.

MUNROE, YVETTE; Hillsboro-Deering HS; Bennington, NH; (S); Teachers Aide; Nwsp Stf; Rep Stu Cncl; Cheerleading; Hon Roll; Prfct Atten Awd; NH Tech Inst; Bus Mgt.

MURDOUGH, REBECCA; Cogswell Memorial HS; Henniker, NH; (Y); Math Clb; Math Tm; Ski Clb; SADD; School Musical; Yrbk Stf; Rep Stu Cncl; Var L Vllybl; Hon Roll; VFW Awd; Fshn Buyg.

MURPHY, ERIN; St Thomas Aquinas HS; Rye Bch, NH; (Y); 12/86; Church Yth Grp; Debate Tm; Sec French Clb; Sec Key Clb; Latin Clb; Yrbk Ed-Chief; Rep Soph Cls; Rep Jr Cls; High Hon Roll; Hon Roll; Frnch Excllnce Awds; Miss NH Natl Teen Title; Hnrs Engl Excllnce Awd; Tufts U; Intl Bus.

MURPHY, KATHLEEN; Kennett HS; N Conway, NH; (Y); 14/205; AFS; Am Leg Aux Girls St; Girl Scts; Ski Clb; Var Co-Capt Crs Cntry; JV Fld Hcky; Co-Capt Var Trk; DAR Awd; French Hon Soc; NHS; Yth In Govt 84, 85 & 86; Skimiester 85; NHS Schlrshp 86.

MURPHY, KIRSTEN; Kennett HS; Intervale, NH; (Y); 7/185; Am Leg Aux Girls St; French Clb; Ski Clb; Variety Show; Rep Frsh Cls; Var Fld Hcky; French Hon Soc; Hon Roll; NHS; Sec NHS 86-87; Vrsty Ski Tm 83-86.

MURRAY, MICHELLE M; Pinkerton Acad; Derry, NH; (Y); Aud/Vis; Library Aide; SADD; Chorus; Soph Cls; Jr Cls; Sr Cls; Stu Cncl; Hon Roll; Comm.

MURRAY, STEVE; Bishop Guertin HS; Nashua, NH; (Y); Computer Clb; FCA; French Clb; Stage Crew; Rep Frsh Cls; Rep Soph Cls; Sec Jr Cls; Rep Sr Cls; Im Bsktbl; Im Ftbl.

MUSIAL, MELISSA; Manchester Memorial HS; Manchester, NH; (Y); 38/350; Girl Scts; Variety Show; Var Capt Sftbl; High Hon Roll; Hon Roll; Vernaculr 82; Merp Ftbl 82-86; Prom Ushr 83; Paraphenia Lit Mag 86; New England Bapts Hosp; Nrsg.

MYERS, HEATHER; High Mowing Schl; Wilton, NH; (Y); 1/28; Drama Clb; Chorus; School Play; Variety Show; Yrbk Stf; Rep Sr Cls; Stu Cncl; St Schlr; Val; Smith College; Thtr Arts.

NADEAU, DEBRA; Berlin HS; Berlin, NH; (Y); Drama Clb; Chorus; School Musical; School Play; Var Trk; Hon Roll; Erly Chldhd Ed.

NADEAU, MATTHEW; Berlin SR HS; Milan, NH; (Y); 47/210; Boys Clb Am; Church Yth Grp; Cmnty Wkr; French Clb; Ski Clb; Yrbk Stf; Var Ftbl; Marines; Welding.

NAMAN, ANANTH; Tilton Schl; Laconia, NH; (S); Cmnty Wkr; French Clb; Library Aide; Mathletes; Math Clb; Math Tm; Nwsp Rptr; Nwsp Sprt Ed; Var Crs Cntry; Var Tennis; Oncologist.

NARASIMHAN, MICHAEL S; Salem HS; Salem, NH; (S); Math Tm; Model UN; Ski Clb; JV Stat Bsktbl; Var L Crs Cntry; High Hon Roll; Hon Roll; Boys Club Yth Yr 84; Rennselaer Polytech; Elec Engr.

NASH, LAURIE; Presentation Of Mary Acad; Kingston, NH; (Y); Church Yth Grp; French Clb; Church Choir; Nwsp Stf; Hon Roll; NEDT Awd; River Coll; Elem Educ.

NAULT, DARLENE; Salem HS; Salem, NH; (Y).

NAULT, SANDRA; Alvirne HS; Hudson, NH; (Y); French Clb; Sec Office Aide; Teachers Aide; Bsktbl; Cheerleading; Coach Actv; Score Keeper; Timer; Cert For Art 83; Cert-Alg I 84; Cert-Ofc Aide 85; Tufts U; Dntstry.

NEAL, PHILIP HAWKINS; Saint Pauls Schl; Richmond, VA; (Y); Pres Schlr; Schl Of Amer Ballet; Pro Dncr.

NEGM, ROBERT S; St Thomas Aquinas HS; Portsmouth, NH; (Y); Political Wkr; Spanish Clb; Varsity Clb; Stu Cncl; JV Bsbl; JV Bsktbl; JV Crs Cntry; Var Ftbl; High Hon Roll; Hon Roll; Biol Awd Hghst GPA; St Anslom Manchester; Med.

NEIL, SARIAH; Monadnock Regional HS; W Swanzey, NH; (Y); Acpl Chr; Swing Chorus; Hon Roll; French Clb; Chorus; Variety Show; Living Color Cert Color Anlyst 85; Church Grls Camp Achvt Awd 83; BYU; Costmtlgst.

NEISTER, KRISTEN; Kingswood Regional HS; Barnstead, NH; (Y); Boy Scts; Chrmn SADD; Gym; Church Yth Grp; Cmnty Wkr; Dance Clb; Debate Tm; Drama Clb; Exploring; Library Aide; Vlntr Amblnce Attndt 85-86; Vlntr Fire Dept 85-86; Vlntr Natl Ski Ptrl 85-86; NE U; Nrsng.

NELSON, DAVID; Pinkerton Acad; East Hampstead, NH; (Y); Boy Scts; Pres Sec 4-H; FBLA; Cit Awd; Dnfth Awd; Cls Rep; 3rd Pl Bus Math 83; Acctng.

NELSON, VICKI; Memorial HS; Manchester, NH; (Y); 40/356; SADD; Drm & Bgl; Powder Puff Ftbl; Hon Roll; Mrn Bio.

NESTOR, ELAINE; Stevens HS; Claremont, NH; (Y); Sec Trs Girl Scts; L Band; Sec Chorus; L Concert Band; Jazz Band; Mrchg Band; Pep Band; Im Bsktbl; JV Sftbl; Hon Roll; Comp Bus.

NEVEU, MIKE; Bishop Guertin HS; Nashua, NH; (Y); FCA; Spanish Clb; JV Socr; JV Var Wrstlng; Spanish NHS; Acad All-Amer 85-86; Sanford Invtnl Wrstlng Tourney 5th Pl 85-86; NHIAA Wrstlng Fnls 5th Pl 85-86; Psych.

NEVEUX, TRACI; Concord HS; Concord, NH; (Y); Church Yth Grp; Drama Clb; Chorus; School Play; Stage Crew; Hon Roll; Prfct Atten Awd; Crista Mc Auliffe Cmmndtn Awd 86; Human Psychlgy Cert Of Rcgntn 86; Top Stu Awd 86; Tchng.

NEWELL III, RONALD; Pembroke Acad; Suncook, NH; (Y); 79/182; Exploring; Red Cross Aide; Capt Socr; High Hon Roll; Hon Roll; Top Stu Frnch/Chem 82-83; Can Canoe Trip 85; Northlnd Coll; Bio.

NEWMAN, TAMI; Alvirne HS; Hudson, NH; (Y); 9/338; Ski Clb; Varsity Clb; Stage Crew; Var Cheerleading; High Hon Roll; Hon Roll; NHS; Hrold Chamberlin Schlrshp 86; U Of NH; Bus.

NEWTON, KRISTINE; Newfound Memorial HS; E Hebron, NH; (Y); 17/57; School Musical; School Play; Nwsp Stf; Yrbk Stf; Sec Sr Cls; VP Trk; Hon Roll; Best Actress Annul Comptv One Act Ply Comptn 86; MV Track 86; Tocca Falls Coll; Flight Atten.

NG, SIU; Laconia HS; Laconia, NH; (Y); Drama Clb; Spanish Clb; Tennis; Hon Roll; Bus.

NICHOLS, DARLENE; Hollis Area HS; Hollis, NH; (Y); 30/130; Church Yth Grp; Dance Clb; French Clb; Ski Clb; SADD; Yrbk Stf; Gym; Trk; Hon Roll; Frnch & Typng Awds 84-85; Nrsng.

NOBLE, JEFF; Franklin JR SR HS; Franklin, NH; (Y); 12/90; French Clb; Hon Roll; NHS; Frank & Laura Tessier Schlrshp Fnd 86; Dllrs For Schlrs 86; NH Tech Inst; Elec Engrng.

NOLAN, DANIEL A; Salem HS; Salem, NH; (S); 10/340; VP Math Tm; Model UN; Ski Clb; Pres Spanish Clb; High Hon Roll; Sec NHS; Ntl Merit Ltr; Spanish NHS; Comp Engrng.

NOLAN, DAVID; Spaulding HS; Union, NH; (S); 10/400; Chess Clb; Church Yth Grp; FCA; Math Clb; Math Tm; School Musical; School Play; JV Bsbl; JV Socr; Hon Roll.

NOLAN, EDWARD G; Milford Area SR HS; Amherst, NH; (Y); Am Leg Boys St; Boy Scts; Quiz Bowl; Teachers Aide; School Musical; School Play; Stage Crew; Tech Theatre Excllnc Awd 86.

NOONAN, SANDRA C; Fall Mountain HS; Alstead, NH; (Y); 3/130; French Clb; Color Guard; Yrbk Stf; Bsktbl; Var L Crs Cntry; Var L Trk; High Hon Roll; Hon Roll; Pres Schlr; Syracuse U; Ad.

NORRIS, CARMEN; Mascoma Valley Regional HS; Enfield Ctr, NH; (Y); Church Yth Grp; Library Aide; Office Aide; Spanish Clb; Chorus; School Musical; School Play; JV Cheerleading; Hon Roll; Ntl Merit Schol; Choral Achvt Lttr 86; Plymouth ST Coll; Englsh.

NOSTROM, KRISTAN; Newmarket HS; Malone, NY; (Y); Math Tm; Pep Clb; Ski Clb; Spanish Clb; Chorus; Yrbk Stf; JV Var Cheerleading; Stat Socr; Var Swmmng; Var Trk; Sprt Awd Chrldg 83-84; Leo Landroche Schlrshp 86; Lampry Rvr Schlrshp 86; Daemet Clg; Psych.

NOVELLO, MARGARET; Academy Of Notre Dame; Pelham, NH; (Y); 10/52; Art Clb; School Musical; Stage Crew; Yrbk Ed-Chief; Yrbk Rptr; Yrbk Stf; Score Keeper; Hon Roll; NHS; Prfct Atten Awd; Natl Hnr Socty Pres 85-86; Northeastern U; Law.

NUTILE, CHRISTOPHER; Bishop Guertin HS; Nashua, NH; (Y); Am Leg Boys St; Church Yth Grp; FCA; Pres SADD; Rep Stu Cncl; Ftbl; Trk; Wt Lftg; Dnfth Awd; Hon Roll; Sadd Schlrshp; American U; Bus.

NYHAN, KEITH; Concord HS; Concord, NH; (Y); 25/345; Bsktbl; JV Var Ftbl; Lcrss; Var Trk; High Hon Roll; Hon Roll; NHS; Pres Schlr; Mark Minichello Schlrshp 86; George Le Brun Mrl Awd 885; Vrsty Ftbl Chs Awd 85; Coll Of Holy Cross.

O BARTON, SUSAN; Epping HS; Epping, NH; (S); 2/50; Drama Clb; Trs French Clb; Teachers Aide; Yrbk Stf; Sec Sr Cls; Var Bsktbl; Vllybl; High Hon Roll; NHS; Intl Frgn Lang Awd 85; Notre Dame Coll-Manchester; Edu.

O BRIEN, CONOR; Bishop Brady HS; Tilton, NH; (Y); 29/80; Am Leg Boys St; Drama Clb; Ski Clb; Varsity Clb; Band; Chorus; Concert Band; Stage Crew; Variety Show.

O CONNOR, PATRICIA; Portsmouth SR HS; New Castle, NH; (Y); Hosp Aide; Latin Clb; Political Wkr; SADD; High Hon Roll; Hon Roll; U NH; Bus Mgmnt.

O CONNOR, SUSAN; Alvirne HS; Hudson, NH; (Y); 11/329; Teachers Aide; Yrbk Stf; Rep Jr Cls; JV Bsktbl; Var Crs Cntry; Im Var Trk; High Hon Roll; Hon Roll; Natl Mrt Spec Schlrp Centronics Cata Comp Co 86; Hudson JR Wmns Clb Schlrp 86; Tufts U; Psych.

O REILLEY, HEATHER; Londonderry HS; Mt Laurel, NJ; (Y); Drama Clb; Hosp Aide; SADD; Rep Frsh Cls; Rep Soph Cls; Trs Jr Cls; JV Bsktbl; Hon Roll; Dollars Schlrs Schrlshp 86; Math Leag Exc Awd 85; Clemson U; Engrng.

O ROURKE II, GERARD P; Alton Central HS; Laconia, NH; (Y); 10/34; Am Leg Boys St; Drama Clb; Pres Intnl Clb; School Play; Stage Crew; Pres Frsh Cls; Pres Jr Cls; Pres Sr Cls; DAR Awd; VP NHS; MP Army.

OCONNELL, BILL; Bishop Brady HS; Concord, NH; (Y); Stu Cncl; JV Bsktbl; Var Ftbl; High Hon Roll; Acad Achvt Awds Spnsh II, Engl 86.

ODUM, CRAIG; Portsmouth HS; Portsmouth, NH; (Y); Boy Scts; Drama Clb; Thesps; Acpl Chr; Chorus; Church Choir; Madrigals; School Musical; School Play; High Hon Roll; U Of NH; Bus.

ORSZAG, PETER; Phillips Exeter Acad; Princeton, NJ; (Y); Debate Tm; Key Clb; Ed Lit Mag; Var L Ftbl; JV Wrstlng; High Hon Roll; Ntl Merit SF; Negley Prz Am Hist 86; Belmont Hill Pub Spkng Prz 84; Pol Sci.

ORVIS, SCOTT J; Stevens HS; Claremont, NH; (Y); Am Leg Boys St; Key Clb; Political Wkr; Yrbk Stf; VP Stu Cncl; Socr.

OSGOOD, KELLEY; Nashua HS; Nashua, NH; (Y); 103/900; Church Yth Grp; Ski Clb; SADD; Varsity Clb; Yrbk Stf; Sec Stu Cncl; JV Var Cheerleading; Im Swmmng; Hon Roll; Phy Thrpy.

OSTERGAARD, PETE; Pelham HS; Pelham, NH; (Y); 32/123; Spanish Clb; Yrbk Stf; VP Sr Cls; Bsbl; Bsktbl; Mgr(s); Socr; Timer.

OUELLETTE, DEBBIE; Winnacunnet HS; Seabrook, NH; (Y); Nwsp Ed-Chief; Nwsp Sprt Ed; Ed Lit Mag; JV Bsktbl; Var Capt Fld Hcky; Var L Trk; High Hon Roll; Kiwanis Awd; NHS; Pres Schlr; Acdmc Excllnc Awd Hon Alg; French II & III Awds Acdmc Excllnc; Outstndg Achvmnt U S Hist; Boston U; Cmmnctns.

OUTRIDGE, STEVEN; Memorial HS; Manchester, NH; (Y); 28/341; Cmnty Wkr; Letterman Clb; Var Crs Cntry; Var L Trk; Hon Roll; Comp Engnrng.

OWEN, AEAN; Manchester HS Central; Manchester, NH; (Y); 79/565; Nwsp Phtg; Nwsp Stf; Yrbk Bus Mgr; Yrbk Ed-Chief; Yrbk Phtg; Yrbk Rptr; Yrbk Sprt Ed; Yrbk Stf; Jr Cls; Hon Roll; NH Outstdng Volunteer 85; Comp Sci.

PABLO, JOHN A; Trinity HS; Manchester, NH; (Y); 1/190; Am Leg Boys St; Math Tm; Model UN; VP Stu Cncl; Var Capt Ftbl; Var Trk; High Hon Roll; NHS; NEDT Awd; US Army Rsrv Natl Schlr Athlt 85-86.

PACKARD, LANCE; Moultonborough Acad; Center Harbor, NH; (Y); 12/44; Boy Scts; Church Yth Grp; Ski Clb; Chorus; Stage Crew; JV Bsktbl; Var Golf; Hon Roll; Astronomy.

PACKARD, TANYA; Kennett HS; N Conway, NH; (Y); 16/185; French Clb; Key Clb; Cheerleading; Hon Roll; Phys Thrpy.

PAIGE, KEVIN; Manchester Central HS; Manchester, NH; (Y); 86/438; Am Leg Boys St; Church Yth Grp; Ed Nwsp Stf; JV Crs Cntry; JV Trk; High Hon Roll; Hon Roll; Yrbk Stf; Nation NH Senator 86; ST Schrlshp 86; Manchester Ed Assn Essay 85; Orthdntcs.

PAINI, CINDY J; Manchester Memorial HS; Manchester, NH; (Y); 49/350; Hst FBLA; Ski Clb; Variety Show; Capt Var Cheerleading; Mgr(s); Im Powder Puff Ftbl; High Hon Roll; Hon Roll; Plymouth ST Coll; Ofc Admin.

PANGRAZE, MELISSA; Memorial HS; Auburn, NH; (Y); 50/350; Red Cross Aide; Ski Clb; Variety Show; Tennis; Hon Roll; Booster Clb Schlrsh P86; Purdue U; Vet-Med.

PAQUETTE, LAURA; Memorial HS; Manchester, NH; (Y); 21/349; French Clb; Variety Show; Var Capt Cheerleading; Hon Roll.

PAQUETTE, MATT; Memorial HS; Manchester, NH; (Y); Band; Concert Band; Mrchg Band; Var JV Trk; Photo.

PAQUETTE, RENE M; Winnisquam Regional HS; Tilton, NH; (Y); 16/98; Drama Clb; Math Tm; Political Wkr; Ski Clb; Thesps; School Play; Lit Mag; Pres Frsh Cls; Rep Soph Cls; Sec Pres Stu Cncl; Bennington Coll; English.

PARENT, DAVE; Londonderry HS; Londonderry, NH; (Y); Ski Clb; Im Bsktbl; JV L Crs Cntry; Var L Tennis; JV Trk; French Hon Soc; High Hon Roll; Hon Roll; NHS; Pres Schlr; Londonderry Schlrshp Comm Schlrshp 86; Var Tennis MVP Awd 86; U Of NH; Pre-Med.

PARENT, MARIE-ANNE; Nashua HS; Nashua, NH; (S); Church Yth Grp; Band; Concert Band; Stu Cncl; Hon Roll; Prfct Atten Awd; Tri ST Guitar Cmpttn 1st Pl 79-80&85; Eagle Cross Awd Outstndg Parish Cntrbtn 86; 1st Peca Cmpttn 86; Johnson & Whales; Trvl Agent.

PARENTEAU, REBECCA; Concord HS; Concord, NH; (Y); 98/360; Drama Clb; Varsity Clb; Yrbk Stf; VP Frsh Cls; Sec Stu Cncl; Capt Trk; Hon Roll; Fred J Hackett Schlrshp Outstndg Trck & Field 86; Var Clb Schlrshp 86; 4 Yr Letter Awd Trck 86; U Of NH.

PARIKH, RAJIV; Goffstown HS; Goffstown, NH; (Y); Ski Clb; VP Sr Cls; Trs Stu Cncl; Var Trk; NHS; Mth, Elec Awd; Granite ST Scholar; Satsang; Nrthn New England Sci & Humanities Sympsm; U NH; Elec Engrng.

PARROTT, TOM; St Thomas Acquinas HS; Durham, NH; (Y); Drama Clb; French Clb; Latin Clb; SADD; School Play; Pres Frsh Cls; Pres Soph Cls; VP Stu Cncl; Var Tennis; Cit Awd; UNH; Bus Admin.

PASHKO, MICHELLE; Cosgswell Memorial HS; Henniker, NH; (Y); 1/24; Computer Clb; Math Tm; Teachers Aide; Yrbk Stf; Pres Jr Cls; Pres Sr Cls; Var Bsktbl; Var Sftbl; High Hon Roll; NHS; 1st Pl Ntl Hstry Dy Cmptn 85 & 2nd Pl 86; St Pauls Advncd Stds Pgm 86; Rlgn.

PATCH, SUZANNE; Stevens HS; Claremont, NH; (Y); Varsity Clb; JV Var Bsktbl; Capt Var Socr; Var Sftbl; Im Vllybl; Im Wt Lftg; Amer H S Athl 84-85; Sccr NH St Selct Tm, Rgnl Camp & St Rnr-Ups; Bsktbl St Champs; Archtctr.

PATRIACCA, TODD; Hopkinton HS; Hopkinton, NH; (Y); 14/68; Drama Clb; French Clb; Math Tm; Model UN; School Musical; School Play; Yrbk Bus Mgr; Frsh Cls; Soph Cls; Jr Cls; Ecnmc & Finance.

PATRICK, MARK; Portsmouth HS; Portsmouth, NH; (S); 3/431; Latin Clb; Var L Crs Cntry; Var L Trk; High Hon Roll; NHS; Schlr Ath Awd; Jr Wrld Cncl; Comp Engrng.

PATTEN, ASHLEE; St Pauls Schl; Flintstone, GA; (Y); Latin Clb; Lit Mag; Ice Hcky; Capt Var Socr; High Hon Roll; Outstndng Athltc & Schlr Awd 85; Cum Laude 85-86; Crw Vrsty Intrschlstc Chmpnships 86; Princeton U; Int Rltns.

PATTEN, PATTY; Stevens HS; Claremont, NH; (Y); Art Clb; Drama Clb; French Clb; Cheerleading; Capt Socr; Swmmng; Trk; Hon Roll.

PEACOCK, CHRIS; Kennett HS; Silver Lk, NH; (Y); #30 In Class; French Clb; VP Soph Cls; Rep Stu Cncl; L Ftbl; L Ice Hcky; Bentley Coll; Bus.

PEARSON, STUART; Concord HS; Bow, NH; (Y); 9/340; Math Tm; Stu Cncl; Im Bsktbl; Var Socr; Var Trk; High Hon Roll; NHS; Pres Schlr; Worcester Polytechnic Inst.

PECKNOLD, BRETT; Manchester West HS; Bedford, NH; (Y); 58/434; Varsity Clb; Variety Show; Sec Stu Cncl; Var Vllybl; Stu Cncl Cert Apprctn 84&85; Stu Cncl Sec Plq 86; Fshn Mrchndsng.

PELCZARSKI, LISA; Memorial HS; Manchester, NH; (Y); 36/341; Nwsp Rptr; Nwsp Stf; Lit Mag; Powder Puff Ftbl; High Hon Roll; Hon Roll; U Of RI; Paralegal.

PELLETIER, SHAWN; Bishop Guertin HS; Houdson, NH; (Y); Ski Clb; Stat Bsbl; Socr; Wt Lftg; Capt Wrstlng; Hon Roll; NEDT Awd; Athlt Wk 85-86.

PENKALA, JOHN; Bishop Guertin HS; Nashua, NH; (Y); JV Bsbl; Im Bsktbl; Ftbl; Im Wt Lftg; Hon Roll; Jr NHS; Spanish NHS; Bus.

PENNYPACKER, BRUCE; Brewster Acad; Stamford, CT; (Y); Aud/Vis; Drama Clb; School Musical; School Play; Stage Crew; Yrbk Phtg; Ed Yrbk Stf; Lcrss; Hon Roll; Stu Trainer Awd 85; Drama Awd 86; Exc Comp Wrk 86; Union Coll; Comp Sci.

PERKINS II, JOHN J; Lin-Wood HS; Lincoln, NH; (Y); 1/25; Math Tm; Teachers Aide; Pres Sr Cls; Rep Stu Cncl; Capt Bsbl; Capt Bsktbl; Capt Socr; Bausch & Lomb Sci Awd; Dnfth Awd; Gov Hon Prg Awd; U Of NH; Comp Engnrng.

PERREAULT, DENISE MARIE; Berlin HS; Berlin, NH; (Y); 2/178; Am Leg Aux Girls St; SADD; Band; Jazz Band; Yrbk Ed-Chief; Var L Cheerleading; NHS; Ntl Merit Ltr; Pres Schlr; Sal; Wellesley Bk Prz 85; James O Neill Meml Schlrshp 86; Berlin Eagles Clb Schlrshp 86; Gov Merit Schlrshp; Wellesley Coll; Biochem.

PERRON, JASON; Fall Mountain Regional HS; Walpole, NH; (Y); Am Leg Boys St; Drama Clb; Chorus; School Musical; School Play; Yrbk Ed-Chief; Trs Sr Cls; Var L Crs Cntry; JV Socr; Var L Trk.

PERRONI, PETER J; Pinkerton Acad; Derry, NH; (Y); 206/616; Am Leg Boys St; Aud/Vis; Boys Clb Am; Political Wkr; Variety Show; Var Ftbl; Var Lcrss; Law.

PERRY, JONATHAN; Keene HS; Keene, NH; (Y); 3/380; Cmnty Wkr; Rep Frsh Cls; Var L Bsktbl; Cit Awd; DAR Awd; High Hon Roll; NHS; Ntl Merit Ltr; Hon Roll; NCTE Awd; Dartmouth Bk Prz; Harvard Bk Prz; 1st Pl NH Concours Ntl De Francais; Eng.

PETERS, DAN; Alvirne HS; Hudson, NH; (Y); Church Yth Grp; FCA; L Bsbl; L Bsktbl; L Socr; Ted Williams Bsbl Cmp Cnslr & Plyr 84.

PETERSON, PAULA; Timberlane HS; Atkinson, NH; (Y); 9/200; Church Yth Grp; German Clb; Hosp Aide; Math Tm; Teachers Aide; Church Choir; Yrbk Stf; High Hon Roll; Hon Roll; NHS; Exc German,Chem,Physics 84-85; U NH; Nrsng.

PETTENGILL, ANN; Salem HS; Salem, NH; (S); #23 In Class; Latin Clb; Band; Concert Band; Drm & Bgl; Jazz Band; Mrchg Band; JV Var Sftbl; High Hon Roll; Hon Roll.

PFEIFFER, SCOTT; Troy HS; Troy, NH; (Y); JV Bsktbl; Engrng.

PHELPS, CHRISTOPHER L; Laconia HS; Laconia, NH; (Y); 28/196; Cmnty Wkr; Pres Key Clb; VP Band; VP Concert Band; VP Mrchg Band; Pres Frsh Cls; Stu Cncl; Var Capt Bsktbl; Var Capt Ftbl; Var Capt Trk; Outstndng Awd-Trk & Fld 84; 2nd Pl-New Englnds Pole Vlt 86; Decathln St Rnr Up 85; Amer HS Athlt 84-85.

PHELPS, DARLENE; Pembroke Acad; Chichester, NH; (Y); Aud/Vis; DECA; Sec Trs 4-H; French Clb; Pres FHA; Library Aide; Sec Frsh Cls; 4-H Awd; High Hon Roll; Natl Hnr Rl 84-86; Auto Mechnc.

PHILIBERT, JEFFREY; Central HS; Manchester, NH; (Y); 58/430; Church Yth Grp; VP Science Clb; Ski Clb; Nwsp Phtg; Yrbk Phtg; High Hon Roll; Hon Roll; Bio.

PHILIPPON, CONNIE; Goffstown HS; Manchester, NH; (Y); Church Yth Grp; FNA; Library Aide; Ski Clb; Cheerleading; High Hon Roll; Hon Roll; NHS; U Of Vermont; Nrsng.

PHILLIPS, JEFFREY; Pembroke Acad; Suncook, NH; (Y); 16/200; French Clb; Pres Key Clb; Service Clb; Varsity Clb; Nwsp Rptr; Nwsp Stf; Frsh Cls; Rep VP Stu Cncl; Trk; Hon Roll; HOBY Ldrshp Awd 84; Boston Coll Smmr Exprnce 85; Diana Schlette Mem Scholar 86; Brandeis U; Psych.

PHIPPARD, MARK; Keene HS; Keene, NH; (Y); 25/365; Var Capt Golf; Var Ice Hcky; Hon Roll; Ntl Merit Ltr; Law.

PICONE, CHRISTOPHER; Bishop Guertin HS; Groton, MA; (Y); 2/150; Cmnty Wkr; Exploring; French Clb; Chrmn Pep Clb; SADD; Chorus; School Musical; Nwsp Phtg; Nwsp Rptr; Stu Cncl; Drtmth Bk Clb Awd 85; Engl Awd 86; Holy Cross Coll; Rsrch Bio.

PIERCE, BRAIN; Bishop Guertin HS; Nashua, NH; (Y); 1/150; Church Yth Grp; VP French Clb; Math Clb; Nwsp Sprt Ed; Sec Soph Cls; VP Jr Cls; VP Sr Cls; Var L Ice Hcky; Var L Socr; Sec NHS; Holy Crss Bk Awd Outstndng Schlstc Achvt 86; Natl Hnr Socty Outstndng Svc Awd 86; Bio.

PIERCE, KIMBERLY; Hanover HS; Hanover, NH; (Y); French Clb; Yrbk Phtg; Yrbk Stf; Lit Mag; Bsktbl; High Hon Roll; Hon Roll; Church Choir; Vllybl; Cnstnt Hgh Achvmnt Biolgy Awd 84-85; 2nd Plc Art Cntst Awd 84-85; HS Clndr 85-86.

PILLSBURY, CANDY; Lebanon HS; Grantham, NH; (Y); SADD; Bsktbl; Hon Roll; Otstndng Awd Elec Cls 86; Elctrncs.

PINARD, ANDREW; Pembroke Acad; Pittsfield, NH; (Y); Aud/Vis; 4-H; Band; Concert Band; Jazz Band; Mrchg Band; Pep Band; 4-H Awd; High Hon Roll; Prfct Atten Awd; Plymouth ST Coll; Music Educ.

PINTAL, ANNMARIE; Pelham HS; Pelham, NH; (Y); Yrbk Stf; Pres Sr Cls; High Hon Roll; Hon Roll; Yth In Govt Stu 86; Comptr Engrng.

PISHON, CRYSTLE; Hopkinton HS; Cantoocook, NH; (Y); VP French Clb; Yrbk Stf; Stat Bsktbl; JV Sftbl; Bausch & Lomb Sci Awd; Hon Roll; NHS; US Acadmc Decathalon Tm 86; Pgm Politics 84; Physics.

PITKIN, MARK; Newport HS; Newport, NH; (Y); Am Leg Boys St; Pres French Clb; JA; Math Tm; Chorus; School Musical; School Play; Nwsp Rptr; VP Jr Cls; Rep Stu Cncl; Princeton; Psych.

PLANTE, CHRIS; Pittsfield HS; Pittsfield, NH; (Y); 13/76; Trs Varsity Clb; Yrbk Sprt Ed; Pres Jr Cls; Pres Sr Cls; L Var Bsbl; Capt Var Bsktbl; L Var Socr; Sec NHS; Quiz Bowl; SADD; Lndn Sheehn Awd-86; Boostrs Clb Awd 86; Merrimack Coll; Comp Sci.

PLANTE, RONALD; Bishop Guertin HS; Nashua, NH; (Y); 5/150; Boy Scts; Rep Church Yth Grp; Nwsp Stf; Im Mgr Bsktbl; JV Crs Cntry; Var L Trk; Im Mgr Vllybl; High Hon Roll; NHS; NEDT Awd; Excptnl Srv In Ntl Hnr Scty 85-86.

PLASCH, KAREN; Portsmouth SR HS; Portsmouth, NH; (Y); Color Guard; Mrchg Band; Variety Show; Var L Vllybl; Hon Roll; Yth Fitnss Achvmnt Awd 84; Clss Marshall Grad Clss 86; Bus.

PLATT, PAIGE; Central HS; Manchester, NH; (Y); 34/430; Cmnty Wkr; Thesps; Nwsp Rptr; Nwsp Stf; Yrbk Phtg; Yrbk Stf; VP Jr Cls; VP Sr Cls; Rep Stu Cncl; High Hon Roll; Praise Inc Peer Cnslng 85-86; Bus.

PLAUTZ, JOHN P; St Thomas Aquina HS; Portsmouth, NH; (Y); Latin Clb; High Hon Roll; Engineering.

PLOURDE, MICHELLE; Concord HS; Concord, NH; (Y); Church Yth Grp; Drama Clb; French Clb; School Play; Stage Crew; Yrbk Ed-Chief; Yrbk Stf; Hstry.

POBLETE, ANNETTE L; Phillips Exeter Acad; Mclean, VA; (Y); French Clb; Service Clb; Chorus; School Musical; Stu Cncl; JV Lcrss; Ntl Merit SF; 1st Prz Hstry 84; 2nd Prz 4th Yr Frnch 85; 4th Pl Locl Div Natl Frnch Cntst 83; Humnts.

POELMAN, CONRAD; Laconia HS; Laconia, NH; (Y); 1/157; Computer Clb; Math Tm; VP Band; Pres NHS; Ntl Merit Schol; Val; VFW Awd; Variety Show; Bausch & Lomb Sci Awd; High Hon Roll; Rickover Sci Inst 85; Westnghse Sci Talnt Srch Wnnr 86; Math Ex Top Scorer 85-86; MA Inst Tech; Engrng.

POIRIER, MARK; Lincoln-Woodstock Cooperative HS; Lincoln, NH; (S); 1/36; Pres Church Yth Grp; Math Tm; Band; Stage Crew; Yrbk Phtg; Pres Frsh Cls; Rep Jr Cls; Pres Stu Cncl; VP NHS; Delgt Hugh O Brien Yth Ldrshp ST Conf 85; Outstndng Stu Awd 85; Princeton U; Law.

POISSON, GINA RE; Winnisquam Regional HS; Franklin, NH; (Y); 3/96; French Clb; Cheerleading; Hon Roll; NHS; Sedgly Schlrshp 86; Almni Assn Schlrshp 86; Ntl Hnr Scty Bk Awd 86; U NH; Lbrl Arts.

POISSON, LORETTA; Newport HS; Newport, NH; (Y); French Clb; Varsity Clb; Nwsp Stf; Yrbk Stf; Trk; Hon Roll; Air Force.

POLISH, SANDIE; Bishop Brady HS; Concord, NH; (Y); French Clb; Spanish Clb; Varsity Clb; Yrbk Stf; Var JV Bsktbl; Var Cheerleading; JV Fld Hcky; JV Sftbl; Hon Roll; Pres 4-H; Rep Eastern ST Expstn 83; U NH; Bus Adm.

POMEROY, MATTHEW; Manchester H S West; Manchester, NH; (Y); 12/420; Boy Scts; Var Trk; High Hon Roll; NHS; Math Clb; Nwsp Rptr; Nwsp Stf; Yrbk Stf; Economics.

PONTZ, BRADFORD S; Phillips Exeter Acad; Lancaster, PA; (Y); Boy Scts; Spanish Clb; Chorus; School Play; Nwsp Stf; High Hon Roll; Jr NHS; Tennis; Amrcn Lgn Pst 34 Awd 84; Tdr-Strt Englnd Hstry Awd 85; Bst Spnsh Stu 85&86.

PORTER, STEPHANIE; Contoocook Valley HS; Temple, NH; (Y); 43/151; Church Yth Grp; Cmnty Wkr; Band; Off Sr Cls; Capt Bsktbl; Crs Cntry; Capt Sftbl; Hon Roll; Temple Schlrshp Awd 86; Wooster Coll; Liberal Arts.

POSNACK, ERIC; Portsmouth HS; Portsmouth, NH; (S); 15/400; Model UN; Varsity Clb; Crs Cntry; JV Var Ice Hcky; JV Var Tennis; High Hon Roll; Hon Roll; Jr NHS; Bus.

POTTER, LISA; Salem HS; Salem, NH; (S); 29/380; Var Capt Trk; Germn Merit Awd-Maintn A Avg.

POTTER, MARK; Salem HS; Salem, NH; (Y); 30/344; Model UN; Ski Clb; Soroptimist; Spanish Clb; Wrstlng; Hon Roll; Kiwanis Awd; Spanish NHS; SADD; Boys Clb Am; Jim Fargon Awd 86; Dllrs For Schlrs Awd 86; RAMS Schlrshp Awd 86; Bentley Coll.

POTVIN, JULIE; Portsmouth SR HS; Portsmouth, NH; (Y); Debate Tm; Office Aide; Stage Crew; Rep Soph Cls; Rep Jr Cls; Rep Sr Cls; Rep Stu Cncl; Var L Cheerleading; Hon Roll; Schlr Athlete Awd 85; 2nd Pl Chrldng Cmpttn Awd 84; UNH; Bus Mgmt.

POULIN, LISE; Berlin HS; Berlin, NH; (Y); 24/260; Church Yth Grp; French Clb; FBLA; Hon Roll; Plymouth ST Coll; Bus.

PRENTICE, PETER; Inter-Lakes HS; Center Sandwich, NH; (Y); Variety Show; Rep Jr Cls; Crs Cntry; Hon Roll; Coll Of Atlantic; Bio.

PREVE, CHRISTINA W; Concord HS; Penacook, NH; (S); DECA; 4-H; Sftbl; 4-H Awd; Hon Roll; Christa Mcauliffe Schrlshp; DECA Schrlshp; 1st Pl Medal ST DECA Conf; Johnson & Wales Coll; Mgmt.

PREVEL, MELINA; Nashua SR HS; Nashua, NH; (Y); 40/843; Spanish Clb; Yrbk Stf; Hon Roll; Jr NHS; NHS; Spanish NHS; KID Players; John Panagoulias Mem Scholar Awd; Cls 1976 Scholar; Clark U; Psych.

PREVIE, PAT; Pembroke Acad; Epsom, NH; (Y); 117/160; Church Yth Grp; Cmnty Wkr; Drama Clb; French Clb; FHA; Latin Clb; SADD; Band; Chorus; Mst Imprvd Schlrshp 83; Psych.

PRIGGE, SEAN; Monadnock Regional HS; Fitzwilliam, NH; (Y); 1/131; Pres Jr Cls; Pres Sr Cls; Socr; Trk; High Hon Roll; Hon Roll; VP NHS; Ski Clb; Yrbk Stf; Englsh Cls Awd; John F Kennedy Amer Hstry Awd; Harvard Bk Awd; St Pauls Advncd Studies Pgm; Engrng.

PRINCE, GREGORY; Hanover HS; E Thetford, VT; (Y); Yrbk Phtg; Capt Crs Cntry; St Lawrence U.

PRIVE, DONNA; Central HS; Manchester, NH; (Y); Advrtsng.

PUTNAM, MARTHA; Fall Mountain Regional HS; Charlestown, NH; (Y); French Clb; Girl Scts; Hosp Aide; Science Clb; Var Cheerleading; Sftbl; Elks Awd; Hon Roll; Cheshire Hosp Schlrshp 86; Moose Ldg Schlrshp 86; Ernest Bixby Schlrshp 86; Elms Coll Hicopee MA; Nrsng.

PYSZ, ANDY; Newport HS; Newport, NH; (Y); French Clb; Letterman Clb; Trs Jr Cls; Co-Capt L Bsbl; L Bsktbl; L Ftbl; Hon Roll; NHS; Bsbl Sprtsmnshp Awd 86.

QUACKENBUSH, NICK W; Contoocook Regional HS; Antrim, NH; (Y); 25/200; Chrmn Am Leg Boys St; Ski Clb; Spanish Clb; Chorus; Var L Bsbl; Im Ftbl; JV Var Socr; Im Vllybl; Im Wt Lftg; High Hon Roll; Embry Riddle; Aviation.

QUIGLEY, SUSAN; Pelham HS; Pelham, NH; (Y); 1/123; French Clb; Model UN; Jr Cls; Stu Cncl; JV Bsktbl; JV Var Sftbl; Bausch & Lomb Sci Awd; High Hon Roll; NHS; Bio.

QUINN, CATHERINE; Bishop Brady HS; Concord, NH; (Y); Intnl Clb; Political Wkr; Ski Clb; School Play; Yrbk Stf; High Hon Roll; NHS; NEDT Awd; Engl Awd 84; Tchr Educ.

QUINN, CHRISTOPHER; Bishop Guartin HS; Nashua, NH; (Y); 58/180; Ski Clb; JV Bsbl; Im Bsktbl; Var L Golf; Wt Lftg; Hon Roll.

QUINT, KERRY; Kennett HS; Conway, NH; (Y); Drama Clb; Thesps; School Musical; School Play; Stage Crew; Hon Roll; Amer Legand Awd 86; Intl Thespian Socy Awd 86; Plymouth Coll; Theatre.

QUIRK, KIMBERLY; Presentation Of Mary Acad; Dracut, MA; (Y); 5/20; Art Clb; VP JA; Pep Clb; Ski Clb; Nwsp Rptr; Rep Soph Cls; Var Bsktbl; Im Sftbl; Im Vllybl; Hon Roll; Acdmc All Amrcn 85; Wrld Hstry Awd 85; Ntl Ed Dvlpmt Tst Awd 85; Bus Adm.

RALPH JR, KENNETH A; Salem HS; Salem, NH; (Y); 41/330; Model UN; Spanish Clb; Hon Roll; Ntl Merit Ltr; Spanish NHS; YMCA All Am Swmng 84-86; New England Champ Swmmng 83-86; Haverhill YMCA Swim Team Capt & MVP 84-86; TX Christian U; Fbus.

RAMIREZ, SONIA; Stevens HS; Claremont, NH; (Y); SADD; Varsity Clb; Chorus; School Musical; Stu Cncl; Bsktbl; Socr; Wt Lftg; DAR Awd; Hon Roll; Ithaca/Penn ST; Optmtry.

RAMSAY, JEFF S; Oyster River HS; Durham, NH; (Y); Am Leg Boys St; Church Yth Grp; Latin Clb; Math Clb; Lit Mag; JV Bsktbl; Var Trk; Hon Roll.

RAMSEY, DAVID; Newmarket Central HS; Newmarket, NH; (Y); Am Leg Boys St; Computer Clb; Exploring; Ski Clb; VP Soph Cls; Var Bsbl; Var Socr; Hon Roll; MIT; Arch.

RAMSEY, KEITH; Alvirne HS; Hudson, NH; (Y); 37/330; Chess Clb; Math Tm; U NH; Elec Engrng.

RAY, KIMBERLY; Dover HS; Dover, NH; (Y); JCL; VP Latin Clb; SADD; Trs Soph Cls; Rep Jr Cls; Rep Stu Cncl; Var Crs Cntry; Co-Capt Var Swmmng; Var Trk; Hon Roll; SEARCH Prog U NH 86; U Sthrn FL Tampa; Poli Sci.

RAY, WILLIAM W; Con Val Regional HS; Peterborough, NH; (Y); Am Leg Boys St; Band; Var L Bsktbl; Var L Socr; Var L Tennis; High Hon Roll; Hon Roll; NHS; Dnl Blnchtt Memrl Tnns Awd; MVP-TNNS; Lbrl Arts.

RAYMOND, PAULA M; Nashua SR HS; Nashua, NH; (Y); 173/837; Aud/Vis; Drama Clb; VP JA; VICA; Cheerleading; Hon Roll; Prfct Atten Awd; Hosp Aide; Library Aide; 1st Pl Preprd Spch VICA Skill Olympcs; Fitchburg ST Coll; Comm.

RAYMOND, TERRI; Pembroke Acad; Epsom, NH; (Y); 18/200; DECA; French Clb; SADD; Yrbk Stf; High Hon Roll; Hon Roll; Voice Dem Awd; Sprague Elec Schlrshp Achvt 86; Mentors 86-87; Bryant Coll; Accntng.

REED, ANGELA; Belmont HS; Canterbury, NH; (S); French Clb; Office Aide; Varsity Clb; Yrbk Ed-Chief; Rep Stu Cncl; Capt Var Cheerleading; Hon Roll; NHS; Var Tnk; Outstndg Achvt Astra Clb 86; Coach Awd Chrldg 86; Oswego ST; Drftg.

REED, JENNIFER; Alvirne HS; Hudson, NH; (Y); 13/350; Band; Concert Band; Pep Band; Var Crs Cntry; JV Trk; Hon Roll; NHS; U Of NH; Cmmnctns.

REMINGTON, PATRICK PAUL; Londonderry HS; Londonderry, NH; (Y); Civic Clb; Math Tm; ROTC; JV Ftbl; Var Trk; High Hon Roll; Pres Acad Fit Awd 86; Booster Clb Schlr Ath Yr 86; U NH; Animl Sci.

RESS, JAMES; Keene HS; Keene, NH; (Y); 10/364; Chess Clb; French Clb; Yrbk Stf; High Hon Roll; Hon Roll; NHS; Natl Frnch Cntst Cert Mrt 84-85; WPI; Mech Engr.

REYNOLDS, D SCOTT; Concord HS; Bow, NH; (Y); 20/356; Yrbk Stf; Var Ice Hcky; Var Socr; High Hon Roll; NHS; Ntl Merit SF; Intl Bus.

REYNOLDS, JENNIFER; Timberlane Regional HS; Sandown, NH; (Y); Church Yth Grp; French Clb; Teachers Aide; Chorus; Church Choir; Madrigals; Swing Chorus; Variety Show; Yrbk Stf; Hon Roll; All ST Music Fstvl Chorus 85; All New Engl Music Fstvl 86; UNH; Voice.

REYNOLDS, KRISTA M; Fall Mtn Regional HS; N Walpole, NH; (Y); 17/150; Am Leg Aux Girls St; SADD; Band; Chorus; Color Guard; Madrigals; Var Swmmng; JV Trk; Trs NHS; Spanish Clb; Outstndng Vol Svc 84; Occuptnl Thrpy.

REYNOLDS, ROBERT A; Nashua SR HS; Nashua, NH; (Y); 159/870; Am Leg Boys St; Ski Clb; Crs Cntry; Socr; Hon Roll; Ski Tm; Sci Pgm At UNH; Air Force Acad; Pilot.

REYNOLDS, TRICIA; Portsmouth SR HS; Rye, NH; (Y); 53/400; Band; Color Guard; Drill Tm; Mrchg Band; High Hon Roll; Hon Roll; U NH; Comm.

RHEAULT, JENNIFER; Manchester HS; Manchester, NH; (Y); 200/420; FBLA; Ski Clb; Chorus; Church Choir; Yrbk Stf; Sec Jr Cls; Sec Sr Cls; JV Socr; Bus Mgmt.

RHEAULT, PATRICIA; Manchester Central HS; Manchester, NH; (S); 376/476; DECA; Hesser U; Bus Mgmt.

RHINEHARDT, MARY; Dover HS; Dover, NH; (Y); 23/289; Am Leg Aux Girls St; French Clb; JV Bsktbl; Var L Crs Cntry; Powder Puff Ftbl; Var L Sftbl; High Hon Roll; Hon Roll; SYRACUSE; Bio.

RICCI, CHRISTINA M; Tilton Schl; Haverhill, MA; (S); 7/83; PAVAS; School Play; Rep Jr Cls; Rep Stu Cncl; Var L Fld Hcky; Var L Ice Hcky; Var Capt Tennis; Robert Dowling Awd-1st In Cls 83; Busnss.

RICE, ANDREA; Hillsboro Deering HS; Hillsboro, NH; (Y); Art Clb; French Clb; Ntl Merit SF; Fine Arts.

RICE, KRISTEN; Portsmouth HS; Portsmouth, NH; (Y); 40/397; Latin Clb; Model UN; Band; Jazz Band; Sftbl; Swmmng; High Hon Roll; Hon Roll; Prtsmth Hosp Schlrshp 86; Drew Schlrs Schlrship 86; Drew U; Pre Med.

RICHARDS, JOHN M; Phillips Exeter Acad; New Ipswich, NH; (Y); Model UN; High Hon Roll; Ntl Merit SF; Hist.

RICHARDS, SANDRA; Fall Mountain Regional HS; Alstead, NH; (Y); #1 In Class; French Clb; Var Capt Crs Cntry; JV Socr; Var Capt Trk; High Hon Roll; Hon Roll; Sec NHS; Prfct Atten Awd; MVP X-Cntry Team 84-85; Stu Of Mnth 86; Girls State Alt 86.

RICHARDSON, DEREK; Timberlane Regional HS; Atkinson, NH; (Y); Church Yth Grp; Teachers Aide; Yrbk Sprt Ed; JV Bsbl; Cheerleading; Var Ftbl; Wt Lftg; Hon Roll; 3rd Pl Sci Fair 85; Pre Med.

RICHARDSON, MELISSA; Hanover HS; Norwich, VT; (Y); 50/167; Cmnty Wkr; Quiz Bowl; Nwsp Phtg; Nwsp Stf; Yrbk Phtg; Yrbk Stf; Lcrss; Swmmng; Vllybl; Mvp Lacrosse Tm 86; Middlebury Coll; Frgn Langs.

RICHER, NATHAN; Newport JR SR HS; Newport, NH; (Y); Am Leg Boys St; French Clb; SADD; Chorus; Jazz Band; School Musical; Pres Sr Cls; Stu Cncl; Bsbl; Ftbl; Grldn Rdnfldt Schlrshp 84; Bst Actr 82-86; Svc Awd 86; Cstltn ST Coll; Cmmnctns.

RICKARD, LYNNE; Salem HS; Salem, NH; (Y); Cmnty Wkr; DECA; 4-H; FBLA; Hosp Aide; Model UN; Office Aide; Teachers Aide; Hon Roll; Rivier Coll; Bus Mgmt.

RICKER, CHERI; Nute HS; Union, NH; (Y); Library Aide; Band; Chorus; Variety Show; JV Cheerleading; Hon Roll; NHS; Ntl Merit Ltr.

RIENDEAU, JACQUELINE; Keene HS; Chesterfield, NH; (Y); Yrbk Stf; Var Socr; JV Sftbl; Hon Roll; MIP Sftbll 82-83; Cmpltd Basic Scuba Divng Course 86; Ushers Club 85-87; U Of NH; Marine Bio.

RIFF, KIMBERLY; Kimball Union Acad; Hanover, NH; (Y); Drama Clb; Key Clb; School Musical; Yrbk Stf; Var Diving; JV Fld Hcky; Var Lcrss; Var Swmmng; High Hon Roll; Hon Roll; MVP Swim Tm 86; Acctg.

RILEY, WANDA G; Nute HS; Milton, NH; (S); JCL; VP Latin Clb; Yrbk Stf; Sec Frsh Cls; Hon Roll; FL Inst Of Tech; Bus Adm.

RIOUX, JAMES; Nashua SR HS; Nashua, NH; (Y); Boys Clb Am; Office Aide; Ski Clb; Rep Frsh Cls; Stu Cncl; Var L Golf; UNH; Bus.

RIVARD, MICHELE; Berlin HS; Berlin, NH; (Y); 18/220; Church Yth Grp; Drama Clb; Office Aide; SADD; Varsity Clb; Chorus; Church Choir; School Musical; School Play; Nwsp Phtg; Rivier Coll; Med Tech.

ROBBINS, MARGARET ELLEN; Keene HS; Keene, NH; (Y); 1/362; Church Yth Grp; Drama Clb; Spanish Clb; Acpl Chr; School Musical; School Play; High Hon Roll; NHS; Chorus; Church Choir; Chesthire Cnty Med Soc Awd Sci 85-86; Wellesley Bk Awd 85-86; BYU.

ROBERGE, PENNY; Berlin HS; Berlin, NH; (Y); 48/205; SADD; Im Bowling; Hon Roll; Mc Donalds Scholar 86; YMCA Yth & Govt Pgm; Plymouth ST Coll; Acctng.

ROBERTS, BETH; Alvirne HS; Hudson, NH; (Y); 60/324; Hosp Aide; Sec SADD; Teachers Aide; Yrbk Stf; Rep Stu Cncl; JV Bsktbl; Var L Crs Cntry; Var L Mgr(s); Var L Trk; Hon Roll; Boston Coll; Eng.

ROBERTS, SHARYN KRISTINA; Littleton HS; Littleton, NH; (Y); #7 In Class; Am Leg Aux Girls St; Drama Clb; Red Cross Aide; SADD; Teachers Aide; Y-Teens; Nwsp Rptr; Yrbk Stf; Pres Stu Cncl; Var Capt Fld Hcky; Keene ST; Elem Ed.

ROBINSON, LYNN; Salem HS; Salem, NH; (Y); 38/316; Pres Church Yth Grp; VP French Clb; Model UN; French Hon Soc; Hon Roll; Rivier Coll; Med Lac Tech.

ROBITAILLE, SCOTT; Manchester Memorial HS; Manchester, NH; (Y); 23/341; VP Exploring; Red Cross Aide; St Anselms; Pre-Dentstry.

ROCHEFORT, SONIA; Concord HS; Bow, NH; (Y); 30/335; Varsity Clb; Lit Mag; Var Capt Fld Hcky; JV Sftbl; High Hon Roll; Hon Roll; NHS; Yrbk Stf; JV Bsktbl; Pres Acad Ftns Awd 86; Exc Engl 84-86; Concord Boostr Fld Hcky Schlrshp 86; Bentley Coll; Bus Mgmt.

ROCHELEAU, LYNNE; St Thomas Aquinas HS; Rochester, NH; (Y); Chess Clb; Church Yth Grp; Computer Clb; Debate Tm; Drama Clb; French Clb; Political Wkr; Church Choir; School Play; Stage Crew; UNH; Business.

ROGERS, KATHLEEN; Spaulding HS; Rochester, NH; (S); 1/397; Math Tm; Pep Clb; Rep Frsh Cls; VP Soph Cls; VP Jr Cls; Capt Vllybl; High Hon Roll; NHS.

ROGERS, TARA; Lebanon HS; W Lebanon, NH; (Y); AFS; Church Yth Grp; Varsity Clb; Chorus; JV Bsktbl; Var Socr; Var Trk; Hon Roll; CPA.

ROGERS, TRACY; Concord HS; Bow, NH; (Y); 1/345; Dance Clb; Yrbk Bus Mgr; L Cheerleading; Gov Hon Prg Awd; NHS; Ntl Merit Ltr; Rotary Awd; Val; Math Tm; Varsity Clb; 4 Yr Merit Schlrshp U Dallas 85-86; Ntl Latin Hnr Scty 84; Acdmc Achvt Awds 83-86; U Dallas; Lbrl Arts.

ROHDE, MONTY; Mascoma Valley Reg HS; Canaan, NH; (Y); Am Leg Boys St; Drama Clb; French Clb; Letterman Clb; Math Clb; Math Tm; Band; Jazz Band; School Play; Socr; Dartmouth Coll Book Awd 86; Drivers Excllnc Participation 86; Architectur.

ROMANCHYK, JENNIE; Lebanon HS; Lebanon, NH; (Y); Spanish Clb; Bsktbl; Fld Hcky; Sftbl; Hon Roll; Law.

ROMANO, CYNTHIA; Memorial HS; Manchester, NH; (Y); 89/489; Dance Clb; French Clb; PAVAS; SADD; Variety Show; Nwsp Stf; Cheerleading; Powder Puff Ftbl; Hon Roll; FL ST; Acctng.

ROMPS, JOHN; Manchester Central HS; Manchester, NH; (Y); 8/430; Math Clb; Math Tm; Rep Jr Cls; Var JV Ice Hcky; JV Socr; High Hon Roll; NHS; Ntl Merit Ltr; US Naval Acad Smr Smnr & Wrkshp 86; St Pauls Schl Advncd Studs Pgm 86.

ROSE, KARYN; Salem HS; Salem, NH; (Y); Ski Clb; Chorus; Capt Cheerleading; High Hon Roll; Model UN; Teachers Aide; Band; School Musical; School Play; Hon Roll; U Of NH; Music Prfrmnc.

ROSE, TODD J; Berlin HS; Dummer, NH; (Y); 9/202; Am Leg Boys St; Drama Clb; Yrbk Stf; Pres Sr Cls; Var Trk; Hon Roll; Jr NHS; NHS; Abbie Sargent Mem Schlrshp 86; Lisa Cavagnaro Mem Schlrshp 86; U Of NH; Electrcl Engr.

ROSEN, JASON M; Milford Area SR HS; Amherst, NH; (Y); 41/308; Boy Scts; ROTC; Yrbk Stf; JV Golf; JV Socr; Var Wrstlng; Hon Roll; Air Frc ROTC-4 Yr Schlrshp 86; Yth & Govt-Cngrsmn 86; PA ST U; Elec Engr.

ROSSON, LOREN; Bishop Geurtin HS; Nashua, NH; (Y); 16/138; SADD; Yrbk Rptr; High Hon Roll; Bowdoin Coll; Chem.

ROULEAU, JAYNE; Pinkerton Acad; Derry, NH; (S); DECA; Pres FBLA; Rep Frsh Cls; Rep Soph Cls; Rep Jr Cls; High Hon Roll; Hon Roll; 3rd Pl Apprl & Accssrs ST SECA Comptn 86; 3rd Pl Econ FBLA ST Comptn 85; 1st Pl Bus Math FBLA ST; Bus.

ROUSSEAU, CRAIG; Memorial HS; Manchester, NH; (Y); 77/341; Am Leg Boys St; Var Ice Hcky; Im Socr; Hon Roll; Rookie Yr Hockey Goalie 85; MVP Hockey 86; All ST Trny Tm Hockey 86.

ROUSSEAU, KIM; Alvirne HS; Hudson, NH; (Y); Hon Roll; Crmnlgy.

ROUSSEL, MICHAEL; Bishop Guertin HS; Dracut, MA; (Y); 68/143; French Clb; JA; SADD; Var Ftbl; Im Wt Lftg; U Of Lowell; Bus.

ROUTHIER, LISA; Laconia HS; Laconia, NH; (Y); 1/200; Math Tm; Concert Band; Mrchg Band; Pep Band; Rep Stu Cncl; Crs Cntry; Trk; High Hon Roll; NHS; GAA; Brown U Bk Awd; Law.

ROUTHIER, MICHAEL R; Nashua HS; Nashua, NH; (Y); 123/783; Am Leg Boys St; High Hon Roll; Hon Roll; NHS; Prfct Atten Awd; U Of NH; Lbrl Arts.

ROW, CHRISTOPHER D; Bishop Guertin HS; Amherst, NH; (Y); 25/141; Boy Scts; Sec Band; Church Choir; Color Guard; Yrbk Stf; God Cntry Awd; NHS; Ntl Merit Ltr; Art Clb; Acpl Chr; St Pauls Schl Advncd Studies Pgm Cncrd NH 86; 1st Crucfr Cnscrtn Of Bhsp Dgls Theuner Epscpl 86; Cthdrl Orgnst.

ROWE, DIANE; Thayer HS; Winchester, NH; (Y); 1/33; FBLA; Latin Clb; Spanish Clb; Teachers Aide; Yrbk Ed-Chief; Stu Cncl; Var Capt Fld Hcky; Hon Roll; NHS; Val; Smith Coll.

ROWE, JENNIFER; Portsmouth HS; Rye, NH; (Y); 112/337; Aud/Vis; Drama Clb; Exploring; Chorus; School Musical; School Play; Stage Crew; Hon Roll; Nwsp Stf; All-New Englnd Drama Cst 86; Bartlett Pblc Spkng Awd 86; Berklee Coll; Audio Engrng.

ROY, DANNY; Gorham HS; Gorham, NH; (Y); 2/39; Drama Clb; School Play; Stage Crew; Variety Show; Rep Soph Cls; Rep Stu Cncl; Var JV Bsktbl; High Hon Roll; Jr NHS; NHS; Bus Mgmt.

ROY, JANNEL A; Manchester H S West; Bedford, NH; (Y); 44/336; Pres Drama Clb; Chorus; School Play; Variety Show; Nwsp Rptr; Yrbk Stf; Rep Stu Cncl; High Hon Roll; NEDT Awd; VFW Awd; SADD 85-86; Artstc Drctr Schl Play 86; NY U; Jrnlsm.

ROY, SHAWN; Bishop Guertin HS; Amherst, NH; (Y); 4/150; Chess Clb; Key Clb; Math Clb; Im Bsktbl; JV Crs Cntry; Im Vllybl; High Hon Roll; Hon Roll; NHS; Ntl Merit Ltr; Pyscs.

RUDD, PAMELA; Salem HS; Salem, NH; (Y); 12/383; French Clb; Model UN; High Hon Roll; Hon Roll; Bus.

RUEL, RICHARD; Gorham HS; Gorham, NH; (Y); Drama Clb; School Play; Stage Crew; Yrbk Phtg; Yrbk Stf; Hon Roll; NHS; Elem Engrng.

RULE, JENNIFER; Trinity HS; Manchester, NH; (Y); Cmnty Wkr; Varsity Clb; Rep Frsh Cls; Rep Soph Cls; JV Var Fld Hcky; Var Capt Tennis; Hon Roll; Variety Show; JV Bsktbl; JV Sftbl; Spnsh Awd; Bio.

RUSSO, NINA; Nute HS; Milton, NH; (S); Art Clb; French Clb; Hosp Aide; Yrbk Stf; Rep Frsh Cls; Rep Soph Cls; Rep Jr Cls; NHS; Balfour Art Awd 83-84.

RYAN, BRIDGET; High Mowing Schl; Cambridge, MA; (Y); Cmnty Wkr; German Clb; Chorus; School Musical; School Play; Yrbk Phtg; Yrbk Stf; Bsktbl; Socr; Vllybl; Freinds Wrld Coll; Anthrplgy.

RYAN, JOHN; Memorial HS; Manchester, NH; (Y); 92/365; Ski Clb; Concert Band; Var Golf; Hon Roll; Lwyr.

RYAN, KELLEY; Portsmouth SR HS; Portsmouth, NH; (Y); Color Guard; Jazz Band; JV Capt Cheerleading; Vllybl; High Hon Roll; Hon Roll; NH Police Assn Honor Cadet 85; St Anselm; Paralegal.

RYAN, TIMOTHY P; Bishop Brady HS; Canterbury, NH; (Y); 27/78; Boys Clb Am; SADD; Band; L Var Bsbl; L Var Bsktbl; L Var Ftbl; Hon Roll; NEDT Awd; All Nw Englnd Bnd 85.

SACKOS, STACEY; Alton Central HS; Alton Bay, NH; (S); 6/37; Trs Leo Clb; Office Aide; OEA; School Play; Sec Jr Cls; Sec Sr Cls; Var Cheerleading; Hon Roll; Nwsp Stf; Yrbk Stf; Outstndng Bus Stdnt Awd 85; Schl Svc Awd 85; Hghst Avg Ofc Proc Awd 85; Burdett Schl; Legl Secy.

SAGLIME, FRANK; Alvirne HS; Hudson, NH; (Y); 7/331; Math Tm; High Hon Roll; Hon Roll; Sci Merit 85; Intrntn Comp Cntst NH Vo-Tech 86; Elec Engrng.

SALTER, KENNETH; Salem HS; Salem, NH; (Y); Aud/Vis; Hon Roll; Ranked 1 Electrncs 84-85; Electro Mech Engr.

SAMA, FRANK; Bishop Guertin HS; Groton, MA; (Y); 30/140; Church Yth Grp; Drama Clb; French Clb; Teachers Aide; Thesps; Varsity Clb; School Musical; School Play; Nwsp Rptr; Nwsp Stf; Outstndng Perf Stu Cncl 84-85; Hon Perf Stu Cncl 85-86; Outstndng Perf Ntl Hnr Scty 85-86; U Of VA; Bus Adm.

SAMICK, BILL; High Mowing Schl; Ghent, NY; (Y); Drama Clb; Orch; School Musical; School Play; Yrbk Phtg; Yrbk Stf; Var Socr; Sftbl; P Smth's Coll; Frstry.

SANBORN, CARRIE L; Plymouth Area HS; Wentworth, NH; (Y); 11/139; Cmnty Wkr; Sec French Clb; Hosp Aide; Math Tm; Yrbk Bus Mgr; VP Sr Cls; Var Capt Tennis; DAR Awd; High Hon Roll; NHS; Chem Awd 85; U VT.

SANBORN, VON; Manchester Memorial HS; Manchester, NH; (Y); 22/351; Yrbk Rptr; JV Ftbl; DAR Awd; Hon Roll; Ntl Merit Ltr; Pres Schlr; Manchester Ed Assn Scholar 86; Stu Govt Scholar 86; Boston U; Intl Law.

SANDERSON, TAWNYA; Stevens HS; Claremont, NH; (Y); Capt Exploring; Var Socr; JV Sftbl; High Hon Roll; Hon Roll.

SANDQUIST, BRETT; St Thomas Aquinas HS; Dover, NH; (Y); JV Bsbl; Var Ftbl; JV Var Ice Hcky; Engrng.

SANG, SOMANA OUM; Dover HS; Dover, NH; (Y); 24/273; Hon Roll.

SANTACRUCE, LORIJO; Concord HS; Concord, NH; (Y); 75/395; Var Bsktbl; L Mgr(s); Var Sftbl; Hon Roll; NHS.

SARETTE, DONNA; Memorial HS; Manchester, NH; (Y); 25/369; Church Yth Grp; FHA; Girl Scts; Church Choir; Variety Show; Hon Roll; Bus Admin.

SARETTE, JULIE; Memorial HS; Manchester, NH; (Y); 35/341; Church Yth Grp; Cmnty Wkr; FHA; Girl Scts; Hosp Aide; Library Aide; Church Choir; Variety Show; Socr; High Hon Roll; Nrsng.

SARGENT, DOUGLAS; Keene HS; Chesterfield, NH; (Y); 65/360; Bsbl; JV Var Bsktbl; JV Var Socr; Var Trk; Hon Roll; NH Cls Soccer Champ 83-86; Slvr Mdlst Frshmn Soph Meet Salem NH 85; NHIAA Boys Cls L Trk Meet 86; U Of NH; Lbrl Arts.

SAUCIER, LINDA; Pembroke Acad; Suncook, NH; (Y); 40/185; Hosp Aide; JV Cheerleading; Hon Roll; NHS; 3rd Pl Trphy For Med Termnlgy Cont 86; Awd Hlth Occptns Stu Of Amer For Overall Great Stu 86; U Of NH; Nrsng.

SAVOIE, STEVEN; Bishop Guertin HS; Dracut, MA; (Y); French Clb; SADD; Im Bsktbl; Var Crs Cntry; JV Trk; High Hon Roll; Hon Roll; Opthmlgst.

SAWYER, STEPHEN R; Phillips Exeter Acad; Hampton, NH; (Y); Radio Clb; Rep Soph Cls; Bsbl; Bsktbl; French Hon Soc; High Hon Roll; Acdmc Excllncd Engl Hons, Geo Hon & Frnch II 84; Pony Bsbll Leag All Star 85; Davis Awd 85; Carleton Coll; Engrng.

SCACCIA, LISA; Salem HS; Salem, NH; (Y); Cmnty Wkr; Rep FBLA; Rep FHA; L JV Cheerleading; High Hon Roll; Hon Roll; Miss Teen Pgnt 3rd Plc 85; Northern Essex CC; Paralgl.

SCHAEFER, CAROLINE P; Phillips Exeter Acad; Bridgeport, CT; (Y); English Clb; German Clb; Library Aide; Yrbk Ed-Chief; Lit Mag; JV Swmmng; High Hon Roll; Ntl Merit SF; 1st Prize 4th Yr Germn 85; English.

SCHALTENBRAND, VICTORIA; Tiberlane Regional HS; Atkinson, NH; (Y); 5/227; Am Leg Aux Girls St; Pres 4-H; Chorus; Concert Band; Jazz Band; Mrchg Band; Yrbk Stf; High Hon Roll; Band; Pep Band; NH All ST Music Fest 86; All New England Music Fest 86; Veterinary Science.

SCHEFFER, TODD A; Tilton Schl; Plymouth, NH; (S); Rep Jr Cls; JV Var Lcrss; JV Var Socr; Hon Roll; Lib Proctor; Dorm Proctor; Brown; Engrng.

SCHIMMOLLER, BRIAN; Concord HS; Bow, NH; (Y); 4/330; Math Tm; Lit Mag; Var L Bsbl; High Hon Roll; NHS; Ntl Merit Ltr; Pres Schlr; Marshall Hahn Engr Merit Schlrshp 86; Gov Schlr Schlrshp 86; Pres Acad Ftns Awd 86; Virginia Tech; Engrng.

SCHMIT, MARK; Bishop Guertin HS; Nashua, NH; (Y); Trs Sr Cls; Var Capt Tennis; JV Trk; Hon Roll; NHS; Prfct Atten Awd; Spanish NHS.

SCHRAMM, THOMAS; Nashua SR HS; Nashua, NH; (Y); 10/738; Am Leg Boys St; Church Yth Grp; SADD; Ed Lit Mag; Var L Crs Cntry; High Hon Roll; Hon Roll; Jr NHS; NHS; Pres Schlr; Sprtsmnshp Awd Intrml Sccr Leag 84.

SCOTT, CHRIS; Pembroke Acad; Pemborke, NH; (Y); Am Leg Boys St; Ski Clb; JV Bsktbl; Var Socr; Hon Roll; Crim Justice.

SCRIPTURE, KAREN; Belmont HS; Canterbury, NH; (Y); 1/75; Math Tm; Teachers Aide; Band; Jazz Band; Pep Band; School Musical; Bausch & Lomb Sci Awd; High Hon Roll; NHS; Val; Pres Acad Ftns Awd 86; Gvrnrs Schlrs Prgm Awd 86; Bay Path JR Clg; Intr Dsgn.

SEVERANCE, DAVID; Pembroke Acad; Suncook, NH; (Y); 10/160; Key Clb; Band; High Hon Roll.

SEYMORE, AUDRA; Concord Christian Hs; Bow, NH; (S); Debate Tm; Drama Clb; Math Tm; Chorus; School Play; Yrbk Stf; Var Bsktbl; Var Vllybl; Hon Roll; Hghst Clss Avg JR Yr 86; Totl Release Awd Vllybl 85; Hofstra; Bus.

SHAFFER, CINDY; Pembroke Acad; Concord, NH; (Y); Latin Clb; Yrbk Stf; Rep Sr Cls; Hon Roll; NHS; Voice Dem Awd; Concord Brd Realtrs Scholar 86; U NH; Bio.

SHARPE, BRIAN D; Pinkerton Acad; Derry, NH; (Y); 70/500; Boy Scts; JV Socr; Var L Trk; Hon Roll; Ntl Merit SF; Pres Schlr; Eagle Scout 85; Hugh Obrien Soph Of Year 84; JR Asst Scout Master Order Of Arrow 85; USNA; Aerospace Engr.

SHEA, KEVIN; Keene HS; Keene, NH; (Y); 18/350; Am Leg Boys St; Latin Clb; JV Var Bsbl; JV Var Bsktbl; JV Socr; Hon Roll; Lion Awd; Boston Coll; Bus Adm.

SHEARER, KARRIE; Londonderry HS; Londonderry, NH; (Y); Varsity Clb; Rep Jr Cls; Rep Sr Cls; JV Cheerleading; Var Gym; Var L Socr; Var L Trk; High Hon Roll; Hon Roll; Womens Clb Schlrshp 86; Embry-Riddle U; Aerontcl Sci.

SHEHORN, CHRISTINA; Trinity Christian Acad; Plaistow, NH; (Y); Art Clb; Church Yth Grp; Cmnty Wkr; FCA; Red Cross Aide; Spanish Clb; Chorus; Church Choir; School Musical; School Play; Computer.

SHELLING, HOPE; Hanover HS; Lyme, NH; (Y); Yrbk Phtg; Fld Hcky; Lcrss; U Of NH-DURHAM.

SHEPARD, JULIE; Keene HS; W Swanbey, NH; (Y); 91/315; Cmnty Wkr; Hosp Aide; Concert Band; Mrchg Band; Yrbk Stf; Nurses Asst Cert & Stu West Swanzey Rascue Hldng 1st Aid Card CPR; NH Vo-Tech Coll; Nrsng.

SHEPHERD, ANN; Stevens HS; Claremont, NH; (Y); Dance Clb; SADD; JV Bsktbl; Var Capt Cheerleading; High Hon Roll; Hon Roll; U Of NH; Comptr Engrg.

SHERMAN, STEPHANIE; Dover HS; Dover, NH; (Y); Key Clb; Yrbk Stf; JV Powder Puff Ftbl; U Of NH.

SHERWOOD JR, KENNETH W; Timberlane Regional HS; Sandown, NH; (Y); Am Leg Boys St; Model UN; Band; Pres Concert Band; Jazz Band; Yrbk Ed-Chief; Stu Cncl; JV Trk; Camera Clb; French Clb; Mc Donald Band 86; New Englnd Camerca Clb Cncl Honb Men Slide 85; SYMS Concrt Band & Jazz Awds 85 &86; Law.

SHIMER, ROBERT J; Phillips Exeter Acad; Armonk, NY; (Y); Chrmn FBLA; Math Tm; Nwsp Rptr; High Hon Roll; Ntl Merit SF; Russn Oral, Wrttn Olympds Awds; Russn Stds.

SHIPLETT, STUART; Manchester West HS; Bedford, NH; (Y); 59/338; Intnl Clb; Latin Clb; Math Clb; Science Clb; Nwsp Stf; Im Bsbl; JV Ftbl; Im Wt Lftg; Hon Roll; Ntl Hnr Soc Prspct 82; Hampden-Sydney Coll; Mgmt Ec.

SHIRLEY, DANIELLE; Manchester Central HS; Deerfield, NH; (Y); 5/500; Debate Tm; Yrbk Stf; Rep Stu Cncl; High Hon Roll; NHS; Ntl Merit Ltr; P Millimet Crtv Wrtng Awd 86.

SHOREY, LISA; Lebanon HS; W Lebanon, NH; (Y); 15/147; Church Yth Grp; Cmnty Wkr; Dance Clb; Band; Concert Band; Mrchg Band; Pep Band; Yrbk Stf; Hon Roll; Bus Mgmt.

SHUFF, CHRISTEN; Kennett HS; N Conway, NH; (Y); 27/184; French Clb; JV Ski Clb; Nwsp Stf; Hon Roll; Creatv Wrtng.

SHUMWAY, KATHLEEN SUSAN; Laconia HS; Laconia, NH; (Y); Am Leg Aux Girls St; Church Yth Grp; Yrbk Stf; VP Soph Cls; Pres Jr Cls; Pres Sr Cls; Rep Stu Cncl; Capt Swmmng; Sec Swmmng; Art Clb; Drtmth Bk Clb Awd 86; Mst Pts Swm 86; MVP Swm Team 86; MVP JR Stu Cncl 86; Pres Awd Swm Team 86; Cmnctns.

SHYNE, KENDRA DENISE; Salem HS; Salem, NH; (Y); 35/350; Sec Exploring; Trs German Clb; Service Clb; High Hon Roll; Hon Roll; NHS; Key Clb; Library Aide; Model UN; Teachers Aide; Grmn Achvts 84-86; Rcknghm Trst Schlrshp 86; Julia Keen Schlrshp 86; Nrtheastrn U; Psych.

SIBLE, JILL C; Timberlane Regional HS; Atkinson, NH; (Y); 1/206; Model UN; Pres Spanish Clb; Yrbk Ed-Chief; Pres Stu Cncl; Var Crs Cntry; High Hon Roll; NHS; Ntl Merit SF; Math Tm; Teachers Aide; NH Rep To US Senate Yth Prog 85; Stu Of Mnth 83-85; Hrvrd Bk Awd; Pre-Med.

SIENKO, FREDERICK J; West HS; Bedford, NH; (Y); 4/340; Math Tm; Nwsp Rptr; Nwsp Stf; Var Golf; High Hon Roll; NHS; Ntl Merit SF; NEDT Awd.

SILER, JULIET; Phillips Exeter Acad; Brookline, MA; (Y); Cmnty Wkr; Drama Clb; French Clb; Acpl Chr; Chorus; Jazz Band; Madrigals; School Musical; School Play; Stage Crew; Latin Prize 84.

SILK, MANDI; Keene HS; Keene, NH; (Y); 125/330; Am Leg Aux Girls St; Cmnty Wkr; Ed Yrbk Stf; Rep Frsh Cls; VP Soph Cls; Pres Jr Cls; Trs Sec Stu Cncl; Cit Awd; DAR Awd; Pres Church Yth Grp; Hugh O Brian Outstndng Soph Ldr 84; Trinity Coll Of VT; Socl Work.

SILVERMAN, CATHY ALICE; Salem HS; Salem, NH; (S); 7/353; Capt Debate Tm; Key Clb; VP Latin Clb; Model UN; Spanish Clb; School Play; Mgr Gym; High Hon Roll; NHS; Spanish NHS; Outstndng Spkr Ntl HS Dbt Trnmnt 84; Schlstc Awd Ms Teen New Engl Pgnt 84; 1st Rnnr Up Century III; Intl Rel.

SILVERMAN, STACEY; Milford Area SR HS; Amherst, NH; (Y); 52/293; Nwsp Ed-Chief; Yrbk Stf; NHS; ANDA Schlstc Jrnlst Awd 85; Quill & Scroll Awd 84; Syracuse U; Lbrl Arts.

SIMKO, KRISTIE; Berlin SR HS; Berlin, NH; (Y); 8/202; Cmnty Wkr; Pep Clb; SADD; Varsity Clb; Band; Nwsp Stf; Yrbk Stf; Var JV Cheerleading; Var Tennis; Cit Awd; Wellesley Bk Prz 86; Phillips Extr Acad Smmr Schl Schlrshp 86; Psych.

SINGER, KAREN B; Phillips Exeter Acad; Exeter, NH; (Y); Cmnty Wkr; Dance Clb; French Clb; Orch; School Musical; School Play; High Hon Roll; Ntl Merit Ltr; James Dwight Arnold Mem Scholar 86; Phillips Exeter Acad Concerto Cont Wnr 86; Harvard Coll; Mth.

SINTROS, SUSAN K; Pelham HS; Pelham, NH; (Y); 8/128; French Clb; Hosp Aide; Yrbk Stf; Trs Frsh Cls; Trs Soph Cls; Trs Jr Cls; Trs Sr Cls; Var Tennis; High Hon Roll; Hon Roll; Natl Hnr Soc Schlrshp 86; HS Schlrshp 86; Philotohos Schlrshp 86; U Of NH; Bus Adm.

SIROIS, AMY B; Nashua SR HS; Nashua, NH; (Y); 87/796; VP Sec FNA; Hosp Aide; High Hon Roll; Hon Roll; Jr NHS; NHS; Stu Yr 85-86; Rivier Coll Schrlshp 86-87; Hillsboro Cty Med Soc Schlrshp 86-87; Rivier Coll; Nrsng.

SIROSKY, MIKE; Newport HS; Newport, NH; (Y); Band; Concert Band; Jazz Band; Mrchg Band; Pep Band; Var L Trk; NHS; 9th Annl Wrld Invtatnl Band Fstvl-FL 86; Comp Info Sys.

SISK, MARK; Concord HS; Concord, NH; (Y); Var Ftbl; Var JV Ice Hcky; Var Tennis; Cit Awd; Wells Tekkey Awd 1st Poster Cntst 82.

SKARIN, CHRISTINE; Newport HS; Newport, NH; (Y); Cmnty Wkr; Trs Letterman Clb; Math Tm; Varsity Clb; Stu Cncl; Bsktbl; Coach Actv; Fld Hcky; Hon Roll; NHS; Stu Cncl Ldrshp Awd 86; Mst Vlbl Plyr Awd Bsktbl 85-86; Sprtsmnshp Awd Sftbl 86; Child Ed.

SKORKO, NANCY; Alvirne HS; Hudson, NH; (Y); 22/332; Cmnty Wkr; Hosp Aide; Art Clb; JV Bsktbl; Var JV Sftbl; Hon Roll; Lion Awd; NHS; Rotary Awd; Engl Prfcncy Awd 86; Boston COLL; Chem.

SKRUCK, KARA; Manchester Central HS; Manchester, NH; (Y); 1/438; Church Yth Grp; Stage Crew; Nwsp Ed-Chief; Socr; Tennis; High Hon Roll; NHS; NEDT Awd; Colby Coll Bk Awd 86.

SLATE, BRENDA; Nashua SR HS; Nashua, NH; (Y); Latin Clb; Library Aide; Office Aide; Amercn Clsscl Leag 86; Natnl JR Clsscl Leag 86; Law.

SLEEPER, WILLIAM D; White Mountain Regional HS; Lancaster, NH; (Y); Am Leg Boys St; Boy Scts; Church Yth Grp; Spanish Clb; Chorus; Var Socr; Var Trk; High Hon Roll; VP NHS; Voice Dem Awd; Engnrng.

SMART, PETER; Coe-Brown Northwood Acad; Northwood, NH; (Y); Drama Clb; SADD; School Musical; School Play; Yrbk Bus Mgr; Stat Bsbl; JV Bsktbl; Var L Socr; Prfct Atten Awd; Lyndon ST Coll; Phys Educ.

SMITH, ANGELA; Newfound Memorial HS; Alexandria, NH; (Y); 43/98; Computer Clb; French Clb; Girl Scts; Library Aide; Office Aide; Band; Chorus; JV Bsktbl; JV Cheerleading; JV Trk; FL Southern; Comp.

SMITH, DEBBY; Pembroke Acad; Epsom, NH; (Y); 15/190; Yrbk Phtg; Trs Jr Cls; Trs Sr Cls; Var Bsktbl; Var Fld Hcky; Var Sftbl; DAR Awd; Hon Roll; NHS; Rotary Awd; Richard Kallgren Memrl Schlrshp 86; Female Athl Yr 85-86; Ithaca Coll; Radio Tv.

SMITH, DOUGLASS M; Phillips Exeter Acad; New York, NY; (Y); Model UN; Lit Mag; Im JV Crs Cntry; Tennis; Ntl Merit SF; Spnsh Prz 83-85; Pres Archlgy Clb 85-86; WA Internship Coll; Philsphy.

SMITH JR, LARRY G; Moultonborough Acad; Center Harbor, NH; (Y); 4/41; Spanish Clb; Trs Stu Cncl; Var Bsbl; Var Bsktbl; Var Capt Socr; DAR Awd; NHS.

SMITH, LAURA; Bishop Brady HS; Penacook, NH; (Y); Yrbk Stf; Var Capt Cheerleading; Coach Actv; Sftbl; St Paul Smr Schl Alt 86; U Of NH; Intl Affrs.

SMITH, SHERI; Concord HS; Concord, NH; (Y); Pres Church Yth Grp; Drama Clb; School Musical; School Play; Stage Crew; Lit Mag; Var Crs Cntry; Im Trk; High Hon Roll; NHS; Challenge Schlrp 86; Awds Engl & Art 85-86; Gordon Coll; Engl Lang.

SMOOT, DAVID M; Phillips Exeter Acad; Raleigh, NC; (Y); Debate Tm; Latin Clb; Library Aide; Trs Science Clb; Var Ftbl; JV Trk; High Hon Roll; Ntl Merit SF; Latin Prz 84-85; Math & Sci Prz 82-83; Hstry.

SNOWDEN, MARK; Portsmouth SR HS; Portsmouth, NH; (Y); Latin Clb; Ski Clb; Nwsp Rptr; Rep Frsh Cls; JV Bsktbl; High Hon Roll; Hon Roll; Lngstcs.

SOCZEWINSKI, RICHARD; Franklin HS; Franklin, NH; (Y); 11/100; Am Leg Boys St; Church Yth Grp; Computer Clb; Debate Tm; Library Aide; Math Clb; Math Tm; Political Wkr; Radio Clb; Rep Stu Cncl; Lions Clb, Tessier & Grange Schlrshps 86; U NH; Engrng.

SOUCY, CELESTE; Memorial HS; Manchester, NH; (Y); 24/341; Church Yth Grp; Drama Clb; Hosp Aide; Political Wkr; VP Boys Clb Am; Trk; High Hon Roll; Hon Roll; Med Tech.

SOWA, KRISTINE LYNN; Keene HS; Spofford, NH; (Y); 62/362; Am Leg Aux Girls St; Pep Clb; Varsity Clb; Acpl Chr; Variety Show; Yrbk Stf; VP Jr Cls; VP Stu Cncl; JV Var Bsktbl; Hon Roll; Awd JV Bsktbl Most Imprvd 84-85; Bus Mgmt.

SOWERS, KENDRA; Keene HS; Keene, NH; (Y); 11/380; Pres Church Yth Grp; Drama Clb; Spanish Clb; Acpl Chr; Chorus; Madrigals; School Musical; Variety Show; Yrbk Stf; Capt Gym; Engl.

SPEAR, RICHARD; Spaulding HS; Rochester, NH; (Y); 49/350; Am Leg Boys St; Key Clb; Yrbk Ed-Chief; Pres Jr Cls; Rep Sr Cls; Kiwanis Awd; Sprngfld Awd 86; U NH.

SPEER, WENDY; Merrimack HS; Merrimack, NH; (Y); Spanish Clb; SADD; Concert Band; Flag Corp; Mrchg Band; School Musical; Rep Jr Cls; Rep Stu Cncl; Mst Outstndng Flag Cls 2 85; Cmnctns.

SPENCER, CYNDI; Bishop Brady HS; Chichester, NH; (Y); Church Yth Grp; Intnl Clb; Chorus; Church Choir; Plymouth ST; Bus M Gt.

SPONAUGLE, KATE; Portsmouth HS; Rye Beach, NH; (S); 26/450; Var L Bsktbl; Var L Fld Hcky; Var L Trk; High Hon Roll; Hon Roll; NHS; JR Wrld Cncl 85-86.

SPRAGGINS, BLAKE; Phillips Exeter Acad; San Angelo, TX; (Y); Church Yth Grp; French Clb; JCL; Political Wkr; Pep Clb; Chorus; Yrbk Stf; Harvard Coll Cambridge; Govt.

SPROULL, WILLIAM J; Hanover HS; Hanover, NH; (Y); AFS; Cmnty Wkr; Stage Crew; Yrbk Stf; Capt Crs Cntry; High Hon Roll.

SRYBNY, JENNIFER; Presentation Of Mary Acad; Haverhill, MA; (Y); Dance Clb; Variety Show; Im Bowling; Im Vllybl; High Hon Roll; Im Hon Roll; Italian Clb; Ecology Clb; Mission Clb; Speedwrtng Awd; Anml Tech.

ST HILAIRE, RICARDO A; Concord HS; Concord, NH; (Y); 3/355; Am Leg Boys St; Pres Debate Tm; VP Intnl Clb; Political Wkr; Pres Jr Cls; Rep Stu Cncl; Gov Hon Prg Awd; NHS; Rotary Awd; Amer Lgn Srv Mdl 86; Clmba U NY; Pltcl Sci.

ST LOUIS, PAULA; Laconia HS; Laconia, NH; (Y); 18/157; Drama Clb; French Clb; Service Clb; JV Fld Hcky; Hon Roll; NHS; Voice Dem Awd; WA & Lee U Smmr Schlrs 85; Soc Stds Dept Awd 86; Yth & Govrn 85-86; U NH; Hist.

STALLINGS, CARLTON; Alvirne HS; Hudson, NH; (Y); 49/335; Pep Clb; School Play; Rep Sr Cls; Var Capt Trk; Hon Roll; Kiwanis Awd; Stu, Athlete & Stu Marshall Of Yr 86; High Point Coll; Sprts Psychlgy.

STANFILL, JACQUELINE; Hanover HS; Hanover, NH; (Y); French Clb; German Clb; JV Lcrss; High Hon Roll; Hon Roll; Physics.

STANIEC, HEATHER; Pelham HS; Pelham, NH; (Y); 15/123; Pep Clb; Spanish Clb; Chorus; Yrbk Stf; Var Fld Hcky; Var JV Sftbl; High Hon Roll; Hon Roll; Jr NHS; NHS; U Lowell; Bus.

STEADMAN, CARRIE; Spaulding HS; Rochester, NH; (S); 29/397; Chorus; Yrbk Stf; Rep Frsh Cls; Cheerleading; Hon Roll; Fash Merch.

STEED, SUZANNE REBECCA; Pembroke Acad; Epmbroke, NH; (Y); 39/155; Varsity Clb; Bsbl; Sftbl; Hon Roll.

STEFANSKI, SCOTT E; Conant HS; Jaffrey, NH; (Y); Am Leg Boys St; Rep Soph Cls; Rep Jr Cls; Pres Stu Cncl; Socr; Hon Roll; NEDT Awd; Frgn Svc.

STEUDLE, KRISTI; Berlin HS; Berlin, NH; (Y); JA; SADD; Chorus; Cheerleading; Trk; Vllybl; Hon Roll; Spcl Ed.

STEVENS, BETSY; Farmington HS; Middleton, NH; (Y); 4/58; Am Leg Aux Girls St; Pres 4-H; French Clb; Teachers Aide; Yrbk Stf; Sec Sr Cls; 4-H Awd; High Hon Roll; Hon Roll; NHS; Wells Coll Aurora NY; Lbrl Art.

STEVENS, BRAD; Concord HS; Concord, NH; (Y); Cmnty Wkr; Letterman Clb; JV L Bsbl; JV Bsktbl; Var Crs Cntry; Hon Roll; Var L Tennis; ST & New England Tm Tnns Titles Mdl 85; World Hist Achvmnt Awd 85; ST Tnns Title Letter & Mdl 86; Bus Mgmt.

STEVENS, ROBYN M; Salem HS; Salem, NH; (Y); Drama Clb; FHA; Key Clb; Model UN; Ski Clb; SADD; Teachers Aide; School Musical; School Play; Trs Sr Cls; FHA Schlrshp 86; Fitchburg ST Coll; Comm.

STEVENS, SHEILA; Exeter Area HS; Stratham, NH; (Y); 40/280; 4-H; Yrbk Stf; Tennis; Hon Roll; Spirit Awd 83; Home Ec Awd 84; Occup Thrpy.

STEVENSON, ROBERT J; Pinkerton Acad; E Derry, NH; (Y); 13/450; Am Leg Boys St; Boys Clb Am; Math Tm; Ski Clb; Capt Crs Cntry; Lcrss; Trk; High Hon Roll; Hon Roll; NHS; Ntl Hnr Soc Schlrshp 86; Coachs Awd Crss Cntry 85; Syracuse U; Cvl Engrng.

STEWART, PETE; Pembroke Acad; Pittsfield, NH; (Y); Ski Clb; Stu Cncl; Amer Legn Schlrshp Awd; Northeastern; Police Work.

STEWART, SHANNON; Laconia HS; Laconia, NH; (Y); Dance Clb; Drama Clb; French Clb; Sec Soph Cls; Stu Cncl; Fld Hcky; Trk; Hon Roll; NHS.

STEWART, SHERRI; Thayer HS; Winchester, NH; (Y); 4/33; Church Yth Grp; Hosp Aide; Teachers Aide; Frsh Cls; Soph Cls; Jr Cls; DAR Awd; Hon Roll; NHS; Apprntce Of Yr 85-86; Leominster Hosp Schl Nrsng; Nrs.

STICKNEY, LINDA; Concord HS; Concord, NH; (Y); 57/390; Hosp Aide; Spanish Clb; Dentl Hygiene.

STINSON, ROSS; Rembroke Acad; Suncook, NH; (Y); Pres Aud/Vis; Chess Clb; Computer Clb; Exploring; FBLA; FFA; Library Aide; Science Clb; Ski Clb; Teachers Aide; Laconia Voc-Tech; Elec Engr.

STONE, BRITAIN; St Pauls Schl; Atlanta, GA; (Y); French Clb; SADD; Nwsp Phtg; Yrbk Phtg; Im Ftbl; JV Lcrss; Im Socr; High Hon Roll; High Hon Roll; Kiwanis Awd.

STREETER, MELISSA J; Goffstown Area HS; Goffstown, NH; (Y); 4/212; Drama Clb; Ski Clb; VP NHS; SADD; School Play; Yrbk Stf; Ntl Merit SF; Ntl Sci Hnr 84; Math Awd 83-84; Psy Bio.

STRICKFORD, DANIEL; Hopkinton HS; Cantoocook, NH; (Y); 1/65; Church Yth Grp; German Clb; Math Tm; Model UN; SADD; Band; Chorus; Concert Band; Pep Band; Stage Crew; NH All ST Chorus 85-86; NH ST Champ Acadmc Decthln 86; St Davis Schl Adv Stds Prog 86; American U; Intl Bus.

STRINO, SHARON M; Alvirne HS; Manchester, NH; (Y); Chorus; NHS; Natl Sci Awd 85 & 86; Intl Drctry Dstngshd Yng Ldrshp 86; Med.

STROBEL, KELLY; Fall Mountain Regional HS; Chalrestown, NH; (Y); Art Clb; 4-H; French Clb; Girl Scts; Band; Chorus; Madrigals; Yrbk Stf; Socr; Var Sftbl; 4-H Awds; Art.

STRUBE, OLIVER; High Mowing HS; South Lyndeboro, NH; (Y); Yrbk Phtg; Capt Var Bsktbl; Var Socr; Photogrphy.

STUART, JOELY; Spaulding HS; Rochester, NH; (S); 9/395; Art Clb; Math Clb; Math Tm; Teachers Aide; Rep Soph Cls; Rep Jr Cls; JV Sftbl; High Hon Roll; NHS; English Clb; Mu Alph Thet 85-86; Srch Pgm U Of NH 85-86; Envrnmntl Engrng.

STURGILL, SCOTT; Central HS; Manchester, NH; (Y); 119/430; Art Clb; Drama Clb; Band; Concert Band; Mrchg Band; Pep Band; School Play; Stage Crew; High Hon Roll; Hon Roll; Boston U; Health.

STYLES, JODI; Spaulding HS; Barrington, NH; (S); 52/400; Hon Roll; Hnrbl Mntn ST Acctg Cont N H Coll 85; Kiwanis Wlk A Thon 84; Bus Adm.

SUBLER, DIANNE; Mount St Mary Seminary; Nashua, NH; (Y); 5/77; Cmnty Wkr; Drama Clb; Hosp Aide; Pres Science Clb; School Play; Bausch & Lomb Sci Awd; High Hon Roll; Hon Roll; NHS; Library Aide; 100 Hrs Vol Time Nashua Mem Hosp 86; High Hnrs U S Hstry I 87; Outstdng Wrk MSMS Sci Clb 87; Vet Med.

SUDOL, KRISTI; Hillsboro-Deering HS; Hillsboro, NH; (S); 2/72; Math Tm; Teachers Aide; Band; Mrchg Band; Pep Band; Yrbk Stf; Sec Frsh Cls; Crs Cntry; NHS.

SUIFT, BRIAN; Hanover HS; Hanover, NH; (Y); Band; Concert Band; Jazz Band; Pep Band; Tennis; Ntl Merit SF; Math Assoc Of Amer Otstndng Ach 83; All-ST Bnd 86.

SULLIVAN, HEATHER; Alvirne HS; Hudson, NH; (Y); SADD; Varsity Clb; School Musical; Im Bsktbl; Var Crs Cntry; Mgr(s); Score Keeper; JV Socr; JV Var Sftbl; Var Trk; STOPP Apprdctn Awd 84.

SULLIVAN, JAMES JOSEPH; Bishop Guertin HS; Lowell, MA; (Y); Spanish Clb; SADD; Band; JV Bsbl; Im Bsktbl; Var Wrstlng; Hon Roll; Spanish NHS; Boys Clb Am; Church Yth Grp; U Lowell; Acctng.

SULLIVAN, TARA; Interlakes HS; Meredith, NH; (Y); 5/83; Drama Clb; Math Tm; Service Clb; SADD; Chorus; School Musical; Variety Show; Yrbk Stf; JV Capt Bsktbl; Var L Trk; Psych.

SUMMERS, AMY; Dover HS; Dover, NH; (Y); 42/289; Yrbk Phtg; Yrbk Stf; Hon Roll; Granite Grls ST 86; Bus.

SUNDEEN, KIM; Manchester Cental HS; Manchester, NH; (Y); 184/430; Church Yth Grp; Drama Clb; German Clb; SADD; Variety Show; Lit Mag; Stu Cncl; Arch.

SUNUNU, JAMES; Salem HS; Salem, NH; (S); 1/350; Math Tm; Model UN; Ski Clb; Pres Jr Cls; Socr; Trk; High Hon Roll; NHS; Engr.

SURETTE, JAMES; Kennett HS; N Conway, NH; (Y); US Rep Frnc 86; Bus.

SVENCONIS, KEVIN; Salem HS; Salem, NH; (Y); Model UN; Bsktbl; Crs Cntry; Hon Roll; Spanish NHS; Coaches Awd Bsktbll 85-86; Grant From Franklin Pierce Coll 86; Franklin Pierce Coll; Law.

SWAIN, DEENA; Newport JR SR HS; Newport, NH; (Y); Am Leg Aux Girls St; Church Yth Grp; Girl Scts; Letterman Clb; Pep Clb; SADD; Varsity Clb; Yrbk Rptr; Yrbk Stf; Rep Jr Cls; Public Rltns.

SWAIN, MICHELLE MARIE; Fall Mountain Regional HS; Walpole, NH; (Y); 25/100; Am Leg Aux Girls St; Math Tm; Color Guard; Gym; Trk; Hon Roll; NHS; Phys Ed Awd 85; Plymouth ST; Bus.

SWAKLA, CHRISTINE; Nashua HS; Newburyport, MA; (Y); 44/782; Latin Clb; Ski Clb; SADD; Var Co-Capt Crs Cntry; Im Sftbl; Var Capt Trk; DAR Awd; Hon Roll; Jr NHS; NHS; Pres Acdmc Ftns Awd 86; Rymnd Chntl Mem Schlrshp 86; MVP Sprng Trck, Crs Cntry, MIP Wntr Trck 85; U Vermont.

SWAN III, THOMAS J; St Pauls Schl; Boston, MA; (Y); Church Yth Grp; Cmnty Wkr; Debate Tm; English Clb; Latin Clb; Political Wkr; Thesps; School Play; Variety Show; Nwsp Bus Mgr; Pres Clsrm Yng Amer 86; ISL Debate Bst Spkr 86; Intrnshp Senator Dole DC 87; Law.

SWIDER, KEITH C; Hollis Area HS; Hollis, NH; (Y); 30/110; Am Leg Boys St; Ski Clb; VP Spanish Clb; Rep Sr Cls; Im Bsktbl; Var Socr; Var Tennis; Var Trk; Hon Roll; Spanish NHS.

SWIFT, ELIZABETH; Inter-Lakes HS; Center Harbor, NH; (Y); Church Yth Grp; French Clb; SADD; Chorus; Yrbk Sprt Ed; Var Capt Vllybl; Hon Roll; Trs Frsh Cls; Trs Soph Cls; Trs Jr Cls; Johnson & Wales Coll; Recrtn.

SWIFT, MARGARET; Inter-Lakes HS; Center Harbor, NH; (Y); Church Yth Grp; SADD; Yrbk Stf; VP Soph Cls; L Stat Mgr(s); L Stat Score Keeper.

SZYMANSKI, PAM; Timberlane Regional HS; Atkinson, NH; (Y); Varsity Clb; Var Bsktbl; Hon Roll; Var Fld Hcky; Var Sftbl; Var Vllybl; Typng Accurcy Hnr Roll 84; Typng Profcncy Cert 84; UNH; Sprts Med.

TANCREL, PAULINE; Manchester Central HS; Hooksett, NH; (Y); 53/430; High Hon Roll; Hon Roll; Med Photo.

TARDIF, GERARD P; Bishop Guertin HS; Nashua, NH; (Y); Pres FCA; SADD; Var Capt Bsbl; Var Ice Hcky; Hon Roll; Hudson Amercn Lgn Bsbl Schlrshp 86; U Of ME Orono; Bus.

TASKER, JUDI; Dover HS; Dover, NH; (Y); 21/273; Church Yth Grp; French Clb; Hosp Aide; JV Var Bsktbl; JV Var Fld Hcky; Var Sftbl; High Hon Roll; Hon Roll; Sci.

TATE, JEFFREY; Bishop Guertin HS; Hudson, NH; (Y); 2/150; Computer Clb; French Clb; Trs Band; Concert Band; Mrchg Band; High Hon Roll; NHS; Phrmcy.

TATINCLAUX, PHILIPPE; Hanover HS; Hanover, NH; (Y); 20/160; German Clb; Im Bsktbl; Var Socr; Var Trk; Hon Roll; Ntl Merit Schol; St Pauls Smr Schl 85; Trk Mst Imprvd Plyr 86; ST Chmpn Sccr Rnr-Up 85; Duke U.

TAYLOR, CORI M; Spaulding HS; Rochester, NH; (Y); 14/400; Am Leg Aux Girls St; Pres Frsh Cls; Pres Soph Cls; Pres Jr Cls; Pres Sr Cls; Var Capt Cheerleading; High Hon Roll; NHS; Hugh O Brian Yth Ldrshp Smnr Ambssdr 85; Ntl Chrg Chmpnshp Stf Stu 86; Eli Mrcx Awd 86.

TAYLOR, MARCY L; Groveton HS; Groveton, NH; (S); 1/44; French Clb; Teachers Aide; Yrbk Phtg; Trs Stu Cncl; JV Var Bsktbl; VP L Fld Hcky; High Hon Roll; NHS; Variety Show; Yrbk Stf; Outstndg Stu Cncl Awd 84; YFU U S Sen-Japan Scholar Semi-Fin 86; Med.

TAYLOR, TROY; Spaulding HS; Rochester, NH; (S); Am Leg Boys St; Hon Roll; Prfct Atten Awd; Mgmt.

TENN, MARY; Manchester Central HS; Manchester, NH; (Y); 12/525; Church Yth Grp; Cmnty Wkr; Debate Tm; Model UN; NFL; Speech Tm; SADD; Nwsp Rptr; Pres Soph Cls; Pres Jr Cls; ST Stu Cncl Pres 86-87; Harvard; Law.

THAYER, JAMES; Woodsville HS; Woodsville, NH; (Y); Scholastic Bowl; SADD; Yrbk Phtg; Yrbk Stf; Ntl Merit Ltr; Voice Dem Awd; Progressv Clb Woodsville Scholar 86; Granite ST Challng Cert Awd 86; Plymouth ST Coll; Engl.

THEROUX, MONICA; Belmont HS; Belmont, NH; (Y); Nwsp Stf; Burdett; Acctng.

THERRIAULT, ANDREA; Mascoma Valley Regional HS; Canaan, NH; (Y); Am Leg Aux Girls St; French Clb; Band; Sec Stu Cncl; Var Bsktbl; Var Fld Hcky; Hon Roll; NHS; Church Yth Grp; Sprtsmnshp Awd 85; Coach Awd 86; Johnson & Wales; Retl/Mrktng.

THERRIEN, MICHELLE; Spaulding HS; Rochester, NH; (S); 36/400; Church Yth Grp; Hosp Aide; Key Clb; Hon Roll; Prfct Atten Awd; Bio.

THIBODEAU, MICHELLE; Fall Mountain Regional HS; Charlestown, NH; (Y); 63/365; Drama Clb; 4-H; Library Aide; Chorus; Yrbk Stf; Lit Mag; Hon Roll; Mstrs Edctn; Spcl Ed Tchr.

THISTLE, PETER; Pinkerton Acad; Camp Hill, PA; (Y); 23/496; Ski Clb; Band; Concert Band; Jazz Band; Mrchg Band; Hon Roll; NHS; Robert F Noonan Schlrshp 86; U Of Miami FL; Music.

THOMAS, BRIAN S; Nashua HS; Nashua, NH; (Y); Am Leg Boys St; High Hon Roll; Hon Roll; NHS; Arch.

THOMAS, GLEN; Concord HS; Concord, NH; (Y); 38/390; Church Yth Grp; Band; Concert Band; Mrchg Band; Im Bsktbl; Im Vllybl; Im Wt Lftg; High Hon Roll; NHS; Prfct Atten Awd; Rnslr Poly Tech; Cvl Engrng.

THOMAS, JOELLE; Spaulding HS; Sanbornville, NH; (Y); 41/350; JV Var Bsktbl; Mgr Sftbl; Hon Roll; Wakefld Wmns Clb Schlrshp 86; Plymouth ST Coll; Acctng.

THOMAS, KRISTEN MARIE; West HS; Bedford, NH; (Y); 21/338; Trs Drama Clb; Ski Clb; Yrbk Stf; DAR Awd; High Hon Roll; NHS; Alpha Delta Kappa Intl Socty For Women 86; Boston Coll; Educ.

THOMPSON, KEVIN; Stevens HS; Claremont, NH; (Y); Dance Clb; Pres SADD; Nwsp Rptr; Nwsp Sprt Ed; Yrbk Rptr; Yrbk Sprt Ed; Yrbk Stf; Stu Cncl; JV L Bsbl; JV Bsktbl; U NH; Hotel Admin.

THOMPSON, LISBETH; Phillips Exeter Acad; Champaign, IL; (Y); Church Yth Grp; French Clb; Service Clb; Church Choir; Var Ice Hcky; Var Sftbl; Var Swmmng; Var Tennis; French Hon Soc; High Hon Roll; Natl Hnr Rl 86; Intl Rltns.

THURBER, MARK; Portsmouth SR HS; Portsmouth, NH; (Y); Church Yth Grp; Cmnty Wkr; Debate Tm; Model UN; Ski Clb; Off Sr Cls; JV Var Ftbl; Ice Hcky; Trk; Hon Roll; UNH; Engrng.

THURSTON, TRACY; Kennett HS; Ctr Conway, NH; (Y); French Clb; JV Capt Sftbl; French Hon Soc; Hon Roll; VP NHS; Engrng.

TIBBETTS, TAMRA; Profile JR SR HS; Bethlehem, NH; (Y); Pres Church Yth Grp; Pres Girl Scts; Chorus; Church Choir; School Musical; School Play; Sec Stu Cncl; JV Fld Hcky; Var Tennis; High Hon Roll; Outstndng SR High Drama Stu 86; Med.

TILTON, JOHN; Portsmouth HS; Portsmouth, NH; (Y); French Clb; Model UN; Band; Concert Band; Jazz Band; Mrchg Band; Med.

TITUS, MICHELLE; Salem HS; Salem, NH; (Y); Debate Tm; Key Clb; Ski Clb; Yrbk Ed-Chief; Stu Cncl; JV Var Fld Hcky; Trk; High Hon Roll; NHS; NEDT Awd; VP NH Assn Stu Cncls 85-86; Wellesley Coll; Lib Art.

TONNESEN, GREGORY; Milford Area SR HS; Amherst, NH; (Y); 48/311; Var Golf; JV Socr; Hon Roll; Solar Energy Awd 82; Brigham Young U; Business.

TOPPING, NOEL; Nashua HS; Nashua, NH; (S); Art Clb; Church Yth Grp; Computer Clb; DECA; Drama Clb; Hon Roll; BYU; Bus.

TOTH, SUSAN MARIE; Salem HS; Salem, NH; (S); 12/340; Ski Clb; Yrbk Ed-Chief; Rep Sr Cls; Trs Stu Cncl; Var JV Bsktbl; JV Trk; Elks Awd; High Hon Roll; NHS; MVP Bsktbl; Cochs Awd JV Bsktbl; Bus Mgmt.

TOWLE, MICHELE; Belmont HS; Canterbury, NH; (S); 3/67; French Clb; Trs Keywanettes; Math Tm; Varsity Clb; Yrbk Ed-Chief; JV Var Cheerleading; Var Trk; High Hon Roll; Hon Roll; NHS; Physcl Thrpy.

TOWNSEND, BENJAMIN; Kimball Union Acad; Canaan, NH; (Y); 3/70; Drama Clb; Math Tm; Ski Clb; Church Choir; School Musical; School Play; Stage Crew; Lit Mag; Var Crs Cntry; High Hon Roll; Biotechnlgy.

TRACY, DONNA; Pelham HS; Pelham, NH; (Y); 10/180; Church Yth Grp; Teachers Aide; Chorus; Rep Soph Cls; High Hon Roll; Hon Roll; NHS; JV Capt Bsktbl; JV Var Fld Hcky; JV Var Sftbl; Adjstmnt Ctr Aide Awd 84; SLATE 85; No Essex Cmmnty Coll; Chld Ed.

TRASATTI, MICHAEL A; Milford Area SR HS; Amherst, NH; (Y); Am Leg Boys St; Teachers Aide; Yrbk Bus Mgr; Yrbk Ed-Chief; Rep Jr Cls; Trs Stu Cncl; Var L Crs Cntry; Var L Trk; Hon Roll; Engrg.

TRASK, ANTHONY; Winnacunnet HS; N Hampton, NH; (Y); 1/325; Jazz Band; Pres Frsh Cls; Pres Soph Cls; Pres Jr Cls; Pres Sr Cls; Var Bsbl; High Hon Roll; NHS; Ntl Merit SF; Math Tm; Harvard Bk Awd 86; All At Orch 85; Aerontcl Engrng.

TRAVIS, BONNIE; Epping JR SR HS; Epping, NH; (S); Drama Clb; Office Aide; Teachers Aide; School Musical; School Play; Yrbk Bus Mgr; Yrbk Phtg; Yrbk Stf; Sec Soph Cls; Var Cheerleading; Pre-Law.

TREMBLAY, JACQUELINE; Portsmouth SR HS; New Castle, NH; (S); #5 In Class; Math Tm; Sec Ski Clb; High Hon Roll; Sec NHS; JWC 84-86; Purdue U; Elec Engr.

TREMBLAY, MARK; Bishop Guertin HS; Amherst, NH; (Y); Church Yth Grp; French Clb; Nwsp Stf; Im Mgr Bsktbl; Var Crs Cntry; Var L Trk; Hon Roll; Jrnlsm.

TRISCIANI, BRENDA LEE; Manchester Memorial HS; Manchester, NH; (Y); 13/343; Am Leg Aux Girls St; Yrbk Stf; Ed Lit Mag; Cheerleading; Sftbl; Stu Cncl; Powder Puff Ftbl; Hon Roll; Wm Loeb Schlrshp 86; AROTC & AFROTC Schlrshp 86; Prestl Schlr 86; Purdue U; Arntcl Engrng.

TROADEC, JEAN-MARC; High Mowing Schl; New London, CT; (Y); French Clb; PAVAS; Ski Clb; Band; Jazz Band; School Musical; School Play; Variety Show; Socr; Hon Roll; Mickey Awd For Schl Spirit 85-86; Music.

TROTTER, KIM; Alvirne HS; Hudson, NH; (Y); 105/338; Art Clb; Church Yth Grp; Drama Clb; Variety Show; Ed Yrbk Stf; Lit Mag; Rep Stu Cncl; Var Crs Cntry; Mgr(s); Hon Roll; Mrymnt NY Coll; Fash Editor.

TUCCOLO, KATRINA; Salem HS; Salem, NH; (Y); 54/380; Church Yth Grp; Model UN; Concert Band; Mrchg Band; Trs Frsh Cls; Stat Bsktbl; Var Fld Hcky; Phys Thrpy.

TUCKER, KATHY; Dover HS; Dover, NH; (S); Camera Clb; VP Pres DECA; 4-H; SADD; 4-H Awd; Hon Roll; Awds DECA Comptn Restrnt & Htl Mgmt 86; UNH; Mktg Ed.

TUEFFERD, NANOOK; Alvirne HS; Hudson, NH; (Y); 13/330; Varsity Clb; Concert Band; Jazz Band; Var Capt Crs Cntry; Var Capt Trk; Hon Roll; VP NHS; Most Impve Wntr Trck 85; Ddctn Awd Spg Trck 85; Engrng.

TURGEON, ANDREA; Keene HS; Keene, NH; (Y); Art Clb; Pep Clb; Ski Clb; Rep Frsh Cls; Rep Soph Cls; Rep Jr Cls; Var Trk; Hon Roll; Adv.

TURNER, DONALD; Spaulding HS; Rochester, NH; (S); 3/350; Key Clb; Math Clb; ROTC; Drill Tm; JV Ftbl; Trk; High Hon Roll; Mu Alp Tht; NHS; Varsity Clb; MIT; Elec Engr.

TUSON, GWEN L; Manchester HS; Manchester, NH; (Y); 12/352; Am Leg Aux Girls St; Trs Drama Clb; Math Tm; SADD; Nwsp Ed-Chief; Ed Lit Mag; Rep Stu Cncl; Var Capt Crs Cntry; High Hon Roll; Ntl Merit SF; Pre-Law.

TUXILL, JOHN; Hopkinton HS; Contoocook, NH; (Y); 1/73; Capt Math Tm; Capt Quiz Bowl; Nwsp Stf; VP Capt Crs Cntry; VP Capt Trk; Bausch & Lomb Sci Awd; High Hon Roll; NHS; Val; French Clb; Colby Coll Book Awd 85; Williams Coll; Bio.

ULRICH, KAREN; Londonderry HS; Londonderry, NH; (Y); Ski Clb; Yrbk Phtg; Yrbk Stf; Pres Stu Cncl; Bsktbl; Socr; Hon Roll; Syracuse U; Phtgrnlsm.

USINGER, EMIL; Contoocook Valley Regional HS; Francestown, NH; (Y); 17/162; Drama Clb; JCL; Band; Yrbk Stf; Pres Frsh Cls; Var Crs Cntry; Var Trk; High Hon Roll; Hon Roll; Ntl Merit Ltr; Colgate U; Chemistry.

VAAS, JEFFREY; Spaulding HS; Rochester, NH; (S); 27/397; Rep Soph Cls; Rep Jr Cls; Ftbl; VP Ice Hcky; Hon Roll.

VACHON, CINDY; Spaulding HS; Rochester, NH; (S); 8/350; Am Leg Aux Girls St; FBLA; Office Aide; High Hon Roll; NHS; NH Coll ST Comp Acctg II 1st Pl 85; Acctg.

VAILLANCOURT, JOSEE; Alvirne HS; Hudson, NH; (Y); Hon Roll; Psych.

VAILLANCOURT, RAY; Bishop Guertin HS; Nashua, NH; (Y); 18/146; Pres Church Yth Grp; Math Clb; SADD; Nwsp Rptr; Lit Mag; High Hon Roll; Jr NHS; NHS; NEDT Awd; Bio.

VAILLANCOURT, TAMMY; Nashua SR HS; Nashua, NH; (Y); 50/936; High Hon Roll; Hon Roll; Jr NHS; NHS; Prfct Atten Awd.

VALDEZ, TRICIA; Hillsboro-Deering HS; Deering, NH; (S); 4/69; Church Yth Grp; Debate Tm; Drama Clb; French Clb; Library Aide; Math Tm; Quiz Bowl; Teachers Aide; Chorus; School Play; Med.

VALDINOCCI, JEAN; Presentation Of Mary Acad; Chelmsford, MA; (Y); 2/20; Church Choir; Trs Frsh Cls; Trs Soph Cls; Rep Jr Cls; Hon Roll; NHS; French Clb; Drm & Bgl; Im Vllybl; Prfct Atten Awd; Cngrsnl Schlr 86; Ambsdr Hugh Obrien Yth Fndtn 85; Chllng Pgm 85-86; Prsntn Mary Acad Schlrshp 83-87; Med Tech.

VALENTI, NANCY; Alvirne HS; Hudson, NH; (Y); 8/333; Band; High Hon Roll; Hon Roll; NHS; Frnch Awd 83-84; HOBY Ldrshp Awd 84-85; Outing Clb 84-85.

VALLANCE, KERRY; St Pauls Schl; Wood Haven, NY; (Y); FTA; Girl Scts; Key Clb; Library Aide; Political Wkr; Spanish Clb; Teachers Aide; Chorus; Church Choir; School Musical; Pell Grant 86-87; U PA Grant 86-87; U PA.

VAN DER LINDE, ROBERT; Hillsboro-Deering Cooperative HS; Deering, NH; (S); 1/75; Chess Clb; Debate Tm; Drama Clb; French Clb; Math Tm; Band; Trs Frsh Cls; Trs Soph Cls; NHS; Rensselaer Polytech; Aero Engr.

VAN MULLEN, WILLIAM F; Trinity HS; Manchester, NH; (Y); Am Leg Boys St; Boys Clb Am; Cmnty Wkr; Exploring; Model UN; Church Choir; Yrbk Stf; Rep Frsh Cls; Trk; Hon Roll; Bys Clb Bsktbll Sprtsmnshp Awd 86; Trnty HS JV Bsktbll Awd 85; Avition.

VAN PELT, JENNIFER; Portsmouth SR HS; Portsmouth, NH; (Y); Band; Concert Band; Jazz Band; Mrchg Band; School Musical; High Hon Roll; Hon Roll; NH All ST Band Percssn 86; U NH; Cmmnctns.

VAN WINKLE, KARI; Hanover HS; Norwich, VT; (Y); Ski Clb; Varsity Clb; Chorus; Orch; Yrbk Stf; Var Capt Crs Cntry; JV Lcrss; Var L Trk; High Hon Roll; Hon Roll; Concord Strng Quart Schlrshp 85; Germ Natl Hnr Soc 86; Frnch Grnd Concrs Exm Lvl 5 86.

VANALSTYNE, MELISSA; Fall Mt Regional HS; Alstead, NH; (Y); Stage Crew; Stat Bsktbl; Mgr(s); Hon Roll; Excllnc-Earth & Spc Sci 84, Fds & Nutrtn 86.

VANDERNOOT, STACY; Laconia HS; Laconia, NH; (Y); French Clb; GAA; Band; Concert Band; Mrchg Band; Pep Band; Bsktbl; NH Rep Ntl Flg Dy Clbrtn Baltmore MD 86; Pre-Law.

VARNEY, KIMBERLY; Spaulding HS; Rochester, NH; (S); 19/397; Office Aide; Yrbk Stf; Rep Frsh Cls; Rep Soph Cls; Rep Jr Cls; High Hon Roll; Hon Roll; NHS; Law.

VERMEULE, CORNELIUS A; St Pauls Schl; Cambridge, MA; (Y); Pres Chess Clb; English Clb; French Clb; Library Aide; Math Tm; Spanish Clb; Lit Mag; Hon Roll; Ntl Merit SF; E Asian Lit.

VERMILYEA, KRISTEN; Bishop Brady HS; Pembroke, NH; (Y); Drama Clb; Ski Clb; Chorus; School Play; Var Cheerleading; Var Sftbl; Var Vllybl; Hon Roll; NHS; Hugh Obrien Yth Fndtn; Miss Am Teenagr NH.

VILLENEUVE, BETTYJO; Berlin HS; Berlin, NH; (Y); Trs FBLA; Yrbk Stf; 1st Plc Typng II 85; Crt Rprtr.

VIOLETTE, LISA; Belmont HS; Laconia, NH; (Y); 29/65; Library Aide; Varsity Clb; Yrbk Sprt Ed; Var Capt Bsktbl; Var Capt Sftbl; Var Capt Vllybl; Cit Awd; Hon Roll; Prfct Atten Awd; Knghts Clmbs Schlrshp 86; Plymouth ST Coll; Bio Sci.

VITALE, GREGORY S; Phillips Exeter Acad; Wayland, MA; (Y); Chess Clb; Orch; School Musical; Rep Jr Cls; Stu Cncl; Im Bsbl; JV Trk; High Hon Roll; Dorm Prctr 85-86; Davis Awd-Goodwl & Enthsm To Respnsblty 85-86; Smfnlst Arts Cmptn 86.

VOLL, S LAYLA; Oyster River HS; Durham, NH; (Y); 1/156; Cmnty Wkr; Drama Clb; Orch; School Musical; School Play; High Hon Roll; Ntl Merit SF; Church Yth Grp; French Clb; Latin Clb; Oystr Rvr Schlstc Hnr Scty 85-86; Chldrn Amer Rvltn Pres 82-84, Treas 84-86; NH ST Myth Exam 83-85; Librl Arts.

VON DREDEN, RICHARD; Fall Mountain Regional HS; Charlestown, NH; (Y); 4-H; 4-H Awd; Hon Roll; Chef.

VON GILLERN, HEATHER; Fall Mountain Regional HS; Charlestown, NH; (Y); 2/150; Cmnty Wkr; Band; Chorus; Concert Band; Drm Mjr(t); Jazz Band; Madrigals; School Musical; Symp Band; Yrbk Stf; NH All ST Bnd 86; Englsh Cmpstn Awds 84 & 85; Chmstry, Algbra II, Trig & Wrld Hstry Awds 85 & 86; Jrnlsm.

VON MOLTKE, DOROTHEA; Hanover HS; Norwich, VT; (Y); 6/100; Dance Clb; Mgr Drama Clb; French Clb; Intnl Clb; Chorus; School Play; Ed Nwsp Ed-Chief; Frsh Cls; Soph Cls; Jr Cls; Frnch Cntst 85; Natl Frnch Compt 85; Hist Recitn Hnrb Mntn 85; Yale College; Theatr Dirctg.

VON ZABERN, MARKUS; High Mowing Schl; Wilton, NH; (Y); 7/28; Acpl Chr; Chorus; School Musical; School Play; Stage Crew; Yrbk Sprt Ed; JV Socr; UNH; Arch.

VONDRA, RICK; Bishop Guertin HS; Warren, IL; (Y); Aud/Vis; JV Var Ftbl; Im Wt Lftg; High Hon Roll; Hon Roll.

VORCE, SHARLENE J; Pembroke Acad; Suncook, NH; (Y); JV Bsktbl; Var L Fld Hcky; Var L Sftbl; Hon Roll; Most Imprvd-Vrsty Fld Hcky 84; Vrsty Pin-2nd Yr Vrsty Softbll 86; Athletic Trnr.

VOSE, JEFFREY S; Fall Mtn Reg HS; Walpole, NH; (Y); Am Leg Boys St; Pres FFA; JV Bsktbl; Ftbl; ME Maritime Acad; Engrng.

WAGNER, MEGAN; Portsmouth HS; Rye, NH; (S); 5/450; Trs Frsh Cls; Trs Soph Cls; Rep Jr Cls; Rep Stu Cncl; Var L Swmmng; NHS; Intl Bus.

WAITE, DAVID; Concord HS; Concord, NH; (Y); 46/375; Rep Frsh Cls; Rep Soph Cls; Im Bsktbl; Im Vllybl; High Hon Roll; Hon Roll; Christa Mc Auliffe Awd Soc Soc 85-86; Physics Achvt Awd 85-86; French Achvt Awd 83-84; Engrng.

WAJDA, STEPH; Alvirne HS; Hudson, NH; (Y); Ski Clb; Varsity Clb; Rep Frsh Cls; Crs Cntry; Trk; Hon Roll; Northeastern U; Engrg.

WALDEN, VICKI; Pinkerton Acad; Derry, NH; (Y); 10/438; Dance Clb; Latin Clb; SADD; Acpl Chr; Chorus; School Musical; School Play; Variety Show; Off Jr Cls; Lion Awd; Wellesley Bk Awd; Stu Cncl Schlrshp; Wesleyan U; Engl.

WALKER, PAULA; Groveton HS; Groveton, NH; (Y); Hosp Aide; Office Aide; Bsktbl; Sftbl; Swmmng; Trk; Hon Roll.

WALKER JR, THOMAS E; Community Baptist Schl; Meadows, NH; (Y); Am Leg Boys St; Church Yth Grp; Political Wkr; Yrbk Ed-Chief; VP Frsh Cls; VP Soph Cls; Pres Jr Cls; Im Socr; Im Sftbl; Hon Roll; Liberty U; Pol Sci.

WALKOWIAK, SCOTT; Portsmouth HS; Portsmouth, NH; (S); Var L Ftbl.

WALLACE, SUSAN L; Franklin HS; Franklin, NH; (Y); 2/86; Math Tm; Trs Frsh Cls; Trs Soph Cls; Trs Jr Cls; Trs Sr Cls; Pres Stu Cncl; Bsktbl; Fld Hcky; Sftbl; DAR Awd; UNH; Pre-Law.

WALLIN, IAN; Centeral HS; Candia, NH; (Y); 65/430; Temple Yth Grp; Yrbk Rptr; Yrbk Sprt Ed; Trs Soph Cls; Trs Jr Cls; Trs Sr Cls; High Hon Roll; Lbrl Arts.

WALSH, CATHERINE M; Newport JR SR HS; Newport, NH; (Y); Church Yth Grp; Drama Clb; French Clb; Political Wkr; SADD; Chorus; School Musical; Nwsp Stf; Yrbk Stf; Stu Cncl; Chld Psych.

WARD, DENNIS M; Spaulding HS; Rochester, NH; (Y); 38/389; Am Leg Boys St; JV Bsbl; Var Ftbl; JV Socr; Var Trk; Hon Roll; NHS.

WARD, KRISTIN; Hopkinton HS; Cantoocook, NH; (Y); #1 In Class; Debate Tm; Drama Clb; Model UN; School Play; Yrbk Ed-Chief; Sec Frsh Cls; Pres Soph Cls; Jr Cls; Dnfth Awd; High Hon Roll; Hugh O Brian Yth Ldrshp Sem; Harvard Book Awd, Dartmouth Book Awd; Selected For St Pauls Schl Studies.

WARE, CHRISTOPHER; Bishop Guertin HS; Nashua, NH; (Y); Boy Scts; French Clb; Key Clb; Ski Clb; SADD; Im Bsktbl; JV Crs Cntry; JV Ftbl; JV Trk; Hon Roll; U NH; Aviatn.

WASHBURNE, DENISE; Spaulding HS; Rochester, NH; (Y); FBLA; Library Aide; Hon Roll; Mc Intosh; Acctng.

WASSERLOOS, JEFFREY A; Tilton Schl; Francestown, NH; (S); Spanish Clb; Var Capt Ftbl; Var Lcrss; Hon Roll.

WASYLAH, RANDY; Bishop Guerth HS; Merrimack, NH; (Y); 78/138; Hosp Aide; SADD; JV Bsbl; JV Var Ftbl; Var Ice Hcky; Hon Roll; 2 Yr Hon Awd 86; Pre-Dentstry.

WATSON, DONALD; Hollis HS; Hollis, NH; (Y); Boy Scts; JA; Library Aide; Office Aide; Spanish Clb; Teachers Aide; Band; Concert Band; Mrchg Band; Rep Soph Cls; Psychlgy.

WAYMAN, TRICIA; Concord HS; Concord, NH; (Y); 100/330; Teachers Aide; Chorus; Ed Lit Mag; Outstndng Effrt In Music Orgnztn 83-84; You & The Law Awd For Outstndng Effrt 85-86; Crmnl Attrny.

WEATHERBEE, MARY-JANE; Mt St Mary Semry; Amherst, NH; (Y); Am Leg Aux Girls St; Cmnty Wkr; Drama Clb; French Clb; Model UN; Sec SADD; Stage Crew; Sec Frsh Cls; Sec Soph Cls; Lib Arts.

WEEKS, STACEY; White Mtns Regional HS; Whitefield, NH; (Y); 5/110; GAA; Spanish Clb; Varsity Clb; Chorus; Yrbk Phtg; Yrbk Stf; VP Soph Cls; VP Jr Cls; Var L Bsktbl; Var L Fld Hcky; Most Vlbl Athlt 86; Whitefld Polc Assc Schlrshp 86; U Of NH.

WEGIEL, MARK P; Pinkerton Acad; Derry, NH; (Y); 112/796; Math Tm; VP Ski Clb; Ntl Merit SF; U Of NH; Ocean Engr.

WELCH, SONJA; Concord Christian HS; Concord, NH; (Y); 5/15; Church Yth Grp; Chorus; Church Choir; Stage Crew; Yrbk Stf; Trs Jr Cls; Pres Sr Cls; Capt Cheerleading; Stat Socr; Vllybl; Tchrs Awd; Ldrshp Chrng Awd; Johnson & Wales; Trvl.

WELLER, KRISTIN; Milford Area SR HS; Amherst, NH; (Y); 32/309; Computer Clb; FBLA; Acpl Chr; Band; Chorus; Concert Band; Flag Corp; Mrchg Band; Variety Show; Hon Roll; All-ST Choir 85; Skiing-IM 82-86; Wheaton Coll; Lbrl Arts.

WELLS, FERMOR; Concord Christian HS; Concord, NH; (Y); Church Yth Grp; Cmnty Wkr; Trs Drama Clb; Chorus; Church Choir; School Play; Yrbk Stf; Var L Cheerleading; Var L Crs Cntry; Hon Roll; Word Of Life Bible Inst Schlrshps 84-86; Most Imprvd Stu Awd 85; Word Life Bible Inst; Psych.

WELLS, THEODORE; Manchester Memorial HS; Manchester, NH; (Y); Boys Clb Am; Political Wkr; Lit Mag; Im Bsktbl; Hon Roll.

WENZEL, ALSEN; Keene HS; Keene, NH; (Y); 56/395; Boy Scts; Pres Church Yth Grp; Acpl Chr; Chorus; Church Choir; Concert Band; Var Debate Tm; JV Var Ftbl; JV Mgr(s); Hon Roll; Daniel Webster; Aerontcs.

WHEELER, CHAROLETTE; Pittsfield HS; Pittsfield, NH; (Y); 19/75; Church Yth Grp; Cmnty Wkr; 4-H; French Clb; Office Aide; Science Clb; SADD; Teachers Aide; Yrbk Sprt Ed; Yrbk Stf; Harvey A Marston Scholar Awd 86; Typg I & II Awd Merit 86; Westbrook Coll; Dntl Hyg.

WHEELER, JESSE; Concord HS; Concord, NH; (Y); 19/369; Church Yth Grp; Drama Clb; Math Tm; Concert Band; Jazz Band; Mrchg Band; School Play; Rep Stu Cncl; Var Crs Cntry; NHS; Cngrss Bndstg Exchng Pgm Schlrshp 86; Cncrd Rtry Exchng Pgm 85; Advncd Stds Pgm 86; Comm.

WHITCHER, REBECCA NOELE; Inter-Lakes HS; Meredith, NH; (Y); Am Leg Aux Girls St; Girl Scts; VP Spanish Clb; VP Band; Mrchg Band; School Musical; Variety Show; Sec Frsh Cls; Sec Soph Cls; Sec Jr Cls; Arion Awd Music 86; Marine Bio.

WHITE, KIMBERLY; Memorial HS; Manchester, NH; (Y); Camera Clb; Drama Clb; French Clb; SADD; Variety Show; Nwsp Phtg; Nwsp Rptr; Var Trk; Hon Roll; Mc Gill U-Montreal; Intrntl Bus.

WHITEHOUSE, SUSAN J; Southeastern NH Christian Acad; Barrington, NH; (S); 1/8; Church Yth Grp; Hosp Aide; Chorus; Church Choir; Pres Soph Cls; High Hon Roll; Prfct Atten Awd; Teachers Aide; Yrbk Stf; Bob Jones U; Educ.

WHITEMAN, KELLY; Concord HS; Concord, NH; (Y); 24/375; Dance Clb; Church Choir; Mgr Stage Crew; Yrbk Stf; Stat Bsktbl; Im Vllybl; High Hon Roll; Hon Roll; NHS; Prfct Atten Awd; UNH; Elem Ed.

WHITMAN, DEBORAH; Moulton Borough Acad; Center Harbor, NH; (Y); 3/41; Band; Concert Band; Mrchg Band; Pep Band; School Musical; Pres Frsh Cls; High Hon Roll; NHS; Prncpls Awd Acadmc Excllnc 86; Marine Semper Fidelis Awd Music 86; Oberlin; Bio.

WHITNEY, BETH; Saint Thomas Aquinas HS; Hampton, NH; (Y); Am Leg Aux Girls St; Yrbk Stf; Var Bsktbl; Socr; Hon Roll; Spanish NHS; ST Treas Am Leg 86.

WHYTE, ANDREW J; Nashua HS; Nashua, NH; (Y); Am Leg Boys St; Trs Frsh Cls; High Hon Roll; NCTE Awd; NHS; Ntl Merit SF; Spanish NHS; Church Yth Grp; Ski Clb; Band; Odyssey Of Mind Natl Finals 2nd Pl In US 86; Acadmc Excllnc Awd 84; Renatra Fusca Awd 86; Engineering.

WICINSKI, DOUGLAS; Concord HS; Bow, NH; (Y); 50/350; Yrbk Phtg; Yrbk Stf; Im Bsktbl; JV Socr; JV Trk; Im Vllybl; Hon Roll; Outstndg Achvt Chem 85; Chem Engrng.

WILBERDING, KURT; Hanover HS; Norwich, VT; (Y); Rep Frsh Cls; Pres Soph Cls; Trs Pres Stu Cncl; Badmtn; Var Tennis; High Hon Roll; Hon Roll; USAC Schlrshp 86; Marion Crss Schlrshp 86; U Of Notre Dame; Philsphy.

WILBUR, KAREN; Dover HS; Dover, NH; (Y); Church Yth Grp; French Clb; Sec Key Clb; SADD; Hon Roll.

WILBY, DAVID; Fall Mountain Regional HS; Charlestown, NH; (Y); 6/150; Boy Scts; Church Yth Grp; Yrbk Stf; Sec Frsh Cls; Var L Bsbl; Var L Bsktbl; Var L Socr; Bausch & Lomb Sci Awd; Hon Roll; NHS; Chrch Diacnate 86; Physcs & Engl Awds 86; Corp Law.

WILCOX, KELLY; Pembroke Acad; Suncook, NH; (Y); French Clb; Science Clb; Ski Clb; Stu Cncl; Cheerleading; Fld Hcky; Sftbl; High Hon Roll; Hon Roll; Mst Imprvd Sftbl 84; U Miami; Physcl Thrpy.

WILDER, KATE; Keene HS; Keene, NH; (Y); 17/362; Drama Clb; JA; Spanish Clb; Band; Concert Band; Mrchg Band; Stage Crew; Yrbk Stf; High Hon Roll; NHS.

WILDER, LORRI; Spaulding HS; Rochester, NH; (S); 42/397; Civic Clb; Cmnty Wkr; FHA; Library Aide; Red Cross Aide; Teachers Aide; High Hon Roll; Hon Roll; NHS; Lukemia Type-A-Thon 84; Child Care.

WILKINSON, SCOTT; Laconia HS; Laconia, NH; (Y); 3/180; Math Tm; Ski Clb; Sec Stu Cncl; Tennis; Trk; Bausch & Lomb Sci Awd; High Hon Roll; Hon Roll; Trs NHS; Boy Scts; Natl Hon Soc Treas 86; Sci.

WILLIAMS, ANDREA; Salem HS; Salem, NH; (S); Key Clb; Spanish Clb; Teachers Aide; Stu Cncl; Fld Hcky; Gym; Trk; High Hon Roll; Hon Roll; Math.

WILLIAMS, CHANDRA L; St Pauls Schl; Brooklyn, NY; (Y); German Clb; Radio Clb; Spanish Clb; Chorus; Concert Band; English Clb; Lit Mag; Im Sftbl; Im Tennis; Im Trk; High Hnrs In Academics 84-85; Foreign Lang.

WILLIAMS, HEATHER; Concord HS; Concord, NH; (Y); Church Yth Grp; Girl Scts; Band; Color Guard; Mrchg Band; Pre Law Pre Med.

WILLIAMS, KATHLEEN; Belmont HS; Belmont, NH; (S); 5/67; French Clb; Math Tm; Yrbk Ed-Chief; Trs Jr Cls; Trs Sr Cls; Mgr Bsbl; Mgr Bsktbl; High Hon Roll; Hon Roll; NHS; Acctg.

WILLIAMS, KRISTI; Alvirne HS; Hudson, NH; (Y); VP Frsh Cls; High Hon Roll; Hon Roll; Bentley Coll; Banking.

WILLIAMS, LAURA; Fall Mountain Regional HS; Walpole, NH; (Y); Pres Trs 4-H; French Clb; Pep Clb; Ed Yrbk Phtg; 4-H Awd; Mrktng.

WILLIAMS, ROBERT; Manchester West HS; Bedford, NH; (Y); Pres Frsh Cls; JV Bsbl; JV Bsktbl; Var Ftbl; Var Lcrss; JV Socr; Var Trk; Wt Lftg; JR Most Athltc Awd 86; Honrbl Mention All ST Ftbl 86; Best Offensive Plyr Ftbl 86; Business.

WILSON, C KELLY; Hanover HS; Irving, TX; (Y); 2/153; Band; Chorus; Church Choir; Jazz Band; Mrchg Band; Orch; School Musical; Swing Chorus; Symp Band; Bsktbl; VT Hnr Schlrshp 86; Music Dept Schlrshp 86; TX All Rgn Bnds New Hamp All ST Bnds 84-86; U TX Austin; Music Ed.

WILSON, SCOTT A; Somersworth HS; Somersworth, NH; (Y); 9/165; Rep Am Leg Boys St; Boy Scts; JCL; Latin Clb; Math Tm; Science Clb; Lit Mag; Hon Roll; Jr NHS; U Of NH; Vet.

WILSON, SHERRY; Fall Mountain Regional HS; E Alstead, NH; (Y); 42/146; FTA; Var Capt Bsktbl; Coach Actv; Var Sftbl; Vllybl; Bsktbll MVP Trphy 85-86; Sftbll Trphy 84-85; Keene ST; Phys Ed.

WILT, MICHELLE; Lebanon HS; Hampton, NH; (Y); 16/144; AFS; French Clb; Office Aide; SADD; Varsity Clb; Band; Rep Sr Cls; Rep Stu Cncl; Bsktbl; Var L Crs Cntry; Bstr Clb Awd 86; Mtlda M Ernst Sci Awd 86; Rookie Of Yr Sftbll 84; U Of NH; Biochem.

WISEMAN, WILLIAM; Portsmouth HS; Portsmouth, NH; (Y); 32/380; Crs Cntry; Trk; High Hon Roll; NHS; Church Yth Grp; Wrstlng; Hon Roll; Schlr-Athl Awd 85; Aviatn.

WISWELL, BRENDA; Pembroke Acad; Concord, NH; (Y); French Clb; Girl Scts; Teachers Aide; Band; Concert Band; Nwsp Rptr; JV Bsktbl; JV Var Sftbl; Im Vllybl; Hon Roll; Denis Clemins Mem Schlrshp Awd 86; Salem ST Coll; Acctng.

WITHAM, ROBERT; Alton Central HS; Alton, NH; (S); 12/32; Aud/Vis; Church Yth Grp; Cmnty Wkr; Drama Clb; Stage Crew; VP Pres Stu Cncl; Var Capt Bsktbl; Var Socr; Hon Roll; Prfct Atten Awd; Schl Svc Awd 83-85; Wentworth Inst; Elec Engr.

WITHYCOMB, ROBIN; Spaulding HS; Gonic, NH; (S); Cmnty Wkr; Drama Clb; Key Clb; Yrbk Stf; Hon Roll; Real Est.

WITTY, SEAN; High Mowing Schl; Wilton, NH; (Y); Var Bsktbl; Var Socr; Var Vllybl.

WOLFE, JENNIFER; Milford Area SR HS; Amherst, NH; (Y); 6/300; Drama Clb; Yrbk Ed-Chief; VP Frsh Cls; Rep Soph Cls; VP Jr Cls; VP Sr Cls; Rep Stu Cncl; Capt Cheerleading; Mgr(s); High Hon Roll; Dollars For Schlrs Schlrshp 86; Rotary Clb Schlrshp 86; Data Prod Schlrshp 86; U Of PA; Foreign Lang.

WOLFF, CRAIG M; Tilton Schl; Laconia, NH; (S); 1/70; Var L Bsbl; Var Bsktbl; L Var Crs Cntry; High Hon Roll; NEDT Awd; Hosea B Burnham Bio Awd 84, Chem Awd 85; Bus.

WOOD, MICHAEL; Spaulding HS; Rochester, NH; (S); 22/356; Computer Clb; UNH; Elec Engrng.

WOODFORD, GINGER A; Hanover HS; Norwich, VT; (Y); Orch; JV Bsktbl; Fld Hcky; Var L Lcrss; High Hon Roll; Hon Roll; School Musical; Yth Of Amer Orchstr European Cncrt Tour 85; Yng Plyrs Chmbr Orchstr 83-86; NH All-St Orchstr 85-86; Sci.

WOODS, KEN; West HS; Bedford, NH; (Y); JV Var Ice Hcky; Im Lcrss; JV Socr; Hon Roll; U New Hampshire.

WOODWARD, JENNIFER; Keene HS; Chesterfield, NH; (Y); 44/388; Church Yth Grp; Cmnty Wkr; Chorus; High Hon Roll; Hon Roll; Messiah Coll; Anmls.

WOODWARD, MARK A; Kearsarge Regional HS; New London, NH; (Y); 13/115; AFS; Drama Clb; French Clb; Model UN; Chorus; Yrbk Stf; Var JV Socr; Hon Roll; NHS; Pres Schlr; St Pauls Advncd Pgm Frnch 85; Boston U; Intl Bus.

WOODWELL, LORI; Keene HS; Keene, NH; (Y); 3/324; Church Yth Grp; Cmnty Wkr; Orch; School Musical; Yrbk Stf; High Hon Roll; Hon Roll; NHS; Govrnrs Schlrshp 86; Pres Acad Ftnss Awd 86; Messiah Coll; Bus Mgmt.

WOODWELL, WENDY; Keene HS; Keene, NH; (Y); Drama Clb; Hosp Aide; Latin Clb; Pep Clb; Pep Band; Yrbk Stf; Rep Stu Cncl; Var JV Bsktbl; Var Fld Hcky; Var JV Sftbl; Psychlgy.

WORRELL, NANCY; Saint Thomas Aquinas HS; Rye, NH; (Y); French Clb; GAA; Key Clb; VP Soph Cls; Pres Jr Cls; Bsktbl; Sftbl; Sociolgy.

WOZNIAK, ANN MARIE; Presentation Of Mary Acad; Hduson, NH; (Y); 2/20; Am Leg Aux Girls St; French Clb; Nwsp Stf; Yrbk Stf; Sec Jr Cls; Sec Stu Cncl; JV Bsktbl; Im Vllybl; High Hon Roll; NHS.

WRIGHT, JANIE MARIE; Kingswood Regional HS; Altoona, PA; (Y); 8/122; Rptr FBLA; Yrbk Stf; VP Stu Cncl; Mgr Sftbl; High Hon Roll; NHS; Hugh O Brien Yth Found Rep; Bentley Clg; Acctg.

WRIGHT, NIKKI; Hanover HS; Etna, NH; (Y); Art Clb; French Clb; Hosp Aide; PAVAS; Nwsp Stf; Yrbk Stf; Bsktbl; RISD; Fine Arts.

WYMAN, ALLEN; Nashua HS; Nashua, NH; (Y); Latin Clb; VICA; Wt Lftg; Wrstlng; Elec Engr.

WYMAN, ANNE B; St Pauls Schl; Quogue, NY; (Y); Church Yth Grp; Dance Clb; French Clb; Intnl Clb; Pres Math Clb; Pres Math Tm; Spanish Clb; Teachers Aide; Stage Crew; DAR Awd; Yale U; Econmcs.

WYMAN, STEVE; Dover HS; Dover, NH; (Y); 75/290; Spanish Clb; Pres Frsh Cls; Pres Soph Cls; JV Bsbl; JV Bsktbl; JV Var Ftbl; Var Gym; Var Trk; Hon Roll; Pilot.

YANDOW, LORI; Londonderry HS; Londonderry, NH; (Y); Band; Concert Band; Mrchg Band; Yrbk Stf; VP Pres Stu Cncl; JV Bsktbl; Var Socr; High Hon Roll; Hon Roll; Stu Cncl Outstndng Svc & Achvt Awd 86; Stu Cncl Scholar 86; U NH; Bus Adm.

YARDLEY, KATHY; Fall Mountain Regional HS; Walpole, NH; (Y); 23/136; Art Clb; Pres 4-H; Pep Clb; Band; Church Choir; Mrchg Band; Pep Band; 4-H Awd; ST 4-H Dairy Judgng Team Trip To Mdsn WI 85.

YEN, TINA; Hanover HS; Hanover, NH; (Y); 2/160; Latin Clb; Orch; Yrbk Stf; Var Capt Swmmng; Cit Awd; High Hon Roll; Ntl Merit Ltr; Cert Merit Hnrs Bio, Chem, Latn I, Intrmed Latn 84-86; Hstry 1st Pl Bruce Essy Awd 85; Ivy League School; Bio.

YOSHINO, KENJI; Phillips Exeter Acad; Cambridge, MA; (S); Cmnty Wkr; French Clb; Acpl Chr; Chorus; School Musical; Ed Lit Mag; Rep Jr Cls; High Hon Roll; Stu Judcry Cmmttee 84-86.

YOUNG, AMY; Fall Mountain Regional HS; Charlestown, NH; (Y); Hosp Aide; Math Tm; Spanish Clb; SADD; Chorus; Color Guard; Madrigals; Yrbk Stf; Sec Sr Cls; Hon Roll; U Of CO; Accntng.

YOUNG, JENNIFER ANNE; Salem HS; Salem, NH; (S); 33/380; Aud/Vis; Hst FBLA; Hosp Aide; Math Clb; Math Tm; SADD; Teachers Aide; Hon Roll; Advrtsng.

YOUNG, KIMBERLY B; Kingswood Regional HS; Wolfeboro, NH; (Y); 6/160; Math Clb; Spanish Clb; Symp Band; Var L Crs Cntry; Var L Trk; High Hon Roll; NHS; Spanish NHS; Womens Clb Schlrshp; Wolfeboro Ski Assn Awd; U Of NH; Sports Medicine.

YOUNG, MARNIE; Mascoma Valley Regional HS; Rumney, NH; (Y); 15/100; Dance Clb; French Clb; Office Aide; High Hon Roll; Hon Roll; Psych.

ZANNINI, JILL; Salem HS; Salem, NH; (S); 32/353; Var Mgr(s); Var Score Keeper; DAR Awd; High Hon Roll; Hon Roll; 2nd Degree Black Belt Tae Kwon-Do; Law.

ZAWIDZIK, SCOTT; Central HS; Hooksett, NH; (S); Acctnt.

ZIMMER, CAROL MARIE; Portsmouth SR HS; Portsmouth, NH; (Y); FHA; VICA; Acpl Chr; Chorus; Stage Crew; High Hon Roll; New Hampshire FHA Mr Prfcncy Evnt Awd 86; NH Voc Tech Coll; Chld Dvlpmnt.

ZIOZE, DEAN; Manchester Central HS; Manchester, NH; (Y); 36/450; Nwsp Phtg; Rep Frsh Cls; Rep Soph Cls; Rep Jr Cls; Rep Stu Cncl; JV Bsktbl; Var Tennis; High Hon Roll; Law.

ZOGOPOULOS, SANDRA; Manchester Central HS; Hooksett, NH; (Y); 106/430; VP Art Clb; Cmnty Wkr; JV Twrlr; High Hon Roll; Hon Roll; Keene ST Coll; Tchr.

ZOGOPOULOS, STACY; Memorial HS; Manchester, NH; (Y); 40/369; Church Yth Grp; Drama Clb; French Clb; Pep Clb; Pres SADD; Powder Puff Ftbl; Mgr Trk; Hon Roll; Ldrshp Awd SADD; Sendoff Commtte; Co-Headed Prjct Grdtn; Spcl Ed.

ZUGER, DEBORAH; Kearsarge Regional HS; Wilmot, NH; (Y); AFS; Cmnty Wkr; Debate Tm; Model UN; Stage Crew; Cheerleading; Sftbl; Cmmnctns.

ZULLO, JASON; Newport HS; Newport, NH; (Y); French Clb; Letterman Clb; Var Bsbl; Var Bsktbl; Var Ftbl; Wt Lftg; Hon Roll; Prfct Atten Awd; Bys ST 86; Brigham Young U; Chem Engnrng.

ZYCH, LORI; Central HS; Manchester, NH; (Y); 28/430; Sec Trs Art Clb; Cmnty Wkr; Dance Clb; Teachers Aide; High Hon Roll; Cert Apprctn Coachng Spec Olym 84-86; Cert Merit For Dncng 85-86; Math.

NEW YORK

AARON, CAREY; Erasmus Hall HS; Brooklyn, NY; (Y); Boys Clb Am; Boy Scts.

AARONSON, MATHEW; Walt Whitman HS; Hunt Sta, NY; (Y); 43/500; Cmnty Wkr; Key Clb; Library Aide; Mathletes; Science Clb; Spanish Clb; Band; Concert Band; Mrchg Band; Trk; Bus.

AASERUD, CHARLOTTE; Pulaski HS; Richland, NY; (S); Church Yth Grp; Drama Clb; French Clb; GAA; Pep Clb; Ski Clb; SADD; Acpl Chr; Band; Chorus; Ntl Outstndng Frnch Awd 85; Music.

ABAD, ROBERT M; St Francis Prep; Hollis, NY; (S); 77/628; Church Yth Grp; Jazz Band; Im Ftbl; Im Sftbl; Im Vllybl; Hon Roll; NHS; Basc Catechst Awd 86; Optmt Socty 82-86; 1st Pl Battl Bands 86.

ABATE, JOSEPH; Farmingdale HS; S Farmingdale, NY; (Y); Boy Scts; Debate Tm; Science Clb; SADD; Hon Roll; NHS; Top In Clss Rcvd Cert & Pin Intl Piano 85; St Marys Coll MD; Laser Srgn.

ABATE, LOUIS; Farmingdale HS; Farmingdale, NY; (Y); Boy Scts; Yrbk Phtg; Jr NHS; NHS; Hofstra; Chrprctcs.

ABATE, PAUL; Christ The King R HS; Richmond Hill, NY; (Y); 138/450; SADD; Athletic Trnr 85-87; Citadel; Pre Med.

ABBATE, JENNIFER; Jamestown HS; Hertford, NC; (Y); Q&S; Color Guard; Nwsp Stf; Yrbk Ed-Chief; Yrbk Phtg; Quill & Scroll Awd 86; VA Cmnwlth U; Fash Dsgn.

ABBATE, KATHLEEN; Curtis HS; Staten Island, NY; (Y); 50/352; Dance Clb; Girl Scts; Intnl Clb; Red Cross Aide; Service Clb; Drill Tm; School Musical; JV Cheerleading; ROTC; School Play; TROA Awd 84-85; Fleet Rsrv Assn Awd; Coll Of Staten Isl; Nrsng.

ABBATIELLO, MICHAEL; Alfred G Berner HS; Massapequa Park, NY; (Y); 132/412; Variety Show; Var Ice Hcky; Var L Socr; Massapequa Sccr Clb Schlrshp Awd 86; US Army MVP Schlr/Athlt Awd 86; Nassau Cnty Sccr Coaches Assoc; Siena Coll.

ABBATIELLO, REGINA; St Raymond Academy For Girls; Bronx, NY; (S); 6/84; Dance Clb; GAA; Library Aide; Office Aide; Teachers Aide; Band; Mrchg Band; Pres Frsh Cls; Stu Cncl; Capt Cheerleading.

ABBOTT, CRAIG; G Ray Bodley HS; Fulton, NY; (Y); 11/250; 4-H; Scholastic Bowl; Science Clb; Capt Ice Hcky; Capt Lcrss; Capt Socr; Elks Awd; Hon Roll; NHS; MVP Athlt Yr 86; Fltn Tchrs Assn Awd 86; Crl Brtn Bstr Awd 86; SUNY Brockport; Indstrl Dist.

ABBOTT, KIMBERLY; Skaneateles Central HS; Skaneateles, NY; (Y); 52/148; High Hon Roll; Hon Roll; NHS; Rochester Inst Of Technlgy; Trv.

ABBOTT, LILLIAN; Centereach HS; Centereach, NY; (S); 23/431; Q&S; Nwsp Ed-Chief; Lit Mag; Sec Frsh Cls; Stu Cncl; Jrnlsm.

ABBOTT, LISA; Cobleskill HS; Cobleskill, NY; (S); 4/120; Trs GAA; Sec Frsh Cls; Sec Soph Cls; Trs Sr Cls; Score Keeper; Socr; Capt Trk; French Hon Soc; High Hon Roll; NHS; NY ST Rgnts Schlrshp 86; Clarkson U; Indstrl Distrbtn.

ABBOTT, MARK; Camden HS; Camden, NY; (Y); AFS; Drama Clb; SADD; Varsity Clb; Band; Chorus; School Musical; School Play; Socr; Hon Roll; HS 3 Letter Awd; Rotary 100 Point Patch; Spec Ed.

ABBOTT, MARY; Lindenhurst HS; Lindenhurst, NY; (Y); Chorus; Yrbk Stf; Sec Frsh Cls; Score Keeper; Trk; Exec Secy.

ABBOTT, MICHAEL R; Middleburgh Central HS; Middleburgh, NY; (Y); 1/54; Am Leg Boys St; Boy Scts; Sec Soph Cls; Sec Jr Cls; Var Capt Bsktbl; Bausch & Lomb Sci Awd; High Hon Roll; Jr NHS; NHS; Math Tm; Elmira Coll Key Awd 86; Bus Admin.

ABBOTT, WILLIAM; Massena Central HS; Massena, NY; (Y); Cmnty Wkr; Band; Church Choir; Concert Band; Mrchg Band; Pep Band; Symp Band; Var Stat Ftbl; Hon Roll; Acad Awd 86; Comp Sci.

ABDULLAH, JOSEPH; East Meadow HS; E Meadow, NY; (Y); FBLA; Key Clb; Band; Chorus; Concert Band; Jazz Band; Mrchg Band; Pep Band; School Musical; Symp Band; LIYO Orch 85-86; SUNY; Music.

ABELE, DIANE; Commack HS South; Commack, NY; (Y); Office Aide; VICA; JV Var Mgr(s); JV Var Score Keeper; Hon Roll; Outstdng Stu Awd-Nrs Asst 86; Vica Nrs Asst Cont 85; Stony Brook; Nrsng.

ABENSOHN, ADAM; Oyster Bay HS; Oyster Bay, NY; (Y); 10/130; Math Tm; Nwsp Stf; Tennis; Hon Roll; Ntl Merit Ltr; Georgetown; Bus.

ABERS, JULIE; Panama Central Schl; Panama, NY; (Y); Quiz Bowl; Band; Chorus; School Musical; Yrbk Stf; Swmmng; Trk; Science.

ABLE, REYNALDO A; Babylon JR & SR HS; W Babylon, NY; (Y); 15/178; Math Clb; Yrbk Stf; Var Lcrss; High Hon Roll; Hon Roll; NHS; Prfct Atten Awd; Babyln Cmnty Schlrshp 86; Rgnts Schlrshp 86; Aero Sp Engrng.

ABOAHAM, BOB; Harry S Truman HS; Bronx, NY; (Y); 36/494; NHS; NY ST Rgnts Schlrshp 86-90; Manhattan Coll Riverdale; Engr.

ABONIA, CLAUDIA; Half Hollow Hills HS West; Dix Hills, NY; (Y); Cmnty Wkr; French Clb; Varsity Clb; Variety Show; Mgr Bsktbl; Score Keeper; High Hon Roll; Jr NHS; NHS; Spanish NHS; Awds In Frnch 84; 2nd Pl Spnsh Poetry Rdng Cntst 86; Advrtsng Art.

ABOUD, KATHY; Fontbonne Hall Acad; Brooklyn, NY; (Y); 25/130; Math Tm; Variety Show; Yrbk Stf; Tennis; NYS Rgnts Schlrshp 86; Manhattan Coll Acad Schlrshp 86; Prfssnl Wmns Org Awd 86; Manhattan Coll; Bus.

ABOULAFIA, CAROL; Commack High School North; Commack, NY; (Y); Office Aide; Temple Yth Grp; Chorus; VP Frsh Cls; Off Soph Cls; Rep Jr Cls; JV Tennis; High Hon Roll; Bio Chem.

ABRAHAM, DAVID P; Liverpool HS; Liverpool, NY; (Y); 52/823; Hon Roll; Jr NHS; Scl Studies Exc; Archtcl Dsgn Exc; Oswego ST U; Comp Sci.

ABRAHAM, JOHN; Wayland Central HS; Wayland, NY; (Y); 4/121; Am Leg Boys St; Varsity Clb; Rep Frsh Cls; Rep Soph Cls; Im Bsbl; JV Bsktbl; Var Socr; Var Tennis; Hon Roll; NHS; Nice Kid Awd 86; Cornell; Engrng.

ABRAHAMSON, JEANNETTE; Grace Dodge Vocational HS; Bronx, NY; (Y); Aud/Vis; Office Aide; Band; Nwsp Stf; Yrbk Stf; Hon Roll; Socl Studies 84; SUNY; Accntng.

ABRAMOSKI, LISA; Southampton HS; Southampton, NY; (Y); 9/115; Spanish Clb; Band; Pres Concert Band; Fld Hcky; High Hon Roll; NHS; Chorus; Mrchg Band; Nwsp Rptr; Rgnts Schlrshp Wnnr 86; Otstndng Music Cls 86; Bard; Ecnmcs.

ABRAMOVICH, SANDRA; Saugerties SR HS; Saugerties, NY; (Y); Church Yth Grp; Cmnty Wkr; Drama Clb; Ski Clb; Pres Spanish Clb; School Musical; Nwsp Stf; Ed Yrbk Stf; Girl Scts; Office Aide; Lang Dept Trip Stdy Spnsh 84; Olympcs Mind 84-85; Bst Grp, Bst Props, Costms, Mkup Lip Sync 86; Kings Coll; Engl.

ABRAMOWITZ, MATTHEW; Sewanhaka HS; Elmont, NY; (Y); Office Aide; Band; Im Bsbl; Im Var Bsktbl; Hon Roll; 100 Pct Atten 85-86; Penn ST; Pre Law.

ABRAMS, ANNETTE; Far Rockaway HS; Far Rockaway, NY; (Y); 17/337; Hosp Aide; Key Clb; Office Aide; High Hon Roll; Hon Roll; Schlrs Awd Cert Merit Comp HOSA 86; Supr Yth Awd 84; Cert Hnr Sci & Frgn Lang 86; Hunter Coll; Med.

ABRAMS, DEBBIE; Monroe Woodbury HS; Monroe, NY; (Y); Crs Cntry; Trk; Outstndng Athl Feml 83-84; NY ST Comptn Indr Trck Hgh Jmp; Grls Outdr Trck & Indr Trck MVP & MIP; Bus.

ABRAMS, KIMBERLY; Half Hollow Hills H S East; Dix Hills, NY; (Y); Cmnty Wkr; Leo Clb; Spanish Clb; SADD; Yrbk Stf; Sftbl; High Hon Roll; Jr NHS; NHS; Spanish NHS; Law 86; Med.

ABRAMS, LAWRENCE; Manhattan Ctr For Science & Math; Bronx, NY; (Y); 1/160; Debate Tm; Teachers Aide; Chorus; Yrbk Ed-Chief; VP Sr Cls; Gov Hon Prg Awd; Hon Roll; Val; Chancllrs Roll Hnr 86; Regents Scholar 86; WABC-TV Bst Cls Awad 86; Yale U; Writer.

ABRAMS, LORI A; John F Kennedy HS; Bellmore, NY; (Y); French Clb; Hosp Aide; Mathletes; Math Tm; Service Clb; SADD; Temple Yth Grp; Nwsp Stf; Yrbk Stf; Off Soph Cls; Hghst Avg Hm Econ 84; Wall Of Hnr 84; Frnch 84; Pediatrcs.

ABRAMS, ROBERT; Centereach HS; Centereach, NY; (Y); Nwsp Rptr; Nwsp Stf; Lit Mag; Im Bsbl; JV Var Trk; Prfct Attndence Awds 84-86; Slvr Mdls In 4 X 400 Mtr Rly & 4 X 100 Mtr Rly 85; St Johns U; Jrnlsm.

ABRAMSON, APRIL; Commack High Schl South; Dix Hills, NY; (S); 56/367; Teachers Aide; Temple Yth Grp; Chorus; Madrigals; School Musical; Variety Show; High Hon Roll; Hon Roll; NHS; NY ST Smmr Schl Of Arts Choral Stds 84-85; Psychlgy.

ABRANTES, ANTONIO ELIAS; Gouverneur Central HS; Gouverneur, NY; (Y); Varsity Clb; Var JV Bsktbl; Var Capt Ftbl; Var Golf; JV Trk; Var Wt Lftg; Hon Roll; Jr NHS; NHS; 3rd Pl Yorker Conv 83; Sci Engrng.

ABREU, ESMILDA M; The Bronx HS Of Science; New York, NY; (Y); Cmnty Wkr; VP JA; Office Aide; Spanish Clb; Teachers Aide; Chorus; Bsktbl; Space Shttl Stu Invlmnt Proj Cert 83; Hampshr Coll; Law.

ABREU, JUDITH; Wiliam Howard Taft HS; Bronx, NY; (Y); Camera Clb; Off Jr Cls; Bsbl; Bsktbl; Sftbl; Vllybl; NCTE Awd; Prfct Atten Awd; Spanish NHS; Comptr 86; Comptrs.

ABUSCH, STEVEN; Commack HS North; E Northport, NY; (Y); Trs Art Clb; Drama Clb; Trs Math Tm; Y-Teens; School Play; Variety Show; Pres Trs Stu Cncl; Crs Cntry; High Hon Roll; NHS; Drct Accptnc Awd NY Smr Schl Arts 86; 5th Pl Cnty Spnsh AATSP Tst 86; Natl Ldrshp Trngn Cnfrnc 85.

ACACIA, SUSAN; Tottenville HS; Staten Island, NY; (Y); 12/871; Band; Nwsp Rptr; Yrbk Sprt Ed; JV Crs Cntry; Var Trk; NHS; Regnts Schlrshp; NYU.

ACAMPORA, ALICE; Port Richmond HS; Staten Island, NY; (Y); Hosp Aide; SADD; Chorus; Pom Pon.

ACAMPORA, KENNETH; Sachem North Campus HS; Lk Ronkonkoma, NY; (Y); Ski Clb; Varsity Clb; Chorus; Var Socr; Im Wrstlng; NYS Rgnts Schlrshp Awd 86; FL Inst Of Tech; Comp Sci.

ACARD, BARBARA; Westhampton Beach HS; W Hampton Bch, NY; (Y); 63/210; Cmnty Wkr; English Clb; French Clb; FBLA; Library Aide; Office Aide; SADD; Teachers Aide; Temple Yth Grp; Drill Tm; Comm Srv Awd Educ 86; Sut Mtn WHB Brd; Suffolk Cnty Creatv Wrtng; Poetry Div 3rd Pl 82; Lesley Coll; Specl Educ.

ACEVEDO, GISELLE; Beach Channel HS; Richmond Hill, NY; (Y); Math Tm; Science Clb; SADD; Yrbk Stf; Coach Actv; Var Capt Socr; Hon Roll; NHS; Prfct Atten Awd; Acdmc All-Amrcn 84; Math Awd Algbra & Trg 85; Athltc Awd Sccr 86; Ocngrphy.

ACEVEDO, LORRAINE; Dominican Commercial HS; New York, NY; (Y); Hosp Aide; Intnl Clb; Latin Clb; Spanish Clb; Rep Jr Cls; Hon Roll; NY U; Lgl.

ACHOLONU, IJEOMA N; Bronx HS Of Science; Bronx, NY; (Y); Library Aide; Office Aide; Trs Science Clb; Teachers Aide; Yrbk Stf; Rep Stu Cncl; NHS; Prfct Atten Awd; Columbia U; Med.

ACKERBAUER, MICHAEL; Lakeland HS; Yorktown Heights, NY; (Y); 92/344; Church Yth Grp; Computer Clb; SADD; Variety Show; Nwsp Ed-Chief; Rep Sr Cls; Stu Cncl; Pace U; Mngmt.

ACKERMAN, BRIAN M; Curtis HS; Staten Island, NY; (Y); 43/330; Am Leg Boys St; Boy Scts; ROTC; Drill Tm; Coach Actv; L Swmmng; NHS; Rgnts Schlrshp 86; Pres Awd 86; Amer Legn ROTC Schltsc Excel Mdl 86; US Mrchnt Mrn Acad; Mrn Engrng.

ACKERMAN, KELLY; Tonawanda JR SR HS; Tonawanda, NY; (Y); Church Yth Grp; French Clb; Varsity Clb; Var L Socr; Hon Roll; Hnrbl Mntn Cncl Of Permng Arts Logo 86; Famly Tanng Saln Logo 86; Art Shw 86; Sec.

ACKERMAN, REBECCA; Spackenkill HS; Poughkeepsie, NY; (Y); Q&S; SADD; Varsity Clb; School Musical; Nwsp Rptr; Yrbk Stf; Fld Hcky; Trk.

ACKERMAN, STACEY; Moravia Central HS; Locke, NY; (Y); Church Yth Grp; Chorus; Church Choir; Golf; Tennis; Trk; Vllybl; High Hon Roll; Hon Roll; Phy Thrpy.

ACKLER, DENISE; Gowanda Central Schl; Gowanda, NY; (Y); Church Yth Grp; 4-H; Girl Scts; Hosp Aide; SADD; VICA; Band; Chorus; Church Choir; Mrchg Band; NY ST Chmpn For Nrsng Asstnt 86; Jmstwn CC; Nrsng.

ACKLES, WAYNE H; Moravia Central Schl; Moravia, NY; (Y); 8/89; French Clb; School Musical; School Play; VP Sr Cls; Rep Stu Cncl; Var Capt Crs Cntry; Var Capt Trk; JV L Wrstlng; Hon Roll; NY ST Regents Schlrshp 86; NY ST U-Geneseo; Scndry Ed.

ACKLEY, KAREN; John H Glenn HS; Huntington, NY; (Y); Yrbk Phtg; Rep Jr Cls; Var Tennis; Var JV Vllybl; Bus.

ACKLEY, MARGARET; Holy Trinity D HS; Syosset, NY; (S); 7/403; French Clb; Math Clb; Stu Cncl; Hon Roll.

ACOCELLA, FRANK X; Iona Prep; Scarsdale, NY; (Y); 80/204; Dance Clb; Exploring; Library Aide; Bsbl; Capt Bowling; Sftbl; Swmmng; Tennis; Trk; Wt Lftg; Penn ST; Bus Admn.

ACOFF, COREY; Marcus Whitman Central HS; Gorham, NY; (Y); Im Bsktbl; JV Ftbl; Var JV Trk; Im Vllybl.

ACOSTA, ABDIEL; Watton HS; Bronx, NY; (Y); 17/542; Aud/Vis; Spanish Clb; Rep Sr Cls; Var Capt Bsbl; Bsktbl; Var Tennis; Prfct Atten Awd; Regents Diploma 86; Hon In 9th Grade; Slectd To All City Bsbll Tm 86; Hunter Coll; Cmmnctns.

ACOSTA, CICELY; Murry Bergtraum HS; Brooklyn, NY; (Y); Ntl Merit SF; Bus.

ACOSTA, JENNY; St Johns Prep; Woodside, NY; (Y); 55/458; Drama Clb; Chorus; School Play; Stage Crew; Yrbk Stf; Lit Mag; Rep Sr Cls; Sec Stu Cncl; Hon Roll; NHS; Hunter College; Bio.

ACOSTA, OLGA; Ellenville HS; Ellenville, NY; (Y); 6/110; Chorus; Yrbk Ed-Chief; Yrbk Stf; Trs Jr Cls; VP Sr Cls; Var Tennis; Var Trk; DAR Awd; High Hon Roll; NHS; Ntl Engl Merit Awd; Ldrshp Svc Awd; Sci Olympid; Vassar Coll; Bio.

ACQUAFREDDA, CHRISTINE; Bellport SR HS; Bellport, NY; (Y); Church Yth Grp; Girl Scts; Ski Clb; Spanish Clb; Teachers Aide; Crs Cntry; Trk; Hon Roll; Spanish NHS; Ed.

ACQUILANO, MICHAEL; Geneva HS; Geneva, NY; (S); 26/173; Am Leg Boys St; Pres Spanish Clb; Pres Band; Jazz Band; Pres Stu Cncl; Var L Ftbl; Var L Lcrss; DAR Awd; NHS; JR Rotarn; Hnr Rl; Vrsty Clb; Poli Sci.

ACQUISTA, ANGELA; Smithtown HS East; St James, NY; (Y); Church Yth Grp; Key Clb; Teachers Aide; Stu Cncl; Tennis; Vllybl; High Hon Roll; Hon Roll; NHS; Italian Hnr Soc Vp 84-86; SUNY Geneseo; Elem Educ.

ADAIR, KEVIN J; Wayne Central HS; Ontario, NY; (Y); 47/200; Church Yth Grp; Computer Clb; Mathletes; Math Tm; Science Clb; Ski Clb; SADD; Teachers Aide; Chorus; School Musical; Art Show Awd & Ntl Sci Olympd Awd 85-86; Gftd & Tlntd Prgm 83-86; Englsh Acdmc Achvt Awd 84-85; NY ST U Oswego; Physics Tchr.

ADAIR, TRACY; St Lawrence Central Schl; Lowville, NY; (Y); Drama Clb; Intnl Clb; Chorus; Cheerleading; L Hon Roll; NHS; Hon Tm Pin & Schl Lttr 84-85; Youth To Youth 85-86; JR Natl Hist Soc 84-85; Bus Club 85-86; Cmmrcl Art.

ADAM, TIMOTHY; Jamestown HS; Jamestown, NY; (Y); 80/400; Church Yth Grp; JA; Pep Clb; Ski Clb; Spanish Clb; SADD; Stu Cncl; Var L Socr; Wt Lftg; Hon Roll; USA Schlrshp 86; Presdntl Acadmc Ftns Awd 86; Jamestown CC; Premed.

ADAM, WILLIAM; Lackawanna SR HS; Lackawanna, NY; (Y); CAP; Drama Clb; ROTC; Color Guard; Concert Band; Drill Tm; Mrchg Band; Pep Band; School Play; Var Ftbl; Law.

ADAMEK, KATHLEEN; North Tonawanda SR HS; N Tonawanda, NY; (Y); DECA; FBLA; Office Aide; Band; Color Guard; Symp Band; Nwsp Stf; Rep Frsh Cls; Bryan & Stratton; Med Doc Asst.

ADAMO, LAURIE A; Performing Arts HS; Glendale, NY; (Y); 28/122; Band; Concert Band; Drm Mjr(t); Orch; Symp Band; Rep Frsh Cls; Rep Stu Cncl; Hon Roll; NHS; NYC Supr Yth 84; Manhattan Schl Music; Pianst.

ADAMO, RICHARD; Archbishop Molloy HS; Forest Hills, NY; (Y); 200/450; Hosp Aide; Intnl Clb; Pep Clb; Quiz Bowl; Nwsp Bus Mgr; Nwsp Rptr; Nwsp Stf; Crmnl Jstc.

ADAMOWICZ, ADAM C; Walt Whitman HS; Huntington Sta, NY; (Y); 77/545; Lit Mag; Hon Roll; Rgnts Coll Schlrshp 86; CO U Boulder.

ADAMOWICZ, MATTHEW; Scio Central Schl; Scio, NY; (S); 1/50; Mrchg Band; School Play; Stage Crew; Yrbk Stf; Pres Stu Cncl; Capt Var Socr; God Cntry Awd; High Hon Roll; NHS; Eagle Scout 4 Palms 82; Soccer Cnty All-Star Tms 84-85 & 85-86; Bus Mngmnt.

ADAMS, AMY; Scotia-Glenville HS; Scotia, NY; (Y); Key Clb; Bus.

ADAMS, BARBARA; Pittsford Sutherland HS; Pittsford, NY; (Y); AFS; Cmnty Wkr; Drama Clb; Exploring; School Musical; School Play; Stage Crew; Nwsp Phtg; Nwsp Stf; Yrbk Phtg; Schlstc Art Awd Phtgrphy 86; Fclty Rcgntn Awd 86; NYU; Flm Prod.

ADAMS, BRIAN BURKE; Columbia HS; Rensselaer, NY; (Y); Off Am Leg Boys St; Pres Debate Tm; Var Capt Crs Cntry; Var L Trk; High Hon Roll; NHS; Ntl Merit SF; Cmnty Wkr; Math Tm; Scholastic Bowl; Harvard Prize Bk For Exclnc 86; Summer Scientific Session AFA 86; Rep Section Ii Leadership Picnic 85; Princeton; Chem Engr.

ADAMS, BRYAN R; Utica Free Acad; Utica, NY; (Y); Trs Church Yth Grp; Spanish Clb; Yrbk Stf; JV Im Bsktbl; Cit Awd; NHS; Natl Merit Cmmnded Stu 85; Comm.

ADAMS, CHERYLL; Frewsburg Central Schl; Frewsburg, NY; (Y); Pep Clb; Chorus; School Musical; Sec Frsh Cls; Cheerleading; Trk; Fshn Dsgn.

ADAMS, DARLENE; Guilderland Central HS; Altamont, NY; (Y); VP Church Yth Grp; Cmnty Wkr; Hghst Avg In Spnsh IV 86; Med.

ADAMS, DAWN; Sacred Heart HS; Yonkers, NY; (S); Church Yth Grp; Chorus; Hon Roll; NHS; NEDT Awd; Cert Achvt Sign Lang 85; Spch Sci.

ADAMS, DEBBIE; Henninger HS; Syracuse, NY; (Y); Hon Roll; Comp Sci.

ADAMS, DONALD D; Clinton Central HS; Clinton, NY; (Y); 28/136; Ski Clb; Stage Crew; Im Badmtn; JV Bsbl; Im Bsktbl; Var Ftbl; Im Lcrss; Var Trk; Im Wt Lftg; Hon Roll; Clarkson U; Engrng.

ADAMS, DOUG; John Jay HS; Brookfield, CT; (Y); Library Aide; Science Clb; Nwsp Stf; Cit Awd; High Hon Roll; NHS; Sci Olympd Tm Gld Medl Cnty Sectnls 86; Layout Edtr Nwspr 85-87; Latn Awd 85; Socl Stds Awd 86; Sci.

ADAMS, FLORELLA; Farmingdale HS; Farmingdale, NY; (Y); Hon Roll; Berkelee Coll Of Music; Music.

ADAMS, JEFFREY R; Faith Heritage Schl; De Witt, NY; (Y); Drama Clb; Political Wkr; School Play; Pres Sr Cls.

ADAMS, KELLY; N Tonawanda SR HS; N Tonawanda, NY; (Y); French Clb; Library Aide; Ski Clb; Band; Mrchg Band; School Play; Cheerleading; French Hon Soc; Hon Roll; NHS; Rsch Engrng.

ADAMS, KIMBERLY; Avon Central HS; Avon, NY; (Y); L AFS; Nwsp Stf; Yrbk Stf; Sec Frsh Cls; Var Cheerleading; Var Diving; JV Sftbl; JV Vllybl; Elem Educ.

ADAMS, MATTHEW J; Royalton Hartland HS; Gasport, NY; (Y); Am Leg Boys St; Letterman Clb; Chorus; Trs Sr Cls; Var L Bsbl; Var L Bsktbl; JV L Ftbl; Var Capt Golf; Aud/Vis; Church Yth Grp; Law.

ADAMS, MICHELLE; Mont Pleasant HS; Schenectady, NY; (Y); JA; Office Aide; Ski Clb; Spanish Clb; Teachers Aide; Band; Concert Band; Mrchg Band; School Musical; Yrbk Ed-Chief.

ADAMS, NORA M; New Hartford Central HS; New Hartford, NY; (Y); Art Clb; Drama Clb; School Play; Stage Crew; Nwsp Stf; Hon Roll; NHS; Yrbk Stf.

ADAMS II, PETER W; Union Springs Acad; Andover, NJ; (S); 4/47; FCA; Chorus; Nwsp Sprt Ed; Rep Frsh Cls; Off Sr Cls; Var Bsktbl; Capt Gym; NHS; Pres Schlr; Andrews U; Ed.

ADAMS, REBECCA; Berlin Central HS; Petersburg, NY; (Y); 10/82; GAA; Chorus; Capt Cheerleading; Score Keeper; Mgr Sftbl; High Hon Roll; NHS; MVP Chrldr 86; FL ST U; Corp Law.

ADAMS, ROSALYN; Kensington HS; Buffalo, NY; (Y); Sec Church Yth Grp; Hosp Aide; Model UN; Spanish Clb; Church Choir; Drm & Bgl; Drm Mjr(t); Flag Corp; Mrchg Band; Tennis; Bus.

ADAMS, TANIA; Tottenville HS; Staten Island, NY; (Y); Ski Clb; School Musical; School Play; Yrbk Sprt Ed; Yrbk Stf; Off Frsh Cls; Sec Sr Cls; Bowling; Gym; Swmmng; Arista 82-83; Citizenship 8-83; Penn ST; Med.

ADAMS, TERRY; Yonkers HS; Yonkers, NY; (Y); Key Clb; Library Aide; Varsity Clb; Chorus; Pres Soph Cls; Pres Jr Cls; Stu Cncl; JV Bsktbl; Var Capt Jr Cls; Var L Trk; Vrsty Clb Awd 86; Dstngsh Ath Awd 86; Natl Cncl Negro Women Inc 86; Bus Mgnt.

ADAMS, TRACY; Mount Vernon HS; Mt Vernon, NY; (Y); Church Yth Grp; Cmnty Wkr; Red Cross Aide; JV Sftbl; Hon Roll.

ADAMS, VICKI; Lansingburgh HS; Troy, NY; (Y); Jr NHS; Elem Ed.

ADAMSHICK, AMY; Tonawanda JR SR HS; Tonawanda, NY; (Y); Cmnty Wkr; Varsity Clb; Ed Nwsp Ed-Chief; Yrbk Stf; Trs Soph Cls; Trs Jr Cls; Trs Sr Cls; Pres Stu Cncl; Dnfth Awd; NHS; Elmira Key Awd 86; US Marine Corp Distngsd Athlt 86; NASC Dlgt Stu Ldrshp 85; Bus Adm.

ADANTI, LAUREL B; Mt Markham HS; Bridgewater, NY; (Y); Church Yth Grp; Drama Clb; Intnl Clb; Band; Chorus; School Musical; School Play; Trk; High Hon Roll; NHS; Clark Schlrshp 86; Rents Schlrshp 86; Summr Traing Corps Schlrshp 86; Word Of Life Bibl Isnt.

ADARI, MARIA; Lincoln HS; Yonkers, NY; (Y); Hosp Aide; Badmtn; Tennis; Hon Roll; Prfct Atten Awd; Awds In Socl Studies, Achvt & Prfct Attndnce 84-85 & 85-86; Nrsng.

ADDEO, GINA; Blessed Sacrament St Gabriel HS; Bronx, NY; (Y); Hon Roll; Berkeley Schl; Prof Secretary.

ADDERLEY, JOANNE; Watertown HS; Watertown, NY; (Y); 86/305; Church Yth Grp; Cmnty Wkr; Dance Clb; Sec Key Clb; Band; School Musical; Variety Show; Var Cheerleading; Var Capt Gym; NY Jr Ms Cmnty Srvc Awd & Tlnt Awd 86; Outstndng Ctznshp Awd 85-86; SUNY Coll Brckprt; Prfsnl Dncr.

ADDONIZIO, SAMANTHA; Fox Ln HS; Bedford, NY; (Y); AFS; Intnl Clb; Ski Clb; Spanish Clb; Variety Show; Stu Cncl; Fld Hcky; Lcrss; High Hon Roll; Outbound Ambssdr Exch Stu Crossrds; Ecologst Conv Wrkshp; Lawyer.

ADDRIZZO, MICHELLE; St Joseph Hill Acad; Staten Island, NY; (Y); 24/106; Drama Clb; Math Tm; Service Clb; SADD; Teachers Aide; Pres Stu Cncl; Co-Capt Cheerleading; High Hon Roll; Hon Roll; NEDT Lttr Of Recmmndtn; Regents Schlrshp; Binghamton; Fin.

ADDUCI, CARLA; St Dominics HS; Bethpage, NY; (S); 4/180; Church Yth Grp; Quiz Bowl; SADD; School Play; Nwsp Rptr; Var Socr; High Hon Roll; NHS; Ntl Merit SF; Engrg.

ADDY, JUNE; Tottenville HS; Staten Island, NY; (Y); 14/820; NHS; Church Yth Grp; Library Aide; Concert Band; High Hon Roll; Jr NHS; NY ST Regents Schlrshp 86; Presdntl Acad Schlrshp 86; Exclnc In Spnsh Awd Grad 86; Susquehanna U.

ADELMANN, CHARLENE; West Seneca West SR HS; West Seneca, NY; (Y); 101/559; Girl Scts; Teachers Aide; Chorus; School Musical; Cit Awd; Hon Roll; NHS; Key Clb; Spanish Clb; Rep Stu Cncl; Grl Sct Gld Awd 85; Natl Cncl Chrstns & Jews 84; Brthrhd Sstrhd Yth Awd 84; Phy Thrpy.

ADESANYA, SHIRLEY; Walton HS; Bronx, NY; (Y); Art Clb; Church Yth Grp; Drama Clb; Girl Scts; Hosp Aide; Speech Tm; SADD; Chorus; Ntl Merit Schol; NEDT Awd; Cert Of Awd Aerobics 86; Schlstc Achvt Bio 85; Drama.

ADINOLFI, MICHAEL T; Msgr Farrell HS; Staten Island, NY; (Y); 117/300; Boy Scts; Computer Clb; Spanish Clb; Bowling; JV Swmmng; Hon Roll; NY ST Rgnts 86; Brooklyn Coll; Pre-Engrng.

ADISSI, THOMAS P; St Francis Prep; Forest Hills, NY; (Y); Service Clb; Var L Bsbl; Var L Bsktbl; Var L Golf; West Point; Engr.

ADIUTORI, ALICIA; Kenmore East HS; Kenmore, NY; (Y); Civic Clb; Dance Clb; German Clb; GAA; Pep Clb; Rep Chorus; Nwsp Sprt Ed; Trs Jr Cls; JV Var Bsktbl; Stat Ftbl.

ADJODHA, MICHAEL EDWARD; Lafayette HS; Brooklyn, NY; (Y); JA; JCL; Library Aide; Math Tm; Service Clb; Yrbk Phtg; Ed Yrbk Rptr; Bio Chem.

ADKINS, ANGELA; L A Webber HS; Lyndonville, NY; (Y); Church Yth Grp; Cmnty Wkr; Teachers Aide; Chorus; Color Guard; Var Capt Cheerleading; JV Vllybl; Rent-A-Kid Of Mnth 86; Typng-Speed & Ablty Cert 86; Elem Tchr.

ADLAM, KAREN; Hillcrest HS; Laurelton, NY; (Y); 50/801; Church Yth Grp; Office Aide; Band; Church Choir; Concert Band; Orch; School Musical; Hon Roll; Hosp Aide; Teachers Aide; Outstndng Musicnshp Awd 86; Hillcrest Sci Cngrss Slvr Medl 83; Regnts Schlrshp 86; SUNY Binghamton; Obstrcl Nrsg.

ADLER, TOMMY; Sachem HS; Holbrook, NY; (Y); 214/1600; Capt Ice Hcky; Mgr(s); Zenith Clb Hrn Soc 85; Blue Knights Ice Hockey Clb Captain 86; Comp Sci.

ADLERMAN, CATHY; Tuckahoe HS; Bronxville, NY; (Y); 1/57; Drama Clb; French Clb; Leo Clb; Ski Clb; Band; Concert Band; Mrchg Band; Ed Lit Mag; Swmmng; High Hon Roll; Mth, Frnch Awds 84-86; Soc Studs Awds 84 & 86; Bio, Latin, Typng Awds 85; Engl, Vassar Bk Awd 86; Frnch.

ADLRICH, JULIE; Beaver River Central Schl; Castorland, NY; (Y); 7/86; French Clb; GAA; JV Var Socr; JV Var Sftbl; High Hon Roll; NHS; Regents Schlrshp 85-86fsprtsmnshp, Bus Awd 86; Jefferson CC; Acctng.

ADOLPH, ANTHONY; Northeastern Acad; Jamaica, NY; (S); Computer Clb; Science Clb; Nwsp Phtg; Yrbk Phtg; VP Frsh Cls; Pres Soph Cls; High Hon Roll; All Amer Acad Schlr Awd 86; Elec Engrng.

ADONIZ, CYNTHIA; Midwoods H S At Brooklyn Clg; Brooklyn, NY; (Y); Chorus; Orch; School Musical; School Play; Nwsp Stf; Ed Yrbk Stf; Var Bsktbl; 2nd Indtl Arts Comptn 86; Med.

ADORNETTO, JOSIE; The Ursuline Schl; New Rochelle, NY; (Y); Cmnty Wkr; JA; Office Aide; Stu Cncl; Cheerleading; Coach Actv; French Hon Soc; High Hon Roll; Jr NHS; NHS; Schlrshp 82; Itln Stds Schlrshp Frdhm U 86; Fordham U; Comp.

ADORNO, KARI; Saugerties HS; Saugerties, NY; (S); Church Yth Grp; Girl Scts; Chorus; Var L Crs Cntry; All Co Chrs 84 & 86; GSA Silver Awd 84; Spec Educ.

ADRIAN, CHARLENE; Perry Central School; Perry, NY; (Y); 5/100; AFS; Trs FHA; Math Tm; Trs Spanish Clb; Im Coach Actv; Var Socr; Cit Awd; High Hon Roll; Hon Roll; NHS; Daemen Coll; Phys Thrpst.

ADRIAN, MICHELLE; Batavia HS; Batavia, NY; (Y); 38/209; Color Guard; Bowling; High Hon Roll; Hon Roll; Acctg.

ADSITT, CATHERINE; Knox Memorial Central Schl; Russell, NY; (S); Spanish Clb; Stage Crew; Yrbk Stf; High Hon Roll; NHS; Forgn Exchng Studnt 84-85; Talntd Jrs At ST Lawrence U 83; Socl Studies Awds 82 & 83; Clarkson U; Mgmt.

ADSITT, KRISTEN; Ononadaga Central HS; Syracuse, NY; (Y); #13 In Class; GAA; Spanish Clb; SADD; Rep Stu Cncl; High Hon Roll; NHS; Chorus; Yrbk Stf; Var Capt Bsktbl; Socr; Mst Outstndg Athlt Schl 85-86; Mst Outstndg MVP Bsktbll & Sftbll 85-86.

ADUKKALIL, MAYBLE; West Genesee HS; Syracuse, NY; (Y); Church Yth Grp; Chorus; Church Choir; Yrbk Stf; Soph Cls; Jr Cls; High Hon Roll.

AEBI, ANTHONY; Laguardia H S Of Music & The Arts; New York, NY; (S); Art Clb; Camera Clb; French Clb; Office Aide; Nwsp Rptr; Nwsp Stf; Rep Jr Cls; Rep Stu Cncl; Hon Roll; NHS; Art Hnrs Leag 85; Physcs.

AEPELBACHER, LOU ANN; Maryvale SR HS; Cheektowaga, NY; (Y); 2/305; Church Yth Grp; German Clb; Girl Scts; Acpl Chr; Band; L Chorus; Church Choir; Drm Mjr(t); Jazz Band; Orch; Regents Schlrshp; Geneseo SUNY; Secndry Math Tch.

AFFINITO, JAMES J; Marlboro Central HS; Marlboro, NY; (Y); NY ST Rgnts Diploma 86; Pitt CC; Radlgc Tech.

AFONSO, MARIA; St John The Baptist HS; Bay Shore, NY; (Y); Interprtr.

AFRICA, DAVID; Liverpool HS; North Syracuse, NY; (Y); DECA; JCL; Latin Clb; VP Frsh Cls; Pres Soph Cls; Pres Jr Cls; Hon Roll; Prfct Atten Awd; Pres Acad Fitness Awd 85-86; Liverpool Hs Class Of 86 Schlrshp 85-86; ST U Of NY; Bus Admin.

AFSHANI, DEBORAH; Williamsville South HS; Williamsville, NY; (Y); VP AFS; Cmnty Wkr; Pres French Clb; Girl Scts; Ski Clb; Orch; Yrbk Stf; Tennis; Hon Roll; Prfct Atten Awd; Psychlgy.

AGAN, LYNETTE; Attica HS; Attica, NY; (Y); Ski Clb; Chorus; Church Choir; Color Guard; Rep Stu Cncl; Var L Mgr(s); JV Capt Socr; JV Vllybl; Hon Roll; NHS; JR All Cnty Chorus 83-84; SR All Cnty Chorus 85-86; Mrktng.

AGCAOILI-BAXTGER, ALISA; St Francis Prep; Astoria, NY; (Y); 219/746; Bowling; Ftbl; Var Trk; Bus.

AGEDAL, BETH; Sauquoit Valley Central HS; Sauquoit, NY; (Y); Am Leg Aux Girls St; GAA; SADD; Variety Show; Yrbk Stf; Var Capt Cheerleading; Var Sftbl; Hon Roll; NHS; Prfct Atten Awd; Elem Educ.

AGGARWAL, ANJUMAN; Clarkstown HS South HS; W Nyack, NY; (Y); Mgr Aud/Vis; VP Cmnty Wkr; Sec Intnl Clb; Math Clb; Stage Crew; Mu Alp Tht; NHS; Intl Bus.

AGGRIPPINO, JEANNE; Hudson HS; Hudson, NY; (Y); Color Guard; Nwsp Stf; Yrbk Stf; Var Gym; Var Pom Pon; Var Score Keeper; JV Sftbl; Var Trk; Hon Roll; Herkimer Cnty CC; Ocptnl Thrps.

AGI, EDIP; Newtown HS; Jackson Heights, NY; (Y); Pres Art Clb; Cmnty Wkr; Drama Clb; Hosp Aide; JA; Office Aide; PAVAS; Red Cross Aide; School Musical; School Play; Arista 85-86; Cooper Union Fll Tutn Excptnc 86; Brklyn Musm Full Tutn Schlrshp Art Hstry 85-86; Cooper Union; Illstrtr.

AGNE, DEBORAH A; Brewster HS; Patterson, NY; (Y); 12/190; Art Clb; Spanish Clb; Yrbk Rptr; Yrbk Stf; Var Trk; JV Vllybl; High Hon Roll; Hon Roll; NHS; Ntl Merit Ltr; Mnhtn Coll Schlrshp 86; Natl Ldrshp & Svc Assoc Mbr 82-86; Hnrs Awd Cmptrs Prjcts 85; Manhattan Coll; Biomed Engnr.

AGNELLO, JOANNA; Gates-Chili SR HS; Rochester, NY; (Y); 63/449; Aud/Vis; Drama Clb; Library Aide; Service Clb; Chorus; School Play; Cit Awd; High Hon Roll; Hon Roll; Prfct Atten Awd; Soc Studs Awd 83-84 & 85-86; Engl & Hlth Awds 83-84; Home Ec & Hstry Awds 85-86; Nazareth Coll; Ed.

AGNES, ADU; Sheepshead Bay HS; Brooklyn, NY; (Y); 89/490; Library Aide; Math Tm.

AGNEW, BRIAN; Marlboro Central HS; Marlboro, NY; (Y); 1/150; Church Yth Grp; VP French Clb; Rep SADD; Varsity Clb; Band; Mrchg Band; Var Tennis; Bausch & Lomb Sci Awd; Dnfth Awd; High Hon Roll; Rensselaer Polytechnic Medl 86; Natl Latn Exm Summa Cum Laude 86; Socl Stds Regnts Awd 86.

AGNONE, NICK; Hicksville HS; Hicksville, NY; (Y); Capt Ice Hcky; Socr; Hon Roll; Deck Hockey Cptn 84-86; NY Inst Tech; Arch.

AGOSTO, LUIS; Saint Agnes Boys HS; Ny, NY; (Y); 7/111; Boys Clb Am; Trs Stu Cncl; Hon Roll; Ntl Merit Ltr; Scnd Hnr Frshmn Yr 84; Scnd Hnrs Sophmr Yr 85; Scnd Hnrs JR Yr 86.

AGRAN, BRYAN; Blind Brook HS; Rye Brook, NY; (Y); Science Clb; Ski Clb; Temple Yth Grp; Variety Show; Mgr Nwsp Phtg; Nwsp Rptr; Nwsp Stf; Frsh Cls; Soph Cls; Golf; Sci Exprmnt U S Space Cmp Selected USA Space Shuttle Mission 85; Sci.

AGRESTA, JOSEPH; Amsterdam HS; Amsterdam, NY; (Y); Varsity Clb; Y-Teens; Im JV Bsbl; Im JV Bsktbl; JV Ftbl; High Hon Roll; Hon Roll; NHS; Prfct Atten Awd; Engrng.

AGRO, PETER; Mc Kee Technical HS; Staten Island, NY; (Y); 15/227; Stage Crew; Lit Mag; Cit Awd; Hon Roll; Prfct Atten Awd; New Paltz ST Coll; Elec Engrng.

AGRON, WENDY; L C Obourn HS; E Rochester, NY; (Y); 24/124; Church Yth Grp; Chorus; Church Choir; Concert Band; School Musical; School Play; Nwsp Ed-Chief; Cmnty Wkr; Debate Tm; Drama Clb; All ST Chrs 84-85; 2nd Pl Natl Soc Studs Olympd 85; Natl Hspnc Schlr Pgm Fnlst 86; Music Educ.

AGUERO, TIMOTHY; Hastings HS; Hastings Hdsn, NY; (Y); Aud/Vis; Boy Scts; Model UN; Ski Clb; Stage Crew; Rep Frsh Cls; Mgr(s); Score Keeper; Tennis; Sullivan County CC; Photo.

AGUIAR, ANA O; St Francis Prep; Jackson Hts, NY; (S); Church Yth Grp; Hosp Aide; Coach Actv; Hon Roll; NHS; Opt Clb Awd; Optimates Lst 83-84; Educ.

AGUILAR, CARLOS; Mount Vernon HS; Mt Vernon, NY; (Y); Band; Concert Band; Mrchg Band; Pep Band; Hon Roll; Prfct Attndnc Awd 79-81; Cert Of Hnr Wrkn Sci & Physcl Educ 81 & 82; Syracuse U; Bio.

AGUILAR, MARLENE; Halfhollow Hills HS East; Melville, NY; (Y); 94/510; Leo Clb; Bsktbl; Vllybl; Cit Awd; French Hon Soc; High Hon Roll; NHS; Spanish NHS; NY ST Schl Music Assn 84-85; Indpndnt Stdy Mndrn Chnse; Wesleyan U; Intl Rltns.

AGUILAR, VIVIAN; Our Lady Of Victory Acad; Yonkers, NY; (Y); French Clb; Mgr Stage Crew; Yrbk Stf; Rep Sr Cls; Tennis; Vllybl; French Hon Soc; Hon Roll; NHS; Ntl Merit SF; Pre-Med.

AGUIRRE, ANITA; Springville Griffith Inst; Springville, NY; (Y); Cmnty Wkr; Var Sftbl; Acad Cmmndtn & Merit Awd-Afro/Asian Cltrs 84; Gregg Typg Awd 86; Acad Cmmndtn Crs IR 84; Arch.

AGUIRRE, LISSETTE; De Witt Clinton HS; Bronx, NY; (Y); Church Yth Grp; FNA; JA; Red Cross Aide; Church Choir; Bsbl; Gym; Trk; Hon Roll; Reg Nrs.

AGUON, IVY ROSE; Hanau American HS; APO, NY; (Y); 1/100; Math Tm; Natl Beta Clb; Nwsp Stf; Pres Jr Cls; NHS; Val; FTA; JA; Sec Math Clb; Nwsp Rptr; 4-Yr Air Frc Schlrp 86; PEAP Schlrp 86; Miss JR 85; U MD Munich.

AGUSTIN, CYNTHIA; Our Lady Of Mercy HS; Dansville, NY; (Y); English Clb; Science Clb; Spanish Clb; Nwsp Rptr; Yrbk Rptr; Ed Yrbk Stf; Ed Lit Mag; Rep Stu Cncl; Hon Roll; NHS; Spnsh 2 Awd 85; Spnsh 3 Awd 86; Genesee Vly HS Chem Achvt Awd 86.

AHL, ELIZABETH; Churchville Chili HS; Rochester, NY; (Y); GAA; Hosp Aide; Ski Clb; Lib Band; Chorus; Concert Band; Mrchg Band; Pep Band; School Musical; Swing Chorus; Music.

AHLERS, CHRISTOPHER D; Bishop Timon HS; Buffalo, NY; (Y); 1/145; Chess Clb; Quiz Bowl; Nwsp Stf; Lit Mag; Vllybl; Bausch & Lomb Sci Awd; High Hon Roll; NHS; Ntl Merit SF; Val; Empire St Schlrshp 86; NYS Rgnts Schlrshp 86; Crnl U Schlrshp/Grnt 86; Cornell U; Ecnmcs.

AHMED, DIAR; Pelham Memorial HS; Pelham, NY; (Y); Debate Tm; Trk Stf; Lit Mag; JV Var Bsbl; Trk; Hon Roll; Prfct Atten Awd; JV Ftbl; Engrng.

AHMED, FARAH; Notre Dame Acad HS; Staten Island, NY; (Y); Cmnty Wkr; French Clb; Math Tm; Science Clb; Teachers Aide; Chorus; Jr NHS; NHS; Natl Frnch Cntst 85-86; Columbia U; Sci.

AHN, KATHLEEN; Bronx HS Of Science; New York, NY; (Y); Church Yth Grp; Yrbk Stf; Lit Mag; Off Frsh Cls; Off Jr Cls; Off Sr Cls; L Trk; Ntl Merit SF; 100 Hr Cert For Vlntr Svc 84-85; Semi-Fnlst Cmmnctns & Ed Schlrshp Cmp 86; Smith; Med.

AHRENS, BARBARA S; Lancaster Central HS; Lancaster, NY; (Y); 11/430; Hosp Aide; Sec Key Clb; Pep Clb; Concert Band; Mrchg Band; Var Trk; Capt Twrlr; French Hon Soc; Hon Roll; VP NHS; Acad Ltr 84; Nrsng.

AHUJA, AJAY; Newton HS; Rego Park, NY; (Y); 14/781; Library Aide; Math Clb; PAVAS; Orch; Yrbk Stf; High Hon Roll; Hon Roll; Mu Alp Tht; Prfct Atten Awd; Cert Hnr 84-85; Cert Awd All Subjcts 84; Bus Adm.

AIELLO, DEBRA; Blessed Sacrament St Gaberials HS; New Rochelle, NY; (Y); 14/136; Yrbk Phtg; Bsbl; Cheerleading; Sftbl; Hon Roll; Berkeley Bus Schl.

AIELLO, JO MARIE; Herkimer SR HS; Herkimer, NY; (Y); Cmnty Wkr; Sec Spanish Clb; SADD; Trs Frsh Cls; Pres Stu Cncl; JV L Bsktbl; Var Capt Cheerleading; Hon Roll; Rep Soph Cls; Rep Jr Cls.

AIELLO, LISA; Frankfort Schuyler Central HS; Frankfort, NY; (S); Key Clb; Pep Clb; Spanish Clb; SADD; Chorus; Rep Stu Cncl; Var Capt Cheerleading; Var L Trk; Hon Roll; NHS; Phys Ther.

AIELLO, SUSAN; Saugerties JR SR HS; Saugerties, NY; (Y); Spanish Clb; Teachers Aide; Hon Roll; NHS; Math.

AIKEN, TAMMI BREDT; Hugh C Williams HS; Potsdam, NY; (Y); 14/115; Girl Scts; Ski Clb; Spanish Clb; Socr; JV Var Trk; Var JV Vllybl; High Hon Roll; Hon Roll; Cmnty Wkr; JA; Hghst Algebra Avg 83; Rgnts Schlrshp 86; U Of VT; Engr.

AILLET, CHRIS; Minisink Valley HS; Westtown, NY; (Y); 34/240; Church Yth Grp; PAVAS; Ski Clb; Varsity Clb; Crs Cntry; Trk; High Hon Roll; U Lowell; Civl Engrng.

AINBINDER, IVY J; Oceanside SR HS; Oceanside, NY; (Y); 122/532; Temple Yth Grp; Thesps; Color Guard; Concert Band; Drm Mjr(t); Madrigals; Mrchg Band; School Musical; Variety Show; Hon Roll; Rgnts Schlrshp 86; Bst Drm Majorette 85; U Miami; Astronaut.

AINEY, RONALD J; Horseheads SR HS; Horseheads, NY; (S); 34/400; 4-H; German Clb; Band; Chorus; Church Choir; Rep Stu Cncl; VP L Crs Cntry; JV Capt Lcrss; L Capt Trk; U Buffalo; Engrng.

AIRO, LOREDANA; St Edmund HS; Brooklyn, NY; (Y); Hon Roll; NHS; Brooklyn Coll; Bus.

AISTARS, SANDRA; Fayetteville-Manlius SR HS; Manlius, NY; (Y); 125/350; Church Yth Grp; Model UN; Chorus; Church Choir; School Musical; School Play; Variety Show; Hon Roll; Ntl Merit SF; Perf Arts Ldrshp 86; Mdl UN Delg Awd 85-86; Rgnts Schlrshp 86; Bard Coll; Polt Sci.

AJAVANANDA, REBECCA; East HS; Rochester, NY; (Y); 22/242; Concert Band; Mrchg Band; Var Crs Cntry; JV Diving; Var L Gym; Var Sftbl; Var Swmmng; High Hon Roll; Hon Roll; NHS; All Star Gym & Swmmng; Nrs.

AKAGI, LANCE; Union-Endicott HS; Endicott, NY; (Y); Computer Clb; Key Clb; Hon Roll; Regents Schlrshp 86; Indstrl Art Awd 86; Broome CC; Elec/Comp Engrng.

AKERS, DARIA; Trott Vocational HS; Niagara Falls, NY; (Y); 3/147; Library Aide; Nwsp Stf; Pres Frsh Cls; Hon Roll; Jr NHS; NHS; Pres Acad Ftnss Awd 86; U Of Buffalo Alumni 86; Otstndng Srv 83; Niagara Cnty CC; Rn.

AKINS, DESIREE; Seward Park HS; New York, NY; (Y); Teachers Aide; Hon Roll; John Jay Coll; Law.

AKLEY, HELEN; Canton Hugh C Williams HS; Canton, NY; (Y); VP Dance Clb; 4-H; FFA; SADD; Nwsp Bus Mgr; Cit Awd; 4-H Awd; Prfct Atten Awd; Empire Farmers Degree FFA 86; Fashion Revue Awd 4-H Modeling 85; Star Chap Farmer Awd 85; Canton ATC; Animal Sci.

AKULA, VIKRAM; Niskayuna HS; Scotia, NY; (Y); Cmnty Wkr; Key Clb; School Musical; Variety Show; Lit Mag; Pres Soph Cls; Pres Jr Cls; Pres Sr Cls; Stu Cncl; Tennis; Prncpls Awd 86; Tufts U.

ALAIMO, THOMAS; Fairport HS; Fairport, NY; (Y); Pre-Dntstry.

ALAMA, ROMMEL S; St Francis Prep; Rosedale, NY; (S); 55/744; Cmnty Wkr; Intnl Clb; Im Tennis; Im Vllybl; Hon Roll; Vrsty Judo Plyr Troph Wnnr 85-86; Optimt Socty Ovr 90 Pct Avg 85; Cmmrcl Dsgn.

ALAMILLA, PETER J; Thomas Edison HS; Richmond Hill, NY; (Y); 72/379; Regents Schlrshp 86; Polytechnic Schlrshp 86; Physics Awd 85; Polytechnic U; Elec Engrng.

ALAMO, DALILA; William Howard Taft HS; Bronx, NY; (Y); CAP; Cmnty Wkr; Drama Clb; English Clb; FBLA; Office Aide; ROTC; Scholastic Bowl; Spanish Clb; SADD; Excell Typng I 84-85; Excell Spnsh IV 85-86; Law.

ALAPECK, SCOTT; Union Endicott HS; Endicott, NY; (Y); Latin Clb; Bsbl; Socr; Wt Lftg; Hon Roll; Ann G Mc Ginness Schlrshp 86; Broome CC; Engrng Sci.

ALBANESE, DAVID; Archbishop Stepinac HS; N Tarrytown, NY; (Y); 87/171; Key Clb; Yrbk Stf; Var Bowling; Var Golf; Var L Ice Hcky; Y-Teens; Intrml Flr Hcky; Ordr Of Arrw Boy Scts 85; PA ST; Bus.

ALBANESE, DAWN; Port Chester SR HS; Port Chester, NY; (Y); 8/220; Ski Clb; Color Guard; Drm & Bgl; Mrchg Band; Stage Crew; Yrbk Stf; Lit Mag; Capt Bsktbl; Mgr(s); Sftbl; Rtry Clb Schlrshp 86; Wmns Sprts Assn Athlt Of Yr 86; U S Army Rsrcs Schlr/Athlt Awd 86; SUNY Oneonta; Corp Law.

ALBANESE, JAMES; Bay Shore HS; Bay Shore, NY; (Y); 56/406; Math Clb; Math Tm; Science Clb; Ed Nwsp Stf; Trs Jr Cls; Im Ice Hcky; Socr; High Hon Roll; Hon Roll; Ntl Merit SF; Med.

ALBANESE, KEVIN; Iona Prep Schl; Yonkers, NY; (Y); Church Yth Grp; Var L Ice Hcky; Im Wrstlng; Hon Roll; Bus Adm.

ALBANESE, LISA MARIE; Academy Of St Joseph; Smithtown, NY; (Y); GAA; Hosp Aide; Library Aide; Model UN; Political Wkr; Science Clb; Spanish Clb; Nwsp Ed-Chief; NHS; Dr Vnct Sllr Ldg Schlrshp 86; NY ST Bar Assn Cert Hon 85 & 86; Cert Spr Acdmc Achvt Spnsh 85; Hofstra U; Law.

ALBANESE, VERONICA A; St Francis Prep Schl; Flushing, NY; (S); Hosp Aide; Ski Clb; SADD; Yrbk Stf; Im Sftbl; Var Twrlr; Im Vllybl; Hon Roll; NHS; Bus.

ALBANEZE, KATHLEEN; Dominican Commercial HS; Flushing, NY; (Y); 102/288; Chorus; Church Yth Grp; Bsktbl; Sftbl; Vllybl; Prncpls List; Bus.

ALBANIS, EFSEVIA; St Francis Preparatory Schl; Jamaica, NY; (S); 26/653; L Am Leg Aux Girls St; Art Clb; Church Yth Grp; Girl Scts; Var JV Trk; Wt Lftg; NHS; Prncpls List 82-85; Pre-Med.

ALBANO, CHRISTINE P; St Francis Prep; Elmhurst, NY; (S); 49/744; Library Aide; Hon Roll.

ALBANO, JEANNE; Our Lady Of Victory Acad; Yonkers, NY; (S); 18/160; Church Yth Grp; Service Clb; Yrbk Phtg; High Hon Roll; NHS; Spanish NHS; Alpha Hnr Soc, Relgn Awd 85; Animal Sci.

ALBANO, VALERIE A; Eastchester HS; Eastchester, NY; (Y); 1/145; Spanish Clb; Ed Yrbk Stf; Sec Sr Cls; DAR Awd; Elks Awd; NHS; Ntl Merit Ltr; Pres Spanish NHS; Val; Rensselaer Math & Sci Medl 85; Fairfield U.

ALBARRAN, MAGDALENA; Eastern District HS; Brooklyn, NY; (Y); 42/333; Church Yth Grp; Library Aide; Teachers Aide; Band; Prfct Atten Awd; Pratt Inst; Photo.

ALBEE, RICHARD; Cohocton Central Schl; Cohocton, NY; (S); 4/28; Am Leg Boys St; French Clb; Band; Sec Pres Stu Cncl; Var Bsktbl; Var Socr; Var Tennis; Trs NHS; 100 Pcnt Geom Regents 83-84; Rochester Inst Tech; Comp Sci.

ALBELO, JOSE; Herbert H Lehman HS; Bronx, NY; (Y); Mgr Aud/Vis; Library Aide; Sec Frsh Cls; Sec Soph Cls; Im Vllybl; Im Wt Lftg; Air Force; Cmmrcl Pilot.

ALBERGO, GIA LYN; Comsewogue HS; Pt Jeff Station, NY; (Y); Church Yth Grp; Cmnty Wkr; Dance Clb; SADD; Teachers Aide; Chorus; Orch; Nwsp Rptr; Yrbk Stf; Rep Frsh Cls; Mst Outstndg Engl Awd 83; St Jsph Acad Grls Schlrshp 83; Stony Brook U; Poly Sci.

ALBERGO, MELISSA; H Frank Carey HS; Franklin Square, NY; (Y); 23/287; Dance Clb; VP FBLA; Pep Clb; Stu Cncl; Capt Cheerleading; High Hon Roll; NHS; Hofstra U; Bus Admin.

ALBERT, BRYAN; North Tonawanda SR HS; N Tonawanda, NY; (Y); Trs Church Yth Grp; Chorus; Hon Roll; Jr NHS; Trs Boy Scts; Outstndng Engl Achvt 84; Bus Admin.

ALBERT, FEROLINE; Catherine Mc Avley HS; Brooklyn, NY; (S); 11/70; Drama Clb; Library Aide; School Play; Nwsp Ed-Chief; Yrbk Ed-Chief; Rep Jr Cls; Rep Stu Cncl; Stat Badmtn; High Hon Roll; Hon Roll; Physical Fitness Awd 83-84; Corp Law.

ALBERT, KIM A; Preston HS; Bronx, NY; (Y); 16/85; Church Yth Grp; Cmnty Wkr; Teachers Aide; Yrbk Stf; Pres Frsh Cls; Sec Soph Cls; VP Jr Cls; Pres Stu Cncl; Cheerleading; Hon Roll; Regents Schlrshp 86; Berkley; Consumer Rltns.

ALBERT, MICHELLE A; Erasmus Hall HS; Brooklyn, NY; (Y); JA; Math Clb; Math Tm; Science Clb; Speech Tm; Chorus; School Play; Rgnts Schlrshp 86; Haverford Coll; Med.

ALBERTELLI, ANN MARIE; Hauppauge HS; Commack, NY; (Y); Cmnty Wkr; SADD; Chorus; Variety Show; Rep Frsh Cls; Chrmn Soph Cls; Rep Chrmn Jr Cls; Rep Chrmn Sr Cls; Rep Stu Cncl; Mgr(s); Bus.

ALBERTI, LAURIE; Gates-Chili HS; Rochester, NY; (Y); Girl Scts; Concert Band; Rep Frsh Cls; Rep Soph Cls; Rep Jr Cls; JV Var Mgr(s); JV Var Score Keeper; JV Var Timer; High Hon Roll; Hon Roll; Bus Adm.

ALBERTINA, LINDA; Sherburne Earlville HS; Norwich, NY; (Y); 6/123; FBLA; SADD; Varsity Clb; Jr Cls; Sr Cls; Stu Cncl; Sftbl; Vllybl; Hon Roll; NHS; Ruth Baxter Hewitt Awd 86; Ntl Bk Trst Co Norwich Awd 86; Merl R Lyon Awd 86; Cazenovia Coll; Acctng.

ALBERTO, NANCY; George Washington HS; New York, NY; (Y); Spanish Clb; School Play; Schlrshp Soc Awd 85; Schltc Excllnc Awd Typng 84; Cert Rcgntn Comprehensive Math & Sci Prog 86; Prfrmng Arts.

ALBOLOTE, BENEDICT; Sachem N Campus HS; Holbrook, NY; (Y); 160/1588; Ski Clb; Yrbk Stf; JV Var Tennis; Im Vllybl; Im Wt Lftg; SCI.

ALBONE, EARL; Royalton HS; Middleport, NY; (Y); 2/150; French Clb; Trs Frsh Cls; Trs Soph Cls; Pres Stu Cncl; Bausch & Lomb Sci Awd; Dnfth Awd; High Hon Roll; Pres NHS; Rensselaer Math-Sci Awd 86; Chem.

ALBOWICZ, DANIELLE; Hoosick Falls Central Schl; Hoosick Falls, NY; (Y); 11/107; French Clb; Pep Clb; Chorus; Yrbk Stf; Rep Soph Cls; Stu Cncl; L Trk; High Hon Roll; Hon Roll; NHS; Regents Schlrshp 86; Obstetrics.

ALBRECHT, ALEXANDRA; Fox Lane HS; Mt Kisco, NY; (Y); 41/277; French Clb; German Clb; Ski Clb; Spanish Clb; JV Powder Puff Ftbl; High Hon Roll; Hon Roll; NHS; Outstndng Achvt Spnsh,German 84-85; Sci.

ALBRECHT, KREGG D; Jarvis Central Schl; Mohawk, NY; (Y); 1/89; Varsity Clb; Im JV Bsktbl; Im JV Ftbl; Bausch & Lomb Sci Awd; NHS; Church Yth Grp; French Clb; Band; Concert Band; Jazz Band; U Rchstr; Chem Engr.

ALBRECHT, LISA; Villa Maria Acad; Cheektowaga, NY; (Y); Cmnty Wkr; Computer Clb; Church Choir; Im Bowling; JV Vllybl; Dnfth Awd; Hon Roll; Bryant & Stratton Bus Inst; Bus.

ALBRIGHT, MARK; Churchville-Chili HS; Churchville, NY; (Y); Trs JCL; Trs Latin Clb; Hon Roll; NHS; Prfct Atten Awd; Cert Prtcptn Mobil & CC Of Fngr Lks Sci Olympcs 85; Chem.

ALBRIGHT, TIM; Coxsackie Athens HS; Athens, NY; (Y); Art Clb; German Clb; Math Clb; Ski Clb; Band; Concert Band; Rep Stu Cncl; High Hon Roll; Dsgnr.

ALBUERNE, CARLOS PEREZ; Mc Quaid Jesuit HS; Rochester, NY; (Y); Church Yth Grp; Letterman Clb; Varsity Clb; Var L Ftbl; Var Trk; Chem Eng.

ALBURY, RUSSELL A; Nazareth Regional HS; Brooklyn, NY; (Y); Boy Scts; Pres Science Clb; Var Socr; NHS; Prncpls List 85; Undrgradt Awds-Engl & Bio 85; Undrgradt Awds-Math, Comp & Chem 86; Pre-Med.

ALCAZAR, CAROL M; St Francis Prep; Woodside, NY; (S); 179/746; Cmnty Wkr; Science Clb; Rep Jr Cls; Rep Stu Cncl; Hon Roll; NHS.

ALCEDO, FRANCIS; Notre Dame-Bishop Gibbons HS; Schenectady, NY; (S); 1/101; Art Clb; Nwsp Rptr; Ed Yrbk Ed-Chief; Lit Mag; Var Trk; High Hon Roll; NHS; Bio Awd 83-84; Chem Awd 84-85; Phy Sci Awd 82-83; Cornell U; Med.

ALCOCK, FRANK; Warwick Valley HS; Warwick, NY; (Y); 12/200; Science Clb; Var JV Bsbl; Var JV Ftbl; Var L Swmmng; Var L Trk; High Hon Roll; NHS; Ntl Merit Ltr; Quiz Bowl; Var JV Tennis; All Orane Cnty Ftbl Tm Def Back 85; Regnl Cahmp Metric Estmtn Natl Sci Olympd 86; NYS Bsbl Cls B 86; Actuarial Sci.

ALCOCK, MELISSA; Waterloo SR HS; Waterloo, NY; (Y); JV Sftbl.

ALCORN, SALLY; Mynderse Acad; Seneca Falls, NY; (Y); 19/126; VP NHS; JV Var Cheerleading; High Hon Roll; Hon Roll; Centenl Schlrshp-Charlston U 86-90; U Charlston; Psych.

ALCOTT, CYNTHIA; Chenango Valley HS; Binghamton, NY; (Y); 37/174; Trs Church Yth Grp; Hosp Aide; Chorus; Church Choir; Color Guard; Flag Corp; Mrchg Band; School Musical; Hon Roll; Jr NHS; Broome CC; Data Proc.

ALCOTT, HOLLY J; Edmeston Central HS; Edmeston, NY; (Y); 1/31; Am Leg Aux Girls St; Girl Scts; Library Aide; Thesps; Trs Frsh Cls; Golf; Cit Awd; High Hon Roll; Church Yth Grp; Math Clb; All-Cnty & All-ST Choirs 84-86; 2nd Pl Legn Aux Amercnsm Essay 86; Poem Publshd World Ptry Anth 86; Geneseo; Engl.

ALDERMAN, STEVE; Fillmore Central HS; Houghton, NY; (Y); SADD; Varsity Clb; Stage Crew; Pres Jr Cls; Rep Stu Cncl; Var L Bsbl; Var L Bsktbl; Var L Socr; Var L Trk; Hon Roll; 1st Tm-All Cnty Bsktbl 86; 2nd Tm-All Cnty Sccr 85; Hnrb Mntn All Cnty Bsbl 86; Bus Adm.

ALDERS, TAMMYLEE; Goshen Central HS; Florida, NY; (Y); SADD; School Play; Nwsp Phtg; Nwsp Stf; Yrbk Phtg; Twrlr; High Hon Roll; Sec NHS; NY ST Rgnts Schlrshp 86; U Of Miami; Biomed Engr.

ALDOUS, BRIGITTE; Hermon-De Kalb HS; Hermon, NY; (Y); 10/45; Drama Clb; Pres French Clb; Varsity Clb; School Play; Yrbk Sprt Ed; Var Capt Bsktbl; Var Capt Socr; L Var Sftbl; High Hon Roll; Hon Roll; Clarkson U; Acctg.

ALDOVINO, NEPTALI; Murry Bergtraum HS; New York, NY; (Y); Church Yth Grp; JA; NHS; Prfct Atten Awd; Med.

ALDRICH, AARON; Hannibal HS; Hannibal, NY; (Y); Band; Color Guard; Concert Band; Mrchg Band; Hon Roll; NHS; Empr ST Gms In Gymnstcs 80-86; Brnz In Allrnt 1st In Vltno 2nd On Brm 84; Phys Thrpy.

ALDRICH, JULIE L; Beaver River Central Schl; Castorland, NY; (Y); French Clb; GAA; Var L Socr; Var L Sftbl; High Hon Roll; NHS; NY ST Regents Coll Schlrshp 86; Jefferson CC; Accntng.

ALDRICH-MOODIE, MARY JANE; Emma Willard Schl; Vineyard Haven, MA; (Y); Cmnty Wkr; Dance Clb; Exploring; Office Aide; Political Wkr; Service Clb; Teachers Aide; Nwsp Rptr; Cit Awd; Hunter Schlr 82-86; Top Latin Stu 83 & 84; Harvard Bk Awd 85; STOP Natl Ldrshp Conf 84; Big Sis 82-83; Soc Sci.

ALDRIDGE, MICHELE; Kenmore East HS; Tonawanda, NY; (Y); Church Yth Grp; Band; Mrchg Band; School Play; Nwsp Rptr; Nwsp Sprt Ed; Hon Roll; Erie County Cmnty; Medcl Asst.

ALDUINO, LEEANNE; Central Islip HS; Central Islip, NY; (Y); 29/329; Cmnty Wkr; Girl Scts; Band; Concert Band; Mrchg Band; School Musical; Nwsp Bus Mgr; Yrbk Stf; Off Soph Cls; Tennis; GS Svlr Awd 84; GS Gld Awd 86; Architect.

ALEKSIEJUK, ERIKA; Troot Vocational HS; Niagara Falls, NY; (Y); Dance Clb; Girl Scts; Hosp Aide; Chorus; Church Choir; Pres Frsh Cls; JV Var Bsbl; JV Var Cheerleading; Score Keeper; JV Vllybl; Nrs.

ALENSTEIN, ABIGAIL J; Briarcliff HS; Briarcliff, NY; (Y); Church Yth Grp; French Clb; Chorus; Church Choir; School Musical; Hon Roll; NY ST Regnts Schlrshp 86; IN U Bloomington; Russn Stud.

ALESANDRO, NICK P; Shaker HS; Latham, NY; (Y); Hosp Aide; Nwsp Phtg; Yrbk Ed-Chief; Yrbk Phtg; Ntl Merit SF.

ALESSI, MARY KATE; Webster HS; Webster, NY; (Y); 20/495; Church Yth Grp; JA; Spanish Clb; Band; Concert Band; Mrchg Band; Var Stat Mgr(s); Var Score Keeper; High Hon Roll; NHS; Outstndng Accomplshmnt Spnsh,Eng 83-84; Regnts Schlrshp NY ST 86; SUNY Binghamton; Bio.

ALESSI, ROBERT; Buffalo Traditional HS; Buffalo, NY; (S); 6/111; Math Tm; Yrbk Bus Mgr; Yrbk Stf; Var Bsbl; Var Bowling; Var Socr; Hon Roll; Trs NHS; Prfct Atten Awd; Buffalo ST; Restrateur.

ALESSIO, DAWN; Kings Park SR HS; Kings Park, NY; (Y); 10/400; Cmnty Wkr; Office Aide; Sec Radio Clb; VP Spanish Clb; SADD; Ed Yrbk Stf; High Hon Roll; Jr NHS; Trs NHS; Full Tuition Pres Schlrshp St Jsphs 86; Rgnts Schlrshp 86; All Amer Acad Schlr Pgm 86; St Josephs Coll; Acctng.

ALESSY, TRACY; Cardinal Spellman HS; Bx, NY; (Y); Dance Clb; Hosp Aide; Pep Clb; Nwsp Stf; Yrbk Stf; Nrs.

ALEXANDER, ANN; Bais Yaakov HS; Monsey, NY; (Y); School Musical; School Play; Stage Crew; Nwsp Ed-Chief; Yrbk Stf; Soph Cls; Capt Bsbl; NHS; St Schlr.

ALEXANDER, ANTHONY; Bishop Ford CC HS; Brooklyn, NY; (Y); Art Clb; Boys Clb Am; Dance Clb; Variety Show; Bsktbl; Lawyer.

ALEXANDER, CHRISTY JO; Whitesboro SR HS; Whitesboro, NY; (Y); 83/301; Church Yth Grp; GAA; Model UN; Ski Clb; Chorus; Concert Band; Mrchg Band; Frsh Cls; Fld Hcky; Trk; Mohawk Vly Review Mag Short Story Publctn 86; Engl.

ALEXANDER, JAMES; Bishop Scully HS; Amsterdam, NY; (Y); JA; JV Bsbl; Var JV Ftbl; Im Wt Lftg; Pre-Law.

ALEXANDER JR, JOSEPH LEE; The Stony Brook Schl; Medford, NY; (Y); Boy Scts; Church Yth Grp; Dance Clb; Office Aide; Spanish Clb; Church Choir; School Play; Sec Jr Cls; L Capt Bsktbl; L Crs Cntry; Martin Luther King Jr Awd 84; Brakenridge Awd 85; Prsdnt Of Studnt Cerenal 86; Bus Admin.

ALEXANDER, JULIE; Thousand Islands HS; Cape Vincent, NY; (Y); Band; Chorus; School Play; Yrbk Stf; JV Var Bsktbl; Var Cheerleading; JV Socr; JV Var Sftbl; JV Var Vllybl; SUNY Albany; Bus.

ALEXANDER, LAUREN; Pittsford Mendon HS; Pittsford, NY; (Y); Girl Scts; School Musical; School Play; Yrbk Stf; Pres Frsh Cls; Rep Soph Cls; VP Jr Cls; Sec Sr Cls; Stu Cncl; Hon Roll; Grl Scouts Silv Awd 84; Black Schlr Monroe Cnty 86; YMCA Yth Yr 86.

ALEXANDER, MATT; Penn Yan Acad; Penn Yan, NY; (S); 4/187; Church Yth Grp; Model UN; Ski Clb; Chorus; Rep Frsh Cls; Rep Soph Cls; Rep Jr Cls; Rep Sr Cls; Var Lcrss; High Hon Roll; Amer Legion Oratorical Cont 82-86; Pennyan Cmnty Choir 86; Physics.

ALEXANDER, MICHAEL; Bishop Ford Catholic HS; Brooklyn, NY; (Y); Art Clb; Church Yth Grp; Computer Clb; Dance Clb; Science Clb; Band; Church Choir; Comp, Dnc & Art Awds 85-86; St Johns U; Adv.

ALEXANDER, SCOTT M; Wayne Central HS; Ontario, NY; (Y); 50/200; Church Yth Grp; Math Tm; Variety Show; Yrbk Stf; Off Frsh Cls; Off Sr Cls; Score Keeper; NHS; Rgnt Schlrshp 86; Monroe CC; Comp Sci.

ALEXANDER, SHEREDA; South Shore HS; Brooklyn, NY; (Y); Cmnty Wkr; DECA; Fncl Anlyst.

ALEXATOS, JOYCE; Archbishop Iakovos HS; Bayside, NY; (S); 2/15; Church Yth Grp; English Clb; Library Aide; Math Clb; Speech Tm; High Hon Roll; St John Chrysostom Oritrcl Fest 84; NY U.

ALFANO, CINDY; Smithtown HS East; Nesconset, NY; (Y); Church Yth Grp; GAA; Hosp Aide; Teachers Aide; Yrbk Stf; Var Bsktbl; Var Fld Hcky; Var Sftbl; Var Vllybl; NHS; Sprts Med.

ALFANO, JASON; Canarsie HS; Brooklyn, NY; (Y); Church Yth Grp; Rep Frsh Cls; JV Bsbl; JV Bsktbl; Gov Hon Prg Awd; High Hon Roll; Hon Roll; Mathletes; Math Clb; Math Tm; 2nd Pl-Borgh Sci Fair 85; 1st Pl-Schl Sci Fair 85; 3rd Pl-Cntnentl Math Leag 84; NY U; Bus Adm.

ALFAYA, GABRIEL; Albertus Magnus HS; Nyack, NY; (Y); JV Bsktbl; Var Ice Hcky; Iona Coll; Bus.

ALFIERI, GRACE; Lawrence HS; Lawrence, NY; (Y); High Hon Roll; Italian Club; Italian Awd 83-84; Accnt.

ALFIERI, LUCINDA; Moore Catholic HS; Staten Island, NY; (Y); Drama Clb; Math Tm; Spanish Clb; Chorus; School Musical; School Play; Nwsp Stf; Yrbk Phtg; High Hon Roll; NHS.

ALFIERI, PAUL; Ed Wilson HS; Spencerport, NY; (Y); Latin Clb; Spanish Clb; Varsity Clb; Var Crs Cntry; Var Trk; Hon Roll; Prfct Atten Awd.

ALFIERI, RENEE; Richmond Hill HS; Richmond Hill, NY; (Y); 4/296; Math Clb; JV Radio Clb; VP Pres Spanish Clb; Chorus; Nwsp Rptr; Hon Roll; NHS; Spanish NHS; Computer Clb; Dance Clb; Spnsh Profcncy Awd 86; NY U Schlrshp Regents Diplma; NYU; Mrktng Mgmt.

ALFINI, LISA; Gloversville HS; Gloversville, NY; (Y); 64/229; Computer Clb; Chorus; Color Guard; Hon Roll; Fulton-Montgomery CC; Trvl Agt.

ALFONSETTI, DAVID L; Solvay HS; Syracuse, NY; (Y); 32/172; Art Clb; SADD; School Musical; Nwsp Stf; High Hon Roll; Hon Roll; Awd 2 Gld Kys Mony Schlstc Art Comp 86; Awd 2nd Tm Blfr Awd Excl Art 86; Cerf Mrt Outstndng Achvt 86; Phtgrphy.

ALFONSO, IVETTE; St Edmund HS; Brooklyn, NY; (S); 10/185; French Clb; Spanish Clb; Gym; Hon Roll; Pres Jr NHS; Pres NHS; Spnsh Cert 82-83; Frnch Cert 83-86; Acadmc All Amer 85-86; St Johns U; Ed.

ALFONSO, MONICA; St John The Baptist HS; Massapequa, NY; (Y); School Play; Hon Roll; Socl Wrk.

ALFORD, BEVERLY; Madrid-Waddington JR SR HS; Madrid, NY; (Y); 2/61; NFL; Yrbk Bus Mgr; Trs Frsh Cls; Trs Soph Cls; Trs Jr Cls; Trs Sr Cls; High Hon Roll; NHS; Sal; Cheerleading; Spch & Debate Rookie Yr 84-85; Potsdam ST U; Secndry Mth Ed.

ALFORD, BRYAN; Irondequoit HS; Rochester, NY; (Y); Art Clb; Cmnty Wkr; Exploring; Intnl Clb; Ski Clb; SADD; Yrbk Stf; SUNY-FASHN Inst Of Tech; Fashn.

ALFORD, YOLANDA; Brooklyn Technical HS; Brooklyn, NY; (Y); Dance Clb; Drama Clb; Math Clb; Chorus; Hon Roll; Nrsng Coll Schlrhsp 86; Boston Coll; Pre-Med.

ALFRED, NICOLE; Adlai E Stevenson HS; New York, NY; (Y); #1 In Class; Church Yth Grp; Teachers Aide; High Hon Roll; Hon Roll; NHS; Achvmnt Lge 86; Acdmc All-Amer 86; Pdtrcs.

ALGIERI, MICHELE; William Floyd HS; Shirley, NY; (Y); Band; Capt Flag Corp; Mrchg Band; Symp Band; JV Cheerleading; High Hon Roll; Hon Roll; Jr NHS; NHS; Sec Frsh Cls; Dntstry.

ALGUERO, ANDRE; Brockport HS; Brockport, NY; (Y); 28/400; Latin Clb; Mathletes; Pres Model UN; Radio Clb; Ski Clb; Var Tennis; Var Trk; High Hon Roll; Robotics Engrng.

ALI, RACHAEL; John Dewey HS; Brooklyn, NY; (Y); Art Clb; Computer Clb; Dance Clb; JA; Math Clb; Chorus; School Musical; Cheerleading; Bus.

ALIA, PHYLLIS; Hall Hollow Hills H S West; Dix Hills, NY; (Y); 36/396; Drama Clb; Spanish Clb; School Musical; School Play; Variety Show; Pres Frsh Cls; Pres Soph Cls; Capt Var Cheerleading; Var Gym; High Hon Roll; US Senate Japan Schlrshp 85; Hugh O Brian Yth Found Rep 84; Ntl Hnr Soc 85-86; Northwestern U; Radio.

ALIBERTI, CARMELA; Colonie Central HS; Albany, NY; (Y); Church Yth Grp; Girl Scts; Rep Frsh Cls; Rep Soph Cls; VP Jr Cls; Rep Sr Cls; Rep Stu Cncl; Vllybl; Hon Roll; NHS; Suny ST U; Law.

ALIOTTA, DINA; Washingtonville HS; Salisbury Mls, NY; (Y); 4/240; Cmnty Wkr; GAA; Varsity Clb; Band; Symp Band; Variety Show; Yrbk Stf; Stat Bsbl; Var Socr; VFW Awd; HS Tchrs Assn Schlrshp 86; Wnnr Of Intrct Vrty Shw 86; Fshn Inst-Tech; Mrktng Csmtcs.

ALISANSKI, CHRISTOPHER F; Marcellus SR HS; Marcellus, NY; (Y); 4/167; Jazz Band; Symp Band; Yrbk Stf; Var L Tennis; High Hon Roll; NHS; Church Yth Grp; Computer Clb; Im Badmtn; All Cnty Band & Wind Ensmbl 83-86; NY ST Regents Schlrshp 86; Var Bowling Awds 85; Allegheny Coll; Chem.

ALITA, JOHN; Centereach HS; Lake Grove, NY; (S); 11/429; Cmnty Wkr; Q&S; Church Choir; Nwsp Stf; Yrbk Stf; Lit Mag; High Hon Roll; Hon Roll; NHS; Brnz Mdl Wnr 1st Annl Acad Dcthln Suffolk Cty 85; Island Drftng & Tech Inst; Comp.

ALIVENTI, THERESA; South Side HS; Rockville Centre, NY; (Y); 21/300; Sec SADD; Trs Frsh Cls; Trs Soph Cls; Trs Jr Cls; Var Capt Badmtn; High Hon Roll; NHS; Cmnty Wkr; Key Clb; Smile Peer Cnslng 86; Yth Part Prog 85; Med Stu At Stony Brk; Dctr.

ALLAN, CHRISTINE; Westlake HS; Thornwood, NY; (Y); Cmnty Wkr; Vllybl; Itln Hnr Socty; Math.

ALLAN, HEATHER; Long Island Luthern HS; Babylon, NY; (S); 11/94; Sec Church Yth Grp; Hosp Aide; Library Aide; Chorus; Church Choir; School Musical; School Play; Cheerleading; High Hon Roll; NHS; Geneseo Coll; Phys Ther.

ALLARD, JAMES EDWARD; St Marys Acad; Glens Falls, NY; (S); Aud/Vis; Computer Clb; Key Clb; Math Clb; Ski Clb; SADD; Concert Band; Nwsp Ed-Chief; High Hon Roll; Boy Scts; Boswell Pash Mem Inst Summr Rsrch Pgm 87; NYS Mth Lg 84-87; MIT; Mech Engrng.

ALLDER, LINDA; Williamsville East HS; Amherst, NY; (Y); AFS; Drama Clb; JA; Stage Crew; Hon Roll; Pre-Law.

ALLEN, BETH; Fairport HS; Fairport, NY; (Y); 43/600; Church Yth Grp; Nwsp Sprt Ed; Trs Soph Cls; Cheerleading; Socr; Trk; Hon Roll; NHS; Dickinson Coll; Pre Law.

ALLEN, CINDY; Canisteo Central HS; Canisteo, NY; (Y); 3/70; Ski Clb; Varsity Clb; Band; Concert Band; Mrchg Band; Variety Show; VP Soph Cls; Rep Stu Cncl; Var JV Bsktbl; Var Crs Cntry; Bus Adm.

ALLEN, CYNTHIA; Union Endicott HS; Endwell, NY; (Y); 21/436; French Clb; SADD; Teachers Aide; Chorus; NHS; Opt Clb Awd; Computer Clb; Drama Clb; School Musical; School Play; Regnts & Robert R Rounds Schlrshps 85-86; Canisius Coll Buffalo; Pre-Med.

ALLEN, DAVID; Green Meadow Waldorf Schl; Nyack, NY; (Y); Chorus; Orch; School Musical; School Play; Yrbk Phtg; Lit Mag; Stu Cncl; Capt Socr; Brown Bk Awd 84-85; RI Schl Dsgn; Fine Arts.

ALLEN, DEBBIE; Northeastern Acad; Mt Vernon, NY; (Y); Church Yth Grp; Chorus; Nwsp Rptr; Nwsp Sprt Ed; Sec Jr Cls; Sec Stu Cncl; Bsbl; Cheerleading; Cert Of Hnr Engl III 86; Cert Of Awd Jrnlsm 86; Awd Of Sci 84; Pediatrics.

ALLEN, ELIZABETH; Gouverneur Central HS; Gouverneur, NY; (Y); Rep Stu Cncl; JV Var Cheerleading; Prfct Atten Awd; MVP Vrsty Ftbl Chrldng 85; Bus.

ALLEN, ERIC N; East Aurora HS; E Aururo, NY; (Y); Am Leg Boys St; Boys Clb Am; Varsity Clb; Stu Cncl; JV Var Bsktbl; JV Var Ftbl; Var Trk; High Hon Roll; NHS; Spcl Achvt Awds Acctng I, Chem & Bus Law 86; US Naval Acad; Aviation.

ALLEN, JACQUELINE; Mt Vernon HS; Mt Vernon, NY; (Y); Key Clb; Latin Clb; JV Vllybl; Hon Roll; Suny At Albany; Pre-Law.

ALLEN, JAMES F; Chittenango HS; Chittenango, NY; (Y); 15/184; FCA; French Clb; Varsity Clb; Stu Cncl; Bsktbl; Ftbl; Trk; High Hon Roll; Jr NHS; NHS; NYS Regnts Schlrshp 86; Chittenango H S Mst Outstndng SR Boy 86; Janus Key Awd 86; SUNY Cortland; Math.

ALLEN, JON; Newfane SR HS; Newfane, NY; (Y); Aud/Vis; VP Sec 4-H; Library Aide; Math Tm; Stage Crew; Swing Chorus; Nwsp Rptr; Cit Awd; 4-H Awd; NYS 4-H Elec Energy Awd 85; Rnnr Up 4-H King Niagara Cnty 85; Niagara Cnty CC; Elec Engr.

ALLEN, KATHLEEN M; Sacred Heart Acad; Baldwin, NY; (Y); Debate Tm; Girl Scts; School Musical; Yrbk Stf; Lit Mag; Ntl Merit Schol; Hofstra U; Cmmnctns.

ALLEN, KELLY; Walt Whitman HS; Huntington Sta, NY; (Y); 160/500; Church Yth Grp; Dance Clb; Library Aide; Office Aide; Teachers Aide; Varsity Clb; JV Cheerleading; Im Coach Actv; Im Diving; Var Gym; Merit Awd 84-86; Stonybrook; Socl Sci.

ALLEN, KIMBERLY; Alexander Hamilton HS; Elmsford, NY; (Y); Key Clb; Yrbk Stf; Var Capt Cheerleading; High Hon Roll; Hon Roll; Jr NHS; NHS; Rochester Inst Tech; Cmptr Sci.

ALLEN, LARA; P V Moore HS; Bernhards Bay, NY; (Y); Sec Drama Clb; Sec French Clb; Intnl Clb; Sec Spanish Clb; French Hon Soc; High Hon Roll; Hon Roll; Jr NHS; NHS; Spanish NHS; Linguistics.

ALLEN, MARK; So Glens Falls Central HS; S Glens Falls, NY; (Y); 11/240; Cmnty Wkr; Varsity Clb; Yrbk Sprt Ed; Pres Jr Cls; Pres Sr Cls; Rep Stu Cncl; Capt Ftbl; Powder Puff Ftbl; Capt Trk; Var Wrstlng; Tri Cnty Multiple Listing Schlrshp 86; Vrsty Clb Pres 85-86; St Lawrence U; Aeroncl Engrng.

ALLEN, MARY; East Syracuse-Minoa HS; Minoa, NY; (Y); DECA; Science Clb; Sec Soph Cls; Sec Jr Cls; Var Socr; Hon Roll; Jr NHS; NHS; Prfct Atten Awd; HOBY Fndtn NY Ambssdr Intl Ldrshp Sem 85; Law.

ALLEN, MELISSA; Albion HS; Medina, NY; (S); 15/180; Band; Concert Band; Mrchg Band; Hon Roll; All Cnty Band 85; Engrng.

ALLEN, MELISSA; Franklin Acad; Malone, NY; (Y); French Clb; Band; Concert Band; Jazz Band; Symp Band; Rep Stu Cncl; Hon Roll; Spnsh Awd 100 Avg 86; Elem Ed.

ALLEN, MEREDITH L; Walton Central HS; Walton, NY; (Y); 21/105; AFS; Church Yth Grp; 4-H; GAA; Key Clb; Varsity Clb; Var Bsktbl; Var Fld Hcky; Var Trk; Hon Roll; Roger Williams Coll; Marine Bio.

ALLEN, NADINE M; Northport HS; Northport, NY; (Y); 120/605; Cmnty Wkr; SADD; Band; Mrchg Band; School Musical; Rep Frsh Cls; NHS; March Of Dimes Awd 86; PTA Awd 86; Quinnipiac Coll; Phys Ther.

ALLEN, PAULA M; Brushton Moira Central HS; North Bangor, NY; (Y); 2/61; VP Pres 4-H; School Play; Yrbk Stf; VP Jr Cls; VP Sr Cls; Capt Var Bsktbl; Var Capt Vllybl; Cit Awd; NHS; Sal; Nrthrn Athltc Conf Div II All Nrthn 1st Tm Vllybl 85-86, Conf Acad 85-86; Natl Hstry/Geog Awd 84-85; Clarkson U; Engrng.

ALLEN, PAULETTE; Wyandanch Memorial HS; Wyandanch, NY; (Y); 5/124; Dance Clb; French Clb; VP Key Clb; Mrchg Band; School Musical; School Play; Nwsp Rptr; Nwsp Stf; Yrbk Stf; Hon Roll; Chem And Frnch Awd 85; Per Arts Awds 86; Serv Awd 86; PA ST; Law.

ALLEN, ROBERT; Solvay HS; Syracuse, NY; (Y); 44/171; Art Clb; Boy Scts; Band; Concert Band; School Musical; Hon Roll; Balfour Awd Excllnc AP Amer Hstry 86; Boy Sct Cmp Stff 84-86; U Of MN; Resrc Mgmt.

ALLEN, ROBIN; Mineola HS; Garden City Pk, NY; (Y); Computer Clb; Cert Of Apprectn 85 & 86; Business.

ALLEN, ROBIN A; Southside HS; Elmira, NY; (Y); 28/319; Cmnty Wkr; Hosp Aide; JA; Latin Clb; Pep Clb; Ski Clb; VP SADD; Varsity Clb; Var Mgr(s); Var Trk; Natl Achvmnt Schlrshp Cmmnded Stu 85-86; Prog For Outstndg Negro Stus; Engrng.

ALLEN, SANDRA; Dodge Vocational HS; Bronx, NY; (Y); Art Clb; Church Yth Grp; Office Aide; Teachers Aide; School Play; Off Jr Cls; Sftbl; Vllybl; High Hon Roll; Prfct Atten Awd; Secy.

ALLEN, SHANNON; Linton HS; Schenectady, NY; (Y); Intnl Clb; JCL; Var Capt Cheerleading; JV Trk; Hon Roll.

ALLEN, TAMMIE; Addison Central HS; Lindley, NY; (Y); Ski Clb; Teachers Aide; Yrbk Stf; Bowling; Tennis; Hon Roll; US Air Frc; Comp Prcssng.

ALLEN, TIMOTHY G; The Harvey Schl; Princeton, NJ; (Y); 1/41; Lit Mag; Var Crs Cntry; Var Wrstlng; Ntl Merit SF; Loeb Cup Hghst Avg 84-85; Greek Prz 83-85; Mst Outstndg Frosh 82-83.

ALLEN, VICKIE; Corcoran HS; Syracuse, NY; (Y); Church Yth Grp; Cmnty Wkr; Hosp Aide; Library Aide; Science Clb; Spanish Clb; Church Choir; Yrbk Stf; Vllybl; Apprctn Svc Awd Candy Striper 85; Rochester Inst Tech; Med Tech.

ALLEYNE, SERVENA; Norman Thomas HS; Brooklyn, NY; (S); 32/597; Sec Church Yth Grp; Pres Exploring; Chorus; Church Choir; Cit Awd; Hon Roll; Acadmc All Am 86; Baruch Clg; Bus Admn.

ALLI, ANTHONY R; John Adams HS; Ozone Pk, NY; (Y); Office Aide; Service Clb; Teachers Aide; Band; NHS; 2ndry Hnrs Schlshp 84-85; Prfct Atten Awd 83-85; Radiolgy.

ALLISON, KRISTIN A; Shaker HS; Latham, NY; (Y); Dance Clb; School Musical; Yrbk Ed-Chief; Yrbk Stf; Hon Roll; NHS; Math And Sci Mdl 85; Harvard Book Awd 85; Union College; Math.

ALLISON, MARY JO; Penn Yan Acad; Penn Yan, NY; (S); 9/174; GAA; Red Cross Aide; Yrbk Stf; Rep Frsh Cls; Rep Soph Cls; Rep Jr Cls; Rep Sr Cls; Rep Stu Cncl; Var L Bsktbl; Var L Socr; Outstndng Stu Awd Spn I; NY ST Regents Scholar; Beneficl Hodson Trst Scholar WA Coll; WA Coll; Pol Sci.

ALLOCCA, GINA; Lindenhurst HS; Lindenhurst, NY; (Y); Band; Concert Band; Orch; Bowling; Hon Roll; Accounting.

ALLOCCO, ANDREA; North Babylon SR HS; North Babylon, NY; (Y); 1/464; Am Leg Aux Girls St; Hosp Aide; Sec Intnl Clb; Mrchg Band; Orch; School Musical; Yrbk Stf; Im Vllybl; Ntl Merit Ltr; Val; Colgate U Alumni Mem Schlrp 86-87; Colgate U; Biol.

ALLPORT, LINDA C; Irvington HS; Tarrytown, NY; (Y); 18/108; Drama Clb; Band; Mrchg Band; Orch; Capt Var Cheerleading; High Hon Roll; Hon Roll; Pres Schlr; Rgnts Schlrshp NYS 86; Gettysburg Coll; Mus Educ.

ALMA, ALISA; Greece Athena HS; Rochester, NY; (Y); 1/310; VP JA; VP Science Clb; Orch; Symp Band; Yrbk Ed-Chief; Stu Cncl; Var Cheerleading; Bausch & Lomb Sci Awd; High Hon Roll; NHS; Sci Stu Of Yr 85-86; Notre Dame JR Of Yr Schl Rep 85-86; Cornell Soc Engrs Excllnc Awd 85-86.

ALMANZAR, FANNY; Erasmus Hall HS; Brooklyn, NY; (Y); Pres Frsh Cls; Hon Roll; NHS; Prfct Atten Awd; Achvmnt Scl Stds,Math & Acctg Bkpg 86; Excllnc Spnsh 85; NY U; Scl Sci.

ALMEIDA, ANGEL LOUIS; Cardinal Hayes HS; Bronx, NY; (Y); 10/258; Dance Clb; Library Aide; Yrbk Stf; Hon Roll; NHS; Prfct Atten Awd; 1st Hnrs 83-85; 2nd Hnrs 84; Svc Awd 84-86; Columbia; Aero Engrng.

ALMSTEAD, FRANK; Germantown Central HS; Germantown, NY; (Y); 15/52; Boy Scts; Varsity Clb; Band; Concert Band; Jazz Band; Var L Bsbl; JV Bsktbl; Var L Socr; Hon Roll; NC ST; Comp Sci.

ALMY, KIMBERLY A; Marion JR SR HS; Williamson, NY; (Y); 11/90; Concert Band; Mrchg Band; School Play; Yrbk Ed-Chief; Sec Jr Cls; Sec Sr Cls; Rep Stu Cncl; Trs NHS; Sec French Clb; All Cnty Band 86; NYS Rgnts Schlrshp 86; Nazareth Coll Rochester; Psych.

ALOIAN, PATRICIA; North Tonawanda SR HS; North Tonawanda, NY; (Y); Trs AFS; Trs Church Yth Grp; Ski Clb; Nwsp Rptr; Yrbk Bus Mgr; Stu Cncl; French Hon Soc; High Hon Roll; NHS; Pres 4-H; Distngushd Stu Yr Awd 85-86; Delg 4 H Clb Cong Cornell U 86; St Bonaventure U; Math.

ALOMAR, PETER; Ossining HS; Ossining, NY; (Y); Church Yth Grp; Letterman Clb; Spanish Clb; SADD; Varsity Clb; JV Var Bsbl; JV Var Ftbl; Wt Lftg; Hon Roll; Prfct Atten Awd; Sec One Inc Achvt Awd Ftbl 85-86; Merit Awd Span 85; NYS Pblc HS Athl Assoc Medal Achvt 86; Fordham U; Bus Econ.

ALONGE, ANTHONY; West Seneca East HS; W Seneca, NY; (Y); Boy Scts; DECA; Ski Clb; Var Stat Bsktbl; Var Capt Socr; Var L Tennis; JV Timer; Hon Roll; MVP JV Soccer 84-85; Coach W Seneca Yth Soccer Lg 84 & 86; Bus Admin.

ALONGI, PAUL ROBERT; Plainedge HS; Massapequa, NY; (Y); 29/316; Rep Jr Cls; Rep Sr Cls; Rep Stu Cncl; High Hon Roll; Hon Roll; NHS; Trs Spanish NHS; Rgnts Schlrshp 86; Binghampton U; Bio.

ALONZI, ACHILLE; Port Chester HS; Port Chester, NY; (Y); 4/230; AFS; Ski Clb; Pres Sr Cls; Rep Stu Cncl; Var Capt Bsbl; High Hon Roll; Hon Roll; Mu Alp Tht; Pres NHS; Ciba Geigy Corp Sci Awd 86; Ntl Schlr Athlete Awd 86; Worcester Poly Tech Inst; Engr.

ALONZO, ANNETTE; W C Mepham HS; Bellmore, NY; (Y); VP Acpl Chr; Madrigals; Yrbk Stf.

ALOUIDOR, FARAH; Cathedral HS; Ny, NY; (Y); 14/272; Intnl Clb; French Hon Soc; High Hon Roll; Hon Roll; Span Awd 83-84; Iona Coll Frnch Cntst 84-85; Frnch Awd 84-85.

ALOUIDOR, MARJORIE; St Edmund HS; Brooklyn, NY; (Y); Church Yth Grp; Sec Cmnty Wkr; Hosp Aide; Church Choir; Hon Roll; French Clb; Science Clb; Im Badmtn; Im Bsktbl; Im Sftbl; Frnch Fshn Shw-Lang Fair-1st Pl 86; Phys Thrpy.

ALPACA, LILIAN; New Rochelle HS; New Rochelle, NY; (Y); Girl Scts; Yrbk Phtg; Sec Soph Cls; Capt Cheerleading; Var Socr; Sftbl; Hon Roll; Bus.

ALPS, JOELLEN; Carmel HS; Carmel, NY; (Y); Intnl Clb; Political Wkr; SADD; Concert Band; Score Keeper; Prfct Atten Awd; Psych.

ALRUTZ, MARGARET; Lockport SR HS; Lockport, NY; (Y); 7/411; French Clb; Latin Clb; Ski Clb; Yrbk Ed-Chief; Pres Stu Cncl; Var Capt Tennis; Var Capt Trk; NHS; NEDT Awd; NYS Regnts Schlrshp 86; Brown U.

ALRUTZ, MICHAEL; De Sales Catholic HS; Lockport, NY; (S); 3/30; French Clb; Var Ftbl; Var Capt Tennis; Var Wrstlng; High Hon Roll; NHS; NEDT Awd; Amer Lgn Awd.

ALSTON, MARK ANTHONY; Hempstead HS; Hempstead, NY; (S); 35/216; Drama Clb; Band; Concert Band; Jazz Band; Mrchg Band; Orch; Pep Band; School Musical; School Play; Stage Crew; Regnts Schlrshp Awd 86; Cert Of Merit 86; Trck Awd 2nd Fstst Mile Rely 86; Fredonia; Acctg.

ALTAMURO, PAUL; Frankfort-Schuyler HS; Frankfort, NY; (Y); Pres Key Clb; Mathletes; Pep Clb; Varsity Clb; Yrbk Phtg; Pres Stu Cncl; Var Trk; Capt Vllybl; High Hon Roll; Hon Roll; Johnson & Wales; Chef.

ALTEMUS, ERIKA; Guilderland Centra HS; Schenectady, NY; (Y); Ski Clb; Church Choir; Variety Show; Rep Frsh Cls; Cheerleading; Trk; High Hon Roll; Hon Roll; Jerome Holland Cornell U 86; Cornell U; Engrng.

ALTER, MIKE; Iona Prep Schl; Scarsdale, NY; (Y); 71/251; Church Yth Grp; Cmnty Wkr; Dance Clb; Drama Clb; Ski Clb; Stage Crew; Yrbk Stf; Lit Mag; Ftbl; Trk; Pub Rel Tm 85-86; Big Brothers Coor Cptn 85-87; Christman Drive 85-86; Colby; Bus.

ALTER, ZENA; Fashion Industries HS; New York, NY; (Y); 46/365; Art Clb; Hosp Aide; Library Aide; Service Clb; Temple Yth Grp; Stage Crew; Im Gym; Vllybl; Prfct Atten Awd; NYU; Micro-Genetc Rsrch Scntst.

ALTERI, ALISSA; Notre-Dame Bishop Gibbons HS; Schenectady, NY; (S); 12/88; French Clb; Hosp Aide; Band; Yrbk Stf; Rep Stu Cncl; JV Cheerleading; JV Vllybl; Hon Roll; NHS; Music Awd 84; Psychlgy.

ALTERIO, SUSANNE; Peekskill HS; Peekskill, NY; (S); Chorus; Trs Soph Cls; Sec Sr Cls; Co-Capt Var Cheerleading; Stat Socr; High Hon Roll; Hon Roll; VP NHS; Law.

ALTHAUS, VIVIAN A; A G Berner HS; Massapequa Pk, NY; (Y); 22/412; Drama Clb; Spanish Clb; SADD; Temple Yth Grp; Chorus; Yrbk Stf; Hon Roll; NHS; Ntl Merit Ltr; Cornell U; Law.

ALTMAN, ERIC; Onteora Central Schl; Woodstock, NY; (Y); 7/201; Chorus; School Musical; School Play; Rep Stu Cncl; High Hon Roll; VP NHS; Dir Talent Show; European Hist Awd Bst Stu; Bard Coll Prize Crtcl Wrtng Course; Swarthmore Coll; Pol Sci.

ALTMAN, VICTOR; Brandeis HS; Brooklyn, NY; (Y); Nwsp Sprt Ed; Capt Bsktbl; Capt Socr; St Johns; Cmmnctns.

ALTSCHUL, ILENE; Port Richmond HS; Staten Island, NY; (Y); Church Yth Grp; Math Tm; Temple Yth Grp; Off School Musical; Off School Play; Yrbk Ed-Chief; High Hon Roll; Trs NHS; Drama Clb; Office Aide; Bus Admn.

ALVARADO, ARLENE; John F Kennedy HS; Bronx, NY; (Y); 114/873; Chorus; Composer For The Metro Opera Guild 83-86; Stu Of The Mnth 84; Singer In Off-Brdway Play-Opera 85; Case Wstrn Reserve U; Comp Sci.

ALVARADO, GLORIA; St Raymond Acad; Bronx, NY; (S); 7/68; Computer Clb; Science Clb; Spanish Clb; Nwsp Stf; High Hon Roll; Steno 85; Spnsh 83; Bronx Community; Paralegal.

ALVARADO, JASMINE; Alfred E Smith HS; New York, NY; (S); 2/217; VICA; Rep Frsh Cls; Pres Sr Cls; NHS; Office Aide; Var Bowling; High Hon Roll; Hon Roll; Network Org Of Bronx Wmn Laureate Awd 85; Rensselaer Polytech; Mech Engrg.

ALVARADO, LESLIE T; St Francis Prep; Whitestone, NY; (S); 106/693; Church Yth Grp; Girl Scts; Mrchg Band; Sec Soph Cls; Vllybl; Hon Roll; NHS; Acad All Amer 85-86; Biol.

ALVARADO, MARGARETT; Rocky Point JR SR HS; Rocky Pt, NY; (Y); 19/190; Debate Tm; Exploring; Science Clb; VP Spanish Clb; Church Choir; Lit Mag; Bowling; Hon Roll; NHS; Hood Coll; Pre-Med.

ALVARADO, MARY; Sacred Heart Acad; Manhasset Hills, NY; (Y); Model UN; SADD; Var L Bsktbl; Var L Socr; Var L Sftbl; Tennis; Hon Roll; NHS; 2nd Hrns Iona Frgn Lang Cntst 86.

ALVAREZ, ANGELA; Clara Barton High School For Health; Brooklyn, NY; (Y); Church Yth Grp; Hosp Aide; Office Aide; Teachers Aide; Church Choir; Color Guard; Prfct Atten Awd; Vlntr Svc Awd-Untd Hosp Fnd 84; Merit Awd-Interfth Med Ctr 84; Cert Awd-Brwn Blt-Shotokon/Ju-Jitsu 85; RN.

ALVAREZ, ANGELINA; Beach Channel HS; Far Rockaway, NY; (Y); Church Yth Grp; Cmnty Wkr; Dance Clb; Math Clb; Pres Spanish Clb; SADD; Church Choir; Gym; High Hon Roll; Prfct Atten Awd; Phys Ftnss Awd 83; Prncpls List For Excllnce In Schlrshp 84; Fash Dsgn.

ALVAREZ, CLOTY; Monroe Woodbury HS; Monroe, NY; (Y); FBLA; JV Vllybl; Hon Roll; Cmnctns.

ALVAREZ, DARLENE; Bronx Science; Bronx, NY; (Y); Key Clb; Teachers Aide; Chorus; Variety Show; Lit Mag; Rep Sr Cls; Rep Stu Cncl; Hon Roll; NHS; Spanish Clb; Acad All Amer 85; Chsn Compete Mrtl Essay Wrtng Cntst 85; Cornell U; Bio Mjr.

ALVAREZ, DOMINGO; Eastern District HS; Brooklyn, NY; (Y); Debate Tm; Hosp Aide; Speech Tm; Teachers Aide; Band; Nwsp Rptr; Stu Cncl; Bsbl; Ntl Merit Schol; Spnsh Clss Awd 84; Tutrng Pgm Merit 85; Pilot.

ALVAREZ, GLORIA; Beacon HS; Beacon, NY; (Y); Key Clb; Yrbk Stf; Pres Sr Cls; Tennis; Hon Roll; Jr NHS; Engl, Phy Ed, Pblc Spkng Awds Excllnc; SUNY Albany; Pre-Law.

ALVAREZ JR, JOSE; Murry Bertgraum HS; Brooklyn, NY; (Y); ROTC; Varsity Clb; Bsbl; Prfct Atten Awd; All-Star Game 1st Baseman 85; 2 Trophies-Best Pitcher Of Tm & League 85; Comp Sci.

ALVAREZ, MICHELLE B; St Francis Prep; Hollis Hills, NY; (S); 127/744; Hosp Aide; Hon Roll; NHS; NYU; Law.

ALVAREZ ROMERO, MARIA V; St Francis Prep; Whitestone, NY; (S); 100/760; Art Clb; Political Wkr; Speech Tm; School Musical; Nwsp Ed-Chief; Nwsp Phtg; Nwsp Rptr; Stu Cncl; Im Coach Actv; JV Var Crs Cntry; Comm.

ALVARO, JASON; Cato-Meridian HS; Cato, NY; (Y); Am Leg Boys St; Drama Clb; French Clb; Model UN; Varsity Clb; School Play; Nwsp Stf; Var Bsbl; Var Crs Cntry; NHS; Comm.

ALVARO, KEVIN J; Colonie Central HS; Albany, NY; (Y); Cmnty Wkr; SADD; Off Frsh Cls; Off Soph Cls; Off Jr Cls; JV Var Bsktbl; JV Trk; High Hon Roll; Hon Roll; NHS; Acctng.

ALWANG, KIM; Richmond Hill HS; Richmond Hill, NY; (Y); Church Yth Grp; Key Clb; Mgr Stage Crew; NHS; English Clb; Intnl Clb; Cheerleading; Hon Roll; Jr NHS; Prfct Atten Awd; St Johns U; Cmmnctns.

AMADEN, JAMES; East Hampton HS; East Hampton, NY; (Y); 26/161; JV Var Socr; Var Tennis; JV Wrstlng; Hon Roll; Ecnmcs.

AMADIO, DEAN M; Sachem HS North; Holtsville, NY; (Y); 199/1579; Y-Teens; Band; Concert Band; Orch; Var Crs Cntry; Var Trk; SUNY Fredonia; Music Educ.

AMADOR, MARIANO; Adlai E Stevenson HS; Bronx, NY; (Y); JA; Band; Mrchg Band; Cit Awd; Hon Roll; NHS; Prfct Atten Awd; Chrctr, Ctznshp, Schlrshp & Srv 84; Engr.

AMAN, TIM; Chruchville-Chili HS; Rochester, NY; (Y); 15/330; French Clb; Letterman Clb; Math Clb; Varsity Clb; Var Bsktbl; Var Socr; Var Swmmng; Hon Roll; NHS; Pres Schlr; Ath Hall Fame 85-86; Distngshd Ath Awd 86; U Buffalo; Engrng.

AMANN, KEN; Pelham Memorial HS; Pelham Manor, NY; (Y); Church Yth Grp; Band; Concert Band; Jazz Band; Mrchg Band; Nwsp Rptr; Nwsp Stf; Lit Mag; High Hon Roll; Mth.

AMAR, DANIEL J; Iona Prep Schl; Bronxville, NY; (Y); 77/192; VP Trs Church Yth Grp; School Play; Nwsp Rptr; Yrbk Stf; Var Bsktbl; Var Ftbl; K Of C Awd 86; SUNY Albany; Bus.

AMAROSA, RICCI; Mount Saint Michael Acad; Bronx, NY; (Y); 89/297; Ski Clb; Im Ftbl; Im Ice Hcky; Sandlot Ftbl & Basbl 83-86; Van Nest Ltl Leag 83-85; St Bonaventure U; Commnctns.

AMAROSO, THOMAS M; Newburgh Free Acad; Newburgh, NY; (Y); Drama Clb; Math Tm; Acpl Chr; Church Choir; Madrigals; School Musical; Lit Mag; Var L Ftbl; Var L Vllybl; Hon Roll; Music Cncl 85-87; RPI; Arch.

AMATO, FRANK; Archbishop Stepinac HS; White Plains, NY; (Y); 30/170; Drama Clb; JA; Nwsp Phtg; Yrbk Phtg; VP Soph Cls; Im Var Bsbl; Im Var Ftbl; NHS; Fordham U; Acctng.

AMATO, MARIANNE; Liverpool HS; N Syracuse, NY; (Y); Civic Clb; Pep Clb; Service Clb; Vllybl; Hon Roll; NHS; Rcvd Hnrs; Comp.

AMATO, MICHAEL; Commack HS North; Commack, NY; (Y); 120/400; Var Trk; Hon Roll; North Eastern U; Bus.

AMATURO, LAWRENCE; St John The Baptist HS; Centereach, NY; (Y); Science Clb; Chorus; French Hon Soc; High Hon Roll; Hon Roll; Jr NHS; NHS; WSUC Schlrshp To NY U 86; NY U.

AMBERGE, KYLE J; Addison Central Schl; Homer, NY; (Y); 5/110; Trs Church Yth Grp; FFA; Varsity Clb; JV L Bsbl; JV Im Bsktbl; Im Bowling; JV Var Socr; Im Swmmng; Im Tennis; Im Wrstlng; Regents Schlrshp; Rensselaer Schlrshp; Rensselaer Plytch; Arntcl Engr.

AMBERSLEY, MICHELLE; Evander Childs HS; Bronx, NY; (Y); Color Guard; School Play; Coach Actv; Mgr(s); Score Keeper; Tennis; Vllybl; Gov Hon Prg Awd; High Hon Roll; Prfct Atten Awd; Big E Clb 85; Merit For Exc In Math 85; Accntng.

AMBERY, REGINA; Acedemy Of Mt St Ursula; Bronx, NY; (Y); 2/126; Drama Clb; Nwsp Bus Mgr; Nwsp Rptr; Yrbk Stf; Bausch & Lomb Sci Awd; Gov Hon Prg Awd; High Hon Roll; Hon Roll; NHS; Church Yth Grp; Mc Shain Schlrshp 86; Prsdntl Schlrshp To Coll Of New Rochelle 86; 2nd Marine Dvsn 86; Coll Of New Rochelle.

AMBLER, DOUGLAS L; The Stony Brook Schl; Selden, NY; (Y); 15/84; Church Yth Grp; Chorus; School Musical; Nwsp Stf; Pres Frsh Cls; Var Socr; Var Capt Trk; Hon Roll; Val; Bio Awd 84; Merit Awd 84; Stephen Philibosian Endowed Memrl Schlrshp 85; Wheaton Coll; Pre-Med.

AMBRISCO, ALAN S; Starpoint Central Schl; Sanborn, NY; (Y); 2/179; Am Leg Boys St; Mathletes; Math Tm; Spanish Clb; VP Soph Cls; Trs Jr Cls; Pres Sr Cls; NHS; Ntl Merit Ltr; Nwsp Stf; Starpnt Schlrs Prog 84; Giftd Math Prog U Buffalo 81; Acadmc Tm 86; Case Western Res; Electrcl Engr.

AMBROISE, CARL H; St Anthony HS; Commack, NY; (Y); 44/240; Church Yth Grp; Cmnty Wkr; Hosp Aide; Chorus; Trs Frsh Cls; VP Soph Cls; Trk; Hon Roll; Ntl Merit SF; Spanish NHS; Spnsh Natl Hnr Soc Awd 85; Acad Achvmnt Awd 83-85; Med.

AMBROSE, BEVERLY; Naples Central HS; Naples, NY; (Y); 12/63; Drama Clb; Chorus; School Musical; Yrbk Stf; Score Keeper; High Hon Roll; Hon Roll; VFW Awd; Voice Dem Awd; Gifted Tlntd Clss Gems 83-86; Bnkng.

AMBROSE, CATHY; John H Glenn HS; Huntington, NY; (Y); JV Socr; Im Trk; Acctg.

AMBROSE, CHRISTOPHER KILLIAN; John A Coleman HS; Kingston, NY; (Y); Church Yth Grp; Drama Clb; French Clb; Key Clb; School Play; Stage Crew; Yrbk Stf; Rep Frsh Cls; Rep Soph Cls; Hon Roll; Mt St Mary Coll; Socl Sci.

AMBROSE, VICTORIA; Nyack HS; Nyack, NY; (Y); 99/250; VICA; Color Guard; Stage Crew; Rep Soph Cls; Socr; Sftbl; Cntrl Nyack Self-Help Proj Recgntn Merit 86; Rockland Negro Scholar Fund Awd 86; Brd Coop Ed Svc Awd; Coburn Schl Fash; Merchndsng.

AMBROSECCHIA, MICHAEL; Mt St Michael Acad; Bronx, NY; (Y); 108/297; Var JV Ftbl; Acctng.

AMBROSINO, ALLEN; Albertus Magnus HS; New City, NY; (Y); Am Leg Boys St; Varsity Clb; Nwsp Rptr; Var L Bsbl; JV Bsktbl; Var Crs Cntry; High Hon Roll; Jr NHS; NHS; Ntl Merit Ltr; Engl.

AMEDIO, BRYAN C; Christian Brothers Acad; Albany, NY; (Y); 13/109; Am Leg Boys St; Boy Scts; ROTC; Band; Rep Stu Cncl; JV Var Bsbl; Capt Var Ftbl; Cit Awd; Hon Roll; NHS; Mcky Mntl ST Chmps East Rgnls Rnnr Up 85; Bg 10 Sect II Ftbll Chmps 3rd In ST 85; Service Acad; Engnrng.

AMELL, FRANCINE; Linton HS; Schenectady, NY; (Y); 41/273; AFS; Drama Clb; Sec Intnl Clb; Pres JA; Service Clb; School Play; Hon Roll; Prfct Atten Awd; Mistress Ceremonies J A Banqust 86; Bst Indvdl Achiever 84; Dale Carnegie Yth Schlrshp 85; SUNY Oswego; Acctg.

AMELL, HOLLY; Tupper Lake HS; Tupper Lake, NY; (Y); Sec Frsh Cls; Rep Stu Cncl; Var JV Cheerleading; Mgr(s); Var JV Socr; JV Vllybl; Hon Roll; NHS; Suny At Albany; Med Tech.

AMENDOLA, PAULA; Sacred Heart HS; Yonkers, NY; (S); 2/270; Church Yth Grp; Hosp Aide; Chorus; High Hon Roll; NHS; 5 Schlrshps Outstndng Grds 83-86; Medcn.

AMENDOLARE, MARYBETH; Frankfort-Schuyler HS; Frankfort, NY; (Y); GAA; Pep Clb; Spanish Clb; Yrbk Stf; Bsktbl; Sftbl; Hon Roll; NHS; MVCC; Acctg.

AMENN, SCOTT; Archbishop Molloy HS; S Richmond Hill, NY; (Y); Kean Coll; Marine Bio.

AMENO, CHARLES J; Lancaster HS; Lancaster, NY; (S); 39/470; VP Pres AFS; Church Yth Grp; VP DECA; Rep Sr Cls; Rep Stu Cncl; NHS; Key Clb; Quiz Bowl; Yrbk Stf; Hon Roll; Hugh O Brian Yth Ldrshp Awd 84; Police Athltc Assoc Schlrshp 85; Regents Schlrshp 86; DECA ST Wnnr 85.

AMENO, DAVID; Lafayette HS; Buffalo, NY; (Y); SUNY At Buffalo; Phrmcst.

AMERA, FELICE E; La Guardia HS Of Music And Arts; New York, NY; (Y); Alvin Ailey Amer Dance Thtre Schlrshp 83-85; Peridance Ctr Schlrshp 85; 2nd Pl Stry Cntst Awd 83; Dance.

AMES, EILEEN; Heuvelton Central Schl; Heuvelton, NY; (S); 1/40; GAA; Latin Clb; Band; Concert Band; Flag Corp; Mrchg Band; Pep Band; Yrbk Stf; JV Var Cheerleading; Score Keeper; Sccr Ofnsv MVP 84; Augsbury N Cntry Schlrshp-St Law U 85-86; Boston Coll.

AMES, KIM; Salamanca Central HS; Salamanca, NY; (Y); DECA; JV Sftbl; Stat Trk; Trvl Toursm.

AMES, NANCI; Massena Central HS; Massena, NY; (Y); Cmnty Wkr; Computer Clb; French Clb; JA; Rep Stu Cncl; Var L Vllybl; Hon Roll; Ntl Merit Ltr; Prfct Atten Awd; Pres Schlr; Knights Columbus Scholar 86; Talented Awd 84; Acad Awd 82 & 84-85; Potsdam ST; Indstrl Engr.

AMES, SHERYL L; Elba Central Schl; Elba, NY; (Y); 1/69; GAA; Math Tm; Sec Trs Science Clb; Var L Crs Cntry; Var L Tennis; Var L Vllybl; DAR Awd; Trs NHS; Ntl Merit Ltr; Val; Mt Union Coll Schlrshp Awd 86; Genesee Cntys Jr Miss Pgnt Cntstnt 86; Mt Union Coll; Bio.

AMES, TODD; Westfield Acad & Central Schl; Westfield, NY; (Y); Ski Clb; Stage Crew; Ftbl; Trk; Wrstlng; Alfred ST Coll; Electrnc Tech.

AMICO, MARIA; Bayport Blue Point HS; Blue Pt, NY; (Y); Sftbl; Vllybl; Suffolk; Bus.

AMICO, SUZANNE; E J Wilson HS; Rochester, NY; (Y); Exploring; 4-H; Mathletes; Band; Nwsp Rptr; Cheerleading; Pom Pon; High Hon Roll; NHS; Pres Acad Ftnss Awd 86; Math & Spnsh Awds 84; U Of Dayton; Crmnl Justc.

AMIDON, SHELLEAN R; Waterloo Central HS; Waterloo, NY; (Y); FTA; Pep Clb; Varsity Clb; Color Guard; Yrbk Stf; Trs Frsh Cls; Sec Soph Cls; Sec Jr Cls; JV Cheerleading; Stat Lcrss; Rgnts Schlrshp Nrsng 85-86; SUNY Plattsburg; Engl.

AMIEL, SARINA; Haftr HS; Island Park, NY; (Y); Pres Art Clb; Sec Debate Tm; French Clb; Hosp Aide; Science Clb; Pres VP Temple Yth Grp; Yrbk Phtg; Var Mgr(s); Rabbi Akva Hon Soc NCSY 86; Boston U; Med.

AMIRA, GREG; Midwood HS; Port Richey, FL; (Y); Aud/Vis; Hosp Aide; Model UN; Office Aide; Teachers Aide; School Musical; Stage Crew; Variety Show; JV Crs Cntry; JV Trk.

AMIRATI, ANTHONY; Stepinac HS; Yonkers, NY; (Y); 43/180; Im Bsktbl; JV Trk; Hon Roll.

AMIRUDDIN, SHALIZA; Evander Childs HS; Bronx, NY; (S); Cmnty Wkr; Hosp Aide; High Hon Roll; Hon Roll; Prfct Atten Awd; Bronx Zodgcl Socty Anml Behvr Awd 85; Daily News Acadmc & Prfct Attndnc Awd 85; Columbia U; Med.

AMODEMO, MARGARET KATHRYN; Newfield HS; Selden, NY; (Y); 16/576; Pres Church Yth Grp; Drama Clb; Sec Intnl Clb; School Musical; School Play; Stage Crew; High Hon Roll; Jr NHS; NHS; Yrbk Stf; Stu Ctzn Mnth 83; Chem Awd 84; Gifted & Tlntd Pgm 83-85; Molloy; Nrsng.

AMODEO, LENNY; John Dewey HS; Brooklyn, NY; (Y); Lawyer.

AMODEO, LORI; Newfield HS; Selden, NY; (Y); Dance Clb; Drama Clb; Spanish Clb; Chorus; School Musical; Hst Stu Cncl; Spanish NHS; Mth.

AMOIA, THOMAS; Msgr Farrell HS; Staten Island, NY; (Y); Letterman Clb; Band; Concert Band; Drm & Bgl; Mrchg Band; Orch; Nwsp Rptr; Nwsp Sprt Ed; Nwsp Stf; Yrbk Rptr; Karate; Manhattan Coll; Engrng.

AMON, GAIL; Tottenville HS; Staten Isld, NY; (Y); Cmnty Wkr; Key Clb; Model UN; Teachers Aide; School Play; Mgr Stage Crew; Lit Mag; Hon Roll; Trs NHS; Prfct Atten Awd; Chrmn Fundraising Mod Congress Clb 85-86; Ed.

AMORES, LIZETTE; Cardinal Spellman HS; New York, NY; (Y); Camera Clb; Chorus; Flag Corp; Mrchg Band; School Play; L JV Vllybl; Pre Vet.

AMOROSI, ANNE; Brewster HS; Mount Vernon, NY; (Y); Sec Spanish Clb; Sec Stu Cncl; Cheerleading; Coach Actv; Score Keeper; Tennis; French Hon Soc; High Hon Roll; Spanish NHS; Hgst Avg Englsh 84-85; French Hnr Awd 85-86; Social Stds Hnr Awd 85-86; Manhatten Coll; Lawyer.

AMOROSO, KIMBERLY; Our Lady Of Mercy HS; E Rochester, NY; (Y); JA; Model UN; Varsity Clb; Chorus; Var Swmmng; Var Trk; Awds Accntg & Amer Chem Soc Achvt 86; Biol Awd; Math & Afro-Asian Awds; Accntg.

AMOROSO, TRACY; Mechanicville HS; Mechanicville, NY; (S); 27/105; Church Yth Grp; Spanish Clb; SADD; Pres Band; Pres Mrchg Band; Pres Pep Band; Symp Band; Yrbk Stf; High Hon Roll; Hon Roll; Omega 83-84; Alpha 84-85; Ariasti 85-86; Russell Sage; Elem Ed.

AMORY, DENISE; De Witt Clinton HS; Bronx, NY; (Y); Key Clb; Chorus; Prfct Atten Awd; Good Guy Awd 85; Arista Hnr Soc 84-86; Gold Metal Psng All Sbjcts 86; Med.

AMPUDIA, MARGOT; Eastern District HS; Bronx, NY; (Y); Sec Dance Clb; Office Aide; Sec Frsh Cls; Bsktbl; Hon Roll 83; Awd Span 83-85; Awd Engl 83-85; Long Island U; Translator.

AMRHEIN, ELEANOR; St Johns Prep; Middle Vlg, NY; (Y); 54/454; Church Yth Grp; Cmnty Wkr; Concert Band; Jazz Band; Hon Roll; SR Yr Attndd St Johns U 5-7 Yrs While Still Stu At Prsnt HS 85-86; St Johns U; Accntng.

AMSLER, DEAN R; Marion JR-SR HS; Marion, NY; (Y); Church Yth Grp; Pres German Clb; Model UN; Variety Show; Yrbk Stf; JV Bsbl; Prfct Atten Awd; Recrdng Arts.

AMUSSEN, KIMBERELY; Port Chester SR HS; Port Chester, NY; (Y); Key Clb; Science Clb; Ski Clb; Band; Concert Band; Mrchg Band; Orch; Yrbk Stf; Lit Mag; Tennis; Sci Hnr Soc 86; Cornell; Vet.

AMYOT, MAUREEN; Keveny Memorial Acad; Clifton Park, NY; (S); 5/40; Q&S; Band; Jazz Band; Mrchg Band; Yrbk Ed-Chief; Yrbk Phtg; DAR Awd; High Hon Roll; NHS; Grl Sct Gold Awd; DAR Essy Regnl Awd Wnr; Grl Sct Wider Opprtntes; St Francis Coll; Jrnlsm.

AMYOT, MICHELE; Keveny Memorial Acad; Clifton Park, NY; (Y); 6/35; Girl Scts; Concert Band; Mrchg Band; Sec Frsh Cls; Var Cheerleading; JV Capt Vllybl; Hon Roll; NHS; Prfct Atten Awd; Natl Bus Hnr Socty 84-86; Acadmc All Amer 86; Elem Ed.

ANANTHAKRISHNAN, DHEERA; John Jay SR HS; Hopewell Junction, NY; (Y); 19/519; Hosp Aide; Math Clb; Math Tm; Model UN; Science Clb; Tennis; High Hon Roll; NHS; Ntl Merit Ltr; AFS; NY ST Rgnts Schlrshp 86; 4 Yr Amry ROTC Schlrshp At MIT 86; MA Inst Of Tech; Physcn.

ANASTASIA, CHARISE; Kensington HS; Buffalo, NY; (Y); Computer Clb; Office Aide; Trs Jr Cls; Sftbl; Swmmng; Church Yth Grp; Yrbk Stf; Score Keeper; MVP Awd Sftbll 84-85; Air Force.

ANASTASIO, ANGELA; Fontbonne Hall Acad; Brooklyn, NY; (Y); 19/132; Math Tm; SADD; Teachers Aide; High Hon Roll; Peer Ldrshp Trng Awd 86; Catholic HS Math Leg Trphy 86; Bus.

ANASTOS, PAULINE; Notre Dame Acad; Staten Island, NY; (Y); Church Yth Grp; Church Choir; Cheerleading; Crs Cntry; Trk; Bus Admin.

ANATOL, LESLIE F; Performing Arts HS; Bronx, NY; (Y); Dance Clb; Drama Clb; Stage Crew; Vassar Coll; Comp Sci.

ANAYA, VICTORIA; Richmond Hill HS; Richmond Hill, NY; (Y); Concert Band; School Musical; Yrbk Stf; Lit Mag; JV Bsktbl; Var Swmmng; Spanish NHS; Hon Roll; Jrnlsm.

ANBAR, SHEREEF; Pelham Memorial HS; New Rochelle, NY; (Y); CAP; Im Bsktbl; Var L Crs Cntry; Capt Var Socr; Im Vllybl; Hon Roll; NHS; NC ST Champ Hgh Point Stars Sccr Team 83; 3rd Pl CAP Drill Team 84; Aerosp Engrng.

ANCKNER, AMY; Gowanda Central HS; Gowanda, NY; (Y); 31/127; Church Yth Grp; Drama Clb; French Clb; Girl Scts; Ski Clb; Thesps; Chorus; School Musical; School Play; Stage Crew; CPA.

ANCONA, LARA JEAN; Earl L Vandermeulen HS; Mt Sinai, NY; (Y); 10/298; Church Yth Grp; Cmnty Wkr; High Hon Roll; NHS; Regnts Schlrshp 86; Union Coll.

ANDER, JEFF; Lyondonville HS; Lyndonville, NY; (Y); Boy Scts; BOCES JR & SR Mech.

ANDERER, KRISTEN; South Side HS; Rockville Centre, NY; (Y); 13/300; Church Yth Grp; Cmnty Wkr; GAA; Key Clb; Pep Clb; Service Clb; Varsity Clb; Yrbk Stf; JV L Bsktbl; Var L Socr; NY ST Soccer Team 85 & 86; Select Soccer Tam 84 & 85; Bus Law.

ANDERLIK, JOELLE; Cicero-North Syracuse HS; Clay, NY; (S); 69/667; Debate Tm; Drama Clb; Science Clb; Stage Crew; Rep Jr Cls; Var Tennis; Var Trk; High Hon Roll; Hon Roll; NHS; Frnch Pronounciatn Cont 83 & 85; Intl Bus Law.

ANDERSEN, CARRIE; Waterloo HS; Waterloo, NY; (S); 2/153; Band; Nwsp Stf; Yrbk Stf; Rep Frsh Cls; Rep Soph Cls; Stu Cncl; JV Var Sftbl; Var Tennis; High Hon Roll; NHS; Ithaca Coll; Phys Thrpy.

ANDERSEN, VICKY; Newfield HS; Centerreach, NY; (Y); 43/515; Church Yth Grp; Chorus; High Hon Roll; Hon Roll; NHS; Pres Schlr; German Awd 83; Peer Grp; High Pt NC; Bus Admin.

ANDERSON, ALLIE; Falconer Central HS; Conewango Vly, NY; (Y); 3/124; Church Yth Grp; Pres Computer Clb; Trs French Clb; JA; Quiz Bowl; Scholastic Bowl; Spanish Clb; Teachers Aide; Pres Orch; Hon Roll; Zonta Clb Schlrshp 86; IN U; Frgn Lang.

ANDERSON, ALLISON; Poughkeepsie HS; Poughkeepsie, NY; (Y); 78/178; Church Yth Grp; Cmnty Wkr; Pep Clb; Teachers Aide; Church Choir; Variety Show; Var Capt Bsktbl; Trk; Vllybl; Hon Roll; Bsktbl Schlrshp U Of Lowell 86; Outstndng Co-Op IBM 86; U Of Lowell; Mech Engr.

ANDERSON, ARLENE; Evander Childs HS; Bronx, NY; (S); 7/383; Church Yth Grp; Cmnty Wkr; Office Aide; Service Clb; Teachers Aide; Chorus; Church Choir; Trk; Cit Awd; Prfct Atten Awd; NY Cty Educ Brd Acad Olympcs 85; Cmprhnsv Math & Sci Pgm 85; Cornell U; Socl Wrk.

ANDERSON, CHANDA; A Philip Randolph Campus HS; New York, NY; (Y); 45/166; Aud/Vis; Cmnty Wkr; Hosp Aide; Office Aide; Political Wkr; Service Clb; Teachers Aide; Nwsp Rptr; Hon Roll; Rep Sr Cls; Stu Svc Hnr Citation From City Cncl 82; Gvnrs Cmmtee On Schltc Achvt Citation 82; CSA Ldrshp Awd 82; Shippensburg U; Econ.

ANDERSON, CHRISTINE; Fairport HS; Fairport, NY; (Y); Church Yth Grp; Girl Scts; Yrbk Stf; Rep Jr Cls; Rep Stu Cncl; Hon Roll; Spanish NHS; Art Instructn Schls Inc Art Awd 83; Intercambio Exchng Stu Pgm To Panama 85; Phys Thrpy.

ANDERSON, CHRISTINE; Washingtonville HS; Rock Tavern, NY; (Y); 4/260; ROTC; Varsity Clb; Yrbk Stf; Rep Frsh Cls; Rep Soph Cls; Rep Jr Cls; Rep Sr Cls; JV Bsktbl; Im Crs Cntry; Im Powder Puff Ftbl; PTSA Schlrhsp Stu/Hlth Fld 86; Longwood Coll; Therapeutic Rec.

ANDERSON, CHRISTOPHER; Falconer Central HS; Kennedy, NY; (Y); 21/125; Church Yth Grp; Debate Tm; Pres Trs 4-H; Pres FFA; JA; Quiz Bowl; Ski Clb; Band; JV Var Ftbl; 4-H Awd; 2nd Pl NY ST JR Hlstn Clb Dry Bwl 84; Wstrn NY Guernsey Cttl Jdgn Chmp 85; Agri.

ANDERSON, CHRISTOPHER; Midlakes HS; Phelps, NY; (Y); Spanish Clb; Yrbk Phtg; Yrbk Stf; Arch.

ANDERSON, CYNTHIA L; Fayetteville-Manlius HS; Fayetteville, NY; (Y); 44/335; Church Yth Grp; Model UN; Variety Show; Stu Cncl; Hon Roll; NHS; NY ST Rgnts Schlrshp 86; SUNY Geneseo; Bus Mgmt.

ANDERSON, DENISE; Tottenville HS; Staten Isld, NY; (Y); Ski Clb; Rep Soph Cls; Rep Jr Cls; NHS.

ANDERSON, DIANE LORRAINE; Holland Patent Central HS; Barneveld, NY; (Y); 18/146; GAA; Chorus; Rep Sr Cls; Var Fld Hcky; Var Vllybl; High Hon Roll; NHS; Rgnts Schlrshp NYS, Pres Acdmc Ftns Awd 86; SUNY Geneseo; Comp Sci.

ANDERSON, ED; Fairport HS; Fairport, NY; (Y); Computer Clb; Var L Swmmng; Hon Roll; Exploring; Engr.

ANDERSON, ERIC; John A Coleman HS; Woodstock, NY; (Y); 18/94; Var Capt Bsbl; Var Capt Bsktbl; Var Capt Golf; Hon Roll.

ANDERSON JR, GARTH ALLAN; York Central Schl; York, NY; (Y); SADD; Variety Show; Var Bsbl; Var Bsktbl; Var Golf; Var Socr; Var Swmmng; Lvngstn Cnty Bsbll All-Star Team 86; Pro Bsbll.

ANDERSON, GLEN; Walter Panas HS; Peekskill, NY; (Y); 10/250; Boy Scts; Concert Band; Mrchg Band; Bsbl; Ftbl; Golf; Var Capt Swmmng; High Hon Roll; NHS; Pres Schlr; Rgnts Schlrshp 86; SUNY Stony Brook; Engr.

ANDERSON, GUSTAV C; Centereach HS; Lk Ronk, NY; (Y); 9/429; Band; Mrchg Band; Variety Show; Capt Bowling; Golf; Tennis; Jr NHS; NHS; Spanish NHS; FL Inst Of Tech; Elec Engr.

ANDERSON, HEIDI; Avon SR JR HS; Avon, NY; (Y); 6/91; Church Yth Grp; 4-H; French Clb; Chorus; High Hon Roll; Hon Roll; Jr NHS; Prfct Atten Awd; All-Cnty Chorus 83; GMI; Engnrng.

ANDERSON, HELENE; Saugerties HS; Saugerties, NY; (S); Flag Corp; Var Trk; High Hon Roll; Hon Roll; Math.

ANDERSON, JOSE; Msgr Mc Clancy Memorial HS; New York City, NY; (Y); 4/300; Var Crs Cntry; Var Trk; Merit Achvmnt Awd 86; Vrsty Athltc Achvmnt Awd 86; Baruch Coll; Accntng.

ANDERSON, JUDITH; Panama Central HS; Niobe, NY; (Y); 3/69; AFS; Library Aide; Office Aide; Quiz Bowl; Spanish Clb; Teachers Aide; Yrbk Stf; Tennis; Hon Roll; NHS; Distgd Riflemn Competitive Smll Bore Shtng 83-86; Panama Fire Dpt Rep For Chautauqua Co Fair 86; New England Coll; Med Lab.

ANDERSON, KIM; Waterford-Halfmoon HS; Waterford, NY; (Y); 6/73; Church Yth Grp; Cmnty Wkr; Math Clb; Pres SADD; Chorus; Church Choir; Yrbk Stf; Stu Cncl; Var Capt Bowling; JV Capt Fld Hcky; Rgnts Nrsg Schlrshp, Awd Excel Hlth, Psych 86; U CT; Phy Thrpy.

ANDERSON, KRISTEN; Briarcliff HS; Briarcliff Mnr, NY; (Y); Band; Concert Band; Yrbk Stf; JV Tennis; Var Trk; Hon Roll; Regis Coll.

ANDERSON, LOREN F; Sanford H Calhoun HS; Merrick, NY; (Y); 23/313; Art Clb; Church Yth Grp; Key Clb; Nwsp Stf; Yrbk Stf; High Hon Roll; NHS; Med Exploreres; Soph Clss Commttee; Its Academic; Le Moyne Coll; Bio.

ANDERSON, LORI; Valley Stream North HS; Franklin Square, NY; (Y); FTA; Mathletes; Office Aide; Chorus; Nwsp Stf; High Hon Roll; Hon Roll; NHS; Bus HNR Soc 84-86; Concern Clb Pres; Bus Mgmt.

ANDERSON, LOUISE; St Anthonys HS; Coramia, NY; (Y); 29/225; GAA; Math Clb; Math Tm; Varsity Clb; Chorus; Variety Show; Nwsp Rptr; Yrbk Stf; Off Jr Cls; Bsktbl; Regents Schrlshp 86; Outstndng Female Athl 83; Stony Brook; Comp Sci.

ANDERSON, MARJORIE A; Maple Grove JRSR HS; Bemus Point, NY; (Y); 1/84; Church Yth Grp; 4-H; French Clb; Girl Scts; Band; Chorus; Church Choir; 4-H Awd; NHS; Val; NY St Rgnts 85; Houghton Schlrshp 86; Houghton Coll; Sci.

ANDERSON, MATT; Randolph Central Schl; Randolph, NY; (Y); 3/86; Scholastic Bowl; Trs Band; School Play; Rep Stu Cncl; L Bowling; L Golf; Ntl Merit SF; Debate Tm; Drama Clb; French Clb; Comm.

ANDERSON, MELISSA; Rinerside HS; Buffalo, NY; (Y); Church Yth Grp; Cmnty Wkr; Drama Clb; Library Aide; Church Choir; Pres Jr Cls; Pres Stu Cncl; Bowling; Coach Actv; Gym; U Buffalo; Dentstry.

ANDERSON, MICHAEL; St Johns Prep; Long Island Cty, NY; (Y); 19/450; Cmnty Wkr; Hosp Aide; Nwsp Rptr; Nwsp Stf; Yrbk Stf; JV Bowling; Im Ftbl; High Hon Roll; Hon Roll; NHS; NS Rgnts Schlrshp 86; Boston U; Bio-Med.

ANDERSON, MICHAEL P; Maple Grove HS; Bemus Pt, NY; (Y); 6/84; Am Leg Boys St; Art Clb; Church Yth Grp; Computer Clb; Quiz Bowl; Varsity Clb; Band; Chorus; Church Choir; School Musical; Fredonia; Bio Ed.

ANDERSON, MICHELE; West Islip HS; W Islip, NY; (Y); Intnl Clb; Spanish Clb; Chorus; Bsktbl; Socr; Trk; Hon Roll; Jr NHS; NHS; Acdmc Achvmnt Awd Math 82-83; Achvmnt Awd Phys Ed 83-84; Hnrs Avg Awds 83-86; Pre-Law.

ANDERSON, MICHELE PATRICE; De Witt Clinton HS; Bronx, NY; (Y); Teachers Aide; Chorus; Church Choir; Orch; School Musical; Variety Show; Var Trk; Cit Awd; Hon Roll; Prfct Atten Awd; Howard U; Law.

ANDERSON, MICHELLE; Avon JR SR HS; Avon, NY; (Y); Drama Clb; French Clb; Pep Clb; Chorus; Yrbk Stf; Rep Jr Cls; Var Tennis; Hon Roll; Jr NHS; Gannon U; Frgn Lang.

ANDERSON, MIKE; Middletown HS; Middletown, NY; (Y); Civic Clb; Key Clb; Ski Clb; Teachers Aide; School Play; Nwsp Sprt Ed; Nwsp Stf; Yrbk Phtg; Yrbk Stf; Stu Cncl; Regents Schrlshp 86.

ANDERSON, PATRICK; Gouveneur HS; Gouverneur, NY; (Y); Band; Concert Band; Mrchg Band; JV Bsbl; Var JV Bsktbl; Var JV Ftbl; High Hon Roll; Hon Roll; Jr NHS; NHS; Band Area Al-ST 86; Math.

ANDERSON, PETAL; Sewanhaka HS; Elmont, NY; (Y); 70/342; Service Clb; Spanish Clb; Chorus; Psych.

ANDERSON, RENEE M; Panama Central HS; Ashville, NY; (Y); 5/66; Debate Tm; Chorus; School Musical; Nwsp Ed-Chief; Yrbk Ed-Chief; Hon Roll; NHS; Am Leg Aux Girls St; Office Aide; Pep Clb; Outstndng Wrtng Awd Lcl Nwsppr 84; 3d Pl Amer Lgn Ortrcl Cntst 85; Music Schlrshp Smmr Vocal Cmp 85; SUNY Geneseo; Jrnlst.

ANDERSON, ROBERT; Delaware Acad; Delhi, NY; (Y); Drama Clb; Ski Clb; Nwsp Rptr; Nwsp Sprt Ed; Nwsp Stf; Var Capt Bsbl; Var Capt Crs Cntry; Hon Roll; Prfct Atten Awd; MVP Bsbl, Sr Cntrl NY Bsbl All St, Sasyenango Bsbl All Star 86; Cmnrl Just.

ANDERSON, SHERRI L; Alden Central HS; Lancaster, NY; (Y); 4/203; VP Art Clb; Trs Church Yth Grp; Science Clb; Pres VP Band; Jazz Band; Mrchg Band; Rep Sr Cls; Trk; High Hon Roll; NHS; Rgnts Schlrshp 86; NY St All St Orch 85; Erie Cnty Band 86; ST U Of NY; Chem.

ANDERSON, SHERYL; Prospect Heights HS; Brooklyn, NY; (Y); Dance Clb; Drama Clb; Intnl Clb; Model UN; Spanish Clb; Teachers Aide; Color Guard; Variety Show; Nwsp Rptr; Swmmng; Natl Jrnlsm Awd 86; Radio Brdcstg.

ANDERSON, TELIA; St Joseph HS; Brooklyn, NY; (S); Drama Clb; NFL; Speech Tm; School Musical; School Play; Variety Show; Nwsp Stf; Hon Roll; NHS; Church Yth Grp; Orl Intrprtn Spch Tm 3rd & 6th Pl 86; Dclmtn Spch Tm 6th Pl & 4th Pl 85; Yale U.

ANDERSON, TODD; Cassadaga Valley HS; Cherry Creek, NY; (Y); 65/130; Am Leg Boys St; Camera Clb; Computer Clb; Math Clb; Ski Clb; Varsity Clb; Yrbk Phtg; Yrbk Stf; Var Tennis; L Var Vllybl; U Of Buffalo; Arch.

ANDERSON, TOM; Mamaroneck HS; Larchmont, NY; (Y); Mgr Church Yth Grp; Ice Hcky; Bus Admin.

ANDERSON, TONY; Churchville-Chili HS; Rochster, NY; (Y); 100/272; Rep 4-H; Ski Clb; SADD; Chorus; Nwsp Ed-Chief; Nwsp Sprt Ed; Nwsp Stf; Lit Mag; JV Var Bsbl; Var Bsktbl; Boston U; Arntcl Engrng.

ANDERSON, VIRGINIA; Westhampton Beach HS; Westhampton Beach, NY; (Y); Computer Clb; FBLA; Pep Clb; Ski Clb; Spanish Clb; Drill Tm; Variety Show; Yrbk Stf; Vllybl; Hon Roll; Math Awd For Highest Avg In Intgrtd 3 85-86; Appld Arts.

ANDERSON, WILLIAM C; Jamestown HS; Jamestown, NY; (Y); 76/380; Drama Clb; Latin Clb; Spanish Clb; Off Frsh Cls; Off Soph Cls; Off Jr Cls; Off Sr Cls; Off Stu Cncl; Hon Roll; St Schlr; Jamestown CC; Spnsh.

ANDINO, LUIS; Alfred E Smith HS; Bronx, NY; (Y); Regnts Coll Schlrshp 86; US Navy.

ANDO, NANCY; St John Villa Acad; Staten Island, NY; (Y); Bus Mgmt.

ANDOR, SHARON; Lindenhurst HS; Lindenhurst, NY; (Y); Cmnty Wkr; German Clb; Teachers Aide; Chorus; Var Capt Badmtn; Var Capt Bowling; Var Fld Hcky; JV Vllybl; Hon Roll; Carl Greenhut Awd 866; Keuka Coll; Occptnl Therapy.

ANDRADES, ANGEL; Park West HS; Bronx, NY; (Y); 68/486; Computer Clb; Library Aide; Math Clb; Hon Roll; Gen Sci, Math 84-85; Bio 85-86; City Coll; Cmptr Engrng.

ANDRE, KEVIN; Bethpage HS; Hicksville, NY; (Y); Spanish Clb; Varsity Clb; Nwsp Sprt Ed; Bsbl; Bsktbl; Ftbl; High Hon Roll; Hon Roll; Worlh Hstry Olympd; Pace U; Bus Admin.

ANDRE, PAUL; Chenango Valley HS; Binghmanton, NY; (Y); Am Leg Boys St; Art Clb; French Clb; Letterman Clb; Yrbk Sprt Ed; VP Jr Cls; Bsktbl; Ftbl; Trk; Wt Lftg; Trk All Star 4x100 Relay 84-85; Trk All Star 4x100, Shot, Discus 85-86; All Star Wrstlng 86; Hobart; Comm Art.

ANDREIUOLO, ANTHONY; Archbishop Molloy HS; Jackson Hts, NY; (Y); SADD; Im Bsktbl; St Johns U; Engrng.

ANDRESEN, LISA; Salmon River Central HS; Brasher, NY; (S); Cmnty Wkr; Drama Clb; Pres 4-H; Teachers Aide; Chorus; School Play; Stage Crew; 4-H Awd; Hon Roll; Rgnts Schlrshp; Coll Of St Rose; Spcl Educ.

ANDREW, NEIL; Hoosick Falls Central HS; Petersburg, NY; (Y); 25/130; Var Ftbl; Hudson Vly CC; Envrmntl Sci.

ANDREWS, ALAN; Gouverneur HS; Gouverneur, NY; (Y); Bsbl; Bowling; Wrstlng; High Hon Roll; Hon Roll; Prfct Atten Awd; Acdmc Ltr; US Navy; Nuc Pgm.

ANDREWS, ALAN; Port Jeruis HS; Westbrookville, NY; (Y); Debate Tm; Yrbk Stf; Hon Roll; Stony Brook; Optmtry.

ANDREWS, ALLISON; Clarkstown HS; W Nyack, NY; (Y); Key Clb; Band; Mrchg Band; Yrbk Ed-Chief; Yrbk Stf; NHS; Hstrcl Soc Rockland Awd Excllnce Amer Hstry 86; Lib Art.

ANDREWS, AUDREY; Gouverneur Central HS; Gouverneur, NY; (Y); Varsity Clb; Bsktbl; Socr; Sftbl; Twrlr; Vllybl; High Hon Roll; Hon Roll; Jr NHS; Prfct Atten Awd; Hghst Spnsh II Avg Awd 84-85; All-Nrthrn Rcgntn Vllybll & Sftbll 85-86; Elec Engnrng.

ANDREWS, CAROLANN; Batavia HS; Batavia, NY; (Y); Ski Clb; SADD; Band; Concert Band; Mrchg Band; Yrbk Stf; Rep Soph Cls; Rep Stu Cncl; Owsego Coll; Elem Ed.

ANDREWS, JAY; Fayetteville-Manlius HS; Manlius, NY; (Y); Pres Exploring; Pres Science Clb; Off Frsh Cls; Off Soph Cls; Off Jr Cls; Off Sr Cls; Off Stu Cncl; Grnd Awd Intl Sci/Engrng Fair 86; Persnl Exprmnt On Space Shttl NASA 85:Hnrs Pgm Brkhvn Natl Labs 85; Aerospc Engr.

ANDREWS, MICHAEL; Cortland JR SR HS; Cortland, NY; (Y); Church Yth Grp; Varsity Clb; Var L Bsbl; Coach Actv; Golf; L Capt Ice Hcky; Sftbl; Tennis; Wt Lftg; Hon Roll; Bsbl Cchs Awd 2nd Tm All STR 85; Bsbl MIP 1st Tm All Str, Mst Hts Sea 86; MVP Hcky Offns 86.

ANDREWS, MICHAEL; Midwood HS; Brooklyn, NY; (Y); Temple Yth Grp; Stu Cncl; Trk; Hon Roll; NHS; Publctn Schl Sci Magzn 86; Publctn Schl Comp Magzn 86; Engr.

ANDREWS, PATRICK; Salamanla HS; Salamanca, NY; (Y); Letterman Clb; Varsity Clb; Pres Frsh Cls; Var Capt Bsbl; Var Capt Bsktbl; Var Capt Bowling; JV Ftbl; Im Golf; Im Tennis; Hon Roll; Bus.

ANDREWS, RICH; Senior HS; Dundee, NY; (Y); 5/80; Am Leg Boys St; Jazz Band; Pres Frsh Cls; Pres Soph Cls; Pres Jr Cls; Var Bsbl; JV Var Bsktbl; Ftbl; High Hon Roll; NHS; Phrmcy.

ANDREWS, SEAN; Hahn American HS; Apo New York, NY; (Y); 1/85; CAP; Model UN; Red Cross Aide; VP Chorus; Jazz Band; Mrchg Band; Pep Band; Symp Band; Var L Tennis; NHS; Percussn Sectn Ldr Regnl Music Festvl 86; Hnr Rl Maint 4.0 GPA 83-85; Superior Ratng ST Music; OK Christian Coll; Elect Engr.

ANDREWS, SUSAN; Grand Island HS; Grand Island, NY; (Y); 22/320; Art Clb; GAA; Ski Clb; Varsity Clb; Variety Show; Var Bowling; JV Coach Actv; Var Diving; Var Swmmng; Im Vllybl; Regnts Schlrshp 86; Canisius Coll Deans Schlrshp 86; 2nd Pl Niagara Frntr Leag Divng Chmpnshp 85; Canisius Coll; Bio.

ANDRIAN, CHRISTINE; Fontbonne Hall Acad; Brooklyn, NY; (Y); 8/130; Church Yth Grp; Cmnty Wkr; Drama Clb; Service Clb; Teachers Aide; School Play; Stu Cncl; Hon Roll; NHS; Prfct Atten Awd; 1st Hnr Iona Coll Language Cntst 85-86; Hnr Magna Cum Laude Natl Latin Cntst 86; Awd Catholic Edu Prog; Edu.

ANDRIANO, CLARE; St Francis Prep; College Point, NY; (Y); Dance Clb; Math Clb; Varsity Clb; Band; Capt Socr; Swmmng; NHS; Opt Clb Awd; Premier Amer Athlt 85-86; Cntntl Tms 86; Excptnl SR 85; St Benaventure; Cmmnctns.

ANDROFF, AMY JO; Mount Mercy Acad; Lackawanna, NY; (Y); Art Clb; Church Yth Grp; Science Clb; Yrbk Stf; Rep Soph Cls; Var JV Sftbl; Var JV Vllybl; Hon Roll; NHS; Vet Sci.

ANDROS, ELEN; Midwood HS At Brooklyn Coll; Brooklyn, NY; (Y); 35/667; Church Yth Grp; Dance Clb; English Clb; Office Aide; Teachers Aide; Band; Concert Band; School Musical; Lit Mag; High Hon Roll; Greek Orthdx Archdcs Catchtcl Schl Awd 85-86; Med.

ANDRULONIS, ANNE MARIA; Shaker HS; Latham, NY; (Y); GAA; Latin Clb; Service Clb; SADD; Var L Gym; Mgr Swmmng; High Hon Roll; NHS; St Schlr; Russian Awd 83; Syracuse U; Spch Path.

ANDRUSCHAT, SUSAN; St Marys HS; E Aurora, NY; (Y); Boys Clb Am; Church Yth Grp; Cmnty Wkr; Girl Scts; SADD; Teachers Aide; Church Choir; Color Guard; Drm & Bgl; Flag Corp; High Hnr Role Name Pblshd In Nwspapr 85; Cert Schlrshp In Engl 85; Law.

ANDRZEJEWSKI, SUSAN; Liverpool HS; Liverpool, NY; (Y); 14/830; Cmnty Wkr; Hosp Aide; School Musical; Rep Soph Cls; Var Capt Crs Cntry; Var L Trk; High Hon Roll; VP Jr NHS; Trs NHS; Ntl Merit Ltr; Most Likely To Succeed 85; Latin Awd 82-883; MIP Cross Cntry 84; Regents Schlrshp 86; Cornell U; Polt Sci.

ANDUJAR, EBELISE; Grace Dodge Voc; Bronx, NY; (Y); 2/29; Church Yth Grp; FBLA; Trk; Hon Roll; Top Ten Bkkpr JR Cls 86; Engl Rcvd Blue Awd 86; AM Stds Blue Awd 86; Fordham U; Accntnt.

ANELLO, ANGELO P; La Salle SR HS; Niagara Falls, NY; (S); 10/260; Boy Scts; Band; Concert Band; Jazz Band; Mrchg Band; Orch; Pep Band; School Musical; NHS; Prfct Atten Awd; Louis Armstrong Awd 85; All Cnty Band 83-86; West Point; Engr.

ANGELICHO, MICHAEL; Geneseo Central HS; Geneseo, NY; (Y); Ski Clb; JV Ftbl; Var Wrstlng; Penn ST; Biomed Engr Gentcs.

ANGELICO, GINA; Tottenville HS; Staten Island, NY; (S); 20/850; Cmnty Wkr; High Hon Roll; NHS; Spanish NHS.

ANGELINO, KRISTIN J; Convent Of The Sacred Heart HS; New York, NY; (Y); Dance Clb; Hosp Aide; Ski Clb; School Musical; Nwsp Stf; Yrbk Stf; Lcrss; Ntl Merit Schol; NEDT Awd; Iona Lang Cntst 2nd Hnrs 85; Cert Apprctn Svc Dctrs Hosp 83; U Of Chicago.

ANGELONE, JESSICA; Corcoran HS; Syracuse, NY; (Y); Church Yth Grp; Dance Clb; French Clb; GAA; Hosp Aide; Ski Clb; SADD; Chorus; Color Guard; School Musical; Natl Latin Exam Magna Cum Laude 86; Psych.

ANGERER, SUSAN; Lansing Central HS; Lansing, NY; (Y); SADD; Band; Concert Band; Orch; L Capt Cheerleading; L Var Trk; L Vllybl; 4-H; Ski Clb; Stu Cncl; Area All-ST Bnd 86; All-Cnty Msc Fst 85-86; Rhode Island Coll; Sprts Med.

ANGERHOFER, TODD E; Pittsford-Mendon HS; Pittsford, NY; (Y); Drama Clb; Sec Exploring; Model UN; Nwsp Ed-Chief; Lcrss; Hon Roll; NHS; Ntl Merit Ltr; Engl Comp Awd 84; Math Ablty Awd 85; MA Inst Of Tech; Elctrcl Engrn.

ANGHEL, MARINA; St Agnsen Academic HS; Elmhurst, NY; (Y); 21/301; Drama Clb; Hosp Aide; Math Clb; SADD; Yrbk Stf; Var Vllybl; High Hon Roll; Hon Roll; NHS; Jewish Found Fed Women Schrlshp 86; Christopher Plunkett Found Schlrshp 86; Vlybl Merit Awd 82-86; PA ST U; Engrng.

ANGILERI, ANGELA; Islip HS; Islip, NY; (Y); 28/246; Cmnty Wkr; Office Aide; High Hon Roll; Hon Roll; Pres Acdmc Ftns Awd 86; Wagner Schlrshp 86; Wagner Coll; Pre-Law.

ANGIOLI, MARK A; Iona Prep; Yonkers, NY; (Y); 17/197; Boy Scts; Hosp Aide; NFL; Yrbk Stf; JV Trk; Hon Roll; Ntl Merit Ltr; Mnhttn Coll Pres Schlrshp 86; NY ST Rgnts Schlrshp 86; Egl Sct 85; Manhattan Coll; Engrng.

ANGLERO, ANGEL; Uniondale HS; Hempstead, NY; (Y); Library Aide; Band; Concert Band; Mrchg Band; Bowling; High Hon Roll; U CA; Tv Studio Oper.

ANGLIM, SEAN; Mynderse Acad; Seneca Falls, NY; (S); 32/138; JV Var Bsbl; JV Var Bsktbl; High Hon Roll; Hon Roll.

ANGONA, ERIKE; Taconic Hills HS; Hillsdale, NY; (Y); Band; Chorus; School Musical; School Play; Stage Crew; Cmnty Wkr; FFA; Political Wkr; Socr; Masonic Awd; Cptl Dist Msnc Ldg Schlrshp 86; Awds Ag; Cazenovia Coll; Soc Wrkr.

ANGORA, EDWARD; John Marshall JR SR HS; Rochester, NY; (Y); Var Bsbl; JV Var Trk; Hon Roll; Chlrns Memrl Schlrshp Fund Inc 85-86; Bus.

ANNA, ROB; Batavia HS; Batavia, NY; (Y); 8/197; Red Cross Aide; Ski Clb; Spanish Clb; Yrbk Phtg; JV Ftbl; JV Golf; Var L Socr; Var L Trk; Var L Wrstlng; Hon Roll; Commercial Art.

ANNA, VAUGHN; Moravia Central Schl; Moravia, NY; (Y); Yrbk Phtg; Yrbk Stf; Bowling; Crs Cntry; Hon Roll; Comm Art.

ANNABLE, MAUREEN; Barker Central Schl; Middleport, NY; (Y); 12/98; AFS; Church Yth Grp; French Clb; FBLA; JV Capt Bsktbl; JV Sftbl; Hon Roll; NY ST Rgnts Schlrshp 86; Sci Achvt Awd 83; Genesee CC; Occptnl Thrpy.

ANNAMALAI, ANGAYURKANNI; Potsdam HS; Nashua, NH; (Y); Trs AFS; Math Tm; Band; Chorus; School Musical; Nwsp Rptr; Yrbk Bus Mgr; High Hon Roll; NHS; Fulham Merit Schlrshp Social Sci 86; Law.

ANNAR, SUSAN; Commack South HS; Commack, NY; (S); Drama Clb; Office Aide; Acpl Chr; Chorus; School Musical; School Play; Stage Crew; Variety Show; Hon Roll; Teachers Aide; Mbr Tri-M Natl Music Hnr Soc 85-86.

ANNESE, MICHELE; Cicero-North Syracuse HS; North Syracuse, NY; (S); 17/623; JA; Letterman Clb; Spanish Clb; Var Bsktbl; Var Socr; Var Capt Sftbl; High Hon Roll; Hon Roll; Boston U; Engrng.

ANNESE, PATRICIA A; Westhill SR HS; Syracuse, NY; (Y); Drama Clb; PAVAS; Thesps; Band; Chorus; School Musical; School Play; Variety Show; Yrbk Ed-Chief; Lit Mag; U Of Buffalo; Engl.

ANNESI, CHRISTOPHER; Naples Central Schl; Naples, NY; (Y); 3/85; Am Leg Boys St; Pres Soph Cls; Pres Sr Cls; JV Var Bsbl; JV Var Bsktbl; JV Var Socr; DAR Awd; High Hon Roll; Pres Schlr; Ethel Foster Gray Schlrshp 86; Eng Awd 86; St Bonaventure U; Accntg.

ANNIBALE, LILLINA; St Johns Prep HS; Astoria, NY; (Y); 33/578; Hon Roll; NHS; Rgnts Dplma; Baroch; Bus.

ANNIS, SUSAN; Union Endicott HS; Endicott, NY; (Y); 19/450; Key Clb; SADD; Concert Band; Capt Flag Corp; Mrchg Band; Yrbk Stf; Stu Cncl; Elks Awd; High Hon Roll; NHS; Salut To Yth Prog Natl Cncl Yth Ldrshp 85; Marin Bio Enrchmnd Prg 85; CYO Chrldr All Star 86; Bucknell U; Elec Engrg.

ANSBACHER, DEBORAH; Wantagh HS; Wantagh, NY; (Y); 5/271; Capt Mathletes; Concert Band; Capt Tennis; CC Awd; High Hon Roll; NHS; Cmnty Wkr; Capt Math Tm; Band; Mrchg Band; Coll William & Mary.

ANSCHULTZ, CHRISTOPHER; Shenendehowa HS; Ballston Lake, NY; (S); Church Yth Grp; Cmnty Wkr; Computer Clb; Pres DECA; Ski Clb; High Hon Roll; Hon Roll; Schlrshp Freed Hardeman Coll 86; Qlfd Natl Comptn DECA 86; Freed Hardeman Coll; Bus Adm.

ANSON, AMY M; Eastchester HS; Scarsdale, NY; (Y); Hosp Aide; Spanish Clb; Nwsp Stf; Yrbk Stf; Lit Mag; Tennis; High Hon Roll; Hon Roll; Jr NHS; NHS; Italian III Wad, Iona Lang Cntst Level III 85; Italian IV Awd, Span I Awd, Natl Span Exam Level I.

ANTALEK, MICHELLE; Beacon HS; Beacon, NY; (Y); Sec Key Clb; Science Clb; Varsity Clb; Trs Band; Mrchg Band; Yrbk Stf; Trs Frsh Cls; Stat Ftbl; Var Sftbl; Capt Vllybl; NYSSMA Awd 84; Marn Bio.

ANTCZAK, KAREN; Bishop Ludden HS; Syracuse, NY; (Y); Hosp Aide; Speech Tm; SADD; Var L Tennis; High Hon Roll; VP NHS; GAA; Lit Mag; Natl Yng Ldrs Conf WA D C 85; Holy Cross Coll Bk Prz 86; Natl Cathlc Forensic Leag Natl Spch 85; Vet Med.

ANTELL, CRAIG; John F Kennedy HS; Bellmore, NY; (Y); Key Clb; SADD; Temple Yth Grp; Y-Teens; Bowling; Im Fld Hcky; Ice Hcky; Hon Roll; Prfct Atten Awd; Socl Stds Achvt Awd; Physcn.

ANTES, TANYA; Croughton HS; Apo, NY; (Y); VP Computer Clb; Debate Tm; Model UN; Speech Tm; Yrbk Stf; Cit Awd; High Hon Roll; Hon Roll; Sec NHS; Micro-Biolgy.

ANTHONY, ANNE MARIE; Aquinas Inst; Rochester, NY; (Y); 19/143; Dance Clb; Office Aide; Red Cross Aide; Ski Clb; Color Guard; Cheerleading; Sftbl; Swmmng; Hon Roll; Pres Schlr; Elmra Coll Key Awd 86; Hamilton Coll; Med.

ANTHONY, DAVID; Canisius HS; Buffalo, NY; (S); Drama Clb; Latin Clb; Pep Clb; Chorus; JV Bsktbl; Hon Roll; NHS; Yrbk Copy Edtr 86-87; Big Brthrs Prog 85-87; Wrng Anncmnts Staff 84-87; Notre Dame; Chem.

ANTHONY, FORMICA; William E Grady HS; Brooklyn, NY; (Y).

ANTHONY, JASON; Smithtown East HS; Nesconset, NY; (S); Pres DECA; Model UN; Radio Clb; Service Clb; SADD; Nwsp Stf; Off Frsh Cls; Off Soph Cls; Off Jr Cls; High Hon Roll; DECA 2nd Pl ST Wnnr 86; DECA 1st Pl Cnty Wnnr 86; DECA Cnty Wnnr 85; Real Estate.

ANTHONY, KIM; Solvay HS; Solvay, NY; (Y); Art Clb; Church Yth Grp; French Clb; Yrbk Stf; Off Soph Cls; Sec Jr Cls; Off Sr Cls; Stu Cncl; Cheerleading; Advtsng Dsgn.

ANTHONY, PATRICIA; Oxford Academy Central HS; Oxford, NY; (Y); 5/80; French Clb; Ski Clb; SADD; Band; Mrchg Band; Rep Frsh Cls; Rep Soph Cls; Rep Jr Cls; Rep Stu Cncl; Score Keeper; Bus Adm.

ANTHONY, SEAN K; Somers HS; Katonah, NY; (Y); 11/196; Pres Computer Clb; Key Clb; Nwsp Stf; Rep Stu Cncl; Bowling; Crs Cntry; Socr; Trk; Vllybl; Wrstlng; Hmltn Coll; Dnstry.

ANTICO, LISA; Preston HS; Bronx, NY; (Y); 4/89; Camera Clb; Teachers Aide; Nwsp Rptr; Yrbk Stf; High Hon Roll; NHS; 4 Yr Schlrshp Preston 83; Rgnts Schlrshp 86; Eng Achvt Awd 86; Fordham U; Mrktg.

ANTKOVIAK, AMY; Maryvale HS; Cheektowaga, NY; (Y); JA; Chorus; Sec Orch; School Musical; Hon Roll; Music.

ANTONACCI, DEANA; Smithtown HS West; Kings Park, NY; (Y); Pres SADD; Chorus; Crs Cntry; Trk; French Hon Soc; Hon Roll; NHS.

ANTONAZZO, ANN MARIE; Maria Regina HS; Hawthorne, NY; (Y); Church Yth Grp; Ski Clb; Chorus; Iona Coll; Bus Admin.

ANTONIO, BARBARA; Cattaraugus Central HS; Cattaraugus, NY; (Y); 15/59; Pep Clb; Varsity Clb; Yrbk Sprt Ed; Var Bsktbl; Var Capt Cheerleading; Var Capt Trk; High Hon Roll; Camera Clb; Church Yth Grp; GAA; Wrstlng Chrldng MVP 85; Vrsty Trk Coaches Awd 86; Vrsty Bsktbl Rgnl Champ Awd 86; US Marine Corps; Jrnlsm.

ANTONIO, JEANNE; Hicksville HS; Hicksville, NY; (Y); Cmnty Wkr; Thesps; School Musical; Variety Show; Lit Mag; Rep Jr Cls; Var Cheerleading; Capt JV Sftbl; Var Tennis; High Hon Roll; SUNY; Perfmg Arts.

ANTONIO, JOSEPH C; Kennedy HS; Plainview, NY; (Y); 11/250; Chess Clb; Hosp Aide; Model UN; Science Clb; High Hon Roll; SUNNY; Prfsnl.

ANTONOVICH, DAVID; Union Springs Acad; Woodside, NY; (Y); 5/50; Ski Clb; Varsity Clb; Pres Soph Cls; Pres Jr Cls; Pres Sr Cls; Var Gym; Var Vllybl; High Hon Roll; NHS; Bus Mgmt.

ANTONUCCI, RUSSELL J; Monsignor Farrell HS; Staten Island, NY; (Y); 77/300; Camera Clb; Pep Clb; Wt Lftg; Wrstlng; Hon Roll; NYS Regents Schlrshp 85-86; SUNY Albany.

ANTONUCCIO, LISA A; Solvay HS; Solvay, NY; (Y); Girl Scts; Spanish Clb; Band; Off Frsh Cls; Off Soph Cls; Off Jr Cls; Stu Cncl; Hon Roll; Bus Awd Keyboardng 85-86; Syracuse U; Mgmt.

ANTONY, BOBBY; Archbishop Stepinac HS; Yonkers, NY; (Y); 15/183; Hon Roll; Doc.

ANTOUN, NICHOLAS; Vestal HS; Binghamton, NY; (Y); Am Leg Boys St; Church Yth Grp; French Clb; Trs FBLA; SADD; JV Bsktbl; High Hon Roll; Var Tennis; NHS; Ntl Merit Ltr; Hstry.

ANTUNES, LISA; Pine Bush HS; Pine Bush, NY; (Y); French Clb; Spanish Clb; Chorus; Hon Roll; Jr NHS; NHS; Ntl Hnr Soc Tres 86-87; Fash Merch.

ANUTH, JAMES; Monsignor Farrell HS; Staten Island, NY; (Y); Computer Clb; Rep Frsh Cls; Im Bowling; Score Keeper; Im Sftbl; Comp Sci.

APARICIO, FRANCES; Saint Vincent Ferrer HS; Astoria, NY; (Y); 40/110; Library Aide; Red Cross Aide; Yrbk Stf; Rep Frsh Cls; Rep Soph Cls; VP Jr Cls; Pres Sr Cls; Stu Cncl; Tennis; Hon Roll; Govs Citation Awd 86; Regnts Schlrp 86; Iona Lg Cntst 2nd Hnrs Native Span 83; Pace U; Comp Sci.

APIADO, MICHELLE; Commack HS South; Dix Hills, NY; (Y); Cmnty Wkr; Math Tm; Teachers Aide; Orch; School Musical; Yrbk Stf; Var Badmtn; JV Tennis; High Hon Roll; NHS; Fencing Tm; NY ST Mock Trail Comptn; Stu Recgntn Day 86; Med.

APICELLA, CHRIS; Pelham Memorial HS; Pelham Manor, NY; (Y); AFS; Am Leg Boys St; Boy Scts; Church Yth Grp; Debate Tm; Intnl Clb; JA; Radio Clb; Ski Clb; SADD; Physician.

APOSTOLIDIS, SOPHIA; Flushing HS; Whitestone, NY; (Y); Church Yth Grp; French Clb; Intnl Clb; Service Clb; Concert Band; School Play; Yrbk Stf; Lit Mag; Trk; Hon Roll; Hellenic Amer Edctrs Medal For Excllnc In Grk 86; Bernard Baruch Coll; Intl Bus.

APPEL, JULIE ANNE; Alden Central SR HS; Alden, NY; (Y); 16/160; Trs French Clb; VP Frsh Cls; Pres Soph Cls; Rep Jr Cls; VP Rep Stu Cncl; Hon Roll; Pres NHS; Church Yth Grp; Cmnty Wkr; Dance Clb; French Frgn Exchng Schlrshp 86; Acadmc Awd 3 Yrs; Med.

APPEL, SHERRI; Commack H S North; Commack, NY; (Y); 24/380; Cmnty Wkr; Spanish Clb; Var Badmtn; Stat Bsktbl; High Hon Roll; NHS; Regents Scholar 86; Pres Acad Fit Awd 86; Cornell U; Pre-Med.

APPELBLATT, JAY; Sheepshead Bay HS; Brooklyn, NY; (Y); 82/430; SUNY.

APPELL, BRECK; Faith Bible Acad; Ames, NY; (Y); Church Yth Grp; Drama Clb; School Play; Stage Crew; Yrbk Phtg; Bsktbl; Socr; Trk; Hon Roll; Prfct Atten Awd; Lawyer.

APPIAH, AMA; Niagara Catholic HS; Niagara Falls, NY; (Y); Drama Clb; French Clb; Hosp Aide; Sec JA; Pres Key Clb; Nwsp Stf; Yrbk Stf; Rep Stu Cncl; Hon Roll; Intrnshp Senator Daly, La Salle Soc Club Schlrshp, Cert Apprctn Fest Lights 86; U FL; Jrnlsm.

APPLEBY, BARBARA; Frontier HS; Lakeview, NY; (S); 13/444; Latin Clb; Ed Yrbk Stf; Off Stu Cncl; Var Capt Socr; High Hon Roll; NHS; Nrsng.

APPLEY, BETH; Hancock Central HS; Fishs Eddy, NY; (Y); Computer Clb; Spanish Clb; VICA; Chorus; Drm Mjr(t); Mrchg Band; Sftbl; Twrlr; Hon Roll; Prfct Atten Awd; Most Cooperative Awd/Cosmetolgy 86; Triple Cities Schl/Bty; Csmtlgy.

APRILE, THERESE; Queen Of The Rosary Acad; South Farmingdale, NY; (S); Drama Clb; Chorus; School Play; Nwsp Rptr; Nwsp Stf; Yrbk Rptr; Yrbk Stf; Hon Roll; NHS; Jrnlsm.

APSON, TRACEY; Dodge Vocational HS; Bronx, NY; (Y); 2/30; Drama Clb; Hosp Aide; Chorus; School Play; Nwsp Rptr; Stu Cncl; Co-Capt Cheerleading; Prfct Atten Awd; Acadmc All Amer Schlr Benfts 87; Close-Up Foundtn 87; Howard U; Busnss Lawyer.

APTAKER, LISA G; The Spence Schl; New York, NY; (Y); Cmnty Wkr; Spanish Clb; Yrbk Phtg; Var Bsktbl; Var Trk; High Hon Roll; Hon Roll; Wshngtn & Lee U Smmr Schlrs Pgm Schlrshp 85; Brown U; Law.

APTHROPE, AMY; Mayville Central Schl; Mayville, NY; (S); 7/36; Girl Scts; Ski Clb; School Musical; Yrbk Ed-Chief; Pres Frsh Cls; Sec Pres Stu Cncl; Capt Var Cheerleading; Var Swmmng; Hon Roll; NHS; Syracuse U; Elem Ed.

APUZZI, ANDREA; Walt Whitman HS; Huntington Sta, NY; (Y); 17/479; GAA; Key Clb; Sec Spanish Clb; Varsity Clb; Band; Concert Band; Mrchg Band; School Musical; Im Cheerleading; Var Tennis.

AQUINO, DENISE; Niagara Catholic HS; Niagara Fls, NY; (Y); Church Yth Grp; French Clb; Key Clb; Yrbk Stf; Rep Jr Cls; Rep Stu Cncl; JV Cheerleading; Var Coach Actv; Hon Roll; NHS; Eng Prof.

AQUINO, MAITE; Moore Catholic HS; Staten Island, NY; (Y); Cmnty Wkr; French Clb; Math Clb; JV Var Bsktbl; NHS; Pre-Law.

AQUINO, ROB; Amherst Central HS; Amherst, NY; (Y); Computer Clb; Latin Clb; Quiz Bowl; Ski Clb; Band; JV Var Socr; High Hon Roll; Hon Roll; Yth Engaged In Svc-Outstndng Studnt 85.

ARAI, YUKO; Rye HS; Harrison, NY; (Y); 5/188; Hosp Aide; Orch; Golf; Tennis; High Hon Roll; Parnts Orgnztn Art Awd 86; Wmns Clb Art Awd 86; Barnard Coll; Art Hstry.

ARATO, CHRISTINE A; Centereach HS; Lake Grove, NY; (Y); 2/439; Math Tm; Capt Scholastic Bowl; Yrbk Rptr; Stu Cncl; Var Tennis; Var Vllybl; French Hon Soc; Pres NHS; Sal; Newsday Hgh Hnrs Cmptn Semi-Fnlst 86; Harvard Radcliffe; Intl Bus.

ARAUZ, BRENDA LEE; Walton HS; Bronx, NY; (Y); 45/545; Chorus; Variety Show; High Hon Roll; Im Vllybl; Art Awd 86; Hnr Mrt Shrthnd I 84; Cert Mrt Awd Math 84; Cert Mrt Awd Accntng I, II, III, & IV 85-86; Baruch Coll; Accntg.

ARBELO, ALBERT L; Dewitt Clinton HS; Bronx, NY; (Y); Library Aide; Science Clb; Teachers Aide; Perfect Attndnc Awd 84-86; Pres Sci Fictnclb 84-86; Stdnt Mnth Awd Sci 85; Bio.

ARBER, MICHELE; Alden Central HS; Alden, NY; (Y); 5/164; SADD; Nwsp Stf; Im Sftbl; French Hon Soc; Hon Roll; VFW Awd; Voice Dem Awd; Church Yth Grp; French Clb; Nwsp Rptr; Rfl Clb-Jnr NRA 83-86; Rfl Clb Sec/Treas 84-85; Acadmc Ltr Awd Wnnr 83-86; Ntl Sci Olympd-Hnrb Mntn; U Of Buffalo; Envrmntl Sci.

ARBETMAN, LORI; Roslyn HS; East Hills, NY; (Y); JV Capt Cheerleading; VP Sftbl; VP Tennis; Dance Clb; Temple Yth Grp; Varsity Clb; Variety Show; All Div Sftbl Soph & JR Yr; Mst Dedctd Chrldr Awd; Coaches Awd Sftbl; Tufts; Law.

ARBITMAN, JACOB; Bronx HS Of Science; New York City, NY; (Y); Aud/Vis; Cmnty Wkr; Computer Clb; Service Clb; School Musical; Variety Show; Yrbk Phtg; Yrbk Stf; Bsktbl; Vllybl; Advrtsng Dir Photogrphy Mag; Big Brother; Bio-Ethics Forum.

ARBOUIN, PETA GAYLE; Bay Shore SR HS; Bay Shore, NY; (Y); 87/400; Library Aide; Office Aide; Hon Roll; NYSSMA Piano Solo 82-85; Studied Piano; Lawyer.

ARCARA, BRIAN; Canisius HS; Williamsville, NY; (Y); Model UN; Political Wkr; Ski Clb; Nwsp Stf; Yrbk Stf; Lcrss; Hon Roll; U Of NH; Bus Adm.

ARCARA, CHRISTOPHER M; Tonawanda SR HS; Tonawanda, NY; (Y); 15/210; Var Socr; High Hon Roll; NHS; Regents Schlrshp 86; Buffalo ST Hnrs Prog Schlrshp 86; AHSME Math Comptns Schl Awd 86; Buffalo ST Coll; Englsh.

ARCARA, MARIA; Tonawanda JR SR HS; Tonawanda, NY; (Y); French Clb; Girl Scts; SADD; Yrbk Phtg; Yrbk Stf; Sec Stu Cncl; High Hon Roll; NHS; Outstdng Math Stu 85-86; 7ath.

ARCARI, CHRISTINE; Walt Whitman HS; Huntington, NY; (Y); Science Clb; Drm Mjr(t); Mrchg Band; Orch; School Musical; Symp Band; Nwsp Ed-Chief; Fld Hcky; VP French Hon Soc; High Hon Roll.

ARCHAMBEAU, ANGELA; St Barnabas HS; Bronx, NY; (Y); Church Yth Grp; Cmnty Wkr; Hosp Aide; Office Aide; Speech Tm; Teachers Aide; Nwsp Rptr; Pres Frsh Cls; Im Swmmng; JV Twrlr; Hunter Coll; Med.

ARCHER, CINDY; Mohawk Central HS; Mohawk, NY; (Y); 12/95; Spanish Clb; Hon Roll; Jr NHS; NHS; Kerkimer County CC; Nrsy Educ.

ARCHER, IAN R; Collegiate Schl; Brooklyn, NY; (Y); Church Yth Grp; Latin Clb; Math Tm; Varsity Clb; Stage Crew; Nwsp Ed-Chief; Lit Mag; JV Var Bsktbl; Var Trk; Ntl Merit Ltr; Carl Andrews Jr Mem Schlr 83-84 & 84-85; Leopold Schepp Fndtn Ny 84-86; Pre-Law.

ARCHIBEE, ANN; Camden HS; Camden, NY; (Y); Chorus; High Hon Roll; Hon Roll; Cazenovia Coll; Bus Mgmt.

ARCUNI, CHRISTINA; Mt Vernon HS; Mt Vernon, NY; (Y); Aud/Vis; Key Clb; Mrchg Band; Capt Cheerleading; Hon Roll; Comp.

ARCUNI, PHYLLIS; Mount Vernon HS; Mount Vernon, NY; (Y); Aud/Vis; Key Clb; Cheerleading; Capt Sftbl; Swmmng; Hon Roll; Berkeley Bus Schl; Word Proc.

ARDITO, JOSEPH; Archbishop Molloy HS; W Hempstead, NY; (Y); Computer Clb; Stu Cncl; Trk; Spanish NHS; Adelphi U; Acctg.

ARDIZZONE, MARIO; Smithtown East HS; Nesconset, NY; (Y); Boy Scts; Math Tm; Hon Roll; Italian Hnr Soc 85; Hi Hnrs LI Sci Congrs 86; Cert Of Exclnc Ll Physcs Tchrs Assn 86; Poly Technic; Elec Engr.

ARDUINI, CHARLES; Clarkstown HS North; New City, NY; (Y); Math Tm; Nwsp Rptr; Yrbk Stf; JV Bsbl; High Hon Roll; NHS; Ntl Merit Ltr; German Clb; SADD; Jr NHS; AHSME 1st Pl Clarkstown N 86; Mu Alpha Theta 85 & 86; Econ.

ARENA, DAWN M; Ward Melville HS; Setauket, NY; (Y); Ed Yrbk Phtg; Hon Roll; Jr NHS; Stony Brook U; Med.

ARENA, DEBORA A; Smithtown H S West; Smithtown, NY; (Y); 8/400; SADD; Yrbk Ed-Chief; Stu Cncl; JV Var Bsktbl; JV Tennis; DAR Awd; French Hon Soc; Trs NHS; Brumman Schlrshp Wnr 86; U Of VA; Mechncl Engr.

ARENA, JOANNE; Bishop Kearney HS; Webster, NY; (Y); Church Yth Grp; Cmnty Wkr; Hosp Aide; Rep Frsh Cls; Rep Soph Cls; Hon Roll; Fshn Merch.

ARENA, JOE; Mc Quaid Jesuit HS; Rochester, NY; (Y); 21/170; Varsity Clb; Im Bsktbl; Var Socr; Var Wrstlng; High Hon Roll; Brighton-Pittsford Post All Star Sccr 85-86; USMA West Point; Engrng.

ARENA, NICOLE J; St Francis Prep; Elmhurst, NY; (S); 141/750; Church Yth Grp; JV Tennis; Hon Roll; NHS; Optimte Soc; Parish Lector; Fordham U; Law.

ARENA, TERESA; John Jay HS; Katonah, NY; (Y); Camera Clb; Church Yth Grp; Cmnty Wkr; Girl Scts; Red Cross Aide; Ski Clb; SADD; Band; Concert Band; Mrchg Band; Accntng.

ARESTOU, JOANNE; Lindenhurst HS; Lindenhurst, NY; (Y); Trs French Clb; JV Bsktbl; JV Sftbl; Var Capt Tennis; JV Vllybl; Hon Roll; NHS; Islip Booster Clb Invtntl For Tnns 85; Bio.

AREZZA, ANGELA; St Raymond Academy For Girls; Bronx, NY; (S); 2/68; Computer Clb; Hon Roll; Wood Bus Schl Scholar 85; Outstndng Achvt Bus Studs Awd 84-85; 1st Hnrs; Wood Bus Schl; Exec Sec.

ARGAMASO, SHARLEEN; Mt Vernon HS; Mount Vernon, NY; (Y); 2/550; Pres Church Yth Grp; Jazz Band; Orch; School Musical; Ed Lit Mag; Capt Pom Pon; Pres NHS; Sal; Computer Clb; Hosp Aide; Rnsslr Awd For Excllence In Math & Sci 85; Theodore Roosevelt Hnr 86; Rgnts Schlrshp 86; Duke U; Bio.

ARGENTINE, STEPHANIE; Oneida SR HS; Oneida, NY; (S); 5/200; Am Leg Aux Girls St; Church Yth Grp; Debate Tm; Drama Clb; Service Clb; SADD; Varsity Clb; Chorus; School Musical; Yrbk Bus Mgr; U Schlr U Of Bufflo SUNY 86; Engrng.

ARGENTINE, SUZANNE M; Homer HS; Cortland, NY; (Y); 2/210; Quiz Bowl; Trs Spanish Clb; Pres Frsh Cls; Pres Soph Cls; VP Stu Cncl; Var Capt Bsktbl; Var Tennis; Bausch & Lomb Sci Awd; Cit Awd; Sal; RPI Awd 85; Snghtly Awd 86; Spnsh Awd 83-86; Coll William & Mary; Chem.

ARGERSINGER, DONALD; Amsterdam HS; Amsterdam, NY; (Y); 42/316; FCA; Pres JA; Varsity Clb; Im Bsktbl; JV Var Ftbl; JV Var Trk; Hon Roll; Prfct Atten Awd; Hotel Mgmt.

ARGINTEANU, MARC S; Tottenville HS; Staten Island, NY; (Y); 11/871; Capt Debate Tm; Scholastic Bowl; School Play; Stage Crew; Lit Mag; Var Trk; Pres NHS; Ntl Merit SF; Yrbk Stf; NCTE Awd; Amer Chem Soc Awd 83; Dramtst Guild Playwrtng Awd 84; Surgn.

ARGIROS, PENELOPI; St Barnabas HS; Bronx, NY; (S); 20/188; Intnl Clb; Library Aide; Teachers Aide; Nwsp Stf; Hon Roll; Jr NHS; NHS; Prfct Atten Awd; Outstndng Svc Awd 85; Math.

ARGYRIS, NICKOLAOS; Sachem N HS; Farmingville, NY; (Y); CAP; Ftbl; High Hon Roll; Hon Roll; NHS; Prfct Atten Awd; Outstndng Achvt Awd 85-86; Dowling Coll; Aviation.

ARIAS JR, CELESTINO; Hendrick Hudson HS; Montrose, NY; (Y); 8/187; Boy Scts; Pres Chess Clb; Sec French Clb; Orch; Nwsp Rptr; Lit Mag; Rep Jr Cls; Rep Sr Cls; NHS; Eagl Sct 83; Ad-Aitare-Dei, Pious XII/Cthlc Relgs Awds 82 & 83; Hstry.

ARIAS, EDDIE; Archbishop Molloy HS; Flushing, NY; (Y); Dance Clb; French Clb; Pep Clb; Church Choir; Var L Crs Cntry; Var L Trk; Hofstra; Indstrl Engrng.

ARIAS, ELIANA; Christ The King HS; Maspeth, NY; (Y); 41/451; ; Psych.

ARIZA, DELFINO; Midwood HS; Brooklyn, NY; (Y); Office Aide; School Musical; Stage Crew; Hon Roll; Awd Ntl Spnsh Exm 85; Med.

ARLETH, ERIKA K; Midwood HS; Brooklyn, NY; (Y); 179/589; Church Yth Grp; Drama Clb; English Clb; Office Aide; Band; Stage Crew; Lit Mag; NY ST Rgntsschlrshp 86; U Of MD.

ARMANDI, BARRY; Sachem North HS; Lake Ronkonkoma, NY; (Y); 7/1558; Science Clb; Ski Clb; Orch; Jr NHS; Ntl Merit Ltr; Prfct Atten Awd; Amer HS Math Exmntn 3rd Schl 86; Med.

ARMELLINO, KENNETH; Archbishop Molloy HS; Fresh Mdws, NY; (Y); 68/383; Computer Clb; SADD; Nwsp Stf; Mgr Bsbl; Mgr Bsktbl; NHS; Ntl Merit Ltr; Cvl Engrg.

ARMENIA, JO ANN; Tonawanda SR HS; Tonawanda, NY; (Y); Am Leg Aux Girls St; Pres Soph Cls; Pres Jr Cls; Pres Sr Cls; Sec VP Stu Cncl; JV Var Cheerleading; Cit Awd; Dnfth Awd; NHS; Church Yth Grp; Hugh O Brian Yth Fndtn Awd; Ntl Stu Cncl Cnfrnc OK; Pre-Law.

ARMENIO, KAREN; Manhasset HS; Manhasset, NY; (Y); French Clb; GAA; Service Clb; Capt Var Tennis; High Hon Roll; Trs Jr NHS; NHS; Rotary Awd; All Cnfrnc, All Cnty & All ST Tns Hnrs 85; Yth Merit Awd For Cmnty Srv 86.

ARMER, LAURA; Ballston Spa HS; Ballston Spa, NY; (Y); 21/236; Cmnty Wkr; FBLA; Office Aide; SADD; JV Trk; High Hon Roll; NHS; Coll Of St Rose Acadmc Schlrshp 85-86; Sartga Bus & Prfssnl Wmns Assn Schlrshp 86; Coll Of St Rose; Bio-Chem.

ARMISON, DIANE; Fillmore Central HS; Fillmore, NY; (Y); 18/60; Pres Church Yth Grp; School Musical; School Play; Variety Show; Var Trk; Hon Roll; Varsity Clb; Chorus; Church Choir; Nwsp Rptr; Cert Of Merit By Sibley, Lindsay & Curr Co 86; 1st Pl Schlrshp Teen N Tlnt 85-86; 3rd Pl Track 84; Monroe CC; Chrstn Sngr.

ARMOLD, JULIE; Geneseo Central HS; Groveland, NY; (Y); Church Yth Grp; Chorus.

ARMSTRONG, AUSTIN; John A Coleman HS; Saugerties, NY; (S); Boy Scts; Band; Chorus; Jazz Band; Stage Crew; Trk; Hon Roll; Ntl Merit Ltr; Order Of Arrow 83; Ad Altarei Dei 84; Northeast Area Coll; Pre-Med.

ARMSTRONG, CHRISTINE; Scio Central HS; Scio, NY; (S); 4/48; Model UN; Chorus; Trs Frsh Cls; Pres Soph Cls; High Hon Roll; Jr NHS; NHS; Bio-Engr.

ARMSTRONG, CRYSTAL; Camden Central HS; Blossvale, NY; (Y); Teachers Aide; High Hon Roll; Hon Roll; Cazenovia Coll; Nrsg.

ARMSTRONG, DIANE; Vestal SR HS; Vestal, NY; (Y); 86/435; Sec Church Yth Grp; Ski Clb; Church Choir; Color Guard; Drill Tm; VP Mrchg Band; Symp Band; Twrlr; Hon Roll; NHS; Faun Wkmn Mem Schlrshp 86; Mrtrs Actvty Awd Stl Band 86; SUNY Cobleskill; Wrd Prcssng.

ARMSTRONG, MICHAEL; Vernon Verona Sherrill Central Schl; Verona, NY; (Y); Pres Church Yth Grp; FCA; Spanish Clb; Church Choir; Drm & Bgl; Var Capt Bsktbl; Var L Trk; High Hon Roll; Hon Roll; NHS; Atlantic COLL; Envrmntl.

ARMSTRONG, RHEA; Lansingburgh HS; Troy, NY; (Y); Drama Clb; Color Guard; School Play; Trk; High Hon Roll; Hon Roll; Jr NHS; Cmpatr Tchnlgy.

ARMSTRONG, TANYA C; F H La Guardia H S Of Music Of Arts; Queensvillage, NY; (Y); Library Aide; Office Aide; Stage Crew; Yrbk Stf; Rep Jr Cls; Rep Sr Cls; Rep Stu Cncl; Cheerleading; Semi-Annl Awds-Partcptn 82-86; Intr Dsgn.

ARMUS, LAUREN; Sachem North HS; Holbrook, NY; (Y); 20/1368; Cmnty Wkr; Science Clb; Ski Clb; Spanish Clb; Sec Temple Yth Grp; Jr NHS; NHS; JV Tennis; Cornell U; Bus.

ARNALDOS, MARIA; Notre Dame Acad; Staten Island, NY; (Y); 4/93; Dance Clb; Intnl Clb; Trs Science Clb; Var Socr; NHS; Notre Dame Awd; Amedal Assoc Lng Instrctr Staten Islnd 86; Mst Imprvd Plyr Sccr 86; NY U; Intl Bus.

ARNAU, MICHAEL; West Hampton Beach HS; Westhampton Beach, NY; (Y); Nwsp Stf; Var Socr; Jrnlsm.

ARNDT, ROBERT; Greece Athena HS; Rochester, NY; (Y); 23/320; Boy Scts; Math Clb; Teachers Aide; JV Ftbl; Im Mgr Socr; Im Mgr Sftbl; High Hon Roll; Hon Roll; NHS; Prfct Atten Awd; Bio.

ARNOLD, CRAIG; Victor Central SR HS; Victor, NY; (Y); 25/228; Boy Scts; Quiz Bowl; Ski Clb; Band; Concert Band; Jazz Band; Mrchg Band; Pep Band; Tennis; High Hon Roll; Pres Physcl Ftns Awds 83-86.

ARNOLD, JENNIFER; Cicero-North Syracuse HS; Mattydale, NY; (S); 20/613; VP Church Yth Grp; Drama Clb; SADD; Chorus; School Musical; School Play; Nwsp Ed-Chief; Stu Cncl; JV Cheerleading; VP CNS Soc 85-86; Perfmg Arts.

ARNOLD, KIM; John F Kennedy HS; Utica, NY; (Y); Cmnty Wkr; Hosp Aide; Yrbk Ed-Chief; Yrbk Stf; Off Stu Cncl; Bowling; Cheerleading; Hon Roll; NHS; Accntnt.

ARNOLD, KIMBERLY; St John The Baptist HS; W Gilgo Beach, NY; (Y); Model UN; Ski Clb; SADD; Hon Roll; Rep Frsh Cls; Pres Soph Cls; Pres Jr Cls; Ldrshp Merit Awd 86; Soc Studies Merit Awd 85; Humanities.

ARNOLD, MELISSA; Watkins Glen HS; Watkins Glen, NY; (Y); 14/111; VP Drama Clb; SADD; Band; Chorus; Nwsp Stf; Sec Sr Cls; Cheerleading; Hon Roll; Prfct Atten Awd; Math Clb; Elmira Key Awd, 4th Rnnr Up Miss Schuylar Co Teenager, 5th Rnnr Up Miss Southern Tier 86; Houghton Coll; Mus.

ARNOLD, PATRICIA H; South Side HS; Rockville Ctr, NY; (Y); 5/297; Exploring; Key Clb; Science Clb; SADD; Band; Yrbk Stf; Cit Awd; High Hon Roll; Jr NHS; Sec NHS; Regents Schlrshp 86; SUNY Binghamton; Psych.

ARNOLD, RICHARD; Schoharie Central Schl; Schoharie, NY; (Y); Cmnty Wkr; FFA; Hon Roll; Prfct Atten Awd; Vlntr Fire Dpt 85-86; Ag.

ARNONE, JENNIFER; Mt Mercy Acad; W Seneca, NY; (Y); Chorus; Off Jr Cls; Off Sr Cls; Var Capt Bowling; JV Var Sftbl; JV Vllybl; All Cath Awd, MVP Bwlng 86; All Cath Awd Sftbl 85.

ARNONE, MICHAEL; Marcellus SR HS; Camillus, NY; (Y); 41/167; Band; JV Bsbl; Var L Bsktbl; Cit Awd; High Hon Roll; Hon Roll; NHS; Rgnts Schlrshp 86; NY ST U Bfl.

ARNZEN, DANIEL; Amityville Memorial HS; Amityville, NY; (Y); 3/200; Chess Clb; Debate Tm; Math Clb; Math Tm; NFL; Science Clb; Band; Concert Band; Mrchg Band; Orch; Presdntl Acad Ftns Awd 86; Rensselaer Schlrshp 86; Rensselaer Polytech Inst; Eng.

AROCHO, JANETTE; Eastern District HS; Brooklyn, NY; (Y); French Clb; Library Aide; Chorus; Gym; French Hon Soc; Hon Roll; NHS; Prfct Atten Awd; Sec Frsh Cls; Rep Jr Cls; Schlstc Achv Bus Ed Awd 85; Schlstc Achvt Engl Awd 86; Sclstc Achvt Hlth Ed Awd 86; NY U; Accntng.

AROCHO, VANCE A; Wallkill SR HS; Wallkill, NY; (Y); 7/193; Boy Scts; Church Yth Grp; Im Mgr Bsktbl; Im Tennis; High Hon Roll; Hon Roll; Ntl Merit Ltr; Regnts Schlrshp 85; Schlrst Fairleigh Dickinson U 86; Schlrshp Stevens Inst Tech 86; Elec Engrng.

ARON, DAVID; Stoyvesant HS; New York, NY; (Y); VP Socr; Hon Roll; Y-Teens; Jr Cls; Gold Pin Jerusalem Culture Test 85; U MI.

AROSTEGUI, CARLOS; Newtown HS; Elmhurst, NY; (Y); Church Yth Grp; Office Aide; Teachers Aide; Orch; Stage Crew; Tennis; Hon Roll; Prfct Atten Awd; 2nd Sci Fair, Cert/Pin Most Svc Credits 84; Cert Merit Civics 86; Comp Engrng.

ARQUETTE, TODD; Hudson Falls Central SR HS; Hudson Fls, NY; (Y); 26/225; JV Var Bsbl; JV Var Ftbl; JV Var Wt Lftg; High Hon Roll; Hon Roll; Jr NHS; Fthlls Cncl All Str Ptchr-Bsbl 86; Fthlls Cncl Att Str Ftbl Tm 85; Marine Bio.

ARRAIZ, LISA; Trott Vocational HS; Niagara Falls, NY; (Y); 75/143; Var Capt Cheerleading; Nrsng.

ARRAS, ANNETTE D; Pittsford Mendon HS; Pittsford, NY; (Y); Church Yth Grp; Model UN; Service Clb; Pres SADD; Church Choir; Yrbk Stf; JV Var Tennis; Var Trk; NY ST Regents Scholar; Boston Coll; Bus Mngmnt.

ARRASJID, DANIEL D; Bennett HS; Buffalo, NY; (Y); #7 In Class; Chess Clb; Pres Computer Clb; 4-H; French Clb; Library Aide; Math Tm; Stage Crew; Nwsp Stf; Hon Roll; NHS; NY St Regents Schlrshp 86; Natl Hnr Soc Of Secondary Schl 86; Buffalo News 84; Suny Ctr Buffalo; Comp Sci.

ARRICALE, FRANCES J M; Saint Francis Prep; Bayside, NY; (S); 226/653; Pres Church Yth Grp; Office Aide; Band; Im Sftbl; Law.

ARRINDELL, LISA C; High School Of Performing Arts; Brooklyn, NY; (Y); 65/551; Dance Clb; Drama Clb; Pres JA; School Play; Nwsp Ed-Chief; Yrbk Stf; Rep Frsh Cls; Rep Sr Cls; Rep Stu Cncl; High Hon Roll; Drama.

ARROYO, ROBERT; Manhasset HS; Manhasset, NY; (Y); Debate Tm; Drama Clb; Speech Tm; Chorus; School Musical; School Play; Nwsp Stf; Ntl Merit SF; St Schlr; Smmr Stud Grnt WA Semnr 85; Poltcs.

ARSENAULT, MARC WM; Niskayuna HS; Schenectady, NY; (Y); Art Clb; Drama Clb; Band; School Musical; School Play; Nwsp Stf; Lit Mag; Ntl Merit Ltr; Rgnts Schlrshp 86; Wmns Clb Awds 86; Schl Off Visual Arts Schlrshp Semi-Fnlst 86; Schl Of Visual Arts; Film.

ARSENAULT, MICHAEL; Naples Central Schl; Naples, NY; (Y); 23/67; Am Leg Boys St; Boy Scts; Ski Clb; Chorus; School Play; Socr; Swmmng; Elec Engrng.

ARTETA, PAUL; Wallkill SR HS; Wallkill, NY; (Y); 37/197; Aud/Vis; Boy Scts; Band; Concert Band; Jazz Band; Pep Band; Symp Band; Rep Soph Cls; JV Var Bsbl; Im Capt Bsktbl; Cortland; Law.

ARTIN, KATHRYN A; Villa Maria Acad; Cheektowaga, NY; (Y); Computer Clb; Girl Scts; Math Clb; Ski Clb; SADD; Chorus; Church Choir; Yrbk Rptr; Yrbk Stf; Rep Jr Cls; Schl West Point; Hist.

ARTINI, MISSY; Solvay HS; Solvay, NY; (Y); Church Yth Grp; Cmnty Wkr; Off Frsh Cls; Off Soph Cls; Off Jr Cls; Gym; Socr; Hon Roll; Geneseo; Acctg.

ARVANS, MARY; Huntington HS; Huntington, NY; (Y); Hosp Aide; Key Clb; Concert Band; Jazz Band; Mrchg Band; Orch; NHS; All ST Band Flute 86; Psych.

ASAAD, KEYSA; St Edmund HS; Brooklyn, NY; (S); Nwsp Stf; Hon Roll; Rlgn Awd 84; Gnrl Excllnc Awd 85; Phrmcy.

ASCIONE, YOLANDA; Gates-Chili HS; Rochester, NY; (Y); Cert Of Merit Diabetes Cntrl 82; Stu Achvt Musc Tchrs Assoc, Stu Audtns Hnrs 84; Psych.

ASDAL, KRISTIN; Susan E Wagner HS; Staten Island, NY; (Y); 19/466; VP Church Yth Grp; Chorus; Church Choir; School Musical; Rep Church Yth Grp; DAR Awd; High Hon Roll; NHS; Soroptmst Intl Yth Ctznshp Awd 86; Rgnts Schlrshp 86; Hofstra U; Cmmnctns.

ASH, BONNIE; Tonawanda JR SR HS; Tonawanda, NY; (Y); Hosp Aide; Library Aide; Ski Clb; Pres Spanish Clb; SADD; Rep Stu Cncl; Marshall U; Ed.

ASH, CHRISTINA; Paul V Moore HS; Cleveland, NY; (Y); Church Yth Grp; Cmnty Wkr; GAA; Band; Rep Stu Cncl; Var L Bsktbl; JV Var Socr; JV Sftbl; Hon Roll; 1st Runner-Up MS Oneida Lake Pageant 85; Social Sci.

ASHBY, HOPE; The Masters Schl; New York, NY; (Y); Lib Chorus; Swing Chorus; Nwsp Rptr; Mgr(s); Cit Awd; Hon Roll; Cornell; Pre-Med.

ASHBY, PHILLIP; Abraham Lincoln Place HS; Brooklyn, NY; (Y); Ftbl; Bio,Gen Sci 84-86; NY U; Pre-Med.

ASHE, CHRISSY; The Franciscan Acad; Syracuse, NY; (Y); VP FBLA; Stage Crew; Nwsp Rptr; Yrbk Stf; VP Sr Cls; Capt Cheerleading; Var Sftbl; Var Vllybl; Hon Roll; NHS; Ntl Bus Hnr Soc 85-87; Mst Achvd Engl Hnrs 85-86; Mst Achvd-Accntng 85-86; Comm.

ASHE, KENDRICK; Frankfort-Schuyler HS; Frankfort, NY; (S); 35/102; Trs Art Clb; Key Clb; PAVAS; Boy Scts; Cmnty Wkr; Drama Clb; Math Clb; Pep Clb; Spanish Clb; SADD; Summer Schl Of The Arts-Fredonia 85; Ad Dsgn.

ASHE, MEGAN M; Southampton HS; Southampton, NY; (Y); 33/115; GAA; Band; Jazz Band; School Musical; Nwsp Stf; Yrbk Stf; Ed Lit Mag; Sec Sr Cls; Rep Stu Cncl; Var Cheerleading; Wstrn MD Coll; Ltry.

ASHER, DEBRA; Canarsie HS; Brooklyn, NY; (Y); Am Leg Aux Girls St; Civic Clb; Key Clb; Pres Service Clb; School Musical; Rep Stu Cncl; Pom Pon; Tennis; Hon Roll; Debate Tm; Citywide Wnnr Apartheid Essay Cntst 86; Intrvwd WABC AM 77 Radio Sta NY 86; Spec Awd Excel Soc Stds; Lawyer.

ASHER, ROBERT; Batavia SR HS; Batavia, NY; (Y); 45/200; Church Yth Grp; English Clb; Rep Political Wkr; Ski Clb; Concert Band; Jazz Band; School Musical; Variety Show; Var L Socr; NCTE Awd; Eng Merit Awd 84-85; Lit.

ASHLEY, EDDIE; Bitburg American HS; Apo Ny, NY; (Y); Am Leg Boys St; Church Yth Grp; Cmnty Wkr; Im Badmtn; Im Bsbl; JV Bsktbl; Var Capt Ftbl; JV Trk; Im Vllybl; Im Wt Lftg.

ASHLINE, LYNN; Franklin Acad; Malone, NY; (Y); 11/266; Church Yth Grp; French Clb; Hosp Aide; Pep Clb; Yrbk Stf; Cheerleading; DAR Awd; Hon Roll; NHS; NY ST Regents Schlrshp 86; Russell Sage Coll; Phy Ther.

ASHMAN, CHERYL; Fairport HS; Fairport, NY; (Y); Library Aide; Ski Clb; Var L Fld Hcky; Var L Sftbl; Var L Swmmng; Hon Roll; Phys Thrpy.

ASHRAF, SABA; Bethpage HS; Bethpage, NY; (Y); 15/303; Cmnty Wkr; French Clb; Office Aide; Science Clb; SADD; Teachers Aide; Chorus; French Hon Soc; High Hon Roll; NHS; Med.

ASIF, M KAMIL; Port Jervis HS; Sparrow Bush, NY; (Y); 3/185; Debate Tm; Math Tm; NFL; Nwsp Rptr; Nwsp Sprt Ed; Ed Nwsp Stf; High Hon Roll; Pres NHS; St Schlr; 3rd Pl Bar Assn Essay Cntst 83; Syracuse U; Elec Engrng.

ASKA-JACKSON, CLAUDE; Park West HS; New York, NY; (Y); Var Bsktbl; Acctg.

ASKEROVA, IRAIDA; Midwood HS; Brooklyn, NY; (Y); 213/667; Office Aide; Band; Concert Band; School Play; Hon Roll; Dntl.

ASPECADA, MARIA; Dominican Commercial HS; Jamaica, NY; (Y); 42/288; Yrbk Rptr; Yrbk Stf.

ASPROMONTI, VINCENT; Smithtown HS West; Smithtown, NY; (Y); Cmnty Wkr; Bsktbl; Ice Hcky; Socr; Trk; 1st Tm All Leag Sccr; Italian Hnr Soc; Marist Coll; Accntng.

ASSANTE, ANTHONY; Valley Stream Central HS; Valley Stream, NY; (Y); Ski Clb; SADD; Variety Show; JV Bsbl; JV Var Bowling; JV Socr; Hon Roll; Accntng.

ASSELTA, GINA; Sacred Heart Acad; Garden City, NY; (Y); Art Clb; Church Yth Grp; Cmnty Wkr; PAVAS; Chorus; School Musical; Hon Roll; NHS; All Cnty Band 84.

ATANASIO, MARC; Ward Melville HS; S Setauket, NY; (Y); 125/735; Church Yth Grp; Cmnty Wkr; Drama Clb; School Musical; School Play; Ice Hcky; Swmmng; High Hon Roll; Hon Roll; Oral Roberts U.

ATHANAS, CHRISTINA HELEN; Commack HS North; E Northport, NY; (Y); Church Yth Grp; Yrbk Stf; Lit Mag; Trs Jr Cls; Trs Sr Cls; JV Tennis; Hon Roll; Bus Manag.

ATHANAS, LAUREN; Northport HS; E Northport, NY; (Y); Cmnty Wkr; Model UN; Political Wkr; Nwsp Rptr; Nwsp Stf; Yrbk Rptr; Yrbk Stf; Lit Mag; Jr Cls; Drama Clb; SUNY Oswego; Crtv Wrtg.

ATHANS, ROBERT; Cicero-N Syracuse HS; N Syracuse, NY; (S); 10/667; German Clb; Math Tm; Ski Clb; Stu Cncl; Bausch & Lomb Sci Awd; High Hon Roll; NHS; Opt Clb Awd; Engrng.

ATHERTON, DUANE; Bolivar Central Schl; Little Genesee, NY; (Y); 3/60; Am Leg Boys St; School Musical; Variety Show; Var L Bsbl; Var L Bsktbl; Var L Ftbl; Var L Wt Lftg; High Hon Roll; Hon Roll; NHS; Cls C Sec V Bsbl Chmpns 85; Allgny Co Hghschl Bsbl 85-86; Math.

ATHERTON, KIMBERLY; Greenwood Central HS; Canisteo, NY; (S); 1/30; 4-H; FFA; Capt Quiz Bowl; Concert Band; Mrchg Band; Yrbk Ed-Chief; Var Capt Bsktbl; Var Capt Socr; High Hon Roll; Pres NHS; Cnty Govt Intrn Prgm 85; Hgh Indivdl NE Dairy Jdgng Cont; Cornell U; Animl Sci.

ATKATZ, JACQUELINE; La Guardia HS; Bronx, NY; (Y); 36/500; Tn Ag Amer Gftd & Tlntd Dnc 84-85; Plc Athltc Lg Ltry Awd 84-85; Natl Fndtn Arts Fnlst 85-86.

ATKATZ, JACQUELINE; La Guardia HS Of Music & Arts; Teaneck, NJ; (Y); 12/121; Trip To NYC-ALL Amer Girl Fnlst 84; 1st Pl Publctn Daily News-Stories Wrttn By Yng Adlts 84; NY U; Concert Dncr.

ATKIN, ANDREW; Rocky Point HS; Rocky Point, NY; (S); 20/175; Drama Clb; FTA; Pres Radio Clb; Thesps; School Musical; School Play; Hon Roll; NHS; Psych.

ATKINS, LARA; Homer HS; Homer, NY; (Y); 13/250; Pres 4-H; French Clb; Orch; Yrbk Phtg; Yrbk Stf; Rep Stu Cncl; JV Var Fld Hcky; JV Var Vllybl; High Hon Roll; NHS; U Of WI; Anthrplgy.

ATKINS, PAUL S; Sheepsherd Bay HS; Brooklyn, NY; (Y); 4/440; Am Leg Boys St; Boy Scts; Nwsp Ed-Chief; Yrbk Stf; VP Sr Cls; Ntl Merit SF; Lynchburg Coll Hopwood Schlrshp 85; Hellraiser Of Month 85.

ATKINSON, FRED; Saranac Central HS; Saranac, NY; (S); 19/127; Computer Clb; Yrbk Ed-Chief; Var Trk; Im Wt Lftg; Var Wrstlng; Hon Roll; Prfct Atten Awd; Rochester Inst Tech; Comp Sci.

ATKINSON, SCOTT; Pulaski JR SR HS; Pulaski, NY; (Y); Varsity Clb; Band; Var Capt Bsbl; Var Capt Bsktbl; Var L Ftbl; Cit Awd; Ntl Merit Ltr; Prfct Atten Awd; Joyce Curry Memrl Awd Bsbl Ldrshp & Ablty 86; Harold B Youker Memrl Awd Athl Mst Desrvg Ltr Wnng 86; SUNY Brockport; Sprts Mgmt.

ATTANASIO, LORI; Wet Hempstead HS; Island Park, NY; (Y); Yrbk Stf; VP Frsh Cls; VP Soph Cls; Rep Jr Cls; Rep Stu Cncl; Capt Cheerleading; NHS; Sec Art Clb; Church Yth Grp; Key Clb; Chem Awd Hgst Avg; Spnch III Awd; Ntl Art Hnr Soc Sec; Pre-Med.

ATTEA, JOEL; Akron Central HS; Akron, NY; (Y); 35/140; Aud/Vis; Ftbl; Capt Swmmng; Trk; NHS; Elec Engrng.

ATTICO, DEREK; William Howart Taft HS; Bronx, NY; (Y); 121/266; Camera Clb; Cmnty Wkr; Hosp Aide; Library Aide; Office Aide; Political Wkr; Teachers Aide; Wt Lftg; Hon Roll; Playwrtg Dramatsts Gld Awd For Exc 84; NYU; Law.

ATTZS, BEVERLEY; St Raymonds Academy; Bronx, NY; (Y); 6/69; Library Aide; Math Clb; Science Clb; Band; VP Stu Cncl; Bsktbl; Crs Cntry; Hon Roll; Prfct Atten Awd; Outstndng Achvt Awd Bio Regnts 84; Outstndng Achvt Chem 85; Biochem.

ATWATER, BOB; Liverpool HS; Liverpool, NY; (Y); DECA; JA; Ski Clb; JV Bsbl; Im Bsktbl; JV Var Ftbl; Im Sftbl; Var Trk; Im Wt Lftg; Ntl Merit Ltr.

ATWOOD, DORA; Corinth Central HS; Corinth, NY; (Y); Church Yth Grp; Cmnty Wkr; Spanish Clb; Band; Chorus; Concert Band; Mrchg Band; JV Bsktbl; Prfct Atten Awd.

ATWOOD, SUSAN; Victor Central HS; Victor, NY; (Y); 77/228; Church Yth Grp; 4-H; SADD; Orch; Stu Cncl; High Hon Roll; Hon Roll; Prfct Atten Awd; Vet.

AUBE, TODD; Shaker HS; Loudonville, NY; (Y); Bus Admin.

AUBEL, LAUREL J; South Lewis JR SR HS; Glenfield, NY; (Y); High Hon Roll; Hon Roll; NYS Rgnts Schlrshp 86; Potsdam Coll; Elem Educ.

AUCHENBAUGH, CARL; Central Islip SR HS; Central Islip, NY; (Y); Boy Scts; SADD; Color Guard; Drill Tm; Stage Crew; C W Post; Vet.

AUDOUIN, ELIZABETH; Nazareth Regional HS; Brooklyn, NY; (Y); 43/267; Church Yth Grp; Hosp Aide; Office Aide; Speech Tm; Teachers Aide; Acpl Chr; Chorus; Nwsp Stf; VP Frsh Cls; Rep Soph Cls; Physics Awd 85-86; St Josephs Coll Schlrshp 86; Religion Awd & Eucharistic Mnstry Awd 86; St Josephs Coll; Pre Med.

AUER, JACQUELINE LEE; Newfield HS; Coram, NY; (Y); 14/576; Boy Scts; Drama Clb; Concert Band; Mrchg Band; School Musical; School Play; Hon Roll; Jr NHS; NHS; NY ST Regnts Schlrshp 86; NC ST U Raleigh; Vet Med.

AUGSTEIN, KAREN; Greenville Central HS; Greenville, NY; (Y); 22/76; Sec Church Yth Grp; 4-H; Sec FFA; Rep Frsh Cls; Var Bsktbl; Var JV Score Keeper; Var Sftbl; JV Vllybl; Hnry Blck Ltr G 86; Str Chtr Grnhd FFA 84; Ag.

AUGSTEIN, TOM; Argyle Central HS; Argyle, NY; (Y); 12/56; Boy Scts; Church Yth Grp; French Clb; Math Clb; Math Tm; Band; Yrbk Bus Mgr; Sec Stu Cncl; Socr; Hon Roll; Ortrcl Cntst 86; Cmptr Sci.

AUGUST, ANDREW; John H Glenn HS; E Northport, NY; (Y); Temple Yth Grp; Varsity Clb; Var Ice Hcky; Var L Tennis; Hon Roll; NHS; Spanish NHS; Bus.

AUGUSTINE, CHRISTOPHER; Watkins Glen HS; Watkins Glen, NY; (Y); Pres Am Leg Boys St; Church Yth Grp; JV Var Bsbl; JV Var Bsktbl; JV Var Ftbl; High Hon Roll; Hon Roll; 5th Pl NYS Math Cmptn 84-85; Corning CC; Engrng.

AUGUSTINE, DENISE B; Hillcrest HS; Laurelton, NY; (Y); 25/801; AFS; Chorus; Hon Roll; NHS; Church Yth Grp; FBLA; Office Aide; Teachers Aide; Rep Frsh Cls; Rep Soph Cls; Spanish.

AUGUSTYNIAK, MARTIN; John F Kennedy HS; Sloan, NY; (Y); 17/145; Boy Scts; Church Yth Grp; Computer Clb; Varsity Clb; Stage Crew; JV Bsbl; Var Bowling; JV Capt Ftbl; Hon Roll; U Buffalo; Elect Engr.

AULET, JENNIFER LEE; East Islip HS; Islip Terrace, NY; (Y); Girl Scts; Band; Chorus; Concert Band; School Musical; Swing Chorus; Hon Roll; E Islip Hs Lttr & Pin 85-86; Girl Scout Slvr Ldrshp & Slvr Awd 86; NUSSMA 86; Elem Ed.

AULETTA, GLENN; Merey HS; Ridge, NY; (Y); Drama Clb; Mathletes; Math Clb; Spanish Clb; JV Var Ftbl; Var Trk; High Hon Roll; Hon Roll; Jr NHS; U Of Miami.

AULICINO, JOE; Centereach HS; Centereach, NY; (S); 12/429; Q&S; Quiz Bowl; Variety Show; Nwsp Bus Mgr; Nwsp Rptr; Nwsp Sprt Ed; Var L Bsbl; JV L Socr; Hon Roll; NHS; Spnsh Awd 85; Bsebl Vrsty Ltr 85; Cornell U; Cmmnctn Arts.

AULT, CHARLES; Torrejon American HS; Blytheville AFB, AR; (Y); Boy Scts; Church Yth Grp; Letterman Clb; Model UN; Office Aide; Varsity Clb; Church Choir; Var Capt Ftbl; Wrstlng; Hon Roll; All Spain-Conf Lnbckr 85-86; 1st Pl All Spain Wrstlg 84-85; Crim Law.

AUMULLER, JOANNE; Bethpage HS; Bethpage, NY; (Y); 13/306; FBLA; Spanish Clb; JV Capt Bsktbl; JV Sftbl; JV Vllybl; High Hon Roll; Hon Roll; Jr NHS; NHS.

AUPONT, MARGALIE; St Edmund HS; Brooklyn, NY; (Y); 21/220; French Clb; Hosp Aide; Im Vllybl; Acad All-Amer 86; Lang Fair-1st Wnrs Of French 86; NY U; Pre-Med.

AURECCHIONE, BARBARA; Long Island City HS; Long Is Cty, NY; (Y); Church Yth Grp; Math Tm; Teachers Aide; Band; School Musical; Pres Sr Cls; Rep Stu Cncl; High Hon Roll; Hon Roll; Val; Daily News Superyouth 85 & 86; NYU; Commnctns.

AURELIA, REGINA; Maple Hill HS; Castleton, NY; (S); Drama Clb; GAA; Spanish Clb; School Play; Rep Frsh Cls; Stu Cncl; Stat Bsbl; JV Bsktbl; Var Capt Vllybl; Hon Roll; Librl Arts.

AURICCHIO, JOSEPHINE; East Meadow HS; East Meadow, NY; (Y); FBLA; JV Lcrss; Var Score Keeper; JV Vllybl; Hon Roll; NHS.

AURINGER, MARLENE; Bainbridge-Guilford HS; Bainbridge, NY; (Y); 11/73; Hosp Aide; Ski Clb; Spanish Clb; Band; Mrchg Band; Orch; Vllybl; High Hon Roll; Hon Roll; Pres Acad Ftns Awd 86; ST U Oneonta; Doctor.

AUSBON, LENORA H; The Fieldston Schl; New Rochelle, NY; (Y); Pres Church Yth Grp; Pres Dance Clb; Sec Radio Clb; Chorus; School Musical; Yrbk Stf; Lit Mag; Var Mgr(s); Var L Trk.

AUSTIN, CAROLYN; Sacred Heart Acad; Bellerose, NY; (S); 3/180; FTA; Math Tm; Pep Clb; SADD; School Musical; School Play; Hon Roll; NHS; Psychlgy.

AUSTIN, CHRISTINE A; Waverly JR SR HS; Waverly, NY; (Y); Art Clb; 4-H; Pep Clb; Nwsp Rptr; Rep Stu Cncl; Var Cheerleading; Bus.

AUSTIN, CRISTINA CRIS; Southwestern Central Schl; Lakewood, NY; (Y); Art Clb; Boys Clb Am; Church Yth Grp; FCA; 4-H; German Clb; Hosp Aide; Pep Clb; Red Cross Aide; Ski Clb; MD.

AUSTIN, DONALD; Paul V Moore HS; Brewerton, NY; (Y); ROTC; Trk; Air Force; Law Enfrcmt.

AUSTIN, EUSTENIA; Erasmus Hall HS; Brooklyn, NY; (Y); Nwsp Stf; Dr Norman W Elliot Awd 86; La Guardia CC; Comp Tech.

AUSTIN, KEVIN; Wellsville HS; Wellsville, NY; (Y); 12/126; Am Leg Boys St; School Play; Stage Crew; Nwsp Rptr; Nwsp Sprt Ed; JV Var Bsbl; JV Var Bsktbl; High Hon Roll; Lion Awd; NHS; NHS Cnty Scholar 86; NMSC Spec Scholar 86; Regents Scholar; Rochester Inst; Biomed Comp.

AUSTIN, MARLO; C-PP West HS; Painted Post, NY; (Y); SADD; Varsity Clb; Stage Crew; Rep Frsh Cls; Rep Soph Cls; Rep Jr Cls; Rep Sr Cls; Rep Stu Cncl; Var Cheerleading; Hon Roll; Sci.

AUSTIN, MICHAEL D; Beaver River Central Schl; Castorland, NY; (Y); 6/86; Church Yth Grp; Band; Jazz Band; JV Var Bsktbl; JV Var Crs Cntry; JV Var Trk; High Hon Roll; Hon Roll; NHS; Exploring; St Rgnts Schlrshp; SUNY Potsdam; Elem Ed.

AUSTIN, PAUL; Spencer Van Etten JR SR HS; Van Etton, NY; (Y); 12/100; Am Leg Boys St; Pres Aud/Vis; Boy Scts; Drama Clb; Pres Radio Clb; Chorus; Stage Crew; Trk; Hon Roll; Elmita Coll Key Awd 86; SUNY; Psychologist.

AUSTIN, RICHARD; Richard Austin HS; Yonkers, NY; (Y); 10/210; NHS; NEDT Awd; Law.

AUSTIN, SHANNEN; Troupsburg Central HS; Troupsburg, NY; (Y); 6/26; Computer Clb; Speech Tm; Teachers Aide; Chorus; Color Guard; School Play; Yrbk Ed-Chief; VP Sr Cls; Coach Actv; Socr; Acad All-Strs 86; Coll Alfred; Bus.

AUTENWIETH, ANN; Stissing Mt JR SR HS; Pine Plains, NY; (Y); AFS; Yrbk Stf; Cheerleading; Trk; 3rd Plc Hrstylng Cmptn 86; Dutchess Community; Dance.

AUTILIO, MELISSA; Gloversville HS; Gloversville, NY; (Y); 9/245; Chorus; Concert Band; Jazz Band; Mrchg Band; Symp Band; Yrbk Sprt Ed; Yrbk Stf; JV Cheerleading; Stat Socr; Trs NHS; NYS Rgnts Schlrshp Wnr 85-86; Union Coll; Pre-Law.

AUYENG, YVETTE; Colonie Central HS; Albany, NY; (Y); 10/496; Hosp Aide; Intnl Clb; Chorus; Yrbk Ed-Chief; Yrbk Stf; Lit Mag; Var Crs Cntry; High Hon Roll; NHS; Pre Law.

AVALLONE, REGINA; H Frank Carey HS; Franklin Square, NY; (Y); 18/228; Capt Dance Clb; High Hon Roll; Trs NHS; Adelphi Trustee Schlrshp 86; SOI Italian Lang Awd 86; Outstndng Achvmnt Italian I II III 83-85; Queens Coll; Accntng.

AVALOS, CHARLES; St John The Baptist HS; Brentwood, NY; (S); 16/560; Chess Clb; JA; JV Socr; High Hon Roll; Jr NHS; Spanish NHS; Spnsh Awd; Math & Spnsh Awd Achvt; Aero Engrng.

AVANT, KRISTEN; Churchville-Chili HS; Churchville, NY; (Y); 14/307; Hosp Aide; JCL; Pres Latin Clb; Ski Clb; JV Capt Sftbl; Var Capt Swmmng; Cit Awd; High Hon Roll; Pres NHS; Presdntl Acadmc Ftns Awd 86; ATAD-GRMNY Exchng Stu 85; Pres Natl Hnr Socty 85-86; Nrsng Rgnts Schlrshp; MI ST U; Emergncy Nrs.

AVEDISIAN, ARTHUR G; Dansville SR HS; Dansville, NY; (Y); Church Yth Grp; Computer Clb; Ski Clb; Varsity Clb; Yrbk Phtg; JV Var Ftbl; Var Capt Trk; Hon Roll; Boys ST 85; Script D-3 Out Of 4 Mkg Periods 85; Clarkson U; Elec Engrng.

AVELLANOSA, KRISTEN; Nardin Acad; Williamsville, NY; (Y); French Clb; Intnl Clb; Model UN; Office Aide; Service Clb; School Play; Nwsp Rptr; Yrbk Stf; Lit Mag; Rep Stu Cncl; Fshn.

AVEN, PATRICIA; John A Coleman HS; Hurley, NY; (Y); Chess Clb; French Clb; Hosp Aide; School Play; Capt Var Cheerleading; Var Crs Cntry; Var Mgr(s); Var Trk.

AVENOSO, KEN; Smithtown HS West; St James, NY; (Y); Am Leg Boys St; Yrbk Phtg; Var Tennis; French Hon Soc; VP NHS; Ntl Merit SF; NY Inst Of Tech Physc Awd 86.

AVENS, DAYNA; Mercy HS; Bridgehampton, NY; (Y); 34/130; Church Yth Grp; Math Tm; Ski Clb; Yrbk Phtg; Yrbk Stf; Trk; High Hon Roll; Hon Roll; Hnrs In Math; Ldrs Clb; Hrsbck Rdng Clb; Med Tech.

AVERILL, PATRICK; Canisius HS; Buffalo, NY; (Y); Bsktbl; Ftbl; Wt Lftg; Canisius Coll; Medcl.

AVERY, ANDREW; Horseheads HS; Horseheads, NY; (Y); Boy Scts; Church Yth Grp; French Clb; Science Clb; Varsity Clb; L Var Bsktbl; High Hon Roll; Mu Alp Tht; NHS; Ntl Merit Ltr; Elec Engr.

AVERY, DAVID; Sherburne-Earvlle Central HS; Earlville, NY; (Y); Art Clb; Hon Roll; NHS; Ntl Merit Ltr.

AVERY, JAMES; South Park HS; Buffalo, NY; (Y); Art Clb; Computer Clb; JA; Math Clb; Math Tm; Nwsp Stf; High Hon Roll; Hon Roll; NHS; Prfct Atten Awd; Buffalo ST; Comp Pgmng.

AVERY, KERRY; Union-Endicott HS; Endicott, NY; (Y); 250/452; Pres Varsity Clb; Var Capt Bsbl; JV Bsktbl; Var Capt Bowling; Var JV Ftbl; Elks Awd; MV Pitcher-Broome Cnty 85; $300 Bwlng Schlrshp-WBWG-TV Champ 85-86; Top Male Athlt; U Of SC-AIKEN; Bus.

AVERY, MICHELLE J; Morris HS; Bronx, NY; (Y); 5/204; Church Yth Grp; Dance Clb; Girl Scts; JA; Church Choir; Vllybl; High Hon Roll; NHS; Prfct Atten Awd; Barnard U; Econ.

AVERY, STANLEY E; New Berlin Central Schl; New Berlin, NY; (Y); 3/48; French Clb; Yrbk Bus Mgr; Yrbk Phtg; Pres Frsh Cls; Trs Jr Cls; Trs Sr Cls; Var Bsbl; Var JV Bsktbl; High Hon Roll; Hon Roll; Rgnts Schlrshp 86; Chem Stu Yr 85; ST U Oneonta; Bio.

AVIGNONE, JESSICA; St Hildas HS; New York, NY; (Y); 1/22; School Play; Nwsp Ed-Chief; Yrbk Stf; Lit Mag; Capt Var Bsktbl; Trk; Capt Var Vllybl; Cit Awd; Pres NHS; Val; Phy Educ Awd 86; Latin Sght Trans Cnts 2nd Pl 86; A P Englsh Awd 85; U Of PA.

AVILA, BENILDA; Potsdam Central HS; Potsdam, NY; (Y); 19/125; AFS; Drama Clb; JA; Pres Spanish Clb; Band; Chorus; Church Choir; School Musical; Hon Roll; NHS; UVM; Phys Thrpy.

AVINO, MARY; Mt Saint Mary Acad; Tonawanda, NY; (Y); Cmnty Wkr; Spanish Clb; Stage Crew; Yrbk Ed-Chief; Yrbk Stf; Var Cheerleading; High Hon Roll; Hon Roll; Cmnctns.

AVITAN, LITA; High School For The Humnties; New York, NY; (Y); Teachers Aide; Temple Yth Grp; Yrbk Stf; Hon Roll; Jr NHS; NHS.

AVOLIO, DAVE; South New Berlin Central Schl; South New Berlin, NY; (Y); Bsktbl; Ftbl; Rochester Inst/Tech; Elec Engr.

AVONDA, PETER; Archbishop Stepinac HS; Chappaqua, NY; (Y); 15/150; Capt L Ftbl; Wt Lftg; Hon Roll; Mech Engrng.

AVRIL, NORMA; Catherine Mcauley HS; Queens Village, NY; (S); 1/70; High Hon Roll; Hon Roll; NHS; Ntl Bus Hnr Soc 85; Pace U; Bus Adm.

AWALD, LAURIE A; North Collins Central HS; N Collins, NY; (Y); 2/68; Drama Clb; VP Trs 4-H; SADD; Capt Color Guard; School Musical; School Play; Yrbk Bus Mgr; Yrbk Stf; 4-H Awd; High Hon Roll; Alfred ST Coll; Exec Secrtry.

AWAN, CYRENA L; Ogdensburg Free Acad; Ogdensburg, NY; (Y); 8/186; Band; Concert Band; Jazz Band; Mrchg Band; Pep Band; Var Trk; High Hon Roll; Trs NHS; NY ST Regnts Schlrshp 86; 6 Yrs Acadmc Banqt 81-86; Cornell U; Lf Sci.

AXEL, LOREY; Lawrence HS; Cedarhurst, NY; (Y); Key Clb; Science Clb; Service Clb; Spanish Clb; Temple Yth Grp; Band; Concert Band; Mrchg Band; Nwsp Ed-Chief; Nwsp Rptr; Vol Jerry Lewis Telethon, Archon Svc Hnr Soc 85-86; Yth Ed Nassau Herald Nwspr 86; Stu Action-Educ 86; Bio.

AXTELL, JODI; Hugh C Williams HS; Canton, NY; (Y); 6/147; Exploring; Pep Clb; Ski Clb; Sec SADD; Thesps; Varsity Clb; Chorus; School Musical; School Play; Stage Crew; Acdmc Let Awds 83-85; U S Sprts Dev Tnns Camp 85; St Lawrence U Tlntd JR Prg 85-86; Med.

AYALA, ANA MARIA; Edison Tech HS; Rochester, NY; (Y); Church Yth Grp; Church Choir; Trs Frsh Cls; Trs Soph Cls; High Hon Roll; Hon Roll; Prfct Atten Awd; Offset Prntng.

AYALA JR, ANIBAL; Aviation HS; Long Island City, NY; (S); 19/416; Church Yth Grp; Computer Clb; Debate Tm; JA; Nwsp Rptr; Hon Roll; Jr NHS; NHS; Sci Medl Awd 84; Bus.

AYALA, AYDE; Msgr Scanlan HS; Bronx, NY; (Y); Leo Clb; Office Aide; Nwsp Rptr; Yrbk Stf; Sftbl; Hon Roll; NHS; Regnts Schlrshp 86; St Johns U; Cmmnctns.

AYALA, LAURIE; John F Kennedy HS; New York, NY; (Y); Office Aide; Band; Jazz Band; Mrchg Band; Hon Roll; Bernard Baruch; Bus Admin.

AYCOCK, KIMBERLY; Williamsville North HS; W Amherst, NY; (Y); Cmnty Wkr; DECA; Drama Clb; Latin Clb; Chorus; School Musical; Yrbk Stf; Trk; Hon Roll; Church Choir; NYSSA 84; N TX ST.

AYDELOTTE, TODD; Pittsford Mendon HS; Pittsford, NY; (Y); Boy Scts; Variety Show; Ed Nwsp Ed-Chief; Ed Nwsp Stf; Yrbk Stf; JV Socr; JV L Trk; Dickinson Coll; Pre-Law.

AYDIN, SUSAN; Warwick Valley HS; Warwick, NY; (Y); Church Yth Grp; Political Wkr; SADD; Var Capt Socr; Hon Roll; 2nd Bst Spnst Stdnt; Cmptr Sci.

AYERS, JODI; Corning West HS; Painted Post, NY; (Y); 16/252; Letterman Clb; Ski Clb; Thesps; Varsity Clb; Mrchg Band; Trs Stu Cncl; Trk; Cit Awd; High Hon Roll; NHS; Pres Acadmc Fit Awd 86; Acadmc & Pres Schlrshps Niagara U 86; Niagara U; Trvl Adm.

AYERS, NANCI L; Dundee Central HS; Dundee, NY; (Y); Sec Soph Cls; Var Capt Cheerleading; Score Keeper; Sftbl; Hon Roll; Double Bars Ltr 83-84; Sportsmnshp Awd Chrldng 84-85; MVP Chrldng 85-86; Treas Vo Schl Cosmtlgy 85-86; Cosmtlgy.

AYOTTE, KATHY; Tupper Lake HS; Tupper Lk, NY; (Y); 13/99; Drama Clb; Sec 4-H; Sec Pep Clb; Science Clb; School Play; Var Socr; JV Trk; 4-H Awd; NHS; Spnsh.

AYOTTE, THOMAS G; Smithtown West HS; Hauppauge, NY; (Y); Am Leg Boys St; Exploring; Rep Soph Cls; Rep Jr Cls; Pres Sr Cls; Pres Stu Cncl; Var Capt Bsbl; Im Vllybl; Cit Awd; Navl ROTC & NY ST Regnts Schlrshps 86; Amer Legn Good Ctznshp Citatn 86; Boston U; Aerosp Engrng.

AYRAULT, KATHY; Olean HS; Olean, NY; (Y); 21/200; Church Yth Grp; Varsity Clb; JV Bsktbl; Var L Bowling; JV Golf; Var Mgr(s); Var Score Keeper; Hon Roll; NHS; AFS; Kent ST; Pilt.

AYRE, OWEN; Unatego JR SR HS; Unadilla, NY; (Y); 11/86; Am Leg Boys St; Trs French Clb; Pres Stu Cncl; Var Crs Cntry; Var Trk; NHS; Trs Frsh Cls; Trs Soph Cls; Oprtn Entrprs David Patchen Schlrshp 85; SUCO Yth Ldrshp 85-86; Union Coll; Intl Bus.

AYRES, SUSAN; John Jay HS; Katonah, NY; (Y); Teachers Aide; Var Capt Tennis; Travel.

AYROSO, ANDREA; Uniondale HS; Uniondale, NY; (Y); FBLA; Yrbk Ed-Chief; VP Frsh Cls; Var Badmtn; Cit Awd; High Hon Roll; Hon Roll; Jr NHS; NHS; Medln Awd 83-84; Fordham U; Psych.

AYTUR, SEMRA; Plattsburgh HS; Plattsburgh, NY; (Y); Trs Frsh Cls; Trs Soph Cls; Trs Jr Cls; Swmmng; Trk; Vllybl; High Hon Roll; NHS; 4-H; Ski Clb; Acdmc Awds Soc Stu, Art, Lang & Scsi 85-86; Acdmc Awd Eng 84&85; Ltr Var Track 86.

AZAR, MICHAEL; Ft Hamilton HS; Brooklyn, NY; (Y); Aud/Vis; Boy Scts; Church Yth Grp; Cmnty Wkr; Drama Clb; Office Aide; Teachers Aide; Chorus; School Play; Variety Show; Untd Fdrtn Of Tchrs Schlrshp 86; Svc Awd 86; Jms J Hckt Spch Awd 86; Brooklyn Coll; Rcrdng Engnr.

AZEEZ, MOHAMED; Eastern District HS; Queens, NY; (Y); 8/333; Nwsp Rptr; Acad Achvt Awd 86; Hunter Coll; Pharm.

AZIMI, SHARENE LISA; White Plains HS; White Plains, NY; (Y); 8/430; Drama Clb; Chorus; School Musical; Yrbk Rptr; Rep Frsh Cls; Sec Stu Cncl; Fld Hcky; High Hon Roll; NHS; Ntl Merit Ltr; Smith Coll Bk Awd 85; Prncpls Rcgntn 86; Pres Acad Ftnss Awd 86; Wesleyan U; Sci.

AZRIA, CAMUNA; William Nottingham HS; Syracuse, NY; (Y); 122/300; Library Aide; Temple Yth Grp; Chorus; SUNY Binghamton U; Law.

AZZARELLA, DARCY LEE; Alexander Central HS; Alexander, NY; (Y); Sec AFS; Church Yth Grp; FNA; Sec Trs Varsity Clb; VP Stu Cncl; Capt Crs Cntry; Capt Trk; Hon Roll; Drama Clb; Sec Trs 4-H; Genesee Co Med Soc Aux Awd, X-Cntry Running Schlrshp Roberts Wesleyan Athl Dept 86; Roberts Wesleyan Coll; Nrsng.

AZZARELLA, PHILIP; Silver Creek HS; Silver Creek, NY; (Y); Library Aide; Math Tm; Spanish Clb; Chorus; Nwsp Sprt Ed; Capt Bowling; Fredonia ST U; Mgmt Accntng.

AZZUE, VINCENT; Middletown HS; Middletown, NY; (Y); Sec Key Clb; Var Ftbl; Var Hon Roll; Tampa U; Dntstry.

BABB, PAUL E; Columbia HS; E Schodack, NY; (Y); Computer Clb; Regents Schlrshp 86; Boys St 85; Suny At Aswego; Comp Sci.

BABBITT, KAREN BETH; Belfast Central Schl; Caneadea, NY; (Y); 1/30; 4-H; Sec VP Stu Cncl; Var Capt Bsktbl; Var Capt Socr; Var Tennis; Var Vllybl; Bausch & Lomb Sci Awd; Cit Awd; 4-H Awd; High Hon Roll; Amer Lg Past Pres Parley Stu Scholar 86; Allegany Cnty NHS Scholar 86; Belfast Bettermnt Scholar 86; St Bonaventure U; Bio.

BABCOCK, AMY; Gowanda Central HS; Gowanda, NY; (Y); 21/135; Rep Frsh Cls; Rep Soph Cls; Var Capt Cheerleading; JV Mgr(s); Var Capt Trk; Bus.

BABCOCK, HEATHER ANN; Mercy HS; Hampton Bays, NY; (Y); 36/125; Am Leg Aux Girls St; Church Yth Grp; Church Choir; JV Var Bsktbl; Var Fld Hcky; Var Sftbl; Var Swmmng; Var Trk; Hon Roll; Ski Clb; Bus.

BABCOCK, KATRINA; Alexandria Central Schl; Alexandria Bay, NY; (Y); Drama Clb; French Clb; Hosp Aide; Co-Capt Color Guard; Mrchg Band; School Play; Stage Crew; Trs Jr Cls; Cheerleading; Score Keeper; Stdnt Govt; Frnch III Hgh Grds Awd; SUNY Geneseo; Spec Ed.

BABCOCK, KIMBERLY S; Linton HS; Schenectady, NY; (Y); 5/296; Church Yth Grp; Key Clb; Chorus; Church Choir; Off Jr Cls; Off Sr Cls; Stu Cncl; Var JV Tennis; Pres Jr NHS; NHS; Regnts Schlrshp 86; Trustee Schlr Stats St Lawrence U 86; Ltr Muscl Cntrbn Schl 86; St Lawrence U; Frnch.

BABCOCK, LERA; St Marys Acad; Hoosick Falls, NY; (Y); 5/17; Nwsp Stf; Yrbk Stf; Trs Soph Cls; Trs Stu Cncl; Var L Bsktbl; Var Powder Puff Ftbl; Var Capt Sftbl; Var Capt Vllybl; High Hon Roll; Hon Roll; Comp Awd 86; All-Arnd Grls Athltc Awd 86; Bttr Crckr Clb 86.

BABCOCK, LYNDA; Tioga Central HS; Smithboro, NY; (S); 10/95; School Musical; Variety Show; Nwsp Stf; Yrbk Stf; Off Frsh Cls; Off Soph Cls; JV Var Cheerleading; VP NHS; Mst Outstndng Chrldr 84-85; Elem Educ.

BABCOCK, ROYALE; Oneida SR HS; Canastota, NY; (S); 10/200; Civic Clb; Pres Trs SADD; Concert Band; Jazz Band; Yrbk Stf; Stat Socr; NHS; Ntl Merit Ltr; Im Vllybl; Rgnts Schlrshp; No 1 Clb; Z Clb; Herkimer Cnty CC; Pre-Law.

BABIAR, DONNA; Gorton HS; Yonkers, NY; (Y); Church Yth Grp; Cmnty Wkr; 4-H; FBLA; Spanish Clb; Varsity Clb; Rep Frsh Cls; Rep Soph Cls; Rep Jr Cls; Rep Stu Cncl.

BABIARZ, DONALD; Hollan Patent Central HS; Barneveld, NY; (Y); Computer Clb; Band; Concert Band; Drm & Bgl; Jazz Band; Symp Band; Hon Roll; Mohawk Valley CC; Microcomp.

BABICHUK, STEPHEN; Monsignor Farrell HS; Staten Island, NY; (Y); Pep Clb; Ski Clb; JV Bsbl; Im Bsktbl; Im Bowling; Im Ftbl; Im Score Keeper; FL Inst Tech; Aviation.

BABIERE, MICHAEL A; Mt St Michael Acad; Bronx, NY; (S); 33/309; Chess Clb; Computer Clb; Lit Mag; Im Bsktbl; Im Ftbl; Hon Roll; NHS; Spanish NHS; Psychlgy.

BABILOT, MICHAEL; Weedsport Central HS; Auburn, NY; (Y); 11/90; Am Leg Boys St; Chess Clb; French Clb; Spanish Clb; Church Choir; Var Capt Crs Cntry; Var Capt Swmmng; Var Capt Trk; Pres NHS; Boy Scts; Congrssnl Mdl Merit 86; Am Leg Scholar 86; West Point Mil Acad; Mech Engr.

BABINO, GIOVANNI; La Salle Acad; Brooklyn, NY; (S); 7/207; Boy Scts; Math Clb; Bowling; NY U; Stats.

BABOWICZ, COLLEEN; John F Kennedy HS; Utica, NY; (Y); 4/140; Aud/Vis; Key Clb; Math Clb; Nwsp Rptr; Hon Roll; Jr NHS; Rgnts Schlrshp; Mohawk Valley CC; Accntng.

BABROWICZ, WENDY; Herkimer HS; Herkimer, NY; (Y); Church Yth Grp; Drama Clb; French Clb; Hst FHA; JA; Library Aide; Pep Clb; Chorus; Yrbk Stf; Var JV Cheerleading; 3rd Rnr-Up Herkimer Cnty Beauty Pagnt 85; Comp Tech.

BABUTS, DIANE; Jamesville-Dewitt HS; Dewitt, NY; (Y); Hosp Aide; Model UN; Chorus; Church Choir; School Musical; Swing Chorus; Var L Swmmng; High Hon Roll; NHS; NY St All St Mixed Chorus 85.

BABY, THOMAS; Chrit The King HS; Queens Village, NY; (Y); Debate Tm; Ski Clb; Hon Roll; NHS; Qns Coll Pres Awd Achvt 84; Comm.

BACCHAS, VERMALYN; George Washington HS; New York, NY; (Y); Art Clb; Camera Clb; Church Yth Grp; Church Choir; School Play; Yrbk Stf; Pace U; Acctnt.

BACCHETTA, CARLO; Angle American HS; Forest Hills, NY; (S); 1/50; Art Clb; Capt Chess Clb; Varsity Clb; Y-Teens; Band; Socr; Tennis; Capt Vllybl; High Hon Roll; NHS; Sci Fair Proj Wnnr 85-86; Mth Achvts 85-86; Excllnce Sci, Art 85-86, Effort Art, Hstry 85-86; Socr Skll; Nuclr Engr.

BACCHUS, ZAID; Long Island City HS; New York, NY; (Y); Stu Cncl; Hon Roll; Daily News Spr Yth Awd 86.

BACETTY, NANCY; Eastern Districk HS; Brooklyn, NY; (Y); Library Aide; Math Clb; Teachers Aide; Variety Show; Nwsp Rptr; Hon Roll; Mary Mount Coll; Bus Mgt.

BACH, MICHAEL; Malverne HS; Malverne, NY; (Y); Art Clb; Camera Clb; Camp Fr Inc; Chess Clb; Computer Clb; SADD; Nwsp Phtg; Nwsp Rptr; Nwsp Stf; Lit Mag; De Vry U; Comp Engr.

BACHMAN, AMY; South Side HS; Rockville Ctr, NY; (Y); 90/285; Drama Clb; Key Clb; Latin Clb; Band; Chorus; Jazz Band; Madrigals; School Musical; Stage Crew; Lit Mag; All Cnty C'rs 84-86; All ST Chrs 85; Intl Thspn Soc 84; Bill Clytn Emerl Schlrshp 86; Syracuse U; Music Prfrmnc.

BACHORIK, MARC; Schalmont HS; Schenectady, NY; (Y); Band; Concert Band; Jazz Band; Mrchg Band; School Musical; School Play; Stage Crew; Symp Band; JV Bsktbl; JV Ftbl; Music.

BACKENSTROSS, KURT; East Syracuse-Minoa HS; Kirkville, NY; (Y); Boy Scts; Cmnty Wkr; Variety Show; Crs Cntry; Lcrss; Paul R Hopkins Mem Awd Most Deserving Stu 86; Adadmc Achvt Awd Drafting 85 & 86; SUNY At Delhi; Drafting.

BACKES, AMY; Cheektowaga Central HS; Cheektowaga, NY; (Y); 42/199; Latin Clb; Color Guard; Yrbk Stf; Stu Cncl; Bsktbl; Capt Cheerleading; Var Capt Fld Hcky; Var Capt Sftbl; Buffalo ST Coll; Office Admin.

BACKUS, CRAIG; Herkimer Central HS; Herkimer, NY; (Y); 1/115; Am Leg Boys St; Band; Chorus; Concert Band; Mrchg Band; Yrbk Stf; Pres Sr Cls; Rep Stu Cncl; Twrlr; NHS; RPI Math & Sci Awds 86; Hugh O Brian Yth Fndntn Ldrshp Seminar Rep 85; All St Band 85; Math.

BACKUS, TAMMY; Indian River Central HS; Oxbow, NY; (Y); Church Yth Grp; Church Choir; Yrbk Stf; Hon Roll; JV Sftbl; Var Tennis; Var Vllybl; Canton Argi; Sec Sci.

BACO, BARBARA; Villa Maria Acad; Buffalo, NY; (Y); Church Yth Grp; Yrbk Stf; Gym; Swmmng; Hon Roll; Villa Maria Coll; Intr Dsgn.

BACON, ANDREW; Sachem HS North Campus; Lake Ronkonkoma, NY; (Y); 116/1556; Radio Clb; Y-Teens; Nwsp Stf; Im Coach Actv; Socr; High Hon Roll; Jr NHS; NHS; Soccr Ref 85-86; Bsbl Umpire 85-86; JR Cnslr 86; Jrnlsm.

BACON, ROBERT; Central Islip HS; Central Islip, NY; (Y); 22/348; Var Bowling; Hon Roll; NHS; Ntl Merit SF; Pres Schlr; SUNY Stony Brook.

BACSARDI, PAUL P; Monroe-Woodburg Central HS; Chester, NY; (Y); 34/360; Am Leg Boys St; Cmnty Wkr; Capt Ice Hcky; High Hon Roll; NHS; Excllnce Soc Stud Awd 85; Natl Phys Ed Awd 86; Coach Awd Litle Rangers Yth Hcky 85-86; Pol Sci.

BADALAMENTI, ANTONIA; Farmindale SR HS; Farmingdale, NY; (Y); Art Clb; Teachers Aide; Church Choir.

BADE, CHRISTOPHER; Mahopac HS; Carmel, NY; (Y); 11/407; Math Tm; Science Clb; Yrbk Sprt Ed; Sec Frsh Cls; Capt Bsbl; Capt Bsktbl; Ftbl; High Hon Roll; Jr NHS; NHS; All Lgu Hnrs Bsbl 85; All Sctn All Lgu Bsbl 86; Yale; Engnr.

BADILLO, SANDRA; N Rockland HS; Garnerville, NY; (Y); Pres Spanish Clb; Yrbk Bus Mgr; Rep Frsh Cls; JV Socr; Bus Admin.

BADOLATO, MARY ANN; Rome Free Acad; Rome, NY; (Y); 35/400; Band; Orch; Co-Capt Socr; NHS; Regents Schlrshp 86; Ben V Smith Schlrshp 86; Suny Albany; Med Tech.

BADORE, VICTORIA; Stissing Mountain JR SR HS; Pine Plains, NY; (Y); 23/83; AFS; Boy Scts; Cmnty Wkr; Library Aide; SADD; Band; Trs Chorus; Hon Roll; Tutrl Awd Svcs 85 & 86; Hnr Key 85-86; Chrl Actvty Cert Area Al-ST 86; Educ Thrpy.

BAE, DAVID; Northport HS; E Northport, NY; (Y); 7/590; Art Clb; Pres Church Yth Grp; Mathletes; Orch; School Play; Lit Mag; High Hon Roll; Jr NHS; NHS; Ntl Merit SF; NYSSMA All Cnty LISFA 83-86; Cngrssnl Awrts Cmpttn 86; All ST Orchstra 85; Archtctr.

BAEHR, LISA; Duanesburg HS; Delanson, NY; (Y); Church Yth Grp; Drama Clb; Intnl Clb; Band; Chorus; Jazz Band; Yrbk Stf; Score Keeper; Socr; Hon Roll; Med Tech.

BAER, CHRIS; Westhampton Beach HS; E Moriches, NY; (Y); VICA; Army; Rest Owrn.

BAER, DAVID; Ramstein American HS; Apo New York, NY; (Y); Boy Scts; Cmnty Wkr; German Clb; Hosp Aide; JA; Ftbl; Trk; Wt Lftg; Prfct Atten Awd; Trvl Agnt.

BAETZHOLD, WILLIAM; Hamburg SR HS; Boston, NY; (Y); 56/384; Var Ftbl; Hon Roll; USAF Acad; Aeronaut.

BAEZ, ANA; St Catharine Acad; New York, NY; (Y); Dance Clb; Variety Show; Yrbk Stf; Diving; Swmmng; Prfct Atten Awd; Excllnc Art; Cmmndtn Art; Wood Schl FIT; Fshn Dsgnr.

BAFFO JR, SAMUEL; Lafayette HS; Brooklyn, NY; (Y); 63/363; Library Aide; Var Socr; Cit Awd; Hon Roll; Ntl Merit Schol; Prfct Atten Awd; Arkon Soc Awd 86; Achvt Acad Cert 82; Cert Hnr Merit Bio 84; OH Northern U; Bio.

BAGDON, TRACY; Amsterdam HS; Amsterdam, NY; (Y); 70/300; VP DECA; Varsity Clb; Yrbk Stf; Rep Frsh Cls; Rep Jr Cls; Trs Stu Cncl; Co-Capt Cheerleading; Pom Pon; Hon Roll; Stu Cncl Schlrshp 86; Maria College; Phys Thrpy.

BAGGIO, CHRIS; Half Hollow Hills HS East; Wheatley Hts, NY; (Y); Varsity Clb; Var Bsbl; Var JV Ftbl; Score Keeper; High Hon Roll; Hon Roll; All Lg Bsbl JR 86; Itln Hnr Soc 85-86.

BAGHDASARIAN, HILDRETH; Port Richmond HS; Staten Island, NY; (Y); Var Socr; Voice Dem Awd; HS Oratrcl Cntst 4th Pl 86; Pdtrcn.

BAGINSKI, JOCELYN; Bishop Ford C C HS; Brooklyn, NY; (Y); French Clb; Science Clb; Spanish Clb; Yrbk Stf; Hon Roll; Bus Admin.

BAGLEY, AMY; Horseheads HS; Big Flats, NY; (S); Pres Church Yth Grp; DECA; Band; Chorus; Mrchg Band; Hon Roll; Emplye Lvl-1st Pl DECA Rgnl Comptn Mrktng 85; CPR Modual 85; Mrktng.

BAGLIN, MARCI; Greece Athena HS; Rochester, NY; (Y); 90/350; Office Aide; Hon Roll; Acad Ltr 86; Geneseo; Comp Sci.

BAGNARDI, VICTOR A; Oneonta HS; Oneonta, NY; (Y); 30/159; Am Leg Boys St; Letterman Clb; Ski Clb; Concert Band; Jazz Band; Pep Band; School Musical; Yrbk Stf; Var L Trk; Hon Roll; Archt.

BAGTAS, MARIA; St John The Baptist D HS; Holbrook, NY; (Y); 33/511; Cmnty Wkr; Hosp Aide; Model UN; Science Clb; Boys Clb Am; Chorus; Yrbk Stf; Hon Roll; Filipino Soc Acad Awd 85; NYSSMA Music Medals Awd 85-86; NY U; Pre-Med.

BAGUIO, MIRIAM; The Stony Brook Schl; Setauket, NY; (Y); 2/80; Library Aide; Ski Clb; Acpl Chr; Madrigals; Orch; School Musical; School Play; Nwsp Phtg; Var Capt Tennis; Trk; Ldng Schltc Achvrs Newsday Hgh Hnrs Comptn 85-86; Bst Contrbtn Fine Arts 85-86; Cum Laude 85-86; U PA; Nrsng.

BAHL, RENEE; Fayetteville-Mahlivs HS; Fayetteville, NY; (Y); 75/335; Art Clb; Model UN; Red Cross Aide; SADD; Nwsp Rptr; Rep Stu Cncl; Var L Swmmng; Var Trk; High Hon Roll; Hon Roll; Luella A Hurdman Awd 83; Coaches Awd 85; Emory U; Math.

BAHLATZIS, DEBBIE; Colonie Central HS; Albany, NY; (Y); Chrch Yth Clb 84-86; Frnch Hnr Soc 84-85; Hnr Roll 84-85; Hdsn Vly Cmnty Coll; Med.

BAIAMONTE, ROSALIA; Bayside HS; Bayside, NY; (Y); 12/686; School Musical; Yrbk Stf; Capt Jr Cls; Capt Sr Cls; High Hon Roll; Jr NHS; NHS; Acdmc Olympics Team 85-86; Latin Mini Schl 83-86; Exec Ed In Chief Law Mag 85-86; Brandeis U; Legal Studies.

BAIATA, CRISTINA; Sachem North HS; Holtsville, NY; (Y); 21/1558; Cmnty Wkr; Intnl Clb; Library Aide; Quiz Bowl; Capt Scholastic Bowl; Service Clb; Spanish Clb; Jr NHS; NHS; Hgh Hnrs LI Sci Cngrss 85; 3rd Pl-NY St Hstry Bwl Tm 85; 2nd Pl-AATSP Natl Cntst LI Chptr 86; Intl Law.

BAILER, LYNN M; Henninger HS; Syracuse, NY; (Y); 10/400; Sec JA; Ski Clb; Band; Chorus; Concert Band; School Musical; Swing Chorus; Nwsp Phtg; Nwsp Rptr; Nwsp Stf; Phtgrphy Awd 85; Mech Drwng Awd 86; Ind Arts Tchrs Awd 86; New Paltz; Grphc Arts.

BAILER, THOMAS; Homer HS; Cortland, NY; (Y); 56/432; Church Yth Grp; Rep Drama Clb; German Clb; SADD; Acpl Chr; Chorus; Church Choir; School Musical; School Play; Stage Crew; Bst Frshmn Actor 84; Drama.

BAILEY, ARLENE; John Dewey HS; Brooklyn, NY; (Y); Library Aide; Teachers Aide; Chorus; Vllybl; Cert Merit Math Schlrshp 83; Eng Achvt Awd Communctns Arts 83; Math Awd Cert Outstndng Achvt Alg 83; Bernard Baruch Coll; Acct.

BAILEY, CURT; Walton HS; Walton, NY; (Y); 10/100; Am Leg Boys St; Key Clb; ROTC; Varsity Clb; VP Jr Cls; VP Sr Cls; Capt Var Crs Cntry; Var Capt Trk; Var Wrstlng; High Hon Roll; MVP Trck 85-86; MVP 86, All STAR Crss Cntry 85-86; Pre Med.

BAILEY, DANIEL; Herkimer SR HS; Herkimer, NY; (Y); Band; Concert Band; Mrchg Band; Pep Band; Stage Crew; Bsktbl; Ftbl; Trk; Hon Roll; Archlgy.

BAILEY, DAVID; Plattsburgh HS; Plattsburgh, NY; (Y); 14/135; Boy Scts; Exploring; Model UN; Ski Clb; School Play; Sec Sr Cls; Rep Stu Cncl; Var JV Swmmng; Var Trk; NHS; Dartmouth Coll; Engr.

BAILEY, HELEN; Catholic Central HS; Troy, NY; (Y); Math Clb; Math Tm; SADD; Teachers Aide; Variety Show; Hon Roll; Yorker Clb 84-85; Cum Ld For Ntl Ltn Exm 85-86; Hghst Aver In 1st Yr Typg 84-86; Hdsn Vly Cmnty Coll; Lab Rsrch.

BAILEY III, JACK S; Jamesville-De Witt HS; Dewitt, NY; (Y); 6/246; Church Yth Grp; Model UN; Orch; School Musical; High Hon Roll; NHS; NYS Lang Tchrs Assn 86; Georgetown; Frgn Svc.

BAILEY, JAMES; Livonia HS; S Lima, NY; (Y); Hon Roll; Draftsmen.

BAILEY, JEANNA; Baldwin SR HS; Roosevelt, NY; (Y); Sec Church Yth Grp; Cmnty Wkr; Teachers Aide; Sec Concert Band; Mrchg Band; Capt Pom Pon; Dr Martin Luther King Jr Hmntrn Awd 86; Pre-Law.

BAILEY, JODI; Avon JR SR HS; Avon, NY; (Y); Church Yth Grp; Ski Clb; Pres SADD; Varsity Clb; Variety Show; Yrbk Stf; Bsktbl; Capt Socr; Trk; Capt Vllybl; Gennesee Vly Pony Clb Riding Tm Capt 84-85; U S Natl Art Awds 84-85; JR Cls Prm Qn 86; Cazenovia Coll; Advrtsng Dsgn.

BAILEY, KEVIN; Huntington Christian Schl; Seaford, NY; (Y); 5/22; Church Yth Grp; Chorus; Var L Bsbl; Var L Bsktbl; Var Crs Cntry; Var L Socr; High Hon Roll; Athlt Of Yr 85-86; Mst Impvd Sccr Plyr 85; Mr Def Bsktbl 85-86; Messiah; Bus Adm.

BAILEY, KIMBERLY R; Elmira Southside HS; Wellsburg, NY; (Y); Pep Clb; VP Spanish Clb; Nwsp Rptr; Yrbk Bus Mgr; High Hon Roll; Hon Roll; NYS Rgnts Nrsg Schlrshp 86; Arnot Ogden Hospital/Nrsg; Nrsg.

BAILEY, LYNN; John F Kennedy HS; Utica, NY; (Y); 5/130; Debate Tm; Exploring; Mathletes; Band; Church Choir; Yrbk Ed-Chief; Yrbk Stf; Var Bowling; High Hon Roll; NHS; Clarkson; Chem Engrng.

BAILEY, MARY-ANN; Averill Park HS; W Sand Lk, NY; (Y); 14/210; GAA; Hosp Aide; JA; Ski Clb; SADD; Varsity Clb; Nwsp Stf; JV Var Tennis; JV Var Vllybl; High Hon Roll; Regents Schlrshp 85-86; Siena Coll; Intl Bnkr.

BAILEY, MICHELLE; Nazareth Acad; Rochester, NY; (Y); French Clb; Varsity Clb; JC Awd; Blck Schlr Urbn League-Rochester 86; Comp Sci.

BAILEY, PAMELA; Newfane SR HS; Newfane, NY; (Y); Exploring; 4-H; Y-Teens; Band; Concert Band; Symp Band; Hon Roll; US Svgs Bond In Soap Bx Drby 81-86; Bus.

BAILEY, REBECCA; Clymer Central HS; Clymer, NY; (Y); AFS; Ski Clb; Band; Stu Cncl; Bsktbl; Sftbl; Vllybl; NHS; FFA Swthrt 86; Pre-Law.

BAILEY, RICHARD D; Walton HS; New York, NY; (Y); Computer Clb; FTA; Office Aide; Yrbk Phtg; Ed Yrbk Rptr; Masonic Awd; Prfct Atten Awd; Pride Yankees Cmmnty Svc 85-86; Supt Schltc Achvt Awd 86; Regents Scholar 86; ST Senate Awd 86; Parks Coll; Aviatn.

BAILEY, SCOTT; Hamburg SR HS; Hamburg, NY; (Y); Rep Frsh Cls; JV Bsktbl; JV Ice Hcky; JV Lcrss; Var Mgr(s); Var Socr; JV Trk; Hon Roll; Yrbk Stf; U Of NH; Bus Mgmnt.

BAILEY, SHARON M; Clara Barton HS; Brooklyn, NY; (Y); Pres Church Yth Grp; Cmnty Wkr; Hosp Aide; Chorus; Church Choir; Nwsp Stf; Rep Sr Cls; Vllybl; Hon Roll; RN.

BAILEY, SHAUNE M; Jamestown HS; Jamestown, NY; (Y); 150/398; Boy Scts; Chess Clb; CAP; Spanish Clb; Stage Crew; Rgnts Schlrshp 86; Jamestown CC; Engr.

BAILEY, SIMON T; Bennett HS; Buffalo, NY; (Y); 55/220; Church Yth Grp; Cmnty Wkr; Debate Tm; DECA; Pep Clb; Speech Tm; SADD; Rep Jr Cls; Pres Sr Cls; Rep Stu Cncl; 1st Pl Schlrshp NY Dist Optmst Intl 84; 4th Pl Ortr At DECA ST Career Cnfrnc 85; Dbtr Of Yr 86; Morehouse Coll; Mass Comm.

BAILEY, SUZANNE; Madrid Waddington HS; Waddington, NY; (Y); Drama Clb; French Clb; Chorus; Mrchg Band; VP Frsh Cls; VP Soph Cls; High Hon Roll; Hon Roll; NHS; Potsdam ST; Elem Educ.

BAILEY, TAMMY; Bradford Central HS; Bradford, NY; (S); 1/29; FBLA; Nwsp Stf; Yrbk Ed-Chief; Trs Sr Cls; DAR Awd; VP NHS; Prfct Atten Awd; Stu Of Year 85; Accntng.

BAILEY, TAMMY; Springville-Griffith Inst; Glenwood, NY; (Y); Pres AFS; FBLA; JV Powder Puff Ftbl; Colorguard Achvt Awd 84; Gregg Typng Awd 86; Alfred A&T; Exec Sec.

BAILIE, JAMES; Saratoga Springs SR HS; Saratoga Sprgs, NY; (Y); 22/491; Computer Clb; Ed Lit Mag; Hon Roll; NHS; NY ST Regnts Schrlshp 86; Clarkson U; Physics.

BAIO, PAUL; Archbishop Stepinac HS; Yonkers, NY; (Y); Key Clb; Var Ice Hcky; Var Lcrss; Wt Lftg; Bus.

BAIR, KATHLEEN; Monticello HS; Kauneonga, NY; (Y); Office Aide; High Hon Roll; Hon Roll; Prfct Atten Awd; Elected Sec Of Bethel CYO 86; Mt Saint Mary Coll; Educ.

BAIRD, BAVAUGHN; Rensselaer HS; Rensselaer, NY; (Y); Art Clb; Boys Clb Am; Church Yth Grp; Cmnty Wkr; SADD; Band; Jazz Band; Nwsp Stf; Yrbk Phtg; Yrbk Rptr; California ST; Soc Wrkr.

BAIRD, MICHAEL; Gloversville HS; Gloversville, NY; (Y); 36/235; Church Yth Grp; JV Ftbl; Im Wt Lftg; High Hon Roll; Regents Scholar 86; SUNY Binghampton; Engrng.

BAIZ, CHRIS; Southside HS; Elmira, NY; (S); French Clb; Intnl Clb; Pep Clb; Ski Clb; Band; Chorus; School Play; Yrbk Stf; Rep Jr Cls; High Hon Roll.

BAJOHR, CHRISTOPHER; La Salle Military Acad; Sebring, FL; (S); 8/92; Capt ROTC; Color Guard; Jazz Band; Yrbk Ed-Chief; Off Sr Cls; JV Bsbl; JV Socr; Hon Roll; NHS; Fordham U; Comm.

BAKEMAN, PAMELA; Carning Painted Post West HS; Lindley, NY; (Y); Church Yth Grp; High Hon Roll; Hon Roll; Bryant-Stratton; Secy Bus.

BAKER, ANDREW J; East Aurora HS; E Aurora, NY; (Y); 19/184; Boy Scts; JA; Rep Frsh Cls; Rep Soph Cls; Rep Jr Cls; Rep Sr Cls; Swmmng; High Hon Roll; Jr NHS; NHS; Gftd & Tlntd Prgm 84-86; NY ST Rgnts Schlrshp 86; SUNY Geneseo.

BAKER, ANDREW S; Greater New York Acad; Brooklyn, NY; (Y); Chess Clb; Computer Clb; Church Choir; Drill Tm; Yrbk Stf; Im Bsktbl; Atlantic Union Coll; Cmptr Pgmr.

BAKER, BERNET; Alexander Hamilton HS; Brooktondale, NY; (Y); Debate Tm; Rep Frsh Cls; Hon Roll; Outstndng Wrk Habit; Acdmc Achvt; Empire ST Coll; Soc Thry.

BAKER, BOBBY; Northeastern Clinton Central HS; Alburg Springs, VT; (Y); 5/153; 4-H; Pres Key Clb; Model UN; Band; Nwsp Stf; Pres Stu Cncl; Socr; High Hon Roll; NHS; Ntl Merit Schol; Prnc JR Prom 85; 1st Pl Troph Karate 85; Embry Riddle Aerontcl U; Pilot.

BAKER, BRANDI JILL; Jeffersonville-Youngsville Ctl HS; Livingston Manor, NY; (Y); 1/60; SADD; Varsity Clb; Chorus; Church Choir; Rep Stu Cncl; Var Co-Capt Socr; Bausch & Lomb Sci Awd; NHS; Prfct Atten Awd; Val; Pres Acad Fit Awd 86; Hnrary Scholar Clarkson U 86; Clarkson U; Chem Engrng.

BAKER, CHRISTINE; Newfane Central HS; Lockport, NY; (Y); 20/160; Girl Scts; Math Tm; Varsity Clb; Band; Var Capt Bsktbl; Var Fld Hcky; JV Sftbl; Var Capt Tennis; Var Vllybl; Wmns Sports Fndtn All Star Awd 85; Boston U; Dentstry.

BAKER, CHRISTOPHER P; Elmira Free Acad; Elmira, NY; (Y); Am Leg Boys St; Church Yth Grp; Ski Clb; Sec Stu Cncl; Var Bsktbl; Var Ftbl; Lcrss; JV Socr; High Hon Roll; NHS; Hamilton Coll; Pol Sci.

BAKER, COLLEEN; Frontier SR HS; Blasdell, NY; (Y); French Clb; FBLA; Pep Clb; Chorus; Hon Roll; Erie CC.

BAKER, CYNTHIA L; Leroy Central Schl; Le Roy, NY; (Y); Spanish Clb; School Musical; Yrbk Stf; Pres Jr Cls; Pres Sr Cls; Var Capt Bsktbl; Var Capt Socr; Var JV Tennis; Var L Trk; Var L Vllybl; U Of Rochester; Psych.

BAKER, DANIEL J; Cambridge Central HS; Cambridge, NY; (Y); Am Leg Boys St; Church Yth Grp; Cmnty Wkr; Band; Mrchg Band; Stage Crew; Hon Roll; VP NHS.

BAKER, DEAN; Northeastern Clinton Central HS; Champlain, NY; (Y); 10/153; 4-H; Key Clb; Model UN; Ski Clb; Nwsp Rptr; Nwsp Sprt Ed; Sec Stu Cncl; Var L Ice Hcky; Var L Socr; High Hon Roll; NYS Regents Scholar 86; Clarkson U; Elec Engrng.

BAKER, DEBRA; Irondequoit HS; Rochester, NY; (Y); 50/385; Church Yth Grp; Hosp Aide; Ski Clb; Church Choir; Rep Soph Cls; JV Diving; Var Gym; Stat Lcrss; Score Keeper; Sftbl; Hnr Roll; NC; Commnctns.

BAKER, DIANE; Dominican Commercial HS; Middle Village, NY; (S); 32/288; Cmnty Wkr; Hosp Aide; Intnl Clb; JV Bsktbl; Hon Roll; Jr NHS; Natl Busnss Honor Soc 86; Busnss Admin.

BAKER, GINA; Newfare Central HS; Lockport, NY; (Y); Church Yth Grp; Varsity Clb; Capt Fld Hcky; Sftbl; Tennis; Capt Vllybl; Cert Of Hon Bus Math 85; Houghton Coll; Bus.

BAKER, HEIDI M; John Jay SR HS; South Salem, NY; (Y); Intnl Clb; Nwsp Ed-Chief; Nwsp Stf; Yrbk Bus Mgr; Yrbk Stf; High Hon Roll; Hon Roll; German Clb; Latin Clb; Library Aide; Rtry Intl Exchng Stu W Grmny 84-85; NY ST Rgnts Schlr 86; Mittelstufe Pruefung Frmn Flncy Exm 86; Tulane U; Intl Jrnlsm.

BAKER, JULIE A; Haverling HS; Bath, NY; (S); French Clb; JCL; Latin Clb; Math Clb; Band; Concert Band; Drm Mjr(t); Mrchg Band; Yrbk Stf; Rep Soph Cls.

BAKER, K LATONIA; Pittsford Merdon HS; Pittsford, NY; (Y); VP JA; Math Tm; Model UN; Var L Bsktbl; Var L Trk; High Hon Roll; Math Clb; Yrbk Phtg; Yrbk Stf; JV L Socr; Urban Lg Of Rochester Early Recog & Blck Schlr 86; Wellesley Coll; Pre-Med.

BAKER, KARL J; Peekskill HS; Peekskill, NY; (Y); Am Leg Boys St; Boy Scts; Teachers Aide; Rep Soph Cls; Rep Jr Cls; Pres Sr Cls; High Hon Roll; Hon Roll; Comp Sci.

BAKER, MARY; Kereny Memorial Acad; Waterford, NY; (Y); 9/40; Drama Clb; Q&S; Red Cross Aide; Capt Color Guard; Mrchg Band; School Play; Variety Show; Yrbk Stf; Rep Frsh Cls; Rep Soph Cls; USNLA 84-86; Schl Sprt Awd Schl Ldrshp Awd Schl Sci Awd 85-86; Suny At Oneonta; Ed.

BAKER, MARY; The Franciscan Acad; Syracuse, NY; (S); 3/26; Pres GAA; Hosp Aide; School Musical; Yrbk Bus Mgr; Sec Soph Cls; Var L Tennis; Var L Vllybl; High Hon Roll; Sec NHS; Ntl Merit Ltr; Franciscan Acadmc Schlrshp 85-86; Italian, Scn, Math & Schl Awds 83-84; Ntl Hnr Roll 85-86; Le Moyne Coll; Comm.

BAKER, OLLI; Penn Yan Acad; Bluff Point, NY; (Y); Am Leg Boys St; Model UN; Varsity Clb; Chorus; Lit Mag; Var Crs Cntry; Var Trk; English.

BAKER, PATRICIA ANN; Kendall JR SR HS; Holley, NY; (Y); Art Clb; VICA; Chorus; Color Guard; Nwsp Rptr; Nwsp Stf; Score Keeper; Socr; Wrstlng; Art Show Sibley Awd 84-86; Brockport; Commercial Art.

BAKER, ROBERT; Sherburne-Earlville Central HS; North Norwich, NY; (Y); Math Tm; Spanish Clb; Stu Cncl; Var Capt Crs Cntry; Var Capt Trk; High Hon Roll; Hon Roll; NHS; Crss Cntry Mst Outstndg Rnnr Yr 84-85; Trck Rcvd Bst Male Prfrmnc & Mst Valuable Rnnr 85-86; Military Acad; Compu.

BAKER, RUSS; Tonawanda JR SR HS; Tonawanda, NY; (Y); 17/220; SADD; JV Bsktbl; Var Ftbl; High Hon Roll; NHS; Pres Schlr; NYS Rgnts Schlrshp 86; Mlln Schlrshp 86; Tn Ythbd Schlrshp 86; Geneseo.

BAKER, SCOTT; Perry Central Schl; Perry, NY; (Y); 1/100; Mathletes; Math Tm; Varsity Clb; Pres Sr Cls; JV Var Bsktbl; Socr; JV Var Tennis; High Hon Roll; NHS; Scholastic Bowl; Hugh O Brien Awd 85; Engrng.

BAKER, SEAN; Cazenovia HS; Cazenovia, NY; (Y); 20/150; Aud/Vis; Church Yth Grp; Cmnty Wkr; Letterman Clb; Mathletes; Math Tm; PAVAS; Acpl Chr; Band; Chorus; ST Schlrshp 86; Engrng.

BAKER, SHANNAN; Warsaw Central HS; Warsaw, NY; (S); 5/90; Pres Sec Drama Clb; Pres French Clb; Pres Band; Pres Chorus; School Musical; School Play; High Hon Roll; NHS; Ntl Merit Ltr; Engl.

BAKER, STEVEN; Cooperstown Central HS; Fly Creek, NY; (Y); Boy Scts; Church Yth Grp; Library Aide; School Play; Stage Crew; Nwsp Stf; JV Var Ftbl; Hon Roll; Law Enfrcmnt.

BAKER, SYDNEY; Midwood HS; Brooklyn, NY; (Y); 15/520; Cmnty Wkr; Service Clb; School Musical; Cheerleading; High Hon Roll; Rgnts, Med Sci Dplma & Rgnts Nrsg Schlrshp 86; Hampton U; Pre-Med.

BAKER, TAMMY; Addison Central HS; Woodhull, NY; (Y); GAA; Color Guard; Trs Soph Cls; Trs Sr Cls; Diving; Mgr(s); Score Keeper; Sftbl; Swmmng; High Hon Roll.

BAKER, TINA; Hancock Central HS; Equinunk, PA; (Y); Church Yth Grp; OEA; Chorus; Yrbk Phtg; Yrbk Stf; Sec Jr Cls; Stat Wrstlng; Pratt Inst; Fshn Dsn.

BAKER, TODD; Attica SR HS; Attica, NY; (S); 1/155; Math Tm; Hon Roll; NHS; Regnts Schlrshp; Buffalo U Two Yr Schlrhsp; Buffalo U; Math.

BAKER, TOM; Thomas A Edison HS; Elmira Hts, NY; (Y); 3/73; Am Leg Boys St; Varsity Clb; Pres Jr Cls; Pres Sr Cls; Var L Bsktbl; Var L Ftbl; Var L Tennis; High Hon Roll; Lion Awd; Acad All-Amer; JR Rtrn; Pres Vrsty Clb; Suny Binghamtor ; Bio Chem.

BAKKE, KRISTIN; Mynderse Acad; Seneca Falls, NY; (Y); 20/139; Church Yth Grp; Drama Clb; Hosp Aide; Color Guard; School Play; Stage Crew; Yrbk Stf; Sec Frsh Cls; Rep Stu Cncl; High Hon Roll; Rgnts Schlrshp 86; Hghst Avrg In Scl Stdys 83; Cayuga CC; Cntrctr.

BAKKER, KAREN A; Newburgh Free Acad; Newburgh, NY; (Y); 3/580; Co-Capt Math Tm; Var Socr; Mgr Vllybl; Bausch & Lomb Sci Awd; Elks Awd; High Hon Roll; Sec NHS; Pres Schlr; Spanish NHS; Aamco Schlrshp 86; Duke U; Biomed Engr.

BAKKO, ERIK; Cortland JR SR HS; Cortland, NY; (Y); Radio Clb; Band; Chorus; Concert Band; Jazz Band; Mrchg Band; Pep Band; Lbrl Arts.

BAKOS, LAURA; Seton Catholic Central HS; Binghamton, NY; (S); 7/162; Drama Clb; Trs French Clb; Mathletes; Band; Chorus; Rep Stu Cncl; Bsktbl; Socr; Trk; NHS; Bio.

BAKSH, JAMAL; Jamaica HS; Queens, NY; (Y); Art Clb; Library Aide; Office Aide; Teachers Aide; Band; Concert Band; School Musical; Yrbk Phtg; Yrbk Stf; High Hon Roll; Arista Awd 83-84; Outstndng Acdmc Achvt 83; Queens Coll.

BALBERA, TODD; Newfield HS; Selden, NY; (Y); Varsity Clb; Im Bsbl; Var Capt Crs Cntry; Var Capt Trk; JV Wrstlng; High Hon Roll; NHS; Spanish NHS; Elec Engrng.

BALCH, MICHAEL; Colonie Central HS; Albany, NY; (Y); 6/467; JV Bsbl; JV Wrstlng; High Hon Roll; NHS; Ntl Merit Ltr; Law.

BALCOM, G TODD; South Glens Falls SR HS; S Glens Falls, NY; (Y); 16/240; Am Leg Boys St; DECA; Yrbk Ed-Chief; VP Soph Cls; Pres Jr Cls; NHS; Hon Roll; Pblc Rltns Chrmn Fthlls Crvtt Clb Inc 86; 3rd Pl ST Lvl DECA Comp 86; 1st Pl Rgnl DECA Comp 86; Bryant Coll; Bus Mang.

BALCOM, THOMAS; Pulaski HS; Pulaski, NY; (S); Crs Cntry; Trk; Hon Roll; John Ben Snow Awd 83 & 85; Acctng Awd 85; Oswego ST; Acctng.

BALCOMB, SOPHIA; Rhinebeck Central HS; Rhinebeck, NY; (Y); 5/103; Drama Clb; Chorus; School Musical; Yrbk Ed-Chief; Yrbk Stf; Var L Fld Hcky; High Hon Roll; NHS; Pres Acad Ftns Awd 86; Rgnts Schlrshp 86; Cornell; Marine Bio.

BALD, CHRISTINE; Clifton-Fine Central HS; Star Lake, NY; (S); 2/43; VP French Clb; Band; Chorus; School Play; Yrbk Stf; Sec Soph Cls; JV Var Cheerleading; JV Var Socr; Var L Trk; High Hon Roll; Aerosp Engrg.

BALDI, STACY; Walton Central HS; Walton, NY; (Y); 15/100; Model UN; Varsity Clb; VP Sr Cls; Tennis; Brd Of Ed Awd 86; Morrisville Ag; Comp Sci.

BALDONADO, HECTOR; Lanarsie HS; Brooklyn, NY; (Y); Computer Clb; Letterman Clb; PAVAS; Science Clb; Varsity Clb; Chorus; Color Guard; Flag Corp; School Musical; School Play; Pace; Law.

BALDRIDGE, KENNETH; Sewanhaka HS; Elmont, NY; (Y); 75/314; Aud/Vis; Boy Scts; DECA; Library Aide; Color Guard; Hon Roll; 2nd Pl DECA 86; St Johns; Acctng.

BALDUCCI, JEANNINE MARIE; Irvington HS; Irvington, NY; (Y); 51/109; Library Aide; Chorus; Var Capt Cheerleading; Var Capt Gym; Var Sftbl; JV Var Trk; Hon Roll; Bloom Awd 86; Awds Bus & Engl 86; SUNY Cobleskill; Secy Sci.

BALDWIN, JENNIFER L; Alexander Central HS; Darien, NY; (Y); 10/90; Drama Clb; Band; Color Guard; Concert Band; Mrchg Band; Sec Frsh Cls; Sec Soph Cls; Sec Sr Cls; Stu Cncl; Cheerleading; Rgt Schlrshp Wnnr Acad All Amer 86; Chrldng Awd 86; Prom Prncss 85; Alfred ST Coll; Math.

BALDWIN, KATHY; John F Kennedy HS; Utica, NY; (Y); 1/100; Pres Church Yth Grp; Key Clb; Mathletes; Yrbk Phtg; Rensselaer Mdl Math & Sci 86; Albany Coll; Phrmcy.

BALDWIN, KEVIN; Union-Endicott HS; Endicott, NY; (Y); 26/435; Computer Clb; Mathletes; SADD; Lit Mag; High Hon Roll; Hon Roll; NHS; Prfct Atten Awd; Jennie F Snapp Schlrshp 86; Earl Brink Schlrshp 86; U Of Rochester; Optcs.

BALDWIN, MARSHA; Mattituck HS; Mattituck, NY; (Y); 2/130; Spanish Clb; Lit Mag; Sftbl; High Hon Roll; Sal; Spnsh Awd High Avrg; St Josephs; Law.

BALDWIN, PATRICIA; St John The Baptist D HS; Brentwood, NY; (S); 5/501; Model UN; Ski Clb; SADD; Band; School Musical; Nwsp Rptr; French Hon Soc; High Hon Roll; Exploring; Girl Scts; Tri-M Music Hnr Soc 84-86; Jr Prom Cmmtte 86; Boston Coll; Bus Admin.

BALDYGO, WILLIAM; Rome Free Acad; Rome, NY; (Y); 55/483; Boy Scts; Ski Clb; Hon Roll; NHS; Pres Schlr; Clarkson U; Elctrcl Engr.

BALEMIAN, RICHARD; Walton HS; Bronx, NY; (Y); Computer Clb; Office Aide; Band; Tennis; U Of IL; Bus Admin.

BALESTRACCI, LISA; Bellport HS; Brookhaven, NY; (Y); 25/304; Drama Clb; Band; Chorus; Madrigals; Soph Cls; Stu Cncl; High Hon Roll; NHS; Newsday Teen Tlnt Wnnr 85; Rotary Stu Mnth 84; Boces Gifted & Tlntd Stu 84; Acting.

BALIAN, JOHN; Nottingham HS; Syracuse, NY; (Y); 26/500; Mathletes; Math Clb; Math Tm; Scholastic Bowl; Bsbl; Bowling; High Hon Roll; NHS; Rgnts Schlrshp; Bnghmtn.

BALINES, MITZY; Evander Childs HS; Bronx, NY; (Y); Exploring; VP Spanish Clb; Band; Diving; Swmmng; Hon Roll; Prfct Atten Awd; CPA.

BALL, JENNIFER L; Immaculata Acad; Orchard Park, NY; (Y); 4/44; JA; PAVAS; Chorus; School Musical; Trs Frsh Cls; Sec Soph Cls; Pres Stu Cncl; JV Var Cheerleading; Cit Awd; NHS; Rgnts Schlrshp 86; D Youville Coll Pres Hnrs Pgm 86; Mnthly Stu Awd 86; D Youville Coll; Accntng.

BALL, KELLY L; Lake Shore Central SR HS; Angola, NY; (Y); 19/284; Sec Stu Cncl; Capt Cheerleading; Hon Roll; NHS; Rgnts Schlrshp; MI ST U; Gnrl Bus Admin.

BALL, MARY; Tioga Central HS; Nichols, NY; (Y); Church Yth Grp; FCA; 4-H; Hosp Aide; Library Aide; School Musical; Nwsp Stf; Cit Awd; Hon Roll; NHS; Smmr Adv Ldrshp Traing 85; Spec Ed.

BALL, MARY; Victor Central Schl; Victor, NY; (Y); JA; Ski Clb; Stage Crew; Yrbk Stf; Stat Mgr(s); Stat Score Keeper; High Hon Roll; Hon Roll; Intl Law.

BALL, TERRI; Wilson Central HS; Ransomville, NY; (Y); 14/111; Red Cross Aide; School Play; Ed Yrbk Stf; Sec Frsh Cls; Var L Fld Hcky; Var Capt Trk; Var L Vllybl; High Hon Roll; VP Pres NHS; Ntl Merit Ltr; NYS Regnst Schlrshp 86; Marymt Acad Schlrshp 86; Athletic Schlrshp 86; Marymount Coll; Fash Desgn.

BALLAGH, ELAINE; North Rose-Wolcott HS; N Rose, NY; (Y); Trs Ski Clb; Trs Sec Cheerleading; JV Socr; Stat Swmmng; Var Trk; Hon Roll; NHS; Prfct Atten Awd.

BALLARD, DOREEN; Milford Central Schl; Milford, NY; (Y); 2/26; Hosp Aide; Drm Mjr(t); School Musical; JV Var Cheerleading; Socr; Bausch & Lomb Sci Awd; NHS; Pres Schlr; Sal; 300 Pt Club Music Milford 86; Clark Schlrshp Wnr 86; Hartwick Coll; Pre-Med.

BALLARD, JACQUELINE; Rome Free Acad; Rome, NY; (Y); Cmnty Wkr; Key Clb; Yrbk Stf; Pres Jr Cls; Pres Stu Cncl; Var Co-Capt Fld Hcky; Hon Roll; Jr NHS; Opt Clb Awd; Corp Law.

BALLARINO JR, SALVATORE A; Monsignor Farrell HS; Staten Island, NY; (Y); 119/288; JA; Office Aide; Stu Cncl; Im Ftbl; Hon Roll; St Johns U; Comp Sci.

BALLES, LAURA L; Pittsford Mendon HS; Pittsford, NY; (Y); Model UN; Chorus; School Musical; School Play; Yrbk Bus Mgr; Lit Mag; Sec NHS; Ntl Merit Schol; Val; Drama Clb; PTSA Ldrshp Awd 86; Yale Book Awd, French Awd 85; Princeton U; Pol Sci.

BALMORI, VANESSA; Susan E Wagner HS; Staten Island, NY; (Y); 30/476; Office Aide; Yrbk Stf; Var Trk; Var Capt Vllybl; Cit Awd; High Hon Roll; NHS; Mrt Rgnts Schlrshp 86-87; Pace Fncl Aid Schlrshp 86-87; Pace U; Pblc Accntng.

BALSAMO, MARK A; Pittsford Mendon HS; Pittsford, NY; (Y); Church Yth Grp; Latin Clb; Model UN; Band; Concert Band; Jazz Band; Pep Band; Yrbk Rptr; Socr; Var L Tennis; Crs Cntry Ski Var Ltr, Capt, MPV 84-86; Middlebury; Econ.

BALSHUWEIT, DODI; Odessa Montour HS; Montour Falls, NY; (Y); 21/86; Drama Clb; FHA; Teachers Aide; VICA; JV Var Cheerleading; Var Sftbl; High Hon Roll; Hon Roll; Voctnl Dipl Hnrs 86; H S Rgnts Dipl Hnr 86; Army.

BALTER, KAREN L A; Cathedral HS; New York, NY; (Y); 9/278; Chess Clb; Drama Clb; French Clb; Library Aide; Political Wkr; Nwsp Rptr; Rep Stu Cncl; Sftbl; High Hon Roll; Voice Dem Awd; 4yr Scl Stds Awd 86; Rgnst Schlrshp 86; Loyola U New Orleans; Pltcl Sci.

BALYSZAK, ROBERT; Auburn HS; Auburn, NY; (Y); Im Wt Lftg; High Hon Roll; Hon Roll; NHS; Engl.

BALZAN, JAMES; Saugerties HS; Saugerties, NY; (S); 3/252; German Clb; Math Clb; Math Tm; Varsity Clb; Symp Band; Var Capt Bsbl; Var Capt Wrstlng; High Hon Roll; NHS; Air Force Acad; Pilot.

BALZANO, LISA; Deer Park HS; Deer Park, NY; (Y); 34/381; FBLA; Hosp Aide; SADD; Mrchg Band; Variety Show; Rep Stu Cncl; Cheerleading; Pom Pon; Hon Roll; NHS; Italian Awd 84; Bus Mrktng.

BAMBERG, IRIS; North Babylon SR HS; N Babylon, NY; (Y); Church Yth Grp; Dance Clb; Church Choir; Var Bsktbl; Var Crs Cntry; Var Capt Trk; JV Vllybl; Coachs Awd 84; Mst Vlbl Rnr-Up Trck 86; Syracus U; Comp Sci.

BANAS, ED; John H Glenn HS; Huntington, NY; (Y); Pres Aud/Vis; Church Yth Grp; Nwsp Rptr; Pres Jr Cls; Pres Sr Cls; Hon Roll; Drama Clb; School Musical; Stage Crew; Variety Show; Cmnctns.

BANCROFT, DEBORAH; York Central HS; Piffard, NY; (Y); Trs AFS; Math Tm; Band; Chorus; Var Trk; Jr NHS; NHS; Ntl Merit Ltr; Cmnty Wkr; French Clb; Cls Rm Hnrs Math 84, Math & Frnch 86; Physcl Ftnss Awd 86; Optcl Engrng.

BANE, SUE; L A Webber HS; Lyndonville, NY; (Y); Band; Chorus; Mrchg Band; Bsktbl; Tennis; Sftbl; Vllybl; Hon Roll; Genessee Comm Coll; Sci & Mth.

BANERJEE, RUKMINI; Clara Barton HS; Brooklyn, NY; (Y); Computer Clb; Dance Clb; Exploring; Hosp Aide; Science Clb; Hon Roll; 1st Essay Black Hist Mnth NY Botanical Grdn/NYC Bd Ed, Outstndng Achvt Acdmc/Extra-Curr Actvts 86.

BANIA, JOHN P; La Salle Inst; Cohoes, NY; (Y); 3/78; Art Clb; Nwsp Stf; Yrbk Stf; Capt Crs Cntry; Golf; Capt Tennis; Trk; High Hon Roll; Sec NHS; Pres Schlr; Accptd US Military Acad 86; Chmstry Mjr.

BANKER, NANCY; Houghton Acad; Plattsburgh, NY; (Y); 3/18; Church Yth Grp; GAA; Varsity Clb; VP Jr Cls; Var Capt Bsktbl; Var Capt Socr; Var Capt Vllybl; Dnfth Awd; Hon Roll; NHS; Sprtsmnshp Awd 85-86; MVP Soccr 85-86; NHS Scholar 85-86; Houghton Coll; Phys Ed.

BANKS, CYNTHIA EUNICE; Hancock Central HS; Fishs Eddy, NY; (Y); German Clb; Chorus; Trs Jr Cls; Var Bsktbl; Var Cheerleading; Var Sftbl; Cit Awd; High Hon Roll; Hon Roll; NHS; Helen Lester Geom Rgnts Awd 85; Radio-Tv Brdcstng.

BANKS JR, FREDERIC W; Roscoe Central HS; Roscoe, NY; (Y); 1/23; Church Yth Grp; Band; Chorus; Church Choir; Yrbk Ed-Chief; Trs Stu Cncl; High Hon Roll; NHS; Val; Lazare Kaplan Schlrshp 86-87; David W Self Schlrshp 86-87; Pres Acdmc Ftns Awd 86-87; Yale U; Lbrl Arts.

BANKS, TEESHALAVONE; Herbert H Lehman HS; Bronx, NY; (Y); Dance Clb; Variety Show; Lit Mag; Bsktbl; Capt Cheerleading; Gym; Score Keeper; Socr; Sftbl; Vllybl; Excllnce Typng Awd 86; Excllnce Tax Bus Law Awd 86; Excllnce Comp Concpts Awd 86; Hofstra Coll; Bus Admin.

BANNAN, LISA; Kenmore East HS; Tonawanda, NY; (Y); 41/330; Sec German Clb; GAA; Math Clb; Var Capt Bowling; High Hon Roll; Hon Roll; NHS; Prfct Atten Awd; St Schlr; Girl Scts; Kenmore E Alumni Assoc Awd 86; 3rd Pl Sectnls Bowling 85; Hnrs Diploma 86; Buffalo ST; Ed.

BANNISTER, CHERYL; Odessa-Montour Central Schl; Montour Falls, NY; (Y); Aud/Vis; SADD; Pres Chorus; Swing Chorus; Variety Show; Yrbk Rptr; Yrbk Stf; Stu Cncl; High Hon Roll; Hon Roll; Educ.

BANNON, ELIZABETH C; Our Lady Of Lourdes HS; Poughkeepsie, NY; (Y); 3/173; Church Choir; Nwsp Rptr; Nwsp Stf; Var Capt Crs Cntry; Var Capt Swmmng; Var Capt Trk; High Hon Roll; Jr NHS; NHS; NY ST Rgnts Schlrshp 86; U CT Frfld; Accntng.

BANNON, LORI; Christ The King R HS; Middle Village, NY; (Y); 93/451; Library Aide; Yrbk Phtg; Yrbk Stf; Media Arts.

BANSE, JOHN; Valley Central HS; Montgomery, NY; (Y); Var L Bsbl; JV Bsktbl; Hon Roll; NHS; NC ST U; Metrlgy.

BANTLE, RICHARD; Frontier Central HS; Blasdell, NY; (Y); Am Leg Boys St; JV Var Bsbl; JV Var Ftbl; JV Var Trk; Bsebll ECIC Div I All Star 86; Richard Bantle; Oceanograph.

BANVARD, TIMOTHY; Long Beach SR HS; Point Lookout, NY; (S); 12/265; Cmnty Wkr; Math Clb; Science Clb; Nwsp Rptr; Var Socr; High Hon Roll; Hon Roll; NHS; Fut Physcns Clb 82-86; Ntl Hosp Ldrshp Svc Awd 84; Secy Fut Physcns Clb Host 85-86; Bio Sci.

BAPTISTE, SANDRA; Elmont Memorial HS; Elmont, NY; (Y); FBLA; Attnd Awd 82 & 86; Pre Med.

BAQUE, GISELLA; Grover Cleveland HS; Brooklyn, NY; (Y); 44/612; Church Yth Grp; Debate Tm; French Clb; Spanish Clb; Teachers Aide; Band; School Musical; Lit Mag; Socr; Hon Roll; Excllnt Certs Engl, Spnsh, Frnch, Scl Study, Math, Photo 84-86; NY U; Intl Bus.

BARABAS, MONICA; Alden SR HS; Alden, NY; (Y); Art Clb; Aud/Vis; Science Clb; SADD; Concert Band; Yrbk Phtg; Yrbk Stf; Hon Roll; Acad Awd; Arch.

BARANELLO, RICHARD; St Marys Boys HS; Merrick, NY; (Y); 37/178; Cmnty Wkr; Trk; Ltr Track 86; 2nd Hnrs Acad 84-86; SUNY; Dentstry.

BARATTA, CHRISTINA; St Dominic HS; Huntington, NY; (S); 14/119; Nwsp Rptr; VP Soph Cls; VP Jr Cls; VP Sr Cls; JV Var Cheerleading; Im Vllybl; High Hon Roll; Hon Roll; Spnsh Awd 84; Elmntry Educ.

BARATTA, CHRISTOPHER; La Salle Military Acad; E Islip, NY; (Y); 33/100; ROTC; Drm & Bgl; Stage Crew; Nwsp Stf; Im Bsktbl; Var Ftbl; JV Tennis; Im Wt Lftg; High Hon Roll; Hon Roll; St John Bptst De La Salle Awd Acad Achvt 85; Stg Crew-Tech Dir 85; Fordham U; Law.

BARAUSKAS, LISA A; Eastport HS; Eastport, NY; (Y); 6/49; Varsity Clb; Concert Band; Stu Cncl; Var Capt Cheerleading; NHS; NEDT Awd; Pres Schlr; Cmnty Wkr; Quiz Bowl; Ski Clb; NY ST Rgnst Schlrshp 85-86; Hugh O Brien Yth Fndtn NY S Ldrshp Smnr 83-84; Presdntl Clsrm 84-85; U Of CT; Ecnmcs.

BARBA, JENNIFER; Roy C Ketcham SR HS; Poughkeepsie, NY; (Y); VP AFS; Church Yth Grp; Cmnty Wkr; Drama Clb; Yrbk Ed-Chief; Yrbk Phtg; Ed Yrbk Stf; High Hon Roll; Hon Roll; Prfct Atten Awd; AFS Smr Exchng Pgm 86; Typng Awd 84; Nrsg.

BARBA, JOHN M; Monsignor Farrell HS; Staten Island, NY; (Y); 4/280; Computer Clb; Teachers Aide; Crs Cntry; Hon Roll; Jr NHS; NHS; Pres Schlr; Frdhm Schlrshp 86; NYU Trst Schlrshp 86; Rgnts Schlrshp 86; NY U; Jrnlsm.

BARBAGALLO, JOHN M; St Francis Prepatory Schl; Bayside, NY; (S); German Clb; Im Bsktbl; Im Fld Hcky; Im Ftbl; Im Sftbl; Im Vllybl; Wt Lftg; Hon Roll.

BARBAGLIA, SUZANNE; Jordan-Elbridge Central HS; Jordan, NY; (Y); 22/143; Hosp Aide; SADD; Concert Band; School Play; Yrbk Stf; Sec Stu Cncl; Var Bsktbl; Var Trk; High Hon Roll; VP NHS; NYSFBC Schlrshp 86; Carnegie Tutorial Schlrshp 86; R Sage Clg Troy Ny; Phys Therpy.

BARBATO, GINA; Hicksville HS; Hicksville, NY; (Y); Dance Clb; Pep Clb; JV Var Cheerleading; Im Gym; Hon Roll; Hlth.

BARBATO, JOHN D; Camden Central HS; Taberg, NY; (Y); 28/211; Ski Clb; Spanish Clb; Lcrss; JV Var Tennis; Hon Roll; Rgnts Schlrshp 86; Le Moyne Coll; Bio.

BARBATSULY, DENISE; West Hempstead HS; W Hempstead, NY; (Y); 28/320; Ski Clb; Concert Band; School Musical; School Play; Yrbk Phtg; NHS; Ntl Merit SF; Drama Clb; Drill Tm; Regents Schrlshp 86; NY Schlrs Pgm 86; NY U; Mgmt.

BARBATSULY, GEORGE; Manhasset HS; Manhasset, NY; (Y); Band; Mrchg Band; Orch; Pep Band; Nwsp Rptr; Nwsp Stf; JV Var Lcrss; JV Var Socr; High Hon Roll; NHS.

BARBEE, WESLEY; Our Saviour Lutheran HS; Bronx, NY; (Y); Office Aide; Rep Soph Cls; Var Sftbl; Im Vllybl; Hon Roll; Prfct Atten Awd; Bus.

BARBER, ALICIA; Hugh C Williams HS; Canton, NY; (Y); 1/130; Sec VP Thesps; Pres Band; Chorus; School Musical; School Play; Yrbk Ed-Chief; Lit Mag; Bausch & Lomb Sci Awd; High Hon Roll; Trs NHS; Area All State Band 85; Northwestern U; Cmmnctns.

BARBER, BRENDA; Bennett HS; Buffalo, NY; (Y); Girl Scts; Yrbk Stf; Cheerleading; Hon Roll; VITA Vlntr Tax Rtrn Assist 86; U Buffalo; Accntng.

BARBER, DEBBIE; Hilton Central HS; Rochester, NY; (Y); Cmnty Wkr; Dance Clb; French Clb; GAA; Girl Scts; Thesps; Yrbk Stf; JV Var Fld Hcky; High Hon Roll; Hon Roll; Bus.

BARBER, KYLE; Ticonderoga HS; Ticonderoga, NY; (Y); Varsity Clb; Var Bsktbl; Var Capt Ftbl; Var Trk; Im Vllybl; Im Wt Lftg; Hon Roll; NHS.

BARBER, LISA; Williamsville North HS; E Amherst, NY; (Y); DECA; Yrbk Bus Mgr; Yrbk Stf; Rep Jr Cls; Jrnlsm.

BARBER, RUSSELL; Fillmore Central HS; Fillmore, NY; (Y); 6/58; Pres Church Yth Grp; Chorus; School Play; Yrbk Stf; JV Var Socr; Var Trk; Hon Roll; NY St Regents Schlrshp 85-86; Daniel Webster Coll; Aviation.

BARBERA, ANTHONY; Palmyra-Macedon HS; Macedon, NY; (Y); 20/180; Church Yth Grp; Library Aide; SADD; Varsity Clb; Acpl Chr; Crs Cntry; Wrstlng; Cit Awd; Hon Roll; Prfct Atten Awd; Sec Ed Hist.

BARBERA, LAURA J; James Madison HS; Brooklyn, NY; (Y); Cmnty Wkr; JA; Office Aide; Office Aide; Service Clb; Teachers Aide; School Play; Lit Mag; NHS; Regents Coll Schlrshp 86; Soc Studies Awd; Spnsh Medal; Brooklyn Coll; Lawyer.

BARBIC, RONALD; Schoharie Central Schl; Central Bridge, NY; (S); 8/115; Math Tm; Varsity Clb; Var Bsbl; JV Bsktbl; Var Socr; High Hon Roll.

BARBIERE, CARMELINA VICTORIA; John Dewey HS; Brooklyn, NY; (Y); Service Clb; School Play; Mgr Stage Crew; Variety Show; Yrbk Stf; Rep Sr Cls; Stu Cncl; Gm Cmng Rcgntn Awd 84; Stu Gvrnmnt Awd 86; Pace U; Comp Sci.

BARBIERI, ELIZABETH; Academy Of St Joseph; Smithtown, NY; (Y); Church Yth Grp; Cmnty Wkr; Dance Clb; Drama Clb; FBLA; Hosp Aide; Science Clb; Chorus; Church Choir; School Play; Bio.

BARBOPOULOS, MARK; Sweet Home SR HS; Tonawanda, NY; (Y); Church Yth Grp; Cmnty Wkr; Chorus; Church Choir; Var JV Socr; Hon Roll.

BARBOSA, STEPHEN; Central Islip SR HS; Central Islip, NY; (Y); 66/365; Drama Clb; Speech Tm; SADD; School Play; Rep Stu Cncl; JV Var Bsbl; Dnfth Awd; Stu Orgnztn Apprec Awd 86; Drama Clb Best Scene Awd 84; Best Supporting Actor 86; Adelphi U; Bus Adm.

BARBOUR, JENNIFER; Vestal SR HS; Vestal, NY; (Y); Drama Clb; Spanish Clb; SADD; Chorus; Church Choir; Color Guard; Drill Tm; Mrchg Band; Stage Crew; Prfct Atten Awd; Mixed Chorus Vcl Awd 84-85; Music.

BARBOUR, RACHEL; Dominican Commercial HS; St Albans, NY; (Y); Art Clb; Computer Clb; Girl Scts; Cheerleading; Princpls List 86; Prfct Atten Awd 84 & 85; Cheyney U; Telecmmnctns.

BARBUSCIA, ANGELA; St Edmund HS; Brooklyn, NY; (Y); Achvmnt Math Awd 86; Achvmnt Kybrd Awd 86; Achvmnt Eng Awd 85; Law.

BARBUTO, AMBROSE; Henninger HS; Syracuse, NY; (Y); Var Socr; High Hon Roll; Engrng.

BARCIA JR, SALVATORE; Monsignor Farrell HS; Staten Island, NY; (Y); Band; Concert Band; Drill Tm; Mrchg Band; Stage Crew; Trk; High Hon Roll; NHS; Bus.

BARCKOW, JOSEPH; Newtown HS; Maspeth, NY; (Y); 8/781; Church Yth Grp; Math Clb; Math Tm; Office Aide; Bowling; High Hon Roll; Hon Roll; Prfct Atten Awd; Bernard Baruch Coll; Acctng.

BARCLAY, DEBORAH; Kenmore East HS; Tonawanda, NY; (Y); 83/330; Pres Pep Clb; PAVAS; School Musical; Swing Chorus; Yrbk Stf; Sec Stu Cncl; Var Cheerleading; Capt Trk; NHS; Rotary Awd; Frank C Densburger Awd 86; Irene Pearson Mrl Awd 86; Otstndng Chrldr Awd 86; Niagara U; Trvl.

BARCOMB, CINDY; Northern Adirondack HS; Altona, NY; (Y); VP 4-H; Band; Concert Band; Mrchg Band; Variety Show; 4-H Awd; Cosmetology.

BARCZAK, KATHLEEN; Villa Maria Acad; Buffalo, NY; (Y); Computer Clb; VP Sec Exploring; French Clb; Chorus; Bowling; High Hon Roll; Hon Roll; NEDT Awd; Canisius Coll; Psych.

BARCZAK, LAURIE; Mercy HS; Riverhead, NY; (Y); 2/180; Cmnty Wkr; Key Clb; Math Clb; Yrbk Stf; Var L Cheerleading; Var L Sftbl; High Hon Roll; Vet.

BARDEN, CHRISTOPHER M; South Glens Falls HS; Gansevoort, NY; (Y); 14/230; Am Leg Boys St; Drama Clb; SADD; Band; Pres Jr Cls; Var L Ftbl; Var L Trk; Var L Wrstlng; Hon Roll; NHS; Faclty Awd Outstndng Frshmn 83-84; Muncpl Ct Judg Boys ST 85-86; Yth Undrstndng Stdnt Exch Japn 85-86; West Point; Engrng.

BARDEN, JAMES; John S Burke Catholic HS; Middletown, NY; (Y); Boy Scts; Pres VP Church Yth Grp; Stage Crew; Var L Trk; Cit Awd; High Hon Roll; Hon Roll; NHS; Prfct Atten Awd; Crdnl Spllmn Yth Awd 86; Manhattan Coll; Chem Engr.

BARDINA, JENNIE; John Jay HS; Brooklyn, NY; (Y); JA; High Hon Roll; Hon Roll; Gladys Howard Meml Awd Ctznshp & Schlrshp 84; Meading Slvr Medal 84; John Jay Spn, Art Schlrshp 85-86.

BARDINA, JOSPHINE; John Jay HS; Brooklyn, NY; (Y); Yrbk Phtg; Yrbk Stf; Bsktbl; Vllybl; Svc Awd Gold Mdl 84; Law.

BARDON, KELLY L; Columbia HS; Castleton, NY; (Y); 148/417; Cmnty Wkr; Lit Mag; Cheerleading; Coach Actv; Powder Puff Ftbl; Score Keeper; NY ST Regnts Schlrshp 86; ST U Of NY Oswego; Frnch Ed.

BARDUNIAS, VALERIE; Marlboro Central HS; Marlboro, NY; (Y); French Clb; GAA; Varsity Clb; Var Bsktbl; Var Sftbl; High Hon Roll; Jr NHS; NHS; Prfct Atten Awd; Busnss Admin.

BARFIELD, ANTHONY; Roosevelt HS; Yonkers, NY; (Y); Church Yth Grp; Computer Clb; Political Wkr; Church Choir; Cit Awd; Mst Outstndng Stu In Sndy Schl 84; Lehman Col6; Comp Anlyst.

BARHITE, LISA; Groton Central JR SR HS; Groton, NY; (Y); 15/68; Pres Church Yth Grp; Ski Clb; VP Jr Cls; Off Stu Cncl; Var Bsktbl; Var Capt Socr; Var Capt Sftbl; High Hon Roll; Hon Roll; NHS; Mst Outstndng Grl Trphy 86; Mst Vlbl Sccr Plyr Awd US Army 86; SUNY Oswego; Tchng Math.

BARICKMAN, CHRISTOPHER M; Fox Lane HS; Bedford, NY; (Y); 84/300; Cmnty Wkr; German Clb; Chorus; Madrigals; School Musical; School Play; High Hon Roll; Hon Roll; Ntl Merit Ltr; WA U.

BARIE, KAREN L; Alexander Central HS; East Bethany, NY; (Y); 6/85; Pres Church Yth Grp; Trs Band; Pres Chorus; Church Choir; Mrchg Band; Swing Chorus; Sec Stu Cncl; Jr NHS; NHS; Genesee Cnty JR Miss Pag 1st Rnnr Up 86; Wstrn NY Draft Horse Queen 85; Wstrn NY All Around Shmn 85; Cornell U; Anml Sci.

BARILE, KIM; Our Lady Of Lourdes; Wappingers Fls, NY; (Y); 57/180; Hosp Aide; Nwsp Ed-Chief; Nwsp Rptr; Nwsp Stf; Bsktbl; Mgr(s); Score Keeper; Sftbl; Our Ldy Of Lrds 1st Acctg I Awd 86; Acctg.

BARILLA, MARIA-LOUISE; Mineola HS; Mineola, NY; (Y); 2/234; Trs French Clb; Keywanettes; Key Clb; Teachers Aide; Nwsp Ed-Chief; Kiwanis Awd; Pres NHS; Rotary Awd; Sal; Church Yth Grp; Harvard Prize Bk 85; John Huston Finley Schlr 86; Dont Drink And Drive Schlrshp 86; Knox College; Bio.

BARISH, ERIC M; Baldwin SR HS; Baldwin, NY; (Y); Aud/Vis; Chess Clb; VP Computer Clb; Latin Clb; Mathletes; Office Aide; Y-Teens; Ntl Merit SF; Mathletes Gold Mdl Wnnr 84-86; Am Invitatnl Math Exam Semi Finlst 86; Accptd To Hampshire Coll Smmr 85; Comp.

BARKAN, PAUL A; South Shore HS; New York, NY; (Y); 5/600; Chess Clb; Capt Debate Tm; Math Tm; Office Aide; Science Clb; Mgr Stage Crew; Nwsp Stf; Trs NHS; SUNY-BINGHAMTON; Hstry.

BARKER, CATRINA; Bennett HS; Buffalo, NY; (Y); Var Trk; RN.

BARKER, WENDY M; Scotia-Glenville HS; Scotia, NY; (Y); Key Clb; Varsity Clb; Yrbk Bus Mgr; Yrbk Stf; JV Var Socr; Var Cmnty Wkr; JV Var Vllybl; Hon Roll; Coll Of St Rose; Accntng.

BARKETT, BARBARA; New Hartford Central HS; Clinton, NY; (Y); Exploring; Spanish Clb; SADD; Teachers Aide; Nwsp Stf; Yrbk Stf; JV Vllybl; Hon Roll; Jr NHS; U Of Southern FL; Psych.

BARKEVICH, ALAN; Gloversville HS; Gloversvl, NY; (Y); Am Leg Boys St; VP Frsh Cls; VP Soph Cls; VP Jr Cls; VP Sr Cls; VP Stu Cncl; Var Crs Cntry; JV Im Trk; High Hon Roll; Ntl Merit Ltr; Engineering.

BARKLEY, MATTHEW I; Richburg Central HS; Friendship, NY; (Y); Am Leg Boys St; Boy Scts; Bsktbl; Jr NHS; NCTE Awd; Alfred ST Coll; Medical Lab.

BARKLEY, SUZANNE; Cicero-N Syracuse HS; Clay, NY; (S); 87/667; Exploring; JA; High Hon Roll; Hon Roll; NHS; Chrstn Yuth Ldrshp Awd, NY ST Music Assn Mdl Piano Solo Exclnt 85; SUNY Geneseo; Med Tech.

BARKOWSKI, JOSEPH; Colonie Central HS; Schenectady, NY; (Y); Trs Drama Clb; School Musical; School Play; Rep Sr Cls; Var Capt Vllybl; High Hon Roll; NHS.

BARKSDALE, LAURA; Maria Regina HS; New Rochelle, NY; (Y); Cmnty Wkr; Hosp Aide; JV Bsktbl; Hon Roll; Schl Svc Awd 84-85; Homrm Svc Awd 84-85; St Johns U; Pharmacy Pgm.

BARLASS, PATRICIA; Royalton-Hartland HS; Gasport, NY; (Y); 24/126; Trs Drama Clb; SADD; Teachers Aide; Chorus; School Musical; School Play; Stage Crew; Solo Comp Vocl Music 5 E Ratgs 84; Wldlf Mgmt.

BARLEBEN, JON; Irondequoit HS; Rochester, NY; (Y); Aud/Vis; Church Yth Grp; Exploring; Latin Clb; Model UN; Ski Clb; Varsity Clb; Var Capt Bsbl; Im Bsktbl; Im Lcrss; NY ST Regenst Schlrshp 86; SUNY Buffalo; Hstry.

BARLOW, SONYA; Rome Free Acad; Rome, NY; (Y); 51/550; Church Yth Grp; FTA; Girl Scts; Intnl Clb; Spanish Clb; Teachers Aide; School Play; Variety Show; Yrbk Stf; Im Vllybl; Elem Educ.

BARNA, MARIETTA; Nazareth Regional HS; Brooklyn, NY; (Y); Itln Awd 83-86.

BARNARD, MICHAEL B; Poland Central Schl; Poland, NY; (Y); Church Yth Grp; Drama Clb; 4-H; French Clb; Band; Chorus; Jazz Band; Cit Awd; 4-H Awd; High Hon Roll; Kings Coll; Mag Wrtr.

BARNARD, MICHELE; Kendall JR SR HS; Kendall, NY; (Y); Church Yth Grp; Cmnty Wkr; 4-H; SADD; Chorus; Concert Band; Mrchg Band; Hon Roll; NHS; Prfct Atten Awd; Hnr Roll Ltr 84; Hnr Roll Bar 85-86; Alfred U; Nrsng.

BARNAS, STAN; Williamsville South HS; Williamsville, NY; (Y); Ftbl; Ice Hcky; Art.

BARNER, KRISTIN M; Brockport Central HS; Hamlin, NY; (Y); 5/355; French Clb; Ski Clb; High Hon Roll; NHS; Fr III Awd 85; Scholar Dnnr 82-86; Regents Scholar 86; Rochester Inst Tech; Biochem.

BARNES, CHRISTINE; Springfield Gardens HS; New York, NY; (S); 15/438; Church Yth Grp; Dance Clb; Drama Clb; 4-H; School Play; Im Vllybl; Hon Roll; Salute To Youth Schlstc Achvt 85; Outstndg Yth Awd 85.

BARNES, DAWN CHERI; Narrowsburg Central HS; Narrowsburg, NY; (Y); 1/25; Pres Church Yth Grp; Band; Trs Frsh Cls; Trs Soph Cls; Trs Jr Cls; Trs Sr Cls; Var Capt Bsktbl; Bausch & Lomb Sci Awd; NHS; Ntl Merit Ltr; Athltc Of Yr 84-85; Pres Schlrshp Grnvl Coll 86; Greenville Coll; Math.

BARNES, DIANA; Scotia-Glenville HS; Scotia, NY; (Y); Church Yth Grp; Cmnty Wkr; French Clb; Girl Scts; JA; Key Clb; Red Cross Aide; Ski Clb; SADD; Church Choir; Trck Awds 85; Optmtst.

BARNES, ERIC; Central Islip HS; Central Islip, NY; (Y); Computer Clb; Band; Mrchg Band; School Musical; Attndnc Awd 81; Bus Adm.

BARNES JR, GARRY E; Marlboro HS; Marlboro, NY; (Y); Variety Show; Nwsp Stf; Yrbk Stf; Trk; Wt Lftg; Wrstlng; Hon Roll; Czehovia Coll Art Schlrshp 86-87; Czenovia Coll; Art.

BARNES, JULIE; Chester HS; Chester, NY; (Y); 4/65; GAA; Varsity Clb; Var L Bsktbl; Coach Actv; Var L Socr; Var L Sftbl; High Hon Roll; Hon Roll; NHS; St Schlr; Pres Schlrshp Morehead ST U 86; Rosemary Desanhs Mem Schlrshp 86; Morehead ST U Grant 86; Morehead ST U; Phy Ed.

BARNES, MELISSA; Bishop Loughlin Memorial HS; Brooklyn, NY; (Y); 3/231; Church Yth Grp; Girl Scts; Science Clb; Jazz Band; Nwsp Stf; Im Vllybl; High Hon Roll; NHS; U Penn; Psych.

BARNES, MICHELLE; Batavia HS; Batavia, NY; (Y); Church Yth Grp; Sec Drama Clb; Capt Color Guard; Drm & Bgl; Mrchg Band; School Musical; Rep Frsh Cls; Rep Soph Cls; Rep Jr Cls; Sftbl; Mst Outstndg Guard Stu 84-85; Area All ST Chrs 82-83; Genesee CC; Pol Sci.

BARNES, PATRICIA; Jordan Elbridge JR SR HS; Elbridge, NY; (Y); Church Yth Grp; Drama Clb; French Clb; Pep Clb; Ski Clb; SADD; Church Choir; Yrbk Stf; Rep Frsh Cls; VP Soph Cls; Hugh O Brien Yth Fndtn Schlrshp 85; Oper Entrps Schlrshp 86; Keuka College; Pre Law.

BARNES, PRISCILLA; Minisink Valley Central Schl; Howells, NY; (Y); Sec Key Clb; SADD; Varsity Clb; Drill Tm; Flag Corp; Mrchg Band; Stu Cncl; Capt Var Vllybl; High Hon Roll; Hon Roll; Cmrcl Art.

BARNES, TAMMY; Kenmore East HS; Kenmore, NY; (Y); Church Yth Grp; Church Choir; Vllybl; Ntl Music Awd 81-84; Bus.

BARNETT, CHERYL; Letchworth Central HS; Portageville, NY; (Y); 3/87; Math Tm; Color Guard; School Musical; Yrbk Ed-Chief; Var Cheerleading; Cit Awd; DAR Awd; High Hon Roll; NHS; Prfct Atten Awd; Trip Washington DC 86; Boston U; Archlgy.

BARNETT, KENNY R; Bronx HS Of Science; Bronx, NY; (Y); Trs Debate Tm; NFL; Trs Speech Tm; Im Bsktbl; Im Mgr(s); Im Sftbl; Im Vllybl; Hon Roll; NHS; Prfct Atten Awd; Law.

BARNETT, SUSAN; Charles O Dickerson HS; Jacksonville, NY; (Y); 3/130; English Clb; Library Aide; Spanish Clb; Nwsp Stf; Sec Stu Cncl; High Hon Roll; NHS; 1st Pl JETS Comp Engl 85-86; 1st Pl Schl Creative Writing Cntst Essay 85-86; Humanities.

BARNETT JR, WILLIAM; Northville Central HS; Mayfield, NY; (Y); 7/53; SADD; Varsity Clb; School Play; Yrbk Stf; Rep Stu Cncl; Var Bsktbl; Var L Trk; NHS; Prtrdg Mem Schlrshp 86; Dvd E Ldr Mem Awd 86; NY SU U Buffalo; Biochem.

BARNEY, HILDA; Franklin Acad; N Bangor, NY; (Y); Hon Roll.

BARNHART, ED; Bainbridge-Guilford HS; Bainbridge, NY; (Y); Boy Scts; Church Yth Grp; Ski Clb; Concert Band; Mrchg Band; Orch; JV Var Ftbl; Var Ice Hcky; Hon Roll; JV Var Score Keeper; Rifle Team Co-Capt 85-86; MVP Rifle Team 85-86; NRAS Exprt Riflemn Awd 85-86; Secndry Tchng.

BARNHART, KIMBERLY; Tioga Central HS; Barton, NY; (S); 17/85; Ski Clb; Var Capt Cheerleading; JV Mgr(s); Var Sftbl; Hon Roll; NHS; Mst Outstndng Fll-Wntr Chrldr 85; 3-Yr Awd Chrldng 85; St Josephs Schl Nrsng; Nrs.

BARNIAK, VICTORIA; Notre Dame HS; Pavilion, NY; (S); 2/80; Ski Clb; Spanish Clb; Var Tennis; High Hon Roll; NHS; Top Wrkng Potntl 85.

BARNNART, KIMBERLY; Tioga Central HS; Barton, NY; (Y); 16/86; Ski Clb; JV Var Cheerleading; JV Mgr(s); JV Var Sftbl; High Hon Roll; Hon Roll; NHS; Mst Outstndng Chrldr Awd 85; Guthrie Clinic Schlrshp 86; Hm Ec Awd 86; Arnot Ogden Hosp Schl Of Nrsng.

BARNUM, DOUG; Fairport HS; Fairport, NY; (Y); 3/605; Computer Clb; Math Tm; Concert Band; Mrchg Band; Orch; Bausch & Lomb Sci Awd; High Hon Roll; NHS; Ntl Merit SF; CO Schl Mines Medl Achvt Math & Sci 85-86; Empire ST Schlrshp Excllnc 85-86; Princeton U; Math.

BAROMETRE, CARINE; Midwood HS At Brooklyn Clg; Brooklyn, NY; (Y); Leo Clb; Library Aide; School Musical; Wt Lftg; Prfct Atten Awd; Bio.

BARON, HOWARD; John Dewey HS; Brooklyn, NY; (Y); Boy Scts; Chess Clb; Orch; Eagle Scout 86; Brooklyn; Pre Law.

BARON, JESSICA; Harry S Truman HS; Bronx, NY; (Y); Girl Scts; Science Clb; Band; Orch; Yrbk Phtg; Yrbk Stf; Trk; Cmnctns.

BARON, NATACHA; Midwood HS; Brooklyn, NY; (Y); Library Aide; Office Aide; Variety Show; Capt Cheerleading; Hon Roll; Prfct Atten Awd; Med.

BARONCELLI, CRAIG A; Christian Brothers Acad; Cazenovia, NY; (Y); Boys Clb Am; Cmnty Wkr; Exploring; Nwsp Rptr; Nwsp Sprt Ed; Nwsp Stf; JV Im Socr; JV Tennis; High Hon Roll; Schl Hnr Scty; Cmmnctns.

BARONE, ANNE; Kenmore West SR HS; Kenmore, NY; (Y); Camera Clb; Service Clb; Acpl Chr; Chorus; School Musical; Nwsp Rptr; Ed Nwsp Stf; High Hon Roll; French Clb; Math Tm; Wellesley Bk Awd 86; Kenmore Town Tonawanda Schls Poetry 86; Marine Sci.

BARONE, DANIELLE; St John Villa Acad; Staten Island, NY; (Y); Yrbk Stf; Achvt Awds-Sci; Achvt Awds-Eng; Yrbk Dsgn Staff; St Johns U; Bus Cmnctns.

BARONE, DANNY; Susan E Wagner HS; Staten Island, NY; (Y); Computer Clb; Awd For Excllnc In Music 84; Computer Programming.

BARONE, LINDA; Carmel HS; Carmel, NY; (Y); 12/350; Ed Yrbk Stf; High Hon Roll; Hon Roll; NHS; Ntl Merit Ltr; Pres Schlr; Syracuse U; Chem Engrng.

BARONE, LISA; West Genesee SR HS; Camillus, NY; (Y); Spanish Clb; Mrchg Band; Yrbk Stf; Sftbl; Hon Roll; SUNY Oswego; Elem Educ.

BARONE, MICHAEL A; Auburn HS; Auburn, NY; (Y); 19/424; Boy Scts; Chrmn Church Yth Grp; VICA; Yrbk Phtg; Trk; Cit Awd; High Hon Roll; Pres Schlr; Sci Dept Awd Chem 85-86; NY ST Rgnts Schlrshp 85-86; Worcester Polytech; Chem Engrng.

BARONE, MIKE; Batavia HS; Batavia, NY; (Y); 32/205; JV Bsbl; Var JV Bsktbl; Var JV Ftbl; Engrng.

BARR, AARON; Savona Central HS; Bath, NY; (Y); Am Leg Boys St; Boy Scts; Ski Clb; Chorus; Concert Band; Mrchg Band; Var JV Bsktbl; JV Var Socr; Var L Trk; Comp Drwng.

BARR, JAMES A; Walton HS; Bronx, NY; (Y); 230/545; CAP; JA; Band; John Jay College; Law Enfrcmnt.

BARR, KENNETH; New Lebanon Central HS; New Lebanon, NY; (Y); Math Tm; Concert Band; VP Sr Cls; Trk; Band Won Lcl Bttl Of Bands Recvd Free Studio Tm 86.

BARR, LISA; Camden Central HS; Camden, NY; (Y); 11/178; Pep Clb; Varsity Clb; Trs Stu Cncl; Var L Cheerleading; Var L Sftbl; High Hon Roll; Hon Roll; NHS; R N Whippe, A Loveonguth Schlrshps, Pres Ftnss Awd 86; SUNY Morrisvill; Acctg.

BARR, MARY ELIZABETH; West Seneca West SR HS; W Seneca, NY; (Y); Debate Tm; Office Aide; Spanish Clb; Yrbk Rptr; Yrbk Stf; Rep Soph Cls; Rep Jr Cls; Rep Stu Cncl; JV Var Socr; JV Var Swmmng; 1st Hnrs Latin & Spn 85 & 86; Hghst Avg Spn 85; Law.

BARR, MICHAEL; Horace Greeley Ny; Chappaqua, NY; (Y); French Clb; Pres JA; School Musical; School Play; Variety Show; Rep Sr Cls; Trk; Vllybl; Outstndng Achiever Of The Yr-Jr Achvmt 84; Grinnell Coll.

BARRAVECCHIO, ANTHONY; Monsignor Farrell HS; Staten Island, NY; (Y); 20/319; Chess Clb; Nwsp Stf; Lit Mag; Im Bsktbl; Im Bowling; Im Ftbl; JV Socr; Hon Roll; Jr NHS; NHS; Italian Poetry Awd Fordham U 86; Amer Schltc Press 1st Pl Awd 86; JR Svc Awd 85; Med.

BARRESI III, ANTHONY V; Hendrick Hudson HS; Croton On Hudson, NY; (Y); 37/187; Var Stu Cncl; High Hon Roll; Hon Roll; Bentley Coll; Bus Admin.

BARRETO, ERNEST; Niskayuna HS; Schenectady, NY; (Y); Art Clb; Pres Chess Clb; Computer Clb; Quiz Bowl; Mrchg Band; Symp Band; Lit Mag; Rep Stu Cncl; Mgr(s); French Hon Soc; Williams Coll Bk Awd 85; Sci Olympd NY ST Brnz Mdl Ntl Brnz Mdl 85; Physcs.

BARRETT, EILEEN; Newtown HS; Elmhurst, NY; (Y); 11/787; Teachers Aide; Yrbk Stf; Rep Stu Cncl; Var Capt Bsktbl; Var Capt Sftbl; Var Capt Vllybl; High Hon Roll; NHS; Arista 86-87.

BARRETT, ERIN G; Clarkstown H S North; Congers, NY; (Y); Nwsp Sprt Ed; Nwsp Stf; Ed Lit Mag; Trs Stu Cncl; JV Socr; Hon Roll; Jr NHS; NCTE Awd; VP NHS; Historical Society Of Rockland County Award 86; Poem Published In Issue Of The Apprentice Writer 86; Eng.

BARRETT, KATHY; Mohonasen HS; Schenectady, NY; (Y); JV Var Cheerleading; Socr; Schenectady CC; Htl Mgmt.

BARRETT, KERRY; Lansingburgh HS; Troy, NY; (Y); French Clb; Varsity Clb; Chorus; Rep Sr Cls; Var Capt Bsktbl; Var Capt Crs Cntry; Var Capt Trk; Hon Roll; NHS.

BARRETT, LARRY; Fayetteville-Manlius HS; Manlius, NY; (Y); Boy Scts; Var Bsktbl; Var Golf; Var Lcrss.

BARRETT, LYNN; Beacon HS; Beacon, NY; (Y); 15/250; Church Yth Grp; Trs French Clb; German Clb; Band; Mrchg Band; Pep Band; Hon Roll; Jr NHS; NHS; All Cty Msc Fest Wind Ensmb 84; Zone 10 Area All-ST NYSMMA Msc Fest 85; NYSMMA Comp 85.

BARRETT, MATT; Dryden HS; Mclean, NY; (Y); Am Leg Boys St; Church Yth Grp; Quiz Bowl; Spanish Clb; School Play; Var L Bsbl; Var L Ftbl; Var L Swmmng; High Hon Roll; NHS; Econ.

BARRETT, MELISSA; Hutchinson Central Technical HS; Buffalo, NY; (Y); 2/260; Natl Beta Clb; Science Clb; Band; Mrchg Band; High Hon Roll; Elec Engrng.

BARRETT, MICHAEL; York Central HS; Piffard, NY; (Y); Math Tm; Ski Clb; Ftbl; NHS; Engrng.

BARRETT JR, ROBERT W; Delaware Academy & Central Schl; Delhi, NY; (Y); 1/85; Am Leg Boys St; Jazz Band; School Musical; Yrbk Phtg; Rptr Lit Mag; High Hon Roll; NHS; Ntl Merit Ltr; Church Yth Grp; German Clb; Gldn Key Awd/Schlstc Art Awd Comp 86; NY ST Snt Stdnt Plcy Frm 86; Trinity U; Engl.

BARRETT, RONALD; Hutch Tech HS; Buffalo, NY; (Y); Color Guard; Var Trk; Cit Awd; High Hon Roll; Hon Roll; Jr NHS; SAR Awd; Navy; Hlcptr Pilot.

BARRETT, STEVEN; Saranac Lake HS; Saranac Lk, NY; (Y); Church Yth Grp; Cmnty Wkr; Stage Crew; Pastors Awd 83, 85; Electrncs.

BARRETT, SUE; Skaneateles HS; Skaneateles, NY; (Y); 28/153; Ski Clb; Variety Show; JV Capt Bsktbl; Swmmng; Tennis; Trk; High Hon Roll; Hon Roll; NHS; Ithaca Coll; Lbrl Arts.

BARRETTE, CHRIS; Saranac Central HS; Plattsburgh, NY; (S); 53/104; Boy Scts; Drama Clb; French Clb; Pres FBLA; Pres SADD; School Musical; School Play; Variety Show; Yrbk Stf; Hon Roll; Hugh O Brien Yth Ambsdr ST Smnr 83-84; Ntl Piano Plyng Audtns 84; Prsdntl Physcl Ftns Awd 84; Johnson & Wales; Rstnt Mgmnt.

BARRINGER, RONALD; Frontier Central HS; Hamburg, NY; (Y); Cmnty Wkr; Spanish Clb; Varsity Clb; L Crs Cntry; JV Var Ftbl; Var Trk; Var Capt Wrstlng; Hon Roll; Engrng.

BARRION, ANTONIO; Archbishop Molley HS; S Ozone Park, NY; (Y); 26/383; Sec Art Clb; French Clb; Chorus; Trk; Hon Roll; NHS; Medicine.

BARRIOS, ELIZABETH; Midwood HS; Brooklyn, NY; (Y); 57/667; Math Tm; Office Aide; Chorus; Yrbk Stf; Jr NHS; NHS; Prfct Atten Awd; Bus.

BARRON, LAURA; Catholic Central HS; Watervliet, NY; (Y); French Clb; Math Clb; SADD; Chorus; Var Bowling; Var Sftbl; Var Tennis; High Hon Roll; NHS; Albany Diocesan Drug Ed Ministry Peer Ldrshp Awd 86.

BARROW, JOSETTE; Preston HS; Bronx, NY; (Y); VP Sr Cls; Var Sftbl; Var Trk; Hon Roll; Variety Show; Im Socr; Im Vllybl; Latin Awd 86; Natl Hnr Scty Axlry 85; St Johns U; Accntng.

BARROWS, SEAN; Oxford Acadamy & Central HS; Oxford, NY; (Y); 21/85; Church Yth Grp; Pres 4-H; VP FFA; Church Choir; 4-H Awd; Hon Roll; Prfct Atten Awd; FFA Empr Frmr Drgr 85; SUNY Morisville; Wdprdcts Tech.

BARRY, BRIAN D; Amherst Central HS; Amherst, NY; (Y); 18/292; Church Yth Grp; Cmnty Wkr; Chorus; Var Golf; Var Capt Ice Hcky; High Hon Roll; L Kent Bergrann Golf 85; MVP Golf 84; SUNY; Bus Mgmt.

BARRY, GREGORY; St John The Baptist D H S; Copiague, NY; (Y); Hon Roll; Cmmnctns.

BARRY JR, JAMES J; Minisink Valley HS; Middletown, NY; (Y); 10/250; Debate Tm; Math Tm; SADD; Ftbl; High Hon Roll; NHS; Prfct Atten Awd; Rotary Awd; Cert Of Hnr-Acadmc Excllnc-Schlrshp 85; Yth In Govt 84-86; SUNY-BINGHAMTON; Chem.

BARRY, JAMES P; Mt St Michael Acad; New York, NY; (S); 36/308; Church Yth Grp; Trk; NHS; NY U; Law.

BARRY, JOHN; Catholic Central HS; Troy, NY; (Y); Church Yth Grp; Cmnty Wkr; French Clb; JA; Math Clb; SADD; Variety Show; Yrbk Phtg; JV Bsktbl; Peer Ldrshp 84-86; Comm.

BARRY, JOHN; Clarkstown S HS; Bardonia, NY; (Y); Aud/Vis; Church Yth Grp; JV Lcrss; Var Socr; Jr NHS; Comm.

BARRY, JOHN; Marlboro HS; Marlboro, NY; (Y); High Hon Roll; Jr NHS; NHS; Prsdntl Acad Ftns Awd 86; Rutgers U; Mchncl Engr.

BARRY, KATHLEEN D; West Babylon HS; West Babylon, NY; (Y); 39/419; Computer Clb; SADD; Yrbk Phtg; Yrbk Stf; Var Crs Cntry; Hon Roll; NHS; Dowling Coll; Biol.

BARRY, KEVIN; Clarence Central HS; Clarence, NY; (Y); 119/250; Church Yth Grp; Church Choir; School Play; Yrbk Stf; Off Jr Cls; Utica Coll; Psych.

BARRY, KRISTEN; St Barnabas HS; Bronx, NY; (S); 12/188; Library Aide; Teachers Aide; Nwsp Stf; Yrbk Stf; JV Sftbl; High Hon Roll; NHS; Spanish NHS; Service Clb; Spanish Clb; Mdl Hghst Mrk In Span; Cert Hnr In Relgn; Natl Sci Olympd Cert Of Merit; Bus.

BARRY, PATRICK; Bishop Cunningham HS; Oswego, NY; (Y); 6/30; French Clb; Variety Show; Rep Frsh Cls; Rep Soph Cls; Trs Jr Cls; Trs Sr Cls; Socr; DAR Awd; Hon Roll; Frgn Exchng Frnc 85.

BARRY, ROBERT J; Chaminade HS; Albertson, NY; (Y); 31/340; Am Leg Boys St; Boy Scts; Hosp Aide; Band; Nwsp Stf; Im Bsktbl; Im Ftbl; Var Trk; Cit Awd; Hon Roll; Eagle Scout Awd 85; Mechanical Engineering.

BARRY, SEAN; Victor SR HS; Victor, NY; (Y); 22/228; Pres Trs Service Clb; Spanish Clb; Varsity Clb; Stu Cncl; Var Crs Cntry; Var L Swmmng; Var Trk; High Hon Roll; NHS; Ntl Merit SF; Mltry Pilot.

BARRY, SENTA; Buffalo Acad Of The Sacred Heart; Amherst, NY; (Y); VP Church Yth Grp; French Clb; JCL; Sec Latin Clb; Ski Clb; Nwsp Stf; Rep Soph Cls; Capt Cheerleading; Hon Roll; NHS; Schlrshp Sacred Heart; Eng.

BARSTOW, BRIAN R; Massena Central HS; Massena, NY; (Y); 3/250; Boy Scts; JV Var Socr; High Hon Roll; Hon Roll; NHS; Ntl Merit Ltr; Prfct Atten Awd; Pres Schlr; St Schlr; Natl Hnr Socty Treas 85-86; Scott Shambo Mst Dedctd Sccr Plyr Awd 85-86; Hnr Grad; VA Tech; Indstrl Engr.

BARTCZAK, DAVID; H C Technical HS; Buffalo, NY; (Y); 2/276; Am Leg Boys St; Boy Scts; Math Tm; Science Clb; Pres Band; Socr; Swmmng; High Hon Roll; NHS; Sal; AFROTC Schlrshp 86; NROTC Schlrshp 86; Regents Schlrshp 86; Rensselaer Plytch Inst; Mech En.

BARTEL, ANNE E; Nottingham HS; Syracuse, NY; (Y); 17/250; Church Yth Grp; Spanish Clb; Yrbk Stf; Var Capt Vllybl; Hon Roll; NHS; Spanish NHS; Regents Schlrshp 85-86; SUNY Binghamton; Bio.

BARTEL, CHERYL; Long Island Lutheran HS; Garden City, NY; (Y); Church Yth Grp; Drama Clb; Exploring; Girl Scts; Math Clb; Math Tm; Pep Clb; Spanish Clb; Acpl Chr; Chorus; Westmont Coll; Engl.

BARTELL, BARRETT; Schoharie Central HS; Schoharie, NY; (S); 2/100; Drama Clb; Latin Clb; Ski Clb; Band; School Musical; Var Bsktbl; Var Golf; Var Socr; Var Tennis; High Hon Roll; U San Diego; Film.

BARTH, CLEA C; William Nottingham HS; Syracuse, NY; (Y); 20/220; Latin Clb; Math Tm; Ski Clb; Yrbk Rptr; Lit Mag; Sr Cls; Stat Lcrss; High Hon Roll; NHS; Slvr Mdl Ntl Latn Axam 85; NYS Regnts Schlrshp 86; Muhlenberg Coll; Chem.

BARTH, DEBORAH; Grand Island HS; Grand Island, NY; (Y); French Clb; Band; Lib Concert Band; Pep Band; Stu Cncl; Hon Roll; Psych.

BARTH, JOHN; Tioge Central HS; Barton, NY; (S); 6/78; Drama Clb; Quiz Bowl; Scholastic Bowl; Thesps; Chorus; School Musical; Variety Show; Rep Stu Cncl; JV Bsbl; Var Crs Cntry; Ntl Latin Exam Gold Mdlst 85; Library Clb VP 85-86; Drama.

BARTH, MIRIAM; New Lebanon Central HS; Nassau, NY; (Y); Var Score Keeper; Var Socr; JV Swmmng; 2nd Pl-Dsgn/Advrtsng Cmptn 85; CDTAA Prjct Exhbt-3 Drwngs 86; Engrng.

BARTKOW, BONNIE; Curtis HS; Staten Island, NY; (Y); Office Aide; Teachers Aide; Var Cheerleading; Var Trk; Hon Roll; Roger Williams Coll; Arch.

BARTKOWSKI, DAVID; Bishop Maginn HS; Albany, NY; (S); 3/86; Latin Clb; Math Clb; Ski Clb; Trs Soph Cls; Stat Bsktbl; Crs Cntry; Golf; High Hon Roll; NHS; Bus.

BARTLETT, BETH; Camden Central HS; Camden, NY; (Y); 55/211; Ski Clb; Varsity Clb; Rep Stu Cncl; Tennis; High Hon Roll; Exec Sec.

BARTLETT, CHRISTOPHER M; East Aurora HS; East Aurora, NY; (Y); 27/184; Boys Clb Am; Church Yth Grp; Letterman Clb; SADD; Varsity Clb; School Musical; Variety Show; Yrbk Stf; Var L Bsbl; Var L Ftbl; Rgnts Schlrshp; NROTC; GMI Engrg & Mgmt Inst; Ind Eng.

BARTLETT, CODY; Bloomfield Central HS; E Bloomfield, NY; (Y); Am Leg Boys St; Chess Clb; French Clb; Ski Clb; SADD; Rep Frsh Cls; Rep Soph Cls; Im Bsktbl; JV Socr; JV Vllybl; Mrt Rl 85-86; Devry Inst Of Tech; Accntnt.

BARTLETT, DENISE; Sheepshead Bay HS; Brooklyn, NY; (Y); 61/439; Church Yth Grp; Band; Concert Band; Variety Show; Yrbk Phtg; Hon Roll; Prfct Atten Awd; Bus Educ Mtl Exclnc Wrd Proc 86; SUNY Buffalo; Bio.

BARTLETT, TERESE; Pembroke Central HS; Corfu, NY; (Y); 10/120; Science Clb; Chorus; School Play; Variety Show; Yrbk Stf; Cheerleading; Hon Roll; NHS; Bus.

BARTLEY, DEBORAH; Midwood HS At Brooklyn College; Brooklyn, NY; (Y); Office Aide; Service Clb; Teachers Aide; Chorus; School Play; Yrbk Stf; Rep Stu Cncl; Cheerleading; Prfct Atten Awd; Handball Tm 84; Bus Mgmt.

BARTO, RICHARD; Ivondequoit HS; Rochester, NY; (Y); 40/400; Church Yth Grp; Spanish Clb; Trs Frsh Cls; Trs Soph Cls; Pres Trs Stu Cncl; JV Tennis; JV Wrstlng; Hon Roll; Bus.

BARTOK, ROBERT; Churchville-Chili HS; Rochester, NY; (Y); Boy Scts; JCL; Latin Clb; Nwsp Stf; Var Wrstlng; NY ST Regents Schlrshp 86; St John Fisher Coll; Accntng.

BARTOKVICH, VICKI; Hamburg SR HS; Hamburg, NY; (Y); 13/389; Am Leg Aux Girls St; Pres Spanish Clb; VP Rep Stu Cncl; Hon Roll; NHS; Cmnty Wkr; Hosp Aide; Library Aide; Ski Clb; Rep Frsh Cls; Bus Awd 84; Soc Studies Awd 84; Richard R Hansen Awd & Studt Cncl Apprectn Awd 84; Syracuse U; Advertising.

BARTOLOMEO, ANDREW; High School Of Art & Design; Brooklyn, NY; (Y); 15/330; Teachers Aide; Nwsp Rptr; Yrbk Stf; Var Bowling; Hon Roll; NHS; SR Grphc Artst & Rgnts Schlrshp Awd 85-86; Ntl Art Hnr Scty 83-86; Cooper Union; Grphc Dsgn.

BARTOLOTTI, CHRISTINE; Whitesboro SR HS; Utica, NY; (Y); GAA; Letterman Clb; Ski Clb; SADD; Varsity Clb; Lit Mag; Rep Stu Cncl; Hon Roll; Whitesboro Tchrs Assoc Awd 86; Capt Ski Tm, MVP Awd; Potsdam Coll; Indstrl Rel.

BARTON, DENA; Notre Dame-Bishop Gibbons HS; Clifton Park, NY; (S); 10/90; French Clb; Trk; High Hon Roll; Hon Roll; NHS; Soc Stud Awd 83; Fr Awd 84; Med.

BARTON, IVY; Hendrick Hudson HS; Peekskill, NY; (Y); Church Yth Grp; Hosp Aide; Mathletes; Office Aide; Stu Cncl; JV Var Bsktbl; Var L Fld Hcky; Var L Socr; High Hon Roll; NHS; Hghst French Avg; All Lgu Hnrbl Mntn Soccer; Accntng.

BARTON, JEFF; Bolivar Central HS; Boliver, NY; (Y); 8/52; Hosp Aide; School Musical; Var L Bsbl; Var L Bsktbl; Mgr(s); Church Yth Grp; Dance Clb; Drama Clb; Spanish Clb; Band; Area All ST Chorus 85; All County Chorus 84-86; All County Swing Chorus 86; Armed Forces; Science.

BARTON, ROBERT P; Red Jacket Central HS; Shortsville, NY; (Y); 3/91; Pres Church Yth Grp; School Musical; Yrbk Sprt Ed; Rep Frsh Cls; VP Stu Cncl; Var L Ftbl; Var L Trk; VP NHS; MVP Of Tracdk 85-86; Marine Corps Dstngshd Athlete Awd 86; NYS All Acdmc Bsktbll Tm 85-86; Ithaca Coll; Accntng.

BARTONE, LISA; Watkins Glen HS; Watkins Glen, NY; (S); Letterman Clb; Nwsp Stf; Trs Frsh Cls; Trs Soph Cls; Trs Jr Cls; Trs Rep Stu Cncl; Swmmng; Tennis; High Hon Roll; NHS; Comm.

BARTONIK, KIMBERLY; Bellport HS; E Patchogue, NY; (Y); 144/251; Nwsp Stf; JV Cheerleading; Var Crs Cntry; JV Tennis; Hon Roll; Suffolk CC; Nrsng.

BARTOSZEK, RONALD J; Eden Senior HS; Hamburg, NY; (Y); 9/166; JV Swmmng; Im JV Vllybl; NHS; NY ST Rgnts Schlrshp Awd 86; NY ST U Bfl; CPA.

BARTOW, CHERYL; Academy Of Saint Joseph; Bayport, NY; (Y); Art Clb; Camera Clb; Church Yth Grp; Cmnty Wkr; Drama Clb; GAA; Model UN; Pep Clb; PAVAS; Service Clb; Advtsng.

BARTUS, GREG; Chenango Forks HS; Chenango Forks, NY; (Y); 19/180; Nwsp Sprt Ed; Bsktbl; Ftbl; Trk; Hon Roll; NHS; Prfct Atten Awd; Perf Atten 82-86; All League Ofensive Guard 84-85; Pres Acad Ftns Awd 86; Cornell U.

BASAK, ADITI; Nichols Schl; Williamsville, NY; (Y); Dance Clb; Drama Clb; School Musical; Swing Chorus; Variety Show; Trk; NHS; Ntl Merit SF.

BASFORD, KIMBERLY; Heuvelton Central HS; Heuvelton, NY; (Y); Sec French Clb; Latin Clb; Band; Color Guard; Concert Band; Mrchg Band; Cheerleading; Area All St Orch 2nd Flute 83; Area All St Cncrt Band 1st Flute-Piecolo 84&85; Csmtlgy.

BASH, LAURIE A; Dansville SR HS; Dansville, NY; (Y); 26/160; Church Yth Grp; Band; SADD; Chorus; Concert Band; Mrchg Band; Capt Swmmng; Hon Roll; Regnts Schlrshp 86; U Of Buffalo; Phy Thrpy.

BASHER, TAMMIE S; Hamilton Central Schl; Hamilton, NY; (Y); 3/56; SADD; Yrbk Bus Mgr; Pres Jr Cls; VP Sr Cls; JV Bsktbl; Var Fld Hcky; Stat Socr; Var Sftbl; Hon Roll; NHS; Nazareth Clg Rochester; Bus Adm.

BASHFORD, KATIE A; Averill Park HS; W Sandlake, NY; (Y); Church Yth Grp; 4-H; Key Clb; Political Wkr; Ski Clb; Band; Chorus; Church Choir; Concert Band; Mrchg Band; All Cnty Band 84-86; 4-H Tm Ambssdr 84-86; Phys Thrpst Asst; Russell Sage; Phys Thrpst.

BASHOFF, SUZANNE; Spackenkill HS; Poughkeepsie, NY; (Y); 1/165; Temple Yth Grp; Thesps; Acpl Chr; School Musical; Ed Nwsp Ed-Chief; High Hon Roll; NHS; Val; Leo Clb; Chorus; AATF Frnch Cntst 3rd Lvl 3rd Pl 84; AATF Frnch Cntst 4th Lvl 3rd Pl 85; AATF Frnch Cntst 5th Lvl 86; Princeton U; Engl.

BASI, MARYROSE; Frankfort Schuyler HS; Frankfort, NY; (S); Church Yth Grp; FBLA; Pep Clb; Spanish Clb; SADD; Sec Jr Cls; Rep Stu Cncl; Cheerleading; High Hon Roll; NHS; SUNY At Oswego; Scndry Math Ed.

BASILE, CARMELLA; Auburn HS; Auburn, NY; (Y); Acpl Chr; Band; Color Guard; Madrigals; Mrchg Band; School Musical; School Play; Vllybl; High Hon Roll; Hon Roll; Chr Awd JR 86; Csmtlgy.

BASILE, ELIZABETH; Lakeland HS; Putnam Valley, NY; (Y); Art Clb; VP Band; Chorus; Concert Band; Jazz Band; Mrchg Band; Nwsp Rptr; Yrbk Stf; Var Trk; High Hon Roll; New Platz; Art.

BASILE, MARIE; Grand Island HS; Grand Island, NY; (Y); Church Yth Grp; Cmnty Wkr; French Clb; Ski Clb; Swmmng; NHS; U Of Buffalo; Psycht.

BASILE, VANESSA; St Francis Prep; Fresh Meadows, NY; (Y); Cmnty Wkr; Computer Clb; Dance Clb; School Play; Pre-Law.

BASKIN, DAWN; Springfield Gardens HS; Springfield Grdns, NY; (Y); Aud/Vis; Church Choir; School Musical; School Play; Rep Soph Cls; Cit Awd; Hon Roll; Prfct Atten Awd; VFW Awd; Voice Dem Awd; Ctznshp Awd 84; VFW Awd 86; Voic Of Demcrcy 86; PACE U; Real Est.

BASS, DIANNE; Lindenhurst HS; Lindenhurst, NY; (Y); Katherine Gibbs Schl; Exctve.

BASS, FARA; Lawrence HS; Lawrence, NY; (Y); AFS; French Clb; VP Temple Yth Grp; Band; Yrbk Stf; Trs Sr Cls; Gym; Socr; Hon Roll; Pre-Med.

BASS, JESSICA; Scarsdale HS; Scarsdale, NY; (Y); Sec Pres Drama Clb; Math Tm; Political Wkr; Lib Chorus; Jazz Band; Madrigals; School Musical; School Play; Ntl Merit Ltr.

BASS, JILL; Syosset HS; Jericho, NY; (Y); 60/481; AFS; Model UN; Political Wkr; Temple Yth Grp; Ed Nwsp Stf; Ed Yrbk Stf; Lit Mag; NHS; NY St Rgnts Schlrshp 86; Gnrl Hnrs 86; U Of Binghampton; Author.

BASS, PAMELA S; Patchogue-Medford HS; Patchogue, NY; (Y); 27/650; DECA; FBLA; Leo Clb; Off Jr Cls; Pres Sr Cls; Jr NHS; NHS; Yrbk Stf; Off Soph Cls; Hon Roll; Mktng Stu Of The Yr; Rotary Stu Of The Mnth; 1st Pl Winner In NY St Deca Comp; SUNY; Bus.

BASSAGE, DENISE; Wayne Central HS; Walworth, NY; (S); 8/193; Sec Church Yth Grp; 4-H; Chorus; School Musical; Var L Socr; Var L Sftbl; Var L Vllybl; 4-H Awd; Hon Roll; NHS; Spnsh, Chors Awds; Math II, Acctg Acad Excl; Outstndg Engl II; Bus Adm.

BASSETTE, TIM; Grand Island SR HS; Grand Island, NY; (Y); 51/290; Pres Church Yth Grp; JV Crs Cntry; Var L Trk; JV Wrstlng; Hon Roll; 1st Pl Physcl Ftns Chllng 84-85.

BASSO, ROBERT D; Peekskill HS; Peekskill, NY; (Y); Ftbl; Golf; High Hon Roll; Hon Roll; Ntl Merit Ltr; NYS Rgnts Schlrshp 86; SUNY New Paltz; Comp Engrng.

BASTIAN, BRETT; Palmyra-Macedon HS; Macedon, NY; (Y); Church Yth Grp; Varsity Clb; Acpl Chr; Concert Band; Symp Band; JV Var Bsktbl; JV Var Ftbl; Var Trk; CC Awd; Hon Roll; Macedon Yth Of Yr Awd 85; Genetics.

BASTY, CHERYL ANN; Hamburg SR HS; Hamburg, NY; (Y); 8/391; 4-H; Chorus; Church Choir; Madrigals; School Musical; Lit Mag; High Hon Roll; Paul Baird Mem Schlrshp 86; Mst Flnt 4-Yr Spnsh Stu 86; Bio Pblshd In Schl Dist Nwspr-Top Ten Stu 86; Schl Of Engrng Suny Bflo; Engr.

BASULTO, DEAN; Fordham Preparatory Schl; Bronx, NY; (Y); Key Clb; Spanish Clb; Varsity Clb; Stat Mgr Bsktbl; JV Var Ftbl; High Hon Roll; Hon Roll; NHS; Mgr(s); Score Keeper; Natl Hispnc Schlr Awds SF 86; AFROTC Scholar 86; Cornell U; Bio.

BATCHEIDER, CHERYL; Brewster HS; Brewster, NY; (Y); Church Yth Grp; Political Wkr; Ski Clb; Chorus; School Play; Stage Crew; JV Cheerleading; JV Sftbl; Hon Roll; Outstndng Librn Aid Awd; Boston U; Pol Sci.

BATCHELDER, DIANE; Vernon-Verona-Sherrill Central HS; Vernon, NY; (Y); Church Yth Grp; Var Bowling; Var Trk; High Hon Roll; Hon Roll; NHS.

BATCHELOR, JACQUELINE; Saint John The Baptist HS; Smithtwn, NY; (Y); Library Aide; Service Clb; School Musical; School Play; Stage Crew; Swmmng; Hon Roll.

BATCHELOR, JACQUELINE KELLIE; John Jay SR HS; S Salem, NY; (Y); Girl Scts; SADD; Variety Show; Yrbk Stf; Sec Sr Cls; JV Crs Cntry; Cit Awd; High Hon Roll; Hon Roll; Cmnty Svc Awd 85-86; Englsh Awd 85-86; Educ.

BATEMARCO, LYNN; Clarkstown High School South; Nanuet, NY; (Y); Band; Concert Band; Mrchg Band; JV Sftbl; Iona ST Lang Cont 2nd Hnrs Itln II 85; Itln Clb 83-85; Frgn Lang.

BATER, RALPH; Liverpool HS; Liverpool, NY; (Y); 31/844; Church Yth Grp; Debate Tm; Exploring; Sec German Clb; VP JA; ROTC; Hon Roll; Jr NHS; NHS; Elec Engrng.

BATES, CASSANDRA; Lake Placid Central Schl; Arnold, MD; (Y); Art Clb; French Clb; Pres Key Clb; Varsity Clb; Yrbk Stf; Trs Lcrss; Var Socr; Cit Awd; High Hon Roll; NHS; Cornll; Engnrng.

BATES, CHARLES H; Brewster HS; Patterson, NY; (Y); 5/190; Yrbk Stf; High Hon Roll; Hon Roll; NHS; Ntl Merit Schol; Prsdtl Schlrshp-Mnhttn Coll 86; Hnrs-Bio, Trigmtry, Comp Pgmmng & Spnsh 84, 85; Schlrshp Erth Sci 83; Manhattan Coll; Comp Sci.

BATES, CORRIE; Glens Falls HS; Glen Falls, NY; (Y); 1/217; Sec AFS; Drama Clb; Key Clb; Pep Clb; SADD; JV Var Cheerleading; Bausch & Lomb Sci Awd; High Hon Roll; NHS; Val; 3rd Pl Eastern NY ST Sci Congrss 86; Renssalaer Polytechnic Inst.

BATES, JULIA; Greensville JR SR HS; Preston Hlw, NY; (Y); FFA; Hon Roll; FFA Chptr Greenhand & Chptr Farmer 83-84 & 84-85; Columbia-Greene; Nursing.

BATES, KANEM; Corcoran HS; Syracuse, NY; (Y); Drama Clb; FBLA; JA; Scholastic Bowl; Variety Show; Cit Awd; JC Awd; Jr NHS; Bus.

BATES, KRISTEN; Greece Athena HS; Rochester, NY; (Y); Ski Clb; Hon Roll; Monroe Coll; Bus.

BATES, STACI; Kendall SR SR HS; Holley, NY; (Y); 26/90; Church Yth Grp; Drama Clb; Ski Clb; Chorus; Concert Band; School Play; Var Socr; Var Sftbl; Hon Roll; Jr NHS; Niagra U; Nrsg.

BATHGATE, JON; Skaneateles Central HS; Skaneateles, NY; (Y); 15/150; Band; Concert Band; Bsktbl; Crs Cntry; Trk; High Hon Roll; NHS; Coaches Wrkhrs Awd 86; 300 Ml Run Clb 85; Geneseo; Comp Sci.

BATISTA, MYRA; Coxsackie-Athens HS; Coxsackie, NY; (Y); Pep Clb; Spanish Clb; Concert Band; Yrbk Stf; Stu Cncl; Var Cheerleading; Score Keeper; JV Var Vllybl; High Hon Roll; NHS; Psych.

BATSCHE, LAUREN; St John The Baptist HS; Central Islip, NY; (Y); JV Cheerleading; Hon Roll; Suffolk Cnty CC; Nrsng.

BATSON, ALEXANDER; Potsdam Central HS; Potsdam, NY; (Y); Aud/Vis; Clarkson U; Bus.

BATSON, ROBERT T; Poland Central HS; Cold Brook, NY; (Y); Varsity Clb; JV Bsktbl; Capt Tennis; High Hon Roll; Hon Roll; NHS; Schlrshp Awd 84; Schlrshp Awd 85; Cert Awd Comp II Achvt 86; Engrng.

BATTAGLIA, GINA; Moore Catholic HS; Staten Island, NY; (Y); Computer Clb; Math Tm; Spanish Clb; SADD; Stage Crew; Crs Cntry; Trk; NHS; Spn Awd 85; Sci.

BATTAGLIA, JOLINE; Le Roy HS; Le Roy, NY; (Y); Latin Clb; SADD; Varsity Clb; Chorus; School Musical; Capt Cheerleading; Coach Actv; Sftbl; Hon Roll; Educ.

BATTAGLIA, KEITH; Christian Brothers Acad; Auburn, NY; (Y); 31/104; Church Yth Grp; NFL; Speech Tm; Yrbk Ed-Chief; Tennis; NYS Regents Schlrshp 86; Brother Adolphus Hnr Cty 82-86; Bus Adm.

BATTAGLIA, LISA; Mount Mercy Acad; W Seneca, NY; (Y); Science Clb; Ski Clb; Spanish Clb; Stage Crew; Swing Chorus; Variety Show; Merit Awd 83-86; Jrnlsm.

BATTAGLIA, STEVE; Moore Catholic HS; Staten Island, NY; (Y); 24/167; Aud/Vis; Boy Scts; Math Tm; School Play; Stage Crew; Nwsp Phtg; Yrbk Phtg; Bowling; Chrmn NHS; NY Rgnts Schlrshp 85; 1st Pl Trphy Math Lge 85-86; Math Awd 86; Rensselear Polytech Inst; Comp.

BATTAGLINI, CHRIS; Union-Endicott HS; Endicott, NY; (Y); Am Leg Boys St; Varsity Clb; Pres Sr Cls; Var Bsbl; Var Crs Cntry; JV Wrstlng; Hon Roll; Broome CC; Engrng.

BATTEN III, FRANK; Torrejon American HS; Woburn, MA; (Y); ROTC; Teachers Aide; Color Guard; Drill Tm; JV Bsbl; Var Ftbl; High Hon Roll; Hon Roll; Military Security.

BATTERS, BETH; Whitesboro SR HS; Whitesboro, NY; (Y); 4/300; Church Yth Grp; GAA; SADD; Yrbk Stf; Bowling; Score Keeper; High Hon Roll; Jr NHS; NHS; Elem Educ.

BATTIG, ROBERT J; Tonawanda SR HS; Tonawanda, NY; (Y); Yrbk Phtg; Bsktbl; Var Trk; Hon Roll; Niagara Frontier League All Star 85; Ntl Ed Dev Test Awd 84; Bus Adm.

BATTISTA, MICHAEL; Archbishop Stepinac HS; Hawthorne, NY; (Y); 50/174; Nwsp Rptr; Lit Mag; Rep Jr Cls; Im Mgr Bsktbl; JV Trk; Hon Roll; NHS.

BATTOE, REBECCA; Liverpool HS; Liverpool, NY; (Y); Church Yth Grp; Var JA; JCL; Var L Socr; Hon Roll; Jr NHS; NHS; Cert Prsnl Achvt Rgnl Schlstc Art Awds 85; Pre-Med.

BATTY, LAUREL C; The Doane Stuart Schl; Gloversville, NY; (Y); Ski Clb; Spanish Clb; Concert Band; Yrbk Stf; Rep Stu Cncl; JV Cheerleading; JV Fld Hcky; Var Sftbl; Var Vllybl; High Hon Roll; James Edward Oglethorpe Scholar 86; Oglethorpe U; Pre-Med.

BATUTIS, DEVIN; White Plains HS; White Plns, NY; (Y); Aud/Vis; Band; Jazz Band; Mrchg Band; Orch; JV Crs Cntry; Hon Roll; Ntl Merit Ltr; Engrng.

BAUER, DAVID; Canisius HS; Williamsville, NY; (Y); 12/150; Computer Clb; Model UN; Ski Clb; Stage Crew; Nwsp Rptr; Yrbk Stf; High Hon Roll; Hon Roll; Boston Coll; Bus Adm.

BAUER, LAURIE; Our Lady Of Mercy HS; Penfield, NY; (Y); Hon Roll; Bus Mgmt.

BAUER, LORAINE T; Saint Frances Prep; College Point, NY; (S); 18/744; Rep Soph Cls; Im Vllybl; High Hon Roll.

BAUER, MARY; Roosevelt HS; Yonkers, NY; (Y); SADD; Flag Corp; Hon Roll; Trophy Flag Squad 85; Westchester CC; Film.

BAUER, NATALIE R; North Collins HS; Springville, NY; (Y); Capt Color Guard; Pres Stu Cncl; Var L Socr; Var L Vllybl; Hon Roll; NHS; 4-H; GAA; Spanish Clb; VP Sr Cls; Pol Sci.

BAUER, ROBERT; Frontier Central HS; Hamburg, NY; (S); 36/441; Chess Clb; Science Clb; SADD; Varsity Clb; Off Frsh Cls; Off Soph Cls; Off Jr Cls; Off Sr Cls; Capt Swmmng; High Hon Roll; Sci Fair Gold Medl 83; Sci Fair Slvr Medl 84; Indstrl Arts Fair-1st & Ind Pl 84; GMI; Mechncl Engrng.

BAUER, SUSAN; Mt St Mary Acad; Tonawanda, NY; (Y); Cmnty Wkr; Political Wkr; Chorus; Outstndng Svc Awd 86; Trvl.

BAUER, TAMMY; Marcus Whitman HS; Stanley, NY; (S); 24/115; DECA; FHA; Yrbk Phtg; Yrbk Stf; Stat Bsktbl; Tennis; Vllybl; High Hon Roll; Hon Roll; Cntrl City Bus Inst; Retl.

BAUER, VICKI; Frankfurt American HS; APO New York, NY; (Y); 82/230; Office Aide; Cit Awd; Hon Roll; Early Grad 86; U Of MD; Bus Mgmt.

BAUERLE, ANDREW; Bainbridge-Guilford Central HS; Bainbridge, NY; (Y); Cmnty Wkr; Varsity Clb; Concert Band; Jazz Band; Mrchg Band; Rep Stu Cncl; Var Bsktbl; Var Ftbl; Var Tennis; Var Vllybl; MVP Awd Vrsty Vllybll 85-86; 2nd Pl Dbls NY Sctn 4 Clss C Tnns Sctnls 85 & 1st Pl-86; Bus.

BAUGH, JOSEPH; Uniondale HS; Hempstead, NY; (Y); JV Var Socr; Trk; High Hon Roll; Hon Roll; Jr NHS; NHS.

BAUGHMAN, ERIC; Niagara Wheatfield HS; Sanborn, NY; (Y); Ski Clb; SADD; Ftbl; Lcrss; Wt Lftg; Bus Mngmnt.

BAUM, RACHEL; Hendrick Hudson HS; Croton On Hudson, NY; (S); 5/187; Pres Debate Tm; Drama Clb; French Clb; NFL; Speech Tm; SADD; Orch; Nwsp Stf; Ed Lit Mag; NHS; Natl Merit Commndtn 85; Pol Sci.

BAUMGARTNER, AMY; Le Roy Central HS; Leroy, NY; (Y); Am Leg Aux Girls St; Math Tm; Trs Chorus; School Musical; Yrbk Ed-Chief; Trs Frsh Cls; Trs Soph Cls; Trs Jr Cls; Trs Sr Cls; NHS; Lab Asst 86-87; JR Miss 86; Natl Lat Hon Men Awd Magna Cum Laude 86; Phrmcy.

BAUSER, DEBORAH A; Brentwood Sonderling HS; Brentwood, NY; (Y); 5/500; Varsity Clb; Band; Yrbk Stf; Off Jr Cls; Off Sr Cls; Stu Cncl; Var L Socr; L Capt Vllybl; Hon Roll; NHS; John Mrowka Mem Awd 83; Outstndng Stu Female Athl 83; Suffolk Zone Awd 85; St John Fisher Coll; Psych.

BAUTISTA, L GRACE; Colonie Central HS; Loudonville, NY; (Y); Ski Clb; Off Sr Cls; Stu Cncl; JV Socr; JV Sftbl; High Hon Roll; NHS; Dntstry.

BAUTZ, JOHN; St Marys Boys HS; Manhasset, NY; (Y); 9/176; Rep Frsh Cls; Rep Stu Cncl; JV Capt Bsktbl; JV Crs Cntry; High Hon Roll; Hon Roll; Mst Imprvd Plyr Hndbl 85.

BAVETTA, MICHELE; Nazareth Regional HS; Brooklyn, NY; (Y); Var Bsktbl; JV Var Sftbl; Var Vllybl; NHS; Bus.

BAXTER, CANDICE; Turner/Carroll HS; Buffalo, NY; (S); Computer Clb; Pep Clb; Teachers Aide; Church Choir; Variety Show; Yrbk Stf; Hon Roll; NHS; Prfct Atten Awd; Omega Psi Phi Frat Awd Talent Hunt 84.

BAXTER, DEANNA; Potsdam Central HS; Potsdam, NY; (Y); 30/136; French Clb; Varsity Clb; Yrbk Stf; Pres Frsh Cls; Rep Stu Cncl; Var JV Socr; Var L Trk; Var JV Vllybl; Hon Roll; Tlntd JRS Cert 86; Clarkson; Psych.

BAXTER, HERMIA Y; Norman Thomas HS; New York, NY; (S); 237/597; Aud/Vis; Computer Clb; DECA; Girl Scts; JA; Office Aide; Teachers Aide; Color Guard; Stage Crew; Nwsp Rptr; City Cncl Citation Schl Svc 85; Data Analysis & Mkt Rsrch Evnt DECA 2nd Pl 86; Mktg Stu Of Mnth 85; Johnson & Wales Coll; Advrtsg.

BAXTER, KIM; Shenendehowa HS; Clifton Park, NY; (Y); Ski Clb; Chorus; High Hon Roll; Hon Roll; Bus.

BAXTER, MARK G; Kendall JR SR HS; Canandaigua, NY; (Y); FFA.

BAXTER, RICHARD C; South Lewis HS; Glenfield, NY; (Y); 5/90; Am Leg Boys St; VP Varsity Clb; Pres Sr Cls; Var Capt Ftbl; Var Swmmng; Var Trk; Pres NHS; NY St Regents Schlrshp 86; St Lawrence U; Pre Med.

BAXTER, SHEILA; Hermon-Dekalb Central HS; Hermon, NY; (Y); Drama Clb; French Clb; Chorus; Concert Band; Mrchg Band; School Play; Stage Crew; Nwsp Stf; CC Awd; High Hon Roll; Stu Of Month 85; Outstndg Stu 2 Yr Prg 86; Scrtrs Awd 86; Accntng.

BAXTER, TERRI; S Glens Falls SR HS; S Glens Falls, NY; (Y); 23/243; Latin Clb; SADD; Varsity Clb; Yrbk Stf; Sec Soph Cls; Rep Sr Cls; Rep Stu Cncl; Var Capt Cheerleading; Hon Roll; Moreau SR Ctzns Schlrshp 86; Amrcn Lgn Schlrshp 86; Ntl Chrldng Cmptn 85; Boston U; Bio.

BAXTER, TIMOTHY; Friendship Central HS; Friendship, NY; (S); 1/30; Boy Scts; Church Yth Grp; Exploring; Model UN; School Play; Rep Stu Cncl; Trk; God Cntry Awd; High Hon Roll; NHS; Rochester Inst Of Tech; Elc Eng.

BAY, MARY; Victor SR HS; Victor, NY; (Y); Art Clb; JA; Ski Clb; Camp Fr Inc; School Play; Yrbk Stf; Stat Score Keeper; Stat Vllybl; High Hon Roll; Hon Roll; Intl Law.

BAYER, BARBARA; Lincoln HS; Yonkers, NY; (S); 1/350; Drama Clb; School Play; Stage Crew; Nwsp Ed-Chief; Nwsp Phtg; Nwsp Rptr; High Hon Roll; Val; Rensallear Polytech Mdlst; Cmmnd Natl Merit; NYU; Intnatl Bus.

BAYER, LORNA E; George W Hewlett HS; Hewlett, NY; (Y); 4/262; Hosp Aide; Mathletes; Math Tm; Science Clb; Chorus; Lit Mag; Var L Gym; Hon Roll; NHS; Ntl Merit Ltr.

BAYES, LISA; Johnstown HS; Johnstown, NY; (Y); Intnl Clb; Chorus; School Musical; Variety Show; High Hon Roll; Hon Roll; NHS; Acctng.

BAYNE, DOUGLAS; Walt Whitman HS; Huntington Stat, NY; (Y); 110/477; German Clb; SADD; Golf; Socr; Vllybl; High Hon Roll; Hon Roll; Albany Bus Coll; Bus Mgt.

BAYS, GAYLE; Fabius-Pompey HS; Fabius, NY; (Y); 1/100; Band; Yrbk Stf; L Var Bsktbl; High Hon Roll; NHS; Jr All Amer Bnd Hl Of Fame 85; NY ST Schl Music Assoc Conf All ST Bnd 85; Dir NY Jr Qtr Hrs Asso.

BAYSE, JUDITH MARIE; Grand Island HS; Grand Island, NY; (Y); 2/325; French Clb; Color Guard; Drm & Bgl; Yrbk Stf; Cit Awd; High Hon Roll; NHS; Ntl Merit Ltr; Sal; St Schlr; Geneseo Almni Schlrshp 86; Empr ST Schlrshp Exclnc 86; SUNY Geneseo; Elem Educ.

BAYUK, MICHELLE; Earl L Vandermeulen HS; Mt Sinai, NY; (Y); Drama Clb; Leo Clb; Mathletes; Math Tm; Band; Mrchg Band; Stage Crew; Nwsp Rptr; Nwsp Stf; High Hon Roll; Bst Math Stu Awd.

BAZATA, RICHARD; St John The Baptist HS; Brentwood, NY; (Y); 34/501; JV Capt Socr; Crtfct Mrt Sci Math Soc Stds 85; Engr.

BAZINET, TERRY L; Sherburne-Earlville HS; Earlville, NY; (Y); 43/146; French Clb; JV Bsktbl; Var Fld Hcky; JV Sftbl; Rgnts Schlrshp-Nrsg 86; SUNY Utica; Nrsg.

BEACH, CHRISTINE; Fairport HS; Fairport, NY; (Y); Cmnty Wkr; Dance Clb; Yrbk Stf; JV Var Cheerleading; Im Coach Actv; Stat Lcrss; Im JV Trk; Hon Roll; Prfct Atten Awd; Hmncng Prncs 84; Area Model; Johnson & Wales Coll; Trsm.

BEACH, MELISSA M; Little Falls HS; St Johnsville, NY; (Y); 28/109; Drama Clb; French Clb; Spanish Clb; Band; Chorus; Concert Band; Mrchg Band; School Play; Hon Roll; Rgnts Schlrshp 85-86; Coll Wooster; Comp Prgmng.

BEACH, MICHAEL; Colonie Central HS; Albany, NY; (Y); 18/490; Chess Clb; Church Yth Grp; Spanish Clb; Var Crs Cntry; Var Trk; High Hon Roll; NHS; Mst Imprvd Rnr Vrsty Crs Cntry 85; Cmptr Sci.

BEACH, SANDI; Liberty HS; Livingston Manor, NY; (Y); Church Yth Grp; Girl Scts; Office Aide; SADD; Chorus; Color Guard; Yrbk Stf; Off Sr Cls; Bowling; Var L Socr; 1st Pl Rnr Up Miss Loyalty Day Pagnt 85; Hnr & Recogntn Shrthnd II, Off Proc 86; Home Econ Awd 86; Krissler Bus Inst; Sec.

BEACHEL, JASON; Letchworth Central Schl; Bliss, NY; (Y); Boy Scts; FFA; Ski Clb; Sec Trs Varsity Clb; Yrbk Stf; Var Ftbl; Var Trk; Var Wrstlng; Hon Roll; Hurdle And Meter Dash Champ 86; 2nd Pl Wrstlr 86; Alfred Ag; Chem Tech.

BEADY, JANIS; Frewsburg Central HS; Frewsburg, NY; (Y); AFS; Chorus; Sec Jr Cls; Var Trk; JV Vllybl; Wilma Boyd Careers Schls; Trvl.

BEAGLE, CLAUDIA; Solvay HS; Solvay, NY; (Y); Church Yth Grp; Frsh Cls; Soph Cls; Jr Cls; Socr; Sftbl; Hon Roll; Alfred ST Coll; Phys Thrpy.

BEAGLE, MARQUIS; Grene Central Schl; Smithville, NY; (Y); Art Clb; Ski Clb; Bowling; Socr; Vllybl; Wrstlng; Hon Roll; Prfct Atten Awd; Broome CC; Art.

BEANER, WILLIAM; Monsignor Farrell HS; Staten Island, NY; (S); #10 In Class; Chess Clb; Church Yth Grp; French Clb; Office Aide; School Play; Pres Frsh Cls; VP Jr Cls; Rep Sr Cls; JV Bsbl; Im Bsktbl; Cert Recog Frm Cngrssmn 86; Monsignor Barnes Outstndg Stu Awd 86; NY ST Assmbly Cert Merit 86; St Johns U; Poli Sci.

BEARD, JANNETTE K; Hampton Bays JR/SR HS; Hampton Bays, NY; (Y); 11/88; Mathletes; Varsity Clb; Chorus; Yrbk Rptr; Yrbk Stf; Cheerleading; Fld Hcky; Vllybl; Hon Roll; Pres Schlr; Rgnts Schlrshp 86; Prsdntl Schlrshp Amrcn & Alfrd U; Amrcn U; Intl Bus.

BEARDSLEE, MATTHEW G; Huntington HS; Huntington, NY; (Y); 131/386; Var Crs Cntry; Var Trk; SUNY Brckprt; Ecology.

BEARDSLEY, JASON; Johnson City SR HS; Johnson City, NY; (Y); Am Leg Boys St; Concert Band; Jazz Band; Mrchg Band; High Hon Roll; NHS; Ntl Merit SF; Prfct Atten Awd; Area All ST Cncrt Bnd; Comp Sci.

BEARDSLEY, MICHAEL G; Mount Morris Central HS; Mt Morris, NY; (Y); Am Leg Boys St; Aud/Vis; Crs Cntry; Swmmng; Hon Roll; Htl Mgmt.

BEASLEY, TAMARA L; Herkimer SR HS; Herkimer, NY; (Y); JA; Pres Pep Clb; Pres SADD; VP Band; Concert Band; Jazz Band; Mrchg Band; Stage Crew; JV Var Fld Hcky; Hon Roll; Regents Schlrshp Awd 86; MVP Fld Hockey 86; CVC All Star 86; Siena Coll Loudonville; Comp.

BEATON, CHUCK; John H Glenn HS; Greenlawn, NY; (Y); Ski Clb; Varsity Clb; Variety Show; Yrbk Stf; Var Bsbl; Var Bsktbl; Var Ftbl; Wt Lftg; Hon Roll; NHS.

BEATTIE, SUSAN M; Norwood-Norfolk HS; Norwood, NY; (Y); 23/130; French Clb; Political Wkr; Teachers Aide; Stage Crew; JV Var Bsktbl; Var Trk; High Hon Roll; Hon Roll; Rgnts Schlrshp Awd 86; Potsdam Coll; Math.

BEATTY, HEATHER; Fox Lane HS; Pound Ridge, NY; (Y); 9/286; Church Yth Grp; Mathletes; Ski Clb; JV Var Fld Hcky; JV Capt Lcrss; High Hon Roll; Sec NHS; Natl Mrt Schlrshp Cmmnd Stu 86; Jsph Fncher Mrl Schlrshp 86; George Tusic Mrl Sci Schlrshp 86; Yale U; Engr.

BEATTY, HOLLY; Fox Lane HS; Pound Ridge, NY; (Y); 17/286; Rep Stu Cncl; Var Capt Fld Hcky; Var Lcrss; High Hon Roll; Ntl Merit Ltr; Geo Tsc Sci Schlrshp, Jos Fnchr Mem Schlrshp 86; Middlebury Coll.

BEAUBRUN, PEPITA; St Joseph HS; Brooklyn, NY; (Y); Church Yth Grp; Cmnty Wkr; Dance Clb; FCA; French Clb; FNA; Hosp Aide; Office Aide; Church Choir; Stage Crew; Bst Cls Attndt 86; Nrs Aide 86; Sch Svc & Actvts 86; LICH; Pdtrc Nrs.

BEAUDIN, CHRISSY; Glens Falls HS; Glens Falls, NY; (Y); 2/217; Dance Clb; Rep Jr Cls; Rep Sr Cls; Sec Sec Stu Cncl; Var L Bsktbl; Var L Cheerleading; Var L Sftbl; Var L Vllybl; NHS; Sal; Sci Stu Qrtr 82; Mth Almn Schlrshp 86; Bg Crs Strt Schl Schlrshp 86; Siena Coll; Math.

BEAUDOIN, NICOLLE; Troy HS; Troy, NY; (Y); 15/425; Trs French Clb; Office Aide; Nwsp Ed-Chief; Nwsp Rptr; Nwsp Stf; Stu Cncl; High Hon Roll; NHS; Fr Clb Awd Excllnce Fr IV; Chockrow Awd Jrnlsm; Toastmstrs Moe Kelly Mem Awd Cmnty Svc; ST U NY Albany; Comm.

BEAULIEU, CHARMAINE; Thomas J Corcoran HS; Syracuse, NY; (Y); French Clb; GAA; Spanish Clb; Yrbk Phtg; Cheerleading; Var Crs Cntry; Var Trk; Hon Roll; Mdcl Tech.

BEAULIEU, MARK; Scotia-Glenville HS; Scotia, NY; (Y); Aud/Vis; French Clb; Varsity Clb; Trk; Hon Roll; Ntl Merit Ltr; U Rochester; Optcs.

BEAULIEU, RENEE; Colonie Central HS; Albany, NY; (Y); Cmnty Wkr; Girl Scts; Band; Bsktbl; Coach Actv; Socr; Sftbl; Vllybl; Hon Roll; Computer Clb; MVP Awd Sftbl 83-84; 110 Pct Awd Bskbtll 83-84; MVP Awd Vlbl 84-85.

BEAUMONT, CYNTHIA; Greenville JR SR HS; Earlton, NY; (Y); 7/76; Key Clb; Spanish Clb; Band; Nwsp Stf; Hon Roll; NHS; Sci Fair Awd 86; Schl Ltr Awd Schltc Achvt 86; Excllnce Awd 86; Publshng.

BEAUMONT, LAUREN; Conastota HS; Canastota, NY; (S); Dance Clb; Intnl Clb; Science Clb; SADD; Nwsp Rptr; Rep Stu Cncl; Cit Awd; High Hon Roll; Jr NHS; NHS; Excllnc Creatv Wrtg 85; Boston Coll; Psychtry.

BEAUREGARD, MARIA; Grand Island HS; Grand Island, NY; (Y); 3/320; French Clb; Ski Clb; Teachers Aide; Variety Show; Trs Soph Cls; Var Cheerleading; Var Gym; Var Trk; Hon Roll; NHS; Wellesley Awd; Awd Acadmc Excllnc Mdl; Charity Fund Schlrshp; Regnts Schlrshp; SUNY Geneseo; Bus.

BEAUREGARD, R; Rome Catholic HS; Rome, NY; (Y); Church Yth Grp; Cmnty Wkr; Ski Clb; Band; Stage Crew; Variety Show; JV Bsbl; Im Bsktbl; Im Crs Cntry; Var Ftbl; Pres Phy Ftnss Awd 86; St John Fisher; Optmtry.

BEBER, JON M; Southside HS; Wellsburg, NY; (Y); Am Leg Boys St; Aud/Vis; Latin Clb; Varsity Clb; Stage Crew; Var Coach Actv; Var L Swmmng; Hon Roll; Val Swmr 86; Schl Rcrds In 200 Im-100 Btryfly 100 Free 86; Bio.

BECAN, DEBORAH; The Bronx High School Of Science; Bronx, NY; (Y); Church Yth Grp; Hosp Aide; Office Aide; Teachers Aide; Socr; Columbia U; Med.

BECCUE, CRAIG; Royalton-Hartland HS; Middleport, NY; (Y); Exploring; VP Spanish Clb; Teachers Aide; VP Band; VP Frsh Cls; VP Jr Cls; VP Sr Cls; Stu Cncl; Capt Golf; Tennis; Fredonia ST; Bus.

BECEIRO, LESLIE; Dominican Commercial HS; Bayside, NY; (Y); 110/273; FBLA; Spanish Clb; Bsktbl; Prfct Atten Awd; Prncpls Lst 82-86; Baruch Coll; Bus Admn.

BECERRIL, DEBORAH; John Dewey HS; Brooklyn, NY; (Y); Church Yth Grp; Exploring; FCA; FNA; GAA; JA; Spanish Clb; Varsity Clb; Chorus; Church Choir; Staten Island Coll; Pedtrc Nrs.

BECHARD, ROBIN; Plattsburgh SR HS; Plattsburgh, NY; (Y); French Clb; Varsity Clb; Capt Var Ftbl; Var Capt Ice Hcky; Var Capt Trk; Var Wt Lftg; Hon Roll; Coach Actv; Art Clb; Camera Clb; Acad Achvt Awd Engl 86; Empire St Games Ice Hockey 84; MVP Vrsty Ftbll 86; Bus Mgmnt.

BECHTEL, ASHLEAH; Cassadaga Valley Central HS; Sinclairville, NY; (Y); 1/110; Spanish Clb; Varsity Clb; Chorus; Yrbk Stf; Sec Frsh Cls; Pres Soph Cls; Pres Jr Cls; Pres Sr Cls; Rep Stu Cncl; Var Capt Cheerleading; U Of NC; Nuclr Physcs.

BECHTEL, TREVOR M; Homer Central HS; Homer, NY; (Y); 26/206; Quiz Bowl; Ski Clb; Nwsp Stf; Socr; Tennis; High Hon Roll; NHS; CA Polytech; Comp Sci.

BECHTELER, HEIDI; Henninger HS; Syracuse, NY; (Y); 35/461; Dance Clb; SADD; Chorus; High Hon Roll; Hon Roll; Jr NHS; NHS; Le Moyne Coll; Bus Mgmt.

BECHTLE, HEIDI; Middletown HS; Middletown, NY; (Y); Key Clb; Flag Corp; Mrchg Band; Yrbk Stf; Rep Stu Cncl; Hon Roll; Teach.

BECK, CONNIE; La Fayette Central HS; Jamesville, NY; (S); 16/96; Drama Clb; Boys Clb Am; Spanish Clb; VP Chorus; School Musical; School Play; Swing Chorus; Yrbk Stf; Off Sr Cls; Var L Cheerleading; Syracuse U; Educ.

BECK, GLORIA; Bethpage HS; Bethpage, NY; (Y); 43/307; Drama Clb; FBLA; Office Aide; Temple Yth Grp; Varsity Clb; Yrbk Stf; Socr; Tennis; High Hon Roll; Hon Roll; Med.

BECK, KAREN S; Pittsford Mendon HS; Pittsford, NY; (Y); Church Yth Grp; Math Clb; Pep Clb; SADD; Var Capt Fld Hcky; Vllybl; Hon Roll; NHS; Phys Ed Awd 84-85; Hamilton Coll.

BECK, KELLY; Bishop Scully HS; Amsterdam, NY; (S); 5/52; Church Yth Grp; French Clb; Math Clb; Chorus; Sec Jr Cls; Bsktbl; High Hon Roll; Mu Alp Tht; NHS; Med.

BECK, MELISSA; East Syracuse-Minoa Central HS; Minoa, NY; (Y); French Clb; Latin Clb; Yrbk Ed-Chief; Yrbk Stf; Capt Var Cheerleading; Jr NHS; NHS; Ntnl Ltn Awd.

BECK, MELISSA; Lafayette HS; Buffalo, NY; (Y); JV Cheerleading; JV Swmmng; Socl Worker.

BECK, NANCY; Hendrick Hudson HS; Peekskill, NY; (Y); SADD; Orch; Yrbk Ed-Chief; Off Stu Cncl; Stat Bsktbl; High Hon Roll; NHS; All Cnty Orchstra 84-85; Spnsh Oral Awd 84-86; Awd For Rgnts Achvt In Mth 84-85; Pre Med.

BECK, TRICIA; Kenmore East SR HS; Kenmore, NY; (Y); Dance Clb; Service Clb; Drill Tm; Yrbk Stf; Cit Awd; High Hon Roll; NHS; Elem Ed.

BECKER, AMY; Wiamsville South HS; Williamsville, NY; (Y); AFS; Cmnty Wkr; Drama Clb; Concert Band; Mrchg Band; Pep Band; School Musical; Amherst YES Vlntr Pgm-Outstndng Vlntr 85.

BECKER, BARBARA; Mayfield Central Schl; Mayfield, NY; (Y); 17/85; Sec Pres 4-H; Concert Band; Mrchg Band; Sec Frsh Cls; Sec Soph Cls; Sec Jr Cls; Cheerleading; 4-H Awd; Hon Roll; NHS; Stu Mth 85; Cobleskill; Dietcn.

BECKER, CHARLES E; Ward Melville HS; Centereach, NY; (Y); 51/725; Rep Soph Cls; Rep Jr Cls; JV Bsbl; JV Ftbl; Var L Swmmng; High Hon Roll; Jr NHS; NHS; Regents Schlrshp 86; GPA 3.89; SUNY Binghamton; Acctg.

BECKER, CHRISTINE LYNN; Johnstown HS; Johnstown, NY; (Y); Intnl Clb; Red Cross Aide; Hon Roll; NHS; Ny St Rgnts Schlrshp 86; Oreonta Coll; Elem Ed.

BECKER, DONNA; Tonawanda JR SR HS; Tonawanda, NY; (Y); Church Yth Grp; VP French Clb; Girl Scts; Office Aide; SADD; Trk; Hon Roll; NHS; 1 Yr Hnr Roll Awd 84 & Again 86; Phys Therapy.

BECKER, JAMES J; Pine Bush HS; Bloomingbur, NY; (Y); 17/300; Spanish Clb; Yrbk Ed-Chief; Rep Stu Cncl; Cit Awd; Hon Roll; NHS; NYS Regents Schlrshp 86; NY U Deans Fllwshp 86; NY U; Pre-Law.

BECKER, JENNIFER; Nardin Acad; Grand Island, NY; (S); Debate Tm; Library Aide; Ski Clb; Orch; School Play; Yrbk Stf; Lit Mag; Hon Roll; Acdmc Schlrshp Nardin Acdmy 83; Bus Admin.

BECKER, JOHN C; Mynderse Acad; Seneca Falls, NY; (Y); 1/140; Am Leg Boys St; Boy Scts; Trs Ski Clb; Band; Jazz Band; Var L Crs Cntry; Var L Golf; NHS; Ntl Merit SF; Rensselaer Medal Wnnr 85.

BECKER, KELLY; Farmingdale HS; Massapequa Park, NY; (Y); Drama Clb; Key Clb; Ski Clb; SADD; Temple Yth Grp; Orch; School Musical; Prfct Atten Awd; Outstndng Svc Green/White Shop 85-86; NYSSMMA Awd Mus 84 & 86.

BECKER, KELLY; Farmingdale SR HS; Massapequa Pk, NY; (Y); Drama Clb; Ski Clb; SADD; Temple Yth Grp; Chorus; Orch; School Musical; Prfct Atten Awd; Schl Store Svc Awd 85-86; NY ST Music Assoc 83-86; Buffalo.

BECKER, KYLE; Hamburg SR HS; Hamburg, NY; (Y); 33/384; French Clb; Tennis; Hon Roll; Cyclng; Boston U; Engrng.

BECKER, LANCE; Earl L Vandermeulen HS; Belle Terre, NY; (Y); 44/333; Art Clb; FBLA; Leo Clb; Ski Clb; Spanish Clb; SADD; Yrbk Stf; Bsktbl; Var Vllybl; High Hon Roll; Pre-Med.

BECKER, LAURA; Jordan-Elbridge HS; Elbridge, NY; (Y); 3/137; Aud/Vis; Camera Clb; Cmnty Wkr; Debate Tm; Drama Clb; English Clb; FBLA; GAA; Girl Scts; Library Aide; U VA; Law.

BECKER, LAURIE; Williamsville North HS; E Amherst, NY; (Y); Intr Dec.

BECKER, RICHARD; Alden HS; Alden, NY; (Y); 24/203; Aud/Vis; Pres Church Yth Grp; Band; Mrchg Band; School Musical; Socr; Var Capt Swmmng; Pres NHS; Eastern Dist Pres Luther Legue Yth Grp 85-87; Nazareth Coll; Pol Sci.

BECKER, STACEY; Glen Cove HS; Glen Cove, NY; (S); 79/266; DECA; Score Keeper; Socr; Sftbl; Trk; 1st Deny Anti-Shplftng Manual, Hnbl Mntn Nassau Co Fin Crdit Test, Parl Glen Cove DECA 86; Acctg.

BECKER, STEPHEN; J C Birdlebough HS; Clay, NY; (Y); 3/165; German Clb; Trs Band; Jazz Band; Mrchg Band; Yrbk Stf; Im Bsktbl; High Hon Roll; NHS; Ntl Merit Ltr; JR All Amer Band 85-86; Techncl Wrtng.

BECKER, TERRY; Unatego JR SR HS; Unadilla, NY; (Y); 3/105; Am Leg Boys St; French Clb; Varsity Clb; School Play; Trk; High Hon Roll; NHS; Ntl Merit SF; Natl Frgn Lang Awd 85-86; West Point Military Acad; Engrg.

BECKER, TIMOTHY; Allegany Central Schl; Allegany, NY; (Y); FFA; Hosp Aide; Library Aide.

BECKERINK, JANNA; Clymer Central HS; Clymer, NY; (Y); 12/45; Church Yth Grp; Pres 4-H; Teachers Aide; Sec Band; Chorus; Mrchg Band; Stage Crew; Yrbk Ed-Chief; Capt Var Bsktbl; 4-H Awd; Tulip Festvl-Ms Congenlty 86; SUNY Fredonia; Elem Educ.

BECKERINK, KELLY; Panama Central HS; Panama, NY; (Y); Aud/Vis; Varsity Clb; Band; Chorus; Concert Band; Mrchg Band; Pep Band; Stat Bsktbl; Swmmng; Stat Trk; Airline Atten.

BECKETT, MARY; Grace Dodge Voc HS; Bronx, NY; (Y); 26/50; Office Aide; Teachers Aide; Nwsp Stf; Hon Roll; Prfct Atten Awd; Gold Awd Eng; Gold Awd Bookpg; Top 10 Bookpg; Albany Bus Clg; Acctnt.

BECKFORD, KAREN V; Bishop Loughlin M HS; Brooklyn, NY; (Y); 2/233; Dance Clb; Math Clb; Teachers Aide; Yrbk Stf; Vllybl; High Hon Roll; Hon Roll; NHS; Lovahlin Gold L Awd 84-86; Acad Schlrshp 85; U Of PA; Elem Educ.

BECKHANS, RONNI; Mercy HS; Watermill, NY; (Y); 26/103; Civic Clb; Cmnty Wkr; SADD; Yrbk Rptr; Yrbk Stf; Var Cheerleading; Var Capt Gym; Hon Roll; Girl Scts; Ski Clb; Gymnstcs Awd 85; Merit Bdg SADD 86; Adelphi U; Acctg.

BECKMAN, JON; Haverling Central Schl; Bath, NY; (Y); 60/150; Boy Scts; Church Yth Grp; JCL; VP Latin Clb; Band; Concert Band; Jazz Band; Mrchg Band; Symp Band; Cit Awd; NYS Amer Legn Ctznshp Awd & Boy Sct Of Yr 85 & 86; Bus.

BECKS, TIFFANY; Aquinas Inst; Rochester, NY; (Y); Office Aide; Science Clb; Ski Clb; Var Sftbl; Var Swmmng; High Hon Roll; Acad All Amer Schlr Pgm 85; Natl Ldrshp & Svc Awd 86.

BECKWITH, KYLE J; Granville Central HS; Granville, NY; (Y); 2/164; Am Leg Boys St; Math Tm; VP Sr Cls; Ftbl; Trk; Wt Lftg; Bausch & Lomb Sci Awd; High Hon Roll; NHS; Most Imprvd 84; Most Outstndg Male Stu 85 & 86; RPI Mdl Most Imprvd In Track 86; RPI; Engineering.

BECKWITH, MICHAEL; Oxford Academy HS; Mc Donough, NY; (Y); Pres FFA; Pres SADD; Varsity Clb; Yrbk Stf; Rep Frsh Cls; Trs Soph Cls; Pres Jr Cls; Pres Stu Cncl; JV Var Bsbl; JV Var Ftbl; All-County Ftbl 1st Tm, All-League Ftbl 1st Tm 85-86; All-County Ftbl 2nd Tm 84-85; Morrisvile Coll; Dairy Farmer.

BECKWITH, NOELLE; Hannibal Central Schl; Hannibal, NY; (Y); 19/114; Church Yth Grp; Pres Sec 4-H; Chorus; School Musical; School Play; Yrbk Stf; Sec Frsh Cls; Sec Soph Cls; Sec Jr Cls; Sec Sr Cls; SUNY Oswego; Psych.

BEDDIA, ANDRA; Westlake HS; Hawthorne, NY; (Y); Ski Clb; Spanish Clb; SADD; Teachers Aide; Nwsp Ed-Chief; Nwsp Rptr; Nwsp Stf; Yrbk Stf; Rep Frsh Cls; Rep Soph Cls; Sccr-All-Leag 3 Yrs, All Sctn-1 Yr 84-86; Bsktbl-All-Sctn 1 86; Engrng.

BEDELL, ANDREA; Bishop Loughlin HS; Brooklyn, NY; (Y); Church Yth Grp; Cmnty Wkr; Library Aide; Band; Church Choir; Sec Stu Cncl; Accntng.

BEDELL JR, GEORGE; Seaford HS; Seaford, NY; (Y); 63/250; Church Yth Grp; Computer Clb; Library Aide; Band; Concert Band; Mrchg Band; Nwsp Rptr; Yrbk Rptr; Trk; Hon Roll; Houghton Coll-Phonathon Grnt $1000 86; LI U At CW Post $1200 86; NYSSMA-CLAIRNET Solo Awd 85; Houghton Coll; Comp Sci.

BEDELL, RICHARD; Gloversville HS; Gloversvl, NY; (Y); #65 In Class; Band; Concert Band; JV Var Bsbl; JV Var Bowling; JV Var Ftbl; Comp Engr.

BEDFORD, CHERYL; St John The Baptist D HS; Amityville, NY; (Y); 126/546; Dance Clb; Girl Scts; Rep Jr Cls; Rep Stu Cncl; Var JV Cheerleading; JV Gym; Var JV Pom Pon; JV Powder Puff Ftbl; Hon Roll; Hampton U; Comp Sci.

BEDFORD, TRINA; Cicero-N Syracuse HS; N Syracuse, NY; (S); 7/662; Mathletes; Chorus; School Musical; Stage Crew; Lit Mag; Stu Cncl; Hon Roll; NHS; Manhattanville Coll; Pol Sci.

BEDNAR, MAURA; Archbishop Walsh HS; Olean, NY; (Y); 1/50; Math Clb; Rep Frsh Cls; Rep Soph Cls; Capt L Bsktbl; Var L Sftbl; High Hon Roll; Sec NHS; French Clb; JA; JV Cheerleading; Cattaraugus Cnty C 1st Al-Star Tm Bsktbl, Sftbl 85 & 86; Mrktng.

BEDNAREK, SARAH ANN; G Ray Bodley HS; Fulton, NY; (Y); Spanish Clb; Band; Concert Band; Mrchg Band; Var Swmmng; Intr Dsgn.

BEDOYA, LINA; Notre Dame-Bishop Gibbons HS; Schenectady, NY; (Y); Art Clb; Spanish Clb; Color Guard; Flag Corp; Mrchg Band; School Musical; Variety Show; Yrbk Stf; Hon Roll; Spnsh Awd, Flg Corp Awd, Clr Gurd Awd 84-86; Med.

BEECHER, DARLENE; Greene Central HS; Harpursville, NY; (Y); Band; Chorus; Concert Band; Jazz Band; Mrchg Band; VP School Play; Swing Chorus; High Hon Roll; Hst NHS; Area All ST Band 84-85; All Cnty Band 83-85; All Cnty Jazz Band 85; Poltcl Sci.

BEECHER, JAMES R; Elmira Free Acad; Elmira, NY; (Y); Boy Scts; Church Yth Grp; Cmnty Wkr; Drama Clb; Latin Clb; Letterman Clb; Political Wkr; SADD; Thesps; Varsity Clb; 1st Lrng Disbld Stu Recv Regns Diplma 86; 1st L D Stu Sch Systm Recv Regnts Schlrshp 86; PA ST U; Telecomm.

BEECHER, ROSLYN; Horseheads HS; Elmira, NY; (Y); French Clb; Ski Clb; Spanish Clb; Color Guard; Yrbk Stf; Swmmng; Hon Roll; Political Sci.

BEER, JOHN; Auburn HS; Auburn, NY; (Y); 1/450; Pres Drama Clb; Jazz Band; Mrchg Band; School Musical; Swing Chorus; Symp Band; Nwsp Rptr; Val; Voice Dem Awd; Bst Spkr Cayuga Cnty Mdl Senate 86; Intl Rltns.

BEER, SANDRA; Lindenhurst HS; Lindenhurst, NY; (Y); 4/550; Art Clb; Church Yth Grp; Dance Clb; German Clb; Science Clb; Ski Clb; SADD; Variety Show; Im Badmtn; Im Bsktbl; Amer Lg Awd 81; Princpls List 85-86; BOCES Gifted & Tlntd Pgm 83 & 84; NYU; Dentstry.

BEERY, BRENDAN T; Ward Melville HS; Setauket, NY; (Y); 45/750; Debate Tm; Political Wkr; Chorus; Nwsp Ed-Chief; Yrbk Ed-Chief; Rep Sr Cls; Var Crs Cntry; High Hon Roll; NHS; Pres Schlr; NYS Cert Of Merit,Regnts Schlrshp Wnnr 86; American U; Intl Stud.

BEERY, CHRISTIAN P; Ward Melville HS; Setauket, NY; (Y); 23/750; Math Clb; Off ROTC; Nwsp Rptr; Yrbk Stf; Var Ftbl; Var Capt Golf; High Hon Roll; NHS; Amer Lgn Awd For Acdmc Studies 85; JROTC Rgmnt 85; Islnd Ftbl Cnfrnc Hnrs 84; U Rchmnd; Bus Adm.

BEETE, PAULETTE ANN; St Francis Prep; Laurelton, NY; (S); 4/746; Church Yth Grp; Drama Clb; Teachers Aide; Chorus; School Musical; School Play; Stage Crew; NHS; Princpls List 83-86; Theatre.

BEFANIS, CHRISSY; Ossining HS; Ossining, NY; (Y); Dance Clb; Band; Concert Band; Mrchg Band; Stat Lcrss; French Hon Soc; High Hon Roll; Hon Roll; OHS Schlrshp Pin Tintnd Brnze, Brnze 85 & 86; Phys Thrpy.

BEGAY, PATRICIA; Bishop Ludden HS; Syracuse, NY; (Y); Church Yth Grp; Trk; NHS; Geneseo; Socl Svc.

BEGHINI, KENNETH P; Cardinal Mooney HS; Rochester, NY; (Y); 43/310; Boy Scts; Band; Concert Band; High Hon Roll; Hon Roll; Eagle Scout Awd 85; Clarkson U; Engr.

BEGIN, KENNETH; Berlin Central HS; Berlin, NY; (Y); Art Clb; Boy Scts; Ski Clb; Yrbk Stf; Wrstlng; Hon Roll; Coll Of St Rose; Grphc Dsgn.

BEGLEY, JANET; Lommack North HS; E Northport, NY; (Y); Cmnty Wkr; English Clb; Hosp Aide; Band; Concert Band; Mrchg Band; Badmtn; Tennis; Vllybl; Hon Roll; All Star Bsktbl Tm 83; 1st Pl-Sftbl All Star Tm 82; Equestrn Awds 82-83; Pace U; Desgn.

BEGY, KAREN; Wayne Central HS; Ontario, NY; (Y); 82/184; Hosp Aide; Library Aide; Red Cross Aide; Chorus; Yrbk Phtg; Yrbk Stf; Rep Stu Cncl; JV Cheerleading; Candy Striping Pin 86; Acad Achvt Eng 86; Law.

BEHAN, SUZANNE; Washington Acad; Cambridge, NY; (Y); Sec French Clb; Math Tm; Pep Clb; Yrbk Stf; Ed Lit Mag; Bsktbl; Capt Rptr Bowling; Var Fld Hcky; Pom Pon; Var Trk; Med.

BEHARI JR, JOSEPH; Savona Central Schl; Savona, NY; (Y); Am Leg Boys St; Church Yth Grp; Stage Crew; Var Socr; L Var Trk; Bausch & Lomb Sci Awd; Hon Roll; NHS; Acadmc All Stars Tm-Capt; NYS Rgnts Schlrshp; Indstrl Arts Awd-Crning Glss Wrks; Masons Math Awd; Army.

BEHR, MAUREEN K; Jamesville HS; Jamesville, NY; (Y); 24/245; Exploring; Hosp Aide; Math Tm; Pep Clb; SADD; Nwsp Stf; High Hon Roll; NHS; Ntl Merit SF; Chorus; Math Teachrs Assn Cert Of Merit 82; Classical Lge Cum Laude Cert 85; Math Awd 85; Pre-Med.

BEHRENS, NANCY; Babylon HS; Babylon, NY; (Y); Drama Clb; Chorus; Lit Mag; Rep Stu Cncl; NHS; Gen Exc Awd 84; Awd Bst Frgn Lang Stu 86; Lang.

BEHRING, ANDREA; Westlake HS; Thornwood, NY; (Y); Church Yth Grp; Hosp Aide; Ski Clb; SADD; Nwsp Phtg; Yrbk Phtg; Yrbk Stf; Hon Roll; Stu Recog Pgm Outstndg Achvt Math 85-86; St Agnes Hosp Vlntrng 322 Hrs 85; Elem Educ.

BEHRMANN, KARIN HOPE; Smithtown East HS; Smithtown, NY; (Y); Church Yth Grp; Cmnty Wkr; Stu Cncl; Cheerleading; Crs Cntry; Var Capt Gym; Var Trk; Pres French Hon Soc; High Hon Roll; NHS; Gold Key Awd Var Athltc 86; Acadmc Achvmnt Hi-Hnrs Awd 86; Wm & Mary Coll; Pre Med.

BEHUNIAK, KATHLEEN; Peekskill HS; Peekskill, NY; (S); Church Yth Grp; Yrbk Stf; Var Socr; Stat Swmmng; High Hon Roll; NHS; All League Varsity Soccer 86; Natl Hnr Soc Treas 86; Bio.

BEIDECK, JAMES; Irondequoit HS; Rochester, NY; (Y); 41/350; Computer Clb; Varsity Clb; Var JV Bsbl; Bowling; Hon Roll; Comp Sci.

BEIJER, SCOTT A; Sachem HS North Campus; Farmingville, NY; (Y); 40/1385; Hst Varsity Clb; Pres Frsh Cls; Pres Soph Cls; Rep Jr Cls; VP Sr Cls; Var L Ftbl; Cit Awd; Jr NHS; Pres NHS; Ntl Merit SF; Rgnts Schlrshp; Cornell U; Ind & Lbr Lrtns.

BEIM, AMY M; Riverdale Country Schl; Riverdale, NY; (Y); Var Crs Cntry; Var Gym; Var Lcrss; Crossroads Africa 86.

BEITCHMAN, LILITH; High School Of The Performing Arts; Brooklyn, NY; (Y); 21/121; Dance Clb; Drama Clb; French Clb; JA; Office Aide; Teachers Aide; Band; Concert Band; Pep Band; School Play; Perfrmng Arts Schlrshp 86; Brooklyn Coll; Actng.

BELAIR, CASSANDRA; Allegany Central Schl; Allegany, NY; (Y); 6/99; Church Yth Grp; Trs Exploring; Concert Band; Mrchg Band; School Musical; Nwsp Ed-Chief; Yrbk Stf; Tennis; High Hon Roll; NHS; Suny At Plattsburgh Pres Schlrshp & Hnrs Prog 86; Jrnlsm Awd 85-86; NY ST U Plattsburgh; Bio Phys.

BELAIR, JOANNA; Allegany Central HS; Allegany, NY; (Y); Church Yth Grp; Hosp Aide; Band; Concert Band; Mrchg Band; School Musical; Yrbk Ed-Chief; Cheerleading; Tennis; High Hon Roll; Diplmtc Stud.

BELANGER, DAVID; Malhopac HS; Mahopac, NY; (Y); 137/409; Nwsp Rptr; Nwsp Stf; Ed.

BELANGER, TODD; Avoca Central HS; Avoca, NY; (Y); 2/41; Am Leg Boys St; Band; Yrbk Phtg; Pres Sr Cls; Crs Cntry; Socr; Tennis; High Hon Roll; NHS; Rochester Inst; Elec Engr.

BELAS, EDWARD; Webutuck Central Schl; Wassaic, NY; (Y); 7/44; Am Leg Boys St; JV Var Bsktbl; Hon Roll; NHS; Schlrshp For Hghr Ed Amenia Lions Clb 86; Alfred U; Ceramic Engrng.

BELCHER, BRETT M; Horseheads HS; Horseheads, NY; (S); 32/380; Church Yth Grp; SADD; Band; Concert Band; Mrchg Band; Orch; Rep Soph Cls; High Hon Roll; Hon Roll; NHS; Comm.

BELDEN, CAROL; Friendship C S HS; Cuba, NY; (S); 3/27; Church Yth Grp; Drill Tm; Variety Show; Rep Jr Cls; Rep Sr Cls; Chrmn Stu Cncl; High Hon Roll; Hon Roll; Masonic Awd; NHS; Scribe 85, Chrmn 86; Girls Guide NYS Baptst 84-86; NYS Champ 4-H Dog Drill 81-84; 1st Pl Masnc Shw 85; Ithica Coll; Physcl Thrpy.

BELDEN, KIM; Warsaw Central Schl; Warsaw, NY; (S); 2/90; Trs Spanish Clb; Yrbk Ed-Chief; Var L Bsktbl; Capt Var Socr; Var L Sftbl; Var L Trk; Var Capt Vllybl; Hon Roll; NHS; Sal; Engl 84-85, Spnsh 83-85 Awds-White W; 4th Rnnr Up-Autumn Fstvl Qn Cont 84-85; Paul Smiths U; Hotel Mgmt.

BELDEN, MARK; Hudson Falls SR HS; Hudson Falls, NY; (Y); 107/260; Church Yth Grp; 4-H; Rep Stu Cncl; Dnfth Awd; 4-H Awd; WA Natl 4-H Conf ST Rep 85; Rprt Cmptn Cnty Wnnr & ST Fnlst 85; Dist 4-H Mtngs Pres 84-86.

BELDNER, JEFFREY M; Lynbrook HS; E Rockaway, NY; (Y); 5/239; Drama Clb; Trs French Clb; Mathletes; Thesps; Chorus; School Musical; Stage Crew; Yrbk Stf; NHS; Ntl Merit SF.

BELDUE, MICHAEL; Churchvill-Chili SR HS; Rochester, NY; (Y); Ski Clb; Bsktbl; JV L Golf; Vllybl; Htl Mngmnt.

BELEC, DAVID A; Honeoye Fals-Lima HS; Uma, NY; (Y); Chorus; Concert Band; Jazz Band; Mrchg Band; Orch; School Musical; Ntl Merit Ltr; Louis Armstrng Jazz Awd; 1st Pl & Bst Vcl Solo In Vrsty Show; Ithaca Coll; Rcrdng Artst.

BELFAY, ANN; Liverpool HS; Liverpool, NY; (Y); 127/816; AFS; Ski Clb; Var Swmmng; Hon Roll; Jr NHS; NHS; St Schlr; Vrsty Rwng; Boston U; Bus.

BELFIORE, VINCENT J; St Francis Prep; Whitestone, NY; (Y); 156/693; JV Crs Cntry; Im Ftbl; Im Sftbl; JV Trk; Im Vllybl; Opt Clb Awd; St Johns U; Bus Adm.

BELFOR, LOREEN; Bishop Loughlin Memorial HS; Brooklyn, NY; (Y); GAA; Band; Concert Band; Jazz Band; School Musical; Trk; Girl Scts; Math Tm; Spanish Clb; Cheerleading; Accntng.

BELILE, MARIE; Massena Central HS; Massena, NY; (Y); Cmnty Wkr; Key Clb; Varsity Clb; Yrbk Stf; Rep Soph Cls; JV Var Cheerleading; Im Mgr Powder Puff Ftbl; Trs Prfct Atten Awd; Herkumer County CC; Nrsng.

BELISLE, MICHELLE ANNE; St Marys Acad; South Glens Falls, NY; (S); Church Yth Grp; Drama Clb; Trs French Clb; Key Clb; SADD; Chorus; School Musical; Nwsp Rptr; Yrbk Ed-Chief; Powder Puff Ftbl; The Rensselaer Medal 86; Engrng.

BELIZAIRE, GUIRLAINE; Midwood H S At Brooklyn College; Brooklyn, NY; (Y); 60/667; Hosp Aide; Chorus; High Hon Roll; Prncpls-Pride Of Ynkees-1985 Ynkees Awd; Pre-Med.

BELL, AMY M; Our Lady Of Mercy HS; Penfield, NY; (Y); 66/172; Exploring; Hosp Aide; Science Clb; SADD; Church Choir; Hon Roll; NY Rgnts Schlrshp 86; Rochester Inst Of Tech; Bio.

BELL, BRETT; Geneseo Central Schl; Geneseo, NY; (Y); Am Leg Boys St; Ski Clb; Varsity Clb; Rep Frsh Cls; Var Capt Bsbl; Var Capt Bsktbl; High Hon Roll; Hon Roll; Jr NHS; Bus.

BELL, ERIN; Brockport HS; Brockport, NY; (Y); 6/315; Church Yth Grp; Exploring; VP Band; Jazz Band; Yrbk Ed-Chief; Crs Cntry; Trk; NHS; Girl Scts; Concert Band; Purdue JR Hl Fame Music 86; Sci.

BELL, ILSE; Bronx H S Of Science; Brooklyn, NY; (Y); Church Yth Grp; Chorus; Church Choir; Cheerleading; Powder Puff Ftbl; Ntl Achvt Schlrshp Pgm Outstndng Negro Stu 85-86; Assoc Schlrshp 85-86; Corp Lawyer.

BELL, JEANINE; Brighton HS; Rochester, NY; (Y); 24/325; Girl Scts; SADD; Thesps; Chorus; Madrigals; School Musical; School Play; Ntl Merit Ltr; NYS Rgnts Schlrshp 86; Northwestern U.

BELL, JEN; Northport HS; E Northport, NY; (Y); 233/572; French Clb; Varsity Clb; Band; Chorus; Concert Band; Variety Show; Im Badmtn; Im Bowling; Var Im Gym; Im Tennis; Bus Ed Dept Typng Awd 84-85; Math.

BELL, JEWEL; Clara Barton HS; Brooklyn, NY; (Y); Church Yth Grp; Cmnty Wkr; Quiz Bowl; Acpl Chr; Chorus; Church Choir; Color Guard; Drm & Bgl; Hon Roll; Andrews U; Pre-Med.

BELL, JOHN; Sperry HS; Henrietta, NY; (Y); Ski Clb; Bsbl; Coach Actv; Socr; Swmmng; Trk; Pottsdam; Comp Sci.

BELL, KEVIN F; Manhasset HS; Plandome, NY; (Y); 1/213; Varsity Clb; School Musical; School Play; Nwsp Rptr; Nwsp Sprt Ed; Yrbk Sprt Ed; Lit Mag; Rep Frsh Cls; Rep Soph Cls; Rep Jr Cls; All Cnfrnc Crs Cntry & Tnns 85 & 86; Duke; Orthpdc.

BELL, MARIA; Harpursville JR SR HS; Harpursville, NY; (S); 7/80; French Clb; Chorus; School Play; Nwsp Rptr; Yrbk Stf; Stu Cncl; JV Var Vllybl; High Hon Roll; Pres NHS; Voice Dem Awd; 9th In ST; Vce Of Democracy 84; Salute To Yth Cntst 85; FL ST U; Crim Just.

BELL, MICHAEL J; Perry Central HS; Perry, NY; (Y); #11 In Class; Am Leg Boys St; 4-H; Trs FFA; Achvt Awd Indtl Arts & Commrcl Arts 86.

BELL, SHAREESE; Grace H Dodge V HS; New York, NY; (Y); Teachers Aide; Nwsp Ed-Chief; Cheerleading; Hon Roll; Pre-Med.

BELL, SHEREE; Cardinal Speilman HS; Bronx, NY; (Y); Flag Corp; Yrbk Phtg; Yrbk Rptr; Yrbk Stf; Var Mgr Bsktbl; Hon Roll; Story Ave Nghbrhd Assn Schlstc Achvt Awd 86; Howard U; Computer Mgmt.

BELL, VANECIA; Greater N Y Acad; Central Islip, NY; (S); 3/35; Pres Church Yth Grp; Yrbk Stf; Off Sr Cls; Pres Stu Cncl; Badmtn; Cit Awd; Hon Roll; NHS; Hampton U; Pltcl Sci.

BELL, WILLETTE T; Notre Dame HS; New York, NY; (Y); Hosp Aide; Math Clb; Science Clb; Bsktbl; NHS; Ntl Merit Ltr; Bio.

BELLADONNA, JOSEPH; La Salle Acad; New York, NY; (S); 6/207; Boy Scts; Hosp Aide; Math Clb; Math Tm; Nwsp Rptr; Trs Stu Cncl; Bowling; Crs Cntry; Trk; NHS; Soc Dstngshd Amer H S 84-86; Bus.

BELLAMY, ANGELA; Henninger SR HS; Jacksonville, NC; (Y); Church Yth Grp; DECA; SADD; Church Choir; Variety Show; Rcvd Cert From DECA 85; Bus Adm.

BELLAMY, SAM; Hugh C Williams HS; Canton, NY; (Y); Nwsp Rptr; Lit Mag; Bsktbl; Golf; Socr; High Hon Roll; NHS; Pres Schlr; MVP 1st Man Golf Tm 85; Capt Bsktbl Tm 84; Cornell U; Bus.

BELLANGER, JANIS; Cicero-North Syracuse HS; North Syracuse, NY; (S); 10/632; SADD; Concert Band; Mrchg Band; Symp Band; Rep Soph Cls; Rep Jr Cls; Hon Roll; Jr NHS; Bio.

BELLANTON, MARTHE; Ramapos HS; Spring Valley, NY; (Y); Church Yth Grp; Computer Clb; DECA; FCA; Hosp Aide; Math Clb; Red Cross Aide; SADD; Concert Band; Nwsp Rptr; Felix Neptune Schlrshp 86; PTA Awd 86; Rockaldn Comm Coll; Comp Analys.

BELLANTONI, RORY J; Blind Brook HS; Rye Brook, NY; (Y); Var Capt Ice Hcky; Elec Engr.

BELLARDINI, THOMAS M; Pulaski JR/SR HS; Pulaski, NY; (S); Math Clb; Ski Clb; Varsity Clb; VP Jr Cls; Rep Stu Cncl; VP Capt Ftbl; Im Wt Lftg; Hon Roll; Canton ATC; Aerontcl Engr.

BELLAS, STEPHEN R; St Marys Boys HS; Manhasset, NY; (Y); 15/178; Am Leg Boys St; L Swmmng; High Hon Roll; Hon Roll; Bus.

BELLAVIA, CHARLENE; Mount St Ursula HS; Bronx, NY; (Y); Art Clb; Var Cheerleading; Hon Roll.

BELLAVIA, MARC; Greece Athena HS; Rochester, NY; (Y); 50/350; Hon Roll; Musical Engr.

BELLAVIA, RAND J; Lyndonville HS; Waterport, NY; (S); 4/100; Band; School Musical; Lit Mag; Pres Frsh Cls; Rep Stu Cncl; Var Socr; Var Trk; Hon Roll; NHS; Stu Of Mnth 84; Engl Lit.

BELLE, DEBORAH; Liverpool HS; Liverpool, NY; (Y); Color Guard; Frsh Cls; Ntl Merit Ltr; Merit Rl; U Of Buffalo-Phrmcy; Phrmcy.

BELLE, MARIA; Mahopac HS; Mahopac, NY; (Y); 55/383; Church Yth Grp; SADD; Pres Soph Cls; Pres Jr Cls; Pres Stu Cncl; Var Stat Bsbl; Var Stat Bsktbl; JV Var Cheerleading; JV Var Sftbl; NHS; Rgnts Schlrshsp 86; Pres Schlrhsp Fit Awd 86; Syracuse U; Comm Arts.

BELLE-OUDRY, DEIRDRE; Centereach HS; Centereach, NY; (Y); 4/428; Yrbk Stf; Stu Cncl; Score Keeper; JV Sftbl; JV Tennis; Im Wt Lftg; French Hon Soc; High Hon Roll; Hon Roll; Jr NHS; PTA Scholar 86; Sons Of Italy 86; Italian Hnr Soc 85; SUNY Stony Brook; Mth.

BELLIA, ANTHONY; Canisius HS; Kenmore, NY; (S); 5/162; Capt Pep Clb; Yrbk Ed-Chief; Yrbk Rptr; Yrbk Stf; Tennis; High Hon Roll; NHS; Hugh O Brien Yth Ldrshp Sem 85.

BELLINGER, JODI; Thomas A Edison HS; Horseheads, NY; (Y); 9/80; Am Leg Aux Girls St; Acpl Chr; Drm Mjr(t); Jazz Band; Mrchg Band; School Musical; Yrbk Ed-Chief; Pres Frsh Cls; VP Soph Cls; Trs Jr Cls; NYS Regnts Schlrshp 86; Utica Coll; Occptnl Thrpy.

BELLINGER, MAGGIE; Clymer Central HS; Findley Lk, NY; (Y); AFS; Church Yth Grp; Pres Girl Scts; Teachers Aide; Yrbk Rptr; Yrbk Sprt Ed; Yrbk Stf; Var JV Cheerleading; Var JV Trk; High Hon Roll.

BELLINGER, PAMELA; Hillcrest HS; Jamaica, NY; (Y); Hosp Aide; Chorus; Church Choir; Coop Educ Awd 86; Syracuse U; Nrsng.

BELLINGER, SARA JANE; Schoharie Central Schl; Howes Cave, NY; (S); 20/108; Sec Church Yth Grp; Pres 4-H; Pres FFA; Key Clb; Trs PAVAS; Concert Band; Drm Mjr(t); Madrigals; School Musical; Rep Stu Cncl; Star Chptr Frmr FFA 85; FFA Slvr Ldrshp Awd 85; FFA WA Ldrshp Schlrshp 85; Cornell U; Ag.

BELLINGER, STEPHANIE; Amsterdam HS; Amsterdam, NY; (Y); Dance Clb; Drama Clb; French Clb; GAA; Girl Scts; Hosp Aide; JA; Office Aide; Ski Clb; Acpl Chr; St Lawrence; Medical Research.

BELLIS, MELANIE; Tioga Central HS; Barton, NY; (Y); 4-H; 4-H Awd; High Hon Roll; Hon Roll; Nrsg.

BELLIS, ROBERT H; Chenango Valley HS; Binghamton, NY; (Y); 1/182; Ski Clb; Concert Band; Mrchg Band; Yrbk Bus Mgr; Var L Socr; Var Trk; High Hon Roll; Trs Jr NHS; NHS; Ntl Merit SF; Rensselaer Mdl Excllnce Mth & Sci RPI 86; Natl Cncl Yth Ldrshp 86; Pres Phys Fit Awd 86; Engrng.

BELLISARIO, STEPHANIE; Sacred Heart HS; Yonkers, NY; (Y); Var Trk; Hon Roll; Track Mdl-By Bros Of Chrstn Schls; Awd For Excllnce In Bio; Iona Coll; Bio.

BELLMAR, MARY T; Our Lady Of Mercy Acad; Plainview, NY; (Y); 2/120; Cmnty Wkr; Pres Computer Clb; SADD; VP Chorus; Church Choir; School Play; Yrbk Stf; High Hon Roll; NHS; Ntl Merit Ltr; USDAN Camp Arts Schlrshp Voice 83; NYSSMA Rating Voice 83-84; Chem Smnr Gifted HS Stu Adelphi U 84.

BELLO, STEPHANIE; Westlake HS; Hawthorne, NY; (Y); Church Yth Grp; Debate Tm; FBLA; Hosp Aide; Library Aide; Yrbk Stf; High Hon Roll; Hon Roll; Wstchstr Bus Inst Achvmnt Awd JR Bus Clss 86; Phrmcy.

BELLO, TOM; Lindenhurst HS; Lindenhurst, NY; (Y); Aud/Vis; Boy Scts; Camera Clb; Cmnty Wkr; Debate Tm; 4-H; Science Clb; SADD; Varsity Clb; Y-Teens; Knights Of Columbus Treasur 84; Ftbl Cptn 86; Swmmng Ldr 86; Bus Admn.

BELLOFATTO, MARY; Port Chester HS; Port Chester, NY; (Y); Key Clb; Stu Cncl; Cheerleading; Gym; Sftbl; Hon Roll; NHS; Spanish NHS.

BELLOS, MARIA; Mahopac HS; Mahopac Falls, NY; (Y); 53/398; Yrbk Stf; Hon Roll; NHS; Albany ST U; Polit Sci.

BELLUCCI, VICTORIA; St Marys Girls HS; Manhasset, NY; (Y); Ski Clb; Spanish Clb; Chorus; Stage Crew; JV Trk; Med.

BELMONTE, JOHN B; Patchogue-Medford HS; Patchogue, NY; (Y); 14/700; Trs Drama Clb; Trs Radio Clb; School Musical; School Play; Stage Crew; Hon Roll; Jr NHS; NHS; Aud/Vis; Math Tm; NY ST Regents Schlrshp 86; Hofstra U; Drama.

BELNA, CHRISTINE; Cicero-North Syracuse HS; Clay, NY; (S); 45/667; Bsktbl; Sftbl; Tennis; Hon Roll; NHS; Schlstc Art Comptn Gold Key & Hmbl Mntn 86; Fashn Dsgn.

BELNA, SUSAN; Cicero North Syracuse HS; Clay, NY; (S); 24/630; Dance Clb; JA; Mathletes; Mrchg Band; Rep Frsh Cls; Bsktbl; Sftbl; Tennis; High Hon Roll; Hon Roll; USAA Govt Awd 85-86; Dstngshd Amrcn Stu 85-86; Pre-Law.

BELROSE, ANNE MARIE; Cooperstown HS; Cooperstown, NY; (Y); 39/105; GAA; Red Cross Aide; Varsity Clb; Chorus; Stage Crew; Yrbk Stf; Stu Cncl; Var JV Fld Hcky; Var Vllybl; Hon Roll; Envrnmntl Lwyr.

BELROSE, GINA; East Islip HS; Great River, NY; (Y); 120/425; Sec DECA; Teachers Aide; Hon Roll; $500 Acdmc Schlrshp & $900 Schlrshp DECA Johnson & Wales Coll 86; Johnson & Wales Coll; Admin Ast.

BELT, KATHERINE; Npt HS; Northport, NY; (Y); 70/585; Art Clb; Cmnty Wkr; Exploring; Pep Clb; SADD; Chorus; Variety Show; Score Keeper; High Hon Roll; Hon Roll; Hnrs In Art 85-86; J Madison U; Art.

BELTON, DAVID; Lafayette HS; Buffalo, NY; (Y); Math Tm; Trk; Prfct Atten Awd; Buffalo Pblc HS Math Legue Awd 85-86; Howard U; Engnr.

BELTON, MICHAEL; Vernon-Verona-Sherrill Central HS; Vernon, NY; (Y); CAP; Ski Clb; JV Bsbl; JV Var Ftbl; Hon Roll; Chrch Lector 84-86; FL Inst Tech; Air Trnsptn Tech.

BELTON, TANYA; White Plains HS; White Plns, NY; (Y); Girl Scts; Office Aide; Teachers Aide; Var Crs Cntry; Var Capt Trk; Hon Roll; Coachs Awd 84; RICH Awd 85; Bus Admin.

BELTRAN, JESUS; All Hallows HS; Brow, NY; (Y); Teachers Aide; JV Bsbl; JV Bsktbl; Wt Lftg; Hon Roll; NHS; Stu Achvt Awd 83-84; Hunter Coll; Ed.

BELTRAN, MIRIAM; Amsterdam HS; Amesterdam, NY; (Y); Church Yth Grp; FNA; Hosp Aide; Hon Roll; Spencer Bus Tech Inst; Exec Sec.

BELTRANI, ANNMARIE; Sachem HS; Farmingville, NY; (Y); Nwsp Ed-Chief; VP Soph Cls; Trs Jr Cls; Cit Awd; NHS; Church Yth Grp; SADD; Socr; Trk; Ntl Merit Schol; Bst Wrtr Jrnlsm; Comm.

BELUSAR, CURT; Oneida SR HS; Oneida, NY; (S); 7/200; Boy Scts; Concert Band; Stage Crew; Yrbk Stf; Var L Socr; Var L Trk; High Hon Roll; Trs NHS; Rotary Awd; Band; NY ST Regents Schlrshp 86; Purdue U; Elec Engr.

BEMISS, DAVID; Chatham Central HS; E Chatham, NY; (Y); 64/148; Boy Scts; Chorus; Var Bsbl; Var Bsktbl; Var Crs Cntry; Hon Roll; Acctg.

BEMPKINS, JENNIFER; West HS; Painted Post, NY; (Y); Church Yth Grp; Ski Clb; Varsity Clb; Band; Concert Band; Mrchg Band; Jr Cls; Stu Cncl; Var L Swmmng; Sec NHS; High Hnr Rl 84-86.

BEN-DOR, ELDAD; Suffern SR HS; Monsey, NY; (Y); 93/393; Drama Clb; Temple Yth Grp; Chorus; Orch; School Musical; School Play; Hon Roll; Ntl Merit Ltr; Prv Pilots Lcnse 85; Drama Clb Awd; FL Inst & Tech; Prof Aviator.

BENACK, GENNY; Stissing Mountain HS; Pine Plains, NY; (Y); AFS; Hon Roll; Jrnlsm.

BENBOW, CURIN; The Knox Schl; East Setauket, NY; (Y); 10/40; Cmnty Wkr; Computer Clb; Drama Clb; Pep Clb; Spanish Clb; SADD; Varsity Clb; Orch; School Musical; School Play; Slctd To Exchng Pgm England 84; Chapman Coll; Cmnctns.

BENCE, CHRISTINE A; Emma Willard Schl; North Adams, MA; (Y); Exploring; PAVAS; SADD; Yrbk Stf; Lit Mag; VP Sr Cls; Cit Awd; High Hon Roll; NYU Tisch; Dance.

BENDELL, BRUCE; New Rochelle HS; New Rochelle, NY; (Y); 248/560; Trs Chess Clb; Pres Ski Clb; Var Golf; Captain Ski Team 85-86; U CO-BOULDER.

BENDER, JILL A; Liverpool HS; Liverpool, NY; (Y); 156/816; Ski Clb; Concert Band; Var L Crs Cntry; Var L Trk; Hon Roll; NHS; NY ST Regents Schlrshp 86; Buffalo ST Coll; Scl Wrkr.

BENEDETTI, PAUL; Newtown HS; Elmhurst, NY; (Y); 84/781; Chorus; Banker.

BENEDETTO, LAWRENCE G; Bayport-Bluepoint HS; Bayport, NY; (Y); 19/222; Pres Key Clb; Mathletes; Political Wkr; SADD; Var Im Bsktbl; Var Golf; NHS; Im Wt Lftg; Lbrl Arts.

BENEDICT, HEATHER; Penn Yan Acad; Pennyan, NY; (S); 16/179; Church Yth Grp; 4-H; Intnl Clb; Ski Clb; Band; Church Choir; Concert Band; Jazz Band; Mrchg Band; Nwsp Stf; Spnsh Awd 83; Yates Cnty Arts Cncl Awd 85; Portfl Schlrshp 86; Syracuse U; Intr Dsgn.

BENEDICT, JANICE; Skaneateles HS; Skaneateles, NY; (Y); 4-H; Girl Scts; Chorus; Yrbk Stf; 4-H Awd; High Hon Roll; Food Svc.

BENEDICT, JOANNE; Immaculata Acad; Derby, NY; (Y); Church Yth Grp; Drama Clb; Ski Clb; Spanish Clb; Chorus; School Musical; Variety Show; Nwsp Rptr; Nwsp Stf; Lit Mag; Gannon U Erie PA; Men Hlth Cns.

BENEDICT, LAEL; Bainbridge-Guilford Central HS; Bainbridge, NY; (Y); Cmnty Wkr; Library Aide; Cit Awd; High Hon Roll; Hon Roll; Prfct Atten Awd; Bus Ed Awd 84; Sec.

BENEDICT, LAURA; James A Beneway HS; Ontario, NY; (Y); Chorus; Yrbk Phtg; Yrbk Stf; JV Bsktbl; Sftbl; Vllybl; Hon Roll; NHS; Law.

BENEDICT, RAE; Newburgh Free Acad; Newburgh, NY; (Y); Cmnty Wkr; Office Aide; Red Cross Aide; Var Stat Score Keeper; Var L Socr; High Hon Roll; Hon Roll; Neighborhood Vllybll Assn-Plyr & Treas 86; Long Island U; Marine Bio.

BENEDICT, TIM; Pleasantville HS; Pleasantville, NY; (Y); 24/105; Drama Clb; Ski Clb; Thesps; Varsity Clb; Band; Chorus; Concert Band; Mrchg Band; Pep Band; School Play; Rnnr Up Sctn 1st Clss Golf Tournmnt 86; MVP Golf 85-86; Liberal Arts Schl; Engl.

BENEROFE, JEFF; Harrison HS; Purchase, NY; (Y); 26/223; Ski Clb; Variety Show; Nwsp Rptr; Nwsp Stf; Yrbk Stf; JV Capt Bsktbl; Var Socr; Tennis; NHS; All Leag Var Soccr 85; Northwestern; Ecnmcs.

BENES, NADINE; Bennett HS; Buffalo, NY; (Y); Cmnty Wkr; Computer Clb; Girl Scts; JA; Varsity Clb; Variety Show; Trk; Miss Natl Teen-Ager Fnlst 85; Buffalo ST; Elem Tchr.

BENESHAN, LARA; Lake Placid Central Schl; Lake Placid, NY; (Y); Church Yth Grp; Spanish Clb; Chorus; School Musical; Yrbk Stf; Var L Cheerleading; Var L Trk; High Hon Roll; Hon Roll; NHS; Bio.

BENINATI, NANCY; Bay Shore HS; Bay Shore, NY; (Y); 7/406; Hosp Aide; Concert Band; Mrchg Band; Nwsp Sprt Ed; Rep Soph Cls; Rep Jr Cls; Bsktbl; Socr; Vllybl; Elks Awd; Islip Yth Of Yr 86; Librl Arts.

BENITEZ, MAUREEN; Moore Catholic HS; Staten Island, NY; (Y); Yrbk Stf; Im Bowling; Hon Roll; Educ.

BENITEZ, RONALD; Msgr Farrell HS; Staten Island, NY; (S); 42/300; Boy Scts; Sec Soph Cls; Pres Jr Cls; Im Bsktbl; Var Ftbl; Var Wt Lftg; Hon Roll; Andrw J Brbri Schlr-Athlt Awd 86; Bob Lwny Memrl Schlrshp 86; SUNY-BINGHAMTON; Biochem.

BENJAMIN, BELINDA LEE; Waterloo SR HS; Waterloo, NY; (S); 5/175; Pres French Clb; FTA; Hosp Aide; Political Wkr; Teachers Aide; Nwsp Stf; Rep Jr Cls; Rep Sr Cls; Pres NHS; High Hon Roll; Adv Plcmnt Hstry 84-85, Engl 85-86; Rgnts Schlrshp Awd 86; Psych.

BENJAMIN, JOHNETTE; John Dewey HS; Brooklyn, NY; (Y); Church Yth Grp; JA; Office Aide; School Play; Yrbk Stf; Im Golf; Im Trk; Im Vllybl; Messiah; Music.

BENJAMIN, PASCALE VIVIANE; Dominican Commercial HS; Flushing, NY; (S); 24/350; Teachers Aide; Var Vllybl; Principals List 84-86; Bus Adm.

BENJAMIN, PATRICIA; Hastings HS; Hastings On Hudso, NY; (Y); 49/108; Church Yth Grp; Key Clb; Chorus; Orch; Stage Crew; Nwsp Rptr; Lit Mag; Martin Luther King Jr Awd Fnlst 86; ACT-SO Natl Cmpttr Regnl Wnnr 85-86; Stony Brook; Ecnmcs.

BENJAMIN, SCOTT S; Oswego HS; Oswego, NY; (Y); 12/385; Am Leg Boys St; Cmnty Wkr; German Clb; Science Clb; Variety Show; Nwsp Ed-Chief; Nwsp Stf; Rep Jr Cls; Sec Sr Cls; JV Bsktbl; Prsdntl Outstndng Acadmc Achvt Ftns Awd 86; OCTA Schlrshp Awd 86; Joanna M Melsbaka Litrcy Schlrshp; ST U Oswego; Pre-Med.

BENN, ALFRED; Our Savior Lutheran HS; Bronx, NY; (Y); 3/32; Bsktbl; Socr; Hon Roll; Ntl Merit Ltr; Iona; Pre-Med.

BENNATI, BRIAN; Vernon-Verona-Sherrill HS; Sherrill, NY; (Y); Am Leg Boys St; JV Var Bsbl; Bsktbl; Var L Socr; High Hon Roll; Hon Roll; NHS; Prfct Atten Awd.

BENNEAR, ELISABETH RUTH; Jamesville-De Witt HS; Dewitt, NY; (Y); 105/245; French Clb; Yrbk Stf; Vllybl; Schlstc MONY Art Awd 86; Schlrshp To RIT; Rochester Inst; Indstrl.

BENNER, MICHAEL J; Canisius HS; Cheektowaga, NY; (Y); Art Clb; Cmnty Wkr; Computer Clb; High Hon Roll; Hon Roll; Regents Schlrshp Wnnr 86; James V Stillwell Schlrshp 86; ST U Of NY Buffalo; Elec Engr.

BENNETT, ALEXANDRA; Skaneateles HS; Skaneateles, NY; (S); Church Yth Grp; Drama Clb; French Clb; Hosp Aide; Red Cross Aide; Stage Crew; Yrbk Stf; Lit Mag; Hon Roll; NHS.

BENNETT, BELINDA; Tioga Central HS; Nichols, NY; (Y); SADD; School Musical; JV Bsktbl; High Hon Roll; Hon Roll; NHS; Prfct Atten Awd; Paul Smiths Coll; Htl/Rst Mgmt.

BENNETT, BRENT; East Hampton HS; E Hampton, NY; (Y); Computer Clb; Quiz Bowl; Scholastic Bowl; Var L Socr; Bausch & Lomb Sci Awd; High Hon Roll; Lion Awd; NHS; Gold Mdls In Math, Sci & Frnch 83-86; Englsh & Scl Stdys Schlrshps & Cert In Phy Ed 83-86; Comp Sci.

BENNETT, DEBORAH; Victor Central HS; Macedon, NY; (S); 43/228; Church Yth Grp; Spanish Clb; Acpl Chr; Chorus; School Musical; Off Stu Cncl; Hon Roll; All Cnty Chrs 84 & 85; All ST Chrs 85-86; NYSSMA 84-86; Engrng.

BENNETT, DERRICK C; Adlai E Stevenson HS; Bronx, NY; (Y); Band; Vllybl; Wt Lftg; Hon Roll; Prfct Atten Awd; Voice Dem Awd; Acdmc All-Amer Awd 86; Pre-Med.

BENNETT, DONNA; Mineola HS; Mineola, NY; (Y); Art Clb; Key Clb; Pres Spanish Clb; SADD; Varsity Clb; Orch; Stage Crew; Nwsp Rptr; Var Bsktbl; Var Socr; Hugh O Brien Yth Awd 84-85.

BENNETT, ELIZABETH M; West Genesee HS; Camillus, NY; (Y); 80/425; Girl Scts; JA; Ski Clb; Pres VP SADD; Chorus; Nwsp Stf; Yrbk Stf; French Hon Soc; High Hon Roll; Hon Roll; Diet Athy Advsry Cncl Themis Awd 86; Outstnd Stu Englsh 86; Outstdng Stu Frng Lang 86; Mc Gill U; Chld Psych.

BENNETT, HEATHER; Warsaw Central Schl; Warsaw, NY; (S); 13/90; Church Yth Grp; French Clb; JV Bsktbl; JV Var Sftbl; JV Vllybl; Hon Roll; Long Island U; Oceanogrphy.

BENNETT, JACKIE; Schoharie Central HS; Esperance, NY; (Y); Teachers Aide; Vllybl; Albany Bus Coll; Comp Pgmr.

BENNETT, JAMES; Rome Free Acad; Rome, NY; (Y); 70/500; Boy Scts; Exploring; NFL; Speech Tm; L Chorus; School Musical; Swing Chorus; L Var Ftbl; Hon Roll; Church Yth Grp; Eagle Scout 84; On My Honor LDS Sctng Achvmnt 83; Brigham Young U; Engr.

BENNETT, JIM; Saint John The Baptist HS; Oakdale, NY; (Y); Chess Clb; Cmnty Wkr; Hosp Aide; Political Wkr; Ski Clb; SADD; Rep Frsh Cls; Rep Soph Cls; Rep Jr Cls; Ftbl; NYU; Law.

BENNETT, JOEL; Gowanda Central HS; Gowanda, NY; (Y); Red Cross Aide; SADD; Varsity Clb; VICA; Rep Jr Cls; Bsktbl; Ftbl; Lcrss; Wt Lftg; Wrstlng; Seneca Lang Outstndng Stu 85-86; Alfred ST; Bldng Trades.

BENNETT, JOLENE; Romulus Central Schl; Romulus, NY; (Y); 4-H; Office Aide; Color Guard; School Musical; Yrbk Stf; Trs Jr Cls; Trs Sr Cls; Var L Socr; 4-H Awd; SUNY Delhi; Vet Sci Tech.

BENNETT, KATHRYN L; Kingston HS; Woodstock, NY; (Y); 1/573; VP Sec Church Yth Grp; Hosp Aide; Teachers Aide; Band; Yrbk Stf; French Hon Soc; Hon Roll; NHS; Ntl Merit Ltr; French Clb; Hghst Avg 83; NYS Rgnts Schlrshp 86; U Of Rochester; Biomed Engr.

BENNETT, KELLY; Eden Central HS; Eden, NY; (Y); GAA; Varsity Clb; Chorus; Coach Actv; Swmmng; Hon Roll.

BENNETT, KERRY A; Baldwin HS; Baldwin, NY; (Y); 34/476; Exploring; Key Clb; VP SADD; Drill Tm; Var Badmtn; High Hon Roll; Hon Roll; Spanish NHS; Rgnts Schlrshp; Amer Studs Outstndng Achvt; Fairfield U; Math.

BENNETT, KRISTIE; Cato Meridian HS; Cato, NY; (Y); 12/72; English Clb; French Clb; Nwsp Stf; Fld Hcky; Sftbl; Trk; High Hon Roll; Hon Roll; Jr NHS; Sec NHS; Robrt & Clara Hrdy Schlrshp 86; SUNY-OSEGO; Pblc Jstc.

BENNETT, MICHAEL; Midwood At Brooklyn College; Brooklyn, NY; (Y); Chorus; School Play; Ftbl; Ntl Merit Ltr.

BENNETT, MICHELLE; Cardinal Spellman HS; Bronx, NY; (Y); 184/486; French Clb; Var Trk; 2nd Hnrs Acadmc; Outstndng Trck Prfrmr-Indr, Outdr CHSAA; Natnly Rnkd Athltc 400m, 600m; Pre-Med.

BENNETT, STEVEN J; Jamesville Dewitt HS; Dewitt, NY; (Y); 53/245; VP Model UN; Political Wkr; Chorus; School Musical; Swing Chorus; Nwsp Rptr; JV Crs Cntry; High Hon Roll; NYS Rgnts Schlrshp 86.

BENNINK, MICHAEL J; East Syracuse-Minoa HS; East Syracuse, NY; (Y); 21/333; Var Capt Bsbl; Var Capt Ftbl; Var Capt Wrstlng; Jr NHS; NHS; Ntl Merit Ltr; Variety Show; Rep Soph Cls; Rep Jr Cls; Rep Sr Cls; NY ST Regents Schlrshp; Rensselaer Polytech; Engr.

BENNS JR, GEORGE; Burgard Vocational HS; Buffalo, NY; (Y); 2/67; Pres Church Yth Grp; Capt Debate Tm; Rep Frsh Cls; Rep Soph Cls; Rep Jr Cls; Rep Sr Cls; Pres Stu Cncl; Bowling; Hon Roll; Sal; Natl Conf Chrstns & Jews Brotherhd Scholar 86; Cntrl Ofc Ed Awd 86; Guid Dept Svc 86; Robert Wesleyan Coll; Relign.

BENSEN, CHRISTINE A; William Floyd HS; Shirley, NY; (Y); 7/455; Ski Clb; Pres Spanish Clb; Chorus; Orch; Nwsp Stf; Pres Stu Cncl; Cheerleading; High Hon Roll; NHS; St Schlr; Boston U; Med.

BENSINK, PAULA; Jamestown HS; Jamestown, NY; (Y); Church Yth Grp; Cmnty Wkr; Latin Clb; Ski Clb; Spanish Clb; SADD; Church Choir; Orch; School Musical; Yrbk Stf; Nazareth Coll; Psych.

BENSON, DONNA; Curtis HS; Staten Island, NY; (Y); 14/400; Pres Church Yth Grp; Hosp Aide; Office Aide; Teachers Aide; Band; Concert Band; Mrchg Band; School Musical; High Hon Roll; NHS; Cert Of Hnr Hnr Key 86; Chld Psych.

BENSON, JEFFREY; Greece Olympia HS; Rochester, NY; (Y); Boy Scts; Pres Church Yth Grp; Cmnty Wkr; Drama Clb; Exploring; JA; SADD; Acpl Chr; Chorus; Church Choir; Comp.

BENSON, KEVIN W; West Islip HS; W Islip, NY; (Y); 6/525; Boy Scts; Church Yth Grp; Cmnty Wkr; Hosp Aide; Band; Hon Roll; NHS; Rgnts ST NY 86; Rchrd Rose Schlrshp Fund 86; PTA Schlrshp Awd 86; Binghamton Coll; Bio.

BENSON III, ROBERT L; Canastota HS; Canastota, NY; (Y); 48/150; Aud/Vis; Band; Concert Band; Mrchg Band; School Musical; Stage Crew; Symp Band; Hon Roll; Frnd Of Educ Schlrshp; Bryant & Stratton; Elctrnc Tech.

BENSON, ROSEANN; Catholic Central HS; Waterford, NY; (S); 3/179; German Clb; Math Clb; Math Tm; Concert Band; School Play; Variety Show; Sftbl; High Hon Roll; NHS; RPI Schlrshp 85; Grmn Awd 83-85; Math Awd 84-85; Engrng.

BENSON, SANDRA; Susan E Wagner HS; Staten Island, NY; (Y); Computer Clb; Math Clb; Teachers Aide; School Musical; Stage Crew; Nwsp Rptr; Lit Mag; High Hon Roll; NHS; Mth.

BENSON, STACEY; Hudson Falls Central HS; Hudson Falls, NY; (Y); 17/214; Trs Church Yth Grp; Key Clb; SADD; Band; Concert Band; Mrchg Band; Stage Crew; Yrbk Stf; Off Frsh Cls; Off Soph Cls; Alfred U; Poly Sci.

BENSON, YVETTE; Cattaraugus Central HS; Cattaraugus, NY; (Y); 2/53; AFS; Cmnty Wkr; FHA; Color Guard; Yrbk Stf; Stat Var Bsktbl; Hon Roll; NHS; Art.

BENTLEY, JACQUELYN; Coipiague HS; Copiague, NY; (Y); 12/312; Cmnty Wkr; Hosp Aide; School Play; Stu Cncl; Gym; Trk; Hon Roll; Trs NHS; Pres Schlr; Rgnts Schlrshp Nrsng 86; Stu Fclty Comm Cmmttee Secy 85-86; JR Leag Amityville Womns Clb Awd 86; Farmingdale U; Nrsng.

BENTLEY, JULIE L; Panama Central Schl; Niobe, NY; (Y); 1/66; Pep Clb; Scholastic Bowl; Spanish Clb; Varsity Clb; Nwsp Sprt Ed; Yrbk Bus Mgr; Cheerleading; Trk; NHS; Val; NY ST Regent Schlrshp 86; U Of Rochester; Optcl Engrng.

BENTLEY, MICHELLE; Albertos Magnus HS; Blauvelt, NY; (Y); 47/192; Sec Church Yth Grp; English Clb; Latin Clb; Math Clb; Service Clb; Varsity Clb; Capt L Socr; Capt L Sftbl; High Hon Roll; Pres Schlr; Lemoyne Coll; Dntstry.

BENTLEY, SHEILA; Hartford Central HS; Granville, NY; (Y); French Clb; Math Tm; Pep Clb; Science Clb; SADD; Chorus; Yrbk Stf; Bsktbl; Vllybl; Lorraine A Reed Meml Schlrshp 86; Pres Schlrshp 86; Mnth Hlth.

BENTON, REBECCA L; Liverpool HS; N Syracuse, NY; (Y); 72/816; Ski Clb; Chorus; Nwsp Ed-Chief; Nwsp Rptr; Stu Cncl; Hon Roll; Masonic Awd; NHS; Rgnts Schlrshp 86; SUNY Binghamton; Comp Sci.

BENTREWICZ, JOHN; Hicksville SR HS; Hicksville, NY; (Y); 86/450; Stage Crew; Variety Show; L Var Bsktbl; Hon Roll; Jr NHS; NHS; Am Legion Cert Schl Awd 80; PTSA Schlrshp 86; Pres Acad Ftns Awd 86; Cazanovia Coll; Arch.

BENVENUTO, DIANA; Tottenville HS; Staten Isld, NY; (Y); School Play; Coll Of Staten Island; Comp.

BENWARE, TODD R; Gouverneur Central HS; Gouverneur, NY; (Y); Computer Clb; Varsity Clb; Var JV Bsktbl; Var Capt Golf; Var Socr; Var Vllybl; Jr NHS; Pres Schlr; 1st Tm All Nthrn Golf Tm 85 & 86; 7th ST Intrsctnl Golf Trnmnt 85, 4th 86; OH Wesleyan U.

BENWITZ, CANDACE; Newark SR HS; Newark, NY; (Y); 31/201; Church Yth Grp; Pres VP 4-H; German Clb; Concert Band; Jazz Band; Mrchg Band; Pep Band; Nwsp Stf; 4-H Awd; NHS; U ME Orono; Ag Engr.

BENZ, DAVE; Henninger HS; Syracuse, NY; (Y); 20/500; Band; Concert Band; Jazz Band; Pep Band; Variety Show; Frsh Cls; Crs Cntry; Var Trk; High Hon Roll; NHS; Comp.

BENZIN, ABBEY; Eden SR HS; Eden, NY; (Y); AFS; Trs Church Yth Grp; SADD; Symp Band; Nwsp Rptr; Im Badmtn; Im Bsktbl; Im Vllybl; Psychlgy.

BENZINGER, ANDREW X; Glen Cove HS; Glen Cove, NY; (Y); 30/270; Varsity Clb; Sr Cls; Bsbl; Ftbl; Art Clb; Socr; Hon Roll; NHS; Rgnts Schlrshp 86; Cmnty Schlrshp 86; Engrng.

BENZONI, LINDA; Herricks SR HS; Albertson, NY; (Y); 25/286; Hosp Aide; Dance Clb; Hosp Aide; Science Clb; Stage Crew; Nwsp Ed-Chief; Nwsp Rptr; Nwsp Stf; Soph Cls; Jr Cls; Cmnty Svc Awd 86; Schl Nwspr Awd 86; SUNY Binghampton; Litrtr.

BERAK, STEPHANIE; Colonie Central HS; Albany, NY; (Y); French Clb; Ski Clb; Varsity Clb; Sftbl; Tennis; Wrstlng; Hon Roll.

BERAUD, KELLY; New Dorp HS; Staten Isl, NY; (Y); Dance Clb; GAA; Girl Scts; Service Clb; Varsity Clb; Nwsp Stf; JV Var Vllybl; Law.

BERCOVICI, MARIUS; Brooklyn Technical HS; New York, NY; (Y); 819/1159; Boy Scts; Cmnty Wkr; Debate Tm; Office Aide; Cit Awd; Masonic Awd; VFW Awd; Eagle Sct Trp 109 86; Wrld Conservation Awd 84; Queens CollLAW.

BERG, JESSICA; Chatham HS; E Chatham, NY; (Y); 1/160; Ski Clb; Nwsp Stf; Yrbk Stf; JV Socr; High Hon Roll; NHS; Sci.

BERG, JONATHAN D; General Douglas Mac Arthur HS; Wantagh, NY; (Y); 27/320; Computer Clb; Debate Tm; Model UN; Science Clb; Var Crs Cntry; JV Socr; High Hon Roll; NHS; Opt Clb Awd; NYS Regnts Schlrshp 86; Carnegie Mellon U; Ecnmcs.

BERG, MICHAEL; Abraham Lincoln HS; Brooklyn, NY; (Y); Debate Tm; Nwsp Rptr; Rep Soph Cls; Rep Jr Cls; Var Bsktbl; Cit Awd; High Hon Roll; NHS; Pride Of Yankees Awd 85; Mock Trl Cert 85; Lincoln Douglas Debate Cert 85; Wrtng.

BERG, SUSAN; Canarsi HS; Brooklyn, NY; (Y); Chorus; Hon Roll; Arista Hnr Soc-Acadmc Hnr Pgm 84 & 86; Archon Hnr Soc-Svc Hnr Pgm 84; Govs Comm Citatn-Schltc Achvt 84.

BERGAMO, KAREN; Mynderse Acad; Seneca Falls, NY; (S); 27/141; Drama Clb; Model UN; SADD; Band; Chorus; Color Guard; Jazz Band; Mrchg Band; School Musical; Stage Crew; SUNY-OSWEGO; Engl.

BERGAMO, KATHERINE A; Pine Bush HS; Thompson Ridge, NY; (Y); 5/286; Church Yth Grp; GAA; Ski Clb; Yrbk Stf; Sec Stu Cncl; Var L Swmmng; High Hon Roll; NHS; VFW Awd; Voice Dem Awd; Regents Schlrshp 86; U NC-CHAPEL Hill; Pre-Med.

BERGAN, BETH; Henniger HS; Syracuse, NY; (Y); 30/400; Pres GAA; SADD; Band; Trs Stu Cncl; Var Capt Tennis; Trk; Var Capt Vllybl; High Hon Roll; Sec NHS; William Smith Coll.

BERGENFELD, SUSAN; Sheepshead Bay HS; Brooklyn, NY; (Y); Drama Clb; Office Aide; Teachers Aide; Orch; Variety Show; Yrbk Stf; Art,Acctng Awd 85-86.

BERGENTHAL, KENNETH A; The Bronx High School Of Science; Bronxville, NY; (Y); Boy Scts; Capt Chess Clb; Library Aide; Band; Concert Band; Jazz Band; Var Capt Tennis; Prfct Atten Awd; Mus Awd 82-86; Math & Frnch Hnr Roll 84-86; MIT.

BERGER, CHRIS; John F Kennedy HS; Mahopac, NY; (Y); 18/220; SADD; Variety Show; JV Capt Bsbl; Ftbl; Wt Lftg; Hon Roll; JC Awd; NHS; Voice Dem Awd; Script Awd 83-84; Cert Of Merit Spnsh 85-86; Springfield Clg; Htlt/Ftns.

BERGER, CHRISTOPHER; Valley Central HS; Walden, NY; (Y); 50/375; Debate Tm; French Clb; Natl Beta Clb; Political Wkr; Tennis; French Hon Soc; Hon Roll.

BERGER, DANIEL; South Side HS; Rockville Centre, NY; (Y); 55/300; Boys Clb Am; Boy Scts; FBLA; Trs Latin Clb; Trs Mathletes; Trs Science Clb; Ed Nwsp Phtg; Ed Yrbk Phtg; Hon Roll; Acctng.

BERGER, GITTIE; Sara Schenirer HS; Brooklyn, NY; (Y); Dance Clb; Spanish Clb; School Musical; Pres Stu Cncl; High Hon Roll; NY U; Law.

BERGER, GLENN; Smithtown West HS; Smithtown, NY; (Y); 1/412; DECA; Capt Quiz Bowl; Band; Mrchg Band; High Hon Roll; Jr NHS; Pres NHS; Spanish NHS; Mathletes; Off Frsh Cls; Japan/US Schlrshp 85-86.

BERGER, HOPE M; Branders Hebrew Day Schl; Oceanside, NY; (Y); Debate Tm; Teachers Aide; Temple Yth Grp; Yrbk Phtg; Yrbk Rptr; Lit Mag; Rep Frsh Cls; Rep Soph Cls; Trs Stu Cncl; NHS; NY St Regents Schlrshp 86; Branders U.

BERGER, JENNIFER; Sacred Heart Acad; Baldwin, NY; (S); Cmnty Wkr; Mrchg Band; Var Bsktbl; NHS.

BERGER, KATIE; Westlake HS; Pleasantvle, NY; (Y); SADD; High Hon Roll; Hon Roll; Spanish NHS; Bus.

BERGER, NEAL T; Spring Valley HS; S Spring Valley, NY; (Y); 80/441; Key Clb; JV Bsbl; Im Bowling; Im Sftbl; JV Tennis; Hon Roll; St Schlr; NYS Regents Schlrshp 86; Gftd Chld Soc; 95 Pct Iowa Stndrd Tsts; Hnr Rl; Key Club & Local Yth Grps; SUNY Albany; Bus Acctg.

BERGER, SCOTT A; Smithtown West HS; Smithtown, NY; (Y); VP CAP; Hosp Aide; Pres JCL; Library Aide; Red Cross Aide; Orch; VP Stu Cncl; Var Capt Powder Puff Ftbl; Sec NHS; Trs Pres Spanish NHS; Amer Legn Citzn Awd 82; NYS Regnts Schlrshp 86; Pres Acad Ftnss Awd 86; Johns Hopkins U; Neurosrgn.

BERGER, SUZANNE; Williamsville South HS; Williamsville, NY; (Y); VP Church Yth Grp; Cmnty Wkr; Sec Pep Clb; Ski Clb; Variety Show; Rep Frsh Cls; Rep Soph Cls; Rep Jr Cls; Rep Sr Cls; Rep Stu Cncl; Fllwshp Chrstn Ath 85; Red Crs Aide; SABAH; Fredonia ST Coll; Comm.

BERGER, THOMAS; Sweet Home SR HS; N Tonawanda, NY; (Y); CAP; Nwsp Ed-Chief; JV Socr; MVP JV Sccr 85-86; Pilot.

BERGIN, TIMMY; New Rochelle HS; New Rochelle, NY; (Y); Church Yth Grp; Var JV Bsbl; Bsktbl; Im Sftbl; Hon Roll; Jr NHS; Spanish NHS; Bus.

BERGIN, WILLIAM; St Marys Boys HS; Port Washington, NY; (S); 1/150; Church Yth Grp; Band; VP Sec Stu Cncl; Im Bsktbl; Im Ftbl; Var Capt Lcrss; Cit Awd; High Hon Roll; NHS; Ntl Merit SF; Amer Leg Amer Awd, Rotary Gen Excel Awd 85; Elec Engrng.

BERGMAN, MICHELLE; Byron-Bergen HS; Churchville, NY; (Y); AFS; Art Clb; Drama Clb; School Play; Lit Mag; Hon Roll; NY ST Art Tchrs Assoc Cert Merit 84; Schlstc Art Awd Cert Merit 84; Intr Dsgn.

BERGSTROM, CARL; Potsdam SR HS; Potsdam, NY; (Y); Yrbk Stf; God Cntry Awd; Vllybl; Hon Roll; Chem.

BERGSTROM, CHRIS; Rome Free Acad; Rome, NY; (Y); 42/440; Church Yth Grp; Band; Concert Band; Jazz Band; Mrchg Band; Orch; Hon Roll; Jr NHS; NHS; 100 Club Alg 9 83; Pres Acdmc Ftns Awd 86; Houghton Coll NY; Bio.

BERHALTER, DEBRA; North Babylon SR HS; No Babylon, NY; (Y); 146/451; DECA; Office Aide; Bronze Merit Awd Gen Merch 86; Farmingdale Coll; Bus Mgmt.

BERHRMANN, KRISTIN; Smithtown HS East; Smithtown, NY; (Y); French Clb; Hosp Aide; Office Aide; SADD; Mgr Sftbl; Sec French Hon Soc; High Hon Roll; NHS.

BERK, MELINDA R; Birch Wathen HS; New York, NY; (Y); Drama Clb; Pep Clb; Chorus; School Musical; School Play; Variety Show; Nwsp Rptr; Nwsp Stf; Lit Mag; JV Cheerleading; Drma.

BERK, MICHELLE; Williamsville South HS; Williamsville, NY; (Y); 10/214; Drama Clb; Office Aide; Pres Temple Yth Grp; School Play; Var L Fld Hcky; Var Sftbl; Tennis; High Hon Roll; NHS; DAR Awd; U Of Toronto; Finc.

BERKELEY, JOEL; West Babylon SR HS; W Babylon, NY; (Y); Art Clb; Church Yth Grp; Computer Clb; 4-H; Key Clb; Church Choir; 4-H Awd; Hon Roll; C W Post; Comp Prgmr.

BERKENFIELD, JAMES; Woodlands HS; Hartsdale, NY; (Y); Art Clb; Boy Scts; Key Clb; Lit Mag; Rep Soph Cls; Rep Jr Cls; Var Golf; Im Socr; High Hon Roll; NHS; Coaches Awd Golf 84-85; Most Improved Player Golf 85-86; Sci Awd Individual Resrch Proj 83-84; Med.

BERKLING, KAY M; Fayetteville-Manlius HS; Fayetteville, NY; (Y); 64/335; Dance Clb; Model UN; Im Fld Hcky; Im Vllybl; High Hon Roll; Hon Roll; NHS; Rgnts Schlrshp 86; Syracuse U; Sci.

BERKOVITS, BAILA; Sara Schenirer HS; Brooklyn, NY; (Y); Cmnty Wkr; Dance Clb; Debate Tm; Drama Clb; FHA; Teachers Aide; School Play; Variety Show; Yrbk Phtg; High Hon Roll; Regnts Schlrshp 86; Miriam Landsky Awd 82; Agudath Israel Comm Svc Awd 84.

BERKSON, MARK D; Hillcrest HS; Queens, NY; (Y); 15/801; Debate Tm; JA; Scholastic Bowl; Temple Yth Grp; Thesps; Jazz Band; Nwsp Ed-Chief; Golf; Capt Gym; NHS; Herman P Mantel Schlrshp JTA 86; Cornell U; Bio.

BERLAN, LISA; Half Hollow Hills H Schl West; Commack, NY; (Y); Art Clb; Camera Clb; SADD; Stage Crew; Nwsp Phtg; Yrbk Phtg; Yrbk Stf; Stu Cncl; Badmtn; Arts Rcngntn & Tlnt Srch Hnrble Mntn 86; Schl Of Visual Arts; Photo.

BERLINER, THERESA; Lindehurst HS; Lindenhurst, NY; (Y); Cmnty Wkr; Key Clb; Leo Clb; Spanish Clb; VP Temple Yth Grp; Y-Teens; Trs Chorus; Var Badmtn; Var Gym; Hon Roll; Audlgy.

BERMAN, ALLAN E; A G Berner HS; Massapequa Park, NY; (Y); #19 In Class; Computer Clb; Science Clb; Rep SADD; Acpl Chr; Mrchg Band; Symp Band; JV Bsktbl; NHS; Pres Schlr; St Schlr; Elec Engr.

BERMAN, JAIME; New Rochelle HS; New Rochelle, NY; (Y); 15/600; Pres Cmnty Wkr; SADD; Temple Yth Grp; Rep Sr Cls; Rep Stu Cncl; Var Socr; Lib Sftbl; High Hon Roll; Hon Roll; NHS; U Of PA; Bus.

BERMAN, LARRY; Sachem North HS; Farmingville, NY; (Y); 602/1558; Boy Scts; Chorus; Socr; Wrstlng; Sagamore Wrstlng Trnmnt 2nd Pl 83; Smmr Enrchmnt Arch Pgm 85; SUNY Geneseo; Comp Pgmmg.

BERMAN, MONICA; Eastchester HS; Eastchester, NY; (Y); Drama Clb; Key Clb; Ski Clb; Concert Band; Mrchg Band; School Play; Yrbk Stf; Var Co-Capt Bsktbl; Trk; Hon Roll; MVP Sprng Trk 86.

BERMAN, SHARON; Commack H S North; East Northport, NY; (Y); 31/390; French Clb; Teachers Aide; Temple Yth Grp; Stat Badmtn; Mgr(s); French Hon Soc; High Hon Roll; NHS; Rensselaer Polytechnc Inst; Bus.

BERMAN, STEVEN L; George W Hewlett HS; Hewlett, NY; (Y); 9/260; Computer Clb; Mathletes; Math Tm; Science Clb; NHS; Ntl Merit SF; Math.

BERNABEL, VICTOR; James Monroe HS; Bronx, NY; (Y); Biology.

BERNADEL, LEVY; Lovis D Brandeis HS; New York, NY; (Y); 14/544; Church Yth Grp; Church Choir; Socr; Hon Roll; Prfct Atten Awd; Fnlst Essy Cnsts 86; Natl Hispnc Schlr Awds Prg 86; Stony Brook.

BERNAGOZZI, ELLEN; Mercy HS; Watermill, NY; (Y); 22/125; Mathletes; SADD; Yrbk Phtg; Yrbk Stf; High Hon Roll; Hon Roll; NHS; Natl Engl Merit Awd; Psychol.

BERNAGOZZI, JOE; Charles O Dickerson HS; Trumansburg, NY; (Y); Letterman Clb; Varsity Clb; Swing Chorus; Var Bsbl; Var Ftbl; Var Wt Lftg; Var Wrstlng; Hon Roll; Masonic Awd; Art Clb; SUNY Bfl.

BERNAL, SARA ELAINE; Alternative Community Schl; Ithaca, NY; (Y); Drama Clb; School Musical; School Play; Ntl Merit Ltr; Mem Reg Ballet Co 84-86; Choregraphed Pieces For Ballet 85-86; U Of Chicago Schlrshp 86; U Of Chicago.

BERNALES, CLARK G; Christian Brothers Acad; Fayetteville, NY; (Y); 25/96; Church Yth Grp; FCA; Hosp Aide; SADD; Chorus; Rep Jr Cls; Rep Sr Cls; Var L Ftbl; Var L Lcrss; High Hon Roll; Brother Adolpus Hnr Soc 80-86; Regnts Schlrshp 85-86; Acadmc All Am Schlr 86; Hofstra U; Hlth Admn.

BERNARD, ANDREW; Sheepshead Bay HS; Brooklyn, NY; (Y); 20/439; Computer Clb; Math Tm; Office Aide; Trk; Prfct Atten Awd; Trck Wll Of Fame 84; Columbia U; Elec Engnrng.

BERNARD, STACI B; Smithtown HS West; Smithtown, NY; (Y); Hon Roll; NHS; Ntl Merit SF; Spanish NHS; Phlsphy.

BERNATZ, FRITZ A; Charlotte JR SR HS; Rochester, NY; (Y); 2/78; Model UN; Yrbk Bus Mgr; Trs Jr Cls; Bausch & Lomb Sci Awd; NHS; Ntl Merit SF; Sal; High Hon Roll; U Of Rochester PLUS Awd Schlrshp 85; Brenda Fraser Mem Schlrshp 85; Hague-Netherlands-Model UN 85; Case Wstrn Reserve U; Chem Engr.

BERNBACH, JASON; New Rochelle HS; Scarsdale, NY; (Y); Nwsp Rptr; Lit Mag; Pres Sr Cls; Var Capt Trk; High Hon Roll; NHS; Spanish NHS; Wnnr Young Wirters Cntst 86; Vet-Med.

BERND, BARBARA; Corning-P P West HS; Corning, NY; (Y); Church Yth Grp; Key Clb; Letterman Clb; Varsity Clb; Church Choir; Crs Cntry; Trk; High Hon Roll; Hon Roll; NHS; Cross-Cntry Qualfd For States 85; Trck Athlete Of Mnth 86.

BERNHARD, AMANADA P; Gates Chili HS; Rochester, NY; (Y); 16/446; German Clb; Ski Clb; Teachers Aide; School Musical; School Play; Var L Crs Cntry; Var L FHA; Var L Trk; High Hon Roll; NHS; Regents Schlrshp NY ST 86; Union Coll; Engl.

BERNHARDT, ROBERT E; Aviation HS; Brooklyn, NY; (S); 26/416; Church Yth Grp; JA; NHS; Acadmc All Am 86; Regents Schlrshp 86; Baruch; Bus.

BERNIER, MARC; Northport HS; E Northport, NY; (Y); 27/570; Nwsp Rptr; Yrbk Rptr; JV Capt Bsktbl; Capt Socr; Jr NHS; Hon Roll; High Hon Roll; Exec Edtr Schl Nwsppr 86-87; Amer Legn Awd 83-84; Capt 9th Grd Sccr Tm 83-84; Wake Forest; Engrng.

BERNS, JON; Mamaroneck HS; Mamaroneck, NY; (Y); JA; Mathletes; Math Tm; Spanish Clb; Yrbk Phtg; Yrbk Stf; JV Socr; Ntl Merit Ltr; Wolfe Mem Amer Lit Awd 86; Outstndng Soc Studs Awd 85; All ST Mth Tm 86; Cornell U; Bio.

BERNSTEIN, CELINE; Harborfields HS; Greenlawn, NY; (Y); French Clb; Trs Spanish Clb; Stage Crew; Nwsp Phtg; Nwsp Rptr; Nwsp Stf; Elmira Coll Key Awd 86; Comp Sci.

BERNSTEIN, DANIEL; Bellport HS; Bellport, NY; (Y); Chess Clb; Computer Clb; Latin Clb; Math Tm; French Hon Soc; High Hon Roll; NHS; French Clb; Chorus; Nwsp Stf; No 1 Suffolk Cnty Math Leag 85-86; Top Stdnt Precalcls Ctr Adv Acdmclly Tlntd Yth 84; Math.

BERNSTEIN, MICHAEL; Fayetteville Manlius HS; Manlius, NY; (Y); School Musical; Stu Cncl; Im Bsktbl; Var Tennis; French Hon Soc; Hon Roll.

BERNSTEIN, MICHAEL E; Bellport HS; Bellport, NY; (Y); 1/325; Civic Clb; Computer Clb; French Clb; Pres Latin Clb; Capt Math Tm; VP Temple Yth Grp; Ed Nwsp Stf; French Hon Soc; NHS; Ntl Merit SF.

BERNSTEIN, VERONICA; Onteora Central HS; West Shokan, NY; (Y); SADD; ST Fnlst Miss Tn NY 84-86; ST Fnlst Miss Co-Ed NY 83-85; Fd The Hngry Orgnzr 83-84; Jrnlsm.

BERROA, JANICE; Seward Park HS; New York, NY; (Y); 77/544; Rep Stu Cncl; John Jay; Lawyer.

BERRY, KRISTIN; Senior HS; Conklin, NY; (Y); SADD; Nwsp Stf; Yrbk Stf; Rep Jr Cls; Rep Stu Cncl; Mgr Trk; Mgr Vllybl; High Hon Roll; Sierra; Accntng.

BERSIN, SCOTT A; Oceanside HS; Oceanside, NY; (Y); 100/530; Mathletes; Varsity Clb; Variety Show; Nwsp Stf; Var Bsbl; Var Bsktbl; Var L Ftbl; Socr; Hon Roll; Regnts Schlrshp 86; All Leag Ftbl 86; Bsbl 86; Washington U St Louis; Bus.

BERTHIAUME, DAWNE; Olean HS; Olean, NY; (Y); Drama Clb; Teachers Aide; Chorus; School Musical; Stage Crew; Yrbk Stf; Cheerleading; Vllybl; High Hon Roll; Hon Roll; Psychlgy.

BERTHOLD, ANITA M; Maryvale SR HS; Cheektowaga, NY; (Y); 33/305; German Clb; SADD; Band; Color Guard; Mrchg Band; Symp Band; Variety Show; Yrbk Phtg; Yrbk Stf; Cheerleading; NY U; Film/TV.

BERTOLDO, JON; Monsignor Farrell HS; Staten Island, NY; (Y); 84/319; Camera Clb; Trs Exploring; Hosp Aide; Im Bowling; Hon Roll; NY ST Rgnts Schlrshp Wnr 86; Empire St Games Bronze Mdl Wnr 85; Northeastern Sts Chmpnshp Mdl Wnr 86; Animal Sci.

BERTOLETTI, ROBERT A; St Francis Prep; Douglaston, NY; (S); 106/744; Cmnty Wkr; Hosp Aide; School Musical; Nwsp Rptr; Lit Mag; French Hon Soc; High Hon Roll; Ntl Merit SF; Merit Schlrshp Portledge Schl 83; Creatv Wrtg Awd 84; Hstry Awd 84; Wrtr.

BERTOLINO, ANDREA; Canasoto HS; Canastoto, NY; (S); 1/150; Drama Clb; Science Clb; SADD; Band; Chorus; School Musical; Yrbk Stf; Cheerleading; VP NHS; Miss Madison Cnty Teen Ager 85; Pre Med.

BERTOLINO, ELENA; Blind Brook HS; Rye Brook, NY; (Y); French Clb; Hosp Aide; Library Aide; Math Tm; Model UN; VP SADD; Acpl Chr; Chorus; School Musical; School Play; Regents College Schlrshp Wnnr 86; Georgetown U; Med.

BERTRAM, AARON; Jamesville-D HS; Jamesville, NY; (Y); Var L Bsktbl; Im Ftbl; Hon Roll; Opt Clb Awd; Bio.

BERTRAM, DAWN M; East HS; Rochester, NY; (Y); 31/242; Dance Clb; Pep Clb; Quiz Bowl; Scholastic Bowl; Varsity Clb; Var Cheerleading; Var Gym; Var Score Keeper; Var Sftbl; PRISM Stu Yr 82-83; Plus Schlrshp Awd 85; Upward Bound Hnr Rl Awd 82-83; U Buffalo; Bio.

BERTRAND, JEAN FRANCOIS; Pleasantville HS; Pleasantville, NY; (Y); AFS; Boy Scts; Church Yth Grp; French Clb; Model UN; PAVAS; Science Clb; School Musical; Capt Var Socr; High Hon Roll.

BERTUCCI, THOMAS J; Dunkirk SR HS; Dunkirk, NY; (Y); Math Tm; Nwsp Rptr; Var L Crs Cntry; Var L Trk; Kiwanis Awd; NHS; St Schlr; Letterman Clb; Rep Frsh Cls; Rep Soph Cls; NY Rgnts Schlrshp 86; Deans Lst SUNY Coll Fredonia 86; Merit Schlrshp Advncd Comps 85; Edinboro U; Math.

BERTUCCIO, MICHAEL J; St Anthonys HS; Tanglewood Hills, NY; (Y); Latin Clb; Varsity Clb; Orch; Symp Band; Yrbk Phtg; Var Ftbl; Var Lcrss; Trk; Pres French Hon Soc; VP NHS; Hmcmng King 85-86; Ftbl All Lg, All Cath Long Isl 85-86; Top 1 Pct IA Standardized Test 82; Harvard U; Eng.

BERTUNA, ISABEL; F D Roosevelt HS; Brooklyn, NY; (Y); Library Aide; Office Aide; Science Clb; Service Clb; Teachers Aide; Chorus; Nwsp Ed-Chief; Nwsp Stf; High Hon Roll; Prfct Atten Awd; Arista 84; NYS Sci Fairs 84-86; Borgh & Ctywide Fairs-1st Pl & Fnlst 84-86; NYU; Sci.

BESCHLER, ANGELA GRACE; Horseheads HS; Horseheads, NY; (Y); Church Yth Grp; German Clb; Hosp Aide; Model UN; Chorus; Church Choir; Orch; Hon Roll; Masonic Awd; Cedarville Coll; Elem Educ.

BESEMER, ELIESE; Union-Endicott HS; Endicott, NY; (Y); Church Yth Grp; Drama Clb; French Clb; Pres Band; Chorus; Church Choir; Concert Band; Drm Mjr(t); Jazz Band; Mrchg Band.

BESHAW, LYNN; De Sales HS; Lockport, NY; (Y); Nwsp Ed-Chief; JV Var Bsktbl; Im Coach Actv; Var Capt Socr; Var Tennis; Hon Roll; NHS; Nazareth Coll; Engl.

BESPECHNY, ALEXANDER; Midwood HS; Brooklyn, NY; (Y); Math Tm; Hon Roll; Math.

BESS, JAMEY; Jamestown HS; Jamestown, NY; (Y); Boys Clb Am; Church Yth Grp; School Play; Nwsp Stf; Ftbl; Engr.

BESSE, KIMBERLY; Queensbury HS; Glens Falls, NY; (Y); 28/250; Ski Clb; Varsity Clb; JV Crs Cntry; Stat Socr; Var Trk; High Hon Roll; Hon Roll; NHS; NYS Regents Schlrshp 86; U VT Grant 86; Margaret Bunn Schlrshp 86; U VT; Med Tech.

BESSER, SHERI L; Batavia SR HS; Batavia, NY; (Y); 4/215; Am Leg Aux Girls St; VP JA; SADD; Band; Concert Band; Mrchg Band; Yrbk Ed-Chief; Yrbk Stf; Sec Trs Soph Cls; Trs Stu Cncl; Chatham Coll Pittsbrgh; Ecnmcs.

BESSETTE, JORJA; Knox Memorial Central Schl; Canton, NY; (S); 3/30; Varsity Clb; Concert Band; Mrchg Band; School Play; Yrbk Stf; Score Keeper; Socr; High Hon Roll; Trs Sec NHS; NYS Rgnts Schlrshp 86; Ithaca Coll NY; Phys Ther.

BESSETTE, SHANNON; Franklin Academy HS; Malone, NY; (Y); AFS; French Clb; Nwsp Rptr; Yrbk Rptr; Yrbk Stf; Stat Ice Hcky; Hon Roll; NHS; Acad All Amer 84 & 85; Vet Med.

BESSEY, JENNIFER; Schroon Lake Central HS; North Hudson, NY; (S); 2/28; SADD; Sec Varsity Clb; School Play; Variety Show; Pres Soph Cls; VP Pres Stu Cncl; Var Capt Cheerleading; Score Keeper; Var Sftbl; High Hon Roll; Writer Mnth Awd 85; Bohrman Hstry Scholar 85.

BESSINGER, ALICE M; John S Burke Catholic HS; Chester, NY; (Y); Pres Camera Clb; Church Yth Grp; JV Bsktbl; Var Co-Capt Socr; Var Sftbl; Hon Roll; NHS; NEDT Awd; Rgnts Schlrshp 86-90; Genl Excllnc 4.0 Avg 83-85; U Of Buffalo; Med Tech.

BEST, CHRISTOPHER; West Hill HS; Syracuse, NY; (Y); Trs Art Clb; Boy Scts; Dance Clb; Drama Clb; Exploring; Library Aide; Science Clb; SADD; High Hon Roll; Hon Roll; Joe Kirby Schl; Graphic Arts.

BEST, KIMBERLEY A; Catholic Central HS; Troy, NY; (Y); Math Clb; Spanish Clb; SADD; Yrbk Stf; Jr Cls; Sr Cls; JV Bsktbl; JV Socr; Trk; High Hon Roll; Schl Engl Awd; Schl Soc Stud Awd; Crmnl Lawyr.

BEST, RHONDA C; Bronx HS Of Sci; Queens, NY; (Y); Drama Clb; Key Clb; Teachers Aide; School Musical; Stage Crew; Yrbk Phtg; NHS; Bio Congrss Awd 84; Boston U; Bio Med Engrng.

BESTINE, JEANNINE; Kenmore East HS; Kenmore, NY; (Y); Cmnty Wkr; Lit Mag; Hon Roll; U Of Bflo; Ansthtst.

BETANCOURT, ALEX; Msgr Mclancy HS; Jackson Hgts, NY; (Y); 24/219; FBLA; Pres Frsh Cls; Socr; Trk; NHS; Ntl Hnr Soc; St Johns U Schlrshp 86-87; St Johns U; Bus.

BETANCOURT, GLORIA E; Uniondale HS; Uniondale, NY; (Y); 5/410; Nwsp Stf; High Hon Roll; Achvmdnt Awd I Frgn Lang 85; English Nrnlsm 86; Hspnc Assn Best Hispanic Stu 86; Hofstra U; Comp Sci.

BETHA, LAURY A; City Honors Schl; Buffalo, NY; (Y); 19/104; French Clb; JA; Latin Clb; Spanish Clb; Chorus; Bsktbl; Trk; Wellesly Bk Awd 84-85; Dvlpmntl Psych.

BETHGE, ROBERT; North Shore HS; Glen Head, NY; (Y); 22/220; Debate Tm; Thesps; Chorus; Stage Crew; NHS; Ntl Merit SF; School Musical; School Play; Hon Roll; Pres Awd For Acad Ftns 86; Fclty Hnr Awd 82; Carnegie-Mellon U; Bus Admin.

BETRUS, MARC; Rome Catholic HS; Rome, NY; (Y); Cmnty Wkr; Rep Jr Cls; Rep Stu Cncl; Hon Roll; Math Hon.

BETTS, KATHRYN M; Auburn HS; Auburn, NY; (Y); German Clb; Ski Clb; High Hon Roll; Jr NHS; NHS; Grmn III Achvmnt Awd 86.

BETZ, CAROLYN; Buffalo Traditional Schl; Amherst, NY; (S); 13/111; Church Yth Grp; Girl Scts; Math Tm; Teachers Aide; Chorus; Hon Roll; Jr NHS; NHS; Prfct Atten Awd; Ntl Tech Inst For Deaf.

BEURKET, MEGAN; Seton Catholic Central HS; Binghamton, NY; (Y); 76/175; Church Yth Grp; GAA; Key Clb; SADD; Varsity Clb; Band; Pep Band; School Musical; Nwsp Stf; Yrbk Stf; All Div Tennis All-Star 83; All STAC Tennis All Star 84-85; Canisius Coll; Fshn Merch.

BEUTEL, LINDA; Niagara Wheatfield HS; Sanborn, NY; (Y); 36/292; Trs Church Yth Grp; Chorus; JV Cheerleading; Hon Roll; Profssnl Secretaries Intl Schlrshp 86; Typing Awd 85 & 86; Shorthand Awd 86; Bryant & Stratton; Exec Sec.

BEVERLY, KERRY; Oakfield-Alabama Central HS; Oakfield, NY; (Y); Trs French Clb; Band; Pres Chorus; Swing Chorus; Pres Jr Cls; Capt L Bsktbl; L Var Socr; Var L Sftbl; Var L Vllybl; NHS; Psychlgy.

BEVILACQUA, JOHN; West Genesee HS; Syracuse, NY; (Y); Cmnty Wkr; SADD; Variety Show; Hon Roll; Syracuse U; Law.

BEVILACQUA, LOUIS; St Peters Boys HS; Staten Island, NY; (Y); 44/163; Wrstlng; Hon Roll; Law.

BEVILACQUA, STEVEN; Saint Francis HS; N Collins, NY; (Y); Ski Clb; Band; Concert Band; Mrchg Band; School Play; VP Frsh Cls; VP Soph Cls; Bsktbl; Socr; NHS; Air Force ROTC Schlrshp 86; Clarkson U; Math.

BEVIVINO, CHRISTINE; Vernon-Verona-Sherrill HS; Vernon, NY; (Y); Church Yth Grp; GAA; Math Tm; Im Swmmng; Var Tennis; Hon Roll; Oneida Lake Sailing Clb Stu 80; Intl Laser Clss Asso Stu 85-86; Physcl Ther.

BEYEA, RENEE; Honeoye Central HS; Honeoye, NY; (S); #8 In Class; French Clb; Band; Concert Band; Jazz Band; Mrchg Band; Pep Band; Rep Stu Cncl; Pom Pon; Socr; Church Yth Grp; Presdntl Awd 81-85; Intnatl Bus.

BEYEA, TAMERA; Wilson Central HS; Ransomville, NY; (Y); Church Yth Grp; VP FBLA; Hosp Aide; SADD; Teachers Aide; Rep Sec Stu Cncl; Trk; High Hon Roll; Computer Clb; Library Aide; Prvt Piano Lssns; 2nd Pl Lcl Assmbly God Teen Tlnt Comptn 85; Med.

BEYER, BETH M; Northport HS; Northport, NY; (Y); 33/585; Sec Camp Fr Inc; Band; Concert Band; Lit Mag; VP Frsh Cls; VP Stu Cncl; Cit Awd; DAR Awd; Hon Roll; Ntl Merit Schol; Sis O Hara Wrtng Awd 83; Art Educ.

BEYER, JEFFREY W; Hamburg SR HS; Hamburg, NY; (Y); 8/384; AFS; Church Yth Grp; Concert Band; Jazz Band; Rep Soph Cls; Rep Jr Cls; Trs Stu Cncl; Var L Bsbl; Hon Roll; NHS; Pre Med.

BEYER, LINDA; Mexico HS; Mexico, NY; (Y); Church Yth Grp; Spanish Clb; Varsity Clb; Rep Stu Cncl; Var L Bsktbl; Var L Socr; Hon Roll; Co-MVP Bsktbl 85.

BEZON, AMANDA; Byron-Bergen Central HS; Byron, NY; (Y); Pres 4-H; French Clb; Yrbk Sprt Ed; Sec Frsh Cls; Sec Soph Cls; Sec Jr Cls; Pres Sr Cls; Capt Cheerleading; Bausch & Lomb Sci Awd; Cit Awd; Bus Adm.

BHAGWAN, SHARON; Stuyvesant HS; New York, NY; (Y); Church Yth Grp; Cmnty Wkr; Debate Tm; Intnl Clb; Library Aide; NFL; Science Clb; Hon Roll; Ntl Merit SF; Sr Jr Sci Acad Achvt Cert 85; Natl Hspnc Schlrshp Fnlst 86; Dbte Trphys 85; Bio.

BHALLA, ANJU; Fairport HS; Fairport, NY; (Y); 11/600; Aud/Vis; French Clb; FBLA; Library Aide; Math Tm; Model UN; Science Clb; Chorus; Yrbk Stf; Lit Mag; 3rd Pl Bus Law Cnty Comptn 85; Best Frnch Stu 85; Natl Soc Of Pro Engrs Schlrshp 86; Soc Of Prof Engrs; GMI; Elec Engrng.

BHANDARI, MEENA; East Syracuse-Minoa HS; Manlius, NY; (Y); 3/333; Cmnty Wkr; Hosp Aide; Pres Latin Clb; Sec Spanish Clb; Variety Show; Yrbk Stf; VP Jr Cls; Pres Stu Cncl; Var JV Socr; Pres NHS; Hugh O Brian Ldrshp Awd 84; Wellesley Bk Awd 85; Syracuse U Schlrshp 85; Harvard; Med.

BHANDARKAR, TEJAS; Monroe-Woodbury SR HS; Harriman, NY; (Y); Aud/Vis; Hon Roll; Comp Engrng.

BHATNAGER, ASHU; Pleasantville HS; Pleasantville, NY; (Y); 36/101; Red Cross Aide; Science Clb; Var Socr; High Hon Roll; Hon Roll; Donald Hermanson Mem Schlrshp 86; SUNY At Stony Brook; Engrn.

BHAUMIK, KAUSHIK; H Frank Carey HS; Franklin Sq, NY; (Y); 10/228; Boy Scts; Pres Mathletes; VP Science Clb; Varsity Clb; Crs Cntry; Bausch & Lomb Sci Awd; Elks Awd; High Hon Roll; Hon Roll; Jr NHS; Hghst Hon Long Island Sci Cngrss 84-85; High Hon NYS Sci Cngrss 84-85; U Of VA; Elec Engrng.

BIAMONTE, JOHN; John F Kennedy HS; Utica, NY; (Y); JV Bsktbl; Mohawk Vly CC; Bus Mgr.

BIANCHET, CHRISTIAN; Smithtown HS East; St James, NY; (Y); Church Yth Grp; Radio Clb; Band; Chorus; Church Choir; Variety Show; JV Tennis; Hon Roll; Jr NHS; Italian Hon Soc 84-86; Bus.

BIANCHI, CHARLES; Bishop Grimes HS; Syracuse, NY; (Y); Art Clb; Debate Tm; JA; Model UN; Ski Clb; Spanish Clb; SADD; Chorus; Yrbk Stf; Rep Frsh Cls; Boston Coll; Art.

BIANCHI, TONY; Maryvale HS; Depew, NY; (Y); Varsity Clb; Var L Ftbl; Var L Trk; Canisius Coll.

BIANCO, GRACE ANN; Nazareth Regional HS; Brooklyn, NY; (S); 11/267; Speech Tm; SADD; Ed Yrbk Ed-Chief; Pres Frsh Cls; Rep Sr Cls; Rep Rep Stu Cncl; NHS; Acad Achvt Schlrshp 83; Hugh O Brian Yth Fndtn Ambssdr 84; Sftbl Coaches Awd 84.

BIANCO, JIM; Bay Port-Blue Point HS; Blue Pt, NY; (Y); 53/259; JV Bsktbl; Var Ftbl; Var Trk; Merit Roll 85 Avg Or Bttr 84-87; Chiroprctc.

BIANCO, JUDI A; T R Proctor HS; Utica, NY; (Y); 78/201; Drama Clb; Pep Clb; Hon Roll; Elizabeth F Bacon Awd 86; Herkimer; Para-Legal.

BIANCO, KENNETH; Williamsville East HS; Williamsvl, NY; (Y); Boy Scts; Sec Chorus; Church Choir; School Musical; Trk; High Hon Roll; NHS; Eagle Sct 85; Rifle Tm Co-Capt 84-87; NY ST All-ST Chrl 85; Bio.

BIANCO, RAYMOND; Marlboro HS; Newburgh, NY; (Y); SADD; JV Wrstlng; High Hon Roll; Hon Roll; NHS; St Schlr; Full Tuition Merit Schlshp UCC 86; Marist Coll; Engrg.

BIANCO, RICHARD; Wheatley HS; E Williston, NY; (Y); SADD; Chorus; Yrbk Bus Mgr; Stu Cncl; JV Bsbl; Tennis; Bus.

BIANCO, STACIE; Corning Painted Past East HS; Corning, NY; (Y); 18/212; Cmnty Wkr; Letterman Clb; Varsity Clb; Yrbk Stf; Rep Soph Cls; Rep Jr Cls; Rep Sr Cls; Cheerleading; High Hon Roll; Hon Roll; Rgnts Schlrshp; U Rchstr; Bio Chmstry.

BIANCULLI, IRENE; Academy Of St Joseph HS; N Babylon, NY; (Y); Art Clb; Dance Clb; Drama Clb; Pep Clb; Variety Show; Dance.

BIASE, ANGELO; Sachem HS North; Lake Ronkonkoma, NY; (Y); 233/1600; Science Clb; Ski Clb; Spanish Clb; Rep Jr Cls; Health Rehtd.

BIAZON, EDGAR; Archbishop Malloy HS; Rosedale, NY; (Y); 15/383; Art Clb; French Clb; Stage Crew; Yrbk Stf; Im Bsktbl; Im Ftbl; Im Sftbl; NHS; NYU; Doc.

BIBAWY, GEORGE A; Haverling Central Schl; Bath, NY; (S); 1/140; Church Yth Grp; French Clb; JCL; Latin Clb; Math Clb; Ski Clb; JV Var Socr; Tennis; High Hon Roll; NHS; Math.

BIBI, KHAN; Far Rockaway HS; Far Rockaway, NY; (Y); Hon Roll; St Johns U; Bus Mgmnt.

BIBIK, BENJAMIN; Fabius-Pompey HS; Fabius, NY; (Y); Computer Clb; VP Exploring; Nwsp Phtg; Nwsp Rptr; Nwsp Stf; Yrbk Bus Mgr; Ed Yrbk Phtg; Yrbk Stf; JV Trk; 2nd Pl Engl Lit Awd 86; SUNY Morrisville; Bus Mgmt.

BICE, TOWANNA; St Catharine Acad; Bronx, NY; (Y); 104/198; Teachers Aide; School Musical; School Play; Hon Roll; Pace U; Broadcasting.

BICHOTTE, MARCELLE; Murry Bengtraum HS; Brooklyn, NY; (Y); Orch; Trk; Bio.

BICKNELL, MELISSA A; Herkimer Central HS; Herkimer, NY; (Y); 19/122; Cmnty Wkr; Hosp Aide; Pep Clb; Capt Color Guard; Yrbk Stf; Var Cheerleading; JV Fld Hcky; Var Gym; Utica Coll; Med Tech.

BICKOM, KURT F; Bishop Grimes HS; N Syracuse, NY; (Y); Art Clb; Ski Clb; Varsity Clb; Rep Frsh Cls; Rep Stu Cncl; Var Ftbl; JV Socr; Hon Mntn Var Ftbl 85; Grphc Dsgn.

BIDAK, DEAN; Lewiston-Porter SR HS; Youngstown, NY; (Y); 39/236; JA; High Hon Roll; Hon Roll; Prfct Atten Awd; Rgnts Schlrshp, Niagara Co Bldrs Assn Women Aux Schlrshp 86; Action Lrngn Intrnshp Pgm 86; SUNY Buffalo; Engrng.

BIDDEMAN, LYNN; Depew HS; Depew, NY; (Y); GAA; Office Aide; Var Socr; Buffal ST Coll; Bus.

BIDDLE, MARY KAY; West Seneca West SR HS; Buffalo, NY; (Y); 41/559; High Hon Roll; Hon Roll; NHS; Prfct Atten Awd; Erie Cmmnty South; Bus.

BIDDLE, RANDY; Saranac Lake Central HS; Saranac Lk, NY; (Y); AFS; Ski Clb; Var Crs Cntry; Var Trk; Rochester Inst Of Tech; Tech.

BIEBER, MICHELE; Mount Mercy Acad; Buffalo, NY; (Y); Boy Scts; Church Yth Grp; FNA; Hon Roll; Eric CC; Nrsng.

BIELEMEIER, ERICA MARIE; Cornwall Central HS; Cornwall, NY; (Y); Concert Band; Yrbk Stf; Rep Stu Cncl; JV Sftbl; Hon Roll; Ntl Merit Ltr; Awd Excllnt NYSSMA 85; Pre-Law.

BIELSKI, HALINA; Sacred Heart HS; Yonkers, NY; (Y); 74/221; Chorus; School Musical; School Play; Med Bus.

BIEN-AIME, GILBERT; Xavier HS; Brooklyn, NY; (Y); Chess Clb; Church Yth Grp; Computer Clb; Dance Clb; Math Clb; Ftbl; Regnts Clg Schlrshp 85; Elec Engrng.

BIER, ELIZABETH M; Bishop Ludden HS; Syracuse, NY; (S); Hosp Aide; JA; High Hon Roll; Hon Roll; NHS; Voice Dem Awd; Biol Merit Mdl 84; Hlth Merit Mdl 85; Vlnteer Cert Apprec 84-85; Le Moyne; RN.

BIERER, MATTHEW K; Sodus Central HS; Williamson, NY; (Y); 11/130; AFS; Boy Scts; 4-H; Model UN; Radio Clb; Science Clb; Spanish Clb; Stu Cncl; God Cntry Awd; NHS; SUNY Oswego; Sec Physcs Educ.

BIERFELDT, PETER; West Seneca West SR HS; Lackawanna, NY; (Y); 30/480; Debate Tm; Ftbl; Trk; High Hon Roll; Hon Roll; Jr NHS; NHS; NY St Rgnts Schlrp 86; Hist.

BIERLING, CHRISTINA; Valley Central HS; Newburgh, NY; (Y); 3/350; Debate Tm; Band; Concert Band; Mrchg Band; School Play; Variety Show; Lit Mag; Sec Frsh Cls; French Hon Soc; NHS; Musc Assoc Medls 84-86; Sec Of Beta Tau Debtg Tm 86; Pre Med.

BIERLY, SANDRA K; Niagra Wheatfield HS; Niagara Falls, NY; (Y); French Clb; Service Clb; Acad Achvt Awd 84-86; Niagara CC; Psych.

BIERNBAUM, MARK; Pittsford Mendon HS; Pittsford, NY; (Y); Debate Tm; VP Drama Clb; French Clb; Pres Model UN; Chorus; School Musical; School Play; Swing Chorus; Yrbk Stf; Ed Lit Mag; Best Delg Nazareth Model Un 85; Alex Malinich Mem Awd; Cornell U.

BIERSTINE, EVE J; John S Burke Catholic HS; Pine Island, NY; (Y); 14/152; Sec Cmnty Wkr; Drama Clb; School Musical; School Play; High Hon Roll; Hon Roll; NHS; NEDT Awd; NYS Regents Scshlrshp 86; Syracuse U Schlrshp 86; Bryant Coll; Mktg.

BIERSTINE, RONALD R; John S Burke Catholic HS; Pine Island, NY; (Y); Trk; High Hon Roll; NHS; NEDT Awd; NY ST Rgnts Schlrshp 86-89; SUNY Geneseo; Envrnmntl Bio.

BIESENBACH, KAREN G; Midlakes HS; Phelps, NY; (Y); 9/167; Pres AFS; Church Yth Grp; German Clb; Model UN; Sec Thesps; Band; School Musical; School Play; Var L Fld Hcky; VP NHS; Lutheran Schlr Awd; Rochester Area Schlr; Wittenberg U.

BIFARELLA, KIM; Our Lady Of Mercy HS; Ontario, NY; (Y); Cmnty Wkr; Hosp Aide; Service Clb; Teachers Aide; Rep Soph Cls; Hon Roll; Nazareth; Med.

BIFULCO, MARYANNE F; The Mary Louis Acad; S Ozone Park, NY; (Y); 7/270; Cmnty Wkr; Math Tm; Office Aide; Hon Roll; Jr NHS; NHS; NEDT Awd; Rgnts Schlrshp 86; Trstee Schlrshp Pace U 86; Coll Of New Rochelle Alumnaeli Assn Bk Awd 85; Pace U; Publc Acctg.

BIGAREL, KRISTY L; Gouverneur JR & SR HS; Hailesboro, NY; (Y); Sec Drama Clb; Speech Tm; Varsity Clb; Pres Acpl Chr; School Musical; Rep Stu Cncl; JV Capt Cheerleading; Var Trk; High Hon Roll; Hon Roll; NY St Rgnts Schlrshp 86; Grad With Hnrs Group 86; Canton ATC; Mech Engr.

BIGELOW, CANDICE; Whitney Point HS; Lisle, NY; (Y); 22/121; Church Yth Grp; Chorus; School Musical; Yrbk Stf; Sec Stu Cncl; Var L Bsktbl; Var L Fld Hcky; Var L Sftbl; High Hon Roll; Hon Roll; Clute Mem Schlrshp 86; SUNY Binghamton; Psych.

BIGELOW, HEATHER; Hoosick Falls Central HS; No Hoosick, NY; (Y); French Clb; Band; Trs Frsh Cls; Trs Jr Cls; Var L Bsktbl; Var L Fld Hcky; Capt Var Trk; High Hon Roll; NHS; Ntl Merit SF; NYSPHSAA Champ Clss C Tm Bsktbll 86; MVP St Marys Bsktbll Tournmnt 86; Most Imprvd Stu Trck 84; Med Engrng.

BIGELOW, SHERRI; Amsterdam HS; Amesterdam, NY; (Y); 35/320; Band; Mrchg Band; Englsh.

BIGGIE, CATHERINE; Cardinal O Hara HS; Kenmore, NY; (S); 3/150; Church Yth Grp; French Clb; Rep Frsh Cls; Trs Soph Cls; Sec Jr Cls; Var Bsktbl; JV Bowling; Var Sftbl; Var Vllybl; High Hon Roll; Mst Imprvd Plyr Vlybl 84; All Cathlc Sftbl Tm 84-85.

BIGGINS, ROXANNE; Le Roy Central HS; Le Roy, NY; (Y); Sftbl; Vllybl; High Hon Roll; Hon Roll.

BIGHAM, CHRISTOPHER H; Attica HS; Attica, NY; (Y); 36/154; AFS; Drama Clb; French Clb; Ski Clb; Spanish Clb; School Play; St Bonaventure U; Spnsh.

BIGHAM, PAMELA; Franklinville Central HS; Franklinville, NY; (Y); 2/48; Church Yth Grp; VP Spanish Clb; Teachers Aide; VP Varsity Clb; Capt L Bsktbl; Capt L Crs Cntry; Capt L Trk; Hon Roll; NHS; Sal; NYS Regents Scholar 86; Houghton Coll SW Paine Scholar 86; Elmira Coll Key Awd 85; Houghton Coll; Elem Ed.

BIGLEY, JOHN; Mount St Michael Acad; Mount Vernon, NY; (Y); 43/297; Computer Clb; Office Aide; Hon Roll; Prfct Atten Awd; Agri.

BILBY, MIKE; Hilton Central HS; Hilton, NY; (Y); 9/316; Bsbl; Ftbl; High Hon Roll; NHS; 100 Prcnt Alg Fnl 83-84; 99 Prcnt Geom Fnl 84-85; Monroe CC; Mech Engr.

BILELLA, CHRIS; Bay Shore HS; Bayshore, NY; (Y); 130/406; Chorus; Jazz Band; School Musical; School Play; Drama Clb; Swing Chorus; Variety Show; Hon Roll; Soc Stds Achvt Awd; Bus Achvt Awd; Music Awd; Crane Potsdam U; Music Tchr.

BILELLO, GARY M; Massapequa HS; Massapequa, NY; (Y); 29/450; Band; Concert Band; Mrchg Band; Var Capt Gym; High Hon Roll; NHS; Prfct Atten Awd; NYS Regents Schlrshp 86; Friars Schlrshp St Bonavendure 86; St Bonaventure; Sci.

BILLA, CHRISTINE; Johnstown HS; Johnstown, NY; (Y); Chorus; Color Guard; School Musical; School Play; Variety Show; Rep Frsh Cls; Rep Soph Cls; Var L Cheerleading; JV Fld Hcky; JV Trk; Radio TV Brdcstng.

BILLINGHAM, FRANK; Massena Central HS; Norcross, GA; (Y); 76/246; Drama Clb; 4-H; Thesps; Chorus; Mrchg Band; School Musical; School Play; Stage Crew; Variety Show; Yrbk Rptr.

BILLITTIER, MARY BETH; Mt Mercy Acad; Hamburg, NY; (Y); Dance Clb; FNA; FTA; Hosp Aide; Pep Clb; Red Cross Aide; Spanish Clb; Gym; Sftbl; Hon Roll; St Bonaventure; Bus Adm.

BILLOTTI, DENA; Hilton Central HS; Hilton, NY; (Y); Ski Clb; Nwsp Stf; Yrbk Bus Mgr; Sec Sr Cls; Stu Cncl; JV Var Fld Hcky; JV Trk; High Hon Roll; NHS; Pres Schlr; NYS Regents Schlrshp 85-86; Syracuse U Davison Mem Trust Schlrshp 86; Suburban News Jrnslsm Awd 86; Syraucse U; Journalism.

BILLS, M SHANNON; Geneva HS; Geneva, NY; (S); 37/175; Cmnty Wkr; Hosp Aide; Spanish Clb; Yrbk Phtg; Yrbk Stf; Powder Puff Ftbl; Trk; High Hon Roll; Hon Roll; Marine Bio.

BILLS, PAULA; Wilson Central HS; Ransomville, NY; (Y); Church Yth Grp; Girl Scts; Bsktbl; Hon Roll.

BILLUPS, RHONDA; Christopher Columbus HS; Bronx, NY; (Y); Office Aide; Service Clb; Color Guard; Stage Crew; Yrbk Stf; Vllybl; Cit Awd; Cmptr Sci.

BILLUPS, TANGELA JAQUET; Irondequoit HS; Rochester, NY; (Y); 39/389; Church Yth Grp; 4-H; Hosp Aide; Intnl Clb; Church Choir; Rep Jr Cls; Rep Sr Cls; Cit Awd; 4-H Awd; Hon Roll; No Truancy Awd 84-86; Outstndg Teen Awd Chrch 86; Comp Engnrng.

BILTNER, JOHN; Solvay HS; Syracuse, NY; (Y); Rep Jr Cls; JV Bsbl; Var JV Bsktbl; Var Capt Ftbl; Hon Roll; All Co Ftbl Hnrs 84-85; All Co Capt,Upstate & All State 85-86; Vrsty Ftbl Capt; Syracuse U; Bus Mngmnt.

BIN, KRISTINA; Maryvale HS; Depew, NY; (Y); Church Yth Grp; 4-H; French Clb; GAA; Chorus; Rep Soph Cls; Rep Jr Cls; Hon Roll; Law.

BINENTI, DOUGLAS; Mount Vernon HS; Mt Vernon, NY; (Y); Boy Scts; Hon Roll; Prdctn Asst Grp W Cbl 84-86; Cert Achvmnt DC & AC Elctrncs 86; Stu Of Mnth Radio & Tv Elctrncs 85; Elec Engnr.

BINGHAM, NIKKI; Salmon River Central HS; Ft Covington, NY; (Y); 13/96; FFA; Var Bsktbl; Var Socr; Var Sftbl; Hon Roll; NHS; NY ST Regnts Shclrshp 86; Canton ATC; Eng Sci.

BINGLEY, STEPHEN E; Newark Valley HS; Newark Valley, NY; (Y); 24/120; Boy Scts; Church Yth Grp; Varsity Clb; Band; Mrchg Band; Var Capt Socr; NHS; Regents Schlrshp 86; Rotary Exchng Stu To Germany 86-87; Long Island U; Marine Bio.

BINI III, DILLIO; Coxsackie Athens Central HS; Coxsackie, NY; (Y); 5/105; Pres Ski Clb; Spanish Clb; Band; Ftbl; Socr; Vllybl; High Hon Roll; NHS; Ntl Merit Ltr; MIT; Aerospace.

BINKLEY, SARAH K; Vestal SR HS; Vestal, NY; (Y); 18/430; Drama Clb; French Clb; Mathletes; Math Tm; SADD; School Play; Cmnty Wkr; Hosp Aide; Library Aide; Ski Clb; Medcl Dr 3rd Wrld Cntry.

BIONDA, DANIELLE; Northport HS; Northport, NY; (Y); 59/596; Pres Cmnty Wkr; Model UN; Chorus; School Musical; VP Frsh Cls; Rep Sr Cls; Rep Stu Cncl; Mgr(s); JV Capt Sftbl; High Hon Roll; Bioengrng.

BIPAT, GEORGE R; Mount Saint Michael Acad; Bronx, NY; (S); 7/309; Chess Clb; Rep Stu Cncl; Im Bsktbl; Im Ftbl; JV Trk; Hon Roll; NHS; Prfct Atten Awd; Acad Exc Awd 84-85.

BIRCH, ANGELA; Midwood HS; Brooklyn, NY; (Y); Aud/Vis; Cmnty Wkr; Hosp Aide; Library Aide; Math Tm; Office Aide; Teachers Aide; Chorus; Color Guard; Hon Roll; Comm Serv Awd 84; Arista 81-84; Archon 86; Med.

BIRD, CHARLES; Midlakes HS; Clifton Spgs, NY; (Y); 16/144; AFS; Am Leg Boys St; Model UN; Bowling; High Hon Roll; Hon Roll; Comp Sci.

BIRD, JOHN; Olean HS; Olean, NY; (Y); 50/216; ROTC; Vllybl; Hon Roll; Bevrg Drnkg Awd 85-86; Water Skiing Champ 86; Hnrd H S Girl Chasing Prgm 86; SUNY Brockport; Lawyr.

BIRD, SHIRLEY; Midlakes HS; Clifton Spgs, NY; (Y); AFS; Church Yth Grp; 4-H; French Clb; GAA; Hosp Aide; Nwsp Rptr; 4-H Awd; Hon Roll; Bryan Stratton; Bus.

BIRDSALL, KIM; Southampton HS; Water Mill, NY; (Y); 6/115; Church Yth Grp; French Clb; GAA; Nwsp Ed-Chief; Yrbk Stf; Pres Sr Cls; Rep Stu Cncl; Var Capt Fld Hcky; Sftbl; Trk; Water Mill Cmmnty Clb Schlrp 86; Buckingham Schlrp Chrch 86; NY Rgnts Schlrp 85; Cornell U.

BIRDSALL, NANCY; Walton Central HS; Walton, NY; (Y); 22/112; AFS; FHA; Girl Scts; Library Aide; VICA; Color Guard; Mrchg Band; Hon Roll; Prfct Atten Awd; Most Outstndng Stu In Boces Sec Course 86; Catskill Area Assn Schlrshp 86; Central City Bus Inst; Word Pro.

BIRDSEY, DARYL JEAN; Fabius-Pompey HS; La Fayette, NY; (Y); 2/57; Am Leg Aux Girls St; Band; Yrbk Ed-Chief; Rep Stu Cncl; High Hon Roll; NHS; Sal; Cortland ST Schlrs Day 85; Amrcn Bus Wmns Assoc Schlrshp 86; Rgnts Schlrshp; ESF At Syracuse; Envrnmtl Chem.

BIRMINGHAM, BRIAN S; Penn Yan Acad; Penn Yan, NY; (Y); Am Leg Boys St; Church Yth Grp; Model UN; VP Varsity Clb; Rep Stu Cncl; JV Ftbl; Var Lcrss; Wt Lftg; JV Wrstlng; High Hon Roll; NY ST Regents Schlrshp 86; ROTC Schlrshp 86; Yorkers Clb VP; Pol Sci.

BIRNBACH, PAMELA; Academy Of The Holy Names; Loudonville, NY; (Y); GAA; Spanish Clb; Nwsp Rptr; Nwsp Stf; Capt Var Cheerleading; Sftbl; Natl Ldrshp & Svc Awds 86; Jrnlsm.

BIRNER, CHRISTOPHER; Eden SR HS; Eden, NY; (Y); Varsity Clb; Band; Concert Band; Jazz Band; Pep Band; School Musical; Symp Band; Bowling; Vllybl; NHS; Comp Repair.

BIRNSTEIN, LARA; Riverhead HS; Riverhead, NY; (Y); Trs Church Yth Grp; JCL; Latin Clb; Orch; Valparaiso U; Educ.

BIRRITTELLA, PATRICIA; Roy C Ketcham SR HS; Wappinger Falls, NY; (Y); Yrbk Stf; Cheerleading; High Hon Roll; Hon Roll; Russell Sage; Pre-Med.

BISAILLON, TERESA; The Franciscan Acad; N Syracuse, NY; (S); 1/26; FBLA; Trs NFL; Ed Yrbk Stf; Stu Cncl; High Hon Roll; NHS; Ntl Merit Ltr; Val; 2nd Pl NY ST Frshmn Of Yr FBLA 82; 4th Pl Pblc Spkng FBLA 83; FBLA ST Ofcr 85-86; Rchstr Inst Of Tech; Math.

BISAILLON, TODD; Mechanicville HS; Mechanicville, NY; (Y); 10/105; Math Tm; Red Cross Aide; Varsity Clb; Off Soph Cls; Sec Jr Cls; Var JV Ftbl; Var Wrstlng; High Hon Roll; NHS; Regnts Schlrshp 86; Albany ST; Dntst.

BISCARO, MICHELLE; Warsaw Central HS; Warsaw, NY; (S); 12/90; Sec Drama Clb; French Clb; Library Aide; Band; Chorus; Church Choir; School Musical; Yrbk Stf; Hon Roll; Prfct Atten Awd; Mdcl Rcrd Tech.

BISCAY, MELISA; West Hempstead HS; Island Park, NY; (Y); Key Clb; Chorus; Yrbk Phtg; Hon Roll; Accntng Awd 85-86; Spnsh Awd 83-84; U Of Albany; Accntnt.

BISCHEL, JULIANNE; Fayetteville-Manlius HS; Manlius, NY; (Y); Cmnty Wkr; Hosp Aide; JCL; SADD; Swmmng; Trk; Hon Roll; NHS; Ntl Merit Ltr; Pres Schlr; Acad Schlrshp CT Coll86; SR Cls Ltry Awd 86; Cum Laude Ntl Latin Exm; CO Coll; Ecnmcs.

BISCHOFF, CATHERINE; Saugerties HS; Saugerties, NY; (Y); French Clb; Ski Clb; Church Choir; Nwsp Stf; Yrbk Stf; Var L Crs Cntry; JV L Socr; L Var Trk; Hon Roll; NHS; Ed.

BISCHOFF, PATRICIA; Sacred Heart Acad; Port Washington, NY; (Y); Church Yth Grp; Hosp Aide; Chorus; Hon Roll; NHS; Semi-Fnlst Ntl Pro-Lf Ortrcl Cntst 86; St Francis Hosp Volntr Awd 86; Comptn NYS Bar Assn Mck Trl 86.

BISCHOPING, PAUL; Mc Quaid Jesuit HS; Rush, NY; (Y); Am Leg Boys St; Am Leg Aux Girls St; Boy Scts; Church Yth Grp; Exploring; Var Crs Cntry; JV Ftbl; Var Trk; JV Vllybl; Ad Atare Dei 86; SUNY Binghamton; Mrktg.

BISH, PAMELA; Mayville Central Schl; Mayville, NY; (S); 2/34; Pres French Clb; Girl Scts; School Musical; Stage Crew; Yrbk Stf; Bausch & Lomb Sci Awd; Dnfth Awd; Trs NHS; VFW Awd; Office Aide; Chautaugua Area Grl Sct WY Trek 84; Math.

BISHARA, ELIZABETH; Niagara Falls HS; Niagara Falls, NY; (S); 3/250; Pres VP Church Yth Grp; VP Sec Drama Clb; VP Band; VP Stu Cncl; NHS; Pres Frsh Cls; VP Jr Cls; JV Sftbl; NY St V Cgrmn Yorkers 85-86; NY St Regents Schlrshp 86; U Of Rochester; Med.

BISHKO, SHERRY; Tuxedo HS; Tuxedo Park, NY; (Y); 1/97; VP AFS; Drama Clb; Intnl Clb; Scholastic Bowl; Science Clb; Spanish Clb; SADD; Chorus; School Musical; School Play; Harvard Bk Awd Outstndg JR 85; Rgnts Schrlshp 86; Outstndg Soc Stds Stu 85; Colgat U; Med.

BISHKOFF, NANCY; Alexander Hamilton HS; New Rochelle, NY; (Y); French Clb; Intnl Clb; Key Clb; Service Clb; Hnrs 82&83; Bus.

BISHOFF, JULIE; Forestville Central HS; Forestville, NY; (Y); Church Yth Grp; Concert Band; Jazz Band; Yrbk Ed-Chief; JV L Bsktbl; Var Trk; Cmrcl Art.

BISHOP, CHANDA; Nazareth Regional HS; Brooklyn, NY; (Y); 64/267; Girl Scts; JA; Office Aide; Teachers Aide; Chorus; Variety Show; Cheerleading; Hon Roll; Prfct Atten Awd; Hmptn U Hmptn VA; Acctng.

BISHOP, EVA; Avoca Central HS; Bath, NY; (Y); Art Clb; Church Yth Grp; GAA; OEA; Var Bsktbl; Hon Roll; Lawyr.

BISHOP, JEFFREY; Anthony A Henninger SR HS; Syracuse, NY; (Y); Drama Clb; Intnl Clb; School Play; Stage Crew; Variety Show; Nwsp Stf; NY ST Regents Schlrshp 86; Cobleskill Ag & Tech; Prof Chef.

BISHOP, JULIE; Tully Central HS; Tully, NY; (Y); Art Clb; Camera Clb; Temple Yth Grp; Varsity Clb; Yrbk Phtg; Var Socr; Rep Frsh Cls; VP Sr Cls; Var Trk; JV Vllybl; Sctn Iii Sccr & Trk Awds 85 & 86; Athltc Awd Chrldng 3rd Pl 84; Yth Chldrns Mnstry.

BISHOP, MELISA; Auburn HS; Auburn, NY; (Y); Cmnty Wkr; Drama Clb; Hosp Aide; Chorus; School Musical; School Play; Stage Crew; JV Sftbl; JV Vllybl; High Hon Roll; Jrnlsm.

BISHOP, SUZANNE; G W Fowler HS; Syracuse, NY; (Y); VP JA; Chorus; Church Choir; Hon Roll; Hnrb Mntn Regents Chem 86; Hnr Rl Comp Sci I Central Tech 86; Bio.

BISHOP, TRACEY; Holy Trinity HS; Hicksville, NY; (S); 10/400; Math Clb; Spanish Clb; Hon Roll; Mu Alp Tht; Ntl Merit Schol; NEDT Awd; Holy Name Scty Schlrsp Awd; Math Best Avg Awd; Elec Engr.

BISKI, BRIAN R; Schelmont HS; Schenectady, NY; (Y); Pres Band; Jazz Band; Mrchg Band; Rep Frsh Cls; Rep Soph Cls; Rep Jr Cls; Rep Sr Cls; Rep Stu Cncl; Var Bsktbl; Var Trk; Merist Coll Schlrshp 86-87; Merist Coll; Comm.

BISOGNO, GLORIA; St Catharine Acad; Bronx, NY; (Y); 18/200; Library Aide; Nwsp Ed-Chief; Hon Roll; NHS; Ntl Merit Ltr; Regnts Coll Schlrshp Awd 86; Manhattan Coll Schlrshp Grnt 86; Manhattan Coll; Hstry Tchr.

BISSAINTHE, CAMILLE; St Edmund HS; Queens Village, NY; (Y); 34/190; Pres Church Yth Grp; Cmnty Wkr; French Clb; Hosp Aide; Science Clb; Church Choir; Im Vllybl; Hon Roll; Lang Fair 1st Pl 86; Christian Svc Awd 86; NYU; Pdtrcn.

BISSESSAR, JASODRA; Sarah J Hale HS; Brooklyn, NY; (Y); Church Yth Grp; Teachers Aide; Chorus; Church Choir; Color Guard; Drill Tm; Swmmng; Cit Awd; God Cntry Awd; High Hon Roll; Brooklyn Coll; Comp Sci.

BISSET, DAVID; Gloversville HS; Gloversvl, NY; (Y); 100/250; Boy Scts; Im Bsbl; JV Var Bsktbl; JV Var Ftbl; Hon Roll.

BISSICK, JILL T; The Brandeis Schl; Baldwin, NY; (Y); Library Aide; Political Wkr; Nwsp Rptr; Nwsp Stf; Yrbk Bus Mgr; Yrbk Stf; Frsh Cls; Soph Cls; Jr Cls; Pres Ntl Merit Schol; Lawyer.

BISWANGER JR, ROBERT; Liverpool HS; Liverpool, NY; (Y); 23/883; Am Leg Boys St; Math Tm; Jazz Band; School Musical; Symp Band; Var Socr; High Hon Roll; NHS; Church Yth Grp; Band; Schlstc Achvmnt Awd 86; All-Cnty Jzz Ensmbl 85&86; Indstrl & Lbr Rltns.

BITELLI, LEN C; Guilderland Central HS; Schenectady, NY; (Y); Chess Clb; High Hon Roll; Hon Roll; Prfct Atten Awd.

BIVETTO, FRED; St Johns Prep; Howard Bch, NY; (Y); Boys Clb Am; JV Coach Actv; Var Crs Cntry; Im Fld Hcky; Im Ftbl; Var Socr; Capt Sftbl; Trk; High Hon Roll; Hon Roll.

BIXBY, ABIGAIL; Libson Central Schl; Heuvelton, NY; (S); 2/47; Camera Clb; VP 4-H; FBLA; FHA; GAA; Rep Stu Cncl; Var Crs Cntry; Capt Vllybl; Hon Roll; Spanish Clb; Whiz Quiz 85-86; Cornell U; Vet Sci.

BIXBY, DAVID A; Owego Free Acad; Endicott, NY; (Y); 1/224; Key Clb; Capt Mathletes; Jazz Band; Nwsp Sprt Ed; Pres Stu Cncl; Var Tennis; Bausch & Lomb Sci Awd; NHS; Ntl Merit Ltr; Val; Thos J Watson Mem Schlrshp IBM 86; H Rodney Sharp Schlrshp U DE 86; Mst Likely Succeed 86; U DE; Chem Engrng.

BIZIK, MIKE; Guilderland Central HS; Guilderland, NY; (Y); Key Clb; Var L Bsbl; JV Crs Cntry; Effrt & Achvt Math III & Soc Stds XI 86; Sprts Mgmt.

BIZZARRO, MICHELLE; Kenmore East HS; Tonawanda, NY; (Y); Band; Rep Color Guard; Drm & Bgl; Mrchg Band; JV Sftbl; Clr Grd Bookie Of Yr 83-84; U Of NY Amherst; Comp Pgmr.

BLAAKMAN, AARON; Mc Quaid Jesuit HS; Rochester, NY; (Y); French Clb; Trs Frsh Cls; Trs Sr Cls; Stu Cncl; High Hon Roll; Teachers Aide; Band; School Musical; Bsbl; Acad Lttr; Frnch Exchng Stu; Intl Financ.

BLACK, BONNIE JEAN; Gates-Chili HS; Rochester, NY; (Y); 29/446; French Clb; Service Clb; Varsity Clb; Color Guard; Rep Sr Cls; Var Tennis; High Hon Roll; Hon Roll; NHS; Pres Schlr; Oneonta Coll; Physcl Thrpy.

BLACK, DAVID THUNEY; Albany Acad; Albany, NY; (Y); 2/43; Am Leg Boys St; Varsity Clb; Nwsp Sprt Ed; Ed Lit Mag; Mgr Bsktbl; Var Trk; High Hon Roll; Sal; NROTC Schlrshp; Cum Laude Soc 86; Worcester Polytech Inst; Engrng.

BLACK, JOY L; Seton Catholic Central HS; Apalachin, NY; (Y); 50/173; French Clb; Key Clb; Varsity Clb; School Play; JV Var Cheerleading; Var Capt Socr; Var L Trk; Sec Jr Cls; Rep Stu Cncl; Regnts Schlrshp 86; Mt Holyoke Clg; Biochem.

BLACK, KAREN M; Smithtown East HS; Nesconset, NY; (Y); Teachers Aide; Nwsp Stf; Stu Cncl; Hon Roll; Jr NHS; NHS; Ntl Merit Ltr; Spanish NHS; NYSSMA Pno A Lvl VI 85; J C Lynn Dnc Cmpny 85-86; Cornell U; Intl Bus.

BLACK, MAX; New Rochelle HS; New Rochelle, NY; (Y); Civic Clb; SADD; Chorus; Swing Chorus; Lit Mag; Lcrss; High Hon Roll.

BLACK, NANCY; Corning-Painted Post West HS; Corning, NY; (Y); Sec Church Yth Grp; JA; Varsity Clb; Stat Mgr Sftbl; High Hon Roll; Hon Roll; Corning CC; Acctng.

BLACK, ROSEMARIE; Dewitt Clinton HS; Bronx, NY; (Y); 64/257; Hosp Aide; Intnl Clb; School Play; Variety Show; Gym; Sftbl; Trk; Vllybl; Wt Lftg; Buffalo U.

BLACK, SAMANTHA P; Nazareth Regional HS; Brooklyn, NY; (S); 5/267; Varsity Clb; School Musical; Yrbk Stf; Pres Frsh Cls; Pres Soph Cls; Pres Stu Cncl; Cheerleading; Vllybl; NHS; NY Super Yth 84; Schl Rep Intl Yth Conf Chrstns & Jews 83; HOBY Natl Conf Schl Rep 84.

BLACKBURN, ELIZABETH; Oakfield Alabama HS; Basom, NY; (Y); 7/94; Art Clb; French Clb; Stu Cncl; JV Socr; Hon Roll; NHS; Deans List Genesee CC 86; Phi Theta Kappa 86; GCC; Bus Adm.

BLACKBURN, PAMALA; Gouverneur Central HS; Gouverneur, NY; (Y); French Clb; Varsity Clb; Chorus; Jr Cls; Stu Cncl; Bsktbl; Sftbl; Hon Roll; Prfct Atten Awd; Cazenovia Coll; Elem Ed.

BLACKMAN, DAVID J; Norwich HS; Norwich, NY; (Y); 64/220; Am Leg Boys St; Church Yth Grp; Spanish Clb; Teachers Aide; Chorus; Jazz Band; Mrchg Band; School Musical; Sr Cls; Hon Roll; Natoli Film Comm 84-87; Guidance Review Comm 85-86; Mock Trial Team 85-86; Educ.

BLACKMON, BERNARD; Far Rockaway HS; Far Rockaway, NY; (Y); English Clb; SADD; Band; Yrbk Stf; Wrstlng; Cprtv Educ Awd Bus Awd 86; Agri & Tech Coll; Bus Admn.

BLACKSHEAR, KAREN; John F Kennedy HS; Utica, NY; (Y); 6/19; Key Clb; Chorus; School Musical; Trk; Hon Roll; MVCC; Nrsng.

BLACKSTONE, BRIAN; Corning-Painted Post W HS; Painted Post, NY; (Y); Am Leg Boys St; Varsity Clb; Var Capt Tennis; High Hon Roll; Pres NHS; Harvard Prize Bk 86; Rensallaer Polytech Inst Math & Sci Awd 86; W High Athlet Of The Month 86.

BLACKWELL, MELISSA; Roosevelt HS; Yonkers, NY; (Y); Church Yth Grp; Hosp Aide; Church Choir; Hon Roll; Comp.

BLACKWOOD, ARIELLA; St Edmund HS; Brooklyn, NY; (Y); French Clb; Hosp Aide; Variety Show; Maritime Coll; Comp Stds.

BLAETZ, ELKE MONIKA; Canajoharie HS; Canajoharie, NY; (Y); 6/83; Am Leg Aux Girls St; Drama Clb; Red Cross Aide; Stat Swmmng; Trs Jr NHS; Sec NHS; Ntl Merit Ltr; Intnl Clb; Hon Roll; Hugh O Brian Yth Found Amb 84; NY ST Regnst Schlrshp 86; Pres Acad Ftns Awds 86; Albany Coll; Phrmcy.

BLAIN, LAURA; Frontier HS; Hamburg, NY; (Y); Yrbk Ed-Chief; Var Bsktbl; Var Sftbl; Capt JV Vllybl; Art Clb; Church Yth Grp; Pep Clb; Varsity Clb; Yrbk Stf; Vrsty Bsktbl & Sftbl Tm 84-85; Capt JV Vllybl Tm 85-86; Sci.

BLAINEY, CHRISTINE; Mineola HS; Mineola, NY; (Y); SADD; Thesps; Chorus; School Musical; School Play; Hon Roll; Theatre Arts.

BLAIR, ALLISON; St Mary Girls HS; Franklin Square, NY; (Y); 42/170; Art Clb; Drama Clb; Ski Clb; Chorus; Stage Crew; Hon Roll; Bus Fnce.

BLAIR, BARBARA; Webster HS; Webster, NY; (Y); 25/540; Church Yth Grp; German Clb; Rep Frsh Cls; Rep Soph Cls; Rep Jr Cls; Rep Sr Cls; Var Cheerleading; High Hon Roll; Hon Roll; Jr NHS; Germn NHS 84; St Bonaventure Pres Scholar 86; Phi Delta Kappa Scholar 86; St Bonaventure; Mth.

BLAIR, CHARMINE M; Northeastern Acad; Bronx, NY; (Y); Chorus; Nwsp Phtg; Yrbk Phtg; Trs Frsh Cls; Pres Soph Cls; Pres Jr Cls; Pres Sr Cls; Var Vllybl; Val; Physcis Mdl 86; Chem Mdl 85; Rgnts Schlrshp 86; Oakwood Coll; Bio.

BLAIR, KIMBERLY; Cortland JR-SR HS; Cortland, NY; (Y); 6/180; Church Yth Grp; Concert Band; Mrchg Band; Orch; Pep Band; School Musical; Lit Mag; High Hon Roll; NHS; Tri-M 84; SUNY Binghamton; Sci Rsrch.

BLAIS, ERIC M; Ogdensburg Free Acad; Ogdensburg, NY; (Y); 25/186; French Clb; Key Clb; Golf; Socr; Trk; Vllybl; Acad Banquet 83; NY St Regents Schlrshp 86; Union Coll; Pre-Med.

BLAIZE, CAROLYN; Mont Pleasant HS; Schenectady, NY; (Y); 22/241; Pres Church Yth Grp; Trs Spanish Clb; Chorus; Church Choir; Yrbk Bus Mgr; Yrbk Stf; Off Frsh Cls; Sec Soph Cls; Trs Jr Cls; Off Sr Cls; Spnsh Hnr Soc Awd 84-85; Spnsh Cls Awd 83-86; Bus Mgmt.

BLAKE, MAUREEN; Sacred Heart Acad; Roslyn Heights, NY; (Y); Church Yth Grp; Cmnty Wkr; Debate Tm; Drama Clb; NFL; Speech Tm; Church Choir; Nwsp Rptr; Nwsp Stf; NYS Lincol-Douglas Debate Tourn 86; Cmnctns.

BLAKE, OSBOURNE; Clara Barton HS; Brooklyn, NY; (Y); Hosp Aide; Co-Capt Science Clb; Concert Band; Rep Jr Cls; Hon Roll; Church Yth Grp; 2nd Prz Borough Sci Fair 85; 6 Flag Fest Band 84; Pride Of The Yankees Awd 85-86; Pre Med.

BLAKE, ROBIN; Chenango Valley JR SR HS; Pt Crane, NY; (Y); 25/175; Drama Clb; French Clb; Spanish Clb; Varsity Clb; Band; Chorus; Mrchg Band; School Musical; School Play; Swing Chorus; Ny St Schl Music Assn Outstndng Rtng 77-85; Rotary Exchg Stu To Belgium 86-87; Frgn Lang.

BLAKE, SHANTEL; St Catharine Acad; Bx, NY; (Y); Chorus; Rep Soph Cls; Var Swmmng; Social Wrkr.

BLAKOWSKI, KATHERINE; Holy Angels Acad; Buffalo, NY; (Y); French Clb; 4-H Awd; High Hon Roll; Hon Roll; Prfct Atten Awd; Comp Litrcy Awd 86; Studio In Art Awd 86; Eucharistic Mnstr 86; Canisius Coll.

BLAM, HOLLY R; East Islip HS; Great River, NY; (Y); 49/425; Church Yth Grp; Hosp Aide; Score Keeper; High Hon Roll; Hon Roll; NY ST Rgnts Schlrshp 85-86; Bus Adm.

BLANCHARD, MICHAEL; Potsdam Central HS; Potsdam, NY; (Y); #4 In Class; AFS; Computer Clb; French Clb; Math Clb; Ski Clb; Hon Roll; NHS; Clarkson U; Elec Engrng.

BLANCHARD, SUZANNE; Clayton A Bouton JR SR HS; Voorheesville, NY; (Y); Pres Church Yth Grp; Drama Clb; Trs 4-H; French Clb; Chorus; Church Choir; Stage Crew; Variety Show; JV Fld Hcky; High Hon Roll; Bus Adm.

BLANCHETTI, IOLANDA; Bishop Grimes HS; Liverpool, NY; (Y); Stage Crew; Yrbk Ed-Chief; Yrbk Sprt Ed; Trs Soph Cls; Var Cheerleading; Hon Roll; NHS; Cmnty Wkr; Hosp Aide; Rep Frsh Cls; Italian Hnr Soc; Bus.

BLANCO, ANNE MARIE; St John The Baptist HS; Brentwood, NY; (S); 25/512; Chrmn Dance Clb; Pres Ski Clb; SADD; Nwsp Stf; Rep Frsh Cls; Rep Soph Cls; Chrmn Stu Cncl; Hon Roll; Spanish NHS; Intl Frgn Lang Awd 86; St Fnlst Miss NY Coed 85; Acctg.

BLANCO, LOURDES; Murry Bergtraum HS; Brooklyn, NY; (Y); Church Yth Grp; VP JA; Band; Concert Band; NHS; Syracuse U; Corp Mgmt.

BLANCO, ROBERT; Archbishop Molly HS; Flushing, NY; (Y); 197/410; Boy Scts; Sec Exploring; French Clb; Science Clb; Spanish Clb; Im Crs Cntry; Capt Swmmng; Im Trk; Cit Awd; Hon Roll; Order Of The Arrow Chap Chf 85; Natl Hspnc Schlr Semi-Fin 85; Eagle Scout Merit Awd 85-86; Biomed Engrng.

BLANCO, SALVATORE F; West Babylon SR HS; West Babylon, NY; (Y); 4/400; Hosp Aide; High Hon Roll; Hon Roll; NHS; Prncpls Awd Outstndng Stdnt Sci 83-84; Regnts Schlrshp 86; 100 Hr Patch & 250 Hr Pin Vlntr Hrs Hosp 86; Stony Brook U; Med.

BLAND, JILL S; Forest Hills HS; Howard Beach, NY; (Y); Debate Tm; English Clb; VP Temple Yth Grp; High Hon Roll; VP NHS; Regnts Schlrshp 86; Oneonta ST U; Phys Thrpy.

BLANDING, KAREN; Chenango Forks HS; Binghamton, NY; (Y); 3/174; Church Yth Grp; Ski Clb; Spanish Clb; Varsity Clb; VP Jr Cls; Var Swmmng; Hon Roll; NHS; Salut Yth 85; Ithaca Coll; Comm.

BLANKENBERG, JENNIFER; Pembroke HS; Corfu, NY; (Y); Hon Roll; Spnsh Awd-99 Pct Avg 83-86; Grmn Awd-Hgh Avg 86.

BLANKENHORN, DAWN; L I Lutheran HS; Lindenhurst, NY; (S); 6/90; Church Yth Grp; French Clb; German Clb; Ski Clb; Spanish Clb; SADD; Var L Trk; Var L Vllybl; High Hon Roll; NHS; Bus.

BLANN, STEPHANIE; Faith Heritage Schl; Baldinsville, NY; (Y); Church Yth Grp; Teachers Aide; Band; Chorus; Church Choir; Im Bsktbl; Im Sftbl; Hon Roll; Color Guard; Concert Band; NYSSMA Awd Excllnc Vocal 84; Educ Of Deaf & Hearing Impair.

BLASCOVI, LEE; St Francis Prep; Whitestone, NY; (Y); 300/750; Aud/Vis; Cmnty Wkr; Computer Clb; Library Aide; Service Clb; Ski Clb; SADD; Teachers Aide; Yrbk Stf; Off Frsh Cls; Italian Natl Hnr Soc 86; Stu Tech Svc 86; Italian Club 86; MA Inst Tech; Engrng.

BLASDEL, BRITTAN; Our Lady Of Mercy HS; Pittsford, NY; (Y); Church Yth Grp; Yrbk Stf; Lit Mag; Swmmng; Vllybl; Hon Roll; Mst Outstndng Artist Cls 86; Art.

BLASI, VALERIE; South Side HS; Rockville Ctr, NY; (Y); Church Yth Grp; 4-H; Church Choir; Orch; Im Socr; Var Trk; Hon Roll; Clark U; Bio.

BLASUCCI, BARBARA; Preston HS; Bronx, NY; (S); 3/89; Drama Clb; Teachers Aide; School Musical; School Play; Stage Crew; Variety Show; Nwsp Rptr; Yrbk Phtg; Yrbk Stf; Ed Lit Mag; 1st Hnrs 83-86; Fordham U.

BLATT, MICHAEL J; Gloversville HS; Gloversville, NY; (Y); 7/235; Cmnty Wkr; Political Wkr; Ski Clb; Temple Yth Grp; Band; Bsktbl; Tennis; Hon Roll; Ntl Merit Ltr.

BLATTO, MICHAEL; St Marys HS; Depew, NY; (Y); Varsity Clb; Bsktbl; JV Crs Cntry; Socr; Var Trk; Cert Schlrshp Math II 85; Cert Rcgntn Mst Imprvd Stdnt Yr 84; Hnr Awd Fund Rsng St Jude 82; Sci.

BLAU, CHERYL; Massapequa HS; Massapequa Park, NY; (Y); 7/440; Drama Clb; French Clb; Pep Clb; SADD; School Musical; School Play; Variety Show; Nwsp Stf; Yrbk Rptr; Yrbk Stf; Cert Merit Bio, Math, Frnch, Italian 82-85; Regents Schlrshp 86; Duke U; Bio-Med.

BLAU, EVELYN; Mahopac HS; Mahopac, NY; (Y); Chorus.

BLAUSTEIN, MICHAEL S; Massapequa HS; Massapequa, NY; (Y); 80/448; Ski Clb; Variety Show; Var Ftbl; Var Mgr(s); Im Socr; Hon Roll; SUNY At Albany; Bio.

BLAUSTEIN, PETER M; Bethlehem Central HS; Delmar, NY; (Y); 15/304; Model UN; Political Wkr; Var JV Socr; High Hon Roll; NHS; Ntl Merit SF.

BLAYER, STEVEN L; Hillcrest HS; Long Island City, NY; (Y); 64/650; Boys Clb Am; Church Yth Grp; Cmnty Wkr; Pres Exploring; Red Cross Aide; Drm & Bgl; Orch; School Play; Boy Scts; Debate Tm; Boys Clb Of Quns Boy Of Yr 85; Queensboro Sci Fr 3rd Pl 84; SUNY Binghamton; Psych.

BLAZE, AILEEN; Frontier Central HS; Hamburg, NY; (Y); Orch; High Hon Roll; Hon Roll; NHS; Ntl Merit Ltr; Hnr Soc Pin & Card 85-86; Hgh Hnrs Pin & Sci Fair Cert Merit 83-84; Hgh Hnrs Cert Merit; Orch Cert Meri; Trocaire Coll; Srgcl Nrsg.

BLECHA, MARK D; Pioneer Central HS; Machias, NY; (Y); Var Capt Bsbl; Var Capt Bsktbl; Var Capt Ftbl; Hon Roll; NY ST Regents Schlrshp Wnnr 86; Big 30 All-Star Div VI & All-Star Ftbl 85-86; 2nd Tm All-Star ECIC; Canisius Coll; Sprts Med.

BLEILER, KATHY; Mynderse Acad; Seneca Falls, NY; (S); #26 In Class; Drama Clb; 4-H; SADD; Band; Chorus; Church Choir; Concert Band; Drm Mjr(t); Jazz Band; Mrchg Band; Music Educ.

BLENCOWE, KATHLEEN; Corning-Painted Post West HS; Coopers Plains, NY; (Y); 25/260; SADD; VP Sec Thesps; Drill Tm; Madrigals; Mrchg Band; Pres Stu Cncl; JV Cheerleading; DAR Awd; NHS; Sec Letterman Clb; Quota Clb Svc Awd 86; Best Actress 86; Oswego ST U; Elem Ed.

BLENIS, ROBERT; Greenville Central JR SR HS; Surprise, NY; (Y); 19/70; Church Yth Grp; Key Clb; Spanish Clb; School Musical; VP Stu Cncl; JV Socr; Hon Roll; Cedarville Coll; Bus Admin.

BLENKER, KRISTIN; Hamburg HS; Hamburg, NY; (Y); 17/384; Dance Clb; JCL; Latin Clb; Band; Concert Band; Mrchg Band; Orch; Pep Band; School Musical; Stage Crew.

BLEWITT, MARGARET A; Saint Francis Prep; Whitestone, NY; (S); 74/744; Art Clb; Nwsp Rptr; Var Capt Sftbl; Hon Roll; NHS; Law.

BLICHT, CARYN; Smithtown HS West; Smithtown, NY; (Y); Temple Yth Grp; Trs Stu Cncl; JV Var Tennis; NHS; Spanish NHS; Decca Clb 84-85.

BLINN, LAURIE; Lake Placid Central Schl; Lake Placid, NY; (Y); 8/43; Key Clb; Varsity Clb; Yrbk Stf; Sec Jr Cls; Sec Sr Cls; Var Sftbl; Var Vllybl; Hon Roll; Prfct Atten Awd; Delhi U; Vet Tech.

BLISH, STEFANIE G; Ravena Coeymans Selkirk HS; S Bethlehem, NY; (Y); #19 In Class; Church Yth Grp; 4-H; Spanish Clb; Yrbk Stf; Var Cheerleading; JV Trk; Im Vllybl; High Hon Roll; NY ST Rgnts Schlrshp 86; Oneonta Coll; Bus Mngmnt.

BLISS, DENISE; Kendall JR SR HS; Hamlin, NY; (Y); Ski Clb; Yrbk Stf; Score Keeper; Socr; JV Vllybl; Hon Roll; Jr NHS; Ntl Merit Ltr; Geo Mason U.

BLISS, ERIC; North Rose-Wolcott HS; Wolcott, NY; (Y); Boy Scts; Church Yth Grp; Concert Band; Jazz Band; High Hon Roll; Hon Roll; Acdmc All Amer Schlr; Engrng.

BLISS, JEFFREY D; Troupsburg Central HS; Troupsburg, NY; (Y); 8/13; Aud/Vis; Letterman Clb; Band; Chorus; Concert Band; Yrbk Sprt Ed; Trs Stu Cncl; Bsbl; Bsktbl; Socr; Leag Mst Vlble Plyr Sccr 85-86; Army Sccr Awd 85-86; Memrl Awd Essay Awd 86; U Of Pittsburgh; Bus Mgmt.

BLISS, JOSEPH M; Holland Patent Central HS; Barneveld, NY; (Y); 2/145; Orch; Pres Stu Cncl; Capt Socr; NHS; Sal; Chorus; School Play; JV Bsbl; Capt Swmmng; High Hon Roll; Phi Delta Kappa Prspctv Eductrs Rgnl Schlrshp 86; DAR Gd Ctzn 85; Hllnd Ptnt Almni Schlrshp 86; Ithaca Coll; Blgy Educ.

BLISS, JULI; Williamsville South HS; Williamsville, NY; (S); Art Clb; Chorus; Hon Roll; Buffalo ST Coll; Advrtsng.

BLISS, LAUREL; North Salem HS; N Salem, NY; (Y); Math Clb; Chorus; Church Choir; Yrbk Rptr; High Hon Roll; NHS; Ntl Merit Ltr.

BLISSETT, AMELIA; Freeport HS; Freeport, NY; (Y); Church Yth Grp; French Clb; Hosp Aide; Leo Clb; Mathletes; Science Clb; Nwsp Rptr; Stu Cncl; High Hon Roll; Hon Roll; Howard; Bio.

BLITSTEIN, MARC A; Jamaica HS; Jamaica Est, NY; (Y); 110/446; Aud/Vis; Computer Clb; SADD; Pres Temple Yth Grp; Capt Wrstlng; NY St Regents Schlrshp 86; Baruch Coll; Fncl Analysis.

BLITZ, ERICA; Carmel HS; Carmel, NY; (Y); 10/350; Camera Clb; Computer Clb; 4-H; Girl Scts; Math Tm; PAVAS; Thesps; School Musical; Stage Crew; Nwsp Phtg; RIT; Photo.

BLIVEN, TRACY; Belmont Central Schl; Belmont, NY; (Y); Church Yth Grp; GAA; Girl Scts; Letterman Clb; Varsity Clb; Band; Chorus; Church Choir; Color Guard; Concert Band; Band Secy 83-86; Chrch Yth Grp Pres 85-86; Al-ST, Cnty Vocl Chorus 83-86; Mgmt.

BLOCKER, WENDY JILL; Kingston HS; Lake Katrine, NY; (Y); 24/573; 4-H; Jazz Band; Ed Nwsp Bus Mgr; Ed Yrbk Bus Mgr; Var Gym; Kiwanis Awd; NHS; UCCC Hnrs Prog Schlrshp 85-86; Temple Emanuel Yth Schlrshp To Natl Conv WA D C 83-84; Rutgers Coll; Mgmt.

BLOK, ANNA; Forest Hills HS; New York, NY; (Y); 61/826; Dance Clb; Mathletes; Office Aide; Science Clb; Service Clb; Teachers Aide; Yrbk Stf; NHS; Hgh Avg 84-86; Cert Partcptn Schl Sci Fair 86; NY U; Bus Mgr.

BLOOD, CHRIS; Greene Central HS; Greene, NY; (Y); 15/151; Church Yth Grp; Cmnty Wkr; Ski Clb; Spanish Clb; Acpl Chr; Band; Chorus; Concert Band; Jazz Band; Mrchg Band; Berklee Coll Of Msc; Music.

BLOODWORTH, DALE; Kendall Central Schl; Kendall, NY; (S); 8/88; Drama Clb; Chorus; Concert Band; Var Bsbl; Var Socr; High Hon Roll; NHS.

BLOOM, PHILIP; Humanities HS; New York, NY; (Y); Boys Clb Am; Badmtn; Bsbl; Bsktbl; Fld Hcky; Gym; Socr; Sftbl; Trk; Vllybl; Brdcstng.

BLOUNT, CHRISTINA; Sperry HS; Rochester, NY; (Y); Trs Church Yth Grp; Exploring; JA; Tennis; Hon Roll; Jr NHS; NHS; Spanish NHS; GAA; Spanish Clb; Smmr Educ Intern, Carnegie Fndtn Grants Pgm HS Imprvmnt 84; Urban Lg Rochester Fut Blck Schlrs 85-86; Acctg.

BLOW, SONJA; Erasmus Hall; Purchase, NY; (Y); Computer Clb; Library Aide; Varsity Clb; Nwsp Stf; Lit Mag; Capt Coach Actv; Sftbl; Hnrs Cert Ecnmcs, Bkkpng 85; Outstndng Stu Awd 85; Manhattanvl Coll; Bus Mgr.

BLUME, ALICE T; St Francis Prep; Flushing, NY; (S); 162/744; Ski Clb; Im Sftbl; Im Vllybl; Im Wt Lftg; Hon Roll; Pre-Law.

BLUME JR, ROBERT W; Ward Melville HS; Centereach, NY; (Y); 192/725; Computer Clb; Band; Mrchg Band; JV Bsbl; Hon Roll; Jr NHS; Rgnts Schlrshp 86; Bus Hnr Soc 86; Adelphi U; Accntng.

BLUMENAUER, CHRISTINE; Bay Shore HS; Bay Shore, NY; (Y); 42/409; Church Yth Grp; Drama Clb; Mathletes; Nwsp Stf; Lit Mag; Rep Sr Cls; Trs Stu Cncl; Hon Roll; Psych.

BLUMENAUER, KATHLEEN A; Bay Shore HS; Bay Shore, NY; (Y); 30/400; Sec Drama Clb; SADD; Sec Thesps; Chorus; School Musical; School Play; Stu Cncl; Cheerleading; NHS; Lit Mag; NYS Rgnts Schlrshp 86; Law.

BLUMENFELD, BRAD; Roslyn HS; Roslyn, NY; (Y); Sec Varsity Clb; Band; Concert Band; Orch; Nwsp Ed-Chief; Ed Nwsp Stf; Trs Frsh Cls; Capt Var Ice Hcky; L Var Trk; Chrmn NHS; Nassau Cnty Exctve Awd 85-86; Rgnts Schlrshp 85-86; Wharton U; Bus.

BLUMENTHAL, SHARI; Fayetteville-Manlius HS; Fayetteville, NY; (Y); Variety Show; Var Capt Cheerleading; JV Socr; Hon Roll; Fshn Mrchdsng.

BLUMER, ROBERT V; Weedsport HS; Weedsport, NY; (Y); 2/81; Am Leg Boys St; VP Spanish Clb; Var Golf; Var Capt Swmmng; High Hon Roll; NHS; Ntl Merit SF; Sal; Rensselaer Mdl 86; Naval Acad Summr Sem 86; Engrng.

BLUMREICH, JANNA; Barker Central HS; Barker, NY; (Y); 15/100; AFS; Drama Clb; French Clb; FBLA; Spanish Clb; Band; Chorus; School Play; Hon Roll; St Fnlst-Miss Amer Co-Ed Pgnt 84; Acctnt.

BLUSTEIN, GLEN; Middletown HS; Middletown, NY; (Y); 16/400; Political Wkr; Ski Clb; SADD; Temple Yth Grp; School Play; Yrbk Phtg; Tennis; High Hon Roll; Hon Roll; NHS; Bio.

BLUTSTEIN, ALLAN; John F Kennedy HS; Old Bethpage, NY; (Y); 6/250; VP Chess Clb; Model UN; Quiz Bowl; Acpl Chr; Nwsp Stf; Stu Cncl; Var Bsbl; Capt Var Bowling; Hon Roll; St Schlr; L I Ches Champ 84-85; V Bowling MVP 83-85; Frankln Marshall; Gov.

BLY, JENNIFER; Southside HS; Pine City, NY; (Y); Church Yth Grp; Hosp Aide; Intnl Clb; Chorus; Concert Band; Madrigals; School Musical; Rep Sr Cls; Hon Roll; L Var Socr; Sherry D White Mem Schlrshp Awd 86; Mercyhurst Coll; Music.

BLY, MICHAEL P; Brentwood Sonderling HS; Brentwood, NY; (Y); Boy Scts; Math Clb; Ski Clb; Stage Crew; JV Bsbl; JV Ftbl; Im Ice Hcky; Im Wt Lftg; Im Wrstlng; Voice Dem Awd; Awd Suffolk Cty Math Cntst 1st Pl 84; Real Est.

BOADWAY, MARY; Franklin Acad; Malone, NY; (Y); Pep Clb; Varsity Clb; Rep Frsh Cls; Var JV Cheerleading; Var Trk; Var Vllybl; Epsilon 84-86; Physcl Educ.

BOARD, TIMOTHY G; Cornwall Central HS; Cornwall Hudson, NY; (Y); Bsbl; Bsktbl; Hon Roll; NHS; Rotary Clb Ldrshp Camp 85; Bio.

BOARDMAN, SUSAN; Woodlands HS; White Plains, NY; (Y); 7/203; Debate Tm; JA; Capt Math Tm; Political Wkr; Teachers Aide; Chorus; Orch; School Play; Stage Crew; Lit Mag; Engl.

BOATE, CHRISTINE; Connetquot HS; Bohemia, NY; (Y); Church Yth Grp; Hosp Aide; Band; Mrchg Band; Symp Band; NHS; Teachers Aide; Chorus; High Hon Roll; Tri-M Ntl Hnr Scty 86; SS Hsptl Auxlty Schlrshp 86; Grdn Coll Chllng Schlrship 86; Gordon Coll; Phycal Thrphy.

BOATWRIGHT, MICHAEL W; Horseheads HS; Horseheads, NY; (Y); Am Leg Boys St; Drama Clb; Band; Chorus; Concert Band; Mrchg Band; Orch; School Musical; Hon Roll; NHS; Engrng.

BOBA, ANASTASIA; Kings Park HS; Kings Park, NY; (Y); 4/397; VP Cmnty Wkr; DECA; Co-Capt SADD; Chorus; Rep Frsh Cls; Trs Soph Cls; Capt Socr; Capt Vllybl; High Hon Roll; NHS; Schl Svc Awd; Plcmnt Ntl Sci Olympd; Binghamton; Ed.

BOBEAR, DANIEL; Catholic Central HS; Latham, NY; (Y); French Clb; Math Clb; Ski Clb; Var Trk; High Hon Roll; Hon Roll; K Of C Scholar 83; Bentley Coll; Bus.

BOBIK, JULIE; Johnson City HS; Binghamton, NY; (Y); 25/190; Key Clb; Pep Clb; Band; Mrchg Band; Yrbk Stf; Rep Stu Cncl; VP L Cheerleading; Score Keeper; JV Var Socr; Hon Roll.

BOBIS, MELISSA; Clarkstown HS North; New City, NY; (Y); FBLA; Hosp Aide; Office Aide; Pep Clb; SADD; Teachers Aide; Temple Yth Grp; Yrbk Phtg; Lit Mag; Bus.

BOBO, JILL; John H Glenn HS; Greenlawn, NY; (Y); Rep Church Yth Grp; French Clb; Chorus; Jazz Band; Orch; School Musical; Rep Frsh Cls; Hon Roll; Band; Church Choir; Pres Mdrn Music Mstrs Dist Chap 86-87; Toured W/Lng Island Yth Orchstr Far E & Scandinavia; All ST 86; Prof French Hrn Plyr.

BOBO, TRACEY; Ramstein American HS; Apo, NY; (Y); 9/230; AFS; Camera Clb; Church Yth Grp; French Clb; German Clb; Natl Beta Clb; Chorus; School Musical; School Play; Rep Jr Cls; Schlrshp Assoc 86; CA ST; Frnch.

BOBO, WINFRED; John Dewey HS; Brooklyn, NY; (Y); Boys Clb Am; Boy Scts; Church Yth Grp; Band; Chorus; Church Choir; Concert Band; Drm & Bgl; Nwsp Phtg; Yrbk Phtg; Brauveh; Bus.

BOBROWSKI, LAURA; Union-Endicott HS; Endicott, NY; (Y); 3/437; Sec Church Yth Grp; Mathletes; SADD; Trs Band; Mrchg Band; School Musical; High Hon Roll; PA ST U; Math.

BOBURKA, JOHN; Seton Catholic Central HS; Endicott, NY; (Y); 10/162; Chess Clb; JV Bsktbl; Var Capt Ftbl; Var Tennis; High Hon Roll; NHS; Ntl Merit Ltr; Seton Schlr 84-85; Broome CC; Engrng.

BOCCIA, VINCENT; Oceanside HS; Oceanside, NY; (Y); #16 In Class; English Clb; French Clb; Var JV Bsbl; Im Bsktbl; JV Im Ftbl; Hon Roll; NHS; Ntl Merit Schol; Pres Schlr; Northeastern U; Engrng.

BOCI, TODD; Royalton-Hartland Central HS; Gasport, NY; (Y); French Clb; Varsity Clb; Stu Cncl; Var Crs Cntry; Capt Var Tennis; Hon Roll; Pres Schlr; NYS Rgnts Schlrshp 86; U Buffalo; Sprts Med.

BOCK, DUANE PHILIP; East Hampton HS; E Hampton, NY; (Y); Church Yth Grp; Spanish Clb; Band; Chorus; School Musical; Pres Frsh Cls; Var Bsktbl; Var Bowling; Var Capt Golf; Asst Sndy Schl Tchr; Hmptn Fstvl Prtcpnt; ST Qulfr Glf, Conf Chmpn, All Leag 85.

BOCKETTI, JOANNE M; Massapequa HS; Massapequa, NY; (Y); 8/440; Trs Spanish Clb; Mrchg Band; Yrbk Stf; Capt Gym; Capt Pom Pon; High Hon Roll; Jr NHS; NHS; Ntl Merit Ltr; Regnts Schlrshp 86; Rennselaer Polytechnic Inst.

BOCKLAGE, MICHAEL; Naples Central Schl; Naples, NY; (Y); 13/83; Var JV Bsbl; Var Socr; Var Vllybl; High Hon Roll; Hon Roll; NYS Rgnts Schlrshp; Prsdntl Acdmc Ftns Awd; Cornell U; Biolgy.

BODAH, MARK; Saranac Lake Central HS; Saranac Lk, NY; (Y); 3/114; Church Yth Grp; Chorus; Trs Frsh Cls; Hon Roll; Rgnts Schlrshp Outstndng SAT Or ACT 86; Saranac Lake Stu Assoc Schlrshp 86; Rcrdng Engr.

BODDIE, DANA; Morris HS; New York, NY; (Y); Camera Clb; Dance Clb; Drama Clb; Spanish Clb; Teachers Aide; School Play; Variety Show; Var Crs Cntry; Var Trk; Var Vllybl; Air Frc; Air Trffc Cntrllr.

BODE, JACQUELINE; St Francis Prep; Corona, NY; (Y); 131/695; JV Vllybl; Hon Roll; Fshn Inst Tech; Mrchndsr.

BODETTE, CAROL LYNN; St Marys Acad; South Glens Falls, NY; (S); 15/57; VP Church Yth Grp; Key Clb; Nwsp Stf; Var Bsktbl; Var Sftbl; Hon Roll; Ed.

BODNAR, LIZ; Washingtonville HS; Washingtonville, NY; (Y); Computer Clb; SADD; Chorus; Nwsp Stf; Var Bowling; JV Var Sftbl; Hon Roll; Mst Imprvd In Sftbl 84-85; Orng Cnty CC; Bus Adm.

BODNICK, MARC; Grand Island HS; Buffalo, NY; (Y); 1/310; Math Tm; Model UN; Political Wkr; Q&S; Quiz Bowl; Stu Cncl; Bausch & Lomb Sci Awd; Cit Awd; High Hon Roll; NHS; Century III Ldrshp Awd 86; Harvard Natl Schlr 86; Pres Schlr Fnlst 86; Harvard; Govt.

BODY, PATRICIA; North Tonawanda HS; N Tonawanda, NY; (Y); Girl Scts; Chorus; JV Var Trk; JV Vllybl; Hon Roll; Jr NHS; Frnch Cert Of Merit 84-85; Lawyer.

BODY, ROBIN; Manhasset HS; Manhasset, NY; (Y); Cmnty Wkr; Rep Frsh Cls; Rep Soph Cls; Rep Jr Cls; Rep Sr Cls; JV Var Fld Hcky; JV Var Lcrss; NHS.

BOEHLERT, CARL J; Vestal SR HS; Vestal, NY; (Y); 55/450; Am Leg Boys St; Boy Scts; Pres Church Yth Grp; French Clb; Varsity Clb; Bsbl; Var L Bsktbl; Var L Ftbl; Var L Trk; NHS.

BOEHM, CAROL; Northport HS; E Northport, NY; (Y); 205/572; Band; Drill Tm; Mrchg Band; Prfsnl Dncr.

BOEHM, KENNETH; Mc Quaid Jesuit HS; Rochester, NY; (Y); 2/165; Boy Scts; Ski Clb; Yrbk Sprt Ed; Ed Lit Mag; Sec Jr Cls; Var Crs Cntry; Var Trk; High Hon Roll; NHS; Prfct Atten Awd; Notre Dame Alum Clb Rochester-Stu Yr 86; Crs Cntry 1000 Mi Clb 85; Mst Imprvd Trck Awd 85; Duke U; Pre-Med Pgm.

BOEHM, KRISTIN A; Our Lady Of Mercy HS; Rochester, NY; (Y); 2/172; Church Yth Grp; Civic Clb; English Clb; Sec Trs Model UN; Science Clb; Service Clb; Ski Clb; Pep Band; Stage Crew; Nwsp Rptr; Amer Assoc Phys Tchrs Outstndng Stu; Amer HS Math Exam 2nd Pl; Schl Awds Ltn 1, 2 & 3; Math & Chem Awd; Bio.

BOEHMCKE, SUZANNE; Cold Spring Harbor HS; Huntington, NY; (Y); 58/140; Hosp Aide; Intnl Clb; Chorus; School Musical; Yrbk Stf; Var Lcrss; JV Socr; Hon Roll; 150 Hrs Awd Hntngtn Hosp 85; NYS Rngts Schlrshp 86; U Ov NC Greensboro; Nrsng.

BOERST, ROBIN; Jamestown HS; Jamestown, NY; (Y); Concert Band; Jazz Band; Mrchg Band; Orch; Symp Band; Nwsp Ed-Chief; Nwsp Rptr; NHS; Church Yth Grp; French Clb; Jrnlsm Schlrshp Bflo Evng Nws 86; Music Cmp Schlrshp SUNY Frdna 86; SUNY Fredonia; Educ.

BOETHCHER, WILLIAM; West Seneca East SR HS; W Eektowaga, NY; (Y); Bowling; Golf; Brdcstng.

BOFFEMMYER, DAWN; Walton Central HS; Walton, NY; (Y); #17 In Class; Church Yth Grp; Key Clb; Varsity Clb; Var L Cheerleading; Var L Tennis; High Hon Roll; Hon Roll; Voice Dem Awd; Pre Dent.

BOFILL, JOANNE; New Rochelle HS; New Rochelle, NY; (Y); Church Yth Grp; 4-H; Girl Scts; Chorus; Tennis; Hon Roll; Fashion Inst Tech; Fshn Merch.

BOGACZ, AMY; Hamburg SR HS; Hamburg, NY; (Y); Service Clb; Yrbk Stf; Var Cheerleading; Var Mgr(s); Var Score Keeper; Swmmng; Hon Roll; Bus Admin.

BOGACZYK, DAVID; Union-Endicott HS; Endicott, NY; (Y); Church Yth Grp; Key Clb; SADD; JV Crs Cntry; Hon Roll; NHS; Rotary Yth Ldrshp Awd 86; Engrng.

BOGARDUS, AMY; Schoharie Central HS; Schoharie, NY; (Y); 2/105; Key Clb; Varsity Clb; Chorus; Sec Frsh Cls; Sec Soph Cls; Sec Jr Cls; Capt Bowling; Socr; Hon Roll; Prfct Atten Awd; Outstndng Stu Awd Ofc Proc 86; Principles Awd Excell 86; Cableskill Ag Tech; Sec.

BOGART, KATRINA; Sodus Central HS; Sodus, NY; (Y); 66/115; French Clb; Model UN; VP Science Clb; Chorus; Yrbk Stf; Rptr Stu Cncl; High Hon Roll; Hon Roll; Prfct Atten Awd; Nyssma Awd 85; Gerontology.

BOGART, MARYANN; Salamanca HS; Salamanca, NY; (Y); 10/150; Trs French Clb; Ski Clb; Varsity Clb; Pres Jr Cls; Rep Stu Cncl; Var Swmmng; French Hon Soc; NHS; Spanish NHS; Languages.

BOGART, ROBERT; Bishop Timon HS; Buffalo, NY; (Y); 30/180; Chrmn Am Leg Boys St; Boys Clb Am; VP Church Yth Grp; Debate Tm; Drama Clb; Pres French Clb; Political Wkr; Lit Mag; Stu Cncl; Var Bsbl; Mayors Yth Achvt Awd 86; Exc Frnch Awd 86; Athletc Schlrshp 85; Law.

BOGARYAN, YEVA; Forest Hills HS; Forest Hills, NY; (Y); 80/829; Math Clb; Quiz Bowl; Science Clb; Y-Teens; High Hon Roll; Hon Roll; Jr NHS; NHS; Gldn Ayin Pin & Crtfct Exclnc 85; Awd Sci Achvmnt 83; Awd Math Achvmnt 83; Rgnts Schlrshp 86; Stoney Brook; Genetic Rsrch.

BOGER, KRISTINE; James Madison HS; Brooklyn, NY; (Y); 23/756; Chorus; Lit Mag; Im Tennis; Hon Roll; Sci Fair-1st Pl Schl Comptn 84; Brooklyn Coll; Bus Adm.

BOGGAN, KATHLEEN; Hamburg HS; Hamburg, NY; (Y); 3/400; Pres 4-H; Yrbk Ed-Chief; Lit Mag; High Hon Roll; NHS; Ntl Merit Ltr; Church Yth Grp; French Clb; Chorus; Yrbk Rptr; Hnbl Mntn Frnch Interpretive Rdng 86; Frgn Lang.

BOGOVICH, JOANNE; Long Island City HS; New York, NY; (Y); Aud/Vis; Church Yth Grp; Hosp Aide; Teachers Aide; Chorus; Tennis; French Hon Soc; Hon Roll; Jr NHS; Prfct Atten Awd; Astoria Civic Spring Bike Race 1st Pl Sr Women Ctgry 86; Mst Imprvd Plyr-Tennis 86; Pt Time Coop 86.

BOGUSLAVSKY, ALLA; John Dewey HS; Brooklyn, NY; (Y); Computer Clb; Dance Clb; Orch; School Play; Yrbk Stf; Im Bowling; Im Tennis; Hon Roll; Jr NHS; Pace U; Intl Bus.

BOHALL JR, JOHN; Weedsport JR SR HS; Weedsport, NY; (Y); 30/90; French Clb; Intnl Clb; Math Tm; Band; Var Capt Swmmng; SUNY Coll Oswego; Comp Sci.

BOHANAN, TODD; Liverpool HS; Liverpool, NY; (Y); 133/850; Boy Scts; Drm Mjr(t); Mrchg Band; Orch; Symp Band; Bsbl; Bsktbl; Hon Roll; Jr NHS; NHS; Best Drum Major 86; Rgnts Schlrshp 86; Onondaga CC; Sci Engr.

BOHAYETS, MELISSA; Auburn HS; Auburn, NY; (Y); Dance Clb; Pep Clb; High Hon Roll; Hon Roll; NHS; Chld Psych.

BOHLI, MARGARET; Bishop Ludden HS; Syracuse, NY; (S); JA; NFL; Speech Tm; Hon Roll; Soc Sci.

BOHLING, KEITH; Owego Free Acad; Owego, NY; (Y); Am Leg Boys St; Boy Scts; Computer Clb; VP German Clb; Stage Crew; High Hon Roll; NHS; Sharpshooter Rank Rifling 85; SUNY Binghampton; Engrng.

BOHLMAN, LAURA M; St Francis Prep; Flushing, NY; (S); JV Cheerleading; Im Sftbl; JV Swmmng; Im Vllybl; Opt Clb Awd; Law.

BOHMAN, KAREN; Mynderse Acad; Seneca Falls, NY; (Y); 31/135; French Clb; Chorus; Mrchg Band; School Musical; Yrbk Stf; Rep Stu Cncl; JV Var Trk; High Hon Roll; NHS; Cvl Engr.

BOHNER, ARLENE M; Sacred Heart Acad; Garden City, NY; (Y); 11/182; Church Yth Grp; Hosp Aide; School Musical; Nwsp Rptr; Trk; Hon Roll; VP Trs NHS; Ntl Merit Ltr; Garden City Intl Stu Exchange Stu Amb 85; VP Stu Cncl 85-86; Villanova U; Eng.

BOHON, KATIE; Northern Adirondack Ctrl; Churubusco, NY; (Y); Art Clb; Computer Clb; VP 4-H; Teachers Aide; Church Choir; Nwsp Stf; Yrbk Stf; Rep Stu Cncl; Var Score Keeper; JV Socr.

BOHON, LARA; Northern Adirondack Central HS; Churubusco, NY; (Y); 6/86; Computer Clb; Drama Clb; French Clb; Variety Show; Nwsp Ed-Chief; Yrbk Phtg; Rep Stu Cncl; High Hon Roll; NHS; Camera Clb; Nrth Cntry Schlr 86; St Lawrence U; Wrtng.

BOHOSIAN, CHARLES SCOTT; West Genesee HS; Syracuse, NY; (Y); Boys Clb Am; Chess Clb; Cmnty Wkr; Exploring; JV Ftbl; JV Trk; High Hon Roll; Hon Roll; SUNY Cortland; Psych.

BOICE, CHRISTINA; Margaretville Central HS; Margaretville, NY; (Y); Art Clb; French Clb; Science Clb; SADD; Yrbk Stf; Off Jr Cls; VP Sr Cls; JV Bsktbl; Var Socr; Var Sftbl; Trea Of Ntl Hnr Scty 86-87; Excllnce In Engl 10 Awd 85; Teach Sci.

BOICE, DON; Bishop Kearney HS; Rochester, NY; (Y); 9/170; Model UN; Varsity Clb; Var Capt Socr; Trk; DAR Awd; High Hon Roll; Pres NHS; Ntl Merit Ltr; Pres Schlr; SUNY Binghamton; Psych.

BOICE, DONALD L; Bishop Kearney HS; Rochester, NY; (Y); 9/141; Church Yth Grp; Model UN; Capt Socr; Capt Trk; Hon Roll; Pres NHS; Ntl Merit Schol; Pres Schlr; Psych.

BOICE, RANDY; Sherburne-Earlville HS; Norwich, NY; (Y); 5/169; Math Tm; Band; Mrchg Band; Rep Stu Cncl; Var L Bsbl; Var L Bsktbl; Stat Ftbl; High Hon Roll; NHS; Olympics Of The Mind Team 84; Ntl Hnr Scty 86; Civil Engr.

BOISE, KIMBERLEY; Marion JR SR HS; Marion, NY; (Y); 4-H; Quiz Bowl; Band; Concert Band; Jazz Band; Mrchg Band; 4-H Awd; Hon Roll; NHS; Pre-Med.

BOISE, MARGE; Shubune-Earlville Central HS; Smyrna, NY; (Y); Drama Clb; Sec 4-H; Trs Pres FFA; SADD; Cit Awd; 4-H Awd; Hon Roll; 4-H Ctznshp Awd 85; Hrdsmnshp 85; Ag Advstsng.

BOJAK, JANICE; Villa Maria Acad; Buffalo, NY; (Y); Computer Clb; Prfct Atten Awd; VFW Awd; Hghst Avg Art 84-85; SUNY Buffalo; Media.

BOKINZ, ROBERT; Riverhead HS; South Jamesport, NY; (Y); German Clb; Letterman Clb; Mathletes; Science Clb; Ski Clb; Varsity Clb; Band; Concert Band; Jazz Band; Mrchg Band; Germn Excllnc Awd; Vrsty Ltr Bsbl & Sccr; Acctg.

BOLAK, ELIZABETH; Auburn HS; Auburn, NY; (Y); 37/450; Drama Clb; Chorus; JV Fld Hcky; Var Vllybl; High Hon Roll; Hon Roll; Teaching.

BOLAND, MARIE S; Our Lady Of Lourdes HS; Poughkeepsie, NY; (Y); 39/191; Church Yth Grp; 4-H; Ski Clb; Church Choir; Nwsp Rptr; Yrbk Rptr; Var Bsktbl; Var Socr; Var Sftbl; Var Tennis; NYS Bkstbl Trny Fnlst 86; New Rochelle Acad Schlrshp; Fordham U; Bus Adm.

BOLAND, SHEILA; Our Lady Of Lourdes HS; Poughkeepsie, NY; (Y); 8/187; Nwsp Rptr; Nwsp Stf; JV Var Bsktbl; Var Socr; Var Tennis; NHS; Ntl Merit Ltr.

BOLANDER, KRYSTINE; John Jay HS; S Salem, NY; (Y); Church Yth Grp; French Clb; Hosp Aide; Intnl Clb; JCL; Latin Clb; Science Clb; Acpl Chr; Church Choir; Variety Show; Sprachdiplom I&II German Culture Ministry Exam 85&86.

BOLDEN, CHRISTOPHER S; Williamsville North HS; Williamsville, NY; (Y); 34/301; Art Clb; Church Yth Grp; VP JA; Trs Spanish Clb; Yrbk Stf; Lit Mag; Rep Stu Cncl; Var Ftbl; Capt Trk; High Hon Roll; 1st Pl Wstrn NY Pole Vault 85-86; Gldn Key Art Awd; U MI Ann Arbor; Aerospc Engr.

BOLDEN, PEGGY LEE; Salem HS; Salem, NY; (Y); 15/55; GAA; Math Tm; Yrbk Stf; Trs Sr Cls; JV Stat Bsktbl; Var L Crs Cntry; Score Keeper; Var L Trk; Hon Roll; Regents Nrsng Schlrshp 86; Air Force; Dntl Lab Tech.

BOLDEN JR, VERNIE; James E Sperry HS; Henderson, NC; (Y); 6/271; JV Bsbl; Var Crs Cntry; Var Trk; Hon Roll; NHS; Church Yth Grp; Rep Sr Cls; Pres Acad Fit Awd 86; Urbn Lg Rochester Blck Schlrs Awd 86; NYS Regents Scholar 86; UNC Greensboro; Art.

BOLDT, DIANE C; West Seneca West SR HS; W Seneca, NY; (Y); VP Church Yth Grp; French Clb; Office Aide; Hon Roll; NHS; Excllnc-Soc Stud 84.

BOLDT, LISA; W Seneca East SR HS; West Seneca, NY; (Y); Ski Clb; Yrbk Stf; Hon Roll; ST U Of NY Bflo; Comps.

BOLES, TAMMIE; Corinth Central HS; Corinth, NY; (S); 8/75; French Clb; Key Clb; Pep Clb; SADD; Yrbk Phtg; Yrbk Stf; Stat Trk; High Hon Roll; Hon Roll; Jr NHS; Stu Of Mnth Engl 85; SUNY Oneonta; Psychlgy.

BOLES, TAMMY; Gloversville HS; Gloversville, NY; (Y); VP Drama Clb; Library Aide; Chorus; School Musical; School Play; Stage Crew; Yrbk Stf; Sftbl; Hon Roll; Radio Communication.

BOLIVAR, AURA; Jane Addams VHS HS; Bronx, NY; (S); 13/266; Dance Clb; Drama Clb; Girl Scts; VICA; School Play; High Hon Roll; Hon Roll; NHS; Un Tchrs Fed Schlrshp 86-87; Dance.

BOLLHOFER, JEAN; Hicksville SR HS; Hicksville, NY; (Y); Spanish Clb; JV Sftbl; Var Trk; High Hon Roll; Hon Roll; NHS; Farmingdale.

BOLLINGER, DIEDRE D; Chatham Central HS; Canaan, NY; (Y); 9/125; Drama Clb; Latin Clb; Chorus; School Musical; Variety Show; Lit Mag; Stu Cncl; High Hon Roll; NHS; NYSSSA Schlrshp Wnnr 85; All ST Chr 85; Fine Arts.

BOLLMAN, LORI; Marcellus HS; Waterford, NY; (Y); #23 In Class; AFS; Debate Tm; Off Band; School Musical; School Play; Pres Jr Cls; Rep Stu Cncl; JV Capt Socr; Vllybl; NHS; AFS Schlrshp; U Schlrshp; Amrcn Lgn Schlrshp; Pace U; Poly Sci.

BOLOGH, GARY D; New Rochelle HS; New Rochelle, NY; (Y); 34/550; Hosp Aide; Math Tm; Var L Bsbl; Coach Actv; Var L Socr; Hon Roll; NHS; Ntl Merit Ltr; Pres Spanish NHS; NY ST Regnts Schlrshp 86; Duke U.

BOLOGNESE, PATRICK J; West Seneca West SR HS; West Seneca, NY; (Y); Chess Clb; DECA; Red Cross Aide; JV Ftbl; JV Ice Hcky; Rgnts Schrshp 86; Canisius Coll; Fnc.

BOLTON, AMY L; Oneida HS; Oneida, NY; (Y); 40/200; Church Yth Grp; Cmnty Wkr; Exploring; French Clb; Chorus; High Hon Roll; Hon Roll; NYS Regents Scholar 86; Utica Coll Syracuse U; Psych.

BOLTON, MIKA; Hutch Tech; Buffalo, NY; (Y); Dance Clb; Library Aide; Drill Tm; Cit Awd; Hon Roll; Roy Wilkins Schlrshp 83; Acctg.

BOLTZ, ANN; South Park HS; Buffalo, NY; (Y); Girl Scts; Hosp Aide; Office Aide; Teachers Aide; Band; Concert Band; Mrchg Band; Orch; Prfct Atten Awd; Girl Scout Silver Awd 85; Modeling Schl-John Robert Powers 84; Beach Boys Chrldr 85; Jewelry Clerk 84; Bus Mgt.

BOLTZ, CATHERINE L; Hamberg SR HS; Hamburg, NY; (Y); 32/374; Cmnty Wkr; German Clb; Service Clb; SADD; Orch; School Musical; Var Tennis; Hon Roll; NHS; Engrng.

BOLUSI, MARIA; Tottenville HS; Staten Island, NY; (Y); Science Clb; Trs SADD; Band; Capt Drm Mjr(t); VP Stu Cncl; Hon Roll; NHS; Ski Clb; Mrchg Band; Psychiatrist.

BOMBARD, DAVID; Franklin Acad; Constable, NY; (Y); Altr Boy; Epsilon; Alfred ST; Auto Rprmn.

BOMMARAJU, UMA; Grand Island HS; Gr Island, NY; (Y); French Clb; GAA; JA; Varsity Clb; L Gym; Hon Roll; U Buffalo; Law.

BONACCIO, CECILIA; Nazareth Acad; Rochester, NY; (Y); 1/158; Latin Clb; Library Aide; Math Clb; Ed Nwsp Stf; Ed Yrbk Stf; Tennis; High Hon Roll; Hon Roll; Pres NHS; Pres Schlr; Engl Awd At Grad For Top Stu 86; Italian Aws At Grad For Top Stu 86; Silver Med Natl Latin Exam 83; U Of Rochester; Jrnlsm.

BONAFEDE, CHRISTOPHER N; Canisius HS; Buffalo, NY; (Y); 22/167; Ski Clb; School Play; High Hon Roll; Hon Roll; Mu Alp Tht; NHS; Ntl Merit Ltr; Spanish NHS; Full Insignis Schlrshp To U Of O 86; NY St Regents Schlrshp 86; U Of Detroit; Mech Engrng.

BONAGURA, THUY; New Paltz HS; Gardiner, NY; (Y); 57/176; Var Bsktbl; Var Sftbl; Var Vllybl; High Hon Roll; Athltc Trng.

BONANNO, MITCHELL J; St Francis Prep; Hollis Hills, NY; (S); 116/653; Church Yth Grp; Cmnty Wkr; Wt Lftg; Hon Roll; NHS; Cptn St Frncs Judo Tm 85-86; Rgnts Schlrshp 86; Elctrl Engr.

BONANNO, VINCENT J; Regis HS; New York, NY; (Y); Mgr Band; Yrbk Phtg; Lit Mag; Im Bowling; Im Wt Lftg; Im Wrstlng; NY ST Regnts Schlrshp 85-86; VASSAR; Engl.

BONAPARTE, LETICIA; Babylon JR SR HS; W Babylon, NY; (Y); Dance Clb; Spanish Clb; JV Mgr(s); Hon Roll; NEDT Awd; Venettes Cultural Wrkshp Voice,Charm Most Imprvd 85; Comm.

BONARRIGO, NICHOLAS; Frankfort-Schuyler Central HS; Frankfort, NY; (S); 2/100; Trs FBLA; Pres Key Clb; Pres Varsity Clb; Nwsp Sprt Ed; Yrbk Sprt Ed; VP Soph Cls; Var Capt Bsktbl; Tennis; Cit Awd; NHS; Natl Math Awd 84; Boys ST-HLD 3 Offcs 85; Key Clb Spirit Awd & 3rd Pl Key Clb Convtn Ten Trnmnt 85; Bus Adm.

BONASIA, DOLORES; Sewanhaka HS; Elmont, NY; (Y); 92/344; Intnl Clb; SADD; Variety Show; Rep Stu Cncl; JV Sftbl; Hon Roll.

BONASIA, ROBERT J; Carle Place HS; Westbury, NY; (Y); 7/118; Chorus; Var Frsh Cls; Var Capt Bsktbl; Var JV Ftbl; Hon Roll; NHS; Ntl Merit Ltr; Verbal Sklls Awd 85; Bucknell; Engr.

BONAVIA, JENNIFER; Groton Central Schl; Groton, NY; (Y); Ski Clb; Band; Sec Soph Cls; Rep VP Stu Cncl; Socr; Trk; Cit Awd; Hon Roll; NHS; Pre-Law.

BONCARO, DAVID; Colonie Central HS; Albany, NY; (Y); 19/475; Aud/Vis; Camera Clb; Drama Clb; High Hon Roll; NHS; Prfct Atten Awd; Pres Schlr; Patrick Angerame Schlrshp 86; Prncpl Prz 86; Nick Costello Meml Awd 86; Hudson Valley CC; Elec Engrng.

BONCI, MICHELLE; Brewster HS; Brewster, NY; (Y); Cert-Geomtry 86; Cert-Drwng & Pntng I 85; Bus Mngmt.

BOND, JOHN; Iona Prep; Mt Vernon, NY; (Y); 18/207; Dance Clb; Teachers Aide; JV Bowling; High Hon Roll; Bus.

BOND, KENNETH; Kenmore East HS; Tonwanda, NY; (Y); Drama Clb; PAVAS; School Musical; School Play; VP Swing Chorus; Yrbk Bus Mgr; JV Wrstlng; High Hon Roll; NHS; Ldrshp Awd 86; Fnlst Washington Wrkshp Prg; NYS Music Assc Voice Rtng 97 86; Poli Sci.

BOND, SUZANNE; Owen D Young HS; Jordanville, NY; (S); 5/23; Q&S; Concert Band; Swing Chorus; Nwsp Ed-Chief; Yrbk Stf; Rep Stu Cncl; Cit Awd; Jr NHS; NHS; Area All St Music Festvl 85; Achvmnt Acad 84; Music.

BOND JR, WILLIAM; Mc Quaid Jesuit HS; Pittsford, NY; (Y); Boy Scts; Church Yth Grp; Computer Clb; French Clb; Ski Clb; Yrbk Stf; JV Bsbl; JV Trk; High Hon Roll; Hon Roll; Elec Engrng.

BONDANZA, DALE; West Seneca West SR HS; W Seneca, NY; (Y); 90/511; Aud/Vis; Computer Clb; Im Tennis; Im Vllybl; Hon Roll; Prfct Atten Awd; FL Inst Tech; Cmptr Sci.

BONDOLILLO, JANALEE; Indian River Central HS; Watertown, NY; (Y); Church Yth Grp; Latin Clb; Ski Clb; Band; Chorus; School Musical; Cheerleading; Gym; Score Keeper; Socr; Bus Admn.

BONELLI, CARMEN; Le Roy Central HS; Leroy, NY; (Y); Hon Roll; Sec.

BONELLO, JEANINE; Sachem H S North; Holbrook, NY; (Y); 87/1579; Girl Scts; Intnl Clb; Service Clb; Chorus; Jr NHS; NHS; 2nd Pl Sci Congress 85; Acctnt.

BONENBERGER, KEVIN; Salamanca Central HS; Salamanca, NY; (Y); 15/150; Concert Band; JV Capt Bsktbl; L Trk; Hon Roll; NHS; Spanish NHS; NC ST U.

BONESTEEL, KIMBERLY; Watervliet HS; Watervliet, NY; (Y); FHA; GAA; Pres Key Clb; Spanish Clb; VP Varsity Clb; Rep Stu Cncl; Var Capt Bsktbl; Var Capt Socr; Var Capt Sftbl; High Hon Roll; Bst Offnsv Sccr Plyr 85; Bst Def Bsktbl Plyr 84-85; Rookie Yr 83.

BONETTI III, ANTHONY; Marion HS; Marion, NY; (Y); 15/96; Am Leg Boys St; Ski Clb; Var Bsbl; Elctd Snt At Boys ST 86; Brdcstng.

BONFIGLIO, MARYANN; St Barnabas HS; Bronx, NY; (S); 14/188; Camera Clb; Church Yth Grp; French Clb; Library Aide; Science Clb; Church Choir; Nwsp Stf; French Hon Soc; High Hon Roll; NHS; Coll Mt St Vincent; Bio.

BONGHI, JOHNNA; Niagara Catholic HS; Youngstown, NY; (Y); French Clb; Var Bsktbl; Var JV Cheerleading; Var Tennis; NHS; Hlth.

BONHOTE, CLAUDIA; Argyle Central HS; Argyle, NY; (Y); Sec 4-H; Sec French Clb; Band; Chorus; Jazz Band; Sec Frsh Cls; Sec Soph Cls; Sec Jr Cls; Stu Cncl; Fld Hcky; Bio.

BONICI, PAULETTE; Curtis HS; Staten Island, NY; (Y); Cmnty Wkr; Dance Clb; Girl Scts; Office Aide; Ski Clb; SADD; Cheerleading; St Johns U; Bus Admn.

BONILLA, MARINA; Great Neck South SR HS; New Hyde Park, NY; (Y); Hspnc Stu Hlpng Awd 85; Bst Crmcs Stu Awd 82; Bst Stu Soc Studys Awd 83; Nassau CC.

BONILLA JR, RENE; Eastern District HS; Brooklyn, NY; (Y); Chess Clb; Church Yth Grp; Cmnty Wkr; Math Clb; Math Tm; Nwsp Rptr; Yrbk Stf; Lit Mag; Crs Cntry; Trk; 1st Pl Ctywide Coll Bnd Essy Cont 85; Hnr Soc Arista 84-86; Jrnlst.

BONILLA, ROSELYN; Newtown HS; Elmhurst, NY; (Y); 7/781; Key Clb; Math Tm; Office Aide; Teachers Aide; Band; Orch; Symp Band; Yrbk Stf; High Hon Roll; Hon Roll; Arista Hnr Soc 85; Super Yth Hnr 85-86; Spcl Dist Attorney Awd 84; Med.

BONINO, RENEE; Tottenville HS; Staten Isld, NY; (Y); Dance Clb; Brkdl CC; Mrkt Mngmnt.

BONK, RONALD; Cicero-North Syracuse HS; Clay, NY; (S); 44/700; Boy Scts; JV Ftbl; Hon Roll; Merit Rll; Lwyr.

BONNER, BARBARA; Tioga Central HS; Candor, NY; (S); 9/90; Variety Show; Nwsp Rptr; Nwsp Stf; Yrbk Stf; High Hon Roll; NHS; Prfct Atten Awd; Broome CC; Acctng.

BONNER, MIKE; Jamestown HS; Jamestown, NY; (Y); Church Yth Grp; Intnl Clb; Latin Clb; Pep Clb; Political Wkr; Ski Clb; Spanish Clb; Chorus; Rep Frsh Cls; Rep Soph Cls; Intl Bus.

BONNETT, CARA; Fairport HS; Fairport, NY; (Y); 9/605; Model UN; Band; School Play; Nwsp Ed-Chief; Nwsp Rptr; Yrbk Stf; Lit Mag; High Hon Roll; NHS; Spanish NHS; Cntrl Wstrn Sctn STANYS Sci Cngrss Hnrs 85; Ntl Hstry & Govt Awd Wnnr 84; Jrnlsm.

BONNEY, LISA; Minisink Valley HS; Pt Jervis, NY; (Y); Trs Key Clb; Sec Spanish Clb; Var Socr; High Hon Roll; Hon Roll; NHS; Cmnty Svc Awd Lukemia Type-A-Thon 85; Peace Corps.

BONO, ELISA; Bethpage HS; Bethpage, NY; (Y); 37/306; Hst FBLA; Spanish Clb; Chorus; Rep Jr Cls; Hon Roll; Jr NHS; SUNY Stonybrook; Med.

BONOMO, ELENA; St Francis Prep; Flushing, NY; (S); 96/750; Art Clb; Cmnty Wkr; Ski Clb; SADD; Yrbk Stf; JV Twrlr; Im Vllybl; High Hon Roll; Hon Roll; NHS; St Johns U; Bus.

BONVENTRE, ERIC; Clarkstown North HS; Congers, NY; (Y); Cmnty Wkr; Hosp Aide; Hon Roll; Mu Alp Tht; Italian Clb; Pre Med.

BOOHER, MARIA; Waltwhitman HS; Hunt Sta, NY; (Y); Dance Clb; Girl Scts; Band; Chorus; Mrchg Band; School Play; Cheerleading; Gym; Mgr(s); Score Keeper; Hghst Avg Spn Awd 83; Dance.

BOOKHART, TRACEY; Avon JR SR HS; Avon, NY; (Y); Cheerleading; Coach Actv; Score Keeper; Trk; Outstndg Acdmc Achvmnt Furture Black Schlrs 85-86; Bus Mgt.

BOOKLESS, CHRISTINA; Cornwall Central HS; Cornwall, NY; (Y); Library Aide; Ski Clb; Teachers Aide; Rep Frsh Cls; Powder Puff Ftbl; Sftbl; High Hon Roll; Hon Roll; Prfct Atten Awd; Med.

BOOKMILLER, DEBBIE; Pioneer Central HS; N Java, NY; (Y); 21/250; Latin Clb; School Musical; School Play; Sec Sr Cls; Var Sftbl; Hon Roll; Engl Educ.

BOONE, DARLENE N; Midwood HS; Brooklyn, NY; (Y); 45/556; Library Aide; Math Tm; Office Aide; Cit Awd; Hon Roll; Prfct Atten Awd; Regents Schlrshp 86; Arista 83-85; Archon 83; Brooklyn Coll; Med.

BOONE, ELIZABETH P G; Smithtown H S East; Saint James, NY; (Y); 25/550; Thesps; Chorus; Stage Crew; Off Frsh Cls; Off Soph Cls; Off Jr Cls; Stat Lcrss; Hon Roll; NHS; Med.

BOONE, JANICE L; Emmanuel Baptist Acad; Prattsburg, NY; (Y); 1/8; Church Yth Grp; Chorus; Church Choir; School Play; Yrbk Ed-Chief; Yrbk Stf; Cheerleading; Socr; Vllybl; Hon Roll; Frndshp Awd 86; Mst Lkly Succeed 86; Chrstn Ldrshp 86; Bob Jones U; Elem Educ.

BOONE, MELISSA; Bishop Grimes HS; Manlius, NY; (S); 5/166; Church Yth Grp; Service Clb; SADD; Chorus; Church Choir; School Play; Yrbk Stf; High Hon Roll; Natl Womns Hall Of Fame Essay Contst-2nd Prz 85; Sci.

BOOS, CAROLE; Our Lady Of Mercy HS; Honeoye Falls, NY; (Y); Church Yth Grp; JA; Rep Stu Cncl; JV Var Socr; Stat Vllybl; High Hon Roll; Ntl Merit Ltr; Yth & Govt Clb; Amer Chem Soc Achvt Awd; 1st & 2nd Yr Mth Hnrs, Engl, Chem, Earth Sci, Afro Asian Awds; Bus.

BOOTH, MARSHA; Brockport HS; Brockport, NY; (Y); Drama Clb; Ski Clb; Concert Band; Mrchg Band; School Musical; School Play; Yrbk Stf; Trk; High Hon Roll; NHS; Sprng Trck-Mst Imprvd Awd 85; Band-Outstndng Imprvmnt Awds 84-85; Frnch Cert For Outstndng Achvt 85.

BOOTHBY, LAURA; Newfield HS; Coram, NY; (Y); Girl Scts; Acpl Chr; Band; Chorus; Concert Band; Mrchg Band; School Musical; Stu Cncl; Jr NHS; Spanish NHS; Music.

BOOTHE, ANN MARIE; Evander Childs HS; Bronx, NY; (S); Church Yth Grp; Office Aide; Swmmng; Hon Roll; Prfct Atten Awd; Daily Rebels Pride Of The Yankees 85; Accntnt.

BOOTHE, LISA; Andrew Jackson HS; St Albans, NY; (Y); 2/400; Church Yth Grp; Chorus; Church Choir; Sec Sr Cls; Cheerleading; Bausch & Lomb Sci Awd; High Hon Roll; Sal; Alpha Kappa Alpha Schlrshp 86; Stony Brook U; Physicians Asst.

BOOTHE, STEPHEN; Salamanca Central HS; Salamanca, NY; (Y); 6/138; Am Leg Boys St; Church Yth Grp; French Clb; Stat Bsktbl; JV Var Trk; French Hon Soc; High Hon Roll; NHS; Ntl Merit Ltr.

BOOZE, DAVID; Hutch Tech; Buffalo, NY; (Y); Drama Clb; School Play; Stage Crew; RIT; Mech Engnrng.

BORDEAU, JOANNE; Coxsackie-Athens Central HS; Coxsackie, NY; (Y); Pres German Clb; Band; Chorus; Yrbk Stf; Var Co-Capt Cheerleading; Rep Frsh Cls; Rep Soph Cls; Rep Jr Cls; Rep Sr Cls; Rep Stu Cncl; Marist Coll-Poughkeepsie; Comm.

BORDEN, VIRGINIA; Kenmore East S HS; Tonawanda, NY; (Y); 3/330; Drama Clb; PAVAS; Pres Service Clb; Band; Color Guard; Concert Band; Mrchg Band; School Musical; School Play; Nwsp Stf; Joseph C Wilson,Alumni Mem Schlrshp 86; Empire ST Schlrshp Exc 86; U Rochester; Bio.

BORDONARO, JACQUIE; Mineola HS; Mineola, NY; (Y); Church Yth Grp; FTA; Key Clb; Spanish Clb; SADD; Chorus; School Musical; Nwsp Stf; Yrbk Stf; VP Frsh Cls; Nassau CC; Ed.

BOREALI, LAWRENCE F; Cobleskill Central HS; Howes Cave, NY; (Y); 7/116; Boy Scts; VP Varsity Clb; Band; Chorus; Mrchg Band; Stu Cncl; Capt Bsbl; Capt Bsktbl; Capt Ftbl; High Hon Roll; Boys ST 85; U Of VT; Elec Engrng.

BORELLA, ANNAMARIE; Sachem HS; Lk Ronkonkoma, NY; (Y); 312/1370; Boy Scts; Drama Clb; Exploring; Ski Clb; Spanish Clb; Chorus; Madrigals; School Musical; School Play; Stage Crew; Suffolk Cnty CC; Vet Med.

BORER, ROBERT; Portville Central Schl; Portville, NY; (Y); AFS; Church Yth Grp; Mgr Ski Clb; Trs Stu Cncl; JV Bsktbl; Var Trk; High Hon Roll; Hon Roll; NHS; Mgr Coach Actv; Med.

BORGES, LUCY; St Catharine Acad; Bronx, NY; (Y); 37/185; Church Yth Grp; Pres GAA; Office Aide; School Play; Rep Frsh Cls; Swmmng; Trk; NHS; Prfct Atten Awd; Eng 10 85; Achvts Music 85; Excllnc NYS Physcl Ftnss Tst 86; Law.

BORGESANO, THERESA; Saint John The Baptist HS; Lindenhurst, NY; (Y); Church Yth Grp; SADD; Concert Band; Pres Frsh Cls; Rep Soph Cls; Ntl Sci Olympiad Bio 85; Pres Physcl Ftns Awd 83; St John Baptist Awd Achvt Bio 85; St Johns U; Bio.

BORGESE, ANTONINO; Hutchinson Central Technical HS; Buffalo, NY; (Y); Im Capt Socr; Hon Roll; Archtctr.

BORGIA, DAWN; St Marys Girls HS; Williston Pk, NY; (Y); #28 In Class; Cmnty Wkr; L Sftbl; Im Vllybl; Hon Roll; NHS; Med.

BORGOS, WILLIAM M; Queensbury HS; Glens Falls, NY; (Y); 1/260; Am Leg Boys St; Debate Tm; Quiz Bowl; Var Capt Crs Cntry; Var L Trk; Bausch & Lomb Sci Awd; High Hon Roll; NHS; Ntl Merit SF; Val; Intl Sprts Exchng Trp-Kenya 85-86; RPI Math & Sci Medal 86; Engrng.

BORIS, SUSAN L; Holland Patent Central Schl; Stittville, NY; (Y); 21/146; Band; Drm & Bgl; Jazz Band; School Play; JV Var Bsktbl; Var L Fld Hcky; High Hon Roll; NHS; Hnr Ltr Pin 83-84; Regents Schlrshp 86; Stu Cncl Recgntn Pin 85; Mohawk Valley CC; Mech Engr.

BORISOFF, MINDY; Scarsdale HS; Scarsdale, NY; (Y); Cmnty Wkr; Office Aide; Pep Clb; Service Clb; Spanish Clb; SADD; Teachers Aide; Chrmn Temple Yth Grp; Varsity Clb; Drill Tm; PTA Svc Awd-Stu Aide 86; PTA Svc Awd-Chldrns Vlg 86; Psych.

BORJA-GORRE, JESSICA; Half Hollow Hills HS East; Dix Hills, NY; (Y); Cmnty Wkr; Dance Clb; Intnl Clb; Red Cross Aide; Service Clb; Nwsp Rptr; French Hon Soc; High Hon Roll; Jr NHS; NHS; Art Dept Awd 84; French Studies.

BORJAS, ASTOR; Cardinal Hayes HS; Bronx, NY; (Y); Camera Clb; Dance Clb; Stage Crew; Socr.

BORKHOLDER, DAVID; Kendall Jr Sr HS; Hamlin, NY; (S); 5/92; AFS; Trs Drama Clb; Model UN; Ski Clb; School Musical; School Play; Stage Crew; VP Stu Cncl; High Hon Roll; Jr NHS; Engrng.

BORLAND, DAVID; Lake Placid Central HS; Lake Placid, NY; (Y); Boy Scts; Cmnty Wkr; Key Clb; Ski Clb; Varsity Clb; Var L Bsktbl; Var Capt Socr; Var L Trk; High Hon Roll; Hon Roll; Life Scout Ordr Of Arrw 86.

BORNKESSEL, SCOTT C; Westhill SR HS; Syracuse, NY; (Y); 30/150; Exploring; Band; Jazz Band; Symp Band; Hon Roll; NHS; NEDT Awd; Stat Bsktbl; JV Computer Clb; Var Tennis; Pres-Jazz Ensmbl; Fnanc.

BORNSTEIN, BRIDGETTE; Jamesville De Witt HS; Dewitt, NY; (Y); Pres Model UN; Ski Clb; Chorus; School Musical; Swing Chorus; Nwsp Bus Mgr; JV Vllybl; High Hon Roll; Political Wkr; Madrigals; Ldrshp Awd 85; Svc Awd 86; Superor Rtng For Piano In Music Fest 84; Pol Sci.

BORNSTEIN, JOANNE; Jamesville Dewitt HS; Dewitt, NY; (Y); 17/245; Latin Clb; Math Tm; Pres Pep Clb; SADD; Temple Yth Grp; Orch; Nwsp Stf; High Hon Roll; NHS; Rotary Awd; Svc Awd 86; Ldrshp Awd 86; Union Coll; Bio.

BORONCZYK, JOSEPH; Fowler HS; Syracuse, NY; (Y); Boys Clb Am; Pep Clb; SADD; Yrbk Stf; JV Var Bsktbl; Coach Actv; JV Crs Cntry; JV Var Tennis; NHS; Sprtndnt Cbnt 85-86; Geneseo Sst; Scndry Educ.

BORRELLI, TONI A; Preston HS; Bronx, NY; (S); Computer Clb; Teachers Aide; Sftbl; Hon Roll; Jr NHS; NHS; NEDT Awd; Pdtrcn.

BORRERO, ARLENE; Cardinal Spellman HS; Yonkers, NY; (Y); Spanish Clb; Trstee Schlrshp Pace U 86; 1st Hnrs 86; Pace U; Mgmt Info Systms.

BORRERO, DENIRA; Moore Catholic HS; Staten Island, NY; (Y); 40/180; Sec Art Clb; Math Clb; Sec Frsh Cls; Sec Soph Cls; VP Jr Cls; Pres Sr Cls; Stu Cncl; Bowling; Acad All-Amer 85; Regents Schlrshp 86; Brighamton SUNY.

BORSKY, THEODORE E; Christian Brothers Acad; Syracuse, NY; (Y); Cmnty Wkr; VP JA; SADD; VP Temple Yth Grp; Var Ftbl; Hon Roll; Law.

BORUCH, MICHAEL; Port Chester SR HS; Port Chester, NY; (Y); Trs Spanish Clb; Band; Rep Jr Cls; Var L Bsbl; Var L Bsktbl; High Hon Roll; NHS; Spanish NHS; SADD; Engrng Mdl Excel Math, Sci 86; Bus.

BORZELLO, JEANNINE; East Islip HS; East Islip, NY; (Y); 32/425; Chorus; Mrchg Band; Orch; School Musical; Yrbk Ed-Chief; Lit Mag; Capt Pom Pon; Jr NHS; NHS; NY ST Regents Schlrshp 86; Long Isl Tchrs Bnvlnt Assoc Schlrshp 86; Freeport Tchrs Assoc Schlrshp 86; Rchstr Inst Tchnlgy; Grphc Dsgn.

BOSA, SANDRA IRIS; St Pius V HS; Bronx, NY; (Y); English Clb; Chorus; Nwsp Stf; Sftbl; Hon Roll; Socl Wrkr.

BOSCHEN, RACHEL; Acad Of Mt St Ursula; Bronx, NY; (Y); Camera Clb; Church Yth Grp; Computer Clb; Chorus; Church Choir; Yrbk Stf; Hon Roll; US Cngrsmn Otstndng Achvt 86; Ust Pl Wnnr; Fshn Dsgn.

BOSCO, LISA; Solvay HS; Solvay, NY; (Y); Chorus; School Musical; School Play; Variety Show; Off Jr Cls; High Hon Roll; Hon Roll; Awd-3 Yrs Of Chrs 86; 2 Musicls That Ernd 1st Pl Awds 84 & 85; Gradtd-Brbzn Mdlng Schl Of Syracuse 83; UCLA; Profsnl Singer.

BOSCO, LISA; V S Central HS; Valley Stream, NY; (Y); Dance Clb; FBLA; Mathletes; Chorus; Socr; Swmmng; Hon Roll; Dancing Awd 85-86; Hofstra; Lawyer.

BOSER, LINDA; A G Berner HS; Massapequa, NY; (Y); German Clb; Intnl Clb; Key Clb; SADD; Teachers Aide; Chorus; Orch; Variety Show; Yrbk Stf; JV Vllybl; Accntng.

BOSIACKI, MICHAEL; Frontier Central HS; Hamburg, NY; (Y); Intnl Clb; Library Aide; Hon Roll; NHS; Prfct Atten Awd; Syracuse U; Arch.

BOSNO, THEODORE; Bradford Central HS; Bradford, NY; (Y); 3/27; Aud/Vis; FBLA; Ski Clb; Band; Chorus; Jazz Band; Mrchg Band; Yrbk Sprt Ed; Rep Frsh Cls; Rep Soph Cls; Ntl Sci Merit Awd 84 & 85; Cnmtgrphy.

BOSS, DENISE; Gowanda Central HS; Collins, NY; (Y); 7/128; Spanish Clb; Sec SADD; Color Guard; Drm Mjr(t); Cheerleading; Score Keeper; Hon Roll; NHS; Prfct Atten Awd; SUNY Geneseo; Math.

BOSSARD, WENDY; Canisteo Central HS; Canisteo, NY; (Y); 14/70; FBLA; Office Aide; Chorus; Yrbk Stf; VP Cheerleading; Stat Sftbl; Cit Awd; Hon Roll; Bus.

BOSSI, DENISE R; Cheektowaga Central HS; Cheektowaga, NY; (Y); 28/199; Latin Clb; Trs Ski Clb; Stage Crew; Yrbk Ed-Chief; Stu Cncl; Co-Capt Fld Hcky; Sftbl; Vllybl; Hon Roll; Rensselaer Polytech Inst Math & Sci Medl 85; SUNY Buffalo.

BOSSUNG, TEAL; Cold Spring Harbor HS; Huntington, NY; (Y); Art Clb; Church Yth Grp; English Clb; Girl Scts; Intnl Clb; Library Aide; Yrbk Stf; JV Bsktbl; JV Socr; Hon Roll; Abstract Art Awd-NY ST 86; Fine Arts.

BOSSY, STEPHEN A; Dwight HS; New York, NY; (Y); Aud/Vis; Stage Crew; Yrbk Phtg; Hon Roll; Regnts Schlrshp 86; Rensselaer Polytech Inst.

BOSTIC, LINDA; Lindenhurst HS; Lindenhurst, NY; (Y); German Clb; Sec Ski Clb; Varsity Clb; Yrbk Phtg; Yrbk Stf; Var L Tennis; JV L Vllybl; Hon Roll; Jr NHS; VP NHS; Mst Imprvd In Vlybl 85; Bst Skier Awd 86.

BOSTON, DIONNE; Erasmus Hall HS; Brooklyn, NY; (Y); 82/687; FBLA; Office Aide; Band; Hon Roll; Long Island U; Sys Anlyst.

BOSTON, ORAL W; Harry S Truman HS; Bronx, NY; (Y); 18/400; Aud/Vis; Library Aide; Church Choir; Yrbk Stf; Lit Mag; Var Bowling; Var Crs Cntry; Var Trk; NHS; Engrg.

BOSWELL, ORVILLE; Allhallows Inst; New York, NY; (Y); Bsktbl; Hon Roll; Comp Engrg.

BOTAITIS, BRENDA; Amsterdam HS; Amsterdam, NY; (Y); 4/350; Am Leg Aux Girls St; Church Yth Grp; Band; Concert Band; Capt Drm Mjr(t); JV Bsktbl; Hon Roll; NHS; Lib Arts.

BOTHWELL, ADRIANNE; Uniondale HS; Uniondale, NY; (Y); French Clb; Sec Key Clb; Nwsp Rptr; Nwsp Stf; Yrbk Phtg; JV Bsktbl; High Hon Roll; Hon Roll; Jr NHS; Gyn.

BOTINDARI, MARY JO; East Syracuse Minoa HS; E Syracuse, NY; (Y); Camera Clb; Church Yth Grp; Yrbk Phtg; Yrbk Stf; Im Vllybl; Hon Roll; Nova U; Psychlgy.

BOTKIN, NAOMI; Huntington HS; Huntington, NY; (Y); Mathletes; SADD; Mrchg Band; VP Orch; Symp Band; Ntl Merit Ltr; Voice Dem Awd; Chorus; Pep Band; School Musical; Mst Outstndng Plyr Awd Band; 4th Cnty Math; 1st Cnty Math.

BOTSCHAGOW, ALEX; Archbishop Molloy HS; Richmond Hill, NY; (Y); 191/383; Off Church Yth Grp; Nwsp Rptr; Im Stat Bsktbl; Im Bowling; Im Stat Ftbl; Im Score Keeper; Im Stat Sftbl; Im Timer; 1st Pl Bwlng Intmrls 85; Rutgers U; Chmcl Engrng.

BOTT, KRISTEN; St John The Baptist HS; Amityville, NY; (Y); Church Yth Grp; Drama Clb; SADD; Nwsp Rptr; Rep Stu Cncl; Swmmng; Educ.

BOTT, MARCELLA; St Barnabas HS; Bronx, NY; (S); 21/188; Pres French Clb; Office Aide; Service Clb; Rep Soph Cls; Rep Stu Cncl; Im Swmmng; Pres French Hon Soc; Hon Roll; NHS; NATL Sci Olympd; Schl Svc Awd.

BOTTI, JAMES J; John Jay HS; Goldens Bridge, NY; (Y); Nwsp Ed-Chief; JV Stat Bsbl; Bsktbl; Coach Actv; Capt Var Crs Cntry; Mgr(s); Var Trk; Cit Awd; Sportsmnshp Awd Cross Cty 84; Most Imprvd Plyr Cross Cty 85; Jrnlsm.

BOTTITTA, GRACE E; Bayport-Blue Point HS; Blue Point, NY; (Y); 14/198; Church Yth Grp; Key Clb; Chorus; School Musical; Yrbk Stf; VP Sr Cls; Capt Var Vllybl; Kiwanis Awd; NHS; Mathletes; Rgnts Schlrshp 86; Kickline Capt 82-86; Ecology Clb 83-84; Vet Med.

BOTTKE, IRENE; Westhampton Beach HS; Westhampton, NY; (Y); 4/210; Computer Clb; French Clb; Hst Latin Clb; Library Aide; Hon Roll; NHS; East End Schlrshp 86; Hgst Avg Math 86; Russian Cls; Southampton Coll; Math.

BOUBOULIS, EVE; Oneonta HS; Maryland, NY; (Y); 20/175; Art Clb; Ski Clb; Spanish Clb; Band; Chorus; Bsktbl; Socr; Sftbl; Trk; Elks Awd; Smith Schlrshp 86; All Cnfrnce All Str Frst Tm 85; All Cnfrnc 82-84; Adelphi U; Arts & Sci.

BOUCHARD, DEBORAH J; John Marshall HS; Rochester, NY; (Y); 1/158; Math Tm; Band; Yrbk Ed-Chief; Socr; Bausch & Lomb Sci Awd; High Hon Roll; NHS; Val; Church Yth Grp; Cmnty Wkr; Rochester Engrg Soc Schlrshp 86; NY ST Regnts Schlrshp 86; Natl Merit Schlrshp Commnd Stu 86; MIT; Elec Engrng.

BOUCHARD, GAIL; Sandy Creek Central Schl; Lacona, NY; (Y); Computer Clb; Drama Clb; Library Aide; Office Aide; SADD; Teachers Aide; Chorus; School Musical; School Play; Stage Crew; CCBI; Legl/Exec Sec.

BOUCHARD, JEANNE; Saratoga Spr SR HS; Greenfield Ctr, NY; (Y); 30/480; Pres Church Yth Grp; Hosp Aide; Red Cross Aide; Orch; Stage Crew; Variety Show; Yrbk Bus Mgr; High Hon Roll; Hon Roll; NHS; Union; Pre-Med.

BOUCHARD, JOHN; New Lebanon Central HS; New Lebanon, NY; (Y); Pres French Clb; Capt Var Bsktbl; Var Capt Crs Cntry; Var L Socr; Var Swmmng; Var Capt Trk; Hon Roll; Band; Concert Band; Mrchg Band; Schl Record 800m Trk; Schl 1600m Relay Tm Trk Record; ST Qlfr Trk; Fairleigh Dickenson U; Math.

BOUCHARD, LYNN; Hillcrest HS; Woodhaven, NY; (Y); Church Yth Grp; Dance Clb; Girl Scts; Hosp Aide; Teachers Aide; Church Choir; Prfct Atten Awd; Grl Scts Slvr Awd 84; Physcl Thrpy.

BOUCHER, LISA; Berne-Knox-Westerlo HS; Berne, NY; (Y); 1/80; Trs Jr Cls; Trs Sr Cls; Capt Crs Cntry; Capt Trk; Co-Capt Vllybl; Bausch & Lomb Sci Awd; High Hon Roll; Ed NHS; Val; (Y ST Regents Schrlshp 86; GE Star Schlrshp Awd 86; Cornell U; Biochem.

BOUCHER, TODD E; Torrejon American HS; APO New York, NY; (Y); Boy Scts; CAP; Drama Clb; Pres Exploring; FTA; Red Cross Aide; Rptr Science Clb; Spanish Clb; Thesps; Acpl Chr; Thtre Arts.

BOUCK, ANDREA; Fort Plain Central HS; Fort Plain, NY; (S); 10/54; Drama Clb; Varsity Clb; Chorus; Yrbk Bus Mgr; Pres Soph Cls; Pres Jr Cls; Pres Sr Cls; Var Capt Cheerleading; NHS; Bus Sqnce Hghst Ave Awd 85; Bus.

BOUDREAU, JOSEPH; Massena Central HS; Massena, NY; (Y); 16/236; Boy Scts; French Clb; Ed Lit Mag; Trk; High Hon Roll; Hon Roll; NHS; Pres Schlr; Dr Wyne T Moses Schlrshp, NY ST Rgnts Schlrshp 86; Clarkson U; Mech Engrng.

BOUEY III, BENKAI EDWARD H; HS For The Humanits; New York, NY; (Y); Color Guard; Pres School Play; Stage Crew; High Hon Roll; Hon Roll.

BOUFFARD, ALEX; Broadalbin Central HS; Broadalbin, NY; (Y); Drama Clb; French Clb; Band; Concert Band; Mrchg Band; School Play; Yrbk Stf; Lit Mag; Rep Stu Cncl; JV Bowling; Chairmn Of Band.

BOUFFARD, BRIAN; Dover JR SR HS; Wingdale, NY; (S); 12/70; Art Clb; Stage Crew; Hon Roll.

BOUGIAMAS, JOHN S; Bronx HS Of Science; Syosset, NY; (Y); Boy Scts; Church Yth Grp; Teachers Aide; Im Bsktbl; Treas-Hellenic Cultrl Socy Of Bronx Sci 85; Altar Boy-St Nicholas Greek Orth Chrch 81; Hofstra U; Pre-Dental.

BOUISSEY, TODD; Franklin Acad; Brushton, NY; (Y); 4-H; Spanish Clb; Acdmc All Amer Awd 83-85; NY ST U Albny; Comp Prgmr.

BOULE, AARON E; Whitehall HS; Whitehall, NY; (Y); Drama Clb; Teachers Aide; Band; School Play; Yrbk Phtg; Var JV Crs Cntry; Var Trk; NHS; Peer Ldrshp Drug Cnclng Grp 84-885; SUNY-PLTTSBRGH; Engr.

BOULE, EUGENE; Fort Ann Central Schl; Ft Ann, NY; (Y); 1/52; Am Leg Boys St; French Clb; Math Clb; Ski Clb; Yrbk Stf; Pres Frsh Cls; Pres Soph Cls; Pres Jr Cls; Pres Sr Cls; JV Var Bsktbl; Army Rsrv Athl Schlr Awd 85; Amer Legn Amer Awd 86; Republ Womns Awd; Syracuse U; Lib Arts.

BOULOUGOURIS, CHRISTINA; Valley Stream Central HS; Valley Stream, NY; (Y); Spanish Clb; SADD; Teachers Aide; Flag Corp; School Musical; Variety Show; JV Var Cheerleading; High Hon Roll; NHS; Spanish NHS; Spn Awd 84; Soc Studs, Engl, Sci Awds 84; Grad Flower Grl 86; Albany; Pre-Law.

BOULRICE, MICHAEL; Northern Adirondack Central HS; Altona, NY; (Y); Key Clb; Band; Mrchg Band; Var Bsbl; JV Var Bsktbl; High Hon Roll; Hon Roll; NHS.

BOUNATSOS, MARIA; St Johns Prep; Woodside, NY; (Y); 82/458; French Clb; Hosp Aide; Intnl Clb; Yrbk Stf; Socr; High Hon Roll; Hon Roll; NHS; NY U; Bio.

BOURBONNAIS, RICHARD; John Marshall HS; Rochester, NY; (Y); 30/160; Rep Stu Cncl; Var Capt Crs Cntry; Var Trk; Prfct Atten Awd; SUNY Morrisville; Mech Engr.

BOURCY, ANNE; Bishop Grimes HS; Syracuse, NY; (S); 16/146; Church Yth Grp; Cmnty Wkr; Political Wkr; Ski Clb; Chorus; School Musical; JV Socr; High Hon Roll; NHS; Ntl Merit Ltr; Spch Pthlgy.

BOURDONY, MICHAEL R; The Bronx HS Of Sci; Bronx, NY; (Y); Debate Tm; NFL; SADD; Orch; Im Ftbl; Tour Dir H S Holocst Ctr; VP Blck Orgnztn Stu Strngth; Chem.

BOURG, ROBERT; Solvay HS; Solvay, NY; (Y); Pres French Clb; Quiz Bowl; School Musical; VP Soph Cls; Pres Jr Cls; Pres Stu Cncl; JV Var Ftbl; High Hon Roll; NHS; Cornell Club Awd 86; 1st Pl Gifted & Talented Proj 86; Accntng.

BOURGAULT, BRIAN; Tamarac HS; Troy, NY; (Y); 3/107; Computer Clb; Debate Tm; Intnl Clb; Math Tm; Science Clb; Var Stat Bsbl; Bausch & Lomb Sci Awd; Hon Roll; NHS; Prfct Atten Awd; Hon Grad 86; Edith Grace Craig Reynolds Schlrshp 86; Alma Gray Meml Schlrshp 86; Siena Coll; Bio.

BOURGAULT, JON; Paul V Moore HS; Brewerton, NY; (Y); AFS; Boy Scts; Church Yth Grp; Drama Clb; Math Tm; School Play; Nwsp Ed-Chief; NHS; Ntl Merit SF; Voice Dem Awd; Stu Mnth 85; Achvt Awd Soc Studies Dept 86; AFS Stu Exc Brazil 86; Tchr.

BOURGEOIS, BRIAN; Ausable Valley Central HS; Keeseville, NY; (Y); Pres 4-H; VP Pres Key Clb; Chorus; VP Stu Cncl; JV Capt Bsktbl; Var Socr; Var Trk; JV Wrstlng; Hon Roll; NHS.

BOURGEOIS, KEITH; Gates-Chili HS; Rochester, NY; (Y); Exploring; Nwsp Rptr; Nwsp Stf; High Hon Roll; Hon Roll; Rochester Inst Of Tech; Engrng.

BOURNS, TRICIA; E J Wilson HS; Spencerport, NY; (Y); 7/350; French Clb; Math Clb; Ski Clb; High Hon Roll; NHS; Schlstc Achvt Soc; Awd Adv Plcmnet Am Hist; Awd Frnch IV.

BOUSQUET, JAMES; Sarawac Central HS; Cadyville, NY; (S); 22/110; Var L Bsbl; Var L Bsktbl; Var L Ftbl; Hon Roll; Aviation.

BOUSSELOT, BRIAN; Liverpool HS; Liverpool, NY; (S); 400/842; Church Yth Grp; DECA; JA; Band; Jazz Band; Stu Cncl; Ftbl; Trk; DECCA Scholar 86; NYS VP DECA 86; Johnson & Wales; Bus Mgmt.

BOUTON, CHRIS; Rome Free Acad; Rome, NY; (Y); Cmnty Wkr; Var Bsbl; Var Ftbl; High Hon Roll; Jr NHS; NHS; Hghst Avg Sci & Soc Stds; Pre-Med.

BOUTON, TAMMY; Harpursville HS; Nineveh, NY; (S); FFA; Spanish Clb; Color Guard; Drill Tm; Yrbk Stf; Var Trk; High Hon Roll; NHS; Voice Dem Awd; NASH; Prof Dog Grmng.

BOUWENS, GINGER LEE; Newark Central SR HS; Palmyra, NY; (Y); 27/201; Aud/Vis; Girl Scts; Color Guard; High Hon Roll; Hon Roll; Prfct Atten Awd; Pres Schlr; Schlrshp Data Prcssng 86; Pres Acdmc Ftnss Awd 86; Crtfct Pub In Mrdn 86; Bryant & Stratton; Data Prcssng.

BOUWMAN, JOYCE; Mamaroneck HS; Larchmont, NY; (Y); VP German Clb; Yrbk Phtg; Yrbk Stf; 1st Hnr Awd Iona Lang Cont German 85; Frshmn SR Advsr 85-86; The Intl Baccalaureate.

BOUZA, GEORGE LOUIS; Herricks HS; New Hyde Prk, NY; (Y); Cmnty Wkr; Computer Clb; DECA; Key Clb; Political Wkr; Teachers Aide; Chorus; Stage Crew; Variety Show.

BOUZA, SUSANA; Academy Of St Joseph; Bayshore, NY; (Y); Aud/Vis; Cmnty Wkr; Drama Clb; Hosp Aide; Pres Pep Clb; Rgnts Schlrhsp 86; Natl Hspnc Schlr Awd Fnlst 86; ST U Of NY-STNY Brk; Math.

BOVA, LISA; Fontbonne Hall Acad; Brooklyn, NY; (Y); 27/133; Drama Clb; Trs SADD; School Musical; Nwsp Sprt Ed; Yrbk Ed-Chief; Pres Frsh Cls; Rep Soph Cls; Rep Jr Cls; Var Capt Tennis; High Hon Roll; Mr Jensen Awd Ldrshp & Outstndng Achvt 85; Peer Ldrshp Training 86; Bus.

BOVA, SHAWN; Frewsburg Central HS; Frewsburg, NY; (Y); Church Yth Grp; Cmnty Wkr; Ski Clb; Pres Jr Cls; Stu Cncl; Var Capt Swmmng; Hon Roll; NHS; JA; JV Ftbl; Optimist JR Ctzn Awd 86; Stu Yr 84; Mth.

BOVA, SUSAN; St Edmund HS; Brooklyn, NY; (S); 8/230; Stage Crew; Variety Show; Yrbk Stf; Prfct Atten Awd; Bio,Italian,Eng Awd; 1st,2nd Hnrs 84-85; Ldrs Clb 85-86; Sci.

BOVAIN, CYNTHIA; Walton HS; Bronx, NY; (Y); Band; Chorus; School Play; Variety Show; Cheerleading; Pom Pon; Twrlr; Vllybl; Prfct Atten Awd; Marist; Acctnt.

BOVERA, CAROL ANN; St John The Baptist HS; Massapequa, NY; (Y); Boy Scts; Drama Clb; French Clb; Girl Scts; Office Aide; Acpl Chr; Chorus; School Musical; Yrbk Stf; Tri-M Music Hnr Scty 85.

BOWDEN, CHRISTA; Academy Of St Joseph; Smithtown, NY; (Y); Debate Tm; Hosp Aide; Speech Tm; SADD; Yrbk Ed-Chief; Yrbk Stf; Natl Frnch Cntst-5th Pl 83; Law.

BOWDREN IV, RICHARD; Earl L Vander Meulen HS; Pt Jefferson, NY; (Y); Computer Clb; Latin Clb; Mathletes; Band; Orch; School Play; Nwsp Stf; Socr; Aerontcl Engrng.

BOWE, KAREN; Our Lady Of Mercy HS; Penfield, NY; (Y); Exploring; Hosp Aide; Ski Clb; Hon Roll.

BOWE, MARIA; Uniondale HS; Uniondale, NY; (Y); Church Yth Grp; Pres Girl Scts; Hosp Aide; Chorus; Church Choir; Rep Stu Cncl; Swmmng; Bus Adm.

BOWEN, BONNIE J; Edmeston Central HS; Burlington Flats, NY; (Y); Chorus; School Musical; School Play; Yrbk Ed-Chief; High Hon Roll; NHS; Val; GAA; Math Clb; Yrbk Stf; Lemoyne Acdmc Schlrshp 86; Rgnts Schlrshp 86; Clrk Schlrshp 86; Lemoyne Coll; English.

BOWEN, DIANNE; Portville Central HS; Portville, NY; (Y); 6/108; Am Leg Aux Girls St; Pep Clb; School Play; Pres Stu Cncl; Capt Cheerleading; Swmmng; Cit Awd; High Hon Roll; NHS; Olean Exchng Club Schlrshp 86; St John Fisher Coll; Mth.

BOWEN, HEATHER; Bishop Ford Central Cath HS; Brooklyn, NY; (S); 12/390; Dance Clb; Drama Clb; Nwsp Rptr; Nwsp Stf; Stu Cncl; Var Bsktbl; Var Crs Cntry; Var Tennis; Hon Roll; NHS.

BOWEN, JAY; Newfane HS; Newfane, NY; (Y); Church Yth Grp; Sftbl; Im Wt Lftg; Scty Distnghd Amer H S Stu 85; NYTT; Osteopath.

BOWEN, JAYNE; John A Coleman HS; Kingston, NY; (S); 1/67; Pres Church Yth Grp; Trs French Clb; Trs Key Clb; Ski Clb; Ed Yrbk Stf; Rep Jr Cls; Rep Sr Cls; VP Cheerleading; High Hon Roll; NHS; Chem.

BOWEN, JULIE; Brockport HS; Brockport, NY; (Y); French Clb; Girl Scts; Ski Clb; SADD; Chorus; Tennis; Trk; High Hon Roll; Hon Roll; CRMNAL Jstc.

BOWEN, MARJORIE; Waterloo SR HS; Phelps, NY; (Y); 18/157; Drama Clb; Pep Clb; Ski Clb; School Musical; School Play; Swing Chorus; Stat Lcrss; Im Sftbl; High Hon Roll; Hon Roll; Accntng.

BOWEN, MICHAEL; Sauquoit Valley Central HS; Sauguoit, NY; (Y); Chess Clb; Computer Clb; French Clb; Varsity Clb; Chorus; Variety Show; Rep Frsh Cls; Rep Soph Cls; Rep Stu Cncl; JV Var Bsbl; Princpls List Pin; Specl Engrng Pgm Stu; French Pin; OH ST U; Comptr Sci.

BOWEN, MIKE; Frontier HS; Hamburg, NY; (Y); Science Clb; Spanish Clb; SADD; Varsity Clb; Nwsp Stf; Bsbl; Var L Trk; ST U Of NY; Law.

BOWEN, PAMELA; Salamanca Central HS; Salamanca, NY; (Y); Church Yth Grp; DECA; Library Aide; Spanish Clb; SADD; Band; Concert Band; Jazz Band; Mrchg Band; Pep Band; Julliard Schl Of Music; Music.

BOWER, AUTUMN; Jamestown HS; Jamestown, NY; (Y); Pres Church Yth Grp; French Clb; Hosp Aide; Hst Acpl Chr; Chorus; Church Choir; Madrigals; School Musical; Lit Mag; Hnrd 300 Hrs Volunteer Wrk 84; CCMTA $100 Schlrshp 86; Pre-Med.

BOWER, BONNI; Sodus Central HS; Sodus, NY; (Y); 18/120; Concert Band; Mrchg Band; Trs Frsh Cls; Trs Soph Cls; Trs Jr Cls; Trs Sr Cls; JV Var Cheerleading; Var Trk; High Hon Roll; Hon Roll; SUNY Buffalo; Int Dsgn.

BOWER, KYLE; Wheatland-Chili HS; Scottsville, NY; (Y); 11/86; Church Yth Grp; Band; Chorus; Church Choir; Concert Band; Mrchg Band; Variety Show; Pres Soph Cls; JV Bsbl; Var Bsktbl; Hugh O Brian Yth Foundtn Ldrshp Awd 85; Peopl To Peopl Stdnt Ambssdr Central Eurp 86; Military Acad; Intl Rel.

BOWER, MICHAEL J; Union Springs HS; Union Springs, NY; (Y); Ski Clb; High Hon Roll; NY Rgnts Schlrshp 86; Alfred ST Tech; Mech Engrng.

BOWER, WILLIAM F; Ilion Central HS; Ilion, NY; (Y); 27/142; Drama Clb; School Musical; Trs Sr Cls; Rep Stu Cncl; Var L Bsktbl; Var L Golf; NHS; Pres Schlr; St Schlr; Jones-Griffith Schlrshp 86; 7th Plc NYS Jr Glf Chmpnshp 85; Clarkson U; Mchncl Engnrng.

BOWERS, DANIEL; Clarence Central HS; Williamsville, NY; (Y); 17/268; Varsity Clb; Var Capt Bsbl; Var Crs Cntry; Var Capt Ice Hcky; Var L Socr; Gov Hon Prg Awd; High Hon Roll; Hon Roll; NHS; Mock Trial Tm 2nd NYS 86; 89.5 Avg Awd; SUNY Buffalo; Lawyer.

BOWERS, GIDGET; Ripley Central Schl; Ripley, NY; (S); Church Yth Grp; Chorus; School Musical; Ed Yrbk Ed-Chief; VP Jr Cls; Cheerleading; Sftbl; Vllybl; Hon Roll; NHS; Natl Chrs Awd 84; NYSSMA Solo Awd Ribbn Mdl 84; Bst Soprano Awd 85; Jamestown CC; Nrsg.

BOWERS, LHAG; Haverling Central HS; Bath, NY; (Y); 7/105; French Clb; JCL; Latin Clb; Math Clb; Yrbk Phtg; High Hon Roll; NHS; Ntl Merit SF.

BOWERS, LYNN D; Horseheads HS; Horseheads, NY; (S); 45/380; Church Yth Grp; Cmnty Wkr; Ski Clb; Varsity Clb; Rep Sr Cls; Mgr Bsktbl; JV Var Sftbl; Var Tennis; High Hon Roll; Hon Roll; Houghton Coll; Occup Ther.

BOWLES, RODNEY; North Babylon Sr HS; North Babylon, NY; (Y); 179/464; DECA; Intnl Clb; Office Aide; Orch; School Musical; Nwsp Stf; Lit Mag; Bowling; Hon Roll; Suffolk Cnty Rgnl Fnlst 86; Sullivan Cnty Coll; Htl Mgmt.

BOWMAN, ALYSON L; Churchville-Chili SR HS; Rochester, NY; (Y); 10/310; Church Yth Grp; JA; JCL; Latin Clb; Math Tm; Ski Clb; School Play; Lit Mag; High Hon Roll; Chorus; NY ST Regnts Schlrshp 86.

BOWMAN, CYNTHIA; Linton HS; Schenectady, NY; (Y); 28/322; Hosp Aide; Trs Frsh Cls; Soph Cls; Jr Cls; Socl Sci Fld.

BOWMAN, DEBORAH L; Faith Heritage Schl; Clay, NY; (Y); Church Yth Grp; Band; Chorus; Church Choir; Var L Socr; Cit Awd; Hon Roll; Stat Trk; Var Vllybl; Southeastern Bible Coll; Educ.

BOWMAN, KIMBERLY; Ichabod Crane HS; Niverville, NY; (Y); Ski Clb; SADD; Band; Concert Band; Mrchg Band; Hon Roll; Outstndng Achvt Bio 85; Outstndng Achvt Math 85; Nuclr Med.

BOWMAN, TODD; Fox Lane HS; Bedford, NY; (Y); 60/300; Camp Fr Inc; Computer Clb; SADD; Varsity Clb; Nwsp Stf; Yrbk Stf; Var Capt Tennis; High Hon Roll; Hon Roll; All Conf, Sectn Ten 85 & 86; Arch.

BOWMAN, TWIGGY; Corcoran HS; Syracuse, NY; (Y); Sec Church Yth Grp; ROTC; Church Choir; Hon Roll; FBLA; GAA; Chorus; Nwsp Bus Mgr; Nwsp Phtg; Yrbk Phtg; ROTC; Bus Mngmnt.

BOYACK, SHARON; Gates Chili SR HS; Rochester, NY; (S); 13/446; Intnl Clb; Band; School Musical; School Play; VP Jr Cls; Capt JV Cheerleading; NHS; Church Yth Grp; Drama Clb; Chorus; Soloist Area All ST Chorus 85; Schlrshp Overseas Frgn Exc Stu 84; Music.

BOYCE, KEVIN; Evander Childs HS; New York, NY; (S); 10/383; Art Clb; Nwsp Rptr; Hon Roll; Barauch U; Bus.

BOYCE, LORI; Elmira Free Acad; Lowman, NY; (Y); 4-H; French Clb; Office Aide; JV Var Mgr(s); High Hon Roll; Hon Roll; Vrsty Lttr For Mgr Of Grls Bsktblr; Rensselaer Union; Cmptr Engrng.

BOYD, LYNNETTE; Louis D Brandcis HS; New York, NY; (Y); JA; Cazenovia Coll; Bus Mngmt.

BOYD, MICHELLE; Southampton HS; Southampton, NY; (Y); Art Clb; Cheerleading; Pom Pon; Score Keeper; Sftbl; Hon Roll; Psych.

BOYD, QUANDA DEIRDRA; Mount Vernon HS; Mt Vernon, NY; (Y); Red Cross Aide; Chorus; Church Choir; Jazz Band; School Musical; School Play; Off Jr Cls; Hon Roll; Church Yth Grp; Teachers Aide; Music Awd 86; Mth Awd 86; Scholar Awd 84; Kings Coll; Orthpdst.

BOYD, RUTH E; Richburg Central Schl; Friendship, NY; (Y); Concert Band; Mrchg Band; Nwsp Stf; Yrbk Ed-Chief; Sec Frsh Cls; Sec Soph Cls; Sec Jr Cls; Sec Sr Cls; Pres NHS; Val; Rgnts Schlrshp 86; ASCA Of Wmn Schlrshp 86; Ntl English Mrt Awd 85; Alfred ST Coll; Accntng.

BOYD, STEPHANIE; Fairport HS; Fairport, NY; (Y); Church Yth Grp; Church Choir; Orch; Rep Jr Cls; Nrsng.

BOYD, STEPHEN; Long Island Lutheran HS; Westbury, NY; (S); 10/90; Church Yth Grp; Drama Clb; French Clb; Mathletes; Thesps; Chorus; School Musical; School Play; Stage Crew; Nwsp Stf; U NY Stny Brook; Osteopath.

BOYD, TIM; Union Springs Acad; Chestertown, MD; (S); 2/45; Ski Clb; Varsity Clb; Concert Band; Pres Frsh Cls; Capt Var Bsktbl; High Hon Roll; JP Sousa Awd; NHS; Sal; U Of DE; Mech Engr.

BOYD, TIM; West Seneca West HS; W Seneca, NY; (Y); Boy Scts; Bsbl; Bowling; Hon Roll; Jr NHS; Vet Med.

BOYD, TYNESE; Hempstead HS; Hempstead, NY; (S); 16/216; Church Yth Grp; Dance Clb; Girl Scts; Office Aide; Teachers Aide; Flag Corp; Sftbl; Hon Roll; Utica Coll Syracuse; Mech Engr.

BOYD, WILLIAM; Scotia-Glenville HS; Scotia, NY; (Y); 7/250; Church Yth Grp; Thesps; Acpl Chr; Chorus; Concert Band; Jazz Band; School Musical; Crs Cntry; Trk; High Hon Roll; NYS Rgnts Schlrshp; Union Coll.

BOYDEN, BRUCE E; Northeastern Clinton Central HS; Rouses Pt, NY; (Y); 1/100; Am Leg Boys St; Chess Clb; Model UN; Scholastic Bowl; Pres Jr Cls; Var Crs Cntry; Bausch & Lomb Sci Awd; NHS; French Clb; Band; Rensselaer Polytechnic Inst Sci & Math Awd 86; Outstndg Delegate N Country Model UN 85; Politician.

BOYEA, TRUDY; Franklin Acad; Malone, NY; (Y); Chorus; Swing Chorus; Crmnlgy.

BOYER, BRYAN; Malone Central Franklin Acad; Malone, NY; (Y); Ski Clb; Prfct Atten Awd.

BOYER, MARY; Rome Catholic HS; Rome, NY; (Y); Hosp Aide; Pres Service Clb; SADD; School Musical; Yrbk Sprt Ed; Var Capt Cheerleading; JV Capt Socr; Capt L Trk; High Hon Roll; NHS; Acadmc All Amer 86; Achvmnt Engl 85; Effort Religion & Math 85-86; Nurse.

BOYER, MICHELE; Tioga Central HS; Nichols, NY; (S); Computer Clb; GAA; Ski Clb; Varsity Clb; Band; Concert Band; School Musical; Variety Show; Fld Hcky; Sftbl; IBM Co-Op; All Cnty Band Muscl Fest; Alfred ST Ag & Tech Coll; Comp.

BOYKO, MICHAEL V; Grand Island HS; Grand Island, NY; (Y); 100/300; Church Yth Grp; Natl Beta Clb; Varsity Clb; Variety Show; Var Capt Lcrss; Var Capt Socr; Im Capt Vllybl; Hon Roll; Bus Mgmt.

BOYLAN, ANN; Our Lady Of Mercy HS; Rochester, NY; (Y); VP GAA; Spanish Clb; SADD; Varsity Clb; Rep Soph Cls; Rep Stu Cncl; Var L Bsktbl; Var L Socr; JV Trk; Hon Roll; US Marine Corp Dstngshd Athlete Awd 86; Le Moyne Coll; Accntng.

BOYLAN, KEVIN; Middletown HS; Middletown, NY; (Y); Var L Tennis; Hon Roll.

BOYLAN, MICHELE; Sacred Heart Acad; Williston Park, NY; (S); Computer Clb; Girl Scts; Math Tm; Science Clb; Ski Clb; SADD; Var Sftbl; Trk; High Hon Roll; NHS; Slvr Awd.

BOYLE, ADAM J; Onteora HS; Bearsville, NY; (Y); Ski Clb; Band; Jazz Band; Mrchg Band; Variety Show; JV L Crs Cntry; Var L Ftbl; Var L Trk; High Hon Roll; Hon Roll; NY ST Rgnts Schlrshp 86; VA Polytech Inst; Aerosp Engr.

BOYLE, COLLEEN; Farmingdale SR HS; Farmingdale, NY; (Y); Capt Sec Dance Clb; Intnl Clb; SADD; Band; Concert Band; Mrchg Band; Symp Band; High Hon Roll.

BOYLE JR, EDWARD G; Sachem HS; Holbrook, NY; (Y); Pres Art Clb; Boy Scts; Pres Church Yth Grp; Cmnty Wkr; Pres Computer Clb; Rep Intnl Clb; Spanish Clb; Yrbk Stf; Lit Mag; Rep Frsh Cls; Pre-Med.

BOYLE, LEIGH; St Peters HS For Girls; Staten Island, NY; (Y); English Clb; FNA; Hosp Aide; Bowling.

BOYNES, THOMAS M; Cathedral Preparatory Seminary; Bronx, NY; (Y); 6/22; Science Clb; Nwsp Ed-Chief; VP Soph Cls; Sec Jr Cls; Sec Sr Cls; Stat Bsbl; Stat Bsktbl; NHS; Cmnty Wkr; Im Fld Hcky; NY ST Regents Schlrshp 86; Comm Art.

BOYNTON, CRAIG; Mayfield HS; Mayfield, NY; (Y); 3/79; AFS; Nwsp Phtg; Pres Sr Cls; Rep Stu Cncl; Capt L Bsktbl; Trs NHS; Crs Cntry; Socr; Trk; High Hon Roll; Exch Stu Uruguay 84-85; Boys St 85; NROTC Schlrshp 86; Old Dominion U; Intl Bus.

BOZAN, ERIK DAVID; Cardinal Hayes HS; New York, NY; (Y); Chess Clb; Cmnty Wkr; Bsktbl; Ftbl; Trk; Wt Lftg; Hon Roll; New Paltz Coll; Bus.

BOZZEY, LEANN; Seton Catholic Central HS; Endwell, NY; (Y); Art Clb; Hosp Aide; Key Clb; Spanish Clb; PA ST U; Psychlgy.

BOZZO, CARISSA; Bronx High School Of Science; New York, NY; (Y); Math Tm; Teachers Aide; School Musical; Nwsp Rptr; Nwsp Stf; Var Stu Cncl; High Hon Roll; NHS; Frnch Merit 86; Dnc 13 Yrs; Psychlgy.

BRABAZON, TARA; Bellport HS; Bellport, NY; (Y); French Clb; NFL; Service Clb; Ski Clb; Spanish Clb; Band; Nwsp Rptr; Yrbk Stf; Jr Cls; Sr Cls; Outstndng Stu Awd 86; 1st Pl Frgn Lang Fair 86; Trinity Coll; Intl Rel.

BRACCINI, ALBERT M; Lakeland SR HS; Putnam Valley, NY; (Y); 86/344; Boy Scts; Nwsp Rptr; Crs Cntry; Golf; Trk; Hon Roll; NYS Regents Scholar 86; SUNY Albany; Spn.

BRACE, MONICA; Watkins Glen HS; Burdett, NY; (S); Dance Clb; Drama Clb; Letterman Clb; PAVAS; Band; School Play; Variety Show; Gym; Tennis; Hon Roll; Physcl Ed.

BRACEY, BEINSON; New Rochelle HS; New Rochelle, NY; (Y); Boys Clb Am; Cmnty Wkr; Bsbl; Bsktbl; Bowling; Ftbl; Sftbl; Swmmng; Wt Lftg; Hon Roll; AL ST U Tskg; Engrng.

BRACEY JR, ROY; Murry Bergtraum HS; Brooklyn, NY; (Y); Boys Clb Am; Cmnty Wkr; Office Aide; Var Bsktbl; Jr NHS; Accntng.

BRACHE, AMIRO; Mc Quaid Jesuit HS; Fairport, NY; (Y); Church Yth Grp; Cmnty Wkr; Model UN; SADD; Varsity Clb; Yrbk Stf; JV Bsktbl; Ftbl; High Hon Roll; Hon Roll; Outstndng Achvt Mdl; Natl Hispnc Schlrshp Awd; Arch.

BRACIKOWSKI, JENNIFER; Springville Griffith Inst; Springville, NY; (Y); 23/200; Camera Clb; Sec 4-H; SADD; Color Guard; Mgr(s); Score Keeper; Vllybl; High Hon Roll; Hon Roll; NHS; SUNY Geneseo; Acctg.

BRACKEN, ANNE; Academy Of Saint Joseph; East Setauket, NY; (Y); Church Yth Grp; Cmnty Wkr; Chrmn SADD; VP Sr Cls; Stu Cncl; Berkeley Clairmont Bus Excllnc Awd 86; Providence Coll.

BRACKEN, MARY L; Mohawk Central Schl; Mohawk, NY; (Y); 8/96; Church Yth Grp; French Clb; Model UN; SADD; Chorus; Concert Band; Mrchg Band; Yrbk Stf; Sec Stu Cncl; JV Bsktbl; Regents Schlrshp 86; Mohawk Vly Businessmens Assoc Distngshd Stu Awd 86; Albany Coll Of Phrmcy; Phrmcy.

BRACKIS, JONATHAN; New Rochelle HS; Scarsdale, NY; (Y); Chess Clb; Nwsp Bus Mgr; Tennis; French Hon Soc; NHS; Emory; Avtg.

BRACKLEY, CHRIS; Hoosic Valley Central HS; Valley Falls, NY; (Y); 2/100; Latin Clb; Red Cross Aide; Band; Concert Band; Jazz Band; Mrchg Band; Pres Frsh Cls; Pres Soph Cls; Off Stu Cncl; Var L Socr; Champ Trck Rely,Long Jump 85-86; Boston U; Med.

BRACKMAN JR, JAMES; Ellenville HS; Napanoch, NY; (Y); AFS; Spanish Clb; Jazz Band; Pep Band; School Musical; Symp Band; Yrbk Bus Mgr; Stu Cncl; Ftbl; Trk; Rgnts Schlrship 86; Bn Slsky Mrch Of Dms Mem 86; Hartwick; Pre Med.

BRACONE, DEBORAH A; Fairport HS; Fairport, NY; (Y); 35/630; Exploring; Pres French Clb; VP Science Clb; SADD; Chorus; Yrbk Stf; Var Fld Hcky; Hon Roll; NHS; NY ST Rgnts Schlrshp 85-86; Miami U Oxford OH; Chld Psychl.

BRACONE, RICHELLE; Fairport HS; Fairport, NY; (Y); Exploring; Latin Clb; Spanish Clb; SADD; Orch; Frsh Cls; Hon Roll; Spanish NHS; Vllybl; Natl Clssc JR Lg Cert Hon Merit Natl Lat Exm Magna Cum Laude 86; Law.

BRADBURY, JEAN; Wayne Central HS; Ontario, NY; (Y); Church Yth Grp; Cmnty Wkr; Girl Scts; Math Tm; SADD; Band; Chorus; Church Choir; Concert Band; Jazz Band.

BRADFIELD, MARK; Alden Central HS; Alden, NY; (Y); Church Yth Grp; Bsbl; Bsktbl; Socr; Tennis; Kiwanis Awd; Army; Cmmnctns.

BRADFORD, TERRY LYNN; Anthony A Henninger HS; Syracuse, NY; (Y); 21/400; GAA; Rep Sr Cls; VP Stu Cncl; Crs Cntry; Trk; Cit Awd; Hon Roll; NHS; Olvr Awd Outstndng SR Athlt 85-86; Rtry Clb Syracuse Yth Rcgntn Awd 86; Alpha Kappa Alpha Schlrshp 86; US Naval Acad; Aerontcl Engrng.

BRADLEY, CASANDRA; Riverside HS; Buffalo, NY; (Y); 55/167; French Clb; Library Aide; Drill Tm; Variety Show; Nwsp Rptr; Hon Roll; MV Worker 86; Bryant & Stratton; H/M Mgmt.

BRADLEY, CINDY; Brewster HS; Brewster, NY; (Y); Stage Crew; Yrbk Phtg; Yrbk Stf; Var Trk; Art Achvmnt 84; Cmmrcl Art.

BRADLEY, COLETTE; Acad Of Mt St Ursula; Bronx, NY; (Y); Hosp Aide; SADD; Yrbk Stf; Nrsng.

BRADLEY, KATHY; Pavilion Central Sch; Pavilion, NY; (Y); #9 In Class; AFS; FTA; Spanish Clb; Teachers Aide; Band; Chorus; School Play; Nwsp Ed-Chief; Nwsp Rptr; Nwsp Stf; Intern Cnty Govt Pgm 86; Ed.

BRADLEY, MICHAEL; La Fayette HS; Lafayette, NY; (Y); Drama Clb; Band; Chorus; School Musical; School Play; Stage Crew; Swing Chorus; Bsktbl; Ftbl; Hon Roll; Charles Bex Schlrshp ,L; La Fayette Firemens Awd 86; Council Of Svc Clubs-Anl Yth Ldrshp Recgntn 86; Suny Morrisville; Electcl Engr.

BRADSHAW, SHEILA; South Park HS; Buffalo, NY; (Y); JA; School Play; Yrbk Stf; Stu Cncl; Trk; Bus Prntng.

BRADT, JAMES; Notre Dame HS; Elmira, NY; (Y).

BRADT, KRISTIN; Broadalbin Central HS; Gloversville, NY; (Y); 3/75; Am Leg Aux Girls St; French Clb; Library Aide; Yrbk Stf; JV Socr; Trk; JV Vllybl; High Hon Roll; FMCC; CPA.

BRADT, LINDA J; Schalmont HS; Schenectady, NY; (Y); Drama Clb; Ski Clb; SADD; Teachers Aide; Chorus; Church Choir; School Musical; School Play; Stage Crew; Swing Chorus; Tuitn Schlrhsp Eastrn U S Music Cmp; Top Teen Voclst NY ST Tlnt Amer Comptn 86; Berklee Coll Of Music; Vocl Per.

BRADWAY, KIMBERLY; G Ray Bodley HS; Fulton, NY; (Y); 4-H; JA; Science Clb; Variety Show; Yrbk Phtg; Yrbk Stf; Var Capt Cheerleading; Var Gym; Var Pom Pon; Var Trk; Herkimer; Bus.

BRADY, CHERYL; Bellport HS; Bellport, NY; (S); #52 In Class; Pres DECA; Yrbk Stf; Rep Frsh Cls; Rep Soph Cls; Rep Jr Cls; Cheerleading; High Hon Roll; Hon Roll; Prfct Atten Awd; Pres Schlr; Pres Schlrshp 86; Briarcliffe Bus Coll; Bus.

BRADY, DEBROAH; Valley Central HS; Walden, NY; (Y); 10/315; Church Yth Grp; Natl Beta Clb; Stage Crew; Rep Stu Cncl; Var Tennis; French Hon Soc; Hon Roll; VP NHS; Ntl Merit Ltr; Intl Yth Confer Rep 85; Pre-Med.

BRADY, ITA; Our Lady Of Victory Acad; Yonkers, NY; (S); 17/159; Hosp Aide; SADD; Variety Show; Yrbk Stf; High Hon Roll; Hon Roll; NHS; NEDT Awd; Spanish NHS; Spanish Clb; Math.

BRADY, JANIS; Frewsburg Central HS; Frewsburg, NY; (Y); AFS; Chorus; Church Choir; Sec Jr Cls; Cheerleading; Trk; Vllybl; Wilma Boyd Schl; Trvl Agnt.

BRADY, KEVIN; All Hallows HS; New York, NY; (Y); Church Yth Grp; Computer Clb; Varsity Clb; Var Crs Cntry; Var Trk; Hon Roll; NHS; Columbia U; Pre-Law.

BRADY, MARGARET L; Catskill HS; Catskill, NY; (Y); 1/140; Drama Clb; Band; Rep Stu Cncl; Vllybl; Bausch & Lomb Sci Awd; DAR Awd; Elks Awd; High Hon Roll; NHS; Ntl Merit Ltr; Deans Schlr-Cornell U 86; NYS Rgnts Schlrshp 86; Outstndg Stu 86; Cornell U; Wrtr.

BRADY, NOREEN; Mynderse Acad; Seneca Falls, NY; (S); 15/138; GAA; Spanish Clb; VP Jr Cls; Var L Bsktbl; Var Capt Socr; Var L Trk; High Hon Roll; Natl Hnr Rl 85-86; Nmcmng Crt 84-85; 3rd Pl 3rd Annl Lang Fair 85.

BRADY, TARA; Hicksville SR HS; Hicksville, NY; (Y); Chorus; Yrbk Stf; Trs Frsh Cls; Rep Soph Cls; Rep Jr Cls; Trs Stu Cncl; Var JV Cheerleading; Pom Pon; Hon Roll; Jr NHS; Soc Studs Achvt Awd Regents 86; Consumer Studs Achvt Awd 86; Hmcmng Princess 85-86; Prom Queen 85-86; Bus.

BRADY, WALT; Mc Quaid Jesuit HS; Rochester, NY; (Y); Im Bsktbl; Im Ftbl; Im Ice Hcky; Im Socr; Im Vllybl; Bus.

BRAGG, EDWARD R; Skaneateles HS; Skaneateles, NY; (S); Nwsp Rptr; Var L Crs Cntry; Var L Trk; High Hon Roll; NHS; Chem Engr.

BRAHM, JAMES E; Naples Central Schl; Canandaigua, NY; (Y); 4/83; Trs Soph Cls; Rep Stu Cncl; JV L Bsbl; JV L Bsktbl; Var L Socr; JV Var Tennis; Var L Vllybl; Cit Awd; High Hon Roll; NHS; Trustees Schlrshp 86; NY ST Regents Schlrshp 86; Presdntl Acadmc Ftnss Awd 86; Brigham Yng U; Elec Engrng.

BRAHM, SHERRY; Naples Central HS; Naples, NY; (Y); 16/85; Spanish Clb; Yrbk Ed-Chief; Var Bsktbl; Var Socr; JV Tennis; JV Vllybl; High Hon Roll; NHS; Teachers Aide; Chorus; Sibley Schlstc Art Awds 84-86; Ntl Schlstc Art Awd 86; Cznvia Coll; Intr Arch Dsgn.

BRAINERD, LORI; Fairport HS; Fairport, NY; (Y); English Clb; 4-H; Ski Clb; SADD; School Musical; Nwsp Sprt Ed; Nwsp Stf; 4-H Awd; JC Awd; Wittenberg U.

BRAITHWAITE, BILLIE; John Dewey HS; Brooklyn, NY; (Y); Drama Clb; Nwsp Stf; Syracuse U; Brdcst Jrnlst.

BRALEY, BETSY; Chatham Central Schl; Chatham, NY; (Y); Drama Clb; VP Pres 4-H; Hosp Aide; Library Aide; SADD; Chorus; JV Capt Bsktbl; Var Trk; High Hon Roll; Hon Roll; Fshn Dsgnr.

BRALEY, TINA; Rensselaer Middle HS; Rensselaer, NY; (Y); Key Clb; JC Of Albany; Nrsng.

BRAM, CAITLIN; Geneva HS; Geneva, NY; (S); 1/175; French Clb; Model UN; Yrbk Stf; High Hon Roll; NHS; Ntl Merit Ltr; Harvard Bk Awd; Bst Frnch I Stu Awd; Bio.

BRAMAN, PAMELA; Moore Catholic HS; Staten Island, NY; (Y); 50/200; Drama Clb; Math Tm; Capt Pep Clb; Ski Clb; Spanish Clb; Thesps; Chorus; School Musical; Yrbk Stf; Var Capt Cheerleading; Geneseo ST SUNY; Lib Arts.

BRAMBLETT, TARA; Rocky Point JR SR HS; Rocky Point, NY; (S); 11/175; Church Yth Grp; Computer Clb; Mathletes; Band; Chorus; Jazz Band; Mrchg Band; Pep Band; Acctnt.

BRAMER, CONNIE; Northville Central Schl; Northville, NY; (Y); Hosp Aide; Jazz Band; School Musical; Swing Chorus; Yrbk Ed-Chief; Sec Stu Cncl; JV Socr; Var Sftbl; Hon Roll; Amer Musical Fndtn Band Hnrs 84; Cert Of Apprctn-Littauer Hosp 85; Pre Med.

BRAMLEY, MELISSA A; Rome Free Acad; Rome, NY; (Y); 55/412; Church Yth Grp; Drama Clb; JA; Concert Band; Mrchg Band; School Musical; Powder Puff Ftbl; Jr NHS; NHS; Prfct Atten Awd; St John Fisher Coll; Lib Art.

BRAMM, KERRI; St Peters HS For Girls; Staten Island, NY; (Y); Math Clb; Math Tm; Pep Clb; SADD; Teachers Aide; Lit Mag; Sec Stu Cncl; Capt Cheerleading; High Hon Roll; Hon Roll; Hnr Medl 85-86; Psychlgy.

BRAMMER, EMILE; Southshore HS; Brooklyn, NY; (Y); Computer Clb; Drama Clb; Exploring; 4-H; Science Clb; Service Clb; Y-Teens; Band; Drill Tm; School Play; Elec Engrng.

BRAMWELL, ROBIN L; Poly Prep CDS; Brooklyn, NY; (Y); Church Yth Grp; Computer Clb; Band; Chorus; Stage Crew; Var L Bsktbl; JV Sftbl; Var L Trk; Ntl Merit SF; Engrng.

BRANCH, DWAYNE; Riverhead HS; Riverhead, NY; (Y); 50/200; VP Church Yth Grp; ROTC; Ski Clb; Spanish Clb; Varsity Clb; Drill Tm; L Var Trk; Cit Awd; Hon Roll; M L King Jr Meritrs Achvt Awd 86; 2nd Pl 1st Baptst Chrch M L K Jr Essay Cntst 85; ROTC Hnr Cdt 86; Engrg.

BRANCH, SCOTT; Th Stony Brook Schl; Stony Brook, NY; (Y); Church Yth Grp; Chorus; Church Choir; Concert Band; Mrchg Band; Symp Band; Variety Show; JV Socr; Yng Artists Competition 1st Pl 85; Taw Law.

BRANCHE, PHILIP; Sackets Harbor HS; Sackets Harbor, NY; (Y); #3 In Class; Quiz Bowl; Trs Frsh Cls; Trs Soph Cls; Trs Jr Cls; VP Stu Cncl; JV Capt Bsktbl; Pres NHS.

BRANCIFORTE, DIANE; St Catharine Acad; Bronx, NY; (Y); 29/189; Teachers Aide; Hon Roll; NHS; Prfct Atten Awd; Chem Engr.

BRANCIFORTE, MICHELLE; Cornwall Central HS; Cornwall, NY; (Y); Church Yth Grp; Ski Clb; Rep Frsh Cls; Rep Soph Cls; Rep Jr Cls; Sec Sr Cls; Rep Stu Cncl; Powder Puff Ftbl; Score Keeper; High Hon Roll; U Of Bridgeport; Cmmnctns.

BRANCIFORTE, SARAH; Mynderse Acad; Seneca Falls, NY; (Y); Sec Spanish Clb; Band; Chorus; Drm Mjr(t); School Musical; Swing Chorus; Yrbk Stf; Stu Cncl; Tennis; Hon Roll; Cmmnctns.

BRAND, JENNIFER; Kenmore East HS; Kenmore, NY; (Y); Cmnty Wkr; Pep Clb; Hon Roll; Ithaca Coll; Elem Educ.

BRAND, TERRANCE A; F D Roosevelt HS; Clinton Corners, NY; (Y); 3/330; Church Yth Grp; Sec Debate Tm; Band; School Musical; Lit Mag; NHS; Ntl Merit Ltr; Boy Scts; Drama Clb; Math Tm; Eagle Scout 84; Mdl For Exc In Math & Sci 85; Rnslr Plytch Inst; Aero Sp Engr.

BRANDMAN, ANDREW; Polytechnic Presparatory CDS; Brooklyn, NY; (Y); Acpl Chr; School Musical; School Play; Yrbk Bus Mgr; Rep Frsh Cls; Rep Soph Cls; Pres Jr Cls; Rep Sr Cls; Var L Trk; Nardi Chautauqua Inst Schlrshp 86; Economics.

BRANDOW, MICHELE; Cairo-Durham HS; Cairo, NY; (Y); Sec Jr Cls; Pres Sr Cls; Rep Stu Cncl; Var JV Cheerleading; Var L Socr; Var L Trk; High Hon Roll; Hon Roll; Jr NHS; Sec NHS; Daffodil Princess Amer Cancer Soc 86; Phrmcy.

BRANDT, CHRISTINE; St Joseph By-The-Sea HS; Staten Island, NY; (Y); Girl Scts; Hosp Aide; Stage Crew; Lit Mag; Bowling; Crs Cntry; Trk; Hon Roll; NHS; NEDT Awd; Soc Studys Mdl Grad 86; Acad Schlrshp 86; Grad With Hnr 86; Mt St Vincent Coll; Pre Med.

BRANDT, ELAINE; North Babylon HS; N Babylon, NY; (Y); Office Aide; Band; Rep Stu Cncl; Capt Cheerleading; JV Gym; Capt Socr; Stat Wrstlng; Jr NHS; FBI.

BRANDT, ELIZABETH; Alexandria Central HS; Redwood, NY; (Y); 2/70; School Play; Stage Crew; Yrbk Stf; Rep Stu Cncl; Var JV Cheerleading; Hon Roll; NHS; US Marine Corps Distngshd Athlete 86; N Cntry Schlr Awd-Augsbury 86; Vet Sci.

BRANDT, ERIKA; Walt Whitman HS; Huntington Stat, NY; (Y); 46/450; Church Yth Grp; German Clb; Band; School Play; Yrbk Stf; JV Socr; Capt Var Trk; Hon Roll; Jr NHS; Grmn Ntl Hnr Soc 85-86; Oral Intrptn Awd 83-84; Phys Thrpy.

BRANDT, KENNETH; Saugerties HS; Saugerties, NY; (Y); Boy Scts; Chess Clb; Church Yth Grp; German Clb; Band; Chorus; Concert Band; Symp Band; JV Crs Cntry; High Hon Roll; Hon Roll; Comp Sci.

BRANDT, KIMBERLY; Bishop Ludden HS; Syracuse, NY; (Y); Cmnty Wkr; Dance Clb; Girl Scts; SADD; Yrbk Stf; Var Cheerleading; JV Vllybl; High Hon Roll; Hon Roll; Elem Educ.

BRANFORD, ANGELICA; Midwood HS; Brooklyn, NY; (Y); 250/589; Chorus; School Musical; School Play; Stage Crew; Rptr Yrbk Phtg; Yrbk Sprt Ed; Pres Stu Cncl; Twrlr; Prfct Atten Awd; Pride Yankees 85; Stu Govrnmnt Awd 86; Outstndng Srvc SGO Awd 86; CW Post Long Island U; Prodcr.

BRANKLINE, KIM; Gates-Chili HS; Rochester, NY; (Y); JV Sftbl; Hon Roll; Var Lttr Sftbl 86; Monroe CC; Adv.

BRANSON, LAURI M; Lajes HS; El Paso, TX; (Y); Church Yth Grp; Teachers Aide; Concert Band; Jazz Band; Mrchg Band; Pep Band; School Musical; Swing Chorus; Variety Show; JP Sousa Awd; Intern 86 Smithsonian Inst 86; Ofcrs Wives Clb Schlrp 86; Hospe-Schmitt Awd Piano 85; U TX El Paso; Educ.

BRANT, CURTIS; John H Glenn HS; Greenlawn, NY; (Y); Boy Scts; Church Yth Grp; Mathletes; Science Clb; Varsity Clb; Var L Crs Cntry; Var L Trk; High Hon Roll; NHS; Spanish NHS; Oscar Ritchie Schlrshp To Kent ST 86; Cert For Exclnc Sci 84; Dickinson; Physcn.

BRANT, PATRICIA; Eden SR HS; Eden, NY; (Y); AFS; French Clb; GAA; Chorus; School Musical; Variety Show; Stu Cncl; JV Bsktbl; Capt Socr; Capt Tennis; 1st Pl Music Tlnt Shw 84; Rgnts Schlrshp 86; Law.

BRANT, PATTI; Holland Central Schl; Holland, NY; (Y); Civic Clb; JA; Spanish Clb; Var JV Cheerleading; Hon Roll; Jr NHS; Fash Merch.

BRASCH, MICHELE; North Babylon SR HS; N Babylon, NY; (Y); Band; Chorus; Concert Band; Mrchg Band; Pep Band; Variety Show; Trs Frsh Cls; Cheerleading; Sftbl; Hon Roll; Cmmnctns.

BRASHIER, BONNIE; Curtis HS; Staten Island, NY; (Y); Teachers Aide; High Hon Roll; Pres NHS.

BRASKETT, MELINDA; John Dewy HS; Brooklyn, NY; (Y); French Clb; Math Tm; Science Clb; Lit Mag; Math.

BRASLOW, MICHELE; White Plains HS; White Plains, NY; (Y); 71/450; Pres Trs Stu Cncl; JA; JCL; Latin Clb; Pep Clb; Political Wkr; Teachers Aide; Temple Yth Grp; Variety Show; Prncpls Awd 86; AZ ST U; Arch.

BRASS, CHRISTINE M; St Francis Prep; Whitestone, NY; (S); 56/700; SADD; Chorus; Concert Band; Hon Roll; NHS; Opt Clb Awd; Bio Sci.

BRASS, STACEY L; Lawrence HS; North Woodmere, NY; (Y); 37/414; Drama Clb; French Clb; Service Clb; Pres Chorus; School Musical; Variety Show; French Hon Soc; High Hon Roll; NHS; Fire Towns Music And Art Foundation Awd 85; NY U; Drama.

BRASSER, JOHN C; Churchville-Chili SR HS; Rochester, NY; (Y); 61/305; Math Clb; Ski Clb; JV Crs Cntry; NY ST Rgnts Schlrshp 86; Gannett Co Inc Mnthly Hnr Carrier Awd 83; Geneseo U; Bus.

BRATCHER, DENINE; Edison HS; Rochester, NY; (Y); Rep Soph Cls; Rep Jr Cls; Var L Vllybl; Hon Roll; Prfct Atten Awd; Comp Prgmmng.

BRATEK, KAREN; Frontier Central HS; Hamburg, NY; (Y); Hon Roll; ECC South; Bus.

BRATHWAITE, JACQUELINE; Cathedral HS; New York, NY; (Y); 62/277; Art Clb; Church Yth Grp; Dance Clb; Intnl Clb; JA; Library Aide; Church Choir; Yrbk Stf; Hon Roll; Johnson & Whales Coll Schlrshp 86; Library Aid Awd 85-86; Nurses Aid Awd 85-86; ST U Of Old Westbury; Accntng.

BRATTA, VITO; St Peters Boys HS; Staten Island, NY; (Y); 18/155; Church Yth Grp; Hon Roll; St Johns Comptv Schlrshp 86; Italian Clb Of Staten Isl Schlrshp 86; St Johns U; Acctng.

BRAUEN, ELIZABETH A; Jamestown HS; Jamestown, NY; (Y); 45/396; Dance Clb; French Clb; Political Wkr; Ski Clb; School Musical; Rep Stu Cncl; JV Cheerleading; Jr NHS; Pres Schlr; Enice Andrsn Awd-Engl II 85; Rgnts Schlrshp-SAT 85; TX Christian U; Dance.

BRAUN, ANDREW; Riverdale Country HS; New York, NY; (Y); Math Tm; Model UN; Nwsp Stf; Yrbk Stf; JV Socr; JV Tennis; Var L Trk; High Hon Roll; Ntl Merit SF; Pssd Amer HS Math Exam Scr 102 86; Math Awd 86; Sci Awd 86; Econ.

BRAUN, SUSAN; Bayport-Bluepoint HS; Bayport, NY; (Y); FBLA; Key Clb; SADD; School Play; Nwsp Stf; Yrbk Ed-Chief; Yrbk Stf; Yrbk Co Edtr In Chf; Molloy; Dntst.

BRAUNFELDS, AIJA; St Catharine Acad; Bx, NY; (Y); 8/185; Dance Clb; GAA; Girl Scts; Chorus; Cheerleading; Vllybl; High Hon Roll; NHS; 4 Yr Fll Schlrshp St Cathrn Acad 83-87; European Stds Awd 85; Frnch Awd 85.

BRAUNSCHEIDEL JR, THOMAS; Frontier HS; Lakeview, NY; (Y); Art Clb; Hon Roll; NHS; Fredonia ST; Ed.

BRAUNSTEIN, TAMARA; Midwood HS; Brooklyn, NY; (Y); 90/660; French Clb; Office Aide; Teachers Aide; Chorus; Madrigals; NCTE Awd; Prfct Atten Awd; Ntl Merit SF; Arista,Archon 86; ASPCA Essy Cntst 2nd Prz 86; Engl.

BRAY, DANIEL; Hermon-Dekalb Central HS; Hermon, NY; (Y); 1/45; Pres Chess Clb; Drama Clb; French Clb; Trs Frsh Cls; Trs Soph Cls; Trs Jr Cls; Trs Sr Cls; Var Capt Socr; Var Capt Wrstlng; Trs NHS.

BRAYER, CHRIS; Bloomfield Central HS; West Bloomfield, NY; (Y); French Clb; Latin Clb; Model UN; Sec Frsh Cls; VP Soph Cls; Trs Jr Cls; Trs Sr Cls; Rep Stu Cncl; JV Bsktbl; JV Var Socr; Geniseo ST U; Scndry Ed.

BRAYER, CINDY; Bloomfield Central HS; W Bloomfield, NY; (Y); 30/125; French Clb; Chorus; Yrbk Stf; Off Frsh Cls; Off Soph Cls; Off Jr Cls; Off Sr Cls; JV Cheerleading; Var JV Socr; Var Vllybl; Physcl Thrpy.

BRAYTON, STEPHEN G; Glens Falls HS; Glens Falls, NY; (Y); 21/220; Key Clb; High Hon Roll; Kiwanis Awd; NHS; NYS Regents Schlrshp 86; U Buffalo; Arch.

BRAZILL, CHRISTINE; Vestal SR HS; Vestal, NY; (Y); Pres Drama Clb; Nwsp Rptr; Yrbk Stf; JV Vllybl; Esspa Nwswrtng Cntst Schlrshp 85; Marywood Coll Pres Schlrshp 85; Marywood Coll; Brdcst Journlsm.

BRAZILL, LAURA CELESTE; Hicksville HS; Hicksville, NY; (Y); Hosp Aide; Chorus; Color Guard; Drill Tm; Mrchg Band; Variety Show; Yrbk Stf; Rep Stu Cncl; JV Cheerleading; Var Pom Pon; Comm.

BRAZILL, LUANN; East-Syracuse-Minoa HS; Minoa, NY; (Y); Spanish Clb; Nwsp Stf; Var Cheerleading; Jr NHS; Prncpls Cabinet Mbr 85-86; Buffalo U; Creatv Wrtng.

BRECHT, KAREN; Gowanda Central Schl; Gowanda, NY; (Y); Spanish Clb; SADD; Yrbk Sprt Ed; Yrbk Stf; Rep Soph Cls; Rep Jr Cls; Rep Stu Cncl; Var L Cheerleading; Var Capt Trk; Hon Roll; Most Vlbl Rnnr Awd Track 86; Sprinter Awd Track 86; Top 10 In Western NY Awd Track 86; U Of Buffalo; Physical Therapy.

BRECK, BRIDGET; Newfield HS; Coram, NY; (Y); 34/576; Cmnty Wkr; Spanish Clb; SADD; Band; Concert Band; Mrchg Band; School Musical; School Play; Variety Show; High Hon Roll; Marywood Coll Grant; Marywood Coll; Dietetics.

BRECKENRIDGE, PAMELA; Vernon Verona Sherrill Central HS; Oneida, NY; (Y); AFS; GAA; Yrbk Ed-Chief; Yrbk Phtg; Yrbk Stf; Rep Stu Cncl; Cheerleading; Fld Hcky; Hon Roll; Am Field Svc Exchg Stu To Japan Smmr Pgm; Art Dsgn.

BREED, BRENDA; Skaneateles Central Schl; Auburn, NY; (S); French Clb; Rep Stu Cncl; JV Var Crs Cntry; Var JV Sftbl; Var Tennis; Var Trk; High Hon Roll; Hon Roll; NHS; Bus.

BREED II, CHARLES L; Chittenango HS; Chittenango, NY; (Y); 20/174; Am Leg Boys St; FCA; Rep Sr Cls; Var Capt Bsbl; Capt Var Crs Cntry; Var Capt Trk; NHS; Pres Schlr; U S Army Schlr/Athlt Awd 86; Rchstr Inst-Tech; Comptatnl Mat.

BREEN, BETH; De Sales HS; Waterloo, NY; (Y); 1/54; Am Leg Aux Girls St; Chorus; School Musical; JV Var Socr; Bausch & Lomb Sci Awd; High Hon Roll; NHS; Voice Dem Awd; JV Cheerleading.

BREEN, NANCY; St Marys Girls HS; Manhasset, NY; (Y); Tennis; NHS; MVP Var Ten 84-86.

BREESE, DOUG; Groton Central HS; Groton, NY; (Y); Boy Scts; Chess Clb; Computer Clb; Science Clb; Prfct Atten Awd; Accntng.

BREHM, KELLY K; Watertown HS; Watertown, NY; (Y); Exploring; Intnl Clb; Ski Clb; Sr Cls; Fld Hcky; Watertown Ed Assn Schlrs 86; SUNY Oswego.

BREINES, KIM; E L Vandermeulen HS; Port Jeff Sta, NY; (Y); Library Aide; Chorus; Hon Roll; Pres Envirnmntl Yth Awd 80; Stony Brook; Chld Psychlgy.

BREITENBACH, MARK; Saugerties HS; Saugerties, NY; (Y); 36/250; Chess Clb; German Clb; Math Tm; Quiz Bowl; Ski Clb; Chorus; Im Bowling; Im Fld Hcky; Var Socr; Var Tennis; Clarkson U; Comp Sci.

BREITENSTEIN, DAVID; Duansburg Central Schl; Delanson, NY; (Y); Camera Clb; VP Drama Clb; Trs Intnl Clb; Ski Clb; Chorus; Yrbk Stf; VP Soph Cls; Var Trk; High Hon Roll; NHS; PA ST; Mod Lang.

BREMM, ANN MARIE; Bishop Maginn HS; Albany, NY; (S); Drama Clb; Latin Clb; Math Clb; School Play; High Hon Roll; Elem Educ.

BRENDEL, STEPHANIE; Lindenhurst HS; Hicksville, NY; (Y); High Hon Roll; Hon Roll; Berkely Outstndng Achvt Awd 86; Lindenhurst Off Persnnl Mem Awd 86; SR HS Prnt Tchr Stu Assoc Awd 86; Sec.

BRENNAN, ALICIA; Manhasset HS; Manhasset, NY; (Y); 17/180; Cmnty Wkr; GAA; Mathletes; Flag Corp; Var Capt Bsktbl; Var Socr; Var Capt Sftbl; High Hon Roll; NHS; All Cnty Bsktbl Plyer 85-86; All Cnfrnc Sccr Plyr 85; Math Hi Scrng Awd 83 & 84; Binghamton; Med.

BRENNAN, BUFFY; Brewster HS; Brewster, NY; (Y); Church Yth Grp; Drama Clb; Pep Clb; Spanish Clb; Chorus; Nwsp Rptr; Nwsp Stf; Bsktbl; Trk; Spanish NHS; Math Achvt Awd 84; SUNY Oneonta; Thtr Arts.

BRENNAN, CANDY; Faith Heritage Schl; Syracuse, NY; (Y); 2/23; Drama Clb; French Clb; Stu Cncl; Cheerleading; Score Keeper; Socr; Hon Roll; Dist Chrstn HS Stu 85-86; Eastern Nazarene Coll; Missnry.

BRENNAN, DAVID C; La Salle Inst; Green Is, NY; (Y); 3/90; Am Leg Boys St; ROTC; Rep Stu Cncl; Golf; Lcrss; High Hon Roll; Jr NHS; NHS; Cmmd Srgnt Mjr In JR ROTC 86; West Point; Engnrng.

BRENNAN, DENA; Bishop Grimes HS; Syracuse, NY; (Y); FBLA; Teachers Aide; Cit Awd; Hon Roll; Var Vllybl; Soclgy.

BRENNAN, EDWARD F; Wyoming Central Schl; Wyoming, NY; (Y); 5/23; Drama Clb; Sec 4-H; School Play; Yrbk Stf; Var Bsktbl; 4-H Awd; Hon Roll; Trs NHS; Natl Mth Awd 85; Regents Scholar 86; Rochester Inst Tech; Bus Sci.

BRENNAN, HEATHER; Clayton A Bouton JR SR HS; New Scotland, NY; (Y); Pres Intnl Clb; Key Clb; VP SADD; Chorus; Concert Band; Jazz Band; Rep Stu Cncl; Var Fld Hcky; High Hon Roll; NHS.

BRENNAN, JENNIFER A; Johnstown HS; Johnstown, NY; (Y); Intnl Clb; SADD; Nwsp Rptr; Yrbk Stf; Rep Soph Cls; Rep Jr Cls; Rep Sr Cls; Regents Schlrshp 85-86; Potsdam U; Anthrplgy.

BRENNAN, JOSEPH; Albion HS; Albion, NY; (S); 3/176; Boy Scts; Church Yth Grp; JCL; Latin Clb; Math Tm; High Hon Roll; Jr NHS; Gen Mtrs/Harrison Radiator Co-Op Prgm; GMI; Mech Engr.

BRENNAN, KELLY; Sacred Heart Acad; Garden City, NY; (Y); Service Clb; SADD; Tennis; Hon Roll; NHS; Essay Cntst 84.

BRENNAN, MAUREEN; Our Lady Of Merch HS; Fairport, NY; (Y); Church Yth Grp; Cmnty Wkr; JA; Ski Clb; SADD; Nwsp Rptr; Rep Stu Cncl; Var Crs Cntry; Var Gym; Im Sftbl; Stud Cncl Crss Cntry Cmmnty Wrkr Gymnstcs Hnr Rll Sftbl Trck Jr Achvt Ski Clb Nwpapr Rprtr; Advrtsng.

BRENNAN, MICHELLE; Brockport HS; Brockport, NY; (Y); 17/315; Cmnty Wkr; Dance Clb; Sec Latin Clb; Office Aide; Yrbk Stf; JV Var Cheerleading; Score Keeper; High Hon Roll; Jr NHS; Sec NHS; Most Improved In Dance Clss 85; Duke U; Marine Bio.

BRENNAN, MOLLY; The Buffalo Seminary; Amherst, NY; (Y); Service Clb; Ski Clb; Stage Crew; Yrbk Bus Mgr; Pres Frsh Cls; Var Lcrss; Var Socr.

BRENNAN, MOLLY E; Cardinal O Hara HS; Buffalo, NY; (S); #26 In Class; Church Yth Grp; Latin Clb; Pep Clb; Spanish Clb; Chorus; Church Choir; Nwsp Stf; VP Frsh Cls; Bowling; Hon Roll; ST U Of NY-BUFFALO; Psyclgy.

BRENNER, ALAN F; Mac Arthur HS; Levittown, NY; (Y); 20/321; Cmnty Wkr; Chorus; L Var Bsbl; JV L Ftbl; High Hon Roll; NHS; NY St Regents Schlrshp 86; Physics Chllng Exam NY Tech 86; Star Of 86 In Hit Grease; SUNY-STONY Brook; Elec Engrng.

BRENNER, CRISSY; Miller Place HS; Miller Place, NY; (Y); 10/250; Church Yth Grp; Pres FTA; Office Aide; Teachers Aide; Var Mgr(s); High Hon Roll; NHS; Elem Ed.

BRENNER, DARREN; Herbert H Lehman HS; New York, NY; (Y); Stage Crew; Yrbk Stf; Wt Lftg; JV Wrstlng; Parsons Fashion Inst Of Tech.

BRENNER, DAVID; Lawrence HS; Woodmere, NY; (Y); Cmnty Wkr; Debate Tm; Model UN; Spanish Clb; Y-Teens; Orch; Nwsp Stf; Lit Mag; Im Bsbl; High Hon Roll; Ecnmcs.

BRENNER, JUDY; W T Clarke HS; Westbury, NY; (Y); 46/200; 4-H; French Clb; FBLA; Model UN; Ski Clb; SADD; Orch; School Musical; Nwsp Bus Mgr; Timer; 1st Orchstra 86; NYSMA Violn 85; 1st FBLA Ecnmcs 86; SUNY Albany; Bus.

BRENNER, PAUL; Smithtown High School East; Nesconset, NY; (Y); Spanish Clb; Temple Yth Grp; Stu Cncl; High Hon Roll; NHS; Prfct Atten Awd; Spanish NHS; Highest Hon Awd 84-86; Math.

BRENNER, ROBERT A; Red Hook Central HS; Red Hook, NY; (Y); AFS; Boy Scts; Sec Church Yth Grp; Pres Jr Cls; Var Tennis; High Hon Roll; Eagle Scout 86; Bard Coll Humanities Awd 86; Egbert Benson Hstrcl Soc Heritage Awd 86; SUNY Binghamton.

BRENON, MARK; East Syracuse-Minoa HS; E Syracuse, NY; (Y); French Clb; JA; Science Clb; Ski Clb; Variety Show; Yrbk Stf; Im Badmtn; Var JV Lcrss; Var Capt Socr; Im Vllybl; Mech Engrg.

BRENT, REGINA; Homell HS; Hornell, NY; (Y); Art Clb; Office Aide; Teachers Aide; Chorus; Color Guard; High Hon Roll; Hon Roll; 1st & 3rd Pl Art/Grphc Awds 84; 3rd Pl Sci Fair Awd 84; Geneseo; Art.

BRESCIA, ANNE MARIE; Our Lady Of Mercy Acad; Huntington, NY; (Y); 1/120; Dance Clb; Hosp Aide; Trs Service Clb; Ed Lit Mag; Elks Awd; High Hon Roll; VP NHS; Val; VFW Awd; Schering-Plough Fndtn Ntl Sci Schlrhshp; Phi Beta Kappa Alumni Assoc Long Islnd Citation 86; Bio Med.

BRESCIA, ANNEMARIE C; Our Lady Of Mercy Acad; Huntington, NY; (Y); 1/120; Church Yth Grp; Cmnty Wkr; Dance Clb; Hosp Aide; Ed Lit Mag; High Hon Roll; VP NHS; Val; Voice Dem Awd; Med.

BRESE, SHARON; Kenmore East HS; Tonawanda, NY; (Y); Church Yth Grp; PAVAS; Orch; School Musical; Swing Chorus; JV Capt Bsktbl; Var Socr; Var Vllybl; High Hon Roll; NHS; Outstndng Math Awd 84; Outstndng Spnsh Stu 84.

BRESLIN, KATIE; St Marys Girls HS; Port Washington, NY; (Y); 39/187; Hosp Aide; Service Clb; Ski Clb; Spanish Clb; SADD; Chorus; Stage Crew; Yrbk Stf; Hon Roll; Law.

BRESLIN, LEE; Northport HS; Northport, NY; (Y); 268/572; Orch; Lit Mag; JV Cheerleading; JV Gym; Var Trk; Liberal Arts.

BRESLIN, MICHAEL; Cathedral Preparatory Seminary; Bronx, NY; (Y); Nwsp Stf; Lit Mag; Var Bsbl; JV Var Bsktbl; Hon Roll; NHS; Sal; Govs Cmmtte Schlstc Achvt; Amer Allinace Hlth, Phy Ed, Recreatn, Dance Achvt Awd; Iona Coll Schlrshp; Cathedral Coll; Psych.

BRESLOW, PAM; Spackenkill HS; Poughkeepsie, NY; (Y); Temple Yth Grp; Yrbk Stf; Trs Soph Cls; Trs Jr Cls; Trs Sr Cls; Trs Stu Cncl; Var Socr; Var Tennis; Rotary Awd.

BRESNAN, CHERYL L; E J Wilson HS; Rochester, NY; (Y); JCL; Latin Clb; Stu Cncl; High Hon Roll; Hon Roll; NHS; NYS Regnts Schlrshp 86; Monroe CC; Actg.

BRESSLER, LARRY; Herbert H Lehman HS; Bronx, NY; (Y); Debate Tm; Drama Clb; Orch; School Play; Bowling; Var Ftbl; Hon Roll; NHS; NY ST Bar Assoc ST Mock Trial Comptn 85; NY ST Bar Assoc ST Mock Trial Champshp 86; Law.

BRETHEN, PATRICK S; Red Creek Central HS; Red Creek, NY; (Y); 3/82; Am Leg Boys St; Camera Clb; Pres French Clb; Band; School Play; Yrbk Sprt Ed; JV Var Socr; Wrstlng; High Hon Roll; VP Sec NHS; Regents Scholar 86; Babe Ruth Sptsmnshp Awd 86; Vrsty Socr ST Co-Champ Tm 85-86; Long Island U; Mar Sci.

BRETT, LISA; Lindenhurst SR HS; Lindenhurst, NY; (Y); French Clb; SADD; Yrbk Stf; Rep Stu Cncl; Stat Socr; High Hon Roll; Hon Roll; Pres NHS; Italian Clb Pres; Stu Soc Respnsblty Treas; Untd HS Stu; Intl Reltns.

BRETTNER, DEBBIE; Auburn HS; Auburn, NY; (Y); Cmnty Wkr; German Clb; Hosp Aide; Red Cross Aide; Ski Clb; Band; Socr; Vllybl; Gov Hon Prg Awd; High Hon Roll; Social Studies Awd 86.

BREUNIG, DAVID; Blessed Sacrament St Gabriel HS; New Rochelle, NY; (Y); Nwsp Stf; Hon Roll; Regents Schrlshp 85; Math Exc; SUNY; Comp Engr.

BREUNIG, MICHAEL D; Sidney Central HS; Sidney, NY; (Y); Am Leg Boys St; Drama Clb; Ski Clb; Varsity Clb; Yrbk Phtg; Var L Crs Cntry; Var L Socr; Var L Tennis; Var L Trk; Hon Roll; Engl.

BREW, JAY; Canisteo Central HS; Hornell, NY; (Y); Boy Scts; Speech Tm; Off Frsh Cls; Bsktbl; Cit Awd; Hon Roll; Wildwood Educ Ctr-Outstndng Effrt 86; Alfred U; Auto Mchncs.

BREWER, JOSEPH; Bishop Grimes HS; Syracuse, NY; (Y); Cmnty Wkr; Exploring; JA; Ski Clb; Lcrss; Socr; Crmnl Justice.

BREWINGTON, MARETTA; Copiague HS; Copiague, NY; (Y); Spanish Clb; Church Choir; Var Capt Cheerleading; Var Gym; Var Sftbl; Church Yth Grp; Yrbk Phtg; Score Keeper; Hon Roll; Prfct Atten Awd; Commended Stu 86; Pembroke U; Psych.

BREWSTER, JEFFREY; Port Jervis HS; Port Jervis, NY; (Y); 23/192; Drama Clb; Varsity Clb; Chorus; School Musical; Yrbk Phtg; Rep Stu Cncl; Var Cheerleading; JV Stat Bsktbl; Var Trk; NHS; Theatre Arts.

BREWSTER, MARION R; Academy Of St Joseph; Brentwood, NY; (Y); SADD; Rotary Awd; Rotary Intl Exchng Stu In Brussels, Belgium 84-85; Nazareth Coll-Rochester; French.

BREWSTER, RHONDA; Evander Childs HS; Bronx, NY; (Y); Typg Awd 86; Nrsg.

BREWTON, DEIRDRE; New Rochelle HS; New Rochelle, NY; (Y); Church Yth Grp; Math Clb; Math Tm; Pep Clb; Science Clb; Spanish Clb; SADD; Varsity Clb; Acpl Chr; Chorus; Howard U; Med.

BREYO, ROBIN; Ballston Spa SR HS; Ballston Spa, NY; (Y); 19/230; 4-H; Varsity Clb; Bsktbl; Fld Hcky; Trk; 4-H Awd; High Hon Roll; NHS; Rgnts Schlrshp 86; Potsdam Coll.

BRICEUS, CARLYNE; Norman Thomas HS; Brooklyn, NY; (S); 19/596; Cmnty Wkr; Drama Clb; VP FBLA; Church Choir; School Play; Trk; Cit Awd; Hon Roll; NHS; SUNY Albany; Acctng.

BRICK, ANDREW; Sayville HS; Sayville, NY; (Y); 60/362; Church Yth Grp; Mathletes; PAVAS; Band; Concert Band; Orch; JV Ftbl; Socr; Wrstlng; Hon Roll; Siena Coll Grant 86-87; Holy Name Province-Friars Awd- 4 Yrs; Siena Coll; Polit Sci.

BRICKLEY, SHAWN; Falconer Central HS; Jamestown, NY; (Y); 25/125; Church Yth Grp; Letterman Clb; Spanish Clb; Stu Cncl; Var L Bsbl; Var L Bsktbl; Var L Ftbl; Hon Roll; Lbrl Arts.

BRICKMAN, SHARI; Lakeland HS; Yorktown Hts, NY; (Y); 66/448; Ski Clb; SADD; Rep Sr Cls; Mgr Cheerleading; JV VP Fld Hcky; Capt Lcrss; Pres Schlr; Natl Ldrshp Merit Awd 86; Oswego St; Bus Admin.

BRIDGE, KAREN; Alexander Central Schl; Batavia, NY; (Y); Drama Clb; Chorus; School Musical; Nwsp Stf; Socr; Stu Cncl, Homeroom Rep, Hmcmng 85-86; All Cnty Chorus, Solo Fstvl 83-84; Ice Sktng Lsns 84-85; Herkimer Coll; Sec.

BRIDGEFORD, ERIN; Cornwall Central HS; Cornwall, NY; (Y); Cmnty Wkr; Drama Clb; Hosp Aide; Math Tm; School Play; Stage Crew; Trk; High Hon Roll; NHS; Ntl Merit Ltr; Schl Rep Yth For Undrstng Scholar 85-86; Duke U.

BRIDGEWATER, ETHELEEN; Peekskill HS; Peekskill, NY; (Y); 7/146; Pres Church Yth Grp; Pres Church Choir; School Play; Rep Stu Cncl; Capt Var Cheerleading; High Hon Roll; Hon Roll; JC Awd; NHS; Principals Awd 86; Stu Of Mnth-Feb 86; Alpha Kappa Alpha Sorority Schlrshp 86 E; Cornell U; Ind & Labor Rltns.

BRIEFS, MARY; Bayport-Blue Point HS; Bayport, NY; (Y); 8/215; Chess Clb; Mathletes; Band; Concert Band; Mrchg Band; Pep Band; Stage Crew; JV Mgr(s); Hon Roll; Jr NHS; Stu Of Wk-Trignmtry 84-85; Stu Of Mnth-Amercn Stds 85-86; Comp Engr.

BRIENZA, ROGER M; Franklin K Lane HS; Wood Haven, NY; (Y); 50/659; Church Yth Grp; Cmnty Wkr; Comm Svc 83-85; Hnr Cert Perf Attndnce 85-86; Hnr Cert Achvt Alg 84-85; Pace U; Comp Sci.

BRIERLEY, JEFF; Brewster HS; Brewster, NY; (Y); Church Yth Grp; Cmnty Wkr; Varsity Clb; Pres Frsh Cls; Rep Stu Cncl; Var Bsktbl; Var Lcrss; Var Socr; Hon Roll; NHS; Bsktbl-MVP Brewster Holiday Tour, WICB All Leag, WICB All Sect 85-86; Ntl Hon Soc 85-86; Hobart Coll; Bus.

BRIGGS, CYNTHIA; Charlotte Valley Central HS; Oneonta, NY; (S); 3/30; Girl Scts; Trs Frsh Cls; Trs Soph Cls; Trs Jr Cls; VP Sr Cls; Var Capt Bsktbl; Var L Sftbl; High Hon Roll; Trs NHS; Elmira Coll Key Awd 85; Schlrs Crtland Day 85; Elmira Coll; Bus Mgmt.

BRIGGS, DAVID D; Dansville SR HS; Arkport, NY; (Y); 9/166; Am Leg Boys St; SADD; Im Vllybl; Im Wt Lftg; Var Wrstlng; High Hon Roll; Hon Roll; St Schlr; Scrpt D Awd 84-85; Rgnts Schlrshp 85; Scl Stdies Rgnts Awd 84; Clarkson U; Cmptr Engnr.

BRIGGS, ERNESTINE; Nazareth Regional HS; Brooklyn, NY; (Y); Cmnty Wkr; Var Math Tm; Spanish Clb; Church Choir; Speech Tm; Rep Sr Cls; JV Sftbl; Hon Roll; NHS; Cert Apprctn-Catholic Charities 84-85; Psych.

BRIGGS, JAMES L; Rome Free Acad; Rome, NY; (Y); 70/462; Intnl Clb; Ski Clb; Yrbk Stf; Var Golf; Hon Roll; Jr NHS; NHS; NYS Regents Scholar 86; Pres Acad Fit Awd 86; Sci Awd 83; Mohawk Vly CC; Elec Engrng.

BRIGGS, JIM; Churchville Chili HS; Spencerport, NY; (Y); 75/325; Cmnty Wkr; Lit Mag; Var L Crs Cntry; Var L Socr; Var L Trk; Var L Wrstlng; High Hon Roll; Hon Roll; NHS; SUNY At Brockport; Phy Ed.

BRIGGS, MARGIE; Glens Falls SR HS; Glens Falls, NY; (Y); 29/217; Girl Scts; Math Tm; Pep Clb; SADD; Band; Mrchg Band; Powder Puff Ftbl; High Hon Roll; NHS; Jackson Hts Schlrshp 86; Accntng & Math Awds 86; ACC; Accntng.

BRIGGS, MICHELE; Mexico Acad HS; Parish, NY; (Y); Church Yth Grp; Pep Clb; Spanish Clb; Varsity Clb; Band; Mrchg Band; Stu Cncl; Var Cheerleading; Hon Roll; Spanish NHS; SUNY Oswego; Psych.

BRIGGS, STACY L; Brocton Central Schl; Brocton, NY; (Y); French Clb; Ski Clb; Nwsp Stf; Yrbk Stf; Pres Jr Cls; Pres Sr Cls; Cheerleading; Bausch & Lomb Sci Awd; DAR Awd; NHS; Stu Of Wk 85; Long Island U; Chem.

BRIGGS, YVETTE; Trott Vocational HS; Niagara Falls, NY; (Y); 11/145; VP Boys Clb Am; Sec Church Yth Grp; Cmnty Wkr; Hosp Aide; Key Clb; Office Aide; Pep Clb; Teachers Aide; Church Choir; Nwsp Stf; John Richarson Awd Outstndng Stu Niagara Cty; Lasalle Soc Clb Schlrshp Awd 86; UTICA Coll; RN Nrs.

BRIGLIO, JEANINE; A G Berner HS; Massapequa Park, NY; (Y); 24/300; Pep Clb; Spanish Clb; NHS.

BRIGNATI, THOMAS G; Half Hollow Hills E HS; Melville, NY; (Y); 15/509; Quiz Bowl; Scholastic Bowl; Varsity Clb; Nwsp Stf; Var Socr; French Hon Soc; High Hon Roll; NHS; Ntl Merit SF; Regents Schlrshp 86; Coll Of Wm & Mary; Ec.

BRILL, CYNTHIA; Queen Of The Roseary Acad; Farmingdale, NY; (S); Art Clb; Teachers Aide; Band; Chorus; JV Bsktbl; JV Var Cheerleading; JV Sftbl; Var Vllybl; Hon Roll; Ldrs Clb 85-86; Nortra Dame Coll; Bus Mngmnt.

BRILL, SHARYN; Clarkstown North HS; New City, NY; (Y); Spanish Clb; Temple Yth Grp; Band; Concert Band; Chrmn Of Holocaust Rmbrnc Prgm 86; Chrmnn Argnl Camp Of Menty Rgn 86.

BRILLI, THERESA; Our Lady Of Mercy HS; Rochester, NY; (Y); Exploring; Ski Clb; SADD; Varsity Clb; Chorus; Hon Roll; Var Gym; JV Trk; Monroe CC; Crim Just.

BRINK, KELLY; Dundee Central HS; Dundee, NY; (Y); Sec FHA; Teachers Aide; Capt Color Guard; Concert Band; Mrchg Band; Yrbk Stf; High Hon Roll; Hon Roll; NHS; Stage Crew; Hm Ec Hgst Achvd; Bryant & Straton; Exec Sec.

BRINK, MICHAEL; Horseheads HS; Horseheads, NY; (S); 17/380; Science Clb; Varsity Clb; Var L Golf; High Hon Roll; Hon Roll; NHS; Engrng.

BRINK, SARA; Our Lady Of Mercy HS; Rochester, NY; (S); 2/13; Sec Church Yth Grp; Drama Clb; Sec Spanish Clb; Chorus; School Play; Stage Crew; Yrbk Stf; Rep Frsh Cls; Rep Jr Cls; Hon Roll; Natl Achvt Schlrshp Prog For Outstdn Negro Stu 86.

BRINKLEY, CHRISTINE; Archbishop Lakovos HS; Jamaica, NY; (S); 3/15; Art Clb; Computer Clb; English Clb; Library Aide; Math Clb; Teachers Aide; Yrbk Stf; Im Wt Lftg; High Hon Roll; Hon Roll; US Air Force Acad; Pilot.

BRINKMAN, JULIE; Batavia HS; Batavia, NY; (Y); 22/200; Am Leg Aux Girls St; Sec Church Yth Grp; Drama Clb; SADD; Var L Socr; Hon Roll; Env Sci.

BRINKMAN, KRISTEN; Bayport Bluepoint HS; Patchogue, NY; (Y); 3/200; Key Clb; Math Tm; Hon Roll; Jr NHS; NHS; Achvt Chem 85-86; Buffalo; Bus.

BRINN, MARK; Penn Yan Acad; Penn Yan, NY; (Y); Am Leg Boys St; Pres Frsh Cls; Pres Soph Cls; Pres Jr Cls; JV Var Bsktbl; JV Var Ftbl; JV Var Lcrss; High Hon Roll; Hon Roll; Church Yth Grp; Hugh O Brian Yth Ldrshp Smnr 85; Coll; Physcl Thrpy.

BRIODY, MARY C; Notre Dame Schl; Rockaway Pk, NY; (Y); 3/49; Drama Clb; Sec Stu Cncl; Capt Bsktbl; Capt Sftbl; Capt Vllybl; Pres NHS; NEDT Hgh Achvt 83; Hopkins Scholar 86; Le Moyne Acad Scholar 86; Boston Coll; Mth.

BRISCOE, AARON; Clara Barton HS; Brooklyn, NY; (Y); Church Yth Grp; Exploring; Hon Roll; Engrng.

BRISSETTE, MICHELLE; Liverpool HS; Liverpool, NY; (Y); 63/884; Church Yth Grp; Concert Band; Mrchg Band; Hon Roll; Jr NHS; NHS; Intl Bus.

BRISTOL, JOHN; Lansingburgh HS; Troy, NY; (S); Math Tm; Red Cross Aide; School Musical; Stage Crew; Yrbk Stf; Cit Awd; High Hon Roll; Jr NHS; Prfct Atten Awd; Hudson Vly CC; Crim Just.

BRITE, HOLLY; Upper Room Christian Schl; Lindenhurst, NY; (S); Church Yth Grp; Hosp Aide; Nrsng.

BRITO, ANTONIO; Christopher Columbus HS; Bronx, NY; (Y); Teachers Aide; Chorus; Hon Roll; Prfct Atten Awd; Daily News Fstvl Voices 84; Acdmc Olympcs Awd, Daily News 86; Comp Prog.

BRITT, AMY; Southampton HS; Southampton, NY; (Y); Art Clb; GAA; Band; Yrbk Stf; Stu Cncl; Sftbl; Hon Roll; Prfct Atten Awd; Art Hnrb Mntn 86; Natl Yng Ldrs Conf 86; Graphc Desgn.

BRITT, BRIDGET; Catholic Central HS; Clifton Park, NY; (S); 21/179; Church Yth Grp; GAA; Math Clb; Pep Clb; Spanish Clb; SADD; School Play; Yrbk Stf; Rep Frsh Cls; Rep Soph Cls; Soc Stud Awd 82; Pres Athltc Awd 80-85; Siera Coll; Bus Mgmt.

BRITTAIN, DAVID; Msgr Farrell HS; Staten Island, NY; (Y); JV Crs Cntry; Im Ftbl; Var L Trk; Marty Celic Schlrshp Awd 86.

BRITTON, CHRISTOPHER; Monsignor Farrell HS; Staten Island, NY; (Y); 65/290; Im Bsktbl; Im Ftbl; JV Capt Socr; Hon Roll; Ntl Merit Ltr; Police Athletic League NY City Soccer Champs 83; NY St Regents Schlrshp Winner 86; Wagner Coll; Physcn.

BRITTON, JACQUELINE; Guilderland Central HS; Altamont, NY; (Y); Exploring; French Clb; Girl Scts; Hosp Aide; Service Clb; SADD; Hon Roll; Censed Amateur Radio Opr 4 Yrs; 100 Hr Pin 100 Hrs Vlntr Wrk 85; Nrs.

BRITTON, MONICA; Westbury SR HS; Westbury, NY; (Y); FBLA; JA; Band; Concert Band; Mrchg Band; Nwsp Rptr; Nwsp Stf; Sec Sr Cls; Rep Stu Cncl; L Cheerleading; Med.

BRIZZI, LEA; Paul V Moore HS; Constantia, NY; (Y); 8/200; GAA; Yrbk Stf; Stu Cncl; JV Socr; High Hon Roll; Karte Cls 2 Yrs; Stu Cncl Wrk; Yrbk Stf 87.

BROADHEAD, WENDY S; Falconer Central HS; Falconer, NY; (Y); 14/121; Church Yth Grp; Pres FBLA; Quiz Bowl; Hon Roll; NHS; Rgnt Schlrshp; Jamestown Prfsnl Bus Wms Clb Schlrshp 86; Viking Schlrshp 84; Our Lady Of Loreto 86; Pace U; Intrnl Mngmnt.

BROADHURST, JEFFREY B; Irvington HS; Irvington, NY; (Y); 45/108; Chess Clb; Church Yth Grp; Cmnty Wkr; JA; Key Clb; Ski Clb; Chorus; Church Choir; School Musical; School Play; CO Schl Of Mines; Engrng.

BROADIE JR II, PAUL; Harry S Truman HS; Bronx, NY; (Y); 94/494; Crs Cntry; Trk; Ntl Merit Ltr; Computer Clb; Math Tm; Teachers Aide; Chorus; Church Choir; Orch; Pres Frsh Cls; Iona Coll; Lawyer.

BROADWATER, ELIZABETH; Columbia HS; Rensselear, NY; (Y); 42/416; Concert Band; Mrchg Band; Orch; School Musical; Symp Band; Crs Cntry; Capt Trk; NHS; Grad Cum Laude; William Smith College.

BROCATO, FRANK; Monsignor Farrell HS; Staten Island, NY; (Y); Chess Clb; Cmnty Wkr; Speech Tm; JV Bsbl; Im Bsktbl; JV Crs Cntry; Im Ftbl; JV Wrstlng; Cert Achvt Publc Schl Cnslr 81-86; Mid Atlantic Regnl Bsbl Tm 87; St Johns U; Ath Adm.

BROCCOLI, KAREN; John F Kennedy HS; Utica, NY; (Y); Cmnty Wkr; Yrbk Phtg; Yrbk Stf; Hon Roll; Sec.

BROCCOLI, RENEE; Whitesboro SR HS; Marcy, NY; (Y); 50/354; GAA; Ski Clb; Powder Puff Ftbl; Var L Sftbl; Var L Tennis; L Vllybl; Hon Roll; Rgnts Schlrshp 86; Union Coll; Bio-Med Engrng.

BROCK, CHRISTINE; Manhasset HS; Manhasset, NY; (Y); 86/205; Debate Tm; JA; Political Wkr; Service Clb; Ski Clb; Spanish Clb; Hon Roll; Jr NHS; 3rd Pl In CA JR Achvt Comp 84; Emory U; Pre Law.

BROCK, EDWARD; Susan Wagner HS; Staten Island, NY; (Y); Teachers Aide; Nwsp Bus Mgr; Sec Frsh Cls; Mgr Socr; Upward Bound At NYU; Bio.

BROCK, MICHAEL; Berlin HS; Petersburg, NY; (S); 5/80; Am Leg Boys St; VP Frsh Cls; Trs Jr Cls; Var L Bsbl; Var L Socr; Var L Wrstlng; Hon Roll; NHS; Ntl Merit Ltr; Prfct Atten Awd.

BROCK, PAMELA; Spring Valley SR HS; Spring Valley, NY; (Y); 39/441; Key Clb; Math Tm; Temple Yth Grp; Thesps; Yrbk Stf; JV Cheerleading; Var L Swmmng; Hon Roll; NHS; Spanish NHS; Regnts Schlrshp 86; Brandeis U; Chem.

BROCKHAUSEN, VICKI; Peekskill HS; Peekskill, NY; (S); Band; Concert Band; Jazz Band; Mrchg Band; Rep Stu Cncl; Stat Golf; Capt Var Swmmng; Bausch & Lomb Sci Awd; High Hon Roll; NHS; Med.

BROCKI, LISA; Frontier Central HS; Hamburg, NY; (Y); French Clb; Chorus; Hon Roll; NHS; Phrmcy.

BROCKS, WILLIAM R; Wellington C Mepham HS; N Bellmore, NY; (Y); 31/360; Political Wkr; JV Bsbl; Var L Ftbl; JV Socr; Hon Roll; NHS; NY ST Regents Schlrshp 86; NY ST U-Albany; Bus.

BROCKWAY, RANDY; Colton-Pierrepont HS; Potsdam, NY; (S); 1/30; Quiz Bowl; School Musical; Pres Frsh Cls; Trs Soph Cls; Trs Jr Cls; Rep Stu Cncl; High Hon Roll; Jr NHS; NHS; Clarkson Univ; Elec/Comp Engrg.

BROCKWAY, TIMOTHY; Nottingham HS; Marcellus, NY; (Y); Church Yth Grp; Latin Clb; Rep Frsh Cls; High Hon Roll; Hon Roll; NHS; Spanish NHS; Latin I 4th Pl Ntl Latin Exam 85; Latin II 3rd Pl Ntl Latin Exam 86; ST U Bringhamton; Geneticist.

BROD, MELISSA A; Irvington HS; Tarrytown, NY; (Y); 13/108; Pres Key Clb; SADD; Pres Temple Yth Grp; Yrbk Bus Mgr; Ed Lit Mag; Rep Soph Cls; Capt Tennis; High Hon Roll; All Conference Tennis 85; U Of MI; Pre-Med.

BRODERICK, ARLENE; Acad Of Mt St Ursula; Bronx, NY; (Y); Church Yth Grp; Dance Clb; SADD; Varsity Clb; Cheerleading; Coach Actv; Psych.

BRODERSEN, LISA; H Frank Carey HS; Franklin Square, NY; (Y); 6/276; Cmnty Wkr; Sec Science Clb; SADD; Thesps; Nwsp Rptr; Yrbk Ed-Chief; Sec NHS; Ntl Merit Ltr; VP German Clb; Hosp Aide; Frgn Lang Hnr Soc; Steuben Awd 86; Tlnt & Gftd Prog.

BRODIN, LAURA M; Mamaroneck HS; Larchmont, NY; (Y); School Musical; School Play; Lit Mag; NHS; Prfrmng Arts Awd 83-84; Russ Lang Awd 86; SR Lang Awd 86; Columbia U; Russ Stud.

BRODKIN, TARA L; Edgemont HS; Scarsdale, NY; (Y); Hosp Aide; Temple Yth Grp; Nwsp Bus Mgr; Stu Cncl; Var Fld Hcky; Lcrss; JV Tennis; St Schlr; Civic & Humantarn Awd Yth In Actn 85; Cornell U.

BRODMAN, DAVID; Bronx H S Of Science; Riverdale, NY; (Y); Y-Teens; Chorus; Hon Roll; Ntl Merit SF; Cert Exclnce Hebrew 84; Gold Ayin Hebrew 83; Hnrs Bio Cls 84; Binghamton ST U; Med.

BRODOWICZ, FRANCINE L; St Francis Prep; New York, NY; (S); 107/749; School Play; Swmmng; Opt Clb Awd; Vlntr Coachg And Hosp 86.

BRODOWSKI, DIANE M; Alexander Central HS; E Bethany, NY; (Y); 16/82; Church Yth Grp; Ski Clb; Spanish Clb; Band; Chorus; Church Choir; Concert Band; Mrchg Band; Rep Stu Cncl; Crs Cntry; NY ST Rgnts Schlrshp; Hmcmng Prncs; SUNY Potsdam; Psychlgy.

BRODSKY, GERI; Canarsie HS; Brooklyn, NY; (Y); Variety Show; Pom Pon; Var Capt Sftbl; Hon Roll; Vrsty Sftbl Awd.

BRODSKY, MATTHEW; Pine Bush HS; Middletown, NY; (Y); JV Bsbl; Var Bsktbl; Var Socr; Hon Roll; Jr NHS.

BRODSKY, SUZANNE R; Hauppauge HS; Hauppage, NY; (S); DECA; Speech Tm; Orch; School Musical; Stage Crew; High Hon Roll; NHS; 1st Pl DECA Pub Spkng 86; 4th Pl Hnrbl Ment Spkng 85; Plattsburgh ST Coll.

BRODY, SUZANNE; South Side HS; Rockville Ctr, NY; (Y); 32/300; Drama Clb; SADD; Band; Chorus; Madrigals; Mrchg Band; School Musical; Yrbk Phtg; Jr NHS; NHS; Latn Hnr Soc 85; Dsgn Musc.

BROMELL, VERNEICE; Monroe JRSR HS; Rochester, NY; (Y); Office Aide; Jr Cls; Stu Cncl; Cheerleading; Sftbl; Hon Roll; Sec Schl Ldrshp Awd; Prisms Acad Recog; NC A&T; Mktg.

BROMIRSKI, JUDY; St Marys Academy HS; Hoosick Falls, NY; (Y); 3/16; Art Clb; Church Yth Grp; Cmnty Wkr; Dance Clb; French Clb; GAA; Math Clb; Pep Clb; SADD; Varsity Clb; Regents Dipl NYS 86.

BROMIRSKI, TIMOTHY; Hoosick Falls Central Schl; Hoosick Falls, NY; (Y); 7/101; French Clb; Stage Crew; Yrbk Stf; Rep Stu Cncl; L Ftbl; Cit Awd; Hon Roll; Kiwanis Awd; NHS; Norwich Military Schl; Cvl Engr.

BROMLEY, HEATHER; Pine Valley Central Schl; Cherry Creek, NY; (Y); AFS; Ski Clb; SADD; Yrbk Phtg; Yrbk Sprt Ed; Trs Frsh Cls; Trs Soph Cls; Trs Jr Cls; Trs Sr Cls; Var Trk; Paul Smits Coll; Trvl.

BRONCATO, BUFFY; Mt St Mary Acad; Tonawanda, NY; (Y); Speech Tm; School Musical; Stage Crew; Nwsp Stf; Cit Awd; High Hon Roll; NHS; Ntl Merit Ltr; NEDT Awd; Debate Tm; Schlrshp Study Abroad France Smmr 85; Altrnte Its Acadmc Team 84; Schl Awd Excllnce French 86; Politics.

BRONITT, MARC; New Rochelle HS; Scarsdale, NY; (Y); Model UN; Spanish Clb; SADD; Nwsp Rptr; Nwsp Stf; Off Sr Cls; Var JV Ice Hcky; Mgr(s); Mgr Capt Socr; High Hon Roll; Arts.

BRONO, LISA; Valley Stream Central HS; Valley Stream, NY; (Y); Dance Clb; Ski Clb; Drill Tm; Sftbl; Hon Roll; NHS; 2nd Pl Piano Awd 85; Bus.

BRONSON, PEGGY SUE; Clymer Central HS; Clymer, NY; (Y); Trs AFS; Band; Chorus; Trs Frsh Cls; Var L Bsktbl; Var Sftbl; Var Capt Vllybl; High Hon Roll; Hon Roll; NHS; Acctng.

BROOKMAN, ANDREA; Silver Creek Central HS; Silver Creek, NY; (Y); 12/87; Church Yth Grp; Dance Clb; Ski Clb; Spanish Clb; Varsity Clb; Trk; Hon Roll; Rochester Inst Tech; Mrktng.

BROOKS, ANNE MARIE; Amsterdam HS; Amsterdam, NY; (Y); 7/316; Band; Concert Band; Mrchg Band; Orch; Nwsp Stf; Mgr Crs Cntry; Hon Roll; NHS; No 1 Club Soc Studies & Sci 83-84, Eng 84-85; Biomed Engrng.

BROOKS, BETH; The Stony Brook Schl; Sewickley, PA; (Y); 17/80; Art Clb; Camera Clb; Pep Clb; Chorus; Stu Cncl; Cheerleading; Fld Hcky; Swmmng; Vllybl; Hon Roll; Gordon Coll; Elem Ed.

BROOKS, BRANDI; Hugh C Williams HS; Canton, NY; (Y); Church Yth Grp; French Clb; Band; Concert Band; Mrchg Band; Orch; Pep Band; School Musical; Yrbk Stf; Stu Cncl; Elem Educ.

BROOKS, CARRIE; Tioga Central HS; Barton, NY; (S); Teachers Aide; Nwsp Rptr; Nwsp Stf; High Hon Roll; NHS; Ntl Merit Ltr; Prfct Atten Awd; Natl Ltn Exm-Slvr Mdlst; Natl Sci Olympd-Bio; Vet Medcn.

BROOKS, DEBORAH; Westbury HS; Westbury, NY; (Y); #5 In Class; Drama Clb; Nwsp Stf; Lit Mag; Im Bowling; High Hon Roll; NHS; Bst Stdnt Spnsh; Wdmn Wrld Life Ins Soc Awd Outstndng Prfcny Amer Hist; Ed.

BROOKS, KELLI; Sweet Home HS; Tonawanda, NY; (Y); Girl Scts; Spanish Clb; SADD; Stu Cncl; High Hon Roll; NHS; Prfct Atten Awd; Silver Awd Girl Scouts 85; Engl Awd-Engl Lit 11r 86; Acctng Awd 85; U Of Buffalo; Bus Admin.

BROOKS, KENT; Northern Adirondack HS; Ellenburg Depot, NY; (Y); Pres Church Yth Grp; VP FFA; Nwsp Stf; Yrbk Sprt Ed; Yrbk Stf; Hon Roll; ST Grnhnd Awd & Dry Prdctn Awd 84; Dry Mngmnt Awd 85; Cobleskill.

BROOKS, MARY B; Alexander Central Schl; Alexander, NY; (Y); 7/85; Pres Sec Band; Pres Sec Concert Band; Jazz Band; Pres Sec Mrchg Band; Symp Band; JV Socr; JV Sftbl; Hon Roll; JP Sousa Awd; Jr NHS; Ithaca Coll.

BROOKS, RODNEY R; Saratoga Springs HS; Saratoga Springs, NY; (Y); 45/491; French Clb; Science Clb; Bowling; High Hon Roll; NHS; Ntl Merit Ltr; Ntl Frnch Cntst Gld Mdlst; NY ST Rgnts Schlrshp; SUNY Buffalo; Arspc Engrng.

BROOKS, ROGER L; Binghamton HS; Binghamton, NY; (Y); Am Leg Boys St; Cmnty Wkr; Rep Frsh Cls; VP Soph Cls; Pres Jr Cls; Rep Sr Cls; Pres Stu Cncl; Var Bsbl; Cit Awd; Hon Roll; Ntl Cncl Yuth Ldrshp 86.

BROOKS, SAMANTHA E; Syosset HS; Woodbury, NY; (Y); Band; Concert Band; Mrchg Band; Orch; Symp Band; Cheerleading; Regnts Schlrshp86; Gradtng Hnrs Math-Engl 86; PA ST U; Bus.

BROOKS, TAMMIE; Mexico Acad; Mexico, NY; (Y); Ski Clb; Yrbk Stf; Trk; Wt Lftg.

BROOKS, TAMMY; Oakfield-Alabama JR SR HS; Alabama, NY; (Y); Art Clb; GAA; Band; Chorus; Concert Band; Mrchg Band; JV Var Cheerleading; High Hon Roll; Hon Roll; Genesee CC; Bus.

BROOKS, THERESA; Sacred Heart Acad; Bellmore, NY; (S); 32/182; Church Yth Grp; FCA; Math Clb; Math Tm; Var Capt Sftbl; Var Capt Vllybl; Hon Roll; Jr NHS; NHS; Bus.

BROOKSHIRE, ANTOINETTE; Hempstead HS; Hempstead, NY; (S); 17/216; Girl Scts; Trs Stu Cncl; Im Gym; High Hon Roll; Hon Roll; NHS; US Natl Ldrshp Merit Awds 86; Martin Luther King Jr Medallion 86; Fshn Merch.

BROOMHALL, STACY; Montpleasant HS; Schenectady, NY; (Y); French Clb; JA; Office Aide; Service Clb; Concert Band; Mrchg Band; JV Bsktbl; French Hon Soc; Hon Roll; SUNY At Albany; Crmnl Jstice.

BROPHY, CHRISTINE; St Francis Prep; Flushing, NY; (Y); 149/653; Chorus; Rep Jr Cls; Rep Sr Cls; Sftbl; Vllybl; Opt Clb Awd; St Johns U; Acctg.

BROSCH, ERIC; Amsterdam HS; Amsterdam, NY; (S); 41/219; Varsity Clb; Jazz Band; Rep Frsh Cls; Rep Soph Cls; Sec Jr Cls; Pres Stu Cncl; Var Capt Ftbl; Swmmng; JV Wrstlng; Hon Roll; Capital Dist All Star Jazz Ensmbl 85; San Diego ST U.

BROSEN, BRIAN; Chatham HS; Chatham, NY; (Y); Cook.

BROSEN, DANIEL; Chatham HS; Chatham, NY; (Y); JV Bsktbl; Chatham Police Dept Crmnl Just Certfct 86; US Marine Corps.

BROSIOUS, LISA; Lakeland HS; Shrub Oak, NY; (Y); Church Yth Grp; Hosp Aide; Intnl Clb; Band; Nwsp Stf; Rep Jr Cls; Stat Bsbl; Stat Bsktbl; High Hon Roll; Jr NHS; Volntr Of Mnth 83; Pre Med.

BROSNAN, MICHELLE; Olean SR HS; Olean, NY; (Y); Band; Chorus; Concert Band; Jazz Band; Mrchg Band; Orch; Pep Band; Yrbk Stf; Var L Crs Cntry; Var Trk; St Bonaventure U; Pblc Rltns.

BROTHERS III, ALFRED S; Plattsburgh HS; Newtonville, MA; (Y); Boy Scts; Church Yth Grp; Pres Exploring; Red Cross Aide; Ski Clb; Mrchg Band; Pep Band; Symp Band; Cit Awd; God Cntry Awd; Eagle Scout 85; Arch.

BROTHERS, AMY; Madrid-Waddington Central HS; Madrid, NY; (Y); Church Yth Grp; Drama Clb; French Clb; NFL; Speech Tm; SADD; School Musical; 2nd & 3rd Pl Trphy Duo Dramatic Spch & Debate Tm 86; Psych.

BROTON, KAREN; Solvay HS; Solvay, NY; (Y); French Clb; Key Clb; Chorus; Yrbk Stf; Rep Frsh Cls; Rep Soph Cls; Rep Jr Cls; Rep Sr Cls; JV Sftbl; Bus.

BROUGH, JIM; Gates-Chili SR HS; Rochester, NY; (Y); Math Clb; High Hon Roll; Hon Roll; Sci.

BROWE, JOHN; Hoosick Falls Central Schl; Hoosick Falls, NY; (Y); Drama Clb; 4-H; Spanish Clb; Band; Mrchg Band; School Play; 4-H Clthng Revue 85; Citadel; Socl Wkr.

BROWER, JOHN; Newburgh Free Acad; Newburgh, NY; (Y); Wrstlng; High Hon Roll; Hon Roll; Jr NHS; Orange Cnty Brd Of Rltrs 1st Pl Arch Dsgn 85; NYS Olympcs Of Vicual Acts In Arch 3rd Pl 86; Syracuse U; Arch.

BROWKA, MELANIE; Rome Catholic HS; Verona, NY; (Y); 4-H; Chorus; Church Choir; School Musical; Sec Stu Cncl; 4-H Awd; High Hon Roll; Dioceses Orgnst Trng Prgrm 85; Cornell U; Vet Sci.

BROWN, ALISON; Potsdam Central HS; West Dummerston, VT; (Y); 11/123; AFS; Latin Clb; Math Tm; Nwsp Rptr; Yrbk Bus Mgr; Lit Mag; Crs Cntry; Trk; Dnfth Awd; NHS; U NC-GREENSBORO.

BROWN, AMY; Wyoming Central Schl; Wyoming, NY; (S); 1/23; Pres AFS; Sec Am Leg Aux Girls St; Debate Tm; Drama Clb; Model UN; School Play; Pres Jr Cls; NHS; Elmira Coll; Chld Psych.

BROWN, AMY ELIZABETH; Arlington Central HS; Poughkeepsie, NY; (Y); Am Leg Aux Girls St; Girl Scts; Spanish Clb; Capt Var Cheerleading; Ntl Merit Ltr; Spanish NHS; Bronze Mdl Natl Wrttn Russian CO 86; Goldmdl NY Olympd Spkn Russian 86; Natl HS Slavic Hon Soc 86; Boston COLL; Intl Bus.

BROWN, ANDREA; Tamarac HS; Melrose, NY; (Y); 14/110; Hosp Aide; SADD; Band; Sec Chorus; Mrchg Band; School Musical; Yrbk Stf; Off Sr Cls; Var JV Cheerleading; Var JV Pom Pon; Bay Path JC; Fash Merch.

BROWN, ANNETTE; South Park HS; Buffalo, NY; (Y); Church Yth Grp; FBLA; Hon Roll; NHS; Prfct Atten Awd; U Of Buffalo; Bus Adm.

BROWN, BABETTE; Campbell Central HS; Campbell, NY; (S); #3 In Class; Sec Church Yth Grp; Sec French Clb; Varsity Clb; Chorus; Drm Mjr(t); Yrbk Stf; Capt L Vllybl; DAR Awd; NHS; Band Pres 85-86; Clss Treas 82-83; Bsktbl Capt 86; Mus.

BROWN, BARON; Mercy HS; Coram, NY; (Y); Cmnty Wkr; Soph Cls; Med Sci.

BROWN, CANDICE; Frontier SR HS; Lakeview, NY; (S); 71/444; Drama Clb; Trs Latin Clb; Political Wkr; Chorus; Sec Soph Cls; Sec Jr Cls; Stu Cncl; Socr; NHS; NEDT Awd; NY ST Bar Assn Cert 84-85.

BROWN, CAROL; Lansingburgh HS; Troy, NY; (Y); 4-H; Key Clb; SADD; Band; Concert Band; Hon Roll; Prfct Atten Awd; Gregg Spd Prodctn & Transcrptn Prodctn & Typg Prodctn Awds 85-86; Bay Path JC; Certf Pro Secy.

BROWN, CHAD; Oxford Academy And Central HS; Oxford, NY; (Y); Cmnty Wkr; Exploring; French Clb; Varsity Clb; JV Var Bsbl; JV Var Bsktbl; Var Ftbl; Var Powder Puff Ftbl; Hon Roll; Prfct Atten Awd; Conficare Awd 85-86; U Of HI Honalulu; Engr.

BROWN, CHARLA; Walton Central Schl; Walton, NY; (Y); Chorus; Color Guard; Mrchg Band; Computer Clb; SADD; Score Keeper; God Cntry Awd; Hon Roll; Bus.

BROWN, CHARLES; Avon JR SR HS; Avon, NY; (Y); Church Yth Grp; Hon Roll; Jr NHS; NHS; Prfct Atten Awd.

BROWN, CHARLES; Dewitt Clinton HS; Bronx, NY; (S); Capt Math Tm; Band; Concert Band; Var Ftbl; Var Wrstlng; Church Yth Grp; SADD; Ursinus Coll; Law.

BROWN, CHARLES; Dundee Central Schl; Dundee, NY; (Y); 2/85; Am Leg Boys St; Pres Sr Cls; Var L Bsbl; JV Bsktbl; DECA; Hon Roll; NHS; Prfct Atten Awd; High Achvt Awd Earth Sci 84; High Achvt Awd European Studies 85; High Achvt Awd Chemistry 86; Bio Chemistry.

BROWN, CHERYL; James Madison HS; Brooklyn, NY; (Y); FBLA; Nwsp Rptr; Lit Mag; Trk; Hon Roll; Prfct Atten Awd; CAM Prog Cert; Askd Rd Poem 86; Cornell; Med.

BROWN, CHERYL; Notre Dame Acad HS; Staten Island, NY; (Y); VP Intnl Clb; Stage Crew; Yrbk Stf; JV Bsktbl; Score Keeper; Spnsh Cont Concurso Natl Lvl III Excllnc 86; Jrnlsm.

BROWN, CHERYLLE; Evander Childs HS; Bronx, NY; (Y); Church Yth Grp; Varsity Clb; JV Fld Hcky; Var Vllybl; Hon Roll; Prfct Atten Awd; Princeton U; Mass Comm.

BROWN, CHRIS; Frankfort Schuyler HS; Frankfort, NY; (Y); 4-H; Bowling; Ftbl; Vllybl; Hon Roll; Bus.

BROWN, CHRIS; Hendrickson HS; Peekskill, NY; (Y); Band; Concert Band; Mrchg Band; Pep Band; Rep Frsh Cls; Rep Soph Cls; JV Bsbl; Im Vllybl; Hon Roll; Marine Bio.

BROWN, CHRIS; Jamestown HS; Jamestown, NY; (Y); French Clb; Quiz Bowl; Concert Band; Mrchg Band; Hon Roll; NHS; Rochester Inst Of Tech; Cmptr.

BROWN, CHRISTINA; The Doane Stuart Schl; Albany, NY; (Y); Service Clb; School Play; Nwsp Rptr; Ed Lit Mag; Rep Frsh Cls; High Hon Roll; NCTE Awd; Ntl Merit Ltr; 1st Prize Wells Coll Poetry Cont 86; Carleton Coll; Engl.

BROWN, CHRISTINE; Gilboa-Conesville HS; Gilboa, NY; (Y); 1/26; Band; Chorus; Yrbk Ed-Chief; Var Cheerleading; Var Capt Socr; DAR Awd; Val; 4-H; GAA; Hosp Aide; Empire ST Petrol Assn Inc Schlrshp 86; Schoharie Cnty Maple Qn 85; Cortland ST; Psych.

BROWN, CLIFF; Westfield Acad; Westfield, NY; (Y); Boy Scts; Church Yth Grp; Debate Tm; Yrbk Rptr; Yrbk Stf; Hon Roll; Prfct Atten Awd; Bus Mngmnt.

BROWN, COLLEEN C; Bishop Kearney HS; Brooklyn, NY; (Y); 69/337; Hosp Aide; Library Aide; Spanish Clb; Ed Nwsp Rptr; Yrbk Stf; Hon Roll; NHS; Wesleyan U; Med.

BROWN, COREY; Dewitt Clinton HS; New York, NY; (Y); Church Yth Grp; Civic Clb; High Hon Roll; LWYR.

BROWN, DAVID A; Ravena-Coeymans-Selkirk Ctrl HS; Selkirk, NY; (Y); 3/185; Var JV Ftbl; Im Sftbl; Var Trk; Im Vllybl; Var Wrstlng; Bausch & Lomb Sci Awd; High Hon Roll; VP NHS; Ntl Merit Ltr; NYS Chem Awd 83; Cobuskill Math Champ 82; Stu Of Yr 86; Cornell U; Chem Eng.

BROWN, DAWN-YVONNE LORRAINE; Sewanhata Central HS; Elmont, NY; (Y); 11/400; Pres Church Yth Grp; Cmnty Wkr; Thesps; Band; Concert Band; Mrchg Band; Yrbk Stf; Rep Jr Cls; Var Cheerleading; Pom Pon; Natl Assn Of Negro Bus & Pro Wmns Clb Inc Yth Recgntn Awd 86; Nassau Cnty H S Tnns All-Star 84; Intl/Corp Law.

BROWN, DENZIL; Our Saviour Lutheran HS; Bronx, NY; (Y); 7/25; Church Choir; JV Var Bsktbl; Var Capt Socr; Concordia Bronxville; Bnkng.

BROWN, DONALD; Bishop Ludden HS; Syracuse, NY; (Y); Cmnty Wkr; Variety Show; Var Golf; Hon Roll; SUNY Potsdam; Mktg.

BROWN, DONNA LYN; Depew HS; Depew, NY; (Y); 75/275; DECA; GAA; Radio Clb; Variety Show; Yrbk Ed-Chief; JV Cheerleading; Var Crs Cntry; Var Socr; Var Trk; Hon Roll; Buffalo ST; Mktg.

BROWN, DOUGLAS; East Hampton HS; E Hampton, NY; (Y); Stu Cncl; Ftbl; Wrstlng; High Hon Roll; Jr NHS; NHS; All Amer Schlr Athl; Econ.

BROWN, DUVAL; Rice HS; New York, NY; (S); Nwsp Stf; Yrbk Stf; Im Bsktbl; Im Ftbl; Trk; Hon Roll; Arch.

BROWN, DWAYNE ANTHONY; Rice HS; New York, NY; (S); Cmnty Wkr; Intnl Clb; Red Cross Aide; Sec Stu Cncl; Var Bsbl; High Hon Roll; Hon Roll; Rcvd Schlrshp Smmr Engrng Pgm 85; MI ST U; Mech Engrng.

BROWN III, EDWARD WESTON; Patchogue Medford HS; E Patchogue, NY; (S); Band; Concert Band; Jazz Band; Mrchg Band; Orch; School Musical; Nwsp Phtg; Yrbk Phtg; Crs Cntry.

BROWN, EILEEN; Sacred Heart Acad; W Hempstead, NY; (S); Capt Debate Tm; NFL; Red Cross Aide; Speech Tm; School Play; Rep Stu Cncl; Var JV Swmmng; Hon Roll; NHS; Century III Ledrshp Awd 85; US Speech & Drama Awd 84; Intl Ec.

BROWN, ELISABET G; H C Williams HS; Canton, NY; (Y); 4/150; Ski Clb; Orch; School Musical; High Hon Roll; NHS; St Schlr; Presdtl Schlrshp St Lwrnc U 86; Stdy-W Grmny 82 & 85; St Lawrence U; Engl.

BROWN, ERIC; Liverpool HS; No Syracuse, NY; (Y); Exploring; JA; JCL; Math Clb; Ski Clb; Orch; Symp Band; NHS; Latin Clb; Stu Cncl; Operation Enterprs 86; Le Moyne Coll-Summer Schlr 86; Engrng.

BROWN, ERIC; Twin Tiers Baptist HS; Breesport, NY; (Y); Church Yth Grp; School Play; Var L Bsktbl; Var L Socr; Comp Sci.

BROWN, EVRICK; Clara Barton HS; Brooklyn, NY; (Y); Hon Roll; Ntl Sci Olympd Slvr Mdl 86; Prncpls Prd Of Ynkees Outstndg Achvmnt Acdmc Actvts 86; Mst Outstndg Stu; Med.

BROWN, GARFIELD; Midwood HS; Brooklyn, NY; (Y); Cmnty Wkr; Band; Chorus; Variety Show; Ftbl.

BROWN, GEOFF; Fayetteville Manlius HS; Fayetteville, NY; (Y); Boy Scts; Church Yth Grp; Cmnty Wkr; German Clb; Intnl Clb; SADD; Varsity Clb; Im Bsktbl; Var L Ftbl; Var L Trk; Natl Germn Awd 83-84; Lib Arts.

BROWN, GEORGE; De Witt Clinton HS; New York, NY; (Y); Church Yth Grp; Computer Clb; ROTC; Church Choir; Color Guard; Drm & Bgl; Crs Cntry; Gym; Trk; Hon Roll; AFROTC Merit Awd 85&86; Superior Prfrmnc 85; Howard; Med.

BROWN, GEORGE; Washingtonville HS; Monroe, NY; (Y); Var Crs Cntry; Var Trk; Hon Roll; Clrksn U; Chem Engrng.

BROWN, GLENN C; Hamburg SR HS; Hamburg, NY; (Y); 22/385; JA; Hon Roll; Prfct Atten Awd; St Schlr; ST U Of NY; Comp Engrng.

BROWN, HILLARY; Hampton Bays HS; Hampton Bays, NY; (Y); Sec Band; Mrchg Band; Orch; Hon Roll; Prfct Atten Awd.

BROWN, JAMES; Bishop Loughlin Memorial HS; Brooklyn, NY; (Y); CAP; Band; Concert Band; Jazz Band; School Musical; Stage Crew; Variety Show; Wt Lftg; Prpl L 3rd Hnr 82 Avg 84-85; NC A&T; Elctrncs.

BROWN, JEFFERY R; Gilboa-Conesville Central HS; Gilboa, NY; (Y); 2/30; Am Leg Boys St; Debate Tm; Capt Quiz Bowl; School Play; Nwsp Ed-Chief; VP Frsh Cls; VP Jr Cls; JV Capt Bsktbl; Crs Cntry; High Hon Roll; Mst Imprvd Wrtng Awd 83-84; Hghst Avg Spnsh III Awd 85-86; Arspc.

BROWN, JENNIE; Mexico HS; Parish, NY; (Y); JV Diving; Var Wt Lftg; Hon Roll; CCBI; Accntng.

BROWN, JENNIFER; Long Island Lutheran JR SR HS; Wantagh, NY; (S); 1/94; Debate Tm; Trs French Clb; Mathletes; Nwsp Ed-Chief; Ed Lit Mag; High Hon Roll; NHS; Ntl Merit SF; Val; Yale; Bio Chem.

BROWN, KATHY; Amstardam HS; Hagaman, NY; (Y); 46/294; Drm Mjr(t); Hon Roll; Acad Schrlshp 86; Century Clb Art Awd 86; St Johns Soc Awd 86; Coll St Rose; Art.

BROWN, KELLEY; Sandy Creek Central HS; Sandy Creek, NY; (Y); 11/87; Pres Sec Church Yth Grp; Pres VP Drama Clb; JCL; Chorus; Church Choir; School Musical; Swing Chorus; Yrbk Ed-Chief; NHS; Intnl Clb; Conf All ST 85; ; Music.

BROWN, KELLY; Amityville Memorial HS; Amityville, NY; (Y); FBLA; Girl Scts; Sec Soph Cls; Sec Jr Cls; Bsktbl; Bowling; Vllybl; Hon Roll; Jr NHS; Cert Schlrshp Math & Shrthnd 86; Cert Of Hnr Blck Achvmnts Engl 86; Maria Regina; Sec.

BROWN, KELLY; Sherburne-Earlville HS; Earlville, NY; (Y); 10/186; Trs Drama Clb; Sec Ski Clb; VP SADD; School Play; Cheerleading; NHS; Oper Enterprise Schlrshp, Natl Sci Merit Awd Wnnr 86.

BROWN, KEVIN; Westmoreland Central HS; Westmoreland, NY; (Y); Boy Scts; Bsbl; Ftbl; High Hon Roll; NHS; Engr.

BROWN, KIMBERLEY; St Marys HS; Depew, NY; (S); Camera Clb; Ski Clb; High Hon Roll; Pres NHS; Canisius Coll Deans Schlrshp 86; Rgnts Schlrshp 86; Canisius Coll; Comm.

BROWN, LAVELL B; Bronx HS Of Sci; New York, NY; (Y); Chorus; Capt Cheerleading; Rgnts Schlrshp 85-86; Mt St Mry Coll; Med Tech.

BROWN, LENNOX W; Newburgh Free Acad; Newburgh, NY; (Y); 50/650; Key Clb; Ski Clb; Var Capt Swmmng; High Hon Roll; Hon Roll; Mdw Hll Schl Prnt Advsry Grp Schlstc Awd 86; Dr James J Flannery Swmmng Awd 86; Clarkson U; Indstrl Dstrbtn.

BROWN, LISA; F D Roosevelt HS; Hyde Park, NY; (Y); 9/465; Sftbl; High Hon Roll; Hon Roll; NHS; NUY Rgnts Schlrshp 86; U Of Binghamton; Bus Mgmt.

BROWN, LISA; Haldane HS; Cold Spring, NY; (S); 9/55; Rep French Clb; VP Intnl Clb; Ski Clb; Rep SADD; Band; Ed Lit Mag; Rep Stu Cncl; Sftbl; Sec Jr NHS; VP NHS; U Of Vermont; Librl Arts.

BROWN, LORI; Lindenhurst SR HS; Lindenhurst, NY; (Y); Hosp Aide; Lit Mag; High Hon Roll; Hon Roll; Civil Engrg.

BROWN, LORI; Palmyra-Macedon Central HS; Palmyra, NY; (Y); Prfct Atten Awd; Bus.

BROWN, LYNETTE; Cicero N Syracuse HS; Clay, NY; (S); 84/667; German Clb; Hon Roll; NHS; Trvl Agt.

BROWN, MARC; Lansingburgh HS; Troy, NY; (S); 12/180; Math Tm; Yrbk Stf; Off Jr Cls; Off Sr Cls; Var Capt Ftbl; Var L Wrstlng; High Hon Roll; Hon Roll; Jr NHS; NHS; Athl & Sprtsmnshp Awd 83; Wrstlng 3rd Pl Clss B Sctnls 85; Ftbl All-City 2nd Tm Offns 85; Rensselaer Polytechnic; Engrng.

BROWN, MARCO; Mynderse Acad; Seneca Falls, NY; (S); 7/142; Yrbk Stf; VP Stu Cncl; JV Bsktbl; Im Ice Hcky; JV Var Lcrss; High Hon Roll; NHS; Ntl Merit Ltr; Highest Avg Chem 85; Math.

BROWN, MARGARET; Valley Central HS; Walden, NY; (Y); Office Aide; Service Clb; Teachers Aide; Chorus; Hon Roll; Walden Swng Awd 84-85; OCCC; Bus.

BROWN, MARK; Hebrew Acad Of The 5 Towns And Rockaway; Belle Harbor, NY; (Y); Chess Clb; Debate Tm; Drama Clb; Spanish Clb; Temple Yth Grp; School Play; Yrbk Stf; NEDT Awd; Rgnts Merit Schlrshp 86; Sci Fair Awd 2nd Pl 85; U Of Albany; Bus.

BROWN, MICHAEL; Bishop Maginn HS; Albany, NY; (Y); Ski Clb; Variety Show; JV Bsbl; JV Var Ftbl; Var Tennis; Niagara U.

BROWN, MICHAEL; Charles O Dickerson HS; Trumansburg, NY; (Y); Band; Jazz Band; Nwsp Ed-Chief; Nwsp Rptr; Nwsp Stf; Yrbk Phtg; Yrbk Stf; Tennis; Wrstlng; RI Schl Dsgn; Art.

BROWN, MICHAEL; Rice HS; Bronx, NY; (Y); Stu Cncl; Bsbl; Bsktbl; Crs Cntry; Ftbl; Swmmng; Trk; NY Inst Tech; Comp Sci.

BROWN, MICHAEL; South Side HS; Rockville Centre, NY; (Y); 5/286; Key Clb; Science Clb; SADD; Nwsp Rptr; Var Bsbl; Var Bsktbl; High Hon Roll; NHS; Chem Awd 85; George Washngtn U Awd Exc In Math & Sci 86; Med.

BROWN, MICHELE; Newfane SR HS; Newfane, NY; (Y); 51/187; Varsity Clb; Yrbk Stf; Trs Jr Cls; Trs Sr Cls; Stat Bsktbl; JV Var Trk; JV Vllybl; Geneseo; Spch Pthlgy.

BROWN, NICOLE; St Joseph HS; Brooklyn, NY; (S); 2/145; Drama Clb; Office Aide; Speech Tm; Hon Roll; NHS; French Clb; Band; Chorus; Variety Show.

BROWN, PAMELA SUE; Cicero North Syracuse HS; North Syracuse, NY; (S); 42/667; Church Yth Grp; Ski Clb; Capt Varsity Clb; Capt Color Guard; Mrchg Band; Nwsp Rptr; Lion Awd; NHS; CNS Soc Pres 85 & 86; Schl Discipline Policy Comm 85; SUNY Geneseo Coll; Chld Psych.

BROWN, PETER; John A Coleman Catholic HS; Prattsville, NY; (Y); 8/92; Boy Scts; Church Yth Grp; Drama Clb; Exploring; French Clb; Ski Clb; School Play; Pres Frsh Cls; Pres Soph Cls; JV Bsktbl; Sci Olympd 86; U Of Notre Dame; Ecnmcs.

BROWN, PRISCILLA; Acad Of Mt St Ursula HS; Bronx, NY; (Y); Cmnty Wkr; Girl Scts; Library Aide; Office Aide; Chorus; Church Choir; Hon Roll; Howard U; Pre-Med.

BROWN, REBECCA; Cincinnatus Christian Acad; Willet, NY; (Y); 1/7; Church Yth Grp; Band; Chorus; Church Choir; School Musical; Capt Cheerleading; Socr; High Hon Roll; Hon Roll; Student Of Year 84-85; Chrstn Ministry.

BROWN, REBECCA; Groton Central Schl; Groton, NY; (Y); 18/75; 4-H; Var Capt Cheerleading; Stat Trk; Stat Wrstlng; Cit Awd; 4-H Awd; Hon Roll; Church Yth Grp; SADD; Rep Stu Cncl; Cngrsnl Mdl Merit 86; Otstndng Fml Achvt Wnnr NY ST Guernsey Assoc 86; Top 10 Fnlst NYS Dry Prncs; Cornell U; Agri Ecnmcs.

BROWN, REGINA T; Hillcrest HS; Laurelton, NY; (Y); 13/801; Church Yth Grp; Girl Scts; Hosp Aide; Science Clb; Band; Church Choir; Orch; Yrbk Rptr; Prfct Atten Awd; Sal; Hnr Roll 84-85; Pre Med.

BROWN, RENE F; Hampton Bays HS; Hampton Bays, NY; (Y); 15/86; SADD; Varsity Clb; Chorus; School Play; VP Jr Cls; Cheerleading; Capt Fld Hcky; Sftbl; Trk; Hon Roll; Loyola Coll; Psychology.

BROWN, ROBERT; Malverne HS; W Hempstead, NY; (Y); #36 In Class; Church Yth Grp; Spanish Clb; JV Ftbl; Howard U; Engrng.

BROWN JR, ROBERT; Corinth Central Schl; Corinth, NY; (S); Church Yth Grp; SADD; Chorus; Church Choir; Philharmonic Awd 84; Scherzo Awd 85; Adirondack Cmnty Coll; Brdcstng.

BROWN, SHANNON; New Paltz HS; New Paltz, NY; (Y); 25/150; Camp Fr Inc; Yrbk Phtg; Var Crs Cntry; Sec NHS.

BROWN, SHARON; Nazareth Acad; Rochester, NY; (Y); Latin Clb; Library Aide; Trs Sr Cls; JV Var Bsktbl; Var Socr; Var Trk; Hon Roll; Engr.

BROWN, SHERYL L; Pine Bush HS; Middletown, NY; (Y); 40/300; Office Aide; Ski Clb; Concert Band; Drm Mjr(t); Mrchg Band; Stu Cncl; JV Fld Hcky; Hon Roll; Jr NHS; NHS; Regents Schlrshp; Orange Cnty CC; Genetic Engrng.

BROWN, SHERYLL; Springfield Gardens HS; Rosedale, NY; (Y); JA; Teachers Aide; Band; Cit Awd; Hon Roll; NHS; Regnts & Merit Diplm 86; Elctd Actv Membr Arista Leag Secy 85; Hnry H S Achvt 86; Adelphi U; Psych.

BROWN, STEPHANIA M; The Masters Schl; Ardsley, NY; (Y); Church Yth Grp; Key Clb; Library Aide; Office Aide; Teachers Aide; Band; Orch; Pep Band; ASPCA Regnls 85-86; AHSA Medal Cls 86; PHA Medal Cls 86; Manhattanville Coll; Econ.

BROWN, STEPHEN; Greenville Central HS; Norton Hl, NY; (Y); VP Church Yth Grp; Pres 4-H; Key Clb; Bsktbl; JV Var Socr; 4-H Awd; Ctznshp 85-86.

BROWN, STEPHEN; Plattsburgh SR HS; Plattsburgh, NY; (Y); 17/170; Var L Ftbl; Var L Swmmng; Var L Trk; High Hon Roll; Hon Roll; Ntl Merit Ltr; Regents Schrlshp 86; Med Pgm Jefferson Med Coll 86; US Military Acad; Chem.

BROWN, STEVEN; Bayside HS; Bayside, NY; (Y); 42/586; Office Aide; Service Clb; Teachers Aide; Band; Orch; Nwsp Rptr; Bsbl; Var Swmmng; High Hon Roll; Hon Roll; NY ST Rgnts Schrshp 86; SUNY Albny; Accntng.

BROWN, SYLVETT; Amityville Memorial HS; Amityville, NY; (Y); Art Clb; Camera Clb; FBLA; Key Clb; Office Aide; SADD; Teachers Aide; Chorus; Nwsp Ed-Chief; Hon Roll; Humn Relations Awd 84; Barbizon Diploma 84; FBLA Awd 85; Key Clb Awd 86; Architecture.

BROWN, TERESA; Deer Park HS; Deer Park, NY; (Y); Computer Clb; FBLA; Spanish Clb; Sftbl; Hon Roll; Farmingdale U; Bus Admin.

BROWN, TERI; Sandy Creek Central HS; Sandy Creek, NY; (Y); Teachers Aide; Chorus; Var Capt Cheerleading; Twrlr; Hon Roll; Bus.

BROWN, TERRI L; La Guardia High Schl Of The Arts; Brooklyn, NY; (Y); 192/437; Church Yth Grp; Chorus; Madrigals; Off Jr Cls; Rep Stu Cncl; Prfct Atten Awd; SUNY-PURCHASE; Opera Singer.

BROWN, TIFFANY; Fairport HS; Fairport, NY; (Y); Church Yth Grp; Dance Clb; Key Clb; Library Aide; Pep Clb; Ski Clb; SADD; Variety Show; Cheerleading; Trk.

BROWN, TIM; Riverhead HS; Riverhead, NY; (Y); Art Clb; Aud/Vis; Ski Clb.

BROWN, TIMOTHY; Christopher Columbus HS; Bronx, NY; (S); Acpl Chr; Band; Church Choir; Concert Band; Jazz Band; Variety Show; SR All Amer Hall Of Fame Bnd Hnrs 86.

BROWN, VALERIE; Camden Central HS; Blossvale, NY; (Y); 60/211; Varsity Clb; Chorus; Orch; School Play; Bowling; Trk; Hon Roll; Madison Oneida Boces Achvt Awd 86; Acad Schrlshp 86; Camden Grange Awd 86; Johnson & Wales Coll; Culnry Ar.

BROWN, VICTORIA; Mercy HS; Lk Ronkonkoma, NY; (Y); 16/125; Mathletes; Office Aide; Nwsp Stf; Yrbk Stf; Coach Actv; Capt Var Crs Cntry; Var Trk; High Hon Roll; Hon Roll; NHS; Trck-110 Prcnt Awd 85; Crs Cntry MVP Awd 84 & 85; Al-Conf Crs Cntry 84; St Josph Coll Patchoque; Jrnlsm.

BROWN, WILLARD R; Marcus Whitman Central Schl; Stanley, NY; (Y); 8/127; Am Leg Boys St; JCL; Ski Clb; Concert Band; Mrchg Band; School Play; Yrbk Stf; Ftbl; Trk; Bausch & Lomb Sci Awd; MI ST U; Chmcl Physcs.

BROWN, YVONNE E; Bishop Kearney HS; Brooklyn, NY; (Y); 77/337; Spanish Clb; Hon Roll; Rgnts Schlrshp & Pace Trustee Schlrshp 86; Pace U.

BROWNE, DEREK; Rice HS; New York, NY; (S); Chess Clb; Church Yth Grp; Computer Clb; Stu Cncl; High Hon Roll; Hon Roll; Comp Sci.

BROWNE, MAUREEN; Valley Central HS; Maybrook, NY; (Y); 35/315; Lit Mag; NHS; Spanish NHS; Med.

BROWNE, MIMI; East Hampton HS; E Hampton, NY; (Y); Nwsp Rptr; Nwsp Stf; Lit Mag; High Hon Roll; Hon Roll; Jr NHS.

BROWNE, ROBERT A; La Guardia H S Of Music & Art; Bronx, NY; (Y); 69/437; Church Yth Grp; Capt Drill Tm; Bsktbl; Hon Roll; Ntl Merit Ltr; Office Aide; Art Awds 83-84; Penn ST; Arch.

BROWNE, URSULA A; Hillcrest HS; Jamaica, NY; (Y); 150/832; Church Yth Grp; Hosp Aide; JCL; Office Aide; Teachers Aide; Drm & Bgl; Yrbk Stf; Rep Frsh Cls; Rep Soph Cls; Rep Jr Cls; NY Cty Spr Yth Awd 84-85; St John U; Phrmcy.

BROWNING, GENE; Tamarac HS; Johnsonville, NY; (Y); 1/103; Intnl Clb; Math Tm; Ed Yrbk Stf; Tennis; High Hon Roll; NHS; Val; Math Clb; Off Frsh Cls; Off Soph Cls; Syracuse U Schlrshp 86; Genl Elec Star Schlrshp 86; Pres Acad Ftns Awd 86; Syracuse U; Arch.

BROWNING, SUSAN; La Guardia H S Of Music; Woodside, NY; (S); 21/437; Teachers Aide; Band; Orch; Nwsp Stf; Wt Lftg; Hon Roll; Jr NHS; NHS; Tutrng Alg Geom, Spnsh 83-85; Svc Tchrs-Asstng Coll Nght 82-85; Lcl HS Nght Rep 85; Psychlgy.

BROWNING, WILLIAM; Patchogue-Medford HS; Medford, NY; (S); Band; Concert Band; Mrchg Band; Orch; School Musical; Stage Crew; Potsdam Coll; Music.

BROZGUL, EVELINA; H S Of Art & Design; Long Island Cty, NY; (Y); 27/406; Art Clb; French Clb; Library Aide; PAVAS; Hon Roll; NHS; Cooper Union Schlrshp 86; Natl Art Hnr Soc 83-85; The Cooper Union; Fine Arts.

BRUBAKER, DINA; Watkins Glen HS; Watkins Glen, NY; (S); 7/135; French Clb; Letterman Clb; Sec Yrbk Stf; Stat Bsbl; Co-Capt Cheerleading; Mgr(s); French Hon Soc; Hon Roll; NHS; Prfct Atten Awd; JR Miss 86; Bucknell U; Mth.

BRUCE, AMANDA; Uniondale HS; Uniondale, NY; (Y); JV Pom Pon; Boosters 85-86 & 86-87; French Cooking Clb 83-84; Business Mgmt.

BRUCE, DEBBIE; Westmoreland Central Schl; Rome, NY; (Y); Pres VP Church Yth Grp; Debate Tm; Math Clb; Speech Tm; Drm Mjr(t); Yrbk Phtg; Yrbk Stf; Socr; High Hon Roll; NHS; Kiwanis Spiritual Aims Awd 85-86; Aeronautical Engrng.

BRUCE, GRETCHEN; Honeoye Falls Lima HS; Honeoye Falls, NY; (S); 6/160; VP Math Clb; Sec Model UN; Trs Soph Cls; Trs Stu Cncl; Var Socr; Var Sftbl; High Hon Roll; NHS; Clsscs.

BRUCE, JAMES D; Watkins Glen HS; Watkins Glen, NY; (Y); 18/135; Am Leg Boys St; Aud/Vis; Boy Scts; Drama Clb; 4-H; Letterman Clb; Math Clb; ROTC; Ski Clb; School Play; ROTC Schlrshp 86; Clarkson U Ed Schlrshp 86; Clarkson U; Mech Engr.

BRUCE, KEVIN; Fort Ann Central HS; Fort Ann, NY; (Y); 3/54; French Clb; Math Clb; Math Tm; Band; High Hon Roll; NHS; Regents Schrlshp 86; Hudson Valley CC; Engr.

BRUCK, JAIME; Riverdale Country Schl; Riverdale, NY; (Y); Yrbk Phtg; Yrbk Stf; Bsktbl; Fld Hcky; Sftbl; Tennis; Trk; Hon Roll; NHS; Ntl Merit SF.

BRUCKNER, HEIDI C; The Masters Schl; Pelham, NY; (Y); French Clb; Chorus; Lit Mag; JV Cheerleading; JV Fld Hcky; JV Var Lcrss; Hon Roll; Ntl Merit SF; Nwsp Stf; Mgr Gym; Drmtry Rpctr; Yrbk Cpy Edtr.

BRUDER, BRIAN; Iona Prep Schl; Yonkers, NY; (Y); 115/204; Aud/Vis; Cmnty Wkr; Teachers Aide; Band; Drm Mjr(t); Bsktbl; Var Capt Lcrss; Trk; Hon Roll; Pub Rel Tm 86-87; Big Brothers Pgm 85-87; Ldrshp Wrkshp Pgm; Providence Coll; Comm.

BRUDER, DEBORA J; Sacred Heart Acad; New Hyde Park, NY; (Y); 37/182; Cmnty Wkr; Debate Tm; VP Math Clb; Crs Cntry; Trk; Hon Roll; NHS; SUNY-BINGHAMPTON.

BRUECKNER, DEBBIE; Onteora HS; Glenford, NY; (S); Sec Church Yth Grp; Sec DECA; Sec 4-H; JA; Library Aide; Office Aide; 4-H Awd; Hon Roll; Bus Dept Hnr Awd 84-85; Mrktg.

BRUEN, HELEN; Ursuline HS; Yonkers, NY; (Y); Cmnty Wkr; Dance Clb; French Clb; Hosp Aide; Intnl Clb; Chorus; Nwsp Rptr; Var Trk; Hon Roll; 2nd-Eastern Rgnls-Irish Dncng 84-85; 2nd-Natl Irish Dncng 84; Amer In Wrld Champs-Irish Dncng 85-86; Sci.

BRUEN, LEANNA; Cortland SR HS; Syracuse, NY; (Y); 14/190; Pres Church Yth Grp; Ski Clb; Thesps; Jazz Band; Mrchg Band; Ed Lit Mag; Rep Stu Cncl; Var L Diving; Var L Swmmng; NHS; Dr Philip S Nason Schlrshp 86; Hrtwck Coll Pres Schlrshp 86; Crtlnd Arts Cncl Awd 3rd Pl 86; Hrtwck Coll; Med Tech.

BRUETSCH, DENNIS M; Maine Endwell HS; Endicott, NY; (Y); 6/234; Mathletes; Spanish Clb; SADD; JV Var Bowling; Stat Ftbl; Var Capt Lcrss; NYS Regents Schlrshp 86; Coaches Yth Lacrosse Tm 86; ST U VA Polytech Inst; Chem.

BRUETSCH, JOHN T; John S Burke Catholic HS; Monroe, NY; (Y); JV Var Crs Cntry; JV Var Trk; Hon Roll; Pres Schlr; Pace U; Accntng.

BRUETSCH, SUE; Susquehanna Valley HS; Conklin, NY; (Y); Drama Clb; Hosp Aide; Service Clb; Pres Spanish Clb; SADD; Orch; Var Fld Hcky; Score Keeper; Spanish NHS; Hon Roll; Chem Lab Tech.

BRUGGEMANN JR, ROBERT H; William Cullen Bryant HS; Astoria, NY; (Y); 168/623; Ed Lit Mag; NYS Rgnts Schlrshp 86; Fiorello H La Guardia CC; Comp.

BRUGGMAN, THOMAS; Alexander Central HS; Alexander, NY; (Y); Art Clb; Aud/Vis; Camp Fr Inc; FFA; Varsity Clb; VICA; Band; School Play; Stage Crew; Yrbk Phtg; 1st Pl Firemans Essay 85.

BRUH, NADINE; Midwood HS; Brooklyn, NY; (Y); 150/670; Church Yth Grp; Model UN; Teachers Aide; Y-Teens; Chorus; Orch; School Musical; Capt Twrlr; Cit Awd; NHS; Myrs Yth Awd; Med.

BRUINSMA, STACIE; York Central Schl; Leicester, NY; (Y); Ski Clb; Temple Yth Grp; Band; Chorus; Concert Band; School Musical; School Play; Nwsp Rptr; Yrbk Stf; Sftbl; LIU Southampton; Creatv Wrtng.

BRUMFIELD, CORY; Kendall JR-SR HS; Kendall, NY; (S); 4/88; Ski Clb; Band; Concert Band; Mrchg Band; Yrbk Stf; Bsbl; Bsktbl; Socr; Jr NHS; NHS; Genesee Rgn All-Str Sccr 2nd Tm 84; US Air Force Acad; Plt.

BRUN-HICKMAN, MIRANDA; Niskayuna HS; Schenectady, NY; (Y); Drama Clb; French Clb; Quiz Bowl; Band; Chorus; Orch; School Musical; School Play; Symp Band; Nwsp Stf; Ntl Sci Olympd 85-86; Shkspr Rctn Eng Spkng Union Cmptn 2nd Pl 86; Amer Tchrs Assoc Of Grmn Ntl 85-86; Wrtng.

BRUNACINI, LAURA; Falconer Central HS; Kennedy, NY; (Y); 13/125; Pres Church Yth Grp; FBLA; GAA; Hosp Aide; Ski Clb; Spanish Clb; Church Choir; Color Guard; Hon Roll; NHS; Jamestwn CC; Phy Ther.

BRUNDAGE, BOBBI JO; Haverling JR SR HS; Bath, NY; (S); 6/136; French Clb; FTA; Girl Scts; Teachers Aide; Concert Band; Mrchg Band; Yrbk Stf; God Cntry Awd; High Hon Roll; NHS; Girl Scout Silvr Awd 84; Prmry Eductr.

BRUNDAGE, MICHAEL C; Chruchville-Chili SR HS; Churchville, NY; (Y); 62/310; Acpl Chr; Chorus; Hon Roll; Rgnts Schlrshp Awd 86; Rchstr Inst Of Technlgy Schlrshp 86; Rchster Inst Tech; Elctrnc Engr.

BRUNDAGE, STEVE; Salamanca HS; Salamanca, NY; (Y); Church Yth Grp; French Clb; Band; Mrchg Band; Var L Bsbl; Score Keeper; High Hon Roll; Prfct Atten Awd; Trophies Sftbl Bsbl 84-86.

BRUNER, KATEY; North Rose-Wolcott HS; Wolcott, NY; (Y); Pres Church Yth Grp; French Clb; Ski Clb; Church Choir; JV Var Socr; High Hon Roll; Hon Roll; NHS; Ntl Merit SF; Arts.

BRUNETTI, JACKI; St Francis Prep; Uniondale, NY; (S); 190/694; Dance Clb; Drama Clb; Band; Chorus; Concert Band; School Musical; School Play; Stage Crew; Crs Cntry; Trk; Hofstra U; Finance.

BRUNK, PAUL; St John The Bapt Diocesan HS; Brentwood, NY; (S); 2/501; Church Yth Grp; Math Clb; Math Tm; Quiz Bowl; Hon Roll; Jr NHS; Natl Sci Olympiad Awd 85.

BRUNNER, CAROLYN; Bishop Ludden HS; Camillus, NY; (S); Exploring; JV Bsktbl; JV Sftbl; Bausch & Lomb Sci Awd; High Hon Roll; NHS; Le Moyne Smmr Schlr 85; Spnsh Awd 82-84; Engl & Earth Sci Awd 82; Pre-Med.

BRUNNER, DOLORES; Jane Addams Vocational HS; Bronx, NY; (S); 8/260; Stage Crew; Rep Sr Cls; Hon Roll; Prfct Atten Awd; Cert Awd Spec Acvht Hnr Bio 84; Cert Profcncy Word Proc 84; Cert Profcncy Century 21 Typwrtng 84; Elec Engrng.

BRUNNER, LISA; Kenmore East HS; Kenmore, NY; (Y); Pep Clb; Jazz Band; School Musical; Nwsp Ed-Chief; Ed Yrbk Stf; Rep Stu Cncl; Var Tennis; NHS; Ntl Merit Ltr; Varsity Clb; WA Congrssnl Wrkshps Pgm 86; Medcn.

BRUNNER, MELISSA J; Morristown Central HS; Morristown, NY; (Y); 2/38; School Play; Yrbk Sprt Ed; Pres Soph Cls; Pres Jr Cls; Var Capt Bsktbl; Var Capt Socr; Var Capt Sftbl; Var Capt Vllybl; High Hon Roll; Hon Roll; Regents Schlrshp.

BRUNNWASSER, JAY; John F Kennedy HS; Merrick, NY; (Y); 3/373; Exploring; Mathletes; Math Tm; Trs Concert Band; Mrchg Band; School Musical; Nwsp Stf; Bausch & Lomb Sci Awd; NHS; Ntl Merit Ltr; Grumman Engrng Schlr 86; George Washington Sici & Engrng Awd 85; U Of PA; Math.

BRUNO, BRENDA; St Barnabas HS; Bronx, NY; (S); 15/187; Office Aide; Teachers Aide; Hon Roll; Jr NHS; NHS; Itln Hnr Socty 84-85; Relgn Awd 84-85; Bio Awd Natl Olympd 83-84; Katharine Gibbs Schl.

BRUNO, DANIELLE; Nardin Acad; Kenmore, NY; (Y); Cmnty Wkr; French Clb; Office Aide; Teachers Aide; Orch; School Musical; Yrbk Stf; Lit Mag; Rep Stu Cncl; Bio Intrnshp ST U Coll Buffalo 86; Empl Sheridn Day Care Ctr 85-86; Music Awd Nardin Acad 85.

BRUNO, LISA; Odessa Montour Central HS; Montour Falls, NY; (Y); Church Yth Grp; Drama Clb; SADD; Stu Cncl; Cheerleading; Sftbl; Htl/Mtl Adm.

BRUNO, LOUIS S; Commack HS South; Commack, NY; (Y); Var Bsbl; Var Socr; High Hon Roll; Hon Roll; Ed.

BRUNO, MARIBETH; Shaker HS; Menands, NY; (Y); Drama Clb; Thesps; School Musical; School Play; Stage Crew; Nwsp Rptr; Nwsp Stf; Hon Roll; Ntl Merit SF; Rcrd Prdcr.

BRUNO, NANCY; Warwick Valley HS; Sugar Lf, NY; (Y); Dance Clb; Drama Clb; FBLA; School Musical; School Play; JV Cheerleading; Cit Awd; Hon Roll; OCCC; Advrtsng.

BRUNO, PAULA; Geneva HS; Geneva, NY; (S); 29/176; Teachers Aide; Trs Sr Cls; Hon Roll; NHS; Geneseo; Elem Ed.

BRUNO, ROBIN; Clarkstown HS North; New City, NY; (Y); FNA; GAA; Girl Scts; Scholastic Bowl; SADD; Varsity Clb; Swing Chorus; Bowling; Score Keeper; Sftbl; Cortland; Pysch.

BRUNSKILL, GORDON; Mayville Central HS; Mayville, NY; (S); #3 In Class; Mathletes; Yrbk Bus Mgr; VP Frsh Cls; Sec Soph Cls; Rep Jr Cls; Var L Bsbl; Stat Bsktbl; JV Var Timer; High Hon Roll; Jr NHS; Arch.

BRUNSWICK, KARRIE; Wayland Central HS; Wayland, NY; (Y); 24/113; Am Leg Aux Girls St; Drama Clb; FBLA; Band; Yrbk Stf; VP Sec Soph Cls; Trs Jr Cls; School Musical; School Play; Phi Delta Kappa Pace U Westchester Chptr Outstndg Schl Achvt Awd 85; Closeup Cert Pgm 86; Nice Kid Awd; Resp Ther.

BRUSCA, LAURA; Oyster Bay HS; East Norwich, NY; (Y); Model UN; Spanish Clb; Yrbk Stf; Mgr(s); Sftbl; Hon Roll; Providence Coll; Fash Mrktng.

BRUSH, THOMAS; Scio Central HS; Scio, NY; (S); 2/50; Model UN; Pres Spanish Clb; Band; Chorus; Drm Mjr(t); Mrchg Band; Pres Sr Cls; Var Bsbl; Var Bsktbl; Var Capt Socr; Soc Dstngshed Amer HS Stdnt 85; Ntl Hnr Soc 84; Hgh Hnr Rll 82-85; Pol Sci.

BRUSIE, ELLEN; Carmel HS; Putnam Valley, NY; (Y); Band; Concert Band; Yrbk Stf; Score Keeper; High Hon Roll; Hon Roll; NHS; Bus Admin.

BRUSKIN, JOY MICHELLE; Harrison HS; Harrison, NY; (Y); 8/215; AFS; VP Temple Yth Grp; Varsity Clb; School Musical; Sec Sr Cls; Crs Cntry; Trk; NHS; Rotary Awd; Spanish NHS; Tufts U.

BRUST, ANN M; Chatham HS; Ghent, NY; (Y); 44/118; Library Aide; Chorus; Yrbk Stf; Rep Stu Cncl; Masonic Awd; Broderick Library Svc Awd 86; Library Cncl Awd 86; Rgnts Dplma Sci, Math, Frnech, 80; SR Ath Awd 86; Columbia Greene CC; Sci.

BRUST, CAROLYN; Sachem North HS; Farmingville, NY; (Y); 196/1558; Mrchg Band; Hon Roll; Briarcliffe Secretarial; Bus.

BRUST, JODY; Cato-Meridian HS; Cato, NY; (Y); Ski Clb; VICA; JV Var Cheerleading; JV Fld Hcky; Hon Roll; Cosmtlgy.

BRUST, LYNAIRE; Chatham HS; Ghent, NY; (Y); 3/147; SADD; Band; Concert Band; Mrchg Band; Orch; Pep Band; Yrbk Phtg; Yrbk Stf; Rep Stu Cncl; NHS; Photo.

BRUST, SUSAN; Division Avenue HS; Levittown, NY; (Y); 90/334; 4-H; Science Clb; SADD; Variety Show; Yrbk Stf; Rep Sr Cls; Stu Cncl; Capt Var Cheerleading; CC Awd; VFW Awd; Humantarium Awd, Mid-Isl Schlrshp 86; PTSA Schlrshp; SUNY Farmingdale; Nrsng.

BRUYN JR, JAMES; Pine Bush HS; Pine Bush, NY; (Y); PAVAS; Hon Roll; NHS; Mst Lkly Succeed, Stdnt Mnth 84; Olympcs Mind Cmpettns 85; Mech Engr.

BRUZZESE, STEPHAN J; Susan E Wagner HS; Staten Island, NY; (Y); Am Leg Boys St; Art Clb; JA; PAVAS; School Play; Lit Mag; Hon Roll; Eugene Greenberg Mem Art Awd 86; PTA Cert Awd Arts 86; Fash Inst Tech; Fine Arts.

BRYAN, DAWN; James Madison HS; Brooklyn, NY; (Y); 99/745; Church Yth Grp; JA; Chorus; Church Choir; School Play; Nwsp Bus Mgr; Rep Stu Cncl; Tennis; Achvt Mnd Your Bus Mgzne 86; Achvt VITA 85; Baruch Coll; Acctng.

BRYAN, DIANE B; St Francci Prep Schl; Corona, NY; (S); 7/744; Art Clb; Library Aide; Im Powder Puff Ftbl; Im Sftbl; High Hon Roll; Bus.

BRYAN, HEWITT; Mt Vernon HS; Mt Vernon, NY; (Y); Computer Clb; FBLA; Key Clb; Spanish Clb; Var Crs Cntry; Var Trk; Hon Roll; Law.

BRYAN, KAREN; Canarsie HS; Brooklyn, NY; (S); 2/500; Capt Bowling; Hon Roll; Prfct Atten Awd; Sal; Arista-Hnr Soc-Tutorng & Fnd Raising; Archon-A Svc Soc; Prncpl Hnr Roll; Bus Admin.

BRYAN, LINDEL; Mount Vernon HS; Mt Vernon, NY; (Y); FBLA; JA; JCL; Math Clb; Radio Clb; SADD; Varsity Clb; Band; Yrbk Stf; Var Trk; Pres Physcl Ftns Awd 86; Track Medals 86; Electrnc.

BRYAN, MARC; HS Of Art & Design; Brooklyn, NY; (Y); Sec Art Clb; Computer Clb; Service Clb; Teachers Aide; Rep Jr Cls; Hon Roll; NHS; Prfct Atten Awd; Natl Art Hnr Soc; Supr Yth Of NY Awd; Arch Clb; Arch.

BRYAN, PAUL; Susquehanna Valley HS; Conklin, NY; (Y); Capt Mathletes; Capt Quiz Bowl; Rep Soph Cls; Rep Jr Cls; Rep Sr Cls; Rep Stu Cncl; Capt Crs Cntry; VP Trk; High Hon Roll; Jr NHS; Trk Div III All Star 84-85; Crs Cntry Div III All Star 84-86; Trk Div III All Star 85-86; Rochester Inst Tech; Cmptr.

BRYAN, YVONNE; Longwood HS; Coram, NY; (Y); Key Clb; Science Clb; Ski Clb; Var Tennis; Outstndg Schlr 80; Stony Brook U; Nrsg.

BRYANT, DEBBIE; Churchville Chili SR HS; Churchville, NY; (Y); Drama Clb; Band; Concert Band; Mrchg Band; Orch; School Play; Symp Band; Hon Roll; Latin Clb; Chorus; Theater.

BRYANT, DIANA; Greene Central HS; Greene, NY; (Y); 25/116; French Clb; Pres Chorus; Trs Frsh Cls; Rep Stu Cncl; JV Co-Capt Bsktbl; Geneseo; Bio.

BRYANT, MARY A; St Johns Prep; Astoria, NY; (Y); 31/457; Chorus; Nwsp Stf; High Hon Roll; Hon Roll; NHS; NYS Regents Schlrshp; Long Island U; Pol Sci.

BRYANT, OTIS; Stony Brook Schl; Central Islip, NY; (Y); 50/80; Varsity Clb; Chorus; School Play; Yrbk Bus Mgr; Off Jr Cls; Stu Cncl; Var L Crs Cntry; Var L Trk; Im Bsbl; Im Bsktbl; Trinity Coll; Chem.

BRYANT, PEGGY; Morain Central HS; Pt Henry, NY; (Y); 11/84; AFS; GAA; Pres Trs Ski Clb; Variety Show; Yrbk Phtg; Yrbk Stf; Var JV Diving; Var JV Sftbl; Var JV Swmmng; High Hon Roll; SUNY At Oneonta; Bus Econ.

BRYANT, TOSHAR; Cathedral HS; Ny, NY; (Y); Church Yth Grp; Exploring; FNA; Radio Clb; Science Clb; Church Choir; Stu Cncl; Amb Genesis Clean Up 83-87; Cert Awd Ldrshp 83; Pace U; Bio.

BRYCELAND, CHARLES; Fordham Prep Schl; Bronx, NY; (Y); Church Yth Grp; Stage Crew; Rep Frsh Cls; Rep Soph Cls; Pres Jr Cls; VP Stu Cncl; Im Bsbl; Im Bsktbl; Coach Actv; Var L Ftbl; Christus Rex Awd 84; Engr.

BRYDALSKI, LISA; Villa Maria Acad; Buffalo, NY; (Y); Hon Roll; Buffalo ST; Psychlgy.

BRYNAERT, RON; Newburgh Free Acad; Newburgh, NY; (Y); Aud/Vis; Drama Clb; School Musical; School Play; Stage Crew; Nwsp Rptr; Nwsp Stf; Lit Mag; Hon Roll; Ntl Merit Schol; Ctzn Of Mnth 86; Syracuse U; Cmnctns.

BRYNIARSKI, MICHELE A; Kenmore East SR HS; Tonawanda, NY; (Y); 50/300; Mrchg Band; High Hon Roll; Hon Roll; NHS; Canisius Coll; Soclgy.

BRZYTWA, STEVE; Wellsville HS; Wellsville, NY; (Y); 16/120; Ski Clb; Var Bsbl; Var Ftbl; High Hon Roll; Southern Tier Schlrshp 86; Alfred U; Cermc Engr.

BUBEL, SANDRA; Jamesville-Dewitt HS; Jamesville, NY; (Y); Exploring; German Clb; High Hon Roll; Opt Clb Awd; Schlstc Awd Scl Studies 85-86; Law.

BUCCI, JONATHAN; Cornwall Central HS; Mountainville, NY; (Y); Church Yth Grp; Hon Roll; Aircrft Mech.

BUCCI, MICHAEL; Union Endicott HS; Endicott, NY; (Y); 57/450; Pep Clb; Varsity Clb; Var Ftbl; Trk; Hon Roll; NHS; MVP Trck 86; Ofnsv Bck Awd 85; CYO MVP 85-86; Alfred U; Crmc Engr.

BUCCI, PATRICIA; Henninger HS; Syracuse, NY; (Y); Girl Scts; Hosp Aide; Spanish Clb; SADD; Yrbk Stf; Lcrss; Score Keeper; Timer; High Hon Roll; Hon Roll; Schlrshp Ithaca Coll 86; Ithaca Coll; Engl.

BUCCOLA, JENNIFER; Lindenhurst HS; Lindenhurst, NY; (Y); SADD; JV Capt Socr; Hon Roll; Hofstra U; Tchr.

BUCERO, GABRIELA; Newtown HS; Elmhurst, NY; (Y); 38/781; French Clb; Orch; Yrbk Stf; Hon Roll; Fit; Fshn Dsgn.

BUCHAL, BETSY; Copenhagen Central Schl; Copenhagen, NY; (Y); 4/43; Am Leg Aux Girls St; Drama Clb; School Play; Yrbk Stf; High Hon Roll; Library Aide; SADD; Hon Roll; Dramtcs Excel 86; St Thomas Aquinas Merit Schlrshp 86; U Of St Thomas; Sec Educ.

BUCHALSKI, ELIZABETH; St Chaterine Acad; Bronx, NY; (Y); 100/185; Dance Clb; Exploring; Girl Scts; Hosp Aide; Office Aide; Teachers Aide; School Play; Bsktbl; Gym; Hon Roll; Cmmndtn Rprt Alge I, Engl 9 84; Superb Asst Aide 85; Excllnce Ny Phys Ftnss Test Svc 86; U Of PA; Realator/Brkr.

BUCHANAN, DEBBIE; Frontier HS; Blasdell, NY; (Y); DECA; Girl Scts; Hosp Aide; Pep Clb; SADD; Teachers Aide; Chorus; School Musical; Mgr(s); Ntl Merit Ltr; Hlth Asst.

BUCHANANAN, MARK T; Fairport HS; Fairport, NY; (Y); Mrchg Band; VP Symp Band; Var Crs Cntry; Var Wrstlng; Tulune U; Arch.

BUCHER, FRED; Pelham Memorial HS; Pelham, NY; (Y); Am Leg Boys St; Church Yth Grp; Drama Clb; Radio Clb; Band; Concert Band; Mrchg Band; School Musical; School Play; Nwsp Stf; Dickinson Coll; Hstry.

BUCHHOLZ, MALTE; Mercy HS; Farmingdale, NY; (Y); Var Bsktbl; Trk; Hon Roll; Cert Of Excllnc 86; Bio.

BUCHINGER, TAMMY; Keshequa Central HS; Dalton, NY; (S); Drama Clb; Pep Clb; School Play; Trs Jr Cls; Cheerleading; High Hon Roll; Chorus; Trs Frsh Cls; Trs Soph Cls; Socr; Bus Mgt.

BUCHINSKI, LAURIE; Union Endicott HS; Endicott, NY; (Y); Drama Clb; French Clb.

BUCK, HEATHER; Auburn HS; Auburn, NY; (Y); High Hon Roll; NHS; Am Studies Awd 86; Cornell U; Arch.

BUCK, JOHN; Deposit Central HS; Deposit, NY; (Y); Am Leg Boys St; SADD; Band; Mrchg Band; Pres Frsh Cls; Trs Soph Cls; VP Stu Cncl; Var L Ftbl; Var L Wrstlng; Bausch & Lomb Sci Awd; Scl Stds Awd 86; US Mltry Acad Wst Pnt NY; Eng.

BUCK, KIM; Cazenovia HS; Cazenovia, NY; (Y); Drama Clb; 4-H; Band; Chorus; Color Guard; Concert Band; Mrchg Band; Orch; School Play; Stage Crew; Bus Mngmnt.

BUCKALEW, LEE; North Rose-Wolcott HS; Wolcott, NY; (S); VP Aud/Vis; Varsity Clb; Mgr Acpl Chr; Chorus; School Musical; Stage Crew; Var L Trk; School Play; Hon Roll; NYSSMA Area All ST Chorus 83-85, All Cnty 83-85; SPEBSQSA-SLD Rep Intl Chorus Comptn 83-85; Tech Theatr.

BUCKENMEYER, LORI; Alexander Central HS; Alexander, NY; (Y); Cmnty Wkr; Ski Clb; Chorus; Variety Show; Rep Frsh Cls; JV L Sftbl; Hon Roll; Jr NHS; Friend Of The Library 83-85; Church Lector 85; Psych.

BUCKENROTH, JENNIFER; St Marys HS; W Seneca, NY; (Y); SADD; Varsity Clb; School Musical; School Play; Stage Crew; Rep Frsh Cls; Var Capt Cheerleading; Var Capt Pom Pon; JV Trk; Hon Roll; Chem Merit Awd 86; Spec Ed.

BUCKING, LISA; Mercy HS; Sag Harbor, NY; (Y); 13/129; Drama Clb; Math Clb; Ski Clb; School Play; Yrbk Stf; Var JV Bsktbl; Hon Roll; Church Yth Grp; Yrbk Phtg; Var Cheerleading; Drmtcs Awd 84; Bus.

BUCKINGHAM, LANCE; Camden Central HS; Tabeig, NY; (Y); Cmnty Wkr; Pep Clb; Varsity Clb; Rep Stu Cncl; Var Bsktbl; Coach Actv; VP Capt Crs Cntry; Hon Roll; Band; Concert Band; Alan Garbarino Dell Awd 86; Camden Alumni Assoc Schlrshp 86; Rotry Clb 86; Morrisville Ag Tech Coll; Engr.

BUCKLAND, MATTHEW; Mc Quaid Jesuit HS; Churchville, NY; (Y); 27/170; Church Yth Grp; Latin Clb; Pep Clb; Im JV Socr; High Hon Roll; NHS; Apptmnt Hd Sprvsr Stu Wrkrs 85-87; Hnds Chrst Wd Cthlc Dcs Rchstr 86-87; St Bonaventure; Pblc Rltns.

BUCKLAND, SANDRA M; Mt St Mary Acad; N Tonawanda, NY; (Y); Cmnty Wkr; VP Computer Clb; Pres Model UN; Red Cross Aide; Sec Chorus; Lit Mag; JV Var Bsktbl; Hon Roll; Church Yth Grp; Hosp Aide; Philadelphia Coll Of Pharm & Sci Inst Schlrshp 86; NYS Rgnts Schlrshp 86; MIP Bsktbl 8485; Philadelphia Coll; Physcl Therp.

BUCKLEY, BRENDA; Commack High School North; Commack, NY; (Y); 29/390; Girl Scts; Sec Math Tm; Chorus; School Musical; Swing Chorus; Variety Show; Off Frsh Cls; Off Soph Cls; Var Trk; High Hon Roll; Pres Ftnss Acad Awd 86; Loyola Coll MD; Elem Ed.

BUCKLEY, COLLEEN; Mount Mercy Acad; W Seneca, NY; (Y); Red Cross Aide; Service Clb; SADD; Chorus; Im Bowling; Hon Roll; Cert Of Distntcn Natl Lang Arts Olympd 84; Cert Of Achvmnt Telephn Assrnc Prog 85.

BUCKLEY, KIMBERLY; Freeport HS; Freeport, NY; (Y); 15/450; Key Clb; Yrbk Stf; Pres Soph Cls; Pres Jr Cls; Pres Sr Cls; JV Cheerleading; Var Sftbl; Var Tennis; NHS; Pres Schlr; Stu Of Mnth Exch Clb 85; Nassau Cnty Execs Acad Exc Awd 86; B Nai Jewish Wmns Awd 86; Gettysburg Coll; Poli Sci.

BUCKLEY, ROCKFORD; Pleasantville HS; Pleasantville, NY; (Y); 6/106; Letterman Clb; Model UN; JP Sousa Awd.

BUCKLEY, TIMOTHY; Alfred G Berner HS; Massapequa Park, NY; (Y); Church Yth Grp; Pep Clb; Variety Show; Var Capt Bsktbl; Coach Actv; Var JV Ftbl; St Schlr; MVP Bsktbl 86; Bsktbl Schlrshp Bentley 86; Bentley Coll MA; Bus.

BUCKNER, STEPHANNIE; Barker Central HS; Appleton, NY; (Y); AFS; Drama Clb; 4-H; French Clb; Spanish Clb; Band; Concert Band; Orch; Pep Band; Stage Crew; Yth Amer Erpn Cncrt Tour 86; Bnd Awd 86; ST U NY New P Altz; Frgn Lang.

BUCKSHAW, LISA; Sachem HS North; Holbrook, NY; (Y); 25/1350; VP Exploring; VP Pres Science Clb; Trs Ski Clb; Y-Teens; Chorus; Rep Jr Cls; Off Sr Cls; Swmmng; Jr NHS; Hst NHS; Soc Studies Proj Local Museum 84; Islip Town Env Awd 86; Parent Tchr Assoc Awd 86; Syracuse U; Env Engr.

BUCKSTAD, ERIK; Washingtonville SR HS; Washingtnvle, NY; (Y); Camera Clb; French Clb; Key Clb; Ski Clb; Chorus; Variety Show; Yrbk Phtg; Yrbk Stf; Socr; Arch.

BUCZAK, KEVIN; Alden Central HS; Lancaster, NY; (S); 44/203; Boy Scts; Exploring; FFA; FTA; Letterman Clb; School Musical; School Play; Rep Jr Cls; JV Var Bsktbl; JV Var Ftbl; Eagl Sct 85; Erie Cnty 1 Dairy Judgng Cntstnt 82; Major Rl Hangmans Noose 85; West Point; Mgmt.

BUDD, EDWARD; St John The Baptst HS; Amityville, NY; (Y); Church Yth Grp; Red Cross Aide; SADD; Chorus; School Musical; Nwsp Stf; Lit Mag; Rep Soph Cls; Pres Jr Cls; Swmmng; Marist Coll; Engl.

BUDD, KEVIN; Valley Central HS; Walden, NY; (Y); 48/313; French Clb; Ski Clb; Rep Jr Cls; Rep Sr Cls; JV Tennis; JV Var Trk; French Hon Soc; NHS; Arch.

BUDDENDECK, KELLY; Victor Central HS; Macedon, NY; (S); 18/228; Spanish Clb; Acpl Chr; Chorus; School Musical; Swing Chorus; Stu Cncl; High Hon Roll; NHS; Prfct Atten Awd; Bio Chemcl Engrng.

BUDHI, RONALD; New Dorp HS; Staten Isl, NY; (Y); Art Clb; Chess Clb; Church Yth Grp; Intnl Clb; Math Clb; Spanish Clb; Pres Stu Cncl; Cit Awd; High Hon Roll; Spanish NHS; St Johns U; Pre-Med.

BUDOFF, KIM B; Lawrence HS; Lawrence, NY; (Y); 12/412; Math Tm; Model UN; Spanish Clb; SADD; Trs Stu Cncl; Var Capt Gym; L Sftbl; High Hon Roll; Pres NHS; Hebrew 3rd Yr Turit Awd 85; Duke U.

BUDREWICZ, SHARON; Niagara Wheatfield SR HS; Niagara Falls, NY; (Y); Girl Scts; Pep Clb; PAVAS; Drm & Bgl; Yrbk Ed-Chief; Var Bowling; Var JV Lcrss; High Hon Roll; Hon Roll; NHS; Acdmc All Amrcn Achvt Awd 84; Grphc Dsgn.

BUDRIES, MARK; Mahopac HS; Carmel, NY; (Y); 94/409; JV Bsbl; Var Capt Bsktbl; Var Golf; Var Capt Socr; Hon Roll; Acctng.

BUDZINSKI, BRENDA; Salamanca Central HS; Killbuck, NY; (Y); 3/150; French Clb; JV Var Bsktbl; JV Var Cheerleading; JV Var Sftbl; French Hon Soc; High Hon Roll; NHS.

BUELL, GREGORY W; Holley JR/SR HS; Albion, NY; (Y); 3/105; Pres Model UN; Red Cross Aide; SADD; Church Choir; Jazz Band; School Musical; Swing Chorus; Yrbk Stf; High Hon Roll; NHS; U Of Rochester Cert Humnties 85; Northwestern U; Mus.

BUEME, JEFFREY; Canisius HS; Buffalo, NY; (S); 11/143; Church Yth Grp; Cmnty Wkr; Teachers Aide; Var Bowling; Im Vllybl; High Hon Roll; NHS; Prfct Atten Awd; Alg II,Eng Hnrs Course 85-87; Pre-Law.

BUERGER, BRUCE; Niagara Wheatfield HS; Sanborn, NY; (Y); Church Yth Grp; Var JV Bsbl; Var JV Bsktbl; High Hon Roll; Hon Roll; NHS; Engrng.

BUETI, GRACE E; Pleasantville HS; Pleasantville, NY; (Y); 12/110; Model UN; PAVAS; Concert Band; School Play; Yrbk Stf; JV Var Fld Hcky; Var Sftbl; High Hon Roll; Hon Roll; NHS; Bus.

BUFANO, MICHAEL; Fairport HS; Fairport, NY; (Y); Concert Band; Jazz Band; Mrchg Band; Ftbl; Hon Roll; All Cnty Band 83-85.

BUFFAMANTI, SUZANNE V; The Nichols Schl; Buffalo, NY; (Y); School Play; Lit Mag; High Hon Roll; Hon Roll; U Of Rochester; Pharmacy.

BUHLER, BRYAN; Northport HS; Northport, NY; (Y); 238/572; Cmnty Wkr; DECA; Hosp Aide; SADD; Stage Crew; Hon Roll; Volunteering Awd-53 Hrs Of Svc At V A Med Ctr 83; IN Inst Of Tech; Bus Admin.

BUHLER, JENNIFER; Walter Panas HS; Peekskill, NY; (Y); FBLA; Ski Clb; Var L Swmmng; Var Tennis; Hon Roll; Law.

BUHSMER, KARLA; Buffalo Acad Of The Sacred Heart; Williamsville, NY; (Y); Cmnty Wkr; German Clb; Hosp Aide; Model UN; Nwsp Phtg; Nwsp Stf; Yrbk Sprt Ed; Yrbk Stf; Trs Soph Cls; Trs Sr Cls; Bst Ice Skatng Coach 83-84; Head Ice Skatng Coach 85-86; Intl Rltns Pgm Georgetwn U 86; Intl Rltns.

BUI, HONG; Mineola HS; Mineola, NY; (Y); Key Clb.

BUI, JIM; The Bronx High Schl Of Science; Elmhurst, NY; (Y); Office Aide; Teachers Aide; Nwsp Rptr; Im Ftbl; Im Capt Socr; Im Sftbl; Im Vllybl; Binghamton ST U; Arch.

BUI, YUNG; Middletown HS; Middletown, NY; (Y); Art Clb; JA; Varsity Clb; Lit Mag; Socr; Hon Roll; Art Club 85-86; Soccer 84-86; Hnr Rll 84; U Buffalo; Arch.

BUJANOW, STEVEN; Chatham HS; Ghent, NY; (Y); 40/150; Debate Tm; Intnl Clb; Radio Clb; Spanish Clb; Hon Roll; SUNY At Albny; Jrnlsm.

BUJOLD, MICHAEL; Martin Van Buren HS; Bayside, NY; (Y); 14/565; Office Aide; Science Clb; Service Clb; Teachers Aide; High Hon Roll; 2nd Pl Sci Fair 84-86; Baruch Incentv Scholar 86; Arista 84-86; Baruch Coll; Acctng.

BULGER, DEANNA-LYNN; Bishop Maginn HS; Albany, NY; (S); Ed Nwsp Ed-Chief; Ed Yrbk Ed-Chief; Pres Frsh Cls; Pres Soph Cls; Pres Jr Cls; Capt Cheerleading; High Hon Roll; VP NHS; Erly Chldhd Ed.

BULL, MICHELLE; Bishop Grimes HS; Manlius, NY; (Y); 32/146; Ski Clb; Yrbk Stf; High Hon Roll; Hon Roll; NHS; Political Wkr; Yrbk Rptr; Yrbk Sprt Ed; Im Swmmng; Prfct Atten Awd; Itln Ntl Hnr Soc; Le Moyne Coll; Lbrl Arts.

BULLARD, REBECCA; Cooperstown Central Schl; Milford, NY; (Y); Chorus; Church Choir; Yrbk Stf; Hon Roll; NHS; Ntl Merit Ltr; Rggls Essy Cntst Fnlst 86; Englsh.

BULLARO, STEPHANIE A; Stella Maris HS; Howard Bch, NY; (Y); Variety Show; Ed Incntv Awd 86; St Johns U; Accntng.

BULLOCK, AMY; Hugh C Williams HS; Canton, NY; (Y); Drama Clb; 4-H; Thesps; Varsity Clb; Chorus; School Musical; School Play; Stage Crew; Nwsp Rptr; Yrbk Stf; Potsdam ST; Elem Ed.

BULLOCK, AMY; West Genesee SR HS; Camillus, NY; (Y); 28/425; Church Yth Grp; Key Clb; Color Guard; Mrchg Band; Off Soph Cls; Off Jr Cls; Off Sr Cls; High Hon Roll; NHS; St Schlr; Clss 86 Schlrshp 86; NY ST Regnts Schlrshp 86; SUNY Buffalo; Bio.

BULLOCK, GLORIA; Cicero-North Syracuse HS; North Syracuse, NY; (S); 14/667; Church Yth Grp; Band; Concert Band; Mrchg Band; Orch; School Musical; Symp Band; High Hon Roll; Hon Roll; NHS; Prncpl Flute Sym Yuth Orch 85-86; Le Moyne Coll; Bio Sci.

BULLOCK, KIMBERLY A; Dominican Commercial HS; Jamaica, NY; (Y); Church Yth Grp; Cmnty Wkr; Political Wkr; Teachers Aide; Nwsp Ed-Chief; Nwsp Rptr; Rep Frsh Cls; Rep Stu Cncl; Pres Stu Cncl; Hon Roll; Tau Gamma Delta Schlrshp 86; Rochdale Black Cult Scty Schlrshp 86; Pan Hellenic Schlrshp 86; Hampton U; Psych.

BULLOCK, MARY JO M; G Ray Bodley HS; Fulton, NY; (Y); Sec Latin Clb; Stat Bsbl; Im Mat Maids; Var Score Keeper; Stat Wrstlng; Phys Thrpst.

BULLOCK, TROY; D E Witt Clinton HS; Bronx, NY; (S); Var Ftbl; Hon Roll; Hist Hnr Awd 84; Arista Hnr Soc 84-85.

BULOW, HEIDI; Rye Neck HS; Mamaroneck, NY; (Y); 6/93; AFS; Key Clb; Quiz Bowl; Ski Clb; Teachers Aide; School Musical; Variety Show; Nwsp Ed-Chief; Hon Roll; Sec NHS; Rgnts Schlrshp 86; Colgate U; Law.

BULSON, JENNIFER; Berlin Central HS; Grafton, NY; (Y); 20/73; Ski Clb; Yrbk Phtg; JV Cheerleading; Mgr(s); Score Keeper; Hon Roll; Intl Rltns.

BULT, SHERRI; Guiderland HS; Guilderland, NY; (Y); Key Clb; Pep Clb; Ski Clb; Varsity Clb; Variety Show; Nwsp Rptr; Rep Jr Cls; Rep Stu Cncl; Sftbl; Capt Swmmng; Mst Vlbl Swmmr Summr Lge Team 83 & 85; Coachs Cup 84; Jr Prom Ct 86; Comm.

BUMBALO, LISA M; Horseheads HS; Horseheads, NY; (S); 40/380; Pres 4-H; German Clb; Hosp Aide; Model UN; Science Clb; Color Guard; Concert Band; Mrchg Band; Yrbk Stf; Rep Stu Cncl.

BUMBULSKY, DENISE; Cohoes HS; Cohoes, NY; (Y); 18/187; Exploring; Im Cheerleading; Hon Roll; Prfct Atten Awd; CSEA Union Scholar 86; U NY Plattsburgh; Acctg.

BUMEDER, GEORGE; H Frank Carey HS; Franklin Sq, NY; (Y); 1/276; Pres Mathletes; Rep Frsh Cls; Rep Soph Cls; Rep Jr Cls; Rep Sr Cls; Trs Stu Cncl; Var L Wrstlng; Jr NHS; NHS; Ntl Merit Ltr; Geo Washington U Engrng Mdl 86; Aerontcl Engrng.

BUMPUS, JENNIFER; Mt Mercy Acad; Depew, NY; (Y); French Clb; Ski Clb; SADD; Chorus; Mgr Var Cheerleading; Var Pom Pon; Hon Roll; Pre-Law.

BUNCE, JOHN; North Spencer Christian Acad; Spencer, NY; (S); 3/7; Computer Clb; School Play; Var Bsktbl; Prfct Atten Awd; Comp Sci.

BUNDSCHUH, BRENDA; Webster HS; Webster, NY; (Y); 7/504; Church Yth Grp; German Clb; Rep Soph Cls; Var Bsktbl; Var Vllybl; High Hon Roll; Jr NHS; NHS; Natl German Hnr Soc 85; Webster Bus & Prof Womens Clb Schlrshp 86; MIP Vllybl Awd 85; Messiah Coll; Acctng.

BUNDY, TARA; Seton Catholic Central HS; Vestal, NY; (Y); Church Yth Grp; Ski Clb; Stu Cncl; Cthrn Fly Mem Awd 86; Kystn JR Coll Educ Grnt 86; Keystone JR Coll; Physcl Thrpy.

BUNISH, STACY; Union-Endicott HS; Endicott, NY; (Y); VP Church Yth Grp; Civic Clb; Key Clb; Service Clb; SADD; Varsity Clb; Band; Flag Corp; Mrchg Band; Socr; Engl.

BUNK, BENSON; Cuba Central Schl; Belfast, NY; (Y); 11/63; FFA; Band; Chorus; Mrchg Band; Pep Band; Hon Roll; NHS; All Cnty Bnd Awd 84.

BUNN II, WARREN M; Sherburne-Earlville Central Schl; Earlville, NY; (Y); Sec Art Clb; English Clb; French Clb; Quiz Bowl; Band; Yrbk Stf; JV Ftbl; Var L Lcrss; Natl Womens Vets Wk 1st Prz 85; Smmr Schl Arts Fredonia 86; Art Awds 83; Art.

BUNNELL, MICHAEL; Cicero-North Syracuse HS; N Syracuse, NY; (S); 37/623; Aud/Vis; Boys Clb Am; Boy Scts; Trs Church Yth Grp; Mathletes; Math Tm; Church Choir; Hst Jr Cls; Bsktbl; Ftbl; Air Force; Elec.

BUNNELL, REBECCA; Sherburne-Earlville HS; Sherburne, NY; (Y); 38/150; FBLA; Ski Clb; Spanish Clb; SADD; Yrbk Phtg; Yrbk Rptr; Yrbk Stf; Trs Jr Cls; Trs Sr Cls; Fld Hcky; Conficare Slctn-Hnr 85; Srch For Tmmrw-Oprtn Entrprs 86; Bus Adm.

BUNTICH, JENNIFER; Hamburg HS; Hamburg, NY; (Y); Cmnty Wkr; Var Capt Bsktbl; Var Capt Fld Hcky; Band; Mrchg Band; Symp Band; Var L Sftbl; Empire ST Fld Hcky Tm 86; U Houston; Htl & Rest Mgmt.

BUONAPONNA, ED; West Islip HS; W Islip, NY; (Y); Ski Clb; SADD; Golf; Socr; Hon Roll; NHS; Chiropractc Med.

BUONICONTO, LISA; Cairo-Durham HS; Cairo, NY; (Y); Band; Pres Jr Cls; Var Bsktbl; Var Socr; Var Sftbl; Var Vllybl; High Hon Roll; Pres NHS; Spec Ed.

BUONINFANTE, TERESA; Cardinal Spellman HS; Yonkers, NY; (Y); 46/500; Hon Roll; St Michaels Coll.

BUONO, DAN; Saugerties HS; Saugerties, NY; (S); Spanish Clb; Variety Show; Wrstlng; High Hon Roll; NHS; Mum Festvl Art Shw 2nd Pl 85.

BUONO, DENISE; Bishop Maginn HS; Rensselaer, NY; (Y); 35/84; Red Cross Aide; Yrbk Stf; Cert Awd Hlth 86; Hudson Valley CC; Word Proc.

BUONO, PATRICK; Saugerties HS; Saugerties, NY; (S); 6/252; Am Leg Boys St; Church Yth Grp; Trs Math Tm; Quiz Bowl; Trs Jr Cls; VP Sr Cls; Trs Stu Cncl; High Hon Roll; NHS; Ntl Merit SF; Pre-Med.

BUONO, VALERIE; Attica Central HS; Attica, NY; (S); 7/156; Girl Scts; Band; Concert Band; Mrchg Band; Capt Swmmng; NHS; Daemen Coll; Physcl Thrpy.

BUQUICCHIO, FRANK; Mc Clancy HS; Richmond Hills, NY; (Y); #89 In Class; Teachers Aide; Yrbk Stf; JV Var Bsbl; Im Bsktbl; Im Ftbl; Hon Roll; NHS; St Johns U; Bus Law.

BURBINE, SARA; Fonda Fulltonville Central Schl; Tribes Hill, NY; (Y); 1/120; 4-H; Co-Capt Hosp Aide; Trs Key Clb; Math Tm; Quiz Bowl; Band; Nwsp Rptr; JV Var Socr; High Hon Roll; NHS; Math.

BURCH, JILL A; West Seneca SR HS; Cheektowaga, NY; (Y); 29/559; Cmnty Wkr; Hosp Aide; Yrbk Stf; Sec Sr Cls; Stu Cncl; L Cheerleading; Hon Roll; Jr NHS; NHS; Art Clb; Vlntr Of Mnth 84; Spnsh Merit Awds 85; 4 Yr Schlrshp 86; Niagara U; Nrsg.

BURCHARD, GREGORY; Camden Central HS; Camden, NY; (Y); Debate Tm; Drama Clb; Spanish Clb; School Musical; School Play; Stage Crew; Ed Nwsp Ed-Chief; Yrbk Stf; NHS.

BURCHARD, RENAE; Canisteo Central HS; Canisteo, NY; (Y); Art Clb; Church Yth Grp; Ski Clb; Band; Yrbk Stf; Powder Puff Ftbl; Socr; Sftbl; Vllybl; DAR Awd; RIT; Comp Arch Dsgn.

BURD, CHRISTINE; Sandy Creek Central HS; Orwell, NY; (S); 3/88; Art Clb; Sec Computer Clb; French Clb; Chorus; Sec Jr Cls; Cheerleading; Socr; Hon Roll; NHS; Schlstc/Mony Phtgrphy Awd 86; Archtr.

BURDA, DOREEN; Sandy Creek Central Schl; Sandy Creek, NY; (S); 5/90; Church Yth Grp; Computer Clb; French Clb; Intnl Clb; JCL; Band; Chorus; Rep Stu Cncl; Capt Var Vllybl; NHS; Lwyr.

BURDASH, ANNMARIE; Susquehanna Valley HS; Binghamton, NY; (Y); Mathletes; Pep Clb; Spanish Clb; Orch; Nwsp Rptr; Yrbk Stf; Fld Hcky; High Hon Roll; NHS; Spanish NHS; Regents Schlrshp 86; Fash Inst Of Tech; Fash Buyng.

BURDASH, PETER T; Highland HS; Highland, NY; (Y); 7/120; Math Tm; Concert Band; Variety Show; Yrbk Stf; Pres Stu Cncl; Var Socr; Var Capt Vllybl; DAR Awd; NHS; Pres Schlr; Rgnts Schlrshp 86; Acad All-Amer 86; US Achvmnt Acad 86; Coll; Engrng.

BURDICK, GINA; P V Moore HS; Central Sq, NY; (Y); AFS; Church Yth Grp; Drama Clb; Radio Clb; Science Clb; Band; Chorus; Church Choir; Concert Band; School Play; Elemetary Education.

BURDITT, CAREY; Richfield Springs Central HS; Schuyler Lake, NY; (Y); Teachers Aide; Chorus; Bus Admn.

BURDO, BRIDGETTE; Cicero-North Syracuse HS; Clay, NY; (S); 59/622; Office Aide; Hon Roll; NHS; St Josephs Schl Of Nrsng; Nrsng.

BUREK, PAUL C; Attica HS; Cowlesville, NY; (Y); 17/155; Computer Clb; Math Tm; Varsity Clb; Var L Bsbl; Var L Socr; Kiwanis Awd; NHS; Plattsburgh; Comp Sci.

BURG, AMY; Penn Yan Acad; Penn Yan, NY; (S); 25/174; GAA; Pep Clb; Band; Drm Mjr(t); Trs Frsh Cls; Trs Soph Cls; Trs Jr Cls; Trs Sr Cls; Rep Stu Cncl; JV Var Cheerleading; SUNY Cobleskill; Acctg.

BURG, KAREN; Grand Island HS; Grand Island, NY; (Y); 46/288; Trs Art Clb; Drama Clb; Sec 4-H; Red Cross Aide; Concert Band; School Musical; Stage Crew; Yrbk Stf; Hon Roll; NHS; Buffalo ST; Elem Ed.

BURG, PATRICIA; Grand Island HS; Grand Island, NY; (Y); Pres Trs Art Clb; 4-H; Mathletes; Quiz Bowl; Yrbk Stf; Hon Roll; NHS; Ntl Merit Ltr; Pres Schlrshp Lk Erie Coll; GI Art Soc Schlrshp Awd; 14 Art Awds Erie Cnty Fr & Expo 82-85; Lake Erie Coll; Equestrn Fac Mg.

BURGAN, A; Springfield Gardens HS; Laruelton, NY; (Y); Aud/Vis; French Clb; Radio Clb; Drm & Bgl; Nwsp Sprt Ed; Bsbl; Trk; Wt Lftg; French Hon Soc; Outstndng Achvt Applied Sci & Hstry Cert 86; NY Tech Coll; Elec.

BURGER, JAMIE; Valley Central HS; Walden, NY; (Y); Dance Clb; Variety Show; Rep Jr Cls; Rep Stu Cncl; Humanities Clb 85-86; Arch Desgn.

BURGER, RACHEL A; Hamburg HS; Hamburg, NY; (Y); 30/385; Drm Mjr(t); Jazz Band; Mrchg Band; Orch; School Musical; Symp Band; NHS; Rep Frsh Cls; Rep Jr Cls; Rgnts Schlrshp 86; NYSSMA Cnfrnc All ST Bnd 85; NYSSMA Sctnl All ST Bnd 85; Ithaca Coll; Msc.

BURGER, WENDY J; Ray C Ketcham HS; Poughkeepsie, NY; (Y); 14/500; Church Yth Grp; Computer Clb; Drama Clb; Math Clb; Church Choir; Yrbk Stf; High Hon Roll; Jr NHS; NHS; Ntl Merit Ltr; Regents Schlrshp 86; Suny Binghamton.

BURGESS, FAITH; Campbell Central HS; Campbell, NY; (S); 6/70; Chorus; Concert Band; Drm Mjr(t); Mrchg Band; Symp Band; Bowling; Capt Vllybl; High Hon Roll; NHS; Prfct Atten Awd; All Cnty Band, Hnr Rll Awds 80-85; HSEWFE.

BURGESS, NANCY A; Lakeshore Central HS; Old Saybrook, CT; (Y); 8/284; Art Clb; Yrbk Phtg; Yrbk Stf; High Hon Roll; NHS; VFW Awd; Alternate On Its Academic 85; NY ST Regents Schlrshp 86; RIT; Graphic Dsgn.

BURGESS, REGINA; Evander Childs HS; Bronx, NY; (S); Church Yth Grp; Sec Exploring; Sec Church Choir; Cit Awd; Hon Roll; Prfct Atten Awd; Pride Yankees 85; Boy Scouts Scout Show Part 84; Cert Apprctn NYC Dept Parks & Rcrtn 84; Pre-Med.

BURGESS, RUPERT; Uniondale HS; Hempstead, NY; (Y); Cmnty Wkr; Yrbk Sprt Ed; JV Var Ftbl; Var Tennis; JV Var Wrstlng; Hon Roll; Church Yth Grp; SADD; Church Choir; Variety Show; Sci Fai Hnrb Mntn 84; Law.

BURGESS, TODD; Addison Central HS; Addison, NY; (Y); Trs Church Yth Grp; Var Letterman Clb; Var L Bsbl; Var Trk; Hon Roll; Math Tchr.

BURGHER, KAREN; Johnson City SR HS; Johnson City, NY; (Y); Capt Science Clb; Teachers Aide; Acpl Chr; Orch; Hon Roll; NHS; Hosp Aide; Latin Clb; Library Aide; Chorus; Helen Pooler Bst Musicn Orchstra 86; 7 NYSSMD Mdls Violn Vcl 84-86; Grinnell; Bio Sci.

BURGIN, CECILIA; The Berkeley Carroll Street Schl; Brooklyn, NY; (S); AFS; Drama Clb; Nwsp Ed-Chief; Yrbk Phtg; VP Stu Cncl; Var Mgr(s); High Hon Roll; Prfct Atten Awd; Chorus; School Musical; Excllnc Awds-Amer Lit, Spansh,Amer Hstry & Visl Arts 85 & 86; Best Actress Awd-Schl Play 85.

BURGIN, MATTHEW A; Delaware Acad; Delhi, NY; (Y); Am Leg Boys St; Church Yth Grp; FFA; German Clb; Var Bsktbl; Var Crs Cntry; Var Trk; NHS.

BURGUN, STEPHEN; Rome Catholic HS; Blossvale, NY; (Y); School Musical; Yrbk Sprt Ed; VP Jr Cls; VP Sr Cls; JV Var Bsktbl; Bausch & Lomb Sci Awd; High Hon Roll; NHS; NEDT Awd.

BURICH, LUCY; St Francis Prep; Elmhurst, NY; (S); 25/653; Church Yth Grp; Cmnty Wkr; Dance Clb; Pres Rep Frsh Cls; Rep Soph Cls; VP Jr Cls; Hon Roll; NHS; Accntng.

BURKE, AMY; Solvay HS; Solvay, NY; (Y); Church Yth Grp; French Clb; Spanish Clb; Sec SADD; Band; Chorus; Church Choir; School Musical; Nwsp Stf; Hon Roll; Trvl.

BURKE, ANN; Hornell HS; Hornell, NY; (Y); 3/170; Pres Frsh Cls; Pres Jr Cls; Rep Stu Cncl; Var Capt Bsktbl; Stat Ftbl; Cit Awd; DAR Awd; High Hon Roll; Pres NHS; St Schlr; Smith Coll; Gvnt.

BURKE, BARBARA A; Garden City HS; Garden City, NY; (Y); 116/345; Hosp Aide; Chorus; Mrchg Band; Yrbk Stf; Mgr(s); Score Keeper; Hon Roll; Pres Schlr; NY St Regents Schlrshp 86; Gettysburg Coll; Bus Adm.

BURKE, CHARLES T; Notre Dame HS; Elmira, NY; (Y); 27/90; Church Yth Grp; Scholastic Bowl; Ski Clb; Rep Jr Cls; Pres Stu Cncl; Stat Bsktbl; JV Var Ftbl; Var Tennis; People To People; Regents Schlrshp; Georgetown U; Bus.

BURKE, COLEY MICHAEL; Saranac Lake HS; Saranac Lk, NY; (Y); Dance Clb; Pep Clb; Band; Concert Band; Pep Band; Bsktbl; Golf; Socr; Tennis; Hon Roll; Villanova U; Bus.

BURKE, DANIEL; Monsigner Farrell HS; Staten Island, NY; (S); 30/400; Computer Clb; Letterman Clb; Yrbk Phtg; Yrbk Rptr; Yrbk Stf; Ntl Frnch Merit Awd 85-87; Engrng.

BURKE, DANIEL C; Sachem HS; Holbrook, NY; (Y); 144/1385; Sec Cmnty Wkr; Science Clb; Ski Clb; Band; Concert Band; Regnts Schlrshp 86; SUNY Albany; Pre-Law.

BURKE, DOREEN; Newburgh Free Acad; Newburgh, NY; (Y); Drama Clb; Key Clb; Spanish Clb; Pom Pon; U Buffalo; Elem Educ.

BURKE, JAMES M; Rye Neck HS; Mamaroneck, NY; (Y); 3/90; Key Clb; Var Trk; High Hon Roll; NHS; George Washington U; Bus Adm.

BURKE, JENNIFER; Nardin Acad; Buffalo, NY; (Y); 4/83; School Musical; Pres Soph Cls; Sec Jr Cls; Hon Roll; NHS; Church Yth Grp; Hosp Aide; Church Choir; Bio.

BURKE, JOHN; Fordham Prep Schl; Rye, NY; (Y); Hosp Aide; School Play; Nwsp Ed-Chief; Lit Mag; Var L Ice Hcky; Var L Tennis; High Hon Roll; NCTE Awd; NHS; Pres Schlr.

BURKE, KATHARINE; Allegany Central Schl; Allegany, NY; (Y); Rep Frsh Cls; Rep Soph Cls; Rep Jr Cls; Pres Sr Cls; Rep Stu Cncl; Var Bsktbl; Var Crs Cntry; Var Trk; High Hon Roll; NHS; Schlrshp Soc 86; Vrsty A Clb 82-86; Pre Law.

BURKE, KATHRYN T; Bayport-Blue Point HS; Bayport, NY; (Y); 55/220; Art Clb; NFL; Office Aide; SADD; Chorus; Orch; VP Frsh Cls; Sec Stu Cncl; JV Var Fld Hcky; JV Trk; Stu Of Mnth; Stu Of Wk; NYSMA Musical Solos-Violin; George Washington U; Intl Rltns.

BURKE, KEVIN; Bethpage HS; Bethpage, NY; (Y); 45/290; Boy Scts; Band; Orch; Var Capt Crs Cntry; Var Capt Trk; Hon Roll; Polc Boys Clb Pres Awd Sportsmnshp 86; Gettysburg Coll; Hstry.

BURKE, KEVIN A; Shaker HS; Latham, NY; (Y); Cmnty Wkr; Computer Clb; French Clb; Ski Clb; Nwsp Ed-Chief; Nwsp Rptr; JV Var Bowling; JV Trk; High Hon Roll; Ntl Merit Ltr; NYS Rgnts Schlrshp 86; Cornell U; Math Engnrn.

BURKE, MATTHEW; Horseheads HS; Horseheads, NY; (Y); Boy Scts; Cmnty Wkr; SADD; Band; Chorus; Nwsp Stf; Pres Jr Cls; Pres Sr Cls; Var L Crs Cntry; Var L Swmmng; HOBY Ldrshp Seminar 84-85; Bus.

BURKE, NANCY ANN; Rocky Point JR SR HS; Rocky Point, NY; (Y); 34/183; Sec FBLA; Band; Concert Band; Mrchg Band; Mgr(s); Hon Roll; Var Gym; Phys Thrpy.

BURKE, ROBERT; Mc Quaid Jesuit HS; Rochester, NY; (Y); Boy Scts; Model UN; School Play; Wrstlng; Law.

BURKE, TIFFANY; Nardin Acad; Williamsville, NY; (Y); 35/79; Model UN; Teachers Aide; School Play; Stage Crew; Yrbk Ed-Chief; Yrbk Phtg; Yrbk Stf; Lit Mag; Cert Of Merit Bio, Geo And Eng 85-86; Pre Med.

BURKE, TIMOTHY; Glens Falls SR HS; Glens Falls, NY; (Y); 17/213; Am Leg Boys St; VP Key Clb; SADD; Capt Diving; High Hon Roll; NHS; Ntl Schlr Athlete Awd 86; Zone I Awd Diving 86; Colgate U Schlrshp 86; Colgate U; Econ.

BURKHARD, LINDA; Eastchester SR HS; Eastchester, NY; (Y); Cmnty Wkr; French Clb; Girl Scts; Hosp Aide; Chorus; Church Choir; Hon Roll; Jr NHS; Candy Strpg 83-84; Chld Devlpmnt Awd 86; Bus.

BURKHOLDER, ANGELA; Greene Central Schl; Greene, NY; (Y); French Clb; VP VICA; Chorus; JV Sftbl; Hon Roll; Stu Of Quarter 85-86; 2 Stsmnshp Awds From Vctn Ind Clbs Of Amer 85-86; 3rd Pl Trphy Ldrshp Cntst 86.

BURKS, APRIL; Owen D Young HS; Van Hornesville, NY; (S); French Clb; Band; Chorus; Rep Stu Cncl; Score Keeper; JV Var Vllybl; Hon Roll; Jr NHS; NHS; Math 100 Pct Regnt Awd 84; Ctznshp & Ed Relgn Awd 85; Pre-Med.

BURKUM, LISA; Potsdam Central HS; Potsdam, NY; (Y); 38/119; Math Clb; Spanish Clb; Canton ATC; Crmnl Jstc.

BURL, TRACY; Salmon River Central HS; Ft Covington, NY; (Y); 2/100; Var Ice Hcky; Bausch & Lomb Sci Awd; DAR Awd; High Hon Roll; Hon Roll; NHS; Prfct Atten Awd; Sal; Rgnts Schlrshp 86; Cornell U; Anml Sci.

BURLEW, KIP; Mynderse Acad; Seneca Falls, NY; (S); 36/142; Var L Bsbl; Im Bsktbl; JV L Ftbl; High Hon Roll; Hon Roll; Rochester Inst Tech; Statistcs.

BURLINGAME, JANET; Churchville-Chili SR HS; Churchville, NY; (Y); Church Yth Grp; Exploring; FTA; JCL; Latin Clb; Office Aide; Church Choir; School Musical; Yrbk Stf; Stu Cncl; Med.

BURLINGAME, JUNE; Paul V Moore HS; Brewerton, NY; (Y); FBLA; Radio Clb; Band; Concert Band; Jazz Band; Mrchg Band; Sftbl; Hon Roll; Rstrnt/Htl Owner.

BURLISON, MIKE; Bainbridge-Guilford Central Schl; Bainbridge, NY; (Y); 4-H; FFA; Nwsp Rptr; Var L Bowling; JV Tennis; 4-H Awd; Hon Roll; Greenhand Chptr Degree-FFA 86; Forestry Awd-FFA 86.

BURMASTER, DANIEL; Wilson HS; Ransomville, NY; (Y); Yrbk Stf; Var L Bsbl; Var L Ftbl; Im Wt Lftg; High Hon Roll; Hon Roll; NHS; Prfct Atten Awd; Pre-Med.

BURMEISTER, KAREN; Fairport Central HS; Fairport, NY; (Y); High Hon Roll; Hon Roll; Prfct Atten Awd; Pres Acdmc Fit Awd 86; SUNY; Accntng.

BURNAM, SCOTT M; St Johns Acad; Plattsburgh, NY; (Y); 13/38; Chess Clb; CAP; Cmnty Wkr; Latin Clb; Model UN; Red Cross Aide; JV Bsktbl; Var Socr; Var Trk; Gold Star Serv Awd 84; Cvl Air Patrl Mitchell Awd 86; NYS Regnts Schlrshp 86; Plattsburgh ST U; Crmnl Just.

BURNAP, KIRSTEN; Sodus Central HS; Sodus, NY; (S); 10/134; VP AFS; Model UN; Ski Clb; Sec Varsity Clb; Band; Mrchg Band; Sec Sr Cls; Var Capt Socr; Var Sftbl; High Hon Roll; Radio Clb Sprtswmn Of Yr 86; Dem & Chrncle Sprts Excllnc Awd 85; St HS Stalom & Giant Stalom Chmp 86; Lib Arts.

BURNET, TIA; Nyack HS; Nyack, NY; (Y); Church Yth Grp; Office Aide; Pep Clb; Drill Tm; Mrchg Band; Pom Pon; Elks Awd; Hon Roll; Shaw U; Soc Wrk.

BURNETT, CHARLES; Rondout Valley HS; Rosendale, NY; (Y); Cmnty Wkr; Science Clb; JV Var Bsktbl; JV Score Keeper; Hon Roll; Tech Schl; Comp Engr.

BURNETT, CHRISTINA L; Gloversville HS; Gloversville, NY; (Y); 14/237; Concert Band; Yrbk Stf; VP Jr Cls; Rep Stu Cncl; Im JV Cheerleading; Var Fld Hcky; Mgr Socr; High Hon Roll; NHS; NY ST Rgnts Schlrshp 86; SUNY-GENESEO.

BURNETT, DAVID THURLOW; John Jay HS; Sunderland, MA; (Y); 110/519; Boy Scts; Chess Clb; Cmnty Wkr; Computer Clb; Science Clb; Ski Clb; Variety Show; Socr; Hon Roll; Rep NYS Socr Tourn Scotland Engl 84; NYS Regents Scholar Wnnr 85-86; U AM; Elec Engrng.

BURNEY, LIZ; Clarkstown High Schl North; New City, NY; (Y); Pres DECA; Pep Clb; Spanish Clb; SADD; Nwsp Stf; 3rd Pl DECCA Local Comp 86; Law.

BURNS, ALISA; Niagara Falls HS; Niagara Falls, NY; (Y); 63/250; Church Yth Grp; Office Aide; Church Choir; Yrbk Stf; Stu Cncl; Hon Roll; Prfct Atten Awd; Nazareth Coll Rochester; Bus.

BURNS, BRADLEY; Gouverneur SR HS; Gouverneur, NY; (Y); 4/139; Pres Soph Cls; Capt Crs Cntry; Var L Socr; 4-H Awd; High Hon Roll; Pres NHS; Pres Schlr; Hannah J Mosher Math,Sci Schlrshp; Regents Schlrshp; Wnnr Yorker Gov Trophy Resrch Cntst; Clarkson U; Elect Engr.

BURNS, BRANDI; Lindenhurst SR HS; Lindenhurst, NY; (Y); French Clb; Spanish Clb; Yrbk Stf; Fld Hcky; Score Keeper; High Hon Roll; NHS; Ntl Merit Ltr; Acdmc All Am 86; Achvt Awd 85; Pre-Law.

BURNS, CINTRY; Murry Bergtraum HS; Bronx, NY; (Y); FHA; Band; Yrbk Stf; Hon Roll; Math Cert 84; Accntg.

BURNS, DAWN; Pioneer Central HS; Delevan, NY; (Y); 25/258; 4-H; French Clb; Pep Clb; Science Clb; Varsity Clb; Capt Var Cheerleading; Var JV Pom Pon; Cit Awd; 4-H Awd; Hon Roll; Lab Tech.

BURNS, GEORGE; Somers HS; Amawalk, NY; (Y); 41/196; SADD; Nwsp Rptr; Rep Stu Cncl; Var Bsktbl; Var Capt Ftbl; Var Golf; Hon Roll; NHS; St Schlr; Soc Stu; NYS Regnts Schlrshp Awd; Boston U; Law.

BURNS, JAMES; Olimpia HS; Rochester, NY; (Y); Computer Clb; 4-H; Ski Clb; Soroptimist; Badmtn; Diving; Ftbl; Sftbl; Swmmng; Vllybl.

BURNS, KAREN; Knox Memorial HS; Russell, NY; (S); 5/30; Mrchg Band; School Play; Yrbk Stf; Sftbl; High Hon Roll; NHS; MVP Vllybl Div; 1st All NAC Bsktbl & Soccr; Ithaca Coll; Phys Ed.

BURNS, LAURA; Sachem HS; Farmingville, NY; (Y); 93/1500; Dance Clb; Service Clb; Concert Band; Mrchg Band; Stage Crew; NHS; Ntl Merit Ltr; Church Yth Grp; Cmnty Wkr; Drama Clb; Sci-Fctn Clb VP 84-85; Yrkr Clb-NY Jnr Hstrcl Soc-Stu Cmmtte 84-86; Engl.

BURNS, LAURA A; Babylon SR HS; Babylon, NY; (Y); 11/180; Hosp Aide; Math Tm; Off Jr Cls; Off Sr Cls; Capt Var Tennis; High Hon Roll; Sec NHS; Lit Mag; Babylon Cmnty Schlrshp 86; Dowling Coll Apttd Schlrshp 86; NY ST Rgnts Schlrshp 86; Dowling Coll; Intl Fin.

BURNS, LISA; Stella Maris HS; Howard Beach, NY; (Y); Library Aide; Math Clb; Hon Roll; Science Clb; Teachers Aide; High Hon Roll; Lib Aide Awd 86; Queens Coll; Doc.

BURNS, MARGARET; Romulus HS; Geneva, NY; (S); Am Leg Aux Girls St; Ski Clb; Spanish Clb; Band; Mrchg Band; Yrbk Ed-Chief; Pres Frsh Cls; VP Soph Cls; Pres Jr Cls; Trs Stu Cncl; Socl Sci.

BURNS, MATTHEW W; Horseheads HS; Elmira, NY; (S); Church Yth Grp; Cmnty Wkr; German Clb; JCL; Latin Clb; Variety Show; Var Trk; High Hon Roll; Hon Roll; Town Yth Comm 85; Pre-Law.

BURNS, MAURA; Mt Mercy Acad; Buffalo, NY; (Y); Cmnty Wkr; French Clb; Quiz Bowl; Rep Jr Cls; Sec Sr Cls; Im Badmtn; Im Tennis; Var Trk; Im Vllybl; Kiwanis Awd; Acad Achvt Awds 84-86; Stu Govt Rep Awd 85-86; Buffalo St Coll; Elem Ed.

BURNS, PATRICIA L; Westhill SR HS; Syracuse, NY; (Y); 26/145; Exploring; Band; Chorus; Jazz Band; Symp Band; Nwsp Stf; Yrbk Stf; Var L Vllybl; NHS; NEDT Awd; NY Rgnts Schlrshp 86; Dlta Kappa Gamma Schlrshp 86; ST U Of NY-GENESEO; Elem Educ.

BURNS, RICHARD; Northstar Christian Acad; Rochester, NY; (S); 3/28; Trs Church Yth Grp; Yrbk Bus Mgr; Rep Jr Cls; VP Stu Cncl; High Hon Roll; Pastorial.

BURNS, ROSEMARY; Hendrick Hudson HS; Verplanck, NY; (Y); Hosp Aide; Office Aide; SADD; Yrbk Stf; Score Keeper; High Hon Roll; Hon Roll; Bsbl; Engrng.

BURNSIDE, DERRICK; De Witt Clinton HS; Bronx, NY; (S); Cmnty Wkr; School Play; Stage Crew; Ftbl; Trk; Wt Lftg; Cit Awd.

BURNSIDE, ELAINE R; Cassadaga Valley Central HS; Sinclairville, NY; (Y); 7/80; Chess Clb; Computer Clb; Drama Clb; Math Clb; Quiz Bowl; Science Clb; Spanish Clb; SADD; Thesps; Chorus; U S Colligt Wind Band Europe Tour 85; NYS Regents Scholar 86; NYS U Geneseo; Secndry Ed.

BURNSIDE, JARED; Attica Central HS; Attica, NY; (S); 10/175; Church Yth Grp; French Clb; Ski Clb; Band; Concert Band; Mrchg Band; Socr; Hon Roll; Ntl Merit Ltr; Envrnmntl Sci.

BUROICK, CORRIE; Alfred-Almond Central HS; Alfred Sta, NY; (Y); French Clb; SADD; Band; Yrbk Stf; Pres Frsh Cls; Rep Soph Cls; Pres Jr Cls; Rep Sr Cls; VP Stu Cncl; Cheerleading; Distngushd Athlete 86; Art.

BURR, GEOFFREY W; Vestal SR HS; Binghamton, NY; (Y); 6/430; Chess Clb; Mathletes; Science Clb; Ski Clb; Band; Concert Band; Jazz Band; Mrchg Band; Orch; Pep Band; Amer Invitatnl Math Exam 85; Interdiscplnry Sci Rsrch Prog 85; Sthrn Tier Mathlete Tm 84; SUNY Buffalo; Elec Engrng.

BURR, MELISSA; West Genesee SR HS; Camillus, NY; (Y); GAA; Mrchg Band; Soph Cls; Jr Cls; Sr Cls; Ice Hcky; Lcrss; Swmmng; Vllybl; Hon Roll; A Rtng NYSSMA Solo Fest Flute 84; Mst Outstndng Female Stu N Am Indian Clb 85-86; Cornell U; Arch.

BURRIDGE, STACEY; Grand Island SR HS; Grand Isl, NY; (Y); 20/300; Trs Church Yth Grp; Hosp Aide; Ski Clb; Yrbk Stf; Rep Stu Cncl; Stat Gym; JV Socr; Var L Trk; High Hon Roll; NHS; Acad Achvt Awd 83-86; GIHS Ftns Awd; Pre-Med.

BURROUGHS, ANN E; Oxford Academy HS; Oxford, NY; (Y); 1/85; Drama Clb; 4-H; French Clb; Ski Clb; SADD; Band; Chorus; Mrchg Band; High Hon Roll; NHS; Rotary Exch Stu New Zealand 84-85; Mock Trial Org 82-83,83-84,85-86; Hugh O Brien Yth Ldrshp Sem 83-84; U PA Wharton Schl; Econ.

BURROUGHS, KRISTEN; Wayland Central HS; Wayland, NY; (Y); 14/104; Drama Clb; Service Clb; Ski Clb; Teachers Aide; Band; Chorus; Concert Band; Jazz Band; Mrchg Band; School Play; Close-Up WA DC Pgm 86.

BURROWS, DAWN; Holland Patent Central HS; Rome, NY; (Y); 43/196; Sec Church Yth Grp; Sec Spanish Clb; Acpl Chr; Band; Chorus; Symp Band; Hon Roll; Worthy Advisor For Intl Order Of The Rainbow For Girls 86; Nazareth Coll; Psych.

BURROWS, JULIE; Fillmore Central Schl; Fillmore, NY; (Y); Office Aide; SADD; Varsity Clb; Nwsp Stf; Stat Bsbl; Stat Bsktbl; Var Socr; JV Var Vllybl; High Hon Roll; Hon Roll; Bus.

BURROWS, SANDRA; Valley Central HS; Montgomery, NY; (Y); 51/286; Service Clb; Off Frsh Cls; Trs Soph Cls; Pres Jr Cls; Off Sr Cls; Stu Cncl; Cit Awd; Hon Roll; NHS; Rotary Awd; John G & Hilda F Sutton Mrl Awd 86; Jennie Marano Ctnzshp Awd 86; HS Schrlshp Cncl 86; Cobleskill; Bus Admn.

BURRUANO, VINCENT D; James I O Neill HS; Garrison, NY; (Y); 35/130; Boy Scts; French Clb; Nwsp Bus Mgr; JV Bsbl; JV Var Ftbl; Var Trk; Hon Roll; Washington Wrkshps Congrssnl Sem 86; Bus Admin.

BURSTEIN, ARI C; Hebrew Academy Fo Nassau County; Plainview, NY; (Y); 5/78; Chess Clb; Cmnty Wkr; Computer Clb; Debate Tm; English Clb; French Clb; NFL; Quiz Bowl; Scholastic Bowl; Temple Yth Grp; NYS Schlrshp 86-87; SUNY Binghamton; Pol Sci.

BURSTEIN, MARK; Fayetteville-Manlius SR HS; Fayetteville, NY; (Y); Pres JCL; Model UN; Variety Show; Nwsp Ed-Chief; Nwsp Stf; Yrbk Phtg; Lit Mag; Stu Cncl; Hon Roll; Outstndng Photo Achvt 84; Outstndng Accomplshmnt Lit Corp 85; Ntl Cncl Tchrs Eng 86; U MI-ANN Arbor; Law.

BURT, CHRISTOPHER; Whitesboro SR HS; Utica, NY; (Y); 3/306; Mathletes; Pres Science Clb; Varsity Clb; Band; Concert Band; Jazz Band; Mrchg Band; Var L Trk; NHS; Ntl Merit Ltr; Elmira Coll Key Awd 86; Engrng.

BURT, JENNIFER; Bishop Ludden HS; Syracuse, NY; (S); Ski Clb; Jr Cls; JV Cheerleading; Var Crs Cntry; Stat Lcrss; Trk; Intr Dsgn.

BURT, KENNETH; Clyde-Savannah HS; Clyde, NY; (Y); Nwsp Stf; Var L Bsbl; Var L Bowling; Var L Ftbl; High Hon Roll; Hon Roll; Hghst Score Mth Cont CCFL 86; Bus Mgmt.

BURT, WALTER M; Ilion Central HS; Ilion, NY; (Y); 15/150; Drama Clb; French Clb; Q&S; Spanish Clb; School Musical; School Play; Nwsp Stf; Lit Mag; Socr; Tennis; Regents 86; Colgate U; Intl Relatns.

BURTNICK, DOUGLAS A; Horseheads HS; Horseheads, NY; (S); 9/380; JA; Model UN; Quiz Bowl; Trs Science Clb; Ski Clb; Band; Yrbk Rptr; NHS; Ntl Merit Ltr; German Clb; Erth Sci Awd 82; Cornell; Chem Engrng.

BURTON, COLLEEN; Murry Bergtraum HS; Brooklyn, NY; (Y); JA; Band; NHS; Acctng.

BURTON, JOHN T; Sachem High Schl North Campus; Farmingville, NY; (Y); 23/1389; Science Clb; Var L Ftbl; Jr NHS; NHS; Im JV Lcrss; Var JV Wt Lftg; Im JV Wrstlng; 17th Natnly Bio Olmpd 85; Regnts Schlrshp 86; Binghamton; Engrng.

BURTON, MARK; De Witt Clinton HS; Bronx, NY; (Y); Teachers Aide; Band; Color Guard; School Musical; Cit Awd; Prfct Atten Awd; Comp Sci.

BURTON, SHERRY A; Westmoreland Central HS; Rome, NY; (Y); 21/81; VP Model UN; SADD; Chorus; Yrbk Stf; Sec Jr Cls; High Hon Roll; Masonic Awd; Pres Acdmc Achvmnt Awd 86; Hnrs Prgrm Stu St Pauls Coll 86; St Pauls Coll; Bus Adm.

BURTON, TERRY L; Schoharie Central HS; Gallupville, NY; (Y); Cmnty Wkr; Varsity Clb; Stage Crew; Yrbk Stf; Sec Sr Cls; Im Badmtn; Var L Crs Cntry; Im Ice Hcky; JV Tennis; Var L Trk; Rgnts Schlrshp 86; SUNY New Paltz; Comm.

BUSACCA, ANTHONY; Monsignor Farrell HS; Staten Island, NY; (Y); Church Yth Grp; Dance Clb; VP Frsh Cls; Bsktbl; Im Ftbl; CYO Bsktbl; UAU Champ; Archtct.

BUSANI, ADRIANA; St Catharine Acad; Bronx, NY; (Y); 1/185; Nwsp Ed-Chief; High Hon Roll; NHS; Ntl Merit Ltr; Cmnty Wkr; Rep Frsh Cls; 1st Hnrs For Itln Iona Coll Lang Cntst 84-85.

BUSCAGLIA, HOLLIE; Frontier Central HS; Blasdell, NY; (Y); Latin Clb; Spanish Clb; Chorus; Var Cheerleading; Im Mgr Diving; JV Vllybl; DAR Awd; 4-H; Hncmng JR Cls Attendt 85-86fJR Cls Prom Attent 85-86; Voluntr Specl Educ Cls 85-86; Buffalo ST; Specl Ed.

BUSCH, GREGORY H; St Anthonys HS; Ronkonkoma, NY; (Y); Spanish Clb; Band; Chorus; Nwsp Rptr; Hon Roll; NHS; Spanish NHS; Br Francis Stelte Awd 86; Prncpls Lst 85; Prncpls Lst 84; Stony Brook; Bio.

BUSCH, STACEY; Connetguoh HS; Bohemia, NY; (Y); 63/700; FBLA; Teachers Aide; Hon Roll; Jr NHS; Craft Clb Pres 82-83; St Josephs Coll; Mgmt.

BUSCHE, STEPHEN M; South Kortright Central HS; South Kortright, NY; (Y); Debate Tm; Drama Clb; SADD; Teachers Aide; Chorus; Color Guard; School Musical; School Play; Nwsp Ed-Chief; Yrbk Bus Mgr; Paul Smiths Comp Schlrshp 86; NYS Rgnts Scshlrshp 86; Paul Smiths Coll; Htl Rest Mgt.

BUSH, ROBERT; Beaver River Central HS; Croghan, NY; (Y); Trs Varsity Clb; Var Bsbl; Var Ftbl; Var Wrstlng; All Star In Bsbl Catcher,Ftbl Quaterback 85-86; All Star In Wrstlng 84-85; Ithaca; Engnrng.

BUSHELL, CRAIG; York Prep Schl; New York, NY; (Y); School Musical; School Play; Nwsp Rptr; Yrbk Stf; Wnnr Ctywd Poetry Art Awd 81; Hrn Rl 83-85; Engr.

BUSHEY, DAVID; Northern Adirondack Central HS; Lyon Mt, NY; (Y); 2/110; French Clb; Band; High Hon Roll; NHS; VFW Awd; Prncpls Awd Math, Chmstry, Frnch III, English III & Typng 86.

BUSHEY, TAMMY; Coxsackie Athens Central HS; W Coxsackie, NY; (Y); Art Clb; 4-H; Spanish Clb; Chorus; VP Frsh Cls; Socr; JV Trk; Var JV Vllybl; 4-H Awd; High Hon Roll; MVP JV Vllybl 86; Commnctns.

BUSHNELL JR, TIMOTHY; Victor SR HS; Farmington, NY; (Y); Off Boy Scts; Trs French Clb; Trs Library Aide; Pres Model UN; Quiz Bowl; Scholastic Bowl; Science Clb; Service Clb; Yrbk Phtg; Mgr Mgr(s); Victor Central H S And Socl Stu 86; Army ROTC Schlrshp 86; Natl Yth Ldrshp Awd 86; Cornell U; Bio.

BUSHORR, LAURIE; Williamsville South HS; Williamsville, NY; (Y); Cmnty Wkr; Ski Clb; Spanish Clb; Rep Frsh Cls; JV Fld Hcky; JV Socr; Hon Roll; NHS; Geneseo ST Coll; Psych.

BUSKEY, CINDY; North Babylon SR HS; N Babylon, NY; (Y); Trs Spanish Clb; Orch; School Musical; Var Bsktbl; High Hon Roll; Jr NHS; NHS; Black Hert Mnth Essay Cntst 3rd 84; Long Isl String Fest Assoc 84; Med.

BUSKEY, TRACI; Fayetteville Manlius HS; Fayetteville, NY; (Y); Church Yth Grp; JCL; Band; Chorus; Concert Band; Mrchg Band; Orch; Pep Band; School Musical; High Hon Roll; Mst Outstndnb And Stu 84-85; JR Natl Hall Fame 86.

BUSKIRK III, MARTIN C; Arlington HS; Pleasant Valley, NY; (Y); 61/550; Church Yth Grp; Im Socr; Hon Roll; NHS; Ntl Merit Ltr; St Schlr; Boys St 85; Regnts Schlrshp 86; ST U NY; Elec Engrng.

BUSSENO, WILLIAM; Amsterdam HS; Amsterdam, NY; (Y); 20/291; Orch; Hon Roll; NY ST Regnts Schlrshp 86; Music Booster Orch Awd 86; Marine Midland Band Awd 86; Buffalo U; Chem Engrng.

BUSSI, CHRISTINE; Frontier HS; Hamburg, NY; (Y); 120/500; Drama Clb; German Clb; Pep Clb; Ski Clb; Concert Band; Mrchg Band; Stu Cncl; Socr; Hon Roll; Prfct Atten Awd; SUNY Oswego; Bus Admin.

BUSSJAGER, REBECCA; East Syracuse-Minoa HS; Minoa, NY; (Y); 8/333; JA; Ski Clb; Pres Soph Cls; Pres Jr Cls; Pres Sr Cls; JV Var Socr; Trk; CC Awd; High Hon Roll; Pres Schlr; Amer Lgn Schlrshp 86; U Of Rochester; Engrng.

BUSSY, KIMBERLY; Roxbury Central HS; Halcottsville, NY; (S); Debate Tm; VICA; Nwsp Stf; Yrbk Stf; High Hon Roll; Hon Roll; Delhi Ag & Tech; Wrd Prcssr.

BUSTOS, PHILIP; Flushing HS; Flushing, NY; (Y); Orch; Nwsp Rptr; Phys Fit In Gym 85-86; US Army.

BUTCHER, LISA RENEE; Washingtonville HS; New Windsor, NY; (Y); SUNY Farmingdale; Vet Tech.

BUTCHER, MARC; Pine Valley Central HS; S Dayton, NY; (Y); Acpl Chr; Chorus; Concert Band; Jazz Band; School Musical; School Play; Stage Crew; JV Var Ftbl; Var Trk; NHS; Bruce & Nancy Garlapow Mem Awd 86; NYS Regents Scholar 86; SUNY Fredonia; Biol.

BUTCHER, SHALUE; Waverly JR SR HS; Waverly, NY; (Y); Church Yth Grp; Trs Sec Pep Clb; Spanish Clb; Variety Show; Nwsp Stf; Var Cheerleading; Var Score Keeper; Im Vllybl; Hon Roll; Varsity Clb; Mst Spirtd Cls Of 87 84-85; Law.

BUTERA, BENNY; Gates Chili SR HS; Rochester, NY; (Y); Exploring; Trk; High Hon Roll; Hon Roll; NHS; Engrng.

BUTKOVICH, STEPHEN; Williamsville North HS; Getzville, NY; (Y); DECA; Teachers Aide; Var Swmmng; Hon Roll; Accntnt.

BUTLER, ALAN; Rice HS; Jamaica, NY; (Y); 2/80; Church Yth Grp; Teachers Aide; Church Choir; Ftbl; Gov Hon Prg Awd; High Hon Roll; Sal; St Johns U; Bio.

BUTLER, AMANDA; Fayetteville-Manlius HS; Manlius, NY; (Y); Hosp Aide; SADD; Yrbk Stf; Socr; High Hon Roll; Hon Roll; NHS.

BUTLER, AMY; Ticonderoga HS; Ticonderoga, NY; (Y); Key Clb; Band; Sec Trs Chorus; Swing Chorus; Yrbk Rptr; Trk; High Hon Roll; NHS; Ntl Merit Ltr; All All ST Chrus 85-86; Hist.

BUTLER, BILL; Union-Endicott HS; Endicott, NY; (Y); Boy Scts; Band; Mrchg Band; Symp Band; Trk; Engrng.

BUTLER, BRIAN; Westhill HS; Syracuse, NY; (Y); Bsktbl; Ftbl; Socr; Trk; Wt Lftg; 1st Tm All-Div Defensive Tackle 85; Bus Mgt.

BUTLER, BRYAN; Lansingburgh HS; Troy, NY; (Y); 10/185; Drama Clb; Varsity Clb; Yrbk Stf; Rep Jr Cls; Rep Sr Cls; Ftbl; Trk; Wrstlng; High Hon Roll; NHS; NYS Rgnts Schlrshp; Plattsburgh ST; Cmmnctns.

BUTLER, CHARLES A; Marcus Whitman HS; Geneva, NY; (Y); 15/115; Boy Scts; Church Yth Grp; Ski Clb; Band; Jazz Band; Mrchg Band; Trk; High Hon Roll; Hon Roll; NY St Rgnts Schlrshp Awd 86; Civil Engr.

BUTLER, CHRISTOPHER; Mount Saint Joseph Acad; Buffalo, NY; (Y); Boy Scts; Church Yth Grp; Chorus; JV Ftbl; JV Mgr(s); Var L Socr; JV Var Wrstlng; 1st Pl Olympics Of The Mind Regional Comp & 9th Pl In ST Competition 84; Envrnmntl Sci.

BUTLER, DAVID; Greece Athena HS; Rochester, NY; (Y); Science Clb; Lit Mag; Hon Roll; Prfct Atten Awd; Acad Lttr 85; Ntl Hon Soc 86; Genesee Valley HS Chem Recog 86; Engr.

BUTLER JR, DONALD; Uniondale HS; Hempstead, NY; (Y); Office Aide; SADD; Bsktbl; Diving; Ftbl; Swmmng; Trk; Mgmt Bus.

BUTLER, GLENN; Bishop Ford Central Catholic HS; Brooklyn, NY; (S); 10/365; Letterman Clb; Nwsp Rptr; Var Bsbl; Var Socr; High Hon Roll; CHSAA All Star Bsbl Tm; Bus.

BUTLER, JEFFERY; Olean HS; Olean, NY; (Y); 25/210; Cmnty Wkr; Hon Roll; NHS; Regents Schlrshp 86; U Buffalo; Phrmcy.

BUTLER, KATHY; Salamanca HS; Salamanca, NY; (Y); DECA; French Clb; Varsity Clb; Bowling; Sftbl; High Hon Roll; Hon Roll; Trvl Agnt.

BUTLER, KENYETTA S; St Nicholas Of Tolentine HS; Bronx, NY; (Y); 12/102; JA; Yrbk Phtg; Yrbk Stf; Sr Cls; Stu Cncl; VP Var Bsktbl; Hon Roll; NY ST Rgnts Schlrshp 86; Pres Eminent Schlrs Awd; Hampton U; Bus Adm.

BUTLER, LISA; The Academy Of Mt St Ursula; Bronx, NY; (Y); 12/134; Church Yth Grp; Drama Clb; Stage Crew; Nwsp Stf; Off Frsh Cls; Off Soph Cls; Off Jr Cls; Stu Cncl; Hon Roll; NEDT Awd; Psych.

BUTLER, MARK; Mineola HS; Mineola, NY; (Y); 35/200; Hosp Aide; Band; Concert Band; Jazz Band; Mrchg Band; School Musical; Hon Roll; Jr NHS; Avtn Mgmnt.

BUTTARAZZI, JOSEPH; Auburn HS; Auburn, NY; (Y); Math Clb; Red Cross Aide; SADD; Varsity Clb; Yrbk Stf; Chrmn Stu Cncl; Var JV Lcrss; High Hon Roll; Hon Roll; NHS; Engrng.

BUTTON, DENELLE M; Avoca Central HS; Cohocton, NY; (Y); 7/45; Church Yth Grp; Drama Clb; 4-H; FBLA; JCL; Latin Clb; Ski Clb; Varsity Clb; Band; Yrbk Stf; Whipple Schlrshp 86; Regents Schlrshp 86; Most Outstndng Female Athlete 86; Morrisville; Animal Sci.

BUTTS, CANDY L; Livonia HS; Geneseo, NY; (Y); 2/135; Church Yth Grp; Computer Clb; Math Tm; Chorus; Rep Sr Cls; Rep Stu Cncl; DAR Awd; High Hon Roll; Sec NHS; Sal; Union Coll; Comp Sci.

BUTTS, LEIGH ANN; Webutuck Central HS; Amenia, NY; (Y); Am Leg Aux Girls St; GAA; Ski Clb; Thesps; Chorus; School Musical; School Play; Pres Stu Cncl; JV Var Bsktbl; Var Fld Hcky; Coach Wtkns Awd Outstndng Cntbtr Athltcs Wbtck; Drma Clb; Yrbk Stff; Acctg.

BUTZER, RITA C; North Collins Central HS; Lawtons, NY; (Y); 1/69; Sec Pres 4-H; Mrchg Band; Trs Sr Cls; Pres Stu Cncl; Stat Bsktbl; Bausch & Lomb Sci Awd; DAR Awd; Elks Awd; NHS; Val; U Of Rochester; Econ.

BUXBAUM, STEVE M; Hunter College HS; New York, NY; (Y); Math Tm; Model UN; Ski Clb; Yrbk Stf; Var Capt Tennis; Ntl Merit SF.

BUXTON, LISA; Newburgh Free Acad; Newburgh, NY; (Y); 73/621; Church Yth Grp; VP Computer Clb; JV Bsktbl; High Hon Roll; Ofc Sklls Coop Educ Wrk Stdy Pgm Awd 85-86; Jms Bst & Rbt Wllms Schlrshp 85-86; Bus & Pro Wmns Schlrsh; Dutchess CC; Bus Admn.

BUYDOS, CAROLYN; Shenendehowa HS; Clifton Pk, NY; (Y); Camera Clb; Dance Clb; Ski Clb; Fld Hcky; Powder Puff Ftbl; High Hon Roll; Seido Karate Brown Blt 86; Regents Diploma 86; Cert Of Merit Awd 86; JC Of Albany; Photogrphy.

BUZBY, BRETT; Grand Island HS; Grand Island, NY; (Y); 60/280; Varsity Clb; Yrbk Phtg; Var L Ftbl; Var L Lcrss; Var L Swmmng; Var L Trk; Hon Roll; Cpt Swm Tm 86-87; Naval Acad.

BUZZETTA, CATHERINE; Adelphi Acad; Brooklyn, NY; (S); Spanish Clb; Nwsp Stf; Yrbk Stf; High Hon Roll; Engl Cert 84; Spnsh & Engl Awd 85; Psychlgy.

BVINGTON, KRISTEN C; Walton Central Schl; Walton, NY; (Y); 4/111; Sec AFS; Girl Scts; Trs Model UN; Chorus; Color Guard; Nwsp Stf; Var Cheerleading; Var Crs Cntry; Var Trk; NHS; Rgnts Schlrshp 86; Schlstc High Hnr Roll 81-85; Hghst Avg Scl Stds 84; SUNY Geneseo; Speech Pathlgy.

BYERS, TAMMY; Paul V Moore HS; Constantia, NY; (Y); 15/266; Trs Church Yth Grp; VP Drama Clb; School Play; Stage Crew; Nwsp Rptr; Nwsp Stf; JV Bsktbl; Var Crs Cntry; High Hon Roll; Zool.

BYINGTON, KRISTEN; Walton Central HS; Walton, NY; (Y); 4/106; Sec AFS; Girl Scts; Trs Model UN; Color Guard; Nwsp Rptr; JV Var Cheerleading; Var L Crs Cntry; Var L Trk; High Hon Roll; NHS; NY ST Regents Schlrshp 86; Hgst Avg Soc Studies 84; Girl Scout Silver Awd; SUNY; Spch Pathlgy.

BYLANCIK, LAURA; Linton HS; Schenectady, NY; (Y); Orch; Off Frsh Cls; Off Soph Cls; Off Jr Cls; Stu Cncl; Var Tennis; Hon Roll; NE; Erly Chldhd Educ.

BYNUM, CARMENA; Holy Trinity HS; Freeport, NY; (Y); Camera Clb; 4-H; Girl Scts; Ski Clb; Spanish Clb; Variety Show; 4-H Awd; NY Inst Of Tech; Comp Sci.

BYRD, DAVID J; South Park HS; Buffalo, NY; (Y); Church Yth Grp; Cmnty Wkr; Color Guard; Drm Mjr(t); Pres Jr Cls; Stu Cncl; Stat JV Bsktbl; L Var Trk; High Hon Roll; Hon Roll; Stu Contrbtn Awd 85-86; 5th Pl Buffalo Publc Schls Trk Relay 85-86.

BYRNE, CHRISTINA; Cardinal Spellman HS; Bronx, NY; (Y); Church Yth Grp; Dance Clb; French Clb; Intnl Clb; Yrbk Stf; Var L Cheerleading; Var Pom Pon; French Hon Soc; Hon Roll; Pre Dent.

BYRNE, DAWN; Our Lady Of Victory Acad; Yonkers, NY; (S); School Play; Lit Mag; Off Frsh Cls; High Hon Roll; NHS; Spanish NHS; Phy Sci Awd 83-84; Rlgn Awd 84-85.

BYRNE, KIM; Henninger HS; Baldwinsville, NY; (Y); Drama Clb; GAA; Rep Stu Cncl; Swmmng; Trk; Hon Roll.

BYRNE, MEGAN; Fort Plain Central HS; Ft Plain, NY; (Y); Spanish Clb; Varsity Clb; Rep Frsh Cls; Rep Soph Cls; JV Var Cheerleading; Var Score Keeper; SUNY Cobleskill Coll; Bus Adm.

BYRNE, MICHAEL; Arch Bishop Molloy HS; Jackson Hts, NY; (Y); 75/383; Pep Clb; Im Bsbl; Im Bsktbl; Im Ftbl; Im Sftbl; Ntl Merit SF; Pre Law.

BYRNES, KAREN; Keshequa HS; Nunda, NY; (Y); 9/62; Church Yth Grp; Spanish Clb; Band; Chorus; Church Choir; Concert Band; Mrchg Band; Stage Crew; Rep Frsh Cls; Rep Soph Cls; Sci.

BYRNES, PATRICK D; Longwood HS; Shirley, NY; (S); 39/500; Drama Clb; Intnl Clb; Key Clb; Q&S; Speech Tm; SADD; Thesps; Chorus; Church Choir; Madrigals; News Edtr Schl Newspr 85-86; Ed-In-Chf Litry Magz & Q S 85-86; Key Clb Trea 85; Jrnslm.

BYRNES, ROBERT; Herbert N HS; Bronx, NY; (Y); 204/561; Debate Tm; Orch; School Musical; Hon Roll; Crtfct Of Hnr NYS Bar Assoc Mock Trl 86; Brnx Mock Trl Chmps 86; Awd Lgl Studies 86; Fordham U; Bus Adm.

BYRNS, AMY; Gouverneur Central HS; Gouverneur, NY; (Y); Pres Sec 4-H; NFL; Speech Tm; Band; Chorus; Yrbk Stf; Rep Stu Cncl; JV Sftbl; 4-H Awd; Jr NHS; Syracuse U; Mktg.

BYRUM, ERIC; Roosevelt JR/SR HS; Roosevelt, NY; (S); Band; Concert Band; Mrchg Band; Pep Band; Nwsp Stf; French Hon Soc; High Hon Roll; Hon Roll; NY Inst Tech; Arch.

CABALLERO, MICHELE; Bishop Kearney HS; Brooklyn, NY; (Y); 1/336; Math Tm; Spanish Clb; Bausch & Lomb Sci Awd; High Hon Roll; Sec NHS; Prfct Atten Awd; Pres Schlr; Harrison Golden Comptrollers Awd Sci 86; Govrnrns Committee Schlstc Achvt 86; Schl Schlrshp 84-86; Pace U; Comp Sci.

CABALLES, RAQUEL; Clarkstown H S South; W Nyack, NY; (Y); Cmnty Wkr; Drama Clb; Var Trk; High Hon Roll; NHS; Ntl Merit Ltr; Pres Schlr; U Of Sthrn CA; Jrnlsm.

CABALUNA, ELEANOR P; Franklin Acad; Malone, NY; (Y); Church Yth Grp; Spanish Clb; Speech Tm; Band; Swing Chorus; Rep Frsh Cls; Vllybl; Berlee College; Perfmg Voice.

CABARCOS, ORLANDO; Bronx High School Of Science; New York, NY; (Y); Boy Scts; Cmnty Wkr; Exploring; JA; Latin Clb; Natl Hspnc Schlr Awd 86; Spec Natl Mrt Schlrshp 86; NY Rgnts Schlrshp 86; Chem.

CABERTO, JULIET A; The Mary Louis Acad; Jamaica, NY; (Y); 42/276; Hosp Aide; Hon Roll; St Schlr; NEDT Achvt Awd 83; Mth 12 Hnrs 84; NY ST Regents Scholar 86; Hunter Coll; Phys Thrpy.

CABLE, GEOFFREY S; Saratoga Springs SR HS; Saratoga Springs, NY; (Y); 55/498; Boy Scts; Church Yth Grp; Hst DECA; Ski Clb; SADD; Varsity Clb; Band; Orch; Yrbk Stf; Lcrss; Bryant Coll; Fin.

CABRAL, CATHERINE; Cato Meridian HS; Cato, NY; (Y); Drama Clb; French Clb; Chorus; Concert Band; Mrchg Band; Yrbk Stf; Trk; Hon Roll; NHS; CMCS Hghst Achvmnt Instrmntl Music 86.

CABRAL, CHRISTINE; Cato-Meridian HS; Cato, NY; (Y); French Clb; Chorus; Concert Band; Mrchg Band; Yrbk Stf; JV Bsktbl; Var Trk; Hon Roll; Jr NHS; NHS; Archtctr.

CABRERA, CARLOS; Archbishop Molloy HS; Levittown, NY; (Y); 69/383; Cmnty Wkr; Hosp Aide; Teachers Aide; Stage Crew; JV Crs Cntry; Var Socr; JV Im Trk; SUNY Stonybrook; Bus Admn.

CABRERA, MANUEL; Cardinal Hayes HS; New York, NY; (Y); 103/292; Latin Clb; VP Frsh Cls; VP Soph Cls; Socr; Wt Lftg; Prfct Atten Awd; Cvl Engnr.

CABRERA, RUTHY; Fashion Inds; Bronx, NY; (Y); 8/386; Art Clb; English Clb; Band; Chorus; Orch; Lit Mag; High Hon Roll; Hon Roll; Prfct Atten Awd; Psych.

CACACE, MATTHEW; South Shore HS; Brooklyn, NY; (Y); Brooklyn Coll; Bus.

CACCAMISE, DINA; Notre Dame HS; Le Roy, NY; (S); 6/61; Yrbk Bus Mgr; Sec Frsh Cls; Sec Soph Cls; Rep Jr Cls; Rep Sr Cls; Pres Stu Cncl; Var Bsktbl; Var Socr; Var Sftbl; NHS; Wkng To Potential; Kent ST U; Telecmnctns.

CACCAMO, JO ANNE; Acad Of The Holy Names; Delmar, NY; (Y); Church Yth Grp; Spanish Clb; Nwsp Stf; Rep Stu Cncl; Var Cheerleading; Var Vllybl; NHS; Ntl Merit Ltr; Spanish Awd 84; Engrng.

CACCUITTO III, MICHAEL J; Scotia-Glenville SR HS; Scotia, NY; (Y); Boy Scts; Key Clb; Acpl Chr; Concert Band; Jazz Band; Orch; Var Crs Cntry; Var Capt Trk; High Hon Roll; NHS; Earth Sci Awd 84; Engr.

CACI, JENNIFER BETH; Pine Buxh HS; Montgomery, NY; (Y); 5/350; Am Leg Aux Girls St; GAA; Ski Clb; Stage Crew; Yrbk Stf; Fld Hcky; Capt Trk; High Hon Roll; Sec Jr NHS; VP NHS; ST Qlyfr Empr ST Gms Hurdles 85; Stdnt Of Yr 84; Vrsty Trck Mvp 85; Vet Med.

CADET, BELLA; Christ The King HS; Hollis, NY; (Y); #20 In Class; Debate Tm; Chorus; Church Choir; Yrbk Stf; Cheerleading; Hon Roll; NHS; Speech Tm 84; Hunter Coll; Sci.

CADET, REGINE; Adalia E Stevenson HS; Bronx, NY; (Y); Hosp Aide; Nwsp Rptr; Off Frsh Cls; Socr; High Hon Roll; Hon Roll; NHS; Co Chrmn NAACP Entertnmnt Comm 86; Chrmn NAACP Fundraisng Comm 86; Edtr Edtrl & News Sectn 86; Jrnlsm.

CADMUS, JUDY; Moriah Central Schl; Moriah Center, NY; (Y); 10/84; Trs AFS; Aud/Vis; French Clb; Ski Clb; Band; Yrbk Stf; Rep Sr Cls; Rep Stu Cncl; High Hon Roll; Concert Band; Alumni Assn Mary K O Brien Scholar 86-87; SR Cls Mem Scholar 86-87; Moria Cntrl Tchrs Assn Scholar; Cobleskill A&T; Data Proc.

CADWALLADER, KATRINA; Christian Central Acad; Buffalo, NY; (S); Church Yth Grp; Chorus; Orch; School Musical; Nwsp Stf; Yrbk Stf; Pres Jr Cls; Rep Stu Cncl; Var Cheerleading; Hon Roll; Music Perfrmnce.

CAFARO, JACQUELINE; Sewanhaka HS; Elmont, NY; (Y); Thesps; School Musical; School Play; Variety Show; Hon Roll; Mst Imprvd Stdnt Math, Sci, Soc Stds Hnr Soc 85-86.

CAFERRO, CHERYL A; Lackawanna SR HS; Lackawanna, NY; (Y); Camera Clb; GAA; Pep Clb; Ski Clb; Spanish Clb; Powder Puff Ftbl; Sftbl; ST Of Buffalo Coll; Psych.

CAFIELO, MICHAEL; Huntington HS; Huntington, NY; (Y); Key Clb; Ski Clb; Varsity Clb; Stage Crew; Variety Show; Im JV Bsktbl; JV Lcrss; Var Capt Socr; All Leag Soccr 85-86; MVP Soccr Tm 85-86.

CAFIERO, MARIA; Moore Catholic HS; Staten Island, NY; (Y); Stu Cncl; High Hon Roll; Hon Roll; Pace U; Psych.

CAGGIANO, MATTHEW; Beacon HS; Chelsea, NY; (Y); 40/217; VP French Clb; Hon Roll; Prfct Atten Awd.

CAGGIANO, PAMELA; Holy Trinity D/ HS; East Meadow, NY; (S); 24/313; Cmnty Wkr; Math Clb; Math Tm; Band; School Musical; JV Var Gym; Im Socr; High Hon Roll; NHS; NEDT Awd; All Star Awd Soccer 82-83; Most Imprvd Gym 84; Pre-Med.

CAGLE, TRACEY; Bradford Central HS; Savona, NY; (Y); 13/29; Church Yth Grp; FBLA; Girl Scts; Color Guard; School Play; Yrbk Stf; Stu Cncl; Cheerleading; Score Keeper; Hon Roll; Cazenovia; Sch Psych.

CAGLIOSTRO, DINA; School Of The Holy Child; Hartsdale, NY; (Y); Hosp Aide; Key Clb; Varsity Clb; Stage Crew; Yrbk Ed-Chief; Rep Frsh Cls; Fld Hcky; Sftbl; High Hon Roll; Hon Roll; Svc Awd & Excllnc Awd.

CAGNETTO, LISA; Central Islip HS; Central Islip, NY; (Y); Church Yth Grp; Math Clb; Mrchg Band; Stage Crew; Pom Pon; Math Tm; Drill Tm; Stu Cncl; Acctng.

CAGNEY, CHRISTINE E; St Barnabas HS; Yonkers, NY; (S); 5/187; Dance Clb; Debate Tm; Hosp Aide; Yrbk Ed-Chief; Yrbk Stf; Stu Cncl; Cheerleading; Sftbl; NHS; Prfct Atten Awd; 1st Hrns 82-86; Acad Awds 82-86; Math.

CAGNINA, CHRISTINA; Bishop Grimes HS; Kirkville, NY; (Y); 64/146; Exploring; Service Clb; SADD; Band; Concert Band; Mrchg Band; School Play; Variety Show; Yrbk Stf; Utica Coll SU; Crimnl Justc.

CAGUIAT, BENJAMIN; Monsignor Farrell HS; Staten Island, NY; (Y); Aud/Vis; Chess Clb; Computer Clb; French Clb; Yrbk Stf; Im Bowling; High Hon Roll; Hon Roll; Alisi Cncrs Natl 85; Med.

CAGUIAT, JOER; Monsignor Farrell HS; Staten Island, NY; (S); Aud/Vis; Chess Clb; Computer Clb; French Clb; Library Aide; Yrbk Stf; Im Bowling; High Hon Roll; Hon Roll; Alisi Concours Natl 85; Med.

CAHILL, ANTHONY T; Regis HS; New York, NY; (Y); Yrbk Rptr; Lit Mag; JV L Crs Cntry; Var L Trk; Ntl Merit Schol; Gen Excel Awd; Heitefus Almni Awd 86; Yale U.

CAHILL, JENNIFER; Northport HS; E Northport, NY; (Y); Church Yth Grp; Science Clb; Acpl Chr; Chorus; Jazz Band; Orch; School Play; Var Socr; Var Vllybl; Hon Roll; Most Vlbl Plyr Awd 84; Var Ltr Awd 85; Math.

CAHILL, MATTHEW C; Clarkstown South HS; New City, NY; (Y); Church Yth Grp; Cmnty Wkr; Computer Clb; SADD; Nwsp Rptr; Nwsp Sprt Ed; Nwsp Stf; Var Swmmng; Intermural Flr Hcky Lg 85-87; Journalism.

CAHILL, ROBERT; Holy Trinity Diocesan HS; Levittown, NY; (S); JV Var Golf; Var JV Socr; High Hon Roll; Hon Roll; Ntl Merit Ltr; Iona Lang Tsts 85; Law.

CAIN, ANDREA; John Marshall HS; Rochester, NY; (Y); Church Yth Grp; Civic Clb; SADD; Church Choir; Prfct Atten Awd; Aud/Vis; Off Frsh Cls; High Hon Roll; Hon Roll; Early Recgntn Black Schlr Pgm 86; Acctng.

CAIN, DONNA; Riverhead HS; Riverhead, NY; (Y); 33/200; FNA; VICA; Band; Concert Band; Mrchg Band; School Musical; Im Vllybl; Nrsng.

CAIN, LIZABETH; Homer SR HS; Cortland, NY; (Y); 21/225; Thesps; Concert Band; Jazz Band; Stage Crew; NHS; Ntl Merit Ltr; French Clb; SADD; Band; Mrchg Band; Empire ST Schlrshp For Exc 86; Area All ST Orchstra & Bnd Cnty Hnr Bnds 84-86; Vassar Coll; Art Hstry.

CAIRES, MICHAEL J; Sewanhaka HS; Bellerose Village, NY; (Y); 40/342; Computer Clb; Mathletes; Science Clb; Hon Roll; NHS; Soc Stds Hon Soc 85; Engrg.

CAIVANO, NANCY; St Barnabas HS; Bronx, NY; (Y); Church Yth Grp; Drama Clb; French Clb; Hosp Aide; NFL; PAVAS; Thesps; School Musical; School Play; Nwsp Rptr; Svc Awd Hosp Vlntr; Coll St Johns; Jrnlsm.

CAJIGAS, JACQUELYN; St John The Baptist HS; Bayshore, NY; (Y); 23/526; Math Clb; Math Tm; SADD; Band; Concert Band; Mrchg Band; Im Bowling; Stat Lcrss; Im Sftbl; Im Vllybl; Pres Schlrshp For Briarcliffe Schl For Bus 86; ST U Of NY; Accntnt.

CALABRESE, CHRISTINE; Tottenville HS; Staten Island, NY; (Y); 76/871; Chorus; Hon Roll; NHS; Merit Awd, Typng Awd; Pace U; Acctg.

CALABRESE, MARIE ANNE; St Peters Girls HS; Staten Island, NY; (Y); Church Yth Grp; Dance Clb; SADD; Varsity Clb; Yrbk Rptr; Yrbk Stf; Trs Frsh Cls; VP Soph Cls; Stu Cncl; JV Var Cheerleading; Law.

CALABRETTA, CATHERINE; Saint Marys Girls HS; Lk Success, NY; (Y); Cmnty Wkr; Service Clb; Spanish Clb; Chorus; School Musical; Stage Crew; Nwsp Phtg; Nwsp Rptr; Im Tennis; Hon Roll; Cmmnctns.

CALABRIA, CARMINE; Albion HS; Waterport, NY; (S); 23/173; Church Yth Grp; Drama Clb; Latin Clb; Chorus; Color Guard; Lit Mag; VP Stu Cncl; Var Ftbl; Var Wrstlng; Ithaca.

CALABRIA, TROY; La Salle Military Acad HS; Dix Hills, NY; (Y); 32/87; ROTC; Lcrss; Wt Lftg; Hon Roll; Army JROTC Cert Of Achvmnt 84; Army Cert Of Trng 84; St Jhns Bptst De La Salle Awd.

CALABRO, PATRICIA I; Sachem HS North; Holbrook, NY; (Y); 50/1400; Orch; Nwsp Ed-Chief; Sec Sr Cls; NHS; Pres Schlr; Color Guard; Lit Mag; Stu Cncl; High Hon Roll; Pres Acdmc Awd 85-86; All Cnty Music Fstvl 85-86; Stu Ldrshp Smnr 85-86; Hofstra U; Bus.

CALAMAN, KEITH; Oswego HS; Oswego, NY; (Y); VP JA; SADD; Regents Schlrshp Wnnr NY ST 86; Law.

CALAMARI, ROBERT; Fordham Preparatory Schl; Bronx, NY; (Y); Office Aide; Var Bsbl; Im Bsktbl; Hon Roll; Itln Clb 85-86; Gen Excllnc; Fordham U; Cmmnctns.

CALAMIA, CHRISTINA; Copiague SR HS; Amity Harbor, NY; (Y); 9/318; English Clb; FBLA; JA; Math Clb; Sec Spanish Clb; Sec Teachers Aide; High Hon Roll; Jr NHS; Prfct Atten Awd; Spanish NHS; SUNY Binghamton; Bus Adm.

CALAMIA, DONNA; Murry Bergtraum HS; Woodside, NY; (Y); Girl Scts; Band; Color Guard; Variety Show; JV Tennis; Cit Awd; French Hon Soc; Hon Roll; NHS; Prfct Atten Awd; French Awd & Mdl 84; Biology, Acctg, Typng Awd 85; Chem, Intrnshp, 100 Pct Attndnc Awd 86; Bus Lawyer.

CALANO, THERESA; Queensburg HS; Glens Falls, NY; (Y); Church Yth Grp; Exploring; Spanish Clb; Stage Crew; Pres Of Spnsh Club 86-87; SUNY Plattsburg; Mass Media.

CALARCO, TAMMI; Odessa-Montour Central HS; Odessa, NY; (Y); 24/86; Office Aide; Teachers Aide; Chorus; JV Bsktbl; Var Crs Cntry; Var Trk; High Hon Roll; Hon Roll; Mark Twain Schlstc Achvt Awd 86; VOOM 84-86; Southeastern Acad; Travel.

CALAY, SHARANJIT; Sacred Heart Acad; Lido Beach, NY; (Y); Computer Clb; Pres Debate Tm; Intnl Clb; NFL; Pres Speech Tm; Rep Stu Cncl; Hon Roll; NHS; Trphs Frnscs; ST Chmpnshps Frnscs; Ntl Chmpshps Frnscs; Hsty.

CALDAIO, DONNA; Susan E Wagner HS; Staten Island, NY; (Y); 40/396; Office Aide; Teachers Aide; High Hon Roll; Hon Roll; NHS; Coll Fo Staten Island; Comp Sci.

CALDARONE, ANN; Babylon HS; Babylon, NY; (Y); 51/170; Capt Bsktbl; Capt Crs Cntry; Sftbl; Var Trk; High Hon Roll; Hon Roll; NYSAHPERD Awd 86; VA Commonwealth U; Bus Adm.

CALDERARO, JOSEPH; Msgr Mc Clancy Memorial HS; Howard Bch, NY; (Y); Chess Clb; Var Bowling; Im Ftbl; Hon Roll.

CALDERON, AARON; Archbishop Molley HS; Forest Hills, NY; (Y); 20/409; Chess Clb; Red Cross Aide; Crs Cntry; L Trk; High Hon Roll; NHS; Computer Clb; Im Bsbl; Im Bsktbl; Im Ftbl; Schlrshp 4 Yrs 86; Dormitory Schlrshp 86; Regents Schlrshp 86; CUNY Med Schl; Med.

CALDERON, FLORA; Richmond Hills HS; Richmond Hill, NY; (Y); 8/289; Rep Frsh Cls; English Clb; JA; Key Clb; Math Clb; Office Aide; Service Clb; Spanish Clb; SADD; Nwsp Rptr; Am U Frshmn Schlrshp 86; Am U Schlrshp 86; NY U Trste Schlrshp 86; Am U; Intrntnl Rltns.

CALDWELL, ANDREA; Honeoye Falls-Lima Central Schl; Mendon, NY; (S); 17/162; Cmnty Wkr; French Clb; Hosp Aide; Intnl Clb; Service Clb; Pres Y-Teens; Band; Mrchg Band; Orch; School Musical; Nrsng.

CALDWELL, DANIELLE; Eden SR HS; Boston, NY; (Y); Pres AFS; Camera Clb; GAA; Ski Clb; Concert Band; Jazz Band; Mrchg Band; Pep Band; Var Socr; Var Sftbl; Intl Rel.

CALDWELL, RAYMOND F; Pulaski JR SR HS; Pulaski, NY; (S); 7/100; Math Clb; Varsity Clb; Var JV Score Keeper; Trk; Cit Awd; Hon Roll; Snow Enrchmnt Awd 83 & 85; Canton ATC; Crmnl Justice.

CALDWELL, RUBEN L; Bronx High Schl Of Science; New York City, NY; (Y); Chess Clb; Computer Clb; Science Clb; Sci Fiction & Fntsy Clb Vp 84-85 & Pres 85-86; Bio Prep Squad Bronx Sci 83-84; U Of MI; Chem Engr.

CALDWELL, SHANNON; Groton Central Schl; Groton, NY; (Y); Spanish Clb; Chorus; Yrbk Bus Mgr; Yrbk Stf; Rep Stu Cncl; Bausch & Lomb Sci Awd; High Hon Roll; JETS Awd; NHS; Spanish NHS; Syracuse U; Cnsrvtn.

CALHOUN, CHUCK; Greene Central HS; Greene, NY; (Y); FBLA; Mathletes; Math Clb; Math Tm; Science Clb; Ski Clb; Computer Clb; VP Varsity Clb; JV Bsktbl; Var Capt Ftbl; Comp Sci.

CALHOUN, COLLEEN; Hartford Central HS; Hartford, NY; (Y); Art Clb; French Clb; Pep Clb; Ski Clb; Varsity Clb; Band; Chorus; Drm & Bgl; Jazz Band; Mrchg Band; Persdntl Acadmc Ftns Awd 86; Music Awd 86; Hudson Vly CC; Mrktng.

CALI III, JOSEPH L; Sayville HS; Sayville, NY; (Y); 60/350; Church Yth Grp; Key Clb; Political Wkr; Concert Band; Mrchg Band; Var Bowling; Var Socr; High Hon Roll; Hon Roll; 1st Pl Innvtv Archtrl Dsgn 84-85; Rgnts Schlrshp 85-86; SUNY; Engr.

CALIENDO, DIANE; Upper Room Christian HS; W Islip, NY; (S); 4/15; Church Choir; Soc Dstngshd Amer H S Stu 86; Cnslg.

CALIFANO, ANDREA; Port Richmond HS; Staten Isld, NY; (Y); 6/500; Cmnty Wkr; Debate Tm; Math Tm; Nwsp Rptr; Yrbk Stf; Sec Stu Cncl; High Hon Roll; NHS; Pres Schlr; Spanish NHS; NY U; Atty.

CALIFANO, CHRISTIN M; Mont Pleasant HS; Schenectady, NY; (Y); Church Yth Grp; JA; Office Aide; Pep Clb; Ski Clb; Mrchg Band; Nwsp Rptr; Off Sr Cls; Cheerleading; High Hon Roll; Regents Scholar; Miss NYS Amer Coed Photogenic Awd; Syracuse U; Advrtsng.

CALISE, LORI; Tottenville HS; Staten Island, NY; (Y); Church Yth Grp; Band; Yrbk Stf; Cheerleading; Hon Roll; Advrtsng.

CALKINS, ANNA; G Ray Bodley HS; Fulton, NY; (Y); 1/260; Sec Church Yth Grp; Latin Clb; Science Clb; Ski Clb; Band; Chorus; Concert Band; Mrchg Band; Orch; School Musical; 4 Yr AFROTC Schlrshp 86; Prm Queen 85; Hmcmng Queen 85; U Of MI; Arspc Engrng.

CALKINS, NANCY; Cato-Meridian Central Schl; Memphis, NY; (Y); 32/72; Cmnty Wkr; Im Badmtn; Im Vllybl; 4-H Awd; Hon Roll; Prfct Atten Awd; 4-H; Jr NHS; Robt & Clara Hrdy Schlrshp 86; Mst Imprvd In Bus Ed 85; Cntrl City Bus Inst; Exec Secy.

CALL, ANDREW; Carmel HS; Carmel, NY; (Y); 4/401; Y-Teens; Nwsp Phtg; Nwsp Rptr; Nwsp Stf; Yrbk Phtg; JV Socr; High Hon Roll; NHS; Pres Schlr; Voice Dem Awd; Alfred U Pres Schlrshp 86-87; Alfred U; Frnsc Med.

CALL, MELISSA; Liverpool HS; Liverpool, NY; (Y); Church Yth Grp; Cmnty Wkr; DECA; Ski Clb; Rep Frsh Cls; Rep Soph Cls; Rep Stu Cncl; JV Powder Puff Ftbl; Bus.

CALL, PAMELA; Indian River Central HS; Evans Mills, NY; (Y); Temple Yth Grp; Band; Drm Mjr(t); Mrchg Band; Stage Crew; Ed Yrbk Stf; Sec Jr Cls; Sec Sr Cls; Hon Roll; NHS; Bus.

CALL, ROBERT; Leroy HS; Stafford, NY; (Y); Am Leg Boys St; Camera Clb; Computer Clb; French Clb; Math Tm; Office Aide; Ski Clb; Socr; High Hon Roll; NHS.

CALL, STACY R; West Hampton Beach HS; East Moriches, NY; (Y); 55/209; French Clb; GAA; Speech Tm; Nwsp Rptr; Yrbk Stf; VP Stu Cncl; Coach Actv; Var Fld Hcky; Capt Var Sftbl; Art Clb; Fld Hockey Rookie Of The Yr 82; Schlrshp To Presdntl Classroom 86; Artist Of The Month 83; Long Island U; Public Rltns.

CALLA, TOM; Mepham HS; N Bellmore, NY; (Y); Bsbl; Ftbl; Hon Roll; Archt.

CALLAGHAN, EDWARD; St Dominic HS; Oyster Bay, NY; (S); 6/118; Quiz Bowl; Im Bsktbl; Var Ftbl; High Hon Roll; NHS; Ntl Merit Ltr; NEDT Awd; Im Vllybl; Im Wt Lftg; Soc Studs & Frnch Awds; Hnrbl Ment Physcs Awd; Engrng.

CALLAGHAN, EILEEN; Sacred Heart Acad; Valley Stream, NY; (S); 2/189; Computer Clb; Intnl Clb; Math Tm; Office Aide; SADD; Band; Trk; High Hon Roll; NHS; Ntl 1st Pl Wnnr AOH Essy Cntst 85; Sci.

CALLAGHAN, KEVIN; Huntington HS; Huntington, NY; (Y); Church Yth Grp; Im Bsktbl; Hon Roll.

CALLAGHAN, SUSAN; Saratoga Central Catholic HS; Saratoga Springs, NY; (S); 8/35; Varsity Clb; Stage Crew; Yrbk Stf; VP Jr Cls; Var Capt Cheerleading; Tennis; Vllybl; High Hon Roll; Hon Roll; NHS; SUNY Buffalo; Mrktng.

CALLAHAN, DAWN; Ichabad Crane Central Sch; Kinderhook, NY; (Y); 40/200; German Clb; GAA; Hosp Aide; Ski Clb; SADD; Teachers Aide; Boy Scts; Color Guard; Concert Band; Mrchg Band; Natl Ldrshp & Svc Awd 85; Phys Ther.

CALLAHAN, ERIN; Franklin Acad; Malone, NY; (Y); Sec AFS; Trs Church Yth Grp; Drama Clb; French Clb; VP Intnl Clb; Model UN; Spanish Clb; School Play; Stage Crew; Sec Stu Cncl; Frnch Awd-100 Avg Frnch I 86; Spnsh Awd-100 Avg Spnsh IV 86; Coll Of St Rose; Spnsh Tchr.

CALLAHAN, GREG H; Corning PP E HS; Beaver Dams, NY; (Y); 39/213; 4-H; Letterman Clb; Ski Clb; Yrbk Stf; Rep Soph Cls; Rep Jr Cls; JV Bsktbl; JV Ftbl; Var L Lcrss; Im Wt Lftg; Regents Schlrshp 86; Alfred U; Ceramic Engrng.

CALLAHAN, JAMES J; W C Mepham HS; N Bellmore, NY; (Y); 50/360; Cmnty Wkr; French Clb; Capt Band; Jazz Band; Mrchg Band; Var Crs Cntry; Var Capt Socr; Var Capt Trk; Im Vllybl; Hon Roll; Rutley Mem Schlrshp 86; All-Div Cross Cntry 84-85; MVP Track & Soccer 83; SUNY At Albany; Bus Mgt.

CALLAHAN, MARK; Dover JR SR HS; Dover Plains, NY; (Y); 2/110; Am Leg Boys St; Math Clb; Math Tm; Varsity Clb; Pres Soph Cls; Bsbl; Bsktbl; Ftbl; High Hon Roll; Pres NHS; All Sectn Awd Bsbl & Bsktbl 86; Hudson Vlys Empire ST Bsktbl Tm 85-86; Math.

CALLAHAN, SEAN; Rocky Point JR SR HS; Rocky Point, NY; (S); 14/175; Church Yth Grp; French Clb; Mathletes; Varsity Clb; Rep Soph Cls; Rep Jr Cls; Var Bsbl; Var Golf; Socr; Hon Roll; Won Math Test; Bus Adm.

CALLAHAN, TODD E; St Athonys HS; Ft Salonga, NY; (Y); 19/240; Chorus; Church Choir; Jazz Band; Stage Crew; Lit Mag; Stu Cncl; High Hon Roll; Hon Roll; NHS; Art Clb; Pres PR; Regnts Schlrshp; Quaker ST Schlrshp; Rensselaer Polytech Inst; El En.

CALLAHAN, TRACEY; St Peters H S For Girls; Staten Island, NY; (Y); Church Yth Grp; Cmnty Wkr; Hon Roll; NHS; Grace Inst; Bus.

CALLAN, DENISE; Pine Bush HS; Pine Bush, NY; (Y); 29/290; Pres 4-H; Ski Clb; Chorus; Drill Tm; School Play; Yrbk Stf; Hon Roll; Jr NHS; NHS; Prfct Atten Awd; Cmmctns.

CALLARI, MARTHA E; Performing Arts HS; Brooklyn, NY; (Y); 48/121; Girl Scts; JA; Teachers Aide; School Play; Hnrbl Mntn-Arts Recog & Tlnt Rsch 85-86; Awds Frm NY Soc Of Deaf For Cmpltn Of Clsses 1-3-Sgn Lang; Actrss.

CALLEN, KEITH; Fredonia HS; Fredonia, NY; (Y); Art Clb; Spanish Clb; Hon Roll; Asst Fund 86; SUNY At Fredonia; Engl.

CALLENDER, NATALIE; Dover JR SR HS; Wingdale, NY; (Y); 7/103; Pres Church Yth Grp; Drama Clb; SADD; Church Choir; VP Stu Cncl; Fld Hcky; Hon Roll; Girl Scts; Spanish Clb; NLSA 85-86; Acadamic All-Am 85; Vassar; Law.

CALLENDER, VERONICA; Port Chester SR HS; Port Chester, NY; (Y); Church Yth Grp; Church Choir; Yrbk Stf; Lit Mag; High Hon Roll; Hon Roll; Jr NHS; NHS; Library Aide; Capt Bsktbl; Exc Math 86; Comp Sci.

CALLENS, DANIEL PRINCE; Ramstein HS; Apo New York, NY; (Y); Church Yth Grp; Letterman Clb; SADD; Varsity Clb; Church Choir; Rep Stu Cncl; Var Bsbl; JV Var Ftbl; Hon Roll; Jr NHS; Stu Of Mnth Spn, Auto Mech 83-84; Stu Of Mnth Engl, Wrld Hstry 84-85; UT Martin; Law Enfrcmnt.

CALLERY JR, PATRICK; Bishop Kearney HS; Rochester, NY; (Y); 17/141; Exploring; Var Lcrss; Im Sftbl; High Hon Roll; Hon Roll; NHS; Prsdntl Acadmc Fitns Awrd 86; Rochester Inst Tech; Elec Engrg.

CALLESTO, REBECCA; Attica Central HS; Attica, NY; (S); 5/150; AFS; Church Yth Grp; Band; Jazz Band; Nwsp Rptr; Jr NHS; Trs NHS; Ntl Merit Ltr; Acad All Amer 85; Intl Frgn Lang Awd 85; Canisius Coll.

CALLIS, SHELLIE; Springfield Gardens HS; Jamaica, NY; (Y); Dance Clb; Drama Clb; FBLA; SADD; Church Choir; School Play; Yrbk Phtg; Off Sr Cls; Vllybl; High Hon Roll; Acctg.

CALMES, AMY; Attica HS; Varysburg, NY; (Y); 36/175; AFS; Ski Clb; Var JV Cheerleading; JV Socr; Syracuse; Cmmnctns.

CALRK, RICK; Alexander Central HS; E Bethany, NY; (Y); Var Wrstlng; Elec Engrng.

CALTABIANO, JAMES P; G Ray Bodley HS; Fulton, NY; (Y); Science Clb; Variety Show; Im Bsbl; Im Bsktbl; Im Score Keeper; Im Sftbl; High Hon Roll; Hon Roll; NHS; Prfct Atten Awd; A P Amer Hstry Awd 85; Math Awd 85; Phy Ed Awd 85; Syracuse U; Fin.

CALVANEZI, GINA; Sacred Heart HS; New York, NY; (Y); School Play; Var JV Cheerleading; Athltc Achvt Awd 86; Trvl.

CALVERT, CAROLYN; Hicksville SR HS; Hicksville, NY; (Y); Camera Clb; Library Aide; Chorus; Crs Cntry; Gym; Comp Prgrmg.

CAMA, EDWARD; John H Glenn HS; E Northport, NY; (Y); Aud/Vis; Boy Scts; Camera Clb; Dance Clb; Ski Clb; Varsity Clb; Stage Crew; Variety Show; Golf; Gym; Schl Emblm In Gymnstcs 84; Cinema.

CAMACHO, EDWIN; De Witt Clinton HS; Bronx, NY; (Y); ROTC; Color Guard; Ntl JR Hnr Soc 83; JR HS Prncpls Awd Merit & Ldrshp 83; Air Force Acad; Aerntcl Engr.

CAMACHO, EMELINA; St Johns Prep; Woodside, NY; (Y); 3/485; Dance Clb; Drama Clb; Chorus; Yrbk Stf; Rep Frsh Cls; Pres Soph Cls; Pres Jr Cls; Pres Stu Cncl; NHS; Sal; Congrssnl Recog Awd 86; Govs Comm On Schlstc Achvt 86; Span Awd 86; Hunter Coll; Psychol.

CAMACHO, GERALYN A; Academy Of St Joseph HS; Melville, NY; (Y); 2/127; Art Clb; Hosp Aide; Science Clb; VP Soph Cls; Trs Stu Cncl; Var Badmtn; Vllybl; High Hon Roll; NHS; NY ST Rgnts Schlrshp 86; Ntl Art Hnr Soc 85-86; Cert Hnr Ntl Frnch Cntst 85; WA U; Pre Med.

CAMACHO, HELAN; Nazareth Acad; Rochester, NY; (Y); Office Aide; Hon Roll; Distngshd Achvt Europen Cltrs Stds 84; Francie Nelan Awd 84; Acadmc Achvt Awd Span85-86.

CAMACHO, NOEL; Cardinal Hayes HS; Bronx, NY; (Y); 4/244; Debate Tm; Library Aide; Service Clb; Nwsp Ed-Chief; Nwsp Phtg; Yrbk Phtg; Hon Roll; NHS; Prfct Atten Awd; Voice Dem Awd; Hofstra U.

CAMACHO, PETER; Riverdale Country Schl; New York, NY; (Y); Capt Chess Clb; Spanish Clb; Chorus; School Musical; Var Capt Crs Cntry; Var Capt Trk; Ntl Merit Ltr; Ntl Hispnc Schlr Awd Prog Semi Fnlst 85-86; Founders Schlrshp 85-86; Economics.

CAMACHO, STEVEN; Fox Lane HS; Mt Kisco, NY; (Y); 70/280; Boys Clb Am; Nwsp Stf; Bsbl; Ftbl; Wt Lftg; Hon Roll; Bus.

CAMAJ, ROSIE; Cathedral HS; New York, NY; (Y); 45/273; Dance Clb; Intnl Clb; Office Aide; Variety Show; Jr Cls; Gym; Socr; Swmmng; Vllybl; Hon Roll; Law.

CAMANN, ELLIE; Hilton Central HS; Hilton, NY; (Y); 1/329; Math Clb; Concert Band; Yrbk Phtg; Rep Soph Cls; Var JV Swmmng; High Hon Roll; NHS; Ntl Merit Ltr; French Clb; Monroe Cnty Tech Ed Assoc Outstndng Photogrphr Awd 85-86; Most Dedictd Swmmr Awd 84-85.

CAMARADA, LISA; Valley Stream North HS; Malverne, NY; (Y); Pres Jr Cls; Pres Sr Cls; Stu Peer Org Cert Recgntn 85-86.

CAMARDELLA, MICHELE L; Harrison HS; Harrison, NY; (Y); 13/211; Band; Chorus; Nwsp Ed-Chief; Yrbk Ed-Chief; Lit Mag; Trs Sr Cls; Rep Stu Cncl; NHS; Ntl Merit Ltr; Spanish NHS; Rtry Stu Of Mnth 85; Cmnctns.

CAMBIO, ELENA M; Notre Dame HS; Elmira, NY; (Y); 11/88; French Clb; Church Choir; Orch; School Musical; Nwsp Ed-Chief; Nwsp Rptr; Lit Mag; High Hon Roll; NHS; Ntl Merit Ltr; Bus & Profssnl Womens Clb Awd 86; Frnch Awd 86; Admssions Schlrshp St John Fisher 86; St John Fisher Coll; Cmmnctns.

CAMBITSIS, JOHN; All Hallows HS; New York, NY; (S); 2/130; Church Yth Grp; Dance Clb; Speech Tm; School Play; Yrbk Stf; Ice Hcky; Var Socr; High Hon Roll; Jr NHS; NHS; 1st Hnr Awds 84-86; Doc.

CAMBRIA, JANE MARIE; St Catharine Acad; Bronx, NY; (Y); 61/185; NHS; Awds Engl & Rlgn 85.

CAMELIO, CARMEN J; Irondequait HS; Rochester, NY; (Y); Var Tennis; Hon Roll; Prfct Atten Awd; Exploring; Science Clb; JV Crs Cntry; Im Vllybl; Bio Achvt Awd 83-84; Physics Final Awd 85-86; Elec Engr.

CAMERON, GREGORY; Queensbury HS; Glens Falls, NY; (Y); 198/240; JV Bsbl; Bsktbl; JV Crs Cntry; Var Capt Ftbl; JV Wrstlng; Hon Roll; St Lawrence U; Ecnmcs.

CAMERON, HEATHER; Auburn HS; Auburn, NY; (Y); Intnl Clb; SADD; Band; Jazz Band; Mrchg Band; Orch; JV Bsktbl; Hon Roll; Concert Band; Achvt Awd Keybrdg Personal Use 86; 1st Tenor All Star Bnd; Music Ed.

CAMERON, JENNIFER; Cairo-Durham Central Schl; Leeds, NY; (Y); 3/86; Cmnty Wkr; Band; Concert Band; High Hon Roll; Jr NHS; NHS; Pres Schlr.

CAMERON, PATTI; William Floyd HS; Mastic Beach, NY; (S); 121/456; Art Clb; Var Capt Cheerleading; Hon Roll; Columbus Coll Art & Design; Art.

CAMEROTA, JOHN M; Stillwater Central HS; Stillwater, NY; (Y); Am Leg Boys St; Camera Clb; French Clb; Key Clb; SADD; School Play; Yrbk Phtg; Socr; Wt Lftg; Hon Roll; Engnrng.

CAMILLE, MAE; Albertus Magnus HS; Nyack, NY; (Y); Second Hnrs 83-86; Fine Art.

CAMILLONE, MICHAEL V; Eastchester HS; Scarsdale, NY; (Y); 3/145; Hst Church Yth Grp; Spanish Clb; Ed Lit Mag; High Hon Roll; Jr NHS; Pres NHS; Prfct Atten Awd; Spanish NHS; St Schlr; Wheaton Coll Pres Schlrshp 86; Wheaton Coll; Comp Math.

CAMINITI, KRISTEN; Union Endicott HS; Endwell, NY; (Y); 107/430; Pres SADD; Trk; Hon Roll; Italian Clb Awd $100 86; Jennie F Snapp Schlrshp $200 86; Rochester Inst Of Tech; Photo.

CAMINITO, LAURA; Academy Of Mt St Ursula; Bronx, NY; (Y); Science Clb; Hon Roll; Acctg.

CAMMARANO, RICHARD; North Babylon SR HS; N Babylon, NY; (Y); Aud/Vis; Computer Clb; Intnl Clb; Band; Concert Band; Jazz Band; Mrchg Band; Orch; School Musical; Jazz Band; Lge Champ-Tnns 86; Engrng.

CAMMARERI, MARIEANN; Our Lady Of Perpetual Help HS; Brooklyn, NY; (Y); Hon Roll; Pace U.

CAMMILLERI, DEBBIE; Roosevelt HS; Yonkers, NY; (Y); Church Yth Grp; Hosp Aide; Band; Drm Mjr(t); Variety Show; Nwsp Stf; Yrbk Ed-Chief; Lit Mag; Stu Cncl; Swmmng; Drtmth Awd 86; Amer Mscl Fndtn Bnd Hnrs 86.

CAMMILLIER, JAMES; Northstar Christian Acad; Brockport, NY; (S); Drama Clb; Rep Frsh Cls; VP Soph Cls; VP Jr Cls; VP Sr Cls; Rep Stu Cncl; Socr; Var Capt Wrstlng; High Hon Roll; Hon Roll; Outstndng Wrstlr 85; Stdnt Amb 86; Rochester Inst Tech; Engrng.

CAMP, ELIZABETH; North Rose-Wolcott HS; Wolcott, NY; (Y); Church Yth Grp; Cmnty Wkr; Ski Clb; Varsity Clb; Chorus; School Play; Variety Show; Yrbk Bus Mgr; Yrbk Stf; Stu Cncl; ST John Fshr; Educ.

CAMPAGIORNI, ANTHONY S; Highland HS; Highland, NY; (Y); Am Leg Boys St; VP Varsity Clb; Yrbk Stf; VP Frsh Cls; VP Soph Cls; VP Jr Cls; Rep Stu Cncl; Var L Ftbl; JV Bsktbl; Spanish NHS.

CAMPAGNINO, ROBERT; La Salle Military Acad; W Hempstead, NY; (S); 1/89; Quiz Bowl; ROTC; Nwsp Rptr; Yrbk Rptr; Pres Frsh Cls; Pres Soph Cls; Pres Jr Cls; Pres Stu Cncl; Var Capt Bsbl; High Hon Roll; Supr Cadt Awd; Assctn U S Army Awd; Amer Legn Mltry Awd.

CAMPANELLA, CHERYL; Mount Marry Acad; Derby, NY; (Y); VP Church Yth Grp; JA; Ski Clb; Spanish Clb; Nwsp Phtg; JV Var Vllybl; Le Moyne Coll; Bus.

CAMPANIE, E JOHN; Vernon Verona Sherill Cntrl HS; Verona, NY; (Y); Computer Clb; JV Bsbl; Im Vllybl; High Hon Roll; Hon Roll; Marine Bio.

CAMPANILE, GUY; Iona Preparatory Schl; Crestwood, NY; (Y); 72/230; Letterman Clb; Nwsp Ed-Chief; Nwsp Rptr; Nwsp Stf; Ed Lit Mag; Im Bowling; Var Crs Cntry; JV Socr; Capt Trk; Hon Roll; All Cnty Rnnr In 3200 Mtr Rly Wstchstr Cnty 86; Crdnl Splmn Yth Awd 86; Cch Of Yr Awd 86; Brdcst Jrnlsm.

CAMPBELL, ANISSA; Central Islip SR HS; Central Islip, NY; (Y); 14/373; Art Clb; Aud/Vis; Camera Clb; School Play; Variety Show; Nwsp Stf; Yrbk Phtg; Gym; Drama Clb; Church Yth Grp; Tech Comp Achvt Awd 85; 3rd Pl Blck Hstry Essay Comp 86; Contstnt Miss Teen Pagnt 86; FIT Manhattan; Advrtsng.

CAMPBELL, BRYAN; St Marys Boys; Floral Pk, NY; (Y); Church Yth Grp; Cmnty Wkr; Exploring; Im Bsktbl; Im Powder Puff Ftbl; St Johns U; Business Admin.

CAMPBELL, CARA E; Shenendehowa HS; Ballston Lake, NY; (Y); 45/675; Intnl Clb; Ski Clb; Varsity Clb; Concert Band; Orch; Yrbk Phtg; JV Powder Puff Ftbl; Socr; Sftbl; JV Trk; Regnts Schlrshp 86; Geneseo; Bio.

CAMPBELL, DAVID; Lake George HS; Lake George, NY; (Y); 7/85; Math Clb; SADD; Yrbk Ed-Chief; Im Bowling; High Hon Roll; Hon Roll; Jr NHS; NHS; Amer HS Math Exam 86; Lndscape Arch.

CAMPBELL, DAWN; Dominican Commercial HS; S Ozone Park, NY; (Y); Rep Church Yth Grp; Cmnty Wkr; Hosp Aide; Intnl Clb; Spanish Clb; Church Choir; Yrbk Stf; Im Swmmng; Im Wt Lftg; Hon Roll; Siena Clb; St Johns U; Comp Sci.

CAMPBELL, ISAAC R; Midwood High Schl At Brooklyn College; Brooklyn, NY; (Y); Drama Clb; OEA; Chorus; Church Choir; School Musical; School Play; Variety Show; Lit Mag; Stu Cncl; Cheerleading; NY ST Rgnts Schlrshp 85; Borough Pres Gldn Rcrd Achvt Awd 83; ST U Of NY-STNYBRK; Corp Lwyr.

CAMPBELL, JOHN; Franklin Central Schl; Franklin, NY; (Y); Boy Scts; Church Yth Grp; 4-H; Ski Clb; VP SADD; Varsity Clb; Rep Stu Cncl; Var Bsbl; Var Bsktbl; Socr.

CAMPBELL, KAREN; Chenango Valley HS; Binghamton, NY; (Y); Drama Clb; French Clb; Sec SADD; Varsity Clb; Church Choir; School Musical; Yrbk Phtg; Yrbk Sprt Ed; Rep Frsh Cls; Rep Soph Cls; Section Iv STAC All Star Swimming 84-85; Hotel Mgnt.

CAMPBELL, KATHLEEN; Acad Of Mt St Ursula; Bronx, NY; (Y); Church Yth Grp; Cmnty Wkr; Sftbl; Mt St Vincent; Nrsng.

CAMPBELL, KAY; Cuba Central Schl; Friendship, NY; (Y); 4/52; Spanish Clb; Varsity Clb; Yrbk Stf; Trs Soph Cls; VP Sr Cls; Var Tennis; JV Vllybl; High Hon Roll; NHS; Rotary Awd; Allegany Cnty Tchrs Assn Schlrshp 86; Trstees Hnr Schlrshp Baldwin Wallace Coll 86; Baldwin-Wallace Coll; Acctg.

CAMPBELL, KICHA; Midwood HS; Bro Klyn, NY; (Y); Hosp Aide; Church Choir; Rep Frsh Cls; Stu Cncl; Hon Roll; Prfct Atten Awd; Val; Howard Golden Awd 84; Bus Admin.

CAMPBELL, LORRAINE; Sanford H Calhoun HS; Merrick, NY; (Y); 36/313; Church Yth Grp; DECA; Chorus; Nwsp Rptr; Nwsp Stf; Rep Soph Cls; Rep Jr Cls; Rep Sr Cls; Var L Socr; Hon Roll; 1st Pl DECA Elmntns Cnty Lvl 85-86; $500 Schlrshp Bellmore Merrick Schlrshp Fund 86; Hofstra U; Mrktng.

CAMPBELL, MARK; Honeoye Central Schl; Holcomb, NY; (S); Yrbk Stf; High Hon Roll; Prfct Atten Awd; Trm Papr Awd 84-85; 1st Pl Fngr Lks Area Typwrtng Cntst 85; Bus.

CAMPBELL, MARTY; Chatham Central HS; Chatham, NY; (Y); 10/150; Pres Ski Clb; JV Var Ftbl; Var Tennis; High Hon Roll; Hon Roll; NHS; Prfct Atten Awd; Trvl Agnt.

CAMPBELL, MARY; Harborfields HS; Greenlawn, NY; (Y); Church Yth Grp; Q&S; Yrbk Stf; Ed Lit Mag; Rep Frsh Cls; Rep Stu Cncl; Outstndng Achvt Art Awd 85-86; Al-ST Exhbtn Albany NY-ART Dsplyd 86; Fine Art.

CAMPBELL, MARY; Trott Vocational HS; Niagara Falls, NY; (Y); Aud/Vis; Church Yth Grp; Hosp Aide; Mrchg Band; Cert Excllnc 84; 2nd Pl Gvrnrs Trphy Rsrch Cntst 84; Nrsng.

CAMPBELL, MELISSA; Madrid Waddington Central HS; Waddington, NY; (Y); Drama Clb; GAA; Spanish Clb; School Play; Sec Jr Cls; JV Var Bsktbl; JV Var Socr; Var Trk; JV Var Vllybl; Hon Roll; Acad Hnr 85-86; Acctng.

CAMPBELL, MIKE; Greece Olympia HS; Rochester, NY; (Y); Ski Clb; Varsity Clb; JV Bsbl; Im Bsktbl; Var Golf; Im Vllybl; Hon Roll; Archtct.

CAMPBELL, RHODA; Dewitt Clinton HS; Bronx, NY; (Y); Church Yth Grp; Chorus; Church Choir; Sci Awd 85; Pedtrcn.

CAMPBELL, SCOTT; Lansingburgh HS; Troy, NY; (Y); Boy Scts; VP Frsh Cls; Trs Soph Cls; Off Jr Cls; Off Sr Cls; Cit Awd; High Hon Roll; NHS; Hghst Earth Sci Avg 84; Eagle Scout 85; Siena; Bus Adm.

CAMPBELL, SEAN; West Hempstead HS; West Hempstead, NY; (Y); Drama Clb; Key Clb; Pres Chorus; Mrchg Band; School Musical; Nwsp Stf; Arts.

CAMPBELL, SHARON; Cardinal Spellman HS; Bronx, NY; (Y); Camera Clb; Chorus; French Hon Soc; High Hon Roll; Pre-Med.

CAMPBELL, SHAUN; Wellsville HS; Garland, TX; (Y); 25/121; Debate Tm; Intnl Clb; Key Clb; Office Aide; Ski Clb; School Play; Stage Crew; Nwsp Bus Mgr; Soph Cls; TX A&M; Aerosp.

CAMPBELL, SHERYL; Norwood-Norfolk Central HS; Raymondville, NY; (Y); 14/130; French Clb; VP Girl Scts; School Play; Nwsp Stf; Yrbk Phtg; Var Capt Trk; High Hon Roll; Drama Clb; Speech Tm; Wm C Cooper Mem Schlrshp 86-87; Hnbl Mntn Wrld Poetry, Golden Poets Awd 86; Canton ATC; Bus Admin.

CAMPBELL, SUSAN J; Walter Panas HS; Peekskill, NY; (Y); 10/240; Rptr FBLA; Ski Clb; SADD; Nwsp Ed-Chief; Sec Frsh Cls; Rep Soph Cls; Rep Jr Cls; Rep Sr Cls; Trk; NHS; 3rd Pl-NYS Ms Fture Bus Ldr 86; Rgnts Schlrshp 85-86; 1st Pl-Schl Poetry Comptn 86; Suny-Binghamton; Engl.

CAMPBELL, TAMMIE M; Franklin Acad; Malone, NY; (Y); 50/265; Art Clb; FBLA; Hosp Aide; Epsilon Hnr Scty 84-85 & 85-86; Cazenovia Coll; Intr Dsgn.

CAMPETELLA, JOHN J; Msgr Farrell HS; Staten Island, NY; (S); Socr; Capt Swmmng; Wrstlng; High Hon Roll; NHS; Regents Schlrshp SAT 86; NY U; Bio.

CAMPION, DAVID; Xavier HS; New York, NY; (Y); 14/231; Church Yth Grp; Math Clb; Science Clb; Spanish Clb; Concert Band; Stage Crew; Hon Roll; NEDT Awd; Hstry.

CAMPISE, KAREN; Kings Park HS; Kings Pk, NY; (Y); 12/382; Hosp Aide; Spanish Clb; SADD; Teachers Aide; Band; Chorus; Color Guard; Concert Band; Mrchg Band; School Musical; NY ST Rgnts Schlrshp 86-90; Vivn P Schmdt Mem Schlrshp 86; Sflk Co Music Educ Assn 1st Chr 84; SUNY Binghamton.

CAMPO, MICHELLE L; Ilion SR HS; Ilion, NY; (Y); 3/148; Trs SADD; Concert Band; Jazz Band; Mrchg Band; Orch; Yrbk Stf; Var Capt Fld Hcky; High Hon Roll; Pres Sec Jr NHS; NHS; NY ST Regents Schlrshp 86; Ctznshp Awd Band Orch 82-85; Mc Donalds All Star Band 85; Cornell U; Ststcs.

CAMPOLI, JAMES; Valley Central HS; Montgomery, NY; (Y); 6/277; Yrbk Sprt Ed; Lit Mag; Capt Crs Cntry; Trk; Hon Roll; NHS; Ntl Merit Schol; Spanish NHS; St Schlr; Union Coll; Comp Sci.

CAMPOLO, PHIL; Bishop Grimes HS; E Syracuse, NY; (S); 11/146; FBLA; SADD; Nwsp Stf; VP Stu Cncl; Var Capt Church Yth Grp; Var Capt Golf; High Hon Roll; Pres NHS; Ntl Merit Ltr; Regents Schlrshp Wnnr 86; Natl Eng Merit Awd Wnnr 85; Acadmc All Amer 85; Boston Coll; Acct.

CAMPS, ANN; Canisteo Central HS; Canisteo, NY; (Y); FBLA; Office Aide; Ski Clb; Color Guard; JV Cheerleading; JV Socr; JV Sftbl; Hon Roll; Typng & Shrthnd Skls Awd Corning CC; BUS.

CAMPS, ELIZABETH; St Vincent Ferrer HS; Woodside, NY; (Y); 4/110; Math Tm; Drm & Bgl; Mrchg Band; High Hon Roll; Hon Roll; Ntl Merit Schol; NEDT Awd; NY Trustees Schrlshp 86; Empire ST Schlrshp Exc 86; Medals Exc Math,Sci 86; NY U; Astrophysics.

CANAGUIER, MICHELE; Sauquoit Valley Central HS; Clayville, NY; (Y); 12/98; Chorus; Nwsp Rptr; Yrbk Stf; Rep Sr Cls; Var L Fld Hcky; L Mgr(s); NHS; NEDT Awd; Prfct Atten Awd; Rotary Awd; Marion R Rosendale Memrl Awd 86; Mohawk Vly CC; Acctnt.

CANALES A, HAYDEE E; St Pius V HS; Bronx, NY; (Y); Chess Clb; Church Yth Grp; French Clb; Intnl Clb; Service Clb; Spanish Clb; Nwsp Sf; Yrbk Stf; High Hon Roll; NHS; Natl Hon Soc Cert 85-86; Yrbk Staff Achvt Awd 85-86; Specl Effort Awd 85-86; Miami Dade CC; Psychology.

CANAVAN, DEIDRE A; St Marys Girls HS; Baldwin, NY; (Y); Church Yth Grp; Drama Clb; Chorus; Church Choir; School Musical; Nwsp Rptr; Nwsp Stf; Hon Roll; NHS; Regents Schlrshp NYS 86-90; Lemoyne Coll; Econ.

CANCEL, MELISSA G; St Johns Prep; Long Island, NY; (Y); 100/459; Church Yth Grp; Dance Clb; Am Leg Boys St; Office Aide; Chorus; Church Choir; Swing Chorus; Variety Show; Yrbk Stf; Stu Cncl; Rgnts Schlrshp 86; Hunter Coll; Educ.

CANCELLARE, MARIE; Wellington C Mepham HS; Bellmore, NY; (Y); Band; Concert Band; Mrchg Band; Symp Band; Yrbk Stf; Hon Roll; NHS; Chem, Bio Olympd Tp 10 Scorer 86; Biochem.

CANDELLA, STEPHENIE; Sacred Heart Acad; Cedarhurst, NY; (Y); FTA; Service Clb; Drm & Bgl; School Play; Yrbk Bus Mgr; Yrbk Phtg; Hon Roll; NHS; Bus.

CANDEROZZI, DENISE; Flora Park Memorial HS; Bellerose Village, NY; (Y); 8/150; Spanish Clb; High Hon Roll; Hon Roll; NHS; Trustee Schlrshp Adelphi U 86; Regents Schlrshp 86; Adelphi U; Certfd Pblc Accntnt.

CANE, TRACY; Saranac Central Schl; Dannemora, NY; (S); 1/102; Trs Church Yth Grp; Sec 4-H; Sec French Clb; Concert Band; School Musical; Yrbk Rptr; Stat Socr; High Hon Roll; Sec NHS; Sec Drama Clb; St Lawrence U; Bio.

CANELL, MELISSA; Ballston Spa SR HS; Ballston Spa, NY; (Y); 99/250; Church Yth Grp; SADD; Yrbk Stf; Twrlr; High Hon Roll; Hon Roll; SUNY Cobleskill; Lib Arts.

CANELL, TAMMY; Thousand Islands HS; Clayton, NY; (Y); 4/80; Varsity Clb; Variety Show; Capt Cheerleading; High Hon Roll; Hon Roll; Jr NHS; Lion Awd; NHS; NEDT Awd.

CANFIELD, JILL M; Lake Shore SR HS; Derby, NY; (Y); 32/284; Church Yth Grp; Chorus; Stage Crew; High Hon Roll; Hon Roll; Jr NHS; Regents Schlrshp 86; Syracuse U; Social Wrk.

CANFIELD, JOHN; G Ray Bodley HS; Fulton, NY; (Y); Art Clb; French Clb; Science Clb; Ski Clb; Chorus; School Play; Bsbl; Ftbl; Wt Lftg; Hon Roll; Fed Bureau.

CANFORA, JOHN L; John H Glenn HS; E Northport, NY; (Y); Drama Clb; Q&S; Chorus; School Musical; School Play; Swing Chorus; Nwsp Ed-Chief; Nwsp Rptr; Nwsp Sprt Ed; Yrbk Rptr; Cmnctns.

CANGIANO, JOSEPH; Valley Stream North HS; Malverne, NY; (Y); Arch.

CANINO, STEVEN; Mc Kee Technical HS; Staten Island, NY; (Y); 3/306; Drama Clb; School Musical; School Play; Stage Crew; Rep Frsh Cls; Rep Soph Cls; Stu Cncl; High Hon Roll; Hon Roll; JETS Awd; Brnz Mdl Rssn Lng Cmptn 86.

CANLAS, JEREMIAS D; St Francis Prep; Queens Village, NY; (S); Im Sftbl; Im Vllybl; Optimate Soc 84-85; Judo 85; Engrng.

CANNATA, FLORENCE JOY; Blind Brook HS; Rye Brook, NY; (Y); Church Yth Grp; French Clb; SADD; Chorus; School Musical; Rep Cheerleading; Tennis; Mathletes; Red Cross Aide; Athlt Achvt Awd Chchs Awd Tnns 84; Westchester Cnty Chrldng Schlrshp 85; Cert Merit Cnty Exec 86; Suny Albany; Bio.

CANNAVO, JACQUELINE; St John Villa Acad; Staten Island, NY; (Y); 30/133; Girl Scts; Hosp Aide; Intnl Clb; Political Wkr; SADD; Stage Crew; Yrbk Phtg; VP Frsh Cls; VP Soph Cls; Pres Stu Cncl; Order Sons Italy Am Merit Awd 84; Am Leg Schl Awd 83; St John U; Bus.

CANNAVO, TAMMI; Buffalo Academy Of The Sacred Heart; Buffalo, NY; (Y); 28/142; Church Yth Grp; Cmnty Wkr; Hosp Aide; JA; Red Cross Aide; Service Clb; Hon Roll; Prfct Atten Awd; Prsh Cncl; :Scl Srvs.

CANNELL, HEATHER L; Guilderland Central HS; Atltamont, NY; (Y); Qlfd AHSA Natl Medal Fnnlst 85 & 86; Qlfd USET Natl Finals 86; Qldf Aaspca Natl Maclay Fnls 86; Horsemanship.

CANNER, PATTI; Oneonta HS; Oneonta, NY; (Y); 26/174; Key Clb; Trs Ski Clb; Trs Varsity Clb; Capt Bsktbl; Var L Socr; Capt Sftbl; Hon Roll; VP NHS; PBA Schlrshp 86; Otsego Co Deputy Sher Schlrshp 86; Stonehill Coll; Crmnl Just.

CANNESTRA, NATALIE; Moore Catholic HS; Staten Island, NY; (Y); Church Yth Grp; Cmnty Wkr; Hosp Aide; School Musical; Nwsp Stf; Yrbk Stf; Bowling; NHS.

CANNIZZARO, CHRISTINA; Bethpage HS; Plainview, NY; (Y); 152/306; Art Clb; Yrbk Ed-Chief; Yrbk Sprt Ed; Yrbk Stf; Rep Jr Cls; Hon Roll; Awd Edtr Yrbk 87; NY Inst Of Tech; Comp Grphcs.

CANNIZZARO, JENNIFER; Christ The King HS; Ozone Park, NY; (Y); 102/451; GAA; Bsktbl.

CANNIZZARO, MARIA; Sacred Heart Acad; S Hempstead, NY; (Y); FHA; Spanish Clb; Lit Mag; Im Tennis; High Hon Roll; NHS; 1st Hnrs In Spnsh II & III 85 & 86; Mrktng.

CANNIZZARO, SCOTT; Niskayuna HS; Scotia, NY; (Y); Cmnty Wkr; JV Bsbl; JV Bsktbl; Var L Ftbl; Im Wt Lftg; Siena Grant 86; Siena Coll; Chem.

CANNON, ANDREW; Curtis HS; Staten Island, NY; (Y); Church Yth Grp; Office Aide; Rep VP Sr Cls; JV Bsktbl; Var Bowling; Pre-Law.

CANNON, JOAN-MARIE; Fontbonne Hall Acad; Brooklyn, NY; (Y); 20/130; Church Yth Grp; Drama Clb; Teachers Aide; Hon Roll; NHS; NEDT Awd; Am Clscl Lg, Natl Jr Clscl Lg 85; Magna Cum Laude-Natl Latin Exam; Peer Grp Ldr 85-86; SUNY Binghamton; Prof Wrtng.

CANNON-UNIONE, JENNIFER; HS For The Humaniti; New York, NY; (Y); Civic Clb; Drama Clb; Office Aide; School Musical; Variety Show; NHS; Hstry.

CANNUSCIO, MICHAEL; Hampton Bays HS; Hampton Bays, NY; (Y); Cmnty Wkr; Letterman Clb; Science Clb; Service Clb; SADD; Varsity Clb; Rep Frsh Cls; Rep Soph Cls; Trs Jr Cls; Pres Trs Stu Cncl; All League Crss Cntry 84-86; All League Trck 86; Htl Mgmt.

CANON, LISA; Middletown HS; Middletown, NY; (Y); School Musical; Symp Band; Var Tennis; Hon Roll; NHS; NY Cnfrnce All-St Band 85.

CANTE, RICHARD C; Wellington C Mepham HS; Merrick, NY; (Y); 26/360; Cmnty Wkr; Exploring; French Clb; Science Clb; Nwsp Stf; Lit Mag; French Hon Soc; High Hon Roll; NCTE Awd; NHS; NY ST Regents Schlrshp 86; Top 10 Of Mepham-Natl Sci Olympiad 85-86; Distngshd Natl Frnch/Itln Cntst; Northwestern U; Pre-Med.

CANTEEN, CHANTAY; Gorton HS; Yonkers, NY; (Y); Church Yth Grp; Cmnty Wkr; Intnl Clb; Lit Mag; Rep Frsh Cls; VP Soph Cls; Rep Jr Cls; CC Awd; Hon Roll.

CANTON, DEMETRIOUS; St John The Baptist HS; Holbrook, NY; (S); 12/550; JV Wrstlng; Hon Roll; Math Hnr Awd-Geom 84-85; Sci Hnr Awd-Bio 84-85; Socl Stud Hnr Awd-Eurpn 84-85.

CANTY, KEVIN; Nottingham HS; Syracuse, NY; (Y); Boys Clb Am; Church Yth Grp; Exploring; Var L Bsktbl; JV Ftbl; VP Trk; Hon Roll; Outstndng Stu Awd Comp Sci 84-85; Hlth Awd 86; Rensselaer Poly Inst; Comp Eng.

CANTY, TRECIA M; St Francis Prep; Jamaica, NY; (S); 202/744; Hosp Aide; Library Aide; Speech Tm; SADD; NHS; Telluride Scholar 85-86; Lwyr.

CAO, HUYEN DIEM; Cicero North Syracuse HS; North Syracuse, NY; (Y); 48/668; Math Clb; Math Tm; NHS; Ntl Merit Ltr; Ntl Hnr Soc 86; Hnr Roll Merit Roll Awd 84-86; Mth Lg Awd 85-86; Chem Rgnts Awd 86; Syracuse U; Chem.

CAPARIS, LAURIE; Pelham Memorial HS; Pelham, NY; (Y); AFS; JA; Ski Clb; Drm Mjr(t); JV Var Diving; Swmmng; Tennis; Twrlr; High Hon Roll; NHS; JR Achvt Awd 86; Divg 80-86; Swmg 82-86; Pre-Law.

CAPASSO, JAMES; Fordham Prepartory Schl; Scarsdale, NY; (Y); Boy Scts; Camera Clb; Computer Clb; Hosp Aide; Latin Clb; Pep Clb; Spanish Clb; SADD; Varsity Clb; Band; Med.

CAPASSO, NETTIE; Roy C Ketcham HS; Wappingers Fls, NY; (Y); School Play; Nwsp Stf; High Hon Roll; Hon Roll; Dncd-NY Cty Bllt Smmrs Of 83 & 84; Schlrshp-Crft Of Chrogrphy 83; NYS Smmr Schl Of The Arts 84-86; Bus.

CAPELLI, PETER; Grand Island SR HS; Grand Island, NY; (Y); Boy Scts; Band; Concert Band; Jazz Band; Mrchg Band; Symp Band; Ice Hcky; Ntl Merit SF; Fndn For Intnl Coopo Forgn Exchng Studnt To Peru 85; Reed Coll; Genetics.

CAPELLUPO, ANTHONY J; Mount St Michael Acad; Bronx, NY; (Y); 3/297; Church Yth Grp; Stu Cncl; Var Capt Bsbl; Im Bsktbl; Im Ftbl; Im Sftbl; Hon Roll; NHS; Spanish NHS; G Pope Meml Schlrshp 86; Villanova U.

CAPELLUPO, LISA ANNE; Fairport HS; Fairport, NY; (Y); Sec JA; SADD; Nwsp Ed-Chief; Nwsp Rptr; Nwsp Stf; Sec Soph Cls; Sec Sr Cls; Rep Stu Cncl; Hon Roll; Spanish NHS; St Bonaventure Friars Scholar 86; St Bonaventure; Mass Cmmnctns.

CAPERS, MICHAEL; Evander Childs HS; Bronx, NY; (Y); Nwsp Rptr; Nwsp Sprt Ed; VP Bsbl; JV Crs Cntry; Im Ftbl; Mgr(s); Score Keeper; Howard U; Comptr Sci.

CAPEZZA, SALVATORE; St John The Baptist HS; Babylon, NY; (S); 10/600; Science Clb; JV Ice Hcky; JV Wrstlng; Hon Roll; Latin Hnrs Awd 85; Social Studies Hnr Awd 85.

CAPITAINE, MIRALINE; Far Rockaway HS; Far Rockaway, NY; (Y); 60/335; Church Yth Grp; Hosp Aide; Office Aide; Teachers Aide; Oneonta; Nrsng.

CAPODANNO, NICOLE; Tottenville HS; Staten Island, NY; (Y); Teachers Aide; Variety Show; Tobe Coburn; Fash Buyr.

CAPOLINO, REMO; Roy C Ketcham HS; Poughkeepsie, NY; (Y); AFS; Ski Clb; Band; Concert Band; Jazz Band; JV Socr; Var Tennis; Im Wt Lftg; High Hon Roll; Hon Roll.

CAPONE, HARRY; Faith Heritaghe HS; Canastota, NY; (Y); Boy Scts; Church Yth Grp; School Play; Nwsp Rptr; Pres Stu Cncl; Var Trk; Trk; Hon Roll; VP NHS; Jr NHS; Dstngshd Chrstn HS Stu 85-86; Schl Vce Ensmbl 86-87; Hdmstrs Lst 85-86; Houghton Coll; Pre Med.

CAPONE, JOHN J; Hampton Bays HS; Hampton Bays, NY; (Y); 2/90; Mathletes; Chorus; Hon Roll; Jr NHS; Ntl Merit SF; NY ST Regnts Schlrshp 86; Boston U; Aerosp Engrng.

CAPONE, RANDY; Lafayette HS; Lafayette, NY; (S); 3/96; Ski Clb; VP Soph Cls; L Capt Ftbl; Var L Ftbl; Cit Awd; High Hon Roll; NHS; Model UN; Band; Concert Band; NYSSMA All ST 84-86; Hghst Avg Band 85; U Rochester; Sci.

CAPONETTO, MARGARET M; The Ursuline Schl; Bronxville, NY; (Y); Chorus; School Musical; Variety Show; Pres Soph Cls; Hon Roll; Jr NHS; Vocl Perf.

CAPORALE, CHRISTOPHER; Saugerties HS; Saugerties, NY; (Y); Am Leg Boys St; Math Tm; VP Soph Cls; Pres Jr Cls; Var Ftbl; High Hon Roll; NHS; Accnting.

CAPORUSCIO, ANDREA; Anthony A Henninger HS; Syracuse, NY; (Y); 22/400; GAA; SADD; Rep Sr Cls; Var Sftbl; Var Capt Swmmng; Var Trk; Var Co-Capt Vllybl; Hon Roll; Exploring; Rep Frsh Cls; Outstndng Jr Female Stu Athlete Awd 84-85; Outstndng Femal Stu Athlete 3 Yrs 85-86; ST U Of New York; Poltcl Sci.

CAPORUSSO, JOSEPH; Monsignor Farrell HS; Staten Island, NY; (Y); Coach Actv; Ftbl; Mgr(s); Wt Lftg; Hon Roll; Karate 84-85; Usher Soc 85-86; NY ST; Pre-Med.

CAPOZZI, CARMELINA; St Barnabas HS; Bronx, NY; (S); 8/188; Office Aide; Teachers Aide; Yrbk Phtg; VP Soph Cls; High Hon Roll; NHS; Itln Hnr Soc.

CAPOZZOLI, ROSE; Sachem HS; Lake Ronkonkoma, NY; (Y); Girl Scts; JA; Stage Crew; Vet Assist.

CAPPA, ROSARIA; Westlake HS; Pleasantville, NY; (Y); Hosp Aide; Chrmn SADD; Thesps; Chorus; School Musical; School Play; Nwsp Rptr; Rep Stu Cncl; High Hon Roll; NHS.

CAPPARELLI, HELENE M; Clarkstown South HS; Spring Valley, NY; (Y); Drama Clb; SADD; School Play; Stage Crew; Yrbk Stf; Stu Cncl; Cheerleading; Lcrss; Intrct Clb Cmnty Svc; St Johns U Cmptv Schlrshp; Peom Pblshd Young Authors Mag 85; St Johns U Jamaica; English.

CAPPELLETTI, MARGARET; Jamesville-De Witt HS; Dewitt, NY; (Y); Church Yth Grp; French Clb; Hosp Aide; Key Clb; SADD; Off Frsh Cls; Off Soph Cls; Socr; Sftbl; Hon Roll; Cmmnctns.

CAPPELLINI, GREG; Hauppauge HS; Hauppauge, NY; (Y); 70/500; DECA; FBLA; Ski Clb; SADD; Bsktbl; Capt Var Socr; High Hon Roll; Hon Roll; NHS; Engrng.

CAPPELLINI, ROBERT; F D Roosevelt HS; Hyde Park, NY; (Y); 50/380; Drama Clb; Ski Clb; Band; Chorus; Concert Band; Drill Tm; Jazz Band; Mrchg Band; School Musical; Stage Crew; Regents Schlrshp 86; U Of Buffalo; Math.

CAPPELLINO, MICHELLE; Pioneer Central HS; Arcade, NY; (Y); 5/258; 4-H; Latin Clb; Band; Orch; Symp Band; Lit Mag; High Hon Roll; High Hon Roll; Jr NHS; Musicn Wk 84; Adv Plcmnt Engl Trsr 85; Chrch Lctr 84; Med.

CAPPELLO, DEBBIE; Solvay HS; Syracuse, NY; (Y); 6/171; VP JA; Sec VICA; Mrchg Band; Ed Yrbk Stf; Sftbl; High Hon Roll; NHS; Pres Schlr; Natl Merit Ltr 84; Exectv Yr Awd JR Achvt 84; Merit Ltr Amercn Study AP 86; William Smith Coll; Poli Sci.

CAPPIELLO, MARY ANN; Pleasantville HS; Pleasantville, NY; (Y); 23/106; Church Yth Grp; Drm Mjr(t); School Musical; Nwsp Ed-Chief; Yrbk Stf; Pres Frsh Cls; Pres Soph Cls; Pres Jr Cls; Pres Sr Cls; Fld Hcky; Rgnts Schlrshp NYS 85-86; Haverford Coll; Jrnlsm.

CAPPIELLO, STEPHANIE; Bay Shore HS; Bay Shore, NY; (Y); 8/406; Church Yth Grp; Math Clb; Chorus; Yrbk Rptr; Lit Mag; Rep Stu Cncl; JV Var Cheerleading; JV Sftbl; High Hon Roll; NHS; Mth, Scl Stds, Eng & Spnsh 83-86.

CAPPUCCI, ROBERT; Scarsdale HS; Bronxville, NY; (Y); FBLA; JV Crs Cntry; JV Trk; Hon Roll; Frdhm U Dns Schlrshp 86; NY ST Rgnts Schlrshp 85; Fordham Coll; Englsh.

CAPRIO, DARLENE E; St Francis Prep; Jamaica, NY; (S); 42/693; Math Clb; Office Aide; Science Clb; Color Guard; Nwsp Rptr; Im Sftbl; Im Vllybl; Hon Roll; NHS; Stu Actvty Awd 85; Biomed Engrng.

CAPRIOLI, MARY; Arlington HS; La Grangeville, NY; (Y); 24/570; French Clb; Varsity Clb; Band; Symp Band; Trk; High Hon Roll; Rgnts Schlrshp 86; Vassar Coll; Mdrn Lang.

CAPRON, MARK; Broadalbin Central Schl; Broadalbin, NY; (Y); 2/80; Am Leg Boys St; French Clb; Yrbk Phtg; Yrbk Stf; Trs Soph Cls; Trs Jr Cls; High Hon Roll; Hon Roll; NHS; Prfct Atten Awd; Tri Vly Math Cntst 85; Awd Exc Photo Mag 85; Rensselaer Ploy Inst; Aerosp En.

CAPUANO, JEFFREY; Mechanicville HS; Mechanicville, NY; (S); 16/105; Church Yth Grp; Spanish Clb; Band; Concert Band; Pep Band; Symp Band; Var Tennis; Hon Roll; NHS; Empire St Yth Orchestra 84-86; Mc Donalds All Amer Marching Band 85-86; LYSSMA Area All St 82-86; Kings Coll; Pre Med.

CAPUANO, LOUIS; Archbishop Molloy HS; Woodhaven, NY; (Y); Im Ftbl; Im Lcrss; Im Sftbl; Iona Coll; Pre-Law.

CAPUTO, ELEONORA; High School For The Hmnties; New York, NY; (Y); 10/150; Chorus; School Play; Stage Crew; Variety Show; Yrbk Ed-Chief; Yrbk Stf; Rep Sr Cls; Rep Stu Cncl; Swmmng; Cit Awd; Gnroso Pope Acadmc Achvt Awd Schlrshp 86; SUNY Binghamton; Biochem.

CAPUTO, GERALDINE; John Adams HS; Howard Bch, NY; (Y); Dance Clb; Office Aide; Service Clb; Teachers Aide; Hon Roll; NHS; Cert 2nd Hnrs 84 & 85; Kings; Bus.

CAPUTO, JANINE; West Babylon HS; Babylon, NY; (Y); SADD; Stu Cncl; JV Var Cheerleading; Stat Lcrss; High Hon Roll; Hon Roll; Jr NHS; Fshn.

CAPUTO, JOHANNA; W Seneca E SR HS; West Seneca, NY; (S); 89/375; DECA; Drama Clb; School Play; Rep Frsh Cls; Stu Cncl; JC Awd; Jr NHS; Lion Awd; Yuth Crt, Bur 84-85; Outstndng Yuth Comm Awd 85; Canisius; Law.

CAPUTO, KAREN; South Shore HS; Brooklyn, NY; (Y); Dance Clb; School Play; Lit Mag; Var Cheerleading; Var Trk; Hunter Coll; Phys Ther.

CAPUTO, STEVEN; Mahopac HS; Putnam Valley, NY; (Y); 120/409; Boy Scts; Ski Clb; Spanish Clb; Var JV Ftbl; Var JV Lcrss; Im Wrstlng; High Hon Roll; Hon Roll.

CAPWELL, AMY; Newark SR HS; Newark, NY; (Y); 30/181; French Clb; SADD; Band; Concert Band; Jazz Band; Mrchg Band; Yrbk Ed-Chief; Ed Yrbk Stf; Tennis; French Hon Soc; NYS Schl Msc Awd; Ltr & Slvr Bar Bnd.

CAPWELL, TODD; Le Roy HS; Leroy, NY; (Y); Church Yth Grp; French Clb; Ski Clb; Golf; L Capt Wrstlng; High Hon Roll; Jr NHS.

CARABALLO, MILLICENT; St Pius V HS; Bronx, NY; (Y); Debate Tm; SADD; VP Frsh Cls; Sec Soph Cls; Stu Cncl; Bsktbl; Sftbl; Hon Roll; Jr NHS; NHS; NY U; Sclgy.

CARACCI, CORINNA; James Madison HS; Brooklyn, NY; (Y); Dance Clb; JA; School Play; Nwsp Stf; Gym; Var Capt Sftbl; Var Capt Vllybl; Hon Roll; Phy Fit Awd 86; MVP Grls Bst Athl 85; Law.

CARACCILO, CHRISTOPHER; Mynderse Acad; Seneca Falls, NY; (Y); 11/140; Am Leg Boys St; Boy Scts; Science Clb; Chorus; Jazz Band; Mrchg Band; Rep Stu Cncl; Trk; Pres NHS; Rotary Awd; Eagle Scout 82; Cornell U; Landscape Arch.

CARACCIOLA, JENNIFER; Dominican Coimmercial HS; Stroudsberg, PA; (Y); Church Yth Grp; Political Wkr; SADD; Chorus; Frsh Cls; Soph Cls; Stu Cncl; Cheerleading; Coach Actv; Swmmng; Pres Awd Gym 85; PA ST; Lawyer.

CARACH, DAVID; Scotia-Glennville HS; Scotia, NY; (Y); Varsity Clb; Frsh Cls; Soph Cls; JV Bsbl; JV Var Bsktbl; Hon Roll; Stu Cncl 83-85; Siena; Accntnt.

CARAMANZANA, JACQUELINE; St Francis Prep; Middle Village, NY; (Y); Computer Clb; Church Choir; Trk; Hon Roll; St Francis Prep Stu Activity Awd Folk Grp 86; Filipino Clb; Retreat Ldrs Clb; Shotokan Martial Arts Ins.

CARANGELO, JOEL; Gloversville HS; Gloversville, NY; (Y); Ski Clb; Spanish Clb; Band; Symp Band; Yrbk Phtg; Yrbk Stf; Rep Soph Cls; Rep Jr Cls; Rep Sr Cls; VP Var Crs Cntry; Cvl Engrng.

CARARA, MATTHEW; Monsignor Farrell HS; Staten Island, NY; (Y); Stage Crew; Im Ftbl; High Hon Roll; Hon Roll; Bus.

CARATSOLE, KATHY; Queensbury HS; Glens Falls, NY; (Y); Spanish Clb; Chorus; Lit Mag; JV Bsktbl; JV Sftbl; JV Vllybl; Hon Roll; Bus.

CARAVELLO, DAWN; Centereach HS; Centereach, NY; (Y); Dance Clb; Hosp Aide; Sec Service Clb; SADD; Rep Soph Cls; Bsktbl; Hon Roll; Hnr Awd Indtl Arts Stu Of Yr 83-84; Resrvd Champ Equestrn Shw 84; Cert Of Awd 85; Geneseo; Elem Ed.

CARBERRY, LISA; Dryden Central HS; Etna, NY; (Y); 95/142; Chorus; Mgr Wrstlng; Tmpkn/Crtlnd CC; Wrd Prcsng.

CARBINO, TERESA; Longwood HS; North Shirley, NY; (Y); Art Clb; PAVAS; Chorus; Ice Hcky; Art 86-87; Intr Dsgnr.

CARBOINE, KAREN; Commack HS South; Commack, NY; (Y); GAA; Office Aide; SADD; Varsity Clb; Var Capt Bsktbl; Var Socr; Var Capt Trk; High Hon Roll; Hon Roll; MVP Awd Vrsty Trk 86; Syracuse U; Ed.

CARBONARO, ANGELA; Half Hollow Hills High S East; Deer Park, NY; (Y); Soph Cls; Sec Jr Cls; Sec Sr Cls; Var Capt Cheerleading; 1st Rnnr Up Hmcmg Qn 85; Nassau CC; Bus Adm.

CARBONARO, STEPHANIE; New Utrecht HS; Brooklyn, NY; (Y); Computer Clb; Dance Clb; Drama Clb; PAVAS; Chorus; School Musical; School Play; Rep Soph Cls; Rep Jr Cls; JV Var Cheerleading; Chrldng Awd 86; Fshn Merch.

CARBONE, LISA; Kings Park HS; Kings Park, NY; (Y); Art Clb; Church Yth Grp; Pep Clb; Radio Clb; Science Clb; Chorus; Crs Cntry; Trk; High Hon Roll; NHS; Psychology.

CARBONE, NINA; Mt Vernon HS; Mount Vernon, NY; (Y); 3/550; Capt Debate Tm; Rep Keywanettes; Math Tm; Sec Science Clb; School Musical; Nwsp Ed-Chief; Ed Lit Mag; L Gym; High Hon Roll; VP NHS; Italian Cvc Assn Awd; Stu ST Senate; Rgnl Chmpn Tm-Mock Trial-Capt; Princeton U; Pre-Law.

CARBONI, LISA; Williamsville South HS; Williamsville, NY; (Y); French Clb; Pep Clb; Sec Chorus; High Hon Roll; NHS.

CARDAMONE, BETH; Eden SR HS; Eden, NY; (Y); GAA; SADD; Varsity Clb; Band; Symp Band; Trs Jr Cls; Stu Cncl; Stat Bsbl; JV Var Cheerleading; NHS.

CARDILLO, MARISA ANN; T R Proctor HS; Utica, NY; (Y); 75/201; Pep Clb; Yrbk Stf; Rep Stu Cncl; Ftbl; Hon Roll; Jr NHS; High Hon Itln Awd 83-84; Herkimer County CC; OT Asst.

CARDINAL, JODY L; Huntington HS; Huntington, NY; (Y); 4/383; Girl Scts; Hosp Aide; Band; School Musical; Camp Fr Inc; NHS; Ntl Merit Ltr; Voice Dem Awd; Drama Clb; Lit Mag; NY ST Regents Coll Scholar 86; 1st Pl Rotary Awd Schl Lit Mag 86; Colgate U; Engl.

CARDINALE, FELICIA; Kenmore East HS; Tonawanda, NY; (Y); Spanish Clb; U Of Buffalo; Bus.

CARDINALE, MARK; Jamestown HS; Jamestown, NY; (Y); Ski Clb; Spanish Clb; Var L Ftbl; Im Golf; Bio Camp Awd 85; Med.

CARDINALE, MATTHEW; Coxsackie-Athes HS; Athens, NY; (Y); 6/135; German Clb; Sec Frsh Cls; Rep Soph Cls; Rep Jr Cls; Rep Stu Cncl; Im Bowling; JV Var Ftbl; High Hon Roll; NHS; Chorus; C-A Tchrs Assc Fighest NY ST Rgnts Exam Bio & Geo 86; Poli Sci.

CARDINO, VALERIE; Commack HS South; Commack, NY; (Y); Mathletes; Math Tm; Teachers Aide; Var Badmtn; Var JV Tennis; High Hon Roll; NHS; JV Tennis Most Valuable Player 84.

CARDON, PAUL; Gowanda Central HS; Perrysburg, NY; (Y); 1/135; Am Leg Boys St; French Clb; Ski Clb; Wrstlng; Bausch & Lomb Sci Awd; NHS; Val; Church Yth Grp; Computer Clb; Gftd Math Prog U Of Buffalo 83-87; Cngrssnl Yth Schlr 86; RPI Math & Sci Awd 86; Elec Engrng.

CARDONE, JENNIFER A; Centereach HS; Centereach, NY; (Y); 10/429; Band; Var Capt Crs Cntry; Trk; NHS; Moreau Schlsrhp-Kings Coll 86; Regents Schlrshp 86; Mst Imprvd Crss Cntry 83; Kings Coll; Bio.

CARELLI, ROXANNE; Berlin Central HS; Berlin, NY; (Y); Am Leg Aux Girls St; Chorus; School Musical; Yrbk Stf; VP Jr Cls; Bsktbl; Score Keeper; Socr; Sftbl; Prfct Atten Awd; Cert Achvt Vlntr Srvc Cmmnty; Prncs Of 86 JR-SR Prm; Bus.

CAREN, CHELSY; Geneseo Central Schl; Geneseo, NY; (Y); Trs Frsh Cls; Trs Soph Cls; Trs Jr Cls; Trs Sr Cls; Var Capt Cheerleading; Var Capt Trk; Var Capt Vllybl; French Hon Soc; High Hon Roll; Jr NHS; Mdcl.

CARETTA, ALAN; Bishop Kearney HS; Rochester, NY; (Y); 19/144; Boy Scts; Rep Frsh Cls; JV Var Ftbl; JV Wrstlng; High Hon Roll; HS Admission Schlrshp 82; Admission Schlrshp St John Fisher Coll 86; St John Fisher Coll; Pre-Law.

CAREY, BRENDAN; Oakfield-Alabama HS; Basom, NY; (Y); Church Yth Grp; Band; Mrchg Band; JV Var Bsbl; JV Var Bsktbl.

CAREY, ELIZABETH; Mt Mercy Acad; Buffalo, NY; (Y); Church Yth Grp; JCL; Latin Clb; Ski Clb; Chorus; Rep Stu Cncl; Im Bowling; Crs Cntry; Tennis; High Hon Roll; 2nd Plc Wstrn NY Frgn Lang Fr 86; Englsh.

CAREY, MELISSA A; Williamsville North HS; E Amherst, NY; (Y); 41/301; Church Yth Grp; Cmnty Wkr; Nwsp Stf; Yrbk Ed-Chief; Sec Soph Cls; Stu Cncl; Cheerleading; Socr; Hon Roll; NHS; U Of MI Ann Arbor; Librl Arts.

CAREY, PATRICIA K; Seton Catholic Central HS; Endwell, NY; (Y); 26/163; Sec French Clb; Key Clb; Ski Clb; Trs Stu Cncl; JV Var Cheerleading; NHS; Seton Schlr Awd 85; PA ST U; Intl Bus.

CAREY, RICHARD; Minisink Valley HS; Port Jervis, NY; (Y); JV Var Ftbl; Var Trk; Eng Lit.

CAREY, VINCENT; H Frank Carey HS; Franklin Square, NY; (Y); JV Ftbl; Var Socr; JV Trk; Vrsty Lttr Sccr; Trck Lttr; Adelphi & Farimsole; Bus.

CARFAGNA, CHRIS; St Marys HS; East Aurora, NY; (S); 11/182; Boy Scts; Hon Roll; Achvt Awds Soc Stud 84-85; Achvt Awds Lat 84; Consrvatn.

CARFORA, DAVID; Mynderre Acad; Seneca Falls, NY; (Y); JV Ftbl; JV Var Ice Hcky; High Hon Roll; Hon Roll; Regents Schlrshp 86; Audio Engnrng.

CARGIN, DALE G; Whitney Point Central HS; Whitney Pt, NY; (Y); 10/128; Am Leg Boys St; Church Yth Grp; Science Clb; Band; Chorus; Concert Band; Jazz Band; Mrchg Band; School Musical; Variety Show; Ntl Army Rsrve Schlr Athltc Awd 86; Wilkes Coll; Tele Cmnctns.

CARGNONI, JIM; Victor Central Schl; Shortsville, NY; (Y); 46/280; Church Yth Grp; JV Ski Clb; Varsity Clb; Stu Cncl; Var JV Bsktbl; JV Var Ftbl; Var Golf; Wt Lftg; High Hon Roll; Hon Roll; Med.

CARGUELLO, TERRENCE; Gates Chili SR HS; Rochester, NY; (S); 21/446; Boy Scts; German Clb; Ski Clb; Band; Jazz Band; School Musical; Socr; Swmmng; Tennis; High Hon Roll; JR Of Yr 85; Soc Stds Awd 84; Syracuse U; Engrng.

CARINGI, TERI; Parishville Hopkinton C S HS; Parishville, NY; (Y); Band; Chorus; Color Guard; School Musical; Yrbk Stf; Socr; Prfct Atten Awd; Tammy Jo Adams Awd; Prfct Attndnce BOCES; Cazenovia Coll; Intr Dsgn.

CARL, ELIZABETH; St Catharine Acad; Bronx, NY; (S); 3/203; GAA; Teachers Aide; Nwsp Rptr; Nwsp Sprt Ed; Var Co-Capt Cheerleading; NHS; Math II Excllnc Awd 85; First Hnrs 82-86; Hstry Clb 85-86; Manhattan Coll; Math Eductn.

CARL, RALPH; Arlington HS; La Grangeville, NY; (Y); Trs Spanish Clb; Mrchg Band; Symp Band; JV Trk; JETS Awd; Jr NHS; Ntl Merit Ltr; Spanish NHS; Spnsh Heritage Homestay Pgm Schlrshp 86; Appt To Rotary Ldrshp Conf 85; Aeronautical Engrng.

CARL, WALTER D; Clarence Central HS; Williamsville, NY; (Y); 1/268; Church Yth Grp; Cmnty Wkr; JCL; Scholastic Bowl; SADD; Rep Sr Cls; Vllybl; High Hon Roll; NHS; Val; RPI Math & Sci Awd; U Of Buffalo; Elec Engr.

CARLBERG, REID; Fairport HS; Fairport, NY; (Y); Sec Boy Scts; Chess Clb; Debate Tm; German Clb; JA; Math Clb; Model UN; NFL; Speech Tm; Nwsp Ed-Chief; Eng.

CARLE, SANDRA; Geneva HS; Geneva, NY; (S); 18/173; Pres Church Yth Grp; Cmnty Wkr; 4-H; Hosp Aide; Ski Clb; Varsity Clb; Band; Concert Band; School Musical; Swmmng; Sci.

CARLEY, CHRISTINE; Vernon Verona Sherrill Central HS; Verona, NY; (Y); 47/200; GAA; Ski Clb; Concert Band; Frsh Cls; Soph Cls; Jr Cls; Stu Cncl; Fld Hcky; Trk; Hon Roll; All Star Field Hocky Tm 85; Dollars Chlrs Schrlshp 86; Athlete Awd Hockey 85; Hartwick Coll; Intl Bus.

CARLIN, BECKY; Union-Endicott HS; Endicott, NY; (Y); French Clb; Pres Key Clb; Mathletes; Ski Clb; Rep Stu Cncl; Var JV Cheerleading; High Hon Roll; Hon Roll; NHS; Biomed.

CARLINEO, DANIEL S; Union Endicott HS; Endicott, NY; (Y); 9/430; Chess Clb; Key Clb; Varsity Clb; Var Lcrss; Var Capt Socr; High Hon Roll; Coach Yth Sccr Tm 86; Westpoint; Nuc Engrg.

CARLINO, CRAIG; Fairport HS; Fairport, NY; (Y); Ski Clb; Im Wt Lftg.

CARLISLE, LORETHA; Maria Regina HS; Mt Vernon, NY; (Y); 12/166; NFL; High Hon Roll; Hon Roll; NHS; Prfct Atten Awd; Gnrl Excel 83; Math Awd 80; US Mltry Acad; Bio.

CARLOCK, DANIELLE; Hicksville HS; Hicksville, NY; (Y); Cmnty Wkr; Lit Mag; JV Var Bsktbl; Hon Roll; NHS; Soc Stds Achvt Awd Advncd Plcemnt Hstry 85-86.

CARLOS, PAUL; Saint Francis Prep HS; Elmhurst, NY; (Y); 350/750; Art Clb; Im JV Ftbl; Im JV Trk; DAR Awd; Artst.

CARLOUGH, COLLEEN; Center Morickes HS; Center Moriches, NY; (Y); 12/92; Cmnty Wkr; French Clb; Ski Clb; Spanish Clb; Chorus; Drill Tm; Variety Show; Hon Roll; Hghst Avg Fr I 83-84; Excllnce Fr II Hghst Avg 84-85; Excllnce Phys Ed Dnce Rout 84-85; C W Post; Fr Intrprtr.

CARLOW, PEGGY; Catholic Central HS; Green Island, NY; (S); 11/178; Math Clb; Drm & Bgl; Yrbk Stf; Cheerleading; Trk; High Hon Roll; NHS; Biomed Engrng.

CARLSEN, LYNN; Union Endicott HS; Endicott, NY; (Y); SADD; Drill Tm; Mrchg Band; Yrbk Stf; Rep Soph Cls; Trs Jr Cls; Trs Sr Cls; Rep Stu Cncl; Stat Lcrss; Hon Roll; Acad All-American 86; Penn ST; Bus Mngmnt.

CARLSON, CARRIE; Chautauqua Central HS; Ashville, NY; (Y); Ski Clb; Teachers Aide; Var Capt Cheerleading; Var L Diving; Var L Sftbl; Var L Swmmng; Var L Vllybl; 4-H Awd; High Hon Roll; Sec 4-H.

CARLSON, COURTNEY; Academy Of The Holy Names; Watervliet, NY; (Y); Art Clb; Spanish Clb; Varsity Clb; Church Choir; Stage Crew; Nwsp Stf; Lit Mag; Cheerleading; Chrldng Excllnce Awd 85; Engl.

CARLSON, DONNA; Jamestown HS; Jamestown, NY; (Y); Church Yth Grp; FCA; Quiz Bowl; Spanish Clb; Teachers Aide; Band; Symp Band; Jamestown CC; Elem Ed.

CARLSON, EDWARD D; Owego Free Acad; Owego, NY; (Y); 11/220; AFS; Boy Scts; Church Yth Grp; Mathletes; School Musical; High Hon Roll; NHS; Ntl Merit SF; NY ST Regents Schlrp 86; Rochester Inst Of Tech; Engrg.

CARLSON, HELEN; Mt Saint Ursula HS; Bronx, NY; (Y); Art Clb; Church Yth Grp; Computer Clb; Drama Clb; Spanish Clb; Nwsp Stf; Yrbk Stf.

CARLSON, JODEL; Frewsburg Central HS; Frewsburg, NY; (Y); AFS; Off Frsh Cls; Off Soph Cls; Trs Jr Cls; Rep Stu Cncl; JCC; Sci.

CARLSON, JOSEPH; Falconer Central Schl; Jamestown, NY; (Y); 1/124; Dnfth Awd; Hon Roll; Val; Mnstr.

CARLSON, KELLY; Chautauqua HS; Stow, NY; (Y); Cmnty Wkr; Ski Clb; Band; Yrbk Bus Mgr; Yrbk Stf; Swmmng; Hon Roll; Jr NHS; Voice Dem Awd; Poetry Pblshd In Local Nwspr 86; Bus.

CARLSON, KRIS; Southwestern Central HS; Jamestown, NY; (Y); Spanish Clb; Golf; Socr; Sftbl; Swmmng; Tennis; Trk; Vllybl; Hon Roll; NHS; Bus Awd 83-84; Math Awd 83-84; Jamestown Bus Coll; Acctg.

CARLSON, MELINDA; John Jay HS; S Salem, NY; (Y); Church Yth Grp; French Clb; Girl Scts; Intnl Clb; Pep Clb; Concert Band.

CARLSON, PENNY; Southwestern Central Schl; Lakewood, NY; (Y); Church Yth Grp; Cmnty Wkr; French Clb; Girl Scts; Pep Clb; Hon Roll; Horse Shws PONY Awds 83; Findly Coll; Hrs Trnr.

CARLSON, REGINALD A; Onteora HS; Boiceville, NY; (Y); Am Leg Boys St; Boy Scts; Varsity Clb; Chorus; Nwsp Rptr; Rep Jr Cls; JV Var Ftbl; Var Trk; Cit Awd; Hon Roll; Eagle Sct Of Trp 63 85; Vigil Hnr Mbr Of Half Mn Ldg No 28 86; Engnrng.

CARLSON, TRACY; Cardinal O Hara HS; Tonawanda, NY; (Y); 35/122; Church Yth Grp; Cmnty Wkr; French Clb; Girl Scts; Pep Clb; Church Choir; School Musical; Stage Crew; Nwsp Rptr; Hon Roll; JR Of Yr Church Yth Grp 86; ST U NY; Soc Wrk.

CARLTON, BETH; Jefferson HS; Rochester, NY; (Y); Nwsp Ed-Chief; Nwsp Rptr; Nwsp Sprt Ed; Nwsp Stf; Var Bsktbl; Co-Capt Var Sftbl; High Hon Roll; Hon Roll; Acad Excel Schl Of Law & Govt 86; ACLU Awd 3rd Pl 84; Air Force Acad; Law.

CARLUCCI, ELEANOR; Riverhead HS; Calverton, NY; (Y); 92/210; DECA; French Clb; FBLA; Spanish Clb; VICA; Chorus; Suffolk CC; Mrktng.

CARLUZZO, EDWARD J; Susan E Wagner HS; Staten Island, NY; (Y); Am Leg Boys St; JV Ftbl; Hon Roll; Prfct Atten Awd; Bus Educ Assn Cert Of Achvt 85; Officer.

CARMAN, CAREN; Charles O Dickerson HS; Trumansburg, NY; (Y); 13/125; Spanish Clb; Varsity Clb; Chorus; Concert Band; Mrchg Band; Nwsp Stf; Yrbk Stf; Var L Bsktbl; Var L Sftbl; 3rd Plc Knights Pythias Essy Cntst 85; Bus Adm.

CARMAN, LISA; Plainedge HS; Massapequa, NY; (Y); 66/315; Office Aide; School Play; Yrbk Stf; Off Sr Cls; Off Stu Cncl; Cheerleading; Socr; Sftbl; High Hon Roll; Hon Roll; Katharine Gibbs Schl Schlrshp 86; PTA Voctnl Career Awd 86; Katharine Gibbs Schl; Lgl Secy.

CARMAN, TRICIA; Vestal SR HS; Vestal, NY; (Y); Church Yth Grp; Drama Clb; Girl Scts; Hosp Aide; Ski Clb; SADD; Band; Concert Band; Mrchg Band; Symp Band; Svc Awd 100 Hrs Vlntrng 85; Med Tech.

CARMEN, DEBORAH; Nazareth Acad; Spencerport, NY; (Y); 3/151; Math Tm; Band; Yrbk Stf; Bausch & Lomb Sci Awd; High Hon Roll; NHS; Ntl Merit Schol; Church Yth Grp; Drama Clb; Exploring; Inst Nuclr Power Opertns Schlrshp 86-87; U VA Dupont Schlrshp 86-87; VA U; Nuclear Engrng.

CARMICHAEL, ANDREW; Le Roy Central HS; Leroy, NY; (Y); 20/140; Ski Clb; Spanish Clb; Varsity Clb; JV Var Ftbl; Wt Lftg; High Hon Roll; Hon Roll; Envrmntl Sci.

CARMICHAEL, KEVIN; Le Roy Central HS; Leroy, NY; (Y); 13/130; Ski Clb; Spanish Clb; SADD; Varsity Clb; Chorus; Yrbk Stf; Rep Jr Cls; Rep Sr Cls; L Bsbl; Co-Capt Ftbl; Acad L Awd 86; All Cnty Tight End-Ftbl & Pitcher-Bsbl 85-86; Amer HS Athlt 85; St Lawurence U.

CARMODY, CAROLYN; Bay Shore HS; Bay Shore, NY; (Y); 75/406; Chorus; Yrbk Stf; Stonybrook U.

CARMODY, KELLY; Frontier Central SR HS; Woodlawn, NY; (Y); Church Yth Grp; Pep Clb; Ski Clb; Spanish Clb; Band; Concert Band; Yrbk Stf; Hon Roll; NHS.

CARMODY, MARIE; New Dorp HS; Staten Island, NY; (Y); Art Clb; Intnl Clb; Chorus; Lit Mag; Rep Jr Cls; Co-Capt Cheerleading; Art.

CARMONA, JENNIFER; Acad Of St Joseph; Brentwood, NY; (Y); Dance Clb; Political Wkr; Chorus; Church Choir; Nwsp Rptr; Nwsp Stf; Lit Mag; High Hon Roll; Hon Roll; Commnctns.

CARNES, VERONICA; Pleasantville HS; Pleasantville, NY; (Y); 3/111; Dance Clb; Drm Mjr(t); Orch; School Musical; Frsh Cls; Soph Cls; Jr Cls; Sr Cls; High Hon Roll; NHS; Acad Awd 85 & 86; Frnch Acad Awd 84; All ST Awd 86; Ed.

CARNESI, LAURA; Oyster Bay HS; Oyster Bay, NY; (Y); Church Yth Grp; Cmnty Wkr; VP Spanish Clb; SADD; Chorus; School Musical; Stage Crew; Yrbk Stf; ROTC; NHS; Pre-Law.

CARNEVALE, ANNE MARIE; Our Lady Of Mercy HS; Rochester, NY; (Y); 7/172; Science Clb; School Play; Stage Crew; Yrbk Stf; JV Var Socr; High Hon Roll; Hon Roll; NHS; Exploring; SADD; Rchstr Diocese Hnds/ Chrst Awd 86; Monroe Cnty All Str Vrsty Sccr Tm 84; Crnll Engrng Coll; Engrng Phycs.

CARNEY, DAVID; Herkimer HS; Herkimer, NY; (Y); 4/110; Church Yth Grp; Key Clb; SADD; Yrbk Ed-Chief; Pres Rep Frsh Cls; Rep Soph Cls; Rep Jr Cls; Rep Sr Cls; VP Stu Cncl; Var Bsbl; Pre-Med.

CARNEY, DEIRDRE; Warwick Valley HS; Warwick, NY; (Y); 6/200; Church Yth Grp; Cmnty Wkr; Band; Concert Band; Variety Show; High Hon Roll; NHS; Prfct Atten Awd; Spnsh Awds 1st 84-86; Natl Sci Olympd Physcs 86; Cert Apprctn Ofc Aging Hnrs 85; Fordham U; Corp Law.

CARNEY, EILEEN S; Our Lady Of Mercy HS; Rochester, NY; (Y); 33/ 172; Cmnty Wkr; Hosp Aide; Pres Service Clb; Sec Trs Spanish Clb; Chorus; School Musical; Nwsp Stf; Yrbk Stf; JV Tennis; NHS; Regents Schlrshp 86; Admssns Schlrshp 86; St John Fisher Coll; Polt Sci.

CARNEY, JAMES; Kenmore East HS; Tonawanda, NY; (Y); 128/330; Aud/Vis; Camera Clb; Yrbk Bus Mgr; Yrbk Phtg; Yrbk Stf; Rep Sr Cls; Rep Stu Cncl; High Hon Roll; Hon Roll; Cert Of Merit Schltc Art Awds 86; Outstndng Photo Art Stu 86; RIT; Acctg.

CARNEY, KRISTIN; New Hyde Park Memorial HS; New Hyde Pk, NY; (Y); French Clb; Mathletes; Band; School Musical; School Play; Var Socr; High Hon Roll; Hon Roll; Jr NHS; Ntl Merit Ltr; Brdcstng.

CARNEY, LYNETTE; Corinth Central HS; Corinth, NY; (S); 3/75; Am Leg Aux Girls St; JA; Spanish Clb; SADD; Varsity Clb; Band; Chorus; Pres Sr Cls; Trs Stu Cncl; Fld Hcky; St Lawrence U; Psych.

CARNICELLI, DAVID; New Rochelle HS; New Rochelle, NY; (Y); Model UN; Crs Cntry; Trk; French Hon Soc; High Hon Roll; NHS; Arch.

CARNIELLO, GLENN; Noth Babylon SR HS; North Babylon, NY; (Y); 39/500; Church Yth Grp; Intnl Clb; Spanish Clb; JV Socr; Var Tennis; Jr NHS; NHS; Pres Schlr; High Hon Roll; Hon Roll; Regnts Schlrshp 86; SUNY Geneseo; Bus.

CARO, DEBORAH A; John F Kennedy HS; Mahopac, NY; (Y); 8/198; Church Yth Grp; Intnl Clb; Math Clb; SADD; Teachers Aide; Chorus; School Musical; Nwsp Stf; High Hon Roll; NHS; Regious Hnr Awd 84-85; Regents Schlrshp 85-86; Hnrs Pgm Syracuse U 86; Syracuse U; Jrnlsm.

CARO, GEORGE; William H Taft HS; Bronx, NY; (Y); Computer Clb; SADD; Concert Band; Rep Stu Cncl; Bowling; Swmmng; Tennis; Wt Lftg; Hon Roll; Prfct Atten Awd; Gyneclgst.

CAROBENE, CHRISTOPHER S; St Francis Prep Schl; Douglaston, NY; (S); Boy Scts; Computer Clb; Ski Clb; Band; Vllybl; Ntl Sci Merit Awd 86; US Ntl Ldrshp Merit Awd 86; Optimate Scty 85; Naval Arch.

CAROLLO, JIM; Rome Free Acad; Rome, NY; (Y); 73/501; 4-H; Ski Clb; Varsity Clb; Ftbl; Lcrss; 4-H Awd; Ind Tech Hnrs Awd 84; Herkimer CC; Auto Engr.

CARON, LISA; Brockport HS; Spencerport, NY; (Y); Drama Clb; Latin Clb; Radio Clb; Ski Clb; Band; Mrchg Band; Orch; Pep Band; School Musical; Symp Band; Sndy Schl Tchr 85-86; Outstndng Mscn 84-85; Bio.

CARON, MELISSA; Hancock Central HS; Hancock, NY; (Y); Church Yth Grp; German Clb; Office Aide; Pep Clb; Chorus; Pres Frsh Cls; Pres Jr Cls; Rep Stu Cncl; Im JV Bsktbl; VP L Fld Hcky; Stdnt Mnth 85-86; Salute Yth 85-86; Susquenango All Str Tm 85-86; Engrng.

CAROVINCI, JOS; John H Glenn HS; E Northport, NY; (Y); Concert Band; Variety Show; Hon Roll; 1st & 3rd Pl Annl Phtgrphy Comptn 85-86; Slvr Metl Indstrl Arts 83-84.

CARPENTER, ANGELA A; Union-Endicott HS; Endwell, NY; (Y); Drama Clb; Girl Scts; Chorus; Church Choir; Concert Band; Drm Mjr(t); Mrchg Band; School Musical; Ed Lit Mag; NHS; Rgnts Schlrshp 86; Blue Rbn & Gld Key Rgnl Schlstc Art Awds 86; Gld Grl Scout Awd 86; Syracuse U; Advrstng Dsgn.

CARPENTER, AYISHA; Yonkers HS; New York, NY; (Y); Dance Clb; Variety Show; VP Frsh Cls; Dance Club Awd 84; Obsttrcn.

CARPENTER, CHRISTINE; Fonda-Fultsville Central HS; Fonda, NY; (Y); Church Yth Grp; Hosp Aide; Intnl Clb; SADD; Chorus; Stage Crew; Yrbk Phtg; Yrbk Stf; Sftbl; Hon Roll; Cdrvil Coll; Bus Admin.

CARPENTER, CLAY; Greece Athena HS; Rochester, NY; (Y); Ski Clb; Band; Jazz Band; School Musical; Symp Band; JV Bsbl; JV Bsktbl; Var Socr; Im Vllybl; Var Wrstlng; Chem Engr.

CARPENTER JR, DAVID; Fort Plain HS; Fort Plain, NY; (S); Church Yth Grp; JV Wrstlng; Hon Roll; Pastorial Ministries.

CARPENTER, JAMES; Dundee Central HS; Dundee, NY; (Y); Capt Bsbl; Ftbl; Trk; High Hon Roll; Hon Roll; Corning CC; Accntng.

CARPENTER, KIMBERLY; Avoca Central HS; Wallace, NY; (Y); 24/ 48; VP FBLA; JCL; School Play; Yrbk Bus Mgr; Yrbk Stf; Var Bsktbl; Var JV Socr; High Hon Roll; Hon Roll; Latin Clb; Spec Svc Awd 86; Alfred ST Coll; Acctng.

CARPENTER, MAGGIE; John Jay HS; Cross River, NY; (Y); Intnl Clb; Ski Clb; Yrbk Ed-Chief; Off Frsh Cls; VP Soph Cls; Rep Stu Cncl; Var Capt Lcrss; Var Capt Tennis; High Hon Roll; NHS; Math 12,Achvt,Chem Achvt 86; Sci And Socl Stu Awd 86; Var Sprtsmnshp Awd 86.

CARPENTER, PAMELA; Wayland Central HS; Wayland, NY; (Y); 14/ 142; Chorus; Color Guard; Swing Chorus; Yrbk Ed-Chief; Yrbk Rptr; Yrbk Sprt Ed; Yrbk Stf; Stueben County Solo Cmpttn; All Cnty Choir; Advrtsng.

CARPENTER, ROBERT; W C Mepham HS; N Bellmore, NY; (Y); Aud/ Vis; Debate Tm; Science Clb; Yrbk Stf; Pres Stu Cncl; French Hon Soc; High Hon Roll; Jr NHS; NHS; Acctg.

CARPENTER, SARA; Keveny Acad; Cohoes, NY; (Y); GAA; Sec Soph Cls; Stu Cncl; Bsktbl; Score Keeper; Tennis; Timer; Vllybl; Hon Roll; NHS; Siena Coll; Accntng.

CARPENTER, WILLIAM; Moriah Central HS; Witherbee, NY; (Y); 1/ 75; Yrbk Stf; VP Frsh Cls; Rep Stu Cncl; JV Bsktbl; Bausch & Lomb Sci Awd; High Hon Roll; NHS; Ntl Merit Ltr; Mth.

CARPENTER, ZANE; Aquinas Inst; Rochester, NY; (Y); 40/205; French Clb; ROTC; Ski Clb; Ftbl; Trk; Hon Roll; NROTC; Pilot.

CARPINELLA, LISA; Sachem HS North Campus; Lake Ronkonkoma, NY; (Y); 63/1558; Art Clb; Science Clb; Ski Clb; Hon Roll; Jr NHS; Prfct Atten Awd; Earth Sci.

CARPINI, LINA DELLI; Preston HS; Bronx, NY; (S); 10/89; Drama Clb; School Play; Nwsp Stf; Sec Frsh Cls; Sec Soph Cls; Sec Jr Cls; Sec VP NHS; Oustndng Perf Volnteer Svc 84; Fash Buying.

CARPIO, LEO; Archbishop Molloy HS; Jackson Hts, NY; (Y); Computer Clb; Math Tm; Im Bsktbl; Im Ftbl; Im Sftbl; NHS; DA Of Queens Essay 1st Pl 86-86; Queens Clg Acad Achvt Awd 86.

CARR, BRIAN; Paul W Moore HS; Bernhards Bay, NY; (Y); Boy Scts; Computer Clb; Radio Clb; Bsbl; Trk; Electrncs.

CARR, CARMEN; Fayetteville Manlius Central Schl; Cleveland, OH; (Y); 67/335; Computer Clb; Debate Tm; Exploring; JA; Office Aide; Teachers Aide; Church Choir; Coach Actv; Mgr(s); Cit Awd; ABC Prg 83-86; Tufts U; Bio.

CARR, CHERYL L; Owego Free Acad; Apalachin, NY; (Y); 39/215; AFS; Church Yth Grp; Girl Scts; Office Aide; Pep Clb; Spanish Clb; SADD; Capt Color Guard; Yrbk Stf; Outstndng Color Guard 84-85; Svc OFA Marchng Band 85-86; Pres Acad Ftns Awd 86; SUNY Coll; Soc Wrk.

CARR, CINDY A; William Cullen Bryant HS; Astoria, NY; (Y); 101/623; JA; Office Aide; Chorus; Nwsp Stf; Hon Roll; Regents Schlrshp 86; Queens Coll; Psych.

CARR, COLLEEN; Liverpool HS; Liverpool, NY; (Y); JA; Drm Mjr(t); Mrchg Band; Trs Orch; Stage Crew; Hon Roll.

CARR, CRAIG A; Westfield Acad And Cen Schl; Westfield, NY; (Y); 15/ 60; Boy Scts; Model UN; Quiz Bowl; Band; Chorus; Concert Band; School Musical; Symp Band; Jazz Band; Rgnts Schlrshp 85-86; SUNY Fredonia; Coop Engnrng.

CARR, DONNA; Centereach HS; Lk Ronkonkoma, NY; (Y); Rep Jr Cls; Prfct Atten Awd; Spanish NHS; St Josephs Coll; Chld Educ.

CARR, JERI; Ripley Central HS; Ripley, NY; (Y); JA; Sec Chorus; Color Guard; Capt Drill Tm; Mrchg Band; Stage Crew; Pres Frsh Cls; VP Soph Cls; JV Var Tennis; NY St Schl Of Visl Arts 86; Best Of Show 2d Category 86; Advtsng.

CARR, KATHLEEN; Liverpool HS; Liverpool, NY; (Y); 99/816; Exploring; VP JA; Latin Clb; Teachers Aide; Mrchg Band; Rep Stu Cncl; L Twrlr; Hon Roll; Jr NHS; NHS; Sunny-Oswego; Elem Educ.

CARR, KELLIE; Gilbertsville Central HS; Gilbertsville, NY; (Y); 8/33; Church Yth Grp; Drama Clb; Pres Sec Varsity Clb; Pres Band; Pres Chorus; Church Choir; Capt Color Guard; Pres Concert Band; Jazz Band; School Play; Music Schlrshp Hartwick Coll 86-87; Exllnc Spnsh Awd 85; Dir Awd Chorus 85-86; Hartwick Coll; Music.

CARR, LAURIE JEAN; Kenmore West SR HS; Kenmore, NY; (Y); Cmnty Wkr; VP Drama Clb; Chorus; School Musical; Swing Chorus; Variety Show; Rep Stu Cncl; Var L Bowling; Hon Roll; Miss Wstrn NY Natl Teengr Pagnt Essy Wnnr, Rnnr Up 84; Theatre.

CARR, LESLIE C; Red Hook SR HS; Red Hook, NY; (Y); 14/135; Church Yth Grp; Quiz Bowl; Concert Band; School Play; Yrbk Stf; Var Tennis; High Hon Roll; Grmn Awd 85; Rgnts Schlrshp 86; Pres Acad Ftnss Awd 86; Lbrl Arts.

CARR, NINA; The Masters Schl; Scarsdale, NY; (Y); Cmnty Wkr; French Clb; GAA; Library Aide; Office Aide; Spanish Clb; Teachers Aide; Varsity Clb; Yrbk Stf; Pres Stu Cncl; Recgntn In Geomtry 85.

CARR, TINA M; Carthage Central HS; Black River, NY; (Y); Drama Clb; Office Aide; Mrchg Band; Nwsp Stf; High Hon Roll; Hon Roll; Regents Scholar 86; Rotary SR 86; Jefferosn CC; Ed.

CARR, VICKY; Lisbon Central Schl; Ogdensburg, NY; (S); 1/50; Camera Clb; Spanish Clb; Chorus; Capt Socr; High Hon Roll; Ed.

CARRANZA, JULISSA; Fashion Industrs; Jackson Hts, NY; (Y); 8/324; Art Clb; Office Aide; Teachers Aide; Yrbk Stf; High Hon Roll; Hon Roll; Prfct Atten Awd; Fshn Inst Tech; Fshn Dsgnr.

CARRARA, DAVID; Roy C Ketcham HS; Wappingers Falls, NY; (Y); Church Yth Grp; Cmnty Wkr; Capt Wrstlng; High Hon Roll; NHS; Ntl Merit Ltr; Fashion Inst Of Tech; Int Desgn.

CARRASCO, RUTH M; Eastern District HS; Brooklyn, NY; (Y); Church Choir; School Musical; School Play; Variety Show; Rep Jr Cls; Vllybl; Lang.

CARRASQUILLO, CARLOS L; Bay Shore HS; Bay Shore, NY; (Y); 180/ 376; Cmnty Wkr; Gym; Trk; High Hon Roll; NVG Gym; Ltr Gym; Trach 86; Med Sci.

CARRASQUILLO, IRENE; St Raymond Acad; Bronx, NY; (S); Computer Clb; Library Aide; Office Aide; Service Clb; Teachers Aide; Hon Roll; Prfct Atten Awd; Spnsh Awd; Bus Educ Awd From Westchester Bus Inst 86; Sec.

CARRASQUILLO, IVAN; Sheepshead Bay HS; Brooklyn, NY; (Y); Boy Scts; FCA; Var Capt Bsbl; Score Keeper; Hon Roll; Athltc Awd Shttl Run; Hon Cls Soc Stds; Embry Riddle Aeronautcl U; Plt.

CARREN, DEBORAH; Northport HS; Northport, NY; (Y); Church Yth Grp; Girl Scts; Chorus; Church Choir; Concert Band; Mrchg Band; Girl Scout Silv Awd 85; Lib Arts.

CARRER, ROBERT; John F Kennedy HS; Bronx, NY; (Y); JA; Wrstlng; Spanish NHS; Rgnts Schlrshp 86; Semi Fnlst Ntl Hspnc Schlrs Awd 85; City U Of NY; Comp Sci.

CARRERAS, MATTHEW; Bayport Blue Point HS; Bayport, NY; (Y); 18/220; Key Clb; Concert Band; Var Tennis; Hon Roll; Sci Stu Of Mo May 86; Medicine.

CARRIER, DEBORAH; Holland Patent HS; Rome, NY; (Y); 4-H; Girl Scts.

CARRIER, MICHAEL; Tuckahoe HS; Bronxville, NY; (Y); 2/60; Computer Clb; Science Clb; Band; Mrchg Band; Orch; Yrbk Stf; Tennis; Var Trk; High Hon Roll; Jr NHS; George Washington U Math & Sci Medal 86; Iona Coll Physics Awd 86; Highst Avg JR Yr 86; Harvard; Math.

CARRIGAN, BRIAN; Corcoran HS; Syracuse, NY; (Y); French Clb; Political Wkr; Band; Mrchg Band; VP Jr Cls; VP Sr Cls; Var Bsbl; High Hon Roll; NHS.

CARRILLO, VERONICA; Pelham Memorial HS; Pelham Manor, NY; (Y); AFS; Church Yth Grp; JA; Spanish Clb; Yrbk Phtg; Lit Mag; Var Sftbl; JV Vllybl; NHS; Spanish NHS; Bus.

CARRINO, DENA; The Franciscan Acad; Syracuse, NY; (Y); 7/25; FBLA; Nwsp Rptr; Nwsp Stf; Yrbk Stf; Cheerleading; Hon Roll; Ntl Merit Ltr; Chorus; 3rd Pl Typg I FBLA ST 86; 1st Pl Typg I FBLA Dist 86; CCBI; Court Steno.

CARRO, ROBERT; Seton Catholic Central HS; Johnson City, NY; (Y); 36/165; Art Clb; French Clb; Ski Clb; Trk; NYS Regents Schlrshp 86; Philadelphia Coll Textls; Mgmt.

CARROLL, CATHY; Fowler HS; Syracuse, NY; (Y); 4/190; Church Yth Grp; 4-H; FBLA; Office Aide; SADD; Stu Cncl; Bowling; Socr; NHS; Prfct Atten Awd; Bus Math Awd 86; Stengrphr I Awd 86; Acctnt.

CARROLL, COLIN J; Amhest Central SR HS; Snyder, NY; (Y); 40/392; Pres Model UN; Quiz Bowl; Varsity Clb; Chorus; School Musical; Capt Socr; Hon Roll; NHS; Ntl Merit SF; Hmcmng Kng 85; Math.

CARROLL, DAWN MARIE; Newfield HS; Selden, NY; (Y); 105/515; GAA; Pep Clb; SADD; Chorus; School Musical; Variety Show; Yrbk Stf; Var Capt Socr; Marist Coll; Bus.

CARROLL, DEW-ANN; Our Lady Of Victory Acad; Yonkers, NY; (S); 5/ 138; Church Yth Grp; Drama Clb; Rep Frsh Cls; Rep Soph Cls; Rep Jr Cls; Rep Stu Cncl; High Hon Roll; NHS; Spanish NHS; Chem Awd OLVA 85; Soc Dstngshd Amer HS Stu 86.

CARROLL, ELLEN; Onondaga Central HS; Syracuse, NY; (S); VP Pres Spanish Clb; SADD; Varsity Clb; VP Jr Cls; VP Stu Cncl; Var Cheerleading; Var Trk; High Hon Roll; Hon Roll; NHS.

CARROLL, JOHN; Salamanca HS; Salamanca, NY; (Y); Church Yth Grp; French Clb; ROTC; Ski Clb; Varsity Clb; Bsktbl; Crs Cntry; Ftbl; Golf; Socr; Math.

CARROLL, MICHELE; Mount St Mary Acad; Buffalo, NY; (Y); Pep Clb; Var Bsktbl; Var Socr; Var Sftbl; Hon Roll; NHS; All Catholic Bsktbl 86; MVP Bsktbl 86; Western New York All Star 86; Norwich U; Crmnl Justice.

CARROLL, PATRICIA; Rensselaer JR SR HS; Rensselaer, NY; (Y); 5/ 75; Trs Intnl Clb; Key Clb; SADD; Yrbk Bus Mgr; Sec Frsh Cls; Sec Jr Cls; Stu Cncl; Var Fld Hcky; Cit Awd; High Hon Roll; Acctng.

CARROLL, PAUL; East Islip HS; East Islip, NY; (S); 65/425; Var Bsktbl; Var Tennis; Hon Roll; NHS; Boys Leaders 85-86; Bsktbl 82; Elec Engr.

CARROWAY, KATHLEEN; Liverpool HS; Liverpool, NY; (Y); Church Yth Grp; Cmnty Wkr; Hosp Aide; Ski Clb; Rep Stu Cncl; Var Capt Fld Hcky; Cit Awd; High Hon Roll; Opt Clb Awd; St Schlr; Empire ST Games Partcpnt Rowng 83-84; Livrpl H S Crew Tm 83-85; Membr NRA 85; Potysdame ST U; Elem Educ.

CARROZZA, ELISABETH; Port Richmond HS; Staten Island, NY; (Y); Pres Church Yth Grp; Cmnty Wkr; Library Aide; Church Choir; Var Socr; Hon Roll; Prfct Atten Awd; Camera Clb; Yrbk Rptr; Yrbk Sprt Ed; Bst Off Plyr Grls Soccr 86; Acad Olympcs 85-86; Sec Bridges-N-Blades Figure Skatng Clb 84-86; Zoolgy.

CARRUBA, LISA; Domininican Commercial HS; S Ozone Park, NY; (S); 28/280; Art Clb; Hon Roll; Natl Bus Hnr Soc 86; Siena Clb 85; Excllnt Attndnc & Pnctlty Awd 83-86; Shrthnd.

CARRYL, RON O; Boys And Girls HS; Brooklyn, NY; (Y); 11/354; Scholastic Bowl; Science Clb; High Hon Roll; Hon Roll; Prfct Atten Awd; JA; Lit Mag; Im Trk; NY Rgnts Schlrshp 86; Rgnts Blgy Awd 84; Rgnts Math Awd 86; Physcn.

CARSELLO, KAREN; Cortland JR & SR HS; Cortland, NY; (Y); 9/194; Hosp Aide; Latin Clb; SADD; Band; Concert Band; Mrchg Band; Orch; Pep Band; School Musical; Yrbk Stf; Cornell U; Hotel Mngmt.

CARSON, CYNTHIA ANN; Patch American HS; Apo New York, NY; (Y); 11/100; FBLA; VP Spanish Clb; Teachers Aide; Hon Roll; Pres Schlr; U Of MD Munich W Grmny.

CARSON, MARY; New Rochelle HS; New Rochelle, NY; (Y); 193/550; FBLA; Nwsp Stf; Yrbk Stf; Bus Educ Awd Outstndng Achvt 86; PTSA Awd Shrthnd And Transcrpt 86; Jnrlsm Awd 86; Outstndng Achvt Eng; IA Clg; Bus Admn.

CARSON, MELISSA; Allegany Central HS; Allegany, NY; (Y); Church Yth Grp; DECA; Drama Clb; FFA; Sec Girl Scts; Library Aide; Y-Teens; Nwsp Stf; Yrbk Stf; FFA Grn Hnd Awd 84; FFA Lab Mgmt 84.

CARSON, MONICA; Geneva HS; Geneva, NY; (S); 31/175; Spanish Clb; Yrbk Stf; Im Powder Puff Ftbl; Hon Roll; Bio.

CARSWELL, RHONDA; Vestal SR HS; Vestal, NY; (Y); Pres Church Yth Grp; Lib Church Choir; Var Crs Cntry; Var Trk; Prfct Atten Awd; Church Sftbl Tm 85-86; Trphy Top Scorer Yth Grp Actvts 85-86; Elem Educ.

CARTAFALSA, VINCENT A; Archbishop Molloy HS; Brooklyn, NY; (Y); 131/383; Intnl Clb; Im Ftbl; Im Sftbl; St Johns U.

CARTAGENA, EVYETTE; John Dewey HS; Brooklyn, NY; (Y); Library Aide; Math Tm; Office Aide; Chorus; Yrbk Stf; Rep Jr Cls; Rep Sr Cls; Bsktbl; Gym; High Hon Roll; Trpl C Awd 83; Baruch; Accntng.

CARTELLA, THERESA; Canisteo Central Schl; Hornell, NY; (Y); 21/77; Ski Clb; Mrchg Band; School Play; Yrbk Stf; Cheerleading; Score Keeper; Socr; Sftbl; Maple City Savings & Loan Awd 86; CC Finger Lakes; Comp Sci.

CARTER, ANNMARIE; Vernon-Verona-Sherrill HS; Sherrill, NY; (Y); Church Yth Grp; Pres 4-H; Chorus; Orch; Yrbk Stf; Rep Frsh Cls; Rep Soph Cls; Rep Jr Cls; Rep Stu Cncl; JV Var Cheerleading; Librl Arts.

CARTER, BENJAMIN CRAIG; Allendale Columbia Schl; Pittsford, NY; (Y); Church Yth Grp; Radio Clb; Bsbl; Ftbl; JV Var Golf; Im Sftbl; JV Wrstlng; French Hon Soc; High Hon Roll; Hon Roll; Cum Laude Scty 86; U Of CA.

CARTER, GLENN; Union Springs Acad; Mercer, ME; (S); 1/29; Capt Drill Tm; Yrbk Phtg; Rep Stu Cncl; Im Ftbl; Gym; Im Sftbl; High Hon Roll; NHS; Cnslr & Instrctr Path Findrs 83-86; Atlantic Union Coll; Mth.

CARTER, JAMIE ALISSA; Long Island Lutheran HS; Roosevelt, NY; (S); 2/94; SADD; Band; Chorus; Concert Band; High Hon Roll; NCTE Awd; NHS; Church Yth Grp; Nwsp Stf; Schltc Awd 85; High Achvrs Awd 85; Frgn Lang Awd 85; Jrnlsm.

CARTER, JIM; Guilderland Central HS; Albany, NY; (Y); Key Clb; Ski Clb; JV Var Ftbl; Im JV Wt Lftg; RIT; Comp Engrng.

CARTER, JOANNE; St Peters High School For Girls; Staten Island, NY; (Y); Hosp Aide; SADD; Pres Frsh Cls; Pres Soph Cls; Pres Jr Cls; Stu Cncl; Capt Var Cheerleading; Gym; Hon Roll; Acad Hon Awd 85; Bst Hosp Vlntr Awd 84; Nrsng.

CARTER, JOEL; Le Roy Central HS; Leroy, NY; (Y); French Clb; Ski Clb; Wt Lftg; Hon Roll; Purdue U; Engrng.

CARTER, JOHN; East Syracuse Minoa HS; E Syracuse, NY; (Y); 26/333; Im Bsktbl; Im Vllybl; Hon Roll; Jr NHS; NHS; Pres Schlr; Trustees Awd 86; VFW Schlrshp 86; Clarkson U; Elect Engrg.

CARTER, JUNE; Prospect Heights HS; Brooklyn, NY; (S); 5/271; Dance Clb; French Clb; Pres JA; School Play; Lit Mag; NYS U; Bus Adm.

CARTER, KATHY; Maple Grove JR SR HS; Dewittville, NY; (Y); 2/75; Pep Clb; Band; Chorus; School Musical; Yrbk Ed-Chief; Sec Jr Cls; Coach Actv; Var L Sftbl; NHS; Sal; Regents Schlrshp 86; Diploma Hnrs 86; Cornell U; Hotel Adm.

CARTER, KATIE; Lockport SR HS; Lockport, NY; (Y); 25/411; Yrbk Stf; Off Frsh Cls; Off Soph Cls; Off Jr Cls; Off Sr Cls; Stu Cncl; Var L Swmmng; Hon Roll; Jr NHS; NHS; Thelma Pies Memrl Schlrshp 86; William T Smith Memrl & Don Richards Memrl Swmg Awds 85-86; SUNY At Geneseo.

CARTER, KELLY; Lake George HS; Fort Ann, NY; (Y); Office Aide; Yrbk Bus Mgr; Bsktbl; Fld Hcky; Vllybl; Hotel Mgt.

CARTER, KEVIN; Saranac Central HS; Cadyville, NY; (S); #10 In Class; Yrbk Stf; Trk; Capt Wrstlng; High Hon Roll; NHS; Air Force Acad.

CARTER, KIM; Holy Trinity HS; Levittown, NY; (S); 19/313; Math Clb; Teachers Aide; Nwsp Stf; Cheerleading; Gym; Trk; High Hon Roll; NHS; Prfct Atten Awd; 2nd Pl NSCHSAA Lg Champ Var Gym 83; 1st Pl Nassau-Suffolk Intrsctnls Hurdls Trk 85; Qualf ST Trk 85; Ed.

CARTER, MICHELE; Grand Island HS; Grand Isl, NY; (Y); Camp Fr Inc; French Clb; GAA; JA; Orch; School Musical; Stu Cncl; Im Badmtn; Var L Bsktbl; Var L Socr; NFL All Star Trck 100 M & 400 Relay 86; Syracuse U; Chem Engr.

CARTER, PETER; Uniondale HS; Uniondale, NY; (Y); Am Leg Boys St; Boy Scts; FBLA; Mgr NFL; Orch; Nwsp Rptr; Pres Soph Cls; Rep Sr Cls; Capt Bowling; NHS; US Natl Math Awd 86; 4th Pl In Impromptu Speech Cmptn FBLA #25 86; Med.

CARTER JR, RICHARD B; Union Springs Central Schl; Union Spgs, NY; (Y); 3/104; Am Leg Boys St; Chess Clb; Cmnty Wkr; Debate Tm; Ski Clb; Spanish Clb; JV Var Golf; JV Var Socr; High Hon Roll; NHS; Aerospc Engr.

CARTER, ROBERT; Hampton Bays HS; Hampton Bays, NY; (Y); Boy Scts; Church Yth Grp; Computer Clb; Science Clb; Band; Jazz Band; Mrchg Band; Hon Roll; Engrng.

CARTER, ROBERT; South Park HS; Buffalo, NY; (Y); Church Yth Grp; Debate Tm; Band; School Play; Nwsp Rptr; Yrbk Sprt Ed; Off Jr Cls; Off Sr Cls; Stu Cncl; Bsktbl; Mech Engr.

CARTER, RUSSELL; Copiaque HS; Copiaque, NY; (Y); 76/312; Computer Clb; Prfct Atten Awd; Howard U; Bus Law.

CARTER, SARAH; Trott Vocational HS; Niagara Falls, NY; (Y).

CARTER, SHANON; Clarence Central HS; Clarence, NY; (Y); Pres Church Yth Grp; Hosp Aide; Pep Clb; SADD; Band; Mrchg Band; Scl Wrkr.

CARTINI, JAY; Bishop Grimes HS; Jamesville, NY; (Y); 35/145; Boy Scts; Exploring; Trs FBLA; VP JA; Model UN; SADD; Nwsp Rptr; Var Golf; Hon Roll; Rotary Awd; Le Moyne Coll; Acctg.

CARTLEDGE, TRACY N; Shenendehowa HS; Clifton Park, NY; (Y); 27/675; Drama Clb; Key Clb; Stage Crew; Yrbk Stf; Off Sr Cls; JV Var Cheerleading; High Hon Roll; Hon Roll; NHS; Ntl Merit Ltr; Rgnts Schlrshp 86; SUNY Geneseo Alumni Flws Schlrshp 86; Top J Prcnt Of Class 85; SUNY Geneseo; Bus Admin.

CARTY, ANNMARIE; Eramus Hall HS; Brooklyn, NY; (Y); Prfct Atten Awd; Culture Club Awds 86; Med Dr.

CARTY, MICHAEL; Glens Falls HS; Glens Falls, NY; (Y); Church Yth Grp; French Clb; Nwsp Sprt Ed; Frsh Cls; Soph Cls; Jr Cls; Stu Cncl; Trk; Wrstlng; Comm.

CARUANA, JOHN; Lindenhurst SR HS; Lindenhurst, NY; (Y); 7/550; Church Yth Grp; High Hon Roll; Hon Roll; NHS; Ntl Merit Ltr; Gld Mdl NYS Sci Olympd 85; Slvr Mdl Sufflk Cnty Acad Decthln 86; NYS Rgnts Schlrshp 86; Hofstra U; Comp Sci.

CARUANA, LORRAINE; Lindenhurst SR HS; Lindenhurst, NY; (Y).

CARUSO, LISA M; West Seneca East SR HS; West Seneca, NY; (Y); 50/375; Cmnty Wkr; French Clb; GAA; Var Socr; Hon Roll; Ntl Merit Schol; Prfct Atten Awd; Ltrcy Vlntr Rcvd Dplma Tch Bsc Rdng 84; Rcvd Svrl Awds Apprctn Mbrshp Yth Engd Svc 84-86; ST U Of NY Buffalo; Psych.

CARUSO, MICHAEL; Henninger SR HS; Syracuse, NY; (Y); French Clb; Latin Clb; Ski Clb; Stage Crew; Var Crs Cntry; Hon Roll; Frnch Tchr.

CARUSO, PATRICIA; Frankfort-Schuyler HS; Frankfort, NY; (S); Art Clb; Exploring; SADD; Nwsp Rptr; High Hon Roll; Hon Roll; NHS; Phrmcy.

CARUSO, RALPH; Mc Quaid Jesuit HS; Henrietta, NY; (Y); Drama Clb; School Musical; JV Trk; High Hon Roll; Hon Roll; Lemoyne; Law.

CARUSO, SUSAN; Frankfort-Schuyler HS; Frankfort, NY; (S); 19/102; VP Exploring; French Clb; Math Clb; Var SADD; Nwsp Rptr; Yrbk Phtg; High Hon Roll; Hon Roll; NHS; Le Moyne Coll; Pre-Dntstry.

CARUSO, TERI-ANN; John H Glenn HS; E Northport, NY; (Y); AFS; Chorus; Drill Tm; School Musical; Stage Crew; Yrbk Stf; Rep Frsh Cls; Var Diving; Pom Pon; Cit Awd; Merit Acdmc Decathln Sffrk Co 85; L I Lang Comptn 1st Cltrl Exhbt 83; NY Inst Of Tech; Arch.

CARY, ELIZABETH; John Marshall JR SR HS; Rochester, NY; (Y); Church Yth Grp; Teachers Aide; Church Choir; Hon Roll; Prfct Atten Awd; All Amercn 85.

CARY, RICHARD; Potsdam Central HS; Potsdam, NY; (Y); 32/122; Varsity Clb; School Musical; School Play; Mgr(s); Trk; Wrstlng; Hon Roll; Talented JR 85; Natl Sci Olympiad High Hons 85; Canton ATC; Engrng Sci.

CARY, SEAN; Albertus Magnus HS; Pearl River, NY; (Y); 82/198; Service Clb; SADD; Varsity Clb; Nwsp Sprt Ed; Var Bsktbl; Var Crs Cntry; Var Lcrss; Hon Roll; Falcon Svc Awd; FL Southern Lakeland; Cmnctns.

CARY, TIMOTHY; Coxsackie-Athens JR SR HS; Coxsackie, NY; (Y); 73/120; Ski Clb; Spanish Clb; Band; Yrbk Stf; Photo.

CASA, DOUGLAS; Newfield HS; Selden, NY; (Y); 60/600; Letterman Clb; SADD; Varsity Clb; Nwsp Rptr; Var Capt Crs Cntry; Var Socr; Var Capt Trk; High Hon Roll; Jr NHS; NHS; Soc Studies Awd 84; Ath Yr 86; MVP Trk 85 & 86; Allegheny Coll; Pre-Med.

CASALE, MARC; Solvay HS; Solvay, NY; (Y); Computer Clb; English Clb; French Clb; Math Clb; Science Clb; Yrbk Stf; Off Soph Cls; Off Jr Cls; Off Sr Cls; Stu Cncl; Rgnts Schlrshp, Cmptr Sci, Soc Stds Awds 86; RIT; Bio Med Cmptng.

CASAMENTO, ANN MARIE; Niagara Wheatfield HS; Niagara Falls, NY; (Y); Drama Clb; Pep Clb; PAVAS; Spanish Clb; Chorus; Color Guard; School Musical; JV Lcrss; Var Swmmng; Prfct Atten Awd.

CASANOVA, MELVA; South Shore HS; Brooklyn, NY; (Y); Aud/Vis; Dance Clb; Varsity Clb; Chorus; Church Choir; Variety Show; Cheerleading; Northwood Inst Of TX; Bus Adm.

CASATELLI, JOLENE; Poland Central HS; Poland, NY; (Y); Off Ski Clb; Pres Spanish Clb; Band; Concert Band; Yrbk Stf; Rep Jr Cls; Rep Stu Cncl; JV Socr; High Hon Roll; Hon Roll; Antl Olympd Awd Hist 86; Golden Awd Typng Bus 84; Mth Awd 85; Mohawk Vlly CC; Lawyr.

CASCIANO, FRANCES ANNE; Wm Floyd SR HS; Shirley, NY; (Y); 26/546; Chorus; Pres Orch; Sec NHS; Spanish Clb; Mrchg Band; Rep Soph Cls; JV Cheerleading; JV Vllybl; Rockette Sqd Capt; Key Clb Exec Brd Dir & Pres; Ldrs Clb; Tri-M VP; Hmcmng Queen Fin; ST U NY Binghamton; Arts.

CASCIO, CYNTHIA; Niskayuna HS; Schenectody, NY; (Y); AFS; French Clb; Key Clb; Pep Clb; Soph Cls; Rep Jr Cls; Cheerleading; Powder Puff Ftbl; High Hon Roll; NHS; RPI; Mngmnt.

CASCONE, JOANNE; Our Lady Of Victory HS; Tuckahoe, NY; (S); 15/160; FBLA; Spanish Clb; Hon Roll; NHS; Spanish NHS; Pace U; Bus.

CASE, BRIAN; Valley Stream North HS; N Val Stream, NY; (Y); Nwsp Stf; Yrbk Stf; L Var Bsbl; L Var Bsktbl; L Var Crs Cntry; JV Wrstlng; Hon Roll; Mu Alp Tht; NHS; PBA Schlrhsp 2nd 83-84; Syracuse; Arch.

CASE, DEBORAH L; Sherburne Earlsville SR HS; Smyrna, NY; (Y); 22/126; Church Yth Grp; Drama Clb; Spanish Clb; SADD; School Play; Stage Crew; Variety Show; Yrbk Stf; High Hon Roll; Hon Roll; NYS Regnts Schlrshp 86; Elim Bible Inst; Nrs.

CASE, KRISTIN J; Cobnie Central HS; Schenectady, NY; (Y); 18/484; DECA; Drama Clb; Sec Key Clb; School Musical; Nwsp Stf; Var Sftbl; Var Tennis; High Hon Roll; NHS; Ntl Merit Ltr; Rgnts Schlrshp 86; U Of VA; Cvl Engrng.

CASE, MONICA; Bradford Central HS; Bradford, NY; (S); 3/30; Sec VP FBLA; School Play; Yrbk Stf; Timer; Capt Vllybl; High Hon Roll; Trs NHS; HNR Mntn In FBLA; Corning CC; Accntng.

CASE, THOMAS; Walt Whitman HS; Huntington Statio, NY; (Y); Computer Clb; German Clb; Ski Clb; Teachers Aide; Stage Crew; Hon Roll; Jr NHS; Bus.

CASELLA, DENISE; East Meadow HS; East Meadow, NY; (Y); 19/340; Key Clb; Band; Mrchg Band; Symp Band; Var Capt Lcrss; Capt Pom Pon; Hon Roll; NHS; US Army Rsrve Natl Schlr Athl Awd, Peter Kostynick Mem Schlrshp & E Meadow Moms & Dad Club Schlrshp; SUNY Farmingdale; Vet Sci.

CASELLA, STEPHANIE; Moore Catholic HS; Staten Island, NY; (Y); French Clb; Hosp Aide; Pep Clb; Varsity Clb; Yrbk Phtg; Yrbk Stf; JV Var Cheerleading; Bernard Baruch Coll; Acctnt.

CASERTO JR, JOSEPH V; Marlboro Central HS; Milton, NY; (Y); French Clb; Hon Roll; NHS; Excllnc In Art 85-86; Ntl Hon Rl 85-86.

CASEY, BRIAN; Trinity Pawling Private Schl; Pawling, NY; (Y); Drama Clb; French Clb; Latin Clb; Ski Clb; SADD; Thesps; Band; Jazz Band; School Play; Yrbk Stf; Nrthestrn Coll; Phys Thrpst.

CASEY, CORINNE M; Ogdensburg Free Acad; Ogdensburg, NY; (Y); 31/186; Pres VP Church Yth Grp; French Clb; Math Clb; School Play; Yrbk Stf; Rep Stu Cncl; Mgr(s); Trk; Hon Roll; SUNY-POTSDAM; Engl.

CASEY, DEBBIE; Huntington HS; Huntington, NY; (Y); Church Yth Grp; Key Clb; Band; JV Bsktbl; Var Capt Socr; Tennis; Bus.

CASEY, JAMES; Lake George HS; Glens Falls, NY; (Y); 4/87; Varsity Clb; Var Bsbl; Var Capt Bsktbl; Var Capt Ftbl; High Hon Roll; Jr NHS; NHS; Biol.

CASEY, JOSEPHINE; Clarkstown South HS; New City, NY; (Y); Church Yth Grp; GAA; Nwsp Rptr; JV Socr; Var L Trk; Villanora U.

CASEY, KRISTINE A; Fayetteville-Manlius HS; Manlius, NY; (Y); 79/335; Thesps; School Musical; School Play; Stage Crew; Symp Band; Variety Show; NHS; Aud/Vis; Nwsp Phtg; Hon Roll; Ntl Schlstcs Photo Cmptn 86; Comms.

CASEY, LAURA; Our Lady Of Victory Acad; White Plains, NY; (S); Nwsp Rptr; Hon Roll; NHS; Spanish NHS; Spn Awd 84; Spn Awd 85.

CASEY, LEIGH; Greece Olympia HS; Rochester, NY; (S); DECA; SADD; Varsity Clb; Pres Concert Band; Yrbk Ed-Chief; Hst Frsh Cls; Pres Soph Cls; Pres Jr Cls; Pres Sr Cls; Hon Roll; Natl DECA Top 10 Wnr 86; NY St DECA Fnlst; Misc Ldrshp Awds & Hnrs; Bus Mrktng.

CASEY, MAUREEN; Mount Mercy Acad; Orchard Park, NY; (Y); 6/198; Church Yth Grp; JCL; Model UN; Ski Clb; Stage Crew; Yrbk Stf; Rep Jr Cls; Var Crs Cntry; Var Sftbl; NHS; Hlth.

CASEY, RITA GABRIELLE; Churchville-Chili SR HS; Churchville, NY; (Y); Chorus; Color Guard; School Musical; Swing Chorus; VP Jr Cls; Rep Stu Cncl; Var Score Keeper; High Hon Roll; NHS; NYSSMA 83-85; Secndry Ed.

CASH, DANIELE; High School Of Fashion Ind; Brooklyn, NY; (Y); 70/324; Chess Clb; Church Yth Grp; Service Clb; Teachers Aide; Band; Church Choir; School Musical; Sec Sr Cls; Hon Roll; Recruiter For H S; Smmr Schl Achvt For Betterment; Syracuse U; Bus Adm.

CASIANO, JOHN; All Hallows HS; Bronx, NY; (Y); 33/92; Crs Cntry; Trk; Wt Lftg; John Jay Coll; Crmnl Jstce.

CASILIO, JULIE; Nardin Acad; Clarence, NY; (S); French Clb; Hosp Aide; Ski Clb; Band; Concert Band; Orch; School Musical; Var Tennis.

CASKO, STEPHEN F; Stuyvesant HS; New York, NY; (Y); Mgr(s); Vllybl; JETS Awd; St Schlr; Ntl Engr Aptitude Search Top 10% 86; JETS 1st Pl Teams Engr Grahics 86; Merit Schlrshp & Hnrs Prog; Cullen Coll; Engr.

CASLER, CHRISTINE; Canastota HS; Canastota, NY; (Y); High Hon Roll; Writer.

CASLER, LORI; Fort Plain HS; Ft Plain, NY; (Y); 12/52; Cmnty Wkr; Dance Clb; Band; Chorus; School Musical; Var Capt Crs Cntry; Dnfth Awd; 4-H Awd; NHS; Hugh O Brian Yth Fndtn Ambssdr 84; Russell Sage Coll; Nutrtn.

CASLER, MAUREEN; Corcoran HS; Syracuse, NY; (Y); Dance Clb; French Clb; Ski Clb; Yrbk Stf; Var Trk; JV Vllybl; High Hon Roll; Hon Roll; Vrsty Ltr Track 83; Physcl Thrpst.

CASO, CHRISTOPHER; Msgr Farrell HS; Staten Island, NY; (S); 15/380; Aud/Vis; Church Yth Grp; Cmnty Wkr; Frsh Cls; Stu Cncl; Bsktbl; Ftbl; Vllybl; High Hon Roll; NHS; Engrng.

CASO, MARIA; St Catharine Acad; Bronx, NY; (Y); Dance Clb; Nwsp Rptr; High Hon Roll; NHS; LIM; Fshn Merch.

CASOLARE, STEPHANIE; Canastota HS; Canastota, NY; (Y); 35/140; Pres Church Yth Grp; Teachers Aide; Band; Drm Mjr(t); Mrchg Band; Pep Band; Var Cheerleading; Hon Roll; Mst Outstndg Music/Bnd 86; Hghst Bus Avg 86; SUNY Cobleskill; Erly Chld Dev.

CASON, CATHERINE; Sacred Heart Acad; Malverne, NY; (S); Debate Tm; FTA; Pep Clb; SADD; VP Sr Cls; Rep Stu Cncl; Tennis; Hon Roll; NHS.

CASONI, DAVA; Amherst Central HS; Amherst, NY; (Y); 67/290; AFS; Drama Clb; Model UN; Chorus; Yrbk Rptr; JV Cheerleading; Swmmng; Hon Roll; Ntl Merit Ltr; Church Yth Grp; Cornell Hotel Schl; Htl Admin.

CASPER, KAREN; Schalmont HS; Schenectady, NY; (Y); Acpl Chr; Band; Chorus; Concert Band; Mrchg Band; School Play; Symp Band; Bsktbl; Socr; Tennis; Hnrs Engl,Scl Stds, Bio.

CASPER, PATRICIA; Tully HS; Apulia Station, NY; (Y); Exploring; French Clb; Varsity Clb; Band; Stage Crew; JV Var Socr; Schl Awd Hghst Avrg-Bus Math & Non-Regents Bio 85; Military Intlgnc.

CASSA, JOANN; John Dewey HS; Brooklyn, NY; (Y); Dance Clb; Im Vllybl; Im Badmtn; Im Gym; Im Sftbl; Im Tennis; Im Trk; Im Wt Lftg; Jhn Dwys HS Intramrl Awd Vllybll 86; Csmtlgy.

CASSAGNOL, PHILIPPE; Union Dale HS; Hempstead, NY; (Y); Drama Clb; School Play; Variety Show; Swmmng.

CASSANI, MARGARET M; General Douglas Mac Arthur HS; Levittown, NY; (Y); 27/321; Pres AFS; Cmnty Wkr; Orch; Variety Show; Nwsp Rptr; Yrbk Stf; Socr; High Hon Roll; Jr NHS; NHS; Hnrbl Recgntn Partcptn Mock Trl Tournmnt 85; Dance.

CASSANO, CHRISTOPHER; Union Springs Acad; Poland, NY; (S); 3/20; Trs Jr Cls; Rep Stu Cncl; Var Bsktbl; Im Sftbl; Var Vllybl; NHS; Acad All-Amer 86; Columbia Union Coll; Bus.

CASSANO, JOHN; New Hyde Park Memorial HS; Garden City Park, NY; (Y); Orch; Trk; High Hon Roll; Jr NHS; Prfct Atten Awd; Stu Mo Sci & Indstrl Arts; Arch.

CASSARA, JOSEPHINE; St Francis Prep; Woodhaven, NY; (S); 23/747; Math Tm; NFL; Speech Tm; SADD; Chorus; Nwsp Rptr; Hon Roll; NHS; Catholic Forn Hon Men Oral Intrprtatn Lit 86; NYU; Acctnt.

CASSARO, JAN; Pelham Memorial HS; Pelham Manor, NY; (Y); Radio Clb; Capt L Socr; Pre-Law.

CASSATA, BARBARA; Bishop Kearney HS; Brooklyn, NY; (Y); Dance Clb; Pace U.

CASSELLA, CHRISTINE; Lake George HS; Glens Falls, NY; (Y); VP SADD; Varsity Clb; Sec Jr Cls; JV Var Bsktbl; JV Var Fld Hcky; Var Score Keeper; High Hon Roll; Hon Roll; Stu Mnth Chem 85-86; MVP Fld Hcky 84-85; Bst Sprtsmnshp Fld Hockey 83-84; Elem Educ.

CASSELLA, STEVE; Churchville Chili HS; Rochester, NY; (Y); 15/280; Computer Clb; French Clb; Math Clb; Math Tm; Ski Clb; JV Swmmng; JV Trk; Im Mgr Vllybl; Im Mgr Wt Lftg; High Hon Roll; Buffalo ST.

CASSELLI, KATHY; Newburgh Free Acad; Newburgh, NY; (Y); Art Clb; GAA; PAVAS; Nwsp Stf; Bowling; Timer; Trk; Cit Awd; Hon Roll; Opt Clb Awd; Bicent Awd 84; Bowlng Awd 85; Shuttl Hurtl Awd 86; Syracuse U; Advtsg Dsgn.

CASSELMAN, MATTHEW; Massena Centyral HS; Massena, NY; (Y); Varsity Clb; Ftbl; Ice Hcky; High Hon Roll; Hon Roll; Ntl Merit Ltr; AZ ST U.

CASSELMAN, MAUREEN; Nazareth Acad; Rochester, NY; (Y); 16/152; French Clb; Math Clb; NFL; Quiz Bowl; Nwsp Phtg; Rep Frsh Cls; VP Soph Cls; Hon Roll; JETS Awd; NHS; St John Fisher Coll Schlrshp; St John Fisher Coll; Pre-Med.

CASSERA, LISA; Linton HS; Schenectady, NY; (Y); 7/296; Sec Intnl Clb; Yrbk Stf; Stu Cncl; High Hon Roll; NHS; Ntl Merit Ltr; J Raymnd Quinn Awd 86; Rgnts Schlrshp 85-86; Spnsh Orl Cmprhnsn Awd 86; Coll Of St Rose; Scndry Educ.

CASSESE, JOHN; Commack HS South; Commack, NY; (Y); Math Tm; SADD; Nwsp Rptr; Yrbk Bus Mgr; Crs Cntry; JV Wrstlng; High Hon Roll; NHS; Ntl Sci Olympd 86; Med.

CASSICK, TERRY; Wilson Central HS; Ransomville, NY; (Y); Library Aide; Hon Roll; Niagara Cnty CC; Engl.

CASSIDY, COLLEEN; Elmira Free Acad; Elmira, NY; (Y); French Clb; Hosp Aide; Color Guard; Mrchg Band; Buffalo ST Coll; Crmnl Justc.

CASSIDY, PAUL; Bishop Maginn HS; Albany, NY; (S); Computer Clb; Latin Clb; Math Clb; High Hon Roll; NHS; Prfct Atten Awd; Latin Awd 83-84; Engrng.

CASSIDY, PAUL; Port Richmond HS; Staten Island, NY; (Y); Nwsp Stf; JV Bsbl; Var Bowling; JV Trk; Law.

CASSORT, MELISSA; Massena Central HS; Massena, NY; (Y); Church Yth Grp; GAA; Leo Clb; Varsity Clb; Church Choir; Bsktbl; VP Capt Sftbl; JV Vllybl; Lion Awd; Crmnl Jstc.

CASSUTO, KIM; Sachem North HS; Holbrook, NY; (Y); 760/1558; Drama Clb; Office Aide; SADD; Chorus; School Musical; School Play; Stage Crew; Drama Prod.

CASTAGNE, CLYDE; Nazareth Regional HS; Brooklyn, NY; (Y); Church Yth Grp; Im Bsktbl; Im Ftbl; NY U; Med.

CASTAGNINO, DINA; St John The Baptist D HS; Brightwaters, NY; (S); 7/546; Church Yth Grp; Hosp Aide; Math Clb; Service Clb; Nwsp Stf; Yrbk Stf; Lit Mag; Stat Bsbl; Jr NHS; NHS; Soc Distngushd Am HS Stu 85.

CASTALDO, LISA; Niskayuna HS; Schenectady, NY; (Y); Spanish Clb; Mrchg Band; Symp Band; VP Frsh Cls; VP Soph Cls; Capt JV Fld Hcky; Stat Lcrss; Hon Roll; Ntl Merit Ltr.

CASTALDO, MARIA; Preston HS; Bronx, NY; (S); 8/89; Drama Clb; School Musical; Trs Soph Cls; Sec Jr Cls; VP Sr Cls; Var Co-Capt Cheerleading; Hon Roll; Pres NHS; Outstndng Vlntr Awd 84; 1-4 HS Tutn Paid 83; Drama.

CASTAN, RENEE; Orchard Park HS; Orchard Park, NY; (Y); Jazz Band; Cmnty Wkr; German Clb; Mrchg Band; Orch; B Rtng NYSSMA Solo Comptn Violin 83; Erie Cnty CC; Dental Lab.

CASTANEDA, EDDIE; Cardinal Hayes HS; Bronx, NY; (Y); 32/258; Capt Var Socr; Hon Roll; Prfct Atten Awd; Diamond H Awd; Frnch Mdl Awd; Comp Sci.

CASTANZA, PAUL A; Frontier Central SR HS; Blasdell, NY; (Y); DECA; Radio Clb; Brdcstng.

CASTELLAN, RITZA; Clara Barton HS; Brooklyn, NY; (Y); 84/487; French Clb; School Musical; High Hon Roll; Hon Roll; Prfct Atten Awd; UFT Awd 83; Oswego U; Lab Tech.

CASTELLANO, GAETANO; Bishop Ford Central Catholic HS; Brooklyn, NY; (S); Debate Tm; Science Clb; Nwsp Sprt Ed; Pres Stu Cncl; Crs Cntry; Capt Socr; Hon Roll; NHS; Computer Clb; Rep Soph Cls; First Hnrs 84-85; Med.

CASTELLANO, JOHN; Curtis HS; New York, NY; (Y); Cmnty Wkr; Debate Tm; Science Clb; Concert Band; Drm Mjr(t); Jazz Band; Lit Mag; Pres Stu Cncl; NHS; Band; Bst Solo Dnc-Tlnt Shw 84 & 85; Rutgers U; Arch.

CASTELLANO, JOHN; John Dewey HS; Brooklyn, NY; (Y); Cmnty Wkr; Lib Service Clb; Concert Band; Yrbk Phtg; Acad Finance 84-86; Baruch Coll; Bus Lawyr.

CASTELLANO, KIM; New Rochelle HS; New Rochelle, NY; (Y); Boys Clb Am; Church Yth Grp; Model UN; Spanish Clb; SADD.

CASTELLANO, MICHAEL; Walt Whitman HS; Hunt Station, NY; (Y); 3/480; Key Clb; SADD; Chorus; Mgr(s); Capt Tennis; High Hon Roll; VP Jr NHS; Chrmn Stu Crt 86-87; Stu Gvt Advsry Brd SR Clss 86-87; Acad Awd Eng 84-85; Bus.

CASTELLANO, RONALD T; Christian Brother Acad; Liverpool, NY; (Y); 2/98; Cmnty Wkr; Ski Clb; JV Ftbl; High Hon Roll; NHS; Rgnts Schlrsp 86; Gnrl Excllnc 83-84; Next In Merit 85-86; Engr.

CASTELLI, MARIA ANGELA; St Francis Prep; Ozone Park, NY; (S); 31/747; Church Yth Grp; Dance Clb; SADD; School Play; Stage Crew; Rep Frsh Cls; Rep Soph Cls; Rep Jr Cls; High Hon Roll; NHS; Psychlgy.

CASTELLINI, JOANNE; Anthony A Henniger HS; Syracuse, NY; (Y); 8/400; Exploring; Intnl Clb; SADD; Yrbk Stf; Sec Sr Cls; JV Var Socr; High Hon Roll; Trs NHS; Schlrshp Gnrl Plski Unt No 1650 86; Wllsly Coll Clb Bk Awd 85; SUNY Geneseo; Comp Sci.

CASTELLINI, LYNN M; Solvay HS; Solvay, NY; (Y); VICA; School Musical; Off Soph Cls; High Hon Roll; Hon Roll; Prfct Atten Awd; Spn Awd Hghst Avg 84; Human Ecolgy Awd 83-84; Cosmtlgy Hnr Rl Awd 85-86.

CASTELLUZZO, DIANE; Plainedge HS; N Massapequa, NY; (Y); Chorus; Yrbk Bus Mgr; JV Sftbl; JV Trk; High Hon Roll; Bus Mngmnt.

CASTIGLIA, CATHERINE; Eden SR HS; Eden, NY; (Y); AFS; GAA; Orch; School Musical; School Play; Nwsp Stf; Rep Jr Cls; JV Bsktbl; Var Swmmng; Hon Roll; NYS Orchstra 85-86; All-Estrn Msc Fstvl 86; Grtr Buffalo Yth Orchstra 83-87.

CASTIGLIA, MARK E; A G Berner HS; Massapequa Park, NY; (Y); 108/416; 4-H; Wrstlng; Ntl Merit Ltr; Regnts Schlrshp 86; NYIT Acadmc Schlrshp 86; NY Inst Tech; Hotl-Restrnt Mgt.

CASTIGLIA, PATRICIA R; Hamburg SR HS; Hamburg, NY; (Y); 2/340; French Clb; High Hon Roll; Hon Roll; NHS; Ntl Merit Ltr; Rotary Awd; Sal; Pres Hnrs Schlrshp U At Buffalo 86; NY ST Rgnts Schlrshp 86; ST U Of NY; Phrmcy.

CASTIGLIA, WENDY; The Nichols Schl; West Falls, NY; (Y); AFS; Cmnty Wkr; Debate Tm; NFL; Ski Clb; Speech Tm; Teachers Aide; Nwsp Rptr; Yrbk Stf; JV L Mgr(s); Rgnts Schlrshp 86; Hnry Mntn Engl Ppr 85; 2nd Pl Nichols Sci Fair 84; Kenyon Coll; Psych.

CASTIGLIONE, DAVID; Jamestown HS; Jamestown, NY; (Y); 7/390; Trs Computer Clb; Capt Quiz Bowl; Band; Concert Band; Mrchg Band; High Hon Roll; Jr NHS; NHS; Rotary Awd; Louis Armstrong Jzz Awd 86; All-ST Wind Ensmbl 85-86; Rensselaer Polytech; Elec Engr.

CASTIGLIONE, RALPH; Sachem HS; Holbrook, NY; (Y); 224/1385; Chess Clb; Office Aide; Q&S; Im Badmtn; JV Bsbl; Im Bsktbl; JV Ftbl; Im Sftbl; Im Vllybl; Im Wt Lftg; Schlrshp Rnoke Coll 86; Awd Dfnsemn Of Yr Hckey 86; Awd MVP Hckey 86; Awd 2nd Yr Awd Otstndng Achvt 86; NY Inst Of Tech; Pre-Chrpractc.

CASTIGLIONE, STEVE L; Corning PP East HS; Corning, NY; (Y); Drama Clb; Exploring; School Musical; School Play; Stage Crew; Yrbk Bus Mgr; Yrbk Phtg; Yrbk Stf; Bsktbl; Mgr(s); Brwn Blt In Karate 86; Corning Comm Coll; Crmnl Jstc.

CASTILLO, DAMIAN; George Washington HS; New York, NY; (Y); 239/320; Drama Clb; Bsktbl; Medal 86; NY City Tech Coll; Elec Engr.

CASTILLO, LISETTE; Eli Whitney V HS; Brooklyn, NY; (Y); 3/212; JA; Sec VICA; Swmmng; High Hon Roll; Jr NHS; NHS; UFT Schlrshp 86; Awd In Ecmncs & Compu Literacy 86; Hunter Coll; Cmmnctns.

CASTILLO, NAIL; Walton HS; Bronx, NY; (Y); Church Yth Grp; Teachers Aide; Cit Awd; Hon Roll; Prfct Atten Awd; Lng Art Awd 83; Bus Adm.

CASTILLO, SANDRA; Nazareth Regional HS; Brooklyn, NY; (Y); Church Yth Grp; Pres Spanish Clb; Chorus; Stu Cncl; Hon Roll; NHS; Math Clb; Spansish Metal Highst Avg 85; Achvt Awd Forn Lang 87; Acctng.

CASTINE, SALLY; Northeastern Clinton HS; Champlain, NY; (Y); 56/153; Ski Clb; Girl Scts; Varsity Clb; Yrbk Bus Mgr; Yrbk Sprt Ed; Yrbk Stf; Bowling; Cheerleading; Crs Cntry; Schlrs For Dllrs 86; Mst Imprvd Engl Stu 86; Awds-Typng, Shrthnd & Flng 86; Clinton CC; Nrsng.

CASTLE, AMANDA; Sacred Heart Acad; Hempstead, NY; (Y); 11/182; Math Tm; Office Aide; Pep Clb; PAVAS; ROTC; Service Clb; SADD; Acpl Chr; Chorus; Church Choir; US Army ROTC Schlrshp, Manhattan Schl Mus Schlrshp 86; NYSSMA Mus Fest 83-86; Johns Hopkins U; Math.

CASTLE, MAUREEN; Catholic Central HS; Troy, NY; (Y); Art Clb; Aud/Vis; German Clb; Math Clb; Variety Show; Crs Cntry; Trk; Hon Roll; NHS; Cert Of Awd Excllnc In Soc Studies 86; Thtr.

CASTNER, KELLY; North Warren Central HS; Brant Lake, NY; (Y); 26/50; SADD; Band; Yrbk Stf; Stu Cncl; Bsktbl; Fld Hcky; Hon Roll; Most Imprvd Fld Hockey Plyr Trphy 83; Most Imprvd Bsktbl Plyr 84; Travel.

CASTO, LOU; Plainedge HS; Seaford, NY; (Y); JV Bsbl; JV Socr; High Hon Roll; Hon Roll; Earth Sci Awd 86; Phys Educ Awd 85; Bus Admin.

CASTOLDI, LORENA; Academy Of Mt St Ursula; Bronx, NY; (Y); Computer Clb.

CASTRANOVA, KELLY; Tottenville HS; Staten Isld, NY; (Y); Teachers Aide; Rep Jr Cls; High Hon Roll; Tobe Coburn; Fash Coord.

CASTRO, BENITO; Molloy HS; Rego Park, NY; (Y); Church Yth Grp; Spanish Clb; Bsktbl; Socr; Fordham; Comp Engr.

CASTRO, CHEA; Westbury SR HS; Westbury, NY; (Y); Art Clb; Drama Clb; French Clb; Library Aide; Spanish Clb; SADD; Chorus; School Musical; School Play; Stage Crew; Fashn Inst Tech; Fshn Illus.

CASTRO, FRANK; Richmond Hill HS; Richmond Hills, NY; (Y); 89/360; Library Aide; Teachers Aide; Hon Roll; Spanish NHS; Cert Of Merit Handbl 85-86; NY Inst Of Tech; Comp Tech.

CASTRO, JERELENE; Richmond Hill HS; Richmond Hill, NY; (Y); Dance Clb; Hosp Aide; Church Choir; Psychtry.

CASTRO, MARISA; Clara Barton HS; New York, NY; (Y); Cmnty Wkr; Computer Clb; Spanish Clb; Teachers Aide; Hon Roll; Pace U; Bus.

CASTRO, MARY-ANN R; Acad Of Saint Joseph; Kings Pk, NY; (Y); Church Yth Grp; Hosp Aide; Library Aide; Service Clb; Spanish Clb; Church Choir; Crs Cntry; NHS; Acad Achvt Schlrshp 85-86; JCL Cum Laude 85-86; Christian Courtesty 84; Med.

CASTRO, ROSANNA; Immaculata HS; New York, NY; (Y); 1/92; Drama Clb; Chorus; High Hon Roll.

CASTRONOVA, RICHARD; Bayshore HS; Bay Shore, NY; (Y); 87/425; Chess Clb; Science Clb; Spanish Clb; VICA; Band; Bsbl; Gym; Socr; High Hon Roll; Hon Roll; Chem.

CASTRONOVO, TONY; Whitesboro SR HS; Whitesboro, NY; (Y); 97/308; Varsity Clb; Pres Sr Cls; Im Coach Actv; JV Ftbl; Var Trk; Var Wrstlng; Hon Roll; Natl Soc Stud Olympd Awd 86; Rgnl Schlstc Art Awd 84; Rgnl Schlstc Art Awd 86; Morrisville Ag & Tech; Hortcltr.

CASUL, MARIA; S Shore HS; Brooklyn, NY; (Y); Chorus; Aviation.

CASVIKES, MARIA; Bronx HS Of Science; Bronx, NY; (Y); Church Yth Grp; Office Aide; Teachers Aide; Im Vllybl; JA; ARISTA 86; NY U; Bio Sci.

CASWELL, GEORGE; Heuvelton Central HS; Heuvelton, NY; (S); Boy Scts; Church Yth Grp; Sec Trs 4-H; Pres French Clb; Varsity Clb; Band; Mrchg Band; Var Socr; NHS; Engrng.

CASWELL III, PAUL D; Ravena-Coeymans-Selkirk Cntrl Schls; Coeymans Hollow, NY; (Y); Boy Scts; Cmnty Wkr; Band; Jazz Band; School Musical; Yrbk Stf; Rep Soph Cls; Rep Jr Cls; High Hon Roll; NHS; Pre-Med.

CAT, TIEN; East-Syracuse Minoa HS; Minoa, NY; (Y); Hosp Aide; Latin Clb; Science Clb; Tennis; High Hon Roll; Hon Roll; NHS; Ntl Hnr Soc 85; Hosp Aid 84; Sci Clb 84; Math & Sci.

CATALANO, MELISSA; Niskayuna HS; Schenectady, NY; (Y); French Clb; Pep Clb; Yrbk Stf; Rep Frsh Cls; Rep Soph Cls; Rep Jr Cls; Rep Stu Cncl; Diving; Mgr(s); Powder Puff Ftbl; Rhode Island.

CATALANO, THOMAS; Oneida HS; Oneida, NY; (S); Varsity Clb; Band; Concert Band; Drm & Bgl; Jazz Band; Mrchg Band; Var L Ftbl; Var L Trk; NHS; Hnrb Mntn All Star Ftbl 87; Engrng.

CATALDO, WILLIAM; Washingtonville HS; Chester, NY; (Y); Ski Clb; Crs Cntry; Trk; High Hon Roll; Hon Roll; NHS; NY St Regents Schlrshp 85-86; Rotarys Let Peace Wrtng Cntst 1st 85-86; ST U NY Binghamton.

CATALFAMO, DINA; Sacred Heart Acad; Floral Park, NY; (S); 3/200; Math Tm; Pep Clb; SADD; Yrbk Stf; High Hon Roll; NHS; Mt St Vincent; Sci.

CATALFAMO, JANINE; St Marys Girls HS; Bayside, NY; (Y); Ski Clb; Chorus; Stage Crew; St Johns; Bus Mgmt.

CATANESE, ELIZABETH; Union-Endicott HS; Endicott, NY; (Y); 11/436; Drama Clb; French Clb; Mathletes; Band; School Musical; Nwsp Ed-Chief; NHS; Church Yth Grp; Cmnty Wkr; Math Clb; Amer Lg Aux Awd 86; Canisius Coll Deans Scholar 86; Rotary Yth Ldrshp Awd 85; Canisius Coll; Mth Ed.

CATANI, MICHELLE; Mt St Mary Acad; Buffalo, NY; (Y); Office Aide; Teachers Aide; Church Choir; School Musical; School Play; Hon Roll; NEDT Awd; Rcvd A NYSSMA Sngng Cntst 85; Grgg Typng Awd 86; Jrnlsm.

CATANIA III, PETER M; Alexander Central HS; Darien Ctr, NY; (Y); 21/87; Letterman Clb; Varsity Clb; Rep Frsh Cls; Rep Soph Cls; Rep Jr Cls; Off Powder Puff Ftbl; Rep Stu Cncl; Var L Golf; Pres NHS; Stat Bsktbl; Pres Acad Fit Awd 86; Spirit Awd 86; Var Clb Scholar 86; U S FL; Financl Mgmt.

CATANZARO, DARA; Kenmore East HS; Buffalo, NY; (Y); Girl Scts; Color Guard; Mrchg Band; Var Pom Pon; Hon Roll.

CATANZARO, JOHN; Lancaster Central HS; Lancaster, NY; (S); 89/461; Church Yth Grp; Pres DECA; Letterman Clb; Pep Clb; Varsity Clb; Rep Stu Cncl; JV Bsktbl; L Ftbl; Hon Roll; Rotary Awd; Outstndng Stdnt 85; Bus Admn.

CATENA, ANN; Amsterdam HS; Amsterdam, NY; (Y); 37/310; Ski Clb; Varsity Clb; Band; Drm Mjr(t); Orch; Yrbk Stf; Sec Soph Cls; Rep Jr Cls; Pres Stu Cncl; Pom Pon; Cmmnctns.

CATENA, JOHN; Amsterdam HS; Amsterdam, NY; (Y); Letterman Clb; Varsity Clb; Rep Frsh Cls; Rep Soph Cls; Sec Sr Cls; Stu Cncl; JV Var Ftbl; Var Hst Trk; Wrstlng; Hon Roll; Acdmc All Am 86; Outstndng Athl Am 86; SUNY Oswego; Bus Sales.

CATER, BETH; Scotia Glenville SR HS; Scotia, NY; (Y); Key Clb; Varsity Clb; Mrchg Band; Frsh Cls; Soph Cls; Jr Cls; Stu Cncl; Gym; Score Keeper; Socr.

CATERINA, ANNIE; St John Villa Acad; Staten Is, NY; (Y); 1/103; Math Tm; Teachers Aide; Stage Crew; Nwsp Rptr; Nwsp Stf; Yrbk Stf; Pres Soph Cls; Pres Jr Cls; Pres Stu Cncl; Gov Hon Prg Awd; Stonehll Schlrshp 86-87; Stone Hill Coll; Engl.

CATHONE, MATTHEW; Pelham Memorial HS; Pelham, NY; (Y); JA; Nwsp Stf; Var Bsbl; JV Var Ftbl; Var Trk; Hon Roll; NHS; Spanish NHS.

CATLIN, GARY R; Averill Park HS; Averill Park, NY; (Y); 3/210; Am Leg Boys St; High Hon Roll; NHS; Gregg Typng Awd 86; 2nd Hghst Avg Scholar Mdl 85-86; Gregg Shorthnd Awd 86; Military Sci.

CATONE, DENA; Sachem North HS; Holbrook, NY; (Y); 186/1400; Church Yth Grp; Cmnty Wkr; DECA; Hosp Aide; Science Clb; Ski Clb; Spanish Clb; Nwsp Phtg; Nwsp Rptr; Nwsp Stf; Hnr Dstngshd Hlth Career Awd & Hnrs $250 86; Awd Of Merit For Peom 86; Awd Of Merit Lfgrd Of Yr 86; Stonybrook U; Phy Thrpy.

CATSADIMAS, MARIA; Midwood HS; Brooklyn, NY; (Y); 215/667; Church Yth Grp.

CATTICH, IRENE C; St Francis Prep; Astoria, NY; (S); 66/746; Library Aide; Band; Concert Band; Madrigals; Mrchg Band; Pep Band; Vllybl; Hon Roll; Med.

CAULIN, MICHELLE MARIE; St Marys Acad; South Glens Falls, NY; (S); Drama Clb; French Clb; Ski Clb; Chorus; School Play; Sec Frsh Cls; Var Cheerleading; Powder Puff Ftbl; JV Sftbl; Hon Roll.

CAVAGLIERE, NADIA M; Half Hollow Hills HS West; Farmingdale, NY; (Y); 10/392; Sec Key Clb; Spanish Clb; Teachers Aide; Yrbk Stf; High Hon Roll; Jr NHS; NHS; Spanish NHS; Untd Itln Amer Prgrss Awd; Itln Hnr Soc VP; Dickinson Coll; Frgn Lang.

CAVALIERI, JAMES; Canisius HS; Williamsville, NY; (Y); 3/161; Model UN; Ski Clb; JV Socr; High Hon Roll.

CAVALLARO, GRACE; Lehman HS; Bronx, NY; (Y); 22/560; Office Aide; Hon Roll; Arista Hnr Soc 86; Sci-Mdcl Tech.

CAVALLARO, KATHY A; Corning-Painted Post East HS; Corning, NY; (Y); 75/222; Cmnty Wkr; Computer Clb; Drama Clb; GAA; JA; Letterman Clb; Office Aide; ROTC; Ski Clb; Spanish Clb; MVP Track 86; ROTC Schrlshp 86; U Tampa; Bus Adm.

CAVALLO, THERESA; Mahopac HS; Putnam Valley, NY; (Y); 48/385; Cmnty Wkr; JA; Leo Clb; Church Yth Grp; Capt Cheerleading; Fld Hcky; High Hon Roll; Hon Roll; NHS; Pres Schlr; SUNY Binghamton; Nrsg.

CAVANAGH, MONICA; Midwood HS; Brooklyn, NY; (Y); 132/556; French Clb; Science Clb; Band; Cit Awd; Hon Roll; Frnch Awd 83; Regents Schlrshp 86; Sci Team Awd 83; NY U; Foreign Lang.

CAVANAUGH, MEGAN M; Niskayuna HS; Schenectady, NY; (Y); Am Leg Aux Girls St; German Clb; Latin Clb; Capt L Socr; Hon Roll; NHS; Sci.

CAVARGNA, JANICE; The Mary Louis Acad; Ozone Park, NY; (Y); Orch; High Hon Roll; Dancing-USTD-GOLD Medal Dance-Tap, Jazz & Ballet 79-86.

CAVE, CATHERINE; Pittsford Mendon HS; Pittsford, NY; (Y); Hosp Aide; Service Clb; Spanish Clb; Trs SADD; Mgr(s); Swmmng; Timer; High Hon Roll; NHS; Awd Of Hnrs 84.

CAVES, JENNY; North Rose-Wolcott HS; N Rose, NY; (Y); Trs Chorus; Church Choir; School Musical; Rep Frsh Cls; Rep Soph Cls; Trs Jr Cls; Trs Sr Cls; Trs Stu Cncl; Cit Awd; VP NHS; Red Cross Ldrshp Awd 85 & 86.

CAVIC, RADE; Richfield Springs Central Schl; Richfield Spgs, NY; (Y); 2/45; Am Leg Boys St; Speech Tm; VP Frsh Cls; Pres Soph Cls; Pres Jr Cls; Pres Stu Cncl; L Bsktbl; L Crs Cntry; L Trk; High Hon Roll; Auto Engr.

CAVOLI, NANCY; Scotia-Glenville HS; Scotia, NY; (Y); Sec JCL; Key Clb; Teachers Aide; Varsity Clb; Var Tennis; Var Trk; JV Vllybl; Hon Roll; NHS; U Of CA Santa Cruz; Law.

CAVOTTA, ANN; Mechanicville HS; Mechanicville, NY; (S); 2/95; Church Yth Grp; French Clb; Ski Clb; Nwsp Rptr; Ed Yrbk Stf; Sec Frsh Cls; VP Soph Cls; Var JV Cheerleading; Capt Crs Cntry; Jr NHS; Omega Hnr Socty 84-85; Alpha Hnr Socty 85-86; Jrnlsm.

CAVOTTA, MICHELE; Mechanicville HS; Mechanicville, NY; (S); 31/106; Church Yth Grp; Pep Clb; Spanish Clb; Rep Stu Cncl; JV Var Cheerleading; Var Trk; Prfct Atten Awd; Earth Sci Awd 83; Plattsburg ST U; Elem Educ.

CAWLEY, CHRISTINE; Kenmore East SR HS; Tonwanda, NY; (Y); Church Yth Grp; Cmnty Wkr; Yrbk Stf; French Hon Soc; Hon Roll; NHS; Brdcst Jrnlsm.

CAYEA, ALLEN; Northern Adirondack Central HS; Lyon Mt, NY; (Y); Am Leg Boys St; Cmnty Wkr; Variety Show; Var Mgr(s); JV Var Socr; Wt Lftg; VFW Awd; Voice Dem Awd; Crmnl Justc.

CAYEA, CHRISTINE; Geneva HS; Geneva, NY; (S); 36/175; Church Yth Grp; Yrbk Ed-Chief; Yrbk Rptr; Yrbk Stf; Rep Stu Cncl; Im Lcrss; JV Var Sftbl; High Hon Roll; Hon Roll; NHS; Cert Of Awd Spanish I, III & Art 82-84; Cortland ST; Bio Med Rsrch Tec.

CAYEA, HEATHER; Cornwall Central HS; Cornwall-On-Hudsn, NY; (Y); 10/216; Church Yth Grp; Pres Intnl Clb; Math Tm; PAVAS; Acpl Chr; High Hon Roll; NHS; Drama Clb; Teachers Aide; Chorus; NY ST Grand Prz Wnnr Frnch Lang 85; Acad All Am 86; Execplry Svc Vol 86; Vocal Perf.

CAZAURANG, CATHY; Earl L Vandermeulen HS; Mt Sinai, NY; (Y); French Clb; Chorus; Fld Hcky; Mgr(s); Score Keeper; High Hon Roll; Hon Roll.

CEACHERELLI, HOLLY; Union-Endicott HS; Endwell, NY; (Y); 2/430; Debate Tm; Pres Key Clb; Sec Concert Band; Sec Mrchg Band; L Trk; High Hon Roll; VP NHS; Sal; Key Club Outstndng Serv Awd 85; Lions Club Schlrshp 85; Jessie Baker Schlrshp 85; SUNY Binghamton; Hist.

CEBRON, LORI A; North Salem HS; Purdys, NY; (Y); 6/95; Var Bsktbl; Var Socr; Hon Roll; Pres NHS; NYS Rgnts Schlrshp 86; Most Lkly To Succeed 86; Franklin & Marshall Coll.

CECCHINI, RONALD D; Pine Bush HS; Madrid, NY; (Y); 3/300; Boy Scts; Computer Clb; 4-H; FFA; Math Tm; Yrbk Stf; Bausch & Lomb Sci Awd; NHS; Church Yth Grp; Var Wrstlng; NYS Chem Awd 85; Schl Awd Exclnc 85; Schlrshp Rensselr Polytech Inst 86; Rensselaer Polytech Inst; Comp.

CECERE, DOMINIC; Eastchester HS; Eastchester, NY; (Y); Varsity Clb; Band; Jazz Band; Pres Stu Cncl; JV Var Bsbl; JV Capt Ftbl; JV Var Wrstlng; Hon Roll; Jr NHS; NHS; Pre-Law.

CECERE, REGINA; Cardinal Spellman HS; Bronx, NY; (Y); Church Yth Grp; Cmnty Wkr; Computer Clb; Dance Clb; Math Tm; Pep Clb; Yrbk Stf; Lit Mag; Bowling; Hon Roll; Regents Scholar 86; Iona Coll Merit Awd 86; Pace U Merit Awd 86; Fordham U; Acctng.

CECH, TERRENCE M; Peru JR SR HS; Plattsburg Afb, NY; (Y); Boy Scts; Band; High Hon Roll; Hon Roll; Nuclr Engrng.

CECI, JULIANNE; Bishop Kearney HS; Brooklyn, NY; (Y); Key Clb; Ski Clb; Chorus; Church Choir; Yrbk Stf; Hon Roll; NHS; World Forum Sec 85-86.

CECIL, RICHARD A; South Jefferson Central HS; Adams Center, NY; (Y); 3/133; Art Clb; Church Yth Grp; Drama Clb; School Musical; School Play; Yrbk Stf; Stu Cncl; Ntl Merit SF; Hon Roll; Gold Keys Art Awds 82-86; Pratt Inst; Fine Arts.

CEDRONE, MICHELE; Westhill HS; Syracuse, NY; (Y); 36/126; Pres Art Clb; Drama Clb; French Clb; SADD; Yrbk Stf; Lit Mag; Trk; Mony Schlr Art Awds 84 & 86; Schl Of Visual Arts In Fredonia NY 85; Grphc Artst.

CEFOLA, CRAIG; Clarkstown South HS; New City, NY; (Y); Nwsp Phtg; Nwsp Rptr; Nwsp Stf; Yrbk Ed-Chief; Yrbk Phtg; Yrbk Rptr; Aud/Vis; Swmmng; Tennis; Schl Visual Arts; Film.

CEGLOWSKI, CAROL; Salem Central Schl; Rupert, VT; (Y); Church Yth Grp; 4-H; French Clb; GAA; SADD; Sec Lit Mag; Fld Hcky; Trk; High Hon Roll; NHS; Hnr Socty 86; Prom Ct Attndt 87; Peer Cnclg 86; Middlebury; Bio.

CELENTANO, KAREN; H Frank Carey HS; Garden City S, NY; (Y); 46/228; Sec Cmnty Wkr; Debate Tm; Thesps; Band; School Musical; School Play; Nwsp Stf; Rep Sr Cls; JV Cheerleading; H Frnk Cry Clss Of 76 Awd For Svc 86; Niagara U Prsdntl Schlrshp 86; Niagara U; Psychlgy.

CELENZA, STEPHANIE; The Ursuline Schl; New Rochelle, NY; (Y); Cmnty Wkr; Hon Roll; Jr NHS; Svc To The Jr Class 85-86; French 3h And 4h 84-86; Advanced Plcmnt Portfolio & Pntng Hnrs 86-87; Art.

CELESTE, GROSSO; Holy Names Acad; Athens, NY; (Y); Math Tm; NFL; Varsity Clb; Nwsp Stf; Trs Jr Cls; Var Cheerleading; Var Pom Pon; Var Sftbl; Acad All Amer; Pre-Med.

CELESTIN, CLAUDE; Uniondale HS; Uniondale, NY; (Y); Cmnty Wkr; FBLA; Key Clb; Mathletes; Quiz Bowl; SADD; Nwsp Stf; Yrbk Stf; Jr NHS; NHS; SUNY Stonybrook; Pre-Med.

CELKUPA, JORDAN S; Hunter College HS; Flushing, NY; (Y); Model UN; Yrbk Phtg; Capt Bowling; Mu Alp Tht; Ntl Merit SF; Awd Excell HS Untd Ntns Conf 85; 2nd Pl Ind PSAL Bowling Comp 85; Vrsty Bowling Team Lttr 84-85; Econ.

CELLA, CHRISTINA; Eldorado HS; Las Vegas, NV; (Y); 154/541; Key Clb; Ski Clb; Thesps; Chorus; Trs Stu Cncl; JV Bsktbl; Var Bowling; Var L Golf; JV Var Socr; Var L Socr; U Of TN Knoxville; Bdcstg.

CELUCH, DIANE M; Kingston HS; Lake Katrine, NY; (Y); 9/573; French Clb; Latin Clb; Pep Clb; Band; Concert Band; Mrchg Band; Yrbk Stf; French Hon Soc; High Hon Roll; Jr NHS; Rgnts Schlrshp 86; Ithaca Coll.

CENDANA, MARIANELLA; Notre Dame Acad; Staten Island, NY; (Y); Church Yth Grp; Computer Clb; Hosp Aide; Intnl Clb; Math Clb; Service Clb; Teachers Aide; Chorus; Yrbk Stf; JV Crs Cntry; Dedctn Awd Karate Tae Kwon Doe 83; Elec Engr.

CENTER, BONNIE JILL; Newfield HS; Selden, NY; (Y); DECA; Y-Teens; Hon Roll; Med.

CENTNER, TINA; Wayland Central Schl; Wayland, NY; (Y); Ski Clb; Chorus; Color Guard; Yrbk Ed-Chief; Yrbk Stf; JV Mgr(s); JV Score Keeper; JV Socr; JV Sftbl; JV Vllybl; Anim Tech.

CERABONE, KAREN; John H Glenn HS; Greenlawn, NY; (Y); Chorus; Concert Band; Jazz Band; Mrchg Band; Orch; French Hon Soc; Hon Roll; NHS; Church Yth Grp; Cmnty Wkr; Modern Music Mstrs Music Hnr Soc 84-86.

CERASUOLO, ANTHONY J; Patchogue-Medford HS; Patchogue, NY; (Y); 31/653; FBLA; Leo Clb; JV Var Ice Hcky; JV Capt Socr; Sftbl; VP French Hon Soc; Hon Roll; Jr NHS; NHS; St Schlr; Boston U; Elec Engnrng.

CERGOL, DENISE; Baldwin HS; Baldwin, NY; (Y); 30/476; SADD; Cheerleading; High Hon Roll; Trs NHS; Spanish NHS; Eclgy Clb 85-86; Sportsnite 82-86; Dickinson Coll; Math.

CERIELLO, MICHAEL; St Marys Boys HS; Glen Cove, NY; (Y); 74/178; Var Bsbl; Var Bowling; JV Trk; Hon Roll; St Johns U; Business.

CERILLI, ANNA R; St Catharine Acad; Bronx, NY; (Y); 22/225; Teachers Aide; Nwsp Rptr; Yrbk Stf; Hon Roll; NHS; Iona Lang Cont 1st Hnrs 86; Fordham U Italian Poetry Cont 2nd Prz 85; Schlrshp To Syracuse Univ 86; Syracuse U; Econ.

CERIO, PAT; Faith Heritage HS; Baldwinsville, NY; (Y); Church Yth Grp; Stage Crew; Yrbk Bus Mgr; Yrbk Phtg; Yrbk Stf; Bsktbl; Lcrss; Hon Roll; RIT; Comp Sci.

CERIO, SHELLY; Canastota HS; Canastota, NY; (S); 3/130; GAA; Leo Clb; Science Clb; Pres Stu Cncl; JV Bsktbl; JV Sftbl; Var Tennis; Jr NHS; NHS; Mst Imprvd Grls Vrsty-Tnns 83-84.

CERNIC, EILEEN; Sacred Heart Acad; N Bellmore, NY; (Y); Dance Clb; Drama Clb; French Clb; FTA; Hosp Aide; PAVAS; Yrbk Stf; Rep Stu Cncl; Hon Roll; NHS; Chld Psych.

CERONE, CELESTE; Marlboro HS; Marlboro, NY; (Y); Church Yth Grp; Girl Scts; SADD; Chorus; Color Guard; JV Var Sftbl; JV Trk; Csmtlgy.

CEROSALETTI, GLENN; Charlotte Valley Central HS; Oneonta, NY; (S); 1/30; Drama Clb; Varsity Clb; Band; Yrbk Bus Mgr; Pres Soph Cls; Pres Jr Cls; Var Bsbl; Stat Bsktbl; High Hon Roll; NHS; Comp Sci.

CEROSKY, ROBERT J; Whitesboro SR HS; Whitesboro, NY; (Y); 33/354; Church Yth Grp; Science Clb; Hon Roll; Rgnts Schlrshp 86; Mohawk Vly CC; Acctg.

CERQUEIRA, ROSA; Yonkers HS; Yonkers, NY; (Y); Cit Awd; Hon Roll; Cert Exclnc 84-85; Achvt Awds 84-85; FIT; Intr Dsgn.

CERRO, SAMUEL; W C Mepham HS; Bellmore, NY; (Y); Art Clb; Debate Tm; Sec Science Clb; Band; Concert Band; Symp Band; Yrbk Stf; Rep Soph Cls; Var Bowling; Var Socr; Bus.

CERRONE, DEBORAH; Johnstown HS; Johnstown, NY; (Y); 12/170; GAA; Sec Frsh Cls; Rep Soph Cls; Rep Jr Cls; Rep Sr Cls; Rep Stu Cncl; Gym; Gov Hon Prg Awd; High Hon Roll; Hon Roll; Coll Of William & Mary.

CERRONE, MIKE; Eden SR HS; Eden, NY; (Y); Aud/Vis; Varsity Clb; Rep Stu Cncl; Var Diving; Var Socr; JV Var Swmmng; Var Trk; Engrng.

CERWECK, FRANCINE; Bethlehem Central HS; Delmar, NY; (Y); Church Yth Grp; GAA; Ski Clb; SADD; Color Guard; Mrchg Band; Var Cheerleading; Lcrss; Stat Sftbl; Var Twrlr; Int Dsgn.

CESARE, ANTHONY; John Glenn HS; E Northport, NY; (Y); Cmnty Wkr; JV Var Bsbl; Hon Roll; Jr NHS; NHS.

CESLIK, NICOLE; St Francis Prep; Bayside, NY; (Y); 313/746; Band; Concert Band; Mrchg Band; Pep Band; Canisius; Frgn Lang.

CESTARO, THOMAS; Sachem HS; Holbrook, NY; (Y); 255/1400; Aud/Vis; Radio Clb; Hon Roll.

CESTERO, TRICIA; St Raymond Acad; Bronx, NY; (Y); 24/73; Computer Clb; Spanish Clb; Band; Mrchg Band; Yrbk Phtg; Pres Jr Cls; Rep Stu Cncl; Capt Pom Pon; 2nd Hnrs; Top 10 Outstndng Stu; ST U New Paltz; Jrnlsm.

CHA, ERICA; Midwood HS; Staten Island, NY; (Y); 15/667; French Clb; JA; Office Aide; Science Clb; Spanish Clb; Teachers Aide; Varsity Clb; Orch; Yrbk Stf; Lit Mag; Sci Awd; Capt Gtwy Vygrs 85; ARISTA Archn Soc; Cornell U; Med.

CHACONA, MICHELLE; Fairport HS; Fairport, NY; (Y); Cmnty Wkr; Ski Clb; Flag Corp; Mrchg Band; Symp Band; Stu Cncl; Hon Roll; U Of Dayton; Medical Technology.

CHACONA, VICKI; Fairport HS; Fairport, NY; (Y); Cmnty Wkr; Key Clb; Chorus; Stu Cncl; Stat Ftbl; Stat Score Keeper; Prfct Atten Awd; Nrsg.

CHACRA, MICHAEL J; Cortland JR SR HS; Cortland, NY; (Y); 15/246; Am Leg Boys St; Church Yth Grp; French Clb; Ski Clb; SADD; Variety Show; Stu Cncl; Var Socr; Var Tennis; Var Vllybl; Aeronautical Engrng.

CHADDERDON, LAUREEN H; Cairo-Durham JR SR HS; Acra, NY; (Y); 2/86; Dance Clb; Girl Scts; Red Cross Aide; School Play; High Hon Roll; Masonic Awd; Trs NHS; Rotary Awd; Sal; CC Awd; Grl Sct Gld Awd 86; NY ST Regnts Schlrshp 86; Vlntr Awds 80-86; Keuka Coll; Elem Ed.

CHADWICK, JENNIFER; Hamburg SR HS; Hamburg, NY; (Y); 4-H; Yrbk Stf; Rep Stu Cncl; Powder Puff Ftbl; Var Capt Vllybl; High Hon Roll; Hon Roll; Jr NHS; Phys Fitns Awd 84; Mst Frndlist 84; MVP ; Jv Vllybl 85; Pol Sci.

CHADWICK, KRISTINE; Mynderse Acad; Seneca Falls, NY; (S); 6/138; Sftbl; Tennis; High Hon Roll.

CHAFFEE, AMY; Hannibal Central HS; Sterling, NY; (S); 9/110; 4-H; Varsity Clb; Sec Frsh Cls; Trs Soph Cls; Trs Jr Cls; Trs Sr Cls; Rep Stu Cncl; Var Capt Bsktbl; Var L Socr; Var Capt Sftbl; Acctg Schlrshp 86; Babe Ruth Awd-Ldrshp In Athl 86; US Army Ntl Schlr/Athl Awd 86; Cazenovia Coll; Acctg.

CHAINANI, ANITA; Hicksville SR HS; Hicksville, NY; (Y); French Clb; Latin Clb; Office Aide; Orch; Nwsp Bus Mgr; Yrbk Ed-Chief; French Hon Soc; High Hon Roll; Jr NHS; NHS; French Poetry Awd 85; Soc Stds Achvt Awd 86.

CHAKRABORTY, RANEN K; Bishop Scully HS; Amsterdam, NY; (S); 2/60; French Clb; Latin Clb; Math Clb; Orch; High Hon Roll; Mu Alp Tht; NHS; Pre-Med.

CHALLICE, LINDA; Valley Stream Central HS; Malverne, NY; (Y); Sec AFS; Church Yth Grp; Computer Clb; Mathletes; Ski Clb; Chorus; Variety Show; Rep Jr Cls; Jr NHS; NHS; Psych.

CHALMERS JR, MARVIN; Walton HS; Bronx, NY; (Y); Computer Clb; Hygiene Merit Awd 86; Barauch Coll; Comp Sci.

CHALONER, JENNIFER; Coxsackie Athens Central HS; Coxsackie, NY; (Y); 20/94; German Clb; Pep Clb; Socr; High Hon Roll; Hon Roll; Eng.

CHALVIRE, ASTRID; Cathedral HS; Ny, NY; (Y); 148/272; Capt Intnl Clb; Spanish Clb; Teachers Aide; Sec Soph Cls; Lbry Aide 84-85; Odontlgst.

CHAMBERLAIN, DAVE; Gloversville HS; Gloversville, NY; (Y); SADD; Yrbk Stf; Var Bsktbl; Var Ftbl; Var Golf; High Hon Roll; NYS Rgnts Schlrshp 86; Siena Coll; Jrnlsm.

CHAMBERLAIN, JEFF; Perry Central HS; Silver Spgs, NY; (Y); 4-H; Varsity Clb; JV Var Bsbl; Var Coach Actv; JV Var Ftbl; 4-H Awd; Hon Roll; Acad Growth Awd Mth; Jrnlsm.

CHAMBERLAIN, LISA S; Richfield Spring Central Schl; Richfield Springs, NY; (Y); 5/58; Red Cross Aide; Band; Concert Band; Mrchg Band; Stat Bsbl; JV Capt Cheerleading; Capt Pom Pon; L Var Tennis; High Hon Roll; NHS; Red Crss Ldrshp Conf Schlrshp 85; Clark Fndtn Schlrshp 86; NYS Rgnts Schlrshp 86; Brockport ST; Bio.

CHAMBERLAIN, MARISSA; Horseheads HS; Elmira, NY; (Y); Yrbk Phtg; Yrbk Stf; Lit Mag; Hon Roll; Ntl Merit Ltr; Lbrl Arts.

CHAMBERLAIN, MICHELLE; Christopher Columbus Bronx; Bronx, NY; (S); Dance Clb; Drama Clb; Office Aide; Teachers Aide; Chorus; School Musical; School Play; Variety Show; Hon Roll; Acadmc All Am Schlr 86; Natl Eng Merit Awd 86; Nrsg.

CHAMBERLAIN, NATHAN W; Cardinal Mooney HS; Hilton, NY; (Y); 98/334; Concert Band; Crs Cntry; Trk; Hon Roll; Rgnts Schlrshp 86; RIT; Comp Engr.

CHAMBERLAIN, VICKY; Clayton A Bouton JR SR HS; Voorheesville, NY; (Y); Pres VP 4-H; Hosp Aide; Key Clb; Chorus; Church Choir; Yrbk Ed-Chief; Cit Awd; Dnfth Awd; High Hon Roll; NHS; NYSSMA Music Awd Lvl 5 Grade A 86; Grtst Contrib To Yrbk 86; 3rd Hghst Avg In Spnsh 85; Nazereth Coll; Bus Ed.

CHAMBERS, CHRIS S; Bronx H S Of Science; New York, NY; (Y); Church Yth Grp; Debate Tm; NFL; Ntl Merit Schol; Columbia; Diplmcy.

CHAMBERS, DAWN; Bainbridge Guilford HS; Bainbridge, NY; (Y); Church Yth Grp; Band; Chorus; Orch; Nwsp Stf; Yrbk Stf; Sr Cls; Bsktbl; Sftbl; Hon Roll; Phys Thrpy.

CHAMBERS, JOHN; Victor Central HS; Farmington, NY; (Y); 40/230; VP Model UN; SADD; Stage Crew; Yrbk Phtg; JV Ftbl; Capt Var Vllybl; High Hon Roll; Hon Roll; Quiz Bowl; Varsity Clb; NY ST Regents Schlrshp 86; All League Boys Vllybl Tm 86; Pres Acad Fitness Awd 86; Elmira Coll; Bus.

CHAMBERS, JONATHAN; Uniondale HS; Hempstead, NY; (Y); Boy Scts; Camera Clb; Var Lcrss; Var Swmmng; High Hon Roll; Hon Roll; Jr NHS; NHS; Achvt Awd 84; Schlrshp Adelphi U 85.

CHAMBERS, MARIE; Hamburg SR HS; Hamburg, NY; (Y); 12/350; Church Yth Grp; JCL; Latin Clb; SADD; Chorus; Color Guard; Madrigals; Orch; School Musical; Lit Mag; Pre Med.

CHAMBLESS, JEFFREY; Southside SR HS; Rockville Centre, NY; (Y); Aud/Vis; Church Yth Grp; Cmnty Wkr; SADD; Church Choir; Ftbl; Wt Lftg; Hon Roll; Canisius Coll; Bus Admin.

CHAMPAGNE, DEREK; Franklin Acad; Malone, NY; (Y); Letterman Clb; Nwsp Phtg; Nwsp Stf; Yrbk Phtg; Yrbk Stf; JV Ftbl; L Capt Swmmng; Trk; Franklin Acad Mst Valuable Swmmr 86; NAC All Nrthrn Swmmr 85-86.

CHAMPAGNE, TAMMY; Saranac Central HS; Cadyville, NY; (S); Concert Band; Arch Drftng.

CHAMPION, BILLY; Central Islip SR HS; Central Islip, NY; (Y); 32/392; Hon Roll; Ntl Merit Schol; Natl Sci.

CHAMPION, JENNIFER; Valley Central HS; Montgomery, NY; (Y); 14/350; VP Debate Tm; Mrchg Band; School Musical; Symp Band; Yrbk Stf; Rep Jr Cls; Var L Trk; Hon Roll; NHS; Spanish NHS; All Cnty Band 85; Bus.

CHAMPLIN, JAMES E; Auburn HS; Auburn, NY; (Y); Church Yth Grp; Letterman Clb; Ski Clb; Varsity Clb; Var Ice Hcky; JV Lcrss; Hon Roll; Church Schlrsph 86; Mst Imprvd Hcky Tm Awd; Ceyoga Cmnty Clg; Engnrng.

CHAMPNEY, MEGAN; Colton-Pierrepont HS; Colton, NY; (S); 3/29; Church Yth Grp; Drama Clb; French Clb; NFL; Quiz Bowl; Scholastic Bowl; Ski Clb; Speech Tm; Band; Concert Band.

CHAN, ANNY; Murry Bergtraum HS; New York, NY; (Y); Art Clb; Camera Clb; Hosp Aide; Intnl Clb; JA; Library Aide; Scholastic Bowl; Hon Roll; NHS; Prfct Atten Awd; Accntng.

CHAN, JOANNE; La Guardia HS Of Music & Art; Elmhurst, NY; (S); Camera Clb; Office Aide; Hon Roll; Art.

CHAN, NANCIE; H S Of Fashion Indust; New York, NY; (Y); 33/324; Aud/Vis; Drama Clb; Teachers Aide; Chorus; Hon Roll; Parsons; Fashion Desgn.

CHAN, PAMELA W; Stuyvesant HS; New York, NY; (Y); Church Yth Grp; Computer Clb; French Clb; Chorus; Church Choir; Yrbk Stf; Sec Frsh Cls; Bsktbl; Vllybl; French Hon Soc; Sentrs Awd Acad & Svc 83; NYU; Psychlgy.

CHAN, PAULA; Preston HS; Bronx, NY; (S); Camera Clb; Computer Clb; Library Aide; Pep Clb; Teachers Aide; Nwsp Rptr; Ed Nwsp Stf; Trk; High Hon Roll; NHS.

CHAN, SANDY; Canarsie HS; Brooklyn, NY; (Y); Chorus; Hon Roll; Ntl Merit Ltr.

CHAN, STEVEN; St Francis Prep; Flushing, NY; (S); 155/655; Crs Cntry; Trk; Wt Lftg; Hon Roll; Karate 83-86; Judo 85; Med.

CHAN, SUK-FAN; James Madison HS; Brooklyn, NY; (Y); 111/756; Chorus; Color Guard; School Play; Gym; Tennis; Hon Roll; Gold Hnr Rl 82; NY U; Accntng.

CHAN, VIRNA; Midwood HS; Brooklyn, NY; (Y); Pre-Dentstry.

CHAN, WILLIAM; Stuyvesant HS; Astoria Li, NY; (Y); Math Tm; Orch; Yrbk Stf; Var Tennis; Hon Roll; NY Regnts Schlrshp 86; NYU; Acctg.

CHANCER, ROBERT; Lakeland HS; Shrub Oak, NY; (Y); 35/385; Chess Clb; PAVAS; Orch; School Musical; Im Bsbl; Im Bsktbl; Var Capt Ftbl; Hon Roll; NHS; Pres Schlr; Natl HS Orchstra Awd 86; James A Thurber Schrlrshp 86; Westchester CC; Music.

CHANCEY, DENISE; Freeport HS; Freeport, NY; (Y); Camera Clb; DECA; Radio Clb; Band; Mrchg Band; Yrbk Stf; JV Var Badmtn; High Hon Roll; Hon Roll; NHS; U Of VA; Phrmclgst.

CHANDLER, CHRIS; Sweet Home SR HS; Amherst, NY; (Y); Chorus; School Musical; Symp Band; Frsh Cls; Off Soph Cls; Off Jr Cls; Capt Socr; High Hon Roll; Pres NHS; Prfct Atten Awd; Schlrshp Awd 84-86; Law.

CHANDLER, JIM; Alexander Central Schl; Darien, NY; (Y); Boy Scts; 4-H; Spanish Clb; Varsity Clb; Co-Capt Drill Tm; VP Jr Cls; Stu Cncl; Var JV Bsbl; Var Capt Ftbl; Eagle Sct 83; MVP-FTBL 85; Coaches Awd-Bsbl 85.

CHANDLER, ROSALIND; Mineola HS; Garden City Park, NY; (Y); Dance Clb; Service Clb; Mrchg Band; JV Bsktbl; Hon Roll; Law.

CHANG, ANNE; Flushing HS; Corona, NY; (Y); 74/392; Chess Clb; Church Yth Grp; Hon Roll; Prfct Atten Awd; AAA Poster Contest 1st Pl NY Metro Area 83; Baruch Coll; Bus.

CHANG, CAROL L; Nazareth Regional HS; Brooklyn, NY; (S); 26/267; Church Yth Grp; Cmnty Wkr; Drama Clb; Chorus; Church Choir; School Play; Stage Crew; Yrbk Stf; Var Bsktbl; Mgr(s); Psychlgy.

CHANG, CHRISTINE I; Vestal SR HS; Vestal, NY; (Y); 11/450; Cmnty Wkr; French Clb; Mathletes; Orch; Yrbk Ed-Chief; Ed Yrbk Stf; High Hon Roll; NHS; Prfct Atten Awd; Thomas J Watson Memorial Schlrsp Wnnr 86; Prof Violinist With BC POPS 86; Binghamton Yth Symphony Con; Stanford U; Comp Sci.

CHANG, CLAUDIA; Huntington HS; Huntington, NY; (Y); 52/383; AFS; Band; Chorus; School Musical; JV Bsktbl; Acpl Chr; Concert Band; Drm Mjr(t); Jazz Band; Mrchg Band; Fnlst NCTE Writing Comp 85; Photo Exhibit Hecksher Art Museum 84; Rgnts Schlrshp Wnnr 86; U MA Amherst; Eng-Frnch.

CHANG, DAVID TSUWEI; Williamsville HS North; Williamsville, NY; (Y); 1/301; Boy Scts; Chess Clb; French Clb; Co-Capt Math Tm; Quiz Bowl; Orch; Var L Tennis; Pres NHS; Pres Schlr; Val; Jostens Yth Ldrshp Awd 86; Natl Bsktbl Assn Scholar 86; Harvard Prize Bk Awd 85; Harvard U; Med Sci.

CHANG, JANICE M; Walter Panas HS; Peekskill, NY; (Y); 1/250; Orch; Variety Show; Nwsp Rptr; Lit Mag; Stu Cncl; Bausch & Lomb Sci Awd; NHS; Ntl Merit Schol; Val; 1st Pl Baldwin Keybd Comptn 82-83; NY All ST Orch 85; IBM Thomas J Watson Mem Schlrshp 86; Yale U; Sci.

CHANG, JERRY; Pt Joseph HS; Brooklyn, NY; (Y); Nwsp Stf; Lit Mag; Rep Stu Cncl; Hon Roll; Glee Clb; Hunter Coll.

CHANG, JULIE Y; Liverpool HS; Liverpool, NY; (Y); 33/816; Cmnty Wkr; Math Tm; Nwsp Stf; Var L Tennis; High Hon Roll; Jr NHS; NHS; Onondaga Comm Schlr 85; Math.

CHANG, LESLIE; John Jay HS; Goldens Bridge, NY; (Y); Cmnty Wkr; Pres Debate Tm; Pres Latin Clb; SADD; Nwsp Rptr; High Hon Roll; NCTE Awd; NHS; Ntl Merit Schol; Brown U Bk Awd; IBM Watson Schlrp; Engl.

CHANG, MING; Norman Thomas HS; New York, NY; (Y); 13/597; Camera Clb; Pres Computer Clb; DECA; FBLA; Math Clb; Office Aide; Teachers Aide; Yrbk Phtg; Yrbk Stf; Badmtn; 2nd Pl FBLA NY City Comptn 86; Acad All Amer 86; Schl Comp Awd 86; SUNY Binghampton; Comp Sci.

CHANG, SHELENE; Union-Endicott HS; Endicott, NY; (Y); Dance Clb; Sec Key Clb; Mathletes; Chorus; Nwsp Sprt Ed; Yrbk Stf; High Hon Roll; NHS; Prfrm In UNICEF Msc Rctl At Stnfrd U For Piano 84; Svrl Math Awds 83-86; Comp Sci.

CHANG, STEPHEN; Seward Park HS; New York, NY; (Y); Hon Roll; Prfct Atten Awd; Cert Of Merit-Meritorious Svc To Schl 86; NY U; Bnkg.

CHANG, WENDY; Canarsie HS; Brooklyn, NY; (Y); Church Yth Grp; Chorus; Hon Roll.

CHANG, WINSLOW; John Dewey HS; New York, NY; (Y); Chess Clb; Math Tm; Science Clb; Comp Sci.

CHANG, Y-LY; Jefferson JR SR HS; Rochester, NY; (S); Math Tm; Science Clb; Stage Crew; Variety Show; Cit Awd; High Hon Roll; Hon Roll; NHS; Prfct Atten Awd; PRISM 85-86; HS Acad Awds 85-86.

CHANG, Y-TING; Jefferson HS; Rochester, NY; (S); 3/85; Tennis; Vllybl; Bausch & Lomb Sci Awd; High Hon Roll; Hon Roll; NHS; Prfct Atten Awd; Math Acad Awd 85; RIT; Elect Engr.

CHANI, HARSHILA; Forest Hills HS; Forest Hills, NY; (Y); 70/900; Exploring; Hosp Aide; VP Intnl Clb; Ed Nwsp Stf; High Hon Roll; Hon Roll; NHS; Prfct Atten Awd; Boys Clb Am; Dance Clb; Natl Art Awd 83; Sci Fair Awd 82-85; Natl Cncl Jewish Wmn Essay Awd 86; NYU; Pre-Med.

CHANIN, DEBBIE; Jericho HS; Westbury, NY; (Y); 69/200; Dance Clb; Key Clb; Office Aide; Ski Clb; Varsity Clb; Drill Tm; Variety Show; Nwsp Stf; Rep Jr Cls; Rep Sr Cls; Achvt In The Prfrmng Arts 83; Suny Albany.

CHANNELL, TONYA; Murry Bergtraum HS; Brooklyn, NY; (Y); Dance Clb; Girl Scts; Teachers Aide; Prfct Atten Awd; Steno Awds 85; Typng Awd 83-86; Hnr Walker Awd From WAMD 85; Cazenovia Coll.

CHAO, ANGELA; Newtown HS; Ridgewood, NY; (Y); 30/781; Church Yth Grp; Math Tm; Church Choir; Hon Roll; NY U; Pre-Med.

CHAO, JEROME D; Sleepy Hollow HS; Scarborough, NY; (Y); 1/186; Math Tm; Pres Model UN; VP Science Clb; Orch; Yrbk Phtg; NCTE Awd; Pres NHS; Val; Pres Jr Cls; Var L Ice Hcky; Westinghouse Sci Talent Srch Semi-Fnlst 86; Intl Sci & Engrng Fair Fnlst 86; Harvard; Med.

CHAO, LINNA; Port Richmond HS; Staten Island, NY; (Y); 18/650; Hosp Aide; Library Aide; Math Tm; Office Aide; Variety Show; Cheerleading; French Hon Soc; Hon Roll; Societe Profssrs Francais Amerique-Frnch Cntst 85; Dntst.

CHAO, MELODY; St Pius V HS; Bronx, NY; (Y); Church Choir; Yrbk Stf; Pres Frsh Cls; Sec Jr Cls; Trs Sr Cls; Sftbl; Hon Roll; NHS; Prfct Atten Awd; Vlnteer Awd-Clrcl Aid; Hnrb Mntn-Relgn; 3rd Hnrs; St Thomas Aquns Coll; Comp Sci.

CHAO, ROBERTA A; The Stony Brook Prep Schl; Poughkeepsie, NY; (Y); 3/83; Art Clb; Hosp Aide; Intnl Clb; Leo Clb; Yrbk Stf; NHS; Ntl Merit SF; A P Bio Awd 86; Cum Laude Awd 86; IBM Regens Scholar 86; Sci.

CHAPIN, JILL; Perry Central HS; Perry, NY; (Y); 1/85; FTA; Chorus; Jazz Band; Yrbk Ed-Chief; Sec Stu Cncl; Pres NHS; Val; 4-H; Math Tm; Varsity Clb; Jostens Ldrshp Fndtn Schlrshp 86; Outstndng Amer Stu 86; Nazareth Coll Schlr Awd 86; Nazareth Coll Rochester; Music.

CHAPIN, MICHELLE; Heuvelton Central HS; Heuvelton, NY; (Y); FHA; GAA; Girl Scts; Latin Clb; Band; Chorus; Mrchg Band; Cheerleading; Socr; Sftbl; 2nd Pl Grl Scts Slvr Awd 84.

CHAPIN, REBECCA; New Berlin Central HS; New Berlin, NY; (Y); 5/53; French Clb; FFA; Office Aide; School Play; Yrbk Stf; Lit Mag; Hon Roll; Jr NHS; Lion Awd; Sec NHS; Mock Trial; Yockers; Cobleskill Ag & Tech; Bus Adm.

CHAPMAN, BEVERLY; T R Proctor HS; Utica, NY; (Y); 18/200; French Clb; Office Aide; Chorus; Nwsp Rptr; Hon Roll; NHS; Prctr Prnts Assoc Awd 86; Bryant & Stration Bus Inst; Trv.

CHAPMAN, BRENDA; Canastota JR SR HS; Canastota, NY; (Y); 4/160; Pres GAA; VP Intnl Clb; Var Bskbtl; Var Fld Hcky; Var Sftbl; High Hon Roll; Hon Roll; NHS; Rcvd $500 Schlrs Schlrshp 86; All Star Fldhcky & Bskbtl 86; SUNY-CORTLAND; Pltcl Sci.

CHAPMAN, GINA; Lansing HS; Lansing, NY; (Y); 6/85; Quiz Bowl; Band; Trs Jr Cls; Trs Sr Cls; Var Capt Bskbtl; Var L Sftbl; Trs Pres NHS; Spanish Clb; Orch; Yrbk Sprt Ed; Ctznshp Awd 84&86; Englsh Awd 85; Scl Stdies Awd 86; Cvl Engr.

CHAPMAN, JOHN; Hoosie Valley Central HS; Schaghticoke, NY; (Y); Spanish Clb; Bausch & Lomb Sci Awd; High Hon Roll; NHS; Comp Engrng.

CHAPMAN, KRISTINE M; Cardinal Mooney HS; Rochester, NY; (Y); 9/305; Exploring; Yrbk Stf; French Hon Soc; High Hon Roll; Rgnts Schlrshp 86; SUNY Oswego.

CHAPPELL, HOLLY; Newark SR HS; Newark, NY; (Y); 29/189; Church Yth Grp; Service Clb; Concert Band; Jazz Band; Nwsp Sprt Ed; Var L Sftbl; Var L Tennis; Var L Vllybl; French Hon Soc; NHS; MVP Vrsty Sftbl Tm 86; MIP Vrsty Sftbl Tm 85; Dely Yth Triennium Purdue U 86; Ed Adm.

CHAR, DANIEL; Clarkstown HS North; New City, NY; (Y); Math Clb; Math Tm; Spanish Clb; JV Lcrss; Mu Alp Tht; NHS.

CHARAK, ROBERTA; Uniondale HS; Uniondale, NY; (Y); Church Yth Grp; Office Aide; Pres Church Choir; Drm & Bgl; Yrbk Stf; JV Var Sftbl; High Hon Roll; Hon Roll; Jr NHS; NHS; Home Ec Achvt Awd 84; Ed.

CHARBONNEAU, LISA; G Ray Bodley HS; Fulton, NY; (Y); Pres Latin Clb; Mrchg Band; Rep Stu Cncl; Var JV Vllybl; High Hon Roll; Hon Roll; Prfct Atten Awd; Albany Coll; Phrmcst.

CHARD, KATHY; Fairport HS; Fairport, NY; (Y); Girl Scts; Ski Clb; Varsity Clb; Chorus; Yrbk Stf; Var Crs Cntry; Var Trk; High Hon Roll; Hon Roll; Prfct Atten Awd; Merit Cert In Frnch Two 84-85; All Leag Awd In Crss Cntry 85; All-Atar Crss Cntry Tm 85; Sprts Med.

CHARETTE, JACQUELINE R; East Syracuse Minoa HS; East Syracuse, NY; (Y); High Hon Roll; Hon Roll; Rgnts Schlrshp 86; OCC/ Lemoyne; Accntng.

CHARLAND, JOHN; Tupper Lake Central Schl; Tupper Lk, NY; (Y); 16/99; Church Yth Grp; SADD; Off Frsh Cls; Off Soph Cls; Off Jr Cls; Off Sr Cls; VP Stu Cncl; Var Capt Bsktbl; Var Capt Ftbl; Wt Lftg; Bio.

CHARLEMAGNE JR, JAMES M; James Monroe HS; Bronx, NY; (Y); Off JA; Math Clb; Orch; Nwsp Rptr; JV Bsbl; Var Bowling; Var Ftbl; Hon Roll; Sal; MVP Trophy Bowling 86, Ftbl 84; Culinary Inst Am; Chef.

CHARLEMONT, ALCENA; Edison Technical HS; Rochester, NY; (Y); High Hon Roll; Hon Roll; Engr.

CHARLES, CAROLENE; Uniondale HS; Uniondale, NY; (Y); Church Yth Grp; Cmnty Wkr; Dance Clb; Key Clb; Yrbk Stf; VP Frsh Cls; Pres Soph Cls; Trs Pom Pon; Hon Roll; Svc Awd 84; Psych.

CHARLES, JOSEPH; Sheepshead Bay HS; Brooklyn, NY; (Y); Cmnty Wkr; Intnl Clb; Service Clb; Teachers Aide; Bsbl; Socr; Law.

CHARLES, KEVIN; Elmira Free Acad; Elmira, NY; (Y); 23/248; Boy Scts; Church Yth Grp; Spanish Clb; Chorus; Church Choir; Stage Crew; Yrbk Stf; Swmmng; High Hon Roll; Pres Schlr; Egl Sct 86; Hnds Of Chrst Awd-Yth 86; Clarkson U; Elec Engr.

CHARLES, MADONNA N; Catherine Mc Auley HS; Brooklyn, NY; (Y); 15/70; Cmnty Wkr; Dance Clb; Hosp Aide; Nwsp Rptr; Var Cheerleading; NY ST Rgnts Schlrshp 86; Brklyn Coll; Med.

CHARLES, MICHELLE; Uniondale HS; Uniondale, NY; (Y); VP Sr Cls; Pom Pon; St Johns U; Law.

CHARLES, RICHARD E; Akron Central HS; Akron, NY; (Y); 2/140; Am Leg Boys St; Cmnty Wkr; Teachers Aide; Band; JV Bsktbl; JV Ftbl; JV Trk; Hon Roll; NHS; Math.

CHARRON, ANDREA; Bloomfield Central Schl; West Bloomfield, NY; (Y); 21/101; Cmnty Wkr; Concert Band; School Musical; Nwsp Stf; Yrbk Stf; Pres Frsh Cls; Pres Soph Cls; Pres Stu Cncl; Hon Roll; AFS; Gftd Stu Pgm, All Co & All St Vocal; Monroe CC; Bus Admin.

CHARTRAW, STEPHEN; Oakfield-Alabama HS; Oakfield, NY; (Y); 9/93; Boys Clb Am; Ski Clb; Bsktbl; Crs Cntry; Ftbl; Tennis; NYS Regents Scholar 85-86; PA ST U; Engrng.

CHARVAT, COLLEEN; Pembroke SR HS; Corfu, NY; (Y); German Clb; Varsity Clb; Color Guard; Variety Show; JV Var Cheerleading; JV Var Socr; JV Var Trk.

CHASE, CATHERINE; Spacenkill HS; Poughkeepsie, NY; (Y); SADD; Yrbk Stf; Co-Capt Sftbl; Vllybl; Regnts Schlrshp 85-86; Schlr Athlt Awd 86; Pres Schlr Athlt Awd 86; Dutchess CC.

CHASE, EDITH; Clara Barton HS; Brooklyn, NY; (Y); 300/487; Church Yth Grp; Hosp Aide; Teachers Aide; Church Choir; Yrbk Stf; Off Sr Cls; Exec Intrnshp Cert 86; Med Sci Cert 86; Adelphi U; Bio.

CHASE, ERICA L; Linton HS; Schenectady, NY; (Y); Acpl Chr; Sec Frsh Cls; Sec Soph Cls; Pres Jr Cls; Sec Stu Cncl; Hon Roll; NCTE Awd; Pres NHS; Pres Church Yth Grp; Drama Clb; Smth Coll Bk Awd 86; Ntl Rep Oprtn Frndshp Nw Englnd Reg 86; Bus.

CHASE, JENNIFER D; Liverpool HS; Liverpool, NY; (Y); 119/817; Rep Sr Cls; Rep Stu Cncl; Var Crs Cntry; Var Trk; High Hon Roll; Hon Roll; Jr NHS; NHS; Rgnts Schlrshp 86; Ithaca Coll.

CHASE, JOHN; Herkimer SR HS; Herkimer, NY; (Y); 52/120; Ski Clb; JV L Bsktbl; Var L Crs Cntry; Var L Trk; Navy; Nclr Engr.

CHASE, ROBIN; Potsdam Central HS; Potsdam, NY; (Y); French Clb; Ski Clb; Varsity Clb; Yrbk Stf; Cheerleading; Crs Cntry; NC ST; Psych.

CHASE, SHANA; Pine Valley Central Schl; South Dayton, NY; (S); 2/55; Drama Clb; Color Guard; Mgr(s); Stat Trk; Hon Roll; Jr NHS; Trs NHS; Med.

CHASE, SUSAN; Liverpool HS; Liverpool, NY; (Y); 16/800; Spanish Clb; Concert Band; School Musical; Symp Band; High Hon Roll; Hon Roll; Jr NHS; NHS; Med.

CHASE, SUSAN C; Gloversville HS; Gloversville, NY; (Y); 102/234; Church Yth Grp; French Clb; Intnl Clb; Spanish Clb; SADD; Yrbk Stf; Hon Roll; Dora Loudon Schlrshp 86-87; Mrn K Smth Bus Awd 86-87; Pell Grnt 86-87; Endicott Coll; Lgl Sectrl.

CHASIN, STEVEN B; The Fieldston Schl; Riverdale, NY; (Y); Aud/Vis; Cmnty Wkr; Computer Clb; Red Cross Aide; Temple Yth Grp; Orch; Coach Actv; Var L Mgr(s); Navl ROTC Schlrshp 86; NY ST Regnts Schlrshp 86; Natl Merit Cmmdtn 86; Northwestern U; Chem.

CHASSAGNE, LUDWIG; Uniondale HS; Uniondale, NY; (Y); Church Yth Grp; Math Clb; Math Tm; Teachers Aide; Varsity Clb; Im Bsktbl; Im Ftbl; Var L Trk; High Hon Roll; Hon Roll; Diocese Of Brooklyn Rgnl Math 83; Pre Med.

CHATEL, LARA L; Glens Falls HS; Glens Falls, NY; (Y); 10/217; Church Yth Grp; French Clb; Political Wkr; Nwsp Stf; Pres Frsh Cls; Stu Cncl; Stat Bsbl; JV Bsktbl; JV Fld Hcky; Powder Puff Ftbl; Regnts Schlrshp 86; St Lawrence U; Govt.

CHATFIELD, LAWRENCE; John Marshall HS; Rochester, NY; (Y); 2/165; Mathletes; Teachers Aide; Trs Jr Cls; JV Bsbl; Var Golf; Var Vllybl; High Hon Roll; Masonic Awd; NHS; Prfct Atten Awd; NY ST Rgnts Schlrshp 86; Gannett Schlrshp 86; Alfred U; Ceramic Engrng.

CHATLAND, CATHY; Franklin Acad; N Bangor, NY; (Y); Church Yth Grp; Cmnty Wkr; 4-H; PAVAS; Spanish Clb; SADD; Varsity Clb; Band; Concert Band; Jazz Band; Music Perfrmnce.

CHATLANI, RESHMA; Glen Cove HS; Glen Cove, NY; (Y); DECA; French Clb; Nwsp Stf; Hon Roll; NHS; Treas-Humn Relatn Clb 86-87; CPA.

CHATMAN, PAULETTE; Nazareth Acad; Rochester, NY; (Y); 41/119; Chorus; Bowling; Score Keeper; Sftbl; Hon Roll; Blck Schlr Awd 86; Buffalo ST Coll; Acctg.

CHATT, JILL; Batavia HS; Batavia, NY; (Y); 24/204; Hosp Aide; Ski Clb; SADD; Band; Concert Band; Mrchg Band; Co-Capt Var Swmmng; High Hon Roll; Hon Roll; Blue Cert 84; Brnz Cert 86.

CHATT, LORI; Oakfield-Alabama C S; Oakfield, NY; (Y); Art Clb; Drama Clb; French Clb; Pep Clb; Ski Clb; Chorus; Swing Chorus; Stu Cncl; Cheerleading; Score Keeper; Med Tech.

CHATTERTON, EILEEN; Hicksville SR HS; Hicksville, NY; (Y); Concert Band; JV Bsktbl; Merit Awd 81; 4-H Awd; Sprts Med.

CHATTERTON, JANINE K; St Jean Baptiste HS; Woodside, NY; (Y); 10/96; Office Aide; Teachers Aide; Nwsp Stf; Yrbk Stf; Trs Sr Cls; Hon Roll; Kiwanis Awd; Pres Phys Ftns Awd 85; Art Exhibit Donnell Library 86; Schl Rep UN 85-86; Hunter Coll; Elem Educ.

CHATTERTON, MICHELE; Cardinal Mooney HS; Rochester, NY; (Y); 110/309; Church Yth Grp; Cmnty Wkr; Dance Clb; Ski Clb; SADD; Rep Frsh Cls; Rep Soph Cls; Rep Jr Cls; VP Sr Cls; Bsbl; Miss Monroe Cnty Tngr 83; St John Fsher Coll; Mgmt.

CHATURVEDI, ANJALI; Homer Central HS; Cortland, NY; (Y); 3/206; VP Service Clb; Sec VP Stu Cncl; Var JV Bsktbl; Var Capt Tennis; DAR Awd; Elks Awd; Sec NHS; Sec Spanish Clb; Sec Varsity Clb; Girls ST Altrnt 85; Cornell Ntl Schlr 86; Regnts Schlrshp 86; Cornell U; Law Field.

CHAU, KING; Murry Bergtraum HS; New York, NY; (Y); Aud/Vis; Stage Crew; Bus Adm.

CHAU, WILLIAM; New Utrecht HS; Brooklyn, NY; (Y); 59/635; French Clb; Capt Math Tm; St Schlr; Natl Merit Roll Of AHSME 86; No 1 Top Screr In NYCIML Comp & H S AHSME 86; SUNY Buffalo; Elec Engrg.

CHAUHAN, ARCHANA; Monsignor Scanlam HS; Bronx, NY; (Y); 1/253; Nwsp Stf; Bausch & Lomb Sci Awd; High Hon Roll; Hon Roll; Sec NHS; Prfct Atten Awd; Pres Schlr; Sal; Schrlshp Berkeley Schls 86; Schlrshp Katherine Gibbs 86; Schlrshp Wood Schl 85; Berkeley Coll; Sec.

CHAUHAN, JENNIFER; Sacred Heart Acad; Malverne, NY; (S); 3/189; Drama Clb; Hosp Aide; Chorus; School Musical; Nwsp Rptr; Yrbk Stf; VP Jr Cls; High Hon Roll; NHS; Iona Lang Cont 2nd Hnrs Fr 85; Acad Scholar.

CHAUVIN, JO-ANN; Saranac Central HS; Saranac, NY; (S); 4/121; Cmnty Wkr; Concert Band; Jazz Band; Mrchg Band; Trk; High Hon Roll; NHS; Prfct Atten Awd; Bio.

CHAVEZ, HECTOR F; Cardinal Hayes HS; Bronx, NY; (Y); 5/258; Sec Church Yth Grp; Ed Yrbk Stf; JV Crs Cntry; JV Swmmng; High Hon Roll; NHS; Aud/Vis; Library Aide; Band; Stage Crew; Gnrl Excllnce Awd 84; Bio Awd Hist Awds 86; Bio Teach.

CHAWLA, SUNJIT; Archbishop Molloy HS; Flushing, NY; (Y); Cmnty Wkr; Computer Clb; VP French Clb; Hosp Aide; Math Clb; Pep Clb; Nwsp Stf; Yrbk Stf; Im Bsktbl; Harvard; Med.

CHAYKA, GINA; Corcoran HS; Syracuse, NY; (Y); French Clb; Latin Clb; Color Guard; Yrbk Stf; Gym; Socr; Hon Roll; NHS; Slvr Mdl & Cert For Natl Latin Exam 85-86; Clarkson; Bio.

CHEATHAM, DEBRA; Holy Trinity HS; Bethpage, NY; (S); 19/313; Math Clb; Yrbk Sprt Ed; Hon Roll; NHS; Cmmnctns.

CHEATHAM, DIANNE A; Manhattan Center For Science & Math; New York, NY; (Y); Pres Church Yth Grp; Ski Clb; SADD; Chorus; Pres Church Choir; School Musical; Yrbk Ed-Chief; Var Bowling; Hon Roll; Miss Black Teen NY Fnlst 85-86; Miss Amer Coed NY St Fnlst 86; Wilberforce U; Math.

CHECKETT, ED H; St Peters HS; Staten Island, NY; (Y); 3/165; Varsity Clb; Socr; Wt Lftg; High Hon Roll; Hon Roll; Trs NHS; Pres Schlr; St Schlr; Full Presdntl Schlrshp St Francis Coll, $3000 Presdntl Schlrshp Scranton U & Faneign Dickenson 86; Scranton U; Dentist.

CHEDZOY, BRET; Watkins Glen HS; Watkins Glen, NY; (S); 7/111; 4-H; Letterman Clb; Ski Clb; Varsity Clb; Var Crs Cntry; Var Ftbl; Wt Lftg; 4-H Awd; Hon Roll; Envrnmntl Engrng.

CHEEK, DANIELLE A; Hillcrest HS; Richmond Hill, NY; (Y); Exploring; 4-H; Hosp Aide; JA; Math Tm; Office Aide; Science Clb; Teachers Aide; Concert Band; Rep Jr Cls; MA Inst Tech; Biomed Engr.

CHEIFETZ, CRAIG; Clarkstown High School North; New City, NY; (Y); 35/500; SADD; Nwsp Rptr; Nwsp Stf; JV Crs Cntry; Var Trk; Jr NHS; Mu Alp Tht; NHS; Spclly Chsn Peer Hlpr 85-86; Marine Corps Physcl Ftns Awd 84-86.

CHEMAN, ERICKA; Eden SR HS; Hamburg, NY; (Y); 16/173; Chorus; Church Choir; Orch; School Musical; Hon Roll; AFS; Church Yth Grp; 4-H; SADD; Acpl Chr; NY ST Conf Mxd Chorus 85; ST U Coll Fredonia; Music Ed.

CHEN, BONNIE; Emma Willard Schl; Limerick, PA; (Y); Exploring; Stage Crew; Yrbk Stf; Ntl Merit Ltr; Cum Laude 86; Warton.

CHEN, DAVID; Arlington HS; Poughkeepsie, NY; (Y); 15/570; Debate Tm; Math Tm; Ed Yrbk Stf; High Hon Roll; Lion Awd; Ntl Merit Ltr; Table Tennis Champs 84; Spnsh Cnslt Gen Awd 85; Georgetown U; Bus.

CHEN, HUMPHREY D; Bronx High Schl Of Science; New York, NY; (Y); Camera Clb; Church Yth Grp; Computer Clb; Math Tm; NFL; Jr NHS; NHS; Ntl Merit Ltr; 1st Pl Affrmtv CFL Debate 84; Bus.

CHEN, JAMES; Mc Quaid Jesuit HS; Penfield, NY; (Y); 12/167; Church Yth Grp; Computer Clb; Debate Tm; Drama Clb; French Clb; Model UN; JV Trk; High Hon Roll; Jr NHS; Chem.

CHEN, JOSEPHINE L; Vestal Central SR HS; Binghamton, NY; (Y); 43/435; Drama Clb; French Clb; Mathletes; Ski Clb; Hon Roll; NHS; Rgnts Schlrshp Awd 86; Cert Merit Ntl Yuth Art, Schlstc Art Awd 83; NYS Schl Music Awd 83-85; Mc Gill U Montreal; Sci.

CHEN, KATHY; Union-Endicott HS; Endicott, NY; (Y); Sec Church Yth Grp; Hosp Aide; Key Clb; Band; Concert Band; Jazz Band; Mrchg Band; Hon Roll; NHS; Ntl Merit Ltr; Intl Rltns.

CHEN, LOUISA; Acad Of Mt St Ursula; Bronx, NY; (Y); Computer Clb; Drama Clb; French Clb; School Play; Nwsp Phtg; Nwsp Rptr; Stu Cncl; Vllybl; 1st Hon French Iona Lang Cont 85; 2dn In Genl Achvt 85; 1st Hon Iona Physic Cont 86; Harvard.

CHEN, MISS DARYL WYNNE; Garden City HS; Garden City, NY; (Y); 3/341; Am Leg Aux Girls St; Drama Clb; French Clb; Art Clb; Nwsp Stf; Yrbk Stf; Lit Mag; L Badmtn; High Hon Roll; Jr NHS; Harvard Bk Awd 86; Renssaeler Polytechnic Inst Mdl Math & Sci 86; Amer Lgn Amer Awd 86.

CHEN, PAULINA E; John Jay HS; Wappingers Falls, NY; (Y); 9/500; Math Clb; Nwsp Stf; Tennis; High Hon Roll; Ntl Merit Ltr; Columbia U Sci Hnrs Pgm 84-86flivingston Mod Cong Pres Of Bst Delegatln 85.

CHEN, T; Clarkstown HS North; New City, NY; (Y); Aud/Vis; Spanish Clb; Nwsp Phtg; Nwsp Rptr; Yrbk Phtg; Yrbk Rptr; Yrbk Stf; Lit Mag; High Hon Roll; Hon Roll; Marine Corp Phy Ftns Awd 83; U Of Chicago; Bus.

CHEN, TEDDY; La Salle Acad; Brooklyn, NY; (S); 19/207; Science Clb; Varsity Clb; Crs Cntry; Trk; High Hon Roll; Pres NHS; US Air Force Acad; Plt.

CHENAILLE, ELIZABETH; Lansingburgh HS; Troy, NY; (Y); VP Socr; Church Yth Grp; French Clb; Band; Chorus; Mrchg Band; High Hon Roll; Hon Roll; Jr NHS; NHS; Elec Educ.

CHENAILLE, JEANETTE; Massena Central HS; Massena, NY; (Y); Church Yth Grp; JV Var Bsktbl; JV Var Sftbl; High Hon Roll; Hon Roll; 2nd Tm All Northern Sftbl 85; Bst Def Plyr Bsktbl 85; Canton ATC; Nrsg.

CHENEY, CATHERINE A; The Chapin Schl; New York, NY; (Y); Cmnty Wkr; JCL; Latin Clb; Science Clb; Boys Clb Am; Teachers Aide; Chorus; Rep Soph Cls; Rep Civic Clb; Im Bsktbl; Magna Cum Laude-Natl Latin Exam 84; Distctn In Natl Sci Olympiad-Chem 85; Regents Schlrshp 86; Child Devlpmt.

CHENEY, CHRISTINE; Liverpool HS; Liverpool, NY; (Y); Girl Scts; Orch; School Musical; Ntl Merit Ltr; Prfct Atten Awd; 1st Woman Pres NY St AIASA 85-86; Local Chptr Pres-AIASA 85-86; Summer Fame Perf Arts 86; Music.

CHENG, CHRISTINE; Hicksville HS; Hicksville, NY; (Y); FBLA; Spanish Clb; Chorus; Yrbk Rptr; Yrbk Stf; Hon Roll; CW Post; Accntng.

CHENG, YA-FANG; Newtown HS; Jackson Hts, NY; (Y); 2/781; French Clb; Math Clb; Service Clb; Hon Roll; NHS; Prfct Atten Awd; Qns Coll Pres Awd Achvt 85 & 86; Daily News Princpls Pride Of The Yankees Awd 85 & 86.

CHEREW, GINA; Avon Central Schl; Avon, NY; (Y); 8/100; AFS; Church Yth Grp; Spanish Clb; SADD; School Play; Yrbk Stf; Swmmng; Tennis; High Hon Roll; Jr NHS; Regents Scholar 86; Alfred ST Coll Ed Fndtn Scholar 86; SUNY; Vet.

CHERIAN, SUSAN; Christ The King R HS; Ridgewood, NY; (Y); 30/462; Church Yth Grp; Hon Roll; Hunter; Pre-Med.

CHERNOSKY, WALT; Smithtown East HS; Smithtown, NY; (Y); Letterman Clb; Var L Ftbl; JV Lcrss; Var Wrstlng; Hon Roll; Avtn.

CHERNOWSKI, JOHN; Canisius HS; Orchard Park, NY; (S); 30/200; Boy Scts; Cmnty Wkr; German Clb; Model UN; Acpl Chr; JV Bsbl; Var Crs Cntry; Var Trk; High Hon Roll; NHS; Eagle Sct 86.

CHERRY, JAMES; Midlakes HS; Clifton Spgs, NY; (Y); 20/145; Boy Scts; French Clb; Hosp Aide; Letterman Clb; Varsity Clb; Yrbk Stf; Bsbl; Ftbl; Wt Lftg; High Hon Roll; Admn.

CHERRY, STEFAN; Bainbridge Guilford HS; Bainbridge, NY; (Y); 25/79; French Clb; Ski Clb; Concert Band; Jazz Band; Mrchg Band; Orch; Stu Cncl; Ice Hcky; Tennis; Trk; Acad Schlrshp 86-87; Ntl Frnch Awd 82-83; SUNY; Acctng.

CHERVAK, STEVEN G; Seton Catholic Central HS; Endicott, NY; (Y); Church Yth Grp; Key Clb; Golf; Wrstlng; Press Carrier Mth 85; Crmnl Jstc.

CHERVENAK, MARY C; Coarning-Painted Post East HS; Corning, NY; (Y); 5/222; Cmnty Wkr; Pres Girl Scts; Quiz Bowl; Chorus; Ed Yrbk Stf; JV L Vllybl; High Hon Roll; NHS; Ntl Merit SF; Voice Dem Awd; GS Awds 84; Pblshd Wrtngs, Hnrbl Mntn Ntl Hist Day 84; Hopwood Schlrshp 85; Biochem.

CHERY, SANDERSON; Prospect Heights HS; Brooklyn, NY; (S); #3 In Class; Debate Tm; French Clb; Math Clb; Office Aide; Scholastic Bowl; Cit Awd; French Hon Soc; High Hon Roll; NHS; NY ST Alt Gen Type Awd; Poly Tech Inst; Elect Engr.

CHESEBRO III, ROBERT ALAN; Central Islip HS; Central Islip, NY; (Y); 3/500; Boy Scts; Chess Clb; Math Clb; Math Tm; Teachers Aide; Orch; Stage Crew; Socr; High Hon Roll; Hon Roll; Bys Sct-Order Of The Arrw 85; Elec Engrng.

CHESHIRE, BONNIE; Riverhead HS; Calverton, NY; (Y); 28/194; Drama Clb; French Clb; Chorus; School Musical; Ed Yrbk Stf; Rep Stu Cncl; Im Wt Lftg; Suffolk Cnty Yth Achvt Awd 85; Asprng Twrds Exc Awd In Bio 84; Frnch Lng Awd 86; U GA; Lndscp Archtctr.

CHESNER, CONSTANCE; Portville JR SR HS; Olean, NY; (Y); 2/108; Concert Band; Var L Swmmng; JV Var Trk; JV Var Vllybl; High Hon Roll; Sec NHS; Ntl Merit Ltr; Prfct Atten Awd; Sal; Church Yth Grp; NY Regents Schlrshp 86; Natl Yth Salute 86; James A Comstock Mem Schlrshp 86; MT Union Coll; Sci.

CHEST, KESHA; De Witt Clinton HS; Bronx, NY; (Y); Red Cross Aide; High Hon Roll; NHS; Prfct Atten Awd; Philosophy.

CHETNEY, GWENN; Hannibal Central HS; Oswego, NY; (Y); Hosp Aide; Vllybl; High Hon Roll; Hon Roll; Bus.

CHEUNG, KAI C; Aviation HS; New York, NY; (S); 24/417; Computer Clb; Math Tm; Band; Cit Awd; Hon Roll; Prfct Atten Awd; UFT Schlrshp 86; Hnr Soc 85-86; Pegasos Soc 84-86; Polytechnic; Elec Engr.

CHEUNG, KAM-YIN; Seward Park HS; New York, NY; (Y); Math Tm; Elect Engr.

CHEUNG, KENT; Malverne HS; Lynbrook, NY; (Y); 8/128; Boy Scts; Chess Clb; Computer Clb; Exploring; Hosp Aide; Office Aide; Science Clb; Ski Clb; High Hon Roll; Hon Roll; Engl,Math Awd 83-85; Med.

CHEUNG, SING; Tottenville HS; Staten Isld, NY; (Y); CAP; Flag Corp; Mrchg Band; Symp Band; Pres Frsh Cls; Trs Sr Cls; Dr.

CHEVALIER, BRENDA; Wells Central HS; Speculator, NY; (S); 5/35; Drama Clb; French Clb; Library Aide; Teachers Aide; Band; Chorus; School Musical; School Play; Yrbk Ed-Chief; Pres Frsh Cls; Potsdam; Psychlgy.

CHEW, KIMBERLY; Newtown HS; Elmhurst, NY; (Y); 52/700; Camera Clb; Computer Clb; JA; Nwsp Rptr; Yrbk Stf; Lit Mag; Cit Awd; Hon Roll; SUNY Stony Brook; Med.

CHEYETTE, DAN; Manhasset HS; Manhasset, NY; (Y); VP Cmnty Wkr; Drama Clb; VP Spanish Clb; Pres SADD; Thesps; Chorus; Var Crs Cntry; Var Trk; NHS; Ntl Merit SF; Part Bst Ensmbl Scene Theatricon 85; Engrng.

CHHABRA, ANITA W; Bronx High Schl Of Science; Holliswood, NY; (Y); Cmnty Wkr; Hosp Aide; Library Aide; Political Wkr; Teachers Aide; Variety Show; Rep Stu Cncl; JV Tennis; Cert Of Recog-Clsscl Indn Danc 83; Clsscl Indn Danc Cont 1st Pl 83; NYS Rgnts Schlrshp 86; Barnard Coll; Pre-Med.

CHI, MARGARET C; Scarsdale HS; Scarsdale, NY; (Y); Ed French Clb; Hosp Aide; Library Aide; Math Tm; Hon Roll; NY ST Regents Schlrshp 86.

CHIAFOLO, CHRISTINA; Hauppauge HS; Hauppauge, NY; (Y); Cmnty Wkr; Hosp Aide; High Hon Roll; NHS; Ntl Merit Ltr; Compltn Marine Bio Boces II Summr Inst 84; Sci Intrnshp SUNY Stonybrook 85; Pre-Med.

CHIANESE, ELIZABETH; Mamoroneck HS; Larchmont, NY; (Y); Church Yth Grp; Dance Clb; Drama Clb; Service Clb; School Musical; School Play; Variety Show; Var Fld Hcky; Hon Roll; Spanish NHS; Perfrmng Arts Curriculem Awd 83; Drama.

CHIANESE, JOANNE M; W Tresper Clarke HS; Westbury, NY; (Y); 29/193; Ed Science Clb; Nwsp Stf; Ed Lit Mag; Var L Bowling; Cit Awd; High Hon Roll; St Schlr; Model UN; Speech Tm; Color Guard; NYS Rgnts Schlrshp 86; Ithaca Coll Schlrshp 86; Ithaca Coll; Cmmnctns.

CHIANG, GRACE; Wheatley Schl; Roslyn Hts, NY; (Y); Hosp Aide; Rep Frsh Cls; Stu Cncl; Math Fair-Brnz Mdl 86; Latin Awd-Gld Mtl 85; Med.

CHIANG, YU-JU; Oyster Bay HS; E Norwich, NY; (Y); Rep Intnl Clb; Rep Chorus; Hon Roll; SUNY Stony Brook; Comp Sci.

CHIANTA, MELISSA; Unatego JRSR HS; Otego, NY; (Y); 2/100; Drama Clb; Church Choir; School Musical; School Play; Capt Trk; High Hon Roll; NHS; French Clb; Mst Enthstc Ldr Rtry Yth Ldrshp Awds Cnfrnc 86; Intl Frgn Lang Awds Frnch 85&86; Mst Imprvd Vrsty Trck; Colgate U; Mnstr.

CHIAPPETTA, DORIS; Blind Brooks HS; Rye Brook, NY; (Y); Cmnty Wkr; Hosp Aide; NFL; Speech Tm; Chorus; Nwsp Rptr; Lit Mag; Cheerleading; Hon Roll; Volnntr/Nrs Aide Awd 84-86; Chrldng & Vcl Grp Awd 83; SUNY; Orthpdc Surg.

CHIAPUSO, MICHELLE; Olean HS; Olean, NY; (Y); 47/200; Spanish Clb; Chorus; Hon Roll; Htl/Rest Mgmt.

CHIARA, JILL; Geneseo Central HS; Genesco, NY; (Y); Church Yth Grp; Cmnty Wkr; French Clb; JA; Pep Clb; Science Clb; Ski Clb; SADD; Varsity Clb; Ltr; Mgr; Running Awds 85; Boston Coll; Bus.

CHIARAMONTE, ANDREA C; Islip HS; Islip, NY; (Y); 11/246; Am Leg Aux Girls St; Acpl Chr; Orch; School Musical; Nwsp Ed-Chief; Sec Stu Cncl; Var Tennis; Var Capt Trk; Jr NHS; NHS; NYS Regents Schlrshp 85-86; U Miami; Psych.

CHIARENZA, CARA-ANTONIA M; Our Lady Of Mercy HS; Henriatta, NY; (Y); 14/165; Chorus; Lit Mag; Hon Roll; NHS; Ntl Merit SF; Paidei Awd Outstndg Achvt Humnities; Artist Of Mnth; Co-Pres JR Wrttrs & Bks; Oberlin; Sculp.

CHIARILLI, CARL; Eden Central SR HS; Eden, NY; (Y); 45/175; Band; Concert Band; Jazz Band; Orch; Pep Band; School Musical; Symp Band; Nwsp Ed-Chief; Yrbk Stf; Mgr(s); 1st Prz-Poetry-Eden Up To Date Clb Crtv Wrtng Cntst 86; Genesco; Crtv Wrtng.

CHIAVAROLI, JEFFREY; Mc Kinley HS; Kenmore, NY; (Y); 7/285; Boy Scts; Church Yth Grp; Cmnty Wkr; Debate Tm; JA; Library Aide; Math Clb; Office Aide; Red Cross Aide; SADD; Jennss Co Schlrshp 86; Tutrl Skls Awd 86; Wrk Study Effrts 85-86; U Of Buffalo-NY; Biochmstry.

CHIAVETTA, KRISTIAN; Hamburg Central HS; Hamburg, NY; (Y); 24/383; Hosp Aide; Varsity Clb; Band; Ed Yrbk Ed-Chief; Yrbk Sprt Ed; Rep Stu Cncl; Trk; Vllybl; Hon Roll; NHS; Phrmcy.

CHICARELLI, CHRISTINE; Centereach HS; Selden, NY; (Y); FTA; Hosp Aide; Spanish Clb; Band; Concert Band; Drill Tm; Yrbk Stf; Prfct Atten Awd; Prtcptd Gifted/Tlntd Music Prg 84-86; Sci.

CHICO, ANGEL; Bushwick HS; Brooklyn, NY; (S); Boy Scts; DECA; Model UN; Chorus; School Musical; School Play; Stu Cncl; Hon Roll; Jr NHS; Natl Mdlng & Actng Awd 84; Mth Hnr Rl 84; DECA 2nd Prize Awd Whlsle Sellng 86; Bus Adm.

CHIDO, LINDA; Cheektowaga Central HS; Cheektowaga, NY; (Y); 32/199; Yrbk Bus Mgr; Yrbk Ed-Chief; Yrbk Phtg; Rep Stu Cncl; JV Bsktbl; Var L Fld Hcky; Var L Trk; JV Vllybl; Hon Roll; Amuetts Buddy Knaus Art Awd 86; Erie CC; Arch Tech.

CHIELLO, CHRISTINE; The Mary Louis Acad; Ridgewood, NY; (Y); 2/270; Teachers Aide; School Play; High Hon Roll; VP NHS; Ntl Merit Ltr; NEDT Awd; Sal; Queens Coll Pres Achvt Awd 83 & 85; Iona Coll Lang Comptn Italn 1st & 2nd Hnrs 84 & 85; Itln Blb 84-85; Siena Coll; Pre-Med.

CHIEN, ALAN; Liverpool HS; Liverpool, NY; (Y); Trs Computer Clb; VP JA; School Musical; Rep Stu Cncl; Im Badmtn; Var Tennis; High Hon Roll; Jr NHS; NHS; Spanish NHS; Micro Tech Awd 85; Math 12 Awd 86; Comp Sci Awd 86; Elec Engrng.

CHILDS, CHRISTIAN J; Binghamton HS; Binghamton, NY; (Y); 10/450; Am Leg Boys St; Hosp Aide; Pres Key Clb; Ski Clb; Varsity Clb; Rep Stu Cncl; JV Var Bsbl; JV Var Golf; High Hon Roll; NHS; Natl Sci Olympd Awd Excllnc 86; Natl Orgnztn Yth Ldrshp 86; Mck Trial Cert Achvt NY Bar Assoc; West Point.

CHILDS, CRYSTAL; Mt Vernon HS; Mount Vernon, NY; (Y); 53/550; Computer Clb; Dance Clb; Sec Drama Clb; Key Clb; Office Aide; Spanish Clb; Mrchg Band; Yrbk Stf; High Hon Roll; Hon Roll; Alpha Kappa Alpha Schrlshp 86; Physcl Ftns Awd 85; Math Hnrs Awds 82-86; ST U NY; Comp Sci.

CHILDS, LORI; Heuvelton Central HS; Heuvelton, NY; (Y); 11/40; Pres French Clb; GAA; Yrbk Stf; Var Sftbl; Lion Awd; Prfct Atten Awd; Canton ATC; Bus Mgmt.

CHILLE, RALPH A; Niagara Falls HS; Niagara Falls, NY; (S); 13/250; Computer Clb; Pres Key Clb; Concert Band; Jazz Band; Var Bsbl; Var Bowling; Var Golf; High Hon Roll; Jr NHS; NHS; Amer Lgn Awd 82-83; Achvt Cert Ntl Histry Day 84-85; Buffalo U; Comp Sci.

CHIM, AMY-YUKLING; Richmond Hill HS; Richmond Hill, NY; (Y); 43/288; Library Aide; Office Aide; Spanish Clb; Teachers Aide; Chorus; High Hon Roll; Hon Roll; Spanish NHS; Pace U; Cmptr Sci.

CHIMENTO, CARA; Albertus Magnus HS; Pomona, NY; (Y); 8/189; Camera Clb; Drama Clb; Hosp Aide; School Musical; Stage Crew; Yrbk Phtg; Yrbk Rptr; Yrbk Stf; High Hon Roll; Hon Roll; Rgnts Nrsng Schlrshp; ST U Of NY-ALBANY; Bio.

CHIMERA, CHARLES; Canisius HS; Clarence, NY; (S); 1/150; Computer Clb; Latin Clb; Yrbk Rptr; Rep Jr Cls; Rep Sr Cls; Var Socr; Var Trk; Hon Roll; NHS; Ntl Merit Ltr; HS Scholar 83-84; Bst Defense JV Soccr 84; Mst Imprvd Var Soccr 85; Georgetown U; Pre-Med.

CHIMIENTI, WILL; Smithtown High School East; Saint James, NY; (Y); Radio Clb; Drill Tm; Bsbl; Ftbl; Ice Hcky; Lcrss; Sftbl; Wrstlng; Culinary Inst Of Amer; Culinary.

CHIMILESKI, ROBERT W; Notre Dame HS; Binghamton, NY; (Y); JV Bsktbl; JV Var Ftbl; Var Trk; High Hon Roll; NY Rgnts Schlrshp 86; Tier Ftbll 1st Tm Ftbll Div 3 85; Tain Tiers Bst Ftbll Sec IV Wntr Trck 85-86; Buffalo U; Engrng.

CHIN, BRYAN; Archbishop Molloy HS; Sunnyside, NY; (Y); 11/401; Cmnty Wkr; Computer Clb; Yrbk Stf; Im Bsktbl; Im Ftbl; Im Sftbl; High Hon Roll; NHS; NYS Rgnts Schlrshp 86; Boston U; Pre-Law.

CHIN, CAROLINE; Franklin D Roosevelt HS; Brooklyn, NY; (Y); Art Clb; Computer Clb; FBLA; Math Clb; Math Tm; Band; Bsktbl; Tennis; Vllybl; Hon Roll; Art Awd 84; Hnrs-Math Awd 86; Sci Prjct Awd 84; NY U; Bus.

CHIN, CEDRIC; Bishop Loughlin Memorial HS; Brooklyn, NY; (Y); 43/233; Chess Clb; Nwsp Rptr; Hon Roll; NYS Regents Diploma/Scholar 86-87; LIU/C W Post Acad Prfrmnce Awd 86; Bishop Loughlin Chess Champ 86; Fordham Coll; TV Brdcst.

CHIN, JAY; Westbury HS; Old Westbury, NY; (Y); Chess Clb; VP Computer Clb; Radio Clb; JV Bowling; High Hon Roll; Var NHS; Merit Achvt Awd 86; Comp Pgmmg.

CHIN, JIM; New Rochelle HS; New Rochelle, NY; (Y); Chess Clb; JV Ftbl; Im Sftbl; Engr.

CHIN, JULIE; HS Of Art And Dsgn; Corona, NY; (Y); Art Clb; FTA; Intnl Clb; Office Aide; Teachers Aide; Variety Show; Yrbk Phtg; Hon Roll; NHS; Art Hnr Soc 86; Parsons Coll; Comm Art.

CHIN, JUNG Y; Aviation HS; Jackson Hts, NY; (S); 23/413; Drama Clb; JA; Library Aide; Math Clb; Model UN; Hon Roll; Silvr Wings; Hnr Soc; Pegasus Clb; Avitn Maintnc Mgmt.

CHIN, MAYLANA; Stuyvesant HS; Queens, NY; (Y); Science Clb; Nwsp Stf; Yrbk Stf.

CHIN, STEPHANIE K; Kings Park HS; Kings Park, NY; (Y); 24/382; Computer Clb; DECA; NHS; Yrbk Phtg; Lit Mag; Capt Var Tennis; Capt Var Vllybl; High Hon Roll; NHS; Natl Yth Coord For Asian Pacific Amer Heritage Wk 83-86; Ten-MVP & John J Flynn Awd; Gold Key Awd; Binghamton; Bus Mgmt.

CHIN, STEVEN; Hillcrest HS; Briarwood, NY; (Y); 229/801; Art Clb; Police Ofcr.

CHIN, STEVEN; Norman Thomas HS; New York, NY; (S); 33/695; Aud/Vis; Computer Clb; FBLA; JA; Math Clb; Math Tm; Yrbk Phtg; Rep Jr Cls; Cit Awd; Hon Roll; Syracuse U; Elctrcl Engrng.

CHIOCCHIO, LUCIA; Our Lady Of Victory Acad; Scarsdale, NY; (S); 2/157; Church Yth Grp; Cmnty Wkr; Spanish Clb; SADD; High Hon Roll; Hon Roll; NHS; Ntl Merit Ltr; Spanish NHS; Our Lady Of Victory Schlrshp; Cartias Awd; Engl Awd.

CHIRELLO, SUSAN; Bishop Cunningham HS; Mexico, NY; (Y); 8/31; French Clb; Trs Frsh Cls; Sec Soph Cls; Rep Jr Cls; Var Socr; Var Capt Sftbl; Var Vllybl; Hon Roll; Bst Ofnse Vllybl 85-86; OHSL South All Leag Awd Vllybl 85-86; Enstnt Effrt Engl Awd 85-86.

CHIRIANI, CHERYL; Albertus Magnus HS; New City, NY; (Y); 16/185; Drama Clb; Service Clb; School Play; Yrbk Ed-Chief; Yrbk Stf; French Hon Soc; Hon Roll; NHS; Accntng.

CHIRUMAMILLA, SREE; Oneida HS; Oneida, NY; (S); VP Debate Tm; Intnl Clb; Varsity Clb; Rep Stu Cncl; Var L Tennis; Var Trk; High Hon Roll; Spanish Clb; Yrbk Stf; Natl Guild Audtns 84; Am Legn Oratrcl Cntst 85; Natl Guild Audtns 85; Law.

CHISOLM, BERNADETTE; De Witt Clinton HS; Bronx, NY; (Y); Church Yth Grp; Church Choir; Color Guard; Howard U; Comp.

CHISOLM, DERRICK; Laguardia HS Of Music & Art; New York, NY; (S); Boys Clb Am; Boy Scts; Office Aide; Teachers Aide; Mgr Bsktbl; Trk; Vllybl; Hon Roll; NHS; Art Ed.

CHISOLM, NAIMA; New Rochelle HS; New Rochelle, NY; (Y); SADD; Rep Jr Cls; Var Trk; NHS.

CHISUM, CRIAG; Franklin Acad; Malone, NY; (Y); French Clb; Ski Clb; Nwsp Sprt Ed; Yrbk Rptr; Yrbk Stf; Trs Jr Cls; Golf; Hon Roll; NHS; U Of MI; Bus.

CHITTENDEN, ALAN; Maple Hill HS; Schodack Landing, NY; (Y); 1/71; 4-H; Math Tm; Spanish Clb; JV Var Bsktbl; Bausch & Lomb Sci Awd; High Hon Roll; Kiwanis Awd; NHS; Ntl Merit Ltr; Pres Schlr; NYS Regents Schlrshp, Cornell Tradition Book Awd; Cornell U; Dairy Sci.

CHIU, CHIN TA; Bronx High School Of Science; Flushing, NY; (Y); Computer Clb; Hosp Aide; Math Tm; Varsity Clb; Nwsp Phtg; Nwsp Rptr; Lit Mag; Sftbl; Vllybl; Hon Roll; JR Artista 84; TIME Educ Pgm Cert Rcgntn 86; 3rd Prz NY Cty Essy Cntst 86; Pre-Med.

CHIU, ELIZABETH; Woodlands HS; Hartsdale, NY; (Y); Trs Key Clb; Trs Service Clb; Sec Stu Cncl; Var Bsktbl; Var Capt Fld Hcky; Var Sftbl; Bausch & Lomb Sci Awd; Hon Roll; NHS; Ntl Merit SF.

CHIU, FRANK; Smithtown High Schl East; Nesconset, NY; (Y); 1/600; Capt Math Tm; Model UN; Orch; Var Tennis; Bausch & Lomb Sci Awd; Ntl Merit SF; Pres Spanish NHS; Princeton Bk Awd 86; Suffolk Co Math Cntst Level 12 2nd 86; Acdmc All Am 86; Brown U; Med.

CHIU, TOOMY; Middletown HS; Middletown, NY; (Y); Boy Scts; Computer Clb; Mathletes; Math Clb; Math Tm; Scholastic Bowl; Science Clb; Ski Clb; Spanish Clb; Var Trk; Art Poster Awd 86; SUNY; Acctng.

CHIU, VICTOR; Locust Valley HS; Bayville, NY; (Y); Am Leg Boys St; Hosp Aide; Library Aide; Chorus; Nwsp Bus Mgr; Nwsp Ed-Chief; Nwsp Rptr; Lit Mag; High Hon Roll; Jr NHS.

CHIVILY, PHILIP S; Lakeland HS; Putnam Valley, NY; (Y); 32/344; Varsity Clb; JV Var Ftbl; High Hon Roll; Hon Roll; NHS; Rgnts Schlrshp 86; Syracuse U; Aerosp Engrng.

CHMIELEWICZ, KIM; Fayettville-Manlius HS; Manlius, NY; (Y); 41/335; Model UN; Orch; School Musical; Ed Lit Mag; NHS; Ntl Merit Ltr; JCL; Math Clb; Stage Crew; 2nd Pl Natl JR Clsscl Leag Creatv Wrtg Cntst 86; Awd Edtg Schl Lit Magz 86; Orch Awd 86; Hamilton Coll; Creatv Wrtg.

CHMIELEWSKI, STEPHEN; Vernon Verona Sherrill HS; Oneida, NY; (Y); Church Yth Grp; Varsity Clb; JV Ftbl; Score Keeper; JV Var Wrstlng; Hon Roll; Oneida Silvercity Stu Achvt Awd 84-85; Air Force; Law Enfrcmnt.

CHO, JANET; Pittsford-Mendon HS; Pittsford, NY; (Y); Sec French Clb; Model UN; Chrmn Pep Clb; Yrbk Ed-Chief; JV Var Trk; NHS; Ntl Merit Ltr; VFW Awd; Art Clb; Boy Scts; NY ST Rgnts Schlrshhp 85-86; U Of Chicago; Bio Sci.

CHO, JENNIE; Niskayuna HS; Schenectady, NY; (Y); Church Yth Grp; Cmnty Wkr; Drama Clb; Latin Clb; Speech Tm; Church Choir; Orch; School Play; Stage Crew; Rep Stu Cncl; Natl Latn Exm Slvr Mdlst 86; Psych.

CHO, JOSEPHINE O; Forest Hills HS; Kew Gardens, NY; (Y); 34/824; Sec Trs Boy Scts; Math Clb; Band; Yrbk Ed-Chief; Var Socr; High Hon Roll; NHS; Westinghouse Sci Talent Srch-Semi Fnlst 86; Annual Cnty Sci Fair 2nd Pl & Hnrb Mntn 85-86.

CHO, TERESA; Norman Thomas HS; New York, NY; (S); 1/597; FBLA; Office Aide; Teachers Aide; Off Jr Cls; Off Sr Cls; Hon Roll; Lion Awd; NHS; Prfct Atten Awd; Val; SUNY Bnghmtn.

CHOATE, CARRIE; Alden Central HS; Alden, NY; (Y); Church Yth Grp; Intnl Clb; Spanish Clb; Color Guard; Flag Corp; Vllybl; 4-H; FTA; Nwsp Rptr; 4-H Awd; Opn Door Exchng Stu Schlrshp 85; Bbystr Awd 83; Bryant & Stratton; Scrtrl Sci.

CHOBAN, MARION; Moore Catholic HS; Staten Island, NY; (Y); Hosp Aide; Ski Clb; Spanish Clb; SADD; Yrbk Stf; Im Cheerleading; Fshn Inst Of Tech; Bus.

CHODAK, JAMES; Bishop Kearney HS; Rochester, NY; (Y); 10/183; Boy Scts; Cmnty Wkr; Drama Clb; Model UN; Band; Chorus; School Musical; Stage Crew; Bowling; Hon Roll; U Of Rchstr Grnt 86; Plsh Flcns Schlrshp Awd 86; Canisius Coll Grnt 86; Canisius Coll; Intl Reltns.

CHOE, SANDY; Eastchester HS; Scarsdale, NY; (Y); Art Clb; Church Yth Grp; Office Aide; Spanish Clb; Teachers Aide; Var Socr; Var Tennis; Hon Roll; Jr NHS; Prfct Atten Awd; Hist.

CHOI, HO; New Rochelle HS; New Rochelle, NY; (Y); Computer Clb; FBLA; Band; Concert Band; Mrchg Band; Symp Band; Var Swmmng; Im Vllybl; High Hon Roll; NHS.

CHOI, KIWON; Herricks HS; Manhasset Hls, NY; (Y); Hosp Aide; Varsity Clb; Orch; Nwsp Stf; Var Tennis; Hon Roll; Jr NHS; NHS; Ntl Merit SF; NYSMA Instrument Comp.

CHOI, SOOJIN; HS Of Art & Design; Elmhurst, NY; (Y); Church Yth Grp; Church Choir; Hon Roll; NHS; NAHS 86; 1st Pl Poster Desn All City Joint Orch 86; Illstrtr.

CHOI, SUNG WON; Mount St Michael Acad; Bronx, NY; (S); 18/309; Chess Clb; Cmnty Wkr; Computer Clb; Lit Mag; Hon Roll; Cornell U.

CHOI, YORHAN; James Madison HS; Brooklyn, NY; (Y); Teachers Aide; Im Socr; Exc Atten 86; NY U; Engrng.

CHOINA, TAMIR; Madison HS; Brooklyn, NY; (Y); Var Tennis; ARISA 86; Mst Imprvd Plyr Ten 86; Cardlgy.

CHONG, CHUN; Aviation HS; New York, NY; (Y); 7/415; Band; Hon Roll; Prfct Atten Awd; Cert Of Excllnc Math,Scl Studies,Bio & Chem 84-86; Cert Of Excllnc Aerospace,Tech Studied 84-85.

CHONG, SUNYOUNG; Academy Of Mount Saint Ursula HS; Bronx, NY; (Y); Church Yth Grp; French Clb; Library Aide; 1st Hnrs Awd 84 & 85; Yth Fit Achvt Awd 85; Bernard; Arch.

CHORAZAK, JENNIFER; Frontier Central SR HS; Blasdell, NY; (S); 64/450; Pres Drama Clb; Library Aide; Pep Clb; Chorus; School Musical; Stage Crew; Stu Cncl; High Hon Roll; Hon Roll; NHS.

CHORAZY, KARI; Palmyra-Macedon HS; Macedon, NY; (S); 3/185; VP SADD; Varsity Clb; Rep Frsh Cls; Rep Trs Jr Cls; JV Bsktbl; JV Var Tennis; Cit Awd; High Hon Roll; Hon Roll; NHS; Phys-Therapy.

CHORBAJIAN, GILBERT; Colonie Central HS; Loudonville, NY; (Y); Chess Clb; Church Yth Grp; High Hon Roll; NHS; Bus.

CHOTTINER, JEFFREY E; Jamesville-De Witt HS; De Witt, NY; (Y); 14/245; Math Tm; Temple Yth Grp; Socr; High Hon Roll; NHS; Outstndng Achvt Erth Sci Awd 82-83; Chem Awd 84-85; Mech Drwng Awd 84-85; Syracuse U; Mech Engrng.

CHOU, DORIS; Herricks SR HS; New Hyde Prk, NY; (Y); Cmnty Wkr; Hosp Aide; Key Clb; Nwsp Stf; Rep Stu Cncl; Hon Roll; NHS; Med.

CHOUDHURY, SAYEED; Jamesville-De Witt HS; Jamesville, NY; (Y); Computer Clb; Model UN; SADD; Yrbk Phtg; Yrbk Stf; Lit Mag; NHS; Elctrnc Engrng.

CHOW, BERNICE; HS Of Art & Design; New York, NY; (Y); FTA; Chorus; Nwsp Stf; Hon Roll; NHS; Prfct Atten Awd; Ntl Art Hnr Scty 85-86.

CHOW, HAROLD; Wallkill SR HS; New Paltz, NY; (S); Chess Clb; Drama Clb; Radio Clb; SADD; Nwsp Rptr; Pres Stu Cncl; Ftbl; Tennis; DAR Awd; VP NHS; Pre-Law.

CHRESOMALES, POTOULA; Newtown HS; Elmhurst, NY; (Y); 35/781; Church Yth Grp; Band; Concert Band; Vllybl; Hon Roll.

CHRISS, BINNIE-AYN; Ballston Spa HS; Mecanicville, NY; (Y); 66/240; Art Clb; Exploring; Rep Soph Cls; High Hon Roll; Hon Roll; JCA; Art Educ.

CHRISTEIN, ERIC; Newburgh Free Acad; Newburgh, NY; (Y); Boy Scts.

CHRISTENSEN, CARENE; Wells Central Schl; Northville, NY; (S); 1/34; Pres Church Yth Grp; Band; Chorus; Church Choir; Trs Sr Cls; Var JV Bsktbl; Var JV Sftbl; Var JV Vllybl; High Hon Roll; Jr NHS; Elem Ed.

CHRISTIAN, AMY JO; Cicero-N Syracuse HS; Clay, NY; (S); 49/623; Color Guard; Mrchg Band; Orch; Hon Roll; Jr NHS; US Hstry-Govt Awd 85; Al-Cnty Orchstra/Viola 84; Hartwick; Pedtrc Nrsng.

CHRISTIAN, ANGIE; Saranac Central HS; Morrisonville, NY; (S); 26/100; Band; Concert Band; Rep Soph Cls; Stu Cncl; Var JV Socr; Var JV Sftbl; Var JV Vllybl; Hon Roll; Phy Thrpy.

CHRISTIAN, ANNA; Penfield SR HS; Penfield, NY; (Y); Art Clb; Cmnty Wkr; Dance Clb; Radio Clb; Yrbk Stf; Lit Mag; Im Bsktbl; Var Trk; Hon Roll; Schlstc Art Awd 86; Advrtsng Dsgn.

CHRISTIAN, DAVID; Beacon HS; Beacon, NY; (Y); 67/205; Model UN; Science Clb; Nwsp Sprt Ed; Yrbk Stf; Var Bowling; Cty Schl Dist Hnr For Logo Cntst 86; Hrvrd Mdl Cngrss Part 86; Pltcl Sci.

CHRISTIAN, RICK; Windsor JR SR HS; Kirkwood, NY; (Y); Varsity Clb; Rep Jr Cls; VP Sr Cls; JV Bsktbl; JV Var Ftbl; Var Trk; Hon Roll; NHS; Ntl Cncl Yth Ldrshp Slt To Yth Pgrm 86; Vrsty Clb All League Awd Trck 86; Archtr.

CHRISTIANA, LAURA; Schenectady Christian HS; Schenectady, NY; (Y); Teachers Aide; School Play; Variety Show; Yrbk Stf; Var L Cheerleading; Trk; Sec Jr Cls; Fshn Merch.

CHRISTIANO, CATHY; Mt St Mary Acad; Tonawanda, NY; (Y); Chorus; Stage Crew; Yrbk Stf; Var Cheerleading; Im Vllybl; Hon Roll; Canisius Coll; Marine Bio.

CHRISTIANSEN, DAWN; Eden Central SR HS; Eden, NY; (Y); GAA; Concert Band; Orch; Pep Band; Symp Band; JV Bsktbl; Var Fld Hcky; Var Sftbl; JV Vllybl; Finger Lakes CC; Chld Psych.

CHRISTIANSEN, MARIA; John F Kennedy HS; Utica, NY; (Y); Key Clb; Variety Show; Sec Stu Cncl; Hon Roll; MVCC; Accntng.

CHRISTIANSEN, MATTHEW; Penn Yan HS; Penn Yan, NY; (S); 10/174; 4-H; FFA; Varsity Clb; Variety Show; Nwsp Sprt Ed; Rep Sr Cls; Im Badmtn; Var Capt Bsktbl; JV Ftbl; 4-H Awd; Regents Scolar 86; Royson N Whipple Scholar 86; PTG Scholar 86; Morrisville Ag Coll; Anim Husb.

CHRISTIE, CERONNE; Port Richmond HS; Staten Island, NY; (Y); Chorus; School Musical; Hon Roll; Merit Roll 85-86; Hunter; Med.

CHRISTIE, EVERTON; Bushwick HS; Brooklyn, NY; (S); 21/233; Computer Clb; Drama Clb; Office Aide; Science Clb; Ski Clb; Teachers Aide; School Musical; School Play; Yrbk Stf; Lit Mag; Biol & Chem Sci Awds 84 & 85; Eng Awd 84 & 85; Sys Anal.

CHRISTIE, KAREN; Midwood HS; Brooklyn, NY; (Y); Hon Roll; Prfct Atten Awd; Medcl Sci Inst 83-84; Bus Adm.

CHRISTIE, MICHELLE; Bay Shore SR HS; Bay Shore, NY; (Y); 28/406; Camera Clb; Hosp Aide; Math Tm; SADD; Color Guard; Mrchg Band; Ed Nwsp Phtg; Yrbk Phtg; High Hon Roll; Hon Roll; Air Force.

CHRISTIE, SEAN; Brewster HS; Brewster, NY; (Y); JV Var Socr; JV Var Trk; Hon Roll; MVP Frshmn Sccr, JV Sccr 83-84; Acctg.

CHRISTINO, PAULA A; Westhill SR HS; Syracuse, NY; (Y); 36/145; Art Clb; Symp Band; Ed Nwsp Stf; Yrbk Stf; Hon Roll; NHS; Ntl Merit Schol; Exploring; Library Aide; 3rd Pl SR Div Stdnt Art Cntst Publ Brdcstg TV 86; 3rd Regnl Schlstc Art Awds 82; Syracuse U; Edtrl Dsgn.

CHRISTMAN, AMY; Duanesburg Central HS; Delanson, NY; (Y); Church Yth Grp; Sec Intnl Clb; Office Aide; Chorus; Nwsp Ed-Chief; Rptr Nwsp Rptr; Yrbk Bus Mgr; Bausch & Lomb Sci Awd; High Hon Roll; NHS; Maxima Cum Laude Slvr Mdl Ntl Latin Exam 85-86; Pharm.

CHRISTNER, JULIE; Perry Central HS; Perry, NY; (Y); 15/100; 4-H; FTA; Spanish Clb; Chorus; Yrbk Stf; Hon Roll; NHS; Nazareth; Deaf Educ.

CHRISTOFORATOS, ALEX; Lehman HS; Bronx, NY; (Y); Boy Scts; School Play; Bsbl; Vllybl; Prfct Atten Awd; Astrnmy.

CHRISTOPHER, JACKIE; Corinth HS; Corinth, NY; (Y); Church Yth Grp; French Clb; Acpl Chr; Im Mgr Bsktbl; Im Mgr Sftbl; NHS; Comp Sci.

CHRISTOPHER, KEVIN; Brockport Central HS; Brockport, NY; (Y); Radio Clb; Capt Crs Cntry; Trk; Hon Roll; Mst Vlbl Rnnr X-Cnty 85-86; Germn I Awd 84-85; Lang.

CHRISTOPHER, LISA; Greece Olympia HS; Rochester, NY; (Y); DECA; Drama Clb; Pres Chorus; Rep Stu Cncl; High Hon Roll; Hon Roll; Schlstc Ltr Acad 85-86; Schlstc Ltr Music 84-85; Comm.

CHRISTOPHER, LISA; St Marys HS; Depew, NY; (Y); Capt Chrmn Dance Clb; VP Exploring; GAA; Ski Clb; SADD; School Musical; JV Bowling; JV Var Sftbl; Bus.

CHRISTOPHER, NANCY; East Syracuse-Minoa HS; East Syracuse, NY; (S); DECA; Variety Show; Yrbk Stf; Hon Roll; Cobleskill Ag & Tech; Elem Educ.

CHRISTY, SCOTT; Bitburg HS; Apo Ny, NY; (Y); Ftbl; Socr; Best Offensive Plyr 86; Sccr All Conf 86; All Tourn Dely 86; Phys Thrpst.

CHRISTY, TRICIA; St Vincent Ferrer HS; Ny, NY; (Y); 19/79; Math Tm; Pep Clb; High Hon Roll; Hon Roll; NEDT Awd; Med.

CHRZANOWSKI, MARK; Camden HS; Camden, NY; (Y); 30/200; Band; Concert Band; Jazz Band; High Hon Roll; Hon Roll; Pedtrcn.

CHU, MICHAEL; Martin Van Buren HS; Bellerose, NY; (Y); 136/562; Computer Clb; JA; Math Tm; Office Aide; Teachers Aide; School Play; Sci Fair 86; St Johns; Law.

CHU, TONY; The Bronx High School Of Science; Brooklyn, NY; (Y); JA; Office Aide; Teachers Aide; Yrbk Phtg; Yrbk Stf; Prfct Atten Awd; Lehigh U; Aerontcl Engrng.

CHU, VICTORIA W; Stuyvesant HS; Flushing, NY; (Y); Cmnty Wkr; Library Aide; Mathletes; Chorus; Orch; Variety Show; NHS; Prfct Atten Awd; Fnlst Queens Symph Aud 85; Solo Piano Recital Juilliard Schl Lincoln Ctr 86; Harvard.

CHUANG, CATHY; Half Holow Hills High Schl East; Dix Hills, NY; (Y); 21/500; Cmnty Wkr; Hosp Aide; Red Cross Aide; Band; Mrchg Band; Orch; Stage Crew; Symp Band; DAR Awd; NHS; NY Rgnts Schlrshp 86; Ntl Jrnlsm Awd 86; Bio.

CHUDASAMA, RANAKDEVI M; St Francis Prep Schl; Whitestone, NY; (S); Girl Scts; Math Clb; Var Tennis; Im Vllybl; Empire ST Gms Fld Hcky; Queens Coll; Med.

CHUN, JOAN; Elmira Free Acad; Elmira, NY; (Y); 2/257; Am Leg Aux Girls St; Cmnty Wkr; Intnl Clb; Trs Key Clb; Orch; Nwsp Ed-Chief; Yrbk Ed-Chief; Tennis; High Hon Roll; Hon Roll; Weis Schlr 86; ST & Rgnl Wnnr Of Esy Cntst On Music 85; Cornell U; Psych.

CHUN, ROBERT; New Rochelle HS; New Rochelle, NY; (Y); Pres Church Yth Grp; Church Choir; Nwsp Phtg; Yrbk Phtg; Ed Lit Mag; JV Socr; Tennis; High Hon Roll; NHS; Prfct Atten Awd.

CHUN, SUN; Roosevelt HS; Yonkers, NY; (Y); 1/245; Trs Band; Yrbk Stf; Off Frsh Cls; Off Soph Cls; Rep Jr Cls; Rep Sr Cls; CC Awd; High Hon Roll; Hon Roll; Sec NHS; Sprntndts Awd Exclln 82-86; CIBA Geigy Excllnc Sci 86; Salute To Youth 86; Suny Binghamton; Law.

CHUNG, EUN SOO; St Francis Prep; Flushing, NY; (S); 48/744; Chess Clb; Chrmn Church Yth Grp; Im Ftbl; Hon Roll; Prfct Atten Awd; Cmptrllrs Awd Sci & Math; Arista Cert; Law.

CHUNG, KAM HUNG; Seward Park HS; New York, NY; (Y); Art Clb; Bureau Of Sci 84; NY City Tech Coll; Archtrl.

CHUNG, KENNETH; Bronx H S Of Science; New York, NY; (Y); Computer Clb; Teachers Aide; VP VICA; Off Jr Cls; Off Sr Cls; Im Mgr(s); Im Vllybl; Prfct Atten Awd; Pride Yankees Ad 85-86; Outstndng Citznshp 86; Early Star Engr 83-86; MA Inst Tech; Mech Engr.

CHUNG, MICHELE M; St Vinccent Ferrer HS; Jackson Heights, NY; (S); 28/78; Cmnty Wkr; Library Aide; Math Tm; Chorus; Nwsp Rptr; Nwsp Stf; Bsktbl; Hon Roll; Awd Excllnc Geom 84-85; Awd Ferrer Minist 84-85; Awd Libry Svc 84-85; Bus Lwyr.

CHUNG, MINA M; Scarsdale HS; Scarsdale, NY; (Y); Cmnty Wkr; Ed French Clb; Hosp Aide; Math Tm; Chorus; School Musical; NHS; Ntl Merit SF; Juilliard Pre-Coll Schlrshp 82-85.

CHUNG, NANCY; Riverdale Country Schl; Flushing, NY; (Y); Church Yth Grp; French Clb; SADD; Orch; Nwsp Bus Mgr; Nwsp Rptr; Nwsp Stf; Lit Mag; Mgr(s); Trk; Arthur Ross Schlrshp 85-87; Law.

CHUNG, PETER; HS For The Hmnities; New York, NY; (Y); 3/30; Boys Clb Am; JV Socr; Hon Roll; Jr NHS; NHS; Prfct Atten Awd; Industrl Art Awd 84; Pre-Law.

CHUNG, WOHN KEE; Port Chester SR HS; Port Chester, NY; (Y); Aud/Vis; Chrmn Church Yth Grp; Band; Concert Band; Mrchg Band; Yrbk Stf; Golf; Hon Roll; Jr NHS; Mu Alp Tht; Science Honor Society 86; Physics.

CHUNG-A-FUNG, RONALD ARTHUR; Regis HS; Brooklyn, NY; (Y); NFL; Speech Tm; Yrbk Stf; Rep Frsh Cls; Rep Jr Cls; JV Var Trk; Ntl Merit Ltr; Natl Achvt Schlrshp 86; Yale U; Econmcs.

CHURCH, DEBORAH; Groton Central Schl; Freeville, NY; (Y); 1/87; Sec Pres 4-H; Trs Spanish Clb; Band; Trs Jr Cls; Rep Trs Stu Cncl; Var Bsktbl; Var Co-Capt Socr; Var Sftbl; Cit Awd; NHS; All IAC All-Str Sccr Bsktbl & Sftbl 83-86.

CHURCH, GLENN ALAN; Onondaga Central HS; Syracuse, NY; (Y); Church Yth Grp; German Clb; Chorus; School Musical; School Play; Stage Crew; JV Stat Ftbl; Hon Roll; Onondaga CC; Arch.

CHURCH, GORDON; Niagara Wheatfield HS; Sanborn, NY; (Y); Math Clb; Chorus; High Hon Roll; Hon Roll; NHS; Elec Engr.

CHURCH, JUDI; Indian River Central HS; Evans Mills, NY; (Y); 27/145; Church Yth Grp; Band; Concert Band; Mrchg Band; Stage Crew; Yrbk Stf; Rep Jr Cls; High Hon Roll; Hon Roll; Indian River Central Schl Schlstc Achvt Awd 85-86; Bus Adm.

CHURCH, SARAH H; Fox Lane HS; Bedford, NY; (Y); 15/286; Intnl Clb; VP JA; Yrbk Stf; JV Fld Hcky; JV Lcrss; High Hon Roll; NHS; Ntl Merit Ltr; Wrld Hunger Clb-Pres; Gold Medl-Natl Sci Olympiad-Sci Bowl; NYS Rgnts Schlrshp; Psych.

CHURCHILL, KRISTEN; Herkimer SR HS; Herkimer, NY; (Y); 11/111; Drama Clb; Concert Band; Jazz Band; Mrchg Band; Var JV Bsktbl; Capt Crs Cntry; Trk; NHS; Band; School Musical; Samuel Woltag Awd Achvt Pop Music 86; Eveng Telegrm Athl Wk Awd Trck 86; Prncpls Awd 86; St Lawrence U.

CHURCHILL, PAMELA; Bishop Scully HS; Johnstown, NY; (Y); 22/48; French Clb; Hosp Aide; Office Aide; Trs Frsh Cls; Sec Soph Cls; JV Var Bsktbl; Yrbk Stf; Coach Actv; Hgst Achvt Int Alg; Most Imprvd Alg; S Ltr Vsktbl; Radiolgic Tech.

CHUTUAPE, ROBERT; Earl L Vandermeulen HS; Pt Jefferson, NY; (Y); 1/333; Latin Clb; Spanish Clb; Varsity Clb; Nwsp Rptr; Yrbk Stf; Pres Frsh Cls; Trs Jr Cls; JV Var Socr; Var Trk; Hon Roll; Sci Supv Assoc Chem Awd 85; Sci Supv Assoc Sci Awd 86; Natl Sci Olympd Physcs 1st Pl 86.

CHWE, CHRISTINE; New Rochelle HS; New Rochelle, NY; (Y); 11/550; Debate Tm; French Clb; Ski Clb; Chorus; Yrbk Bus Mgr; Var Socr; French Hon Soc; High Hon Roll; NHS; Val; Charles Dickens Englsh Awd 86; NY ST Regents Schlrshp 86; Frnch Awd 83; Tufts U; Bus.

CHYUNG, HENRY; Corning West HS; Painted Post, NY; (Y); 2/250; Key Clb; Jr Cls; Stu Cncl; Var Bsktbl; JV Ftbl; JV Socr; Var Tennis; Bausch & Lomb Sci Awd; NHS; Ntl Merit SF; Bus.

CIACCIARELLI, MICHAEL; Port Richmond HS; State Island, NY; (Y); Cmnty Wkr; Math Clb; Math Tm; Teachers Aide; Nwsp Rptr; High Hon Roll; Hon Roll.

CIACCIO, MICHELLE M; St Joseph Hill Acad; Staten Island, NY; (Y); 10/107; Math Tm; NFL; Pres Science Clb; Nwsp Ed-Chief; Var L Socr; High Hon Roll; NHS; Ntl Merit SF; NEDT Awd; Cmnty Wkr; JR Acad Sci; Westinghouse Sci Fair; NY Ctywde Sci Fair Navy Sci Awd; Biochem.

CIACH, LUISA; Mount Saint Joseph Acad; Buffalo, NY; (Y); 4/44; Church Yth Grp; Teachers Aide; School Musical; Yrbk Stf; Off Sr Cls; Hon Roll; NHS; Acad All Amer 85-86; Canisius Coll; Lwyr.

CIAFONE, JOHN J; Long Island City HS; Long Is Cty, NY; (Y); 2/35; Pres Chess Clb; Science Clb; Orch; Nwsp Ed-Chief; Pres Jr Cls; Mu Alp Tht; NHS; Ntl Merit Schol; Voice Dem Awd; Pres Acad Fitness Awd 86; NY U Med Sch; Immurologist.

CIALONE, LAURA; St Catharine Acad; Bronx, NY; (S); 1/205; Cmnty Wkr; Nwsp Ed-Chief; Yrbk Ed-Chief; VP Jr Cls; Pres Sr Cls; Rep Stu Cncl; Gov Hon Prg Awd; High Hon Roll; NHS; 4 Yr Acadmc Schlrshp 82; Hnrs-Iona Coll Lang Contst 84; Math.

CIAMPA, DEBRA; E Meadow HS; E Meadow, NY; (S); Key Clb; Band; Concert Band; Mrchg Band; Symp Band; Cit Awd; Hon Roll; Jr NHS; NHS; NYSSMA 82 & 84-85; All Cnty Nassau 84; Woodland JR Hgh Band Awd 83-84; Hofstra U; Law.

CIAMPI, JOHN; Onondaga Central HS; Syracuse, NY; (Y); 11/75; Am Leg Boys St; Spanish Clb; Varsity Clb; JV Var Bsbl; JV Bsktbl; JV Ftbl; High Hon Roll; Hon Roll; NHS; Prfct Atten Awd; Elec Engrng.

CIANCIOSI, HELEN ANNE; Hornell HS; Hornell, NY; (Y); AFS; SADD; Nwsp Rptr; Yrbk Rptr; Rep Jr Cls; JV Var Socr; High Hon Roll; NHS; Acad Ltr Awd 85-86; Crtifct Mrt Ltn III 86; Crtfct Mrt Chmstry 86.

CIANCIOSI, NICHOLAS P; Hornell HS; Hornell, NY; (Y); 6/190; Am Leg Boys St; Latin Clb; Rep Soph Cls; L Socr; L Swmmng; High Hon Roll; NHS; Wake Forest U; Bus Mgt.

CIANCIOTTA, LAURIE; Bishop Kearney HS; Brooklyn, NY; (Y); 81/356; Cmnty Wkr; Hon Roll; NHS; Natl Bus Hnr Scty Secy 85-86; Brooklyn Coll; Edu.

CIANCIULLI, MICHAEL; New Rochelle HS; New Rochelle, NY; (Y); Boys Clb Am; Acpl Chr; Im Bsktbl; Im Ftbl; Im Swmmng; Wt Lftg; Hon Roll; Prfct Atten Awd; Perfect Attndnc Awd 84; Hon Roll 84; Iona Coll; Criminal Justice.

CIANFLONE, ANTHONY; Carmel HS; Stormville, NY; (Y); Service Clb; Var Bsbl; JV Ftbl; JV Ftbl Mst Imprvd Plyr 85; AZ ST; Psych.

CIANFROGNA, RON; Copiague HS; Copiague, NY; (Y); Am Leg Boys St; Debate Tm; Mathletes; SADD; Im Bsktbl; JV Var Ftbl; JV Var Lcrss; Hon Roll; NHS; Prfct Atten Awd; Soc Stu Awd 82-83; Peer Assistance Pgm 85-86; US Tennis Assn 84-85; Stanford; Pre-Law.

CIANO, KATHERINE; Academy Of St Joseph; Dix Hills, NY; (Y); Cmnty Wkr; Dance Clb; Hosp Aide; Science Clb; Teachers Aide; Yrbk Stf; Ntl Merit Ltr; FL Inst Tech; Marine Bio.

CIANO, LINDA; Benjamin N Cardozo HS; Little Neck, NY; (Y); 16/531; Orch; School Musical; Nwsp Rptr; Nwsp Stf; Var Vllybl; NHS; Ntl Merit SF; Drama Clb; Key Clb; Math Clb; Wstnghs Sci Tlnt Srch 86; Hnrb Mntn/Ung Plywrtrs Cntst 86; Outstndng Achvt & Exc In Englsh Awd 86; SUNY Bnghmtn.

CIARAMITARO, GIROLAMA; St John The Baptist HS; Massapequa, NY; (Y); Hosp Aide; Yrbk Stf; High Hon Roll; Hon Roll; Jr NHS; Med.

CIARDIELLO, DEBRA; New Rochelle HS; Scarsdale, NY; (Y); 130/550; FBLA; Spanish Clb; SADD; Rep Sr Cls; SUNY Albany; Lwyr.

CIARICO, ROBIN; James E Sperry HS; Henrietta, NY; (Y); Drama Clb; Pres Thesps; School Musical; School Play; Stage Crew; Jr Cls; Jr NHS; Pres NHS; Latin Hnr Soc 86; Ntl Acad Dcthln Cmptr 86.

CIARLANTE, NADENA; Saugerties HS; Glasco, NY; (S); Library Aide; Office Aide; Spanish Clb; Hon Roll; Pres Spnsh Clb 85-86; Bus.

CIAVATTA, MICHAEL; Connetquot HS; Oakdale, NY; (S); 51/730; Boy Scts; Band; Concert Band; Jazz Band; Mrchg Band; Pep Band; School Musical; Symp Band; Jr NHS; NHS; Rgnts Schlrshp; SUNY-FRDNIA; Music.

CICCARELLA, JOE; Frontier Central SR HS; Lakeview, NY; (S); 21/444; JA; Science Clb; Ski Clb; Spanish Clb; SADD; Trs Varsity Clb; Var Ftbl; Var Ice Hcky; Im Trk; U Of Rochester; Mechncl Engrng.

CICCARELLA, MARK; Maryvale SR HS; Depew, NY; (Y); 22/305; Am Leg Boys St; French Clb; Var L Vllybl; NHS; Pres Schlr; Northwood Inst Acad Scholar 86-87; NYS Regents Scholar 86-87; Northwood Inst; Acctng.

CICCI, STEPHEN A; Fayetteville-Manlius HS; Fayetteville, NY; (Y); 62/340; Church Yth Grp; JCL; SADD; Variety Show; Var JV Bsbl; Im Bsktbl; Var JV Ftbl; Hon Roll; NHS; Cornell U.

CICCONE, JESSICA; Glen Cove HS; Glen Cove, NY; (Y); Church Yth Grp; VP French Clb; Political Wkr; SADD; Stage Crew; Boys Clb Am; Nwsp Stf; Var Crs Cntry; Stat Score Keeper; Var Trk; Ad Edtr Schl Paper; Vars Trck 4 Yrs; Frnch Clb VP; Hist.

CICHANOWICZ, SARA; Mattituck HS; Cutchogue, NY; (Y); 13/124; 4-H; French Clb; German Clb; Ski Clb; Variety Show; JV Fld Hcky; NHS; Delta Epsln Phi Grmn Hnr Soc 83; Boston U; Bus Mgmt.

CIECZKA, DIANE; Villa Maria Acad; Cheektowaga, NY; (S); Computer Clb; French Clb; School Play; Yrbk Stf; Var Vllybl; High Hon Roll; Mock Trl Trnmnt 86; Comp Engrng.

CIESLAK, LYNN; St Marys HS; Cheektowaga, NY; (S); 1/164; Hosp Aide; Science Clb; Ski Clb; Nwsp Stf; High Hon Roll; NHS; Voice Dem Awd; Cmnty Wkr; Rep Stu Cncl; Awd Acad Achvt Eng,Bio,Chem 84-85; Canisius Coll; Bio Chem.

CIFELLI, SCOTT; Alexander Central HS; Alexander, NY; (Y); 12/89; Boy Scts; Math Tm; Ski Clb; Band; Concert Band; Jazz Band; Mrchg Band; Bsktbl; Tennis; Hon Roll; SUNY Buffalo; Mech Engrng.

CIFERRI, ROD; Our Lady Of Lourdes HS; Millbrook, NY; (Y); 70/180; Drama Clb; Pres Stu Cncl; Var L Ftbl; Var L Trk; High Hon Roll; Hon Roll; US Naval Acad; Political Sci.

CIFONE, CHRISTINE; Glens Falls HS; Glen Falls, NY; (Y); AFS; Ski Clb; Orch; Var Crs Cntry; Var Trk; High Hon Roll; Hon Roll; Cazenovia Coll; Fash Dsgn.

CIFUENTES, SANTIAGO; Newtown HS; Jackson Hts, NY; (Y); 43/781; Hon Roll; Baruch Coll; Bus Mgmt.

CIGALE, GEORGE; Bronx H S Of Science; Jamaica, NY; (Y); Camera Clb; Rep Frsh Cls; L Socr; Ntl Merit Ltr; Suny At Binghamton:Entrprnr.

CILIOTTA, JEANNINE; Poly Prep CDS; Brooklyn, NY; (Y); Am Leg Aux Girls St; Cmnty Wkr; Dance Clb; Drama Clb; Pep Clb; Science Clb; SADD; Teachers Aide; School Musical; School Play; Cnclmn NW Serv Awd 84; Chitagua Prfrmng Arts Schlrshp 86; Grnt Resrch Alcohol Energy 84; Law.

CILUFFO, DIANNE; Nazareth Acad; Rochester, NY; (Y); Church Yth Grp; Dance Clb; Drama Clb; Exploring; French Clb; Chorus; School Musical; Swing Chorus; Rep Jr Cls; Hon Roll; French High Hnrs 85; Dance Merits 83; St Bonaventure U; Elem Ed.

CIMBRICZ, JOHN R; Salamanca Central HS; Killbuck, NY; (Y); 15/138; Model UN; JV Bsbl; Var Capt Bsktbl; Var Crs Cntry; Im Socr; Var Capt Trk; Prfct Atten Awd; Mst Imprvd-Vrsty Bsktbl 84-85; Mst Dedctd-Vrsty Crss Cntry 85; Rgnts Schlrshp 86; Syracuse U; Fnanc.

CIMINERA, ANDREA; St John Baptist HS; Lindenhurst, NY; (Y); Dance Clb; FBLA; FHA; Hosp Aide; Chorus; Fashn.

CIMMINO, DOMENICO; Mont Pleasant HS; Schenectady, NY; (Y); Cmnty Wkr; French Clb; Service Clb; Pres SADD; Rep Frsh Cls; Rep Soph Cls; Rep Jr Cls; Rep Sr Cls; Var L Bsktbl; Var L Mgr(s); RIT Scholar 86; RIT; Bus Adm.

CINDEL, LAURA; Nyack HS; Nyack, NY; (Y); 12/300; Math Clb; Math Tm; Ski Clb; Spanish Clb; Drill Tm; Yrbk Stf; Capt Cheerleading; Var Fld Hcky; Var Lcrss; High Hon Roll; Natl Hnr Soc 86; Natl Spn Hnr Soc 86; NYS La Crosse Sec Champ Tm 86; Sci.

CINQUANTI II, PHILIP; Cortland HS; Cortland, NY; (Y); Ski Clb; Ftbl; Trk; Wt Lftg; Boys State 86; Aeronautical Engrng.

CINQUEMANI, KELLY; Central Islip HS; Central Islip, NY; (Y); 7/360; French Clb; Nwsp Ed-Chief; Off Sr Cls; Stat Sftbl; Var Tennis; Cit Awd; Hon Roll; NHS; NEDT Awd; NY RGNTS Schlrshp 85-86; Pres Acdmc Ftns Awd 86; SUNY Bnghmtn; Law.

CINTRON, MICHELLE; Academy Of Mt St Ursula; Bronx, NY; (Y); Cmnty Wkr; Spanish Clb; Yrbk Stf; Stu Cncl; Bsktbl; Score Keeper; Sftbl; Hon Roll; Spanish NHS; Crmnl Justice.

CINTRON, RICHARD P; Mt St Michael Acad; Bronx, NY; (Y); Var Capt Socr; Rgnts Scshlrshp, NYC All Star Soccer Tm, NYS Select, Empire Select Tm NYC 83-86; Pace U; Bus Mgt.

CINTRON, RUTH; Seward Park HS; New York, NY; (Y); Church Yth Grp; Cmnty Wkr; Girl Scts; Church Choir; Orch; High Hon Roll; Prfct Atten Awd; Med Tech.

CIONI, JOE; Garden City HS; Garden City, NY; (Y); Aud/Vis; Stage Crew; L Ftbl; L Golf; Score Keeper; Timer; Hon Roll.

CIOTOLI, ED; Union-Endicott HS; Endicott, NY; (Y); Varsity Clb; JV Var Bsbl; JV Var Ftbl.

CIOTOLI, MARY; Notre-Dame-Bishop Gibbons HS; Schenectady, NY; (S); 5/98; French Clb; Var Bsktbl; Var Socr; JV Sftbl; Var Swmmng; Var Trk; NHS; French Clb; High Hon Roll; Hstry Awd 85; Med.

CIPOLLA, KIM; Union Endicott HS; Endicott, NY; (Y); 2/450; Key Clb; Mathletes; Concert Band; Mrchg Band; Yrbk Stf; Var L Gym; Var L Trk; High Hon Roll; NHS; Sal; Broome Cnty Kopernik Soc Schlrhsp 86; Thoms J Woetson Schlrshp Fnlst 86; Colgt U Alumni Awd 86; Bucknell U; Mech Engrng.

CIPOLLONE, ANTONIA; Monsignor Scanlan HS; Bronx, NY; (Y); 1/256; Math Tm; Hon Roll; Pres NHS; Prfct Atten Awd; Val; Govrnrs Comm On Schlstc Achvmt 86; Regnts Schlrshp 86; Adelphi U; Law.

CIPOLLONE, ROSA; Monsignor Scanlan HS; Bronx, NY; (Y); Math Tm; Hon Roll; FIT; Merchndsng.

CIPOLLONE, TONI; Monsignor Scanlan HS; Bronx, NY; (Y); Math Tm; Gov Hon Prg Awd; High Hon Roll; Pres NHS; Val; Gldn Awd Math, Sci; NYS Rgnst Schlrshp 85-86; Phi Beta Kappa Schlrshp; Pres Awd; Soc Wmn Engrs Awd; Adelphe U.

CIPRIANI, MICHAEL; Copiague SR HS; Copiague, NY; (Y); SADD; Yrbk Stf; Hon Roll; Criminal Justice.

CIPRIANO, ALISSA; Canarsie HS; Brooklyn, NY; (S); 6/500; Cmnty Wkr; Dance Clb; Math Tm; Teachers Aide; Varsity Clb; Band; School Musical; Var Bowling; High Hon Roll; Prfct Atten Awd; Sec Aritsa Hnr Schltc Soc 85-86; Archon Svc Hnr Soc 85-86; NYC Peer Tutor Pgm 85-86.

CIRACO, WILLIAM; Westhampton Beach HS; East Quogue, NY; (Y); Nwsp Sprt Ed; Yrbk Sprt Ed; Pres Sr Cls; Var Capt Bsbl; Var Capt Bsktbl; Var Capt Ftbl; Ski Clb; Lit Mag; Sfflk Cnty Ocean Lfgrd Crtfd; Amrcn Hrtlnd Lung Assoc CPR Crtfd; Arch.

CIRELLA, TRACY; Half Hollow Hills E HS; Melville, NY; (Y); GAA; SADD; Chorus; Variety Show; Rep Frsh Cls; Stu Cncl; Capt Badmtn; Bsktbl; Coach Actv; Mgr(s); Girls Raiders Clb 83; Amer Liver Fndtn Chrmn 86; Boston U; Ed.

CIRENZA, EMANUEL N; Cornwall Central HS; Cornwall, NY; (Y); 10/200; Am Leg Boys St; Church Yth Grp; Teachers Aide; Variety Show; Var Capt Bsktbl; Coach Actv; Var L Ftbl; Im Wt Lftg; High Hon Roll; Hon Roll; Cls Spkr 86; Gentleman Ath Awd 85; Siena Coll; Pre-Med.

CIRICILLO, MINDY; Bishop Grimes HS; Liverpool, NY; (Y); Art Clb; Drama Clb; Ski Clb; Spanish Clb; SADD; School Musical; School Play; Yrbk Stf; Trk; Hon Roll.

CIRILLO, CARIN; Catholic Central HS; Troy, NY; (S); 4/178; Cmnty Wkr; French Clb; Red Cross Aide; SADD; Variety Show; High Hon Roll; NHS; Frnch Awd; Socl Stds Awd; St Rose; Rcrdng Engrng.

CIRILLO, DONNA L; Cardinal Spellman HS; Bronx, NY; (Y); 53/500; High Hon Roll; 1st Hnrs 85-86; Pres Schlrshp 85; Iona Coll; Educ.

CIRONE, VITO; Bishop Ford Central Catholic HS; Brooklyn, NY; (Y); 31/416; Nwsp Rptr; JV Var Bsbl; Im Bsktbl; Hon Roll; SUNY; Bus.

CIRRITO, RICK; Trott Vocational HS; Niagara Falls, NY; (Y); Exploring; Var Bsbl; Var Capt Bowling; Var Ftbl; Var Wrstlng; Hon Roll; Stu Mnth 86; Crimnl Justc.

CISEK, PAUL E; Carmel HS; Carmel, NY; (Y); Computer Clb; Yrbk Stf; Tennis; High Hon Roll; Hon Roll; Conrell; Comp Sci.

CISYK, PETER; New Dorp HS; Staten Island, NY; (Y); 94/600; DECA; NFL; Office Aide; Teachers Aide; Var Crs Cntry; Var Trk; Hon Roll; Pace; Acctng.

CISZ, MARK MICHAEL; Greene Central HS; Greene, NY; (Y); 4/120; Am Leg Boys St; Computer Clb; Ski Clb; VP Pres Varsity Clb; Trs Jr Cls; Var L Bsbl; Var Capt Ftbl; High Hon Roll; VP NHS; Socl Stds Key Awd; MVP Vrsty Bsbl; Boys ST Bar Exm; Med.

CISZAK, LYNN; Springville-Griffith Inst; Springville, NY; (Y); Pres Trs Church Yth Grp; Pres VP 4-H; Yrbk Ed-Chief; JV Var Bsktbl; Powder Puff Ftbl; 4-H Awd; Hon Roll; NHS; SUNY-GENESEO; Bus.

CIUFO, BRIAN; Greenville Central HS; Greenville, NY; (Y); 3/80; Church Yth Grp; Spanish Clb; Band; Chorus; Church Choir; Concert Band; Jazz Band; Pep Band; School Musical; NHS; Alice Hedges Moore Meml Awd-Instrmntl Music 86; Music.

CIUFO, PAIGE; Greenville Central HS; Greenville, NY; (Y); Church Yth Grp; Band; Sec Frsh Cls; Rep Stu Cncl; JV Bsktbl; Excllnce Awd For Bnd 84; Excllcne Aws Srvce To Schl 86; Lttr G 86.

CIUITANO, SUSAN; Ursuline HS; New Rochelle, NY; (Y); Spanish Clb; Spnsh 3h 84-85; Iona Coll; Fshn Mrktng.

CIVELLO, PATRICIA; Cicero-North Syracuse HS; Clay, NY; (S); 42/667; Church Yth Grp; JA; Stu Cncl; JV Var Cheerleading; Stat Ftbl; JV Var Powder Puff Ftbl; JV Socr; Hon Roll; NHS; Le Moyne Coll; Bus.

CIVITELLA, ANTONIO; Mount Pleasant HS; Schenectady, NY; (Y); 26/263; Key Clb; Pep Clb; Ski Clb; Spanish Clb; Yrbk Bus Mgr; Yrbk Phtg; Yrbk Stf; Pres Frsh Cls; Pres Soph Cls; Pres Sr Cls; Coll; Comp Sci.

CIVLLO, CARA; Sachem HS; Farmingville, NY; (Y); 41/1700; Cmnty Wkr; Debate Tm; Intnl Clb; Yrbk Stf; Stu Cncl; Im Mgr Bsktbl; High Hon Roll; Hon Roll; Jr NHS; NHS; Sci Fair Awds, Scl Stys Fair & Poetry Cntst Awds; Ed.

CIZDZIEL, JAMES V; West Seneca East SR HS; West Seneca, NY; (Y); 29/375; Boy Scts; Varsity Clb; Capt Golf; Hon Roll; Natl Hnr Soc Membr 86; Syracuse; Envrnmntl Sci.

CLABEAUX, DAWN; St Marys HS; E Aurora, NY; (Y); Boys Clb Am; Hosp Aide; JV Sftbl; Damen Coll; Socl Wrk.

CLABEAUX, ROBERT; Hutchinson Central Technical HS; Buffalo, NY; (Y); 15/300; Band; Concert Band; Jazz Band; Rep Stu Cncl; Var Bsbl; Var Bsktbl; Hon Roll; NHS; SAR Awd; Kappa Sigma Phi Frtrnty 85-87; Syracuse U; Mech Engrng.

CLACKETT, CHERY; Hauppauge HS; Hauppauge, NY; (Y); Church Yth Grp; FCA; GAA; VICA; Church Choir; Variety Show; JV Socr; JV Trk; Hon Roll; 2nd Pl LI Rgnl VICA, Photo Cmptn 86.

CLAIR, BONNIE; Williamsville East HS; E Amherst, NY; (Y); 18/302; Pres NFL; Chorus; Sec Rep Stu Cncl; Var L Crs Cntry; Var L Trk; High Hon Roll; NHS; Ntl Merit Ltr; AFS; Drama Clb; Ntl Assn Stu Cncls 1987 Ntl Conf Preprtry Cmmtte; Dist Inter-H S Cncl; Duke U; Bio.

CLAIRE, KAREN; Hornell HS; Hornell, NY; (Y); French Clb; Yrbk Stf; Rep Stu Cncl; JV Capt Vllybl; Bausch & Lomb Sci Awd; NHS; Ntl Merit Ltr; Rensselaer Polytechnic Inst Math & Sci Awd 86; Elmira Key Awd 86; Acadmc All Str Tm 86.

CLANCY, BRENDAN T; Alfred Almond Central Schl; Hornell, NY; (Y); Am Leg Boys St; Church Yth Grp; Yrbk Sprt Ed; Trs Jr Cls; Var Bsbl; High Hon Roll; Trs NHS; Prfct Atten Awd; 4-H; Stat Bsktbl; Youth Action Floor Hockey Sportsmanship Awd 85-86; Youth Action Floor Hockey Champions 85-86.

CLANCY, BRIDGET; Haverling Central Schl; Bath, NY; (Y); French Clb; Math Clb; Ski Clb; Band; Color Guard; Yrbk Stf.

CLANCY, HEATHER; Plattsburgh HS; Plattsburgh, NY; (Y); French Clb; Chorus; School Play; Yrbk Stf; Hon Roll; Psych.

CLANCY, KYLE; Mount Mercy Acad; Buffalo, NY; (Y); Pres Church Yth Grp; French Clb; Hon Roll; 3r Dpl Frgn Lang Fair Frnch 85; Canisius Coll.

CLAPP, BRIAN; Clarkstown HS South; New City, NY; (Y); Cmnty Wkr; Math Clb; Stage Crew; Jr NHS; Pace; Acctg.

CLAR, SUZANNE; Our Lady Of Mercy HS; Webster, NY; (Y); Church Yth Grp; Exploring; French Clb; Pres Science Clb; SADD; Church Choir; School Musical; Variety Show; Rep Stu Cncl; High Hon Roll; Engrng.

CLARCQ, MATTHEW; Eastridge HS; Rochester, NY; (Y); 14/235; Boys Clb Am; Teachers Aide; Band; Mrchg Band; Orch; School Musical; Rep Jr Cls; Rep Sr Cls; High Hon Roll; NHS; Phi Dlta Kppa Schlrshp 86; Rgnts Schlrshp Awd 86-90; NYS Chmpnshp Cls A Fld Band Solost 86; NY ST Coll-Geneseo; Hstry.

CLARE, JACQUELINE; Amsterdam HS; Amsterdam, NY; (Y); Ski Clb; Var Bowling; Var JV Cheerleading; Var Mgr(s); Hon Roll; Natl Art Hnr Soc; NY St Smmr Sch Of Arts 85; Rgnl Olympcs Of Vis Arts Gld Mdl 2nd Pl Paintg; Arts Adm.

CLARE, SUZANNE; Williamsville South HS; Williamsville, NY; (Y); AFS; Drama Clb; VP French Clb; Girl Scts; Pep Clb; SADD; Acpl Chr; School Musical; Cheerleading; NHS.

CLARIDGE, EMILY; Fayetteville Manlivs HS; Woodinville, WA; (Y); 34/400; 4-H; Model UN; Orch; Nwsp Rptr; 4-H Awd; Hon Roll; NHS; US Pony Clb Natls 84 & 85; Music Awd-4 Yrs Orchstra 86; Wellesley Coll; Bio.

CLARK, ANDRE; St Raymonds HS For Boys; Bronx, NY; (Y); 41/160; CAP; Computer Clb; Drill Tm; Crs Cntry; Sftbl; Trk; Manhattan Coll; Aero Sp.

CLARK, BETSY; Groton Central HS; Groton, NY; (Y); Church Yth Grp; Drama Clb; Chorus; School Play; Variety Show; Yrbk Bus Mgr; Yrbk Ed-Chief; Yrbk Phtg; Yrbk Stf; VP Frsh Cls; Delegt Eastern European Peace Tr 86; Finance.

CLARK, BRIAN; Lake Placid Central Schl; Lake Placid, NY; (Y); Key Clb; Varsity Clb; Yrbk Stf; Sec Frsh Cls; JV Var Bsbl; Im JV Ice Hcky; Var Socr; High Hon Roll; Hon Roll; Awd Hockey For Sprtsmnshp Bantam Lvl 84.

CLARK, CHARLES; Johnson City HS; Binghamton, NY; (Y); Mgr(s); Poli Geog.

CLARK, CHERYL; Waverly JR-SR HS; Waverly, NY; (Y); Hst FHA; Pep Clb; SADD; Variety Show; Rep Stu Cncl; JV VP Cheerleading; JV VP Trk; Im Vllybl; High Hon Roll; Hon Roll; Corning CC; Sec.

CLARK, CHRISTINE; Geneva HS; Geneva, NY; (S); 14/175; Cmnty Wkr; Pres French Clb; Chorus; School Musical; Yrbk Stf; JV Capt Cheerleading; NHS; Frnch III Compstn Awd 1st Pl 85; Nazareth Coll; Spch Path.

CLARK, DAVE; New Berlin Central Schl; New Berlin, NY; (Y); Yrbk Sprt Ed; JV Var Bsbl; JV Var Bsktbl; Var L Trk; Media.

CLARK, DAVID M; Geneseo Central Schl; Geneseo, NY; (Y); 8/43; Boy Scts; Church Yth Grp; Computer Clb; French Clb; VP JA; Ski Clb; VP SADD; Rep Frsh Cls; Rep Soph Cls; Var JV Bsbl; USAF Acad; Comp Pgmr.

CLARK, EARL; Rice HS; New York, NY; (Y); Art Clb; Computer Clb; Dance Clb; FBLA; Pep Clb; Yrbk Stf; Rep Stu Cncl; Bsktbl; Ftbl; Gym; Hampton U; Bus Mgmnt.

CLARK III, EARL R; Hicksville HS; Hicksville, NY; (Y); JV Bsbl; High Hon Roll; Hon Roll; NHS; Cert Outstndng Achvmnt U S Hstry & Soc Stud 85-86; Bsbl Trphy Bst Wn-Ls Rcrd 85; Bsbl Trphy MVP 86; Comp Sci.

CLARK II, FREDERICK G; Monsignor Farrell HS; Staten Island, NY; (S); Boy Scts; Band; Concert Band; Drm Mjr(t); Jazz Band; Mrchg Band; Orch; Communications Music.

CLARK, GARY; Mexico HS; Mexico, NY; (Y); Debate Tm; Pres 4-H; Pres FFA; German Clb; Quiz Bowl; Varsity Clb; Stage Crew; Var JV Debate Tm; Var L Ftbl; 4-H Awd; Dry Jdgng Tm 4-H Top Indvdl At ST 83; Dry Cattle At Cnty & ST Fairs 78-86; Won Shwmnshp & 1st Prz; Morrisville; Vet-Sci.

CLARK, GEORGE; Archbishop Molley HS; Queens Vlg, NY; (Y); 76/383; Boys Clb Am; Teachers Aide; Bsktbl; Swmmng; CC Awd; Cit Awd; High Hon Roll; Hon Roll; NHS; SAR Awd; Eagle Scout Pres 85; Merit Gov Cuomo 85; Recgntn U S Cong; Phrmcy.

CLARK, GREG; Skaneateles Central HS; Skaneateles, NY; (Y); 34/140; Church Yth Grp; Varsity Clb; Bsbl; Var Coach Actv; Var Ice Hcky; Var Socr; Var Tennis; Hon Roll; NHS; Mst Imprvd Plyr Ice Hcky 86; Geneseo; Poli Sci.

CLARK, JAMES P; St Anthonys HS; Northport, NY; (Y); 50/430; Am Leg Boys St; Office Aide; Political Wkr; Teachers Aide; Nwsp Rptr; JV Ftbl; Pres NHS; Library Aide; Nwsp Stf; Duns Scts Hnr Soc 84-86; Amer Lgn Ctznshp Awd 86; Pltcl Sci.

CLARK, JENNIFER; Broadalbin HS; Broadalbin, NY; (Y); 12/71; Computer Clb; Dance Clb; Library Aide; Chorus; Church Choir; Mrchg Band; Symp Band; Cheerleading; Pres Acad Ftns Awd 86; Fulton Montgomery CC Schrlshp 86; Music Assoc Prz 86; Fulton Montgomery CC; Arts.

CLARK, JENNIFER; Whitestone Acad; Beechhurst, NY; (S); 2/30; Art Clb; Teachers Aide; Chorus; Church Choir; Nwsp Stf; Yrbk Stf; Hon Roll; Hnr Engl & Sci 82-83; Awd Engl II, Hist, Typng I, Spnsh II & III & Chmstry 85; Adelphi U; Engl.

CLARK, JOANNA; Haverling Central HS; Bath, NY; (Y); 49/139; Art Clb; Girl Scts; Chorus; Grl Sct Gold Awd 85; Accntng.

CLARK, JUDITH A; Owego Free Acad; Apalachin, NY; (Y); 101/224; Art Clb; Drama Clb; Church Choir; Pres Madrigals; Mrchg Band; School Musical; Swing Chorus; AFS; Church Yth Grp; Concert Band; Gldn Rule Schlrshp Attndng Toronto Smmr In Dance 85; All St Chorus 84-85; Arts Rcgntn & Tlnt Srch 86; Phila Coll Per Arts; Dance.

CLARK, JULIAN; Cazenovia Central Schl; New Woodstock, NY; (Y); Boy Scts; Church Yth Grp; JV Ftbl; High Hon Roll; Hon Roll; Engrng.

CLARK, JULIE; Pinebush HS; Bullville, NY; (Y); SADD; Band; Color Guard; Concert Band; Drill Tm; Drm & Bgl; Mrchg Band; School Musical; School Play; Hon Roll; Envrnmntl Sci Pgm 85; Sci.

CLARK, KATHERINE ANN; Hilton Central HS; Rochester, NY; (Y); 8/315; Drama Clb; Chorus; School Musical; School Play; Stage Crew; Variety Show; High Hon Roll; NHS; Ski Clb; Concert Band; Schl Trp Frnce 86; Music.

CLARK, KATHLEEN; North Shore HS; Glen Head, NY; (Y); 4/208; Library Aide; Mathletes; Math Clb; Nwsp Rptr; Rep Stu Cncl; High Hon Roll; Hon Roll; NHS; TX A & M; Vet.

CLARK, KIM; Fillmore Central HS; Fillmore, NY; (Y); Church Yth Grp; Office Aide; SADD; Chorus; Nwsp Stf; Cheerleading; Cit Awd; Dnfth Awd; High Hon Roll; Hon Roll; Comp Prgmr.

CLARK, KRISTEN; Auburn HS; Auburn, NY; (Y); 26/387; Pres Chorus; Capt Color Guard; Madrigals; Swing Chorus; High Hon Roll; NHS; Ntl Merit SF; Cnfrnce All ST Wmns Chr 85; Fld Bnd Cnfrnce Schlrshp 86; Dir Awd Music 86; Cayaga CC; Lbrl Arts.

CLARK, KRISTINA S; Elmira Free Acad; Elmira, NY; (Y); Intnl Clb; Key Clb; Sec Ski Clb; Trs Spanish Clb; Yrbk Stf; Rep Frsh Cls; Rep Soph Cls; Rep Sr Cls; Stu Cncl; Var Bsktbl; Rgnts Schlrshp 86; Villanova U; Acctg.

CLARK, LEE; Gouverneur Central HS; Gouverneur, NY; (Y); Pres 4-H; Pres FFA; JV Bsktbl; Cit Awd; 4-H Awd; High Hon Roll; Hon Roll; Jr NHS; Lion Awd; Masonic Awd; NY ST Star Farmer FFA 85; NYS Grange Schlrshp 86; Cornell U; Anml Sci.

CLARK, MARYBETH; Eastridge HS; Rochester, NY; (Y); #72 In Class; Art Clb; Office Aide; SADD; Teachers Aide; School Play; Im Bsktbl; JV Cheerleading; Var Socr; JV Var Sftbl; Im Vllybl; Imprv Achvt Awd 83; Csmtlgy.

CLARK, MATTHEW; Hudson HS; Hudson, NY; (Y); Letterman Clb; Varsity Clb; Ftbl; SUNY New Paltz; Elec Engrng.

CLARK, MATTHEW; Leroy Central Schl; Leroy, NY; (Y); Ski Clb; Varsity Clb; School Musical; Bsktbl; Socr; Tennis; Trk; Wrstlng; High Hon Roll; NEDT Awd; St John Fisher; Acctg.

CLARK, MATTHEW V; Pawling JR SR HS; Pawling, NY; (Y); Latin Clb; Spanish Clb; Varsity Clb; Stage Crew; Var Bsbl; Capt L Ftbl; Trk; High Hon Roll; Hon Roll; NHS; (YS Regnts Schlrshp 86; U Of VT; Engr.

CLARK, NATE; John C Birdlebough HS; Phoenix, NY; (Y); Drama Clb; Pres 4-H; Radio Clb; School Musical; Stage Crew; Hon Roll.

CLARK JR, RICHARD; Kendall JR SR HS; Hamlin, NY; (S); 5/88; Spanish Clb; Yrbk Stf; Var Capt Bsbl; Var Capt Bsktbl; Var Capt Socr; High Hon Roll; Pres Jr NHS; NHS; Natrl Sci.

CLARK, RONALYN; Hornell HS; Hornell, NY; (Y); Sec AFS; Art Clb; Church Yth Grp; Pres Library Aide; Band; Concert Band; Drm Mjr(t); Symp Band; Hon Roll; Exec Sec.

CLARK, SHELBY; Groton HS; Locke, NY; (Y); Ski Clb; Nwsp Stf; Yrbk Stf; Typwrtng Keybrd I Awd 85; Typwrtng Keybrdng II Awd 86; Tompkins County CC; Sec.

CLARK, SUSAN; Franklin Acad; Constable, NY; (Y); 46/256; 4-H; Hosp Aide; Ski Clb; Spanish Clb; Chorus; Var Swmmng; Var Vllybl; Hon Roll; NHS; Malone Fed Tchrs Schlrshp 86; Plattsburgh ST; Elem Ed.

CLARK, TERRENCE P; Westhill HS; Syracuse, NY; (S); Boy Scts; Computer Clb; Letterman Clb; Math Tm; Political Wkr; Varsity Clb; Rep Stu Cncl; JV Var Bsktbl; JV Var Ftbl; Var Capt Trk; Full Athltc Schlrshp-U Of CT; Ftbl-MVP, 1st Tm All Upstate, 3rd Tm All ST 85-86; Track MVP 83-86; U Of CT; Economics.

CLARK, THERESA L; Faith Heritage Schl; Syracuse, NY; (Y); Pep Clb; Ed Nwsp Stf; Var L Cheerleading; Hon Roll; NHS; Cortland ST; Bio.

CLARK, TIA; Wantagh HS; Seaford, NY; (Y); Cmnty Wkr; Dance Clb; Girl Scts; Concert Band; Badmtn; Capt Pom Pon; Trk; Hon Roll; Outstndng Typst Cert 83; Outstndng Ldrshp/Kickline 86; Stock Broker.

CLARK, TOM; West Genesee HS; Syracuse, NY; (Y); Nwsp Rptr; Nwsp Sprt Ed; Nwsp Stf; Bsktbl; Capt Bowling; Hon Roll; Hghst Avg Bwlg Leag 86; Sprts Wrtr Locl Papr 86; Jrnlst.

CLARK, ZACHARY; Lake Placid HS; Lake Placid, NY; (Y); Church Yth Grp; Key Clb; Varsity Clb; Trs Frsh Cls; Var L Bsbl; Capt Ice Hcky; JV Socr; Hon Roll; Kiwanis Awd; Prfct Atten Awd; Arch.

CLARKE, ALISON; Holy Trinity Diocesan HS; East Meadow, NY; (Y); 9/315; Math Clb; Cheerleading; Gym; High Hon Roll; Mu Alp Tht; NHS; NEDT Awd; Quinnipiac Coll Deans Schlrshp; Mt St Vincent Alumnae Comptv Schlrshp; Hofstra Recgntn Schrlshp; Quinnipiac Coll; Intl Bus.

CLARKE, AMY J; Earl L Vandermeulen HS; Mt Sinai, NY; (Y); 30/330; FBLA; SADD; Band; Mrchg Band; Yrbk Stf; Stu Cncl; Vllybl; NHS; Trk; High Hon Roll; Outstndng Eng Stu; Stu Cncl Svc Awd; James Madison U; Bus Mgt.

CLARKE, DAVID W; Alden Central HS; Elma, NY; (Y); 2/203; Am Leg Boys St; Capt Quiz Bowl; Spanish Clb; Kiwanis Awd; Trs NHS; Pres Schlr; Sal; U Schlrs Prgm UTM 86-89; Ampco Pitts Emply Schlrshp 86-89; U TN At Martin; Chem.

CLARKE, JANNETH; Jane Addams HS; Bronx, NY; (S); 18/260; Drama Clb; Office Aide; Chorus; Church Choir; School Play; Cheerleading; Hon Roll; Prfct Atten Awd; Accntng.

CLARKE, LARRY; Southampton HS; Southampton, NY; (Y); Band; Concert Band; Jazz Band; Mrchg Band; Pep Band; School Musical; Stage Crew; Variety Show; Ski Clb; Bus.

CLARKE, LYNN; Mount Mercy Acad; Buffalo, NY; (Y); 49/163; French Clb; JA; Science Clb; SADD; Church Choir; Stage Crew; Hon Roll; Kings Coll; Intl Bus.

CLARKE, MIA; Clara Barton HS; Brooklyn, NY; (Y); Dance Clb; Chorus; Hon Roll; Med.

CLARKE, NYLPHIA; Mt Vernon HS; Mount Vernon, NY; (Y); Ski Clb; Band; Chorus; Church Choir; Concert Band; Mrchg Band; School Play; Yrbk Stf; High Hon Roll; Hon Roll; Duchess CC; Med Asst Tech.

CLARKE, SUSAN; Keshequa Central HS; Dalton, NY; (Y); 2/62; French Clb; Math Tm; Band; Concert Band; Mrchg Band; Nwsp Rptr; High Hon Roll; NHS; Prfct Atten Awd; IFLA Awd 86.

CLARRETT, SHARON; Queen Of The Rosary Acad; Amityville, NY; (S); Camera Clb; Math Clb; Spanish Clb; SADD; Yrbk Stf; Trs Frsh Cls; High Hon Roll; NHS; Mu Alp Tht; NHS.

CLARY, AMY; Cato-Meridian HS; Cato, NY; (Y); VICA; Hon Roll; Hghst Achvmnt Occptnl Ed & Outstndg Achvmnt Occptnl Ed 86; Compu Prgr.

CLATYON, GREGORY; Shaker HS; Latham, NY; (Y); Church Yth Grp; Band; Sftbl; JV Trk; NYS Regents Scholar 86; 1st Prz Sienna Coll Art/Hstry Cont SR Div 86; Exhibits Albany Inst 86; Alfred U; Photo.

CLAUDE, DAWN; Sandy Creek Central Schl; Redfield, NY; (Y); Computer Clb; French Clb; Math Tm; Political Wkr; Spanish Clb; Teachers Aide; Boys Clb Am; Yrbk Stf; NHS; Rgnt Schlrshp 86; SUNY-ALBANY; Bus Admin.

CLAUDIO, MELISSA; HS For Humaniti; New York, NY; (Y); Art Clb; Dance Clb; Drama Clb; Chorus; School Play; Variety Show; Lit Mag; Hon Roll; Prfct Atten Awd; Excllnc In Art Awd 84; Excllnc In Spnsh Awd 84; Prfssnl Mdl.

CLAUER, JOHN; Connetquot HS; Bohemia, NY; (Y); 102/700; Nwsp Rptr; Lit Mag; Mgr Bsbl; Mgr(s); Hon Roll; Bus.

CLAUSEN, CAROLYN; John Jay SR HS; Hopewell Jct, NY; (Y); 111/519; Dance Clb; Drama Clb; Stage Crew; High Hon Roll; Hon Roll; Pres Schlr; Wpngrs Cntrl Schl Dstrct Ofc Prsnl Mem Schlrshp Awd 86; Sullivan CC; Trvl & Trsm.

CLAUSSEN, KENDRA; Our Lady Of Victory Acad; New York, NY; (S); 6/128; French Clb; SADD; Var Cheerleading; French Hon Soc; High Hon Roll; NHS; Math Awd 84.

CLAVELO, EDWARD; All Hallows HS; Bronx, NY; (Y); 65/135; Rep Stu Cncl; Var Bsbl; JV Ftbl; Var Ice Hcky; Hon Roll; Comp.

CLAY, CLAIRESA; Wm H Maxwell Vocational HS; Brooklyn, NY; (Y); 10/210; Computer Clb; Pres FBLA; Band; Concert Band; Yrbk Phtg; Yrbk Stf; Pres Soph Cls; Sec Jr Cls; Rep Sr Cls; Hon Roll; NYS Rgnts Schlrshp 86; Bernard Baruch; Bus Adm.

CLAY, JENNIFER; South Side HS; Rockville Ctr, NY; (Y); 50/278; VP Key Clb; Yrbk Stf; Mgr(s); JV Sftbl; Trk; Var JV Vllybl; High Hon Roll; Hon Roll; Archt.

CLAYDON, MELINDA A; Akron Central JR SR HS; Akron, NY; (Y); 7/136; Trs Church Yth Grp; Sec Band; Sec Concert Band; Sec Mrchg Band; School Musical; Stat Swmmng; NHS; VP Sr Cls; Pres Schlrshp U Of Rchstr 86-87; Rgnts Schlrshp 86; U Rchstr; Med Rsrch.

CLAYTON, JANEEN; St Catharine Acad; Bx, NY; (Y); Hosp Aide; Office Aide; Rep Frsh Cls; Rep Soph Cls; Rep Jr Cls; Rep Stu Cncl; Cheerleading; High Hon Roll; NHS; Outstndg Svc Guidnce Dept.

CLAYTON, JUDITH; Trott Vocational & Tech Schl; Niagara Falls, NY; (Y); 10/142; Am Leg Aux Girls St; Office Aide; Political Wkr; School Play; Nwsp Rptr; Nwsp Stf; Yrbk Ed-Chief; Yrbk Rptr; Yrbk Stf; Prfct Atten Awd; Berkley; Psych.

CLAYTON, THEODORE M; Queensbury HS; Glens Falls, NY; (Y); 24/253; Church Yth Grp; Cmnty Wkr; Key Clb; Var L Socr; Var L Tennis; JV L Trk; High Hon Roll; NHS; Clrksn U Trstees Schlrshp 86-87; NYS Rgnts Schlrshp 86-87; Clarkson U; Mchncl Engr.

CLEARY, BRIAN; Hicksville SR HS; Hicksville, NY; (Y); JV Im Bsbl; Var Bowling; Im Score Keeper; High Hon Roll; Hon Roll; Jr NHS; NHS.

CLELAND, THOMAS; G Ray Bodley HS; Fulton, NY; (Y); French Clb; Office Aide; JV Bsbl; Capt Var Bsktbl; Var Coach Actv; Golf; JV Var Socr; Sftbl; Hon Roll; Prfct Atten Awd; Bus Adm.

CLEMENT, DARRIN; Beacon HS; Beacon, NY; (Y); Boy Scts; Math Tm; Variety Show; Im Ftbl; High Hon Roll; Hon Roll; Jr NHS; NHS; Music.

CLEMENTE, ARNOLD; Archbishop Molloy HS; Hollis, NY; (Y); Art Clb; Camera Clb; Church Yth Grp; Computer Clb; French Clb; Pep Clb; Science Clb; Yrbk Phtg; Yrbk Stf; Hon Roll.

CLEMENTE, LENA; Solvay HS; Solvay, NY; (Y); Church Yth Grp; Cmnty Wkr; Hosp Aide; Key Clb; Spanish Clb; SADD; Stage Crew; Off Soph Cls; Off Jr Cls; Off Sr Cls; Service Stu Cncl 85-86; Key Clb 85-86; Cmmnty Svc 83-84; Bus.

CLEMENTE, MARCO; Anthony A Henninger HS; Syracuse, NY; (Y); JV Ftbl; JV Lcrss; Hon Roll.

CLEMENTS, AMY J; Newark SR HS; Lyons, NY; (Y); 11/201; Am Leg Aux Girls St; Latin Clb; Service Clb; Varsity Clb; Var Capt Socr; JV Trk; Capt Var Vllybl; High Hon Roll; Pres NHS; Section V Clss B All Tourn Tm Selectn Vllybl 85-86; Mst Imprvd & Bst Defns Plyr Sccr 84-85; SUNY Buffalo; Phy Thrpy.

CLEMENTS, DOUG; Hugh C Williams HS; Canton, NY; (Y); Ski Clb; Thesps; Lcrss; Socr; High Hon Roll; Hon Roll; Duke; Libl Arts.

CLEMENTS, GILLIAN; Lindenhurst SR HS; Lindenhurst, NY; (Y); Church Yth Grp; Chorus; Var Badmtn; Hon Roll; Stony Brook; Psych.

CLEMENTS, JENNIFER; E J Wilson HS; Spencerport, NY; (Y); Latin Clb; Ski Clb; Spanish Clb; Sftbl; Vllybl; High Hon Roll; Hon Roll; NHS; Math Engr.

CLEMENTS, KELLEY A; Lakenheath HS; Palo Alto, CA; (Y); Drama Clb; French Clb; Latin Clb; Library Aide; Model UN; Chorus; Church Choir; School Musical; School Play; Stage Crew; U S Hstry Awd 85; Frnch Awd 85; Advncd Bio Awd 85.

CLERICI, LISA; West Seneca East SR HS; Cheektowaga, NY; (Y); 58/375; German Clb; Stu Cncl; Capt Var Sftbl; Hon Roll; JC Awd; Prfct Atten Awd; Ger NHS 85; SUNY Geneseo; Med Tech.

CLERMONT, FREDERIQUE; Bronx H S Of Science; Queens Village, NY; (Y); Cmnty Wkr; Rep Soph Cls; Rep Jr Cls; Off Sr Cls; L Bsktbl; Vllybl; Office Aide; Teachers Aide; Varsity Clb; School Play; Bronx Champs Handball; Genetic Cnslr.

CLEVELAND, BETSY JO; Greece Olympia HS; Rochester, NY; (S); Dance Clb; DECA; Ski Clb; SADD; Varsity Clb; L Var Mgr(s); Var Score Keeper; Var Timer; L Var Trk; Hon Roll; Trvl.

CLIFFORD, BRENDAN; La Salle Military Academy; Syosset, NY; (Y); 20/90; Computer Clb; ROTC; Ski Clb; School Play; Yrbk Phtg; JV Crs Cntry; Marist College; Computer Sci.

CLIFFORD, KERRI L; Bolton Central HS; Bolton Landing, NY; (Y); 3/23; School Play; Yrbk Ed-Chief; JV Var Bsktbl; Var Socr; Var Sftbl; JV Var Vllybl; Bausch & Lomb Sci Awd; St Johns U; Athltc Admin.

CLIFFORD, MAUREEN E; Copiague HS; Copiague, NY; (Y); 1/325; FBLA; School Musical; Yrbk Ed-Chief; Trs Frsh Cls; Trs Soph Cls; Trs Jr Cls; Var Fld Hcky; JV Vllybl; High Hon Roll; NHS; Suffolk Cnty All Lg Fld Hcky 85-86; NY Rgnts Schlrp 86; SUNY Binghamton; Accntg.

CLIFT, MICHELLE; Cathedral HS; New York, NY; (Y); 10/277; Drama Clb; Intnl Clb; Library Aide; Nwsp Rptr; Nwsp Stf; Sec Sr Cls; Hon Roll; Miami JR Schrls Prgm 85; Ascnt Prgm 85-86; Hnrb Mntn Engl, Religion, Soc Studies 85-86; Syracuse U; Jrnlsm.

CLIFT, TIMOTHY J; Glens Falls HS; Glens Falls, NY; (Y); 33/217; Am Leg Boys St; Church Yth Grp; SADD; Ftbl; Lcrss; Wrstlng; Hon Roll; St Schlr.

CLINCH, CHRIS; Saugerties JR SR HS; Saugerties, NY; (S); Art Clb; Church Yth Grp; Girl Scts; SADD; Band; Mrchg Band; Sec Frsh Cls; Sec Stu Cncl; JV Var Cheerleading; Powder Puff Ftbl.

CLINCH, CHRISTEN; Auburn HS; Auburn, NY; (Y); 10/400; Sec Drama Clb; SADD; Chorus; School Musical; School Play; Stage Crew; Jr NHS; NHS; Soc Stu Am Stu 86; Eng II Awd 86; Dntst.

CLINE, BRAD; East Hampton HS; E Hampton, NY; (Y); Yrbk Stf; JV Bsktbl; Hon Roll; Rep For Freshman Class Homecoming 83-84; Penn ST; Math.

CLINGAN, BRIDGET; Churchville-Chili HS; Rochester, NY; (Y); GAA; Pep Clb; Radio Clb; Ski Clb; School Play; Nwsp Stf; Yrbk Stf; Rep Stu Cncl; JV Cheerleading; JV Socr; Advrtsng.

CLINTON, CRYSTAL; Ben Franklin HS; Rochester, NY; (Y); Girl Scts; Yrbk Stf; Bsktbl; Var Sftbl; CC Awd; Hon Roll; Hon Roll 2nd & 3rd Mrkng Period 85-86; Tchng.

CLIVE, JEFFREY M; Ilion HS; Ilion, NY; (Y); Boy Scts; Church Yth Grp; JA; Library Aide; Model UN; Spanish Clb; SADD; Score Keeper; Wt Lftg; Hon Roll; Mohawk Valley CC; Aero Engr.

CLODOMIR, ELSIE; John Dewey HS; Brooklyn, NY; (Y); Church Yth Grp; Drama Clb; FNA; Chorus; School Play; CC Awd; Prfct Atten Awd; Teachers Aide; Color Guard; Stage Crew; Nrsng.

CLOEN, LYNNETTE; Hutchinson Central Tech; Buffalo, NY; (Y); Library Aide; Natl Beta Clb; Stage Crew; Variety Show; Nwsp Rptr; Bowling; Hon Roll; Cmptr Electrncs.

CLOOKEY, HEATHER; Madrid Waddington HS; Waddington, NY; (Y); Camera Clb; Church Yth Grp; Cmnty Wkr; Drama Clb; French Clb; GAA; Girl Scts; Pep Clb; Red Cross Aide; Spanish Clb; Lib Arts.

CLOR, JANET; Le Roy HS; Leroy, NY; (Y); Socr; Girl Scts; Ski Clb; Varsity Clb; Chorus; Coach Actv; Score Keeper; Trk; High Hon Roll; Hon Roll.

CLOSE, KATHRYN M; Johnstown HS; Johnstown, NY; (Y); 3/200; Dance Clb; Drama Clb; Girl Scts; Hosp Aide; Teachers Aide; Stage Crew; Variety Show; JV Var Cheerleading; Candy Striper Of Yr-Nathan Littuer Hosp 84; Fashion Inst Of Tech; Fash Merc.

CLOSSER, MIKE; Charles H Roth HS; Rochester, NY; (Y); Chess Clb; Lit Mag; Cit Awd; French Hon Soc; Rochester Inst Of Tech; Phtgrph.

CLOUSER, KIMBERLY; Niagara Wheatfield HS; Sanborn, NY; (Y); 5/291; Hst Pres Latin Clb; Math Clb; VP Pres Band; Drm Mjr(t); VP Stu Cncl; Var L Swmmng; Dnfth Awd; High Hon Roll; VP Pres NHS; Prfct Atten Awd; Police Athl Lg Svc Awd 86; NY St Legsltr Rep Cert 86; NY St Rgnts Schlrp Wnr 86; Fredonia St; Engrg.

CLOUTING, JENNIFER M; Arlington HS; Pleasant Valley, NY; (Y); 32/575; Pres Sec 4-H; Sec SADD; Variety Show; Nwsp Rptr; Yrbk Phtg; Rep Soph Cls; Rep Jr Cls; Pres Stu Cncl; Hon Roll; Lion Awd; NY ST Rgnts Schlrshp 86; SUNY Binghamton; Jrnlsm.

CLOW, DERRICK; Trumansburg HS; Trumansburg, NY; (Y); Exploring; Yrbk Phtg; Yrbk Stf; Ftbl; Trk; Wrstlng.

CLUNA, JAMIE; Farmingdale HS; Farmingdale, NY; (Y); Drm & Bgl; Ntl Merit Ltr; Care & Share Fstvl For L I Devlpmntl Ctr Volunteer 84; Stu Ldrshp Training Prgm; Psych.

CLUNIE, JACQUELYN; Kenmore West SR HS; Kenmore, NY; (Y); 166/424; Pres Trs Girl Scts; Math Tm; Political Wkr; Concert Band; Mrchg Band; Im Vllybl; Im Wt Lftg; Hon Roll; GSA Silver Ldrshp & Slvr Awds 85 & 86; SUNY Buffalo ST Coll; Comp.

CLYNE, ROSEMARY K; Saint Marys Acad; Cambridge, NY; (Y); 1/23; Nwsp Phtg; Rptr Nwsp Stf; Yrbk Stf; VP Frsh Cls; Trs Jr Cls; Var Powder Puff Ftbl; Var Sftbl; High Hon Roll; Kiwanis Awd; NHS; Gnrl Exc Awd 84-86.

CO, JOHN PATRICK; Vestal SR HS; Vestal, NY; (Y); Cmnty Wkr; Hosp Aide; Mathletes; Spanish Clb; SADD; High Hon Roll; NHS; Ntl Merit Ltr; Ski Clb; Bsktbl; Cert Of Rcgntn Broome Dvlpmntl Srvs 86; Cert Of Prtcptn Atlantic-Pacific Math Leag 86; Med.

COAKLEY, JEFFERY; G R Bodley HS; Fulton, NY; (Y); JV Lcrss; JV Socr; Htl Mgmt.

COAN, TIM; Fox Lane HS; Bedford, NY; (Y); Im Badmtn; Var Ftbl; JV Trk; Im Wt Lftg; High Hon Roll; Hon Roll; Ntl Merit Ltr.

COAR, MARILYN; Union-Endicott HS; Endwell, NY; (Y); French Clb; Key Clb; Ski Clb; Concert Band; Drill Tm; Mrchg Band; School Musical; High Hon Roll; Hon Roll; NHS; U Of VT; Psych.

COATES, CHRIS; Corcoran HS; Syracuse, NY; (Y); Boy Scts; Church Yth Grp; Stu Cncl; Var Bsbl; Var Bsktbl; JV Ftbl; JV Lcrss; Hon Roll.

COATES, ROBBIE; Camden Central HS; Camden, NY; (Y); Church Yth Grp; Drama Clb; Band; School Musical; School Play; Stage Crew; Hon Roll; Oswego ST Coll; Engl.

COATS, JENNIFER; Randolph Central HS; E Randolph, NY; (Y); 4/81; Art Clb; French Clb; Girl Scts; Quiz Bowl; Ski Clb; Acpl Chr; Yrbk Sprt Ed; Cit Awd; Pres Schlr; Voice Dem Awd; Excllnce Smmr Coll Schlrshp 85; Allegheny Mtn Sci Fair Wnnr 86; Rgnts Schlrshp Wnnr 86; Wells.

COBB, CHERYL; Ticonderoga HS; Hague, NY; (Y); Drama Clb; French Clb; Hosp Aide; Key Clb; SADD; School Musical; School Play; Cheerleading; Vllybl; Hon Roll; Mrn Bio.

COBB, JENNIFER; Spencer Van Etten Central HS; Spencer, NY; (Y); 22/87; Cmnty Wkr; Girl Scts; Pep Clb; Varsity Clb; Band; Chorus; Church Choir; Concert Band; Mrchg Band; School Musical; Acctg Awd 85; All Cnty Awds Band Chorus 83-86; Ntl Choral Awd 86; Cazenovia Coll; Acctng.

COBB, JUDITH; Hermon-Dekalb Central Schl; De Kalb Jct, NY; (Y); 3/40; Band; Chorus; Concert Band; Mrchg Band; Stage Crew; Nwsp Rptr; Ed Yrbk Stf; High Hon Roll; JP Sousa Awd; NHS; Regents Schlrshp 86; Houghton Coll.

COCCA, CARLA M; St Catharine Acad; Bronx, NY; (S); 27/205; Office Aide; Teachers Aide; VP Soph Cls; VP Jr Cls; VP Stu Cncl; Capt Cheerleading; Hon Roll; Most Active Hmrm Rep 82-83; Vet.

COCCA, MICHAEL; Tamarac HS; Troy, NY; (Y); 19/125; German Clb; Intnl Clb; Math Tm; Var Ftbl; JV Wrstlng; Ntl Merit Ltr; Regents Schlrshp 86; Rochester Tech Inst; Mech Engr.

COCHRAN, KATHERINE A; Elmira Free Acad; Elmira, NY; (Y); VP Pres French Clb; Intnl Clb; Hst Key Clb; Chorus; School Musical; Yrbk Stf; Tennis; Lion Awd; NHS; Ntl Merit Ltr; 3rd Natl Frnch Exm Levl 2 And 3 84-85; GA Inst Of Tech; Engrng.

COCHRANE, CHERYL; De Sales Catholic HS; Lockport, NY; (Y); 12/33; Hosp Aide; Hon Roll; NHS; Plc Athltc Lg Inc For Srv Awd 86; Prfssnl Sec Intrnl Awd 86; Francis & Agnes Schimscheiner Mrl Schlrsh; Trvl.

COCHRANE, FRED T; Smithtown High Schl West; Smithtown, NY; (Y); Chorus; Swing Chorus; Lit Mag; Bowling; Hon Roll; James Madison U.

COCHRANE, SAMUEL; Hoosic Valley Central Schl; Johnsonville, NY; (S); 7/98; Boy Scts; Drama Clb; Latin Clb; Band; Chorus; Church Choir; School Musical; Pres Stu Cncl; Crs Cntry; Trk; Mgt.

COCKAYNE, SCOTT; Brockport HS; Brockport, NY; (Y); 90/310; Boy Scts; Ski Clb; Yrbk Phtg; Swmmng; Hon Roll.

COCKERELL, KRISTEN; Mount St Mary Acad; Kenmore, NY; (Y); Art Clb; Debate Tm; Science Clb; Spanish Clb; School Play; Stage Crew; Variety Show; Cheerleading; Hon Roll; NHS; Wstrn NY Sci Cngrs 83; U Of Buffalo; Grphc Arts.

COCKLE, JANET; Fillmore Central HS; Fillmore, NY; (Y); 4/55; 4-H; FFA; Office Aide; SADD; Nwsp Sprt Ed; Var Socr; 4-H Awd; High Hon Roll; Hon Roll; NHS; Olean Bus Inst; Accntng.

COCOLICCHIO, BRIAN; Valley Central HS; Montgomery, NY; (Y); 8/313; Debate Tm; Hosp Aide; Capt Math Tm; Trs Science Clb; Var L Socr; Var L Trk; Hon Roll; NHS; Spanish NHS; Walden Svgs Bnk Hist Awd 85; Chem Engrng.

COCOZZO, CHRISTINA; Mechanicville HS; Mechanicville, NY; (S); 4/100; Ski Clb; Spanish Clb; SADD; Band; Nwsp Ed-Chief; Yrbk Stf; Stu Cncl; Bsktbl; Cheerleading; Trk; Dntl.

CODERRE, MICHELLE; Smithtown East HS; Nesconset, NY; (Y); Cmnty Wkr; Key Clb; Spanish Clb; Bsktbl; Hon Roll; Spanish NHS; Mdrn Lang Awd 86; Suffolk County CC; Frgn Lang.

CODONER, CHRISTOPHER; Monsignor Farrell HS; Staten Island, NY; (Y); 40/300; French Clb; Yrbk Stf; Var Bowling; JV Swmmng; French Hon Soc; High Hon Roll; NHS; Dntstry.

CODY, JENNIFER; Charles H Roth HS; W Henrietta, NY; (Y); Church Yth Grp; Cmnty Wkr; Dance Clb; Drama Clb; Trs French Clb; GAA; Girl Scts; Library Aide; Office Aide; Pep Clb; Ldrshp Awd 84; Schltc Ltr 86; Comm Serv Ltr 86; Ithica; Stage Perfrmr.

COENEN, ANDREW; Alfred G Berner HS; Massapequa Park, NY; (Y); German Clb; Trs Key Clb; JV Var Ftbl; JV Wrstlng; High Hon Roll; Hon Roll; NHS; Ntl Sci Olympiad Awd 86; Nation Physics Challenge 86; Sci.

COFFEY, DANNY; St Agnes HS; New York, NY; (Y); Bsktbl; Ice Hcky; Hon Roll; Iona Coll; Cmmnctns.

COFFEY, JEANNE M; Avoca Central HS; Avoca, NY; (Y); 8/44; Pres Church Yth Grp; Trs French Clb; Pres Band; Chorus; Yrbk Phtg; Sec Stu Cncl; Capt Tennis; Sec Frsh Cls; Sec Soph Cls; Rep Sr Cls; Regnts Schlrshp Recpnt 86; Rotry Exchng Stu 86; Clarkson; Engrg.

COFFEY, JOHN; St Pauls Schl; Malverne, NY; (Y); 6/35; Latin Clb; Varsity Clb; Nwsp Rptr; Nwsp Sprt Ed; Lit Mag; Pres Soph Cls; Stu Cncl; Crs Cntry; VP Tennis; Classics.

COFFEY, MIKE; Lindenhurst HS; Lindenhurst, NY; (Y); Band; Jazz Band; Socr; Sony Purchase; Music.

COFFEY, MONICA; Sacrea Heart Acad; Malverne, NY; (S); 15/189; French Clb; SADD; Chorus; Stage Crew; Yrbk Stf; Pres Jr Cls; Stu Cncl; Tennis; Hon Roll; NHS.

COFFMAN, CAROLYN; Generd HS; Generd, NY; (S); 8/175; Am Leg Aux Girls St; Band; Church Choir; Concert Band; Mrchg Band; School Musical; Lit Mag; Var L Crs Cntry; High Hon Roll; NHS; Dickinson Clg; Poli Sci.

COGAN, SEAN; Curtis HS; Staten Island, NY; (Y); Art Clb; Boy Scts; Pres Church Yth Grp; Cit Awd; Order Of Arrow Hon Soc Scouting 85.

COGAN, TRACY; C O Dickerson HS; Trumansburg, NY; (Y); 6/126; French Clb; SADD; Varsity Clb; Yrbk Sprt Ed; Yrbk Stf; VP Stu Cncl; Var Bsktbl; Var Socr; High Hon Roll; NHS; Hist.

COGER, TIMOTHY P; Corning East HS; Corning, NY; (Y); Am Leg Boys St; Model UN; Rep Soph Cls; Rep Jr Cls; Crs Cntry; Capt Var Lcrss; Var L Socr.

COHEN, ADAM I; Scarsdale HS; Scarsdale, NY; (Y); JV Var Lcrss; NY ST Rgnts Schlrshp 85-86; Wslyn U.

COHEN, ADAM S; Sachem High Schl North; Holbrook, NY; (Y); 86/1381; Science Clb; Ski Clb; Temple Yth Grp; Band; Concert Band; Jazz Band; Mrchg Band; Orch; School Musical; Symp Band; Regents Schlrshp 86; NY Telephone Schlrshp 86; Brandeis U.

COHEN, ALYSSA; Emma Willard Schl; Annapolis, MD; (Y); Ski Clb; School Play; Yrbk Stf; JV Socr; Im Tennis; Var Tennis; Emma Wllrd Schl Drm Prctr 86-87; Echo Hll Otdr Schl Intrn 86; Coord Oxfm AM Emma Wllrd 84-87; Envrnmnt Sci.

COHEN, BETH; Blink Brook HS; Rye Brook, NY; (Y); Math Tm; Ski Clb; Concert Band; JV Socr; JV Sftbl.

COHEN, BRIAN A; Lakeland HS; Yorktown Hts, NY; (Y); 17/350; Debate Tm; NFL; SADD; Stage Crew; Yrbk Phtg; Golf; Hon Roll; NHS; Ntl Merit SF; Jr NHS; Cmnctns.

COHEN, BRIAN S; Lynbrook HS; East Rockaway, NY; (Y); 10/240; Mathletes; Temple Yth Grp; Varsity Clb; Lit Mag; JV Bsktbl; Var Capt Lcrss; JV Socr; Var Wrstlng; High Hon Roll; Hon Roll; Regents Scholar 86; U Binghampton.

COHEN, CHAD; Mahopa HS; Goldens Bridge, NY; (Y); 12/383; Math Tm; Temple Yth Grp; JV Bsktbl; Im Ftbl; Var Capt Tennis; High Hon Roll; NHS; Ntl Merit Ltr; Pres Schlr.

COHEN, DANIEL E; The Bronx High School Of Science; Jackson Heights, NY; (Y); 2/750; Library Aide; Hon Roll; Truste Schlrshp 86; Rgnts Schlrshp 86; Jose Martel Essy Cntst 1st Pl 85; Chem.

COHEN, DARIN E; Ward Mehville HS; South Setauket, NY; (Y); Cmnty Wkr; Computer Clb; Ski Clb; Concert Band; Crs Cntry; Trk; Vllybl; High Hon Roll; NHS; Regents Scholar Wnnr 86; Gold Achvt Awd 84; 2nd Pl Plaq County Mth Cont 83; Biochem.

COHEN, DAWN S; Midwood HS; Brooklyn, NY; (Y); 11/556; Math Tm; Science Clb; Concert Band; School Musical; Yrbk Stf; Gov Hon Prg Awd; High Hon Roll; NCTE Awd; Ntl Merit Ltr; Val; Natl Womans Wk Essay Wnnr, NYC Mayor Awds 83 & 85; Brklyn Jew Pstl Empl Wlfre Lg Schlrshp & Rgnst 86; Vassar Coll; Corp Law.

COHEN, DREW H; Riverdale Country Schl; New York, NY; (Y); 2/110; Pres Camp Fr Inc; Chrmn 4-H; VP Girl Scts; Keywanettes; Mathletes; Office Aide; Q&S; Red Cross Aide; Pres VICA; Mrchg Band; Westinghse Sci Achvt SF 85; Manhattan Coll; Supervisor.

COHEN, ELISE; Half Hollow Hills East HS; Melville, NY; (Y); Cmnty Wkr; SADD; JV Vllybl; Hon Roll; Suffolk Cnty CC; Bus Adm.

COHEN, ERIK; Wellington C Mepham HS; North Bellmore, NY; (Y); Computer Clb; Debate Tm; Math Tm; Science Clb; Im Wt Lftg; JV Wrstlng; Hon Roll; Ntl Merit Schol; Chem Ntl Sci Olympd Awd 86; Soc Stdies Ntl Olympd Awd 84; Psych.

COHEN, GREGORY; Newtown HS; Cambria Hgts, NY; (Y); 181/790; Pep Clb; Varsity Clb; Band; Concert Band; Jazz Band; Mrchg Band; Symp Band; Bsbl; Bsktbl; 21 Trhophies Comm Activtes 83-86; Hampton Inst; Law.

COHEN, HARVEY; Corning-Painted Post West HS; Painted Post, NY; (Y); 25/257; Exploring; Pres Trs Key Clb; Ski Clb; Trs Thesps; Varsity Clb; School Play; Socr; Var L Tennis; High Hon Roll; NY ST Regents Schlrshp 86; Donavan Acad Schlrshp Cornell Smr Coll 85; Tns Inter Sectnl Trnmnt 85; WA U St Louis; Bus.

COHEN, HELAINE; Tottenville HS; Staten Island, NY; (S); 9/800; Cmnty Wkr; Teachers Aide; High Hon Roll; Jr NHS; NHS; Psychlgy.

COHEN, HOWARD; Truman HS; Bronx, NY; (Y); 87/494; Office Aide; Chorus; Prfct Atten Awd; Rgnts Schlrshp Awd 86; Bus Educ Awd 86; Super Yth NYC Awd 85; Tax Prep Awd 85; Baruch Coll; Comp Statstcs.

COHEN, JANE E; Emma Willard Schl; Menands, NY; (Y); Ski Clb; Temple Yth Grp; Varsity Clb; Nwsp Ed-Chief; Rptr Nwsp Rptr; Nwsp Stf; Sec Soph Cls; Rep Stu Cncl; JV Sftbl; Var Tennis; Wellesley Coll; Intl Rltns.

COHEN, JEFF; West Hempsted HS; West Hempstead, NY; (Y); Ski Clb; JV Var Ftbl; Hon Roll; Aerntcl Engrng.

COHEN, JODI; East Meadow HS; E Meadow, NY; (Y); Key Clb; Rep SADD; Temple Yth Grp; Yrbk Stf; JV Cheerleading.

COHEN, JONATHAN; Port Richmond HS; Staten Island, NY; (Y); Camera Clb; Ski Clb; Temple Yth Grp; Yrbk Rptr; Var Bowling; High Hon Roll; Pre Dntstry.

COHEN, KRISTY; Gowanda Central HS; Collins, NY; (Y); AFS; Church Yth Grp; Ski Clb; Spanish Clb; Band; Chorus; Concert Band; Drm Mjr(t); Jazz Band; Mrchg Band; Grove City Coll; Elem Educ.

COHEN, LAURIE; Centereach HS; Centereach, NY; (S); 80/429; Chess Clb; Computer Clb; DECA; Q&S; Scholastic Bowl; Temple Yth Grp; Nwsp Rptr; Nwsp Stf; Ed Lit Mag; Slvr & Brnz Mdlst Suffolk Cty Acad Dcthln 84-85; Kids For Kids Prodctn Oliver & Loves Lbrs Lst 83-86; Oswego; Poli Sci.

COHEN, LESLEY; Briarcliff HS; Briarcliff, NY; (Y); Yrbk Stf; Cmnty Wkr; Sec Soph Cls; Trs Stu Cncl; Capt Cheerleading; DAR Awd; Hon Roll; Irwin Bed Klein Schlrshp 85-86; George Washington U; Politcl Sc.

COHEN, LISA M; Roy C Ketchm SR HS; Poughkeepsie, NY; (Y); 7/500; AFS; Temple Yth Grp; Sec Frsh Cls; Sec Soph Cls; Sec Sr Cls; Stu Cncl; Var Capt Cheerleading; NHS; Ntl Merit SF; Rotary Awd; Andrew Erdreich Mem Essay Awd 83.

COHEN, MICHELLE L; John H Glenn HS; Greenlawn, NY; (Y); 20/268; Jazz Band; School Musical; School Play; Yrbk Ed-Chief; French Hon Soc; Pres Jr NHS; NHS; Drama Clb; French Clb; Chorus; NY ST Schl Music Assn-All ST Voice 84, 85; NY ST Smmr Schl Thtr Pgm 85; Rgnt Schlr 86; Sarah Lawrence.

COHEN, NANCI A; Clarkstown North HS; New City, NY; (Y); French Clb; Spanish Clb; Varsity Clb; Yrbk Stf; Fld Hcky; Mat Maids; Trk; Hon Roll; Jr NHS; NHS; 2nd Hnrs Iona Lang Cont French 86; Regents Schlrshp 86; Suny Albany.

COHEN, NANCY R; Bronx HS Of Science; Flushing, NY; (Y); Cmnty Wkr; Key Clb; Office Aide; Service Clb; Teachers Aide; Temple Yth Grp; Hon Roll; NHS; Prfct Atten Awd; Arista Hnr Soc 86; Rgnts Schlrshp 86; Schlrshp In Hebrew 84; NY U; Doc.

COHEN, NEAL W; Oceanside HS; Oceanside, NY; (Y); 73/537; Debate Tm; Pres French Clb; French Hon Soc; Hon Roll; Ntl Jr Hnr Soc 82-83; SUNY.

COHEN, SCOTT P; Gen Douglas Mac Arthur HS; Levittown, NY; (Y); 24/326; Boy Scts; Computer Clb; Debate Tm; Science Clb; Ski Clb; SADD; Nwsp Stf; Yrbk Ed-Chief; High Hon Roll; Hon Roll; 1st Pl Mac Arthr Comp Fair 84, 85; NY ST Rgnts Schlrshp 86; 1st Pl Pratt U Comp Cntst 85; Buffalo ST U; Comp Sci.

COHEN, SETH H; Lynbrook HS; E Rockaway, NY; (Y); 37/260; Drama Clb; Mathletes; Pres Spanish Clb; School Play; Sec Frsh Cls; Var Capt Lcrss; JV Socr; Wt Lftg; High Hon Roll; Hon Roll; Rgnts Schlrshp 86; Profssnl Modl 84-86; Vassar Coll; Med.

COHEN, SUSAN BETH; New Rochelle HS; Scarsdale, NY; (Y); Drama Clb; French Clb; PAVAS; Temple Yth Grp; Thesps; Chorus; School Musical; Yrbk Rptr; Soph Cls; Jr Cls; Psych.

COHEN, TANYA; Moriah Central HS; Mineville, NY; (Y); 4/93; AFS; Hosp Aide; Ski Clb; Pres Frsh Cls; Sec Trs Stu Cncl; Co-Capt Cheerleading; VP NHS; NYS Regents Scholar 86; Govnr Conway Scholar 86; JR Miss Schltc Awd 85; SUNY Albany; Bus.

COHEN, TODD; Roy C Ketcham HS; Wappingers Falls, NY; (Y); Var Bowling; Var Ftbl; Northwestern; Acctg.

COHEN, TODD; Valley Stream Central HS; Valley Stream, NY; (Y); Computer Clb; Mathletes; Math Clb; Math Tm; JV Wrstlng; Hon Roll; Jr NHS.

COHEN, WILLIAM; Edgemont HS; Hartsdale, NY; (Y); Jazz Band; Stu Cncl; Var Bsktbl; Var Crs Cntry; Var Trk; Bausch & Lomb Sci Awd; Ntl Merit SF; CAP; Pres Computer Clb; Math Tm; Cum Laude Soc 86; NYS Sci Sprvsrs Assoc Physics Awd 86; Empire ST Schlrshp 86; Princeton U.

COHICK, CHARLENE; Gates Chili HS; Rochester, NY; (Y); FCA; Var Bsktbl; High Hon Roll; Hon Roll; Bus.

COHN, JODY L; Lawrence HS; Inwood, NY; (Y); 44/500; AFS; Drama Clb; French Clb; Band; Orch; Nwsp Rptr; VP Sr Cls; Score Keeper; CC Awd; Cit Awd; Most Spirited SR Girl In Grad Clss; Cornell U.

COISMAN, JAMES; Marion Central HS; Marion, NY; (Y); 4-H; German Clb; Model UN; Natl Beta Clb; Quiz Bowl; Band; 4-H Awd; Hon Roll; Roberts Wesleyan Coll; Vet Med.

COIT, LAMAR; Fiorello Laguardia HS Music & Arts; Bronx, NY; (S); 17/43; VP JA; Office Aide; Service Clb; Jazz Band; Off Sr Cls; Hon Roll; NHS; Teachers Aide; Band; Music Hnr Leag; Cornell U; Engrng.

COKE, JACQUELINE; James Monroe HS; Bronx, NY; (Y); Church Yth Grp; Cmnty Wkr; FCA; Temple Yth Grp; Chorus; Church Choir; High Hon Roll; Hon Roll; Ntl Merit SF; Prfct Atten Awd.

COKER, CRAIG A; Hampton Bays JR SR HS; Hampton Bays, NY; (Y); 26/106; Am Leg Boys St; Varsity Clb; Band; Concert Band; Mrchg Band; Var Capt Ftbl; Var Trk; Var Wrstlng; Hon Roll; Hnrbl Mntn Suffolk Cnty Lgue VI Ftbll 85-86; Mst Otstndng Offnsv Lnmn 85; Cvl Engnrng.

COKER, LAURA; Center Moriches HS; Center Moriches, NY; (Y); 4/107; Debate Tm; VP Pres French Clb; Latin Clb; Sec Pres Service Clb; Ed Nwsp Rptr; Ed Lit Mag; Hon Roll; NHS; Ntl Merit Ltr; Cmmnctns.

COLABELLA, DORINE; New Rochelle HS; New Rochelle, NY; (Y); Boys Clb Am; Dance Clb; Pres SADD; Sec Stu Cncl; Hon Roll; French Clb; Political Wkr; School Play; Variety Show; Rep Soph Cls; Merrit Schlrshp Wnnr; Modl Cngrss; Psych.

COLABELLO, BRIDGET; The Franciscan Acad; N Syracuse, NY; (S); FBLA; GAA; Yrbk Ed-Chief; Yrbk Phtg; Sec Frsh Cls; VP Frsh Cls; VP Jr Cls; Stu Cncl; Tennis; Pres NHS; Le Moyne Coll.

COLANDRO, TINAMARIE; New Hyde Pk Memorial HS; New Hyde Pk, NY; (Y); Spanish Clb; Pom Pon; High Hon Roll; Hon Roll; Bus Adm.

COLANGELO, CARRIE; Ossining HS; Ossining, NY; (Y); Cmnty Wkr; Model UN; Variety Show; Yrbk Stf; Off Stu Cncl; Gym; Powder Puff Ftbl; Socr; High Hon Roll; NHS.

COLANGELO, CHRISTINE; Notre Dame Acad; Staten Island, NY; (Y); Church Yth Grp; Cmnty Wkr; Computer Clb; Dance Clb; French Clb; Hosp Aide; Library Aide; Science Clb; Teachers Aide; Jr NHS; Mst Imprvd Dncr Awd 84.

COLANGELO, DAVID; Cicero-North Syracuse HS; North Syracuse, NY; (S); 35/622; VP Church Yth Grp; Exploring; Math Tm; Jazz Band; Orch; Symp Band; Var Trk; Hon Roll; NHS; Bst Soloist KY St Fld Band Champs 85; Clarkson; Mech Engr.

COLANGELO, MARIA; Nanuet SR HS; Nanuet, NY; (Y); 28/230; NHS; 1st Hnrs, Excllnc Spanish; 1st Hnrs In Spanish Comp; Iona; Lang.

COLANTINO, CHRIS; Eden SR HS; Eden, NY; (Y); SADD; Varsity Clb; Rep Jr Cls; Rep Stu Cncl; JV Var Bsbl; JV Var Ftbl; Im Vllybl; Im Wt Lftg; JV Var Wrstlng; Prfct Atten Awd; 2nd Pl St Frncs Trnmnt Wrstlng 84-85; 2nd Pl W Snca Trnmnt Wrstlng 85-86; 1st Pl Frntr Trnmnt Wrstlng; Engrng.

COLAO, JOHN; Port Richmond HS; Staten Island, NY; (Y); Bsbl; Bsktbl; St Johns U.

COLAPIETRO, CHRISTOPHER P; Union-Endicott HS; Endicott, NY; (Y); 12/450; Church Yth Grp; Cmnty Wkr; Computer Clb; Mathletes; Varsity Clb; Rep Frsh Cls; Rep Soph Cls; Rep Jr Cls; Rep Sr Cls; Rep Stu Cncl; 2nd Pl Lcl DPMA-CCC Prgrmng Cntst 85; Williams Coll; Math.

COLASANTE, DANA; Mahopac HS; Mahopac, NY; (Y); 149/409; GAA; Varsity Clb; Chorus; Socr; Vllybl; Hon Roll.

COLASANTE, DAVID G; Friends Acad; Mill Neck, NY; (Y); Spanish Clb; Band; Concert Band; Jazz Band; School Musical; School Play; Yrbk Rptr; Yrbk Stf; Bsbl; Bsktbl; Villanova; Econ.

COLASANTI, MARY PATRICIA; Bishop Ludden HS; Liverpool, NY; (S); Dance Clb; French Clb; NFL; Speech Tm; SADD; School Musical; High Hon Roll; HOBY Ambssdr 85; Langs.

COLASURDO, KELLY; Homer HS; Cortland, NY; (Y); Nwsp Rptr; Sec Frsh Cls; JV Var Bsktbl; Var Capt Sftbl; JV Tennis; Cit Awd; Elks Awd; High Hon Roll; NHS; Latin Club Awd 85 & 86; Putnam Prize Soc Stud 85; Lib Arts.

COLATARCI, ALISA; Tonawanda SR HS; Tonawanda, NY; (Y); French Clb; SADD; Nwsp Stf; Stu Cncl; Cheerleading; Coach Actv; Sftbl; Tennis; Hon Roll; NCA All Star Chrldg Sqd 86; Niagara U; Pre-Law.

COLAZZI, BRYAN; York Central Schl; Leicester, NY; (Y); 16/103; Boy Scts; Church Yth Grp; Band; Concert Band; Drm Mjr(t); Jazz Band; Mrchg Band; Pep Band; School Musical; Symp Band; AD & ALTARE & Dei Awd 86; Yth Fit Achvt Awd 86; Comp Sci.

COLB, DAVID; Mamaroneck HS; Larchmont, NY; (Y); 95/390; Cmnty Wkr; Science Clb; Service Clb; Stage Crew; Nwsp Bus Mgr; JV Lcrss; Hon Roll; Chem Awd 10th.

COLBATH, MICHAEL R; Suffern HS; Suffern, NY; (Y); 81/397; Am Leg Boys St; Var L Bsbl; Var L Bsktbl; Var L Ftbl; Cit Awd; Hon Roll; Concert Band; Outstndng Male Athlete 85-86; MVP Var Ftbll 85-86; Var Athlete Agnst Subst Abuse; Gettysburg Coll; Bus.

COLBERT, DAVID; Amsterdam HS; Amsterdam, NY; (Y); 20/316; Computer Clb; Band; Jazz Band; Mrchg Band; Pep Band; Var Crs Cntry; Var Trk; High Hon Roll; NHS; Prfct Atten Awd; Syracuse U; Bio.

COLBERT, ILENE; St Barnabas HS; Bronx, NY; (Y); 90/189; Church Yth Grp; Computer Clb; Drama Clb; Office Aide; Teachers Aide; Church Choir; Georgetown U; Law.

COLBERT, MELISSA; John C Birdlebough HS; Phoenix, NY; (Y); 12/250; Church Yth Grp; Drama Clb; Latin Clb; Band; Chorus; Concert Band; Mrchg Band; School Musical; Swing Chorus; Socr; Music Ed.

COLBURN, DANIELLE; Saint Catherine Acad; Bronx, NY; (Y); 31/185; Dance Clb; Hosp Aide; Teachers Aide; Hon Roll; NHS; St Johns U; Comp Sci.

COLBURN, LISA; Frewsburg Central HS; Frewsburg, NY; (Y); 3/86; Pres Church Yth Grp; Sec 4-H; Concert Band; Jazz Band; Sec Stu Cncl; Capt Var Bsktbl; JV Cheerleading; Capt Var Trk; Var Vllybl; Sec NHS; Mrch Dms Medcl Fld Schlrshp 86; Vac Aic Schlrshp 86; Natl Hnr Soc Math Awd 86; U Of Buffalo; Phy Thrpy.

COLBURN, MARY; Whitesboro SR HS; Whitesboro, NY; (Y); Cmnty Wkr; GAA; Hosp Aide; Red Cross Aide; SADD; Chorus; Var L Bsktbl; Var L Sftbl; Hon Roll; MVCC; Bus Admn.

COLBY, KAREN JANINE; Wellsville HS; Wellsville, NY; (Y); 28/126; Aud/Vis; Debate Tm; Office Aide; Speech Tm; Chorus; School Musical; School Play; Hon Roll; Drama Clb; Intnl Clb; Rgnts Schlrshp 86; Arion Awd-Excllnc-Chr 86; Geneseo; Comm.

COLCLOUGH, PATRICK; Saugerties HS; Saugerties, NY; (S); 4/250; VP French Clb; German Clb; Yrbk Ed-Chief; Pres Frsh Cls; Var L Crs Cntry; Var L Trk; High Hon Roll; Mid Atl Ntl JR Olymp Ski Tm 85; Gftd, Tlntd Pgm; Lang.

COLDEN, ANGELA; Schroon Lake Central HS; Schroon Lake, NY; (S); 1/22; French Clb; Chorus; School Musical; VP Soph Cls; Trs Stu Cncl; Var Cheerleading; Var Socr; High Hon Roll; I Care Awd 85; Natl Hnr Scty 85-86; Bus Mgmt.

COLDEN, DARYL; Earl L Vandermeulen HS; Port Jefferson, NY; (Y); 1/350; Latin Clb; SADD; Nwsp Stf; Yrbk Sprt Ed; Yrbk Stf; Trs Stu Cncl; Var Socr; NHS; Sfflk Cnty Mthmtcs Cntst 2dn Plc Schl Lvl 12 86-86; Sfflk Cnty Mthmtcs Cntst 1st Plc Lvl II.

COLE, AMY; Livonia Central HS; Lima, NY; (Y); Dance Clb; GAA; Teachers Aide; Varsity Clb; Var Capt Bsktbl; Coach Actv; Var Sftbl; Stat Vllybl; Hon Roll; Umpire Smmr Sftbll 84&85; Trp To Europe Grmn Clb 85; Antq Car Buff Ownr 56 Ford PU; Purdue; Aviation.

COLE, C BRENDON; W Genesee HS; Camillus, NY; (Y); Variety Show; Bsktbl; Ftbl; High Hon Roll; NHS.

COLE, CAROL; St Catharine Acad; Bronx, NY; (Y); Church Yth Grp; Exploring; Hosp Aide; JA; Yrbk Stf; Stu Cncl; Trk; Hon Roll; Prfct Atten Awd; Rgnts Nrsng Schlrshp 86; Mt St Vincent; Nrsng.

COLE, CHRISTINA; The Buffalo Seminary; Orchard Pk, NY; (Y); VP Church Yth Grp; Hosp Aide; Pres Frsh Cls; VP Jr Cls; Pres Sr Cls; Rep Stu Cncl; Var Socr; Var Capt Sftbl; Hon Roll; NHS.

COLE, CHRISTOP E; Miller Place HS; Sound Beach, NY; (Y); Chess Clb; Quiz Bowl; Hon Roll; NHS; Regnts Schlrshp 86; SUNY Stonybrook; Med.

COLE, CHRISTOPHER; New Rochelle HS; New Rochelle, NY; (Y); Pres FBLA; SADD; Concert Band; Mrchg Band; Symp Band; NHS; 2nd Pl NY ST FLBA Accntng I 86; Bus Adm.

COLE, CRAIG; Middletown HS; Circleville, NY; (Y); Boy Scts; Computer Clb; Mathletes; Math Tm; Drm & Bgl; Im Fld Hcky; Im Vllybl; Hon Roll; Astro.

COLE, DIANNA; Portville Central HS; Portville, NY; (Y); 26/108; Cmnty Wkr; Band; Concert Band; Mrchg Band; High Hon Roll; Hon Roll; NHS; U Of NV Las Vegas; Spnsh.

COLE, ENID; Nazareth Regional HS; Brooklyn, NY; (Y); Dance Clb; Chorus; Variety Show; Dnc Exclnce Awd 83-84; Dnc Mdl/Chrs Cert/Spec Chrs Cert 84-85 & 85-86; Hunter; Journalism.

COLE, ERICKA L; Bronx HS Of Science; Bronx, NY; (Y); Cmnty Wkr; Chorus; Church Choir; School Musical; Variety Show; Cheerleading; Pres Ntl JR Hnr Soc 83; NYU; Bio.

COLE, HEATHER; Fairport HS; Fairport, NY; (Y); Church Yth Grp; Drama Clb; Girl Scts; Key Clb; Rep Jr Cls; Rep Stu Cncl; Var Tennis; Hon Roll; Prfct Atten Awd; Sparkplug Awd Vrsty Tennis 86.

COLE, HOLLY; Williamsville South HS; Williamsville, NY; (Y); Church Yth Grp; Band; Chorus; Concert Band; Jazz Band; Madrigals; Mrchg Band; School Musical; Hon Roll; Erie Cnty Chorus 86; All St Choir 86; Socl Wrk.

COLE, JEFF; Irondequoit HS; Rochester, NY; (Y); 32/389; Am Leg Boys St; Boy Scts; Model UN; Rep Stu Cncl; Hon Roll; Church Yth Grp; School Musical; NACEL Exchg Stu To France 86; Alpine Ski Tm 83-86; Us Acadmc Decathalon 1st Pl 86; US Military Acad.

COLE, JONATHAN; Port Chester SR HS; Port Chester, NY; (Y); 1/245; Boy Scts; Hosp Aide; Yrbk Stf; Jr NHS; Mu Alp Tht; NHS; Pres Spanish NHS; AFS; Pres Aud/Vis; Rensselaer Math & Sci Awd 86; Sci Hnr Soc 86; Pre Med.

COLE, JUDITH; E J Wilson SR HS; Spencerport, NY; (Y); 12/350; Pres Church Yth Grp; French Clb; Math Tm; Ski Clb; Symp Band; Rep Frsh Cls; Rep Soph Cls; Chrmn Jr Cls; High Hon Roll; NHS; Indstrl Engrng.

COLE, LAURA; Torrejon American HS; Apo, NY; (Y); Aud/Vis; VP Ski Clb; Speech Tm; Yrbk Ed-Chief; Var Capt Bsktbl; Var Sftbl; Var Tennis; Var Vllybl; High Hon Roll; Hon Roll; Althlt Of Yr 86; All Trnmnt All Cnfrnce Bsktbll 86; Hnrs Eng 85-86; U Of AZ; Cmmnctn.

COLE, MARNIE; West Babylon HS; Babylon, NY; (Y); 20/413; Drama Clb; Pres Intnl Clb; School Play; Yrbk Stf; Var Stat Bsktbl; High Hon Roll; Pres NHS.

COLE, MARY ANNE; Walter Panas HS; Peekskill, NY; (Y); 13/220; Band; Mrchg Band; School Play; Rep Stu Cncl; Stat Bsktbl; JV Socr; Tennis; High Hon Roll; NHS; NYS Regents Schlrshp 86; SUNY Binhamton; Frgn Lang.

COLE, MELISSA; Herricks HS; Roslyn Hts, NY; (Y); Aud/Vis; Cmnty Wkr; Drama Clb; Hosp Aide; Key Clb; Temple Yth Grp; Chorus; Orch; Stage Crew; Hon Roll; Bus Admn.

COLE, MELISSA R; La Salle SR HS; Niagara Falls, NY; (S); 19/258; Drama Clb; Library Aide; Trs Sr Cls; Hon Roll; NHS; Bst Publcty Chrmn Drama Clb 84-85; U NH; Marine Stds.

COLE, NINA; Plattsburgh HS; Plattsburgh, NY; (Y); Cmnty Wkr; Hosp Aide; Political Wkr; Yrbk Stf; Hon Roll; Vlntr Of Mnth 84; Socl Wrk.

COLE, ROBERT J; Chenango Forks Central HS; Chenango Forks, NY; (S); Band; Jazz Band; Mrchg Band; Orch; School Play; Symp Band; Rep Stu Cncl; JV Socr; Hon Roll; All ST Band 86; All Cnty Band 84; Outstndng Nyssma Awd 83-85; Law.

COLE, SEAN R; West Genesee SR HS; Camillus, NY; (Y); 125/450; French Clb; Var Crs Cntry; JV Var Ftbl; Var Capt Gym; Var Capt Trk; High Hon Roll; Hon Roll; Varsity Clb; Wegmans Schlrsdhp 86-87; MVP Awd Vrsty Gym 85; Mst Imprvd Athlt 86; Suny; Accntnt.

COLE, TODD; Tioga Central HS; Tioga Center, NY; (Y); 5/80; Boy Scts; Variety Show; Var Ftbl; Var Wrstlng; High Hon Roll; Hon Roll; NHS; SADD; School Musical; Prfct Atten Awd; Gold Key Rgnl Art Awd 84; Order Of The Arrw 83; 4th Pl Class D Wrstlng Trnmnt 86; Phys Thrpy.

COLEGROVE, DAVID P; Skaneateles Central HS; Skaneateles, NY; (Y); Band; Concert Band; Jazz Band; Mrchg Band; Pep Band; Symp Band; Variety Show; Lcrss; Bausch & Lomb Sci Awd; High Hon Roll; Architecture.

COLELLA, MELISSA; Auburn HS; Auburn, NY; (Y); Symp Band; Drama Clb; Band; Chorus; Concert Band; Jazz Band; Mrchg Band; Orch; School Musical; Hon Roll; Elem Ed.

COLEMAN, ALLISON; Our Lady Of Mercy HS; Rochester, NY; (Y); Church Yth Grp; Spanish Clb; SADD; School Musical; School Play; Stage Crew; Hon Roll; English Clb; Hosp Aide; PAVAS; Yth For Undrstndg Exch Stu/Japan 8 Wks 85; Chrch Parish Cncl; Monroe Cnty Lilac Teen Semiflnst; Intl Affrs.

COLEMAN, ANDREA; Grover Cleveland HS; Buffalo, NY; (Y); English Clb; Library Aide; Pep Clb; Red Cross Aide; Chorus; Yrbk Stf; Rep Frsh Cls; Rep Jr Cls; Off Stu Cncl; Crs Cntry; Psych.

COLEMAN, DANIELLA; Bishop Ford HS; Brooklyn, NY; (S); 16/439; Cmnty Wkr; Nwsp Rptr; Nwsp Stf; Var Bsktbl; Mgr Var Sftbl; Var Tennis; High Hon Roll; NHS; Msgr Altman Memrl Awd-Commnty Svc 84; Holy Name Soc Schlrshp & Emerald Soc Schlrshp 83; Physcl Thrpy.

COLEMAN, DAVID; Rice HS; New York, NY; (Y); Boy Scts; Computer Clb; Nwsp Rptr; Vllybl; Lbrl Arts.

COLEMAN, ERIC; Caro-Meridian HS; Cato, NY; (Y); Boy Scts; French Clb; Model UN; School Play; JV Wrstlng; Hon Roll; Jr NHS; NHS.

COLEMAN, JOSEPHINE A; St Francis Preparatory HS; Jamaica, NY; (S); 164/744; Church Yth Grp; Drama Clb; Hosp Aide; Band; Church Choir; Concert Band; Mrchg Band; Orch; School Musical; Hon Roll; Optimate List 90 Avg & Above; Engl.

COLEMAN, KARI; Vestal SR HS; Vestal, NY; (Y); 61/430; Mathletes; Varsity Clb; Capt Mrchg Band; Im Capt Vllybl; High Hon Roll; Hon Roll; Ntl Merit Ltr; Regents Schlrshp 85-86; Vrsty Lttr Mrchng Band 84-85; Rensselaer Plytech Inst; Physcs.

COLEMAN, KELLIE; Roosevelt HS; Yonkers, NY; (Y); Sec SADD; Band; Color Guard; Drm Mjr(t); Mrchg Band; Yrbk Stf; Var Sftbl; High Hon Roll; Htl Mngmnt.

COLEMAN, KELLY; Sachem HS; Farmingville, NY; (Y); 96/1659; Stat Ftbl; Fash Inst Tech; Fash Indstry.

COLEMAN, KRISTINE; Albertus Magnus HS; New City, NY; (Y); 48/190; Church Yth Grp; Math Tm; Office Aide; Service Clb; Teachers Aide; Hon Roll; Fedrtn Of Polc Tri-Cnty NY Schlrshp 86; Echrstc Mnstr 85-86; Manhattan Coll; Med.

COLEMAN, LISA; Union Endicott HS; Owego, NY; (Y); 197/459; SADD; Band; Color Guard; Concert Band; Drill Tm; Flag Corp; Mrchg Band; Symp Band; Rep Frsh Cls; Rep Soph Cls; MV Rifl Mrchg Band 86; NYSSMA Excllnc Awd; Utica Coll Of Syracuse U; Thrpy.

COLEMAN, MARK H; Vestal SR HS; Binghamton, NY; (Y); 59/430; Exploring; VP Varsity Clb; Lit Mag; JV Bsktbl; Var Trk; High Hon Roll; Pres NHS; Ntl Merit Ltr; Rotary Awd; 2nd Natl Cncl Yth Ldrshp Yth Salute 85; Rotary Yth Ldrshp Awd 85; Natl Inst Hlth Mnrty Sci Apprnt 85; Biochem.

COLEMAN, MICHELLE; Notre Dame Acad; Staten Island, NY; (Y); Variety Show; Lit Mag; Var Crs Cntry; Var Score Keeper; Var Trk; Prfct Atten Awd; Most Improved Varsity Rnnr 86; Bus Adm.

COLEMAN, THORNTON; Hutch-Tech HS; Buffalo, NY; (Y); Rep Soph Cls; Rep Jr Cls; Stu Cncl; JV Var Bsktbl; Hon Roll; Elctrncs.

COLEY, KIM; Mt Vernon HS; Mt Vernon, NY; (Y); Office Aide; Drill Tm; Orch; Rep Sr Cls; Rep Stu Cncl; Capt Cheerleading; Hon Roll.

COLIC, MICHELE; Dominican Commercial HS; Brooklyn, NY; (Y); VP Pres Hosp Aide; Citation Svc To Greenpoint Vol Amb Corps 85.

COLISTRA, CHRISTINE ANN; Troy HS; Troy, NY; (Y); 19/427; Drama Clb; Radio Clb; Band; Chorus; Color Guard; Mrchg Band; School Musical; School Play; Nwsp Rptr; Hon Roll; Smmns Coll; Cmmnctns.

COLLADO, MARIE; Queens Vocational HS; Brooklyn, NY; (Y); Teachers Aide; Vllybl; Cit Awd; Mech Engrng.

COLLAR, MELISSA; Gloversville HS; Gloversvl, NY; (Y); 10/250; Intnl Clb; Key Clb; Mrchg Band; Band; Jazz Band; Mrchg Band; Yrbk Stf; Bsktbl; Bowling; Mgr(s); Ntl Sci Merit Awd; Math Sci Flds.

COLLARD, ELIZABETH; Manhasset HS; Plandome, NY; (Y); Band; Rep Soph Cls; Rep Jr Cls; Rep Sr Cls; Var Fld Hcky; Var Gym; JV Lcrss; Var Trk; High Hon Roll; NHS; Law.

COLLAZO, JANET; Albertus Magnus HS; Stony Point, NY; (Y); 82/175; Cmnty Wkr; Girl Scts; Spanish Clb; Teachers Aide; Hon Roll; Prfct Atten Awd; Campus Mnstry Cert Svc Awd; Devonshire Coll Outstndng Acadmc Achvt; Socty Propgtn Faith; St Thomas Aquinas; Ed.

COLLAZO, MICHAEL; Cathedral Prep Seminary; Brooklyn, NY; (Y); 8/36; Lit Mag; NHS; NY ST Rgnts Schlrp 86-87; Engl Mdl 85-86; Gen Exclnc Mdl 82-86; SUNY Stonybrook; Engl.

COLLAZO, SANDRA; St John Villa HS; Staten Island, NY; (Y); 62/123; Varsity Clb; Crs Cntry; Tennis; Trk; Pre Med.

COLLEA, MARIA; John F Kennety HS; Utica, NY; (Y); Sec Debate Tm; Rep FBLA; Hosp Aide; Key Clb; SADD; Yrbk Bus Mgr; Yrbk Stf; Sec Stu Cncl; Var Bowling; Bus Admin.

COLLERAN, COLLEEN; Saint John The Baptist HS; Copiague, NY; (Y); Office Aide; Pep Clb; SADD; Yrbk Stf; Off Frsh Cls; Rep Soph Cls; Off Jr Cls; Pres Stu Cncl; Gym; Bus Adm.

COLLETTI, ANGELA; New Dorp HS; Staten Island, NY; (Y); FTA; Teachers Aide; Tennis; Early Childhd Ed.

COLLIER, HELENE A; Bronx HS Of Science; City Island, NY; (Y); Girl Scts; Office Aide; Teachers Aide; Band; Yrbk Ed-Chief; High Hon Roll; NHS; Ntl Merit Ltr; Deans Schlr 86; Rgnts Schlr 86; Fordham U; Law.

COLLIER, JULIE; Sherburne-Earlville HS; Norwich, NY; (Y); 37/156; Concert Band; Jazz Band; Mrchg Band; JV Vllybl; Prfct Atten Awd; Field Band 83-84; Intl Bus.

COLLIGAN, ROBERT T; Cazenovia Cenral HS; Erieville, NY; (Y); 3/150; Am Leg Boys St; Var L Ftbl; Var L Trk; High Hon Roll; NHS; Ntl Merit SF; Crnll Clb Bk Awd 86; AM Mngmnt Assn Oprtn Entrprs 86; Math.

COLLINS, ANDY; Rhinebeck Central HS; Rhinebeck, NY; (Y); Boy Scts; Ski Clb; Im Golf; Im Vllybl; Comp Sci.

COLLINS, BECKY; Hugh C Williams HS; Canton, NY; (Y); 2/115; Trs Church Yth Grp; Cmnty Wkr; Yrbk Stf; Stat Bsktbl; Score Keeper; Stat Socr; Bausch & Lomb Sci Awd; Dnfth Awd; Elks Awd; High Hon Roll; Clarkson U; Indstrl Hygn.

COLLINS, CRAIG CLIFTON; Cobleskill Central HS; Cobleskill, NY; (S); 9/116; Drama Clb; Band; Chorus; School Play; Swing Chorus; Rep Sr Cls; Sec Stu Cncl; Bsktbl; High Hon Roll; Sec NHS; Natl Fnlst Ful-NROTC Schlrshp 86; NYS Rgnts Schlrshp 86; SUNY Geneseo; Drmtc Arts.

COLLINS, DAVID A; Kenmore West SR HS; Tonawanda, NY; (Y); 90/424; Math Tm; Rep Stu Cncl; JV Bsbl; Var L Bsktbl; Var Capt Vllybl; Hon Roll; NHS; Vllybl All Wstrn NY 1st Tm All-Star 85-86; Niagara Frntr Lg 1st Tm All-Star 84-86; Pres Awd 86; U Of Buffalo; Mth Tchr.

COLLINS, ELIZABETH; The Ursuline Schl; Yonkers, NY; (Y); Rep Sec Church Yth Grp; Ski Clb; Yrbk Stf; JV Sftbl; High Hon Roll; Hon Roll; Cert Exclnc AP Bio 86; Cum Laude Natl Ltn Exm 86.

COLLINS, ERIC; E J Wilson HS; Spencerport, NY; (Y); 20/300; Latin Clb; Math Clb; Math Tm; NHS; SUNY Oswego; Math.

COLLINS, JACK; Tioga Central HS; Barton, NY; (Y); Cmnty Wkr; Ski Clb; Ftbl; Wrstlng; Broome CC; Crmnl Jstc.

COLLINS, JERAMIE; Vernon-Verona-Sherrill HS; Verona, NY; (Y); Art Clb; Boy Scts; Church Yth Grp; Drm & Bgl; JV Bsktbl; JV Var Ftbl; Trk; Wt Lftg; Hon Roll; MVP Trk, Bsktbl 84-85; Lyncchburg; Cty Fire Fghtr.

COLLINS, JOSEPH; Moore Catholic HS; Staten Island, NY; (Y); Speech Tm; SADD; VP Chorus; School Musical; Yrbk Stf; Rep Frsh Cls; Rep Soph Cls; Rep Jr Cls; VP Stu Cncl; Ntl Merit Ltr; Acad All Amer.

COLLINS, KATHLEEN; Nottingham HS; Syracuse, NY; (Y); Church Yth Grp; Cmnty Wkr; French Clb; Latin Clb; Ski Clb; Concert Band; School Musical; Nwsp Stf; Socr; Hon Roll; All City Concert Band 86.

COLLINS, KATHY; Odessa-Montour HS; Montour Falls, NY; (Y); Am Leg Aux Girls St; VP Band; Concert Band; Mrchg Band; Pep Band; VP Sr Cls; Var Capt Bsktbl; Var Capt Swmmng; High Hon Roll; Hon Roll.

COLLINS, KEVIN E; Clinton Central HS; Clinton, NY; (Y); 1/130; Sec Trs Drama Clb; Band; School Musical; School Play; Nwsp Ed-Chief; Var L Tennis; Aud/Vis; Boy Scts; Key Clb; Letterman Clb; Grand Prize Wnnr Regnl Sci Fair 84.

COLLINS, MARK; Half Hollow Hills High School West; Dix Hills, NY; (Y); Band; Mrchg Band; Socr; Wrstlng; High Hon Roll; Jr NHS; Ntl Merit Ltr; Genetcs.

COLLINS, MICHAEL S; Nottingham HS; Syracuse, NY; (Y); 66/222; Church Yth Grp; Exploring; Latin Clb; Science Clb; Stu Cncl; Var L Crs Cntry; Var L Trk; Hon Roll; Regents Schlrshp 86; Whipple Schlrshp 86; U Buffalo; Elect Engr.

COLLINS, ROBERT; Sauquoit Valley HS; Chadwicks, NY; (Y); 8/100; 4-H; Varsity Clb; Pres Frsh Cls; Var L Bsktbl; Var L Socr; 4-H Awd; High Hon Roll; Hon Roll; Jr NHS; NHS; Engrng.

COLLINS, SUSAN; Center Moriches HS; Mastic, NY; (Y); Dance Clb; Pres DECA; Drama Clb; FBLA; Pres Chorus; Capt Cheerleading; Hon Roll; Mktg Mgt.

COLLINS, TAMMY; Saranac Central HS; Morrisonville, NY; (S); 20/105; Pres SADD; VP Frsh Cls; VP Soph Cls; JV Var Cheerleading; High Hon Roll; Hon Roll; Clinton CC; Medcl Lab Tech.

COLLINS, TRACY E; Sachem HS North; Holbrook, NY; (Y); 120/1500; VP Drama Clb; VP PAVAS; Political Wkr; Ski Clb; SADD; Church Choir; School Musical; Lit Mag; NHS; Voice Dem Awd; Outstndng Muscnshp 83-84; Attny NYS Mock Trl Teams 85; Fredonia; Poltcl Sci.

COLLORA, SANDY; St Peters Boys HS; Staten Island, NY; (Y); 6/163; Var Bsbl; Crs Cntry; Trk; Hon Roll; NHS.

COLLUMB, CHRISTOPHER; Archbishop Molloy HS; Middle Vlg, NY; (Y); 10/383; Pep Clb; SADD; Var L Crs Cntry; Var L Trk; NHS; Ntl Merit Ltr; Pre-Med.

COLLURA, CHRISTEN; Notre Dame Acad; Staten Island, NY; (Y); Dance Clb; Drama Clb; School Musical; School Play; Stage Crew; Yrbk Phtg; Yrbk Rptr; Yrbk Stf; Cheerleading; Swmmng; St Johns; Law.

COLLURA, SCOTT; Bay Shore HS; Bay Shore, NY; (Y); 68/404; Art Clb; Sec Sr Cls; Trk; High Hon Roll; Hon Roll; Suffolk Cnty Film & TV Comp 86; Film Theory.

COLLVER, JEFF; Frewsburg Central HS; Frewsburg, NY; (Y); SADD; Nwsp Sprt Ed; Yrbk Stf; Var Capt Bsktbl; Var Ftbl; Var Trk; Var Wt Lftg; King Of Sports 85-86; Roberts Westeyan Coll; Art.

COLOMBO, MARK; Solvay HS; Solvay, NY; (Y); 24/130; Church Yth Grp; Key Clb; Ski Clb; Yrbk Stf; Off Frsh Cls; Off Soph Cls; Off Jr Cls; Bsbl; Ftbl; High Hon Roll; Elec Engrng.

COLON, ALEX XAVIER; All Hallows Inst; New York, NY; (Y); 38/119; Cmnty Wkr; Computer Clb; Ice Hcky; Trk; Hon Roll; John Jay Coll; Police Sci.

COLON, DAVID; Dobbs Ferry HS; Dobbs Ferry, NY; (Y); 29/80; AFS; Key Clb; Yrbk Stf; Rep Soph Cls; L Bowling; L Wrstlng; Natl Hspnc Schlrshp SF 86; U Of AZ; Aerosp Engrng.

COLON, DIANA; Clara Barton HS; Brooklyn, NY; (Y); Hon Roll; Jr NHS; Med.

COLON, DOREEN; Bishop Loughlin Memorial HS; Brooklyn, NY; (Y); Dance Clb; PAVAS; Chorus; Prpl L 85 Avg 83-84; Bus Mgmt.

COLON, EDWIN; St John The Baptist HS; Wyandanch, NY; (Y); 3/546; Chess Clb; Computer Clb; ROTC; Spanish Clb; Chorus; Trk; High Hon Roll; Hon Roll; Jr NHS; NHS; Ntl Sci Awd; Cornell U; Elec Engrng.

COLON, ELIZABETH; Murry Bergtraum HS; Bronx, NY; (Y); Church Yth Grp; FCA; Teachers Aide; Temple Yth Grp; Church Choir; Orch; Missionettes Clb 84-86; Lifesaver 81; Barauch Coll; Bus.

COLON, ERWIN; Bronx HS; Bronx, NY; (Y); 20/539; Library Aide; Chorus; JV Swmmng; High Hon Roll; Hon Roll; NY ST Rgnts Schlrshp 86; Embry-Rdl Arntcl U; Avtn Tech.

COLON, GREGORY; All Hallows HS; Bronx, NY; (Y); ROTC; Teachers Aide; Stage Crew; Nwsp Rptr; Nwsp Sprt Ed; Nwsp Stf; Vllybl; Wt Lftg; Wrstlng; NHS; 1st Hnr Awds 83-86; Stu Achvmnt Awd 83-86; Mltry.

COLON, HERNAN; Eastern District HS; Brooklyn, NY; (Y); Office Aide; Teachers Aide; Band; Hon Roll; Cert Prtcptn Sci Fair 84; Arsta 85; Hlth Educ 85.

COLON, IVELISSE; Adlai Stevenson HS; Bronx, NY; (Y); Church Yth Grp; GAA; Vllybl; Hon Roll; NHS; Bst Typst Awd; Cmmnctns.

COLON, JEANNETTE L; ST Joseph HS; Brooklyn, NY; (S); 3/104; Capt Drama Clb; Office Aide; School Play; Nwsp Rptr; Soph Cls; Sec Jr Cls; Rep Sr Cls; Hon Roll; NHS; St Johns U; Bus Adm.

COLON, JUAN; Walton HS; Bronx, NY; (Y); Computer Clb; Mathletes; Spanish Clb; School Play; Off Soph Cls; Bsbl; Cit Awd; High Hon Roll; Prfct Atten Awd; Stu Yr 83; Comp Tech.

COLON, JULIO; George Washington HS; New York, NY; (Y); Office Aide; Band; Orch; Nwsp Rptr; Nwsp Stf; Yrbk Stf; Rep Sr Cls; Trk; Vllybl; Wt Lftg; Empire ST Chalngr Schlrshp 86; Marist Coll; Bio.

COLON, MARITZA; Clara Barton HS; Brooklyn, NY; (Y); 7/485; Cmnty Wkr; Hosp Aide; Chorus; Hon Roll; NHS; St Gauders Mdl For Fine Draftsmanship 84; Super Yth Awd 84-85; Pace U; Pre-Med.

COLON, MICHAEL R; Mt St Michael Acad; Bronx, NY; (S); 20/310; Boy Scts; Church Yth Grp; L Bsbl; L Bowling; Hon Roll; Law.

COLONNA, DANIELLE F; St Francis Prep; Bayside, NY; (S); 254/744; Church Yth Grp; Dance Clb; Teachers Aide; Varsity Clb; Drm & Bgl; Var Crs Cntry; JV Gym; Powder Puff Ftbl; Var Trk; Vllybl; Fordham; Law.

COLONNA, PHILIP; Monsignor Farrell HS; Staten Island, NY; (Y); Cmnty Wkr; Yrbk Ed-Chief; Yrbk Stf; VP Jr Cls; Bsbl; Im Bsktbl; Im Bowling; Var Coach Actv; Im Ftbl; High Hon Roll.

COLOSI, SANTINA; Aquinas HS; Bronx, NY; (Y); School Musical; School Play; High Hon Roll; Hon Roll; NHS; Prfct Atten Awd; 2nd Hnrs Italn Iona Coll Lang Cntst 85; Iona Coll Merit Awd 86; 1st Prz Sci Fair 83; Iona Coll; Accntg.

COLSON, ROBERT; Yonkers HS; Yonkers, NY; (Y); Art Clb; School Play; Off Jr Cls; Wt Lftg; Math.

COLTON, CHRISTINE; Fayetteville-Manlius HS; Brookfield, WI; (Y); 22/335; Hosp Aide; JA; Model UN; SADD; Nwsp Stf; Lit Mag; High Hon Roll; NHS; Ntl Merit Ltr; Hon Roll; Outstndng Achvt French III-A 85; U WI Madison; Pre-Med.

COLUCCI, JAMIE; West Genesee SR HS; Camillus, NY; (Y); Boy Scts; French Clb; Key Clb; Ski Clb; Concert Band; Drm Mjr(t); Jazz Band; Mrchg Band; NHS.

COLUCCI, ROBERT; Cadinal O Hara HS; Kenmore, NY; (S); 12/127; Am Leg Boys St; Boy Scts; Church Yth Grp; French Clb; Pres Frsh Cls; VP Soph Cls; Pres Jr Cls; Rep Sr Cls; Rep Stu Cncl; Im Badmtn; Med.

COLUDRO, JESUS; High School For The Humnts; New York, NY; (Y); Art Clb; Boy Scts; Camera Clb; Computer Clb; Dance Clb; Drama Clb; Service Clb; Teachers Aide; Y-Teens; Band; Fashion Inst; Phtgrphy.

COLUMBIA, THOMAS J; St Anthonys HS; Nesconset, NY; (Y); 45/270; Am Leg Boys St; Boy Scts; Ski Clb; SADD; Nwsp Rptr; Ed Nwsp Stf; Yrbk Stf; JV Ice Hcky; Cit Awd; Hon Roll; Bus.

COLWELL, HOLLY; Coxsackie-Athens HS; Catskill, NY; (Y); 24/107; Sec German Clb; Hosp Aide; Red Cross Aide; Chorus; Stu Cncl; Hon Roll; Albany Med Schl Nrsg; Nrs.

COLWELL, LORRAINE; Stissing Mt JR SR HS; Pine Plains, NY; (Y); Camera Clb; Drama Clb; Pep Clb; PAVAS; SADD; Chorus; VP Frsh Cls; Sec Soph Cls; Law.

COLYER, JULIE; Schoharie Central HS; Schoharie, NY; (S); 1/116; Key Clb; Pres Varsity Clb; Band; Chorus; School Musical; Pres Soph Cls; Var Bsktbl; Var Trk; Val; Hugh O Brian Mst Outstndng Awd 84-85; William Prescott Mdl Hstry 84-85; Brigham Young U.

COMBATTI, MARGARET; Patchogue-Medford HS; Patchogue, NY; (Y); 23/653; Leo Clb; Spanish Clb; Yrbk Stf; JV Tennis; Hon Roll; NHS; Spanish NHS; NYS Rgnts Schlrshp 86; SUNY Albany.

COMBS, ISAAC; Cardinal Hayes HS; Bronx, NY; (Y); 91/258; AFS; Boy Scts; Computer Clb; JA; Library Aide; Nwsp Ed-Chief; Wt Lftg; Hon Roll.

COMEAU, MICHELLE; Westhampton Beach HS; Quogue, NY; (Y); 11/232; Concert Band; Mrchg Band; School Musical; Yrbk Ed-Chief; Yrbk Stf; Trs Soph Cls; JV Bsktbl; Var Cheerleading; Var JV Sftbl; Var JV Tennis; MVP Sftbl 84; Sprtsmnshp Awds In Sftbl & Tennis 85 & 86; Pre-Med.

COMEGYS, ELEANOR; Monroe HS; Rochester, NY; (Y); Math Tm; Model UN; Orch; School Musical; School Play; Lit Mag; High Hon Roll; NHS; NY ST Smmr Schl Of Arts, Schl Of Theatr 84; Hochstein Schlrp Woodwnd Quntet Prog 84-87; Theatr.

COMERFORD, KAREN; Jamesville-Dewitt HS; Fayetteville, NY; (Y); 116/256; Church Yth Grp; French Clb; Key Clb; Pep Clb; Ski Clb; SADD; Sftbl; Vllybl; Hon Roll; Sclr Art Awd 83; St Marys Coll; Elem Educ.

COMIS JR, JOHN; Bishop Ford Central Catholic HS; Brooklyn, NY; (Y); 18/426; Hosp Aide; Science Clb; Pres Soph Cls; Dnfth Awd; Pres NHS; Zoo Svc Sqd; Lab Aide; Spcl Chldrns Cmp Vlntr; Brooklyn Coll; Pre-Med.

COMITINI, MANNY; Moore Catholic HS; Staten Island, NY; (Y); Intnl Clb; Math Clb; Ski Clb; Stage Crew; Yrbk Rptr; Yrbk Stf; Swmmng; Trk; Pace U; Accntng.

COMMERFORD, KELLEY; Rome Free Acad; Rome, NY; (Y); 95/400; Intnl Clb; Key Clb; Ski Clb; Nwsp Sprt Ed; Yrbk Stf; Lit Mag; Sec Soph Cls; Sec Jr Cls; Var Capt Fld Hcky; Pres Jr NHS; Miami U Oxford; Mass Cmnctns.

COMMEY, KIMBERLEY D; Julia Richman HS; Bronx, NY; (Y); Library Aide; Acpl Chr; Chorus; Rep Stu Cncl; Cit Awd; Hon Roll; Jr NHS; Prfct Atten Awd; Sal; Capt Debate Tm; Daily News Acad/Extracrrclr Awd 85; Acad Olympcs Awd 84 & 85; Ltr Recommndtn Coll 85; Prof Nrsg.

COMMISSO, MARIA; St Marys Grils HS; Floral Park, NY; (Y); Pres English Clb; Sec Teachers Aide; Variety Show; Hon Roll; NHS; St Johns U; Phrmcy.

COMO, TAMMY; Rome Free Acad; Rome, NY; (Y); Church Yth Grp; Drama Clb; Chorus; Church Choir; Languages.

COMPAS, MARIE; Nyack HS; Nyack, NY; (Y); Church Yth Grp; Rep Exploring; Orch; Var JV Trk; Hon Roll; Prfct Atten Awd; Amer Chem Soc Achvt 86; 1st Pl Stu Energy Exhib 86; Stu Wk Sci 86; Med.

COMPAS, PAM; Academy Of St Joseph HS; Holbrook, NY; (Y); French Clb; Service Clb; Hon Roll; Acad Awd French.

COMPEAU, LAURA; Indian River Central HS; Philadelphia, NY; (Y); 2/122; Church Yth Grp; Latin Clb; Band; Chorus; Concert Band; Jazz Band; Swing Chorus; JV Vllybl; Hon Roll; NHS; Math.

COMPITELLO, JOSEPH; Mc Quaid Jesuit HS; Rochester, NY; (Y); Camera Clb; Church Yth Grp; Drama Clb; Model UN; Ski Clb; School Musical; School Play; Stage Crew; Nwsp Stf; Var Swmmng.

COMPOLO, FRANK; Herkimer SR HS; East Herkimer, NY; (Y); 7/100; SADD; Yrbk Sprt Ed; Yrbk Stf; Rep Stu Cncl; Bsktbl; Crs Cntry; Trk; High Hon Roll; Hon Roll; NHS; Accptd NY Acad Sci 86; Vet Med.

COMPSON JR, RICHARD G; Clinton Central Schl; Clinton, NY; (Y); 13/136; French Clb; Concert Band; Symp Band; VP Frsh Cls; Ice Hcky; Socr; Hon Roll; Jr NHS; NHS; St Schlr; Stu Of Mnth 85; Franklin & Marshall; Polit Sci.

COMUNALE, TERESA MARIE; Kings Park HS; Ft Salonga, NY; (Y); 20/382; Church Yth Grp; Cmnty Wkr; Debate Tm; NFL; Speech Tm; Varsity Clb; Concert Band; Orch; Symp Band; Rep Stu Cncl; All-ST Band NY 85; Army ROTC Schlrshp 86; U Of Richmond; Poly Sci.

CONANT, DARRIN; Union Endicott HS; Endicott, NY; (Y); Boy Scts; Church Yth Grp; Cmnty Wkr; Socr; Vllybl; Hon Roll; Ntl Merit Ltr; Hnr Carrier 85; Elect Engr.

CONATY, SIOBHAN; Academy Of St Joseph; Bohemia, NY; (Y); Aud/Vis; Hosp Aide; Teachers Aide; Yrbk Stf; JV Socr; Intl Stds.

CONAWAY, PAMELA; Perry Central HS; Perry, NY; (Y); Am Leg Aux Girls St; Pres French Clb; Hosp Aide; Ski Clb; Pres SADD; Band; Stu Cncl; 4-H Awd; High Hon Roll; Hon Roll; Runner Up HOB Awd 85; Psych.

CONBOY, BRIDGET; Our Lady Of Mercy HS; Walworth, NY; (Y); Model UN; Crs Cntry; Hon Roll; Nwsp Rptr; Jrnlsm.

CONBOY, LISA; Cohoes HS; Cohoes, NY; (Y); 12/186; Exploring; French Clb; GAA; Pres Frsh Cls; Pres Soph Cls; Pres Jr Cls; Var Capt Crs Cntry; Var Capt Trk; DAR Awd; NHS; St John Fisher Schlrshp 86; Span Lang Awd 86; Vrsty Xcntry Indoor & Outdorr Trck Mst Vlbl Plyr 86; St John Fisher Coll; Intl Stds.

CONCANNON, CATHY; Greece Athena SR HS; Rochester, NY; (Y); 47/322; Church Yth Grp; Cmnty Wkr; French Clb; Hosp Aide; Ski Clb; SADD; Yrbk Ed-Chief; Rep Jr Cls; Var JV Socr; JV Var Sftbl; Physcl Thrpy.

CONCEICAO, ANTHONY; Iona Preparatory HS; New Roch, NY; (Y); 83/204; Boys Clb Am; Boy Scts; Y-Teens; Nwsp Stf; Yrbk Stf; Im Bowling; Im Ftbl; Trk; Hon Roll; St Johns U; Bus.

CONCEICAO, ERMELINDA; Charles E Gorton HS; Yonkers, NY; (Y); 8/196; Intnl Clb; Yrbk Stf; Lit Mag; Var Socr; Var Trk; 4-H Awd; High Hon Roll; NHS; Supt Awd Clb 90 83-86; Iona Coll; Frgn Lang.

CONCEPCION, MIKE; Port Jervis HS; Port Jervis, NY; (Y); Varsity Clb; Rep Soph Cls; Rep Jr Cls; VP Stu Cncl; Var Ftbl; Var Wrstlng; Hon Roll.

CONDE, STEVEN L; Alfred Almond C S HS; Alfred Station, NY; (Y); 3/66; JCL; Varsity Clb; Band; Jazz Band; Yrbk Bus Mgr; Trs Stu Cncl; Var Capt Crs Cntry; Var L Swmmng; L Trk; High Hon Roll; Engrng.

CONDON, KATHLEEN; Seton Catholic Central HS; Endicott, NY; (Y); 100/165; Church Yth Grp; Key Clb; Varsity Clb; Nwsp Stf; Sec Frsh Cls; VP Soph Cls; VP Jr Cls; Stu Cncl; JV Var Cheerleading; Science Clb; Prnts Clb Awd; Marywood Coll; Soclgy.

CONDOS, PANAYOTA; High Schl Of Art & Design; Long Island City, NY; (Y); 14/222; Church Yth Grp; Debate Tm; Nwsp Ed-Chief; Pres Sr Cls; Hon Roll; NCTE Awd; NHS; NY U Prtl Schlrshp 86; Hellenic U Clb Schlrshp 86; Regents Coll Schlrshp 86; NY U.

CONERTY, MICHELLE; Mehcanicville HS; Mechanicville, NY; (S); 2/105; Math Tm; Spanish Clb; SADD; Band; Yrbk Stf; Pres Sr Cls; Bsktbl; Sftbl; NHS; NEDT Awd; Spn Awd; Mth Awd; Biomed Engrng.

CONEY, E CHRISTINE; T J Corcoran HS; Syracuse, NY; (Y); Exploring; French Clb; JA; Model UN; Nwsp Rptr; Yrbk Stf; High Hon Roll; NHS; Boys Clb Am; Trk; Jrnlsm.

CONFORTI, LORIANN; Uniondale HS; Hempstead, NY; (Y); Rptr FBLA; Hon Roll; NHS; Bus.

CONGDON, LISA; Elmira Christian Acad; Pine City, NY; (Y); 1/13; Church Yth Grp; Hosp Aide; Chorus; School Musical; Pres Frsh Cls; Var L Socr; High Hon Roll; Church Choir; School Play; Sec Soph Cls; Roberts Wesleyan Coll; Nrsg.

CONGDON, LISA; Granville Central Schl; Wells, VT; (Y); 32/140; Nwsp Rptr; Nwsp Sprt Ed; Nwsp Stf; Var Capt Bsktbl; Capt Sftbl; Prfct Atten Awd; Delta Kappa Gamma Hnr Soc Awd 86; Sm Eppltto Mem Awd 86; MVP Bsktbll 86; Coachs Awd Sftbll 86; Castleton ST Coll; Phy Ed.

CONGDON, MELISSA; Pine Valley Central Schl; Forestville, NY; (Y); Dance Clb; Sec 4-H; Chorus; Drill Tm; Mrchg Band; Cheerleading; Gym; Twrlr; Hon Roll; Jr NHS; Phy Ed.

CONGELLI, SARAH; Wayland Central Schl; Wayland, NY; (Y); 8/113; VP Church Yth Grp; Drama Clb; Math Tm; Science Clb; Stage Crew; Stat Bsktbl; Golf; Tennis; High Hon Roll; Mar Biol.

CONGIMI, JOYCE; Christ The King R HS; Middle Village, NY; (Y); 155/448; GAA; JV Var Bsktbl; JV Sftbl; JV Vllybl; Athlt Of Yr Bsktbl 84-85; CYO Chrstn Ldrshp For Mrcls Mdl 84-85; Chrstn Ldrshp Chrst The King 85-86.

CONHEADY, KELLY A; East HS; Rochester, NY; (Y); 11/242; Pres Church Yth Grp; Cmnty Wkr; Var Capt Socr; Var Swmmng; Hon Roll; NHS; Rgnts Schlrshp 86; Nazareth Coll Schlr 86; Syrcs U Ctznshp Ed Cnfrnc Schlrshp 86; Syrcs U; Scl Wrk.

CONIBER, CONSTANCE; Cato-Meridian HS; Memphis, NY; (Y); French Clb; Band; Chorus; Mrchg Band; School Musical; Yrbk Stf; Sec Jr Cls; High Hon Roll; Jr NHS; NHS; CORPRT Law.

CONKLIN, CARYN S; Kingston HS; Kingston, NY; (Y); 3/573; Band; Nwsp Rptr; Nwsp Sprt Ed; Var L Swmmng; French Hon Soc; NHS; Ntl Merit Ltr; Computer Clb; VP French Clb; Mrchg Band; Natl Hnr Scty Schlrshp 86; Thomas Watson Schlrshp 86; Area All ST Band 85; U Of PA; Engr.

CONKLIN, KAREN; Yonkers HS; Yonkers, NY; (Y); Key Clb; Office Aide; Pep Clb; Nwsp Rptr; Nwsp Stf; Yrbk Stf; Hon Roll; Athlon Soc 86; SUNY; Spcl Ed.

CONKLIN, MARK; Churchville-Chili HS; Rochester, NY; (Y); 3/310; Math Tm; Ski Clb; School Play; JV Var Tennis; NHS; Ntl Merit Ltr; OH Nrthrn U Hnr Schlrshp 86; NYS Rgnts Schlrshp 86; Prsdntl Acdmc Ftns Awd 86; OH Nrthrn U; Corprt Law.

CONKLIN, VANESSA; Bay Shore HS; Bay Shore, NY; (Y); 61/425; Art Clb; Hosp Aide; Office Aide; Chorus; Stage Crew; Var Crs Cntry; Var Socr; Var Trk; Hon Roll; Pres Schlr; St Bonaventure U; Bus Admin.

CONLEE, BILL; Hoosic Valley HS; Schaghticoke, NY; (Y); Latin Clb; Var Bsbl; Var Capt Bsktbl; 2nd Tm All Area Bsktbl 85-86; Thrw No-Htr Bsbl 86; 2nd League Scrng Bsktbl 85-86; Phys Ed.

CONLEY, CHRISTOPHER S; Garden City HS; Garden City, NY; (Y); 105/346; Boy Scts; Nwsp Stf; Var Capt Crs Cntry; Var Swmmng; Var Capt Trk; Hon Roll; Lehigh; Bus.

CONLEY, COLLEEN; Lansingburgh HS; Troy, NY; (Y); SADD; Trs Jr Cls; Trs Sr Cls; Var Capt Bsktbl; JV Var Coach Actv; Var Sftbl; High Hon Roll; Hon Roll; Jr NHS; NHS; Nrsng.

CONLEY, KELLY; Frankfort-Schuyler HS; Frankfort, NY; (S); GAA; Band; Concert Band; Mrchg Band; School Play; Yrbk Phtg; Var JV Bowling; High Hon Roll; Hon Roll; NHS; Herkimer Cnty CC; Comp Sci.

CONLEY, LAWRENCE; Scotia-Glenville HS; Schenectady, NY; (Y); 54/255; Aud/Vis; JA; Library Aide; Concert Band; Mrchg Band; Hon Roll; Pres Acdmc Ftns Awd; American U; Pol Sci.

CONLEY, MAUREEN; Irondequoit HS; Rochester, NY; (Y); 43/368; Girl Scts; Hosp Aide; Latin Clb; SADD; Band; Chorus; Nwsp Stf; Lit Mag; Rep Frsh Cls; Rep Soph Cls; Rgnts Schlrshp 86; Le Moyne Coll; Soclgy.

CONLEY, NANCY S; Liverpool HS; Liverpool, NY; (Y); 24/816; VP JCL; Orch; Sec Stu Cncl; Var Fld Hcky; High Hon Roll; Jr NHS; NHS; Ntl Merit Ltr; Yth Orch; Regnts Schlrshp; All Cnty Orch,Confrnc All ST Orch,All Eastern Conf Orch; Ithaca Clg; Musc Perfrmnc.

CONLEY, STEPHEN; North Babylon SR HS; North Babylon, NY; (Y); Art Clb; VICA; Nwsp Stf; Hon Roll; NHS; Prfct Atten Awd; 2nd Pl-Slvr Mdlst VICA St Conf-Advtsng Art 86; 1st Pl-South Shr VICA Rgnl-Advtsng Art 86; Farmingdale; Advrtsng.

CONLIN, CHERYL A; West Seneca West HS; West Seneca, NY; (Y); 45/559; Art Clb; GAA; Spanish Clb; SADD; Var Socr; Capt Var Swmmng; DAR Awd; Hon Roll; Jr NHS; NHS; MVP Swmng 83-85; NY ST Rgnts Schlrshp 85-86; Outstndng Achvt In Frgn Lng 83, 84 & 86; Grgtwn U; Russian Intrptn.

CONLON, BERNADETTE P; St Francis Prep; Glendale, NY; (S); 35/744; Hosp Aide; Band; Concert Band; Mrchg Band; Im Ftbl; Im Sftbl; High Hon Roll; NHS; Tutrng 86-87; Retrt Ldng 86-87; Acctng.

CONN, CATHLEEN; Kings Park SR HS; Kings Park, NY; (Y); Church Yth Grp; SADD; Rep Soph Cls; Rep Stu Cncl; Var L Socr; Var L Trk; Hon Roll; Leukma Soc Of Am 83; Natl Sci Olympd 84; Outstndg Achvt SADD Clb 85-86; Dsgn.

CONN, RENEE M; Ballston Spa HS; Ballston Spa, NY; (Y); 8/244; Chorus; School Musical; Sec Frsh Cls; Pres Soph Cls; Pres Jr Cls; Rep Stu Cncl; JV Var Cheerleading; NHS; Pres Schlr; Drama Clb; NY ST Rgnts Schlrshp 86; Siena Coll; Bio.

CONNELL, AVON; Exander Childs HS; Bronx, NY; (S); Office Aide; Hon Roll; Outstndng Achvt Soc Studs, Spn Awd 84; Med.

CONNELL, MICHAEL BRIAN; Notre Dame-Bishop Gibbons HS; Albany, NY; (S); 10/90; Ski Clb; Var L Ftbl; Var L Trk; High Hon Roll; Hon Roll.

CONNELL, NOREEN; Manhasset JR SR HS; Manhasset, NY; (Y); 21/180; Church Yth Grp; VP Cmnty Wkr; Mathletes; Band; Rep Frsh Cls; Stu Cncl; Var Cheerleading; JV Fld Hcky; JV Lcrss; Med.

CONNELL, PATRICIA; Hamburg SR HS; Hamburg, NY; (Y); 16/374; 4-H; Hosp Aide; Pres Service Clb; Ed Yrbk Stf; Hon Roll; NHS; Microbio.

CONNELL, SHARON; Babylon SR HS; Babylon, NY; (Y); Spanish Clb; Chorus; Cheerleading; Coach Actv; Gym; Mgr(s); Score Keeper; High Hon Roll; NHS; Berkeley; Secty.

CONNELL, THOMAS A; Delaware Valley Central Schl; North Branch, NY; (Y); 2/42; Quiz Bowl; Var L Bsbl; Trk; High Hon Roll; NHS; Ntl Merit Ltr; Sal; Trs Church Yth Grp; Colgate U.

CONNELLY, SHANNON; Mechanicville HS; Mechanicville, NY; (S); 44/92; VP French Clb; Nwsp Ed-Chief; Yrbk Stf; Pres Frsh Cls; Pres Soph Cls; Sec Stu Cncl; Var Cheerleading; High Hon Roll; SADD; Physcl Ftnss Awd; Pres Awd; Ms Frshmn; Jrnlsm.

CONNERY, SHAWN; Ticonderoga HS; Ticonderoga, NY; (Y); Exploring; Im Badmtn; Var L Bsbl; JV Ftbl; Im Sftbl; Im Vllybl; JV Wrstlng; ARSPCE Engrng.

CONNOLLY, DIANNE; James Madison HS; Brooklyn, NY; (Y); 229/756; Art Clb; Dance Clb; Drm & Bgl; Orch; Hon Roll; Stenotype Acad; Court Stngrphr.

CONNOLLY, EILEEN; Maria Regina HS; Crestwood, NY; (Y); Pres Church Yth Grp; Cmnty Wkr; Rep Key Clb; Rep Soph Cls; Rep Sr Cls; Stu Cncl; Capt Swmmng; Var Trk; Hon Roll; Hnrs Convctn 84 & 85; Achvts Ldrshp Awd 85; Engrng.

CONNOLLY, ELIZABETH; Valley Stream North HS; Malverne, NY; (Y); 4-H; French Clb; Office Aide; Ski Clb; SADD; Yrbk Stf; JV Badmtn; Im Gym; 4-H Awd; Trvl Agnt.

CONNOLLY, JAMES; Garden City HS; Garden City, NY; (Y); 130/341; Church Yth Grp; JV Var Bsktbl; Var L Ftbl; JV Var Socr; Hon Roll; St Johns; Bus.

CONNOLLY, MARK D; Bishop Ford CC HS; Brooklyn, NY; (Y); 195/441; Computer Clb; Debate Tm; Drama Clb; Quiz Bowl; Speech Tm; School Play; Stage Crew; Var L Socr; NYS Regents Scholar 86; U Dayton; Comp Sci.

CONNOLLY, MATTHEW; Msgr Mc Clancy HS; Richmond Hill, NY; (Y); 104/219; Boys Clb Am; Math Clb; Ski Clb; Band; JV Var Bsbl; JV Im Bsktbl; Im Capt Ftbl; Coaches Awd Var Bsbl 86; Wrld Champ Violin Plyr 82; Bsbl Scholar Wagner Coll 86; Wagner Coll; Acctng.

CONNOLLY, MICHAEL J; John A Coleman HS; Woodstock, NY; (Y); VP Exploring; School Play; Var Socr; Var Trk; Hon Roll; NY ST Regents Schlrshp 86; Villanova U; Elect Engrng.

CONNOLLY, SHANE P; John C Birdlebough HS; Phoenix, NY; (Y); 1/180; Trs Church Yth Grp; Church Yth Grp; Nwsp Bus Mgr; Yrbk Ed-Chief; Pres Sr Cls; Val; Yrbk Stf; Var Golf; High Hon Roll; Lrkn Schlrshp 86; Ntl Dllrs Fr Schlrs Schlrshp 86; Mrn Mdlnd Bk Math Awd 86; Suny Buffalo; Engnrng.

CONNOR, ANN E; Honeoye Falls-Lima Central HS; Honeoye Falls, NY; (Y); #34 In Class; 4-H; Girl Scts; Math Tm; Yrbk Stf; Score Keeper; Trk; High Hon Roll; Hon Roll; NHS; Pep Clb; Natl Latn Exm Awd 85; SUNY Geneseo; Bio.

CONNOR, ELIZABETH; Thomas R Proctor HS; Utica, NY; (Y); Am Leg Aux Girls St; GAA; Mathletes; Spanish Clb; Yrbk Stf; JV Sftbl; Hon Roll; Jr NHS; NHS; Prfct Atten Awd; Comp Sci.

CONNOR, JAMES; Marlboro Central HS; Marlboro, NY; (Y); 14/150; Church Yth Grp; French Clb; Band; Chorus; Concert Band; Mrchg Band; JV Crs Cntry; Var L Trk; Var Wt Lftg; NHS; Mgna Cum Laude-Ntl Ltn Exam 86; NYS Trk & Fld Chmpnshps 2nd Pl Pole Vlt 86; All ST Band Frnch Hrn 86; Baylor U; Music.

CONNOR, MATTHEW; Clarkstown HS North; New City, NY; (Y); Natl Beta Clb; Band; Mu Alp Tht.

CONNORS, BERNADETTE; Seton Catholic Central HS; Binghamton, NY; (Y); Art Clb; Church Yth Grp; Cmnty Wkr; Latin Clb; DAR Awd; Hon Roll; Colgate U; Med.

CONNORS, CHARLES; Archbishop Stepinac HS; Yorktown, NY; (Y); 35/182; Church Yth Grp; Cmnty Wkr; Key Clb; Pep Clb; Ski Clb; Nwsp Rptr; Nwsp Stf; Yrbk Ed-Chief; Lit Mag; Var L Lcrss; Boston Coll; Bio.

CONNORS, CIRSTIN M; Sayville HS; Sayville, NY; (Y); 17/335; FTA; Key Clb; SADD; Color Guard; Nwsp Bus Mgr; Nwsp Stf; Yrbk Phtg; Lit Mag; Im Bsktbl; Im Tennis; Intl Affrs.

CONNORS, KARIN; Stissing Mt JR SR HS; Pine Plains, NY; (Y); 8/100; Church Yth Grp; 4-H; Hosp Aide; SADD; Band; Yrbk Rptr; JV Capt Bsktbl; Sftbl; Hon Roll; Bio Rsrch.

CONNORS, KATHLEEN J; Maine Endwell SR HS; Endwell, NY; (Y); 5/234; Spanish Clb; SADD; Yrbk Stf; Var Trk; Hon Roll; NHS; Ntl Merit Ltr; Blue Ribbn Art Exhbtn 83-85; Hallmark Art Awd 86; Regnts Schlrshp 86; Cornell U.

CONNORS, MARCY; West Seneca West SR HS; Buffalo, NY; (Y); 17/559; Hosp Aide; Key Clb; Office Aide; Red Cross Aide; Pres Jr Cls; Pres Sr Cls; NHS; Cmnty Wkr; GAA; Mathletes; Jaycees Outstndng Yng NY 86; SR Prom Qn 86; Dghtrs Of Am Revltn Ctznshp Awd 86; Ithaca College; Phys Thrpy.

CONNORS, TRACEY M; Tri-Valley Central Schl; Sundown, NY; (Y); 14/85; Church Yth Grp; Drama Clb; SADD; Chorus; School Musical; High Hon Roll; NHS; Regnts Schlrshp 86; Sullivans Schlr Awd; Sullivan Cty CC; Librl Arts.

CONNORS, YVONNE; St John The Baptist D HS; Seaford, NY; (S); 13/502; Ski Clb; Var Bsktbl; Var Sftbl; Var Vllybl; High Hon Roll; Outstndng Ath Awd 85; Cert Merit Outstndng Perfrmnce Soc Studs 85; Siena.

CONRAD, BONNIE; Victor SR HS; Farmington, NY; (Y); 55/225; Quiz Bowl; Spanish Clb; Stu Cncl; High Hon Roll; Hon Roll; Pres Acadmc Ftns Awd 86; Dept Schlrshp Awd 86; Daemen Coll; Elem Ed.

CONRAD, CATHERINE; Tuckahoe HS; Bronxville, NY; (Y); 3/66; Drama Clb; French Clb; Trs Intnl Clb; Trs Leo Clb; Math Clb; Band; Chorus; Concert Band; Nwsp Ed-Chief; Nwsp Rptr; Frnch Cont Awd 1st Hnrs 86; DAR Awd 84; Hnr Soc & Leo Clb Awd 86; Lawyer.

CONRAD, KATHLEEN J; Faith Bible Acad; Fort Plain, NY; (S); Church Yth Grp; Drama Clb; Radio Clb; Church Choir; School Musical; School Play; Yrbk Stf; Vllybl; Hon Roll; Cedarville Coll; Elem Ed.

CONRAD, MELISSA; Mount Mercy Acad; Hudson, OH; (Y); Art Clb; French Clb; School Play; Stage Crew; Hon Roll.

CONRAD, NANCY; Ravena-Coeymans-Selkirk Cntrl HS; Ravena, NY; (Y); Computer Clb; French Clb; SADD; Stat JV Bsktbl; Score Keeper; Var Trk; JV Vllybl; Highest Av Math 83-84; Bio-Chem.

CONRAD, SHARON D; E J Wilson HS; Spencerport, NY; (Y); 2/360; Am Leg Aux Girls St; Hst Sec Latin Clb; Ski Clb; Nwsp Stf; Yrbk Stf; High Hon Roll; NHS; Church Yth Grp; French Clb; JCL; Outstndng Achvt Frnch, Latn 83-85; William And Mary; Frgn Rltns.

CONRAD, WENDY S; Newark Valley HS; Newark Valley, NY; (Y); 10/120; Pres VP Ski Clb; Pres Chorus; School Musical; Trs Jr Cls; Stu Cncl; High Hon Roll; Trs NHS; Drama Clb; Swing Chorus; Salute Yth Hnre 85; Rgnts Schlrshp 86; SUNY Binghamton; Bus Adm.

CONROE, SHELLEY; Skaneateles Central HS; Skaneateles, NY; (S); French Clb; Hosp Aide; Acpl Chr; Band; Chorus; Concert Band; Mrchg Band; Orch; School Musical; Yrbk Stf; Ink Drwng At Mony Art Show 85; Gold Key Awd Art Show 86; NYSSMA Solos 83-84; All Cnty Chorus 79-84; Comm Art.

CONROY, JOHN W; St Anthonys HS; Farmingville, NY; (Y); 118/580; JV Var Ftbl; JV Lcrss; Hon Roll; U Of Dayton; Bus Admin.

CONROY, KELLY; Riverhead HS; Riverhead, NY; (Y); 116/211; Girl Scts; Acpl Chr; Chorus; JV Sftbl; Im Wt Lftg; Stat Wrstlng; Police Acad; Law Enfrcmnt.

CONROY, ROBERT; Warwick Valley HS; Warwick, NY; (Y); 30/200; Drama Clb; Band; Jazz Band; Off Soph Cls; VP Jr Cls; Stu Cncl; Var JV Crs Cntry; JV L Socr; Var L Trk; High Hon Roll; Mst Imprvd Rnnr 85; SUNY; Musicn.

CONSAGA, TONY; Ossining HS; Ossining, NY; (Y); Var Capt Ice Hcky; High Hon Roll; Hon Roll; Italian Achvmnt Awd 86; Pace U; Bus Mgmt.

CONSAVAGE, JENNIFER; Sacred Heart HS; Yonkers, NY; (S); Church Yth Grp; Chorus; School Musical; Nwsp Rptr; Rep Jr Cls; Rep Stu Cncl; Stat Score Keeper; JV Vllybl; Hon Roll; NHS; Educ.

CONSIDINE, WILLIAM J; Fordham Prep; Bronx, NY; (Y); JA; Library Aide; Varsity Clb; Rep Jr Cls; Var Bsktbl; Var Ftbl; Var Wt Lftg; Hon Roll; Francis Griffin Schlrshp.

CONSLER, CHRISTY; Honeoye Central HS; Honeoye, NY; (S); 4/64; French Clb; VP Soph Cls; VP Stu Cncl; JV Socr; Dnfth Awd; High Hon Roll; NHS; Ntl Merit Ltr; Ski Clb; Off Frsh Cls; Bst Trmpapr Cls 84; Smmr Schlr Pgm St John Fisher Coll 85; Cornell U; Bus.

CONSTABLE, JULIE; Geneva HS; Geneva, NY; (Y); Church Yth Grp; Ski Clb; Spanish Clb; Rep Jr Cls; Stu Cncl; Cheerleading; Mgr(s); Score Keeper; Socr; Sftbl; Hotel Mgmt.

CONSTABLE, MICHAEL; Walton HS; Walton, NY; (Y); 4-H; FFA; VICA; Var Crs Cntry; Var Trk; Wt Lftg; Vrsty Lttr In Trck & Crss Cntry 85-86; William Anslow Memrl Awd For Indstrl Arts 85; Crpntr.

CONSTABLE, SETH; Wallkill SR HS; Newburgh, NY; (S); 2/173; Am Leg Boys St; Boy Scts; Rep Jr Cls; Ftbl; Wrstlng; High Hon Roll; NHS; U S Achvt Acad Ldrshp & Svc Awd 84; Natl Sci Merit Awd 83; Intl Forgn Lang Awd 86.

CONSTANTATOS, GUS; Commuck HS South; Commack, NY; (Y); Camera Clb; Computer Clb; Varsity Clb; Ftbl; Score Keeper; Wt Lftg; Wrstlng; High Hon Roll; Med.

CONSTANTINE, AMY; William Cullen Bryant HS; Woodside, NY; (S); 18/623; Pres Key Clb; Science Clb; Pres Service Clb; Band; Symp Band; Nwsp Rptr; Nwsp Stf; Tennis; NHS; Prfct Atten Awd; Georgetown U; Law.

CONSTANTINE, KIMBERLY A; Babylon HS; Babylon, NY; (Y); Intnl Clb; Science Clb; Spanish Clb; Mgr(s); Hon Roll; Chrldr.

CONSTANTINE, THEA; William Cullen Bryant HS; Woodside, NY; (S); Drama Clb; Key Clb; Concert Band; Variety Show; Nwsp Rptr; French Hon Soc; Hon Roll; Jr NHS; NHS; Prfct Atten Awd; Phys Educ Awd 85.

CONSTANTINO III, MICHAEL; Friends Acad; Glen Cove, NY; (Y); SADD; Band; Yrbk Phtg; Var L Socr; Var L Timer; Ntl Merit Schol; Varsity Clb; Concert Band; Jazz Band; Parades All Am Soccer Tm 86; Friends Acad V Soccer MVP 83-85; Yth Soccer Assoc Region 83-86; U PA; Finance.

CONSTANTINOU, MARIA; Newtown HS; Elmhurst, NY; (Y); 45/781; Computer Clb; Chorus; Church Choir; Stage Crew; Yrbk Ed-Chief; Var Capt Bsktbl; Var Cheerleading; Var Capt Vllybl; Prfct Atten Awd; City Cncl Citatn Awd; St Johns U; Comp.

CONTA, ANDY; Grand Island SR HS; Grand Island, NY; (Y); Boys Clb Am; Teachers Aide; Chorus; Bowling; Crs Cntry; Gym; Sftbl; Trk; NCC; Sci Tech.

CONTE, CHRISTOPHER; Uniondale HS; Uniondale, NY; (Y); Church Yth Grp; School Play; Stage Crew; Lit Mag; CC Awd; Turtle Hook JR HS Art Awd 84; Yth On Parade Afro-Amer Hertg Assn 86; Pratt U; Pro Illustrtr.

CONTE, DEANNA; Holy Trinity HS; Hicksville, NY; (Y); Math Clb; Cheerleading; Gym; Hon Roll; Mu Alp Tht; NASSAU CC.

CONTE, ELIZABETH; Henninger HS; Syracuse, NY; (Y); GAA; Intnl Clb; Key Clb; SADD; Rep Jr Cls; Var Socr; Hon Roll; NHS; Ptcpnt Oprtn Entrprise; Henninger Fth Ctr; Italian Clb.

CONTE, JEFF; Smithtown West HS; Smithtown, NY; (Y); Cmnty Wkr; Hosp Aide; Math Tm; Spanish Clb; Varsity Clb; Concert Band; Mrchg Band; Symp Band; Rep Soph Cls; Rep Jr Cls; All-Lg Wrstlng 85; All-Lg Wrstlng 2nd Pl 86; Pre-Med.

CONTE, THOMAS J; Smithtown West HS; Smithtown, NY; (Y); 79/387; Cmnty Wkr; Computer Clb; Science Clb; Spanish Clb; Band; Stu Cncl; Var Golf; Var Socr; Var Trk; Hon Roll; All League Suffolk Cnty Soccer Team 86; Rgnts Schlrshp 86; Pres Acdmc Ftns Awd 86; James Mdsn U; Comp Sci.

CONTENT, STEPHEN; Earl Vandermeulen HS; Port Jefferson, NY; (Y); #1 In Class; FBLA; Pres Leo Clb; Political Wkr; Spanish Clb; Nwsp Rptr; Golf; L Wrstlng; High Hon Roll; NHS; Ntl Merit Schol; WST NY Bus Dynmcs Awd; Atty.

CONTI, ALICIA; Linton HS; Schenectady, NY; (Y); 27/326; Key Clb; Office Aide; Yrbk Sprt Ed; Frsh Cls; Soph Cls; Jr Cls; Sr Cls; Bsbl; Var Cheerleading; Stat Ftbl; Mnhtn Coll Pres Schlrshp 86-87; Nzrth Coll & Ithaca Coll Schlrshp 86-87; Ithaca Coll; Bus.

CONTI, ANDREW; Johnn Jay HS; S Salem, NY; (Y); High Hon Roll; Hon Roll; Art, Math And Chem Awds 84-86; Vet Med.

CONTI, CAMILLE; Cardinal O Hara HS; Tonawanda, NY; (Y); 16/150; Cmnty Wkr; Drama Clb; French Clb; JA; Pep Clb; Teachers Aide; Varsity Clb; School Play; Var Cheerleading; Var Pom Pon; Child Psychlgy.

CONTI, CLAUDINE; Franklin D Roosevelnt HS; Brooklyn, NY; (Y); Library Aide; Teachers Aide; Yrbk Stf; Lit Mag; Cheerleading; Hon Roll; Tchng.

CONTI, LAURA; Brocton Cenral HS; Brocton, NY; (Y); 4/48; Pep Clb; School Musical; Nwsp Bus Mgr; Nwsp Stf; Yrbk Stf; Trs Jr Cls; Stat Bsktbl; High Hon Roll; SADD; Teachers Aide; LIU Acadmc Excell Awd 86; NY ST Regents Schlrshp 86; LIU Southampton Coll; Oceangry.

CONTI, MICHAEL; Union Endicottt HS; Endwell, NY; (Y); 36/432; Wrstlng; NHS; Turstee Awd Clarkson U 86; Clarkson U; Elect Engr.

CONTI, VINCENT; Garden City SR HS; Garden City, NY; (S); Boy Scts; Church Yth Grp; French Clb; Office Aide; Drm Mjr(t); Madrigals; Nwsp Rptr; Yrbk Stf; SADD; Concert Band; Garden Cty Intl Stu Exch Ambssdr 85; NYS Regents Scholar 86; Loyola Coll.

CONTINO, MICHELLE; St Jean Baptiste HS; Long Island City, NY; (S); 7/99; Yrbk Stf; Jr Cls; Stu Cncl; High Hon Roll; Computer Clb; Jr NHS; NHS; Princpls Awd Ldrshp 86; Relgn 10 Recgntn Excllnce Scholar 85; Japan-US Senate Scholar Pgm 86; Cazenovia Coll; Fash Merch.

CONTOIS, ALBERT; Ticonderoga HS; Ticonderoga, NY; (Y); Stu Cncl; Crs Cntry; Trk; Hon Roll; Engrng.

CONTRERAS, SHARON; Uniondale HS; Uniondale, NY; (Y); Debate Tm; Drama Clb; NFL; Speech Tm; Chorus; School Play; Rep Jr Cls; Rep Sr Cls; JV Pom Pon; High Hon Roll; Cornell U; Crdlgsts.

CONTRINO, PATRICIA; Smithtown HS West; Smithtown, NY; (Y); Art Clb; Spanish Clb; Chorus; Hon Roll; Spanish NHS; Graphic Art.

CONVERSE, CARRI; Irondequoit HS; Rochester, NY; (Y); 17/393; Church Yth Grp; Ski Clb; Chorus; Church Choir; JV Vllybl; Hon Roll; NHS; Class 85 Grad Ceremonies Usher 85; Miami U; Bus Mngmnt.

CONVEY, MAURICE J; Garden City HS; Garden City, NY; (Y); 110/346; SADD; Orch; School Musical; School Play; Nwsp Rptr; Off Jr Cls; Off Sr Cls; JV Socr; Var Capt Swmmng; High Hon Roll; Msc Guild Awd 84forchstra Drctrs Awd 85; Rgnts Schlrshp 86; Adelphi Univ Trustee & Honors Scholarship; EMORY; Dntstry.

CONVISER, LENORE; Pelham Memorial HS; Pelham, NY; (Y); Am Leg Aux Girls St; Drama Clb; School Musical; School Play; Stage Crew; Nwsp Rptr; Nwsp Stf; NHS; Mt Holyoke Bk Awd 86; Columbia Sci Hnr Prog 85-86.

CONWAY, ELIZABETH; Out Lady Of Perpetual Help HS; Brooklyn, NY; (Y); 10/69; Camp Fr Inc; Exploring; Chorus; Hons Hist & Engl 84; Accntng.

CONWAY, MICHELLE; Tamarac HS; Johnsonville, NY; (Y); 20/106; Intnl Clb; Chorus; Yrbk Stf; Stu Cncl; Socr; Trk; Hon Roll; Brunswick Bus Assoc Awd 86; Admnstrtv Mgmnt Society Awd 86; Hudson Vly CC; Bus Admin.

CONWAY, THERESA; Dominican Commercial HS; Brooklyn, NY; (Y); 5/288; Church Yth Grp; Political Wkr; Wt Lftg; Cit Awd; High Hon Roll; NHS; Siera Clb; Prncpls Lst; Bio.

CONYERS, FRANKIE; Bishop Loughlin Memorial HS; Brooklyn, NY; (Y); Church Yth Grp; Science Clb; Band; Church Choir; Concert Band; Variety Show; Cmmnctn Engr.

CONYERS, MARSHALL; All Hallows HS; Bronx, NY; (Y); Im Bsktbl; Hon Roll; IN Inst Of Tech; Acctng.

COOGAN, CHRISTINE; Hicksville HS; Hicksville, NY; (Y); Hosp Aide; Chorus; Variety Show; Stu Cncl; NHS; James Madison U; Psych.

COOK, ANDREW; Cornwall Central HS; Highland Mills, NY; (Y); Ski Clb; Var Ftbl; Var Trk; Var Wt Lftg; Hon Roll; Undrclssmn Awd Ftbll 85; Blgy.

COOK, BRIAN F; Oriskany Central HS; Oriskany, NY; (Y); 3/70; Varsity Clb; Concert Band; Stage Crew; Nwsp Ed-Chief; Yrbk Phtg; Var Bsbl; High Hon Roll; Pres Jr NHS; VP NHS; Rep Stu Cncl; Rgnts Schlrshp NY ST 86; SR Yr Awd St Stephens Chrch 86; Leag Chmpns In V Bsbll 86; Rnsslr Polyt Inst; Med.

COOK, DARRYL; P V Moore HS; Brewerton, NY; (Y); Debate Tm; Math Tm; Radio Clb; ROTC; Var Ftbl; Var Lcrss; Hon Roll; Engr.

COOK, DAVE; Fayetteville-Manlius HS; Manlius, NY; (Y); Boy Scts; Pres Church Yth Grp; Off JCL; Sec Model UN; Var Socr; High Hon Roll; NHS; Cmnty Wkr; Hosp Aide; Political Wkr; Cum Laude Natl Latn Exm Awd 84; Outstndng Delgt Modl UN 85; Ldrs Of Tomrw 86; Electrcl Engrng.

COOK, JENNIFER; Midwood HS; Brooklyn, NY; (Y); 183/556; Church Yth Grp; Service Clb; Chorus; Church Choir; Madrigals; School Musical; Stage Crew; Rep Stu Cncl; Var Socr; Mchl J Qll Schrlshp Fnd 85-86; Ntl Phy Ed Awd By U S Achvmnt Acad 85-86; Hunter Coll; Bio Sci.

COOK, JENNY LYNN; Mechanicville HS; Mechanicville, NY; (S); Pres French Clb; Ski Clb; SADD; Band; Nwsp Rptr; Ed Yrbk Stf; Rep Stu Cncl; High Hon Roll; Hon Roll; Jr NHS; Omega Hon Soc 84-85; Alpha Hon Soc 85-86; Boston Coll; Pre-Med.

COOK, LARRY; Ramstien American HS; Apo New York, NY; (Y); Boy Scts; Science Clb; Spanish Clb; Varsity Clb; Band; Concert Band; JV Bsktbl; Var Socr.

COOK, LARRY; Victor Central HS; Farmington, NY; (Y); 27/230; Debate Tm; Model UN; SADD; High Hon Roll; Hon Roll; Pres Acad Ftns Awd; NYS Regnts Schlrshp; Industrl Arts Awd; CC; Elect Tech.

COOK, LAURA; Schoharie Central Schl; Schoharie, NY; (S); FHA; Hosp Aide; Teachers Aide; Yrbk Stf; Pres Soph Cls; High Hon Roll; Hon Roll; Bus.

COOK, MARY ANN; Corning Painted Post East HS; Corning, NY; (Y); Drama Clb; Hosp Aide; Spanish Clb; Thesps; Concert Band; Mrchg Band; Orch; School Musical; JP Sousa Awd; NHS; NY ST Rgnts Schlrshp 86; NY ST Rgnts Dplm With Hnrs 86; U Rchstr; Bio.

COOK, MICHELLE; Johnstown HS; Johnstown, NY; (Y); Band; Concert Band; Mrchg Band; Pep Band; JV Bsktbl; JV Fld Hcky; JV Sftbl; High Hon Roll; Hon Roll; VFW Awd; Prm Crt 86; U Of GA; Pltcl Sci.

COOK, RENEE D; Niskayuna HS; Schenectady, NY; (Y); 3/330; Cmnty Wkr; School Musical; Variety Show; Off Frsh Cls; Off Soph Cls; JV Var Socr; Sftbl; Cit Awd; Elks Awd; Pres Schlr; Zonta Clb Awd; Rotary Awd; Girls Clb Awd; Tchrs Assoc; Comm Svc; Oneonta; Lib Arts.

COOK, SHELLY; Groton Central Schl; Groton, NY; (Y); Ski Clb; Color Guard; Nwsp Stf; Yrbk Stf; Hon Roll; Secretary.

COOK, WILLIAM; Bainbridge-Guilford HS; Bainbridge, NY; (Y); 12/80; Boy Scts; French Clb; Band; Chorus; Mrchg Band; JV Var Bsbl; Var Capt Vllybl; High Hon Roll; Prfct Atten Awd; Ithaca Coll; Chem.

COOKE, CATHERINE; W C Mepham HS; Wantagh, NY; (Y); VP Mathletes; Sec Scholastic Bowl; Mgr Concert Band; Capt Tennis; French Hon Soc; NHS; Ntl Merit Ltr; Debate Tm; French Clb; Science Clb; Natl Hist Day Awds 1st Lcl & 2nd ST 84; Cncours Natl De Francais Awd 86; Nassau Cnty Mathlete Comp; Phrmcy.

COOKE, DAMIEN N; Harry S Truman HS; Bronx, NY; (Y); CAP; Computer Clb; Spanish Clb; Teachers Aide; Im Wt Lftg; Hon Roll; De Vry Inst; Aerosp Engrng.

COOKE, ELEANOR; Francis Lewis HS; Bayside, NY; (Y); Sec Church Yth Grp; Cmnty Wkr; French Clb; FTA; Service Clb; Concert Band; Jazz Band; Mrchg Band; School Play; Rep Stu Cncl; Prid Of Yankees Outstng Yth Awd 86; Phy Asst.

COOKE, JANA; Indian River Central HS; Philadelphia, NY; (Y); 8/140; AFS; Band; Chorus; Jazz Band; School Musical; Swing Chorus; JV Var Bsktbl; JV Var Socr; JV Var Sftbl; Hon Roll; All Str Bsktbl 85-86.

COOKE, STEPHEN; Saugerties HS; Saugerties, NY; (Y); Debate Tm; JA; SADD; Acpl Chr; Chorus; Church Choir; Mrchg Band; School Musical; School Play; Var Ftbl; Awd $100 Svngs Bnd From SHSC 86; Awd $25 From Mens Catskill Glee Clb 86; A NYSSMA All St Solo 86; Army; Law.

COOKE, WINIFRED; Lafayette HS; Brooklyn, NY; (Y); Orch; Yrbk Stf; Twrlr; NHS; Awd Excllnc Advncd Plcmnt Europn Hstry 85; Excllnc Chem & Psychbio 86; Excllnc Svc & Chrctr 85-87; Psychlgy.

COOKHOUSE, FAYE; Fayetteville-Monlius HS; Manlius, NY; (Y); Aud/Vis; Thesps; School Musical; Mgr Stage Crew; Lcrss; Var L Trk; High Hon Roll; Hon Roll; Rotary Awd; Awd Excelnc Spnsh 85; John Godleski Schlrshp 86; LIU-C W Post; Commnctns.

COOLIDGE, GARY; Waverly JRSR HS; Waverly, NY; (Y); Boy Scts; French Clb; Scholastic Bowl; Concert Band; Mrchg Band; School Play; Var L Crs Cntry; Var L Trk; NHS; Regents Schlrshp 86; Suny Geneseo; Bio Chem.

COOMA, I; Dodge Vocational HS; Bronx, NY; (Y); FNA; Cit Awd; Hon Roll; Prfct Atten Awd.

COOMBS, BRIAN E; Bishop Ludden HS; Clay, NY; (Y); English Clb; VP French Clb; VP German Clb; Ski Clb; Chorus; L Crs Cntry; L Ice Hcky; L Trk; Hon Roll; NHS; Music Ed.

COOMBS, JOAL; Pulaski JR SR HS; Pulaski, NY; (Y); FBLA; GAA; SADD; Chorus; Color Guard; Mrchg Band; Twrlr; Hon Roll; Canton ATC; Exec Sec.

COOMBS, ROBERT; Sayville HS; W Sayville, NY; (Y); Key Clb; Band; JV Capt Golf; Pres NHS; Key Clb Serv Awd 86.

COON, DALE L; Madison Central HS; Oriskany Falls, NY; (Y); Am Leg Boys St; FFA; Varsity Clb; Bsbl; Socr; Wrstlng; Hon Roll; Won 2 Bronze Mdls At JR Pan Am Wrstlng Games 84; USA Natl JR Olympic Freestyle Wrstlng Tem 85; Penn ST; Physical Education.

COON, LYNETTE; Charles O Dickerson HS; Trumansburg, NY; (Y); Spanish Clb; SADD; Band; Mrchg Band; Cheerleading; High Hon Roll.

COON, MICHELE; Our Lady Of Mercy; Fairport, NY; (Y); Drama Clb; Intnl Clb; JA; Model UN; PAVAS; Science Clb; Spanish Clb; SADD; School Musical; Nwsp Rptr; Siena Coll Schlrshp 86; Siena Coll; Pltcl Sci.

COONEY, BRIAN; Lyons Central Schl; Lyons, NY; (Y); 18/100; 4-H; Quiz Bowl; Band; Concert Band; Jazz Band; Mrchg Band; School Musical; Im Ftbl; Cit Awd; Dnfth Awd; FFA Awd 86; WA DC 4-H Ctznshp Shortcourse 85; Wayne Cnty Holstein Clb Distngshd Stu 85; Alfred ST Coll; Bldg Constrctn.

COONEY, JAMES; Mt Upton Central HS; Mt Upton, NY; (Y); 6/24; Church Yth Grp; Ski Clb; Nwsp Stf; L Bsbl; Bsktbl; Socr; Hon Roll; Regents Schlrshp NOPA Schlrshp 86; Keith Clark Achvt Awd 86; Drew U; Pre Law.

COONEY, LISA; Nooside Falls Central HS; Hoosick Falls, NY; (Y); Computer Clb; Exploring; Pep Clb; Off Stu Cncl; Score Keeper; Ntl Merit Ltr; HVCC; Bus Admin.

COONEY, MICHAEL JUDE; Lansingburgh HS; Troy, NY; (S); 2/196; Trs Jr Cls; Capt Sr Cls; Var Capt Crs Cntry; Capt Ice Hcky; Var L Trk; Cit Awd; DAR Awd; High Hon Roll; Pres Jr NHS; NHS; Earth Sci, Frnch I Outstndng Achvt 83; Bio.

COONRAD, CINDY; Chatham HS; Ghent, NY; (Y); 24/117; Chorus; Yrbk Stf; Hon Roll.

COONRADT, KIMBERLY; Stissing Mt JR SR HS; Clinton Corners, NY; (Y); 24/89; Church Yth Grp; Cmnty Wkr; 4-H; Capt Bsktbl; Var Coach Actv; L Var Crs Cntry; JV Sftbl; Var L Trk; 4-H Awd; Hon Roll; Cmnty Svc Awds 86; Keene ST Coll; Home Econ.

COONS, BRADFORD; Pine Plains Central HS; Pine Plains, NY; (Y); 28/101; Boy Scts; Varsity Clb; Yrbk Stf; Var Capt Bsbl; Var Capt Bsktbl; Var Ftbl; JV Socr; High Hon Roll; Hon Roll; Bttng Chmpn Trphy All-Sctn I All-Str 84; Bsktbl MV Trphy Hnrbl Mntn 85; Bttng Chmpn Trphy 86; Springfield; Bus Mgmt.

COONS, DARLENE; Watkins Glen HS; Watkins Glen, NY; (S); 3/135; Am Leg Aux Girls St; Band; VP Sr Cls; VP Rep Stu Cncl; Var Bsktbl; Var Swmmng; High Hon Roll; Hon Roll; Pres NHS; Church Yth Grp; Engr.

COONS, JOHN M; Hoosick Falls Central HS; Hoosick Falls, NY; (Y); Aud/Vis; Spanish Clb; Stage Crew; Var L Bsbl; Tennis; Hon Roll; NHS; CSF 83.

COONS, SHAWN; Lansingburgh HS; Troy, NY; (Y); 5/145; French Clb; Off Sr Cls; Rep Stu Cncl; High Hon Roll; Jr NHS; Rgnts Schlrshp 86; Pres Acdmc Ftns Awd 86; Magna Cum Laude 86; Air Force; Aviation.

COOPER, ALISA; Smithtown West HS; Smithtown, NY; (Y); Ski Clb; Spanish Clb; SADD; Yrbk Stf; Off Frsh Cls; Off Soph Cls; Off Jr Cls; Off Sr Cls; High Hon Roll; Hon Roll; Spnsh & Natl Hnr Socty 84-86; Pre-Law.

COOPER, ANGELINA; Sewanlake HS; Elmont, NY; (Y); Drama Clb; Library Aide; Red Cross Aide; School Play; JV Bsktbl; JV Twrlr; High Hon Roll; Hon Roll; Nassau CC.

COOPER II, DAVID D; Glen Cove HS; Glen Cove, NY; (Y); Debate Tm; Hst Drama Clb; PAVAS; Spanish Clb; Thesps; Chorus; School Musical; School Play; Ntl Merit SF; Spanish NHS; Carnagie-Mellon U Schlrshp 85; Intl Thspn Soc 85; Masquers Soc Vrsty Lttr; NY U; Prdcr.

COOPER, DENISE; Park West HS; Brooklyn, NY; (Y); 105/483; Church Yth Grp; Office Aide; Teachers Aide; Church Choir; Hon Roll; Prfct Atten Awd; Engl Hnrs 85-86; Vlntr Wrk Awd 86; Acctnt.

COOPER, J JAMES; Dryden Central HS; Freeville, NY; (Y); Chess Clb; Pres 4-H; Band; Color Guard; 4-H Awd; Hon Roll; Prfct Atten Awd; Cnty Mdl Art Crfts 4h 83-85.

COOPER, JEFFREY A; Ardsley HS; Ardsley, NY; (Y); 2/159; Band; Mrchg Band; Nwsp Ed-Chief; Pres Soph Cls; Pres Jr Cls; Var Capt Golf; Bausch & Lomb Sci Awd; Ntl Merit SF; Sal; Political Wkr; Brwn U Bk Awd 85; Amer Chem Soc Awd 84; Wrtng Awds Excllnc 84-85; MBA; Ecnmcs.

COOPER, KAREN M; Queen Of The Rosary Acad; Amityville, NY; (Y); 16/50; Hosp Aide; Library Aide; Nwsp Rptr; Var Trk; St Johns U; Amer Hstry.

COOPER, KATHLEEN; West Genesee SR HS; Warners, NY; (Y); Church Yth Grp; Girl Scts; Acpl Chr; Chorus; Church Choir; School Musical; Off Sr Cls; Var Gym; High Hon Roll; NHS; Semifnlst Cngrss Bndstg Yth Exchng Pgm 85; Sci.

COOPER, MARIE; Smithtown H S East; Smithtown, NY; (S); Trs DECA; FBLA; Fld Hcky; Hon Roll; Bus.

COOPER, SAMANTHA E; Tottenville HS; Staten Island, NY; (Y); Drama Clb; JA; Spanish Clb; Chorus; School Play; Cheerleading; Ntl Merit SF; Regents Scholar 86; Brooklyn Coll; Video Prod.

COOPER, SANDRA; Bishop Kearney HS; Brooklyn, NY; (Y); Spanish Clb; NHS; Regents Schlrshp 86; Pace U Trustees Schlrshp 86; Pace U; Compu Sci.

COOPER, TRESSA; Uniondale HS; Hempstead, NY; (Y); Concert Band; Mrchg Band; Orch; Badmtn; Pom Pon; Trk; Vllybl; High Hon Roll; Jr NHS; All Co Awd Band 84; Engrng.

COOPER, ZARA; The Dwight Schl; New York, NY; (S); Debate Tm; Model UN; Temple Yth Grp; Nwsp Ed-Chief; Yrbk Ed-Chief; Lit Mag; Mgr(s); Hon Roll; Key Clb; Nwsp Rptr; Comms.

COOPERMAN, KEN; John F Kennedy HS; Bellmore, NY; (Y); Art Clb; SADD; Nwsp Ed-Chief; Lit Mag; Hon Roll; Treas Of Yorker Clb 85-86; 3rd Pl Ntl Hstry Day Cmptn 84.

COOPERMAN, RANDI; South Shore HS; Brooklyn, NY; (Y); Bowling; Accntng.

COPE, BETH; Sacred Heart Acad; Merrick, NY; (Y); Church Yth Grp; Cmnty Wkr; FHA; PAVAS; Political Wkr; SADD; Acpl Chr; Chorus; Church Choir; Orch; Pre-Law.

COPELAND, HORACE; New Lebanon Central HS; W Lebanon, NY; (Y); Bsbl; Socr; Boy Scts; Variety Show; Gym; Sftbl.

COPELAND, JANIQUE; Half Hollow Hills East HS; Wheatley Hts, NY; (Y); Pres Sec Church Yth Grp; Cmnty Wkr; Teachers Aide; Varsity Clb; Nwsp Rptr; Nwsp Stf; Rep Stu Cncl; Var Crs Cntry; Stat Ftbl; Var Capt Trk; Cert Of Appreciatn Teachg Law To Elem Schl Stud 86; Part In Debutante Cottillion 86; Soc Work.

COPELAND, KIMBERLY A; Huntington HS; Huntington, NY; (Y); 44/383; AFS; Key Clb; Band; Concert Band; Mrchg Band; Trk; Vllybl; High Hon Roll; Hon Roll; Jr NHS; Regnts Schlrshp NY ST; Le High U; Lib Arts.

COPELAND, MOLLY; Webster HS; Webster, NY; (Y); Camp Fr Inc; Church Yth Grp; Cmnty Wkr; Dance Clb; 4-H; Hosp Aide; Library Aide; Office Aide; SADD; Chorus; Hnds Of Chrst Rchstr Dioscese 86; Hrsbck Rdng Awds; 4-H Hghpt Awd 84; Cazanovia Coll; Farm Mgmt.

COPLAND, BETH; Harrison HS; Harrison, NY; (Y); 34/200; Ski Clb; Chorus; Yrbk Stf; JV Tennis; NHS; St Schlr; Regents Schlrshp 86; Rotary Stu Mnth 86; American U; Cmmnctns.

COPPA, STEVEN J; Park West HS; Bronx, NY; (Y); 8/511; CAP; Orch; School Musical; VP Sr Cls; Stu Cncl; Cit Awd; Hon Roll; Rgnts Schlrshp 86; Excllnc Earth Sci 83; Supr Achvmnt Flight 85; Embry-Riddle Aero U; Aero Sci.

COPPEDGE, TIFFANY; Mt Vernon HS; Mt Vernon, NY; (Y); 118/550; High Hon Roll; Hon Roll; Cert Of Mert From Asmbly Of NY ST 86; Hwrd U; Pdtrcn.

COPPING, TERENCE; Bayport-Blue Point HS; Bayport, NY; (Y); 91/222; FBLA; Political Wkr; Science Clb; Bsbl; Bsktbl; Socr; Tennis; Merit Rl 84-85; FL Inst Tech; Comp.

COPPOLA, CARMELINA; Mont Pleasant HS; Schenectady, NY; (Y); JA; Pep Clb; Spanish Clb; Capt Cheerleading.

COPPOLA, JANINE; Auburn HS; Auburn, NY; (Y); Varsity Clb; Gym; High Hon Roll; Hon Roll; Liberal Arts.

COPPOTELLI, CORENE; Sacred Heart Acad; Rockville Centre, NY; (Y); Church Yth Grp; Dance Clb; Drama Clb; Rep Yrbk Bus Mgr; Rep Lit Mag; Swmmng; Tennis; Hon Roll; NHS; Psych.

CORACI, NATALE; Nazareth HS; Brooklyn, NY; (Y); Math Tm; Im Bsktbl; Var Ftbl; NHS.

CORBET, JENNIFER; Tottenville HS; Staten Island, NY; (Y); 1/871; Service Clb; Var Gym; Bausch & Lomb Sci Awd; Gov Hon Prg Awd; NHS; Ntl Merit Ltr; Val; Teachers Aide; School Play; Yrbk Stf; Rensselaer Awd Math & Sci 85; Ntl Hisp Schlr Awd 86; NY Regnts Schlrshp 86.

CORBETT, BETH; Saugerties HS; Saugerties, NY; (Y); French Clb; SADD; Teachers Aide; Band; Concert Band; Mrchg Band; Symp Band; Nwsp Rptr; Nwsp Stf; Hon Roll; Vision Of One World-Lit Awd 85; Bio.

CORBETT, CHRISTINE; Franciscan HS; Peekskill, NY; (Y); 19/58; Drama Clb; Chorus; School Musical; School Play; Variety Show; Nwsp Bus Mgr; Yrbk Bus Mgr; French Hon Soc; Pace U; Mrktng.

CORBETT, MICHELLE; Onondago Central HS; Syracuse, NY; (S); 2/70; Art Clb; Spanish Clb; Varsity Clb; Chorus; Rep Frsh Cls; Stu Cncl; Var Crs Cntry; Var Socr; NHS; Sal; 2nd Pl Mony Schlstc Art Comp 84-85; Cross Cty ST Champ Tn 5th Rnnr Div III 82-83; Pol Sci.

CORBETT, MICHELLE; Potsdam HS; Potsdam, NY; (Y); Drama Clb; French Clb; Math Clb; Stat Bsktbl; JV Var Cheerleading; JV Var Vllybl; Hon Roll; Potsdam ST U; Accntng.

CORBI, CAROLINE; Cardinal Spellman HS; Bronx, NY; (Y); Pep Clb; Yrbk Stf; Im Bsktbl; Hon Roll; Manhattan Coll; Civil Engrng.

CORBISIERO, MARK; Archbishop Mollory HS; Douglaston, NY; (Y); 37/383; Teachers Aide; Y-Teens; Capt Swmmng; Hon Roll; NHS; Coachs Awd Vrsty Swmng 86; Acadmc Excllnce Awd 85; Bus.

CORCHADO, MARIBEL; Murry Bergtraum HS; Brooklyn, NY; (Y); Computer Clb; John Joy Fr Crmnl Jstc; Law.

CORCHIA, LINDA A; St Francis Prep; Astoria, NY; (S); 3/746; Cmnty Wkr; Color Guard; Hon Roll; NHS; Bnd Cncl & Movie Clb; Cornell; Pre-Med.

CORCORAN, ANNE ELIZABETH; Keshequa Cenral HS; Nunda, NY; (Y); 4/73; Am Leg Aux Girls St; French Clb; Math Clb; Pep Clb; Capt Flag Corp; Nwsp Ed-Chief; VP Pres Stu Cncl; JV Score Keeper; High Hon Roll; Hon Roll; JR Yr 86; Med.

CORCORAN, BRIDGET; Frontier Central HS; Hamburg, NY; (S); 92/449; Library Aide; Office Aide; NHS; NEDT Awd; Acadmc Schlrshp Hilbert Coll 86; Hilbert Coll; Bus Adm.

CORCORAN, BRIGID; Academy Of Saint Joseph; Sayville, NY; (Y); Art Clb; Church Yth Grp; Dance Clb; SADD; School Musical; School Play; Stage Crew; Yrbk Stf; Trk; Prtl Schlrshp Acad St Joseph 83-87; Villanova U.

CORCORAN, COLEEN; Bishop Ludden HS; Baldwinsvile, NY; (Y); Exploring; Rep Jr Cls; Var Cheerleading; Var Trk; High Hon Roll; NHS; Schlrshp Coll Crs For Le Moyne Coll 86; 3rd Pl Prtnr Cmbntn Div At Chrldng Cmptn 86; Lbrl Arts.

CORCORAN, COLLEEN MARIE; Shenendehowa HS; Clifton Park, NY; (Y); 150/675; Cmnty Wkr; English Clb; Intnl Clb; Ski Clb; High Hon Roll; NHS; Cert Merit-Concours Natl Francais 85; Presdntl Acadmc Ftns Awd 86; Wells Coll; Econmcs.

CORCORAN, COURTNEY LYN; Medina SR HS; Medina, NY; (Y); 15/175; Band; Concert Band; Jazz Band; Mrchg Band; Orch; Hon Roll; NHS; Daisy Chain 85; U Of Rochester; Bio.

CORCORAN, JASON; Henninger High HS; Syracuse, NY; (Y); Spanish Clb; Var Bsktbl; Var Lcrss; Var Socr; Htl Mgmt.

CORCORAN, LISA; Olean HS; Olean, NY; (Y); 48/200; Hosp Aide; Ski Clb; Spanish Clb; Chorus; Color Guard; Flag Corp; Psych.

CORCORAN, MARGARET; Albertus Magnus HS; Pearl River, NY; (Y); 15/200; Cmnty Wkr; Library Aide; Spanish Clb; SADD; Teachers Aide; Cheerleading; Hon Roll.

CORCORAN, PAMELA; Bishop Grimes HS; Liverpool, NY; (Y); 6/143; Hosp Aide; Chorus; School Musical; Bowling; High Hon Roll; NHS; Pres Schlr; NEMA 84-85; Hrsmnshp 83-86; St Lawrence U; Bio.

CORCORAN JR, THOMAS; Monsignor Farrell HS; Staten Island, NY; (Y); Im Bsktbl; Crs Cntry; Im Ftbl; Var Trk; High Hon Roll; Athltc Admin.

CORDA, FRANK; North Babylon SR HS; N Babylon, NY; (Y); Boy Scts; Pres Computer Clb; Exploring; Letterman Clb; Science Clb; Rep Frsh Cls; JV Trk; High Hon Roll; Hon Roll; NY Tech Inst; Comp Sci.

CORDARO, KAREN L; William Floyd HS; Shirley, NY; (Y); Cmnty Wkr; Leo Clb; Band; Concert Band; Flag Corp; Mrchg Band; Im Vllybl; Hon Roll; NY ST Regents Schlrshp 86; Farmintdale Tech; Anml Sci.

CORDARO, STEPHEN G; St Francis Prep; Whitestone, NY; (S); 22/653; Church Yth Grp; Ski Clb; Im Ftbl; Var Tennis; Var Trk; High Hon Roll; NHS; Ntl Merit Ltr; Pre Med.

CORDERO, PABLO; South Park HS; Buffalo, NY; (Y); Im Wt Lftg; Prfct Atten Awd; Bryant & Stratton; Lwyer.

CORDERO, PATRICIA; St Catharine Academy; Bronx, NY; (Y); Dance Clb; GAA; Ski Clb; School Musical; School Play; Variety Show; Sftbl; Swmmng; Hon Roll; NHS; Iona Coll; Mrktng.

CORDIER, BRUCE; West Seneca West SR HS; W Seneca, NY; (Y); Boy Scts; Hon Roll; Ntl Merit Ltr; Pres Schlr; SR Ptrl Ldr Of Sct Trp 138 85; Elctrcl Engrng.

CORDIS, RHONDA; Springfield Gardens HS; Rosedale, NY; (Y); #13 In Class; Teachers Aide; Lit Mag; Rep Frsh Cls; Rep Soph Cls; Rep Jr Cls; Hon Roll; NHS; Daily News Pride Yankees Awd 86; 2nd Pl Awd Sci Fair 86; John Jay; Corp Lawyer.

CORDOVA, AMY; Abraham Lincoln HS; Brooklyn, NY; (Y); Aud/Vis; Key Clb; Pep Clb; SADD; Chorus; School Play; Nwsp Stf; Yrbk Ed-Chief; Rep Sr Cls; Rep Stu Cncl; NY U; Elem Ed.

CORDOVA, VIVIAN; Shaker HS; Latham, NY; (Y); #9 In Class; Dance Clb; JA; Science Clb; Hon Roll; German Clb; Intnl Clb; Chorus; Cornell U; Vet.

COREY, HEATHER; Sherburne-Earlville HS; Earlville, NY; (Y); 5/167; Pres Drama Clb; School Play; Stage Crew; JV Cheerleading; High Hon Roll; NHS; OM Cmptn 86; Mck Trl 86; Ntl Sci Merit Awd 86.

CORKERY, TODD E; Jamestown HS; Jamestown, NY; (Y); 104/390; Cmnty Wkr; Ski Clb; Hon Roll; St Bonaventure U; Acctg.

CORKWELL, KEITH; Pine Valley HS; South Dayton, NY; (S); 2/63; Bausch & Lomb Sci Awd; Hon Roll; NHS; Sal; Penn-York Chem Awd 84-85; JR Schlrshp Awd 84-85; PTA Awd 84-85; Engr.

CORLITO, DAYNA; James Madison HS; Brooklyn, NY; (Y); Teachers Aide; Band; Chorus; School Musical; Var Twrlr; Arista-Archon 83-84; COLL Now Prog; Bus Mgnt.

CORN, GAVIN ALEXANDER; Bellport HS; Bellport, NY; (Y); 25/293; Cmnty Wkr; Ski Clb; Varsity Clb; Yrbk Phtg; Ftbl; Var Capt Trk; Wt Lftg; NHS; NY ST Rgnts Schlrshp & Physcs Olympcs Team 86; All Cnfrnc In Track 85; Dcknsn Coll; Archlgst.

CORNA, LIZ; Franklin Central HS; Franklin, NY; (Y); GAA; Pep Clb; SADD; Varsity Clb; Nwsp Sprt Ed; Nwsp Stf; Yrbk Phtg; Yrbk Rptr; Yrbk Sprt Ed; Yrbk Stf; Most Imprvd Plyr-Scr 8384; Most Vlbl Plyr-Scr 85; Bus.

CORNACCHIA, ANTHONY J; John F Kennedy HS; Utica, NY; (Y); Boy Scts; Church Yth Grp; Exploring; Key Clb; Math Clb; Spanish Clb; Drm & Bgl; JV Var Ftbl; JV Golf; Var Vllybl; Comp Engr.

CORNACCHIO, DIANE; Mahopac HS; Mahopac, NY; (Y); 111/375; VP Pres Dance Clb; Hosp Aide; Hon Roll; Bridgeport U; Fash Merch.

CORNEILSON, CHRISTINE; Unatego JR SR HS; Bainbridge, NY; (Y); 17/86; Church Yth Grp; Letterman Clb; Spanish Clb; Varsity Clb; Chorus; Capt Crs Cntry; Sftbl; Score Keeper; Capt Var Vllybl; Hon Roll; ST U Of NY Geneseo; Sec Educ.

CORNELES, KAREN; Waterloo SR HS; Waterloo, NY; (Y); Pep Clb; Ski Clb; Spanish Clb; Color Guard; Mrchg Band; Var Socr; Im Sftbl; High Hon Roll; Hon Roll; Prfct Atten Awd; Med Lab Tech.

CORNELL, ANGELA; Jasper Central HS; Greenwood, NY; (Y); Varsity Clb; Yrbk Stf; Off Soph Cls; Off Jr Cls; Off Sr Cls; Capt Var Bsktbl; Capt Var Socr; Capt Var Vllybl; Hon Roll; Prfct Atten Awd; All-Str Tm Vllybl & Bsktbl 85-86; Steuben Cnty Dairy Prncs 86-87; Physclly Chlngd Kds.

CORNELL, CHARLENE; Broadalbin Central Schl; Broadalbin, NY; (Y); 16/71; French Clb; Trs Varsity Clb; Mrchg Band; School Play; Var Cheerleading; Capt Var Socr; Var Trk; High Hon Roll; NHS; 2nd All Star Soccr Tm Tri Vly Lg 85 & 86; Mst Dedicated Chrldng 85; Kennyetto Fire Co Aux Awd Effrt 86; Herkimer Cnty CC; Sec Sci.

CORNELL, JOHN H; Westhampton Beach HS; East Quogue, NY; (Y); 16/261; Camera Clb; Computer Clb; Ski Clb; Band; Mrchg Band; Var L Crs Cntry; Var L Trk; NHS; Varsity Clb; Concert Band; U Of CO Boulder; Aerspc Engr.

CORNELL, KENNETH; Perry Central HS; Perry, NY; (Y); Pres 4-H; Varsity Clb; Chorus; Var Capt Socr; 4-H Awd; Math & Sci.

CORNELL, MICHAEL A; Johnson City HS; Johnson City, NY; (Y); 77/198; Boys Clb Am; French Clb; Ski Clb; Sec Jr Cls; Var L Bsbl; Var L Ftbl; Var Ice Hcky; Rgnts Schlrshp; NY ST U Bnghmtn; Elec Engrng.

CORNETT, HOWARD G; Paul V Moore HS; Bernhard Bay, NY; (Y); Am Leg Boys St; Math Tm; Sec Varsity Clb; JV Var Bsbl; Var Socr; Var Trk; High Hon Roll; NHS; Boy Scts; Pres Clssrm 86; Ltr Bsbl, Sccr And Indr Trk 86; Georgetown; Poltcl Sci.

CORNETTE, PAUL; Msgr Farrell HS; Staten Island, NY; (Y); Cmnty Wkr; Exploring; Varsity Clb; Stu Cncl; Bsbl; Var L Bsktbl; Im Ftbl; Var Trk; Bus.

CORNISH, JEFF; Solvay HS; Solvay, NY; (Y); JV Var Bsktbl; Im Vllybl; Bus Mgt.

CORNISH, ROBIN; Onondaga Central HS; Nedrow, NY; (S); Pres Trs Exploring; GAA; Spanish Clb; SADD; Teachers Aide; School Play; Yrbk Stf; Var Sftbl; Var Capt Vllybl; High Hon Roll; SUNY; Elem Educ.

CORNO, RICHARD; Babylon JR SR HS; Babylon, NY; (Y); Chorus; Nwsp Phtg; Nwsp Rptr; Yrbk Phtg; Off Frsh Cls; Off Soph Cls; Stat Stu Cncl; Im Mgr Bsktbl; Im Mgr Vllybl; Atlantic Union Coll; Hist.

CORNWALL, CHRISTINE A; St Francis Prep; Little Neck, NY; (S); 190/744; Church Yth Grp; Cmnty Wkr; Concert Band; Mrchg Band; School Musical; St Johns U; Elem Eductn.

CORP, THOMAS; Liverpool HS; Liverpool, NY; (Y); 144/816; Var JV Bsbl; Var JV Ftbl; JV Wrstlng; NHS; Hnrb Mntn All Leg Bsbl 86; Clarkson U; Indstrl Engrng.

CORRADINO, MICHELLE; Sachem North HS; Holbrook, NY; (Y); 98/1376; Teachers Aide; High Hon Roll; Pres Schlr; Pres Acad Achvt Awd 86; 2nd Pl NY ST Natl Hstry Day Cert Of Achvt Natl Cntst Natl Hsty Day 83; SUNY Stony Brk NY; Phys Ther.

CORRADO, JOSEPH; Marlboro Cen HS; Marlboro, NY; (Y); 23/156; Dutchess CC; Elect Engrng.

CORRADO, PATRICIA; Central Islip SR HS; Central Islip, NY; (Y); Cmnty Wkr; Drama Clb; French Clb; Library Aide; Office Aide; SADD; Varsity Clb; Band; Concert Band; Mrchg Band; PTA Cncl Schlrshp 85-86; NYSSMA Fstvl Awd; Kent ST U; Pol Sci.

CORRAL, HENRY; Southampton HS; Southampton, NY; (Y); Cmnty Wkr; Drama Clb; French Clb; Ski Clb; Yrbk Stf; Rep Frsh Cls; Rep Stu Cncl; JV Bsbl; Var Socr; Hon Roll.

CORRALL, KIMBERLY; Garden City HS; Garden City, NY; (Y); 23/350; VP Spanish Clb; Church Choir; Stage Crew; Nwsp Stf; Lit Mag; Off Frsh Cls; Off Soph Cls; L Tennis; NHS; Debate Tm; NY All ST Mixed Chorus 85-86; Spn Awd Excllnce 85-86; Soloist Nassau All Cnty Music Fest 85-86; Music.

CORRARO, STEVE; Oneonta HS; Oneonta, NY; (Y); Art Clb; Boys Clb Am; Boy Scts; Letterman Clb; Ski Clb; Varsity Clb; Yrbk Stf; Off Stu Cncl; Var Bsbl; Var Capt Bsktbl; Athltc Of The Yr Oneonta Bys Clb 86; Sprtsmn Of The Yr Oneonta Bys Clb 85; Dvsn III All Star 85; Morrisville; Acctg.

CORREA, ALFONSO; Immaculata HS; Bronx, NY; (Y); Boys Clb Am; Capt Coach Actv; Im Ftbl; Im Sftbl; Im Swmmng; High Hon Roll; Hon Roll; U S Achvmnt Acad Ntl Awd Wnnr 85; Ntl Scndry Educ Cncl Acdmc All Amrcn 85; NY U; DDS.

CORREA, MARIA; Park West HS; Bronx, NY; (Y); Chorus; School Play; Off Sr Cls; The Wood Schl; Word Proc.

CORREIA, STEPHEN C; Vestal SR HS; Vestal, NY; (Y); 51/430; Concert Band; Mrchg Band; Orch; Var Capt Bsbl; Var Capt Golf; Var Capt Ice Hcky; High Hon Roll; NHS; Ntl Cncl Yth Ldrshp 84-85; Pres Schlr Ptsdm Coll-NY 85-86; Rgnts Schlrshp; Potsdam Coll; Engrng.

CORRICA, KEVIN; Prospect Heights HS; Brooklyn, NY; (S); 13/271; Debate Tm; FBLA; Math Clb; Office Aide; Pres Soph Cls; Daily News-Pride Of Yankees Awd-85; Mech Engrng.

CORRIERE, ANTHONY; Monsignor Farrell HS; Staten Island, NY; (Y); Yrbk Stf; Im Bsktbl; Im Bowling; Coach Actv; JV Var Socr; High Hon Roll; Hon Roll; Ldng Scorer Awd Soccr 85-86; NYU; Lawyer.

CORRIERO, DAVID; Bishop Grimes HS; Manlius, NY; (Y); Ski Clb; Band; Chorus; Var Golf; Capt Socr; MVP Soccr 85; FL ST U; Htl/Rest Mngmnt.

CORRIGAN, BRYAN; Beacon HS; Beacon, NY; (Y); Varsity Clb; Band; Var Capt Socr; Var Tennis; High Hon Roll; Hon Roll; Jr NHS; Arch.

CORRIGAN, CLAUDIA; A G Berner HS; Massapequa Park, NY; (Y); 52/470; Political Wkr; Stage Crew; Hon Roll; Ntl Merit Schol; Schl Vsl Arts NYC; Ilstrtn.

CORRIGAN, JEANNINE; Mary Louis Acad; Jackson Heights, NY; (Y); 32/270; Church Yth Grp; French Clb; Library Aide; Service Clb; Teachers Aide; High Hon Roll; Rgnts Schlrshp-Alt 86; Dominican Acadmc Schlrshp 86; Mt St Vncnt Comptv Schlrshp 86; Molloy Coll; Nrsng.

CORSALE, ANNMARIE; Moore Catholic HS; Staten Island, NY; (Y); Dance Clb; Drama Clb; Hosp Aide; School Musical; School Play; Yrbk Stf; Cheerleading; Hon Roll; Prfct Atten Awd; Law.

CORSELLO, LINDA A; St Francis Prep; Little Neck, NY; (S); 140/744; Church Yth Grp; Hosp Aide; Band; Concert Band; Mrchg Band; Im Ftbl; Im Sftbl; Im Vllybl; Hon Roll; NHS; Med.

CORSO, REGINA A; Marymount School Of New York; New York City, NY; (Y); Cmnty Wkr; Drama Clb; FTA; Teachers Aide; Acpl Chr; Chorus; School Musical; School Play; Nwsp Bus Mgr; Nwsp Stf; Rgnts Schlrshp; Skidmore Coll; Psychlgy.

CORSO, STACI; Division Avenue HS; Levittown, NY; (Y); 69/335; Band; Spanish Clb; Mrchg Band; Variety Show; Yrbk Stf; Score Keeper; Hon Roll; ST U Of NY.

CORSON, JANE; West Genesee SR HS; Syracuse, NY; (Y); 67/520; Ski Clb; Concert Band; Mrchg Band; Orch; Symp Band; Off Sr Cls; Sec Stu Cncl; Bsktbl; High Hon Roll; Opt Clb Awd.

CORTALE, MARK; North Shore HS; Glen Head, NY; (Y); 8/225; Pres Drama Clb; Pres Thesps; Chorus; Madrigals; School Musical; School Play; Nwsp Bus Mgr; Sec Stu Cncl; Hon Roll; Pres NHS; All-St Mixed Choir 84-85; All-Eastern Mixed Choir 85; Mannes Coll Of Music; Voice.

CORTAZZI, JOSEPH; Nazareth Regional HS; Brooklyn, NY; (Y); English Clb; Speech Tm; Hon Roll; Top Freshman Art Awd 83-84; Journalism.

CORTES, CLAUDIA; Holy Trinity Diocesan HS; Plainview, NY; (S); 9/328; Cmnty Wkr; Drama Clb; SADD; Stage Crew; Rep Frsh Cls; Rep Soph Cls; Rep Jr Cls; Rep Sr Cls; Rep Stu Cncl; High Hon Roll; Spnsh Awd-Iona Coll Cntst 84; Math Awd 83; Stoneybrook; Psychlgy.

CORTEZ, RENEE; De Witt Clinton HS; Bronx, NY; (Y); Band; Mrchg Band; Orch; Variety Show; Hon Roll; Syracuse U; Nrsng.

CORTI, KIM; Mamaroneck HS; Mamaroneck, NY; (Y); Church Yth Grp; Cmnty Wkr; Latin Clb; Service Clb; Chorus; Psychol.

CORTINA, LISA; St Mary Girls HS; New Hyde Park, NY; (Y); 23/180; Cmnty Wkr; Library Aide; Spanish Clb; Teachers Aide; Chorus; Camera Clb; High Hon Roll; Hon Roll; NHS; St Johns U; Bus.

CORTO, RONNIE JEAN; Sweethome HS; Amherst, NY; (Y); Camp Fr Inc; Church Yth Grp; Cmnty Wkr; 4-H; Girl Scts; Hosp Aide; Library Aide; Spanish Clb; Varsity Clb; Chorus; Physcl Fitness Awd 83-84; U Of NY; Bus Admin.

CORTRIGHT, BRENDA; Newark Valley HS; Newark Vly, NY; (Y); 29/114; 4-H; Girl Scts; Chorus; Color Guard; 4-H Awd; High Hon Roll; Hon Roll; Broome Cmnty Coll; Dntl Hygnst.

CORVATO, MIKE; Bay Shore HS; Bayshore, NY; (Y); 166/380; Cmnty Wkr; Intnl Clb; Varsity Clb; JV Bsktbl; Var Ftbl; JV Lcrss; Im Wt Lftg; Achvt Math 84; Excllnc Phy Ed Outstndng Achvt 85-86; Acctg.

CORVINO, RACHEL; Mohanasen HS; Schenectady, NY; (Y); Rep Key Clb; Spanish Clb; Band; Concert Band; Mrchg Band; Var Trs Cheerleading; Socr; High Hon Roll; Field Show Band Comptn 83-85; Math.

CORVO, AMY; Rye HS; Rye, NY; (Y); Church Yth Grp; High Hon Roll; Soclgy.

CORZA, ANA; Seward Park HS; New York, NY; (Y); School Musical; Prfct Atten Awd; Intln Lang Awd 86; Arista Clb 86; Nutrtn.

COSCIA, MELISSA; Niagara Catholic HS; Niagara Fls, NY; (Y); Dance Clb; French Clb; Hosp Aide; Key Clb; Yrbk Bus Mgr; Yrbk Phtg; Yrbk Stf; Pres Stu Cncl; JV Vllybl; High Hon Roll; Father Kroupa Mem 86; Vol Svc 83; Physcl Thrpy.

COSCIA, VERONICA; Academy Of Saint Joseph HS; Sayville, NY; (Y); Art Clb; Dance Clb; Drama Clb; Service Clb; SADD; Teachers Aide; School Musical; School Play; Stage Crew; Swing Chorus; Vrsty Ltr & Achvt In La Salle Living Theatre 85; Art Effort Awd 85; Trinity Coll; Education.

COSENTINO, APRIL; Bronx High School Of Science; Bronx, NY; (Y); German Clb; Library Aide; Church Choir; Ap Hist And Eng 86; Rgnts Schlrshp 86; Geneseo.

COSENTINO, CYNDI; Amsterdam HS; Amsterdam, NY; (Y); Yrbk Bus Mgr; Stu Cncl; Hon Roll; Awd Of Bus Excllnc 86; Rgnts Schlrshp 86; SUNY At Albany; Bus.

COSGROVE, JOSETTE; Ward Melvill HS; Setauket, NY; (Y); Dance Clb; Vllybl; Hon Roll.

COSGROVE, NOREEN; Maria Regina HS; Crestwood, NY; (Y); 25/727; Intnl Clb; Yrbk Stf; Lit Mag; Var Swmmng; High Hon Roll; Sec VP NHS; Trs Church Yth Grp; Exploring; Key Clb; NY ST Regnts Schlrshp 86; Chase Manhattan Ldrshp Awd 86; Catholc U Gibbons Hnrs Schlrshp 86; Fairfield U.

COSMAN, DIANE; Marlboro Central HS; Newburgh, NY; (Y); Church Yth Grp; Church Choir; Swmmng; High Hon Roll; Hon Roll; NHS; Intr Dsgn.

COSME, MARTHA; Bushwick HS; Bronx, NY; (S); Office Aide; Stu Cncl; Cit Awd; Doctor.

COSS, DARNELL; Whitesboro Central Schl; Marcy, NY; (Y); Exploring; Chorus; Hon Roll; Utica Schl Of Cmrc; Scrtry.

COSSENTINO, MARK; East Hampton HS; Montauk, NY; (Y); ROTC; Spanish Clb; SADD; Band; Mrchg Band; Var Socr; Var Trk; Var Wrstlng; High Hon Roll; NHS; Intrct Vstng SR Ctzns Cmnty Hlp 85-86; U Of MI; Med Dr.

COST, SCOTT; Elmira Free Acad; Elmira, NY; (Y); Am Leg Boys St; Pres Spanish Clb; Orch; Trs Stu Cncl; Var Bsbl; Var Bsktbl; Var Golf; Var Mgr(s); High Hon Roll; Ntl Merit Ltr; All ST Orch NY; Stu Senate Cmmttee-Albany; Elec Engr.

COSTA, ARIANNE D; Fontbonne Hall Acad; Staten Island, NY; (Y); 16/121; Drama Clb; GAA; Math Clb; Math Tm; Nwsp Rptr; Yrbk Stf; High Hon Roll; Hon Roll; Jr NHS; NHS; 2nd Hnrs, 1st Hnrs, Acdmc Awds In Hist, Math, Bio 82-85; St Johns U; Bus Mgmt.

COSTA, DEBORAH; North Babylon HS; North Babylon, NY; (Y); 5/454; Acpl Chr; Concert Band; Capt Flag Corp; Madrigals; Off Mrchg Band; Orch; Symp Band; Nwsp Stf; Yrbk Stf; High Hon Roll; SCMEA Perfmg Arts Schlrshp 84; Lions Intl All ST Band 86; Fnlst Miss Natl Teen Pgnt 86.

COSTA, FRANK; Leroy HS; Leroy, NY; (Y); Church Yth Grp; French Clb; Ski Clb; SADD; Varsity Clb; Stage Crew; Var Capt Ftbl; Trk; Wt Lftg; Var L Wrstlng; U Of CT; Pharm.

COSTA, KAREN; New Paltz Central HS; New Paltz, NY; (Y); Debate Tm; Spanish Clb; Band; Chorus; Concert Band; Mrchg Band; School Musical; Fld Hcky; High Hon Roll; Hon Roll; NYSSMA 3rd Pl Duet Medl & 2nd Pl Quart Medl Flute 84-85; NYSSMA 1st Duet Medl & 1st Trio Medl 86; Law.

COSTA, WILLIAM; North Babylon SR HS; North Babylon, NY; (Y); 61/464; Cmnty Wkr; DECA; JV Socr; Var Tennis; Hon Roll; Jr NHS; NHS; Pres Acad Ftnss Awd 86; DECA-BRONZE Merit Awd; DECA-SUFFOLK Cnty Cont-Job Interview 1st Pl 86; Oneonta; Accntng.

COSTANTINI, AMY; Solvay HS; Syracuse, NY; (Y); #2 In Class; Pres French Clb; Key Clb; Band; Chorus; Swing Chorus; Variety Show; Yrbk Stf; Sec NHS; Sal; Voice Dem Awd; Balgour Engl Awd 86; Cvc Ctr Thtr Fstvl Ind Cmmndtn 86; Musical Piano Awd 86; U Of Notre Dame.

COSTANTINI, VALERIE; Fairport HS; Fairport, NY; (Y); Mgr Aud/Vis; Drama Clb; Pres SADD; Chorus; School Musical; School Play; Stage Crew; Swing Chorus; Mgr Fld Hcky; Hon Roll; Ldrshp Awd 86; Prfct Attndnce Awd 86; Music.

COSTANZO, MARIALISA; South Shore HS; Brooklyn, NY; (Y); Concert Band; Jazz Band; School Musical; Var L Cheerleading; Var L Gym; Outstndng Perf Awd 86; Physcl Thrpst.

COSTELLO, DAVID; Archbishop Molloy HS; New York, NY; (Y); 12/385; Computer Clb; Science Clb; Ftbl; NHS; Engr.

COSTELLO, JOANNE; Fayetteville-Manlius HS; Fayetteville, NY; (Y); FBLA; JCL; Flag Corp; Mrchg Band; Sibleys Star Of Wk 85; SUNY Coll-Buffalo; Busnss Mgmt.

COSTELLO, KEVIN; Salamance HS; Killbuck, NY; (Y); Boy Scts; Spanish Clb; Band; Concert Band; Mrchg Band; Pep Band; Nwsp Bus Mgr; Nwsp Rptr; Nwsp Stf; Hon Roll; Comp Systms Anlyst.

COSTELLO, MICHELLE L; Bayport-Blue Point HS; Blue Point, NY; (Y); 3/209; Key Clb; Mathletes; Orch; School Musical; School Play; Yrbk Ed-Chief; Var Capt Cheerleading; Twrlr; High Hon Roll; NHS; Lng Isl Tchrs Bnvlnt Fnd Schlrshp 86; Blue Pnt Violin Schlrshp 86; Rgnts Schlrshp; Accntng.

COSTELLO, PATRICK; Oneida SR HS; Oneida, NY; (Y); 27/200; Aud/Vis; Mathletes; School Musical; Yrbk Sprt Ed; JV Var Ftbl; Var Capt Wrstlng; Rotary Awd; Boy Scts; Church Yth Grp; Cmnty Wkr; NY ST Rgnts Schlrshp 86; Mst Vlbl Wrstlr Tri Vly Leg All Str 86; Myrs Yth Advsry Cncl 85-86; U Notre Dm; Med.

COSTELLO, SARAH; Union Springs Central HS; Auburn, NY; (Y); 4/100; Ski Clb; School Play; Ed Yrbk Ed-Chief; Yrbk Phtg; Yrbk Stf; Soph Cls; Jr Cls; Sr Cls; Cheerleading; High Hon Roll; Phrmcy.

COSTELLO, THERESA; Our Lady Of Perpetual Help; Brooklyn, NY; (Y); 8/156; Stu Cncl; Mgr(s); Sftbl; High Hon Roll; Hon Roll; NHS; Pres Schlr; Regents Coll Scholar 86; LIU Full Acad Scholar 86; LIU; Phys Ther.

COSTIC, KENNETH; Port Jervis HS; Port Jervis, NY; (Y); Pres Aud/Vis; Band; Chorus; Concert Band; Drm Mjr(t); Jazz Band; Mrchg Band; Orch; School Musical; Symp Band; Music.

COSTLEY, SCOTT J; Horseheads HS; Horseheads, NY; (S); 27/380; Boy Scts; Band; Mrchg Band; Rep Church Yth Grp4; JV Crs Cntry; Var Trk; High Hon Roll; NHS; 4-H; Hon Roll; Army ROTC Conditnl Scholar Fin 85; Eagle Scout 85; Med.

COTA, ARNOLD; Canton Central HS; Hermon, NY; (Y); 55/120; Boy Scts; Computer Clb; Thesps; Lit Mag; Var Ftbl; Var Lcrss; Hon Roll; Ntl Merit Schol; Prfct Atten Awd; Rgnts Schlrshp 86; Potsdam ST; Comp.

COTE, LISA; Le Roy Central HS; Le Roy, NY; (Y); 11/125; Spanish Clb; Yrbk Stf; Trs Frsh Cls; Trs Soph Cls; Trs Sr Cls; JV Var Sftbl; Var Twrlr; JV Var Vllybl; AFS; French Clb; Calvin Noyes Keeney Schlrshp 86; Mary Frances Cromwell Meml Awd; Beta Sigma Phi Awd 86; Carusius Clg; Bus Adm.

COTE, STEPHEN A; Shenendehowa HS; Clifton Park, NY; (Y); Am Leg Boys St; Leo Clb; Symp Band; Pres Frsh Cls; Pres Soph Cls; Pres Jr Cls; Pres Sr Cls; Trs Stu Cncl; Var Golf; Var Trk; Engrng.

COTHRAN, DAVID; Onondaga HS; Nedrow, NY; (Y); 9/69; Spanish Clb; SADD; Yrbk Stf; Bsktbl; Var Crs Cntry; Var Trk; High Hon Roll; NHS; Ntl Merit Ltr; Schlrshp Syracuse U Pre Clg Prog 86; Accptd Cornell U Summr Clg Prog 86; Law.

COTHRAN, TRACI; Onondaga Central HS; Nedrow, NY; (S); 1/69; German Clb; Sec Spanish Clb; SADD; Rep Stu Cncl; Var Capt Crs Cntry; DAR Awd; Pres NHS; Trs FBLA; GAA; Varsity Clb; HOBY Ldrshp Fndtn 84; Century III Ldrshp 86; Syracuse U Pre-Coll Scholar 85; Allegheny Coll; Polit Econ.

COTON, WADE; Amsterdam HS; Amsterdam, NY; (Y); 12/290; Am Leg Boys St; Boy Scts; 4-H; Varsity Clb; Rep Stu Cncl; Var L Bsbl; Var L Bsktbl; Var Capt Ftbl; 4-H Awd; High Hon Roll; Schls Mst Outstndng Athlt 86; Mrn Crps Dstngshd Athlt Awd 86; Bsktbl Art Ofs Sprtmnsp Awd 86; SUNY Buffalo; Mech Engrng.

COTRONEO, CATHY; Rome Free Acad; Rome, NY; (Y); 33/500; Intnl Clb; Yrbk Stf; Var JV Tennis; JV Vllybl; Hon Roll; Jr NHS; NHS; Ntl Merit SF; Engr.

COTTER, SHARON; West Seneca East SR HS; West Seneca, NY; (Y); 16/375; Pres Trs GAA; Yrbk Sprt Ed; Var Capt Bsktbl; Var Capt Fld Hcky; Var JV Vllybl; High Hon Roll; JC Awd; NHS; Prfct Atten Awd; Grmn Ntl Hnr Soc; Buffalo ST Coll; Crmnl Jstc.

COTTON, JAMES; Victor SR HS; Victor, NY; (Y); Boys Clb Am; Boy Scts; Varsity Clb; Bsktbl; Capt Socr; Trk; Law Enf.

COTTRELL, JAMES; Hutchinson Central Tech HS; Buffalo, NY; (Y); 34/266; JA; Rep Sr Cls; Stu Cncl; Var Ftbl; Var Capt Trk; Hon Roll; NYS Rgnts Schlrshp 86; U Of Buffalo; Comp Sci.

COTUGNO, AARON; Amsterdam HS; Amsterdam, NY; (Y); 28/312; Orch; Rep Soph Cls; Rep Jr Cls; Stu Cncl; Var Bsbl; JV Capt Ftbl; Var Socr; High Hon Roll; Jr NHS; All St Orchestra 85; Union Coll; Bio.

COUCH, DEBRA; Grand Island HS; Grand Island, NY; (Y); Dance Clb; Political Wkr; Ski Clb; Yrbk Stf; Stu Cncl; JV Swmmng; Ntl Merit SF; Beloved Queen Of Aries Traingle #131 85-86; Sweetheart Of Isle De Molay 84-85; Ny St Rgnts Schlrshp 85; UCLA; Psych.

COUCH, SCOTT; Thousand Islands Central HS; Clayton, NY; (Y); JV Ftbl; Hon Roll; Comm Diver.

COUCHE, ALYCE; Frontier Central HS; Blasdell, NY; (Y); 4-H; FBLA; Pep Clb; Red Cross Aide; Spanish Clb; JV Mgr(s); Score Keeper; Sch Hlth Offc Aide 84; Trvl Agnt.

COUDERT, SANDRA; The Masters Schl; Ossining, NY; (Y); Chorus; Swing Chorus; Ed Yrbk Phtg; Fld Hcky; Lcrss; Hon Roll; Ntl Merit SF; Cum Laude Soc 85; Cmmnty Svc Advsry Bd 85-86; Wms Bk Awd 85; Engl, Fr & Math Awds 85.

COUGHLIN, CECELIA; Seaford HS; Seaford, NY; (Y); Church Yth Grp; Concert Band; Nwsp Stf; High Hon Roll; Hon Roll; Newsday Carrier 83-85; Sales Person 85-86; Fairfield; Attorney.

COUGHLIN, JUDY; The Ursuline Schl; New Rochelle, NY; (Y); 36/122; Church Yth Grp; French Clb; Spanish Clb; Stage Crew; Variety Show; Hon Roll; Schrlshp New Rochelle 86; Coll New Rochelle; Comm.

COUGHLIN, MAUREEN; Johnson Cith HS; Johnson City, NY; (Y); French Clb; SADD; Chorus; Color Guard; Mrchg Band; Orch; Trk; Hon Roll; SUNY Binghamton; Frgn Lang.

COULSTING, MARIAN K; Smithtown HS West; Smithtown, NY; (Y); Spanish Clb; Yrbk Stf; Off Soph Cls; Sec Jr Cls; Off Sr Cls; Capt Co-Capt Cheerleading; Pom Pon; Twrlr; Hon Roll; Spanish NHS; Bus.

COULTER, JUNE; Sweet Home SR HS; Tonawanda, NY; (Y); Drama Clb; French Clb; Science Clb; Teachers Aide; Stage Crew; French Hon Soc; Hon Roll; Buffalo ST Tchrs Coll; Elem Ed.

COUMOUTSEAS, JOSEPHINE; St Edmund HS; Brooklyn, NY; (Y); Art Clb; Pres Jr Cls; Hon Roll; Religion 86; Am Studies 86; Physcl Ed 86; Tabe Coburn; Fash Merch.

COUNTRYMAN, MIKE; Rush-Henriett Roth HS; Honeoye Falls, NY; (Y); Church Yth Grp; 4-H; Ski Clb; Varsity Clb; Var Bsbl; JV Var Bsktbl; JV Var Ftbl; JV Lcrss; Sftbl; Var Wt Lftg; Ag.

COUNTS, TODD; John Marshall HS; Rochester, NY; (Y); Aud/Vis; French Clb; Office Aide; Ftbl; Trk; Hon Roll; Comp Sci.

COURTEMANCHE, ELEANOR C; Huntington HS; Huntington, NY; (Y); 1/383; AFS; Cmnty Wkr; Drama Clb; SADD; Chorus; Lit Mag; Rep Stu Cncl; NHS; Ntl Merit SF; Val; Newspaper Mngng Edtr 85-86; U S Stu Cncl Awd Wnnr-Achv Acad 85; Town Of Huntington Vol Svc Awd 84.

COURTNEY, JENNIFER; Elmira Free Acad HS; Elmira, NY; (Y); Pres Church Yth Grp; Cmnty Wkr; French Clb; Latin Clb; Band; Church Choir; School Play; Cheerleading; Crs Cntry; Lcrss; Langs.

COURTNEY, KAREN; Sachem H S North Campus; Lake Ronkonkoma, NY; (Y); 15/1558; Drama Clb; Quiz Bowl; Service Clb; Spanish Clb; Stage Crew; Nwsp Rptr; Yrbk Stf; Rep Jr Cls; VP Jr NHS; NHS.

COURTNEY, STEVE; Hamburg SR HS; Hamburg, NY; (Y); Var Capt Ftbl; Var L Gym; Var Capt Lcrss; Empire ST Games La Crosse/All Western NY 86.

COUSIN, LOLITA; Sacred Heart Acad; Cambria Hts, NY; (Y); Library Aide; NFL; Science Clb; Speech Tm; Chorus; Hon Roll; NHS; 4th Pl Awd 83; Pre-Med.

COUSINS, MARY LYNN; Brockport HS; Brockprot, NY; (Y); 28/353; Latin Clb; Chorus; Yrbk Stf; JV Var Cheerleading; High Hon Roll.

COUTANT, LYNDA; John A Coleman HS; Ruby, NY; (Y); 23/92; 4-H; JA; Key Clb; Trs Spanish Clb; School Play; Yrbk Ed-Chief; Yrbk Stf; JV Bsktbl; JV Var Vllybl; Hon Roll; Bio.

COUTINHO, ARMANDO; Christ The King HS; Jamaica, NY; (Y); 74/374; Varsity Clb; School Play; Var Bsbl; Im Ftbl; Var Socr; Im Sftbl; St Johns U; Lib Arts.

COUTTS, ANDREW; Vestal SR HS; Vestal, NY; (Y); 44/430; Trs Church Yth Grp; Varsity Clb; Var L Socr; Var Capt Tennis; Hon Roll; NHS; Ntl Merit Ltr; Prfct Atten Awd; Pres Schlr At St Lawrence U 86; All-Conf Tnns 85-86; Intl Frgn Lang Awd Frnch 84; St Lawrence U; Hstry.

COV, RENEE; Fillmore Central HS; Fillmore, NY; (Y); Church Yth Grp; Varsity Clb; Band; Chorus; Church Choir; School Play; Stage Crew; Nwsp Stf; Cheerleading; Teachers Aide; Monroe CC; CPA.

COVELL, MICHAEL; Mynderse Acad; Seneca Falls, NY; (Y); Boy Scts; Model UN; Band; Yrbk Stf; L Var Lcrss; Var JV Wrstlng; Hon Roll; Eagle Scout 86; Comm Art.

COVELL, WILLIAM; South Side HS; Rockville Centre, NY; (Y); 90/300; Computer Clb; Ice Hcky; Trk; Hon Roll; Lehigh; Engrng.

COVELLO, TERRIANN; H Frank Carey HS; Garden Cy S, NY; (Y); 25/276; Varsity Clb; JV Var Bsktbl; Var Sftbl; JV Var Vllybl; High Hon Roll; Hon Roll; Jr NHS; NHS; Spanish NHS; All-Cnty Awd Vllybl 85; All-Div Sftbll 86; Pre-Med.

COVENEY, KIMBERLEE; Sewanhaka HS; Elmont, NY; (Y); Church Yth Grp; Cmnty Wkr; Hosp Aide; Office Aide; Service Clb; SADD; Chorus; Church Choir; School Musical; School Play; Arnold M Wagner Commnty Svc Awd 86; Music Awd 86; Stu Supprt Svcs Stu Month 85; Roberts Wesleyan Coll; Socl Wrk.

COVERDALE, ALYSSA; Gorton HS; Yonkers, NY; (Y); Am Leg Aux Girls St; Church Yth Grp; Hosp Aide; Library Aide; Office Aide; Chorus; Church Choir; Rep Jr Cls; Hon Roll; Nrsng.

COVERT, BARBARA A; Newburgh Free Acad; Newburgh, NY; (Y); 23/621; Key Clb; Sec Band; Sec Concert Band; Sec Mrchg Band; School Musical; High Hon Roll; Jr NHS; Spanish NHS; Band Secy; Schl Musical; All Cnty Fests 82-86; All ST Area Fests 84-85; Le High U; Bio Sci.

COVERT, CHRISTINE; De Ruyter Central Schl; De Ruyter, NY; (S); Concert Band; Jazz Band; Mrchg Band; Bsktbl; Socr; Sftbl; High Hon Roll; Hon Roll; NHS.

COVEY, LONN C; Arthage Central HS; Carthage, NY; (Y); High Hon Roll; Hon Roll; Rotary Awd; NY ST Regents Schlrshp 86; Ind Engr.

COVINO, DANIEL; Blind Brook HS; Rye Brook, NY; (Y); AFS; Boy Scts; Var Bsbl; Var Crs Cntry; Ntl Merit Ltr; Eagle Sct 86.

COWAN, EDWARDYNE V; Hillcrest HS; Ozone Park, NY; (Y); 75/832; Thesps; Chorus; School Musical; Rep Jr Cls; Rep Sr Cls; Stu Cncl; Natl Englsh Merit Schlr 85; NY ST Regents Sclrsp 86; Partcpnt In Arts Recgntn & Tlnt Srch Prog 85-86; Coll Of New Rochelle.

COWAN, KIMBERLY; John Jay SR HS; Hopewell Juncti, NY; (Y); 81/519; Church Yth Grp; Var Capt Cheerleading; Var Swmmng; High Hon Roll; Hon Roll; NHS; Tri Cnty Fedrtn & Deans Schlrshps 86; Gordon Coll; Psych.

COWAN, LISA; Westfield Central HS; Westfield, NY; (Y); 15/58; Teachers Aide; Rep Jr Cls; JV Var Cheerleading; Var Sftbl; Hon Roll; Elem Tchr.

COWEN, MARK; Randolph Central Schl; Conewango Valley, NY; (Y); Church Yth Grp; 4-H; FFA; 4-H Awd; Empire Fmr Awd 86; Ntl FFA Dairy Prod Awd 86; Va Bro Holstein Awd 86; Alfred Tech; Agri.

COWIE, KIM; Alexander Central HS; Alexander, NY; (Y); Spanish Clb; Band; Concert Band; Mrchg Band; Socr; Jr NHS; Equestrian.

COWIN, JENNIFER L; Stillwater Central HS; Stillwater, NY; (Y); 15/90; VP Jr Cls; Hon Roll; NHS; NY ST Rgnts Schlrshp 86; Suny Oswego; Cmnctns.

COWING, DAVID T; Binghamton HS; Binghamton, NY; (Y); 17/450; Boy Scts; Pres Computer Clb; Key Clb; School Play; Var L Crs Cntry; Var L Trk; Var Vllybl; High Hon Roll; Trs NHS; Mathletes; Regents Schlrshp 86; Cornell U; Comp Sci.

COWLES, STACY; Tully JR SR HS; Marietta, NY; (Y); Pres Church Yth Grp; French Clb; Varsity Clb; Band; Chorus; Church Choir; Yrbk Stf; Var JV Vllybl; High Hon Roll; NHS; Lang Scholar Frnch 86.

COWLES, TRICIA; Corinth HS; Corinth, NY; (Y); 18/75; GAA; Girl Scts; SADD; Varsity Clb; Band; Chorus; Concert Band; Mrchg Band; JV Var Bsktbl; JV Var Fld Hcky; Mst Vlbl Plyr Awd JV Sftbl 84; Hst Btng Avrg V Sftbl 86; New Paitz; Cmrcl Art.

COX, CARRIE; Albion HS; Waterport, NY; (S); 11/169; Latin Clb; Rep Spanish Clb; Teachers Aide; Capt Color Guard; Rep Sr Cls; Hon Roll; NHS; SUNY Clg Geneseo; Mth.

COX, CHERYL; Hillcrest HS; Sp Gdns, NY; (Y); 321/801; Frsh Cls; Soph Cls; Jr Cls; Sr Cls; Sec Stu Cncl; Mgr Bsktbl; JV Var Mgr(s); Score Keeper; Pace U; Corp Lawyr.

COX, CHERYL M; Boys And Girls HS; New York City, NY; (Y); VP Chess Clb; Debate Tm; 4-H; JA; Teachers Aide; Band; Variety Show; Off Jr Cls; Off Sr Cls; Stu Cncl; JA Awd 85; Essay Wrtng Comptn Awds 82-85; Ithaca Coll.

COX, CRAIG; St Mary Boys HS; Garden City, NY; (S); 4/170; Teachers Aide; Socr; Trk; High Hon Roll; Hon Roll; Jr NHS; NHS; Med.

COX, CRISTAL; Rome Catholic HS; Blossvale, NY; (Y); 25/77; SADD; School Musical; Nwsp Stf; VP Frsh Cls; Var Capt Cheerleading; JV Var Socr; Var Trk; Hon Roll; 4-H; Med Tech.

COX, DAWN; Keshequa HS; Nunda, NY; (Y); 7/62; Varsity Clb; Trs Band; Concert Band; Drm Mjr(t); Mrchg Band; Sec Frsh Cls; Sec Soph Cls; Sec Jr Cls; Rep Stu Cncl; JV Var Bsktbl; Awd Bst Dfnsv Plyr Bsktbl 85-86; Wldlf Mgmt.

COX, DENISE; Keshequa HS; Dalton, NY; (Y); 8/62; Library Aide; Band; Concert Band; Mrchg Band; JV Vllybl; Hon Roll; Med Rcrds Tech.

COX, GEOFFREY; Nyack HS; Nyack, NY; (Y); 15/263; Concert Band; Jazz Band; Ed Lit Mag; Rep Sr Cls; JV Tennis; French Hon Soc; High Hon Roll; NHS; Math Tm; Band; Pres Natl Acad Fit Awd 86; NY Rgnts Schlrp Wnr 86; Creatv Wrtng Awd 86; Carnegie-Mellon U; Engrg.

COX, JESSICA; Lynbrook HS; Lynbrook, NY; (Y); 20/239; Church Yth Grp; Pres Trs Leo Clb; Pres Library Aide; Church Choir; Hon Roll; Masonic Awd; Trs NHS; Pres Schlr; NY ST Rgnts Schlrshp 86; Stu Of Mnth 84 & 85; Nassau Cnty Cnslrs Assn Schlrshp 86; Alfred U; Elem Ed.

COX, JILL; Le Roy Central HS; Leroy, NY; (Y); 15/135; Ski Clb; Varsity Clb; Sec Frsh Cls; Sec Soph Cls; Sec Jr Cls; Sec Sr Cls; Sec Rep Stu Cncl; Cheerleading; Trk; High Hon Roll; Regents Schlrshp 86; John F Kennedy Awd 86; Niagara U; Nrsng.

COX, JOANNE; Spackenhill HS; Poughkeepsie, NY; (Y); Co-Capt Math Tm; Spanish Clb; Thesps; Flag Corp; Nwsp Rptr; Hon Roll; NHS; Ntl Merit Schol; Drama Clb; Office Aide; Manhattan Coll; Elect Engr.

COX, KIM; Remsen Central HS; Remsen, NY; (Y); Teachers Aide; Color Guard; Concert Band; Mrchg Band; Yrbk Phtg; Socr; Sftbl; Cit Awd; High Hon Roll; Gov Hon Prg Awd; Stu Mnth 86; Schlrshp Nrsng Alumni Assoc 86; High Hnr,Hnr Rl 85-86; St Elizabeths Schl Nrsng; Nrsng.

COX, MARILYN; Maple Hill HS; Schatack Lnd, NY; (Y); Aud/Vis; French Clb; Temple Yth Grp; School Play; Stage Crew; Yrbk Stf; JV Var Sftbl; JV Capt Vllybl; Pace U; Acctg.

COX, MATTHEW; Charles O Dickerson HS; Trumansburg, NY; (Y); French Clb; Ski Clb; Band; Chorus; Socr; Trk; Hon Roll; Awd Short Stry 85; Ithaca Coll; Music.

COY, VANESSA; Mt Vernon HS; Mt Vernon, NY; (Y); Sec Church Yth Grp; Sec Computer Clb; Office Aide; Band; Church Choir; Concert Band; Mrchg Band; High Hon Roll; Hon Roll; NHS; Syst Anlyst.

COYLE, JAY; Geneseo Central Schl; Geneseo, NY; (Y); 3/90; French Clb; Mathletes; Ski Clb; Pres Frsh Cls; Pres Soph Cls; Pres Jr Cls; Pres Sr Cls; Capt Bsbl; Capt Ice Hcky; Capt Socr; Georgetown; Bus.

COYLE, KEVIN; Archbishop Molloy HS; Rosedale, NY; (Y); 28/383; Boy Scts; Ed Lit Mag; L Crs Cntry; L Trk; High Hon Roll; NHS; Knights Columbus Schlar 83-87; NYPD Holy Name Soc Scholar 83.

COYLE, KEVIN; Geneseo Central HS; Geneseo, NY; (Y); 8/90; Capt Varsity Clb; JV Var Bsbl; Var Ice Hcky; Var Capt Socr; High Hon Roll; Jr NHS; NHS; Bstr Clb Treas 85-87; Villanova; Bus Admin.

COYLE, SHANNON; Huntington HS; Huntington, NY; (Y); AFS; Hosp Aide; Key Clb; Varsity Clb; Chorus; Var Capt Crs Cntry; Var Trk; Hon Roll; Jr NHS.

COYLE, SHEILA; Frontier Central HS; Lake View, NY; (Y); FBLA; Chorus; Color Guard; High Hon Roll; Hon Roll; Law.

COYNE, CHRISTOPHER; Holy Trinity HS; N Massapequa, NY; (S); 6/319; Math Clb; Var Crs Cntry; Var Capt Trk; Hon Roll; NHS; NEDT Awd; Coaches Awd 85facad All Am 85; RPI; Aero Sp Engr.

COYNE, JOHN J; Johnson City HS; Johnson City, NY; (Y); French Clb; Key Clb; VP Pep Clb; Ski Clb; Rep Frsh Cls; Rep Soph Cls; Trs Jr Cls; Trs Sr Cls; Hon Roll; Trs NHS; SUNY Binghamton.

COYNE, KATHLEEN; Cornwall Central HS; Cornwall, NY; (Y); Hosp Aide; Ski Clb; Chorus; JV Cheerleading; JV Vllybl; High Hon Roll; Hon Roll; NHS.

COZART, TINA; Nyack SR HS; Nyack, NY; (Y); 51/256; Sec Church Yth Grp; Band; Chorus; Church Choir; Color Guard; Concert Band; Mrchg Band; School Musical; Mgr Cheerleading; Hon Roll; Acctnt.

COZZIE, KAREN; Immaculate Heart Central HS; Watertown, NY; (Y); Cmnty Wkr; Sec FBLA; Variety Show; Ed Yrbk Stf; Pres Frsh Cls; Pres Soph Cls; Stu Cncl; JV Var Socr; JV Sftbl; Hon Roll; Regents Scholar 86; Natl Latin Exam Wnnr 83; SUNY Geneseo; Elem Ed.

COZZOLINO, MELINDA; Hudson HS; Claverack, NY; (Y); Debate Tm; Drama Clb; GAA; Pep Clb; SADD; Band; Chorus; Concert Band; Jazz Band; Mrchg Band; Rotary Ldrshp Conf 84; Reginald Kline Mem Sportsmnshp Awd 86; Kenka Coll; Occuptnl Thrpy.

CRABB, MARLENE; Carthage Central HS; Black River, NY; (Y); 40/177; AFS; French Clb; Band; Chorus; Concert Band; Jazz Band; Mrchg Band; School Musical; School Play; Nwsp Stf; NY ST Regnts Schlrsh P86; Math.

CRAGG, DEBORAH; Nazareth Acad; Churchville, NY; (Y); 31/152; Cmnty Wkr; FBLA; Hon Roll; Monroe CC; Lbrl Arts.

CRAGNOLIN, MIKE; John F Kennedy HS; Utica, NY; (Y); Aud/Vis; Boy Scts; 4-H; FBLA; Key Clb; Math Clb; SADD; Band; Chorus; Concert Band; MVP Vllybl 85; Grand Lodge Knights Pythias Mst Imprvd Stu 86; Mohawk Vly CC; Acctg.

CRAIB, CRISTI; Berlin Central Schl; Berlin, NY; (S); Ski Clb; Band; Chorus; School Musical; School Play; Swing Chorus; Stu Cncl; Bsktbl; Cheerleading; Socr; Hopwood Schlrshp-Lynchburg Coll 85; Pre-Law.

CRAIG, JENNIFER N; Pulaski HS; Pulaski, NY; (S); 25/100; Drama Clb; GAA; Ski Clb; SADD; Concert Band; Mrchg Band; Yrbk Ed-Chief; Rep Stu Cncl; Snow Incntv Awd; Le Moyne Coll; Bus Admin.

CRAIG, SCOTT M; Mc Quaid Jesuit HS; Henrietta, NY; (Y); 11/170; Cmnty Wkr; Letterman Clb; Varsity Clb; Stage Crew; Coach Actv; JV Socr; Var Trk; Var Vllybl; High Hon Roll; Jr NHS; Acadmc Ltr & Bar 84 & 86; Regnts Schlrshp 86; Mech Engrng.

CRAMER, KIMBERLY; Kensington HS; Buffalo, NY; (Y); Chorus; Stu Cncl; Trk; Home Ec Awd 85; Chrs Awds 84.

CRAMER, RICHARD T; Red Jacket Central HS; Palmyra, NY; (Y); 8/92; Chess Clb; Ski Clb; Spanish Clb; Varsity Clb; Madrigals; School Musical; Yrbk Rptr; JV Bsbl; Var L Trk; Hon Roll; NYS Regents Schlrshp 86; Lock Haven U; Athl Trng.

CRAMER, SHERRI; Cicero-North Syracuse HS; Clay, NY; (S); 19/676; Ski Clb; Concert Band; Mrchg Band; School Musical; Swing Chorus; Symp Band; Var L Tennis; High Hon Roll; NHS.

CRAMER, STEVE; Southwestern HS; Celacon, NY; (Y); Boy Scts; Cmnty Wkr; FCA; French Clb; Band; Bsbl; Gym; High Hon Roll; Hon Roll; Jamestown Bus Coll; Acctg.

CRANDALL, JOEL; Oxford Acad; Mcdonough, NY; (Y); 29/89; Am Leg Boys St; French Clb; Varsity Clb; VP Frsh Cls; Pres Soph Cls; VP Jr Cls; Rep Stu Cncl; Bsbl; Bsktbl; Capt Var Ftbl; SUNY Cortland; Phy Ed.

CRANDALL, LARRY; Fort Ann Central HS; Fort Ann, NY; (Y); 9/57; French Clb; Mathletes; Math Clb; Math Tm; High Hon Roll; Hon Roll; NYS Regents Schlrshp 86.

CRANDALL, LAURIE A; Pualski JR SR HS; Pulaski, NY; (S); 2/98; Drama Clb; French Clb; GAA; Math Clb; Color Guard; Trs Sr Cls; High Hon Roll; Sec NHS; Schlrshp-LI U 86; Hghst Sci Rgnts Mark Awd-100 Pct Bio 84; Long Island U; Marine Bio.

CRANDALL, MICHAEL T; Granville Central HS; Hampton, NY; (Y); 15/126; AFS; Civic Clb; Pres Spanish Clb; SADD; Rep Stu Cncl; JV Bsktbl; JV Crs Cntry; JV Var Golf; Hon Roll; Regents Sclrp 86; Siena Coll; Poli Sci.

CRANDALL, MIKE; Granville Central HS; Hampton, NY; (Y); 15/120; AFS; Civic Clb; Political Wkr; Pres Spanish Clb; Rep Stu Cncl; Bsktbl; Crs Cntry; Golf; Hon Roll; Pres Schlr; Rgnts Schlrshps 86; Siena Coll; Poli Sci.

CRANE, JEFF; Avon JR SR HS; Avon, NY; (Y); 1/90; Ski Clb; Spanish Clb; Var Golf; Var Capt Socr; Bausch & Lomb Sci Awd; High Hon Roll; Jr NHS; NEDT Awd; Prfct Atten Awd; Comp Sci.

CRANE, JEFF; Haverling HS; Bath, NY; (Y); Church Yth Grp; French Clb; JCL; Latin Clb; Ski Clb; Yrbk Stf; Airline Profssn.

CRANE, JUDY; Middletown HS; Middletown, NY; (Y); 34/315; Sec 4-H; Symp Band; Lit Mag; 4-H Awd; Hon Roll; Tamarack Grove 6116 Wfmn Of Wrld Awd 86; Drctrs Awd Music 86; Instrmntlst Mgzn Music Awd 86; Orange Cnty Comm Coll.

CRANER, FRAN; Catholic Central HS; Cohoes, NY; (Y); Math Clb; JV Bsktbl; JV Var Ftbl; Hon Roll; NHS; NY St Cert Merit 86.

CRANER, GARREN T; North Shore HS; Glenwood Landg, NY; (Y); 15/196; Am Leg Boys St; Boy Scts; Bowling; Score Keeper; Timer; Cit Awd; Eagle Scout Order Of The Arrow 85; VP PTA 86-87; Camping Hiking; Medicine.

CRANER, JOHN; Jamesville Dewitt HS; Jamesville, NY; (Y); Boy Scts; Church Yth Grp; Snd Engr.

CRANEY, BRENDA; Tamarac HS; Troy, NY; (Y); Cmnty Wkr; Intnl Clb; SADD; Acpl Chr; Band; Pres Chorus; School Musical; Var Capt Cheerleading; JV Sftbl; Hon Roll; Outstndg Schlstc Achvmnt Awd 86; Outstndg Stu Ind Bus Awd 86; Hudson Valley CC; Mrktng.

CRANEY, CHRIS; Fairport HS; Fairport, NY; (Y); Chess Clb; Math Tm; Trs Model UN; Ski Clb; Im Bsktbl; Im Ftbl; Hnrb Mntn Sci Congress 85; Mdl UN Bst Delg Awd-Hnrb Mntn 85; Cornell; Bio.

CRANS, TAMMY; Dundee Central HS; Dundee, NY; (Y); Pep Clb; Band; Chorus; Color Guard; Concert Band; Mrchg Band; Capt Var Cheerleading; Var Pom Pon; High Hon Roll; Hon Roll; Sprtsmnshp Awd Chrldng Awd 86; Pensacola JC; Bus Mgmt.

CRAPARO, JOSEPH; Seton Catholic Central HS; Binghamton, NY; (S); 5/165; Am Leg Boys St; Sec Church Yth Grp; Band; Pep Band; School Musical; Var L Ftbl; JV Socr; High Hon Roll; NHS; Pres Schlr; Natl Sci Merit Awd 86; Regents Schlrshp 86; Seton Schlr With Distnctn 85; Engrng.

CRAPSER, KAREN; New Paltz HS; New Paltz, NY; (Y); Church Yth Grp; Cmnty Wkr; 4-H; SADD; Chorus; 4-H Awd; High Hon Roll; Hon Roll; NHS; Albny Cptl Dys Trp 4-H 85; Paul Smith Schlrshp 86; Lcs Tree Inn Awd 86; Paul Smiths; Htl Mgmt.

CRARY, DAVID; Hugh C Williams HS; Canton, NY; (Y); 10/150; VP Sr Cls; Im Bsbl; JV Ftbl; Var Trk; High Hon Roll; Acad Ltr Awd 85-86; Natl Merit Schlrp Hgh Scorer 85-86; Tlntd Jrs Prog At St Lawrence U 85-86; Princeton U; Engrg.

CRAST, DANIEL; Sandy Creek Central Schl; Lacona, NY; (Y); Church Yth Grp; Drama Clb; JCL; Chorus; Var Capt Bsbl; JV Var Ftbl; Wrstlng; Osweg Coll; Envrnmntl Sci.

CRAWFORD, ANGELENE; Avon Central HS; Avon, NY; (Y); 17/104; FBLA; Library Aide; Rep Stu Cncl; Var Swmmng; High Hon Roll; Hon Roll; Bryant & Stratton Bus Inst Schlrshp 86; Dist & St Champ In FBLA Comp 86; Outstndng Stu-Voc Class 86; Bryant-Stratton Bus Inst.

CRAWFORD, CHRIS R; Elmont Memorial HS; Elmont, NY; (Y); 3/241; Aud/Vis; Boy Scts; Computer Clb; Science Clb; Socr; Hon Roll; NHS; Prfct Atten Awd; Spanish NHS; Long Isl Sci Cngrs Hnrs 84; Rensselaer Polytech Inst; Engr.

CRAWFORD, ELLEN; Unatego JR SR HS; Otego, NY; (Y); French Clb; FHA; Band; Concert Band; Mrchg Band; Pep Band; JV Sftbl; High Hon Roll; Hon Roll; NHS; Jostens Key Frnch II 85; Engrng.

CRAWFORD, GERALD; Grand Island SR HS; Grand Island, NY; (Y); Art Clb; Drama Clb; Ski Clb; Chorus; Concert Band; Madrigals; School Musical; Variety Show; Yrbk Phtg; Hon Roll; NYSSMA Hi Score A Level 6 86; MVP Choir & Spotlghtrs 84-86; Sibleys Tlnt Srch Fnlst 84; Musical Thtr.

CRAWFORD, JENIFER; Sodus Central HS; Sodus, NY; (Y); 19/120; Drama Clb; Ski Clb; Varsity Clb; Band; Chorus; Concert Band; Mrchg Band; School Musical; School Play; Vllybl; Eastman Schl Music; Music Tchr.

CRAWFORD, KIM MARIE; Vincent Smith Schl; Port Charlotte, FL; (Y); Art Clb; Hosp Aide; Service Clb; Chorus; Church Choir; JV Crs Cntry; Trk; Hon Roll; Ldr Arts & Crafts Clb 83; Anna Maria Coll; Bio.

CRAWFORD, LYNDA A; St Marys Acad Of The North Country; Glens Falls, NY; (Y); 5/46; Drama Clb; Ski Clb; Teachers Aide; Crs Cntry; Tennis; High Hon Roll; NHS; School Play; Stage Crew; Outstndng Achvt Scl Studies Awd; Raymond A Balcom Schrlshp; Upstate Med Ctr; Radiolgc Tech.

CRAWFORD, REVONDA; Turner-Carroll HS; Buffalo, NY; (S); 14/109; JA; Pep Clb; Sec Frsh Cls; Sec Sr Cls; Sec Stu Cncl; Hon Roll; Hnr Rl; Niagara U; Bus.

CRAWFORD, STACEY L; Johnson City HS; Binghamton, NY; (Y); 12/198; VP SADD; Capt Color Guard; Mrchg Band; Nwsp Rptr; Yrbk Ed-Chief; Stat Trk; Hon Roll; NY ST Regents Schlrshp 85-86; Maxima Cum Laude-Natl Latin Exam 86; SUNY Binghamton; Psych.

CRAWFORD, STEPHEN; St Josephs Collegiate Inst; Kenmore, NY; (Y); 10/200; Dance Clb; Pep Clb; Acpl Chr; School Musical; Swing Chorus; Lit Mag; Sec Sr Cls; Rep Stu Cncl; NHS; St Schlr; Courier Exprss Clg Schlrshp 86; Vocl Arion 86; St U Of Buffalo; Eng.

CRAWFORD, TIMOTHY; St John The Baptist Diocesan HS; W Babylon, NY; (S); Boy Scts; Cmnty Wkr; Chorus; Church Choir; Hon Roll; Rgnt Hnrs In Frnch 85; US Navy.

CRAWFORD, WANDA L; Flushing HS; Cambria Heights, NY; (Y); 29/372; Library Aide; Office Aide; Service Clb; Teachers Aide; Band; Chorus; School Musical; Variety Show; High Hon Roll; Hon Roll; NYS Regents Schlrshp 86; Penn ST Blck Achvt Awd 86; Svc Awd 83; PA ST U; Acctg.

CREA, NATINA; Christopher Columbus HS; Bronx, NY; (Y); 4/642; Key Clb; Cit Awd; High Hon Roll; Hon Roll; Jr NHS; NHS; Prfct Atten Awd; SUNY Binghamton; Acctg.

CREARY, GEORGIA; Erasmus Hall HS; Brooklyn, NY; (Y); #224 In Class; Cmnty Wkr; Computer Clb; FNA; Hosp Aide; Intnl Clb; JA; Library Aide; Off Sr Cls; Swmmng; FTA; Phillip Exetor Acad Schlrshp 83; Boston U; Nrsng.

CREARY, JEMAL; New Rochelle HS; New Rochelle, NY; (Y); French Clb; Model UN; Varsity Clb; Chorus; JV Var Tennis; French Hon Soc; Hon Roll; NHS; Moorehouse; Corprt Lwyr.

CREAVEN, MARTIN; Archbishop Molloy HS; Jamaica Est, NY; (Y); 110/400; Intnl Clb; Off Frsh Cls; Off Soph Cls; Im Bsktbl; Var L Crs Cntry; Var L Trk; Hon Roll; St Johns U; Law.

CREEN, SHARI; Saugerties HS; Saugerties, NY; (Y); 9/256; Band; Chorus; Concert Band; Symp Band; Trk; High Hon Roll; NHS.

CREGAN, KAREN; West Genesee SR HS; Camillus, NY; (Y); Church Yth Grp; Cmnty Wkr; Dance Clb; Rep Frsh Cls; Sec Soph Cls; Pres Jr Cls; Rep Sr Cls; Rep Stu Cncl; Bsktbl; Score Keeper; Sec Educ.

CREHAN, SUSAN; Mt St Mary Acad; Tonawanda, NY; (Y); 6/113; Church Yth Grp; VP Cmnty Wkr; Computer Clb; NFL; VP Service Clb; Speech Tm; Acpl Chr; Lit Mag; Hon Roll; Hon Roll; NY ST Rgnts Schlrshp 86; Twn Svc Awd 85-86; U Cntr NY Buffalo; Occup Thrpy.

CREIGHTON, JAMES; Xavier HS; Middle Vlg, NY; (Y); 50/250; Computer Clb; Drama Clb; Math Tm; ROTC; Ski Clb; School Musical; School Play; Ed Yrbk Ed-Chief; Ed Yrbk Stf; Rep Frsh Cls.

CREIGHTON, KELLY; South Jefferson Central HS; Lorraine, NY; (Y); 69/155; Trs Art Clb; Church Yth Grp; FTA; Girl Scts; Stage Crew; Yrbk Stf; Stu Cncl; Stat Socr; Gold Key Mony Schlstc Art Show 84; Art.

CREMEAN, MICHAEL; North Rose-Wolcott Central HS; Wolcott, NY; (Y); Boy Scts; Church Yth Grp; Ski Clb; Pres Spanish Clb; Church Choir; Var Trk; Hon Roll; Ntl Merit SF; NHS Awd Mth 85; Rochester Inst Tech; Engrng.

CREQUE, PATRICIA; Adlai E Stevenson HS; Bronx, NY; (Y); 111/487; Hosp Aide; Office Aide; Teachers Aide; Capt Color Guard; Drm & Bgl; Drm Mjr(t); Capt Mrchg Band; Nwsp Phtg; Yrbk Phtg; Hon Roll; Trphy & Cert For 85 Pct Avg Or Bttr-Nrsg 86; Cert-Gd Attndnc 86; Medls Trphys & Certs-Drm & Bugle Crps; Coll Of Mt Saint Vincent; Nrsg.

CRESPI, RACQUEL; Port Richmond HS; Staten Island, NY; (Y); Cmnty Wkr; Hosp Aide; Math Tm; Office Aide; Scholastic Bowl; Temple Yth Grp; Orch; Nwsp Rptr; High Hon Roll; NHS; NY Super Yth 85; Yrbk Stu Life Edtr 86-87; VP Belle Brummels 86-87.

CRESPO, CHRISTOPHER L; Fordham Preparatory Schl; Bronx, NY; (Y); Boys Clb Am; Spanish Clb; JV Swmmng; Spanish NHS; Natl Hispanic Schlr Awd Fnlst 86; NY ST Regent Schlrshp 86; Fordham U; Pre-Med.

CRESPO, JOHN; St Marys Boys HS; Pt Washington, NY; (S); 3/146; Ed Nwsp Stf; Yrbk Sprt Ed; Var Trk; High Hon Roll; NHS; Ntl Merit Ltr; Mst Imprvd Trckmn 84; Engrng.

CREWS, CHRISTOPHER; Kingston HS; Kingston, NY; (Y); 118/574; Key Clb; Chorus; Church Choir; Ftbl; Trk; Hon Roll; St Schlr; 1st Tm All ST NY 86; All Amer Hnbl Mntn 86; Full Athl Schlrshp U Of VA 86; U Of VA; Bus.

CRIMI, CHRISTINA A; St Francis Prep; Maspeth, NY; (S); 158/746; Im Bowling; Im Ftbl; Im Sftbl; Im Vllybl; Law.

CRINKLAW, CINDY; Franklin Acad; N Bangor, NY; (Y); Hosp Aide; SADD; Varsity Clb; JV Var Crs Cntry; Hon Roll; Church Yth Grp; Cmnty Wkr; Pep Clb; Var Timer; JV Var Trk; Epsilon Mst Imprvd In Crss Cntry; For Hldng 90 Avg; Red Nrs.

CRISCI, JAMES; Lakeland HS; Mohegan Lk, NY; (Y); Boy Scts; Cmnty Wkr; Library Aide; Variety Show; Im Ftbl; Jr NHS; Eagle Sct 86; Bus Adm.

CRISCUOLO, PAULA; Mamaroneck HS; Larchmont, NY; (Y); Pres Trs Key Clb; Var Capt Tennis; Stonehill Coll; Engl.

CRISPELL, CAROLYN; L D Luthern HS; N Bellmore, NY; (S); Church Yth Grp; Band; Church Choir; Pep Band; High Hon Roll; Hon Roll; NHS; U S Achvt Acad Natl Engl Merit Awd 86; Med.

CRISPI, JEFF; South Side HS; Rockville Centre, NY; (Y); Church Yth Grp; Computer Clb; School Play; Hon Roll.

CRISPIN, TRACEY; Cicero-North Syracuse HS; N Syracuse, NY; (S); 26/623; Church Yth Grp; Drama Clb; SADD; Concert Band; Mrchg Band; School Musical; School Play; Nwsp Stf; High Hon Roll; NEDT Awd; Bio.

CRISPINO, CAROLYN; Notre Dame Acad HS; Staten Island, NY; (Y); Drama Clb; Hosp Aide; School Musical; School Play; Yrbk Stf; Lit Mag; Trk; Pres-Christian Life Orgnztn Notre Dame HS 85-86; Engl.

CRISPINO, PETER; Monsignor Farrell HS; Staten Island, NY; (S); Church Yth Grp; Cmnty Wkr; Pep Clb; Im Bsktbl; Im Bowling; Im Ftbl; Hon Roll; NY St Regnts Schlrshp; Fairfield U; Business.

CRISS, THOMAS N; Cato-Meridian HS; Cato, NY; (Y); 21/72; Boy Scts; Church Yth Grp; Letterman Clb; Model UN; Varsity Clb; VICA; Band; Variety Show; Rep Stu Cncl; JV Bsktbl; U S Air Force; Elctrncs.

CRISSEY, MARISA; Groton Central HS; Freeville, NY; (Y); 3/87; Drama Clb; Sec Spanish Clb; Chorus; School Musical; Ed Yrbk Ed-Chief; Yrbk Stf; Stu Cncl; High Hon Roll; NHS.

CRISTAL, BEN; Westhampton Beach HS; Westhampton Beach, NY; (Y); Wrstlng; Hon Roll; MVP Wrstlng 84; Acadmc Decathln Acadmc Clb 85-86; Electrcl Engr.

CRISTODERO, CHRISTINE; H Frank Carey HS; Franklin Square, NY; (Y); 36/225; Trs Church Yth Grp; Cmnty Wkr; Debate Tm; School Musical; School Play; Ed Nwsp Stf; Ed Yrbk Stf; Hst Stu Cncl; Hon Roll; Lioness Clb Awd 86; Adelphi U; Theatre Tech.

CRO, ROBERT; Monsignor Farrell HS; Staten Island, NY; (Y); Church Yth Grp; Cmnty Wkr; Service Clb; Lit Mag; Im Ftbl; Var Trk; High Hon Roll; NHS; Ntl Merit Ltr; Arch.

CROAD, THERESA; Frontier Central SR HS; Blasdell, NY; (Y); French Clb; Girl Scts; Hon Roll; Nrsng.

CROBAR, KIMBERLEY L; Liverpool HS; Liverpool, NY; (Y); 119/884; Mgr DECA; Ed Exploring; FBLA; VP JA; Lit Mag; JV Crs Cntry; JV Trk; Hon Roll; Jr NHS; NHS; 2nd Pl Trophy Job Interview 85; 3rd Pl Ja VP Prod 85; Psychlgy.

CROCE, CARLA; Hamburg HS; Hamburg, NY; (Y); Church Yth Grp; JCL; Trs Latin Clb; SADD; Trs Chorus; Capt Color Guard; Orch; School Musical; Variety Show; Nwsp Stf.

CROCE, SUSAN; Lindenhurst SR HS; Lindenhurst, NY; (Y); Ski Clb; Yrbk Stf; Var Badmtn; Var Gym; Hon Roll; Most Impvd Gymnst 83-84; Stonybrook U; Law.

CROCEVERA, JOHN; Xavier HS; Jackson Hgts, NY; (Y); Computer Clb; Math Tm; Hon Roll; Ntl Merit Ltr; Bus Mgmt.

CROCKENBERG, CHRISTINE; Berkeley Carroll St Schl; Brooklyn, NY; (Y); Chess Clb; Library Aide; Math Clb; Teachers Aide; Varsity Clb; Chorus; Variety Show; Nwsp Ed-Chief; Nwsp Phtg; Nwsp Rptr; Merit Schlrshp 83; Columbia College; Pre Med.

CROCKER, KIMBERLY; Granville Central HS; Granville, NY; (Y); Camera Clb; Church Yth Grp; Cmnty Wkr; FBLA; GAA; Ski Clb; SADD; Var Capt Fld Hcky; Var Capt Sftbl; Elks Awd; Lorrie A Reed Meml Schlrshp Awd 86; Slate Vly Grdn Clb Awd 86; Delhi A&T; Vet Sci Tech.

CROCKER, LAURIE; Haverling Central Schl; Bath, NY; (Y); Pres FTA; JCL; Latin Clb; Math Clb; Teachers Aide; School Play; Stage Crew; Nwsp Stf; Yrbk Ed-Chief; Yrbk Rptr; George & Mary Atanesian Schlrshp 86; Letter H FFA 86; Actvties Ed Yrbk 86; Corning CC; Lib Arts.

CROCKETT, DIANA; West Genesee SR HS; Camillus, NY; (Y); Cmnty Wkr; French Clb; Ski Clb; Chorus; Yrbk Stf; Rep Soph Cls; Rep Jr Cls; High Hon Roll; Jr NHS; Opt Clb Awd; Optmst Ortrcl Awd 84; Pres Syrcs Symphny JR Gld 85-87; Law.

CROCKETT, JENI R; The Mary Louis Acad; Douglaston, NY; (Y); Sec Pres Drama Clb; Teachers Aide; Chorus; Madrigals; School Musical; School Play; Stage Crew; Variety Show; Service Clb; Music Schlrshp 82-86; Thtre.

CRODERO, LIZETTE; Cathedral HS; Ny, NY; (Y); 61/272; Church Yth Grp; Intnl Clb; JA; Red Cross Aide; Science Clb; VICA; NHS; Prfct Atten Awd; Sal; 2nd Hnrs 84 & 86; NY U; Phys Thrpy.

CROFF, JOHN; Niagara Catholic HS; Niagara Fls, NY; (Y); 15/95; Church Yth Grp; Ski Clb; Nwsp Sprt Ed; Bsbl; JV Var Ftbl; Sftbl; Wt Lftg; Hon Roll; Ftbl Captn 85; Hnrbl Ment 84-86; Houghton Coll; Bio.

CROFOOT, LAURIE; G Ray Bodley HS; Fulton, NY; (Y); Pres Church Yth Grp; Hosp Aide; Office Aide; Color Guard; Stu Cncl; Gym; Mat Maids; Vllybl; Cit Awd; Prfct Atten Awd; Bus.

CROFT, KERRI; Dundee Central HS; Bradford, NY; (Y); Ski Clb; Sec SADD; Varsity Clb; Sec Band; Trs Soph Cls; VP Sr Cls; JV Bsktbl; Var Socr; Var Trk; Hon Roll; Bus.

CROKE, ROBERT; Miller Place SR HS; Miller Place, NY; (Y); 14/248; Am Leg Boys St; VP Computer Clb; Varsity Clb; Var L Crs Cntry; Var L Trk; High Hon Roll; NHS; Mathletes; Ntl Merit Ltr; Engrng.

CROLLE, JAMES; Westfield Central Schl; Westfield, NY; (Y); 6/60; Quiz Bowl; Chorus; School Musical; VP Stu Cncl; Var Bsktbl; JV Var Ftbl; Tennis; Hon Roll; NHS; Model UN; Pre-Law.

CROMARTIE, JOSEPH; Far Rockaway HS; Far Rockaway, NY; (Y); Cmnty Wkr; Varsity Clb; Chorus; Color Guard; Var Bsbl; Var Ftbl; Hon Roll; Prfct Atten Awd; Sci Achvt Awd; FL ST; Comp Pgmmg.

CROMER, SHARON; Erasmus Hall HS; Brooklyn, NY; (Y); Dance Clb; Teachers Aide; Chorus; Var Frsh Cls; Trk; Vllybl; Cert Apprctn Outstndng Poem, NYC HS Poetry Cont Chncllrs Rll Hnr 84; Dly News Awd Chrstmn Cncrt 85; Bkkpng.

CROMEYN, CHRIS; Bayport-Bluepoint HS; Bayport, NY; (Y); 16/122; Band; Church Choir; Jazz Band; Orch; Pep Band; Nwsp Rptr; Lit Mag; Crs Cntry; Hon Roll; NHS; Messiah Coll; Jrnlsm.

CROMPWELL, SUE; East Syracuse Minoa HS; Kirkville, NY; (Y); Church Yth Grp; Science Clb; Spanish Clb; Trs SADD; Band; Color Guard; Concert Band; Mrchg Band; Hon Roll; Prfct Atten Awd; Culinary Inst Amer; Cheif.

CRONIER, NICOLE; John C Birdlebough HS; Pennellville, NY; (Y); 18/186; Art Clb; Exploring; Latin Clb; SADD; Teachers Aide; Stage Crew; Yrbk Stf; Stu Cncl; High Hon Roll; Prfct Atten Awd; Schlrshp Frm Ntl Dlrs For Schlrs 86; Blvd Qun Of Frndshp Trngl 83; Irvng Nrsng; RN.

CRONIN, ALICIA; Catholic Central HS; Troy, NY; (Y); Math Clb; SADD; Chorus; Rep Soph Cls; Rep Jr Cls; Stu Cncl; JV Cheerleading; Pom Pon; High Hon Roll; Hon Roll; Natl Assn Stu Cncls 85; Engl Ed.

CRONIN, CAROLINE; New Hyde Park Memorial HS; New Hyde Pk, NY; (Y); French Clb; FBLA; VP German Clb; Library Aide; Chorus; Church Choir; School Musical; Tennis; Dist Musicl Awd 86; Cert Grmn Amrcn Schl Assn Grad 86; Bus Cmmnctns.

CRONIN, ELIZABETH; Dominican Comercial HS; Bellerose, NY; (Y); 40/273; Art Clb; Church Yth Grp; Library Aide; Pep Clb; Teachers Aide; High Hon Roll; NHS; Ntl Bus Hnr Soc 85-86; Schlstc Excel Awd 86; St Johns U; Educ.

CRONIN, JAMES; Sacred Heart HS; Yonkers, NY; (S); 18/213; Nwsp Ed-Chief; Rep Soph Cls; Rep Jr Cls; Trs Stu Cncl; JV Bsktbl; Mgr(s); NHS; Iona Coll; Corp Law.

CRONIN, JOSEPH P; Wellington C Mepham HS; Merrick, NY; (Y); 7/360; Science Clb; Hon Roll; Jr NHS; NCTE Awd; NHS; Ntl Merit SF; Italian Awd 83; Polit Forum-Schlrshp To Adelphi U 85-86; Its Acad-Trivia Tm 85-86; Pre Med.

CRONIN, KATHLEEN M; St Franics Prep HS; Bayside, NY; (S); 73/744; Math Clb; JV Var Bsktbl; Im Ftbl; Capt Var Sftbl; High Hon Roll; Hon Roll; NHS; Prfct Atten Awd.

CRONIN, LOREEN; Cardinal Spellman HS; Bronx, NY; (S); 52/520; Cmnty Wkr; Drama Clb; Pep Clb; Science Clb; Stage Crew; Yrbk Stf; Hon Roll; NHS; Regents Schlrshp 86; Private Coll Schlrshp 86; SUNY-STONY Brook; Polt Sci.

CRONIN, MICHELLE; Lafayette HS; Nedrow, NY; (Y); 26/96; Church Yth Grp; GAA; Trs Spanish Clb; Varsity Clb; Var Socr; Var Sftbl; Hon Roll; Asst Cptn Vly Grls Hcky Tm 82-84; Hnrbl Mntn All Star 84-85; Red Grn Memrl Awrd Sprtsmnshp 85-86; Cornell U; Indstrl Lbr Rltns.

CRONIN, SUSAN; Sachem HS; Farmingville, NY; (Y); 315/1532; Camera Clb; Cmnty Wkr; Teachers Aide; Band; Concert Band; Mrchg Band; Pep Band; Vrsty Lttr Marching Band 84-86; Accounting.

CRONOQUE, KELLI; St Josephs Acad; Centereach, NY; (Y); Girl Scts; SADD; Nwsp Phtg; Nwsp Stf; Psychology.

CROOK, DAVID; G Ray Bodley HS; Fulton, NY; (Y); Science Clb; Bsktbl; Ftbl; Lcrss; Poltcl Sci.

CROPLEY, RALPH; Dover JR SR HS; Windgale, NY; (Y); 10/110; Am Leg Boys St; Science Clb; Spanish Clb; Varsity Clb; Var Bsbl; JV Bsktbl; Var Ftbl; Hon Roll; Wrld Lit Clss 85-86; Advncd Plcmnt Socl Stu And Eng 86; Poltc Sci.

CROSBY, DAN; Chatham HS; Chatham, NY; (Y); 1/130; Am Leg Boys St; Math Tm; Jazz Band; Stu Cncl; Capt Crs Cntry; Gym; Capt Trk; Val; Orch; School Musical; All ST String Orchestra 84-85; Cross Cnt Ry MOP 85; Dartmouth Coll; Math.

CROSBY, DAWN; Ossining HS; Ossining, NY; (Y); Hosp Aide; JA; Office Aide; Trk; Hon Roll; Cert Merit 86; Bus.

CROSBY, JUNE; Our Lady Of Mercy HS; Penfield, NY; (Y); Church Yth Grp; Cmnty Wkr; SADD; Church Choir; School Musical; Var Trk; High Hon Roll; Hon Roll; Drama Clb; French Clb; Ecnmcs.

CROSBY, KAREN; Our Lady Of Mercy HS; Rochester, NY; (Y); Church Yth Grp; Cmnty Wkr; Girl Scts; Hosp Aide; Spanish Clb; SADD; School Musical; School Play; Stage Crew; Yrbk Stf; Intl Affairs.

CROSIER EDICK, DEBORA; Owen D Young Central HS; Jordanville, NY; (Y); 2/21; Band; Chorus; Trs Jr Cls; High Hon Roll; NHS; Sal; Norstar Bank Bus Awd 86; Pres Acad Ftns Awd 86; St Assmbly Of NY Cert Of Merit 86; Trvl.

CROSS, BILL; Lafayette Central HS; Jamesville, NY; (Y); 48/109; Church Yth Grp; French Clb; VICA; Hon Roll; Embry-Riddle Aero U; Sci.

CROSS, CHERYL; Bishop Grimes HS; Liverpool, NY; (S); Office Aide; Var Bsktbl; Hon Roll; Natl Phys Educ Awd 86.

CROSS, COLLEEN SHEEHAN; Cardinal Mooney HS; Rochester, NY; (Y); 30/304; Church Yth Grp; Hosp Aide; Ski Clb; School Musical; Ed Yrbk Stf; Trs Soph Cls; Stu Cncl; JV Vllybl; Hon Roll; VFW Awd; NY Rgnts Coll Schlrshp 85; Acadmc Decthln Tm; Boston U; Cmnctns.

CROSS, JULIE; Berne-Knox-Westerlo HS; Berne, NY; (Y); 20/80; Band; Chorus; Concert Band; Mrchg Band; Pep Band; School Musical; School Play; Stage Crew; Variety Show; NHS; Hudson Vly CC; Radiolgc Tech.

CROSS, MARK; John Marshall HS; Rochester, NY; (Y); Hosp Aide; Math Tm; Yrbk Stf; Pres Stu Cncl; Trk; NHS; Eagle Scout 85; 1st Pl Citywide Spelling Bee 85; Childrens Mem Schlrshp 85; Brigham Youn U; Lawyer.

CROSS, TANYA; Gloversville HS; Gloversville, NY; (Y); Church Yth Grp; 4-H; French Clb; Girl Scts; Key Clb; SADD; Chorus; JV Capt Bsktbl; Hon Roll; Prfct Atten Awd; Mater Dei Coll; Scl Wrk.

CROSS, WENDY; Hoosic Valley Central HS; Melrose, NY; (Y); Camp Fr Inc; Church Yth Grp; Pres 4-H; Girl Scts; Hosp Aide; Quiz Bowl; Ski Clb; 4-H Awd; Hon Roll; Mary Slocum Scrtrl Awd 86; Hdsn Vly CC; Accntnt.

CROSSAN, SEAN; Rhinebeck Central Schl; Rhinebeck, NY; (Y); JV L Crs Cntry; Var L Trk; Hon Roll; Winter Trck MVP Awd 85; Section I Conf C All Star Tm Winter Trck 85; Engr.

CROSSWAY, MATTHEW B; Hamilton Central HS; Hamilton, NY; (Y); 18/58; Boy Scts; Varsity Clb; L Bsktbl; L Socr; L Trk; Hon Roll; NHS; Rgnts Schlrshp 85-86; SUNY Cobleskill; Lndscp Dev.

CROSTON, KEVIN; Canisteo Central HS; Canisteo, NY; (Y); Pres 4-H; Alfred ST Coll; Comp Sci.

CROTHERS, STEPHANIE A; Chruchville-Chili HS; N Chili, NY; (Y); Church Yth Grp; Teachers Aide; Hon Roll; Roberts Wesleyan Coll; Humnts.

CROTHERS, WALTER; Newark HS; Newark, NY; (Y); 20/201; Am Leg Boys St; Church Yth Grp; Service Clb; Varsity Clb; Variety Show; Nwsp Stf; Off Frsh Cls; Var Bsbl; Var Socr; Var Capt Swmmng; ST Tourn Swmmng 86; Rutgers U; Engrg.

CROTTY, MAURA; Hamburg SR HS; Hamburg, NY; (Y); 9/384; Chorus; School Musical; Yrbk Stf; Rep Soph Cls; Rep Jr Cls; Sec Sr Cls; Rep Stu Cncl; Var Capt Cheerleading; Trk; Rotary Awd; Vars Ltr Awds Trck & Chrldg 85-86.

CROUCHER, HEATHER; Ward Melville HS; Stony Brook, NY; (Y); German Clb; Letterman Clb; Var Vllybl; Hon Roll; Jr NHS.

CROUCHER, MARK; Bishop Cunningham HS; Oswego, NY; (S); Yrbk Ed-Chief; Yrbk Stf; Capt Bsbl; Bsktbl; Capt Ftbl; Wt Lftg; DAR Awd; High Hon Roll; Hon Roll; Jr NHS; All Lgu Ftbl Offns & Dfnse 85; FBI.

CROUGH, DAN; Liverpool HS; Liverpool, NY; (Y); Art Clb; Chess Clb; Exploring; Rep German Clb; Ski Clb; Im Tennis; Var Trk; Im Vllybl; High Hon Roll; Acdmc Exclnc Awd Englsh 84-85; Brnz Rqttbl Lge 85; Middleberry; Biolgy.

CROWE, ALISSA; G Ray Bodley HS; Fulton, NY; (Y); Science Clb; Spanish Clb; Nwsp Rptr; High Hon Roll; Hon Roll; Acdmc Exc Awd In Math 85 & 86; Acdmc Exc Awd In Comp Math 86; Chmcl Engrng.

CROWE, JOHN W; Mc Quaid Jesuit HS; Rochester, NY; (Y); 33/170; Cmnty Wkr; Nwsp Stf; Im JV Ftbl; High Hon Roll; Hon Roll; NHS; St Schlr; Notre Dame U; Bus.

CROWE, JUSTIN; Naples Central Schl; Naples, NY; (Y); Trs DECA; Chorus; Madrigals; School Play; JV Bsbl; Var Socr; Im Sftbl; Hon Roll; Prfct Atten Awd; Brockport ST; Real Estate Brkr.

CROWELL, KRISTIN; Forestville Central HS; Forestville, NY; (Y); 3/46; Am Leg Aux Girls St; Girl Scts; Chorus; Capt Color Guard; Mrchg Band; Score Keeper; High Hon Roll; Hon Roll; Pres NHS; Rgnts Schlrshp 86; Smmnr Stay Spain Schlrshp 84; Outstndng Achvts Spnsh I, II & III 83-85; Jamestown CC; Comp Sci.

CROWELL, LYNNE B; Wallkill SR HS; Wallkill, NY; (Y); Am Leg Aux Girls St; Band; Chorus; Mrchg Band; Rep Stu Cncl; JV Bsktbl; Var Capt Socr; Var Trk; High Hon Roll; Pres NHS; U Of CT; Elem Ed.

CROWELL, SCOTT; Cattaraugus Central HS; Otto, NY; (Y); L Var Bsbl; L Var Bsktbl; L Var Ftbl; Cortland ST; Bus Admin.

CROWLEY, DENNIS; Regis HS; Wilton, CT; (Y); Chess Clb; Cmnty Wkr; Computer Clb; NFL; Speech Tm; Teachers Aide; Nwsp Rptr; Lit Mag; Bowling; Tennis; Harvard Invtnl Spch Trnmt Qrtr Fnlst 85-86; Semifnlst M Bump Inv Sp Trnmt 85-86; Engl.

CROWLEY, EDWARD; Archbishop Molloy HS; Belle Harbor, NY; (Y); Cmnty Wkr; French Clb; Service Clb; SADD; Crs Cntry; Trk; Hon Roll; NHS; Intl Bnkg.

CROWLEY, KELLIE; Perry Central HS; Perry, NY; (Y); French Clb; Math Tm; Concert Band; Mrchg Band; Var JV Socr; Hon Roll; SUNY Geneseo; Bus.

CROWLEY, ROBERT N; Bellport SR HS; Bellport, NY; (Y); Nwsp Sprt Ed; Rep Soph Cls; Rep Jr Cls; Rep Sr Cls; Var Bsbl; Var Bsktbl; Hon Roll; Cmnty Wkr; Teachers Aide; Stage Crew; NY ST Rgnts Schlrshp Wnr 86; Nvl ROTC Natl Schlrshp Wnr 86; Suffolk Cnty Cls A Bsktbl Chmpn Tm 85; SUNY Cortland; Educ.

CROWLEY, TRACI; Olean HS; Olean, NY; (Y); Drama Clb; Letterman Clb; Thesps; Chorus; Orch; School Musical; School Play; Var Cheerleading; JV Score Keeper; Hon Roll; Art.

CROWNINGSHIELD, YVONNE; Northville Central HS; Northville, NY; (Y); 24/44; GAA; Chorus; School Musical; Sec Stu Cncl; Capt Cheerleading; Socr; Drama Clb; SADD; Swing Chorus; Yrbk Stf; Chrldng Mst Outstndng 86; Dir Awd For Music 86; Byron Schyler Awd $1000 86; Lbry Clb VP; Long Island U; Music.

CRUCES, ROBERT; Woodlands HS; Hartsdale, NY; (Y); French Clb; Sec Trs Key Clb; Nwsp Bus Mgr; Nwsp Rptr; Ed Yrbk Bus Mgr; Yrbk Sprt Ed; Var Tennis; NHS; Jrnlsm.

CRUDELE, MELINDA; Midlakes HS; Clifton Spgs, NY; (Y); 40/140; French Clb; German Clb; GAA; SADD; Varsity Clb; Yrbk Stf; Var L Bsktbl; Var Socr; Var Trk; Hon Roll; Pre-Law.

CRUM, GEORGE M; Seton Catholic Central HS; Binghamton, NY; (Y); 50/164; Computer Clb; Letterman Clb; Stage Crew; L Crs Cntry; Capt Wrstlng; St Schlr; NY Rgnts Schlrshp 85-86; Columbia Coll NY; Pre Law.

CRUMP, SONYA; Buffalo Traditional HS; Buffalo, NY; (S); 13/122; Camera Clb; 4-H; French Clb; Intnl Clb; JA; Spanish Clb; Teachers Aide; Chorus; School Play; Nwsp Ed-Chief; Fashion Inst Tech; Fash Merch.

CRUNDEN, JIM; Union-Endicott HS; Endicott, NY; (S); Am Leg Boys St; Church Yth Grp; Rep Frsh Cls; Rep Soph Cls; Rep Stu Cncl; JV Capt Bsbl; JV Var Ftbl; Im Trk; JV Wrstlng; Phy Thrpy.

CRUZ, ALEXANDRA; Midwood HS; Brooklyn, NY; (Y); 76/667; Math Tm; Band; School Musical; Hon Roll; Trs Jr NHS; Arista Stu 86.

CRUZ, CECILY; St Raymond Academy For Girls; Bronx, NY; (S); Mrchg Band; Cheerleading; Pom Pon; NHS; Prfct Atten Awd; Spnsh & Relgn Hnrs 84-85; Mandl Schl; Lab Tech.

CRUZ, DENISE; La Guardia HS Of Music & The Arts; Brooklyn, NY; (S); 5/650; Teachers Aide; Chorus; Church Choir; Rep Soph Cls; Hon Roll; NHS; Prfct Atten Awd; Val; Music Hnr Lg 86; Med.

CRUZ, EVELYN; Sheepshead Bay HS; Brooklyn, NY; (Y); Intnl Clb; Sec Frsh Cls; Sec Soph Cls; Sec Jr Cls; Cert Of Schlrshp In Acctng I & Typng 4 86.

CRUZ, GINA; Liverpool HS; Liverpool, NY; (S); 244/816; DECA; Off Soph Cls; Off Jr Cls; Off Sr Cls; Stu Cncl; JV Cheerleading; Var Tennis; Hon Roll; Rochester Inst; Bus Mgmt.

CRUZ, GINA; St Raymonds Acad; New York, NY; (Y); 30/74; Mrchg Band; Sec Stu Cncl; Prfct Atten Awd; Cert Merit Phy Ed 81-86; Cert Awd Art 80; Cert Merit Stdt Art Comptn 81; Sci.

CRUZ, HECTOR; Eastern Dist HS; Brooklyn, NY; (Y); Math Tm; Science Clb; Hon Roll; NHS; Yng Dplmts Exchng Prgm Madrid Spain & NY 86; Cornell; Engrng.

CRUZ, JEANNETTE; Grace H Dodge Voc HS; New York, NY; (Y); #46 In Class; Church Yth Grp; Cmnty Wkr; Dance Clb; Hosp Aide; Prfct Atten Awd; Engl, Glb Hist, Spnsh 83-84; Engl, Hlth Career 84-85; Grwth, Dev, Engl Amer Stds 85-86; Ped RN.

CRUZ, JOSE; Uniondale HS; Uniondale, NY; (Y); Art Clb; Church Yth Grp; Computer Clb; Debate Tm; NFL; Speech Tm; SADD; VICA; Nwsp Stf; Var Ftbl; Trphy & Cert Art Awd 83-84; Blue Hon Mntn Rbn For Sci Fair 83-84; Tm Trphy 3rd Pl Frnscs Tm 85-86; CO Air Frc Acad; Engrng.

CRUZ, LILY; Eastern District HS; Brooklyn, NY; (Y); Office Aide; Service Clb; Jr Cls; Phy Ed, Typng & Englsh 85; Hygiene, Phy Ed & Spnsh 86.

CRUZ, LISA; James E Sperry HS; Rochester, NY; (Y); 63/277; Exploring; Spanish Clb; Hon Roll; Spanish NHS; Pres Crmnl Justc Explrs Pst 722 85; Syracuse U; Crmnl Law.

CRUZ, LOURDES; Dundee Central HS; Dundee, NY; (Y); English Clb; French Clb; FHA; Intnl Clb; Spanish Clb; SADD; Teachers Aide; Chorus; School Musical; School Play; Track Awd; Art Awds; New Paltz; Comp.

CRUZ, LUCESITA; Herbert H Lehman HS; Bronx, NY; (Y); 97/561; Dance Clb; Band; Variety Show; Cit Awd; High Hon Roll; Prfct Atten Awd; Spanish NHS; JR Arista Awd 83-84; Bus Mgmt.

CRUZ, MARIA; Beach Channel HS; Arverne, NY; (Y); Band; Concert Band; Mrchg Band; Arista Awd 84; Psych.

CRUZ, MELISSA; Connetquot HS; Ronkonkoma, NY; (S); 19/699; Church Yth Grp; Band; Mrchg Band; Symp Band; Nwsp Stf; Rep Stu Cncl; Cheerleading; Jr NHS; NHS; Ntl Merit Ltr; Soclgy.

CRUZ, TINA; Central Islip HS; Central Islip, NY; (Y); 4/348; SADD; Stage Crew; Lit Mag; Rep Soph Cls; VP Jr Cls; Rep Sr Cls; Chrmn Stu Cncl; Hon Roll; Sec NHS; Pres Schlr; Regents Schlrshp 85-86; Stu Orgnztn Schlrshp 85-86; NE U; Accntng.

CRUZ-ARELLANO, GLORIA; Aquinas HS; Bronx, NY; (Y); 68/170; Art Clb; Church Yth Grp; Cmnty Wkr; Computer Clb; Office Aide; Speech Tm; Bsbl; Gym; High Hon Roll; Hon Roll; Sec Hnrs 86; Awd Maria Regina Clg 86; Maria Reginia Clg; Sec Studies.

CRYDERMAN, AMY L; Massena Central HS; Massena, NY; (Y); 27/250; Hon Roll; Ntl Merit SF; Regents Schlrshp 86; Acdmc Ltr 85; Piano Diplomas Montreal Cnsrvtry Mus 83-86.

CRYVOFF, CATHERINE MARY; Our Lady Of Lourdes HS; Pleasant Vly, NY; (Y); 3/180; Church Yth Grp; Drama Clb; Ski Clb; Teachers Aide; Nwsp Stf; Yrbk Stf; Var Stat Bsbl; Var Capt Vllybl; High Hon Roll; NHS; 1st Math, Math II 84-85; 3rd Calculs I, II, 2nd Chem, Spnsh III Awds 86; Math.

CTORIDES, CHRISTINA; Wm Cullen Bryant HS; New York, NY; (S); 4/623; Key Clb; Mathletes; Teachers Aide; Concert Band; Nwsp Ed-Chief; French Hon Soc; Jr NHS; NHS; Pol Sci.

CUCCHIARA, DONALD; Valley Central HS; Newburgh, NY; (Y); 43/300; French Clb; Band; Concert Band; Im Bsbl; Im Bsktbl; Im Swmmng; French Hon Soc; Hon Roll; NHS; Ntl Merit Ltr; Scuba Diving Clb 86; U Of Miami; Marine Bio.

CUCCIA, CATHERINE; Dover HS; Dover Plains, NY; (Y); French Clb; Pres Band; Chorus; Church Choir; Pres Concert Band; Drm Mjr(t); Jazz Band; Mrchg Band; Pep Band; School Play; Music Schlrshp Wilkes Coll 86; SR All Amer Hall Of Fm Band Hnrs 86; Grad Awd 86; Wilkes Coll; Music Ed.

CUCCIA, MICHELE; Sacred Heart Acad; Garden City, NY; (S); Art Clb; Math Clb; Science Clb; SADD; Concert Band; High Hon Roll; Jr NHS; NHS; Madrigals; School Play; Italian Hnr Soc; Fine Arts Clb; Hrsbck Riding Clb; Bio.

CUCCINIELLO, MARY; St Raymond Acad; Bronx, NY; (S); 4/69; Dance Clb; English Clb; French Clb; Latin Clb; Pres Frsh Cls; Stu Cncl; Cheerleading; High Hon Roll; Hon Roll; U Rome; Pol Sci.

CUCINOTTA, ELIZABETH M; St Francis Prep; Woodside, NY; (S); 148/744; Cmnty Wkr; Bowling; Powder Puff Ftbl; Sftbl; Hon Roll; Mst Imprvd 3rd Pl Bwlng Tm 83-84; Hgh Avg, Hgh Series Bwlng 84-85; Dean Lst 83-85.

CUDAHY, KERRY; Sacred Heart Acad; Floral Park, NY; (Y); Office Aide; SADD; Nwsp Rptr; Nwsp Stf; JV Bsktbl; JV Cheerleading; Var Capt Socr; Hon Roll; NHS; LI Cath HS Athltc Assn Vrsty Sccr All-Star Awd 86; Tm Capt-Sccr League Sprtsmnshp Wnnrs 86; Bus.

CUDDEBACK, CAROLYN; Union Springs Central HS; Cayuga, NY; (Y); 14/106; Church Yth Grp; PAVAS; Spanish Clb; Chorus; School Musical; Var Fld Hcky; JV Var Sftbl; High Hon Roll; Yorkers Hstry Clb 85-86; Mth.

CUDDEBACK, HEATHER; Auburn HS; Auburn, NY; (Y); Drama Clb; SADD; Chorus; School Musical; School Play; Nwsp Stf; Yrbk Stf; High Hon Roll; Jr NHS; NHS; Med.

CUDDY, JENNIFER; Bayside HS; Bayside, NY; (Y); 28/561; Teachers Aide; Band; Concert Band; Jazz Band; Orch; Nwsp Rptr; High Hon Roll; NHS; Bus.

CUDDY, WILLIAM; Trinity Pawling HS; Pawling, NY; (Y); Aud/Vis; French Clb; Letterman Clb; Ski Clb; Varsity Clb; Yrbk Stf; Stu Cncl; Var Bsbl; L Var Bsktbl; L Var Golf; Effrt & Achvt Clsses 84-87; Forgn Bus Affrs.

CUDECK, KATHY; Maryvale HS; Cheektowaga, NY; (Y); Band; Chorus; Concert Band; Jazz Band; Mrchg Band; School Musical; School Play; Symp Band; Rep Frsh Cls; Sec Soph Cls; Accntng.

CUEVAS, DIEGO; Newtown HS; Elmhurst, NY; (Y); Latin Clb; Math Clb; PAVAS; Radio Clb; Chorus; Concert Band; Jazz Band; Mrchg Band; Orch; Symp Band; Bst Band Musicn 85; Bst Trmpt Plyr 86; Schl Chorus Awd Music Accmpnmt 86; Med.

CUEVAS, EVELYN; Erasmus Hall HS; Brooklyn, NY; (Y); Jazz Band; Nwsp Rptr; JV Gym; Biology Honors 85; Brooklyn Coll; Bio.

CUFF, COLLEEN; Auburn HS; Auburn, NY; (Y); Dance Clb; Varsity Clb; School Musical; Var L Gym; High Hon Roll; Hon Roll; Amer Studies Awd 86; Ftns Achvt Awd 86; Jrnlsm.

CUFFARO, CATHERINE; Union-Endicott HS; Endicott, NY; (Y); Concert Band; High Hon Roll; Hon Roll; Broome CC; Med Asst.

CUGINI, CHRISTINE; Moore Catholic HS; Staten Island, NY; (Y); Math Tm; Pres Spanish Clb; Pres SADD; Pres Chorus; School Musical; Nwsp Stf; Yrbk Stf; Rep Jr Cls; VP Stu Cncl; NHS; Ecnmcs.

CUIFFO, DEBORAH; The Masters Schl; Bronxville, NY; (Y); Office Aide; Teachers Aide; Chorus; School Musical; Rep Stu Cncl; Church Yth Grp; Cmnty Wkr; Stage Crew; Nwsp Rptr; Hon Roll; Semi-Fin Natl Hrse Shw 85; Mth Awd 84; Pre-Vet.

CUILLA, JAMES; Argyle Central HS; Argyle, NY; (Y); Am Leg Boys St; French Clb; Math Tm; Trs Varsity Clb; Off Stu Cncl; Bsbl; Bsktbl; Socr; High Hon Roll; Hon Roll; Arch.

CUILLA, JOHN; Argyle Central HS; Argyle, NY; (Y); Am Leg Boys St; Math Tm; VP Varsity Clb; Yrbk Sprt Ed; Pres Sr Cls; VP Stu Cncl; Var Capt Bsbl; Var Capt Bsktbl; Coach Actv; Var Capt Socr; Sprngfld Coll Schlrshp 86; JMS Argyle Cntrl Schl 86; FWMA 86; Springfield Coll; Phy Ed.

CULBERT, CHRISTINA; Fillmore Central HS; Fillmore, NY; (S); 7/60; Am Leg Aux Girls St; 4-H; Yrbk Stf; Sec Sr Cls; Var Vllybl; NHS; Office Aide; Ski Clb; Sec Jr Cls; Psych.

CULHANE, TIMOTHY R; Newburgh Free Acad; Newburgh, NY; (Y); 17/600; Pres 4-H; Science Clb; CC Awd; High Hon Roll; Hon Roll; Regnts Schlrshp 86; Yth Ct Membr Apprectn 86; ST U Of NY; Corp Lwyr.

CULLEN, ANNE; Westhill HS; Syracuse, NY; (Y); Camera Clb; Drama Clb; Exploring; Hosp Aide; Spanish Clb; Yrbk Stf; Lit Mag; Centrl Acad Deca Awd 86; Cert Apprectn 84; Nrsng.

CULLEN, ANTHONY; St Pauls Schl; Garden City, NY; (Y); Service Clb; Varsity Clb; Nwsp Ed-Chief; VP Soph Cls; Rep Jr Cls; Var Bsktbl; JV Ftbl; Var Capt Tennis; Hon Roll.

CULLEN, CHRISTINE A; Academy Of St Joseph HS; Bay Shore, NY; (Y); Church Yth Grp; Cmnty Wkr; Drama Clb; School Play; Stage Crew; Variety Show; NEDT Awd; Rotary Awd; NY ST Rgnts Schlrshp 86; Mnhttnvll Coll Hnrs Schlrshp 86; Exchng Stdnt Brzl 84-85; Manhattanville Coll; Intl Rel.

CULLEN, KATRINA; Pine Valley Central HS; Conawango, NY; (Y); Trs AFS; 4-H; Stat Bsktbl; Score Keeper; St Bonaventure U; Med Tech.

CULLEN, MOIRA; Seton Catholic Central HS; Endicott, NY; (S); 1/162; Cmnty Wkr; Mathletes; Nwsp Ed-Chief; JV Var Socr; L Trk; Bausch & Lomb Sci Awd; Pres NHS; Ntl Merit Ltr; Telluride Schlrshp 85; Cornell U; Pre-Med.

CULLEN, PETER; Tully HS; Tully, NY; (Y); Spanish Clb; Ftbl; Trk; Hon Roll; NHS; Prfct Atten Awd; Comp Sci.

CULLEY, EMILY C; Chatham HS; Chatham, NY; (Y); 20/120; Drama Clb; 4-H; Hosp Aide; Acpl Chr; Chorus; School Musical; School Play; JV Vllybl; 4-H Awd; High Hon Roll; NY ST Wldlf Rhbltr & Smr Stck Thtr Aprntc; Amer Intl Coll; Vtrntn.

CULLEY, MATTHEW P; Alfred-Almond Central Schl; Alfred, NY; (Y); Ski Clb; Chorus; Mrchg Band; School Musical; School Play; Yrbk Stf; Var L Bsbl; L Var Crs Cntry; Co-Capt Var Swmmng; High Hon Roll; Rgnts Schlrshp Nrsg 86; Alfred U; Nrsg.

CULLINAN, TERRI-ANN; Sachem HS; Holtsville, NY; (Y); 100/1400; Girl Scts; Science Clb; Chorus; Fld Hcky; Jr NHS; 2nd Pl Soc Stds Fair 83-84; 2nd Pl Sci Fair 82-83; Grl Sct Slvr Awd 82-83; Syracuse U; Spcl Educ.

CULLINAN, THOMAS; St Marys Boys HS; Port Washington, NY; (S); Ntl Hnr Soc 86; Regents Schlrshp 86; Accntng.

CULLON, JOSEPH; The Wheatley Schl; E Williston, NY; (Y); Cmnty Wkr; Capt Quiz Bowl; SADD; Varsity Clb; Nwsp Rptr; Rep Frsh Cls; Rep Soph Cls; Rep Jr Cls; Var Ftbl; NHS; Pres Inter Cultrl Unity 85-86; Yuth Cnf 86; Engl Ed.

CULLUM, DAVID; Lakeland HS; Putnam Valley, NY; (Y); Church Yth Grp; Rep Stu Cncl; Socr; Trk; High Hon Roll; Hghst Achvmnt In Math & Soc Stud Awd 84; Elec Engr.

CULVER, TODD; Seward Park HS; New York, NY; (Y); Chess Clb; Computer Clb; Office Aide; Teachers Aide; Variety Show; NYU; Bus Admn.

CUMBERBATCH, CLEON E; Andrew Jackson HS; Laurelton, NY; (Y); 14/479; Church Yth Grp; Band; Concert Band; Jazz Band; Mrchg Band; School Musical; School Play; Yrbk Stf; Lit Mag; Rgnts Schlrshp 86; Amer Musical Fndatn Band Hnrs 86; Jr All-Amer Hll Of Fame Band Hnrs 85; Hamilton Coll; Art.

CUMELLA, JEAN; Sacred Heart Acad; Westbury, NY; (Y); Church Yth Grp; Hosp Aide; Pep Clb; SADD; Im Cheerleading; Mgr(s); Score Keeper; Capt Var Socr; Captn Sprtsnite 85; Missn Commssn Rep 84-86; Physcl Ed.

CUMMER, MIKE; Sweet Home SR HS; N Tonawanda, NY; (Y); Model UN; Science Clb; Spanish Clb; JV Socr; High Hon Roll; NHS; Spanish NHS; Sci Hon Soc; Med.

CUMMINGS, CHRISTINE A; E L Vandermeulen HS; Port Jeff Station, NY; (Y); 35/330; Leo Clb; Spanish Clb; SADD; Yrbk Rptr; Rep Sr Cls; Cheerleading; Vllybl; High Hon Roll; NHS; Regnts Schlrshp 86; Geneseo.

CUMMINGS, D MICHAEL; Newfane SR HS; Burt, NY; (Y); Hon Roll; Cert Hnr Vhcl Pwr I & II, Mfg & Cnstrctn 85.

CUMMINGS, DEANNA; Keveny Memorial Acad; Watervliet, NY; (S); 7/42; Cmnty Wkr; Band; Mrchg Band; Stu Cncl; Crs Cntry; Stat Socr; High Hon Roll; Trs NHS; Ntl Merit Schol; Serv Awd; Phys Ther.

CUMMINGS, JENNIFER; South Side HS; Rockville Centre, NY; (Y); 53/300; Band; Mrchg Band; Hon Roll.

CUMMINGS, LAURIE; Berlin Central JR & SR HS; Stephentown, NY; (S); 6/83; Pres Church Yth Grp; Ski Clb; Band; Chorus; Church Choir; Concert Band; Mrchg Band; School Musical; School Play; Var L Bsktbl; All-Cnty Wind Ensmbl, Bnd & Chorus 82-86; SYNOD Of N E Yth Advsry Delegate 85; Coll Of Wooster; Elglsh.

CUMMINGS, SUSANNE; Newfield HS; Selden, NY; (S); 128/515; Pres Camera Clb; Q&S; Chorus; Stage Crew; Pres Nwsp Ed-Chief; Nwsp Phtg; Nwsp Rptr; Nwsp Stf; Yrbk Phtg; Sec Yrbk Stf; Spllng Bee Chmp 83; Prop Mgr 85; St Johns U; Athltc Adm.

CUMMINGS, TIMOTHY I; Monsignor Farrell HS; Staten Island, NY; (Y); 63/290; Boy Scts; Chess Clb; Stage Crew; Im Bsktbl; Im Bowling; Im Ftbl; JV Var Swmmng; Ntl Merit SF; Ntl Merit Semi-Fnlst; Boy Scouts Ldrshp Corps.

CUMMINGS, WILLIAM; Dundee Central HS; Himrod, NY; (Y); Library Aide; Chorus; Nwsp Stf; Bowling; Acctg.

CUMMO, CHRISTOPHER; Longwood HS; Middle Island, NY; (Y); 69/485; Boy Scts; Chess Clb; Church Yth Grp; Varsity Clb; Bsbl; Coach Actv; Crs Cntry; Ftbl; Golf; Trk; Brkhvn Chmbr Of Cmrc Awd 86; Coll St Rose; Chmstry.

CUMPSTON, ANGELA; Scio Central HS; Scio, NY; (S); 3/50; FBLA; Model UN; Chorus; School Play; Sec Frsh Cls; Sec Soph Cls; Sec Jr Cls; Var L Tennis; High Hon Roll; Jr NHS; Acad All Amer Engl 85; St Bonaventure U; Econ.

CUNEO, JOHN; Valley Central HS; Montgomery, NY; (Y); Church Yth Grp; JV Bsbl; JV Var Ftbl; Var Wt Lftg; Soc Studies Hnr Soc 85-86.

CUNNEEN, CHRISTINE M; Sachem SR HS North Campus; Holtsville, NY; (Y); 45/1375; Trs GAA; Var Stat Bsktbl; Var Capt Fld Hcky; Mgr(s); Var Sftbl; Var Trk; NHS; NYS Regents Schlrshp 86; Frshmn Rec Schlrshp Hofstra U 86; Actvty Grant Fld Hcky Hofstra U 86; Hofstra U; Acctg.

CUNNINGHAM, GERALDINE; Bronx HS Of Science; Bronx, NY; (Y); Pres Intnl Clb; Teachers Aide; Lit Mag; Cert Of Merit Excllnc In Latin By NY Classical Clb 86; Cert Of Honbl Merit On Natl Latin Exam 86; Librl Arts.

CUNNINGHAM, JENNIFER R; Blind Brook HS; Rye Brook, NY; (Y); Drama Clb; French Clb; Math Tm; Rep Soph Cls; Ntl Merit SF; Bio.

CUNNINGHAM, JOSEPH B; St Francis Prep; Little Neck, NY; (Y); Drama Clb; School Musical; School Play; Stage Crew; NY ST Regents Schlrshp 86; St Johns U; Jrnlsm.

CUNNINGHAM, KARLA; Aquinas Inst; Rochester, NY; (Y); Drama Clb; Hosp Aide; Scholastic Bowl; Science Clb; School Musical; Nwsp Stf; Yrbk Phtg; Rep Sr Cls; Hon Roll; Ntl Merit Schol; Chatham Merit Schlrshp Sci 86; Acad Achvt Awd Bio,Engl,Physcis 86; Chatham Coll; Bio.

CUNNINGHAM, KRISTEN M; Pittsford Sutherland HS; Pittsford, NY; (Y); Church Yth Grp; Latin Clb; Service Clb; SADD; Chorus; Stage Crew; JV Var Fld Hcky; NHS; Var Mgr Bsktbl; Hon Roll; NYS Rgnts Schlrshp 86; Bst Defnsv Plyr-V Fld Hcky 86; Coll Of The Holy Cross-Pre-Med.

CUNNINGHAM, LORI; New Rochelle HS; New Rochelle, NY; (Y); Cmnty Wkr; Drama Clb; Spanish Clb; Socr; JV Vllybl; High Hon Roll; Jr NHS; NHS; Ntl Merit Schol; Spanish NHS; Bio.

CUNNINGHAM, REBECCA L; Southside HS; Horseheads, NY; (Y); Church Yth Grp; Cmnty Wkr; Hosp Aide; JCL; Key Clb; Latin Clb; Nwsp Rptr; Yrbk Stf; High Hon Roll; NHS; NY ST Rgnts Schlrshp 85-86; Pre-Med.

CUNNINGHAM, SCOTT D; Sayville HS; Sayville, NY; (Y); 54/360; Mathletes; School Play; Swmmng; High Hon Roll; Boston U; Bus.

CUNNINGHAM, STACEY; Salmon River Central HS; Bombay, NY; (S); 7/88; Pres Church Yth Grp; Sec Drama Clb; Pres 4-H; Pres French Clb; Band; Pres Church Choir; Concert Band; Pres Stu Cncl; Capt Swmmng; 4-H Awd; Schl Stu Of Mnth 85; Rgnts Schlrshp Wnr 86; Plattsburgh ST U.

CURANAJ, THERESA UCAJ; St Catharine Acad; Bx, NY; (Y); Dance Clb; Office Aide; Teachers Aide; School Play; Hon Roll; Prfct Atten Awd; Steno Awd 85-86; Fordham U; Bus Mgmt.

CURCHAR, RICHARD; Erasmus Hall HS; Brooklyn, NY; (Y); Socr; Trk.

CURCIO, LISA; Bishop Ford CC HS; Brooklyn, NY; (Y).

CURLEY, DENNIS M; Nottingham HS; Syracuse, NY; (Y); 2/220; Drama Clb; Latin Clb; Chorus; Concert Band; Madrigals; School Musical; Swing Chorus; Pres NHS; Sal; Computer Clb; Harvard Bk Awd 85; Outstndg Music Stu 85; U Rochester; Music.

CURLEY, PAUL; Ravena-Coeymans-Selkirk HS; Selkirk, NY; (Y); 2/200; Cmnty Wkr; Spanish Clb; Band; Nwsp Rptr; Var Capt Crs Cntry; Var Trk; Var Wrstlng; High Hon Roll; NHS; Econmst.

CURLEY, SUE; John Jay HS; Katonah, NY; (Y); 1/250; Hosp Aide; Pep Clb; Ski Clb; SADD; Var Bowling; JV Var Cheerleading; JV Var Pom Pon; JV Powder Puff Ftbl; JV Sftbl; Im Trk; Mst Imprvd Sftbl Plyr JV Tm 86; Accntnt.

CURLEY, WILLIAM S; St Anthonys HS; Kings Park, NY; (Y); 8/240; Computer Clb; Service Clb; Ski Clb; Band; Symp Band; Nwsp Rptr; French Hon Soc; High Hon Roll; NHS; Ntl Merit Ltr; Schlrshp 85; Rensselaer Polytech Inst; Engr.

CURNS, DAN; Elmira Free Acad; Elmira, NY; (Y); Art Clb; Church Yth Grp; Variety Show; Stat Bsktbl; Mgr(s); High Hon Roll; Psych.

CURRAN, BRIDGET; Ursuline Schl; Bronxville, NY; (Y); Church Yth Grp; Ski Clb; Yrbk Stf; Jr NHS; Arch.

CURRAN, CHRISTOPHER; Saranac Lake Central HS; Saranac Lk, NY; (Y); 18/135; AFS; Key Clb; Ski Clb; School Play; Nwsp Stf; Yrbk Stf; Var L Bsktbl; Var L Socr; Hon Roll; NHS; NY ST Rgnts Schlrshp 86; Womens Coll Schlrshp Clb Awd 86; St Lawrence U; Intl Rltns.

CURRAN, PETER; Margaretville Central Schl; Arkville, NY; (Y); 5/44; Boy Scts; Chess Clb; French Clb; JA; Math Clb; Bsbl; Ftbl; Lcrss; Wt Lftg; Wrstlng; Phy Geolgy Rgnts Coll Exm 86; Rgnts HS Diplma 86; Engl, Jrnlsm Awds/Roswell Sandford Memrl Awd 86; Utica Coll; Crmnl Jstc.

CURRAN, TIMOTHY; La Salle Military Acad; Kings Park, NY; (Y); 16/89; Computer Clb; Radio Clb; ROTC; Chorus; Church Choir; School Musical; Swing Chorus; Nwsp Phtg; Var L Bsbl; Var L Ftbl; Outstndng Sr Actor 86; St Michaels Coll; Civil Engrng.

CURREY, JOYCE; De Witt Clinton HS; Bronx, NY; (Y); Cmnty Wkr; Intnl Clb; Key Clb; Chorus; School Play; Sftbl; Vllybl; Cit Awd; Gd Gal Awd 85; 2nd Plc Wrtng Cntst 86; Art.

CURRIE, FRANCHESCO; Kensington HS; Buffalo, NY; (Y); Variety Show; Ftbl; Trk; Hon Roll; Cert Apprctn Awds IRS, NY ST Dpt Tax 86; IN Inst Tech; Acctg.

CURRIE, JILL K; Newfane HS; Newfane, NY; (S); 8/181; Church Yth Grp; Dance Clb; Math Tm; Varsity Clb; Band; Var L Bsktbl; Var Trk; JV Vllybl; Hon Roll; NHS; Ed.

CURRIE, SUE; Hudson Falls SR HS; Hudson Fls, NY; (Y); Exploring; Pep Clb; SADD; Y-Teens; Acpl Chr; Chorus; Stu Of Qrtr Sci 84-85; Adirondack CC; Nrsg.

CURRIER, EDWARD; Auburn HS; Auburn, NY; (Y); Art Clb; Boy Scts; Bowling; Ftbl; Score Keeper; Hon Roll; Harvard Law Schl; Lawyer.

CURRIER, KAREN L; Massena Central Schl; Saranac Lake, NY; (Y); Powder Puff Ftbl; High Hon Roll; Hon Roll; Acdmc Banq Ltr 85; Acdmc Banq 2 Strs 86; Anyamous Hmkrs Awd 86; North Cnty CC; Bus Adm.

CURRIER, LYNN; Lindenhurst HS; Lindenhurst, NY; (Y); Cmnty Wkr; Exploring; Crs Cntry; Trk; Hon Roll.

CURRY, ALICIA; Walt Whitman HS; Huntington, NY; (Y); 46/479; Drama Clb; SADD; School Play; Yrbk Stf; Pres Sr Cls; Var Fld Hcky; Hon Roll; Trs Jr NHS; Spanish NHS; Key Clb; Comm.

CURRY, ANGIE; Hanau HS; Apo Ny, NY; (Y); Office Aide; Rep Stu Cncl; JV Tennis; JV Capt Vllybl; Hon Roll; Bus.

CURRY, CHRISTOPHER J; Goshen Central HS; Florida, NY; (Y); Boy Scts; VP Exploring; Jazz Band; God Cntry Awd; Hon Roll; VP Jr NHS; VP NHS; Prfct Atten Awd; Church Yth Grp; French Clb; Amer Lgn Awd 86; Govt Yth Chrmn & Cnty Lgsltr 85-86; Dickinson Coll; Psychlgy.

CURRY, FRANCES; Ichabod Crane HS; Stuyvesant, NY; (Y); Drama Clb; German Clb; SADD; Thesps; Chorus; School Musical; School Play; Swing Chorus; Church Yth Grp; Cmnty Wkr; Area All ST Chorale 85; NY ST Schl Of Music Assn 85; Mst Prmsng Actrs Schl Awd 85; Dramatic Arts.

CURRY, JONATHAN; Edison HS; Rochester, NY; (Y); 44/281; Band; Chorus; Church Choir; Jazz Band; School Musical; Variety Show; High Hon Roll; Hon Roll; Prfct Atten Awd; Hobart & Wm Smith Coll; Mus Ed.

CURRY, KEVIN M; Clarence HS; Clarence, NY; (Y); 2/272; Drama Clb; Nwsp Sprt Ed; VP Stu Cncl; Var Capt Bsbl; Var Bsktbl; Var Ftbl; High Hon Roll; NHS; Sal; U Notre Dame; Bus.

CURTH, GEORGE W; Ward Melville HS; Stony Brook, NY; (Y); 130/725; Nwsp Rptr; Rep Jr Cls; Rep Sr Cls; Trs Stu Cncl; L Golf; L Capt Socr; High Hon Roll; Jr NHS; Ski Clb; Rep Frsh Cls; NROTC Schlrshp-Marine Option 86; Coached Cmmnty Yth Sccr Tms 85-86; Schl Rcrd Of 25 Assts In 12 Games; Accntng.

CURTIN, JEANNE; Minisink Valley HS; Middletown, NY; (Y); 18/222; Church Yth Grp; Hosp Aide; Concert Band; Mrchg Band; Yrbk Stf; Tennis; High Hon Roll; Hon Roll; NHS; Orange Cnty CC; Accntg.

CURTIN, JOHN J; Smithtown H S West; Smithtown, NY; (Y); Rep Stu Cncl; JV Var Tennis; Wt Lftg; JV Var Wrstlng; High Hon Roll; Jr NHS; NHS; Ntl Merit SF; Spanish NHS; Med.

CURTIN, KATHERINE; Mahopac HS; Mahopac, NY; (Y); 121/405; Girl Scts; Red Cross Aide; Varsity Clb; Chorus; Church Choir; Bsktbl; Sftbl; Hon Roll; Long Island U; Marine Bio.

CURTIS, DIANA; Cazenovia Central Schl; Cazenovia, NY; (Y); Debate Tm; Trs 4-H; Trs FFA; Quiz Bowl; Cit Awd; 4-H Awd; Madison Cnty Altrnt Dairy Prncss 86; NYS Future Frmr Empire Degree 85-86; Dstngshd JR Stu Fnlst 86; SUNY; Agri.

CURTIS, JODI; Churchville Chili SR HS; North Chili, NY; (Y); Am Leg Aux Girls St; Drama Clb; JA; Library Aide; Model UN; Y-Teens; Nwsp Rptr; Nwsp Sprt Ed; High Hon Roll; Hon Roll; Intl Stud.

CURTO, MARK; Kenmore West SR HS; Kenmore, NY; (Y); 6/443; High Hon Roll; Hon Roll; Prfct Atten 83-84; U Of Buffalo; Comp Sci.

CURTO, ROBERT; Herricks HS; New Hyde Park, NY; (Y); Chorus; Concert Band; Jazz Band; Mrchg Band; Orch; School Musical; Hon Roll; NHS; Ntl Merit Ltr.

CURULLA, JULIE; East Syracuse-Minoa CHS; Minoa, NY; (Y); Debate Tm; Latin Clb; Ski Clb; Concert Band; Drm Mjr(t); High Hon Roll; NHS; Exploring; Band; Mrchg Band; Wellsley Book Awd 86; Schlrshp Syracuse Us Pre-Coll Pgm 86; Schlrshp Attnd Oprtn Entrz 86; Cornell U; Civil Engrng.

CUSACK, CATHY; Acad Of St Jsph; Kings Pk, NY; (Y); Art Clb; Church Yth Grp; Dance Clb; Pep Clb; Church Choir; Hon Roll; Natl Art Hon Scty 86; Awd Natl Art Hon Scty Outstndng Achvt Art 86.

CUSACK, CONOR; Mc Quaid Jesuit HS; Rochester, NY; (Y); Church Yth Grp; Varsity Clb; Lit Mag; Var Capt Crs Cntry; JV Var Trk; JV Vllybl; Hon Roll; Capt Vrsty X-Cntry Tm 86; X-Cntry Lttr 85; Cmmnctns.

CUSACK, MURIEL; John A Coleman HS; Saugerties, NY; (S); Church Yth Grp; French Clb; JA; Key Clb; Ski Clb; Chorus; Church Choir; School Play; Var Capt Cheerleading; Crs Cntry; Accntnt.

CUSATO, KRISTEN; Pine Bush HS; Pine Bush, NY; (Y); 6/289; Pres Band; Mrchg Band; VP Trs Stu Cncl; Var L Bsktbl; Hon Roll; NHS; Pres Schlr; Voice Dem Awd; Office Aide; Rep Frsh Cls; Brd Drctrs Pine Bush Arts Cncl; Band Schlrshp; Stu Senate Ldrshp Awrd; SUNY At Geneseo; Radio TV.

CUSHEN JR, MICHAEL J; Sleepy Hollow HS; Tarrytown, NY; (Y); 8/180; Math Tm; Varsity Clb; Chorus; Orch; Im Badmtn; Capt Tennis; High Hon Roll; Hon Roll; NHS; Cert Of Achvt Spnsh 82-86; SUNY Binghamton.

CUSICK, BETH; Bainbridge-Guilford HS; Unadilla, NY; (Y); Chorus; Bus Adm.

CUSICK, DANIEL; Seaford HS; Seaford, NY; (Y); Boy Scts; Varsity Clb; Band; Concert Band; Mrchg Band; Yrbk Ed-Chief; Yrbk Stf; Stu Cncl; Socr; Cit Awd; Eagle Scout Awd 84; NYSMMA Metal 83-86; Ad Altare Dei Metal 84; Architecture.

CUSIMANO, KELLIE; Jamestown HS; Jamestown, NY; (Y); 5/399; Pres Trs French Clb; Intnl Clb; Pres Latin Clb; L Var Swmmng; French Hon Soc; High Hon Roll; NHS; Rotary Awd; Debate Tm; JA; Natl Hon Rl; Natl Hon Soc Awd; Maude Kent Schlrp; Boston U; Intl Rltns.

CUSTER, KRISTINE; Tonawanda JR SR HS; Tonawanda, NY; (Y); SADD; Stu Cncl; JV Socr; Cit Awd; Hon Roll; Bus.

CUSUMANO, LINDA; Hicksvill HS; Hicksville, NY; (Y); Hosp Aide; Ski Clb; Mrchg Band; Nwsp Stf; Rep Stu Cncl; Var Capt Gym; Pom Pon; Var Swmmng; Var Trk; MVP Gymnstcs 86; Hon Mntn L I Poster Cont 86; Phy Thrpy.

CUSUMANO, LUISA; Bishop Grimes HS; Liverpool, NY; (Y); 29/146; FBLA; School Musical; High Hon Roll; Hon Roll; NHS; Grnde Ldg Ordr Of Son Of Itly Schlrshp 86; Le Moyne Coll; Bus.

CUTAIA, ANNA; Mahopac HS; Mahopac, NY; (Y); 40/409; Var Sftbl; High Hon Roll; NHS; Prfct Atten Awd; Stu Of Mnth Italian 85; Stu Of Mnth Bus 85; Bus Adm.

CUTILLO, LUCILLE; Carmel HS; Carmel, NY; (Y); Capt Math Tm; Sec SADD; Orch; Trs Frsh Cls; Trs Soph Cls; Pres Jr Cls; Pres Sr Cls; Vllybl; High Hon Roll; NHS; Bus.

CUTLER, BEN; Spackenkill HS; Poughkeepsie, NY; (Y); 14/175; Art Clb; Drama Clb; Leo Clb; Thesps; School Musical; School Play; Yrbk Phtg; High Hon Roll; NHS; Ntl Merit Ltr.

CUTLER, BETH A; Norwood-Norfolk Central HS; Norwood, NY; (Y); 47/128; Aud/Vis; FTA; Office Aide; Teachers Aide; Band; Chorus; Concert Band; Jazz Band; Yrbk Stf; Vllybl; Cazenovia Coll; Studio Art.

CUTLER JR, KENNETH B; Bronxville HS; Bronxville, NY; (Y); 2/118; Boy Scts; Concert Band; Jazz Band; Orch; School Musical; Var Capt Crs Cntry; JV Socr; Var Trk; High Hon Roll; Geo Wshngtn U Schl Of Engrng & Apld Sci Awd 85; NY ST Rgnts Schlrshp 86; CIBA-GEIBY Sci Awd 86; Amhrst Coll.

CUTLER, KIMBERLY R; Cassadaga Valley HS; Gerry, NY; (Y); 1/75; Science Clb; Ski Clb; Stage Crew; Nwsp Stf; Yrbk Bus Mgr; Trs Frsh Cls; Rep Stu Cncl; Hon Roll; NHS; Val; Grove City Coll; Bus Adm.

CUTLER, SUZANNE M; Saratoga Springs SR HS; Gansevoort, NY; (Y); 41/465; Church Yth Grp; GAA; Band; Church Choir; Orch; High Hon Roll; Hon Roll; NHS; Pres Schlr Gettysburg Coll 86; Regents Sclrp 86; Gettysburg Coll; Hist.

CUTRONA, MICHAEL A; La Salle Military Acad; Brooklyn, NY; (Y); 25/90; Chess Clb; Dance Clb; Math Tm; ROTC; Chorus; Yrbk Rptr; L Bsbl; Im Bsktbl; L Bowling; Im Ftbl; NYS Rgnts Schlrshp; JROTC Oprtns Ofcr Btln Stf; 1st Plc Rgmntl Mnl Of Arms Cmptn; Alfred U; Attrny.

CUTRONE, NICHOLAS; Port Richmond HS; Staten Island, NY; (Y); Elec Engr.

CUTTER, CHRISTIAN; Bellport HS; Brookhaven, NY; (Y); Am Leg Boys St; Drama Clb; School Musical; School Play; Stage Crew; Variety Show; Var Capt Crs Cntry; Var Trk; Cmnty Wkr; SADD; Sailng Trphy 84-85; Nvl Arch.

CUYLER, STEPHANIE; G Ray Bodley HS; Fulton, NY; (Y); Drama Clb; French Clb; Hosp Aide; Science Clb; Chorus; Concert Band; School Musical; Ed Yrbk Ed-Chief; Var Cheerleading; NHS; Dance.

CUZZUPOLI, MARK; Brockport HS; Hamlin, NY; (Y); 105/320; Trs Jr Cls; Rep Trs Stu Cncl; Bus Adm.

CWUDZINSKI, ELIZABETH; Villa Maria Acad; Buffalo, NY; (Y); Computer Clb; Math Clb; Ski Clb; High Hon Roll; Hon Roll; Prfct Atten Awd; Hghst Aver In Mth Crs II Rgnts 84; U Of Bflo; Med Tech.

CYPHER, JONATHAN; Brewster HS; Brewster, NY; (Y); Boy Scts; Nwsp Stf; Im Bowling; Var Trk; Hon Roll; NHS; Comp Sci.

CYR, RITA; Queen Of The Rosary Acad; Westbury, NY; (S); 3/50; Library Aide; Yrbk Stf; High Hon Roll; Hon Roll; Sec Frsh Cls; Busnss Hnr Soc 84-86; Nassau CC; Chld Stdy.

CYRCZAK, LISA; Bradford Central Schl; Savona, NY; (S); FBLA; Band; Chorus; Ed Nwsp Ed-Chief; Stu Cncl; Stat Bsktbl; Socr; Var Sftbl; Var Vllybl; High Hon Roll; Law.

CYRUS, SHEILA; Senior HS; Bronx, NY; (Y); Church Yth Grp; Cmnty Wkr; Office Aide; Church Choir; Swing Chorus; Nwsp Rptr; Var Bowling; Var Socr; Hon Roll; Prfct Atten Awd; Citation Of Mrt 84; Bus Mgmt.

CYRUS, TONYA; St Raymond Acad; Bronx, NY; (Y); 1/68; Math Clb; Pep Clb; Science Clb; Nwsp Stf; Yrbk Stf; Pres Jr Cls; VP Stu Cncl; NHS; Val; Regents Scholar 86; Cornell U; Pre-Med.

CYWINSKI, JOHN; Maryvale SR HS; Cheektowaga, NY; (Y); Spanish Clb; Varsity Clb; Bsbl; Ftbl; Hon Roll; NHS; Prfct Atten Awd; Alfred; Acctng.

CZAK, HELENA; Westfield Acad; Westfield, NY; (Y); Ski Clb; Y-Teens; Chorus; School Musical; School Play; Swing Chorus; Yrbk Stf; Stat Bsktbl; Nrsng.

CZAMARA, KENNETH J; Gates Chili SR HS; Buffalo, NY; (Y); Jazz Band; Nwsp Ed-Chief; Pres Jr Cls; High Hon Roll; NHS; Boy Scts; Computer Clb; Drama Clb; Exploring; German Clb; Sci Cngrs Hghst Hnrs Awd 84; Kdk Intl Sci & Engrng Fair Awd 83-85; Nvy & Marine Sci Awds Spr Achvt 84; SUNY Bfl; Sci.

CZAPLA, DAWN M; Lancaster HS; Lancaster, NY; (Y); AFS; French Clb; VP JA; French Hon Soc; High Hon Roll; Pres Schlr; Spanish NHS; 1st Pl Hnr Rll 85 & 86; Canisius Coll; Accntng.

CZAPLICKI, AMY; West Seneca East SR HS; Cheektowaga, NY; (Y); Intnl Clb; Library Aide; Teachers Aide; Stage Crew; Hon Roll; Concours Natl De Francais Cert Merit 84 & 85; Frnch II & III Awd 83-85; Buffalo ST; Ed.

CZAPLYSKI, JULIE; Smithtown HS East; St James, NY; (Y); French Clb; Hosp Aide; Var L Badmtn; Hon Roll.

CZARNECKI, HEDYANNE; Buffalo Acad For Visual Arts; Buffalo, NY; (Y); 1/109; Drama Clb; Math Clb; Capt Math Tm; School Play; Stage Crew; Yrbk Stf; Hon Roll; NHS; Val; Regents Schlrshp; Creative Achvt Awd 86; Acad Merit Awd 86; Awd For Achvt In Free Enpertpreise 86; Boston U; Pre-Med.

CZARNIAK JR, DAVID F; Depew HS; Depew, NY; (Y); 27/272; JV Var Bsbl; Hon Roll; Ntl Merit Schol; NY ST U Buffalo; Law.

CZARNIECKI, MARIA; St Dominic HS; E Norwich, NY; (S); 1/119; Hosp Aide; Model UN; Q&S; School Musical; Nwsp Ed-Chief; Rep Stu Cncl; High Hon Roll; NHS; Ntl Merit Ltr; Church Yth Grp; Holy Cross Coll Bk Awd 85; George Washington U Engr Awd 85; Most Likely To Succeed 86.

CZARTORYSKI, SHARON; Christ The King Regional HS; Middle Village, NY; (Y); Art Clb; Girl Scts; Intnl Clb; Red Cross Aide; Nwsp Ed-Chief; Cert Apprectn 85; Press Awd Best Column 3rd Pl 85; Gazett Cert 85-86; Vet.

CZEBINIAK, DAN; Whitney Point HS; Binghamton, NY; (Y); 42/124; Church Yth Grp; Dance Clb; Hon Roll; Broome CC; Comp Tech.

CZEKAI, LYNN M; Charles H Roth HS; Rush, NY; (Y); 4/197; GAA; Hosp Aide; Pres Sr Cls; Rep Stu Cncl; Var Tennis; JV Vllybl; DAR Awd; NHS; Spanish NHS; VFW Awd; Rochester Pnhlnc Schlrshp 86; Amer Legion Schlrshp 86; Siena Coll; Pre-Med.

CZERWINSKYJ, CHRYSTINA D; Marymount School Of New York; Bronx, NY; (Y); Church Yth Grp; Drama Clb; Intnl Clb; Library Aide; Math Clb; Model UN; High Hon Roll; Hon Roll; NHS; Ntl Merit Ltr; 1st Hnrs Iona Lang Cntst Spnsh III 85; Outstndng Achvt Shkspear Festvl; Med.

CZUBA, PAULETTE; Frontier HS; Athol Springs, NY; (Y); Church Yth Grp; Latin Clb; Library Aide; Office Aide; Chorus; School Musical; School Play; Stage Crew; Hon Roll; NHS; Buffalo ST Coll; Chld Care.

CZUBA, PAULETTE; Frontier SR HS; Hamburg, NY; (S); Church Yth Grp; Latin Clb; Library Aide; Office Aide; Chorus; School Musical; Stage Crew; Hon Roll; NHS; Dyouville; Nrs.

CZVEKUS, DAWN; Cardinal Spellman HS; Bronx, NY; (Y); Camera Clb; Computer Clb; French Clb; High Hon Roll; Hon Roll; Bio Sci.

D AGOSTINO, ANNE MARIE; Brockport HS; Brockport, NY; (Y); Church Yth Grp; Latin Clb; Chorus; Yrbk Phtg; Yrbk Stf; Pres Frsh Cls; Rep Soph Cls; Rep Jr Cls; Rep Sr Cls; Var Swmmng; All Cnty Swim 82-83; PTSA Stu Bdy Rep 85-86; Sectnl Champ Swim 84; UCLA; Sales.

D AGOSTINO, LISA; Notre Dame Academy HS; Staten Island, NY; (Y); Camera Clb; GAA; School Play; Stage Crew; Yrbk Stf; Rep Stu Cncl; Var Cheerleading; Var Crs Cntry; Capt Trk; Fairfield; Bus Mgmt.

D AGOSTINO, MARIA; Mineola HS; Mineola, NY; (Y); Dance Clb; Concert Band; Jazz Band; Mrchg Band; Sec VP Stu Cncl; Var Bsktbl; Score Keeper; Socr; High Hon Roll; NHS; Mineola Booster Clb Athltc Schlrshp 86; Mineola Music Prnts Undrclssmn Schlrshp 86; Phy Ed.

D ALESSANDRO, CARL; Farmingdale HS; Farmingdale, NY; (Y); Computer Clb; Socr; Elec.

D AMELIA, KIM T; Holy Trinity HS; Hicksville, NY; (S); Var Gym; Capt JV Sftbl; High Hon Roll; Hon Roll.

D AMELIO, MICHELLE; St Marys Girls HS; Port Washington, NY; (Y); 12/180; Spanish Clb; Teachers Aide; Chorus; High Hon Roll; Jr NHS; NHS; NY U; Frgn Lang.

D AMELIO, ROSANNA; St Joseph HS; Brooklyn, NY; (S); 2/109; Yrbk Bus Mgr; Yrbk Stf; Cit Awd; High Hon Roll; Trs NHS; Sal; Polc Athltc Leag Awd 85; Natl Eng Merit Awd 85; Acadmc All Am 85; Hunter College; Poltc Sci.

D AMICO, KURT A; Paul V Moore HS; Central Square, NY; (Y); 2/200; Am Leg Boys St; Math Tm; Ski Clb; Yrbk Stf; Var L Bsktbl; Var L Tennis; High Hon Roll; NHS; JR Achvt Awd 85-86; Defnsve Awds For Bsktbll 85-86; Rebndng Trophy 85-86; MIT; Elec Engr.

D AMORE, ROBB A; Rome Free Acad; Rome, NY; (Y); 40/610; Am Leg Boys St; Intnl Clb; Rep Stu Cncl; Var Bsbl; Capt Var Ftbl; DAR Awd; Pres Jr NHS; NHS; Opt Clb Awd.

D ANDREA, JONAS J; Saratoga HS; Greenfield Center, NY; (Y); 15/480; Am Leg Boys St; Math Tm; Var L Lcrss; Var L Wrstlng; High Hon Roll; NHS; Ntl Merit SF; AF Acad; Physcs.

D ANGELO, JENNIFER; School Of The Holy Child; Pelham, NY; (Y); Drama Clb; Hosp Aide; Model UN; Service Clb; Nwsp Rptr; Yrbk Phtg; Fld Hcky; NSEC Acad All Americn Schlr 84; NY ST Math League Finalst 85; Theatre Arts.

D ANGELO, JOHN K; North Babylon SR HS; No Babylon, NY; (Y); 23/273; French Clb; Intnl Clb; Mathletes; Varsity Clb; Chorus; Var Ftbl; Im L Gym; Im Trk; Im JV Wrstlng; French Hon Soc; Ntl JR Hnr Soc Pres 84; Math.

D ANTONI, GUY; Monsignor Farrell HS; Staten Island, NY; (Y); Cmnty Wkr; Band; Lit Mag; Im Capt Bowling; Im Ftbl; Merit Cert Natl Frnch Cntst 84 & 85; Coach Of Ltl Lge Bsbl Tm 84 & 85; Med.

D ANTONIO, ROBERT; Foxlane HS; Bedford Hills, NY; (Y); 48/277; Boys Clb Am; Spanish Clb; JV Bsbl; Socr; High Hon Roll; Hon Roll; Sprtsmn Awd Soccer 85-86; Dplma Merit Spnsh 84-86.

D ANTONIO, VALERIE J; Liverpool HS; Liverpool, NY; (Y); 18/824; Ski Clb; Stage Crew; Variety Show; Rep Stu Cncl; Crs Cntry; Swmmng; Trk; Hon Roll; NHS; Pres Schlr; Regents Scholar 86-87; Ger II Awd 83; Ger III Awd 84; Penn ST U; Pre-Med.

D AQUISTO, LISSA; West Hampton Beach HS; East Quogue, NY; (Y); 71/209; FBLA; Hosp Aide; Office Aide; VICA; Drill Tm; Stat Bsbl; Score Keeper; Rgnts Schlrshp 85-86.

D ARBANVILLE, STEPHANIE A; Notre Dame Academy HS; Staten Island, NY; (Y); Church Yth Grp; Chorus; School Musical; Stage Crew; Nwsp Stf; Yrbk Stf; Ed Lit Mag; NY St Rgnts Schlrshp 86; St Johns U; Teacher.

D ARCANGELIS, KELLY; Dodgeville Central HS; Salisbury Ctr, NY; (S); 4/70; Pres German Clb; Band; Yrbk Stf; VP Soph Cls; VP Stu Cncl; Cheerleading; Socr; Sftbl; Hon Roll; Jr NHS; Sccr All Star Tm 85-86; Phys Educ.

D ARPINO, CARLA; St Marys Girls HS; Roslyn Heights, NY; (Y); 30/170; Church Yth Grp; Cmnty Wkr; Hosp Aide; Chorus; Sec Soph Cls; Sftbl; JV Capt Vllybl; Hon Roll; NHS; Fnlst In Miss Ntl Tngr 84; Wnr Spch Cmpt N Miss Ntl Tngr Pgnt 84; Adlphi U; Nrsg.

D ARRIGO, ELIZABETH; Williamsville East HS; Williamsvl, NY; (Y); AFS; Drama Clb; Latin Clb; Yrbk Stf; Powder Puff Ftbl; High Hon Roll; Hon Roll; U Buffalo; Arch.

D AVERSA, MIKE; East Meadow HS; East Meadow, NY; (Y); 85/340; JV Bsbl; JV Var Ftbl; Rgnts Schlrshp 86; Hofstra U; Bus.

D ELIA, GIAN; Archbishop Molloy HS; Glendale, NY; (Y).

D ELIA, ROBERT; St Francis Prep; Flushing, NY; (S); Pep Clb; JV Trk; Opt Clb Awd; Trk Lttr & Mdls 82-83; Brooklyn Poly Tech; Elec Engr.

D ESPOSITO, FRAN J; Preston HS; Bronx, NY; (Y); 29/106; High Hon Roll; Hon Roll; Jr NHS; NHS; Berkeley Schl Manhattn; Med Sec.

D ESPOSITO, MARY LOU; Preston HS; Bronx, NY; (Y); 32/106; Yrbk Stf; Trs Sr Cls; High Hon Roll; Hon Roll; Berkeley Schl; Legal Sec.

D ISABEL, DEBORAH L; Niskayuna HS; Schenectady, NY; (Y); AFS; French Clb; Orch; Symp Band; French Hon Soc; High Hon Roll; Hon Roll; NCTE Awd; NHS; Ntl Merit Ltr; Hnbl Mntn Amer Assoc Tchrs Frnch; Boston Coll.

D ONOFRIO, TONIANN; Pelham Memorial HS; Pelham Manor, NY; (Y); Cmnty Wkr; Yrbk Stf; VP Frsh Cls; VP Soph Cls; Pres Jr Cls; Var Capt Cheerleading; Hon Roll; NHS; Teachers Aide; Rep Stu Cncl; Tarah Lentner Awd 86; Peer Cnslng 85-86; Bus.

D SOUZA, KIM; Arlington HS; La Grangeville, NY; (Y); 27/566; Chess Clb; Pres 4-H; Ntl Merit Ltr; Cornell U.

D URSO, ROSANNA; Sacred Heart Acad; New Hyde Park, NY; (Y); Church Yth Grp; Cmnty Wkr; SADD; Stage Crew; Nwsp Sprt Ed; Yrbk Phtg; Lit Mag; Rep Stu Cncl; Socr; JV Var Sftbl; Sccr All Stars Most Outstndng; Sprtsmnshp Awd; Bus.

D URSO, TINA; Sacred Heart Acad; East Williston, NY; (S); #4 In Class; Church Yth Grp; FNA; Hosp Aide; Math Clb; Math Tm; Tennis; High Hon Roll; NHS; Pediatrcs.

DA SILVA, MARIA FERNANDA; West Babylon HS; W Babylon, NY; (Y); High Hon Roll; Hon Roll; Jr NHS; NHS; Frnch Embssy Awd 86; PTA Schlrshp Awd 86; SUNY Stony Brook; Physcl Thrpy.

DABNEY, HUGH; Elmira Southside HS; Elmira, NY; (Y); 5/319; French Clb; Spanish Clb; Varsity Clb; JV Var Ftbl; Trk; High Hon Roll; NHS; Rotary Awd; Thomas Hurley Mem Awd 86; Regents Schlrshp 86; Alfred U; Engr.

DABROWSKI, CHRISTINA H; St Francis Prep; Flushing, NY; (Y); 240/690; Church Yth Grp; Civic Clb; Cmnty Wkr; Intnl Clb; Stage Crew; Variety Show; Bsktbl; Vllybl; NYS Regents Nrsng Schlrshp 86; St Johns U; Pharmacy.

DABROWSKI, RONALD; Kenmore East SR HS; Tonawanda, NY; (Y); Computer Clb; German Clb; Math Clb; Scholastic Bowl; Stu Cncl; High Hon Roll; Hon Roll; NHS; Mrchg Band; School Musical; Hgh Obrn Yth Ldrshp Awd 84-85; 1st Pl U Of WI Ntl Comp Cntst 84-86; Wstrn NY Amer Yth All Str 85-86; Engrng.

DABY, DONNA; Lake Placid Central Schl; Lake Placid, NY; (Y); 8/43; AFS; Church Yth Grp; GAA; Library Aide; Varsity Clb; Chorus; Yrbk Bus Mgr; Yrbk Stf; Capt Crs Cntry; Trk; Grand Schlrshp 86; Jean Corneau Schlrshp 86; Ed Schlrshp 86; D Yaiville; Elem Ed.

DABY, JENNIFER; Ticonderoga HS; Ticonderoga, NY; (Y); 9/100; Drama Clb; Sec Key Clb; Varsity Clb; Pres Band; Chorus; Color Guard; Concert Band; Mrchg Band; School Musical; Yrbk Stf; Stephen J Potter Ed Awd 86; Mary Keogh Paniccia Mem Prz 86; Bus Profssnl Womens Clb Prz 86; Cntrl City Bus Inst; Ex Sec.

DADD, TISHA; Attica Central HS; Attica, NY; (Y); AFS; Political Wkr; Nwsp Ed-Chief; VP Stu Cncl; Var Bsktbl; Var Tennis; Teenage Rpblcn Schl Of Politics TAR 82-83; Natl Rpblcn Cnvntn In Dallas 84; Pltcl Sci.

DADDABBO, NICK; Auburn HS; Auburn, NY; (Y); 125/450; Drama Clb; Chorus; School Musical; School Play; Stage Crew; JV Bsbl; JV Coach Actv; JV Ftbl; JV Sftbl; High Hon Roll; Gvrnrs Accmdtn Prfrmnc Mrtn Lthr Kng Clbrtn 86; Physcl Educ.

DADDESA, LISA A; Tottenville HS; Staten Island, NY; (Y); 31/871; Church Yth Grp; Debate Tm; Teachers Aide; Color Guard; Mrchg Band; School Musical; Variety Show; Yrbk Stf; NHS; High Hon Roll; Rgnts Schlrshp 86; Cert Of Merit Borourde Sci Fair 84; U Of Rochester.

DADDIS, BRIAN; Deposit Central HS; Deposit, NY; (Y); Cmnty Wkr; Band; Jazz Band; Mrchg Band; Pep Band; Var L Ftbl; Archeolgy.

DADY, JOELLA; Little Falls JR SR HS; Little Falls, NY; (Y); 2/103; VP GAA; Nwsp Ed-Chief; Sec Sr Cls; Var Capt Bsktbl; Var Capt Fld Hcky; Var Capt Sftbl; Elks Awd; High Hon Roll; Trs NHS; Sal; NYS Rgnts Schlrshp 85-86; U Of Rochester; Optcl Engr.

DAGAMA, ANA S; Notre Dame HS; New York City, NY; (Y); Cmnty Wkr; Drama Clb; Chorus; School Play; Sftbl; Regents Schlrshp; Law.

DAGNINO, VICKI; Herbert H Lehman HS; Bronx, NY; (Y); Art Clb; Dance Clb; Hosp Aide; Office Aide; Chorus; School Musical; Engl Awd, Social Awd 84 & 85; Nrsng.

DAHL, JULIE; Frontier Central HS; Lake View, NY; (Y); 20/500; Am Leg Aux Girls St; French Clb; Ski Clb; Nwsp Ed-Chief; Hon Roll; Pres NHS; Nwsp Rptr; Nwsp Stf; Frnch.

DAHL, KIM; John H Glenn HS; E Northport, NY; (Y); Church Yth Grp; Spanish Clb; School Play; Nwsp Stf; Sec Bowling; Sftbl; Hon Roll; Jr NHS; NHS; Spanish NHS; RIT; Comp Sci.

DAHL, SHEREE; Bonanza HS; Las Vegas, NV; (Y); 57/551; Church Yth Grp; Debate Tm; Key Clb; NFL; Ski Clb; Speech Tm; Teachers Aide; Thesps; School Play; Hon Roll; 1st Rnr-Up NV Miss TEEN 84; Cmmrcl Pilot.

DAHL, THERESA; Dominican Commercial HS; Brooklyn, NY; (S); 12/288; Church Yth Grp; Cmnty Wkr; GAA; Political Wkr; JV Var Bsktbl; Swmmng; Wt Lftg; High Hon Roll; Jr NHS; NHS; Prncpls List 83-86; Siena Clb 83-86; Natl Hnr Soc 86-87; St Johns U; Sci.

DAHN, MICHELE; Rome Free Acad; Rome, NY; (Y); Intnl Clb; Chorus; Var L Bsktbl; Hon Roll; Jr NHS; Specl Ed.

DAI, CHARLES; Susan E Wagner HS; Staten Island, NY; (Y); Am Leg Boys St; Var Ftbl; JV Ice Hcky; JV Trk; Var Wt Lftg; Var Wrstlng; Hon Roll; Naval Aviator.

DAIGLE, BRAD; Catholic Central HS; Clifton Pk, NY; (Y); School Musical; Yrbk Stf; Var Capt Socr; Var L Trk; Hon Roll; NHS; Church Yth Grp; French Clb; Math Clb; Mcgill U; Engl.

DAIKUHARA, NOZOMI; Blind Brook HS; Rye Brook, NY; (Y); AFS; Band; Concert Band; Jazz Band; School Musical.

DAILEY, CRAIG; East Syrcause-Minoa HS; E Syracuse, NY; (Y); Cmnty Wkr; Drama Clb; JA; Ski Clb; Chorus; School Musical; School Play; Stage Crew; Swing Chorus; Var Tennis; Syracuse U; Arch.

DAILEY, ELIZABETH T; Skaneateles HS; Skaneateles, NY; (S); Church Yth Grp; French Clb; Model UN; VP Soph Cls; Rep Stu Cncl; Var Golf; Var Trk; High Hon Roll; Hon Roll; NHS.

DAILEY, KIMBERLEY; Uniondale HS; Uniondale, NY; (Y); VP Frsh Cls; Hon Roll; Law.

DAILEY, MARY; Jamestown HS; Jamestown, NY; (Y); Church Yth Grp; French Clb; Intnl Clb; Pep Clb; Ski Clb; Stu Cncl; DAR Awd; High Hon Roll; Hon Roll; NHS; Engrng.

DAILEY, PATRICK; Glen Cove HS; Glen Cove, NY; (Y); 25/250; Computer Clb; Nwsp Rptr; Nwsp Stf; High Hon Roll; Hon Roll; NCTE Awd; Ntl Merit Ltr; Bst Wrtr Achvt Awd 86; Bst Spnsh III Stu Awd 86.

DAKE, RENEE C; Saratoga Springs SR HS; Saratoga Springs, NY; (Y); 30/492; Dance Clb; Sec Key Clb; SADD; Varsity Clb; Y-Teens; VP Rep Stu Cncl; L Tennis; High Hon Roll; Ntl Merit Schol; Cmnty Wkr; YMCA Youth & Govt 83-86; Cornell U; Mech Engr.

DAL FIUME, LUKE R; Tioga Central HS; Nichols, NY; (Y); 5/96; Church Yth Grp; Cmnty Wkr; Computer Clb; Debate Tm; Scholastic Bowl; SADD; Variety Show; Nwsp Stf; Off Frsh Cls; Off Soph Cls; Ltr Cmmndtn Ntl Merit Schlrshp Fndtn 86; Rgnt Schlrshp; IN U Bloomigton; Exploratory.

DALAL, RAGINI; Brighton HS; Rochester, NY; (Y); 65/315; Ski Clb; Pres Spanish Clb; Nwsp Stf; Yrbk Stf; Var Fld Hcky; Spanish NHS; Margaret Wojnowski Crump Awd Exclnc Spnsh 86; Colgate U; Lbrl Arts.

DALE, ANTHONY; Arlington HS; Poughkeepsie, NY; (Y); Boy Scts; Drama Clb; Key Clb; Latin Clb; Chorus; School Musical; School Play; Variety Show; Bsbl; Psych.

DALEO, ROY; Westhampton Beach HS; Mastic, NY; (Y); 6/243; Civic Clb; Drama Clb; FBLA; JA; SADD; School Play; Nwsp Bus Mgr; Yrbk Bus Mgr; Yrbk Phtg; Yrbk Stf; Achvmnt In Scl Stud 84-85, Engl 84; All Around Stu 84; Brown; Law.

DALESSIO, JEFF; Westhill HS; Syracuse, NY; (Y); 30/130; Boys Clb Am; Exploring; Spanish Clb; Nwsp Sprt Ed; Nwsp Stf; JV Bsbl; JV Bsktbl; Score Keeper; High Hon Roll; Hon Roll; Sports Jrnlsm.

DALEY, AMANDA; Linton HS; Schenectady, NY; (Y); Drama Clb; Intnl Clb; Key Clb; Chorus; Off Jr Cls; JV Var Cheerleading; JV Var Pom Pon; Empire St Winter Games Silver Mdl 84; Amer All-Star Chrldng Awd 85; Pittsfield Figure Skating Comp 86; Sprts Psych.

DALEY, DESRENE; De Witt Clinton HS; Bronx, NY; (Y); Church Yth Grp; Hosp Aide; Key Clb; Church Choir; Sec Stu Cncl; JV Trk; Var Vllybl; Prfct Atten Awd; Med.

DALEY, DONNA; Uniondale HS; Uniondale, NY; (Y); French Clb; Girl Scts; Hosp Aide; Band; Concert Band; Mrchg Band; Symp Band; Columbia U; Pre Med.

DALEY, JEANNE M; Ichabod Crane HS; Valatie, NY; (Y); 3/182; Debate Tm; Drama Clb; Ski Clb; SADD; Yrbk Stf; Var Trk; High Hon Roll; NHS; Pres Schlr; French Clb; Intl Rela.

DALFIUME, LUKE; Tioga Central HS; Nichols, NY; (S); 5/96; Church Yth Grp; Ski Clb; SADD; Stage Crew; Variety Show; Pres Frsh Cls; Pres Soph Cls; JV Bsbl; JV Bsktbl; High Hon Roll; IN U.

DALL, MARC S; Warsaw Central Schl; Warsaw, NY; (Y); 14/92; French Clb; Spanish Clb; Varsity Clb; JV Var Bsbl; JV Var Bsktbl; JV Var Socr; Hon Roll; NYS Regents Schlrshp 86; SUNY-GENESEO; Bus Mgmt.

DALLAS, KEITH; W C Mepham HS; N Bellmore, NY; (Y); Church Yth Grp; JV Crs Cntry; Trk; NHS; Ntl Sci Olympd Chem 86; Cornell U; Chem.

DALLOLIO, THOMAS; East Meadow HS; E Meadow, NY; (Y); Nassau Cmnty Coll; Poltcl Sci.

DALMAZIO, JENNIFER; St Edmunds HS; Brooklyn, NY; (Y); Dance Clb; Chorus; School Play; Stage Crew; Nwsp Stf; Yrbk Rptr; Yrbk Stf; Lit Mag; St Johns U; Bus Admin.

DALPHINIS, DELTINA; Graphic Communications Arts; Brooklyn, NY; (Y); Church Yth Grp; Natl Beta Clb; Columbia; Jrnlsm.

DALTON, MAJITA; Park West HS; New York, NY; (Y); Church Yth Grp; Girl Scts; Hosp Aide; Library Aide; Variety Show; Elks Awd; Hon Roll; Pace; Travel.

DALTON, SEAN; Msgr Farrell HS; Staten Island, NY; (Y); Im Bsktbl; Im Bowling; JV Im Ftbl; JV Wrstlng; Pre-Med.

DALY, BERNADETTE; Martin Van Buren HS; Floral Pk, NY; (Y); 78/506; Girl Scts; JA; Service Clb; School Play; Hon Roll; Haney Medal For Art 86; Humanities & Hnrs Prog 83-86; Artist.

DALY, BRIAN E; La Salle Acad; New York, NY; (S); 6/38; JV Var Bsktbl; Crs Cntry; Hon Roll; Jr NHS.

DALY, CHRISTINE C; Tappan Zee HS; Sparkill, NY; (Y); 32/245; SADD; Ed Yrbk Stf; Trs Rep Soph Cls; Rep Stu Cncl; Hon Roll; Trk; NY ST Rgnts Schlrshp 86; Loyola Coll Pres Schlrshp 86; James Madison U; Fin.

DALY, DANTE; Bishop Grimes HS; Baldwinville, NY; (Y); JA; Math Clb; Orch; Sec Stu Cncl; Socr; Tennis; High Hon Roll; Hon Roll; Jr NHS; Amanda Sugar Awd 84; Pre-Law.

DALY, EILEEN; Cicero-North Syracuse HS; Clay, NY; (S); 15/627; Church Yth Grp; German Clb; Hosp Aide; Yrbk Ed-Chief; Yrbk Phtg; Yrbk Rptr; L Var Tennis; Hon Roll; Sci.

DALY, EILEEN MARY; Floral Park Memorial HS; Floral Park, NY; (Y); 21/150; Cmnty Wkr; Pres 4-H; FBLA; Mathletes; Political Wkr; Band; Chorus; Church Choir; Concert Band; VP Mrchg Band; NY ST Home Mgmt Wnnr 85; Estrn Dist Home Ec Conf 85; All Dist Music Fest 83-86; Elem Educ.

DALY, KELLY J; Cheektowaga Central HS; Cheektowaga, NY; (Y); 9/199; JCL; Trs Latin Clb; Trs Chorus; Capt Color Guard; Capt Flag Corp; School Musical; Rep Stu Cncl; Var Cheerleading; Jr NHS; NHS; NY ST Regents Schlrshp; Brckprt Alumni Schlrshp; SUNY-BROCKPORT.

DALY, SHARON; Frontier SR HS; Hamburg, NY; (Y); 4-H; FBLA; ROTC; Swmmng; 4-H Awd; Hon Roll; NHS; Math & Sci.

DALY, SHAWN; Union Springs Central Schl; Auburn, NY; (Y); Yrbk Sprt Ed; Yrbk Stf; Sec Frsh Cls; Var L Bsbl; JV Bsktbl; Var JV Ftbl; IAC Hnrb Mntn-Vrsty Ftbl 85; Mst Imprvd Vrsty Bsbl 86; Bus Adm.

DALY, SUSAN; North Babylon SR HS; N Babylon, NY; (Y); 28/451; JV Bsktbl; Var Fld Hcky; Var Vllybl; High Hon Roll; NHS; All-Lg Hnrbl Mntn Vllybll 86; Capt & MVP JV Vllybll 85; Capt & MVP JV Fld Hcky 84; Mrktg.

DALY, SUSAN; Smithtown High School East; Smithtown, NY; (Y); DECA; Hosp Aide; Stage Crew; Badmtn.

DAMASK, JAY N; Bellport HS; Bellport, NY; (Y); 16/270; Computer Clb; Math Tm; Concert Band; Jazz Band; Mrchg Band; Pep Band; Variety Show; High Hon Roll; NHS; Ntl Merit Ltr; MIT; Elec Engrng.

DAMATO, ANGELA; Newtown HS; Elmhurst, NY; (Y); 37/781; Key Clb; Math Tm; Band; Jazz Band; School Play; Nwsp Stf; Yrbk Stf; Hon Roll; Prfct Atten Awd; Church Yth Grp; Arista Awd 85; Oritorical Awd 84; Hunter Coll; Comm.

DAMATO, DIANA H; Arlington HS; Pleasant Valley, NY; (Y); 92/576; Intnl Clb; Concert Band; Orch; Hon Roll; Virtuoso Prgrss W/Hudson Vly Philhrmnc Orch 84; NY ST Schl Music Assn-Conf Al-ST Band 85; Mercy Coll; Librl Arts.

DAMERAU, ELAINE M; North Salem HS; Purdys, NY; (Y); 21/94; Pres Sec Drama Clb; School Musical; School Play; Variety Show; Yrbk Stf; NHS; Church Yth Grp; Chorus; Madrigals; High Hon Roll; NYSSA Cert Of Merit/Schl Of Visual Arts 85; Theater.

DAMICO, JEFF; Clarence Central SR HS; Williamsville, NY; (Y); 34/250; Latin Clb; Ski Clb; Varsity Clb; Yrbk Sprt Ed; Rep Sr Cls; JV Var Bsbl; JV Var Bsktbl; JV Var Ftbl; Capt Powder Puff Ftbl; Im Wt Lftg; Pdtrcs.

DAMKOHLER, LISA; St Francis Prep; Whitestone, NY; (S); 141/744; SADD; Sftbl; Optimate Soc.

DAMMEIR, PEGGY; New Paltz HS; New Paltz, NY; (Y); 90/187; Spanish Clb; Chorus; Var Fld Hcky; Var Capt Gym; Suny Brockport; Liberal Arts.

DAMMERT, JOE; Edison HS; Rochester, NY; (Y); Tool & Die Mkr.

DAMON, CHERYL; Panama Central HS; Panama, NY; (Y); 21/66; Aud/Vis; Church Yth Grp; Cmnty Wkr; Drama Clb; 4-H; Letterman Clb; Office Aide; Pep Clb; Red Cross Aide; Spanish Clb; 4-H Exhbtng Hrs Awd 84; Lab Tech.

DAMON, ELLEN J; Dunkirk HS; Dunkirk, NY; (Y); 18/293; Church Yth Grp; German Clb; Library Aide; Lit Mag; NHS; Ntl Merit Ltr; Pres Hon Schlrshp Ednboro U 86; Rgnts Schlrshp 86; Jhn L Kreider Schlrshp 86; Edinboro U PA; Bio.

DAMONE, SCOTT R; Ward Melville HS; E Setauket, NY; (Y); 320/711; Variety Show; Bsktbl; Capt Ice Hcky; JV Lcrss; Rgnts Schlrshp 86; Cert Of Merit For Aprctn Of Work W/Cmnty Yth Srvs 85; Iona Coll; Mrktng.

DANA, DEBORAH L; Ogdensburg Free Acad; Ogdensburg, NY; (Y); 60/180; Band; Var Capt Bsktbl; JV Crs Cntry; JV Socr; Var L Sftbl; Im Vllybl; Acad Banquet 83; NYS Regents Schlrshp Nrsng 86; Suny Plattsburgh; Nrsng.

DANA, MICHAEL; Bishop Ludden HS; Liverpool, NY; (Y); Am Leg Boys St; Pres Frsh Cls; Var L Bsbl; Var L Ftbl; Var L Lcrss; Hon Roll; NYS Regnts Schlrshp 86; Hubert Coll; Pre-Med.

DANAHY, JENNIFER; Mt Mercy Acad; Buffalo, NY; (Y); Girl Scts; SADD; Trk; Hon Roll; Socl Wrk.

DANBOISE, ROXANE; George W Fowler HS; Syracise, NY; (Y); Dance Clb; Drama Clb; School Musical; School Play; Stage Crew; Variety Show; Nwsp Phtg; Nwsp Rptr; Nwsp Stf; Socr; Athltc Awds Scr & Sftbl 85-86; Acdmc Awds Rgnts, Chem, Photo & Englsh II 85-86; SUNY Oswego; Brdcst Jrnlsm.

DANCA, GERIANNE; Sacred Heart Acad; Long Beach, NY; (S); 11/186; Church Yth Grp; Math Clb; Math Tm; Pep Clb; SADD; School Play; Stage Crew; Hon Roll; NHS; St Johns U Compttv Schlrshp 85; Acad All Amer 85; Natl Hnr Roll 85; Bus.

DANDREA, LISA; Sachem HS; Farmingville, NY; (Y); 76/1385; FHA; Hosp Aide; Spanish Clb; Color Guard; Lit Mag; Frsh Cls; Sr Cls; Stu Cncl; Jr NHS; NHS; Svc Awd Stu Gvt 85; Sci Cngrss Hnrbl Mntn 84; Mdaille Schlrshp 86; St Josephs Coll; Spec Educ.

DANDREA, MARY LYNN; Nazareth Acad; Rochester, NY; (Y); 3/135; Church Yth Grp; VP Latin Clb; Library Aide; Math Tm; Pres VP Concert Band; Jazz Band; Stage Crew; Yrbk Stf; Hon Roll; NHS; Magna Cum Laude Ntl Latn Exm 83; Silvr Mdl JETS Tms Comptn 86.

DANDREA, PAYTON; Thomas A Edison HS; Elmira, NY; (Y); Church Yth Grp; Cmnty Wkr; Drama Clb; English Clb; JA; Office Aide; Red Cross Aide; School Play; Nwsp Ed-Chief; Nwsp Rptr; Frances B Watts Crtve Wrtng Awd 86; Regents Schlrshp 86; Corning CC; Humn Serv.

DANG, ANH STEVE; Williamsville South HS; Williamsville, NY; (Y); French Clb; Pep Clb; Concert Band; Yrbk Phtg; Bsbl; Bsktbl; Hon Roll; Natl Hnr Rll; George Washington U; Sci.

DANGELO, JANET; Moore Catholic HS; Staten Island, NY; (Y); VP Frsh Cls; Pres Soph Cls; Pres Jr Cls; Rep Stu Cncl; High Hon Roll; Hon Roll; Cmnty Wkr; Nwsp Ed-Chief; Nwsp Stf; NHS; Moore Cthlc Sci Fair Bsdt Prjct 86; Fleet Rsrv Assoc Awd 85; Staten Is Sci Fair Hnrbl Mntn 86; Sec Ed.

DANGLADE, RHEINHOLD; Prospect Heights HS; Brooklyn, NY; (Y); 69/271; Teachers Aide; Trk; Wt Lftg; Hon Roll; Bus.

DANIEL, DEBRA; Midwood HS; Brooklyn, NY; (Y); Cmnty Wkr; Model UN; Chorus; Orch; School Musical; NHS; Pre-Med.

DANIEL, MICHAEL J; Irondequoit HS; Rochester, NY; (Y); 8/350; Math Clb; Ski Clb; High Hon Roll; Ntl Merit Ltr; Cornell U.

DANIELE, STACY; Blessed Sacrament-St Gabriel HS; New Rochelle, NY; (Y); Teachers Aide; Yrbk Stf; Sec Jr Cls; Rep Sr Cls; Stu Cncl; Cit Awd; High Hon Roll; Hon Roll; NHS; Jeffrey & David Sutton Mem Schlrshp; Spectmur Agndo Awd-Schl Spirit 86; Ctznshp Awd-Westchester 86; Coll Of Mt St Vincent; Nrsng.

DANIELLO, MICHELE; St Francis Prep; Howard Bch, NY; (Y); Dance Clb; Stage Crew; St Johns U; Bus.

DANIELS, BEVERLY; A Phillip Randolph Campus HS; New York, NY; (Y); 34/166; Cmnty Wkr; Library Aide; Hon Roll; Prtcptn Meck Cngrs Brooklyn Coll 85; Howard U; Bus.

DANIELS, JOHN; Mount St Michael Acad; New York, NY; (Y); Im Bsktbl; Im Ftbl; Im Ice Hcky; Im Sftbl; Hon Roll; Sci.

DANIELS, NEVA; Coxsackie-Athens Central HS; West Coxsackie, NY; (Y); 22/109; Church Yth Grp; Computer Clb; Girl Scts; Spanish Clb; Chorus; Rep Frsh Cls; Rep Soph Cls; Rep Jr Cls; Rep Stu Cncl; High Hon Roll; Comp Engrng.

DANILOWICZ, BRET; Whitesboro SR HS; Whitesboro, NY; (Y); Exploring; Stu Cncl; Cit Awd; High Hon Roll; NHS; Ntl Merit SF; Pres Schlr; Boy Scts; Science Clb; Ski Clb; Amer Cntrct Bridge Lge Josephs Trphy 83; Prsdntl Acdmc Ftns Awd 86; Rgnts Schlrshp 86; Utica Coll; Marine Biolgst.

DANK, AMELIA T; Mattituck HS; Cutchogue, NY; (Y); 37/112; Art Clb; Church Yth Grp; French Clb; Church Choir; School Play; Stage Crew; Nwsp Rptr; Yrbk Stf; Score Keeper; Vllybl; Frnch Awd Outstndng Stu 84-85; Art Hnr Soc 84-85; Pre-Law.

DANN, ERIC; Fairport HS; Fairport, NY; (Y); Trs French Clb; Math Tm; Model UN; Concert Band; Jazz Band; Orch; Rep Stu Cncl; Bausch & Lomb Sci Awd; NHS; Ntl Merit Ltr; Biolgy.

DANN, MICHAEL P; Liverpool HS; Liverpool, NY; (Y); VP JA; Band; Concert Band; Jazz Band; School Musical; Nwsp Rptr; Nwsp Stf; Trs Stu Cncl; Trk; Hon Roll; 1st Seal All Cnty Cncrt Jzz Bnds; 1st Seat All ST Bnd; Rgnts Schlrshp; Potsdam Coll; Msc Educ.

DANNELS, COLLEEN; Grand Island HS; Grand Isl, NY; (Y); VP Pres Art Clb; Church Yth Grp; Hst Drama Clb; Mathletes; Concert Band; School Musical; Stage Crew; High Hon Roll; Hon Roll; NHS; AATG PAD German Trvl Study Awd 87.

DANNENBERG, CAROL; Charlotte HS; Rochester, NY; (Y); #1 In Class; Church Yth Grp; Exploring; Girl Scts; Model UN; Bausch & Lomb Sci Awd; High Hon Roll; NHS; Val; Elmira Key Awd 86; Harvard Bk Awd 86; Notre Dame JR Of Yr; Med Mcrblgst.

DANNENBERG, LISA; Riverhead HS; Aquebogue, NY; (Y); 16/211; Cmnty Wkr; JCL; Pres Key Clb; Latin Clb; Science Clb; Chorus; NHS; Parents/Alumni/Friends Wrtg & Svc Awds 85 & 86; 3rd Pl Mth Awd 84; 2 Lat Cum Laude Awds 84; U FL; Eng.

DANNI, TRACI; Williamsville South HS; Williamsville, NY; (Y); Sec French Clb; Pep Clb; Acpl Chr; School Play; Var Swmmng; NCTE Awd; Awd Hrdst Wrkr On Swim Tm 85-86; Engnrng.

DANO, PAUL; Henninger HS; Syracuse, NY; (Y); Boy Scts; Exploring; Ski Clb; Off Jr Cls; Var Ftbl; Capt Lcrss; JV Socr; Hon Roll; Indust Arts Awd 86; ESF Syracuse; Forstry.

DANOSKI, JEFFREY R; Chenango Valley JR SR HS; Binghamton, NY; (Y); 86/100; Am Leg Boys St; Stu Cncl; Bsbl; Bsktbl; Ftbl; Trk; Wt Lftg; Hon Roll; Jr NHS; All Stac Div III 4x100 Meter Rely Tm 86; Law Enforcement.

DANTONIO, CHRISTINE; Hicksville HS; Hicksville, NY; (Y); Drama Clb; Chorus; Variety Show; Lit Mag; Hon Roll; Jr NHS; NHS; Itln Hnr Soc 86; Law.

DANTONIO, MARK; Fox Lane HS; Bedford Hills, NY; (Y); 68/277; Boys Clb Am; Var Bsbl; Var Socr; Hon Roll; Spnsh Dipl Merit 84-85; Bus Mgmt.

DANTUONO, BETH; Liverpool HS; Liverpool, NY; (S); DECA; JA; Spanish Clb; DECA 1st Pl NYS Phillips Free Entrprs Proj 86; DECA Hnbl Mntn Regl Comptn 86; Fshn Merch.

DANZIG, FARA; Glen Cove HS; Glen Cove, NY; (Y); French Clb; Key Clb; Temple Yth Grp; School Musical; Stage Crew; High Hon Roll; Hon Roll; 3rd In Class 84-85; Law.

DAO, LINH T; Norman Thomas HS; New York, NY; (S); 45/597; Pres FBLA; VP JA; Im Vllybl; Hon Roll; 1st Pl Ping Pong 84; Future Bus Ldrs Of Amer 1st & 3rd Pl 86; Triple Cs Awd 83; Penn ST; Bus Mngmnt.

DARCY, ALICIA M; John F Kennedy HS; Yorktown Hts, NY; (Y); Chess Clb; Band; Chorus; Church Choir; School Musical; Yrbk Stf; NY ST Rgnts Schlrshp 86; Le Moyne; Bio.

DARDE, CLAUDIA; John Dewey HS; Brooklyn, NY; (Y); French Clb; Intnl Clb; Band; Concert Band; School Musical; Nwsp Ed-Chief; Nwsp Rptr; Nwsp Stf; Lit Mag; Congrss Bundestg Atltrnt 85-86; Lang.

DARDEN, GAIL; Hempstead HS; Hempstead, NY; (S); 12/235; Am Leg Aux Girls St; Church Yth Grp; Dance Clb; Church Choir; School Musical; School Play; Hon Roll; Jr NHS; NHS; Ntl Merit Schol; Cert Excllnce NHS 85; Cert Merit Amer Lg Auxlry 85; Cert Partcptn Martin L King Pgm 84; Hampton U.

DARK, JULIE; John C Birdlebough HS; Phoenix, NY; (Y); 17/200; FBLA; Varsity Clb; Band; Concert Band; Socr; Vllybl; Hon Roll; Prfct Atten Awd; Bryant & Straton; Ex Secr.

DARLAK, JOSEPH R; Clarence Central HS; Clarence, NY; (Y); 6/286; Drama Clb; Concert Band; Symp Band; VP Soph Cls; Pres Jr Cls; Ftbl; Trk; Bausch & Lomb Sci Awd; High Hon Roll; NHS; USN Acad; Mech Engrng.

DARLING, DANE M; Perth Central HS; Johnstown, NY; (Y); 7/44; Am Leg Boys St; Pres Jr Cls; Bsbl; High Hon Roll; Hon Roll; NHS; Air Force; Military.

DARLING, JULIE; Sodus Central HS; Sodus, NY; (Y); 5/125; Am Leg Aux Girls St; Pres Spanish Clb; Pres Varsity Clb; Sec Jr Cls; Capt Bsktbl; Capt Crs Cntry; Capt Trk; Vllybl; NHS; Prfct Atten Awd; Regents Schrlshp Wnnr 86; Hope Coll Pres Schlrshp 86; Wayne Finger Lakes Lang Ed Schrlshp 86; Hope Coll; Lang.

DARLING, KELLY A; South Lewis HS; Brantingham, NY; (Y); GAA; SADD; Rep Stu Cncl; Var Capt Bsktbl; JV Golf; Var Socr; Var Sftbl; Var Trk; JV Vllybl; Hon Roll; NYS Rgnts Schlrshp 85-86; Rep Stu Cncl 83-86; ST U Oneonta; Math.

DARLING, MOLLY; Leroy HS; Stafford, NY; (Y); AFS; Church Yth Grp; French Clb; Capt Color Guard; Yrbk Bus Mgr; Yrbk Stf; JV Stat Bsktbl; Cit Awd; High Hon Roll; Hon Roll; Appld Art.

DARLING, NAOMI; Northville Central Schl; Northville, NY; (Y); 3/50; Computer Clb; Teachers Aide; Yrbk Stf; High Hon Roll; NHS; Ntl Merit SF; NY ST Regls Schlrshp 86; Grad Hnr Stdnt 86; Pres Acdmc Fit Awd 86; Nyack Coll; Arch Engrng.

DARROW, BRUCE J; Woodlands HS; White Plains, NY; (Y); 3/203; Capt Debate Tm; Co-Capt Math Tm; Chorus; Jazz Band; Yrbk Phtg; Crs Cntry; High Hon Roll; Ntl Merit SF; Columbia U Sci Hnrs Prog 84-85; Union Carbide Schlr WA Wrkshp Smnr 85; Hnrb Mntn Poetry Cntst 83; Bio Chem.

DARROW, RACHEL; Horseheads SR HS; Horseheads, NY; (Y); 135/374; Art Clb; Church Yth Grp; 4-H; Letterman Clb; Science Clb; Ski Clb; Varsity Clb; Band; Concert Band; Mrchg Band; St Josephs Schl Of Nrsng; RN.

DARTT, CHRISTOPHER; Hugh C Williams HS; Canton, NY; (Y); 5/147; Math Tm; Teachers Aide; Rptr Lit Mag; Trs Sr Cls; Var Socr; Var Trk; Dnfth Awd; High Hon Roll; NHS; Ntl Merit Ltr; Engrng.

DARVISHIAN, MELISSA; Williamsville South HS; Williamsville, NY; (Y); AFS; Art Clb; Drama Clb; Pep Clb; Chorus; Nwsp Phtg; Bus.

DAS, BIBHASH; Pelham Memorial HS; Pelham Manor, NY; (Y); Cmnty Wkr; Hosp Aide; Nwsp Bus Mgr; Lit Mag; Var L Socr; Var L Trk; Hon Roll; NHS; AFS; Computer Clb; Achvt Awd Pelham Guidance Cncl 85-86; Pre-Med.

DASHEFSKY, LANCE; Roslyn HS; Roslyn, NY; (Y); Chess Clb; Cmnty Wkr; Computer Clb; Office Aide; Teachers Aide; Temple Yth Grp; Rep Jr Cls; Rep Sr Cls; Rep Stu Cncl; Var JV Crs Cntry; Sci Engr Sympsm Hnry Spkr 86; Franklin & Marshall Coll.

DASKIEWICH, DARLENE J; Adirondack Central HS; Boonville, NY; (Y); 3/127; Dance Clb; Concert Band; School Musical; School Play; Sftbl; Swmmng; Vllybl; High Hon Roll; NHS; Pres Schlr; Regnts Schlrshp 86; Jeanette Talcott Ptchr Memrl Prz Hghst SR Avg 86; Harold P Seamon SR Schlrshp 86; Mohawk Vly CC; Comp Sci.

DATES, LISA E; Red Creek Central HS; Wolcott, NY; (Y); Camera Clb; Church Yth Grp; SADD; Yrbk Phtg; Yrbk Sprt Ed; Yrbk Stf; JV Var Socr; Hon Roll; French Clb; Girl Scts; Frnch Compstn Awd 85; Psyclgy.

DAUBE, KATHLEEN; Holland Patent Central HS; Marcy, NY; (Y); 5/150; Chorus; Orch; Rep Sr Cls; JV Var Cheerleading; JV Var Fld Hcky; Var L Trk; NHS; Ntl Merit Ltr; GAA; Math Tm; Rnsslr Mdl Math, Sci 85; Hugh O Brian Yth Fndtn Rep 84; All ST Choir 85; Rensselaer Polytech Inst; El En.

DAUCHER, KIM; Alden Central Schl; Alden, NY; (Y); Church Yth Grp; Letterman Clb; Varsity Clb; Yrbk Stf; Rep Frsh Cls; Rep Jr Cls; JV Var Cheerleading; Gym; JV Var Trk; Var Vllybl; Liberty U; Bus Ad.

DAUER, JULIE; Brockport HS; Brockport, NY; (Y); Pres SADD; Pres Y-Teens; Nwsp Rptr; Ed Yrbk Stf; Trs Frsh Cls; Hon Roll; YMCA Yth Yr 85; Springfield Coll; YMCA Prfssn.

DAUGHERTY JR, JAMES JOHN; Elmira Free Acad; Elmira, NY; (Y); Church Yth Grp; Cmnty Wkr; Red Cross Aide; Chorus; Bsbl; Ftbl; Hon Roll; NO SO Invtnl Clssc Trnmnt Tm Ctchrs Awd 86; Vlntr Awd Hd Strt Prgm 86; Vrsty Bsebl & Ftbl Ltrs & Mdl; Phy Ed.

DAUMEN, MICHAEL J; Canisius HS; Buffalo, NY; (Y); 10/169; Boy Scts; Chess Clb; Computer Clb; Model UN; Political Wkr; Varsity Clb; Lit Mag; Hon Roll; Ntl Merit SF; Intl Law.

DAVAN, MELISSA; Garden City HS; Garden City, NY; (Y); 40/350; Cmnty Wkr; VP Latin Clb; Ed Spanish Clb; Pres Orch; Nwsp Stf; Yrbk Phtg; Rep Stu Cncl; Capt Vllybl; NHS; Ntl Merit SF; Regents Schlrshp 86; Amer Legion Essay Cont Winner 85; Pres Acad Fitness Awd 86; Biomed Engrng.

DAVENPORT, LIEN LYNN; Lansingburgh HS; Troy, NY; (Y); High Hon Roll; Hon Roll; Ntl Merit Ltr; Mktg Hghst Schlstc Achvt 85; Cert Merit 84-85; HVCC; Wrtng.

DAVENPORT, MARYELLA; Cobleskill Central Schl; Cobleskill, NY; (Y); FFA; Science Clb; Varsity Clb; School Musical; Stu Cncl; Bsktbl; Gym; Trk; Vllybl; NHS; NY ST Regents Schlrshp 86; Cobleskill Ag & Tech; Rsrch Bio.

DAVEY JR, ROBERT; Auburn HS; Auburn, NY; (Y); 23/423; DECA; SADD; Socr; Trk; High Hon Roll; NHS; 1st Team All Conf Soccr 84; MVP Soccr 85; Clark U; Cmmnctns.

DAVEY, STEVE; Nyack HS; Nyack, NY; (Y); 8/250; Church Yth Grp; Church Choir; Bsbl; Bsktbl; Sftbl; High Hon Roll; Chem Awd Achvt 86; Bst Lkng 86; Bus.

DAVI, STEVEN; AG Berner SR HS; Massapequa, NY; (Y); 20/400; Cmnty Wkr; SADD; Symp Band; Rep Sr Cls; Var Bsktbl; Var Lcrss; Var Socr; High Hon Roll; NHS; Ntl Merit Schol.

DAVICO, CHRIS; John Jay SR HS; Goldens Ridge, NY; (Y); Cmnty Wkr; Lit Mag; Ftbl; JV Golf; Var Swmmng; Hon Roll; Stanford U; Suprm Crt Jstc.

DAVID, AMY BETH; Bishop Grimes HS; E Syracuse, NY; (Y); 44/146; Cmnty Wkr; Political Wkr; SADD; Sec Soph Cls; Crs Cntry; Trk; Vllybl; High Hon Roll; Jr USVBA 86; Brockport SUNY; Spcl Ed Psych.

DAVID, DANA; Taconic Hills HS; Hillsdale, NY; (Y); 5/114; Am Leg Aux Girls St; Church Yth Grp; 4-H; Jazz Band; VP Stu Cncl; Var Capt Cheerleading; Var Socr; Cit Awd; High Hon Roll; NHS; Tnagr Mnth 86; Tnagr Yr 86; Hnrs Schlrshp Stonehill Coll 86; Stonehill Coll; Intl Bus.

DAVID, DONALD; Lyndonville Central Schl; Lyndonville, NY; (Y); Boy Scts; Church Yth Grp; Varsity Clb; Chorus; Pres Frsh Cls; Pres Soph Cls; Pres Jr Cls; Rep Stu Cncl; Var L Bsbl; Var L Bsktbl; Stu Of Mnth 82 & 83; Phys Ed.

DAVID, GRACE; Henninger HS; Syracuse, NY; (Y); Im Cheerleading; U Of Oswego; Teacher.

DAVID, KENDALL B; Geneva HS; Geneva, NY; (S); 16/175; Church Yth Grp; Computer Clb; Drama Clb; Varsity Clb; Band; School Musical; School Play; Lcrss; Swmmng; NHS; Printing.

DAVID, LAFLEUR; Sheeps Head Bay HS; Brooklyn, NY; (Y); Band; Chorus; Ebony Clb; John Jay; Corp Lwyr.

DAVID, RAJA; Dobbs Ferry HS; Dobbs Ferry, NY; (S); VP AFS; Drama Clb; Key Clb; Band; Pres Chorus; Concert Band; Jazz Band; Mrchg Band; School Musical; Stage Crew; Instrmntl Magzn Awd 83-84; Psychlgy.

DAVIDE, CHRIS; Bay Shore HS; Bay Shore, NY; (Y); 13/430; Church Yth Grp; Orch; School Musical; Nwsp Ed-Chief; Nwsp Rptr; Lit Mag; Off Frsh Cls; Off Soph Cls; Off Jr Cls; Socr; Hrvrd Prize Bk Awd 86; Eng.

DAVIDOFF, SCOTT; H S For The Humanits; New York, NY; (Y); Chess Clb; Pres Jr Cls; Var Trk; Hon Roll; Albany ST; Law.

DAVIDSON, ANTHONY S; Bronx High School Of Science; New York, NY; (Y); NCTE Awd; NHS; Ntl Merit Ltr; St Schlr; Var L Bsbl; Im Bsktbl; Im Sftbl; Im Vllybl; Best Spkr Cmmttee Model Congress 84 & 86; Lttr Merit Concours Natl De Francais; Williamns Coll; Polt Sci.

DAVIDSON, BERNADETTE; Wallkill SR HS; Wallkill, NY; (S); 15/190; Church Yth Grp; Socr; Sftbl; Wt Lftg; High Hon Roll; Hon Roll; NHS; Intnatl Frgn Lang Awds 85-86; Sci.

DAVIDSON, CARLA; Chautauqua Central HS; Mayville, NY; (Y); 1/32; Band; JV Var Cheerleading; Var Diving; Var Sftbl; Var Swmmng; JV Var Vllybl; High Hon Roll; Jr NHS; A Pg Locl Nwsppr Poem Publ 86; WJTN Read Poem 85; Art.

DAVIDSON, CATHLEEN; Clarkstown SR High School South; New City, NY; (Y); Chorus; Var Socr; Var Trk; Vet.

DAVIDSON, CHRIS; Wheatland-Chili Central Schl; Scottsville, NY; (Y); #1 In Class; Model UN; Ski Clb; Chorus; Jazz Band; Yrbk Stf; JV Var Tennis; JV Var Vllybl; Ntl Merit Ltr; Voice Dem Awd; Church Yth Grp; Sci Hgst Avg Awd 84-86; Spnsh II,Hist Hgst Avg Awd 84-86; Evn Ed.

DAVIDSON, CRAIG; Wallkill Central HS; Walden, NY; (S); 1/200; Band; Jazz Band; VP Stu Cncl; Var L Socr; Var L Trk; High Hon Roll; NHS; Concert Band; Mrchg Band; Pep Band; Area All ST Band 85-86; Accptnc U S Navl Acad 86; Engrng.

DAVIDSON, TERRI L; Bennett HS; Buffalo, NY; (Y); 5/220; Var Sftbl; Var Vllybl; High Hon Roll; NHS; Regents Schlrshp 86; Erie CC; Bus Educ.

DAVIES, ANDREW; Fairport HS; Fairport, NY; (Y); Exploring; Latin Clb; Lit Mag; Im Bsbl; Im Lcrss; Var Wrstlng; French Hon Soc; Hon Roll; Chem.

DAVIES, ANNA; Wilson Magnet HS; Rochester, NY; (Y); Sec Church Yth Grp; Pres JA; Red Cross Aide; Ski Clb; Pres Jr Cls; Var Crs Cntry; Var Gym; High Hon Roll; NHS; Rep Frsh Cls; Red Cross Ldrshp Conf 85.

DAVIES, BRIAN F; Williamson SR HS; Williamson, NY; (Y); 1/94; AFS; Am Leg Boys St; Church Yth Grp; Ski Clb; Pres Frsh Cls; Pres Soph Cls; JV Socr; Bausch & Lomb Sci Awd; High Hon Roll; NHS; Best Of Show-Sci Fair 83; Advncd Pgm In Schl Comm 85; 1st Red Cross Ldrshp Dev Conf Wayne Co 86; Arch.

DAVIES, HEATHER; John C Birdlebough HS; Phoenix, NY; (Y); 13/197; Exploring; French Clb; Sec Stu Cncl; Var Crs Cntry; Var Capt Trk; High Hon Roll; Hon Roll; NHS; Otstndng Achvt Awd Mth 86; Cnsci Stu Awd Amer Hstry 86; Frnch Awd 85; Albany ST; Accntng.

DAVIES, JEANNINE M; Pulaskie Acad & Central HS; Pulaski, NY; (S); #10 In Class; Math Clb; VICA; Pres Frsh Cls; Trk; Vllybl; Gold Mdl Natl Schltc Awd Art 85; 1st Pl VICA Regnl Comm Art 86; RI Schl Dsgn; Grphc Art.

DAVIES, JOHN; Midlakes HS; Clifton Spgs, NY; (Y); 80/167; FCA; 4-H; Red Cross Aide; Varsity Clb; Y-Teens; Var Bsktbl; Var Capt Ftbl; Var Wrstlng; 4-H Awd; Hon Roll; U FL; Phys Ed.

DAVIES, JULIE; Frontier Central HS; Blasdell, NY; (Y); Pep Clb; Sec Spanish Clb; Chorus; School Play; Nwsp Stf; Yrbk Stf; High Hon Roll; Hon Roll; Prfct Atten Awd; St Boneventure U; Jrnlsm.

DAVIES, MONICA; Academy Of The Resurctn; White Plains, NY; (Y); Church Yth Grp; Hosp Aide; Office Aide; Chorus; Pres Jr Cls; Var Capt Cheerleading; Var JV Coach Actv; Var Tennis; Var Capt Vllybl; Hon Roll; Srv Awd St Agnes Hosp 85; Rosemont Coll; Hist.

DAVIES, PAT; E J Wilson HS; Spencerport, NY; (Y); French Clb; Letterman Clb; Varsity Clb; Var Golf; JV Socr; French Hon Soc; High Hon Roll; NHS; Pres Schlr; Mst Imprvd Var Golf; St Bonaventure; Sci.

DAVIES, PETER; Brewster HS; Brewster, NY; (Y); 3/200; Band; Jazz Band; Mrchg Band; Symp Band; Var L Bsktbl; Var L Golf; Var L Socr; High Hon Roll; VP NHS; Atnd Rtry Yth Ldrshp Cnfrnce 85; Psych.

DAVIES, TAFFY; Middletown HS; Middletown, NY; (Y); Trs Church Yth Grp; Key Clb; Scholastic Bowl; SADD; Yrbk Stf; Stu Cncl; Var Cheerleading; Jr NHS; NHS; EAGLET 86; U Of NC; Intl Rltns.

DAVIES, TODD; Fayetteville-Manlius HS; Manlius, NY; (Y); Chess Clb; 4-H; Model UN; Nwsp Rptr; Nwsp Stf; Lit Mag; Hon Roll; Ntl Merit Lr; St Schlr; Regents Schlrshp NY 86; Empire ST Schlrshp NYS 86; ST U NY Albany; Psychlgy.

DAVILA, LUIS O; Evander Childs HS; Bronx, NY; (Y); 39/383; Var Bsbl; SUNY New Paltz; Dntstry.

DAVILA, TANIA; Fontbonne Hall Acad; Brooklyn, NY; (Y); Am Leg Aux Girls St; Camera Clb; Cmnty Wkr; Hosp Aide; Library Aide; Pep Clb; SADD; Nwsp Phtg; Yrbk Ed-Chief; Yrbk Phtg; Certifcte Of Acad Hnr 85; Certifcte Of Apprctn 86; US Air Force Acad; Intnal Law.

DAVIS, ADAM; Greene Central HS; Greene, NY; (Y); 2/112; VP Frsh Cls; Rep Jr Cls; Rep Sr Cls; Im Bsktbl; High Hon Roll; Sal; Engl & Bio Key Awd; VP & 3 Yr Mbr Natl Hnr Soc; 3 Yr Mbr Stu Cncl; Cornell U; Animal Sci.

DAVIS, ANDREA R; Uniondale HS; Hempstead, NY; (Y); 3/410; Sec Mathletes; SADD; Band; Jazz Band; Yrbk Rptr; High Hon Roll; Lion Awd; NHS; Pres Schlr; Jack & Jill Amer Fndtn Schlrshp 86; Faculty Memrl Schlrshp 86; SUNY; Phrmcy.

DAVIS, ANN; Auburn HS; Auburn, NY (Y); 10/428; Cmnty Wkr; Teachers Aide; High Hon Roll; NHS; NY St Assn For Retrded Chldrn Schlrshp 86; Superntndnts Awd 86; Christopher Columbus Schlrshp 86; Marywood Coll; Spec Ed.

DAVIS, BARBARA J; Henninger HS; Syracuse, NY; (Y); 13/400; Church Yth Grp; Cmnty Wkr; Spanish Clb; High Hon Roll; Hon Roll; NYS Regnts Schlrshp 85-86; Round Table 85-86; Liberty U Lynchburg VA; Bio.

DAVIS, BERTHA ANN; Monticello HS; Monticello, NY; (Y); 10/178; Sec Church Yth Grp; Library Aide; Cit Awd; High Hon Roll; NHS; Ntl Merit Ltr; Prfct Atten Awd; Luis De Hayes Mem Awd/Spnsh 86; Pres Acad Ftns Awd 86; Humntrn Awd 86; Mount ST Mary Coll; Nrs.

DAVIS, BRIAN; Burgard VHS HS; Buffalo, NY; (Y); #2 In Class; JA; Red Cross Aide; High Hon Roll; Hon Roll; Spartans U; Aviatn Mchncs.

DAVIS, BRIAN; Williamsville South HS; Williamsville, NY; (Y); Art Clb; Church Yth Grp; Drama Clb; Acpl Chr; Madrigals; School Musical.

DAVIS, BRONWEN; Dindee Cntrl HS; Lakemont, NY; (Y); #11 In Class; AFS; French Clb; Ski Clb; Yrbk Stf; High Hon Roll; Hon Roll; NHS.

DAVIS, CHENORA; George W Wingate HS; Brooklyn, NY; (Y); Cmnty Wkr; Office Aide; Teachers Aide; Prfct Atten Awd; Englsh Hnrs 84-86; Hampton Inst; Comp Tech.

DAVIS, COREY; All Hallows Inst; New York, NY; (Y); Church Yth Grp; Church Choir; Trk; Hon Roll; Prfct Atten Awd; NROTC; Engrng.

DAVIS, CYNTHIA S; Wayne Central HS; Walworth, NY; (Y); Dance Clb; Chorus; Concert Band; School Musical; Pres Soph Cls; Pres Jr Cls; Var Capt Vllybl; 4-H Awd; NHS; Merit Schlrshp NY St Summer Schl Choral Studies 84; Syracuse U; Vocal Perfrmnc.

DAVIS, DAWN; City AS Schl; New York, NY; (Y); Hosp Aide; Office Aide; Hon Roll; Cert Essy Fnlst Kiss Radio 86; Rnnr Up Fctn Cntst NYC Pr 85; Lbrl Arts.

DAVIS, DEBRA; East Islip HS; East Islip, NY; (Y); Teachers Aide; Hon Roll; Sec.

DAVIS, DEBRA; Hempstead HS; Hempstead, NY; (Y); #11 In Class; Library Aide; Yrbk Stf; Vllybl; High Hon Roll; Hon Roll; NHS; Ntl Merit Schol; Bus Admin.

DAVIS, DIANE; East Islip HS; E Islip, NY; (Y); 31/425; Cmnty Wkr; Service Clb; High Hon Roll; Hon Roll; Spanish NHS; SUNY At Stony Brook.

DAVIS II, DONALD T; Mc Graw HS; Marathon, NY; (Y); 8/42; Am Leg Boys St; Varsity Clb; Pres Chorus; Concert Band; Mrchg Band; School Musical; Pres Stu Cncl; Var Bsbl; High Hon Roll; NHS; Rtry Yt Ldrshp Cnfrnc 86; Yth Svcs 85; Ostndng Vcl Mscn 86; Coll; Music.

DAVIS, ELENA T; Bronx H S Of Science; Bronx, NY; (Y); Office Aide; Natl Achvt Scholar SF 85-86; Cornell; Vet Med.

DAVIS, ERIC; Gloversville HS; Gloversvl, NY; (Y); French Clb; Band; Jazz Band; Mrchg Band; Stage Crew; Trs Frsh Cls; Rep Soph Cls; Rep Jr Cls; JV Socr; Aerontcl Engr.

DAVIS, GLENN C; West Islip HS; W Islip, NY; (Y); Church Yth Grp; Church Choir; Stat Bsktbl; JV Var Diving; Stat Ftbl; Var Golf; SUNY Oneonta.

DAVIS, HODARI B; Ithaca HS; Ithaca, NY; (Y); Am Leg Boys St; Aud/Vis; Ski Clb; Spanish Clb; Chorus; Nwsp Ed-Chief; Im Bsktbl; Im Ftbl; Im Vllybl; Crnll U, Blck Grdt Stdnts Assoc Awd Acdmc Achvt 85; Mrtn Lthr Kng Jr Ortrcl Cntst 1st Pl 86; Econ.

DAVIS, JAMES; Bitburg American HS; APO, NY; (Y); Chess Clb; Computer Clb; German Clb; Math Clb; Math Tm; Science Clb; Yrbk Phtg; Wrstlng; Exctllnce Awd Mth 84; Mth Cont Awds 85; U IL U/C; Aerontcl Engrng.

DAVIS, JAMES S; Wison Magnet HS; Rochester, NY; (Y); Church Yth Grp; Teachers Aide; Trs Jr Cls; Trs Sr Cls; JV Var Bsbl; Var Bsktbl; Var Socr; High Hon Roll; Hon Roll; Comp Kit Dsgn Cntst 83; Wrtr Wk 83; Natl Sci Olympd 82 & 83; Nazareth Coll; Hstry.

DAVIS, JEFF; Burgard HS; Buffalo, NY; (Y); Cmnty Wkr; School Play; Variety Show; Yrbk Rptr; Yrbk Stf; Off Frsh Cls; Off Jr Cls; Bsbl; Bsktbl; Trk; Memphis ST U.

DAVIS, JEFF; Hornell HS; Hornell, NY; (Y); NHS; Acctg.

DAVIS, JIM; Addison Central HS; Addison, NY; (Y); 2/120; JCL; Latin Clb; Ski Clb; Socr; Swmmng; Vllybl; High Hon Roll; Hon Roll; NHS; Sal; Acdmc All Stars; Med.

DAVIS, JIM; Whitesboro SR HS; Whitesboro, NY; (Y); SADD; Varsity Clb; Rep Stu Cncl; JV Var Bsktbl; JV Var Ftbl; Var Trk; Hon Roll; Aviation.

DAVIS, JOEL; Sherburne-Earlville HS; Earlville, NY; (Y); 6/165; Debate Tm; Drama Clb; VP Trs FFA; SADD; School Play; Trs Stu Cncl; Hon Roll; NHS; Ntl Merit Ltr; Won Natl Sci Merit Awd & Acdmc All Amer 86; Rcvd ST Office FFA 86; Military Acad; Pilot.

DAVIS, JOHN FRANCIS; Johnson City SR HS; Johnson City, NY; (Y); Boys Clb Am; Boy Scts; Church Yth Grp; Cmnty Wkr; Computer Clb; Exploring; Church Choir; Bsktbl; Hon Roll; NHS; Biolgcl Stds.

DAVIS, JULIE; Vernon-Verona-Sherrill Central HS; Vernon, NY; (Y); Pres Church Yth Grp; GAA; Thesps; Chorus; Church Choir; School Play; Yrbk Stf; Law.

DAVIS, KARINA L; William Nottingham HS; Syracuse, NY; (Y); French Clb; Latin Clb; SADD; School Musical; Stage Crew; Yrbk Stf; VP Frsh Cls; VP Soph Cls; Var JV Sftbl; Var Capt Swmmng; Ntl Latin Exam Soma Cum Laude 83; Syracuse U; Psych.

DAVIS, KIM; Curtis HS; Staten Island, NY; (Y); Camp Fr Inc; Church Yth Grp; Office Aide; Teachers Aide; Swmmng; Cit Awd; Hon Roll; Prfct Atten Awd; Wgnr Coll; Nrsng.

DAVIS, KRISTIN M; Kenmore East HS; Tonawanda, NY; (Y); Chrmn Church Yth Grp; GAA; Pep Clb; Chorus; Church Choir; School Musical; Yrbk Stf; Stat Ftbl; JV Var Vllybl; Hon Roll.

DAVIS, LA SHAN; Newburger Free Acad; New Windsor, NY; (Y); Church Yth Grp; Trs Computer Clb; Library Aide; Math Tm; Office Aide; Varsity Clb; Trs Church Choir; Yrbk Stf; Hon Roll; Val; Ottoway Fndtn Schlrshp 86; Vldctrn Upwrd Bnd 86; SUNY Albany; Bus Adm.

DAVIS, LASHAWN; Grace Dodge Voc HS; Bronx, NY; (Y); School Play; Sftbl; Prfct Atten Awd; Physcl Educ Hon 84; Bus Math Hon 85; Engl Hon 86; Nrsng.

DAVIS, MARIE; Riverhead HS; Riverhead, NY; (Y); FBLA; VICA; Comp Pgmr.

DAVIS, MARK A; Cicero North Syracuse HS; N Syracuse, NY; (Y); 201/667; Boy Scts; Exploring; Var L Lcrss; Var L Socr; Regents Schlrshp 86; ROTC; Miltry Pilot.

DAVIS, MELANIE; Nazareth Acad; Rochester, NY; (Y); 4/129; Church Yth Grp; Cmnty Wkr; Latin Clb; Band; Chorus; Church Choir; Concert Band; Jazz Band; Mrchg Band; Orch; Area All ST Band 84-85; All Cty Orch 85; Anderson Coll; Music.

DAVIS, MELISSA; Neward Senior HS; Newark, NY; (Y); Cmnty Wkr; Hosp Aide; Red Cross Aide; Pres SADD; Acpl Chr; Chorus; Church Choir; Swing Chorus; Variety Show; Red Cross Ldrshp Devlpmnt Conf 84-86; Natl Ldrshp Awd 84; SUNY Oswego; Zoolgy.

DAVIS, MICHAEL; Archbishop Molloy HS; Richmond Hill, NY; (Y); JV Crs Cntry; Im Ftbl; Im Sftbl; Var Trk; 2nd Hnrs 83-84; Pre-Med.

DAVIS, MICHAEL; Midwood HS; Brooklyn, NY; (Y); Boy Scts; Debate Tm; Teachers Aide; Temple Yth Grp; Chorus; Hon Roll; NCTE Awd; Music Supv Awd 84; Soc Studs Cert 84; Apieta 86; Law.

DAVIS, MICHELLE; Canisteo Central Schl; Canisteo, NY; (Y); 6/76; Ski Clb; Orch; Yrbk Stf; Var L Swmmng; Var L Vllybl; High Hon Roll; NHS; Ny ; St Rgnts Schlrshp 86; Sunny At Plattsburgh; Med Tech.

DAVIS, MICHELLE; Sacred Heart Acad; Bellerose, NY; (Y); Hosp Aide; Math Clb; Tennis; Hon Roll; NHS; Med.

DAVIS, PAUL M; Hillcrest HS; Cambria Heights, NY; (Y); 103/801; Church Yth Grp; Exploring; Hosp Aide; Chorus; Hon Roll; Volunteer Svc Awd 85; Chem Engr.

DAVIS, PENNY; Hamburg HS; Hamburg, NY; (Y); 56/350; French Clb; Varsity Clb; Band; Concert Band; Mrchg Band; Var L Socr; Var L Swmmng; Hon Roll; Bio.

DAVIS, ROBERT; Babylon HS; Babylon, NY; (Y); Cmnty Wkr; Spanish Clb; Chorus; School Musical; Swing Chorus; Variety Show; Nwsp Stf; JV L Crs Cntry; Var L Trk; Hon Roll; Vlntr Cmnty Awd 86; Tlnt Shw Awds 83 & 84; Bus.

DAVIS, ROBYN; Wallkiu SR HS; Plattekill, NY; (Y); Band; Concert Band; Symp Band; Rep Frsh Cls; Rep Soph Cls; Var Gym; Stat Score Keeper; Tennis; Hon Roll; England; Intl Bus.

DAVIS, ROSE A; Dundee Central Schl; Lakemont, NY; (Y); Pres Church Yth Grp; Science Clb; Spanish Clb; Chorus; Church Choir; Hon Roll; Prtcl Nrsng Course FIAVC 84-86; FLAVC; Nrs.

DAVIS, ROXANA; Canisteo Central HS; Canisteo, NY; (Y); 10/74; FBLA; Office Aide; Teachers Aide; School Play; Yrbk Stf; Powder Puff Ftbl; Socr; Vllybl; Hon Roll; NHS; 1/2 Yr Schlrshp Bryant & Stratton 86; Acad Ftns Awd 86; Bryant & Stratton; Exec Sec.

DAVIS, ROY J; Harrisville Ctr HS; Harrisville, NY; (Y); 1/52; Art Clb; Boy Scts; Trs Computer Clb; Chorus; High Hon Roll; Trs NHS; Prfct Atten Awd; Val; N Cntry Schlr 86; NY St Rgnts Schlrshp 86; Clrksn Trstee Schlrshp 86; Clarkson U; Elec Engr.

DAVIS, SABRINA; Bishop Loughlin HS; Brooklyn, NY; (Y); Art Clb; Dance Clb; English Clb; FBLA; GAA; Math Tm; Spanish Clb; Vllybl; John Jay Coll; Law.

DAVIS, SANDRA A; Bishop Kearney HS; Brooklyn, NY; (Y); Dance Clb; Hosp Aide; Library Aide; Variety Show; Hon Roll; NYS Schrlshp 86; SAY Pgm St Josephc Coll 85-86; Pre-Med Resrch Ed Pgm 85-86; Howard U; Microbio.

DAVIS, SCOTT; Corning-Painted Post West HS; Painted Post, NY; (Y); 34/252; Letterman Clb; Thesps; Acpl Chr; Madrigals; School Musical; L Var Golf; Capt Var Lcrss; High Hon Roll; Pres Schlr; St Schlr; Lehigh U; Elec Engrng.

DAVIS, SHAEMANE; John Dewey HS; Brooklyn, NY; (Y); Church Yth Grp; Drama Clb; Chorus; Church Choir; School Musical; School Play; Cit Awd; SCI.

DAVIS, SHAWN; Oakwood Schl; Middletown, NY; (Y); Var Bsbl; Socr; Wrstlng; Hon Roll; Mst Imprvd Wrstlr 83-84; Schl Dorm Prctr 85-86; Psych.

DAVIS, SHEILA; Harry S Truman HS; Bronx, NY; (Y); Hosp Aide; Library Aide; Office Aide; Teachers Aide; Pres Soph Cls; Mgr Ftbl; Fash Merch.

DAVIS, SHERRI; Corning Painted Post West HS; Painted Post, NY; (Y); Church Yth Grp; Band; Chorus; Var Capt Bsktbl; Co-Capt Twrlr; Hon Roll; Bus.

DAVIS, STEVEN; Baldwin SR HS; Baldwin, NY; (Y); Aud/Vis; Key Clb; Tennis; Bus.

DAVIS, SUSAN; Uratego JR SR HS; Otego, NY; (Y); Church Yth Grp; Drama Clb; Ski Clb; Spanish Clb; Chorus; Church Choir; School Musical; School Play; Stage Crew; Hon Roll; JR Ptrlr Ntl Ski Ptrl Systm 85; Ldrshp Cnfrncs 86; Bus Admin.

DAVIS, TRACY L; Whitney Point SR HS; Lisle, NY; (Y); 1/124; Pres Latin Clb; Ski Clb; Yrbk Ed-Chief; Var Capt Cheerleading; 4-H Awd; High Hon Roll; NHS; Val; Pres Trs 4-H; JCL; NYS Rgnts Schlrshp 86; Excllnc Awds 83-86; Rtry Yth Ldrshp Awd 85; Rochester Inst; Elec Engnrng.

DAVIS, VICKIE; Avoca Central Schl; Avoca, NY; (Y); 11/44; Pres French Clb; FBLA; Band; Chorus; Church Choir; Yrbk Stf; Rep Frsh Cls; Var Cheerleading; Var Trk; Hon Roll; E TX Baptist U; Elem Ed.

DAVIS-DALE, AMY; Potsdam Central HS; Potsdam, NY; (Y); French Clb; SADD; Orch; Pres Frsh Cls; Pres Soph Cls; Pres Jr Cls; Rep Stu Cncl; JV Var Cheerleading; JV Var Socr; JV Sftbl; Cherldng Sprtsmnshp Awd 85; 1st Wnnr Chrldng Squd Cntst 84-86; Ldrshp Awd Soccer 85; Lawyer.

DAVITT, JOHN; Westhill HS; Syracuse, NY; (Y); 40/150; Ski Clb; Chorus; Im Bsktbl; Var L Crs Cntry; Var L Ftbl; Var L Trk; Im Vllybl; St Schlr; Oswego ST U; Med.

DAWE, STEPHEN A; Mcquaid Jesuit HS; Rochester, NY; (Y); 67/179; Church Yth Grp; Nwsp Stf; Im Bsktbl; Bowling; JV Im Ftbl; JV Var Socr; JV Var Trk; High Hon Roll; Hon Roll; NHS; NYS Rgnts Schlrshp 86; St John Fisher Coll Schlrshp 86; Ithaca Coll Schlrshp 86; Acctg.

DAWKINS, AUDREY; Evander Childs HS; Bronx, NY; (S); 4/383; Math Tm; Office Aide; Concert Band; Trk; Vllybl; VP High Hon Roll; Ntl Merit Ltr; Prfct Atten Awd; Borough Pres Stanley Cert Achvt 85; Extra Circular Actvts; Pride Yankees Awd 84-85; Stanford; Sci.

DAWLEY, STERLING; Jamesville-Dewitt HS; Fayetteville, NY; (Y); 52/275; Boy Scts; Church Yth Grp; Chorus; Var Lcrss; Im JV Socr; God Cntry Awd; High Hon Roll; Cmnty Wkr; School Musical; Ordr Of Arrw 81; Eagl Sct 84; NY ST Lacrosse Champs 86; Cvl Engrng.

DAWSON, ADAM; Shenendehowa HS; Clifton Park, NY; (Y); Boy Scts; Sec Church Yth Grp; Ski Clb; Band; Church Choir; Concert Band; Symp Band; Hon Roll; Prfct Atten Awd.

DAWSON, DAWN; Randolph Central HS; Randolph, NY; (Y); 8/85; Art Clb; Dance Clb; Trs Spanish Clb; Varsity Clb; Yrbk Stf; Trs Frsh Cls; Trs Soph Cls; Cheerleading; Hon Roll; NHS; Jamestown CC; Bus.

DAWSON, DERRICK; Mount Saint Joseph Acad; Buffalo, NY; (Y); Art Clb; JA; Math Clb; Varsity Clb; Bsktbl; Socr; Tennis; Hon Roll; U At Buffalo; Econmcs.

DAWSON III, JOHN F; Northeastern Clinton Central HS; Champlain, NY; (Y); Am Leg Boys St; French Clb; Intnl Clb; Trs Key Clb; Red Cross Aide; Var L Golf; JV Socr; Im Swmmng; Mrktng.

DAWSON, KENNY; Minisink Valley HS; Middletown, NY; (Y); Math Tm; SADD; JV Var Bsbl; JV Var Bsktbl; JV Var Ftbl; High Hon Roll; NHS; U Of MD; Engrng.

DAY, ATRICIA; Mt Vernon HS; Mt Vernon, NY; (Y); Library Aide; Teachers Aide; Hon Roll; U Of SC; Accntnt.

DAY, DAWN MARIE; Central Islip SR HS; Central Islip, NY; (Y); Church Yth Grp; Library Aide; Church Choir; Cmnty Wkr; Girl Scts; Office Aide; SADD; Chorus; Hon Roll; Cznva Coll; Horse Care.

DAY, DWAYNE; Greece Arcadia HS; Rochester, NY; (Y); 48/285; Am Leg Boys St; Model UN; Science Clb; Nwsp Bus Mgr; High Hon Roll; Hon Roll; NHS; Aud/Vis; School Play; Nwsp Stf; NYS Regents Scholar 86; Pres Acad Fit Awd 86; Pres Clsrm Young Amer 86; U Rochester; Pol Sci.

DAY, JENNY; Shenendehowa Central HS; Clifton Park, NY; (Y); Varsity Clb; Var Cheerleading; Var Gym; JV Trk; High Hon Roll; Empire St Games Gymnastic Tm 83.

DAY, JIM; Midlakes HS; Phelps, NY; (Y); VP FFA; Varsity Clb; Band; JV Var Bsktbl; JV Var Ftbl; Var Trk; Hon Roll; Loc And ST Awds FFA 82-86; Alfred; Ag.

DAY, KIMBERLY; Sherburne-Earlville HS; Smyrna, NY; (Y); Sec Church Yth Grp; Civic Clb; Band; Chorus; Church Choir; School Musical; High Hon Roll; NHS; Prfct Atten Awd; Natl Sci Merit Awd 86.

DAY, KRISTEN; Rome Free Acad; Rome, NY; (Y); 25/500; Hosp Aide; Intnl Clb; Twrlr; High Hon Roll; Jr NHS; NHS; Cazenovia; Bus.

DAY, LEE M; Roy C Ketcham HS; Wappingers Falls, NY; (Y); 100/500; VP Computer Clb; French Clb; Hosp Aide; Science Clb; Ski Clb; School Play; High Hon Roll; Hon Roll; NHS; NY ST Rgnts Schlrshp 86; SUNY Albany; Comp Sci.

DAY, MICHELE; Churchville-Chili HS; Dundee, NY; (Y); Letterman Clb; Ski Clb; Varsity Clb; Band; Jazz Band; Var Bsktbl; Var Socr; Var Trk; Var Vllybl; High Hon Roll; Southeastern Acad; Trvl.

DAY, MICHELLE; Sweet Home HS; Tonawanda, NY; (Y); Cmnty Wkr; French Clb; GAA; Off Soph Cls; Stu Cncl; Var Crs Cntry; Var Trk; French Hon Soc; Hon Roll; MVP Indr Trck 85-86; Mst Imprvd Rnnr Crss Cntry 85-86; Psych.

DAY, TODD; Bloomfield Central School; East Bloomfield, NY; (Y); 15/105; Am Leg Boys St; Chess Clb; Church Yth Grp; French Clb; Rep Stu Cncl; Vllybl; Hon Roll; Engrng.

DAYTON, CATHY; Our Lady Of Mercy HS; Rochester, NY; (Y); Cmnty Wkr; Hosp Aide; Intnl Clb; Ski Clb; Spanish Clb; SADD; Rep Stu Cncl; Bsbl; Sftbl; Swmmng; FL Inst Tech; Marine Bio.

DAYTON, SHAWN; Catholic Central HS; Troy, NY; (Y); 46/189; Cmnty Wkr; Latin Clb; Math Clb; SADD; Variety Show; Var L Tennis; Ntl Merit Ltr; Arch Engrng.

DE ALMEIDA, NELLIE; H Frank Carey HS; Franklin Square, NY; (Y); 27/228; Sec Camera Clb; Cmnty Wkr; Hst FBLA; Pres Spanish Clb; Ed Yrbk Rptr; High Hon Roll; Spanish NHS; Faculty Svc Awd 86; Hofstra U; Intl Bus.

DE ANGELIS, JODI; East Meadow HS; East Meadow, NY; (Y); Civic Clb; Computer Clb; FBLA; Key Clb; Orch; Sec Jr Cls; C W Post Mus Awd 86-87; Key Club Awd 86; C W Post; Mus.

DE ASLA, MICHAEL; Sachem North HS; Ronkonkoma, NY; (Y); 45/1500; Math Tm; Ski Clb; Yrbk Phtg; Lcrss; Var Tennis; Trs NHS; Ntl Merit Ltr; Mech Engnrng.

DE AVEIRO, ROBERT; Lafayette HS; Brooklyn, NY; (Y); 16/48; JA; Math Tm; Socr; High Hon Roll; Untd Fdrtn Tchrs Schlrshp 86; Cert Of Merit Data Prcssng 86; PACE U NYC; Comp Sci.

DE BADTS, RICHARD K; North Rose-Wolcott HS; Wolcott, NY; (S); Acpl Chr; Band; Chorus; School Musical; School Play; Stage Crew; Variety Show; Rep Stu Cncl; Trs Aud/Vis; Concert Band; All Cnty Msc Fstvl & All ST Msc Fstvl.

DE BARTOLO, STEPHANIE; Mamaroneck HS; Larchmont, NY; (Y); FBLA; Service Clb; Trs Spanish Clb; Hon Roll; NHS; Twn Of Mamaroneck Cert For Dedicated Volunteer Svc 85; Acad Merit Schlrshp From Iona 86; Iona Coll; BBA.

DE BELLA, STEPHEN; Bishop Ford C C H S; Brooklyn, NY; (Y); Computer Clb; High Hon Roll; Bus.

DE BENEDETTO, GINA; Fontbonne Hall Acad; Brooklyn, NY; (Y); 38/130; Drama Clb; School Musical; School Play; Variety Show; Hon Roll; Prfct Atten Awd; Prtl Schlrshp To Tisch NY U 86; Tisch Schl Arts; Actress.

DE BETTA, JOSEPHINE; St John Villa Academy HS; Staten Is, NY; (Y); Dance Clb; Teachers Aide; Chorus; Schltc Merit Awd 86; St Johns U; Bus Mgmt.

DE BONET, CYNTHIA; Patchogue-Medford HS; Patchogue, NY; (S); 49/621; Exploring; Leo Clb; Concert Band; Mrchg Band; Hon Roll; Jr NHS; NHS; Geneseo Coll SUNY; Phy Thrpy.

DE BROWN, STACY; Uniondale HS; Uniondale, NY; (Y); Drama Clb; Key Clb; Office Aide; Mgr Bsktbl; Score Keeper; Own Choclt Bus 86; Hme Eco 83-84; Howard U; Bus.

DE CARLO, ERIC; Millbrook HS; Millbrook, NY; (Y); Cmnty Wkr; Drama Clb; Ski Clb; Coach Actv; Var L Crs Cntry; Var L Trk; Hon Roll; Chorus; 1st & 2nd Pl Sci Olympd Physcs & Chmstry 85-86; Hghst Avg Rgnts Erth Sci 85-86; Keene ST Coll; Comp Math.

DE CARLO, MICHAEL M; St Francis Prep; Middle Village, NY; (S); 114/744; Office Aide; JV Var Bsbl; JV Bsktbl; Crs Cntry; Hon Roll; NHS; Opt Clb Awd; Math Hnrs 83-86; Engr.

DE CELESTINO, BLASE; Herbert Lehman HS; Bronx, NY; (Y); 41/347; Ed Yrbk Stf; Hon Roll; NHS; Prfct Atten Awd; NY Rgnts Schlrshp 86; Comp Hnr Roll 85 & 86; Acad Olympcs 85; NY Inst Of Tech; Comp Sci.

DE CICCO, MARK J; Sachem HS; Farmingville, NY; (Y); 61/1350; Church Yth Grp; Science Clb; Ski Clb; Band; Concert Band; Off Frsh Cls; Im Bowling; JV Tennis; Im Vllybl; Cit Awd; Prsdntl Acadmc Ftns Awd 86; Mbershp Dir Intrct Clb 84-86; NY ST Stony Brook; Bio.

DE CLERCG, PATRICIA; John Marshall HS; Rochester, NY; (Y); 8/170; Church Yth Grp; Exploring; Math Tm; Ski Clb; Co-Capt Color Guard; Rep Jr Cls; Rep Stu Cncl; Im Bowling; High Hon Roll; NHS; Regents Schlrshp 86; SUNY-BUFFALO; Mech Engr.

DE FABIO, DANIEL; Catholic Central HS; Clifton Park, NY; (S); 19/179; Band; Jazz Band; School Musical; School Play; Nwsp Rptr; Yrbk Stf; Lit Mag; Chrmn Sr Cls; NHS; Ntl Merit Ltr; Orgnlty-Wrtng Play 84-85; All Amercn Hall Fame Band 84-85; Alfred U; Cermc Engrng.

DE FANTI, LUCY; Preston HS; Bronx, NY; (S); 1/89; Hosp Aide; Stage Crew; Nwsp Rptr; Trs Frsh Cls; Im Vllybl; Hon Roll; NHS; NEDT Awd; Val; SF Natl Hispnc Schlr Awds Prog 85; Awd Natl Socty Autistic Chldrn 83-85; Schlrshp St Catherines 82; Cornell U; Pre-Med.

DE FAZIO, CHRISTIAN; Lockport SR HS; Lockport, NY; (Y); 2/411; Latin Clb; Var L Bsbl; Var L Ice Hcky; JV Capt Socr; High Hon Roll; NHS; Sal; Loraine Altro Deitz Schlrhsp 86; Charles H Kennedy Awd; Princeton; Pre-Med.

DE FAZIO, TINA; Batavia HS; Batavia, NY; (Y); 24/211; VP Chorus; Drm Mjr(t); Variety Show; Lit Mag; Rep Soph Cls; Cheerleading; Hon Roll; Mst Outstndng Drum Mjrt 85 & 86; 4th Rnnr Up JR Miss Pag 86; St Bonaventure U; Bus Mktng.

DE FEDERICIS, TONI; Pembroke JR SR HS; Corfu, NY; (Y); 8/110; Church Yth Grp; Drama Clb; German Clb; Science Clb; Band; Church Choir; Concert Band; Mrchg Band; Pres School Musical; Variety Show; Chld Psychlgy.

DE FILIPPO, ELIZABETH; John Jay SR HS; Hopewell Junction, NY; (Y); 8/519; VP Church Yth Grp; Drama Clb; Model UN; School Musical; Yrbk Stf; High Hon Roll; Lion Awd; NHS; Cmnty Wkr; Computer Clb; Pres Acad Ftns Recpnt 86; NYS Regnts Schrlshp 86; Math Stu Wk 85; Bucknell U; Elect Engr.

DE FOREST, CHAD; South Jefferson Central HS; Lorraine, NY; (Y); Boy Scts; German Clb; Band; Concert Band; Jazz Band; Mrchg Band; Trs Jr Cls; Trk; Hon Roll; NHS; Biochem.

DE FOREST, ERIC; Tupper Lake HS; Tupper Lk, NY; (Y); 14/102; VP Drama Clb; Pres Science Clb; Band; Pres Chorus; School Musical; School Play; Yrbk Ed-Chief; Yrbk Stf; L Crs Cntry; Var Trk; NYSSMA All ST Conf Choir 84-85; Achvt Acad Awd Trig 84; Essay Cty Music Schlrsh P 86; Ithaca Coll; Music.

DE FRANCO, LAURA; Massena Central HS; Massena, NY; (Y); 30/246; French Clb; Var Capt Bsktbl; JV Socr; JV Sftbl; Hon Roll; NHS; Ntl Merit Schol; North Cntry & Clarkson U Schlrshps 86; Clarkson U; Engrng.

DE GAETANI, PATRICIA; F D R HS; Brooklyn, NY; (Y); #7 In Class; Office Aide; Teachers Aide; Chorus; Lit Mag; Var Bsktbl; Score Keeper; High Hon Roll; Hon Roll; Prfct Atten Awd; Rgnts Schlrshp 86; UFT Schlrshp 86; FDR Schl Schlrshp 86; Brooklyn Coll; Pre-Med.

DE GIULE, ERIC; Rensselaer HS; Rensselaer, NY; (Y); 1/70; Varsity Clb; Yrbk Stf; Stu Cncl; JV Ftbl; Var L Trk; Hon Roll; VP NHS; Prfct Atten Awd; Scndry Ed.

DE GRAY, SCOTT; Gates-Chili SR HS; Rochester, NY; (Y); Aud/Vis; Boy Scts; Chess Clb; Computer Clb; Drama Clb; French Clb; Mathletes; Math Clb; Science Clb; Chorus; Audio Visual Serv Awd 86; Math League Compttn Awd 84; Monroe CC; Compu Sci.

DE GROAT, ROBIN; Wallkill HS; Wallkill, NY; (Y); Band; Chorus; Color Guard; Concert Band; Drill Tm; Mrchg Band; Variety Show; Yrbk Rptr; Stat Bsktbl; Stat Ftbl; SUNY Buffalo; Dntst.

DE GROOT, MARY; Cicero N Syracuse HS; N Syracuse, NY; (S); 46/623; Speech Tm; Nwsp Rptr; Rep Frsh Cls; Pres Jr Cls; Rep Stu Cncl; Stat Bsbl; JV Var Bsktbl; Var Socr; Jr NHS; Opt Clb Awd; Natl Hstry & Govt Awd 85; Elem Tchr.

DE GRUSHE, MATTHEW; Edward R Murrow HS; Brooklyn, NY; (Y); 78/669; Nwsp Stf; Off Soph Cls; French Hon Soc; Hon Roll; Prfct Atten Awd; St Schlr; Frnch Natl Cntst Lvls I, III 83 & 85; Soc Frnch Prfssrs Cert 86; Gld Medl Excllnc Frnch 86; IN U; Bus.

DE HAAS, CAROLINA; North Babylon SR HS; N Babylon, NY; (Y); 14/484; Dance Clb; Intnl Clb; Office Aide; Teachers Aide; Band; School Musical; Variety Show; High Hon Roll; Jr NHS; NHS; Hofstra U; Acctg.

DE IASI, LISA M; Floral Park Memorial HS; Bellerose, NY; (S); 5/150; GAA; Stage Crew; Nwsp Ed-Chief; Yrbk Stf; Cheerleading; Trk; High Hon Roll; Hon Roll; NCTE Awd; NHS; Rgnts Schlrshp 86; Med.

DE JAGER, PHILIP; Riverdale Country HS; Bronx, NY; (Y); Math Tm; Science Clb; Nwsp Rptr; Nwsp Stf; Ntl Merit Ltr; Dept Awd Outstndng Achvt Sci, Hstry, Engl & Latn 85-86; Bio.

DE JESUS, DIMAS; Bishop Ford C C HS; Brooklyn, NY; (Y); Computer Clb; Dance Clb; Off Jr Cls; Hon Roll; Comp Tech.

DE JESUS, MADELINE; Murry Bergtraum HS; Brooklyn, NY; (Y); Church Yth Grp; Church Choir; High Hon Roll; Hon Roll; NHS; Bio Achvt Awd & 100% Atndnc Awd 85; St Johns U; Bus Adm.

DE JESUS, TERESA; Bishop Ford CC HS; Brooklyn, NY; (S); 8/439; Computer Clb; Dance Clb; Rep Jr Cls; Gym; High Hon Roll; Hon Roll; NHS; Bus Adm.

DE JESUS, TODD; Sutyvesant HS; Howard Beach, NY; (Y); Cmnty Wkr; Computer Clb; Drama Clb; Mathletes; Math Tm; Office Aide; Pres Temple Yth Grp; School Musical; Lit Mag; Semfnlst Ntl Hspnc Schlr Awd Pgm 85-86; Sci Mdl 9th Yr Grad 83; Avsta Hnr Soc 85-86; Appld Math.

DE JOHN, DANIEL; Eastridge HS; Rochester, NY; (Y); 14/196; Exploring; Spanish Clb; Concert Band; Jazz Band; Mrchg Band; Var L Swmmng; Var L Trk; High Hon Roll; Hon Roll; NHS; NY ST Fld Bnd Chmpns 85; Rchster Inst Of Tech; Elec Engr.

DE LA CRUZ, ANGEL; Clinton Central HS; Clinton, NY; (Y); 2/147; Computer Clb; Key Clb; Math Tm; SADD; Nwsp Ed-Chief; Ed Yrbk Stf; VP Soph Cls; JV Trk; High Hon Roll; NHS; Natl Hspnc Awds Fnlst 86; 36th Intl Sci Fair Fnlst 85; MA Inst Of Tech; Engrng.

DE LA OSA CRUZ, STEVEN MARCO; Thomas A Edison HS; Elmira Hts, NY; (Y); 14/86; Am Leg Boys St; Letterman Clb; Model UN; Varsity Clb; Var L Bsbl; Var Capt Ftbl; Hon Roll; Regnts Schlrshp 86; Cornell U; Indstrl Rltns.

DE LA ROSA, LYNN; Division Ave HS; Levittown, NY; (Y); 120/300; Spanish Clb; Band; Church Choir; Concert Band; Drm & Bgl; Jazz Band; Mrchg Band; Orch; School Musical; School Play.

DE LEON, ANGEL; Gorton HS; Yonkers, NY; (Y); Church Yth Grp; Sci Tchr.

DE LEON, RACHEL A; St Francis Prep; Jamaica Estates, NY; (S); 84/744; Hosp Aide; Chorus; Church Choir; VP Jr Cls; Im Capt Powder Puff Ftbl; Im Capt Sftbl; Im Capt Vllybl; Hon Roll; NHS; Optimate Soc 85 & 86; Bus.

DE LONG, JOE; Whitesboro SR HS; Whitesboro, NY; (Y); 98/306; Exploring; Ski Clb; Varsity Clb; Rep Stu Cncl; Var L Golf; Var L Ice Hcky; JV Socr; Hon Roll; Compu.

DE LORENZO, GEORGE; Homer Central HS; Cortland, NY; (Y); 15/210; Am Leg Boys St; Ski Clb; Thesps; Varsity Clb; Var L Crs Cntry; Var L Lcrss; Bausch & Lomb Sci Awd; Cit Awd; High Hon Roll; NHS.

DE LOS SANTOS, CARLOS; Eastern District HS; Brooklyn, NY; (Y); 4/330; Church Yth Grp; Math Tm; Color Guard; Capt Vllybl; Hon Roll; Tchrs Clb NY Awd Excllnce Physcs 86; Excllnce Spn Mdl 86; Excllnce Soc Studs Mdl 86; Rensselaer Polytech; Chem Engr.

DE LOSH JR, WALTER M; Camden Central HS; Taberg, NY; (Y); 27/189; Am Leg Boys St; Yrbk Stf; Hon Roll; NHS; Pres Acad Awd 86; Elizabeth Dorance Creatv Wrtng Awd 86.

DE LUCA, KEVIN; Amsterdam HS; Amsterdam, NY; (Y); 11/302; Computer Clb; Mrchg Band; Yrbk Stf; Trs Soph Cls; Trs Jr Cls; Rep Sr Cls; Var Capt Bsbl; Var Ftbl; NHS; St Schlr; Siena Coll; Comp Sci.

DE LUCIA, JULIE; Solvay HS; Solvay, NY; (Y); Church Yth Grp; Ski Clb; Chorus; Pres Frsh Cls; Off Jr Cls; Off Sr Cls; Sftbl; Vllybl; High Hon Roll; Math Iir Trignmtry 85; Engl IIR Creative Wrtng Skills 86; Shrthnd I 86; Accntng.

DE LUCIA, MARIA; St Agnes HS; Westbury, NY; (Y); Teachers Aide; Variety Show; Hon Roll; NHS; Art Awd 86; Trustee Scholar 86; Adelphi U; Elem Ed.

DE MAILLE, GREGORY A; St John The Baptist HS; W Babylon, NY; (Y); 9/546; Computer Clb; Math Tm; Var Ftbl; Wt Lftg; Trs NHS; Spanish NHS; Regents Schlrshp 86; All League Hnrs-Ftbll 86; Athltc Schlr Awd 86; Poly-Tech Inst; Elec Engnr.

DE MAIO, PATRICIA; St Edmund HS; Brooklyn, NY; (S); Spanish Clb; Nwsp Stf; Hon Roll; NHS; Brooklyn Coll; Lib Arts.

DE MAIO, ROBERT; St John The Baptist DHS; Massapequa, NY; (Y); Boy Scts; Church Yth Grp; Ski Clb; Var JV Ftbl; Var JV Trk; JV Wrstlng; Hon Roll; Catholic Dghtrs Art Awd 84; Bus.

DE MARCO JR, ANTHONY L; Newark SR HS; Newark, NY; (Y); Chrmn Am Leg Boys St; Church Yth Grp; Cmnty Wkr; Latin Clb; Political Wkr; Service Clb; Varsity Clb; Lib Band; Concert Band; Drm & Bgl; Latn Nat Hnr Socty; Joseph Hanel Latn Awd; 2nd Hnrs Awd; U S Military Acad; Law.

DE MARCO JR, ROBERT C; Lockport SR HS; Lockport, NY; (Y); 107/460; Boy Scts; Camera Clb; Radio Clb; Band; Mrchg Band; Stage Crew; Symp Band; Yrbk Phtg; JV Var Swmmng; Lifegrd BSA 83; Newspapr Carrier Mnth 86; Ad Altare Dei 82; Engr.

DE MARCO, THOMAS J; Bronx HS Of Science; Bronx, NY; (Y); Aud/Vis; Cmnty Wkr; Key Clb; Office Aide; Teachers Aide; Italian Frgn Lang Awd 86; NYU Trustee Schlrshp 86; Georgetown U; Hist.

DE MARTINO, LAURA; School Of The Holy Child HS; Bronxville, NY; (Y); Hosp Aide; Key Clb; Political Wkr; Teachers Aide; Nwsp Ed-Chief; Lit Mag; Hon Roll.

DE MARZIO, KIM; West Seneca West SR HS; West Seneca, NY; (Y); DECA; Sec Trs French Clb; Office Aide; Teachers Aide; Hon Roll; Jr NHS; French Hons Awd 84-85 & 85-86; Regents Bio Hons Awd 84-85; St Bonaventure; Bus Mgmt.

DE MASI, OLIMPIA; Preston HS; Bronx, NY; (S); 9/106; Stage Crew; Nwsp Rptr; Yrbk Phtg; Yrbk Stf; Trs Sr Cls; Hon Roll; NHS; Compt Prgrmg.

DE MASI, OLYMPIA; Preskon HS; Bronx, NY; (Y); 9/106; Stage Crew; Nwsp Rptr; Yrbk Phtg; Yrbk Rptr; Trs Sr Cls; Hon Roll; NHS; Drama Clb; Yrbk Stf; Italian Awd 86; Regents Scholar 86; Amer Lg Awd 86; Fordham U.

DE MELLO, DOMINIC L; Holy Cross HS; Bellerose, NY; (S); 27/332; Sec Debate Tm; Library Aide; PAVAS; Scholastic Bowl; Sec Speech Tm; Nwsp Rptr; Ed Lit Mag; VP Stu Cncl; NHS; Queens Dist Rep Cmmssnr Educ Stu Advsry Commtt 85-87; Med.

DE MIGUEL, CARLOS; John A Coleman HS; Kingston, NY; (S); JV Bsktbl; JV Var Socr; 1st Hnrs In Drwng/Pntng 84-85; 1st Hnrs In Bsc Geo 84-85; Woodstock Schl Of Art Schlrshp 84-85; Arch.

DE MOORS, TAMARA; Weedsport Central HS; Weedsport, NY; (Y); 7/86; French Clb; Concert Band; Drm Mjr(t); Jazz Band; Mrchg Band; Var Capt Fld Hcky; Trk; JP Sousa Awd; Lion Awd; NHS; Elmira Key Awd 85; Weedsprt Msc Booster Schlrshp 86; Alumni Asso Schlrshp SUNY Cortland 86; SUNY Coll Cortland; Spch Pathl.

DE MORAS, MATHIEU; Penn Yan Acad; Penn Yan, NY; (Y); Boy Scts; Drama Clb; Model UN; Ski Clb; School Musical; Lit Mag; High Hon Roll; NHS; Ntl Merit SF; NEDT Awd; Archt.

DE OLIVEIRA, MARTHA; Newtown HS; Flushing, NY; (Y); Chess Clb; Church Yth Grp; Rep Jr Cls; Rep Sr Cls; Capt Vllybl; Vllybll & Chess Awd 82-83; CUNY City Coll; Cvl Engr.

DE PALMA, CHARLES A; Southside HS; Elmira, NY; (Y); 7/319; Pres Aud/Vis; Model UN; Yrbk Sprt Ed; Swmmng; Trk; NHS; Ntl Merit Ltr; Chess Clb; Key Clb; Latin Clb; U Of Redlands CA.

DE PAUW, MIKE; Newark SR HS; Newark, NY; (Y); 15/220; Concert Band; Jazz Band; Mrchg Band; Pep Band; Symp Band; High Hon Roll; NHS; Spanish NHS; JV Bsktbl; Boys ST Alt 86; Comp Sci.

DE PRIMO, VINCENT; Long Island City HS; Astoria, NY; (Y); Intnl Clb; Library Aide; Office Aide; Service Clb; Teachers Aide; Cit Awd; High Hon Roll; Hon Roll; Ntl Merit Schol; Prncpls List Awd; Mario Biaggi Awd; Sci, Majr Art & Itln Hnr Awds; Bus Mgmt.

DE PRISCO, LAURA; Walt Whitman HS; Hunt Sta, NY; (Y); SADD.

DE PUTRON, RENEE; Susan Wagner HS; New York, NY; (Y); Var Gym; Var Socr; Coll Of Boca Raton; Comps.

DE PUY, KELLY; Holy Trinity HS; Eastmeadow, NY; (S); Math Clb; Ski Clb; Teachers Aide; Nwsp Stf; Capt Socr; High Hon Roll; Hon Roll; NHS; Ntl Merit Ltr; NEDT Awd; Al-Leag Sccr Plyr 83; U Of CT; Phrmcy.

DE RIGGI, CATHERINE; Queen Of The Rosary Acad; Wantagh, NY; (Y); 20/49; Art Clb; School Musical; Nwsp Ed-Chief; Yrbk Ed-Chief; Rep Stu Cncl; Var Badmtn; Capt Cheerleading; Hon Roll; Long Isl Cath Jrnlsm Awd 86; Trvl/Trsm.

DE RITIS, JOSEPH; Binghamton HS; Binghamton, NY; (Y); Art Clb; Boys Clb Am; Camera Clb; Concert Band; Broome CC; Elec Engr.

DE ROBERTS, LISA; East Syracuse Minoa HS; E Syracuse, NY; (Y); 38/333; Variety Show; Sec Soph Cls; VP Jr Cls; VP Sr Cls; Var L Socr; JV Sftbl; JV Vllybl; High Hon Roll; NHS; Peer Cnslg Fremont Elem Awd 85; Merit MONY Schlstc Art Awd Blu Rbbn 2 Hnbl Mntn 86; SUNY Buffalo Coll; Fine Arts.

DE RONDE, SCOTT; Guilderland HS; Schenectady, NY; (Y); Ski Clb; Varsity Clb; Ftbl; Trk; Im Wt Lftg; Var Wrstlng; Math Tchr.

DE ROOS, TIMOTHY; Union Springs Cen HS; Auburn, NY; (Y); Math Clb; Var JV Golf; Var L Socr; High Hon Roll; VP NHS; Mchncl Engrng.

DE ROSA, BETH; Gloversville HS; Gloversville, NY; (Y); 46/235; French Clb; Yrbk Bus Mgr; Yrbk Stf; Rep Stu Cncl; Var Cheerleading; Powder Puff Ftbl; Hon Roll; NHS; SUNY Cortland; Elem Educ.

DE ROSA, JULIET; Moore Catholic HS; Staten Island, NY; (Y); Computer Clb; Library Aide; Math Clb; Math Tm; Ski Clb; Crs Cntry; Trk; Ded, Effrt Trck Awd 85; Math.

DE ROSA, MARGARET; Hoosick Falls Central Schl; Hoosick Falls, NY; (Y); Drama Clb; Spanish Clb; School Musical; School Play; Stu Cncl; Powder Puff Ftbl; Score Keeper; Hon Roll; NHS; Christian Action Awd 86; Dewey Schlrshp 86; Hnr Stu Pin & Cert 84-86; SUNY.

DE ROSA, STEPHEN V; Bronx HS Of Science; Whitestone, NY; (Y); Pres PAVAS; School Musical; School Play; Stage Crew; Yrbk Stf; Lit Mag; Pres Sr Cls; NHS; NYS Rgnts Schlrshp 86; Georgetown U; Frgn Svc.

DE ROSA, THOMAS A; Iona Preparatory Scl; New Rochelle, NY; (Y); Teachers Aide; Nwsp Rptr; Crs Cntry; JV Var Ftbl; Var Lcrss; Wt Lftg; High Hon Roll; NHS; All League Ftbll 85-86; NY ST Rgnts Schlrshp; Lehigh U; Cmptr Sci.

DE ROSA, TONY; Gloversville HS; Gloversville, NY; (Y); Var JV Ftbl; Wt Lftg; Hon Roll; Accntng.

DE RUE, MICHAEL J; E J Wilson HS; Rochester, NY; (Y); Exploring; Trs Mathletes; High Hon Roll; Hon Roll; NHS; Prfct Atten Awd; Rgnts Schlrshp-NYS 86; Outstndng Achvt Rgnts Bio 85; High Screr Math Leag 85-86; Monroe CC; Comp Pgmmng.

DE RUE, MICHELE; E J Wilson HS; Rochester, NY; (Y); French Clb; Mathletes; Varsity Clb; Church Choir; Mrchg Band; Yrbk Stf; JV Tennis; Var L Trk; High Hon Roll; NHS; Geom Awd 84; Trigmtry Awd 85; Math 12 86; Scndry Ed.

DE RUE, SHANE; Palmyra Macedon SR HS; Macedon, NY; (Y); 62/174; Var JV Ftbl; Im Wt Lftg; JV Wrstlng; St Schlr; Paul Smiths Coll; Forestry.

DE RYCKE, KIM; Fairport HS; Fairport, NY; (Y); Chorus; Yrbk Bus Mgr; Yrbk Stf; Cheerleading; Var Diving; Hon Roll; Prfct Atten Awd; Wegmans Schlrshp 86; ST U Of NY; Accntrrng.

DE SANTIS, JENNIFER; Nardin Acad; Hamburg, NY; (S); French Clb; Ski Clb; Spanish Clb; Nwsp Stf; Lit Mag; Stu Cncl; Bsktbl; Crs Cntry; Socr; Sftbl; Exclnce Span I 85; Dedication & Lylty Bsktbl Tm 85; Bus.

DE SANTIS, KESSA; Bronx HS Of Science; New York, NY; (Y); Office Aide; Teachers Aide; Chorus; Madrigals; Stage Crew; Prfct Atten Awd; NY U; Sci.

DE SARRO, JOE; T R Proctor HS; Utica, NY; (Y); Pep Clb; Bsbl; Bsktbl; Bowling; Ftbl; Hon Roll; Jr NHS; Accntng.

DE SCETTO, KRISTINA A; Baldwin SR HS; Flanders, NJ; (Y); 17/476; Band; Chorus; Concert Band; Mrchg Band; Orch; NHS; Halian Ntl Hnr Scty 86; Bstn U; Astronaut.

DE SIMONE, JEFFREY; Liverpool HS; Liverpool, NY; (Y); 2/884; Am Leg Boys St; Exploring; JA; Math Tm; School Musical; Bsktbl; Coach Actv; Bausch & Lomb Sci Awd; High Hon Roll; NHS; Math Leag 6th Pl Onordaga Cnty 86; RPI Math & Sci Awd 86; AHSME 20th Pl NY ST 86; Engrng.

DE SIMPLICIIS, ALICE; Central HS; Valley Stream, NY; (Y); Hon Roll; Jr NHS; Italian Hnr Soc Sec 85; Hofstra U; Law.

DE SOCIO, NICOLETTE; Auburn HS; Auburn, NY; (Y); Varsity Clb; JV Var Sftbl; L Var Swmmng; Cit Awd; NHS; High Hon Roll; Hon Roll; Swmmng MIP 84-85.

DE SOUSA, BENITA; Mount Vernon HS; Mt Vernon, NY; (Y); Aud/Vis; French Clb; FBLA; Key Clb; Ski Clb; Spanish Clb; Teachers Aide; Hon Roll; Computer Clb; Girl Scts; Fordham U; Frgn Lang.

DE SOUSA, DIANE; Schoharie Central HS; Schoharie, NY; (S); 3/85; Church Yth Grp; Hosp Aide; Concert Band; Yrbk Stf; Sec Frsh Cls; Pres Sr Cls; Capt L Socr; Capt L Trk; NHS; Amer Legion Socl Studies Awd; Russell Sage; Nrsng.

DE STAEBLER, DOUGLAS; Manhasset HS; Manhasset, NY; (Y); Cmnty Wkr; Service Clb; JV Var Bsbl; Var L Bowling; JV L Socr; High Hon Roll; Hon Roll; Bus.

DE STAFENO, BARBARA; Warwick Valley HS; Warwick, NY; (Y); 9/195; Math Tm; Science Clb; Drm & Bgl; Yrbk Stf; Soph Cls; Sr Cls; Var Capt Cheerleading; Var Trk; High Hon Roll; NHS; Rgnts Schlrshp Rcpnt 86; Vp Stu Senate 86; Hgst Spnsh Level I Avg 82; Comp Svc.

DE STENO, DAVID A; Highland HS; Highland, NY; (Y); #1 In Class; Math Tm; Quiz Bowl; Spanish Clb; Yrbk Stf; High Hon Roll; NHS; Ntl Merit Ltr; Pres Schlr; Spanish NHS; Val; Pres Acad Fit Awd 86; Vassar Coll; Biopsych.

DE SZALAY, KRISZTINA; Farmingdale HS; Farmingdale, NY; (Y); Art Clb; Cmnty Wkr; Trs German Clb; Ski Clb; SADD; Hon Roll.

DE TORE, TAMMY; Frankfort Schuyler Central HS; Frankfort, NY; (S); French Clb; Key Clb; SADD; Concert Band; School Musical; Rep Stu Cncl; Var JV Cheerleading; Hon Roll; Vrsty Awd Chrldg 84-85; Phrmcy.

DE TOUCHE, AMELIA C; Dominican Commercial HS; Jamaica, NY; (Y); Art Clb; Church Yth Grp; Rep Soph Cls; Hon Roll; Prfct Atten Awd; USA SR Ftnss Aahperd Awd 85 & 86; Queensborough Coll; Data Prssng.

DE VAY, SUSAN M; North Rose-Wolcott HS; N Rose, NY; (Y); 13/142; Ski Clb; VP Spanish Clb; Rep Jr Cls; Rep Sr Cls; VP Sec Stu Cncl; Var Swmmng; High Hon Roll; Hon Roll; NHS; Rotary Awd; SUNY Oswego; Elem Ed.

DE VINCENZI, ELIZABETH; Franklin Delano Roosevelt HS; Brooklyn, NY; (Y); Chorus; Hon Roll; Couples Dncng Awd 86; Italian Lang Awd 86; Bio Awd, Chem Awd 85-86; Brooklyn Coll.

DE VINNEY, TARA M; Charlotte HS; Rochester, NY; (Y); 4/78; High Hon Roll; Hon Roll; NYS Regnts Schlrshp 86; Monroe CC; Humn Svcs.

DE VITO, ANGELINA; St Edmund HS; Brooklyn, NY; (S); High Hon Roll; Hon Roll; Prfct Atten Awd; Princpls List 86; Mth Awd 85.

DE VITO, DANIEL JOHN; Palmyra-Macedon HS; Palmyra, NY; (S); Church Yth Grp; High Hon Roll; NHS.

DE VITO, MICHAEL A; St Marys Boys HS; Rockville Ctr, NY; (Y); Chess Clb; Ski Clb; School Musical; Stage Crew; Nwsp Rptr; Var L Crs Cntry; Var L Trk; Hon Roll; Manhattan Coll; Engrng.

DE VITO, ROSARIO; Monsignor Farrell HS; Staten Island, NY; (Y); Science Clb; Teachers Aide; Varsity Clb; Ftbl; Socr; Hon Roll; Ntl Merit Ltr; Med.

DE VITO, SINA; Bishop Kearney HS; Brooklyn, NY; (Y); 52/337; GAA; Hosp Aide; Library Aide; Political Wkr; Rep Jr Cls; Rep Sr Cls; Hon Roll; NHS; Cmnty Wkr; Rep Stu Cncl; NY ST Rgnts Schlrshp 86; NY U Trstees Schlr 86; Prncpls Lst 82-83; Frst Hnrs 83-86; NY U; Comm.

DE VIVIO, LORI; South Shore HS; Brooklyn, NY; (Y); Office Aide; Var Bsktbl; Var Sftbl; Sftbl Rookie Of Yr 84; Sftbl Dly News All Str Hon Mntn 85; Htl Rstrnt Mgmt.

DE VIVO, MARGARET; Beacon HS; Beacon, NY; (S); 5/205; Hosp Aide; Key Clb; Sec Spanish Clb; Band; Sec Frsh Cls; Sec Soph Cls; VP Jr Cls; Var Bowling; VP Cheerleading; US Bus Educ Awds 86; Vlntr Yr Awd-Cndystrpng 85; Comp Pgm.

DE VONISH, KIM; Murry Bergtraum HS; Brooklyn, NY; (Y); Math Tm; NHS; Sec.

DE VORE, ANITA; Jasper Central HS; Cameron, NY; (Y); VP Church Yth Grp; Drama Clb; French Clb; Library Aide; Teachers Aide; Chorus; Stage Crew; Vllybl; Hon Roll; NHS; Elem Educ.

DE VRIES, DONNA; Brewster HS; Brewster, NY; (Y); Chorus; School Musical; JV L Bsktbl; Var L Fld Hcky; Hon Roll; NHS; Social Work.

DE WATER, MICHAEL; Southside HS; Elmira, NY; (S); Church Yth Grp; Band; Chorus; Jazz Band; Orch; School Musical; School Play; Stage Crew; Symp Band; Variety Show; US Army; Musicn.

DE WITT, BURTON F; Cardinal O Hara HS; Buffalo, NY; (Y); Church Yth Grp; Cmnty Wkr; Yrbk Stf; Crs Cntry; Var Trk; Var Wrstlng; Hon Roll; JC Awd; Drama Clb; Exploring; Cert Apprectn Yuth Engagd Svc, Cath Yuth Org 86; CCAF; Emerg Med.

DE YULIO, SANDRA A; Geneva HS; Geneva, NY; (S); 26/175; Cmnty Wkr; Yrbk Stf; High Hon Roll; Hon Roll; Med Asst.

DEACY, CHRISTA; Liverpool HS; Liverpool, NY; (Y); 53/884; Art Clb; Church Yth Grp; VP SADD; School Musical; Rep Stu Cncl; High Hon Roll; Hon Roll; Jr NHS; NHS; Rgn Schlstc Art Awds 84; Psych.

DEAL, RAYMOND R; Marcus Whitman Central Schl; Stanley, NY; (Y); 6/140; Am Leg Boys St; Pres Frsh Cls; Pres Soph Cls; Pres Jr Cls; Rep Stu Cncl; Var Bsktbl; Var Ftbl; Var L Tennis; High Hon Roll; NHS; Econ.

DEAN, ANGELA; Charles O Dickerson HS; Trumansburg, NY; (Y); 4/120; Cmnty Wkr; Science Clb; Spanish Clb; Var Sftbl; Cit Awd; High Hon Roll; NHS; Engrng.

DEAN, KAREN; West Genesee HS; Camillus, NY; (Y); Sec Soph Cls; Sec Jr Cls; JV Var Socr; Var Sftbl; Stat Wrstlng; High Hon Roll; Hon Roll; MVP Var Sftbl 86; 1st Tm All Cnty 86; MVP JV Soccr 86; Child Psych.

DEAN, KIMBERLY; Cardinal O Hara HS; Kenmore, NY; (Y); Church Yth Grp; VP French Clb; School Musical; Bsktbl; Sftbl; Vllybl; Trvl.

DEAN, TERESA; Newfane SR HS; Newfane, NY; (Y); 12/152; VICA; Chorus; JV Sftbl; Hon Roll; Prfct Atten Awd; Certf Hon Key Brdng Bus Commnctns 84-85; Union Coll; Bio.

DEAN, TERRI; Holland Patent Central HS; Holland Patent, NY; (Y); GAA; Varsity Clb; Chorus; Stage Crew; Symp Band; Yrbk Stf; Rep Sr Cls; Var Diving; Var Swmmng; Hon Roll.

DEANGELIS, SHANIE; Hicksville HS; Hicksville, NY; (Y); NY U; Psych.

DEANGELO, MARIA A; Schalmont HS; Schenectady, NY; (Y); 9/166; Drama Clb; Nwsp Rptr; Yrbk Stf; Capt Crs Cntry; Capt Trk; High Hon Roll; JC Awd; VP NHS; Prfct Atten Awd; Voice Dem Awd; New Paltz; Fine Arts.

DEANGELO, PHILIP; John F Kennedy HS; Utica, NY; (Y); Church Yth Grp; Pres Stu Cncl; Var Bsbl; Var Bowling; Var Coach Actv; Capt Var Socr; Var Tennis; Hon Roll; Jr NHS; Vrsty Awd Mst Vlbl Plyr Dfns 85; 2 Yr Vrsty Bwlng Pin 86.

DEANS, ANN M; Harry S Truman HS; Bronx, NY; (Y); 85/400; Office Aide; Yrbk Stf; Hon Roll; NHS; Prfct Atten Awd; Comp Engr.

DEARBORN JR, RICH E; Troy HS; Troy, NY; (Y); 10/500; Boy Scts; German Clb; Band; School Musical; JV Capt Socr; High Hon Roll; Hon Roll; NHS; Ntl Merit Ltr; Rgnts Schlrshp NYS 86; ST U Of NY Albany; Sci.

DEATON, BRANTLEY; Pulaski Acad & Central Schl; Pulaski, NY; (Y); Pres Church Yth Grp; French Clb; Math Clb; SADD; Varsity Clb; Stage Crew; Ftbl; Trk; Wt Lftg; Tp Scr Math Lge Cntst 86-87; Pstrl.

DEBALD, ANDREA; St Francis Prep; Bayside, NY; (Y); 34/653; SADD; Im Vllybl; Hon Roll; NHS; Ntl Merit Ltr; Boston College; Bio.

DEBIQUE, NICOLE; Uniondale HS; Uniondale, NY; (Y); Church Yth Grp; Girl Scts; Hosp Aide; Red Cross Aide; Orch; Vllybl; Hon Roll; Prfct Atten Awd; Pre Med.

DEBLER, KRISTA; Ctr Moriches HS; Center Moriches, NY; (Y); 28/104; GAA; Girl Scts; Ski Clb; Spanish Clb; Varsity Clb; Band; Jazz Band; Mrchg Band; Var L Bsktbl; Var L Socr; All Lg Sccr 85; Phys Thrpy.

DEBRETTI, FRANK; New Rochelle HS; New Rochelle, NY; (Y); Church Yth Grp; Cmnty Wkr; Band; Concert Band; Flag Corp; Mrchg Band; Pep Band; Symp Band; NHS; Rlgn Chrstn Action Awd 86; Berklee Music Schl; Music Perfm.

DEBROFF, ROBERT; Union Springs Central HS; Auburn, NY; (Y); Ftbl; High Hon Roll; Hon Roll; High Hnr Boces 85-86; Drive Trk.

DEBS, CHRISTINA; Fontbonne Hall Acad; Brooklyn, NY; (Y); French Clb; Chorus; Nwsp Rptr; Yrbk Phtg; Yrbk Stf; Hon Roll; Pre-Law.

DEBYAH, MELISSA J; Franklin Acad; North Bangor, NY; (Y); 10/266; Debate Tm; NFL; Speech Tm; Thesps; School Play; Stage Crew; Hon Roll; NHS; Franklin Co Dairy Princess 85-86; Rgnts Schlrshp 86; Mary Flanagan Mem Schlrshp 85; St Lawrence U; Psych.

DEC, FRANCIS P; Auburn HS; Auburn, NY; (Y); CAP; Pres German Clb; Thesps; Jazz Band; Orch; School Musical; School Play; Swing Chorus; Symp Band; Hon Roll; Musical Theater.

DEC, REBECCA; Auburn HS; Auburn, NY; (Y); 4-H; Hosp Aide; Intnl Clb; JV Var Bsktbl; 4-H Awd; High Hon Roll; Hon Roll.

DECAMBRE, TRACIA; Mount Vernon HS; Mt Vernon, NY; (Y); Drama Clb; Hosp Aide; Key Clb; Pres Science Clb; Mrchg Band; School Play; Gym; Trk; Hon Roll; NHS; Amer Teen Mdl Yr USA 86; 2nd Rnnr Up Teen Mdl Yr NY ST 86; Actng Scholar Barizon Schl 85; George Washington; Bio Sci.

DECARO, RICHARD J; Division Ave HS; Levittown, NY; (Y); 25/335; Boy Scts; German Clb; Math Clb; Nwsp Rptr; Var Fld Hcky; Var Ftbl; High Hon Roll; Jr NHS; NHS; NY ST Rgnts Schlrshp 86; St Johns U Cmptv Schlrshp Awd 86; St Johns U; Pltcl Sci.

DECENSI, ESTHER; Hoosick Falls Central Schl; No Petersburg, NY; (Y); 21/110; Mst Imprvd Stu Of Yr Kawana Clb 85; Merit Awd Hnr Rll 85&86; Devry Tech; Comp.

DECHICK, CAROLYN; Mynderse Acad; Seneca Falls, NY; (S); 40/144; Church Yth Grp; Cmnty Wkr; Cit Awd; Hon Roll; Intr Dsgn.

DECK, MARY M; Mt St Mary Acad; Williamsville, NY; (Y); 8/112; Church Yth Grp; Computer Clb; Ski Clb; Chorus; School Musical; Nwsp Stf; Lit Mag; High Hon Roll; Ntl Merit Ltr; NEDT Awd; NY ST Rgnts Schlrshp 86; Pres Acadmc Ftns Awd 86; SUNY At Buffalo.

DECK, PAMELA; Fairport HS; Fairport, NY; (Y); French Clb; Intnl Clb; Latin Clb; Varsity Clb; Yrbk Ed-Chief; Yrbk Stf; Rep Soph Cls; Rep Jr Cls; Var L Fld Hcky; Hon Roll; Hofstra U; Pre-Med.

DECKER, BRENDA LYNN; Mynderse Acad; Seneca Falls, NY; (S); 40/143; Spanish Clb; Band; Color Guard; Concert Band; Jazz Band; Mrchg Band; Orch; Pep Band; School Musical; School Play; All-Str Jz Bnd; All-Cnty Bnd; Cazenovia Coll; Bus Mngmnt.

DECKER, DANIEL C; Alfred Almond Central Schl; Belmont, NY; (Y); Pres 4-H; FFA; JCL; Nwsp Rptr; Var Wrstlng; Cit Awd; 4-H Awd; High Hon Roll; NHS; St Schlr; Elmira Coll Key Awd 85; Alfred U Schl Ceramics; Ceramic.

DECKER, DAWN; Port Jervis HS; Huguenot, NY; (Y); 5/180; Cmnty Wkr; Key Clb; Rep Jr Cls; Var Trk; High Hon Roll; Hon Roll; Jr NHS; NHS; Regnts Schlrshp; Pace U; Pre Law.

DECKER, DEAN; Clayton A Bouton HS; Voorheesville, NY; (Y); Key Clb; JV Bsbl; JV Var Bsktbl; JV Ftbl; JV Bsktbl Ideal Teamate Awd 85; Bus.

DECKER, ELLEN; Keveny Memorial Acad; Troy, NY; (S); 6/40; Cmnty Wkr; Q&S; Service Clb; Yrbk Bus Mgr; Yrbk Stf; High Hon Roll; NHS; Natl Bus Hnr Soc 84-85; Acctg.

DECKER, JOSEPH; Maple Hill HS; Schodack Landin, NY; (Y); Drama Clb; 4-H; Spanish Clb; Wrstlng; Hon Roll; Hnr Roll; Bus.

DECKER, KATHLEEN; Queensburg HS; Glens Falls, NY; (Y); 8/248; French Clb; Key Clb; Math Clb; Ski Clb; Varsity Clb; Band; Yrbk Sprt Ed; Sec Stu Cncl; Var Swmmng; Ntl Merit Ltr; US Air Force Acad 86; Eonta Clb Schlrshp 85; USAF Acad; Elec Engrng.

DECKER, KATHY; New Paltz HS; Tooele, UT; (Y); 34/122; 4-H; Color Guard; Ed Yrbk Phtg; Yrbk Rptr; Yrbk Sprt Ed; Yrbk Stf; Sec Soph Cls; Rep Jr Cls; Stat Bsktbl; Var Fld Hcky; U Of UT; Cmnctns.

DECKER, LAURIE; Lindenhurst HS; Lindenhurst, NY; (Y); 9/512; German Clb; Girl Scts; Varsity Clb; Color Guard; Mrchg Band; Orch; Var Tennis; Var Twrlr; High Hon Roll; Jr NHS; Hofstra U; Acctng.

DECKER, MELISSA; Deposit HS; Windsor, NY; (Y); Church Yth Grp; Cmnty Wkr; GAA; Varsity Clb; Rep Stu Cncl; Var Capt Bsktbl; Var Fld Hcky; Im Sftbl; Var Capt Trk; High Hon Roll; Rotary Yth Ldrshp Assn 86; Sports Med.

DECKER, RANDY; Cambridge Central HS; Shushan, NY; (Y); 11/77; Trs 4-H; VP FFA; Library Aide; Rep Stu Cncl; Hon Roll; NHS; Ag.

DECKER, SANDRA; Sherburne-Earlville Central HS; North Norwich, NY; (Y); 5/117; Drama Clb; Hosp Aide; Mrchg Band; Orch; School Musical; School Play; Variety Show; JV Var Vllybl; NHS; NYS Schrlshp 86; William Resch Hnr Soc Mem Awd 86; Jerome Olds Mem Awd 86; Cazenovia Coll; Adv.

DECOSTA, ALISON; Midlakes HS; Phelps, NY; (Y); #14 In Class; Varsity Clb; Pres Soph Cls; Pres Jr Cls; JV Var Socr; JV Var Vllybl; Med.

DECRESCENZO, ROBERT; Copiague HS; Copiague, NY; (Y); Computer Clb; Math Clb; Yrbk Stf; Boces Smmr Clses Schlrshp 85-86; Comp Prgrmr.

DEDRICK, AMY; Keveny Memorial Acad; Troy, NY; (S); 14/41; Q&S; Spanish Clb; Band; Chorus; Concert Band; Drm Mjr(t); Jazz Band; Mrchg Band; School Musical; Yrbk Ed-Chief; St Rose; Public Comm.

DEEGAN, MARY; Our Lady Of Mercy Acad; Sea Cliff, NY; (Y); French Clb; Pres Band; Chorus; NY ST Regnts Schlrshp 86; Cert Of Merit 86; Providence Coll.

DEEGAN, WILLIAM P; Huntington HS; Huntington, NY; (Y); 43/383; Am Leg Boys St; Computer Clb; Mathletes; Political Wkr; High Hon Roll; Hon Roll; Jr NHS; NHS; Ntl Merit Ltr; Rgnts Schlrshp 86; Elec Engr.

DEELY, GREGORY; Clarkstown So HS; New City, NY; (Y); Spanish Clb; Varsity Clb; Band; Jazz Band; Mrchg Band; Symp Band; Capt Trk; Jr NHS; Lion Awd; Pres Schlr; Band Parents Sclrshp 86; Itln Amrcn Schlrshp 86; Mark Kolesar Mem Schlrshp 86; Suny New Paltz NY; Elec Engrng.

DEELY, MIKE; Pittsford Mendon HS; Pittsford, NY; (Y); Church Yth Grp; Drama Clb; Chorus; School Musical; Rep Jr Cls; Rep Sr Cls; Rep Stu Cncl; Ftbl; Trk; Hon Roll; MVP-TRK Tm 85; Engrng.

DEEP, AMY BETH; Clinton Central HS; Clinton, NY; (Y); 18/136; Concert Band; School Musical; Variety Show; Var L Cheerleading; JV Crs Cntry; Var L Fld Hcky; Var L Trk; Var L Vllybl; Jr NHS; NHS; US Rmy Rsve Natl Schlr Ahtl Awd 86; US Marine Corps Dist Athl Awd 86; Clinton-Clark Mills PTA 86; U Of Rochester.

DEES, ERIC; Elmira Free Acad; Elmira, NY; (Y); Am Leg Boys St; Spanish Clb; VP Jr Cls; Pres Sr Cls; JV Var Bsktbl; Var Golf; High Hon Roll; Hon Roll; NHS; Civil Engr.

DEES, RAMON; H C Technical HS; Buffalo, NY; (Y); Computer Clb; SAR Awd; 3rd Pl Wstrn NY Sci Congress 82; SUNY Buffalo; Aerospc Engrng.

DEFAZIO, KATIA; Sweet Home SR HS; Amherst, NY; (Y); Church Yth Grp; GAA; SADD; School Musical; Stage Crew; JV Socr; High Hon Roll; NHS; Prfct Atten Awd; Italian Hnr Soc 85-86; Ilalian Club 82-86; SUNY Buffalo; Math.

DEFAZIO, MELANIE; St Peters HS; Staten Island, NY; (Y); Cheerleading; Bus Awds 86; SECRETARY.

DEFAZIO, SANDRA; St Peters High For Girls; Staten Island, NY; (Y); JV Cheerleading; Grace Inst; Para Lgl.

DEFENDINI, PATRICIA; Farmingdale HS; Farmingdale, NY; (Y); Church Yth Grp; Cmnty Wkr; Office Aide; SADD; Varsity Clb; Band; Church Choir; Concert Band; Orch; Var Mgr(s); Educ.

DEFEO, MICHAEL J; Monticello HS; Rockhill, NY; (Y); 9/195; Church Yth Grp; French Clb; Math Tm; JV Bsbl; JV Trk; High Hon Roll; Hon Roll; NHS; Regents Schlrshp 86; Pres Schlrshp-U Of Tampa 86; U Of Tampa; Marine Bio.

DEFEO, SUZANNE; Mt Vernon HS; Mt Vernon, NY; (Y); Church Yth Grp; Trs Keywanettes; School Musical; VP Soph Cls; VP Jr Cls; Stu Cncl; Score Keeper; Var Swmmng; High Hon Roll; NHS; Keyette Awd Svc Dedication 85; MIP Swim 84.

DEFILIPPIS, CHRIS; Fox Lane HS; Pound Ridge, NY; (Y); Boy Scts; Church Yth Grp; Exploring; JA; Ski Clb; Stu Cncl; Bsbl; Diving; Socr; Hon Roll; Mktg.

DEFOREST, EVETTE; Hamburg Central HS; Boston, NY; (Y); Church Yth Grp; JCL; Political Wkr; Lit Mag; Rep Frsh Cls; Sec Soph Cls; Rep Jr Cls; Rep Stu Cncl; Var Fld Hcky; Stat Wrstlng; Boston Coll; Pre Law.

DEFRANCO, DOUGLAS A; The Wheatley Schl; Old Westbury, NY; (Y); 56/133; Chess Clb; Drama Clb; Exploring; SADD; Varsity Clb; Acpl Chr; Chorus; School Musical; School Play; Yrbk Stf; NY Rgnst Schlrshp 86; Hofstra U; Bus.

DEFREITAS, SIMONE; Baldwin SR HS; Freeport, NY; (Y); Church Yth Grp; Cmnty Wkr; Key Clb; SADD; Chorus; Rep Jr Cls; Sec Sr Cls; Rep Stu Cncl; Fordam; Bus.

DEFRIEST, JODI; Riverhead HS; Riverhead, NY; (Y); 35/230; Art Clb; French Clb; Spanish Clb; Band; Mrchg Band; Var Tennis; Im Wrstlng; French Hon Soc; Rotary Awd; A P Am Hist Cls 85-86; Wrkd Schl Flts & Mrls 83-87; Interior Dsgn.

DEGAETANO, ANNA; Sachem HS; Holbrook, NY; (Y); 110/1500; Church Yth Grp; French Clb; Orch; Hst Frsh Cls; Off Soph Cls; Off Jr Cls; Stat Score Keeper; Socr; French Hon Soc; Hon Roll; Outstndng Perf Trck-Fld, Sccr 82-83; Orvall Acad Achvt 80-81; Music Awd 80-81; Bucknell; Jrnlsm.

DEGALA, REX; Xavier HS; Brooklyn, NY; (Y); Boy Scts; ROTC; Var Trk; DAR Awd; Hon Roll; Archtctr.

DEGELLEKE, JANA; Lyons HS; Sodus, NY; (Y); Church Yth Grp; Girl Scts; Ski Clb; Band; Chorus; Concert Band; Mrchg Band; JV Trk; Hon Roll; Prfct Atten Awd; Agrnmy.

DEGELLEKE, JENELL; Clyde-Savannah HS; Lyons, NY; (Y); Sec Jr Cls; Sec Sr Cls; Rep Stu Cncl; Var Tennis; Var JV Vllybl; High Hon Roll; Hon Roll; Hnrs Engl 84-87; Hnr Currclm 87; Daytona Bch CC; Bus Adm.

DEGEN, ANDREW; Abraham Lincoln HS; Brooklyn, NY; (Y); 100/440; Letterman Clb; Varsity Clb; Capt Wrstlng; Ira Towbin Physcl Ftns Awd 82-83; St Johns; Sprts Mgmt.

DEGILIO, PETER; G Ray Bodley HS; Fulton, NY; (Y); SADD; VICA; Chorus; Drm & Bgl; Yrbk Phtg; Yrbk Stf; Rep Stu Cncl; Im Ftbl; Var Swmmng; Var Trk; Elctrncs.

DEGNI, RICHARD; H Frnak Carey HS; Franklin Square, NY; (Y); 28/338; Camera Clb; SADD; Yrbk Phtg; Yrbk Sprt Ed; Sec Frsh Cls; VP Soph Cls; Pres Jr Cls; Pres Sr Cls; JV Bsktbl; NHS; James A De Sonne Prncpls Awd 86; Fclty Schlrshp 86; Outstndng Art Stu Awd 86; Schl Of Visual Arts; Adv.

DEGRANGE, MICHELE; Dominican Commercial HS; Woodhaven, NY; (Y); 53/280; Teachers Aide; Yrbk Stf; High Hon Roll; Hon Roll; NHS; Siena Clb 83; Natl Hnr Bus Soc 86; Schlstc Achvt Awd 86; Bus Mngmnt.

DEHAQUIZ, CLAUDINE; Tottenville HS; Staten Island, NY; (Y); 80/875; Church Yth Grp; Library Aide; Office Aide; Teachers Aide; Church Choir; Orch; Socr; Timer; High Hon Roll; Hon Roll; Coll Statn Islnd Schlrshp 86; Trphy Schlr Athlt Sccr 86; Ntl Hnr Soc Awd 86; Coll Staten Islnd; Lbrl Arts.

DEHLINGER, HEIDI; Wilson Central HS; Lockport, NY; (Y); Art Clb; 4-H; Stage Crew; Nwsp Phtg; Yrbk Stf; 4-H Awd; Hon Roll; Attnd NY ST Smmr Schl Arts 86; Bst Bus & Art Stu; Art.

DEIBEL, ANN MARIE; St John The Baptist HS; Islip, NY; (S); Church Yth Grp; Hosp Aide; Hon Roll; Regents Coll Nrsng Schlrshp 86; Hnr Rll 82-86; Albany Med Ctr; Nrs.

DEICHMAN, PAM; Half Hollow Hills HS East; Melville, NY; (Y); Leo Clb; SADD; Temple Yth Grp; Nwsp Rptr; Nwsp Stf; Yrbk Stf; Mgr(s); JV Tennis; High Hon Roll; Hon Roll; MD U; Cmmnctns.

DEIDAN, DIANA J; St Francis Prep; Woodside, NY; (S); 168/744; Church Yth Grp; Cmnty Wkr; Office Aide; Service Clb; SADD; Teachers Aide; Ftbl; Trk; Hon Roll; Opt Clb Awd; Arch.

DEITZ, TRINA; Bethlehem Central HS; Delmar, NY; (Y); 21/305; GAA; Key Clb; School Play; Yrbk Stf; JV Var Cheerleading; High Hon Roll; NHS; Pres Schlr; Pres Acad Ftns Awd 86; Russell Sage Fndrs Schlrshp & Spgfld Coll Schlrshp 86; Best All-Arnd Chrldr 86; Springfield Coll; Phys Ther.

DEL BALSO, CHRISTINE; Westfield Acad; Westfield, NY; (Y); Pres Model UN; Band; VP Chorus; Concert Band; School Musical; Pres Frsh Cls; Sec Stu Cncl; Score Keeper; High Hon Roll; NHS.

DEL BALZO, DENISE; Pelham Memorial HS; Pelham, NY; (Y); 26/157; Church Yth Grp; Drama Clb; School Musical; School Play; Stage Crew; Lit Mag; NHS; Ladies Aux Pelham Cvc Assn Schlrshp 86; Manhattanville Coll; Langs.

DEL CASALE, KAREN; St Catharine Acad; Bronx, NY; (Y); 25/205; Ski Clb; Teachers Aide; Yrbk Ed-Chief; Rep Frsh Cls; Rep Soph Cls; Rep Jr Cls; Rep Sr Cls; Rep Stu Cncl; JC Awd; NHS; Trstee Schlrshp Pace U 86; Schlrshp Grnt Iona Coll 86; Fordham; Acctg.

DEL EVEILLE, LORI; Andrew Jackson HS; Hollis, NY; (Y); 29/539; Aud/Vis; Concert Band; Jazz Band; Mrchg Band; Wt Lftg; Hon Roll; NHS; Regents Scholar Awd 86-87; St Johns U; Modlng.

DEL GUIDICE, DIANA; Mary Louis Acad; Middle Village, NY; (Y); Cmnty Wkr; Office Aide; Queens Coll; Bus Mgmt.

DEL MONTE JR, EDWARD J; Port Chester HS; Port Chester, NY; (Y); 2/250; Am Leg Boys St; Pres Key Clb; VP Spanish Clb; Yrbk Ed-Chief; VP Sr Cls; JV Bsbl; Cit Awd; Mu Alp Tht; NHS; Sal; Hugh O Brien Yth Ldrshp 84; Duracel Sci Cntst SF 83; Lehigh U; Engrng.

DEL NEGRO, SUSAN; Albertus Magnus HS; Garnerville, NY; (Y); 69/189; Camera Clb; Service Clb; School Musical; JV Var Socr; JV Capt Vllybl; U Of Scranton; Frgn Lang.

DEL PILAR, DEBBIE; Newfield HS; Selden, NY; (Y); Cmnty Wkr; FBLA; Service Clb; SADD; Rep Frsh Cls; Rep Soph Cls; Rep Jr Cls; JV Sftbl; Hon Roll; Jr NHS; 1st Pl Spnsh Prod In Longislnd Lng Fr 86; Nrsng.

DEL POPOLO JR, JOSEPH; Manlius Pebble Hill HS; Liverpool, NY; (Y); 10/36; Political Wkr; SADD; Yrbk Ed-Chief; Ed Lit Mag; Stu Cncl; L Bsbl; L Bsktbl; L Ftbl; Socr; L Trk; NY ST Rgnts Schlrshp; All League Goalie Ltr; MVP Team Dfnsv In Ftbl; Lehigh U; Attorney.

DEL PRADO, ALONA; Academy Of Mt St Ursula; Bronx, NY; (Y); Boys Clb Am; Drama Clb; Hosp Aide; Library Aide; School Musical; Stage Crew; Nwsp Stf; Yrbk Stf; Stu Cncl; Hon Roll; 1st Hnr, Scl Studies Awd 83-84; Nrsng.

DEL RIO, MICHAEL; Stuyvesant HS; New York, NY; (Y); Office Aide; Teachers Aide; NYS Regents Scholar 86; Trustee Scholar 86; Semi Fin Natl Hspnc Schlrs Awds Pgm 85; Columbia Schl Engrng; Engrng.

DEL ROSARIO, MARC; Valley Stream Central HS; Valley Stream, NY; (Y); 140/349; Im Lcrss; Var Capt Socr; All Division Sccr Plyr 84-85; All Leag Sccr Plyr 85-86; MVP Vs Cntrl Sccr Plyr 85-86; NY Inst Tech; Mech Engr.

DEL ROSSI, CHRISTINE; Bayport Blue Pnt HS; Blue Point, NY; (Y); 42/240; Office Aide; Ice Hcky; JV Vllybl; Hon Roll.

DEL SIGNORE, PETER; Gloversville HS; Gloversville, NY; (Y); AFS; VP SADD; Stage Crew; Nwsp Stf; Yrbk Sprt Ed; Var Crs Cntry; Hon Roll; Prfct Atten Awd; Sci.

DEL VALLE, ANGEL; All Hallows HS; Bronx, NY; (S); 4/90; Stage Crew; Yrbk Phtg; Yrbk Stf; Stu Cncl; Bowling; Crs Cntry; High Hon Roll; Ntl Merit Ltr; Iona Coll; Bus Mngmnt.

DEL VECCHIO II, ANTHONY J; West Genesee SR HS; Syracuse, NY; (Y); FCA; Rep Frsh Cls; Rep Jr Cls; Rep Stu Cncl; JV Var Bsbl; DAR Awd; Hon Roll; JR Sent; Sci.

DEL VECCHIO, MARIA T; Preston HS; Bronx, NY; (S); Science Clb; Teachers Aide; Stage Crew; Pres Frsh Cls; Pres Soph Cls; Cheerleading; High Hon Roll; Jr NHS; NHS; Drama Clb; NYU; Psychlgy.

DELA ESPRIELLA, JUAN CARLOS; Msgr Mc Clancy HS; Queens, NY; (Y); Hon Roll; Law.

DELA ROSA, JACQUELINE; Morris HS; Bronx, NY; (Y); 2/30; JA; Scholastic Bowl; Spanish Clb; Teachers Aide; Stu Cncl; NHS; Prfct Atten Awd; Aeronaut Engrng.

DELAFUENTE, KARA; Dundee Central HS; Dundee, NY; (Y); Hon Roll; Engl Hnrs Course 86; Art.

DELAND, MOYA H; Portville Central HS; Portville, NY; (Y); 28/109; Pres Frsh Cls; Pres Soph Cls; Pres Jr Cls; Pres Sr Cls; Cheerleading; NHS; Mass Comm.

DELANEY, COLLEEN; South Park HS; Buffalo, NY; (Y); Hosp Aide; Band; Mrchg Band; Rep Stu Cncl; Var Sftbl; Typng Awd 86; Merit Awd 86; Nrsng.

DELANEY, DARCY; Thousand Islands HS; Clayton, NY; (Y); Girl Scts; Band; Chorus; Color Guard; Concert Band; Jazz Band; Mrchg Band; School Musical; School Play; Var Capt Cheerleading; ROTC; Teacher.

DELANEY, JOE; Skaneateles Central HS; Skoneateles, NY; (S); Church Yth Grp; Latin Clb; SADD; Var Ftbl; Var Golf; Var Ice Hcky; High Hon Roll; Jr NHS; Varsity Clb; Law.

DELANEY, STACEY; Berne-Knox-Westerlo HS; Glenmont, NY; (Y); Yrbk Stf; Trs Frsh Cls; Pres Soph Cls; Rep Stu Cncl; JV Cheerleading; Stat Socr; High Hon Roll; Hon Roll; Bus.

DELANGO, DAWN; Roosevelt HS; Yonkers, NY; (Y); Camera Clb; JA; Math Clb; Pep Clb; Nwsp Phtg; Nwsp Stf; Yrbk Phtg; Yrbk Rptr; Yrbk Stf; Cheerleading; Elizabeth Seton Coll; Lgl Sec.

DELEEL, ROXANE; Marion Central Schl; Marion, NY; (Y); Sec German Clb; Concert Band; Jazz Band; Mrchg Band; School Musical; Yrbk Stf; Tennis; Hon Roll; NHS; Prfct Atten Awd.

DELEIS, SHAWN; Alexander Hamilton HS; Elmsford, NY; (Y); Cmnty Wkr; Drama Clb; Key Clb; Office Aide; Off Jr Cls; Cheerleading; Pom Pon; Hon Roll; Outstndng Awd Most Imprvd Chrldr 84-86; Howard U; Comm.

DELESSIO, ANN; Valley Central HS; Maybrook, NY; (Y); 60/313; Church Yth Grp; Hon Roll; IBM Sec Co-Op Wrk E Niskkill Ny 86-87; Bus.

DELGADO, BELINDA; St Raymond Acad For Girls; Bronx, NY; (Y); Boys Clb Am; Church Yth Grp; Library Aide; Church Choir; Drm Mjr(t); Mrchg Band; Yrbk Phtg; Yrbk Stf; Prfct Atten Awd; Pre-Med.

DELGADO, JOHN; Newfield HS; Selden, NY; (Y); 5/510; Trs Church Yth Grp; Computer Clb; Math Tm; Science Clb; Nwsp Rptr; French Hon Soc; NHS; Spanish NHS.

DELGADO, RAFAEL E; Adela Stevenson HS; Bronx, NY; (Y); Church Yth Grp; JA; Office Aide; PAVAS; Concert Band; Orch; Nwsp Rptr; Cit Awd; Mck Trl, Crt Lwyr 86; Law.

DELGAN, JEFFRY; Mahopac HS; Mahopac, NY; (Y); 8/409; Pres Frsh Cls; JV Wrstlng; High Hon Roll; NHS; Ntl Merit SF; Schl Wnnr AHSME 85 & 86; MIT; Elec Engrng.

DELGAUDIO, ANDREA; Charles H Roth HS; Rochester, NY; (Y); 2/195; Church Yth Grp; Ski Clb; Lit Mag; French Hon Soc; High Hon Roll; Jr NHS; NHS; Sal; Prix D Honneur Frnch Awd 84; NYSSSA Visl Arts 85; Boston Coll; Biol.

DELGAUDIO, MICHAEL J; Loyola HS; New York City, NY; (Y); 11/50; Pres Stu Cncl; Var Bsbl; Var Capt Bsktbl; Var Capt Socr; Hon Roll; Boston Coll; Lib Arts.

DELIA, LAURIE; Mynderse Acad; Seneca Falls, NY; (S); 14/138; Church Yth Grp; GAA; Spanish Clb; Var Bsktbl; Var Socr; Var Trk; High Hon Roll; Natl Merit Hnr Rll 84; SADD 85.

DELIBERT, MICHELE; Edison Tech HS; Rochester, NY; (Y); Ski Clb; JV Var Bsktbl; Var Socr; Var Capt Sftbl; JV Var Vllybl; High Hon Roll; Hon Roll; Outstndng Achvt Math 84-86; Outstndng Achvt Sci 84; Mech Engr.

DELILLO, MARK; Monsignor Farrell HS; Staten Island, NY; (Y); Ftbl; NHS; Aud/Vis; SADD; Yrbk Stf; VP Soph Cls; Rep Jr Cls; Rep Sr Cls; Rep Stu Cncl; Im Bsktbl; Chrmn Sprdnc MDA 86-87; Catholic HS Cnfrnce 84-86; Actn Ldrshp Cnvctn 86.

DELIMA, MARGARET; Acad Of St Joseph; Sayville, NY; (Y); Art Clb; School Musical; School Play; Stage Crew; NHS; Hnrb Mntn Congrssnl Art Cont 86; Excllnce Art 85-86; Art.

DELLA BOVIE, LOUIS; James Madison HS; Brooklyn, NY; (Y); 28/756; JA; Nwsp Stf; Lit Mag; Im Bsbl; Im Bsktbl; Golf; Im Ice Hcky; Pre-Law.

DELLA ROCCA, GREGORY J; Maple Hill HS; Castleton, NY; (S); 1/100; Math Tm; Jazz Band; Symp Band; VP Frsh Cls; Pres Soph Cls; Var Socr; High Hon Roll; Masonic Awd; NHS; Computer Clb; Lorenz W Peter Gen Sci Awd 84; Med.

DELLA VALLE, CRAIG; West Hempstead HS; West Hempstead, NY; (Y); Boy Scts; Ski Clb; Pres Frsh Cls; JV Lcrss; Wt Lftg; Hon Roll; Pres Jr NHS; Pres NHS; Ntl Merit Ltr; Outstndg Prfrmnc Advncd Bio 85-86; Pre-Med.

DELLA VALLE, DAVID; Monsignor Farrell HS; Staten Island, NY; (Y); Boy Scts; Drama Clb; Letterman Clb; Ski Clb; Spanish Clb; Y-Teens; Stage Crew; Stu Cncl; Bsktbl; Crs Cntry; ST U At Albany; Law.

DELLACONTRADA, DAVID; Rome Catholic HS; Rome, NY; (Y); Bsktbl; Prfct Atten Awd; Math Achvt 83-84; Bio Achvt 84-85; Math II Achvt 85-86; Busnss Admin.

DELLACORTE, DANIELLE; Roy C Ketcham HS; Wappingers Falls, NY; (Y); Church Yth Grp; Sec Drama Clb; Thesps; Ed Nwsp Phtg; Yrbk Ed-Chief; High Hon Roll; NHS; Columbia; Educ.

DELLHEIM, MIRIAM R; Arlington HS; Poughkeepsie, NY; (Y); Exploring; Hosp Aide; Red Cross Aide; Teachers Aide; Temple Yth Grp; Orch; School Play; Yrbk Stf; St Schlr; Nrsng.

DELLI CARPINI, JOSEPH; Pelham Memorial HS; Pelham, NY; (Y); Pres Computer Clb; Band; Concert Band; Jazz Band; Mrchg Band; Pep Band; Nwsp Rptr; Hon Roll; Prfct Atten Awd; Tri-M Music Hnrs Soc Chptr VP 85-86; Meteorlgy.

DELLI PIZZI, ANN MARIE; St Catherines Acad; Bronx, NY; (S); 2/200; Dance Clb; Hosp Aide; Office Aide; Teachers Aide; Nwsp Ed-Chief; Rep Soph Cls; Stu Cncl; Gov Hon Prg Awd; NHS.

DELLICARPINI, LINA; Preston HS; New York, NY; (Y); 10/89; Drama Clb; School Play; Nwsp Stf; Sec Frsh Cls; Sec Soph Cls; Sec Jr Cls; Hon Roll; Sec VP NHS; Rgnts Schlrshp Cert 86; Cert App & Grat Vlntr Svc 84; Fash Inst Of Tech; Fash Byng.

DELMAGE, JI; Candor Central HS; Willseyville, NY; (Y); Camera Clb; Chorus; Yrbk Stf; Trk; Hon Roll; NHS.

DELMONTE, TONY; St Marys HS; Depew, NY; (Y); 11/169; Pres Frsh Cls; Pres Soph Cls; Pres Jr Cls; Pres Stu Cncl; Var L Bsbl; Var L Ftbl; Var L Ice Hcky; High Hon Roll; NHS; Stu Ldrshp Inst 85-86; MVP Bsbl 84-85; All Catholics Ftbl 85-86; US Navl Acad; Med.

DELONGCHAMP, JAMES; Bishop Scully HS; Amsterdam, NY; (Y); 15/48; Math Clb; Trs Soph Cls; Trs Jr Cls; Trs Sr Cls; Var JV Bsbl; JV Bsktbl; Score Keeper; Hotel Mgmt.

DELORENZO, DAVID; Trott Voc HS; Niagara Falls, NY; (Y); Stage Crew; Hon Roll; NHS; Electrn.

DELPRINCIPE, VICTORIA A; St Catharine Acad; Bronx, NY; (Y); Girl Scts; Library Aide; Teachers Aide; Yrbk Stf; NHS; Iona Coll; Intl Stud.

DELSIGNORE, CINDY; Cicero-North Syracuse HS; North Syracuse, NY; (S); 40/667; Trs JA; SADD; Rep Soph Cls; Trs Jr Cls; Stu Cncl; JV Socr; Hon Roll; NHS; Actg.

DELSOIN, MARC A; Springfield Gardens HS; Rosedale, NY; (Y); Computer Clb; Office Aide; Comp Sci.

DELSOIN, PIERRE; John Dewey HS; Brooklyn, NY; (Y); Dance Clb; Teachers Aide; School Musical; School Play; Bsktbl; Coach Actv; Ftbl; Sftbl; Trk; Vllybl; Law.

DELUCA, DANIEL L; Penn Yan Acad; Penn Yan, NY; (Y); Church Yth Grp; Drama Clb; Varsity Clb; School Musical; School Play; Variety Show; Yrbk Stf; Var L Bowling; Var L Ftbl; Hon Roll; NY ST Rgnts Schlrshp 86; Cmrcl Art.

DELUCA, DEBBY; Tottenville HS; Staten Isld, NY; (Y); Aud/Vis; Ski Clb; Band; Prfct Atten Awd; Music.

DELUCA, JULIANNE; Alexander Hamilton HS; Elmsford, NY; (Y); Key Clb; Spanish Clb; Var Capt Cheerleading; Var Sftbl; Var Trk; Hon Roll; 2nd Hnrs 83-86; Merch Bus.

DELVECCHIO, DANIEL; Charlotte HS; Rochester, NY; (Y); Aud/Vis; Debate Tm; FBLA; Office Aide; Varsity Clb; Concert Band; Rep Stu Cncl; Var Bowling; Var Tennis; Hon Roll; Standard Bearer 86; Hugh O Brien 85; Elmira Coll Key 86; Acctnt.

DELVICARIO, CARMELA; Bethpage HS; Bethpage, NY; (Y); FBLA; Mathletes; SADD; Concert Band; Drm Mjr(t); Jazz Band; Orch; School Musical; Lcrss; High Hon Roll; Tri M Music Hnr Scty Treasr 85-86; Italian Scty 85-86; Princpls Cabinet 85-86; Psychtry.

DELWO, KRISTI; Herkimer HS; Herkimer, NY; (Y); 1/126; Sec Drama Clb; Pep Clb; VP SADD; School Musical; Yrbk Stf; VP Stu Cncl; Var Cheerleading; Var Gym; Vllybl; Cit Awd; Regents Schlrshp NYS; Albany ST; Pre Med.

DELZOTTO, JEANMARIE; Harborfields HS; Greenlawn, NY; (Y); Art Clb; Camera Clb; Church Yth Grp; Dance Clb; Pep Clb; Ski Clb; Chorus; School Play; Variety Show; Yrbk Stf; Mrt Trck Mst Efrt Shwn 84; Law.

DEMARCO, JOSEPH; Mechanicville HS; Mechanicville, NY; (S); 29/105; Red Cross Aide; Spanish Clb; Pres Band; Pres Concert Band; Pres Mrchg Band; Pres Orch; Pres Pep Band; Symp Band; Golf; Cit Awd; Aris Toi 85-86; Hudson Valley CC; Elect.

DEMARCO, MATTHEW; Archbishop Stepinac HS; Harrison, NY; (Y); 19/175; Sec Exploring; JA; Nwsp Rptr; Rep Stu Cncl; L Ftbl; Hon Roll; Jr NHS; NHS; Schl Ltr Acadmc Achvt; Pre Med.

DEMARCO, MICHAEL; Hannibal Central HS; Martville, NY; (Y); JV Crs Cntry; Var Tennis; Var Trk; High Hon Roll; Hon Roll; NHS; Prfct Atten Awd; FL Inst Tech; Actg.

DEMARE, JAMES; Rome Free Acad; Rome, NY; (Y); 16/400; Intnl Clb; High Hon Roll; NHS; Actg.

DEMAREE, MARIA L; Maine-Endwell SR HS; Endwell, NY; (Y); 13/240; Rep Church Yth Grp; GAA; Office Aide; SADD; Yrbk Bus Mgr; Tennis; Twrlr; DAR Awd; NHS.

DEMARIA, KAREN; West Genesee HS; Syracuse, NY; (Y); Library Aide; Teachers Aide; Hon Roll; Stu Rcgntn Awd Home Ec 86; Early Chldhd Educ.

DEMARIA, LAURA; S H Calhoun HS; Merrick, NY; (Y); Cmnty Wkr; Nwsp Phtg; Yrbk Phtg; Physcl Ed Awd; Rochester Ist Of Tech; Advstng.

DEMARIA, LINDA; Amsterdam HS; Amsterdam, NY; (Y); 46/310; VP FBLA; Hosp Aide; JA; VP JA; Orch; Yrbk Phtg; Yrbk Stf; Off Stu Cncl; Hon Roll; JR Achvt-Outstdng Slsprsn & Bst Indvdl Achvr 83-84; Comm.

DEMARTE, ANTHONY J; Angelica Central HS; Belmont, NY; (Y); 7/37; Am Leg Boys St; Trs Drama Clb; Pres 4-H; Ski Clb; Pres Frsh Cls; Pres Jr Cls; Pres Stu Cncl; Var Capt Bsktbl; Socr; 4-H Awd; Ntl Hnr Soc & JR Ntl Hnr Soc 82-87; Ntl Awd Photogrphy 4-H 85; Bys ST Lgsltr & Cnclmn; U Of Buffalo; Bus.

DEMATTEO, LEANN; Rome Free Acad; Rome, NY; (Y); Intnl Clb; Key Clb; Ski Clb; SADD; Yrbk Bus Mgr; Yrbk Stf; JV Capt Fld Hcky; Var Gym; Score Keeper; Im Swmmng; All Str Trk & Fld 83; JV Fld Hocky Mst Imprvd 84; Crmnl Jstc.

DEMATTEO, LESLIE; New Paltz HS; New Paltz, NY; (Y); Yrbk Phtg; Ulster Cnty Cmnty; Bus Admin.

DEMBSKI, LINDA; Frontier Central HS; Hamburg, NY; (Y); Political Wkr; Spanish Clb; SADD; Jazz Band; Orch; Rep Jr Cls; Rep Stu Cncl; JV Var Swmmng; Hon Roll; Church Yth Grp; St Boniventure U; Law.

DEMER, DAVID; Chenango Valley HS; Binghamton, NY; (Y); Aud/Vis; Yrbk Phtg; Yrbk Stf; L Socr; Im Vllybl; Hon Roll; Jr NHS; Boy Scts; Church Yth Grp; VP Rep Frsh Cls; Cmnctns.

DEMERI, MARY A; Saint Francis Prep; Middle Village, NY; (S); 36/744; Church Yth Grp; Civic Clb; Library Aide; Science Clb; Nwsp Rptr; Nwsp Stf; High Hon Roll; Hon Roll; NHS; Crim Lwyr.

DEMERS, KELLY; Skaneateles HS; Skaneateles, NY; (Y); 6/152; Pres Stu Cncl; Capt Var Bsktbl; Capt Var Socr; Var Trk; NHS; ROTC Awd-Natl Schlr/Athltc 86; West Point.

DEMICCO, JULIE; Beacon HS; Fishkill, NY; (Y); Key Clb; Ski Clb; Spanish Clb; Varsity Clb; School Play; Stage Crew; Yrbk Stf; Var Bowling; Jr NHS; NHS; Bio.

DEMING, JOANNE; Hoosic Valley Central HS; Valley Falls, NY; (Y); Dance Clb; Band; Chorus; School Musical; Rep Stu Cncl; Stat Bsktbl; JV Cheerleading; JV Fld Hcky; JV Sftbl; Danced With Berkshire Ballet 84 & 85; Busnss Admin.

DEMINO, TRACEY I; Brockport HS; Spencerport, NY; (Y); 7/335; Mathletes; Ski Clb; Jazz Band; Mrchg Band; Symp Band; Golf; Socr; High Hon Roll; Hon Roll; NHS; Rgnts Schlrshp 86; Effrt Cmmndtn 86; Cornell; Pre-Med.

DEMIRJIAN, JANET; Christopher Columbus HS; Bronx, NY; (Y); 179/763; Office Aide; Teachers Aide; Chorus; Nwsp Ed-Chief; Nwsp Rptr; Cit Awd; Chancellors Hnr Roll-100 Pct Atten 4 Yrs 86; NY Schltc Press Assn 86; Bd Of Ed Cert-Continous Schl Sv; Fordham U.

DEMIS, ROBERT; Ravena-Coeymans-Selkirk HS; Feura Bush, NY; (Y); Varsity Clb; Wrstlng; Gnrl Cntrctng.

DEMME, NILS; Mahopac HS; Mahopac, NY; (Y); Radio Clb; Science Clb; Nwsp Rptr; Lcrss; Socr; Boston U; Cmmnctns.

DEMMIN, TRACY; Wilson Central HS; Lockport, NY; (Y); Art Clb; Church Yth Grp; 4-H; Band; Var Bsktbl; Powder Puff Ftbl; Stat Wrstlng; 4-H Awd; Hon Roll; Art Mjr 83-87; Cmrcl Art.

DEMON, KEITH; Troupsburg Central HS; Troupsburg, NY; (Y); Computer Clb; 4-H; French Clb; FFA; Mathletes; Nwsp Stf; Var L Bsktbl; JV Mgr(s); Var Socr; 4-H Awd; FFA Jdgng Cttl 84-86; Grnhnd Frmr & Chapt Frmr 85; Anml Hsbndry.

DEMONACO, JAMES; Tottenville HS; Staten Island, NY; (Y); 96/900; Camera Clb; Var L Bsbl; High Hon Roll; Hon Roll; Jr NHS; NHS; Stu Athlt Awd 84&86; Knny Srg Mem Schlrshp 86; Rutgers U; Cmmnctn Art.

DEMORE, WYNNE; Corcoran HS; Syracuse, NY; (Y); Cmnty Wkr; Exploring; Girl Scts; Color Guard; Nrsg.

DEMOURA, ANITA; Mt Vernon HS; Mount Vernon, NY; (Y); 75/530; Dance Clb; French Clb; Library Aide; Teachers Aide; Hon Roll; Iona Coll; Lang.

DEMPSEY, CAROLINE; Moore Catholic HS; Staten Island, NY; (Y); SADD; Stage Crew; Yrbk Phtg; Yrbk Stf; Score Keeper; Sftbl; Hon Roll; Pre-Law.

DEMPSEY, JOE; Bolivar Central Schl; Boliver, NY; (Y); 5/60; Am Leg Boys St; Ski Clb; Band; Chorus; Bsbl; Bsktbl; Ftbl; High Hon Roll; Hon Roll; NHS; Engrng.

DEMPSEY, PAULA; Oceanside HS; Oceanside, NY; (Y); 19/535; Dance Clb; Library Aide; Model UN; Service Clb; Trs Spanish Clb; VP Band; School Musical; Nwsp Stf; Hon Roll; NHS; Frgn Lng Awd In Spnsh II, III, IV 82-85; HIP Prgm For Excptnly Brght Stu 82-83; Hofstra U.

DENAPOLE, TRACEY; Herkimer HS; E Herkimer, NY; (Y); 5/110; Church Yth Grp; Model UN; Sftbl; High Hon Roll; NHS; Psych.

DENCE, TRACY L; Pulaski JR SR HS; Pulaski, NY; (S); French Clb; GAA; Intnl Clb; Ski Clb; SADD; Variety Show; Mgr(s); Score Keeper; Timer; Hon Roll; Concours De Francais-Fr Cont 85.

DENDY, DAVID; Valley Central HS; Montgomery, NY; (Y); 170/313; Yrbk Stf; Trk; Ntl Merit Ltr; Pace U; Arch.

DENEEN III, JAMES E; Valley Stream South HS; Valley Stream, NY; (Y); 49/168; Computer Clb; Mathletes; JV Var Socr; NY ST Regents Coll Schlrshp 86; Nassau CC; Bus Adm.

DENENKAMP, MICHELLE L; Miller Palce HS; Miller Place, NY; (Y); 30/210; Church Yth Grp; Sftbl; Trk; Hon Roll; NHS; SUNY Binghamton; Mngmt.

DENERO, JOSEPH A; Bishop Grimes HS; Syracuse, NY; (Y); 71/146; Church Yth Grp; Band; Concert Band; Pep Band; All Amer Hall Of Fame Bond Hnrs 85; MA Coll Of Pharm Schlrshp 86; MA Coll Of Pharmacy; Pharm.

DENESHA, STACY; Hermon-Dekalb Central HS; De Kalb Jct, NY; (Y); 13/42; Pres Drama Clb; Nwsp Ed-Chief; Yrbk Sprt Ed; VP Jr Cls; VP Stu Cncl; Co-Capt Bsktbl; Var Socr; Var Sftbl; Capt Var Vllybl; Hon Roll; Masonic Schlrshp 86; Potsdam ST; Advtstng.

DENGAL, WAYNE; Mc Quaid Jesuit HS; Henrietta, NY; (Y); Boy Scts; French Hon Soc; High Hon Roll; Hon Roll; Schl Acad Let 86; Comp Sci.

DENGEL, PETER T; Newfield HS; Selden, NY; (Y); 50/515; Boy Scts; Varsity Clb; Ftbl; Wt Lftg; Wrstlng; High Hon Roll; Hon Roll; Prfct Atten Awd; Pres Schlr; Rgnts Schlrshp 86; Syracuse U; Arch.

DENGER, LYNN; Seaford HS; Seaford, NY; (S); Band; Mrchg Band; Symp Band; VP Soph Cls; VP Stu Cncl; Bsktbl; Cheerleading; Pom Pon; Sftbl; Hon Roll; Luthrn Chrch Bsktbl Leag 84; Al-Star Bsktbl Gm MVP 84; Elem Ed.

DENGLER, ROBERT; Hauppauge HS; Hauppauge, NY; (Y); Nwsp Stf; JV Var Bsbl; Im Bsktbl; JV Trk; High Hon Roll; NHS; Ntl Merit Ltr; Engrng.

DENGOS, PAMELA; Hamburg HS; Hamburg, NY; (Y); French Clb; Chorus; Socr; Vllybl; Hon Roll.

DENICOURT, SCOTT; Potsdam Central HS; Potsdam, NY; (Y); 5/123; French Clb; Math Clb; Varsity Clb; Rep Frsh Cls; Rep Soph Cls; Rep Stu Cncl; Bsbl; Ftbl; Ice Hcky; High Hon Roll; Schl Mem Scholar 86; Clarkson U; Elec Engrng.

DENIG, KELLY; Academy Of Saint Joseph; Massapequa, NY; (Y); Art Clb; Church Yth Grp; Pep Clb; Red Cross Aide; Chorus; NHS; Supr Acad Achvt Sci & Spnsh 84 & 85; Supr Acad Achvt Spnsh 84; Columbia U; Elem Educ.

DENIS, SHELLY; Burnt Hills Baylston Lake HS; Scotia, NY; (Y); Pres Church Yth Grp; High Hon Roll; Hon Roll; Stu Of Mth-Ind Arts 86; Org Of Trngls-Onistagrawa Chptr 83-85; Crmnl Jstc.

DENIS, TIMOTHY; Tupper Lake Central HS; Piercefield, NY; (Y); 18/99; Camera Clb; Chess Clb; JV Var Bsbl; Hon Roll; Chem Awd 86; Accelerated Mth 83-86; Regents Grade 100 NYS Regents Bio 85; Chem Engrng.

DENK, ERIC; Seton Catholic Central HS; Binghamton, NY; (Y); 43/163; Service Clb; SADD; School Play; Capt L Trk; Cit Awd; St Schlr; Am Leg Boys St; Church Yth Grp; Band; Nwsp Rptr; Pope Jhn XXII Chrstn Ctznshp Awd 86; Broome Cty Cyo/Le Moyne Coll Schlrshp 86; Yth Ctznshp Awd 86.

DENKO, JULIE; Granville Central HS; Pawlet, VT; (Y); 2/136; GAA; VP Spanish Clb; Var L Crs Cntry; Var L Trk; Bausch & Lomb Sci Awd; Cit Awd; Elks Awd; High Hon Roll; NHS; Prfct Atten Awd; RPI Mdl-Excllnc-Math & Sci 85; Coaches Awd-Outdr Trck 86; U S Army Rsrv Schltc Athlt Awd 86; U Of VT; Psychlgy.

DENMARK, BECKY; Waterloo Central HS; Waterloo, NY; (Y); Spanish Clb; Mrchg Band; Chess Clb; Twrlr; Hon Roll; Intermdt Strut Champ NY 85; 1st Rnnr Up Adv Miss Mjrt NY 86; Adv Plcmnt Soc Studs & Engl 85-86; Pol Sci.

DENNER, STEPHEN; HS For The Humants; New York, NY; (Y); Drama Clb; School Play; Bsbl; Drama Awd 84; Atten Awd 85.

DENNEY, GENEA; Romulus Central HS; Romulus, NY; (Y); Office Aide; Pep Clb; VP Spanish Clb; Chorus; Rep Stu Cncl; Var Capt Cheerleading; Var Socr; High Hon Roll; Hon Roll; NHS; Varsity & Jv Lttrs; Math.

DENNIE, TREVOR; Gloversville HS; Gloversville, NY; (Y); 1/234; French Clb; Math Tm; Nwsp Ed-Chief; JV Var Socr; Var Capt Tennis; NHS; Ntl Merit Ltr; Val; Empire ST Schlrshp 86; Brown U Area Almn Awd 85; Amherst Coll; Engl.

DENNING, JULIE; Bolivar Central HS; Bolivar, NY; (Y); 8/59; Chorus; Nwsp Rptr; Nwsp Stf; High Hon Roll; Hon Roll; NHS; Pres Schlr; OBI; Exec & Lgl Sec.

DENNIS, CHASSITY; Benjamin Franklin HS; Rochester, NY; (Y); Cmnty Wkr; 4-H; JA; Office Aide; Pep Clb; Mrchg Band; Variety Show; Pres Jr Cls; Var Capt Bsktbl; Mgr(s); Key Schl 85-86; Howard U; Law.

DENNIS, JEFF; Victor Central HS; Victor, NY; (Y); Boy Scts; Church Yth Grp; Spanish Clb; Band; Jazz Band; Mrchg Band; Pep Band; School Musical; Stage Crew; High Hon Roll; Eagle Scout 84; Embry Riddle Aeronatcl U; Engr.

DENNIS, JODIE ANN; Roy C Ketcham HS; Poughkeepsie, NY; (Y); 164/520; Art Clb; Spanish Clb; High Hon Roll; Hon Roll; Fine Arts Awd 86; Dutchess CC; Art.

DENNIS, PHILLIP; Nalverne HS; Rockville Ctr, NY; (Y); Key Clb; SADD; Trs Pres Stu Cncl; JV Ftbl; Var Trk; Cit Awd; Boys Clb Am; Boy Scts; Chess Clb; Church Yth Grp; Syracuse U; Bus Admin.

DENNISON, CRAIG; Pittsford Sutherland HS; Pittsford, NY; (Y); Boy Scts; Church Yth Grp; Exploring; Band; Jazz Band; Swmmng; Wooster Coll; Mnstry.

DENNISON, PATRICIA; Cardinal Ohara HS; Kenmore, NY; (Y); 5/123; GAA; Pep Clb; Varsity Clb; Rep Stu Cncl; JV Var Bsktbl; Var L Sftbl; Var L Vllybl; High Hon Roll; NHS; Pres Schlr; 1st Tm All Cathlc Vllybl 85; MIP Sftbl 85; Treas NHS 86-87; Engrng.

DENOYERS, MICHELLE L; Ravena Coeymans Selkirk SR HS; New Baltimore, NY; (Y); Pres DECA; Political Wkr; Ski Clb; Off Jr Cls; Off Sr Cls; Stu Cncl; Rngl Wnnr DECA 85; Lib Arts.

DENSON, JENNY; St Marys Girls HS; Pt Washington, NY; (Y); 49/150; Art Clb; Drama Clb; Pep Clb; SADD; Chorus; School Play; Stage Crew; Yrbk Stf.

DENTLINGER, AMY; E J Wilson HS; Spencerport, NY; (Y); 28/320; Math Clb; VP Spanish Clb; High Hon Roll; Hon Roll.

DENZ, MARY ANN; St Marys HS; Amherst, NY; (S); 8/166; Computer Clb; English Clb; Office Aide; Political Wkr; Teachers Aide; Rptr Nwsp Rptr; Nwsp Stf; Lit Mag; Hon Roll; NHS; 1st Pl Beawny Comptn Typng; Svc Awd; Top Stu Offc Procdrs; 3rd Pl Bryant/Straton Typng Comptn; Erie CC; Comp Systms Analyst.

DEPACE, NICK; Sachem HS; Lk Ronkonkoma, NY; (Y); DECA; JV Ice Hcky; Coaches Awd Hockey 85; MVP JV Ice Hockey 86; Suffolk All Star Ice Hockey Tm 86; Platsberg; Mktng.

DEPENA, RITA; Nazareth Regional HS; Brooklyn, NY; (Y); 76/249; Science Clb; Boys Clb Am; Chorus; Church Choir; Cheerleading; Sftbl; Chors, Singng, & Ckng Clb Awds 82-86; Sci Clb 82-83; Chrldng 84-86; Long Island U; Med.

DEPEW JR, ROBERT D; Geneva HS; Geneva, NY; (S); 12/175; JV Bsbl; High Hon Roll; Hon Roll; Natl Sci Merit Awd-Bio 83-84; Natl Sci Merit Awd-Chem 84-85; Natl Sci Merit Awd Physics 85-86; Engrng.

DEPFERD, MICHELLE; Brockport HS; Brockport, NY; (Y); 39/350; Cmnty Wkr; Trs Latin Clb; JV Tennis; High Hon Roll; NHS; Spnsh.

DEPIETRO, DIANA L; Manhasset HS; Manhasset, NY; (Y); 62/195; Drama Clb; Service Clb; Teachers Aide; Thesps; Chorus; School Musical; School Play; Stage Crew; VP Frsh Cls; VP Soph Cls; Regents Schlrshp 86; Bucknell.

DEPIETTO, DAVID; Half Hollow Hills H S West; Dix Hills, NY; (Y); Boy Scts; Service Clb; SADD; Stu Cncl; Crs Cntry; Ftbl; Lcrss; Swmmng; Hon Roll; NHS.

DEPINA, SABRINA; Cathedral HS; Ny, NY; (Y); 92/370; Dance Clb; Drama Clb; FNA; Girl Scts; Library Aide; Church Choir; Cheerleading; Gym; Howard U; Actress.

DEPUTAT, MYRON J; Clarence Central HS; Clarence, NY; (Y); Pres Computer Clb; Rep Drama Clb; JCL; Model UN; PAVAS; SADD; Chorus; School Musical; Socr; NHS; GMP Suynab 80-86; Media Study Smmr Film Schl 83; Best Filmmaker Awd 83; SUNY; Comp Engr.

DERACO, LORENZO; Nyack HS; Nyack, NY; (Y); Var Ftbl; Drama Clb; FBLA; Ski Clb; School Play; Rep Frsh Cls; Rep Soph Cls; Rep Jr Cls; JV Lcrss; Socr; Psychlgst.

DERBY, MICHELLE; De Sales HS; Waterloo, NY; (Y); 12/54; French Clb; Band; Concert Band; Jazz Band; Mrchg Band; School Musical; Var Sftbl; Hon Roll; NHS; Mth Educ.

DERBY, THOMAS; Pine Valley Central HS; Cherry Creek, NY; (Y); Band; Concert Band; Jazz Band; Mrchg Band; School Musical; School Play; Bsktbl; Hon Roll; Solo Fstvl Bnd Drms 85 & 86; Jamestown Cmnty Coll; Comp Wrk.

DEREFINKO, DONNA; Brockport HS; Brockport, NY; (Y); Ski Clb; Band; Concert Band; Jazz Band; Mrchg Band; Trk; High Hon Roll; Hon Roll; Latin Clb; Radio Clb.

DERELLA, MICHAEL; Mohawk Central Schl; Mohawk, NY; (Y); 10/96; Am Leg Boys St; Pres French Clb; Model UN; Concert Band; Var Capt Golf; DAR Awd; High Hon Roll; NHS; Ntl Merit Schol; Mrchg Band; NYS Regents Scholar 85; Utica Coll; Jrnlsm.

DERFLER, MICHELE; Alexander Hamilton HS; White Plains, NY; (Y); 1/53; Office Aide; Science Clb; Lit Mag; Off Jr Cls; Pres Sr Cls; High Hon Roll; Jr NHS; NHS; Ntl Merit Schol; VFW Awd; Valedictorian 86; Stu Govt Pres 86; Natl Hnr Soc 85-86; SUNY Binghamton; Pre-Med.

DERICK, RUSSELL; Avoca Central HS; Avoca, NY; (Y); Boy Scts; Pres Trs 4-H; FBLA; Band; Concert Band; Mrchg Band; School Play; Crs Cntry; Socr; Trk; Coaches Awd Outstndng Stu 85-86; Alfred ST Coll; Constructn.

DERIENZO, DAWN; Northport HS; East Northport, NY; (Y); 374/605; Art Clb; Band; Mrchg Band; Yrbk Stf; Hgh Achvt & Extnsv Partcptn In Arts 83; C W Post LIU; Fine Arts.

DERITO, MICHAEL; Elmira Free Acad; Elmira, NY; (Y); Church Yth Grp; Spanish Clb; Variety Show; Rep Frsh Cls; Rep Soph Cls; Off Jr Cls; Rep Sr Cls; Sec Stu Cncl; Capt Var Bsktbl; Capt Socr; Kiwanis Athl Of Mnth Awd Trck 86; Yth Mnstry Diocese Of Rochester Ldrshp 86; WENY Sprts Awd Trk 85-86; Mowhawk Valley CC; Bus Adm.

DEROUCHIE, MARC; Massena Central HS; Massena, NY; (Y); Golf; Var Capt Ice Hcky; Cit Awd; Hon Roll; Potsdam ST College.

DERR, ROBYN; Penn Yan Acad; Bellona, NY; (S); 16/174; Church Yth Grp; Cmnty Wkr; Drama Clb; Intnl Clb; Chorus; Church Choir; High Hon Roll; Hon Roll; NHS; St Schlr; Frsh Spn Awd 83; Psych.

DERRENBACHER, JAMES R; Dansville SR HS; Dansville, NY; (Y); 25/160; Am Leg Boys St; Varsity Clb; Band; Yrbk Stf; Ftbl; Golf; Swmmng; Wt Lftg; NHS; Ntl Merit Ltr; Lock Haven U; Spts Med.

DERUSHIA, KELLY; Lisbon Central HS; Heuvelton, NY; (S); 3/40; Am Leg Boys St; Computer Clb; Stage Crew; Yrbk Ed-Chief; Trs Frsh Cls; Trs Soph Cls; Cit Awd; High Hon Roll; NHS; Prfct Atten Awd; Mech Engrng.

DESAI, ANJALI; Roy C Ketcham SR HS; Wappingers Fls, NY; (Y); 33/500; Drama Clb; Thesps; School Play; Yrbk Stf; Off Stu Cncl; High Hon Roll; NHS; Masque & Mime Schlrshp 86; NY St Regents Schlrshp 86; Brd Of Educ Let Of Comdtn In French 86; Cornell U; Microbio.

DESAI, RAVI; Vestal SR HS; Binghamton, NY; (Y); Trs Exploring; French Clb; Hosp Aide; Yrbk Sprt Ed; Rep Soph Cls; Rep Jr Cls; Stu Cncl; High Hon Roll; VP NHS; Ntl Merit Ltr; Med.

DESAMOUR, JOSEPH; George W Wingate HS; Brooklyn, NY; (Y); Math Clb; Science Clb; Teachers Aide; City Coll; Elec Engrng.

DESANDO, COLLEEN; Newark SR HS; Walworth, NY; (Y); Sec VP 4-H; FHA; Library Aide; Yrbk Stf; Crs Cntry; Trk; Bus.

DESANTIS, ANTHONY; Bishop Ford HS; Brooklyn, NY; (Y); Hon Roll.

DESANY, BRIAN A; Waterville Central HS; Waterville, NY; (Y); 8/95; Am Leg Boys St; Church Yth Grp; Mathletes; Pep Clb; Varsity Clb; Chorus; School Musical; Socr; High Hon Roll; NHS; RPI; Elect Engrg.

DESBOROUGH, GINA; De Sales HS; N Tonawanda, NY; (Y); 9/30; VP Church Yth Grp; Cmnty Wkr; French Clb; Nwsp Stf; Yrbk Stf; Vllybl; French Hon Soc; Hon Roll; NHS; A J Mulane Mem Schlrshp 83; De Sales Lay Fclty Schlrshp 85; Bio.

DESCARTES, LARA JAN; Berne-Knox-Westerlo HS; West Berne, NY; (Y); 4/76; Drama Clb; Hosp Aide; SADD; Band; Var L Trk; JV Capt Vllybl; NHS; NEDT Awd; Library Aide; Quiz Bowl; Albany Panhellenic Assoc Schlrshp 86; NY ST Rgnts Schlarshp 86; MA Inst Tech; Physcs.

DESCH, JULIE; Sasugertiesd HS; Mt Marion, NY; (Y); Church Yth Grp; Nwsp Rptr; Bsktbl; Powder Puff Ftbl; Tennis; Trk; Vllybl; Hon Roll; NHS; Berkley Bus Schl; Bus.

DESCHAINES, SUZETTE; F D Roosevelt HS; Staatsburg, NY; (Y); Hosp Aide; Hon Roll; Jeffrey C Obanesian Memrl Awd 86; CSEA Sectrl-Clrcl Awd 86; Dutchs Cnty Assn Educ Secys Schlrshp 86; Dutchess CC; Offc Tchnlgs.

DESENSI, IRENE; St Edmund HS; Brooklyn, NY; (Y); 40/200; Art Clb; Stu Cncl; Italian Clb.

DESEPOLI, KAREN A; Smithtown H S East; Nesconset, NY; (Y); French Clb; Key Clb; Teachers Aide; Yrbk Stf; Var L Mgr(s); Var L Trk; French Hon Soc; High Hon Roll; NHS; St Schlr; SUNY Geneseo.

DESHPANDE, MADHAVI NARAYAN; Penfield HS; Penfield, NY; (Y); 14/351; Cmnty Wkr; Exploring; Hosp Aide; VP JA; Sec Math Tm; Pres Temple Yth Grp; Cit Awd; High Hon Roll; NHS; Exploring; JR Achvmnt Shclrshp 86; Frtrnl Ordr Egls Schlrshp 86; Rgnts Schlrshp 86; Purdue U; Engr.

DESIDERIO, RALPH; Moore Catholic HS; Staten Island, NY; (Y); 59/180; Am Leg Boys St; JV Var Bsbl; Hon Roll; MVP Vrsty Bsbl, MVP Babe Rth All Str Comptn Bsbl 86; Arizona ST; Mgt.

DESIMONE, DEBRA; Domican Commercial HS; Rosedale, NY; (Y); Cmnty Wkr; FCA; Sec Office Aide; Teachers Aide; Adelphi U; Wrk With Deaf.

DESIMONE, JODI; Frankfort Schuyler HS; Frankfort, NY; (Y); Dance Clb; FBLA; Spanish Clb; Pres SADD; School Musical; Variety Show; Yrbk Bus Mgr; Rep Stu Cncl; High Hon Roll; Hon Roll; A 10 Yr Dance Studio Awd 84; 1st Pl Dancng Awd For Tlt Show 83; Sppd Take Awd Of 42 Wrds-Min Typng 85; Bus Ed.

DESIR, JUDITH; Queen Of The Rosary Acad; Freeport, NY; (S); 4/50; Math Clb; Service Clb; Yrbk Stf; Pres Sr Cls; Rep Stu Cncl; Hon Roll; NHS; Widener U; Psychtry.

DESMOND, JENNIFER; Albertus Magnus HS; Spring Valley, NY; (Y); Church Yth Grp; Stage Crew; Var Crs Cntry; Var Trk; Elks Awd; High Hon Roll; NHS; Chemcl Bank Art Comptn Schlrshp 86; Falcon Svc Awd 86; Natrlst.

DESMOND, SHEILA M; Fairport HS; Fairport, NY; (Y); Church Yth Grp; French Clb; Intnl Clb; Chorus; Yrbk Stf; JV Bsktbl; JV Sftbl; Hon Roll; Prfct Atten Awd.

DESNOYERS, PHILIP; Lansingburgh HS; Troy, NY; (Y); 2/175; Var L Crs Cntry; Var L Trk; JV L Wrstlng; High Hon Roll; NHS; Rensselaer Medl Math & Sci 86; Engrng.

DESORMEAUX, MICHELLE; Berlin Central HS; Stephentown, NY; (Y); 18/82; GAA; Ski Clb; Trs Band; Trs Chorus; School Musical; School Play; Trs Swing Chorus; Yrbk Ed-Chief; Lit Mag; Bsktbl; Marist Coll; Fash Design.

DESPAIGNE, LUIS A; Manhattan Center For Science & Math; Bronx, NY; (Y); 4/159; Letterman Clb; Varsity Clb; Stage Crew; JV Var Bsktbl; High Hon Roll; Hon Roll; NHS; Prfct Atten Awd; Untd Fed Tchrs Col Schlrshp Fund $4000 86; David M Winfield Fndtn Schlrshp-Acad Excllnc 84; Wesleyan U; Econ.

DESPOSITO, DAWN; South Side HS; So Hempstead, NY; (Y); 78/280; Cmnty Wkr; Drama Clb; Key Clb; Science Clb; SADD; Band; Hon Roll; Advrtsg.

DESSIBOURG, URSULA; St Johns Prep; Astoria, NY; (Y); 66/458; Church Yth Grp; French Clb; Rep Frsh Cls; Rep Soph Cls; Rep Jr Cls; Pres Sr Cls; Pres Stu Cncl; Bsktbl; Hon Roll; NHS; NY ST Rgnts Schlrshp 86; 2nd Hnrs 83-86; Pltcl Sci.

DESTITO, JOSEPH C; Rome Free Acad; Rome, NY; (Y); JV Ftbl; Elctrnc Engr.

DESTITO, MARIANNE; Rome Free Acad; Rome, NY; (Y); 171/462; Church Yth Grp; Cmnty Wkr; GAA; Intnl Clb; School Musical; Stage Crew; Im Bsktbl; Var Capt Golf; Im Score Keeper; Im Timer; Art Awd Schlrshp 86; NY ST Sctn III Golf Champ TM 85; Mst Imprvd Golfer Rome Free Acad 84-85; Mohawk Valley CC; Fine Arts Tc.

DETELICH, RICHARD R; Smithtown West HS; Smithtown, NY; (Y); Chess Clb; Computer Clb; Math Clb; Math Tm; Science Clb; Spanish Clb; Concert Band; Orch; Hon Roll; Spanish NHS; Geneseo NY; Engrng.

DETHOMASIS, ANNA; Rensselaer Middle HS; Rensselaer, NY; (Y); #11 In Class; DECA; Key Clb; SADD; Yrbk Stf; JV Sftbl; Hudson Vly Comm Coll; Chld Devl.

DETMAR, SHIRLEY A; Averill Park HS; Sand Lake, NY; (Y); 3/210; Drama Clb; Pres 4-H; Hosp Aide; Ski Clb; SADD; Varsity Clb; School Musical; Nwsp Stf; Var L Tennis; Bausch & Lomb Sci Awd; Rochester Inst Of Tech.

DETRANI, GEOFFREY; HS For The Humanit; New York, NY; (Y); Art Clb; Aud/Vis; Chess Clb; School Musical; Stage Crew; Nwsp Ed-Chief; Ntl Merit Schol; Social Studies 85-86; SUNY.

DETWEILER, BONITA; Ticonderoga HS; Putnam, NY; (Y); 9/130; Church Yth Grp; SADD; Sec Chorus; School Play; Yrbk Stf; Lit Mag; High Hon Roll; Hon Roll; NHS; Messiah Coll; Elem Ed.

DETWEILER, JOHN A; Pittsford Sutherland HS; Pittsford, NY; (Y); 2/240; Boys Clb Am; Model UN; Ski Clb; Hon Roll; NHS; St Schlr; Natl Frnch Cntst Awd-5th In Cnty 7th In NY St 84; Slvr Tst Tube Awd-Rgnts Chem-Hghst Avg In Cls 83; Middlebury Coll; Math.

DEUTSCH, CHRISTINE; Division Avenue HS; Levittown, NY; (Y); 22/335; Pres Math Clb; SADD; Variety Show; Nwsp Rptr; Rep Soph Cls; Trs Jr Cls; Var Badmtn; NHS; FBLA; Stat Ftbl; Rgnts Schlrshp 86; Dstngshd Acdmc Scchlrshp Hofstra 86; Hofstra U; Corprt Law.

DEVER, MARION K; Nazareth Regional HS; Breezy Point, NY; (S); 16/267; Ed Yrbk Stf; Off Sr Cls; Bsktbl; Capt Sftbl; Capt Vllybl; High Hon Roll; Hon Roll; NHS; US Army Rsrv Ntl Schlr/Athlt Awd 85; Englsh Mdl 84-85; Coaches Awd In Bsktbl 85; Coaches Awd In Sftbl; Physcl Thrpst.

DEVEREAUX, SCOTT; Solvay HS; Syracuse, NY; (Y); Var Bsbl; Var Bsktbl; Var Capt Ftbl; Hon Roll; Rotary Awd; 1st Tm Al-Cnty Lnbckr, Outfldr 85-86; Advrtsng.

DEVERS, BARBARA; Valley Stream North HS; Franklin Square, NY; (Y); Church Yth Grp; Mathletes; High Hon Roll; Hon Roll; Nassau Coll; Bus.

DEVERTER, JEFF; Saugerties HS; Saugerties, NY; (S); Exploring; German Clb; Symp Band; VP Jr Cls; Comp Sci.

DEVINE, MARGARET M; The Mary Louis Acad; Whitestone, NY; (Y); 3/270; French Clb; Hosp Aide; Teachers Aide; Nwsp Stf; Yrbk Stf; High Hon Roll; Sec NHS; Ntl Merit SF; NEDT Awd; Acad H S Schlrp 82-86; Dartmouth Coll; Bus.

DEVITA, CHARLES; Brooklyn Technical HS; Flushing, NY; (Y); Boy Scts; Cmnty Wkr; Eagle Scout 86; Am Inst Aeronautics & Astronautics 85-86; Plattsbuarg SUNY; Crim Just.

DEVITA, JACK; Pelham Memorial HS; Pelham, NY; (Y); Church Yth Grp; JA; Yrbk Stf; Pres Sr Cls; Rep Stu Cncl; Var JV Bsbl; Im JV Trk; High Hon Roll; Hon Roll; NHS; Blgy.

DEVLEN, NANCY; Groton Central Schl; Groton, NY; (Y); Ski Clb; Spanish Clb; Concert Band; Mrchg Band; Var Bsktbl; Var Socr; Var Sftbl; High Hon Roll; NHS; Schlstc Art Awd Gld Key-Blue Rbn 85; Schlstc Art Awd Hnbl 86; Scndry Ed.

DEVLIN, BARBARA; Lansingburgh HS; Troy, NY; (Y); Hosp Aide; Office Aide; Chorus; Yrbk Stf; Rep Stu Cncl; High Hon Roll; Hon Roll; NHS; Awd Hghst Avg Yr In Studio Art 84; Cazenovia Coll; Adv Grphcs.

DEVLIN, BETH; St Dominic HS; E Norwich, NY; (Y); Var Capt Cheerleading; Var Sftbl; High Hon Roll.

DEVLIN, SHARON; Pelham Memorial HS; Pelham, NY; (Y); AFS; Cmnty Wkr; Yrbk Stf; JV Fld Hcky.

DEVOE, CHRISTY; Shenendehowa Central HS; Clifton Park, NY; (Y); GAA; Varsity Clb; Coach Actv; Var Gym; High Hon Roll; Hon Roll; Pres Schlr; Phys Ed.

DEVOE, CRAIG; Hauppauge HS; Hauppauge, NY; (S); 2/491; FBLA; Math Tm; ROTC; Orch; Crs Cntry; Var Trk; Bausch & Lomb Sci Awd; High Hon Roll; Hon Roll; NHS; All ST All Estrn Music Awds-Viola 85 & 86; Smns Fllwshp SUNY Stny Brk-Physcs 85; Wlsn Schlrshp 86; Physcs.

DEVRIES, JENNIFER; John Jay HS; Wappingers Fls, NY; (Y); Ski Clb; Yrbk Ed-Chief; Yrbk Phtg; Yrbk Stf; Var Bsktbl; Var Capt Sftbl; Var Vllybl; High Hon Roll; Hon Roll; Jr NHS; AAU Hudsn Vly Grls Bsktbl Clb 86; St Johns; Bus Admin.

DEWERT, KAREN; Corning Painted Post West HS; Beaver Dams, NY; (Y); Pres JA; SADD; Varsity Clb; Rep Jr Cls; Var L Tennis; High Hon Roll; Hon Roll; Cttn Clb JR Achvmnt 85; Stut Lbrty Cntrbutn Crtfct 85.

DEWEY, DAVID K; St Francis HS; Eden, NY; (Y); 95/159; Church Yth Grp; PAVAS; Nwsp Rptr; Pres Stu Cncl; Var L Ftbl; Hon Roll; St Schlr; Spanish Clb; School Musical; Stage Crew; Mdl ST Assn For Scndry Schls & Col Schl Comm 85-86; Outstndng Srv Awd For Fine Arts Prgm 82-86; Bwlng Grn ST OH; Bus Mngmnt.

DEWEY, LAURA; Eastridge HS; Rochester, NY; (S); Cmnty Wkr; DECA; Girl Scts; SADD; Rep Frsh Cls; JV Gym; CC Awd; 2nd Pl Monroe Cnty Food Mrktng Evnt DECA 86; 1st Pl NY ST Food Mrktng Evnt DCA 86; Monroe Coll; Bus.

DEWING, PRISCILLA; Valley Stream Central HS; Valley Stream, NY; (Y); Church Yth Grp; Mathletes; SADD; Church Choir; Var Badmtn; JV Bsktbl; High Hon Roll; Jr NHS; NHS; Spanish NHS; Hnr Ushr 86; Math Awds 84; Spnsh & Engl Awds 83; Accntng.

DEXTER, JENNIFER; Gowanda Central Schl; Gowanda, NY; (Y); French Clb; Ski Clb; SADD; Stu Cncl; Cheerleading; Sftbl; Wt Lftg; Hon Roll; NHS; Bus.

DEYETTE, DAVID; Glens Falls SR HS; Glens Falls, NY; (Y); 21/208; Key Clb; Rep Math Clb; SADD; High Hon Roll; NHS; Pres Schlr; NYS Rgnts Schlrshp 86; Rochester Inst Tech; Bio.

DEYETTE, JOHN; Scotia-Glenville HS; Scotia, NY; (Y); Im Ftbl; Arntcl Engrng.

DEYETTE, MICHELLE A; Shenendehowa HS; Round Lake, NY; (Y); 146/675; GAA; Girl Scts; Leo Clb; SADD; Varsity Clb; Chorus; Yrbk Stf; Soph Cls; Jr Cls; Sr Cls; Co Knlls Wmns Clb Acad Schlrshp 86; Mjr Hnr Ltr 86; SR Athltc Awd 86; Geneseo; Acctng.

DEYO, MARY E; Northern Adirondack Central HS; Altona, NY; (Y); 9/87; Drama Clb; Band; School Play; Variety Show; Bsbl; Capt Cheerleading; Score Keeper; Vllybl; High Hon Roll; Hon Roll; SUNY Potsdam; Bio.

DEZA, PATRICE; Dominican Commercial HS; Jamaica, NY; (S); Im Swmmng; Tennis; Hon Roll; NHS; Prfct Atten Awd; Hunter Coll; RN.

DHANDARI, ANGELETA; St Francis Prep; Jamaica, NY; (Y); Church Yth Grp; Cmnty Wkr; Debate Tm; Hosp Aide; Library Aide; Office Aide; Service Clb; SADD; Teachers Aide; Band; NYU; Psychlgy.

DHANRAJ, SEAN; New Hyde Park Memorial HS; Garden City Pk, NY; (Y); Concert Band; Orch; Var Tennis; High Hon Roll; NHS; Brnz, Silv, Gold Plqs Acad Hnrs 84-86; NYSSMA Solo Awd 86; Mst Imprvd Plyr Awd Ten 84; Surgeon.

DI BELLO, PAUL; Cicero North Syracuse HS; North Syracuse, NY; (S); 1/667; Am Leg Boys St; Mathletes; VP Sr Cls; VP Stu Cncl; JV Capt Bsktbl; Var Capt Ftbl; Var L Lcrss; High Hon Roll; Hon Roll; NHS; Cornell Bk Awd 85; Oper Enterprise Scholar 85; NYS Mth Awd 85; UMASS; Biol.

DI BENEDETTO, ANDREA KIM; Earl L Vandermeulen HS; Pt Jeff Sta, NY; (Y); 66/333; Art Clb; Capt Chess Clb; Mathletes; Color Guard; Mrchg Band; Stage Crew; Symp Band; Nwsp Stf; Var Trk; Hon Roll; Mt St Marys Coll; Law.

DI BENEDETTO, DANIELA; Hicksville HS; Hicksville, NY; (Y); Office Aide; Band; Concert Band; Jazz Band; Mrchg Band; Symp Band; Variety Show; Hon Roll; NY ST Music Assn 81; Music Educ.

DI BENEDETTO, JAMES J; Mt St Michael HS; Yonkers, NY; (S); 13/306; Pres Computer Clb; Hon Roll; Co-Op Schlrp; MIT; Aerospc Engr.

DI BENEDETTO, LISA A; St Francis Prep; Flushing, NY; (S); 120/744; Red Cross Aide; Hon Roll; NHS.

DI BERNARDO, LISA; Bethlehem Central HS; Glenmont, NY; (Y); 136/304; Key Clb; Nwsp Rptr; Rep Soph Cls; Rep Jr Cls; Vllybl; Phtgrphy Achvmnt Awd 86; Prsdntl Acdmc Ftns Awd 86; Bthlhm Bkng Cntst 2nd Plc 84; SUNY Oneonta; Blgy.

DI BIASE, JUDITH; Notre Dame-Bishop Gibbons HS; Schenectady, NY; (Y); French Clb; Tennis; Hon Roll; Frnch Awd; Rlgn Awd; Accntng.

DI BIASE, MARISA; Brockport HS; Brockport, NY; (Y); 7/320; Computer Clb; Latin Clb; Mathletes; Radio Clb; Ski Clb; Stage Crew; Yrbk Phtg; Yrbk Stf; High Hon Roll; VP Frsh Cls; Latin I Awd 84; Latin II Awd 85.

DI BLASI, GLORI ANN; Southwestern Central HS; Jamestown, NY; (Y); 11/145; Pres Church Yth Grp; FCA; Spanish Clb; Band; Concert Band; Mrchg Band; Rep Stu Cncl; DAR Awd; Hon Roll; NHS; US Stu Cncl Awd 85; Houghton Coll; Educ.

DI BONO, PAOLA; Commack South HS; Commack, NY; (Y); Teachers Aide; Chorus; School Musical; Hon Roll; Farmingdale; Sec.

DI CARLO, MARGARET; Mount Saint Mary Acad; Buffalo, NY; (Y); 1/113; Hosp Aide; Nwsp Rptr; Ed Lit Mag; Pres VP Stu Cncl; Var Capt Vllybl; Kiwanis Awd; NHS; Pres Schlr; Val; Schl Awd 86; Alpah Kappa Alpha Sorority Schlrshp 86; Wellesley Coll Ldrshp/Schlrshp Awd 85; Loyola Coll MD; Psych.

DI CARLO, NEIL; Mount Vernon HS; Mt Vernon, NY; (Y); Nwsp Phtg; Yrbk Phtg; Hon Roll; Center For The Media Arts.

DI CARLO II, VINCENT; Grand Island HS; Grand Isl, NY; (Y); 36/325; Drama Clb; Varsity Clb; Chorus; School Musical; School Play; Stu Cncl; JV Crs Cntry; Var Swmmng; Hon Roll; Acad Var Lttr 85-86; Accntng.

DI CATERINO, LISA; Gloversville HS; Gloversville, NY; (Y); Cmnty Wkr; Ski Clb; JV Var Crs Cntry; JV Var Trk; Arch.

DI CRISTOFARO, ALBERT; Lackawanna SR HS; Lackawanna, NY; (Y); Cmnty Wkr; French Clb; Varsity Clb; Rep Jr Cls; JV Var Bsbl; JV Var Ftbl; Hon Roll; NHS; U Buffalo; Mechncl Engr.

DI CRISTOFARO, DAVID P; Linton HS; Schenectady, NY; (Y); 15/296; JV Var Socr; Hon Roll; NHS; NYS Sci Supv Assn Earth Sci Awd 83; Natl Merit Scholar 85; Siena Coll; Acctng.

DI CUFFA JR, ALDO; Utica Free Acad; Utica, NY; (Y); 9/300; Model UN; Spanish Clb; SADD; Nwsp Rptr; Nwsp Stf; Stu Cncl; High Hon Roll; Hon Roll; Jr NHS; NHS; Boston U Schlrshp 86; Dorothy Hurd Memrl Schlrshp 86; Alumni Spnsh Prz 86; Boston U; Cmmnctns.

DI DONATO, GERARD; Canarsie HS; Brooklyn, NY; (Y); Band; JV Bsbl; JV Ftbl; High Hon Roll; Hon Roll; Arista Socty 85-86.

DI FLAVIO, GINA; Frontier Central HS; Hamburg, NY; (S); 40/444; French Clb; Varsity Clb; Yrbk Stf; Rep Jr Cls; Rep Stu Cncl; Var Capt Bsktbl; Stat Socr; JV Capt Sftbl; Stat Vllybl; High Hon Roll; Hnrbl Mntn Div I Bsktbl; 1st Tm All Stars Bsktbl.

DI FLAVIO, MARTHA ANN; Mount Mercy Acad; Buffalo, NY; (Y); Camp Fr Inc; Dance Clb; SADD; School Play; Lit Mag; Im Vllybl; 3rd Lang Fair 85; Spnsh II 85; Melodrs 85; Silvr Mdl 86; Merit Mdl 86; Phrmcy.

DI FONZO, CAROLYN; Niagara Catholic HS; Lewiston, NY; (Y); Hosp Aide; Key Clb; Yrbk Stf; Trs Soph Cls; Sec Sr Cls; JV Var Cheerleading; Co Chrmn Cathlc Charties Appl 86; Niagara U; Comp Sci.

DI FRANCESCO, CHRISTINA; Clarence Central HS; Clarence, NY; (Y); 22/250; Church Yth Grp; JCL; Latin Clb; Band; Concert Band; Orch; Pep Band; School Musical; Symp Band; Nwsp Rptr; Most Imprvd Musician 85.

DI FRANCO, GARY; Monsignor Farrell HS; Staten Island, NY; (Y); Cmnty Wkr; French Clb; Hosp Aide; Red Cross Aide; Acpl Chr; Band; Church Choir; Mrchg Band; French Hon Soc; High Hon Roll; Vlntr Of Yr Staten Isl Hosp 84; NY U; Cardio-Thoracic Surg.

DI FRANCO, ROSS C; Hutchinson Central Tech HS; Buffalo, NY; (Y); Letterman Clb; High Hon Roll; Hon Roll; Clarkson Trustee Schlrshp 86; NY ST Regenst Schlrshp 86; Top 10 Hnr Awd 85; Clarkson U; Comp Sci.

DI FUSCO, DAVID; Baldwin HS; Baldwin, NY; (Y); 5/476; Acpl Chr; Pres Orch; School Play; Stu Cncl; Var Capt Socr; Capt Var Trk; DAR Awd; Elks Awd; High Hon Roll; NHS; Long Island JR Sccr Lg Schlrshp 86; Elks Mst Vlbl Stu Awd 86; Kathy Robertson Mem Awd 86; Wharton; Crprt Fncn.

DI GENNARO, DAVID J; East Syracuse Minoa HS; Minoa, NY; (Y); 12/333; Latin Clb; Band; Concert Band; Jazz Band; Mrchg Band; School Musical; Variety Show; High Hon Roll; Jr NHS; NHS; NY ST Rgnts Schlrshp 86; Music Educ.

DI GIACOMO JR, VINCENT PAUL; Gloversville HS; Gloversville, NY; (Y); Cmnty Wkr; SADD; Var Bsbl; Var Bsktbl; Var Capt Ftbl; Hon Roll; Sci.

DI GIANTOMMASO, JENNIFER; Port Jervis HS; Port Jervis, NY; (Y); Varsity Clb; Rep Frsh Cls; Rep Soph Cls; Rep Stu Cncl; JV Bsktbl; Var L Socr; Var L Sftbl; Pre Law.

DI GIORGIO, PAUL; Warwick Valley HS; Warwick, NY; (S); CAP; Dance Clb; VP Pres Drama Clb; Acpl Chr; Band; Capt Chorus; Jazz Band; Mrchg Band; School Musical; School Play; Theatrc Perfrmg.

DI GREGORIO, ANDREW L; North HS; N Valley Stream, NY; (Y); 18/128; Chess Clb; Computer Clb; Drama Clb; Exploring; Thesps; Varsity Clb; School Play; Variety Show; Nwsp Rptr; Nwsp Stf; NY Regnts 86; Rensselaer Schlrshp 86; Rennsselaer; Engrng.

DI GRIGOLI, MARIA; Farmingdale HS; Massapequa Park, NY; (Y); Intnl Clb; Var L Badmtn; Var Trk; JV L Vllybl; Hofstra; Bus Admin.

DI IOIA, STEVEN; Cortland JR SR HS; Dryden, NY; (Y); 4/186; School Musical; Yrbk Phtg; Pres Jr Cls; Pres Sr Cls; Rep Stu Cncl; Capt L Socr; DAR Awd; Kiwanis Awd; NHS; Pres Schlr; Ldrshp Cup Boys Cls 86; Rep Natl Asso Stu Cncls Conf 85; Ldrhsp Awd Soccer Tm 85; U Buffalo; Aerontcl Engr.

DI IULIO, RENEE; Ou Lady Of Mercy; Fairport, NY; (Y); Exploring; Hosp Aide; Model UN; Science Clb; SADD; Yrbk Stf; High Hon Roll; Hon Roll; NHS; Ntl Merit Ltr; William J Stolze Schrlshp 83; Am Chem Assoc Awd 2nd Pl 86; Math Awd 86; Med.

DI LORENZO, BRIAN E; Walton Central Schl; Walton, NY; (Y); Aud/Vis; Computer Clb; Band; Concert Band; Jazz Band; Mrchg Band; Orch; Pep Band; Rep Frsh Cls; Rep Soph Cls; Rgnts Schlrshp 86; Norwich U; Crmnl Jstc.

DI MARIA JR, JOSEPH F; Mc Quaid Jesuit HS; Fairport, NY; (Y); 20/176; Church Yth Grp; Cmnty Wkr; Varsity Clb; Capt Im Bsktbl; Capt Im Ftbl; Var L Trk; Capt Im Vllybl; High Hon Roll; Acad Lttr & Bar; Notre Dame Clb Of Rochester Schlrshp; U Of Notre Dame; Engrng.

DI MATTEO III, ALEXANDER R; Nottingham HS; Syracuse, NY; (Y); Church Yth Grp; Latin Clb; Varsity Clb; Yrbk Stf; Pres Frsh Cls; Pres Sr Cls; Rep Stu Cncl; JV Var Bsbl; Var Socr; Sftbl; Rochester Inst Of Tech; Engrng.

DI MEGLIO, LORI; Port Jervis HS; Port Jervis, NY; (Y); 20/186; VP Key Clb; Math Tm; Pres SADD; Varsity Clb; Mrchg Band; Yrbk Phtg; Yrbk Stf; Var Tennis; JV Vllybl; High Hon Roll; Anthy Dllr Schlrshps 86; Hnr Soc Schlrshp 86; Prncpls Prstgious Excllnc Awd 86; U Of Scranton; Pltcl Sci.

DI MODICA, ITALO J; St Francis Prep; Middle Village, NY; (S); Art Clb; Arch.

DI NAPOLI, GINA ANNE; Msgr Scanlan HS; Bronx, NY; (Y); 21/257; Church Yth Grp; Intnl Clb; JA; Nwsp Rptr; Incentive Grant Mercy Coll 86; Mercy Coll; Psych.

DI NATALE, ANTHONY; New Dorp HS; Staten Island, NY; (Y); FBLA; Ski Clb; Gym; Socr; Wt Lftg; Hon Roll; Bus Admn.

DI NITTO, CHRISTINE; Gates Chili HS; Rochester, NY; (Y); Office Aide; School Musical; Variety Show; Pres Trs Stu Cncl; High Hon Roll; Hon Roll; Dancworks Studio Scholar 86; Dance.

DI PAOLA, PATRICIA; The Franciscan Acad; Syracuse, NY; (S); 2/24; FBLA; GAA; NFL; Nwsp Stf; Var Sftbl; Var Vllybl; High Hon Roll; NHS; Englsh 10 Hnrs Achvt Awd 84-85; Frnch Awd For Hghst Grds Frnch II 84-85; Hnr Rll Awd 4 Qtrs 84-85; Educ.

DI PASQUA, CRISTINA; Notre Dame HS; Sauquoit, NY; (Y); 17/170; Cmnty Wkr; French Clb; Hosp Aide; Office Aide; Chorus; Yrbk Stf; Lit Mag; NHS; St Schlr; Mohwk Vlly Wrld Trcd Cncl Intl Bus Schlrshp; Utica Coll; Intl Bus.

DI PAULO, MATTHEW; Liverpool HS; Liverpool, NY; (Y); 100/987; Church Yth Grp; Debate Tm; Drama Clb; FBLA; Ski Clb; Speech Tm; SADD; Variety Show; Nwsp Stf; Yrbk Stf; Cert Apprctn Vlntr Svc 84-86; Indctn NJHS & NHS 84-86; Colgate U; Bus.

DI PIETRANTONIO, MARIA; St Catharine Acad; Bronx, NY; (Y); 40/185; Hon Roll; Cmmndtn Geo 84-85; Bus.

DI PIETRO, ADRIANA; Ossining HS; Ossining, NY; (Y); High Hon Roll; Hon Roll; Itln Awd 83-86; North Eastern-Boston; Bus.

DI RAFFAELE, MARY M; Sachem HS North Campus; Lk Ronkonkoma, NY; (Y); 276/1360; Band; Concert Band; Mgr Mrchg Band; Ed Yrbk Stf; Mgr(s); Im Vllybl; Suny At Stony Brook; Phy Thrpy.

DI RITO, PAUL; Ossining HS; Ossining, NY; (Y); Band; Jazz Band; Mrchg Band; Orch; School Musical; School Play; Symp Band; JV Lcrss; Italian Awd 84-86; Music.

DI RUBBO, ANTHONY M; Liverpool HS; Liverpool, NY; (Y); 32/886; Teachers Aide; Band; Concert Band; Jazz Band; Im Bsktbl; JV Ftbl; Lcrss; Im Sftbl; Var L Trk; High Hon Roll; Ntl Sci Found Pgm 86-87; All Cty Band All Cty Jazz Band 84-83; NYSSMA Music Solo Awd 83-85; Med.

DI RUSSO, ANNA; St Catharine Acad; Bronx, NY; (Y); 34/185; Teachers Aide; Stage Crew; Rep Soph Cls; Rep Stu Cncl; Hon Roll; Prfct Atten Awd; Ntl Hnr Rll 86; Pre-Dntstry.

DI SANTO, SUE ANNE; Clyde-Savannah HS; Clyde, NY; (Y); Drama Clb; Girl Scts; Band; Concert Band; School Musical; School Play; Nwsp Stf; Yrbk Stf; Sec Frsh Cls; High Hon Roll; Schlrshp Awd 85; Social Wrk.

DI SAVERIO, ANTONELLA; Wilham Cullen Bryant HS; Woodside, NY; (S); Drama Clb; Hosp Aide; Key Clb; Library Aide; Band; Nwsp Rptr; Var Trk; Hon Roll; Princeton U; Crim Law.

DI SIENA, MARIA A; Saint Francis Prep; Whitestone, NY; (S); 51/744; Art Clb; Service Clb; Ski Clb; SADD; Yrbk Stf; High Hon Roll; Opt Clb Awd; Prfct Atten Awd.

DI STEFANO, CHRISTINE; Briarcliff HS; Briarcliff Mnr, NY; (Y); AFS; Library Aide; Chorus; Rptr Lit Mag; High Hon Roll; Hon Roll; Sec NHS; Span Awd; Quill & Scrll Awd; Trinity Coll; Engl.

DI STEPHAN, RAYMOND; Archbishop Molloy HS; Jamaica, NY; (Y); Church Yth Grp; Pep Clb; Service Clb; Church Choir; Queens College; Psych.

DI TEODORO, JACK; Monsignor Farrell HS; Staten Island, NY; (Y); Im Bsktbl; Im Bowling; Im Ftbl; Engnrng.

DI VERONICA, JEFFREY PAUL; Canastota JR SR HS; Canastota, NY; (Y); Am Leg Boys St; Science Clb; Nwsp Sprt Ed; Yrbk Sprt Ed; Pres Soph Cls; VP Jr Cls; Var L Bsbl; Var L Socr; Hon Roll; Jr NHS; Most Imprvd Awd Var Sccr 86; Most Dedicated Awd Var Bsbl 86; Cmmnctns.

DI VESTEA, JOSEPH L; Carmel HS; Carmel, NY; (Y); 19/350; French Clb; Pres Intnl Clb; Leo Clb; Tennis; Dnfth Awd; High Hon Roll; JC Awd; Sec NHS; Service Clb; Jr NHS; Sons Italy Grnd Lodge Scholar ST NY 86; Wake Forest U; Bus Adm.

DI VIRGILIO, SARAH E; St Johns Preparatory HS; Astoria, NY; (Y); 21/458; Church Yth Grp; School Play; Rep Soph Cls; Rep Jr Cls; Rep Sr Cls; High Hon Roll; NHS; Val; Principals Svc Awd 86; Hunter Coll; Elem Ed.

DIACHUN, JUSTIN; Wilson HS; Youngstown, NY; (Y); 1/125; Computer Clb; Var Tennis; High Hon Roll; NHS; Prfct Atten Awd; ST U NY Buffalo; Biochem.

DIACHUN, NATHAN A; Wilson HS; Youngstown, NY; (Y); 1/120; Trk; High Hon Roll; Pres Trs NHS; Ntl Merit SF; Gftd Math Pgm SUNY Buffalo 80-86; Brkhvn Ntl Lab Envrnmntl Sci Hnrs Wrkshp 85; SUNY At Buffalo; Chem.

DIADEMA, DEBRA; Paul D Schreiber HS; Port Washington, NY; (Y); 22/403; Model UN; SADD; Chorus; Madrigals; School Musical; Nwsp Phtg; High Hon Roll; Sec NHS; Drama Clb; Church Choir; Natl Choir Awd 86; Fairfield U; Bio.

DIAMOND, DINA; Smithtown High School West; Smithtown, NY; (Y); High Hon Roll; Hon Roll; Spanish NHS; Law.

DIAMOND, JENNIFER; Garden Schl; Rego Park, NY; (S); 2/35; NFL; Nwsp Stf; Ed Yrbk Stf; Rep Stu Cncl; Capt Cheerleading; Var Sftbl; Var Tennis; Var Vllybl; NHS; NEDT Awd; Brdcst Cmmnctns.

DIAMOND, PAUL; General Douglas Macarthur HS; Levittown, NY; (Y); 21/365; VP Computer Clb; Rptr Yrbk Stf; High Hon Roll; Jr NHS; NHS; Pol Chrmn Mdl Cngrss 85-86; Johns Hopkins U.

DIAMOND, RACHEL; Christopher Columbus HS; Bronx, NY; (Y); 26/746; Math Tm; Temple Yth Grp; Thesps; Band; Concert Band; School Musical; Hon Roll; NHS; Prfct Atten Awd; J P Morgan Spcl Schlrshp 86; Rgnts Schlrshp 86; Otto P Burgdorf Awd 86; Queens Coll; Bus.

DIAMOND, RICHARD; Schoharie Central HS; Howes Cave, NY; (Y); VP FFA; Wshngtn Schlrshp FFA, Chptr Frmr FFA 86; Hog Prvcncy FFA 85; Law.

DIANA, PATRICIA; Fayetteville-Manlius HS; Manlius, NY; (Y); 73/335; Church Yth Grp; Girl Scts; Varsity Clb; Orch; Variety Show; Yrbk Stf; Off Jr Cls; Var Capt Cheerleading; Hon Roll; MONY Schlstc Art Awd, Pres Acdmc Ftns Awd 86; HS Athl Awd 84-86; SUNY Albany; Bus.

DIANETTI, DON; Victor Central HS; Farmington, NY; (Y); Comptrs.

DIAZ, BRENDA; Riverhead HS; Riverhead, NY; (Y); 50/200; Church Yth Grp; Pres Dance Clb; French Clb; Spanish Clb; Chorus; Church Choir; School Play; Stage Crew; Variety Show; Hon Roll; LIBEC Cert 86.

DIAZ JR, CHARLES A; Susan Wagner HS; Staten Island, NY; (Y); Camera Clb; Cmnty Wkr; JA; Stu Cncl; JV Ftbl; Var Ice Hcky; St John S U; Law.

DIAZ, DANIEL; Trinity Schl; New York, NY; (Y); VP Chess Clb; Math Clb; Trs Spanish Clb; Nwsp Ed-Chief; Trk; Ntl Merit SF; Math.

DIAZ, ELVIS; St Marys Boys HS; New Hyde Park, NY; (Y); Varsity Clb; JV Var Bsbl; JV Trk; Comp.

DIAZ, LUCY; Far Rockaway HS; Far Rockaway, NY; (Y); Church Yth Grp; Spanish Clb; Teachers Aide; Chorus; Church Choir; Yrbk Stf; Diving; Gym; Swmmng; Vllybl; 2 Mdls In Bus & Schlrshp 86; 3 Hnrs 86; Schlrshps, Hnrs, Awds 83-85; Katherine Gibbs; Exec Sec.

DIAZ, OMAR; Cardinal Spellman HS; Bronx, NY; (Y); 59/509; Computer Clb; Science Clb; Nwsp Rptr; Stu Cncl; Bsbl; JV Ftbl; Wt Lftg; Hon Roll; NHS; NEDT Awd; Natl Hispnc Scholar SF 85-86; Aerospc Engrng.

DIAZ, RAYMOND A; St Francis Prep; Waldron, NY; (S); 195/653; Debate Tm; Hosp Aide; Math Clb; Science Clb; Band; Wt Lftg; Hon Roll; Mr Congenlty 85; Karate; Judo; Physcn.

DIAZ, ROBERT; Archbishop Stepinac HS; Port Chester, NY; (S); 13/200; JA; High Hon Roll; NHS; Knight Of Col Schlrshp 82; Elec Engr.

DIBBLE, PATRICIA; Vestal Central SR HS; Vestal, NY; (Y); Drama Clb; French Clb; Intnl Clb; Sec SADD; Lib Chorus; School Musical; School Play; High Hon Roll; Hon Roll; Art Cmmnctns.

DIBBLE, SUSAN; Bellport HS; E Patchogue, NY; (Y); 1/300; French Clb; Ski Clb; Yrbk Sprt Ed; Trs Jr Cls; Var Socr; Var JV Vllybl; French Hon Soc; High Hon Roll; Jr NHS; NHS; Varsty Vllybl & Soccr Schlr Athlete Awds 83-87; Med.

DIBERARDINO, DAVID; Elmira Free Acad; Elmira, NY; (Y); Ski Clb; Spanish Clb; Rep Frsh Cls; Rep Soph Cls; Off Jr Cls; Stu Cncl; Var Ice Hcky; High Hon Roll; NHS; Engrng.

DIBLBLE, DENISE; Connetquot HS; Ronkonkoma, NY; (Y); 155/689; GAA; Math Clb; Variety Show; Yrbk Stf; Bowling; JV Cheerleading; Var Sftbl; High Hon Roll; Hon Roll; Jr NHS; SUNY Brockport; Pre-Law.

DICE, JOHN P; Mcquaid Jesuit HS; Fairport, NY; (Y); 2/172; Cmnty Wkr; French Clb; Varsity Clb; Chorus; Ed Yrbk Stf; Lit Mag; Var L Trk; NHS; Ntl Merit Ltr; Val; Air Frc ROTC Shclrshp 86; Empr ST Schlrshp Of Excllnc 86; Bst Of Cls Awd 86; U Of Ntr Dm; Med.

DICERBO, CHERI; Manhasset HS; Manhasset, NY; (Y); 35/190; Cmnty Wkr; GAA; Trs Soph Cls; Trs Jr Cls; Trs Sr Cls; Capt Lcrss; Cit Awd; Hon Roll; Hosp Aide; Var Bsktbl; All Cnty Lacrosse 85-86; All Conf Soccr 85; Robert Ryan Mem Scholar 86; U VA; Arts.

DICESARE, JAMES; Mynderse Acad; Seneca Falls, NY; (Y); Rep Am Leg Boys St; Trs Boy Scts; Model UN; Spanish Clb; Yrbk Ed-Chief; Rep Stu Cncl; Cit Awd; DAR Awd; Kiwanis Awd; Hghst Avg Bio & Trig; Spec Awd Arch Svc Cntst In Yrkr Clb; Intl Affairs.

DICICCIO, JODIE; Lake George HS; Lake George, NY; (Y); Church Yth Grp; Chorus; Church Choir; Yrbk Stf; Im Golf; Im Swmmng; High Hon Roll; Hon Roll; NHS; Adirondack CC; Vet Med.

DICICCO, DONNA; Lindenhurst HS; Lindenhurst, NY; (Y); 230/580; Art Clb; Yrbk Stf; Sftbl; Hon Roll; Nassau Com7; Advtsg Dsgn.

DICK, MARGARET; Washingtonville HS; Monroe, NY; (Y); Church Yth Grp; Cmnty Wkr; Ski Clb; Band; JV Bsktbl; Var Tennis; WV U; Int Design.

DICKENS JR, FRANK T; Evander Childs HS; Bronx, NY; (Y); Math Clb; Math Tm; Band; Concert Band; Drm & Bgl; Drm Mjr(t); Jazz Band; School Musical; Variety Show; Prfct Atten Awd.

DICKENS, JAMES; Letchworth Central HS; Castile, NY; (Y); Cmnty Wkr; Drama Clb; Chorus; School Musical; Stage Crew; Yrbk Bus Mgr; Yrbk Phtg; Yrbk Stf; Var L Swmmng; Hon Roll; Elem Education.

DICKERSON, CATHERINE; Notre Dame Bishop Gibbons HS; Schenectady, NY; (S); 2/90; Cmnty Wkr; Nwsp Rptr; Lit Mag; JV Capt Bsktbl; Var Sftbl; Var Vllybl; High Hon Roll; NHS; Math Awd; Chem.

DICKERSON, CHERYL; Jamesville-Dewitt HS; Dewitt, NY; (Y); 10/235; Model UN; Band; Chorus; Stage Crew; Rep Jr Cls; Var L Vllybl; High Hon Roll; Hon Roll; NHS; German Clb; Psych.

DICKERSON, JENNIFER; Notre Dame Bishop Gibbons HS; Schenectady, NY; (S); 1/90; French Clb; Church Choir; Nwsp Rptr; Rep Stu Cncl; JV Bsktbl; Var Crs Cntry; JV Sftbl; High Hon Roll; NHS; Psych.

DICKERSON, ROBERT; Cicero-North Syracuse HS; N Syracuse, NY; (S); 5/623; Spanish Clb; Hon Roll; Prfct Atten Awd; Pre Med.

DICKERSON, SONDRA; Union Springs Acad; Riverside, CA; (Y); 3/46; FCA; VP Jr Cls; Pres Stu Cncl; L Gym; VP Vllybl; NHS; Loma Linda U; Dntstry.

DICKERSON, SONNIE; Unica Springs Acad; Riverside, CA; (S); 3/46; Varsity Clb; VP Jr Cls; Pres Stu Cncl; L Gym; Vllybl; NHS; Loma Linda U; Dnstry.

DICKHAUS, DEBORAH L; Auburn HS; Auburn, NY; (Y); 14/426; Church Yth Grp; SADD; Varsity Clb; Acpl Chr; Band; Church Choir; Orch; Nwsp Stf; Bsktbl; Crs Cntry; Acdmc All Amer 85; Medallion Tuition Schlrshp To Wstrn MI U 86; Wstn MI U; Cert Physcn Asstnt.

DICKINSON, DONNA LYNN; Cicero N Syracuse HS; Kirkville, NY; (Y); German Clb; JV Cheerleading; SUNY Coll Brockport; Psych.

DICKINSON, JENNIFER; Sodus Central HS; Sodus Pt, NY; (Y); Yrbk Bus Mgr; Yrbk Ed-Chief; Yrbk Phtg; Yrbk Rptr; SADD; VICA; High Hon Roll; Hon Roll; Prfct Atten Awd; Chef.

DICKINSON, JONATHAN; Lockport SR HS; Lockport, NY; (Y); Latin Clb; Var Capt Bsktbl.

DICKLER, PHILIP S; Valley Stream South HS; Valley Stream, NY; (Y); Computer Clb; Red Cross Aide; Pres SADD; Temple Yth Grp; Y-Teens; Swmmng; High Hon Roll; Pres NHS; Ntl Merit Schol; SUNY.

DICKSON, JACQUELYN; Royalton-Hartland Central Schl; Gasport, NY; (Y); JV Var Cheerleading; Hon Roll.

DICOCCO, JENNIFER; Schalmont HS; Schenectady, NY; (Y); Church Yth Grp; Dance Clb; Yrbk Stf; Sec Frsh Cls; Sec Soph Cls; Sec Jr Cls; Sec Sr Cls; VP Stu Cncl; Oral Roberts U; Med.

DICOSOLA, LISA A; St Catharines Acad; Bronx, NY; (Y); Church Yth Grp; Dance Clb; Pep Clb; Stage Crew; Variety Show; Nwsp Rptr; Yrbk Rptr; Pres Frsh Cls; VP Jr Cls; Rep Sr Cls; Hnrs In Englsh, Hlth & Svc To Schl 83-85; Schlrshp To Wood Schl-Bus; Schlrshp To NY U; Fordham U; Law.

DICUPE, DENISE; Queens Vocational HS; Brooklyn, NY; (Y); 20/335; SADD; Church Choir; Cit Awd; Hon Roll; NHS.

DIDAS, MARK; Wayland Central HS; Perkinsville, NY; (Y); 10/120; Art Clb; Math Tm; Varsity Clb; Var Socr; Var Trk; Var Wrstlng; NHS; Art Awd 86; NYS Smmr Schl Art Fredonia 86; Close-Up Pgm Washington DC 86; Syracuse U; Fine Arts.

DIDIE, KATHLEEN; Acad Of St Joseph; Stony Brook, NY; (Y); Cmnty Wkr; Dance Clb; Hosp Aide; Math Clb; Math Tm; Service Clb; SADD; Yrbk Rptr; Yrbk Stf; High Hon Roll; NYSSMA NY ST Schl Music Assn 85-86; Lbrl Arts Coll; Bus.

DIECKHOFF, RICHARD; La Salle Military Acad; Babylon, NY; (Y); ROTC; Drill Tm; Var L Diving; Var L Ftbl; Lcrss; Var L Trk; Silver Hnrs 85-86; Mount St Marys Coll; Bus Adm.

DIECKMAN, DAWN; Mechanicville HS; Mechanicville, NY; (S); SADD; Concert Band; Var Bsktbl; Capt Socr; Var Sftbl; Sect II Record Most Shutouts-Soccer Goalie 85-86; Locl Nwspr & Locl TV Athlt Of Wk 85-86.

DIEFENDORF, KIRSTEN; Cazenovia HS; Cazenovia, NY; (Y); AFS; Drama Clb; Acpl Chr; Chorus; Church Choir; Madrigals; School Musical; Swmmng; Hon Roll; NHS; Theatre.

DIEFES, RICHARD; Blind Brook HS; Pt Chester, NY; (Y); Hosp Aide; Teachers Aide; Concert Band; Jazz Band; School Musical; JV Var Crs Cntry; NYS Rgnts Schlrshp 86; Awd-Outstndng & Sustnd Svc To Cmnty 86; Hnrb Mntn-Sci Awd 86; Boston U; Engrng.

DIEHL, AMY; Our Lady Of Mercy HS; Rochester, NY; (Y); Cmnty Wkr; Diving; Hon Roll; Teach.

DIEHL, MARGARET A; Liverpool HS; Liverpool, NY; (Y); 9/816; Ski Clb; School Musical; Variety Show; Stu Cncl; Var Capt Gym; High Hon Roll; Sec Jr NHS; NHS; Ntl Merit Ltr; MVP Awd Gymnstc 82-85; Summa Cum Laude Natn Latn Exm 85; Oper Enterp 85; PA ST U; Med.

DIEHR, JEAN; Northport HS; E Northport, NY; (Y); Dance Clb; VP FBLA; Sec Office Aide; Teachers Aide; Band; Chorus; School Musical; School Play; Variety Show; Sec Stu Cncl; 1st Pl Bus Dynmcs Awd 84; 2nd Pl Short Hand Awd 85; 1st Pl Word Proc Awd 86; Hofstra U; Bus.

DIEKMAN, STACY; North Salem HS; N Salem, NY; (Y); JV Var Cheerleading; JV Vllybl; High Hon Roll; Hon Roll; Assist Ed 86-87; I Care Clb Schlrshp Gen Exell 84-85.

DIELLO, KIMBERLY; Fabius Pompey HS; Pompey, NY; (Y); Trs Frsh Cls; Trs Soph Cls; Trs Jr Cls; JV Var Bsktbl; JV Var Socr; JV Var Sftbl; Hon Roll; Bus.

DIENER, GREGORY P; Oneonta SR HS; Oneonta, NY; (Y); 30/186; Ski Clb; Spanish Clb; Band; Concert Band; Mrchg Band; Hon Roll; NHS; Ntl Merit Ltr; Lehigh U; Sci.

DIEP, LOU; Midwood HS; Brooklyn, NY; (Y); French Clb; Math Tm; Yrbk Phtg; Hon Roll; Columbia U; Arch.

DIETEMAN, DIANE; Allegany HS; Allegany, NY; (Y); Art Clb; Church Yth Grp; Teachers Aide; Var L Bsktbl; Mgr(s); Var L Sftbl; Hon Roll; Grls Guild Vice Chrmn 85-87; VP Area I Yth 85-86; Jamestown CC; Tchr.

DIETRICH, JOSEPH; Canisius HS; Amherst, NY; (Y); Church Yth Grp; Model UN; Ski Clb; Pep Band; Ntl Amer & Canadian Rwng Champ 85-86; Drexel U; Bus Mgmt.

DIETRICH, LISA; Warwick Valley HS; Warwick, NY; (Y); 34/200; Science Clb; Spanish Clb; SADD; Trk; High Hon Roll; Hon Roll; Stu Ldr 86; Comp Sci.

DIETZEN, BRAD; Dunkirk HS; Dunkirk, NY; (Y); 29/194; Boy Scts; Socr; Wt Lftg; High Hon Roll; NY ST Rgnst Schlrshp, Indstrl Union Schlrshp 86; Lang Awd 86; Hofstra U; Intl Bus.

DIFFENDORF, MARY; Susquehanna Valley HS; Kirkwood, NY; (Y); 82/188; Cmnty Wkr; Varsity Clb; Variety Show; Nwsp Rptr; Nwsp Stf; Yrbk Sprt Ed; Rep Sr Cls; Capt Bowling; Socr; Capt Sftbl; Broome; Elmntry Ed.

DIFIORE, ELENA M; New Utrecht HS; Brooklyn, NY; (Y); Key Clb; Ed Nwsp Stf; Ed Yrbk Stf; Lit Mag; Hon Roll; Sal; U Fed Tchrs Schlrshp 86; Rgnts Schlrshp 86; Fordham U; Jrnlsm.

DIGENNARO, DOUGLAS; East Syracuse-Minoa HS; Minoa, NY; (Y); Band; Color Guard; Concert Band; Jazz Band; Mrchg Band; Pep Band; School Musical; Swing Chorus; Jr NHS; NHS; Music.

DIGGS, ERIKA; White Plains HS; White Plns, NY; (Y); Church Yth Grp; Cmnty Wkr; Office Aide; Chorus; Var JV Bsktbl; Trk; Var JV Vllybl; Hon Roll; Crmnl Jstc.

DIGGS, KELLY; Middletown HS; Middletown, NY; (Y); Band; Church Choir; Concert Band; Mrchg Band; Capt Var Crs Cntry; Capt Var Trk; High Hon Roll; NHS; Arch Engr.

DIGIOVANNI, ROSE; Cheektowaga Central HS; Buffalo, NY; (Y); VP FTA; Spanish Clb; Teachers Aide; Yrbk Stf; Rep Stu Cncl; Fut Tchrs Amer Scholar 86; ST U Coll Buffalo; Elem Ed.

DIGNAM, LYNN; St John The Baptist D HS; W Babylon, NY; (S); 35/547; VP Chorus; Color Guard; School Musical; School Play; Nwsp Rptr; Bowling; High Hon Roll; NHS; Spanish NHS; Barbizon Grad; Modern Music Mstrs-VP; Med.

DIIOIA, STEVEN J; Cortland JR SR HS; Dryden, NY; (Y); 4/194; Varsity Clb; Yrbk Phtg; Yrbk Stf; Pres Jr Cls; Pres Sr Cls; Rep Stu Cncl; Var Capt Socr; DAR Awd; High Hon Roll; Jr NHS; 1st Cntrl NY Nwppr Prss Day Phtgrphy 85; Hnrbl Mntn Cortland Arts Cncl Phtgrh 86; NY ST Schlshp 86; U Of Buffalo; Aerontcl Engr.

DIKEMAN, GEORGE; Bethpage HS; Bethpage, NY; (Y); 2/290; Bsbl; Swmmng; Elks Awd; Hon Roll; Jr NHS; NHS; Sal; NYS Rgnts Schlrshp 86; All ST Swim Tm 85-86; Schlr/Athlt Awd 86; West Point.

DILAPI, DONNA; Sacred Heart Acad; N Bellmore, NY; (S); 18/182; FTA; Hosp Aide; Math Clb; Math Tm; Spanish Clb; Hon Roll; NHS; Acad All Amer 85; Natl Scty Of Distngshd Ldrs 85; Natl Ldrshp & Svc Awd 85; Acctng.

DILEO, SALVATORE; Mt St Michael Acao HS; Bronx, NY; (Y); 15/340; Camera Clb; Stu Cncl; Hon Roll; Jr NHS; NHS; Spanish NHS; St Johns U; Pharmcy.

DILL, JENNIFER; Brockport HS; Brokcport, NY; (Y); Boy Scts; Var Capt Crs Cntry; Var Capt Trk; High Hon Roll; Hon Roll; NHS; Alt-Cmnty Ambassador 86; Rgnts Schlrshp 86; Bus.

DILLILLO, LINDA; Susan E Wagner HS; Staten Is, NY; (Y); 113/498; Hon Roll; Bus Ed Assoc Cert Achvt 86; Hgst Standing Word Proc; Susan E Wagner Cert Awd Typng 86; Baruch Coll; Acctng.

DILLINGER, STEPHEN; Kings Park SR HS; Ft Salonga, NY; (Y); Church Yth Grp; Pres Computer Clb; Pres Debate Tm; Political Wkr; Rep Frsh Cls; Rep Soph Cls; Rep Jr Cls; Rep Stu Cncl; Var Ftbl; Var Trk; Bkng.

DILLMAN, JANICE; Sweet Home HS; N Tonawanda, NY; (Y); Pres 4-H; Sec SADD; Orch; 4-H Awd; High Hon Roll; NHS; Prfct Atten Awd.

DILLMAN, KEITH; Mc Quaid Jesuit HS; Pittsford, NY; (Y); 5/175; Model UN; Radio Clb; Spanish Clb; Im Fld Hcky; High Hon Roll; NHS; Ntl Merit SF; Rensselaer Math & Sci Awd 86; 1st Pl-Monroe Cnty Spnsh Assn Tst 85; Engrng.

DILLON, JEANETTE; Odessa-Montour HS; Montour Falls, NY; (Y); 19/86; SADD; Pres Varsity Clb; VP Jr Cls; VP Sr Cls; Rep Stu Cncl; Var L Bsktbl; Var L Swmmng; Var L Trk; High Hon Roll; Sec NHS; Wmns Sprts Fndtn HS All STAR Awd 86; Athlt Of Yr 86; Keuka Coll.

DILLON, JULIA E; Spring Valley SR HS; Nanuet, NY; (Y); 29/441; Computer Clb; Hosp Aide; Office Aide; Nwsp Stf; Yrbk Stf; Mu Alp Tht; NHS; Ntl Merit SF; Mth Supr Achvt Awd 84-85; Comp Sci Supr Achvt Awd 82-83; Soc Stud Supr Achvt Awd 82-83; Elec Engrng.

DILLON, MICHAEL; Wallkill SR HS; Wallkill, NY; (S); JV Var Bsbl; JV Var Ftbl; Wt Lftg; High Hon Roll; NHS; Spanish NHS; Bus.

DILLON, ROSEMARIE; Moore Catholic HS; Staten Island, NY; (Y); Art Clb; Girl Scts; Intnl Clb; Nwsp Rptr; Var Crs Cntry; Var Trk; High Hon Roll; NHS; NY Fire Dept Holy Nm Scty Schlrshp 83; Biochem.

DILLUVIO, ANNAMARIA; St Catharine Acad; Bronx, NY; (Y); Cmnty Wkr; Dance Clb; Teachers Aide; NHS; 2nd Hghst Acad Avg 84-85; 4 Yr Schlrshp To St Catharine Acad 83; Excllnc Sqntl Math III 86; Comp Sci.

DILTS, JOHN; Watkins Glen HS; Burdett, NY; (S); Computer Clb; Spanish Clb; Nwsp Rptr; Nwsp Stf; Rep Jr Cls; Stu Cncl; Ftbl; Trk; High Hon Roll; Hon Roll.

DILUCCI, CARMELA; Cominican Commercial HS; Richmond Hill, NY; (Y); Spanish Clb; Queens Coll.

DILUZIO, NICHOLAS J; Susquehanna Valley HS; Conklin, NY; (Y); Computer Clb; Mathletes; Rep Soph Cls; Pres Stu Cncl; Crs Cntry; Trk; High Hon Roll; Hon Roll; NHS; Comp Sci.

DILWORTH, MAUREEN; Cllyde-Savannah Central Schl; Savannah, NY; (Y); Drama Clb; SADD; Band; Jazz Band; Nwsp Rptr; Pres VP Stu Cncl; Var Capt Cheerleading; High Hon Roll; Hon Roll; Voice Dem Awd; Quest; Comm.

DIMAGGIO, ROSARIO; La Salle Military Acad; Flushing, NY; (S); 8/99; ROTC; Ski Clb; Yrbk Phtg; Ftbl; Swmmng; Trk; Wt Lftg; High Hon Roll; Hon Roll; NHS; All Honors Cls 83-86; Busnss.

DIMARTINO, LUCY; Yonkers HS; Yonkers, NY; (Y); 35/250; Intnl Clb; Key Clb; Off Jr Cls; Off Sr Cls; Mgr(s); Hon Roll; NHS; Achvmnt Awds 82-86; Iona Coll; Bus Adm.

DIMATTEO, RICHARD A; Amsterdam HS; Amsterdam, NY; (Y); 26/294; Yrbk Stf; Var Tennis; Hon Roll; Ntl Merit Schol; U Center Of Binghamton; Pol Sci.

DIMATTIA, RACHELE; New Rochelle HS; New Rochelle, NY; (Y); Church Yth Grp; Hon Roll; NHS; Medcl Technlgst.

DIMICELI, CHRISTINE; New Dorp HS; Staten Island, NY; (Y); Computer Clb; Drama Clb; Hosp Aide; Intnl Clb; Office Aide; Science Clb; Teachers Aide; Yrbk Phtg; Tennis; Coll Sarasota; Marine Bio.

DIMITROV, BARBARA; Bishop Kearney HS; Rochester, NY; (Y); 28/130; Pres JA; Ski Clb; Mrchg Band; Bsktbl; Var Bowling; Pres Twrlr; Hon Roll; Wegmans Schlrshp 86; Albany Coll; Phrmcst.

DIMOPOULOS, STAVROS; All Hallows HS; New York, NY; (Y); Church Yth Grp; FCA; Im Bsbl; Im Bsktbl; Im Bowling; Im Coach Actv; Im Ftbl; Im Ice Hcky; Im Socr; Im Sftbl; NY U; Finc.

DIMORA, GARY; Greece Athena HS; Rochester, NY; (Y); Exploring; Office Aide; Rep Frsh Cls; Rep Soph Cls; Rep Stu Cncl; Hon Roll; Ntl Merit Ltr; Outstndng Indstrl Arts Awd Plstcs 84-85; Monroe Comm Coll.

DIN, JAY; Union Springs Acad; Blauvelt, NY; (S); 18/45; Ski Clb; Band; Im Bsktbl; Im Capt Ftbl; Hon Roll; Acad All Amer Awd 86; Atlantic Union Coll; Bio.

DINDYAL, RENNY; Central Islip SR HS; Central Islip, NY; (Y); 4/300; Cmnty Wkr; Math Tm; Lit Mag; Var Swmmng; NHS; NEDT Awd; Pilot.

DINEEN, KERRY; Guilderland Central HS; Guilderland, NY; (Y); 4-H; Key Clb; Chorus; School Musical; Variety Show; Bowling; Hon Roll; Outstndng Music Stu Voice 85-86; Russell St Coll; Bio.

DINEHART, CAREY; Naples Central Schl; Naples, NY; (Y); Church Yth Grp; Dance Clb; Girl Scts; Teachers Aide; Chorus; Cheerleading; SUNY Coll Brockport; Elem Educ.

DINGEE, JOSEPH; Dover JR SR HS; Dover Plains, NY; (Y); Cmnty Wkr; High Hon Roll; Hon Roll; Bus.

DINGLE, JEFFREY MARK; West Hempstead SR JR HS; W Hempstead, NY; (Y); 99/330; Rep Frsh Cls; Rep Soph Cls; Rep Jr Cls; Rep Sr Cls; Var Ftbl; Var Trk; Hon Roll; Rotary Awd; All ST Ftbl-Hnrb Mntn All Amercn 85; All ST-400-M & 300-M 86; Fll-Schlrshp-U Of Villvna 86; Villanova U; Bus Adm.

DINGMAN, ALAN; Hudson HS; Hudson, NY; (Y); 24/166; Art Clb; Cmnty Wkr; Intnl Clb; Yrbk Stf; Crs Cntry; Trk; Hon Roll; Kiwanis Awd; Parsons Inst Schlr 86; Parsons Schl Desgn; Graphic Des.

DINGMAN, FLOYD; Broadalbin Central HS; Gloversville, NY; (Y); Drama Clb; Varsity Clb; School Play; Pres Soph Cls; Pres Jr Cls; Pres Sr Cls; VP Pres Stu Cncl; Var L Bsktbl; Var L Socr; Hon Roll; Bus Admin.

DINH, TRANG; Union-Endicott HS; Endicott, NY; (Y); Church Yth Grp; Computer Clb; Debate Tm; Drama Clb; French Clb; Trs Key Clb; Mathletes; High Hon Roll; NHS; Rotary Awd; Salute Yth Pgm 86; Mnrty Stu Apprntcshp Pgm SUNY Bnghmtn 86; Rgn II Wnnrs NY ST Mck Trl Pgm 85; Elec Engnrng.

DINNOCENZO, ANTHONY; Lackawanna SR HS; Lackawanna, NY; (Y); Computer Clb; French Clb; Varsity Clb; Var Bowling; Var Golf; Var Tennis; Law.

DINO, LESLIE; Union Endicott HS; Endwell, NY; (Y); Ski Clb; SADD; Varsity Clb; Band; Concert Band; Mrchg Band; Symp Band; Var L Trk; High Hon Roll; Hon Roll; Comp Engr.

DINOLFO, ANNE; Bishop Kearney HS; Rochester, NY; (Y); Pres Boy Scts; Pres Exploring; JA; Var Bowling; JV Socr; High Hon Roll; Hon Roll.

DINOLIS, JOEY; All Hallows HS; Bronx, NY; (Y); Boys Clb Am; Computer Clb; FCA; Varsity Clb; Var L Bsktbl; Wt Lftg; High Hon Roll; Hon Roll; Acctg.

DIO GUARDI, SARAH; Mt Morris Central Schl; Mt Morris, NY; (S); Am Leg Aux Girls St; Key Clb; Stage Crew; Yrbk Ed-Chief; Sec Frsh Cls; Pres Jr Cls; Var Cheerleading; Cit Awd; DAR Awd; Hon Roll; JR Cup Awd 85; Achvt Awd 84; Elem Ed.

DIOGUARDI, MARY; North Babylon SR HS; N Babylon, NY; (Y); 36/480; Cmnty Wkr; Political Wkr; Spanish Clb; Rep Frsh Cls; Rep Soph Cls; JV Cheerleading; Mgr(s); High Hon Roll; Jr NHS; NHS; Nvl.

DIOGUARDI, THOMAS; Avon JR SR HS; Avon, NY; (Y); Am Leg Boys St; Varsity Clb; Var JV Bsbl; Hon Roll; Jr NHS; Prfct Atten Awd; Dayton U.

DION, DAVID A; Northeastern Clinton Central Schl; Rouses Point, NY; (Y); 6/153; Am Leg Boys St; Key Clb; Var Golf; Var Capt Ice Hcky; Var Capt Socr; Var Tennis; High Hon Roll; NHS; Yrbk Stf; Trs Stu Cncl; Cls VP 84-85; Model UN 83-85; Mst Well Rounded Stu Awd 84-85; Clarkson U; Indstrl Dstrbtn.

DIPIAZZA, FRANK; Lehman HS; Bronx, NY; (Y); 41/536; Intnl Clb; Orch; School Musical; Stat Bowling; Cit Awd; High Hon Roll; Hon Roll; 86 Arista Hnr Scty; Arch.

DIPIPPO, ROSEANN; New Rochelle HS; New Rochelle, NY; (Y); Hon Roll; NHS.

DIPPOLD, JOHN; Solvay HS; Syracuse, NY; (Y); Church Yth Grp; Band; Pres Frsh Cls; Var Capt Bsbl; Var Capt Ftbl; Hon Roll; All Cty Ftbl Hnrbl Mntn 85-86; Acctg.

DIPTEE, ANGELINE R; The Mary Louis Acad; Jamaica, NY; (Y); 57/270; NFL; Trs Spanish Clb; Speech Tm; Orch; Nwsp Rptr; Sec Sr Cls; Hon Roll; St Schlr; NY U Schlrshp 86; Bnjmn Frnkln Schlrshp 86; NY U; Intl Bus.

DIRLAM, KARI; Hauppauge HS; Hauppauge, NY; (Y); 57/499; Ski Clb; Varsity Clb; Band; Var Capt Bsktbl; Var Capt Socr; Var L Sftbl; Vllybl; Hon Roll; NHS; Prfct Atten Awd; Rgnts Schlrshp 86; St Francis Coll Of PA; Jrnlsm.

DISAPIA, NUNZIO; New Rochelle HS; New Rochelle, NY; (Y); Hon Roll; Auto Bdy Achvt Awd 86; Westchester CC; Data Prcsng.

DISBROW, LISA M; Dundee Central HS; Dundee, NY; (Y); Drama Clb; French Clb; Ski Clb; Chorus; School Musical; Yrbk Phtg; Hon Roll; Ntl Englsh Merit Awd 86; Achvt In Frnch Awd 86; Theater.

DISCHNER, JANE; Bishop Ludden HS; Syracuse, NY; (Y); Ski Clb; Var JV Socr; JV Sftbl; High Hon Roll; Hon Roll; NHS; Bus.

DISENA, KAREN C; Wm Floyd HS; Mastic Beach, NY; (Y); 8/544; Ski Clb; Spanish Clb; Band; Mrchg Band; Symp Band; JV Fld Hcky; High Hon Roll; Trs NHS; Spanish NHS; NY Regents Schlrshp 86; Stony Brook U; Math.

DISENHOUSE, MASADA R; Yeshiva Of Flatbush HS; Staten Island, NY; (Y); Cmnty Wkr; Library Aide; Chorus; Color Guard; Orch; Yrbk Stf; Lit Mag; Hon Roll; Jr NHS; Ntl Merit Ltr; Engrng.

DISHAW, MARJORIE; Potsdam Central HS; Potsdam, NY; (Y); Math Clb; Varsity Clb; Orch; Nwsp Rptr; Yrbk Stf; JV Var Crs Cntry; JV Var Trk; High Hon Roll; Hon Roll; Prfct Atten Awd; Sprtsmnshp Trphy 83-84; Erth Sci Achvt Awd 83-84; Engl Achvt Awd 84-85; Clarkson Coll-Potsdam; Bio.

DISHAW, RICHARD; Massena Central HS; Massena, NY; (Y); Boy Scts; Exploring; Canton ATC; Math.

DISKIN, LEE; St John The Baptist HS; N Babylon, NY; (S); 10/524; High Hon Roll; Hon Roll.

DISKIN, MARY; Academy Of Mount Saint Ursula; New York, NY; (Y); SADD; Rep Frsh Cls; 1st Hnrs 83 & 86; Bus.

DISMUKE, BARBARA L; Midwood HS; Brooklyn, NY; (Y); Cmnty Wkr; Girl Scts; Teachers Aide; School Play; Badmtn; Bsktbl; Vllybl; Wt Lftg; Handbl 85-86; Navy; Arch.

DISPENZA, ARI; John Jay HS; S Salem, NY; (Y); Lit Mag; Ftbl; Lcrss; Wrstlng; Hnrbl Ment In Wrld Of Poetry Cntst 85; Psych.

DISPIRITO, MELISSA; Montcello HS; Monticello, NY; (Y); Key Clb; Temple Yth Grp; Yrbk Stf; JV Socr; JV Trk; Var Vllybl; High Hon Roll; Hon Roll; Jr NHS; Christmas Toy Drv 85; Fashion Inst Of Tech; Rtlng.

DISTEFANO, FRANCINE; H Frank Carey HS; Franklin Square, NY; (Y); 45/320; Sec Art Clb; Mgr Camera Clb; Mgr Orch; Rptr Yrbk Phtg; Mgr Yrbk Stf; Mgr High Hon Roll; Mgr Hon Roll; Mgr Girl Scts; Mgr Latin Clb; Mgr Science Clb; Most Friendly 84; Homcmg Dutchess 85; Radio & TV.

DISTEFANO, JOSEPH; W Tresper Clarke HS; East Meadow, NY; (Y); 13/193; Key Clb; Quiz Bowl; Scholastic Bowl; NHS; 86 NYS Schlrshp Wnnr 86; SUNY Strong Brook; Elec Engr.

DISTEFANO, LEIGH; Eden SR HS; Eden, NY; (Y); AFS; Chorus; School Musical; Yrbk Stf; Im Badmtn; Tennis; Vllybl; Hon Roll; NHS; Prfct Atten Awd; Art Achvt Awd 84; Athltc Rcgntn Awd 83; U Of Buffalo; Jrnlsm.

DITE, PATRICIA; Rome Catholic HS; Rome, NY; (Y); School Musical; Nwsp Stf; Yrbk Stf; Rep Frsh Cls; Rep Soph Cls; Rep Jr Cls; Var Cheerleading; Var Socr; High Hon Roll; NHS; Prfct Attnd; Spnsh Awds; Rsltn Cmmn Cncl Rome NY Drg Abs Pgm; Spnsh.

DITMORE, MELISSA; Curtis HS; New York, NY; (Y); 10/215; Debate Tm; French Clb; Yrbk Stf; Jr NHS; Ntl Merit SF; Band; Concert Band; Mrchg Band; Stage Crew; ALISI Ntl Frnch 83 & 84; Cornell U; Lngstcs.

DITTENHOEFER, TIM; Roy C Ketcham HS; Wappingers Falls, NY; (Y); Ski Clb; Bsbl; Ftbl; High Hon Roll; Hon Roll; USFNA Ftbl Awd; Phys Ther.

DITTMAN, JOEL; Southwestern Central HS; Ashville, NY; (Y); French Clb; Ski Clb; Varsity Clb; Stage Crew; Yrbk Stf; Im Bsktbl; Var Trk; Var Vllybl; St Schlr; Rochester Inst/Tech; Comp Engr.

DIVANNA, PRESLEY; Thomas A Edison Vo Tech; Richmond Hill, NY; (Y); Band; School Musical; Mth, Engl, Sci Hnr Rl; Elec Engrng.

DIVINO, MARIA; Saint Francis Prep; Queens Village, NY; (Y); Coll Fndtn Schlrshp 86; SUNY-PLATTSBURGH-ENGL.

DIVINO, RALPH; Archbisop Molloy HS; Rosedale, NY; (Y); 38/383; Dance Clb; Trs Intnl Clb; Service Clb; Acpl Chr; Church Choir; Yrbk Stf; Off Soph Cls; Off Jr Cls; JV Crs Cntry; Im Fld Hcky; Queens Coll Pres Awd Achvt 84; Bus.

DIX, DOREEN; Jamesville De Witt HS; Jamesville, NY; (Y); Cmnty Wkr; Hosp Aide; Library Aide; Lit Mag; Hon Roll; Crtfct Apprctn 84-86; Extcrprl Tech.

DIX, DOREEN; Lindenhurst HS; Lindenhurst, NY; (Y); 117/500; Aud/Vis; Orch; Variety Show; Yrbk Stf; Var Badmtn; JV Fld Hcky; Hon Roll; NYSSMA 81-86; SCEMEA 84; Psych.

DIXIT, SADHANA; Fairport HS; Pittsford, NY; (Y); JV Var Gym; Trk; Hon Roll; Mech Engrng.

DIXIT, SANAT; Tottenville HS; Staten Island, NY; (Y); 65/800; Cmnty Wkr; French Clb; Quiz Bowl; SADD; Jazz Band; School Musical; School Play; Sec Sr Cls; NHS; Brown U Bk Awd-Eng Achvt 86; NYC Sci Fair, Mc Graw Hill Awd-Marine Corps Awd 85; CTE Wrtng Achvt 86; Med Surg.

DIXON, CASSANDRA; Sacred Heart Acad; Hempstead, NY; (Y); Drama Clb; French Clb; FTA; Library Aide; Office Aide; Pep Clb; Hon Roll; NHS; Law.

DIXON, JEANETTE; Kenmore East HS; Tonawanda, NY; (Y); 85/300; Church Yth Grp; GAA; Bsktbl; Vllybl; Hon Roll; Prfct Atten Awd; VP Of Bkstore Clb 85-86; U Of Buffalo; Law.

DIXON, MAUREEN; Sacred Heart Acad; Merrick, NY; (Y); Cmnty Wkr; Library Aide; Office Aide; SADD; Chorus; School Musical; Stage Crew; Hon Roll; NHS; Ntl Piano Plyng Adtns ACM 84-87; Bus.

DIXON, MICHAEL; Dannemora HS; Dannemora, NY; (Y); Art Clb; Cmnty Wkr; French Clb; FBLA; Bsktbl; Socr; MVP Dfnsve Var Sccr 86; MVP Dfnse JV Bsktbl 83; Arch.

DIXON, PATRICIA; Erasmus Hall HS; Brooklyn, NY; (Y); Church Yth Grp; 4-H; Acpl Chr; School Play; Bowling; Gym; Swmmng; 4-H Awd; Prfct Atten Awd; Spnsh Awd 84; Ptmn Shrtrhnd 85 & 86; Math 84 & 85; NY City Coll; Bus.

DIXON, TROY; All Hallows HS; Bronx, NY; (Y); Boys Clb Am; Var Bsktbl; Var Wt Lftg; Hon Roll; MIP Bsktbl 85; Cmnctns.

DIZON, ROWENA-FRANCESCA I; Sachem HS; Holbrook, NY; (Y); 35/1300; Art Clb; Cmnty Wkr; Dance Clb; Intnl Clb; Mrchg Band; Orch; Nwsp Rptr; Lit Mag; Jr NHS; NHS; NY Regents Schlrshp 86; NY U Trustree Sclrshp 86; 1st Pl Prose Wrtng Cont 83; Syracuse U; Comm.

DJORDJEVIC, MARK; Mt St Michael Acad; Bronx, NY; (S); 21/309; Church Yth Grp; French Clb; French Hon Soc; Hon Roll; Jr NHS; NHS; Prfct Atten Awd; St Johns U; Phrmcy.

DLHOPOLSKY, CHARLES; Holy Trintiy Diocesan HS; Lindenhurst, NY; (S); 2/313; Computer Clb; Math Clb; Math Tm; Yrbk Ed-Chief; Pres Soph Cls; Var L Bsbl; High Hon Roll; NHS; Ntl Merit Ltr; Mathletes; 1st Pl Math Leag 84-85; MIT; Comp Engrng.

DLHOSH, WILLIAM J; Royt C Ketcham HS; Wappingers Falls, NY; (Y); 103/500; Latin Clb; Math Clb; Ski Clb; Im Bowling; JV Ftbl; Im Golf; Im Wt Lftg; High Hon Roll; Hon Roll; Rgnts Schlrshp 86; Emby-Rdl Arntcl U; Avtn Engr.

DLUGOLENSKI, THOMAS J; Liverpool HS; Liverpool, NY; (Y); Pres Frsh Cls; Rep Soph Cls; Rep Jr Cls; Rep Sr Cls; Rep Stu Cncl; Im Bsktbl; Im Vllybl; High Hon Roll; Hon Roll; NHS; Acad Achvt Excllnc Awd 82-83; Yng Wmns Chrstn Assoc Apprctn Cert 85; Stonybrook Coll; Pltcl Sci.

DOAN, MELORA A; Hilton Central HS; Hilton, NY; (Y); 17/325; Cmnty Wkr; Spanish Clb; Concert Band; Mrchg Band; Symp Band; Var Sftbl; JV Vllybl; High Hon Roll; NHS; Ntl Merit SF; 1st Tm All Cnty Sftbl 84; Cornell; Biol.

DOAR, JULIE S; John S Burke Catholic HS; Greenwood Lake, NY; (Y); Math Clb; School Play; Stage Crew; Mgr(s); JV Trk; High Hon Roll; Hon Roll; NEDT Awd; Accntnt.

DOBBIN, NANCY; Union Endicott HS; Endwell, NY; (Y); 7/436; Cmnty Wkr; Key Clb; Ski Clb; Rep Stu Cncl; Var L Swmmng; High Hon Roll; NHS; Ntl Merit Ltr; Hosp Aide; Varsity Clb; Thomas J Watson Schlrshp 86; Regents Schlrshp 86; Cornell U; Bio Sci.

DOBBINS, EVAN; Greece Athena HS; Rochester, NY; (Y); 11/300; Church Yth Grp; Drama Clb; Ski Clb; Concert Band; Jazz Band; Symp Band; Sec Soph Cls; High Hon Roll; Hon Roll; NHS; Louis Armstrong Jazz Awd 86; Ntl Merit Lttr 86; Schlrshp Estmn Schl Of Music 86; Cornell U; Physcs.

DOBBS, DIANE; Bitburg American HS; Apo Ny, NY; (Y); Church Yth Grp; Teachers Aide; Rep Stu Cncl; Cert Of Merit French Dramatics ENMU 85; Bus.

DOBE, MELISSA; Bishop Ludden HS; Syracuse, NY; (S); Church Yth Grp; Ski Clb; Chorus; Church Choir; School Musical; Swing Chorus; Trk; High Hon Roll; Jrnlsm.

DOBEK, CAROL; Academy Of St Joseph; Ft Salonga, NY; (Y); Art Clb; Cmnty Wkr; Dance Clb; Pres Spanish Clb; Stage Crew; Yrbk Stf; Hon Roll; Natl Art Hnr Socy; Sup Acad Achvt In Art Awd; Arch.

DOBERT, JULIE; Rensselaer JR SR HS; Rensselaer, NY; (S); Church Yth Grp; Computer Clb; Bsktbl; Crs Cntry; Trk; Vllybl; NHS; SUNY-PLATTSBURGH; Acctng.

DOBIESZ, TRACEY; Nardin Acad; Orchard Pk, NY; (Y); Bsktbl; Score Keeper; Sftbl; Timer; Hon Roll; Hobart William & Smith; Pre Vet.

DOBLES, CHRISTOPHER A; E J Wilson SR HS; Spencerport, NY; (Y); 1/290; JCL; Latin Clb; JV Bsbl; Var L Vllybl; High Hon Roll; Hon Roll; NHS; Regents Schlrshp 86; Voc Indstrl Clubs Am Skill Olympics Wnnr 85 & 86; Mohawk Vly CC; Advrtsng.

DOBLES, JEFF; E J Wilson HS; Spencerport, NY; (Y); Church Yth Grp; Ski Clb; Bsbl; Mgr(s); Score Keeper; Vllybl; High Hon Roll; Hon Roll; Prfct Atten Awd; Auto.

DOBOSIEWICZ, ELIZABETH J; Depew HS; Depew, NY; (Y); 13/273; GAA; Sec Spanish Clb; School Musical; Yrbk Ed-Chief; Yrbk Stf; JV Swmmng; Stat Vllybl; Hon Roll; NHS; Canisius Coll Deans Schlrshp & NYS Rgnts Schlrshp 86; Canisius Coll; Law.

DOBRANSKY, ERIC R; Maine-Endwell SR HS; Johnson City, NY; (Y); 18/234; Trs Church Yth Grp; Im Bsktbl; High Hon Roll; Hon Roll; NHS; Hon Awd Pin & Outstndg Srv Awd 83-84; Cert Of Mmbrshp Natl Hon Soc & Employee Of Month 8; Clarkson U; Compu.

DOBRASZ, STANLEY J; La Salle SR HS; Niagara Falls, NY; (Y); Am Leg Boys St; Boy Scts; Socr; Wrstlng; Hon Roll; NHS; Bowling Lg; Biological Engineering.

DOBRIC, LAURA; Saint Johns Prep; Astoria, NY; (Y); Dance Clb; FTA; Sftbl; Hon Roll; School Play; 1st Hnr Roll 85 & 86; Hntr Coll; Chld Dvlpmnt.

DOBRY, EMILY; The Mary Louis Acad; Jamaica Estates, NY; (Y); Cmnty Wkr; Dance Clb; Hosp Aide; Office Aide; Political Wkr; DAR Awd; Church Yth Grp; Teachers Aide; Stage Crew; Athlc Awd 85 & 86; Cert Hon Math 83-84 & 84-85; Cert Recgntn Svcs Rendered 85; St Johns U; Bus.

DOBSON, CRYSTAL; Sacred Heart Acad; Corona, NY; (Y); Church Yth Grp; Cmnty Wkr; Math Tm; Office Aide; Church Choir; Nwsp Rptr; Nwsp Stf; Lit Mag; Trk; NHS; Church Yth Grp; Cmmnty Wrkr; Mth Tm; NHS; Church Choir; Nwsp Rptr, Staff; Pep Clb; Mth Tm; Lit Mag; Bus.

DOBSON, SCOTT; Randolph Central HS; Randolph, NY; (Y); 30/120; Drama Clb; Ski Clb; Spanish Clb; Var Bsktbl; Var Ftbl; Var L Golf; OH ST U; Vet Med.

DOBULER, ANDREW; Saint Francis Prep; Bayside, NY; (Y); Art Clb; Church Yth Grp; Cmnty Wkr; Variety Show; Im Bowling; Regents Scholar 86; Art Awd 86; Bowling Trophy 85; Bus.

DOCKENDORF, PAMELA; Bitburg HS; Apo Ny, NY; (Y); French Clb; Office Aide; Pep Clb; Hon Roll; Schiller Intl; Psych.

DODDS, MARIE; Heuvelton Central HS; Heuvelton, NY; (Y); 9/38; French Clb; Chorus; School Play; Yrbk Stf; Badmtn; Crs Cntry; Swmmng; Vllybl; Vocal Music Awd 85; Acad Achvt 86; Embry-Riddle Coll; Pilot.

DODDS, MICHELLE; Hudson HS; Hudson, NY; (Y); 7/158; Pres Sec Science Clb; JV Gym; Var Pom Pon; High Hon Roll; NHS; Regents Schlrshp 86; Pres Fit Awd 86; Berkley Schl; Fshn Mrktng.

DODDS, SUSAN; Potsdam SR HS; Potsdam, NY; (Y); 24/147; AFS; Church Yth Grp; 4-H; French Clb; Math Clb; Varsity Clb; Chorus; Crs Cntry; Trk; Mgr Vllybl; SUNY Oswego; Zoolgy.

DODGE, BECKY; Canandaigua Acad; Naples, NY; (Y); Varsity Clb; Chorus; Concert Band; Jazz Band; Mrchg Band; Bsktbl; Cheerleading; Socr; Sftbl; High Hon Roll; Annl Genesee Valley H S Chem Achvt 86.

DODGE, ERIC; Royalton-Hartland Central HS; Middleport, NY; (Y); Boy Scts; Sec French Clb; Chrmn Red Cross Aide; Rep Stu Cncl; JV Var Trk; High Hon Roll; Lion Awd; Exploring; Stage Crew; JV Ftbl; Squad Mem Tri-Town Volntr 84-86; Middleprt Volntr Fire Dept 86; NY ST Cert 1st Respndr 85; Niagara Cnty CC; Nrsng.

DODGE JR, GEORGE; St Lawrence Central HS; Brasher Fls, NY; (Y); Pres Church Yth Grp; Yrbk Phtg; JV Var Bsktbl; Hon Roll; Prfct Atten Awd; Pres Schlr; AAHPERD Ftnss Awd 85; Cnmtgrphr.

DODGE, MICHAEL; Maryvale HS; Cheektowaga, NY; (Y); Church Yth Grp; Varsity Clb; Var L Crs Cntry; Mgr(s); Var Capt Swmmng; Var L Trk; Hon Roll; NHS.

DODGE, SCOTT; York Central HS; Leicester, NY; (Y); FFA; Crs Cntry; Trk.

DODGE, TERESA; Frewsburg Central HS; Frewsburg, NY; (Y); Jr Cls; Stu Cncl; JV Sftbl; JV Var Vllybl; Hon Roll; NHS; Comp Oprtr.

DODSON, ZAK; Skaneateles HS; Skaneateles, NY; (S); Aud/Vis; Ftbl; Wrstlng; High Hon Roll; NHS; Rochester Inst Tech; Comp Sci.

DOELGER, TERESA; Lindenhurst SR HS; Lindenhurst, NY; (Y); Art Clb; German Clb; Political Wkr; Yrbk Stf; Hon Roll; Med.

DOELL, KEVIN V; Warwick Valley HS; Warwick, NY; (Y); 15/20; Am Leg Boys St; Church Yth Grp; Drama Clb; SADD; Band; School Musical; Var Bsbl; Var Golf; High Hon Roll; NHS; Mediatr 40 Hrs Inst, Chrmn Dscpln Comm 85-86; ROTC Schlrshp; Rutgers; Pilot.

DOGGETT, KERRY; Saugerties HS; Saugerties, NY; (S); 2/249; Church Yth Grp; French Clb; Math Tm; Var Capt Bsktbl; Var L Trk; Var High Hon Roll; Var Hon Roll; 10th Yr Mth Awd Maintain Bst Avg Schl Yr 84-85; Mth.

DOHERTY, BRIAN; Mahopac HS; Mahopac, NY; (Y); 24/409; Church Yth Grp; Political Wkr; Band; Concert Band; Jazz Band; Mrchg Band; Nwsp Rptr; High Hon Roll; NHS; Ntl Merit Ltr; Intl Rltns.

DOHERTY, DANIELLE; James Madison HS; Brooklyn, NY; (Y); Tennis.

DOHERTY, ERIN ANNE; East Meadow HS; East Meadow, NY; (Y); 205/340; Debate Tm; FBLA; Concert Band; Mrchg Band; Stage Crew; Yrbk Bus Mgr; Church Yth Grp; Drama Clb; Girl Scts; Key Clb; 3rd Pl Prne Pstn Rfl Coachs Comptn 86; Prfct Attnd Awd Mrchng Bnd Awd 86; Yrbk Achvt Awd Asst Edtr 86; Nassau CC; Bus Admn.

DOHERTY, KAREN; Hauppauge HS; Smithtown, NY; (Y); Church Yth Grp; Chorus; Orch; JV Var Pom Pon; High Hon Roll; Hon Roll; NHS; Rgnts Schlrshp 86; SUNY Binghamton; Pre Law.

DOHERTY, MICHAEL; Hicksville HS; Hicksville, NY; (Y); Boy Scts; Cmnty Wkr; Drama Clb; School Musical; School Play; Nwsp Sprt Ed; Im Ice Hcky; Var L Trk; Hon Roll; NHS; Duke; Bus.

DOHERTY, WENDY; Groton Central HS; Locke, NY; (Y); 6/100; Pres Church Yth Grp; Sec Trs 4-H; Girl Scts; Ski Clb; Spanish Clb; School Play; Variety Show; Rep Stu Cncl; Socr; Sftbl; Cornell; Envrnmntl Sci.

DOIN, KAREN; Lansingburgh HS; Troy, NY; (Y); Chorus; School Musical; Sec Soph Cls; Im Mgr Cheerleading; Var Crs Cntry; JV Var Trk; High Hon Roll; Hon Roll; Jr NHS; Prfct Atten Awd; Hm Rm Cap 85-86; Marshall SR Grad 86; Prom Cmmtte 86.

DOIN, KATHLEEN; Lansingburgh HS; Troy, NY; (S); 13/185; Chorus; School Play; JV Var Bsktbl; Capt Var Trk; High Hon Roll; Pres NHS; Hmrm Capt 85-86; Mgmt.

DOLAN, ALLISON; Moore Catholic HS; Staten Island, NY; (Y); Hosp Aide; Speech Tm; Nwsp Stf; Yrbk Stf; Stu Cncl; Var L Crs Cntry; Hon Roll; NHS; French Clb; Ski Clb; Bst Prjct Moore Cthlc Sci Fair 85; Amer Inst Schl Sci Fair Hnrb Mntn 86; Psychlgy.

DOLAN, JACK; Niskayuna HS; Schenectady, NY; (Y); Church Yth Grp; Cmnty Wkr; Latin Clb; Pep Clb; Spanish Clb; JV Var Ftbl; JR Ftbl Mst Vlble Dfnsve Plyr 84; Vrsty Ftbl Coaches Awd 85; Engrng.

DOLAN, KAREN; Garden City HS; Garden City, NY; (Y); 169/356; Cmnty Wkr; French Clb; Hosp Aide; Political Wkr; SADD; Nwsp Stf; Frncs C Hly Memrl Awd-Outstndng Svc-Winthrp U Hosp 86; Chrmn Vlntr Supvsiors-Wnthrp U Hosp 85-86; Hofstra U; Psychlgy.

DOLAN, KATHLEEN A; St Anthonys HS; Massapequa, NY; (Y); Cmnty Wkr; Drama Clb; Hosp Aide; SADD; Nwsp Rptr; Yrbk Sprt Ed; Var Capt Badmtn; Mu Alp Tht; Ntl Merit Ltr; NEDT Awd; Rgnts Schlrshp 86; Sienna Coll; Math.

DOLAN, KERRY; Dobbs Ferry HS; Dobbs Ferry, NY; (S); 6/80; JA; Key Clb; Band; Jazz Band; Yrbk Bus Mgr; Capt Tennis; Pres French Hon Soc; High Hon Roll; NHS; Louis Armstrong Jazz Awd; Intl Busnss.

DOLAN, SEAN; Christ The King HS; Middle Village, NY; (Y); Im JV Bsbl; Im Var Ftbl; Var Golf; Im Sftbl; USAF Acad; Aerontcs.

DOLBECK, JASON; Ticonderoga HS; Ticonderoga, NY; (Y); 11/110; Am Leg Boys St; Boy Scts; Trs FCA; Varsity Clb; Yrbk Stf; Pres Jr Cls; Off Stu Cncl; Var JV Bsktbl; Var JV Ftbl; Var Golf; Cvl Engnrng.

DOLENUCK, COLLEEN; Buffalo Traditional HS; Buffalo, NY; (S); 2/111; Math Tm; Spanish Clb; Hon Roll; Sec NHS; Prfct Atten Awd; Sal; Bus Adm.

DOLGAS, LANCE; Hoosic Valley HS; Schaghticoke, NY; (S); 11/99; Band; Chorus; Trs Frsh Cls; Trs Soph Cls; Trs Jr Cls; Var L Bsbl; Bowling; Var L Socr; NHS; Boy Scts; NY ST Schl Music Assn Area All-ST Symphnc Band 85; Math.

DOLGOFF, ELIANA D; John F Kennedy HS; Old Bethpage, NY; (Y); Trs Model UN; Stage Crew; Var Crs Cntry; Var Trk; Hon Roll; Undrsecrtry Gnrl Met Mdl UN Cnfrnc 85; Europn Hstry Awd 84; Spnsh Awd 85; Barnard.

DOLINS, LAURA; Guilderland Central HS; Schenectady, NY; (Y); Aud/Vis; Cmnty Wkr; Chorus; Symp Band; JV Crs Cntry; Hon Roll; Ctznshp Awd Wrk Hearing Imprd 84; 7th Plc Natl French Exam 84; 4th Plc Eqtn Cap Dist Hntr Jmpr Cncl 85; Training & Brdng Horses.

DOLL, DAVID; Hornell HS; Hornell, NY; (Y); Boy Scts; Band; Chorus; Concert Band; Mrchg Band; Ftbl; Wrstlng; Elec.

DOLPH, LARRY; Bishop Cunningham HS; Oswego, NY; (Y); 4/40; Am Leg Boys St; Yrbk Ed-Chief; VP Jr Cls; Var Bsktbl; Var Capt Socr; Elks Awd; Hon Roll; Pres NHS; Voice Dem Awd; Le Moyne Coll; Bus Adm.

DOLPHIN JR, JOHN P; Lafayette HS; Buffalo, NY; (Y); Boys Clb Am; Computer Clb; Office Aide; Varsity Clb; Var Bsbl; Var Ftbl; Var Socr; Var Wt Lftg; Hon Roll; Prfct Atten Awd; Crim Law.

DOLPHIN, WENDY; Union Endicott HS; Endicott, NY; (Y); Church Yth Grp; Dance Clb; Pep Clb; Varsity Clb; Band; Color Guard; Concert Band; Mrchg Band; Orch; Symp Band; Penn ST; Sec Ed.

DOLSON, FAY ANN; Minisink Valley HS; Otisville, NY; (Y); 42/224; SADD; Flag Corp; Mrchg Band; High Hon Roll; Hon Roll; Natl Merit Cmmnded Negro Stu 84; Bus Mgmt.

DOMAGALA, MICHAEL R; John F Kennedy HS; Cheektowaga, NY; (Y); 1/150; Aud/Vis; Computer Clb; VP DECA; FHA; Hst Letterman Clb; Pres Trs PAVAS; Trs Varsity Clb; Band; Stage Crew; Nwsp Stf; RIT & NYS Regnts Schlrshps 86; Gftd Math Prgrm SUNY 80-86; Rochester Inst Of Tech; Statstc.

DOMAGALA, PENNY L; Southlewis Central HS; Glenfield, NY; (Y); 4/86; Sec Pres 4-H; Church Choir; School Musical; Var L Vllybl; 4-H Awd; High Hon Roll; Hon Roll; NYS Rgnts Schlrshp 86; Sci Stu Recog 85; Le Moyne Coll; Math Mgmt.

DOMAGALSKI, DONNA CATHERINE; Orchard Park HS; Orchard Park, NY; (Y); Am Leg Aux Girls St; Chorus; Concert Band; School Musical; Nwsp Rptr; Yrbk Stf; Lit Mag; Rep Stu Cncl; Var Fld Hcky; Hon Roll; Empire Grls ST Awd Recog 86; Schlrshp Awd Hnr Rll 86; Supr Grd Adv Plcmt Amer Hstry Exm 86; Notre Dame; Hstry.

DOMBAL, LISA; Minisink Valley HS; State Hill, NY; (Y); Stage Crew; Rep Soph Cls; High Hon Roll; Hon Roll; Educ.

DOMBROSKI, MARY; G Ray Bodley HS; Oswego, NY; (Y); 85/261; Pep Clb; Science Clb; Yrbk Stf; Rep Frsh Cls; Rep Soph Cls; Hon Roll; Herkimer Coll; Trvl.

DOMBROW, RUSSELL W; Bishop Ludden HS; Syracuse, NY; (Y); Am Leg Boys St; French Clb; Model UN; Political Wkr; Var L Ice Hcky; Var L Socr; High Hon Roll; Hon Roll; Cmnty Wkr; Intnl Clb; OH ST U Cls 68 Schlrshp 85-86; NYS Rgnts Schlrshp 85-86; Hnbl Mntn CNY Model UN 86; ST U NY Buffalo; Bus Admin.

DOMBROWSKI, CYNTHIA; Wst Seneca East SR HS; West Seneca, NY; (Y); Art Clb; Dance Clb; Trs Spanish Clb; SADD; School Musical; Lit Mag; Stu Cncl; High Hon Roll; JC Awd; NHS.

DOMBROWSKI, DENISE; Attica SR HS; Cowlesville, NY; (S); 10/154; Pres VP AFS; Church Yth Grp; Sec Band; Nwsp Stf; Yrbk Stf; Trs Soph Cls; JV Var Cheerleading; Var Trk; NHS; Most Valuable Chrldr For Vrsty Soccer 85; Frnch Awd 83-85; Ntl Ldrshp Awd 84; Houghton Coll; Lang.

DOMBROWSKI, LORI; Aiden Central HS; Elma, NY; (Y); 26/203; Spanish Clb; School Musical; Yrbk Stf; Pres Sr Cls; Rep Stu Cncl; Hon Roll; Kiwanis Awd; Alden Hook & Ldr Schlrshp 86; V Gebhard Mem Schlrshp 86; NY ST U Buffalo; Physcl Thrpy.

DOMECILLO, MARTIN; Greater New York Acad; Brooklyn, NY; (S); 2/25; Boys Clb Am; FCA; Science Clb; Varsity Clb; School Musical; Nwsp Stf; Var Bsktbl; Cit Awd; High Hon Roll; Sec Frsh Cls; Hnr Rll 83-86; Gym Awd 85; Rlgn Awd 85; Atlantic Union Coll; Med.

DOMICK, TIM; Thomas J Corcoran HS; Syracuse, NY; (Y); Aud/Vis; Nwsp Rptr; Nwsp Stf; NHS; Comp Sci.

DOMICO, KAREN; Alexander Central Schl; Darien, NY; (Y); 16/84; FNA; FTA; Chorus; Color Guard; Nwsp Stf; Yrbk Stf; NHS; D Youville Coll; Sec Ed.

DOMINICK, DANA F; Newburgh Free Acad; Newburgh, NY; (Y); 50/625; Spanish Clb; Acpl Chr; Concert Band; High Hon Roll; Hon Roll; Jr NHS; Band; Chorus; Mrchg Band; Margaret B Bunn Scholar 86; Robert D Williams Music Awd 83; Hartwick Coll; Phrmcy.

DOMINO, VANESSA; Stissing Mt Pine Plains HS; Red Hook, NY; (Y); AFS; Ski Clb; Yrbk Phtg; Yrbk Stf; Trs Soph Cls; Fld Hcky; Score Keeper; Tennis; Trk; Hon Roll; Franklin Pierce Coll NH; CPA.

DONAGHY, JOHN; Mewfield HS; Selden, NY; (Y); Bsbl; Ice Hcky; Hon Roll; Real Estate.

DONAHUE, JACK; St Marys Boys HS; Pt Washington, NY; (Y); 30/180; Ski Clb; Yrbk Stf; Stu Cncl; JV Var Bsktbl; JV Crs Cntry; Im Ftbl; JV Var Lcrss; High Hon Roll; Hon Roll; Bus.

DONAHUE, MARIANNE; Queen Of The Rosary Acad; Farmingdale, NY; (Y); Teachers Aide; Im Badmtn; Im Bsktbl; Im Sftbl; Im Tennis; Im Vllybl; Hon Roll; Nassau CC; Nrsng.

DONAHUE, THOMAS C; Red Hook Central HS; Red Hook, NY; (Y); 4/137; Church Yth Grp; Drama Clb; Exploring; School Play; Variety Show; Nwsp Phtg; Nwsp Rptr; High Hon Roll; NHS; Pres Schlr; Regents Schrlshp 86; SUNY; Filmmkng.

DONARUMA, TRACY; Commack South HS; Dix Hills, NY; (Y); Chorus; Stage Crew; Cheerleading; Hon Roll; Bus.

DONARUNNA, TRACY; Commack South HS; Dix Hills, NY; (Y); Office Aide; Chorus; Stage Crew; Cheerleading; Hon Roll; Bus.

DONATELLI, SANDY; Oriskany Central HS; Oriskany, NY; (Y); Hosp Aide; Sec Key Clb; SADD; Varsity Clb; Chorus; Color Guard; VP Jr Cls; Im Bowling; Var Capt Cheerleading; Var Sftbl; Ution Coll.

DONATI, LISA; Henninger HS; Syracuse, NY; (Y); GAA; Intnl Clb; Key Clb; SADD; Sec Frsh Cls; VP Soph Cls; Pres Jr Cls; Pres Sr Cls; Var Socr; Elks Awd; Le Moyne Coll; Englsh.

DONATI, MICHAEL J; Shaker HS; Latham, NY; (Y); Church Yth Grp; Cmnty Wkr; Lit Mag; Socr; Hon Roll; NY ST Rgnts Schlrshps 85-86; Rochester Tech Inst; Bio-Tech.

DONATO, CHRISTINE ANN; John Jay HS; Katonah, NY; (Y); Chorus; Variety Show; Yrbk Stf; Capt Var Crs Cntry; Var Trk; Cit Awd; High Hon Roll; NHS.

DONATO, JOANNE; Bishop Maginn HS; Albany, NY; (S); School Play; Bsktbl; Sftbl; Vllybl; High Hon Roll; Hon Roll.

DONATO, VINCENT; Bishop Maginn HS; Albany, NY; (S); 4/86; Math Clb; Nwsp Stf; Trs Jr Cls; High Hon Roll; NHS; Elmira Coll Key Awd Schlrshp 85; Holy Cross Bk Awd 85; U Of PA; Fince.

DONER, MARNIE L; Hinsdale Central Schl; Hinsdale, NY; (Y); Pres Church Yth Grp; Pres Library Aide; Spanish Clb; Nwsp Ed-Chief; Rep Stu Cncl; Stat Bsktbl; Stat Sftbl; High Hon Roll; NHS; Allegheny Coll; Intl Stu.

DONG, HELEN H; Hillcrest HS; Briarwood, NY; (Y); 17/800; Cmnty Wkr; Computer Clb; Sec Intnl Clb; Teachers Aide; Yrbk Stf; High Hon Roll; Hon Roll; Prfct Atten Awd; Rgnts Schlrshp Awd 86; NY U; Bus Mgmt.

DONLAN, ANDREW K; James I O Neill HS; Highland Falls, NY; (Y); 22/135; Pep Clb; Band; Jazz Band; Lit Mag; Stu Cncl; Crs Cntry; Swmmng; Trk; Hon Roll; Rotary Awd; Siena; Sci.

DONLON, LYNEE; Waterville HS; Waterville, NY; (Y); 12/90; Church Yth Grp; Pep Clb; Varsity Clb; Chorus; Concert Band; School Musical; JV Cheerleading; High Hon Roll; Hon Roll; NHS; Gftd & Tlntd Prg 84; Drama Awd Local Arts Clb 85; Score Of 99 Out Of 100 NY ST Solo Fstvl 86; Elec Educ.

DONNELLY, CHRISTINA; Sacred Heart Acad; Floral Park, NY; (S); 10/189; FTA; SADD; Tennis; High Hon Roll; NHS.

DONNELLY, ELIZABETH A; Bishop Grimes HS; Morrisville, NY; (S); GAA; Ski Clb; Band; Concert Band; Mrchg Band; JV Var Bsktbl; JV Var Fld Hcky; Var Sftbl; Var Tennis; Var Trk; JV Bsktbl Trnmtn Al-Star; Vrsty Fld Hcky Leag Al-Star; Starter 84-85; NYS Bsktbl ST Chmps Morrisvl.

DONNELLY, GERARD J; Kings Park SR HS; Kings Park, NY; (Y); 32/393; Church Yth Grp; Cmnty Wkr; Computer Clb; Exploring; Math Clb; Math Tm; ROTC; Science Clb; Spanish Clb; SADD; Wm T Rogers Achvt Awd 83; Bsebl Coaches Awd 83; PAL Natl Wrld Srs Slvr Mdl Wnnr 84 Sci Olympd Mdl 83; U Of Notre Dame; Pre-Law.

DONNELLY, JACQUELI; Cardinal Mooney HS; Rochester, NY; (Y); 52/318; Cmnty Wkr; Library Aide; Nwsp Rptr; Rep Jr Cls; Rep Sr Cls; Var Cheerleading; Im Socr; Hon Roll; Ntl Merit Schol; Spanish NHS; Schlrshp U Of Chrlstn 86; Rgnts Schlrshp Nrsng 86; U Of Rochester; Nrsng.

DONNELLY, JAMES; Mngr Farrell HS; Staten Island, NY; (Y); Aud/Vis; Cmnty Wkr; Letterman Clb; Lit Mag; Pres Soph Cls; Rep Stu Cncl; Im Bsktbl; JV Im Ftbl; JV Wt Lftg; Pre-Med.

DONNELLY, JANET; Canisteo Central Schl; Canisteo, NY; (Y); 1/73; School Play; Yrbk Ed-Chief; Pres Sr Cls; Elks Awd; NHS; Ntl Merit Ltr; Val; Art Clb; Church Yth Grp; Girl Scts; Intern With ST Assmblymn 86; Steuben Cnty Yth In Govt Intern 86; 2nd Pl-Aimee Garman Mem Spkg Cont 84; Syracuse U; Advtg.

DONNELLY, JOANNE; Canisteo Central HS; Canisteo, NY; (Y); 1/75; Church Yth Grp; Ski Clb; Color Guard; Yrbk Stf; Trs Frsh Cls; Trs Soph Cls; Capt L Socr; L Trk; Cit Awd; High Hon Roll; Lcl Hnr Scty 83-86; Math.

DONNELLY, KATHLEEN; Bishop Ludden HS; Auburn, NY; (Y); Cmnty Wkr; Hosp Aide; Intnl Clb; Speech Tm; SADD; Off Sr Cls; High Hon Roll; NHS; Le Moyne Stu Schlrshp 86; Frontiers Sci Syracuse U 86.

DONNELLY, KEVIN; Archbishop Molloy HS; Floral Park, NY; (Y); CAP; SADD; Off Stu Cncl; Score Keeper; Bus.

DONNELLY, KEVIN; Chester HS; Chester, NY; (Y); 6/69; JV Var Bsbl; JV Var Bsktbl; Regnts Schlrshp Math 86; Clarkson U; Elect Engrg.

DONNELLY, MABEL; Jamesville De Witt HS; Jamesville, NY; (Y); Sec Church Yth Grp; Opt Clb Awd.

DONNELLY, PATRICK; Carmel HS; Hudson, NY; (Y); Church Yth Grp; JV Im Ftbl; JV Var Trk; Outstndng & Dedicated Svc Awd 86; Columbian Squire Awd 86; ST Deputy Chief Squire NY 86; Bus Mgmt.

DONNINI, DARCI; Cohoes HS; Cohoes, NY; (Y); Church Yth Grp; Exploring; Spanish Clb; SADD; Trs Frsh Cls; Cheerleading; Score Keeper; Timer; Hon Roll.

DONNINI, LISA; Cohoes HS; Cohoes, NY; (Y); 2/184; Art Clb; Math Tm; Science Clb; Nwsp Rptr; JV Bsktbl; Var Bowling; Var Trk; Var L Vllybl; High Hon Roll; NHS; Coll Of St Rose Acadmc Schlrshp 86; St Rose; Chemistry.

DONOFRIO, ANNA; Mynderse Acad; Seneca Falls, NY; (Y); Drama Clb; Girl Scts; Band; Chorus; Church Choir; Concert Band; Mrchg Band; School Musical; Rep Stu Cncl; Var Crs Cntry; Mst Insprtnl Crs Cntry 86; Var Ltr Crs Cntry 86; Nyssma Awds Vocal Solos 84-86.

DONOFRIO, CHRIS; Arch Bishop Stepinac HS; Hawthorne, NY; (Y); 60/200; Ski Clb; Socr.

DONOHUE, JEANNETTE; Delaware Valley C S HS; Hortonville, NY; (S); 3/42; Pres AFS; Pres Drama Clb; Pres 4-H; Hosp Aide; Q&S; Sec Spanish Clb; School Musical; Nwsp Stf; Yrbk Stf; NHS; Regents Schlrp 86; Syracuse U; Pub Reltns.

DONOHUE, JENNIE; Delaware Valley Central HS; Hortonville, NY; (Y); 3/42; Pres Drama Clb; Pres 4-H; Hosp Aide; Pres Intnl Clb; Q&S; Sec Spanish Clb; Trs Chorus; Nwsp Stf; Yrbk Rptr; NHS; Syracuse U Schlrshp & Grant 86; USA Natl Jrnlsm Awd 83; Sawyer Thorwelle Kautz Schlrshp 86; Syracuse U; Publ Rel.

DONOHUE, NOEL; Stissing Mnt JR SR HS; Red Hook, NY; (Y); 15/83; Nwsp Stf; Trs Jr Cls; Trs Sr Cls; Var JV Bsktbl; Var Trk; Var Vllybl; Hon Roll; NHS.

DONOHUE, RICHARD; Hicksville HS; Hicksville, NY; (Y); 42/445; Cmnty Wkr; Spanish Clb; Nwsp Stf; Rep Stu Cncl; Hon Roll; NHS; Pres Schlr; St Schlr; Dstngushd Acdmc Schlrshp 86; Hofstra U; Invstmt Bnkg.

DONOVAN, EILEEN; Holy Trinity HS; Wantagh, NY; (S); 3/403; Ski Clb; Spanish Clb; SADD; Var Badmtn; Trk; Hon Roll; Dartmouth; Bus.

DONOVAN, JOSEPH; Elmira Free Acad; Elmira, NY; (Y); Capt Church Yth Grp; Cmnty Wkr; Varsity Clb; Bsbl; Bsktbl; Ftbl; Wt Lftg; Hon Roll; People To People Ambssdr Pgm 85-86; Sprts Med.

DONOVAN, KATHLEEN; Hicksville SR HS; Hicksville, NY; (Y); Church Yth Grp; Drama Clb; Band; Church Choir; Color Guard; Mrchg Band; School Play; Stage Crew; Symp Band; Variety Show; Music.

DONOVAN, KELLI; Newburgh Free Acad; New Windsor, NY; (Y); Jr NHS; Bio.

DONOVAN, MARY; Sacred Heart Acad; Malverne, NY; (Y); VP FTA; Pep Clb; Service Clb; Chorus; Yrbk Stf; Hon Roll; NHS; Bus Adm.

DONOVAN, NATALIE; Dominican Commercial HS; Jamaica, NY; (Y); Art Clb; Drama Clb; School Musical; School Play; Cheerleading; Gym; Swmmng; Hon Roll; Prfct Atten Awd; Advrtsng.

DONUS, ANDREW GEORGE; South Side HS; Rockville Ctr, NY; (Y); Church Yth Grp; Political Wkr; SADD; Varsity Clb; Var Bsbl; JV Ftbl; Var Ice Hcky; Wt Lftg; Var Wrstlng; Hon Roll; U Of Buffalo; Sprts Med.

DOODIAN, SHARON M; Shaker HS; Latham, NY; (Y); French Clb; SADD; Variety Show; Yrbk Sprt Ed; Var Fld Hcky; Hon Roll; NHS; Ntl Merit SF; VP Frsh Cls; Pres Soph Cls; Engl.

DOODY, MARYNA B; St Joseph Hill Acad; Brooklyn, NY; (Y); 65/107; Cmnty Wkr; French Clb; FTA; Speech Tm; Nwsp Stf; Yrbk Stf; Hon Roll; NY ST Regnts Schlrshp 86; NY U; Eng.

DOOHER, KATHY; Rome Catholic HS; Rome, NY; (Y); 10/70; Trs Jr Cls; Trs Sr Cls; Am Leg Aux Girls St; Church Yth Grp; Library Aide; Nwsp Rptr; Yrbk Stf; JV Var Socr; Var Trk; NEDT Awd; Le Moyne Coll; Psych.

DOOHER, MICHELLE; Rome Catholic HS; Rome, NY; (Y); 15/68; Church Yth Grp; School Musical; Nwsp Rptr; Yrbk Rptr; Bsktbl; Socr; Trk; High Hon Roll; Hon Roll; Pres Schlr; Acad All Amer 86; St Josephs Hosp Schl Nrsng.

DOOLEY, BRENDAN; Fordham Prep; Bronx, NY; (Y); Cmnty Wkr; French Clb; JA; JCL; Ski Clb; JV Capt Bsktbl; JV Var Ftbl; Golf; High Hon Roll; NHS; Howard U; Aerontcs.

DOPSOVIC, BETH; Bay Shore HS; Brightwaters, NY; (Y); 36/380; Nwsp Sprt Ed; Nwsp Stf; Rep Stu Cncl; Var L Socr; Var L Sftbl; NHS; Tom Short Awd/Outstndng Stu 84; Outstndng Achvt Athltc Schrshp 84; Hnrb Mntn All Cnty Sftbl 86; Pltcl Sci.

DORAN, CATHERINE; Sachem HS; Lake Grove, NY; (Y); 229/1558; Church Yth Grp; French Clb; Ski Clb.

DORAN, JULIA C; Our Lady Of Mercy HS; Rochester, NY; (Y); 69/172; Church Yth Grp; Debate Tm; Girl Scts; JA; Model UN; SADD; Nwsp Rptr; Yrbk Stf; Rep Stu Cncl; Cheerleading; Acad Schlrshp-Our Lady Of Mercy HS 82; NYS Regnts Schlrshp 86; U Of Rochester; Lawyr.

DORAN, JUSTIN B; Chatham Central HS; Old Chatham, NY; (Y); 5/130; Am Leg Boys St; Church Yth Grp; Ski Clb; Pres Soph Cls; Rep Stu Cncl; JV Bsktbl; Socr; Tennis; High Hon Roll; NHS; Var Lttrs Sccr & Tnns; Bus Adm.

DORAN, TERRY; Argyle Central Schl; Argyle, NY; (Y); Hon Roll; Electrncs.

DORE, CATHERINE JOANNE; Holy Trinity HS; Bethpage, NY; (Y); 21/314; High Hon Roll; Hon Roll; Cert Achvt Algb 83; Schlrshp Cert Geom 84; Farmingdale Ag & Tech; Vet.

DORE, JEANINE CANDACE; Middletown HS; Middletown, NY; (Y); Cmnty Wkr; Math Tm; Mrchg Band; Lit Mag; Rep Jr Cls; Rep Stu Cncl; Var L Bsktbl; Var L Socr; High Hon Roll; NHS; Acad Awd Soc Stds 84-85; Acad Awd Soc Stds & Engl 85-86; Pol Sci.

DORESTANT, SHIRLEY; John Dewey HS; Brooklyn, NY; (Y); Church Yth Grp; Dance Clb; Debate Tm; French Clb; Church Choir; Orch; Bsktbl; Vllybl; Cit Awd; Hon Roll; Glee Clb Awd 80; Schlrshp Awd 80; ST Of Albany; Psych.

DORETY, MICHELE; Duanesburg HS; Esperance, NY; (Y); 11/50; Cmnty Wkr; Drama Clb; 4-H; GAA; Girl Scts; Intnl Clb; SADD; Teachers Aide; Band; Chorus; NYS Regnts Schlrshp 86; Mrs Forbes Memrl Awd 86; Recrd Hldr 400 M Hurdles 86; Sec Ed.

DOREY, LISA; Plattsburgh HS; Plattsburgh AFB, NY; (Y); 9/170; Hosp Aide; Red Cross Aide; Ski Clb; Var Crs Cntry; Var Diving; Var Swmmng; High Hon Roll; NHS; Soc Stud Achvmnt Awd Psych 83-84; Plattsburgh AFB Ofcrs & Enlstd Wvs Clbs Schlrshp 86; Physcs Achvmnt; U Of Vermont; Bio.

DORF, SHIRLEY B; Blind Brook HS; Rye Brook, NY; (Y); AFS; French Clb; Math Tm; Sec Trs SADD; Pres Temple Yth Grp; Concert Band; School Musical; Rep Stu Cncl; JV Tennis; NY ST Regnts Schlrshp 86; Columbia U; Gentcs.

DORLON III, DANIEL A; Amsterdam HS; Amsterdam, NY; (Y); 29/296; Varsity Clb; Rep Sr Cls; Var Ftbl; Var Trk; Var Wrstlng; 4-H Awd; Hon Roll; NHS; Pres Schlr; Regents Schlrshp 86; Union Coll; Mech Engrng.

DORNEY, CHRIS; Kendall JR SR HS; Hamlin, NY; (Y); 6/87; Cmnty Wkr; Drama Clb; Model UN; Ski Clb; Varsity Clb; Chorus; Var Capt Bsbl; High Hon Roll; Jr NHS; NHS; Bst Offensive & Deffensive Plyr Bsbll 84-85; Schlstc Letter 84-86; Engrng.

DORNEY, JEANETTE; Academy Of St Joseph HS; Oakdale, NY; (Y); Hosp Aide; Science Clb; Varsity Clb; Nwsp Rptr; Nwsp Stf; Badmtn; Hon Roll; 9th Pl In Natl Frnch Cntst 84; Outstndng Acad Achvmt In Art 86; Excllnc In Art & Math 86; Cornell U; Hstry.

DORR, NANCY; Sweet Home SR HS; Tonawanda, NY; (Y); Church Yth Grp; German Clb; Girl Scts; Mathletes; Science Clb; Concert Band; Mrchg Band; Tennis; High Hon Roll; NHS; Psych.

DORR, STEPHANI R; Doane Stuart HS; W Sand Lake, NY; (Y); Church Yth Grp; Girl Scts; Ski Clb; Spanish Clb; Stage Crew; Yrbk Stf; Socr; High Hon Roll; Hon Roll; Syracuse U; Intr Dsgn.

DORRIES, JOANN MARIE; Deer Park HS; N Babylon, NY; (Y); 68/468; FBLA; Intnl Clb; Library Aide; Political Wkr; Service Clb; SADD; Stage Crew; Yrbk Phtg; Yrbk Stf; Lit Mag; St Johns U; Scndry Math Educ.

DORSCHUG, SARITA K; St Francis Prep; Fresh Meadows, NY; (S); 67/744; Sec German Clb; Var Gym; Opt Clb Awd; 2nd And 3rd All Arnd Gymnstc Champs 83-85; Acadmc All Am 85-86.

DORSET, ERIK L; Williamsville South HS; Williamsville, NY; (Y); 18/210; VP Orch; School Musical; Ed Yrbk Phtg; Yrbk Stf; Hon Roll; NHS; Obrln Coll Cnsrvtry-Music; Musi.

DORSEY, CHRISTINE; John Jay HS; Fishkill, NY; (Y); Concert Band; High Hon Roll; Hon Roll; Jr NHS.

DORTCH, KATRINA; Hutch Tech; Buffalo, NY; (Y); 23/270; Hon Roll; NHS; Alpha-Kapa Boule Schlrshp 86; Canisius Coll; Acctg.

DORWAY, DAVID P; Midwood HS; Brooklyn, NY; (Y); Computer Clb; Hosp Aide; Orch; School Musical; Stu Cncl; Stu Med Sci Inst 82-86; Med.

DOSCHER, DREW; Xavier HS; New York, NY; (Y); Boys Clb Am; Cmnty Wkr; Dance Clb; Rep Soph Cls; Rep Jr Cls; Rep Sr Cls; Rep Stu Cncl; Var Capt Socr; Hon Roll; Utsngr Awd NY Athltc Clb 83; Magna Cum Laude Ntl Ltn Exm Amer Clscl Lg 85; Scr Svc Awd NY Bys Clb 86.

DOSCHER, SUSAN; Spackenkill HS; Poughkeepsie, NY; (Y); Sec Pres Girl Scts; Concert Band; Pep Band; Rep Stu Cncl; Cit Awd; Pres Schlr; Miss New Ntl Teenager Pgnt ST Fnlst; Girl Scout Ldrshp Vol Svc Silver Awds 86; Outstndng Dedctn Music; Bryant Coll; Comp Sys.

DOSS, CHERYL; Onondage Central HS; Syracuse, NY; (Y); Church Yth Grp; German Clb; Band; Chorus; Sec Jr Cls; Crs Cntry; JV Socr; Trk; High Hon Roll; Sec NHS; Law.

DOTEGOWSKI, TRACY; Gowanda Central HS; Collins, NY; (Y); 11/130; Ski Clb; VP Spanish Clb; SADD; Yrbk Stf; Rep Soph Cls; Rep Jr Cls; Stu Cncl; Var Cheerleading; Hon Roll; Aud/Vis; Russell Sage; Law.

DOTY, KATHERINE; Fairport HS; Fairport, NY; (Y); Hosp Aide; Ski Clb; SADD; Concert Band; Mrchg Band; School Musical; Var Capt Tennis; Hon Roll; NHS; Spanish NHS; Sci.

DOTY, MARY C; John S Burke Catholic HS; Middletown, NY; (Y); 17/130; Drama Clb; Yrbk Stf; Rep Sr Cls; Rep Stu Cncl; Var Vllybl; High Hon Roll; NHS; Law.

DOTY, STEPHANIE; Cortland JR SR HS; Cortland, NY; (Y); Church Yth Grp; Latin Clb; Red Cross Aide; Var L Fld Hcky; High Hon Roll; Hon Roll; Nrsng.

DOTY, VALERIE; Glenns Falls SR HS; Glen Falls, NY; (Y); 8/217; Drama Clb; Girl Scts; Key Clb; Pep Clb; SADD; Stage Crew; High Hon Roll; NHS; Regnts Schrlshp 86-90; Alexander S Gillan Mem Schlrshp 86; Acad Exc Awd 86; Long Island U; Marine Bio.

DOUCETTE, MARIE; Clarkstown South HS; New City, NY; (Y); Art Clb; French Clb; Art.

DOUD, MICHELLE; Twin Tiers Baptist HS; Lawrenceville, PA; (Y); 5/18; School Play; Mgr Stage Crew; Var Bsktbl; Hon Roll; Sci Fair Awd; Secdry Ed.

DOUGAN, JAMES; Tully Central HS; Tully, NY; (Y); Art Clb; Spanish Clb; SADD; Varsity Clb; Bsktbl; Ftbl; Lcrss; Gov Hon Prg Awd; Hon Roll; Clarkson U; Engrng.

DOUGHER, WENDY; Queensbury HS; Glens Falls, NY; (Y); 44/262; Chorus; School Musical; Yrbk Bus Mgr; Yrbk Ed-Chief; Im Gym; JV Trk; High Hon Roll; Hon Roll; Prfct Atten Awd; Sec & Treas Aviation Clb 83-85; Hotel Mgr.

DOUGHERTY, JENNIFER E; School Of The Holy Child; Rockville Cntr, NY; (Y); Art Clb; Hosp Aide; Library Aide; Pres SADD; Nwsp Bus Mgr; Nwsp Ed-Chief; Nwsp Rptr; Ed Yrbk Stf; Rep Frsh Cls; Rep Soph Cls; Fll Acadmc Schlrshp 82-86; Prtl Schlrshp Sdy Abrd-U Of Madrd 85; Vrsty Allstr Scrr Tm; Notre Dame; Bus.

DOUGHERTY, JILL; Tioga Central School; Candor, NY; (S); 2/96; Church Yth Grp; Scholastic Bowl; Church Choir; Variety Show; Nwsp Stf; Yrbk Stf; Trs Sr Cls; VP Stu Cncl; Cheerleading; Vllybl; Comp Sci.

DOUGHERTY, MARK; Brockport HS; Brockport, NY; (Y); 14/350; Cmnty Wkr; Var L Crs Cntry; Var L Trk; High Hon Roll; Ntl Merit Ltr; Mc Ginnis Awd Srv Awd Crss Cntry 85; Democrat & Chronicle Carrier Month 84-85; Carrier Hnr Roll 83-86; Chem Engrng.

DOUGHERTY, ROBERT; Glen Cove HS; Glen Cove, NY; (Y); Church Yth Grp; Science Clb; SADD; Band; Concert Band; Jazz Band; Orch; School Musical; Symp Band; Hon Roll; Musician.

DOUGHERTY, STEPHEN; Brockport HS; Brockport, NY; (Y); 10/350; Cmnty Wkr; Var L Crs Cntry; Var L Trk; High Hon Roll; Ntl Merit Ltr; Democrat & Chronicle Carrier Hnr Roll 83-86; William A Elston Jr Mem Awd 83.

DOUGHERTY, WILLIAM A; Alfred G Berner HS; Massapequa Park, NY; (Y); 4/412; Computer Clb; Ed Nwsp Ed-Chief; Var Socr; Hon Roll; NHS; Ntl Merit Ltr; Robotics Club 83-85; Clarkson U; Elec Engr.

DOUGHERTY, WILLIAM K; Christian Brothers Acad; Fabius, NY; (Y); Church Yth Grp; 4-H; Service Clb; Ski Clb; Variety Show; Var Crs Cntry; Var Socr; Var Trk; DAR Awd; Hon Roll; Regents Schlrshp 86; Hnr Roll 82-86; Northeastern U; Mfg Engrng.

DOUGHNEY, KEVIN; Archbishop Molloy HS; Douglaston, NY; (Y); Computer Clb; Ski Clb; Yrbk Stf; Capt Var Diving; Var Swmmng; Power Mem HS Schlrshp 83; Empire ST Games/Diving 84-86; Diving Record 85.

DOUGHTY, DAWN; F D Roosevelt HS; Poughkeepsie, NY; (Y); Chorus; Cheerleading; Hon Roll; Sci.

DOUGLAS, DAVID; Niagara Falls HS; Niagara Falls, NY; (Y); 24/250; Computer Clb; Drama Clb; JA; Spanish Clb; Teachers Aide; Thesps; School Musical; School Play; Stage Crew; Natl Spch And Drama Awd 85; Hnr Membr Intl Thespn Soc 85; ST U Of NY; Flm.

DOUGLAS, JENNIFER L; Peekskill HS; Peekskill, NY; (Y); 20/146; Church Yth Grp; Pres Drama Clb; Concert Band; Mrchg Band; School Play; Yrbk Phtg; Var Capt Socr; Var Vllybl; High Hon Roll; All Leag Hnrb Mntn Sccr 84; Potsdam Coll; Math Educ.

DOUGLAS, MELISSA; Amsterdam HS; Ft Johnson, NY; (Y); 22/294; FBLA; Ed Yrbk Stf; Tennis; High Hon Roll; Hon Roll; NHS; John P Gomulka Dem Schlrshp 86; NYS Rgnst Schlrshp 86; NY ST U Buffalo; Intl Lawyer.

DOUGLAS, TRACEY; Bishop Loughlin HS; Queens, NY; (Y); 6/234; Computer Clb; Office Aide; Service Clb; Nwsp Ed-Chief; Nwsp Rptr; Nwsp Stf; 4-H Awd; Gov Hon Prg Awd; High Hon Roll; NHS; Dist Attnry Awd 86; Gen Excllnc Awd Nwsp 85-86; St Johns U; Comp Sci.

DOUGLAS, YVETTE; George W Wingate HS; Brooklyn, NY; (Y); Teachers Aide; Vllybl; Hon Roll; Utica Coll; Math.

DOUGLASS, JAMES; Gouverneur HS; Gouverneur, NY; (Y); 3/143; Quiz Bowl; Stu Cncl; Var Golf; JV Var Socr; Var Trk; Var Vllybl; NHS; NROTC Scholar 86; US Coast Grd Acad.

DOUGLASS, KEVIN; Gouverneur HS; Gouverneur, NY; (Y); Trs Jr Cls; Trs Sr Cls; JV Var Bsktbl; Var L Golf; Var L Socr; High Hon Roll; Hon Roll; Jr NHS; NHS; Rcvd 1st Team All Nrthn Athlt Cnfrnce Golf 86.

DOUROS, TIMOTHY J; Oyster Bay HS; Oyster Bay, NY; (Y); 5/123; Cmnty Wkr; German Clb; Trs Model UN; SADD; Nwsp Phtg; Nwsp Rptr; Nwsp Sprt Ed; Nwsp Stf; Yrbk Ed-Chief; Yrbk Stf; Regents Schrlshp 86; Schlr Athlete Ntl Ftbl Found Hall Fame 86; Dartmouth; Chem.

DOUTHIT, JOHN W; John S Burke Catholic HS; Monroe, NY; (Y); Church Yth Grp; Rep Jr Cls; JV Var Bsbl; JV Var Bsktbl; JV Var Socr; High Hon Roll; Pres Schlr; U Scrntn; Bus.

DOUVLOS, MARIA; Oakfield-Alabama HS; Batavia, NY; (Y); French Clb; Sec Sr Cls; High Hon Roll; Hon Roll; NHS; Hlth Awd-Hghst Avg 86; Frnch III Awd-Hghst Avg 86; SUNY; Pharm.

DOVIDIO, MARK; Walton Cntrl HS; Walton, NY; (Y); AFS; Aud/Vis; Drama Clb; Library Aide; Chorus; School Play; Stage Crew; Yrbk Phtg; Yrbk Stf; Bowling.

DOW, MATTHEW J; Sweet Home SR HS; Tonawanda, NY; (Y); 49/410; Am Leg Boys St; Boy Scts; Science Clb; Varsity Clb; Chorus; Capt Var Crs Cntry; Capt Var Trk; High Hon Roll; NHS; Insign Schlrshp U Detroit 86; U Detroit; Bio.

DOW, WILLIAM H; Croton-Harmon HS; Croton-On-Hudson, NY; (Y); 4/107; AFS; Concert Band; Drm Mjr(t); Jazz Band; School Musical; Yrbk Ed-Chief; Var Socr; NHS; Var Capt Trk; Cornell U; Engrng.

DOWARD, MATT; Batavia HS; Batavia, NY; (Y); Varsity Clb; Chorus; Church Choir; School Play; Capt Var Bsktbl; Capt Var Ftbl; Capt Var Trk; Wrstlng; Mcdonalds Athlt Yr Schlrshp 86; Eddie Meath All Str Ftbll Gm Splt End 86; NYS Trck Fld Mt 4th ST 86; Brockport ST U; Crimnl Just.

DOWD, KATHLEEN; Mercy HS; Loudonville, NY; (Y); Church Yth Grp; Drama Clb; Hosp Aide; Ski Clb; School Play; Rep Frsh Cls; Rep Soph Cls; High Hon Roll; Hon Roll; NHS.

DOWD, MEGHAN; Bellport HS; Bellport, NY; (Y); 11/375; French Clb; Band; Rep Soph Cls; Rep Jr Cls; Var Bsktbl; Var Socr; Var Capt Vllybl; High Hon Roll; Jr NHS; NHS; Empire ST Vllybl Team 86; All Leage & Conf Vllybl Hnrs 85-85; MVP Middle Cntry Vllybl Tournmnt 86; Pol Sci.

DOWD, MICHAEL; Johnstown HS; Johnstown, NY; (Y); Boy Scts; Band; Concert Band; Jazz Band; Mrchg Band; Variety Show; JV Bsktbl; Var Ftbl; JV Swmmng; Var L Trk; Culinary Arts.

DOWD, SHANNON; Northern Adirondack HS; Lyon Mt, NY; (Y); 25/86; Camera Clb; French Clb; Variety Show; Nwsp Phtg; Swmmng; Vllybl; Hon Roll; CVPH Schl Rad Tech; Radiology.

DOWEJKO, KRISTIN M; Hilton HS; Rochester, NY; (Y); 49/390; Fld Hcky; Swmmng; Boston U; Busnss.

DOWLEARN, DEANNA; Sandy Creek Central HS; Lacona, NY; (Y); Church Yth Grp; JCL; Stat Bsbl; Var Capt Bsktbl; Coach Actv; Stat Ftbl; Mgr(s); Var L Socr.

DOWLEY, KATHERINE; Kingston HS; Kingston, NY; (Y); 100/570; Sec Ski Clb; SADD; Y-Teens; Stu Cncl; Var Diving; Var Capt Gym; Hon Roll; NY ST Rgnts Schlrshp, Prsdntl Acad Ftnss Awd 86; U VT.

DOWLING, BARBARA R; Calhoun HS; N Merrick, NY; (Y); 256/313; Sec Key Clb; Chorus; Crs Cntry; Mgr(s); Trk.

DOWLING, JOSEPH A; Watervliet HS; Watervliet, NY; (Y); #1 In Class; Art Clb; German Clb; School Play; Nwsp Stf; Yrbk Stf; Var JV Vllybl; Bausch & Lomb Sci Awd; High Hon Roll; NHS; Ntl Merit SF; Cartooning.

DOWLING, MICHAEL; Bishop Scully HS; Amsterdam, NY; (Y); 13/47; Latin Clb; Letterman Clb; Math Clb; Ski Clb; SADD; Yrbk Stf; JV Ftbl; Hon Roll; Mu Alp Tht; NHS; Mu Alpha Theta 85; Latin Clb Awd 86; Colgate; Dentstry.

DOWLING, STACEY; Greenwich Central HS; Greenwich, NY; (Y); 55/87; AFS; Chorus; School Play; Nwsp Stf; Yrbk Stf; Capt Var Cheerleading; Var Crs Cntry; Var Pom Pon; Trk; High Hon Roll; Hudson Valley CC; Hlth Ser.

DOWNEY, CHRISTOP S; Briarcliff HS; Briarcliff Manor, NY; (Y); Mathletes; JV Im Bsktbl; JV Var Ftbl; High Hon Roll; NHS; Ntl Merit Ltr; Rensselaer Medal 85; Golden Dozen Schlr Athlt Awd 85; All League Ftbl 85; Cornell U.

DOWNEY, KRISTINE; A G Berner HS; Massapequa, NY; (Y); Key Clb; Pep Clb; Spanish Clb; Var Fld Hcky; Var Trk; Hon Roll; NHS; All Conf Fld Hcky 86; All Conf Winter Track 86; MVP Winter Track 86; Educ.

DOWNEY, MARK J; John S Burke Catholic HS; Montgomery, NY; (Y); Aud/Vis; Stage Crew; Hon Roll; Amer Stds Olympd 85; Coll Of Engrng Rutgers; Cvl Eng.

DOWNING, MATTHEW M; Canisius HS; Orchard Park, NY; (Y); 40/165; Model UN; Pep Clb; Nwsp Stf; Yrbk Bus Mgr; Rep Frsh Cls; Soph Cls; U Of MI; Bus Mgmt.

DOWNS, JOHN; New Rochelle HS; New Rochelle, NY; (Y); 127/550; French Clb; Var Capt Bsbl; Var L Ice Hcky; NHS; William Brud Flwrs Memrl Schlrshp 86; Cassara Family Mrmrl Awd 86; ST U NY Cortland; Law.

DOXBECK, HEATHER; Kenmore West SR HS; Buffalo, NY; (Y); 15/421; Sec Trs Girl Scts; Math Tm; Band; Mrchg Band; Stage Crew; High Hon Roll; Hon Roll; NHS; Math Awds; Bio Awd; Rensselaer Polytech; Comp Sci.

DOYEN, PATTI; Niagara Wheatfield HS; Sanborn, NY; (Y); AFS; Pres VP Church Yth Grp; FCA; Pep Clb; Nwsp Ed-Chief; Yrbk Stf; Hst Soph Cls; Hst Jr Cls; Tennis; Trk; Cmmnctns.

DOYKA, DENISE; Hamburg SR HS; Hamburg, NY; (Y); #120 In Class; Church Yth Grp; JCL; Latin Clb; Service Clb; Off Lib Band; Off Lib Mrchg Band; Nwsp Stf; Ed Yrbk Ed-Chief; Yrbk Stf; Lit Mag; Psych.

DOYLE, AMY; Copenhagen Central HS; Copenhagen, NY; (S); 6/45; SADD; Color Guard; Yrbk Stf; Score Keeper; JV Var Socr; Var Sftbl; NHS; Sec Soph Cls; Sec Jr Cls; Sec Sr Cls; Bio.

DOYLE, AMY; Skaneateles Central Schl; Skaneateles, NY; (S); Yrbk Phtg; Stu Cncl; Coach Actv; Powder Puff Ftbl; Socr; Sftbl; Tennis; High Hon Roll; Hon Roll; NHS; Photogrphy Awd 84 & 86; Pre-Law.

DOYLE, JAMES P; Mount Saint Michael Acad; The Bronx, NY; (S); 4/308; Camera Clb; Church Yth Grp; Stu Cncl; Crs Cntry; High Hon Roll; NHS; Ntl Merit SF; Stu Mnth 85; Engl.

DOYLE, JIM; Pine Bush HS; Pine Bush, NY; (Y); JV Var Bsbl; JV Var Bsktbl; JV Socr; Hon Roll; Athlete Of Wk Bsbll 86; 2nd Tm All Star Tm Orange Cnty Bsbll 86; Sprts Med.

DOYLE, JOHN J; West Seneca West SR HS; Cheektowaga, NY; (Y); 25/559; Key Clb; Spanish Clb; VP Varsity Clb; Var Capt Socr; Var Swmmng; Hon Roll; JC Awd; Jr NHS; NHS; Regents Schlrp 86; Bus.

DOYLE, KIMBERLY A; Pine Plains Central Schl; Stanfordville, NY; (Y); 1/101; Pres Trs AFS; Pres Band; Rep Jr Cls; Rep Sr Cls; Trs Stu Cncl; Var Cheerleading; Swmmng; Trk; NHS; Val; Amer Fld Svc Exch Stdnt Turkey 85; Hghst Acadmc Awd Chrldg 83-86; Rensselaer Polytechnic Inst.

DOYLE, MARY M; John F Kennedy HS; Purdys, NY; (Y); 1/198; Hosp Aide; Pres Service Clb; Cit Awd; NHS; Val; Church Yth Grp; Cmnty Wkr; Stage Crew; High Hon Roll; Holy Cross Bk Awd 85; Coll Of Holy Cross; Tchr.

DOYLE, MARYELLEN; Dominican Commercial HS; Brooklyn, NY; (Y); 88/288; Church Yth Grp; Cmnty Wkr; Girl Scts; Service Clb; Soroptimist; Varsity Clb; Chorus; Church Choir; Rep Jr Cls; Bsktbl; Siena Awd 83-86; Spirit Awd 83-86; Psych.

DOYLE, PATTY; St Marys Girls HS; Port Washington, NY; (Y); 1/178; Math Clb; Ski Clb; Spanish Clb; SADD; Stage Crew; Yrbk Ed-Chief; Rep Stu Cncl; High Hon Roll; Trs NHS; Iona Coll Lang Cntst Span 86; Enrg.

DOYLE, REBECCA; Somers HS; Katonah, NY; (Y); School Musical; Stage Crew; Nwsp Ed-Chief; JV Var Sftbl; JV Capt Vllybl; VP NHS; Chorus; Nwsp Sprt Ed; Nwsp Stf; Lit Mag; Tusker Tms Awd Schl Nwspr Achvmnt Awd 85-86; Otstndng Acmplshmnt Engl 84; Otstndng Acmplshmnt Soc Stds; Archt.

DRAEGER, DEANNE L; St Joseph Hill Acad; Staten Island, NY; (Y); French Clb; FTA; Girl Scts; Hosp Aide; Latin Clb; Math Tm; Nwsp Rptr; Nwsp Stf; Cheerleading; Swmmng; Rgnts Schlrshp 86; St Johns Coll.

DRAGO, MARK; Archbishop Molloy HS; Ridgewood, NY; (Y); 85/383; Cmnty Wkr; Varsity Clb; Im Crs Cntry; Var Trk; Hon Roll; Awds Trk; Hofstra U; Bus.

DRAGOTTA, NANCY; Salamanca Central HS; Salamanca, NY; (Y); Drama Clb; Spanish Clb; Thesps; Varsity Clb; Band; Chorus; Color Guard; Concert Band; Drill Tm; Drm & Bgl; Bfflo Evng Nws Spllng Bee Chmpn 83-84; All-ST & Cnty Bnd & Chrs 82-86; Clr Grd Wintr Grd Intl Chmpshp; NY Inst Of Tech; Pre-Law.

DRAJEM, CHRISTOPHER R; St Josephs Collegiate Inst; Buffalo, NY; (Y); 25/200; Pres Church Yth Grp; School Play; Nwsp Bus Mgr; Lit Mag; High Hon Roll; Pres NHS; Model UN; Swmmng; Yth Mo Awd Exchng Clb 86; Amer Vlus & Pres Hon Schlrshp Jhn Crrll U 86; Br Crnls Awd Rlgn St Joes Coll; John Carroll U.

DRAKE, ANDREW J; Clinton Central HS; Clinton, NY; (Y); 13/141; Am Leg Boys St; Pres Key Clb; Var L Ftbl; JV Im Socr; Var L Trk; Trs Jr NHS; NHS; Model UN; Timer; Im Vllybl; Physical Educ Stu Of Yr 84 & 86; Schl Rcrd 4x100 Relay 85 & 86; Presdntl Physcl Fittness Awd 85 & 86; Marine Corps; Political Science.

DRAKE, JENNY; Sweet Home SR HS; N Tonawanda, NY; (Y); Drama Clb; Latin Clb; Library Aide; Science Clb; SADD; Color Guard; Flag Corp; School Play; Stage Crew; Yrbk Stf; U Of NY; Lbrl Arts.

DRAKE, LAURENDA M; Newfane SR HS; Newfane, NY; (S); 8/180; Chorus; Hon Roll; NHS; ST U NY Buffalo; Marine Bio.

DRAKE, MALIK; Wilson Magnet HS; Rochester, NY; (Y); JA; Math Tm; Science Clb; JV Ftbl; Var Trk; High Hon Roll; NHS; Excllnc Photo-Optics 84; Excllnc German Ii 85; Chem Engrng.

DRAKE, MARK; Elmira Free Acad; Elmira, NY; (Y); Drama Clb; Intnl Clb; Latin Clb; Model UN; Ski Clb; SADD; Thesps; Chorus; School Musical; Swing Chorus; Music.

DRAKE, MELISSA; Jasper Central HS; Jasper, NY; (Y); 4-H; FHA; Teachers Aide; Chorus; Trk; Cit Awd; 4-H Awd; Hon Roll.

DRAKE, MICHAEL P; Pittsford Mendon HS; Pittsford, NY; (Y); Boy Scts; Church Yth Grp; Radio Clb; Service Clb; Ski Clb; Nwsp Rptr; Nwsp Stf; Yrbk Phtg; Yrbk Stf; Trk; Exchange Stu Sweden 85; Engrng.

DRAKE, STEVEN A; Stockbridge Valley Central Schl; Oneida, NY; (Y); 17/48; Am Leg Boys St; 4-H; FFA; Science Clb; Concert Band; Mrchg Band; Yrbk Stf; Stu Cncl; Church Yth Grp; National 4-H Congress Woodworking Awd 85; 4-H Citizenship Awd Washington Focus 84; Morrisville Ag & Tech; Engr.

DRALLIOS, XENIA; The Mary Louis Acad; Flushing, NY; (Y); 63/270; Art Clb; Church Yth Grp; Cmnty Wkr; Library Aide; Yrbk Stf; Bowling; St Johns U; Mktg.

DRAPER, MICHELE; Indian River Central HS; Antwerp, NY; (Y); 15/142; AFS; Sec Church Yth Grp; Latin Clb; Variety Show; JV Sftbl; Var Tennis; High Hon Roll; NHS; Schlstc Achvt Awd 87.

DRASNER, LISA; Kings Park SR HS; Kings Park, NY; (Y); 99/382; Hosp Aide; Spanish Clb; SADD; Temple Yth Grp; Yrbk Stf; High Hon Roll; Hon Roll; Drama Clb; Office Aide; Radio Clb; Interact Clb Vice Pres 85-86; NYS Rgnts Nrsng Schlrshp 86; Karen Morrell Awd Cndystrpng 86; Oswego U; Elem Educ.

DRAWBRIDGE, TIM; Riverhead HS; Baiting Hollow, NY; (Y); 12/235; Church Yth Grp; JCL; Latin Clb; ROTC; Chorus; Orch; Trs Jr Cls; Var Ftbl; Cit Awd; Jr NHS; Awds For Irish Dncng & Plyng Bagpipes 67-84.

DRAZKA, FRANK J; Sanford H Calhoun HS; Merrick, NY; (Y); 5/313; VP Mathletes; SADD; Pres Concert Band; Nwsp Rptr; Var Capt Bowling; Var Capt Golf; Var Capt Trk; Cit Awd; NHS; Pres Schlr; Knights Columbus Awd 86; Cooper Union Engr Schrlshp 86; NY ST Regents Schlrshp 86; Yale U; Mathmtcs.

DREANEY, TERESA; Amsterdam HS; Amsterdam, NY; (Y); Church Yth Grp; FBLA; JA; Church Choir; Flag Corp; Orch; Hon Roll; Area All Cnty All ST Orchestra; CPA.

DREEKE, ROBIN; Carmel HS; Carmel, NY; (Y); Trs Spanish Clb; VP Band; Mrchg Band; Yrbk Bus Mgr; Trs Jr Cls; VP Stu Cncl; Ftbl; Trk; High Hon Roll; NHS; Outward Bnd ME Sea 85; Rotary Intl Yth Rep 86; Peer Ldrshp Cnslr 86; Math.

DREHER, JOSEPH; Thomas J Corcoran HS; Syracuse, NY; (Y); Pres Chess Clb; VP Latin Clb; Pres Model UN; Capt Quiz Bowl; Concert Band; Jazz Band; Pep Band; School Musical; Mgr School Play; Var Tennis; Cum Laude Natl Latin Exam Lvl II 85; 3rdpl Latin Prof Lvl II Oswego Lang Fair 85; 15th Pl NY ST 84.

DREHER, K; T J Corcoran HS; Syracuse, NY; (Y); Spanish Clb; Concert Band; Mrchg Band; School Musical; Nwsp Stf; Yrbk Stf; Lit Mag; Swmmng; Trk; NHS; Dept Awd Excllnc Span NYS Regents Exam 85-86; Dept Awd Excllnc Eng NYS Regents Exam 86; Liberal Arts.

DREISBACH, DAWN; Our Lady Of Mercy HS; Honeoye Falls, NY; (Y); Ski Clb; Spanish Clb; Stu Cncl.

DREITZER, RICHARD; Canovsie HS; Brooklyn, NY; (S); 7/500; Debate Tm; Math Tm; Quiz Bowl; Science Clb; Soroptimist; Speech Tm; Acpl Chr; Chorus; School Play; Yrbk Ed-Chief; Natl Endolment For The Humanities Schlr; Regents Schlrshp Wnnr; Soroptimist Awd Schlrshp Wnnr; Cornell U; Pre-Law.

DRENGERS, ANDREW; St Agnes HS; Bayside, NY; (Y); 9/98; Chess Clb; Hon Roll; NHS; St U Of NY; Meteorlgy.

DRENNAN, LYNDA; Tottenville HS; Staten Island, NY; (Y); 137/891; Office Aide; Teachers Aide; Stage Crew; NHS; Starr Foundtn Schlrshp 85-86; SUNY-STONY Brook; Stage Mgmt.

DRESCHER, DONNA; Watervliet HS; Watervliet, NY; (Y); GAA; Spanish Clb; Varsity Clb; VP Frsh Cls; VP Soph Cls; Pres Stu Cncl; Var L Cheerleading; Var Socr; Var Vllybl; High Hon Roll; Psych.

DREW, BRIAN; Horseheads Central HS; Horseheads, NY; (Y); Concert Band.

DREW, STEVE; Southside HS; Elmira, NY; (S); Church Yth Grp; Dance Clb; Debate Tm; Drama Clb; French Clb; Intnl Clb; Pep Clb; Thesps; Chorus; Jazz Band; Music.

DREW, TAMMY; Grover Cleveland HS; Buffalo, NY; (Y); Pep Clb; Spanish Clb; Varsity Clb; Yrbk Stf; Sec Jr Cls; Cheerleading; Hon Roll; NHS; Acctg.

DREWES, STEVEN; St John The Baptist; Pt Jeff Sta, NY; (Y); Bsbl; Ftbl; Trk; Wt Lftg; Wrstlng; All Lg Discus; Bus.

DREWS, HANS W; Little Falls JR SR HS; St Johnsville, NY; (Y); Am Leg Boys St; Chess Clb; Church Yth Grp; VP SADD; Concert Band; Mrchg Band; Pep Band; Yrbk Stf; Hon Roll; Systms Anlyst.

DRIER, MICHELE L; Lansing HS; Groton, NY; (Y); 4-H; French Clb; Band; Var Ice Hcky; Var Score Keeper; Var Swmmng; Im JV Vllybl; Intr Dsgnr.

DRIMAK, JEFF; Johnson City SR HS; Johnson City, NY; (Y); 8/250; Key Clb; Mathletes; VP Jr Cls; Var L Ftbl; Var L Trk; Capt L Wrstlng; NHS; VP Soph Cls; High Hon Roll; Yrh Cncl On Smkng; Cornell U; Elctrcl Engr.

DRISCOLL, BENJAMIN; Whitney Point SR HS; Whitney Pt, NY; (Y); 4/123; Yrbk Stf; Stu Cncl; Crs Cntry; Trk; DAR Awd; High Hon Roll; Hon Roll; Ntl Merit Schol; Clute Mem 86; U Of PA; Elec Engr.

DRISCOLL, JENNIFER; Horseheads HS; Hoseheads, NY; (Y); Drama Clb; Ski Clb; Spanish Clb; Band; Chorus; Concert Band; Mrchg Band; Rep Stu Cncl; Hon Roll; Bus Admin.

DRISCOLL, JOHN; Holy Trinity HS; East Meadow, NY; (S); 19/313; Church Yth Grp; Cmnty Wkr; Math Clb; Math Tm; Ski Clb; Yrbk Stf; Ftbl; Lcrss; Hon Roll; NHS; Acadmc All Amer; Alumni Jdgng Pnl Awd; Ntl Merit Ldrshp Awd.

DRISCOLL, SHEILA; St Peters HS For Girls; Staten Island, NY; (Y); 2/101; Exploring; Math Tm; Trs Soph Cls; JV Bsktbl; JV Sftbl; Timer; Var Trk; High Hon Roll; NHS; Pres Schlr; Wrld Of Poetry Hnrbl Mntn 86; Staten Isl Fed Cthlc Schl Merit Cert 86; Ms Ntl Tnagr Pagnt Fnlst 84; Maritime Coll; Elec Engr.

DROBINSKI, JULIE; Greece Olympia HS; Rochester, NY; (Y); Church Yth Grp; DECA; Ski Clb; Rep Soph Cls; Rep Jr Cls; Rep Sr Cls; Vllybl; Hon Roll; Local DECA Cmptns 1st Pl 86; Mrktng.

DROGALIS, NORA; Sacred Heart Acad; Floral Park, NY; (S); 11/181; Math Clb; Math Tm; Pep Clb; Bus Mgr; Rep Frsh Cls; High Hon Roll; NHS; Acad All Amer 85; Natl Hnr Roll 85; Amer HS Stu Dstngshd Soc 85; Bus Mgmt.

DROHAN, MATTHEW; G Ray Bodley HS; Fulton, NY; (Y); Boys Scts; French Clb; Var Bsbl; JV Bsktbl; High Hon Roll; Hon Roll; Prfct Atten Awd.

DROISEN, RACHEL L; Shoreham-Wading River HS; Shoreham, NY; (Y); Mathletes; Ski Clb; SADD; School Play; Ed Lit Mag; Wt Lftg; NHS; Ntl Merit Ltr; Bellport Sr Poetry Cntst Hnrbl Mntn 85; Shrhm Wdng Rvr Poetry Cntst 1st Pl 85; Columbia U; Pre-Med.

DROLLETTE, AMY; Saranac Central HS; Saranac, NY; (S); 10/103; Office Aide; JV Socr; Var L Trk; Im Vllybl; NHS; Clinton CC; Med Lab Tech.

DROLLETTE, KRISTINA; Saranac HS; Morrisonville, NY; (S); 43/106; Band; Ed Trk Stf; Rep Frsh Cls; Trs Soph Cls; Trs Jr Cls; Trs Sr Cls; Cheerleading; Socr; Sftbl; Auburn U; Aviatn Mgmt.

DROP, DIANE; Our Lady Of Lourdes HS; Poughkeepsie, NY; (Y); 1/180; Church Choir; Ed Nwsp Stf; Ed Yrbk Stf; Stat Trk; Hon Roll; NHS; Rensselaer Mdl 86; Math.

DROPPERS, ANN F; Alfred-Almond Central Schl; Alfred, NY; (Y); #4 In Class; Church Yth Grp; Church Choir; Variety Show; Yrbk Stf; High Hon Roll; NHS; Ntl Merit Ltr; NY ST Regents Schlrshp 86; Natl Latin Exam Cum Laude 83-84; Gordon Coll; Lbrl Arts.

DROSMAN, VICKI; Canarsie HS; Brooklyn, NY; (Y); Math Tm; Teachers Aide; Concert Band; School Play; Yrbk Stf; Var Capt Bowling; Hon Roll; Spnsh Awd 84.

DROWN, MARY ELLEN; Bainbridge-Guilford HS; Masonville, NY; (Y); 17/70; French Clb; Ski Clb; Score Keeper; Hon Roll; Prfct Atten Awd; Dr Thomas Many Nursing Schlrshp, Pres Acdmc Ftns Awd, Outstndng Achvt Awd 86; Crouse-Irving Mem Hosp Schl.

DROZD, SOPHIA E; Aviation HS; Glendale, NY; (Y); 1/416; Pres Debate Tm; Math Tm; Nwsp Ed-Chief; Var Crs Cntry; Var Trk; Var Wt; Drama Clb; JA; Library Aide; Queens Coll Pres Awd For Achvt 82-86; Schlrshp-York Coll 85; PAL Illstrd Poetry 1st Pl 82-86; Mit; Aerosp Engrng.

DRUAR, JOHN; Randolph Central HS; Randolph, NY; (Y); Drama Clb; French Clb; Ski Clb; School Play; Yrbk Stf; Rep Frsh Cls; Rep Stu Cncl; Var Trk; Var Wrstlng; 1st Pl Amer Lgn Ortrcl Cntst 86; Engrng.

DRUBIN, RANDI; Kings Park SR HS; Kings Pk, NY; (Y); 121/397; Drama Clb; Spanish Clb; Varsity Clb; Band; Chorus; Concert Band; Drm & Bgl; School Play; Nwsp Ed-Chief; Nwsp Rptr; Bst Imprvd Musician 83; New Paltz; Engl.

DRUCKENMILLE, DANIEL H; Hoosic Valley Central HS; Valley Falls, NY; (Y); 2/101; Am Leg Boys St; 4-H; Concert Band; Jazz Band; Swing Chorus; Pres Sr Cls; Var Crs Cntry; Var Trk; Bausch & Lomb Sci Awd; NHS; NROTC Schlrsp 85-86; GE Star Prog Schlrshp 85-86; U Of Rochester; Optical Engr.

DRUM, MARGARET; St Marys Acad; Glens Falls, NY; (S); Drama Clb; Spanish Clb; Chorus; School Musical; School Play; Variety Show; Yrbk Stf; Var Cheerleading; Gym; Var Pom Pon; Music.

DRUM, MICHAEL T; Garden City HS; Garden City, NY; (Y); 87/353; Boy Scts; Ntl Merit Ltr; NYS Regents Nrsng Schlrshp; Merit Schlrshp Pgm; Queens Coll; Med.

DRUMM, JOHN; Plattsburgh SR HS; Plattsburgh, NY; (Y); Computer Clb; Ski Clb; Var JV Ftbl; Im Wt Lftg; FL Inst Of Tech; Cmmrcl Scuba.

DRUMMOND, LORNA; Walt Whitman HS; Huntington, NY; (Y); 65/500; German Clb; GAA; Band; Yrbk Ed-Chief; Socr; Sftbl; Swmmng; Vllybl; High Hon Roll; Jr NHS; German Hnr Soc 86; Most Athletic 84; Intl Bus.

DRURY, THOS; Sodus Central HS; Sodus, NY; (Y); Chess Clb; Model UN; Science Clb; Socr; Prfct Atten Awd.

DRUS, CLAUDIA; New Dorp HS; Staten Island, NY; (Y); Church Yth Grp; Debate Tm; Hosp Aide; Pep Clb; Nwsp Stf; Hon Roll; Jr NHS; NHS; Qrtr Fnlst-Lincoln Douglass Debates 86; Bio.

DRUSIN, CAMI L; Clarkstown High School North; New City, NY; (Y); 91/435; Service Clb; Spanish Clb; Pres SADD; Yrbk Stf; Rep Stu Cncl; Var Fld Hcky; Jr NHS; Mu Alp Tht; NYS Regents Schlrshp 86; Emory U.

DRYGAS, JOHN C; Nyack HS; Valley Cottage, NY; (Y); 8/247; Drama Clb; Math Tm; Ski Clb; Varsity Clb; Band; Concert Band; Jazz Band; Mrchg Band; School Play; JV Bsbl; PTA Schlrshp 86; Assn Of Sons Of Poland Schlrshp 86; Binghamton U; Biochem.

DRYGULA, GEORGIANN; Amsterdam HS; Amsterdam, NY; (Y); FBLA; Socr; Sftbl; Vllybl; Hon Roll; Csmtlgy.

DU BOFF, KEITH; Lakeland HS; Shrub Oak, NY; (Y); Var L Swmmng; Jr NHS; Comp Sci.

DU BOIS, RICHARD; Earl L Vandermeulen HS; Mt Sinai, NY; (Y); 26/333; French Clb; Band; Jazz Band; Nwsp Stf; Yrbk Stf; Var Bsbl; JV Var Bsktbl; Im Ftbl; JV Socr; Partcpnt Sci Apprtnshp Prgm 84; Phys Ed Awd 84; Lead Prgm 86; Librl Arts.

DU BOIS II, THOMAS E; G Ray Bodley HS; Fulton, NY; (Y); 51/270; French Clb; Science Clb; JV Ftbl; Var L Golf; Hon Roll; Prfct Atten Awd; NY ST Rgrnts Schlrshp 86; Philip Morris Schlrshp; Canton U; Engr.

DU BREY, TRICIA; Northern Adirondack Cntrl HS; Chazy Lake, NY; (Y); Aud/Vis; Computer Clb; French Clb; Library Aide; Chorus; Nwsp Stf; Yrbk Stf; Var Capt Cheerleading; High Hon Roll; Hon Roll; Math.

DU PONT, SUE; Averill Park HS; Troy, NY; (Y); 27/210; GAA; Varsity Clb; Prfct Atten Awd; Rep Soph Cls; Rep Jr Cls; JV Var Bsktbl; JV Powder Puff Ftbl; Var Capt Socr; Var JV Trk; High Hon Roll; 85 Clb 82-86; Outstndng Stu 86; Hudson Valley CC; Bus Admin.

DU PUY, CLAUDINE; Fontbone Hall Acad; Brooklyn, NY; (Y); 15/135; French Clb; Math Tm; High Hon Roll; Hon Roll; NEDT Awd; Rep Soph Cls; Math Achvt Awd 83-84; Socl Stds Awd 83-85; NE Regnl Figr Sktg Champ 83; Acctg.

DU RON, ERIK; H S For The Humanits; New York, NY; (Y); School Musical; School Play; English.

DU VERNAY, JANINE; Haverling HS; Bath, NY; (Y); Art Clb; Church Yth Grp; 4-H; French Clb; SADD; Band; Yrbk Stf; Cheerleading; Pom Pon; Socr; Bryant; Med Sec.

DU-PONT, BETHANY; Emma Willard Schl; Newburyport, MA; (S); Mgr Orch; Nwsp Sport Ed; Yrbk Phtg; Trs Sec Frsh Cls; JV Tennis; Huntr Schlrshp 83; Prctr 86; Alumni Exec Comm 86.

DUARTE, DORIS; Seeward Park HS; New York, NY; (Y); Latin Clb; Office Aide; Teachers Aide; Band; Concert Band; Stage Crew; Variety Show; French Hon Soc; Hon Roll; Frnech Outstndg Mdl 86; SUNY; French.

DUBE, GREGORY; Greenwood Central Schl; Greenwood, NY; (S); 2/30; Varsity Clb; Yrbk Stf; Rep Stu Cncl; L Bsbl; L Ftbl; L Socr; L Trk; High Hon Roll; Pres JETS Awd; NHS; Syracuse U; Aero Engr.

DUBEL, MARK; Canisius HS; Lancaster, NY; (Y); Nwsp Stf; JV Var Ftbl; Capt Golf; Im Vllybl.

DUBERT, MICHELE J; Brocton Central HS; Portland, NY; (Y); 14/50; Am Leg Aux Girls St; SADD; Varsity Clb; Nwsp Sport Ed; Nwsp Stf; Var Sftbl; Var Vllybl; Hon Roll; NHS; Portland Fire Dept Miss Portland 86; Brockport Coll; Cmmnctns.

DUBEY III, RICHARD D; Hamburg SR HS; Hamburg, NY; (Y); 68/377; Red Cross Aide; Pres Stu Cncl; Im JV Bsbl; JV Bsktbl; Im JV Ftbl; Hon Roll; Rchrd R Hnsn Awd For Ldrshp 83-84; MVP Awd Mdfd Ftbl 83-84; Sprtsmn Awd Mdfd Bsbl 83-84; Ithaca Coll; Phys Thrpy.

DUBINSKY, HANIA; Potsdam Central HS; Potsdam, NY; (Y); 2/136; AFS; Drama Clb; French Clb; JCL; Model UN; Var Crs Cntry; Var Trk; High Hon Roll; NHS; All Conf Trk & Indoor Trk, Hnrb Mntn All Nac-X Cntry; Amer HS Athlt Trk; Natl Piano Guild Dist Wnnr; Liberal Arts.

DUBOIS, TRAVIS; Sherburne-Earlville Central HS; Earlville, NY; (Y); Ski Clb; Spanish Clb; Band; Crs Cntry; Engrng.

DUBOVY, DARIN; South Side HS; Rockville Centre, NY; (Y); 29/290; VP Latin Clb; SADD; Jazz Band; Nwsp Stf; JV Bsbl; JV Bsktbl; Var Capt Crs Cntry; Var Capt Trk; High Hon Roll; Silv Mdl Natl Latin Exam 86.

DUBROWSKY, CARIN L; Clarkstown High Schl North; New City, NY; (Y); 20/425; Math Tm; Spanish Clb; Yrbk Stf; Rep Soph Cls; Rep Jr Cls; JV Tennis; High Hon Roll; Hon Roll; Jr NHS; Mu Alp Tht; Regnts Schlrshp 86; U Of MI.

DUCA, JOHN; Henninger HS; Syracuse, NY; (Y); 20/350; Band; Concert Band; Jazz Band; Mrchg Band; Pep Band; Symp Band; JV Var Socr; High Hon Roll; Italian III Awd Daugh 86; Engrng.

DUCAR, JULIE; Catholic Central HS; Stillwater, NY; (Y); Cmnty Wkr; Math Clb; Math Tm; Ski Clb; SADD; Variety Show; Cheerleading; Trk; Awd Exclln Scl Stds II Regents 86; ST U Geneseo; Journlsm.

DUCHARME, BETSY; Salem Central HS; E Greenwich, NY; (Y); 7/50; Ski Clb; Band; Yrbk Stf; VP Capt Bsktbl; Bowling; Sftbl; Marine Bio.

DUDA, KAREN; Guilderland HS; Schenectady, NY; (Y); Girl Scts; Hosp Aide; Key Clb; Office Aide; Red Cross Aide; Yrbk Stf; Score Keeper; Vllybl; High Hon Roll; NHS; Cmmnty Svc Awd 84; Guilderland Brd Ed Schlstc Awd 86.

DUDASH, SHEILA; Bishop Ludden HS; Liverpool, NY; (S); Cmnty Wkr; Speech Tm; Band; Sec Chorus; School Musical; Rep Jr Cls; High Hon Roll; NHS; Intl Ldrshp Conf Notre Dame 85; Cmmnty Svc Cndystrpr Awd 83; Mastrs Music Prog Tri-M 85; Le Moyne Coll; Ed.

DUDKA, PAUL; Amsterdam HS; Amsterdam, NY; (Y).

DUDZIAK, ROBERT; East Syracuse-Minoa HS; E Syracuse, NY; (Y); Boy Scts; Concert Band; Mrchg Band; Ski Clb; Soroptimist; Band; NYSSMA 83; Ordr Of Arrw BSA 84; Comm Air Pilot.

DUEBEN, JEANNINE; Marlboro HS; Newburgh, NY; (Y); Church Yth Grp; Color Guard; Mrchg Band; Tennis; Vllybl; Hon Roll; Vrsty M Athltc Awd 85; Acctg.

DUEL, KELLY A; Marcus Whitman JR SR HS; Rushville, NY; (Y); 15/115; Sec 4-H; Quiz Bowl; Chorus; Drill Tm; School Musical; Variety Show; Yrbk Stf; 4-H Awd; High Hon Roll; Prfct Atten Awd; Royson Whipple Schlrshp 86; Morrisville Coll; Mgmnt & Prod.

DUELL, KIMBERLY; Corinth Central Schl; Corinth, NY; (Y); 4/95; SADD; Varsity Clb; Variety Show; Yrbk Ed-Chief; Var Cheerleading; Var Fld Hcky; High Hon Roll; NHS; Spanish NHS; Math Honor Society 86-87; Science Honor Society 86-87.

DUERR, WERNER R; Stissing Mountain HS; Stanfordville, NY; (Y); 25/84; AFS; Aud/Vis; Boy Scts; FL Inst Of Tech; Engrng.

DUESLER, STACEY; Oppenheim Ephratah Central HS; St Johnsville, NY; (S); Church Yth Grp; Drama Clb; 4-H; Color Guard; Yrbk Stf; Score Keeper; Socr; 4-H Awd; High Hon Roll; Sec Trs Jr NHS; Cnslr.

DUFF, CAROLYN; Sacred Heart Acad; Garden City, NY; (Y); Cmnty Wkr; FTA; Hosp Aide; Intnl Clb; Service Clb; SADD; Yrbk Stf; Rep Soph Cls; Hon Roll; NHS; Natl Svc/Ldrshp Awd 85.

DUFF, DAVID A; Regis HS; Forest Hills, NY; (Y); Boy Scts; Cmnty Wkr; Debate Tm; Drama Clb; NFL; Speech Tm; Teachers Aide; School Play; Im Bsktbl; Hon Roll; Forensic Catgry Orig Oratory ST Champ 85; US Naval Acad.

DUFF, GREG; Smithtown H S West; Smithtown, NY; (Y); Boy Scts; Dance Clb; Debate Tm; Letterman Clb; Political Wkr; Yrbk Phtg; Yrbk Rptr; Yrbk Stf; Bsktbl; Lcrss; Engrng.

DUFF, JENNIFER; The Franciscan Acad; Manlius, NY; (Y); Church Yth Grp; Girl Scts; SADD; Bowling; Tennis; Cit Awd; High Hon Roll; Hon Roll; NHS.

DUFFELMEYER, MICHELLE E; Academy Of Our Lady Of Good Counsel; E White Plains, NY; (Y); 3/70; Dance Clb; Drama Clb; JA; Latin Clb; Sec Science Clb; Service Clb; SADD; Yrbk Stf; Var Swmmng; Var Trk; High Hon Roll; Sec NHS; Binghamton; Med.

DUFFIN, PATRICK; Henninger HS; Syracuse, NY; (Y); JV Bsbl; JV Var Bsktbl; Syracuse U; Engr.

DUFFY, KELLY A; East Hampton HS; Montauk, NY; (Y); 2/115; Aud/Vis; Drama Clb; Band; Chorus; Mrchg Band; School Play; Nwsp Ed-Chief; Yrbk Stf; Lit Mag; Sec Stu Cncl; Brown U Bk Awd 85; Ladies Vlg Imprvmnt Soc Acdmc Achvt Awd 83 & 84; Long Isl Soc Stu Achvt Awd 84; Boston Coll.

DUFFY, KERRY; Academy Of St Joseph; St James, NY; (Y); Church Yth Grp; Sec Sr Cls; Sec Stu Cncl; Var Crs Cntry; High Hon Roll; Hon Roll.

DUFFY, PATRICK; Pelham HS; Pelham, NY; (Y); AFS; Am Leg Boys St; Aud/Vis; Camera Clb; Church Yth Grp; Debate Tm; JA; Radio Clb; Ski Clb; Yrbk Phtg; MVP Track 86; Ath Of Wk; Rensselaer Polytech Inst Smmr Coll Prtl Schlrshp; Sci.

DUFFY, PATRICK J; Franklin D Roosevelt HS; Hyde Park, NY; (Y); 11/335; VP Frsh Cls; VP Soph Cls; Var Bsbl; Var Capt Bsktbl; Var Crs Cntry; Socr; High Hon Roll; NHS; Regents Schlrshp 86; Ganet Pblshng Schlrshp 81; Comp Sci.

DUFOUR, KAREN; Mexico HS; Mooers, NY; (Y); Church Yth Grp; Crs Cntry; Var Sftbl; Grm Hnr Soc 85-86.

DUFRESNE, ANN MARIE; Bishop Scully HS; Amsterdam, NY; (S); 1/47; Latin Clb; Red Cross Aide; Yrbk Ed-Chief; VP Frsh Cls; Sec Stu Cncl; Var Bowling; Var Vllybl; High Hon Roll; Hon Roll; Mu Alp Tht; NHS; Jpn/US Snt Schlrshp Pgm 85; Biochem.

DUFRESNE, ELIZABETH M; Arlington HS; Pleasant Valley, NY; (Y); 46/565; Political Wkr; Variety Show; Yrbk Stf; Hon Roll; Acadmc Hnr Key; NY ST Regents Schlrshp; Syracuse U; Envrnmntl Dsgn.

DUFRESNE, ROBERT; Hamburg HS; Hamburg, NY; (Y); 84/374; Boy Scts; Exploring; Chorus; School Musical; School Play; Im Ftbl; Hon Roll; Spanish Clb; Ntl Sci Olympiad Bio 84; Staff Engr TV Station 85-86; Math.

DUGAN, CHRIS; Hauppauge HS; Hauppauge, NY; (Y); Ski Clb; Golf; Capt Socr; High Hon Roll; NHS; Prfct Atten Awd; Hauppauge Art Shw Juried Drwng Exhbtd 84-85; Bio.

DUGAN, CHRISTINE; Notitingham HS; Syracuse, NY; (Y); 83/200; Hosp Aide; Spanish Clb; SADD; Stage Crew; Lit Mag; Var Cheerleading; JV Socr; Psych.

DUGAN, COLLEEN F; Scotia-Glenville HS; Scotia, NY; (Y); 19/250; Pres AFS; Church Yth Grp; Co-Capt Dance Clb; SADD; Var Capt Sftbl; High Hon Roll; NHS; SUNY Albany; Frgn Lang Ed.

DUGAN, JAMES C; St Francis Prep; College Point, NY; (S); Boy Scts; Office Aide; Im Ftbl; Im Vllybl; Ntl Merit Ltr; Optimate Soc 85; NYS Regents Schlrp 86; Penn ST.

DUGAN III, JOHN; Skaneateles HS; Skaneateles, NY; (Y); 48/150; SADD; Var Bsbl; Var Crs Cntry; Var Capt Trk; Hon Roll; NHS; Mst Vlble Runnr Indr Trck 86; Mst Imprvd Runnr Crs Cntry 85; U Of Buffalo; Aerospace Engrng.

DUGAN, LAURA; Cicero North Syracuse HS; Clay, NY; (S); 83/677; Exploring; JA; Key Clb; Stage Crew; Powder Puff Ftbl; Hon Roll; NHS.

DUGAN, MARK; Fayetteville-Manlius HS; Fayetteville, NY; (Y); Trs JCL; Trs Latin Clb; SADD; Rep Stu Cncl; JV Var Ftbl; Wt Lftg; JV Var Wrstlng; High Hon Roll; Hon Roll; NHS; Am Legn Schlr Athlt Awd 84.

DUGAN, MARY; Archbishop Walsh HS; Olean, NY; (Y); Civic Clb; French Clb; Latin Clb; Pep Clb; Nwsp Rptr; Nwsp Stf; Yrbk Stf; High Hon Roll; NHS; Olean Area Sth Salut 86; Frnch Awd 86; Lwyr.

DUGAN, MAUREEN; Colonie Central HS; Albany, NY; (Y); 40/584; Intnl Clb; High Hon Roll; NHS; Ntl Merit Ltr; NY ST Regnts Schlrshp 85-86; Siena Clg Acdmc Schlrshp 85-86; Pres Acdmc Fit Awd 85-86; Siena Coll; Socl Wrk.

DUGGAN, AMY; Mount Mercy HS; Orchard Pk, NY; (Y); Cmnty Wkr; Hosp Aide; Science Clb; Spanish Clb; SADD; Im Badmtn; Var Co-Capt Cheerleading; Gym; Im Vllybl; Prfct Atten Awd; WNY Lang Fair 2nd Pl; Niagra U; Nrsng.

DUGGAN, KEVIN; Hamburg SR HS; Hamburg, NY; (Y); Letterman Clb; Red Cross Aide; Ski Clb; Varsity Clb; Var L Ftbl; Im Wt Lftg.

DUGGINS, KIMBERLY M; Msgr Scanlan HS; Bronx, NY; (Y); Chorus; Morris Brown U; Pre-Med.

DUHAMEL, KRISTINE M; Oyster Bay HS; Oyster Bay, NY; (Y); 23/122; Debate Tm; SADD; Var Bsktbl; Var Crs Cntry; NHS; French Clb; Band; Chorus; Yrbk Phtg; Rep Stu Cncl; Lehigh U; Pedtrcn.

DUHART, SUSAN A; Cardinal Spellman HS; Bronx, NY; (Y); Chess Clb; Sec Computer Clb; Teachers Aide; Lit Mag; NY St Regents Schlrshp 86; SUNY.

DUHOSKI, LEE ANN; Bishop Ludden HS; Syracuse, NY; (S); Exploring; GAA; Model UN; JV Bsktbl; Var Capt Socr; High Hon Roll; Sec NHS; Church Yth Grp; Varsity Clb; DAR Awd; Wllerley Coll Bk Awd 85; Chem Engr.

DUKAT, CHRIS; Sweet Home HS; Buffalo, NY; (Y); SADD; Varsity Clb; Chorus; Symp Band; Rep Stu Cncl; Var Trk; JV Vllybl; Hon Roll; SUNY Buffalo; Dntstry.

DUKAT, KAREN; Villa Maria Acad; Buffalo, NY; (S); 1/87; JCL; Latin Clb; Math Clb; Quiz Bowl; SADD; Var Swmmng; Vllybl; NEDT Awd; Prfct Atten Awd; Schlrshp-Hghst Avg 85; Biochem.

DUKE, SAMANTHA MANDY; Troy HS; Troy, NY; (Y); 23/425; Spanish Clb; Varsity Clb; Var L Bsktbl; Var L Trk; High Hon Roll; NHS; NY ST Regents Schlrshp 86; Russell Sage Coll Fndrs Schlrshp 86; Union Coll Smmr Exper Abroad 85; Russell Sage Coll; Phy Thrpy.

DUKES, DARLENE; HS Of Fashion Industry; Bronx, NY; (Y); 25/364; Church Yth Grp; Dance Clb; Office Aide; Teachers Aide; Band; School Musical; Yrbk Stf; Cit Awd; Hon Roll; Jr NHS; Fshn Merch.

DUKES, LATONIA; Canarsie HS; Brooklyn, NY; (Y); Science Clb; Teachers Aide; Color Guard; School Musical; Var Twrlr; Hon Roll; 1st Pl Awd Brooklyn Borough Sci Fair 85; Schls Arista Hnr Soc 85-86.

DUKETTE, JAMES; Saranac Central HS; Cadyville, NY; (S); 2/125; Chrmn French Clb; High Hon Roll; NHS; Ntl Merit Ltr.

DUKETTE, MICHELINE; Liverpool HS; Liverpool, NY; (Y); Church Yth Grp; Chorus; JV Var Cheerleading; 4-H Awd; Hon Roll.

DULANEY, DEBORAH; Cornwall Central HS; Cornwall, NY; (Y); 24/186; Band; Concert Band; Drm & Bgl; Tennis; Hon Roll; Pres Schlr; Regents Schlrshp, Frank Dimiceli Mem Awd 86; SUNY Albany; Econ.

DULAY, RACHEL; Columbia HS; E Greenbush, NY; (Y); 13/417; Art Clb; Church Yth Grp; Church Choir; Crs Cntry; High Hon Roll; Art Dept Awd For Exclllnc 86; De Noad Awd No 13 Rank 86; Labyrinth Awd/Exclllnc & Litrary Awd 86; Colgate U.

DULBERG, JEFFREY W; Longwood HS; Coram, NY; (Y); 2/700; Am Leg Boys St; Key Clb; Math Tm; Nwsp Stf; Rep Soph Cls; Rep Jr Cls; Tennis; High Hon Roll; NHS; Lawyr.

DUMAS, ARTHUR; Franklin Acad; Malone, NY; (Y); Church Yth Grp; Computer Clb; French Clb; Wt Lftg; Hon Roll; Trig Awd 86; Comp Awd 86; Sci Fair Awd; Comp Engnrng.

DUMAS, ROBERT; Franklin Acad; Malone, NY; (Y); French Clb; Ski Clb; Elctrcl Engr.

DUMAS, TRACEY; G Ray Bodley HS; Fulton, NY; (Y); Pres French Clb; Yrbk Phtg; Yrbk Stf; Sec Jr Cls; Sec Sr Cls; Var Capt Cheerleading; High Hon Roll; Church Yth Grp; Cls Ldrshp & Respnsblty 86; Engl 9 Awd 84.

DUMLAO, GENEVIEVE; Hackley Schl; Orangeburg, NY; (Y); Debate Tm; French Hon U; Pep Clb; Stage Crew; Yrbk Stf; JV Fld Hcky; Hon Roll; NYS Rgnts Schlrshp 86; Econ.

DUMOFF, MICHELE; Union Endicott HS; Endwell, NY; (Y); 45/450; Key Clb; VP Temple Yth Grp; Concert Band; Mrchg Band; Hon Roll; NHS; SUNY Binghamton; Lib Arts.

DUNAHOO, LANA; Ramstein American HS; Apo New York, NY; (Y); Church Yth Grp; Computer Clb; German Clb; Var JV Socr; Sci.

DUNALEWICZ, CHRISTINA; Hicksville SR HS; Hicksville, NY; (Y); Hosp Aide; Spanish Clb; Band; Orch; School Musical; Stage Crew; Symp Band; Nwsp Phtg; Nwsp Rptr; Nwsp Stf; NYSSMA Exclnt 83 & 84; LIMTA Gold Mdl 83-84 & 86; Silv Mdl 85; Photo Jrnlsm.

DUNATOV, ANNEMARIE; Lindenhurst SR HS; Lindenhurst, NY; (Y); 49/550; Pres Civic Clb; Pres Cmmty Wkr; VP Debate Tm; Drama Clb; French Clb; Girl Scts; PAVAS; Political Wkr; Science Clb; VP Speech Tm; Bst Debatr 85-86; Engl.

DUNAWAY, MELISSA; Greece Olympia HS; Rochester, NY; (Y); Exploring; Hon Roll; Schlstc Art Awd 85; Bus.

DUNCAN, BETH; Lansingburgh HS; Troy, NY; (Y); German Clb; Varsity Clb; Chorus; Stat Bsktbl; Socr; High Hon Roll; Jr NHS; NHS.

DUNCAN, GEORGINE; Villa Maria Acad; Buffalo, NY; (Y); Church Yth Grp; Computer Clb; Girl Scts; Math Clb; Chorus; Trs Soph Cls; Hon Roll; School Musical; Variety Show; Wmns Fed Awd 86; Lnks Schlrshp, Alpha Kappa Alpha Awd 86; Yngst Stu Bfflo Schlcntrm 85-86; Baldwin-Wallace Cnsvtry; Voice.

DUNCAN, GLEN; Aquinas Inst; Rochester, NY; (Y); Science Clb; School Musical; JV Ftbl; Var Trk; Wt Lftg; Hon Roll; Al Brocuto Mem Awd Bxng 86; Achvt Awd Chem & Math; Bio Engrng.

DUNCAN, JAMES; Hutchinson Central Technical HS; Buffalo, NY; (Y); SADD; Rep Jr Cls; Var Bsbl; L Var Bowling; Hon Roll; Jr NHS; Kappa Sigma Phi Boys Hon Frtrnty; Bowling Clb; BEAM; Air Force Acad; Engrng.

DUNCAN, KAREN; Evander Childs HS; Bronx, NY; (Y); Church Yth Grp; Office Aide; Teachers Aide; Prfct Atten Awd; Law.

DUNCAN, KATHERINE; Maryvale SR HS; Cheektowaga, NY; (Y); Spanish Clb; Band; Chorus; Mrchg Band; Symp Band; Rep Stu Cncl; Var Pom Pon; Hon Roll; Intl Bus.

DUNCAN, KRISTIN; Valley Stream Central HS; Malverne, NY; (Y); AFS; Computer Clb; Mathletes; Ski Clb; Chorus; Var Sftbl; Hon Roll; NHS; Natl Bus Hnr Soc 84-85; Bus.

DUNCAN, LISA; Dover JR SR HS; Dover Plains, NY; (S); Teachers Aide; Varsity Clb; Color Guard; Drm & Bgl; Drm Mjr(t); Var Capt Bsktbl; Var JV Sftbl; High Hon Roll; Hon Roll; NHS; Cmmnctns.

DUNCAN, STACY A; Greenville Central HS; Medusa, NY; (Y); 5/90; Girl Scts; Teachers Aide; High Hon Roll; NHS; Spartan Excllnc Awd 85; Schl Ltr Awd 85; Rotry Spnsh Awd 83; Coll Of St Rose; Elem Ed.

DUNCAN, STEVEN; Canisteo Central HS; Canisteo, NY; (Y); Ski Clb; Var JV Bsbl; Var Bsktbl; Im Bowling; Var JV Ftbl; Wt Lftg; Hon Roll.

DUNDON, ELIZABETH A; Faith Heritage HS; Syracuse, NY; (Y); Camera Clb; Church Yth Grp; Chorus; Nwsp Rptr; Yrbk Stf; L Var Socr; L Var Trk; L Var Vllybl; MVP Sccr 85, Trk 86; Engl.

DUNGIE, CHRIS D; Mt St Michael Acad; Bronx, NY; (Y); 63/291; Chess Clb; Sec Computer Clb; Hon Roll; Spanish NHS; Pa ST U; Cmptr Sci.

DUNHAM, BRIDGET; Henninger HS; Syracuse, NY; (Y); 20/450; Exploring; Band; Concert Band; Jazz Band; Pep Band; Jr Cls; Mgr(s); Hon Roll; Regnts Schlrshp 86; Potsdam College; Librl Arts.

DUNLAP, FAITH; Hannibal Central HS; Oswego, NY; (S); 15/118; Sec Church Yth Grp; Teachers Aide; Var Score Keeper; Var Trk; High Hon Roll; Hon Roll; Ntl Merit Ltr; Bus Stu Yr 86; Natl Hon Soc 86; Highst Avg Shrthnd II 98 86; Leg Sec.

DUNLOP, DESIREE; Grand Island SR HS; Gr Island, NY; (Y); Art Clb; Dance Clb; French Clb; Ski Clb; SADD; Trs Stu Cncl; Cheerleading; Hon Roll; Natl Inst Of Hlth Schlrshp & Roswell Pk Mem Inst 33rd Smr Res Prog 86; Med.

DUNMYER, DAVID; Hutchinson Central Tech HS; Buffalo, NY; (Y); Band; Concert Band; Mrchg Band; Bsktbl; Bowling; Mech Engrng.

DUNN, CHRISTOPHER; Seton Catholic Central HS; Endicott, NY; (Y); Am Leg Boys St; Key Clb; SADD; Varsity Clb; Stu Cncl; Ftbl; Spts Adm.

DUNN, CHRISTOPHER R; Mt Morris SR HS; Mt Morris, NY; (S); 10/52; Am Leg Boys St; Church Yth Grp; Key Clb; Thesps; Varsity Clb; Band; Chorus; Church Choir; Concert Band; Jazz Band; All ST Chori 85; Boys ST 85; NY ST U Cortland; Physcl Ed.

DUNN, DANIEL P; Oneida HS; Oneida, NY; (Y); 22/205; Drama Clb; Ski Clb; Chorus; Yrbk Stf; Pres Stu Cncl; Socr; Trk; Hon Roll; St Schlr; Spanish Clb; Jr Rotarion; Mayors Yth Advsry Cncl; Top 10 Pct Cls.

DUNN, EILEEN; Copiague HS; Copiague, NY; (Y); Church Yth Grp; Cmnty Wkr; FBLA; Spanish Clb; Teachers Aide; Capt Color Guard; School Play; Stage Crew; Hon Roll; Svc Copiague Yth Leag 84; Elem Ed.

DUNN, GEORGIA M; Evanderchilds HS; Bronx, NY; (Y); 63/254; Church Yth Grp; Cmnty Wkr; Orch; School Play; Nwsp Rptr; Nwsp Stf; Prfct Atten Awd; Theatre Mngmnt.

DUNN, GLORIOUS; De Witt Clinton HS; Bronx, NY; (Y); 5/257; Church Yth Grp; FCA; Service Clb; Teachers Aide; Varsity Clb; Band; Church Choir; School Play; Yrbk Stf; Vllybl; UFT, G Lane Mem Schlrshps, Engl, Physcs, Vis Arts, Math, Hlth Awds 86; Psych.

DUNN, KATHERINE; South Lewis Central Schl; Glenfield, NY; (Y); 7/103; Pres FHA; GAA; Quiz Bowl; Golf; Swmmng; Hon Roll; NHS; Chorus; HOBY Fndtn Ldrshp Sem; Semi-Fin Cngrss-Bundestag Exch Pgm; Tutor; Dent.

DUNN, KELLEY; Tottenville HS; Staten Island, NY; (Y); School Musical; Trk; Hon Roll.

DUNN, KEVIN; The Albany Acad For Boys; Chatham, NY; (Y); Church Yth Grp; Intnl Clb; Ski Clb; Nwsp Stf; Lit Mag; Var L Crs Cntry; Var L Trk; Ntl Merit Ltr; Library Aide; Math Tm; Cum Laude Awd 86; Natl Fr Cont Awd 86; Georgetown U; Intl Econ.

DUNN, LISA; Oneida HS; Oneida, NY; (S); Church Yth Grp; Drama Clb; Intnl Clb; Spanish Clb; Chorus; Yrbk Stf; DAR Awd; High Hon Roll; Myrs Yth Cncl 85-87; Englsh.

DUNN, PHILIP; Commack HS North; E Northport, NY; (Y); 53/390; Ftbl; Trk; High Hon Roll; Hon Roll; Pres Schlr; SUNY Binghampton.

DUNN, TOM; Smithtown High Schl West; Smithtown, NY; (Y); Church Yth Grp; Hosp Aide; Science Clb; Art Clb; Band; Concert Band; Jazz Band; Mrchg Band; Pep Band; Bsbl; Siena Coll; Chem.

DUNN, VICTORIA; Grand Island SR HS; Grand Island, NY; (Y); 27/325; Art Clb; Church Yth Grp; Cmnty Wkr; Church Choir; Hon Roll; Pres Acdmc Fit Awd 86; Regents Schlrshp 86; G I Letter & Cert Acdmc Excllnc Cert 83-86; U Of Steubenville; Math.

DUNNE, CHRISTOPHER E; Fordham Prep; Bronx, NY; (Y); Church Yth Grp; French Clb; Hosp Aide; Im Mgr Bsktbl; Engr.

DUNNE, DEIRDRE; Commack South HS; Dix Hills, NY; (Y); Hosp Aide; Chorus; Variety Show; French Hon Soc; Hon Roll.

DUNNING, DAVID; Voorheesville JR-SR HS; Voorheesville, NY; (Y); Church Yth Grp; Yrbk Phtg; Yrbk Stf; Rep Stu Cncl; Var Bsktbl; Var Socr; Dnfth Awd; High Hon Roll; Bus.

DUNPHY, CHRISTINE; St Marys Girls HS; Manhasset, NY; (Y); Ski Clb; Yrbk Sprt Ed; Capt Var Cheerleading; JV Capt Vllybl; Hon Roll; NHS; Psych.

DUNSTER, TOM; Waterville JR/SR HS; Waterville, NY; (Y); 40/110; Church Yth Grp; French Clb; Ski Clb; Varsity Clb; Var Capt Bsktbl; Im Coach Actv; Var L Crs Cntry; Stat Ftbl; Mgr(s); Var L Socr; Physcl Educ.

DUONG, MAI; Newtown HS; Elmhurst, NY; (Y); Math Clb; Science Clb; Hon Roll; Prfct Atten Awd; Phrmcy.

DUPEE, SUZANNE N; Warwick Valley HS; Warwick, NY; (Y); 16/195; Ski Clb; Stage Crew; Yrbk Stf; High Hon Roll; Hon Roll; Ntl Sci Olympd Awd-Bio 83-84; Bst Stu-Math 10-Geomtry 83-84; Hstry.

DUPEE, TAMI; Northeastern Clinton Central HS; Champlain, NY; (Y); Trs Key Clb; Model UN; Yrbk Stf; Hon Roll; NHS; Prfct Atten Awd; Physc.

DUPREE, CAROLE; Roosevelt HS; Yonkers, NY; (Y); SADD; Stu Cncl; Acad Achvt Awd Ntl Cncl Negro Wmn 85; Bus Admin.

DUPREY, CHARMAIN; Crown Point Central HS; Crown Point, NY; (Y); 4/31; Drama Clb; Hosp Aide; Varsity Clb; School Play; Nwsp Stf; Stat Bsbl; Scrkpr Bsktbl; Scrkpr Socr; Hon Roll; Prfct Atten Awd; Moses Ludington Hsop Awd 86; Odd Fellows Schlrshp 86; Onondaga CC Syracuse; Surg Tec.

DUQRE, CHRISTINE; Beth Page HS; Bethpage, NY; (Y); 87/291; Cmnty Wkr; GAA; Mathletes; Office Aide; Im Coach Actv; Var Fld Hcky; JV Sftbl; Hon Roll; Rochester Inst Of Tech $3000 86; Herman Slavin Awd $150 86; Stony Brook U; Bio Sci.

DUQUELLA, ANDRE; Seton Catholic Central HS; Binghamton, NY; (Y); Cmnty Wkr; Var Capt Ftbl; Var Capt Trk; Var L Wrstlng; 3 Sprt All Star Ftbl, Wrstlng Trk 85-86; All Star Trk & Ftbl 84-85; Bus Admin.

DUQUETTE, DIANE; NCCS HS; Champlain, NY; (Y); 33/156; Church Yth Grp; Key Clb; Ski Clb; Yrbk Stf; Bowling; John T Zurlo Schlrshp Awd 86; Svc Awd Bus 86; Recog Outstndng Bus 86; Clinton CC; Bus.

DUQUIN, MONICA; Turner/Carroll HS; Buffalo, NY; (Y); Yrbk Stf; Vets Asst.

DURAKU, INDIRA; Curtis HS; Staten Island, NY; (Y); Art Clb; Office Aide; Teachers Aide; 1st Pl Awd In Mslm Hstry 85; Tobe Coburn; Fash Dsgn.

DURAND, PAULA; Cicero North Syracuse HS; N Syracuse, NY; (S); 199/776; DECA; Drama Clb; Color Guard; Stage Crew; Regnl DECA Comptn-1st Pl Genrl Mrktng 86; ST DECA Career Conf-4th Pl Genrl Mrktng 85; SUNY-OSWEGO; Busnss.

DURANT, CONSTANCE; Stockbridge Valley Central HS; Oneida, NY; (S); 4/43; FFA; Cit Awd; High Hon Roll; NHS; FFA Chap Sec 85-86; Ag.

DURANT, DIANNE; Potsdam Central HS; Potsdam, NY; (Y); 31/120; Church Yth Grp; French Clb; Math Clb; Acpl Chr; Band; Chorus; Church Choir; Hon Roll; Lion Awd; Masonic Awd; Cert Of Achvt For Hvng 25 1/2 Crdts 86; Potsdam ST; Mjr Bio.

DURFY, JENNIFER; Pleasantville HS; Pleasantville, NY; (Y); 20/111; Church Yth Grp; Hosp Aide; PAVAS; Stage Crew; Nwsp Stf; Yrbk Stf; High Hon Roll; Hon Roll; Kings Coll; Nrsg.

DURHAM, JEANNE; Mineola HS; Mineola, NY; (Y); 52/234; Key Clb; Office Aide; SADD; Band; Chorus; Church Choir; Concert Band; Mrchg Band; Off Frsh Cls; Hon Roll; Berkeley Secretarial; Secry.

DURIEUX, MONIQUE; Monsignor Scanlan HS; Bronx, NY; (Y); 87/276; Hon Roll; Prfct Atten Awd; Math Awd 83-84; Hist Awd 83-84; Spanish I Awd 84-85; Johnson ST Coll; Accntng.

DURKEE, STEPHEN; Henninger HS; Syracuse, NY; (Y); Church Yth Grp; Band; Chorus; Concert Band; Jazz Band; Mrchg Band; Pep Band; Lcrss; Hon Roll; Prodctn Engrng.

DURKIN, DARLENE ANN; Depew HS; Depew, NY; (Y); 2/260; Hon Roll; Jr NHS; NHS; Ntl Merit Ltr; Sal; NY ST Regents Schlrshp 86; Depew Pol Clb Awd 86; Presdntl Acadmc Fitness Awd 86; ST U NY; Pre Med.

DURKIN, MAURA; Academy Of St Joseph; Sayville, NY; (Y); SADD; Orch; Rep Frsh Cls; Im Fld Hcky; Im Sftbl; Var JV Vllybl; Prfct Atten Awd; Accomdtns Effort Lit,Chem 86; FASH Merch.

DURKIN, MICHAEL P; St Francis Prep; College Point, NY; (S); 96/740; Capt Bowling; Im Ftbl; Im Sftbl; Optimate Soc 86; Acad All Amer 86; Astrnmy.

DURKO, KRISTIN; Briarcliff HS; Briarcliff, NY; (Y); 2/100; AFS; Hosp Aide; Band; Ed Nwsp Stf; Var Socr; Var Trk; High Hon Roll; NHS; Sal; JV Vllybl; Camp Cnslr Of Yr Awd 85; ST U Of NY Brmnghm; Bus.

DURNFORD, REBECCA; Scotia Glenville HS; Scotia, NY; (Y); Cmnty Wkr; Hosp Aide; VP Key Clb; Teachers Aide; Varsity Clb; Band; Drm Mjr(t); Trs Jr Cls; Trs Sr Cls; Var Capt Sftbl; Russell Sage; Ed.

DUROCHER, BETH; Elmira Free Acad; Elmira, NY; (Y); JA; Trs Latin Clb; Spanish Clb; Trs Frsh Cls; Co-Capt Var Cheerleading; Gym; Hon Roll; NYU; Engl.

DUROCHER, LISA; Saranac Central HS; Saranac, NY; (S); #6 In Class; 4-H; French Clb; Hosp Aide; Band; School Musical; Trs Frsh Cls; VP Jr Cls; High Hon Roll; NHS; Phys Thrpy.

DUROW, SUSAN; La Webber JR SR HS; Lyndonville, NY; (Y); 16/75; VICA; JV Bsktbl; JV Var Socr; Hon Roll; Prfct Atten Awd; Won VICA Cmptn For The Infmtn; Prcssng Sectrl Cls Hld At Niagra-Orleans Ctr 86; Sec.

DURR, MICHAEL; Rome Catholic HS; Lee Center, NY; (Y); 9/80; Nwsp Stf; Capt Bsktbl; High Hon Roll; NHS; Latn Achvt Awd 86; Engrng.

DURSI, KIMBERLY; Rome Catholic HS; Rome, NY; (Y); Hosp Aide; Service Clb; School Musical; Yrbk Stf; Var L Trk; High Hon Roll; NHS; Ntl Merit Ltr; Acad Achvt Awd Soc Stud 84; Bio-Chem.

DURSO, JAMES; Longwood HS; Yaphank, NY; (S); 36/500; High Hon Roll; 1st Hnrs 84-85; SUNY Albany; Music.

DURSO, JEANIENE; Beacon HS; Beacon, NY; (Y); Drama Clb; Girl Scts; Library Aide; School Play; Stage Crew; Hon Roll; Prfct Atten Awd; Awd Englsh Rgnts Top 4 Stu 86; Envrnmntl Sci.

DURSO, SUSAN; Walt Whitman HS; Huntington Statio, NY; (Y); 115/478; Key Clb; Mathletes; Spanish Clb; Orch; School Musical; Yrbk Stf; JV Bsktbl; JV Socr; JV Vllybl; Spanish NHS; Natl Span Exm Awd 85; Accntg.

DURYEA, MARIA C; Park Schl Of Buffalo; Orchard Park, NY; (Y); Chess Clb; Drama Clb; Quiz Bowl; Chorus; School Musical; School Play; Ed Lit Mag; Var Lcrss; Var Socr; Sftbl; Helen Long Schlrshp; Rgnts Schlrshp; Mt Holyuke; Sci.

DUSKAS, WILLIAM; Hugh C Williams HS; Canton, NY; (Y); 5/115; Pres Church Yth Grp; Trs Soph Cls; Pres Jr Cls; VP Sr Cls; Sec Stu Cncl; Var Golf; Var Capt Ice Hcky; NHS; Ntl Merit Ltr; Natl Schlr-Athltc Awd 86; US Air Frce Acad; Air Frce Plt.

DUSSING, KAREN; Frontier Central SR HS; Lakeview, NY; (Y); Pep Clb; Spanish Clb; Stage Crew; Yrbk Stf; Hon Roll.

DUSTIN, TERRI; Southwestern Central HS; Celoron, NY; (Y); 122/148; French Clb; Hosp Aide; Chorus; Color Guard; Hon Roll; Pres Schlr; Acadmc Prfrmnc Awd-LIU Sthhmptn 86; Cmmns Engn-Jmstwn Plnt-Schlrshp 86; Chtqa Rgn Cmnty Fndtn Schlrsh; LIU-SOUTHAMPTON; Mrn Bio.

DUTCHER, COREY; Schoharie Central HS; Schoharie, NY; (S); Boy Scts; Church Yth Grp; Band; Concert Band; Jazz Band; Mrchg Band; School Musical; Var Socr; Var Tennis; Var Wrstlng; Scholar U S Eastern Music Cmp 85 & 86; Instrmntlst Mag Merit Awd 82 & 83; Music Ed.

DUTTON, KELLY; Tioga Centra HS; Nichols, NY; (S); 71/96; Church Yth Grp; Chorus; Church Choir; Variety Show; Cheerleading; Hon Roll; Grd A For Piano; Cobleskill; Erly Chldhd Ed.

DUTTON JR, PETER ALAN; Westhampton Beach HS; Manorville, NY; (Y); 3/261; Quiz Bowl; Scholastic Bowl; Band; Lit Mag; JV Socr; Var L Trk; Hon Roll; Jr NHS; NHS; Concert Band; Scty Of Mayflower Dscndnts Hstry Awd 86; MIT; Engr.

DUTZER, THOMAS M; Garden City SR HS; Garden City, NY; (Y); 46/346; Key Clb; Speech Tm; Nwsp Sprt Ed; Yrbk Sprt Ed; Sr Cls; Stu Cncl; Var Capt Bsbl; Tennis; Cit Awd; Hon Roll; Pres Ftnss Awd 86; NY ST Rgnts Schlrshp 86; Spnsh Nwspr Sprts Edtn; Coll Of Holy Cross; Lbrl Arts.

DUVAL, KIMBERLY; Berlin Central Schl; Petersburg, NY; (Y); Camera Clb; 4-H; Chorus; Drill Tm; School Musical; School Play; Yrbk Phtg; Yrbk Stf; Cit Awd; 4-H Awd; Lab Techncn.

DUVAL, ROXANNE; Crown Point Central HS; Crown Point, NY; (S); Varsity Clb; VP Frsh Cls; Pres Soph Cls; Pres Jr Cls; JV Var Cheerleading; Socr; Cit Awd; DAR Awd; High Hon Roll; NHS.

DUVAL, TIMOTHY; Archbishop Milly HS; Maspeth, NY; (Y); Art Clb; Cmnty Wkr; Pep Clb; SADD; Chorus; Church Choir; Stat Crs Cntry; Stat Trk; U Of Dayton; Spcl Educ-Deaf.

DUVALL, TAMMY; Addison Central Schl; Cameron Mills, NY; (Y); JCL; Latin Clb; SADD; Color Guard; High Hon Roll; Hon Roll; Alfred ST Coll; Sec.

DUWE, KEVIN; Pleasantville HS; Pleasantville, NY; (Y); 1/101; Yrbk Stf; JV Crs Cntry; Var Ftbl; Var Socr; Var Tennis; High Hon Roll; NHS; Colby Coll Awd 85-86; Chmstry Awd 85-86; Math Awd 83-85; Pre-Med.

DWORSKY, AMY LYNN; Troy HS; Troy, NY; (Y); 1/406; Sec French Clb; Yrbk Ed-Chief; Bausch & Lomb Sci Awd; Elks Awd; NHS; Ntl Merit Schol; Val; Varsity Clb; Band; Chorus; Empr ST Schlrshp Of Excllnc Awd 86; RPI Mdl For Mth & Sci 85; Hrvrd Bk Prz 85; Ntl Frnch Cntst Wnr 83; Williams Coll.

DWYER, JENNIFER; Holy Trinity Diocesan HS; Bethpage, NY; (S); 7/403; Math Clb; Cheerleading.

DWYER, JENNIFER; Sodus Central HS; Sodus, NY; (S); 15/135; Trs VP AFS; English Clb; French Clb; Model UN; Science Clb; Sec Varsity Clb; Trs Band; Mrchg Band; School Play; Rep Stu Cncl; Rgnts Schlrshp 86; Cornell U; Bus Mngmt.

DWYER, JOEL; Oxford HS; Oxford, NY; (Y); Band; Concert Band; Mrchg Band; Pep Band; Hon Roll; NYSSMA Blu Rbbn Lvl 6 Duet Perf Score 85-86; Music.

DWYER, JOHN M; Ichabod Crane HS; Hudson, NY; (Y); Letterman Clb; Varsity Clb; VP Frsh Cls; Rep Stu Cncl; Var Trk; Var Vllybl; Hon Roll; Contrbtng To Clss 84.

DWYER, KELLY; Saranac Lake Central HS; Saranac Lk, NY; (Y); Off Jr Cls; Stu Cncl; Bsktbl; Powder Puff Ftbl; Socr; Sftbl; Vllybl; Hon Roll; MVP Soccer 84; 2nd Team All Nrthrn Soccer 85.

DWYER, KIM; Catholic Central HS; Troy, NY; (Y); Church Yth Grp; French Clb; Chorus; Variety Show; Hon Roll; St Lwrnce U; Lwyr.

DWYER, MICHAEL; Mount Vernon HS; Mount Vernon, NY; (Y); 18/550; Church Yth Grp; Cmnty Wkr; Office Aide; Spanish Clb; Stu Cncl; High Hon Roll; Hon Roll; Jr NHS; NHS; Acad Hnrs 86; Tau Eplsn Phi 86; SUNY Buffalo; Accntng.

DWYER, PATRICK J; Homer Central HS; Truxton, NY; (Y); 27/150; Am Leg Boys St; Varsity Clb; Pres Soph Cls; Bsbl; Bsktbl; Capt Ftbl; Wt Lftg; Cit Awd; Hon Roll; Phys Ther.

DWYER, SHARON; Liverpool HS; Liverpool, NY; (Y); 140/816; Church Yth Grp; Varsity Clb; Nwsp Sprt Ed; Bsktbl; Coach Actv; Socr; Sftbl; Hon Roll; Jr NHS; NHS; 1st Tm All Cnty Sccr, Bsktbl, & Sftbl 82-86; Alfred U; Nrsng.

DYBDAHL, SONIA; Midwood HS At Brooklyn College; Brooklyn, NY; (Y); French Clb; German Clb; Concert Band; Lit Mag; Off Frsh Cls; 1st Pl Achvt Tst Natl Assoc Tchrs Germ 85; Placemnt From Essay Soc Profs Frnch 87; Intl Fest 84-86; Lingstcs.

DYBDAL, DAVID; Xavier HS; Staten Is, NY; (Y); Dance Clb; Teachers Aide; Rep Stu Cncl; Var JV Bsbl; JV Ftbl; Hon Roll; Ntl Merit Ltr; NEDT Awd; Rep Frsh Cls; Rep Soph Cls; Acad Scholar 83-87; Spec Cnslr; Pre-Med.

DYCKES, MICHELINE; St Dominic HS; Huntington, NY; (Y); 24/119; SADD; Chorus; Nwsp Rptr; Co-Capt Var Cheerleading; Socr; High Hon Roll; SUNY-CORTLAND; Elem Eductn.

DYE, MELISSA; Tri-Valley Central Schl; Grahamsville, NY; (Y); Pres Church Yth Grp; Pres Exploring; Office Aide; Teachers Aide; Chorus; Crs Cntry; Cit Awd; High Hon Roll; Hon Roll; Cazenovia Coll; Spec Ed.

DYETT, MICHELLE; George Washington HS; Brooklyn, NY; (Y); 10/382; Church Yth Grp; Cmnty Wkr; Teachers Aide; Stu Cncl; Tennis; Vllybl; High Hon Roll; NHS; Ntl Merit Ltr; Pres Schlr; Pres Acad Fit Awd 86; Assn Tchrs Soc Stud United Fed Tchrs Awd 86; Hnr Soc Wmn Engrs 86; Baruch Coll; Acctg.

DYKE, JENNIFER J; St Lawrence Central HS; Brasher Falls, NY; (Y); Pres Trs Girl Scts; Band; Yrbk Ed-Chief; VP Stu Cncl; Var L Bsktbl; Var L Socr; Bausch & Lomb Sci Awd; Hon Roll; NHS; Ntl Merit Ltr; Masonic Lodge Zonta Schlrshp, Regents Schlrshp, Clarkson Schl Phalanx Awd 86; Clarkson U; Indstrl Dist.

DYKEMAN, KARIN; Stissin Mt JR SR HS; Red Hook, NY; (Y); 7/90; Pres VP Church Yth Grp; SADD; Band; Pres Soph Cls; Pres Jr Cls; Pres Sr Cls; NHS; Ntl Merit SF; AFS; AFS Intl Exchng-Iceland 85; Summer Schlrs Regional HS Of Excllnc 86; Arch.

DYKEMAN, TERESSA; Seton Catholic Central HS; Binghamton, NY; (S); 20/165; Church Yth Grp; French Clb; Varsity Clb; School Musical; Variety Show; Stu Cncl; Cheerleading; NHS; Var Ltrs Recog 84-85; Seton Schlr 85; Chrldng Comp 85; Math.

DYKSEN, JAMES R; Ichabod Crane HS; Stuyvesant, NY; (Y); 3/189; Am Leg Boys St; Spanish Clb; Varsity Clb; Yrbk Stf; Sec Frsh Cls; Var L Bsbl; Var L Bsktbl; High Hon Roll; NHS; Ntl Merit Ltr; Engl.

DYLAG, EDWIN M; Pembroke Central HS; Corfu, NY; (Y); 3/115; Math Tm; Varsity Clb; JV Ftbl; JV Golf; High Hon Roll; Hon Roll; NHS; NY ST Regents Schlrshp 86; SUNY; Engrng.

DYSINGER, BRIAN; Royelton Hartland HS; Lockport, NY; (Y); Boy Scts; JV Ftbl; Church Yth Grp; 4-H; WY Tech Inst; Auto Mech.

DYSON, APRIL Y; North Babylon SR HS; North Babylon, NY; (Y); 44/464; French Clb; Intnl Clb; Yrbk Stf; Cheerleading; French Hon Soc; High Hon Roll; Jr NHS; NHS; Bus Stu Of Mnth 85; Ntl Merit Cmmnd Stu 85; Long Island Bus Inst; Wrd Prcsg.

DYSON, NANCY; Attica Central Schl; Attica, NY; (Y); 15/152; Sec Church Yth Grp; Chorus; Church Choir; Yrbk Stf; Var Bsktbl; Var Capt Crs Cntry; Var Trk; Stat Vllybl; NHS; Houghton Coll; Engl.

DZANOUCAKIS, GEORGE; William Cullen Bryant HS; Woodside, NY; (S); 131/623; Key Clb; SADD; Orch; Nwsp Ed-Chief; Nwsp Rptr; Yrbk Stf; Hon Roll; NHS; Prfct Atten Awd; Forgn Lang Hnr Soc 84; Greek Clb 83-86; Schl Svc 83-85.

DZIALAK, JENNIFER; Sweet Home SR HS; Amherst, NY; (Y); GAA; Spanish Clb; Band; Symp Band; JV Crs Cntry; JV Fld Hcky; JV Socr; Hon Roll; NYSMA Solo Awds 83 & 84; Soc Studs Hnr Awd 85; Drama Hnr Awd 86; Med.

DZIEKAN, CHERYL; Holland Central Schl; Holland, NY; (Y); Varsity Clb; Nwsp Stf; Yrbk Stf; Var Bsktbl; Var Capt Fld Hcky; Var Socr; Var JV Vllybl; NHS; Hilbert Coll; Bus Admin.

DZIEL, ANDREW; George W Fowler HS; Syracuse, NY; (S); 1/200; Boys Clb Am; Cmnty Wkr; Debate Tm; Library Aide; Spanish Clb; SADD; Band; Nwsp Rptr; Yrbk Stf; Rep Stu Cncl; U Of Rochester; Engrng.

DZIELSKI, MARK; Canisius HS; Grand Island, NY; (Y); Pres Church Yth Grp; Hosp Aide; Stage Crew; Variety Show; Im Bsktbl; JV Socr; Hon Roll; NHS; Diocesan Cath Yth Orgnztn 85-86; Bishops Diocesan Pastrl Cncl 85-86; Cathlc Yth Orgnztn Tm Spirit 85; Fordham U; Acctng.

DZIERZANOWSKI, LYNETTE; Alexander Central HS; Darien Ctr, NY; (Y); Math Tm; Science Clb; Varsity Clb; Chorus; Nwsp Ed-Chief; Capt Crs Cntry; Capt Trk; Lion Awd; NHS; Voice Dem Awd; Natl TAC Jr Olympcs 84; Am Chem Soc Stu Of Yr 86; Math Ed.

DZIEWIONTKOWSKI, AMY B; Performing Arts HS; Flushing, NY; (Y); 34/121; Aud/Vis; Drama Clb; Office Aide; PAVAS; School Play; Stage Crew; Yrbk Bus Mgr; Yrbk Ed-Chief; Yrbk Phtg; Yrbk Stf; Hnrbl Mentn-Arts Recgntn & Talnt Search 86; Juilliard; Actress.

DZIEZYNSKI, JOSEPH F; Utica Free Acad; Utica, NY; (Y); 14/325; Am Leg Boys St; Debate Tm; Trs Key Clb; Latin Clb; Rep Stu Cncl; JV Crs Cntry; Var L Tennis; Im Vllybl; High Hon Roll; NHS; Physcn.

DZIOMBA, MICHAEL; St John The Baptist HS; Central Islip, NY; (Y); JV Bsktbl; Hofstra U; Real Estate.

DZIUBA, PATRICIA; Auburn HS; Auburn, NY; (Y); Church Yth Grp; Drama Clb; Acpl Chr; Chorus; Church Choir; School Musical; Nwsp Stf; Hon Roll; Music Ed.

DZIWIS, DAVE; Whitesboro SR HS; Whitesboro, NY; (Y); Varsity Clb; Band; Concert Band; JV Var Bsbl; JV Var Ftbl; JV Golf; Hon Roll; Arch.

DZURILLA, DAVID E; Freeport HS; Freeport, NY; (Y); Boy Scts; Camera Clb; Church Yth Grp; Key Clb; Varsity Clb; Band; Variety Show; Off Frsh Cls; Off Soph Cls; Off Jr Cls; St Johns; Mktg.

DZYGUN, DIANNE M; Kenmore West HS; Kenmore, NY; (Y); 74/443; Church Yth Grp; Acpl Chr; Chorus; School Musical; High Hon Roll; Hon Roll; NHS; Prfct Atten Awd; Spnsh Awd 86; ST U Coll Buffalo; Bus Adm.

EADE, ALICIA; Archbishop Walsh HS; Olean, NY; (Y); Art Clb; Latin Clb; Pep Clb; Spanish Clb; Nwsp Stf; Yrbk Stf; High Hon Roll; NHS; Nwsp Rptr; Olean Yth Court 86; Nrsng.

EADER, LISA; Southampton HS; Southampton, NY; (Y); Art Clb; Yrbk Phtg; Yrbk Stf; Fld Hcky; Gym; Tennis; Trk; High Hon Roll; Hon Roll; Jr NHS; Regents Schlrshp SATS 86; Arch.

EADES JR, RICHARD E; Dansville HS; Dansville, NY; (Y); 6/172; Boy Scts; Band; Jazz Band; Mrchg Band; Stu Cncl; Golf; God Cntry Awd; Hon Roll; NHS; Paideia Awd U Rochester 86; Script D Awd 83-86; MVP Var Golf 84-85 & 85-86; U Rochester; Pol Sci.

EADIE, NICOLE; Cathedral HS; Ny, NY; (Y); 79/272; Teachers Aide; Hon Roll; Bus Adm.

EAGAN, COLLEEN; Bishop Ludden HS; Syracuse, NY; (Y); Var Capt Socr; JV Sftbl; Var Capt Vllybl; High Hon Roll; Hon Roll; NHS; Spnsh & Bus & Secy Awds; SUNY Coll; Ed.

EAGEN, LYNNETTE A; Arlington HS; Poughkeepsie, NY; (Y); 36/565; Church Yth Grp; French Clb; Ski Clb; Stat Socr; Vllybl; Rotary Awd; NY ST Regents Schlrshp 86; Hnr Key Scty 86; Siena Coll; Intl Bus.

EAGER, TIFFANNY E; Jamestown HS; Jamestown, NY; (Y); Art Clb; Boys Clb Am; Cmnty Wkr; Political Wkr; Lit Mag; Stat Bsktbl; Hon Roll; Jr NHS.

EAGLE, TODD; Roslyn HS; Roslyn, NY; (Y); Chess Clb; Jazz Band; Symp Band; Var L Crs Cntry; Var L Tennis; Jr NHS; Spnsh Northeast Conf Awd 86; Long Isl Sci Cong Awd 85; Dartmouth.

EAGLETON, MATTHEW; North Rose-Wolcott HS; Wolcott, NY; (Y); 1/135; Pres Varsity Clb; Pres Stu Cncl; Var Capt Crs Cntry; Var Capt Swmmng; Var Trk; Bausch & Lomb Sci Awd; NHS; Val; Intl Yth Achvmnt Awd 85-86; U Of Rochester.

EARICH, CRAIG; Dannemora HS; Dannemora, NY; (Y); Am Leg Boys St; French Clb; Var L Bsktbl; Var Socr; High Hon Roll; Engrng.

EARLY, JOHN D; Niskayuna HS; Schenectady, NY; (Y); French Clb; Nwsp Rptr; Var Capt Vllybl; Kiwanis Awd; NHS; Ntl Merit Schol; Rotary Awd; Pres Acdmc Ftns Awd, Tchr Assoc Schlrshp, NYS Rgnts Schlrshp 86; U Notre Dame; Chem Engrng.

EASON, MILES; Malverne HS; W Hempstead, NY; (Y); 15/121; Cmnty Wkr; JA; Political Wkr; Var Capt Bsktbl; Capt Wt Lftg; High Hon Roll; Hon Roll; Excllnce Mth 85; Cert Merit 84; Bus Adm.

EASTWOOD, BRUCE; Christ The King HS; Queens Village, NY; (Y); Bsktbl.

EASTWOOD, LORNA-MARIE; Commack H S South; Commack, NY; (Y); 100/364; Office Aide; Pep Clb; Band; Concert Band; Mrchg Band; Pep Band; Symp Band; Nwsp Stf; Yrbk Stf; Lit Mag; Pres Awdacdmc Achvt&phys Ftns 86; SUNY Cortland; Eng Educ.

EASTWOOD, LORRIE; Canastota JR SR HS; Canastota, NY; (S); 6/150; French Clb; GAA; Intnl Clb; Leo Clb; Science Clb; SADD; Rep Stu Cncl; Stat Fld Hcky; JV Sftbl; Var Vllybl; Al-Star Vllybl 84; Mst Imprvd Sftbl 85; Lions Tp 4 83; Math.

EATMAN, TIMOTHY K; Mt Pleasant Christian Acad; New York, NY; (Y); 1/14; Church Yth Grp; Drama Clb; PAVAS; Teachers Aide; Band; Chorus; Church Choir; School Play; Variety Show; Nwsp Phtg; Mt Pleasant Christian Acad Stu Of Yr 82-83; Harlem Schl Of Arts Dir Schlrshp Piano & Comp 85-86; Pace U; Lawyer.

EATON, CAROLYN J; Troy HS; Troy, NY; (Y); 17/435; Sec German Clb; Ski Clb; Concert Band; Yrbk Ed-Chief; Hon Roll; Sec NHS; Prfrmng Arts Dept Smr Msc Schlrshp 84-85; Lois C Smith Schlrshp For Chmstry; NY ST U Bnghmtn; Bio Chmstry.

EATON, JACQUELYN; Greene Central HS; Willet, NY; (Y); 32/110; Sec Trs Chorus; Swing Chorus; Trk; L Vllybl; Hon Roll; Prfct Atten Awd; Sec Soph Cls; Trs Sr Cls; Rep Stu Cncl; Fclty Key Awd For Chrs & Art 86; Prfrmg Arts Awd 86; Broome CC; Phys Ther.

EATON, MICHAEL; Clinton Central HS; Clinton, NY; (Y); Art Clb; Intnl Clb; SADD; JV Bsbl; JV Var Ftbl; JV Golf; Var Trk; Hon Roll; Adv Plcmnt Art 85-86; Hartwick Coll; Psych.

EATON, OLIVIA M; John Vay HS; South Salem, NY; (Y); JV Var Lcrss; Hon Roll; Studio In Art & Drwng & Pntng Awd 85; Schlrshp To NYSSSA 85; Dsgnr.

EATON, PATRICK; Geneseo Central HS; Geneseo, NY; (Y); 4/87; Am Leg Boys St; Cmnty Wkr; Stage Crew; Pres Soph Cls; VP Jr Cls; VP Sr Cls; Rep Stu Cncl; L Socr; L Trk; High Hon Roll; Cst Guard AIM Pgm 86; U S Naval Acad; Chmcl Engrng.

EATON, RENEE; Liverpool HS; Liverpool, NY; (Y); 200/884; Hon Roll; Jr NHS; Sec.

EATON, THOMAS; Frewsburg Central HS; Frewsburg, NY; (Y); Pres AFS; Church Yth Grp; Drama Clb; Chorus; School Musical; School Play; Stage Crew; Rptr Nwsp Ed-Chief; Rptr Yrbk Ed-Chief; Swmmng; NYC; Acting.

EBERHARD, JENNIFER; Grand Island HS; Grand Isl, NY; (Y); Pres Trs Church Yth Grp; Hosp Aide; Ski Clb; SADD; Varsity Clb; Variety Show; Yrbk Stf; Powder Puff Ftbl; JV Socr; Var Trk; Red Crs Cert Lifgrd 85; John Casablancas Mjr Prfsnl Mdlng 86; Hosptl Admns.

EBERLE, DEAN; Canisius HS; Amherst, NY; (Y); 23/160; Boy Scts; Church Yth Grp; Cmnty Wkr; JV Capt Ftbl; JV Capt Trk; High Hon Roll; Hon Roll; Spanish NHS; Im Mgr Bsktbl; Im Mgr Sftbl; Scholar Buffalo Fndtn 86-87; Alumni Grant 85-86; Pre-Med.

EBERLE, SCOTT; Archbishop Stepinac HS; New Rochelle, NY; (Y); Boys Clb Am; Chorus; School Musical; School Play; Nwsp Stf; Yrbk Phtg; High Hon Roll; Hon Roll; NHS; Educ.

EBERLY, STACY; Indian River Central HS; Philadelphia, NY; (Y); 9/150; Church Yth Grp; Latin Clb; Chorus; Swing Chorus; Sftbl; Hon Roll; NHS; Prfct Atten Awd; NYSSMA Solo Fstvl Sngng Scr 96/100 84-86; All-ST Chrs 84-86; Bi-Cnty Chrs 84-86; Jzz Rck Chrs 84-86; Messiah; Tchng.

EBERT, CARLA; Allegany Central Schl; Allegany, NY; (Y); 4/100; Pres Church Yth Grp; Drama Clb; Church Choir; Concert Band; Mrchg Band; School Musical; School Play; Nwsp Ed-Chief; Nwsp Phtg; Ed Yrbk Phtg; Schlrshp Scty; Nmn Natl Cncl Tchrs Eng Awd; Oqlfyng Natl Mrt Schlrshp.

EBERT, MICHELLE LYNN; Brockport SR HS; Brockport, NY; (Y); 65/335; French Clb; Ski Clb; Drill Tm; Drm & Bgl; Yrbk Phtg; Yrbk Stf; Rep Sr Cls; Rep Stu Cncl; High Hon Roll; Hon Roll; Alfred Ag & Tech.

EBERWEIN, NANCY; Wilson Central HS; Wilson, NY; (Y); 9/125; SADD; Jazz Band; Symp Band; Nwsp Stf; Yrbk Stf; Hon Roll; NHS; JR Band Hall Fame; Sec Ed.

ECCLESTON, LINETTE; Addison Central Schl; Addison, NY; (Y); Exploring; GAA; Ski Clb; JV Var Socr; JV Sftbl; Var Vllybl; High Hon Roll; Hon Roll; Bowling Club; Cntrl City Bus Inst; Exec Sec.

ECHAN, MARTHA; Union Endicott HS; Endicott, NY; (Y); French Clb; Key Clb; Pep Clb; Var Flag Corp; JV Bsktbl; High Hon Roll; Hon Roll; Schlstc Art Awd 84; Art.

ECHEVERRIA, ROWENA; St Raymond Academy For Girls; Bronx, NY; (S); 2/84; Computer Clb; Drm & Bgl; Mrchg Band; Yrbk Stf; Pres Frsh Cls; VP Soph Cls; Stu Cncl; High Hon Roll; NHS; ITV Grphcs Awd 84-85; Hghtst Avg In Regents Bio, Gen Sci & Afro-Asian 84-85; Fordham U; Acctng.

ECK, JOHN S; Ward Melville HS; Stonybrook, NY; (Y); 65/711; Boy Scts; Ski Clb; High Hon Roll; Hon Roll; Jr NHS; NHS; Ntl Merit Ltr; Eagle Sct Awd 86; Ad Altair Dei & Pope Ps XII Rlgs Emscms BSA; Webb Inst Of Nvl Archtr; Archtr.

ECKARDT, JAMES W; Massapequa HS; Massapequa, NY; (Y); 16/454; Church Yth Grp; Band; Concert Band; Jazz Band; Mrchg Band; Co-Capt Tennis; High Hon Roll; NHS; Ntl Merit Schol; U Of Buffalo; Elec Engr.

ECKARDT II, JORGE L; Holy Cross HS; Jackson Hts, NY; (Y); 35/312; Church Yth Grp; Radio Clb; Nwsp Sprt Ed; Nwsp Stf; Bsbl; Hon Roll; NHS; Tablet Jrnlsm Awd 2nd Pl Best; Ntl Hspnc Schlrshp Awd $100; Boston U; Engr.

ECKARDT, SCOTT; North Babylon HS; N Babylon, NY; (Y); Civic Clb; Varsity Clb; Band; Var Capt Crs Cntry; Var Capt Trk; Hon Roll; Jr NHS; NHS; Ntl Merit Ltr; MVP X-Cntry 84 & 85; All Conf I X-Cntry 85; Comp Sci.

ECKBERG, KELLEY S; Southwestern Central HS; Jamestown, NY; (Y); 33/162; Church Yth Grp; Cmnty Wkr; Pep Clb; Red Cross Aide; Rep Art Clb; FCA; Sec Girl Scts; Library Aide; Var Gym; Slvr Awd In Grlsctng 83; Geneseo; Spec Ed.

ECKELBERGER, WAYNE A; Gates Chili SR HS; Rochester, NY; (Y); 47/446; Chess Clb; French Clb; High Hon Roll; NHS; NYS Regnts Schlrshp 86; Rochester Inst Of Tech; El Engr.

ECKERLIN, SUZANNE; Tully Central HS; Tully, NY; (Y); Varsity Clb; Band; Chorus; Jazz Band; Cheerleading; Crs Cntry; Trk; Vllybl; High Hon Roll; Hon Roll; Marine Bio.

ECKERT, GREG; Cuba Central HS; Cuba, NY; (Y); 14/60; Model UN; Quiz Bowl; Ski Clb; Capt L Crs Cntry; Var L Golf; Var Capt Vllybl; NHS; French Clb; Letterman Clb; Varsity Clb; NY ST Regnts Schlr 86; Allegany Cnty Natl Hnr Socty Schlrshp 86; Mnrty Ldr 1st Pl Awd Allegany 85; St Bonaventure U; Acctg.

ECKERT, LISA; Frontier Central HS; Lake View, NY; (Y); Rep Art Clb; High Hon Roll; Hon Roll; NHS; Schrlshp Immaculata 83-84; Most Artistic Stu 83-84; Adv.

ECKERT, SUZETTE; Greece Arcadia HS; Rochester, NY; (Y); Math Tm; Ski Clb; Teachers Aide; JV Sftbl; Hon Roll; Acadmc Ltr & Pin 86; Cert Vlntr Wrk Spcl Ed Bwlng 84-86; SUNY-BROCKPORT; Elem Ed.

ECKES, DAVID; Port Jervis HS; Sparrow Bush, NY; (Y); 60/212; Art Clb; Cmnty Wkr; Spanish Clb; Bowling; Hon Roll; Wst Pnt Gn 83-85; Art.

ECKHARDT, DAVID; Hamburg SR HS; Hamburg, NY; (Y); 191/390; Church Yth Grp; Band; Concert Band; Mrchg Band; Orch; Symp Band; Im Bsktbl; JV Var Tennis; JV Var Vllybl; Hon Roll; ECIC Divisn I All Str Vllybll Plyr 86; Bowling Gree ST U; Sprts Mgmt.

ECKHARDT, LISA; Pinecrest Christian HS; Salisbury Center, NY; (S); Drama Clb; Office Aide; Yrbk Stf; Pres Sr Cls; Hon Roll; Pinecrest Bible Traing Ctr.

ECKHOFF, DANA; Haverling Central HS; Bath, NY; (Y); 20/130; Boy Scts; Pres French Clb; Math Clb; Scholastic Bowl; Ski Clb; Nwsp Stf; Socr; Capt Swmmng; High Hon Roll; Mst Imprvd Swmr-Leag 84-85; Mst Vlbl Al-Star Swmng Leag 85-86.

ECKLER, IVY M; Poland JR SR HS; Poland, NY; (Y); 8/60; Pres Jr Cls; Pres Stu Cncl; Var Bsktbl; Var Capt Socr; Var Capt Sftbl; Hon Roll; NHS; Prfct Atten Awd; Doc.

ECKLUND, MELVIN; Mayville Central Schl; Mayville, NY; (S); 1/44; Church Yth Grp; Pres Frsh Cls; Rep Stu Cncl; Var Bsbl; Var Bsktbl; Var Ftbl; Bausch & Lomb Sci Awd; High Hon Roll; Jr NHS; NHS; Elec Engrng.

ECKMAN, JENNIFER; Frontier Central HS; Blasdell, NY; (S); 10/444; Church Yth Grp; French Clb; Ski Clb; SADD; Im Bsktbl; Sftbl; Im Vllybl; High Hon Roll; Hon Roll; Jr NHS; Bus Adm.

ECKSTEIN, RACHEL; Smithtown HS; Smithtown, NY; (Y); Cmnty Wkr; DECA; Temple Yth Grp; Band; Concert Band; Symp Band; Yrbk Stf; Tennis; High Hon Roll; NHS; Bus.

ECKSTRAND, KYA; Chautauqua Central HS; Ashville, NY; (Y); 3/37; Band; Chorus; School Play; Yrbk Phtg; Sec Stu Cncl; Var L Cheerleading; Var Capt Trk; High Hon Roll; Pres NHS; Voice Dem Awd; Rgnts Schlrshp-NYS 85; Jnr Miss Fnlst 85; Presdntl Acadmc Ftns Awd 86; Kenyon Coll; Math.

EDDINGER, SHELLEY; Marcus Whitman Central HS; Stanley, NY; (Y); 27/125; Capt Crs Cntry; Var L Trk; Stat Wrstlng; Color Guard; Mrchg Band; School Play; Stage Crew; Yrbk Phtg; Yrbk Stf; Hon Roll; Accntnt.

EDDY, JILL A; Pulaski JR SR HS; Pulaski, NY; (S); 10/85; GAA; Math Tm; Ski Clb; Band; Sec Frsh Cls; JV Var Bsktbl; JV Var Socr; JV Var Trk; Hon Roll; NHS; Snow Incntv Awd 85; All Leag 10 Mtr Hgh Hurdles 85; Cortland ST; Phys Educ.

EDDY, JULIA; Alexander Central HS; Alexander, NY; (Y); 14/84; Church Yth Grp; FNA; Ski Clb; Chorus; Color Guard; Mrchg Band; Yrbk Stf; Trk; High Hon Roll; Jr NHS; Regnts Nursng Schlrshp 86; Alfred ST Coll; Nursng.

EDELMAN, BILL; H Frank Carey HS; W Hempstead, NY; (Y); 11/176; Nwsp Sprt Ed; Var JV Bsbl; Var JV Bsktbl; French Hon Soc; High Hon Roll; VP NHS.

EDELMAN, MARY JEAN; Churchville-Chili SR HS; N Chili, NY; (Y); JCL; Latin Clb; Var Capt Bsktbl; High Hon Roll; Hon Roll; MIP Bsktbl Var 84-85; MVP Bsktbl Var 85-86; Natl JR Clsscl Lg Cert 83-84; Zoologist.

EDENS, JEANNE; Nazareth Acad; Rochester, NY; (Y); Dance Clb; FBLA; Chorus; Yrbk Stf; Hon Roll; Shorthand Awds 86; Ledrshp Awd 86; Grade Pt Avg 88.6 86.

EDESESS, MARIE E; Convent Of The Sacred Heart; New York, NY; (Y); Cmnty Wkr; Dance Clb; Hosp Aide; Model UN; Ski Clb; Nwsp Rptr; Yrbk Ed-Chief; Cit Awd; Ntl Merit SF; Stuart Awd Indpndnt Thinkng 83; Summa Cum Laude Natl Latin Cont 82.

EDGAR, CHRIS; West Genesee SR HS; Camillus, NY; (Y); Trs Church Yth Grp; 4-H; French Clb; Key Clb; Band; Concert Band; Mrchg Band; High Hon Roll; NHS; Chess Clb; Ntl Sci Olympiad Chem 86; All Cty Concert Band 86; Chem Engr.

EDGAR, JAMES; Bethlehem Central HS; Glenmont, NY; (Y); 4/304; Boy Scts; Pres Exploring; Lit Mag; JV Golf; High Hon Roll; NHS; Ntl Merit Ltr; Pres Schlr; Head Acolyte St Andrews Episcopal Church 85-86; Dartmouth Coll; Engrng.

EDGAR, VICTORIA; Smithtown East HS; St James, NY; (Y); French Clb; Stu Cncl; French Hon Soc; High Hon Roll; Hon Roll; NHS; Stu Mnth Awd 85; Mst Artistc Cls Awd 86; Hnrsb Mntn NFAA Arts Awd; Dance.

EDGERTON, ELLEN; West Genesee HS; Syracuse, NY; (Y); Exploring; Nwsp Rptr; High Hon Roll; Ntl Merit SF; NY Rgnts Schlrshp 86-90; Gld Ky Awd Crrnt Evnts 86; Otstndng Stu Englsh Awd 86; Syracuse U; Wrtng Tlcmmnctns.

EDICK, BEATRICE; Westmoreland HS; Clinton, NY; (Y); Church Yth Grp; Model UN; Church Choir; Nwsp Rptr; Nwsp Stf; Yrbk Stf; Powder Puff Ftbl; High Hon Roll; Hon Roll; CCBI; Med Rcptnst.

EDINGER, HENRY F; Corcoran HS; Syracuse, NY; (Y); Am Leg Boys St; Chess Clb; French Clb; Hosp Aide; Key Clb; Science Clb; Yrbk Ed-Chief; Yrbk Stf; VP Stu Cncl; Bsktbl; NY ST Spcl Scl Stds Awd 86; Co-Sprtmn Of Yr 86; Oswego ST; Hstry.

EDIP, DERIN; John Jay SR HS; Stormville, NY; (Y); Cmnty Wkr; Pep Clb; Ski Clb; Var Cheerleading; Hon Roll; Pltcl Sci.

EDKINS, JODI; Rush-Henrietta Roth HS; Rush, NY; (Y); Pres 4-H; VP GAA; Latin Clb; Red Cross Aide; SADD; Concert Band; Ed Yrbk Stf; VP Frsh Cls; VP Soph Cls; Rep Jr Cls; Svc Ltr 86; GAA Sport Ltr 86; Speech.

EDLER, DEBORAH; Gowanda Central HS; Irving, NY; (Y); 2/126; Am Leg Aux Girls St; Pres Spanish Clb; Trs SADD; Rep Frsh Cls; Sec Soph Cls; Rep Jr Cls; VP Stu Cncl; High Hon Roll; NHS; AFS; Amer Chem Soc Awd 86; SUNY; Pre-Med.

EDMISTER, ANGEL; Elmira Free Acad; Elmira, NY; (Y); Church Yth Grp; Girl Scts; Hosp Aide; JA; Red Cross Aide; Vllybl; Hon Roll; Bantum Bowlng 80; Bus.

EDMISTER, BILL; Dundee Central HS; Dundee, NY; (Y); Boy Scts; 4-H; Pep Clb; Varsity Clb; Chorus; Yrbk Bus Mgr; Yrbk Phtg; Rep Stu Cncl; Var L Ftbl; Golf; Old Dominion U; Pltcl Sci.

EDMISTON, DAWN; John F Kennedy HS; Utica, NY; (S); 9/130; Pres Church Yth Grp; Key Clb; Trs Band; Nwsp Ed-Chief; Rep Stu Cncl; Var Capt Cheerleading; DAR Awd; VP NHS; Cmnty Wkr; Qlty Lt Gov Awd 86; 2nd Outstndng Young New Yorker 85; Key Club Dist Adm Awd 86; Hamilton Coll; Pre-Law.

EDMONDSON, JILL; Uniondale HS; Hempstead, NY; (Y); Pres Church Yth Grp; Mathletes; Thesps; Concert Band; Orch; Pres Frsh Cls; Rep Sr Cls; Pres Stu Cncl; High Hon Roll; Jr NHS; Yth Yr Awd 86; Ywn Hempstead Yth Achvt Awd 86; Outstndng Stdnt Svc Awd 84; Duke; Intl Corp Law.

EDMONSON, MAUREEN J; Newfield HS; Selden, NY; (Y); 29/550; Drama Clb; Pres SADD; School Play; Pres Frsh Cls; Sec Soph Cls; Pres Sr Cls; Fld Hcky; Sftbl; Jr NHS; Trs NHS; NYS Rgnts Schlrshp 86; Mddl Cntry Admin Awd 86; Hofstra Ldrshp Grnt 86; Hofstra U; Cmmnctn Arts.

EDMONSTON, DAPHNE; Bronx HS Of Science; New York, NY; (Y); Y-Teens; Yrbk Stf.

EDSON, DEE; Massena Central HS; Massena, NY; (Y); 12/246; Pres Sec 4-H; Rep Stu Cncl; Stat Wrstlng; 4-H Awd; High Hon Roll; NHS; Henry P Clark Schlrshp 86; NYS Rgnt Schlrshp 86; U Of CT; Animal Sci.

EDSON, JOSEPH; Maple Hill HS; Castleton, NY; (Y); 7/72; Debate Tm; Band; Jazz Band; School Musical; Ed Yrbk Phtg; Rptr Stu Cncl; Var Tennis; Elks Awd; High Hon Roll; NHS; Schodack Tchrs Assn Schlrshp 86; NYS Rgnts Schlrshp 86; SUNY Binghamton; Lib Arts.

EDWARDS JR, ARTHUR L; Regis HS; Brooklyn, NY; (Y); Latin Clb; Lit Mag; Off Frsh Cls; Off Soph Cls; Trs Jr Cls; Sec Stu Cncl; Capt Bowling; Trk; Admssn To Bishops Ldrshp Proj 85; Cert Of Merit Natl Frnch Cont 85; Englsh.

EDWARDS, CAROLINE; Our Lady Of Mercy HS; Rochester, NY; (Y); English Clb; Spanish Clb; Stage Crew; Yrbk Stf; Lit Mag; Tennis; High Hon Roll.

EDWARDS, CHARLAINA; Turner-Carroll HS; Buffalo, NY; (S); 5/116; Hosp Aide; Hon Roll; Hghst Afro-Asn Avg Awd & Amer Stds 83 & 86; Hnr Hghst Avg Nrsng Cls 85; 1st Hnrs 86; Trocaine Coll; Sci.

EDWARDS, CHRISTIAN; Walt Whitman HS; Huntington Statio, NY; (Y); 63/500; Boy Scts; German Clb; Im Wt Lftg; High Hon Roll; Jr NHS; Comp Engrng.

EDWARDS, DAVID J; Mc Quaid Jesuit HS; Rochester, NY; (Y); 13/172; Pres Camera Clb; Cmnty Wkr; Nwsp Phtg; Ed Yrbk Phtg; Yrbk Stf; Tennis; NHS; 1st Hnrs; Acad Awds; Coll Of Holy Cross; Hist.

EDWARDS, DAVID L; Silver Creek Central HS; Silver Creek, NY; (Y); 4/92; Sec Key Clb; Pres Spanish Clb; Pres Chorus; School Musical; Pres Sr Cls; Sec Stu Cncl; Var L Bsbl; Var L Crs Cntry; Sec NHS; Voice Dem Awd; Presdntl Schlrshp-KSU; Honors Schlrshp-KSU Honors Coll; NCTE Achvt Awds-Writng Wnnr 85; Kent ST U; Telecomm.

EDWARDS, DENISE; L A Webber HS; Lyndonville, NY; (Y); Church Yth Grp; Teachers Aide; Yrbk Stf; JV Cheerleading; Stat Trk; Jr NHS; Bus.

EDWARDS, DENNIS C; East Syracuse Minoa HS; Minoa, NY; (Y); 39/340; Am Leg Boys St; Variety Show; Var Ice Hcky; Var Capt Lcrss; Var Capt Socr; NHS; Pres Schlr; Exploring; Im Bsktbl; Im Vllybl; Army ROTC Schlrshp 86; Amrcn Lgn Schlrshp 86; Corneil U; Agri Engnrng.

EDWARDS, DOTTIE; Whitney Point HS; Lisle, NY; (Y); 14/124; JCL; Latin Clb; Ski Clb; Yrbk Ed-Chief; Hon Roll; NHS; Excllc In Soc Studies 10 Rgnts 84; SUNY Geneseo; Pre Med.

EDWARDS V, FRANKLIN G; West Islip HS; West Islip, NY; (Y); 100/525; Debate Tm; Band; Concert Band; Jazz Band; School Musical; Var L Socr; Hon Roll; Prfct Atten Awd; Computer Clb; Lib Arts.

EDWARDS, IAN ROY; Uniondale HS; Uniondale, NY; (Y); 102/400; Score Keeper; Socr; Hnr Roll 84-85; NY Tech Inst; Phys Thrpy.

EDWARDS, JENNIFER; Letchworth HS; Castile, NY; (Y); Am Leg Aux Girls St; FBLA; Yrbk Stf; Pres Frsh Cls; Pres Jr Cls; Pres Sr Cls; Var JV Cheerleading; Var JV Sftbl; Hon Roll; Prfct Atten Awd; Bus Adm.

EDWARDS, JENNIFER ANN; Grand Island HS; Gr Island, NY; (Y); 56/320; Cmnty Wkr; FNA; Hosp Aide; Red Cross Aide; Hon Roll; Pres Acad Fit Awd 86; Regents Scholar Nrsng 86; Niagara U Pres Scholar 86; Niagara U; Nrsng.

EDWARDS, JULIE C; Norwood Norfolk Central HS; Raymondville, NY; (Y); 42/133; French Clb; Yrbk Phtg; Yrbk Stf; Rep Stu Cncl; JV Capt Socr; JV Var Sftbl; Hon Roll; Regents Schlrshp 86; Accntng.

EDWARDS, KARYN; Irvington HS; Irvington, NY; (Y); 23/108; Pres Church Yth Grp; Key Clb; Nwsp Rptr; Yrbk Ed-Chief; Cheerleading; Fld Hcky; Socr; Kiwanis Awd; Ldrs Club Girls Vrsty Club Co-Fndr & Capt 85-86; Chldrns Vlg Tutors At Boys Shelter 84-86; St Lawrence U.

EDWARDS, KRISTIN M; Shenendehowa HS; Clifton Park, NY; (Y); 80/675; Am Leg Aux Girls St; Church Yth Grp; Pres GAA; ROTC; Ski Clb; Varsity Clb; VP Capt Crs Cntry; Var Socr; Var Trk; High Hon Roll; Empire ST Games 1st & 2nd Ski Orntng 85-86; Estrn HS Cross-Cntry Ski Champ 8th Pl 86; UNCAS Fmle 86; US Military Acad W Pt; Engrng.

EDWARDS, LAURA; Southampton HS; Southampton, NY; (Y); 21/110; Drama Clb; School Play; Nwsp Stf; Yrbk Stf; Score Keeper; Var Sftbl; Var Tennis; High Hon Roll; Hon Roll.

EDWARDS, MARLON; Mt Vernon HS; Mt Vernon, NY; (Y); Church Yth Grp; Socr; Trk; Hon Roll; Pres Schlr; All Cnty Socr Empire ST Games 86; Hnrb Mntn Trk 86; Acctg.

EDWARDS, MARY ANN JOAN; Frankfort-Schuyler HS; Frankfort, NY; (S); French Clb; FBLA; GAA; SADD; Chorus; Yrbk Stf; Var Fld Hcky; High Hon Roll; Hon Roll; NHS; Commrcl Airpln Pilot.

EDWARDS, MYREI; Brooklyn Technical HS; Brooklyn, NY; (Y); 500/1159; Library Aide; Chorus; Church Choir; Nwsp Phtg; Nwsp Rptr; Lit Mag; Rep Stu Cncl; Crs Cntry; Trk; NCTE Awd; NY ST Regents Scholar 86; Black Incentive Awd; Syracuse U.

EDWARDS, PAMELA; West Genesee SR HS; Syracuse, NY; (Y); Church Yth Grp; French Clb; Var Cheerleading; Im Lcrss; High Hon Roll; Hon Roll; School Play; Variety Show; Psych.

EDWARDS, POLLY; Mercy HS; Castleton, NY; (Y); Girl Scts; Church Choir; Yrbk Stf; High Hon Roll; Hon Roll; Jr NHS; Ntl Merit Schol.

EDWARDS, RICHARD; Elmira Free Acadamy; Elmira, NY; (Y); Boy Scts; Church Yth Grp; Latin Clb; Ski Clb; Spanish Clb; SADD; JV Var Socr; Hon Roll; NYS Rgnts Schlrshp 86; Slng Clb B Flt Chmpn Open Flt Chmpn 82-85; Ordr Of St Vncnt; Hobart Coll.

EDWARDS, SCOTT; John Jay Sr HS; Wappingers Fls, NY; (Y); FBLA; Ski Clb; Trs Soph Cls; Trs Jr Cls; Trs Sr Cls; High Hon Roll; NHS; FBLA Conf Hnrb Mntn Acctng II 86; Finance.

EDWARDS, SEAN; Southwestern Central Schl; Lakewood, NY; (Y); Pres French Clb; Ski Clb; Varsity Clb; Nwsp Ed-Chief; Nwsp Rptr; Nwsp Stf; Gym; Var Tennis; Hon Roll; NHS; Bus,Engl Awd 84-86; Boston Coll; Law.

EDWARDS, SHONNA; Sheepshead Bay HS; Brooklyn, NY; (Y); Dance Clb; Capt Cheerleading; Trk; Pilot.

EDWARDS, SUE; Saugerties HS; Woodstock, NY; (Y); 10/220; Library Aide; Ski Clb; Band; Concert Band; Orch; Yrbk Stf; Score Keeper; Trk; High Hon Roll; Cmptr Sci.

EDWARDS, VALERIE; New Rochelle HS; New Rochelle, NY; (Y); Cmnty Wkr; Achvmnt Awd Home Arfts 83; Voctnl Fund Awd Outstndg Bus Stu 86; $100 Schlrshp Awd Yng Womens Leag 86; Pace U; Compu Sci.

EDWARDSON, ERIC; Smithtown High School East; Saint James, NY; (Y); Church Yth Grp; Model UN; VP Frsh Cls; VP Soph Cls; VP Jr Cls; VP Sr Cls; Rep Stu Cncl; JV Var Socr; Var L Trk; High Hon Roll; YMCA Yth & Govt Conf 85-86; Pol Sci.

EFRON, LEAH; La Guardia H S For Music & The Arts; Brooklyn, NY; (S); Band; Concert Band; Jazz Band; Orch; School Musical; Symp Band; Cit Awd; NHS; Spanish NHS; Hon Roll; Arista 85-86; Music Hnr Soc 86; Capt Mth-Sci Acad Tm 86; Med.

EGAN, ANNE C; The Spence Schl; New York, NY; (Y); Rep GAA; Political Wkr; Nwsp Phtg; Nwsp Rptr; Var Fld Hcky; Var Socr; Hon Roll; St Schlr; Debate Tm; Drama Clb; Intrnshp-Senatr Moynihans Ofc 85-86; Barnard Coll; Invstmnt Bkg.

EGAN, CONSTANCE; Colonie Central HS; Albany, NY; (Y); Camera Clb; Cmnty Wkr; Hosp Aide; Library Aide; Ski Clb; Spanish Clb; Teachers Aide; School Play; Yrbk Phtg; JV Bowling; SUNY Plattsburgh; Psych.

EGAN, JILL; Orchard Park HS; Orchard Park, NY; (Y); Office Aide; Ski Clb; Church Choir; Rep Jr Cls; Score Keeper; Var JV Swmmng; Hon Roll; Engl.

EGAN, RAYMOND; Curtis HS; New York, NY; (Y); Nwsp Stf; Ftbl; Bus Mngmnt.

EGAN, ROBERT; Mercy HS; Center Moriches, NY; (Y); Math Clb; Ski Clb; Varsity Clb; Rep Jr Cls; Rep Stu Cncl; Var Bsbl; Rep Ftbl; Rep Wt Lftg; High Hon Roll; Hon Roll.

EGAN, TRACY; Catholic Central HS; Watervliet, NY; (Y); Cmnty Wkr; Math Clb; Pep Clb; SADD; Chorus; Variety Show; Lit Mag; Var Trk; Geneseo U; Elem Ed.

EGGERS, DREW; Ward Melville HS; Stony Brook, NY; (Y); Art Clb; Intnl Clb; Ski Clb; Spanish Clb; SADD; Chorus; Nwsp Phtg; Rep Frsh Cls; Rep Stu Cncl; Im Badmtn; Acdmc Art Awd 84; Stu Cncl Awd Art & Goals 84; U MA Amherst; Mngmnt.

EGGERT, NEIL; Jamesville-De Witt HS; Dewitt, NY; (Y); 44/235; Spanish Clb; Band; Concert Band; Jazz Band; Orch; School Musical; Variety Show; JV Capt Bsbl; High Hon Roll; Pepe Bnd Stu Cndctr 86-87; Srv Awd 84-85; All-Cnty Bnd 85-86; BUS Mgmnt.

EGLOFF, JENNIFER; John Jay SR HS; S Salem, NY; (Y); SADD; Variety Show; Nwsp Rptr; Yrbk Phtg; Var Capt Bsktbl; Trk; Hon Roll; Fshn Mdse.

EGNER, DIONNE; Villa Maria Acad; Buffalo, NY; (Y); Computer Clb; FBLA; Red Cross Aide; Sftbl; Swmmng; Canisius; Pre Law.

EHJEM, TONY; Whitesboro SR HS; Whitesboro, NY; (Y); Church Yth Grp; Ski Clb; Band; Concert Band; Jazz Band; Mrchg Band; Orch; Pep Band; JV Lcrss; JV Socr; Bus Admin.

EHLERS, CHRISTINA; Tully Central HS; Tully, NY; (Y); French Clb; Varsity Clb; Rep Sr Cls; Var Score Keeper; JV Var Socr; Var Sftbl; Var Trk; Var Vllybl; Bst Efrt Blgy 84-85; Bst Efrt Frnch 84-85; Bst Effrt Soc Stds 84-85; Engr.

EHRENSTEIN, CATHARINE; New Rochelle HS; New Rochelle, NY; (Y); Church Yth Grp; Math Tm; Church Choir; Mrchg Band; Pep Band; Symp Band; Im Sftbl; Hon Roll; NHS; Spanish NHS; Princeton; Mktng.

EHRLICH, JODIE; Schoharie Central HS; Schoharie, NY; (Y); DECA; Girl Scts; Varsity Clb; Chorus; JV Crs Cntry; JV Socr; Var Sftbl; JV Wt Lftg; Albany Bus Clg.

EIBS, SHANNON; Huntington HS; Huntington, NY; (Y); AFS; Church Yth Grp; Cmnty Wkr; Hosp Aide; Var Swmmng; Frgn Exchng Stu Peru 86.

EICHELE, JILL; Charles H Roth HS; Honeoye Falls, NY; (Y); Sec Pres GAA; Ed Yrbk Stf; Var Pres Stu Cncl; Var Socr; Var Capt Vllybl; High Hon Roll; Hon Roll; Jr NHS; NHS; Spanish NHS; MIP Soccer & Sftbll 84-86; Psychlgy.

EICHENLAUB, ROBERT D; East Syracuse Minoa Central HS; East Syracuse, NY; (Y); 30/333; Exploring; Var L Crs Cntry; Var Trk; Hon Roll; Jr NHS; NHS; Ntl Merit SF; Wildlf Bio.

EICHNER, STEWART E; Lawrence HS; Lawrence, NY; (Y); Cmnty Wkr; Key Clb; Spanish Clb; Im Bsktbl; Socr; High Hon Roll; Hon Roll; NHS; Rgnts Schlrshp 86; Johns Hopkins U; Law.

EICK, JULIE; Royalton Hartland Central HS; Middleport, NY; (Y); 6/140; Pres VP Church Yth Grp; Spanish Clb; Chorus; School Musical; Yrbk Stf; Rep Stu Cncl; High Hon Roll; NHS; Pres Schlr; Suny Geneseo.

EIDELMAN, MICHAEL E; Oceanside HS; Oceanside, NY; (Y); 32/530; Boy Scts; Cmnty Wkr; Hosp Aide; Key Clb; Model UN; Nwsp Bus Mgr; Hon Roll; Jr NHS; NHS; Best Spkng Awds-Model Congress 84-85; Cornell; Hlth Fld.

EIGNOR, AMY; Roxbury Central HS; Halcottsville, NY; (Y); Art Clb; Drama Clb; Pep Clb; Spanish Clb; Chorus; Drm Mjr(t); Capt Cheerleading; Socr; Sftbl; Hon Roll; Musci Awds Solo 85-86; Sci.

EILL, JULIE; Westhampton Beach HS; Remsenburg, NY; (Y); 5/212; Hosp Aide; SADD; Chorus; School Musical; Yrbk Stf; Stat Bsktbl; Fld Hcky; High Hon Roll; NHS; Val; Hampshire Coll.

EINHORN, NEIL; W C Mepham HS; N Bellmore, NY; (Y); Debate Tm; Math Tm; Band; Yrbk Stf; Stu Cncl; Var L Socr; Hon Roll; NHS; Math Clb; Temple Yth Grp.

EIPP, BILLY; Northville Central HS; Northville, NY; (Y); Computer Clb; French Clb; Ski Clb; SADD; Pres Varsity Clb; Band; Yrbk Sprt Ed; Pres Soph Cls; Bsbl; Capt Socr; 2nd Tm Tri-Valley Lg Soccr All Stars 86; Off Awd Soccr 86; Bus Exec.

EIPP, MARIANNE; Lafayette HS; Lafayette, NY; (Y); 21/96; GAA; Band; Orch; Pres Frsh Cls; Pres Soph Cls; Trs Jr Cls; Rep Stu Cncl; Cheerleading; High Hon Roll; Hon Roll; Hghst Avg Algebra 82; Ldrshp Gym 85; Buffalo ST Coll; Soc Wrkr.

EISCH, AMELIA J; Vestal SR HS; Vestal, NY; (Y); 14/437; Am Leg Aux Girls St; Pres SADD; VP Orch; School Play; Nwsp Sprt Ed; Pres Stu Cncl; Cheerleading; Var Capt Fld Hcky; Stat Vllybl; Trs NHS; Founding Stu Against Driving Drunk 84-86; Binghamton Yth Symp 81-86; Captain Hockey 84-86; Yale Coll; Prof.

EISELEN, KARL; Mc Quaid Jesuit HS; Rochester, NY; (Y); 11/168; AFS; Drama Clb; Pres French Clb; Model UN; School Play; Lit Mag; Var Tennis; Trk; High Hon Roll; Mc Quaid Mdl Outstndg Achvt 83; Natl Hon Soc 86; Vrsty Nordic Skiing 84-86; Darmouth Coll; Polit Sci.

EISENBERG, HAVA; East Syracuse-Minod HS; E Syracuse, NY; (Y); Drama Clb; Latin Clb; Science Clb; Spanish Clb; SADD; Temple Yth Grp; Stage Crew; Yrbk Stf; Lit Mag; Stat Gym; Soc Stds Merit Cert; Colgate U; Pre Med.

EISENBERG, OSMAN; Newfield Central HS; Newfield, NY; (Y); 18/48; Boy Scts; Band; Concert Band; Jazz Band; Mrchg Band; L Var Ftbl; Var Trk; L Var Wrstlng; Hon Roll; Hrry Jms Mem Awd; SUNY Alfrd; Frst Engnrng.

EISENHART, CHRISTINE; Sutherland HS; Pittsford, NY; (Y); Exploring; French Clb; JA; Im Bsktbl; Hon Roll; Pittsford Firemns Schlrshp 86; Gannon U; Crmnl Jstc.

EISENHAUER, JOHN; Immaculate Heart Central HS; Watertown, NY; (Y); 2/78; Am Leg Boys St; Boy Scts; Variety Show; Nwsp Sprt Ed; Pres Stu Cncl; JV Var Bsktbl; JV Var Ftbl; JV Var Lcrss; NHS; Hon Roll; Hoby Ldrshp Sem 84; Am Legion Outstndng Stu 86; US Military Acad; Elec 1 Comp.

EISINGER, SILVIA E; St Francis Preparatory Schl; Flushing, NY; (S); 69/744; Hosp Aide; Vllybl; Optimate Soc; Med.

EISNER, MOISHE; Torah Temimah HS; Brooklyn, NY; (Y); Art Clb; Aud/Vis; Chess Clb; Civic Clb; Computer Clb; Debate Tm; Math Tm; Science Clb; Nwsp Ed-Chief; Hon Roll; Comp Prgmmr.

EK, KIRSTEN L; Horseheads HS; Horseheads, NY; (S); 12/385; Spanish Clb; Varsity Clb; Concert Band; Mrchg Band; Nwsp Rptr; Stu Cncl; Co-Capt Gym; High Hon Roll; NHS; Ntl Merit SF; Span Awd Hghst Avg 83; USGF Clss III NY Gymnstcs Meet 1st Pl Blnc Beam & 2nd Pl All-Arnd 83; Lib Arts.

EKELAND, TOR B; Fairport HS; Fairport, NY; (Y); Aud/Vis; Drama Clb; Model UN; Radio Clb; Chorus; School Musical; School Play; Stage Crew; VP Jr Cls; Pres Sr Cls; Perinton Blck Hstry Essay Cont 3rd Pl 84; Minerva Deland Schl Essay Cont 2nd Pl 85; Film.

EKHOLM, JENNIFER L; Cortland SR HS; Cortland, NY; (Y); 40/194; Church Yth Grp; Church Choir; Rep Stu Cncl; Var L Trk; JV Vllybl; Hon Roll; NHS; Regents Scholar 86; U NY Albany; Acctng.

EKLUND, BOBBY; Stamford HS; Stamford, NY; (Y); Debate Tm; Ski Clb; SADD; Varsity Clb; Chorus; School Play; Stage Crew; Stu Cncl; Bsbl; Bsktbl; Cornell; Bio-Chemst.

EL SHAKRY, OMNIA; Somers HS; Somers, NY; (Y); Intnl Clb; SADD; Chorus; Lit Mag; French Hon Soc; High Hon Roll; NHS; Ntl Merit Ltr; Spanish NHS; Intl Rltns.

ELAM, TERESA; Lyndonville Central HS; Albion, NY; (Y); 19/81; AFS; Hosp Aide; Spanish Clb; Varsity Clb; Church Choir; Yrbk Stf; Stat Bsktbl; Score Keeper; JV Socr; Var Capt Sftbl; Ashland Coll; Sprts Med.

ELBAUM, LAURENCE B; Hackley Schl; Rye, NY; (Y); 51/89; Band; Jazz Band; Var Crs Cntry; Var Capt Golf; Im Ice Hcky; JV Capt Lcrss; NY Rgnts Schlrshp 85-86; Franklin & Marshall; Bus Admin.

ELDRED, MARK; Galway HS; Galway, NY; (Y); 5/180; SADD; Varsity Clb; Pres Band; Jazz Band; Mrchg Band; Pep Band; Var Bsbl; JV Var Bsktbl; Var Crs Cntry; Var Socr; Music Perf.

ELFLEIN, KAREN; Kenmore East SR HS; Tonawanda, NY; (Y); 44/330; GAA; Orch; Var Capt Tennis; Hon Roll; NHS; Smith Coll; Phd In Hist.

ELIA, SUSAN; Nardin Acad; N Tonawanda, NY; (S); Drama Clb; Spanish Clb; Speech Tm; Acpl Chr; School Musical; School Play; Lit Mag; Rep Stu Cncl; Ntl Engl Merit Awd 85.

ELIACIN, PATRICIA; John Dewey HS; Brooklyn, NY; (Y); Dance Clb; Hosp Aide; Teachers Aide; Orch; School Musical; Nwsp Rptr; Nrsng.

ELIACIN, PATRICK; Win Gate HS; Brooklyn, NY; (Y); 6/35; Vllybl; Engrng.

ELIAS, MELISSA; Utica Free Acad; Utica, NY; (Y); Church Yth Grp; DAR Awd; Hon Roll; Law.

ELIAS, PETE; Pine Bush HS; Pine Bush, NY; (Y); Office Aide; Stage Crew; Rep Frsh Cls; Var Socr; JV Trk; Hon Roll; Prfct Atten Awd; Hghst Aver Math 84-85; MIP, Ltr Sccr 85-86; Cvl Engr.

ELIAS, SUSAN; Mount Saint Mary Acad; Kenmore, NY; (Y); Church Yth Grp; Pep Clb; School Musical; Variety Show; Ed Nwsp Rptr; Var L Sftbl; High Hon Roll; NHS; Ntl Merit Ltr; NEDT Awd; MIP-VRSTY Sftbl 86; Pre-Law.

ELINSKAS, KATHLEEN A; Westhill SR HS; Syracuse, NY; (Y); 23/150; Art Clb; Key Clb; Library Aide; Ski Clb; Spanish Clb; Band; Chorus; School Musical; Symp Band; Nwsp Stf; NY ST Rgnts Schlrshp 86; U Of MO Columbia; Mag Publshr.

ELISAFIDIS, JOHN; Newtown HS; Elmhurst, NY; (Y); Teachers Aide; Band; Orch; Hon Roll; Advanced Placement Bio Test Grade 4 85-86; Med.

ELKIN, JENNIFER R; Sanford H Calhoun HS; Merrick, NY; (Y); 31/313; Aud/Vis; Drama Clb; Key Clb; SADD; Teachers Aide; Temple Yth Grp; Nwsp Ed-Chief; Var Mgr(s); Var Score Keeper; Hon Roll; Natl Merit Schlr 85; Rgnts Schlrshp 86; Brandeis U; Jewish Hstry Tchr.

ELKIN, LISA; Brighton HS; Rochester, NY; (Y); VP Temple Yth Grp; Rep Soph Cls; Rep Jr Cls; Trs Sr Cls; JV Cheerleading; Sst U Of Oswego; Psych.

ELLIOTT, ALTHEA; East Meadow HS; East Meadow, NY; (Y); FBLA; Intnl Clb; JV Sftbl; Var Trk; Hon Roll; Ntl Merit SF; Prfct Atten Awd; Prsdntl Physcl Ftns Awd 81-85; Actg.

ELLIOTT, ANTHONY; Mount Vernon HS; Mt Vernon, NY; (Y); Boy Scts; Key Clb; Varsity Clb; Ftbl; Hon Roll; Math Hon Awd 86; Good Sprtmnshp Awd 84; Fine Work In Art Awd 84; USAF Acad; Drafting.

ELLIOTT, CHRISTOPHER; Perry Central HS; Wyoming, NY; (Y); 2/100; Boy Scts; Pres VP Church Yth Grp; VP Jr Cls; Sec Sr Cls; Var Socr; Capt Var Wrstlng; Bausch & Lomb Sci Awd; Cit Awd; High Hon Roll; NHS; Top Score Natl Sci Olympiad Chem Test 86; Cert Of Achvt 2nd Pl Editorial-Gannett Rochester Nwspr 84; :Biochem.

ELLIOTT, JOHN WOLLNY; Huntington HS; Huntington, NY; (Y); Church Yth Grp; Cmnty Wkr; Key Clb; Band; Pres Chorus; Church Choir; Jazz Band; Stu Cncl; Var Swmmng; NHS.

ELLIOTT II, LEWIS; Lisbon Central HS; Lisbon, NY; (Y); 4/38; Debate Tm; French Clb; Trs Jr Cls; Trs Sr Cls; Capt Socr; Vllybl; High Hon Roll; Hon Roll; Ntl Merit SF; MVP Soccr 86; MIP Soccr 84; Clarkson; Elec Engrng.

ELLIOTT, MATTHEW; Mynderse Acad; Seneca Falls, NY; (S); 30/140; Boy Scts; Band; Concert Band; Jazz Band; Mrchg Band; Orch; Pep Band; School Musical; Yrbk Stf; Rep Frsh Cls; Boys ST 85.

ELLIOTT, RICHARD; Uniondale HS; Hempstead, NY; (Y); Rep Math Tm; Varsity Clb; Ed Yrbk Stf; Rep Stu Cncl; JV Socr; Gov Hon Prg Awd; High Hon Roll; High Hon Roll 85-86; Aeronautical Engrng.

ELLIOTT, RIVA; Turner/Carroll HS; Buffalo, NY; (Y); Girl Scts; Pep Clb; Chorus; Yrbk Stf; Score Keeper; Cert Of Atten 84-85; U Of Bflo; Pre-Med.

ELLIOTT, WILLIAM S; Massapequa HS; Massapequa Park, NY; (Y); 60/440; Chess Clb; Church Yth Grp; Cmnty Wkr; NHS; Ntl Merit Ltr; NYS Rgnts Schlrshp 86; SUNY At Stoneybrook; Engnrng.

ELLIS, DEBORAH; Kingston HS; Kingston, NY; (Y); 28/575; Key Clb; Ski Clb; Spanish Clb; SADD; Soph Cls; Jr Cls; Stu Cncl; JV Bsktbl; Var L Swmmng; High Hon Roll; Rgnts Schlrshp 86; Northeastern U; Math.

ELLIS JR, JAMES; Bishop Timon HS; Buffalo, NY; (Y); Bsbl; Ftbl; Wt Lftg; Cit Awd; Hon Roll; Ntl Merit Schol; Gannon U; Elec Engrng.

ELLIS, JONATHAN A; Holland Patent Central HS; Remsen, NY; (Y); Chess Clb; Church Yth Grp; Debate Tm; Chorus; School Musical; School Play; Var Crs Cntry; JV Wrstlng; Cit Awd; God Cntry Awd; Arch.

ELLIS, KIM; Berlin Central Schl; Stephentown, NY; (S); 1/91; Ski Clb; School Musical; School Play; JV Bsktbl; NHS; Ntl Merit Ltr; Pres Church Yth Grp; Chorus; Frgn Lang Dept Awd 85; U S Army Rsrve Natl Schlr/Ath Awd 84.

ELLIS, KIMBERLY; Glens Falls HS; Glens Falls, NY; (Y); 44/217; Pep Clb; Chorus; Yrbk Stf; Mgr(s); JV Powder Puff Ftbl; JV Vllybl; Stat Wrstlng; High Hon Roll; Hon Roll; Prfct Atten Awd; SUNY Cortland; Frnch.

ELLIS, LISA M; Plattsburgh HS; Plattsburgh, NY; (Y); 1/170; Drama Clb; Sec French Clb; Pres Band; Chorus; Mrchg Band; Pres Orch; Pep Band; Hon Roll; Pres NHS; Ntl Merit SF; Bio Sci.

ELLIS, PAUL; Hilton Central HS; Hilton, NY; (Y); Ski Clb; Spanish Clb; NHS; Ntl Merit Ltr; SUNY Buffalo; Engrng.

ELLIS, RAE; Wallkill SR HS; Wallkill, NY; (Y); Camera Clb; Computer Clb; Drama Clb; Library Aide; SADD; Nwsp Phtg; Yrbk Phtg; Yrbk Stf; High Hon Roll; Hon Roll; Wallkills Home Econ Awd-Cooking 84-86; Pre-Law.

ELLIS, SOFIA; Harry S Truman HS; Bronx, NY; (Y); 33/750; Art Clb; Debate Tm; Drama Clb; JA; Chorus; Church Choir; Color Guard; School Play; Yrbk Rptr; Yrbk Stf; Miss Am Coed ST Fnlst 85; Actg Schlrshp 85; Cert Of Achvt 86; Milwaukee Sch Engrg; Elec Engr.

ELLIS, STACEY; Greenwich Central HS; Greenwich, NY; (Y); Var Bsktbl; Trk; Hon Roll; Girl Scts; Yrbk Stf; JV Crs Cntry; Var Fld Hcky; Var Sftbl; Coll At Cazenovia; Nursing.

ELLIS, THOMAS G; Johnstown HS; Johnstown, NY; (Y); Band; Chorus; Jazz Band; Mrchg Band; School Musical; School Play; Variety Show; Rep Stu Cncl; Var Tennis; Best Actr 83-85; Sch Of Summr Thtr 85; SUNY Purchase; Theatr.

ELLISON, DOUGLAS A; Arlington SR HS; Poughkeepsie, NY; (Y); Chess Clb; Church Choir; Orch; School Musical; NY ST Rgnts Coll Schlrshp 86; Manhattan Music Schl Parnts Assoc Excllnc Awd/Music 85-86; Prof Musician.

ELLISON, JACQUELINE; Edison Tech HS; Rochester, NY; (Y); Church Choir; Hon Roll; Prfct Atten Awd; Cmptr Op.

ELLISON, TESSA; Stuyvesant HS; Brooklyn, NY; (Y); Aud/Vis; Boy Scts; Church Yth Grp; Cmnty Wkr; Dance Clb; Exploring; Hosp Aide; Latin Clb; Library Aide; Service Clb; German Ntl Hnr Soc Spcl Events Commtte 85-86; Engr Tech Bio Engl Awds; Long Island U; Med.

ELLISON, TRACY; Friendship Central HS; Friendship, NY; (S); 4/30; 4-H; Spanish Clb; Chorus; Drill Tm; Yrbk Stf; Sec Soph Cls; Sec Jr Cls; Cheerleading; Socr; Sftbl; Sectn 5 Cls D Champs Sftbl 85; Med Lab Tech.

ELLITHORPE, SARAH; Jamesville-Dewitt HS; Fayetteville, NY; (Y); Key Clb; Swmmng; Trk; Hon Roll.

ELLOR, CHRIS; Ticonderoga HS; Ticondderoga, NY; (Y); 17/91; Boy Scts; Church Yth Grp; Ski Clb; JV Ftbl; Regents Schlrshp 86; New England Coll; Engr.

ELLSWORTH, CRAIG; Oneida HS; Oneida, NY; (S); 3/200; CAP; Band; Capt Crs Cntry; L Trk; High Hon Roll; NHS; Ntl Merit Ltr; Rotary Awd; Rgnts Schlrshp 86; Vrsty Indr Trck 83-86; West Point USMA; Army.

ELLSWORTH, TONIA; Plattsburgh HS; Plattsburgh, NY; (Y); 10/175; Art Clb; French Clb; High Hon Roll; NHS; Soc Stud Awd 85-86; Brown U Bk Awd Englsh 86; Prsdntl Acdmc Ftns Awd 86; Union Coll; Psych.

ELMAN, ANDREW; Roy C Ketcham HS; Wappinger Falls, NY; (Y); Drama Clb; PAVAS; Thesps; School Musical; School Play; Stage Crew; Stu Cncl; Crs Cntry; Robert Leaden Memrl Schlrshp 86; Rgnts Schlrshp NYS 86-90; SUNY; Theatre.

ELNASSER, FARRIS M; Fredonia HS; Fredonia, NY; (Y); 19/198; Am Leg Boys St; Band; Nwsp Sprt Ed; Pres Frsh Cls; Pres Soph Cls; Pres Jr Cls; Pres Stu Cncl; Var Capt Bsbl; Capt L Socr; Capt L Vllybl; Engineering.

ELSWICK, RICHARD; Torrejon HS; APO, NY; (Y); Letterman Clb; VICA; Yrbk Phtg; Rep Jr Cls; Var Crs Cntry; Var Ftbl; Var Trk; Hon Roll; Jr NHS; NHS.

ELY, GREGORY; Alexandria Central Schl; Alexandria Bay, NY; (Y); Var Ice Hcky; NHS; Math.

ELY, SHANE M; Granville HS; Granville, NY; (Y); 51/134; Rgnts Schlrshp 86; Adirondack CC; Cmptr Sci.

EMAM, SUZANNE; Bronx HS Of Science; Bronx, NY; (Y); Cmnty Wkr; Intnl Clb; Office Aide; Service Clb; Teachers Aide; Rep Stu Cncl; Psycholgy.

EMANUEL, DOUGLAS J; Wantagh HS; Wantagh, NY; (Y); 6/300; Am Leg Boys St; Political Wkr; Band; Jazz Band; Nwsp Sprt Ed; Pres Frsh Cls; Trs Jr Cls; Ntl Merit SF; JV Capt Bsktbl; Hon Roll; Hugh Obrn Yth Fndtn ST Smnr Ambssdr 85; Hugh Obrn Assoc Liason 86-87.

EMANUEL, LAURA; Herricks HS; Williston Park, NY; (S); Pres DECA; Varsity Clb; Concert Band; Mrchg Band; Yrbk Stf; Rep Stu Cncl; Var Capt Bsktbl; Var Socr; Var Sftbl; NHS; Orgnzd Bowl-A-Thon For MDA 85; ST Cnfrnce For Gen Merch 1st Pl Awd 86; DECA & Data Analysis Mrk Res; Bus.

EMANUELE, DANIEL; Albion HS; Albion, NY; (S); Sec Latin Clb; Band; Concert Band; Drm Mjr(t); Jazz Band; Mrchg Band; Orch; Pep Band; Lit Mag; Co-Capt Bsbl; Most Musical Freshman 83; Most Musical Junior 85; Mcdonalds All-Amer Band 86; Pol Sci.

EMENS, CHERYL; West Seneca East HS; Cheektowaga, NY; (Y); #20 In Class; Church Yth Grp; VP German Clb; JA; Key Clb; Orch; Nwsp Stf; JV Socr; JC Awd; NHS; Ger Natl Hnr Soc 85; UNY Geneseo; Biol.

EMENS, SHELLY; Romulus Central HS; Romulus, NY; (Y); 1/34; Am Leg Aux Girls St; Pres Varsity Clb; Capt Color Guard; Yrbk Sprt Ed; VP Stu Cncl; Var Socr; Var Capt Sftbl; Bausch & Lomb Sci Awd; Pres NHS; Val; Grswld Awd 86; Acdmc Athlt Of Yr 86; Cornell U; Appld Ecnmcs.

EMENY, SUZANNE; Fabius-Pompey HS; Fabius, NY; (Y); Church Yth Grp; Pres Drama Clb; 4-H; Band; Concert Band; Yrbk Stf; Vllybl; NYSMA Solo Cmptn; Tompkins CC.

EMERICK, THERESA; N Tonawanda HS; N Tonawanda, NY; (Y); 14/398; Am Leg Aux Girls St; Cmnty Wkr; JA; Office Aide; Radio Clb; Spanish Clb; Varsity Clb; Band; Concert Band; Jazz Band; Youth Mnth 85; Acad Scholar 86; Niagara Gazette Jrnlsm Scholar 86; Niagara U; Cmmnctns.

EMERSON, CARRIE; Tonawanda JR SR HS; Tonawanda, NY; (Y); Drama Clb; French Clb; SADD; Band; Chorus; Concert Band; Jazz Band; School Musical; Stage Crew; Hon Roll; Jr All Amer Band Awd 86; Bio.

EMERSON, DAWN; Cuba Central Schl; Black Creek, NY; (Y); 1/52; Spanish Clb; Varsity Clb; Yrbk Stf; Sec Soph Cls; Trs Jr Cls; Sec Sr Cls; Socr; Vllybl; High Hon Roll; NHS; 1st Rnd Wnnr NY ST Engy Rsrch Comp 84-85; Outstndng Schlrs Awd 86; Highest Avg Schl Yr Plaque 83-84; Baldwin-Wallace Coll; Bus Adm.

EMERSON, DAWN; Tonawanda JR SR HS; Tonawanda, NY; (Y); 40/197; Sec Aud/Vis; Pres Church Yth Grp; Girl Scts; Spanish Clb; Band; Pres Chorus; Concert Band; Trs Jazz Band; School Musical; Stage Crew; Villa Maria; Erly Chldhd Educ.

EMERSON, JILL M; Geneva HS; Penn Yan, NY; (Y); 34/155; Latin Clb; Varsity Clb; Chorus; Yrbk Stf; Var L Socr; Var L Sftbl; Var L Vllybl; NHS; School Musical; Var L Bsktbl; GTA Tchrs Assn Schlrshp 86; Sftbl 1st Tm Sctn 5 All Stars & MVP Awd 86; ST U Of NY Plattsburgh; Bio.

EMERSON, LORI; Auburn HS; Auburn, NY; (Y); 29/490; Church Yth Grp; Drama Clb; Pres French Clb; Chorus; Yrbk Stf; Cheerleading; High Hon Roll; NHS; Pres Acad Ftnss Awd 86; Dept Hnr In Behvrl Sci 86; Regents Schlrshp 86; Hamilton Coll; Intl Bus.

EMERSON, MICHAEL; Penn Yan Acad; Penn Yan, NY; (Y); 26/200; Am Leg Boys St; Rep Frsh Cls; Rep Soph Cls; Rep Jr Cls; Var JV Bsbl; Var JV Bsktbl; Var JV Ftbl; High Hon Roll; Hon Roll; Prfct Atten Awd.

EMERSON, SHARON; Blind Brook HS; Rye Brook, NY; (Y); AFS; Art Clb; Cmnty Wkr; Ed Yrbk Stf; Schlrshp Art Life Studios 86; Spnsh Awd 85; Painting Awd 84; Visual Art.

EMERSON, TIMOTHY O; Churchville-Chili SR HS; Rochester, NY; (Y); Boy Scts; Exploring; Latin Clb; Math Tm; Ski Clb; Capt Ice Hcky; Im Socr; Im Swmmng; Wrstlng; Hon Roll; Bio.

EMERY, LYNETTE; Pioneer Central Schl; Delevan, NY; (Y); 5/261; Cmnty Wkr; Key Clb; Math Clb; School Musical; Nwsp Rptr; Lit Mag; Var Socr; High Hon Roll; NHS; Prfct Atten Awd; Hugh O Brian Yth Ldrshp Ambssdr 85; NY ST B-B Gun Champ Tm 84; Gentc Engrng.

EMIG, KELLI; Williamsville-South HS; Williamsville, NY; (Y); AFS; Cmnty Wkr; Math Tm; Ski Clb; Chorus; Rep Jr Cls; Stu Cncl; JV Vllybl; High Hon Roll; Hon Roll; James Madison U; Commnctns.

EMMANUELLIS, JOANNA; George Washington HS; New York, NY; (Y); Church Yth Grp; Dance Clb; FBLA; Office Aide; Teachers Aide; Swmmng; Hon Roll; Radford U; Pltcl Sci.

EMPIE, KRISTEN; Hendrick Hudson HS; Montrose, NY; (Y); 1/180; Ed Yrbk Stf; Ed Lit Mag; Trs Stu Cncl; Var Socr; Var Tennis; High Hon Roll; NHS; 1st Plc Non-Fctn Gannett Wstchstr Nwspaprs Yng Wrtrs Cntst 86; Nabisco Brnds Schlrshp 85; Cmmnctns.

EMPIE, LORENA; Frankfort-Schuyler HS; Frankfort, NY; (S); Math Tm; Spanish Clb; SADD; Chorus; Vllybl; High Hon Roll; NHS; Utica Coll; Nrs.

EMRICH, MEG; Spackenkill HS; Poughkeepsie, NY; (Y); Sec Church Yth Grp; Cmnty Wkr; Hosp Aide; Thesps; Trs Chorus; School Musical; School Play; Swing Chorus; Tennis; Prfct Atten Awd.

EMSING, COLLEEN; Bethlehem HS; Selkirk, NY; (Y); 45/304; Church Yth Grp; Cmnty Wkr; Girl Scts; Hosp Aide; Ski Clb; Stage Crew; Rep Stu Cncl; Var Cheerleading; Hon Roll; NHS; Albny Fncl Plnnrs Schlrshp 86; Pres Ftns Awd 86; Bthlhm Bus Wmns Schlrshp 86; Siena Coll; Bus.

ENDLICH, MELISSA; Midwood HS; Brooklyn, NY; (Y); 69/669; Office Aide; Chorus; Orch; Prfct Atten Awd.

ENDRESS, KAROL; Sherman Central Schl; Sherman, NY; (S); 6/29; Church Yth Grp; French Clb; Band; Variety Show; Yrbk Bus Mgr; Yrbk Stf; Sec Frsh Cls; Hon Roll; NHS; Nrs.

ENG, BRYAN; Bayside HS; Bayside, NY; (Y); 83/658; Office Aide; Variety Show; Yrbk Phtg; Yrbk Stf; Hon Roll; Jr NHS; NY St Rgnts Schlrshp 86; Hrbl Mntn-Sci Fair Of Amer Inst Of Sci & Tech Of Cty Of NY 81; SUNY; Acctng.

ENG, JOAN; Hicksville HS; Hicksville, NY; (Y); 62/550; Am Leg Aux Girls St; Church Yth Grp; Cmnty Wkr; Spanish Clb; Church Choir; Stu Cncl; High Hon Roll; NHS; 1st Pl Wrtng Essy On Schl Sprit 84; Lt Crl Kzma Memrl Schlrshp 86; Stoney Brook U; Engrng.

ENGEL, CHRIS; Jamestown HS; Jamestown, NY; (Y); 24/350; French Clb; Q&S; Spanish Clb; Nwsp Rptr; Nwsp Stf; Hon Roll; NHS; Outstndng Spnsh Stud 86; Ltn Spnsh Ortrcl Awds 83; Prsdntl Acad Awd 86; Lake Erie Coll; Spnsh.

ENGEL, JULIE; Jamesville-Dewitt HS; Fayetteville, NY; (Y); 22/250; Cmnty Wkr; Pres French Clb; SADD; Temple Yth Grp; Rep Stu Cncl; Capt Cheerleading; High Hon Roll; NHS; Key Clb; Hon Roll; Mony Schlstc Art Awds 85-86; Acdmc Art Awd 86; 1st Rnnr Up Miss Cherry Vly NYS Cmptn 86.

ENGEL, KRISTIN L; Riverhead HS; Riverhead, NY; (Y); 8/200; Church Yth Grp; Spanish Clb; Church Choir; Concert Band; Orch; Symp Band; Mgr(s); Score Keeper; Jr NHS; NHS; Regents ST Schlrshp; De Vry Inst Tech GA; Elect.

ENGEL, LAUREN; Clarktown North HS; New City, NY; (Y); Drama Clb; Hosp Aide; Spanish Clb; Temple Yth Grp; Band; Concert Band; Mrchg Band; Orch; Stage Crew; Symp Band; Bio Sci.

ENGEL, MARC; Irondequoit HS; Rochester, NY; (Y); 3/390; Exploring; Pres Temple Yth Grp; Nwsp Ed-Chief; Trs Jr Cls; VP Stu Cncl; Im Bsktbl; JV Socr; Cit Awd; High Hon Roll; Ntl Merit Ltr; Dartmouth Clb Book Awd 86; Med.

ENGEL, MICHAEL; Hahn American HS; Apo New York, NY; (Y); 7/75; Boy Scts; Cmnty Wkr; JA; Spanish Clb; Teachers Aide; Trs Jr Cls; Capt Var Crs Cntry; Var Socr; High Hon Roll; Jr NHS; FFA Pilot License 86; Eagle Scout 84; USAF Acad; Engr.

ENGEL, TED; Oakfield-Alabama HS; Oakfield, NY; (Y); Chorus; Yrbk Stf; Var Crs Cntry; Var Trk; High Hon Roll; Cmmnctns.

ENGELFRIED, DEBORA A; Pittsford HS; Pittsford, NY; (Y); Drama Clb; Math Clb; Ski Clb; Sec SADD; Chorus; Yrbk Ed-Chief; Var Capt Fld Hcky; Hon Roll; Math Tm; Spanish Clb; Schlrshp-Piano 1 Yr From Teacher 86; Awd-Superior Rating In Natl Piano Auditions 77-85; Penn ST U; Liberal Arts.

ENGELHARDT, BAMBI; Savgerties HS; Saugerties, NY; (Y); Drama Clb; Ski Clb; Spanish Clb; Var Bsktbl; Var Vllybl; Nwsp Stf; Rep Frsh Cls; Rep Soph Cls; Stat Ftbl; Trk; Military Air Frce; Bus.

ENGELHARDT, KRISTIN; Guilderland HS; Voorheesville, NY; (Y); Exploring; Crs Cntry; High Hon Roll; Hon Roll; NHS; NTID Rochester; Math.

ENGELS, YVONNE; Kaiserslautern American HS; APO, NY; (Y); VP French Clb; German Clb; Concert Band; Mrchg Band; Sec Soph Cls; JV Sftbl; JV Trk; Hon Roll; Jr NHS; NHS; Bus.

ENGLE, CATHERINE; Highland HS; Clintondale, NY; (Y); 18/124; 4-H; Varsity Clb; Band; Mrchg Band; Yrbk Stf; Var Trk; Hon Roll; NHS; Spanish NHS; Crnll Trdtn Fllwshp 86; Cornell U; Plnt Sci.

ENGLE, DAVID; Hannibal Cntrl HS; Hannibal, NY; (Y); French Clb; Band; Trs Chorus; Concert Band; Drm Mjr(t); Jazz Band; Mrchg Band; School Musical; School Play; Symp Band; Med.

ENGLE, DOUG; Waterville Central HS; Oriskany Falls, NY; (Y); Am Leg Boys St; Spanish Clb; Var Capt Bsbl; JV Var Bsktbl; Var Socr; Var Trk; Al-Star Tm Sccr 85-86; Hnrbl Mntn Sccr 84-85; Al-Star Tm Bsbl 85-86; MVCC; Police Sci.

ENGLE, MARK A; Honeoye Central HS; Honeoye, NY; (Y); Boy Scts; 4-H; Radio Clb; Ski Clb; Spanish Clb; Stu Cncl; JV Bsbl; Rgnts Schlrshp 86; CC Of Fngr Lakes; Polc Sci.

ENGLE, ROBIN; Albion Central HS; Albion, NY; (S); #11 In Class; Latin Clb; Chorus; School Play; Swing Chorus; Lit Mag; JV Var Cheerleading; Pres Jr NHS; Mgr NHS; Paralegal Asst.

ENGLER, BRIAN; Rocky Point JRSR HS; Rocky Point, NY; (S); 1/200; Mathletes; Voice Dem Awd; Mark Twain Lit Cont Hon Men Prose 84; Mark Twain Lit Cont 1st Pl Prose 85; Mst Outstndg Inst Gft & Tal.

ENGLERT, JOHN; Aquinas Inst; N Chili, NY; (Y); 3/145; Church Yth Grp; JA; Math Clb; Stage Crew; Prfct Atten Awd; Cornell U Hnr Fllw 86; NYS Rgnts Schlrshp 86; Cornell U; Hrtcltr.

ENGLERT, SCOTT G; Dansville SR HS; Dansville, NY; (Y); 28/115; Am Leg Boys St; Church Yth Grp; Var L Tennis; NHS; Astronomy.

ENGLESBERG, BARI SUE; Newfield HS; Coram, NY; (Y); 84/514; Q&S; Yrbk Stf; Var Capt Swmmng; High Hon Roll; Hon Roll; Jr NHS; Vrsty Swm Schlrshp 85-86; Mst Vlbl Swmmr 80-85; Florida ST U.

ENGLISH, CAMILLE A; Midwood HS; Brooklyn, NY; (Y); 248/589; Library Aide; Office Aide; Band; Chorus; Concert Band; Lit Mag; Prfct Atten Awd; Regents Schlrshp 86; Cmmndbl Art Wrk Martin Luther King Art Cont 86; Med Sci Inst 83-86; ST U-Oswego; Bio.

ENGMANN, SCOTT; Longwood HS; Coram, NY; (Y); 12/600; Mathletes; Math Tm; Var L Bsbl; High Hon Roll; NHS; Engrg.

ENGQUIST, LORIN; Midwood HS; Brooklyn, NY; (Y); 60/667; Math Tm; Var Capt Tennis; Hon Roll; Ntl Merit Ltr.

ENGRAM, CLINTON; Midwood HS; Brooklyn, NY; (Y); Chorus; Var Bsbl; JV Var Ftbl; Duke U.

ENKVIST, KRISTINE A; Pittsford Mendon HS; Pittsford, NY; (Y); Exploring; Ski Clb; Band; Yrbk Stf; Var L Swmmng; Hon Roll; NY St Regents Schlrshp 86; Temple U; Arch.

ENNIS, DAVID L; DansvilleSR HS; Dansville, NY; (Y); 15/147; Am Leg Boys St; Computer Clb; Yrbk Stf; Jr Cls; Stu Cncl; High Hon Roll; Hon Roll; Script D Schl Acadmc Lttr 84-85; Bar For Script D 85-86; Awd For DAR For Highest Grd On NY Soc Stud; Computer.

ENNIS, DAVID T; Bayside HS; New York, NY; (Y); 53/750; Art Clb; Aud/Vis; Teachers Aide; Nwsp Rptr; Nwsp Stf; Yrbk Stf; Lit Mag; Cit Awd; High Hon Roll; Hon Roll; Sci Fr Cmndtn 83; U Of Miami; Bus.

ENOS, JACQUELINE; Oriskany Central HS; Oriskany, NY; (Y); Capt GAA; Trs Key Clb; Spanish Clb; SADD; Varsity Clb; Band; Color Guard; Mrchg Band; Stage Crew; Nwsp Sprt Ed; Mohawk Vly CC; Human Svcs.

ENRIGHT, JEANETTE; Mount Mercy Acad; Buffalo, NY; (Y); VP SADD; Chorus; Capt Crs Cntry; Capt Trk; Hon Roll; Inter Msc Fest 84-86; Mst Vlbl Plyr Vrsty Crss Cntry 85-86; Spec Ed.

ENSERRO, ROBERT; Jamestown HS; Jamestown, NY; (Y); Am Leg Boys St; Church Yth Grp; Intnl Clb; Latin Clb; Pres Ski Clb; Spanish Clb; Chorus; Frsh Cls; Soph Cls; Pres Jr Cls; Prendergast Awd 86; Law.

ENSLOW, TRACY; Waterloo SR HS; Waterloo, NY; (Y); 7/154; Church Yth Grp; Drama Clb; Sec 4-H; FTA; Library Aide; Spanish Clb; Teachers Aide; School Play; High Hon Roll; NHS; Geneseo ST; Scndry Ed.

ENSMINGER, KAREN; Grand Island HS; Grand Island, NY; (Y); 26/325; Rptr 4-H; Hosp Aide; ROTC; Concert Band; Var Tennis; JV Trk; NHS; Regents Scholar; Clarkson U; Civil Engrng.

ENSSLIN, CHRISTINE; Hilton Central HS; Rochester, NY; (Y); Exploring; Girl Scts; Ski Clb; Trk; Pres Phy Ftnss Awd 86.

ENTERLEIN, DAWN; Fox Lane HS; Bedford Hills, NY; (Y); AFS; Pres Jr Cls; Var Capt Crs Cntry; Var Capt Swmmng; Var Capt Trk; Hon Roll; Lion Awd; Dllwd Awd 86; Athlt Of Yr 86; Amercn Assn Of U Wmn Awd 86; U Of NH.

ENTLER, CHERYL; John Dewey HS; Brooklyn, NY; (Y); Dance Clb; Rep Frsh Cls; Rep Soph Cls; Rep Jr Cls; Athltc Ldrs 84-85; St Johns U; Bus Cmnctns.

ENTRESS, SHARON; Gates-Chili HS; Rochester, NY; (Y); Service Clb; Spanish Clb; School Musical; Stage Crew; High Hon Roll; Pres Schlr; U Of Rochester; Bio.

ENZIEN, PETRA; Mechanicville HS; Mechanicville, NY; (S); French Clb; Math Tm; SADD; Nwsp Stf; Yrbk Stf; Rep Soph Cls; Rep Jr Cls; Rep Stu Cncl; High Hon Roll; Hon Roll; Med.

EPHRAIM, CAMILLE; Sewanhanka HS; Elmont, NY; (Y); Art Clb; Camera Clb; Church Yth Grp; Dance Clb; English Clb; GAA; Office Aide; SADD; VICA; Band; Stu Of Mnth Awds 85; Mst Imprvd Stu Awd 85; Hnr Soc; Nrsng.

EPPERSON, LLOYD; Hahn Americna HS; Apo New York, NY; (Y); 24/72; Exploring; French Clb; Library Aide; Speech Tm; School Play; Var L Cheerleading; Var L Ftbl; Var L Mgr(s); Var L Socr; Voice Dem Awd; Stu Of Qrtr 85-86; All Conf Regn Ftbl 85-86; Bst Def Lnmn 85-86; Fed.

EPPICH, GREGORY; St Marys Acad; Glens Falls, NY; (Y); 10/55; Boy Scts; Chess Clb; French Clb; Scholastic Bowl; Pres Ski Clb; Nwsp Bus Mgr; Yrbk Bus Mgr; Golden Gaueon Awd Otstndng Contri To Yrbk Pub 86; Adirondack Comm Coll; Bus Admin.

EPPIG, LORIANN; Bayport-Blue Point HS; Bayport, NY; (Y); 23/269; FBLA; Library Aide; Political Wkr; Science Clb; Church Choir; Color Guard; Flag Corp; Hon Roll; Jr NHS; NHS; Bus.

EPPS, KIMBERLY Y; Bronx HS Of Science; New York, NY; (Y); Ed Camera Clb; Library Aide; Science Clb; Speech Tm; Yrbk Phtg; Lit Mag; Ntl Merit SF; Natl Merit Semi Fnlst; Astrophysicist.

EPPS, MARJORIE; Franklin Central Schl; Oneonta, NY; (Y); Trs FHA; Trs Letterman Clb; SADD; Trs Varsity Clb; Trs Frsh Cls; Trs Soph Cls; VP Stu Cncl; Var L Cheerleading; Score Keeper; Socr; TTC Srty Pres 82-87; 150th Anvrsry Cmpstn Awd 85; Ftr Hmmkrs Of Amer Treas; Ltrmn Clb Treas; Vrsty Clb; Endicott Coll; Rstrnt Mgmt.

EPSTEIN, ALYSE K; Syosset HS; Jericho, NY; (Y); 28/492; Hosp Aide; NFL; Service Clb; Teachers Aide; Nwsp Stf; Sec Rep Stu Cncl; Capt Bsktbl; High Hon Roll; NHS; All Div Girls V Bsktbl II-1 84-85; Columbiana Awd Jrnlsm 82-83; Engl Svc Awd 83-84; Rgnts Schlrshp; Barnard Coll; Pre-Med.

EPSTEIN, CURTIS S; Midwood HS; Staten Island, NY; (Y); 260/556; Drama Clb; Office Aide; Service Clb; Ski Clb; School Musical; School Play; Rep Soph Cls; Rep Jr Cls; Rep Stu Cncl; Bsbl; Regents Schlrshp 86; Arch Hnr Soc 86; Stonybrook; Bio.

EPSTEIN, ELENA; La Guardia HS Of The Arts; New York, NY; (S); Hon Roll; NHS; Hnr Cert 95.71 Avg 84; Liberal Arts Coll; Arts.

EPSTEIN, MILES Z; Pleasantville HS; Pleasantville, NY; (Y); Model UN; Band; Concert Band; Mrchg Band; Pep Band; Nwsp Bus Mgr; Ed Nwsp Rptr; Ed Lit Mag; High Hon Roll; Hon Roll; Soc Studies Citznshp Awd 86; 1st Pl WERPGA Essay Cont 84; Nwspr Journ Awd 85.

ERB, GREGORY; Uniondale HS; Uniondale, NY; (Y); AFS; Debate Tm; Mathletes; Service Clb; Band; Concert Band; Mrchg Band; Orch; School Musical; Nwsp Rptr; Spec Awd 86; Writer.

ERBE, AARON; Avon JR SR HS; Avon, NY; (Y); 13/91; Computer Clb; Drama Clb; Band; Chorus; School Play; Nwsp Stf; Trs Stu Cncl; Socr; High Hon Roll; NHS; NYU; Soviet Studs.

ERBLAND, PHILIP; Mc Quaid Jesuit HS; Fairport, NY; (Y); 61/183; Camera Clb; Church Yth Grp; Cmnty Wkr; Ski Clb; Im Fld Hcky; JV Trk; High Hon Roll; Hon Roll; Prfct Atten Awd; FL Inst Of Tech; Marine Bio.

ERENFRYD, MICHELE; Port Richmond HS; Staten Island, NY; (Y); Dance Clb; Drama Clb; Math Tm; Temple Yth Grp; School Musical; Yrbk Stf; Off Sr Cls; Sec Stu Cncl; Cheerleading; Psych.

ERGIN, AYSEGUL; Greece Olympia HS; Rochester, NY; (Y); 54/287; Dance Clb; Debate Tm; Intnl Clb; Nwsp Rptr; Nwsp Stf; High Hon Roll; Hon Roll; Smmr Comp Camp Tchr Assist 83fyrbk Typing Edtr 85-86; Acdmc Achvt Awd Econ, German & Photo 82-83; Rochester Inst Tech; Comp Engr.

ERHARD, JAMES; St Marys Boys HS; Valley Stream, NY; (Y); 30/178; Boy Scts; Exploring; Color Guard; Socr; Trk; Wt Lftg; High Hon Roll; Hon Roll; Law.

ERIAN, NEIL; Liverpool HS; Liverpool, NY; (Y); 59/864; Am Leg Boys St; Nwsp Rptr; JV L Crs Cntry; JV Trk; High Hon Roll; Jr NHS; NHS; Crew 83-87; Ntl Champ Schlstc Rowng Assoc 86; Engrng.

ERICKSON, BRIAN; Long Island Lutheran HS; Plainview, NY; (S); 8/96; Mathletes; Chorus; School Musical; School Play; Nwsp Stf; Yrbk Stf; Sec Jr Cls; VP Stu Cncl; Var Crs Cntry; Capt Tennis; Aero Engr.

ERICKSON, COURTNEY A; Linton HS; Schenectady, NY; (S); 3/332; Cmnty Wkr; Drama Clb; Chorus; Concert Band; Rep Sr Cls; Rep Stu Cncl; Stat Bsktbl; High Hon Roll; Trs NHS; Spanish NHS; Area All St Chorus 85; Languages.

ERICKSON, SCOTT; Saint John The Baptist HS; Copiague, NY; (Y); Band; Concert Band; Mrchg Band; Pep Band; Stage Crew; Math Hnrs 84-86; Stony Brook U; Engrng.

ERICKSON, SUZANNE; Cairo-Durham HS; E Durham, NY; (Y); Band; Bsktbl; Pres Cheerleading; Socr; Sftbl; Twrlr; DAR Awd; 4-H Awd; High Hon Roll; Jr NHS; Buyng.

ERICSON, TIMOTHY; Binghamton HS; Binghamton, NY; (Y); AFS; Key Clb; Ski Clb; Varsity Clb; Var L Lcrss; High Hon Roll; Hon Roll.

ERKENBECK, MARIE; Valley Central HS; Walden, NY; (Y); 85/312; Church Yth Grp; Acpl Chr; Band; Mrchg Band; School Musical; Rep Soph Cls; Rep Jr Cls; Off Sr Cls; Rep Stu Cncl; NY ST Schl Music Assn Awds; Music.

ERLICH, LORI; Sheepshead Bay HS; Brooklyn, NY; (Y); 23/439; Office Aide; Band; School Musical; Arista & Archon 85-86; Acdmc All Amer Schlr 85-86; Hnr Schl 82-86; Brooklyn Coll; Acctng.

ERMER, JEFF; Depew HS; Lancaster, NY; (Y); Natural Sci.

ERMI, BRETT; Eden SR HS; Eden, NY; (Y); 12/168; Chorus; Stu Cncl; Var L Bsbl; Var L Bsktbl; Var Capt Ftbl; Im Trk; Im Vllybl; Im Wt Lftg; Hon Roll; NHS; Chem Engr.

ERNENWEIN, PAUL; Newburgh Free Acad; Newburgh, NY; (Y); Sec Debate Tm; VP Key Clb; Ski Clb; Chorus; Var Crs Cntry; Var Trk; Pre-Law.

ERNST, CARYN; Huntington HS; Huntington, NY; (Y); Sec VP AFS; Orch; Crs Cntry; Trk; Church Yth Grp; Key Clb; Socr; Hon Roll; Cross Cntry Medls Awds 84-85; Trk Medls Awds 84-85; Bus.

ERNST, DEBORAH; Sayville HS; Sayville, NY; (Y); 6/340; Trs Key Clb; Orch; Ed Nwsp Stf; Yrbk Sprt Ed; Capt Tennis; NHS; SADD; Chorus; JV Sftbl; JV Vllybl; Lincoln Ave PTA Schlr Athl Svc Awd; Stdnts Awd Schlrshp; All Conf Tennis Tm; Lehigh U; Bus Adm.

ERNST, JOSEPH; Maryvale SR HS; Cheektowaga, NY; (Y); Church Yth Grp; German Clb; Varsity Clb; Var L Crs Cntry; Mgr(s); Capt Var Swmmng; Var L Trk; Hon Roll; Canisius; Chem.

ERNSTHAUSEN, MARK; E J Wilson HS; Spencerport, NY; (Y); French Clb; Jazz Band; Symp Band; Var Swmmng; Var Tennis; Hon Roll; NHS; Educ.

ERRICHETTI, CHRIS; Washingtonville HS; Rock Tvn, NY; (Y); Church Yth Grp; School Musical; JV Bsbl; Var Golf; Hon Roll; Rgnts Schlrshp 86; Hrtwck Coll.

ERRICO, DEANNA MAE; Maple Grove HS; Bemus Point, NY; (Y); 8/76; Am Leg Aux Girls St; Church Yth Grp; L Var Bsktbl; Var L Trk; Var L Vllybl; Stat Wrstlng; NHS; Spanish Clb; Hon Roll; Jr NHS; Hugh Obrian Yth Fndtn Ldrshp Semnr 84; Jamestown CC Emphasis On Excel Pgm 85; Jr Ms Schlrshp Pgm 85; Buffalo U; Physcl Thrpy.

ERSING, RICHARD; Canisius HS; East Aurora, NY; (S); Aud/Vis; Church Yth Grp; Teachers Aide; Yrbk Ed-Chief; Yrbk Phtg; Hon Roll; NHS; Cmmnctns.

ERSKINE, JOHN; Westfield Central HS; Westfield, NY; (Y); Fine Arts Hnr Soc 86-87.

ERWAY, VICTOR M; Cherry Valley HS; Cherry Valley, NY; (Y); 5/27; Am Leg Boys St; Drama Clb; Pres Varsity Clb; Chorus; Yrbk Stf; VP Soph Cls; Pres Jr Cls; Pres Sr Cls; Var Bsbl; Var Bsktbl; Stu Of Mnth; Outstndng SR Ath Awd; MVP Sccr, Bsbl; Syracuse U; Bus Mgmt.

ERWIN, GAYLE; Edison Tech; Rochester, NY; (Y); Pres Girl Scts; Science Clb; Ski Clb; VP SADD; Varsity Clb; Sec Jr Cls; Var Swmmng; NHS; Exploring; Letterman Clb; City Writg Awd 86; Brd Locl Girl Sct & Grass Roots Schl Dist 85 & 86.

ESBIN, KEITH; James Madison HS; Brooklyn, NY; (Y); Boy Scts; Camera Clb; Temple Yth Grp; Thesps; Nwsp Ed-Chief; Nwsp Phtg; Nwsp Rptr; Nwsp Sprt Ed; Nwsp Stf; Yrbk Phtg; Egl Sct 85; FL Inst Of Tech; Avtn Mngmt.

ESCOBEDO, JUAN A; Christ The King Regional HS; Ozone Park, NY; (Y); 167/451; Boy Scts; Cmnty Wkr; Y-Teens; Stage Crew; Coach Actv; JV Var Fld Hcky; Ftbl; Mgr(s); Score Keeper; Hon Roll; Astronaut.

ESCOS, ANDREA; Aquinas Inst; Rochester, NY; (Y); Church Yth Grp; Cmnty Wkr; French Clb; Nwsp Rptr; Cheerleading; Socr; Swmmng; Trk; Hon Roll; Cert Of Achvt 84; Cornell U; Biopsychology.

ESCOTT, BRIAN; Port Jervis SR HS; Sparrow Bush, NY; (Y); Varsity Clb; Bsbl; Ftbl; Hon Roll; Engrng.

ESPERTO, PATTY; Hicksville SR HS; Hicksville, NY; (Y); Variety Show; Rep Soph Cls; Rep Jr Cls; Rep Stu Cncl; Var Capt Bsktbl; Var Gym; Var Socr; Var Trk; High Hon Roll; Hon Roll; 4th Pl Pnthln Mdl Nassau Cnty 86; Rcd 100m Hrdls & Lng Jmp 86; Hld Schl Rcd Pnthln; North Carolina U; Plce Ofcr.

ESPINOSA, LISA; Central Islip HS; Central Islip, NY; (Y); Stage Crew; Bus.

ESPINOZA, MILTON; Archbishop Molloy HS; Rego Pk, NY; (Y); Pep Clb; Spanish Clb; Yrbk Stf; Im Mgr Bsktbl; Im Mgr Ftbl; JV Var Socr.

ESPIRITU, MELLINA; Tottenville HS; Staten Island, NY; (Y); 8/871; Debate Tm; Yrbk Rptr; Yrbk Stf; Hon Roll; NHS; Brd Tsrstees Fl Tuitn Schlrshp Plytchnc U 86; Staten Isl Scl Stdies Fr 2nd Plc 85; Rgnts Schlrshp 86; Polytechnic U; Eltrcl Engr.

ESPOSITO, CAROL; Port Chester HS; Port Chester, NY; (Y); Ski Clb; Ed Yrbk Stf; Ed Lit Mag; Var Sftbl; High Hon Roll; Hon Roll; Jr NHS; Mu Alp Tht; NHS; Spanish NHS; Port Chester Sci Hnr Soc 86; Med.

ESPOSITO, JOE; John F Kennedy HS; Utica, NY; (Y); Ski Clb; Band; Jazz Band; Pep Band; Bowling; Nclr Engr.

ESPOSITO, JOHN; Berlin Central HS; Stephentown, NY; (Y); JV Var Bsbl; JV Capt Socr; Var Wrstlng; 2nd Pl Wrstlng Tr 84; 3d Pl Wrstlng Tr 85; 3rd Pl Duanesburg Wrstlng Tr 85; US Army; Cmptr Mech.

ESPOSITO, LORI; St Peters HS For Girls; Staten Island, NY; (Y); FNA; Math Tm; Rcrd Of Achvt Awd Of Merit 86; Med Secy.

ESPOSITO, MARK R; Shaker HS; Latham, NY; (Y); Art Clb; PAVAS; School Play; Stage Crew; Nwsp Stf; Yrbk Stf; Trs Sr Cls; Var Capt Gym; Hon Roll; NHS; All Am Gymnstc 85-86; Ful Tuitn Schlrshp 86; Art Schlrshp 86; Syracuse U; Ill.

ESPOSITO, MICHAEL; Monsignor Farrell HS; Staten Island, NY; (Y); Cmnty Wkr; Office Aide; Ski Clb; Spanish Clb; Im Bsktbl; Im Bowling; Im Ftbl; Im Sftbl; Hon Roll; Great Kills Babe Ruth Lg All-Str 85; Law.

ESPOSITO, NICOLE; Clarkstown HS North; New City, NY; (Y); Church Yth Grp; Pep Clb; Color Guard; Spec Olymp Awd 86; Piano Awd 85; Psych.

ESPOSITO, RICHARD; Onteora Central HS; Woodstock, NY; (Y); 7/201; Math Tm; Science Clb; Varsity Clb; School Play; Var Bsbl; Var Socr; Hon Roll; NHS; Cornell; Elctrcl Engr.

ESPOSITO, ROBERT; Bishop Ford Central Catholic HS; Brooklyn, NY; (S); 23/493; Church Yth Grp; Cmnty Wkr; Yrbk Stf.

ESPOSITO, SAMUELA; Northport HS; E Northport, NY; (Y); Cmnty Wkr; French Clb; Nwsp Stf; Hon Roll; Sons Itly Awd 86; Lang.

ESPOSITO JR, THOMAS P; Saratoga Springs HS; Saratoga Springs, NY; (Y); 57/534; Boy Scts; Church Yth Grp; Lit Mag; JV Wrstlng; High Hon Roll; Hon Roll; NHS; NYS Rgnsts Schlrshp 86; ROTC Army Schlrshp; Saratoga Spgs Jaycees Org 85; SUNY Geneseo; Mgt.

ESQUIVEL, MICHELLE; Clarkstown South HS; New City, NY; (Y); French Clb; Stage Crew; Nwsp Stf; Yrbk Stf; Lit Mag; Jr NHS; NHS; 2nd Hnrs Iona Lang Cont Frnch 85 & 86; Fshn Inst Of Tech; Fash Dsgn.

ESSOM, ROBERTA; Fayetteville-Manlius HS; Manlius, NY; (Y); 28/335; Exploring; Office Aide; Chorus; Orch; School Musical; Camp Fr Inc; High Hon Roll; Hon Roll; NHS; Bio.

ESTABROOK, NANCY; Greene Central HS; Oxford, NY; (Y); Chorus; Drm Mjr(t); Jazz Band; Var L Fld Hcky; Var L Sftbl; Var L Vllybl; Hon Roll; Prfct Atten Awd; 1st Tm Al-Star SUS W Div IV Vllybl 86; 2nd Tm Al-Star SUS W Div IV Fld Hcky 85-86; SUNY Brockport; Phy Ed.

ESTAY, ANDRES; White Plains HS; White Plains, NY; (Y); CAP; JA; Yrbk Phtg; JV Crs Cntry; JV Trk; Cert Of Merit 86; Syrause U; Sci.

ESTERLINE, MARK; Greece Athena HS; Rochester, NY; (Y); 60/282; DECA; Nwsp Phtg; Nwsp Rptr; Yrbk Phtg; Bsbl; Bsktbl; Hon Roll; Church Yth Grp; Socr; 2nd St DECA Conf RE 85; 1st St DECA Conf Mgt Decision Making 86; DECA Ofcr Bk Store Mgr 86; The Kings Coll; Econ RE.

ESTIGARRIBIA, DIANA; The Mary Louis Acad; S Ozone Park, NY; (Y); Aud/Vis; Spanish Clb; School Play; Hon Roll; Svc Rendrd Cert; Film.

ESTILO, ALVIN E; St Francis Prep Schl; Howard Beach, NY; (S); 159/744; JA; Band; Concert Band; Mrchg Band; Golf; Wrstlng; Hon Roll; Opt Clb Awd; Acad All Amer Awd 86; Med.

ESTIME, LUNIQUE; Nazareth Regional HS; Brooklyn, NY; (Y); Varsity Clb; Bsktbl; Ftbl; Hon Roll; Howard U; MED.

ESTIN, BETH; Sachem High School North; Lake Grove, NY; (Y); 105/1389; French Clb; Science Clb; Service Clb; SADD; Temple Yth Grp; Band; Concert Band; Mrchg Band; Orch; NHS; Pres Acad Achvt Awd 85-86; SUNY Binghamton; Chld Psych.

ESTROW, JOHN; Walter Panas HS; Peekskill, NY; (Y); Computer Clb; 4-H; FBLA; Ski Clb; Socr; Bus.

ESTUS, MICHELE; Stamford Central Schl; Harpersfield, NY; (Y); FBLA; Var Capt Socr; Var Sftbl; Hon Roll; Var Bsktbl; Albany Bus Coll; Bus.

ETERNO, SANDY; Utica Free Acad; Utica, NY; (Y); JA; Pep Clb; Nwsp Stf; Cheerleading; Pom Pon; Hon Roll; Hghst Avg 86; Hghst Avg Intro Cosm 86; Hghst Avg Engl II 86; Hrsmnshp.

ETKIN, MARNIE A; Clarence Center HS; Clarence Center, NY; (Y); 50/270; Pep Clb; School Play; Yrbk Stf; High Hon Roll; Hon Roll; Prfct Atten Awd; Rbbns For Particptn In Numerous Horse Shws 80-84; SUNY Geneseo; Spch Commnctns.

ETOLL, THOMAS M; Bishop Ludden HS; Syracuse, NY; (Y); Church Yth Grp; Cmnty Wkr; FBLA; Variety Show; Im Bsktbl; Var JV Socr; Im Tennis; Wt Lftg; Im Wrstlng; Hon Roll; Bus Mgmt.

ETTINGER, KATHERINE L; John S Burke Catholic HS; Monroe, NY; (Y); 1/152; Drama Clb; Chorus; School Musical; School Play; Variety Show; Rep Frsh Cls; NHS; NEDT Awd; Dance Clb; High Hon Roll; Hnrs Englsh Awd 85; Phy Ed Awd 83; NY U Kisch Schl; Dance.

ETTINGER, TALEE; Oakfield-Alabama HS; Oakfield, NY; (Y); Church Yth Grp; Drama Clb; Library Aide; Chorus; Church Choir; School Musical; Var Sftbl; JV Var Vllybl; Clnry Arts.

ETU, MICHAEL; Cardinal O Hara HS; Buffalo, NY; (Y); 29/150; Am Leg Boys St; Ski Clb; Nwsp Phtg; Nwsp Rptr; Yrbk Phtg; Yrbk Stf; Crs Cntry; Trk; High Hon Roll; Pre-Law.

EUDALY, CARRIE; HS For The Humanities Humanity; New York, NY; (Y); Cmnty Wkr; VP Political Wkr; Varsity Clb; SADD; Speech Tm; Stage Crew; OEA; Nwsp Stf; Rep Frsh Cls; Rep Soph Cls; Daily News Awd 86; Outstndng In Stu Govt 86; Spkrs Bureau Awd & Recog 86; Pre Law.

EUFEMIO, MARTHA; New Rochelle HS; New Rochelle, NY; (Y); Computer Clb; Yrbk Stf; JV Var Vllybl; High Hon Roll; NHS.

EUGENE, JUDE E; Polytechnic Prep Country Day Schl; Elmont, NY; (Y); Art Clb; Church Yth Grp; Cmnty Wkr; Computer Clb; French Clb; Office Aide; Bsktbl; Lcrss; Socr; Ntl Merit SF; NYU; Comp Sci.

EUGENE, MARJORIE; Dominican Commercial HS; Rosedale, NY; (Y); Science Clb; Chorus; Church Choir; Sienna Clb 84-85; Prncpls List 84-86; Nrsng.

EURE, JOSEPH D; Poly Prep CDS; Brooklyn, NY; (Y); Church Yth Grp; Intnl Clb; SADD; Varsity Clb; Stu Cncl; Bsktbl; Ftbl; Trk; Schl Svc Awd 86; Heisman Comm Hnree 86; All City Ftbl 86; U PA; Finance.

EUSUFZAI, SEHRA; Jamesville-De Witt HS; Dewitt, NY; (Y); 15/243; Cmnty Wkr; Debate Tm; Pres German Clb; Key Clb; SADD; Variety Show; Ed Lit Mag; High Hon Roll; NHS; Ntl Assctn Tchrs Of German-Comptn Fnlst 84; German Awd 85 & 86; Cmnty Shclr 86; Engrng.

EVANGELISTA, ANGELA; St John Villa Acad; Staten Island, NY; (Y); 9/100; JV Cheerleading; Hon Roll; Soc Studs Fair 2nd Pl; Achvt Awds Ital & Hist; Italn Clb; Law.

EVANS, ARTHUR; Monsignor Farrell HS; Staten Island, NY; (Y); 35/356; Letterman Clb; Varsity Clb; Im Mgr Bsktbl; JV Diving; JV Swmmng; JV Var Trk; High Hon Roll; NHS; Ntl Merit SF.

EVANS, CAMILLE LITITIA; Holy Trinity Diocesan HS; Uniondale, NY; (Y); Civic Clb; Hosp Aide; Math Clb; Science Clb; SADD; School Musical; School Play; Rep Stu Cncl; Var Trk; Hon Roll; Nassau Cnty Med Ctr Volunteer Awd 85; Slippery Rock U Bd Govnrs Scholar 86; Slippery Rock U PA; Biol.

EVANS, CAROL; Holland Central HS; Holland, NY; (Y); Teachers Aide; Rep Frsh Cls; Rep Jr Cls; Sftbl; Buffalo; Spec Educ.

EVANS, DELEON; Hutchinson Central Tech HS; Buffalo, NY; (Y); Rep Frsh Cls; Rep Soph Cls; Rep Jr Cls; Rep Stu Cncl; JV Bsktbl; Sec Ftbl; Var Mgr(s); Hon Roll; RLT; Micro Elec Engrng.

EVANS, ERIC; South Park HS; Buffalo, NY; (Y); Hon Roll; NHS; Church Yth Grp; Niagara U; Cmnctns.

EVANS, GARY; Sarah J Hale HS; Brooklyn, NY; (Y); Computer Clb; JA; Math Tm; Chorus; JV Capt Bsktbl; Trk; Wt Lftg; Hon Roll; NHS; Prfct Atten Awd; Latimerwoods Merit Award 83; Elec Engr.

EVANS, GEORGE; Bishop Timon HS; Buffalo, NY; (Y); 3/160; Sec SADD; VP Sr Cls; Jr NHS; NHS; Prfct Atten Awd; Pres Schlr; St Schlr; Boy Scts; Pep Clb; Chorus; Navy ROTC Schlrp 86; Cornell Frosh Tradtn Flwshp 86; U Dayton Pres Schlrp 86; Cornell U; Hotel Mgmt.

EVANS, HEATHER; Greene Central HS; Greene, NY; (Y); 5/110; Pres Church Yth Grp; French Clb; Ski Clb; Chorus; Color Guard; Mrchg Band; Yrbk Stf; Sec Jr Cls; JV Sftbl; Var Tennis; Sal Army Schlrshp, Pres Acdmc Ftns Awd, Prin Awd 86; Utica Coll Syracuse U; Oc Ther.

EVANS, JOAN M; Frankfort-Schuyler Central HS; Frankfort, NY; (Y); 22/95; FBLA; GAA; Girl Scts; Spanish Clb; Yrbk Stf; Bsktbl; Sftbl; Hon Roll; NHS; Stacy Weston Mem Awd Sftbl 86; Geneso ST U; Acctng.

EVANS, JOANNE; Argyle Central Schl; Argyle, NY; (Y); 8/58; Sec 4-H; French Clb; GAA; Math Tm; Rep Stu Cncl; JV Bsktbl; JV Sftbl; 4-H Awd; High Hon Roll; NHS; SUNY Cobleskill; Ag Bus.

EVANS, KELLY; Cardinal Ohara HS; Tonawanda, NY; (S); Drama Clb; French Clb; Rep Soph Cls; Rep Jr Cls; Rep Stu Cncl; Var Cheerleading; Score Keeper; High Hon Roll.

EVANS, LONNIE; Cardinal Hayes HS; Bronx, NY; (Y); 50/258; PAVAS; Band; Concert Band; Jazz Band; Mrchg Band; Orch; Pep Band; School Musical; Symp Band; Rep Frsh Cls; Ltr Bsbl 85; Band Svc Clb 86; Ntl Soc Childrens Awd 86; U FL; Law.

EVANS, MAURICE; Malverne HS; W Hempstead, NY; (Y); Art Clb; Bsktbl; Wt Lftg; High Hon Roll; Hon Roll.

EVANS, MEREDYDD; Jamesville-Dewitt HS; Fayetteville, NY; (Y); 16/245; French Clb; Model UN; Nwsp Ed-Chief; Nwsp Rptr; Nwsp Stf; High Hon Roll; NHS; Cmnty Wkr; Debate Tm; Quiz Bowl; Barnard Clg; Pltcl Sci.

EVANS III, ROBERT C; Hunter College HS; New York City, NY; (Y); Boy Scts; Computer Clb; Model UN; Stage Crew; Ntl Merit SF; Cert Distnctn Natl Socl Stds Olymp 85; Stanford; Engr.

EVANS, SABRINA; Midwood HS; Brooklyn, NY; (Y); Chorus; Cheerleading; Daily News Prncpls Pride For Outstndng Achvt Acdmc & Extrcurrclr Actvties 86; Ed Adm.

EVANS, STACY; Edison Tech; Rochester, NY; (Y); 160/270; Cmnty Wkr; Office Aide; SADD; Teachers Aide; Chorus; Variety Show; Varsity Clb; Rep Sr Cls; JV Vllybl; High Hon Roll; Fingerlakes CC; Theatre.

EVANS, TANYA; Eastchester HS; Eastchester, NY; (Y); Art Clb; Debate Tm; School Musical; School Play; Nwsp Stf; Drama Clb; Gym; Art.

EVANS, TRACY; Frontier Central HS; Hamburg, NY; (Y); French Clb; JA; Office Aide; Pep Clb; Off Frsh Cls; Off Jr Cls; Co-Capt Cheerleading; Sftbl; Hon Roll; NHS; Math.

EVANS, TRINA; Whitesboro HS; Whitesboro, NY; (Y); Church Yth Grp; Girl Scts; Hosp Aide; Spanish Clb; Temple Yth Grp; Chorus; Church Choir; Depickett Span Awd 83-84; Sem Awd Church 82-84; BYU; Pschlgy.

EVERETT, KORRIE; Smithtown West HS; Hauppauge, NY; (Y); Hosp Aide; Chorus; Capt Color Guard; Mrchg Band; Orch; Hon Roll; Outstndng Achvt Orch 86; NYSSMA Mdl 86; Wilkes College; Musc Ed.

EVERETT, LYNN MARIE; Chenango Forks HS; Binghamton, NY; (Y); 5/172; Church Yth Grp; Ski Clb; Cheerleading; Sftbl; High Hon Roll; Masonic Awd; NHS; Prfct Atten Awd; Pres Schlr; Rgnts Schlrshp Jssie Baker Schlrshp; Chrngo Frks Tchrs Assoc Schlrshp; Broome; Math.

EVERLING, SCOTT; Honeoye Falls-Lima HS; Honeoye Falls, NY; (S); 3/168; Math Clb; Ski Clb; Bsktbl; Capt Ftbl; Wt Lftg; High Hon Roll; NHS.

EVERNHAM, JEFFREY T; Williamsville North HS; East Amherst, NY; (Y); Am Leg Boys St; Pres VP Computer Clb; Ski Clb; Ed Yrbk Stf; Var L Vllybl; High Hon Roll; VP NHS; Ntl Merit SF; Prfct Atten Awd; Church Yth Grp; 1st Pl Natl Sci Olympiad In The Password Event $1000 Schlrshp 86; Engineering.

EVEROSKI, MIKE; Sachern North HS; Farmingville, NY; (Y); 43/1579; Jr NHS; Hnrs & Aclrtd Prgm 82-87; Pre-Med.

EVERSON, DIANNA REIDA; Tuxedo HS; Greenwood Lake, NY; (Y); 14/97; Am Leg Aux Girls St; Church Yth Grp; Drama Clb; Pres Spanish Clb; Yrbk Stf; Trs Soph Cls; Trs Sr Cls; Var Capt Cheerleading; Hon Roll; NHS; Cmmnty Schlrshp 86; Slvr Acad Awd 86; Grnwd Lk PTA Awd 86; SUNY-CORTLAND; Engl.

EVERSON, ERIC; Lakenheath HS; Apo New York, NY; (Y); Boy Scts; Computer Clb; Debate Tm; FCA; Letterman Clb; Ski Clb; Varsity Clb; Rep Jr Cls; Var Crs Cntry; Capt Var Socr; John Hitchcok Mem Awd 84; Pol Sci.

EVERSON, JOE; Henninger SR HS; Syracuse, NY; (Y); 25/370; Boys Clb Am; SADD; Bsktbl; Crs Cntry; Lcrss; High Hon Roll; Hon Roll; NHS; Elec Engr.

EVERTS, PAMELA; Hudson HS; Hudson, NY; (Y); AFS; Hosp Aide; SADD; Orch; Nwsp Ed-Chief; Nwsp Rptr; Var Bowling; NHS; Vrsty Bwlng Schlrshp 86; HTA Schlrshp 86; Syracuse U; Jrnlsm.

EVON, ALBERT; Guilderland Central HS; Altamont, NY; (Y); 23/366; Vllybl; U Of Notre Dame; Law.

EWALD, SHANE; Wilson Central HS; Ransomville, NY; (Y); High Hon Roll; Hon Roll; Art.

EWERT, HEATHER; Wayland Central Schl; Wayland, NY; (Y); 26/140; FBLA; Pep Clb; Yrbk Rptr; Mgr JV Socr; Var Mgr Trk; Close-Up 86; Amrcn Mgmt Assoc Oprtn Entrprs; Central FL CC; Lgl Sec.

EWING III, FLOYD T; Westbury HS; Westbury, NY; (Y); 23/250; Church Yth Grp; Cmnty Wkr; Varsity Clb; Acpl Chr; Var L Bsbl; Var JV Bsktbl; Var L Ftbl; Capt L Wrstlng; Hon Roll; Bus Admin.

EXCELL, CHARLES; Brockport HS; Hamlin, NY; (Y); Boy Scts; Church Yth Grp; Cmnty Wkr; Dance Clb; Drama Clb; Radio Clb; Var Ftbl; Var Swmmng; Var Wt Lftg; SUNY Brockport.

EXELBERT, MICHELLE; Half Hollow Hills East HS; Dix Hills, NY; (Y); 297/499; Y-Teens; Chorus; Phys Ftnss Tm; NY Inst Of Tech; Htl Mgmt.

EXELBERT, RENEE; Half Hollow Hills HS East; Dix Hills, NY; (Y); Cmnty Wkr; SADD; Chorus; School Musical; School Play; Swing Chorus; Sec Jr Cls; Sec Sr Cls; High Hon Roll; NHS; Prfsnl Med Intrnshp Prgm 86; Vogue Intl Mdlng Pageant 85; Med.

EXFORD, ALICIA A; Pine Valley Central HS; Conewango Vly, NY; (Y); Cmnty Wkr; Pres 4-H; Band; Chorus; Stage Crew; Rptr Nwsp Rptr; Yrbk Phtg; Yrbk Sprt Ed; Yrbk Stf; JV Score Keeper; Qualified Tap 86; SUNY; Art.

EXNER, KRISTINE; Cicero-North Syracuse HS; Clay, NY; (S); Church Yth Grp; Church Choir; Hon Roll; Chrstn Yth Ldrshp Awd 85; Bryant & Strttn Bus Schl; Sec.

EXTON, MARY JO; Palmyra-Macedon HS; Palmyra, NY; (Y); 44/174; Drama Clb; 4-H; Chorus; School Musical; School Play; 4-H Awd; Mnr Cncl Hrs Show Brl Rcng Rsrv Chmpn 85.

EYCHNER, KYLE; Vernon-Verona-Sherrill Central HS; Rome, NY; (Y); Var High Hon Roll; Var Hon Roll; Navy; Helcptr Pilot.

EYER, MARK E; Liverpool HS; N Syracuse, NY; (Y); 212/848; Pres Church Yth Grp; VP JA; Ski Clb; Nwsp Ed-Chief; Stu Cncl; Var L Bsbl; Im Bsktbl; Rgnts Schlrshp 86; Vrsty Ltr Bsbl 85 & 86; George Washington U; Cmnctns.

EYTH, VICKI; Port Jervis HS; Port Jervis, NY; (Y); Spanish Clb; Varsity Clb; Trs Frsh Cls; Trs Soph Cls; Trs Sr Cls; Stu Cncl; JV Var Socr; Var JV Sftbl; High Hon Roll; Hon Roll; Mst Imprvd & Dedctd Athltc Sftbl 84; NY ST Cls B Vrsty Sftbl Chmps 85; Bus.

EZARD, LISA; Wilson SR HS; Spencerport, NY; (Y); Varsity Clb; Band; Mrchg Band; Symp Band; Cheerleading; Trk; Buffalo ST; Intr Dcrtng.

EZER, GAYE; Oyster Bay HS; Oyster Bay, NY; (Y); French Clb; Sec Model UN; Spanish Clb; Chorus; School Musical; Stage Crew; Yrbk Stf; Rep Stu Cncl; Mgr Crs Cntry; High Hon Roll; Selctd Study Prog Adelphi U 86; Doc.

EZZO, LYNN; G Ray Bodley HS; Fulton, NY; (Y); JV Var Cheerleading; Var Gym; High Hon Roll; Acadmc Achvt Awd In Soc Studies 85-86; Herkimer CC; Paralegal.

FABER, BETH; Hauppauge HS; Hauppauge, NY; (Y); Hosp Aide; Model UN; SADD; Stage Crew; Rep Soph Cls; Off Jr Cls; High Hon Roll; Hon Roll; NHS; Ntl Merit Ltr; Engrg.

FABER, ROSALIE; Schoharie Central Schl; Schoharie, NY; (Y); Key Clb; Hosp Aide; Spanish Clb; Teachers Aide; Chorus; School Musical; Yrbk Ed-Chief; Stat Bsktbl; Outstndng Stu-WSCM Radio Stat Spnsr 85-86; Coll Of St Rose; Scndry Math.

FABIANO, DENISE; Saugerties HS; Saugerties, NY; (S); 21/252; French Clb; Hosp Aide; Band; Yrbk Stf; Cheerleading; Elks Awd; High Hon Roll; Sec NHS; Voice Dem Awd; Teenager Of Yr 82-83; Poem Pblshd Amer Poetry Anthlgy 85; Eng.

FABRIZIO, GINA; Geneva HS; Geneva, NY; (S); 9/175; Spanish Clb; Band; Concert Band; Mrchg Band; Rep Frsh Cls; Sec Soph Cls; Sec Jr Cls; JV Bsktbl; Var Cheerleading; JV Socr; Mst Outstndng Spnsh II 83-84; Mst Outstndng Spnsh III 84-85; Math.

FABRIZIO, PAULA; Bay Shore HS; Bayshore, NY; (Y); Art Clb; Church Yth Grp; Dance Clb; Drama Clb; Girl Scts; Intnl Clb; Nwsp Rptr; Hrtcltr.

FABRYKANT, ADRIANA J; Hillcrest HS; Kew Gardens, NY; (Y); 150/801; Dance Clb; VICA; Sec Y-Teens; Variety Show; Cit Awd; French Hon Soc; Lit Mag; Stat Badmtn; Wt Lftg; Hon Roll; Hnr Roll 85-86; Rgnts Endrsmnt On Dplma 86; Awd Frm Amer Assoc Of Tchers 86; Oneonta ST; Acctng.

FACEY, DONNAH; Evander Childs HS; New York, NY; (S); #1 In Class; Debate Tm; Girl Scts; Hosp Aide; Lit Mag; Stu Cncl; Hon Roll; Ntl Merit Schol; Prfct Atten Awd; Pride Of The Yankees Awd 84; Rensselaer Medal Excell Math & Sci 84.

FACEY, PAUL; St Francis Preparatory Schl; Ny, NY; (Y); 210/720; Spanish Clb; Band; Concert Band; Pep Band; School Musical; Law.

FACKLAM, PAUL; Grand Island HS; Grand Isl, NY; (Y); Crs Cntry; Bus Mgmt.

FACTOR, CRAIG H; George W Hewlett HS; Woodmere, NY; (Y); 13/260; Quiz Bowl; Science Clb; SADD; Nwsp Stf; Yrbk Phtg; Lit Mag; VP Frsh Cls; JV Socr; NHS; Ntl Merit SF; Brown U.

FADER, PATRICIA; Valley Stream No HS; N Valley Stream, NY; (Y); Jrnlsm.

FAERY, LISA; Wilson Central HS; Ransomville, NY; (Y); FBLA; Political Wkr; Ski Clb; School Play; Yrbk Stf; VP Frsh Cls; Sec Sr Cls; Stu Cncl; High Hon Roll; Hon Roll; Gregg Typng Awd 86; Movng-Up Day 84; Fsh Inst FL; Fshn Mrchndsng.

FAERY, NICOLE; Wilson Central HS; Ransomville, NY; (Y); Sec 4-H; Ski Clb; SADD; Teachers Aide; Chorus; School Musical; School Play; Swing Chorus; Variety Show; Yrbk Ed-Chief; Fash Merch.

FAERY, SHANNON; Wilson Central HS; Ransomville, NY; (Y); FBLA; School Play; Variety Show; Yrbk Stf; Trs Frsh Cls; Trs Soph Cls; Stu Cncl; Cheerleading; Powder Puff Ftbl; Hon Roll.

FAGAN, ARLENE; Miller Place HS; Miller Place, NY; (Y); Art Clb; Camera Clb; Church Yth Grp; FBLA; Stat Bsktbl; Var JV Cheerleading; Score Keeper; Socr; JV Sftbl; Wt Lftg; Art.

FAGAN, LISA; Midwood HS; Brooklyn, NY; (Y); Church Yth Grp; Band; Church Choir; Concert Band; Hon Roll.

FAGAN, STACEY; Valley Central HS; Montgomery, NY; (Y); Church Yth Grp; Cmnty Wkr; 4-H; FFA; Office Aide; Service Clb; Teachers Aide; Chorus; Hon Roll; Mount Saint Mary Coll; Elem Ed.

FAGAN, THERESA; St Barnalas HS; Yonkers, NY; (S); 16/188; Cmnty Wkr; Intnl Clb; Library Aide; Math Tm; Office Aide; Teachers Aide; VP Stu Cncl; French Hon Soc; Hon Roll; NHS; Bus.

FAGELLO JR, WILLIAM; La Salle Acad; New York, NY; (Y); Var Bsktbl; Im Sftbl; NHS; Buffalo U; Psychology.

FAGEN, DOUG; Smithtown HS East; Nesconset, NY; (Y); SADD; Nwsp Stf; Var Tennis; High Hon Roll; NHS; Spanish NHS.

FAGEN, JEFFREY; Half Hollow Hills West HS; Dix Hills, NY; (Y); Debate Tm; Quiz Bowl; Trs Radio Clb; Scholastic Bowl; Nwsp Ed-Chief; Yrbk Sprt Ed; VP Stu Cncl; Var Capt Swmmng; NHS; Key Clb; Dartmouth Bk Awd 86; 1st Pl H S Natl Sci Olymp Biol 86.

FAGLEY, JOANNE; Cardinal O Hara HS; Kenmore, NY; (Y); Church Yth Grp; Cmnty Wkr; Hosp Aide; Yrbk Stf; Rep Jr Cls; Rep Stu Cncl; Hon Roll.

FAGNAN, ELIZABETH; South Park HS; Buffalo, NY; (Y); Church Yth Grp; Band; Church Choir; Concert Band; Mrchg Band; Orch; Merit Rll Awd 85-86; Music Achvmnts Awd 85; Cert Apprctn 82.

FAGNAN, KAREN; Cardinal Mooney HS; Rochester, NY; (Y); 12/330; Church Yth Grp; Library Aide; Ski Clb; Stage Crew; Capt Cheerleading; Hon Roll; NHS; Spanish NHS; Engrng.

FAHERTY, MICHAEL T; Desales HS; Shorsville, NY; (Y); Am Leg Boys St; Drama Clb; Pres Chorus; Mrchg Band; School Musical; Mgr Stage Crew; Ed Nwsp Stf; Gold D Awd Desales Ctznshp Awd; Exlnc Mech Drawng & Phys Sci; Arch Engr.

FAHEY, JONATHAN T; Half Hollow Hills High School East; Melville, NY; (Y); 91/500; Church Yth Grp; Chorus; Var Gym; Var Trk; High Hon Roll; 2nd Pl-Ronald Wrase Arch Dsgn Comp 85; NYS Rgnts Schlrshp 86; Ambassador Coll; Frnch.

FAHY, THOMAS M; North Rockland HS; Thiells, NY; (Y); 10/600; Am Leg Boys St; Debate Tm; Math Tm; Speech Tm; Nwsp Rptr; Lit Mag; Var Capt Socr; High Hon Roll; NHS; Ntl Merit Ltr; Math Assn Of Amer Hghst Scoring Soph; Rep Rockland Cnty NY St Math League Tourn; All Sctn Sccr Plyr.

FAILEY, LYNN E; Auburn HS; Auburn, NY; (Y); Camera Clb; Ski Clb; Color Guard; Var Capt Fld Hcky; Regents Scholar Awd 86; Cazenovia Coll; Fash Merch.

FAILLA, CHRISTOPHER; Centereach HS; Centereach, NY; (Y); Varsity Clb; Var Bsbl; Var Ftbl; Boys Ldrs Corps 86-87; Presdntl Physcl Ftns Awd; Actng.

FAILLA, FRANCES; F D Roosevelt HS; Brooklyn, NY; (Y); Camera Clb; Ed Lit Mag; Hon Roll; Prfct Atten Awd; Club Arkon 85-86; Club Atista 86-87; Brooklyn Coll; Elem Educ.

FAILLA, FRANCES; Preston HS; Bronx, NY; (Y); 2/89; Church Yth Grp; Drama Clb; Church Choir; Symp Band; Nwsp Ed-Chief; Sftbl; Vllybl; Hon Roll; NHS; Sal; Regents Schlrshp 86; Govrnrs Committee Schlrshp 86; NY U; Bio.

FAINA, LORAINE; Mynderse Acad; Seneca Falls, NY; (Y); Pres GAA; Band; Color Guard; Jazz Band; Off Stu Cncl; Crs Cntry; Socr; Sftbl; Hon Roll; NY U-Outstdng Perf, Natl Assn Of Jazz Eductrs-Outstdng Mscnshp & Union-Endicott Jazz Festvl Drums; SUNY; Comm.

FAIOLA, MARIA; Romulus Central Schl; Romulus, NY; (Y); Pres Ski Clb; Varsity Clb; Cheerleading; Golf; Gym; Socr; Capt Sftbl; Teachers Aide; Band; Color Guard; Ntl Phy Ed Awd 83-84; Coachs Awd Sftbl 86; Hmcmng Crt 85-86; ROTC.

FAIRBANKS, JOHN DANIEL; Union Springs Acad; Jamestown, NY; (Y); Drama Clb; Ski Clb; Concert Band; Yrbk Ed-Chief; Vllybl; High Hon Roll; NHS; Presdntl Acad Fitness Awd 86; Andrews U; Pre-Med.

FAIRCLOTH, SUZANNE; Eden SR HS; Eden, NY; (Y); AFS; Church Yth Grp; Computer Clb; FHA; GAA; SADD; Band; Concert Band; Pep Band; Symp Band; Phys Ed.

FAIRLIE, KRISTI; Noth Dome Academy HS; Staten Island, NY; (Y); Church Yth Grp; Var Swmmng; Engl.

FAIRWEATHER, JULIAN; Clara Barton HS; Brooklyn, NY; (Y); Church Yth Grp; GAA; Varsity Clb; Band; Drm Mjr(t); School Play; Var Bsktbl; Var Bowling; Var Sftbl; Hon Roll; Pre-Med.

FAIZARANO, LISA; Pine Bush HS; Bloomingburg, NY; (Y); French Clb; Girl Scts; Band; Chorus; Stage Crew; Yrbk Stf; Var Swmmng; Silver Awd,Ldrshp Scouting 84; Berklee Coll; Audio Engr.

FALANGA, JEANNE; Batavia HS; Batavia, NY; (Y); 30/200; Sec Church Yth Grp; Drama Clb; SADD; Yrbk Stf; JV Tennis; Hon Roll; Spnsh Awd 86; Prft Atten 83-84; Spcl Ed Tchr.

FALBO, CHRISTINA; Greece Athena HS; Rochester, NY; (S); 16/300; DECA; FBLA; Intnl Clb; JV Sftbl; 1st Pl, 4th Pl NYS FBLA Conf-Prlmntry Prcdrs 85 & 84; 4th Pl NYS DECA Conf-Dcsn Mkg 86.

FALCO, PATRICK; Christ The King HS; Howard Beach, NY; (Y); Boy Scts; Church Yth Grp; Chorus; Yrbk Stf; Bsbl; Bsktbl.

FALIS, NEIL D; Clarkstown HS North; New City, NY; (Y); French Clb; Math Tm; SADD; Band; Nwsp Rptr; Var Capt Crs Cntry; Var Capt Trk; High Hon Roll; Mu Alp Tht; NHS; PTA Schlrshp 86; NY Rgnts Schlrshp; Duke U.

FALKOFF, ADAM S; Bayside HS; Beechhurst, NY; (Y); 24/658; Math Tm; Capt Scholastic Bowl; Orch; Nwsp Rptr; Yrbk Ed-Chief; Rep Frsh Cls; Var Golf; Gov Hon Prg Awd; High Hon Roll; NCTE Awd; BSC Cttn Hnr Music 83; Gld Mdlst NYCAO Comp 85-86; Gov Comm Schlstc Achvmnt 85; Duke U; Pre-Law.

FALKOWSKI, AGATHA; Ichabod Crane HS; Valatie, NY; (Y); 35/170; Ed Yrbk Stf; High Hon Roll; Hon Roll; NHS; Prfct Atten Awd; Effrt & Achvt-Bus 84-86; Effrt & Achvt-Math 85; Schlrshp-Lbany Bus Coll 86; Schlrshp-IC HS Tchrs Assn; Albany Bus Coll; Acctng.

FALLACE, LOURDES; The Franciscan Acad; Liverpool, NY; (S); 1/26; Exploring; Speech Tm; Yrbk Stf; Pres Frsh Cls; Pres Soph Cls; Pres Jr Cls; Im Swmmng; Hon Roll; NHS; USAF Acad; Aero Engrng.

FALLETTI, CHRISTINA; Sacred Heart Acad; West Hempstead, NY; (Y); Drama Clb; Math Clb; Service Clb; School Musical; Hon Roll; NHS.

FALLON, CHRISTINA; Fairport HS; Fairport, NY; (Y); Drama Clb; Intnl Clb; Stage Crew; Yrbk Phtg; Yrbk Stf; Lit Mag; Ntl Merit Ltr; Smifnlst Tllurde Assn Smmr Prgrm 86; Eugene Lang Coll.

FALLON, CLAIRE; John A Coleman HS; Kingston, NY; (Y); Hosp Aide; VP JA; Key Clb; Ski Clb; School Play; Bsktbl; Coleman Vsts Agng CVA 85-86; Awd B Avrg Rlgn 83-84; Fshn Rtl.

FALSETTA, MICHAEL; East Meadow HS; East Meadow, NY; (S); Off Computer Clb; Mathletes; Math Tm; Trs Science Clb; Nwsp Stf; Ed Lit Mag; High Hon Roll; Jr NHS; Frnch Awd 84; MIT; Engrng.

FALTYN, LAURA; South Park HS; Buffalo, NY; (Y); French Clb; German Clb; Chorus; Hon Roll.

FALVEY, BRENDAN; Hampton Bays HS; Hampton Bays, NY; (Y); Pres Computer Clb; Quiz Bowl; Varsity Clb; Trs Soph Cls; Var L Crs Cntry; Var L Trk; Hon Roll; NHS; Engr.

FALVEY, SCOTT P; Penn Yan Acad; Penn Yan, NY; (Y); 1/190; Am Leg Boys St; Boy Scts; Scholastic Bowl; Band; Concert Band; Mrchg Band; Var Golf; Var Tennis; High Hon Roll; NHS; Cert Of Merit-Frnch I & II; Sci.

FALVO, DAVIA; Linton HS; Schenectady, NY; (Y); Spanish Clb; Mgr(s); Tennis; Timer; Trk; Ntl Merit Ltr; Spanish NHS; SUNY-ALBANY; Human Sci.

FALVO, DAWN; Proctor HS; Utica, NY; (Y); Drama Clb; GAA; Chorus; Drm & Bgl; School Play; Yrbk Stf; Trs Soph Cls; Trs Jr Cls; Stu Cncl; JV Vllybl; Prfct Attndnc 84-85.

FAMA, ANTHONY; Sewanhaka HS; Elmont, NY; (Y); 2/383; Boy Scts; Computer Clb; Mathletes; Math Clb; Math Tm; School Play; Variety Show; Nwsp Rptr; Off Stu Cncl; Bsbl; L I Math Fair Champ 85; Math And Sci Awds 85; Pres Of Math Hnr Soc 85-86; Elec Engrng.

FAMA, SEAN; Mynderse Acad; Seneca Falls, NY; (S); 8/138; Rep Stu Cncl; High Hon Roll; Hon Roll; Comp Sci.

FAMULARO, EILEEN M; Maria Regina HS; Yonkers, NY; (Y); 1/126; Key Clb; Nwsp Stf; Rep Pres Stu Cncl; NHS; Ntl Merit Ltr; Val; NY ST Rgnts Schlrshp 86; CYO Yth Svc Awd 85; Enrico Fermi Schlrshp 86; Fordham U.

FANARA, PETER J; West Seneca West SR HS; West Seneca, NY; (Y); 47/559; Boy Scts; Key Clb; Math Tm; Spanish Clb; Varsity Clb; Band; Concert Band; Mrchg Band; Bsbl; Bowling; NYS Rgnts Schlrshp 86; Eagle Scout 85; SUNY Buffalo; Comp Engrng.

FANCHER, BARBARA; Hamburg SR HS; Hamburg, NY; (Y); 136/350; Church Yth Grp; DECA; Symp Band; Stat Bsktbl; Bus.

FANCHER, LORI; Walton Central HS; Walton, NY; (Y); 9/111; Pres 4-H; Girl Scts; Key Clb; Trs Model UN; Varsity Clb; Orch; Rep Stu Cncl; Var Bsktbl; 4-H Awd; Operation Enterprise 85; Siena Coll; Finc.

FANELLI, ALANA; St Raymond Acad; Bronx, NY; (Y); 27/73; Yrbk Phtg; Pres Frsh Cls; Var Sftbl; Hon Roll; Pre-Med.

FANG, LICHUAN; Kingston HS; Kingston, NY; (Y); 5/573; AFS; Sec Trs German Clb; Hosp Aide; Math Tm; Ski Clb; Chorus; Orch; Nwsp Rptr; Yrbk Ed-Chief; Rep Stu Cncl; NYSSM Awd Piano; U Of PA; Pre Med.

FANNING, ROYACE H; Cicero N Syracuse HS; N Syracuse, NY; (S); 60/622; Boy Scts; Latin Clb; Math Clb; Jazz Band; Mrchg Band; Symp Band; Ftbl; Var L Golf; High Hon Roll; NHS; U Of AR; Chem Engrng.

FANNUCCI, DARCIE; Keveny Memorial Acad; Ballston Lake, NY; (S); 3/40; Math Clb; VP Spanish Clb; Color Guard; Rep Soph Cls; VP Jr Cls; VP Stu Cncl; VP Capt Cheerleading; Crs Cntry; Score Keeper; Dnfth Awd; Natl Bus Hnr Soc 83-84; Engl, Typg Awds 8; Elem Ed.

FANOS, DEIRDRE; St Marys Girls HS; Floral Pk, NY; (Y); Chorus; Comp Pgmmng.

FANTINATO, TRICIA; Eat Syracus-Minoa HS; E Syracuse, NY; (Y); 70/359; Latin Clb; Chorus; Var Tennis; Var Trk; Hon Roll; Jr NHS; NHS; Jesuit Schlrshp; NY St Regents Schlrshp; Dr Bishop Mem Schlrp 86; NYSMA 1st Pl Awd Concert Choir 84-5; Le Moyne Coll; Chem.

FANTINI, SUSAN E; Clarkstown North HS; New City, NY; (Y); Chorus; Concert Band; Orch; School Musical; Stage Crew; Gym; Intnl Clb; Band; Mrchg Band; Hon Roll; NSOA Orch Awd 86; Coaches Vrsty Gymnstcs 86; Schl Cnslrs Of Rockland Cnty Schlrfshp 86; IN U; Chem.

FANTON, RICHARD J; Hutchinson Central Technical HS; Buffalo, NY; (Y); 8/266; Math Clb; Math Tm; Hon Roll; NHS; Ntl Merit SF; SAR Awd; Jesse Kethcum Memrl Awd 82; MI ST; Elctrcl Engrng.

FARACE, TODD; Eden HS; Eden, NY; (Y); Am Leg Boys St; Math Tm; SADD; Varsity Clb; Pres Soph Cls; Pres Jr Cls; JV Var Bsbl; JV Var Bsktbl; JV Var Ftbl; High Hon Roll; BUS Mgmt.

FARANELLO, GREGORY; Valley Stream Central HS; Valley Stream, NY; (Y); 23/347; Church Yth Grp; Debate Tm; Drama Clb; Chorus; Swing Chorus; Nwsp Rptr; Nwsp Stf; Lit Mag; Pres Sr Cls; Stu Cncl; Class Of 1960 Schlrshp 86; Srv To Schl Life Blue & Wht Plaque 86; W Pt Awd 86; US Mltry Acad; Pub Affrs.

FARBANIEC, DAVID; Glens Falls SR HS; Glens Falls, NY; (Y); 9/204; Am Leg Boys St; Boy Scts; Key Clb; Band; Rep Jr Cls; Var Crs Cntry; JV Socr; JV Trk; High Hon Roll; NHS; Stu Of Quarter Engl & French 85; Empire St Games X-Cntry Skiing 86.

FARBER, DARREN; Liberty HS; Liberty, NY; (Y); 1/105; Teachers Aide; Pres Sr Cls; Rep Stu Cncl; Var Bsbl; JV Bsktbl; Var Ftbl; Wt Lftg; Wrstlng; High Hon Roll; NHS; Western Sull League Awd Ftbl 85; Spec Hnr Honrs Courses Spnsh,Eng,Comp,Chem Hist II 85-86; Engrng.

FARBER, LEONARD; Bronx HS Of Science; Queens Village, NY; (Y); Teachers Aide; Band; Tennis; Wt Lftg; High Hon Roll; ARISTA 85-86; Regents Hon 86; Pres Acad Fit Awd 86; SUNY Binghamton; Bio-Chem.

FARBER, SHARON; Herkimer SR HS; Herkimer, NY; (Y); 6/110; Church Yth Grp; Drama Clb; Band; Chorus; School Musical; VP Frsh Cls; Trs Sr Cls; Rep Stu Cncl; High Hon Roll; NHS; Stu Of Mnth 86; Math.

FARBERMAN, LEWIS E; Horace Mann-Barnard HS; New York, NY; (Y); Aud/Vis; Orch; School Musical; School Play; Yrbk Stf; Hon Roll; Ntl Merit Ltr; Regents Schlrshp 85-86; Exclnce Theatre 84-85; Bst Sci Stu 82-83; U Rochester.

FARELLA, MARIE M; Central HS; Valley Stream, NY; (Y); 15/349; AFS; Church Yth Grp; Service Clb; SADD; Nwsp Stf; JV Sftbl; Mu Alp Tht; NHS; Spanish NHS; Girl Scts; Fordham U; Chld Psych.

FARIA, GARY; Westmoreland Central HS; Rome, NY; (Y); Golf; Socr; Vllybl; High Hon Roll; Hon Roll; NHS; Engnrng.

FARIETTA, TATYANA; Adai E Stevenson HS; Bronx, NY; (Y); Band; Concert Band; Mrchg Band; Yrbk Stf; Hon Roll; NHS; Prfct Atten Awd; Exclinc Sequential Math 84; Exclinc Math 86; Achvmnt Spanish II 84; Bus Admin.

FARINA, KAREN; Smithtown HS; Smithtown, NY; (Y); Church Yth Grp; Hosp Aide; Ski Clb; Sftbl; Hon Roll; ST U Cortland.

FARKOUH, NICK G; Susan E Wagner HS; Staten Island, NY; (Y); 1/400; Am Leg Boys St; Math Tm; Ed Nwsp Stf; Stu Cncl; Capt Crs Cntry; Capt Tennis; French Hon Soc; High Hon Roll; NHS; Val; 1st Pl NY Cty Indstrl Arts Cntst Arch Dsgn 86; Pride Of Ynkees Awd Extracrrclr Actvts 85&86; MIT; Engnrng.

FARLEY, CARA; Port Richmond HS; Staten Isld, NY; (Y); 79/491; AFS; Intnl Clb; Ski Clb; Lit Mag; Cit Awd; Hon Roll; Rotary Awd; Office Aide; Yrbk Stf; Var Trk; Presdntl Acadmc Fitnss Awd 86; Regnts Diploma With Merit 86; Exchng Studnt To Chile 85; Baruch Coll; Intl Busnss.

FARLEY, JILL; Horseheads HS; Horsehdads, NY; (Y); DECA; Spanish Clb; SADD; Band; Color Guard; Nwsp Rptr; JV Sftbl; Hon Roll; Bus.

FARLEY, JO ANN D; Centereach HS; Centereach, NY; (Y); 19/429; Hosp Aide; SADD; Mrchg Band; School Musical; Rep Sr Cls; Im Vllybl; NHS; Prfct Atten Awd; Drama Clb; Band; Svc Recog Awd Cndy Strpg 85-86; Regnts Schlrshp 86; Svc Recogntn Mrch Of Dimes 84-86; Fairfield U; Pre-Med.

FARLEY, JONATHAN; Brockport HS; Brockport, NY; (Y); 3/315; Chess Clb; Computer Clb; Latin Clb; Trs Mathletes; VP Math Clb; Model UN; Radio Clb; Nwsp Rptr; L Crs Cntry; Trk; Wn 3 Schl Math Awds 84-86; Pyscis Prz 84; Wn Prz 1st Pl Frshmn Clss 84; Pblsh ANALOG Cmptng Mgzn 86; :Doctral Sty.

FARLEY, NICOLE; Beacon HS; Beacon, NY; (Y); Hosp Aide; Key Clb; Latin Clb; Math Tm; Office Aide; Capt Bsktbl; Trk; High Hon Roll; Hon Roll; NHS; Math,Track,Basketball Awd 86; Electrical.

FARMER, DOLORES; St Catherine Acad; Bx, NY; (Y); Dance Clb; Office Aide; Teachers Aide; School Play; Rep Stu Cncl; Cheerleading; Trk; Prfct Atten Awd; Outstndng Slsmnshp; Jmp Rop Hrt Fnd Raisng; Comp Pgmng.

FARNELLA, ELIZABETH; Jamestown HS; Jamestown, NY; (Y); Cmnty Wkr; Pep Clb; Ski Clb; Yrbk Stf; Pres Frsh Cls; Hst Jr Cls; Hst Sr Cls; Stu Cncl; JV Cheerleading; Tennis; Glf & Tnns Awds 80-85; Math.

FARNSWORTH, SUZAMIE J; Midlakes HS; Clifton Springs, NY; (Y); 11/167; Pres Stu Cncl; Capt Vllybl; NHS; Pres French Clb; GAA; Ski Clb; Trs SADD; Trs Jr Cls; Socr; High Hon Roll; Regents Schlrshp; Hamilton Coll; Med.

FARONE, CARLA; Our Lady Of Mercy HS; Rochester, NY; (Y); 27/172; Cmnty Wkr; Intnl Clb; Ski Clb; JV Tennis; Hon Roll; St Schlr; Hghst Avg Math, Ital I, II & III; Villanova U; Bio.

FARONE, TONI ANN; Liverpool HS; Liverpool, NY; (Y); Ski Clb; Chorus; Color Guard; Rep Stu Cncl; JV Bsktbl; Newscaster.

FARR, EVE; Gloversville HS; Gloversville, NY; (Y); 13/240; Sec Drama Clb; Band; Chorus; Church Choir; Jazz Band; School Musical; Swing Chorus; Symp Band; Stu Cncl; High Hon Roll; Ithaca Coll; Musical Theatre.

FARR, SAMARA; Horseheads HS; Big Flats, NY; (S); 32/380; Cmnty Wkr; Drama Clb; SADD; Chorus; Concert Band; Mrchg Band; Orch; School Play; VP Stu Cncl; NHS; NYS Wind Ensmbl 85; Philharmonic Yth Orch 82-86; Elmira Yng Artsts Cmptn Wnnr 84; Mus.

FARR, STACEY; Whitney Point Central HS; Maine, NY; (Y); 10/122; French Clb; Key Clb; Chorus; Yrbk Stf; Trs Soph Cls; Cheerleading; Hon Roll; Masonic Awd; NHS; Cazenoria Coll; Fshn Merch.

FARR, VIRGINIA H; Auburn HS; Auburn, NY; (Y); 21/423; Ski Clb; Varsity Clb; JV L Fld Hcky; JV Trk; High Hon Roll; NHS; Ntl Merit Ltr; Coll Schlrshp Hamilton Coll 86; NYS Rgnts Schlrshp 86; Hamilton Coll Clinton NY; Engr.

FARRAND, JULIEANNE; Seton Catholic Central HS; Endwell, NY; (Y); 95/163; Art Clb; Church Yth Grp; JV Var Bsktbl; Trk; Broome CC; Physcl Educ.

FARRANTO, AMY; Jamesville Dewitt HS; Dewitt, NY; (Y); Band; Chorus; Concert Band; School Musical; School Play; Stage Crew; Socr; High Hon Roll; Hon Roll; Schlstc Art Awd Blue Rbbn, Gld Key 85-86; Music.

FARRAR, VICTORIA A; Ballston Spa HS; Ballston Spa, NY; (Y); 37/247; Chorus; Church Choir; Color Guard; Sec Drill Tm; Nwsp Rptr; Nwsp Stf; Yrbk Rptr; Yrbk Stf; Off Sr Cls; Stu Cncl; Lat Hnr Soc 86; Saratoga Cnty Lgl Sec Assn Scholar 86; Russell Sage; Polit Sci.

FARRELL, CLARE; St Vincent Ferrer HS; Rego Park, NY; (Y); 13/110; Art Clb; Church Yth Grp; Hosp Aide; Math Tm; Pep Clb; Q&S; Yrbk Ed-Chief; Yrbk Stf; Hon Roll; St Johns U; Med Asstnt.

FARRELL, DAVID; Columbia HS; Rensselaer, NY; (Y); Im Bsbl; Im JV Ftbl; Var L Tennis; Var L Vllybl; Im Wt Lftg; Hon Roll; Captn Trck Tm 84; Vrsty Tnns 3 Yrs 85-87; Amth & Sci Hons Clsses 85-87; Cvl Engr.

FARRELL, DEBORAH; Brockport HS; Brockport, NY; (Y); 60/315; Drama Clb; Spanish Clb; Chorus; Color Guard; Rep Frsh Cls; Rep Soph Cls; JV Var Cheerleading; High Hon Roll; Hon Roll; Nmnts.

FARRELL, GINA; W C Mepham HS; N Bellmore, NY; (Y); Cultural Arts Dance Pgm 84-85; Shore Dance Co 83; Comm.

FARRELL, JOHN; Xavier HS; Belle Harbor, NY; (Y); 24/260; Latin Clb; Ski Clb; Nwsp Rptr; Yrbk Stf; Off Jr Cls; Im Bsbl; Im Bsktbl; Im Ftbl; JV Trk; Hon Roll.

FARRELL, KERRI L; Cambridge Central Schl; Cambridge, NY; (Y); 30/80; French Clb; Yrbk Ed-Chief; Yrbk Phtg; JV Fld Hcky; Regnts Clg Schlrshp; Syracuse U; Russn Stud.

FARRELL, STEPHANIE; Guilderland Central HS; Guilderland, NY; (Y); Cmnty Wkr; Hosp Aide; Key Clb; Ski Clb; Varsity Clb; Variety Show; Nwsp Stf; Off Jr Cls; Var Tennis; Russell Sage; Early Chld Ed.

FARRELL, TRACY; Niskayuna HS; Schenectady, NY; (Y); AFS; Church Yth Grp; Drama Clb; SADD; Acpl Chr; Church Choir; Orch; School Musical; School Play; Stu Cncl; Boston U Schlrshp 86; Niskayuna Frnds Of Musc Schlrshp 86; Sch Musc Assoc 86; Musc Perf.

FARRELLY, JOHN J; Mount St Michael Acad; Bronx, NY; (Y); 171/292; Computer Clb; Ski Clb; Im Bsbl; Im Capt Bsktbl; JV L Crs Cntry; Var Capt Ftbl; Var L Trk; Wt Lftg; Regents Schlrshp 86; U Of MA.

FARRELLY, SEAN P; Cardinal Spellman HS; Bronx, NY; (Y); 13/500; Cmnty Wkr; Nwsp Rptr; High Hon Roll; Ntl Merit Ltr; Schl Awd For Exc In Scl Studies 83; NY U; Gvnmnt/Ecnmcs.

FARRINGTON, KAREN; Bellport HS; E Patchogue, NY; (Y); 4/300; VP French Clb; Capt Scholastic Bowl; Ed Yrbk Stf; Var Tennis; Bausch & Lomb Sci Awd; High Hon Roll; VP Jr NHS; NHS; Ntl Merit Ltr; French Hon Soc; Wnnr Simons Fllwshp At Stony Brook U For Chem 86.

FARRO, JOHN; Eastchester HS; Eastchester, NY; (Y); JV Var Bsbl; JV Bsktbl; Bus Mgmt.

FARROW, ELISSA; La Guardia School Of Arts; New York City, NY; (S); Office Aide; Teachers Aide; Hon Roll; NHS; Fine Art.

FARRUGGIO, THOMAS P; Lancaster Central HS; Depew, NY; (Y); 99/463; PAVAS; Chorus; Concert Band; Jazz Band; Mrchg Band; Symp Band; Ftbl; Wt Lftg; Hon Roll; Jr NHS; Mrchng Band Schlrshp 86; SUNY Fredonia; Music.

FARRUGIA, JOSEPH G; Xavier HS; New York, NY; (Y); 15/250; Aud/Vis; Computer Clb; VP JA; Math Clb; Ski Clb; Im Bsbl; Im Ftbl; High Hon Roll; Ntl Merit Ltr; NEDT Awd; NYS Regnts Schlrshp; Fnlst Polytech Full Tuitn Schlrshp; A P Am Hist,A P Bio,A P Calcus Hnrs Eng; Rensselaer Polytech; Elec Engrg.

FARRUGIA, LINDA; Commack HS South; Commack, NY; (Y); Girl Scts; VICA; Y-Teens; Chorus; Swing Chorus; JV Bsktbl; Trk; NEDT Awd; Prepared Speech Awd VICA-WILSON Tech 86; Farmingdale Coll; Dntl Hygn.

FARRY, KRISTEN; Linton HS; Schenectady, NY; (Y); Key Clb; Rep Jr Cls; Hon Roll; Schenectady CC; Hotel Mgmt.

FARTHING, JOAN M; Lafayette HS; Buffalo, NY; (Y); 19/220; Hon Roll; Rgnts Schlrshp 86; U Of Buffalo.

FARTHING, WILLIAM B; Niagara Wheatfield HS; Niagara Falls, NY; (Y); 11/292; JA; Band; Concert Band; Jazz Band; Ftbl; Wt Lftg; High Hon Roll; NHS; Bucknell U Prtl Stu Athl Grnt 86; NY ST Rgnts Schlrshp 86; Ftbl All Str Tm, All Cnty, & All Lge 85; Bucknell U; Engrng.

FARWELL, MICHAEL; Roy C Ketcham HS; Poughkeepsie, NY; (Y); Var L Bsktbl; Hon Roll.

FARZAN, PETER; Williamsville South HS; Williamsville, NY; (Y); Bsbl; Im Ice Hcky; Hon Roll; Regents Schlrshp; Engrng.

FASANELLA, LILIANA; Hillcrest HS; Queens, NY; (Y); 156/850; Art Clb; Office Aide; Stage Crew; Yrbk Stf; Most Promsng Art Stu Awd; PA Awd Achcdmsh Achvmnt In Art; NY U; Lang.

FASANO, MARIA; Notre Dame HS; Batavia, NY; (S); Nwsp Stf; Yrbk Ed-Chief; Hon Roll; NHS; NEDT Awd; Daemen Coll; Engl.

FASCIANA, JOSEPH; Frontier Central HS; Blasdell, NY; (Y); Church Yth Grp; Math Clb; Science Clb; SADD; Varsity Clb; Band; Chorus; Church Choir; Concert Band; Jazz Band; ECIC Div II Ftbl All ST 85; Sports Med.

FASCIGLIONE, JOSEPH P; Mount St Michael HS; Bronx, NY; (Y); 90/297; Church Yth Grp; Im Bsktbl; Im Ftbl; Regnts Schlrshp; Iona College; Psych.

FASONE, SHANNON; John F Kennedy HS; Utica, NY; (Y); Capt Church Yth Grp; JV Bsktbl; JV Fld Hcky; Herkimer Cnty CC; Crt Steno.

FASS, SAMUEL; Eastchester HS; Eastchester, NY; (Y); French Clb; Math Tm; Temple Yth Grp; Band; Rep Frsh Cls; Hon Roll; Jr NHS; Biolgcl Sci.

FASSELL, AMY; Greenwich Central HS; Greenwich, NY; (S); 4-H; Trs FFA; Rptr FHA; Ski Clb; Varsity Clb; Nwsp Rptr; Var Cheerleading; Sftbl; Trk; 4-H Awd; Mrchng Bnd Flute 82; Schl Plays 80-82; Cornell U; Vet Med.

FASSNACHT, TINA; Valley Central HS; Montgomery, NY; (Y); 33/360; Rep Soph Cls; Rep Jr Cls; Rep Sr Cls; JV Bsktbl; Var Tennis; Hon Roll; NHS; Pres Schlr; Spanish NHS; Spanish Clb; NYS Regents Scholar 86; Co-Pres Natl Spn Hnr Soc 85-86; PA ST; Bus.

FATOUSH, GEORGE; East Meadow HS; East Meadow, NY; (Y); Church Yth Grp; Library Aide; Office Aide; Rep Jr Cls; Rep Stu Cncl; Bsbl; Bsktbl; Diving; Swmmng; Tennis; NY Inst Of Tech; Bus Exec.

FAUCETTE, WILLIAM R; Mc Quaid Jesuit HS; Fairport, NY; (Y); Camera Clb; Model UN; Political Wkr; Varsity Clb; Variety Show; Yrbk Phtg; Var Ftbl; Var Trk; High Hon Roll; NHS; Ftr Blck Schlr Rochester Urban Lg 85; Pre-Law.

FAUCI, JENNIFER; Seton Catholic Central HS; Endwell, NY; (Y); Church Yth Grp; French Clb; Hosp Aide; Key Clb; Political Wkr; Ski Clb; Varsity Clb; Tennis; Trk.

FAUL, JENNIFER; John Jay SR HS; S Salem, NY; (Y); Cmnty Wkr; Dance Clb; Intnl Clb; SADD; Teachers Aide; Yrbk Phtg; Lit Mag; Var Diving; Cit Awd; Jr NHS; Excllnc Chem & Sci Awd, Cmnty Svc Awd 86; 2nd Pl Awd Sci Fair 84; Med.

FAULER, LAURA; G Ray Bodley HS; Fulton, NY; (Y); French Clb; Latin Clb; Science Clb; Chorus; High Hon Roll; Hon Roll; NHS; Chem.

FAULER, TIMOTHY; Hoosick Falls Central Schl; Hoosick Falls, NY; (Y); Boy Scts; Cmnty Wkr; French Clb; VP Stu Cncl; Var Bsktbl; Var Ftbl; Trk; Citizenship Awd 85; Svc Awd 86; Aero Engrng.

FAULKNER, DENISE; Clymer Central Schl; Clymer, NY; (Y); 2/47; Pres Soph Cls; Sec Jr Cls; Pres Sr Cls; Var Capt Cheerleading; Var Trk; Var Capt Vllybl; NHS; Sal; Sec AFS; FFA; Jostens Fndtn Ldrshp Schlrp 86; Miss Chautauqua Cnty Schlrp Wnr 85; Rgnts Schlrp 86; Syracuse U; Brdcstng.

FAULKNER, MARK; Lasalle Military Acad; Brooklyn, NY; (Y); 23/90; Church Yth Grp; ROTC; Spanish Clb; Chorus; Church Choir; Drm & Bgl; Var Trk; Hon Roll; Color Guard; Concert Band; Mst Outstndg Percussnst 85; Empire ST Karate Chmpnshp Green Blt Champ 85.

FAULKNER, SANDRA; John Dewey HS; Brooklyn, NY; (Y); Cert Excllnc Hlth Asst 86; Med.

FAULS, BRIAN; Smithtown HS West; Smithtown, NY; (Y); Trs Chess Clb; Drama Clb; Hosp Aide; Thesps; Chorus; School Musical; School Play; Stage Crew; Hon Roll; NYS Regents Scholar 86; Pres Acad Fit Awd 86; SUNY Binghamton.

FAUST, CARLETTA; Uniondale HS; Baldwin, NY; (Y); Pres Church Yth Grp; Hosp Aide; Chorus; Pres Church Choir; Yrbk Ed-Chief; Yrbk Phtg; Trs Stu Cncl; Cheerleading; Hon Roll; Jr NHS; Natl Ldrshp & Svc Awd 85; U Of SC; Pre-Med.

FAUSTIN, ALISON; Murry Bergtraum HS; Jamaica, NY; (Y); Girl Scts; Hosp Aide; JA; Prfct Atten Awd; Elizabeth Seton Col; Comp Sci.

FAUSTIN, SNYDER; Dominican Commercial HS; St Albans, NY; (Y); 75/288; Hosp Aide; Science Clb; Chorus; Hunter Coll; Med.

FAVA, ANITA; Hicksville SR HS; Hicksvl, NY; (Y); Church Yth Grp; SADD; Church Choir; Stage Crew; Nwsp Stf; Rep Stu Cncl; Law.

FAVARO, JENNIFER; Saranac HS; Cadyville, NY; (S); 15/105; Pres Church Yth Grp; Pres Drama Clb; Trs French Clb; VP SADD; Church Choir; School Musical; Rep Sr Cls; Pres Stu Cncl; High Hon Roll; NHS; Utica Coll Syracuse; Psychlgy.

FAVARO, TESS; Saranac Central HS; Morrisonville, NY; (S); Yrbk Stf; Hon Roll.

FAVATA, TOM; Catholic Central HS; Watervliet, NY; (Y); German Clb; Math Clb; SADD; School Musical; Variety Show; Yrbk Stf; JV Var Bsktbl; JV Var Ftbl; Var Trk; Hon Roll; Aerrontcl Engnrng.

FAVILLE, MICHAEL; James E Sperry HS; Rochester, NY; (Y); 5/271; Exploring; VICA; High Hon Roll; Hon Roll; JETS Awd; Jr NHS; NHS; Spanish NHS; NY St Regents Schlrshp 86; 1st Pl NY St Indus Arts Cmpttn-Tech Drwng 86; J E Sperry Indus Art Awd 86; General Motors Inst; Mech Engrg.

FAVUZZA, ROSANNE; Sheepshead Bay HS; Brooklyn, NY; (Y); Hon Roll; Hm Ec Awd 83-84; Prfct Attndnc Hnr 85-86; Transcrptn Hnr; Baruch; Bus.

FAWWAZ, MARC; Pelham Memorial HS; Pelham, NY; (Y); JA; Radio Clb; Ski Clb; JV Bsbl; Bsktbl; Ftbl; Comm.

FAY, BRIAN G; Fayetteville-Manlius HS; Manlius, NY; (Y); 107/330; Badmtn; Ntl Merit Ltr; Clarkson U; Elec Engrng.

FAY, JASON; Watkins Glen HS; Watkins Glen, NY; (S); 2/130; Nwsp Bus Mgr; Yrbk Bus Mgr; Yrbk Ed-Chief; Var L Trk; Bausch & Lomb Sci Awd; French Hon Soc; High Hon Roll; NHS; Ntl Merit SF; Prfct Atten Awd; Elmira Coll Key Awd, W Pt Acad Wrkshp 85; Geo Washington U; Engrng.

FAY, MARGARET; Liverpool HS; North Syracuse, NY; (Y); Stu Cncl; Var L Cheerleading; Var JV Pom Pon; JV Socr; Hon Roll; Jr NHS; Opt Clb Awd; NY St Stu Senete Rep 85; Miss NY Amer Co-Ed St Fnlst-Top 20 85; Syracuse U.

FAY, THERESA; Colonie Central HS; Colonie, NY; (Y); 23/498; Teachers Aide; Score Keeper; Socr; High Hon Roll; Hon Roll; NHS; Ntl Merit Ltr; NY ST Regnts Schlrshp 86; Pres Acadmc Fitnss Awd 86; Cornell U; Natrl Res.

FAY, TRACY; Mechanicville HS; Mechanicville, NY; (S); 2/100; Church Yth Grp; Girl Scts; Ski Clb; VP Spanish Clb; Nwsp Stf; Yrbk Bus Mgr; Yrbk Stf; Rep Frsh Cls; Rep Soph Cls; Rep Stu Cncl; Sbstnc & Drg Abuse Cnslr 84-86; Skidmore Coll 5th Annl Achvt Awd 85; Boston U; Med.

FAYETTE, MARLENE E; Massena Central HS; Massena, NY; (Y); 44/250; Cmnty Wkr; Key Clb; Stat Bsktbl; Var Capt Cheerleading; Var Trk; High Hon Roll; Hon Roll; Regnts Schlrshp 86; Ithaca; Phy Thrpst.

FAZ, ANISSA; Smithtown HS East; St James, NY; (Y); Art Clb; Drama Clb; Chorus; School Musical; School Play; Variety Show; Yrbk Stf; Off Frsh Cls; Off Soph Cls; Off Jr Cls; FL Intl U; Music Ed.

FAZIO, JENNIE; Academy Of St Joseph; St James, NY; (Y); Church Yth Grp; Cmnty Wkr; Church Choir; Orch; Yrbk Stf; Awd For Excllnc Italn 84; Pre-Law.

FAZIO, KRISTEN; Frankfort Schuyler Central HS; Frankfort, NY; (S); 41/102; Church Yth Grp; FBLA; Chorus; School Musical; Fld Hcky; Trk; High Hon Roll; Hon Roll; NHS; French Clb; Gregg Shothnd Awds 85; Exec Sec.

FAZIO, ROY; Cazenovia Central Schl; Cazenovia, NY; (Y); Var L Ftbl; Var L Trk; Hon Roll; Slvr Mdltst Wnnr 85 Empr ST Gms 85; Cmplt Empr Sst Gms Wghtlftng 86; Rnkd 11th 85 JR Wghtlftng 85; Morrisville Coll; Mech Engrng.

FAZZOLARI, FRANK; Niagara Wheatfield HS; Niagara Falls, NY; (Y); Church Yth Grp; French Clb; Math Clb; Varsity Clb; Var Bsbl; JV Bsktbl; Var Bowling; Var Capt Vllybl; High Hon Roll; NHS; Math.

FEAGLES, JUDY; St Johnsville Central HS; St Johnsville, NY; (Y); 6/26; VP Sec 4-H; Sec Chorus; Concert Band; Yrbk Stf; Cit Awd; Dnfth Awd; 4-H Awd; Hon Roll; English Clb; French Clb; Montgomery Cnty Dairy Prncs 85-86; MENC Interst Chrl Fstvl 85; SUNY Cobleskill; Anml Sci.

FEARMAN, DANIEL; Fredonia HS; Fredonia, NY; (Y); Lit Mag; JV Trk; Smmr Enrchmnt Pgm Comp 85; SUNY Fredonia; Comp Sci.

FEARY, PEGGY; Alexander Central HS; Batavia, NY; (Y); Band; Concert Band; Mrchg Band; Off Jr Cls; Rep Stu Cncl; Var Cheerleading; JV Var Socr; JV Var Sftbl; Stat Wrstlng; Scl Wrk.

FEATHERS, NEIL; New Lebanon Central HS; Hancock, MA; (Y); 10/52; Pres Church Yth Grp; Band; Chorus; Church Choir; Mrchg Band; Yrbk Phtg; Var Trk; Hon Roll; NHS; Northern Columbia Cnty Rotary Clb-Svc Abov Self Awd; Nellie Camaron Schlrshp; All-ST Chorus; Hampshire Coll; Lbrl Arts.

FECK, MATHEW; James E Sperry HS; Henrietta, NY; (Y); Computer Clb; Ski Clb; Varsity Clb; Rep Frsh Cls; Var Bsbl; Im Mgr Bsktbl; Var Ftbl; Var Ice Hcky; French Hon Soc; Jr NHS; Psych.

FECURA, MICHELLE; Hoosic Valley Central HS; Melrose, NY; (Y); 20/94; Church Yth Grp; SADD; Band; JV Fld Hcky; Mgr(s); Score Keeper; JV Var Sftbl; SUNY; Writing.

FEDDO, THOMAS P; North Tonawanda SR HS; N Tonawanda, NY; (Y); 1/398; Am Leg Boys St; Boy Scts; Var L Ftbl; Var L Swmmng; Bausch & Lomb Sci Awd; Trs NHS; Val; Ftbl All League Hnrbl Ment 85; Rensellaer Ply Tech Math,Sci Awd 85; NROTC Schlrshp 86; Aero Sp Engr.

FEDERICI, CONNIE; Sweet Home SR HS; Tonawanda, NY; (Y); Church Yth Grp; 4-H; JA; Ski Clb; Cornell; CPA.

FEDERICO, CARMEN J; Liverpool HS; Liverpool, NY; (Y); 64/816; Exploring; Hosp Aide; Pep Clb; Band; Church Choir; Concert Band; Jazz Band; Mrchg Band; Orch; Pep Band; NY ST Rgnts Schlrshp 86; All ST Wnd Ensmbl 85; Onondaga Cnty Med Auxilry Schlrshp 86; ST U Of NY-BNGHMTN; Pre-Med.

FEDOCKS, HEATHER A; Spencer-Van Etten Central HS; Van Etten, NY; (Y); Art Clb; Cmnty Wkr; Debate Tm; Drama Clb; French Clb; Science Clb; Pres Ski Clb; Band; Chorus; Nwsp Ed-Chief; NYS Rgnts Schlrshp 86; Alfred ST Coll; Med Lab Tech.

FEDYNAK, STEPHANIE A; Wellington C Mepham HS; North Bellmore, NY; (Y); 4/360; Cmnty Wkr; Yrbk Stf; Off Soph Cls; Sec Jr Cls; Rep Sr Cls; Stu Cncl; Badmtn; Var Socr; Hon Roll; NHS; NY ST Rgnts Schlrshp 86; Adelphi U Pres Schlrshp 86; Adelphi U.

FEDYSZEN, PETER JOSEPH; Massapequa HS; Massapequa, NY; (Y); 33/450; Am Leg Boys St; Cmnty Wkr; Key Clb; Rep Jr Cls; Bsktbl; Var Lcrss; Cit Awd; High Hon Roll; NHS; Pres Schlr; Spnsh Hnrs; Wake Forest U; Pre-Med.

FEE, EILEEN; Clarkstown North HS; Congers, NY; (Y); Exploring; GAA; Spanish Clb; Yrbk Stf; Lit Mag; Var Capt Crs Cntry; Var Capt Trk; Regents Schlrshp Wnnr 86; Coaches Awd Crs Cntry 85; Varsity Athl Against Substance Abuse Rep 85-86; Advertising.

FEE, SANDY; Jordan-Elbridge HS; Elbridge, NY; (Y); Art Clb; Camera Clb; Computer Clb; Ski Clb; Var JV Bsktbl; Var Capt Socr; Var Capt Sftbl; NHS; Cortland; Phy Ed.

FEELEY, BRIDGET MARY; Mount Mercy Acad; Buffalo, NY; (Y); JCL; Latin Clb; Chorus; Church Choir; Hon Roll; U Buffalo; Acctg.

FEELEY, FRANCIS A; Canisius HS; Buffalo, NY; (Y); 3/162; VP Church Yth Grp; Latin Clb; Ski Clb; Acpl Chr; School Musical; School Play; Ed Yrbk Sprt Ed; Rep Soph Cls; High Hon Roll; NHS; Mu Slpha Theta 85-86; Scty Of Distngshd Amer H S Stu 85-86; Presdntl Schlr 85-86; U Of Notre Dame; Pre-Med.

FEELEY, WILLIAM A; Bishop Timon HS; W Seneca, NY; (Y); Church Yth Grp; Chorus; Im Bsktbl; JV Crs Cntry; Var Socr; Var Trk; Im Vllybl; Hon Roll; NHS; Pres Schlr; Engl, Latn, Math Awds; Canisus; Acctg.

FEELY, MARTIN; Earl L Vandermeulen HS; Mt Sinai, NY; (Y); Cmnty Wkr; SADD; JV Bsktbl; JV Var Socr.

FEELY, PATRICK; Cohocton Central HS; Cohocton, NY; (Y); 5/27; French Clb; Band; Yrbk Stf; Pres Sr Cls; Var Bsktbl; Capt Bsktbl; Var Socr; High Hon Roll; VP NHS; Rochester Inst Of Tech; Htl Mgt.

FEENEY, BARBARA JEAN; Massena Central HS; Massena, NY; (Y); Church Yth Grp; Cmnty Wkr; French Clb; Rep Frsh Cls; Score Keeper; JV Capt Sftbl; High Hon Roll; NHS; Womens Clb Outstndng Stu Awd 86; Robert Engstrom Awd 86; Pres Acad Ftns Awd 86; Plattsburgh ST; Acctng.

FEENEY, MARY; St Patricks CCHS; Coxsackie, NY; (Y); 3/25; Drama Clb; Pres Jr Cls; NHS; US Nvl Sea Cadets Mstr Arms 85; Hnr Cadet TRC Davisville NCBC 85; Rgnts Diploma/Schlrshp 86; US Nvl Acad Annapolis; Engrng.

FEGAN, ROBERT J; W C Mepham HS; Bellmore, NY; (Y); 14/380; Trs Band; Pres Jr Cls; Pres Sr Cls; Bsktbl; Ftbl; Capt Trk; Wrstlng; Kiwanis Awd; NHS; Sal; U Of PA.

FEGER, CHRISTOPHER; Pembroke JR SR HS; Akron, NY; (Y); 3/117; Drama Clb; Pres Trs German Clb; Math Tm; Pres Trs Science Clb; Band; Mrchg Band; School Musical; Var Swmmng; Var Tennis; NHS; Amer Chem Soc Awd 86.

FEGGLER, MARK H; East Meadow HS; East Meadow, NY; (Y); 78/340; Computer Clb; Concert Band; Mrchg Band; Yrbk Stf; Lit Mag; Regents Schlrshp 86; SUNY Plattsburgh; Creat Eng.

FEHLING, BARBARA; Sacred Heart Acad; New Hyde Park, NY; (S); 10/200; Church Yth Grp; Math Clb; Math Tm; Chorus; Coach Actv; High Hon Roll; NHS; Med.

FEHLMAN, BILL; Falconer Central Schl; Falconer, NY; (Y); 16/122; Am Leg Boys St; Var Capt Bsbl; Var L Ftbl; Bausch & Lomb Sci Awd; Cit Awd; Hon Roll; NHS; USA Schlrshp 86; All Conf Hgst Battng Avg Bsbl 84-86; MVP Bsbl 85-86; JCC; Surveyng Officer.

FEIFER, FELICIA; West Hempstead HS; W Hempstead, NY; (Y); Temple Yth Grp; Orch; Pom Pon.

FEILEN, DEBRA A; Jamaica HS; Hillcrest, NY; (Y); 74/507; Pres Debate Tm; PAVAS; Band; School Musical; Camp Fr Inc; Rptr Yrbk Stf; VP Frsh Cls; Swmmng; NHS; Ntl Merit Schol; Yth & Govt Bill Spnsr 84-86; Jewish Identity Clb Pres 83-86; Stock Mrtk Tm Co-Capt 84-86; Bard Coll; Econ.

FEIN, GENE F; The Bronx HS Science; Bronx, NY; (Y); Political Wkr; Y-Teens; Jr NHS; Screen Actors Guild Cmmrcl Actor; Advncd Astrophysics Lehman Coll 85-86; Fordham U; Cmmnctns.

FEINBERG, JOHN; Minisink Valley HS; Middleton, NY; (Y); 1/250; Chess Clb; Computer Clb; Capt Math Tm; Scholastic Bowl; Chorus; Yrbk Phtg; Yrbk Stf; Rep Stu Cncl; Bausch & Lomb Sci Awd; High Hon Roll; Bst Score On Annuual HS Math Exam 86.

FEINSTEIN, JEFFREY; John F Kennedy HS; Merrick, NY; (Y); Boy Scts; Computer Clb; Hosp Aide; Mathletes; Math Clb; Math Tm; Red Cross Aide; SADD; Y-Teens; Chorus; UCLA; Med.

FEIST, DAWN; St Joseph By The Sea HS; Staten Island, NY; (Y); Art Clb; Church Yth Grp; Cmnty Wkr; Computer Clb; Drama Clb; Hosp Aide; Church Choir; School Musical; School Play; Nwsp Stf; Nrsng.

FEISTHAMEL, KAREN; Poland Central Schl; Cold Brook, NY; (Y); French Clb; Ski Clb; Varsity Clb; Band; Yrbk Stf; JV Var Socr; High Hon Roll; Hon Roll; VP NHS.

FEIT, DAVID E; Oceanside HS; Oceanside, NY; (Y); 35/550; Pres Model UN; Sec Chorus; Nwsp Ed-Chief; Lit Mag; Var L Trk; Trs NHS; Ntl Merit SF; SADD; Temple Yth Grp; Madrigals; Cntry III Ldrshp Schlrshp 85; All ST Chr 85; All Cnty Trk 85.

FEKLER, DAVID; Union Endicott HS; Endicott, NY; (Y); Am Leg Boys St; Exploring; Vllybl; High Hon Roll; Hon Roll; Syracuse U; Electr Engr.

FELAKOS, JAMES G; Somers HS; Granite Springs, NY; (Y); Am Leg Boys St; Exploring; Model UN; SADD; Bsktbl; Var JV Ftbl; JV Wrstlng; High Hon Roll; Hon Roll; Bio.

FELD, AMY R; Bay Shore SR HS; Bay Shore, NY; (Y); 7/375; Camera Clb; Church Yth Grp; Cmnty Wkr; Drama Clb; Hosp Aide; Color Guard; School Musical; Stage Crew; Lit Mag; Crs Cntry; Pres Envrnmntl Awd Bch Capt 84-85; Worcester Polytech Inst; Biomed.

FELDBORG, ERIC K; Spackenkill HS; Poughkeepsie, NY; (Y); 60/178; Off Am Leg Boys St; Boy Scts; Sec Church Yth Grp; Exploring; Thesps; Orch; School Musical; Yrbk Phtg; Socr; Trk.

FELDGOISE, JEFFREY; Auburn HS; Auburn, NY; (Y); 2/450; Drama Clb; Ski Clb; School Musical; Rep Frsh Cls; VP Soph Cls; VP Stu Cncl; Var Lcrss; L Socr; Bausch & Lomb Sci Awd; NHS.

FELDIS, KEVIN; South Side HS; Rockville Centre, NY; (Y); 13/270; Yrbk Phtg; Trs Sr Cls; Swmmng; High Hon Roll; Jr NHS; NHS; Ntl Merit Ltr; Yale; Lbrl Arts.

FELDMAN, DANA; Canarsie HS; Brooklyn, NY; (Y); Dance Clb; Service Clb; School Play; Variety Show; Stu Cncl; Cheerleading; Sftbl; Hon Roll; Borough Sci Fair 2nd Pl 85; Canarsie Sci Fair 3rd Pl 85.

FELDMAN, DEBORAH I; Southside HS; New York, NY; (Y); 31/285; VP Exploring; Hosp Aide; Key Clb; Chorus; Nwsp Rptr; Rptr Lit Mag; Var L Badmtn; High Hon Roll; Hon Roll; NHS; Rgnts Schlrshp 86; U Of Rochester; Pre-Med.

FELDMAN, ELIZABETH M; Green Meadow Waldorf Schl; Spring Valley, NY; (Y); Drama Clb; Chorus; Orch; School Musical; School Play; Nwsp Rptr; Lit Mag; Bsktbl; Lcrss; Socr; German Awd 83; NY U.

FELDMAN, MARC; Half Hollow Hills West HS; Wheatley Hts, NY; (Y); French Clb; Letterman Clb; SADD; Varsity Clb; JV Bsbl; Var Bsktbl; Var Socr; Var Tennis; French Hon Soc; Hon Roll; All-Cntry 4th Dbls Tm 86; Albany; Bus.

FELDMAN, MATTHEW; Cararsie HS; New York, NY; (Y); Math Spnsh Chem Physcs Cmptr Sci 86; Cmptr Prgrmng.

FELDMAN, NICOLE; Broadalbin Central HS; Johnstown, NY; (Y); 25/73; 4-H; French Clb; SADD; Chorus; Yrbk Bus Mgr; Cit Awd; Dnfth Awd; 4-H Awd; High Hon Roll; Hon Roll; Leeland Reed Awd Yrbk 86; Cobleskill Ag & Tech; Acctng.

FELDMAN, ROSS; Smithtown East HS; Nesconset, NY; (Y); Computer Clb; FBLA; Math Clb; Math Tm; Spanish Clb; SADD; Temple Yth Grp; Rep Frsh Cls; Rep Soph Cls; Rep Jr Cls; Bus.

FELDMAN, SHEILA; New Paltz HS; New Paltz, NY; (Y); 1/176; SADD; Chorus; Pres Frsh Cls; Pres Soph Cls; VP Lib Jr Cls; Stu Cncl; JV Var Bsktbl; JV Var Socr; JV L Sftbl; High Hon Roll.

FELDMETH, RENEE; St Raymond Acad; Bronx, NY; (Y); 25/73.

FELICE, JEFFREY; Waterloo SR HS; Waterloo, NY; (S); 32/157; Rep Frsh Cls; Trs Soph Cls; Rep Stu Cncl; JV Bsbl; Var Capt Bsktbl; Var Trk; High Hon Roll; Hon Roll; Hstry.

FELICE, MIA; Onondage Central HS; Syracuse, NY; (Y); GAA; Spanish Clb; SADD; Pres Jr Cls; Var Bsktbl; Var Cheerleading; Var Socr; Var Trk; Hon Roll; NHS; Elem Ed.

FELICELLO, MIA; Marlboro HS; Marlboro, NY; (Y); 13/150; Office Aide; SADD; Yrbk Stf; High Hon Roll; Hon Roll; Jr NHS; NHS; Bus Awd $25 84-85; Shrthnd 85-86; Krissler Bus Inst; Secretary.

FELICETTI, LAURA; St John The Baptist HS; Lindenhurst, NY; (Y); 85/530; Intnl Clb; SADD; Ed Nwsp Bus Mgr; Yrbk Stf; Lit Mag; Var Crs Cntry; Hon Roll; Lion Awd; Cmnty Wkr; Drama Clb; Creative Excllnc Awd Engl 86; Natl Engl Merit Awd 86; Salve Regina; Educ.

FELICETTI, LOUISE; Walt Whitman HS; Melville, NY; (Y); 24/479; Key Clb; Mathletes; Band; Im Cheerleading; JV Tennis; High Hon Roll; VP Jr NHS; Spanish NHS; Girls Ldrs Club 85-86; Math Awd 84; Bus Adm.

FELICIANO, DEBBIE; Immaculata HS; New York, NY; (Y); 2/96; Church Yth Grp; Variety Show; Rep Stu Cncl; Hon Roll; Drama Clb; Chorus; Church Choir; VP Soph Cls; Im Bsktbl; Im Bowling; Ped.

FELICIANO, FELIX; Aviation HS; Bronx, NY; (S); 10/416; CAP; JA; Yrbk Phtg; Yrbk Stf; Rep Sr Cls; Hon Roll; Prfct Atten Awd; Manhattan Coll Pres Schlrshp 86; Tech Hnr Soc-Pegasus Soc 85; Manhattan Coll; Mech Engrng.

FELICIANO, MICHELLE; High Of Fashion Industry; Bronx, NY; (Y); Fashn Desgnr.

FELICIANO, VIVIAN; John Dewey HS; Brooklyn, NY; (Y); Chorus; Vllybl; Nrs.

FELIO, SCOTT; Sandy Creek Central HS; Lacona, NY; (Y); Camera Clb; Varsity Clb; Ice Hcky; Wt Lftg; Wrstlng; Phy Fit 80-86; Outstndng Mile Run 82; Farm.

FELL, PATRICIA; Beacon HS; Beacon, NY; (Y); 44/160; Math Tm; Chorus; School Musical; Pres Frsh Cls; VP Soph Cls; Pres Stu Cncl; Hon Roll; Otstndng Stu Hlth & Mth Awds 86; Accntng.

FELLER, SCOTT D; Eden Central SR HS; Eden, NY; (Y); 1/163; AFS; Computer Clb; Varsity Clb; Nwsp Sprt Ed; Trs Stu Cncl; Var Capt Swmmng; Bausch & Lomb Sci Awd; Pres NHS; Prfct Atten Awd; Val; NYS Rgnts Schlrshp 86; U Of Rochester; Gnrl Sci.

FELLION, LORI; Franklin Acad; Malone, NY; (Y); 3/256; Drama Clb; Pres Spanish Clb; Chorus; School Play; Swing Chorus; Pres Stu Cncl; Hon Roll; NHS; Natl Sci Merit Awd Bio 84; Natl Sci Merti Awd Chem 85; Knights Pithias Awd 86; Russell Sage; Lib Arts.

FELLOWS, WILLIAM C; Argyle Central HS; Argyle, NY; (Y); Boy Scts; French Clb; Math Tm; Political Wkr; Yrbk Phtg; Yrbk Stf; Rep Stu Cncl; Hon Roll; Outstndng Achvt Engl 86; NYS Regnts Schlrshp 86; Mst Imprvd Socl Stds 84; SUNY Plattsburg; Cmmnctns.

FELMET, ROBIN; Mount Saint Josephs Acad; Buffalo, NY; (S); Cmnty Wkr; Debate Tm; Quiz Bowl; Science Clb; Var L Badmtn; Bsktbl; Mgr(s); Score Keeper; Mgr Sftbl; Tennis; Sister Sylvia Awd Engl 83-84; Boston U; Bio.

FELSO, ALICE; Lyndonville Central HS; Medina, NY; (S); #8 In Class; AFS; Sec Church Yth Grp; Sec Spanish Clb; Band; Concert Band; Mrchg Band; School Musical; Sec Frsh Cls; Sec Stu Cncl; Hon Roll; Proj Adept 84-86.

FELSTEAD, KEITH; Medina HS; Medina, NY; (Y); 6/147; Am Leg Boys St; Church Yth Grp; Band; Concert Band; Jazz Band; Mrchg Band; Pres Soph Cls; Rep Stu Cncl; JV Bsktbl; Var Lcrss; Engrng.

FELT, ANGELA; Salamanca Central HS; Salamanca, NY; (Y); 16/158; VP DECA; Drama Clb; French Clb; Concert Band; Mrchg Band; Var Capt Sftbl; JV Capt Vllybl; French Hon Soc; High Hon Roll; Hon Roll; Cattaraugus Cnty Intrnshp 86-87; Mrktng.

FELTER, ANDREW L; Ravena-Coeymans-Selkirk Centrl Schl; Coeymans Hollow, NY; (Y); 35/177; Camera Clb; Church Yth Grp; Debate Tm; Drama Clb; Key Clb; Ski Clb; School Musical; Nwsp Phtg; Yrbk Phtg; Pres Soph Cls; NY ST Rgnts Schlrshp 85-86; Cobleskill Coll; Marine Bio.

FELTON, MARK; Rockland Country Day Schl; Palisades, NY; (S); Drama Clb; Math Tm; NFL; Capt Scholastic Bowl; Capt Varsity Clb; School Musical; Yrbk Ed-Chief; Yrbk Phtg; Lit Mag; Trs Jr Cls; Cornell Club Most Outstndng Stu; Stanford; Med.

FEMINELLA, KAREN T; St Francis Prep; Maspeth, NY; (S); 16/744; Church Yth Grp; Cmnty Wkr; Dance Clb; Teachers Aide; Chorus; Concert Band; JV Var Vllybl; High Hon Roll; NHS; Math.

FENNELL, CHRISTINE; Kenmore East HS; Kenmore, NY; (Y); Dance Clb; Girl Scts; Hosp Aide; Pres Band; Chorus; Color Guard; Orch; Bausch & Lomb Sci Awd; High Hon Roll; NHS; Engr.

FENNELL, LAURA; West Babylon SR HS; W Babylon, NY; (Y); 7/411; SADD; Cit Awd; High Hon Roll; Jr NHS; NHS; Ntl Merit Ltr; West Babylon PTA Cncl Schlrshp 86; Excllnc In Hmnties & Excllnc In Eng Awds 86; Rgnts Schlrshp 86-90; SUNY Stony Brook; Pre Med.

FENNESSY, MARY BETH; Auburn HS; Auburn, NY; (Y); Letterman Clb; Varsity Clb; Bsktbl; Var Socr; Var JV Sftbl; Cayuga County CC.

FENNESSY, STEVE; Auburn HS; Auburn, NY; (Y); Drama Clb; Ski Clb; JV Golf; High Hon Roll; Hon Roll.

FENOCCHI, MICHAEL G; Liverpool HS; Liverpool, NY; (Y); Boy Scts; CAP; Lit Mag; JV Ftbl; Lcrss; Hon Roll; St Schlr; Alfred ST; Frstry.

FENSON, SARAH; John Jay HS; Katonah, NY; (Y); Ski Clb; Variety Show; Var Lcrss; Var Swmmng; Hon Roll; Prfct Atten Awd; Corporate Law.

FENTON, COLLEEN; Burnt Hills Ballston Lake HS; Ballston Lake, NY; (Y); 35/300; Church Yth Grp; Hosp Aide; Latin Clb; Chorus; Yrbk Rptr; Rep Frsh Cls; Rep Soph Cls; Rep Stu Cncl; JV Socr; High Hon Roll; Skidmore Coll Acad Achvt Awd 85; Alcohol & Substnc Abuse Educ Prog Hnrs 86; Middlebury Coll; Bio.

FENTON, NEIL; Archbishop Molloy HS; Middle Vlg, NY; (Y); 45/400; Computer Clb; Nwsp Rptr; Var L Crs Cntry; Var L Trk; NHS; Fordham U; Pre Law.

FEOLA, MICHELLE; Central HS; Valley Stream, NY; (Y); Dance Clb; Drama Clb; Drill Tm; School Musical; School Play; Variety Show; JV Sftbl; Nassau CC; Accntnt.

FERBER, JILL; Delaware Valley Central HS; Callicoon, NY; (S); 6/42; AFS; Trs Drama Clb; Library Aide; Quiz Bowl; Pres Spanish Clb; SADD; Teachers Aide; Capt Color Guard; School Play; Score Keeper; W H Stengal Memrl Lib Prze 83-85; Hofstra U; Elem Educ.

FERER, DARREN; North Babylon SR HS; N Babylon, NY; (Y); 58/455; Intnl Clb; Library Aide; Temple Yth Grp; Mrchg Band; Yrbk Stf; High Hon Roll; Hon Roll; Jr NHS; Prfct Atten Awd; ST U Of NY; Pharmacy.

FERGUSON, ALFRED; Monsignor Farrell HS; Staten Island, NY; (S); Boy Scts; Im Bsktbl; Im Bowling; Hon Roll; St Johns U; Law.

FERGUSON, ANDREW; Gloversville HS; Gloversville, NY; (Y); Am Leg Boys St; Band; Pres Soph Cls; Pres Jr Cls; Pres Sr Cls; Var Bsbl; Var Bsktbl; Var Capt Ftbl; Hon Roll; NHS; Law.

FERGUSON, DAVID T; Bishop Grimes HS; No Syracuse, NY; (Y); 30/190; Art Clb; Church Yth Grp; PAVAS; Ski Clb; Teachers Aide; Lit Mag; Tennis; Hon Roll; NHS; U Of Tampa; Grphc Dsgn.

FERGUSON, JEFFREY; Oppenheim Ephiatah Central Schl; St Johnsville, NY; (S); 3/24; Art Clb; Band; Concert Band; Mrchg Band; Trs Frsh Cls; Trs Soph Cls; Trs Jr Cls; Bsktbl; Mgr(s); Score Keeper; Elec Engrng.

FERGUSON, JOHN; Sodus Central Schl; Alton, NY; (Y); 16/111; Am Leg Boys St; Church Yth Grp; Wrstlng; High Hon Roll; Hon Roll; Perfct Attndnc 5 Yrs; Comp Sci.

FERGUSON, LLATETRA; Boro Bay Acad; Brooklyn, NY; (S); 1/30; OEA; Political Wkr; Nwsp Stf; Yrbk Stf; Stu Cncl; High Hon Roll; Hon Roll; Val; Arista Awd 83; Law.

FERGUSON, PATRICE L; Williamson SR HS; Williamson, NY; (Y); 5/101; Sec Pres AFS; Girl Scts; Pres Latin Clb; Pres Science Clb; Trs Band; Chorus; Pres Stu Cncl; JV Sftbl; Var Capt Vllybl; NHS; Girl Scout Gold Awd 86; NYS Rgnts Schlrshp 86; Cornel Trdtnl Bk Awd 86; Cornell U; Anml Sci.

FERGUSON, PATRICK; Msgr Mc Clancy HS; Long Islnd City, NY; (Y); Church Yth Grp; Rep Sr Cls; Rep Stu Cncl; Im Bsktbl; Im Bowling; Im Fld Hcky; Im Ftbl; Hon Roll; Cert Catechist Tech 86; Yth Minstry Pgm 85-86; Bus.

FERGUSON, PAUL; Riverhead HS; Riverhead, NY; (Y); 19/200; Church Yth Grp; Im Ice Hcky; Hon Roll; SUNY Canton ATC; Mortry Sci.

FERGUSON, REGINALD V; Our Saviour Lutheran HS; Bronx, NY; (Y); 2/24; Computer Clb; Drama Clb; Spanish Clb; Pres Sr Cls; Pres Stu Cncl; Socr; Trk; Sal; NYS Regnts Schlrshp 86; NYU; Mktg.

FERGUSON, SULEICA; Fashion Industries HS; Brooklyn, NY; (Y); 89/324; Dance Clb; JA; Acpl Chr; Chorus; School Play; Variety Show; Yrbk Stf; Vllybl; Engl Hon Rl 85; Baruch Coll; Bus Adm.

FERGUSON, TANYA; Bishop Kearney HS; Rochester, NY; (Y); Debate Tm; Drama Clb; Model UN; Y-Teens; Chorus; Church Choir; School Musical; School Play; Socr; JC Awd; Blck Schlr Awd 86-87; Law Explr Mck Trl Comptn 86; Prjct Bus Fn Achvt 83; Georgetown; Pre Law.

FERGUSON, THOMAS; Regis HS; New York, NY; (Y); Church Yth Grp; Cmnty Wkr; Variety Show; Var JV Bsbl; Var JV Bsktbl; Im Fld Hcky; Im Sftbl; Merit Cards 83-86; Boston Coll; Bus.

FERLITO, LAURA; Mineola HS; Mineola, NY; (Y); Cmnty Wkr; Drill Tm; Mrchg Band; Hon Roll.

FERLO, DESIREE; Rome Catholic HS; Rome, NY; (Y); 16/68; Library Aide; Yrbk Stf; Rep Frsh Cls; JV Cheerleading; Var Mgr(s); High Hon Roll; Hon Roll; Hartwick Coll Grnt 86; Hartwick Coll; Eng.

FERM, DOUGLAS; Chatham HS; Spencestown, NY; (Y); 42/125; Boy Scts; Church Yth Grp; Library Aide; Ski Clb; Chorus; School Musical; Mgr(s); Tennis; Stat Bsktbl; Arch.

FERMON, DAN; Penfield HS; Penfield, NY; (Y); Ski Clb; School Play; Rep Frsh Cls; Rep Soph Cls; VP Stu Cncl; JV Ftbl; High Hon Roll; Hon Roll; NHS; Prfct Atten Awd; GA Tech; Aerospace Engrng.

FERNANDES, DAWN; Brewster HS; Brewster, NY; (Y); Pep Clb; Band; Color Guard; Fostering Schl Spirit 85; Spec Achvt Occ Ed 86; Bus Sec.

FERNANDES JR, MANUEL D; Iona Prep; Yonkers, NY; (Y); 134/191; Boy Scts; Camp Fr Inc; Church Yth Grp; Cmnty Wkr; Office Aide; Service Clb; Variety Show; Coach Actv; Var Crs Cntry; Var Trk; Eagle Sct By Scts 86; 1st Pl Mdl Cooleys Anemia Bike-A-Thon 82; Ad & Altari & Dei Rltns Mdl 83; Iona Coll; Bus.

FERNANDEZ, CAROLINE; St Edmund HS; Brooklyn, NY; (Y); 36/188; Science Clb; Spanish Clb; Spnsh I & Sci 82-83; Spnsh II & Socl Stds 83-84; Spnsh III 84-85; Brooklyn Coll; Tchr.

FERNANDEZ, CHERIE L; Mac Arthur HS; Levittown, NY; (Y); 10/321; Trs Computer Clb; Mathletes; Nwsp Stf; Socr; Vllybl; High Hon Roll; Jr NHS; NHS; Ntl Merit Ltr; Prfct Atten Awd; 1st Pl Schl Shrt Stry & Poetry Cntsts 83; Schlstc Achvt Awd 83; Comp Rsrch.

FERNANDEZ, DAVID; Aviation HS; Woodside, NY; (Y); 55/415; Camera Clb; VP JA; Off Color Guard; Rep Frsh Cls; Rep Soph Cls; Rep Jr Cls; VP Sr Cls; VP Stu Cncl; Hon Roll; Prfct Atten Awd; Baruch Coll Of Bus; Accntncy.

FERNANDEZ, EDITH; Newtown HS; Corona, NY; (Y); 33/781; Hon Roll; Schlrshp Prep Stu Highest Acdmc Av 84; BUS Admin.

FERNANDEZ, EVETTE; Our Lady Of Perpetual Help HS; Brooklyn, NY; (Y); 71/150; Art Clb; Church Yth Grp; Teachers Aide; Lion Awd; Prfct Atten Awd; Prfct Atten 86; Brooklyn Coll; Psych.

FERNANDEZ, FRANCINE; HS Of Art And Design; Astoria, NY; (Y); Office Aide; Teachers Aide; Band; Drm Mjr(t); Rep Jr Cls; High Hon Roll; Hon Roll; Prfct Atten Awd; Art & Dsgn Medl Advrtsg & Grphc Dsgn 86; Exec Intrnshp Prog Advrtsg 85-86; Fnlst Miss Amer Co Ed 84; Fashion Inst Tech; Advrtsg Dsgn.

FERNANDEZ, IRIS; Jane Addmas Vocation HS; Bronx, NY; (S); 4/260; Cmnty Wkr; FBLA; Office Aide; Stage Crew; Yrbk Stf; Trs Stu Cncl; Gym; High Hon Roll; Hon Roll; Hnr Soc 85-86; Ldrs Clb 85-86; Coop Educ Pgm 85-86; Pace U; Sec Sci.

FERNANDEZ, LUIS; Bishop Scully HS; Amsterdam, NY; (Y); Art Clb; Spanish Clb; Yrbk Stf; JV Var Bowling; Hon Roll; Prfct Atten Awd; Spanish NHS; Mr & Mrs Furda Art Hnr Awd 86; JC Coll Albany; Grphc Dsgn.

FERNANDEZ, MARLENA; Bay Shore HS; Bay Shore, NY; (Y); 86/406; Computer Clb; Drama Clb; Pep Clb; Band; Chorus; Concert Band; Mrchg Band; Orch; Pep Band; Nwsp Stf; Medl Acdmc Decthln 86; Wrtg Cntst Long Island Wide 86; Spec Smmr Coll Prog Adelphi U 86; Govt.

FERNANDEZ, VICKY; St Francis Prep; College Point, NY; (Y); 342/694; Cmnty Wkr; Dance Clb; Hosp Aide; Ski Clb; Varsity Clb; Band; Socr; Trk; Peer Cnclng; Daily Nws Excptnl SR; SUNY Stony Brook; Phy Thrpy.

FERNANDEZ, WILLIAM; Jame Monroe HS; Bronx, NY; (Y); Boys Clb Am; Boy Scts; Church Yth Grp; Church Choir; Bsbl; Bsktbl; Ftbl; Vllybl; Wt Lftg; High Hon Roll; Hon Roll; Elec Spec.

FERNANDEZ, ZENIA C; St Agnes Acad; Littleneck, NY; (Y); School Play; Variety Show; Spnsh Hnrs 85-86; Englsh & Hlth Hnrs 85-86; Psychlgy.

FERNSEBNER, KAREN; Depew HS; Cheektowaga, NY; (Y); 30/272; VP French Clb; Band; Chorus; Color Guard; School Musical; Variety Show; NHS; GAA; Concert Band; Drill Tm; NY Rgnts Schlrshp 86; Buffalo ST Coll; Elem Ed.

FERRADINO, CECILIA; Notre Dame-Bishop Gibbons HS; Schenectady, NY; (Y); 21/90; SADD; Band; Mrchg Band; Lit Mag; JV Bsktbl; Var Socr; Var Sftbl; Hstry.

FERRAIOLI, JODIE; Saugerties HS; Saugerties, NY; (Y); Camera Clb; Church Yth Grp; 4-H; Spanish Clb; Rep Frsh Cls; Stu Cncl; Score Keeper; Var Score Keeper; Wt Lftg; Hon Roll; US Army.

FERRAIOLI, KIM MARIE; Washingtonville HS; Salisbury Mills, NY; (Y); 3/286; FBLA; Ski Clb; Band; Capt Var Sftbl; Hon Roll; Art Clb; JV Socr; Alum Assn-Luella Delavan Schlrshp 86; Orange-Ulster BOCES Awd 86; Amer Mgmt Assn Awd-Operatn Entrprs; Orange Cnty CC; Comp Prgmng.

FERRAIUOLO, PETER; Msgr Farrell HS; Staten Island, NY; (Y); Cmnty Wkr; Varsity Clb; Rep Frsh Cls; Rep Soph Cls; Rep Jr Cls; Rep Sr Cls; Rep Stu Cncl; Im Bsktbl; Var Socr; Var Trk; MOA Awd Sprdnc 84-86.

FERRANDO, CHRIS; Pembroke Central HS; Batavia, NY; (Y); Varsity Clb; Powder Puff Ftbl; Var JV Sftbl; JV Vllybl; Hon Roll; Bus.

FERRANDO, REGINA M; Adlai E Stevenson HS; Bronx, NY; (Y); Orch; Nwsp Ed-Chief; Hon Roll; Marymount Coll; Bus Adm.

FERRANTE, MICHAEL; Long Beach HS; Long Beach, NY; (S); 5/250; Key Clb; School Play; Yrbk Stf; Trs Sr Cls; Var Lcrss; Var Socr; Hon Roll; Pres Schlr; NYS Rgnts Schlrshp 86.

FERRARA, ANNA; The Wheatley Schl; E Williston, NY; (Y); Church Yth Grp; Mathletes; Orch; Rep Stu Cncl; Var JV Fld Hcky; Var Lcrss; NHS.

FERRARA, DANIEL J; Monsignor Farrell HS; Staten Island, NY; (Y); 41/290; Ftbl; NYS Regents Schlrshp 86; Manhattn Coll Pres Schlrshp 86; Manhattan Coll; Engr.

FERRARA, JAMI; Henninger HS; Syracuse, NY; (Y); Band; Concert Band; Jazz Band; Pep Band; Yrbk Stf; Var Swmmng; NCTE Awd; NHS; Oprtn Entrprse 2-Day Smnr 86; Engl.

FERRARA, JANE; South Side HS; Rockville Centre, NY; (Y); 2/300; Sec Key Clb; Trs Latin Clb; Chorus; Nwsp Stf; High Hon Roll; Jr NHS; NHS; Prfct Scor Natl Latn Exm-Awd 86; 90 Avg Latn Awd-Natl Latn Hnr Soc 85 & 86; Elec Engr.

FERRARA, LISA; St Marys Girls HS; Roslyn, NY; (Y); 48/178; Ski Clb; Sftbl; Trk; Vllybl; NHS; St Johns U; Law.

FERRARA, MARIANN; Perry Central HS; Perry, NY; (Y); 6/89; Band; Chorus; Church Choir; Concert Band; Mrchg Band; Sec Jr Cls; Sec Sr Cls; High Hon Roll; Hon Roll; NHS; Roberts Wesleyan Coll; Nrsng.

FERRARA, SAMUEL; Victor Central HS; Victor, NY; (Y); Letterman Clb; Varsity Clb; Stu Cncl; Capt Socr; Capt Trk; High Hon Roll; NHS; Ntl Merit SF; Prfct Atten Awd; Pres Schlr; ROTC Schlrshp 86; Rgnts Schlrshp 86; Bstn U; Intl Rltns.

FERRARI, ERIC; Johnstown HS; Johnstown, NY; (Y); Im JV Bsktbl; Var L Ftbl; CC Awd; Cit Awd; High Hon Roll; Hon Roll; NHS; Oneonta ST U; Bio Sci.

FERRARO, ANTOINETTE; Roosevelt HS; Yonkers, NY; (Y); SADD; Teachers Aide; Rptr VICA; Variety Show; Hon Roll; Westchester CC; Advrtsg.

FERRARO, JEAN; Central HS; Valley Stream, NY; (Y); Dance Clb; Flag Corp; School Musical; School Play; Jr Cls; Pom Pon; Molloy; Psych.

FERRARO, JOHN J; Northport HS; E Northport, NY; (Y); 61/572; Am Leg Boys St; Pres Exploring; Red Cross Aide; Science Clb; Var Crs Cntry; JV Socr; JV Trk; JV Wrstlng; High Hon Roll; NHS; NY St Dlgt NASC Ldrshp Conf 85; WA Wkshp Cngrssnl Smnr 86.

FERRARO, JOHNEEN; Southwestern Central HS; Lakewood, NY; (Y); 22/149; French Clb; Girl Scts; Pep Clb; Ski Clb; Varsity Clb; Band; Chorus; School Play; Rep Stu Cncl; Var JV Cheerleading; Hgh Jump Cnty Champ 84; Stdnt Cncl Awd 85-86; Geneseo; Ed.

FERRARO, JULIE; Saugerties HS; Saugerties, NY; (S); Office Aide; Hon Roll; Acctng.

FERREIRA, ANTONIO M; Mohawk Central HS; Mohawk, NY; (Y); 18/96; Am Leg Boys St; French Clb; Red Cross Aide; Mrchg Band; Yrbk Phtg; L Bsktbl; Hon Roll; JETS Awd; NHS; St Schlr; NY ST Rgnts Schlrshp; NY ST Fld Band Cnfrnc Schlrshp; U S Naval Acad; Aerospc Engnrng.

FERRELL, STEPHENSON M; Uniondale HS; Uniondale, NY; (Y); Boy Scts; Church Yth Grp; Office Aide; Band; Church Choir; Concert Band; Mrchg Band; Var Ftbl; Var Trk; Columbia U; Med.

FERRER, LIDIA; George Washington HS; Bronx, NY; (Y); Office Aide; Chorus; Yrbk Stf; Rep Stu Cncl; Capt Socr; Hon Roll; 80 Pct Awd Gym; John Jay; Crimnl Justc.

FERRER, MONICA; The Barnard Schl; Bronx, NY; (Y); 1/8; Spanish Clb; School Musical; Yrbk Stf; Lit Mag; Pres Jr Cls; Sec Pres Stu Cncl; Vllybl; Bausch & Lomb Sci Awd; Pres Frsh Cls; Pres Soph Cls; 1st Pl 84; 1st Pl 85; Sci.

FERRERA, DOREEN E; Walt Whitman HS; Huntington Sta, NY; (Y); 34/549; Pres Debate Tm; Key Clb; Nwsp Stf; Mgr(s); French Hon Soc; High Hon Roll; NHS; Ntl Merit Ltr; School Musical; Mrazeks Mdl Cngrssn WA; Blood Drv Cpt; Intl Corpt Law.

FERRERO, VINCENT M; Newburgh Free Acad; Newburgh, NY; (Y); 10/644; Am Leg Boys St; Co-Capt Math Tm; Concert Band; JV Bsbl; Bsktbl; VP Jr NHS; NHS; Ntl Merit Ltr; Mrchg Band; High Hon Roll; John Du Baldi Mem Awd 84; C Y O Bsktbl Capt & Leading Scorer 84-86; New Burgn Free Acad Italian Club; Engineering.

FERRETTI III, PAUL F; Lindenhurst SR HS; Lindenhurst, NY; (Y); Aud/Vis; Thesps; Varsity Clb; Band; Chorus; Jazz Band; Orch; Bsbl; Ftbl; Wt Lftg; Subboda Dance Studios 86; Physcl Thrpy.

FERRETTI, THERESA; Shenendehowa HS; Clifton Park, NY; (Y); 252/675; DECA; GAA; Varsity Clb; Chorus; Var Mgr Fld Hcky; Mgr Stat Ftbl; Capt Powder Puff Ftbl; Capt Var Sftbl; Mgr Wrstlng; High Hon Roll; Army Awd 86; SUNY At Albany; Accntng.

FERRI, IMMACOLATA; Hutchinson Central Tech; Buffalo, NY; (Y); Boys Clb Am; Nwsp Stf; Grls Hcky Leag 84-86; N Bonifaccio Awd 86; Arch Engrng.

FERRI, MARYLU; Notre Dame-Bishop Gibbons HS; Schenectady, NY; (Y); Am Leg Aux Girls St; Church Yth Grp; Drama Clb; Pres French Clb; Hosp Aide; School Musical; School Play; Variety Show; Im Tennis; Rst Wrk Of Yth Undr 18 Awd Altmnt Fair 85; 3rd Pl Clnl Cncl Hme Ecnmcs Fair 85; Frnch Awd Bshp Gbns 86; Russell Sage Coll; Bus Admin.

FERRICK, MOLLY; Nardin Acad; E Amherst, NY; (Y); GAA; Girl Scts; Library Aide; Service Clb; Varsity Clb; Stage Crew; JV Cheerleading; JV Swmmng; JV Trk.

FERRIS, JESSICA; Riverside HS; Buffalo, NY; (Y); Hon Roll; Prfct Atten Awd; Comp Tech.

FERRIS, LEE M; Fonda-Fultonville Central Schl; Fultonville, NY; (Y); 20/111; Boy Scts; Band; Chorus; Church Choir; Concert Band; Mrchg Band; Yrbk Rptr; Yrbk Stf; Var Swmmng; Hon Roll; Natl Boy Sct Jamboree 85; ST U Of NY-MRTME; Nvl Arch.

FERRIS, SAMANTHA L; Liverpool HS; Liverpool, NY; (Y); 112/815; Computer Clb; JA; JCL; Latin Clb; Ski Clb; JV Var Sftbl; Var Swmmng; Hon Roll; NHS; NY ST Regents Schlrshp 86; SUNY-BUFFALO; Elect Engr.

FERRIS, SHARON; Liverpool HS; Liverpool, NY; (Y); 240/884; Ski Clb; Bus Ad.

FERRIS, SYLVIA; Heuvelton Central Schl; Ogdensburg, NY; (S); 4/40; GAA; Girl Scts; Latin Clb; Chorus; Yrbk Stf; Var Cheerleading; Var Socr; High Hon Roll; NHS; Mth & Sci Awd 84; U NH.

FERRIS, TRACI R; Lanarsie HS; Brooklyn, NY; (Y); Teachers Aide; School Musical; School Play; Cheerleading; Hon Roll; NHS; Pres Arista; Archon.

FERRO, DANIELLE; Middletown HS; Berwick, PA; (Y); Math Tm; Sec Science Clb; Swmmng; High Hon Roll; Ntl Merit SF; Natl Sci Achvt Awd 85; Bloomsburgh U PA; Stock Brooke.

FERRO, LAURIEANN; Pine Bush HS; Middletown, NY; (Y); 4-H; Hosp Aide; SADD; Chorus; Drill Tm; Drm Mjr(t); School Musical; School Play; Stage Crew; Variety Show; Amer Essy Cntst Ladies Aux 83; OCCC; Elem Ed.

FERRO, MARIA; Christ The King R HS; Middle Village, NY; (Y); 11/451; Yrbk Stf; Rep Frsh Cls; Hon Roll; NHS.

FERRONE, GEORGE; Archbishop Molloy HS; Flushing, NY; (Y); 25/383; Cmnty Wkr; Computer Clb; French Clb; Pep Clb; Red Cross Aide; Science Clb; Ski Clb; SADD; Chorus; Pep Band; Stanner Spirit Awd 84.

FERRUGGIA, MICHAEL A; Half Hollow Hills HS East; Melville, NY; (Y); Camera Clb; Church Yth Grp; Cmnty Wkr; Trk; Cit Awd; High Hon Roll; Hon Roll; Kiwanis Awd; SUNY-STONY Brk; Psychlgy.

FERRUZZA, JEFFREY; Aquinas Inst; Rochester, NY; (Y); 8/146; Spanish Clb; Stage Crew; Yrbk Sprt Ed; Var Bowling; JV Var Socr; JV Var Trk; Hon Roll; Prfct Atten Awd; Pres Acdmc Ftns Awd 86; Clrksn; Engrng.

FERRUZZO, CATHERINE; Canarsie HS; Brooklyn, NY; (Y); Dance Clb; Hosp Aide; SADD; Chorus; School Play; Nwsp Phtg; Cheerleading; Vllybl; Hon Roll; NHS; Arkon Schrll Serv To The Schl Arista Schrll 84; St Johns; Acctng.

FERRY, JENNIFER; Alexander Central HS; Darien, NY; (Y); Math Tm; Spanish Clb; Varsity Clb; Chorus; JV Var Bsktbl; Var Tennis; JV Var Vllybl; Bausch & Lomb Sci Awd; High Hon Roll; Hon Roll; Drexel U; Bus.

FERRY, LAURA; Kenmore West SR HS; Kenmore, NY; (Y); 5/420; French Clb; Math Tm; Trs Soph Cls; VP Sr Cls; Rep Stu Cncl; Var Vllybl; Bausch & Lomb Sci Awd; High Hon Roll; NHS; Pres Schlr; Buffalo Alumnae Pnhllnc Awd 86; Roy E Freeman Plq Outstndng Acad & Serv 86; Bausch & Lomb Sci Schlrshp; U Of Rochester; Pre Med.

FERRY, PATTY; John A Coleman HS; Tillson, NY; (Y); Sec Church Yth Grp; Drama Clb; French Clb; Capt Bsktbl; 4-H Awd; 2nd Hnrs In Advrtsg, Dsgn, & Grphcs 85-86; 1st Hnrs Engl 84-85; 2nd Hnrs Rlgs Stds 85-86; Mt St Mary Coll; Elem Ed.

FERTUCCI, JOSEPH; Archbishop Stepinac HS; Putnam Vly, NY; (Y); 50/175; Var Socr; Hon Roll; Boston U; Med.

FESTA, ANNEMARIE; Riverhead HS; Aquebogue, NY; (Y); 3/200; Art Clb; Church Yth Grp; Cmnty Wkr; Hosp Aide; Math Tm; Teachers Aide; Church Choir; NHS; Elem Educ.

FESTA, CAROL; Richmond Hill HS; Howard Beach, NY; (Y); 8/259; English Clb; Key Clb; Math Clb; Nwsp Rptr; Yrbk Phtg; Yrbk Stf; High Hon Roll; Jr NHS; NHS; Spanish NHS; Pres Acad Ftns Awd 86; NYC Assoc Tchrs Soc Studys Awd 86; Spnsh Mdl 86; Hofstra U; Intl Bus.

FESTA, SUSAN J; St Francis Prep; Middle Village, NY; (S); 11/653; Hosp Aide; Math Tm; Office Aide; Teachers Aide; Rep Stu Cncl; High Hon Roll; NHS; Acad All Amer 85; Nrsng.

FETTEROLF, ROBERT; Union Endicott HS; Endicott, NY; (Y); Boys Clb Am; Church Yth Grp; Key Clb; SADD; Band; Concert Band; Jazz Band; Mrchg Band; Im Vllybl; JV Wrstlng; Regents Schlrshp 86; SUNY-GENESEO; Busnss Admin.

FETTEROLFS, ELIZABETH; Cold Spring Harbor HS; Huntington, NY; (Y); Church Yth Grp; Cmnty Wkr; Intnl Clb; Varsity Clb; Band; Jazz Band; School Play; Sccr MVP,All County, High Scorer, NY ST Select Tm Capt 85; Sccr Hall Of Fame, All County 86.

FETZER, LISA; Saugerties HS; Saugerties, NY; (Y); 5/250; Band; Symp Band; Bowling; Elks Awd; High Hon Roll; NHS; Ntl Merit Ltr; Natl Soc Studs Olympd 86; Acad All Amer 86; Mth.

FEUER, ALLEN H; Vestal HS; Vestal, NY; (Y); 19/430; Cmnty Wkr; Pres FBLA; High Hon Roll; NHS; Ntl Merit SF; 2nd Plc NYS FBLA Entrprnrshp I 84; Hnrbl Mntn NYS FBLA Accntng I 84; NYS Dstrct VP FBLA 85; Brandeis.

FEUER, SCOTT; John Dewey HS; Brooklyn, NY; (Y); Math Tm; Nwsp Stf; Bsktbl; Var Tennis; High Hon Roll; Untd Fed Of Tchrs Schlrshp 86; Rgnts Schlrshp 86; Dly News Spr Yth Awd 84-85; SUNY Bngmtn; Econ.

FEUERMAN, MARY; Riverhead HS; Riverhead, NY; (Y); Hst Pres FBLA; JA; VICA; Nwsp Stf; Assso Long Iland Voc Ed Outstndng SR 86; Riverhd Rotry Schrlshp 86; Outstndng Female SR HB Ward 86; Suffolk Cnty CC; Bus Adm.

FEUERSTEIN, KIMBERLY; Niskayuna HS; Schenectady, NY; (Y); Pep Clb; Trs Spanish Clb; Rep Stu Cncl; JV Var Fld Hcky; JV Var Vllybl; NHS; Hosp Aide; Latin Clb; Powder Puff Ftbl; Ntl Merit Ltr; Semi Fnlst In Natl Hispanic Hnr Socy Schlrshp 86; U Of MI Achvt Awd 86; Diploma De Merito 85; Georgetown U; Intl Rltns.

FEUZ, LISA; Springville-Griffith Inst; Springville, NY; (Y); 21/197; Church Yth Grp; French Clb; Yrbk Ed-Chief; Yrbk Stf; NHS; U Of Ptsbrgh At Brdfrd Pres Schlrshp 86; Rgnts Schlrshp 86; Pres Acad Ftns Awd 86; Ptsbrgh U-Brdfrd; Elec Engrng.

FEVOLA, KEITH; Clarkstown SR HS South; New City, NY; (Y); Art.

FEY, DANIEL R; Briarcliff Manor HS; Briarcliff Manor, NY; (Y); Band; Jazz Band; Pres Sr Cls; Var JV Bsbl; Var Capt Socr; Ntl Merit SF; St Schlr; Pep Band; Hon Roll; NYS Rgnts Schlrshp 86; All Sect & All Lg Skiing 86; Colgate U; Engrng.

FEY, KIMBERLY; Sachem HS; Lake Ronkonkoma, NY; (Y); 26/1550; Ski Clb; Orch; Sec Frsh Cls; Sec Soph Cls; Sec Jr Cls; Sec Sr Cls; Stu Cncl; NHS; Service Clb; Spanish Clb; Schl Hsty Lng Islnd Sci Cngrss 85; Suffolk All Cnty Orchstr Mbr 84-86; NY All ST Orchstr 85-86.

FIALA, ERIC; Archbishop Molloy HS; Ridgewood, NY; (Y); 215/383; Wt Lftg.

FIANDACH, MICHELLE; Penfield HS; Penfield, NY; (Y); Church Yth Grp; Exploring; Chorus; Im Fld Hcky; Im Socr; Im Sftbl; Im Tennis; Im Vllybl; High Hon Roll; Hon Roll; Chld Care.

FIASCHETTI, JOELY; Catholic Central HS; Troy, NY; (Y); Math Clb; SADD; School Musical; Stage Crew; Yrbk Stf; Rep Jr Cls; Sec Sr Cls; Hon Roll; NHS; Excllnc Music Theory; Engrng.

FIASCHETTI, ROMONA; Rome Free Acad; Rome, NY; (Y); Church Yth Grp; Girl Scts; Library Aide; Sec Office Aide; Hon Roll; Paulette Mumpton Mem Schrlshp 86; Ctzns Schlrshp Fndtn Amer 86; Anna & Meyer Gardner Schlrhsp 86; Utica Schl Commerce; Exec Secy.

FICAZZOLA, MICHAEL; St Peters Boys HS; Staten Island, NY; (Y); 1/155; VP SADD; VP Stu Cncl; JV Trk; Debate Tm; Drama Clb; Gov Hon Prg Awd; Hon Roll; NHS; Val; NY U Schlrshp, C W Post Schlrshp, Italian Schlrshp 86; 1st Hnrs 85-86; Sci Awd, Gen Excllnc Engl 86; NY U; Pre Med.

FICHERA, MICHAEL; Archbishop Molly HS; Flushing, NY; (Y); 6/383; Art Clb; Science Clb; Teachers Aide; Nwsp Stf; Lit Mag; High Hon Roll; NHS; Rensselaer Polytec Inst Math & Sci Awd 85-86; Acad Excllnc Schl Awd 85-86; Chem Engrng.

FIEBKE, KEVIN M; Columbia HS; East Greenbush, NY; (Y); 12/417; Boy Scts; Church Yth Grp; JA; Math Tm; Radio Clb; School Musical; School Play; High Hon Roll; NHS; Hgst Grd Earth Sci 83; Outstndng Achvmnt In 11 R Social Studies 85; Hudson Valley CC; Elec Engr.

FIEDLER, CONNIE; Brushton-Moira Central HS; Moira, NY; (Y); Hon Roll; NHS; Recgntn Excllnce Ltr & Badge 86; Med.

FIEDLER, PAMELA; Gloversville HS; Gloversvl, NY; (Y); Latin Clb; SADD; Concert Band; Orch; Nwsp Stf; Yrbk Stf; Swmmng; High Hon Roll; Hon Roll; Ntl Merit Ltr; Capt Glvrsvl YMCA Swm Tm 85-8.

FIEGE, MIKE; Beacon HS; Beacon, NY; (Y); German Clb; Key Clb; Math Clb; Science Clb; Varsity Clb; VP Soph Cls; Pres Jr Cls; Var L Socr; VFW Bys ST Slctn 86; Phys Thrpy.

FIELD, DERRICK; Madrid-Waddington HS; Waddington, NY; (Y); Church Yth Grp; Drama Clb; Thesps; School Musical; School Play; Variety Show; Hon Roll; Socl Activities Dir-Madrid-Waddington Yth Cncl 85-86; Harold Hill In The Music Man 85; HS Of Excllnce.

FIELD, TRACY; Midwood HS; Brooklyn, NY; (Y); Office Aide; Varsity Clb; School Play; Yrbk Stf; Rep Stu Cncl; Bowling; Cheerleading; Cornell U; Bus Adm.

FIELDING, CRAIG E; Bayside HS; Whitestone, NY; (Y); 32/658; Debate Tm; Math Tm; Nwsp Ed-Chief; Lit Mag; Rep Stu Cncl; Cit Awd; Hon Roll; Jr NHS; NHS; Prfct Atten Awd; NY ST Rgnts Schlrshp 86; Ltn Hnrs Pgm 83-86; US Army Rsrv Natl Essay Cntst 85; UN Peace Mdl 85; Law.

FIELDS, CINDY; Prospect Heights HS; Brooklyn, NY; (Y); #22 In Class; Debate Tm; FBLA; Office Aide; Teachers Aide; Band; School Play; Nwsp Rptr; Nwsp Stf; Hon Roll; NHS; Super Yth Awd 86; NY ST Bar Assoc Mock Trl Trnmnt 86; Recgntn NYC Mentrng Prg; Pltcl Sci.

FIELDS, PATRICK; Watertown HS; Watertown, NY; (Y); Boy Scts; Ski Clb; Tennis; Hon Roll; Arch.

FIELDS, ROY; Pulaski HS; Pulaski, NY; (Y); Varsity Clb; Var Capt Bsktbl; Var L Crs Cntry; Var L Trk; Hon Roll; All Star Bsktbl Tm 86; All Leag Trk 86.

FIELDS, SALENA; Hempstead HS; Hempstead, NY; (S); Trs Variety Show; Off Soph Cls; Trs Jr Cls; Hon Roll; NHS; Coed Clb 83-84; Bus Mngmnt.

FIEN, MARK A; Pittsford Mendon HS; Pittsford, NY; (Y); Pres Chess Clb; Tennis; High Hon Roll; Hon Roll; Rgnts Schlrshp 86; Lafayette Coll; Engrng.

FIERRO, DOREEN L; Acad Of The Rsrctn; Port Chester, NY; (Y); 1/82; Art Clb; Church Yth Grp; Math Clb; Service Clb; Yrbk Ed-Chief; High Hon Roll; NHS; Val; Christine A Nolan Mrl Gld Mdl Awd Gnrl Exel 86; Hghst Hnr Scty Wmn Engrs Mrt SCI & Math 86; U Of NY; Chld Psychlgy.

FIERRO, MICHAEL ROBERT; Kings Park SR HS; Kings Park, NY; (Y); Varsity Clb; Band; Concert Band; Mrchg Band; School Musical; Ftbl; Trk; Wt Lftg; Wrstlng; High Hon Roll; Mech Engrng.

FIFIELD, BARBARA; Linton HS; Schenectady, NY; (Y); Intnl Clb; Key Clb; Church Choir; Off Soph Cls; Off Jr Cls; Hon Roll; Jr NHS; NHS; Ntl Merit SF; Spanish NHS; Erth Sci Awd 84; Columbia U; Intl Reltns.

FIFIELD, CHRISTINA; Lindenhurst HS; Lindenhurst, NY; (Y); Church Yth Grp; Drama Clb; Spanish Clb; Thesps; Chorus; Color Guard; Drm & Bgl; Drm Mjr(t); School Musical; School Play; Psych.

FIG, MICHELE; William Floyd HS; Shirley, NY; (Y); VP DECA; Concert Band; Jazz Band; Bus Stu Mnth 86; Bus Awd 86; Oswego; Acctng.

FIGARI, JACK N; Msgr Farrell HS; Staten Island, NY; (Y); 41/289; Math Tm; Capt Im Bowling; Im Ftbl; Ntl Merit Ltr; Polytechnic U Trstees Brd Schlrshp 86; NY ST Rgnts Schlrshp 86; Polytechnic U; Mech Engrng.

FIGLIOLI, DIANE; Valley Stream Central HS; Valley Stream, NY; (Y); 145/349; Drill Tm; Hon Roll; Ntl Bus Hnr Sco 83-85; Cls Wk 83-85; Streamers Champ 84-86; St Johns U.

FIGLOW, JODI; Batavis SR HS; Batavia, NY; (Y); 13/213; Church Yth Grp; Drama Clb; SADD; Color Guard; Cheerleading; Score Keeper; Tennis; Hon Roll; NHS; Mst Outstndng Clrgrd 85-86; Gntc Engrng.

FIGUEROA, ANGEL LUIS; Thomas Edison HS; Brooklyn, NY; (Y); Boy Scts; Band; Concert Band; Drm Mjr(t); Bsktbl; Ftbl; Vllybl; Air Force; Plt.

FIGUEROA, IRENE; St Raymond Acad; Bronx, NY; (Y); Yrbk Stf; NYS Rgnts Schlrshp 86; Hunter Coll; Comp Sci.

FIGUEROA, JOHANNA; St Pius V HS; Bronx, NY; (Y); 3/80; Hosp Aide; Service Clb; Chorus; Nwsp Stf; Stu Cncl; Cheerleading; Twrlr; High Hon Roll; Hon Roll; Sec Trs NHS; Mth & Frnch Awd 84-85; Ntl Hnr Soc 85-86; Columbia U; Bio.

FIGUEROA, LIZBETH; Monsignor Scanlan HS; Bronx, NY; (Y); 21/277; Gym; Trk; Hon Roll; 1st Hnr Awd 85; Acdmc Certs 83-86; Comp Statistics.

FIGUEROA, NELSON; Cathedral Prep Seminary; Brooklyn, NY; (Y); Church Choir; Variety Show; Yrbk Ed-Chief; Lit Mag; Hon Roll; Elect Engr.

FIGUEROA, SEAN; Central Islip HS; Central Islip, NY; (Y); 11/380; Church Yth Grp; Math Tm; Mrchg Band; Variety Show; Ftbl; Lcrss; Hon Roll; NHS; Law.

FIGUEROA, SHARON; Preston HS; Bronx, NY; (S); 13/89; Camera Clb; Leo Clb; Teachers Aide; Soph Cls; High Hon Roll; NHS; Fordham U; Bus Adm.

FIK, EDWARD; Lackawanna SR HS; Lackawanna, NY; (Y); Yrbk Phtg; Yrbk Rptr; Yrbk Stf; Tennis; Trk; Comm Art.

FILARECKI, LAURIE; Lansingburgh HS; Troy, NY; (Y); 106/185; Hosp Aide; Key Clb; Varsity Clb; Chorus; Concert Band; Mrchg Band; Stage Crew; Var JV Tennis; High Hon Roll; Hon Roll; Suny U Oneonta; Phy Thrpy.

FILASKI, DAVID; John Jay HS; Waccabuc, NY; (Y); Ski Clb; SADD; Variety Show; Var Capt Golf; High Hon Roll; Hon Roll; NHS; Spanish NHS; ST Champ Tm FPSP 81-85; 13th Pl Scenario Wrtng FPSP 84; 2nd Pl Fin ST Champnshp FPSP 83-84; Bus.

FILEY, CHRISTINE M; Canastota HS; Canastota, NY; (Y); 28/147; Camera Clb; Church Yth Grp; Drama Clb; Pres 4-H; Trs FTA; VP GAA; Chrmn Intnl Clb; Library Aide; Science Clb; Chrmn Spanish Clb; Regents Schlrshp Wnnr NYS 86; CTA Schlrshp Wnnr 86; Dollars Schlrshp 86; Cortland ST; Ed.

FILINGERI, ANDREA; Franckfort-Schuyler Central Schl; Frankfort, NY; (S); 7/100; Pres Art Clb; Sec Trs GAA; Yrbk Ed-Chief; Rep Stu Cncl; JV Var Bsktbl; Var Capt Fld Hcky; Capt Trk; Var Vllybl; High Hon Roll; Sec NHS; NY ST Smmr Schl Visual Arts 85; Adv Desgn.

FILIPE, STEVEN; La Salle Acad; New York, NY; (S); 7/165; Church Yth Grp; Computer Clb; Dance Clb; Office Aide; Teachers Aide; Orch; Hon Roll; Cmmndtn Excllnce Mth 84; Cert Excllnce Sci 84; Comp Advrtstg.

FILIPELLI, LAURIE A; Gloversville HS; Gloversville, NY; (Y); 8/237; Intnl Clb; Nwsp Stf; Yrbk Stf; Sec Frsh Cls; Sec Soph Cls; Sec Jr Cls; Sec Sr Cls; Sec Stu Cncl; NHS; Opt Clb Awd; Stu Of Mnth 86; Geneseo Coll; Engl.

FILIPPETTI, MIA; Watkins Glen HS; Watkins Glen, NY; (Y); 16/130; Aud/Vis; Dance Clb; Drama Clb; French Clb; Letterman Clb; Band; Chorus; School Musical; School Play; Variety Show; Stu Media Fstvl 1st, 2nd & 3rd 86; Alfred Drm Fstvl Awd Instrmnt 86; Danny Hactors Dnc Crvn 86; Suny; Cinma.

FILIPSKI, DORIE; Springville Griffith Inst; Colden, NY; (Y); 10/192; GAA; Spanish Clb; Rep Sr Cls; Rep Stu Cncl; JV Var Cheerleading; Var Swmmng; Var Tennis; High Hon Roll; JC Awd; NHS; NY ST Rgnts Schlrshp 86; NY ST U Buffalo; Psychlgy.

FILKINS, MICHELE; Berne-Knox-Westerlo HS; E Berne, NY; (Y); Sec SADD; Stage Crew; Sec Frsh Cls; Sec Jr Cls; JV Vllybl; High Hon Roll; NHS; Trvl Agnt.

FILKINS, RON; Rensselaer HS; Rensselaer, NY; (Y); Varsity Clb; Band; Concert Band; Jazz Band; Rep Stu Cncl; Bowling; Hon Roll; Prfct Attndnc 85-86; Elec.

FILKORN, EMIL J; Hamburg SR HS; Hamburg, NY; (Y); 20/391; CAP; Debate Tm; German Clb; Model UN; Var Capt Tennis; Var Trk; Var Vllybl; Bausch & Lomb Sci Awd; NHS; 4 Yr Air Force ROTC Scholar 86-90; Rensselaer Polytech; Aero Engrn.

FILOSA, JENNIFER ANNE; Sachem HS; Farmingville, NY; (Y); 50/1506; Drama Clb; Science Clb; Spanish Clb; SADD; Chorus; Capt Var Bowling; Jr NHS; NHS; Mst Vlbl Bwlr Var Bwlng 83-86; Socl Stds Fair Wnnr 83; Bryant Coll; Accntng.

FILOSA, SUSAN; Port Richmond HS; Staten Isld, NY; (Y); 15/500; AFS; Art Clb; Intnl Clb; Office Aide; Science Clb; Spanish Clb; Temple Yth Grp; Nwsp Stf; Yrbk Stf; Lit Mag; Columbia Assn Schlrshp Awd 86famer Fld Srv Schlrshp 85; Axlry To Rchmnd Med Assn Awd 86; NY U; Doctor.

FILOSETA, DANIELLE; Valley Stream Central HS; Valley Stream, NY; (Y); Dance Clb; Pep Clb; Ski Clb; Drill Tm; Variety Show; Mgr Lcrss; Danc Coordntr Skit Nite 85; Jr Prm Cmmtee 86; Prfrm Suprstar Drl Tm Aloha Bwl 85; Advrtsng.

FINAN, CATHLEEN M; Stella Maris HS; Belle Harbor, NY; (Y); 3/213; Art Clb; Var Math Tm; Nwsp Ed-Chief; High Hon Roll; NHS; Ntl Merit Ltr; Pres Schlr; Sal; St Schlr; Phi Beta Kappa Schlrshp 86; Trstee Schlr/Schlrshp NY U 86; St La Salle Hnr Scty 86; Tablet Achvmnt Awd; Adelphi U; Biolgy.

FINAN, COLLEEN M; Stella Maris HS; Belle-Harbor, NY; (Y); 2/213; Var Math Tm; Nwsp Ed-Chief; Gov Hon Prg Awd; High Hon Roll; NHS; Ntl Merit Ltr; Pres Schlr; Sal; Spanish NHS; Phi Beta Kappa Schlrshp 86; Trstee Schlr/Schlrshp NY U 86; St La Salle Hnr Scty 86; Nwsdy Hi Hnr Smfnl; Adelphi U; Biology.

FINAZZO, GERRY; Lindenhurst Senior HS; Lindenhurst, NY; (Y); French Clb; Intnl Clb; Spanish Clb; SADD; Chorus; Stat Socr; High Hon Roll; Hon Roll; Jr NHS; Spanish NHS; Prncpls Lst 92% Or Btr Avg All 4 Qtrs 85-86; NY U; Languages.

FINCH, ALTON; Nottingham HS; Syracuse, NY; (Y); Exploring; Latin Clb; L Var Golf; L Var Trk; Wt Lftg; Hnr To Prtcpt Prfc Pgm At RPI 85; Smmr Schlr Lemoyne Coll 86; Cornell U; Bio.

FINCH, JANICE; Murry Bergtraum HS; Bronx, NY; (Y); 200/601; Red Cross Aide; Rep Sr Cls; Rep Stu Cncl; Morgan ST U; CPA.

FINCH JR, JOHN A; Hannibal Central HS; Sterling, NY; (Y); Varsity Clb; Band; JV Var Bsbl; JV Var Bsktbl; JV Var Ftbl; High Hon Roll; Hon Roll; MVP Bsbl 86.

FINCH, JULIE; North Rose-Wolcott HS; Clyde, NY; (Y); 18/140; Pres Sec Church Yth Grp; Ski Clb; Spanish Clb; Chorus; Yrbk Stf; Stu Cncl; JV Var Socr; Hon Roll; Sec NHS; NY ST U Geneseo; Elem Ed.

FINCH, KAREN; Ravena-Coeymans-Selkirk HS; Ravena, NY; (Y); 17/184; Art Clb; Exploring; Spanish Clb; Yrbk Stf; Rep Sr Cls; Im Vllybl; High Hon Roll; Hon Roll; Prncpls Advsry Comm 85-86; Ithaca Clg Schlrshp 85-86; Regnts Schlrshp 85-86; Ithaca College; Cinma Dir.

FINCH, MARC; Camden Central HS; Camden, NY; (Y); 7/211; AFS; Ski Clb; Varsity Clb; Var L Bowling; JV Ftbl; Var Capt Golf; Jr NHS; NHS; Pres Schlr; Pgnts Schlrshp 86; Frank Harden Schlrshp 86; Amer Lgn Schlrshp 86; Rchstr Inst Of Tech; Image Sci.

FINCHER, ERIK; Falconer Central HS; Jamestown, NY; (Y); 13/125; Boy Scts; Spanish Clb; Pres Stu Cncl; Var JV Bsktbl; Var Tennis; God Cntry Awd; Hon Roll; Prfct Atten Awd; Egl Awd 86; Engrng.

FINCHER, KIMBERLY; Falconer HS; Jamestown, NY; (Y); 9/123; Am Leg Aux Girls St; Varsity Clb; Pres Stu Cncl; Var Capt Bsktbl; Var Capt Sftbl; Var Capt Vllybl; Dnfth Awd; Hon Roll; NHS; Opt Clb Awd; NY Rgnts Schlrshp 86; Pres Acad Ftnss Awd 86; Amer Legn Schl Awd 86; Allegheny Coll; Bio.

FINDLAY, LANCELOT; Christopher Columbus HS; Bronx, NY; (S); 147/690; Drama Clb; Key Clb; Chorus; School Play; Stage Crew; Off Jr Cls; Off Sr Cls; Stu Cncl; Ftbl; Grambline ST U; Bus Adm.

FINE, BRIAN; Hendrick Hudson HS; Montrose, NY; (Y); 62/195; Im Bsbl; Pace U; Acctnt.

FINE, NATALIE; H S For The Humaniti; New York, NY; (Y); Band; Nwsp Ed-Chief; Nwsp Rptr; VP Soph Cls; Stu Cncl; Gov Hon Prg Awd; High Hon Roll; NHS; Sal; Mayors Super Yth; CSA Stu Ldrshp Awd 84; NYC Assn Assist Princpls Cert 84; Jrnlsm.

FINELLI, CHRISTOPHER M; Roy C Ketcham HS; Poughkeepsie, NY; (Y); Church Yth Grp; Ski Clb; Var L Socr; Var L Trk; High Hon Roll; Jr NHS; Pres NHS; Marn Bio.

FINER, MARC; East Meadow HS; East Meadow, NY; (S); Key Clb; Mathletes; Math Tm; SADD; Temple Yth Grp; Band; Yrbk Stf; Bsbl; Bsktbl; Socr; Schlr/Athlt Awd; MD.

FINGER, JULIE; Mc Kinley HS; Buffalo, NY; (Y); 21/216; FFA; Girl Scts; Library Aide; Hon Roll; SUNY Fredonia; Radio Brdcstng.

FINGERHUT, LORI; Longwood HS; Coram, NY; (S); 33/487; Yrbk Stf; JV Cheerleading; High Hon Roll; Hon Roll; NHS; Rgnts Schlrshp 86; Acctng.

FINGERLING, MARYELLEN; Academy Of St Joseph; Northport, NY; (Y); Church Yth Grp; GAA; Orch; Variety Show; Nwsp Rptr; Nwsp Stf; Yrbk Stf; Bsktbl; Capt Socr; NEDT Awd; Fordham U.

FINI, GINA; St Francis Prep; Douglaston, NY; (S); 52/746; Dance Clb; Chorus; Cheerleading; Powder Puff Ftbl; Vllybl; Wt Lftg; High Hon Roll; NHS; Prfct Atten Awd; Studnt Athlt-JV Cheerldrs 85; JV Cheerldrs Capt 84-85; Freshmn Cheerldrs Capt 83-84.

FINISTER, LISA; Brewster HS; Brewster, NY; (Y); Church Yth Grp; French Clb; Ski Clb; School Musical; Yrbk Phtg; Rep Stu Cncl; Var L Bsktbl; Var L Tennis; Var L Trk; FL Inst Tech; Mktng.

FINK, JILL; Fayetteville-Manlius HS; E Northport, NY; (Y); Art Clb; Debate Tm; Hosp Aide; JA; Model UN; SADD; Temple Yth Grp; Yrbk Stf; Photo Awd 83; Outstndg Vlntr 82; American U; Chld Psych.

FINK, KELLY; Saranac Central Schl; Cadyville, NY; (S); VP Soph Cls; VP Jr Cls; JV Var Bsktbl; JV Sftbl; Socl Svcs.

FINK, SHARI; Commack HS; Commack, NY; (Y); Cmnty Wkr; Teachers Aide; Temple Yth Grp; Y-Teens; Hon Roll; Pres Frsh Cls; Pres Soph Cls; Pres Jr Cls; Rep Stu Cncl; Cmmnctns.

FINK, THEODORE; Ravenda-Coeymans-Selkirk HS; Coeymans Hollow, NY; (Y); Church Yth Grp; Computer Clb; German Clb; Library Aide; High Hon Roll; Hon Roll; Comp Sci.

FINKE, LINDA; Columbia HS; E Greenbush, NY; (Y); JV Bsktbl; JV Var Sftbl; Var Trk; Hon Roll; Plymouth ST Coll; Bus.

FINKEL, LAURA; Lansingburgh HS; Troy, NY; (Y); Chorus; Jazz Band; School Musical; Nwsp Rptr; High Hon Roll; Hon Roll; Math.

FINKEL, RICHARD A; Yeshivah Of Flatbush HS; Staten Island, NY; (Y); Band; Chorus; Mrchg Band; Orch; Ed Lit Mag; Ntl Merit SF; Med.

FINKELSTEIN, ADAM; Long Beach HS; Lido Beach, NY; (S); 23/273; DECA; Key Clb; Temple Yth Grp; Band; Mrchg Band; School Musical; Nwsp Rptr; Nwsp Stf; Var Swmmng; NHS; Bus.

FINKELSTEIN, ELLIOT; Middletown HS; Middletown, NY; (Y); 1/400; Capt Math Tm; Capt Scholastic Bowl; Acpl Chr; Jazz Band; Swing Chorus; Var Trk; High Hon Roll; NHS; Achvt Awd In Math, Comp Sci & Soc Studies 86; Achvt Awd In Engl & Chem 84; U Of PA; Mgmt.

FINKELSTEIN, PHILIP M; The Bronx Science; Woodside, NY; (Y); NFL; Speech Tm; Band; Jr Cls; Jr NHS; Regnts Schlrshp 86; Prncpl Cmndtn Prfrmnc Frnch Comdy 85; Hunter Col; Actr.

FINKELSTEIN, STUART; Middletown HS; Middletown, NY; (Y); 2/360; Scholastic Bowl; Acpl Chr; Jazz Band; School Musical; Yrbk Bus Mgr; Kiwanis Awd; NHS; Drama Clb; French Clb; Math Tm; Chem Achvt Awd 84; Engl Achvt Awd 85 & 86; NROTC Scholar 86; Rice U; Mech Engrng.

FINKLE, THEODORE L; Margaretville Central Schl; Kelly Corners, NY; (Y); Am Leg Boys St; Chess Clb; Drama Clb; Letterman Clb; Spanish Clb; SADD; Varsity Clb; Band; Chorus; Concert Band; All Leag All Str Sccr, All Leag All Str Bsktbl; Pre-Med.

FINKNEY, JOHN; Oakfield-Alabama C S HS; Batavia, NY; (Y); Art Clb; 4-H; L Var Crs Cntry; JV Im Swmmng; JV Im Trk; 4-H Awd; Hon Roll; JV Im Wt Lftg; Genessee Cnty Crs Cntry No 1 85-86; MVP Crs Cntry 85-86.

FINLAY, MICHELLE; Evander Childs HS; Bronx, NY; (S); 16/353; Church Yth Grp; Cmnty Wkr; English Clb; Key Clb; Office Aide; Teachers Aide; Hon Roll; Comprhnsv Mth & Sci Pgm 84; Columbia U; Pre-Med.

FINLEY, ROSE M; Clifton-Fine Central Schl; Star Lake, NY; (S); 1/40; French Clb; Band; Yrbk Stf; High Hon Roll; NHS; Clarkson U; Elec Engrng.

FINLEY, SARAH; Fairport HS; Fairport, NY; (Y); Church Yth Grp; Drama Clb; Key Clb; Math Tm; Band; Mrchg Band; Tennis; High Hon Roll; Hon Roll; NHS; Pre-Med.

FINN, CATHERINE; Valley Stream Central HS; Valley Stream, NY; (Y); Art Clb; Church Yth Grp; FBLA; Girl Scts; Var Socr; Cooking Cont Grl Scts 1st Pl Pear Pie 85; 3rd Pl Lemon Meringe Pie 84.

FINN, SUSAN; St Barnabas HS; Yonkers, NY; (S); 19/188; Drama Clb; NFL; PAVAS; School Play; Nwsp Rptr; Stu Cncl; NHS.

FINNERTY II, GARY H; Altmar-Parish-Williamstown HS; Williamstown, NY; (Y); Am Leg Boys St; French Clb; Concert Band; Pres Jr Cls; Pres Sr Cls; Trs Stu Cncl; Var Bsbl; Var Bsktbl; NHS; Pres Schlr; Regnts Scholar Hnrs Sci 86; Snow Scholar 86; N-P-W Alumni Awd Mst Congenial 86; Le Moyne Coll; Pre-Med.

FINNEY, DAVID; West Genesee HS; Syracuse, NY; (Y); Aud/Vis; Church Yth Grp; French Clb; Letterman Clb; Variety Show; Var Trk; Hon Roll; MVP Track 86; The Citadel; Officer.

FINNIE, LORIE; Gouverneur HS; Gouverneur, NY; (Y); Library Aide; Bryant & Stratton Coll; Lgl Sec.

FINOCCHARIO, FRANCINE E; Geneseo Central HS; Groveland, NY; (Y); 13/86; Yrbk Stf; Rep Stu Cncl; Var Capt Bsktbl; Var L Socr; Var L Sftbl; High Hon Roll; Jr NHS; NHS; MVP Awd Sftbl 84; Excptnl Srs Bsktbl Game 86; Daemen College; Phys Thrpy.

FINSTER, LAURA; Vernon Verona Sherrill Central HS; Durhamville, NY; (Y); Sec Church Yth Grp; Mathletes; Church Choir; Mgr Var Bsktbl; High Hon Roll; Hon Roll; MVCC; Med.

FINUCANE, STEPHANIE; North Rockland HS; Garnerville, NY; (Y); Drama Clb; NFL; Chorus; Orch; School Musical; JV Var Socr; High Hon Roll; Hon Roll; NCTE Awd; Hst NHS; Writng.

FINZ, DAVID; Valley Stream North HS; Valley Stream, NY; (Y); 22/128; Debate Tm; Political Wkr; Speech Tm; Temple Yth Grp; Nwsp Ed-Chief; Var Capt Crs Cntry; JV Socr; Var L Trk; Ntl Merit SF; Chess Clb; Div All Star X-Cntry 84; NY ST U; Pblc Affrs.

FIORAVANTI, CLAYTON L; Ithaca HS; Ithaca, NY; (Y); Am Leg Boys St; Office Aide; Ski Clb; Pres Spanish Clb; Variety Show; Off Frsh Cls; Rep Soph Cls; Stu Cncl; Stu Fllwshp Awd 86; Buffalo ST Coll; Pltcl Sci.

FIORE, ANTHONY; Christ The King HS; Ridgewood, NY; (Y); 10/455; Computer Clb; Key Clb; Ski Clb; School Musical; School Play; JV Bsktbl; Im Fld Hcky; High Hon Roll.

FIORE, KATERINA; Herkimer SR HS; Herkimer, NY; (Y); Drama Clb; Pep Clb; SADD; Band; Chorus; Mrchg Band; Stage Crew; Yrbk Stf; Mgr(s); Tennis; Grace Pelton Awd 86; Larr Knapp Art Schlrshp Most Imprvd Art 86; Larry Knapp Art Schlrshp 86; Munson/Williams/Proctor; Art.

FIORE, KATHERINE M; Tuxedo HS; Greenwood Lake, NY; (Y); 8/98; Drama Clb; French Clb; Math Tm; Var Ski Clb; Chorus; Yrbk Stf; VP Sr Cls; NHS; Boston U; Comp Info.

FIORE, LISA; St Marys Girls HS; Glen Cove, NY; (Y); Camera Clb; Service Clb; Ski Clb; Accntg.

FIORE, MICHAEL J; Sachem North HS; Farmingville, NY; (Y); 96/1400; Science Clb; Ski Clb; Spanish Clb; Teachers Aide; Stage Crew; JV Lcrss; Hon Roll; NYS Regents Schlrshp 86; Penn ST; Engrng.

FIORELLA, BRIAN C; South Western HS; Jamestown, NY; (Y); Ski Clb; Spanish Clb; Band; Concert Band; Jazz Band; Mrchg Band; Stage Crew; Socr; Trk; Wrstlng; Fredonia; Music.

FIORELLO, CHRISTINE; Westlake HS; Hawthorne, NY; (Y); 3/168; Art Clb; Cmnty Wkr; Sec Debate Tm; English Clb; French Clb; Hosp Aide; Science Clb; Variety Show; Nwsp Stf; Lit Mag; Natl Hispanic Schlr Awd 85; Vetrnry Med.

FIORELLO, STACIE A; Midwood HS; Brooklyn, NY; (Y); 101/538; Drama Clb; Math Tm; Office Aide; School Play; Capt Cheerleading; Archon Svc Awd 85-86; Arista Acadmc Awd 85-86; SUNY Bimghamton; Indstrl Psych.

FIORETTA, MARK; West Hempstead HS; W Hempstead, NY; (Y); 25/325; Church Yth Grp; Computer Clb; Pres Radio Clb; Science Clb; Ski Clb; SADD; Stu Cncl; Hon Roll; NHS; Bus Law Achvt Awd 84; Bus Dynamcs Achvt Awd 84; Bio Achvt Awd 84; Fairfield U; Bus.

FIORETTI, THOMAS; Mc Kee HS; Staten Island, NY; (Y); Teachers Aide; Ntl Merit Ltr; Coll Of Staten Island; Bus.

FIORI, CARA; Solvay HS; Solvay, NY; (Y); Church Yth Grp; Exploring; Spanish Clb; Teachers Aide; Band; Chorus; School Play; Off Jr Cls; Achvt Chorus 86; Schlstic Art Appreciation Awd 85; Psych.

FIORITO, KELLY; Le Roy HS; Leroy, NY; (Y); Hon Roll; Genesee CC.

FISCHER, CARA; Walt Whitman HS; Huntington Stat, NY; (Y); 23/500; Church Yth Grp; German Clb; Chorus; Church Choir; School Musical; School Play; Stage Crew; Yrbk Stf; Hon Roll; Jr NHS; Sci Awd 84; German Spkng Awd 84.

FISCHER, CAROLINE R; Brewster HS; Patterson, NY; (Y); 11/209; Drama Clb; SADD; Band; Jazz Band; Yrbk Bus Mgr; JV Var Vllybl; Hon Roll; Trs NHS; Regents Scholar 86; Bucknell U; Lib Arts.

FISCHER, HEIDI; Hamburg SR HS; Hamburg, NY; (Y); 141/384; German Clb; Spanish Clb; Color Guard; VP Jr Cls; VP Sr Cls; Stu Cncl; Im Wt Lftg; 3 Yr Ctlna Clb Mbr Secy Of Clb 86-87; Mgmt.

FISCHER, JUDD; John Dewey HS; Brooklyn, NY; (Y); Ski Clb; Teachers Aide; Concert Band; Jazz Band; Ed Nwsp Bus Mgr; Lit Mag; Bsbl; Bsktbl; Bowling; Ftbl; Envrnmntl Studies.

FISCHER, KATHLEEN; Dominican Commercial HS; Woodside, NY; (Y); 5/288; Intnl Clb; Political Wkr; Teachers Aide; Yrbk Rptr; High Hon Roll; Hon Roll; Jr NHS; NHS; Siena Clb 82-86; NY U Schlrshp 86; Schlr Encllnc Mdl Otstndng Achvt Englsh Rgnts Schlrshp 86; NY U; Jrnlsm.

FISCHER, KATHLEEN; Tuckahoe HS; Eastchester, NY; (Y); Art Clb; Drama Clb; Girl Scts; Math Clb; Science Clb; Band; Chorus; High Hon Roll; Jr NHS; NHS; Chorus Awd 84; Arch.

FISCHER, LAUREN; Hamburg SR HS; Hamburg, NY; (Y); 33/387; 4-H; Sec JCL; Latin Clb; Band; Concert Band; Mrchg Band; Orch; Pep Band; Symp Band; Pres Jr Cls; Intrnshp Phrmcy 86-87; PAVAS; U Of Buffalo; Phrmcy.

FISCHER, LYNN M; Cheektowaga Central HS; Cheektowaga, NY; (Y); 5/199; Drama Clb; Band; Concert Band; Mrchg Band; School Musical; School Play; Stage Crew; Hon Roll; Jr NHS; NHS; Regnts Schlrshp 86; Erie Cty Band 86; U Of Buffalo; Phrmcy.

FISCHER, MARGUERITE C; Ward Melville HS; Stony Brook, NY; (Y); 29/725; Service Clb; Spanish Clb; SADD; Nwsp Rptr; Chorus; JV Gym; High Hon Roll; Jr NHS; NHS; Ntl Merit Ltr; Duke U; Atrny.

FISCHER, PETER; Dunkirk HS; Dunkirk, NY; (Y); 3/192; Letterman Clb; Q&S; Radio Clb; Nwsp Rptr; Nwsp Sprt Ed; Var L Ftbl; Capt L Trk; Im Wt Lftg; High Hon Roll; NYS Regnts Schlrshp 86; NYU Fredonia; Comp Engr.

FISCHER, SHARON; Wayne Central HS; Ontario, NY; (S); 8/193; JV Bsktbl; Var Capt Socr; Var Sftbl; Var Capt Vllybl; Hon Roll; NHS; MVP Sccr 85-86; Acadmc Excllnc Awd Amer Stud 85; Acadmc Achvt Awd Chem 85; St John Fisher; Cmnctns.

FISCHER, THOMAS; Sewanhaka HS; Stewart Manor, NY; (Y); Hst Church Yth Grp; VP Band; Jazz Band; Mrchg Band; School Musical; Hon Roll; Pre-Med.

FISCINA, EVELYN; Stella Maris HS; Maspeth, NY; (Y); Girl Scts; Band; Prncpls List 82; 1st Hnrs 2nd Hnrs 83; 1st Hnrs 86; St Johns U; Law.

FISER, LORETTA; Port Jervis HS; Pt Jervis, NY; (Y); Dance Clb; Drama Clb; 4-H; French Clb; Ski Clb; Spanish Clb; Varsity Clb; Band; School Play; Yrbk Stf; Awd For Mst Dedctd & Imrpvd Skier 84-85; Var Ski Tm 83-86; Sci.

FISH, LORI; Norwood-Norfolk HS; Norfolk, NY; (Y); Church Yth Grp; Key Clb; Chorus; Church Choir; Var Socr; Var JV Sftbl; High Hon Roll; Hon Roll; Jr NHS; Latin Clb; Clarkson Univ; Engrng.

FISH, MICHELE; Saratoga Springs HS; Saratoga Sprgs, NY; (Y); 12/460; Key Clb; Orch; L Mgr Crs Cntry; L Mgr Trk; High Hon Roll; Hon Roll; NHS; NYS Regnts Schlrshp 86; Rochester U; Chem Engrng.

FISHER, AMY; Plattsburgh SR HS; Plattsburg, NY; (Y); 4/172; Church Yth Grp; Drama Clb; Band; Jazz Band; Orch; School Musical; L Var Cheerleading; Lion Awd; NHS; Ntl Merit Ltr; Navy ROTC Schlrshp 86; Acadmc Achvt Awds 83 & 85; Penn ST U; Elctrcl Engrng.

FISHER, ANNE; Middleburgh Central HS; Middleburgh, NY; (S); 2/74; Teachers Aide; Chorus; Mrchg Band; Elks Awd; High Hon Roll; Hon Roll; NHS; BBW Kybrdng, Shrthnd Awd 85; Adirondack CC; Lgl Sec.

FISHER, CAROL ANN; Bishop Ludden HS; Syracuse, NY; (S); 3/124; Church Yth Grp; Model UN; Acpl Chr; Band; Chorus; Pep Band; School Musical; Variety Show; Cornell U; Scientist.

FISHER, DAVID; Marion Central Schl; Marion, NY; (Y); 11/100; Exploring; SADD; JV Bsbl; Im Bowling; JV Crs Cntry; Prfct Atten Awd; Alfred Tech; Comp Engrng.

FISHER, ELIZABETH; Pelham Memorial HS; Pelham, NY; (Y); AFS; JA; Math Tm; Spanish Clb; Twrlr; Hon Roll; NHS; Spanish NHS; Church Yth Grp; Math Clb; Alg Awd 83; JA Awd 86; Mth Tm Awd 85; Mth.

FISHER, EMANUEL; Burgard Voc HS; Buffalo, NY; (Y); Merit Roll; Prfct Attndnce; Engrng.

FISHER, HELENE; Clarkstown North HS; New City, NY; (Y); 97/500; Spanish Clb; Temple Yth Grp; Band; Concert Band; Mrchg Band; Yrbk Stf; Rep Soph Cls; Rep Stu Cncl; Pres Jr NHS; Mu Alp Tht; SUNY Albany; Law.

FISHER, JAMES; Guilderland Central HS; Slingerlands, NY; (Y); ROTC; SADD; Varsity Clb; Off Frsh Cls; Off Soph Cls; Off Stu Cncl; Var L Ftbl; Bus Adm.

FISHER, JENNIFER; Johnstown HS; Johnstown, NY; (Y); Color Guard; Fulton Montgomery CC; Lib Arts.

FISHER, KIM; Fabius-Pompey HS; Fabius, NY; (Y); Band; Concert Band; Pres Frsh Cls; Pres Soph Cls; Pres Jr Cls; Var Bsktbl; Var Socr; Var Sftbl; Hon Roll; All Cnty 83-84; NYSSMA Solo Mdl 83-84; All ST 83-84; Franklin-Pierce; Cmrcl Art.

FISHER, KIMBERLY; Alexander HS; Alexander, NY; (Y); FTA; Intnl Clb; Spanish Clb; Band; Concert Band; Mrchg Band; Nwsp Rptr; Prim Educ.

FISHER, KIMBERLY; Amsterdam HS; Amsterdam, NY; (Y); 65/297; Church Yth Grp; DECA; Intnl Clb; Ski Clb; Drm Mjr(t); Yrbk Stf; Rep Stu Cncl; Bowling; Hon Roll; Prfct Atten Awd; Bus Awd-Rpd Clcltn-10th Pl 85; DECA Awd-Genrl Merch-2nd Pl 85; Cntry Clb Awd-Prose Cntst 1st Pl 86; ST U Of Oswego; Bus Educ Tchr.

FISHER, LINDA; South Park HS; Buffalo, NY; (Y); German Clb; Girl Scts; Hosp Aide; Spanish Clb; Church Choir; Yrbk Stf; Prfct Atten Awd; Erie CC; Nurse.

FISHER, MARIA; Lindenhurst SR HS; Lindenhurst, NY; (Y); VP Sec German Clb; Thesps; Concert Band; Mrchg Band; School Musical; Yrbk Stf; High Hon Roll; Hon Roll; NHS; Band; Tchrs Assoc Awd 86; Med.

FISHER, MAUREEN E; E J Wilson HS; Rochester, NY; (Y); Drama Clb; French Clb; Math Tm; Band; Chorus; Mrchg Band; School Musical; School Play; Stage Crew; Swing Chorus; Regents Schlrshp 86; Ithaca Coll; Cmmnctns.

FISHER, MICHELE B; Harrison HS; Harrison, NY; (Y); 11/211; Debate Tm; Math Tm; SADD; Yrbk Stf; Rep Stu Cncl; Var Socr; Var JV Tennis; NHS; Ntl Merit Schol; Drama Clb; NY ST Rgnts Schlr; Awd-Mntning 90 Avg Frgn Lang-Spnsh 83, 84; Awd Mst Imprvd Tnns Plyr 85; Northwestern U; Poltcl Sci.

FISHER, ROBERT; West Seneca East SR HS; Cheektowasa, NY; (Y); Boys Clb Am; DECA; Bsktbl; Ftbl; Hon Roll; Spanish NHS; 1st Pl ST & Ntl Fnlst-Entrprnshp Prtcptng Evnt 86; U Of Buffalo; Bus.

FISHER, SUZETTE; Greenwich Central HS; Greenwich, NY; (Y); AFS; Art Clb; GAA; Ski Clb; Band; Concert Band; School Musical; JV Var Cheerleading; JV Crs Cntry; Var Fld Hcky; Franklin Pierce; Fine Arts.

FISHER, TAMMY; Franklin Acad; Malone, NY; (Y); Trs Art Clb; Hon Roll; NCTE Awd; Epsilon 85-86; Bus.

FISHKIN, MARK; Blind Brook HS; Rye Brook, NY; (Y); AFS; Boy Scts; French Clb; Math Tm; SADD; Nwsp Stf; Rep Stu Cncl; TV.

FISHMAN, DAWN; Laguardia HS Of Music & Art; Brooklyn, NY; (S); Library Aide; Office Aide; Yrbk Stf; Hon Roll; Jr NHS; NHS; Val; Cooper Union; Art.

FISHMAN, RACHEL; Brooklyn Friends Schl; Brooklyn, NY; (Y); Cmnty Wkr; Dance Clb; Exploring; Service Clb; School Musical; Nwsp Phtg; Ed Yrbk Stf; Var Vllybl.

FISK, KATHLEEN; Marion JR SR HS; Marion, NY; (Y); 25/99; Band; Concert Band; Mrchg Band; School Musical; Stage Crew; Yrbk Stf; Stat Bsktbl; JV Var Sftbl; Arch.

FISK, KEVIN; Mannheim American HS; Apo New York, NY; (Y); 12/100; FBLA; German Clb; Teachers Aide; Outstndng Achvt Chmstry 85-86; U Of AZ; Aerntcl Engr.

FISKE, GREGG; Cortland HS; Cortland, NY; (Y); 24/200; Am Leg Boys St; Aud/Vis; Boys Clb Am; Var Bsbl; Var Bsktbl; Var Ftbl; Jr NHS; NHS; Deke Mc Evoy Awd 83; Coaches Awd In Ftbl 85; Linda Claiborn Mem Awd 86; De Camp Memschlrp 86; Shafer Awd; Manhattan Coll; Phy Ed Tchr.

FISLER, KATHRYN; Tottenville HS; Staten Island, NY; (S); 2/850; Am Leg Aux Girls St; Scholastic Bowl; Jazz Band; School Musical; Lit Mag; High Hon Roll; NHS; Ntl Merit SF; Prfct Atten Awd; Rprsnt NYS Natl Grl Sct Ldrshp Conf Wash DC 85; Rprsnt Schl NYS Hugh Obrien Ldrshp Conf 85.

FITCH, CHRISTINE; Chenango Valley HS; Binghamton, NY; (Y); Spanish Clb; Varsity Clb; Band; Concert Band; Jazz Band; Mrchg Band; School Musical; Symp Band; Swmmng; Hon Roll.

FITCH, DAWN; Kensington HS; Buffalo, NY; (Y); Yrbk Stf; Cit Awd; D Youville; Med Tech.

FITCHPATRICK, KIM; Trumansburg HS; Trumansburg, NY; (Y); Varsity Clb; Color Guard; Mrchg Band; Var L Socr; Var L Trk; Var Capt Vllybl; High Hon Roll; MVP JV Vlybl 83-84; MVP Vrsty Trck 86; Mst Dedictd Awd-Colorgrd 86; Acctng.

FITE, DEIDREA L; Wheatland-Chili HS; Scottsville, NY; (Y); 3/74; Ski Clb; SADD; School Musical; Pres Frsh Cls; VP Jr Cls; VP Sr Cls; Pres Stu Cncl; Sftbl; High Hon Roll; NHS; Phi Beta Kappa 86; MI ST U Grant 86; MI ST U; Htl Mgmt.

FITZ GERALD, SUZANNE; Cornwall Central HS; Cornwall Hudson, NY; (Y); JV Bsktbl; JV Var Sftbl; Var Capt Swmmng; High Hon Roll; Hon Roll; NHS; MVP Awd Vrsty Swmng 85.

FITZAGERALD, MEG; Henninger HS; Syracuse, NY; (Y); 28/500; Art Clb; Cmnty Wkr; Computer Clb; GAA; Spanish Clb; SADD; Varsity Clb; Band; Concert Band; Jazz Band; Mst Vlbl Plyr Tnns Tm 85-86; Ptrck Spadafora Awd 85-86; Cmptr Sci.

FITZGERALD, AMY; Henninger HS; Syracuse, NY; (Y); 12/400; Am Leg Aux Girls St; Off GAA; SADD; Band; Yrbk Stf; Trs Sr Cls; JV Bsktbl; Var Capt Tennis; Var Trk; High Hon Roll; St Lawrence U.

FITZGERALD, BRIAN; Iona Preparatory Schl; New Rochelle, NY; (Y); 20/192; Ski Clb; Nwsp Rptr; Crs Cntry; Trk; Hon Roll; NHS; NY St Regents Schlrshp 86; Drew U Fresh Schlrshp 86; Fairfield U Schlrshp 86; Boston Coll; Ecnmcs.

FITZGERALD, COLLEEN; Liverpool HS; Liverpool, NY; (Y); 92/806; Ski Clb; High Hon Roll; Hon Roll; Jr NHS; NHS; Essy Pblshd Lvrpl Rvw 86; SUNY Albany; Crmnl Jstc.

FITZGERALD, DOROTHY A; John Jay SR HS; Katonah, NY; (Y); Church Yth Grp; Ski Clb; Variety Show; JV Bsktbl; Var Sftbl; Hon Roll; Girl Scts; Im Powder Puff Ftbl; Im Swmmng; Im Tennis; All Conf Vrsty Sftbl Tm 86; Mst Vlbl Plyr JV Sftbl Tm 85; Bus.

FITZGERALD, GERALDINE; Lincoln HS; Yonkers, NY; (Y); 4/340; Nwsp Rptr; Nwsp Stf; Lit Mag; Bsktbl; Crs Cntry; Trk; Cit Awd; High Hon Roll; NHS; Pres Schlr; Super Encllnc Awd 83-84-85-86; Manhattan Pres Schlrshp 86; Schlr Athl Awd 86; Manhattan Coll; Bio Educ.

FITZGERALD, JOHN; Clarkstown HS North; New City, NY; (Y); Church Yth Grp; Exploring; Math Clb; Natl Beta Clb; Spanish Clb; SADD; Mu Alp Tht.

FITZGERALD, KATHLEEN M; Fontbonne Hall Acad; Brooklyn, NY; (Y); Cmnty Wkr; Drama Clb; Library Aide; Political Wkr; SADD; Teachers Aide; Chorus; School Play; Stage Crew; Cit Awd; Vincent P Kassenbrock Schlrshp 86; NYS Regnts Schlrshp 86; St Josephs Coll Alumni Schlrshp 86; St Josephs Coll; Tchr.

FITZGERALD, KRISTINE M; William Floyd HS; Shirley, NY; (Y); 77/454; French Clb; Thesps; School Musical; School Play; Stage Crew; Lit Mag; Hon Roll; NHS; Spanish NHS; Drama Clb; Pres William Floyd Ldrs Clb 85-86; Stu Dirc Schl Muscl 86; ST U NY; Bio.

FITZGERALD, NORA; Oriskany Central Schl; Rome, NY; (Y); Cmnty Wkr; Sec SADD; Teachers Aide; Chorus; VP Stu Cncl; Cit Awd; High Hon Roll; Jr NHS; Pres NHS; SAR Awd; Stdnt Cncl Awd 85; Utica Coll; Bio.

FITZGERALD, STEPHANIE; Ticonderoga HS; Ticonderoga, NY; (Y); Church Yth Grp; Drama Clb; Key Clb; Latin Clb; School Musical; School Play; Stage Crew; Stu Cncl; Capt Var Bsktbl; Var Score Keeper; Bio.

FITZGERALD, THERESA; Holy Trinity HS; West Hempstead, NY; (Y); 25/315; Cmnty Wkr; Hon Roll; Math Awd 83; Adelphi U; Liberal Arts.

FITZPATRICK, ANNE C; Whitesboro SR HS; Whitesboro, NY; (Y); 36/354; Drama Clb; GAA; Acpl Chr; Chorus; Rep Stu Cncl; Var Fld Hcky; Var Trk; High Hon Roll; Jr NHS; NYS Rgnts Schlrshp 86; VA Tech; Bio-Med.

FITZPATRICK, CRISTY BETH; West Islip HS; West Islip, NY; (Y); Hosp Aide; Ski Clb; Concert Band; JV Swmmng; Var Tennis; NHS; Outstndng Achvmnt In Soc Stud 85; 90 Overall Avg 84.

FITZPATRICK, ERIC; Watertown HS; Watertown, NY; (Y); 48/305; Intnl Clb; Key Clb; Concert Band; Mrchg Band; Yrbk Stf; NY ST Rgnts Schlrshp 86; Bi-Cnty Band 85; Area Al-ST Band 85; Jefferson CC; Math.

FITZPATRICK, FIDELMA; Nardin Acad; Hamburg, NY; (Y); 3/85; Model UN; Ski Clb; School Musical; Yrbk Stf; Lit Mag; Rep Stu Cncl; High Hon Roll; Ntl Merit Ltr; Rensselaer Math & Sci Awd 86; Med.

FITZPATRICK, JACQUELINE; Dominican Commercial HS; Woodhaven, NY; (Y); Cmnty Wkr; GAA; Chorus; Rep Stu Cncl; JV Bsktbl; Gym; Sftbl; Hon Roll; NHS; Vlntr Spec Olympcs 86; Bus Mgt.

FITZPATRICK, LORNA K; Wardin Acad; Hamburg, NY; (Y); Hosp Aide; Model UN; Orch; School Musical; Stage Crew; Lit Mag; Trs Jr Cls; Golf; High Hon Roll; Clscl Assn Of Wstn (Y Ltn Awd 85; Sci Fair/Cngrs Of Wstrn NY 84 & 85; Canisius Coll; Pre-Med.

FITZPATRICK, MATT; Franklin Acad; Malone, NY; (Y); Church Yth Grp; 4-H; Trs French Clb; Bsktbl; Mgr(s); Score Keeper; Hon Roll; Hnr Roll Awd 84-85; CYO Bsktbl MIP Awd 84-85; Biol.

FITZPATRICK, MAUREEN; Auburn HS; Auburn, NY; (Y); Pep Clb; Ski Clb; SADD; Varsity Clb; Rep Frsh Cls; Rep Soph Cls; Rep Jr Cls; Var L Diving; JV Capt Pom Pon; NHS.

FITZSIMMONS II, PATRICK J; Saugerties HS; Saugerties, NY; (S); French Clb; Concert Band; JV Var Bsbl; JV Var Bsktbl; JV Var Ftbl; Powder Puff Ftbl; Hon Roll; Prfct Atten Awd; NY ST Cls B Vrsty Bsbl 85; Frmn All Star Hnrb Mntn Ftbl 85; Cert Lfgrd, Ltl League Umpire 84-85; Comp Sci.

FITZSIMMONS, STACEY; Leroy HS; Stafford, NY; (Y); FTA; Girl Scts; Chorus; Trs Stu Cncl; Var Score Keeper; JV Sftbl; JV Vllybl; High Hon Roll; Genesee CC; Sec Sci.

FIX, MARY; Cleveland HS; Cheektowaga, NY; (Y); GAA; JCL; SADD; Var Capt Vllybl; Full Sport Schlrshp Vllybll Villa Maria 86; US Marine Corp Dstngshd Athlete Awd 86; Villa Maria Coll; Bus Admin.

FIX, MATTHEW; East Aurora HS; East Aurora, NY; (Y); 50/185; Varsity Clb; Band; Orch; Var Crs Cntry; Capt Swmmng; Var Trk; Hnrs Eng Pgm 82-85; NY ST Regents Schlrshp 86; Won Swmmng Schlrshp 86; St Bonaventure U; Pre-Med.

FIX, SHARON; Eden SR HS; Eden, NY; (Y); 6/170; AFS; GAA; Ski Clb; Var Diving; Var L Score Keeper; Var L Trk; Var L Vllybl; Hon Roll; NHS; Prfct Atten Awd; Swmmg MIP 1st ECIC Fnls 85; Hghst Avg Fr 84; Schl Rcd & Secnl Trk 86; Hghst Avg Fr 84; Chiro.

FIXLER, MITCHELL DAVID; Somers HS; Tarrytown, NY; (Y); 26/212; VP AFS; Intnl Clb; Yrbk Ed-Chief; Rep Stu Cncl; Bsbl; High Hon Roll; NHS; St Schlr; Church Yth Grp; Political Wkr; Olympcs Mind Tm 3rd & 4th ST; Yrbk Undrclssmn Sectn Edtr 85; NYS Mck Trial Comptn; Brandeis U; Pltcl Sci.

FLADD, DAVID; Victor Central SR HS; Victor, NY; (Y); Camera Clb; Ski Clb; Concert Band; Mrchg Band; Pep Band; Yrbk Phtg; Var Crs Cntry; Var Trk; Cit Awd; High Hon Roll; Engrng.

FLAHERTY, CHRISTINE; Onondaga Central Schl; Nedrow, NY; (Y); Hosp Aide; SADD; Band; Sec Frsh Cls; Sec Soph Cls; Sec Jr Cls; Bsktbl; Crs Cntry; Sftbl; Trk; Onondago CC.

FLAHERTY, GWYNNE; Bishop Ludden HS; Syracuse, NY; (Y); Ski Clb; Chorus; Church Choir; Trk; High Hon Roll; NHS; Tri-M Music Hnr Soc 85-87; Bus.

FLAHERTY, JOHN; Seaford HS; Seaford, NY; (Y); Cmnty Wkr; Computer Clb; Yrbk Stf; Bsbl; Socr; High Hon Roll; NHS; Prfct Atten Awd; Natl Soc Stds & Sci Olympiad 84-85; Outstndng Achvt European Stds 85; Engrng.

FLAHERTY, MICHAEL F; General Douglas Mac Arthur HS; Levittown, NY; (Y); Mathletes; School Musical; Nwsp Rptr; VP Jr Cls; VP Sr Cls; VP Crs Cntry; Var Trk; NY ST Rgnts Schlrshp 86; Mdl Cngrss Pres 86; Bld Drive Chrmn 86.

FLAHERTY, NEVA; Harley HS; Rochester, NY; (Y); French Clb; Varsity Clb; Chorus; Yrbk Stf; Lit Mag; Sec Rep Stu Cncl; Var Diving; Var Socr; Williams Coll Bk Awd 85-86; Schls Cafe 85-86.

FLAMENBAUM, MINDY; Sachem HS North; Holbrook, NY; (Y); 56/1396; FBLA; Math Clb; SADD; Temple Yth Grp; Nwsp Stf; Hon Roll; Jr NHS; NHS; SUNY Albany.

FLAMMER, DEBORAH; Bay Shore HS; Bay Shore, NY; (Y); Church Yth Grp; Girl Scts; Sec SADD; Sec Chorus; Rep Soph Cls; Rep Jr Cls; Stu Cncl; Var Socr; Trk; NHS; Trvl To Europe W/Sccr Tm 85; Girl Scout Silvr Awd 83; Acctg.

FLAMMIA, KENNETH; St Francis Prep; Bayside, NY; (Y); 451/700; Art Clb; Tampa U; Comm.

FLANAGAN, KELLY; Tonawanda HS; Tonawanda, NY; (Y); Trs Church Yth Grp; Civic Clb; French Clb; SADD; Pep Band; Hon Roll; NHS; 1 Yr Hnr Roll Awd 84 & 86; David Lipscomb Coll; Art.

FLANAGAN, KRISTINE; Mechanicville HS; Mechanicville, NY; (S); 32/106; Church Yth Grp; Trs French Clb; Pres Ski Clb; SADD; Varsity Clb; Yrbk Ed-Chief; Yrbk Phtg; Yrbk Sprt Ed; Yrbk Stf; JV Var Bsktbl; Colonial Cncl All Str Sccr Tm 84; Sectn II All Str Sccr 2nd Tm 84; MVP Colonial Cncl 85; SUNY Cortland; Athl Trnr.

FLANAGAN, MICHAEL; Iona Prep; Larchmont, NY; (Y); 121/204; Capt Crs Cntry; Hon Roll; Bus Adm.

FLANAGAN, MIKE; Aquinas Inst; Rochester, NY; (Y); Boy Scts; Church Yth Grp; Var Capt Bsbl; Var Capt Ftbl; Var Swmmng; JV Var Wt Lftg; Hon Roll; Theology Achvt Awd 82; Hist Achvt Awd 85; Engl, Mech Drwng Achvt Awd 86; St Bonaventure U; Math.

FLANAGAN, RICHARD; St John The Baptist HS; Bayshore, NY; (S); 30/550; DECA; Model UN; Political Wkr; Speech Tm; Nwsp Rptr; Lit Mag; Bowling; Hon Roll; Natl Mdl UN Mrt Awd 85; Law.

FLANDERS, JONATHAN; Voorheesville Central HS; Voorheesville, NY; (Y); 8/110; Am Leg Boys St; Boy Scts; Ski Clb; Band; Im Bsktbl; Var L Socr; Var L Tennis; Var L Vllybl; High Hon Roll; Law.

FLANIGAN, JEFFREY; Brewster HS; Brewster, NY; (Y); Church Yth Grp; Nwsp Stf; VP Sr Cls; Im JV Bsktbl; Var Tennis; High Hon Roll; Hon Roll; Prfct Atten Awd; Mech Drwng Awd Top Stu 83-85; Arch.

FLANNERY, KRISTIN; Academy Of The Holy Names; Albany, NY; (Y); Dance Clb; GAA; Pep Clb; Cheerleading; Gym; Pom Pon; Cls IV NY St Champ Gymnstcs 83; All Amer Chrldr 85; Physical Educ.

FLANNERY, RAYMOND L; Canisius HS; Orchard Park, NY; (Y); 23/169; Pres Sec Church Yth Grp; VP JA; Stage Crew; Nwsp Sprt Ed; Nwsp Stf; Yrbk Sprt Ed; Var Capt Bsktbl; Var Tennis; Mu Alp Tht; NHS; AFROTC Schlrp Awd 86; Bsktbl MVP, Mr Mack Awd, 1st Tm All-Cthlc, Hon Mtn All-Wstrn NY 86; Rgts Schl; U Notre Dame; Elec Engrng.

FLANSBURG, KRISTEN; Hoosick Falls Central HS; Hoosick Falls, NY; (Y); 1/110; Cmnty Wkr; French Clb; Ski Clb; Band; Rep Stu Cncl; Bausch & Lomb Sci Awd; High Hon Roll; NHS; Church Choir; School Musical; RPI Mth & Sci Mdl 86; Schlrshp Awds 84-86.

FLANSBURG, LAURIE; Corinth Central HS; Greenfield Ctr, NY; (Y); FHA; FHA Awd 86; Bus.

FLASHBURG, SANDRA; Sheepshead Bay HS; Brooklyn, NY; (Y); Model UN; SADD; Chorus; School Play; Stage Crew; Yrbk Stf; Rep Stu Cncl; Cit Awd; Kingsbay Schlrshp Svc 86; Socl Stds Suprvsrs Assn NYC Awd 86; Hlth & Phys Ed Svc Awd 86; Brooklyn Coll; Engl.

FLATH, LORI; Connetquot HS; Ronkonkoma, NY; (Y); 122/746; Chorus; Pres Frsh Cls; Pres Soph Cls; Rep Jr Cls; Pres Sr Cls; Rep Stu Cncl; JV Stat Ftbl; Var Capt Sftbl; Hon Roll; Laurie Mcnl Awd Outstndng Stu Cncl Grl 84; Elem Educ.

FLAXMAN, GREGORY; Mamaroneck HS; Larchmont, NY; (Y); English Clb; Intnl Clb; Latin Clb; Political Wkr; Service Clb; Ski Clb; Ed Nwsp Rptr; Yrbk Stf; Var Capt Socr; Hon Roll; NY ST Cncl Socl Stds Cert Hnr 86; Engl.

FLECK, ALYSSA; Deruyter Central HS; Deruyter, NY; (S); Band; Concert Band; Mrchg Band; Pres Frsh Cls; Rep Soph Cls; Bsktbl; Cheerleading; Socr; Sftbl; Hon Roll; Schlrshp Cup.

FLECKENSTEIN, CAROL; Westhampton Bch HS; East Quogue, NY; (Y); Art Clb; Spanish Clb; School Play; Stage Crew; Nwsp Rptr; Nwsp Stf; Yrbk Phtg; Yrbk Rptr; Yrbk Stf; Lit Mag; Atst Wk 84-86; Artwk Exhbtd 82-86; Fashion Inst Of Tech; Adv Dsgn.

FLEET, SARA E; Haverling Central HS; Bath, NY; (S); Church Yth Grp; Exploring; French Clb; Hosp Aide; Intnl Clb; Math Clb; Red Cross Aide; Ski Clb; Spanish Clb; SADD; Pres Explrers Clb 85; Stu Govt Intrnshp Cnty Leg 85; Colgate U; Psych.

FLEICHER, TOMILYNN; Greene Central HS; Chenango Forks, NY; (Y); 6/115; Computer Clb; French Clb; JV Sftbl; High Hon Roll; Masonic Awd; NHS; Principals Awd 86; Brcome CC; Mental Hlth.

FLEISCHER, PAUL; John Jay SR HS; S Salem, NY; (Y); Leo Clb; Trs Jr Cls; Trs Sr Cls; JV Var Bsktbl; JV Var Socr; Cit Awd; High Hon Roll; NHS.

FLEISCHER, STACY; North Rockland HS; Garnerville, NY; (Y); Cmnty Wkr; French Clb; Spanish Clb; Mat Maids; JV Swmmng; New Paltz; Frgn Lng.

FLEISCHMAN, NANCY; Long Beach HS; Long Beach, NY; (S); 4/251; Political Wkr; Mrchg Band; Nwsp Stf; Stat Lcrss; Capt Tennis; CC Awd; High Hon Roll; NHS; Ntl Merit Ltr; Pres Schlr.

FLEISHMAN, BETH; Islip HS; Islip, NY; (Y); Cmnty Wkr; Dance Clb; Hosp Aide; Chorus; Concert Band; Nwsp Rptr; Rep Frsh Cls; Rep Soph Cls; Rep Jr Cls; Stu Cncl; Vet.

FLEISIG, LOREN B; Wantagh HS; Wantagh, NY; (Y); 10/291; Band; Orch; Yrbk Phtg; Capt Cheerleading; Gym; High Hon Roll; Hon Roll; NHS; Regents Schlrp 86; Cornell U; Pre-Med.

FLEMING, CHRISTINE A; Westhill HS; Syracuse, NY; (Y); 8/145; VP Church Yth Grp; Nwsp Rptr; Yrbk Bus Mgr; Lit Mag; Capt Cheerleading; High Hon Roll; Hon Roll; NHS; NEDT Awd; Spanish NHS; Cornell U.

FLEMING, KRISTEN; Curtis HS; Staten Island, NY; (Y); Pres Church Yth Grp; Teachers Aide; Chorus; Lit Mag; Twrlr; Hon Roll; NHS.

FLEMING, MICHAEL A; Huntington HS; Huntington Sta, NY; (Y); 20/384; Boy Scts; Band; Jazz Band; Trs Orch; Variety Show; Lit Mag; Var L Ftbl; Var L Lcrss; NHS; DECA; Rgnts Schlrshp 86; Rensselaer Polytech Inst; Engr.

FLEMING, RITA; Far Rockaway HS; Far Rockaway, NY; (Y); Church Yth Grp; Hosp Aide; Key Clb; Yrbk Stf; Sec Trs Sr Cls; Sec Trs Stu Cncl; Hon Roll; Prfct Atten Awd; Hlth Assist 85; Coop Awd 86; St Johns U; Law.

FLETCHER, CHERYL; Cardinal O Hara HS; Tonawanda, NY; (S); 16/122; Church Yth Grp; Cmnty Wkr; French Clb; Ski Clb; Sec Frsh Cls; Rep Soph Cls; Rep Stu Cncl; VP Socr; JV Sftbl; Hon Roll; Natl Hist Day Awd 85; Psych.

FLETCHER, CHRISTINE; Schoharie Central Schl; Schoharie, NY; (Y); Library Aide; Teachers Aide; Chorus; Pres Jr Cls; Socr; Hon Roll; March Of Dimes Schlrshp 86; Tchrs Assn Schlrshp 86; Alumni Awd 86; Maria Coll Of Albany; Nrsng.

FLETCHER, JEFFREY; Naples Central HS; Naples, NY; (Y); 30/85; Rep Stu Cncl; JV Var Score Keeper; High Hon Roll; Hon Roll; Prfct Atten Awd; Most Imprvd Stu 85; Most Congnl Stu 86; James Moore Meml Awd 86; Cayuga CC; Telecomm.

FLETCHER, JENNIE; Columbia HS; Nassau, NY; (Y); Art Clb; Girl Scts; Hon Roll; Outstndng Achvmnt Local Hist $100 86; SUNY; Home Ec Tchr.

FLETCHER, JERRY; Avoca Central HS; Avoca, NY; (Y); Varsity Clb; Var Capt Bsbl; Var Crs Cntry; JV Socr; Var Wrstlng; 1st Tm All Star Cls C Bsbl 86; MVP San Burke Bsbl Trnmnt 86; Elec Tech.

FLETCHER, MEGAN; T J Corcoran HS; Syracuse, NY; (Y); 15/206; Church Yth Grp; GAA; Red Cross Aide; SADD; Rep Sr Cls; Cheerleading; Swmmng; Trk; Hon Roll; Pltcl Sci.

FLETCHER, ROBERT; Warwick Valley HS; Warwick, NY; (Y); 25/200; Drama Clb; Ski Clb; School Play; Jr Cls; Crs Cntry; Ice Hcky; Trk; High Hon Roll; Hon Roll; NHS; Bus Mgmt.

FLETCHER, ROBERT A; Falconer Central HS; Jamestown, NY; (Y); 7/127; Church Yth Grp; Pres Computer Clb; FBLA; JA; Ski Clb; Yrbk Stf; Rep Stu Cncl; Bowling; Golf; Hon Roll; Vkng Schlrshp 86; AARP Schlrshp 86; Pres Acad Ftns Awd 86; Jmstwn Cmnty Coll; Acctng.

FLETCHER, THOMAS; Xavier HS; Brooklyn, NY; (Y); Cmnty Wkr; Capt ROTC; Var L Swmmng; Cadet/Capt Xavier JROTC 86; NYS Regents Scholar 86; Fordham U; Crimnl Justc.

FLETCHER, TIMOTHY J; St Johnsville HS; St Johnsville, NY; (Y); Am Leg Boys St; Boy Scts; VP Sec FFA; Nwsp Sprt Ed; Yrbk Stf; L Bsbl; L Socr; VFW Awd; Hugh O Brien Yth Ldrshp Smnr 85; Cmnty Svc Awd-Rescue Sqd Vlntr 86; Miltry Sci.

FLEURY, CHRISTINE; Paul Y Moore HS; Constantia, NY; (Y); FBLA; Var Capt Cheerleading; Outstndng Achvt Bus 85-86; Corning; Paralegal.

FLEVRY, MICHELLE; Keveny Memorial Acad; Waterford, NY; (Y); Color Guard; Frsh Cls; Jr Cls; Stu Cncl; Hon Roll; Natl Bus Hnr Socty 86; Maria Coll; Bus Adm.

FLICK, TABATHA; Allegany Central HS; Olean, NY; (Y); Chorus; Color Guard; Yrbk Stf; Im Vllybl; High Hon Roll; Hon Roll; Elem Tchr.

FLIERL, STACY; Frontier Central HS; Blasdell, NY; (Y); Cmnty Wkr; Drama Clb; French Clb; Hosp Aide; Concert Band; Stage Crew; Rep Stu Cncl; Hon Roll; Church Yth Grp; Pep Clb; NYSSMA Solo Awd Clrnt 84; Law.

FLINT, LAURA; Berlin Central HS; Petersburg, NY; (S); 2/100; Band; Chorus; School Play; Trs Sr Cls; JV Bsktbl; Var Socr; Var Sftbl; High Hon Roll; NHS; Lynchburg Hopwood Schlrshp 85.

FLINT, MATT; Amsterdam HS; Amsterdam, NY; (Y); 41/320; Church Yth Grp; Varsity Clb; Rep Stu Cncl; Var JV Bsbl; Var JV Bsktbl; Im Sftbl; Im Vllybl; Cmnty Wkr; 4-H; Stage Crew; Educ.

FLINT, SHANNON; Hannibal Central HS; Hannibal, NY; (Y); Trs 4-H; Varsity Clb; Var Vllybl; 4-H Awd; Hon Roll; Acctng.

FLOOD, CHRIS; Pleasantville HS; Pleasantville, NY; (Y); Church Yth Grp; Hosp Aide; Model UN; PAVAS; Science Clb; School Play; Stage Crew; Hon Roll; NHS; Outstndng Soc Stu Awd 84-85.

FLOOD, MICHAEL B; Archbishop Stepinac HS; Rye, NY; (Y); Camera Clb; Pep Clb; Band; Chorus; School Musical; Yrbk Phtg; Sec Frsh Cls; JV Ftbl; Var Trk; JV Wrstlng; St Vincents Hosp Spec Apprectn Aws 84; Focus On Excellnc 85; Columbia; Engrng.

FLORA, KENT P; North Rose-Wolcott HS; Wolcott, NY; (Y); 25/139; Chess Clb; Spanish Clb; Yrbk Stf; Im Bsktbl; Co-Capt Golf; High Hon Roll; Hon Roll; Awd Excllnc Soc Studies 86; Marine Corps.

FLORCZYK, KEITH; Liverpool HS; Liverpool, NY; (Y); JCL; Latin Clb; Ski Clb; Stage Crew; Yrbk Phtg; Rep Stu Cncl; Var L Gym; JV Lcrss; Im Tennis; Comp Prog.

FLORCZYKOWSKI, DENISE; Liverpool HS; Liverpool, NY; (Y); 97/884; Hosp Aide; Yrbk Phtg; Yrbk Stf; Stu Cncl; Bowling; Sftbl; Hon Roll; JR Hon Soc 83-85; Bus Mgt.

FLORENDO, MELISSA; Bishop Scully HS; Amsterdam, NY; (S); 6/45; Latin Clb; Yrbk Stf; High Hon Roll; Mu Alp Tht; NHS.

FLORES, CARLOS; Newtown HS; Jackson Heights, NY; (Y); 66/781; English Clb; Lit Mag; Hon Roll; Prfct Atten Awd; Health Ed Awd 84; Soc Studs Awd 83-84; Engl Awd 83; Engrng.

FLORES, DENNISSE; Academy Of Mt St Ursula HS; Bronx, NY; (Y); Computer Clb; Trs Science Clb; Lit Mag; Hon Roll; Columbia U; Psych.

FLORES, ERIC DUNCAN; Xaverian HS; New York, NY; (Y); 28/370; Cmnty Wkr; Computer Clb; Teachers Aide; Crs Cntry; JV Trk; JV Wrstlng; Hon Roll; NHS; Spanish NHS; Ntl Hispnc Schlr Awd 86; NY ST Regents Schlrshp 86; Elec Engr.

FLORES, GUILLERMO; Bushwick HS; Brooklyn, NY; (S); 6/233; Chess Clb; Computer Clb; Office Aide; Service Clb; Teachers Aide; Stage Crew; Yrbk Stf; Lit Mag; Trs Sr Cls; Rep Stu Cncl; Bio Awd; Cmptr Sci.

FLORES, LINDA; St Joseph HS; Brooklyn, NY; (Y); 5/150; Sec Science Clb; Sec Spanish Clb; Chorus; School Play; Bausch & Lomb Sci Awd; Hon Roll; Sec NHS; Hnds Acrss Amer 86; Sci.

FLORES, NELSON; Ft Hamilton HS; Brooklyn, NY; (Y); 85/500; Spanish Clb; Varsity Clb; Chorus; Var Crs Cntry; VP Trk; Var Wt Lftg; Phys Ftnss Awd 84; Mst Achvmnt Italian 84; Brooklyn Coll; Bus Mngmt.

FLOWER, KRISTINE; Glens Falls HS; Glen Falls, NY; (Y); 55/217; Girl Scts; SADD; Yrbk Ed-Chief; Sr Cls; Rep Stu Cncl; Mgr Fld Hcky; High Hon Roll; Hon Roll; Yrbk Awd 86; Elizabeth P Davis Schlrshp 86; Crary Educ Fnd Awd 86; Suny At Geneseo; Spcl Educ.

FLOWERS, AMY; Churchville Chili HS; Churchville, NY; (Y); 35/320; Color Guard; School Musical; Pres Soph Cls; Pres Jr Cls; Dnfth Awd; High Hon Roll; NHS; Am Leg Aux Girls St; Cmnty Wkr; Brckprt Alumni Assn Schlrshp 86; Wm J Cox Schlrshp 86; Brckprt ST U; Dance.

FLOWERS, LAURA; Sacred Heart Acad; Lynbrook, NY; (S); 18/218; Dance Clb; Library Aide; Service Clb; Chorus; Church Choir; Concert Band; Orch; School Play; Hon Roll; NHS; Psych.

FLOYD, MARNITA Y; Christopher Columbus HS; Bronx, NY; (Y); 22/792; Nwsp Ed-Chief; Nwsp Rptr; Var Capt Cheerleading; Tennis; High Hon Roll; NHS; UFT Schlrshp 86; NYS Cncl Supv & Adm Awd Excptnl Spirit Ldrshp; Wesleyan U.

FLOYD, TAMMY; Monroe HS; Rochester, NY; (Y); 55/175; Band; Chorus; Concert Band; Mrchg Band; School Play; Swing Chorus; Hon Roll; Prfct Atten Awd; Byrant; Accntng.

FLUMARO, JAMES; Valley Stream Central HS; Valley Stream, NY; (Y); Church Yth Grp; 4-H; Mathletes; JV Capt Bsktbl; Hon Roll; Acctng.

FLUSCHE, PAMELA A; F D Roosevelt HS; Hyde Park, NY; (Y); 7/336; Ski Clb; Band; Mrchg Band; Var L Trk; Var L Vllybl; Hon Roll; NHS; Ntl Merit SF; Notre Dame; Elec Engr.

FLYNN, ANDREW; Tupper Lake HS; Tupper Lk, NY; (Y); 15/99; Art Clb; Camera Clb; Debate Tm; Drama Clb; Chorus; School Musical; Trs Frsh Cls; Stat Crs Cntry; Var Timer; NHS; Area All ST Chorus; SUNY; Thtr.

FLYNN, BARBARA; G Ray Bodley HS; Fulton, NY; (Y); 30/280; Band; Rep Jr Cls; VP Stu Cncl; Im Sftbl; Var Capt Swmmng; Var Trk; High Hon Roll; Hon Roll; Prfct Atten Awd; Hnr Awd Gym 83; Achvt Awd Engl 83; Oswego St; Teaching.

FLYNN, CAROLINE; Northport HS; Northport, NY; (Y); Cmnty Wkr; Drill Tm; School Play; Variety Show; Rep Frsh Cls; Rep Soph Cls; Rep Jr Cls; Off Sr Cls; Rep Stu Cncl; JV Cheerleading.

FLYNN, CHRISTINE; Hauppauge HS; Hauppauge, NY; (Y); Sec Church Yth Grp; DECA; German Clb; Model UN; VP Service Clb; Rep Frsh Cls; Rep Soph Cls; Rep Jr Cls; JV Tennis; Chrmn NHS; Acdmc Ltr 85; DECA Advrtsng Design Awd 2nd Co/St 86.

FLYNN, DEBORAH; Beacon HS; Beacon, NY; (Y); Math Clb; Office Aide; Science Clb; Spanish Clb; Jr NHS; Rgstrd Nrs.

FLYNN, DEBORAH; Newark Valley HS; Owego, NY; (Y); 9/114; Library Aide; Ski Clb; Varsity Clb; Band; Off Jr Cls; Stu Cncl; Mgr(s); Trk; High Hon Roll; Jr NHS; Slte To Youth 85; Clarkson U; Elec Engnrg.

FLYNN, EDWARD W; Westlake HS; Thornwood, NY; (Y); Am Leg Boys St; Pres Chess Clb; Spanish Clb; Stage Crew; Nwsp Stf; VP Sr Cls; JV Bsktbl; Var Socr; Var Tennis; NHS; Delaware U; Arch.

FLYNN, KENNETH; New Dorp HS; Staten Isl, NY; (Y); Debate Tm; JV Var Bsbl; JV Bsktbl; Im Trk; High Hon Roll; Hon Key 86; Physcl Sci.

FLYNN, KEVIN P; Newark Valley HS; Owego, NY; (Y); 19/114; Boy Scts; Varsity Clb; Band; Concert Band; Drm Mjr(t); Mrchg Band; Hon Roll; NHS; JV Ftbl; Var L Socr; Regents Schlrshp 86; Broune CC; Lib Arts.

FLYNN, MARY A; Red Creek Central HS; Red Creek, NY; (Y); #5 In Class; VP French Clb; Sec Ski Clb; Band; Rep Stu Cncl; Socr; High Hon Roll; NHS; NY Rgnts Schlrshp 86; SUNY Oswego; Envrnmntl Sci.

FLYNN, NICOLE; Sacred Heart HS; Yonkers, NY; (Y); 2/215; Ed Yrbk Stf; High Hon Roll; Hon Roll; Sal; Enrico Fermi Schlrshp 86; Excllnce Awds Eng And Socl Stu 86; Awd Excllnce Am Hist 86; SUNY Purchase; Eng.

FLYNN, SIOBHAN P; St Francis Prep; Fresh Meadows, NY; (S); 59/744; Cmnty Wkr; Girl Scts; Library Aide; SADD; Band; Chorus; Church Choir; Color Guard; School Play; NHS; Psych.

FLYNN, STEPHEN; Tupper Lake JR SR HS; Tupper Lk, NY; (Y); 1/100; Art Clb; 4-H; Sec Jr Cls; Sec Sr Cls; Ftbl; Trk; Wt Lftg; High Hon Roll; NHS; Acad All Amer 84; Math & Sci Rensselaer Mdl For Excel 86; Cazenovia Coll; Adv Dsgn.

FLYNN, THERESA; Central Islip HS; Central Islip, NY; (Y); Chorus; Variety Show; Rep Sr Cls; JV Sftbl; Hon Roll; Hnry Splln Awd Outstndng Sprtsmnshp 84; Psych.

FLYNN, THOMAS J; Geneva HS; Geneva, NY; (S); 23/175; Ski Clb; Varsity Clb; Rep Sr Cls; Var L Ftbl; Im Ice Hcky; Var L Lcrss; High Hon Roll; Hon Roll; NHS; Rotary Awd; Empire ST Games Westrn Regn Lacrosse Tm 85; Dartmouth; Engrng.

FLYNN, TIMOTHY; Mcquaid Jesuit HS; Rochester, NY; (Y); 6/175; Pres Exploring; Hosp Aide; Yrbk Stf; L Var Ftbl; High Hon Roll; Acdmc Ltr 84-86; Natl Frnch Cntst 5th Plc Natly 85; Frnkln & Mrshll Coll Bk Awd 86; Biochem.

FLYNN, TRACY; Owen D Young Central HS; Van Hornesville, NY; (S); AFS; Band; Chorus; Nwsp Stf; Sec Jr Cls; Stat Bsbl; Var JV Cheerleading; Var Socr; Var JV Vllybl; High Hon Roll.

FOBARE, WILLIAM; H C Williams HS; Rensselaer Falls, NY; (Y); Debate Tm; Trs FFA; Rep Soph Cls; Im Badmtn; JV Ftbl; Im Swmmng; Hon Roll; Grnhd Degr & Chptr Frmr Degr & Empire Degr FFA 85-86; Canton; Ag.

FOCARILE, CHRISTINA; North Rockland HS; Van Alstyne, TX; (Y); 8/528; Sec Bowling; Sec Pres Band; Sec Pres Chorus; Pres Sec Concert Band; Flag Corp; Pres Sec Mrchg Band; Swing Chorus; High Hon Roll; JP Sousa Awd; NHS; Itln-Amer Clb Schlrshp 86; Tchrs Assoc Schlrshp 86; Baylor U Waco TX; Spcl Ed.

FODERA, JOHN; Sewanhaka HS; Elmont, NY; (Y); Socr; MVP Sccr 85-86; Bus.

FOELS, PATRICIA; Tonawanda SR HS; Tonawanda, NY; (Y); 3/220; French Clb; Church Choir; Jazz Band; School Musical; Swing Chorus; Stu Cncl; Cheerleading; Kiwanis Awd; NHS; Val; Henry Wells Schlrshp 86-88; St Marys Slf-Discpln Awd 85; Exch Stu Of Mnth 86; Wells Coll; Hlth Psych.

FOGARTY, MICHAEL; Newburgh Free Acad; Newburgh, NY; (Y); Debate Tm; Key Clb; Latin Clb; Rep Soph Cls; Rep Jr Cls; Var Golf; Var Capt Swmmng; NHS; Pres Rotary Awd; High Hon Roll.

FOGLE, DONNA; Midwood HS; Brooklyn, NY; (Y); Doctor.

FOISY, JOEL S; Brasher Falls Central HS; Winthrop, NY; (Y); 1/71; Am Leg Boys St; French Clb; Math Tm; Band; Pres VP Stu Cncl; Var L Ice Hcky; Var L Lcrss; Bausch & Lomb Sci Awd; NHS; Val.

FOLAND, PENNY; Faith Heritage Schl; Brewerton, NY; (Y); 3/23; VP Church Yth Grp; Chorus; Nwsp Sprt Ed; Rep Stu Cncl; Capt Socr; Trk; Capt Vllybl; DAR Awd; Hon Roll; Pres NHS; Army Res Schlr Ath Awd; Headmstrs Awd; Distngshd Chrstn HS Stu; Nrthestrn Christian JC; Pre-Md.

FOLEY, ANN; Ripley Central Schl; Ripley, NY; (S); 3/26; Pep Clb; VP Frsh Cls; Sec Jr Cls; Var Capt Vllybl; Hon Roll; NHS; Comp Engr.

FOLEY, BURTON J; Town Of Webb HS; Old Forge, NY; (Y); Am Leg Boys St; Var L Ski Clb; Band; Sec Frsh Cls; Trs Soph Cls; Trs Jr Cls; Var L Crs Cntry; Var L Golf; High Hon Roll; NHS; Lib Art.

FOLEY, CHRIS; Auburn HS; Auburn, NY; (Y); 26/450; Ski Clb; Nwsp Ed-Chief; Rep Frsh Cls; Rep Soph Cls; Sr Cls; JV L Lcrss; High Hon Roll; Ntl Merit SF; Church Yth Grp; Band; HS Sci Awd 85-86.

FOLEY, MAUREEN; Mac Arthur HS; Levittown, NY; (Y); 14/321; AFS; Bsktbl; Socr; Trk; High Hon Roll; NHS; Cornell U; Comp Prgmng.

FOLEY, MICHAEL; Victor Central HS; Victor, NY; (Y); 88/240; Quiz Bowl; Ski Clb; Varsity Clb; Im Badmtn; Var Socr; Var Swmmng; Var Trk; Sec Treas Of Boys Ldrs Clb 86-87; Chiropratic.

FOLEY, PATRICK; Monsignor Farrell HS; Staten Island, NY; (Y); Cmnty Wkr; VP Soph Cls; Var Capt Bsktbl; Church Yth Grp; Teachers Aide; JV Bsbl; Im Ftbl; Co MVP JV Bsktbl 84-85; Adv Hnrs Mth 83-85; Cmmnctns.

FOLEY, RACHEL A; Dunkirk HS; Dunkirk, NY; (Y); 8/200; Sec Computer Clb; Pres French Clb; Sec Trs Key Clb; Trs Science Clb; School Play; Trs Stu Cncl; JV Var Vllybl; Hon Roll; NHS; Rgnts Schlrshp NYS 86; Allegheny Coll.

FOLEY, ROGER W; Gregory B Jarvis Schl; Mohawk, NY; (Y); Am Leg Boys St; Exploring; French Clb; Varsity Clb; Chorus; Var Crs Cntry; JV Golf; Var Trk; JV Wrstlng; High Hon Roll; Semnr Authr Nat Hentoff 85; Attnd Legl Profssn Semnr 86; Law.

FOLEY, SHAWN; Newfield HS; Selden, NY; (S); Aud/Vis; Camera Clb; Church Yth Grp; Cmnty Wkr; Computer Clb; Library Aide; Office Aide; Service Clb; Varsity Clb; Nwsp Rptr; 1st Pl NY ST U-19 Fncng USFA 86; Capt Fncng Tm 85-86; Mst Imprvd Fncr 86; St Johns U.

FOLEY, SHEILA; Our Lady Of Mercy HS; Webster, NY; (Y); Camera Clb; Cmnty Wkr; Intnl Clb; Model UN; Ski Clb; Variety Show; Trk; Hon Roll.

FOLEY, SHIOBAN M; Goshen Central HS; Goshen, NY; (Y); Band; Concert Band; Mrchg Band; Sec Sr Cls; Rep Stu Cncl; Var L Crs Cntry; Var L Trk; NHS; Prfct Atten Awd; Rgnts Schlrshp; SUNY Albany; Law.

FOLGER, JENNIFER; Mamaroneck HS; Larchmont, NY; (Y); JV Bsktbl; JV Fld Hcky; Var Mgr Sftbl; Bus Mngmnt.

FOLK, TAMMY JO; South Seneca Central Schl; Interlaken, NY; (Y); Am Leg Aux Girls St; Church Yth Grp; Varsity Clb; Nwsp Rptr; Yrbk Phtg; Yrbk Stf; Sec Jr Cls; VP Stu Cncl; Var Vllybl; Cit Awd; Moody Bible Inst; Commctns.

FOLLETT, COLLEEN; Kenmore E HS; Tonawanda, NY; (Y); Church Yth Grp; GAA; Pep Clb; JV Capt Bsktbl; JV Var Socr; Capt Var Sftbl; Var Trk; Im Vllybl; Erie CC; Dntl Hygnst.

FOLLIERO, LISA M; Sachem HS North; Farmingville, NY; (Y); 166/1385; Radio Clb; Hofstra U; Commnctns.

FOLMER, CHRISTINE; Bronx High School Of Science; Bronx, NY; (Y); Cmnty Wkr; Debate Tm; JA; Teachers Aide; Chorus; Nwsp Rptr; Rep Jr Cls; Ftbl; Bus.

FOLSTER, DENISE; L A Webber HS; Gasport, NY; (Y); Art Clb; Girl Scts; Yrbk Stf; Cheerleading; Vllybl; NCCC Coll; Phycology.

FOMINA, ELENA; F D Roosevelt HS; Brooklyn, NY; (Y); 4/592; Teachers Aide; Hon Roll; Ntl Merit Schol; Daily News Yankees Awd 85; NY U; Doc.

FONDA, ANNE; Mount Pleasant HS; Schenectady, NY; (Y); 19/262; Color Guard; Mrchg Band; French Hon Soc; Hon Roll; Jr NHS.

FONDA, BRAD; Schoharie Central Schl; Central Bridge, NY; (S); 18/115; Varsity Clb; JV Var Bsktbl; JV Var Socr; High Hon Roll; Hon Roll; Arch.

FONDA, JILL E; Mayfield HS; Gloversville, NY; (Y); 14/85; Church Yth Grp; Socr; High Hon Roll; Hon Roll; NYS Rgnts Schlrshp 86; Schenectady CC; Accntng.

FONG, NANCY; Immaculata HS; New York, NY; (Y); Mrchg Band; Hon Roll; Accntng.

FONG, STEVEN; Bronx High School Of Science; Bronx, NY; (Y); Cmnty Wkr; NYS Regnts Schlrshp 86; U Of Buffalo SUNY; Lib Arts.

FONG, WINIFRED; Canarsie HS; Brooklyn, NY; (Y); Boys Clb Am; Teachers Aide; Band; Concert Band; School Musical; School Play; Stage Crew; High Hon Roll; Hon Roll; NHS; Chancellors Fellwshp 86.

FONKEN, OSWALDO; Immaculata HS; New York, NY; (Y); Drill Tm; Bsktbl; Diving; Ftbl; Swmmng; Hon Roll; Lawyer.

FONTAINE, MONIQUE; Uniondale HS; Uniondale, NY; (Y); Drama Clb; Trs Key Clb; Acpl Chr; Chorus; Jazz Band; School Musical; High Hon Roll; Hon Roll; NHS; All-Cnty Chorus 86; Syracuse U; Pre-Law.

FONTANA, FRANK A; Bronx HS Sci; Bronx, NY; (Y); Chess Clb; Cmnty Wkr; Nwsp Stf; Rep Frsh Cls; Var Bsbl; Prfct Atten Awd; Math Fair Metrpltn Cert Merit 85; Rgnts Schlrshp 86; Rensselaer Polytech Inst; Arch.

FONTANA, JEAN; Commack High School North; Commack, NY; (Y); High Hon Roll; Hon Roll; Fshn Insti Of Tech; Fshn Byng.

FONTANAROSA, MARC; Monsignor Farrelkl HS; Staten Island, NY; (Y); Band; Concert Band; Drill Tm; Jazz Band; Mrchg Band; Symp Band; Lit Mag; Hon Roll; Law.

FONTANES, LILLIAN; Dominican Commercial HS; Jamaica, NY; (Y); 75/259; Dance Clb; High Hon Roll; Hon Roll; Prfct Atten Awd; Spanish NHS; Siena Clb 83-84; Prncpls List 83-86; Queens Cathlc Med Ctr; Nrs.

FONTENELLE, MICHELLE A; Bishop Ford Central Catholic HS; Brooklyn, NY; (S); #1 In Class; Church Yth Grp; Debate Tm; Nwsp Rptr; Yrbk Stf; Ed Lit Mag; Capt Im Bowling; High Hon Roll; NHS; Med.

FOODY, KEVIN; Thomas J Corcoran HS; Syracuse, NY; (Y); Math Tm; Ski Clb; School Play; Yrbk Sprt Ed; VP Stu Cncl; JV Var Bsbl; Capt Crs Cntry; Trk; NHS; SADD; Hugh P Sarf Awd 86; Pres Mock Trial Tm 86; Med.

FOOTE, DEBORAH; Altmar-Parish-Williamstown HS; Parish, NY; (Y); Drama Clb; VP French Clb; Ski Clb; Band; Mrchg Band; Rep Stu Cncl; Capt Cheerleading; Var Socr; High Hon Roll; Hst NHS; Natl Dollars Schlrs Scholar 86; NYS Regents Scholar 85-86; Herkimer Cnty CC; Trvl.

FOOTE, JOHN H; La Fayette HS; Lafayette, NY; (Y); Boy Scts; French Clb; Band; Rep Stu Cncl; Var Capt Crs Cntry; Lcrss; Cit Awd; USN; Engrng.

FOOTMAN, MONET; Dewitt Clinton HS; Bronx, NY; (Y); Church Yth Grp; GAA; Library Aide; Office Aide; Church Choir; Var Bsktbl; Bourough Of Manhanttan; Accntnt.

FORASTIERO, DONNA; Cicero-North Syracuse HS; Clay, NY; (S); 47/623; Chorus; Trs Drill Tm; Mrchg Band; School Musical; Swing Chorus.

FORAY, STEPHEN; Connetquot HS; Oakdale, NY; (S); 119/700; Aud/Vis; Chess Clb; Pres Trs DECA; FBLA; Cit Awd; Hon Roll; Prfct Atten Awd; DECA Sfflk Cnty Sales Demo Wnnr 84-86; DECA NY ST Career Conf 2nd Pl Sales Demo 85-86; SUNY-GENESEO; Bus Mgmt.

FORBES, BRENDA; Westfield Central HS; Westfield, NY; (Y); Hosp Aide; Band; Chorus; Rep Stu Cncl; Cheerleading; High Hon Roll; Hon Roll; Flght Attndnt.

FORBES, FYRN S; Northeastern Acad; Brooklyn, NY; (S); Church Yth Grp; Cmnty Wkr; Quiz Bowl; Science Clb; Chorus; Church Choir; Drill Tm; Trs Jr Cls; Cit Awd; Hon Roll; Spnsh Awd 84-85; Schltc Awd 83-84; Eng Awd 83-84; Atlantic Union Coll; Obstet.

FORBES, JULIE A; Utica Free Acad; Utica, NY; (Y); Church Yth Grp; Cmnty Wkr; Hosp Aide; Latin Clb; Red Cross Aide; Spanish Clb; NHS; NYS Rgnts Schlrshp 86; Colgate Semnr 85; Utica Coll; Biotchnlgst.

FORBES, SEAN C; Susquehanna Valley HS; Binghamton, NY; (Y); 4/187; Key Clb; Letterman Clb; Political Wkr; Scholastic Bowl; Science Clb; Ski Clb; Pres Spanish Clb; Varsity Clb; Nwsp Ed-Chief; Rep Sr Cls; Offered Appointments West Point & US Nvl Acad 86; MENSA 84; Cornell Coll Engrng; Engrng.

FORCADA, JOAO M; Edgemont HS; Scarsdale, NY; (Y); Off Computer Clb; Mathletes; Frsh Cls; Var L Tennis; NYS Regnts Schlrshp 86; Amer Comptr Sci Leag 85-86; Comptr Comptn 85-86; Carnegie-Mellon U; Comp Sci.

FORCE, LAURA; Liverpool HS; Liverpool, NY; (Y); 264/800; Band; Concert Band; Mrchg Band; Pep Band; Off Sr Cls; Stu Cncl; Sftbl; Physcl Thrpst.

FORCUCCI, TONY; W Seneca West SR HS; West Seneca, NY; (S); 153/559; DECA; Key Clb; Spanish Clb; Band; Jazz Band; School Musical; School Play; Yrbk Phtg; Lit Mag; JV Vllybl; DECA 2nd Pl Awd-Food Mrktng Comptn 85; ST Comptn Cncrd NY DECA 85; Bowling Green ST U; Mngmnt.

FORD, CHRISTOPHER; Amsterdam HS; Amsterdam, NY; (Y); 53/293; Boy Scts; VP JA; Orch; Rep Stu Cncl; Bowling; NY ST Rgnts 86; Egl Sct 86; Vgl-Ordr Of Arrw 85; Rochester Inst Of Tech; Physcs.

FORD, DANIELLE; Waterloo SR HS; Waterloo, NY; (Y); #1 In Class; Church Yth Grp; Drama Clb; Pres French Clb; FTA; Model UN; Capt Color Guard; Yrbk Stf; Bausch & Lomb Sci Awd; NHS; Voice Dem Awd; Geochem.

FORD, JENNIFER; Ocford Acad; Mcdonough, NY; (Y); 2/70; Am Leg Aux Girls St; French Clb; Ski Clb; Varsity Clb; Trs Jr Cls; Var Bsktbl; Var Fld Hcky; High Hon Roll; NHS; Scholastic Bowl; Rtry Exchng Stu Of Swdn 86-87; Bioengr.

FORD, KRISTIN A; Bloomfield Central HS; Holcomb, NY; (Y); 4/96; Rep Stu Cncl; Socr; Trk; High Hon Roll; Trs NHS; Prfct Atten Awd; Regents Schlrshp 86; Acdmc All Am 86; Monroe CC; Bus Law.

FORD, MARTINA; The Masters Schl; Roseburg, OR; (Y); 4-H; Hosp Aide; Nwsp Bus Mgr; Nwsp Ed-Chief; Yrbk Bus Mgr; Yrbk Ed-Chief; Capt JV Socr; Var Sftbl; 4-H Awd; Top 10 OR Qurtr Horse Assoc 13 & Under 84; Outstndg Newspr Stff Mbr 84; Hgh Hnr Athl Clb 86; Bus.

FORD, MELISSA; Honeoye Falls-Lima HS; Honeoye Falls, NY; (S); 13/164; Cmnty Wkr; SADD; Varsity Clb; Variety Show; Trs Frsh Cls; JV Bsktbl; VP Golf; Capt Socr; High Hon Roll; NHS; Spnsh II Stu Of Hnr 84; Phys Ther.

FORD, NANCY; Lindenhurst HS; Lindenhurst, NY; (Y); Sec Varsity Clb; Nwsp Stf; Capt Bsktbl; High Hon Roll; NHS; Fld Hcky; Sftbl; Trk; Capt Vllybl; High Hnr Roll 86; Bsktbl All League 86; Ntl Hnr Scty 86; Pre-Med.

FORD, ROBERT; Fordham Prep Schl; Yonkers, NY; (Y); Var JV Bsktbl; High Hon Roll; Hon Roll; NHS; Pres Schlr.

FORD, SHARON; Palmyra-Macedon HS; Macedon, NY; (S); 2/170; Church Yth Grp; Math Tm; Chorus; JV Var Bsktbl; JV Var Tennis; JV Vllybl; Hon Roll; NHS; Prfct Atten Awd; Acad Achvt Awd 84-85; JV & Vrsty Mst Impvd Tnns Plyr 84-85.

FORD, TOBIAS D; Massena Central HS; Massena, NY; (Y); Am Leg Boys St; Church Yth Grp; Yrbk Stf; JV Bsktbl; Capt Var Socr; Var Trk; High Hon Roll; Hon Roll; NHS; Rosenbaum Physics Awd 86; Engrng.

FORD, VALERIE C; Susan E Wagner HS; Staten Island, NY; (Y); Debate Tm; NFL; School Musical; Rep Stu Cncl; JV Pom Pon; Swmmng; Hon Roll; Dance Clb; St Schlr; Co-Op Ed Prog 86; NYS Rgnt Dplma 86; NYS Rgnt Schlrshp 86; Creighton U; Finance.

FORDE, MAXINE; Erasmus Hall HS; Brooklyn, NY; (Y); 72/474; Church Yth Grp; Debate Tm; Church Choir; Kingsborough CC; Psychology.

FORIAN, MARGARET; Onondaga HS; Syracuse, NY; (S); Spanish Clb; SADD; Band; Chorus; Church Choir; Trs Jr Cls; Cheerleading; Crs Cntry; Trk; NHS; All Cnty Chorus 85 & 86.

FORMAN, REGINA; HS Of Fashion Ind; Bronx, NY; (Y); 32/324; Art Clb; Dance Clb; Debate Tm; Hon Roll; Fit; Fshn Dsgn.

FORMAN, STUART; Tottenville HS; Staten Island, NY; (Y); Band; Coach Actv; Crs Cntry; Timer; Trk; Jr NHS; Prfct Atten Awd.

FORMOZA, JOHN W; Solray HS; Syracuse, NY; (Y); Bsbl; Im Bsktbl; Im Wrstlng; Hon Roll; Church Yth Grp; Math Clb; Band; Concert Band; Jazz Band; NYSMA Trumpet & Drums 84-85; NYSMA Trumpet 83-84; Potsdam; Elec Engr.

FORNARO, VICTORIA; Liverpool HS; Liverpool, NY; (Y); 11/856; Ski Clb; Color Guard; Mrchg Band; Tennis; Hon Roll; NHS; Math Awd 82; Rgnts Schlrshhp 86; Clarkson U; Physics.

FORNES, MARYLEE; Springville Griffith Inst; Springville, NY; (Y); 2/197; VP Pres Key Clb; Acpl Chr; Band; Chorus; Concert Band; Mrchg Band; Orch; JV Var Bsktbl; Var Diving; Capt Swmmng; Outstndng Orchstra 85; Amer Lg Ldrshp Awd 85; Wstrn NY Swmmrs Assn Scholar 85; Mst Imprvd Swmmr 81; U NC Chapel Hill; Vet Med.

FORRETT, KELLEY; Northern Adirondack HS; Ellenburg, NY; (Y); 7/90; Church Yth Grp; Debate Tm; Key Clb; Bsktbl; Swmmng; High Hon Roll; NHS; MCC; Elec Engnrng.

FORSBERG, JULIE; Jamestown HS; Jamestown, NY; (Y); 12/396; Church Yth Grp; Sec Acpl Chr; Band; Church Choir; Concert Band; Madrigals; Mrchg Band; Orch; School Musical; Nwsp Stf; Jamestown Winter Swthrt 86; Rgnts Schlrp 86; Weston Schlrp 86; Hamilton Coll; Crtv Wrtng.

FORSTER, MIKE; Liverpool HS; Liverpool, NY; (Y); Wrstlng; Alfred ST Coll; Bus Mgmnt.

FORSTER, SAMANTHA; Midwood MSI HS/Brooklyn Coll HS; Brooklyn, NY; (Y); 100/667; Teachers Aide; Chorus; Lit Mag; Hon Roll; Jr NHS; NCTE Awd; Prfct Atten Awd; Val; Ntl Energy Found Awd 83; Am Assoc Tchrs Spnsh 84; Tchrs Engl Awd 83; Psychtry.

FORSYTH, MELISSA; Valley Central HS; Montgomery, NY; (Y); 26/316; Lion Awd; Spanish NHS; NHS; Hon Roll; Stu Cncl; School Musical; Cmnty Wkr; Color Guard; Service Clb; Yrbk Stf; Pre-Law.

FORTE, ANDRE; Archbishop Molloy HS; Ozone Park, NY; (Y); 77/413; Chess Clb; Dance Clb; Sec Intnl Clb; Pep Clb; SADD; Var Capt Bsbl; JV Crs Cntry; Tennis; JV Var Trk; Hon Roll; Grgtwn; Lawyer.

FORTE, ANNE MARIE; St Joseph Hill HS; Staten Island, NY; (Y); Drama Clb; Hosp Aide; Intnl Clb; Science Clb; Trs Chorus; School Musical; Sci Projct Hnrbl Ments 83; Rgnts Nrsng Schlrshp 86; St Johns U.

FORTE, CAROLINE; St Francis Prep; Flushing, NY; (S); 184/744; Ski Clb; Spanish Clb; Nwsp Stf; Yrbk Stf; Vllybl; Hon Roll; NHS; Cert Tutoring Pgm, Stnd Glass Clss.

FORTE, DONNA; High Schl East; Saint James, NY; (Y); Camera Clb; German Clb; Hosp Aide; Teachers Aide; Hon Roll; 100 Hrs Vlntr Svcs Cndy Strpr 85; Stony Brook SUNY; Law.

FORTE, DONNA; St Peters H S For Girls; Staten Island, NY; (Y); Mgr Church Yth Grp; FNA; Hosp Aide; Math Tm; Red Cross Aide; Teachers Aide; Im Coach Actv; S Johns U; Accntnt.

FORTE, ETHEL; Christ The King Regional HS; Middle Village, NY; (Y); 111/452; GAA; Girl Scts; Spanish Clb; Varsity Clb; JV Var Bsktbl; JV Var Sftbl.

FORTE, JOSEPH; Churchville-Chili HS; Rochester, NY; (Y); Church Yth Grp; Chorus; Yrbk Stf; JV Bsktbl; Embry Riddle; Airline Pilot.

FORTE, MARK; Horseheads SR HS; Horseheads, NY; (Y); Pres Trs 4-H; JCL; Trs Latin Clb; Band; Concert Band; Jazz Band; Mrchg Band; Yrbk Stf; JV Trk; Hon Roll; Busnss.

FORTE, MICHAEL J; Syosset HS; Syosset, NY; (Y); 48/481; Boys Clb Am; Computer Clb; 4-H; Library Aide; Political Wkr; Radio Clb; Red Cross Aide; Science Clb; SADD; School Play; Rgnts Schlrshp Cert 86; SUNY; Surgeon.

FORTE, SUSAN; Huntington HS; Huntington, NY; (Y); Key Clb; Varsity Clb; Sec Sr Cls; Var L Bsktbl; Var L Sftbl; Var L Tennis; Hon Roll; Jr NHS; NHS; Band; Mst Sprtsmnlk 83; Miss Tm Sprt Vrsty Bsktbl 85-86; Acctnt.

FORTH, KARY; York Central HS; Pavilion, NY; (Y); Boy Scts; Pres Church Yth Grp; 4-H; Pres Science Clb; Ski Clb; Spanish Clb; Stage Crew; Tennis; Hon Roll; Bilgcl Engr.

FORTIER, JOE; Mexico HS; Mexico, NY; (Y); Art Clb; Varsity Clb; Rep Frsh Cls; Rep Soph Cls; Rep Stu Cncl; Var Bsktbl; Var L Socr; Var L Trk; Wt Lftg; Prfct Atten Awd; MVP Awd Sccr 86; Slvr Mdl Empr ST Gms 85; Drftng.

FORTIN, ROBERT; Bishop Grimes HS; N Syracuse, NY; (Y); Church Yth Grp; JV Bsbl; JV Var Socr; Babe Ruth Mst Outstndg Plyr 85; Envrnmntl Sci.

FORTMEYER, JAMES; Lindenhurst SR HS; Lindenhurst, NY; (Y); 45/548; Ski Clb; Yrbk Stf; Socr; JC Awd; NHS; Archtrl.

FORTNAM, KATHERINE; Oriskany Central HS; Oriskany, NY; (Y); 4/65; Sec Key Clb; Spanish Clb; Band; Symp Band; Yrbk Stf; Stu Cncl; Hon Roll; Jr NHS; NHS; Anthony A Rybicky Bus Awd 86; Mohawk Vly CC; Accounting.

FORTON, KENNETH; Grand Island HS; Grand Island, NY; (Y); 20/325; Pres Church Yth Grp; Mathletes; Model UN; Rep Stu Cncl; High Hon Roll; NHS; Ntl Merit Ltr; Boy Scts; Chess Clb; Cmnty Wkr; Egl Sct 86; Tchrs Assn Schlrshp 86; SR Ctzn Of Mnth 86; Boston Coll; Mrktng.

FORTUNA, DON; Hornell HS; Hornell, NY; (Y); 60/210; FCA; SADD; Varsity Clb; Pres Frsh Cls; Pres Soph Cls; Pres Jr Cls; Var L Bsbl; Var L Bsktbl; Var L Socr; Hon Roll; Sllvn Trl Conf All-Star-Bsbl-Shrtstp 86; Bus Adm.

FORTUNATO, JAY; Farmingdale HS; Farmingdale, NY; (Y); 11/560; Boy Scts; Yrbk Stf; High Hon Roll; Ntl Merit Ltr; Regents Schlrshp NY ST; Rensselaer Polytech Inst; Engrg.

FORTUNATO JR, LOUIS P; Newburgh Free Acad; Newburgh, NY; (Y); VP Church Yth Grp; Var Golf; Im Ice Hcky; Var JV Socr; High Hon Roll; Jr NHS; NHS; RPI Mth & Sci Awd 86; Seq III-I Mth Awd 86; Lat Awd 85; Engr.

FORWAND, RACHEL; John H Glenn HS; Huntington, NY; (Y); Rep Jr Cls; Capt Lcrss; Score Keeper; Hon Roll; JR Prom Queen.

FORYS, ALBERT; Bishop Kearney HS; Rochester, NY; (Y); 3/141; Var Im Bowling; Var Golf; Im Sftbl; High Hon Roll; Hon Roll; NHS; Coaches Awd Bowling 85; RIT Alumni Schrlsh P86; Pres Acad Ftns Awd 86; Rochester Inst Tech; Bus Adm.

FOSE, KENNETH; Churchville-Chili SR HS; Churchville, NY; (Y); Computer Clb; Ski Clb; Bsktbl; Tennis; Trk; Wt Lftg; High Hon Roll; Hon Roll; U NY Rchstr; Comp Sci.

FOSHAY, MARIANNE; Walter Panas HS; Peekskill, NY; (Y); Cmnty Wkr; Hosp Aide; Ski Clb; SADD; Var JV Bsktbl; Score Keeper; JV Vllybl; Bus.

FOSHER, APRIL; Nazareth Acad; Hilton, NY; (Y); French Clb; SADD; Nwsp Stf; Lit Mag; High Hon Roll; Hon Roll; Outstndng Svc Nazareth Acad 86; Monroe CC; Exec Sec.

FOSSEL, STEVEN L; John Jay HS; Katonah, NY; (Y); Capt Math Tm; Science Clb; Var Capt Crs Cntry; Var Capt Trk; High Hon Roll; NHS; Ntl Merit Ltr; Middlebury Clg.

FOSSETT, PAUL; Center Moriches HS; Center Moriches, NY; (Y); Church Yth Grp; French Clb; Spanish Clb; Variety Show; Lit Mag; Sec Sr Cls; Hon Roll; Prfct Atten Awd; Young Scholars 86; Stony Brk ST U; Med.

FOSTER, CHRISTOPHER; Rice HS; New York, NY; (Y); Church Yth Grp; Office Aide; Church Choir.

FOSTER, ELAINE; George W Wingate HS; Brooklyn, NY; (Y); JV Stat Badmtn; Capt Swmmng; JV Trk; JV Vllybl; Exploring; Band; Chorus; Socr; Tennis; Prfct Atten Awd; Survival Swmmng Mdls 82; Trk & Fld Wnr 82; Hunter U; RN.

FOSTER, GILLIAN; St Catharine Acad; Bronx, NY; (Y); 59/185; Cmnty Wkr; Hosp Aide; Office Aide; Hon Roll; NHS; Prfct Atten Awd; Pace U; Pre Law.

FOSTER, JEANETTE; Keveny Memorial Acad; Clifton Park, NY; (S); 1/35; Cmnty Wkr; Drama Clb; Band; School Play; Pres Soph Cls; Rep Stu Cncl; JV Capt Cheerleading; Vllybl; Acad All Amer 83 & 84; Natl Bus Hnr Soc 83 & 84; Brown U; Pre-Med.

FOSTER, JOHANNA; Arlington HS; Wappingers Falls, NY; (Y); Cmnty Wkr; Band; Concert Band; Mrchg Band; Nwsp Phtg; Nwsp Rptr; Nwsp Stf; Lit Mag; Pres Frsh Cls; Rep Soph Cls; Engl.

FOSTER, JON P; Hilton Central HS; Hilton, NY; (Y); Am Leg Boys St; Ftbl; Wrstlng; History.

FOSTER, KELLEY; Easthampton HS; Montauk, NY; (Y); JA; JV Tennis; JV Vllybl; High Hon Roll; Jr NHS; Lion Awd; NHS; Stu Of Mo Jan; Psychology.

FOSTER, LEE; Valley Central HS; Walden, NY; (Y); Church Yth Grp; Hosp Aide; Acpl Chr; Band; Chorus; Church Choir; Concert Band; Mrchg Band; School Musical; School Play; All Cnty Band 85-86; Navy; Naval Aviator.

FOSTER, MATTHEW; Gouverneur Central HS; Gouverneur, NY; (Y); Church Yth Grp; School Musical; VP Jr Cls; Socr; High Hon Roll; Hon Roll; VP Jr NHS; Chorus; Rep Hgh O Brn Yth Fndtn 84-85; Rep HS Of Excllnc 85-86; Math.

FOSTER, MONIQUE M; Fashion Industries HS; New York, NY; (Y); 54/365; Aud/Vis; Drama Clb; Office Aide; Yrbk Stf; Tennis; Hon Roll; Regents Schlrshp 86; Penn ST; Adv.

FOSTER, STEVEN R; New Berlin Central HS; New Berlin, NY; (Y); 24/48; Concert Band; Jazz Band; Mrchg Band; Pep Band; Nwsp Ed-Chief; Yrbk Stf; Pres Stu Cncl; Cit Awd; Computer Clb; Band; Rgnts Schlrshp 86; Auburn Jazz Fstvl All Str Awd 86; Morrisville Ag & Tech; Comp Sci.

FOTINO, GIA; Warwick Valley Central HS; Warwick, NY; (Y); 20/186; Ski Clb; SADD; Yrbk Phtg; Yrbk Stf; VP Sr Cls; Cit Awd; High Hon Roll; Hon Roll; NHS; Empire ST Winter Game Skiing 85-86; Plattsburgh ST; Math.

FOUCHT, CRAIG; Victor SR HS; Victor, NY; (Y); 16/225; Church Yth Grp; French Clb; Thesps; Varsity Clb; Band; School Musical; School Play; Socr; Swmmng; Trk; Northwestern U; Cmmnctns.

FOURMAN, BRUCE; Raverna Coeymans Selkirly HS; Glenmont, NY; (Y); Chess Clb; Church Yth Grp; Spanish Clb; Varsity Clb; Stage Crew; Var Bsktbl; Var Ftbl; Cit Awd; High Hon Roll; Hon Roll; Architecture.

FOUTS, ANNA; Stissing Mtn JR SR HS; Stanfordville, NY; (Y); AFS; VP 4-H; Sec Chorus; Crs Cntry; Trk; 4-H Awd; Hon Roll; Hnr Key 84-86; Lbrl Arts.

FOWLER, DANA; Walter Panas HS; Peekskill, NY; (Y); Teachers Aide; Band; Concert Band; Mrchg Band; Var Bowling; Stat Swmmng; Hon Roll; Miss Westcher Cnty Teen Ager 85-86; ST Pgnt Semi Fnlst 85; Teen Wrld Beauty Semi Fnlst 86; Flght Atten.

FOWLER, KAREN; Wilson Central HS; Wilson, NY; (Y); 2/110; Am Leg Aux Girls St; School Musical; Rep Stu Cncl; Im Powder Puff Ftbl; DAR Awd; NHS; Sal; Natl Sci Merit Awds 84-86; LIU U Schlr Awd 86; Pres Acadmc Fitnss Awd 86; Long Island U; Psychlgy.

FOWLER, KIMBERLEY A; Archbishop Walsh HS; Olean, NY; (Y); Church Yth Grp; Drama Clb; Hosp Aide; Latin Clb; Pep Clb; Spanish Clb; School Musical; Nwsp Stf; Diving; Sftbl; Psych.

FOWLER, PATRICIA; Holy Trinity Diocesan HS; Wantagh, NY; (S); 7/403; Math Clb; Math Tm; Ski Clb; VP Soph Cls; Var Cheerleading; Var Gym; JV Sftbl; High Hon Roll; Frsh Cls; Rep Jr Cls; Math Awd 84-85; Sportsnight 83-85; Boston Coll; Acctnt.

FOWLER, SANDRA L; South Jefferson Central HS; Lorraine, NY; (Y); 1/125; Cmnty Wkr; French Clb; FTA; German Clb; Nwsp Stf; Yrbk Stf; High Hon Roll; Hon Roll; Jr NHS; NHS; Regents Schlrshp 86; JCC; Tchr.

FOX, ARMANDO; Regis HS; Rego Park, NY; (Y); Computer Clb; Ski Clb; Band; High Hon Roll; Hon Roll; Ntl Merit SF; Natl Assoc Of Teachers Of French 85; Cert Progrm Mannes Coll Of Music 78-86; Gen Excellence Awd 85; MIT; Aerosp Engrng.

FOX, BETHANY; Pine Valley Central Schl; Conewango Valley, NY; (S); AFS; FHA; Ski Clb; VP Jr Cls; Rep Stu Cncl; Var Sftbl; Var Capt Vllybl; Hon Roll; NHS; Voice Dem Awd; PTA High Cls Avg Awd 85; High Math & Eng Avg Awds 84; Engrng.

FOX, BRIDGET E; Newfane SR HS; Newfane, NY; (Y); 12/175; Church Yth Grp; Drama Clb; Intnl Clb; Math Clb; School Play; Stage Crew; Yrbk Stf; Sec Stu Cncl; Tennis; Hon Roll; Rgnts Schlrshp; Daemen Coll; Arch.

FOX, C PATRICK; Duanesburg Central HS; Delanson, NY; (Y); Boy Scts; Pres Chess Clb; Drama Clb; Math Clb; SADD; Chorus; School Play; Nwsp Rptr; Var Trk; Var Wrstlng; Comp Pgmmg.

FOX, CAROL; Hamburg SR HS; Hamburg, NY; (Y); 4/356; Church Yth Grp; JCL; Acpl Chr; Band; Chorus; Church Choir; Concert Band; Orch; School Musical; Symp Band; Pre-Med.

FOX, COLLEEN; Villa Maria Acad; Depew, NY; (S); 1/87; JCL; Latin Clb; Pep Clb; Quiz Bowl; Nwsp Rptr; Nwsp Stf; Rep Stu Cncl; High Hon Roll; Girl Scts; SADD; Schl Schlrshp 84-85; Full Schlrhsp 83.

FOX, DAVID; Holy Trinity HS; Roosevelt, NY; (Y); Aud/Vis; Camera Clb; Chess Clb; French Clb; Math Clb; Math Tm; Office Aide; Ski Clb; SADD; Teachers Aide; NYS Nrsng Schlrshp 86; Ecnmcs.

FOX, ERIC J; Centereach HS; Centereach, NY; (Y); 40/469; Teachers Aide; Variety Show; Pres Frsh Cls; Pres Soph Cls; VP Jr Cls; Rep Sr Cls; Var Golf; Var Socr; Var Capt Wrstlng; Hon Roll; NYS Ashperd Schlr Athl Sr Cls 85-86; NYS Rgnts Schlrshp 86; AAA Outstndng Drvr Educ Awd 85; Rutgers U; Meteorology.

FOX, IAN M; United Nations International Schl; Queens, NY; (Y); 2/110; Chess Clb; Church Yth Grp; Computer Clb; Ski Clb; Orch; School Musical; Lit Mag; Ntl Merit SF; Concert Band; Yrbk Stf; Accptnc Sci Hnrs Prog Columbia U 84; Comm Orgnzg Conf Untd Ntns 83-86; Oxford U; Physcs.

FOX, JILL H; Southwestern Central HS; Jamestown, NY; (Y); 15/142; Am Leg Aux Girls St; Pep Clb; Political Wkr; Ski Clb; Sec Band; School Musical; Nwsp Ed-Chief; Rep Sr Cls; Sec Stu Cncl; NHS; U Buffalo; Lawyer.

FOX, JOHN C; Newark SR HS; Newark, NY; (Y); 13/186; Am Leg Boys St; Boy Scts; Capt L Swmmng; High Hon Roll; Hon Roll; Ntl Merit Ltr; Tech Orientd Coll; Engrng.

FOX, JONATHAN PATRICK; Attica SR HS; Cowlesville, NY; (Y); 31/154; Band; Concert Band; Jazz Band; Mrchg Band; Orch; Hon Roll; Youth Amer; US Collgt Wind Band; Fluff Reynolds Mem Marchng Awd; Geneseo ST.

FOX, KURT A; Attica Central Schl; Athica, NY; (Y); Math Clb; Math Tm; Science Clb; JV Ftbl; Hon Roll; NHS; Devils Cup-Hcky All Star 84-85.

FOX, NANCY; Silver Creek Central HS; Silver Creek, NY; (Y); Spanish Clb; Band; Concert Band; Mrchg Band; Pep Band; JV Var Trk; Erly Chldhd Ed.

FOX, PENNY; Bablylon HS; Babylon, NY; (Y); Drama Clb; French Clb; Concert Band; School Musical; School Play; Symp Band; Variety Show; Var Gym; High Hon Roll; NHS; Comm.

FOX, RICHIE; Salamanca JR SR HS; Salamanca, NY; (Y); Spanish Clb; Var Bsktbl; High Hon Roll; Hon Roll; Prfct Atten Awd; Spanish NHS; Seton Hall; Crim Jstc.

FOX, SHAWN; Marion Central HS; Walworth, NY; (Y); Church Yth Grp; Chorus; Color Guard; Secy Chrch Yth Grp 85 & 86; Sndy Schl & Bible Schl Tchr 85 & 86; Teachng.

FOX, TIMOTHY; North Rockland HS; Stony Point, NY; (Y); Am Leg Boys St; Cmnty Wkr; Drama Clb; NFL; Political Wkr; Trs Spanish Clb; Band; VP Chorus; Concert Band; Jazz Band; SCI.

FOXWORTH, SHERI; New Rochelle HS; New Rochelle, NY; (Y); FBLA; Chorus; Hon Roll; Achvmnt Awds Engl & Home Arts 84; FL Inst U; Fshn Mrchndsng.

FRACCALVIERI, MARYANNA; Lindenhurst HS; Lindenhurst, NY; (Y); Pres Church Yth Grp; French Clb; German Clb; Ski Clb; Varsity Clb; Var L Tennis; Stat Wrstlng; NHS; Twn Babyln Wmns Tnns Dbls Chmpn 86; VP Italian Clb; Brdcstng.

FRACCHIA, SUSANNE; Elmira Free Acad; Elmira, NY; (Y); Church Yth Grp; Spanish Clb; Trs SADD; Varsity Clb; Band; School Play; Off Jr Cls; Var Capt Cheerleading; Vllybl; Hon Roll; Bus.

FRACENTESE, MARY; Bishop Kearney HS; Brooklyn, NY; (Y); Spanish Clb; Bowling; Hon Roll; NY St Rgnts Schlrshp 86; Brooklyn Coll; Med.

FRADELLA, HENRY F; The Searing Schl; Morganville, NJ; (S); Hosp Aide; Chorus; VP Jr Cls; Pres Sr Cls; Pres Stu Cncl; High Hon Roll; Pres Schlr; Val; Cngrssnl Yuth Ldrshp Cncl 86.

FRAIDKIN, ELISA; Tottenville HS; Staten Isld, NY; (Y); Teachers Aide; Chorus; Stage Crew; NHS; Natl Writing Contest 86; French Cntst 7th NYC Area 84.

FRAINA, CHRIS; E J Wilson HS; Spencerport, NY; (Y); 24/300; French Clb; JCL; Latin Clb; Math Tm; Varsity Clb; Var L Diving; Var L Gym; Var L Trk; High Hon Roll; Hon Roll; Mktg.

FRAIOLI, CHRIS; Iona Prep; Larchmont, NY; (Y); 13/198; Ski Clb; Var Capt Lcrss; Boston Coll; Bus Adm.

FRALEIGH, KIMBERLY J; Our Lady Of Lourdes HS; Poughkeepsie, NY; (Y); 1/200; Teachers Aide; Chorus; Yrbk Stf; NHS; Skidmore Coll; Child Psych.

FRALIEGH, LAURIE; Dover JR SR HS; Dover Plains, NY; (Y); Pres Varsity Clb; Yrbk Bus Mgr; Trs Frsh Cls; VP Jr Cls; Pres Stu Cncl; Stat Bsktbl; Var Fld Hcky; Var Sftbl; Cit Awd; Hon Roll; Stu Mnth 85; Pace; Bus Adm.

FRAMENT, TIMOTHY; Scotia-Glenville HS; Scotia, NY; (Y); Key Clb; Varsity Clb; Rep Stu Cncl; Capt Var Socr; Var Vllybl; High Hon Roll; Trs NHS; RPI Math, Sci Mdl 86; All ST Sccr Tm 85; Engrng.

FRAMPTON, BONNIE; Sachem HS; Holtsville, NY; (Y); Ski Clb; Stage Crew; Stat Ftbl; C W Post; Cmmnctns.

FRANCE, BONNIE L; Lancaster Central HS; Lancaster, NY; (Y); 46/452; Library Aide; Office Aide; Pep Clb; Yrbk Stf; Var Cheerleading; Jr NHS; Pres Schlr; Spanish NHS; Acdmc L Hon Roll; SUNY.

FRANCE, CHRISTIAN R; Hornell HS; Hornell, NY; (Y); Boy Scts; Cmnty Wkr; Pep Clb; Ski Clb; SADD; Teachers Aide; Acpl Chr; Band; Chorus; Church Choir; Physics.

FRANCESCHELLI, CAROL; Auburn HS; Auburn, NY; (Y); JV Socr; JV Sftbl; Math.

FRANCESCOTT, THOMAS; Germantown Central HS; Germantown, NY; (S); 2/43; Church Yth Grp; Varsity Clb; School Play; Rep Stu Cncl; Bsbl; Socr; Vllybl; High Hon Roll; Art Awds 85; Spnsh Awds 84-85; Engr.

FRANCHETTI, SUZANNE P; St Franics Prep; Manhasset, NY; (S); 87/746; Church Yth Grp; Cmnty Wkr; Drama Clb; Chorus; Church Choir; School Musical; Stage Crew; JV Gym; Hon Roll; NHS; Presdntl Citation-Manhasset Yth Councl 85; Optimates Soc 84-85; Psych.

FRANCIA, DANA; Carmel HS; Pawling, NY; (Y); 77/350; Var JV Cheerleading; Var Hon Roll; Var JV Prfct Atten Awd; SUNY Cortland; Elem Ed.

FRANCIA, LISA; Norwood Norfolk Central HS; Norfolk, NY; (Y); French Clb; Girl Scts; Pep Clb; JV Capt Bsktbl; JV Sftbl; High Hon Roll; Hon Roll; Canton ATC; Crmnl Justc.

FRANCIONE, KIM; Valley Stream Central HS; Valley Stream, NY; (Y); Ski Clb; JV Var Sftbl; Hon Roll; NHS; Hofstra; Nrsng.

FRANCIS, BEATRICE; St Edmund HS; Brooklyn, NY; (Y); Cmnty Wkr; French Clb; Library Aide; Service Clb; Yrbk Stf; Rep Jr Cls; Hon Roll; Prfct Atten Awd; Outstndg Achvt Engl Awd 86; 1st Pl Troph Lang Fair 86; NY U; Biol.

FRANCIS, BRENDA; Malverne HS; W Hempstead, NY; (Y); Church Yth Grp; Computer Clb; Dance Clb; Debate Tm; Drama Clb; Girl Scts; PAVAS; Band; Chorus; Church Choir; Law.

FRANCIS, CHRISTINA; Hahn American HS; Apo New York, NY; (Y); Yrbk Stf; Pres Frsh Cls; Sec Stu Cncl; JV Bsktbl; Var Capt Sftbl; Var Capt Vllybl; High Hon Roll; Scholastic Bowl; Jr NHS; Trs Sec NHS; Exc Acctng,Math 83-85; Am Hist Acad Achvt 85-86; Acctng.

FRANCIS, DAWN; Wilson Magnet HS; Rochester, NY; (Y); JA; Math Tm; Science Clb; Concert Band; Mrchg Band; Yrbk Ed-Chief; Tennis; Hon Roll; NHS; Prfct Atten Awd.

FRANCIS, DWAYNE; William E Grady HS; Brooklyn, NY; (Y); Boy Scts; Church Yth Grp; Math Clb; Teachers Aide; Concert Band; JV Bsktbl; Yth Awd KWOA Inc Brooklyn Branch 83; Elec Engr.

FRANCIS, JIM; Roy C Kethcam HS; Poughkeepsie, NY; (Y); 150/550; Varsity Clb; Band; Concert Band; Jazz Band; Symp Band; Rep Stu Cncl; Var Crs Cntry; Var Swmmng; Var Trk; Hon Roll; SUNY Cobleskill; Htl Mgt.

FRANCIS, JOEL; Rice HS; New York, NY; (Y); School Play; Nwsp Rptr; Yrbk Rptr; Im Bsktbl; Im Ftbl; Baruch Coll.

FRANCIS, KATHRYN L; Akron HS; Akron, NY; (Y); 4/143; Cmnty Wkr; French Clb; FFA; Letterman Clb; Math Clb; Teachers Aide; High Hon Roll; Hon Roll; NYS Rgnts Schlrshp 86; Bryant; Info Processing.

FRANCIS, MICHAEL M; Haverling Central HS; Bath, NY; (S); 7/140; Church Yth Grp; Mrchg Band; Symp Band; Var Bsktbl; Capt JV Socr; Tennis; High Hon Roll; NHS; French Clb; Math Clb; Soccer Invtnl MVP 85; Acdmc All St Tm 85 & 86; Sci.

FRANCIS, OMAR; Rice HS; Bronx, NY; (Y); Cmnty Wkr; Ed Yrbk Stf; Rep Stu Cncl; Var Bowling; Im Ftbl; High Hon Roll; Rev Brthr John M Shea Awd Bus 86; Iona Coll; Bus.

FRANCIS, RUDOLPH; Adlai E Steenson HS; Bronx, NY; (Y); Church Yth Grp; Cmnty Wkr; Debate Tm; Political Wkr; Speech Tm; Concert Band; Drm Mjr(t); Mrchg Band; Orch; Nwsp Rptr; Most Court Coach Trphy 86; Law.

FRANCIS, SHERONNA; Park West HS; Bronx, NY; (Y); Cmnty Wkr; Girl Scts; JA; Math Clb; Sec Office Aide; Service Clb; Teachers Aide; Temple Yth Grp; Drill Tm; Hon Roll; Awd Acad Exc Math Regnts 86; Engrng.

FRANCIS, VALBERT; Evander Chilos HS; Bronx, NY; (S); Church Yth Grp; Office Aide; Quiz Bowl; Church Choir; Rep Stu Cncl; Hon Roll; Prfct Atten Awd; Engrng.

FRANCISCO, DANIEL; Tupper Lake HS; Tupper Lk, NY; (Y); 15/135; 4-H; Teachers Aide; Wt Lftg; Dnfth Awd; 4-H Awd; Hon Roll; Lion Awd; Am Leg Awd Voice Of Dem 82; CSEA Schlrshp 86; Paul Smith COLL Schlrshp 86; Paul Smiths COLL; Frstry.

FRANCO, CARLOS; Sacred Heart HS; New York, NY; (Y); Science Clb; Church Yth Grp; Computer Clb; Chorus; Cornell U; Vet-Med.

FRANCO, JOSEPH; Port Richmond HS; Staten Island, NY; (Y); Im Trk; Aerospace Repair.

FRANCO, MICHAEL A; Walter Panas HS; Peekskill, NY; (Y); 17/247; Computer Clb; VP Drama Clb; FBLA; Ski Clb; SADD; Chorus; School Musical; Stage Crew; Nwsp Rptr; Lit Mag; Ithaca Coll; Brdcst Jrnlsm.

FRANCO, NICHOLAS; Lake George HS; Glens Falls, NY; (Y); #17 In Class; Church Yth Grp; SADD; Rep Frsh Cls; JV Bsbl; Var Ftbl; Wt Lftg; High Hon Roll; Hon Roll; Jr NHS; Bio Engrng.

FRANCO, SHELLEY; Horseheads SR HS; Horseheads, NY; (S); 35/380; DECA; Ski Clb; Spanish Clb; Varsity Clb; Nwsp Rptr; JV Var Cheerleading; Gym; Stat Lcrss; Trk; Im Wt Lftg; Hpwd Schlrshp Frm Lynchbrg Coll 85; Miss Hsptlty Awd; Bus.

FRANDINA, MARTINA; St Francis Prep; Howard Beach, NY; (S); 93/744; Church Yth Grp; Cmnty Wkr; Hosp Aide; NHS; Opt Clb Awd; Itln Clb Co-Fndr & Co Pres 85-86; Fshn Dsgn.

FRANK, ALISON; Riverdale Country Schl; Bronx, NY; (Y); Science Clb; SADD; JV Fld Hcky; Var Lcrss; Swmmng; High Hon Roll; Fndrs Schlrshp 86-87; Ski Rcng Awds 83-86; Med.

FRANK, AMY; Oppenheim Ephratah CS HS; Johnstown, NY; (S); 1/32; GAA; Trs Spanish Clb; Band; Nwsp Ed-Chief; Trs Sr Cls; VP Stu Cncl; Bausch & Lomb Sci Awd; DAR Awd; High Hon Roll; NHS; Engrng.

FRANK, ANDREW; Fayetteville-Manlkius HS; Manlius, NY; (Y); Church Yth Grp; Cmnty Wkr; JCL; SADD; JV Lcrss; Var Socr; Natl Latn Exm Magna Cum Laude 86; Bus.

FRANK, AUDREY; Chatham HS; Chatham, NY; (Y); Yrbk Phtg; Yrbk Stf; Trk; Vllybl; High Hon Roll; Hon Roll; Elem Ed.

FRANK, BARBARA J; Marcus Whitman HS; Stanley, NY; (Y); 2/135; 4-H; Yrbk Ed-Chief; Swmmng; DAR Awd; 4-H Awd; High Hon Roll; NHS; Ntl Merit Ltr; Sal; Ski Clb; Ntl 4-H Conf 86; Cornell U; Biol.

FRANK, BRADLEY R; Martin Van Buren HS; Hollis Hills, NY; (Y); 13/565; English Clb; Math Tm; Science Clb; Service Clb; Temple Yth Grp; Variety Show; Trs Sr Cls; Bsktbl; Hon Roll; NHS.

FRANK JR, DOMINICK G; Amsterdam HS; Amsterdam, NY; (Y); Concert Band; Mrchg Band; Crs Cntry; Trk; Geneseo; Math Tchr.

FRANK, JEFF; Mayfield Central HS; Mayfield, NY; (Y); 2/72; Teachers Aide; Nwsp Ed-Chief; Bausch & Lomb Sci Awd; High Hon Roll; NHS; Prfct Atten Awd; Pres Schlr; Sal; Church Yth Grp; Nwsp Rptr; Sci Awd 86; Hstry Awd 86; Regents Diploma With Hnr 86; Suny Cortland; Psychology.

FRANK, LAURIE; Holland Patent HS; Stittville, NY; (Y); Aud/Vis; FTA; Chorus; JV Cheerleading; JV Sftbl; Hon Roll; JR Vrsty Awd 85-86; Bio Tchr.

FRANK, LISA; Whitesboro SR HS; Whitesboro, NY; (Y); Drama Clb; Chorus; School Musical; School Play; Yrbk Stf; Rep Frsh Cls; Rep Soph Cls; Rep Stu Cncl; Hon Roll; Accntnt.

FRANK, LORI; Cardinal Mooney HS; Rochester, NY; (Y); 38/304; Hosp Aide; Library Aide; Nwsp Rptr; JV Var Cheerleading; French Hon Soc; Hon Roll; Pres Schlr; Regents Nrsg Sclrp 86; Alfred U; Nrsng.

FRANK, MATTHEW; Cardinal Mooney HS; Hilton, NY; (Y); Church Yth Grp; Cmnty Wkr; School Musical; Stage Crew; Variety Show; Hon Roll; Regnts Schlrshp 86; Potsdam ST Clg; Comptr Sci.

FRANK, NANCY; Frontier SR HS; Hamburg, NY; (S); 14/450; Chorus; VP Concert Band; Jazz Band; School Musical; Sec Stu Cncl; Var Capt Bsktbl; Var Socr; Var Capt Vllybl; High Hon Roll; NHS; Vlybl MVP Bulldog Trnmnt 85; Bsktbl-Most Steals 83-84; All Around Athl 83; Music Educ.

FRANK, RACHEL; Baldwin SR HS; Baldwin, NY; (Y); Drama Clb; Thesps; Chorus; Orch; School Musical; School Play; Stage Crew; Variety Show; Hon Roll; NHS; Nassau HS All Cnty Choir 86; Long Island String Fest 84 & 86; VP Lighting Crew 85-86; Music Ed.

FRANK, ROBIN; Fairport HS; Fairport, NY; (Y); Drama Clb; Girl Scts; VICA; Chorus; Stage Crew; Yrbk Stf; Cosmtlgy.

FRANK, SAMANTHA; The High Schl Of Music & Art; New York, NY; (S); Chorus; Madrigals; Hon Roll; NHS; Prfrmng Arts.

FRANK, SCOTT LARRY; Springville-Griffith Instit & CS; Springville, NY; (Y); 2/197; NHS; Ntl Merit Ltr; Sal; Its Acad Tm; NALC William C Doherty Schlrshp Wnnr 86; ST U Of NY; Hnrs Pgm.

FRANK, SCOTT R; Canisius HS; E Aurora, NY; (Y); Church Yth Grp; Model UN; School Musical; Yrbk Stf; JV Var Ftbl; JV Trk; Wt Lftg; Hon Roll; Law.

FRANK, SYLVIA K; Fonda Fultonville Central Schl; Esperance, NY; (Y); 2/111; VP Intnl Clb; Key Clb; SADD; Concert Band; Mrchg Band; Trs NHS; Ntl Merit Ltr; Sal; Hghst Acdmc Avg Fr Grl 83-85; Phi Theta Kappa Early Admt 86; SUNY Buffalo; Biochmstry.

FRANK, TRACEY; Alexander Central HS; Batavia, NY; (Y); 21/83; Cmnty Wkr; Dance Clb; Trs 4-H; French Clb; Band; Sec Chorus; Concert Band; Jazz Band; Mrchg Band; School Musical; Al-Cnty Chorus 84-86; Al-Cnty Band 84 & 86; Bst Sctn Mrchng Band 838 85 & 86; Bst Sctn Cncrt Band 85; LIU; Spcl Educ.

FRANK, WILLIAM; Cicero-North Syracuse HS; N Syracuse, NY; (S); 40/623; German Clb; JA; Letterman Clb; Capt Var Bsbl; JV Bsktbl; Var Capt Ftbl; Hon Roll; Stanford; Pro Baseball.

FRANKE, JUDY; Wilson Central Schl; Wilson, NY; (Y); 28/111; Library Aide; Teachers Aide; Powder Puff Ftbl; Hon Roll; Perfect Attndnc; Bryant/Stratton Bus Inst; CPA.

FRANKEL, GLENN; Williamsville East HS; Buffalo, NY; (Y); Am Leg Boys St; Boy Scts; Drama Clb; Model UN; School Musical; School Play; Pres Stu Cncl; NHS; Williams Coll Bk Awd 86.

FRANKEL, STEPHEN; Lawrence HS; Woodmere, NY; (Y); 1/400; Pres Key Clb; Orch; Nwsp Ed-Chief; Capt Sftbl; Ntl Merit SF; Val; Computer Clb; Mathletes; Math Tm; RITEC Awd 86; Adelphi U Smmr Acad Intl Stds Schlrshp 85; Archon Svc Hnr Socty 86; Intl Rel.

FRANKINO, NANCY; St Marys HS; Buffalo, NY; (S); 16/166; Computer Clb; Pres Exploring; Sec Teachers Aide; Ed Nwsp Stf; Lit Mag; Var Mgr(s); JV Vllybl; High Hon Roll; NHS; Treas/Sec NCHA Teens 82-86; Co-Chrprsn Schl Fund Raiser 85-86; SUNY Buffalo; Comp Sci.

FRANKLIN, DARLENE M; Woodlands HS; White Plains, NY; (Y); 51/203; Church Yth Grp; Cmnty Wkr; Hosp Aide; Math Tm; Rep Frsh Cls; Rep Soph Cls; Rep Jr Cls; Rep Sr Cls; Capt Vllybl; Ntl Merit Schol; Hwrd U Schlrshp 85; Howard U; Micro-Bio.

FRANKLIN, KIM; Uniondale HS; Uniondale, NY; (Y); Chorus; Yrbk Stf; Capt Cheerleading; Score Keeper; Hon Roll; Comp Sci.

FRANKLIN, MARIE C; St John The Baptist HS; N Babylon, NY; (Y); 29/540; FTA; Hosp Aide; Science Clb; SADD; Nwsp Stf; Stu Cncl; Socr; High Hon Roll; Spanish NHS; Bio.

FRANKLIN, PATRICIA A; West Islip HS; W Islip, NY; (Y); Library Aide; Office Aide; Service Clb; Var Chorus; High Hon Roll; Hon Roll; NHS; Acctng I,II Exc Awds 85-86; Medalie Schlrshp 86; Soc Studies Exc Awd 86; St Josephs Coll; Acctng.

FRANKS, TOM M; Maine Endwell HS; Endwell, NY; (Y); 2/234; Cmnty Wkr; JV Bsbl; Bausch & Lomb Sci Awd; High Hon Roll; NHS; Sal; Am Leg Outstndng Frshmn 83; Thomas J Watson Mem Schlrshp 86; Cornell U; Engrng.

FRANQUI, BEN; Cardinal Spellman HS; Bx, NY; (Y); Drama Clb; Off Latin Clb; SADD; School Musical; Variety Show; Lit Mag; Pres Stu Cncl; JV Var Ftbl; NROTC Scholar Fin 86-87; Aerospc Engrng.

FRANTINO, MICHAEL J; Mt St Michael Acad; Bronx, NY; (Y); 6/300; Im Bsktbl; Im Fld Hcky; Im Ftbl; Im Sftbl; NHS; SUNY Albany; Mktng.

FRANTZESKAKIS, OLIVIA; Port Richmond HS; Staten Island, NY; (Y); Art Clb; Teachers Aide; Stage Crew; Yrbk Stf; 2nd Prz Prntmakng Comptn Portland Schl Art 85; Alexander Awd Art League NY 85; Pratt; Fine Arts.

FRANZ, PAMELA S; Garden City HS; Garden City, NY; (Y); 58/346; Church Yth Grp; Girl Scts; Capt Color Guard; Mrchg Band; Albright Clg; Psych.

FRANZA, ALFRED; Archbishop Molloy HS; Woodhaven, NY; (Y); 180/400; Im Ftbl; Im Sftbl; High Hon Roll; Hon Roll; Acctng.

FRANZEN, SCOTT; Jamestown HS; Jamestown, NY; (Y); Boy Scts; Church Yth Grp; French Clb; Var Swmmng; Hon Roll; NHS; Eagle Scout 85; Boy Scouts Youth Leadership In America Award 85; Rochester Inst Tech; Elec Engr.

FRANZESE, JULIE; Watkins Glen HS; Watkins Glen, NY; (S); 14/130; Rep Soph Cls; Rep Jr Cls; Rep Stu Cncl; Capt Cheerleading; Diving; Swmmng; French Hon Soc; Hon Roll; NHS; Ntl Merit Ltr; Elmira Key Awd 85; Chrldr Yr 84; Bio.

FRANZESE, MINDY; Watkins Glen HS; Watkins Glen, NY; (S); Chorus; Concert Band; Jazz Band; Nwsp Rptr; Rep Soph Cls; Var Cheerleading; Diving; French Hon Soc; Hon Roll; Ntl Merit Ltr; 1st Pl SR Jazz Solo 85; 3rd Pl JV Indv All Amer Natl Chldg Comp 85; Educ.

FRANZESE, PAUL; West Hempstead HS; Island Park, NY; (Y); Church Yth Grp; Cmnty Wkr; Hon Roll; Natl Art Hnr Socty 85; Psych.

FRANZITTA, JACK; Valley Stream Central HS; Valley Stream, NY; (Y); Art Clb; Computer Clb; Science Clb; School Musical; JV Bsbl; JV Ftbl.

FRASCHILLA, DARCY; St John Villa Acad; Staten Island, NY; (Y); Church Yth Grp; Stage Crew; Yrbk Phtg; Yrbk Rptr; Yrbk Sprt Ed; Yrbk Stf; Var Capt Crs Cntry; Var Capt Trk; Excllnc Studio Art, Achvt Studio Art 85; Excllnc Intro Art, Achvt Intro Art 84; Wnnr Ch 13 Stu Art Fst; Grphc Dsgnr.

FRASE, ROSEANNE; Sweet Home SR HS; Tonawanda, NY; (Y); Church Yth Grp; GAA; Ski Clb; Var JV Fld Hcky; Var JV Socr; Dental Lab Tech.

FRASER, DAVID; Mynderse Acad; Seneca Falls, NY; (S); 7/138; Spanish Clb; Band; Concert Band; Jazz Band; Stu Cncl; JV Crs Cntry; Var Trk; High Hon Roll; JV Bowling; Telecomm.

FRASER, KAREN E; Kenmore East HS; Tonawanda, NY; (Y); 11/330; Color Guard; Mrchg Band; High Hon Roll; NHS; Full Tuitn Schlrshp 86; Regents Schlrshp 86; Bryant & Stratton; Bus.

FRASER, THOMAS G; Lewiston-Porter SR HS; Youngstown, NY; (Y); Key Clb; Political Wkr; Orch; Rep Frsh Cls; Rep Soph Cls; Rep Jr Cls; Rep Sr Cls; Rep Stu Cncl; Var Capt Bsktbl; Var Capt Tennis; Rbt F Curry Outstndng Athlt Stu; Lamp Of Lrng Exc Awds; Rgnts Schlrshp; U Notre Dame; Life Sci.

FRASIER, CELESTE; Northville Central HS; Northville, NY; (Y); Am Leg Aux Girls St; Library Aide; SADD; Chorus; School Play; Yrbk Stf; Stu Cncl; Hon Roll; NHS; Vocal, Mus, Boosters, Library Awds; Club Awds & Frgn Lang Span Awds; Marist Poughkeepsie NY; TV.

FRASIER, GARY; Gloversville HS; Gloversville, NY; (Y); Church Yth Grp; Fulton Montgomery Coll Trustees Scholar 86; Cobleskill A&T; Med.

FRATANGELO, MICHAEL R; Johnstown HS; Johnstown, NY; (Y); 3/190; Am Leg Boys St; Math Tm; School Play; VP Frsh Cls; Var L Bsktbl; Var Capt Golf; Var Capt Tennis; NHS; Prfct Atten Awd; Chemistry Awd Highest Avg 86; Golf MVP 84 & 85; Tennis MVP 84; Accounting.

FRATARCANGELO, CATHERINE; Haverling Central HS; Bath, NY; (Y); 3/114; French Clb; Latin Clb; Ski Clb; Trs Yrbk Stf; Sec Frsh Cls; Sec Soph Cls; JV Var Cheerleading; Co-Capt Tennis; High Hon Roll; NHS; Regents Schlrshp; St John Fisher Coll; Intl Stds.

FRATESCHI, RACHEL; Solvay HS; Syracuse, NY; (Y); FNA; Hosp Aide; Band; Yrbk Ed-Chief; Yrbk Phtg; Sec Soph Cls; Hon Roll; Svc Awd Ldrshp Awd 83-84; Band Awd 84-85; Nrsng Schlrshp 86; Irving Schl Nursing; Nrs.

FRATOLILL, GIRARD R; John F Kennedy HS; Yorktown Heights, NY; (Y); 95/200; Camera Clb; Church Yth Grp; 4-H; JA; Office Aide; SADD; Teachers Aide; JV Wrstlng; 4-H Awd; NYS Rgnts Schlrshp 86; CO ST U; Pre-Vet.

FRATTO, ADAM J; Maulius Pebble Hill HS; Syracuse, NY; (Y); Drama Clb; Pres Model UN; Political Wkr; Quiz Bowl; Scholastic Bowl; Varsity Clb; Acpl Chr; Band; Chorus; Madrigals; RPI Medal Math & Sci 85; David Edwards Awd Engl 85; Schl Select Century III Ledrshp Comptn 86; Swarthmore Coll.

FRATTO, FRANK; Middletown HS; Middletown, NY; (Y); SADD; SUNY Albany; Intl Bus.

FRATTURA II, DAVID E; Archbishop Stepinac HS; Yonkers, NY; (Y); Exploring; Key Clb; Im Crs Cntry; Im JV Trk; High Hon Roll; Hon Roll; NHS; Westchester Cnty JR Lgsltr 86; Yth For Life 85-86; Rep HS Natl Physcs Cmpttn 86; Engrng.

FRAWLEY, LIAM T; Mount Saint Michael Acad; New York, NY; (Y); 105/290; JV Var Bsbl; Rgnts Schlrshp 86; Manhattan Coll; Physcl Educ.

FRAZIER, JEFFREY; Fillmore Central HS; Fillmore, NY; (Y); FFA; Varsity Clb; JV Var Bsbl; Wrstlng; Hon Roll.

FRAZIER, KELLY; Catholic Central HS; Menands, NY; (S); 6/179; Church Yth Grp; Math Tm; Ski Clb; Band; Church Choir; Cheerleading; Tennis; High Hon Roll; NHS; Excl Afro-Asian, Spnsh I & Earth Sci 82-83; Excl Engl 83-84; Am Assoc Tchrs Awd 84-85; Law.

FRAZIER, MAUREEN; Catholic Central HS; Menands, NY; (Y); Math Tm; Ski Clb; Band; Church Choir; Concert Band; Bsktbl; Tennis; Hon Roll; NHS; Ntl Merit Ltr; 2nd Pl Mixed Doubles Ten Lipton Amtrs Trnmnt 86; Pre-Med.

FRAZIER, MELISSA A; Whitehall JR-SR HS; Whitehall, NY; (Y); 8/76; Sec Stu Cncl; Var Bsktbl; JV Golf; JV Sftbl; Var Stat Vllybl; Cit Awd; Trs NHS; NY ST Regnts Schlrshp 86; Acctng.

FREANEY, JAMES; Shoreham-Wading River M S HS; Shoreham, NY; (Y); 4/220; Scholastic Bowl; Science Clb; Sec Soph Cls; Sec Jr Cls; Rep Stu Cncl; Crs Cntry; Trk; NHS; Ntl Merit Ltr; Outstndng Stdnt Engrng Drwg 85; U S Naval Acad Smmr Smnr 86; Physcs Olmpcs Tm 1st Cnty 86; U S Naval Acad; Navl Ofcr.

FRECHETTE, MICHELLE; Hilton Central HS; Hilton, NY; (Y); 23/316; Sec Trs Drama Clb; Band; Trs Chorus; Mrchg Band; School Musical; School Play; Stage Crew; Symp Band; Variety Show; NHS; Roberts Wesleyan; Phlsphy.

FREDA, BILLY; St John The Bapt; Middle Island, NY; (S); Math Tm; ROTC; Var Crs Cntry; Var Trk; High Hon Roll; Hon Roll; Jr NHS; Mu Alp Tht; Spanish NHS; Bio Olympiad; Math Sci Socl Studies Cert Of Merit; Schlr Athlete Awd; Navy ROTC; Math.

FREDA, BILLY; St John The Baptist HS; Middle Isld, NY; (Y); Math Clb; Math Tm; Crs Cntry; Trk; Hon Roll; Jr NHS; NHS; Sci Olympia; Spnsh Hon Soc; Math Hon Soc.

FREDENBURGH, STEPHANIE A; Roy C Ketcham SR HS; Poughkeepsie, NY; (Y); 21/500; Chorus; Lib Orch; Symp Band; Nwsp Rptr; High Hon Roll; Jr NHS; NHS; Rgnts Schlrshp; Stony Brook; Mus.

FREDERICK, CALVIN; Centereach HS; Centereach, NY; (Y); 21/481; Pres Varsity Clb; Band; Jazz Band; Mrchg Band; Ftbl; Trk; Wt Lftg; Hon Roll; Jr NHS; NCTE Awd; Air Force Acad; Elec Engrng.

FREDERICK, MICHELE; Shoreham-Wading River HS; Shoreham, NY; (Y); Dance Clb; Ski Clb; Mgr(s); JV Tennis; Phys Thrpy.

FREDERICK, MICHELLE R; Morris Central HS; Morris, NY; (Y); 10/36; 4-H; GAA; Chorus; School Play; Yrbk Ed-Chief; Yrbk Phtg; Socr; High Hon Roll; NHS; Church Yth Grp; NY St Regents Schlrshp 85-86; Hartwick Coll; Nrsng.

FREDERICK, PAMELA; Johnstown HS; Johnstown, NY; (Y); Intnl Clb; Trs Frsh Cls; JV Var Fld Hcky; JV Var Sftbl; JV Vllybl; High Hon Roll; NHS; Regents Schlrshp 86; Potsdam Coll; Pol Sci.

FREDERICK JR, SCHIMEON; Thomas Edison HS; Rosedale, NY; (Y); Boy Scts; Church Yth Grp; Drama Clb; PAVAS; Science Clb; Variety Show; Off Stu Cncl; Cit Awd; High Hon Roll; Hon Roll; HS Queens Borough Sci Fr 2nd Plc Wnnr 84; Pop Warner Ftbll Leag Bst Defnsv Linemn 84; ROTC; Comp Engr.

FREDERICKSEN, ALICE; Oakwood Friends Boarding Schl; White Plains, NY; (Y); Church Yth Grp; Cmnty Wkr; French Clb; Band; Chorus; Mrchg Band; School Musical; School Play; Stu Cncl; Var L Sftbl; Farlham; Educ.

FREDLUND, BETH; Randolph Central HS; Randolph, NY; (Y); Art Clb; Drama Clb; Ski Clb; Acpl Chr; Chorus; School Play; Jamestown CC; Hotel Mgmr.

FREDRICKSON, SERENA; Tottenville HS; Staten Island, NY; (Y); 30/800; French Clb; GAA; Ski Clb; Var Crs Cntry; Var Gym; Var Trk; French Hon Soc; Hon Roll; Jr NHS; NHS; 5th Pl NYC Ntl Frnch Cntst 84; U NC Chpl Hl; Cmnctns.

FREEBORN, MICHELE; Cazenovia HS; New Woodstock, NY; (Y); Church Yth Grp; Acpl Chr; Chorus; Concert Band; Jazz Band; School Musical; Symp Band; High Hon Roll; Hon Roll; NHS; Nmntd Mcdonalds All Am Mrchng Bnd 86; Messiah Coll; Accntnt.

FREED, ANDREW; White Plains HS; White Plains, NY; (Y); 14/500; Nwsp Bus Mgr; Capt Swmmng; Elks Awd; NHS; Ntl Merit SF; St Schlr; Frgn Plcy Assn Awd 86; Capt Empire Sts Games Wtr Polo 85; VP Nrth House Govt 85; Harvard U; Govt.

FREEDELL, LAURA; Sachern HS; Holtsville, NY; (Y); 68/1585; Church Yth Grp; Cmnty Wkr; German Clb; Girl Scts; Ski Clb; Orch; Nwsp Rptr; Lit Mag; High Hon Roll; NHS; A Violin Solo NYSSMA 85; 1st Pl Long Isl Lang Fair German Poem 86; Gold Awd Girl Scouts 84-86; Eng.

FREEL, MIKE; Albertus Magnus HS; Pearl River, NY; (Y); 40/172; Service Clb; Stage Crew; JV Lcrss; SUNY; Commnctns.

FREELAND, ERIC PRESTON; Hutch-Tech HS; Buffalo, NY; (Y); Chess Clb; Band; Concert Band; Trk; Hon Roll; Prfct Atten Awd; Chem Engnrng.

FREELAND, MAXINE; George Wingate HS; Brooklyn, NY; (Y); Math Tm; Teachers Aide; Hon Roll; NHS; Prfct Atten Awd; Harvard U; Law.

FREELAND, TERRY; Cato-Meridian HS; Cato, NY; (Y); Girl Scts; Library Aide; Ski Clb; Chorus; Yrbk Stf; Pres Jr Cls; VP Stu Cncl; Vllybl; Hon Roll; NHS; Geneseo; Chem Engr.

FREEMAN, ANDREA; Alfred-Almond Central HS; Alfred Sta, NY; (Y); Sec JCL; SADD; Band; School Musical; Yrbk Sprt Ed; JV Var Sftbl; Var Tennis; NHS; JA; Latin Clb; Allegany Cnty Intern Hon Mntn On Proj 85-86; NYS JCL 2nd Pl Vocab/Derivitive Tst 85; Pol Sci.

FREEMAN, CHARLIE; North Salem HS; Purdys, NY; (Y); Math Tm; Varsity Clb; Band; Jazz Band; School Musical; Symp Band; JV Var Bsbl; Bausch & Lomb Sci Awd; High Hon Roll; NHS.

FREEMAN, JACQUELINE M; Grover Dleveland HS; Buffalo, NY; (Y); Spanish Clb; Band; Mrchg Band; Nwsp Stf; Yrbk Stf; Stu Cncl; Bsktbl; Tennis; Vllybl; Varsity Clb; Canisius; Pre-Law.

FREEMAN, LAUREEN ANN; Liverpool HS; Liverpool, NY; (Y); 172/821; AFS; Ski Clb; Spanish Clb; Mrchg Band; Nwsp Ed-Chief; Stu Cncl; High Hon Roll; Hon Roll; Jr NHS; NHS; SUNY Geneseo; Lbrl Art.

FREEMAN, MARGARET E; Garden City HS; Garden City, NY; (Y); 24/325; Cmnty Wkr; GAA; SADD; Stu Cncl; Diving; Fld Hcky; Swmmng; High Hon Roll; Ntl Merit SF; Trinity Clg; Arts.

FREEMAN, MARTHA; Randolph Central HS; Randolph, NY; (Y); Art Clb; Drama Clb; Ski Clb; Spanish Clb; Yrbk Stf; Var Cheerleading; Big 30 All Star Chrldng Awd 86; Bus Adm.

FREEMAN, RENEE; Porspect Heights HS; Brooklyn, NY; (S); Cmnty Wkr; Drama Clb; FBLA; Library Aide; Office Aide; Hon Roll; Prfct Atten Awd; Cert Of Merit Amer Hstry II & Emergency Med Care 85; Cert Of Hnr Englsh 84; Air Force; Law.

FREEMAN, ROBERT; Ossining HS; Briarcliff, NY; (Y); 5/255; Ski Clb; Varsity Clb; Nwsp Rptr; Var Bsbl; JV Bsktbl; Var Ftbl; High Hon Roll; NHS; Ntl Merit Ltr; Pres Schlr; Natl Ftbl Fndtn Gldn Dozen Awd, Schlrshp, Con Edison Athl Wk Awd 85; All Sect Ftbl & Bsbl 85-86; Princeton U; Econ.

FREEMAN, SUSAN; Heuvelton Central HS; De Peyster, NY; (S); Sec Trs Church Yth Grp; 4-H; Latin Clb; Band; Concert Band; Mrchg Band; Variety Show; Pres Jr Cls; NHS.

FREEMIRE, STEVE; Vernon-Verona-Sherrill Cntrl HS; Vernon Ctr, NY; (Y); 22/199; Boy Scts; Computer Clb; Var Golf; High Hon Roll; NY ST U; Chem Engrng.

FREER III, ROY; Cairo-Durham JR SR HS; Leeds, NY; (Y); 24/102; VP Pres Church Yth Grp; Cmnty Wkr; 4-H; Concert Band; School Musical; JV L Bsktbl; 4-H Awd; High Hon Roll; Jr NHS; Comp Sci.

FREGOE, LISA; Saranac Centeral HS; Morrisonville, NY; (S); SADD; Band; Chorus; Yrbk Stf; Hon Roll; Civil Engrng.

FREIERT, MICHELLE; Livonia HS; Conesus, NY; (Y); Church Yth Grp; French Clb; Ski Clb; Chorus; Lit Mag; Stu Cncl; Stat Wrstlng; Jr NHS; Psych.

FREILICH, JEFFREY; Clarkstown South HS; Nanuet, NY; (Y); Math Clb; Math Tm; Science Clb; Temple Yth Grp; Mu Alp Tht; Pres NHS; Law.

FREIN, REBECCA; Freeport HS; Freeport, NY; (Y); 2/450; VP Key Clb; Pres Ski Clb; Var Capt Gym; Capt Lcrss; Var Capt Socr; Elks Awd; High Hon Roll; Kiwanis Awd; NHS; Pres Schlr; Cornell U; Engrg.

FREITAG, CAROL; Sewanhaka HS; Elmont, NY; (Y); 65/342; Church Yth Grp; Office Aide; Chorus; School Musical; Variety Show; Hon Roll; Chorus Awd; Ed.

FREITAG, CURTIS E; Owego Free Acad; Owego, NY; (Y); 12/220; Church Yth Grp; Key Clb; Mathletes; Math Clb; Var Stu Cncl; Var L Tennis; High Hon Roll; Hon Roll; NHS; Ntl Merit Ltr; Colgate U; Math.

FRELIER, KAREN; Eastridge HS; Rochester, NY; (Y); 3/13; Trs Church Yth Grp; Cmnty Wkr; Library Aide; Spanish Clb; JV Im Bsktbl; JV Socr; JV Sftbl; High Hon Roll; Hon Roll; Niagara U; Crim Just.

FRELIGH, JOHN; Saugerties HS; Saugerties, NY; (S); Spanish Clb; Bsbl; Bsktbl; Hon Roll; Acctg.

FREMGEN, JENNIFER; St Francis Prep; Glendale, NY; (Y); Dance Clb; Sftbl; Bus Mgmt.

FRENCH, CYNTHIA J; Art & Design HS; New York, NY; (Y); 58/411; Art Clb; PAVAS; Variety Show; Yrbk Stf; Rep Sr Cls; Rep Stu Cncl; Hon Roll; NHS; Prfct Atten Awd; Natl Arts Rcgntn & Tlnt Search 85-86; Natl Art Hnr Soc 86; Phila Coll Arts; Animator.

FRENCH, JENNIFER; L A Webber Schl; Lyndonville, NY; (S); 5/81; AFS; Computer Clb; Math Clb; Science Clb; Spanish Clb; Varsity Clb; Concert Band; Mrchg Band; Trs Frsh Cls; Trs Soph Cls; Law.

FRENCH, JENNY; Waverly JR & SR HS; Waverly, NY; (Y); 6/120; Pres Trs 4-H; Pep Clb; Ski Clb; Pres Spanish Clb; JV Var Bsktbl; Var L Crs Cntry; JV Sftbl; Im Vllybl; 4-H Awd; Hon Roll; Engrng.

FRENCH, SARA L; Chatham HS; Chatham, NY; (Y); 9/117; Library Aide; Band; Church Choir; Mrchg Band; Orch; School Musical; Variety Show; High Hon Roll; NHS; NY ST Scty Chldrn Of Amer Rvltn 86-67; Wells Coll Aurora NY.

FRENCH, SUE ANN; Haverling Central HS; Bath, NY; (Y); 19/117; Exploring; Girl Scts; JCL; Trs Latin Clb; Math Clb; Band; Concert Band; Mrchg Band; Orch; School Musical; Cole & Latham Bus Law Awd 86; Corning Comm Coll; Parlegal.

FRESCH, JOSEPH; G Ray Bodley HS; Fulton, NY; (Y); Church Yth Grp; Science Clb; Chorus; Hon Roll; Arch.

FRESHMAN, MATTHEW E; Shaker HS; Menands, NY; (Y); Debate Tm; JA; Ski Clb; Temple Yth Grp; Orch; School Play; Frsh Cls; JV Socr; JV Trk; NHS; Cnty Gvrnmnt Intrn 85-86; Phtgrphy Dsply 86; Cornell U Smr Explrtn Archctr 85; Dartmouth Coll; Legal Sci.

FRETTO, KIMBERLY; Lansingburgh HS; Troy, NY; (Y); Church Yth Grp; Drama Clb; French Clb; Chorus; School Play; Yrbk Stf; Sec Frsh Cls; Capt Cheerleading; Hon Roll; HVCC; Human Svc.

FREVERT, PATRICIA; St Edmunds HS; Brooklyn, NY; (S); Sec Church Yth Grp; Drama Clb; Library Aide; Speech Tm; Band; Nwsp Stf; Bowling; JV Cheerleading; French Hon Soc; High Hon Roll; Mscl Bnd Awd 84; Engl Excllnc Awd 85; Excllnc Soc Studs 85; Cmmnctns.

FREW, LISA; Jamestown HS; Jamestown, NY; (Y); Trs French Clb; Trs Concert Band; Mrchg Band; Orch; School Musical; Symp Band; Yrbk Stf; Stat Var Bsktbl; Jr NHS; NHS; Law.

FREY, ALANNA M; Garden City SR HS; Garden City, NY; (Y); German Clb; Key Clb; Var Socr; Var Sftbl; Hon Roll; NY St Regents Coll Schlrshp 86; Intl Stu Exchng Pgm-Germany 85; Gettysburg Coll; German.

FREY, DIANA; Dominican Commercial HS; Brooklyn, NY; (Y); Hosp Aide; Im Sftbl; Var Swmmng; Hon Roll.

FREY, JEFFREY; Tonawanda SR HS; Tonawanda, NY; (Y); JV Bsbl; Var L Bsktbl; JV Socr; Buffalo ST; Math.

FREY, SCOTT; John F Kennedy HS; Bellmore, NY; (Y); Pres Mathletes; Quiz Bowl; Scholastic Bowl; Orch; Ed Nwsp Stf; Lit Mag; Hon Roll; NHS; Ntl Merit Ltr; AATF Natl French Contst 1st Co 3rd Reg 86; Bausch & Lomb Sci Awd 86; Pres Yorker Clb Schl 86-87.

FREY, TINA; Somers HS; Lincolndale, NY; (Y); Art Clb; Church Yth Grp; Dance Clb; Yrbk Stf; Cheerleading; Sftbl; Communications.

FREYTAG, CHRISTINE; Whitesboro SR HS; Utica, NY; (Y); 63/354; Church Yth Grp; Drama Clb; SADD; Band; School Play; Variety Show; Stu Cncl; Cheerleading; Mgr(s); Hon Roll; Mohawk Valley CC; Bus Ed.

FRICHNER, JASON M; Bronx H S Of Science; New York, NY; (Y); Cmnty Wkr; Teachers Aide; Lit Mag; High Hon Roll; Hon Roll; NHS; Cornell U; Psych.

FRICKER, TAMARA; Batavia SR HS; Batavia, NY; (Y); 37/211; Pres Drama Clb; Chorus; School Musical; School Play; Variety Show; Lit Mag; Stu Cncl; Cheerleading; Perfrmg Arts Schlrshp 86; Sherwin Publc Spkg Awd 86; Outstndng Achvt Spch And Drama Awd 86; Fredonia ST Clg; Eng.

FRIDAY, MATT; Walter Panas HS; Peekskill, NY; (Y); Band; Jazz Band; Mrchg Band; JV Tennis; High Hon Roll; Hon Roll; NHS; Sci Stu Of Mnth 86; Vrsty Ltr Mrchg Bnd 84; Engrng.

FRIDDELL, PAMELA; Frontier Central HS; Blasdell, NY; (Y); Drama Clb; Library Aide; Chorus; Color Guard; Stage Crew; Off Soph Cls; Off Jr Cls; Diving; Swmmng; Trk; Jamestown Bus Coll; Bus Admin.

FRIDMANN, JULIE; Williamsville South HS; Williamsville, NY; (Y); Cmnty Wkr; Drama Clb; Pep Clb; Ski Clb; SADD; Acpl Chr; School Musical; Yrbk Stf; Stu Cncl; Gym; U Of Buffalo; Bio.

FRIEDEL, DAVID; Lindenhurst HS; Lindenhurst, NY; (Y); VFW Awd; Voice Dem Awd; Princpls List 86; Fnlst Kodak Cntst Photo 85; Hofstra U; Acctng.

FRIEDLAND, DONNA REGINA; New Paltz HS; New Paltz, NY; (Y); 1/130; French Clb; Hosp Aide; Math Clb; SADD; Temple Yth Grp; Yrbk Stf; Bausch & Lomb Sci Awd; NHS; Ntl Merit Ltr; Val; SUNY; Pre-Med.

FRIEDLAND, TERRI; Earl L Vandermeulen HS; Mt Sinai, NY; (Y); 15/333; Drama Clb; SADD; Temple Yth Grp; Chorus; School Musical; Yrbk Stf; Rep Jr Cls; Mgr Cheerleading; High Hon Roll; NHS; Suny Schl; Bio.

FRIEDLANDER, PHILIP; Hebrew Acad Of The Five Towns; N Woodmere, NY; (Y); 5/57; Math Clb; Math Tm; Pres Temple Yth Grp; Ed Yrbk Stf; Rep Sr Cls; Rep Stu Cncl; Var Capt Bsktbl; VP NHS; Rgnts Schlrshp 85; Awd For Excllnc In Sci 86; Brown U; Med.

FRIEDMAN, ADRIA R; Tottenville HS; Staten Island, NY; (Y); 19/800; Am Leg Aux Girls St; GAA; Band; Concert Band; Gym; Hon Roll; Jr NHS; NHS; Prfct Atten Awd; Law.

FRIEDMAN, ALAN; Clarkstown North HS; New City, NY; (Y); 20/500; Math Clb; Math Tm; SADD; Temple Yth Grp; JV Bsbl; Var Socr; Var Trk; High Hon Roll; Mu Alp Tht; NHS; Engr.

FRIEDMAN, ANDREA; Dominican Commercial HS; Richmond Hill, NY; (Y); 15/273; Cmnty Wkr; Dance Clb; JA; Service Clb; Gov Hon Prg Awd; High Hon Roll; Hon Roll; Jr NHS; NHS; Pres Schlr; St Johns U; Poltc Sci.

FRIEDMAN, ERIK; Charles H Roth HS; Henrietta, NY; (Y); Varsity Clb; Band; Jazz Band; Var Socr; Var Tennis; Jr NHS; NHS; Spanish NHS; Ski Clb; JV Lcrss; Bob Perkins Ftr Chmpns Sprtsmnshp Awd 86; Outstndng Cmpr Awd YMCA Cmp Gorhm 85; Mst Imprvd Plyr Tns; Pltcl Sci.

FRIEDMAN, MATTHEW J; Half Hollow Hills HS East; Dix Hills, NY; (Y); 39/499; Quiz Bowl; SADD; Acpl Chr; Chorus; Jazz Band; School Musical; Lit Mag; French Hon Soc; High Hon Roll; Jr NHS; Music Hnr Soc; Ntl Soc Stds Olympd Gld Mdl, All ST Chorus 85; Pre Med.

FRIEDMAN, PERRY B; Sachem HS North; Holbrook, NY; (Y); 1/1387; Pres Cmnty Wkr; Pres Math Tm; Trs Science Clb; Ski Clb; Rep Sr Cls; Jr NHS; NHS; Ntl Merit SF; Val; Simons Flwshp SUNY Stonybrook 86; Outstndng Math & Chem Stu 83-85; Bst Phys Stu 85; Stanford; Math.

FRIEDMAN, SONDRA; Mamaroneck HS; Larchmont, NY; (Y); Art Clb; Hosp Aide; Service Clb; Spanish Clb; SADD; Yrbk Stf; Lit Mag; JV Socr; JV Vllybl; Spanish NHS.

FRIEDMAN, SUSAN; James Madison HS; Brooklyn, NY; (Y); School Play; Variety Show; Cheerleading.

FRIEDMAN-TORRES, ALISSA; The Mary Louis Acad; Flushing, NY; (Y); AFS; Computer Clb; Debate Tm; French Clb; NFL; Orch; Hon Roll; Govrnrs Citation Schlstc Achvt 86; 100% Attndnc 86; Alvin Ailey Amer Dance Tr Tr Div Schlrshp 84; Cornell U; Anml Sci.

FRIEL, LAURA; Our Lady Of Mercy HS; Rochester, NY; (Y); Service Clb; Spanish Clb; SADD; Tennis; Pblc Rel.

FRIELLO, STEPHEN A; Aviation HS; Richmond Hill, NY; (S); 38/413; JA; Office Aide; Ski Clb; Drill Tm; Variety Show; Trs Sr Cls; Stu Cncl; Var Tennis; NHS.

FRIEND, NATHAN; Greenwich Central HS; Greenwich, NY; (Y); Yrbk Phtg.

FRIEND, NICOLE; Oyster Bay HS; Oyster Bay, NY; (Y); French Clb; Model UN; Temple Yth Grp; Yrbk Stf; VP Frsh Cls; VP Soph Cls; VP Jr Cls; VP Sr Cls; Rep Stu Cncl; JV Cheerleading; Mst Imprvd Plyr Ten Tm 85-86; Med.

FRIES, PATRICIA; John Marshall JR SR HS; Rochester, NY; (Y); Aud/Vis; Boy Scts; French Clb; FBLA; Teachers Aide; Capt Color Guard; Mgr Vllybl; High Hon Roll; NHS; Moore CC; Bus Admn.

FRIES, SYLVIA; Longwood HS; Yaphank, NY; (Y); 19/450; Math Tm; Ski Clb; Trs Varsity Clb; Capt Drill Tm; Stage Crew; Yrbk Ed-Chief; Bsktbl; Sftbl; Jr NHS; NHS; Natl Hnr Soc Acad Scholar 86; White Ltr 86; MVP Lionettes 86; Villanova U; Mech Engrng.

FRIETSCH, BARBARA; Dominican Commercial HS; Glendale, NY; (Y); 114/274; Art Clb; Girl Scts; Pep Clb; Yrbk Sprt Ed; Var L Swmmng; Timer; Hon Roll; Siena Clb 82-86; Queens Coll; Accntng.

FRIGULETTO, MICHAEL; Notre Dame Bishop Gibbons HS; Schenectady, NY; (S); 8/100; Computer Clb; Nwsp Rptr; Lit Mag; Var Capt Golf; High Hon Roll; NHS; Knights Ordr Of Lance; Comp Sci.

FRINK II, CLIFFORD H; Oriskany Central HS; Whitesboro, NY; (Y); 24/69; School Play; Stage Crew; JV Bsbl; JV Bsktbl; JV Var Ftbl; Var Golf; Im Vllybl; Hon Roll; Outstndng Achvt Awd 86; Prnt-Tchr Awd 86; Alfred ST Coll; Elec Cnstrctn.

FRINK, DAVID; Niskayuna HS; Schenectady, NY; (Y); Drama Clb; ROTC; School Play; Stage Crew; Yrbk Stf; Var Socr; Hon Roll; U Of VT; Bus Adm.

FRINK, JOHN; Canisius HS; Buffalo, NY; (Y); Aud/Vis; Church Yth Grp; Pep Clb; Political Wkr; Music Forum Piano Solo Awd 85; Psych.

FRIOL, MICHAEL; Eden SR HS; Angola, NY; (Y); Var JV Ftbl; Var Socr; Var Trk.

FRISBEE, MICHAEL P; Guilderland Central HS; Schenectady, NY; (Y); School Musical; School Play; JV Crs Cntry.

FRISBEE, SHAWN; Berne-Knox-Westerlo HS; E Berne, NY; (Y); 30/99; Drama Clb; Math Clb; Ski Clb; School Play; Stage Crew; Yrbk Rptr; Trs Stu Cncl; Bsbl; Golf; Vllybl; Rochester Inst Tech; Comp Sci.

FRISBIE, PATRICIA; Bethpage HS; Bethpage, NY; (Y); 30/306; Sec FBLA; Spanish Clb; Yrbk Stf; Off Soph Cls; High Hon Roll; Jr NHS; NHS; Lbrl Arts.

FRISCHMANN, TODD A; Mc Quaid Jesuit HS; Rochester, NY; (Y); Drama Clb; Varsity Clb; Chorus; School Musical; Var Capt Socr; High Hon Roll; Hon Roll; NHS; Ntl Merit SF; Acdmc Lttr; NYSR Schlrshp Wnnr; Rutgers U; Lib Arts.

FRISINA, MARCY; Bishop Scully HS; Gloversville, NY; (S); 4/50; Drama Clb; Girl Scts; Varsity Clb; Concert Band; Jazz Band; Mrchg Band; School Musical; Variety Show; High Hon Roll; NHS.

FRITCH, DAVID; Msgr Farrell HS; Staten Island, NY; (S); Debate Tm; Intnl Clb; Lit Mag; Bsktbl; Bowling; Ftbl; Trk; Hon Roll.

FRITTS, MICHAEL; Herkimer HS; Herkimer, NY; (Y); 9/120; Boy Scts; VP Drama Clb; Pres Model UN; Trs Chorus; School Play; Nwsp Rptr; Var Bowling; Ntl Merit Ltr; Computer Clb; French Clb; BSA Lfgrd 85-86; Elks JR Bwlng Sngls Chmpn 83; Crtv Wrtr.

FRITZ, JILL M; E J Wilson HS; Rochester, NY; (Y); Ski Clb; Sec Spanish Clb; Sec Band; Concert Band; Mrchg Band; Symp Band; Hon Roll; Trs NHS; VFW Awd; Rep Frsh Cls; NY ST Regnts Schlrshp 86; Natl Merit Schlrshp Ltr Of Commndtn 86; VFW Merit Awd 86; PA ST U; Bus Admin.

FRITZ, TODD; Abraham Lincoln HS; Brooklyn, NY; (Y); Chorus; Nwsp Sprt Ed; Pres Sr Cls; Var Tennis; Hon Roll; Sal; Police Comm For A Day Essay Cntst Wnnr 84; NY Daily News Prncpls Pride/Yankees Awd 85-86; Law.

FRITZEN, KATRINA; Duanesburg Central HS; Quaker St, NY; (Y); Art Clb; Drama Clb; Hosp Aide; Intnl Clb; Office Aide; Pep Clb; Spanish Clb; Varsity Clb; Color Guard; Capt Drm Mjr(t); Vrsty Let & Pin-Chrldr 85; Hd Majorette 83-85; Outstndng Sr Artist Awd 86; Art For Womens Fed 1st Pl 86; Mohawk Vlly Coll; Ad Design.

FRITZMEIER, DAVID S; Hugh C Williams HS; Canton, NY; (Y); 19/145; Drama Clb; Model UN; Ski Clb; Trs Thesps; Band; Concert Band; Jazz Band; School Musical; School Play; High Hon Roll; Natl Mrt High Scr 86; Nyssma Band Solo 86.

FRITZSCHE, CHRISTINE; Bayport Bluepoint HS; Bayport, NY; (Y); 38/249; Art Clb; Science Clb; Chorus; Stage Crew; Score Keeper; Ntl Merit Ltr; SEA-BBS Smmr Stdy Prg Art 84; Art.

FRODYMA, KEVIN; Columbia HS; E Greenbush, NY; (Y); Wt Lftg; Hon Roll; SUNY Albany; Accntg.

FROMAGET, KIMBERLY; Washingtonville HS; Monroe, NY; (Y); French Clb; Ski Clb; Varsity Clb; Symp Band; Yrbk Ed-Chief; Trs Jr Cls; Sftbl; Tennis; Trk; NHS; Siera Coll; Acctg.

FROMBGEN, DIANE; Barker Central HS; Barker, NY; (Y); 4/108; AFS; Pres Spanish Clb; Band; Pres Frsh Cls; VP Stu Cncl; DAR Awd; Hon Roll; Masonic Awd; Mu Alp Tht; VP NHS; ROTC Schlrshp Air Frce 86; Plce Athltc Leag Awd Svc 86; Jstns Fndtn Ldrshp Awd 86; U Rochester; Math.

FRONCKOWIAK, AMY-ANN T; Buffalo Acad Of Vsl & Prfrmng Arts; Buffalo, NY; (Y); 6/110; Drama Clb; School Musical; School Play; Stage Crew; Frsh Cls; Var L Sftbl; NHS; NY ST Rgnts Schlrshp 86-90; Nancy Jo Abeles Schlrshp 86-87; SUNY Buffalo Dept Thtre& Dnc Apprntc 84; SUNY Coll-Prchs; Thre Dsgn.

FRONCZAK, KIM; Villa Maria Acad; Buffalo, NY; (S); Pres Church Yth Grp; JCL; Latin Clb; Pep Clb; Ski Clb; Nwsp Stf; Sec Jr Cls; Rep Stu Cncl; Gym; Hon Roll; Pre-Med.

FRONCZAK, LISA; Villa Maria Acad; Buffalo, NY; (Y); Church Yth Grp; Trs Computer Clb; Math Clb; SADD; Rep Trs Stu Cncl; Hon Roll; St U Of NY Buffalo; Pharm.

FRONK, TABITHA; Maple Hill HS; Castleton, NY; (Y); Drama Clb; Sec Spanish Clb; School Play; Variety Show; Hon Roll; Var Score Keeper; Dsplyr Art Wrk At Hyde Cllctn 85; NYSSSA SUNY At Fredonia 86; Rensselaer Co Cncl Of Arts Drwg Exhb; Art Ther.

FROSINA, ANTHONY; Archbishop Molloy HS; Glendale, NY; (Y); 130/383; Church Yth Grp; Computer Clb; Chorus; High Hon Roll; Law.

FROST, DERRICK; Eastern District HS; Brooklyn, NY; (Y); Science Clb; Teachers Aide; Church Choir; Hon Roll; Arista Hnrs Clb 84-85; Stu Govt Orgnztn 83-86; Med.

FROUDE, SHARON E; Bay Shore HS; Bay Shore, NY; (Y); 13/363; Hosp Aide; Math Tm; Concert Band; Mrchg Band; Orch; Var Gym; High Hon Roll; NHS; Math Clb; Band; Full Tuition Bd Trustees Schlr 86; Lehigh U Acad Schlrshp 86; NY St Regents Schrlshp Wnnr 86; Wilkes Coll; Biolgy.

FROUXIDES, VIVIAN; Farmingdale HS; Farmingdale, NY; (Y); 160/620; Church Yth Grp; Cmnty Wkr; Pres Debate Tm; French Clb; FBLA; Key Clb; SADD; Flag Corp; Camp Fr Inc; Yrbk Bus Mgr; Greek Schl Hnr Awd 82; Hlth Ed Awd 86; Hofstra; Bus.

FRUEHWIRTH, ELIZABETH; Bellport HS; E Patchogue, NY; (Y); Church Yth Grp; Pres French Clb; Symp Band; Yrbk Stf; Rep Stu Cncl; Var Bowling; Var Tennis; French Hon Soc; VP Jr NHS; NHS; Pres Clssrm 85-86; Rotary Stu Of Mnth 85; Brd Ed Awd Outstndg Acad & Music Achvt 86; Pre-Med.

FRUGONE, BRIGIETTE; Lindenhurst HS; Lindenhurst, NY; (Y); Varsity Clb; Yrbk Stf; Sec Soph Cls; Sec Jr Cls; Sec Sr Cls; Var Capt Cheerleading; Hon Roll; Jr NHS; Girl Scts; Spanish Clb.

FRUSCIANTE, WILLIAM; Cornwall Central HS; Cornwall Hudson, NY; (Y); Sec Computer Clb; JV Crs Cntry; Var L Trk; Hon Roll; Comp Sci.

FRY, LAURIE J; Pavilion Central HS; East Bethany, NY; (Y); 8/62; Trs AFS; Math Tm; Band; Chorus; Drm Mjr(t); Nwsp Bus Mgr; Yrbk Sprt Ed; High Hon Roll; NHS; Pres Church Yth Grp; NY ST Regents Schlrshp Wnr; SUNY Geneseo; Bus.

FRYAR, MICHAEL; Poughkeepsie HS; Poughkeepsie, NY; (Y); Church Yth Grp; Chorus; Church Choir; Jr Cls; Hon Roll; Prfct Atten Awd; Comp Op Prgmmr.

FRYDMAN, RONK; Shulamith HS; Brooklyn, NY; (S); Library Aide; Office Aide; Chorus; Yrbk Stf; High Hon Roll; Hon Roll.

FRYE, DONALD; Broadalbin HS; Broadalbin, NY; (Y); 17/74; Am Leg Boys St; Drama Clb; Letterman Clb; Library Aide; Math Clb; Varsity Clb; School Play; Yrbk Phtg; Yrbk Stf; Rep Jr Cls; Lgn Schlrshp 86; Kennyetto Auxlry Fire Co Awd 86; Rgnts Schlrshp 86; Clarkson U; Comp Tech.

FRYE, TRISHA; Thomas J Corcoran HS; Syracuse, NY; (Y); Am Leg Aux Girls St; Art Clb; Teachers Aide; Yrbk Stf; Lit Mag; High Hon Roll; NHS; Ntl Ltn Exm MCL Slv Medl 86; Drwng Ctgrycrcrn-Syrcs Annl Tng Art Cmpttn 84; Math.

FRYSCAK, FRANCIS M; Roosevelt HS; Crestwood, NY; (Y); 16/287; Lit Mag; Rep Soph Cls; Off Jr Cls; NHS; Ntl Merit Ltr; Ynkrs Educ Brd Sprintndnts Awd 85; NY U Univ Schlr 86; NY U; Pltcl Sci.

FUCHEK, CAROLYN; Walter Panas HS; Peekskill, NY; (Y); Hosp Aide; Orch; School Musical; Hon Roll; Larry Burns Memrl Awd 86; All-Cnty Orch 82; Suny Potsdam; Music.

FUCHS, ADAM; East Hampton HS; E Hampton, NY; (Y); Art Clb; Lit Mag; Var Socr; Var Trk; High Hon Roll; NHS; Ntl Merit Ltr; Exc Stu To Japan; Archlgy.

FUCHS, PAMELA IVY; Centereach HS; Lake Grove, NY; (S); 55/429; Q&S; Temple Yth Grp; Thesps; Chorus; Church Choir; School Musical; Swing Chorus; Variety Show; Rptr Nwsp Rptr; Yrbk Phtg; Actg.

FUEGLISTER, VALERIE; Hicksville HS; Hicksville, NY; (Y); 55/435; Cmnty Wkr; French Clb; German Clb; Hosp Aide; Pres Latin Clb; Nwsp Stf; Ed Yrbk Stf; French Hon Soc; 1st Prz Orgnl Frnch Poetry 83; Latin Hnr Soc 85-86; Creighton U; Bio.

FUEHRER, KURT; Charles H Roth HS; Rochester, NY; (Y); 38/200; Boy Scts; Pres Trs Ski Clb; Varsity Clb; Yrbk Phtg; Rep Stu Cncl; Lcrss; Socr; Hon Roll; Jr NHS; Church Yth Grp; NY ST Rgnts Schlrshp 86; Alfred U; Indstrl Engrng.

FUENTES, ALBERTO DAVID; Charlotte Valley HS; East Meredith, NY; (Y); Church Yth Grp; Hon Roll; Rgnts Schlrshp 86; Syracuse U; Arch.

FUENTES, JOSE L; Park West HS; Brooklyn, NY; (Y); 16/483; JA; Office Aide; Teachers Aide; Hon Roll; Prfct Atten Awd; Comp Sci.

FUENTES, MICHELLE G; Kings Park SR HS; Kings Pk, NY; (Y); 127/392; Cmnty Wkr; Concert Band; Nwsp Ed-Chief; Nwsp Phtg; Nwsp Rptr; Nwsp Stf; JV Var Mgr(s); JV Var Sftbl; Office Aide; Band; CP Tag Dag Chairprsn Awd 83-84; Nwspr Hnry Awd 85; Comm.

FUERST, ROBERT C; Lakeshore Central HS; Angola, NY; (Y); 75/284; Am Leg Boys St; Ski Clb; Trs Frsh Cls; Var JV Swmmng; Hon Roll; Regents Scholar 86; Sci Olympd 83-84 & 86; Alfred U; Ceramic Engr.

FUERTES, MICHELLE A; Birch Wathen HS; New York, NY; (Y); Debate Tm; Drama Clb; Model UN; Ski Clb; School Musical; School Play; Nwsp Phtg; Nwsp Stf; Yrbk Ed-Chief; Yrbk Phtg; NY U; Econ.

FUETTERER, JEANINE H; Riverside HS; Buffalo, NY; (Y); Office Aide; OEA; Radio Clb; Red Cross Aide; SADD; Y-Teens; Band; Variety Show; Yrbk Phtg; Lit Mag, Newspr Rptr, Photgrphr; Secy.

FUHRMANN, KATHARIN R; The Chapin Schl; New York City, NY; (Y); Church Yth Grp; Cmnty Wkr; Sec Drama Clb; French Clb; Political Wkr; School Play; Rep Frsh Cls; Sec Jr Cls; Trs Sr Cls; JV Capt Vllybl; Margaret Emerson Bailey Mem Prz Exc Crtv Wrtng 85; NY ST Regents Schlrshp 86; Harvard U.

FUHST JR, ROBERT F; Mt St Michael Acad; Bronx, NY; (Y); 25/296; Spanish Clb; Off Stu Cncl; Var L Bsbl; Im Mgr Bsktbl; Im Mgr Ftbl; High Hon Roll; Hon Roll; NHS; Ntl Merit Ltr; Spanish NHS; Syracuse U Schlrshp 86; Legn Hnr Medl Grad 86; Syracuse U; Cmmnctns.

FUIERER, TRISTAN A; Holley JR SR HS; Holley, NY; (Y); 7/100; Ski Clb; Stage Crew; Rep Frsh Cls; Rep Soph Cls; Rep Jr Cls; Rep Stu Cncl; High Hon Roll; Hon Roll; NHS; St John Fisher Coll; Chem.

FUJIWARA, FUYUKI; Briarcliff HS; Briarcliff Manor, NY; (Y); Pres Debate Tm; Mathletes; NFL; Teachers Aide; Jazz Band; Orch; Nwsp Stf; High Hon Roll; Hon Roll; NHS; Harvard Alumni Bk Awd 85; Columbia Sci Hnrs Prog 84-85; NY ST All-ST Orch 84.

FULFARO, ANNA MARIA; Sweet Home SR HS; N Tonawanda, NY; (Y); Cmnty Wkr; GAA; Orch; Fld Hcky; Mgr(s); Socr.

FULLAGAR, MOLLY; Penn Yan Acad; Penn Yan, NY; (Y); 30/174; GAA; Pep Clb; Ski Clb; Yrbk Ed-Chief; Rep Soph Cls; Rep Jr Cls; Rep Sr Cls; JV Var Cheerleading; JV Socr; Hon Roll; NYS Regnts Schlrshp 86; Hnrs Soc Stds 85; SUNY Geneseo; Psychlgy.

FULLER, BARBARA; Gouverneur Central Schl; Gouverneur, NY; (Y); Trs Church Yth Grp; Girl Scts; Band; Concert Band; Mrchg Band; Orch; CC Awd; Hon Roll; Pep Band; Grl Scout Gold Awd 85; Non Instrctnl Employees Scholar 86; Mater Dei Coll; Legal Sec.

FULLER, DANIEL J; Chenongo Forks HS; Binghamton, NY; (Y); 5/200; Am Leg Boys St; Cmnty Wkr; Ski Clb; Rep Soph Cls; Rep Jr Cls; VP Stu Cncl; Hon Roll; NHS; Ntl Merit Ltr; Yth Ldrshp Awd 86; Engrng.

FULLER, DONNA FAYE; Mount Vernon HS; Mount Vernon, NY; (Y); 106/600; Cmnty Wkr; Girl Scts; Office Aide; Political Wkr; Pres Band; Concert Band; Drm Mjr(t); Stage Crew; Variety Show; Stu Cncl; Spelman Coll; Educ.

FULLER, JODI L; Carthage Central HS; Felts Mills, NY; (Y); 17/190; Spanish Clb; Nwsp Stf; Yrbk Stf; Trs Sr Cls; JV Socr; High Hon Roll; Hon Roll; NHS; Rotary Awd; St Schlr; SUNY; Hlth-Sci Field.

FULLER, KERRIE; Olean HS; Olean, NY; (Y); Ski Clb; Acpl Chr; Chorus; Orch; School Musical; School Play; Yrbk Stf; High Hon Roll; Hon Roll; JR Vrsty Ltr Rifle Tm 83-84; Paul Smiths; Chef.

FULLER, LISA; Salamanca Central HS; Killbuck, NY; (Y); 22/136; Camera Clb; Drama Clb; French Clb; Ski Clb; SADD; High Hon Roll; Hon Roll; Prfct Atten Awd; Homecomg Attn; Seneca Nation Acad Achvt; 3rd Hghst Avg Seneca Nation; Fredonia SUNY; Intl Rel.

FULLER, MARCY A; Cuba Central Schl; Cuba, NY; (Y); 11/55; Teachers Aide; Chorus; Yrbk Stf; Tennis; JV Vllybl; High Hon Roll; NHS; NYS Rgnts Schlrshp 86; Art Awds 83-85; Cngrsnl Art Cmptn Crtfct Achvmnt 84; Mohawk Valley CC; Advrtsng.

FULLER, ROBERT; Brockport HS; Hamlin, NY; (Y); 69/335; Church Yth Grp; Var Capt Ftbl; Var Capt Wrstlng; Hon Roll; NYS Rgnts Schlrshp 86; 1st Tm All Lg Wrstlng 85; 1st Tm All Lg Ftbl 85; Syracuse U; Bio-Engrng.

FULLER, SHELLI; Gowanda Central HS; Collins, NY; (Y); Church Yth Grp; French Clb; Ski Clb; SADD; Chorus; Church Choir; VP Sr Cls; Rep Stu Cncl; Hon Roll.

FULLER, STACEY; Narrowsburg Central HS; Cochecton, NY; (Y); 2/30; Church Yth Grp; Pep Clb; Spanish Clb; Band; Chorus; Concert Band; Drm Mjr(t); Pep Band; School Musical; School Play; Pres Clssrm For Young Amer 86; Mst Vlbl Sccr 85; Psych.

FULLONE, LISA; South Park HS; Buffalo, NY; (Y); French Clb; Chorus; Hon Roll; Tchr.

FULTON, FELICIA; Pine Bush HS; Middletown, NY; (Y); Cmnty Wkr; French Clb; Ski Clb; Yrbk Stf; Hon Roll; Jr NHS; Law.

FULTON, KIMBERLY; Academy Of St Joseph; Kings Pk, NY; (Y); Orch; Yrbk Stf; Rep Jr Cls; Var Badmtn; Capt Var Trk; NHS; Church Yth Grp; Service Clb; Spanish Clb; James F Tynion Schlrshp 83-87; Sprior Acad Achvt In Hmnties II 84-85; Sprior Acad Achvt In Math 85-86; Yale U.

FULTON, MELISSA; Churchville-Chili HS; Churchville, NY; (Y); Am Leg Aux Girls St; Church Yth Grp; JCL; Sec Latin Clb; Ski Clb; Church Choir; School Musical; Nwsp Stf; High Hon Roll; VP NHS; Excllnc Latn 84; Mst Imprvd Stdnt Sci 85.

FUNG, AUDREY S; Sacred Heart Acad; Westbury, NY; (Y); 24/190; Art Clb; Cmnty Wkr; French Clb; Pres Math Clb; Service Clb; Hon Roll; NHS; NY U; Pre Med.

FUNGAFAT, JILL; A G Berner HS; Massapequa, NY; (Y); SUNY Stny Brk; Engrng.

FUNK, MICHELLE; Lansingburgh HS; Troy, NY; (Y); Hosp Aide; High Hon Roll; NHS; Comp Sci.

FUNNY JR, JOHN; Seward Park HS; New York, NY; (Y); Boys Clb Am; Teachers Aide; School Musical.

FUOCO, THERESA A; Patchogue Medford HS; Patchogue, NY; (Y); Church Yth Grp; ROTC; Church Choir; Drill Tm; Yrbk Stf; Cheerleading; Hon Roll; NHS; Amer Legn Schlstc Excllnc Awd 85; Achvtmt Awd LIU Southampton 86; Regnts Schlrshp 86; Long Island U; Psych.

FUORI, VINCENT; Central Islip HS; Central Islip, NY; (Y); Computer Clb; Drama Clb; Pres Math Clb; Math Tm; Boy Scts; Drm Mjr(t); Mrchg Band; School Musical; School Play; Stage Crew; Tempo Music Awd Wnnr 86; NY Inst Tech; Comp Sci.

FUREY, DANIEL J; Rhinebeck HS; Rhinebeck, NY; (Y); 34/104; AFS; Boy Scts; CAP; Ski Clb; Band; School Play; Stage Crew; Yrbk Phtg; Yrbk Stf; Wrstlng; Jdsn Mem Art Awd 86; Rchster Inst Tech; Grphs Dsgn.

FURINO, JOS; John H Glenn HS; E Northport, NY; (Y); Band; Jazz Band; School Musical; Rep Stu Cncl; Var Bsbl; Var Ftbl; High Hon Roll; NHS; Spanish NHS; Modern Music Masters Tri-M 86.

FURMAN, BYRON; Delaware Acad; Delhi, NY; (Y); Spanish Clb; Trk; Hon Roll; Prfct Atten Awd; Regnts Schlrshp 86; Presdntl Acadmc Ftns Awd 86; Acadmc Achvt Awd-Hnr Grad 86; Pfeiffer Coll; Theatr Art.

FURMAN, NANCY; Blind Brook HS; Rye Brook, NY; (Y); Drama Clb; Math Tm; VP Temple Yth Grp; Concert Band; School Play; Nwsp Ed-Chief; U PA Westchester Alumni Achvt Awd, Am HS Math Comp Schl Wnnr, IA Lang Cntst Hnrs Span IV 86.

FURNESS, RICHARD; Kendall JR SR HS; Kent, NY; (Y); Art Clb; Stage Crew; Bsbl; Hon Roll; Ntl Merit Ltr.

FURST, MICHAEL C; Oceanside HS; Oceanside, NY; (Y); Cmnty Wkr; Pres Church Yth Grp; Nwsp Ed-Chief; Cit Awd; HOBY Yth Found Ambassdr 84; NY ST Chief Squire Columbian Squires 86; NY Inst Technology.

FURST, SUSAN; Midwood HS; Brooklyn, NY; (Y); Hosp Aide; Orch; Hon Roll; Doctor.

FUSARI, MATTHEW; John Jay SR HS; Wappinger Fls, NY; (Y); Aud/Vis; Prfct Atten Awd; Productvty Awd 86; MIT; Engrng.

FUSCO, ANGELA; Kings Park SR HS; Kings Park, NY; (Y); 147/383; Church Yth Grp; Cmnty Wkr; Office Aide; Spanish Clb; Variety Show; Mgr(s); Vllybl; Outstndng Medal Vlybl 84; Cert Typethon 83; Oral Roberts U; Nrs.

FUSCO, JOHN; Central Islip SR HS; Central Islip, NY; (Y); Aud/Vis; Boy Scts; Stage Crew; Nwsp Bus Mgr; Nwsp Rptr; Nwsp Stf; Lit Mag.

FUSCO, LAURA; New Utrecht HS; Brooklyn, NY; (Y); 35/600; Key Clb; Yrbk Bus Mgr; Yrbk Stf; NHS; Cathl Tchrs Assc Awd 86; Arista Natl Hon Soc 84-86; St Johns U; Cmmnctn Arts.

FUSS, LISA; Hilton Central HS; Hamlin, NY; (Y); 10/300; Drama Clb; Math Clb; Var Crs Cntry; Var Trk; High Hon Roll; NHS; Oswego ST U; Acctg.

FUSS, SUSAN; Hannibal Central HS; Hannibal, NY; (Y); 6/106; Church Yth Grp; French Clb; Key Clb; Varsity Clb; Chorus; School Play; JV Var Bsktbl; Var Sftbl; High Hon Roll; Hon Roll; Oswego Coll.

FUSSTEIG, ROBIN L; Somers HS; Katonah, NY; (Y); 4/198; Sec AFS; Intnl Clb; Nwsp Ed-Chief; Sec Sr Cls; Stu Cncl; JV Var Fld Hcky; JV Var Socr; Var Trk; French Hon Soc; NHS; NY ST Rgnts Schlrshp 86; Chase Mnhttn Bnk Awd 86; Soc Studs Mnth Stu 84; Frnch Schltc Achvt Awd 84; Cornell U; Pre-Med.

FUTRELL, PENNY; Middletown HS; Middletown, NY; (Y); Hon Roll; Acad Achvt Awd In Engl 84-85.

GABALSKI, RONALD; Alden SR HS; Alden, NY; (Y); 56/203; Aud/Vis; Pres Radio Clb; Trs Band; Concert Band; Jazz Band; Trs Mrchg Band; Stage Crew; Rep Stu Cncl; Capt Score Keeper; Capt Timer; Admin Acknwldgmnt Outstndg Sci 86; Vis MVP Awd 86; Mst Unappreciated SR 86; NCCC; Rad Prod.

GABAY, JACQUELINE E; Stuyvesant HS; Rego Park, NY; (Y); NFL; Chorus; Jazz Band; Lit Mag; High Hon Roll; NHS; NEDT Awd; Cmnty Wkr; Debate Tm; French Clb; Young Artists Music Comp-1st Prize 84; Manhattan Schl Of Music 81-86; NY U Med Ctr 84-86.

GABBUR, NAGARAJ; The Wheatley Schl; E Williston, NY; (Y); Trs Chess Clb; Hosp Aide; Orch; Yrbk Rptr; Stu Cncl; Var Crs Cntry; Var Trk; NHS; Ntl Merit Ltr; Computer Clb; Rnd 1 Wnr & Stwd Stu Enrgy Rsrch Cmptn 86; Chrls H Dvs Music Schlrshp Awd 85; AATF Ntl Frnch Fnlst 85; Med.

GABELMAN, DEBRA B; East Meadow HS; E Meadow, NY; (Y); 27/350; FBLA; Mathletes; Temple Yth Grp; Varsity Clb; Orch; Nwsp Stf; Yrbk Stf; Rep Frsh Cls; Rep Soph Cls; Sec Jr Cls; Orchstra Achvmnt Awd 86; SUNY Binghmtn.

GABIZON, GUY; South Shore HS; Brooklyn, NY; (Y); Brooklyn Coll.

GABOR, MARY; Mineola HS; Mineola, NY; (Y); 73/250; Church Yth Grp; Key Clb; Chorus; Church Choir; Badmtn; Swmmng; Vllybl; Kiwanis Awd; Rotary Awd; Hofstra U; Bio.

GABRIEL, JAMES V; Liverpool HS; Liverpool, NY; (Y); 138/816; Ski Clb; Chorus; Mrchg Band; School Musical; Pres Stu Cncl; Var Gym; NHS; St Schlr; Church Yth Grp; Cmnty Wkr; Crew Tm 83-84; Crew Tm Mgr 84-85; Clarkson U; Elec Engrg.

GABRIEL JR, MICHAEL J; Huntington HS; Huntington Sta, NY; (Y); 35/383; Am Leg Boys St; Pres Computer Clb; Mrchg Band; Socr; Trk; Hon Roll; NHS; Mathletes; Band; U S Naval Acad Annapolis MD 86; U S Naval Acad; Comp Sci.

GABRIEL, NICK H; Xavier HS; Brooklyn, NY; (Y); Yrbk Stf; Chess Clb; Dance Clb; Math Clb; Capt ROTC; NY ST Regents Awds 86; Kings Coll Moreau Awd 86-87; JROTC Gold Schltc Exclnc, Schltc Achvt; Kings Coll; Med.

GABRIEL, YVES; Midwood HS; Brooklyn, NY; (Y); 109/660; Art Clb; French Clb; Math Tm; Color Guard; Ftbl; Wt Lftg; French Hon Soc; High Hon Roll; NHS; Prfct Atten Awd; Columbia U; Pre-Med.

GABRIELE, BARBARA; Mercy HS; Bridgehampton, NY; (Y); 29/129; Hosp Aide; Ski Clb; SADD; Yrbk Rptr; Var L Fld Hcky; JV Sftbl; Var L Trk; High Hon Roll; Hon Roll; NHS.

GABRIELE, CATHERINE A; Mercy HS; Bridgehampton, NY; (Y); 7/101; Church Yth Grp; Mathletes; Office Aide; Ski Clb; Spanish Clb; Rep Jr Cls; VP Stu Cncl; JV Capt Fld Hcky; High Hon Roll; Trs NHS; Rgnts Schlrshp 86; Marymt Coll Trrytwn; Foods.

GABRIELE, KATHLEEN; Glen Cove HS; Glen Cove, NY; (Y); 40/270; Hosp Aide; Pres Key Clb; Varsity Clb; Band; Concert Band; Mrchg Band; Yrbk Phtg; Var Cheerleading; Var Crs Cntry; Var Socr; Pre Med.

GABRIELLI, PAULA; Richmond Hill HS; Ozone Pk, NY; (Y); 6/250; English Clb; JA; Math Clb; Spanish Clb; Var Bowling; High Hon Roll; Hon Roll; Nrs.

GADALETA, ANTHONY; Henninger HS; Syracuse, NY; (Y); Band; Chorus; Jazz Band; School Play; Merit Cert Outstndng Musicianshp; Most Imprvd Musicn Awd; Schrlshp Music Smmr Schl; Syracuse U; Musician.

GADHIA, ROOMA V; Fairport HS; Fairport, NY; (Y); 140/600; Model UN; JA; Model UN; Band; Mrchg Band; Symp Band; Fld Hcky; Rgnts Schlrshp 86; U Of Pittsburgh; Engrng.

GADWAY, STEPHEN; Moriah Central HS; Mineville, NY; (Y); French Clb; Rep Stu Cncl; Var JV Bsktbl; High Hon Roll; Hon Roll; Plattsburgh ST U; Bus Mgmt.

GADZINSKI, KAREN; Babylon HS; Babylon, NY; (Y); SADD; Church Choir; Variety Show; Var Bsktbl; JV Var Fld Hcky; JV Var Vllybl; Church Yth Grp; Political Wkr; Grls Bsktbl & Vllybl All Lg V All Cnfrnc Iii 85 & 86; Grp W Cbl Tv Athlt Wk 86; Princeton Coll Chr 84; Elem Educ.

GADZINSKI, LAURA; Riverhead HS; Riverhead, NY; (Y); 42/218; French Clb; Band; Mrchg Band; Sec Jr Cls; Stat Crs Cntry; Stat Trk.

GAEBEL, RICHARD; Immaculate Heart Central HS; Watertown, NY; (Y); NFL; Nwsp Ed-Chief; Var Ftbl; Var Golf; High Hon Roll; Hon Roll; Trs NHS; Augbrg N Cntry Schlr 86; Rgnts Schlrshp 86; Bishps Awd Outstndng Cthlc Sch Grad 86; St Lawrence U; Engnrng.

GAETA, MARK E; Msgr Farrell HS; Staten Island, NY; (Y); 80/330; Boy Scts; Chess Clb; Debate Tm; Drama Clb; School Play; VP Frsh Cls; Im Bsktbl; Im Fld Hcky; Im Ftbl; Im Sftbl; 3rd Pl Sci Awd; Pre Med.

GAETA, MICHAEL; Archbishop Molloy HS; Glendale, NY; (Y); 203/409; Chess Clb; Computer Clb; Dance Clb; Science Clb; Band; Chorus; Church Choir; Rep Stu Cncl; NY ST Regents Schlrshp 86; Hofstra U.

GAFF, PATTY; Tupper Lake HS; Tupper Lake, NY; (Y); Var Cheerleading; Hon Roll; Hudson Vly Esthn Coll; Csmtlgst.

GAFFNEY, DIANA; Newfield HS; Coram, NY; (Y); Yrbk Stf; Trs Soph Cls; Trs Jr Cls; VP Sr Cls; Rep Stu Cncl; JV Fld Hcky; Var Trk; Hon Roll; NHS; Spanish NHS.

GAFFNEY, EILEEN M; St Catharine Acad; Bronx, NY; (Y); Church Yth Grp; Dance Clb; Office Aide; Service Clb; Church Choir; Variety Show; High Hon Roll; Hon Roll; Ntl Merit Ltr; NY St Regents Schlrshp 86; Chairperson Secy & Treas Of Self Help Group 84-86; Lehman Coll; RN.

GAFFNEY, ELLYN; Huntington HS; Huntington, NY; (Y); DECA; Key Clb; SADD; Varsity Clb; Variety Show; Crs Cntry; Trk; 3 Vrsty Lttrs; MA U; Psych.

GAFFNEY, KELLEY; The Franciscan Acad; Fayetteville, NY; (Y); 4/25; Civic Clb; GAA; Hosp Aide; Ski Clb; Spanish Clb; SADD; Nwsp Rptr; Rep Stu Cncl; Var L Cheerleading; JV Socr; Ntl Lang Arts Olympd Awd 83-84; All Lge Awd Hnbl Mntn Softbll 85-86; Acadmc Awds Spnsh & Engl 86; Pol Sci.

GAFFNEY, MARGARET E; Guilderland Central HS; Albany, NY; (Y); 76/370; Political Wkr; Varsity Clb; School Musical; Rep Soph Cls; Rep Jr Cls; Off Sr Cls; Score Keeper; Capt Socr; Sftbl; Hon Roll; PTA Schlrshp 86; Ldrshp Cert-Stu Govt 86; Wittenberg U; Mrn Bio.

GAGE, ALLEN; Hebrew Acad Of Nassau County; W Hempstead, NY; (Y); 12/80; Aud/Vis; Chess Clb; Cmnty Wkr; Math Tm; Temple Yth Grp; Nwsp Sprt Ed; Yrbk Stf; Rep Stu Cncl; Var Fld Hcky; Tennis; Rgnts Schlrshp Awd 86; Svc Awd Sci 84.

GAGE, JENNIFER; Bishop Scully HS; Fultonville, NY; (Y); Art Clb; Drama Clb; Trs Rptr 4-H; School Play; Yrbk Ed-Chief; Yrbk Phtg; Yrbk Stf; 4-H Awd; Hon Roll; Wheaton Coll; Advrtsng.

GAGE, THERESA A; Ilion HS; Ilion, NY; (Y); Yrbk Stf; Rep Stu Cncl; Var JV Cheerleading; Var Trk; High Hon Roll; NHS; Pres Schlr; Church Yth Grp; GAA; Pep Clb; Fnlst Outstndng Yng New Yorker 86; Stu Yr 85-86; Queen Winter Weekend; FL ST U; Intl Pub Rel.

GAGLIANO, CHARLES; Archbishop Molloy HS; Floral Pk, NY; (Y); 24/383; Boy Scts; Teachers Aide; Im Bsktbl; JV Crs Cntry; Im Ftbl; Im Sftbl; JV Trk; High Hon Roll; Hon Roll; Aerntcl Engrng.

GAGLIANO, DENISE; Churchville-Chili SR HS; Rochester, NY; (Y); Office Aide; Accntnt.

GAGLIARDI, MICHAEL; Eastchester HS; Scarsdale, NY; (Y); Cmnty Wkr; Band; Chorus; Commnctn Wrks Amerca 86; IA Coll; Bus.

GAGLIARDO, CYNTHIA M; Plainedge HS; Massapequa, NY; (Y); 14/304; Mathletes; Orch; Stage Crew; Ed Yrbk Phtg; Capt Bsktbl; High Hon Roll; NHS; Spanish NHS; St Schlr; Camera Clb; Long Isl Sci Congrss Hnrb Mntn 84; Contintl Mth Lg 2nd Pl 83-84; Cornell U; Engrng.

GAGLIARDO, DANIEL; Port Chester HS; Port Chester, NY; (Y); Lit Mag; JV Bsbl; Hon Roll; Jr NHS; Mu Alp Tht; NHS; Prfct Atten Awd; Itln Ntl Hnr Soc 85; Math.

GAGLIO, MICHELE; Moore Catholic HS; Staten Island, NY; (Y); 38/170; Church Yth Grp; Intnl Clb; Math Tm; Teachers Aide; Var Bowling; High Hon Roll; Hon Roll; NHS; Wagner Coll Schlrshp 86-87; St Johns U SI; Elem Ed.

GAGLIOTTI, JEAN; New Dorp HS; Staten Isl, NY; (Y); Hosp Aide; Math Tm; Spanish NHS; Rep Soph Cls; JV Capt Gym; Var Sftbl; Hon Roll; NHS; Hnr Ky; Cmmnctns.

GAGNIER, KIMBERLY; Beaver River Central HS; Croghan, NY; (Y); 2/90; Church Yth Grp; French Clb; GAA; Band; Ed Yrbk Stf; Sec Soph Cls; Pres Sr Cls; Var Capt Trk; High Hon Roll; NHS; Gftd Tlntd Awd 86; Math Awd Sequential Math III 86; Alfred U; Art Ed.

GAGNIER, PAUL; Chittenango HS; Chittenango, NY; (Y); 1/200; Am Leg Boys St; Drama Clb; Ski Clb; SADD; Band; Sec Chorus; School Musical; School Play; Swing Chorus; VP Stu Cncl; Cornell Clb Bk Awd 86; All ST Choir 86; Bio.

GAGNON, DENISE; Tonawanda JR SR HS; Tonawanda, NY; (Y); Church Yth Grp; French Clb; Ski Clb; SADD; Yrbk Phtg; Rep Stu Cncl; JV Var Bsktbl; JV Var Socr; JV Var Vllybl; Hon Roll; :Bus Admn.

GAHR, THOMAS; Notre Dame HS; Batavia, NY; (S); 3/62; Ski Clb; Trs Jr Cls; Pres Sr Cls; Stu Cncl; Var Ftbl; Capt Wrstlng; Hon Roll; Jr NHS; NHS; Ntl Merit Schol; Clarkson U; Engrng.

GAIDASZ, LORI; York Central HS; Mt Morris, NY; (Y); Dance Clb; Drama Clb; Library Aide; Science Clb; Service Clb; Spanish Clb; Teachers Aide; Acpl Chr; Chorus; School Musical; Soc Stud Cls Hnrs 85; Pre-Law.

GAILIS, LINDA; Pine Bush Central HS; Circleville, NY; (Y); Sec 4-H; Library Aide; Varsity Clb; Yrbk Stf; Var Socr; Var Trk; 4-H Awd; Hon Roll; Sec Jr NHS; NHS.

GAINES, CARLA; The Masters Schl; Dobbs Ferry, NY; (Y); 8/80; Church Yth Grp; Cmnty Wkr; Pres Dance Clb; French Clb; Teachers Aide; School Musical; Nwsp Stf; Yrbk Stf; Lit Mag; Rep Jr Cls; Natl Latn Awd 84; Westchester Chpt Jack & Jill Of Amer Sec, Delegate To Teen Conference; Lbrl Arts.

GAINES, VALERIE; Carthage Central HS; Carthage, NY; (Y); 20/175; VP Drama Clb; Key Clb; Chorus; School Musical; Swing Chorus; Swmmng; High Hon Roll; NHS; Pres Schlr; AFS; Ithaca Coll Schlrshp, Miss NYS Talent Title 85; Theatre Awd, Mus Awd, Excllnce Eng 86; Rotary Sr 86; Ithaca Coll NY; Mus Educ.

GAINEY, LAURA; Lackawanna HS; Lackawanna, NY; (Y); 6/249; Am Leg Aux Girls St; GAA; Office Aide; Red Cross Aide; Spanish Clb; Var Crs Cntry; Var Trk; NHS; Rgnts Schlrshp 86; Amer Lgn Grls ST Rep 85; X-Cntry ST Cmptn 82; Canisius Coll; Law.

GAINOR, SHAWN; Prospect Heights HS; Brooklyn, NY; (S); 4/271; Sec Church Yth Grp; Debate Tm; FBLA; Hosp Aide; Office Aide; Teachers Aide; Nwsp Ed-Chief; Nwsp Rptr; Ed Yrbk Stf; Pres Stu Cncl; Regnts Schlrshp 86; UFT 86; Arista Pres 85-86; Pre Med.

GAISO, MICHAEL A; Saint Francis Prep; Howard Beach, NY; (Y); 301/653; Boy Scts; Cmnty Wkr; JA; Wt Lftg; St Johns U; Bus Admin.

GAJDOS, ALENA; John Dewey HS; Brooklyn, NY; (Y); Office Aide; Im Bowling; Business.

GALAGARZA JR, JULIO; Park West HS; New York, NY; (Y); 37/483; JA; Concert Band; Orch; Hon Roll; Acad Olympic Sq 86; Embry Riddle; Aviation.

GALANAKIS, ALEXANDRA; The Stony Brook Schl; Stony Brook, NY; (Y); 4/84; Art Clb; Camera Clb; Drama Clb; English Clb; Hosp Aide; Chorus; School Play; Yrbk Ed-Chief; Yrbk Phtg; Var Cheerleading; Engl Mdl AP Engl 86; King Awd Deramics 85; Bryn Mawr Coll; Bio.

GALANEK, CHARLENE; The Acad Of The Resurrection HS; New Rochelle, NY; (Y); 9/81; Camera Clb; Math Clb; NFL; Pres Stage Crew; Yrbk Phtg; Trs Soph Cls; JV Var Score Keeper; Var Sftbl; Hon Roll; NHS; U Of San Diego Schlrshp Acad 86; Std Star Carrier Of Yr 85; U Of San Diego; Accntng.

GALANTY, CAROL A; Hampton Bays HS; Hampton Bays, NY; (Y); 5/85; SADD; Varsity Clb; Chorus; School Musical; Var Bsktbl; Hon Roll; NHS; Schlrshp Dstnctn 86-1990; Schlrshp Achvt 86-87; NY ST Schlrshp 86-1990; Marymount-Tarrytwn; Fshn Byng.

GALARNEAU, DANIELLE; Catholic Central HS; Waterford, NY; (Y); Band; Concert Band; Mrchg Band; School Musical; VP Frsh Cls; Bsktbl; Hon Roll; NHS; Partcpt Empire ST Games Bsktbl; Cert Merit ST Assmbly & Senate Rep; Ed.

GALARZA, SANE C; Southside HS; S Hempstead, NY; (Y); Church Yth Grp; Dance Clb; Band; Orch; Gym; Sftbl; Swmmng; Hon Roll; Engnrng.

GALASSO, ALISON; West Hampton Beach HS; Manorville, NY; (Y); Church Yth Grp; FBLA; Office Aide; Varsity Clb; Yrbk Phtg; Var Cheerleading; Var L Trk; Hon Roll; Peer Grp Ldrshp Awd 85; Spec Ed.

GALASSO, ANNETTE; Glen Cove HS; Glen Cove, NY; (Y); Sec DECA; Drama Clb; School Musical; Hon Roll; French Clb; Key Clb; Variety Show; Cheerleading; Twrlr; 2nd Pl Rd Advrtsng Rgnl Evnt 86; Aawd Oscar Dstrbtv Educ Clbs Of Amer 86; Psych.

GALBATO, RICK; Auburn HS; Auburn, NY; (Y); Model UN; SADD; Varsity Clb; School Play; JV Socr; Var L Tennis; Most Impvd Plyr-Ten 9th Grd; MVP Vrsty Ten Tm 10th-11th Grds; Pol Sci.

GALE, RACHEL; Brockport HS; Brockport, NY; (Y); Church Yth Grp; Ski Clb; Spanish Clb; Varsity Clb; Var Coach Actv; Var Score Keeper; Var Swmmng; Capt Var Tennis; Timer; Hon Roll; All Cnty Tnns Team 85; Swim Team Won Sectnls 84; Ldrshp Awd Trophy 85; Tennis Pro.

GALEANO, ANA MARIA; Roy C Ketcham HS; Poughkeepsie, NY; (Y); 30/510; Political Wkr; Ski Clb; SADD; Pres Frsh Cls; VP Jr Cls; VP Sr Cls; Rep Stu Cncl; Capt Var Cheerleading; High Hon Roll; Hon Roll; Gannett Schlrshp 86; Roy C Ketcham Hmcmng Queen 85-86; 2nd Rnr-Up Amer Hmcmng Queen 86; SUNY Binghamton; Lngstcs.

GALEK, DENISE; Sodus Central HS; Sodus, NY; (Y); 2/120; Model UN; Science Clb; Spanish Clb; Off Stu Cncl; High Hon Roll; Bausch & Lomb Sci Awd; NHS; Rotary Club Acadmc Awd; Acadmc Lttr & Pin; TNAOL By Women; Chem.

GALES, MIKE; Hancock Central HS; Hancock, NY; (Y); 2/75; German Clb; Stu Cncl; Var Ftbl; Var Wrstlng; Hon Roll; NHS; Ntl Merit Ltr; Pres Elect Natl Hnr Soc 86-87; Engrng.

GALGANSKI, MICHELE; Alexander Central Schl; Alexander, NY; (Y); 1/83; Math Tm; Band; Rep Soph Cls; Rep Sec Stu Cncl; Var Capt Trk; Pres Jr NHS; Lion Awd; Sec NHS; Ntl Merit Ltr; Val; Empr ST Gms Slvr Mdlst Schlstc Heptthln 85; US Army Rsrv Schlr/Athlt Mdl 85-86; U Of Rochester; Hlth Sci.

GALIFI, ROBERT; Msgr Farrell HS; Staten Island, NY; (Y); 191/319; Ski Clb; Band; Mrchg Band; Stage Crew; Rep Stu Cncl; JV Crs Cntry; Awd Muscular Distrophy Assoc; Mech Engnrng.

GALIK, CYNTHIA; Sacred Heart HS; Yonkers, NY; (Y); VP Church Yth Grp; Hosp Aide; Hon Roll; Intl Womens Leag For Peace Essay Cont 84; Sacred Heart High Nwspr Spring Wrtng Cont 83; Regents Diplmt; NYU; Spec Ed.

GALISKI III, JOHN A; S S Seward Inst; Florida, NY; (Y); 1/45; Am Leg Boys St; Pres Art Clb; VP Camera Clb; SADD; Band; Pres Jr Cls; Var L Socr; High Hon Roll; NHS; Nwsp Rptr; Gatewys Pgm 83-86; King 86 Jr Prom 86; Physcl Sci.

GALIZIA, FELICIA; Brewster HS; Brewster, NY; (Y); Pep Clb; Spanish Clb; Rep Jr Cls; Rep Sr Cls; Rep Stu Cncl; Cheerleading; Mgr(s); High Hon Roll; Hon Roll; Spanish NHS; Schlrshp Gym 84-85; Foreign Lang Awd 85-86; Social Studies Awd 85-86; Aivary U; Cmmnctns.

GALLAGHER, COLLEEN; Bayport Bluepoint HS; Bayport, NY; (Y); Cmnty Wkr; Office Aide; Teachers Aide; Prfct Atten Awd; Merit Roll 84-85; Achvt In Advncd Typg 86; Meritorious Svc In Guidance Ofc 86; Bus Mgmt.

GALLAGHER, DANIELLE; West Babylon HS; W Babylon, NY; (Y); 34/415; Varsity Clb; Yrbk Stf; Capt Var Bsktbl; JV Fld Hcky; JV Sftbl; Var Tennis; Cit Awd; High Hon Roll; NHS.

GALLAGHER, DONNA; Holy Trinity HS; N Massapequa, NY; (S); 35/403; Camera Clb; Dance Clb; Girl Scts; Math Clb; Math Tm; Ski Clb; Chorus; Stage Crew; Yrbk Stf; Rep Frsh Cls; Hofstra U; Bus Comp.

GALLAGHER JR, JOHN; Irondequoit HS; Rochester, NY; (Y); 51/346; Church Yth Grp; Latin Clb; Letterman Clb; Model UN; Scholastic Bowl; Varsity Clb; Off Soph Cls; Off Jr Cls; Off Sr Cls; JV Var Bsktbl; U Buffalo; Elec Engr.

GALLAGHER, ROD; Marlboro Central HS; Marlboro, NY; (Y); 1/160; Letterman Clb; Varsity Clb; Var L Bsbl; Var Capt Bsktbl; High Hon Roll; NHS; Val; Thomas J Watson Mem Schlrshp 86; Rnslr Polytchnc Inst Mth & Sci Awd 85; Tms Herald Rcrd 86 Schlr Athlt; Cornell U; Elec Engrng.

GALLAGHER, THOMAS B; Mahopac HS; Mahopac, NY; (Y); Cmnty Wkr; JV Var Ftbl; JV Var Lcrss; JV Wrstlng; Hon Roll.

GALLAGHER, TIMOTHY A; Monsignor Farrell HS; Staten Island, NY; (Y); 53/300; Im Bsktbl; Var L Crs Cntry; Im Ftbl; Stat Ice Hcky; Var L Trk; Hon Roll; NHS; 2nd Tm Crss Cntry All ST 85; Schlrshp-St Peters Coll 86; Rgnts Schlrshp-Baruch Coll Schlrshp 86; St Peters Coll; Bus.

GALLAGHR, MARIA L; Queensbury HS; Glens Falls, NY; (Y); 18/256; Var Crs Cntry; Var Trk; High Hon Roll; Rgns Schlrshp 86; Acad Schlrshp 86; Hartwick; Pre-Vet.

GALLANTER, TISHA; Stamford Central HS; Stamford, NY; (S); 1/39; Intnl Clb; Band; Chorus; Drm Mjr(t); Flag Corp; Mrchg Band; Var Capt Bsktbl; Var Capt Socr; High Hon Roll; NHS; Med.

GALLARDO, SERENA M; Adlai E Stevenson HS; Bronx, NY; (Y); Office Aide; Teachers Aide; Chorus; Nwsp Stf; Yrbk Stf; Sec Sr Cls; Rep Stu Cncl; Hon Roll; NHS; Rgnts Schlrshp 86; PCA.

GALLE, LISA; Wayne Central HS; Ontario, NY; (Y); 3/190; Band; Concert Band; Mrchg Band; High Hon Roll; Hon Roll; NHS; Frnch Excllnce 85; Bio Achvt 85.

GALLELLO, ANGELA; Blessed Sacrament-St Gabriel HS; New Rochelle, NY; (Y); 2/138; Stu Cncl; High Hon Roll; NHS; Sal; Yrbk Stf; Rep Jr Cls; Rep Sr Cls; Full Schlrshp Iona Coll 85-86; Ntl Scl Stud Cont Awd; Iona Coll.

GALLELLO, KATHLEEN; Dominican Commercial HS; Queens Village, NY; (S); 24/288; Church Yth Grp; Vllybl; High Hon Roll; NHS; Peer Grp Cnclng Music 83-86; Intl Lookg Sci Clb 84-85; Assist Staf Yth Ctr 83-86; Adelphi; Pre-Law.

GALLER, SHERYL BETH; Yeshivah Of Flatbush HS; Brooklyn, NY; (Y); Cmnty Wkr; Nwsp Rptr; Yrbk Ed-Chief; Ed Lit Mag; High Hon Roll; Jr NHS; NHS; Ntl Merit SF; 46th Schl Sci Fair Hnrb Mntn 84; 2nd Prize Schl Wide Hebrew Lit Cont 85.

GALLERY, DAWN; St Agnes Acad; Queens Village, NY; (Y); Drama Clb; SADD; School Musical; Nwsp Ed-Chief; Lit Mag; Hon Roll; Rgnts Schlrshp 86; English Awd 86; Amer Lgn Jrnlsm Awd 86; Queens Coll.

GALLETTA, JACQUELINE; Bishop Ford CC HS; Brooklyn, NY; (S); 20/390; Computer Clb; Dance Clb; JA; Math Tm; Var Bsktbl; Mgr(s); Hon Roll; Jr NHS; NHS; Fash Buyer.

GALLETTI, KERRYANNE; Ward Melville HS; Centereach, NY; (Y); Chorus; Church Choir; Bsktbl; Socr; Sftbl; Tennis; Exc NYSMA 83-85; Tnns Var Ltr Trphy 83 & 85; Hofstra U; Bus.

GALLIGAN, MAUREEN; Clarkstown South HS; New City, NY; (Y); 52/475; Cmnty Wkr; Girl Scts; Math Clb; Math Tm; Office Aide; Service Clb; High Hon Roll; Hon Roll; VP Jr NHS; NY ST Rgnts Schlrshp 86; SUNY Bnghmtn; Math.

GALLIPEAU, DAVID; Albion HS; Albion, NY; (S); 29/186; Crmc Engnrng.

GALLIVAN, COLEEN; Frontier Central HS; Lakeview, NY; (Y); French Clb; FBLA; Pep Clb; Ski Clb; Cheerleading; Bus Mgr.

GALLIVAN, ERIN; Byron-Bergen Central HS; Bergen, NY; (Y); 38/104; Drama Clb; Band; Color Guard; Concert Band; Drill Tm; Drm Mjr(t); Yrbk Phtg; Cheerleading; Socr; Kiwanis Awd; Bryant & Stratton; Lgl Sec.

GALLO, ANITA; Pelham Memorial HS; Pelham, NY; (Y); AFS; Church Yth Grp; Drama Clb; Capt Pep Clb; Varsity Clb; Chorus; Church Choir; School Play; Stage Crew; Var JV Sftbl; Vrsty Ltr Twrlg & Awds 84-87; Pre-Med.

GALLO III, FERDINAND J; Mercy HS; Riverhead, NY; (Y); 1/101; Mathletes; Political Wkr; Scholastic Bowl; SADD; Nwsp Ed-Chief; High Hon Roll; NHS; Ntl Merit Ltr; Rotary Awd; Riverhead Lions Clb Schlrshp 86; Deans Schlr 86-87; NY Rgnts Schlrshp 86; Corenll U; Policy Analysis.

GALLO, FRANCES; Mahopac HS; Mahopac, NY; (Y); 62/383; SADD; Nwsp Stf; Yrbk Stf; Sec Sr Cls; Stu Cncl; Bsktbl; Var Socr; Var Capt Vllybl; High Hon Roll; NHS; All-Leag Varsity Bllybl All Sctn Hnrb Mntn Varsity Sccr 86; Nwspr Sptlght On A Athltc Ablty 84; Siena Coll; Bus Admin.

GALLO, JOSEPH G; St Anthonys HS; N Babylon, NY; (Y); 12/350; Im Bsktbl; NHS; Spanish NHS; NYS Regnts Schlrshp 86-90; Amer Exprss Spec Schlrshp 86-90; SUNY Binghamton; Law.

GALLO, LAURA; Bishop Kearney HS; Brooklyn, NY; (Y); Girl Scts; Nwsp Stf; Bowling; Hon Roll; Katharine Gibbs Founders Schlrshp 86; Katharine Gibbs; Secr.

GALLO, LAURIEANN; St Edmunds HS; Brooklyn, NY; (Y); Cmnty Wkr; Library Aide; Hon Roll; Law.

GALLO, LEIGH; Nyack HS; Upper Nyack, NY; (Y); 4/255; Am Leg Aux Girls St; Mrchg Band; School Musical; Swmmng; Var Capt Vllybl; French Hon Soc; High Hon Roll; NHS; Itln Am Schlrshp 86; Clg Of William And Mary.

GALLO, LISA; Iroquois Central HS; Lancaster, NY; (Y); 58/273; Church Yth Grp; French Clb; Ski Clb; Stu Cncl; JV Fld Hcky; JV Mgr(s); Var Trk; Hon Roll; Gifted & Talnted Pgm 83-86; Wellesley Coll.

GALLO, SANDRA; New Covenant Christian Schl; Ontario, NY; (S); Church Yth Grp; Drama Clb; Office Aide; Pres Spanish Clb; Chorus; Stage Crew; Var Socr; Var Trk; Var Vllybl; Hon Roll; Good Samaritan 85; Soccer Trophy 84; Soccer Appreciation 85; Bus.

GALLO, SUZANNE E; St Francis Prep; Whitestone, NY; (S); 54/746; Hosp Aide; Color Guard; Im Bowling; Im Sftbl; Hon Roll; NHS; Opt Clb Awd.

GALOSIC, JANE; St Johns Prep; Astoria, NY; (Y); 10/458; Dance Clb; Hon Roll; Jr NHS; Pace U; Mrktng Res.

GALSTER, CATHY; Alexander Central Schl; Alexander, NY; (Y); Church Yth Grp; Drama Clb; FNA; Hosp Aide; Library Aide; SADD; Varsity Clb; Yrbk Stf; Socr; Emrgncy Med Doc.

GALURA, DONNA; Sacred Heart HS; Yonkers, NY; (S); 8/214; Capt Crs Cntry; Capt Trk; Mgr Vllybl; High Hon Roll; NHS.

GALUSHA, LESLIE A; Horseheads HS; Big Flats, NY; (S); 44/385; Ski Clb; Varsity Clb; Chorus; Stu Cncl; Capt Cheerleading; Hon Roll; People To People Stu Ambssdr Pgm 85; Bus.

GALVIN, BRIDGET; Berne-Knox-Westerlo Central HS; Delanson, NY; (Y); 11/76; Sec FBLA; Band; Color Guard; Capt Co-Capt Drm Mjr(t); Mrchg Band; Yrbk Stf; Twrlr; Hon Roll; Rep Stu Cncl; Stu Of Mnth Nov 86; Fml Stu Hghst Avg Bus 86; Dean JC; Exec Sec.

GALVIN, EDWARD M; Miller Place HS; Miller Place, NY; (Y); 7/205; Drama Clb; SADD; Thesps; Band; Concert Band; Jazz Band; Pep Band; School Play; Stage Crew; Trk; NY ST Rgnts Schlrshp 86; IIT IL; Aerontcl Engrng.

GALVIN, SUE; Mount Saint Joseph Acad; Buffalo, NY; (S); Art Clb; Stage Crew; Yrbk Stf; Lit Mag; High Hon Roll; Hon Roll; NHS; Prfct Atten Awd.

GALVIN, TRACY ANN; Smithtown HS East; Smithtown, NY; (Y); Church Yth Grp; Teachers Aide; Chorus; Church Choir; Stage Crew; Stu Cncl; JV Var Mgr(s); Score Keeper; Hon Roll; VP Stat Bsktbl; Bus.

GAMA, LISA; St Joseph By The Sea HS; Staten Island, NY; (Y); Exploring; Variety Show; Capt Var Socr; Pace U.

GAMACHE, LAWRENCE W; Warwick Valley HS; Warwick, NY; (Y); 30/197; Cmnty Wkr; Drama Clb; French Clb; Math Tm; SADD; Band; Jazz Band; School Musical; School Play; Nwsp Ed-Chief; Natl Sci Olympd Chmstry 1st Plc 84-85; US Hstry & Gvrnmnt Awd 85-86; NYS Rgnts Schlrshp 85-86; George Washington U; Intl Affrs.

GAMAR, DANIELLE; New Dorp HS; Staten Isl, NY; (Y); Church Yth Grp; Teachers Aide; Church Choir; Stage Crew; Hon Roll; Gymnstc Awd 85; Suny Stoney Brook; Sci.

GAMBA, JASON; Saint Francis Prep; Middle Village, NY; (S); 70/653; Art Clb; Cmnty Wkr; L Im Ftbl; Im Sftbl; Trk; Im Vllybl; Hon Roll; NHS; Ntl Merit Ltr; Optimate Soc; Bus Mgmt.

GAMBACORTA, MARIA; Buffalo Acad Of The Sacred Heart; Buffalo, NY; (Y); Church Yth Grp; Cmnty Wkr; Hosp Aide; Political Wkr; Pres Service Clb; Sec Spanish Clb; Stage Crew; Tennis; Hon Roll; Daemen Clg Dept Schlrshp 86-90; Daemen Clg; Physcl Thrpy.

GAMBER, FRANCES; Nottingham HS; Syracuse, NY; (Y); 54/307; Drama Clb; French Clb; Latin Clb; Ski Clb; SADD; Chorus; Yrbk Phtg; Yrbk Stf; Off Stu Cncl; Schlrp From Readers Digest Recog Of Wrk With SADD 86; Bus.

GAMBINO, CHERISE; H C Technical HS; Buffalo, NY; (Y); Math Tm; Var Cheerleading; Math.

GAMBINO, KATHRYN; Christ The King Regional HS; Glendale, NY; (Y); 76/451; Cmnty Wkr; Computer Clb; Dance Clb; English Clb; Office Aide; Political Wkr; Acpl Chr; Chorus; Natl Svc Lg 83-84; Choraleer 83-84; John Jay Coll Of Criminal Just.

GAMBINO, MARY ANN; John Adams HS; Ozone Park, NY; (Y); Hon Roll; Cert Merit Italn Stds 86; 2nd Hnrs 86; Wrd Procssg Awd 86; St Johns U; Bus.

GAMBOA, LIZETTY; George Washington HS; New York, NY; (Y); 13/321; Hon Roll; ESL Schlrshp 83; Teresa Humanan Mdl 86; Baruch Coll; Acctngn.

GAMBOIAN, NANCY; Lewiston Porter SR HS; Lewiston, NY; (Y); 26/240; Church Yth Grp; Dance Clb; Drama Clb; PAVAS; Teachers Aide; Orch; School Play; High Hon Roll; NHS; Flippll Shcl Of Clsscl Rllt 82-84; Fredonia.

GAMERMAN, ELLEN; Mamaroneck HS; Larchmont, NY; (Y); Cmnty Wkr; Dance Clb; Drama Clb; School Play; Stage Crew; Nwsp Stf; High Hon Roll; NHS; Ntl Merit Ltr; Wellsly Bk Awd 85; Deptmntl Awds Engl & Hstry 86; Swarthmore Coll; Engl.

GAMLIEL, SHLOMIT; Sephardic HS; Brooklyn, NY; (S); Cmnty Wkr; Political Wkr; Orch; Hon Roll; Barilan U; Med.

GANDINI, CHRISTINE; East Meadow HS; E Meadow, NY; (Y); 133/340; Church Yth Grp; Cmnty Wkr; FBLA; Band; Concert Band; Mrchg Band; Pep Band; Symp Band; JV Cheerleading; Var JV Sftbl; MVP Awd Sftbl 86; All Div Vrsty Sftbl 86; Nassau CC; Bus.

GANDOLFO, ANGELA; Dominican Commercial HS; Glendale, NY; (Y); Sec Church Yth Grp; Cmnty Wkr; Hon Roll; Jr NHS; NHS; Prncpls Lst 82-86; Ntl Bus Hnr Soc 85-86; Rgnts Dplma 86; Bus.

GANDY, TONIA L; White Plains HS; White Plains, NY; (Y); PAVAS; Yrbk Phtg; Natl Fndtn Advncmnt Arts 85-86; Moore Coll; Photography.

GANEY, CHRISTINE; Frontier Central HS; Hamburg, NY; (Y); 100/450; Pres Church Yth Grp; Drama Clb; Girl Scts; Library Aide; Spanish Clb; Chorus; Church Choir; Stage Crew; Rep Stu Cncl; Hon Roll; Erie Cty Chorus 79; Sci Fair Awd 82; Ferdonia; Educ.

GANG, DAVID; Lawrence HS; Woodmere, NY; (Y); DECA; Key Clb; Capt Math Tm; Spanish Clb; Bsktbl; High Hon Roll; NHS; Ntl Merit Ltr; 1st Pl Long Is Lang Fair Spn Poetry 86; U MI; Bus.

GANJIAN, EMIL; Anglo American HS; Forest Hills, NY; (S); Boy Scts; Pres Chess Clb; Capt Math Tm; Varsity Clb; Var Socr; Swmmng; Vllybl; High Hon Roll; NHS; Excllnc-Sci, Math & Hdmstr Hgh Hnr Rll; Harvard; Doctr.

GANNETT, SARAH; Newark SR HS; Newark, NY; (Y); 16/193; Church Yth Grp; Hosp Aide; Math Tm; Varsity Clb; Yrbk Stf; French Hon Soc; High Hon Roll; Hon Roll; Lion Awd; NHS; VA Polytech Inst; Engnrng.

GANNON, EILEEN M; Lackawanna SR HS; Lackawanna, NY; (Y); 26/265; Church Yth Grp; Drama Clb; French Clb; Library Aide; Ski Clb; Concert Band; Mrchg Band; School Play; Stage Crew; Symp Band; Amer Lgn Post 63-Amer Hstry Awd 85; Awd Excllnc-Frnch 85; NY ST Rgnts Schlrshp 86; MI ST U; Pre-Med.

GANNON, KELLY; Greenwich HS; Greenwich, NY; (Y); Nwsp Stf; Yrbk Stf; Sec Frsh Cls; VP Soph Cls; Pres Jr Cls; Stu Cncl; Fld Hcky; Sftbl; Hon Roll; Cmmnctns.

GANOE, VICTOR; Mc Kinley HS; Buffalo, NY; (Y); 30/216; Band; U Of Buffalo; Engrng.

GANSER, MARGARET; Frontier SR HS; Lakeview, NY; (Y); Art Clb; FBLA; Pep Clb; Varsity Clb; Var JV Bsktbl; Var Socr; Im Sftbl; Var JV Vllybl; Hon Roll.

GANSHAW, JOEL D; Marlboro Central HS; Milton, NY; (Y); 26/160; Letterman Clb; Varsity Clb; Band; Concert Band; Pep Band; Nwsp Stf; Var L Crs Cntry; Var L Trk; High Hon Roll; Hon Roll; NYS Rgnts Schlrshp 86; SUNY Buffalo.

GANTT, CALVIN; Walton HS; Bronx, NY; (Y); Computer Clb; FTA; Teachers Aide; Coach Actv; Var JV Vllybl; Hon Roll; Prfct Atten Awd; Varsity Clb; Color Guard; Score Keeper; Daily News Awds Outstndng Achvt Acad & Extra Currclr Actvts 85 & 86; Engrng.

GANTZ, AMY; Ossining HS; Ossining, NY; (Y); Church Yth Grp; Cmnty Wkr; Band; Concert Band; Orch; Coach Actv; Score Keeper; Sftbl; Vllybl; Hon Roll; Athl Traing.

GANZ, JULIE; Mahopac HS; Mahopac, NY; (Y); 4-H; Girl Scts; Hon Roll; Westchester CC; Legal Sec.

GARA, STEVEN J; Great Neck North SR HS; Great Neck, NY; (Y); Temple Yth Grp; Varsity Clb; Band; Stage Crew; Nwsp Rptr; Nwsp Stf; Rep Stu Cncl; Var Trk; Wt Lftg; Sci Fair Awds 84; Vrsty G Track Awds 85-86; Temple U; Psych.

GARAFALO, JULIE; Bishop Ford Central HS; Brooklyn, NY; (Y); 2nd Honors 84-85; Katherine Gibbs; Bus.

GARAU, ANNMARIE; Fox Lane HS; Mt Kisco, NY; (Y); Church Yth Grp; Pep Clb; Ski Clb; Chorus; School Musical; JV Lcrss; Vllybl; Hon Roll.

GARAVUSO, THOMAS; Aviation HS; Brooklyn, NY; (Y); 120/418; Boy Scts; JA; Drm & Bgl; Cit Awd; Ntl Merit Schol; Prfct Atten Awd; Cert Excllnc Physcs 85; Prfct Attnd Awd 83-886; Cmndtn Hnsty & Cncrn Prprty Othrs 85; Airln Mchnc.

GARAY, GENE; Freeport HS; College Pt, NY; (Y); Aud/Vis; Pres Sec Drama Clb; Chorus; VP Orch; School Musical; Stage Crew; Hon Roll; NHS; Violin.

GARBARINO, ELLEN; St Johns Prep; Flushing, NY; (Y); Church Yth Grp; Cmnty Wkr; Nwsp Rptr; Rep Stu Cncl; JV Cheerleading; Hon Roll; Ntl Merit Ltr; Queens Coll; Educ.

GARBUTT, KIM; Massena Central HS; Massena, NY; (Y); 17/246; Church Yth Grp; Cmnty Wkr; Yrbk Bus Mgr; Cheerleading; Trk; Gov Hon Prg Awd; High Hon Roll; NHS; Pres Schlr; Gym; Educ Sec Awd 86; Tlntd JR 85; Hnr Grad 86; VA Plytchnc; Bus.

GARCES, JAVIER; Sacred Heart HS; Yonkers, NY; (Y); 6/225; Nwsp Rptr; Stat Bsktbl; Mgr(s); High Hon Roll; Hon Roll; NHS; Pres Schlrshp To U Of Tampa 86; Ntl Hspnc Schlr Awds Pgm Semi Fnlst 86; U Of Tampa; Comp Sci.

GARCIA, AMANDA; North Babylon SR HS; N Babylon, NY; (Y); Debate Tm; Nwsp Rptr; Rep Stu Cncl; Hon Roll; Intnl Clb; Office Aide; Spanish Clb; Teachers Aide; Stage Crew; JV Sftbl; Bus.

GARCIA, ANDREW; La Salle Military Acad; Bayonne, NJ; (S); 4/99; ROTC; Drill Tm; Nwsp Rptr; Ftbl; High Hon Roll; Hon Roll; Jr NHS; NHS; Ntl Merit Ltr; Prfct Atten Awd; Best Drl Tm Cmmndr 85; H S Chmpnshps 85; Natl Ldrshp And Sci Merit Awds 85; Boston Clg; Bus Mgmt.

GARCIA, CARMEN; Walton HS; Bronx, NY; (Y); Drama Clb; FTA; Office Aide; Teachers Aide; School Play; Nwsp Sprt Ed; Nwsp Stf; Yrbk Phtg; Yrbk Stf; Sftbl; Outstndng Achvt Pride Of Yankees Acadmc And Extra Curtclr Actvties 85; Partptd Acadmc Olympcs 86.

GARCIA, CESAR; Richmond Hill HS; Richmond Hill, NY; (Y); Chess Clb; Computer Clb; Debate Tm; School Play; Var Tennis; Jr NHS; NHS; French Hon Soc; High Hon Roll; Prfct Atten Awd; Engrng.

GARCIA, CHARLIE; Bronx HS Of Science; Bronx, NY; (Y); Regnts Schlrshp 86; CO ST U; Biol.

GARCIA, DAVID; Evander Childs HS; Bronx, NY; (S); Debate Tm; Speech Tm; Nwsp Ed-Chief; Nwsp Rptr; Stu Cncl; Ftbl; High Hon Roll; Hon Roll; Cert Of Merit Hnr Schl, Soc Stu & Engl 85-86; Binghamton U; Bus Adm.

GARCIA, DENISE; Murry Bergtraum HS; Brooklyn, NY; (Y); Girl Scts; Math Clb; Math Tm; Hon Roll; Rep NHS; Pace U Of Hefstra; Psyclgy.

GARCIA, GERALDINE; Franciscan HS; Mohegan Lake, NY; (Y); 5/58; Hosp Aide; Church Choir; School Musical; Rep Frsh Cls; Pres Soph Cls; VP Jr Cls; Rep Sr Cls; Pres Stu Cncl; Var Vllybl; Outstndng Ldrshp Awd 86; Natl Hnr Soc 84-86; Spanish Natl Hnr Soc 85-86; Villanova U; Dentistry.

GARCIA, GRACE; Academy Of St Joseph; E Islip, NY; (Y); Hosp Aide; Model UN; Science Clb; Yrbk Phtg; Var Tennis; High Hon Roll; NHS; Ntl Latin Exam Cum Laude 84-86; Magna Cum Laude Slv Mdl 86.

GARCIA, JEANNETTE; St Pius V HS; Bronx, NY; (Y); Hosp Aide; Service Clb; Yrbk Stf; Hon Roll; NHS; Manhattan Coll; Bus.

GARCIA, JEANNY; St Vincent Ferrer HS; Jackson Hts, NY; (Y); 3/110; Art Clb; Library Aide; Math Tm; High Hon Roll; NHS; Iona Lang Cntst 1st Hnrs Natv Spnsh 85; NEDT Awd 84; Pace U; Pblc Acctng.

GARCIA, JUAN A; Westbury HS; Westbury, NY; (Y); 11/25; Varsity Clb; JV Bsbl; Var Capt Socr; Comp Engr.

GARCIA, LETTY; Dominican Commercial HS; Richmond Hill, NY; (S); Church Yth Grp; Dance Clb; Y-Teens; Ntl Bus Hnr Soc; Sci Clb Stu; NY Tech; Legal Sec.

GARCIA, LIZZETTE; Dominican Commercial HS; Brooklyn, NY; (Y); Art Clb; Drama Clb; Chorus; School Play; Gym; Penn St; Advrtsng.

GARCIA, LUIS; Walton HS; Bronx, NY; (Y); Computer Clb; FTA; Office Aide; Scholastic Bowl; Teachers Aide; Yrbk Stf; Hon Roll; Cornell U; Engrng.

GARCIA, MARCO; Poughkeepsie HS; Poughkeepsie, NY; (Y); Computer Clb; Intnl Clb; Spanish Clb; Nwsp Stf; Elec Engrng.

GARCIA, MARK; Midwood HS; Brooklyn, NY; (Y); 393/667; Ftbl; Communications.

GARCIA, MARK; Saugerties HS; Mt Marion, NY; (S); Church Yth Grp; Band; Concert Band; Jazz Band; Mrchg Band; Pep Band; Symp Band; Var L Socr; Im Vllybl; Hon Roll.

GARCIA, MARY; N Babylon SR HS; North Babylon, NY; (Y); 117/471; Pres Intnl Clb; Thesps; Mrchg Band; School Play; Nwsp Phtg; Yrbk Phtg; French Hon Soc; Hon Roll; NHS; Pres Schlr; Castleton ST Coll VT; Elem Ed.

GARCIA, MICHELE; Herbert H Lehman HS; New York, NY; (Y); Cmnty Wkr; Office Aide; Chorus; Stage Crew; Nwsp Rptr; Nwsp Stf; Hon Roll; Prfct Atten Awd; Psych.

GARCIA, NANCY; Yonkers HS; Yonkers, NY; (Y); Church Yth Grp; Dance Clb; Girl Scts; Latin Clb; Spanish Clb; Teachers Aide; Varsity Clb; Y-Teens; School Play; Score Keeper; Chatham Coll; Med.

GARCIA, NOEL; St Francis Preparatory HS; Elmhurst, NY; (Y); Ski Clb; Spanish Clb; Variety Show; Tennis; Trk; Vllybl; NY U; Systms Anlyst.

GARCIA, RALPH; Cardinal Hayes HS; New York, NY; (Y); Latin Clb; Math Clb; Math Tm; Spanish Clb; Bsbl; Crs Cntry; Trk; Hon Roll; JETS Awd; Prfct Atten Awd; Stony Brook Man Coll; Engrng.

GARCIA, RAMON; Archbishop Molloy HS; Sunnyside, NY; (Y); Computer Clb; Hosp Aide; Spanish Clb; Teachers Aide; Hon Roll; Elec Engrng.

GARCIA, RAPHAEL; Park West HS; Bronx, NY; (Y); 71/492; Ski Clb; Yrbk Phtg; Yrbk Stf; Hon Roll; Embry-Riddle Aero U; Pilot.

GARCIA, SORAYA; St Raymond Academy For Girls; Bronx, NY; (Y); 11/68; Computer Clb; Library Aide; Office Aide; Science Clb; Teachers Aide; VP Soph Cls; Rep Stu Cncl; Hon Roll; Prfct Atten Awd; Fordham U; Acctng.

GARDEPE, PAULA; Stockbridge Valley Central Schl; Pratts Hollow, NY; (S); 2/45; Church Yth Grp; Drama Clb; 4-H; French Clb; Mathletes; Math Clb; Office Aide; Pep Clb; Science Clb; Spanish Clb; Herkimer Cnty CC; Trvl.

GARDNER, DANA; Andes Central Schl; Andes, NY; (Y); 1/18; Drm Mjr(t); Trs Yrbk Stf; Pres Frsh Cls; Pres Soph Cls; VP Jr Cls; Var Cheerleading; Var Socr; Hon Roll; Val; Natl Englsh Merit 84-85; Natl Frnch Merit 83-84; Russell Sage Coll; Med Tech.

GARDNER, JEFF M; Pine Valley Central Schl; Gerry, NY; (Y); Am Leg Boys St; Band; Chorus; Mrchg Band; School Musical; School Play; Var Trk; NHS; Voice Dem Awd; 3-1-3 Coll Pgm 85-86; Regents Scholar 86; Fredonia ST; Engl.

GARDNER, JEFFREY V; Hugh C Williams SR HS; Canton, NY; (Y); Boy Scts; Church Yth Grp; CAP; Exploring; Letterman Clb; Model UN; ROTC; Color Guard; Ftbl; Trk; NYS Stu Senate Forum 86; Order Arrow Area I Chief 86; H L Williams SOAR Ldrshp Grp 86; Pol Sci.

GARDNER, KEITH; Nazareth Regional HS; Brooklyn, NY; (Y); SADD; Varsity Clb; Drm Mjr(t); Stage Crew; Nwsp Rptr; Bsbl; Bsktbl; Trk; Cit Awd; High Hon Roll; Seton Hall; Law.

GARDNER, KEVIN; Columbia HS; Rensselaer, NY; (Y); Trs Church Yth Grp; Drama Clb; SADD; Thesps; Church Choir; School Musical; School Play; High Hon Roll; NHS; VP Art Clb; Cert Of Merit Sntr Jsph L Bruno 86; Intrnshp ESIPA 86; Thtre.

GARDNER, MARY ELLEN; Horseheads HS; Horseheads, NY; (Y); 58/376; Drama Clb; Girl Scts; Varsity Clb; Band; Chorus; Church Choir; Capt Color Guard; Orch; School Musical; Nwsp Stf; Regents Schlrshp Wnnr 86; Rep To Chemung Cnty JR Miss Prog 86; Mst Promising Acresss Awd Drama Clb 84; ST U Of NY; Englsh.

GARDNER, NANCY C; Odessa-Montour Central Schl; Montour Falls, NY; (Y); 20/88; FBLA; SADD; Teachers Aide; School Play; VP Frsh Cls; JV Cheerleading; JV Vllybl; Hon Roll; Cngrssnl Yth Ldrshp Cncl Schlr 86; Alfred U Ag & Tech; Rtl Bus.

GARDNER, SCOTT C; Franklin Acad; Constable, NY; (Y); Band; Concert Band; Jazz Band; Frnkln Acdmy Schlrshp 84; Rgnts Schlrshp 86; SUNY Plattsburgh; Bus Adm.

GARDNER, VERONICA; Cattaraugus Central Schl; Little Valley, NY; (Y); 4-H; Girl Scts; Hosp Aide; Band; Chorus; Church Choir; Concert Band; L Cheerleading; 4-H Awd; Hon Roll; MIP Wrstlng Chrldng 83-84; Dry Shwmnshp 6th Pl 85; Dry Jdgng 7th Pl 85; Jamestown Cmnty Coll; RN.

GARELICK, LORI J; Wantagh HS; Wantagh, NY; (Y); 3/271; Cmnty Wkr; Pres Debate Tm; Off Soph Cls; Mgr Vllybl; Hon Roll; Sec NHS; Rgnts Schlrshp 86; E Roeling Schlrshp 86; U Of PA; Mgmt.

GAREY, JOHN; Niagara Wheatfield SR HS; Niagara Falls, NY; (Y); 146/292; Latin Clb; PAVAS; Varsity Clb; Nwsp Rptr; Var Ice Hcky; Stat Score Keeper; Var Tennis; Var Vllybl; JV Wrstlng; Hon Roll; ST U Of NY Fredonia; Educ.

GARGAN, MOLLY; Auburn HS; Auburn, NY; (Y); Y-Teens; High Hon Roll; Marine Blgst.

GARGANO, ANGELINA; High School Of Fashion Ind; Bronx, NY; (Y); 3/324; Drama Clb; Office Aide; Teachers Aide; Variety Show; Nwsp Rptr; Pres Sr Cls; Hon Roll; NHS; Pace U; Accntnt.

GARGUILO, MICHAEL G; Oriskany Central HS; Oriskany, NY; (Y); 2/67; Am Leg Boys St; Key Clb; Spanish Clb; Varsity Clb; School Play; Yrbk Stf; JV Bsbl; JV Var Bsktbl; Im Bowling; Var Ftbl; NYS Rgnts Schlrshp, Rgnst Dipl Hmr 86; Syracuse U; Pharm.

GARGUILO, NANCY; Yonkers HS; Yonkers, NY; (Y); 32/217; Nwsp Rptr; Off Sr Cls; Cheerleading; Vllybl; NHS; Socl Awds Amercn Hstry 85; Iona Coll.

GARIBOLDI, JOHN; Commack South HS; Dix Hills, NY; (Y); 190/356; Camera Clb; JA; Varsity Clb; Bsbl; Ftbl; Wt Lftg; Wrstlng; High Hon Roll; Hon Roll; Cmnty Ldr 83-85; MVP Ftbl 84; All Lg Ftbl, Bsbl 85-86; NYIT; Arch.

GARIGEN, DANIEL; Alexander Central HS; Attica, NY; (Y).

GARIL, SCOTT E; Martin Van Buren HS; Queens Village, NY; (Y); 31/565; English Clb; Math Clb; Math Tm; Science Clb; Chorus; Hon Roll; SUNY.

GARLO, MARIE E; Acad Of St Joseph; Amityville, NY; (Y); 2/125; Science Clb; SADD; Yrbk Stf; Lit Mag; Ntl Merit Ltr; NEDT Awd; Englsh Awd 84-85; Latin Awd 82-83; Cert Mrt Latn Amer Clsscl Lge; Cornell U; Vet Med.

GARNER, ANGELA; Mt Vernon HS; Mt Vernon, NY; (Y); Cmnty Wkr; Computer Clb; FBLA; Office Aide; Color Guard; Drm & Bgl; Mrchg Band; Rep Sr Cls; Hon Roll; Jr NHS; Howard U; Bus Admin.

GARNETT, LORA; Romulus Central HS; Romulus, NY; (Y); Church Yth Grp; Ski Clb; L Var Cheerleading; L Var Gym; L Var Socr; L JV Sftbl; High Hon Roll; NHS; Ntl Merit Ltr; Grmn Hnr Soc 84-85; U Of VA; Pre-Med.

GARNIER, ROSEMARIE; West Hempstead HS; Island Pk, NY; (Y); 129/333; Drm & Bgl; JV Badmtn; JV Swmmng; Mc Gill U; Bus.

GARNOT, MARY; Beacon HS; Beacon, NY; (Y); Yrbk Stf; Hon Roll; Army Recrtng Awd For Achvmnt 84; Acctng.

GARNSEY, MONIQUE; Avon JR SR HS; Avon, NY; (Y); Library Aide; SADD; Varsity Clb; Pres Sec VICA; Church Choir; Variety Show; Var L Cheerleading; CC Of/Finger Lakes; Psych.

GARRA, JODY; Frontier Central HS; Lake View, NY; (Y); Church Yth Grp; 4-H; French Clb; Latin Clb; Pep Clb; Yrbk Stf; 4-H Awd; High Hon Roll; Hon Roll; NHS; Engrng.

GARRAN, CHRISTINA; Spackenkill HS; Poughkeepsie, NY; (Y); Leo Clb; SADD; Thesps; Concert Band; Yrbk Bus Mgr; Sec Stu Cncl; Fld Hcky; Mgr(s); Trk; Nwsppr Stf 84; Stg Crew Hse Mgr 85-86; Psych.

GARRETT, CHRISTOPHER; Linton HS; Schenectady, NY; (Y); 77/322; Intnl Clb; JA; Off Frsh Cls; Rep Soph Cls; Rcvd A Pssng Grade In Comp Sci At Coll Lvl; Bus Adm.

GARRETT, DERRICK; Archbishop Molloy HS; Queens Vlg, NY; (Y); 4/401; Computer Clb; Yrbk Stf; Im Bskstbl; Im Ftbl; Im Sftbl; Gov Hon Prg Awd; High Hon Roll; NHS; Service Clb; Ntl Merit SF; Ntnl Achvt Prgrm Outstndng Negro Stu & Colrd People Schlrshp 86; Yale U; Comp Sci.

GARRETT, EUFAULA K; The Harley Schl; Rochester, NY; (Y); Cmnty Wkr; Yrbk Stf; Rep Frsh Cls; Rep Soph Cls; Rep Jr Cls; Rep Stu Cncl; Var Socr; Var Trk; NY ST Sec 5 Chmp Trk 83, Socr 84-85; Cmmnded Stui Natl Merits Achvt Scholar Pgm 86; Arch Engrng.

GARRETT, JAMES; Lansingburgh HS; Troy, NY; (S); 8/185; Pres Sec Church Yth Grp; Band; Jazz Band; Mgr Stage Crew; Trk; NHS; Ntl Merit Ltr; All ST Symphnc Band 83; All Cntys Mdls; West Point; Engrng.

GARRETT, KELLY; Linton HS; Schenectady, NY; (Y); Key Clb; Yrbk Stf; Off Sr Cls; Var Capt Cheerleading; Var Socr; Capital Rgn All-Star Soccer 85; Saber Classic All-Star Soccer 85; Cortland ST; Phys Ed.

GARRETT, LIANA; Monticello HS; Wurtsboro, NY; (Y); Intnl Clb; Ski Clb; SADD; Band; Stage Crew; Yrbk Stf; Sec Stu Cncl; Var Crs Cntry; Var Tennis; Var Trk; Social Work.

GARRI, RICHARD; Scarsdale HS; Scarsdale, NY; (Y); Church Yth Grp; Spanish Clb; Trk; NHS.

GARRIDO, ANABELLA; Eastern District HS; Brooklyn, NY; (Y); Art Clb; Church Yth Grp; Debate Tm; FCA; Math Clb; Office Aide; Political Wkr; Teachers Aide; Church Choir; Wt Lftg; John Jay Coll; Law Enfrcmnt.

GARRIGAN, MICHELLE; Spring Valley SR HS; Monsey, NY; (Y); French Clb; Yrbk Stf; French Hon Soc; High Hon Roll; NY U Trstees Schlrshp 86-90; NY U; Pltcl Sci.

GARRISON, BLAKE; St Patricks HS; Palenville, NY; (Y); Ski Clb; Nwsp Stf; Yrbk Stf; Trs VP Stu Cncl; Var Capt Bsbl; L Socr; Central Hudson Vlly Leag SR Athlt Of Yr 85-86; MP Sccr 85; Slvr Mdlst NASTAK Skiing 84; Castleton ST Coll; TV Brdcst.

GARRISON, LAURIE; John Jay HS; Cross River, NY; (Y); Church Yth Grp; Ski Clb; Band; Chorus; Mrchg Band; Variety Show; Var L Sftbl; Var L Vllybl; Hon Roll; Prfct Atten Awd; Law.

GARRISON, NAOMI; Penn Yan Acad; Penn Yan, NY; (Y); 19/171; Trs Sec 4-H; GAA; Sec Service Clb; Nwsp Ed-Chief; Var L Bowling; Stat Mgr(s); JV Socr; 4-H Awd; NHS; Finger Lakes Lf Undrwrtrs Tngr Of Yr 86; Chase Lincoln 1st Bnk Bus Awd 86; Carol Chambers Mem Awd 86; St John Fisher; Accntng.

GARRITY, DAVID G; Corning-Painted Post West HS; Painted Post, NY; (Y); 18/252; Boy Scts; Key Clb; Varsity Clb; Rep Soph Cls; Rep Sr Cls; Rep Stu Cncl; JV Bsbl; JV Var Bsktbl; High Hon Roll; Var NHS; Egl Sct Awd 83; Elwd Smmrs Mem Awd 86; Mr Hstl Awd Bsktbll 86; Bucknell U; Bus.

GARTNER, MARIE; Rensselaer HS; Rensselaer, NY; (Y); Key Clb; SADD; Nwsp Ed-Chief; Yrbk Ed-Chief; Trs Sr Cls; Stu Cncl; Fld Hcky; Hon Roll; Hudson Valley; Tchg.

GARVELLI, KEVIN; Minisink Valley HS; Westtown, NY; (Y); Varsity Clb; Rep Jr Cls; Var Wrstlng; 3rd Sec 9 Wrstlg 86; 3rd Orang Cnty Wrstlg 86; 1st Mid Hudson Tourn Wrstlg 85.

GARVER, CARRIE; Lockport SR HS; Lockport, NY; (Y); Girl Scts; VICA; Nwsp Ed-Chief; Rep Sr Cls; Rep Stu Cncl; CC Awd; Cit Awd; Hon Roll; Prfct Atten Awd; Camera Clb; Occuptnl Advsry Cncl Outstndng Stu 85-86; Grl Sct Slvr Awd; Comp Pgmng.

GARVIN, DIANE; Frontier Central HS; Blasdell, NY; (S); 81/444; Girl Scts; Pep Clb; Spanish Clb; Chorus; Hon Roll; NHS; Ntl Merit Ltr; Creatv Wrtng.

GARZON, DAVID; Hauppauge HS; Commack, NY; (Y); 4-H; 4-H Awd; Hon Roll; Prfct Atten Awd; Boy Scts; Stonybrook; Pre-Med.

GASBARRINI, ANGELA RAE; Pioneer Central HS; Arcade, NY; (Y); Church Yth Grp; Latin Clb; Off VICA; Prfct Atten Awd; Air Force; Aireal Photo.

GASKIN, NICOLE; George Wingate HS; Brooklyn, NY; (Y); Church Yth Grp; Teachers Aide; Church Choir; Variety Show; Nwsp Ed-Chief; Nwsp Rptr; Nwsp Stf; Camera Clb; Hon Roll; Prfct Atten Awd; Crmnl Law.

GASNER, KELLY; Boradalbin Central Schl; Gloversville, NY; (Y); 2/74; Dance Clb; Yrbk Stf; Trs Jr Cls; Trs Sr Cls; Rep Stu Cncl; Cit Awd; DAR Awd; High Hon Roll; NHS; Sal; Fulton Montgomery CC.

GASSLER, JOHN P; Pelham Memorial HS; Pelham, NY; (Y); 7/153; Am Leg Boys St; Aud/Vis; Cmnty Wkr; Computer Clb; Capt JV Bsbl; Var Ftbl; Golf; High Hon Roll; NHS; Ntl Merit Ltr; SUNY Stony Brook; Crdlgst.

GATELEY, DEIRDRE; St Marys Girls HS; Plandome, NY; (Y); Cmnty Wkr; Ski Clb; Spanish Clb; Chorus; Stage Crew; Rep Frsh Cls; Rep Stu Cncl; L JV Crs Cntry; Trk; Hon Roll; Psych.

GATES, ANDREW; Byron Bergen Central Schl; Bergen, NY; (Y); 9/100; Math Tm; Model UN; Trs Stu Cncl; Socr; Swmmng; High Hon Roll; Hon Roll; Jr NHS; NHS; Ntl Merit Ltr; Pres Acdmc Fit Awds 86; Regents Schlrshp Awd 86; Byron Bergen Stu Cncl Schlrshp 86; U Of Buffalo; Ecnmcs.

GATES, BILL; Frankfort Schuyler HS; Frankfort, NY; (Y); Boy Scts; Spanish Clb; Chorus; Leather Stocking Swim Tm 84-87; CMNCTNS.

GATES, COLLIN; Honeoye Central HS; Honeoye, NY; (S); 1/67; French Clb; Stu Cncl; Bsbl; Socr; High Hon Roll; Secndry Staff Awd, Bd Ed Awd; Engrng.

GATES, DANIEL J; Eden SR HS; Eden, NY; (Y); 9/170; Aud/Vis; Varsity Clb; Var L Ftbl; Var L Trk; Var L Wrstlng; Hon Roll; NHS; NY ST Rgnt Schlrshp 86; Rochester Inst Tech Schlrshp 86; Rochester Inst Tech; Comp Tech.

GATES, DOUG; Spackenkill HS; Poughkeepsie, NY; (Y); 10/170; Yrbk Stf; VP Soph Cls; Pres Jr Cls; Pres Sr Cls; Stu Cncl; Capt Var Ftbl; Golf; Hon Roll; NHS; 5th Frnch Cntst 84; Rotry Intl Ldrshp Camp Rep 85; NY ST Stu Sent Rep 86; Bio Chem.

GATES, GARY; Carmel HS; Carmel, NY; (Y); 14/400; School Play; Var Capt Ice Hcky; Var Capt Socr; High Hon Roll; Hon Roll; NHS; St Schlr; Texaco Philanthropic Scholar 86; Regents Scholar 86; SUNY Buffalo; Chem Engr.

GATES, JOLENE; Binghamton HS; Binghamton, NY; (Y); Key Clb; Nwsp Rptr; Nwsp Stf; Var Trk; Broome CC; Phys Ther.

GATES, ROBERT C; Livonia SR HS; Lakeville, NY; (Y); 25/131; Am Leg Boys St; Spanish Clb; Yrbk Ed-Chief; Yrbk Phtg; Lit Mag; Hon Roll; Jr NHS; Ntl Merit Ltr; Sibleys Schlstc Art Shw Hnrbl Mention 84; Biology.

GATES, WYLEY; Chatham HS; E Chatham, NY; (Y); 2/150; Concert Band; Jazz Band; Mrchg Band; Orch; Nwsp Ed-Chief; VP Stu Cncl; High Hon Roll; NHS; Sal; Chem Engrng.

GATLIFF, JENNIFER; Hahn HS; Apo New York, NY; (Y); Church Yth Grp; Varsity Clb; Yrbk Phtg; Powder Puff Ftbl; Socr; Swmmng; Tennis; Trk; Jr NHS; Cmmnctns.

GATT, ANDREW; Coxsackie-Athens Central HS; W Coxsackie, NY; (Y); 2/118; Quiz Bowl; Pres Sr Cls; Rep Stu Cncl; Var L Bsktbl; Var L Socr; Capt Trk; Bausch & Lomb Sci Awd; Trs NHS; Sal; Mensa Intl 85; Colgate U; Physcs.

GATTO, DIANE M; ST Joseph Hill Acad; Brooklyn, NY; (Y); 34/107; Art Clb; FTA; Library Aide; Nwsp Rptr; Yrbk Ed-Chief; Var Capt Tennis; Hon Roll; Ntl Merit Ltr; NEDT Awd; St Schlr.

GATTO, LISA; Hampton Bays JR SR HS; Hampton Bays, NY; (Y); Church Yth Grp; Girl Scts; Science Clb; SADD; Stat Bsktbl; JV Var Fld Hcky; JV Var Sftbl; Hon Roll; Future Scientists Of Amer 85-86; Psych.

GAUDET, PETER W; Harrison HS; Harrison, NY; (Y); 23/227; Am Leg Boys St; Spanish Clb; Nwsp Rptr; Nwsp Sprt Ed; Off Soph Cls; Off Jr Cls; Var Bsbl; Var Capt Ftbl; NHS; JV Bsktbl; US Svc Acad; Bus.

GAUDETT, MICHELLE; Connetquot HS; Ronkonkoma, NY; (S); 6/700; Band; Color Guard; Drill Tm; Mrchg Band; Symp Band; Yrbk Stf; Pres Frsh Cls; JV Capt Cheerleading; Hon Roll; NHS; Geneseo Coll; Bioengrng.

GAUDINO, JOHANNA; Haverling Central HS; Bath, NY; (Y); Art Clb; French Clb; FBLA; Chorus; Color Guard; Yrbk Stf; Stu Cncl; Bsktbl; Vllybl; Hon Roll; Bus.

GAUGHAN, JOHN E; Norwich SR HS; Norwich, NY; (Y); 22/200; Am Leg Boys St; Church Yth Grp; Spanish Clb; SADD; Bsktbl; Score Keeper; Var Vllybl; Cit Awd; High Hon Roll; Pres Schlr; Shonosky Mem Awd Srv & Ctznshp 86; John Charles Mc Mullen Mem & Dr H Lynn Wilson Schlrshps 86; Colgate; Pre Med.

GAULIN, JENNIFER LYNN; St Marys Academy; S Glens Falls, NY; (S); 2/58; Sec Church Yth Grp; SADD; School Musical; Nwsp Ed-Chief; Yrbk Rptr; Capt Var Cheerleading; Drama Clb; Key Clb; Spanish Clb; Chorus; Cathlc Yth Org Sec 85-86; Altar Servr 83-86; St Bonaventure U; Chld Psych.

GAUS, RUSS; Schalment HS; Schenectady, NY; (Y); Band; Concert Band; Jazz Band; Mrchg Band; Symp Band; High Hon Roll; Hon Roll; NHS; Prfct Atten Awd; Cvl Engrng.

GAUTHIER, JEANNINE; Owen D Yount Central Schl; Mohawk, NY; (S); 1/21; Sec Trs French Clb; Sec Trs Intnl Clb; Chorus; Yrbk Ed-Chief; Pres Jr Cls; Var Capt Cheerleading; High Hon Roll; NHS; Prfct Atten Awd; Herkimer Cnty Dairy Maid 85-86; Lang Awd 82; Rochester Bus Inst; Sec.

GAUVIN, THOMAS; Columbia HS; Troy, NY; (Y); Pep Clb; Bsbl; Bsktbl; Ftbl; Lcrss; High Hon Roll; Hon Roll; Jr NHS; Avtn.

GAVALOS, JIMMY; H Frank Carey HS; Franklin Square, NY; (Y); 107/288; Art Clb; 4-H; Ftbl; High Hon Roll; Hon Roll; Stonybrook; Med.

GAVAZZI, JENNIFER E; Newfane SR HS; Lockport, NY; (S); 10/181; Church Yth Grp; Band; Church Choir; Concert Band; School Musical; High Hon Roll; Hon Roll; NHS; Houghton; Early Child Ed.

GAVEY, BARBARA C; Albertus Magnus HS; Spring Valley, NY; (Y); 4-H; Latin Clb; Math Tm; Hon Roll; NHS; Ntl Merit Ltr; Natl Mth Hnr Soc; Natl Sci Hnr Soc; Regents Scholar; NYU; Entrprnrshp.

GAVICH, GREG; Odessa-Montour HS; Montour Falls, NY; (Y); Am Leg Boys St; Capt Scholastic Bowl; Pres Varsity Clb; Pres Band; Jazz Band; Mrchg Band; Yrbk Rptr; Pres Frsh Cls; Trs Jr Cls; Trs Sr Cls; Brdcst Jrnlsm.

GAVIGAN, CATHERINE A; St Joseph Hill Acad; Staten Island, NY; (Y); 8/107; Pres Drama Clb; Pres Spanish Clb; Mgr Stage Crew; Variety Show; Yrbk Phtg; JV Capt Bsktbl; Coach Actv; VP NHS; Ntl Merit Ltr; Spanish NHS; U Of Scranton; Intl Affrs.

GAVIGAN, THOMAS; Hilton Central HS; Hilton, NY; (Y); 15/299; Computer Clb; SADD; Bowling; Ice Hcky; Var L Trk; NHS; Long Island U; Sec Ed.

GAVILANES, JESSICA; Queen Of The Rosary Acad; Farmingville, NY; (S); Hosp Aide; Rep Frsh Cls; Rep Soph Cls; Socr; Sftbl; Hon Roll; NHS; C W Post; Bus.

GAVIN, BILLY; Tottenville HS; Staten Isld, NY; (Y); Band; School Musical; Symp Band; Ftbl; Wt Lftg; High Hon Roll; Engrng.

GAVNEY, KATHLEEN A; Sachem HS North Campus; Holbrook, NY; (Y); 138/1578; Church Yth Grp; Cmnty Wkr; French Clb; Intnl Clb; Church Choir; Orch; Yrbk Rptr; NHS; Civic Clb; Computer Clb; Most Outstndng Orchstra 84-85; NY St Summer Schl Arts 85.

GAVRILUK, NICOLE; Ossining HS; Briarcliff Manor, NY; (Y); Cmnty Wkr; Sftbl; High Hon Roll; Hon Roll; Edwin G Michaelian Schlrshp Awd Westchstr CC 86; Bus Stdnt 86; Frnch 84-85; Westchester CC; Acctg.

GAVRIN, MEREDITH; Scarsdale HS; Scarsdale, NY; (Y); Teachers Aide; School Musical; Ed Lit Mag; High Hon Roll; NHS; Creat Wrtg.

GAWENUS, KEVIN; Horseheads HS; Horseheads, NY; (Y); Boy Scts; Chess Clb; German Clb; Ski Clb; Band; Jazz Band; Mrchg Band; Hon Roll; Engrng.

GAWINSKI, DIANE; West Seneca West SR HS; W Seneca, NY; (Y); 77/559; Q&S; Capt Color Guard; Drm & Bgl; Orch; School Musical; Nwsp Rptr; Hon Roll; JC Awd; Jr NHS; NHS; Buffalo ST Coll; Intr Dsgn.

GAWLAK, MARY; Frontier HS; Blasdell, NY; (S); 16/449; Church Yth Grp; SADD; Pres Stu Cncl; Capt Var Bsktbl; Var Sftbl; Capt Var Vllybl; Hon Roll; JP Sousa Awd; NHS; NEDT Awd; Phy Ed.

GAWRONSKI, KELLY; Mount Mercy South Park & BVTC; Buffalo, NY; (Y); Church Yth Grp; Cmnty Wkr; French Clb; Ski Clb; Rep Jr Cls; Hon Roll; Trvl.

GAYHART, BRIAN; South Park HS; Buffalo, NY; (Y); Boy Scts; Exploring; JA; ROTC; SADD; Drm Mjr(t); Bsbl; Ice Hcky; Wt Lftg; Prfct Atten Awd; Combat Pilot.

GAYLE, ERIC; Evander Childs HS; Bronx, NY; (S); 30/383; Boy Scts; Church Yth Grp; Math Tm; Rep Stu Cncl; Socr; Hon Roll; St Schlr; Math Awd Of Yr 85; Pride Of The Yanks 85; Biochem.

GAYLE, NADINE; Guander Childs HS; Bronx, NY; (Y); VP Leo Clb; Sftbl; Trk; Hon Roll; Prfct Atten Awd; Trk And Fld; Sftbl; Leo Clb Vice Pres; Hnr Rl; Perfct Attndc Awd; Med.

GAZZALEY, ADAM H; Bronx HS Of Science; Howard Beach, NY; (Y); Debate Tm; Key Clb; NFL; Teachers Aide; Y-Teens; Yrbk Stf; Lit Mag; Off Soph Cls; Off Jr Cls; Off Sr Cls; ST U Binghamton; Biochem.

GEARSBECK, JOANNE; Paul V Moore HS; Central Sq, NY; (Y); AFS; FBLA; Var Cheerleading; Trk; High Hon Roll; Hon Roll; Mst Imprvd Vars Ftbl Chrldr 85; Alfred ATC; Csmtc Chem.

GEARY, KATHERINE M; St Joseph Hill Acad; Brooklyn, NY; (Y); 12/106; French Clb; FTA; Hosp Aide; Intnl Clb; Math Tm; Ed Yrbk Stf; Var Tennis; VP French Hon Soc; Hon Roll; NHS; Fordham U Schlrshp 86; ST Josephs Coll Pres Schlrshp 86; Manhattan Coll Schlrshp 86; Fordham U; Bus Fin.

GEARY, ROY; York Central Schl; East York, NY; (Y); 3/88; Am Leg Boys St; Trs Pres Key Clb; Trs Pres Band; Chorus; Concert Band; Jazz Band; Mrchg Band; Pep Band; School Musical; School Play; Anthony Lariton Awd 85; St John Fisher Coll; Psych.

GEBHARD, MICHELLE; Roxbury Central HS; Grand Gorge, NY; (S); Church Yth Grp; Library Aide; Pep Clb; Spanish Clb; School Musical; School Play; High Hon Roll; NHS; Trs Jr Cls; Socr; 2nd Pl Amer Lgn Ortrcl 85; Elem Schl Tchr.

GEBHARDT, MARK; E J Wilson HS; Spencerport, NY; (Y); 54/331; Boy Scts; Church Yth Grp; JV Var Socr; JV Var Wrstlng; God Cntry Awd; Hon Roll; Soccr Tm-Europe Trip 85; Engrng.

GEDDE, JOHN; Bayport-Blue Point HS; Bayport, NY; (Y); Elec Engrng.

GEDDIS, JACQUELINE; Lansingburgh HS; Troy, NY; (Y); German Clb; Hosp Aide; Var Tennis; Hon Roll; Jr NHS; NHS; Nrsng.

GEDEON, WLADIMIR; Uniondale HS; Uniondale, NY; (Y); 39/410; Boy Scts; French Clb; PAVAS; Varsity Clb; VP Frsh Cls; JV Bsktbl; JV Var Socr; Stony Brook; Bio.

GEDZ, ROBERT; Valley Stream North HS; N Valley Stream, NY; (Y); Ski Clb; Var JV Bsbl; JV Ftbl; Hon Roll; Bus Hnr Soc 86; Mchncl Drwng 85; Bus.

GEE, EDMUND; Dundee Central HS; Dundee, NY; (Y); Band; Concert Band; Mrchg Band; Bsbl; Ftbl; Mgr(s); Hon Roll; Prfct Atten Awd; Hghst Ovrll Av For Wdwrkng 85-86; Indust Arts.

GEE, STACEY; Herricks SR HS; New Hyde Park, NY; (Y); SADD; Var Cheerleading; JV Sftbl; Hon Roll; Jr NHS; NHS; Bus.

GEELAN, SIOBHAN; St Agnes Academic HS; Whitestone, NY; (Y); Trk; Ed.

GEERTGENS, TIM; Unatego Central HS; Wells Bridge, NY; (Y); Church Yth Grp; Band; Concert Band; Jazz Band; Mrchg Band; Pep Band; Var Bowling; Golf; High Hon Roll; NHS; Cornell U; Vet Sci.

GEGA, KIM; Lindenhurst HS; Lindenhurst, NY; (Y); 48/580; Church Yth Grp; German Clb; Science Clb; Band; Concert Band; Mrchg Band; Hon Roll; NHS; Tuitn Schlrshp Adelphi 86; Adelphi U; Nrsg.

GEGA, KIRSTEN; Lindenhurst HS; Lindenhurst, NY; (Y); Camera Clb; VP Church Yth Grp; German Clb; Hosp Aide; Science Clb; Ski Clb; Orch; Yrbk Stf; Var L Tennis; High Hon Roll; Sci.

GEHAN, MARY; Our Lady Of Mercy HS; Rochester, NY; (Y); JA; Political Wkr; Chorus; Nwsp Rptr; Rep Stu Cncl; Socr; Hon Roll; Bus Mngmt.

GEHL, DAN; Albion HS; Albion, NY; (Y); 24/178; Boys Clb Am; Church Yth Grp; Nwsp Ed-Chief; JV Var Ftbl; Var Capt Trk; Prfct Atten Awd; Pres Schlr; Knights Of Columbus Schlrshp 86; Track MVP 85-86; BSA Yth Ldrshp Awd 85; Alfred ST Coll; Arch.

GEIL, PATRICIA; Our Lady Of Victory Acad; Mt Vernon, NY; (S); 5/157; Computer Clb; Science Clb; SADD; Nwsp Stf; Yrbk Stf; Lit Mag; Rep Stu Cncl; NHS; Ntl Merit Ltr; Spanish NHS; St Thomas Aquinas Chemstry 1st Pl Tm; Sci Awd; Eng Awd; Neurlgst.

GEISELMAN, ANN MARIE; Pine Bush HS; Middletown, NY; (Y); Art Clb; Band; Concert Band; Jazz Band; Mrchg Band; Var Diving; Var Swmmng; Im Wt Lftg; Hon Roll; 2nd Plc Sch Art Cntst; Flager Coll; Arts.

GEISER, JOSEPH; Seton Catholic Central HS; Endwell, NY; (Y); 8/162; Pres Church Yth Grp; Var L Ftbl; Var Trk; High Hon Roll; NHS; Ntl Merit Ltr; German Awd For Excllnc 86; NYS Rgnts Schlrshp 86; Math Achvt Awd 86; RIT.

GEITTER, GRETCHEN; Alden Central HS; Lancaster, NY; (Y); Church Yth Grp; Pres 4-H; Chrmn GAA; Science Clb; Spanish Clb; Chorus; Mrchg Band; School Musical; Yrbk Stf; Rep Jr Cls; 1st Frgn Lang Fair 83; 2 Yrd Acadmc Ltr 83-84; Var Band Ltr 84; Nrsg.

GELFAND, DOUGLAS M; Commack H S North; E Northport, NY; (Y); 135/390; Office Aide; Red Cross Aide; SADD; Band; Concert Band; Mrchg Band; Symp Band; AFS; NHS; U MD; Bus.

GELFUSO, THOMAS J; Frankfort Schuyler HS; Frankfort, NY; (S); Var Golf; Var Vllybl; Hon Roll; NHS; Mohawk Vly CC; Elec Engrng.

GELIN, JOAN K; Half Hollow Hills HS East; Melville, NY; (Y); 32/516; Chorus; Orch; School Musical; Variety Show; High Hon Roll; NHS; Ntl Merit Ltr; All ST String Orch Viola 85; A-Plus Awd For Lvl VI Piano Solo 85; Asst Prncpl 2nd Violin Sctn 85; Med.

GELINSON, ROBIN; Cobleskill HS; Cobleskill, NY; (Y); 12/116; Drama Clb; Girl Scts; Hosp Aide; Temple Yth Grp; School Play; Nwsp Stf; Yrbk Stf; Hon Roll; NHS; Var Tennis; Girl Scout Slvr Awd 86; Ithaca Coll; Lbrl Arts.

GELL, JULEE; Chenango Forks HS; Binghamton, NY; (Y); 9/181; School Musical; School Play; Rep Soph Cls; Pres Sr Cls; Rep Stu Cncl; Stat Bsbl; JV Cheerleading; Var Socr; High Hon Roll; NHS; Presdntl Acadmc Fitnss Awd 86; Teachrs Assn Schlrshp 86; SUNY Albany; Eng.

GELLER, AMY F; Yeshiva University HS For Girls; Flushing, NY; (Y); NY ST Rgnts Schlrshp 86; Brnrd Coll; Englsh.

GELLER, ANDREA; Oyster Bay HS; E Norwich, NY; (Y); 4/122; Spanish Clb; SADD; Temple Yth Grp; Chorus; School Musical; School Play; Nwsp Rptr; Yrbk Stf; Rep Frsh Cls; Rep Soph Cls; Regnts Schlrshp 86; Cornell Deans Schlr 86; Hnrs Pgm 86; U MI.

GELLER, BETH; Midwood HS At Brooklyn College; Brooklyn, NY; (Y); 11/667; French Clb; Office Aide; Nwsp Rptr; Nwsp Sprt Ed; Swmmng; Girls Swm Tm MVP 85; Arista Hnr Soc 85; Archon Svc Soc 86.

GELLER, ELISA; West Hempstead HS; W Hempstead, NY; (Y); 95/320; Art Clb; Key Clb; Political Wkr; Trs Spanish Clb; Lit Mag; Trs Soph Cls; Var Vllybl; Hon Roll; JV Bowling; JV Sftbl; Natl Art Hnr Socty 82-86; Bnai Brith Yth Orgnztn VP & Sec 82-86; Hofstra U; Pol Sci.

GELLER, PAUL S; Lawrence HS; Cedarhurst, NY; (Y); 133/414; Science Clb; Band; Mrchg Band; Nwsp Rptr; Yrbk Phtg; Yrbk Stf; Sftbl; High Hon Roll; NHS; Svc Hnr Soc Pres 85-86; NY ST Rgnts Schlrshp Wnnr 86; In Action Sntr Govt 83-86; U Of WI-MADISON; Bus.

GELLER, THOMAS M; Fox Lane HS; Mt Kisco, NY; (Y); 53/250; Acpl Chr; Band; Chorus; Jazz Band; Madrigals; Orch; School Play; Lit Mag; High Hon Roll; Hon Roll; Operetta Chorus Awd 85; Music.

GELLIS, GREGORY; Babylon JR SR HS; Babylon, NY; (Y); 7/175; Math Tm; Orch; JV Bsbl; JV Var Socr; JV Wrstlng; High Hon Roll; Hon Roll; NHS; Bus.

GELSEY, ALEX; Niagara Falls HS; Niagara Falls, NY; (Y); Ski Clb; NHS; Ntl Merit Ltr; Rochester Inst Tech; Micro-Elec.

GEMMA, TINA; Smithtown HS East; Nesconset, NY; (Y); Key Clb; Hon Roll; Itln Hnr Scty; Hofstra U; Accntnt.

GENDEBIEN, MICHELLE; Lisbon Central Schl; Ogdensburg, NY; (Y); 1/40; Am Leg Aux Girls St; Girl Scts; Pres Chorus; Pres Swing Chorus; Ed Yrbk Stf; VP Sr Cls; Cheerleading; Capt Socr; NHS; Val; St Alwrence Cnty Dairy Prncs 85; Area Al-ST Chorus NY 85; Colgate U; Psychtrst.

GENDUSO, GERALD J; Marcus Whitman HS; Rushville, NY; (Y); 6/130; Trs Model UN; Ski Clb; School Play; Trs Frsh Cls; Trs Sr Cls; JV Var Ftbl; Im Vllybl; High Hon Roll; NHS; NYS Regnts & Allegheny Schlrs-Cmptv Exam Schlrshps 86; Allegheny Coll PA; Litry.

GENN, VINCENT; Monsignor Farrell HS; Staten Island, NY; (Y); Church Yth Grp; Ski Clb; Spanish Clb; Yrbk Stf; Im Bsktbl; Im Ftbl; Manhattan Coll; Engrng.

GENNA, JOANNE; Canarsie HS; Brooklyn, NY; (S); 12/500; Church Yth Grp; Church Choir; Concert Band; Hon Roll; Prfct Atten Awd; Regents Scholar 85; Illustr.

GENNARELLI, HOLLY; Chenango Forks HS; Binghamton, NY; (S); 14/181; Church Yth Grp; Pres Band; Chorus; Mgr Mrchg Band; Hon Roll; NHS; Prfct Atten Awd; Church Choir; Concert Band; Pep Band; NY ST Regnts Schlrshp 86; ST Smnr Sch Arts, Schl Chrl Stds 85; Tlnt Christ Schlrshp 85; Army.

GENNATTASIO, ANNMARIE; Tottenville HS; Staten Island, NY; (Y); 24/871; Hosp Aide; Office Aide; SADD; Teachers Aide; Band; Concert Band; Flag Corp; Mrchg Band; Stage Crew; Symp Band; Amer Fed Tchrs 86; Regnts Schlrshp 86; Haney Medl Awd Met Museum Art 83; ST U Binghamton NY; Pre-Med.

GENNUSO, PAUL; Kenmore East HS; Tonwanda, NY; (Y); Varsity Clb; Var Bowling; Var Capt Tennis; Hon Roll; Vrsty Ltrs 3 Yrs Bwlng & Tnns 83-86.

GENO, JOHN; Saranac Central HS; Plattsburgh, NY; (S); 44/107; Am Leg Boys St; Church Yth Grp; VP Library Aide; Band; Church Choir; VP Concert Band; Jazz Band; Mrchg Band; Variety Show; Hon Roll; RPI; Arch.

GENOCESE, MARK A; Monsignor Farrell HS; Staten Island, NY; (Y); 144/289; JV Var Ice Hcky; ST U Of NY-ALBANY; Bus Mgmt.

GENOVA, ANDREW; Bishop Kearney HS; Rochester, NY; (Y); Aud/Vis; Boy Scts; Chess Clb; Computer Clb; Band; Concert Band; Jazz Band; Mrchg Band; School Musical; Im Bowling; St John Fisher Coll.

GENOVA, CAMELIA; John Dewey HS; Brooklyn, NY; (Y); Capt Art Clb; Chorus; School Musical; School Play; Yrbk Phtg; Yrbk Stf; Gym; Tennis; Vllybl; Wt Lftg.

GENOVA, KIMBERLY; Southampton HS; Southampton, NY; (Y); 14/115; GAA; Spanish Clb; Nwsp Rptr; Yrbk Stf; Rep Stu Cncl; Capt Cheerleading; Fld Hcky; Trk; High Hon Roll; Hon Roll; All Trnmnt Hcky Awd 85; Fairfield U; Jrnlsm.

GENOVA, MATTHEW; Archbishop Molloy HS; Middle Village, NY; (Y); SADD; Crs Cntry; Trk; St Schlr; Ntl Grnd Cncl Clmbn Schlrshp Assn 86; NY ST Rgnt Schlrsh& 86; ST U NY Buffalo; Med.

GENOVESE, PHIL; Voorhesville JR SR HS; Slingerlands, NY; (Y); 4-H; Red Cross Aide; Ski Clb; Im Bsktbl; Score Keeper; Var L Trk; Var L Vllybl; 4-H Awd; Hon Roll; Engrng.

GENS, JOHN SCOTT; Liverpool HS; Liverpool, NY; (Y); 1/884; Boy Scts; Math Tm; Speech Tm; Mrchg Band; Yrbk Stf; Elks Awd; High Hon Roll; Jr NHS; NHS; Church Yth Grp; Cornell Bk Awd 86; Schl Bio Awd 85; Natl Soc Daughters Fndrs & Patriots Amer Awd Social Stds 86; Bio Sci.

GENSLER, BILLIE; Oyster Bay HS; Oyster Bay, NY; (Y); 3/123; Pres Model UN; SADD; Ed Yrbk Stf; Var Badmtn; High Hon Roll; Lion Awd; NHS; Ntl Merit Ltr; Trs AFS; Spanish Clb; Mar Dms Dstngshd Stu Hlth Carr Awd 86; Hon Hmnts Pgm U CA Irvine 86-87; U Of CA Irvine; Bio.

GENSLER, CYNTHIA M; Lyons Central HS; Lyons, NY; (Y); 2/100; Church Yth Grp; Trs Latin Clb; Library Aide; Ski Clb; Stu Cncl; Bowling; Hon Roll; NHS; Prfct Atten Awd; Regents Schlrshp 86; Alabany Clg; Phrmcy.

GENSON, RAYMOND JOHN; Mc Graw HS; Cortland, NY; (Y); Var Socr; Hon Roll; Bus Educ Frm Crtlnd Svngs Bnk 86; Elec.

GENTILE, JOHN; Solvay HS; Syracuse, NY; (Y); Pres Quiz Bowl; Yrbk Stf; Sec Frsh Cls; Sec Soph Cls; Rep Jr Cls; Im Bsbl; Im Bsktbl; Im Wt Lftg; Hon Roll; NHS.

GENTILE JR, JOSEPH B; Oswego HS; Oswego, NY; (Y); 44/400; Am Leg Boys St; VP SADD; Variety Show; Nwsp Sprt Ed; JV Bsbl; Coach Actv; Var Capt Ftbl; Var Trk; Wt Lftg; High Hon Roll; Buccaneer Booster Scholar 86; Rita Gimmie Scholar 86; Ernest R Behrend Scholar Alt 86; Canisius Coll; Phys Ed.

GENTILE, WENDY; Roosevelt HS; Yonkers, NY; (Y); 70/245; Concert Band; Mrchg Band; Nwsp Phtg; Yrbk Stf; Lit Mag; Var Sftbl; Hon Roll; Band; NY St Regnts Diploma 86; Pace U; Theatre.

GENTIN, ANDREW N; J L M Great Neck North SR HS; Great Neck, NY; (Y); 17/236; Cmnty Wkr; Hosp Aide; Political Wkr; Pres Spanish Clb; Nwsp Rptr; Rep Stu Cncl; Var Capt Tennis; Ntl Merit SF; E Ten Assn Rnked 24th 18 & Undr 85; Stu Rep H S Goals Comm 85-86.

GENUNG, JEFFREY; Oxford Acad; Oxford, NY; (Y); 5/86; Am Leg Boys St; Drama Clb; French Clb; Mrchg Band; Nwsp Rptr; High Hon Roll; NHS; Amer Legn Ortrcl Cntst 1st Pl 85; SUNY Oswego; Cmmnctns.

GEOBEL, STEPHANIE; Christopher Columbus HS; Bronx, NY; (Y); 46/600; Hon Roll; Jr NHS; NHS; Regnts Schlrshp 86; Hunter Merit Schlrshp 86; Hunter Coll; Psychlgst.

GEORGE, ANN MARGARET; George Wingate HS; Brooklyn, NY; (Y); Church Yth Grp; Cmnty Wkr; JV Crs Cntry; Tennis; Span 4 Hnr Cert 85; Merit Awd Fashion Technlgy 86; Cert Grad Coll Bound Prog 86; Foreign Lang.

GEORGE, AUDREY M; John Dewey HS; Brooklyn, NY; (Y); Art Clb; Church Yth Grp; Debate Tm; Variety Show; Pres Sr Cls; Rep Stu Cncl; CC Awd; Cit Awd; God Cntry Awd; High Hon Roll; Miami Dade CC; Psych.

GEORGE, CHERYLANN; Dominican Commercial HS; Middle Vlge, NY; (Y); Office Aide; Pep Clb; Teachers Aide; Sftbl; St Johns U; Psych.

GEORGE, CHRISTINA; Notre Dame HS; Batavia, NY; (S); Drama Clb; Ski Clb; School Musical; JV Var Cheerleading; High Hon Roll; NHS; Englsh Awd 84-85; Frnch Awd 85; Stu Wrkng Potntl Awd 84.

GEORGE, DEREK; Catherdral Prep; Bronx, NY; (Y); Library Aide; NFL; Speech Tm; Teachers Aide; Nwsp Rptr; Trs Sr Cls; Rep Stu Cncl; Im Bowling; Im Fld Hcky; Im Vllybl; Mngmnt Inf Systms.

GEORGE, DEVON; Evander Childs HS; New York, NY; (S); 22/383; Math Tm; Office Aide; Teachers Aide; Coach Actv; Vllybl; High Hon Roll; VP Hon Roll.

GEORGE, JENNIFER M; Ogdensburg Free Acad; Ogdensburg, NY; (Y); 2/186; Church Yth Grp; French Clb; Nwsp Ed-Chief; Yrbk Stf; Rep Stu Cncl; CC Awd; High Hon Roll; NHS; Sal; Watertown Daily Times Schl Press Inst Schlrshp 85; Skidmore Coll; Art.

GEORGE, MICHAEL; Williamsville South HS; Williamsville, NY; (Y); Boy Scts; Var L Trk; Hon Roll; NHS; Sci.

GEORGE, MICHELLE; Solvay HS; Solvay, NY; (Y); Pres Art Clb; Church Yth Grp; Spanish Clb; Chorus; Concert Band; School Musical; Yrbk Stf; Im Mgr(s); Im Score Keeper; JV Sftbl; Art Ed.

GEORGE, SHANNON; Mt St Mary Acad; N Tonawanda, NY; (Y); Model UN; Chorus; School Musical; Swing Chorus; Rptr Nwsp Rptr; High Hon Roll; Hon Roll; Jr NHS; NEDT Awd; Cmmnctns.

GEORGE, SUSAN; Hillcrest HS; Jamaica, NY; (Y); Church Yth Grp; Girl Scts; Church Choir; School Play; Lit Mag; Queens Coll; Med.

GEORGE, TERESSA; Nazareth Acad; Rochester, NY; (Y); 22/154; Church Yth Grp; Dance Clb; French Clb; Hosp Aide; Radio Clb; Chorus; School Play; Var Crs Cntry; Var Vllybl; Hon Roll; Urbn Lg Acad Excllnc Awd 86; Bio.

GEORGIANIS, MARIA V; St Francis Prep; Flushing, NY; (S); 2/653; Library Aide; Science Clb; Chorus; Im Vllybl; Hon Roll; Jr NHS; NHS; Ntl Merit Ltr; Eng.

GEORGIANO, JEANMARIE; Hicksville HS; Hicksville, NY; (Y); Church Yth Grp; Thesps; Chorus; School Musical; High Hon Roll; Jr NHS; NHS; Drama Clb; Stage Crew; Variety Show; Italian Hnr Soc 86; Intl Bus.

GEORGIS, VENICE; Garden Schl; Woodside, NY; (S); 10/32; Nwsp Sprt Ed; Trs Stu Cncl; Var Capt Bsktbl; Cheerleading; Var Sftbl; Baruch Coll; Accntng.

GEPPI, SARAH; Keveny Memorial Acad; Watervliet, NY; (S); 7/40; Q&S; Spanish Clb; Ed Yrbk Stf; JV Bsktbl; Var Sftbl; JV Var Vllybl; Hon Roll; Niagara; Socl Wrk.

GERACE, BARBARA J; Our Lady Of Mercy HS; Fairport, NY; (Y); 10/172; French Clb; VP Model UN; Science Clb; Ski Clb; Ed Yrbk Ed-Chief; Yrbk Sprt Ed; Stu Cncl; Var Capt Trk; High Hon Roll; Hon Roll; NY St Rgnst Schlrshp; French 2-3 Awds; High Jump Schl Rec; Boston Coll; Pol Sci.

GERACE, DANA M; New Hartford SR HS; New Hartford, NY; (Y); Intnl Clb; Spanish Clb; Concert Band; Symp Band; Score Keeper; Timer; Hon Roll; Engr.

GERACE, JOSEPH S; Frontier Central HS; Raleigh, NC; (Y); 47/445; Art Clb; VP Aud/Vis; Yrbk Phtg; Off Frsh Cls; Off Soph Cls; Off Jr Cls; High Hon Roll; Hon Roll; Ntl Merit Ltr; Franklin Pierce Schlrshp 86; Buffalo ST Coll Internshp 85; U NC-RALEIGH; Microbio.

GERACE III, THOMAS P; Lake Shore Central HS; Irving, NY; (Y); 39/284; Boy Scts; Drama Clb; School Musical; School Play; Stage Crew; Nwsp Stf; Yrbk Stf; Hon Roll; Jr NHS; NHS; NYS Regents Schlrshp 86; ST U Fredonia; Grphc Dsgnr.

GERALD, JEFFREY FITZ; Scotia Glenville SR HS; Scotia, NY; (Y); Spanish Clb; Band; Concert Band; Mrchg Band; Yrbk Stf; High Hon Roll; Aerontcl Engrng.

GERARD, BRAD; Mc Quaid Jesuit HS; Rochester, NY; (Y); 26/150; Letterman Clb; Model UN; Nwsp Stf; Yrbk Stf; Im Bsktbl; Im Ftbl; Var L Ice Hcky; Socr; Hon Roll; Aud/Vis; Natl Champ USET Driving Single Pony 81-83; MVP Hockey 84; 1st Tm All Star W Genesee Trnmt 85; Mechanical Engineering.

GERARDI, SUSAN; Lindenhurst SR HS; Lindenhurst, NY; (Y); Service Clb; School Musical; School Play; Var Socr; Var Trk; High Hon Roll; Hon Roll; NHS; Mst Imprvd Plyr In Soccer 84; U NC Chpl Hl; Crtv Wrtng.

GERASIMCZYK, LEE; Richmond Hill HS; Richmond Hill, NY; (Y); 68/320; Church Yth Grp; Drama Clb; Radio Clb; School Musical; School Play; Nwsp Rptr; Yrbk Rptr; Crs Cntry; Swmmng; Prfct Atten Awd; Spryth 84-85; Prfct Attnd 83-86; Engl Hon 84-86; St Johns U; Chld Pysch.

GERAZOUNIS, PETER; Holy Cross HS; New Hyde Park, NY; (Y); 4/300; Chess Clb; Library Aide; Var L Trk; High Hon Roll; NHS; Ntl Merit Ltr; Cooper Union; Mech Engrng.

GERBER, NICOLE; Grand Island HS; Grand Island, NY; (Y); 4-H; Band; Concert Band; Var JV Bsktbl; Var JV Tennis; High Hon Roll; Hon Roll; NHS; Cert Acad Excllnce & Acad Ltr Awd 86; Daemen Coll; Vet.

GERBER, ROBERT; Shenendehowa HS; Clifton Park, NY; (Y); Computer Clb; Science Clb; Nwsp Rptr; Nwsp Stf; Yrbk Phtg; Yrbk Stf; Var Tennis; Hon Roll; Senatrs Awd 86; Rochester Inst Of Tech; Comp.

GERBER, SUSAN E; Midwood HS At Brooklyn Coll; Brooklyn, NY; (Y); 4/589; Debate Tm; Capt Math Tm; Orch; School Musical; Nwsp Stf; Rptr Lit Mag; Var Swmmng; Gov Hon Prg Awd; Ntl Merit SF; Rnsslr Plytchnc Inst Math & Sci Mdl 85.

GERDINE, LAUREL L; Emma Willard Schl; Troy, NY; (Y); French Clb; Intnl Clb; Library Aide; Pep Clb; SADD; School Play; Stage Crew; Nwsp Rptr; Yrbk Rptr; Ntl Merit Ltr; Econ.

GEREMITA, LISA; Riverhead HS; Wading River, NY; (Y); Spanish Clb; Chorus; Prfct Atten Awd; Intr Dsgn.

GEREMSKI, ANDY; West Genesee SR HS; Camillus, NY; (Y); Yrbk Phtg; Off Jr Cls; Ice Hcky; Var Socr; High Hon Roll; Hon Roll; NHS; JR Sympsm Sci Albany NY 86; Bio Chmstry.

GERENA, CHARLES; Abraham Lincoln HS; Brooklyn, NY; (Y); 30/431; NY Regents Schlrshp 86; NY Inst Tech; Comp Sci.

GERENCSER, MARY; Nyack HS; Valley Cottage, NY; (Y); 49/250; Concert Band; Variety Show; Var Co-Capt Fld Hcky; Var Co-Capt Sftbl; Hon Roll; All Sec Hnr Mntn Sftbl; Fordham; Bus.

GERGAL, MARY ANN; Wilson Central HS; Ransomville, NY; (Y); Debate Tm; 4-H; SADD; Chorus; Nwsp Rptr; Nwsp Stf; Hon Roll; Niagara U; Travel.

GERGEN, JENNIFER A; Amityville Memorial HS; Massapequa, NY; (Y); 1/210; Drama Clb; Band; Orch; Pres Stu Cncl; Var Tennis; DAR Awd; NHS; Ntl Merit Ltr; Val; Georgetown U; Intl Rel.

GERING, BRETT M; Friends Acad; Oyster Bay, NY; (Y); Pres SADD; School Musical; Nwsp Rptr; Nwsp Stf; Yrbk Phtg; Rep Frsh Cls; Trs Soph Cls; Rep Jr Cls; Stu Cncl; Bsktbl; Rgnts Schlrshp 86; Trinity Coll.

GERMACK, CHRISTINA M; Keshequa Central HS; Nunda, NY; (Y); 10/70; AFS; Drama Clb; Sec Varsity Clb; Band; Chorus; Concert Band; Mrchg Band; School Play; Var Capt Cheerleading; JV Socr; Hnr Rl; SUNY Clg Fredonia; Bus Admn.

GERMAIN, VICKI; Schuylerville Central HS; Greenwich, NY; (Y); Cmnty Wkr; 4-H; French Clb; SADD; Band; Yrbk Stf; JV Var Cheerleading; Hon Roll; Jr NHS; Mgr(s); Natl Frnch Cont Awd 84; Math.

GERMAN, LISA; Windham-Ashland-Jewett Central HS; Prattsville, NY; (S); 7/41; Teachers Aide; Band; Yrbk Ed-Chief; Yrbk Stf; Trs Jr Cls; Trs Sr Cls; Hon Roll; Sec NHS; Prfct Atten Awd; DAR Awd; Certified Pblc Accntnt.

GERMAN, TOM; Cairo-Durham HS; Durham, NY; (Y); Boy Scts; Concert Band; Jazz Band; Pep Band; School Musical; Yrbk Stf; Var Crs Cntry; Var Trk; High Hon Roll; NHS; Marist Coll; Comp Sci.

GERMANI, ANTHONY; Mahopac HS; Mahopac, NY; (Y); 71/409; AFS; Aud/Vis; Science Clb; Nwsp Stf; Yrbk Stf; Lit Mag; Var Vllybl; Hon Roll; NHS; Bus.

GERMANO, FRANCINE; Watervliet HS; Watervliet, NY; (Y); SUNY Albany; Bus Adm.

GERMANO, MICHELE; Bishop Kearney HS; Rochester, NY; (Y); 17/140; Church Yth Grp; VP JA; Varsity Clb; Nwsp Stf; Yrbk Rptr; Mgr Bsktbl; Bowling; JV Var Mgr(s); Mgr Sftbl; Hon Roll; Rochester Yth Am Bowling Alliance Scholar 86; Outstndng Ath Awd 86; Schlr Ath Awd 86; St John Fisher Coll.

GERO, DEBBIE; Commack HS North; Commack, NY; (Y); 3/390; Spanish Clb; Mrchg Band; Symp Band; Nwsp Rptr; Yrbk Stf; Off Soph Cls; Off Church Yth Grp2; Off Sr Cls; Chrmn Stu Cncl; High Hon Roll; Mst Outstndng Sci Stu Awd Wnnr 84; Rgnts Schlrshp Wnnr 86; Pres Acad & Ftns Awd Wnnr 86; Emory U; Bus Admin.

GEROULD, PAMELA; Naples Central Schl; Naples, NY; (Y); 26/63; Girl Scts; Office Aide; Chorus; Hon Roll; Chld Care.

GERRINGER, KELLY; Chenango Forks HS; Chenango Forks, NY; (Y); 6/174; Band; Concert Band; Mrchg Band; High Hon Roll; NHS; NY Stu Senate Forum 86; NY Rgnts Schlrshp 86; Engnrng.

GERRISH, AMY; Charles O Dickerson HS; Jacksonville, NY; (Y); Church Yth Grp; French Clb; Varsity Clb; Yrbk Stf; Var Bsktbl; Var Socr; Var Trk; Phys Thrpy.

GERSON, MARIBEL; Walton HS; Bronx, NY; (Y); Dance Clb; GAA; Library Aide; Office Aide; Spanish Clb; Teachers Aide; Chorus; Color Guard; Lit Mag; Rep Jr Cls; Bus Mgmt.

GERST, GREG; Skaneateles HS; Skaneateles, NY; (S); Pres Jr Cls; JV Golf; Var Ice Hcky; Lcrss; Var Socr; NHS; Empire ST Hockey Tm 86; 2nd Tm All Sectn Hockey 86; MVP Soccr Def 85; Elec Engrng.

GERUASI, SALVATORE; North Babylon HS; N Babylon, NY; (Y); Wrstlng; Stoneybrook; Lawyr.

GERVAIS, LEE ANN; Lansingburgh HS; Troy, NY; (Y); Church Yth Grp; JV Sftbl; High Hon Roll; Hon Roll.

GERWIG, R S; Williamsville North HS; Kenmore, NY; (Y); 36/301; Cmnty Wkr; Math Clb; Ski Clb; Band; Concert Band; Var Crs Cntry; JV Socr; Capt Trk; Hon Roll; NHS; Regents Schlrshp 86; ROTC Schlrshp 86; Lehigh U; Acoustical Sci.

GERWIN, ELIZABETH; Port Richmond HS; Staten Island, NY; (Y); Drama Clb; Math Tm; Spanish Clb; School Play; Variety Show; Lit Mag; High Hon Roll; NHS; Spanish NHS; Dietcn.

GESCHWENDER, PAULA ANN; Grand Island HS; Buffalo, NY; (Y); Yrbk Stf; Swmmng; High Hon Roll; Ntl Merit SF; Pres Schlr; St Johns Fisher Coll; Pre-Law.

GESSNER, CLAIRE; Sacred Heart Acad; Rockville Centre, NY; (Y); Cmnty Wkr; Drama Clb; Office Aide; Chorus; School Musical; School Play; Im Tennis; Lawyer.

GETTMAN, MARY; Faith Heritage HS; Syracuse, NY; (Y); Church Yth Grp; Drama Clb; Ski Clb; Spanish Clb; Band; Chorus; Church Choir; VP Jr Cls; Socr; High Hon Roll; Citznshp Awd 85-86; Natl Hnr Soc 84-86; Soc Distingshed Amer HS Stu 84-86; Nyack.

GETZLER, JOSHUA G; Horace Mann Schl; New York, NY; (Y); Drama Clb; Political Wkr; Temple Yth Grp; Band; School Play; Nwsp Rptr; Pres Frsh Cls; Rep Soph Cls; Rep Jr Cls; Rep Sr Cls; Jrnlst.

GEWIRTZ, JEFFREY B; Baldwin SR HS; Baldwin Harbor, NY; (Y); 60/500; Boy Scts; Key Clb; Temple Yth Grp; Varsity Clb; VP Frsh Cls; Bsktbl; Capt Var Tennis; Hon Roll; NHS; Ntl Merit Ltr; Eastern Tennis Assn 85-86; Eastern Tennis Assn Doubles 84-85; Eastern Tennis Assn Dist 6 85-86; Tufts U; Dentistry.

GHARTEY, MBIABAH LISA; Mount Vernon HS; Mt Vernon, NY; (Y); Pres Church Yth Grp; Hosp Aide; Key Clb; Sec Trs Latin Clb; L Orch; Rep Stu Cncl; Var Tennis; Hon Roll; Sec NHS; Natl Cncl Of Negro Wmn For Perfrmng Arts Awd 86; Law.

GHENT, GINA; St Joseph By-The-Sea HS; Staten Island, NY; (Y); 10/248; Aud/Vis; Varsity Clb; Nwsp Stf; Pres Sr Cls; Var Capt Bsktbl; Var Capt Sftbl; Tennis; Hon Roll; VP NHS; NEDT Awd; Jrnlsm Awd-Staten Isl Advnc 86; Bsktbl Schlrshps-Concrdia Coll & St Frncs Coll 86; Concordia Coll; Pltcl Sci.

GHERSI, LINDA; North Shore HS; Glen Head, NY; (Y); 21/210; French Clb; Model UN; Varsity Clb; Yrbk Stf; Capt Cheerleading; Var Pom Pon; Var Trk; Pres Schlr; Rotary Awd; Sci Schlr Mnth 85; Typng Awd 84; SUNY Binghamton; Bus.

GHEZZI, CHRISTOPHER; Cicero North Syracuse HS; Clay, NY; (S); 2/623; Computer Clb; Math Clb; Spanish Clb; Stu Cncl; Hon Roll; VP Jr NHS; Mth Lg Awd 85; Hnr Roll Ltr 85; Trnd Driver & Trffc Ed 85; Genetics.

GHEZZI, LEA; John Jay SR HS; Hopewell Jct, NY; (Y); Art Clb; Ski Clb; Stage Crew; Yrbk Phtg; Yrbk Stf; Stu Cncl; Gym; High Hon Roll; Jr NHS; NHS; Nutritn.

GHINGO, LAUREN E; St Francis Prep; Flushing, NY; (S); 245/653; Drama Clb; Ski Clb; SADD; Band; Ftbl; Tennis; Cit Awd; Ntl Merit Ltr; Hmntrn Srv Awd For Crbl Plsy 85; Retreat Ldr 84-85; Mrktng & Sls.

GHOLSON, RONALD L; Bridgehampton HS; Bridgehampton, NY; (Y); 3/12; French Clb; Band; Chorus; Church Choir; Mrchg Band; Sec Frsh Cls; Sec Soph Cls; Off Jr Cls; Var Bsktbl; Var Crs Cntry; Bus Mgnt.

GHOORAH, CHARLES V; Orchard Park HS; Orchard Park, NY; (Y); 20/421; VP AFS; Am Leg Boys St; Boy Scts; Pres Intnl Clb; Trs Science Clb; Orch; Stage Crew; Yrbk Phtg; Trs Soph Cls; Pres Jr Cls; Pre Med.

GIACINTO, MARIA VICTORIA; Cardinal Spellman HS; Bronx, NY; (Y); 60/506; Art Clb; Church Yth Grp; Cmnty Wkr; Library Aide; Pep Clb; Pep Band; Stage Crew; Nwsp Stf; Hon Roll; NHS; Manhattan Coll; Law.

GIAGRANDE, JOSEPH T; St Anthonys HS; Commack, NY; (Y); Computer Clb; Ski Clb; SADD; Concert Band; Orch; Pep Band; Capt Trk; High Hon Roll; NHS; Sec Spanish NHS; Trck-Al Leag, Al Rgn, Al Cnty, Al ST 85-86; U Of PA; Engrng.

GIAMBRA, RENEE; Niagara Wheatfield HS; North Tonawanda, NY; (Y); 22/190; Church Yth Grp; Hosp Aide; VICA; Chorus; School Play; High Hon Roll; Hon Roll; NHS; Ntl Merit SF; Prfct Atten Awd; 1st Plc Nrsng Comptn Niagara Orleans Boces 85; 2nd Plc All ST Nrsng Comptn 86; Distgshd Stu Schlrshp; Niagara Cnty CC; RN.

GIAMBRA, TRISH; Franklin Central Schl; Oneonta, NY; (Y); Trs FHA; Ski Clb; Varsity Clb; Rep Frsh Cls; Rep Soph Cls; Rep Jr Cls; Var Capt Cheerleading; Socr; Sftbl; Bio.

GIAMBRONE, MICHAEL A; Pine Valley Central HS; Leon, NY; (Y); 13/70; Am Leg Boys St; FHA; Band; Concert Band; Var Capt Ftbl; Var Capt Wrstlng; Rgnts Schlrp 86; SUNY Fredonia; Engrg.

GIAMBRUNO, AMY; Plattsburgh HS; Plattsburgh, NY; (Y); French Clb; Ski Clb; Sec Jr Cls; Cheerleading; Swmmng; French Hon Soc; High Hon Roll; NHS; Acad Awd Socl Stds 85; Acad Awd Frgn Lang 86; Acad Awd Hgh Avg-Acad Hnrs 86; Plattsburgh ST U Coll.

GIANNAKIS, ANNA; Archbishop Jakovos HS; Bayside, NY; (S); 1/16; Computer Clb; Math Clb; Teachers Aide; Yrbk Stf; Capt Vllybl; High Hon Roll; Art Clb; Cmnty Wkr; English Clb; French Clb; Qns Coll Pres Awds 82-85; MA Inst Tech; Comp Sci.

GIANNELLI, LAURA; Smithtown High Schl East; Smithtown, NY; (S); VP DECA; SADD; Stu Cncl; Var Badmtn; JV Fld Hcky; High Hon Roll; Hon Roll; Prtcptn Anl Rgnl Cntst DECNY Sflk CC 86; Pltcl Sci.

GIANNETTINO, FRANK; Somer HS; Yorktown Hgts, NY; (Y); JV Bsbl; Var Ftbl; Bus Cmptrs.

GIANNI, CARLA; Bethpage HS; Bethpage, NY; (Y); Drama Clb; Band; Concert Band; Jazz Band; Mrchg Band; School Musical; School Play; Sec Jr Cls; Hon Roll; Ntl Merit Ltr; Hnr Soc; Nrsng.

GIANNITSAS, NICK; Lindenhurst HS; Lindenhurst, NY; (Y); Trs Pres Church Yth Grp; Dance Clb; Im JV Ftbl; JV Var Lcrss; JV Var Wt Lftg; 1st Pl Sci Fair 83; Outstndng Dfnsv Plyr Ftbl 83; Hofstra U; Dntstry.

GIANNOLA, JOSEPH; Bishop Ford CC HS; Brooklyn, NY; (Y); Dance Clb; Hon Roll; Pre-Law.

GIANNOTTI, MARYANN; Smithtown HS East; Nesconset, NY; (Y); Church Yth Grp; Trs GAA; Key Clb; Office Aide; Var L Fld Hcky; Var L Trk; Hon Roll; NHS; Italian Hnr Soc 84; Lifegrd Certfctn 84; Elmntry Ed.

GIARAFFA, DANA; Kenmore East SR HS; Kenmore, NY; (Y); Nwsp Rptr; Nwsp Stf; Yrbk Ed-Chief; Yrbk Phtg; Yrbk Rptr; Yrbk Stf; Sftbl; Trk; High Hon Roll; Hon Roll; Canisius Coll; Acctg.

GIARDIELLO, GREGORY J; St Peters Boys HS; Staten Island, NY; (Y); 3/155; NFL; Chorus; School Musical; School Play; Variety Show; Nwsp Rptr; Yrbk Stf; Lit Mag; Stu Cncl; High Hon Roll; Pres Ntl Hnr Soc 85-86; St Johns; Accntng.

GIARDINA, CARA; Eastchester HS; Eastchester, NY; (Y); Key Clb; Latin Clb; Leo Clb; Chorus; Rep Jr Cls; Finance.

GIARDINA, ELIZABET K; Sacred Heart Acad; Valley Stream, NY; (Y); Drama Clb; FTA; Office Aide; Pep Clb; SADD; Chorus; Hon Roll; NHS; NY St Regents Nrsng Schlrshp 86; Fordham U; Englsh.

GIARDINA, ESTHER MARIE; Bishop Ford C C HS; Brooklyn, NY; (Y); Dance Clb; Science Clb; High Hon Roll; Hon Roll; NYC Regents Nrsng Schlrshp; Brooklyn Coll; Bio.

GIARDINO, LUCY; Rome Free Acad; Rome, NY; (Y); 27/500; Intnl Clb; Band; JV Tennis; NHS; Prfct Atten Awd; Potsdam ST Coll; Comp Sci.

GIARRATANO, LINDA; Tappan Zee HS; Tappan, NY; (Y); 19/245; French Clb; VP SADD; Nwsp Rptr; Ed Nwsp Stf; Yrbk Bus Mgr; Yrbk Ed-Chief; Rep Stu Cncl; Sec NHS; NY ST Regnts Schlrshp 86; Ioha Coll Lang Cntst 83 & 86; Fairfield U; Psych.

GIARRATANO, LOUISA; Susan E Wagner HS; Staten Island, NY; (Y); 14/466; Church Yth Grp; Teachers Aide; Chorus; NHS; Teen Tlnt Comp Kybrd Div 85; Nyack Coll.

GIBBONS, BARBARA; Farmingdale HS; Farmingdale, NY; (Y); 134/600; Office Aide; Yrbk Stf; Lit Mag; Var Gym; Hon Roll; Mid Island Hosp Mem Schlrshp 86; Rgnts Nrsng Schlrshp 86; Keywanettes Schlrshp & March Of Dimes Awd 86; Nassau CC; Nrsng.

GIBBONS, DANIEL; Newfield HS; Centereach, NY; (Y); DECA; Hon Roll; Prfct Atten Awd; Spanish NHS; Spn Hnr Soc; Ger Hnr Soc; ST Fnls DECA Clb 2 Yrs; Frgn Policy.

GIBBONS, DEIRDRE; Roy C Ketcham HS; Wappingers Falls, NY; (Y); Church Yth Grp; FBLA; Ski Clb; Yrbk Phtg; Yrbk Stf; Im Bsktbl; Hon Roll; Bus.

GIBBONS, MELLISA; St Edmund HS; Brooklyn, NY; (S); 23/187; Church Yth Grp; Pres Spanish Clb; Yrbk Stf; Lit Mag; Awd Exc Soc Studies 83-84; Awd Exc Spnsh,Eng,Relgn 83-85; Wagner Coll; Spcl Ed.

GIBBONS, RACHEL R; Shaker HS; Latham, NY; (Y); Girl Scts; Rgnts Schlrshp 86; SUNY New Paltz; Textiles Dsgn.

GIBBONS, TOM; Grand Island SR HS; Grand Isl, NY; (Y); Church Yth Grp; Red Cross Aide; Y-Teens; Variety Show; Yrbk Stf; Stu Cncl; JV Swmmng; Hon Roll; Cornell; Vet Med.

GIBBS JR, ARNOLD; Longwood HS; Coram, NY; (Y); Boy Scts; Key Clb; Band; Mrchg Band; Orch; Var JV Bsbl; Var JV Ftbl; Peer Ldrshp Clb 84-86; Eagle Boy Scout 86; Farmingdale; Librl Arts.

GIBBS, LISA; Kereny Memorial Acad; Troy, NY; (Y); Pres Art Clb; Pres Ski Clb; VP Soph Cls; Rep Jr Cls; Pres Sr Cls; Pres Stu Cncl; Var Capt Sftbl; Var Capt Tennis; Hon Roll; NY ST Nwspapr Crrier Of The Yr 84-85; Art Dept Awd 86; Tnnis & Art Schlrshp @ Cazenovia 86; Cazenovia Coll; Advrtsng Dsgn.

GIBBS, TIMOTHY; Hudson Falls SR HS; Hudson Fls, NY; (Y); 16/250; Drama Clb; SADD; Thesps; School Musical; School Play; Stage Crew; High Hon Roll; NHS; L Var Crs Cntry; Acpl Chr; Drama Clb & Thspn Clb 84-86.

GIBIDES, CARY; J C Birdlebough HS; Mesa, AZ; (Y); Trs Jr Cls; Stu Cncl; JV Bsbl; JV Var Ftbl; JV Wrstlng; High Hon Roll; Hon Roll; NHS; Highest Avg On Football Team 85; Syracuse U; Comp Engr.

GIBNEY, DANIELLE; James I O Neill HS; Fort Montgomery, NY; (Y); Am Leg Aux Girls St; Church Yth Grp; Sec Jr Cls; Rep Stu Cncl; JV Cheerleading; VP NHS; Pres Schlr; Fordham U.

GIBSON, ANDREW J; Whitesville Central HS; Whitesville, NY; (Y); 6/20; Am Leg Boys St; Chorus; Stage Crew; Yrbk Ed-Chief; Rep Stu Cncl; JV Var Bsktbl; JV Var Socr; High Hon Roll; Hon Roll; NHS; US Army; Phrmcy.

GIBSON, DANIEL W; Colonie Central HS; Albany, NY; (Y); Aud/Vis; Chess Clb; Exploring; Orch; Hon Roll; Prfct Atten Awd; Schl Cntmpry Radio; Radio Ancr.

GIBSON, DAVID; Charles H Roth HS; W Henrietta, NY; (Y); FBLA; Ski Clb; Spanish Clb; Hon Roll; Tax Atty.

GIBSON, DONALD; John Dewey HS; Brooklyn, NY; (Y); Am Leg Boys St; Cmnty Wkr; Office Aide; PAVAS; Teachers Aide; Chorus; Wt Lftg; Hon Roll; School Musical; Stage Crew; Irving Gershon Mem Awd For Chrctr Dvlpmnt 84; Return Of Last Property Recmndtn 83; Prof Sprts.

GIBSON, JON E; Bethlehem Central HS; Voorheesville, NY; (Y); 21/304; Boy Scts; Chess Clb; Pres Church Yth Grp; Exploring; High Hon Roll; NHS; Ntl Merit SF; Harvard Smmr Schl Scndry Schl Stu; Brown; Econmcs.

GIBSON, KELLY; Dundee Central HS; Dundee, NY; (Y); 15/80; Spanish Clb; JV Bsktbl; Var Socr; L Sftbl; JV Vllybl; Hon Roll; Natl Englsh Mrt Awd 86; Slctn Fr Englsh Hnrs Crs 86; Acad Ptry Awd 86.

GIBSON, KIM; Jamestown HS; Jamestown, NY; (Y); Church Yth Grp; Hosp Aide; Spanish Clb; Vlntry Wrk-50 Hrs 84; Grove City Coll; Acctng.

GIBSON, LAURA; Beacon HS; Beacon, NY; (Y); 7/217; Chorus; Nwsp Rptr; Nwsp Stf; Var Bowling; High Hon Roll; Jr NHS; NHS; Prfct Atten Awd; Cmmndrs Cert Hnr Schlstc Excllnc 84; Cert Hnr Seq II Math 85; Cert Hnr Phy Ed 86; Engrng.

GIBSON, LAURA MARGARET; Seton Catholic Central HS; Binghamton, NY; (Y); 21/162; Church Yth Grp; GAA; Key Clb; Bsktbl; Cheerleading; Socr; Sftbl; Hon Roll; NHS; Jessie Baker Schlrshp Awd 86; Harold C & C Burns Schlrshp Awd 86; Broome CC.

GIBSON, LISA; Dundee Central Schl; Dundee, NY; (Y); 2/86; 4-H; GAA; Quiz Bowl; Teachers Aide; Bsktbl; Score Keeper; Sftbl; Vllybl; 4-H Awd; High Hon Roll; Frnch II DTA Awd 85; ST Fr Wnr 86; Frnch III DTA Awd 86; Mansfield; Home Ec.

GIBSON, LORRI JO; Bishop Kearney HS; Pittsford, NY; (Y); 9/140; Math Tm; Band; Concert Band; Drill Tm; Jazz Band; Mrchg Band; School Musical; Hon Roll; VFW Awd; St John Fisher Coll; Engrng.

GIBSON, LYNDA; Sachem HS; Farmingville, NY; (Y); 26/1383; Science Clb; Spanish Clb; Off Sr Cls; Hon Roll; NHS; Ithaca Coll Scholar 86; Regents Scholar 86; Ithaca Coll; Mgmt.

GIBSON, SHARON; Livingston Manor Central Schl; Livingston Manor, NY; (S); 2/55; Chorus; Concert Band; School Musical; Pres Frsh Cls; Pres Soph Cls; Pres Jr Cls; Capt Bsktbl; Sftbl; High Hon Roll; Sec NHS; Acad All Amer 86; Stanys & NASA Selectn Witnss Chllngr Launch 85; Outstndng Chrldng 83-84; Math.

GIBSON, STEVEN T; Lewiston Porter SR HS; Youngstown, NY; (Y); #1 In Class; Pres JA; Ski Clb; Pres Band; Orch; School Play; Hon Roll; NHS; Navy ROTC Schlrshp 86; Boston U; Bio-Med Engr.

GIELLA, LAURA; Holy Trinity HS; East Meadow, NY; (Y); 50/320; Var Capt Vllybl; High Hon Roll; Hon Roll; Alt Regents Nrsng Schlrshp 86; MIP Vllybl 83-84; Lemoyne Coll.

GIERKE, LORI; Fillmore Central HS; Fillmore, NY; (Y); 4/58; Church Yth Grp; Spanish Clb; SADD; Teachers Aide; Church Choir; Timer; Stat Vllybl; High Hon Roll; Hon Roll; NHS; Nrsg.

GIESELER, JUDI; Amsterdam HS; Amsterdam, NY; (Y); Church Yth Grp; VP FBLA; Girl Scts; Chorus; Church Choir; High Hon Roll; Bus Admin.

GIESIN, PETER W; Gilboa Conesville Central HS; N Blenheim, NY; (Y); 1/28; School Play; Yrbk Stf; Pres Frsh Cls; JV Bsbl; Var Bsktbl; High Hon Roll; NHS; Pres Schlr; Sal; Regnts Schlrshp 86; Plattsburgh ST U; Physcs.

GIETL, DONNA; Ten Broeck Acad; Cuba, NY; (Y); 9/50; Band; Chorus; Yrbk Stf; VP Frsh Cls; Sec Soph Cls; Trs Sr Cls; Sec Stu Cncl; Var Cheerleading; Var Crs Cntry; NHS; Pennysaver Ad Craft Hnrb Mntn 4th Pl 83-84; Faculty Tchrs Assn Awd 86; St Bonaventure U; Secndry Music.

GIETL, JESSIE; Franklinville Central HS; Cuba, NY; (Y); 2/60; Band; Chorus; Jazz Band; Mrchg Band; Yrbk Stf; Var L Cheerleading; Var L Crs Cntry; Var L Trk; High Hon Roll; NHS; JR Marshall Grad 86.

GIFFIN, ROSEMARY; Riverhead HS; Riverhead, NY; (Y); 45/192; Dance Clb; JCL; Latin Clb; Library Aide; Chorus; Nwsp Ed-Chief; Nwsp Rptr; Nwsp Stf; Rep Stu Cncl; Bar Assoc Crimnl Law 85; Spcl Stu Awd 86; Spcl Ed.

GIFFORD, HEIDI; Greece Athena HS; Rochester, NY; (S); 22/265; DECA; Spanish Clb; Rep Frsh Cls; Rep Soph Cls; Rep Jr Cls; Rep Sr Cls; VP Stu Cncl; Socr; Trk; Hon Roll; DECA 2nd Pl Hnrb Mntn Awds 86; SUNY Geneseo; Mngmnt.

GIFFORD, MICHAEL; Mayfield JR SR HS; Mayfield, NY; (Y); Drama Clb; Varsity Clb; Chorus; School Play; Stage Crew; Variety Show; Pres Stu Cncl; Capt Var Socr; Im Vllybl; Im Wt Lftg; Herkimer Cnty CC; Cnst Tech.

GIFFORD, VICTORIA; Bronx High School Of Science; New York, NY; (Y).

GIGLIA, CHERYL; St Dominic HS; Huntington, NY; (S); Hosp Aide; SADD; School Play; Capt Cheerleading; High Hon Roll; NHS; Acadmc All Amer 84; NEDT Cert 84; Chem Achvt Cert 85; Bus Adm.

GIGLIA, DEBORAH; St Dominics HS; Huntington, NY; (S); 10/120; SADD; Yrbk Stf; High Hon Roll; NHS; Accntng Achvt Cert 85; St Johns U; Busnss Mgmt.

GIGLIA, JOYCE; North Tonawanda SR HS; N Tonawanda, NY; (Y); Trs FBLA.

GIGLIO, ALEXANDRA; Brockport HS; Brockport, NY; (Y); 6/335; Church Yth Grp; Drama Clb; Ski Clb; Band; Concert Band; JV Var Socr; High Hon Roll; St John Fisher Coll Admssns Schlrshp 86; Nazareth Acad Tuitn 82; St John Fisher Coll; Bio.

GIGLIOTTI, SAMUEL S; Waterloo SR HS; Waterloo, NY; (Y); 1/170; Jazz Band; Mrchg Band; Pres Frsh Cls; Pres Sr Cls; Pres Stu Cncl; L Golf; NHS; Ntl Merit SF; St Schlr; Val; Rochstr Inst Of Tech Outstndng Schlrshp 86; Veronica Maher Mem Schlrshp 86; Paul Schaffer Jazz Bnd Awd; Rochester Tech Inst; Comp Engr.

GIGLIOTTI, SANDRA; Geneva HS; Geneva, NY; (S); 15/175; School Musical; Sec Trs Varsity Clb; Yrbk Stf; Trs Soph Cls; Rep Stu Cncl; Var Cheerleading; High Hon Roll; Hon Roll; NHS; Latn III Most Outstndt Awd 85; Aeronaut Engrng.

GIL, ROBERT; John F Kennedy HS; Bronx, NY; (Y); 312/873; Off Frsh Cls; Elctrcl Engrng.

GILBERT, AL; Liverpool HS; Liverpool, NY; (Y); Art Clb; Camera Clb; Nwsp Phtg; Nwsp Stf; Im Bsktbl; Syracuse U; Cmmnctns.

GILBERT, DANIEL; Oakfield-Alabama Central HS; Oakfield, NY; (Y); 4-H; JV Var Bsbl; JV Var Ftbl; 4-H Awd; Hon Roll; Brockport ST Coll; CPA.

GILBERT, JAMES; Rocky Point JR SR HS; Rocky Point, NY; (Y); 21/205; Varsity Clb; Yrbk Stf; Var Capt Bsktbl; Var Capt Golf; NHS; All-League Bsktbll 85-86; All Lg Glf 83-86; All-Cnfrnc All Cnty Gulf 85-86; Stetson U; Bus Mngmnt.

GILBERT, LACRETIA; North Rose-Wolcott HS; Wolcott, NY; (Y); Church Yth Grp; Drama Clb; Girl Scts; Band; Chorus; Church Choir; Concert Band; Mrchg Band; School Musical; School Play; All Cnty Chorus 86; 2nd Yth Delegate To Church Session & Of Church PNC 86; Music.

GILBERT, MONICA E; Mc Graw HS; Mc Graw, NY; (Y); 1/46; Am Leg Aux Girls St; Capt Color Guard; Jazz Band; Mrchg Band; Swing Chorus; Sec Soph Cls; Score Keeper; VP Jr NHS; Mgr NHS; Mst Outstndng Yth In Diocese 83; Phrmcy.

GILCHICK, STACEY; North Babylon SR HS; North Babylon, NY; (Y); 7/464; Intnl Clb; Pep Clb; Nwsp Rptr; Yrbk Stf; Rep Soph Cls; Pom Pon; French Hon Soc; High Hon Roll; Jr NHS; NHS; Pres Physcl Fit Awd 86; Muhlenberg Coll; Bus.

GILCHRIST, ANGELA M; Plainedge HS; Bethpage, NY; (Y); 6/304; DECA; Mathletes; SADD; Yrbk Phtg; Sftbl; High Hon Roll; NHS; Ntl Merit Ltr; VP Spanish NHS; 4-H; NY Rgnts Schlrshp 86; Physcs Stu Of Yr 84-85; SUNY Stony Brook; Engrng.

GILCHRIST, THOMAS; Mahopac HS; Mahopac, NY; (Y); 18/402; Aud/Vis; Church Yth Grp; FBLA; Band; Stage Crew; Nwsp Rptr; Nwsp Stf; Lit Mag; Rep Frsh Cls; Rep Soph Cls; Yale; Law.

GILEBARTO, PHILIP J; Jamestown HS; Jamestown, NY; (Y); JV Bsktbl; Im Crs Cntry; JV Ftbl; Im Sftbl; Var Trk; Hon Roll; Jr NHS; NHS; Case Western Rsrv U; Biochem.

GILELS, DORI; Fayetteville-Manlius HS; Manlius, NY; (Y); VP Trs SADD; Yrbk Stf; Gym; Socr; Hon Roll; Dale Carnegie Pblc Spkng Crs 86.

GILES, DAWN; N Babylon SR HS; N Babylon, NY; (Y); Office Aide; Spanish Clb; NHS.

GILES, LA SHAWN; St Pius V HS; Bronx, NY; (Y); Pres JA; Pres Y-Teens; Rep Variety Show; Pres Jr Cls; Rep Stu Cncl; Hon Roll; NHS; Hghst Avg Engl II 85-86; 2nd Hghst Avg Trig 85-86; Cert Of Hnr 85-86; John Jay Coll; Frncsc Psychlgy.

GILES, LEAH; Franklin Acad; Malone, NY; (Y); AFS; Intnl Clb; Pep Clb; Varsity Clb; Var Cheerleading; Var Trk; Mabne Ctr Arts Scshlrshp Dance 85; Dance.

GILES, PETER; Oyster Bay HS; Oyster Bay, NY; (Y); Boy Scts; FBLA; Variety Show; Yrbk Rptr; Rep Frsh Cls; Rep Soph Cls; Rep Jr Cls; Rep Sr Cls; VP Stu Cncl; Bsbl; SUNY Albany; Pol Sci.

GILFILIAN, MELISSA; Tully Central Schl; Preble, NY; (Y); Hosp Aide; Spanish Clb; Hon Roll; NHS; Tompkins Cortland CC; Trvl.

GILHOOLY, CAROL; Mount Mercy Acad; Buffalo, NY; (Y); 57/163; Art Clb; Cmnty Wkr; 4-H; Red Cross Aide; SADD; Nwsp Stf; Yrbk Stf; 4-H Awd; Hon Roll; CCD Tchr 85-86; Retreat Grp; Villa Maria Coll; Grphc Art.

GILHOOLY, SHANNON M; St Joseph Hill Acad; Staten Island, NY; (Y); 7/107; Math Tm; Science Clb; Teachers Aide; Color Guard; Mrchg Band; Yrbk Phtg; Pres Frsh Cls; Trs Soph Cls; Pres Sr Cls; Hon Roll; NEDT Test Commdntn; Bio.

GILISON, DINA; Academy Of St Joseph; St James, NY; (Y); Art Clb; Dance Clb; Hosp Aide; Chorus; Church Choir; Nwsp Rptr; Nwsp Stf; Lit Mag; Hon Roll; Natl Art Hnr Soc 85-86; Natl Fr Cont 85-86; Huntington Twp Art Lg 86.

GILL, AVERILL L; Jamaica HS; Flushing, NY; (Y); Computer Clb; Debate Tm; Math Tm; Band; Concert Band; Nwsp Rptr; Var Golf; Hon Roll; Jr NHS; NHS; Creatv Arts Soc 84-86; Queens Coll; Muscn.

GILL, DONALD C; Msgr Farrell HS; Staten Island, NY; (Y); Boy Scts; Church Yth Grp; Computer Clb; Science Clb; Spanish Clb; Im Bsktbl; Hon Roll; NY ST Rgnts Schlrshp 86; Brklyn Coll NY; Sci.

GILL, ELIZABETH; Our Lady Of Mercy HS; Penfield, NY; (Y); Camera Clb; Exploring; Science Clb; SADD; Church Choir; School Musical; School Play; Stage Crew; Ed Yrbk Phtg; Hon Roll.

GILL, KATHLEEN; Farmingdale HS; Farmingdale, NY; (Y); Girl Scts; SADD; Concert Band; Mrchg Band; Mort Sci.

GILL, RICHARD; Port Jervis HS; Sparrow Bush, NY; (Y); Boy Scts; Im Bsktbl; God Cntry Awd; Hon Roll; SUNY Delhi; Arch.

GILLANDERS, JAMES G; John Jay Senior HS; S Salem, NY; (Y); Chess Clb; French Clb; Orch; Hon Roll; Prfct Atten Awd; Pltcl Sci.

GILLEECE, DIANNE; Oneida SR HS; Oneida, NY; (S); Drama Clb; Intnl Clb; SADD; Varsity Clb; Concert Band; School Play; Crs Cntry; Trk; High Hon Roll; Jr NHS; NHS; Pres Fit Awd 85; Hamilton Coll; Anthrplgy.

GILLEN, LAURA; Sacred Heart Acad; Baldwin, NY; (S); Cmnty Wkr; Dance Clb; Hosp Aide; SADD; School Musical; Yrbk Stf; Trs Sec Stu Cncl; JV Cheerleading; Hon Roll; NHS.

GILLEN, NELSON; Frankfort-Schuyler Central HS; Frankfort, NY; (Y); Spanish Clb; Varsity Clb; JV Var Bsbl; JV Bsktbl; Var Ftbl; Lib Arts.

GILLESPIE, DANIELLE; Attica Central HS; Varysburg, NY; (S); 9/150; AFS; Church Yth Grp; Dance Clb; Drama Clb; French Clb; Spanish Clb; Chorus; Church Choir; JV VP Cheerleading; Gym; GPA Awd 83-84; Nuc Med.

GILLESPIE, LANETTE; Valley Central HS; Maybrook, NY; (Y); FBLA; Lit Mag; Hon Roll; Lawyer.

GILLETTE, CARRIE M; C-Pp East HS; Corning, NY; (Y); Exploring; French Clb; Hosp Aide; SADD; VICA; Color Guard; Cit Awd; High Hon Roll; Lion Awd; NHS; Pres Acad Ftnss Awd 86; BOCES Mst Outstndng Emplybl Stu 86; Coll Schlrshp Locl Odd Fllws Asso 86; Corning CC; Nursing.

GILLETTE, GARY; Fillmore Central HS; Fillmore, NY; (S); 12/61; Aud/Vis; French Clb; Drill Tm; High Hon Roll; Hon Roll; NHS; Prfct Atten Awd; Cnty Govt Intern 84-85; Outstndng Carrier Of Yr 85; Govt Intrshp Albany NY 85; Suny U Geneseo; Engr.

GILLETTE, HEATHER; Alden HS; Alden, NY; (Y); Church Yth Grp; Cmnty Wkr; 4-H; Library Aide; Science Clb; Spanish Clb; Teachers Aide; Church Choir; Swmmng; 4-H Awd; Bio.

GILLETTE, JACQUELI A; Susquchanna Valley HS; Conklin, NY; (Y); Chorus; Nwsp Sprt Ed; Nwsp Stf; Trs Soph Cls; Trs Jr Cls; Trs Sr Cls; JV Var Bsktbl; Var Capt Fld Hcky; Var Capt Sftbl; Hon Roll; NY ST Regents Schlrshp 86; All Conf Field Hockey Team 84; MVP Sftbl Leag 85; SUNY-CORTLAND; Bio Sci.

GILLETTE, SUZANNE; Franklin Acad; Malone, NY; (Y); Hon Roll; Prfct Atten Awd; Acdmc All Amer 84-86.

GILLIES, JEFF; Albertus Magnus HS; Congers, NY; (Y); 17/175; Ski Clb; Yrbk Bus Mgr; Yrbk Stf; Im Ice Hcky; High Hon Roll; NHS; Cornell; Jrnslm.

GILLIGAN, JANICE; Alexander Central HS; Darien, NY; (Y); Science Clb; Spanish Clb; Yrbk Stf; Geneseo.

GILLIGAN, MARYBETH; Glens Falls HS; Glen Falls, NY; (Y); 56/218; Yrbk Phtg; Yrbk Sprt Ed; Capt Bsktbl; Fld Hcky; Capt Powder Puff Ftbl; Capt Sftbl; High Hon Roll; Yrbk Phtg; Yrbk Sprt Ed; Trs Frsh Cls; Alpha Epsln Chptrs Dlta Kppa Gmma Soc Intl Wmn Edctrs 86; US Mrn Cps Athl Awd 86; Fthls Cncl 83-86; St John Fisher Coll; Elem Tchr.

GILLILAND, GREGG; Berlin Central Schl; E Nassau, NY; (Y); SADD; Chorus; School Musical; School Play; Stage Crew; Yrbk Phtg; Yrbk Stf; Rep Stu Cncl; JV Var Socr; JV Wrstlng.

GILLIS, JOSEPH; Greenwich Central HS; Schaghticoke, NY; (Y); JV Var Ftbl; Var Wt Lftg; Hon Roll; Hudson Valley CC.

GILLMAN, ILYSSA; Bronx High Schl Of Science; Bronx, NY; (Y); Office Aide; Temple Yth Grp; Hon Roll; NHS; Marn Bio 86; Anml Behvr & Psych 86; U Of NH; Zoolgy.

GILLMORE, JAMES; Skaneateles Central HS; Skaneateles, NY; (Y); Church Yth Grp; JV Bsbl; Var L Ice Hcky; Var L Lcrss; Var L Socr; Hon Roll; Boston U; Engrng.

GILLS, KAREN; Bishop Loughlin HS; Brooklyn, NY; (Y); 79/233; Var Trs Cheerleading; Trk; High Hon Roll; Hon Roll; Slvr Lghln L 84-85; Prpl Lghln L 85-86; Chrng Sqd Treas Awd 85-86; John Jay Coll; Law.

GILMAN, ARTHUR J; Kendall JR SR HS; Holley, NY; (Y); 16/90; Boy Scts; Rptr FFA; FFA Empire Degree 86; Elec Engrng.

GILMAN, LYNLY; Norwood Norfolk Central HS; Raymondville, NY; (Y); Boy Scts; Color Guard; JV Crs Cntry; VP Trk; Hon Roll; Sectn X Cls B Champ Trk 84-85; Boy Scouts Hon Unit Troop 12 84.

GILMAN, TIMOTHY; Kendall JR-SR HS; Holley, NY; (Y); Trs FFA; Yrbk Stf; Sr Cls; High Hon Roll; NHS; Schl Schlrshp 86; Rtry Clb Awd Frm Holley Rtry 86; Alfred Ag & Tech; Ag.

GILMARTIN, KARA A; Massapequa HS; Massapequa, NY; (Y); 14/440; Pep Clb; Spanish Clb; Variety Show; Yrbk Phtg; Ed Yrbk Stf; Var Capt Fld Hcky; Var Lcrss; High Hon Roll; NHS; St Schlr; Franklin & Marshall Coll; Med.

GILMARTIN, KATHLEEN A; Hamburg HS; Hamburg, NY; (Y); 17/391; AFS; Church Yth Grp; Dance Clb; JA; Acpl Chr; Chorus; Church Choir; Color Guard; Madrigals; School Musical; Regents & Cornell Schlrshp 86; Cornell U; Applied Econ.

GILMARTIN, NONA; H Frank Carey HS; Franklin Sq, NY; (Y); 15/250; Var Cheerleading; High Hon Roll; Hon Roll; Jr NHS; NHS.

GILMORE, KATHY; John F Kennedy HS; Utica, NY; (Y); Art Clb; Drama Clb; SADD; Chorus; Gym; Hon Roll; Artst.

GILMORE, KERIN ANNE; Sacred Heart Acad; Malverne, NY; (S); 29/182; Spanish Clb; SADD; Yrbk Stf; Hon Roll; Jr NHS; NHS; Ntl Merit Ltr; Church Yth Grp; 2nd Hnrs Iona Coll Lang Cont 85; Clin Psych.

GILMORE, LOUIS; Oswego HS; Oswego, NY; (Y); 113/380; Aud/Vis; Church Yth Grp; VP JA; Rep Soph Cls; Rep Jr Cls; Capt L Crs Cntry; Var L Tennis; Var L Trk; Hon Roll; NEDT Awd; HOBY Ldrshp Ambssdr 84; Central Cty Bus Inst; Accntng.

GILMORE, MICHAEL; John Dewey HS; Brooklyn, NY; (Y); Cmnty Wkr; Exploring; Chorus; Yrbk Ed-Chief; Yrbk Stf; Wt Lftg; Pres Exploring Grp 85; Hnr Doing Cmmty Work 84; Awd Volenteer Work 84; Compu Engr.

GILMORE, RICK; Northern Adirondack Central HS; Ellenburg Center, NY; (Y); Church Yth Grp; 4-H; FFA; Key Clb; Stage Crew; JV Var Bsktbl; JV Var Socr; Dekalb Awd 86; Taylor Scholar 86; Canton ATC; Crimnl Justc.

GILMOUR, TRICIA; Freeport HS; Freeport, NY; (Y); 7/450; Church Yth Grp; Key Clb; Ski Clb; Variety Show; Nwsp Rptr; Yrbk Phtg; Gym; Capt Lcrss; Socr; High Hon Roll; Blanck Schlrshp Awd, Caroline Atkinson Awd 86; Mrch Dimes Hlth Awd 86; Moser Athletic Awd 86; Suny Binghampton; Phys Thrpy.

GILSON, CHRIS; Middletown HS; Middletown, NY; (Y); VP Key Clb; Band; Symp Band; Yrbk Phtg; Sec Sr Cls; Var JV Ftbl; Hstry.

GILSON, JENNIFER; Canarsie HS; Brooklyn, NY; (Y); Debate Tm; Varsity Clb; Acpl Chr; Chorus; Madrigals; School Musical; School Play; Sftbl; Vllybl; High Hon Roll; Honrry Archon Stu & Arista Stu 86; NY Acad Of Sci Stu 85-86; Cornell U; Med.

GILYARD, DENISE; Lehman HS; New York, NY; (Y); Science Clb; Chorus; Rep Jr Cls; JV Cheerleading; Hon Roll; Prfct Atten Awd; Slvr Arista Awd 86; Stngrphy 1 Awd 86; SAT Prep Awd 86; Hofstra U; Acctg.

GINES, X; Yonkers HS; Yonkers, NY; (Y); FBLA; Library Aide; Bus Awd Rcrdkpng 86; Ctznshp; Sci; Bus.

GINGERICH, DEBRA; Indian River Central HS; Philadelphia, NY; (Y); Chorus; School Musical; School Play; Yrbk Stf; Stu Cncl; Cheerleading; Hon Roll; NHS; AFS; Conf All ST Chorus 85; Area All ST Chorus 83-85; Natl Chrldg Awd 85; Jefferson CC; Bus Mgmt.

GINSBURG, KAREN A; The Masters Schl; Briarcliff, NY; (Y); Drama Clb; Key Clb; Spanish Clb; School Musical; School Play; Rptr Lit Mag; Cheerleading; High Hon Roll; Ntl Merit SF; Cum Laude Soc 85; Engl Awd 3rd Pl 85; Drama.

GIOFFRE, TONY; Blind Brook HS; Rye Brook, NY; (Y); Ski Clb; Variety Show; Var Bsbl; Im Bsktbl; Var Socr; Vrsty Ski Tm 84 & 85; Vrsty 86 Chmpnshp Hocky Tm 84-86; Cptn Blades Ice Hcky Tm 87.

GIORDANO, ANDREW; South Shore HS; Brooklyn, NY; (Y); Var Wrstlng; LIU; Cmnctns.

GIORDANO, DENISE; Northport HS; E Northport, NY; (Y); Cmnty Wkr; Hofstra; Accntng.

GIORDANO, JEANINE M; Fontbonne Hall Acad; Brooklyn, NY; (Y); VP Church Yth Grp; Dance Clb; Drama Clb; French Clb; Service Clb; Teachers Aide; School Play; Nwsp Rptr; Hon Roll; Prfct Atten Awd; St Johns U Comp Schlrshp 86; Regents Schlrshp 86; Mt St Vincent Coll; Law.

GIORDANO, JOHN R; St Francis Prep Sch; Whitestone, NY; (S); 195/744; Im Bsktbl; Im Ftbl; Im Sftbl; Im Vllybl; Opt Clb Awd; Bus.

GIORDANO, JOSEPH; Abraham Lincoln HS; Brooklyn, NY; (Y); Key Clb; Math Tm; Lit Mag; JV Bsbl; Cit Awd; Italian Tchr 85; Bus.

GIORDANO, KIM; Mount Saint Mary Acad; Buffalo, NY; (Y); Intnl Clb; Ski Clb; Teachers Aide; Stage Crew; Yrbk Stf; Rep Stu Cncl; Swmmng; High Hon Roll; Hon Roll; Awd For Develop Of Schl 86; Niagra U; Nrsng.

GIORDANO, LOUIS; Lindenhurst HS; Lindenhurst, NY; (Y); 6/550; Chess Clb; VP Debate Tm; Pres German Clb; Mathletes; Spanish Clb; VP Speech Tm; Nwsp Rptr; Capt Tennis; High Hon Roll; Hon Roll; Dr Buscareno Mem Awd 86; Rep Tom Downey Cert Of Merit 86; Pres Acad Ftnss Awd 86; SUNY Binghamton; Lwyr.

GIORDANO, MARIA; Mt Vernon HS; Mt Vernon, NY; (Y); High Hon Roll; Hon Roll; Iona Coll.

GIORDANO, MARIA; St Marys HS; New Hyde Park, NY; (Y); 26/171; Service Clb; Stage Crew; High Hon Roll; Hon Roll; NHS; Bus.

GIORDANO, RENEE; Beacon HS; Beacon, NY; (Y); Am Leg Aux Girls St; Drama Clb; Thesps; Varsity Clb; School Play; Stage Crew; Sec Stu Cncl; Var L Tennis; NHS; Peggy Wood Awd Bst Sprtng Actrs 86; Thtr Arts.

GIORDANO, TAMMY; Frontier Central HS; Lake View, NY; (Y); German Clb; Pep Clb; Science Clb; SADD; School Play; Yrbk Rptr; Stu Cncl; JV Swmmng; High Hon Roll; NHS; Sci Awd 83-84; Pre Law.

GIORLANDO, NICKY; Valley Stream Central HS; Valley Stream, NY; (Y); Boy Scts; Computer Clb; Exploring; Key Clb; Radio Clb; Science Clb; Ski Clb; SADD; Stage Crew; Yrbk Stf.

GIORNO, RUSSELL; Pt Chester SR HS; Port Chester, NY; (Y); Ski Clb; Band; Concert Band; Jazz Band; Mrchg Band; Variety Show; Tennis; Hon Roll; Jr NHS; NHS; Itln & Sci Hnr Scty; Cchs Awd Tnns; Law.

GIOVANNINI, ROBERT; Mc Quaid Jesuit HS; Fairport, NY; (Y); Boy Scts; Camera Clb; Church Yth Grp; Trs Debate Tm; Model UN; Ski Clb; Trs Soph Cls; Crs Cntry; Trk; High Hon Roll; Egl Sct Awd 83; Chrmn Of Lbst Cmmtt 86; Ltn Awd Ntl Ltn Exm 86; Law.

GIPSON, ANTHONY; John Jay HS; Brooklyn, NY; (Y); Plc Offcr.

GIRANDOLA, LAURA; Rocky Pt JR Ssr HS; Rocky Point, NY; (Y); 1/186; Cmnty Wkr; VP Sec German Clb; Pres SADD; Chorus; School Musical; Symp Band; DAR Awd; NHS; Val; English Clb; Cornell Ntl Schlr 86; Cornell U; Med.

GIRARDI, NICOLE; Longwood HS; Coram, NY; (S); 42/479; Art Clb; Aud/Vis; Hosp Aide; Chorus; Stage Crew; High Hon Roll; Hon Roll; Jr NHS; Fine Art.

GIRAUD, ANDREW; Oneida SR HS; Oneida, NY; (Y); 31/206; Church Yth Grp; Library Aide; Spanish Clb; Chorus; Church Choir; Rep Soph Cls; Rep Stu Cncl; Crs Cntry; Wrstlng; Grove City Coll.

GIRESI, MICHAEL; Monsignor Farrell HS; Staten Island, NY; (S); Cmnty Wkr; Frsh Cls; Sr Cls; Stu Cncl; Ftbl; Wt Lftg; Wrstlng; Hnr Stu 86; Engrng.

GIRGENTI, DOUG; H Frank Carey HS; Franklin Sq, NY; (Y); 5/228; Boy Scts; Var Socr; Var L Wrstlng; Jr NHS; NHS; Spanish NHS; VFW Awd; Brown Book Awd 85; Dakin Mem Awd 86; Talntd & Gftd Assn 83-86; Cornell U; Chem.

GIRIS, JANET J; Plainedge HS; N Massapequa, NY; (Y); 12/304; Mathletes; SADD; Band; Chorus; School Musical; Ed Yrbk Stf; Stu Cncl; Trk; Sec NHS; NYS Yorker Chairprsn Hghst Hnr 85-86; SUNY Binghamton; Law.

GIRLEA, FLORIN; Aviation HS; New York, NY; (Y); Aud/Vis; Debate Tm; Drama Clb; Math Tm; Capt Socr; Cit Awd; NY Polytech; Aerospace Engr.

GIRMUS, ANNETTE; Cato-Meridian Central HS; Cato, NY; (Y); 11/75; Church Yth Grp; Drama Clb; French Clb; GAA; Girl Scts; Ski Clb; Spanish Clb; Varsity Clb; Concert Band; Jazz Band; N Alantic Leag Exchng Stu France 85; Allen Benton Mem Schlrshp 86; Female Schlr Athlt Awd 86; SUNY Geneseo; Pol Sci.

GIROUX, THOMAS J; Trinity-Pawling Schl; Wapp Fls, NY; (Y); 8/79; Church Yth Grp; Trs French Clb; L Var Bsbl; Var L Bsktbl; Capt Socr; High Hon Roll; Brdfrd N Abbott Awd 86; WNEPPSA Slct Tm 85; VA Tech; Elctrcl Engrng.

GITTER, RUSSELL; Abraham Lincoln HS; Brooklyn, NY; (Y); JA; Key Clb; Math Tm; Service Clb; SADD; Nwsp Stf; Var Capt Crs Cntry; Var Capt Trk; Schlrshp Trip Isreal 84; SUNY; Phrmcst.

GITTLEMAN, MARNI; John M Glenn HS; Greenlawn, NY; (Y); Cmnty Wkr; Teachers Aide; Temple Yth Grp; Nwsp Stf; Yrbk Stf; High Hon Roll; Jr NHS; NHS; Ntl Merit Ltr; Spanish NHS; Bus.

GITTLITZ, LEAH; Spring Valley SR HS; Spring Valley, NY; (Y); 34/441; Cmnty Wkr; Math Clb; Co-Capt Math Tm; Science Clb; Temple Yth Grp; Thesps; Band; Concert Band; Drm Mjr(t); Mrchg Band; Brandeis U.

GITTO, TINA; Guilderland Central HS; Albany, NY; (Y); Key Clb; Varsity Clb; Symp Band; Rep Soph Cls; Rep Stu Cncl; Var Cheerleading; Hon Roll; Engl Spec Awd 84; Acad Achvt Mth I Spec Awd 84; Bus Adm.

GIULIANI, FRANCA; Moore Catholic HS; Staten Island, NY; (Y); Art Clb; Drama Clb; Intnl Clb; Science Clb; Speech Tm; Chorus; School Musical; Rep Soph Cls; VP Jr Cls; ECBS Coll; Fash Desgn.

GIULIANO, ANTHONY; Beach Channel HS; Howard Beach, NY; (Y); Concert Band; Yrbk Stf; Pride Of Yankees Awd Extra Crrclr Actvts 84-85; 4 Yrs Svc In Math Dept 83-87; Elec Engrng.

GIUNTA, JOANNE; Marlboro Central HS; Marlboro, NY; (Y); 34/164; Camera Clb; Cmnty Wkr; 4-H; FTA; Varsity Clb; Nwsp Phtg; Swmmng; 4-H Awd; High Hon Roll; Dtchs Cnty CC; Math Tchr.

GIUNTA, MICHAEL; Holy Trinity HS; Bethpage, NY; (S); 35/403; Cert Achvt Math 84-85; Cert Achvt Math 83-84.

GIUNTI, JOHN A; Tottenville HS; Staten Island, NY; (Y); 71/871; Am Leg Boys St; Cmnty Wkr; Ski Clb; SADD; Orch; Symp Band; Rep Frsh Cls; Rep Soph Cls; Pres Jr Cls; Pres Stu Cncl; Daily News Music Excllnc 85; Principals Pride Yankees 86; Brooklyn Coll Schlrs; Pre-Med.

GIURA, MARIA T; Bishop Kearney HS; Staten Island, NY; (Y); Camera Clb; Cmnty Wkr; FTA; Ski Clb; Teachers Aide; Nwsp Stf; Lit Mag; High Hon Roll; NHS; NY St Rgnts Schlrshp 86; Cert Of Merit-Poetry Awd-Fordham U Dept Of Itln Stus 84; Wrld Poetry Cntst; Wagner Coll; Ed.

GIUSTI, EVELYN; Hillcrest HS; Woodside, NY; (Y); 91/830; Church Yth Grp; Trs Exploring; Hosp Aide; Regents Schlrshp 87; Pre Med Pgm 83-87; Columbia; Math.

GIUTTARI, SUSAN; Hicksville HS; Hicksville, NY; (Y); Spanish Clb; SADD; Mrchg Band; Orch; Rep Frsh Cls; Rep Soph Cls; Rep Jr Cls; Capt Var Bsktbl; Var Mgr(s); Tennis.

GIVEN, PATRICIA; Knox Memorial Central Schl; Russell, NY; (S); 1/29; French Clb; Library Aide; Ski Clb; Chorus; Rep Stu Cncl; JV Bsktbl; Mgr(s); Var Socr; Var Sftbl; High Hon Roll; RN.

GIZZIE, JON; Baldwin SR HS; Roosevelt, NY; (Y); Key Clb; Pres Latin Clb; Mathletes; Science Clb; Trs SADD; School Musical; High Hon Roll; NHS; Hgh Hnrs Blue Rbn 86 Lng Islnd Sci Cngrs 86; NY Clscl Clbs Exclnc Latn Awd 84-86; Exclnc Soc Stud 85; Bio.

GJELAJ, GEORGE; Cardinal Spellman HS; Bronx, NY; (Y); Bsktbl; Rgnts Schlrshp 86; Fordham U; Bus.

GLACY, KURT; South Glens Falls SR HS; S Glens Falls, NY; (Y); 12/300; Church Yth Grp; Key Clb; Chorus; Church Choir; Stu Cncl; Hon Roll; NHS; Church Sply Orgnst 84-86; Paul H Howe Mem Schlrshp Rcpnt 86; Union Coll; Engrng.

GLADYSZ, MICHELE; Newark Valley HS; Berkshire, NY; (Y); Church Yth Grp; Drama Clb; 4-H; Spanish Clb; SADD; Color Guard; Flag Corp; Stage Crew; Trk; Twrlr; Reg Nrs.

GLANCY, ELIZABETH J; Nazareth Regional HS; Brooklyn, NY; (S); 35/267; Yrbk Sprt Ed; Bsktbl; Vllybl; Boston Coll; Psych.

GLANTZ, ANITA; Walter Panas HS; Crompond, NY; (Y); 4/250; Debate Tm; French Clb; NFL; Nwsp Stf; Stu Cncl; JV Sftbl; High Hon Roll; NHS; Ntl Merit Schol; Pres Schlr; NY ST Rgnts Schlrshp 86; WA U.

GLANZEL, LYNN; Avon Central HS; Avon, NY; (Y); Sftbl; Vllybl; High Hon Roll; Hon Roll; Jr NHS; Bryant & Stratton; Lgl Assnt.

GLANZER, SUSAN; Boces Cultral Arts Ctr; Lynbrook, NY; (Y); 1/26; Dance Clb; Drama Clb; 4-H; Chorus; Drill Tm; School Musical; School Play; Variety Show; VP Sr Cls; Ntl Merit Ltr; Schlrshp NY Acad Theatrical Arts 86; Cert Recgntn Drama Awd; NY Acad Theatrical Arts; Theat.

GLASER, LAUREN M; Christopher Columbus HS; Bronx, NY; (Y); 16/671; Concert Band; Nwsp Ed-Chief; Yrbk Stf; Ed Lit Mag; High Hon Roll; Jr NHS; NCTE Awd; NHS; Spanish NHS; St Schlr; NY Lib Clb Awd Wrtng 85; Engl, Spnsh, Psych Awds 85; Global & Amer Hist, Econ Awds 84-85; NY ST U; Pre-Law.

GLASER, ROBERT; Christopher Columbus HS; Bronx, NY; (Y); 91/671; Bsbl; Scl Stds Awd Hghst Grd 85; Awds Hghst Grds Math & Psychlgy 86; John Jay Coll; Lgl.

GLASS, DEBRA; Waterford-Halfmoon HS; Waterford, NY; (Y); 8/73; Dance Clb; French Clb; SADD; Chorus; Madrigals; Yrbk Stf; JV Bsktbl; Var Fld Hcky; High Hon Roll; NHS; Pres Acdmc Ftns Awd; Cortland ST; Hist.

GLASS, JEFFREY R; Midwood High Schl At Blyn Coll; Brooklyn, NY; (Y); 7/530; Math Tm; Band; School Musical; School Play; Nwsp Rptr; Pres Sr Cls; Stu Cncl; Var JV Bsbl; Var Capt Bowling; Tennis; Faraday Medl-Chem; Morty Gunty Awd-Prfmg Arts; Midwood Schlrshp Ldrshp; Amherst Coll.

GLASS, MATTHEW; Patchague-Medford HS; Patchogue, NY; (Y); 61/608; Am Leg Boys St; Band; Concert Band; School Musical; Yrbk Phtg; Rep Sr Cls; Capt Socr; Var Capt Tennis; NHS; Drama Clb; Stu Of Yr 86; Thlma M Tmpl Awd 86; Fclty Awd 83; U Of VT.

GLASSMAN, SUZANNE; Mineola HS; Mineola, NY; (Y); Hosp Aide; Key Clb; Pres Spanish Clb; SADD; Nwsp Stf; Rep Stu Cncl; NHS; Nwsp Rptr; JV Sftbl; High Hon Roll; Studnt Spnsr In Studnt Svc Ctr 84-86; V P & Dist Histrn Key Club 85-86; Proclamatn 86; Bio.

GLATT, SHIRA; Yeshiva University High Schl For Grls; Flushing, NY; (Y); Art Clb; Cmnty Wkr; Drama Clb; Teachers Aide; School Musical; School Play; Yrbk Stf; Sec Soph Cls; Hon Roll; St Schlr; Michalah Coll-Israel.

GLATZ, CHRISTINE; Rensselaer Middle HS; Rensselaer, NY; (S); 3/92; Am Leg Aux Girls St; Trs Computer Clb; Math Tm; Pres Varsity Clb; Yrbk Stf; Rep Stu Cncl; Var Capt Vllybl; High Hon Roll; NHS; Acadmc All Amer 85; Siena Coll; Chem Engrng.

GLATZ, JAMIE; Jamestown HS; Jamestown, NY; (Y); Letterman Clb; Bsktbl; Golf; Gym; Wrstlng; Prendergast Lib Awd Excllnc In Am Hist 86; Berkley.

GLAVE, SUZETTE; Auburn HS; Auburn, NY; (Y); Sec Pres 4-H; FBLA; Office Aide; Chorus; Hon Roll; Achvt Awd In Rcrdkpng 86; Prfncy Awd In Kybrdng 86; Mrsvl Coll; Hrs Trnr.

GLAVEY, PATRICIA; Mount Mercy Acad; Buffalo, NY; (Y); Art Clb; Dance Clb; SADD; School Play; Stage Crew; Badmtn; Fld Hcky; Stat Score Keeper; Hon Roll; Jr NHS; Rochester Inst; Tech Dsgn.

GLAVIANO, ANTHONY; Arbishop Molloy HS; Woodhaven, NY; (Y); 97/386; Hon Roll; BUS.

GLAZER, KIM F; Walt Whitman HS; Huntington, NY; (Y); Computer Clb; Library Aide; Office Aide; Spanish Clb; High Hon Roll; Hon Roll; Spanish NHS; Am Hert Club VP 86; Natl Span Exam 85; Rgnsts Schlrshp 86; Nova U; Psych.

GLAZIER, DANIEL; Sandy Creek Central Schl; Lacona, NY; (Y); 20/91; Drama Clb; French Clb; Band; Chorus; Church Choir; Concert Band; Jazz Band; Mrchg Band; School Musical; Variety Show; Dollars For Schlrs Schlrshp, Natl Funeral Dir Am Schlrshp 86; Canton ATC; Funeral Dir.

GLAZIER, DAVID; Ithaca HS; Ithaca, NY; (Y); 4-H; JA; Lit Mag; Rep Soph Cls; Rep Jr Cls; JV Var Ftbl; JV Trk; JV Wrstlng; 4-H Awd; AZ ST U; Accntng.

GLEASON, AMY; Waterloo SR HS; Waterloo, NY; (Y); 13/157; Sec Exploring; FTA; Girl Scts; Spanish Clb; Concert Band; Jazz Band; Mrchg Band; Score Keeper; Hon Roll; NHS; Silvr Awd Grl Scts 84; Elem Ed.

GLEASON, GLORIA; Indian River Central HS; Philadelphia, NY; (Y); AFS; Pres Church Yth Grp; Pres 4-H; Pres Latin Clb; Band; Chorus; Church Choir; School Musical; School Play; Variety Show; Med.

GLEASON, JAMES W; Horseheads HS; Horseheads, NY; (S); 1/380; German Clb; Model UN; Scholastic Bowl; VP Science Clb; Var Tennis; Hon Roll; Pres NHS; Ntl Merit SF; Rensselaer Medal 85; NY Sci Olympd Gold Medal 85; Corning Chem Bwl Silver Medal 85; Engrng.

GLEASON, JEFF; Thomas A Edison HS; Elmira Hts, NY; (Y); 33/79; Camera Clb; Drama Clb; Drill Tm; School Musical; JV Bsbl; JV Bsktbl; JV Ftbl; Var Trk; Hon Roll; US Army.

GLEASON, LORI; Indian River Central Schl; Philadelphia, NY; (Y); 6/147; AFS; Latin Clb; Chorus; Color Guard; Stage Crew; Jr Cls; JV Var Cheerleading; JV Vllybl; Hon Roll; NHS.

GLEASON, SCOTT; Hamburg HS; Boston, NY; (Y); 29/380; Chess Clb; Computer Clb; Ski Clb; High Hon Roll; Hon Roll; Math.

GLEASON, TAMMY; Granville Central HS; Granville, NY; (Y); 11/125; Girl Scts; Mathletes; Math Tm; Spanish Clb; SADD; Yrbk Phtg; Yrbk Stf; Hon Roll; Clcls Awd 86; Clarkson U; Mthmtcs.

GLEBA, MICHAEL C; Bronx HS Of Science; Bronx, NY; (Y); Church Yth Grp; Im Bsktbl; Manhattan College Prsdntl & NY ST Regents Schlrshps 86; Natl Assoc Socl Stud Thcrs Clb Awd 86; Manhattan Coll; Urbn Affrs.

GLEISSNER, ROBERT; Wantagh HS; Wantagh, NY; (Y); 88/271; Boy Scts; Computer Clb; Mathletes; Math Clb; Math Tm; Ski Clb; Slvr Math Awd 84; Bst HS Math Awd 84; Hofstra U; Accntng.

GLENN, SHERRIE; Edison Tech; Rochester, NY; (Y); Aud/Vis; Camp Fr Inc; Computer Clb; Girl Scts; Library Aide; Office Aide; Pep Clb; Band; Chorus; Pep Band; Guidnce Aid Awd 83-86; Seans Aid Awd 84-86; Engl Awd 86; Cazenova U; Comp.

GLENNON, DAVID; Stissing Mountain HS; Elizaville, NY; (Y); 3/83; AFS; Chess Clb; Chorus; Variety Show; Nwsp Rptr; Lit Mag; VP Sr Cls; Var L Trk; NHS; Principals Stu Of The Week Awd 85; Natl Sci Olympiad Awd In Bio 85; Outstndng Runner 86; Lawyer.

GLENNON, JENNIFER; New Rochelle HS; New Rochelle, NY; (Y); Model UN; Band; Concert Band; Mrchg Band; Orch; Symp Band; Lit Mag; Mu Alp Tht; NCTE Awd; NHS; U PA Book Awd Excllnce Engl 86; Frgn Policy Assn Consrtm 86-87; Legsltv Conf 86; Engl.

GLICKMAN, EMILY; Hunter College HS; New York, NY; (Y); Model UN; Nwsp Ed-Chief; Nwsp Rptr; Nwsp Stf; Lit Mag; Sec Stu Cncl; Ntl Merit Ltr; Frgn Policy Assn Essay Wnnr; Model UN, NY Conf Delegation Awd Wnnr; Intl Rel.

GLIDDEN, HEIDI; Fairport HS; Fairport, NY; (Y); Exploring; Key Clb; Library Aide; Ski Clb; SADD; Chorus; School Musical; Swing Chorus; Yrbk Stf; DAR Awd; Psychlgy.

GLIDDEN, SUSAN; Hugh C Williams HS; Canton, NY; (Y); 9/115; Orch; Sec Frsh Cls; Sec Soph Cls; VP Jr Cls; Pres Sr Cls; Var L Socr; Trs NHS; Pres Schlr; JV L Bsktbl; Lcrss; N Cntry Schlr St Lawrence U 86; Franklin/Marshll Coll Bk Awd 86; Regents Schlrshp 86; Bucknell U.

GLIKAKIS, ANASTASIA; Newtown HS; Elmhurst, NY; (Y); 62/781; Church Yth Grp; Library Aide; Band; Symp Band; Coach Actv; Score Keeper; Sftbl; Trk; Hon Roll; Psych.

GLINKA, DARRA JEAN; Roy C Ketcham HS; Poughkeepsie, NY; (Y); 130/600; Art Clb; Cmnty Wkr; Band; Chorus; Church Choir; Bsktbl; Crs Cntry; Swmmng; Hon Roll; Dutchess Comm Coll; Mrchndsng.

GLINSKI II, DAVID LEE J; Sweet Home SR HS; Tonawanda, NY; (Y); Boy Scts; Computer Clb; Chorus; Off Soph Cls; Off Jr Cls; Im Mgr Ftbl; Var Mgr(s); JV Score Keeper; JV Tennis; Hon Roll; Comp Sci.

GLINSKI, MICHAEL; Turner/Carroll HS; Buffalo, NY; (Y); Computer Clb; JV Var Bsbl; Im Var Bowling; JV Var Ftbl; Im Vllybl; Turner/Carroll Schlrshp 83; U Of Buffalo; Comp Sci.

GLITCH, CHERYL; Victor Central HS; Victor, NY; (Y); GAA; Varsity Clb; VP Soph Cls; Rep Stu Cncl; Var Bsktbl; Var Capt Socr; Var Trk; Cit Awd; Sftbl; Hon Roll; Ldrs Clb Awd 86; Pres Phy Ftnss Awd 85; Brockport Coll; Psych.

GLOBERMAN, KENNETH A; Midwood HS; Brooklyn, NY; (Y); Cmnty Wkr; Drama Clb; Math Tm; School Musical; Math.

GLOECKNER, BETH; Shaker HS; Loudonville, NY; (Y); Key Clb; Ski Clb; Socr; Sftbl; Trk; Hon Roll; Acctng.

GLOSENGER, JAMES; Elmira Free Acad; Elmira, NY; (Y); Boy Scts; JA; Hon Roll; Corning CC; Data Prcsng.

GLOVER, JILL; Linton HS; Schenectady, NY; (Y); JCL; Key Clb; Rep Jr Cls; Var Trk; Hon Roll; Syracuse U; Spcl Educ.

GLOVER, MARJORIE; New Dorp HS; Staten Island, NY; (Y); Church Yth Grp; Exploring; Intnl Clb; Key Clb; Teachers Aide; Band; Church Choir; School Musical; Off Sr Cls; Pom Pon; Howard Hampton U; Lawyer.

GLOVER, RODELL H; La Guardia Schl For Performing Arts; New York, NY; (Y); Aud/Vis; Church Yth Grp; Church Choir; School Musical; School Play; Stage Crew; Variety Show; Rep Jr Cls; Rep Sr Cls; Schlrshp To Natl Horn Muscl Theatr 83; SUNY Purchase; Drama.

GLOW, KATHLEEN; Morrisville-Eaton HS; Morrisville, NY; (Y); 10/60; GAA; Math Tm; Band; Chorus; Concert Band; Mrchg Band; Bsktbl; Cheerleading; Crs Cntry; Fld Hcky; Art Awd 86; Syracuse U; Rtlng.

GLOWKA, TAMMY; Alden Central HS; Elma, NY; (Y); Church Yth Grp; Cmnty Wkr; 4-H; Spanish Clb; SADD; Ed Yrbk Stf; 4-H Awd; Hon Roll; NHS; Prfct Atten Awd.

GLOWNY, REBECCA; Mt Mercy Acad; Buffalo, NY; (Y); Church Yth Grp; Quiz Bowl; SADD; Chorus; Church Choir; Swing Chorus; Variety Show; Hon Roll; 4 Yr 1/2 Schlrshp To HS 83; Silvr Mdl Intl Music Festvl 85; Mdl Of Merit In Intl Music Festvl 86; Buffalo U; Commnctns.

GLUC, ANN; Villa Maria Acad; Buffalo, NY; (Y); Variety Show; Trs Frsh Cls; VP Soph Cls; Rep Jr Cls; Sec CAP; Var Bsktbl; JV Bowling; Var Sftbl; Im Vllybl; Hon Roll.

GLUCK, DAVID L; Great Neck South SR HS; Great Neck, NY; (Y); 7/234; Boy Scts; Nwsp Ed-Chief; Rep Stu Cncl; Var Capt Crs Cntry; Var Capt Trk; Ntl Merit SF; Harvard U; Jrnslsm.

GLUCK, JOHN; St John The Baptist D HS; Ronkonkoma, NY; (Y); Church Yth Grp; JV Crs Cntry; JV Trk; Crmnl Justice.

GLUCK, JULIE B; Port Richmond HS; Staten Island, NY; (Y); Band; Variety Show; Yrbk Stf; Var Sftbl; NHS; Hugh O Brien Ldrshp Sem 85; New Schl Flwshp 86; Pres Belle Brummels, Capt Acdmc Olympics 86-87.

GLUCKMAN, STEVE; The Harley School; Bergen, NY; (Y); Debate Tm; Jazz Band; Mgr Mrchg Band; Orch; School Play; Ed Nwsp Phtg; Pres Frsh Cls; Rep Stu Cncl; Hon Roll; Pres NHS; Comp Law.

GLUS, NINA; Stony Brook Schl; Hauppaughe, NY; (Y); Am Leg Aux Girls St; Church Yth Grp; Orch; School Musical; Nwsp Rptr; Nwsp Stf; Var Crs Cntry; High Hon Roll; Ntl Merit Schol; Orchestra Awd 85; German Awd 84; Columbia U Of Barnard; Nat Sci.

GLYNN, TOM; South Side HS; Rockville Centre, NY; (Y); 4/278; Aud/Vis; Boy Scts; Camera Clb; Computer Clb; Key Clb; Math Clb; Pep Clb; Spanish Clb; SADD; Ice Hcky; Niagra U; Law.

GMELIN, DENISE; Hauppauge HS; Hauppauge, NY; (Y); Church Yth Grp; Cmnty Wkr; Teachers Aide; Orch; School Musical; JV Trk; High Hon Roll; Hon Roll; NHS; NYSSMA Violin Solo 84 Awds 84 & 85.

GNAGE, JENNIFER; Groton Central Schl; Groton, NY; (Y); 12/68; VICA; Stat Bsktbl; Hon Roll; Pres Acad Ftnss Awd 86; Gld Key Awd 86; Outstndng JR Cosmtlgy Stu 84-85; Cosmtlgy.

GNERRE, MARIA; Bishop Ford Central HS; Brooklyn, NY; (Y); Drama Clb; School Play; Nwsp Stf; Yrbk Bus Mgr; Var Trk; Var Vllybl; High Hon Roll; Retarded Chldrn Camp Cnslr 83 & 86; Fash Merch.

GO, GENEVIEVE; Francis Lewis HS; Flushing, NY; (Y); 18/351; Drama Clb; French Clb; Library Aide; Teachers Aide; School Play; Var L Crs Cntry; Hon Roll; NHS; Stat Gym; Trk; NY ST Rgnst Schlrshp 86; Mead Sci Essy Comptn Chem Awd 85; New York U; Med.

GOBERN, EUGENE; De Witt Clinton HS; Bronx, NY; (Y); Prfct Atten Awd; Cert Of Merit Bookkeeping Acctng 85-86; Sut Of Mo Aqd 85-86; Accounting.

GODEK, EDWARD J; St Francis Prep; Middle Village, NY; (S); 82/690; Boy Scts; Ski Clb; Band; Im Bsktbl; Im Ftbl; Im Socr; Im Sftbl; Im Vllybl; Wt Lftg; Opt Clb Awd; Rengents 86; Cooper Union; Engr.

GODEK, TARA; Henninger HS; Syracuse, NY; (Y); Art Clb; Stage Crew; Hon Roll; Pratt U; Illistrtn.

GODINEZ, BRADLEY; Franklin Acad; Malone, NY; (Y); Hon Roll; Prfct Atten Awd; Epsilon 84; Acdmc All Amer 86.

GODSELL, GLORIA; Smithtown West HS; Hauppauge, NY; (Y); Cmnty Wkr; DECA; Stu Cncl; Mgr Gym; High Hon Roll; Jr NHS; NHS; SUNY Binghampton; Law.

GODSEN, MICHAEL; Westhill SR HS; Syracuse, NY; (S); 31/145; Boy Scts; Exploring; Var Capt Crs Cntry; Var Trk; Hon Roll; NHS; Awds Excllnc Crss Cntry 84; Qualf ST Mt Crss Cntry 85; Qualf NY ST Fed Mt Crss Cntry 85; Elctrcl Engrng.

GOEBEL, DONNA; Warwick Valley HS; Warwick, NY; (S); 14/195; Pres Band; Concert Band; Drm Mjr(t); Jazz Band; Symp Band; High Hon Roll; Sec NHS; All ST Band 84-86; Engrng.

GOERGEN, BELINDA; Hamburg Sr HS; Hamburg, NY; (Y); 23/384; Cmnty Wkr; French Clb; Hosp Aide; Service Clb; SADD; Band; Chorus; Mrchg Band; School Musical; Sftbl; Bus Mgmt.

GOERKE, BRIAN; Hicksville HS; Hicksville, NY; (Y); 10/400; Spanish Clb; Symp Band; Bsbl; Fld Hcky; High Hon Roll; Jr NHS; NHS; Prfct Atten Awd; Spanish NHS; Achvt Awd Amer Hstry II Regents 86; Achvt Awd Consumr Studs 86; Prfct Atten 85 & 86; Hofstra U; Bus.

GOERLITZ, RICHARD; Plattsburgh SR HS; Plattsburgh, NY; (Y); Boy Scts; Ski Clb; School Musical; Stage Crew; Crs Cntry; Swmmng; Trk; Hon Roll; Blck Lttr Awd-Swmmg 85-86; Acad Awd Engl 86; Soc Sci.

GOES, JOANNE; Ravena-Coeymans-Selkirk Centl HS; Selkirk, NY; (Y); Church Yth Grp; Cmnty Wkr; Commnctns.

GOETCHIUS, KAREN; Faith Heritage Schl; Jamesville, NY; (Y); 1/23; Church Yth Grp; Drama Clb; Ski Clb; School Play; Nwsp Ed-Chief; Nwsp Stf; VP Frsh Cls; Sec Soph Cls; VP Stu Cncl; Trk; NYS Regents & Coll Deans Schlrshp 86; Cornell U; Human Devlpmnt.

GOETZ, ROBERT; Lincoln HS; Yonkers, NY; (S); 35/350; Drama Clb; Band; Chorus; Concert Band; Mrchg Band; School Play; Capt L Ftbl; NHS; Math Clb; Math Tm; Honrbl Mentn-Westchester & Putnam Cnty Golden Dozen Schlr/Athlt Awd; U Of PA; Intl Busnss.

GOETZE, VICKI; Lyndonville Central HS; Lyndonville, NY; (Y); 20/90; Computer Clb; GAA; Math Clb; Science Clb; Spanish Clb; Varsity Clb; Chorus; Yrbk Stf; Bsktbl; Socr; MVP Awd 86; Bus Admin.

GOFF, MARY KATHLEEN; Fairport HS; Fairport, NY; (Y); Office Aide; Band; Color Guard; Concert Band; Drill Tm; Flag Corp; Mrchg Band; Twrlr; Hon Roll; Ideal Miss Tlnt Wnnr 83; Physcl Thrpy.

GOGGIN, CHRISTOPHER; Liberty JR SR HS; Liberty, NY; (Y); Debate Tm; Band; Jazz Band; School Play; Stage Crew; Nwsp Phtg; Nwsp Stf; Yrbk Phtg; Yrbk Stf; Var L Golf; Intl Bus.

GOHDE, HEATHER; Unatego JR SR HS; Otego, NY; (Y); FHA; SADD; Band; Color Guard; Pep Band; Yrbk Phtg; Rep Stu Cncl; Var Bsktbl; Var Fld Hcky; Var Sftbl; Linda Russ Mem Sprts Awd 83; Trvl/Tourism.

GOJCAJ, IRENE GO; Dominican Commercial HS; Scarsdale, NY; (Y); Accntnt.

GOLA, RON; Jamesville De Witt HS; Jamesville, NY; (Y); CAP; Cmnty Wkr; Computer Clb; Exploring; Im JV Ftbl; Piloting.

GOLBIN, JENNIFER; Huntington HS; Huntington, NY; (Y); Cmnty Wkr; Trs Girl Scts; Hosp Aide; Orch; Var Trk; Cit Awd; High Hon Roll; Jr NHS; NHS; Sufflk Cnty Yth Brd 85; Cert Apprec Cty Exec 86; NYS Yth Cncl 86; Law.

GOLD, JENNIFER; Roy C Ketcham HS; Wappingers Falls, NY; (Y); Cmnty Wkr; Hosp Aide; Chrmn Temple Yth Grp; Nwsp Stf; Yrbk Stf; JV Trk; High Hon Roll; Sec NHS; AJH Hnrs Scty 86-87; Micrblgy.

GOLD, MICHAEL; Canarsie HS; Brooklyn, NY; (S); 19/500; Cit Awd; High Hon Roll; Hon Roll; Hnr Lgn 83; Arista 83-86.

GOLD, VIRGINIA; John Jay SR HS; Katonah, NY; (Y); Trs Church Yth Grp; Latin Clb; Band; Orch; School Musical; Bowling; Var Swmmng; High Hon Roll; Sec Jr NHS; NHS; Psych.

GOLDBACH, JOHN H; Binghamton HS; Binghamton, NY; (Y); Am Leg Boys St; Art Clb; Boy Scts; Computer Clb; Scholastic Art Awds Gold Key 84 & 85; National Honorable Mention Scholastic Art Awds 84.

GOLDBERG, ABBE; Janesville-Dewitt HS; Fayetteville, NY; (Y); VP Exploring; Sec Pres Key Clb; SADD; Teachers Aide; Temple Yth Grp; Sec Frsh Cls; Pres Soph Cls; Rep Jr Cls; Var Capt Cheerleading; High Hon Roll; Elmira Key Awd 86; Schlstc Art Awd Hnrbl Mntn 85; Ldrshp Awd 86.

GOLDBERG, ANDREA; Sanford H Calhoun HS; Merrick, NY; (Y); 2/313; Key Clb; Mathletes; Math Clb; Pres Math Tm; Band; School Play; Off Soph Cls; Hon Roll; NHS; Sal; Union Coll; Physician.

GOLDBERG, BETH; Hebrew Academy Of Nassau County; Great Neck, NY; (Y); Art Clb; Model UN; Office Aide; Temple Yth Grp; Nwsp Stf; Yrbk Stf; High Hon Roll; Hon Roll; NHS; NEDT Awd; NYS Rgnts Schlrshp, NYU Trustee Schlrshp, Stern Coll Bd/Lin Schlrshp 86; Barnard Coll; Law.

GOLDBERG, CRAIG; Valley Stream North HS; Malverne, NY; (Y); 1/140; Mathletes; Model UN; Ed Nwsp Stf; Chrmn Soph Cls; Trs Jr Cls; Trs Sr Cls; JV Bsbl; Bausch & Lomb Sci Awd; Mu Alp Tht; Spanish NHS; RPI Medal 86; George Washington U Medal 86; Long Isnald Math Fair Bronze, Gold & Slvr Mdls 84-86.

GOLDBERG, FAYE; Commack HS North; Commack, NY; (Y); Library Aide; 1st Pl Hrsbckrdng 84; Bwlng Trphs; Typng Cert 85; Comp Sci.

GOLDBERG, FELICIA S; Plainview Old-Bethpage HS; Plainview, NY; (Y); 23/194; Cmnty Wkr; Key Clb; Model UN; Teachers Aide; Temple Yth Grp; Chorus; Yrbk Stf; High Hon Roll; Hon Roll; NHS.

GOLDBERG, GREGG; Commack High Schl South; Commack, NY; (Y); Math Tm; Jazz Band; Mrchg Band; Orch; School Musical; Symp Band; Golf; Tennis; High Hon Roll; NHS; Bus.

GOLDBERG, LORI; Central Islip HS; Central Islip, NY; (Y); 20/530; Stage Crew; Ed Nwsp Ed-Chief; Lit Mag; Sec Stu Cncl; Hon Roll; NHS; 1st Pl Nwswrtng Ctgry Lng Islnd Prs Cntst 86; 2nd Pl Entrl Ctggry 86; 3rd Pl Untd Prs Ass Wmn Wrtng 86.

GOLDBERG, MARCIE; Jamesville Dewitt HS; Dewitt, NY; (Y); 36/250; French Clb; Key Clb; SADD; Temple Yth Grp; Var Cheerleading; High Hon Roll; NHS; Community Svc Awd 85; ST U Of NY Albany.

GOLDBERG, MEREDITH; Commack HS South; Dix Hills, NY; (Y); Math Tm; Temple Yth Grp; Sec Soph Cls; Cheerleading; Var Tennis; JV Vllybl; High Hon Roll; NHS; Ntl Merit Ltr; All Conf & All Cnty Tnns 84 & 85; Pre Law.

GOLDBERG, MIRIAM R; The Brandeis Schl; Levittown, NY; (Y); Service Clb; Temple Yth Grp; Nwsp Ed-Chief; Nwsp Rptr; Yrbk Rptr; Yrbk Stf; Sec NHS; Ntl Merit SF; A J Caplow Schlrshp 85; Awds Merit Achvt Piano 82-85; Lib Arts.

GOLDBERG, STACY; Smithtown HS East; Nesconset, NY; (Y); Cmnty Wkr; Hosp Aide; Service Clb; SADD; Chrmn Jr Cls; Rep Stu Cncl; JV Tennis; Hon Roll; Jr NHS; NHS; Natl Hnr Socty 84-86; Awd 100 Hrs Svc Hosp 84-85; Psych.

GOLDBERG, WARREN K; Bethpage HS; Plainview, NY; (Y); 44/290; Hon Roll; NY ST Rgnst Schlrshp 86; Bowling Coll; Aerospace.

GOLDBLATT, MICHAEL; Valley Central HS; Newburgh, NY; (Y); 109/325; Drama Clb; Intnl Clb; Service Clb; Chorus; School Musical; School Play; Yrbk Stf; Off Frsh Cls; Off Soph Cls; Off Jr Cls; Soc Studies 10r Fnl Exm 85; Awd Part Svc Clb 86; Advncd Soc Studies Ii & Engl Ii 85-86; Johnson & Wales; Hotel Mgnt.

GOLDE, MICHAEL J; St Anthonys HS; East Northport, NY; (Y); 11/240; Nwsp Rptr; Yrbk Rptr; Var L Ftbl; Var L Trk; VP French Hon Soc; High Hon Roll; Sec NHS; Ntl Merit Ltr; St Schlr; Msgr Peter Nolan Acad Schlrshp 84-85; Rensselaer Polytech Inst Medl-Math & Sci 85; Pace U; Fin.

GOLDEN, JOY; Aubum HS; Auburn, NY; (Y); Varsity Clb; Nwsp Stf; Lit Mag; Tennis; High Hon Roll; Hon Roll; Pres Schlr; 1st Pl Nws Story Syracuse Prss Day Awds 86; Jrnlsm.

GOLDEN, PAUL; Shenendehowa HS; Clifton Park, NY; (Y); 60/700; AFS; Exploring; Intnl Clb; Key Clb; Political Wkr; Yrbk Phtg; Rep Stu Cncl; JV Var Trk; High Hon Roll; NHS; NYS Energy Comp 2nd Pl 86; Ind Rel.

GOLDENBERG, DAVID; Central HS; Valley Stream, NY; (Y); 5/300; Art Clb; Camera Clb; Computer Clb; Var Wt Lftg; Hofstra U; Accntng.

GOLDFARB, MICHELLE; Walt Whitman HS; Huntington, NY; (Y); 131/522; Orch; Off Jr Cls; Fld Hcky; Gym; High Hon Roll; Hon Roll; Spanish NHS; Elem Ed.

GOLDFEDER, STEVEN; Abraham Lincoln HS; Brooklyn, NY; (Y); 46/465; Computer Clb; Key Clb; Hon Roll; Sr Actvts Trs 86; Arista 84-86; Akiva-VP 85; Vol Hosp 84-85; HS Biol/Hebrew Mdls; SO & Yth Serv Awds; Brooklyn Coll; Dentistry.

GOLDGEWERT, RONALD; Hebrew Acad Of Nassau Cnty; Greenlawn, NY; (Y); 1/78; Debate Tm; CAP; Math Tm; Quiz Bowl; Ed Nwsp Stf; Yrbk Stf; Bsbl; High Hon Roll; NHS; Sal; NY St Rgnts Schlrshp 85; Cornell U; Bus.

GOLDIN, ADAM; Baldwin SR HS; Baldwin, NY; (Y); Exploring; Key Clb; SADD; Band; Concert Band; Jazz Band; Pep Band; Wrstlng; High Hon Roll; Hon Roll; Bus.

GOLDMAN, ELIZABETH E; Kenmore East HS; Tonawanda, NY; (Y); 1/300; Capt Dance Clb; Pep Clb; Band; Color Guard; Mrchg Band; Ed Yrbk Stf; Stat Vllybl; High Hon Roll; NHS; Peer Tm 85-86; Bio Sci.

GOLDMAN, JEFFREY D; Clarkstown HS North; New City, NY; (Y); Aud/Vis; Cmnty Wkr; Computer Clb; JV Trk; Hon Roll; Mu Alp Tht; NY ST Rgnts Schlrshp 86; SUNY-ALBANY.

GOLDMAN, LEE; Harley Schl; Rochester, NY; (Y); Aud/Vis; Debate Tm; Model UN; Trs Thesps; Pres Stage Crew; Yrbk Stf; Var Bsktbl; NY ST Rgnts Schlrshp 86; Trinity Coll Hrtfrd.

GOLDMAN, SCOTT; The Wheatlex Schl; Old Westbury, NY; (Y); Rep Jr Cls; Coach Actv; Tennis; Trk; Bstn U; Pre-Law.

GOLDSAND, ALYSSA; Brewster HS; Brewster, NY; (Y); Teachers Aide; Temple Yth Grp; Varsity Clb; School Play; Var Capt Bsktbl; Var JV Fld Hcky; Var JV Socr; Hon Roll; NHS; MVP JV Bksthl; Cert Of Appreciation In Field Hcky; Class B Field Hcky Champ; Cert Of Honor Euro Hist; Child Psych.

GOLDSCHMIDT, JEAN; Spackenkill HS; Poughkeepsie, NY; (Y); Thesps; School Musical; Yrbk Bus Mgr; Yrbk Stf; Rep Sr Cls; Rensselaer Polytech; Physics.

GOLDSTEIN, AILEEN; Mahopac HS; Mahopac, NY; (Y); 49/409; Am Leg Aux Girls St; Teachers Aide; Nwsp Bus Mgr; Yrbk Bus Mgr; Ed Lit Mag; Var L Tennis; JV Vllybl; High Hon Roll; Hon Roll; NHS; HOBY Ldrshp Awd 84; Most Imprvd Tennis Plyr 85; Physcl Thrpy.

GOLDSTEIN, BROOK J; E L Vandermeulen HS; Pt Jefferson Sta, NY; (Y); 120/330; SADD; Temple Yth Grp; Chorus; Rep Stu Cncl; Stat Ftbl; Mgr(s); Score Keeper; Stat Socr; Stat Wrstlng; Hon Roll; NYS Rgnts Schrlshp 86; U S FL; Marine Bio.

GOLDSTEIN, DAVID J; Lakeland HS; Yorktown Hts, NY; (Y); 28/344; Pres Computer Clb; Hosp Aide; Pres Science Clb; School Musical; Nwsp Ed-Chief; Yrbk Bus Mgr; High Hon Roll; Hon Roll; Jr NHS; NHS; CIBA-GEIGY Awd 86; Case Western Reserve U; Med.

GOLDSTEIN, ELIZABETH; Lawrence HS; N Woodmere, NY; (Y); AFS; Pres Hst DECA; Spanish Clb; Temple Yth Grp; Chorus; Yrbk Bus Mgr; Yrbk Phtg; Hon Roll; NHS; Rep Frsh Cls; Job Intrvw 1st Pl Nassau Cnty Levl DECA 86; Outstndng Chptr Hnbl Mntn DECA 86; Invstmt Bnkr.

GOLDSTEIN, ERIN; Islip HS; Bayshore, NY; (Y); 5/250; Mathletes; Quiz Bowl; Sec Temple Yth Grp; Chorus; School Musical; Yrbk Stf; Rep Soph Cls; Trs Stu Cncl; High Hon Roll; Jr NHS; Outstndng Achvt In Bio 83-84; Psych.

GOLDSTEIN, GREGORY M; Mc Kee Vocational & Technical HS; Staten Island, NY; (Y); 11/227; Pres Sr Cls; Rep Stu Cncl; Capt Bowling; Capt Vllybl; Hon Roll; Prfct Atten Awd; Stu Athltc Train Ftbl,Bsktbl 83-86; SR Day Comm 86; NYS Regnt Schlrshp 86; SUNY Farmingdale; Elec Engrng.

GOLDSTEIN, JEFFREY D; Niskayuna HS; Schenectady, NY; (Y); Am Leg Boys St; Cmnty Wkr; Pres Stu Cncl; Capt Trk; DAR Awd; Hon Roll; NHS; Ntl Merit Schol; St Schlr; Cntry III Schl Wnr; Cornell U; Industrl.

GOLDSTEIN, KAREN; Half Hollow Hills HS East; Melville, NY; (Y); 202/500; Cmnty Wkr; Hosp Aide; Leo Clb; Service Clb; Orch; Stage Crew; Yrbk Phtg; Yrbk Stf; Lit Mag; High Hon Roll; Emerson; Film.

GOLDSTEIN, LORI; White Plains HS; White Plns, NY; (Y); Office Aide; Teachers Aide; Temple Yth Grp; Capt Drill Tm; Capt Pom Pon; Hon Roll; Liberty Weekend Closing Ceremonies-Drill Tm 86; SUNY-CORTLAND; Math Educ.

GOLDSTEIN, PETER L; Huntington HS; Huntington, NY; (Y); 3/383; AFS; Key Clb; SADD; Variety Show; Yrbk Stf; Trs Frsh Cls; Var L Socr; High Hon Roll; Pres NHS; Dartmouth Coll.

GOLDSTEIN, STEVEN L; New Rochelle HS; New Rochelle, NY; (Y); 64/550; Cmnty Wkr; 4-H Awd; VP Service Clb; NHS; NY ST Regents Schlrshp 86.

GOLDSTOCK, DEBORAH; Mamaroneck HS; Larchmont, NY; (Y); French Clb; Political Wkr; SADD; Chorus; French Hon Soc; Hon Roll; NHS; Ntl Merit Ltr; Cornell U; Law.

GOLDWIRE, CELESTE; Springfield Gardens HS; Queens, NY; (Y); Debate Tm; Service Clb; Band; Symp Band; Rep Frsh Cls; Off Soph Cls; Bsktbl; Corporate Law.

GOLDWYN, THEODORE J; Riverhead HS; Baiting Hollow, NY; (Y); 11/216; Math Tm; Chorus; Jazz Band; Orch; Ed Yrbk Stf; Var Crs Cntry; Var Tennis; High Hon Roll; NHS; Ntl Merit SF; NYSSMA All-St String Orch 84-85; Cornellu; Elec Engr.

GOLEBIEWSKI, JEANNE; Hamburg SR HS; Eden, NY; (Y); 40/374; Pres French Clb; Concert Band; Symp Band; Stu Cncl; Var JV Bsktbl; Var Swmmng; Var Tennis; Hon Roll; NHS; Phys Thrpy.

GOLIBERSUCH, DANA; Linton HS; Schenectady, NY; (Y); Key Clb; Ski Clb; Teachers Aide; Off Frsh Cls; Off Soph Cls; Trs Jr Cls; Off Sr Cls; Stu Cncl; Hon Roll; NHS; Ntl French Exam Hnrble Mntn 84; Regents Schlrshp 86; 3rd Rnnr Up Miss Teen NY Pgnt; Boston U; Chldhd Ed.

GOLL, CHRISTOPHER; Cassadaga Valley HS; Cassadaga, NY; (Y); Am Leg Boys St; Acpl Chr; Chorus; Trs Jr Cls; Trs Rep Stu Cncl; Var JV Bsktbl; Var Crs Cntry; Var Golf; Var JV Vllybl; NHS; Engrng.

GOLL, DARYL W; Williamsville East HS; Buffalo, NY; (Y); Drama Clb; Chorus; School Musical; School Play; Swing Chorus; Schlstc Exc Awd Music 83 & Vcl Msc 84; Bstn Cnsrvtry; Mscl Thtr.

GOLLANCE, RORI; Commack HS North; Commack, NY; (Y); Cmnty Wkr; GAA; Office Aide; Rep Frsh Cls; Rep Soph Cls; Rep Jr Cls; Rep Sr Cls; Var Fld Hcky; JV Sftbl; High Hon Roll; Rgnts Schlrshp 86; Pres Grls Ldr Clb 86-87; Bus Mgmnt.

GOLOMBEK, PAULA; Villa Maria Acad; Cheektowaga, NY; (Y); 10/85; High Hon Roll; Hon Roll; Bryant & Stratton Bus Schl; Bus.

GOLOVE, JEFF; James Sperry HS; Pittsford, NY; (Y); 45/277; JA; Band; Jazz Band; Bsktbl; Socr; Hon Roll; Intrnshp Prog Cert Persnnl & Engr 84-86; Coach 2 Bsbll Tms Ages 7-13 84-86; Personnel.

GOLUB, ARNOLD P; Wantagh HS; Wantagh, NY; (Y); 18/271; Debate Tm; Math Tm; Temple Yth Grp; Band; Jazz Band; Nwsp Stf; Yrbk Phtg; Sr Cls; NHS; Amer U Prsdntl Schlrshp 86; NY ST Rgnts Schlrshp 86; American U; Accntng.

GOLUB, MICHAEL; Smithtown HS West; Smithtown, NY; (Y); VP Cmnty Wkr; Science Clb; Bsbl; Wrstlng; Hon Roll; Psych.

GOMES, ERIC; Monsignor Farrell HS; Staten Island, NY; (Y); 1/320; Cmnty Wkr; VP Math Tm; Spanish Clb; Sec Jr Cls; JV Crs Cntry; Var Trk; Cit Awd; High Hon Roll; VP NHS; Rensselaer Medal Math,Sci 86; George Washington U Medal Math,Sci 86; Tchr CCD Pgm 86-87; Pre-Med.

GOMES, MARIA; Yonkers HS; Yonkers, NY; (Y); Math Tm; SADD; High Hon Roll; NHS; Bus Adm.

GOMEZ, ALEX; Herbert H Lehman HS; Bronx, NY; (Y); Church Yth Grp; Nwsp Rptr; Nwsp Stf; Pres Frsh Cls; VP Soph Cls; Wrstlng; Hon Roll; NHS; Hstry Relig Eng & Sci 84; Spn Biol Eng & Hstry 85; NYU; Jrnlsm.

GOMEZ, ALEX; Port Chester HS; Port Chester, NY; (Y); Ski Clb; Band; Concert Band; Mrchg Band; Yrbk Stf; Mu Alp Tht; Spanish NHS; Hon Roll; Sci Hnr Soc, Paperboy Mnth, TV Prod Awd; Elec Engrng.

GOMEZ, ALICIA; John Dewey HS; Brooklyn, NY; (Y); Library Aide; Office Aide; Spanish Clb; Chorus; Yrbk Stf; Cit Awd; Hon Roll; Trophy Dist Span Spelling Bee 83-84; Teach English.

GOMEZ, BELITZA; Clara Barton HS; Brooklyn, NY; (Y); Pres Spanish Clb; Off Frsh Cls; Off Soph Cls; Off Jr Cls; Hon Roll; NY U; Pre-Med.

GOMEZ, CLAUDIA; Saint Francis Prep; Woodside, NY; (S); 131/744; Science Clb; DAR Awd; AATSP Ntl Cntst Long Isl Chptr 1st Pl 85; Pre-Med.

GOMEZ, ELISSA; St Joseph By The Sea HS; Staten Island, NY; (Y); 79/239; Art Clb; Aud/Vis; Cmnty Wkr; Computer Clb; Girl Scts; Chorus; Nwsp Stf; Bowling; No Smoking Poster Award From American Lung Association 84; New Paltz; Marketing.

GOMEZ, FREDDY; Sachem North HS; Ronkonkoma, NY; (Y); 194/1400; Church Yth Grp; German Clb; Hosp Aide; Chorus; Church Choir; Jazz Band; Madrigals; School Musical; School Play; Socr; Perf Publ Schl Attndnc K-12 86; Adelante 86; SUNY Stony Brook; Med.

GOMEZ, JANIS MARY; Peekskill HS; Peekskill, NY; (Y); 1/146; Nwsp Sprt Ed; Trs Rep Stu Cncl; Stat Ftbl; Var Vllybl; Stat Wrstlng; Elks Awd; High Hon Roll; Trs NHS; Val; VP Frsh Cls; CIBA-GEIGY Sci Awd 86; Bank NY Schlrshp 86; Rotary Clb Acadmc Awd 86; Yale U; Ec & Poly Ci.

GOMEZ, MARYBEL; John Dewey HS; Brooklyn, NY; (Y); Cmnty Wkr; Hosp Aide; JA; Spanish Clb; Chorus; Color Guard; Yrbk Stf; Rep Jr Cls; Hon Roll; Prfct Atten Awd; Sci Awd 84; Schlrshp Awd 84; Arista 84; Columbia U; Organic Chemst.

GOMEZ, PATTY; Richmond Hill HS; Richmond Hill, NY; (Y); 86/200; English Clb; Library Aide; Ftbl; Cit Awd; Engl Hnr Awd 85; Miami ST U; Ctrng.

GOMEZ, ROSA; St Edmund HS; Brooklyn, NY; (S); Hon Roll; Jr NHS; Prfct Atten Awd; Math Awd; Ntl Lang Arts Olympd Awd; Katherine Gibbs; Exec Sec.

GOMEZ, TANYA; De Witt Clinton HS; Bronx, NY; (Y); Drama Clb; Library Aide; Office Aide; ROTC; Science Clb; Chorus; Stage Crew; Variety Show; Cit Awd; Vlntr Awd-Jewish Hm & Hosp For Aged 85; Crmnl Alw.

GOMEZ, THERESA; Doninican Comm HS; Brooklyn, NY; (Y); St Johns U; Bus Mgmt.

GOMMENGINGER, CHRISTINA; Kendall JR SR HS; Albion, NY; (Y); Art Clb; Color Guard; JV Var Cheerleading; Hon Roll; Prfct Atten Awd; Prfct Attndnc At Occptnl Schl 85-86; Awd For 3rd & 4th In Frmns Pgnt 84-86; Monroe CC; Comp Prog.

GONELL, JENNIFER; H Frank Carey HS; Franklin Square, NY; (Y); 2/276; Church Yth Grp; Hosp Aide; SADD; Thesps; Band; Nwsp Ed-Chief; Rep Stu Cncl; Var Capt Crs Cntry; NHS; Sal; HOBY Rep 85; Frgn Lang Hnr Soc 84; Fnlst Voice Dem 86; Chem Engr.

GONGORA, GERALDINE; Attica SR HS; Attica, NY; (Y); Stage Crew; Nwsp Rptr; Yrbk Stf; Rep Frsh Cls; Rep Soph Cls; Hon Roll; NHS; Bus.

GONGORA, RAFAEL C; Christian Brothers Acad; Syracuse, NY; (Y); 23/93; Exploring; Hosp Aide; Political Wkr; Nwsp Stf; Yrbk Stf; JV Ftbl; Var L Tennis; Hon Roll; NEDT Awd; NYS Regnts Schlrshp 86; 2dn Pl NY Mensa Schlrshp 86; Syracuse U; Pre-Med.

GONSALVES, ANDREW; Geneva HS; Geneva, NY; (S); 33/175; Am Leg Boys St; Church Yth Grp; Varsity Clb; Concert Band; Jazz Band; Mrchg Band; Variety Show; Lcrss; Hon Roll; All Cnty Jazz Band 85; Cmmnctns.

GONYEA, GINA; Whitesboro SR HS; Whitesboro, NY; (Y); 45/300; GAA; Nwsp Rptr; Nwsp Stf; Var Bowling; Var Socr; Hon Roll; Accntng.

GONYEA, KEN; Madrio-Waddington HS; Lisbon, NY; (Y); French Clb; JV Bsbl; High Hon Roll; Hon Roll; NHS; Coble Skill; Bus Adm.

GONZALES, MICHELE; Fairport HS; Fairport, NY; (Y); Church Yth Grp; French Clb; Office Aide; Pep Clb; Bsktbl; Tennis; Hon Roll; Jr NHS; NHS.

GONZALEZ, ALEJANDRO; Holy Cross HS; Bayside, NY; (Y); 1/310; Cmnty Wkr; Intnl Clb; Library Aide; SADD; Nwsp Rptr; Yrbk Ed-Chief; JV VP Trk; Trs NHS; Val; Queens Coll Pres Schlr 83-85; Colgate U Alumni Mem Schlrshp 86; NY St Rgnts Schlrshp 86; Lib Arts.

GONZALEZ, ALEX; Amsterdam HS; Amsterdam, NY; (Y); 67/159; JA; Varsity Clb; Rep Frsh Cls; Rep Soph Cls; Rep Jr Cls; Off Sr Cls; Stu Cncl; JV Bsbl; Var Ftbl; Var Wrstlng; Arch.

GONZALEZ, AMMIE; William Floyd HS; Mastic, NY; (Y); 5/455; Spanish Clb; SADD; Drill Tm; Hon Roll; NHS; St Schlr; Adelphi U; Nrsng.

GONZALEZ, ANGELA; Hamburg SR HS; Hamburg, NY; (Y); Girl Scts; Hosp Aide; Red Cross Aide; Stage Crew; Yrbk Stf; Lit Mag; Rep Frsh Cls; Rep Soph Cls; Stu Cncl; Hon Roll.

GONZALEZ, AURORA; The Hewitt Schl; New York, NY; (Y); Drama Clb; Chorus; School Musical; School Play; Stage Crew; Scholastic Bowl; Ntl Merit Schol; Nwsp Rptr; Yrbk Stf; Grtst Cntrbtn Drama Awd 84; Bst Actrss Awd 84; Bst Spprtng Actrss 85; Drama.

GONZALEZ, BARBARA; Torrejon HS; Apo, NY; (Y); Art Clb; Exploring; Library Aide; ROTC; Teachers Aide; Chorus; Yrbk Sprt Ed; Yrbk Stf; Off Frsh Cls; Hon Roll; Outstndng Art Stu 85-86; Food Svcs Outstndng Wrk 84-85; Mst Outstndng Library Aide 84-85; Comp Opertr.

GONZALEZ, BARRY; Valley Central HS; Newburgh, NY; (Y); Boy Scts; JV Ftbl; Acctg.

GONZALEZ, DANIEL; Wallkill SR HS; Wallkill, NY; (Y); 6/200; Cmnty Wkr; Nwsp Stf; Ed Yrbk Ed-Chief; Lit Mag; High Hon Roll; NHS; Socr; Hon Roll; Pres Schlr; MITE Prtcpnt GA Tech,Spanish Awds 2 Yr 85; Natl Hispanic, Cornell Tradtnl &regents Schlrshps 86; Cornell U; Mech Engrng.

GONZALEZ, ERIC; John Dewey HS; Brooklyn, NY; (Y); Cmnty Wkr; Computer Clb; Latin Clb; Political Wkr; Scholastic Bowl; Science Clb; Teachers Aide; Nwsp Stf; Stu Cncl; Dave Winfield Awd 84-85; Daily News Pride Yankees Awd 84-86; Law.

GONZALEZ, GINA; Niagara Catholic HS; Niagara Falls, NY; (Y); VP French Clb; Teachers Aide; Yrbk Ed-Chief; VP Trs NHS; Cmnty Wkr; Drama Clb; Hosp Aide; Key Clb; Science Clb; School Play; Amer Legion Awd; Fr Kroupa Awd Rnnr Up; ST U Of NY; Intl Rltns.

GONZALEZ, GLORIA; Central Islip HS; Central Islip, NY; (Y); JV Vllybl; 1st Pl AATSP Natl Cont Long Isl Chptr 85; Suffolk Cnty CC; Acctng.

GONZALEZ, GUILLERMO; John Jay HS; Brooklyn, NY; (Y); Art Clb; Science Clb; Stage Crew; Variety Show; Bsbl; Swmmng; Cntrl Diesel Schl Hnr Awd 85-86; John Jay Auto Cls Awd 83-84; Diesel Mech.

GONZALEZ, GUSTAVO; Newtown HS; Jackson Heights, NY; (Y); 56/781; Church Yth Grp; Math Clb; Socr; Hon Roll; Prfct Atten Awd; Admin & Fclty Schlrshp 84; Jr Arista Soc-Wm Cowper Jr HS 84; Air Force Acad; Pilot.

GONZALEZ, HECTOR L; Aviation HS; Bronx, NY; (S); 29/416; Yrbk Stf; Rep Stu Cncl; Wings Awd-85 Avg Btr Shop 85-86; Pegasus Soc/Aviatn Technen Hnr Soc 85-86; Aircrft Maint Technen.

GONZALEZ, IVAN; Walton HS; Bronx, NY; (Y); #75 In Class; Boys Clb Am; Camera Clb; Church Yth Grp; Computer Clb; Latin Clb; Natl Beta Clb; Scholastic Bowl; Spanish Clb; Church Choir; School Play; Founder Schlrshp 86; Acad Of Aerntcs; Avioncs Technl.

GONZALEZ, JAMES R; Valley Stream South HS; Valley Stream, NY; (Y); 43/168; Chess Clb; Computer Clb; Chorus; School Musical; Swing Chorus; Variety Show; Nwsp Ed-Chief; Lit Mag; Ntl Merit Ltr; Drama Clb; Chess Clb Champ 84-86; Comp Clb 86; All Dist Chrs, NYS Exclnce; Schl Mus Stage Mgr; Rgnts Schlrshp 86; Manhattanville Coll; Acting.

GONZALEZ, JANET; Sacred Heart HS; Yonkers, NY; (Y); Service Clb; Rep Frsh Cls; Rep Soph Cls; Rep Jr Cls; Cheerleading; Hon Roll; NEDT Awd; Intnl Clb; Pep Clb; Yrbk Stf; Fordahm U; Bus Mgmt.

GONZALEZ, JOANNE; Dominican Commercial HS; Brooklyn, NY; (Y); Church Yth Grp; Spanish Clb; Teachers Aide; JV Var Bsktbl; NHS; Sclstc Exclnce Awd, Pres Acdmc Ftns Awd 86; St Johns U.

GONZALEZ, KAREN; Torrejon HS; Apo, NY; (Y); Band; Chorus; Variety Show; Yrbk Stf; Bowling; Trk; Hon Roll; Outstndng Cosmtlgst 85-86; Outstndng Job 401st/Sply 84-85; Nrs.

GONZALEZ, LISA; Erasmus Hall HS; Brooklyn, NY; (Y); Math Tm; Office Aide; Bsktbl; Sftbl; Vllybl; March Dimes Awd 86; Leukemia Awd 85; Comp.

GONZALEZ, LIZETTE; Adlai E Stevenson HS; Bronx, NY; (Y); Dance Clb; JA; Office Aide; School Play; Variety Show; Gov Hon Prg Awd; Hon Roll; Jr NHS; Prfct Atten Awd; Cert Hnr Achvt Lge 86; Bus.

GONZALEZ, LUIS; Roscoe Central HS; Roscoe, NY; (Y); Boy Scts; Computer Clb; FHA; Spanish Clb; Varsity Clb; Chorus; Sec Sr Cls; VP Capt Bsbl; VP Bsktbl; VP Ftbl; Ldrshp Awd-Bsbl 85-86; ITESM Hermosillo; Fncl Accntng.

GONZALEZ, MARIE; St Peters Girls; Staten Island, NY; (Y); Cmnty Wkr; FNA; Hosp Aide; JV Var Sftbl; Nrsg.

GONZALEZ, MONIQUE; Acad Of Mt St Ursula; Bronx, NY; (Y); Church Yth Grp; Drama Clb; Spanish Clb; VP Chorus; School Play; Cheerleading; Lbrl Arts.

GONZALEZ, MYRA; Cathedral HS; Brkyn, NY; (Y); 52/314; Dance Clb; Drama Clb; Intnl Clb; School Play; Variety Show; Yrbk Stf; Hon Roll; Acad Of Aeronautics; Cmmrcl Plt.

GONZALEZ JR, OSCAR; Lindenhurst SR HS; Lindenhurst, NY; (Y); Cmnty Wkr; Ski Clb; Spanish Clb; Hon Roll; NHS; Prelaw.

GONZALEZ, SAMANTHA; Christ The King Regional HS; Maspeth, NY; (Y); JV Gym; High Hon Roll; Hon Roll; Lion Awd; Nrsg.

GONZALEZ, STEVEN; Shenendehowa HS; Clifton Park, NY; (Y); 101/675; Intnl Clb; Socr; High Hon Roll; Natl Hispanic Merit Schlrshp 86; Long Island U; Marine Bio.

GONZALEZ, SUZANNE; John Jay HS; Katonah, NY; (Y); Girl Scts; Latin Clb; Math Tm; Ski Clb; JV Socr; High Hon Roll; Chemcl Engr.

GONZALEZ, THOMAS; Shoreham-Wading River HS; Shoreham, NY; (Y); Computer Clb; Science Clb; School Musical; School Play; Stage Crew; Im Bsktbl; Im Wt Lftg; Ntl Merit SF; St Schlr; NY ST Rgnts Schlrshp 86; NY ST Enrgy Rsrch & Dvlpmnt Achvt Cert 84; Lng Islnd Sci Cngrss 84; U Of CA-SAN Diego; Comp Engr.

GOOCH, MICHELLE; Bishop Loughlin Memorial HS; Brooklyn, NY; (Y); Computer Clb; Dance Clb; Teachers Aide; Rep Stu Cncl; Crs Cntry; Gym; Tennis; Vllybl; Hon Roll; Outstndng Srvc 81st Precnct Cmmnty Cncl 85; Ed.

GOOD, LAURIE; Waterloo SR HS; Waterloo, NY; (S); 17/170; Ski Clb; SADD; Yrbk Stf; Rep Jr Cls; Trs Sr Cls; Stu Cncl; Trk; High Hon Roll; Masonic Awd; Prfct Atten Awd; Upstate Med Ctr; Phys Thrpy.

GOOD, WILLIAM; Grand Island SR HS; Grand Island, NY; (Y); 78/324; Boy Scts; Chess Clb; L Ftbl; L Trk; High Hon Roll; JV Socr; Math Comptn Cert Of Merit 84; Regnts Schlrshp Recpnt 86; Rochester Inst; Elect Engr.

GOODALE III, HAL; Riverhead HS; Riverhead, NY; (Y); Boy Scts; Church Yth Grp; 4-H; Ski Clb; VICA; VP Soph Cls; Wrstlng; Jr NHS; Phys Fit Awd 84-86; 4th Wrstlng 86; Engrng.

GOODE, DAVE; Faith Heritage HS; Syracuse, NY; (Y); Church Yth Grp; Band; Variety Show; Var L Bsktbl; JV Bsbl; Var L Socr; Var L Trk; Hon Roll; Jr NHS; NHS; Coachs Awd Bsktbl 84; All-League Trck 85/Hnr Mntn 86; All-League Hnr Mntn Bsktbl 86; Psychlgy.

GOODEMOTE, GREG; Gloversville HS; Gloversville, NY; (Y); 65/229; Bsktbl; Socr; Hon Roll; JV Soccer MVP 83-84; Co MVP Vrsty Bsktbl 86; Math Tchr.

GOODEN, KEN; Iona Prep; Bronx, NY; (Y); 116/204; JV Var Bsktbl; JV Var Ftbl; Hon Roll; VP Of Afro-Amer Cultr Clb 85-86; Big Bros Prgm 85-86; Yng Chrstn Soc 85-86; Avtg.

GOODERMOTE, PATRICIA A; Chatham HS; Chatham, NY; (Y); 11/120; Drama Clb; Pres Latin Clb; Library Aide; SADD; Orch; School Musical; Yrbk Stf; High Hon Roll; NHS; U Hartford; Music Ed.

GOODFELLOW, JENNIFER; Jordan Eldridge HS; Elbridge, NY; (Y); Drama Clb; Mrchg Band; School Musical; Yrbk Ed-Chief; Var Crs Cntry; Var Trk; Hon Roll; NHS; VFW Awd; Voice Dem Awd; IATSE Locl 9 Schlrshp Awd Cvc Ctr Theatr Fest 86; Prfrmg Arts.

GOODIE, CAROL; Charles O Dickerson HS; Trumansburg, NY; (Y); SADD; Var JV Bsktbl; Var JV Sftbl; Hon Roll.

GOODIER, BECKY; Frontier HS; Blasdell, NY; (Y); Church Yth Grp; FCA; Hon Roll; Bus.

GOODING, LAURA; Union Endicott HS; Endicott, NY; (Y); Mathletes; Ski Clb; Color Guard; Flag Corp; Trk; Hon Roll; Law.

GOODLESS, STEPHEN J; New Rochelle HS; Scarsdale, NY; (Y); Y-Teens; Ny St Rgnts Coll Schlrshp 86.

GOODLOE, PAUL; Archbishop Stepinac HS; New Rochelle, NY; (Y); 34/193; Key Clb; Ski Clb; Rep Soph Cls; Rep Jr Cls; Im Bsktbl; Var L Ftbl; Im Vllybl; NHS; NROTC Schlrshp 86; NY Rgnts Schlrshp 86; U TX Astn; Med Dctr.

GOODMAN, ALLISON; Greenwich Central HS; Greenwich, NY; (Y); Band; Jazz Band; Orch; Var L Crs Cntry; Var L Trk; Bausch & Lomb Sci Awd; DAR Awd; High Hon Roll; NHS; Ntl Merit Ltr; Area All-St Orch 85-86; Empire St Jr Orch 85-86; St Record-Track 50 Mtr Hurdles 83-84; Chem.

GOODMAN, BONNIE B; Spring Valley SR HS; Spring Vly, NY; (Y); Drama Clb; Girl Scts; Key Clb; PAVAS; SADD; Chorus; School Musical; School Play; Stage Crew; Yrbk Phtg.

GOODMAN, JESSICA; The Dwight Schl; New York, NY; (S); Chorus; Stage Crew; Variety Show; Nwsp Ed-Chief; Wt Lftg; High Hon Roll; Regents Schlrshp 86; Mount Holyoke Coll; Bio.

GOODMAN, KIM; Franklin Acad; Malone, NY; (Y); Band; Concert Band; Jazz Band; Rep Soph Cls; Prfct Atten Awd; NYSMMA Awd Lev 5 85, 6 86; Marine Bio.

GOODMAN, YVETTE; Batavia HS; Batavia, NY; (Y); 59/84; Church Yth Grp; Chorus; Church Choir; School Musical; Variety Show; Yrbk Stf; Var Trk; The Kings Coll; Acctg.

GOODNIGHT, THOMAS; Wilson Central HS; Wilson, NY; (Y); Aud/Vis; Church Yth Grp; Teachers Aide; Band; Chorus; Church Choir; Concert Band; Jazz Band; Madrigals; Mrchg Band; 2nd Pl In NY St For Teen Tlnt 85; Outstndng Band & Chorus Person 86; Fother Schl; Accntnt.

GOODNOUGH, TINA MARIE; Brasher Falls Central HS; Brasher Fls, NY; (Y); Drama Clb; French Clb; Library Aide; Spanish Clb; SADD; Chorus; Rep Stu Cncl; Var Socr; Hon Roll; NHS; Lang & French II Cert 85; JETS & NEAS Merit Rcgntn Cert 85; Crim Justice.

GOODRICH, ALISON; Rome Catholic HS; Rome, NY; (Y); Debate Tm; Drama Clb; Speech Tm; Teachers Aide; Thesps; School Musical; School Play; Stage Crew; Variety Show; High Hon Roll; Languages.

GOODRICH, MARGARET; Hicksville HS; Hicksville, NY; (Y); French Clb; Band; Symp Band; Yrbk Stf; Rep Frsh Cls; Var L Crs Cntry; Var L Trk; Hon Roll; Crs Cntry All Cnfrnc & All Dvsn 84-85; Crs Cntry NYS Fed Chmpnshp 85; UNLV; Bus Mngmnt.

GOODSON, TRACEY; Freeport HS; Freeport, NY; (Y); DECA; Library Aide; Sec Science Clb; Sec Orch; School Musical; Nwsp Rptr; Rptr Nwsp Stf; Rptr Yrbk Stf; High Hon Roll; NHS; Law.

GOODSPEED, KIM; Mt Mercy Acad; W Seneca, NY; (Y); Ski Clb; Spanish Clb; Chorus; School Musical; School Play; Stage Crew; Rep Frsh Cls; Sr Cls; Crs Cntry; Prfct Atten Awd; Melodears Pres; Psych.

GOODSTEIN, KIM; Oyster Bay HS; East Norwich, NY; (Y); French Clb; Chorus; School Musical; Lit Mag; Psych.

GOODWIN, DANIEL J; Kendall JRSR HS; Hamlin, NY; (Y); Aud/Vis; High Hon Roll; Sibleys Schltc Art Awds 86; Nazareth Coll 1st Pl Sculptr Div 86; Omegi Sci Fi Frat Tlnt Hnr Wnnr 86; Alfred U; Art.

GOODWIN, DEIDRE; Pittsford Sutherland HS; Rochester, NY; (Y); Model UN; Chorus; School Musical; JV Var Sftbl; Var Capt Vllybl; NHS; Rep Frsh Cls; Var Capt Bsktbl; Var Capt Socr; High Hon Roll; RPI Math/Sci Awd; AHSME Schl Wnnr; AATG Germ Cntst 2nd; Slvr Mdl Natl Latin Exam; PTSA Germ/Latin.

GOODWIN, MICHELLE; Hoosick Falls Central HS; Hoosick Falls, NY; (Y); 16/117; Band; Concert Band; Mrchg Band; Rep Stu Cncl; JV Bsktbl; Hon Roll; NHS; All-Cnty Bnd 85 & 86; Cmmnty Bnd 83-84; Engrg.

GOODY, BENJAMIN; Wellington C Mempham HS; Wantagh, NY; (Y); Drama Clb; Math Tm; Temple Yth Grp; Band; Concert Band; Mrchg Band; Hon Roll; NHS; Pre-Vet Sci.

GOODZEIT, CAROLYN; Bellport HS; Brookhaven, NY; (Y); 6/375; Pres French Clb; Orch; Symp Band; Variety Show; Yrbk Stf; Var Capt Tennis; French Hon Soc; High Hon Roll; Sec French Hon Soc; NHS; Rtry Stu 86; Prsdntl Clssrm For Yng Amrcns 86; Pre-Law.

GOOLDEN, GEOFFREY G; Ogdensburg Free Acad; Ogdensburg, NY; (Y); 10/186; Church Yth Grp; Key Clb; Math Clb; JV VP Bsbl; JV VP Ftbl; Capt JV Ice Hcky; JV Socr; Im Vllybl; Hon Roll; NHS; Clarkson U; Elec Engrng.

GOOLDEN, SUSAN L; Hugh C Williams HS; Canton, NY; (Y); Drama Clb; French Clb; Ski Clb; Spanish Clb; Speech Tm; Varsity Clb; School Musical; School Play; Nwsp Stf; Yrbk Stf; Tlntd JR; Outstndng Author Awd; Bus Mgnt.

GOOLEY, JODY; Newark Valley HS; Owego, NY; (Y); 17/121; Church Yth Grp; Varsity Clb; Var Bsktbl; JV Ftbl; Var Golf; Hon Roll; NHS; Led Tm Wnng IAC Leag Golf Champ 86; Broome CC; Engrg Sci.

GOOLSBY, SABRINA; John Dewey HS; Queens Village, NY; (Y); Church Yth Grp; Hosp Aide; JA; School Musical; Cmmndtn Awds 84; Cert Of Excllnc 86; Lgl Sec.

GOOSLEY, SUSAN; Brockport HS; Brockport, NY; (Y); 100/350; Girl Scts; Trs Sr Cls; Mgr Bsktbl; Var JV Mgr(s); Niagara; Trvl.

GOPAL, SUNIL; Half Hollow Hills HS East; Dix Hills, NY; (Y); 141/517; Hosp Aide; SADD; Crs Cntry; Socr; Trk; High Hon Roll; Hon Roll; NHS; SUNY; Pre-Med.

GOPIE, KIRK; Midwood HS; Brooklyn, NY; (Y); Chorus; Albany ST; Med.

GORBEA, ELYSE; G Ray Bodley HS; Fulton, NY; (Y); Pres 4-H; Girl Scts; Science Clb; Spanish Clb; Chorus; Orch; Nwsp Rptr; 4-H Awd; High Hon Roll; Hon Roll; Syracuse U Frontiers Sci 86; Parent Agnst Drug Abuse Essay Cont Wnr 84; Cornell U; Biol.

GORCZYNSKI, CATHERINE; Wanwickvalley HS; Pine Isld, NY; (Y); 44/198; Church Yth Grp; Cmnty Wkr; Girl Scts; Ski Clb; Church Choir; Yrbk Stf; Trk; Cit Awd; High Hon Roll; Hon Roll; Hm Ec Awd 86; Hgh Hnr Rll Awd 85; Hnr Rll Awd 86; Worcester ST Coll; Bus Adm.

GORDDARD, JEFFREY P; Farmingdale HS; Farmingdale, NY; (Y); Key Clb; Letterman Clb; SADD; Varsity Clb; Frsh Cls; Stu Cncl; Ftbl; Lcrss; Wrstlng; Voice Dem Awd.

GORDNER, TRACY; Midlakes HS; Seneca Castle, NY; (Y); 34/134; 4-H; German Clb; GAA; Concert Band; Mrchg Band; Var Cheerleading; JV Trk; Hon Roll; Acctnt.

GORDON, CORINNE; Ward Melville HS; Stony Brook, NY; (Y); Art Clb; Cmnty Wkr; DECA; SADD; Temple Yth Grp; Chorus; Nwsp Stf; Yrbk Phtg; Lit Mag; Rep Jr Cls; Cmnty Svc Awd 85; Art Awd 86; Johnson & Wales; Fshn Mrchndsg.

GORDON, ELIZABETH; York Preparatory Schl; New York, NY; (Y); Art Clb; Spanish Clb; SADD; Nwsp Rptr; Yrbk Stf; Soph Cls; Vllybl; High Hon Roll; NHS; Hstry Awd 84; Hstry, Engl & Gen Excllnc 85; Engl, Spanish, Art, Sci & Gen Excllnc 86.

GORDON, GIDEON; Bronx HS Of Science; New York, NY; (Y); Concert Band; Nwsp Stf; Stu Intrnshp Rsrch Mt Sinai Med Ctr 85-86; Life Sci.

GORDON, ISA-JILL; Woodlands HS; Hartsdale, NY; (Y); Drama Clb; Pres Radio Clb; School Play; Ed Nwsp Stf; Ed Yrbk Stf; Ed Lit Mag; Trs NHS; School Musical; Nwsp Phtg; Nwsp Rptr; Dramatist Glds Yng Playwrights Fest Fnlst-Staged Rdng Of Play 86; Theatre Arts.

GORDON, KIRK; Evander Chips HS; Bronx, NY; (Y); Capt Ftbl; Mgr(s); Score Keeper; Trk; Hgst Grade Eng,Sci 86; TX A & M; Pilot.

GORDON, LISA; John Jay SR HS; Fishkill, NY; (Y); VP SADD; Nwsp Stf; Ed Yrbk Stf; Stu Cncl; High Hon Roll; Jr NHS; NHS; Stu Wk 84-85; John Jay Columbian Relief Co-Formng Recgntn 85-86; Med.

GORDON, LORI; Frewsburg Central Schl; Frewsburg, NY; (Y); Pep Clb; SADD; Stu Cncl; Cheerleading; Sftbl; Swmmng.

GORDON, MARJI L; Half Hollow Hills East HS; Wheatley Heights, NY; (Y); 78/500; Leo Clb; Sr Cls; JV Var Cheerleading; Sftbl; JV Vllybl; High Hon Roll; Jr NHS; NHS; Spanish NHS; U Of MI; Bus.

GORDON, SAMUEL; Erasmus Hall Acad Of Arts; Brooklyn, NY; (Y); Aud/Vis; Drama Clb; Library Aide; Variety Show; Nwsp Rptr; Rep Soph Cls; Rep Jr Cls; Cit Awd; Spr Yth Citznshp, Acad 86; Scrd Hrt Sum Prgm 85-86; Thtre.

GORDON, VIOLET; Springfield Gardens HS; Queens, NY; (Y); 6/440; Math Clb; Math Tm; Teachers Aide; Nwsp Stf; Off Jr Cls; High Hon Roll; Queens Bridge Med Pgm 86-87; City U NY; Med.

GORDON, WENDY; Middletown HS; Middletown, NY; (Y); Key Clb; Nwsp Phtg; Yrbk Phtg; Stu Cncl; Var Capt Cheerleading; Hon Roll; Acdmc Awd Achvmnt Englsh 83-84; MVP Awd Chrldng 85-86; SUNY Oneonta; Psych.

GORDY, ANN; Williamsville South HS; Williamsville, NY; (Y); Church Yth Grp; Drama Clb; Girl Scts; Hosp Aide; Pep Clb; Chorus; Church Choir.

GORELCZENKO, WALTER; St Francis Prep; Elmhurst, NY; (Y); Cmnty Wkr; Office Aide; Political Wkr; Rep Soph Cls; JV Var Tennis; JV Var Trk; Intl Assn Machnst & Aerospc Wrkrs Scholar 86; Fordham U; Pol Sci.

GORENFLO, DENISE; John Jay HS; Hopewell Jct, NY; (Y); FFA; OEA; Krissler Bus Inst; Computer Sci.

GORENSTEIN, ANDREW; E Meadow HS; E Meadow, NY; (Y); VP FBLA; Key Clb; Math Clb; SADD; Temple Yth Grp; Nwsp Stf; Yrbk Stf; Var L Golf; JV L Lcrss; JV L Socr; Law Bus.

GORGA, PETER; Galway HS; Galway, NY; (Y); 7/84; Aud/Vis; Drama Clb; French Clb; Library Aide; Chorus; Variety Show; High Hon Roll; NHS; Rgnts Schlrshp 86; Union Coll.

GORGAN, CHRISTINE; Hicksville HS; Hicksville, NY; (Y); Spanish Clb; School Play; Variety Show; Var Bowling; Elks Awd; High Hon Roll; Jr NHS; NHS; Ntl Merit SF; Spanish NHS; Amer Legn Awd Outstndng Amer Pgm 84; Bernard H Braun Mem Schlrshp Awd 84; Hi Achvmnt Hlth/Math 84; Intl Law.

GORHAM, ANNE; Ichabod Crane HS; Valatie, NY; (Y); Trs Drama Clb; SADD; School Play; Sec Ed Lit Mag; Elks Awd; VP NHS; Prfct Atten Awd; Srv To Schl 85 & 86; Efrt In Englsh 86; Miami U Oxfrd OH.

GORHAM, BERNADETTE K; Our Lady Of Good Counsel Acad; Scarsdale, NY; (Y); 6/66; Drama Clb; School Play; Nwsp Rptr; Lit Mag; Pres Soph Cls; Trs Stu Cncl; Trk; Hon Roll; Sec Trs NHS; 4 Yr Academic Schlrshp 82-86; Awd-NEDT 84; Natl Merit Semi-Fnlst 85; Biochem.

GORHAM, CHRISTINA; Jordan Elbridge HS; Elbridge, NY; (Y); Church Yth Grp; Spanish Clb; Chorus; Rep Jr Cls; Var L Bsktbl; Powder Puff Ftbl; Var L Sftbl; Var L Tennis; Hon Roll; GAA; Stu Cncl Cert Achvt 84-86; Bus Mgmt.

GORIN, BETHEL S; Lawrence SR HS; Lawrence, NY; (Y); 13/414; Pres French Clb; Math Tm; Pres Temple Yth Grp; Chorus; School Musical; Ed Yrbk Stf; Var L Tennis; High Hon Roll; NHS; Drama Clb; NY ST Regnts Schlrshp 86; Wesleyan U; Invstmt Bkg.

GORKA, DONNA; St Peters High School For Girls; Staten Island, NY; (Y); Hosp Aide; Trk; High Hon Roll; Fin Miss Teen USA Pgnt 86; Partcptn In Fund Raisers For MDA & March Of Dimes 85-86; Pre-Med.

GORMAN, CINDY; Bronx High School Of Science; Bronx, NY; (Y); Yrbk Ed-Chief; Htl Mgmt.

GORMAN, COLLEEN A; Hamburg HS; Hamburg, NY; (Y); 72/374; Ski Clb; Chorus; Yrbk Stf; Rep Frsh Cls; Rep Soph Cls; Rep Jr Cls; Sec Sr Cls; Rep Stu Cncl; Hon Roll; VP Catalina Clb 86-87; Enrolled Two Adv Plcmnt Courses 85-87; St Bonaventure U; Bus.

GORMAN, ERIC D; Cardinal Mooney HS; Rochester, NY; (Y); 11/370; Am Leg Boys St; Boy Scts; Yrbk Stf; Lit Mag; JV Trk; JV Wrstlng; High Hon Roll; NHS; Chess Clb; Exploring; Am Chemical Soc Achvt Awd 86; US Acdmc Decathlon Tm 86; Pre-Calculus Math Awd 86; Aerospace Engrng.

GORMAN, MAUREEN; North Babylon SR HS; N Babylon, NY; (Y); 22/473; French Clb; Intnl Clb; Sec Frsh Cls; Sftbl; Vllybl; French Hon Soc; High Hon Roll; VP Jr NHS; NHS; Pres Schlr; Bus Admin.

GORMAN, MICHAEL; Amsterdam HS; Amsterdam, NY; (Y); 5/316; Quiz Bowl; Varsity Clb; Concert Band; Jazz Band; Mrchg Band; Ftbl; Golf; Trk; High Hon Roll; NHS; No 1 Clb For Socl Stud; Sci.

GORMAN, PATRICIA; East Meadow HS; East Meadow, NY; (S); 41/340; Sec Ski Clb; Chorus; Var Bsktbl; Var Cheerleading; Capt Fld Hcky; Var Lcrss; Hon Roll; ROTC Schlrshp; ST Johns U; Pharmcy.

GORMAN, PETER; Msgr Farrell HS; Staten Island, NY; (Y); 155/320; Im Bsktbl; Im Bowling; Im Ftbl; Ntl Merit Schol; Regents Schlrshp 86; Italion Colture Clb 84; Avtn.

GORNEY, STACEY; Kenmore East HS; Tonawanda, NY; (Y); 161/330; Sec GAA; Var Capt Socr; Var Capt Sftbl; MVP JV & V Sccr 83-86; MVP JV & V Sftbl 83-86; All Westrn NY Grls Sftbl 86; Buffalo ST Coll; Bus.

GOROSTIOLA, MARIA; New Dorp HS; Staten Island, NY; (Y); Spanish Clb; Varsity Clb; Yrbk Stf; Var Vllybl; Hon Roll; Prfct Atten Awd; Spanish NHS; Arista 85-86; Hnr Key Recpnt 86; Girls ST Candt 86; Clemson U; Elem Ed.

GORTON, CLAY; Tri-Valley HS; Liberty, NY; (Y); 3/53; FFA; Varsity Clb; JV Var Ftbl; Trk; High Hon Roll; NHS; Prfct Atten Awd; Nuclr Chem.

GOSS, DEIRDRE; James Madison HS; Brooklyn, NY; (Y); Gym; Vllybl.

GOSSELIN, ANGELA; Saranac Central HS; Saranac, NY; (S); 25/121; Church Yth Grp; Band; Concert Band; Jazz Band; Mrchg Band; Orch; Capt Var Socr; Trk; Stat Wrstlng; Hon Roll; Pre-Vet Med.

GOSSIN, THOMAS; T R Proctor HS; Utica, NY; (Y); Trk; Delhi; Crpntry.

GOSSMANN, LAURA; St Johns Preparatory HS; Woodside, NY; (Y); 106/458; Cmnty Wkr; French Clb; Latin Clb; Letterman Clb; Office Aide; Teachers Aide; Varsity Clb; Band; Concert Band; Jazz Band; 2nd Hnrs SR Yr 86; Retreat Ldr Awd Grp Cnslng 86; Tchrs Aide Awd Field Psychlgy 86; Harren Wilson Coll; Intr Dsgn.

GOTTESFELD, SANDY; James I Oneill HS; Putnam Vly, NY; (Y); Camera Clb; Office Aide; Teachers Aide; Temple Yth Grp; Yrbk Phtg; Yrbk Stf; Acad Awd In Art 86.

GOTTESMAN, LINDA; Mac Arthur HS; Seaford, NY; (Y); 13/321; Computer Clb; English Clb; French Clb; Hosp Aide; Mathletes; Science Clb; Acpl Chr; Chorus; School Musical; Variety Show; Mst Outstndg Thtr Stdnt 85; Nrsng Schlrshp 86; 1st Pl Art Cmpntn 85; All Cnty Chorus 86; Bnghmtn U; Math Sci.

GOTTFRIED, DINA; Smithtown High School East; Nesconset, NY; (Y); Cmnty Wkr; Girl Scts; SADD; Temple Yth Grp; Rep Frsh Cls; Rep Soph Cls; Rep Jr Cls; Rep Stu Cncl; JV Stat Mgr(s); Hon Roll.

GOTTHELF, GREG; Sweet Home SR HS; N Tonawanda, NY; (Y); Latin Clb; Science Clb; Var Socr; Wt Lftg; Hon Roll; NHS; Prfct Atten Awd; Latin Hnr Scty 85-86; Sci Hnr Scty 85-86.

GOTTLER, DAVID; Cardinal O Hara HS; Tonawanda, NY; (Y); Aud/Vis; Drama Clb; Chorus; School Musical; School Play.

GOTTLIEB, DAPHNE; Cazenovia HS; Manlius, NY; (Y); 10/150; Drama Clb; Chorus; School Musical; Stage Crew; High Hon Roll; Ntl Merit SF; Outstndng Jr 85; Poetry Cntst Wnnr 85; Outstndng Creative Wrtng In Eng II Regents 85; Filmmaking.

GOTTOVI, SARA; Brockport HS; Spencerport, NY; (Y); 5/315; Computer Clb; Sec Debate Tm; Sec VP Girl Scts; Latin Clb; Mathletes; Trs Sec Model UN; Speech Tm; High Hon Roll; NHS; Amer Hstry Awd 85-86; Alene Butler Awd For European Stds 84-85; Artcl Prchsd For Pblctn 17 Mgzne 84-86; Intrntnl Rltns.

GOTTSTEIN, AMY; Colonie Central HS; Albany, NY; (Y); Hon Roll; Siena Coll; Bio.

GOUDAS, PAUL; Midwood HS; Brooklyn, NY; (Y); 15/700; Intnl Clb; Math Clb; Math Tm; ROTC; Var Swmmng; High Hon Roll; Hon Roll; Engrng.

GOULD, ANNE E; Pulaski HS; Pulaski, NY; (S); 1/98; Church Yth Grp; Drama Clb; French Clb; Ski Clb; SADD; Band; Mrchg Band; School Musical; Stage Crew; Yrbk Stf; Elmira Coll Key Awd Outstndg JR 85; DAR Awd 86; Show Incntv Awd 83; Chem.

GOULD, ELIZABETH; Tioga Central HS; Nichols, NY; (S); 6/96; Camp Fr Inc; Church Yth Grp; Library Aide; High Hon Roll; NHS; Ntl Merit Ltr; Prfct Atten Awd; Silver Mdl Natl Latin Exam 84; SUNY Geneseo.

GOULD, JIM; Ichabod Crane HS; Valatie, NY; (Y); 10/190; Boy Scts; Bsbl; Bsktbl; Socr; Rep Faclty Stu Review Brd 84-86.

GOULDIN, MICHAEL H; Binghamton HS; Binghamton, NY; (Y); 26/460; Am Leg Boys St; Church Yth Grp; Key Clb; Letterman Clb; Varsity Clb; Band; Mrchg Band; Stu Cncl; Ftbl; Swmmng; Ftbl Capt 86; All-Conf Swmmr-Sect 4 ST Relay 86; Med.

GOULTE, MELANIE; Bishop Ludden HS; Camillus, NY; (Y); Sec Intnl Clb; Ski Clb; Rep Frsh Cls; Stat Lcrss; High Hon Roll; Hon Roll; NHS; Volntr Svc Awd-Commnty Genrl Hosp 84-85; Med.

GOURDINE, NATASHA PAULETTE; Dominican Commercial HS; Cambria Heights, NY; (Y); 88/273; Girl Scts; Chorus; Church Choir; Stu Cncl; Var Bsktbl; NHS; Pres Schlr; Prncpls Lst 82-86; Siena Clb 83-86; Mrgn ST U; Bus Admin.

GOURJI, RITA; Smithtown West HS; Smithtown, NY; (Y); Art Clb; French Clb; Chorus; French Hon Soc; JC Awd; Brown Belt/Karate 85; Sec Of Ecology Clb 85-86; NYSSMA-PIANO 85-86; Tchg.

GOURNELOS, TINA; New Utrecht HS; Brooklyn, NY; (Y); 11/635; Key Clb; School Play; Yrbk Stf; Lit Mag; Rep Stu Cncl; NHS; Ntl Merit Ltr; Nwsp Ed-Chief; NYS Regnts Schlrshp 86; NYU; Dntstry.

GOVENER, PAMELA; North Rose-Wolcott HS; Wolcott, NY; (Y); Pres Church Yth Grp; Sec Ski Clb; Trs Varsity Clb; Madrigals; Var L Sftbl; Var L Swmmng; High Hon Roll; NHS; Sec French Clb; Prsdntl Acdmc Fit Awd 86; Messiah Coll; Ped Dntst.

GOVER, BRIAN; Seaford HS; Seaford, NY; (S); Am Leg Boys St; Boy Scts; Var Bsbl; Var Socr; Cit Awd; High Hon Roll; NHS; Prfct Atten Awd; Computer Clb; Science Clb; Eagle Scout 86; Fuller Awd 84; USN Acad; Engrng.

GOW, ANDREW; Hamburg Central HS; Hamburg, NY; (Y); AFS; Am Leg Boys St; Var Capt Ice Hcky; JV L Lcrss; Var Capt Socr; 4-H; Letterman Clb; Spanish Clb; Jazz Band; Hon Roll; 1st US Marine Phy Ftnss, Schlrshp AFS Jpn, JR Prm Crt 86; Bus.

GOWE, SHANNON; Candor HS; Candor, NY; (Y); 11/87; Varsity Clb; VP Frsh Cls; Var L Bsktbl; Var L Sftbl; Var L Vllybl; High Hon Roll; NHS; Bus Admn.

GOWELL, COLLEEN; Bishop Ford HS; Brooklyn, NY; (S); 13/420; Computer Clb; JV Mgr Sftbl; Var Tennis; Hon Roll; NHS.

GOWIE, AMY; Columbia HS; Rensselaer, NY; (Y); Church Yth Grp; Key Clb; Teachers Aide; Stage Crew; Score Keeper; High Hon Roll; Hon Roll; NHS; Tchrs Assoc Schlrshp 86; Hudson Valley CC; Ed.

GRABER, MICHAEL; John H Glenn HS; Greenlawn, NY; (Y); French Clb; Hosp Aide; Temple Yth Grp; L Bsbl; L Bsktbl; Im Sftbl; Hon Roll; Jr NHS; NHS; Sprts Admin.

GRABIEC, JENNIFER; Turner-Carroll HS; Buffalo, NY; (S); 1/124; Sec Church Yth Grp; Var Cheerleading; Var Sftbl; Im Vllybl; High Hon Roll; Hon Roll; NHS; Ntl Merit Schol; NEDT Awd; Schlstc Awds High Avg; Awds Athletic Abilities; Schlrshp; Cosmetic Chem.

GRABNER, GERALD; H C Technical HS; Buffalo, NY; (Y); 25/320; Boys Clb Am; Church Yth Grp; Stage Crew; Im Bsktbl; Var Im Bowling; Hon Roll; Knghts Altr 84; Rochester Inst Tech; Elec Engr.

GRABO, MELINDA; Unatego JR SR HS; Otego, NY; (Y); French Clb; FHA; Ski Clb; French Hon Soc; Hon Roll.

GRABOSKY, ZACHARY; Cazenovia Central HS; Cazenovia, NY; (Y); Boy Scts; Acpl Chr; Band; Chorus; Jazz Band; School Musical; Symp Band; JV Trk; Hon Roll; Prfct Atten Awd; SUNY Oswego Coll; Eng.

GRABOWSKI, KAREN; Mount Mercy Acad; W Seneca, NY; (Y); Church Yth Grp; Latin Clb; Model UN; Rep Soph Cls; Var Cheerleading; Sftbl; Hon Roll; Prfct Atten Awd; Buffalo ST; Med Tech.

GRABOWSKI, LYNDA J; St Joseph Hill Acad; Staten Island, NY; (Y); Computer Clb; FTA; Spanish Clb; Yrbk Stf; Vllybl; Ntl Merit Ltr; NY ST Regnts Schlrshp 86; St Johns U.

GRABOWSKI, MARY P; Bishop Grimes HS; Liverpool, NY; (S); Church Yth Grp; Science Clb; Speech Tm; Chorus; School Musical; Trs Jr Cls; JV Var Cheerleading; Var Tennis; 1st Pl Natl Wmns Hall/Fame Essy Cntst 85; 1st Pl Natl Hstry Day Essy Cntst 85; Psychlgy.

GRACE, KEVIN; St John The Baptist HS; Oakdale, NY; (Y); Church Yth Grp; Ski Clb; SADD; Band; Socr; Tennis; Hon Roll; Law.

GRACE, MARK R; Newfield HS; Selden, NY; (Y); 10/576; Boy Scts; Church Yth Grp; Exploring; Library Aide; Band; Concert Band; Jazz Band; Mrchg Band; Rep Sr Cls; High Hon Roll; Franklin Coll; Pre-Healing Arts.

GRACEY, DIANE; Washingtonville SR HS; Campbell Hall, NY; (Y); Church Yth Grp; GAA; Hosp Aide; Varsity Clb; Band; Concert Band; Orch; Capt Crs Cntry; Capt Trk; Hon Roll; Mst Imprvd Track 84; Mst Imprvd X-Cntry 85; NY ST Chmpns X-Cntry Twice 83-85; Bus.

GRACIA, BARBARA; Bishop Ford Central Catholic HS; Brooklyn, NY; (Y); Camera Clb; Church Yth Grp; Cmnty Wkr; Hosp Aide; Bowling; Cheerleading; Hon Roll; York Coll; Engl.

GRACIA, ROSELYNE; John Dewey HS; Brooklyn, NY; (Y); Dance Clb; Spanish Clb; Chorus; Color Guard; School Musical; Off Jr Cls; Gym; Trk; Vllybl; Wt Lftg; Hnr 84; A Restor Stu 84; Merit Stu 86; Chld Dvlpmnt.

GRADY, BARBARA; Our Lady Of Mercy HS; Macedon, NY; (Y); Church Yth Grp; Civic Clb; Latin Clb; Science Clb; Church Choir; Hon Roll; Women Engr Pgm 86; Space Camp Rocket Ctr 84; U Dayton; Aernutcl Engr.

GRADY, DEBRA; M C S M HS; New York, NY; (Y); 15/159; JA; Office Aide; Teachers Aide; School Musical; Nwsp Rptr; Yrbk Stf; Tennis; Cit Awd; Hon Roll; Chem Awd 84; Trig Awd 85; Skidmore Coll; Pdtrcn.

GRADY, JULIE O; St Joseph By The Sea HS; Staten Island, NY; (Y); 9/215; Red Cross Aide; Yrbk Stf; Lit Mag; Tennis; High Hon Roll; NHS; Concours Natl De Francois Cert Mrt 85.

GRADZEWICZ, TRESA; Grover Cleveland HS; Buffalo, NY; (Y); Church Yth Grp; Pep Clb; Science Clb; Spanish Clb; Score Keeper; Hon Roll; ST U Buffalo; Pre Med.

GRAEF, CHRISTINE M; Mount St Mary Acad; Buffalo, NY; (Y); Sec Computer Clb; Model UN; Ski Clb; Band; VP Chorus; School Play; Var Tennis; DAR Awd; High Hon Roll; NHS; Superior Frnch Fluncy Awd 83-86; 2nd Pl Art Show Awd 83-84; Shcl Svc Awd 85-86; Intl Comm.

GRAF, HEIDI; Monroe HS; Rochester, NY; (Y); Math Tm; Concert Band; Mrchg Band; Swmmng; High Hon Roll; Hon Roll; Trs NHS.

GRAF, LAURA; Bishop Ludden HS; Syracuse, NY; (Y); Church Yth Grp; NHS.

GRAFFEO, GAIL; Midwood HS; Brooklyn, NY; (Y); 63/586; Library Aide; Math Tm; Chorus; Orch; School Musical; School Play; Variety Show; Lit Mag; Hon Roll; Jr NHS; Math Medal 83; SUNY Buffalo; Vet.

GRAFFIGNA, NORMA; Fashion Industries HS; Brooklyn, NY; (Y); Art Clb; Girl Scts; Office Aide; Service Clb; Yrbk Stf; Hon Roll; FIT Coll; Fashion Design.

GRAHAM, COURTNEY; Middletown HS; Middletown, NY; (Y); 14/316; Dance Clb; Drama Clb; Acpl Chr; Band; Chorus; Church Choir; Madrigals; School Musical; School Play; Swing Chorus; Lillian Holland Lannigan Memrl Cmmnty Svc Awd 86; Middletwn Tchrs Assn Schlrshp 86; Pennsylvania ST U; Ed.

GRAHAM, DENNINE; Beacon HS; Glenham, NY; (Y); 54/205; Sec French Clb; Sec German Clb; Library Aide; JV Sftbl; Hon Roll.

GRAHAM, ERIC; Tri Valley Central Schl; Grahamsville, NY; (Y); Boy Scts; Church Yth Grp; Ftbl; Cit Awd; God Cntry Awd; High Hon Roll; Hon Roll; Prfct Atten Awd; Comp Sci.

GRAHAM, HEATHER; Mount Mercy Academy; Buffalo, NY; (Y); French Clb; FHA; JA; Latin Clb; SADD; Teachers Aide; Yrbk Bus Mgr; Prfct Atten Awd; Chorus; 3rd Pl Frnch-Frgn Lang Fair 86; Buffalo ST Coll; Scndry Ed.

GRAHAM, IAN; Great Neck South HS; Great Neck, NY; (Y); 6/234; Debate Tm; Model UN; NFL; Speech Tm; School Play; Nwsp Stf; Lit Mag; Tennis; Cit Awd; Ntl Merit Ltr; Geo Washington U Mth & Sci Awd 85; PTA Mth Excllnc Awd 86; Amer Lgn Schl Awd 83; Yale U; Pltcl Sci.

GRAHAM, JAMES; Bishop Grimes HS; Syracuse, NY; (Y); Hosp Aide; Concert Band; Jazz Band; Hon Roll; Schl Musical Awd; Bus.

GRAHAM, JANET; Bishop Ludden HS; Syracuse, NY; (S); Dance Clb; Exploring; JA; NFL; Sec Speech Tm; SADD; Hon Roll; SUNY Brockport:Attrny.

GRAHAM, JOHN; Argyle Central HS; Argyle, NY; (Y); 1/60; Am Leg Boys St; Chorus; Yrbk Ed-Chief; Pres Frsh Cls; Pres Soph Cls; Pres Jr Cls; Trs Stu Cncl; JV Var Socr; High Hon Roll; NHS; Math Tm Rnnr Up Leag High Scorer 85-86; Area All St Music Fstvl Chrs 85.

GRAHAM, JOHN; Bishop Timon HS; Buffalo, NY; (S); Am Leg Boys St; JA; Nwsp Rptr; Yrbk Sprt Ed; Stat Bsbl; Stat Bsktbl; Stat Ftbl; Hon Roll; Engl & Spnsh Awds 85; Svc Awd 85; Sci Cngrss Awd 84-85; Math.

GRAHAM, JOSEPH; Lyons Central HS; Lyons, NY; (Y); Art Clb; Yrbk Stf; JV Ftbl; Schltc Key Awd 85; Fredonia ST U Summr Schl Visual Arts Pgm 86; Comm Art.

GRAHAM, KAREN; Saint Josephs HS; Brooklyn, NY; (Y); 1/106; Nwsp Stf; Yrbk Stf; Lit Mag; NHS; Val; Schl Scholar 82-86; Princpls Lst 82-86.

GRAHAM, KIMBERLY L; Honeoye Central Schl; Honeoye, NY; (S); 2/70; Teachers Aide; Chorus; School Musical; Yrbk Ed-Chief; VP Sr Cls; Rep Stu Cncl; High Hon Roll; NHS; Spanish Clb; Swing Chorus; Williams Coll Bk Awd 85; Schl Wrtng Awd 83; Pre-Law.

GRAHAM, KRISTIN; Catholic Central HS; Waterford, NY; (Y); Dance Clb; SADD; Variety Show; Rep Stu Cncl; Var L Pom Pon; High Hon Roll; NHS; Outstndng Achvt Soc Stds 84 & 85; Pltcl Sci.

GRAHAM, MARY; Lowville Central Schl; Lowville, NY; (Y); 1/117; French Clb; Sec VP FTA; Science Clb; Teachers Aide; Nwsp Stf; Var L Bsktbl; Var L Socr; Var L Sftbl; Kiwanis Awd; NHS; Augsbury Schlr Awd 869; Kraft Inc Schlrshp 86; NYS Regents Schlrshp 86; St Lawrence U; French Trch.

GRAHAM, SHARON; Skaneateles Central HS; Skaneateles, NY; (Y); 7/143; Intnl Clb; Pres Sec Band; Chorus; Var Capt Cheerleading; Tennis; High Hon Roll; NHS; Pres Schlr; ST Chmpns Olympcs Of The Mind 85; Boston Coll; Bus.

GRAHAM, SHARON; Tri-Valley Central HS; Grahamsville, NY; (Y); 6/58; High Hon Roll; Hon Roll; NHS; Acadmc All Amer Schlr 85; Ntl Sci Olympd Awd 84; Cert Of Merit Engl 83-85; Comm.

GRAISON, DEBORAH; Holy Trinity HS; Hempstead, NY; (S); 7/403; French Clb; Math Clb; Ski Clb; Stage Crew; Stu Cncl; Cheerleading; High Hon Roll; Ntl Merit Ltr; NEDT Awd; Shoppers Vlg Maureen Nolan Schlrp 83.

GRAJEK, THOMAS C; West Seneca West HS; West Seneca, NY; (Y); 35/550; Aud/Vis; Chess Clb; Church Yth Grp; Cmnty Wkr; Computer Clb; Political Wkr; Spanish Clb; Varsity Clb; Ice Hcky; U Buffalo; Elec Engr.

GRAMBLE, LISA; Yonkers HS; Yonkers, NY; (Y); VICA; Hon Roll; Cert Of Excllnc Soc Studies 83-84; Celebration Of Excllnc Achvt Awd 85; Cosmetologist.

GRAMMAS, MARIE; Saugerties Public HS; Mt Marion, NY; (S); Church Yth Grp; Office Aide; Church Choir; High Hon Roll; Hon Roll; NHS; Bapt Bible Coll; Engl.

GRAMMATICO, LAURA J; E J Wilson HS; Spencerport, NY; (Y); Church Yth Grp; Ski Clb; Yrbk Stf; Rep Sr Cls; Rep Stu Cncl; JV Cheerleading; Hon Roll; NHS; ST U Of NY-BUFFALO; Bus Mngmt.

GRAMMENOS, MARIA; Long Island City HS; Astoria, NY; (Y); Debate Tm; Bowling; Gym; Hon Roll; Jr NHS; Mu Alp Tht; NHS; Prfct Atten Awd; Pin Outstndng Achvmnt & Schlrshp French 84; Pin For Excllnce In Foods & Nutri Hm Ec 84; Soc Stu Awd 84; St Johns U; Pharm.

GRAMZA, NANCY ANN; Emerson Vocational HS; Buffalo, NY; (Y); 2/95; Yrbk Stf; Sec Sr Cls; Capt Bowling; Mgr Socr; Capt Tennis; High Hon Roll; NHS; Sal; Nwsp Rptr; Mgr(s); NY ST Grnts Schlrshp Wnr 86; Statler Fndtn Awd Schlrshp Wnr 86; Erie CC North; Fd Svc Admin.

GRAN, RICHARD; Catholic Central HS; Latham, NY; (S); 12/179; Aud/Vis; JA; School Play; Hon Roll; NHS; Arch.

GRANA, STEPHANIE; Sacred Heart Acad; Malverne, NY; (S); Dance Clb; Sec Debate Tm; NFL; Spanish Clb; Sec Speech Tm; School Play; Stu Cncl; Swmmng; Trk; High Hon Roll; NY ST Debat Trnmnt Albany; NY ST Stu Congrs Trnmnt Albany; JV MVP Swmmng; Law.

GRANBOIS, TOM; Weedsport HS; Weedsport, NY; (Y); 2/90; Math Clb; Spanish Clb; Var L Ftbl; Var L Trk; Bausch & Lomb Sci Awd; Cit Awd; High Hon Roll; Sal; APT Sci Prize 85; Clarkson U; Mech Engrng.

GRANBY, MICHELLE; Hilton HS; Hamlin, NY; (Y); 80/316; Boy Scts; Church Yth Grp; Office Aide; High Hon Roll; Hon Roll; SUNY; Elem Ed.

GRANDINETTI, THOMAS; Hudson HS; Hudson, NY; (Y); Boys Clb Am; Church Yth Grp; Varsity Clb; Var L Bsbl; Var L Ftbl; Hon Roll; Norwich U; Crmnl Jstc.

GRANDISON, DEBORAH; Amityville Memorial HS; Amityville, NY; (Y); Camera Clb; Trs Church Yth Grp; FTA; VP Key Clb; Office Aide; VP Church Choir; Crs Cntry; Trk; JV Vllybl; High Hon Roll; Comp.

GRANER, LAURA D; Pittsford Sutherland HS; Pittsford, NY; (Y); Church Yth Grp; Cmnty Wkr; Debate Tm; Drama Clb; Model UN; Red Cross Aide; Spanish Clb; Trs SADD; Chorus; Stage Crew; Cornell U; Ind Rltns.

GRANER, SUSANNE; Ward Melville HS; E Setauket, NY; (Y); Church Yth Grp; Cmnty Wkr; Hosp Aide; Ski Clb; Band; Capt Flag Corp; Stat Bsktbl; Sftbl; Vllybl; Jr NHS; Natl Piano Plyng Auditions Guild 84; Winter Comptn Flag Corps 85-86; Spcl Olympics 85; Spts Med.

GRANEY, JENNIFER; Rome Free Acad; Rome, NY; (Y); Red Cross Aide; DAR Awd; Hon Roll; NHS; Vet-Med.

GRANEY, JENNIFER; St Francis Prep; Bellerose, NY; (S); 50/800; Am Leg Aux Girls St; Pres Church Yth Grp; Drama Clb; Office Aide; Political Wkr; SADD; Teachers Aide; Rep Stu Cncl; Hon Roll; NHS; Pblc Rltns.

GRANEY, PATRICIA M; E J Wilson SR HS; Rochester, NY; (Y); 70/300; Drama Clb; VP Exploring; Trs Girl Scts; Trs Latin Clb; Sec Model UN; Symp Band; Var L Bsktbl; Var L Crs Cntry; Var Capt Trk; NYS Regnts Schlrshp 86; Coll & Hgh Schl Combnd 1 Yr With Coll Part Time Both 86; U Of Sil Urbana Champaign; Bio.

GRANGE, NADINE; St Catharine Acad; Bronx, NY; (Y); 7/180; Nwsp Ed-Chief; Nwsp Rptr; Nwsp Stf; Hon Roll; NHS; Prfct Atten Awd; Awd Excllnce Spn III 86; Boston U; Jrnlsm.

GRANT, ALICIA R; La Guardia H S Of Music & The Arts; New York, NY; (Y); JA; Teachers Aide; Chorus; Prfct Atten Awd; Natl Fndtn Advncmnt Arts 85-86; Boston Conservtry; Entertainer.

GRANT, CARL; Springfield Gardens HS; Laurelton, NY; (S); 27/438; JA; Yrbk Stf; Frsh Cls; Sr Cls; Im Vllybl; Hon Roll; Cert Of Achvt FEGS Spec Tst Prep Prog 85; Merit Awd Cert 85; Cert Clss Achvt Amer Stds Sdv Plcmt 85; Bus Adm.

GRANT, CAROL ANNETTE; Trumansburg Central HS; Trumansburg, NY; (Y); Teachers Aide; JV Score Keeper; Stat Vllybl; Hon Roll; Prfct Atten Awd; Awd Cmpltn Data Entry, Wrd Proc & Comp Oper At Tompkins-Seneca-Tioga 85-86; Adm Spprt.

GRANT, CYNTHIA; North Babylon SR HS; N Babylon, NY; (Y); Office Aide; Hon Roll; Nasau CC; Mdcl Lab Tech.

GRANT, DANIEL PATRICK; Minisink Valley HS; Middletown, NY; (Y); Yrbk Phtg; Yrbk Rptr; Rep Frsh Cls; Rdng, Wrtng, & Arthmtc Awds; Bus Law.

GRANT, DIANE; Columbia HS; Castleton, NY; (Y); 32/417; Trs Soph Cls; Trs Jr Cls; VP Sr Cls; Stu Cncl; Capt Socr; Var Sftbl; JV Vllybl; Hon Roll; NHS; Powder Puff Ftbl; Rgnts Coll Schlrshp NY ST 86; ST U Of NY Albany; Bus Adm.

GRANT, ELAINE; Sarah J Hale HS; Brooklyn, NY; (Y); 51/218; Library Aide; Sec Math Tm; Teachers Aide; Drill Tm; Cit Awd; High Hon Roll; Prfct Atten Awd; Church Yth Grp; Sec Office Aide; Nwsp Rptr; Triple C Atty Gen Awd 86; Bus Achvt Awd 83; Comp Lit Cert 86; John Jay; Law.

GRANT, ELISE K; Green Meadow Waldorf Schl; Upper Saddle Ri, NJ; (Y); Drama Clb; Chorus; Orch; School Musical; School Play; Painting Awds 84-85; Arts Recgntn & Talent Search 85; Fine Arts.

GRANT, GARY; Oriskany Central HS; Oriskany, NY; (Y); Boy Scts; Model UN; NFL; Varsity Clb; Stage Crew; Nwsp Stf; Ftbl; Capt Trk; Mgr Wrstlng; Hon Roll; Psych.

GRANT, JACQUALINE; Bishop Kearney HS; Rochester, NY; (Y); 4/140; Exploring; Library Aide; Math Tm; Nwsp Stf; Yrbk Stf; Trk; High Hon Roll; Hon Roll; NHS; Ntl Merit Ltr; Marshall Hahn Engrng Merit Schlrshp 86; Natl Merit Ltr Cmmndtn 85; NYS Rgnts Schlrshp 86; VA Tech; Engrng.

GRANT, JODI; Oyster Bay HS; Oyster Bay, NY; (Y); 2/123; Trs SADD; Trs Chorus; Nwsp Ed-Chief; Yrbk Ed-Chief; VP Stu Cncl; Var Badmtn; Capt Bowling; Bausch & Lomb Sci Awd; High Hon Roll; VP NHS; Harvard Alumni Bk Awd 85; Empr ST Schlrshp 86; Cornell Natl Schlr 86; Yale U.

GRANT, KEVIN; Uniondale HS; Hempstead, NY; (Y); Boy Scts; Trs Frsh Cls; JV Bsbl; Var Socr; Var Swmmng; High Hon Roll; Hon Roll; Jr NHS; NHS; Prfct Atten Awd; Hghst Medal Of Merit 84; MVP Swmmng 84; Bus.

GRANT, MARLENE; York Central HS; Piffard, NY; (Y); Teachers Aide; Varsity Clb; Var JV Bsktbl; Var Cheerleading; Var JV Score Keeper; Var Capt Socr; Var Trk; JV Vllybl; Hon Roll; Kiwanis Awd; Bus.

GRANT, MICHAEL J; Alden HS; Alden, NY; (Y); 33/203; FFA; Rep Jr Cls; Rep Sr Cls; Rep Stu Cncl; Var Bsbl; Var Ftbl; Var Capt Wrstlng; Kiwanis Awd; Athl Yr, Cnty Fair Schlrshp 86; Kent ST U; Arch.

GRANT, SUSAN M; Newark SR HS; Lyons, NY; (Y); 1/201; Am Leg Aux Girls St; Drama Clb; 4-H; French Clb; Girl Scts; Math Tm; Concert Band; Drm Mjr(t); Jazz Band; School Musical; S T Comstock Awd 84; Rensslr Medl Excl Math & Sci 85; E J Cunningham Schlrshp 86; U Of MI; Mus.

GRANT JR, THOMAS; Rice HS; New York, NY; (S); 2/100; Rep Church Yth Grp; Rep Computer Clb; Rep Chorus; Rep Nwsp Rptr; Rep Nwsp Stf; Bsktbl; Im Ftbl; JV Trk; High Hon Roll; Hon Roll; Schl Scholar 83-86; Word Proc & Visicale Awd 85; Boston Coll; Comp Sci.

GRANT, VIVECA; St John The Baptist HS; Central Islip, NY; (Y); Drama Clb; French Clb; Band; Concert Band; School Play; Stage Crew; Yrbk Stf; Off Soph Cls; Off Stu Cncl; Pom Pon; Hampton U; Fashion Merch.

GRASSMANN, ROBERT J; Cicero North Syracuse HS; Clay, NY; (Y); Am Leg Boys St; Key Clb; Ski Clb; Var Gym; Im Socr; Var Cmnty Wkr; Jr NHS; NHS; Oswego ST U; Bus Adm.

GRASSO, KRISTINA; North Rockland HS; Stony Point, NY; (Y); Debate Tm; French Clb; Capt Quiz Bowl; VP Spanish Clb; SADD; Stage Crew; Lit Mag; JV Socr; Hon Roll; NHS; Iona Lang 1st Hnrs 86; Stdnt Mnth, Hghst Aver Spnsh II 84; Biotechnlgy.

GRAU, JENNFER; Newfield HS; Selden, NY; (Y); 54/576; Cmnty Wkr; SADD; Varsity Clb; Chrmn Stu Cncl; Var Fld Hcky; Var Sftbl; Var Capt Vllybl; NHS; Gold Key Awd All-Lge All-Conf Vlybl 85-86; Athltc/Schlr Awd 83-84; Scl Stud Awd 83-84; Albright Coll; Hstry.

GRAUBMAN, LISA; Lackawanna HS; Lackawanna, NY; (Y); 52/324; Drama Clb; FBLA; FHA; Office Aide; School Play; Lit Mag; High Hon Roll; Jr NHS; NHS; 5th Pl ST Acctng Cont 85; SUNY Buffalo; Acctng.

GRAUER, DEBORAH L; W Seneca W SR HS; W Seneca, NY; (Y); 10/559; Pres Church Yth Grp; Sec SADD; Capt Drill Tm; Orch; School Musical; JC Awd; NHS; Nwsp Phtg; French Clb; Color Guard; JAYCEES Awd/Mchncl Drwng 85; Ntl Orchstra Awd 85; VA Poly Tech Inst; Archtctr.

GRAULICH, PATRICIA A; St Joseph Hill Acad; Staten Island, NY; (Y); 20/107; French Clb; Math Tm; Teachers Aide; Color Guard; Mrchg Band; Yrbk Stf; Rep Stu Cncl; Hon Roll; NHS; NEDT Awd; St Johns U; Comp Sci.

GRAULICH, TIMOTHY; Monsignor Farrell HS; Staten Island, NY; (Y); Band; Color Guard; Mrchg Band; Stage Crew; Im Bsktbl; Im Bowling; JV Capt Socr; JV Trk; Hon Roll; NHS; Alisi Concours Ntl 2nd Pl 84-85; Monsgnr Farrel JV Sprt Awd 86.

GRAVANTE, BARRY; Cicero North Syracuse HS; North Syracuse, NY; (S); 65/667; Church Yth Grp; JV Bsbl; Var Capt Socr; Hon Roll; NHS; Oswego; Mth.

GRAVELINE, PENNY; Holland Patent Central HS; Northwestern, NY; (Y); Am Leg Aux Girls St; Long Island; Csmtlgy.

GRAVENESE, PAUL; Roosevelt HS; Yonkers, NY; (Y); Varsity Clb; Variety Show; Yrbk Stf; Var JV Bsbl; Var JV Ftbl; Spring Sprts Awd 86; Mercy Coll; Bus Admin.

GRAVES, CHERIE; John C Birdlebough HS; Clay, NY; (Y); Church Yth Grp; 4-H; Band; Concert Band; Mrchg Band; Orch; School Musical; 4-H Awd; Hon Roll; Prfct Atten Awd; Speech Pathology.

GRAVES, DIANE; Vernon-Verona Sherrill HS; Sherrill, NY; (Y); Church Yth Grp; Spanish Clb; Rep Jr Cls; Im Bowling; High Hon Roll; Hon Roll; Spanish NHS; Elem Ed.

GRAVES, JACQUELINE M; Bronx High School Of Science; New York, NY; (Y); Yrbk Stf; Lit Mag; Capt Sftbl; Ntl Merit SF.

GRAVES, TAIFA; Erasmus Hall HS; Brooklyn, NY; (Y); 115/667; Capt Varsity Clb; Band; Concert Band; Rep Soph Cls; Rep Jr Cls; Var Capt Bsktbl; Var Mgr(s); Var Score Keeper; Var Sftbl; Prfct Atten Awd; Math Team 83; Physcl Educ 83-86; Law.

GRAVLIN, AUDREY; Chateaugay Central HS; Chateaugay, NY; (Y); 5/60; FBLA; Nwsp Stf; Off Jr Cls; Off Sr Cls; Socr; Sftbl; High Hon Roll; Hon Roll; NHS; Psych.

GRAY, AMEENA; Fayetteville-Manlius HS; Manlius, NY; (Y); Pres Church Yth Grp; Pep Clb; CPA.

GRAY, ANDREA; East Meadow HS; East Meadow, NY; (Y); Drama Clb; Key Clb; Thesps; Band; Chorus; School Musical; School Play; Variety Show; Yrbk Stf; Psychlgy.

GRAY, CASEY; Pulaski HS; Pulaski, NY; (S); 20/100; Aud/Vis; Varsity Clb; Pres Sr Cls; Stu Cncl; Var L Trk; Wrstlng; Hon Roll; Canton U; Crmnl Justice.

GRAY, CHARMAINE; Holy Trinity Diocesan HS; Hempstead, NY; (S); 20/322; Teachers Aide; Nwsp Rptr; Yrbk Stf; Rep Stu Cncl; High Hon Roll; Hon Roll; Trs NHS; NEDT Awd; Johns Hopkins U; Cardlgst.

GRAY, DOUG; Le Roy HS; Bergen, NY; (Y); Boy Scts; Hnrb Mntn Genesee CC Art Show 85 & 86.

GRAY, ELIZABETH; Bethlehem Central HS; Delmar, NY; (Y); 89/304; GAA; Key Clb; Ski Clb; Band; Concert Band; Stage Crew; Sec Frsh Cls; Rep Soph Cls; Rep Jr Cls; Rep Sr Cls; U Delaware; Txtls.

GRAY, JANICE; Pulaski HS; Pulaski, NY; (S); 9/98; 4-H; Math Clb; Ski Clb; Sec SADD; Pres Band; Chorus; Concert Band; Mrchg Band; School Musical; NHS; Natl Ldrshp Merit Awd 86; Psych.

GRAY, JASON; De Witt Clinton HS; New York, NY; (Y); Phys Ftnss Achvt Awd 84; Sci Hnr Cert 84; Attndnc Hrn Cert 84.

GRAY, LATRICE; Kensington HS; Buffalo, NY; (Y); Computer Clb; Drill Tm; Off Frsh Cls; Stu Cncl; Cmptr Oper.

GRAY JR, LEON; Cardinal Spellman HS; Bronx, NY; (Y); Band; Concert Band; Jazz Band; Mrchg Band; Orch; School Musical; Symp Band; Trk; NY St Regents Schlrp 86; SUNY Farmingdale; Elec Engr.

GRAY, MARGARET P; Sacred Heart Acad; Merrick, NY; (Y); Cmnty Wkr; Pres Spanish Clb; School Musical; Yrbk Rptr; Stu Cncl; Bowling; Var Trk; Hon Roll; Sec NHS; Champs Moc Trl Trnmnt 85; Regnts Schlrshp Recpt 86; Lafayette College; Math.

GRAY, MICHELLE; Immaculata HS; New York, NY; (Y); Chorus; Capt Color Guard; Capt Drill Tm; Yrbk Stf; Sec Soph Cls; VP Sec Jr Cls; VP Sr Cls; Rep Stu Cncl; High Hon Roll; Schl Srv Awd 86; Debutante Ball 86; Judo Awd 85-86; Mt St Vincent; Sprm Crt Jstc.

GRAY, QUEENIE LORETTE; Lafayette HS; Brooklyn, NY; (Y); Hosp Aide; Teachers Aide; Office Aide; Yrbk Stf; Vllybl; Cit Awd; Sci Schlrshp Tea 86; SR Of Mnth 84; NC U Chapel Hill; Med.

GRAY, SABRINA; Boys & Girls HS; Brooklyn, NY; (Y); 175/354; Hosp Aide; JA; Office Aide; Chorus; Gym; Socr; Sftbl; Trk; Vllybl; Hon Roll; Intrfaith Mdcl Ctr Cert Merit 86; Phy Ed Certfct 83; Certfct Excllnc-Peer Ldrshp Reach Out Pgm 82; Morrisvl Coll; Lgl Secy.

GRAY, SHELLY; Lackawanna SR HS; Lackawanna, NY; (Y); Spanish Clb; Swmmng; Hnr Rl 84-85; Sci.

GRAY, STACY; Whitesboro SR HS; Whitesboro, NY; (Y); 78/368; Church Yth Grp; Cmnty Wkr; Intnl Clb; Science Clb; Spanish Clb; Chorus; Stage Crew; Nwsp Rptr; Powder Puff Ftbl; Trk; Rgnts Schlrshp 86; SUNY Albany; Acctg.

GRAY, THERESA; Hamburg SR HS; Hamburg, NY; (Y); 46/374; Quiz Bowl; Teachers Aide; Band; Concert Band; Mrchg Band; Orch; Symp Band; Hon Roll; Phys Ther.

GRAY, TRINA; Thousand Islands HS; Cape Vincent, NY; (Y); Cmnty Wkr; Varsity Clb; Yrbk Ed-Chief; Yrbk Stf; Sec Sr Cls; Gym; JV Var Socr; JV Vllybl; Hon Roll; Bus.

GRAY, WILLIAM J; Westhill HS; Syracuse, NY; (Y); FBLA; Ski Clb; Trs Frsh Cls; Var Bowling; JV Crs Cntry; St Schlr; ST FBLA Comptn-4th Pl Accntng 86; Morrisville CC; Busnss Mgmt.

GRAYMAN, TOM C; Horace Mann Schl; Yonkers, NY; (Y); Variety Show; Var Crs Cntry; Var Trk; Ntl Merit SF; U Of PA; Bus Adm.

GRAZIANO, ANTHONY M; MSGR Farrell HS; Staten Island, NY; (Y); 31/248; Math Clb; Spanish Clb; Varsity Clb; Im Bsktbl; Im Bowling; Im Ftbl; Var Socr; Hon Roll; Ntl Merit Ltr; Regents Schlrshp 86; Pace U Trustee Schlrshp 86; Pace U; Accntng.

GRAZIANO, MILDRED; Nazareth HS; Brooklyn, NY; (Y); Medl Itln 84; Medl Stngrphy 85; Cert Engl 85; Kingsborough CC; Trvl.

GRAZIANO, REGINA; Wallkill SR HS; Wallkill, NY; (Y); 66/194; SADD; Chorus; Nwsp Rptr; Yrbk Rptr; Rep Soph Cls; Rep Jr Cls; Trs Stu Cncl; Var Vllybl; Hon Roll; Prfct Atten Awd; Suny Cortland; Cmnctns.

GRAZIE, MARY DELLE; Bishop Kearney HS; Brooklyn, NY; (Y); 30/338; Cmnty Wkr; Latin Clb; Library Aide; Teachers Aide; Hon Roll; NHS; Charles Johnson Jr Mem Schlrshp 86; Pace Univ Trustee Schlrshp 86; Acadmc All-Amer 86; Pace U; Mrktng.

GREABELL, JEFFREY; Onondaga Central HS; Nedrow, NY; (S); German Clb; SADD; Band; Chorus; VP Frsh Cls; Var Bsbl; Var Ftbl; Var Wrstlng; Hon Roll; Hugh O Brian Yuth Fed 85; Aerontcs.

GREALISH, ANNE MARIE; Maria Regina HS; Yonkers, NY; (Y); 15/186; Key Clb; Nwsp Rptr; Yrbk Stf; Trk; Hon Roll; NHS.

GREANEY, LAURA; Hicksville HS; Hicksville, NY; (Y); 115/540; Art Clb; Aud/Vis; Church Yth Grp; Cmnty Wkr; 4-H; Political Wkr; Ski Clb; Yrbk Stf; Sftbl; 4-H Awd; Nassau CC; Crmnl Law.

GREAVES, PAUL; A Philip Randolph Campus HS; Brooklyn, NY; (Y); 25/166; Pres JA; Capt Var Bsktbl; Var Capt Tennis; Band; L Chorus; L Concert Band; Mrchg Band; Hon Roll; NY Daily News Super Yth 85; NYC PSAL 1st Tm All Cty Bsktbl Plyr 86; A Philip Randolph Schlr Ath 86; Boston Coll; Comp Sci.

GREAVES, SCOTT; Herbert H Lehman HS; Bronx, NY; (Y); Var Bsktbl; Hon Roll; Prfct Atten Awd; Elec Hnr Rll 84-86; Arista Hnr Soc 86; NY Inst Tech; Engrng.

GRECCO, JEANNIE; Clarkstown H S North; Congers, NY; (Y); Cmnty Wkr; Spcl Plympics Recgntn Awd 86; Spcl Training Cert Comptn 86; Tchng.

GRECO, CARMINE J; Sachem High School North; Holbrook, NY; (Y); Computer Clb; Science Clb; Bsbl; Lynchbrg Coll 86; Pace U 86; Seton Hall U 86; Seton Hall U; Comp Sci.

GRECO, CLAUDINE; Bishop Kearney HS; Brooklyn, NY; (Y); 25/332; Spanish Clb; Yrbk Stf; Hon Roll; NHS; Regent Schlrshp 86; Drexel Burnham Lambert Schrlshp 86; 2nd Hnrs Spnsh 84; St Johns U; Comp Pgmr.

GRECO, FRANK; Massena Central HS; Massena, NY; (Y); Y-Teens; Yrbk Stf; Crs Cntry; Vllybl.

GRECO, FRED; Grand Island HS; Grand Island, NY; (Y); 19/300; Chess Clb; Latin Clb; VP Model UN; Political Wkr; JV Bsbl; Im Vllybl; Hon Roll; NHS; Ntl Merit SF; Natl Hnr Soc 86; U Of NY-BUFFALO; Pre-Med.

GRECO, JASON; La Salle Military Acad; Huntington, NY; (Y); 17/83; ROTC; Var Capt Bsbl; Var Bsktbl; Var Socr; High Hon Roll; NHS; All Leag Sfflk Cnty Bsbl Coaches Assn 86, Sfflk Cnty Scer Coaches Assn 85.

GRECO, LORI; Clinton Central HS; Clinton, NY; (Y); 24/136; Pep Clb; Yrbk Stf; JV Sftbl; JV Vllybl; Hon Roll; NHS; VFW Awd; Stu Mnth 85; Geneseo; Mgt Sci.

GRECO, PATRICIA R; Rome Free Acad; Rome, NY; (Y); 4/500; Intnl Clb; Band; Concert Band; Mrchg Band; DAR Awd; High Hon Roll; Jr NHS; Schlrshp Math, Sci, Spn Awds 84; Clrksn U; Engrng.

GRECO, RICHARD; Pelham Memorial HS; Pelham Manor, NY; (Y); Trs Computer Clb; Drama Clb; Model UN; Nwsp Rptr; Lit Mag; Trs Stu Cncl; NHS; Hrvrd Bk Awd 86; Fndr & Prvs Schl Astrnmy Clb 84; Edward Hary Awd Excel Sci & Ctznshp 86; Pre Med.

GRECO, VICTORIA; Smithtown HS East; Nesconset, NY; (Y); Cmnty Wkr; Orch; Off Soph Cls; Off Jr Cls; Off Sr Cls; Var Mgr(s); Cit Awd; GAA; Badmtn; Score Keeper; Schl Svc Awd 86; Jacksonvl U Brd Trstees Schlrshp 86; SUNY Albany; Acctg.

GRECO, VITO J; Rome Free Acad; Rome, NY; (Y); 5/470; JV Socr; High Hon Roll; JETS Awd; Jr NHS; NHS; Pres Schlr; Gilman Awd Comp Sci Hgh Avg 86; Dyett Awd Outstndng Acad Perf 86; AFCEA Schlrshp Awd 86; Clarkson U; Elect Engr.

GREDDER, DARLEEN J; Baldwin SR HS; Baldwin, NY; (Y); Variety Show; Var Capt Bsktbl; Var Capt Sftbl; Var Capt Vllybl; NHS; Pres Schlr; Spanish NHS; Church Yth Grp; Dance Clb; Spanish Clb; Hgh Hnrs, Cert Merit, M M Waldman Awd, W Publshng Co Schlrshp 86; Albany; Bus.

GREELEY, DIANE; Hoosick Falls Central HS; Buskirk, NY; (Y); 27/113; Drama Clb; Chorus; School Musical; School Play; Lit Mag; Merit Achvt Awds; Sullivan Cnty CC; Paralgl Asst.

GREEN, AMY; Thousand Islands HS; Clayton, NY; (Y); Yrbk Stf; Stat Ftbl; Timer; Stat Vllybl; Hon Roll; Bus.

GREEN, AMY; Warwick Valley HS; Warwick, NY; (Y); Church Yth Grp; Hosp Aide; JA; Nwsp Bus Mgr; Yrbk Stf; Bsktbl; Cheerleading; Crs Cntry; Tennis; Trk; Northeastern U; Bus.

GREEN, CATHERINE; Mechanicville HS; Mechanicville, NY; (S); 5/105; Church Yth Grp; Trs French Clb; SADD; Concert Band; Yrbk Stf; Crs Cntry; Trk; High Hon Roll; NHS; Music Cmptn Awd 85; Omega 84; Alpha 85; Mc Gill; Engrng.

GREEN, CHERI; Victor Central HS; Macedon, NY; (Y); Church Yth Grp; Ski Clb; Varsity Clb; Stu Cncl; Var Swmmng; Var Trk; NHS; Phy Ther.

GREEN, CHERYL; Amsterdam HS; Amsterdam, NY; (Y); 110/294; Church Yth Grp; 4-H; FBLA; Church Choir; Yrbk Stf; JV Cheerleading; Hon Roll; FMCC; Law.

GREEN, CHRISTINA; Fabius-Pompey HS; Apulia Station, NY; (Y); 3/60; Drama Clb; Var L Varsity Clb; Trk; High Hon Roll; Hon Roll; Clarkson U $4000 86; Clarkson U; Bus.

GREEN, CYNTHIA; John Jay HS; Katonah, NY; (Y); Church Yth Grp; Cmnty Wkr; Dance Clb; Drama Clb; Girl Scts; Latin Clb; Thesps; School Musical; Variety Show; Cheerleading; Acting.

GREEN, DAMON; Hutchinson Central Technical HS; Buffalo, NY; (Y); SADD; Concert Band; Drill Tm; Mrchg Band; Trs Jr Cls; Im Bowling; Var Capt Trk; Im Vllybl; High Hon Roll; Hon Roll; Our Best In 84; Air Force ROTC; Aerosp Tech.

GREEN, DARRIN; Cardinal Hayes HS; New York, NY; (Y); Bsktbl; Coach Actv; Mgr(s); Score Keeper; Swmmng; Vllybl; Off Soph Cls; Comp.

GREEN, DAVID C; Franklin Delano Roosevelt HS; Hyde Park, NY; (Y); 58/336; Capt Math Tm; SADD; School Musical; Nwsp Rptr; Rep Stu Cncl; Var Capt Crs Cntry; Var Capt Trk; Hon Roll; VP NHS; ROTC Navy Schlrshp 86; NYS Regents Schlrshp 86; Rep NYS Stu Sen Forum 85; Le Moyne Coll; Pol Sci.

GREEN, DONALD; Bishop Kearney HS; Rochester, NY; (Y); Rep Frsh Cls; Rep Sr Cls; JV Var Ftbl; Im Wt Lftg; JV Wrstlng; High Hon Roll; Hon Roll; Nacy; Machine Repairst.

GREEN, HARRY; Rice HS; New York, NY; (Y); Yrbk Stf; Rep Frsh Cls; Rep Soph Cls; Rep Jr Cls; Rep Sr Cls; Im Ftbl; Hon Roll; U Of Charleston; Comp Sci.

GREEN, JAMES; Herkimer SR HS; Herkimer, NY; (Y); 31/113; Library Aide; Hon Roll; Voice Dem Awd; Avionics.

GREEN, JAMIE; Auburn HS; Auburn, NY; (Y); Cmnty Wkr; Intnl Clb; Ski Clb; Capt Lcrss; Hon Roll; Hist Clb; Bio.

GREEN, JENNIFER; Marlboro HS; Milton, NY; (Y); 8/160; Drama Clb; 4-H; Chorus; Church Choir; School Musical; Variety Show; Yrbk Stf; 4-H Awd; High Hon Roll; Pres NHS; Wittenberg U; Psych.

GREEN, JENNIFER; Smithtown HS East; Saint James, NY; (Y); Church Yth Grp; FBLA; Thesps; Church Choir; Sec Concert Band; Sec Mrchg Band; School Musical; Stu Cncl; Hon Roll; Jr NHS; Accntng.

GREEN, KAREN; Cardinal O Hara HS; Tonawanda, NY; (S); 4/122; Art Clb; Drama Clb; French Clb; Ski Clb; Stage Crew; Stat Crs Cntry; Stat Trk; High Hon Roll; Ntl Hstry Day-Hnrb Mntn 85; Prncpls Schlrshp 83; Psych.

GREEN, LAUREN H; Walt Whitman HS; Melville, NY; (Y); Intnl Clb; Key Clb; Spanish Clb; Sec SADD; Yrbk Stf; Off Sr Cls; Stu Cncl; High Hon Roll; NHS; Trs Spanish NHS; NYS Rgnts Schlrshp 86; U Of MA Amherst; Bus.

GREEN, MARAH; Middletown HS; Middletown, NY; (Y); 60/400; Pres Church Yth Grp; Math Tm; Office Aide; Sec Political Wkr; Sec Jr Cls; Var Capt Vllybl; MVP Vrsty Vlbl 86.

GREEN, MICHELLE; Dominican Commercial HS; Flushing, NY; (Y); Cheerleading; Stat Swmmng; Hon Roll; Lawyer.

GREEN, MICHELLE A; James Madison HS; Brooklyn, NY; (Y); 48/748; Office Aide; Service Clb; Color Guard; Drill Tm; Mrchg Band; Orch; Lit Mag; Var L Gym; Var L Swmmng; Hon Roll; Regnts Schlrshp 86; NYU; Pre Med.

GREEN, STACEY; Clarkstown High Schl North; Congers, NY; (Y); JV Trk; Hon Roll; Jr NHS; Enrlld All Hnrs Clss 84-87; Bio.

GREEN, TAMMY; Unatego HS; Wells Bridge, NY; (Y); VP FHA; SADD; Capt Color Guard; Sec Soph Cls; Sec Jr Cls; Sec Sr Cls; JV Var Cheerleading; Hon Roll; French Clb; Girl Scts; Vrsty Ltr 83-86; Jsters Key Awd 86.

GREEN, THOMAS G; E J Wilson HS; Spencerport, NY; (Y); Am Leg Boys St; Church Yth Grp; Exploring; French Clb; Ski Clb; Concert Band; Jazz Band; Var Tennis; JV Vllybl; Hon Roll; Schltc Achvt Soc 85-86.

GREEN, WENDY SOPHIA; Mt Vernon HS; Mount Vernon, NY; (Y); 97/550; Aud/Vis; Key Clb; Library Aide; Office Aide; Spanish Clb; Chorus; Hon Roll; Jr NHS; Yng Athrs Awd Cert 85; Hunter Coll.

GREENAN, MAUREEN A; Our Lady Of Mercy Acad; Seaford, NY; (Y); 24/122; Cmnty Wkr; French Clb; Im Ftbl; Trk; Hon Roll; Ntl Merit Ltr; NEDT Awd; Rgnts Schlrshp; U Of Richmond; Finance.

GREENAUER, GEORGE; Churchville-Chili SR HS; Churchville, NY; (Y); 25/200; Math Clb; Math Tm; Ski Clb; JV Bsbl; Hon Roll; Monroe CC; Police Det.

GREENAWAY, ANDREA; Northeastern Acad; Jamaica, NY; (Y); 4/35; Church Yth Grp; Cmnty Wkr; Spanish Clb; Drill Tm; Drm Mjr(t); Rep Stu Cncl; Cheerleading; Score Keeper; Ntl Merit Ltr; Art Awd 83; Spnsh Awd 84; Andrewus U MI; Pre-Law.

GREENBAUM, ROBERT; East Hampton HS; Montauk, NY; (Y); 1/116; Political Wkr; Lit Mag; Rep Frsh Cls; Cit Awd; High Hon Roll; Jr NHS; NHS; Rotary Awd; Val; NYS Regnts Schlrshp 86; Cornell U; Pre-Vet.

GREENBAUM, YONATAN; Baldwin HS; Riverdale, NY; (Y); Chess Clb; Debate Tm; Drama Clb; Service Clb; Temple Yth Grp; School Play; Nwsp Ed-Chief; Yrbk Stf; Rep Jr Cls; Rep Stu Cncl; NY ST Bar Assc Mock Trl 83-85; Dept Awd Social Studies 86; Educ.

GREENBERG, ALEX B; Vestal SR HS; Binghamton, NY; (Y); 68/430; Concert Band; Var Bsktbl; Var L Socr; Im Vllybl; Wt Lftg; Hon Roll; NHS; U Of Rochester; Mediation.

GREENBERG, EMILY; Half Hollow Hills HS; Dix Hills, NY; (Y); Drama Clb; Trs Key Clb; Leo Clb; SADD; Chorus; School Musical; Variety Show; Nwsp Rptr; High Hon Roll; NHS; Pres Arts & Tlnt Recog Srch 86.

GREENBERG, JAY; Tottenville HS; Staten Island, NY; (Y); 43/871; Chorus; Orch; School Musical; Yrbk Phtg; Hon Roll; NHS; Prfct Atten Awd; Dave Winfield Fdn Schlrshp Music 86; Rgnts Schlrshp 86; SUNY Bnghmtn; Am Hstry.

GREENBERG, LOREN; Tottenville HS; Staten Island, NY; (S); 7/957; Key Clb; School Musical; School Play; French Hon Soc; High Hon Roll; NHS; Natl Frnch Cntst Awd 84; Modl Congrs 85; Womn In Hist Awd 85; Sci.

GREENBERG, MICHAEL; New Rochelle HS; Scarsdale, NY; (Y); Cmnty Wkr; FBLA; JA; Ski Clb; VP Temple Yth Grp; Hon Roll; Sci.

GREENBERG, MITCHELL; Roosevelt HS; Yonkers, NY; (Y); Computer Clb; Spanish Clb; JV Bsbl; JV Var Bsktbl; JV Var Ftbl; Med.

GREENBERG, THOMAS; South Side HS; Rockville Centre, NY; (Y); 11/300; Chess Clb; Trs Sec Latin Clb; Mathletes; Orch; Nwsp Rptr; Var L Socr; Var L Tennis; NHS; Ntl Merit Ltr; All ST Orch 87; Gold Mdl Summa Cum Laude Natl Lat Exam 86; Cmnty Svc Awd 85; Chem.

GREENBLATT, MITCHELL; Clarkstown North HS; New City, NY; (Y); Teachers Aide; Yrbk Stf; Bsktbl; Coach Actv; Mgr(s); Helped Run Spec Olympics, DECA 1st Co & 3rd St 86; Bus.

GREENBLATT, RICK; Churchville-Chili HS; Spencerport, NY; (Y); Capt JV Bsbl; Capt Var Socr; High Hon Roll; NHS; High Score Acctng Awd 85-86; Socl Wrkr.

GREENE, CHRIS; John H Glenn HS; E Northport, NY; (Y); 81/268; Varsity Clb; Socr; Rotary Awd; Bwmn Ashe Schlrshp U Of Miami 86-87; U Of Miami; Arch.

GREENE, DIANA; Holladn Patent HS; Remsen, NY; (Y); Art Clb; Church Yth Grp; Hosp Aide; Chorus; School Play; Stage Crew; JV Var Score Keeper; Pres Phys Fit Awd 86.

GREENE, ERINN; Fayetteville-Manlius HS; Manlius, NY; (Y); Thesps; Chorus; School Musical; Rep Stu Cncl; Var JV Fld Hcky; High Hon Roll; Hon Roll; NHS; Model UN; SADD; Eng Lit Awd 84; Cert Excllnce Spnsh Awd 84-86; Sanford Seltzer Schlrshp Israel 85.

GREENE, ILYSSA; Half Hollow Hills West HS; Dix Hills, NY; (Y); Sec French Clb; Hosp Aide; Key Clb; Leo Clb; Chorus; School Play; JV Tennis; Var Trk; NHS; Ntl Merit Ltr.

GREENE, JOSEPH; Uniondale HS; Uniondale, NY; (Y); Church Yth Grp; FBLA; Cpa.

GREENE, KAREN; Uniondale HS; Hempstead, NY; (Y); Camera Clb; Cmnty Wkr; Key Clb; Library Aide; Office Aide; Radio Clb; Speech Tm; SADD; Acpl Chr; Chorus; NAACP 85-86; Hotel Mgmt.

GREENE, KEVIN; Greenwich Central HS; Schaghticoke, NY; (Y); FFA; Varsity Clb; Yrbk Stf; Var L Crs Cntry; Var L Trk; High Hon Roll; Hon Roll; Prfct Atten Awd; Math.

GREENE, KEVIN; Niagara Catholic HS; Lewiston, NY; (Y); 1/87; Spanish Clb; Var Capt Bsktbl; Var Capt Crs Cntry; Var L Trk; High Hon Roll; NHS; X-Cntry All Cathlc 85; Elec Engrng.

GREENE, LAURA M; Martin Luther HS; St Albans, NY; (Y); Church Yth Grp; French Clb; Concert Band; Yrbk Bus Mgr; Trs Soph Cls; Trs Sr Cls; Stu Cncl; JV Bsktbl; Var L Cheerleading; High Hon Roll; Uppr 7 Pct PSAT NMSQT SF Comptn 86; Natl Achvt Prog Outstndng Negro Stdnts 86; Lwyr.

GREENE, LISA; New Rochelle HS; New Rochelle, NY; (Y); Key Clb; SADD; Nwsp Stf; Lit Mag; Rep Soph Cls; VP Jr Cls; VP Sr Cls; Cit Awd; NHS; Spanish NHS; Excllnc Spanish Awd 84.

GREENE, PAM; Sodus Central HS; Sodus, NY; (Y); Chorus; Sftbl; Hon Roll; Comp Pgmmng.

GREENE, PAUL; Midwood HS; Brooklyn, NY; (Y); Office Aide; Service Clb; Teachers Aide; Var Bsbl; Lincoln U; Psych.

GREENE, PAULA LYNN; Holy Angels Acad; Kenmore, NY; (Y); Drama Clb; French Clb; Math Tm; Chorus; School Musical; School Play; Variety Show; Yrbk Stf; Vllybl; Hon Roll; Buffalo ST Coll; Sysms Mgt.

GREENE, RAEANN; Mexico HS; Oswego, NY; (Y); French Clb; German Clb; Ski Clb; High Hon Roll; Hon Roll; NHS; Voice Dem Awd; Sprts Med.

GREENE, RAYMOND; HS For The Humanities HS; New York, NY; (Y); Cmnty Wkr; Band; Concert Band; School Musical; School Play; Var Bsbl; JV Im Bsktbl; Im Bowling; Hon Roll; Cardinal Hayes Hnr Soc 84.

GREENE, RICHARD; Bishop Ford HS; Brooklyn, NY; (Y); JA; Office Aide; JV Bsktbl; Golf; Mgr(s); Score Keeper; JV Var Swmmng; Intl Trade.

GREENE, ROBERT E; Clarkstown HS North; New City, NY; (Y); Cmnty Wkr; SADD; Off Frsh Cls; Off Soph Cls; Off Jr Cls; Off Sr Cls; Stu Cncl; Var L Debate Tm; Var L Bsktbl; Law.

GREENE, SANDRA; Grace Dodge V HS; Bronx, NY; (Y); Girl Scts; Office Aide; SADD; Teachers Aide; Chorus; Sftbl; John Jay CC; Paralegal.

GREENE, TANYA; High Schl For The Humaniti; New York, NY; (Y); Political Wkr; Q&S; Acpl Chr; School Musical; Nwsp Stf; Lit Mag; VP Sr Cls; VP Jr NHS; NHS; Art Clb; Mst Intelligent Girl; Mst Outstndng Alto; Law.

GREENFIELD, AMELIA; Wm Nottingham HS; Syracuse, NY; (Y); 83/200; Latin Clb; Ski Clb; VP Spanish Clb; SADD; Sec Soph Cls; Tennis; Rotary Awd; 1st Altrnt Rotry Yth Exch 84-85; Schlrshp Rotry Yth Exch 86-87; Miami U; Pltcl Sci.

GREENFIELD, MICHAEL; Fairport HS; Fairport, NY; (Y); Capt Math Tm; Sec Model UN; Trs Temple Yth Grp; Band; Jazz Band; NHS; Monroe Cnty Math Lg 1st Pl 85-86; Navl Aviatn Art Sax Qrtet 86; Amer Chem Soc 3rd Pl Cnty 85; Johns Hopkins U; Engrng.

GREENFIELD, MICHAEL B; Roslyn HS; Roslyn Heights, NY; (Y); Cmnty Wkr; Pres Temple Yth Grp; Chorus; Nwsp Rptr; Ed Lit Mag; NCTE Awd; NHS; Author.

GREENING, JENNIE; Valley Central HS; Maybrook, NY; (Y); Sec Church Yth Grp; Yrbk Stf.

GREENLEAF, EARL; Ballston Spa HS; Ballston Spa, NY; (Y); Boy Scts; Church Yth Grp; Science Clb; Ski Clb; JV Crs Cntry; Var Trk; High Hon Roll; Hon Roll; NHS; Clarkson U; Engrng.

GREENLEAF, KIMBERLY; Whitesboro SR HS; Utica, NY; (Y); Hosp Aide; Orch; Stu Cncl; Powder Puff Ftbl; JV Trk; Var Vllybl; Hon Roll; Mohawk Vly CC; Bio.

GREENLEAF, MICHAEL; Westfield Academy And Central Schl; Westfield, NY; (Y); AFS; Ski Clb; Yrbk Stf; Var Golf; Var Socr; Var Tennis; JV Trk; High Hon Roll; Hon Roll.

GREENMAN, C RONALD; Byron-Bergen Central HS; Bergen, NY; (Y); 21/89; Cmnty Wkr; Math Tm; Rep Stu Cncl; Var Capt Bsbl; High Hon Roll; Hon Roll; Prfct Atten Awd; NYS Rgnts Schlrshp 86-90; Mynhn Mem Schlrshp 86-90; Stfl Fmly Cmmnty Svc Awd 86; St Bonaventure U; Acctng.

GREENOUGH, JANE; Ticonderoga HS; Ticonderoga, NY; (Y); Pres Church Yth Grp; Varsity Clb; Rep Soph Cls; Rep Jr Cls; Var L Socr; High Hon Roll; Hon Roll; NHS; Bus.

GREENOUGH, LAURA; St Johns Prep; Astoria, NY; (Y); 45/478; Drm & Bgl; Hon Roll; Jr NHS; Pres NHS; Prncpls Svc Awd 86; Pace U; Finance.

GREENQUIST, KIRK; Eden SR HS; Eden, NY; (Y); 4/173; Nwsp Rptr; JV Var Ftbl; Trk; Im Vllybl; Hon Roll; NHS; Rochester Inst Of Tech; Comp.

GREENSPAN, MIREET S; Yeshiva Univ High School For Girls; Flushing, NY; (Y); Temple Yth Grp; Nwsp Ed-Chief; Yrbk Stf; Lit Mag; High Hon Roll; Ntl Merit Ltr; Max Stern Schlrshp 85; Queens Coll Schlr 85; Stern Coll; Attrny.

GREENSTEIN, JENNIFER; Riverdale Country Schl; New York, NY; (Y); Cmnty Wkr; French Clb; Model UN; School Play; Nwsp Bus Mgr; Nwsp Ed-Chief; Nwsp Rptr; Lit Mag; Var Capt Trk; Hon Roll; Outstndng Stu Of Englsh Awd 86; All Ivy Trck Tm 86; Englsh.

GREENSTEIN, JESSICA; Watkins Glen HS; Watkins Glen, NY; (Y); 8/135; Math Clb; Concert Band; Jazz Band; School Play; Nwsp Rptr; Var Swmmng; French Hon Soc; NHS; Ntl Merit Schol; Im Sftbl; Cornell U.

GREENWALD, AVROMIE; Yeshiva Torah Temimah HS; Brooklyn, NY; (Y); Library Aide; Office Aide; Scholastic Bowl; NY ST Regents Schlrshp 85-86; Talmudic Law.

GREENWALD, BRIAN; South Shore HS; Brooklyn, NY; (Y); Cmnty Wkr; Hosp Aide; Stonybrook; Doc.

GREENWALD, DAVID N; Hunter College HS; Brooklyn, NY; (Y); Variety Show; Pres Soph Cls; Pres Jr Cls; Mu Alp Tht; Ntl Merit SF; Columbia Sci Hnr Pgm 84-85; Clsscs.

GREENWELL, BETSY; Royalton-Hartland Central HS; Middleport, NY; (Y); Church Yth Grp; French Clb; Girl Scts; SADD; Yrbk Stf; JV Mgr(s); JV Score Keeper; God Cntry Awd; Hon Roll; Bus.

GREENWICH, GRACE; Mt Vernon HS; Mount Vernon, NY; (Y); 91/600; Church Yth Grp; Chorus; Church Choir; Mrchg Band; Orch; School Musical; Symp Band; Cheerleading; Trk; Hon Roll; Myrs Cty-Wd Essy Cont 86; Cecil H Parker Schlrshp 86; Pres Physcl Ftnss 82-86; U IL; Bus.

GREENWOOD, JODIE; Frewsburg Central HS; Jamestown, NY; (Y); 2/87; Am Leg Aux Girls St; 4-H; Spanish Clb; Band; Yrbk Stf; JV Sftbl; Var Swmmng; Var Trk; Bausch & Lomb Sci Awd; NHS; Mrch Of Dms Schlrhsp 86; Cmmns Engn Schlrshp 86; ACT Schlrshp-Andrws U 86; Andrews U; Physcn.

GREENWOOD, VICTORIA; Frankfort-Schuyler Central Schl; Frankfort, NY; (Y); Church Yth Grp; Hosp Aide; Political Wkr; SADD; Yrbk Stf; Hon Roll; Gegg Shorthnd Awd Achvmnt 60 Wrds A Minute & 80 Wrds A Minute 86; Dntl Hygnst.

GREER, LAURIE D; La Salle SR HS; Niagara Falls, NY; (S); 1/250; Library Aide; Yrbk Bus Mgr; Yrbk Stf; Rep Stu Cncl; Var L Bowling; Var Mgr(s); Var L Swmmng; Bausch & Lomb Sci Awd; Hon Roll; Val; Case Western Rsrv U; Biotech.

GREER, MARK; Hannibal Central HS; Sterling, NY; (Y); 13/114; Key Clb; Math Clb; Fld Hcky; Trk; High Hon Roll; Hon Roll; NHS; Prfct Atten Awd; SUNY Coll Oswego; Engrng.

GREER, STEVEN; Cicero-North Syracuse HS; Clay, NY; (S); 6/667; Mathletes; Math Tm; Ski Clb; Bsktbl; Bowling; Swmmng; High Hon Roll; NHS; Clarkson; Bio.

GREEVY, DONNA MARIE; Roy C Ketcham HS; Wappingers Falls, NY; (Y); Dance Clb; Chorus; Rep Stu Cncl; Var Trk; Hon Roll; Prfct Atten Awd; Bus Mgmt.

GREGES, JANINE; Northport HS; E Northport, NY; (Y); 50/590; Church Yth Grp; DECA; Yrbk Stf; Rep Soph Cls; Rep Jr Cls; Hon Roll; Jr NHS; Camera Clb; Dance Clb; Rep Stu Cncl; Outstndng Achvt Amercn Hstry & Constnl Law 86.

GREGG, DEBORAH; White Plains HS; White Plains, NY; (Y); 35/420; French Clb; Nwsp Stf; Rep Frsh Cls; Rep Soph Cls; Rep Jr Cls; Im Lcrss; JV Socr; Var Swmmng; Hon Roll.

GREGG, TAMMIE; Amityville Memorial HS; Massapequa, NY; (Y); Key Clb; Office Aide; Teachers Aide; Nwsp Stf; Cit Awd; High Hon Roll; NHS; Psych Bio.

GREGOR, MARY B; St Francis Prep; Ridgewood, NY; (S); 111/744; Band; Hon Roll; Opt Clb Awd; Aerobcs Clb 84-85; Acctg.

GREGOR, SUSAN; Villa Maria Acad; Buffalo, NY; (Y); Gym; Prfct Atten Awd; Hghst Avg Math 3 Non Regnts 85-86; 2nd Hnrs Made Merit Rll 85-86; Gregg Typg Awd Achvt 85-86; ECC; Math Tchr.

GREGORY, AMY; Charles H Roth HS; Henrietta, NY; (Y); Radio Clb; Ski Clb; Chorus; School Play; Nwsp Stf; Lit Mag; High Hon Roll; Hon Roll; Jr NHS; NHS; Social Stud Hnr Roll 85-86; S U N Y; Hstry Prof.

GREGORY, BETH; Pulaski JR SR HS; Pulaski, NY; (Y); Church Yth Grp; Girl Scts; Var Capt Vllybl; Drama Clb; French Clb; Math Clb; Office Aide; Chorus; Rep Stu Cncl; Var Crs Cntry; Erly Chldhd Educ.

GREGORY, JOYCE; Cathedral HS; Brkn, NY; (Y); 43/277; Chess Clb; Intnl Clb; Library Aide; Chorus; Hon Roll; Prfct Atten Awd; Piano Achvt Awd 85; Regnts Coll Schlrsahp 86; Pres Acadmc Fitns Awd 86; Marymount Coll; Med.

GREGORY, MARY; Nanuet SR HS; Nanuet, NY; (Y); 40/162; Church Yth Grp; DECA; SADD; School Play; Variety Show; Ed Yrbk Stf; Sec Soph Cls; Sec Jr Cls; Sec Sr Cls; Rep Stu Cncl; Fr Peter Malet Svc To Yth Awd 86; PTA Schlrp & Svc Merch Schlrp 86; Jesse Kaplan Awd 86; Bryant Coll; Mrktng.

GREIN, JEANINE; Spackenkill HS; Poughkeepsie, NY; (Y); Exploring; Girl Scts; Leo Clb; Stage Crew; Nwsp Stf; Lit Mag; Tennis; High Hon Roll; NHS; Phys Sci.

GREINER, DINA; Marlboro HS; Marlboro, NY; (Y); 8/150; Chorus; Stat Bsktbl; Var Trk; High Hon Roll; Jr NHS; NHS; Prfct Atten Awd; Band; Concert Band; Mrchg Band; Solo Comptn Awd Piano 81-86; Accompnst 85-86; Siena College; Acctg.

GREINER, LYNN; Marlboro HS; Newburgh, NY; (Y); 63/130; Church Yth Grp; Band; Concert Band; Mrchg Band; Pep Band; Swmmng; Trk.

GRELL, CRAWFORD; Prospect Heights HS; Brooklyn, NY; (Y); 10/278; Debate Tm; French Clb; FBLA; Band; School Musical; Nwsp Rptr; VP Frsh Cls; Socr; High Hon Roll; Hon Roll; Untd Fdrtn Tchrs Schlrshp 86; Roothbert Schlrshp 86; Hunter Coll; Poli Sci.

GRENZY, CASSANDRA; Niagara Catholic HS; Niagara Fls, NY; (Y); Yrbk Phtg; Yrbk Stf; JV Vllybl; Prjct Bus 85; Niagara Cmnty Coll; Bus.

GRESIS, TRACY; Somers HS; Somers, NY; (Y); Yrbk Stf; Stu Cncl; JV Bsktbl; JV Sftbl; High Hon Roll; Hon Roll; NHS; Spanish NHS; Bus.

GRESKO, JOYCE; South Park HS; Buffalo, NY; (Y); Rep Sr Cls; Hon Roll; Prfct Atten Awd; Med.

GRESOCK, GREGORY G; Horseheads HS; Horseheads, NY; (S); 4/380; Boy Scts; Model UN; Pres Science Clb; Jazz Band; Mrchg Band; Rep Stu Cncl; JV L Crs Cntry; Trk; High Hon Roll; NHS; Eagle Scout Awd 85; Alfred U Summer Inst Sci & Engrng 85; 2nd & 3rd Es Sagts Germ Conf 83; Cornell U; Biomed Engrng.

GRESSLER, KATHRYN; Mohawk Central HS; Mohawk, NY; (Y); 6/100; Art Clb; Pep Clb; Spanish Clb; Teachers Aide; Varsity Clb; Band; Concert Band; Mrchg Band; Variety Show; Sec Soph Cls; Elmira Coll Key Awd $4000 Schlrshp 86; Elmira Coll; Elem Educ.

GRETKA, SHERRY; Frontier Central HS; Blasdell, NY; (Y); Hosp Aide; Latin Clb; Pep Clb; JV Var Cheerleading; Powder Puff Ftbl; Wt Lftg; Hon Roll; Prfct Atten Awd; U Buffalo; Gen Surg.

GRETZINGER, CHRISTEN; E J Wilson HS; Rochester, NY; (Y); 25/340; French Clb; Math Tm; Ski Clb; Trs Frsh Cls; Trs Soph Cls; Trs Jr Cls; High Hon Roll; Hon Roll; NHS; Prfct Atten Awd; Med.

GREUBEL, KIRK; S H Calhoun HS; Merrick, NY; (Y); Boy Scts; Var Lcrss; Capt Var Swmmng; Egl Sct 86; MVP-VRSTY Swmmng-All Cnty 86; All Div All Leag Lacrss Cmp Ave Almns Awd 86; Slippery Rock U-PA; Elem Ed.

GREVEN, ADRIANNE; Mt St Ursula HS; New York, NY; (Y); Drama Clb; Girl Scts; Stage Crew; The Wood Schl; Sec.

GREW, CHRISTOPHER; Arlington HS; Poughkeepsie, NY; (Y); Aud/Vis; Bsbl; Bowling; Ftbl; Socr; Sftbl; Trk; Vllybl; High Hon Roll; Hon Roll; U PA; Bus.

GREY, BONNIE; Alleghany Central HS; Allegany, NY; (Y); Church Yth Grp; SADD; Chorus; Color Guard; School Play; Nwsp Rptr; Yrbk Phtg; Sec Stu Cncl; Cheerleading; High Hon Roll; Med Lab Tech.

GREY, TARA; Frankfort - Schuyler HS; Frankfort, NY; (S); Drama Clb; Sec French Clb; Key Clb; Pep Clb; Sec SADD; Chorus; Color Guard; Mrchg Band; Sec Frsh Cls; High Hon Roll; All-Cntry Chorus; Accntng.

GREY, TERESA; Rome Free Acad; Rome, NY; (Y); 7/58; Church Yth Grp; Drama Clb; Chorus; Nwsp Rptr; Trk; High Hon Roll; Hon Roll; NHS; Church Choir; School Musical; Headmasters List 85; Linguistics.

GRIBBINS, JEAN A; Floral Park Memorial HS; Floral Park, NY; (Y); 20/157; Trs FBLA; GAA; SADD; Varsity Clb; Chorus; Sec Stu Cncl; Bsktbl; Capt Socr; Sftbl; NHS; NY ST Regnts Schlrshp; Siena; Bus.

GRIDLEY, TOBY; Addison Central HS; Addison, NY; (Y); Am Leg Boys St; Exploring; Yrbk Ed-Chief; High Hon Roll; NHS; Intrnshp Lcl Govt 85-86; Elmira Coll; Comp Sci.

GRIECO, DANIELLE; Manhasset HS; Manhasset, NY; (Y); Service Clb; Yrbk Stf; Var JV Fld Hcky; Var JV Lcrss; Vllybl; High Hon Roll; Ntl Merit Ltr; Sec Girls Athltc Cncl 86-87; Cum Laude Awd Outstndg Perfrmance Natl Latin Exam 86; Awd Natl Scie Olymp; Medicine.

GRIER, SHELBY; Union Springs Central HS; Union Spgs, NY; (Y); 2/130; VP Spanish Clb; Yrbk Phtg; Yrbk Stf; Pres Frsh Cls; Pres Jr Cls; Var L Tennis; Var Trk; High Hon Roll; NHS; Diploma Merit Excllnce Spn 86; Engrng.

GRIESBACH, ELIZABETH; Our Lady Of Victory Acad; Bronx, NY; (S); 10/157; French Clb; Nwsp Rptr; Yrbk Stf; Lit Mag; Sftbl; Tennis; French Hon Soc; NHS; Commissioners Awd Sftbl 83.

GRIESE, LAURI; Morrisville-Eaton Central Schl; Morrisville, NY; (Y); 16/50; VP 4-H; VP Science Clb; Band; Chorus; Mrchg Band; Nwsp Stf; JV Vllybl; 4-H Awd; Hon Roll; SUNY Fredonia; Comm.

GRIESEMER, KRISTEN C; Hoosick Falls Central Schl; Hoosick Falls, NY; (Y); 5/104; Rep 4-H; Quiz Bowl; Ski Clb; Off Frsh Cls; Off Soph Cls; Off Jr Cls; Var Cheerleading; 4-H Awd; High Hon Roll; Hon Roll; Edth Crg Rynlds Schlrshp 85-86; Rgnts Schlrshp 85-86; Outstndng Engl Achvt & Engl Rgnts Awd 85-86; Carnegie Mellon U; Engrng.

GRIFFATON, MICHAEL C; St Anthonys HS; Central Islip, NY; (Y); Art Clb; Chess Clb; Yrbk Phtg; Lit Mag; High Hon Roll; NHS; Spanish NHS; Pblc Rltns Clb VP 84-86; NY ST Rgnts Schlrshp 86; OH Wesleyan U; Physcn.

GRIFFIN, BILLY; Beach Channel HS; Breezy Point, NY; (Y); Math Tm; Stage Crew; Yrbk Stf; Wt Lftg; Hon Roll; NHS; VFW Awd; Arista 85-86; Annapolis; Med.

GRIFFIN, CHRISTOPHER A; Locust Valley HS; Bayville, NY; (Y); 11/220; Am Leg Boys St; Mathletes; SADD; Nwsp Bus Mgr; Nwsp Phtg; Nwsp Rptr; Nwsp Stf; Var Capt Bsktbl; Im Coach Actv; Ftbl; Exclnc In Sci & Soc Studies 84; Georgetown; Engrng.

GRIFFIN, DIANE; Tottenville HS; Staten Island, NY; (Y); GAA; Var Crs Cntry; Var Trk; Hon Roll; Jr NHS; Natl Hnr Socy 83-86; Crss Cntry, Indoor & Outdoor Trck; Model Cngrss.

GRIFFIN, DJOY; Mt Vernon HS; Mt Vernon, NY; (Y); Nwsp Stf; Lawyer.

GRIFFIN, GREGORY; West Genesee SR HS; Camillus, NY; (Y); Am Leg Boys St; Art Clb; Cmnty Wkr; Exploring; French Clb; Ski Clb; Nwsp Rptr; Nwsp Stf; Yrbk Stf; Jr Cls; Brdcstng.

GRIFFIN, JEFF; Potsdam Central HS; Potsdam, NY; (Y); JV Var Bsbl; Var Capt Ftbl; Elks Awd; Hon Roll; All Northrn Ftbl 85.

GRIFFIN, JENNIFER; John Dewey HS; New York, NY; (Y); Intnl Clb; PAVAS; Band; Orch; School Musical; School Play; Stage Crew; Nwsp Stf; Yrbk Stf; Im Tennis; Arista 84.

GRIFFIN, JOSEPH T; Ballston Spa HS; Ballston Spa, NY; (Y); 11/245; Math Clb; SADD; Varsity Clb; Orch; Var Capt Socr; High Hon Roll; Sec NHS; Var L Bsbl; Var L Bsktbl; Ganett Sartgn Mrt Awds Dnr 84; JV Bsktbl MVP 85; NYS Rgnts Schlrshp 86; Syracuse U; Cmmnctns.

GRIFFIN, KEITH; Iona Prep; Scarsdale, NY; (Y); 49/204; Church Yth Grp; Hosp Aide; Band; School Play; High Hon Roll; Hon Roll.

GRIFFIN, KELLY; Saugerties HS; Saugerties, NY; (S); 32/250; Church Yth Grp; French Clb; Ski Clb; Band; Chorus; Concert Band; Rep Mrchg Band; Rep Symp Band; Variety Show; Stat Ftbl; St Lawrence U; Chld Advocate.

GRIFFIN, KIM; Warrensburg HS; Warrensburg, NY; (Y); 1/57; Pres French Clb; Varsity Clb; Sec Jr Cls; Var Capt Bsktbl; Var Capt Fld Hcky; Var Vllybl; Bausch & Lomb Sci Awd; NHS; Pres Schlr; Val; Rgnts Schlrshp Awd Wnnr 86; W Point; Engrng.

GRIFFIN, MARY JEAN; Salamanca Central HS; Salamanca, NY; (Y); 1/133; Trs Band; Sftbl; Vllybl; French Hon Soc; NHS; Ntl Merit Ltr; Pres Schlr; Spanish NHS; St Schlr; Val; Athl Yr 86; NY ST Regnts Schlrshp 86; Dr Ruth Knobloch Physcn Memrl Schlrshp 86; St Bonaventure U; Bio.

GRIFFIN, SAMANTHA; Andrew Jackson HS; Cambria Hts, NY; (Y); English Clb; Science Clb; Band; Chorus; Church Choir; Mrchg Band; School Musical; Nwsp Rptr; Nwsp Stf; Rep Jr Cls; NY Yth Connectn 84-85; Queens Coll; Nrsg.

GRIFFING, GEOFFREY; Lingwood HS; Coram, NY; (S); 25/500; Math Tm; Band; School Musical; School Play; Stage Crew; Nwsp Phtg; Nwsp Rptr; Nwsp Stf; Yrbk Phtg; Yrbk Stf.

GRIFFING, JOCELYN; The Chapin Schl; New York City, NY; (S); Cmnty Wkr; Drama Clb; French Clb; NFL; Red Cross Aide; Speech Tm; Teachers Aide; Chorus; Badmtn; Prfct Atten Awd; Law.

GRIFFING, MEREDITH; Hampton Bays JR SR HS; Hampton Bays, NY; (Y); VICA; JV Fld Hcky; JV Vllybl; Briarcliffe Bus Coll; Csmtlgy.

GRIFFITH, CHARON; Erasmus Hall HS; Brooklyn, NY; (Y); Church Yth Grp; Office Aide; Political Wkr; Teachers Aide; Church Choir; School Play; Rep Frsh Cls; Rep Soph Cls; Rep Jr Cls; Rep Stu Cncl; Timmy Swaggert Bible; Jrnlsm.

GRIFFITH, GREGORY; Archbishop Molloy HS; Cambria Hts, NY; (Y); 130/383; Church Yth Grp; Cmnty Wkr; Debate Tm; Hosp Aide; Nwsp Stf; Rep Frsh Cls; Rep Soph Cls; Rep Jr Cls; Im Bsktbl; Im Score Keeper; U NC Chapel Hill; Pre-Law.

GRIFFITH, JOSEPH W; Garden City HS; Garden City, NY; (Y); 34/341; Church Yth Grp; VP Frsh Cls; Var L Bsktbl; Var L Ftbl; Var L Lcrss; Jr NHS; NHS; Letterman Clb; Varsity Clb; High Hon Roll; Ltrd Div Champ Ftbl Tm Qtrbk 84-85; 1st Midfld NYS Cls A Champ La Crosse Tm 86.

GRIFFITH, JULIE; Massena Central HS; Massena, NY; (Y); JV Var Socr; Oswego ST Coll; Educ.

GRIFFITH, KRISTEN; Mercy HS; Schen, NY; (Y); Dance Clb; Pep Clb; Ski Clb; School Play; Stage Crew; Yrbk Rptr; Yrbk Stf; Stu Cncl; Cheerleading; Hon Roll; CW Post Long Island; Fshn Dsgn.

GRIFFITH, LEASIAH; Franlyn Delano Roosevelt HS; Brooklyn, NY; (Y); Debate Tm; Drama Clb; Nwsp Rptr; Ed Lit Mag; High Hon Roll; Prfct Atten Awd; Acad Olympcs 86; Mock Trial 86; 1st Pl Poem Wmns Week 86; Med.

GRIFFITH, PAUL E; Amsterdam HS; Fort Johnson, NY; (Y); 5/320; Cmnty Wkr; Band; Concert Band; Drm Mjr(t); Jazz Band; Mrchg Band; Orch; High Hon Roll; NHS; Ntl Merit Ltr; Air Force ROTC 86; NY ST Regnts Schlrshp; Clarkson U; Comp Engr.

GRIFFITHS, JEFF; Milford Central HS; Milford, NY; (Y); 1/27; Am Leg Boys St; Pres Computer Clb; Pres Spanish Clb; Band; Jazz Band; Mrchg Band; Stage Crew; Nwsp Sprt Ed; L Bsbl; L Socr; Clark Fndtn Schlrshp 85; Rgnts Schlrshp 86; Vldctrn Awd 86; Mohawk Valley CC; Engrng.

GRIFFO, ANTHONY; New Rochelle HS; New Rochelle, NY; (Y); Chess Clb; Computer Clb; Hon Roll; NHS; Earth Sci Awd 83-84; 6 Coll Crdts Earth Sci NY Rgnts Exms 83-84; Engnrng.

GRIFIN, KIMBERLY L; Warrensburg Central Schl; Warrensburg, NY; (Y); 1/50; French Clb; Varsity Clb; Var Capt Bsktbl; Var Capt Fld Hcky; Var Vllybl; NHS; Pres Schlr; Val; US Military Acad.

GRIGGSBY, COLETTE; Cathedral HS; Ny, NY; (Y); 90/291; Art Clb; Drama Clb; Intnl Clb; Office Aide; Pep Clb; Chorus; Nwsp Rptr; Lit Mag; Im Gym; Im Sftbl; Htl Rstrnt Mgt.

GRIGOLI, JOHN; Oneonta SR HS; Oneonta, NY; (Y); Boys Clb Am; Church Yth Grp; Computer Clb; Spanish Clb; Varsity Clb; Chorus; Yrbk Phtg; Bsbl; Bsktbl; Hon Roll; Employee Yr 84; Oneonta ST; Comp Sci.

GRILES, ALLYSON; Brewster HS; Brewster, NY; (Y); Church Yth Grp; Teachers Aide; Stage Crew; Trs Frsh Cls; Trs Soph Cls; Trs Jr Cls; Rep Stu Cncl; JV Var Fld Hcky; Stat Socr; Frnch Merit Cert 86; U RI; Int Des.

GRILL, PAMELA M; Delhi Central HS; De Lancey, NY; (Y); FHA; Var Tennis; Var Twrlr; DAR Awd; Hon Roll; Bus & Po Wmns Clb Delhi 86; Jss Brktt Schlrhsp 86; Rgna Armndy Mem Art Awd 86; Jhn Smth Engl Awd 83; SUC Oneonta; Fshn Dsgn.

GRILLI, BARBARA; Spacekenkill HS; Poughkeepsie, NY; (Y); 42/158; Cmnty Wkr; Hosp Aide; Leo Clb; SADD; Temple Yth Grp; Yrbk Stf; Var Tennis; Hon Roll; Pres Ftnss & Acdmc Awd 86; Boston U; Accntnt.

GRIMALDI, ANGELA; Bethpage HS; Bethpage, NY; (Y); 25/290; Drama Clb; Exploring; SADD; School Play; Yrbk Stf; High Hon Roll; Regnts Schlrshp 86; Acadmc Achvt And Exclnc Awd 86; C W Post; Comm Arts.

GRIMALDI, CLAUDIA; The Ursuline HS; Bronx, NY; (Y); Art Clb; French Clb; School Musical; Yrbk Phtg; Lit Mag; Hon Roll; Advncd Placement Art Portfolio; Fren Hnrs Classes; Svc JR Cls Awd; Cooper Union; Photogrphy.

GRIMALDI, MARGARET M; Bishop Kearney HS; Brooklyn, NY; (Y); Library Aide; Im Bowling; Im Sftbl; St Schlr; Oneonta SUNY; Bus.

GRIMALDI, MARIA; West Seneca East SR HS; W Seneca, NY; (Y); 45/376; Church Yth Grp; Civic Clb; DECA; French Clb; FBLA; German Clb; JA; Spanish Clb; Nwsp Rptr; Nwsp Stf; German NHS 86; U Buffalo; Intl Bus.

GRIMES, JACKIE; Depew HS; Depew, NY; (Y); French Clb; Nrsng.

GRIMES, PAMELA; Medina SR HS; Medina, NY; (Y); 5/165; VP Church Yth Grp; Model UN; Teachers Aide; Acpl Chr; Rep Frsh Cls; Rep Soph Cls; Rep Stu Cncl; Coach Actv; Var Score Keeper; Capt L Sftbl; NY ST Rgnts Schlrshp 86; Rotary Clb Howard Brown & Dr John Roach Mem 86.

GRIMINS, STACY; West HS; Corning, NY; (Y); Corning Comm; Elem Ed.

GRIMM, JOHN W; Charles H Roth HS; Industry, NY; (Y); 12/195; Am Leg Boys St; Boy Scts; Church Yth Grp; SADD; Varsity Clb; Pres Soph Cls; Stu Cncl; God Cntry Awd; NHS; VFW Awd; Henrietta Yth Hall Fame 85; Eagle Scout 85; Harvard U.

GRIMM, MICHAEL J; Clarkstown H S North; New City, NY; (Y); Am Leg Boys St; Church Yth Grp; JV Capt Ftbl; Socr; High Hon Roll; Hon Roll; Jr NHS; Mu Alp Tht; NHS; Mu Alpha Theata 84-85/85-86; Physcs Tm 84-85; Teen Republcns 85/86; US Naval Acad; Aero Engrng.

GRIMSHAW, PAUL; Bishop Cunningham HS; Fulton, NY; (Y); Yrbk Phtg; Sec Sr Cls; JV Bsktbl; Hon Roll; Amer Bus Awd 86; Advrtsng.

GRINDER, ANN MARIE; Frontier Central HS; Blasdell, NY; (Y); 12/430; French Clb; JA; Pep Clb; Band; Concert Band; Mrchg Band; Crs Cntry; Socr; Tennis; Trk; NYS Rgnts Schlrshp, Laura B Cole Schlrshp SUNY Fredonia, ARW Fndtn Schlrshp 86; SUNY Fredonia.

GRINDER, JENNIFER; Chautauqua Central HS; Ashville, NY; (Y); 5/31; Ski Clb; Band; Yrbk Ed-Chief; Yrbk Stf; Sec Frsh Cls; Sec Soph Cls; Sec Jr Cls; Score Keeper; Swmmng; Trk; Awdpoetry Publshd Loc Stu Publctn 86; Pres Of Natl Hnr Soc 86.

GRIPPER, ADRIAN; Canarsie HS; Brooklyn, NY; (Y); Drama Clb; FHA; Mathletes; Teachers Aide; Yrbk Stf; Vllybl; Hon Roll; Health Careers Awd 86; Engl Awd 86; Binghampton; Pre-Med.

GRISAFI, ANDREW; Alexander Hamilton HS; Whitelns, NY; (Y); 14/176; Aud/Vis; Cmnty Wkr; Key Clb; Band; Yrbk Ed-Chief; Stu Cncl; Bsbl; Socr; High Hon Roll; Biolgcl Sci Awd 86; Ntl Sci Merit Awd 86.

GRISMORE, DANA; Liverpool HS; Liverpool, NY; (Y); Exploring; Varsity Clb; Yrbk Phtg; Rep Stu Cncl; JV Capt Socr; JV Mgr Swmmng; Var Capt Vllybl; Wt Lftg; Hon Roll; NHS; Ntl Merit Ltrs; 4 H Awds; Ithaca; Physcl Thrpy.

GRISWOLD, DEANNA; Sherman Central HS; Clymer, NY; (S); 2/29; Cmnty Wkr; Library Aide; Teachers Aide; Nwsp Rptr; Yrbk Stf; L Sftbl; High Hon Roll; NHS; JV Bsktbl; L Vllybl; Chem All-Amer 84-85; Engl All-Amer 84-85; Jamestown CC; Math.

GRISWOLD, JOSEPH N; Homer Central HS; Preble, NY; (Y); 33/210; 4-H; School Musical; Symp Band; Rep Stu Cncl; Var Ftbl; High Hon Roll; NHS; Ntl Merit SF; Rochester Inst Of Tech; Engr.

GRITZMACHER, RUTH; De Sales Catholic HS; Lockport, NY; (Y); Church Yth Grp; Cmnty Wkr; Library Aide; Varsity Clb; Nwsp Rptr; Nwsp Stf; Var Tennis; Hon Roll; NHS; Ntl Merit Ltr; Niagara CC; Bus.

GRIZZAFFI, JOSEPH A; Mt St Michael Acad; Bronx, NY; (S); 43/309; High Hon Roll; Hon Roll; Jeweler.

GRIZZAFFI, LAURALEE; Adlai E Stevenson HS; Bronx, NY; (Y); Cmnty Wkr; Office Aide; Church Choir; Rptr Soph Cls; Hon Roll; NHS; Achvt Lg 86; Chem Awd 86; Frnch Awd 86; Astrontcl Engrg.

GROAT, EVAN A; Hamburg SR HS; Hamburg, NY; (Y); 84/363; Aud/Vis; Var Socr; Hon Roll; NHS; Gannon; Elec Engrg.

GROAT, JOHN; T J Corcoran HS; Syracuse, NY; (Y); Ski Clb; Nwsp Phtg; Nwsp Rptr; Yrbk Ed-Chief; Yrbk Phtg; Pres Sr Cls; Var JV Lcrss; Trk; High Hon Roll; NHS; Syracuse U; Cmmnctns.

GROB, DAVID; West Islip HS; W Islip, NY; (Y); Pres Aud/Vis; Church Yth Grp; Computer Clb; Stage Crew; Hon Roll; Long Isl Sci Congrss Excllnce Awd 86; Rifle Tm Var Capt 86; Vlg Babylon Aux Police Radio Oper 85-86; Bio Sci.

GROBELNY, JUDE; South Park HS; Buffalo, NY; (Y); Cmnty Wkr; Band; Concert Band; Jazz Band; Mrchg Band; Yrbk Stf; Bowling; Vllybl; High Hon Roll; NHS; 2dn Hghst Grd Engl I Exam 84; Outstndng 1st Yr Band Awd 85; Med.

GROCKI, BRIAN; Wilson Central HS; Wilson, NY; (Y); 18/250; Trs Am Leg Boys St; Pres Chess Clb; Computer Clb; Trs SADD; Stu Cncl; Var Ftbl; Var Trk; Var Wrstlng; Hon Roll; Math Awd 84; Coach Awd 85; Compu Sci.

GROENEVELD, JAMES; Smithtown West HS; Smithtown, NY; (Y); Pres DECA; Yrbk Sprt Ed; Yrbk Stf; Rep Soph Cls; Rep Jr Cls; Rep Sr Cls; Rep Stu Cncl; Bsktbl; Tennis; Vllybl; Italian Honor Society; Italian Club; Bryant; Bus.

GROENING, BRUCE; Jamesville Dewitt HS; Dewitt, NY; (Y); 37/251; AFS; Church Yth Grp; Cmnty Wkr; Ski Clb; Concert Band; Jazz Band; Pep Band; Im Mgr Crs Cntry; Im Mgr Socr; High Hon Roll; Rgnts Schlrshp 86; Binghamton; Bio-Psych.

GROETZ, STEVEN J; East Syracuse-Minoa Central HS; East Syracuse, NY; (Y); 23/333; Computer Clb; Exploring; German Clb; JA; Variety Show; Rep Sr Cls; Var Trk; Im Vllybl; High Hon Roll; Hon Roll; Rgnts Schlrshp 86; SUNY Canton; Ppr Sci Engrng.

GROGAN, COLETTE; Uniondale HS; Uniondale, NY; (Y); Cmnty Wkr; 4-H; Girl Scts; Orch; Hon Roll; Jr NHS; NHS; Bus Adm.

GROHMAN, HENRY L; St Francis HS; Buffalo, NY; (Y); 2/150; Math Tm; PAVAS; Quiz Bowl; Nwsp Ed-Chief; Lit Mag; JV Ice Hcky; Stat Trk; Im Vllybl; NHS; Ntl Merit Ltr; Rensl Polytech Inst Mdl Math & Sci 85; Rensselaer Polytech; Bio Engr.

GROHOVAC, DORIS; Freeport HS; Freeport, NY; (Y); Key Clb; Ski Clb; SADD; Yrbk Stf; JV Var Lcrss; Mgr Sftbl; High Hon Roll; Hon Roll; Oneonta; Bus Admin.

GROLL, CHRIS; Monsignor Farrell HS; New York, NY; (Y); Ski Clb; SADD; Bsbl; JV Crs Cntry; Stat Ftbl; Var JV Trk; Var Wt Lftg; Busd.

GRONICH, AMANDA J; High School Of Performing Arts; New York, NY; (Y); 9/121; JA; Teachers Aide; School Play; Stage Crew; Variety Show; Hon Roll; Pride Of Yankees/Dly Nws Schlr 82-83; Arts Recog & Tlnt Srch-Drama Semi-Fnlst 85-86; Drama.

GRONO, ANTHONY; Arch Bishop Stepinal HS; Yonkers, NY; (Y); 42/174; Dance Clb; Exploring; Off CAP; Im Bsktbl; Bowling; Fld Hcky; Hon Roll; Prfct Atten Awd; Natl Sci Olympd 84; Acad Ltr 85; Bowling Ltr 85; Fordam U; Bus.

GRONONNIEX, JOHNNY; Beacon HS; Beacon, NY; (Y); 30/250; Key Clb; VP Varsity Clb; Bsbl; Ftbl; Wrstlng; Jr NHS; Arch Work.

GROOM, CHAD; Adlai E Stevenson HS; Bronx, NY; (Y); JA; Chorus; School Musical; Nwsp Rptr; Im Crs Cntry; Im Trk; Prfct Atten Awd; Lawyr.

GROSE, JENNA E; Ballston Spa HS; Ballston Spa, NY; (Y); 31/244; VP French Clb; School Musical; School Play; Stage Crew; Ed Lit Mag; NHS; Rotary Awd; Nwsp Rptr; Hon Roll; NY ST Regnts Schlrshp 85-86; NY U; Dramtc Wrtg.

GROSMAN, RAQUEL L; Horace Mann Schl; Bronx, NY; (Y); Cmnty Wkr; Office Aide; SADD; Yrbk Stf; Lit Mag; JV VP Mgr(s); Mgr Socr; Mgr Trk; High Hon Roll; Ntl Merit Ltr; Cornell U.

GROSS, ALLISON J; Onteora HS; West Hurley, NY; (Y); 31/201; Concert Band; Mrchg Band; Bsktbl; Fld Hcky; Sftbl; Hon Roll; NHS; U Of VT; Bio Sci.

GROSS, CHRISTINE; Scotia-Glenville HS; Amsterdam, NY; (Y); Church Yth Grp; Spanish Clb; Varsity Clb; Church Choir; Rep Stu Cncl; Capt Bsktbl; Var JV Fld Hcky; Hon Roll; NHS; Dickinson; Pre-Law.

GROSS, DANIEL E; Pavilion Central Schl; Stafford, NY; (Y); Am Leg Boys St; Band; Jazz Band; Mrchg Band; Pep Band; School Play; Var Capt Crs Cntry; Var Trk; High Hon Roll; NHS.

GROSS, GARRETT; Lafayette HS; Brooklyn, NY; (Y); Bsbl; Bsktbl; Ftbl; Tennis; Stu Org Lttr Eligibility Cert-Tnns 86; PSAL NYC Sngls Champs-Gld Mtl-Tnns 86; Phy Ed.

GROSS, LAUREN; St John Villa Acad; Staten Island, NY; (Y); Sftbl; Spnsh Awd 84; St Johns U; Accntng.

GROSS, RONALD; Spring Valley SR HS; Spring Valley, NY; (Y); 108/441; Key Clb; Temple Yth Grp; Band; Orch; School Musical; Lit Mag; Bsbl; High Hon Roll; Hon Roll; Regents Schlrshp 86; Babson Coll; Bus.

GROSS, SUZANNE D; Clarkstown North HS; New City, NY; (Y); Temple Yth Grp; Band; Lit Mag; Hon Roll; NHS; Mu Alpha Theta-Math Hnr Soc; Rgnts Schlrshp; SUNY Albany; Accntng.

GROSS, THOMAS; Canisius HS; Amherst, NY; (Y); Computer Clb; JCL; Model UN; JV Ftbl; JV Trk; Wt Lftg; Pol Sci.

GROSS, TIMOTHY J; Churchville-Chili SR HS; Rochester, NY; (Y); JV Bsbl; Im Vllybl; JV Wt Lftg; JV Wrstlng; Systms Analyst.

GROSS, TRINA; Eastridge HS; Rochester, NY; (Y); 42/216; Band; Orch; Hon Roll; Chtqua Yth Orch 86; Hchstn Merit Schlrshp 86; Rchstr Phlhrmnc Yth Orch 86; Eastman School Music; Music.

GROSSBARD, JEREMY; Williamsville South HS; Williamsville, NY; (Y); Boy Scts; French Clb; Red Cross Aide; Temple Yth Grp; Nwsp Stf; Hon Roll; Arch.

GROSSFELD, SCOTT; Commack South HS; Commack, NY; (Y); 81/359; Band; Concert Band; Mrchg Band; Symp Band; Yrbk Phtg; High Hon Roll; Hon Roll; NHS; Pres Schlr; Temple Yth Grp; Yrbk Photo Edtr 85-86; Muhlenberg Coll; Accntg.

GROSSI, JULIANNE; Webster HS; Webster, NY; (Y); 201/530; Dance Clb; JA; Spanish Clb; Bsktbl; Socr; Sftbl; Hon Roll; Alfred; Spnsh.

GROSSO, ED; Washingtonville HS; Monroe, NY; (Y); Boy Scts; JA; Ski Clb; SADD; Rep Sr Cls; Var Capt Socr; JV Var Trk; Hon Roll; FL Inst T Ech; Mech Engr.

GROTH, KRISTINA A; Liverpool HS; Liverpool, NY; (Y); 38/816; Chorus; Capt Ice Hcky; High Hon Roll; NHS; Church Yth Grp; GAA; Ski Clb; Spanish Clb; Varsity Clb; School Musical; Pres Acad Fit Awd; HOBY; Amer Soccr Ambssdrs MVP; Regents Scholar; Spn 5 Excllnce Awd; MVP Var Soccr; St Lawrence U; Lang.

GROVER, KIM; Newfield Central HS; Newfield, NY; (Y); 11/50; Drama Clb; Varsity Clb; Band; Concert Band; Jazz Band; Mrchg Band; School Play; Pres Jr Cls; Fld Hcky; Trk; Arion Musicianshp Awd 86; Ithaca Coll; Radio Cmnctns.

GROVER, STEVE; York Central Schl; Leicester, NY; (Y); Art Clb; Boy Scts; Nwsp Rptr; Nwsp Stf; JV Ftbl; High Hon Roll; Hon Roll; NYS Hist Assc Cert Of Merit Gov Trophy Rsrch Cntst 86; Schlstc Art Awd Cert Of Merit 86; Art.

GROVER, TAMMY; Watkins Glen HS; Montour Falls, NY; (Y); Aud/Vis; Math Clb; Yrbk Stf; Hon Roll; Elmira; Acctg.

GROVER, TIM; Kenmore East HS; Tonawanda, NY; (Y); Im Ftbl; Var Vllybl; Elec Engr.

GROVES, ANDREW; Unatego JR SR HS; Otego, NY; (S); 1/101; Church Yth Grp; Drama Clb; Ski Clb; Jazz Band; School Musical; School Play; Symp Band; Trs Stu Cncl; High Hon Roll; NHS; Awd Hghst Avg 84; Hghst Avg Engl 84-85; Hghst Avg Bio 85; Pol Sci.

GROVES, DEBORAH A; Goshen HS; Goshen, NY; (Y); VP Spanish Clb; Band; School Play; Nwsp Ed-Chief; Nwsp Stf; Yrbk Ed-Chief; Yrbk Rptr; Yrbk Stf; NHS; NEDT Awd; Outstndng Perfrmnc Engl 83-85; Outstndng Imprvmt Bnd 83; Outstndng Perfrmnc Soc Stds 85; Middlebury Coll; Engl.

GROWE, CHERYL; John C Birdlebough HS; Fulton, NY; (Y); AFS; Drama Clb; 4-H; FBLA; Band; Chorus; Concert Band; Mrchg Band; School Musical; School Play; Oswego Cnty Dairy Prncss 85-86; Oswego Cnty 4-H Exec Cmmtte 84-86; Teen Cncl Off 82-86; Air Frc.

GRUBE, JOSEPH; Cattaraugus HS; Cattaraugus, NY; (Y); 3/60; Spanish Clb; Concert Band; Pres Trs Stu Cncl; Ftbl; Trk; Bausch & Lomb Sci Awd; High Hon Roll; NHS; Computer Clb; 4-H; Manley Mem Schlrshp 86; NYS Rgnts Schlrshp 86; STY U Of NY; Elec Engrng.

GRUBER, STUART; Ripley Central HS; Ripley, NY; (Y); Boy Scts; Debate Tm; School Play; Stage Crew; Yrbk Bus Mgr; Bsbl; Bsktbl; Crs Cntry; Hon Roll; Jamestown Cmnty Coll; Comp Sci.

GRUBIAK, MARY; Sacred Heart HS; Yonkers, NY; (S); 1/350; Cmnty Wkr; High Hon Roll; NHS; Scholar Awd 83-85; Natl Sci Olympd Awd 83; Concordia; Elem Ed.

GRUEBMEYER, KATHRYN A; Ramstein American HS; San Antonio, TX; (Y); 15/230; Church Yth Grp; Intnl Clb; Model UN; Band; Church Choir; School Musical; Lit Mag; High Hon Roll; Jr NHS; NHS; Pres Acdmc Fit Awd & Lutheran Schlr Awd 86; Combnd Schlrshp Assn Acdmc 86; Wittenberg U.

GRULLON, CESAR A; All Hallows Inst; Bronx, NY; (S); 3/90; Drama Clb; Math Clb; School Play; Stu Cncl; Bsbl; Bowling; Ice Hcky; High Hon Roll; NHS; 11 1st Hnr Awd 82-86; 2 Stu Achvt Awd 84-85; Cthlc HS Math Leag Trphy Outstndng Achvt 85; NY Inst Of Tech; Pre Med.

GRUMER, ELISA H; Bronx HS Of Sci; Bronx, NY; (Y); Office Aide; Teachers Aide; Temple Yth Grp; Y-Teens; Lit Mag; NHS; Ntl Merit Ltr; Prfct Atten Awd; Deans Schlr Cornell U 86; NYS Regnts Schlrshp 86; Cornell U.

GRUMMONS, EDWARD D; Vestal HS; Apalachin, NY; (Y); Boy Scts; Church Yth Grp; Orch; Var Trk; God Cntry Awd; Rgnts Schlrshp 86; Eagl Sct 85; Broome CC; Microelctrnc Engr.

GRUNDEN, JOANNE; Henninger HS; Syracuse, NY; (Y); GAA; Nwsp Rptr; Var Diving; Var Swmmng; Var Trk; Bausch & Lomb Sci Awd; High Hon Roll; NHS; Ntl Merit SF; SADD; Cornell Clb Bk Awd Wnr 86; Elec Engr.

GRUNDNER, KEITH; Clarence Central HS; Clarence, NY; (Y); 112/250; 4-H; Hon Roll; Actuary.

GRUNER, ELLEN; John A Coleman HS; Kingston, NY; (S); Drama Clb; French Clb; Key Clb; Ski Clb; Rep Soph Cls; Fld Hcky; Trk; Val; Trk Ltr 84 & 85; Acctng.

GRUNWOOD, LORI; Frewsburg Central Schl; Jamestown, NY; (Y); 3/80; Am Leg Aux Girls St; 4-H; GAA; Pres Spanish Clb; Chorus; Rep Stu Cncl; Var Bsktbl; Var Sftbl; Var Capt Swmmng; 4-H Awd; Bus.

GRUOSSO, DIANE; St Edmund HS; Brooklyn, NY; (S); English Clb; Spanish Clb; Hon Roll; NHS; Hnr Awd 1st Hnrs; Social Studies, Engl, & Spanish Awds.

GRUPP, LAWRENCE; East Meadow HS; E Meadow, NY; (Y); 80/340; Band; Var VP Bsbl; Acad All-Amercn Awd 86; AZ ST U.

GRUPP, VIRGINIA; East Meadow HS; East Meadow, NY; (S); FBLA; GAA; Key Clb; Mathletes; SADD; Band; JV Bsktbl; JV Lcrss; JV Sftbl; Hon Roll.

GRUSZKOS, KIMBERLY A; Cohoes HS; Cohoes, NY; (Y); 7/176; French Clb; Key Clb; School Play; Nwsp Stf; Cheerleading; High Hon Roll; Hon Roll; Jr NHS; Lois C Smith Schlrshp 85; Rgnts Schlrshhp 86; Geneseo ST; Bio.

GRYNIEWICH, LORRAINE; Hauppauge HS; Smithtown, NY; (Y); Varsity Clb; Orch; Yrbk Stf; Var Capt Bsktbl; Var Capt Crs Cntry; JV Socr; Var Capt Trk; Hon Roll; NHS; Ltr Orch 83; Psychlgy.

GRZANKOWSKI, SUSAN; Villa Maria Acad; Checktowaga, NY; (S); 5/98; Computer Clb; JCL; Latin Clb; Ski Clb; Pres Jr Cls; High Hon Roll; NHS; Prfct Atten Awd; Prtl Schlrshp Overal Avg 95.07 85-86; Cert Merit Soc Profssnl Engrs 84-85; Hghst Avg Math Hnrs 84-85; Medcn.

GRZEGORCZAK, JILL M; Immaculata Acad; Orchard Park, NY; (Y); 1/40; French Clb; Hosp Aide; Teachers Aide; Nwsp Rptr; Trs Stu Cncl; High Hon Roll; NHS; NEDT Awd; Val; SUNY Geneseo; Elem Ed.

GRZELECKI, MICHAEL; Notre Dame Bishop Gibbons HS; Schenectady, NY; (S); 14/96; Hosp Aide; Band; Church Choir; Mrchg Band; School Musical; Swing Chorus; Variety Show; Nwsp Rptr; High Hon Roll; Cmnty Wkr; Service Awd 84-85; Engl Awd 84-85; Theatre Arts Awd 85; Siena; Theatre Arts.

GRZESIK, JOSEPH C; Massapequa HS; Massapequa, NY; (Y); Chess Clb; Computer Clb; Mathletes; Ntl Merit Ltr; NY ST Regnts Schlrshp 85; 2nd Pl Untd Cerebral Palsy Trivia Chllng 86; Hofstra U; Engl.

GRZESKOWIAK, LORIANN; Hamburg Central HS; Hamburg, NY; (Y); 4-H; Ski Clb; SADD; Chorus; Yrbk Ed-Chief; Rep Stu Cncl; U Buffalo; Psych.

GRZYWACZEWSKI, ANN; Goshen Central HS; Goshen, NY; (Y); Office Aide; JV Socr; Hon Roll; Prfct Atten Awd; Enrhcmnt Clb 85-86; SUNY Oneonta; Elem Ed.

GUADAGNO, CINDY; Fonda-Fultonville HS; Fonda, NY; (S); #2 In Class; Key Clb; Library Aide; Yrbk Stf; Hon Roll; Bio.

GUADALUPE, GLADYS; Grace Dodge Voc HS; Bronx, NY; (Y); #37 In Class; Nrsng.

GUALTIERI, CATHERINE A; Anthony A Henninger HS; Syracuse, NY; (Y); #1 In Class; Sec Intnl Clb; Pres SADD; Yrbk Phtg; Off Jr Cls; Var Cheerleading; Cit Awd; NHS; Key Clb; High Hon Roll; Oper Enterprise AMA 86; Syracuse U; Psych.

GUALTIERI, EUGENE; Anthony A Henninger HS; Syracuse, NY; (Y); 2/400; Var Capt Crs Cntry; Var Capt Trk; Bausch & Lomb Sci Awd; High Hon Roll; NHS; Ntl Merit Schol; Sal; Oliver Awd 86; Gen Elec Star Pgm Schlrshp 86; NYS Regents Schlr 86; U Of PA; Physics.

GUALTIERI, THOMAS P; Fayetteville-Manlius HS; Manlius, NY; (Y); 27/335; SADD; Pres Soph Cls; Pres Jr Cls; Pres Sr Cls; JV Lcrss; Cit Awd; High Hon Roll; Hon Roll; NHS; Rep Frsh Cls; Onondaga Comm Schlr 85; Apprctn Awd Stu Bvt Wrk 84; Outstndng Ldrshp Awd 86; Holy Cross Coll.

GUANCIALE, W SCOTT; Solvay HS; Syracuse, NY; (Y); Aud/Vis; Boy Scts; Library Aide; Drm & Bgl; Bowling; NHS; Forestry.

GUARASCI, DENISE; Oyster Bay HS; Oyster Bay, NY; (Y); GAA; SADD; Varsity Clb; Trs Frsh Cls; Rep Jr Cls; Var L Bsktbl; Var L Sftbl; Var L Vllybl; Hon Roll; Mst Imprvd Plyr Bsktbl 85; All-Conf Bsktbl 86; Lib Arts.

GUARDINO, STACEY; Bishop Kearney HS; Brooklyn, NY; (Y); 9/330; Church Yth Grp; Intnl Clb; Key Clb; Math Tm; Spanish Clb; High Hon Roll; NHS; Prfct Atten Awd; Pres Schlr; Mnhtn Coll Pres Schlrshp 86; Rgnts Schlrshp 86; Generoso Pope Schlrshp 86; Manhattan Coll; Accntnt.

GUARIGLIA II, MICHAEL A; Half Hollow Hills East HS; Dix Hills, NY; (Y); Var Bsktbl; Var Socr; NHS.

GUARIN, MARC F; Bayside Latin Honor Schl; Whitestone, NY; (Y); 6/658; Church Yth Grp; German Clb; Quiz Bowl; Church Choir; Nwsp Stf; Yrbk Stf; Lit Mag; Hon Roll; NHS; Sal; Govs Commtt Schlstc Achvt Awd 86; NYS Regnts Schlrshp 86; Dartmouth Coll; Engl.

GUARINI, ANDREA; North Babylon SR HS; N Babylon, NY; (Y); 1/460; Am Leg Aux Girls St; Computer Clb; Nwsp Rptr; High Hon Roll; NHS; Prfct Atten Awd; Church Yth Grp; Spanish Clb; Teachers Aide; Band; Medl Sci And Math 86; Acad Intl Studies 86; Sentr For A Day 86; Comp Engrng.

GUARINO, DIANA; Unatego SR HS; Otego, NY; (Y); 13/86; Cmnty Wkr; Dance Clb; French Clb; Hosp Aide; Spanish Clb; Cheerleading; NHS; Ntl Merit Ltr; Mgr(s); Regents Schlrshp; Intl Foreign Lang Awd; Intl Srv & Ldrshp Awd; Wells Coll; Frnsc Psychtry.

GUARINO, JAMES F; Park West HS; New York, NY; (Y); 26/505; Exploring; School Play; High Hon Roll; Hon Roll; Regnts Schlrshp 86; RPI Schlrshp Math & Sci 86; Elctrcl Engrng.

GUARINO, MICHAEL; Jamestown HS; Jamestown, NY; (Y); Concert Band; Jazz Band; Mrchg Band; School Musical; Stu Cncl; Hon Roll; NHS; Ntl Merit SF; Chess Clb; French Clb; James Prendergast Prz Math Fnl 84; Natl Hnr Soc Pres Elect 86-87; JHS Bnd Asst Treas 85-86; Pre-Med.

GUARINO, PAUL; Clarkstown South HS; Nyack, NY; (Y); Ski Clb; Var Capt Golf; Indep Insur Open, MVP Golf 86; Pinehurst JR Ntl Trmnt Wnnr 85; FL Intl U; Htl Mgmnt.

GUARNERI, DANIELLE; Fontbonne Hall Acad; Brooklyn, NY; (Y); 12/132; Hosp Aide; High Hon Roll; Hon Roll; Jr NHS; NHS; Prfct Atten Awd; Rep Stu Cncl; Outstndng Awd Bio & Mth 84-85; Cert Vlntrng & Mdl 85 & 86; NYU; Pre-Med.

GUARNOTTA, JACQUELINE; Dominican Commercial HS; Middle Village, NY; (Y); Art Clb; Cmnty Wkr; Hosp Aide; Teachers Aide; Rep Jr Cls; Hon Roll; Peer Grp Ldr 86-87; Criminal Justice.

GUARRACINO, NICHOLAS; Art And Design HS; Brooklyn, NY; (Y); Art Clb; Yrbk Stf; Hon Roll; NHS; Natl Art Hnr Soc 85-86; Illustration.

GUARRERA, CHRIS; G Ray Bodlye HS; Fulton, NY; (Y); Off Soph Cls; Bsktbl; Crs Cntry; Trk; High Hon Roll; Hon Roll; NHS; Prfct Atten Awd; Math Educ.

GUARRERA, MARGARET; G Ray Brodley HS; Fulton, NY; (Y); 42/261; Rep Frsh Cls; Rep Soph Cls; Rep Jr Cls; Rep Sr Cls; Rep Stu Cncl; Capt Cheerleading; Elks Awd; Pres HOSA Chptr 85-86; Wmns Clb Fulton Schlrshp; Paul E Bradshaw Schlrshp; Hudson Vly CC; Dntl Hygn.

GUAY, JEFFREY D; Glens Falls HS; Glens Falls, NY; (Y); 41/217; Boy Scts; High Hon Roll; Hon Roll; NY ST Rgnts Schlrshp 86; Engrng.

GUBER, STEPHANIE; Canarsie HS; Brooklyn, NY; (Y); Band; Concert Band; School Musical; Yrbk Stf; Co-Capt Bowling; Sftbl; Bus Admn.

GUBERNICK, HOLLY; Cornwall Central HS; Highland Mills, NY; (Y); Girl Scts; Varsity Clb; Nwsp Rptr; Nwsp Sprt Ed; Nwsp Stf; Var Capt Crs Cntry; Im Sftbl; Var Capt Trk; Hon Roll; Mst Vlbl Grl Athlt 85; Mst Imprvd Grl Athlt 84-85; Won Sctnl & Cnty Mdls 85; ST U Of Albany; Accntng.

GUBIN, VINCENT; St John The Baptist HS; Holbrook, NY; (Y); Chess Clb; Rep Sr Cls; Rep Stu Cncl; Im Coach Actv; Im Score Keeper; Im Socr; Im Timer; Hon Roll; Bio Olympd Awd 84-85; Chrstn Fllwshp Schlrshp 83; Hofstra U; Bus.

GUBITOSI, ANTHONY; Mc Kee Tech; Staten Island, NY; (Y); 29/306; Prfct Atten Awd; Engr.

GUCCIARDI, SCOTT P; Auburn HS; Auburn, NY; (Y); 24/425; Am Leg Boys St; ROTC; Swmmng; High Hon Roll; NHS; Drama Clb; School Musical; AFROTC 4 Yr Schlrshp 85-86; Vrsty Swim Team Co-Cptn 85-86; AFJROTC Schlstc Excllnce Mdl 85-86; Clarkson U; Mech Engr.

GUCCIARDO, ANNETTE; Port Richmond HS; Staten Island, NY; (Y); Dance Clb; Math Tm; Service Clb; Church Choir; Orch; Pres Frsh Cls; Pres Soph Cls; Pres Jr Cls; Pres Sr Cls; Cheerleading; Ldrshp Awd 83; Miss Richmond Cty 85; Mrktng.

GUCHE, MICHAEL; Fairport HS; Fairport, NY; (Y); High Hon Roll; Hon Roll; Prfct Atten Awd; Mth.

GUCHEK, LEA ANN; Fontbonne Hall Acad; Brooklyn, NY; (Y); 14/132; Cmnty Wkr; French Clb; Math Tm; SADD; Yrbk Stf; Var Sftbl; Hon Roll; NHS; Magna Cum Lauda In Ltn Cont 86.

GUDELL, VALERIE; Commack South; Commack, NY; (Y); Varsity Clb; Mrchg Band; Orch; Symp Band; Yrbk Sprt Ed; Stu Cncl; Var Cheerleading; Var Gym; High Hon Roll; NHS; All Cnty Band 84; All Cnty Band,Gldn Quill Awd,Hnr Soc 85; MVP Chrldg 86; Musc Perfmnc.

GUENTHER, DAVID; Kensington HS; Buffalo, NY; (Y); Boy Scts; Chess Clb; Computer Clb; FBLA; JA; Yrbk Stf; Stu Cncl; Crs Cntry; Hon Roll; Ntl Campers & Hikers Assn; NY St Mr Citizen 84-86; Air Force; Electrncs.

GUENTHER, THERESA M; Homer HS; Cortland, NY; (Y); 8/218; Church Yth Grp; French Clb; Hosp Aide; Quiz Bowl; Thesps; School Play; Nwsp Stf; Rep Stu Cncl; Elks Awd; NHS; Centennial Prize Scholar; Regents Scholar; U Rochester; Pre-Med.

GUERCIO, JONELL; Kenmore East HS; Kenmore, NY; (Y); GAA; Pep Clb; Cheerleading; Hon Roll; Niagra CC; Lgl Sec.

GUERIN, CHRISTINE B; Fairport HS; Fairport, NY; (Y); 60/600; Band; Concert Band; Flag Corp; Jazz Band; Mrchg Band; Orch; Hon Roll; NHS; Prfct Atten Awd; Princ Flutist All Co HS Orch 86; Solo Piccolo All St Bnd 84; Bnd Awd 83; PA ST U; Bus Acctg.

GUERIN, PETER; Connetquot HS; Bohemia, NY; (Y); 283/712; Nwsp Stf; Hon Roll; Scl Stds Mdl 84; Dowling.

GUERNELLI, GIANELIA F; Cardinal Spellman HS; Bronx, NY; (Y); 2/800; Church Yth Grp; Computer Clb; Radio Clb; Science Clb; Nwsp Rptr; Gov Hon Prg Awd; High Hon Roll; Hon Roll; Ntl Merit SF; NEDT Awd; Manhattan Coll-Pres Schlrshp 86; La Salle Hnr Soc 86; Manhattan Coll.

GUERNERO, KATYA; H S For The Humanity; New York, NY; (Y); School Musical; School Play; Stage Crew; NHS; Hstrn.

GUERON, NICOLE L; The Dalton Schl; New York, NY; (Y); Debate Tm; Model UN; Pres Chorus; Pres Madrigals; School Play; Capt Sftbl; Ntl Merit SF.

GUERRA, LOUIS J; Locust Valley HS; Bayville, NY; (Y); 7/203; Am Leg Boys St; Chorus; Madrigals; School Musical; School Play; Nwsp Phtg; Nwsp Rptr; Frsh Cls; JV Bsbl; NHS; Cmnty Schlrshp 86; Ntl Chrl Awd, Engl Awd 86; Sthrn Rgnl Nwspr Carrier NY ST 84; Northwestern U; Film Mkg.

GUERRERA, JEFFREY ALLEN; Huntington HS; Huntington, NY; (Y); Rep VP Band; Concert Band; Drm Mjr(t); Mrchg Band; Orch; Symp Band; NHS; Rep Frsh Cls; Rep Soph Cls; Rep Jr Cls; JR All-Am Hall Fame Band Hnrs 86; Instrmntlst Mag Merit Awd 86; Vrsty Ltr, Gold Star Band Hnrs 86; UCLA; Engl.

GUERRERO, JOSE; Queens Vocational HS; New York, NY; (Y); Boy Scts; Band; Sec Frsh Cls; Church Yth Grp; Hon Roll; Excllnt Acad Skills 85-86; Best Stu Of Year Elec Shop 85-86; City Coll; Elec Engrng.

GUERRERO, SANDRA; The Mary Louis Acad; Flushing, NY; (Y); French Clb; Hosp Aide; Spanish Clb; Yrbk Stf; Rep Stu Cncl; Hon Roll; NHS; Cert Merit Ntl Frnch Cntst 85; Math Cert Hnr 84-86; Cert Svc 85; Acctng.

GUERRIERO, ROBERT A; La Salle Inst; Kinderhook, NY; (Y); Boy Scts; Chess Clb; Chrmn Church Yth Grp; Drm & Bgl; Nwsp Rptr; Yrbk Phtg; Var Trk; High Hon Roll; NHS; Army ROTC Scholar 86; Regents Scholar 86; West Point; Astrnmy.

GUEST, ARLENE; Central Islip HS; Central Islip, NY; (Y); Nwsp Rptr; Var L Cheerleading; Var L Tennis; Intl Bus.

GUEVARA, ELSIE; Grace Dodge Voc HS; Bronx, NY; (Y); 27/50; Hosp Aide; Office Aide; Teachers Aide; Nwsp Rptr; Nwsp Stf; Sec Stu Cncl; Bsktbl; Sftbl; Vllybl; Hon Roll; Certct Awd Span 84; Hons Schlrshp Jrnlsm 85; Hons Engl 86; Cazenovia Coll; Nursing.

GUGLIELMO, STEVEN; Saint Francis Preparatory Schl; Floral Park, NY; (Y); Boy Scts; Band; Trk; Im Vllybl; Stu Actvty Awd Outstndng Achvt Sci Fctn Clb 86; Sci Fctn Clb Pres 82-86; FUN Volntr 83-84; U Southern CA; Wrtr.

GUGLIUZZA, MICHAEL; Williamsville South HS; Williamsville, NY; (Y); Boy Scts; Church Yth Grp; Computer Clb; JV Ftbl; High Hon Roll; Hon Roll; Aerospc Engnrng.

GUGSA, EMEYE; Martin Van Buren HS; Queens Village, NY; (Y); Art Clb; Church Yth Grp; Drama Clb; GAA; Hosp Aide; Math Clb; Math Tm; Office Aide; Science Clb; Service Clb; JR Sci Acad NY Acad Of Sci 84-86; Irwin Tobin Awd 86; Cert Of Merit Excllnce Bio 84; Wellesley Coll; Engrng.

GUICE, ADRIENNE; Westbury SR HS; Westbury, NY; (Y); #63 In Class; Church Yth Grp; Dance Clb; Office Aide; Chorus; Church Choir; School Musical; School Play; Yrbk Stf; Hon Roll; Spellman; Pre-Law.

GUIDIE, MICHAEL; Alden Central HS; Alden, NY; (Y); French Clb; Trs Letterman Clb; Science Clb; SADD; Nwsp Rptr; Nwsp Stf; Rep Frsh Cls; Rep Soph Cls; Rep Jr Cls; High Hon Roll; Athltc Vrsty Rifle Ltr 83; Comp Engrng.

GUIDIE, STEPHAN; Alden SR HS; Alden, NY; (Y); 22/204; Aud/Vis; French Clb; Science Clb; Band; Chorus; Mrchg Band; School Musical; Rep Soph Cls; Rep Sr Cls; Var Crs Cntry; Acdmc Ltr Awd 83-86; Pres Acdmc Ftns Awd 85-86; SUNY Buffalo; Comp Sci.

GUIDO, MAUREEN; Northport SR HS; Northport, NY; (Y); 111/572; Stage Crew; Lng.

GUIFFRIDA, GRACE; Hauppauge HS; Hauppauge, NY; (Y); 5/400; Aud/Vis; Hosp Aide; Rep Soph Cls; Rep Sr Cls; High Hon Roll; Lion Awd; Chrmn NHS; Ntl Merit Ltr; NYS Video Comp 86; M Nicholls Awd 86; Lib Art.

GUIGLIANO, LISA; Smithtown H S East; Smithtown, NY; (Y); Nwsp Sprt Ed; Chrmn Soph Cls; Capt Jr Cls; Stu Cncl; Var L Socr; Sftbl; Hon Roll; NHS; Itln Clb & Itln Hnr Soc.

GUIGNARD, ALEXANDRA; Dominican Commercial HS; Laurelton, NY; (S); 32/273; Cmnty Wkr; Hosp Aide; Teachers Aide; NHS; Principals List 82-86; Sienna Clb 82-86; Hunter Coll; Pre-Med.

GUIHEEN, JAMES; St Marys Boys HS; Malverne, NY; (S); Boy Scts; Ski Clb; Stage Crew; Nwsp Rptr; Lit Mag; Im Ftbl; JV Var Socr; Var Swmmng; JV Trk; NHS.

GUILE, TAMMY; Victor SR HS; Farmington, NY; (S); Church Yth Grp; VP DECA; Chorus; Stu Cncl; Var Bowling; Hon Roll; Rochester Business Inst; CPA.

GUILFU, JOHN; Oyster Bay HS; Glen Cove, NY; (Y); 32/150; Church Yth Grp; Dance Clb; Debate Tm; Quiz Bowl; Ski Clb; Spanish Clb; SADD; Teachers Aide; Varsity Clb; Chorus; Choral Awd 83-84 & 86; NVP Ftbl, Wrstlg, Bsktbl 85-86; Brake ST Track HS Record 200 Yrds 85; Penn ST; Political Science.

GUINEY, CHRIS; Mahopac HS; Mahopac, NY; (Y); Camera Clb; Chorus; Ed Nwsp Phtg; Nwsp Rptr; Nwsp Stf; Yrbk Phtg; JV Ftbl; JV Var Lcrss; Hon Roll; Photo.

GUINEY, PATRICE; Mahopac HS; Mahopac, NY; (S); VP JA; Capt Cheerleading; Stat Lcrss; Phy Ed.

GUINEY, THERESA; Albertus Magnus HS; Palisades, NY; (Y); 3/175; Church Yth Grp; Debate Tm; Girl Scts; Trs Spanish Clb; JV Cheerleading; JV Sftbl; High Hon Roll; Hon Roll; Mu Alp Tht; NHS; Math.

GUINYARD, MELANIE; Queen Of The Rosary Acad HS; Roosevelt, NY; (S); 6/50; Camera Clb; Pres Math Clb; Pep Clb; Red Cross Aide; Spanish Clb; SADD; Nwsp Phtg; Nwsp Rptr; Yrbk Stf; VP Soph Cls; Cpt Gld Tm Calithenics 84-86; Pre Law.

GULBRANDSEN, JOHN; Guilderland Central HS; Schenectady, NY; (Y); Art Clb; Church Yth Grp; Ski Clb; Varsity Clb; Var Bsbl; Var Ftbl; High Hon Roll; Hon Roll; Jr NHS; NHS; Spcl Awd In Advrtsng Art 86; Achvmnt Awd Math I II & III 84-86; Sco Stud & Engl 84; Army Reserve; Adv Art.

GULI, STACEY; St John Villa Acad; Staten Island, NY; (Y); VP Capt Socr; MVP Soccer 84-85; Achvt Awd Physcl Ed 86; Acctnt.

GULICK, JOANN A; Oneida SR HS; Oneida, NY; (Y); 37/215; Pres Trs Church Yth Grp; Dance Clb; Pres Debate Tm; Drama Clb; Pres Exploring; Intnl Clb; Political Wkr; Spanish Clb; SADD; Varsity Clb; Regnts Schlrshp Wnr 86; Clarkson U; Corp Law.

GULISANO, JUNE; Eastridge HS; Rochester, NY; (Y); Office Aide; Chorus; School Musical; Hon Roll; St John Fischer; Spcl Ed Tchr.

GULLICKSEN, AMY; Saranac Lake HS; Saranac Lk, NY; (Y); FBLA; Mary Mullin Wood Scholar 86; SUNY Canton; Sec Sci.

GULOTTY, ERIC S; Chatham HS; Albany, NY; (Y); 23/125; Latin Clb; Library Aide; Chorus; Orch; School Musical; Swing Chorus; Yrbk Stf; VP Frsh Cls; VP Soph Cls; VP Jr Cls; NY U; Theatr.

GUMBS, COLIN; Freeport HS; Freeport, NY; (Y); 6/450; Church Yth Grp; Radio Clb; Band; Concert Band; Mrchg Band; High Hon Roll; NHS; Pres Schlr; St Schlr; Regents Scholar NYS 86; Burger King Scholar 86; U Notre Dame; Engrng.

GUMBS, RHONDA J W V; Hillcrest HS; St Albans, NY; (Y); 140/865; Church Yth Grp; Cmnty Wkr; FNA; Hosp Aide; Teachers Aide; Church Choir; Nwsp Rptr; Nwsp Stf; Yrbk Stf; Hillcrest HS Prfct Attndnc Awd 84; Frncis Lewis HS Comp Cmp Awd 83; Hunter Coll; Nrsng.

GUMPPER, MICHAEL; Paul V Moore HS; Brewerton, NY; (Y); 10/350; Yrbk Phtg; Sec Soph Cls; Bsktbl; JV Var Golf; Im Socr; Im Trk; High Hon Roll; NHS; Econ.

GUNDLACH, EMILY; Tuckahoe HS; Bronxville, NY; (Y); Church Yth Grp; Church Choir; Trk; High Hon Roll; NHS; Art Clb; Leo Clb; Tennis; Assmbly ST NY Merit Cert 86; Cert Merit Spnsh 85; Vrsty Ltr 84-85; Nrsng.

GUNKEL, LAURIE; De Sales Catholic HS; Newfane, NY; (Y); Sftbl; Vllybl; Crmnl Justice.

GUNNING, NANCY; Herricks HS; Williston Prk, NY; (Y); Church Yth Grp; Dance Clb; VP Varsity Clb; Band; Concert Band; Mrchg Band; Var Crs Cntry; Var Capt Trk; Key Clb; Jr NHS; All Cnty Varsity Winter & Sprg Track A Ll Cnty & Track; Top 10 All ST Sprg Track 86; Jrnlst Reporting.

GUNNING, ROBERT; Liverpool HS; Liverpool, NY; (Y); 52/900; Church Yth Grp; FBLA; VP JA; High Hon Roll; Hon Roll; Jr NHS; NHS; Ntl Merit Ltr; Poltc Sci.

GUNNING, TERESA; Odessa-Montour Central HS; Trumansburg, NY; (Y); 4-H; Pep Clb; Quiz Bowl; Spanish Clb; SADD; Stu Cncl; Cheerleading; Sftbl; 4-H Awd; Hon Roll; SUNY Buffalo; Cmmnctns.

GUNUSKEY, SARAH; Vernon-Verona-Sherrill HS; Rome, NY; (Y); Church Yth Grp; SADD; Rep Frsh Cls; Rep Stu Cncl; Var JV Cheerleading; High Hon Roll; NHS; Bio.

GUPIT, BERNADINE; Tottenville HS; Staten Isld, NY; (Y); 35/1000; Band; Color Guard; Mrchg Band; Orch; Pep Band; School Musical; School Play; Symp Band; Stu Cncl; Twrlr; NYS Schl Music Assn-All ST 85 & 86; Wmns Hstry Mnth Borgh & Cty Wnnr 85; Pre-Law.

GUPTA, EVA; Beacon HS; Beacon, NY; (S); 4/200; Library Aide; Spanish Clb; Nwsp Ed-Chief; Var Crs Cntry; Var Tennis; Var Trk; NHS; Ntl Merit Ltr; Regents Scholar 86; Comp Sci.

GURAK, MICHAEL; Greece Olympia HS; Rochester, NY; (Y); 48/287; Drama Clb; Chorus; School Musical; School Play; Swing Chorus; Im Socr; Hon Roll; Morrisville Tech; Elec Engnrng.

GURALNY, JENNIFER S; Pulaski JR SR HS; Pulaski, NY; (S); Church Yth Grp; Drama Clb; GAA; Math Clb; Ski Clb; SADD; Chorus; School Musical; Yrbk Phtg; Hon Roll; Snow Schlrshp Awd 83.

GUREL, OZAN; Stuyvesant HS; New York, NY; (Y); Chorus; Orch; Symp Band; Pres Sr Cls; Var L Socr; NHS; Ntl Merit Ltr; Hnrs Grp 1986 Wstnghs Sci Tlnt Srch 86; Ntl Wnr NATO Essay Cntst 85; Harvard Coll.

GURLEY, DWAYNE; Sewanhaka HS; S Floral Pk, NY; (Y); Exploring; Var Bsbl; Var Bsktbl; Var Ftbl; Trk; MIP Awd 85-86; Stu Cncl Awd 85-86; MIP Awd 84-85; Comp Pgmmr.

GURLEY, STEPHEN G; William Nottingham HS; Syracuse, NY; (Y); 28/220; Ski Clb; Bsbl; Socr; Hon Roll; NHS; Embry-Riddle Aero U; Pilot.

GURMAN, BONNIE; Wantagh HS; Wantagh, NY; (Y); 48/271; Drama Clb; Library Aide; School Play; Stage Crew; Bowling; Hon Roll; Am Leg Cert Awd 86; Exc Tech Ed 86; Ind Art Awd 84-85; Maryland U; Arch.

GURNEE, JOHN; Naples HS; Naples, NY; (Y); 9/64; Am Leg Boys St; Band; Concert Band; Jazz Band; Mrchg Band; School Musical; Stage Crew; Pres Stu Cncl; Bsktbl; Socr; Alfre Tech; Auto Tech.

GURRERI, MARIA; Sweet Home HS; Amherst, NY; (Y); GAA; Chorus; School Musical; Bsktbl; Fld Hcky; Sftbl; Vllybl; Hon Roll; Italian Hnr Soc 86; Nrsng.

GURTOWSKI, STEPHANIE; Solvay HS; Syracuse, NY; (Y); 18/177; Capt Color Guard; Yrbk Ed-Chief; Rep Soph Cls; Sec Jr Cls; VP Sr Cls; Capt Cheerleading; Hon Roll; NHS; Pres Schlr; Solvay HS Tchr Ldrshp Awd 85-86; Solvay Tchrs Assoc Awd & Schlrshp 86; Advnc Plcmnt Am Hstry Awd 86; Oswego ST Coll; Elem.

GURVICH, DAVID; Hunter College HS; New York, NY; (Y); Boys Clb Am; Chess Clb; Library Aide; Office Aide; Ntl Merit SF; Engrng.

GURWITZ, DEBORAH; Onteora HS; West Hurley, NY; (Y); 28/201; Band; NHS; Regnts Schlrshp 86; U MA Amherst; Psych.

GUSHLAW, CONSTANCE; Pulaski JR SR HS; Pulaski, NY; (Y); Chorus; Color Guard; Bryant Stratton; Word Proc.

GUSS, KAREN R; Tottenville HS; Staten Island, NY; (Y); 2/871; School Musical; Ed Lit Mag; DAR Awd; NHS; Ntl Merit Ltr; Sal; Lib Clb Awd,Dramats Gld,Bar Assoc 85; SUNY Binghamton.

GUSTAFSON, TARA; Newfield HS; Coram, NY; (S); 114/515; Church Yth Grp; Debate Tm; Trs FBLA; Trs Q&S; Band; Concert Band; Mrchg Band; Nwsp Rptr; Trs Ed Nwsp Stf; Mst Imprvd Fncr Awd & Vrsty Ltr 84-85; Acctng.

GUSTAS, BRIAN; Bishop Scully HS; Amsterdam, NY; (Y); Pres 4-H; Math Clb; Math Tm; School Play; Yrbk Stf; Trs Jr Cls; Trs Sr Cls; Bsbl; Bsktbl; NHS; Plattsburgh ST U; Math.

GUSTUM, TAMMY; Rome Free Acad; Gunter AFS, AL; (Y); Church Yth Grp; GAA; Intnl Clb; Varsity Clb; Bsktbl; Crs Cntry; Trk; Hon Roll; Jr NHS; Mth.

GUTAUSKAS, JULIE; Mount Mercy Acad; Blasdell, NY; (Y); French Clb; Model UN; Ski Clb; Stage Crew; French Hon Soc; High Hon Roll; Hon Roll; ST U Of NY Buffalo.

GUTELIUS, KENNETH; Auburn HS; Auburn, NY; (Y); JA; Band; School Musical; Crs Cntry; Trk; High Hon Roll; NHS; Mech Engrng.

GUTER, MARLENE; Rochester Christian HS; Webster, NY; (S); 1/13; Sec Church Yth Grp; Drama Clb; Pres Spanish Clb; Chorus; Yrbk Ed-Chief; Trs Sr Cls; Bsktbl; Var Socr; Trk; High Hon Roll; Calvin Coll; Cvl Engr.

GUTH, BRAD; Cold Spring Harbor HS; Pound Ridge, NY; (Y); 14/140; Drama Clb; Intnl Clb; Mathletes; Jazz Band; Yrbk Sprt Ed; Trs Stu Cncl; Var Socr; DAR Awd; NHS; Ntl Merit Schol; Schl Math Awd 86; Harvard U; Ecnmcs.

GUTHEIL, KRISTIN M; Sanford H Calhoun HS; Merrick, NY; (Y); 10/313; Pres Church Yth Grp; Science Clb; Nwsp Stf; Jr Cls; Trs Stu Cncl; Var L Badmtn; Capt Cheerleading; Var L Tennis; Hon Roll; NHS; Schlrshp For Effort & Perf-Donna Carbones Dance Arts 83; NASTAR Ski Race Brnz Mdl 86; Washington U; Pre-Med.

GUTIERREZ, DEBORAH; Catholic Central HS; N Troy, NY; (Y); 4-H; Math Clb; Red Cross Aide; Sec Spanish Clb; Chorus; School Musical; Stage Crew; Lit Mag; Trk; Prfct Atten Awd.

GUTIERREZ, EVELYN; John Dewey HS; Brooklyn, NY; (Y); Church Yth Grp; Cmnty Wkr; Prfct Atten Awd; Kingsborough; Secy Sci.

GUTIERREZ, GIOVANNI; William Cullen Bryant HS; Jackson Hts, NY; (Y); 120/580; French Clb; Office Aide; Service Clb; Teachers Aide; French Hon Soc; High Hon Roll; NHS; Juan Acosta Schlrshp 86; Amer Assn Of Frnch Tchrs-Strlng Shld Pin 86; J K Hackett Mdl-Profcncy In Ortr; US Naval Acad; Aerosp.

GUTIERREZ, GRISSEL; George Washington HS; Bronx, NY; (Y); Band; Chorus; Hon Roll; The Wood Schl; Busnss Admin.

GUTIERREZ, PABLO; Huntington HS; Huntington, NY; (Y); Boy Scts; Chess Clb; Band; Concert Band; Mrchg Band; Pep Band; Var Socr; Hon Roll; Honors Collegua; Astronomy.

GUTOWSKI, TRACY; Amsterdam HS; Amsterdam, NY; (Y); DECA; Band; Concert Band; Mrchg Band; Hon Roll; Heth Coons Schrlshp; Herkimer CC; Trvl.

GUTOWSKI, WENDY A; E Seneca SR HS; W Seneca, NY; (Y); 21/365; DECA; Spanish Clb; Chorus; Rep Stu Cncl; Var Capt Bowling; High Hon Roll; Hon Roll; NHS; Camp Fr Inc; JA; Regnts Schlrshp 85-86; DECA Cmptn Wnnr 85-86; St Bonaventure; Mktg.

GUY, LAURA; Shoreham-Wading River HS; Shoreham, NY; (Y); Church Yth Grp; Cmnty Wkr; 4-H; Science Clb; Ski Clb; Band; Yrbk Phtg; Yrbk Stf; 4-H Awd; Bio.

GUY, NEVAR; Erasmus HS; Brooklyn, NY; (Y); Church Yth Grp; Computer Clb; Church Choir; Color Guard; Drill Tm; Drm & Bgl; Flag Corp; Mrchg Band; Ftbl; Long Island U; Comp Pgmng.

GUYBURU, SILVIA; Ossining HS; Ossining, NY; (Y); Church Yth Grp; Sec Exploring; Pres VP 4-H; French Clb; Hosp Aide; Spanish Clb; Acpl Chr; Chorus; 4-H Awd; High Hon Roll; Hm Ec.

GUYER, JOLYNN; Mexico Academy & Central Schls; Fulton, NY; (Y); 4-H; Spanish Clb; Color Guard; Mgr(s); Mat Maids; 4-H Awd; Hon Roll; Cazenovia Coll; Soc Svc.

GUYETTE, DANIELLE; Queensbury HS; Glens Falls, NY; (Y); Debate Tm; Drama Clb; 4-H; French Clb; Library Aide; Pep Clb; Band; Chorus; Jazz Band; Sec Frsh Cls; Crmnl Justice.

GUYETTE, MATT; Ticonderoga HS; Ticonderoga, NY; (Y); 3/100; Church Yth Grp; VP Soph Cls; Trs Jr Cls; Var Ftbl; Var Trk; High Hon Roll; Hon Roll; Union; Engrng.

GUYTON, TRACIE; Carthage Central HS; Carthage, NY; (Y); Pres Computer Clb; French Clb; SADD; VP Cheerleading; JV Var Vllybl; High Hon Roll; Hon Roll; Excllnc Eng Awd 86; Jefferson CC; Eng.

GUZIEC, SHARON L; Jamestown HS; Jamestown, NY; (Y); Spanish Clb; Acpl Chr; Band; Chorus; Concert Band; Mrchg Band; Stat Bsktbl; Hon Roll; NHS; Mus Schlrshp 84 & 86; Chautauqua Cty Mus Tchrs Assn Schlrshp 85; Engr.

GUZMAN, GLORIA; Saint Raymond Acad For Girls; Bronx, NY; (S); 3/84; Office Aide; VP Band; Mrchg Band; Pres Soph Cls; Pres Stu Cncl; High Hon Roll; NHS; Columbia U; Lwyr.

GUZMAN, SALLY; Central Islip SR HS; Central Islip, NY; (Y); Stage Crew; Var Cheerleading; Var Trk; Coaches Awd Trck 86; Med Lab Tech.

GWIN, ALISON; Alden Central HS; Alden, NY; (Y); GAA; Spanish Clb; SADD; Trk; Vllybl; Bus.

GWINN, ROBERT J; Averill Park Central HS; Troy, NY; (Y); Am Leg Boys St; Yrbk Phtg; JV Bsktbl; Hon Roll; Sienna Coll; Bus.

HA, GLEN JUNGHO; Bethpage HS; Plainview, NY; (Y); Am Leg Boys St; Cmnty Wkr; FBLA; Spanish Clb; Var Lcrss; Cit Awd; High Hon Roll; Jr NHS; Trs NHS; Prfct Atten Awd; Med.

HA, JULIAN; The Bronx HS Of Science; New York City, NY; (Y); Pres Art Clb; Boy Scts; Computer Clb; Math Tm; Science Clb; Lit Mag; Var Tennis; Jr NHS; NHS; Slvrstn Schlr 86; Coll Of Arts & Sci Crnl U.

HAACKER, WENDY; North Tonawanda SR HS; North Tonawanda, NY; (Y); AFS; Art Clb; Church Yth Grp; Drama Clb; Hosp Aide; JA; Chorus; School Play; Swing Chorus; Schrlshp NY Smmr Schl Arts 83; Crmnl Jstce.

HAAKMAT, DANIELLE; Notre Dame Acad; Staten Island, NY; (Y); 8/93; Civic Clb; Hosp Aide; Library Aide; Swmmng; Hon Roll; Jr NHS; NHS; Villanova U; Accntnt.

HAAS, BARBARA ANN; Seton Catholic Central HS; Endicott, NY; (Y); 16/160; Church Yth Grp; French Clb; School Musical; Nwsp Rptr; Nwsp Stf; Yrbk Ed-Chief; Rep Jr Cls; Rep Sr Cls; Rep Stu Cncl; Hon Roll; Hrld C & Clr Brns Schlrshp 86; Yrbk Awd 86; Amer Assn U Wmn 86; SUNY Genesco.

HAAS, ELIZABETH; Coxsackie-Athens HS; Cixsackie, NY; (Y); 26/104; Church Yth Grp; German Clb; Chorus; Hstry.

HAAS, JENNIFER; Cardinal Spellman HS; Bronx, NY; (Y); Dance Clb; Pep Clb; Yrbk Stf; High Hon Roll; Hon Roll.

HAAS, JENNY; Churchville-Chili HS; Churchville, NY; (Y); Chorus; Nwsp Stf; Var Capt Swmmng; High Hon Roll; Hon Roll; American U; Pre-Law.

HAAS, PAULA; Buffalo Acad Of The Sacred Heart; East Amherst, NY; (Y); Cmnty Wkr; Model UN; Red Cross Aide; Ski Clb; Chorus; Yrbk Stf; Rep Stu Cncl; Var Badmtn; Hon Roll; NHS; Outstndng Volntr Awd 85-86.

HABBERFIELD, KAREN; Scio Central HS; Wellsville, NY; (Y); 9/47; Pres FHA; Girl Scts; Spanish Clb; Band; Chorus; Concert Band; Mrchg Band; High Hon Roll; Hon Roll; NHS; Allgny Co Dry Prncss 86-87; Acad All-Amer 85-86; Grl Sct Slvr Ldrshp Awd 84-85; Gdnc Cnslr.

HABER, ELIZABETH A; Kingston HS; Kingston, NY; (Y); 16/573; Cmnty Wkr; Teachers Aide; Rep Jr Cls; Trs French Hon Soc; French Clb; Pres Girl Scts; Hosp Aide; Nwsp Rptr; High Hon Roll; Hon Roll; Regnts Schlrshp 86; Skidmore Coll; Librl Arts.

HABER, JEANNE; New Lebanon Central HS; Old Chatham, NY; (Y); 3/56; Sec Church Yth Grp; Sec Spanish Clb; Band; Chorus; Concert Band; Mrchg Band; Yrbk Stf; Rep Frsh Cls; Rep Soph Cls; Var Mgr(s); Rssll Sage Coll Fndrs Schlrshp 86; Tuitn Asst Pgm 86; Russell Sage Coll; Bus Mngmt.

HABER, MICHAEL; Catholic Central HS; Troy, NY; (Y); German Clb; Math Clb; High Hon Roll; Hon Roll; NHS; Ntl Merit Ltr; JCL; Math Tm; ACL NTCL Natl Latin Exam-Maxima Cum Laude; Excllnc-Eng; Excllnc-German; Astronomy.

HABEREK, WENDY; Fabius-Pompey HS; Jamesville, NY; (Y); Cmnty Wkr; SADD; Band; Sftbl; Co-Capt Vllybl; Hon Roll; NHS; All ST Orch 85; Coachs Awd 86; 1st Tm All Cnty Sftbl 86; Sci.

HABERLY, BRIAN; Babylon JR/SR HS; Babylon, NY; (Y); Boy Scts; Drama Clb; Acpl Chr; Chorus; Church Choir; School Musical; School Play; Stage Crew; JV Socr; JV Wrstlng; Crmnnl Jstc.

HACIC, CAROL; Frontier Central HS; Blasdell, NY; (S); 52/444; French Clb; FBLA; Pep Clb; Ski Clb; Chorus; Socr; Hon Roll; NHS; NEDT Awd; U Buffalo; Acctng.

HACKAL, WENDY; Riverhead HS; Calverton, NY; (Y); JCL; Latin Clb; Ski Clb; JV Capt Cheerleading; Trk; MVP Chrldng 83-84.

HACKER, CANDICE; St Hildas & St Hughs HS; New York, NY; (Y); Drama Clb; Teachers Aide; Chorus; Madrigals; School Play; Hon Roll; Chem Awd 85-86; Math Awd 86; Actng Awd 85; Lib Arts Coll; Indust Chem.

HACKETT, JAMES; Newfield HS; Selden, NY; (Y); Computer Clb; Dance Clb; VICA; School Musical; Stage Crew; Trk; Jr NHS; Spanish NHS; Math Awd 84; Indstrl Arts Awd 84; Presdntl Physcl Ftns Awd 84 & 85; Law.

HACKETT, LAURIE; Plattsburgh HS; Plattsburgh, NY; (Y); Yrbk Stf; Var Capt Cheerleading; Sftbl; Hon Roll; Ntl Merit Ltr; Sec.

HADDAD, AYDA; Kenmore West HS; Kenmore, NY; (Y); VP French Clb; Sec Math Tm; Model UN; Quiz Bowl; Nwsp Rptr; Yrbk Rptr; High Hon Roll; Voice Dem Awd; 7th Pl Wstrn NY Frnch Cntst 86; Wstrn NY Sci Cngrs Brnz Mdl 86; Olypmcs Of Mnd Fnlst 85.

HADDAD, GEORGE; Kenmore West HS; Kenmore, NY; (Y); 3/410; Debate Tm; Math Tm; Model UN; Quiz Bowl; Scholastic Bowl; Science Clb; Yrbk Stf; High Hon Roll; NHS; Ntl Merit Ltr; 1st Pl Wstrn NY Sci Congress 86; Hnrs Grp 86; Kenmore Exch Clb Yth Yr 86; SUNY Buffalo; Pre-Med.

HADDLETON, CINDY; Gates Chili HS; Rochester, NY; (Y); 5/442; Am Leg Aux Girls St; Office Aide; Service Clb; Spanish Clb; School Musical; Ed Yrbk Stf; High Hon Roll; NHS; U Of Charleston.

HADELMAN, MINDY B; John Jay SR HS; Pound Ridge, NY; (Y); 2/253; Debate Tm; Hosp Aide; VP Latin Clb; Temple Yth Grp; Variety Show; Rep Stu Cncl; JV Var Cheerleading; High Hon Roll; NHS; Ntl Merit Ltr; Soc Studies Awds; NY St Rgnts Schlrshp; Tufts U; Intl Law.

HADELMAN, REBECCA; John Jay HS; Pound Ridge, NY; (Y); Art Clb; Cmnty Wkr; Hosp Aide; Temple Yth Grp; Rep Stu Cncl; Hon Roll; Cert Achvt Wrkng Dsabld 86; Physcl Thrpy.

HADLOW, CHRISTINE; St Agnes Academic HS; Flushing, NY; (Y); 63/301; Cmnty Wkr; Spanish Clb; SADD; Chorus; Nwsp Rptr; Ed Yrbk Rptr; Lit Mag; Hon Roll; Iona Coll Frgn Lang Cntst Spnsh; Intl Studies Abroad Spain Prog; Columbia U Pblctns Wrkshp; NY U; Jrnlst.

HAEGELAND, MICHELLE; Smithtown High Schl East; St James, NY; (Y); Church Yth Grp; Chorus; High Hon Roll; Hon Roll; Rgnts Schlrshp 86; Pres Acdmc Fit Awd 86; Oral Roberts U; Psych.

HAEICK, MICHELLE; Clarence SR HS; Akron, NY; (Y); Church Yth Grp; 4-H; Girl Scts; Latin Clb; Color Guard; Orch; Bowling; Cheerleading; Sftbl; Vllybl; UB; Ed.

HAENLIN, ANDREA; Mexico Acad; Mexico, NY; (Y); Spanish Clb; Trs Soph Cls; Trs Jr Cls; Trs Stu Cncl; Socr; Sftbl; Vllybl; 1st Team All Stars Soccer-Onadoga Cnty 85; 1st Team All Stars Vlybl-Onadoga Cnty 86; Mud Vlybl 86; Psy Educ.

HAFFER, JILL; Sachem North HS; Centereach, NY; (Y); Drama Clb; GAA; Ski Clb; Spanish Clb; Im Bsktbl; Im Cheerleading; Im Crs Cntry; Im Socr; Im JV Trk; Im JV Vllybl; MVP Vllybl & Trck 84-85; Psych.

HAGADORN, STACEY; Jamestown HS; Jamestown, NY; (Y); Sec Church Yth Grp; Ski Clb; Trs Acpl Chr; Concert Band; Mrchg Band; Nwsp Stf; Rep Frsh Cls; Rep Soph Cls; Swmmng; Tennis; Bus.

HAGAN, MARY PATRICIA; Irondequoit HS; Rochester, NY; (Y); 4/389; Band; VP Frsh Cls; Off Soph Cls; Off Sr Cls; Var Capt Gym; High Hon Roll; Ntl Merit SF; MVP Gymnstcs Var 84-85; JR Law Clerk Intrnsp 85-87; Harvard; Intl Finance.

HAGELBERGER, JAMES; Attica HS; Darien Center, NY; (S); 3/175; Math Tm; Band; Concert Band; Jazz Band; Mrchg Band; JV Socr; Hon Roll; Elect Engr.

HAGEMANN, EILEEN; Corcoran HS; Syracuse, NY; (Y); Trs GAA; Hosp Aide; Sec Spanish Clb; Pres Frsh Cls; Pres Soph Cls; Pres Jr Cls; Trs Sr Cls; Var Sftbl; Var Capt Swmmng; Vllybl; Phy Thrpy.

HAGENAH, JOHN; Brockport HS; Brockport, NY; (Y); French Clb; German Clb; Chorus; School Play; French Hon Soc; High Hon Roll; Hon Roll; Special SR Yr Prog SUNY Coll 86; Lang Intrpeter.

HAGER, AMY; Haverling Central Schl; Bath, NY; (Y); Sec Church Yth Grp; French Clb; Ski Clb; Chorus; Nwsp Stf; Socr; Sftbl; Hon Roll; ADMNSTVE Sec.

HAGER, CHARLES; Msgr Mc Clancy Mem HS; Forest Hills, NY; (Y); Boy Scts; Church Yth Grp; Cmnty Wkr; Variety Show; Nwsp Rptr; Forest Hls Vlntr Amblnc Corp 84-86; Cert Of CPR & AFA 86; St Johns U NY; Phys Asst.

HAGER, ISAAC M; Williamsville South HS; Williamsville, NY; (Y); 3/230; Trs Soph Cls; Trs Jr Cls; Trs Sr Cls; Im Ice Hcky; NHS; Ntl Merit SF; Harvard Bk Awd.

HAGERMAN, JASON D; Midlakes HS; Clifton Springs, NY; (Y); 16/186; Church Yth Grp; French Clb; Band; Concert Band; Jazz Band; Mrchg Band; JV Var Bsktbl; JV Var Socr; High Hon Roll; Hon Roll; Regents Scholar 86; Clarkson U; Elec Engrng.

HAGGERTY, ANDREW; Regis HS; Baysie, NY; (Y); English Clb; Exploring; Nwsp Rptr; Lit Mag; Dnfth Awd; Ntl Merit Ltr; Opt Clb Awd; JR Chmpn Estrn Queens Archry Leag 86; Crtve Wrtng Medl Merit 85; Nvlst.

HAGGERTY, JOHN; Msgr Scanlan HS; Flushing, NY; (Y); 41/276; Am Leg Boys St; Church Yth Grp; Drama Clb; School Play; Stage Crew; Variety Show; Accntng 86; Atndnce 85-86; Mltry.

HAGGERTY, KATHLEEN A; Shenendehowa HS; Clifton Park, NY; (Y); 193/675; FBLA; Girl Scts; Key Clb; Leo Clb; Library Aide; Yrbk Stf; Trk; High Hon Roll; NYS Regents Diploma 86; Concours Natl Frnch Cont Cert Merit 86; NY Senator Cert Merit 86; Oneonta ST; Lang.

HAGIPADELIS, MARIA S; Abraham Lincoln HS; Brooklyn, NY; (Y); 19/417; VP JA; Math Tm; Concert Band; Nwsp Ed-Chief; Hon Roll; Jr NHS; NHS; Prfct Atten Awd; Art Clb; Rgnts Schlrshp 85-86; Dly News Cert Art Mrt 83; Itln Awd Cert 83; St Johns U; Law.

HAGIWARA, SUMI; Fashion Industries HS; Flushing, NY; (Y); 51/365; Hosp Aide; Office Aide; Teachers Aide; Yrbk Stf; Rep Soph Cls; VP Sr Cls; Tennis; FIT; Bus Merch.

HAGUES, BRIAN S; Whitesboro SR HS; Utica, NY; (Y); 40/354; Varsity Clb; Band; Concert Band; Jazz Band; Mrchg Band; Orch; Pep Band; Var L Socr; Var Tennis; Hon Roll; Rgnts Schlrshp NYS 86; Amer Lgn Essy Cont 83; SUNY Buffalo; Aerosp Engrng.

HAHN, BELINDA; Jamesville Dewitt HS; Syracuse, NY; (Y); German Clb; Chorus; Crs Cntry; Trk; High Hon Roll; NHS; Ntl Merit SF; Syracuse China Awd 86; Brown U.

HAHN, HOWARD S; Bronx Science; New York, NY; (Y); Drama Clb; Office Aide; Political Wkr; Teachers Aide; VP Temple Yth Grp; Nwsp Rptr; Nwsp Stf; NHS; Prfct Atten Awd; St Schlr; Drama Awd 83; Cmpltn Of Intensive Jrnlsm Wrkshp At Nwsppr 85; Jrnslsm.

HAHN, LORI; Byron-Bergen HS; Bergen, NY; (Y); Church Yth Grp; Drama Clb; Spanish Clb; Band; Concert Band; Mrchg Band; Score Keeper; Trk; Hon Roll; Duane Streeter Memrl Awd 86; Brockport ST U; Nrsng.

HAHN, LYNN; Central Islip HS; Central Islip, NY; (Y); 25/373; Art Clb; Chorus; Lit Mag; Hon Roll; Accntng.

HAHN, MATTHEW; Mc Quaid Jesuit HS; Fairport, NY; (Y); 83/187; Cmnty Wkr; Ski Clb; Spanish Clb; JV Bsbl; Im Bsktbl; JV Ftbl; Im Ice Hcky; Acctg.

HAHN, NANCY LYNN; Mercy HS; Lake Ronkonkoma, NY; (Y); 62/130; Church Yth Grp; SADD; Yrbk Stf; JV Var Bsktbl; Hon Roll; Art.

HAIG, WALTER; Saranac Lake HS; Saranac Lk, NY; (Y); 17/131; JV Var Ftbl; Var Trk; Var Wt Lftg; Hon Roll; Canton ATC; Engnrng.

HAIGH, RICHARD W; Lakeland HS; Putnam Valley, NY; (Y); 4/344; Boy Scts; Cmnty Wkr; Nwsp Ed-Chief; Socr; High Hon Roll; Pres NHS; JV Bsbl; JV Bsktbl; Church Yth Grp; Outstndg Achvt Hgh Avg, Forgn Lang & Math 83; Gettysburg Coll; Econs.

HAIGHT, KELLY; Union-Endicott HS; Endicott, NY; (Y); Key Clb; Sec Trs SADD; Band; Color Guard; Flag Corp; Mrchg Band; Rep Stu Cncl; High Hon Roll; NHS; Church Yth Grp.

HAILE, MONICA; Dominican Commercial HS; St Albans, NY; (Y); Pep Clb; Teachers Aide; Rep Soph Cls; Rep Jr Cls; L Cheerleading; NY Inst Tech; Comp Sci.

HAILEY, DEXTER; Midwood HS; Brooklyn, NY; (Y); 109/667; Church Yth Grp; Band; Church Choir; Orch; School Musical; Symp Band; Trk; Hon Roll; Arista 83; Comp Engr.

HAILSTON, DENNIS; Owen D Young Central HS; Richfield Springs, NY; (S); 3/21; Boy Scts; Church Yth Grp; VP Sr Cls; Var Bsbl; Bausch & Lomb Sci Awd; Cit Awd; High Hon Roll; Jr NHS; NHS; Salem Coll; Phy Ed.

HAINES, DAVID; Auburn HS; Auburn, NY; (Y); VP Trs Church Yth Grp; Ftbl; Trk; High Hon Roll; Hon Roll; Lake Forest Coll Chgo; Comp Eng.

HAINES, LINDA; Frontier Central SR HS; Hamburg, NY; (Y); SADD; Varsity Clb; Yrbk Stf; Stu Cncl; JV Var Socr; Hon Roll; NHS; Intrnshp Pgm Arch 86-87; Stu Govt 84-87; Arch.

HAIRSTON, JOHN; Hutchison Central Technical HS; Buffalo, NY; (Y); Chess Clb; Debate Tm; SADD; Teachers Aide; Yrbk Stf; Bowling; Pres Blk Enrchmnt Soc 86-87; Ortrcl Fnlst 83; NAACP Rcgntn Awd 84-85; Med.

HAIZLIP, VIOLA; Mercy HS; Albany, NY; (Y); Hosp Aide; Library Aide; Chorus; Yrbk Stf; Vllybl; Hon Roll; Excllnc In Spnsh II 84-85; Excllnc In Snpnsh III 85-86; Excllnc In Social Studies 83-84; Coll Of New Rochelle; Spnsh.

HAJDUK, ANN M; St Francis Prepratory HS; Hollis, NY; (S); Cmnty Wkr; Capt Hosp Aide; Band; Concert Band; Mrchg Band; Pep Band; Hon Roll; NHS; Optmate Soc Awd; Salutn Army 100 Hrs Pin Awd; Cornell; Med.

HAKE, ANN MARIE; South Shore HS; Brooklyn, NY; (Y); Teachers Aide; Band; School Musical; JV L Socr; Natl Fdrtn Msc Clbs Natl Hnr Jr Div 85; Math & Sci Acad Jr Div Achvmnt Awd 84; At Achvmnt Awd 86; Oneonta; Musc Indstry.

HAKIEL, ANGELIQUE; Lindenhurst HS; Lindenhurst, NY; (Y); 14/550; VP French Clb; Thesps; Orch; School Musical; Rep Sr Cls; Rep Trs Stu Cncl; Stat Gym; French Hon Soc; Hon Roll; Jr NHS; Rgnts Schlrshp 85; NYSSMA Awds Music; Hofstra U; Fin.

HAKIEL, KRISTIN; Lindenhurst HS; Lindenhurst, NY; (Y); Drama Clb; Pep Clb; Thesps; Varsity Clb; Band; School Musical; School Play; Variety Show; Rep VP Stu Cncl; Cheerleading; Physcl Thrpy.

HAKIM DIN, AFZAL; Smithtown West HS; Smithtown, NY; (Y); Band; Concert Band; Mrchg Band; Symp Band; Nwsp Phtg; Var L Tennis; Hon Roll; Ntl Merit Ltr; Spanish NHS; Physcs.

HALABY, FARAH; Dominican Commercial HS; Queens Village, NY; (Y); 68/256; Intnl Clb; Prfct Atten Awd; Prncpls List; Sports Awd; U Rochester; Med.

HALADY, THERESA; Mt Mercy Acad; Blasdell, NY; (Y); Pres Church Yth Grp; French Clb; Math Clb; Science Clb; Stat Bsktbl; Var Sftbl; Var Vllybl; Catholic Yth Orgnztn Tm Spirt Awd 84; Dioceson Board CYO 86; 2nd Pl Sci Fair Mt Mercy Acad 84; Med Lab Tech.

HALBEISEN JR, PETER W; South Lewis Central HS; Boonville, NY; (Y); 13/86; Quiz Bowl; Varsity Clb; Var L Trk; Im Trs Wt Lftg; High Hon Roll; Hon Roll; NHS; Prfct Atten Awd; NY ST Sen Stu Policy Forum 86; Acadmc Schlrshp Rochester Inst Ot Tech; Presdnetl Acadmc Fitness Awd; Rochester Inst Of Tech; Mech.

HALBFINGER, DAVID; Baldwin SR HS; Freeport, NY; (Y); 6/476; Pres Debate Tm; Orch; Nwsp Ed-Chief; French Hon Soc; High Hon Roll; Kiwanis Awd; Drama Clb; Q&S; Speech Tm; Thesps; Concrtmstr-All Cnty Orch Long Islnd String Fstvl 86; Asstnt Concrtmstr-Long Isl Yth Orch; Yale Coll.

HALDEMAN, DAVID; Lowville Academy & Central Schl; Lowville, NY; (Y); Church Yth Grp; 4-H; Pres FFA; Cit Awd; 4-H Awd; Hon Roll; NHS.

HALDEMAN, KAAREN; Catholic Central HS; Troy, NY; (Y); Church Yth Grp; German Clb; Spanish Clb; Pres Frsh Cls; Pres Soph Cls; Var Capt Cheerleading; JV Var Sftbl; High Hon Roll; NHS; Library Aide; Exclnc Grm 1, 2 & 3 84-86; Exclnc Amer Hstry Wrld Hstry 85-86; Exclnc Englsh 9 84; Blgy.

HALE, ANDREW; Liverpool HS; Liverpool, NY; (Y); Church Yth Grp; Exploring; Concert Band; Mrchg Band; Pep Band; Trk; Hon Roll; NHS; Airway Cmpter Sci.

HALE, MARGARET ANN; Chittenango HS; Bridgeport, NY; (Y); 10/182; Am Leg Aux Girls St; Concert Band; School Musical; Var Capt Tennis; DAR Awd; JP Sousa Awd; Sec NHS; Pres Schlr; Armys Schlr Ath Awd 86; Outstndng Grl Awd 86; Navys Semper Fidelis Music Awd 86; Allegheny Coll; Cmmnctns.

HALES, JOHN; Albion HS; Albion, NY; (S); 12/176; Boy Scts; Sec Church Yth Grp; Church Choir; Jazz Band; Mrchg Band; Symp Band; High Hon Roll; NHS; Exploring; 4-H; Harrison Radiator BOCES Coop Pgm 84-86; Rgnts Schlrshp, Henry King Staford 1/2 Schlrshp 86; U Miami; Bio Tchr.

HALESKI, LISA; Minisink Valley HS; Pt Jervis, NY; (Y); Sec Ski Clb; SADD; Varsity Clb; Yrbk Stf; Sec Frsh Cls; Rep Soph Cls; Sec Jr Cls; Trs Sr Cls; Rep Stu Cncl; Var Socr; Cmnctns.

HALEY, JULIE; Dover JR SR HS; Wingdale, NY; (Y); SADD; Concert Band; Stage Crew; Fld Hcky; Hon Roll; NYSSMA 83-84; Stu Cncl; Spec Educ.

HALEY, MARY; St Joseph By The Sea HS; Staten Island, NY; (S); Var JV Bsktbl; Im Bowling; Var Trk; Sprtmnshp 85; MVP Bsktbll & Trck 84; Nrsng.

HALFIN, MARCIA ALEXANDRA; Colonie Central HS; Albany, NY; (Y); 11/484; Art Clb; Red Cross Aide; Yrbk Stf; High Hon Roll; NHS; Office Aide; Teachers Aide; Awd Essay Cntst 83; Pres Acad Ftns Awd 86; Physcl Ftns Awd 83; Union Coll; Engrng.

HALL, AMY; Uniondale HS; Uniondale, NY; (Y); Church Yth Grp; Girl Scts; Orch; School Musical; Hon Roll; Stwrdss.

HALL, ANJEANETTE; Vestal SR HS; Vestal, NY; (Y); Pres Church Yth Grp; Pep Clb; Concert Band; Mrchg Band; Symp Band; Im Socr; Im Vllybl; High Hon Roll; Jr NHS; 50 Pct Schlrshp To Lake Tahoe Music Camp 84; Schlrshp To Drum Major Camp At UNR 84; Biology.

HALL, AVIAN; Camden Central Schl; Blossvale, NY; (Y); 81/187; Drama Clb; 4-H; Hosp Aide; Chorus; School Musical; School Play; Stage Crew; Swing Chorus.

HALL, COLLEEN M; Johnson City HS; Johnson City, NY; (Y); 76/198; Science Clb; SADD; Pres Varsity Clb; Color Guard; Yrbk Phtg; Yrbk Sprt Ed; Rep Sec Stu Cncl; Stat Ftbl; Capt Trk; Hon Roll; Lycoming Grant In-Aid 86-90; U Wmn Loan 86-90; Broome Cnty Bsnss Wmns Assn Awd 86-87; Lycoming Coll; Ed.

HALL, DAHLIA; Mount Vernon HS; Mt Vernon, NY; (Y); 4/500; French Clb; Hosp Aide; Keywanettes; Pres Latin Clb; Math Tm; Science Clb; High Hon Roll; NHS; Pres Medcl Opprtnty Clb 86; Pres New Frontiers Clb 85-86; Treas NHS 86; Bio.

HALL, DENISE; Portville Central Schl; Olean, NY; (Y); Pep Clb; Ski Clb; Lib Chorus; Sec Frsh Cls; Sec Soph Cls; Sec Jr Cls; Var Trk; Var Vllybl; High Hon Roll; Hon Roll; Gftd-Tlntd Pgm 84-86; Lwyr.

HALL, DENISE D; Amsterdam HS; Amsterdam, NY; (Y); 17/296; Drm Mjr(t); Yrbk Stf; Sec Soph Cls; Rep Stu Cncl; High Hon Roll; Hon Roll; NHS; Rgnts Schlrhsp 86; Siena Coll.

HALL, DONNA; St Johns Prep HS; Middle Vlg, NY; (Y); Church Yth Grp; Cmnty Wkr; Teachers Aide; Band; JV Sftbl; Bus Mgmt.

HALL, DOUGLAS; Geneva HS; Geneva, NY; (S); 2/170; Boy Scts; French Clb; Rep Stu Cncl; Var Socr; Var Trk; High Hon Roll; NHS; Ntl Merit Ltr; Church Yth Grp; RPI Mdl 85; Egl Sct 84; Engrng.

HALL, ELIZABETH; Roy C Ketcham HS; Wappingers Falls, NY; (Y); Computer Clb; Girl Scts; Math Clb; Church Choir; Var Crs Cntry; Var Trk; High Hon Roll; Jr NHS; NHS; Intl Bus.

HALL, HUGH; Dover JR SR HS; Dover Plains, NY; (Y); 8/90; Band; Jazz Band; JV Debate Tm; Stat Bsktbl; Var Capt Golf; High Hon Roll; Hon Roll; Jr NHS; NHS; Prfct Atten Awd.

HALL, JASON; Edison Tech HS; Rochester, NY; (Y); Var Wrstlng; High Hon Roll; NHS; Auto Mech.

HALL, JEFF; Maryvale HS; Cheektowaga, NY; (Y); Pres Trs Church Yth Grp; Sec FFA; Spanish Clb; Hon Roll; Middle East Stud.

HALL, JEFFREY C; Newfane Central Schl; Lockport, NY; (S); 9/181; Pres Church Yth Grp; Var Bsbl; Var Ftbl; Hon Roll; NHS; Comp Sci.

HALL, JENNIFER; Herricks HS; Manhasset Hls, NY; (Y); Dance Clb; SADD; Nwsp Stf; Yrbk Stf; Actress.

HALL, KENNETH; Polytechnic Prep County Day Schl; Brooklyn, NY; (Y); Pres Aud/Vis; Chess Clb; Church Yth Grp; Computer Clb; Math Clb; Band; Church Choir; Stat Var Bsktbl; Var Mgr(s); Hon Roll; Arch.

HALL, KIM; Liverpool HS; Brewerton, NY; (Y); 280/800; Rep Stu Cncl; JV Bsktbl; Var Lcrss; Lacrosse All Cnty Awd 86; Bus Mgmt.

HALL, LAUREN S; Pittsford Sutherland HS; Rochester, NY; (Y); Cmnty Wkr; JA; Ed Yrbk Stf; Rep Stu Cncl; Powder Puff Ftbl; Stat Socr; Hon Roll; NHS; Ntl Merit Schol; 1st Pl Rochester, 2nd Pl Nation Spnsh Exam 82-83; Hnrbl Mntn Ntl Spnsh Exam 84-85; U Of MI.

HALL, SANDRA; Uniondale HS; Uniondale, NY; (Y); 60/410; Sec Church Yth Grp; Church Choir; Badmtn; High Hon Roll; Hon Roll; Jr NHS; Pres Schlr; Elizabeth Maria Muller Mem Schlrshp 86; Pres Schlrshp Niagara U 86; Niagara U; Nrsng.

HALL, SCOTT; Newdorp HS; Staten Island, NY; (Y); Art Clb; Computer Clb; Science Clb; Hon Roll.

HALL, VANESSA; Mount Vernon HS; Mt Vernon, NY; (Y); Drama Clb; Latin Clb; Office Aide; Political Wkr; Spanish Clb; Capt Color Guard; Capt Pom Pon; Hon Roll.

HALL, WENDY LYNN; Canastota HS; Canastota, NY; (Y); 36/150; Church Yth Grp; Variety Show; Cit Awd; High Hon Roll; Hon Roll; Mohawk Valley CC; Pol Ofcr.

HALLAHAN, RICHARD; Pelham Memorial HS; Pelham, NY; (Y); Boy Scts; Spanish Clb; JV Socr; Var Tennis; Var Trk; NHS; Spanish NHS.

HALLAHAN, SHEILA A; St Francis Prep; Whitestone, NY; (S); 36/746; Church Yth Grp; Dance Clb; Hosp Aide; Nwsp Stf; Im Ftbl; Im Sftbl; Im Tennis; High Hon Roll; Hon Roll; NHS.

HALLENSTEIN, CHARLES; Ramstein HS; Apo New York, NY; (Y); Church Yth Grp; Exploring; Model UN; Quiz Bowl; SADD; Y-Teens; Trs Stu Cncl; Bsbl; Ftbl; Elks Awd; 1st Tm Ldrshp Frmt US Air Frce Acadmy 86; Rcvd 5 Crdt Hrs Advncd Plcmnt GA 85-86; Tn Ctr Bd 85-86; U Of GA; Arch.

HALLER, CHRISTOPHER; Horseheads SR HS; Horesheads, NY; (S); Pres VP DECA; 4-H; Pres VP JA; Ski Clb; Band; Yrbk Stf; JV Ftbl; Im Ice Hcky; Natl Jr Achvt Conf 83-85; High Sellr Statue Of Liberty JA 84-85; DECA Regnl Champ 2nd Mgmt Achvt Dec; St Bonaventure U; Bus Admn.

HALLERAN, COLLEEN; Northport HS; E Northport, NY; (Y); 5/600; Spanish Clb; Band; Mrchg Band; Var Crs Cntry; Var Trk; High Hon Roll; Jr NHS; NHS; Amer Leg Athl Achvt Crss Cntry, All Leag Awd Crss Cnty, Trk 86; Phy Thrpy.

HALLERAN, RAYMOND; Uniondale HS; Uniondale, NY; (Y); Aud/Vis; Boy Scts; Church Yth Grp; Cmnty Wkr; Drama Clb; PAVAS; Drm Mjr(t); School Play; Stage Crew; Comp.

HALLETT, ROBIN; Avon JR SR HS; Avon, NY; (Y); 14/85; Church Yth Grp; French Clb; Band; Chorus; High Hon Roll; Hon Roll; NEDT Awd; Wildlife Bio.

HALLETT, WILLIAM L; Addison Central Schl; Addison, NY; (Y); 1/104; JCL; Latin Clb; School Play; Pres Frsh Cls; Pres Soph Cls; Pres Jr Cls; Pres Sr Cls; Var Bsbl; Var Bsktbl; NHS; Penn ST.

HALLIDAY, JAMES; Mamaroneck HS; Larchmont, NY; (Y); 1/406; Church Yth Grp; Capt Math Tm; Concert Band; Jazz Band; Capt Lcrss; Capt Socr; Trk; Bausch & Lomb Sci Awd; Sec NHS; Val; Outstndg Ml Athlt Awd 86; Schlr Athlt Awd 86; AP Chem Awd 86; Princeton; Engnrng.

HALLINGER, CAROL A; St Francis Prep; Glendale, NY; (S); 51/653; Computer Clb; Math Clb; JV Trk; Hon Roll; Acad All Amer 85; Bio.

HALLISSY, MARIA; St Francis Prep; Flushing, NY; (Y); 23/693; Chorus; School Musical; Nwsp Stf; Im Ftbl; Im Sftbl; Im Vllybl; High Hon Roll; NHS; Pres Schlr; Adelph U.

HALLIT, ANN; Coxsackie-Athens JR SR HS; Coxsackie, NY; (Y); 18/118; SADD; Band; Jazz Band; Nwsp Stf; Trs Jr Cls; Rep Stu Cncl; JV Var Cheerleading; High Hon Roll; NHS; Bus Prof Womens Assoc 86; Utica Coll; Med Tech.

HALLORAN, JOHN J; Troy HS; Troy, NY; (Y); Political Wkr; Concert Band; Jazz Band; Mrchg Band; School Musical; Yrbk Phtg; Pres Jr Cls; Pres Sr Cls; Hon Roll; NHS; NY ST Rgnts Schlrshp 86; Occdntl Coll Schlrshp 86; Ntl Merit Schlrshp Ltr Cmmndtn 85; Occdntl Coll; Pltcl Sci.

HALLORAN, MARY B; Williamsville East HS; East Amherst, NY; (Y); 29/304; Drama Clb; Trs French Clb; Rep Model UN; Trs Band; Orch; School Play; Var Swmmng; High Hon Roll; NHS; Outstndng Vlntr Amherst YES 82; U MI Alumni Annual Giving Scholar 86; U MI; Lawyer.

HALPIN, ABIGAIL; Brockport HS; Brockport, NY; (Y); Cmnty Wkr; Concert Band; Jazz Band; Mrchg Band; Pep Band; Symp Band; JV Var Socr; Var Trk; NHS; Church Yth Grp; All Amer Hall Of Fame Band Hnr 85; Music.

HALPIN, MARTINA; Hamburg SR HS; Hamburg, NY; (Y); 124/374; Orch; Yrbk Phtg; Sftbl; Hilbert; Legl Asst.

HALPIN, ROSEMARY; Cornwall Central HS; Cornwall, NY; (Y); Church Yth Grp; Cmnty Wkr; Hosp Aide; Chorus; Yrbk Stf; Var L Socr; Var L Trk; High Hon Roll; Sec NHS.

HALPIN, SHANNON; Nardin Acad; Orchard Pk, NY; (Y); Drama Clb; School Musical; Lit Mag; Church Yth Grp; Scholastic Bowl; Ski Clb; Spanish Clb; Speech Tm; Teachers Aide; Yrbk Stf; 2nd Pl-Schl Sci Fair 84; Cmnctns.

HALSEY, BEN; Sandy Creek Central HS; Lacona, NY; (Y); 15/80; Computer Clb; French Clb; SADD; Chorus; Camp Fr Inc; Pres Frsh Cls; Stu Cncl; Var Capt Bsbl; Var Bsktbl; Var Capt Ftbl; Music Awd 84; Sprtsmnshp Awd Bsbl MVP 84; Ftbl Ldrshp Awd 86; Educ.

HALSEY, DARRIN; Southampton HS; Water Mill, NY; (Y); 10/100; Spanish Clb; Band; School Play; JV Var Ftbl; Var Golf; Var Trk; Hon Roll; Jr NHS; NHS; Ntl Merit Ltr.

HALSEY, JOCIE; Southampton HS; Water Mill, NY; (Y); French Clb; Yrbk Stf; Lit Mag; Pres Frsh Cls; Rep Soph Cls; Pres Stu Cncl; Capt Fld Hcky; Capt Trk; Jr NHS; NHS; Scl Psych.

HALSTEAD, LORI; Sandy Creek Central Schl; Pulaski, NY; (Y); Drama Clb; French Clb; Chorus; JV Sftbl; Var Vllybl; Bus Mngmnt.

HALSTED, CURTIS; Cairo-Durham HS; Leeds, NY; (Y); 4/100; Church Yth Grp; VP Sec 4-H; School Musical; Sec VP Stu Cncl; JV Var Socr; Var Tennis; Cit Awd; 4-H Awd; High Hon Roll; Jr NHS; Cornell U; Vet Sci.

HALVORSEN, KIRSTEN; Huntington HS; Huntington, NY; (Y); AFS; Church Yth Grp; Hosp Aide; Key Clb; Varsity Clb; Band; Rep Frsh Cls; Rep Jr Cls; Var Swmmng; Var Trk; Swmg Vrsty Mst Imprvd 84.

HAM, SHEILA; Potsdam HS; E Lebanon, ME; (Y); Computer Clb; Latin Clb; Nwsp Rptr; Nwsp Stf; Yrbk Rptr; Yrbk Stf; High Hon Roll; Hon Roll; NHS; Hstry Fair Awd 83-84; Govt & Ltn Awd 84-85; Gldswrthy Schlrshp 85-86; MI ST U; Physics.

HAMANN, TRACEY; Alden HS; Alden, NY; (Y); Letterman Clb; Spanish Clb; SADD; Band; Trs Frsh Cls; Trs Soph Cls; Trs Stu Cncl; JV Var Cheerleading; JV Var Trk; JV Vllybl.

HAMANN, WENDY; Alden Central HS; Alden, NY; (Y); Letterman Clb; Spanish Clb; SADD; Varsity Clb; Band; School Musical; Rep Jr Cls; JV Sftbl; Var Capt Tennis; Var JV Vllybl; Long Island U; Mar Biol.

HAMBERGER, JOHN; Fayetteville-Manlius HS; Manlius, NY; (Y); SADD; JV Bsbl; Im Bsktbl; Var L Socr; Hon Roll; Spanish NHS; Outstndg Dfndr Sccr 86; Htl Mgmt.

HAMBLIN, BARB; Fort Ann Central Schl; Fort Ann, NY; (Y); 6/51; Drama Clb; Band; School Play; Yrbk Stf; Score Keeper; Hon Roll; NHS; Ft Ann Tchrs Assn Awd, Hys Fuel Svc Cmrcl Awd, Crmn Btlr Mem Bus Awd 86; US Air Force; Acctg.

HAMBLIN, PENNY L; Addison Central HS; Cameron Mills, NY; (Y); 19/104; 4-H; JCL; Latin Clb; Chorus; Color Guard; Yrbk Stf; JV Var Cheerleading; 4-H Awd; High Hon Roll; NHS; Rgnts Nrsng Schlrshp 86; SUNY At Pltsbrg; Nrsng.

HAMBURG, BARB; Churchville-Chili HS; N Chili, NY; (Y); Ski Clb; Chorus; Hon Roll; Bus Mgmt.

HAMER, LILLIAN; Dominican Commercial HS; South Ozone Pk, NY; (S); Church Yth Grp; JA; Yrbk Stf; Hon Roll; NHS.

HAMER, MARCEL; George Wingate HS; Brooklyn, NY; (Y).

HAMER, MARNIE; Oneida HS; Oneida, NY; (S); Trs Pres Church Yth Grp; Varsity Clb; Concert Band; Mrchg Band; Symp Band; Pres Jr Cls; L Var Tennis; High Hon Roll; Hon Roll; Var Trk; ST Solo Cmptn Flute 1st Pl & 2nd Pl 84-85; Pre-Med.

HAMETZ, SHARON R; Massapequa HS; Massapequa, NY; (Y); 11/450; Drama Clb; French Clb; Orch; School Musical; Nwsp Ed-Chief; NHS; Ntl Merit Ltr; Vassar Coll.

HAMILL, KEVIN; Sachem HS; Farmingville, NY; (Y); 18/1576; Science Clb; Jazz Band; Orch; Symp Band; Variety Show; Lit Mag; Socr; Trk; NHS; Ntl Merit Ltr; 3rd Pl In ATTSP Ntl Cntst 86; All St Band 84-86; Middle Island Band Fstvl 85-86; Cornell U; Vet Med.

HAMILTON, ANTOINETTE; George W Wingate HS; Brooklyn, NY; (Y); Cmnty Wkr; Hosp Aide; Teachers Aide; Church Choir; Nwsp Ed-Chief; Lit Mag; Trk; Hon Roll; Prnctn; Comp Sci.

HAMILTON, ASHLEY; Nazareth Regional HS; Brooklyn, NY; (Y); Art Clb; Church Yth Grp; Cmnty Wkr; Math Tm; Science Clb; Church Choir; Trk; Achvmnt Awd 84; Loyola U; Med Srgy.

HAMILTON, BETSY; Eastchester HS; Scarsdale, NY; (Y); Co-Capt Aud/Vis; Key Clb; Latin Clb; Nwsp Sprt Ed; Nwsp Stf; Yrbk Stf; Lit Mag; Rep Frsh Cls; Rep Soph Cls; Rep Jr Cls; Al-Sctn, Daily Nws Al-Star Sftbl 85; Al-Sctn Vllybl 85; Wmns Clb Awd-Poem 86; USAF Acad; Astrnaut.

HAMILTON, CHRISTOPHER R; Saratoga Springs SR HS; Greenfield Center, NY; (Y); 67/470; SADD; Chorus; Orch; Var Capt Bsktbl; Var Ftbl; Var Socr; Var Capt Trk; High Hon Roll; NHS; St Schlr; NYS Rgnts Hnrs 86; Union Coll; Elec Engrng.

HAMILTON, CLIO; Midwood HS; Brooklyn, NY; (Y); 238/667; Cmnty Wkr; Dance Clb; Intnl Clb; Library Aide; Office Aide; Yrbk Stf; Prfct Atten Awd; Psych.

HAMILTON II, DAVID BRIAN; Gouverneur Central HS; Gouverneur, NY; (Y); Hon Roll; Adv Metl Awd 86; Canton ATC; Engrng Tech.

HAMILTON, DAVID M; East Aurora HS; East Aurora, NY; (Y); JA; Rep Frsh Cls; Rep Soph Cls; Tennis; ST Rgnts Schlrshp 86; Syracuse U; Transptn Mgmt.

HAMILTON, EDWARD; Letchworth Central HS; Castile, NY; (Y); Am Leg Boys St; Boy Scts; Drama Clb; Math Tm; Ski Clb; Spanish Clb; Chorus; Var Bsktbl; Var Trk; Wt Lftg; Egl Sct 84.

HAMILTON, LYNN; Pembroke HS; Corfu, NY; (Y); 9/100; Varsity Clb; Variety Show; Pres Jr Cls; Var Capt Bsktbl; JV Var Sftbl; JV Var Vllybl; Hon Roll; NHS; Stu Choice Awd 86; MVP Bsktbl & Vlybl, All-Star Tm V B & B B 85-86.

HAMILTON, MICHELE; Our Lady Of Mercy HS; E Rochester, NY; (Y); Art Clb; Church Yth Grp; Cmnty Wkr; Model UN; Ski Clb; SADD; Chorus; Variety Show; Im Gym; Hon Roll.

HAMILTON, MICHELLE; Shoreham Wading River HS; Wading River, NY; (Y); Cmnty Wkr; Intnl Clb; Science Clb; Band; Concert Band; Stage Crew; Yrbk Phtg; Im Badmtn; Bowling; Mgr Gym; Awd For Excllnc In Span 84; Hon Acceptnc In LI HS Smmr Acad Intl Studies Gifted HS Studs 86; Science.

HAMILTON, MONTRESE; Niagara Falls HS; Niagara Falls, NY; (Y); 38/250; Computer Clb; Model UN; Pep Clb; Spanish Clb; SADD; Ed Yrbk Ed-Chief; Var Cheerleading; Hon Roll; Prfct Atten Awd; Natl Merit Schlrshp Outstndg Negro Stu Fnlst 86; U Of MI; Finance.

HAMILTON, RANDY; The Anglo American Schl; New York, NY; (Y); Computer Clb; Drama Clb; Varsity Clb; Band; School Musical; Lit Mag; Stu Cncl; Gym; Socr; St Schlr; 6th Karate 85; Regnts Schlrshp 86; Musc Compstn.

HAMILTON, SHERRY; Eas Syracuse-Minola HS; Kirkville, NY; (Y); Church Yth Grp; Drama Clb; 4-H; Thesps; Acpl Chr; Chorus; Church Choir; School Musical; School Play; Stage Crew; Chrs Advsry Brd 85-86; Peer Cnslr 85-86; People To People H S Stu Ambass Europe 86.

HAMILTON, TAMAR; Hugh C Williams HS; Canton, NY; (Y); FCA; Girl Scts; Pep Clb; Varsity Clb; Stage Crew; Im Gym; Var Capt Socr; Var Sftbl; Var Capt Trk; Var Im Vllybl; Boce Hgh Achvt Awd-Nrsng 86; MVP-SPRNG Trk 84; Nrsng.

HAMLETT, DONNIE; North Babylon SR HS; N Babylon, NY; (Y); Art Clb; Chess Clb; Computer Clb; Spanish Clb; Variety Show; JV Gym; JV Trk; Im Wt Lftg; Martial Arts 84-86; Elect Engr.

HAMLIN, DARCIE; Marion JR SR HS; Marion, NY; (Y); 8/96; French Clb; Ski Clb; Band; Concert Band; Mrchg Band; Orch; Var Sftbl; Var Tennis; Hon Roll; NHS; Ntl Math Awd 84; Acad All-Amer 84; Ntl Ldrshp & Srvice Awd 85; Aviation.

HAMM, ELLYN; Flushing HS; College Point, NY; (Y); Library Aide; Teachers Aide; Chorus; Yrbk Stf; Queensboro CC; Secrtrl Sci.

HAMM, JOEL L; Oakfield Alamba HS; Oakfield, NY; (Y); Band; Jazz Band; Mrchg Band; School Musical; Trs Jr Cls; VP Sr Cls; Bsktbl; Ftbl; Trk; God Cntry Awd; Babe Ruth Schlrshp Awd 86; SR Athltc Awd 86; NY ST Physcl Fitness Awd; Genesee CC; Bus Admin.

HAMM, MICHELLE; Corinth Central HS; Corinth, NY; (Y); Aud/Vis; VICA; Hon Roll; Bus.

HAMMEL, BARBARA A; St Francis Prep; Flushing, NY; (S); 17/653; Library Aide; Office Aide; Drm & Bgl; Im Sftbl; Im Tennis; Var Twrlr; Im Vllybl; Hon Roll; Sec NHS; Ntl Sci Merit Awd 86; Ntl Ldrshp Merit Awd 86; Law.

HAMMEL, STEVEN; Attica Central HS; Attica, NY; (S); 2/154; Math Tm; ROTC; Var L Socr; Var Capt Tennis; Bausch & Lomb Sci Awd; Lion Awd; NHS; Ntl Merit SF; Sal; Am Leg Svc Awd 82; MVP Tnns 83-85; Soccer MVP 82; Canisius Coll; Biochem.

HAMMER, MICHELE J; St Francis Prep; Ozone Park, NY; (S); #83 In Class; Hosp Aide; Math Tm; Office Aide; Teachers Aide; Hon Roll; NHS; Optmt Soc Awd 84 & 85; Hofstra U; Educ.

HAMMERSMITH, ANN; Mt Mercy Acad; Buffalo, NY; (Y); Hosp Aide; Ski Clb; Chorus; School Musical; School Play; Stage Crew; Coach Actv; Vllybl; Hon Roll; Dance Clb; Intl Music Fest Awd Silv Mdl 85; Canisius Coll; Pedtrcn.

HAMMES, TARA; Hoosic Valley Central HS; Troy, NY; (Y); VP French Clb; Band; Chorus; Mrchg Band; JV Bsktbl; Mgr(s); Score Keeper; Trk; Hon Roll; NHS; Misc Cmnty Svc Awds 84-86; Mdrn Lang.

HAMMILL, DEBORAH; Charles O Dickerson HS; Trumansburg, NY; (Y); 19/120; VP Drama Clb; French Clb; Thesps; Ed Yrbk Stf; Sec Stu Cncl; Socr; Vllybl; NHS; Hstry.

HAMMON, SUSAN; Liverpool HS; Liverpool, NY; (Y); 45/885; Church Yth Grp; Spanish Clb; Church Choir; Concert Band; Mrchg Band; Hon Roll; Jr NHS; NHS.

HAMMOND, BRENDA; Avoca Central Schl; Cohocton, NY; (Y); 3/44; Sec FBLA; Yrbk Ed-Chief; VP Frsh Cls; Pres Soph Cls; Pres Jr Cls; Trs Stu Cncl; Cheerleading; Trk; High Hon Roll; NHS; Acctng I, Hgh Hnr & Stu Cncl Awds 86; Bryant S Stratton; Accntng.

HAMMOND, DANIEL; Alexandria Central Schl; Alexandria Bay, NY; (Y); Band; Chorus; Concert Band; Mrchg Band; Pep Band; School Play; Stage Crew; Variety Show; Hon Roll; NHS; Union Coll; Elec Engrng.

HAMMOND, MEEGAN; Beacon HS; Beacon, NY; (Y); Science Clb; Band; Pep Band; Yrbk Phtg; Yrbk Stf; Stat Bsktbl; JV Sftbl; Var L Tennis; Hon Roll; Jr NHS; Engrng.

HAMMOND, MICHELLE L; Tioga Central HS; Owego, NY; (S); 9/96; Dance Clb; Ski Clb; Varsity Clb; Variety Show; Bsktbl; Crs Cntry; Fld Hcky; Sftbl; High Hon Roll; NHS; Natl Ltn Exm Slvr & Gld Mdls; Broome CC; Engl.

HAMMOND, R GREGORY; Southwestern Central HS; Jamestown, NY; (Y); 17/149; Am Leg Boys St; Trs German Clb; Trs JA; Trs Band; Chorus; School Musical; JV Var Socr; JV Var Tennis; NHS; Pres Acadmc Fit Awd 86; Miami U OH; Acctg.

HAMMOND, WARREN R; Rhinebeck HS; Rhinebeck, NY; (Y); 11/120; Chess Clb; Yrbk Bus Mgr; Bsktbl; Tennis; High Hon Roll; Hon Roll; NHS.

HAMOU, DANIEL; Iona Prep; Mt Vernon, NY; (Y); Computer Clb; Dance Clb; JA; Pep Clb; Ski Clb; Varsity Clb; Yrbk Stf; Lit Mag; Rep Sr Cls; JV Var Bsbl; Opthmlgy.

HAMPTON, CYNTHIA M; Bronx High School Of Science; Bronx, NY; (Y); Drama Clb; Key Clb; NFL; VP Spanish Clb; Speech Tm; Im Ftbl; H S Diplm For Piano Frm Natl Gld Of Piano Tchrs 86; Advncd Bach Mdl 83; Poli Sci.

HAMPTON, DAWN M; Haverling Central HS; Bath, NY; (S); 13/140; Pres French Clb; FBLA; FTA; Math Clb; Off Stu Cncl; Capt Var Cheerleading; Var Sftbl; High Hon Roll; Langs.

HAMPTON, LAURA; Babylon HS; Babylon, NY; (Y); Cmnty Wkr; Drama Clb; French Clb; Girl Scts; Chorus; School Musical; School Play; Stage Crew; Variety Show; Crs Cntry; Cross Cntry Awds 82-86; Home Ec Clb 83; Farmingdale Coll; Chld Dvlpmnt.

HAMPTON, TRACY; Saint John The Baptist HS; Amityville, NY; (Y); Cmnty Wkr; Chorus; Bsktbl; Hon Roll; Psychlgy.

HAMWI, GAYLE; Polytechnic Prep Country Day Schl; Brooklyn, NY; (Y); Camera Clb; Cmnty Wkr; Letterman Clb; Spanish Clb; Chorus; Yrbk Phtg; Yrbk Stf; Var L Bsktbl; Var L Mgr(s); Var L Tennis; Math.

HAN, HYE SUN; Flushing HS; Flushing, NY; (Y); 7/410; Church Yth Grp; Math Tm; Church Choir; School Play; Ed Nwsp Stf; Ed Yrbk Stf; Co-Capt Var Vllybl; NHS; Assmbls God Tn Tlnt, Vcl Ensmbl Dist Lvl 1st Pl 86; Arch.

HAN, SEONG SIM; Newtown HS; Corona, NY; (Y); #11 In Class; Chess Clb; Cmnty Wkr; Intnl Clb; School Play; Ed Lit Mag; VP Sr Cls; Gov Hon Prg Awd; Jr NHS; NHS; Prfct Atten Awd; Regnts Schlrshp 86-90; Chncllrs Awds 86; Fincl Awd, Schlrshp Boston 86-87; Boston U; Law.

HANACHI, ESSYA; Mercy HS; East Hampton, NY; (Y); 15/126; Church Yth Grp; Ski Clb; SADD; Chorus; Yrbk Stf; Tennis; High Hon Roll.

HANCHETT, LORI A; Shaker HS; Latham, NY; (Y); GAA; Latin Clb; School Musical; Diving; Var Gym; NHS; Cornell U; Vet Med.

HANCOCK, GREGORY T; Skaneateles HS; Skaneateles, NY; (Y); Boy Scts; Church Yth Grp; Yrbk Phtg; JV Crs Cntry; Im Socr; Var L Trk; Hon Roll; NHS; Eagle Awd By Scts 86; Engr.

HANCOCK, IRA A; Poughkeepsie HS; Poughkeepsie, NY; (Y); 21/300; Scholastic Bowl; Cit Awd; Am Leg Boys St; Cmnty Wkr; 4-H; Library Aide; Office Aide; Radio Clb; Teachers Aide; Y-Teens; Psych.

HANCOCK, MARY C; Thomas Edison HS; Elmira, NY; (Y); 3/75; Am Leg Aux Girls St; Church Yth Grp; French Clb; Girl Scts; Model UN; Band; Chorus; Church Choir; Concert Band; Drm Mjr(t); Outstndng Musician 80-83 & 85-86; Corning CC; Ed.

HAND, BRIAN; Southern Cayuga Central HS; Genoa, NY; (Y); French Clb; JV L Bsbl; Capt L Crs Cntry; Bausch & Lomb Sci Awd; High Hon Roll; NHS; Engrng.

HAND, DIANA; Belmont Central HS; Belmont, NY; (Y); 5/21; Trs GAA; Sec Spanish Clb; Trs Band; Yrbk Rptr; Pres Frsh Cls; Trs Stu Cncl; Var Cheerleading; Var Socr; Var Sftbl; Pres NHS; ST U Of Geneseo; Frgn Lang.

HAND, RONALD G; Walt Whitman HS; Huntington, NY; (Y); 108/549; Trk; Regents Coll Schlrshp 86; JV Let 84; Mem Athletic Awd 83.

HANDEL, JACQUELINE M; Bronx HS Of Science; Flushing, NY; (Y); SADD; Temple Yth Grp; Sftbl; DAR Awd; Law.

HANDLEY, RICHARD; Arlington HS; Poughkeepsie, NY; (Y); 78/576; Spanish Clb; Thesps; School Musical; School Play; Stage Crew; Variety Show; Nwsp Stf; Spanish NHS; Oneonta SUNY; Wrtr.

HANDY, PATRICIA M; Brewster HS; Brewster, NY; (Y); Spanish Clb; Cheerleading; Trk; Hon Roll; Stu Congress Rep; Psych.

HANEIN, SHIRLEY; Abraham Lincoln HS; Brooklyn, NY; (Y); 22/416; Key Clb; Teachers Aide; Band; Nwsp Ed-Chief; Nwsp Phtg; High Hon Roll; Jr NHS; NCTE Awd; NHS; Mass Cmmnctns.

HANER, MICHELLE L; Owego Free Acad; Nichols, NY; (Y); 21/224; Key Clb; Concert Band; Jazz Band; Trs Madrigals; Mrchg Band; School Musical; 4-H Awd; VP NHS; Ntl Merit SF; Drama Clb; Tioga Cnty 1st Altrnt Dairy Prncss 85-86; SUNY Plattsbrgh; Pblc Rel.

HANESIAN, LAUREL A; Niagara Wheatfield HS; Lewiston, NY; (Y); 37/292; Latin Clb; PAVAS; Band; Chorus; Mrchg Band; School Musical; School Play; Socr; NYS Rgnts Schlrshp 85; SUNY At Fredonia; Music Educ.

HANEY, MICHELLE; Cardinal O Hara HS; Kenmore, NY; (S); French Clb; High Hon Roll; Hon Roll; Ed.

HANEY, ROY; Rye HS; Rye, NY; (Y); VP Church Yth Grp; ROTC; Var Ftbl; Wt Lftg; Var Wrstlng; High Hon Roll; Hon Roll; Amer Legion ROTC Medal 86; Retired Officers Assoc Mdl 86.

HANEY, STEPHEN; Franklin Delanor Roosevelt HS; Brooklyn, NY; (Y); 50/634; Civic Clb; Computer Clb; Science Clb; Var Ftbl; High Hon Roll; Pres Schlr; Pres Acdmc Fit Awd 86; Assmbly ST NY Citation 84; NYS Enrgy Rsrch/Dvlpmnt & Sen Achvmnt Awd 84; John Jay Coll; Law.

HANFORD, BETH; Onondaga Central HS; Marietta, NY; (Y); GAA; Spanish Clb; SADD; Varsity Clb; Band; Concert Band; L VP Bsktbl; VP L Crs Cntry; VP L Trk; Hon Roll; Sprts Educ.

HANG, DIANA; H S Of Fashion Indstry; Flushing, NY; (Y); 4/324; French Clb; JA; Library Aide; Office Aide; Service Clb; Teachers Aide; VICA; School Play; Swing Chorus; Ntl Merit Ltr; Englsh Awd 85; Frnch Awd 84.

HANKERSON, ANDRE; Cardinal Hayes HS; Bronx, NY; (Y); 17/289; Band; Concert Band; Jazz Band; Mrchg Band; Rep Stu Cncl; Var JV Ftbl; Hon Roll; Aeronautics.

HANKS, KATHLEEN; Dominican Commercial HS; Glendale, NY; (S); 9/279; Art Clb; Chess Clb; Cmnty Wkr; Nwsp Ed-Chief; Nwsp Rptr; Nwsp Stf; High Hon Roll; Hon Roll; NHS; Prfct Atten Awd; Mayorial Vlntr Awd 85; Workmens Benefit Fund Comm Vlntr Wrk 85; NY Food/Htl Mgmt Schl; Cooking.

HANLEY, CHRISTINE; Walton Central HS; Walton, NY; (Y); 15/100; Rep AFS; Rep Key Clb; Chorus; Ed Yrbk Phtg; Yrbk Stf; VP Rep Stu Cncl; Var Cheerleading; Var L Fld Hcky; High Hon Roll; Hon Roll; Regents Schlrshp Awd 86; Field Hcky Ltr; Chorus Ltr; Teaching.

HANLEY, KATHY J; Hackley Schl; Congers, NY; (Y); 16/89; Church Yth Grp; Math Clb; Band; Mrchg Band; Socr; High Hon Roll; Hon Roll; Jr NHS; Mu Alp Tht; NHS; GA Inst Of Tech; Engrng.

HANLON, DOUG; Centereach HS; Lake Ronkonkoma, NY; (S); 72/429; Q&S; Band; Concert Band; Drm Mjr(t); Jazz Band; Mrchg Band; Nwsp Sprt Ed; Nwsp Stf; Crs Cntry; Trk; Cmmnctns.

HANLON, FRANCES; Longwood HS; Middle Island, NY; (S); 20/500; Intnl Clb; Key Clb; Sec Band; Concert Band; Mrchg Band; School Musical; High Hon Roll; Jr NHS; NHS; BOCES Smmr Inst For Gftd & Tlndt Yth 83; Gold Mdl Lng Is Music Tchrs Assn Piano Solo 85; SUNY Stony Brook; Music Educ.

HANNA, ANN MARIE; Cardinal Mooney HS; Rochester, NY; (Y); 166/359; Yrbk Stf; Hon Roll; Spnsh Awd 86; Bryant & Stratton; Bus Adm.

HANNA, CRAIG; Franklin Acad; Malone, NY; (Y); Var L Ice Hcky; Hon Roll; Jr NHS; NHS; Acad All Amer & Natl Sci Merit Awds 84; Amer H S Ath 85; Canton; Elec Tech.

HANNA, GIHAN; Fayetteville Manlius HS; Manlius, NY; (Y); Hosp Aide; Model UN; SADD; Concert Band; Nwsp Rptr; Rep Stu Cncl; Mgr Sftbl; Hon Roll; NHS; Cert Of Excllnc French IIIA 85-86.

HANNA, MICHELLE; Williamsville North HS; E Amherst, NY; (Y); Computer Clb; French Clb; Math Tm; U Chicago; Mth.

HANNA, MOLLY; Avon JRSR HS; Avon, NY; (Y); 20/91; Church Yth Grp; 4-H; Girl Scts; Ski Clb; Spanish Clb; Trk; High Hon Roll; Hon Roll; Grl Scout Silv Awd 84; Grl Scout 10 Yr Pin 86; Grl Scout Natl Wider Opprtnty 84; Mth Ed.

HANNA, THOMAS; Franklin Acad; Malone, NY; (Y); 1/250; Church Yth Grp; Spanish Clb; Bsbl; High Hon Roll; Jr NHS; NHS; Ntl Merit Schol; Prfct Atten Awd; Acad All Amer Hgh Hnrs 83-85; Natl Sci Recog Day Awd 84; Acad All Amer Spn 84.

HANNAN, CARRIE; Lynbrook SR HS; Lynbrook, NY; (Y); Drama Clb; FBLA; Spanish Clb; SADD; Varsity Clb; Var Capt Badmtn; Var Bsktbl; Var Cheerleading; JV Stat Lcrss; Boston Coll; Psych.

HANNAN, KELI; Cornwall HS; Cornwall Hudson, NY; (Y); Cmnty Wkr; Ski Clb; Acpl Chr; Chorus; Church Choir; School Play; Var Im Socr; Var Capt Vllybl; Hon Roll; Estrn Orng Cnty Chmbr Of Cmrc Yth Bus Smnr 86; Bus.

HANNAN, LISA; Canastota JR SR HS; Canastota, NY; (S); Chess Clb; FBLA; Teachers Aide; High Hon Roll; NHS; Math.

HANNIGAN, KIM; North Salem HS; N Salem, NY; (Y); Library Aide; Nwsp Ed-Chief; Nwsp Rptr; Mgr Jr Cls; Var Tennis; Hon Roll; Psych.

HANNIGAN, MATT; St John The Baptist DHS HS; Central Islip, NY; (Y); Var Ice Hcky; JV Lcrss; Var Socr; Elec Engr.

HANNIGAN, ROBERT; Regis HS; Brooklyn, NY; (Y); Varsity Clb; Bsbl; JV Fld Hcky; Ftbl; Sftbl; $11000 HS Schlrshp 84; Harvard; Medcn.

HANNIGAN, THERESE; De Sales Catholic HS; Lockport, NY; (Y); 12/30; Ski Clb; Nwsp Rptr; Yrbk Stf; Pres Stu Cncl; Var Bsktbl; Var Cheerleading; Var Socr; Var Tennis; High Hon Roll; NEDT Awd.

HANNIS, ERIC R; Chenango Valley HS; Binghamton, NY; (Y); 6/180; Am Leg Boys St; Church Yth Grp; Pres Latin Clb; Ski Clb; Varsity Clb; Nwsp Sprt Ed; Var L Socr; Capt Var Tennis; High Hon Roll; NHS; Hon Grad BOCES SCOPE Mrn Bio Pgm 84; Asst Dir Cmnty Yth Smmr Schl Pgm 85; Ltn Clb Awd 86; Hamilton Coll; Law.

HANNON, CHRISTINE; Thomas A Edison HS; Elmira Hts, NY; (Y); 2/74; French Clb; Concert Band; Drm Mjr(t); School Musical; High Hon Roll; JP Sousa Awd; Sal; Church Yth Grp; Girl Scts; JA; Chemung Vly JR Womns Clb Schlrshp 86; Chem Bwl 2nd Pl 86; Piccolo Area All ST Band Fest 86; Dickinson Coll; Sci.

HANNON, JOHN F; Archbishop Walsh HS; Angelica, NY; (Y); 1/55; Math Clb; Yrbk Stf; Pres Sr Cls; Rep Stu Cncl; High Hon Roll; NCTE Awd; NHS; Ntl Merit Ltr; Colgate U; Physcs Mjr.

HANNON, TIMOTHY; Bishop Timon HS; Cheektowaga, NY; (S); 7/70; Cmnty Wkr; Quiz Bowl; Boys Clb Am; Nwsp Rptr; Yrbk Stf; Var L Socr; High Hon Roll; Estblshd Chem Clb 86; Stdnt Tutr 84; SUNY; Pre-Dntl.

HANOUSEK, JANET; Westhill Central HS; Syracuse, NY; (S); 7/145; Pres Drama Clb; ROTC; Trs SADD; School Play; Nwsp Ed-Chief; Var Capt Bsktbl; Var Capt Socr; Var Capt Sftbl; Hon Roll; NHS; MVP Vrsty Bsktbl 84; MVP Vrsty Sftbl-1st Tm Al-Cnty 84; ROTC Schlrshp Wnnr 86; Biomed Engr.

HANRAHAN, JOHN; Whitesboro SR HS; Whitesboro, NY; (Y); 118/306; Var Stat Bsktbl; Hon Roll; Cvl Engrng.

HANRAHAN, PATRICIA; Our Lady Of Victory HS; Bronx, NY; (S); 13/148; Church Yth Grp; Sec Frsh Cls; Rep Jr Cls; Hon Roll; NHS; Spanish NHS; Busnss.

HANSELMAN, DAVID; Waterloo SR HS; Waterloo, NY; (Y); Am Leg Boys St; Hon Roll; Prfct Atten Awd.

HANSEN, ANN; Catholic Central HS; Troy, NY; (Y); French Clb; Math Clb; SADD; Band; School Musical; Stage Crew; L Tennis; Hon Roll; NHS; Untd Way Vlntr Awd 84; Coll Of St Rose; Elem Ed.

HANSEN, BRIAN; Trott Vocational HS; Niagara Falls, NY; (Y); Library Aide; Stage Crew; Hon Roll; NHS; Elctncs.

HANSEN, EVE; Corning-Painted Post E HS; Corning, NY; (Y); Ski Clb; JV Bsktbl; Var JV Swmmng; Var Trk; JV Var Vllybl; High Hon Roll; Hon Roll; Jr NHS; NHS; Girl Scts; Pres Acad Ftns Awd 85-86; SUNY; Bio.

HANSEN, HILLARY SCOTT; The Masters Schl; Ardsley On Hdsn, NY; (Y); French Clb; Teachers Aide; JV Capt Bsktbl; JV Capt Socr; Var Trk; Wrk Prg Proctor 86-87; Marine Bio.

HANSEN, KAREN-LEE; Washingtonville HS; New Windsor, NY; (Y); Church Yth Grp; Debate Tm; French Clb; Girl Scts; Ski Clb; Rep SADD; School Play; Stage Crew; Yrbk Stf; Rep Jr Cls; Law.

HANSEN, KRISTIN; Queen Of The Rosary Acad; Bellmore, NY; (S); 3/38; Drama Clb; Variety Show; Gym; High Hon Roll; Hon Roll; NHS; Cert For Super Perf Natl Educ Dev Tests 83; Fairfield U; Psych.

HANSEN, LISA; Hoosick Falls Central HS; Hoosick Falls, NY; (Y); Church Yth Grp; Drama Clb; Sec VP SADD; Teachers Aide; Stage Crew; Rep Stu Cncl; Stat Var Bsktbl; Im Vllybl; Hon Roll; NHS; Merit List 84-86; Hnrs/Rcgntn Tchng Sunday Schl 84-86.

HANSEN, MARGARETE; Walt Whitman HS; Huntington, NY; (Y); 5/479; German Clb; Key Clb; Chorus; Yrbk Stf; Var L Badmtn; High Hon Roll; Jr NHS; Scrtry Grmn Hnr Scty 86-87; Mst Outstndng Dbl Ply In Badminton 86; Frgn Lang Awd In Grmn 83-84; Frgn Lang.

HANSEN, MELANIE; St John Villa Acad; Staten Island, NY; (Y); 6/120; Church Yth Grp; Math Tm; Bowling; Swmmng; Hon Roll; Achvt Engl,Clsscl Orgn Plyng 85; Achvt Amrcn Stds 86; Accntng.

HANSEN, MICHAEL; Hicksville SR HS; Hicksville, NY; (Y); 40/400; Computer Clb; Drama Clb; Thesps; Orch; Var L Trk; High Hon Roll; Jr NHS; NHS; Pres Schlr; Science Clb; Italn Hon Soc 84; Rochester Inst Of Tech; Chem.

HANSLICK, NICOLE; Mynders Acad; Seneca Falls, NY; (S); 11/138; French Clb; Boys Clb Am; Stage Crew; Yrbk Stf; Stu Cncl; Crs Cntry; Tennis; Trk; High Hon Roll; VFW Awd; DAR 84; Intl Bus.

HANSON, CURT; Geneseo Central HS; Geneseo, NY; (Y); Var Capt Bsbl; Var Capt Bsktbl; Var Capt Ftbl; High Hon Roll; Hon Roll; Jr NHS; NHS; Pres Schlr; St Lawrence U Schlrshp & Presdntl Schlrshp To Alfred U 86-87; St Lawrence U; Bus.

HANSON, CYNTHIA; Potsdam Central HS; Potsdam, NY; (Y); AFS; French Clb; Varsity Clb; Band; Nwsp Rptr; Yrbk Stf; Var L Cheerleading; High Hon Roll; Hon Roll; NHS; St Lawrence U.

HANSON, JANET; Hillcrest HS; S Ozone Pk, NY; (Y); Pres Church Yth Grp; Hosp Aide; Intnl Clb; Office Aide; Chorus; Church Choir; NHS; Pre-Med.

HANSON, JASON; York Central Schl; Geneseo, NY; (Y); Mathletes; Trs Frsh Cls; VP Tennis; VP Wrstlng; Bausch & Lomb Sci Awd; High Hon Roll; Jr NHS; NHS; Ntl Merit SF.

HANSON, JOHN; Shape American HS; APO, NY; (Y); Exploring; ROTC; Yrbk Phtg; Hon Roll; Pres Schlr; KS U; Aerspc Engr.

HANSON, KEN; Fonda-Fultonville HS; Tribes Hill, NY; (Y); 9/110; Bsbl; Ftbl; Wt Lftg; Capt Wrstlng; High Hon Roll; Hon Roll; VP NHS; Alfred ST Coll; Arch.

HANSON, LISA; Our Lady Of Mercy HS; Pittsford, NY; (Y); Cmnty Wkr; French Clb; JA; Model UN; Service Clb; Ski Clb; Varsity Clb; Stu Cncl; Capt Crs Cntry; Trk; MVP Crs Cntry 85; Magazine Modl 85 & 86; Child Psych.

HANSON, PETER C; Greenville Central Schl; Rensselaerville, NY; (Y); Am Leg Boys St; SADD; Nwsp Ed-Chief; Nwsp Rptr; Pres Stu Cncl; NHS; UCLA; Flm.

HANSON, SARAH K; W C Mepham HS; Bellmore, NY; (Y); 28/360; Drama Clb; Lib Band; Mrchg Band; School Musical; School Play; Symp Band; Yrbk Stf; Off Jr Cls; Off Sr Cls; Stu Cncl; NY ST Rgnts Schlrshp 86; Muhlenbeg Coll PA; Music.

HANSON, TIMOTHY; Monroe HS; Rochester, NY; (Y); 9/156; Ski Clb; Var L Bsbl; Var L Bsktbl; L Golf; Hon Roll; NHS; St Schlr; The American U; Econs.

HAPANOWICZ, SHAWN; Whitesboro Central HS; Whitesboro, NY; (Y); 104/350; Ski Clb; Varsity Clb; JV VP Ftbl; Var JV Lcrss; Im Wt Lftg; Acadmc All Am 86; Am Conf 1st Tm Defensv And Ftbl Indepnd Lg 1st 86; Ed Synakowski Awd 86; Ithaca; Accounting.

HAPEMAN, DONNA; Horseheads SR HS; Horseheads, NY; (Y); Pres 4-H; French Clb; Library Aide; Hon Roll; Continentl Schl Of Beauty Cult.

HARA, KEVIN O; E J Wilson HS; Rochester, NY; (Y); VP French Clb; Hon Roll; Jr NHS; NHS; Cinematgrphy.

HARA, MARY; Moore Catholic HS; Staten Island, NY; (Y); Camera Clb; Cmnty Wkr; French Clb; Stage Crew; Nwsp Phtg; Yrbk Phtg; Lit Mag; Hon Roll; Psychlgy.

HARBAUGH, BRIDGET; Manhasset HS; Manhasset, NY; (Y); 63/187; Church Yth Grp; Cmnty Wkr; Dance Clb; Drama Clb; GAA; Chorus; Drill Tm; School Musical; Soph Cls; Jr Cls; Hmcmng Queen 85-86; Ldrs Clb 83-86; PA ST U; Fash Buyer.

HARBERT, TERENCE L; Nottingham HS; Syracuse, NY; (Y); 52/220; Boys Clb Am; Exploring; JA; Bowling; Outstndng Negro Stdnts 85; Engrng.

HARBOUR, JANICE; Midwood HS; Brooklyn, NY; (Y); 224/589; Cmnty Wkr; Teachers Aide; Chorus; Concert Band; Rep Stu Cncl; Rgnts Schlrshp Nrsng 86; Chrch Wrkr; Thomas Hunter Coll; Nrsng.

HARCLEROAD, BRENDA; Letchworth HS; Silver Springs, NY; (Y); Hosp Aide; RN.

HARDEN, DINA; Murry Bergtraum HS; Brooklyn, NY; (Y); Church Yth Grp; Math Tm; Band; Church Choir; Yrbk Stf; Hon Roll; Comp Sci.

HARDEN, SAMUEL ANDRE; Uniondale HS; Hempstead, NY; (Y); Church Yth Grp; Cmnty Wkr; Computer Clb; FCA; Speech Tm; Varsity Clb; Var JV Trk; Wrstlng; High Hon Roll; Hon Roll; Am Leg Awd 83-84; Black Studies Clb 85-86; JR Black Belt Tae Kwon Do 84; Adv Plcmnt Adelphi U; Pre-Law.

HARDENSTINE, TAMMY; Rome Free Acad; Rome, NY; (Y); 62/445; Chorus; Church Choir; Flag Corp; Nwsp Bus Mgr; Nwsp Rptr; Nwsp Stf; High Hon Roll; Hon Roll; NHS; Pres Schlr; LA Coll; Englsh.

HARDIMAN, CATHERINE; Royalton Hartland Central HS; Middleport, NY; (Y); 5/127; French Clb; Varsity Clb; Bsktbl; Fld Hcky; Sftbl; High Hon Roll; Hon Roll; NHS; MVP Fld Hcky; MIP JV Sftbl.

HARDY, GLENN F; Walt Whitman HS; Melville, NY; (Y); 33/549; Trs Drama Clb; School Play; Ed Nwsp Stf; Rep Jr Cls; Rep Sr Cls; High Hon Roll; NHS; Ntl Merit Ltr; VP Spanish NHS; Intl Acad 85; Model Cngrss 86; Senatr For A Day 85; Binghampton SUNY; Hstry.

HARDY, LAURA; Leroy JR SR HS; Leroy, NY; (Y); 8/135; French Clb; Chorus; Concert Band; Jazz Band; Mrchg Band; School Musical; Nwsp Ed-Chief; High Hon Roll; NHS; JR Miss Schlrshp 85; Regents Schlrshp NYS 85; Bowlig Green ST U; Mag Jrnlsm.

HARGESHIMER, HEATHER; Hamburg HS; Hamburg, NY; (Y); AFS; Sec Trs 4-H; Trs Girl Scts; JCL; Ski Clb; Band; Concert Band; Mrchg Band; School Musical; Stage Crew; Silver Awd-Girls Scouts 86; Carnegie-Mellon; Archtctr.

HARGRAVE, KEVIN; Mexico Acad; Mexico, NY; (Y); 10/180; Pres FFA; Concert Band; Mrchg Band; Hon Roll; Lion Awd; NHS; Pres Schlr; NY ST Regents Schlrshp 86; Ctzns Schlrshp Fdn Am Schlrshp 86; Canton ATC Alumni Schlrshp 86; Canton Agri & Tech Coll; Engr.

HARGRAVE, KYLE; Charles H Roth HS; Rochester, NY; (Y); SADD; Varsity Clb; Band; Rep Stu Cncl; Bsbl; Var Capt Bsktbl; Var JV Socr; High Hon Roll; Hon Roll; Jr NHS; Urban Lg Blck Schlr 86; All Cnty Scor Awd 85-86; All Tourn Tm Awd Bsktbl 86; Sec Tchr.

HARGRAVES, DEIDRA E; Hillcrest HS; St Albans, NY; (Y); 102/835; Hosp Aide; Pres Jr Cls; Rep Sr Cls; Stu Cncl; Capt Cheerleading; Church Yth Grp; Dance Clb; Teachers Aide; Church Choir; Badmtn; Sci Fair Awd 82; Vol Svc Awd 83; Regents Schlrshp 86; Hofstra U; Acctg.

HARGREAVES, CHARLES; Mahopac HS; Mahopac, NY; (Y); 55/409; Bsktbl; Var Ftbl; Var Im Lcrss; Im Wt Lftg; High Hon Roll; Hon Roll; NHS; Elec Engrng.

HARGROVE, PAUL; La Salle Acad; Brooklyn, NY; (S); 4/256; Am Leg Boys St; Rep Stu Cncl; NHS; Crs Cntry; Trk; Rep Frsh Cls; Rep Soph Cls; Rep Jr Cls; Rep Sr Cls; Acctg.

HARGROVE, SOPHIE; Roosevelt JR SR HS; Freeport, NY; (Y); 2/160; FBLA; Band; Concert Band; Mrchg Band; Orch; Yrbk Stf; Pres Jr NHS; VP NHS; Sal; C W Post; Actg.

HARINSKI, JAMES M; St Francis Prep; Maspeth, NY; (S); Boy Scts; Var Diving; Var Trk; Wt Lftg; NHS; Im Vllybl; Eagle Sct 84.

HARINSKY, KARYN; Smithtown H S East; Nesconset, NY; (Y); Yrbk Stf; Rep Stu Cncl; Var Capt Badmtn; Var L Socr; Hon Roll; Girls Ldrs Clb Treas 86-87.

HARKE, RUSSELL; Genesco Central Schl; Geneceo, NY; (Y); 3/86; Mathletes; Varsity Clb; Lit Mag; Bsbl; Ice Hcky; Socr; Hon Roll; Jr NHS; NHS.

HARKIN, SUSAN; Haverling HS; Bath, NY; (Y); VP Church Yth Grp; French Clb; FBLA; FTA; Teachers Aide; Yrbk Sprt Ed; Yrbk Stf; Bsktbl; Socr; Trk; Mst Imprv Trck Rnnr 86; Mst Imprv Bsktbll Plyr 86; Herkimer CC; Sports Med.

HARLEY JR, COLIN EMILE; The Anglo-American Schl; New York, NY; (Y); French Clb; Key Clb; Teachers Aide; Chorus; Yrbk Phtg; Lit Mag; Ntl Merit Ltr; Franklin Coll.

HARLEY, ERINN; New Rochelle HS; Scarsdale, NY; (Y); Hosp Aide; Rep Soph Cls; Rep Jr Cls; High Hon Roll; Hon Roll; NHS; Pres Spanish NHS; Alpha Kappa Alpha Srty Awd 85-86; MLKCDCI Awd Vlnteer Svc 85; Harvard; Pediatrics.

HARLEY, KASANDRA; Seward Park HS; New York, NY; (Y); Cmnty Wkr; Office Aide; Political Wkr; Teachers Aide; Variety Show; Yrbk Rptr; Yrbk Stf; Rep Frsh Cls; Hon Roll; Martin Luther King Humanitarian Awd 84; Cert Of Svc 86; Pride Of The Yankees Awd 86; Elem Educ.

HARLEY, LAURA; Sacred Heart Acad; Rockville Centre, NY; (S); Trs Debate Tm; Math Tm; NFL; Spanish Clb; Chorus; Orch; High Hon Roll; NHS; All Cnty HS Music Fstvl 85-86.

HARLOS, TAIA; Sweet Home SR HS; N Tonawanda, NY; (Y); Latin Clb; VP Orch; Rep Soph Cls; Rep Jr Cls; Stat Vllybl; Var Wt Lftg; Hon Roll; Miss NY Ntl Teen Ager Fnlst 86; Latin Hnr Soc 86; Eastman Schl Music; Music.

HARMAN, JEFFREY; Geneva HS; Geneva, NY; (S); 35/175; Boy Scts; Church Yth Grp; Cmnty Wkr; Computer Clb; Crs Cntry; High Hon Roll; Hon Roll; Achvt Awd Algbr Regnts 83; Achvt Awd Bio 84; Achvt Awd Amer Hstry Regnts 85; Cornell; Bio.

HARMAN, KAREN; Eden SR HS; Eden, NY; (Y); AFS; Church Yth Grp; Drama Clb; Band; Chorus; Church Choir; Concert Band; Orch; School Musical; Im Badmtn; Cmnctns.

HARMAN, REBECCA; Unatego JR SR HS; Otego, NY; (Y); 4/100; Church Yth Grp; Ski Clb; Spanish Clb; Band; Concert Band; Mrchg Band; Orch; Pep Band; School Musical; Crs Cntry; Volntr Staff DEC Camp Colby 85; FHV Mecklenburg Consrvtn Fellowshp 86; Biochem.

HARMER, TERRY; Spackenkill HS; Poughkeepsie, NY; (Y); Pres Church Yth Grp; Exploring; Church Choir; Color Guard; Var Wrstlng; God Cntry Awd; Hon Roll; Var Ntl Merit Ltr; Var Rotary Awd; Boy Scts.

HARMON, MISSY; Auburn HS; Aubrn, NY; (Y); Intnl Clb; Var Capt Bsktbl; Var Golf; Socr; JV Sftbl; High Hon Roll; Hon Roll; Jr NHS; NHS; Law.

HARMS, DREA; Huntington HS; Huntington, NY; (Y); Key Clb; Trs Varsity Clb; Orch; VP Sr Cls; Var Bsktbl; Var Socr; Var Sftbl; Hon Roll; NHS; NY ST Slct Sccr Team 85-86; Pre-Med.

HARNED, RAYMOND T; Cicero-North Syracuse HS; Clay, NY; (Y); Church Yth Grp; School Play; Rep Stu Cncl; Coach Actv; Im Golf; NYS Rgnts Schlrshp 85-86; Onondaga CC; Music.

HARNER, KENNETH; Livonia HS; Livonia, NY; (Y); 1/154; Computer Clb; German Clb; Math Tm; Science Clb; Varsity Clb; Nwsp Stf; Var L Bsbl; JV Bsktbl; High Hon Roll; Jr NHS; Amer Soc Chmcl Engrs 86.

HARNICK, JOEL; Baldwin HS; Baldwin, NY; (Y); Pres Key Clb; SADD; Trs Temple Yth Grp; Trs Stu Cncl; High Hon Roll; NHS; Ntl Merit SF; Drama Clb; Exploring; Long Is Sci Cngrss Red Rbbn 84; Eurpn Hstry Achvt Awd 85; Drftng I & Engrng Grphcs Achvt Awd 85; Med.

HARNLY, ANN MARIE; Fairport HS; Fairport, NY; (Y); French Clb; Intnl Clb; Latin Clb; Stu Cncl; Cheerleading; Hon Roll; Cum Laude Natl Latin Exam 85; Hnrb Mntn CLAWNY Exam 86; Frgn Lang.

HARONER, HEIDI; Lyndonville Central HS; Lyndonville, NY; (S); 1/65; Trs Computer Clb; School Musical; School Play; Var Socr; Bausch & Lomb Sci Awd; Pres NHS; Ntl Merit Ltr; Val; Church Yth Grp; ACS Chem Test Fnlst 85.

HAROW, JAY SCOTT; Brentwood Ross HS; Brentwood, NY; (Y); 29/500; Aud/Vis; Boy Scts; Radio Clb; Temple Yth Grp; Stage Crew; Nwsp Rptr; Cit Awd; Hon Roll; NHS; Prfct Atten Awd; Eagle Scout 84; Medal Creatv Wrtng Eng 83-84; Calman Lasky Mem Awd 84; Ithaca Coll; Radio.

HARP, KIMBERLY; Cicero-N Syracuse HS; Clay, NY; (S); Am Leg Boys St; Ski Clb; Color Guard; Hon Roll; NHS; NY Regnts Schlrshp; Presdntl Acad Ftnss Awd; SUNY; Arch.

HARPER, HOLLY; Prospect Heights HS; Brooklyn, NY; (S); 6/300; Dance Clb; Model UN; Hon Roll; Prospect Hts Sci Awd 85; Regnts Schlrshp 86; Med.

HARPER, JAMES; Westfield Central HS; Westfield, NY; (Y); 4/60; Am Leg Boys St; SADD; Yrbk Sprt Ed; Var L Bsbl; Var L Bsktbl; Var L Ftbl; Var L Golf; High Hon Roll; Hon Roll; NHS; Bus Mgmt.

HARPER, MAGGIE; Grace Dodge V HS; Bronx, NY; (Y); Dance Clb; FTA; Library Aide; Mathletes; Office Aide; Teachers Aide; Chorus; Nwsp Stf; Trk; Btty Crckr Awd; Sec Stud Hnrs Awd 83; Atten Awd 85; Fiorello H La Guardia CC; Sec.

HARPER, PATTI; Rome Free Acad; Rome, NY; (Y); 87/450; GAA; Sec Trs Ski Clb; Varsity Clb; Yrbk Sprt Ed; Rep Stu Cncl; Capt Crs Cntry; Trk; Jr NHS; Ntl Merit Ltr; Alfred ST Coll; Sectrl Sci.

HARPER II, ROBERT W; Norwood-Norfolk Central HS; Norwood, NY; (Y); Am Leg Boys St; Church Yth Grp; Pres 4-H; VP Latin Clb; Sec Frsh Cls; Var Trk; Cit Awd; 4-H Awd; High Hon Roll; NHS; JR Ldrshp Awd 85; Cptl Days Awd Trp 85; Phrmcy.

HARRAGAN, SUSIE; School Of The Holy Child; Pelham, NY; (Y); Service Clb; School Play; Yrbk Stf; Rep Frsh Cls; Rep Jr Cls; Rep Stu Cncl; Crs Cntry; Fld Hcky; Hon Roll; Cmnty Wkr.

HARRALSON, NANCY B; Sauquoit Valley HS; Sauquoit, NY; (S); 13/104; Church Yth Grp; Service Clb; Chorus; Yrbk Phtg; Sec Trs Frsh Cls; Sec Soph Cls; Rep Sr Cls; Rep Sec Stu Cncl; JV Fld Hcky; Hon Roll; Syracuse U.

HARREN, PAUL; Bakyport-Blue Point HS; Bayport, NY; (Y); 2/220; Am Leg Boys St; Key Clb; Library Aide; Scholastic Bowl; Science Clb; SADD; Crs Cntry; Trk; Bausch & Lomb Sci Awd; Mech Engrng.

HARRIAN, TODD; Bradford Central Schl; Bradford, NY; (S); 4/32; FBLA; Nwsp Stf; Bsktbl; Hon Roll; Rep NHS; SS Awd 84.

HARRIC HARAN, GREGORY; St Agnes HS; New York, NY; (Y); Variety Show; Bsbl; Im Bsktbl; High Hon Roll; Hon Roll; Acad Excllnc Jr Achvt Prjct Bus 84-3; Achvt In Effort-Hstry Mdl 81-83; Track Mdls 83; Marines.

HARRIGAN, ANN MARIE J; Rensselaer Middle HS; Rensselaer, NY; (Y); 13/90; Cmnty Wkr; DECA; Hosp Aide; Key Clb; Yrbk Stf; Var JV Score Keeper; Hon Roll; Coll Of St Rose.

HARRIGAN, DAVID; Elmira Free Acad; Holiday, FL; (Y); Church Yth Grp; Letterman Clb; Spanish Clb; Varsity Clb; Variety Show; Rep Frsh Cls; Rep Soph Cls; Rep Jr Cls; Rep Sr Cls; Rep Stu Cncl; US Army Res Natl Schlr Ath Awd 86; All Lg Ftbl 86; Yth Cnty 85; U S FL; Bus Adm.

HARRIGAN, KATHLEEN; Northern Adirondack Central HS; Chateaugay, NY; (Y); 4-H; French Clb; Yrbk Stf; Rep Stu Cncl; JV Cheerleading; Comp Sci.

HARRIGAN, MARY; St John The Baptist DHS; Deer Pk, NY; (Y); SADD; Rep Frsh Cls; Rep Soph Cls; Rep Jr Cls; JV Cheerleading; Var Diving; Var Gym; Trk; Hon Roll.

HARRIGER, SHELLEY; Dundee HS; Dundee, NY; (Y); 5/88; Letterman Clb; Lib Band; Trs Chorus; Jazz Band; Var L Bsktbl; L Var Socr; Var L Trk; Var L Vllybl; High Hon Roll; Pres NHS; Ntl Eng Merit Awd 86.

HARRIMAN, AMY; Scotia-Glenville HS; Scotia, NY; (Y); Church Yth Grp; Key Clb; Office Aide; Ski Clb; Hon Roll; JV Cheerleading; JV Trk; Pol Sci.

HARRIMAN, JAMES; Northern Adirondack Central Schl; Churubusco, NY; (Y); Chess Clb; Band; Jazz Band; Mrchg Band; Yrbk Phtg; Yrbk Sprt Ed; Yrbk Stf; Bsktbl; Score Keeper; Socr; RIT; Phtgrphy.

HARRING, SUSAN; Fayetteville Manlius HS; Manlius, NY; (Y); JCL; SADD; Im Bsktbl; JV Var Sftbl; Vet Med.

HARRINGTON, BRIAN; Copiague HS; Lindenhurst, NY; (Y); JV Bsbl; Var Lcrss; Mst Imprvd Ply Lacrosse 86; Plyd Ice Hocky Police Athltc Leag 3 Yrs; Wrks Print Shop Smmr; St Johns U; Accntng.

HARRINGTON JR, BRUCE E; Robert St JR SR HS; Canastota, NY; (Y); 12/150; Am Leg Boys St; Pres FBLA; Pres Leo Clb; Pres Science Clb; Ftbl; Trk; Wrstlng; Intnl Clb; Nwsp Phtg; Nwsp Rptr; Rgnts Schlrshp 86; Cert Of Mert Ctznshp Awd 86; FBLA 86; St John Fisher Coll; Bus Admin.

HARRINGTON, CHRISTOP J; MSGR Farrell HS; Staten Island, NY; (Y); Im Bsktbl; Var Trk; St Schlr; NYCPD Holy Name Schlrshp, NYCPD Emerald Scty Schlrshp 82; St John U; Law.

HARRINGTON, CONSTANCE; Fillmore Central HS; Fillmore, NY; (Y); Cmnty Wkr; SADD; Chorus; Stu Cncl; Var Socr; Var Sftbl; Var Trk; Var Vllybl; High Hon Roll; Hon Roll; Olean Bus Inst; Sec.

HARRINGTON, ERIK F; Newfane SR HS; Appleton, NY; (S); 6/158; Var Bsbl; Var Bsktbl; Hon Roll; NHS; Comp Prgmng.

HARRINGTON, MAUREEN; West Genesee SR HS; Syracuse, NY; (Y); Cmnty Wkr; Key Clb; Ski Clb; Color Guard; Mrchg Band; Rep Jr Cls; Rep Stu Cncl; Im Sftbl; JV Vllybl; Hon Roll; Intl Bus.

HARRINGTON, MELISSA; Akron Central HS; Akron, NY; (Y); 19/140; Church Yth Grp; Drama Clb; Chorus; Church Choir; School Musical; School Play; Swing Chorus; Variety Show; Lit Mag; Buffalo ST Coll; Engl Educ.

HARRINGTON, MICHELE; Amsterdam HS; Amsterdam, NY; (Y); 26/326; Concert Band; Mrchg Band; Var Cheerleading; Hon Roll; NHS; Physcl Thrpy.

HARRINGTON, SCOTT; Naples Central Schl; Naples, NY; (Y); 3/63; Bowling; Var JV Socr; Var JV Vllybl; High Hon Roll; Med Doc.

HARRINGTON, THOMAS; North Babylon SR HS; No Babylon, NY; (Y); Church Yth Grp; Computer Clb; DECA; Political Wkr; Golf; Bus.

HARRIS, BENEDICTE; Paul V Moore HS; Constantia, NY; (Y); Church Yth Grp; GAA; Hosp Aide; Ski Clb; Yrbk Phtg; Stu Cncl; Golf; Score Keeper; Socr; Trk; Comm.

HARRIS, CAROLYN; Scotia-Glenville HS; Scotia, NY; (Y); 4/250; AFS; Church Yth Grp; German Clb; Key Clb; SADD; Chorus; High Hon Roll; NHS; Ntl Merit Ltr; Pres Schlr; Wellesley.

HARRIS, CHRIS T; E Aurora HS; E Aurora, NY; (Y); 16/186; Boys Clb Am; Boy Scts; Yrbk Stf; Pres Frsh Cls; Pres Soph Cls; Bsbl; Ftbl; High Hon Roll; Hon Roll; NHS; Ithaca Coll; Accntng.

HARRIS, CHRISTINE; Academy Of St Joseph; Brightwaters, NY; (Y); Art Clb; Hosp Aide; Pep Clb; Science Clb; Church Choir; JV Capt Bsktbl; Var Socr; Trk; Sistr Mary Hnr Schlrshp 83-86; Mst Imprvd Plyr JV Bsktbl 86; Acctg.

HARRIS, DONYALE K; Notre Dame Schl; New York, NY; (Y); 1/49; Model UN; Science Clb; Yrbk Phtg; Tennis; High Hon Roll; VP NHS; Prfct Atten Awd; Regents Nrsng Schlrshp 86; Georgetown U; Bio.

HARRIS, ELLEN; Irondequoit HS; Rochester, NY; (Y); 55/360; Ski Clb; Pres Varsity Clb; Var L Bsktbl; Var L Socr; Var Capt Trk; Mgr Vllybl; Hon Roll; NHS; Ntl Merit Ltr; Mgr(s); Regents Scholar 86; Maynard Hall Awd 86; U NH; Engrng.

HARRIS, HOLLY; Greenwich Central HS; Greenwich, NY; (Y); 28/86; Pres 4-H; FFA; Trs Service Clb; School Play; Bowling; Var JV Score Keeper; High Hon Roll; Adrndck Coll; Bus.

HARRIS, JOY; Highland HS; Highland, NY; (Y); 15/120; French Clb; Trs Yrbk Stf; L Var Tennis; Var Trk; French Hon Soc; High Hon Roll; NHS; Pres Schlr; Hghst Acadmc Achvt-Rgnts Engl 85; Hghst Acadmc Achvt 4th Yr Frnch 86; Rgnts Schlrshp 86; ST U Of NY Buffalo; Hotl Mgmt.

HARRIS, KATHLEEN M; St Marys HS; Manhasset, NY; (Y); 40/171; Hosp Aide; Library Aide; Chorus; School Musical; School Play; Stage Crew; Hon Roll; NHS; Extnsv Hrs Vlntr Wrk Awd 83; Rgnts Schlrshp 86; Providena Coll; Bus Admin.

HARRIS, KATRINA; Penn Yan Acad; Penn Yan, NY; (S); 7/174; Pres Sec 4-H; Intnl Clb; Ski Clb; Sec Band; Concert Band; Jazz Band; Mrchg Band; 4-H Awd; High Hon Roll; NHS; 4-H Yr Awd 85; Ithaca Coll; Human Sci.

HARRIS, KENERSON; Tonawanda HS; Tonawanda, NY; (Y); 8/220; Sec French Clb; Band; Trs Jazz Band; Mrchg Band; Pep Band; School Musical; Var Capt Socr; Hon Roll; NHS; Pres Awd; Buffalo ST U.

HARRIS, KIMBERLY A; Salamanca Central HS; Little Valley, NY; (Y); 13/135; Drama Clb; 4-H; French Clb; Red Cross Aide; Speech Tm; Mrchg Band; Swmmng; Trk; NHS; NYS Rgnts Schlrshp 86; Walter/Beatrice J Beigel Schlrshp 86; Unfd Stu Asst Prg Fll Tuiutn Schlrshp 86; Jamestown CC; Nrnsg.

HARRIS, KIMBERLY L; Ward Melville HS; Stony Brook, NY; (Y); 165/725; Camera Clb; Pres Church Yth Grp; Nwsp Phtg; Yrbk Phtg; Mgr Cheerleading; Fld Hcky; Trk; High Hon Roll; Hon Roll; Jr NHS; Gettysburg Coll; Lbrl Arts.

HARRIS, LATRELL; Edison Techical Occupational Schl; Rochester, NY; (Y); Church Yth Grp; Church Choir; Rep Frsh Cls; Rep Soph Cls; Rep Jr Cls; JV Bsktbl; Hon Roll; Comp Sci.

HARRIS, LAURA; Ward Melville HS; Stony Brook, NY; (Y); Hosp Aide; Spanish Clb; Teachers Aide; Chorus; Nwsp Stf; Yrbk Stf; Hon Roll; Soph Awds 84; U Of RI; French Tchr.

HARRIS, LESLIE; Midwood HS; Brooklyn, NY; (Y); Church Yth Grp; Library Aide; SADD; Concert Band; School Musical; Stage Crew; Var Crs Cntry; Var Trk; Martin Luther King Essy Wrtng Cntst 86; Fash Coord.

HARRIS, MARK; Fayetteville-Manlius HS; Fayetteville, NY; (Y); Camera Clb; Cmnty Wkr; Math Clb; Nwsp Stf; Lit Mag; Var L Swmmng; High Hon Roll; Hon Roll; NHS; Natl Sci Olympd Chem Distnctn 85-86; Achvt Photo-Bst Stu 85-86; Schlrshp-Israel 84-85; 2nd Slide Yr 84.

HARRIS, MARLA; Hempstead HS; Hempstead, NY; (S); Drama Clb; Chorus; Variety Show; Pres Jr Cls; Cheerleading; Sftbl; Psych.

HARRIS, MELISSA; Dundee Central Schl; Dundee, NY; (Y); Sec French Clb; Sec Hst FHA; Girl Scts; Sec Spanish Clb; Teachers Aide; Chorus; Stage Crew; Yrbk Stf; Hon Roll.

HARRIS, MICHELE; Mount Vernon HS; Mt Vernon, NY; (Y); Church Yth Grp; Cmnty Wkr; Intnl Clb; Chorus; Rep Sr Cls; Rep Stu Cncl; JV Lcrss; Computer Clb; 4-H; Am Leg Aux Girls St; Acadmc Hnr-Grace Baptist Chrch 86; Hnr-Chance To Stdy Abroad-Africa 86; Deans Forum 84-86; Wellesley Coll; Cmnctns.

HARRIS, O P; Lyndonville Central HS; Lyndonville, NY; (Y); 7/80; AFS; Computer Clb; Math Clb; Math Tm; Science Clb; Spanish Clb; JV Var Socr; Var Capt Trk; Hon Roll; NHS; MVP & All Star Trck 86; Engrng.

HARRIS, PATRICE R; Bitburg HS; Apo Ny, NY; (Y); Sec Church Yth Grp; Girl Scts; Sec Chorus; Church Choir; School Musical; Variety Show; Bsktbl; Powder Puff Ftbl; Hon Roll; Prfct Atten Awd; Outstndng Choir Stu Trphy 86; U TX Austin; Music.

HARRIS, RAVONDA; Bushwick HS; Brooklyn, NY; (S); 1/233; Hosp Aide; JA; JCL; Office Aide; Teachers Aide; Y-Teens; Chorus; School Musical; School Play; Yrbk Stf; Bio.

HARRIS, REXFORD M; Mayville Central Schl; Mayville, NY; (S); 4/42; Spanish Clb; High Hon Roll; Hon Roll; Jr NHS; NHS; Var L Bsbl; Var Bsktbl; Var L Ftbl; Engrng.

HARRIS, SAMANTHIA; Bay Shore HS; Bayshore, NY; (Y); 107/400; Church Yth Grp; Dance Clb; Teachers Aide; Bsktbl; Mgr(s); Hon Roll; Engl Awd 85; Chem Outstndng Stu Awd 86; Socl Sci.

HARRIS, SANDRA F; Waterville Central Schl; Sangerfield, NY; (Y); GAA; VICA; Chorus; Stage Crew; Yrbk Stf; Bsktbl; Trk; Cmmrcl Art-Advrtsng.

HARRIS, SHARON N; A Philip Randolph Campus HS; New York, NY; (Y); 69/166; Cmnty Wkr; Yrbk Stf; Rep Frsh Cls; Ntl Merit SF; Prfct Atten Awd; Prefect Atten Awd 82; Macy Med Prof Pgm Hnr Soc 82-86; Beth Israel Schl Nrsng; RN.

HARRIS, SONJA L; Lackawanna SR HS; Lackawanna, NY; (Y); 81/244; FBLA; Church Choir; Bsktbl; Trk; Vllybl; Hon Roll; Tobis Harter Schlrshp 86; Buffalo ST; Info Systms Mgmt.

HARRIS, TAMI; Newark SR HS; Newark, NY; (Y); Boy Scts; Cmnty Wkr; Office Aide; Teachers Aide; Band; Chorus; Color Guard; Yrbk Stf; Var Mgr(s); Hon Roll; Teen Pgnts Trophy & Cert 85-86; Comm Cert 83-86; Cub Scout Ldr Pins & Cert 84-85; Law Enforcement.

HARRIS, TRACIE; Mt Vernon HS; Mt Vernon, NY; (Y); Church Yth Grp; Cmnty Wkr; Girl Scts; Office Aide; Political Wkr; Science Clb; Ski Clb; Spanish Clb; Chorus; VP Church Choir; Syracuse U; Pre-Med.

HARRIS, TROY; Morris HS; Bronx, NY; (Y); Nwsp Ed-Chief; Nwsp Stf; Cit Awd; Hon Roll; Prfct Atten Awd; Academic All American Schlr Prog 84; Law.

HARRIS JR, WILLIAM R; Chenango Valley JR SR HS; Binghamton, NY; (Y); 20/173; Boy Scts; Concert Band; Mrchg Band; Stage Crew; Vllybl; High Hon Roll; Hon Roll; Jr NHS; NHS; Band; NYSSMA-SOLO Awd-Percssn-Snare Drm 85; U At Buffalo; Engrng.

HARRISON, ALYSSA D; Lawrence HS; Woodmere, NY; (Y); Debate Tm; Drama Clb; Temple Yth Grp; School Play; Nwsp Rptr; Yrbk Stf; Stu Cncl; High Hon Roll; Sec NHS; Lng Isl Math Fair Brnz Mdl 84-85; NY ST Rgnts Schlrshp 86; Rutgers U.

HARRISON, DANIEL A; Niskayuna HS; Schenectady, NY; (Y); Am Leg Boys St; Church Yth Grp; Computer Clb; French Clb; Ed Nwsp Ed-Chief; Nwsp Rptr; Rptr Nwsp Stf; French Hon Soc; NHS; Lawyer.

HARRISON, DAVID; Carmel HS; Stormville, NY; (Y); Nwsp Rptr; Bsbl; Hon Roll; Jrnlsm.

HARRISON, JOHN; Laffayette HS; Buffalo, NY; (Y); Prfct Atten Awd; Sci.

HARRISON, LAURINDA S; Avoca Central HS; Prattsburg, NY; (Y); Pres Church Yth Grp; VP Exploring; Library Aide; Office Aide; Teachers Aide; Chorus; School Play; JV Var Score Keeper; JV Var Socr; Var Trk; Avoca Fire Queen Rnr-Up 85; Englsh Awd 83-84; Csmtlgy.

HARRISON, NATHALIE; Dominican Commerical HS; St Albans, NY; (Y); 47/259; Hosp Aide; Political Wkr; Chorus; Hon Roll; Ftns Awd 85; Stoney Brook; Med.

HARRNACKER, MICHAEL; Mynderse Academy SR HS; Seneca Falls, NY; (S); Cmnty Wkr; 4-H; Band; Chorus; Concert Band; Jazz Band; Mrchg Band; Pep Band; School Musical; School Play; Engnrng.

HARRON, CHRISTINE; St John The Baptist Diocesan HS; Deer Park, NY; (S); 6/512; Concert Band; Mrchg Band; High Hon Roll; Jr NHS; Spanish NHS; Modern Music Masters Hnr Scty 84-86; Elem Educ.

HARRSCH, CYNTHIA; Clyde-Savannah HS; Clyde, NY; (Y); 1/75; Sec Jr Cls; Sec Sr Cls; Bausch & Lomb Sci Awd; Elks Awd; High Hon Roll; Lion Awd; Masonic Awd; NHS; Ntl Merit Ltr; Pres Schlr; NY ST Schlrshp Of Excell 86; Rotary Clb Schlstc Achvmnt Awd 86; Parma Richmnd Tatle Engl Awd; SUNY Binghamton; Acctng.

HART, DOUGLAS; Victor Central HS; Victor, NY; (Y); 60/235; JV Var Bsktbl; Var L Ftbl; Golf; Hon Roll; Clss Offcr 85; Clss VP 87; Boys Ldrs Pres 87; St Bonneventure; Scl Stds.

HART, LAURA; Ossining HS; Ossining, NY; (Y); Church Yth Grp; Rep Sr Cls; Var L Bsktbl; Var JV Sftbl; High Hon Roll; Hon Roll; All Dvsn In Sftbl 86; Bus Stu Of Mnth 86; Jr Prm Queen Awd 86.

HART, LAURA J; Huntington HS; Huntington, NY; (Y); 13/385; SADD; Nwsp Bus Mgr; Ed Nwsp Rptr; Yrbk Stf; Lit Mag; Socr; High Hon Roll; NHS; VFW Awd; Rgnts Schlrshp Wnnr 85-86; Bryn Mawr Coll.

HART, LUCINDA; Watkins Glen HS; Beaver Dams, NY; (Y); Church Yth Grp; 4-H; Church Choir; Concert Band; Mrchg Band; Yrbk Stf; 4-H Awd; United Wesleyan Coll; Engl.

HART, RACHAEL; Scotia-Glenville HS; Scotia, NY; (Y); Church Choir; Var Crs Cntry; Var Mgr(s); Var Trk; High Hon Roll; Hon Roll; English.

HART, RAYMOND L; Peekskill HS; Peekskill, NY; (Y); 26/146; Am Leg Boys St; Band; Jazz Band; Mrchg Band; VP Rep Stu Cncl; Var L Ftbl; Var L Lcrss; Var L Trk; High Hon Roll; NHS; Roanoke Coll; Comp Sci.

HART, STEPHANIE; Cardinal O Hara HS; North Tonawanda, NY; (S); 6/122; Girl Scts; Spanish Clb; Chorus; Stat Bsbl; Stat Socr; High Hon Roll; Hugh Obrien Yth Ldrshp Smnr 84-85; Slvr Awd-Grl Sctng 85; Cmpus Mnstry-Sec 84-86; Elem Ed.

HART, VICTORIA; H Frank Carey HS; Franklin Square, NY; (Y); 36/276; Art Clb; Dance Clb; Chorus; Yrbk Phtg; Yrbk Stf; Hon Roll; Fash Merch.

HARTE, KATHLEEN; St John The Baptist HS; Lk Grove, NY; (Y); FBLA; Yrbk Stf; Rep Frsh Cls; Sec Soph Cls; Jr Cls; Pres Stu Cncl; Pom Pon; Dance Clb; Girl Scts; Service Clb; Prncpls Awd Stu Bst Exmplf St Jhns Baptst Stu Ldrshp Acadm Sprt Chrstn Vls 85; Bus.

HARTE, KEVIN; Mount St Michael HS; Yonkers, NY; (Y); 33/297; Computer Clb; Crs Cntry; Trk; Hon Roll; Spanish NHS.

HARTEL, ERIC; Woodbridge American HS; Apo, NY; (Y); CAP; L Model UN; NFL; L Yrbk Stf; Rep Soph Cls; Pres Jr Cls; JV Capt Bsktbl; Var L Ftbl; Var L Socr; Trs NHS; Most Imprvd Bsktbl 85; Pol Sci.

HARTEL, PAUL; Frontier Central HS; Blasdell, NY; (Y); German Clb; Hosp Aide; Math Clb; Band; Concert Band; Jazz Band; Mrchg Band; School Musical; Crs Cntry; Hon Roll; Psychtry.

HARTELL, MARK; Susan E Wagner HS; Staten Is, NY; (Y); 87/466; Hosp Aide; Office Aide; Red Cross Aide; Boys Clb Am; School Musical; Hon Roll; NHS; Amer Lgn Hsptl Vlnt Ctznshp Awd 86; Drs Hsptl Schrlshp Awd 86; PTA Awd Sci & Mth 86; 1st Pl Sci Fr 84; SUNY Oswego; Med Tech.

HARTENSTINE, PAUL J; Hunter College HS; Flushing, NY; (Y); Chess Clb; German Clb; Math Clb; Math Tm; Model UN; Ski Clb; Im Wrstlng; Mu Alp Tht; Ntl Merit Ltr; Rgnts Schlrshp 86; Dartmouth Coll; Comp Sci.

HARTIG, ZANDY; The Spenche Schl; New York, NY; (Y); Drama Clb; French Clb; School Play; Swing Chorus; Nwsp Rptr; Yrbk Rptr; Lit Mag; Hon Roll; Ntl Merit Ltr; Englsh Depts Anthlgy Of Wrtng 85; Actress.

HARTIGAN, MAUREEN ANNE; Fairport HS; Fairport, NY; (Y); Church Yth Grp; Cmnty Wkr; 4-H; School Play; JV L Trk; 4-H Awd; Hon Roll; Spanish NHS; JV Ltr & Pin For Trck & Fld 85; Hnr Rll Avg 90 All Yr 86; Dntstry.

HARTL, JENNIFER; Clarence Central HS; Clarence Center, NY; (Y); Cmnty Wkr; Drama Clb; SADD; School Musical; School Play; Stage Crew; Nwsp Ed-Chief; Socr; Hon Roll; Grwth & Dedication 84-85; Pblcty Crew Chrprsn 85-86.

HARTLEB, CHRISTOPHER F; Saunders Trade & Technical HS; Bronxville, NY; (Y); 4/204; Boy Scts; Church Yth Grp; VICA; Lit Mag; Mgr Sftbl; Trk; High Hon Roll; NHS; Prfct Atten Awd; Sprntndnts Acdmc Awd 82-86; Ciba-Geigy Sci Awd 86; Rensselaer Plytech Inst; Biomed.

HARTMAN, CHRIS; Vernon Verona Sherrill Central HS; Verona, NY; (Y); Church Yth Grp; Cmnty Wkr; Spanish Clb; Church Choir; High Hon Roll; Hon Roll; Bio Med Engrng.

HARTMAN, EVELYN M VIVI; Roy C Ketcham HS; N Hamburg, NY; (Y); 54/500; Aud/Vis; Computer Clb; Chorus; Stage Crew; High Hon Roll; NHS; RIT Alumni Schlrshp 86; RIT; Comp Anmtn.

HARTMAN, JACQUELINE V; Sachem HS; Lake Grove, NY; (Y); 125/1600; Cmnty Wkr; Girl Scts; Ski Clb; Spanish Clb; Chorus; NHS; York Coll PA; Pdtrcn.

HARTMANN, AMY MARIE; Buffalo Acad Of The Sacred Heart; Buffalo, NY; (Y); 2/140; Pres Church Yth Grp; German Clb; Hosp Aide; Red Cross Aide; Rep Jr Cls; Stat Bowling; High Hon Roll; NHS; Prfct Atten Awd; Natl Ldrshp & Svc Awd 86; ST U NY Buffalo; Phrmcy.

HARTMANN, HEIDI; Sachem HS North; Farmingville, NY; (Y); Art Clb; Church Yth Grp; Dance Clb; French Clb; Girl Scts; Jr NHS; Slvr Ldrshp Awd Grl Scts 85.

HARTMANN, LORI C; Brockport HS; Brockport, NY; (Y); 20/335; Church Yth Grp; Exploring; French Clb; Ski Clb; Im Badmtn; Im Vllybl; High Hon Roll; Hon Roll; Rgnts Schlrshp 86; Effrt Cmndtn 86; U Of Buffalo; Chem.

HARTMANN, WINIFRED; Bellport HS; Bellport, NY; (Y); 106/395; French Clb; Sec Girl Scts; Spanish Clb; Church Choir; High Hon Roll; Hon Roll; Prfct Atten Awd; Sctng Awd 85-86; Frnch Achvt Awd 83-84; Art Awd 83; Frnch Ed.

HARTMARK, LAURA; Guilderland Central HS; Schenectady, NY; (Y); Debate Tm; English Clb; Orch; School Musical; School Play; Lit Mag; Crs Cntry; 2nd Pl Poem Lit Mag 86; Simons Rock Bard Coll Scholar 86; Simons Rock Bard Coll; Crtv Wrt.

HARTNEY, LYNN; Salem Central Schl; Salem, NY; (Y); 14/62; Aud/Vis; Church Yth Grp; Cmnty Wkr; GAA; Teachers Aide; Yrbk Stf; Var Capt Bsktbl; Var L Crs Cntry; Mgr(s); Var L Trk; Amer HS Ath Awd 85-86; Le Moyne Coll; Bio.

HARTREY, JOHN; Carmel HS; Carmel, NY; (Y); Bsbl; JV Bsktbl; JV Var Ftbl; High Hon Roll; Hon Roll; Bus.

HARTS, MELISSA L; St Francis Prep; Hollis, NY; (S); 100/653; Library Aide; Church Choir; Drm & Bgl; Nwsp Rptr; NHS; Opt Clb Awd; Ms Amer Coed ST Fnlst 86; Ms Teen-Ag Amer Semi-Fnlst 85; Fordham U; Cmnctns.

HARTUNG, CHRISTOPHER; Fayetteville-Manlius HS; Manlius, NY; (Y); 28/335; Church Yth Grp; Pres Debate Tm; Model UN; NFL; Political Wkr; Pres Speech Tm; Im Bsktbl; High Hon Roll; Trs NHS; Ntl Merit Ltr; Cornell U; Bus Mgt.

HARTZ, ROBERT P; Wilson Central Schl; Wilson, NY; (Y); 3/111; VP Band; School Musical; VP Stu Cncl; Var Capt Bsbl; Var Capt Bsktbl; Var Capt Ftbl; High Hon Roll; NHS; Spanish Clb; Chorus; Sci Fair Wnnr; Regents Scholar; U Rochester; Engrng.

HARTZEL, GREG; Sayville HS; Sayville, NY; (Y); Pres Church Yth Grp; Key Clb; Band; Jazz Band; Mrchg Band; Var Tennis; Timer; High Hon Roll; Hon Roll; Trs NHS; Engr.

HARTZELL, CYNTHIA; Guilderland Central HS; Albany, NY; (Y); Aud/Vis; Cmnty Wkr; Church Choir; Stage Crew; JV Trk; High Hon Roll; Hon Roll; Church Yth Grp; Girl Scts; Variety Show; Achvt Excllnc Amer Hstry 86; NYSSMA Vcl Adtn Lvl 5 86; Ltr & Pin Schl Chr 86; Aerospc Engr.

HARVEY, ANDREA; Kendall JR SR HS; Kendall, NY; (S); Church Yth Grp; Drama Clb; Band; Chorus; Concert Band; Mrchg Band; Sec Soph Cls; Sec Jr Cls; NHS; Stat Wrstlng; Orleans Cnty Yth Rcgntn Awd 84.

HARVEY, AUDREY; Erasmus Hall HS; Brooklyn, NY; (Y); Church Yth Grp; FBLA; Math Clb; NY Regents Schlrshp 86; Syracuse U; Comp Sci.

HARVEY, BECKIE; Bishop Grimes HS; Clay, NY; (S); Rep Stu Cncl; Var Bsktbl; Var Capt Socr; Var Sftbl; High Hon Roll; 1st Tm All Cntry Soccr 84-85; Ntl Ldrshp Merit Awd 86.

HARVEY, JENNIFER; Tioga Centeral HS; Owego, NY; (Y); Church Yth Grp; Dance Clb; 4-H; FBLA; Girl Scts; Teachers Aide; VICA; Band; Chorus; Drm & Bgl; IBM; Sec.

HARVEY, JOY; De Witt Clinton HS; Bronx, NY; (Y); Church Yth Grp; Drama Clb; Chorus; Church Choir; School Musical; School Play; Variety Show; Yrbk Ed-Chief; Yrbk Stf; Sftbl; Ldrshp; Scl Wrk.

HARVEY, RICH; Williamsville South HS; Williamsville, NY; (Y); Im Bsbl; Var L Ftbl; Wt Lftg; High Hon Roll; Hon Roll; Engrng.

HARWELL, LETITIA; Hutchinson-Central Technical HS; Buffalo, NY; (Y); Natl Beta Clb; Rep Jr Cls; Rep Stu Cncl; Mgr(s); Trk; Hon Roll; Awd For Black Enrchmnt Soc 86; Modlng Clb 85-86; Hon Rl Awd 84-86; Syracuse U; Comp Sci.

HARWOOD, LISA; Olean HS; Olean, NY; (Y); 64/206; Science Clb; Ski Clb; Orch; Yrbk Stf; JV Var Cheerleading; Var Stat Sftbl; Hon Roll; Syracuse U; Cmnctns.

HASAN, CINDY; Lafayette HS; Buffalo, NY; (Y).

HASBROUCK, WENDY; Hutchinson Central Tech HS; Buffalo, NY; (S); Church Yth Grp; Natl Beta Clb; SADD; Rep Stu Cncl; Var Capt Cheerleading; Cit Awd; Hon Roll; 2dn Rnr-Up Mst Sprtd Chrldr Awd NY ST Cmptn 85-86; U Of Buffalo; Media.

HASELEY, DARYL; Niagara Wheatfield SR HS; Sanborn, NY; (Y); Bowling; Cit Awd; High Hon Roll; Hon Roll; NHS; Civil Engrng.

HASELEY, LAURIE A; Niagara Wheatfield HS; Sanborn, NY; (Y); 12/291; Hosp Aide; Pep Clb; Sec PAVAS; Chorus; School Musical; Var Tennis; JV Trk; High Hon Roll; Lion Awd; NHS; Judge Gamble Schlrshp 86; Geneseo; Phy Thrpy.

HASELHOFF, OTTO L; St Francis Prep HS; Fresh Meadows, NY; (S); 87/653; JV Im Tennis; Opt Clb Awd; AATG Ermn Awd; Tutrng Prgrm, Cresthaven Dbls Trny Wnnr; Bus Mgt.

HASENFELT, KAREN; Royalton-Hartland Central HS; Middleport, NY; (Y); Trs Church Yth Grp; Latin Clb; Teachers Aide; Yrbk Phtg; JV Fld Hcky; Jr NHS; Nrsng.

HASKINS, TERRI; Midlakes HS; Phelps, NY; (Y); French Clb; Pres FHA; Pep Clb; Varsity Clb; Yrbk Rptr; Yrbk Sprt Ed; Yrbk Stf; Var Capt Cheerleading; Var Pom Pon; Var Powder Puff Ftbl; Mst Imprvd Bsktbl Chrldr 86; FHA Dist Pres 86; U Of FL; Rl Est.

HASLER, KAREN; York Central Schl; Leicester, NY; (Y); AFS; Sec Pres Boy Scts; 4-H; Library Aide; 4-H Awd; High Hon Roll; Hon Roll; NHS; Med.

HASPETT, PATTI; Tonawanda JR-SR HS; Tonawanda, NY; (Y); Teachers Aide; Jazz Band; School Musical; Sec Frsh Cls; Sec Soph Cls; Rep Stu Cncl; JV Var Cheerleading; High Hon Roll; NEDT Awd; Mrchg Band; Outstndng Achvt Art Awd 84; Mth & Engl Tutor 84-85; Art.

HASSAN, SAMAR; Evander Childs HS; Bronx, NY; (S); 15/383; Office Aide; Teachers Aide; Concert Band; Bsbl; Bsktbl; Ftbl; Sftbl; Vllybl; Hon Roll; Cert Merits Excel Engl, Soc Stds, Arts, Music, Gym, Tpyewrtng, Alg 84-85; American U Cairo; Comm.

HASSETT, KATHLEEN; Churchvill-Chili HS; Rochester, NY; (Y); Latin Clb; Ski Clb; Chorus; School Musical; School Play; Lit Mag; High Hon Roll; NHS; Ntl Merit Ltr; Church Yth Grp; Pres Awd Acad Ftns 86; NY ST Regents Schlrshp 86; Ntl Latin Exm Cum Laude 83; Wooster Coll.

HASSON, HELEN M; St Joseph Hill Acad; Staten Island, NY; (Y); 34/107; Drama Clb; FTA; Library Aide; Chorus; School Play; Yrbk Stf; Im Vllybl; NY ST Regents Schlrshp 86; Fordham U.

HASTEE, LORI; Oakfield-Alabama HS; Alabama, NY; (Y); 11/90; Hosp Aide; Ski Clb; Band; Concert Band; Drm Mjr(t); Mrchg Band; Sec Stu Cncl; JV Var Cheerleading; JV Socr; Hon Roll; B J Mancuso Mem Awd Outstndng Achvt Nrsng Asst 86; Merit Tuition Schlrshp Genesee CC 86-88; Nrsng Sci.

HASTINGS, BETH; Solvay HS; Solvay, NY; (Y); Art Clb; Church Yth Grp; Chorus; School Musical; Off Jr Cls; Stu Cncl; Cheerleading; Btty Crckr Awd; High Hon Roll; Awd In Comp Engl 86; Awd In Soc Studies 86; Syracuse U; Law.

HASTINGS, JONATHAN; Sandy Creek Central HS; Sandy Creek, NY; (S); French Clb; Chorus; Rep Frsh Cls; Pres Soph Cls; Var JV Bsbl; Var JV Bsktbl; Hon Roll; NHS; Brdcstng.

HASTINGS, KELLY; Vernon-Verona-Sherrill HS; Vernon Ctr, NY; (Y); Pres Sec Church Yth Grp; Cmnty Wkr; Chorus; Church Choir; Yrbk Stf; High Hon Roll; Hon Roll; NHS; Phys Thrpy.

HASTINGS, MICHELLE M; Lewiston & Porter SR HS; Youngstown, NY; (Y); 12/236; Pres Church Yth Grp; Drama Clb; Pres Girl Scts; School Musical; School Play; Sec Stu Cncl; Mgr(s); Capt Var Swmmng; High Hon Roll; Jr NHS; Drama Awd 84; Acadmc Pin 84; Lamp Of Lrng Math And Spnsh 85; Clarkson U; Engrng.

HASTINGS, SUSANNE; Our Lady Of Mercy HS; Honeoye Falls, NY; (Y); Dance Clb; Fld Hcky; Gym; Socr; Tennis; Vllybl; Wt Lftg; Acctng.

HATCH, BOB; Tioga SR HS; Barton, NY; (Y); 17/72; Computer Clb; Ski Clb; SADD; School Play; Stage Crew; Variety Show; Var L Ftbl; Var L Trk; Wt Lftg; Prfct Atten Awd; Engrng.

HATCH, DAWN; Gowanda Central HS; S Dayton, NY; (Y); Chess Clb; French Clb; Spanish Clb; Chorus; High Hon Roll; Hon Roll; Steno.

HATCH, KAREN J; Chatham HS; Canaan, NY; (Y); 7/126; Church Yth Grp; 4-H; Girl Scts; Cit Awd; 4-H Awd; High Hon Roll; Masonic Awd; NHS; 2d ST Art, Awd Hghst Aver 86; Art Awds 82-86; Berkshire CC; Elem Ed.

HATCHER, CHRIS L; La Guardia HS Of Music & Art; Queens Village, NY; JA; Chorus; School Musical; Vllybl; Hon Roll; Jr NHS; Prfct Atten Awd; Natl Arista Hnr Scty 83-84; Hartt Schl Music; Vcl Music.

HATCHER, RICHARD; Uniondale HS; Hempstead, NY; (Y); Art Clb; Camera Clb; Library Aide; Office Aide; Spanish Clb; Varsity Clb; Church Choir; Yrbk Stf; VP Frsh Cls; VP Stu Cncl; Crmnl Jstc.

HATEM, SHARON; Lackawanna HS; Lackawanna, NY; (Y); Cmnty Wkr; GAA; Sec Ski Clb; Sec Spanish Clb; Band; Concert Band; Mrchg Band; Stat Sftbl; Hon Roll; NHS; U Buffalo.

HATHAWAY, ANDREW; Franklin Acad; St Regis Falls, NY; (Y); Band; Chorus; Swing Chorus; VP Frsh Cls; Var Swmmng; Aerosp Engrng.

HATHAWAY, BRYAN; Seton Catholic Central HS; Little Meadows, PA; (S); 17/167; Boy Scts; Bsbl; Wrstlng; Hon Roll; NSMA; Phys Ther.

HATHAWAY, LEE; Royalton-Hartland Central HS; Gasport, NY; (Y); 6/124; High Hon Roll; Hon Roll; Chem/Elec Engrng.

HATLEE, MATTHEW; Tioga Central Schl; Owego, NY; (S); 24/80; Pres Jr Cls; Stu Cncl; Var L Ftbl; Var L Wrstlng; Ag.

HATT, GREGORY A; East Rochester HS; East Rochester, NY; (Y); Am Leg Boys St; Aud/Vis; Camera Clb; FCA; Latin Clb; Varsity Clb; Stage Crew; Jr Cls; Bsktbl; Trk; MO ST U; Aviatn Tech.

HATTEMER, THERESA; Bellport SR HS; E Patchogue, NY; (Y); 10/395; Jazz Band; Symp Band; Rep Soph Cls; Var Socr; Var Capt Sftbl; High Hon Roll; NHS; Ntl Merit Ltr; Band; Mrchg Band; All Cty Band 85; All League,All Conf Sftbl 85-86; Brkhaven Lab Smmr Pgm Altrnte 84; U VA; Engr.

HAUBER, J ELIZABETH; Honeoye Falls-Lima HS; Lima, NY; (S); 9/160; Trs Church Yth Grp; Trs Model UN; Yrbk Stf; Sec Stu Cncl; Var Swmmng; DAR Awd; High Hon Roll; NHS; Mechanical Drawing Awd 83; Arch Dsgn Awd 85; Arch.

HAUCK, ANGELA; Union-Endicott HS; Endicott, NY; (Y); Key Clb; SADD; Hon Roll; NHS; Salute To Yth 86; Rochester Inst Of Tech; Engrng.

HAUCK, JUNE MARIE; H Frank Cavey HS; Garden City S, NY; (Y); 3/228; Hosp Aide; Concert Band; Yrbk Bus Mgr; Sec Soph Cls; Sec Jr Cls; High Hon Roll; Sec Jr NHS; Sec NHS; Pres Schlr; Varsity Clb; Frgn Lang Hnr Society; SUNY; Med.

HAUG, ANDREA; The Waldorf Schl; Oceanside, NY; (Y); Drama Clb; School Musical; School Play; Yrbk Ed-Chief; Jr NHS; Ntl Merit Ltr; NYS Rgnts Schlrshp 86; Colgate U; Eng.

HAUG, SHERI; Nardin Acad; Buffalo, NY; (Y); 26/83; Church Yth Grp; Office Aide; Ski Clb; Spanish Clb; School Musical; School Play; Stage Crew; Lit Mag; Var Trk; Hon Roll; Spnsh Awd; Interntl Studies.

HAUGHNEY, TRICIA; Catholic Central HS; Troy, NY; (Y); Church Yth Grp; French Clb; Math Clb; Pep Clb; Church Choir; School Musical; Stage Crew; Variety Show; Lit Mag; Hon Roll; Pedtctn.

HAUGHTON, JUDITH; John Dewey HS; Brooklyn, NY; (Y); Church Yth Grp; JA; PAVAS; Teachers Aide; Band; Chorus; Church Choir; School Musical; Stage Crew; Variety Show; Dance Awd 86; Cncrt Choir Prfrmnce Awd 86; Gospl Chorus Prfrmnc Awd 86; Long Island U; Music.

HAUGLAND, GORDON; Tottenville HS; Staten Island, NY; (Y); 31/871; Debate Tm; Science Clb; Ski Clb; Speech Tm; School Musical; Yrbk Phtg; Crs Cntry; Capt Swmmng; High Hon Roll; NHS; Lehigh U; Med.

HAUK, WILLIAM; Wallkill SR HS; Newburgh, NY; (S); 3/191; Church Yth Grp; Band; Concert Band; Jazz Band; Im Bsktbl; Var Capt Socr; Var Trk; High Hon Roll; NHS; Instrmntl-Music Awd 84 & 85; SUNY Binghamton; Engrng.

HAUMAN, GLENN; Earl L Vandermeulen HS; Pt Jefferson, NY; (Y); Chess Clb; Mathletes; SADD; Thesps; Acpl Chr; Chorus; School Musical; School Play; Nwsp Ed-Chief; Ed Yrbk Phtg; Acad Tm Capt 85-86; Cmmnctns.

HAUNSS, KAREN A; St Francis Prep; Flushing, NY; (S); 5/653; German Clb; Hosp Aide; Library Aide; Im Tennis; Im Vllybl; High Hon Roll; NHS; Ntl Merit Ltr; Pres Schlr; George Washington U Engrng & Appld Sci Mdl 85; Govrs Commt Schltc Achvt Citation 86; Med Doctor.

HAUPT, DEBORAH; Riverhead HS; S Jamesport, NY; (Y); Cmnty Wkr; Hosp Aide; JCL; Latin Clb; Ski Clb; VICA; Ftbl; Score Keeper; Vllybl; Prfct Atten Awd; RN.

HAUPT, JENNIFER; Guilderland HS; Albany, NY; (Y); CAP; Varsity Clb; Var Capt Trk; Hon Roll; Meteorology.

HAURY, MADALYN; Paul V Moore HS; W Monroe, NY; (Y); 10/220; AFS; Math Tm; Chorus; Church Choir; Stu Cncl; Gym; High Hon Roll; NHS; Rotary Awd; Pres Acad Fit Awd 86; Empire ST Scholar Excllnce 86; Regents Scholar 86; Le Moyne Coll; Secndry Ed Tchr.

HAUSER, DONNA; St Dominics HS; Oyster Bay Cove, NY; (S); Quiz Bowl; SADD; Nwsp Rptr; Trs Soph Cls; High Hon Roll; NHS; NEDT Awd; Acad All Amer & Natl Ldrshp & Svc Awd; Cert Of Achvt Engl, Math & Soc Stud; Cert Of Achvt Fr, Chem; Bus.

HAUSER, PAM; Frontier Central HS; Hamburg, NY; (Y); Pres 4-H; Latin Clb; Varsity Clb; Yrbk Stf; Gym; Mgr(s); JV Socr; Tennis; Trk; Hon Roll; ACCTNG.

HAUSLADEN, MICHAEL; West Irondequoit HS; Rochester, NY; (Y); 44/351; Church Yth Grp; Orch; School Musical; Swmmng; Hon Roll; NHS; Co-Chrmn Diocesan Yth Cmmssn 85-86; Diocesan Pastrl Cncl 85-86; JR Engrng Tech Soc Test 85-86; Elec Engrng.

HAUSMAN, SETH A; Plainedge HS; North Massapequa, NY; (Y); 10/304; Cmnty Wkr; Mathletes; Red Cross Aide; Temple Yth Grp; School Play; Rep Sr Cls; Var Capt Crs Cntry; Var Capt Trk; High Hon Roll; NHS; HPM Schlrshp 86; Rgnts Schlrshp 86; Sci Fair Awd 84; Cornell U; Bio.

HAUSNER, SONYA; Scotia-Glenville HS; Scotia, NY; (Y); 16/250; Key Clb; Ski Clb; Teachers Aide; Band; Mrchg Band; Var Capt Swmmng; High Hon Roll; NHS; Pres Schlr; Rea Hwrd & St Jsphs Schl Prnts Clb Awds 86; Butler U.

HAUTER, ANTER; John Dewey HS; Brooklyn, NY; (Y); Off Soph Cls; Off Jr Cls; Off Sr Cls; Bsbl; Ftbl; Gym; Score Keeper; Socr; Vllybl; Wt Lftg.

HAUTMANN, KEN; Hampton Bays HS; Hampton Bays, NY; (Y); Aud/Vis; Church Yth Grp; Band; Concert Band; Jazz Band; Mrchg Band; Bryant Coll; Bus Adm.

HAUVER, SCOTT E; Skaneateles HS; Skaneateles, NY; (Y); Am Leg Boys St; Boy Scts; Church Yth Grp; Band; JV Var Bsbl; JV Var Bsktbl; Var JV Ftbl; Im Vllybl; Im Wt Lftg; Hon Roll; Communctns.

HAVASY, CHARLES K; Burnt Hills-Ballston Lake HS; Scotia, NY; (Y); 5/325; Am Leg Boys St; Boy Scts; Pres Key Clb; Rep Soph Cls; Rep Jr Cls; Var L Crs Cntry; JV Trk; High Hon Roll; NHS; Bio & Chem Stu Yr 85 & 86; 1st Pl Div Comp Pgmmng Cont 86; RPI; Elec Engrng.

HAVENS, MARTHA; Pulaski Acad; Pulaski, NY; (Y); Drama Clb; French Clb; GAA; Ski Clb; SADD; Chorus; Church Choir; School Musical; School Play; Var JV Cheerleading; Tourism.

HAVERLY, JON; Schoharie Central Schl; Schoharie, NY; (S); Nwsp Phtg; Yrbk Phtg; Yrbk Stf; Hon Roll; Prfct Atten Awd; Schls No 1 Clb For Mnth.

HAVRANEK, RICHARD; Cazenovia HS; Cazenovia, NY; (Y); 19/160; AFS; Church Yth Grp; Mathletes; SADD; Sec Rep Jr Cls; Trs Sr Cls; Rep Stu Cncl; Capt L Wrstlng; NHS; Ntl Merit Ltr; Spnt Time In Mexpico With Amigos De Los Americas Doing Publc Hlth Wrk 86; Yale; Pre Law.

HAWK, JAMES D; Haverling Central HS; Bath, NY; (S); 5/140; French Clb; Math Clb; Ski Clb; Band; Rep Jr Cls; Var L Golf; Var L Socr; High Hon Roll; NHS; 5th Pl Alfred U Wm Varrick Nevins Math Cmptn 85.

HAWK, KATHY; Weedsport Central Schl; Pt Byron, NY; (Y); French Clb; Math Clb; Spanish Clb; Var Bsktbl; Var Fld Hcky; Var Sftbl; NHS; Prfct Atten Awd; Church Yth Grp; Leo Pinckney Schlrshp 86; Warrior Booster Clb Schlrshp 86; Herkimer County CC; Rsrc Mgmt.

HAWKINS, EUGENE A; St Francis Prep; Springfield Grdns, NY; (S); Church Yth Grp; Rep Stu Cncl; Im Bsktbl; JV Crs Cntry; Im Var Ftbl; JV Var Trk; Wt Lftg; Air Force Acad; Aerntcl Engr.

HAWKINS, JENIFER; Minisink Valley HS; Middletown, NY; (Y); 52/250; FBLA; Nwsp Stf; Cert Of Merit 86; Orange County CC; Psych.

HAWKINS, JENNIFER; Amsterdam HS; Amsterdam, NY; (Y); FBLA; Girl Scts; Hosp Aide; JA; Bio.

HAWKINS, KATHLEEN M; Shoreham-Wading River HS; Wading River, NY; (Y); Church Yth Grp; Cmnty Wkr; Mathletes; Yrbk Sprt Ed; Yrbk Stf; Rep Soph Cls; Var Fld Hcky; Var Sftbl; High Hon Roll; NHS; Athlt-Schlr Zone Awd 85-86; All-Cnty Fld Hcky 84-85; Fld Hcky MVP 84; Duke U; Bio.

HAWKINS, KIMBERLY; Albion SR HS; Albion, NY; (S); 14/181; Girl Scts; Latin Clb; Band; Chorus; Jazz Band; Mrchg Band; VP Frsh Cls; VP Soph Cls; VP Jr Cls; Rep Stu Cncl; Amer Red Cross Yth 85-86; Georgetown U; Bus Adm.

HAWKINS, MIRANDA; Sacred Heart HS; Mt Vernon, NY; (Y); Church Yth Grp; Trk; High Hon Roll; :Dntstry.

HAWKINS, RODNEY; Samuel J Tilden HS; Brooklyn, NY; (Y); Art Clb; Computer Clb; Var Ftbl; Var Trk; NY U; Comp Anlyst.

HAWKINS, SHEILA J; Owego Free Acad; Apalachin, NY; (Y); 3/221; Sec German Clb; Mrchg Band; Orch; JV Socr; High Hon Roll; NHS; Ntl Merit SF; Rgnts Schlrshp 86; ST U Buffalo NY; Chem Engnrng.

HAWKINS, VOLANDA; Springfield Gardens HS; W Mifflin, PA; (Y); 4/300; Drama Clb; School Play; Nwsp Stf; Cheerleading; High Hon Roll; Jr NHS; 1st Pl Essay Cntst/Mntl Rtrdtn 83; Trphy & Cert For Acdmc Achvt In Schl 86; Jrnlsm.

HAWKINS, WILLIAM; West Babylon HS; Babylon, NY; (Y); 40/439; Boy Scts; Church Yth Grp; Computer Clb; Drama Clb; Leo Clb; Red Cross Aide; Varsity Clb; School Play; Var Crs Cntry; Var Golf; Egl Sct BSA 87; Pre-Med.

HAWLEY, VALERIE; Hancock Central HS; Equinunk, PA; (Y); Pep Clb; Spanish Clb; Chorus; JV Sftbl; Hon Roll; Excllnc Attndc 83-86.

HAWTHORNE, ADRIENNE; Uniondale HS; Hempstead, NY; (Y); Pres Girl Scts; Acpl Chr; Band; Chorus; Orch; Pep Band; School Musical; Cheerleading; Vllybl; Hon Roll; Trphy Hempstead NAACP Apprctn Awd 86; Top 10 Miss HUB Beauty Pgnt Miss Cngnlty 85; Cornell; Msc.

HAWTHORNE, MICHAEL J; Harrisville Central HS; Harrisville, NY; (Y); 2/52; Chess Clb; Computer Clb; Concert Band; Mrchg Band; Orch; Var L Bsbl; Var L Bsktbl; High Hon Roll; NHS; Sal; NY ST Regnts Schlrshp 86; NAC Div III Bsktbl All Nrthrn 86; Sectn X All Acadmc Sqd 86; Clarkson U; Elec Engrng.

HAWTHORNE, STACEY E; Columbia HS; Castleton, NY; (Y); Cmnty Wkr; Key Clb; Library Aide; Office Aide; Swmmng; Trk; Hon Roll; Rgnts Schlrshp Awd 85-86; Siena; Accntng.

HAY, BRUCE; F D Roosevelt HS; Hyde Park, NY; (Y); 6/336; Am Leg Boys St; Drama Clb; Mathletes; ROTC; Boy Scts; Concert Band; Jazz Band; Mrchg Band; School Musical; Stage Crew; Hgh Obrn Ldrshp Fndtn; Union Coll; Engrng.

HAYE, CHRISTIAN J; Jericho HS; Jericho, NY; (Y); Drama Clb; Mathletes; Chorus; School Play; Nwsp Stf; Lit Mag; Off Stu Cncl; Ftbl; Swmmng.

HAYES, DIANE; Hudson Falls HS; Hudson Falls, NY; (Y); 5/210; 4-H; Key Clb; SADD; Yrbk Stf; Rep Soph Cls; Rep Sr Cls; Var Tennis; JV Trk; Hon Roll; NHS; Med Engr.

HAYES, DORINDA; Grover Cleveland HS; Buffalo, NY; (Y); Red Cross Aide; Spanish Clb; Rep Stu Cncl; Crs Cntry; Trk; Hon Roll; NHS; Reneassler Ply Tech Awd 86; Wrld Rgns Awd Hghst Exam Mrk 84; Spnsh Awd Hnrs 83-86; CPA.

HAYES, ERIC S; Homer SR HS; Homer, NY; (Y); German Clb; Ski Clb; Pres Varsity Clb; School Play; Rep Stu Cncl; Var Capt Crs Cntry; Var Trk; High Hon Roll; Hon Roll; NHS; NYS Rgnts Schlrshp 8; Hobart Coll Schlrshp 86; Hobart Coll; Engrng.

HAYES, JAMIE; John Jay HS; S Salem, NY; (Y); Band; Chorus; School Musical; Variety Show; JV Var Fld Hcky; JV Var Lcrss; High Hon Roll; NHS; Ntl Merit Ltr; Drama Clb; Excllnc Sci Awd 86.

HAYES, JANE; Sacred Heart HS; Yonkers, NY; (Y); 34/210; Yrbk Bus Mgr; Sec Stu Cncl; Var Capt Cheerleading; Model UN; Yrbk Stf; Rep Jr Cls; Var Sftbl; Cit Awd; Hon Roll; U Of CT; Acctng.

HAYES, JENNIFER; Jamesville Dewitt HS; Jamesville, NY; (Y); 87/243; Church Yth Grp; Key Clb; Math Tm; JV Bsktbl; JV Trk; High Hon Roll; Hon Roll; Gold Key Award Art 86; Honorable Mention Award Art 83-84,86; Lemoyne Coll; Educ.

HAYES, JOHN; Mahopac HS; Mahopac, NY; (Y); 3/141; AFS; Exploring; Science Clb; Nwsp Stf; Trk; Wrstlng; Hugh O Brien Yth Fndtn Ldrshp Smnr 85; Peer Ldrshp Grp 86.

HAYES, KAREN; Hamburg SR HS; Hamburg, NY; (Y); 8/360; AFS; 4-H; Service Clb; Spanish Clb; Mrchg Band; Symp Band; Var Socr; JV Tennis; 4-H Awd; Hon Roll; Wellesley Book Awd; Bio.

HAYES, KIMBERLY; St Edmund HS; Brooklyn, NY; (S); 2/187; Girl Scts; Science Clb; Spanish Clb; Nwsp Ed-Chief; Yrbk Stf; Rep Stu Cncl; High Hon Roll; NHS; Schlrshp St Edmund 83; Ntl Eng Merrit Awd 84; Princpls List; Fordham U; Lib Arts.

HAYES, LAURA; Jasper Central HS; Cameron, NY; (Y); 1/25; Drama Clb; Chorus; Yrbk Ed-Chief; Var Capt Bsktbl; Var Capt Socr; Var Capt Trk; DAR Awd; Pres NHS; St Schlr; Val; Houghtin Coll; Bio.

HAYES, LISA A; Beaver River Central Schl; Croghan, NY; (Y); French Clb; GAA; SADD; Teachers Aide; Chorus; School Musical; Variety Show; JV Var Cheerleading; Hon Roll; Rgnts Schlrshp 86; Jefferson CC; Elem Ed.

HAYES, MARC; Herman-Dekalb HS; Richville, NY; (Y); 5/45; Nwsp Ed-Chief; Stu Cncl; Var Capt Bsbl; Var Capt Bsktbl; Var Capt Socr; NHS; Rgnts Schlrshp 86; TDS Esy Awd 85; Syracuse U; Cmnctns.

HAYES, MICHAEL G; Our Lady Of Lourdes HS; Poughkeepsie, NY; (Y); 19/180; Chess Clb; Church Yth Grp; Cmnty Wkr; Varsity Clb; Nwsp Rptr; JV Bsktbl; JV Var Ftbl; Golf; Hon Roll; Jr NHS; Parish CYO Teen Clb Pres & VP 84-86; Dutchess Cnty RYO Pres 85-86; Archdiocese Of NY CYO Pres 86; Iona Coll; Accntng.

HAYES, PAULA; Hutchinson Central Technical HS; Buffalo, NY; (Y); Pres Church Yth Grp; Varsity Clb; Pres Church Choir; Trs Drill Tm; Rep Jr Cls; Stat Bsktbl; Im Trk; Mech Engr.

HAYES, POLLY; Union Endicott HS; Endicott, NY; (Y); Am Leg Aux Girls St; Key Clb; Nwsp Ed-Chief; Yrbk Sprt Ed; VP Frsh Cls; Gym; Var Tennis; Capt Var Trk; High Hon Roll; NHS; Eng.

HAYLE, BRIAN W; Mont Pleasant HS; Schenectady, NY; (Y); 29/206; Ski Clb; Concert Band; Mrchg Band; Orch; Yrbk Stf; French Hon Soc; Hon Roll; NHS; Aud/Vis; Key Clb; Cthlc U Of Amer; Law.

HAYMES, JENNIFER; Alfred-Almond Central Schl; Almond, NY; (Y); 1/68; GAA; JCL; Spanish Clb; Chorus; Yrbk Stf; Var L Tennis; High Hon Roll; NHS; Pltcl Sci.

HAYNAM, RICHARD; Liverpool HS; Liverpool, NY; (Y); 15/884; JA; Math Tm; Chorus; Stage Crew; High Hon Roll; NHS; Computer Clb; Exploring; Jr NHS; Cornell U Smmr Coll 86; Scty Myflwr Dcndnts Awd 86; Cmptr Sci.

HAYNER, TARA; Sharon Springs Central HS; Cherry Valley, NY; (S); 5/24; Ski Clb; Varsity Clb; Band; Chorus; Drm Mjr(t); School Musical; Yrbk Stf; Stu Cncl; Var Cheerleading; Var Capt Socr; Soccer All-Star Tm 83-85; Soccer MVP 84; Elem Educ.

HAYNES, ALLISON; Mt Vernon HS; Mt Vernon, NY; (Y); Church Yth Grp; FBLA; Hosp Aide; Key Clb; Latin Clb; Math Tm; Science Clb; Nwsp Stf; Yrbk Stf; Lit Mag; Medcn.

HAYNES, CATHERINE T; Tottenville HS; Staten Island, NY; (Y); 74/864; Ski Clb; Band; Concert Band; Drm Mjr(t); Mrchg Band; School Musical; School Play; Stage Crew; Symp Band; NHS; U MA; Bus Adm.

HAYNES, CATHLEEN M; Westhill SR HS; Syracuse, NY; (Y); 2/145; Spanish Clb; Concert Band; Jazz Band; JV Var Vllybl; Hon Roll; NHS; NEDT Awd; Spanish NHS; NY St Rgnts Schlrshp 86; U Of Notre Dame.

HAYNES, ROBERT; Union Endicott HS; Endicott, NY; (Y); Boys Clb Am; Varsity Clb; Rep Stu Cncl; JV Bowling; Var L Trk; Hon Roll; NHS; Med Doc.

HAYNES, SONJA; Hillcrest HS; Cambria Hgts, NY; (Y); Church Yth Grp; Chorus; Rep Frsh Cls; Var Cheerleading; Hon Roll; Jr NHS; Prfct Atten Awd; Howard U; Accntng.

HAYNESWORTH, ELAINE; John Dewey HS; Brooklyn, NY; (Y); Art Clb; Camera Clb; Computer Clb; English Clb; FHA; Service Clb; Spanish Clb; Nwsp Stf; Lit Mag; Im Badmtn; Fshn Illust Cert Of Excllnc 86; Fshn Dsgn Cert Of Excllnc 86; Fshn Dsgn Cert Of Achvt 86; Phil Coll Of Txtles; Bus Admin.

HAYS, DAVID; Fairport HS; Fairport, NY; (Y); Pres Church Yth Grp; Drama Clb; Trs French Clb; Pres Jazz Band; Pres Orch; Sec Stu Cncl; Hon Roll; NHS; Ntl Merit Schol; Pres Schlr; PTA Schlrshp Wnnr 86; Harvard U; Gvrnmnt.

HAYS, ROB; Lansing HS; Ithaca, NY; (Y); 8/80; Spanish Clb; Stage Crew; Var Capt Socr; Var L Trk; High Hon Roll; Ntl Merit Schol; Regns Schlrshp 86; Pres Acadmc Ftnss Awd 86; Hnrbl Mntn Soccr Leag 86; Rochester Inst Tech; Appld Math.

HAYWARD, JAMES C; Le Roy HS; Le Roy, NY; (Y); 9/126; Am Leg Boys St; Computer Clb; French Clb; Math Tm; SADD; Varsity Clb; Var Bsbl; JV Bsktbl; Var Ftbl; Wt Lftg; Coaches Awd Ftbll 85; Rochester Inst Tech; Elec Engr.

HAZARD JR, EDWIN; Gates Chili HS; Rochester, NY; (Y); 36/446; Trs Church Yth Grp; Trs German Clb; Concert Band; Jazz Band; Mrchg Band; JV Var Wrstlng; God Cntry Awd; High Hon Roll; NHS; NE Regnl Royl Ranger Of Yr 82; NYS Ranger Of Yr 82-86; Royl Ranger Gold Mdl Achvt 84; Rochester Inst Tech; Micrelctrn.

HAZEL, SIMONE S; Art & Design HS; New York, NY; (Y); 42/406; Hon Roll; Merit Amer Studs II 85; Exec Intrnshp 85-86; Schl Visual Arts; Advrtsng.

HAZELTON, JANET; Fairport HS; Fairport, NY; (Y); Cmnty Wkr; Drama Clb; SADD; Stage Crew; Yrbk Stf; Hon Roll; Ntl Merit Ltr; 2nd Pl Rtry Essay Cntst 86; Archtctr.

HAZEN, ELLEN K; Hilton Central HS; Hilton, NY; (Y); 3/310; Sec Math Clb; Symp Band; Nwsp Stf; Var Capt Crs Cntry; Var Capt Trk; NHS; Ntl Merit Ltr; Pres Schlr; Computer Clb; Math Tm; NY St Regents Schlrshp 85-86; Cntry Rdrs Club Awd 85-86; Williams Coll; Comp.

HAZLE, ALEATHA; Jefferson JR SR HS; Rochester, NY; (Y); Debate Tm; JA; Office Aide; High Hon Roll; Hon Roll; Prfct Atten Awd; Corp Law.

HAZUCHA, CHRISTOPHER; Nanvet HS; Pearl River, NY; (Y); Cmnty Wkr; Mathletes; Math Clb; Y-Teens; Im JV Bsbl; High Hon Roll; NHS; Rockland Cnty JR Gldn Pins Schlrshp 84.

HEAD, HOLLY; Attica HS; Darien Center, NY; (S); 11/175; AFS; Drama Clb; Chorus; Law.

HEADD, MARK; Corcoran HS; Syracuse, NY; (Y); Computer Clb; Variety Show; Yrbk Stf; Crs Cntry; Golf; Gym; Trk; Computer Sci.

HEADY, LEE ANN; Dover JR SR HS; Dover Plains, NY; (S); 7/75; Church Yth Grp; Yrbk Phtg; Yrbk Stf; Rep Jr Cls; Mgr Cheerleading; JV Fld Hcky; Mgr(s); High Hon Roll; Hon Roll; NHS; Nrsry Schl Tchr.

HEALEY, KATHY; Hicksville HS; Hicksvl, NY; (Y); Drama Clb; FBLA; School Musical; Stage Crew; Hon Roll; Church Yth Grp; Girl Scts; Office Aide; SADD; Teachers Aide; SUNY Oswego; Econmcs.

HEALEY, MARK; Holy Cross HS; Flushing, NY; (S); 167/360; Art Clb; Church Yth Grp; NFL; Pres Speech Tm; School Musical; Lit Mag; Rep Frsh Cls; Var Score Keeper; Im Sftbl; Var Swmmng; Queens Coll; Cmmnctn Arts.

HEALEY, RALPH; St John The Baptist HS; Massapequa, NY; (Y); Computer Clb; Exploring; PAVAS; Ski Clb; Stage Crew; Lit Mag; Wt Lftg; Wrstlng; Hon Roll; HS Merit Cert-Hstry & Sci 85; Knights Of Columbus Corps Delite Awd 85; Poltcl Sci.

HEALY, ANDREW D; Center Moriches HS; Center Moriches, NY; (Y); Boy Scts; Drama Clb; Band; Mrchg Band; School Musical; Yrbk Stf; JV Var Bsbl; Var Crs Cntry; Bausch & Lomb Sci Awd; Hon Roll; US Air Force Acad.

HEALY, JAMES M; Clinton Central HS; Clark Mills, NY; (Y); 6/136; Boy Scts; Yrbk Ed-Chief; Var Capt Crs Cntry; High Hon Roll; Hon Roll; Jr NHS; NHS; Prfct Atten Awd; Bernie Club-Life Mbr 83; Eagle Scout 84; Clarkson U; Elec Engrng.

HEALY, TIMOTHY W; Onteora Cnt HS; West Hurley, NY; (Y); 42/201; Boy Scts; Church Yth Grp; Quiz Bowl; Radio Clb; Hon Roll; Rgnts Schlrshp 86; U Meth Lay Spkr 85-86; Order Of Arrow 82-86; Pre-Med.

HEALY, TOM; Schem North Campus; Farmingville, NY; (Y); 92/1558; Computer Clb; Im Bsbl; JV Var Ftbl; Var L Trk; Im Wt Lftg; High Hon Roll; Hon Roll; Jr NHS; U Of AZ; Accntng.

HEANEY, ARAN S; Belfast Central HS; Belfast, NY; (Y); 3/34; Am Leg Boys St; Boy Scts; Political Wkr; Pres Stu Cncl; Var Bsktbl; Var Golf; Var Socr; High Hon Roll; NHS; Close Up Prtcpnt 86; Union Coll; Pltcl Sci.

HEANEY, ELIZABETH; Anthony A Henninger SR HS; Syracuse, NY; (Y); Var Crs Cntry; Mgr(s); Score Keeper; Var Trk; Hon Roll; Prfct Atten Awd; Exclnce Span, Rgnts Diploma 86; SUNY Buffalo; Phys Ther.

HEANEY, TRACI; Valley Central HS; Walden, NY; (Y); 92/313; Yrbk Stf; Lit Mag; Rep Jr Cls; Rep Stu Cncl; JV Sftbl; JV Vllybl; Bus Admin.

HEAPHY, TIMOTHY; Corcoran HS; Syracuse, NY; (Y); School Musical; Yrbk Sprt Ed; Trs Frsh Cls; Trs Soph Cls; Trs Jr Cls; Var Capt Swmmng; Var Capt Tennis; Hon Roll; Jr NHS; NHS; Supertndnt Cabnt 84-86; Empire ST Games Waterpolo Gld Slvr Brnz 83-86.

HEARD, PETER; Mattituck HS; Mattituck, NY; (Y); 29/117; German Clb; JA; VICA; Variety Show; Yrbk Phtg; Yrbk Stf; Off Frsh Cls; Off Stu Cncl; 50 Dllrs For Achvmnt; Crpntry.

HEARN, JOSEPH; Bishop Ludden HS; Syracuse, NY; (Y); Church Yth Grp; Cmnty Wkr; Political Wkr; Var JV Socr; Var Tennis; Hon Roll; NHS; Ski Clb; SADD; JV Lcrss; Schlrshp Le Moyne Coll 86; Psych.

HEARY, JON; Friendship Central HS; Friendship, NY; (S); 5/25; Model UN; School Play; Stage Crew; Rep Stu Cncl; VP Capt Bsktbl; Var JV Socr; Hon Roll; NHS; Cls Pres 81.

HEASLIP, DEIRDRE; Mahopac HS; Mahopac, NY; (Y); 37/409; Radio Clb; Science Clb; Orch; Nwsp Ed-Chief; Lit Mag; JV Capt Fld Hcky; Socr; High Hon Roll; NHS; Crtv Wrtng.

HEBERER, CATHERINE; Hicksville HS; Hicksville, NY; (Y); Church Yth Grp; Drama Clb; Pep Clb; Thesps; Acpl Chr; Chorus; Church Choir; Drill Tm; Madrigals; School Musical; Adelphi U; Acctg.

HEBERLE, JENNIFER L; Ou Lady Of Mercy HS; Macedon, NY; (Y); 49/145; Church Yth Grp; English Clb; Science Clb; Color Guard; School Play; Stage Crew; Yrbk Bus Mgr; Trk; Varsity Clb; School Musical; NY ST Regent Scholar 86; Merit Roll 83-86; U S Pony Clb Wny Regnl Champ 84; U MA; Equine Rsrch.

HEBERT, KRISTIN; Acad Of The Holy Names; Troy, NY; (Y); VP Drama Clb; Varsity Clb; Ed Yrbk Stf; Ed Lit Mag; VP Frsh Cls; Sec Sr Cls; Ntl Merit Ltr; Var Socr; Engl Awd 85 & 86; St Michaels Coll; Jrnlsm.

HEBERT, LISA; Lansingburgh HS; Troy, NY; (Y); Camp Fr Inc; Chorus; Yrbk Stf; High Hon Roll; Hon Roll; Jr NHS; Prfct Atten Awd; Maynard G Noble Mem Awd 86; Cert Merit 85-86; Plattsburgh; Engl.

HEBERT, NADINE; Lansignburgh HS; Troy, NY; (Y); 20/180; French Clb; VP Frsh Cls; VP Soph Cls; VP Jr Cls; VP Sr Cls; Var Capt Bsktbl; Var Capt Socr; Var Trk; Jr NHS; NHS; Intl Bus.

HEBERT, TERRY; Co'oes HS; Cohoes, NY; (Y); 12/171; Varsity Clb; Nwsp Stf; Trs Sr Cls; Rep Stu Cncl; Var Bowling; JV Var Cheerleading; French Hon Soc; High Hon Roll; NHS; 5th Pl Acctg Tst-HS Day At Cobleskill 85; Siena Coll; Acctg.

HEBERT, TROY; Carthage SR HS; Natural Bridge, NY; (Y); Computer Clb; Pep Clb; Variety Show; Ftbl; Hon Roll; NY St Regents Schlrshp 86; JCC Watertown; Crmnl Justice.

HECHT, GARY; Bellmore-Merrick F Kennedy HS; Merrick, NY; (Y); FBLA; SADD; Temple Yth Grp; Nwsp Rptr; Pres Sr Cls; Pres Stu Cncl; Var JV Socr; VP Yorker Clb; Albany; Law.

HECK, GREGORY E; Bishop Scully HS; Amsterdam, NY; (Y); Drama Clb; Stage Crew; Hon Roll; Hudson Vly CC; Elec Tech.

HECKSTALL, ROBERT; Clara Barton HS; Brooklyn, NY; (Y); Boy Scts; Cmnty Wkr; Computer Clb; Office Aide; Hon Roll; Ntl Merit SF; Podiatry.

HECTOR, PATRICIA J; Hamburg SR HS; Hamburg, NY; (Y); 51/389; Girl Scts; Spanish Clb; NHS; NY ST Rgnts Schlrshp 85-86; SNUY Buffalo; Phrmcy.

HECTOR JR, THEODORE E; Saratoga Central Catholic HS; Schuylerville, NY; (Y); Church Yth Grp; Radio Clb; Ski Clb; Varsity Clb; Chorus; Nwsp Stf; Yrbk Sprt Ed; Im Capt Badmtn; Var L Golf; Capt Im Ice Hcky; Green Mountain; Comm.

HEDDERMAN, MARY KATE; Bishop Maginn HS; Albany, NY; (S); French Clb; Ski Clb; Bsktbl; Sftbl; Tennis; Vllybl; Hon Roll; NHS.

HEDGEMOND, FELICIA; Morris HS; New York, NY; (Y); 5/30; Varsity Clb; Nwsp Rptr; Nwsp Stf; Yrbk Rptr; Yrbk Stf; Rep Soph Cls; Rep Jr Cls; Var Bsktbl; Hon Roll; Prfct Atten Awd; Old Wstbry; Med.

HEDRICK, YVONNE; Cicero-North Syracuse HS; Mattydale, NY; (S); Hon Roll; NHS; Hnbl Mntn & Cert Of Merit Recog MONY Schlstc Art Awds Cntst 85; Achvt Assmbly ST NY 85; Grphc Artst.

HEDSTROM, ARTHUR; Uniondale HS; Hempstead, NY; (Y); Boy Scts; Pres Exploring; Capt Lcrss; Socr; Capt Swmmng; Hon Roll; Cmmrcl Art.

HEEGER, BRIAN; Northport HS; E Northport, NY; (Y); Computer Clb; Ski Clb; School Play; Nwsp Rptr; Yrbk Stf; Hon Roll; Jrnlsm.

HEENEY, BRIAN J; Ward Melville HS; Stony Brook, NY; (Y); 147/725; Church Yth Grp; Ski Clb; Chorus; Nwsp Phtg; Var Trk; High Hon Roll; Hon Roll; St Schlr; U DE; Engrng.

HEERS, KRISTEN; Hornell HS; Hornell, NY; (Y); Pres AFS; Am Leg Aux Girls St; Church Yth Grp; Hosp Aide; JCL; Ski Clb; Pres SADD; Band; Concert Band; Mrchg Band; Amer Abroad Stu AFS Intl 86; 1st Annl Upstate NY Humanities & Sci Symposium 86; Biomed Engrng.

HEERY, STEPHANIE; A G Berner HS; Massapequa Park, NY; (S); 1/450; Exploring; French Clb; Hosp Aide; Key Clb; Red Cross Aide; Nwsp Ed-Chief; Rep Stu Cncl; Hon Roll; NHS; Val; Adelphi U Smr Prgm Schlrshp Awd 85; Natl Hstry Day Excllnc Awd 86; Princeton Bk Awd Semi Fnlst 85 & 86; Law.

HEFFEREN, CAROLYN; Seaford HS; Seaford, NY; (S); 30/251; Computer Clb; Orch; Yrbk Ed-Chief; Yrbk Stf; VP Jr Cls; Pres Sr Cls; Bsktbl; Trk; High Hon Roll; NHS; Yrbk Awd 84-85; Oswego Coll; Acctg.

HEFFERNAN, ANN; Fabius-Pompey HS; Fabius, NY; (Y); 13/65; Cmnty Wkr; Drama Clb; 4-H; Girl Scts; Chorus; Cit Awd; Hon Roll; NHS; Oper Enterprs 86; Syracuse U; Med.

HEFKE, JENNIFER; Bay Shore HS; Bay Shore, NY; (Y); 75/400; Cmnty Wkr; Drama Clb; Sec Band; Sec Concert Band; Jazz Band; Sec Mrchg Band; Orch; School Musical; School Play; Socr; Outstndng Achvt Band,Spnsh 84-86; Cornell U; Vet.

HEFTER, MICHELE; Riverhead HS; Riverhead, NY; (Y); 19/230; JCL; Key Clb; Latin Clb; Pep Clb; Ski Clb; Temple Yth Grp; Yrbk Phtg; Yrbk Stf; JV Var Cheerleading; Im Gym; Cheerng & Ten Var Athltc Awd 83 & 86; Lib Arts.

HEGARTY, MATTHEW; Amsterdam HS; Hagaman, NY; (Y); Ski Clb; Band; Concert Band; Jazz Band; Mrchg Band; Swmmng; Hon Roll; Elec Engrng.

HEGEDUS, PETER; Canisius HS; Buffalo, NY; (Y); 15/200; Pep Clb; Stage Crew; Nwsp Rptr; Var L Socr; JV Trk; High Hon Roll; Schl Radio Sta; Wtr Polo; Dr.

HEGENER, ELLEN; Catholic Central HS; Clifton Pk, NY; (Y); Cmnty Wkr; Drama Clb; German Clb; Hosp Aide; Math Tm; PAVAS; Chorus; Church Choir; School Musical; School Play; Med Tech.

HEGGINS, AMY N; Laguardia H S Of Performing Arts; Jamaica, NY; (Y); Church Yth Grp; Cmnty Wkr; Dance Clb; Hosp Aide; Church Choir; School Play; Cheerleading; Hon Roll; Ntl Merit SF; Jazz Dance Mrt Arts 86; SMU-DALLAS; Dance.

HEGQUIST, SUSAN M; Bishop Kearney HS; Brooklyn, NY; (Y); 10/337; Debate Tm; Girl Scts; Library Aide; Math Tm; NFL; Political Wkr; Speech Tm; Band; High Hon Roll; NHS; Trustee Schlrshp 86; New Rochelle Bk Awd 85; NY U; Comp Sci.

HEGSTROM, KRISTYN L; Liverpool HS; Liverpool, NY; (Y); 80/816; Pres Dance Clb; Debate Tm; German Clb; Pres Sec Girl Scts; NFL; Speech Tm; Color Guard; Drill Tm; Flag Corp; NHS; Degree Of Distnctn Ntl Frnscs Lge 85; Slvr Ldrshp Awd 84; 1st Pl NCFL Qlfrs Debate 86; BYU; Bio.

HEICK, DANIEL L; Bishop Grimes HS; Syracuse, NY; (Y); 51/143; FBLA; Ski Clb; SADD; Stage Crew; Ftbl; Golf; Wt Lftg; High Hon Roll; SUNY Cortland.

HEIDELBERGER, SUZANNE; Garden City SR HS; Garden City, NY; (Y); 103/355; French Clb; German Clb; Key Clb; SADD; Color Guard; School Play; Variety Show; Rep Soph Cls; Rep Jr Cls; Mgr(s); Lng Islnd Rest & Catr Assoc; Rgnts Schlrshp; Slng Awds; Cornell U; Htl Adm.

HEIER, JEFFREY; Mepham HS; N Bellmore, NY; (Y); Temple Yth Grp; Mgr Band; Stu Cncl; Crs Cntry; Trk; Hon Roll; NHS; Cert Of Merit-Nassau Reading Cncl Yng Authors Cont 86.

HEIGLE, NANCY; East Syracuse-Minoa HS; Kirkville, NY; (Y); Church Yth Grp; Drama Clb; Girl Scts; Chorus; School Musical; School Play; Swing Chorus; JV Cheerleading; High Hon Roll; Hon Roll; All Cnty Chrs 83-86; 11 Area-All ST Chrs 85-86; Yth Ambssdr Egypt 86; Acctg.

HEIL, SHELLY ELEANOR; Falconer HS; Jamestown, NY; (Y); 13/127; Am Leg Aux Girls St; Ski Clb; Sec Band; Mrchg Band; School Play; Sec Jr Cls; Sec Stu Cncl; Var Capt Cheerleading; Golf; Var Capt Tennis; MVP W Tnns Tm 86; Wmns Chrstn Assoc Schlrshp 86; Fredonia U; Elem Educ.

HEILMAN, TODD; Pine Bush HS; Middletown, NY; (Y); Acctg.

HEIMERL, SUSAN L; Williamsville East HS; Williamsville, NY; (Y); 58/302; Cmnty Wkr; Drama Clb; French Clb; Girl Scts; JA; Latin Clb; School Musical; High Hon Roll; Hon Roll; Magna Cum Laude Ltn Awd 85; Nwsp Mnthly Carrier Awd 82; Rgnts Schlrshp 86; ST U Of NY-BNGHMTN.

HEIMILLER, DIANA; Kenmore East HS; Kenmore, NY; (Y); Dance Clb; GAA; Speech Tm; Drill Tm; Nwsp Rptr; Yrbk Rptr; Var JV Bsktbl; Var JV Sftbl; Hon Roll; NHS; German Scrapbk Awd 1st Pl NY ST 83; 5 Yr Pin For Attndng Camp 85; Syracuse U; Comm.

HEIN, CAROLYN; St Joseph By-The-Sea HS; Staten Island, NY; (Y); Rep Computer Clb; PAVAS; Spanish Clb; Nwsp Phtg; Nwsp Rptr; Yrbk Phtg; Yrbk Stf; Bowling; Capt Tennis; High Hon Roll; Tnns Chs Awd 84-86; Prft Attndc Grad 83-86; Schlrshp Wagner Coll 86; Wagner Coll; Bus.

HEIN, CHRISTINA K; Rocky Point JR SR HS; Sound Bch, NY; (Y); Aud/Vis; Camera Clb; Church Yth Grp; Band; Mrchg Band; Yrbk Phtg; Fld Hcky; Mgr(s); Vllybl; Ntl Merit Ltr; Schl For Vis Arts; Prof Photo.

HEINEMAN, SUSAN; Hornell HS; Hornell, NY; (Y); AFS; Spanish Clb; Band; Concert Band; Mrchg Band; Symp Band; Cheerleading; Pom Pon; High Hon Roll; NHS; Bus.

HEINEMEIER, SARAH E; Bronx HS Of Science; Bronx, NY; (Y); Church Yth Grp; Cmnty Wkr; Science Clb; Teachers Aide; Orch; High Hon Roll; Regents Schlrshp 86; SUNY Frshmn Schlrshp 86; ST U-Stony Brook; Bio Sci.

HEINEN, TOM; Alfred G Berner HS; Massapequa Park, NY; (Y); Var Bsktbl; Var Bowling; Acctng.

HEININGER, JONATHAN M; Franklin Acad; Constable, NY; (Y); 2/266; Math Tm; Quiz Bowl; Varsity Clb; JV Bsktbl; Var L Trk; Im Vllybl; Bausch & Lomb Sci Awd; High Hon Roll; Hon Roll; NHS; NY ST Rgnts Schlrshp 86; Sci Awd 84; Hghst Avrg In Class 85; CPA.

HEINLEIN, VIRGINIA C; Sayville HS; Sayville, NY; (Y); 40/310; Sec Drama Clb; Service Clb; Chorus; Jazz Band; School Musical; School Play; Capt Var Cheerleading; Hon Roll; Key Clb; SADD; Music Ed Awd 84; Nyssma Comp 78-83; Washington U; Intl Bus.

HEINRICH, SUZANNE A; Scarsdale HS; Scarsdale, NY; (Y); Hosp Aide; SADD; School Musical; Cheerleading; Im Powder Puff Ftbl; Capt Sftbl; Var Swmmng; Hon Roll; All Sctn Sftbl 85; U TV; Pre-Med.

HEINS, HILDEGARD; Huntington HS; Huntington Sta, NY; (Y); Church Yth Grp; German Clb; Band; Church Choir; Concert Band; Drm Mjr(t); Jazz Band; Mrchg Band; Orch; Pep Band; Music Educ.

HEINTZ, ANDREE; Gates Chili HS; Rochester, NY; (S); 6/460; VP German Clb; Math Tm; Service Clb; Concert Band; Mrchg Band; Rep Soph Cls; Rep Jr Cls; High Hon Roll; NHS; Ntl Merit Ltr; Top 9th Grade Stu GPA 83; MST Val Percussion Plyr Mrch Bnd; Rsrch Bio.

HEINTZ, JAMES; Polattsburgh SR HS; Plattsburgh, NY; (Y); 6/161; Cmnty Wkr; Drama Clb; Model UN; Jazz Band; Mrchg Band; Orch; School Musical; Symp Band; High Hon Roll; Ntl Merit Ltr; B Congress/Bundestag Schlrshp Altrnt 85; Acadmc Awd Schlstc Excllnc 85-86; Hnrs Recital NYSSMA; Cornell U; Animal Sci.

HEINTZ, JOB; Skaneateles Central HS; Skaneateles, NY; (Y); 21/153; Church Yth Grp; Var Capt Ice Hcky; Var Capt Lcrss; Var JV Socr; Hon Roll; Jr NHS; NHS; Cmnty Wkr; Variety Show; NY ST Rgnts Schlrshp 86; Vncnt Vnse Ltn Schlr Awd 86; Cntrl NY All Str Hcky Team All Leag 1st Team; U New Hampshire; Engl.

HEINZELMAN, STACY; Minisink Valley HS; Otisville, NY; (Y); 12/243; Cmnty Wkr; Ski Clb; Band; Mrchg Band; Pep Band; Trs Yrbk Stf; High Hon Roll; NHS; Prfct Atten Awd; Mercy Comm Hosp Schlrshp 85-86; Albany ST; Pharm.

HEINZMAN, TODD; Newark SR HS; Newark, NY; (Y); 76/201; German Clb; Band; Concert Band; Variety Show; Lcrss; High Hon Roll; Hon Roll; CC Finger Lakes; Bus Adm.

HEISER, TRAVIS M; Christian Brothers Acad; Fayetteville, NY; (Y); 5/91; Church Choir; Var Ice Hcky; Var L Socr; High Hon Roll; NHS; St Schlr; Hugh O Brian Fndtn; Mst Vlbl Plyr Hockey & Mst Imprvd Plyr Soccer; Hmltn Coll NY; Bus Adm.

HEISER, WESLEY; Pittsford Sutherland HS; Pittsford, NY; (Y); Cmnty Wkr; French Clb; JA; Model UN; Ski Clb; Mrchg Band; Yrbk Stf; JV Socr; High Hon Roll; NHS; Monroe Cty Hnr Carrier Mnth 86; Ldng Tone Awd NY ST Music Tchrs Assoc 85; Cert Hnr 85.

HEISLER, JOHN R; Watertown HS; Watertown, NY; (Y); 4/305; Am Leg Boys St; SADD; Nwsp Sprt Ed; VP Stu Cncl; Im Bsktbl; Im Vllybl; NHS; Band; Voice Dem Awd; Key Bank Cup Awd 86; A Presdntl Clssrm For Yng Amer 85; US Air Force ROTC 4 Yr Schlrshp 86; Penn ST U; Engrng.

HEISS, GERARD; Miller Place HS; Miller Place, NY; (Y); 46/248; Mathletes; Concert Band; Nwsp Stf; Lit Mag; Crs Cntry; Trk; Wt Lftg; Hon Roll; Journ.

HEITKAMP, DONNA; Scotia-Glenville HS; Scotia, NY; (Y); Art Clb; VP French Clb; Library Aide; SADD; Bowling; Sftbl; Swmmng; Tennis; Prfct Atten Awd; Hudson Valley; Cpa.

HEITZHAUS, CAROLE; Mount Mercy Acad; Buffalo, NY; (Y); 69/196; Art Clb; Cmnty Wkr; Hosp Aide; Model UN; Ski Clb; Spanish Clb; Off Soph Cls; Off Jr Cls; Off Sr Cls; Crs Cntry; Art.

HELD, JO ANNE; Polytechnic Prep; Brooklyn, NY; (Y); Hosp Aide; Library Aide; Acpl Chr; Chorus; Church Choir; Nwsp Rptr; Nwsp Stf; Yrbk Rptr; Yrbk Stf; Lit Mag; Outstndng Comm Srv Schl Awd 86; Psych.

HELDMAN, MARY; Holland Patent HS; Rome, NY; (Y); Rep Jr Cls; Rep Sr Cls; Rep Stu Cncl; Var Cheerleading; JV Fld Hcky; Var Trk; Hon Roll; 1st Pl Prtnr 85; Cosmtlgy.

HELDT, NICOLE; Watertown HS; Watertown, NY; (Y); Ski Clb; Varsity Clb; JV Bsktbl; JV Socr; Var Trk; SCI.

HELENBROOK, BRIAN; Grand Island HS; Gr Island, NY; (Y); 3/300; Model UN; Ski Clb; VP Soph Cls; VP Jr Cls; VP Sr Cls; L Socr; L Tennis; NHS; Varsity Clb; High Hon Roll; Outstndng Bio Stu; Rensselaer Medal; Outstndng Math,Sci Stu; Engrng.

HELFAND, DEBRA C; Valley Stream South HS; Valley Stream, NY; (Y); 2/168; Yrbk Phtg; Ed Lit Mag; Var L Bsktbl; Var L Socr; Var L Sftbl; Sec NHS; Ntl Merit Ltr; Sal; Art Clb; Mathletes; NYS Rgnts Schlrshp 85-86; Bio Awd 83; Sccr All Conf-All Lg 84,85 & 86; Cornell U.

HELFERT, MICHELLE A; Nortre Dame Ny; Utica, NY; (Y); 16/158; Cmnty Wkr; French Clb; FBLA; Hosp Aide; School Play; Yrbk Stf; Lit Mag; High Hon Roll; NHS; St Schlr; 1st Pl FBLA Accntng I; 1st Pl FBLA Bus Cmnctns; Fash Inst Of Tech; Fash Dsgn.

HELLDORFER, SUSAN A; Out Lady Of Mercy Acad; Bethpage, NY; (Y); 2/115; Church Yth Grp; Computer Clb; Hosp Aide; Pres Spanish Clb; Chorus; Yrbk Bus Mgr; Yrbk Stf; Var Badmtn; Sftbl; High Hon Roll; Comptv St Johns Schlrshp,Acadmc Exclnc Schlrshp And Regnts Schlrshp 86; St Johns U; Acctg.

HELLEIS, LISA; Longwood HS; Coram, NY; (S); 3/487; Hosp Aide; Key Clb; Office Aide; Q&S; Chorus; Variety Show; Nwsp Stf; Lit Mag; Jr NHS; NHS; Natl Ldrshp-Sci Awd 86; Acadmc Amer Awd 85; Hosptl Svc Awd 84; St Josephs Coll; Chld Stdy.

HELLER, CLIFFORD; Hicksville HS; Hicksville, NY; (Y); Art Clb; German Clb; Ski Clb; Varsity Clb; Jr Cls; Ice Hcky; Lcrss; Socr; High Hon Roll; Hon Roll; NY Inst Of Tech; Archtctr.

HELLER, DENNIS M; Mechanicville HS; Mechanicville, NY; (Y); 14/105; Spanish Clb; Rep Stu Cncl; Var Capt Crs Cntry; Var L Trk; High Hon Roll; Hon Roll; NHS; Regents Schrlshp 86; SUNY Found Schrlshp 86-87; SUNY; Env Sci.

HELLER, MATTHEW; Hauppauge HS; Hauppauge, NY; (Y); 9/498; Symp Band; Nwsp Ed-Chief; Mgr Stat Bsbl; Var Ftbl; Var Wrstlng; Ntl Merit Schol; St Schlr; Varsity Clb; Orch; School Musical; US Army Rsrv Schlr Athl Awd, Sflk Co Gld Key Awd Athltc Prfmnc, WA Crsng Fndtn Smifnlst 86; U Of Virginia; Intrntl Rltns.

HELLERMAN, MARY; Leroy Central HS; Leroy, NY; (Y); AFS; DECA; FTA; Office Aide; Spanish Clb; Drm Mjr(t); Mrchg Band; Pres Frsh Cls; Pres Soph Cls; Stu Cncl; Brockport ST.

HELLGOTH, JOHN; Maripac HS; Carmel, NY; (Y); 21/383; Boy Scts; Church Yth Grp; Computer Clb; Band; Concert Band; Mrchg Band; Orch; Im Bsktbl; High Hon Roll; NHS; Steuben Awd For Grmn Lng 86; Villanova U; Engrng.

HELLRIEGEL, CAROLINE; Academy Of Saint Joseph; Bayshore, NY; (Y); Hosp Aide; Science Clb; Trs Spanish Clb; Yrbk Stf; Var Socr; NHS; Church Yth Grp; Cmnty Wkr; Service Clb; Town Of Islps Awd For Oustndng Achvt & Exc In Sci 86; Gen Exc Awd 86; MIP Vrsty Scr 85; Psych.

HELLRIEGEL, JENNIFER J; The Nichols Schl; Buffalo, NY; (Y); Office Aide; Yrbk Stf; L Bsktbl; Fld Hcky; Trk; Hon Roll; French Exchange Student 86; NY ST Summer School Of The Arts 85; RI Schl Of Dsgn; Painting.

HELM, ELIZABETH; St Peters H S For Girls; Staten Island, NY; (Y); Hosp Aide; Pep Clb; Pres Frsh Cls; Pres Rep Soph Cls; Pres Jr Cls; VP Stu Cncl; Capt Cheerleading; Coach Actv; Pom Pon; Hon Roll; St Johns U.

HELMAN, MAXINE; Smithtown HS; Smithtown, NY; (Y); DECA; Exploring; 4-H; Sec Leo Clb; Science Clb; SADD; Acpl Chr; Chorus; JV Socr; DAR Awd; Orgnztn Of Triangles Beloved Qn Nissequogue Triangle No 137 86-87; Behavioral Sci.

HELMAN, STEVEN; Roslyn HS; East Hills, NY; (Y); 25/250; Science Clb; Temple Yth Grp; Off Soph Cls; Off Soph Cls; Trs Sr Cls; Var Crs Cntry; Var Trk; Trs NHS; Otto P Burgdorf Rsrch Comptn Fnlst 86; NY St Rgnts Schlrp Awd 86; US Stu Cncl Awd 86; Williams Coll; Soc Sci Rsrch.

HELMBOLD, KRISTEN; Avon JR SR HS; Avon, NY; (Y); Sec Church Yth Grp; 4-H; French Clb; Ski Clb; Swing Chorus; Yrbk Stf; Swmmng; Hon Roll; Paul Smiths; Hotel-Motel Mgt.

HELMER, GLEN; Mynderse Acad; Seneca Falls, NY; (Y); Chess Clb; French Clb; High Hon Roll; Accntng.

HELMS, LILLIAN; Livingston Manor Central Schl; Livingston Manor, NY; (S); 4/46; Cmnty Wkr; Dance Clb; Speech Tm; Varsity Clb; Chorus; Variety Show; Nwsp Ed-Chief; Nwsp Rptr; Cheerleading; Capt Crs Cntry; Stu Cncl Achvt Awd 83-86; Bus Mgmt.

HELSTEIN, RICHARD; Commack HS North; E Northport, NY; (Y); 33/366; Spanish Clb; Yrbk Stf; High Hon Roll.

HELVOIGT, HEIDI; Sherburne-Earlville HS; Earlville, NY; (Y); 10/117; Am Leg Aux Girls St; Drama Clb; 4-H; Chorus; Concert Band; Mrchg Band; School Musical; Stage Crew; Hon Roll; NHS; Allegheny Coll; Math.

HEMEDINGER, CHRISTOPHER; St Josephs Collegaite Inst; Williamsville, NY; (Y); 60/193; Pres Church Yth Grp; Cmnty Wkr; Nwsp Stf; Im Tennis; JV Trk; Hon Roll; Comp Sci.

HEMMER, CHRISTOPHER; Monsignor Farrell HS; Staten Island, NY; (Y); Im Bsktbl; Im Ftbl; Psych.

HEMMER, SUEANE; Brockport SR HS; Brockport, NY; (Y); 10/325; Ski Clb; Off Band; Church Choir; School Musical; Swing Chorus; JV Cheerleading; Var Tennis; Var Trk; High Hon Roll; NHS; Monroe Cnty 2nd Pl Dbls Tnns Chmpnshp 85; Math.

HEMMERLY, SANDRA; John Marshall HS; Rochester, NY; (Y); Intnl Clb; Math Tm; High Hon Roll; Hon Roll; NHS.

HENDERSON, ELIZABETH; Tri-Valley HS; Grahamsville, NY; (Y); Rptr SADD; VP Band; Chorus; Jazz Band; Yrbk Ed-Chief; Yrbk Stf; Pres Frsh Cls; VP Soph Cls; Pres Jr Cls; Rep Sec Stu Cncl; SUNY Fredonia; Prof Musician.

HENDERSON, ERIK; Perry Central HS; Perry, NY; (Y); 25/120; Varsity Clb; Band; Mrchg Band; Socr; Trk; Hon Roll; NHS; Spanish NHS; Bus.

HENDERSON, JAMES; St John The Baptist D HS; Ronkonkoma, NY; (Y); Boy Scts; Church Yth Grp; Cmnty Wkr; Var Trk; Hon Roll; Brdcstg.

HENDERSON, JENNIFER M; New Hartford HS; New Hartford, NY; (Y); Cmnty Wkr; Sec Spanish Clb; Teachers Aide; Band; Concert Band; Yrbk Sprt Ed; Var L Fld Hcky; Im Sftbl; Hon Roll; Jr NHS; Stu Recog Awd PASS Pgm 84; Mth.

HENDERSON, MARGARET; Aquinas Inst; Rush, NY; (Y); 20/207; Exploring; Band; Concert Band; Jazz Band; Mrchg Band; High Hon Roll; Hon Roll; Leah Marlowe Scholar 83-85; Fin.

HENDERSON, MATTHEW; John C Birdlebough HS; Phoenix, NY; (Y); 2/194; VP Latin Clb; Concert Band; Jazz Band; Mrchg Band; School Musical; Pres Soph Cls; VP Jr Cls; JV Var Bsbl; JV Ftbl; Pres Trs NHS; Engrng.

HENDERSON, ROBERT T; Liverpool HS; Liverpool, NY; (Y); 80/816; SADD; Nwsp Sprt Ed; Rep Stu Cncl; Var Golf; Var Capt Ice Hcky; JV Lcrss; Hon Roll; Jr NHS; NHS; NY ST Rgnts Schlrshp 86; Carnegie-Mellon U; Elec Engrng.

HENDERSON, ROBIN; Palmyra-Macedon HS; Macedon, NY; (Y); Pres Church Yth Grp; SADD; Varsity Clb; Rep Soph Cls; Rep Jr Cls; Var Capt Cheerleading; Var Score Keeper; Var Sftbl; Im Vllybl; Cit Awd; Maria Coll; Sec Stds.

HENDERSON, SUE; Tully Central Schl; Tully, NY; (Y); 2/69; Church Yth Grp; Drama Clb; French Clb; Hosp Aide; Chorus; School Musical; Elks Awd; High Hon Roll; NHS; Sal; Regents Scholar 86; Meth Conf Scholar 86; Area All ST Chorus 84 & 86; SUNY Potsdam; Comp Sci.

HENDERSON, THOMAS G; Xavier HS; Brooklyn, NY; (Y); 45/250; Church Yth Grp; Computer Clb; Math Clb; ROTC; Teachers Aide; Var Tennis; Gov Hon Prg Awd; Hon Roll; Pres Schlr; Gvnrs Achvt Awd/Mnhtn Schlrshp; Rgnts Schlrshp/Poly Tech Schlrshp; PRATT Schlrshp For Ftr Engrs; Mnhtn Schl Of Engrng; Cvl Engr.

HENDERSON, WINSTON E; Baldwin SR HS; Baldwin, NY; (Y); 12/476; Cmnty Wkr; Chorus; Pres Frsh Cls; Pres Soph Cls; Trk; High Hon Roll; NHS; School Musical; Stage Crew; Hon Roll; Ntl Achvt Schlrshp Outstndng Negro Stu 85; Ntl Lab Excptnl Sci Abilty Awd 85; Hugh O Brien Youth Found; Biomed.

HENDERSON-KILTS, MARILYN; Mexico Acad And Central HS; Parish, NY; (Y); Art Clb; German Clb; Hon Roll; Delta Eipsilon Phi Otstndng Grmn Stu Awd 83; Phtgrpgr.

HENDRICKS, JUANICE; N Babylon SR HS; N Babylon, NY; (Y); Intnl Clb; Spanish Clb; Chorus; Swing Chorus; Nwsp Rptr; Nwsp Stf; Bsktbl; Mgr(s); Communications.

HENDRICKS, MICHELLE; New Berlin Central HS; New Berlin, NY; (Y); 8/66; Trs Church Yth Grp; Dance Clb; French Clb; Girl Scts; Bsktbl; Socr; Sftbl; Prfct Atten Awd; Delhi A&t; Bio-Tech.

HENDRICKS, STEPHANIE L; Maine-Endwell SR HS; Endwell, NY; (Y); 3/230; GAA; Sec Key Clb; SADD; Chorus; Var L Fld Hcky; Var Sftbl; High Hon Roll; NHS; PAVAS; Recog By Natl Cncl Yth Ldrshp 85; Bd Of Ttees Schlrshp-Wilkes Coll 86; PA ST U; Pre-Med.

HENDRIX, ELIZABETH; Gowanda Central HS; Gowanda, NY; (Y); 1/121; Church Yth Grp; Concert Band; School Musical; Stu Cncl; Mgr(s); Capt Vllybl; Bausch & Lomb Sci Awd; NHS; Ntl Merit Ltr; Val; RPI Math & Sci Awd 85; Clemson U; Engrng.

HENEGHAN, ELIZABETH C; Our Lady Of Mercy; Rochester, NY; (Y); Church Yth Grp; Model UN; Science Clb; Ski Clb; Church Choir; Stage Crew; Thesps; Nwsp Sprt Ed; Nwsp Stf; Alumni Scholar 83-85; Aviatn Awareness Essay Cont 3rd Pl 86.

HENKE, CHARLES; Huntington HS; Huntington, NY; (Y); Church Yth Grp; FCA; Key Clb; Varsity Clb; Variety Show; JV Ftbl; JV Capt Lcrss; Var Capt Wrstlng; Hon Roll.

HENKE, KENNY; Eden SR HS; Eden, NY; (Y); Church Yth Grp; SADD; Varsity Clb; Var L Bsbl; Var L Bsktbl; Var L Ftbl; Im Vllybl; Prfct Atten Awd; Sales.

HENKE, SUSAN; Bayport-Blue Point HS; Blue Pt, NY; (Y); Key Clb; Math Tm; Political Wkr; Band; Chorus; Jazz Band; Nwsp Rptr; Yrbk Ed-Chief; Sec Stu Cncl; Jr NHS.

HENKEL, CAROL A; Our Lady Of Mercy HS; Rochester, NY; (Y); 4/172; Exploring; French Clb; Hosp Aide; Chorus; School Musical; Yrbk Rptr; Yrbk Stf; NHS; Ntl Merit Ltr; Allegheny Schlr, Comp Exam Schlrshp 86; Regents Schlrshp 86; Allegheny Coll; Psych.

HENKEL, JOHN; Gorton HS; Yonkers, NY; (Y); Im Mgr Bsbl; Im Mgr Bsktbl; Im Mgr Socr; Im Mgr Sftbl; High Hon Roll; Hon Roll; Econ.

HENLEY, VIRGINIA; Johnstown HS; Johnstown, NY; (Y); 4-H; Hosp Aide; Intnl Clb; Yrbk Stf; Hon Roll; Prfct Atten Awd; Atlantic Union Coll; Bus Adm.

HENLEY, WENDY MARLO; St Anne Inst; Mount Vernon, NY; (Y); English Clb; French Clb; Pep Clb; Nwsp Ed-Chief; Yrbk Rptr; High Hon Roll; Hnr Hgst Typng Speed; Columbia U; Soc Svc.

HENNEBERG, STACY; Attica SR HS; Attica, NY; (Y); Church Yth Grp; Cmnty Wkr; Church Choir; Color Guard; Nwsp Stf; Yrbk Ed-Chief; NHS; Merit Tuition Asstnc Pgm 86; Attica Cntrl Schl Faclty Schlrshp 86; Lions Clb Cmnty Svc Awd 86; Genesee CC; Dental Hygenist.

HENNEDSSEY, SUSAN; Bishop Ludden HS; Syracuse, NY; (Y); Church Yth Grp; French Clb; German Clb; Chorus; Rep Frsh Cls; Rep Jr Cls; Trs Stu Cncl; Var L Bsktbl; Var L Socr; Var L Tennis; Polit Sci.

HENNEL, DEBORAH; Scotia-Glenville HS; Scotia, NY; (Y); Sec French Clb; Hosp Aide; Key Clb; Trs Varsity Clb; Concert Band; Orch; Var L Bsktbl; Var L Socr; High Hon Roll; Pres NHS.

HENNESSEY, SUSAN; Bishop Ludden HS; Syracuse, NY; (S); Church Yth Grp; French Clb; German Clb; Chorus; Rep Frsh Cls; Rep Jr Cls; Var Capt Bsktbl; JV Var Socr; JV Var Sftbl; JV Capt Vllybl; Boston Coll; Frgn Svc.

HENNESSY, ELISABETH; Walt Whitman HS; Melville, NY; (Y); 71/535; SADD; Band; Concert Band; Mrchg Band; School Musical; Variety Show; Yrbk Stf; Var Cheerleading; Socr; High Hon Roll; Fordham U; Lib Arts.

HENNESSY, HELEN; Vernon-Verona-Sherrill Central HS; Vernon, NY; (Y); Spanish Clb; Var Cheerleading; JV Var Fld Hcky; High Hon Roll; Hon Roll; NHS; Bus.

HENNING, CATHLEEN J; Tully Central Schl; Lafayette, NY; (Y); 1/72; Drama Clb; Pres Library Aide; Math Tm; Spanish Clb; SADD; VP Chorus; School Musical; Swing Chorus; NHS; Val; Regnts Schlrshp 86; C W Post Univ Schlr Awd; Long Island U.

HENNING, CHRISTINE; Manhasset HS; Manhasset, NY; (Y); 3/185; VP Church Yth Grp; Co-Capt Trs GAA; Band; Yrbk Bus Mgr; Var Fld Hcky; Var Capt Trk; NHS; Ntl Merit Ltr; Concert Band; Brnz Medal LI Math Fair 85; Supts Sprts Awd 86; MVP Indr Trck 84; Dartmouth; Socl Sci.

HENNING, DAWN; Wayland Central HS; Wayland, NY; (Y); 12/115; Art Clb; Pep Clb; Yrbk Rptr; Rep Jr Cls; JV Var Cheerleading; JV Socr; Hon Roll; Bus Adm.

HENNINGHAM, MICHELLE; Tonawanda SR HS; Tonawanda, NY; (Y); French Clb; Hosp Aide; SADD; Stu Cncl; Trk; Flight Atten.

HENRICE, JAMES; Cardinal Hayes HS; Bronx, NY; (Y); 18/244; Aud/Vis; Church Yth Grp; Exploring; Church Choir; Drm & Bgl; Mrchg Band; Vllybl; High Hon Roll; Prfct Atten Awd; NY Inst Of Tech; Ind Engrng.

HENRICH, MICHELLE; Frontier HS; Hamburg, NY; (Y); French Clb; Varsity Clb; Rep Frsh Cls; Rep Soph Cls; Rep Jr Cls; Rep Stu Cncl; Var Socr; Var Swmmng; Var Trk; JV Vllybl.

HENRICHS, SANDRA; Mineola HS; Mineola, NY; (Y); SADD; Chorus; School Musical; Hon Roll; Barbarettes 84-85; Lunch Bunch 85-86.

HENRIGUEZ, MARY; George Washington HS; New York, NY; (Y); Office Aide; Spanish Clb; High Hon Roll; Hon Roll; Comp Sci.

HENRIQUEZ, MAGDA; Cardinal Spellman HS; Ny, NY; (Y); Computer Clb; Debate Tm; Drama Clb; Spanish Clb; Teachers Aide; Hon Roll; Cornell U; Htl Admin.

HENRY, AMY; Liverpool HS; Liverpool, NY; (Y); 240/882; Red Cross Aide; Thesps; Chorus; Yrbk Phtg; Trs Frsh Cls; Trs Stu Cncl; Swmmng; Trk; Hon Roll; Prfct Atten Awd; Syracuse Art Gld Schlrshp 86; Advtsng Dsgn Hon Awd 86; Mony Schlstc Art Shw 86; Syracuse U; Vsl Advrtsng Dsgn.

HENRY, ANDREW; St John The Baptist HS; Amityville, NY; (Y); Art Clb; Boy Scts; Var Ftbl; JV Wt Lftg; Art Shw Ms Lbrty 10th 86; Howard U; Archtr.

HENRY, CHARLES E; Hunter College HS; New York, NY; (Y); Church Yth Grp; Math Clb; Teachers Aide; Church Choir; Trk; Natl Achvt SF 85; Acctng.

HENRY, JAVA; James Madison HS; New York, NY; (Y); #12 In Class.

HENRY, JENNIFER B; West Seneca West SR HS; Cheektowaga, NY; (Y); 62/559; Art Clb; Key Clb; Spanish Clb; Rep Frsh Cls; Var Fld Hcky; Hon Roll; JC Awd; Jr NHS; NHS; Pres Schlr; Adv Bio Awd 86; Regents Chem Awd 84; Niagara U; Vet.

HENRY, KATHY; Sweet Home HS; Tonawanda, NY; (Y); Hon Roll; U Of Buffalo; Dntst.

HENRY, MELISSA; Liverpool HS; Liverpool, NY; (Y); 179/867; Onondaga CC; Hmnts.

HENRY, MICHAEL; A G Berner HS; Massapequa Park, NY; (Y); 5/375; Band; Concert Band; Jazz Band; Mrchg Band; Orch; Variety Show; Ed Nwsp Stf; JV Crs Cntry; JV Var Trk; Hon Roll.

HENRY, MICHAEL; Grace H Dodge HS; Bronx, NY; (Y); Boys Clb Am; Church Yth Grp; CAP; Cmnty Wkr; FCA; FBLA; FNA; Hosp Aide; JA; Church Choir; Bronx Week 86; Hunter Coll; Nrsng.

HENRY, MICHAEL; Stuttgart American HS; Apo, NY; (Y); Boy Scts; Cmnty Wkr; French Clb; Ski Clb; Hon Roll; U Of S MS; Acctg.

HENRY, MICHELLE; John H Glenn HS; Huntington, NY; (Y); Intnl Clb; Science Clb; Variety Show; Nwsp Rptr; Ed Nwsp Stf; Rep Soph Cls; Secndry Educ.

HENRY, NICOLE A; St Francis Prep Schl; S Ozone Park, NY; (S); 58/746; Dance Clb; Ski Clb; Spanish Clb; Band; Color Guard; Variety Show; Hon Roll; NHS; Karate 7 Trphs; Retreat Ldr; Med.

HENRY, RENEE; Scotia Glenville HS; Amsterdam, NY; (Y); Church Yth Grp; Hosp Aide; Rep Frsh Cls; Rep Soph Cls; Rep Stu Cncl; JV Capt Bsktbl; Im Socr; Var L Sftbl; Hon Roll; NHS; :Scl Work.

HENRY, RENITA; St Pius V HS; Bronx, NY; (Y); Church Yth Grp; Computer Clb; Dance Clb; JA; Math Clb; Office Aide; Pep Clb; SADD; School Play; Cheerleading.

HENRY, ROBERT; Gates-Chili SR HS; Rochester, NY; (Y); Bsktbl; Hon Roll; Urbn League Outstndng Acdmc Awd 86; Northeastern U; Bioengnrng.

HENRY, SHANNON D; Mc Graw Central HS; Mc Graw, NY; (Y); Am Leg Boys St; Ski Clb; Trs Varsity Clb; Pres Concert Band; Pres Jr Cls; Rep Stu Cncl; JV Socr; Cit Awd; Pres Jr NHS; NHS; Syracuse U; Finance.

HENRY, TEDD; Ripley Central HS; Ripley, NY; (Y); Boy Scts; Church Yth Grp; Band; Concert Band; Mrchg Band; Yrbk Bus Mgr; Yrbk Stf; VP Sr Cls; Rep Stu Cncl; Bsbl; Star Scout 84; Mech Tech.

HENRY, TIMOTHY J; Caledonia-Mumford Central Schl; Caledonia, NY; (Y); #11 In Class; Am Leg Boys St; FCA; 4-H; Math Tm; Jazz Band; Rep Stu Cncl; Var L Bsbl; Capt Var Ftbl; NHS; Ntl Merit Ltr; Vet.

HENRY, WAYNE A; Erasmus Hall HS; Brooklyn, NY; (Y); Chess Clb; Church Yth Grp; Cmnty Wkr; Debate Tm; Office Aide; Science Clb; Nwsp Rptr; Nwsp Stf; High Hon Roll; NHS; Physics Clb NY Awd 86; Physcis Awd 2nd Rnkng Physcis Stu 86; Erasmian Staff Awd 86; Oakwood Coll; Med.

HENS, SAMANTHA M; Mc Kinley HS; Amherst, NY; (Y); 4/216; Church Yth Grp; JA; Yrbk Stf; Hon Roll; Pres Acad Fit Awd 85-86; Buffalo Tchrs Fed Awd 85-86; SUNY Buffalo; Chem Engrng.

HENSAL, LEIGH; Lockport SR HS; Lockport, NY; (Y); 57/463; Latin Clb; Var L Bsktbl; Var L Socr; Hon Roll; Jr NHS; Math Tchr.

HENSCHKE, CHARLES; Bushwick HS; Brooklyn, NY; (S); Cmnty Wkr; Library Aide; Office Aide; Teachers Aide; Wt Lftg; Cit Awd; Hon Roll; NHS; Data Proc Awd 85; Econ Awd 85; Fin.

HENSHAW, TAMMY; Campbell Central HS; Campbell, NY; (S); 17/70; French Clb; Band; Chorus; Mrchg Band; School Musical; Swing Chorus; Yrbk Stf; VP Sr Cls; Var Score Keeper; Var Socr; Corning CC; Human Svcs.

HENSON-MC DONALD, BRIAN K; Osterholz American HS; Wasco, CA; (Y); Pep Clb; ROTC; VP Frsh Cls; Rep Stu Cncl; Coach Actv; Capt L Ftbl; L Trk; Wt Lftg; L Wrstlng; CA ST-BAKERFIELD; Hist.

HENST, JENNIFER VANDER; Berne-Knox-Westerlo HS; Berne, NY; (Y); Trs Key Clb; Band; Concert Band; Mrchg Band; Yrbk Ed-Chief; Yrbk Stf; Score Keeper; Hon Roll; NHS; Schl Ltr & Cert Girls Bsktbl Statstcn 85-86; Bus.

HEPPARD, JOHN; Sheepshead Bay HS; Brooklyn, NY; (Y); JV Bsktbl; JV Trk; Hon Roll; Progrs Awd 84; Home Arts Awd 84; Aviation.

HEPPNER, CHRIS; John Jay SR HS; Katonah, NY; (Y); Church Yth Grp; Cmnty Wkr; Debate Tm; SADD; Variety Show; Im Bsktbl; Var Tennis; Var Wrstlng; Cit Awd; Eco.

HERAGHTY, CATHERINE; Marymount Schl Of New York; Bronx, NY; (Y); Mgr Drama Clb; Sec French Clb; Math Clb; Pres Model UN; NFL; Nwsp Rptr; Yrbk Stf; Hon Roll; NHS; Ntl Merit Ltr; Regents Scholar 85-86; NY Bldg Indstry Assn Scholar 85-86; Barnard Coll; Pol Sci.

HERBERT, CARLA; Fairport HS; Fairport, NY; (Y); 148/605; Intnl Clb; Mrchg Band; Symp Band; Yrbk Stf; Hon Roll; Prfct Atten Awd; Assn Of Rtrded Ctzns Schlrshp 86; Suny Genesen; Pre School Ed.

HERBERT, CHRISTINE; West Hempstead HS; Island Pk, NY; (Y); 63/300; Debate Tm; Office Aide; JV Cheerleading; Var Crs Cntry; Var Trk; Hon Roll; Astrnmy Awd Outstndng Stu 84-85; Pre-Calc Outstndng Stu Awd 85-86; Pace U; Math.

HERBERT, JEANNE; South Park HS; Buffalo, NY; (Y); Office Aide; Swmmng; Hon Roll; Pres NHS; Med.

HERBERT, SOPHIA; St Francis Prep HS; Cambria Hts, NY; (Y); Church Yth Grp; Cmnty Wkr; Dance Clb; Library Aide; Variety Show; Hon Roll; NHS; Ntl Merit Ltr; Presdntl Schlrshp 86; Manhattan Coll; Law.

HERBST, ALLISON B; Horace Mann Schl; New Rochelle, NY; (Y); Math Tm; Temple Yth Grp; Lib Orch; Yrbk Stf; Var Sftbl; Var Swmmng; Ntl Merit Ltr; Awd Hghst Excllnc 84; Rgnts Schlrshp 85-86; Boston U; Phys.

HERBST, ROBERT J; Shaker HS; Latham, NY; (Y); 23/403; Boy Scts; Church Yth Grp; God Cntry Awd; Hon Roll; Rochester Inst/Tech; Micro Engr.

HERCHENRODER, LYNN; Colonie Central HS; Albany, NY; (Y); GAA; High Hon Roll; Hon Roll; Phy Thrpy.

HERDE, CHRISTINE; Carmel HS; Carmel, NY; (Y); Intnl Clb; Mathletes; Math Tm; VP SADD; High Hon Roll; NHS; Med.

HERDEMAN, CHRIS; Victor Central HS; Victor, NY; (Y); 21/210; Band; Color Guard; Mrchg Band; High Hon Roll; Hon Roll.

HERENDEEN, DEBORAH M; Royalton-Hartland Central HS; Gasport, NY; (Y); Camera Clb; Church Yth Grp; Drama Clb; French Clb; Chorus; School Musical; School Play; Swing Chorus; Hon Roll; NHS; Niagara County Legislative Intern Program; Niagara County Youth Bureau Borad Of Directors; Amer Hist.

HERETH, DEBRA L; Williamsville East HS; Williamsville, NY; (Y); 86/260; Math Tm; Hon Roll; Prfct Atten Awd; Rgnts Schlrshp 86; SUNY Buffalo; Cvl Engrng.

HERHOLZ, KELLY MARIE; Sharon Springs Central HS; Sharon Springs, NY; (S); 2/24; Art Clb; Aud/Vis; Computer Clb; Drama Clb; FBLA; Ski Clb; Spanish Clb; SADD; Teachers Aide; Trs Varsity Clb; Genesee; Comp Repr.

HERKENHAM, MICHELLE; Mercy HS; Albany, NY; (Y); Cmnty Wkr; Ski Clb; School Play; Yrbk Stf; Bowling; Tennis; High Hon Roll; Ntl Sci Merit Awd; Gregg Typng Awd; Bus Mgmt.

HERKERT, CAROL ANN; Cardinal O Hara HS; Kenmore, NY; (Y); French Clb; Pep Clb; Quiz Bowl; Nwsp Rptr; Yrbk Phtg; Yrbk Sprt Ed; Yrbk Stf; Rep Stu Cncl; JV Im Badmtn; JV Stat Bsktbl; Schlrshp Natl Hnr Scty 82; Tonawanda Yth Brd Outstndng Stu 86; Dusquesne U; Phrmcy.

HERKO, SUZANNE; Ossining HS; Ossining, NY; (Y); Mathletes; Math Tm; Model UN; SADD; Trs Concert Band; Jazz Band; Mrchg Band; Orch; Swing Chorus; Nwsp Bus Mgr.

HERLE, ARAVIND; Canisius HS; West Seneca, NY; (S); Drama Clb; Model UN; Ski Clb; School Musical; Yrbk Stf; Var Capt Golf; Var Tennis; High Hon Roll; NHS; Williams Coll Book Awd 86; Med.

HERLIHY, KAREN M; W Melville SR HS; Stony Brook, NY; (Y); Capt Dance Clb; Mgr Ski Clb; Band; Chorus; School Musical; Rep Sr Cls; Cheerleading; High Hon Roll; Jr NHS; NHS; NY Rgnts Schlrshp Awd 86; Outstndg Effrt-Drg Abuse Prvntn In Elem Schls 86; Natl Chrldr Achvt Awd 86; PA ST U; Elec Engrng.

HERMAN, FRED; Bronx H S Of Science; Bronx, NY; (Y); Chess Clb; Cmnty Wkr; Library Aide; Nwsp Rptr; Lit Mag; Ntl Merit SF; Pol Sci.

HERMAN, PAUL; Holy Trinity HS; Levittown, NY; (S); JV Crs Cntry; JV Trk; Wrstlng; Vrsty Wrstlng Coaches Awd 84-85; Frgn Sci.

HERMAN, THOMAS; Union-Endicott HS; Endicott, NY; (Y); Church Yth Grp; Varsity Clb; Var JV Bsktbl; JV Ftbl; Var JV Lcrss; Mech Engrng.

HERMANN, JULIE; Indian River Cntrl HS; Evans Mills, NY; (Y); Cmnty Wkr; Library Aide; Office Aide; Red Cross Aide; Ski Clb; Teachers Aide; Band; School Play; Stage Crew; Hon Roll; Jefferson CC; Exec Secty.

HERMANN, MECHAEL; Greenville JR SR HS; Medusa, NY; (Y); VP FFA; Pres VICA; Yrbk Ed-Chief; JV Cheerleading; Var Socr; Var Trk; 4-H Awd; Computer Clb; Drama Clb; 4-H; Nalt Poultry Sci Cntst Bronze Mdl, St 2nd 85; St FFA Chorus 85; Acting.

HERMANS, DAVID J; Cardinal Mooney HS; Rochester, NY; (Y); 29/315; Church Yth Grp; Cmnty Wkr; Church Choir; School Play; Nwsp Rptr; Hon Roll; NY ST Regents Coll Schlrshp 86-87; St John Fisher Coll Schlrshp 86-87; St John Fisher Coll; Chem.

HERMITT JR, LESLIE C; Gorton HS; Yonkers, NY; (Y); Varsity Clb; Nwsp Stf; Yrbk Stf; Lit Mag; Rep Soph Cls; Rep Jr Cls; Rep Sr Cls; Diving; Ftbl; Score Keeper; Pace Bus Schl Acadmc Schlrshp 86; PTSA Awd Groton HS 86; Ctzn Yr Govrnr Awd 86; Albany ST U; Comp Sci.

HERMOSO, RAFAEL M; St Francis Prep; Jamaica Ests, NY; (S); 42/744; Im Fld Hcky; Im Vllybl; High Hon Roll; Comp Sci.

HERMS, MICHAEL; Eden SR HS; Eden, NY; (Y); Computer Clb; German Clb; Varsity Clb; Rep Jr Cls; Var L Ftbl; Comp Sci.

HERNANDEZ, DAVID; Regis HS; Bronx, NY; (Y); Church Yth Grp; Computer Clb; Latin Clb; SADD; Yrbk Stf; Im Bsktbl; Hon Roll; ST Rgnts Schlrshp 86; Weslyan Schlrshp 86; Chrls Ray Schlrshp 86; Weslyan U; Econmcs.

HERNANDEZ, DIANA; Bronx High School Of Science; Queens, NY; (Y); Lit Mag; Natl Hspnc Schlrs Awd Smi-Fnslt 86; Rgnts Schlrshp 86.

HERNANDEZ, JEFFREY; De Witt Clinton HS; Bronx, NY; (Y); 3/31; Am Leg Boys St; Library Aide; ROTC; Band; Drm Mjr(t); Lit Mag; Bsbl; Wrstlng; Cit Awd; Hon Roll; Law.

HERNANDEZ JR, JOSEPH; All Hallows HS; Bronx, NY; (Y); Chess Clb; Computer Clb; Crs Cntry; Hon Roll; Hstry Clb; Boston Coll; Crim Law.

HERNANDEZ, LISSETTE; Adlai E Stevenson HS; Bronx, NY; (Y); Orch; Hon Roll; NHS; Supr Achvt Sci Cert Awd, Outstndng Achvt Soc Stds Cert Merit, Music Awd, Cert Awd Achvt Spnsh II 84; Chld Psychlgst.

HERNANDEZ, MARIA P; St Francis Prep; Jackson Heights, NY; (S); 138/744; Dance Clb; Library Aide; Science Clb; Hon Roll; Optimate Soc 84-85; Ntl Piano Plyng Adtns 84-85; NY U; Tchr.

HERNANDEZ, ROLANDO; John A Coleman HS; Ulster Park, NY; (Y); Cmnty Wkr; Key Clb; Ski Clb; Spanish Clb; Socr; Hon Roll; Natl Sci Olympd-Chem 86; Pilot.

HERNER, JENNIFER; Scardsale HS; Scarsdale, NY; (Y); AFS; Trs Church Yth Grp; Girl Scts; Band; JV Fld Hcky; JV Trk; Stat Wrstlng.

HEROLD, ETTA; Onondaga Central HS; Nedrow, NY; (S); 10/73; VP German Clb; SADD; Band; Jazz Band; School Play; Yrbk Phtg; Pres Sr Cls; JV Tennis; Var Capt Vllybl; High Hon Roll; St John Fisher; CPA.

HEROLD, KENNETH A; Liverpool HS; Liverpool, NY; (Y); 25/800; Concert Band; Lit Mag; Var Gym; Jr NHS; NHS; Regents Schlrshp 86; Engrng Schlrshp Clarkson U 86; MIP Gymnast Awd 84; Clarkson U; Elec Engrng.

HERON, ALISON H; Half Hollow Hills West HS; Dixhills, NY; (Y); Lit Mag; Arts Cont Outstndng Perfrmnce 85-86; Writer.

HEROUX, JOSEPH FRANCIS; Cohoes HS; Cohoes, NY; (Y); 33/170; VP Exploring; French Clb; JV Var Bsbl; Hudson Vly Comm Coll; Accntng.

HEROW, ANDREA J; Newfield HS; Terryville, NY; (Y); 95/579; Hosp Aide; Band; Chorus; Concert Band; Mrchg Band; Orch; Pep Band; School Musical; Variety Show; Hon Roll; All Cty Bands; NYMSA; Music.

HERR, CINDY; L I Lutheran HS; E Northport, NY; (S); 2/92; Pres German Clb; Trs Mathletes; Chorus; School Musical; Stat Bsktbl; Var Vllybl; High Hon Roll; VP NHS; Sal; Chem Engr.

HERR, ROBERT; Frontier Central HS; Blasdell, NY; (S); 72/444; Aud/Vis; Chess Clb; German Clb; Yrbk Stf; Trk; Hon Roll; NHS; Merit Awd Audio Visual 80-82; U Buffalo; Dntstry.

HERRADOR, HELEN A; Academy Of St Joseph HS; Bay Shore, NY; (Y); 1/137; Drama Clb; Hosp Aide; Library Aide; Chorus; Stage Crew; Yrbk Stf; Hon Roll; NHS; Natl Hispnc Schlrs Awd Pgm 86; NY Regents Schlrshp 86; Doctors Tmrrw Pgm 86; Cornell U; Pre-Med.

HERRERA, BRIAN; Charles H Roth HS; Henrietta, NY; (Y); Ski Clb; Spanish Clb; Varsity Clb; JV Lcrss; Var L Socr; High Hon Roll; NHS; Spanish NHS; Schlrshp Letter 86; Writing Awd 84; Sci.

HERRERA, MAURICE; Archbishop Molloy HS; Richmond Hill, NY; (Y); 120/390; Boys Clb Am; French Clb; Math Tm; Pep Clb; Science Clb; Service Clb; Spanish Clb; Chorus; Im Bsktbl; High Hon Roll; NYS Regents Schlrshp 86; Bsktbl Intramural Champs 84; Hndbl JV CHSAA Champs 85.

HERRERA, MAURICIO F; St Francis Prep; Jackson Heights, NY; (S); 200/750; Latin Clb; Spanish Clb; JV Im Ftbl; JV Vllybl; Wt Lftg; JV Wrstlng; All Amer Stdnt Awd 86; New York U; Nutrtn.

HERRERO, MARIE; White Plains HS; White Plns, NY; (Y); Church Yth Grp; Dance Clb; FBLA; Girl Scts; Hosp Aide; Pom Pon; High Hon Roll; Hon Roll; Traind Peer Ldr 85-86; Pre-Med.

HERRICK, DIANE; Randolph Central HS; Little Valley, NY; (Y); 3/83; Pres 4-H; Quiz Bowl; Spanish Clb; VP Band; Nwsp Stf; Yrbk Stf; High Hon Roll; JP Sousa Awd; NHS; Pres Schlr; Regnts Schlrshp 85; Emphasis Excllnc Schlrshp 85; March Dimes Schlrshp 86; Daemen Coll; Phys Therpy.

HERRICK, NANCY; Hamilton Central Schl; Hamilton, NY; (Y); 21/56; Art Clb; Drama Clb; Band; Chorus; Concert Band; Mrchg Band; Orch; School Musical; Yrbk Phtg; Yrbk Stf; Regents Schlrshp 86; CO ST U; Vet.

HERRICK SANFORD, KAMMI S; Friendship Central HS; Almond, NY; (Y); 1/25; Spanish Clb; Band; Chorus; Mrchg Band; School Play; Yrbk Bus Mgr; Yrbk Ed-Chief; Socr; Sftbl; NHS; Regents Schrlshp 86; Alfred U; Elem Ed.

HERRIMAN, ERIC E; Wayne Central HS; Walworth, NY; (Y); 44/153; Church Yth Grp; Mathletes; Math Tm; Stage Crew; Yrbk Bus Mgr; Var Crs Cntry; Var Trk; Hon Roll; NHS; Prfct Atten Awd; Rgnts Schlrshp 86; Wrld Cmptn-Olympcs Of Mind 84; U Of Buffalo; Comp Sci.

HERRING, CAROL M; Eastridge HS; Rochester, NY; (Y); 17/214; Ski Clb; Spanish Clb; Varsity Clb; Band; Trs Frsh Cls; Sec Jr Cls; Golf; Hon Roll; NHS; Rochester Inst/Tech; Elec Engr.

HERRING, CHRISTOPHER C; Newburgh Free Acad; New Windsor, NY; (Y); Am Leg Boys St; ROTC; JV Socr; Var Trk; Hon Roll; Church Choir; Prfct Atten Awd; Air Frc Citation Awd 86; Ldrshp Excllnc Awd 86; Acdmc Excllnc Awd 85; U S Service Acad; Aerospc Engnr.

HERRINGTON, ERIC; Newfane Central Schl; Newfane, NY; (Y); 61/185; Boy Scts; Varsity Clb; Var L Bsbl; Var L Bsktbl; Var L Ftbl; Var JV Mgr(s); Arch.

HERRMANN, AMY; Maryvale HS; Cheektowaga, NY; (Y); Cmnty Wkr; VP German Clb; Spanish Clb; Varsity Clb; Rep Stu Cncl; Stat Var Bsktbl; Var L Trk; Hon Roll; NHS; Ntl Merit SF; Zoolgy.

HERRMANN, KRISTIN; Sweet Home SR HS; Tonawanda, NY; (Y); Girl Scts; Spanish Clb; Rep Soph Cls; Rep Jr Cls; Hon Roll; Spanish NHS; Soc Sci.

HERRON, JEFFREY; Mynderse Acad; Seneca Falls, NY; (S); 48/150; Church Yth Grp; Letterman Clb; Varsity Clb; Yrbk Stf; VP Jr Cls; VP Sr Cls; Var L Ftbl; Var L Lcrss; Wt Lftg; Cit Awd; St John Fischer; Engrng.

HERRON, JIM; Central HS; Valley Stream, NY; (Y); Leo Clb; Variety Show; Nwsp Stf; Off Stu Cncl; Nassau CC; Geology.

HERSCH, JONATHAN; Commack HS North; Commack, NY; (Y); 7/390; Pres Temple Yth Grp; Mrchg Band; School Musical; Symp Band; Elks Awd; French Hon Soc; High Hon Roll; Pres NHS; Pres Schlr; PTA Scholar 86; Duke U; Med.

HERSEE, MARK; West Seneca West SR HS; W Seneca, NY; (Y); Camera Clb; Church Yth Grp; Band; Mrchg Band; Yrbk Stf; Var Ftbl.

HERSHEY, MARK; Fairport HS; Fairport, NY; (Y); Church Yth Grp; Cmnty Wkr; German Clb; Intnl Clb; Mathletes; Math Clb; Math Tm; JV Bsbl; JV Bsktbl; Hon Roll; Bus.

HERSHINSON, ARLA; Port Richmond HS; Staten Island, NY; (Y); Pres Church Yth Grp; Drama Clb; Office Aide; Teachers Aide; Temple Yth Grp; Band; School Musical; School Play; Yrbk Stf; Twrlr; Law.

HERSHMAN, KARYN; Lawrence HS; Cedarhurst, NY; (Y); 68/414; Stage Crew; Ed Yrbk Stf; U Of Miami; Marine Bio.

HERSHON, ANDREW; Niskayuna HS; Schenectady, NY; (Y); VP Exploring; French Clb; Hosp Aide; Ski Clb; Jazz Band; Orch; Symp Band; Pres NHS; Temple Yth Grp; French Hon Soc; Downhill Ski Var Ltr 83-86; Natl Frnch Comptn 6th Pl Natl, 2nd Regnl 86; Cornell U; Bio.

HERSON, ANNE; Saint Barnabas HS; Bronx, NY; (Y); 42/189; Dance Clb; Drama Clb; School Musical; School Play; Variety Show; SUNY; Dance.

HERTE, BRIAN G; St Anthonys HS; E Northport, NY; (Y); 150/500; Var Capt Bsktbl; Hon Roll; Duns Scts Acad Awd 84-86; Marist Coll; Acctg.

HERTER, KAREN; Vernon-Verona-Sherrill HS; Verona, NY; (Y); Mathletes; Math Tm; Ski Clb; Varsity Clb; Stu Cncl; Fld Hcky; Socr; Sftbl; High Hon Roll; NHS; Vtd Mst Intlgnt In Schl By Stu Srvy 86; Mthmtcs.

HERTIG, HEIDI A; Westhill SR HS; Syracuse, NY; (Y); 14/155; Church Choir; Stage Crew; Symp Band; Vllybl; Cit Awd; NHS; NEDT Awd; Church Yth Grp; Cmnty Wkr; Ski Clb; Onondaga CC Schlr Awd 85; NY ST U-Albany; Bus Admin.

HERTLEIN, PAUL; St Marys Boys HS; Glen Head, NY; (S); 2/145; Ski Clb; Nwsp Stf; Yrbk Stf; Rep Stu Cncl; Var Trk; High Hon Roll; Hon Roll; NHS; Ntl Merit Ltr; MA Inst Tech; Engrng.

HERTRICH, CHRISTINE; Baldwin SR HS; Baldwin, NY; (Y); High Hon Roll; Hon Roll; Nassau Comm; Sec Sci.

HERTZ, PATRICIA; Hamburg SR HS; N Boston, NY; (Y); 49/374; Var 4-H; Soph Cls; Jr Cls; Sr Cls; Stu Cncl; L Var Bsktbl; Capt Var Fld Hcky; L Var Socr; 4-H Awd; Hon Roll; Bio.

HERTZOG, BRIAN D; Canisius HS; East Aurora, NY; (Y); 20/169; Church Yth Grp; Cmnty Wkr; Model UN; Quiz Bowl; Drm & Bgl; Yrbk Rptr; Yrbk Stf; Ftbl; Hon Roll; NHS; Georgetown U; German.

HERZ, SETH JEREMY; Binghamton HS; Binghamton, NY; (Y); 6/453; Sec Trs Spanish Clb; SADD; Temple Yth Grp; Var L Trk; High Hon Roll; NHS; Prfct Atten Awd; Salute To Yth 84-85; Elnr Rsvlt Cmmnty Svc Awd 86; Prsdntl Acdmc Ftnss Awd 86; Carnegie-Mlln U; Bus Admin.

HERZFELD, DAVID; Hauppauge HS; Smithtown, NY; (Y); Hon Roll; Vet Med.

HERZOG, DENISE; Smithtown HS; Smithtown, NY; (Y); Office Aide; Service Clb; SADD; Off Jr Cls; High Hon Roll; Hon Roll; NHS; Clss Chrprsn JR SR Sprts Evnt 86; Ed.

HERZOG, ELAINE; Academy Of Saint Joseph; Hauppauge, NY; (Y); 3/130; Church Yth Grp; Girl Scts; Hosp Aide; Band; Pres Orch; Rep Sr Cls; Var Badmtn; Var Capt Bsktbl; Sftbl; Hon Roll; All League In Vrsty Bsktbl 86; Mt St Mary Pres Schlrshp 86; SUNY Bnghmtn; Nrs.

HESKIN, KAROLYN; Solnay HS; Solvay, NY; (Y); Church Yth Grp; Intnl Clb; Pep Clb; Spanish Clb; Off Frsh Cls; Off Soph Cls; Off Jr Cls; Var Cheerleading; Pom Pon; Var JV Socr; Oswego ST COLL.

HESLER, CHRISTOPHER J; Christian Brothers Acad; Liverpool, NY; (Y); 23/101; Cmnty Wkr; Band; Stage Crew; Variety Show; Nwsp Stf; Yrbk Stf; High Hon Roll; Hon Roll; Ntl Merit SF; De Paul U; Psychlgy.

HESLOP, GARFIELD; South Shore HS; Brooklyn, NY; (Y); Chess Clb; Math Tm; Pres Schlr; Embry Riddle Aero U; Aero Sci.

HESPENHEIDE, AMY L; Arlington HS; Poughkeepsie, NY; (Y); 6/560; Church Yth Grp; Pres French Clb; Band; Color Guard; Mrchg Band; Orch; Yrbk Stf; Rep Frsh Cls; Ntl Merit SF; Drama Clb; E Coast Champions-Marching Bnd 83-85; Womens Champion Table Tennis; 2nd Pl Orchstrintl Yth/Music Fstvl; Engl.

HESS, KRISTIN; Commack High School North; E Northport, NY; (Y); 18/364; SADD; Chorus; School Musical; Off Sr Cls; Var Socr; Var Vllybl; French Hon Soc; High Hon Roll; NHS; Off Jr Cls; Modern Music Masters VP 86-87; Phy Thrpy.

HESS, MELANI; Walter Panas HS; Peekskill, NY; (Y); 22/250; Spanish Clb; SADD; Jr Cls; Sr Cls; Var JV Cheerleading; High Hon Roll; Hon Roll; Jr NHS; NHS; Pres Acdmc Fit Awd 86; Awd Excllnc Spnsh 86; Stdnt Mnth Sci, Engl, Spnsh 84-85; SUNY Stonybrook; Spnsh.

HESS, PAMELA; Farmingdale HS; Farmingdale, NY; (Y); Aud/Vis; Drama Clb; SADD; Thesps; Chorus; Church Choir; Flag Corp; School Musical; School Play; Stage Crew; Tech Thtr.

HESS, ROBERT A; Ellenville Central HS; Ellenville, NY; (Y); 1/170; Am Leg Boys St; French Clb; Science Clb; Ski Clb; Band; Jazz Band; Yrbk Stf; Var Golf; NHS; Ntl Merit SF; Bio Med.

HESSELBIRG, FRANCES; Queen Of The Rosary Acad; Hauppauge, NY; (S); 1/50; Cmnty Wkr; Varsity Clb; Yrbk Stf; VP Sr Cls; Rep Stu Cncl; Var Capt Pom Pon; High Hon Roll; NHS; Church Yth Grp; Physcl Ftnss Awd.

HESSING, RENEE; Holy Trinity D HS; Westbury, NY; (Y); Dance Clb; Drama Clb; French Clb; Girl Scts; JA; Acpl Chr; Chorus; Church Choir; Pep Band; School Musical; NEDT Achvt Awd 84; Hnr Rl 84-86; NY U; Pre-Med.

HESSION, STEVE; Sachem North HS; Holbrook, NY; (Y); 152/1550; Church Yth Grp; French Clb; Ski Clb; Stage Crew; Bowling; Socr; NHS; Hofstra U; Pre Law.

HESTER, DONNA; Albany HS; Albany, NY; (Y); 144/625; DECA; Intnl Clb; JA; Pep Clb; Variety Show; Var Trk; Hon Roll; Ntl Merit Ltr; Black Hstry Mnth Cont Awd 82; Lawyr.

HETZLER, MARY JEANNE; Commack HS North; Commack, NY; (Y); Sec SADD; Rep Frsh Cls; Rep Soph Cls; Rep Jr Cls; Rep Stu Cncl; Var Bsktbl; Var Capt Socr; Var Sftbl; High Hon Roll; NHS; All Cnfrnc-All Lg Sfflk Cnty Sftbl 86; Prtcpnt Of Sci Fair Frmngdl Coll 84; Comp Sci.

HEW, ADRIENNE N; The Ursuline Schl; Bronx, NY; (Y); 48/121; Chorus; Stage Crew; Hon Roll; Russian Excllnc Cert 85; NY U ; Frgn Lang.

HEWES, GINA; Charles O Dickerson HS; Trumansburg, NY; (Y); 1/85; VP Stu Cncl; Var L Trk; Bausch & Lomb Sci Awd; High Hon Roll; NHS; Prfct Atten Awd; Val; French Clb; Science Clb; Sec Jr Cls; Coaches Awd Trk 85; Mst Stds 86; Yale U; Archlgy.

HEWETT, KERRI; Tonawanda SR HS; Tonawanda, NY; (Y); Church Yth Grp; Girl Scts; Hon Roll; Bryant & Stratton; Acctng.

HEWITT, CHRISTINE; Vernon Verona Sherrill Central HS; Verona, NY; (Y); Trs Church Yth Grp; Chorus; Color Guard; Concert Band; Drm & Bgl; Mrchg Band; Pep Band; High Hon Roll; Hon Roll; Elem Educ.

HEWITT, DEBORAH L; Garden Schl; Astoria, NY; (Y); 1/32; VP Drama Clb; Office Aide; Pres Spanish Clb; School Musical; Nwsp Ed-Chief; Yrbk Ed-Chief; Cit Awd; Ntl Merit SF; NEDT Awd; Val; Math.

HEWITT, ELIZABETH; Amsterdam HS; Amsterdam, NY; (Y); Am Leg Aux Girls St; Cmnty Wkr; Rep Jr Cls; Stu Cncl; Pom Pon; Stat Wrstlng; Hon Roll; NHS; Cert For Tv Shows 85-86; Brdcstng.

HEWLETT, KATHY; Westhampton Beach HS; East Quogue, NY; (Y); 50/269; FBLA; Library Aide; Ski Clb; Band; Concert Band; Mrchg Band; Pep Band; Bsktbl; Var Trk; Hon Roll; Bus Adm.

HEWLETTE, FRANCISCO; West Islip HS; W Islip, NY; (Y); 190/525; Boy Scts; Ski Clb; Bsktbl; Ftbl; Lcrss.

HEXIMER, CHRISTOPHER; Kenmore East HS; Tonawanda, NY; (Y); Varsity Clb; JV Capt Bsbl; Im Bsktbl; JV Var Ftbl; Im Vllybl; Im Wt Lftg; JV Var Wrstlng; Hon Roll; Penn ST U; Spch Pthlgy.

HEYWARD, CHARESE; St Chatharine Acad; Bx, NY; (Y); Girl Scts; Rep Frsh Cls; Rep Soph Cls; Rep Jr Cls; Rep Stu Cncl; Awd Perf Atten 83-85; Comp Anlyst.

HEYWARD, MICHELLE R; Troy HS; Troy, NY; (Y); Trs French Clb; Hon Roll; NHS; Boston U; Lib Arts.

HIBBARD, DAVID; Colonie Central HS; Albany, NY; (Y); 98/499; Ski Clb; Band; Mrchg Band; JV Var Ftbl; Var Capt Lcrss; Im Wt Lftg; Hon Roll; Bio.

HIBBERT, MARCIA; Evander Childs HS; Bronx, NY; (Y); Drama Clb; Teachers Aide; Chorus; School Play; Rep Frsh Cls; VP Soph Cls; Prfct Atten Awd; Office Aide; Awds Engl & Keybrdng 85-86; Harvard; Law.

HIBBERT, NELLITA; HS Of Fashion Indust; Brooklyn, NY; (Y); 47/324; Drama Clb; JA; Office Aide; Chorus; Var Tennis; NHS; NHS; Prfct Atten Awd; Hnr Cert Englsh Lng Arts 86; Fhsn Dsgnr.

HIBBERT, SETH L; Liverpool HS; Liverpool, NY; (Y); 26/816; Am Leg Boys St; JCL; Latin Clb; Hon Roll; NHS; Ntl Merit Ltr; Boy Scts; Socr; Clsscl League Schlrshp 86-87; Latin Outstndng Achvt 85-86; Niagara U; Crimnlgy.

HIBBS, DONA; Sewanhaka HS; Elmont, NY; (Y); Girl Scts; Office Aide; Band; Mrchg Band; Hon Roll; Artist.

HICKEY, ANN; Royalton-Hartland HS; Middleport, NY; (Y); Dance Clb; Varsity Clb; Yrbk Stf; Var Capt Bsktbl; Var Fld Hcky; Var JV Sftbl; MIP & MVP JV Bsktbll 84-85; Hon Ment All Leag Field Hockey & Sftbl 86; Trvl.

HICKEY, BRIAN; Notre Dame-Bishop Gibbons HS; Schenectady, NY; (S); 23/101; Boy Scts; Band; Mrchg Band; Nwsp Rptr; Var Capt Crs Cntry; Var Capt Trk; Dnfth Awd; Rensselaer Polytech Inst; Mth.

HICKEY, ELLEN; Olean HS; Olean, NY; (Y); 10/210; Church Yth Grp; Pres Science Clb; VP Varsity Clb; Var Diving; Var Capt Swmmng; NHS; AFS; French Clb; Orch; JV Var Cheerleading; Antl Yth Salute 86; SUNY Geneseo; Spch Pthlgy.

HICKEY, JOHN; Tappan Zee HS; Blauvelt, NY; (Y); VP Pres JA; Math Tm; Rep Stu Cncl; Var L Golf; NHS; Chess Clb; Im Socr; Prfct Atten Awd; Celtic Golf Clb Singles Champ 84; Ntl Math Hnr Soc 85 & 86; Outstndng Yng Busns Man Awd-Jr Achvt 85-86; Rensselaer Polytech Inst; Math.

HICKEY, KERRI; Mahopac HS; Mahopac, NY; (Y); 125/409; Capt GAA; Color Guard; Var Capt Socr; Hon Roll; Prfct Atten Awd.

HICKEY, KEVIN D; Oneonta SR HS; Oneonta, NY; (Y); Church Yth Grp; Computer Clb; French Clb; Key Clb; Library Aide; Red Cross Aide; Temple Yth Grp; Bowling; Socr; Vllybl; St Bonaventure.

HICKEY, LIZ; White Plains HS; White Plains, NY; (Y); Boy Scts; Church Yth Grp; Cmnty Wkr; French Clb; Hosp Aide; Office Aide; Pep Clb; Red Cross Aide; Service Clb; Church Choir; Blood Drv 83-86; Cmnty Svc With Retarded Chldrn 85; Telethn For Cystic Fibrosis 85; Bus.

HICKEY, NAOMI; Holy Child HS; Larchmont, NY; (Y); Pres GAA; Rep Frsh Cls; Stu Cncl; Hon Roll; Var Bsktbl; JV Capt Fld Hcky; Var Capt Socr; Var Sftbl; Var Capt Trk.

HICKMAN, DARIN; August Martin HS; Springfield Grdns, NY; (Y); Aud/Vis; CAP; Pres Cmnty Wkr; Office Aide; Band; Concert Band; Stage Crew; Rep Frsh Cls; Stu Cncl; NYS Regents Scholar 86; NY City Super Yth 85; Sthrn Queens Park Assn Awd Ldrshp & Merit 84; Hamilton Coll; Pre-Med.

HICKMAN, VIVIAN C; St Jean Baptiste HS; Jamaica, NY; (S); 10/98; Art Clb; Camera Clb; Trs Jr Cls; Sftbl; Vllybl; Hon Roll; NHS; Bus.

HICKOK JR, DONALD; South Park HS; Buffalo, NY; (Y); Hon Roll; Comp Tech.

HICKOK JR, ROY KEITH; Massena Central HS; Massena, NY; (Y); Band; Concert Band; Mrchg Band; Var JV Socr; Var Trk; Var JV Wrstlng; Hon Roll; Prfct Atten Awd; AFS; French Clb.

HICKS, ANDREW P; Homer SR HS; Cortland, NY; (Y); 19/210; Intnl Clb; Bsbl; Hon Roll; VP NHS; Rotary Yth Ldrshp Conf 85; Boys ST 85; Rgnts Schlrshp Awd 86; Fredonia ST U; Elec Engrng.

HICKS, ANNE; Haverling Central Schl; Bath, NY; (Y); 33/115; JCL; Latin Clb; Math Clb; Chorus; Yrbk Bus Mgr; Yrbk Stf; Off Sr Cls; JV Var Tennis; Var Vllybl; Hon Roll; Bus Stf Mgr 85-86.

HICKS, BONNIE; Haverling HS; Bath, NY; (Y); JCL; Rep Latin Clb; Ski Clb; Yrbk Stf; Stu Cncl; Sftbl; Vllybl; Hon Roll; Rep Sr Cls; All Star Vllybl All Lg Plyr 85; Natl Soc Stud Olympd 84; SUNY; Phys Ed.

HICKS, CHERE; Cortland SR HS; Cortland, NY; (Y); Chorus; Chld Studies.

HICKS, DONALD; Cortland HS; Cortland, NY; (Y); Church Yth Grp; Ski Clb; Varsity Clb; Im Mgr Bsbl; JV Var Bsktbl; JV Var Ftbl; Im Mgr Lcrss; Wt Lftg; High Hon Roll; Hon Roll; Arch.

HICKS, FRANCINE; Port Jervis HS; Port Jervis, NY; (Y); 32/195; Church Yth Grp; Capt Math Tm; Band; Concert Band; Jazz Band; Mrchg Band; Yrbk Ed-Chief; Hon Roll; NY ST Schl Music Assoc 85 & 86; Prfct Attndnc; Math.

HICKS, SHELLEY D; Hammondsport Central HS; Hammondsport, NY; (Y); 15/68; Church Yth Grp; Sec Chorus; Drm Mjr(t); Jazz Band; School Play; Yrbk Phtg; Girl Scts; Rep Stu Cncl; Trk; High Hon Roll; Distngshd Acadmc Schlrshp Hofstra U 86; Regnts Schlrshp 86; Hofstra U; Appld Psych.

HICKS, STEVE; Dryden HS; Dryden, NY; (Y); Boy Scts; Church Yth Grp; Spanish Clb; JV Var Bsbl; JV Var Bsktbl; JV Var Ftbl; Im Sftbl; Im Vllybl; Im Wt Lftg; High Hon Roll; Bus.

HIDALGO, GILDA; Babylon JR SR HS; W Babylon, NY; (Y); Hosp Aide; Office Aide; Hon Roll; Schlstc Awd Frgn Lang 84-85; Acctng.

HIDARY, JACK D; Yeshivah Of Flatbush HS; Brooklyn, NY; (Y); Chess Clb; Math Tm; Orch; School Musical; Symp Band; Ed Lit Mag; Pres Soph Cls; Var Swmmng; Hon Roll; Ntl Merit SF; JR Arista Soc 84-85; Yeshina U; Ed.

HIDDESSEN, MARK; Holy Trinity HS; Seaford, NY; (S); Boys Clb Am; Boy Scts; Scholastic Bowl; Ski Clb; Bsbl; L Bowling; L Ftbl; High Hon Roll; Hon Roll; NEDT Awd; NEDT Cert 84; Princeton; Math.

HIEBER, JENNIFER; Garden City HS; Garden City, NY; (Y); Art Clb; Pres Church Yth Grp; Drama Clb; French Clb; Church Choir; Stage Crew; Yrbk Stf; Badmtn; Swmmng; Jr NHS; NHS; Mastr Acolyte 85.

HIGBEE, JAMES; Kenmore West HS; Kenmore, NY; (Y); 103/440; Boy Scts; JA; Concert Band; Mrchg Band; Hon Roll; NHS; Ntl Merit Ltr; Pres Schlr; Paul Steimle Awd Outstndng Industrl Arts Stu 86; Clarkson U; Elect Engr.

HIGGINS, BONNIE; Columbia HS; Rensselear, NY; (Y); Trs Art Clb; Sec Concert Band; Mrchg Band; Ltr Concert Band,Marchng Band 86; Mildred Elly Bus Schl; Secrtcl.

HIGGINS, JOYCE B; Dundee Central HS; Dundee, NY; (Y); 1/78; Science Clb; Varsity Clb; Trs Concert Band; Trs Mrchg Band; Var L Sftbl; Scrkpr Vllybl; High Hon Roll; VP NHS; Val; Pres Church Yth Grp; NY Regnts Schlrshp Awd 86; Cornell U; Biochem.

HIGGINS, KELLI; Jordan Elbridge HS; Elbridge, NY; (Y); 8/140; Sec Church Yth Grp; Drama Clb; Drm Mjr(t); Mrchg Band; School Musical; Trs Soph Cls; Sec Jr Cls; JV Var Sftbl; High Hon Roll; NHS; Prom Queen 86; Pres SR Hnr Scty 86-87.

HIGGINS, KURT; Gouverneur Central HS; Gouverneur, NY; (Y); Computer Clb; Quiz Bowl; Var Crs Cntry; Var Trk; High Hon Roll; Hon Roll; NHS; 1st Pl Awd Clrksn Schls Sci Stu Rcgntn Day 86; 2dn Pl Awd Trdtnl Spch Cntst 86; Clrksn Schl; Comp Prgmng.

HIGGINS, MARY; Dominican Commercial HS; Richmond Hill, NY; (S); 3/288; Cmnty Wkr; Intnl Clb; Teachers Aide; JV Score Keeper; Socr; Wt Lftg; High Hon Roll; Jr NHS; Cthlc War Vets Pst 666 Schlrshp 83-87; Prncpls List 83-84; Sienna Clb 84-85; St Johns U; Math.

HIGGINS, MELISSA; E Syracuse-Minoa HS; E Syracuse, NY; (Y); Science Clb; Chorus; Sec Frsh Cls; Var Cheerleading; Coach Actv; Hon Roll; Jr NHS; NHS; Phrmctcl Rsrch.

HIGGINS, PAMELA; Hanau American HS; Fayetteville, NC; (Y); 10/120; Cmnty Wkr; Keywanettes; SADD; Teachers Aide; Hon Roll; Hlth Occptn Stu Of Amer 85; Omega Psi Phi Frtrnty Schlrshp 86; Outstndng Ldrshp-Chem 86; Fayetteville ST U; Dntstry.

HIGGINS, TERRI; Jordan Elbridge HS; Elbridge, NY; (Y); 14/150; Sec Church Yth Grp; Chorus; Church Choir; Yrbk Bus Mgr; Var JV Bsktbl; Powder Puff Ftbl; Var Capt Sftbl; High Hon Roll; Jr NHS; Sec NHS; Dorthea Deitz Mem Schlrshp 86; Dollars For Scholars Schlrshp 86; MVP Var Sftbl 86; Ithaca Coll; Phy Ed.

HIGHSMITH, TAMARA; Skaneateles HS; Skaneateles, NY; (S); Yrbk Stf; Crs Cntry; Socr; Tennis; Trk; High Hon Roll; NHS; Vet.

HIGHT, ADRIENNE; St John The Baptist HS; Amityville, NY; (Y); Hosp Aide; Trk; Hon Roll; Jr NHS; Cert Merit Math & Sci 85.

HIGHTOWER, CHANDA; Canarsie HS; Brooklyn, NY; (Y); Concert Band; Pres Frsh Cls; Pres Sr Cls; Capt Cheerleading; Var Pom Pon; Var Vllybl; High Hon Roll; Hon Roll; NHS; Prfct Atten Awd; Golden Recd Achvt Awd 84; Serv Awd 84; Hnry Phys Ed Ldrs Clb 85-86; Arch.

HIGLEY, DARLENE; Onteora HS; West Shokan, NY; (Y); 17/201; Concert Band; Mrchg Band; High Hon Roll; Hon Roll; NHS; High Hnr Rl Awd 84; Spnsh Hnr Awd 84; Awd Cert Exc Engl 83; Ulster County CC; Soc Sci.

HIGMAN, KERRY L; Niagara Catholic HS; Niagara Falls, NY; (Y); 16/81; Spanish Clb; Stat Vllybl; Hon Roll; NY ST Rgnts Schlrshp 86; Niagara U; Accntng.

HILARIO, ARTHUR; MSGR Farrell HS; Staten Island, NY; (Y); Intnl Clb; Math Tm; Im Bsktbl; High Hon Roll; Hon Roll; Philippien Jr Sci Lge Amer 86; Non-Schl Bsbl, Bsktbl & Hcky Tm 83-86.

HILBERT, JACK; John Jay HS; S Salem, NY; (Y); Church Yth Grp; Var Bsktbl; JV Socr; Var Tennis; High Hon Roll; Hon Roll; NHS; Prfct Atten Awd; John Jay Coaches Awd 84; Booster Clb Sportsmnshp Awd Soccer 83; Most Imprvd Bsktbl 85-86.

HILBERT, JANE; Mount Saint Mary Acad; Kenmore, NY; (Y); 8/96; Cmnty Wkr; Pep Clb; Nwsp Ed-Chief; Nwsp Stf; Yrbk Stf; High Hon Roll; Hon Roll; NHS; E Zone Athltc US Synchrnzd Swm 86; Fnlst SR Ntls Synchrnzd Swmmg 86.

HILEY, MELISSA; Tioga Central HS; Nichols, NY; (Y); 3/80; Spanish Clb; SADD; Teachers Aide; Varsity Clb; Variety Show; Rep Stu Cncl; JV Bsktbl; Wt Lftg; Stat Wrstlng; High Hon Roll; Natl Merit Awd Spn 85; Schlrshp For Coll Exprnce 86.

HILKEN, DAWN; Mt Morris Central Schl; Mt Morris, NY; (Y); Ski Clb; High Hon Roll; Hon Roll; Jr NHS; NHS; Merit Tuition Assist Pgm 86; Genesee CC; Chem.

HILL, CHRISTINE; Chenango Valley HS; Binghamton, NY; (Y); 11/180; Sec Art Clb; French Clb; SADD; Varsity Clb; Ed Nwsp Stf; Ed Yrbk Stf; Var L Tennis; Var L Vllybl; High Hon Roll; NHS; NY St Regents Schlrshp 86-87; SUNY Binghamton; Art.

HILL, DANIEL; Frewsburg Central HS; Frewsburg, NY; (Y); 15/85; Boy Scts; Church Yth Grp; Stat Bsktbl; JV Var Ftbl; Im Ice Hcky; Im Wt Lftg; Hon Roll; Prfct Atten Awd; Var JV Score Keeper; Hnr Soc Awd Exc Ind Arts 86; Mst Imprvd Plyr Awd Ftbl 84-86; Jamestown CC; Bus Adm.

HILL, DEBORAH; Holland Central HS; Holland, NY; (Y); 50/142; AFS; Library Aide; Teachers Aide; Chorus; Yrbk Sprt Ed; Yrbk Stf; Vllybl; Hon Roll; Prfct Atten Awd; Ldrshp Prog Awd 85; Erie CC S; Exec Sec.

HILL, HEATHER; Newburgh Free Acad; Newburgh, NY; (Y); Church Yth Grp; Cmnty Wkr; French Clb; Science Clb; High Hon Roll; Opt Clb Awd; VFW Awd; Voice Dem Awd; Ski Clb; Chorus; 2-A Ratngs Nyssma Piano Solo 80-82; Sci Congrs-2nd Pl 85-86; Colorado Schl Mines; Geolgy.

HILL, HEATHER L; Columbia HS; E Greenbush, NY; (Y); 20/417; Chorus; School Musical; Symp Band; Rep Frsh Cls; Rep Soph Cls; Rep Jr Cls; Trs Sr Cls; JV Bsktbl; Hon Roll; NHS; NY ST Rgnts Schlrshp 86; Bucknell U; Lbrl Arts.

HILL, JAMES; M L King Jr HS; New York, NY; (Y); Band; Var Bsbl; Hon Roll; St Johns U; Comp Prgmr.

HILL, JASON; Letchworth Central HS; Silver Springs, NY; (Y); Am Leg Boys St; Varsity Clb; Wrstlng; Genesee CC; Model Mkng.

HILL, JEFF; Hugh C Williams HS; Rensselaer Fls, NY; (Y); Pres FFA; NYS Empire Degree Diary Prod FFA 85; Hgh Hnr Roll 85-86; Hnr Roll 83-85; Ag.

HILL, JENNIFER; Bay Shore HS; Bay Shore, NY; (Y); 3/375; Nwsp Bus Mgr; Ed Yrbk Stf; Rep Stu Cncl; JV Tennis; VP Trk; Project AIM US Coast Guard Acad 86; Cheryl De Genaro Academic Excellence Awd 83-84; Economics.

HILL, JOHN; Cardinal O Hara HS; Tonawanda, NY; (S); 4/140; French Clb; Rep Stu Cncl; Im Badmtn; Var Bsktbl; Var Ftbl; Var Capt Socr; High Hon Roll; NHS; Ntl Merit Ltr; 1st Tm Soccr 85; US Air Force Acad; Engr.

HILL, JOHN; East Syracuse-Minoa Central HS; E Syracuse, NY; (Y); Boy Scts; Trs Drama Clb; Thesps; School Play; Yrbk Stf; High Hon Roll; NHS; Latin Clb; Office Aide; Yrbk Rptr; Prncpls Cbnt; Systms Anlyst.

HILL, KIMBERLY A; John Jay HS; Goldens Bridge, NY; (Y); SADD; School Musical; School Play; Stage Crew; Sec Frsh Cls; Rep Soph Cls; Rep Sr Cls; Cmnty Wkr; Computer Clb; Dance Clb.

HILL, KRISTINE C; East Islip HS; Great River, NY; (Y); Pres Church Yth Grp; Red Cross Aide; Sec Service Clb; VP Band; Jazz Band; Orch; Var Fld Hcky; High Hon Roll; Jr NHS; NHS; Frgn Lang Hon Soc Itln 84-85; Pres Physcl Ftn 81-86; Sci Fair Awds 84 & 85.

HILL, LISA; Whitesboro SR HS; Whtiesboro, NY; (Y); 34/306; Church Yth Grp; GAA; Chorus; Stu Cncl; JV Var Cheerleading; JV Capt Fld Hcky; Hon Roll; Engr.

HILL, MARIA; Bayport Blue Point HS; Blue Point, NY; (Y); 5/200; Church Yth Grp; Key Clb; Mathletes; Yrbk Stf; Crs Cntry; Trk; Hon Roll; NHS; NYS Rgnts Schlrshp 86; SUNY Binghamton; Acctg.

HILL, MELODY; Brewster HS; Brewster, NY; (Y); High Hon Roll; Hon Roll; Westchester CC; Bus.

HILL, MICHAEL S; Forest Hills HS; Rego Park, NY; (Y); 101/826; Debate Tm; Letterman Clb; Varsity Clb; Concert Band; School Musical; High Hon Roll; NHS; Vrsty Fencing-Capt; NY St Regents Schlrshp; UFT Svc Awd; US Military Acad; Aerosp Engrg.

HILL, MIKEL; Sodus Cental HS; Williamson, NY; (Y); 8/114; VP French Clb; Model UN; Pres Science Clb; Varsity Clb; Var JV Bsbl; JV Bsktbl; Var JV Socr; High Hon Roll; NHS; Chess Clb; Hgh Hnr Rll 84-86; Aerontcl Engr.

HILL, NICHOLLE; Sweet Home SR HS; Amherst, NY; (Y); Cmnty Wkr; DECA; Pep Clb; School Musical; School Play; Variety Show; Soph Cls; Jr Cls; Stu Cncl; Mgr(s); U Of Buffalo; Advrtsng.

HILL, RALPH; Saranac Lake HS; Saranac Lk, NY; (Y); JV Bsbl.

HILL, ROMAN; Wayland Central HS; Perkinsville, NY; (Y); Drama Clb; German Clb; Hon Roll.

HILL, SCOTT; Williamsville South HS; Williamsville, NY; (Y); Church Yth Grp; Pep Clb; Ski Clb; VP Sr Cls; Bsbl; Capt JV Bsktbl; Capt Var Ftbl; High Hon Roll; Hon Roll; Ftbl All Western NY Hon Mntn 85; Arch.

HILL, TAMMY; Ticonderoga HS; Ticonderoga, NY; (Y); 7/107; Drama Clb; French Clb; Key Clb; School Musical; School Play; Stage Crew; Yrbk Stf; High Hon Roll; Hon Roll; NHS; Madame Grandchamps Awd Frnch 87; Sci.

HILL, TIM; Camden Central HS; Camden, NY; (Y); Am Leg Boys St; Mathletes; VP Science Clb; Spanish Clb; Varsity Clb; Yrbk Stf; JV Bsbl; Bsktbl; Var JV Socr; High Hon Roll; Med.

HILLABRANDT JR, LARRY L; Honeoye Falls Lima Central HS; Honeoye Falls, NY; (Y); 38/184; Am Leg Boys St; Science Clb; Pres Church Yth Grp; Var L Ftbl; Var L Trk; High Hon Roll; Hon Roll; NHS; Prfct Atten Awd; Ducks Unlmtd Essay Cont Wnnr 83; Bus Dynamcs & French Outstndng Stu 84; Cross Cntry Ski Tm 83-86; Forestry.

HILLABUSH, TAMARA; Byron-Bergen Central HS; Byron, NY; (Y); 5/100; Church Yth Grp; Band; Chorus; Yrbk Stf; Lit Mag; Pres Sr Cls; Rep Stu Cncl; Pres NHS; French Clb; FTA; Ithaca Schlrshp 86; U Rchster Padeia Awd 85; Rgnst Schlrshp 86; Ntl Yth Cncl For Ldrshp 85; Ithaca Coll; Cmnctns.

HILLEN, BRIAN; Moore Catholic HS; Staten Island, NY; (Y); Boy Scts; Science Clb; Ski Clb; Teachers Aide; Church Choir; Swmmng; Annopolis Naval Acad; Engr.

HILLICK, AMY; Unatego Central HS; Unadilla, NY; (Y); French Clb; NHS.

HILLIKER, JANET L; Dunkirk HS; Dunkirk, NY; (Y); 21/197; Computer Clb; French Clb; Chorus; VP Frsh Cls; VP Soph Cls; VP Jr Cls; Rep Stu Cncl; Hon Roll; Regents Schlrshp 86; Bryant Stratton Schlrshp 86; Bryant Stratton; Exec Sec Sci.

HILLIS, ANNE; Binghamton HS; Binghamton, NY; (Y); 4-H; Key Clb; SADD; Trs Frsh Cls; VP Soph Cls; Jr Cls; Pres Stu Cncl; Capt Swmmng; Var Vllybl; Ntl Merit Ltr; Mst Outstndg Stu 85; Rotry Yth Ldrshp Awd 85; West Point; Intl Reltns.

HILLIS, JOHN T; Binghamton HS; Bingmanton, NY; (Y); Am Leg Boys St; Church Yth Grp; Key Clb; Spanish Clb; Varsity Clb; VP Trs Stu Cncl; Var Capt Swmmng; Prfct Atten Awd.

HILLS, JERRY; Union-Endicott HS; Endicott, NY; (S); 130/450; Rep Soph Cls; JV Var Bsbl; JV Bsktbl; Var L Ftbl; Hon Roll; MIP Lgn Bsbll 85; MCP Vrsty Ftbl 85; CYO Bsktbll 85-86; U Of Buffalo; Elec Engr.

HILLS, TRISHA; Hancock Central HS; Fishs Eddy, NY; (Y); Camera Clb; Teachers Aide; Chorus; Church Choir; ST Trooper.

HILOW, FRANK; Rome Catholic HS; Rome, NY; (Y); Church Yth Grp; School Musical; Lit Mag; Var Bsktbl; Hon Roll; CYS Spch Spr 83; Essay Wnnr Itln Amer Assn 81, 83; Psych.

HILS, WENDY; North Tonawanda HS; N Tonawanda, NY; (Y); AFS; Church Yth Grp; Church Choir; JV Var Bsktbl; U Of Buffalo; Specl Ed.

HILSER, SUZANNE B; Masters Schl; Rhinebeck, NY; (Y); Cmnty Wkr; Key Clb; High Hon Roll; Hosp Aide; Yrbk Stf; JV Bsktbl; JV Capt Fld Hcky; JV Sftbl; Ntl Merit Ltr; Cum Laude Soc 86; U NC Chapel Hill; Psych.

HILSON, ELIZABETH; Guilderland Central HS; Schenectady, NY; (Y); JA; Band; Educ Schlrshp Awrd 86; Outstndng Achvt Data Prc 86; Comp Sci.

HILTBRAND, LISA M; Liverpool HS; Liverpool, NY; (Y); 42/816; Mrchg Band; Orch; JV Sftbl; Hon Roll; Jr NHS; NHS; RPI; Arch.

HILTON, LAURA; Whitesboro SR HS; Marcy, NY; (Y); 44/363; 4-H; Girl Scts; Science Clb; Chorus; Im Bsktbl; Im Sftbl; Im Trk; Im Vllybl; High Hon Roll; Hon Roll; Accntng.

HILTON, MONICA; A-P-CO HS; Altmar, NY; (Y); Trs French Clb; Girl Scts; JV Vllybl; Cit Awd; High Hon Roll; Hon Roll; NHS; Dllrs Schlrs Schlrshp, APW Fclty Schlrshp 86; Soc Stds Awd, Amrcnsm Awd 86; SUNY Oswego; Elem Educ.

HILTON, RICHARD; Whitesboro SR HS; Marcy, NY; (Y); 33/346; Boy Scts; Exploring; Hon Roll; Jr NHS; Regents Schlrshp 85-86; Herkimer Co CC; Engrng Sci.

HILTS, BARBARA; Morrisville-Eaton Central HS; Eaton, NY; (Y); Library Aide; Office Aide; Band; Chorus; Concert Band; Nwsp Stf; Cheerleading; Hon Roll; Paul J Head Attd Achvmnt Awd 85-86; AZ Western; Law.

HILTS, BRADLEY; Vernon-Verona-Sherrill HS; Verona, NY; (Y); Church Yth Grp; Bsktbl; Trk; Hon Roll; Morrisvl Ag Schl; Anml Husbdry.

HILTS, SUSAN; Veron-Verona-Sherrill HS; Verona, NY; (Y); Church Yth Grp; GAA; Sec Frsh Cls; Rep Soph Cls; Rep Jr Cls; Stu Cncl; Bsktbl; Socr; Sftbl; High Hon Roll; Art Sch; Adv Design.

HIN, JADE; Hillcrest HS; College Point, NY; (Y); 97/801; Library Aide; Office Aide; Band; Rgnts Schlrshp 86; Hunter; Nrsng.

HINDMAN, CRAIG; Mayville Central HS; Dewittville, NY; (S); Church Yth Grp; Ski Clb; Spanish Clb; Var Trk; High Hon Roll; Lion Awd; Pres NHS.

HINDS, MAXINE; Nazareth Regional HS; Brooklyn, NY; (Y); Dance Clb; Intnl Clb; Office Aide; Spanish Clb; Varsity Clb; Chorus; Variety Show; Crs Cntry; Trk; Hon Roll; Dnc Awd 86; Chorus Awd 86; Nzrth Kngsmn Sngrs Awd 86; FL ST U; Spnsh.

HINE, WENDY; Fredonia HS; Fredonia, NY; (Y); 7/181; French Clb; Ski Clb; Chorus; School Musical; Lit Mag; Var L Swmmng; L JV Trk; High Hon Roll; Pres Schlr; St Schlr; Connecticut Coll; Psych.

HINKELMAN, JEANNE M; Nazareth Acad; Rochester, NY; (Y); 15/157; Church Yth Grp; Exploring; Ski Clb; Concert Band; Jazz Band; Nwsp Phtg; Stu Cncl; High Hon Roll; Hon Roll; St Schlr; St John Fisher Coll Max Schlrshp 86; Le Moyne Coll 86; Nazareth Acad H S Partl Tuitn 82; St John Fisher & Siena; Intl St.

HINKLE, NANCY; Portville Central Schl; Westons Mills, NY; (Y); AFS; Camp Fr Inc; Cmnty Wkr; Drama Clb; 4-H; Library Aide; Spanish Clb; Band; Concert Band; Mrchg Band; Air Force; Nrsng.

HINKLEY, JODI LYNNE; Susquehanna Valley HS; Kirkwood, NY; (Y); 9/186; French Clb; Girl Scts; Service Clb; Pres SADD; Chorus; Rep Sr Cls; Rep Stu Cncl; Bowling; Tennis; High Hon Roll; Cazenovia Coll; Fash Mech.

HINMAN, LISA J; Union Springs Central Schl; Skaneateles, NY; (Y); 10/94; Cmnty Wkr; French Clb; German Clb; Spanish Clb; Teachers Aide; Var L Socr; High Hon Roll; NYS Rgnts Schlrshp 86; Loyola U; Intl Bus.

HINMAN, STEPHANIE; Columbia HS; E Greenbush, NY; (Y); 37/417; Trs Key Clb; Band; Mrchg Band; Var L Tennis; JV Trk; NY ST Regents Schrlshp 85-86; SUNY Albany; Pol Sci.

HINOJOSA, TANYA; Bishop Ludden HS; Syracuse, NY; (Y); Quiz Bowl; Red Cross Aide; Band; High Hon Roll; Phrmcy.

HINSDALE, BRENDA; Southwestern Central HS; Jamestown, NY; (Y); French Clb; FTA; Home Ec Achvt 86; Elem Ed.

HINSKEN, AMY; Attica SR HS; Cowlesville, NY; (Y); 110/175; AFS; Church Yth Grp; Drama Clb; Spanish Clb; Chorus; JV Cheerleading; Var Trk; JV Vllybl; School Play; Stat Bsktbl; NYSSMA Solo Fstvl 85; NYSSMA All Cnty Fstvl 84; Psychlgy.

HINTON, ASHLEY; Westbury HS; Westbury, NY; (Y); 12/250; Chorus; Cheerleading; Hon Roll; Acctg.

HINZ, TIMOTHY F; Alexander Central HS; Batavia, NY; (Y); Boy Scts; Pres Church Yth Grp; Spanish Clb; Chorus; JV Var Bsktbl; Miltry Police.

HIPP, BILL; Riverhead HS; Calverton, NY; (Y); 43/210; Acpl Chr; Chorus; Concert Band; Jazz Band; Orch; School Musical; Yrbk Stf; Var Crs Cntry; Socr; Im Wt Lftg; Undrclssmn Music Schlrshp 84; Outstndg Musical Prfrmnc 84; Mst Imprvd Band 85; Music Educ.

HIPPOLYTE, GREGORY; Archbishop Molloy HS; Kew Gardens, NY; (Y); 136/383; Computer Clb; Latin Clb; Science Clb; Spanish Clb; JV Trk; Hon Roll; JV Wt Lftg; NY U; Pre Med Stu.

HIRALDO, LIZ MARYLAND; Bronx HS Of Science; Bronx, NY; (Y); Pres Church Yth Grp; Cmnty Wkr; Science Clb; Spanish NHS; U Of Rochester; Pre-Med.

HIRN, RUSSELL; Valley Central HS; Maybrook, NY; (Y); Aud/Vis; Chess Clb; Hon Roll.

HIRSCHEY, LISA; Watertown HS; Watertown, NY; (Y); Band; Concert Band; Mrchg Band; Capt Ice Hcky; Potsdam; Elem Ed.

HIRSHBERG, JAY; Hebrew Acad Of The Five Towns; W Hempstead, NY; (Y); 14/57; Boy Scts; Chrmn Ski Clb; Temple Yth Grp; Var Sftbl; Tennis; Ntl Merit Ltr; 2nd Bsmn Sftbl Tm 85-86; Captain Tennis Tm 85-86; SUNY; Chem.

HIRST, BRAD; Harpursville Central HS; Port Crane, NY; (S); 10/90; Church Yth Grp; Chorus; School Play; Off Stu Cncl; JV Capt Bsbl; JV Var Bsktbl; JV Var Ftbl; NHS; Drama Clb; Spanish Clb; Activities Awd 84-85; NYSSMA Solo Excllnt 84-85; Area All-ST Music Fest 84-85.

HIRVONEN, HEIDI; Lansing HS; Lansing, NY; (Y); 6/85; Pres 4-H; French Clb; Concert Band; Jazz Band; Orch; 4-H Awd; Sec NHS; Powder Puff Ftbl; Timer; Frnch Acad Awd 84-85; Area All ST Orch 85-86; NYSSMA Music Comptn 85-86; Int Design.

HISE, PATRICIA; Gates-Chili SR HS; Rochester, NY; (S); 24/411; Service Clb; Band; Rep Jr Cls; Rep Sr Cls; Var JV Bsktbl; Var L Crs Cntry; Var L Trk; Var L Vllybl; High Hon Roll; Hon Roll; Soc Stds Achvt Awd, JR Cls Svc Awd, Cptn Awd Trk 85; Bio Sci.

HISE, SANDRA LEE; Gates-Chili SR HS; Rochester, NY; (S); 7/411; Math Tm; Concert Band; Jazz Band; Rep Sr Cls; JV Bsktbl; Var L Crs Cntry; Var L Trk; High Hon Roll; Pres NHS; Mathletes; Stu Rep Genesee Vly Schl Brd Inst Conf 83; Sprts Boostr Clb Athltc Schlrshp 84; Cls Svc Awd 85; Geneseo ST Coll; Elem Ed.

HITCHCOCK, APRIL; F D Roosevelt HS; Poughkeepsie, NY; (Y); Ski Clb; Church Yth Grp; Dance Clb; Band; Concert Band; Jazz Band; Mrchg Band; Var Cheerleading; Bst NYS 4th Out Of U S Chrldng Squad 84-85; Casinovia; Theatr.

HITCHCOCK, CELINA M; Mt Mercy Acad; W Seneca, NY; (Y); Science Clb; SADD; School Play; Stage Crew; Yrbk Ed-Chief; Yrbk Stf; Bowling; Hon Roll; Acad Schlrshp 86; Hilbert Coll; Exec Secy.

HITCHCOCK, GREG; Faith Heritage Schl; Syracuse, NY; (Y); Church Yth Grp; Computer Clb; 4-H; French Clb; Band; Rep Frsh Cls; Capt Bsktbl; Golf; Socr; Trk; Houghton Coll; Bus Admin.

HITCHCOCK, JAMES; Fairpot HS; Fairport, NY; (Y); Im Bsktbl; Im Coach Actv; JV Ftbl; JV Im Lcrss; Im Sftbl; Bus.

HITCHCOCK, STACEY L; Pulaski JR SR HS; Pulaski, NY; (S); Am Leg Aux Girls St; Church Yth Grp; Drama Clb; French Clb; GAA; Math Clb; Chorus; Church Choir; Color Guard; School Musical; Snow Incentv Awd 84; SUNY-PLATTSBURGH; Deaf Educ.

HITT, CHRISTOPHER; Bay Shore HS; Bay Shore, NY; (Y); Computer Clb; Debate Tm; SADD; Teachers Aide; Nwsp Sprt Ed; Yrbk Stf; Sec Frsh Cls; JV Var Gym; Hon Roll; LEAD 85; US Naval Acad.

HITT, JULIE; Walton JR SR HS; Walton, NY; (Y); 46/107; GAA; Key Clb; SADD; VP Varsity Clb; VICA; Sec Soph Cls; Crs Cntry; Socr; Capt Trk; Capt Vllybl; Hmcmg Ct 86; Joan Mc Graghan Awd-Most Outstndg Dtrmntn Vlybl 86; Acad Achvt Awd 86; Cobleskill Coll; Early Chld Dev.

HLADIK, MELISSA L; Johnstown HS; Johnstown, NY; (Y); 2/167; Yrbk Stf; Sec Jr Cls; Sec Sr Cls; Powder Puff Ftbl; Capt L Sftbl; Capt L Vllybl; High Hon Roll; Hon Roll; Sec NHS; Sal; Rgnts Schlrshp 86; Levi Parsons Schlrshp-Union Coll 86; Latn I Awd 85; Union Coll; Mech Engrng.

HO, ANNETTE; Seward Park HS; New York, NY; (Y); Library Aide; Office Aide; Teachers Aide; Frnch Awd 82-83; Jrnlsm.

HO, DAVID; Aviation HS; New York, NY; (Y); 14/415; Library Aide; Office Aide; Teachers Aide; Chorus; Nwsp Stf; Prfct Atten Awd; Aviation H S Pegasus Soc 86; Law.

HO, DAW; Midwood HS; Brooklyn, NY; (Y); Office Aide; Spanish Clb; Variety Show; Lit Mag; Prfct Atten Awd.

HO, GORDON; Seward Park HS; New York, NY; (Y); 6/5044; Regnts Schlrshp; Engrng.

HO, RODNEY; Oyster Bay HS; Oyster Bay, NY; (Y); 1/132; Trs Computer Clb; Capt Mathletes; VP SADD; Band; Jazz Band; Nwsp Ed-Chief; Lit Mag; Var Tennis; NHS.

HOAD, LISA M; Wayland Central Schl; Wayland, NY; (Y); 2/110; Trs FTA; Math Tm; Trs Varsity Clb; Pres Concert Band; Jazz Band; Tennis; DAR Awd; NHS; Sal; Regnts Schlrshp 86; Hnrs Clb 82-86; Geneseo ST U; Elem Ed.

HOAD, STEVE; Wayland Central HS; Wayland, NY; (Y); 23/137; Varsity Clb; Var L Bsbl; Hon Roll; Var L Socr; Physcl Educ.

HOAGE, DEBORAH A; Kenmore West SR HS; Kenmore, NY; (Y); Cmnty Wkr; Capt Debate Tm; French Clb; Teachers Aide; Varsity Clb; Yrbk Stf; Rep Stu Cncl; Var JV Socr; High Hon Roll; Hon Roll; Schl Ltr Soccer 84-86; Recntn Cert NY ST Bar Assoc 85; Recgntn Cert Black Rock Riverside Pantry; Law.

HOAGLAND, KIM; Kenmore West HS; Kenmore, NY; (Y); 144/420; GAA; Varsity Clb; Color Guard; Bsktbl; Capt Tennis; Vllybl; Hon Roll; St Bonaventure; Psych.

HOAK, SUSAN J; Notre Dame HS; Byron, NY; (S); #6 In Class; Art Clb; Cmnty Wkr; 4-H; French Clb; FNA; Math Clb; Science Clb; Service Clb; Ski Clb; Teachers Aide; Genesee Soc Prevntn Cruelty Animals; Vol NYS Schl Blind; Private Piano,Art Lessng; U ME; Vet.

HOBAN, KELLY L; Hamburg SR HS; Hamburg, NY; (Y); 26/382; Pres AFS; French Clb; Mrchg Band; School Musical; Stage Crew; Lib Symp Band; Co-Capt Cheerleading; NHS; Lib Band; Color Guard; Ny St Rgnts Schlrshp 86; GA ST U; Chiroprctr.

HOBART, KIM; Le Roy Central HS; Leroy, NY; (Y); Camera Clb; Ski Clb; Yrbk Stf; Trk; Hon Roll; Human Svcs.

HOBBES, JOSHUA; Ward Melville HS; Stony Brook, NY; (Y); DECA; Im Trk; Hon Roll; Bus Hnr Soc 85-86; Hnrb Mntn Suffolk Cnty Dera Cmptn 86; Bus.

HOBBS, LISA; Far Rockaway HS; Brooklyn, NY; (Y); 8/338; VP Key Clb; Quiz Bowl; Yrbk Bus Mgr; VP Stu Cncl; High Hon Roll; NHS; Prfct Atten Awd; Office Aide; Service Clb; Teachers Aide; Assoc Black Ed Schlrshp 86; Teachers Schlrshp 86; NY ST Regents Schlrshp 86; Polytechnic U; Engrng.

HOBERG, CYNTHIA ANN; Kingston HS; Kingston, NY; (Y); 51/573; 4-H; Chorus; Church Choir; Jr Cls; 4-H Awd; High Hon Roll; Hon Roll; Jr NHS; NHS; NYS Regnts Schlrshp 86; Fshn Merch.

HOCH, KITTIE; Canastota JR SR HS; Canastota, NY; (S); 4-H; Band; Concert Band; Mrchg Band; Tennis; 4-H Awd; High Hon Roll; Jr NHS; NHS; Comp Prog.

HOCHREITER, JO ELLYN; Brockport Central HS; Brockport, NY; (Y); Church Yth Grp; Dance Clb; Ski Clb; Spanish Clb; SADD; Bsktbl; Im Bowling; Var JV Cheerleading; JV Diving; Im Sftbl; Stu Tchr 85-86; Cmnty Ambass 85; Genesee CC; Elem Ed.

HOCKER, JOHN D; Southold HS; Southold, NY; (Y); 3/75; Am Leg Boys St; ROTC; Ski Clb; Color Guard; Drill Tm; Yrbk Stf; Pres Stu Cncl; Socr; Tennis; High Hon Roll; Sci.

HODGE, EDITH; St Joseph HS; Brooklyn, NY; (S); 3/153; French Clb; Girl Scts; Office Aide; Science Clb; School Musical; Gym; Hon Roll; NHS; Speech Tm; Brookhaven Smmr Sci Hnrs Prog Cert 85; Sci.

HODGE, RHONDA; Fairport HS; Fairport, NY; (Y); Key Clb; Ski Clb; Band; Hon Roll; Med.

HODGSON, DOREEN; St John The Baptist HS; Central Islip, NY; (Y); FNA; Hosp Aide; SADD; Band; High Hon Roll; Ntl Merit Ltr; Merit Awd Sci & Social Stds 86; Top Hon Roll; Loretto Hts; Nursing.

HODNE, DANIEL; Clarkstown HS South; New City, NY; (Y); Chess Clb; Sec German Clb; Im Bsktbl; Mu Alp Tht; NHS; Iona Lng Cont 1st Hnrs 86; Arch.

HODNE, THOMAS; Clarkstown HS; New City, NY; (Y); Sec Chess Clb; Cmnty Wkr; German Clb; Math Tm; Service Clb; Trk; NHS; Ntl Merit Ltr; US Naval Acad; Aerospc Engr.

HOEFER, JON; James E Sperry HS; Henrietta, NY; (Y); 20/300; French Clb; VP JA; Ski Clb; School Musical; Yrbk Ed-Chief; VP Stu Cncl; High Hon Roll; NHS; Art Clb; Drama Clb; Henrietta Yth Brd Hall Of Fame 83; 3 Blue Rbbn Key Awds Sibleys Art Shw 83-85; Natl Hon Mntn 85; Syracuse U; Adv.

HOEFFNER, DONNA; Valley Central HS; Montgomery, NY; (Y); 18/286; Natl Beta Clb; Service Clb; Stu Cncl; JV Var Bsktbl; JV Var Socr; JV Var Sftbl; Hon Roll; Spanish NHS; Regents Schlrshp 86; Binghamton.

HOEFLER, PETER MICHAEL; James Madison HS; Brooklyn, NY; (Y); 49/756; Debate Tm; JA; Office Aide; Political Wkr; Speech Tm; Teachers Aide; Band; School Musical; Lit Mag; Hon Roll; Pre-Law.

HOEFLICH, MIKE; St Marys HS; Lancaster, NY; (S); 7/163; Boys Clb Am; SADD; Pres Jr Cls; Trs Sr Cls; Capt L Bsktbl; L Ftbl; L Tennis; Hon Roll; NHS; NY ST Regnts Schrlshp 86; Canisius Coll Friars Schlrshp 86; Canisius Coll; Engrng.

HOELTZEL, BRYCE W; Schroon Lake Central Schl; Schroon Lake, NY; (Y); 6/28; Aud/Vis; Chess Clb; Exploring; Model UN; School Play; Yrbk Stf; VP Jr Cls; VP Sr Cls; Var Socr; Im Swmmng; Oneonta; Biol.

HOELZER, DAVID; Central Islip SR HS; Central Islip, NY; (Y); Boy Scts; Chess Clb; Math Tm; Scholastic Bowl; School Musical; Nwsp Rptr; Lit Mag; Swmmng; High Hon Roll; Trs NHS; JV Swim Team Captn 83; 2nd Pl Regnl Amercn Legn Speech Cntst 86; W Point; Sci.

HOEN, CYD; Bishop Maginn HS; Rensselaer, NY; (S); 13/86; Ski Clb; Spanish Clb; School Play; Cheerleading; Sftbl; Tennis; Vllybl; High Hon Roll; Hon Roll; SUNY Coll; Math.

HOERBELT, MARK D; Batavia HS; Batavia, NY; (Y); 28/204; Chorus; Church Choir; Jazz Band; Orch; School Musical; Swing Chorus; Variety Show; Im Var Bsktbl; Im Ftbl; Var Socr; 2 Yr All Leg Ten Tm 85-86; All ST Chorus 86; Talent Schlrshp Ithaca Coll 86; Ithaca Coll; Music.

HOF, JENNIFER M; The Waldorf Schl; Forest Hills, NY; (Y); Am Leg Aux Girls St; Church Yth Grp; Drama Clb; Exploring; Service Clb; School Musical; School Play; Stage Crew; Yrbk Stf; Tennis; Regents Schlrshp 86; Smith Coll; Gov.

HOFF, DARCI; Southside HS; Pine City, NY; (S); 15/250; AFS; Church Yth Grp; Drama Clb; French Clb; Acpl Chr; Band; Church Choir; Madrigals; School Musical; Var Diving.

HOFF, JENNIFER; Mount Mercy Acad; Buffalo, NY; (Y); 44/198; JCL; Math Clb; Ski Clb; SADD; Stage Crew; Trs Frsh Cls; Rep Soph Cls; Rep Jr Cls; Trs Sr Cls; NHS; Bus Admin.

HOFFBERG, AMY SUE; Wantagh HS; Wantagh, NY; (Y); 17/279; Drama Clb; Mathletes; Math Clb; Math Tm; Ski Clb; Teachers Aide; School Musical; School Play; Stage Crew; Variety Show; Rgnts Schlrshp Awd 86; Bstn U; Music Thry.

HOFFELDER, CAROLYN; Garden City HS; Garden City, NY; (Y); 150/376; Church Yth Grp; French Clb; GAA; Hosp Aide; Pep Clb; Rep Soph Cls; JV Bsktbl; Fld Hcky; Lcrss; Rgnts Schlrshp Awd Wnr; Fordham U; Bus.

HOFFMAN, BROCK; Clarence HS; Clarence, NY; (Y); Socr; Hon Roll; Prfct Atten Awd; Sccr Ltr 85; Archtctr.

HOFFMAN, CAROL J; Walt Whtiman HS; Melville, NY; (Y); 50/549; Drama Clb; Political Wkr; Spanish Clb; Stage Crew; NHS; Ntl Merit Ltr; Spanish NHS; SUNY Binghamton; Law.

HOFFMAN, DAVID; Hamburg Central HS; Hamburg, NY; (Y); Am Leg Boys St; Chess Clb; VP German Clb; Model UN; Quiz Bowl; Im Bsktbl; L Trk; Regnl Chmp State Olympd Russn 86; 1st Pl Germn Rdng NY Forgn Lang Fair 86; 6th Pl Indr Trck 86.

HOFFMAN, DAVID A; Kenmore West HS; Kenmore, NY; (Y); 33/425; Boy Scts; JA; Pres Math Tm; Quiz Bowl; Orch; Cit Awd; Hon Roll; NHS; St Schlr; Princpls Awd 86; Mock Trial Team 85-86; Tonawanda Yth Ct 83-86; Hamilton Coll; Pol Sci.

HOFFMAN, DEBBIE E; The Bronx HS Of Science; New York, NY; (Y); Cmnty Wkr; JA; Library Aide; Temple Yth Grp; Nwsp Ed-Chief; Nwsp Rptr; High Hon Roll; Exclince Jrnlsm 86; NYU; Jrnlsm.

HOFFMAN, GLEN L; Floral Park Memorial HS; Floral Park, NY; (Y); 3/150; Computer Clb; Mathletes; Variety Show; Nwsp Stf; High Hon Roll; NHS; Aud/Vis; Lit Mag; Hon Roll; Prfct Atten Awd; NYS Rgnts Schlrshp 86; Nassau Cnty Math Slvr Pin Awd 86; Natl Sci Olympiad Awd-Bio 85; Bucknell U; Math.

HOFFMAN, HEIDI; Valley Central HS; Montgomery, NY; (Y); 43/315; Sec Exploring; Concert Band; Mrchg Band; Symp Band; Lit Mag; French Hon Soc; Hon Roll; NHS; Psych.

HOFFMAN, JENNIFER; Kenmore East HS; Kenmore, NY; (Y); 65/330; Trs Church Yth Grp; Off Frsh Cls; Off Soph Cls; French Hon Soc; High Hon Roll; NHS; Amherst YES Outstndng Vlntr 83-85; Natl Conf Of Christians & Jews Brothrhd/Sistrhd Awd 86; Physcl Thrpy.

HOFFMAN, JOHN P; Marcus Whitman Central HS; Gorham, NY; (Y); 11/113; Am Leg Boys St; Latin Clb; Band; Concert Band; Mrchg Band; Var Bsbl; Var Co-Capt Bsktbl; Var Socr; High Hon Roll; NHS; Outstndng SR Athlt 86; Daniel Harris Mem Bsktbll Awd 86; Hobart Coll Schlrshp 86; Hobart Coll; Politcl Sci.

HOFFMAN, JULIE; South Shore HS; Brooklyn, NY; (Y); 50/729; Drama Clb; English Clb; Model UN; Science Clb; SADD; Chorus; School Play; High Hon Roll; Buffalo U; Lwyr.

HOFFMAN, MAUREEN; Tappanzee HS; Orangeburg, NY; (Y); 14/245; Concert Band; Orch; Yrbk Stf; Sec Frsh Cls; Sec Soph Cls; Sec Jr Cls; Sec Sr Cls; Var Capt Crs Cntry; Capt Trk; NHS; NYS Rgnts Schlrshp 86; Boston Coll.

HOFFMAN, MEMRAY; New Rochelle HS; New Rochelle, NY; (Y); Church Choir; Flag Corp; Orch; Twrlr; NHS; Black Cult Clb; NAACP Yth Cnsl Sec 86; Natl Musc Hnr Soc Vice Pres 86.

HOFFMAN, NANCY; Lindenhurst HS; Lindenhurst, NY; (Y); Thesps; Varsity Clb; School Play; Yrbk Phtg; Rep Sr Cls; VP Pres Stu Cncl; JV Var Cheerleading; Var Trk; JV Vllybl; Hon Roll; Elem Educ.

HOFFMAN, NANCY; Liverpool HS; Liverpool, NY; (Y); 36/816; Spanish Clb; Orch; School Musical; Symp Band; Crs Cntry; Hon Roll; NHS; U Of Rochester; Hosp Adm.

HOFFMAN, PHILIP; Hillcrest HS; Rosedale, NY; (Y); Debate Tm; VP JA; Temple Yth Grp; Rep Jr Cls; Gym; JR Achvt Ldrshp Trainng Awd 83; Debat Tm-Lincoln Douglas Debats 85; Exec Intrnshp, Spkr Assmbly 85-86; Queens Coll; Cmnctns.

HOFFMAN, SAMUEL; United Nations International Schl; Forest Hills, NY; (Y); 2/120; Model UN; Symp Band; Nwsp Stf; Lit Mag; Var Tennis; NHS; Ntl Merit Schol; Estrn Tnns Assoc Rnkd Plyr 83-85; Orgnzr Nuclear Issue Dy Cnfrnc NY Area Schls At UN 86; Hrvrd Coll; Ecnmcs.

HOFFMANN, KENNETH; La Salle Military Acad; Stony Brook, NY; (S); 4/99; Am Leg Boys St; ROTC; Chorus; Drill Tm; Nwsp Ed-Chief; Capt Socr; Hon Roll; NHS; Most Dedicated Awd Drill Team 84-85; Natl Sci Merit Awd 85-86; Polt Sci.

HOFFMANN, PAULINE; Alden Central HS; E Aurora, NY; (Y); Science Clb; SADD; Sec Band; Yrbk Bus Mgr; Yrbk Stf; JV Var Bsktbl; High Hon Roll; Art Clb; Concert Band; Mrchg Band; All Co Band; 1st Pl Ntl Hstry Day; Sci Fair Exhbtr; Mrn Bio.

HOFMAN, JOHN P; Bishop Ford Central Catholic HS; Brooklyn, NY; (Y); 10/441; Math Tm; Yrbk Phtg; Regnts Schlrshp 86; NY U; Comp Sci.

HOFMANN, GREGORY; Attica HS; Attica, NY; (S); 5/154; Am Leg Boys St; Varsity Clb; Bsbl; Bsktbl; Socr; Hon Roll; Jr NHS; NHS.

HOFMANN, RENEE; Sewanhaka HS; Floral Pk, NY; (Y); Church Yth Grp; FBLA; GAA; Spanish Clb; JV Bsktbl; Var Socr; JV Var Sftbl; Hon Roll; Varsity Clb; Bus Hnr Socty; Bus Mgmt.

HOGAN, CHERYL A; Catherine Mc Auley HS; Brooklyn, NY; (S); 3/70; Church Yth Grp; Dance Clb; Girl Scts; Church Choir; Stage Crew; Rep Frsh Cls; Sec Stu Cncl; Capt Cheerleading; Var Sftbl; High Hon Roll; JV Sftbl Bst Bttr 83; Vrsty Sftbl MIP 84; Boostr Clb Mst Dedctd 82.

HOGAN, CHRISTOPHER; Seton Catholic Central HS; Johnson City, NY; (Y); French Clb; Ski Clb; Varsity Clb; Var JV Ftbl; MVP Awd St Jms CYO Bsktbl Team 85-86; Bnghmtn Press & Snblltn Paper Carrier Mo 86.

HOGAN, KATIE; Charles O Dickerson HS; Trumansburg, NY; (Y); 13/115; Church Yth Grp; Cmnty Wkr; French Clb; Political Wkr; Yrbk Stf; Socr; Vllybl; High Hon Roll; NHS; PTO Awd 83; Frnch.

HOGAN, KRISTIN; Cohoes HS; Cohoes, NY; (Y); Hosp Aide; Mathletes; Office Aide; Red Cross Aide; Y-Teens; Chorus; School Musical; High Hon Roll; Hon Roll; Prfct Atten Awd; Nrsng.

HOGAN, MARY A; John S Burke Catholic HS; Warwick, NY; (Y); 10/153; Drama Clb; Math Tm; School Play; Sec Stage Crew; Ed Lit Mag; High Hon Roll; NHS; Ntl Merit SF; NEDT Awd; Niagara U Acad Schlr 86; Niagara U; Acctng.

HOGANCAMP, RACHEL; Elmira Southside HS; Pine City, NY; (S); 5/385; Varsity Clb; School Musical; Ed Yrbk Stf; Pres Soph Cls; VP Stu Cncl; Bsktbl; Sftbl; Vllybl; High Hon Roll; Aud/Vis; Bus.

HOGENBOOM, TIMOTHY; Berne-Know-Westerlo Centrl Schl; Knox, NY; (Y); French Clb; Quiz Bowl; VP Sr Cls; Var Capt Bsktbl; Var L Crs Cntry; Var Golf; Var L Tennis; High Hon Roll; NHS; Ntl Merit SF; Math Tchr.

HOGLE, KAREN; Knox Memorial Central HS; Hermon, NY; (S); 2/30; French Clb; Varsity Clb; Concert Band; Mrchg Band; Yrbk Ed-Chief; VP Sr Cls; Socr; Vllybl; High Hon Roll; NHS; St John Fisher Coll; Gerntlgy.

HOGLE, ROGER; Knox Memorial Central HS; Hermon, NY; (S); 3/28; Varsity Clb; Yrbk Stf; Bsbl; Socr; Vllybl; High Hon Roll; Engrng.

HOHL, JAMES; Liverpool HS; Liverpool, NY; (Y); 3/884; Boy Scts; Off Church Yth Grp; VP JA; Math Tm; NFL; Stage Crew; Jr NHS; Pres NHS; Cert Exc Frnch Amb 84; AATF Ntl Frnch Cntst 1st Pl 84; Intl Bus.

HOHLOWSKI, SEAN; E L Vandermeulen HS; Port Jefferson, NY; (Y); 51/300; Computer Clb; Ski Clb; SADD; Varsity Clb; JV Var Bsktbl; Var Golf; Var Trk; High Hon Roll; JV Crs Cntry; NYS Rgnts Schlrshp 86; 1st Pl Physcs Cntst 86; Clemson U; Engrng.

HOHN, REBECCA; Hoosick Falls Central Schl; Hoosick Falls, NY; (Y); Chorus; Hon Roll; Bus Adm.

HOILETT-BARRETT, ALTHEA; St Raymond Acad For Girls; Bronx, NY; (S); 3/85; Cmnty Wkr; Computer Clb; Dance Clb; Library Aide; Math Clb; Spanish Clb; Swmmng; Hon Roll; NHS; Engl Awd; Bio.

HOKE, BRIAN; Susquehanna Valley HS; Kirkwood, NY; (Y); Mathletes; Quiz Bowl; Varsity Clb; Band; Jazz Band; Mrchg Band; Var Ftbl; Var L Trk; High Hon Roll; NHS; Area All St Awd Band; Hamilton Coll; Physics.

HOKE, HEATHER-MARIE; Owen D Young HS; Jordanville, NY; (Y); Q&S; Band; Yrbk Stf; Sec Stu Cncl; Var Capt Jr Cls; Var Capt Sftbl; Var Capt Vllybl; Jr NHS; Drama Clb; Varsity Clb; Gvnrs Trophy Rsrch Cont Awd 85; Mst Imprvd Awd Soccer 84-85; Clark Schlrshp 86; Wstrn New Englnd Coll; Bus Mgmt.

HOKE, THOMAS A; North Eastern Clinton HS; Mooers, NY; (Y); 16/126; CAP; Radio Clb; Band; Jazz Band; High Hon Roll; Rgnts Scshlrshp 86; NY; Clarkson; Elec Engrng.

HOLAHAN, T SCOTT; Victor Central Schl; Victor, NY; (Y); Bsktbl; Golf; High Hon Roll; Hon Roll; Athltc Achvt Awds Glf 83-86; Engrng.

HOLBEN, JILL; Hamburg SR HS; Hamburg, NY; (Y); Service Clb; Yrbk Phtg; Yrbk Stf; Rep Frsh Cls; Mgr(s); Score Keeper; Swmmng; Trk; NY Schl Of Design; Intr Dsgn.

HOLBROOK, MICHELLE; Chateaugay Central Schl; Chateaugay, NY; (Y); 3/63; French Clb; GAA; Varsity Clb; Rep Jr Cls; Rep Sr Cls; Pres Stu Cncl; Capt Cheerleading; Var Socr; High Hon Roll; NHS; Law.

HOLCOMB, DAWN; Auburn HS; Auburn, NY; (Y); Cmnty Wkr; Dance Clb; High Hon Roll; Hon Roll; Oswego U; Erly Chldhd Educ.

HOLCOMBE, JON; Bishop Ludden HS; Syracuse, NY; (S); Art Clb; Spanish Clb; Nwsp Phtg; Yrbk Phtg; Yrbk Stf; Var Tennis; High Hon Roll; NHS; Ntl Merit Ltr; Lbrl Arts.

HOLCOMBE, LAURA; Bayport Blue Point HS; Bayport, NY; (Y); Art Clb; Key Clb; Science Clb; Ed.

HOLDEN, GREG M; Shoreham Wading River HS; Shoreham, NY; (Y); Computer Clb; School Play; Stage Crew; Yrbk Bus Mgr; Yrbk Stf; Rep Frsh Cls; Rep Soph Cls; Rep Stu Cncl; JV Socr; JV Var Trk; NYS Regnts Schlrshp 85-86; Phys Olmpcs 85-86; Bradley U; Bio.

HOLDEN, MEGAN; Shoreham-Wading River HS; Shoreham, NY; (Y); Mathletes; Science Clb; SADD; Chorus; Orch; Var Crs Cntry; Var Trk; NHS; Ntl Merit Ltr; Athlt Of Yr Awd 85-86; Brnz Mdlst In Pswrd In NY ST Sci Olympics 84-85; Sprts Med.

HOLDEN, STEVE; Blind Brook HS; Port Chester, NY; (Y); Boy Scts; NY Acad Of Sci Intrnshp 85-86; Bio.

HOLDEN, WILBUR; Myndersc Acad; Seneca Falls, NY; (Y); 9/138; Am Leg Boys St; French Clb; Ski Clb; JV Bsktbl; JV Var Lcrss; High Hon Roll; NHS; Block M Athltc Clb.

HOLDER, CHERYL ANNE; Chenango Forks HS; Binghamton, NY; (Y); 8/182; Church Yth Grp; Drama Clb; SADD; School Musical; School Play; Yrbk Stf; Sec Sr Cls; High Hon Roll; NHS; Pres Schlr; Prsdntl Outstndng Acdmc Ftns Awd 86; Prsdntl Schlrshp Shenandoah Coll & Msc Cnsrvtry 86; Broome CC; Performance.

HOLDER, CHRISTINE; John Marshall HS; Rochester, NY; (Y); Aud/Vis; FBLA; Office Aide; Spanish Clb; Teachers Aide; Acpl Chr; Color Guard; Yrbk Stf; Stu Cncl; Var Bowling; Lawrence R Kiepper Mst Promising Stu Ath Awd 84-85; Bus.

HOLDER, STACY O; Westbury HS; Westbury, NY; (Y); 87/250; Cmnty Wkr; Spanish Clb; Teachers Aide; Chorus; Yrbk Stf; Lit Mag; Mgr(s); Stat Socr; Hon Roll; Jrnlsm.

HOLDERER, DAVID; Greece Athena HS; Rochester, NY; (Y); 10/300; Exploring; Radio Clb; High Hon Roll; Hon Roll; NHS; French Stu Of Yr 85-86; Comp Cntst Wnnr 85; Comp Telecomm.

HOLFELDER, PETER J; Lakeland HS; Yorktown Heights, NY; (Y); 19/350; SADD; Stage Crew; Variety Show; Chrmn Jr Cls; JV Trk; Hon Roll; Jr NHS; NHS; Ntl Merit SF; Renssealer Poly Inst; Physcis.

HOLICKY, WILLIAM G; New Hartford HS; New Hartford, NY; (Y); Boys Clb Am; Jazz Band; Yrbk Sprt Ed; Capt L Socr; L Var Swmmng; Trk; Hon Roll; JETS Awd; Jr NHS; Ntl Merit Ltr; Archtctr.

HOLIHAN, MELISSA; Solvay HS; Solvay, NY; (Y); Political Wkr; Chorus; Socr; Vllybl; Soc Wrk.

HOLL, DOUG; Queensbury HS; Glens Falls, NY; (Y); Ski Clb; Var Ftbl; JV Wt Lftg; High Hon Roll; Hon Roll; Stu Of Qrtr In Indl Arts 84; Engr.

HOLLAMBY, MARK; Portville Central HS; Olean, NY; (Y); Am Leg Boys St; Pres Church Yth Grp; Pres Concert Band; Mrchg Band; Yrbk Stf; God Cntry Awd; High Hon Roll; Trs NHS; Prfct Atten Awd; DAR Awd; Cnty Gvmnt Intrnshp Prgm 86; Area Yth Salute 86.

HOLLAND, LYNN; Union Springs Acad; Coudersport, PA; (S); 1/46; Drama Clb; Church Choir; Rep Sr Cls; Cheerleading; Gym; High Hon Roll; Sec NHS; Val; Pres Acdmc Ftns Awd 86; Atlantic Union Coll; Nrsng.

HOLLAND, MICHAEL; Franklin Acad; N Bangor, NY; (Y); 4-H; French Clb; Varsity Clb; JV Var Bsbl; Var L Ftbl; Var L Ice Hcky; Wt Lftg; High Hon Roll; Hon Roll; NHS; St Lawrence; Pre-Law.

HOLLAND, TIM; Candor Central HS; Candor, NY; (Y); Varsity Clb; Bsbl; Bsktbl; Coach Actv; Ftbl; Mgr(s); Wrstlng; Hon Roll; NCTE Awd; Prfct Atten Awd; Criminal Law.

HOLLANDER, STACEY; Tohenville HS; Staten Island, NY; (Y); Hosp Aide; SADD; Teachers Aide; Band; Hlth Career Awd 86; Staten Island; Spec Educ.

HOLLENBECK, KAREN; East Hampton HS; E Hampton, NY; (Y); Band; Tennis; Vllybl; Hon Roll; Spanish NHS.

HOLLENBECK, KRISTINA; Westmoreland Ctnrl Schl; Rome, NY; (Y); Trs Church Yth Grp; Hosp Aide; Model UN; SADD; Pres Band; Rep Chorus; Yrbk Stf; VP Stu Cncl; High Hon Roll; NHS; Retl Bus Mngmnt.

HOLLENBECK, LAURA S; Hamburg HS; Hamburg, NY; (Y); 29/376; Dance Clb; French Clb; Hosp Aide; Rep Soph Cls; Rep Jr Cls; Rep Sr Cls; Var Capt Cheerleading; Var Gym; Var Capt Socr; Hon Roll; NY ST Rgnts Schlrshp 86; U Rchstr; Srgn.

HOLLER, SCOTT; St Francis Prep; Flushing, NY; (Y); Drama Clb; Stage Crew; Arch.

HOLLERAN, BETHANN; Vestal Senior HS; Apalachin, NY; (Y); French Clb; JA; Lit Mag; Sr Cls; Var Cheerleading; Var Diving; Var Gym; Var Trk; High Hon Roll; NHS; NY ST Vaultng Champ 85; Ranked 14th Gym 86; Schlrshp Walnut Hill Prep Schl 84-85; Math.

HOLLEY, KEITH; Long Island Lutheran HS; Levittown, NY; (S); Aud/Vis; Band; Stage Crew; Yrbk Stf; Var Bsbl; Var Ftbl; Hon Roll; NHS; Phys Ther.

HOLLIDAY, MARGARET; Fairport HS; Fairport, NY; (Y); Latin Clb; Office Aide; Varsity Clb; Rep Sr Cls; Var Capt Cheerleading; Hon Roll; NHS; NY ST Rgnts Schlrshp 86; Prsdntl Acad Ftnss Awd 86; Ldrshp Awd Vrsty Chrldng 85; Syracuse U; Bio-Med Engrng.

HOLLINS, SHEILA M; The Anglo American Schl; New York, NY; (Y); Drama Clb; JA; Office Aide; School Play; Yrbk Ed-Chief; Rep Sr Cls; Rep Stu Cncl; VP Cheerleading; Ntl Merit Ltr; Lawyer.

HOLLOWAY, DAVID; Potsdam Centeral HS; Potsdam, NY; (Y); Boy Scts; Camera Clb; Chess Clb; Church Yth Grp; Computer Clb; Drama Clb; German Clb; Key Clb; Math Clb; Nwsp Rptr; Potsdam; Comptrs.

HOLLOWAY, SHERWOOD; White Plains HS; White Plains, NY; (Y); 78/425; Church Yth Grp; Cmnty Wkr; Computer Clb; English Clb; Hosp Aide; Math Clb; Spanish Clb; Mrchg Band; Howard U; Bio Sci.

HOLLOWAY, VICTORIA; Woodlands HS; White Plains, NY; (Y); 2/203; Hosp Aide; Math Tm; Band; Concert Band; Orch; Cit Awd; High Hon Roll; NHS; Ntl Merit Schol; Pres Schlr; CIBA Sci Awd 86; Sci Hnrl Pgm 84-86; NY ST Regnts Schlr 86; Harvard U; Bio.

HOLLWEDEL, DEBRA; Islip HS; Islip, NY; (Y); #17 In Class; Church Yth Grp; Sec SADD; Concert Band; School Musical; Capt Pom Pon; High Hon Roll; Jr NHS; NHS; Frnch Awd 83; VA Wesleyan Schlr 86; VA Wesleyan Coll; Elem Ed.

HOLM, AMY; Thomas J Corcoran HS; Syracuse, NY; (Y); Church Yth Grp; French Clb; Latin Clb; Library Aide; Color Guard; Yrbk Stf; Hon Roll; Pres NHS; Magna Cum Laude Natl Latin Exm 86; Marine Biol.

HOLMAN, TANIA M; Norman Thomas HS; Flushing, NY; (S); 18/597; Church Yth Grp; Drama Clb; Pres Church Choir; Hon Roll; NHS; Dollars For Scholars 86; Acad Perf Awd 86; Long Island U; Accntng.

HOLMBERG, ERNEST; Moore Catholic HS; Staten Island, NY; (Y); Im Bowling; Hon Roll; Engr.

HOLMES, BRENNAN; Bay Shore HS; Brightwaters, NY; (Y); Scholastic Bowl; Crs Cntry; Trk; High Hon Roll; Hon Roll; Bay Shore JR Fire Dept 77-87; Acad Decath 85; Atty.

HOLMES, CAROL; John H Glenn HS; Huntington, NY; (Y); Science Clb; Socl Wrk.

HOLMES, DARIN; Franklin Academy HS; N Bangor, NY; (Y); 20/270; Church Yth Grp; VP 4-H; Crs Cntry; Swmmng; 4-H Awd; Hon Roll; NHS; Blue Top Farm Awd ST Fair Jdgng Dairy Cattle 86; 4th Pl Jdgng & 9th Pl Rsns ST Fair Dairy Jdgng 85; ST U Geneseo; Physcl Thrpst.

HOLMES, FELICIA; Romulus Central Schl; Romulus, NY; (Y); Church Yth Grp; Cmnty Wkr; 4-H; Hosp Aide; Pres SADD; VICA; Rep Stu Cncl; Var Vllybl; Pep Clb; Red Cross Aide; BOCES Cosmtlgy Prfct Atten & Cls Pres; Fash Merch.

HOLMES, GREG; Archbishop Molloy HS; Flushing, NY; (Y); SADD; Im Bsbl; Im Bsktbl; Crmnl Justc.

HOLMES, KELLI; Wilson Central HS; Ransomville, NY; (Y); 1/140; Am Leg Aux Girls St; Sec Acpl Chr; School Musical; Yrbk Stf; VP Soph Cls; Sec Stu Cncl; JV Var Cheerleading; Var Tennis; Sec NHS; Area All ST Chorus 85; All Cnty Swng Choir 85; MVP & Coachs Chrldng Awd 84-85; Lbrl Arts.

HOLMES, KELLY; Mercy HS; Albany, NY; (Y); Pep Clb; Spanish Clb; Lit Mag; High Hon Roll; NHS; Church Yth Grp; Accntng.

HOLMES, KIMBERLY; Royalton-Hartland HS; Middleport, NY; (Y); 21/131; Camera Clb; Drama Clb; FTA; Orch; School Play; Hon Roll; NHS; Mddlprt, Mdna, & Lyndnvl AAUW Schlrshp 86; Gemma Awd For Eng 86; Announcers Clb 86; NY ST U Buffalo; Elem Ed.

HOLMES, LINDA; Warsaw Central Schl; Warsaw, NY; (S); 1/90; Sec French Clb; Mathletes; Band; Chorus; JV Var Bsktbl; JV Var Socr; JV Var Sftbl; JV Vllybl; Hon Roll; NHS; USWLM Awds-Frnch, Ldrshp & Outstndng Prfrmnc 84; Band & Ovrall Achvt, Bio, Engl & Frnch Acadmc 84; Pre Med.

HOLMES, MICHELLE; Pavilion Central Schl; East Bethany, NY; (Y); 2/63; AFS; 4-H; Spanish Clb; Chorus; Color Guard; School Play; Nwsp Stf; Yrbk Bus Mgr; JV Bsktbl; Im Gym; NY Sec V Vlybl All STAR 85; Pres Acad Ftnss Awd, Fac Mem Schlrshp 86; Ithaca Coll; Phy Thrpy.

HOLMES, RENAE; Canisteo Central HS; Canisteo, NY; (Y); 28/76; Drama Clb; Ski Clb; Chorus; Concert Band; Mrchg Band; Pep Band; School Musical; Yrbk Stf; Stu Cncl; Hon Roll; Drama.

HOLMES, ROBIN; Hartford Central Schl; Fort Ann, NY; (Y); 2/39; Church Yth Grp; Drama Clb; 4-H; French Clb; Math Tm; Pep Clb; Science Clb; Ski Clb; SADD; Band; CIBA-CEIGY Sci Awd Rcpnt 86; Woodmn Wrld Otstndng Schlstc Achvmnt Hstry 86; Syracuse U; Cmptr Prgmng.

HOLMSTROM, GAIL; Clymer Central HS; Clymer, NY; (Y); 8/45; Trs AFS; Sec Trs Church Yth Grp; Chorus; Church Choir; School Play; Yrbk Ed-Chief; Cheerleading; High Hon Roll; Hon Roll; NHS; Exec Sctrl Sci Schlrshp 86; Chautauqua Cnty Assn Educ Offc Prsnnl Schlrshp 86; Bryant & Stratton; Exec Secy.

HOLOHAN, RAYMOND; St Marys Boys HS; Bellmore, NY; (S); Chess Clb; Nwsp Rptr; Im Bsktbl; Im Bowling; JV Golf; NHS; Ntl Merit Ltr; Med.

HOLOHAN, TARA; Brockport HS; Hamlin, NY; (Y); Ski Clb; Score Keeper; High Hon Roll; Spnsh III Awd 85-86; Boston U; Comp Sci.

HOLOWKA, JAMES; Orchard Park HS; Orchard Park, NY; (Y); Boys Clb Am; Debate Tm; JCL; Latin Clb; Varsity Clb; Rep Soph Cls; Rep Jr Cls; Var Lcrss; Boys Clb Orchard Pk Yr 86; Bus Adm.

HOLSEY, MICHAEL; Herbert H Lehman HS; Bronx, NY; (Y); Cmnty Wkr; Computer Clb; Service Clb; Teachers Aide; Stage Crew; Yrbk Stf; Var Bsbl; Im Wt Lftg; Ntl Merit Ltr; Prfct Atten Awd; Bronze Mdl Awd Excllnc In Drafting 86; Cert Of Excllnc In Phy Ed 86; Queensborough CC; Comp Tech.

HOLST, JOHN; Beach Channel HS; Brooklyn, NY; (Y); Computer Clb; Math Tm; Science Clb; Yrbk Phtg; Hon Roll; Marine Bio.

HOLST, RAYMOND JOHN; Connetquot HS; Oakdale, NY; (Y); 32/700; Math Tm; Rep Frsh Cls; Pres Jr Cls; Pres Sr Cls; Var Capt Lcrss; Jr NHS; NHS; Pres Schlr; Idle Hr PTA Schlrshp, Outstndng AP Am Hist Stu 86; Union Coll; Econ.

HOLSTEAD, CATHY; Valley Stream Central HS; Valley Stream, NY; (Y); 76/350; Red Cross Aide; Ski Clb; Band; Mrchg Band; Variety Show; Socr; Sftbl; Swmmng; Vllybl; Jr NHS; All Amer Leag Awd Sccr 85-86; Nassau CC; Physcl Therpy.

HOLT, BECKY JEANNE; Fort Ann Central HS; Glens Falls, NY; (Y); 5/52; Drama Clb; Library Aide; Red Cross Aide; Teachers Aide; Lit Mag; High Hon Roll; Hon Roll; NHS.

HOLT, JACK; Aquinas Inst; Rochester, NY; (Y); 28/146; Boy Scts; Exploring; JA; JV Crs Cntry; Empire ST Schlrshp Of Exc 86; NY ST Rgnts Schlrshp 86; Rchstr Inst Of Tech Alumni Schlrshp 86; Rchstr Inst Of Tech; Engrng.

HOLT, LAURA; Fairport HS; Fairport, NY; (Y); Church Yth Grp; Yrbk Stf; Fshn Merch.

HOLT, SHAUN DASSELLE; De Witt Clinton HS; Bronx, NY; (Y); Boys Clb Am; Debate Tm; Drama Clb; Key Clb; Office Aide; SADD; Varsity Clb; Chorus; Color Guard; School Musical; Bus Adm.

HOLTHAUS, KEVIN; Le Roy Central HS; Leroy, NY; (Y); 10/125; Am Leg Boys St; Vrsty Clb; JV Var Ftbl; JV Var Wrstlng; High Hon Roll; Jr NHS; NHS; Vrsty Clb Pres 86-87; Amer Legn Boys ST 86.

HOLTHOUSE, BETHANN; Clymer Central Schl; N Clymer, NY; (Y); 5/45; Church Yth Grp; Sec 4-H; Library Aide; Chorus; Church Choir; Yrbk Bus Mgr; High Hon Roll; NHS; Acdmc Achvt Schlrshp 86-87; Villa Maria.

HOLTZAPPLE, GRETCHEN WYNNE; Jamesville-Dewitt HS; Jamesville, NY; (Y); 46/229; French Clb; Hosp Aide; Key Clb; SADD; Orch; Yrbk Stf; Tennis; High Hon Roll; NHS; Church Yth Grp; Schlstc Art Awd Gold Key 84; Graphic Desgn.

HOLVIK, SHARON; Huntington HS; Huntington Sta, NY; (Y); 37/383; Church Yth Grp; Hosp Aide; Band; Church Choir; JV Cheerleading; JV Var Fld Hcky; High Hon Roll; Jr NHS; NHS; St Schlr; Messiah Coll; Nrsng.

HOLWAY, KELLY; Grand Island SR HS; Grand Island, NY; (Y); 3/320; Yrbk Sprt Ed; Hst Jr Cls; Hst Sr Cls; Var Capt Bsktbl; Var Capt Socr; Var L Sftbl; Hon Roll; Sec NHS; Ntl Merit Ltr; PTSA Schlrshp 86; Empr ST Schlrshp & Regnts Schlrshp 86; Pres Acadmc Ftnss Awd 86; U Of VT; Elem Ed.

HOLZBERG, ADAM; East Meadow HS; East Meadow, NY; (S); FBLA; Key Clb; Mathletes; Math Tm; SADD; Temple Yth Grp; Chorus; Nwsp Stf; Trk; Hon Roll; Med.

HOLZMAN, DANIEL B; Garden Schl; Long Island City, NY; (Y); 9/32; Computer Clb; Debate Tm; Model UN; School Musical; Im Fld Hcky; High Hon Roll; Hon Roll; NMSQT Cmndtn 85; SAT Cmndtn 86; Rgnts Schlrshp Elgblty 84; Antioch; Physics.

HOM, DANNY; La Salle Acad; Long Island City, NY; (S); Camera Clb; Chess Clb; Hosp Aide; Nwsp Phtg; Bowling; NHS; Soc Amer Distngshd H S Stu; Biochem Engr.

HOMA, DAVID E; The Stony Brook Schl; Selden, NY; (Y); Art Clb; Thesps; Orch; School Musical; School Play; Stage Crew; Yrbk Phtg; Var Bsktbl; Var Trk; NHS; NY ST Regents Schlrshp 86; Natl Merit Cmmnd Stu 86; Le High U; Elec Engr.

HOMAN, DONNA; Baldwin HS; Baldwin, NY; (Y); Art Clb; Church Yth Grp; Dance Clb; Hosp Aide; SADD; Cheerleading; Trk; Prfct Atten Awd.

HOMER, MARY; Scotia-Glenville HS; Scotia, NY; (Y); French Clb; Girl Scts; JA; Chorus; Yrbk Stf; JV Fld Hcky; Mgr(s); Score Keeper; High Hon Roll; Masonic Awd.

HOMIN, PAUL V; Newburgh Free Acad; New Windsor, NY; (Y); 57/621; Computer Clb; Math Tm; ROTC; Rep Soph Cls; Rep Jr Cls; Rep Sr Cls; Im Vllybl; High Hon Roll; Hon Roll; Jr NHS; Ntl Sojourners Awd 85; NY ST Regents Schlrshp 86; Air Force ROTC Schlrshp 86; Clarkson Coll; Elec.

HONAN, JAMES; Churchville-Chili SR HS; Rochester, NY; (Y); Church Yth Grp; Math Tm; Jazz Band; School Musical; Trs VP Symp Band; Nwsp Stf; Lit Mag; Rep Stu Cncl; Trs NHS; Band Mbr Of Yr 84-85; Amer Chem Soc Achvt, Notre Dame Clb Rochester Jr Of Yr Fnlst 85-86; Chem Engrng.

HONG, ANH; Bishop Kearney HS; Rochester, NY; (Y); High Hon Roll; Hon Roll; ESOL Engl Awd 83-84; Rochester Inst Tech; Mth.

HONG, MAY; Jamaica HS; Queens Village, NY; (S); 33/537; Church Yth Grp; Cmnty Wkr; Computer Clb; Intnl Clb; Math Tm; Science Clb; Lit Mag; Vllybl; Hon Roll; Queens Coll; Bio.

HONG, MICHELE H; Scarsdale HS; Stamford, CT; (Y); Church Yth Grp; Cmnty Wkr; French Clb; Hosp Aide; Teachers Aide; Rep Jr Cls; JV Socr; JV Trk; NHS; Columbia U; Educ.

HONG, ROBERT; Williamsville South HS; Williamsville, NY; (Y); Pres Church Yth Grp; Math Tm; Ski Clb; Trs Chorus; Church Choir; VP Orch; Var L Socr; Var L Swmmng; High Hon Roll; NHS; Brown Coll; Chem.

HONG, YUHOE; Newark HS; Newark, NY; (Y); 7/190; Am Leg Aux Girls St; Red Cross Aide; SADD; Band; Yrbk Ed-Chief; Trk; High Hon Roll; NHS; Spanish NHS; NYSSMA Gld Mdl; JR Hnr Grl 86; Cmstck Awd 85; Pre Med.

HONIG, DEBRA; Wantagh HS; Wantagh, NY; (Y); Political Wkr; Spanish Clb; Y-Teens; Variety Show; Nwsp Ed-Chief; Yrbk Stf; Rep Frsh Cls; Hon Roll; NHS; Prfct Atten Awd; Scrpps Hwrd Nwsppr Fndtn Schlrshp 86; Pres Acdmc Ftns Awd 86; Amer Assn U Wmn Awd 86; Union Coll; Engl.

HONIGMANN, GLORIA MARIE; Bethpage HS; Bethpage, NY; (Y); 68/291; French Clb; Girl Scts; Intnl Clb; Mathletes; Office Aide; High Hon Roll; Hon Roll; Manhattan Coll; Cvl Engr.

HONOR, DAVID; Tottenville HS; Staten Isld, NY; (Y); Drama Clb; SADD; Trs Sr Cls; Var Bsbl; JV Bsktbl.

HONORE, LOUIS; Art And Design HS; Ozone Park, NY; (Y); Pratt Inst Of Tech; Indtl Dsgn.

HONS, WENDY; Harpursville HS; Nineveh, NY; (S); 46/85; Sec 4-H; Band; Concert Band; Jazz Band; Mrchg Band; Pep Band; Nwsp Stf; Yrbk Stf; Hon Roll; Amer Mscl Fndtn Bnd Hnrs 83; Amer Lgn Poppy Qun 83; Smmr Mrchng Bnd Trphy For Mst Sprtf 85; Music Ed.

HOOCK, MICHELLE; West Seneca East SR HS; Cheektowaga, NY; (Y); French Clb; Nwsp Stf; Rep Stu Cncl; Hon Roll; JC Awd; NHS; Merit Cert Ntl Frnch Cntst 84; Merit Cert Achvt In Frnch 84-86; Hlth Cr Admin.

HOOD, ED; Lake Placid HS; Lake Placid, NY; (Y); 3/60; Am Leg Boys St; Key Clb; Varsity Clb; Stage Crew; VP Soph Cls; Pres Jr Cls; L Socr; L Tennis; L Trk; NHS; Sports Doctor.

HOOPER, BEN; Union Endicott HS; Endicott, NY; (Y); Boy Scts; Mathletes; Yrbk Phtg; Hon Roll; NHS; Natl Order Arrow Treas 85.

HOOPER, DAVID M; Hannibal HS; Hannibal, NY; (Y); 4/120; Am Leg Boys St; Chess Clb; Chorus; Concert Band; Jazz Band; School Musical; Var Capt Tennis; High Hon Roll; NHS; Mrchg Band; Red Creek Am Lg Band 86; Biomedical Engineering.

HOOVER, SHELLEY; Indian River Central HS; Theresa, NY; (Y); Sec AFS; Chorus; School Musical; School Play; Stage Crew; Yrbk Stf; Bryant & Stratton; Lgl Asst.

HOPE, BARBRA; Tottenville HS; Staten Isld, NY; (Y); Crs Cntry; Trk; Hon Roll; NHS; Oswego; Nutrtnst.

HOPKINS, EILEEN; Moore Catholic HS; Staten Island, NY; (Y); Math Tm; SADD; Nwsp Sprt Ed; Yrbk Sprt Ed; JV Var Bsktbl; JV Capt Sftbl; NHS; Ntl Merit Ltr; Science Clb.

HOPKINS, HEATHER; Newburgh Free Acad; Vails Gate, NY; (Y); #115 In Class; Drama Clb; Spanish Clb; Chorus; Variety Show; High Hon Roll; Hon Roll; Music Dept Svc Cert Chorus 84; Cert Prfrmnc Outstndng Accmplshmt All Cnty Music Fest 84; Cmmnctns.

HOPKINS, JAMES R; Angelica Central Schl; Angelica, NY; (Y); Am Leg Boys St; French Clb; Science Clb; Trs Frsh Cls; Trs Soph Cls; Trs Jr Cls; Trs Sr Cls; Bausch & Lomb Sci Awd; High Hon Roll; NHS; Navy; Nuclr Pwr Pgm.

HOPKINS, JOANN; G Ray Bodley HS; Fulton, NY; (Y); Church Yth Grp; Latin Clb; Ski Clb; Spanish Clb; Trs Sr Cls; Rep Stu Cncl; Var Gym; JV Socr; Stat Bsbl; JV Cheerleading; Prom Queen 86; Fash Merch.

HOPKINS, KIMBERLY; Monsignor Scanlan HS; Bronx, NY; (Y); 14/276; Norris Browm Coll; Compu Anlyst.

HOPKINS, ROBERT J; Sachem HS North; Ronkonkoma, NY; (Y); Boy Scts; Spanish Clb; Teachers Aide; Band; Orch; Rep Frsh Cls; Coach Actv; JV Ftbl; Var JV Lcrss; NHS; Ldrs Clb 83-85; Perfmg Fclty Danc Band 84-86; Med.

HOPKINS, SEAN; Franklin Acad; Malone, NY; (Y); Church Yth Grp; Spanish Clb; Bsbl; Hon Roll; Arch.

HOPKINS, STEPHANIE; Mynderse Acad; Seneca Falls, NY; (S); French Clb; GAA; JV Var Bsktbl; JV Sftbl; Var L Tennis; Var L Vllybl; Hon Roll; NHS; Jrnlsm.

HOPKO, JOE; Union-Endicott HS; Endicott, NY; (S); Rep Stu Cncl; JV L Bsbl; Im Bsktbl; Var L Ftbl; Wt Lftg; Hon Roll; Pres Phy Ftns Awd 83-84; Arch.

HOPLER, CARRIE; Mercy HS; Shelter Island, NY; (Y); 23/128; Church Yth Grp; Cmnty Wkr; Trs FFA; Mathletes; VICA; Yrbk Phtg; Yrbk Rptr; JV Socr; High Hon Roll; Hon Roll; JR Achvt Awd Horticulture 86; Landscape.

HOPPE, BRONWEN; Rome Free Acad; Rome, NY; (Y); 100/476; Trs Drama Clb; GAA; Red Cross Aide; Speech Tm; School Play; Yrbk Stf; Cit Awd; Hon Roll; Jr NHS; Opt Clb Awd; Rgnts Schlrshp 86; Fred & Blanche Griffiths Schlrshp 86; Doc Hans Zutraun Memrl Fund Awd 86; Utica Coll; Nrsng.

HOPPE, SUZANNAH JANE; Kingston HS; Ulster Park, NY; (Y); 120/573; AFS; Art Clb; French Clb; Hosp Aide; Key Clb; Crs Cntry; French Hon Soc; Pres Acdmc Ftns Awd 86; R R Grvs Mem Schlrshp 86; Niagara U; Tourism.

HOPPENTHALER, LINDA; Coxsackie-Athens HS; W Coxsackie, NY; (Y); Computer Clb; 4-H; German Clb; Band; Chorus; Yrbk Stf; Var Cheerleading; Var Gym; 4-H Awd; Hon Roll.

HOPPENTHALER, SANDRA; Coxsackie-Athens HS; W Coxsackie, NY; (Y); 4-H; German Clb; Band; Cheerleading; Gym; 4-H Awd; Hon Roll; Hudson Valley CC; Trvl.

HOPPER, DAWN; Connelquot HS; Ronkonkoma, NY; (S); 3/699; Art Clb; Nwsp Rptr; Rep Frsh Cls; Rep Stu Cncl; Mgr Crs Cntry; Im Trk; Hon Roll; Jr NHS; Rgnts Schlrshp 86; Syracuse U; Aerospc Engrng.

HOPSON, DANIELLE; Southampton HS; Southampton, NY; (Y); Dance Clb; Debate Tm; Drama Clb; French Clb; GAA; Thesps; Band; Chorus; Mrchg Band; School Play; Schlrshp Crtv & Prfrmg Arts 84.

HORAN, DAVID F; Haneoye Central Schl; Haneoye, NY; (Y); Am Leg Boys St; Art Clb; Acpl Chr; Chorus; Swing Chorus; Yrbk Phtg; Yrbk Stf; Pres Stu Cncl; Hon Roll; NYS Rgnts Schlrshp 86; CC Of Finger Lakes; Music Rcdg.

HORAN, HOLLI; Union Endicott HS; Endicott, NY; (Y); Dance Clb; Key Clb; Latin Clb; Mrchg Band; Symp Band; Yrbk Stf; Bsktbl; Crs Cntry; Trk; Hon Roll; NYSSMA Mdl Wnnr Solo Cntst 84; Physics Club Egg-Drop Fnlst 86; Arch.

HORBAS, BRIAN; G Ray Bodley HS; Fulton, NY; (Y); French Clb; VP Science Clb; Ski Clb; Var Capt Bowling; Var L Tennis; High Hon Roll; Hon Roll; NHS; Bus Mgmt.

HORBATUK, ELISA L; St Joseph Hill Acad; Staten Island, NY; (Y); 3/107; Library Aide; Variety Show; Nwsp Stf; Yrbk Phtg; Co-Capt Bowling; NHS; Ntl Merit SF; Drm Mjr(t); VP Computer Clb; FTA; 1st Pl JV Div B Cath H S Math Leag 85; 1st Pl Police Athl Leag Essy Cntst & Hon Mntn Borough Sci Fr.

HORBOYCHUK, DEBBIE; Arlington HS; Hopewell Jct, NY; (Y); 91/556; Office Aide; Teachers Aide; Chorus; Variety Show; Trs Jr Cls; Trs Sr Cls; Hon Roll; Bst Dressed 85-86; Dutchess CC; Bus Adm.

HORDGE, CYNTHIA; G Ray Bodley HS; Fulton, NY; (Y); Pres Church Yth Grp; Drama Clb; Church Choir; School Play; Hon Roll; Messiah Coll; Commun.

HORDINES, CARL; Cohoes HS; Cohoes, NY; (Y); Math Tm; Spanish Clb; High Hon Roll; NHS; Intl Frgn Lang Awd 86; Comp Sci.

HORDLOW, KARA; Garden City HS; Garden City, NY; (Y); 30/346; Church Yth Grp; GAA; SADD; Nwsp Ed-Chief; Ed Yrbk Stf; Var Capt Fld Hcky; Var Capt Sftbl; High Hon Roll; Pres Jr NHS; NCTE Awd; Brown U Bk Awd Excl Engl 85; Columbia U Prss 1st Pl Sprtswrtng; Ntl Yng Ldrs Conf 85.

HORGAN, ANGELA MICHELLE; Sutherland HS; Pittsford, NY; (Y); Am Leg Aux Girls St; French Clb; Model UN; Chorus; Im Fld Hcky; Capt Powder Puff Ftbl; JV Socr; Hon Roll; NHS; 3rd Pl Ntl Frnch Cntst; Genetic Engrng.

HORGAN, TERESA; St Marys Acad; Glens Falls, NY; (S); 1/60; French Clb; Girl Scts; Library Aide; Service Clb; SADD; Teachers Aide; Nwsp Stf; Yrbk Stf; Bausch & Lomb Sci Awd; Val; Boston Coll; Elem Tchr.

HORMOZDI, STEVEN; Manhasset HS; Manhasset, NY; (Y); Hosp Aide; Yrbk Stf; Trs Frsh Cls; Trs Soph Cls; Rep Sr Cls; JV Socr; Var Swmmng; High Hon Roll; Ntl Merit SF.

HORN, ANDREA; Dover JR SR HS; Dover Plains, NY; (S); 3/70; Am Leg Aux Girls St; Varsity Clb; Pres Jr Cls; Trs Sr Cls; Bsktbl; Fld Hcky; High Hon Roll; NHS; Voice Dem Awd; Hmcmng Crt.

HORN, KAREN; Avoca Central HS; Avoca, NY; (S); 2/50; Sec Trs JCL; Pres Trs Latin Clb; Ski Clb; Chorus; Tennis; Vllybl; Cit Awd; DAR Awd; High Hon Roll; NHS; Intl Frgn Lang Awd 85; Natl Engl Mrt Awd; Alfred U; Hlth Care.

HORNAUER, MICHELE LEE; Sharon Springs Central HS; Sharon Springs, NY; (S); 1/24; FBLA; Yrbk Ed-Chief; VP Sr Cls; VP Stu Cncl; Cit Awd; Hon Roll; NHS; Val; Art Clb; SUNY Cobleskill; Accntng.

HORNBECK, SEAN; Liberty Central HS; Liberty, NY; (Y); Debate Tm; Library Aide; NFL; Speech Tm; Nwsp Rptr; Trs Jr Cls; Trs Sr Cls; High Hon Roll; NHS; Stu Cncl; Karate Black Belt 85; Acadmc Block L Dv Comp; Acadmc Block L Spnsh III, Chem, Histry & Math.

HORNBERGER, CATHERINE; Bronx HS Of Science; New York, NY; (Y); Civic Clb; Key Clb; Library Aide; Rep Jr Cls; NCTE Awd; Ntl Merit Schol; UFT Schlrshp 86; Rgnts Schlrshp 86; Acdmc Fit Awd 86; Clmbia U; Wrtng.

HORNE, DENISE; Frontier Central SR HS; Blasdell, NY; (Y); French Clb; Girl Scts; Spanish Clb; Trs SADD; School Play; Rep Jr Cls; Stu Cncl; Mgr(s); Hon Roll; Pre-Med.

HORNE, PAMELA; Uniondale HS; Hempstead, NY; (Y); Cmnty Wkr; Debate Tm; English Clb; FBLA; Key Clb; NFL; Political Wkr; Service Clb; SADD; Yrbk Stf; Brown U; Crimnl Law.

HORNER, MARY; Scotia-Glenville HS; Scotia, NY; (Y); French Clb; Girl Scts; JA; Chorus; Yrbk Stf; JV Fld Hcky; Mgr(s); Score Keeper; High Hon Roll; Masonic Awd.

HORNIK, KATHRYN; St John The Baptist HS; Deer Park, NY; (S); 1/550; Var Capt Cheerleading; Var Powder Puff Ftbl; Hon Roll; Engrng.

HORNQUIST, BENJAMIN; Eden Central HS; Eden, NY; (Y); SADD; Off Jr Cls; JV Ftbl.

HORNUNG, CHRISTOPHER A; Depew HS; Depew, NY; (Y); 1/272; Cmnty Wkr; Pres Computer Clb; Concert Band; Mrchg Band; School Musical; JV Ftbl; High Hon Roll; Jr NHS; NHS; Ntl Merit SF; JR All-Amer Hll Of Fm Bnd Hnrs 85; Outstndg Stu Of Mnth Awd Depew-Lancaster Rotary Clb 85; Aerosp Engrng.

HORNUNG, JOHN; Gloversville HS; Gloversvl, NY; (Y); Band; Trs Soph Cls; Trs Jr Cls; Trs Sr Cls; Rep Stu Cncl; JV Bsktbl; JV Var Ftbl; Var Tennis; Im Wt Lftg; High Hon Roll.

HOROHOE, TIMOTHY J; Msgr Farrell HS; Staten Island, NY; (Y); Boy Scts; Political Wkr; Mrchg Band; Yrbk Phtg; Yrbk Rptr; Yrbk Sprt Ed; Yrbk Stf; Ftbl; Trk; Law.

HOROWITZ, AMY; Lynbrook HS; Lynbrook, NY; (Y); 32/239; Drama Clb; French Clb; NFL; Speech Tm; Thesps; Chorus; School Musical; School Play; Stage Crew; Nwsp Rptr; U Of MA.

HOROWITZ, AMY B; Susan E Wagner HS; Staten Island, NY; (Y); 40/466; Art Clb; Computer Clb; Teachers Aide; School Musical; Stu Cncl; Hon Roll; NHS; NY ST Regents Schlrshp Wnnr 86; Fash Merch.

HOROWITZ, KAREN G; Ramaz HS; Bronx, NY; (Y); Art Clb; Cmnty Wkr; Debate Tm; Hosp Aide; Math Tm; Spanish Clb; Teachers Aide; Stage Crew; Nwsp Ed-Chief; Ntl Merit SF; Untd Hosp Fnd Awd; Lenox Hill Hosp Awd; Engrng.

HORTA, JACQUELINE; Midwood HS; Brooklyn, NY; (Y); Drama Clb; Hosp Aide; Office Aide; Political Wkr; Red Cross Aide; Orch; School Musical; Lit Mag; Rep Frsh Cls; Prfct Atten Awd; Prncpls Pride Yankees Awd 85; Cert Of Hnr Indvdl Effrt Mock Trl 85; Brooklyn Coll; Law.

HORTON, CYNTHIA; F D Roosevelt HS; Hyde Park, NY; (Y); JV Var Cheerleading; JV Sftbl; Natl Chrldng Cmptn 85; Bus Mgt.

HORTON, ROBERT; Bellport HS; Brookhaven, NY; (Y); Pres Drama Clb; PAVAS; School Musical; School Play; Variety Show; Nwsp Phtg; Nwsp Rptr; Rep Frsh Cls; Rep Soph Cls; Rep Jr Cls; Gftd & Tlntd Theatre Arts 84; TV & Film.

HORVATH, KRISTY M; Rye Country Day Schl; Ryebrook, NY; (Y); CAP; Cmnty Wkr; Debate Tm; Hosp Aide; Political Wkr; Chorus; Nwsp Stf; Im Mgr Badmtn; Var Capt Cheerleading; Im Mgr Golf; Brown U Bk Awd/Excellnc-Engl 85; Engl Awd 8; Edtr-Schlspltcl Mewspapr 86; Brown U; Biochem.

HORWITZ, JOSH; Midwood HS; Brooklyn, NY; (Y); 45/672; French Clb; Model UN; Orch; Stage Crew; High Hon Roll; Prfct Atten Awd; Bcycl Racing Clb-Pres 84-86; Astrphyscs.

HOSEY, BRIAN; Valley Stream Central HS; Valley Stream, NY; (Y); Debate Tm; School Play; Rep Frsh Cls; Trs Soph Cls; Rep Stu Cncl; Var L Ftbl; Var L Lcrss; Var Capt Wrstlng; Hon Roll; NHS; Earl Awd & Compu Math 83-84.

HOSKINS, MICHAEL D; Cato-Meridian HS; Hannibal, NY; (Y); Computer Clb; Radio Clb; Hon Roll; 1st NAR Essy Cntst 85; Regnts Acadmc Schlrshp 86; Math And Sci Schlrshp 86; ASU; BSEE.

HOSMER, KELLY; Hannibal HS; Hannibal, NY; (Y); French Clb; Band; Color Guard; Orch; School Musical; Yrbk Ed-Chief; Yrbk Phtg; Yrbk Rptr; Ed Yrbk Stf; Score Keeper; Bio.

HOSMER, TERENCE; Mahopac HS; Mahopac, NY; (Y); 89/409; SADD; Nwsp Ed-Chief; Vllybl; Chorus; Nwsp Rptr; Hon Roll; Marist Coll; Comp Sci.

HOTALING, MICHAEL; Jordon-Elbridge JR SR HS; Jordan, NY; (Y); Am Leg Boys St; Drama Clb; Jazz Band; School Musical; Nwsp Stf; Yrbk Stf; Stu Cncl; Bsktbl; Golf; High Hon Roll; Chem Engrng.

HOTALING, RICHARD; Newburgh Free Acad; New Windsor, NY; (Y); Drama Clb; Radio Clb; Spanish Clb; School Musical; School Play; Stage Crew; Variety Show; Awd Excel By Mst Actv Drama 86; Acknwldgmnt Poder Spnsh Assn Acad Achvt 86; NY U; Comm.

HOTCHKISS, PETER; Cicero North Syracuse HS; N Syracuse, NY; (S); Church Yth Grp; Stu Cncl; Capt Socr; Ithaca Coll; Lwyr.

HOTCHKISS, TERESA; Randolph Central HS; Randolph, NY; (Y); 11/77; Art Clb; Drama Clb; Ski Clb; Varsity Clb; Rep Stu Cncl; Var Crs Cntry; Var Trk; High Hon Roll; Fredonia; Acctg.

HOTCHKISS, TRACY L; West Seneca West SR HS; W Seneca, NY; (Y); NYS Rgnts Schlrshp 86; Deans Schlrshp-Canisius Coll 86; Clsscl Music Achvt Awd Piano 85; Canisius Coll Buffalo NY; Med.

HOTELING, ANDREW J; Little Falls JR SR HS; Little Falls, NY; (Y); 13/95; Am Leg Boys St; Letterman Clb; Spanish Clb; Band; Var JV Bsbl; Var JV Bsktbl; Var Socr.

HOTELLING, MISTY; Columbia HS; Nassau, NY; (Y); Latin Clb; Bsktbl; Sftbl; Trk; Vllybl; Cit Awd; High Hon Roll; Ntl Merit Ltr; Prfct Atten Awd; Marine Corps Leag Phys Ftns Awd 83-84; OH ST U; Vet.

HOTSKO, JOHN; Union Endicott HS; Endwell, NY; (Y); 13/430; Key Clb; Mathletes; Quiz Bowl; JV Bowling; Var L Tennis; NHS; Ntl Merit Ltr; Empr ST Schlrshp Excllnc 86; Jessie Bkr Schlrshp 86; Soc Stds Plq 86; Cornell; Microbio.

HOTTER, DAVID; Westfield Central HS; Westfield, NY; (Y); Ski Clb; Band; Concert Band; Mrchg Band; Pres Jr Cls; Var Ftbl; Var L Tennis; High Hon Roll; NHS; Ntl Merit Ltr; Geroge E Plmb Mem Schlrshp 84; George S Knt Mem Math Schlrshp 84; Comp Engnrng.

HOTZELT, DIANE JOY; Uniondale HS; Uniondale, NY; (Y); 15/410; Am Leg Aux Girls St; Trs Drama Clb; NFL; Acpl Chr; Band; Chorus; Nwsp Ed-Chief; Var Swmmng; Var Tennis; Pres Schlr; Brwn U Bk Awd 84-85; Bst Actrs 85-86; Achvt Soc Stds 85-86; SUNY New Paltz; Jrnlsm.

HOU, ERNIE; Hunter College HS; Forest Hills, NY; (Y); Math Tm; Model UN; Teachers Aide; Band; Yrbk Stf; Var L Bowling; Bausch & Lomb Sci Awd; Ntl Merit SF; Rennsselaer Math & Sci Awd 84; Amer HS Math Exam Hnr Rll 84; Natl Olympiad In Chem Hnr Rll 84; Bio.

HOUGH, GERALD E; Mahopac HS; Mahopac, NY; (Y); Aud/Vis; Drama Clb; Science Clb; Thesps; Trs Chorus; School Play; Nwsp Stf; High Hon Roll; NHS; AFS; Purdue U; Med Bio-Chem.

HOUGH, KIMBERLY A; Solvay HS; Solvay, NY; (Y); School Musical; High Hon Roll; Hon Roll; NHS; Church Yth Grp; Drama Clb; French Clb; Girl Scts; Chorus; Gftd, Tlntd Pgm 85-87; Onodaga Cnty Math Awd 85; Socl Stud Awd 86; Geom Awd 85; Chorus Al-Arn 86; Acctng.

HOUGHTALING, PATTY; Lansing HS; Lansing, NY; (Y); Church Yth Grp; Library Aide; Chorus; Nwsp Rptr; High Hon Roll; Hon Roll; Paralegal.

HOUGHTLING, RICHARD; Cardinal O Hara HS; Kenmore, NY; (S); 15/122; Drama Clb; French Clb; Hosp Aide; Quiz Bowl; Red Cross Aide; School Musical; Nwsp Stf; Stat Ftbl; Hon Roll; NHS; Med.

HOUGHTON, CALVIN; Schoharie Central Schl; Esperance, NY; (S); VP 4-H; Math Tm; Hon Roll; Prfct Atten Awd; Rep Frsh Cls; Rep Soph Cls; Rep Jr Cls; Rep Stu Cncl; Acctng.

HOUGHTON, JAMES; Liberty HS; Liberty, NY; (Y); 5/115; Varsity Clb; Acpl Chr; Band; Chorus; Concert Band; Drill Tm; Jazz Band; Mrchg Band; Orch; Pep Band; All Leag Ftbll Tm 86; 6-A Vocal Solo Rtng 86; Gold Mdl ST Qlfyng Mt Trck 86; USAF Acad; Aerontcl Engr.

HOUGHTON, KRISTIN; Clayton A Bouton JR SR HS; Voorheesville, NY; (Y); Church Yth Grp; French Clb; Intnl Clb; Key Clb; Speech Tm; SADD; Nwsp Rptr; Yrbk Stf; JV Var Cheerleading; Hon Roll; Advrtsg.

HOUK, RACHEL; Plainview-Old Bethpage HS; Plainview, NY; (S); 73/200; Art Clb; Rptr Aud/Vis; Pres Church Yth Grp; Pres DECA; Drama Clb; Key Clb; Sec Mrchg Band; Thesps; Band; VP Chorus; Mem Art Schlrshp 86; Awd ST Resolution 86; Outstndg JR & SR Bus Awd; Buffalo ST Coll; Design.

HOULE, FAWN; Penn Yan Acad; Pennyan, NY; (S); 15/174; 4-H; GAA; Intnl Clb; Ski Clb; SADD; Yrbk Stf; Sec Var Bsktbl; Var Mgr(s); JV Var Socr; 4-H Awd.

HOULIHAN, MARK M; Ballston Spa HS; Ballston Spa, NY; (Y); 6/275; Math Tm; Science Clb; Varsity Clb; Var L Crs Cntry; Var L Trk; High Hon Roll; NHS; Skdmore Coll Acdmc Achvmnt Awds Dnr; NYS Rgnts Schlrshp; Hudson Valley CC; Elctrcl Engr.

HOULIHAN, THOMAS; Berne-Knox-Westerlo HS; Berne, NY; (Y); Ski Clb; SADD; Rep Frsh Cls; Rep Soph Cls; Capt Jr Cls; Rptr Stu Cncl; High Hon Roll; Hon Roll; NHS; SUNY; Med.

HOUNG, LINDY C; Jamaica HS; Flushing, NY; (Y); 34/507; Hosp Aide; Intnl Clb; Office Aide; Teachers Aide; Nwsp Rptr; Hon Roll; NHS; Regnts Schlrshp 86; ARISTA 86; UCLA; Med.

HOURIGAN, RACHEL; Onondaga Central Schl; Syracuse, NY; (S); GAA; Spanish Clb; VP Varsity Clb; Band; Capt Socr; Trk; Vllybl; High Hon Roll; Hon Roll; NHS.

HOURIGAN, TRACY; Jordon-Elbridge JR SR HS; Elbridge, NY; (Y); 1/141; Am Leg Aux Girls St; VP Frsh Cls; Var Capt Bsktbl; Var Powder Puff Ftbl; Var JV Socr; JV Sftbl; Var Trk; Cit Awd; High Hon Roll; Hon Roll; Hugh O Brian Yth Fndtn Ambssdr 84-85; Law.

HOURIHAN, LIZ; Potsdam HS; Potsdam, NY; (Y); French Clb; JA; Varsity Clb; Band; L Var Crs Cntry; Var L Trk; High Hon Roll; Jr NHS; NSMA Sci Merit, Smmr Excllnce Art Camp 85-86; Sci.

HOUSE, MELISSA; Pulaski HS; Parish, NY; (S); 4-H; French Clb; GAA; Math Clb; Math Tm; Ski Clb; Var Bsktbl; Socr; Var Sftbl; Dnfth Awd; Math.

HOUSE, MICHELLE; Canisteo Central HS; Canisteo, NY; (Y); 2/73; Band; School Play; Var Capt Cheerleading; Stat Crs Cntry; Stat Ftbl; Var Trk; High Hon Roll; NHS; Sal; VP Soph Cls; Acdmc Achvt Awd 85; Pres Acdmc Ftns Awd 86; Fredonia; Comp.

HOUSE, WILLIAM; Gloversville HS; Gloversvl, NY; (Y); Var Bsktbl; JV Ftbl; Hon Roll; Acctg.

HOUSEKNECHT JR, JAMES D; Frontier Central HS; Hamburg, NY; (Y); Boy Scts; Church Yth Grp; Socr; Buffalo ST; Comp Repair.

HOUSEL, TODD; Marion JR SR HS; Marion, NY; (Y); Church Yth Grp; School Musical; School Play; Stage Crew; Yrbk Stf; Rep Jr Cls; Rep Stu Cncl; Wrstlng; Avtn Spec.

HOUSEMAN, JILL J; Williamsville North HS; East Amherst, NY; (Y); Camp Fr Inc; Cmnty Wkr; Red Cross Aide; Spanish Clb; Yrbk Stf; JV Swmmng; Hon Roll; ST U Of NY-BFFLO.

HOUSER, JOSEPH; Cicero-North Syracuse HS; Clay, NY; (S); 85/676; Church Yth Grp; Var L Bsbl; Bsktbl; Socr; Hon Roll; NHS; U Of Binghamton; Sci.

HOUSTON, ANTHONY; Pelham Memorial HS; Pelham, NY; (Y); Cmnty Wkr; Mrchg Band; SADD; Off Jr Cls; Off Sr Cls; JV Bsktbl; Var JV Ftbl; Trk; Northwestern; Engrg.

HOUSTON, MICHELLE; Tonawsanda SR JR HS; Tonawanda, NY; (Y); Var Bsktbl; JV Sftbl; Hon Roll; Pre-Law.

HOUSTON, PAUL; Grand Island HS; Grand Island, NY; (Y); 53/295; Pres Model UN; Varsity Clb; Var JV Ftbl; Var Capt Tennis.

HOVATER, CHERYL; Liverpool HS; Liverpool, NY; (Y); Ski Clb; Band; Concert Band; Sec Sr Cls; Rep Stu Cncl; Powder Puff Ftbl; JV Vllybl; Cosmtlgy Practical Awd 85-86; Soph Cls Princess 83-84; Cosmetologist.

HOVEL, KEVIN; John Jay SR HS; Katonah, NY; (Y); Boys Clb Am; Im Bsktbl; JV Lcrss; Var Swmmng; Cit Awd; Hon Roll; NHS; Var Swmmng Mst Outstndng Swmr 86; Bio.

HOVER, KATHY; Hornell HS; Hornell, NY; (Y); 24/168; Art Clb; Church Yth Grp; Color Guard; Concert Band; Mrchg Band; Pep Band; Symp Band; Yrbk Phtg; Yrbk Stf; Bowling; NY ST Rgnts Schlrshp 86; Area All Cnty Bnd 82-86; Area All ST Bnd 85; Alfred Ag Tech; Comp Grphcs.

HOVER, TRACY; Hudson HS; Hudson, NY; (Y); Drama Clb; Band; Chorus; Concert Band; Mrchg Band; Pep Band; School Musical; Stage Crew; Cheerleading; Var Ftbl; Chrltn Awd; Outstndng Vclst; George Mason U; Pltcl Sci.

HOVEY, ELIZABETH; Geneva HS; Geneva, NY; (S); 4/175; Am Leg Aux Girls St; Trs French Clb; Latin Clb; Ski Clb; Yrbk Stf; Rep Stu Cncl; High Hon Roll; Sec NHS; Ntl Merit Ltr; Wellesley Bk Awd; Outstndng Latin; Lib Arts.

HOWANSKY, PETRUSIA; Roosevelt HS; Yonkers, NY; (Y); 15/245; Chess Clb; Church Yth Grp; Drama Clb; Hosp Aide; Key Clb; Service Clb; Nwsp Stf; Soph Cls; Jr Cls; Cit Awd; Dartmouth Clb Bk Awd 84-5; United Slavonian-Amer League Schlrshp 86; New York U; Pre-Med.

HOWARD, ALLISON; New Lebanon HS; New Lebanon, NY; (Y); 6/60; Drama Clb; Rep French Clb; Hosp Aide; Ski Clb; Chorus; School Play; Stage Crew; Yrbk Phtg; Sec Frsh Cls; Pres Stu Cncl.

HOWARD, AMY; Fairport HS; Fairport, NY; (Y); 2/600; Cmnty Wkr; Model UN; Ski Clb; SADD; Chorus; Nwsp Rptr; Rep Stu Cncl; Hon Roll; Prfct Atten Awd; Rotary Awd; 1st All Cnty Arts Shw 85.

HOWARD, AMY; Mexico HS; Maple View, NY; (Y); Dance Clb; Sec German Clb; Band; Mrchg Band; Sec Stu Cncl; Var Trk; JV Vllybl; Mst Actv Grmn Stu 85-86; Stu Cncl Sec 83-86; 90 Avg In Grmn & All Sbjcts 85-86; Grmn Clb Sec 85-86; Cmptr Sci.

HOWARD, ANDREW B; Pulaski Academy & Central Schl; Pulaski, NY; (S); 5/97; Band; Chorus; Nwsp Rptr; L Bsktbl; L Crs Cntry; Capt Ice Hcky; Hon Roll; NHS; Voice Dem Awd; Drama Clb; Schlrshp To WA Wrkshp Semnr On Wrkngs Of Fed Govt 85; Ind Labor Relations.

HOWARD, ARLENE; Cardinal O Hara HS; Kenmore, NY; (Y); French Clb; Nwsp Rptr; Stat Ftbl; Cmptv Rllr Sktr Awds; Engrng.

HOWARD, BARB; Warsaw HS; Silver Springs, NY; (S); 9/92; Debate Tm; Drama Clb; Sec Trs French Clb; Ski Clb; SADD; Sec Trs Chorus; School Musical; Rep Jr Cls; Pres Stu Cncl; Capt Socr; Warsaws 84 Autumn Festvl Pgnt 84; Sfty Cncl 85-86; SUNY Geneseo; Psych.

HOWARD, CHARISSE; Hutch Tech HS; Buffalo, NY; (Y); 97/243; Dance Clb; Exploring; Girl Scts; JA; Stu Cncl; High Hon Roll; Hon Roll; Top 10 SR 86; Buffalo ST Coll; Engrng.

HOWARD, DONNA; Kendall JR SR HS; Kendall, NY; (Y); 35/87; AFS; Exploring; 4-H; FHA; Spanish Clb; SADD; Band; Chorus; Concert Band; Mrchg Band; Hon Roll 84-86; Med.

HOWARD, DOUG; Alden Central HS; Alden, NY; (Y); Letterman Clb; Science Clb; Nwsp Stf; Var Swmmng; Hon Roll; Acad Ltr 86; Natl Sci Olympd 84; Med.

HOWARD, HENRY; Victor Central HS; Fairport, NY; (Y); 92/238; Computer Clb; Spanish Clb; Variety Show; Im Socr; Im Sftbl; Var Wrstlng; 2nd,1st Pl Victor Film Soc Cntst 83-86; Bethany; Comm.

HOWARD, JAMES; George W Wingate HS; Brooklyn, NY; (Y); Church Yth Grp; Radio Clb; Stage Crew; JV Crs Cntry; JV Ftbl; Capt JV Trk; JV Wt Lftg; Ldr Sundy Schl Clss 85-86; Recvd Outstndng Prfrmnc 84-85; VA Commonwealth U; Bus Fndtn.

HOWARD, JOHN; West Genesee HS; Camillus, NY; (Y); JV Bsbl; Im Bsktbl; JV Ftbl; High Hon Roll; NHS; Natl Sci Olympd 85; Hi-Quiz Clb 85; Onondoga CC; Acctng.

HOWARD, JONATHAN; Cazenoula HS; Cazenovia, NY; (Y); Mathletes; Stage Crew; Coach Actv; Swmmng; Var Trk; Bausch & Lomb Sci Awd; High Hon Roll; NHS; Ntl Merit Qrtr Anlst 86; Sci.

HOWARD, JUSTINE; South Jefferson Central HS; Adams, NY; (Y); French Clb; Ski Clb; Varsity Clb; Band; Concert Band; Jr Cls; Sr Cls; Stu Cncl; Bsktbl; Socr; Soccer All Star-Frntr Lge 85; Bsktbl All Star-Frntr Lge 86fAPW Bsktbl Trny All Star 86; Syracuse U; Pre Law.

HOWARD, KATHLEEN; Manhassett HS; Manhasset, NY; (Y); 1/189; Hosp Aide; Service Clb; Mrchg Band; Ed Nwsp Stf; Lit Mag; Stu Cncl; Capt Fld Hcky; Capt Gym; Cit Awd; NHS; Bauch & Lomb Sci Awd, Amer Lgn Poppy Queen & Manhasset Cmnty Clb 86; Princeton; Chmcl Rsrch.

HOWARD, KATHLEEN; St John Baptist Diocesan HS; N Babylon, NY; (S); 6/521; Girl Scts; Hosp Aide; Ski Clb; Yrbk Stf; Var Cheerleading; French Hon Soc; High Hon Roll; Ntl Sci Olympd 3rd Pl Chem 85; Ntl Sci Olymd Bio 84; Math.

HOWARD, LISA; George Wingate HS; Brooklyn, NY; (Y); Office Aide; Sftbl; Hon Roll; Prfct Atten Awd; Comptr Prgmg.

HOWARD, MARGARET S; Midwood HS; Brooklyn, NY; (Y); 76/556; Hosp Aide; Math Tm; Ed Yrbk Stf; Ed Lit Mag; Hon Roll; Math Clb; Office Aide; Teachers Aide; Chorus; Arista Soc 85; Archon Soc 85; Senatrs Vlntr Achvt Awd 83; SUNY Albany; Psych.

HOWARD, MAURA; St Marys Girls HS; Manhasset, NY; (Y); 1/176; Cmnty Wkr; French Clb; Mathletes; Math Tm; Ski Clb; Teachers Aide; Chorus; Stage Crew; Yrbk Stf; Var Tennis; 2nd Pl Iona Coll Lang Comptn Frnch 5; JR Sngl Dbl & Mxd Dbls Champ Plandome Cntry Clb 83-84; Bus.

HOWARD, MELISSA M; Chenango Valley HS; Port Crane, NY; (Y); Band; Color Guard; Drm Mjr(t); Trs Frsh Cls; Pres Soph Cls; Pres Jr Cls; Trs Stu Cncl; Cheerleading; Hon Roll; Jr NHS; Ntnl Slt To Yth Prog 86; Coll; Ed.

HOWARD, REBECCA; Marcus Whitman HS; Middlesex, NY; (Y); Church Yth Grp; 4-H; Hosp Aide; Acpl Chr; Band; Chorus; Mrchg Band; School Musical; Cit Awd; High Hon Roll; NY ST Regnts Schlrshp 86; Houghton Coll; Pedtrctn.

HOWARD, RICHARD P; Kenmore West HS; Kenmore, NY; (Y); 96/420; Var Socr; Var Trk; Hon Roll; ROTC Schlrshp 3 Yrs 87-89; Regent Schlrshp; Canisius Coll.

HOWARD, ROBERT; Valley Central HS; Walden, NY; (Y); 80/410; Letterman Clb; Varsity Clb; Yrbk Stf; Rep Stu Cncl; Var Wrstlng; Prfct Atten Awd; Intl Reltns.

HOWARD, SCOTT; John Jay HS; S Salem, NY; (Y); VP Church Yth Grp; Science Clb; Chorus; Var L Diving; Var L Ftbl; Var L Swmmng; Var L Trk; Cit Awd; Hon Roll; Boy Scts; Mech Engr.

HOWARD, SOPHIA; Fowler HS; Syracuse, NY; (Y); 31/153; Church Yth Grp; FBLA; JA; Pep Clb; Church Choir; Trs Frsh Cls; High Hon Roll; Prfct Atten Awd; 4-H; Hon Roll; Engl Hnrs Cls 85; Co-Op MONY 85-87; Hofstra U; Legal Sec.

HOWARD, WILLIAM BRADLEY; Randolph Central Schl; Randolph, NY; (Y); 5/86; Am Leg Boys St; Boy Scts; Var L Bsbl; Var L Ftbl; Var L Wrstlng; Hon Roll; NHS; Marine ROTC Scholar 86; U Rochester; Math.

HOWARD, YOLANDA; Mount Vernon HS; Tuckahoe, NY; (Y); Key Clb; Library Aide; Nwsp Stf; Cheerleading; Hon Roll; Bridgeport U; Med.

HOWE, ALAN; East Islip HS; E Islip, NY; (Y); 3/425; Cmnty Wkr; French Clb; Mathletes; Math Clb; Math Tm; SADD; Varsity Clb; JV Gym; JV Lcrss; Var L Tennis.

HOWE, CRAIG A; Oneida SR HS; Oneida, NY; (Y); Am Leg Boys St; Letterman Clb; SADD; Varsity Clb; Yrbk Stf; Pres Frsh Cls; Var L Bsbl; Var Capt Bsktbl; Var L Socr; Tri Vly Lg Bsktbl All Star Tm 86; Colgate U Semnr Pgm 86 & 87; Mayors Yth Advsry Cncl 86 & 87; U Of NC; Broadcast Comm.

HOWE, DEBORAH L; Dansville SR HS; Dansville, NY; (Y); Drama Clb; Band; Mrchg Band; Yrbk Stf; Soph Cls; JV Var Bsktbl; Var Cheerleading; Socr; Sftbl; Vllybl; Regnts Schlrshp 86; James Madison U; Comms.

HOWE, HEATHER A; Hamburg SR HS; Hamburg, NY; (Y); 32/390; Church Yth Grp; Service Clb; Chorus; Church Choir; Capt Color Guard; Orch; JV Cheerleading; Stat Vllybl; Hon Roll; Sec NHS; Mercyhurst Coll; Fshn Merch.

HOWE, KARA; Chautaugua Centeral HS; Mayville, NY; (Y); Teachers Aide; Band; Concert Band; Bsktbl; Sftbl; High Hon Roll; High Hon Roll; Jr NHS; Pres Schlr; Bus.

HOWE, LAURIE A; Westhill HS; Syracuse, NY; (Y); 19/150; Art Clb; Yrbk Stf; JV Var Socr; Hon Roll; NHS; Leag All Stars-V Sccr 85; Sprtsmnshp Awd V Sccr 85; Schltc MONY Awd-Art 86; Fredonia.

HOWE, NANCY; Niskayuna HS; Schdy, NY; (Y); Latin Clb; Symp Band; Rep Frsh Cls; Rep Soph Cls; Rep Jr Cls; Rep Sr Cls; Rep Stu Cncl; High Hon Roll; NHS; Ntl Merit SF; Empir ST Shclrshp 86; U Of PA; Engrng.

HOWELL, ALAN W; Johnson City SR HS; Johnson City, NY; (Y); 2/198; Chorus; Jazz Band; Orch; Symp Band; JP Sousa Awd; NHS; Sal; Nwsp Rptr; High Hon Roll; NY Conf All St Mxd Chorus 85; Bst Mscn Cls B Union Endicott Jazz Fest 86; NY St Regents Schlrshp 86; St U Of NY Buffalo; Music Ed.

HOWELL, BRYAN; Dundee Central HS; Dundee, NY; (Y); Boy Scts; Varsity Clb; VP Jr Cls; JV Bsktbl; Var Bowling; Var JV Ftbl; Var JV Trk; Var JV Wt Lftg; Hon Roll; Wood Shop Tchr.

HOWELL, DEBRA; Lansing HS; Lansing, NY; (Y); VP Spanish Clb; Chorus; School Musical; Stage Crew; Pres Frsh Cls; Cheerleading; Trk; High Hon Roll; Lion Awd; NHS; Awd Outstndg Achvmnt Spnsh 86; Physcl Thrpy.

HOWELL, DETREL; Uniondale HS; Hempstead, NY; (Y); 125/415; VP Key Clb; Office Aide; Band; Chorus; Mrchg Band; Orch; Nwsp Sprt Ed; Hon Roll; Cmnty Wkr; Girl Scts; Allysia Janene Allen Meml Schlrshp 86; US Envrnmntl Prtctn Agcy Schlrshp 86; Cert In Typg/Shrthnd 85; Bufalo Coll; Brdcst Cmmnctns.

HOWELL, GINA; Mount Vernon HS; Mt Vernon, NY; (Y); Pres Church Yth Grp; Trs 4-H; VP FBLA; Key Clb; Latin Clb; Office Aide; Yrbk Stf; Tennis; Hon Roll; Comp Sci.

HOWELL, KEVIN; Sayville HS; W Sayville, NY; (Y); SADD; Varsity Clb; Band; Concert Band; Mrchg Band; Orch; Var Ftbl; Var Trk; Var Wt Lftg; Hon Roll; Hist.

HOWELL, LILLI; Northeastern Acad; White Plains, NY; (Y); Teachers Aide; Acpl Chr; Church Choir; Nwsp Phtg; Nwsp Rptr; Nwsp Stf; Pres Frsh Cls; Soph Cls; Pres Jr Cls; Cheerleading; Oakwood Coll; Math.

HOWELL, PETER J; The Nichols Schl; Buffalo, NY; (Y); Var Capt Crs Cntry; Var Capt Trk; Hon Roll; Ntl Merit Ltr; Rgnts Schlrshp 86; 2nd Pl Schl Sci Fair 84; U Of Rochester; Bus.

HOWES, CHRIS; Jordan Elbridge JR SR HS; Memphis, NY; (Y); 18/142; Pres Church Yth Grp; Trs Girl Scts; Concert Band; Mrchg Band; School Play; Trs Sr Cls; Var Cheerleading; Hon Roll; NHS; Drama Clb; Silvr Ldrshp Awd Girl Scts 84; Bio.

HOWES, STEVE; Royalton Hartland HS; Lockport, NY; (Y); 40/135; Boy Scts; Church Yth Grp; Pres Sr Cls; Var JV Bsbl; Var JV Bsktbl; Var JV Ftbl; Var Swmmng; Hon Roll; Arch.

HOWEY, MELINDA; Smithtown East HS; St James, NY; (Y); Church Yth Grp; Cmnty Wkr; Hosp Aide; Key Clb; SADD; Off Frsh Cls; Off Soph Cls; Off Jr Cls; Stu Cncl; Jr NHS.

HOWICK, CHARLES; Hamburg SR HS; Hamburg, NY; (Y); Church Yth Grp; Socr; Trk; Vllybl; Aerospace Engr.

HOWIE, DONNA L; John Jay HS; Cross River, NY; (Y); 2/253; Ski Clb; VP Frsh Cls; Rep Soph Cls; Rep Jr Cls; Rep Sr Cls; Trs Stu Cncl; Var Capt Bsktbl; JV Var Fld Hcky; Var Capt Lcrss; Var Cit Awd; Sprtmnshp Awd Bsktbll 84-85; All Assoc La Cross Plyr Awd 84-85; Villanova U; Bus.

HOWLAN, CHRISTOPHER; Colonie Central HS; Albany, NY; (Y); Church Yth Grp; Civic Clb; Cmnty Wkr; Library Aide; Political Wkr; Var JV Bsbl; Var JV Bsktbl; Hon Roll; NHS; Schl Record Varsity Schl Bsbl 86; Varsity Bsktbl 85; Babe Ruth All-Star Trnmnt MVP & Bst Pitchng Awd; Arch.

HOWLAND, JANNA; Moravia Central HS; Locke, NY; (Y); 9/89; Color Guard; Mrchg Band; Stage Crew; Yrbk Stf; Trs Soph Cls; Rep Stu Cncl; Im Bowling; Var JV Fld Hcky; Var JV Vllybl; Hon Roll; Acdmc Achvmnt Awd 86; Stdy Awd 86; Long Island U; Marine Bio.

HOWLAND, PAUL; Guilderland HS; Esperance, NY; (Y); Aud/Vis; Ftbl; Hon Roll; Mth, Soc Studs, Sic, Bio Awds; Media Prod.

HOWLEY, JOHN; Auburn HS; Auburn, NY; (Y); Pres Intnl Clb; JA; Letterman Clb; Varsity Clb; JV Var Crs Cntry; Var Ice Hcky; Var Trk; Hon Roll; Aviatn.

HOWSON, CHARLOTTE M; F D Roosevelt HS; Hyde Park, NY; (Y); 17/336; PAVAS; Band; Concert Band; Jazz Band; Mrchg Band; Symp Band; Lit Mag; High Hon Roll; NHS; St Schlr; Franklin & Marshall; Medcn.

HOXIE, KIM; New Berlin Central HS; S Edmeston, NY; (Y); 1/60; Spanish Clb; Yrbk Bus Mgr; Cheerleading; Socr; Trk; Bausch & Lomb Sci Awd; Jr NHS; Lion Awd; Sec NHS; VP Frsh Cls; Arch.

HOYT, JAMES M; Notre Dame HS; Elmira, NY; (Y); 22/87; VP Church Yth Grp; Pres Computer Clb; Scholastic Bowl; Var Crs Cntry; Var Trk; STC All-Str Crs Cntry Tm 85-86; Cntntl Math Lge 82; Mst Imprvd Crs Cntry 84-86; Stonehill Coll; Math.

HOYT, RICHARD; Salem Central HS; Rupert, VT; (Y); Capt Bowling; Hon Roll; Prfct Atten Awd; Bus.

HOYT, RICK; Elmira Free Academy; Elmira, NY; (Y); Church Yth Grp; JV Bsktbl; Comp Prgrmg.

HOYT, TAMARA; Geneva HS; Geneva, NY; (S); 21/175; Church Yth Grp; Cmnty Wkr; Hosp Aide; Yrbk Stf; Var Cheerleading; Var Tennis; Hon Roll; Engl Achvt Awd 84; Hnrs Engl Achvt Awd 85; Sprtsmnshp Awd-Tnns 85; Engl.

HOYT, WENDY; Columbia HS; Castleton, NY; (Y); 66/425; Chorus; Church Choir; Mrchg Band; Orch; School Musical; Symp Band; NHS; Church Yth Grp; 4-H; Hon Roll; Music Dept Awd 86; SUNY; Music Ed.

HRYNIEWICZ, CHRISTINA; Maspeth HS; Maspeth, NY; (Y); 18/451; Camera Clb; Computer Clb; Hon Roll; Nrsg.

HSIA, MIN; Norman Thomas HS; Flushing, NY; (Y); 29/598; Chorus; Nwsp Ed-Chief; Nwsp Rptr; Trs NHS; St Johns Comptv Scholar 86; Regents Coll Scholar 86; Cert Excllnce 84-86; St Johns U; Jrnlsm.

HSIA, TAIN YEN; Long Beach SR HS; Long Beach, NY; (S); 2/256; Sec Hosp Aide; Capt Math Tm; School Musical; Nwsp Stf; Var Trk; Bausch & Lomb Sci Awd; CC Awd; VP NHS; Prfct Atten Awd; Pres Schlr; Semi-Fin Westinghouse Sci Talnt Srch 86; Fnlst Long Islnd Sci & Engrng Symp 86; Lng Bch Ambass HOBY; Med.

HSIEH, JOANNE; Manhasset HS; Manhasset, NY; (Y); Dance Clb; Girl Scts; Service Clb; Variety Show; Nwsp Rptr; Yrbk Stf; Gym; Hon Roll; Latin Awd Magna Cum Laude 85-86; Ballet Comptn Fnlst Awd 85-86; Bus.

HSU, HANK; Edward R Murrow HS; Brooklyn, NY; (Y); 4/669; Math Tm; Teachers Aide; School Play; Nwsp Ed-Chief; Nwsp Phtg; Bausch & Lomb Sci Awd; NCTE Awd; Westinghouse Honors Grp 85; Govnrs Commtt On Schlstc Achvt 85.

HSU, KENNETH D; Newtown HS; Elmhurst, NY; (Y); 5/667; Chorus; Lit Mag; Rep Sr Cls; Var Bowling; Mu Alp Tht; VFW Awd; Voice Dem Awd; Church Yth Grp; Jazz Band; Orch; Chncllrs Awd 86; NYU; Mus Tech.

HSU, MARGARET; Clarkstown H S North; New City, NY; (Y); Art Clb; Sec Mathletes; Capt Science Clb; Orch; School Musical; Nwsp Stf; Yrbk Stf; Lit Mag; High Hon Roll; Hon Roll; Hall Fame Awd; Frnch Awd; Mth Awd; Art Awd; Typng Awd; Mth Lg Cert; Italian Clb Rep; Acad Tm; QED; Mth.

HU, CHIMING; Newtown HS; Corona, NY; (Y); 22/667; Chess Clb; Math Clb; Office Aide; Teachers Aide; Chorus; Lit Mag; Hon Roll; Prfct Atten Awd; Acad All-Amer 86; Assoc Tchrs Of Math Of NY Schlrp 86; SUNY Stony Brook; Elec Engrg.

HUANG, ARNOLD; The Wheatley Schl; Albertson, NY; (Y); VP Chess Clb; Computer Clb; Library Aide; Mathletes; Stu Cncl; JV Bowling; Ntl Merit Ltr; 1st Pl Newfane 10th Yr Math Cont 84; 3rd Pl Pratt Ins Computer Cont 84; Math.

HUANG, BIN BIN; Stuyvesant HS; Jackson Hts, NY; (Y); Cmnty Wkr; Debate Tm; Hosp Aide; Library Aide; Teachers Aide; Nwsp Stf; Rep Frsh Cls; Elks Awd; Jr NHS; Ntl Merit Schol; Washington Cross Fdtn 86; Psych.

HUANG, CHEIH; Scarsdale HS; Scarsdale, NY; (Y); Hosp Aide; Varsity Clb; Var Wrstlng; 1st Pl Beacon Wrstlng Trnmnt 86; MV Wrstlr Beacon Trnmnt 86; All-League Wrstlr 86.

HUANG, HENRY; Aviation HS; Corona, NY; (S); 17/416; Computer Clb; Math Tm; Teachers Aide; Cit Awd; Hon Roll; NHS; Ntl Merit Schol; Pegasus Scty 85-86; Brd Educ Achvt Awd 85; City Yth 85; Cornell U; Elec Engr.

HUANG, JENNIFER; Avoca Central Schl; Avoca, NY; (Y); 1/42; French Clb; Sec Latin Clb; Math Tm; Quiz Bowl; Ski Clb; Band; Var Tennis; High Hon Roll; Lion Awd; NHS; The Clarkson Schl; Physcs.

HUANG, LORDER P; Bayside HS; Brooklyn, NY; (Y); 34/700; Intnl Clb; Math Clb; Math Tm; Yrbk Phtg; Lit Mag; Hon Roll; NHS; Queens Sci Fair Hnrbl Ment 85; NY Jr Sci Acad Smmr Hnr Rsrch 85; Natl Chinese Essy Cntst 4th Pl 85; ST U Of NY-BNGHMTN; Biochem.

HUANG, SHERMAN; Avoca Central Schl; Avoa, NY; (Y); ROTC; Ski Clb; Band; Pep Band; High Hon Roll; JP Sousa Awd; NHS; Ntl Merit SF; Headmasters Schlr 86; MA Inst Of Tech; Mech Engr.

HUANG, WESLEY; Unin Endicott HS; Endicott, NY; (Y); Boy Scts; Key Clb; Mathletes; Quiz Bowl; Science Clb; Yrbk Phtg; Rep Jr Cls; High Hon Roll; NHS; Amer Legn Schl Awd 84; Black Blt Karate 83.

HUBBARD, CHERI; Williamsville East HS; Williamsville, NY; (Y); 17/300; Church Yth Grp; Cmnty Wkr; Latin Clb; Math Clb; Church Choir; JV Bsktbl; Hon Roll; NHS; Prfct Atten Awd; Commnty Vlntr Of Yth Awd 86; Slvr Mdl Latin Cntst 84; SUNY Geneseo; Sec Educ.

HUBER, LISA; Preston HS; Bronx, NY; (S); 16/89; Red Cross Aide; Stage Crew; Bowling; Diving; Swmmng; High Hon Roll; Fordham U; Comp Prog.

HUBER, MARIA; Sweet Home SR HS; Amherst, NY; (Y); Church Yth Grp; Rep Frsh Cls; Rep Soph Cls; Stu Cncl; JV Socr; Hon Roll; Ntl Merit Schol; Panthers Pause 85; Syracuse; Arch.

HUBERT, MICHELE; George Washington HS; New York, NY; (Y); 110/321; Office Aide; Teachers Aide; Stage Crew; Variety Show; Yrbk Phtg; Yrbk Stf; Crs Cntry; Trk; Wt Lftg; Cit Awd; Schlstc Excllnc Awd In Bus Mth 86; Coll Bnd Pgm Cert 86; BMCC; Bus Mgmt.

HUBMAN, MARK; Romulus Central Schl; Romulus, NY; (S); 14/54; Church Yth Grp; Band; Chorus; Concert Band; Jazz Band; Mrchg Band; School Musical; Pres 4-H; Trs Spanish Clb; Stat Bsbl; Alfred Ag & Tech Coll; Bus Admi.

HUCK, TERESA; Mercy HS; Wading River, NY; (Y); 11/101; Nwsp Ed-Chief; High Hon Roll; Hon Roll; NHS; Briarcliffe Acadmc Schlrshp; Briarcliffe Pres Schlrshp 86; Briarcliffe Clg; Bus.

HUCKABEE, ANDY; Lafayette HS; Jamesville, NY; (S); 1/96; 4-H; Math Clb; Math Tm; Quiz Bowl; Ski Clb; Spanish Clb; High Hon Roll; NHS; Ntl Merit Ltr; Val; Hghst Avg Eng Soc Stud & Bus Dynmcsd 82-83; Hghst Avg Eng Biol & Hlth 83-84; Hghst Avg Eng Spn 84-85.

HUDAK, PETER; St John The Baptist DHS; Central Islip, NY; (Y); 119/546; Buds Natl Hnrs Scty 85-86; Hofstra U; Accntng.

HUDD, BARBARA ANN; Maria Regina HS; White Plains, NY; (Y); 11/126; Key Clb; Trs Service Clb; Nwsp Stf; Yrbk Ed-Chief; Rep Sr Cls; Fld Hcky; Cit Awd; Hon Roll; NHS; Chorus; Generoso Pope Awd 86; Iona Coll; Cmmnctns.

HUDDERS, NEAL; Williamsville South HS; Williamsville, NY; (Y); Church Yth Grp; Quiz Bowl; Acpl Chr; Concert Band; Orch; Crs Cntry; Trk; Hon Roll; NHS; Math Tm; All-ST Bnd 85.

HUDSON, ERIK M; Monsignor Farrell HS; Staten Island, NY; (Y); 18/289; Wt Lftg; High Hon Roll; Ntl Merit Ltr; NY ST Regnts Schlrshp 86; Alt Bd Of Trustees Schlrshp Polytech U 86; SUNY Stony Brook; Aerosp Engrg.

HUDSON, GLORIA A; Patchoque-Medford HS; Patchogue, NY; (Y); 10/620; VP Leo Clb; Spanish Clb; Rep Frsh Cls; VP Soph Cls; VP Jr Cls; Rep Sr Cls; Trs Stu Cncl; Var Stat Bsbl; NHS; Mathletes; Jr Prom Queen; Homecmng Court; Bucknell U; Engrng.

HUDSON, HEATHER; Cato-Meridian HS; Cato, NY; (Y); Computer Clb; Ski Clb; Stage Crew; Nwsp Stf; Yrbk Stf; Var Fld Hcky; Var Sftbl; Var Vllybl; Hon Roll; NHS; Sports Camp Schlrshp; All Star Tm-Vllybl; Bio.

HUDSON, JUNE A; N Babylon HS; No Babylon, NY; (Y); Sec French Clb; Intnl Clb; Political Wkr; Variety Show; Cheerleading; Vllybl; Stony Brook; Acctnt.

HUDSON, LYNNE; Maple Hill HS; Castleton, NY; (Y); 5/71; Debate Tm; Model UN; Ski Clb; Spanish Clb; Fld Hcky; Trk; DAR Awd; High Hon Roll; NHS; Scholar Panhellenic Assn Albany NY 86; Pres Acad Fit Awd 86; L G Balfour SR Awd 86; Lndscpe Archit.

HUDSON, SONIA; Harry S Truman HS; Bx, NY; (Y); Girl Scts; Church Choir; JV Bsktbl; Var Sftbl; JV Trk; Baruch; Accntng.

HUDSON, YOLANDA; White Plains HS; White Plns, NY; (Y); Art Clb; Dance Clb; Girl Scts; Spanish Clb; SADD; Church Choir; Yrbk Stf; Var Capt Cheerleading; JV Vllybl; Hon Roll; Spelman Coll; Bus Mgmt.

HUDY, JENNIFER; Kendall JR SR HS; Holley, NY; (Y); 32/100; Church Yth Grp; Pep Clb; Color Guard; Nwsp Stf; Yrbk Stf; Hon Roll; Bus.

HUE, HENRY; Hicksville SR HS; Hicksville, NY; (Y); Computer Clb; ROTC; Band; Drm & Bgl; Jazz Band; Orch; Hon Roll; NHS; Polytechnic Inst Of Tech; Engrg.

HUEMPFNER, JOHN; Syosset HS; Syosset, NY; (Y); 28/48; Radio Clb; Chorus; Lit Mag; JV Socr; JV Var Swmmng; High Hon Roll; NHS; Rensselaer; Elec Engr.

HUERTA, LUPE; Acad Of Mt St Ursola; Bronx, NY; (Y); Chorus; JV Bsktbl; Iona Coll; Busnss Mgmt.

HUESTER, DAVE; John Jay HS; Katonah, NY; (Y); Boy Scts; Church Yth Grp; SADD; Band; Jazz Band; Mrchg Band; Variety Show; Yrbk Phtg; Stu Cncl; Lcrss; Egl Sct Awd 86; Mrn Trnprtn.

HUESTIS, AMY; Ticonderoga HS; Ticonderoga, NY; (Y); 1/100; Trs SADD; VP Jr Cls; Var Bsktbl; Coach Actv; Var Socr; Var Trk; Bausch & Lomb Sci Awd; Elks Awd; NHS; Val; Clarkson U; Engrg.

HUFF, AMY; Alexander Central HS; Darien, NY; (Y); Church Yth Grp; Ski Clb; School Play; JV Cheerleading; JV Socr; JV Vllybl; Hon Roll; Bookkeeping Excllnt Wrk 86; Acctng.

HUFF, CHERYL; South Lewis Central HS; Brantingham, NY; (Y); 7/92; Sec Church Yth Grp; Cmnty Wkr; Sec Hosp Aide; SADD; Rep Stu Cncl; High Hon Roll; Hon Roll; Library Aide; Band; Chorus; U Mthdst Chrch Offcrs & Dstrct Yth Sctry 84-86; Stu Tr Hstry 83-84; Cmmnctns.

HUFF, JULIE; E J Wilson HS; Spencerport, NY; (Y); 36/327; Drama Clb; French Clb; Jazz Band; Stage Crew; Symp Band; Tennis; Hon Roll; Med.

HUFF, SANDRA E; Cherry Valley Central HS; Cherry Valley, NY; (Y); 2/26; Drama Clb; Varsity Clb; Score Keeper; Var Socr; Var Sftbl; High Hon Roll; NHS; Chorus; Concert Band; Yrbk Stf; Stu Of Mnth 86; Delhi Agr & Tecn Coll; Htl Mngm.

HUFFER, BOBBI; Kendall JR-SR HS; Hamlin, NY; (Y); GAA; VICA; Concert Band; Mrchg Band; Trs Jr Cls; Var Capt Bsktbl; Var Socr; Var Capt Sftbl; Var Vllybl; Hon Roll; V Bskbtl, MVP Defense, Y Vlybl MVP 86, Y Sftbl, MVP Defense 86; JV Sftbl MVP Offense 84; Monroe CC; Media Comm.

HUFFMAN, KIM; Randolph Central HS; Randolph, NY; (Y); Pres Sec Church Yth Grp; Drama Clb; Sec VP 4-H; French Clb; Sec Acpl Chr; Sec Chorus; Yrbk Phtg; JV Var Cheerleading; Var Crs Cntry; Var Trk.

HUFFMAN, MELISSA; Royalton-Hartland Central HS; Gasport, NY; (Y); 28/132; CAP; Girl Scts; Spanish Clb; SADD; Band; Chorus; Pep Band; Yrbk Stf; Stu Cncl; Bsktbl; Blue Rbn In Bnd 86; Cvl Air Ptrl Currie Rbn 85; Trck & Bskbtl Vrrssty Ltr & Pins 84-85; Oswego; Chld Psychlgy.

HUFLAND, COURTNEY; Shenendehowa HS; Clifton Park, NY; (Y); Varsity Clb; JV Trk; High Hon Roll; Hon Roll; JV Cheerleading; Fld Hcky; Im Socr; Nazareth Coll; Art.

HUGG, MELISSA; Elmira Free Acad; Lowman, NY; (Y); French Clb; Chorus; Sftbl; Hon Roll; USAF; Bus.

HUGGINS, PETER; Mc Quaid Jesuit HS; Lima, NY; (Y); #59 In Class; Church Yth Grp; Drama Clb; Chorus; School Musical; Nwsp Rptr; Nwsp Stf; Yrbk Stf; JV Im Crs Cntry; Var JV Trk; NHS; NY ST Choir/Schl Choral Study 86; Ctznshp Awd/Dghtrs Amercn Rvltn 81; Jrnlsm.

HUGGLER, ANDREA; Copiague SR HS; Amityharbor, NY; (Y); Art Clb; Hon Roll; Arts.

HUGHES, ALISSA; Frontier SR HS; Hamburg, NY; (S); 41/444; Hosp Aide; Pep Clb; Stu Cncl; High Hon Roll; Hon Roll; Trs NHS; NEDT Awd; Med Tech.

HUGHES, ANGEL; Greenwich HS; Middle Fls, NY; (Y); Service Clb; Hon Roll; Lawyer.

HUGHES, BONNIE; Chazy Central Rural Schl; Chazy, NY; (Y); 1/35; Model UN; School Play; Yrbk Ed-Chief; VP Sr Cls; JV Var Cheerleading; High Hon Roll; NHS; Val; Pep Clb; Ski Clb; N Country Schlrshp 85; NY ST Regents Schlrshp 86; St Lawrence U; Psych.

HUGHES, CAROLYN; St Dominic HS; N Bellmore, NY; (Y); 9/143; Camera Clb; Mathletes; Math Clb; Quiz Bowl; Ski Clb; Yrbk Stf; Swmmng; High Hon Roll; Mu Alp Tht; NHS; Awds Exclnc Accntng Spnsh 86; 1st Plc Mdl Exclnc Theolgy 86; NEDT Hgh Achvmnt Awd 84; Biolgy.

HUGHES, CHRISTINE; Indian River Central HS; Evans Mills, NY; (Y); #4 In Class; JCL; Latin Clb; Band; Mrchg Band; Hon Roll; Elmira Coll Key Awd 86.

HUGHES, DUNCAN; De Sales Catholic HS; Lockport, NY; (S); 8/32; Var Bsbl; Var Ftbl; Var Wrstlng; U Of IL Chicago; Arch.

HUGHES, ELIZABETH; Oxford Acad & Central HS; Oxford, NY; (Y); Drama Clb; SADD; Teachers Aide; Color Guard; Concert Band; Nwsp Rptr; Rep Jr Cls; Trs Stu Cncl; Cheerleading; Hon Roll; Rtry Yth Ldrshp Awd 86; Mst Dedctd Stu Govt Awd 85-86; Hofstra U; Elem Educ.

HUGHES, JULIE; Scotia-Glenville HS; Scotia, NY; (Y); French Clb; Key Clb; Ski Clb; Yrbk Stf; Rep Jr Cls; Stu Cncl; Cheerleading; Sftbl; Hon Roll; NHS.

HUGHES, KATHLEEN; Tully Central HS; Lafayette, NY; (Y); 4-H; French Clb; Math Tm; Varsity Clb; Yrbk Stf; Trk; Vllybl; Hon Roll; NHS; Math.

HUGHES, KERRY A; Kings Park SR HS; Kings Park, NY; (Y); 51/395; Church Yth Grp; Cmnty Wkr; Computer Clb; Service Clb; Speech Tm; Rep Soph Cls; Rep Stu Cncl; Var Tennis; High Hon Roll; Sec NHS; Cath Leag Awd-Religious & Cvl Rghts 86; Medl-Faithful Svc To Schl & Stu 85; Hugh O Brien Ldrshp Awd 84; Marymount Coll; Bus Admin.

HUGHES, LESLIE; Saratoga Central Catholic HS; Ballston Lake, NY; (S); Drama Clb; SADD; Chorus; Stage Crew; Sftbl; Hon Roll; Skidmore Saratogian Outstndng JR Awd 85; Sci.

HUGHES, LOLENE; Jordan-Elbridge HS; Elbridge, NY; (Y); 1/143; Church Yth Grp; ROTC; Band; Chorus; Concert Band; Drm Mjr(t); Jazz Band; Mrchg Band; School Musical; Yrbk Stf; NROTC Schlrshp Marine Oper 86; Elmira Key Awd 85; Dllrs Schlrs Schlrshp 86; Cornell U; Biolgy.

HUGHES, PATRICK; Twin Tiers Baptist HS; Lawrenceville, PA; (Y); Pres Church Yth Grp; Pres 4-H; Chorus; Jr Cls; Bsktbl; High Hon Roll; Church Choir; School Play; Stage Crew; Socr; Soaches Awd In Soccer 85; Sci Awd In Bio 85; 2d Pl Sxphn Soloist At Fine Arts Fstvl 85.

HUGHES IV, RICHARD J; La Salle Military Acad; Massapequa, NY; (S); 7/97; Cmnty Wkr; Capt ROTC; Chorus; Coach Actv; Var Lcrss; Var Socr; Var Swmmng; Wrstlng; NHS; Math & Ctznshp Awds 80; Lwyr.

HUGHES, SARA; Bishop Ludden HS; Syracuse, NY; (S); Church Yth Grp; Spanish Clb; Band; Concert Band; Cheerleading; Crs Cntry; Socr; Trk; High Hon Roll; Middlebury; Interpreter.

HUGHES, TADD; Aquinas Inst; Rochester, NY; (Y); Concert Band; Drm & Bgl; Jazz Band; Mrchg Band; Pep Band; Symp Band; Yrbk Phtg; Yrbk Stf; Hon Roll; Mst Outstndng Musicn 85-86; Comp Sci.

HUGHES, TERENCE W; Mount Saint Michaels Acad; Pelham, NY; (S); 1/309; Am Leg Boys St; Nwsp Sprt Ed; Rep Stu Cncl; Im Bsktbl; JV Var Ftbl; Wt Lftg; Hon Roll; NHS; Spanish NHS; Columbia U; Pre-Med.

HUGHES III, THOMAS F; Camisius HS; Orchard Park, NY; (Y); Hosp Aide; Model UN; Stage Crew; Hon Roll; Rowng Tm Slvr Mdlst Empire ST Games 85; Canadn Schlstc Rowng Chmpnshp Slvr Mdl 85; Boston Coll; Pre-Law.

HUGHES, VINCENT; Roy C Ketcham HS; Wappingers Fls, NY; (Y); Var Bsbl; Ftbl; Sectn 1 Bsbl All Star Southeastern Conf Bsbl All Star 86; Poughkeepsie Jrnl 2nd Tm Bsbl 86.

HUGHEY, JESSICA; Hamburg SR HS; Hamburg, NY; (Y); Red Cross Aide; School Musical; JV Cheerleading; Var Swmmng; UNC; Elem Educ.

HUGHNER, LISA; Naples Central Schl; Naples, NY; (Y); VICA; Hon Roll; Southeastern Acad; Travel.

HUGHSON, BARB; Wayne Central HS; Ontario, NY; (Y); 2/200; Math Tm; Chorus; Concert Band; School Musical; Cit Awd; High Hon Roll; NHS; Sal; French Clb; Mathletes; Hchstn Msc Schl Schlrshp 84-86; Hmltn Coll; Lbrl Arts.

HUGHSON, BARBARA A; Wayne Central HS; Ontario, NY; (Y); 2/189; Math Tm; Chorus; Concert Band; Mrchg Band; School Musical; Cit Awd; High Hon Roll; Prfct Atten Awd; Sal; French Clb; Hocstein Music Schlrshp 84-86; Hamilton Coll; Librl Arts.

HUHTALA, DAVID A; Norwich HS; Norwich, NY; (Y); Pres Intnl Clb; Spanish Clb; School Musical; Var L Ftbl; Var Vllybl; Hon Roll; St Schlr; Ithaca Clg; Bus Mgmt.

HUI, BENNY S K; Thomas A Edison HS; Richmond Hill, NY; (Y); 5/40; High Hon Roll; Elctrncs.

HUKEY, KRISTINE; Guilderland HS; Altamont, NY; (Y); Church Yth Grp; Girl Scts; Chorus; Church Choir; Orch; School Musical; Off Sr Cls; Cit Awd; God & Church Awd 84; Girl Scout Silver & Gold Awd 83&86; St Olaf Coll; Music.

HULBERT, CHRIS; Johnson City SR HS; Johnson City, NY; (Y); French Clb; Ski Clb; Golf; Tennis; Wt Lftg; High Hon Roll; Hon Roll; Broome CC; Crml Just.

HULBERT, JULIE; Sodus Central HS; Sodus, NY; (Y); AFS; Pep Clb; Science Clb; Ski Clb; JV Var Cheerleading; Im Gym; JV Var Pom Pon; JV Socr; JV Sftbl; JV Tennis; Brockport; Psychlgst.

HULBERT, KENNETH; Cicero-North Syracuse HS; Clay, NY; (S); 55/667; Mathletes; Math Clb; Math Tm; JV Socr; Var L Trk; NHS; RIT; Engr.

HULBERT, SHARON; Johnstown HS; Johnstown, NY; (Y); AFS; Sec Trs 4-H; Band; Mrchg Band; Mgr(s); Score Keeper; JV Capt Swmmng; Trk; 4-H Awd; Hon Roll; Lawyer.

HULBERT, TODD; Minisink Valley HS; Middletown, NY; (Y); 9/230; Capt Math Tm; Red Cross Aide; Capt Scholastic Bowl; Service Clb; Varsity Clb; Var L Bsbl; Capt L Socr; High Hon Roll; Pres NHS; Ntl Merit Ltr; Cntl Schlrshp For Exclinc 86; NW ST Rgnts Schlrshp 86; 7th Pl Ntl Acad Chmpnshps 86; SUNY-BINGHAMPTON ; Comp Sci.

HULL, BONNIE J; Unatego JR SR HS; Otego, NY; (Y); 13/86; Church Yth Grp; Drama Clb; Ski Clb; JV Bsktbl; JV Sftbl; Var L Trk; High Hon Roll; NHS; Prfct Atten Awd; Schlrshps-Presdtl, Biglw & Rgnts; Albany Coll Of Phrmcy; Phrmcy.

HULL, MICHELLE E; Belfast Central Schl; Caneadea, NY; (Y); #2 In Class; Yrbk Ed-Chief; Pres Soph Cls; VP Stu Cncl; Vllybl; Cit Awd; High Hon Roll; NHS; Sal; Houghton Coll; Comp Sci.

HULL, TERRENCE; Southampton HS; Southampton, NY; (Y); Church Yth Grp; French Clb; Stu Cncl; Bsktbl; Socr; Tennis; Invstmnts.

HULL, TIMOTHY H; Southampton HS; Southampton, NY; (Y); Church Yth Grp; French Clb; Letterman Clb; Rep Frsh Cls; Rep Soph Cls; Rep Jr Cls; JV Bsktbl; Var Socr; Var Tennis; Hon Roll; Bus.

HULL-RYDE, BETSY; Charlotte Valley Central Schl; Davenport Center, NY; (S); Drama Clb; GAA; Ski Clb; Spanish Clb; Stu Cncl; Bsktbl; Socr; Sftbl; High Hon Roll; NHS; JV Bsktbl Trphy 84; Spnch Excllnc Awds 84 & 85; Suny At Cortland; Elem Educ.

HULSE, BETH; Greenwood Central HS; Greenwood, NY; (S); 3/30; Yrbk Stf; Trs Soph Cls; Trs Jr Cls; Trs Sr Cls; Score Keeper; Socr; High Hon Roll; Hon Roll; Sec NHS; Varsity Clb; Alt Co Dairy Princess 85-86; Phys Ther.

HULSEN, CHRISTINE; North Babylon HS; N Babylon, NY; (Y); Drama Clb; Mathletes; Chorus; School Play; Score Keeper; High Hon Roll; Hon Roll; Jr NHS; NHS; Italian Natl Hnr Soc 85; Fshn Mrchndsng.

HULSLANDER, BILL; Elmira Free Acad; Elmira, NY; (Y); Service Clb; Ski Clb; Spanish Clb; Band; Concert Band; Drm Mjr(t); Mrchg Band; High Hon Roll; Hon Roll; Bio.

HULTS, WENDY; Lindenhurst SR HS; Lindenhurst, NY; (Y); 30/600; Cmnty Wkr; French Clb; Band; Concert Band; Mrchg Band; Stage Crew; High Hon Roll; Hon Roll; NHS; Elem Educ.

HUMBACH, THOMAS; Vernon HS; Mount Vernon, NY; (Y); 34/550; Boy Scts; Letterman Clb; Ski Clb; Band; Concert Band; Jazz Band; Mrchg Band; Pep Band; Lit Mag; Cheerleading; Schlr Ath Awd 86; NY Regents Scholar 86; PA ST U; Aerontcl Engrng.

HUMBERT, PHILIPPE; Amherst Central HS; Amherst, NY; (Y); 55/295; Pres German Clb; Radio Clb; Pres Orch; School Play; Im Badmtn; JV Crs Cntry; Im Socr; Im Sftbl; High Hon Roll; Hon Roll; Rgnts Schlrshp 86; ST U Of NY Buffalo; Bus.

HUMBERT, SHERI; North Rose Wolcott HS; Clyde, NY; (Y); 3/143; Pres Church Yth Grp; Pres 4-H; Teachers Aide; Lib Band; Church Choir; Var Vllybl; 4-H Awd; High Hon Roll; NHS; 4-H Schlrshp 86; NYSSMA Solo Comptn Music Awd 82-83; Delhi Ag & Tech; Vet Sci Tech.

HUME, MAUREEN; Keveny Memorial Acad; Cohoes, NY; (S); 2/41; Hosp Aide; Math Clb; Band; Chorus; Sec Sr Cls; Stu Cncl; Co-Capt Cheerleading; Pres NHS; Ntl Merit Ltr; RDI Math & Sci Awd 85; Schl Srv Awd 85; Phrmcy.

HUME, SHARYLL; Le Roy Central HS; Leroy, NY; (Y); Computer Clb; 4-H; French Clb; Girl Scts; SADD; Color Guard.

HUMIG, KATHERINE; Hutch Tech; Buffalo, NY; (Y); SADD; Rep Jr Cls; Acctng.

HUMMEL, KRISTIN; The Franciscan Acad; Syracuse, NY; (S); 4/25; GAA; Hosp Aide; NFL; Chorus; School Play; Yrbk Stf; VP Jr Cls; Rep Stu Cncl; Var Bsktbl; Var Sftbl; Frnch, Latin Awds 84-85; Phy Ed Awd 83-84; Boston U; Pub Rel.

HUMPHREY, DAVID L; Watkins Glen HS; Beaver Dams, NY; (Y); 23/129; Letterman Clb; School Play; Nwsp Stf; Yrbk Stf; Crs Cntry; Trk; Wrstlng; High Hon Roll; NY ST Rgnts Schlrshp Wnr 86; Pee Wee Wrstlng Instrctr 86; Alfred ST Ag & Tech; Paper Sci.

HUMPHREY, RENA; Hoosick Falls Central HS; Hoosick Falls, NY; (Y); Church Yth Grp; Drama Clb; French Clb; Band; Chorus; Church Choir; Concert Band; Mrchg Band; School Musical; School Play; Army.

HUMPHREY, SHAY; Lake George HS; Lake George, NY; (Y); 6/84; Dance Clb; Drama Clb; Key Clb; SADD; School Musical; Rep Stu Cncl; Capt Cheerleading; High Hon Roll; NHS; Bst Supprtng Actrss 85; Outstndg Work In Dance 83; Theat.

HUMPHREYS, BEVERLY; St Raymonds Acad Por Girls; Bronx, NY; (Y); 39/73; Computer Clb; Capt Color Guard; VP Soph Cls; Prfct Atten Awd; Cert For Outstndng Achvt From US Navy 86; St Joseph; Law.

HUMPHREYS, COLLEEN; Lockport SR HS; Lockport, NY; (Y); 139/400; Bus.

HUMPHREYS, KELLY; Lyndonville Central Schl; Lyndonville, NY; (Y); 15/83; Math Clb; Spanish Clb; Mrchg Band; Varsity Clb; School Play; Sec Frsh Cls; JV Score Keeper; JV Capt Socr; JV Var Wrstlng; Spanish NHS; Cortland ST; Pyschlgy.

HUMPHRIES, PATRICIA R; Julia Richman HS; Glendale, NY; (Y); 10/246; Hosp Aide; Teachers Aide; Pres Temple Yth Grp; Band; Chorus; Church Choir; School Play; Rep Frsh Cls; Hon Roll; Rgnts Schlrshp 86; Nrsng Awd 83-84; Hln Field Schl Of Nrsng; Nrs.

HUNDEMER, BRETT D; Midwood HS; Brooklyn, NY; (Y); 127/649; Hosp Aide; Orch; Nwsp Rptr; Lit Mag; High Hon Roll; NHS; St Schlr; Vet Tech Cert Scholar Sci Eng Comp Sci Spn & Hstry 83; Mod Cngrss 86; Clark U; Corp Law.

HUNDLEY, CARLA; Kensington HS; Buffalo, NY; (Y); 22/238; Cmnty Wkr; FBLA; Varsity Clb; Chorus; Church Choir; Drill Tm; Variety Show; Yrbk Stf; Sec Soph Cls; Sec Jr Cls; Feyler Awd 86; Daemen Coll; Acctg.

HUNG, JEFFERY K; Kingston HS; Kingston, NY; (Y); 73/573; Boy Scts; Band; Chorus; Concert Band; Drm & Bgl; Drm Mjr(t); Jazz Band; Mrchg Band; Orch; Pep Band; Ulster Cnty CC; Bus Admin.

HUNGER, ELIZABETH; Cardinal Mooney HS; Hilton, NY; (Y); 65/304; Sec VP 4-H; 4-H Awd; Hon Roll; Regents NY ST Schlrshp 86; Grnd Cham Yth Mare Qrtr Horse Erie Cnty 84-85; U Buffalo; Bus Mgmt.

HUNKINS, ALAIN; La Guardia HS Of Music & Art HS; Flushing, NY; (S); 1/437; French Clb; JA; Scholastic Bowl; Orch; Nwsp Rptr; Wt Lftg; Gov Hon Prg Awd; Hon Roll; NHS; Val.

HUNT, CHRISANN; Auburn HS; Auburn, NY; (Y); Dance Clb; Girl Scts; Sec JA; Hon Roll; Achvt Awd 86; CCBI; Exec Secty.

HUNT, DARRYL; Perry Central HS; Perry, NY; (Y); Art Clb; Boy Scts; Church Yth Grp; Ski Clb; Varsity Clb; Church Choir; JV Bsbl; JV Var Ftbl; Hon Roll; Acdmc Ftbll Awd; Natl Chem Merit Awd; Caseroptics.

HUNT, KELLY; Shoreham Wading River HS; Shoreham, NY; (Y); French Clb; Varsity Clb; Nwsp Bus Mgr; Nwsp Ed-Chief; Lit Mag; JV Var Bsktbl; Tennis; Vllybl; Church Yth Grp; Ski Clb; Bus.

HUNT, MARY ALICE; Niskayuna HS; Niskayuna, NY; (Y); AFS; Civic Clb; Drama Clb; German Clb; Library Aide; Church Choir; Stage Crew; Powder Puff Ftbl; High Hon Roll; Hon Roll; NY ST Rgnts Schlrshp 86; ST U Of NY; Hstry.

HUNT, NOREEN; Moore Catholic HS; Staten Island, NY; (Y); Art Clb; French Clb; Teachers Aide; Bowling; Crs Cntry; Hon Roll; NHS; Sci Awd 1st Pl 86; Amer Lgn Awd Essay Cntst 84; Vtrns Of Frgn Wars Essy Cntst 85.

HUNT, RONALD; George W Wingate HS; Brooklyn, NY; (Y); Church Yth Grp; Crs Cntry; Trk; NHS; US Air Force Acad; Economics.

HUNT, SUSAN F; Ausable Valley Central Schl; Ausable Forks, NY; (Y); 2/130; French Clb; Library Aide; Ski Clb; Stage Crew; Yrbk Stf; Var Sftbl; Im Vllybl; High Hon Roll; NHS; Sal; NYS Regnts Schlrshp 86; Cortland Clg; Librl Arts.

HUNTER, AMY; Oakwood Schl; Poughkeepsie, NY; (Y); Camera Clb; Intnl Clb; Letterman Clb; Pep Clb; Political Wkr; Varsity Clb; School Play; Stage Crew; Variety Show; Nwsp Phtg; Hdsn Vly Athltc Leag All Str Team Sccr, Bkstbl, Sftbl 84-86; Nrthn CA Athltc Leag Grls JV X-Cntry; Hstry.

HUNTER, DAWN; East Meadow HS; East Meadow, NY; (Y); Church Yth Grp; Hosp Aide; Library Aide; Teachers Aide; Band; Chorus; Church Choir; Hon Roll; Prsdntl Physcl Ftnss Awd 83; Hnr Rll 83-84; Assn Chldrn W/Dwns Syndrm 83; Navy; Mltry Nrs.

HUNTER, JOANNE; Hoosic Valley Central Schl; Johnsonville, NY; (Y); 18/94; Hon Roll; NHS; Prfct Atten Awd; Allen Bassett Mem Awd; Hdsn Vly Comm Coll; Crmnl Psych.

HUNTER, MATTHEW J; Notre Dame HS; Bath, NY; (Y); 13/88; Am Leg Boys St; Key Clb; School Musical; Rep Stu Cncl; JV Var Bsbl; JV Var Ftbl; Var Wrstlng; High Hon Roll; Hon Roll; Pres NHS; Altrnt US Coast Guard Acdy 85-86; Altrnt NROTC Schlrshp 85-86; NYS Rgnts Schlrshp Rcpnt 85-86; Clarkson U; Engr.

HUNTER, MELISSA; De Sales HS; Waterloo, NY; (Y); 13/54; French Clb; Ski Clb; Chorus; Yrbk Stf; JV Bsktbl; Var Cheerleading; High Hon Roll; Hon Roll; NHS; Engl.

HUNTER, SEAN; Mechanicsville HS; Mechanicville, NY; (S); 26/104; Bsktbl; Var Crs Cntry; Var Socr; NHS; Aristoi Hnr Socty 86; Ithaca Coll; Phy Ed.

HUNTER, WILLIAM; John Dewey HS; Brooklyn, NY; (Y); Math Clb; Math Tm; Bsktbl; Sftbl; Trk.

HUNTINGTON, SALLY; Wilson Central HS; Ransomville, NY; (Y); Church Yth Grp; Cmnty Wkr; Library Aide; Office Aide; SADD; Teachers Aide; Varsity Clb; Nwsp Rptr; Nwsp Stf; Var Cheerleading; Dmncn Rpblc Mssnry 86; Robts Wslyn Coll; Chrstn Mnstry.

HUNTINGTON, STACEY; Barker Central HS; Barker, NY; (Y); AFS; Church Yth Grp; Trs 4-H; VP Sec French Clb; VP FBLA; Teachers Aide; Chorus; Rep Stu Cncl; Var Trk; Hon Roll; Rodney Bunting Schlrshp 86; Niagara Cnty CC; Lbrl Arts.

HUNTINGTON, TED; Jamesville-Dewitt HS; Syracuse, NY; (Y); Jazz Band; Var Ftbl; Crtfct Mrt Accntng 86; Engr.

HUNZINGER, SCOTT; Deer Park HS; Deer Park, NY; (Y); Intnl Clb; Math Tm; Chorus; School Musical; JV Var Bsktbl; High Hon Roll; Hon Roll; NHS; Pre Law.

HUPKA, LISA; Port Jervis HS; Sparrowbush, NY; (Y); Trs Key Clb; Math Tm; Office Aide; Varsity Clb; Chorus; School Musical; Var L Trk; Hon Roll; Prfct Atten Awd; Key Clb Schlrshp 86; Math Educ.

HUPPUCH, BIRGIT; Ossining HS; Ossining, NY; (Y); Cmnty Wkr; Acpl Chr; Pres Chorus; School Musical; Yrbk Stf; Pres Frsh Cls; Pres Soph Cls; Pres Stu Cncl; Var Fld Hcky; NHS; Smith Bk Awd 86; Wellesley Book Awd 86.

HURD, KELLY; Camden HS; Camden, NY; (Y); AFS; Church Yth Grp; SADD; Band; Chorus; Concert Band; School Musical; Yrbk Stf; High Hon Roll; NHS; AFS Stu Spain 86; Stu Band Condctr 86; Cornell.

HURD, NATALIE; Horseheads HS; Erin, NY; (Y); Hon Roll.

HURD, PATTI; Gloversville HS; Glovesville, NY; (Y); Office Aide; Pep Clb; Band; Concert Band; Mrchg Band; Pep Band; School Musical; Stage Crew; Symp Band; Nwsp Rptr; GATE.

HURD, SCOTT; East Aurora HS; East Aurora, NY; (Y); Boy Scts; SADD; JV Bsktbl; JV Ftbl; Var Socr; Forestry.

HURD, SHERRY; Camden HS; Camden, NY; (Y); AFS; Church Yth Grp; 4-H; Trs SADD; Band; Yrbk Stf; VP Sr Cls; 4-H Awd; High Hon Roll; Ntl Merit SF; Rgnt Schlrshp 86; MONY Art Merit 86; Art.

HURD, SHURMAN M; Alfred-Almond Central HS; Almond, NY; (Y); 1/67; Trs Soph Cls; Pres Jr Cls; Var L Bsktbl; Var L Crs Cntry; Var L Trk; High Hon Roll; NHS; Ntl Merit Ltr; Val; 4-H; US Hse Reps Page 84-85; Natl Latin Exam Magna Cum Laude 83-84; Georgetown U; Frgn Svc.

HURLBURT, DAVID A; Pioneer Central HS; Arcade, NY; (Y); Church Yth Grp; French Clb; Acpl Chr; Chorus; Church Choir; School Musical; School Play; Swing Chorus; Variety Show; JV Var Socr; NYS Music Assc All ST Chorus 86; Alfred U; Sci.

HURLBURT, TODD; Perry Central HS; Perry, NY; (Y); Church Yth Grp; Computer Clb; Varsity Clb; Band; Concert Band; Jazz Band; Mrchg Band; JV Var Bsktbl; JV Var Golf; Hon Roll; Comp Achvt Awd; Sci Achvt Awd; Comp Sci.

HURLEY, AMASTASI; Westhampton Beach HS; Westhampton Beach, NY; (Y); Lit Mag; Rep Soph Cls; Ntl Merit Ltr; Rgnts Schlshp Awd; Hist.

HURLEY, CHRISTINE; Valley Stream North HS; Malverne, NY; (Y); Varsity Clb; Capt Var Tennis; High Hon Roll; Hon Roll; Prfct Atten Awd; MVP Ten 86; Ten Awd 86.

HURLEY, GERALD; Bishop Timon HS; Buffalo, NY; (S); 6/150; Boy Scts; Spanish Clb; SADD; Im Bsktbl; Im Ftbl; JV Var Socr; Im Vllybl; Hon Roll; Rochester Tech; Engr.

HURLEY, JAMIE; Elmira Free Acad; Elmira, NY; (Y); Boy Scts; French Clb; Rep Frsh Cls; Rep Soph Cls; Rep Jr Cls; Capt Socr; Capt Wrstlng; Hon Roll.

HURSON, JANICE; East Syracuse-Minoa HS; Kirkville, NY; (Y); Church Yth Grp; Mathletes; Chorus; Color Guard; Mrchg Band; School Musical; NHS; Scndry Educ.

HURST, AMY; Groton Central Schl; Groton, NY; (Y); 17/72; High Hon Roll; Hon Roll; Pres Acad Fit Awd 86; Civil Svc Cert 86; Bus.

HURST, MATTHEW; Commack High Schl South; Commack, NY; (S); 234/352; Chorus; Concert Band; Jazz Band; Mrchg Band; Orch; School Musical; Pres Symp Band; Im Bsktbl; Natl Music Hnr Soc 85-86; Schlrshp NJ Schl Of Arts-Montclair ST U 85; All-Cnty Chrs 85; Music Edu.

HURST, PATRICIA; Fillmore Central HS; Fillmore, NY; (S); 6/56; 4-H; Nwsp Stf; 4-H Awd; High Hon Roll; Hon Roll; NHS; Jamestown CC; Acctng.

HURT, AMOS; Roosevelt HS; Yonkers, NY; (Y); Church Yth Grp; Cmnty Wkr; Office Aide; Teachers Aide; VP VICA; Acpl Chr; Chorus; Church Choir; Nwsp Rptr; High Hon Roll; Awd Excllnc Acdmcs, Tlnt, Cvl Dedctn 83; PTSA Awd Outstndng Schl Ctznshp 86; Cert Merit RHS Mgnt Pgm; Pace U; Elem Educ.

HURTEAN, DAVID; Franklin Acad; N Bangor, NY; (Y); French Clb; Pep Clb; Varsity Clb; Crs Cntry; Trk; Hon Roll; NHS; Epsilon 83-86; Crs Cntry & Trk Awds 83-84 & 85-86; Bio.

HURTEAU, DAVID; Franklin Acad; N Bangor, NY; (Y); French Clb; Pep Clb; SADD; Varsity Clb; Crs Cntry; Trk; Hon Roll; NHS; Epsilon 84-86; 5th Pl In NYS Trck Chmpnshps 86; 1600 Mt Run 86.

HURTGEN, MATTHEW T; Dunkirk HS; Dunkirk, NY; (Y); 13/240; Am Leg Boys St; Computer Clb; Letterman Clb; Ski Clb; VP Sr Cls; L Diving; L Socr; L Tennis; Hon Roll; NHS; Boys 13 & 14 3 Meter Champ-NNYDA 83; Superior-Natl Piano Plyng Audtns 83-84; Gld Mdl-Nastar Ski Race; Automtv Engrng.

HURTUBISE, MARY; Unatego JR SR HS; Unadilla, NY; (Y); 34/110; Church Yth Grp; Pres French Clb; Ski Clb; Chorus; Church Choir; School Musical; Swing Chorus; Fld Hcky; Timer; Radiologic Tech.

HURWITZ, LAURIE; Tottenville HS; Staten Island, NY; (S); 25/850; Dance Clb; Key Clb; Scholastic Bowl; Spanish Clb; Teachers Aide; School Play; Symp Band; High Hon Roll; NHS; Concert Band; Tchng.

HUSAIN, TANJILA; John H Glenn HS; Huntington, NY; (Y); French Clb; Mathletes; Q&S; Nwsp Stf; French Hon Soc; High Hon Roll; Hon Roll; NHS; Talntd & Gftd 84-87; Nwspr Ed 86-87; VP Mthlts 85-86; Sci.

HUSFELDT, ANNMARIE; Lindenhurst HS; N Lindenhurst, NY; (Y); Spanish Clb; JV Sftbl; High Hon Roll; Hon Roll; Principals List 93.3 Avg 86; Teacher.

HUSSAIN, AYLA; Bronxville HS; Bronxville, NY; (Y); 9/115; Chorus; Madrigals; School Musical; Stage Crew; Variety Show; Nwsp Rptr; Yrbk Stf; Var L Socr; Var L Tennis; Var L Vllybl; Georgetown U; Intl Jrnlsm.

HUSSEIN, AYESHA; Long Island City HS; Long Island City, NY; (Y); Aud/Vis; Dance Clb; Drama Clb; Math Tm; PAVAS; Service Clb; School Musical; Cit Awd; Hon Roll; Ntl Merit Ltr; 1st Runnr-Up U N Speech Cntst 83; NYU; Sci.

HUSSEIN, DEBORAH; Maryvale SR HS; Cheektowaga, NY; (Y); Church Yth Grp; French Clb; Intnl Clb; Spanish Clb; Am Leg Boys St; Drama Clb; GAA; Chorus; Stage Crew; Lit.

HUSSER, KRISTINE E; Fairport HS; Fairport, NY; (Y); Ski Clb; Var Capt Vllybl; Rotary Awd; Wittenberg U.

HUSSEY, KATHLEEN; Monticello HS; Monticello, NY; (Y); 111/191; Church Yth Grp; Office Aide; Var Capt Vllybl; Sullivan Co CC.

HUSSEY, KIMBERLY J; Fairport HS; Fairport, NY; (Y); 5/600; Math Tm; Science Clb; Ski Clb; Band; VP Jazz Band; Var Swmmng; High Hon Roll; NHS; Prfct Atten Awd; VFW Awd; Monroe Prfsnl Engrs Soc Schlrshp 86; Purdue Pres Awd 86; Rgnts Schlrshp 86; Purdue U; Aerospace Engrng.

HUSSEY, ROBERT M; Dansville SR HS; Dansville, NY; (Y); 5/163; Am Leg Boys St; Math Tm; Ski Clb; Band; Chorus; Capt Crs Cntry; Trk; NHS; Boy Scts; Church Yth Grp; Lions NY ST Yth Band 86; 3 Crs Cntry Schlrshps 85 & 86; Clarkson U; Elec Engr.

HUSTED, REBECCA; Barker Central HS; Appleton, NY; (Y); 8/102; VP AFS; High Hon Roll; Hon Roll; NHS; Pres Schlr; Odyssey Of Mind 1st Rgnl Comptn 85-86; Westminster Coll.

HUSTIS, BRENDA; John Jay HS; Fishkill, NY; (Y); 11/519; AFS; Political Wkr; Yrbk Ed-Chief; Im Vllybl; High Hon Roll; VP Jr NHS; NHS; Patriot Of Yr 86; Acad Exclnc Awd-US Hse Page Schl 85; Outstndg Stu-HOBY Yth Ldrshp Smnr 84; Boston Coll; Law.

HUSTON, CARLA; Park West HS; Brooklyn, NY; (Y); Church Choir; Bsktbl; Cheerleading.

HUSTON, MICHELLE R; Watkins Glen HS; Burdett, NY; (Y); Drama Clb; 4-H; FHA; Band; Chorus; Nwsp Stf; Yrbk Stf; Hon Roll; Ntl Merit Schol; Corning CC.

HUSTON, TODD W; Mc Quaid Jesuit HS; Rochester, NY; (Y); 29/169; Church Yth Grp; Letterman Clb; Ski Clb; Varsity Clb; Capt Bowling; Cheerleading; High Hon Roll; NHS; Regnts Schlrshp Wnnr 86; Wheaton Clg; Bus.

HUTCHESON, MARK F; Horseheads HS; Horseheads, NY; (S); 30/380; Boy Scts; Science Clb; Band; Chorus; Mrchg Band; School Musical; School Play; Variety Show; Nwsp Stf; Yrbk Stf; Engrng.

HUTCHINGS, LISA; Webster SR HS; Webster, NY; (Y); 180/500; Hosp Aide; Chorus; Color Guard; Mrchg Band; Var Crs Cntry; JV Swmmng; Var Trk; Mst Vlbl Swmmr Vrsty Ltrs 83-85; Schlrshp Encllnc Englsh 85; Hmcmng Cmty; Suny Brockport.

HUTCHINS, JAMIE M; Brushton-Moira Central HS; Brushton, NY; (Y); 4/64; French Clb; Ski Clb; Stage Crew; Pres Soph Cls; Pres Jr Cls; Pres Sr Cls; JV Bsbl; JV Var Bsktbl; JV Crs Cntry; Hon Roll; Hudson Valley CC; Laser Tech.

HUTCHINSON, CANDICE; Friendship HS; Friendship, NY; (S); Chorus; Socr; High Hon Roll; Hon Roll; Bus.

HUTCHINSON, DANA; Auburn HS; Auburn, NY; (Y); Drama Clb; Ski Clb; Chorus; Ntrl Sci.

HUTCHINSON, JACKIE; Paul V Moore HS; Cleveland, NY; (Y); Church Yth Grp; 4-H; GAA; Science Clb; Yrbk Stf; Sftbl; 4-H Awd; Kiwanis Awd; Sci.

HUTCHINSON, KERRY; Fayetteville-Manlius HS; Fayetteville, NY; (Y); 23/335; Church Yth Grp; SADD; Var Swmmng; JV Var Vllybl; Cit Awd; High Hon Roll; Hon Roll; NHS; Xi Gamma Chi Cptr Beta Sigma Phi Awd 86; Pasto Mem Awd 86; Alumni Schrlshp 86; St Lawrence U.

HUTCHINSON, STACI; Belleville Henderson Central HS; Pierrepont Manor, NY; (Y); French Clb; Var Crs Cntry; JV Trk; Cit Awd; Hon Roll; Jr NHS; Natl Splng Comptn Awds 84.

HUTCHINSON, VICKI; Watervliet HS; Watervliet, NY; (Y); Cit Awd; Hon Roll; Prfct Atten Awd; Beautcn.

HUTCHISON, DONNA M; Amherst Central HS; Buffalo, NY; (Y); Pres Latin Clb; VP Model UN; Chorus; Nwsp Rptr; Lit Mag; Im Socr; High Hon Roll; Ntl Merit Ltr; JCL; Im Bsktbl; NY ST Rgnts Schlrshp 85-86; Natl Latn Clsscl Leag-Magna Cum Laude-2nd Pl 84-85; SUNY Buffalo; Aeronaut Engrng.

HUTCHISON, GARY; Brockport Central HS; Spencerport, NY; (Y); 122/315; Boy Scts; Radio Clb; Stage Crew; Var Trk; French Clb; JV Socr; JV Swmmng; Civil Engr.

HUTCHISON, TAMMY; Geneva HS; Geneva, NY; (S); 24/177; Church Yth Grp; Hosp Aide; Spanish Clb; Yrbk Stf; High Hon Roll; Hon Roll; NASA Sci Awd; Psychlgy.

HUTH, DAVID; Jordan-Elbridge JR & SR HS; Elbridge, NY; (Y); Art Clb; Church Yth Grp; Drama Clb; Concert Band; Mrchg Band; School Musical; School Play; Pep Clb; Nwsp Stf; Yrbk Stf; Smmr Perfrmng Arts Prog Syracuse Cvc Cntr; Anonymous Donor Cash Schlrshp Outstndng Dramtc Perfrmnc; Art.

HUTT, BONNIE; Marion Central HS; Marion, NY; (Y); 8/81; Trs Chess Clb; Pres 4-H; School Musical; School Play; Chess Clb; Yrbk Stf; Sftbl; 4-H Awd; High Hon Roll; NHS; NYS Rgnts Schlrshp, Pres Acdmc Ftns Awd, Marion Historic Awd 86; Calvin Coll; Lib Arts.

HUTT, DAVE; Bishop Grimes HS; North Syracuse, NY; (S); 9/200; Exploring; Speech Tm; Band; Concert Band; Jazz Band; Rep Stu Cncl; Trk; Hon Roll; Comp Sci.

HUTTLESTON, TIMOTHY; Greene Central HS; Smithville Flats, NY; (Y); 13/112; French Clb; Ski Clb; Yrbk Stf; Rep Soph Cls; Pres Stu Cncl; High Hon Roll; Hon Roll; Prfct Atten Awd; Regents Schlrshp 86-87; SUNY Binghamton; Pre-Med.

HUTTON, BEVERLY; Gouverneur HS; Gouverneur, NY; (Y); French Clb; Chorus; Church Choir; Sec Soph Cls; Rep Stu Cncl; 4-H Awd; Hon Roll; Elem Educ.

HUTTON, BRIAN; Williamsville South HS; Williamsville, NY; (Y); DECA; Hosp Aide; Golf; High Hon Roll; Treas PTSA 86-87; BUS Mgmt.

HUTTON, LISA; Saugerties HS; Saugerties, NY; (Y); 8/244; French Clb; Chorus; High Hon Roll; Hon Roll; NHS; Mrn Bio.

HUVANE, PATRICK; Cardinal Spellman HS; Bronx, NY; (Y); Church Yth Grp; Dance Clb; Pep Clb; Ski Clb; Var JV Bsktbl; JV Im Ftbl; Im Sftbl; Hon Roll; Regents Scholar 86; Manhattan Coll; Bus.

HUXTA, CHRISTIE; Our Lady Of Victory Acad; Yonkers, NY; (S); 1/157; Computer Clb; Hosp Aide; Spanish Clb; SADD; Yrbk Stf; Lit Mag; Rep Stu Cncl; High Hon Roll; VP NHS; Gen Excllnce Awd 83-85; Natl Sci Merit Awd 84; Biol Sci.

HUYEN, DIEM CAO; Cicero North Syracuse HS; N Syracuse, NY; (S); 48/667; Math Clb; Math Tm; Teachers Aide; Off Sr Cls; Cornell U; Chem.

HUYNH, HUNG; Susan E Wagner HS; Staten Island, NY; (Y); Math Tm; Science Clb; Nwsp Rptr; NHS; Prfct Atten Awd; 1st Pl Staten Isl Soc Studs Cont 84-85; Alumnus NY HOBY Fndtn Ldrshp Sem 85; Bio-Chem.

HUYNH, MY PHUONG; Troy HS; Troy, NY; (Y); French Clb; Hon Roll; NHS; Plant Engrs Exec Schlrshp 86; Acvht Awd Math 86; Frgn Lang Dept Awd 86; Hudson Valley CC; Math.

HUYNH, MYNGOC J; Forest Hills HS; Long Island City, NY; (Y); 24/8260; Church Yth Grp; Exploring; Math Clb; Science Clb; Hon Roll; Jr NHS; NHS; Cornell U; Bio.

HUYNH, NGANH P; White Plains HS; White Plains, NY; (Y); 34/432; Hosp Aide; Sec JETS Awd; JV Socr; NHS; Pres Schlr; Westchester Art Pgm Schlrshp 82-86; Sci Awd, Prncpls Rcgntn Awds 86; Phillips Acad Schlrshp 85; Union Coll; Med Dr.

HWANG, DANIEL; La Salle Military Acad; Huntington Sta, NY; (Y); 4/84; ROTC; Nwsp Ed-Chief; Rep Jr Cls; Rep Sr Cls; Im Bsbl; Im Ftbl; High Hon Roll; Hon Roll; NHS; SAR Awd; Amer Revltn Awd 84; Acdmc Excllnc 1st In Merit 85; Mltry Ordr Wrld Wars 85; Pre-Med.

HWANG, DAVID H; Cortland JR SR HS; Cortland, NY; (Y); 2/210; Am Leg Boys St; Church Yth Grp; Pres Latin Clb; Ski Clb; Orch; School Play; Nwsp Rptr; Var Tennis; NHS; Sal; 4th Pl 2nd Sngls Sect 3 Tnns Tourn 86; Mediatr Afro-Asian Stds Conf 84; 4 Area All-St Orch 2nd Violn; Elec Engr.

HWANG, EMMIE; Hauppauge HS; Smithtown, NY; (Y); 9/479; Orch; Lit Mag; Rep Frsh Cls; Chrmn Stu Cncl; VP Chrmn NHS; Ntl Merit Ltr; Prfct Atten Awd; Yrbk Stf; High Hon Roll; Hon Roll; NY ST Smmr Schl Orchstrl Stds-85&86 & Vsl Arts-86; Awd Excllnc & Jdgs Awd Art Accent 85&86; Fine Arts.

HWANG, FELICIA; East Islip HS; East Islip, NY; (Y); 2/427; Art Clb; Church Yth Grp; FBLA; Math Tm; SADD; Orch; Ed Nwsp Rptr; Yrbk Ed-Chief; Lit Mag; Trs Stu Cncl; NY ST Assn Suffolk Zone Rcpnt Of Outstndng Phys Perfmng Schlrshp & Ctznshp; Hugh Obrien Ldrshp Smnr.

HWANG, HAESIN; La Guardia H S Of Music & Arts; Elmhurst, NY; (S); Library Aide; Orch; Variety Show; High Hon Roll; Jr NHS; Prfct Atten Awd; Music Hnr Lg 85; Daily News Salute Supr Yth 85; 1st Pl Wnr Piano Comp BACA 85.

HWANG, VICTOR; Hauppauge HS; Sithtown, NY; (Y); 1/500; Exploring; Hosp Aide; Symp Band; Rep Frsh Cls; VP Soph Cls; Rep Jr Cls; JV Var Crs Cntry; NHS; Ntl Merit SF; Prfct Atten Awd; Schlstc Wrtng Awd Hnrbl Ment For Sht Stry 86; Docts Of Tmmrw Schlrshp 86; Sci Awd Suffolk Cnty 86; Stanford U; Med.

HWANG, YOUNG; Port Richmond HS; Staten Isld, NY; (Y); Church Yth Grp; Chorus; Church Choir; Excllnt Jap Studies 86; NY Inst Tech; Mech Engr.

HYCHKA, STACEY; Saranac Lake HS; Paul Smiths, NY; (Y); 5/110; AFS; Jazz Band; JV Var Cheerleading; Var Swmmng; High Hon Roll; NHS; Concert Band; School Musical; Yrbk Stf; Im Diving; 3rd Chr All ST Rgnl Band 84-86; 95 On Grd Six Solo 86; AFS Stu Indonesia 86-87; Smith Coll; Intrntnl Trd.

HYDE, MARIANN; Hendrick Hudson HS; Peekskill, NY; (Y); Office Aide; Yrbk Sprt Ed; Off Frsh Cls; Off Soph Cls; Off Jr Cls; Off Sr Cls; Trs Stu Cncl; JV Stat Bsktbl; JV Fld Hcky; JV Capt Socr; All-Leag Sccr; Hghst Spnsh Avg; Athltc Training.

HYDE, PATRICE; Deer Park HS; Deer Park, NY; (Y); Hosp Aide; Office Aide; Band; Concert Band; Drill Tm; Drm & Bgl; Mrchg Band; Var Capt Bsktbl; Sftbl; Hon Roll; Booster Clb Sports Schlrshp 86; Rochester Inst Tech; Bio.

HYLAND, CATHLEEN; Oneida HS; Oneida, NY; (S); Pres Intnl Clb; Spanish Clb; Band; Var L Cheerleading; Hon Roll; NHS; Pep Band; Nwsp Rptr; VP Frsh Cls; Rep Soph Cls; Z Club Treas 85-86; JV Chrldng Capt 85-86; MIP Vrsty Chrldng 86; Htl Mgmt.

HYLAND, KARA; Scotia-Glenville HS; Scotia, NY; (Y); French Clb; Key Clb; Yrbk Stf; Stat Bsktbl; Scrkpr Socr; High Hon Roll; Hon Roll; NHS; Business Administration.

HYLAND, KIM; Lindenhurst SR HS; Lindenhurst, NY; (Y); Thesps; Sec Band; Concert Band; Jazz Band; Mrchg Band; School Play; High Hon Roll; NHS; Cmnty Wkr; Drm Mjr(t); Acad All Amer Awd 86; Recvd A NYSSMA Clrnt All ST Ctgry 86; Accptd BOCES III Smmr Inst Plywrtng 86; Music.

HYLLA, LAURA; Oneida HS; Oneida, NY; (S); 12/200; Computer Clb; Spanish Clb; Yrbk Stf; Rep Soph Cls; Im Vllybl; High Hon Roll; NHS; Regnts Schlrshp 86; Cornell; Elec Engrng.

HYMAN, DEBORAH; Shulamith HS; Rochester, NY; (S); Art Clb; Stage Crew; Yrbk Stf; Lit Mag; Mgr(s); Hon Roll; NHS.

HYNES, CHRIS; Greenville Central HS; Greenville, NY; (Y); 7/85; Am Leg Boys St; Boy Scts; Exploring; Key Clb; Spanish Clb; Trs Jr Cls; Rep Stu Cncl; JV Bsbl; Co-Capt Bsktbl; Var Crs Cntry; Eagl Sct 84; Frgn Exch Stu Of Swedn 84-85; Bio.

HYNES, KATHY; Mahopac HS; Mahopac, NY; (Y); 25/409; Dance Clb; Political Wkr; Orch; Nwsp Sprt Ed; Nwsp Stf; Var Bsktbl; JV Var Fld Hcky; Var Socr; High Hon Roll; NHS; Area All ST Orch 83-85; Ed.

HYSER, HEATHER; Frontier Central HS; Lancaster, PA; (Y); 8/470; French Clb; FBLA; Library Aide; Ski Clb; Orch; School Musical; Rep Stu Cncl; Hon Roll; NHS; Rochester Inst Tech Alumni Scholar; Rochester Inst Tech; Bus Adm.

I LIOU, OLYMPIA; Dominican Commercial HS; Cambria Heights, NY; (Y); 66/281; Church Yth Grp; Girl Scts; Chorus; Nwsp Rptr; Rep Frsh Cls; Rep Soph Cls; Var Swmmng; Lawyr.

IACCARINO, JENNIFER; Moore Catholic HS; Staten Island, NY; (Y); Cmnty Wkr; JA; Math Tm; VICA; Mgr Bsbl; Mgr Bsktbl; Co-Capt Cheerleading; Mgr(s); Sftbl; High Hon Roll; Natl Math Awd; Natl Chem Awd; Law.

IACOBELLIS, MICHAEL; Hicksville HS; Hicksville, NY; (Y); Hon Roll; NHS.

IACOBELLIS, VINCENT; East Meadow HS; East Meadow, NY; (Y); Intnl Clb; Key Clb; Varsity Clb; Band; Yrbk Stf; Var Bsktbl; Var Crs Cntry; JV Lcrss; Var Socr; Var Trk; Hofstra; Art.

IACONO, ANN MARIE; Moore Catholic HS; Staten Island, NY; (Y); Art Clb; Dance Clb; Math Tm; Science Clb; Chorus; Yrbk Stf; Lit Mag; Cheerleading; Tennis; High Hon Roll; Rgnts Schlrshp 86; St Johns U Comp Schlrshp 86; St Johns U Staten Isl.

IACONO, CARL; Monsignor Farrell HS; Staten Island, NY; (Y); Church Yth Grp; Cmnty Wkr; Hosp Aide; VP Frsh Cls; Pres Soph Cls; Pres Jr Cls; Rep Stu Cncl; JV Var Wrstlng; High Hon Roll; Hon Roll; Schlrs/Ahtl Awd 86; Itln Poetry Awd 86; Vlntr Awd/50 Hrs Srv 86; SUNY Bnghmtn; Bus.

IACOVELLI, VINCENT; Commack South HS; Commack, NY; (Y); Band; Concert Band; Mrchg Band; Symp Band; Hon Roll.

IADEVAIO, CHRISTINE; Valley Stream Central HS; Valley Stream, NY; (Y); Dance Clb; Ski Clb; Spanish Clb; SADD; Flag Corp; Yrbk Stf; Hon Roll; NHS; Spanish NHS; Variety Show; St Johns U; Tchg.

IAFALLO, DEANNA; Frontier Central HS; Hamburg, NY; (Y); FBLA; Pep Clb; Spanish Clb; Yrbk Stf; Hon Roll; Bus.

IAFE, GEORGE A; Tottenville HS; Staten Island, NY; (Y); 122/872; Political Wkr; Pres Ski Clb; Teachers Aide; School Play; Stage Crew; Yrbk Phtg; Cit Awd; Hon Roll; NHS; Rgnts Schlrshp Awd 86.

IANNO, DOMINIC A; Liverpool HS; Liverpool, NY; (Y); 48/816; Exploring; SADD; Trs Varsity Clb; Band; Rep Sr Cls; Var Ftbl; Var Golf; Capt Var Wrstlng; High Hon Roll; NHS; NY St Regents Schlrshp 86; Carnegie-Mellon U; Ind Mgt.

IANNONE, LISA A; Shenendehowa HS; Waterford, NY; (Y); 1/675; Drama Clb; Key Clb; SADD; High Hon Roll; NCTE Awd; NHS; Val; Amy D Delo Actng Awd 82-83; Outstndng Achvt Bio 83-84; Syracue U; Bio.

IANNOTTA, MARIA; Westbury SR HS; Westbury, NY; (Y); 8/250; Aud/Vis; Drama Clb; Mgr Stage Crew; Nwsp Rptr; Hon Roll; NHS.

IANNOTTI, PATRICIA; John H Glenn HS; Huntington, NY; (Y); Cmnty Wkr; Office Aide; Teachers Aide; Chorus; Church Choir; Stage Crew; Hon Roll; NHS; Bus.

IANNUCCI, ANTHONY; Carle Place HS; Westbury, NY; (Y); Am Leg Boys St; Debate Tm; NFL; Lit Mag; Hon Roll; Superior Acdmc Awds Engl, Spnsh & Scl Stds 86; Med.

IARROBINO, LISA; Curtis HS; Staten Island, NY; (Y); Key Clb; Office Aide; Varsity Clb; Stage Crew; Yrbk Stf; Stu Cncl; Swmmng; Capt Vllybl; CC Awd; Fndtn For Excptnl Chldrn 86; Northeastern U; Bus.

IARUSSO, JOHN; Bishop Scully HS; Amsterdam, NY; (Y); 11/47; Am Leg Boys St; Latin Clb; Math Clb; SADD; Yrbk Stf; VP Jr Cls; VP Sr Cls; Var Bsktbl; Hon Roll; NHS; Engr.

IBELLI, STEPHEN; Eastchester HS; Eastchester, NY; (Y); Aud/Vis; Drama Clb; Key Clb; Ski Clb; SADD; Band; Concert Band; Drm Mjr(t); Jazz Band; Mrchg Band; Chem Awd Audio Visual 85; Cornell U Summr Coll 86.

IBIETATORREMENDIA, JOSE; La Salle Military Acad; W New York, NJ; (Y); 2/87; Boy Scts; Camera Clb; Camp Fr Inc; Chess Clb; Computer Clb; Drama Clb; English Clb; ROTC; Scholastic Bowl; School Musical; George Washington U Medl Engrng Aplld Sci 85; Full Schlrshp La Salle Militry Acadm 82; Princeton U; Pol Sci.

IDA, JAMES; Tottenville HS; Staten Island, NY; (S); 4/850; Boy Scts; Chess Clb; Model UN; Scholastic Bowl; Teachers Aide; Mrchg Band; Stage Crew; Symp Band; High Hon Roll; NHS; Ntl Italn Awds 85-86; Med.

IDEMAN, CATHERINE; Caroning-Painted Post West HS; Holcomb, NY; (Y); 168/252; Church Yth Grp; Trs FBLA; SADD; Crning Ldg #94-IOOF; Brynt/Strttn Bus Schl; Exec Sec.

IDICULLA, SAJI; Geneseo Central HS; Geneseo, NY; (Y); 9/96; Church Yth Grp; Yrbk Bus Mgr; Var Tennis; High Hon Roll; Jr NHS; NHS; Pres Schlr; Cmnty Wkr; Drama Clb; SADD; 1st Jr Edtr In Chf Yrbk 84-85; Chf Frgn Edtr Indian Pblctd Vidyarthi 85; Geneseo Fclty Assn Schlrshp; U Of Rochester; Corp Law.

IDZI, CAMI; Waterville Central HS; Oriskany Falls, NY; (Y); Art Clb; Cmnty Wkr; GAA; Band; Concert Band; Mrchg Band; Coach Actv; Socr; Cit Awd; Prfct Atten Awd; ADV Dsgn.

IEHLE, DARRELL; Center Moriches HS; Center Moriches, NY; (Y); Electrncs.

IERARDI, THOMAS; Cornwall Central HS; Highland Mills, NY; (Y); 20/180; Im Bsbl; Var Golf; JV Wrstlng; Hon Roll; Mech Engr.

IGLESIAS, MARGARITA; The Mary Louis Acad; Jackson Heights, NY; (Y); Cmnty Wkr; Dance Clb; Yrbk Stf; Gym; NHS; Bus Admin.

IGNASZAK, KEVIN; Albion HS; Albion, NY; (S); 13/176; Art Clb; Aud/Vis; Church Yth Grp; Ski Clb; JV Var Bsbl; JV Ftbl; Hon Roll; NHS; Engrng.

IGNATOWSKI, KIMBERLY; West Seneca East SR HS; Cheektowaga, NY; (Y); Church Yth Grp; Cmnty Wkr; Nwsp Stf; Jr NHS; Prfct Atten Awd; Pres Schlr; Deans Schlrshp 86; Dept Schlrshp 86; Daemen Coll; Phys Thrpy.

IGNATZ, JULIE; Wyoming Central HS; Wyoming, NY; (S); 2/22; Debate Tm; Drama Clb; School Play; Yrbk Phtg; Off Sr Cls; VP Stu Cncl; Cheerleading; Socr; Hon Roll; NHS; Chem Awd 85; U Buffalo; Elec Engrng.

IGNAZIO, GINA-MARIA; Bishop Ford Ctl Catholic HS; Brooklyn, NY; (Y); Girl Scts; Office Aide; Spanish Clb; Band; School Play; Yrbk Phtg; Bowling; Sftbl; Hon Roll; NHS; Rgnts Schlrshps 86; St Johns U; Sports Admn.

IHDE, DENISE; Longwood HS; Middle Island, NY; (Y); FNA; Hosp Aide; Office Aide; Chorus; Vllybl; Suffolk CC; Nrsng.

IKEDA, EMI; Mamaroneck HS; Larchmont, NY; (Y); Girl Scts; JA; Model UN; Spanish Clb; Church Choir; Stu Cncl; Var Vllybl; Interschlstc Achvt Awd Math 86; Ntl Guild Couty Music 84-86.

ILARDI, MARGARET; St Catherine Acad; Bx, NY; (Y); Art Clb; Teachers Aide; Off Frsh Cls; Off Soph Cls; Stu Cncl; Hon Roll; NHS.

ILARDO, MARY BEA; Hamburg SR HS; Hamburg, NY; (Y); 59/374; JCL; Latin Clb; Orch; Hon Roll; Arch.

ILES, MARY; Vernon-Verona Sherrill HS; Vernon, NY; (Y); GAA; Var JV Fld Hcky; Var VP Vllybl; High Hon Roll; Hon Roll; Math.

ILEY, KELLY; Gloversville HS; Gloversvl, NY; (Y); Church Yth Grp; Mrchg Band; Symp Band; Bsktbl; Hon Roll; Med.

ILLIG, ROBERT; Pittsford Sutherland HS; Rochester, NY; (Y); VP Trs French Clb; Model UN; Bsktbl; Var Tennis; NHS; Rep Intl Model UN 86; Yngr Scshlrs Grant Natl Endowment Humanities 86; Rotary UN Schlrshp 87; Hist.

ILLIG, TRACI; Kenmore West SR HS; Kenmore, NY; (Y); 53/424; Band; Trs Concert Band; Mrchg Band; School Musical; Rep Stu Cncl; JV Var Sftbl; Var Capt Vllybl; High Hon Roll; Hon Roll; NHS; Sprtmnshp Awd Vllybll 85-86; Spirit Awd Cncrt Band; U Of Buffalo; Physcl Thrpy.

ILUKOWICZ, CRISTINA; E L Vandermeulen HS; Pt Jefferson, NY; (Y); Pep Clb; SADD; Rep Soph Cls; Rep Jr Cls; Var Cheerleading; JV Fld Hcky; Var Tennis; Hon Roll; NHS; Acdmc All-Amer.

IM, SYLVIA; Herricks SR HS; Mnahasset Hls, NY; (Y); Drama Clb; Pres Key Clb; Radio Clb; Nwsp Stf; Yrbk Stf; JV Cheerleading; Hon Roll; NHS; Pre-Med.

IMBERT, CORINNE; Nazareth Regional HS; Brooklyn, NY; (Y); Camera Clb; Math Tm; NHS; Pre-Law.

IMBESI, FORTUNATO; Cicero-North Syracuse HS; Clay, NY; (S); 22/667; JA; Math Tm; JV Socr; Capt Tennis; High Hon Roll; JETS Awd; NHS; Ntl Merit Ltr; Math.

IMBESI, TINO; Liverpool HS; Liverpool, NY; (Y); Exploring; JV Lcrss; JV Socr; High Hon Roll; Hon Roll; SUNY Buffalo; Engrg.

IMBROGNO, LISA; Port Chester HS; Port Chester, NY; (Y); Key Clb; Ski Clb; Color Guard; Mrchg Band; Yrbk Bus Mgr; High Hon Roll; Mu Alp Tht; NHS; Ntl Merit Ltr; Spanish NHS; Sci Hnr Soc 86.

IMIOLA, KAREN; Mount Mercy Acad; W Seneca, NY; (Y); Ski Clb; Chorus; Swing Chorus; Hon Roll; Bus.

IMMANUEL, DAVID; St Pauls Schl; Mineola, NY; (Y); 1/27; Chess Clb; Computer Clb; Spanish Clb; Var Trk; Bishops Awd Top Hnrs 83-85; Math, Sci Achvt Awds, Engrng Mdl 85-86; Med.

IMMEDIATO, MARIE; Mount Vernon HS; Mount Vernon, NY; (Y); 27/590; Sec FTA; Office Aide; Pres SADD; Teachers Aide; High Hon Roll; Hon Roll; Jr NHS; Iona Coll; Elem Ed.

IMMERMAN, GABY; Mamaroneck HS; Larchmont, NY; (Y); Hosp Aide; Nwsp Ed-Chief; French Clb; Office Aide; Nwsp Rptr; Yrbk Rptr; Yrbk Stf; JV Socr; JV Sftbl; Var Capt Vllybl; Natl French Cntst-4th In USA 85; Amer Chem Tchrs Exam-5 Mbr Tm 85; NCTE Partcpnt In Writing Comp 86; Harvard; Astrnmr.

IMPELLIZZERI, JOHN A; Jamesville De Witt HS; Jamesville, NY; (Y); 79/245; Boy Scts; Chess Clb; Capt Math Tm; Band; Hon Roll; Faculty Recgntn Awd Bus 86; NYS Regents Scholar 85-86; Bristol-Myers Career Ed Awd 86; Onondaga CC; Engrng Sci.

IMPELLIZZERI, WENDI; Colonie Central HS; Albany, NY; (Y); Band; Im Bowling; Hon Roll; Key Clb; Temple Yth Grp; Marine Biologist.

IMPERATI, SONDRA; Our Lady Of Mercy HS; Henrietta, NY; (Y); Exploring; Intnl Clb; Spanish Clb; SADD; Chorus; School Play; Variety Show; VP Trs Sr Cls; Rep Stu Cncl; Hon Roll; St John Fisher Coll; Attrny.

IMPERATI, STEPHANI E; Our Lady Of Victory Acad; Bronx, NY; (Y); 32/158; SADD; Yrbk Ed-Chief; Yrbk Stf; Lit Mag; Bsktbl; Tennis; French Hon Soc; NHS; French Clb; Acad Al-Amer 85-86; Rgnts Schlrshp 86; U Of Stoneybrook; Poli Sci.

IMPERATO, MARY; St Joseph By The Sea HS; Staten Island, NY; (Y); Art Clb; Dance Clb; Drama Clb; French Clb; Girl Scts; Hosp Aide; Library Aide; Office Aide; Teachers Aide; School Musical; 1st Hnr Awd 82-86; St Johns U.

IMPERIO, ANTOINETTE; Herbert H Lehman HS; Bronx, NY; (Y); 43/500; Orch; Symp Band; High Hon Roll; Jr NHS; Hnrs In Englsh, Social Studies, & Typing Awds 84-86; Awd Crmnlgy & Lgl Studies 85-86; St Johns U; Legal Studies.

IMPERIO, CRISTINA; St Barnabas HS; Mt Vernon, NY; (S); Hosp Aide; Library Aide; Office Aide; Nwsp Rptr; VP Jr Cls; Rep Stu Cncl; High Hon Roll; NHS; Cumulative 3 Yr Rnk 1 Out Of 188 Stu 82-85; Italian Ntl Hnr Scty 85; Nrsng.

INCE, LESLIE; Midwood HS; Brooklyn, NY; (Y); Hosp Aide; Chorus; Church Choir; Madrigals; School Musical; Lit Mag; Acad Olympc Sqd 84; Cty Coll Brdg Med Pgm 86-87; Med.

INCE, MICHAEL; East Syracuse-Minoa HS; East Syracuse, NY; (Y); JA; Ski Clb; Variety Show; JV Var Socr; Var Trk; Jr NHS; Acctng.

INCORVAIA, DENISE; Middletown HS; Middletown, NY; (Y); Drama Clb; 4-H; Hosp Aide; Teachers Aide; Band; Chorus; Btty Crckr Awd; 4-H Awd; Middletown Beauty Schl; Csmtlgy.

INCORVAIA, JOSEPH S C A; Bishop Ford HS; Brooklyn, NY; (Y); Ski Clb; Yrbk Phtg; St Schlr; NY ST Rgnts Schlrshp 86; U Of Hartford; Elec Engr.

INDELICATO, ANTHONY; Moore Catholic HS; Staten Island, NY; (Y); Bsbl; Bowling; Hon Roll; St Johns U; Acctg.

INDERMILL, ALICIA; Spackenkill HS; Poughkeepsie, NY; (Y); 40/167; Church Yth Grp; Bsktbl; Var L Socr; Cit Awd; Hon Roll; Outstndng Bus Stu 85-86; Pres Acad Fit Awd 85-86; Northeastern U; Intl Bus.

INDILICATO, VICKI; Guilderland Central HS; Schenectady, NY; (Y); Chrmn Key Clb; Varsity Clb; Rep Jr Cls; Chrmn Stu Cncl; Capt Cheerleading; Var Tennis; High Hon Roll; Pres Jr NHS; VP NHS; Prfct Atten Awd; Bus Admin.

INDYKE, DANIELLE; Glen Cove HS; Glen Cove, NY; (Y); 71/267; French Clb; Pres Key Clb; SADD; Thesps; Band; Nwsp Rptr; Yrbk Rptr; Rep Stu Cncl; JV Var Cheerleading; Hon Roll; Psychol.

INFANTE, BRIDGID A; John S Burke Catholic HS; New Windsor, NY; (Y); Cmnty Wkr; Drama Clb; 4-H; Model UN; School Play; Stage Crew; Variety Show; Lit Mag; 4-H Awd; High Hon Roll; Theron Crawford Vet Sci Awd 83-84; Cornell U.

INFANTE, JOSE; Mamaroneck HS; Larchmont, NY; (Y); Latin Clb; Spanish Clb; Varsity Clb; Chorus; Lit Mag; JV Var Socr; Vllybl; Spanish NHS; Empr St Games In Vlybl 84 & 85; All Cnty Choir 85-86; Soccer Schlrshp 86; New Pltz Coll; Crtv Wrtr.

INGEBRETSEN, KIRK; East Islip HS; East Islip, NY; (Y); Church Yth Grp; Band; Mrchg Band; Orch; Lcrss; Hon Roll; Physcl Sci.

INGENERI, CLAUDINE; Westhampton Beach HS; E Moriches, NY; (Y); Aud/Vis; FBLA; Ski Clb; Lit Mag; Fld Hcky; JV Var Tennis; Var Trk; Law.

INGERSOLL, MELISSA R; Alden Central HS; Alden, NY; (Y); 40/160; Art Clb; Letterman Clb; SADD; Yrbk Stf; Crs Cntry; Lion Awd; Ntl Merit Ltr; VFW Awd; Arabian Horse Assn Of NY JR Exhibtr High Score 84 & 85; NRA JR Sec Champ 1st Pl Schlstc 3 Pos 86; Villa Maria Of Buffalo; Graphic.

INGERSON, AMY L; Kensington HS; Buffalo, NY; (Y); 6/239; Office Aide; Yrbk Stf; Rep Frsh Cls; Rep Church Yth Grp; Rep Jr Cls; Rep Sr Cls; VP Stu Cncl; Var Sftbl; Pres NHS; NY ST Rgnts Schlrshp 86; Geneseo Coll; Bus Adm.

INGHER, STACY; Commack HS South; Commack, NY; (Y); Computer Clb; Teachers Aide; Varsity Clb; Y-Teens; Nwsp Stf; Var L Badmtn; JV Tennis; Hon Roll; SUNY; Bio.

INGRAHAM, DEANA; Groton Central School; Groton, NY; (Y); Chorus; Concert Band; School Musical; Swing Chorus; NHS; Ntl Merit Ltr; Girl Scts; Library Aide; Seneca Tompkins Cnty Music Tchrs Assn Schlrshp 83-85; Tompkins Cnty JR Music Clbs Schlrshp 85-86; Music Ed.

INGRAHAM, KRISTINE; Sandy Creek Central Schl; Pulaski, NY; (S); SADD; Var Cheerleading; Stat Ftbl; Twrlr; Hon Roll; NHS; Cazenovia Coll; Socl Svcs.

INGRAM, DEBBIE; Farmingdale HS; Farmingdale, NY; (Y); Computer Clb; Dance Clb; French Clb; Vclst 86.

INGRAM, MELANIE; Pelham Memorial HS; Pelham, NY; (Y); AFS; Cmnty Wkr; Dance Clb; FBLA; Girl Scts; Hosp Aide; JA; Library Aide; Office Aide; Speech Tm; Real Est.

INGRAM, RACQUEL; Our Saviour Lutheran HS; Bronx, NY; (Y); Church Yth Grp; Library Aide; Chorus; Church Choir; School Musical; Yrbk Stf; Off Soph Cls; Stu Cncl; Sftbl; Cit Awd; Med.

INGRAM, RICHARD M; Ballston Spa HS; Ballston Spa, NY; (Y); 15/200; Am Leg Boys St; Latin Clb; Varsity Clb; Var JV Bsktbl; Var JV Ftbl; Var Tennis; Var Trk; High Hon Roll; NHS; Natl Ltn Hnr Socty 86; Pre-Med Physiothrpy.

INMAN, DEBORAH K; Mt Markham SR HS; West Winfield, NY; (Y); 15/115; GAA; Yrbk Stf; Var Trk; High Hon Roll; NHS; Trck MVP 84; St Rose Coll; Elem Educ.

INMAN, GORDIE; Ichabod Crane Central HS; Valatie, NY; (Y); Drama Clb; Ski Clb; Varsity Clb; School Play; Rep Jr Cls; Var Bsbl; Var L Socr; Hon Roll; Ithaca Coll.

INNOCENZI, LYNDA; Hastings HS; Hastings Hdsn, NY; (Y); 26/110; JA; Spanish Clb; Band; Chorus; Concert Band; Jazz Band; Mrchg Band; Orch; Yrbk Stf; Var L Pom Pon; Fordham Coll Bus; Bus Adm.

INSCHO, JUDY; Wayland Central HS; Dansville, NY; (Y); 31/110; Church Yth Grp; FBLA; FHA; Chorus; Church Choir; Prfct Atten Awd; Comp Pgmmng.

INSERRO, ALLISON M; The Mary Louis Acad; Flushing, NY; (Y); 91/270; Art Clb; Cmnty Wkr; Hosp Aide; Office Aide; Nwsp Ed-Chief; Lit Mag; Engl.

INSETTA, JENNIFER; Oneonta SR HS; Oneonta, NY; (Y); 42/186; Church Yth Grp; Drama Clb; French Clb; Key Clb; Q&S; Thesps; Varsity Clb; Chorus; Church Choir; Madrigals; Mlnri Fmly Awd 86; FL Sthrn Fndrs Schlrsrhp 86; Jrnlsm Awd 86; FL Sthrn Coll; Comm.

INSETTA, JOHN-MICHAEL; Oneonta HS; Oneonta, NY; (Y); Am Leg Boys St; Art Clb; Spanish Clb; Varsity Clb; Chorus; Yrbk Ed-Chief; Yrbk Phtg; Stu Cncl; Var Crs Cntry; Var Trk; Poltcl Sci.

INSINNA, EMANUEL; Monsignor Farrell HS; Staten Island, NY; (Y); 48/319; Am Leg Boys St; Boy Scts; Camera Clb; Church Yth Grp; Yrbk Stf; Crs Cntry; Trk; High Hon Roll; NHS; BMT Holy Name Soc Scholar 83; Military.

INSINNA, THOMAS; Kenmore East HS; Tonawanda, NY; (Y); Varsity Clb; Band; Concert Band; Mrchg Band; Tennis; High Hon Roll; Hon Roll; NHS; Med.

INSLER, TODD; Mt Vernon HS; Mt Vernon, NY; (Y); 80/550; Aud/Vis; Pres Key Clb; Concert Band; Mrchg Band; Swmmng; Wrstlng; High Hon Roll; Kiwanis Awd; FL Inst Tech; Flght Technlgy.

INTILE, JOHN; Sachem HS North; Holbrook, NY; (Y); 99/1558; Computer Clb; Math Tm; Bsbl; Im Wt Lftg; Wrstlng; NHS; Engr.

INTINI, FRANK; Sachem HS; Farmingville, NY; (Y); VP German Clb; JV Gym; JV Swmmng; Long Island Lang Fair 2nd German Ptry 86; Acad Excel Engl 85; Long Island Regnl Hstry Fair 84; Stony Brook U; Med.

INTRIERI, THOMAS; Walt Whitman HS; Huntington Statio, NY; (Y); 61/479; Aud/Vis; Church Yth Grp; Mathletes; Varsity Clb; Band; Church Choir; Mrchg Band; Var Socr; High Hon Roll; Jr NHS; Acctg.

INZANA, ANTHONY; Aquinas Inst; Rochester, NY; (Y); 7/215; Drama Clb; School Musical; School Play; Nwsp Stf; Rep Frsh Cls; Rep Soph Cls; JV Bsktbl; Capt Var Tennis; Im Vllybl; Hon Roll; Bio Med.

INZERILLO, ANGELA; Oyster Bay HS; Oyster Bay, NY; (Y); 8/122; Model UN; Spanish Clb; Sec SADD; Nwsp Stf; Yrbk Bus Mgr; Yrbk Stf; Var Badmtn; Var Bowling; High Hon Roll; NHS; Spnsh Awd Bst Spnsh Stu 86; U Of Richmond; Bus.

IOELE, SARAH; Gloversville HS; Gloversvl, NY; (Y); Pres DECA; SADD; Cheerleading; Mgr Socr; Natl Hnr Socty 86; DECA Regl Ofcr; Advrtsg.

IPPOLITO, CYNTHIA; Avon Central HS; Caledonia, NY; (Y); AFS; Church Yth Grp; Dance Clb; French Clb; Trs VP Girl Scts; Band; Color Guard; Concert Band; Drm Mjr(t); Jazz Band; Niagara U; Trnsptatn.

IPPOLITO, JOHN M; Tottenville HS; Staten Island, NY; (S); 5/850; High Hon Roll; Jr NHS; NHS; Delia P King Schlrshp 84; Med.

IPPOLITO, JUSTINA; Silver Creek Central HS; Silver Creek, NY; (Y); Yrbk Stf; Var Bsktbl; Score Keeper; Var Co-Capt Sftbl.

IPPOLITO, TONYA M; Avon Central HS; Avon, NY; (Y); 1/101; Am Leg Aux Girls St; Sec Pres Church Yth Grp; Drama Clb; Chorus; Pres Sr Cls; Elks Awd; NHS; Ntl Merit Ltr; Val; Exploring; Harvard Bk Awd 85; Sr Apprctn Music Awd 86; Cornell Tradtn Fllwshp 86-87; Cornell U; Pre Med.

IRAM, STEPHEN; Vernon-Verona-Sherrill Central Schl; Verona, NY; (Y); 29/189; Am Leg Boys St; Pres Latin Clb; Band; Drm & Bgl; School Musical; Rep Stu Cncl; Capt Crs Cntry; Var Socr; Capt Trk; Cit Awd; NYS Rgnts Schlrshp, Stu/Athl Yr, Pres Acdmc Ftns Awd, US Mltry Acad Schlrshp 86; W Point Mltry Acad; Elec Engrng.

IRBE, AINA; Lafayette SR HS; Jamesville, NY; (S); 2/96; Math Clb; Model UN; Spanish Clb; Chorus; School Musical; Yrbk Ed-Chief; Yrbk Phtg; High Hon Roll; NHS; Sal; Soc Mayflower Ed Awd 85; Syracuse Cncl Svc Annual Yth Ldrshp Recgntn 85; Georgetown U; Intl Rel.

IRBY, LEIGH; Lawrence HS; Inwood, NY; (Y); Pres Church Yth Grp; Sec Exploring; VP Key Clb; Band; Chorus; Orch; JP Sousa Awd; Kiwanis Awd; NHS; Jack Jill Awd 86; U DE.

IRFANI, HANA; Blind Brook HS; Rye Brook, NY; (Y); Art Clb; Cmnty Wkr; Socr; Hosp Aide; SADD; Pol Wrtg.

IRIZARRY, BERNADETTE; Academy Of Saint Joseph; Brentwood, NY; (Y); Art Clb; Cmnty Wkr; Drama Clb; Service Clb; Spanish Clb; Nwsp Rptr; Yrbk Stf; Pres Sr Cls; Badmtn; NHS; Acdmc Achvt Awd, Smns Fllwshp Awd, Hgh Obrn Yth Ldrshp Awd 85-86; Frgn Lang.

IRVINE, ANN; Watervliet HS; Watervliet, NY; (Y); Art Clb; GAA; Mathletes; Var Bowling; Hon Roll; Air Force.

IRVINE, KERRY; Huntington HS; Huntington, NY; (Y); Drama Clb; Chorus; School Play; Var Swmmng; Hon Roll; Coaches Awd Swmmng 84; Providence Coll; Psychlgy.

IRVING, JACQUELINE T; St Francis Prep; Whitestone, NY; (S); 177/746; Drama Clb; Church Choir; School Play; Opt Clb Awd; Cert Of Recog 83-85.

IRVING, RUFFINO; Poughkeepsie HS; Poughkeepsie, NY; (Y); Im Badmtn; JV Var Bsktbl; Im Golf; Hon Roll; Hgst Avg 85; Hist Cert; Acctng.

IRVING, STEPHANIE; Uniondale HS; Uniondale, NY; (Y); FBLA; Trk; MVP-GIRLS Trck; Spirit Awd Girls Trck; Howard U; Bus Admin.

IRWIN, ELIZABETH; John Dewey HS; Brooklyn, NY; (Y); Math Tm; Ntl Merit Ltr; Natl Hnr Rl 86; MIT; Physcst.

ISAAC, KIM; St Pius V HS; Bronx, NY; (Y); Church Yth Grp; Dance Clb; Girl Scts; JA; Radio Clb; Cheerleading; Fld Hcky; Sftbl; Prfct Atten Awd; Drama Dnc.

ISAAC, TRACEY L; Clarkstown North HS; New City, NY; (Y); French Clb; SADD; Stu Cncl; Twrlr; Yth Court 83-86; Yth Agnst Cncr 84; SUNY Albany; Law.

ISAACS, ASHER; Kenmore East HS; Kenmore, NY; (Y); 17/330; Intnl Clb; Pres Band; Concert Band; Jazz Band; Pres Frsh Cls; Var Tennis; Var Capt Vllybl; NHS; Math Tm; Varsity Clb; Princpls Svc Awd Excptnl Schl Svc 86; Natl Achvt Scholar Pgm Wnr 86; All Cnty H S Bnd 3rd Chr Clrnt 86; Colgate U; Pre-Law.

ISAACSON, TODD; Jamestown HS; Jamestown, NY; (Y); CAP; Varsity Clb; Band; Concert Band; Mrchg Band; Var Capt Socr; JV Wrstlng; Prfct Atten Awd; Private Pilot Training 86; U Rochester; Pilot.

ISAKSSON, KIMBERLY; Sachem HS; Holbrook, NY; (Y); 116/1385; Drama Clb; VP Science Clb; Band; Mrchg Band; School Musical; Rptr Lit Mag; Stu Cncl; NHS; Ntl Merit SF; Suffolk Rdg Cncl Poetry Cont 1st Pl 85; Hofstra U Spnsh Poetry Rdg Cmptn 3rd Pl 86; Roanoke Coll; Engl.

ISALES, CYNTHIA; Park West HS; Bronx, NY; (Y); 8/505; Church Yth Grp; Cmnty Wkr; Debate Tm; English Clb; JA; Office Aide; Service Clb; Church Choir; Color Guard; Concert Band; Rgnts Schlrshp Awd 86; Franklin Coll; Jrnlsm.

ISAMAN, ANNETTE; Perry Central HS; Perry, NY; (Y); Church Yth Grp; FHA; FTA; Girl Scts; Math Tm; Spanish Clb; Chorus; Church Choir; Concert Band; Mrchg Band; Alfred Ag & Tech; RN.

ISAMAN, BRENDA; Olean HS; Olean, NY; (Y); 52/246; Library Aide; Chorus; Hon Roll; Jrnlsm.

ISERNIA, JOANN; Bethpage HS; Brthpage, NY; (Y); 32/307; Church Yth Grp; Cmnty Wkr; FBLA; Spanish Clb; Yrbk Stf; Rep Jr Cls; Var L Badmtn; High Hon Roll; Hon Roll; NHS; HSTRY.

ISERNIA, RALPH A; Sachem HS; Lake Ronkonkoma, NY; (Y); 16/1600; Ski Clb; Pres Frsh Cls; Pres Soph Cls; Pres Jr Cls; Pres Sr Cls; JV Var Bsbl; JV Bsktbl; JV Var Ftbl; Jr NHS; NHS; Law.

ISHAM, JOSEPH R; Lancaster Central HS; Lancaster, NY; (Y); 185/464; JA; Varsity Clb; JV Ftbl; Var Capt Ice Hcky; SUNY Fredonia; Pol Sci.

ISLAS, KRISTEN; Saranac Central HS; Saranac, NY; (S); Pres French Clb; Yrbk Stf; Pres Frsh Cls; Pres Soph Cls; Pres Church Yth Grp; Pres Sr Cls; Capt Socr; High Hon Roll; Hon Roll; NHS; Socr All Star Tm 84 & 85; North Country CC; Comp Sci.

ISMAIL, DEEMA; Fontbonne Hall Acad; Brooklyn, NY; (Y); 20/131; Cmnty Wkr; Drama Clb; Office Aide; Variety Show; High Hon Roll; Hon Roll; NHS; Prfct Atten Awd; NY ST Regents, NYU Partial & Pace Trustees 86; Baruch Coll CVNY Incentive Awd & Pres Acad Awd 86; NY U; Acctng.

ISOM, DICK; Rome Catholic HS; Rome, NY; (Y); 2/90; Drama Clb; FNA; Keywanettes; Math Clb; Math Tm; Service Clb; Soroptimist; Teachers Aide; Church Choir; Flag Corp; Hard Up Crew 85-86; Old Mill Crew Pres 85-86; Sylvan Beach U; Gynecologist.

ITHIER, ODARIS MARIE; Dominican Commercial HS; Queen Village, NY; (S); Computer Clb; English Clb; FBLA; JA; Latin Clb; Math Clb; OEA; Red Cross Aide; SADD; Stu Cncl; Prncpls List 83-86; Sienna Clb 85-86; St Johns U; Crt Stnogrphr.

ITTNER, JOHN B; Millbrook Schl; New York City, NY; (Y); Aud/Vis; Math Tm; Model UN; Quiz Bowl; JV Bsktbl; JV Tennis; NY ST Rgnts Schlrshp; Media Cmmndtn; Columbia U; Engrng.

ITZKOWITZ, MICHELLE; E Meadow HS; E Meadow, NY; (S); FBLA; SADD; VP Temple Yth Grp; Nwsp Stf; Yrbk Ed-Chief; Var Tennis; Hon Roll; Jr NHS; NHS; Art Dept Awd Excllnce 84.

IULG, TRACY; Tonawanda SR JR HS; Tonawanda, NY; (Y); GAA; Boys Clb Am; SADD; Varsity Clb; Var L Bsktbl; Score Keeper; Var L Sftbl; JV Tennis; Hon Roll; Bus Mgmt.

IVANOV, CHRISTINE; Dominican Commercial HS; Richmond Hill, NY; (S); Church Yth Grp; Chorus; Church Choir; Hon Roll; NHS; Math.

IVANOVIC, IRENA; High Schl Of Art And Design; Long Islnd City, NY; (Y); Computer Clb; Drama Clb; FTA; Teachers Aide; School Play; Variety Show; Lit Mag; Stu Cncl; NHS; Int Design.

IVERS, KEVIN D; East Islip HS; Great River, NY; (Y); 8/425; Political Wkr; Chorus; Color Guard; Mrchg Band; School Musical; School Play; Nwsp Rptr; NHS; Intnl Clb; Swing Chorus; Jazz Rock Ensmbl; Rotary Intl Frgn Exch Stu 84-85; Russian.

IVERY, LAUREN; West Genesee SR HS; Camillus, NY; (Y); Cmnty Wkr; Girl Scts; Key Clb; Ski Clb; Color Guard; Mrchg Band; Jr Cls; Sr Cls; Sftbl; Swmmng.

IVES, CHARLENE; G Ray Bodley HS; Fulton, NY; (Y); Pres Church Yth Grp; Pres 4-H; French Clb; Latin Clb; Science Clb; Socr; Dnfth Awd; High Hon Roll; Hon Roll; NHS; Sci.

IVES, JODI; Canisteo Central HS; Hornell, NY; (Y); GAA; Ski Clb; Band; Bsktbl; Socr; Trk; Vllybl; NHS.

IVES, JULIE; Charlotte Valley Central HS; Charlotteville, NY; (S); Art Clb; Trs Yrbk Stf; Sec Jr Cls; JV Bsktbl; High Hon Roll; Hon Roll; NHS; Bus Adm.

IVES, RICK; Clymert Central HS; Wayland, NY; (Y); Church Yth Grp; Pres Exploring; Trs Band; Trs Chorus; Rep Frsh Cls; Rep Soph Cls; Rep Jr Cls; JV L Bsktbl; Var L Tennis; NHS; Am Leg Cont 3rd Cnty 86; Scholar Ldrshp Char & Svc Awd 85; Houghton Coll; Real Est Brkr.

IVEYS, COREY; Trott Voc HS; Niagara Falls, NY; (Y); Boys Clb Am; Boy Scts; Cmnty Wkr; Bsbl; Bsktbl; Ftbl; GA ST; Elec.

IZZO, DARCY LYNN; Northville Central HS; Northville, NY; (Y); 9/50; Computer Clb; Drama Clb; Ski Clb; School Musical; Yrbk Sprt Ed; Sec Sr Cls; Var Capt Cheerleading; Var L Socr; Var L Sftbl; Debate Tm; Outstndng Sportsmnshp, Enthusm, Tm Spirit 86; Drama Awd 86; SUNY Oceonta.

IZZO, MARIE; Rome Free Acad; Rome, NY; (Y); Drama Clb; Intnl Clb; Library Aide; SADD; Yrbk Stf; Var Gym; JV Var Socr.

IZZO, NANCY N; John S Burke Central HS; Washingtonville, NY; (Y); 48/152; Drama Clb; Math Tm; Concert Band; School Musical; School Play; VP Stage Crew; Lit Mag; Teachers Aide; Mgr(s); High Hon Roll; SUNY Albany; Comp Sci.

JABBS, STEPHANIE A; Liverpool HS; Liverpool, NY; (Y); 100/874; VP Church Yth Grp; Exploring; Math Tm; Chorus; Church Choir; Mrchg Band; Orch; Symp Band; Hon Roll; Jr NHS; U Of Rochester; Biolgcl Rsrch.

JABIR, MARK; Bishop Ford HS; Brooklyn, NY; (Y); Var Bsktbl; Var Tennis; Var Vllybl.

JABLONSKI, CHARLES T; St Anthonys HS; Deer Park, NY; (Y); 17/224; Computer Clb; Im Bowling; High Hon Roll; Hon Roll; Jr NHS; NHS; Spanish NHS; NY ST U-Stony Brk; Elec Engr.

JABLONSKI, LYNN M; Hamburg SR HS; Hamburg, NY; (Y); 4/390; Cmnty Wkr; French Clb; Band; Mrchg Band; School Play; Hon Roll; VP NHS; NY ST Rgnts Schlrshp 86; Purdue U; Aero Spc Engrng.

JABS, STACEY; Saugerties HS; Saugerties, NY; (Y); 13/270; Pres French Clb; Math Tm; Ski Clb; School Play; Yrbk Phtg; Stat Socr; Var Trk; High Hon Roll; NYS Rgnts Schlrshp 86; Erly Admssns/Hnrs Pgm 86; Bio.

JACHIM, JOE; Solvay HS; Solvay, NY; (Y); Pep Clb; Bus Mgmt.

JACKINO, JENNIFER; Pelham Memorial HS; Pelham Manor, NY; (Y); SADD; Yrbk Ed-Chief; JV Var Bsktbl; JV Var Lcrss; Var Vllybl; NHS; Spanish NHS; Church Yth Grp; Cmnty Wkr; Model UN; Dante Mdl Of Hon 86; Outstndng Achvt Lng 86; Cum Laude Ntl Ltn Exam; Villanovale; Lbrl Arts.

JACKLITSCH, ERIC; St Marys Boys HS; Hicksville, NY; (S); 17/158; Var JV Swmmng; High Hon Roll; Hon Roll; NHS; Acctg.

JACKMAN, MARK; New Rochelle HS; New Rochelle, NY; (Y); #3 In Class; Computer Clb; Math Tm; Lit Mag; Bausch & Lomb Sci Awd; High Hon Roll; Hon Roll; NCTE Awd; NHS; Ntl Merit Ltr; NEDT Awd; 1st-Wstchstr Cnty 85 & 86; 1st-Math Tm 85 & 86; Princeton; Engrng.

JACKMAN, ROSEANN; Moore Catholic HS; Staten Island, NY; (Y); Dance Clb; Hosp Aide; Ski Clb; SADD; School Musical; Yrbk Stf; Lit Mag; Stu Cncl; Hon Roll; Nrsng.

JACKOB, RICHARD; Lincoln HS; Yonkers, NY; (S); 47/400; Drama Clb; Key Clb; Stage Crew; Ed Nwsp Stf; Pres Stu Cncl; Var L Crs Cntry; Var L Trk; CO Outward Bound Schl 85.

JACKOWICZ, STEPHEN J; Baldwin SR HS; Baldwin, NY; (Y); 1/476; Boy Scts; Chess Clb; Sec Computer Clb; Science Clb; Varsity Clb; Nwsp Stf; High Hon Roll; NHS; Ntl Merit SF; Val; Hrvra Book Awd 85; Rnslr Poly Tech Inst Mdl For Math & Sci 85fsteuben Scty Mdl For Grmn 85; Harvard.

JACKOWSKI, MICHELLE; Solvay HS; Solvay, NY; (Y); Art Clb; Pres Intnl Clb; Spanish Clb; Pres SADD; School Musical; Nwsp Stf; Yrbk Phtg; Yrbk Stf; Off Frsh Cls; Off Soph Cls; Mst Outstndg Ldrshp Awd 86; Humn Eclgy Awd 84.

JACKSON, AMY S; Homer Central HS; Homer, NY; (Y); Vllybl; Hon Roll; NHS; Geneseo; Psych.

JACKSON, BRIAN; Skaneateles Central HS; Skaneateles, NY; (S); Band; Pep Band; Ftbl; Wrstlng; God Cntry Awd; NHS; Ftbl Ltr 84-85, Wrstlng 83; 4th Pl Cazenovia Wrstlng Trnmnt 83; Elec Engr.

JACKSON, CATHERINE; Riverdale Country HS; New York, NY; (Y); Hosp Aide; Acpl Chr; Chorus; Orch; Boston U; Engl.

JACKSON, CHRISTINE; Salamanca Central HS; Limestone, NY; (Y); French Clb; FHA; JV Sftbl; JV Trk; JV Var Vllybl; Schlrshp SCOPES Clrksn U 86.

JACKSON, DEBRA; Grand Island HS; Grand Island, NY; (Y); Art Clb; Sec Church Yth Grp; Varsity Clb; Swmmng; Vllybl; Hon Roll; Varsity Ltr Vlybl 85-86; Awd For Vlybl 85-86; Erie CC; Sec Sci.

JACKSON, DONALD; Coxsackie Athens JR SR HS; Athens, NY; (Y); Chess Clb; Church Yth Grp; Computer Clb; Variety Show; Crs Cntry; High Hon Roll; Hon Roll; Prfct Atten Awd; Comp Lang.

JACKSON, DONNA; Charlotte JR SR HS; Rochester, NY; (Y); Capt Cheerleading; Trk; Hon Roll; Outstndng Achvt Readng 85; Cert Cmmndtn Pract Chem 86; Natl Yth Phys Fit Pgm Marine Corps Lg 86; U Pittsburgh; Sci.

JACKSON, EDNA; Lackawanna SR HS; Lackawanna, NY; (Y); JV Cheerleading; JV Var Trk; VP Jr Cls; JV Crs Cntry; Comp Pgmr.

JACKSON, FRED T; Norman Thomas Commercial HS; Brooklyn, NY; (Y); 21/597; DECA; Band; School Play; Rep Frsh Cls; Rep Soph Cls; Rep Jr Cls; High Hon Roll; NHS; Ntl Merit Schol; Sal; Regnts Schlrshp 86; Pace U; Mktg.

JACKSON, JENNIFER; Brasher Falls Central HS; Winthrop, NY; (Y); Sec Pres Church Yth Grp; FBLA; Chorus; Church Choir; Drm Mjr(t); Stu Cncl; Twrlr; Hon Roll; Girl Scts; Library Aide; Perfct Attndnc 83 & 84; Outstndng Achvt Math 83; Legl Secy.

JACKSON, JENNIFER; Niagara Wheatfield HS; Niagara Falls, NY; (Y); 37/292; French Clb; PAVAS; Sec Jazz Band; School Musical; Symp Band; Stu Cncl; Var Tennis; High Hon Roll; NHS; Pres Schlr; Niagara U Pres Schlrp & Acad Schlrp 86-90; Merit Awd 86; Niagara U; Pharm.

JACKSON, JEUANITA; South Park HS; Buffalo, NY; (Y); 66/356; Church Yth Grp; Drama Clb; Teachers Aide; School Play; Yrbk Stf; Hon Roll; Jr NHS; Stu Cntrbtn Awd 86; Merit Roll 85; U Of NY-BUFFALO; Engl.

JACKSON, JULIA; Sodus Central HS; Williamson, NY; (Y); 38/112; Sec Church Yth Grp; Varsity Clb; Church Choir; Var Bsktbl; Var Trk; Hon Roll; Prfct Atten Awd; Urban Lge-Blk Schlr Erly Recog Nom 86; Wayne Cnty All St 2nd & 3rd Tm-Trk 84 & 86; Pentathln Champ 86; Acctng.

JACKSON, JULIE; Frontier Central HS; Blasdell, NY; (Y); FBLA; German Clb; Pep Clb; Band; Concert Band; Mrchg Band; High Hon Roll; Hon Roll.

JACKSON, JUNIOR R; North Babylon SR HS; North Babylon, NY; (Y); Art Clb; Church Yth Grp; Computer Clb; Drama Clb; French Clb; Mathletes; SADD; Varsity Clb; Acpl Chr; Chorus; NE; Biotech.

JACKSON, KAREN E; Hicksville HS; Hicksville, NY; (Y); Church Yth Grp; Cmnty Wkr; Teachers Aide; Church Choir; Orch; School Musical; Var L Gym; Hon Roll; 7th Pl NYS USGF Clss III C&o Gymnstcs 85; NYTSSMA Lvl 5 85-86; Vlntr & Staff Hndcppd Chldrn 86; Nassau CC; Tchr.

JACKSON, KELLY; Mynderse Acad; Seneca Falls, NY; (S); 10/135; FHA; Spanish Clb; SADD; Band; Chorus; Color Guard; Mrchg Band; School Musical; Yrbk Stf; Rep Soph Cls; Ntl Hnr Roll; Bio-Chem.

JACKSON, KELLY; Unatego JR SR HS; Otego, NY; (Y); 13/104; Church Yth Grp; Cmnty Wkr; Dance Clb; Spanish Clb; Varsity Clb; Band; Color Guard; Concert Band; Mrchg Band; Pep Band; Outstndng Def Awd Field Hcky 85; Mst Imprvd Field Hcky 86; Jostens Key Awd Chem 86; Intl Bus.

JACKSON, KERRY; Academy Of St Joseph; Coram, NY; (Y); Drama Clb; Hosp Aide; School Musical; Nwsp Rptr; Nwsp Stf; Hon Roll; Departmental Excellence In Italian 83-85; Journalism.

JACKSON, KIMBERLY; Henniger HS; Syracuse, NY; (Y); Sec Church Yth Grp; Chorus; Church Choir; Hon Roll; Otstndng Achvt Awd 86; Syracuse U; Comp Engr.

JACKSON, LEON; Hutchinson Central Technical HS; Buffalo, NY; (Y); Church Yth Grp; Howard U; Comp Elec.

JACKSON, MATTHEW; Pelham Memorial HS; Pelham, NY; (Y); Church Yth Grp; Model UN; Band; Concert Band; Jazz Band; Mrchg Band; Pep Band; JP Sousa Awd; School Musical; Stage Crew; Nmntd For Mcdnls Bnd 85; US Mrn Corps Semper Fidelis Bnd Awd 86; Pelham Tchrs Assoc Schlrshp 86; Amherst Coll; Pltcl Sci.

JACKSON, MAUDETTE; Jefferson JR SR HS; Rochester, NY; (S); 1/134; Nwsp Rptr; Pres Soph Cls; VP Stu Cncl; Var L Bsktbl; Var L Sftbl; Var L Tennis; Var Capt Vllybl; High Hon Roll; Rchstr Area Fndtn Lwr R Klepper Mst Prmsng Stu Atlt 84-86; PRIS2M Outstndng Team Awd 83-85; Engrng.

JACKSON, MELVIN; Lackawanna SR HS; Lackawanna, NY; (Y); French Clb; Varsity Clb; Band; JV Var Bsktbl; Var Ftbl; Var Trk; Hon Roll; Elec Engr.

JACKSON, MEREDITH; Fonda Fultonville Central HS; Fonda, NY; (Y); 15/111; Intnl Clb; Sec SADD; Band; Chorus; Yrbk Stf; VP Frsh Cls; Var L Swmmng; Hon Roll; Pres Schlr; Rcrdr Swmmr Of Yr 84; Marist Coll; Pre-Law.

JACKSON, MICBELLE; Uniondale HS; Uniondale, NY; (Y); Art Clb; Orch; Var JV Vllybl; High Hon Roll; Hon Roll; Jr NHS; Advtsng Dsgn.

JACKSON, ORLANDRO GIAVANTE; South Park BVTC HS; Buffalo, NY; (Y); Cmnty Wkr; Hosp Aide; Library Aide; Model UN; Spanish Clb; Chorus; VP Stu Cncl; NHS; Long Island U; Pre-Med.

JACKSON, PHYLLIS H; Sonderling HS; Brentwood, NY; (Y); 55/500; FNA; Spanish Clb; Varsity Clb; Chorus; School Musical; Stage Crew; Rep Frsh Cls; Rep Soph Cls; Rep Jr Cls; Rep Stu Cncl; Cert Compltn Peer Cnslng Plnned Parenthd 85; Pre-Med.

JACKSON, REGINA; Mynderse Acad; Seneca Falls, NY; (S); Chorus; NHS; Nrsg.

JACKSON, REGINA; St Edmund HS; Brooklyn, NY; (S); Hon Roll; Jr NHS; Religion Awd; Spllng Awd; History Awd; UCLA; Dietician.

JACKSON, REGINALD; Mt Vernon HS; Bronx, NY; (Y); Orch; Var JV Crs Cntry; Var Trk; UCLA.

JACKSON JR, RICHARD E; Saugerties HS; Saugerties, NY; (Y); French Clb; Ski Clb; School Musical; High Hon Roll; NHS; SUNY Albany; Mth Ed.

JACKSON, RODNEY L A; Spring Valley SR HS; Spring Valley, NY; (Y); Am Leg Boys St; Pres Church Yth Grp; Trs German Clb; Church Choir; Drm Mjr(t); Mrchg Band; Orch; High Hon Roll; Jr NHS; NHS; Grmn Hnr Soc; Intl Bus.

JACKSON, SHANIN; Herbert H Lehman HS; Bronx, NY; (Y); 100/561; Science Clb; Awd For Excllnc In Soc Studies 84; SELH Prog 86; ASCENT Prog John Joy Coll 86; U Of S FL; Med.

JACKSON, SHIRLEY; John F Kennedy HS; Utica, NY; (Y); Church Yth Grp; 4-H; SADD; Concert Band; Bsktbl; Trk; 4-H Awd; Hon Roll; Law.

JACKSON JR, SYLVESTER; Canisius HS; Buffalo, NY; (Y); 11/169; Boys Clb Am; Boy Scts; Bsktbl; Ftbl; Trk; High Hon Roll; Hon Roll; NHS; Ntl Merit Ltr; Mst Imprvd Sprntr Trk 85; AKA Gama Phi Omega Chptr Hghst Acad Ath Achvt Awd 85; Cornell; Bus Mngmnt.

JACKSON, VALERIE; Eastern District HS; Brooklyn, NY; (Y); Science Clb; Teachers Aide; Band; Var Sftbl; Hon Roll; Jr NHS; NHS; Pride Yankees Awd Outstndng Achvt 85; Howard Golden Outstndng Essay Awd 86; Phys Fit Awd 86; Lawyer.

JACKSON, VINCENT; Bishop Ford Cchs; Brooklyn, NY; (Y); Var L Bsktbl.

JACOB, JOSEPH; Tonawanda JR SR HS; Tonawanda, NY; (Y); 1/220; Am Leg Boys St; Var L Bowling; Bausch & Lomb Sci Awd; NHS; Ntl Merit Ltr; Pres Schlr; Val; Boys Clb Am; Im Wrstlng; High Hon Roll; Rensselaer Medal Math,Sci; Regnts Schrlshp; Soc Descendnts; ST U; Comp Sci.

JACOB, MICHAEL; Vernon Verona Sherrill Central HS; Sherrill, NY; (Y); Church Yth Grp; Varsity Clb; Var Socr; JV Tennis; Hon Roll; Archtctr.

JACOBELLIS, LAURA; Hauppauge HS; Smithtown, NY; (Y); Dance Clb; Office Aide; SADD; Chorus; Cheerleading; Coach Actv; Gym; Score Keeper; Tennis; Vllybl; Accntng.

JACOBS, BETH; Amsterdam HS; Amsterdam, NY; (Y); FBLA; JA; Spanish Clb; Teachers Aide; Rep Frsh Cls; Prfct Atten Awd; JR Achvt Sls Awd 86; St Bonaventure; Acctg.

JACOBS, BRENDA; Springfield Gardens HS; Jamaica, NY; (Y); FBLA; Bowling; Vllybl; Cit Awd; High Hon Roll; Hon Roll; Class Achvt Art Awd 86; Merit Awd 86; Eng Honor Awd 85; Bernard N Baruch Coll; Bus.

JACOBS, CINDY; Evander Childs HS; Bronx, NY; (S); 5/383; Cmnty Wkr; Hosp Aide; Letterman Clb; Service Clb; Teachers Aide; Varsity Clb; Trs Sr Cls; Vllybl; Hon Roll; Prfct Atten Awd; Prid Yankee Awd 84 & 85; Cert Merit Al Acadmc Sbjcts 82-85; Medcn.

JACOBS, DANIEL; New Rochelle HS; New Rochelle, NY; (Y); Chess Clb; Computer Clb; Band; Nwsp Rptr; Lit Mag; Im Sftbl; Im Vllybl; NHS; Spanish NHS.

JACOBS, JEANNE; Culson Central HS; Lockport, NY; (Y); 4-H; Teachers Aide; Y-Teens; Band; Pep Band; Powder Puff Ftbl; Trk; Bryant & Stratton; Data Proc.

JACOBS, JENNIFER; Long Island Lutheran HS; Wantagh, NY; (S); 4/90; Ski Clb; SADD; Nwsp Rptr; Yrbk Stf; Var Capt Socr; JV Sftbl; Var Trk; Stat Wrstlng; NHS; Church Yth Grp; 2 Acadmc Schlrshps; Natl Engl Merit Awd; Hmcmng Crt.

JACOBS, LEONARD A; Jamaica HS; Flushing, NY; (Y); 52/537; PAVAS; Q&S; Chorus; School Musical; School Play; Nwsp Ed-Chief; Yrbk Ed-Chief; Lit Mag; Stu Cncl; NHS; NYS Rgnts Schlrshp 86; NY U; Theatre.

JACOBS, LINDA; New Rochelle HS; New Rochelle, NY; (Y); Drama Clb; Var Socr; Var Vllybl; NHS; Russian Clb 85-86; Model Congress Hospitality Staff 84-86; Helpng Hand 85-86; Brown; Law.

JACOBS, LORI; Clarkstown HS; Spring Valley, NY; (Y); Cmnty Wkr; Dance Clb; Drama Clb; PAVAS; Ski Clb; SADD; Temple Yth Grp; Chorus; Church Choir; School Musical; Natl Sci & Socl Studies Olympiad 84; Bus.

JACOBS, MARIA E; Schalmont HS; Schenectady, NY; (Y); 18/168; Capt Mrchg Band; Mrchg Band; Rep Sr Cls; Stat Socr; Var Capt Vllybl; NHS; Le Moyne Coll; Math Mgt.

JACOBS, MARK; Pelham Memorial HS; Pelham, NY; (Y); 5/180; Concert Band; Jazz Band; Mrchg Band; Golf; High Hon Roll; NHS; Ntl Merit Schol; Presdntl Ftns 86; Clark U; Phlsphy.

JACOBS, PAUL; Half Hollow Hills HS West; Dix Hills, NY; (Y); JV Bsbl; Im Bowling; Var Diving; JV Ftbl; Var Swmmng; Im Wt Lftg; Italian Natl Hon Soc 84-86; Townson ST; Accntng.

JACOBS, ROBERT; P V Moore HS; Cleveland, NY; (Y); Bsbl; JV Bsktbl; JV Var Ftbl; NHS; Aerospc Engrng.

JACOBS, SUSAN D; South Jefferson Central HS; Rodman, NY; (Y); 8/135; Aud/Vis; French Clb; FHA; Hon Roll; NHS; Rgnts Schlrshp Wnnr 86; Syracuse U Schlrshp-Proj Advnc 85-86; Marist Coll; Cmmnctns.

JACOBSEN, GORDON; John Jay HS; Fairfield, CT; (Y); Stat Bsktbl; Var Ftbl; Var Wt Lftg; Hon Roll; Awd Prctcl Geo, Awd Spnsh Cnvrstnl 85.

JACOBSEN, INGER C; Newark SR HS; Newark, NY; (Y); 39/202; Aud/Vis; Service Clb; Concert Band; Variety Show; Nwsp Rptr; Lit Mag; Sec Trs Frsh Cls; Sec Trs Jr Cls; JV Tennis; German Clb; Stu Excl Awd 85; Regnts Schlrshp 86; Buffalo ST Coll; Grphc Dsgn.

JACOBSON, ADAM; The Gow HS; Huntington, WV; (Y); 10/37; Aud/Vis; Key Clb; Letterman Clb; SADD; Temple Yth Grp; Varsity Clb; Nwsp Ed-Chief; Nwsp Sprt Ed; Yrbk Phtg; Var Capt Bsktbl; Marshall U; Brdcstg.

JACOBSON, AMY; Waterville Central HS; Deansboro, NY; (Y); 1/96; Drama Clb; NFL; Chorus; School Musical; Swing Chorus; Stu Cncl; Fld Hcky; Var JV Tennis; Hon Roll; NHS; Colgate Sem; Sahger High Avg Awd; Brainard Math; Zoolgy.

JACOBSON, CHERYL; Commack HS; Commack, NY; (Y); Concert Band; Mrchg Band; Symp Band; Yrbk Stf; Var L Trk; Bausch & Lomb Sci Awd; High Hon Roll; NHS; Ntl Merit Ltr; Rensslr Mdl/Excllnc Math & Sci 86; Pre-Med.

JACOBSON, LISA R; Lewiston Porter HS; Ransomville, NY; (Y); 10/236; Sec JA; Band; Concert Band; Mrchg Band; Yrbk Stf; High Hon Roll; NHS; Lamp Of Learning Awd For Art 84-85; Lamp Of Learning Awd For Englsh 85; NY ST Regents Schlrshp 86.

JACOBSON, LYN S; The Fieldston Schl; New York, NY; (Y); Cmnty Wkr; Chrmn Drama Clb; Chorus; School Musical; School Play; Stage Crew; Yrbk Phtg; Ihaca Schl Of Music; Voice.

JACOBSON, PAUL; James Madison HS; Brooklyn, NY; (Y); Kings Boro; Acctng.

JACOBSON, THORVALD; H S Of The Humnties; New York, NY; (Y); JV Crs Cntry; JV Diving; Pres/Fndr Rifle Club 84-85; VP/Co-Fndr Russian Club 84-85; Tae-Kwon-Do 85-86; Lang.

JACOBY, JAYME; Newfield HS; Selden, NY; (Y); Pres Band; Chorus; Concert Band; Jazz Band; Mrchg Band; Orch; School Musical; Stu Cncl; High Hon Roll; Spanish NHS; All Cnty Band 85; Music.

JACOBY, KENNETH L; Oceanside SR HS; Oceanside, NY; (Y); 69/530; Pres Church Yth Grp; Pres French Clb; VP SADD; Chorus; Nwsp Stf; Yrbk Ed-Chief; Rep Stu Cncl; NHS; Rep Frsh Cls; Rep Soph Cls; Did Most For Schl Awd 83; Franklin & Marshall Coll; Econ.

JACQUES, STEPHEN; Catholic Central HS; Troy, NY; (Y); Art Clb; Church Yth Grp; Math Clb; Spanish Clb; Variety Show; Bsbl; Picotte Galary Art Show 84; Art Awd 84-86; Mass Committe Lect Mass 84-86; Schl Comm Art; Illustrator.

JAEGER, LYNDA J; Baldwin SR HS; Baldwin, NY; (Y); 55/492; Church Yth Grp; Civic Clb; SADD; Band; Chorus; Mrchg Band; Tennis; Hon Roll; NHS; Pres Schlr; Wmns Advnc Clb Schlrshp 86; Stephen Barry Mem Schlrshp 86; OH Wslyn U; Psychlgy.

JAENISCH, CARIN; Coxsackie Athens HS; Hannacroix, NY; (Y); 32/111; Spanish Clb; Trs Frsh Cls; Stu Cncl; High Hon Roll; Hon Roll; Nurses Aide 83-84; CPR 83-84; Nrsng.

JAENTSCHKE, VAL; Abraham Lincoln HS; Brooklyn, NY; (Y); Church Yth Grp; Library Aide; Teachers Aide; Color Guard; Yrbk Stf; Stu Cncl; Prfct Atten Lincoln HS 84; Kings Borough Coll; Comp.

JAFFE, MICHAEL ELIOT; Hewlett HS; N Woodmere, NY; (Y); Debate Tm; Orch; Hon Roll; NHS; Law.

JAFFE, RUSSELL; Smithtown HS; Nesconset, NY; (Y); Pres Key Clb; SADD; Var L Socr; Var L Trk; French Hon Soc; NHS; Hosp Aide; Off Frsh Cls; Off Soph Cls; Off Jr Cls.

JAFFEE, KIM; Farmingdale HS; Farmingdale, NY; (Y); Girl Scts; Trk; Elem Educ.

JAFFIER, RAYDON; George W Wingate HS; Brooklyn, NY; (Y); Office Aide; Teachers Aide; Hon Roll; Prfct Atten Awd; Mktg.

JAGODZINSKI, ANDREW J; Brockport Central HS; Hamlin, NY; (Y); Ski Clb; Socr; Swmmng; Private Pilot 86; Monroe CC; Cmmrcl Pilot.

JAIKISSOON, JEET; Newtown HS; Corona, NY; (Y); 97/667; Boys Clb Am; Bsktbl; Sftbl; Trk; Hon Roll; Straus Excllnc Awd In Coop Ed 86; Outstndng Schlrshp Trng Merit Awd 86; Achvt Cert In Bus Ed 86; St Johns U; Bus Admin.

JAIME, AMANDA; Laguardia H Schl Of The Arts; New York, NY; (Y); JA; Wt Lftg; Hon Roll; Ntl Merit SF; Fash Edtr.

JAIME, VIRGINIA; Saint Raymond Acad For Girls; Bronx, NY; (S); 10/74; Spanish Clb; Band; Pres Soph Cls; Pom Pon; Hon Roll; Westchstr Bus Inst Bus Awd; NY U; Bus Mgmt.

JAIN, ARVIND; Kingston HS; Kingston, NY; (Y); 17/576; French Clb; Latin Clb; Pep Clb; Quiz Bowl; Scholastic Bowl; Science Clb; Socr; Tennis; Wrstlng; French Hon Soc; Ldrshp Recgntn 85-86; Regnts Schlrshp 86; Sci Awd 83; Carnegie-Mellon U; Engr.

JAISON, DENA; Shulamith HS; Brooklyn, NY; (S); 5/28; Temple Yth Grp; Chorus; School Musical; Nwsp Stf; NHS; Natl Bibl Cntst 83-85; Michlalah & Brooklyn Coll; Ed.

JAITIN, AILEEN R; Jamaica HS; Flushing, NY; (Y); 5/537; Computer Clb; Service Clb; Band; Sec Orch; School Musical; Yrbk Stf; High Hon Roll; Chorus; Church Choir; Pep Band; Bnjm S Chancy Citation Of Msc 83; St Jhns U Sci Rsrch Schlrshp 85; Crtv Arts Scty 83-86; Crng-Mellon U.

JAKAB, WILLIAM; Iona Prep; New Roch, NY; (Y); 56/204; Cmnty Wkr; Service Clb; Stage Crew; Variety Show; Yrbk Stf; Hon Roll; NHS; Prfct Atten Awd.

JAKUBCZYK, LISA; Mount Mercy Acad; Lackawanna, NY; (Y); 31/201; Church Yth Grp; French Clb; Model UN; Ski Clb; Stage Crew; Im Fld Hcky; Hon Roll; Law.

JAKUC, CHRISTINA LYNN; Shenendehowa HS; Clifton Park, NY; (Y); Am Leg Aux Girls St; Leo Clb; Trs SADD; VP Trs Varsity Clb; Rep Frsh Cls; Rep Soph Cls; Rep Jr Cls; Rep Sr Cls; Sec Stu Cncl; Var Capt Bsktbl; PTSA Schlrshp 86; Harrison Hubbard Vrsty Club Spts Schlrshp 86; Shenendehowa Rtry Ctznshp Awd 84; IN U Bloomingham; Bus.

JAKUC, PETER A; Shenendehowa Central HS; Clifton Park, NY; (Y); Am Leg Boys St; Debate Tm; Leo Clb; VP SADD; Rep Stu Cncl; Im Bsktbl; JV Var Lcrss; High Hon Roll; NHS; Moot Ct Law 1st Pl 86; Sup Hnr Rll 84-86; Engrng.

JAKYMIW, NICOLE; Carmel HS; Carmel, NY; (Y); Yrbk Stf; JV Var Cheerleading; High Hon Roll; Hon Roll; NHS; Prfct Atten Awd; Hmcmng Queen; Mst Vlbl Var Chrldr; Comm.

JALALZAI, ZUBEDA; Gouvernew Central HS; Gouverneur, NY; (Y); Computer Clb; High Hon Roll; Jr NHS; Gnrl G Awd 83-86; Ntl Soc Stds Olympd 86; Shkspr Clb Engl Awd 86; St Lawrence U; Pre-Med.

JAMES, BILL; Wallkill HS; Newburgh, NY; (Y); Boy Scts; Chess Clb; Band; Concert Band; Jazz Band; Mrchg Band; Pep Band; Bsktbl; Ftbl; Trk; Orng Cnty CC; Psychlgy.

JAMES, BRIAN; West Hempstead HS; Long Island, NY; (Y); Computer Clb; Office Aide; Ski Clb; VP Temple Yth Grp; Y-Teens; Lit Mag; Hon Roll; NHS; Yrbk Stf; Sci Awd Astrnmy 85-86; S Nassau Untd Synag Yth Div Genrl Brd SR Prgrmmr 86-87; Comp Engrng.

JAMES, CARL L; Mount Saint Michael Acad; Bronx, NY; (S); 5/309; Chess Clb; Computer Clb; High Hon Roll; Hon Roll; Prfct Atten Awd; Mt Saint Michael Acad Schlrshp Awd 83-86; Engrng.

JAMES, CONNIE; De Ruyter Central Schl; De Ruyter, NY; (S); Drama Clb; SADD; Chorus; Church Choir; School Play; Nwsp Stf; Yrbk Stf; Var Bsktbl; Hon Roll; NHS; 2nd Highest Avg Jr Cls 85; Stu Of Mnth 83-85; CPA.

JAMES, IAN R; James I O Neill HS; West Point, NY; (Y); 27/135; Boy Scts; Computer Clb; Ski Clb; Concert Band; Nwsp Rptr; Var Crs Cntry; JV Socr; NHS; West Point Acad; Engrng.

JAMES, JENNIFER; Chenango Forks HS; Binghamton, NY; (S); Cmnty Wkr; VP Key Clb; Ski Clb; Chorus; Church Choir; Concert Band; Orch; Rep Jr Cls; Swmmng; Hon Roll; 3rd Pl Natl Frnch Cont 86; Area All ST 83-85; Acad Achvt Awds 84-85; Med.

JAMES, JOHN H; Poland Central Schl; Poland, NY; (Y); Am Leg Boys St; Varsity Clb; Band; Concert Band; Var Badmtn; Bsktbl; Var Socr; Var Capt Tennis; Cit Awd; Babe Ruth Awd 86; Mohawk Vly CC; Engrng.

JAMES, JULIE; William G Nottingham HS; Syracuse, NY; (Y); 15/220; Latin Clb; Var L Sftbl; Var L Trk; High Hon Roll; NHS; NYS Rgnts Schlrshp, Outstndng Achvt Latin Hnr Awd 86; Summa Cum Laude 83 & 84; Maxima Cum Laude 85; SUNY Binghamton; Bio.

JAMES, LLOYD; Walton HS; Bronx, NY; (Y); Church Yth Grp; Cmnty Wkr; Computer Clb; Debate Tm; FBLA; Teachers Aide; Drill Tm; Yrbk Phtg; Yrbk Stf; Vllybl; Bus.

JAMES, PATTY; Poland Central Schl; Poland, NY; (Y); Drama Clb; French Clb; SADD; Varsity Clb; Chorus; Yrbk Stf; Crs Cntry; Score Keeper; Tennis; NHS; Mohawk Vly CC; Engrng.

JAMES JR, RALPH L; Archbishop Molloy HS; West Hempstead, NY; (Y); 26/383; School Play; Yrbk Stf; VP Stu Cncl; Var Bsktbl; Var Trk; High Hon Roll; VP NHS; 1st Tm All-City Slctn Bsktbl 86; Cthlc HS City Chmpn In Long Jump 84-86; Pre-Med.

JAMES, TIMOTHY; White Plains HS; White Plns, NY; (Y); JV Ftbl; Wt Lftg; Hon Roll; Mamie Haynes Schlrshp Awd 86; Comp Sci.

JAMIESON, DEBBIE; Royalton-Hartland HS; Middleport, NY; (Y); Cmnty Wkr; Pep Clb; Varsity Clb; Stu Cncl; Bsktbl; Fld Hcky; Sftbl; Daemen; Bus Admin.

JAMIESON, DONNIE D; Newburgh Free Acad; Newburgh, NY; (Y); Camera Clb; Library Aide; Political Wkr; ROTC; Color Guard; Nwsp Phtg; Yrbk Phtg; Hon Roll; Am Lgn Mltry Excllnt Awd 85-86; Ldrshp Awd 85-86; Acad Awd 85-86; Syraccuse U.

JAMIESON, JULIE; Royalton-Hartland Central HS; Middleport, NY; (Y); 1/120; Am Leg Aux Girls St; French Clb; Var Capt Bsktbl; Var L Fld Hcky; Var L Trk; High Hon Roll; NHS; Varsity Clb; JV Sftbl; JV Vllybl; Hgst Acad Avg Awd; Bio Awd; Williams Coll Bk Awd; Elem Ed.

JAMISON, CHARLENE; High School Of Fashion Industri; Bronx, NY; (Y); 6/432; Trs Church Yth Grp; Drama Clb; Office Aide; Capt Quiz Bowl; Trs Church Choir; Yrbk Stf; Off Stu Cncl; Hon Roll; Jr NHS; NHS; Eng Hnr Rll 83-86; Pride Of Yankees Awd 85-86; Acadmc All Am 86.

JAMISON, JACK; Bayport-Blue Point HS; Bayport, NY; (Y); Bsbl; Ftbl; Wrstlng; Emil Mazzei Awd 86; Coaches Awd For Wrstlng & Bsbl 86; Bus.

JAN, NANCY Y; Forest Hills HS; New York, NY; (Y); 63/826; Church Yth Grp; PAVAS; Church Choir; Orch; Ed Yrbk Stf; High Hon Roll; Hon Roll; Office Aide; Teachers Aide; Dorothy Richard Starling Fndtn Schlrshp 85-86; Violin Solo Perfrmnc 83-86; Trio Cncrt 83-86; Music.

JANACK, JAMES; Solvay HS; Syracuse, NY; (Y); 1/180; French Clb; Key Clb; Nwsp Stf; Yrbk Phtg; Yrbk Rptr; Yrbk Sprt Ed; Sec Soph Cls; VP Jr Cls; Pres Sr Cls; JV Var Bsktbl; WA Wrkshp Union Carbide Schlr 86; Chem.

JANAS, ROBERT; Auburn HS; Auburn, NY; (Y); Nwsp Sprt Ed; Nwsp Stf; Law.

JANAWITZ, JAMISON; Mc Quaid Jesuit HS; Pittsford, NY; (Y); Boy Scts; Varsity Clb; Trs Frsh Cls; Var Ftbl; JV Wrstlng; Hon Roll; Cert Of Merit In Span Region Roch NY 85; Aeronatuical Engrng.

JANDREAU, CHRISTINE M; Niagara Wheatfield SR HS; Niagara Falls, NY; (Y); 13/292; Pep Clb; PAVAS; Varsity Clb; Chorus; Swing Chorus; Var Tennis; High Hon Roll; Hon Roll; NHS; Prfct Atten Awd; Rgnts Schlrshp 85-86; Fredonia ST U; Indstrl Mgmt.

JANES, MARY; Attica Central HS; Attica, NY; (S); 3/150; Am Leg Aux Girls St; Color Guard; Yrbk Stf; Off Stu Cncl; JV Var Cheerleading; JV Sftbl; Var Capt Swmmng; Lion Awd; NHS.

JANETSKY, KATHLEEN; Duanesburg HS; Delanson, NY; (Y); Drama Clb; 4-H; Intnl Clb; Office Aide; Chorus; School Play; Yrbk Ed-Chief; Var Cheerleading; Var Score Keeper; L Trk; Phys Thrpy.

JANGER, MICHAEL C; Hastings HS; Hastings-On-Hud, NY; (Y); AFS; Boy Scts; Intnl Clb; Latin Clb; Library Aide; Model UN; Temple Yth Grp; Yrbk Stf; Stu Cncl; Var L Socr; Brown U; Polit Sci.

JANGRO, RHONDA; Schoharie Central HS; Schoharie, NY; (S); 9/85; Sec 4-H; VICA; Var Bowling; Var Trk; 4-H Awd; Hon Roll; Bwlng Awds 77; Wnr Of Stu No 1 Clb 85; Wrd Procsng Fld.

JANICKI, CHRISTOPHER M; Utica Free Acad; Utica, NY; (Y); Pres Church Yth Grp; Pres Computer Clb; Model UN; Pres Spanish Clb; Bsbl; JV Bsktbl; NHS; Exploring; Mathletes; SADD; Intrnshp NY Acad Sci 84; Notre Dame JV Bsktbl Tourn 84; 1st Pl Comp Prgrmg Cntst 86; Clarkson U; Elctrcl Engrng.

JANIDLO, PETE; Shaker HS; Latham, NY; (Y); Ski Clb; Hon Roll; Comp Engrng.

JANISH, TIMOTHY D; Clarence SR HS; Clarence, NY; (Y); 9/250; Am Leg Boys St; Computer Clb; Math Tm; Ski Clb; Concert Band; Jazz Band; Mrchg Band; Socr; Hon Roll; NHS; R I T; Elec Engrng.

JANISZEWSKI, MARK; Seneca Voc HS; Buffalo, NY; (Y); 2/150; Hon Roll; NHS; Ntl Merit Ltr; Pres Acad Ftnss Awd, Excel Diplma Spnsh, Bus Moniter Awd 86; U Buffalo; Elec Engr.

JANKE, KELLIANNE; Lindenhurst SR HS; Lindenhurst, NY; (Y); Church Yth Grp; Cmnty Wkr; Pres Key Clb; Leo Clb; Political Wkr; Trs Service Clb; Trs Orch; Yrbk Phtg; Yrbk Stf; Hon Roll; Katharine Gibbs Ldrshp Awd 86; Gregg Shrthnd Achvt Awd 86; NY ST Music Assn Awds 84 & 85; Katherine Gibbs Schl; Med Sec.

JANKE, TRACY A; Waterloo HS; Waterloo, NY; (Y); 6/170; French Clb; FTA; Model UN; Teachers Aide; Varsity Clb; JV Bsktbl; Var L Vllybl; DAR Awd; High Hon Roll; NHS; Regnts Schlrshp; Advncd Plcmnt Eng; Advncd Plcmnt Socl Stu; SUNY Oswego; Libl Arts.

JANKNER, TARA; South Shore HS; Brooklyn, NY; (Y); Model UN; Temple Yth Grp; Chorus; School Play; Variety Show; Ed Yrbk Rptr; Super Yth Daily News 85-86; Music Hnr Soc 84-86; Close Up Rep 86.

JANKOWIAK, JACQUELYN M; Turner Carroll HS; Buffalo, NY; (S); 1/103; Quiz Bowl; Nwsp Sprt Ed; Yrbk Ed-Chief; Yrbk Stf; Stat Bsbl; Stat Bsktbl; Score Keeper; High Hon Roll; NHS; Val; SUNY Buffalo; Nrsg.

JANKOWSKI, JENNIFER; Linton HS; Schenectady, NY; (Y); Band; Chorus; Concert Band; Mrchg Band; Orch; Frsh Cls; Soph Cls; Acctg.

JANKOWSKI, MELISSA; West Seneca East SR HS; Cheektowaga, NY; (Y); 121/396; French Clb; JA; Q&S; Science Clb; SADD; Nwsp Stf; French Hon Soc; Hon Roll; Prfct Atten Awd; Frnch Awd Positive Attitude 85-86; Frnch Awd 90 Or Above Avg 82-86; Buffalo ST Coll; Scl Wrk.

JANMAAT, RENEE; Copiague HS; Copiague, NY; (Y); DECA; High Hon Roll; Hon Roll; Trk; JV Var Timer; Socr; Color Guard; Mathletes; GAA; Cmnty Wkr; DECA Chptr Proj Awd & Natl Germn Hnr Soc 85-86; Pace U; Bus Admin.

JANNOTTI, JULIANNE; Newburgh Free Acad; Newburgh, NY; (Y); 31/620; Computer Clb; Girl Scts; Math Tm; Stage Crew; JV Var Socr; Var Swmmng; High Hon Roll; Jr NHS; NHS; Ntl Merit SF; Educ.

JANSEN, TRACY; Westbury SR HS; Westbury, NY; (Y); 31/275; Capt Dance Clb; Drama Clb; Orch; School Musical; School Play; Yrbk Stf; JV Var Cheerleading; Var Gym; Tennis; VP Jr Cls; Med Tech.

JANSON, ALISSA; Tully HS; Tully, NY; (Y); Spanish Clb; Varsity Clb; Trs Jr Cls; Stu Cncl; JV Var Bsktbl; Prom Committe 86; Speech Pathology.

JANSSEN, CHRISTINE A; St Francis Prep; Elmhurst, NY; (Y); Computer Clb; Hosp Aide; Var Tennis; Rgnts Nrsg Schlrshp 86; SUNY Oneonta; Engl.

JANTZI, LARRY; Panama Central HS; Panama, NY; (Y); 30/65; Church Yth Grp; Pep Clb; Pres Spanish Clb; Varsity Clb; Rep Sr Cls; VP Stu Cncl; Coach Actv; Ftbl; Capt Ice Hcky; Capt Wrstlng; Alfred ST; Agri Bus.

JANUARY, ANNE J; Pleasantville HS; Pleasantville, NY; (Y); 6/110; AFS; Church Yth Grp; Pres Intnl Clb; Science Clb; Band; Mrchg Band; School Musical; VP Jr Cls; VP Sr Cls; Var Socr; Ciba-Geigy H S Sci Awd 86; Hghst Avg Math 12 X 85.

JANUCHOWSKI, DENNIS; Grand Island SR HS; Grand Island, NY; (Y); 41/320; Mathletes; ROTC; Ski Clb; Band; Concert Band; Mrchg Band; Masonic Awd; Var L Tennis; Naval Rsrv Off Trnng Corp 4 Yr Schlrsp 86-87; Stephen H Jamieson Mem Schlrshp 86-87; U Of Rochester; Pre-Law.

JANULEWICZ, MARK; Maryvale HS; Cheektowaga, NY; (Y); Chorus; Ftbl; Trk; NHS; Canisuis; Acctng.

JAQUAYS, COLIN P; Mohawk Central HS; Mohawk, NY; (Y); 20/95; Am Leg Boys St; Math Tm; Var Bowling; NHS; Am Lg Schl Awd 86; Bnai Brith Comm Svc Awd 86; Regent Schlrshp 86; Utica Coll Syracuse; Astrophysc.

JAQUEWAY, DEBORAH; Schoharie Central Schl; Schoharie, NY; (S); 5/102; Church Yth Grp; Key Clb; Latin Clb; Ski Clb; Trs Varsity Clb; Band; Chorus; Church Choir; Mrchg Band; School Musical; Medcn.

JAQUISH, MARY; Moriah Central Schl; Moriah, NY; (Y); 4-H; GAA; Co-Capt Cheerleading; Gym; High Hon Roll; Hon Roll; Clinton CC; Bus.

JARCZYK, WENDY; West Seneca East SR HS; Buffalo, NY; (Y); 68/350; Rep Frsh Cls; Rep Soph Cls; Rep Jr Cls; Trs Stu Cncl; Mrt Schlrshp 86; Trocaire; Bus Fld.

JARMAN, MARTIN W; Locust Valley HS; Bayville, NY; (Y); Am Leg Boys St; Var Bsbl; Var Bsktbl; JV Ftbl; Pre Law.

JAROKER, JON; Susan E Wagner HS; Staten Island, NY; (Y); 4/573; Chess Clb; Computer Clb; Math Clb; Math Tm; Office Aide; Science Clb; Teachers Aide; Nwsp Rptr; Nwsp Stf; Lit Mag; Mbr Columbia U Sci Hnrs Proj 85-86; Princeton U; Engrng.

JAROSH, NADJA; Saratoga Central Catholic HS; Saratoga Springs, NY; (S); 1/40; School Play; Yrbk Stf; Rep Frsh Cls; Sec Jr Cls; Sec Stu Cncl; Cheerleading; Sftbl; Vllybl; High Hon Roll; Jr NHS; Engl, Math Awd 84; Skidmore Acad Achvt Awd 85; Bus Mgmnt.

JAROSZ, BILL; Lansingburgh HS; Troy, NY; (Y); Boy Scts; Church Yth Grp; 4-H; Bsbl; Bsktbl; Crs Cntry; Trk; 4-H Awd; God Cntry Awd; NHS; Daemen Coll; Physcl Thrpy.

JAROSZ, JENNIFER A; Trott Vocational HS; Niagara Falls, NY; (Y); 6/147; JA; Stage Crew; VP Jr Cls; VP Stu Cncl; Sftbl; Vllybl; Hon Roll; NHS; Rgnts Schlrshp 86; Dstngshd Stu Schlrshp Niagara CC 86; Niagara CC; Elec Tech.

JAROSZ, WILLIAM; Lansingburgh HS; Troy, NY; (Y); Boy Scts; Church Yth Grp; 4-H; Bsbl; Bsktbl; Crs Cntry; Trk; 4-H Awd; God Cntry Awd; High Hon Roll; Daemen; Physcl Therapy.

JARRETT, GERI; Nebutuck Central HS; Millerton, NY; (Y); 15/42; Am Leg Aux Girls St; Quiz Bowl; Chorus; Madrigals; School Play; Rep Jr Cls; Rep Sr Cls; JV Var Bsktbl; Var Cheerleading; Var Fld Hcky; Coach Watkins Awd 85; Hawthorne Coll NH; Aeronctcs.

JARRETT, JEFFREY; Mynderse Acad; Seneca Falls, NY; (Y); 6/138; Am Leg Boys St; Boy Scts; Science Clb; Band; Concert Band; Jazz Band; Mrchg Band; Var L Crs Cntry; Var L Trk; High Hon Roll; Regents Schlrshp 86; N Amer Philips Schlrshp 86; Yorkers Clb Pres 85-86; Suny Genesco.

JARUSZEWSKI, ANTOINETTE; Depew HS; Depew, NY; (Y); Trs French Clb; GAA; Color Guard; Var Bowling; Hon Roll; Jr NHS; NHS; Cosmtlgy.

JARVIS, DENNIS; Norwood-Norfolk Central HS; Norwood, NY; (Y); Boy Scts; Church Yth Grp; Computer Clb; French Clb; SADD; Chorus; Nwsp Sprt Ed; Nwsp Stf; Rep Soph Cls; Im Bsbl; MVP Massena Hcky Tourn Mnr Hcky 82; Babe Ruth Bsbl All Strs Tm 82-83; ATC; Data Proc.

JARVIS, ERNESTO; Art & Design HS; Brooklyn, NY; (Y); Boys Clb Am; Boy Scts; Church Yth Grp; Debate Tm; Library Aide; Quiz Bowl; Service Clb; Band; Chorus; Church Choir; Math & Art Hnr Rll 85; Sci Hnr Rll 85; Socl Stu Hnr Rll 86; Arch.

JARVIS, LOUIS; Hilton Central HS; Hilton, NY; (Y); 83/300; Yrbk Phtg; Ftbl; Trk; High Hon Roll; Hon Roll; Pres Schlr; Stu Exc In Prntng 86.

JARVIS, STEVEN; Northville Central HS; Northville, NY; (Y); 8/45; Am Leg Boys St; Boy Scts; Jazz Band; School Musical; School Play; Yrbk Stf; Stu Cncl; Bsbl; Bsktbl; DAR Awd; Regents Schrlshp 86; SR Ldrshp Awd 86; Eagle Sct 86; St Bonaventure; Bus.

JARZABEK, PAUL; Bishop Scully HS; Amsterdam, NY; (S); 5/65; JA; Math Clb; Mu Alp Tht; NHS; Spcl Awd US Svngs Bnd 81; Catechst Tchr-Cert Svc 82; Smmr Excllnc Crs FMCC 85; Bio-Chem.

JASINSKI, DEBORAH; West Seneca East SR HS; Buffalo, NY; (Y); Church Yth Grp; DECA; 4-H; German Clb; Hon Roll; NHS; Nalt Germ Hnr Soc; St John Fisher Clg; Comm.

JASINSKI, ROBERT; West Seneca East SR HS; Cheektowaga, NY; (Y); DECA; Spanish Clb; Im JV Ftbl; U Of Buffalo; Comp Pgmmr.

JASS, KENNETH P; Pleasantville HS; Pleasantville, NY; (Y); 44/112; CAP; FBLA; Keywanettes; Letterman Clb; Model UN; Q&S; Soroptimist; Thesps; School Play; Stage Crew.

JASSY, ANDREW R; Scarsdale HS; Scarsdale, NY; (Y); Pres Radio Clb; Varsity Clb; VP Socr; Var Capt Tennis; NHS; Pres Schl Radio Sta 85-86; Presdntl Clsrm 86; NYS Regents Scholar; Harvard Coll; Pre-Law.

JASTRAB, DAVID; Whitesboro HS; Whitesboro, NY; (Y); 5/350; Aud/Vis; NHS; William S Barnes Frosh Awd 86-87; SUNY; Comm.

JASTREMSKI, KIMBERLY; Fayetteville Manlius HS; Chittenango, NY; (Y); 20/332; Model UN; VP Thesps; Chorus; School Musical; School Play; Swing Chorus; Variety Show; Lit Mag; High Hon Roll; Sec NHS; Fayeteville Manlius Dollars Schlrs Scholar 86; Mt Holyoke Coll; Russn.

JAVED, ZARQA; Eastport HS; Eastport, NY; (Y); 2/47; AFS; Am Leg Aux Girls St; Trs Soph Cls; Trs Jr Cls; Bausch & Lomb Sci Awd; High Hon Roll; NHS; Prfct Atten Awd; Rotary Awd; Sal; SUNY Stony Brook.

JAWORSKI, PATRICIA; Mc Kinley HS; Buffalo, NY; (Y); 3/216; Debate Tm; Rptr FFA; JA; Ski Clb; Nwsp Rptr; Rep Stu Cncl; Tennis; Hon Roll; NHS; Pres Acadmc Fitnss Awd 86; Aldo Leopold Ecolgy Awd 86; Regents Schlrshp 86; Cornell U; Natrl Resrcs.

JAWORSKI, PETER; Germantown Central HS; Ancram, NY; (S); 2/40; Radio Clb; Varsity Clb; Band; Chorus; Concert Band; Jazz Band; JV Bsbl; JV Bsktbl; Var L Socr; JV Vllybl; Elec Engr.

JAWORSKI, SCOTT M; Westhill HS; Syracuse, NY; (Y); Art Clb; Exploring; Ftbl; Trk; Hon Roll; Alfred ST Coll; Elec Engr.

JAY, JEFFREY A; Cicero N Syracuse HS; Clay, NY; (Y); 125/667; Key Clb; Ski Clb; Lit Mag; Stu Cncl; JV Ftbl; NYS Regnts Schlrshp 86; St Bonaventure; Mass Comms.

JAYNE, AMY L; Union Springs JR SR HS; Auburn, NY; (Y); 4-H; German Clb; Hosp Aide; Leo Clb; PAVAS; ROTC; Stage Crew; Yrbk Stf; 4-H Awd; NYS Rgnts Schlrshp 86; Loyola U New Orleans; Elem Educ.

JAYNE, LORA E; Dundee Central Schl; Dundee, NY; (Y); 11/73; FNA; Varsity Clb; Yrbk Stf; Pres Jr Cls; Sec Sr Cls; Socr; Trk; Vllybl; High Hon Roll; NHS; Rgnts Schlrshp Nrsng; Hmcmg Qun JR Prm Qun; SUNY Alfred; Med Asst.

JAYNES, TIFFANY; Watkins Glen HS; Watkins Glen, NY; (S); Church Yth Grp; Rep Jr Cls; JV Capt Vllybl; Hon Roll; SUNY Cortland; Erly Chldhd Ed.

JEAN PIERRE, PASCALE S; St Fracis Prep; Laurelton, NY; (Y); 40/653; Mgr Cmnty Wkr; Hosp Aide; Intnl Clb; Library Aide; Science Clb; Service Clb; Color Guard; Concert Band; Nwsp Rptr; Yrbk Stf; Prncpls List Awd 85-86; Ped.

JEAN-BART, DOROTHY; Catherine Mc Auley HS; Brooklyn, NY; (S); 2/70; JA; Yrbk Stf; Badmtn; Vllybl; High Hon Roll; Hon Roll; NHS; Physcl Ftns Awd 83-84; Elem Ed.

JEAN-FELIX, DIANE; St Francis Prep; Laurelton, NY; (S); 162/744; Drama Clb; Service Clb; Band; Chorus; School Musical; School Play; Stage Crew; Wrstlng; Hon Roll; Opt Clb Awd; Sci.

JEAN-JACQUES, NORMA; Maria Regina HS; White Plains, NY; (Y); 10/168; Hosp Aide; NFL; Lit Mag; Hon Roll; NHS; NY Cath Frnsc Lge Fnlst 86; Awd White Plns Hosp Cert Of Apprctn For Vlntr Wk 85; Bio.

JEAN-ROMAIN, DJENO; Nazareth Regional HS; Brooklyn, NY; (S); 9/267; JA; Math Clb; Teachers Aide; Concert Band; Var Socr; High Hon Roll; Hon Roll; NHS; Gen Mdl Achvt Schlrshp, Mdl Achvt Phy Sci 83; Mdl Achvt Bio, Spnsh II 84; Mdl Achvt Chem, MIP Scr; Elec Engrng.

JEANBAPTISTE, RIGAL; Eramus Hall HS; Brooklyn, NY; (Y); 9/455; Church Yth Grp; Trs Math Clb; Math Tm; Science Clb; Orch; Sec Sr Cls; Erasmus Hall Fndtn Schlrshp-Orchestra 86; Chem Tchrs Clb 86; Brnze Mdl Math-Fleur De Lys Awd 86; CT Coll; Med.

JEDLICKA, PAUL J; Greece Athena HS; Rochester, NY; (Y); 1/264; Varsity Clb; Var Tennis; Bausch & Lomb Sci Awd; High Hon Roll; Hon Roll; NHS; Val; Spanish Clb; Phi Beta Kappa Outstndng Sr Schlr Awd 86; Ogden Bio Schlrshp Comptn Wnnr 86; J C Wilson Schlrshp 86; U Of Rochester; Med.

JEDREICICH, STEVE; St Johns Prep; Woodside, NY; (Y); 27/478; Am Leg Boys St; Church Yth Grp; Concert Band; Jazz Band; Hon Roll; Jr NHS; NHS; 4 Yr Full St Johns Prep Scholar 82-86; Regents Scholar 86; NYIT Hnr & Chllnge Scholar 86; NY Inst Tech; Archit.

JEDRICH, CHRISTOPHER J B; South Lewis JR SR HS; Constableville, NY; (Y); Varsity Clb; Capt L Bsktbl; Capt L Golf; Hon Roll; VP NHS; Leag All Star Glf 85; Regents Schlrshp 85-86; Drexel U; Arch Engrng.

JEFFE, LUCINDA A; Hamburg SR HS; Hamburg, NY; (Y); 44/390; Sec AFS; VP Church Yth Grp; FTA; Color Guard; Madrigals; Orch; School Musical; NHS; Chorus; Church Choir; Regents Schlrshp 86; Allegheny Coll; Ed.

JEFFER, TIM; Corning-Painted Post West HS; Painted Post, NY; (Y); 47/256; Key Clb; JV Bsbl; JV Bsktbl; JV Ftbl; High Hon Roll; Hon Roll; Ntl Merit Ltr; Pres Schlr; U SC; Mechcl Engr.

JEFFERSON, DENISE; Patchogue-Medford HS; Medford, NY; (Y); 13/650; Leo Clb; Scholastic Bowl; SADD; Pres Frsh Cls; Sec Pres Stu Cncl; Mgr Tennis; Kiwanis Awd; NHS; Ntl Merit SF; Spanish NHS; Hugh O Brian Yth Ldrshp Pgm; Hmcmg Qn; Century III Ldr Cert Of Merit; Soc Sci.

JEFFERSON, JAMES; Springfield Gardens HS; Queens, NY; (Y); 53/440; Boy Scts; Church Yth Grp; Computer Clb; Band; VP Soph Cls; VP Stu Cncl; Bowling; Tennis; Hon Roll; Elec Engrng.

JEFFERSON, ROKEL; St Joseph HS; Brooklyn, NY; (Y); Chorus; School Musical; Gym; Hon Roll; Comp Sci.

JEFFERY, JENNIFER; Brasher Falls Central HS; Brasher Falls, NY; (Y); 3/101; Aud/Vis; French Clb; Nwsp Stf; Yrbk Phtg; Stu Cncl; Swmmng; High Hon Roll; NHS; Ntl Merit Ltr; Pres Schlr; NYS Regents Schlrp 86; SUNY Geneseo; Envrnmntl Sci.

JEFFORDS, ANDREA; Niagara Catholic HS; Niagara Fls, NY; (Y); Church Yth Grp; Dance Clb; Hosp Aide; JA; Key Clb; Yrbk Stf; Sec VP Stu Cncl; JV Cheerleading; Hon Roll; Awd Jr Vlntr 83-84; Athltc Awd Chrldg 84-85; Robert Rougeaux Meml Schlrshp Fund 84; Comm.

JEFFORDS, MARCIA; Niagara Falls HS; Niagara Falls, NY; (Y); 50/250; Church Yth Grp; Dance Clb; Hosp Aide; Key Clb; Spanish Clb; Cheerleading; Ntl Merit SF; Pres Schlr; Niagara U; Comp Sci.

JEFFREY, RANDAL; Midwood HS; Brooklyn, NY; (Y); 6/667; Sec Chess Clb; Capt Math Tm; Quiz Bowl; Orch; Lit Mag; Rensselaer Mdl 86; Scientist.

JEFFRIES, JENNIFER; Maryvale HS; Cheektowaga, NY; (Y); French Clb; Varsity Clb; Chorus; Stu Cncl; Var Capt Cheerleading; Var JV Socr; Var Trk; Hon Roll; Jr NHS; NHS; U Of Buffalo.

JEMETZ, BOHDAN; West Genesee SR HS; Warners, NY; (Y); 36/450; Im Socr; High Hon Roll; NHS; German Clb; Quiz Bowl; NYS Regnts Schlrshp 85; Outstndng Stdnt Forgn Lang 85; Syracuse U; Elctrcl Engrng.

JEMISON, LASHAWN; Yonkers HS; Yonkers, NY; (Y); SADD; Chorus; Yrbk Stf; Soc Studies Achvt Awd 85; Englsh Achvt Awd 85; Acctnt.

JENICK, DAVID; Archbishop Stepinac HS; Yonkers, NY; (Y); 62/174; Soph Cls; Rep Jr Cls; Var Ftbl; JV Socr; JV Trk; Elctrcl Engr.

JENKINS, CHRISTOPHER; Turner Carroll HS; Buffalo, NY; (S); 26/101; VP Drama Clb; PAVAS; School Musical; Nwsp Ed-Chief; Cheerleading; Capt Tennis; Vllybl; Hon Roll; NHS; Regents Schlrshp 86; Buffalo ST Clg; Theatre.

JENKINS, DANIEL; Altmor-Parish-Williamstown HS; Parish, NY; (Y); Boy Scts; Concert Band; Jazz Band; Mrchg Band; Pep Band; Golf; High Hon Roll; Hon Roll; NHS; NYS Regents Schrlshp 86; SUNY; Acctnt.

JENKINS, JAMES; Fairport HS; Columbia, MD; (Y); 15/650; Var Im Bsktbl; Var L Lcrss; High Hon Roll; Regents Schlrshp 86; Bucknell U; Elec Engrng.

JENKINS, JASON; Mc Quaid Jesuit HS; Fairport, NY; (Y); Varsity Clb; Var Capt Ftbl; Wt Lftg; Sec V AAA Champ Game Outstndng Offc 85.

JENKINS, KELLY; J A Coleman-Kingston HS; Bearsville, NY; (Y); French Clb; Eng Hnrs 85-86; Bus.

JENKINS, MARY A; Dover JR SR HS; Dover Plains, NY; (S); Color Guard; Drm & Bgl; Mrchg Band; Rep Stu Cncl; JV Sftbl; JV Vllybl; Hon Roll; Spnsh I 90 Avg 3 Out Of 4 Qtrs Yr 83-84; Navy.

JENKINS, MICHAEL D; Maple Hill HS; Castleton, NY; (Y); Boy Scts; Debate Tm; French Clb; Math Tm; Jazz Band; Var L Socr; Var L Trk; Hon Roll; NHS; Aud/Vis; Empire STSCHLRSHP Excellence 86; Dartmarth Coll; Math.

JENKINS, SAUNDRA; Uniondale HS; Uniondale, NY; (Y); Dance Clb; Office Aide; Band; Orch; Pres Sr Cls; Var Cheerleading; High Hon Roll; Hon Roll; PA ST; Bus.

JENKS, JOANNE; Colton-Pierrepont Central HS; Colton, NY; (S); 2/22; 4-H; French Clb; Yrbk Phtg; Yrbk Stf; Var JV Sftbl; Var JV Vllybl; High Hon Roll; Hon Roll; Jr NHS; NHS; Hghst Avg 83; NYS H S Art Awd 84; Potsolam Coll; Art Ed.

JENKS, JONATHAN; North Spencer Christian Acad; West Danby, NY; (S); 1/3; Church Yth Grp; Band; Chorus; Church Choir; Yrbk Stf; Pres Frsh Cls; Trs Soph Cls; Trs Jr Cls; Var L Bsktbl; Var Crs Cntry; Boostr Clb 83-86; Sec Ed.

JENNIFER, ZORN; Frontier Central HS; Hamburg, NY; (Y); German Clb; Band; Concert Band; Mrchg Band; Socr; Tennis; Hon Roll; Mrn Bio.

JENNINGS, CHARLES; Eastchester HS; Eastchester, NY; (Y); Rep Frsh Cls; Rep Soph Cls; Pres Jr Cls; Pres Sr Cls; Capt Socr; Var Trk; Vllybl; Hon Roll; NHS; Spanish NHS; Lat Clb Slvr Maxima Cum Laude Lat Natl Cont 85-86; Empire ST Games Vllybl 86.

JENNINGS, JAMES; Broadalbin Central HS; Broadalbin, NY; (Y); Boys Clb Am; Boy Scts; Church Yth Grp; High Hon Roll; Hon Roll; Prfct Atten Awd; Hudson Valley CC; Mchncs.

JENNINGS, MELISSA; Cicero-North Syracuse HS; Brewerton, NY; (S); 73/667; DECA; Political Wkr; Hon Roll; NHS; Oswego ST; Mrktng.

JENNINGS, REBECCA RANIA; Riverhead SR HS; Riverhead, NY; (Y); Pres Church Yth Grp; French Clb; Chorus; Church Choir; Variety Show; Hon Roll; VP Of Riverhead HS Tlnt Srch 84; Sec Of Tlnt Srch 83; Rcvd Hnrb Mntn Awd In Martin Luther King 85; Boston U; Philosophy.

JENNINGS, SHARON ANDREA; Harry S Truman HS; Cambria Heights, NY; (Y); 5/600; Dance Clb; Debate Tm; Hosp Aide; JA; Teachers Aide; Chorus; Yrbk Ed-Chief; Yrbk Stf; Rep Frsh Cls; Rep Stu Cncl; Arista 86; Natl Sci Awd 84; Mathematics.

JENNINGS, THERESA; Villa Maria Acad; Buffalo, NY; (S); 17/90; Church Yth Grp; FBLA; Church Choir; Yrbk Stf; Rep Frsh Cls; Stu Cncl; Swmmng; Hon Roll; Prfct Atten Awd; Crmnl Just.

JENSEN, BARBARA; The Wheatley Schl; East Williston, NY; (Y); Am Leg Aux Girls St; Girl Scts; Math Clb; Concert Band; Orch; Stu Cncl; Socr; Sftbl; Trk; Bd Dir Cty Teenage Newspaper 86; Engrng.

JENSEN, DAREN T; Penn Yan Acad; Penn Yan, NY; (Y); Am Leg Boys St; 4-H; FFA; JV Var Ftbl; Ag.

JENSEN, DAVID; Smithtown H S East; Smithtown, NY; (Y); Boy Scts; Church Yth Grp; Concert Band; Mrchg Band; Nwsp Phtg; Nwsp Rptr; Nwsp Stf; Vet Sci.

JENSEN, DEBORAH L; Shoreham-Wading River HS; Shoreham, NY; (Y); 1/180; Ski Clb; SADD; Chorus; Orch; School Musical; School Play; Yrbk Sprt Ed; Var Capt Fld Hcky; NHS; Ntl Merit Ltr; Fld Hockey Tm MVP & All-Cnty Hnrb Mntn Plyr 84-85; Faculty Schlrshp-Emory U 86; Emory U; Pre-Med.

JENSEN, JULIE; Northville HS; Northville, NY; (Y); 2/51; Am Leg Aux Girls St; Library Aide; Red Cross Aide; Yrbk Ed-Chief; Cheerleading; Socr; High Hon Roll; NHS; Rdng Club Sec; WGY Xmas Wish; Bio Engr.

JENSEN, SUSAN; Colonie Central HS; Albany, NY; (Y); 90/462; Cmnty Wkr; Intnl Clb; JA; Office Aide; Red Cross Aide; SADD; Yrbk Stf; High Hon Roll; Hon Roll; Prfct Atten Awd.

JENSON, MARK; Greenville Central Schl; Greenville, NY; (Y); 6/76; Boy Scts; Im Crs Cntry; Im Trk; Hon Roll; NHS; Cert Merit Schltc Achvt 84; Athltc Awd 85; Cert Recog Scholar 86; Comp Sci.

JEONG, DANNY; West Hempstead HS; West Hempstead, NY; (Y); Bsktbl; Hon Roll; St Johns U; Bus Mgmt.

JERABEK, JEFFREY J; Lackawanna SR HS; Lackawanna, NY; (Y); 4/250; Am Leg Boys St; ROTC; Varsity Clb; Rep Stu Cncl; JV Var Bsbl; Var Bowling; Var Tennis; Var Vllybl; High Hon Roll; Hon Roll; Air Frc ROTC, Plsbry, & Rgnts Schlrshps; Rchstr Inst Tech; Electrcl Engr.

JEREZ, IVAN; St Agnes HS; Corona, NY; (Y); 15/111; Im Bsktbl; Im Ftbl; Hon Roll; NHS; Prfct Atten Awd; Embry Riddle; Avtn.

JERGE, JEANNE M; Grand Island SR HS; Grand Island, NY; (Y); 60/320; Girl Scts; Ski Clb; Trs Chorus; Sec Madrigals; School Musical; Stu Cncl; Bowling; CC Awd; Hon Roll; NHS; Rgnts Schlrshp 86; Niagara U; Htl Mgt.

JERMAN, JOHN; Mount Vernon HS; Mount Vernon, NY; (Y); 4/550; Chess Clb; Yrbk Stf; Off Soph Cls; High Hon Roll; NHS; Stu Mnth Latin,Sco Studies,Bio 83-84; Acad Awd 86; Womens Welfare Clb Awd 86; Yale U; Law.

JERMYN, SCOTT; Gates-Chili SR HS; Rochester, NY; (Y); 50/460; Boy Scts; Chess Clb; Ski Clb; Spanish Clb; Off Frsh Cls; Stu Cncl; Bsbl; Ftbl; High Hon Roll; NHS; U Of Rochester; Pre-Med.

JEROSE, CAROLYN; Onondaga HS; Nedrow, NY; (S); 3/100; Sec 4-H; Sec Spanish Clb; SADD; Varsity Clb; Band; Chorus; Var Socr; Var Sftbl; Var Vllybl; High Hon Roll.

JERRY, RHONDA; Saranac Central HS; Cadyville, NY; (S); 6/113; 4-H; SADD; Yrbk Stf; VP Soph Cls; VP Jr Cls; VP Sr Cls; Stu Cncl; Bsktbl; Socr; Sftbl; Meritorous Awd/Svng Child Life; NYS Amer Hmng Queen Pgnt; Siena; Bio.

JESKE, ANNETTE; Avon Central HS; Avon, NY; (Y); French Clb; Radio Clb; Yrbk Stf; Sftbl; High Hon Roll; Jr NHS; NHS; Gym; Acctg.

JESMER, ROBERT; Jordan-Elbridge SR HS; Jordan, NY; (Y); Var Bsbl; Hon Roll; Bus Mgmt.

JESMER, SHARON; Cicero-North Syracuse HS; N Syracuse, NY; (S); 13/623; Mathletes; Band; Concert Band; Mrchg Band; Symp Band; Jr NHS.

JETT, ROBERT; Stissing Mountain HS; Stanfordville, NY; (Y); Aud/Vis; Boy Scts; Dance Clb; PAVAS; Science Clb; SADD; Band; Yrbk Stf; Bsktbl; Ftbl; US Martines; Arch.

JETTE, LESLIE; Nardin Acad; W Seneca, NY; (Y); 19/85; Model UN; Ski Clb; Orch; Nwsp Rptr; Nwsp Stf; Lit Mag; Sftbl; Vllybl; Hon Roll; NHS; Eng III Hnrs; Outstndng Achvt Bio; Exclnt Amer Coll Musicians Paino Hobbyist; Bio.

JEUDY, FARAH; Sheepshead Bay HS; Brooklyn, NY; (Y); Intnl Clb; Library Aide; Service Clb; Spanish Clb; Teachers Aide; Concert Band; Orch; School Play; Cit Awd; Hon Roll; Cert Of Merit Pan Am Soc 84; Cert Of Serv Trnsit Authrty 85; Awd Of Merit 86; Brooklyn College; Sec Sci.

JEW, KERRI; Sanford H Calhoun HS; Merrick, NY; (Y); 3/313; Cmnty Wkr; Hosp Aide; Science Clb; Rep Sr Cls; VP Stu Cncl; Tennis; NHS; Drama Clb; JA; Key Clb; Amer Pstl Wrkrs Un, Host Comm Svc Awd Schlrshps, Dakin Chem Awd 86; Cornell U; Pre Med.

JEWETT, GREGORY; Solvay HS; Solvay, NY; (Y); Church Yth Grp; French Clb; Yrbk Stf; Off Soph Cls; Off Jr Cls; Stu Cncl; JV Bsktbl; Var Trk; High Hon Roll; NHS; Sci Awd 84; Culture Awd 85; Am Hist Awd 86; Law.

JEZICK, JEANETTE; Sachem HS; Holtsville, NY; (Y); 175/1380; Cmnty Wkr; Dance Clb; Drama Clb; Science Clb; School Musical; Lit Mag; Hon Roll; Camera Clb; Church Yth Grp; PAVAS; Joe Mascolo Mem Schlrshp 86; 15 Yr Dance Awd 86; Pres Acadmc Achvmnt Awd 86; Radford U; Librl Arts.

JHUN, JEANNIE; G Ray Bodley HS; Fulton, NY; (Y); Exploring; French Clb; Science Clb; High Hon Roll; Trs NHS; Police Benevolent Awd 84-85; Frontiers Sci Pgm 86-87; Bio.

JIGGETTS, SABRINA; De Witt Clinton HS; Bronx, NY; (Y); VP Boys Clb Am; Hosp Aide; VP Key Clb; Math Tm; Chorus; Nwsp Rptr; Hon Roll; Prfct Atten Awd; Arista Hnr Socty Treas & Pres 83-87; Pinkerton Achvt Awd Ed 85; Yng Womn Yr 85; Cornell; Pre-Med.

JIMENEZ, DAVID; St Francis Prep; Brooklyn, NY; (S); 105/693; Church Yth Grp; Cmnty Wkr; Band; Concert Band; Jazz Band; NHS; Opt Clb Awd; Acdmc All Amer 85; Ntl Hspnc Awds Prgm 86; Stny Brook; Med.

JIMENEZ, JOSEPH A; Arcbishop Molloy HS; Kew Gardens Hills, NY; (Y); 103/383; Trs Church Yth Grp; French Clb; Hosp Aide; Pep Clb; Chorus; Rep Jr Cls; Crs Cntry; Trk; Psychtry.

JIMENEZ, MARTIN; All Hallows Inst; New York, NY; (S); 1/90; Chess Clb; Drama Clb; Math Clb; Yrbk Ed-Chief; Stu Cncl; Var Bowling; High Hon Roll; NHS; Val; All Amer Schlr 85; Mech Engrg.

JINKS, ROBERT; Gloversville HS; Gloversvl, NY; (Y); French Clb; Concert Band; Yrbk Stf; Rep Frsh Cls; Rep Soph Cls; Rep Jr Cls; Rep Sr Cls; Pres Stu Cncl; Var Crs Cntry; High Hon Roll; Bio-Med Elec Engr.

JIRANEK, KATHRYN M; Miller Place HS; Miller Pl, NY; (Y); 40/196; Church Yth Grp; Drama Clb; FBLA; Thesps; VICA; School Musical; School Play; Yrbk Stf; High Hon Roll; Hon Roll; BOCES Cert Of Commendation 85-86; Math High Hons Level 3 84-85; Bryant Coll; Accounting.

JISHL, REEM; Jamesville De Witt HS; Fayetteville, NY; (Y); 9/243; Cmnty Wkr; Band; Orch; Trs Soph Cls; Pres Jr Cls; Var JV Socr; Var L Trk; NHS; German Clb; Chorus; Ldrshp, Svc & Phy Ed Awds; Teacher.

JIVRAJ, HANIFMOHAMED; Forest Hills HS; Elmont, NY; (Y); Boy Scts; Office Aide; Teachers Aide; Wt Lftg; Hon Roll; Prfct Atten Awd; Rgnts Schlrshp 86; Mosque Vlntr 80dbtng Tm 82.

JOACHIM, FARAHNAZ; Nazareth Regional HS; Brooklyn, NY; (Y); Math Tm; Concert Band; Jazz Band; Var Bsktbl; Var Crs Cntry; JV Var Sftbl; Var Trk; Hon Roll; NHS; Achvmnt Awd Eng 84-85.

JOACHIM, JUNIE; Holy Trinity HS; Hempstead, NY; (S); Math Clb; Math Tm; SADD; Yrbk Stf; JV Vllybl; Hon Roll.

JOBE, SHONIA; Curtis HS; Staten Island, NY; (Y); Drama Clb; School Play; JV Sftbl; JV Trk; Var Vllybl; Hon Roll; Bus Educ Awd 86; Data Proc Awd 86; Attndnc Awd; Norfolk ST U; Bus Mgmt.

JOBMANN, KARL; Union-Endicott HS; Endicott, NY; (Y); Computer Clb; Exploring; Broome CC; Comp Sci.

JOCELYN, CARINE; Elmont Memorial HS; Elmont, NY; (Y); 67/244; Sec FBLA; FNA; Spanish Clb; SADD; VICA; Chorus; Stu Cncl; Cheerleading; Frgn Lang Hnr Soc Awd 84; Acadmc Merit Schlrshp Long Islnd U 86; Lng Islnd U; Hosp Hlth-Care Adm.

JOE, DENNIS; Far Rockaway HS; Far Rockaway, NY; (Y); 2/338; Math Tm; L Var Bowling; Gov Hon Prg Awd; High Hon Roll; NHS; Pres Schlr; Sal; Key Clb; Sec Ftbl; Queens Coll Pres Awd Achvt 83 & 85-86; Anita Dalberg Outstndng Schlr Awd 86; Chancllrs Roll Hnr 86; Polytech U; Mechncl Engrng.

JOELL, DAWN; Alexander Hamilton HS; White Plains, NY; (Y); 7/53; Church Yth Grp; Intnl Clb; Key Clb; Flag Corp; Yrbk Stf; Stat Bsktbl; Stat Trk; Cit Awd; Hon Roll; Pres Schlr; Patrick A Digilio Mem Schlrshp 86; White Plains Stu Aid Soc Inc 86; Var Awds 86; Parsons Schl/Dsgn; Illstrtr.

JOHANEMAN, KELLY; Livingston Manor Central HS; Livingston Manor, NY; (S); 4/47; Drama Clb; Girl Scts; Varsity Clb; Chorus; Yrbk Stf; Sec Jr Cls; Var Capt Bsktbl; Var Socr; Var Capt Sftbl; High Hon Roll; Stu Cncl Achvt Awd 84 & 85; Western Sullivan Lg Awd All Lg; Mth.

JOHANNESSEN, JENNIE; Bishop Maginn HS; Glenmont, NY; (S); Drama Clb; Math Clb; Yrbk Ed-Chief; Trs Jr Cls; Stat Bsbl; High Hon Roll; NCTE Awd; Prom Cmmttee; Fin.

JOHANSEN, PATRICE N; Dominican Commercial HS; Woodhaven, NY; (S); 9/288; Church Yth Grp; Varsity Clb; JV Var Bsktbl; Wt Lftg; NHS; Sienna Clb 83-84; Prncpls List 83-86; Math.

JOHANTGEN, BRET; Wayland Central HS; Perkinsville, NY; (Y); 1/120; German Clb; Math Tm; Ski Clb; Yrbk Stf; Soph Cls; Bsktbl; High Hon Roll; NHS; Secntl Trk Awd 85; Mth Awd 85; Close-Up 86; Sci.

JOHN, ALEXIA; Salamanca Central HS; Salamanca, NY; (Y); DECA; French Clb; FHA; Band; Chorus; Church Choir; Mrchg Band; Pep Band; Score Keeper; Swmmng; Polc Woman.

JOHN, BURTON; Sachem North HS; Farmingville, NY; (Y); 23/1387; French Clb; Letterman Clb; Mathletes; Math Tm; Im JV Ftbl; Im JV Lcrss; JV Var Wt Lftg; JV Wrstlng; NHS; Pres Schlr; Spagnoli Bros Mem Schlrshp Sachem Touchdown Club, Rgnts Schlrshp Wnnr 86; U Miami; Engrng.

JOHN, CEBEY; Adlai E Stevenson HS; Bronx, NY; (Y); Church Yth Grp; Library Aide; Office Aide; Teachers Aide; Band; Mrchg Band; High Hon Roll; Hon Roll; NHS; Val; Achvt Leag Awd 86; Dr Albert G Oliver Cmmnty Svc Awd 86; Psych.

JOHN, DOUGLAS E; Salamanca JR SR HS; Steamburg, NY; (Y); Cmnty Wkr; DECA; Drama Clb; French Clb; Model UN; Ski Clb; Rep Soph Cls; Var L Trk; Hon Roll; Prfct Atten Awd; Recrtnl Mgn.

JOHN, JOLLY; Yonkers HS; Yonkers, NY; (Y); Church Yth Grp; Church Choir; Lit Mag; Hon Roll; Prfct Atten Awd; Pre-Med.

JOHN, PAUL; Yonkers HS; Yonkers, NY; (Y); 4/281; Trs Church Yth Grp; VP Math Clb; Nwsp Rptr; Vllybl; High Hon Roll; NHS; Pres Schlr; Rgnts Schlrshp NYS 86; Manhattan Coll; Elctrc Engr.

JOHN, RENEE; Chitterango HS; Chittenango, NY; (Y); French Clb; SADD; Chorus; Cheerleading; Socr; High Hon Roll; Hon Roll; Jr NHS; NHS; U Of Miami; Marine Bio.

JOHN, SAM; De Witt Clinton HS; Bronx, NY; (Y); 36/300; Art Clb; Debate Tm; FCA; Key Clb; Math Clb; Science Clb; School Musical; Yrbk Rptr; Sec Sr Cls; Capt Bsktbl; Sci Awd 86; Biol Sqd Awd 86; Excllnce Atten Awd 85; NY Inst Tech; Elec Engrng.

JOHN, SUJA; Hererricks HS; New Hyde Prk, NY; (Y); Library Aide; Yrbk Stf; Hon Roll; Prfct Atten Awd.

JOHN, SUSAMMA; Domminican Commercial HS; Jamaica, NY; (Y); Church Yth Grp; Cmnty Wkr; Hosp Aide; Intnl Clb; Office Aide; Teachers Aide; High Hon Roll; Hon Roll; NHS; WA Cngrsnl Wrkshps Schlrshp; Ntl Hstry & Govt Awd; Schlstc Exc Awd.

JOHN, VINOJ A; Wellsville HS; Wellsville, NY; (Y); 25/120; Var Badmtn; Var Socr; Var Trk; Var Vllybl; MIP Sccr; Track 2nd Long Jump; Dfnsve Plyr Yr, Co All Star Sccr; All Cty Hnbl Mntn; NYS Vllybl Champ; Embry Riddle U; Pilot.

JOHN, VINU; Susan E Wagner HS; Staten Island, NY; (Y); Chorus; Bus Mgmt.

JOHNCOX, JULIE; John F Kennedy HS; Utica, NY; (Y); 25/130; Church Yth Grp; SADD; Trs Soph Cls; Stu Cncl; Sftbl; Trk; Hon Roll; Prfct Atten Awd; 1st Rnnr Up Miss Mohwak Vly Teen Pag 85; 2nd Miss Oneida Cnty Teen 84; 2nd Miss Leatherstckng Teen 84; Mohawk Vly CC; Acctng.

JOHNS, ANDREW W; Archbishop Walsh HS; Machias, NY; (Y); 3/56; French Clb; Library Aide; Math Clb; High Hon Roll; Mu Alp Tht; NHS; Ntl Merit SF; NEDT Awd; Sci Awd PSPE 85; Ntl Yth Awd 85; Knghts Of The Alter 82; Elec Engr.

JOHNSN, CHARLES L; Onteora Central HS; Woodstock, NY; (Y); 80/209; VP JA; Library Aide; Office Aide; Regents Schlrshp 86; VP Finance Of Yr 84; Dale Carnegie 83; SUNY; Comp Sci.

JOHNSON, ANDY; Cazenovia Central HS; Cazenovia, NY; (Y); 10/140; Church Yth Grp; French Clb; Orch; Bsbl; Bsktbl; Ftbl; Score Keeper; Trk; High Hon Roll; Hon Roll; All Star Bsktbl; St Johns; Bus.

JOHNSON, ARLENE; Monsignor Scanlan HS; Bronx, NY; (Y); 35/276; Cit Awd; Hon Roll; Intrmdt Algbra 85; Amer Lit 86; Atten 85; Bkkpng.

JOHNSON, BETH; Union-Endicott HS; Endicott, NY; (Y); Church Yth Grp; Debate Tm; Drama Clb; Girl Scts; Key Clb; Library Aide; Mathletes; Pep Clb; Speech Tm; Orch; Cert Awd Binghamton Psychtr Ctr Volntr 85; Pre-Med.

JOHNSON, BETSY; Jamestown HS; Jamestown, NY; (Y); Church Yth Grp; Spanish Clb; SADD; Lib Band; Concert Band; Drm Mjr(t); Mrchg Band; Orch; School Musical; High Hon Roll; Chautauqua Cnty Music Teachers Assoc Summer Schlrshp 86; Suny Fredonia; Snd Recrdng Tech.

JOHNSON, BILL; Bishop Cudden HS; Syracuse, NY; (Y); NHS.

JOHNSON, CAROL; Acad Of Mount Saint Ursula; Bronx, NY; (Y); Art Clb; Computer Clb; Dance Clb; Drama Clb; Hosp Aide; SADD; School Play; Yrbk Phtg; Rep Jr Cls; Rep Stu Cncl; Drama Club Awd For Best Actress 83-84; Phy Ftnss Awd 85-86.

JOHNSON, CATRINA; Mamaroneck HS; Mamaroneck, NY; (Y); Mktng.

JOHNSON, CHADWICK; Hutchinson Central Tech HS; Buffalo, NY; (Y); Ftbl; Trk; Pittsburgh U; Elec.

JOHNSON, CHARLENE; New Rochelle HS; New Rochelle, NY; (Y); 45/550; Teachers Aide; Hon Roll; NHS; Prfct Atten Awd; Spanish NHS; Pres Acad Awd 86; Yng Wmns Lg Schlrp 86; Cornell U; Ind & Lbr Rltns.

JOHNSON, CHERIE; Geneva HS; Geneva, NY; (S); 21/176; French Clb; JV Var Vllybl; Hon Roll; Acad Achvt Awd 83-86; U Of MN.

JOHNSON, CHRISTOPHER; Newark Valley HS; Willseyville, NY; (Y); 26/114; Church Yth Grp; VP Ski Clb; Chorus; Flag Corp; Swing Chorus; Yrbk Rptr; Ed Yrbk Stf; Socr; Trk; Hon Roll; All Star Soccr 85; USAF; Astro Engr.

JOHNSON, CHRISTOPHER W; Scarsdale HS; Scarsdale, NY; (Y); Am Leg Boys St; Rep SADD; Varsity Clb; Rep Frsh Cls; Rep Soph Cls; Rep Jr Cls; Rep Sr Cls; Var Capt Lcrss; Var Socr; Letterman Clb; Georgetown.

JOHNSN, CLAUDINE; Dminican Commercial HS; Brooklyn, NY; (S); 65/288; Drama Clb; Chorus; Church Choir; School Musical; School Play; Yrbk Stf; Rep Frsh Cls; Rep Stu Cncl; Cheerleading; Wt Lftg; Prncpls List; Sienna Club; Natl Bus Hnr Scty; Bus.

JOHNSON, CORRIE J; Southwestern Central HS; Jamestown, NY; (Y); 26/145; Church Yth Grp; German Clb; Chorus; Color Guard; School Musical; Stage Crew; Yrbk Stf; Var Cheerleading; Ntl Merit Ltr; NYS Regnts Schlrshp 86; WV U; Engr.

JOHNSON, CYNDI; Cazenovia Central Schl; Cazenovia, NY; (Y); Drama Clb; Hosp Aide; Chorus; Church Choir; School Musical; Stage Crew; Var Cheerleading; Hon Roll; Hamilton Coll; Soc Wrk.

JOHNSON, CYNTHIA A; Camden Central HS; Westdale, NY; (Y); 17/189; Red Cross Aide; High Hon Roll; Elizabeth Dorrance Englsh Awd 86; Rome Brd Rltrs Schlrshp 86; Eleanor Ischia Mmrl Bus Stu Sch 86; Mohawk Vly Comm Coll; Ex Sec.

JOHNSON, DAHLIA; Midwood HS; Brooklyn, NY; (Y); 125/625; Science Clb; Teachers Aide; School Musical; Cheerleading; Hon Roll; Hampton Inst; Engrg.

JOHNSON III, DAVID E; Sidney HS; Unadilla, NY; (Y); 5/104; Am Leg Boys St; Boys Clb Am; Church Yth Grp; Math Clb; Varsity Clb; Band; Yrbk Phtg; Yrbk Sprt Ed; Rep Stu Cncl; Crs Cntry; Schlrshp Citizens Schlrshp Fndtn Of Amer 86; Schlr Athlete 86; Cornell U; Pre Med.

JOHNSON, DEANNA; Grand Island SR HS; Grand Island, NY; (Y); Hon Roll; Niagara CC; Nrsg.

JOHNSON, DERRICK; Hanau American HS; Jackson, MS; (Y); Capt Bsktbl; Cit Awd; Hon Roll; Jr NHS; Jackson ST U; Bus Adm.

JOHNSON, DONALD; Cardinal Spellman HS; Bronx, NY; (Y); Computer Clb; Sec Debate Tm; NFL; Trs Science Clb; SADD; Ed Nwsp Stf; Im Bsbl; Im Vllybl; Hon Roll; Art Clb; Hendrick Hudson Spch & Debt Clb Awd 85; Voice Of Demcy Commdtn 85; Featrd Edtrl 85; Med.

JOHNSON, EILEEN; Saugerties HS; Saugerties, NY; (Y); 52/250; French Clb; Girl Scts; JA; Math Clb; Math Tm; Ski Clb; Varsity Clb; Band; Variety Show; Powder Puff Ftbl; SUNY Oswego.

JOHNSON, ELAINE; Erasmus Hall HS; New York, NY; (Y); 58/667; Hosp Aide; Concert Band; Orch; Prfct Atten Awd; Cheerleading; Trk; Math Awd 84; Benjamin S Chancey Cittn Of Hon 83; Ntl Hon Soc Awd-Scndry Schls 85; Snd Brdcstg.

JOHNSON, ERIC S; Shenendehowa HS; Bailston Lake, NY; (Y); 72/684; Ski Clb; Band; Concert Band; Jazz Band; Orch; Symp Band; Trk; High Hon Roll; JP Sousa Awd; NHS; Intl Assoc Schlrshp 85; MENC Ntl HS Hnrs Orchstra 86; Prfrmnc Larsson Concertino 86; New England Cnsrvtry; Orchstrl.

JOHNSON, EVA; Maple Hill HS; Castleton On H, NY; (Y); Nwsp Stf; Yrbk Stf; JV Score Keeper; French Clb; Library Aide; Crmnl Jstc.

JOHNSON, GRANT A; Cassadaga Valley Central Schl; Gerry, NY; (Y); Boy Scts; Pres Church Yth Grp; Varsity Clb; Church Choir; Pres Concert Band; School Musical; Trs Soph Cls; Trs Jr Cls; Rep Stu Cncl; JV Var Bsbl; Dfnsve Plyr Yr Bsbl 84; Houghton Coll; Comp Sci.

JOHNSON, GREG; Wayland Central Schl; Wayland, NY; (Y); Rptr FFA; Var Bsbl; Wt Lftg; Var Wrstlng; Mst Outstndng JR Cnsrvtn Cls, Chrls G May FFA 85-86; Good Kid Awd Wylnd Cntrl 85-86; Morrisville; Cnsrvtn.

JOHNSON, JENNIFER; Middleburgh Central HS; Middleburgh, NY; (S); 1/75; Sec 4-H; Office Aide; Quiz Bowl; Teachers Aide; Band; School Play; High Hon Roll; NHS; Church Yth Grp; Val; Dressage, Equitatn Class Rbbns; Halter Driving Draft Horse Cls Rbbns 85; Vet Sci.

JOHNSON, JOANNE; Catholic Central HS; Averill Park, NY; (Y); 19/179; French Clb; Math Clb; Capt Sftbl; French Hon Soc; High Hon Roll; Hon Roll; Leo D Doherty Schlrshp 86; Athl Schlrshp Sftbl 86; Womns Sprts Fndtn All Str Awd 86; Le Moyne Coll.

JOHNSON, JOHNANNE R; Sweet Home SR HS; N Tonawanda, NY; (Y); Church Yth Grp; 4-H; Library Aide; Science Clb; Spanish Clb; Teachers Aide; Nwsp Rptr; Ntl Merit SF; Spanish NHS; Med.

JOHNSON, JUDY; Moriah Central HS; Port Henry, NY; (Y); 15/84; Bsktbl; Socr; Sftbl; High Hon Roll; Hudson Valley CC; Acctng.

JOHNSON, JULIA L; Chittenango Central HS; Chittenango, NY; (Y); 1/174; Church Yth Grp; Nwsp Stf; Yrbk Stf; Bausch & Lomb Sci Awd; NHS; Val; Cmnty Wkr; French Clb; Science Clb; Ski Clb; Outstndng Achvt-Jrnlsm Awd 86; Schl Art Svc Awd 86; Outstndng Achvt Physcs 86; U Of Rochester.

JOHNSON, KAREN; Louis D Brandeis HS; New York, NY; (Y); Church Yth Grp; Office Aide; Service Clb; Teachers Aide; Church Choir; Vllybl; Cit Awd; Hon Roll; Brdcstng.

JOHNSON, KARIN; Saugerties HS; Saugerties, NY; (S); Trs Church Yth Grp; Girl Scts; Key Clb; Library Aide; Spanish Clb; Chorus; Church Choir; School Play; Symp Band; Girl Sct Slvr Awd 84.

JOHNSON, KELLY; Half Hollow Hills HS East; Wheatley Hts, NY; (Y); Varsity Clb; Band; Rep Sr Cls; Stu Cncl; Capt Var Ftbl; Var Trk; Capt Var Wrstlng; Hon Roll.

JOHNSON, KEMPTHORNE; Albany HS; Albany, NY; (Y); 51/576; Pres FBLA; VP JA; VP Church Choir; Var Co-Capt Bsktbl; Hon Roll; Church Yth Grp; Computer Clb; Wt Lftg; U Of Rochstr Schlrshp 86; U Of Rochester; Mchncl Engr.

JOHNSON, KENNETH; Hillcrest HS; Jamaica, NY; (Y); 200/900; Am Leg Boys St; Art Clb; Boys Clb Am; Cmnty Wkr; SADD; Band; Yrbk Phtg; Yrbk Stf; Rep Frsh Cls; Rep Soph Cls; Queens Coll; Comp Sci.

JOHNSON, KIM-MONIQUE; Holy Trinity Diocesan HS; Wyandanch, NY; (S); 6/312; Math Clb; Nwsp Rptr; Co-Capt Yrbk Ed-Chief; Mgr Bsktbl; High Hon Roll; Hon Roll; NHS; NEDT Awd; Psych.

JOHNSON, KRISTINA; Earl L Vandermeulen HS; Mt Sinai, NY; (Y); 100/318; Art Clb; FBLA; Pep Clb; SADD; Rep Stu Cncl; Cheerleading; Var Mgr(s); Hon Roll; Swimming Awd 85; Fairfield; Psych.

JOHNSON, LADY CAROL; James Monroe HS; Bronx, NY; (Y); Drama Clb; Chorus; Church Choir; Variety Show; Nwsp Ed-Chief; Yrbk Stf; Prfct Atten Awd; Cmnty Wkr; Nwsp Rptr; Bronx Borough Pres Citation 86; Schl Svc 85-86; Acad Olympcs 86; Htl Mgmt.

JOHNSON, LIESNER J; Niagara Wheatfield HS; Sanborn, NY; (Y); Boy Scts; Rep Church Yth Grp; JV Socr; Hon Roll; Elctrncs Engr.

JOHNSON, LISA; Byron-Bergen HS; Bergen, NY; (Y); FCA; Band; Color Guard; Trs Sr Cls; Var Cheerleading; Hon Roll; NHS; Faclty Asso Schrlshp 86; Flora Watson Awd 86; Roberts Wesleyan; Bus Adm.

JOHNSON, LISA; Nazareth Regional HS; Brooklyn, NY; (Y); Hosp Aide; SADD; Chorus; Hon Roll; Regents Nrsng Schlrshp 86; Med.

JOHNSON, LYNN; Poughkeepsie HS; Poughkeepsie, NY; (Y); Church Yth Grp; Cmnty Wkr; Drama Clb; Library Aide; Office Aide; Nwsp Ed-Chief; Varsity Clb; Church Choir; JV Bsktbl; Mgr(s); Morgan ST U; Sociology.

JOHNSON, MARK; Southampton HS; Southampton, NY; (Y); 51/115; Cmnty Wkr; School Musical; School Play; Nwsp Rptr; Jr Cls; Stu Cncl; Bsktbl; Cit Awd; Kiwanis Awd; Rotary Awd; Suffolk County Yth Awd 85; All Lg Awd 86; Canisius Coll; Marketing.

JOHNSON, MARK; West Hempstead HS; West Hempstead, NY; (Y); Computer Clb; Mathletes; Quiz Bowl; Radio Clb; Ski Clb; Jazz Band; JV VP Bowling; Trs Chess Clb; Sec German Clb; Band; David Cayton Mem Awd Math 85 & 86; Natl Soc Stds Olym Mdl Eur Hist 85; Hon Mtn Spkr Senat Armd Svcs 86; Rochester Inst Tech; Comp Math.

JOHNSON, MARK D; Johnson City HS; Johnson City, NY; (Y); 3/198; Exploring; Latin Clb; Mathletes; Var L Tennis; High Hon Roll; NHS; Ntl Merit Ltr; Prfct Atten Awd; Acdmc Achvmnt Awd; Olympcs Of Mnd Crtvty Awd; Cornell U; Biolgcl Sci.

JOHNSON, MELANIE; Aquinas HS; Bronx, NY; (Y); 57/170; Computer Clb; French Clb; Girl Scts; Hon Roll; Pace U 86; Svc Awd 86; Pace U; Bus Admin.

JOHNSON, MICHAEL; Corning-Painted Post West HS; Painted Post, NY; (Y); Boy Scts; Key Clb; Ski Clb; Varsity Clb; JV Ftbl; Var Tennis; High Hon Roll; NHS; Amer Legn Gd Ctznshp Citatn 85; Engrng.

JOHNSON, MICHAEL B; Pine Valley HS; Forestville, NY; (Y); Am Leg Boys St; Chorus; Stage Crew; JV Var Bsktbl; JV Bowling; JV Var Ftbl; JV Trk; Outstndng Achvt Awd Auto Repair 86; Engr.

JOHNSON, MICHAEL R; Carle Place HS; Carle Place, NY; (Y); 13/120; AFS; Boy Scts; Quiz Bowl; Nwsp Sprt Ed; Yrbk Stf; JV Ftbl; Hon Roll; Ntl Merit Ltr; Boston U; Engrng.

JOHNSON, MICHELLE A; St Francis Prep; Hollis, NY; (Y); 322/653; Library Aide; Office Aide; Teachers Aide; Var L Trk; Ntl Merit Ltr; Comp Sci.

JOHNSON, MIKE A; Olean SR HS; Olean, NY; (Y); 19/203; Hon Roll; NHS; ST Stdnt Enrgy Rsrch Comptn 5th Pl 85; Alleghny Mtn Engn & Implmt Assoc 84-86; RR Engr.

JOHNSON, NICOLE; Mount Vernon HS; Mt Vernon, NY; (Y); Girl Scts; Intnl Clb; Keywanettes; Library Aide; Office Aide; Church Choir; Tennis; Fisk U; Opthlmgst.

JOHNSON II, OTIS T; Rome Free Acad; Omaha, NE; (Y); Intnl Clb; Var Trk; Jr NHS; NHS; USAF Acad; Comp Pgmmng.

JOHNSON, PATRICIA; Naples Central HS; Naples, NY; (Y); Bsktbl; Socr; Sftbl; High Hon Roll; Amer Ambassador Sccr Tour In Europe 85; All-Star 1st Teams For Sccr & Bsktbl Bsktbl & Sccr Capt 85-86; Wilma Boyd Creer Schl; Fld Trvl.

JOHNSON, PATTY; Jamestown HS; Jamestown, NY; (Y); Church Yth Grp; Hst Acpl Chr; Concert Band; Sec Mrchg Band; Sec Symp Band; Stat Bsktbl; Hon Roll; Jr NHS; NHS; Educ.

JOHNSON, RAE; Allegany Central HS; Allegany, NY; (Y); 12/101; Camp Fr Inc; Church Yth Grp; Hosp Aide; Red Cross Aide; SADD; Band; Concert Band; Mrchg Band; Yrbk Stf; Im Vllybl; Elizabethtown Acdmc & NY ST Regnts & Dresser Clark Employee Benefit Schlrshps 86-87; Elizabethtown Coll; Occptnl Thr.

JOHNSON, REBECCA; Oneonta SR HS; Oneonta, NY; (Y); 7/180; Drama Clb; Ski Clb; Thesps; Varsity Clb; Stage Crew; Yrbk Sprt Ed; Var L Socr; High Hon Roll; NHS; Rotary Awd; Rgnts NYS 86; Rotary Exch Brazil; Intl Stds.

JOHNSON, RUTH; Chenango Valley HS; Binghamton, NY; (Y); Church Yth Grp; FHA; Spanish Clb; Church Choir; Concert Band; Symp Band; Hon Roll; Jr NHS; Philadelphia Coll-Bible; Music.

JOHNSON, SHAWN; Franklin Acad; Burke, NY; (Y); 15/280; Varsity Clb; Concert Band; Var Capt Ftbl; Var Capt Trk; Hon Roll; NHS; Ntl Merit Ltr; Prfct Atten Awd; St Lawrence U; Engrng.

JOHNSON, SHEILA; Marion Central HS; Marion, NY; (Y); 13/93; French Clb; Model UN; Chorus; School Musical; Yrbk Stf; JV Var Tennis; NHS; Ithaca; Acctg.

JOHNSON, SHERI; Unatego JR SR HS; Otego, NY; (Y); 11/106; Drama Clb; French Clb; Ski Clb; Band; Jazz Band; School Musical; High Hon Roll; NHS; Rotary Awd; Rotry Intl Schlrshp Frnc 86; Rep-Hugh O Brien Yth Fndtn ST Ldrshp Semnr 85; Pre-Med.

JOHNSON, SHONDELLA; Lehman HS; Bronx, NY; (Y); Dance Clb; English Clb; Teachers Aide; Chorus; Nwsp Stf; Im Trk; Cit Awd; Hon Roll; Prfct Atten Awd; Earn Coll Credts-Grad & Undrgrad Crses-Jhn Jay Coll Of Crmnl Jstc 85-87; Music.

JOHNSON, SONYA D; Midwood HS; Brooklyn, NY; (Y); 113/589; Pres Church Yth Grp; Debate Tm; Acpl Chr; Chorus; Church Choir; School Musical; Yrbk Stf; Lit Mag; Stu Cncl; Cit Awd; Rgnts Schlrshp 86; Cornell U; Corp Lwyr.

JOHNSON, SUSAN; Nardin Acad; East Amherst, NY; (S); 6/81; AFS; Model UN; Service Clb; Speech Tm; Acpl Chr; Orch; School Musical; Var Socr; Hon Roll; Partl Schlrshp To Nardin Acad 83; 1st Pl Schl Sci Fair 85; Partptd In Sci Congrss Of Western NY 85; Med.

JOHNSON, TAMMI; Albion HS; Kent, NY; (S); Church Yth Grp; Library Aide; Church Choir; Var Crs Cntry; Mgr(s); Capt Var Trk; Var Vllybl; Cit Awd; High Hon Roll; Sheriffs Dept Cert Apprctn 84.

JOHNSON, THERESA; Glens Falls HS; Glen Falls, NY; (Y); 56/208; Dance Clb; Key Clb; Variety Show; Gym; Powder Puff Ftbl; High Hon Roll; Hon Roll; Glens Falls Alumni Schlrshp 86; SUNY-DELHI; Vet Sci.

JOHNSON, TIM; Torrejon American HS; Apo, NY; (Y); Aud/Vis; Boy Scts; Church Yth Grp; Debate Tm; German Clb; Pep Clb; Speech Tm; Im Golf; Im Var Socr; Hon Roll; UCLA; Cnmtgrphy.

JOHNSON, TIMOTHY; Hutchinson Central Tech HS; Buffalo, NY; (Y); Rep Pres Stu Cncl; Var Bsbl; Var L Bowling; High Hon Roll; Hon Roll; NHS; Comp Sci.

JOHNSON, TODD H; Liverpool HS; Liverpool, NY; (Y); 94/816; Boy Scts; VP Church Yth Grp; Exploring; VP JA; Ski Clb; Variety Show; Cit Awd; Hon Roll; Jr NHS; VP NHS; U Of FL-GAINESVILLE; Pre Med.

JOHNSON, TRINA; Erasmus Hall HS; Brooklyn, NY; (Y); 12/626; Chess Clb; Computer Clb; FBLA; Math Clb; Acpl Chr; Chorus; Church Choir; Hon Roll; NHS; Miss Northeastern Yth Conf Church 86; Cornell; Bus.

JOHNSON, VICKI; Gloversville HS; Gloversvl, NY; (Y); Intnl Clb; Pep Clb; SADD; Band; Nwsp Stf; Yrbk Phtg; Yrbk Stf; Rep Frsh Cls; Hon Roll; Drama Clb; Elem Educ.

JOHNSON, VICKI; Oppenheim Ephratah Central Schl; St Johnsville, NY; (S); GAA; Pres Spanish Clb; Bsktbl; Cheerleading; Capt Socr; Sftbl; Capt Vllybl; Hon Roll; Jr NHS; VP Sr Cls; Spnsh Natl Hnr Socty 84; Sci.

JOHNSON, WAYNE; Cicero North Syracuse HS; Syracuse, NY; (S); 90/667; Am Leg Boys St; Var Socr; Hon Roll; NHS; NY ST U; Chem.

JOHNSTON, CHRISTIAN E; Way Land Central HS; Wayland, NY; (Y); Art Clb; Church Yth Grp; Cmnty Wkr; FCA; 4-H; Spanish Clb; JV Bsktbl; Var Crs Cntry; Var Trk; Ntl Merit Schol; Florence Brasser Merit Schlrshp 85-86; Polk CC FL; Comp Sci.

JOHNSTON, CHRISTINE; Charles O Dickerson HS; Trumansburg, NY; (Y); French Clb; SADD; Concert Band; Mrchg Band; Yrbk Bus Mgr; Yrbk Stf; Var L Socr; Var L Vllybl; High Hon Roll; NHS; Psych.

JOHNSTON, CORINNA; Schoharie Central HS; Schoharie, NY; (S); 13/106; Girl Scts; Key Clb; Varsity Clb; Band; Concert Band; Var L Bsktbl; Var L Socr; Var L Vllybl; Hon Roll; Hotel Tech.

JOHNSTON, DALE; Wilson Central HS; Ransomville, NY; (Y); Ski Clb; Band; JV Var Bsbl; JV Var Bsktbl; JV Var Ftbl; Hon Roll; Hotl-Rest Mgmt.

JOHNSTON, DAMIAN P; Arlington North Campus HS; Lagrangeville, NY; (Y); 47/570; Cmnty Wkr; Ftbl; Mgr(s); NHS; St Schlr; Clarkson U; Engr.

JOHNSTON, DAVID; Holy Trinity Diocesan HS; Hicksville, NY; (S); 13/313; Math Clb; Math Tm; Ski Clb; Yrbk Stf; JV Var Lcrss; Trk; JV Wrstlng; High Hon Roll; NHS; Cornell; Biol Sci.

JOHNSTON, HENRY; Cold Springs Harbor HS; Huntington, NY; (Y); School Musical; Lit Mag; Pres Frsh Cls; Pres Soph Cls; Trs Sr Cls; Var Lcrss; Var Socr; Drama Clb; SADD; Chorus; Advanced Plcmnt Latin Achvmnt Awd 86; All Nassan Cnty Chorus 84-86; Achvmnt Cmmnty Peer Ldrshp Prg 86.

JOHNSTON, IAN; Sewanhaka HS; Elmont, NY; (Y); 22/350; Mathletes; Variety Show; Nwsp Sprt Ed; Var L Bsktbl; Var L Ftbl; NHS; Natl Achvt Progrm For Outstndng Negro Stu 85-86; Natl Hispanic Schlr Awds Progrm 85-86; U Of PA; Engrng.

JOHNSTON, KELLY; Niagara Falls HS; Niagara Falls, NY; (S); 6/250; Church Yth Grp; Hosp Aide; Key Clb; Red Cross Aide; SADD; Yrbk Ed-Chief; Yrbk Phtg; Yrbk Sprt Ed; Rep Frsh Cls; Rep Soph Cls; Schlr Athlt Sccr 86; Cornell U; Vet.

JOHNSTON, KIM; Allegany Central HS; Allegany, NY; (Y); 6/100; Debate Tm; Pres Band; Concert Band; Jazz Band; Mrchg Band; Orch; Pep Band; School Musical; School Play; Nwsp Bus Mgr; Syracuse U; Chem.

JOHNSTON, LAURIE; G Ray Bodley HS; Fulton, NY; (Y); Latin Clb; Science Clb; NHS; SUNY Coll Oswego; Pre-Law.

JOHNSTON, ROBERT; Tottenville HS; Staten Island, NY; (Y); 17/871; Jazz Band; Orch; School Musical; Symp Band; High Hon Roll; NHS; NY ST Rgnts Schlrshp 86; John E Schroeder Meml Awd 86; 2nd Pl Music Awd; Manhattan Schl Of Music; Music.

JOHNSTON, RODNEY; Marlboro Central HS; Marlboro, NY; (Y); Church Yth Grp; Varsity Clb; Concert Band; Variety Show; Var L Bsbl; Stat Bsktbl; Var JV Ftbl; Cit Awd; Hon Roll.

JOHNSTON, TERI; Colonie Central HS; Loudonville, NY; (Y); 20/475; Band; JV Cheerleading; High Hon Roll; Hon Roll; Ntl Phys Ed Awd 85-86; Plattsburgh ST.

JOHNSTON, WENDY; Colonie Central HS; Schenectady, NY; (Y); Key Clb; Yrbk Stf; Rep Frsh Cls; Rep Stu Cncl; JV Bsktbl; Score Keeper; JV Var Sftbl; Capt Vllybl; High Hon Roll; Hon Roll; Psychlgy.

JOKHAN, LARRY V; St Francis Prep; Queens Village, NY; (S); 170/725; Math Clb; Band; Concert Band; Jazz Band; Mrchg Band; Im Bowling; Im Sftbl; Music Trophies 83 & 85; Comp Sci.

JOLANE, TORO; John Jay HS; Brooklyn, NY; (Y); De Vry; Comp Pgmr.

JONES, ADRIAN; Buffalo Traditional HS; Buffalo, NY; (S); 10/100; Boys Clb Am; Boy Scts; Church Yth Grp; Debate Tm; 4-H; French Clb; FBLA; Math Clb; Model UN; PAVAS; Ordnd JR Deacon Chrch 85; St Lawrence; Law.

JONES, ADRIENNE; Uniondale HS; Roosevelt, NY; (Y); Church Yth Grp; Civic Clb; Cmnty Wkr; Office Aide; Cheerleading; Trk; Twrlr; Hon Roll; Rep Frsh Cls; Rep Soph Cls; Pres Central Nassau Yth Clb 85-86; Pre-Law.

JONES, ALICIA; Vernon-Verona-Sherrill HS; Sherrill, NY; (Y); Red Cross Aide; Band; Yrbk Stf; Var Bowling; JV Golf; High Hon Roll; NHS; Accntnt.

JONES, ANNE M; Hendrick Hudson HS; Peekskill, NY; (Y); Church Yth Grp; SADD; Crs Cntry; Trk; Vllybl; Foreign Lang.

JONES, BARBARA A; Smithtown West; Smithtown, NY; (Y); Exploring; Spanish Clb; Sec Jr Cls; Sec Sr Cls; High Hon Roll; NHS; VICA; Spanish NHS; Providence Clg; Bus.

JONES, CAROLINE; St Catharine Acad; Bronx, NY; (Y); 79/198; Church Yth Grp; Girl Scts; Chorus; Church Choir; FL A&M U; Soc Wrk.

JONES, CHARI; Schoharie Central HS; Howes Cave, NY; (S); 18/85; Key Clb; Library Aide; Office Aide; SADD; Chorus; Yrbk Stf; Stu Cncl; Teachers Aide; Most Artistc SR 85-86; Siena Coll; Engl.

JONES, CHARLES EDWARD; Brooklyn Technical HS; S Ozone Park, NY; (Y); 444/1159; Church Yth Grp; Var Capt Ftbl; Var L Trk; Wt Lftg; Hon Roll; Prfct Atten Awd; Howard U; Cvl Engrng.

JONES, CHARMAINE; Springfield Gardens HS; Springfield Gdns, NY; (S); 24/438; Church Yth Grp; Teachers Aide; High Hon Roll; Hon Roll; Prncpls Hnr Socty 85; Cmmnctns.

JONES, CHRIS; Olean HS; Olean, NY; (Y); 97/197; Boy Scts; L Bsktbl; L Ftbl; Wt Lftg; Accntng.

JONES, CHRISTINE; Roy C Ketcham HS; Wappingers Falls, NY; (Y); Drama Clb; School Play; Stage Crew; Nwsp Rptr; High Hon Roll; Hon Roll; Jr NHS; NHS; Psychlgy.

JONES, CHRISTOPHER; Binghamton HS; Binghamton, NY; (Y); 23/456; Church Yth Grp; VP Computer Clb; Im Bowling; Cit Awd; High Hon Roll; NHS; Hstry Clb; Clarkson U; Comp Engrng.

JONES, DAMARIS; Lawrence HS; Inwood, NY; (Y); GAA; Varsity Clb; Chorus; JV Bsktbl; Hon Roll; Howard U; Bus Admin.

JONES, DANA; Plattsburgh HS; Plattsburgh, NY; (Y); Church Yth Grp; Cmnty Wkr; Hosp Aide; Red Cross Aide; Mgr(s); Chld Stdies.

JONES, DARCY; La Fayette HS; Manlius, NY; (S); 5/96; Cmnty Wkr; Drama Clb; Math Tm; Model UN; Stage Crew; Nwsp Stf; High Hon Roll; NHS; Mgr(s); Mst Improved Art 83-84; Top 10 Srs; SUNY Potsdam; Tchr.

JONES, DEREK; Onondaga HS; Syracuse, NY; (S); 6/72; Exploring; Quiz Bowl; Spanish Clb; Yrbk Stf; Trs Jr Cls; Trs Sr Cls; Bausch & Lomb Sci Awd; SUNY ESF; Chem.

JONES, DIONNE; Hempstead SR HS; Hempstead, NY; (S); Office Aide; Variety Show; Yrbk Ed-Chief; JV Cheerleading; Var Trk; JV Vllybl; Ntl Ldrshp Merit Awd 86; U ME; Jrnlsm.

JONES, ERIC; Saratoga Central Catholic HS; Saratoga Springs, NY; (S); 12/38; Boy Scts; Ski Clb; Fld Hcky; Sienna; Mech Engrng.

JONES, FRANK; Babylon JR SR HS; W Babylon, NY; (Y); High Hon Roll; Hon Roll; Principls Hgh Hnr List Plq 81-83; Lwyr.

JONES, GARY; Jamesville De Witt HS; Jamesville, NY; (Y); 90/240; Trs Exploring; SADD; Off Jr Cls; Lcrss; Capt Socr; Capt Wrstlng; Dnfth Awd; Hon Roll; Opt Clb Awd; US Stu Council Awd 86; J-D Fac Awd 86; Naval Acad.

JONES, GEORGE P; Williamsville South HS; Williamsville, NY; (Y); 27/210; Boy Scts; Church Yth Grp; French Clb; Concert Band; Rep Frsh Cls; Capt Var Crs Cntry; Capt Var Trk; Capt Im Bsbl; Capt JV Bsktbl; Eagle Boy Sct 85; Engrng.

JONES, GERI L; G Ray Bodley HS; Fulton, NY; (Y); Sec Frsh Cls; Sec Soph Cls; Pres Jr Cls; Pres Sr Cls; Rep Stu Cncl; Stat Var Lcrss; Cit Awd; High Hon Roll; NHS; Ntl Merit Ltr; Regnts Schlrshp 86; Outstndng Stdnt 82-86; Prom Qn Cand 85; Hamilton Coll; Corp Law.

JONES, GINA; Salmon River Central HS; Ft Covington, NY; (S); 15/88; Band; Trk; Incntv Awd St Regis Mhwk Comm 82 & 83; Ptr Dctr Memrl Indn Schlrshp 86; SUNY Ptsdm; Data Prcsr.

JONES, GREGORY; Albion HS; Albion, NY; (S); 15/170; Church Yth Grp; Spanish Clb; Band; Concert Band; Jazz Band; Mrchg Band; Capt Var Golf; Hon Roll; Ntl Merit Ltr; Regnts Schlrshp 86; St Bonaventure U; Marketing.

JONES, GREGORY; Uniondale HS; Uniondale, NY; (Y); 18/410; Stu Cncl; Ftbl; Trk; High Hon Roll; Hon Roll; NHS; Ltr Ftbl, Trk, Nassau Blkmn, Blk Prof Coaltn Schlrshps 86; Stony Brook U; Phy Thrpy.

JONES, HEATHER; Palmyra-Macedon Central HS; Palmyra, NY; (Y); Girl Scts; Concert Band; Mrchg Band; Symp Band; Var L Cheerleading; JV Sftbl; Hon Roll; JC Awd; Good Ctznshp Citatn Am Leg 83; SUNY; Child Psych.

JONES, JACKIE; Niagara Wheatfield HS; Sanborn, NY; (Y); 80/292; Pres Church Yth Grp; French Clb; Pep Clb; Capt Swmmng; NY ST Regents Schlrshp 86; Niagara County CC; Elec Enceph.

JONES, JANINE; Curtis HS; Staten Island, NY; (Y); Key Clb; Office Aide; Yrbk Phtg; Yrbk Stf; Coach Actv; Score Keeper; Swmmng; Ntl Merit Ltr; Business Mgmt.

JONES, JENNIFER; Corinth Central HS; Corinth, NY; (Y); Church Yth Grp; Drama Clb; SADD; School Play; Trs Sr Cls; JV Var Fld Hcky; High Hon Roll; Hon Roll; Jr NHS; NHS; JR Of The Yr 86; Lang Clb; Social Studies Clb; French.

JONES, JENNIFER; Lansingburgh HS; Troy, NY; (Y); French Clb; Chorus; Stu Cncl; High Hon Roll; Hon Roll; NHS; Prfct Atten Awd; Gregg Typng Awd 86; JC Albany; Acctng.

JONES, JENNIFER ANN; Tuxedo HS; Tuxedo Park, NY; (Y); 6/97; AFS; Drama Clb; Spanish Clb; SADD; Chorus; School Musical; Yrbk Stf; Pres Jr Cls; VP Stu Cncl; NHS; Sci Fair Hon Mntn; Ithaca Coll Schlrshp; Hgh Hnr Roll Awd; Ithaca Coll; Bio.

JONES, JENNIFER L; Iroquois Central Schl; Lockport, NY; (Y); AFS; Church Yth Grp; Pep Clb; Yrbk Ed-Chief; Yrbk Stf; JV Bsktbl; JV Var Fld Hcky; Var Mgr(s); JV Socr; Trk; Regent Schlrshp 86; Keuka Coll Awd 86; Keuka Coll; Psych.

JONES, JOELLE; Waterloo SR HS; Waterloo, NY; (Y); 30/154; Cmnty Wkr; Girl Scts; Band; Concert Band; Mrchg Band; Pep Band; Hon Roll; 3rd Hnrbl Ment NYS Art Poetry Cntst 86; Crtv Writer.

JONES, JOHN; Walton Central Schl; Walton, NY; (Y); 7/120; Pres VP AFS; Trs Key Clb; Model UN; Yrbk Ed-Chief; Trs Jr Cls; Trs Sr Cls; Tennis; High Hon Roll; NHS; Chiro Med.

JONES, KENNETH; La Salle Military Acad; Queens, NY; (S); 10/89; ROTC; Nwsp Rptr; Capt Var Bsktbl; Capt Var Crs Cntry; Var Trk; High Hon Roll; NHS; Supr Cadet 85; LEAD 85.

JONES, KENNETH; Nutch-Tech HS; Buffalo, NY; (Y); JV Bsktbl; Var Trk; Black Hist Wk Merit Awd 84; GA Tech; Comp Arch.

JONES, KENRICK; Bishop Loughlin Memorial HS; Brooklyn, NY; (Y); 4/240; Science Clb; Bausch & Lomb Sci Awd; High Hon Roll; NHS; Envrnmntl Sci Hnrs Wrkshp 85; Math Achvt Awd 86; Loma Linda U; Med.

JONES, KERRY; South Side HS; Rockville Centre, NY; (Y); 114/285; Church Yth Grp; Drama Clb; SADD; Chorus; School Musical; School Play; Stage Crew; Sec Frsh Cls; Hon Roll; Psych.

JONES, KIMMARIE; Dominican Commercial HS; St Albans, NY; (Y); Art Clb; Cmnty Wkr; 1st Pl Proctr & Gamble Natl Art Cont 85; Art Cet Merit NYS Assn Frgn Lang Tchrs 85; Art Cert WNET 86; St Johns U; Art Ed.

JONES, KIRSTIN A; Liverpool HS; Liverpool, NY; (Y); 16/816; AFS; JCL; Latin Clb; Stage Crew; Yrbk Phtg; Yrbk Stf; Hon Roll; Jr NHS; NHS; MONY Reg Schlstc Art Awd 86; Rgnts Schlrshp 86; Ntl Latin Exam Cum Laude & Maxima Cum Laude 83-86; Rochester Inst Of Tech; Phtgrph.

JONES, KRISTEN; Vicotr SR HS; Victor, NY; (Y); Art Clb; Stage Crew; Yrbk Stf; Im Badmtn; Var Crs Cntry; Var Trk; Var JV Vllybl.

JONES, KRISTIE; York Central HS; York, NY; (Y); Sec AFS; Library Aide; Band; Chorus; Jazz Band; School Musical; Nwsp Rptr; Stat Crs Cntry; Var Trk; NHS; Frnch Clsrm Hnrs 85.

JONES, LAURIE; Holland Central HS; Holland, NY; (S); 23/100; Pres Varsity Clb; Nwsp Stf; Yrbk Stf; VP Sr Cls; Var Capt Bsktbl; Var Capt Fld Hcky; Var Capt Trk; Var Capt Vllybl; Hon Roll; Jr NHS; Athl Yr 84-85; Intl Cable Mst Outstndng 85; Capt Fld Hkcy 85-86; Sprts Med.

JONES, LISA; Chateaugay Central HS; Chateaugay, NY; (Y); 4-H; Chorus; Yrbk Phtg; Yrbk Rptr; Yrbk Stf; JV Var Cheerleading; Gym; JV Var Socr; Chrldng-Mst Spirited 85 & 86; X-Ray Tech.

JONES, LYNN G; Cambridge Central Schl; Buskins, NY; (Y); Yrbk Ed-Chief; Pres Sr Cls; Vllybl; Hon Roll; NHS; Ntl Merit Schol.

JONES, MAHVA; Linton HS; Schenectady, NY; (Y); 45/257; Intnl Clb; Service Clb; Spanish Clb; Stu Cncl; Hon Roll; European Cultr Stud Awd 85; Cazenovia; Exec Sec.

JONES, MARCI; Potsdam HS; Etna, NY; (Y); 43/120; GAA; Pep Clb; Varsity Clb; Chorus; Bsktbl; Mgr(s); Trk; Vllybl; Ntl Merit Ltr; Tad Awd 86; Topkins CC; Acctg.

JONES, MARK; Kensington HS; Buffalo, NY; (Y); Boy Scts; Spanish Clb; Jr Cls; Bsktbl; Cit Awd; Prfct Atten Awd; Med.

JONES, MICHELLE; Franklin Acad; Malone, NY; (Y); French Clb; Band; Concert Band; Jazz Band; School Musical; Variety Show; High Hon Roll; Hon Roll; Lion Awd; NHS; Schlrshp 86; Band Lttr & Pin Allgro Clb VP 84&86; Epsln Soc Sec 85-86; Music.

JONES, MICHELLE; South New Berlin Central HS; S New Berlin, NY; (Y); 14/40; Church Yth Grp; Office Aide; VICA; Concert Band; Jazz Band; Mrchg Band; School Play; Variety Show; Yrbk Stf; Pres Frsh Cls; 2nd NYS VICA Comp Sec, Mst Outstndng Stu BOCES Awd 86; Female Athl Yr 85-86; Johnson/Wales Prov RI; Bus Adm.

JONES, NICHOLAS; Mepham HS; Bellmore, NY; (Y); Art Clb; Debate Tm; Math Clb; VP Science Clb; Chorus; Var Trk; JV Wrstlng; Hon Roll; NHS; Prfct Atten Awd; 3rd Pl Sci Cngrs Merit Awd 85; 5th Pl In Wrstlng 86; P Shea Awd 84.

JONES, NICOLE; Louis D Brandeis HS; New York, NY; (Y); Chorus; Church Choir; School Musical; TEI Inst; Prfrmg Arts.

JONES, PAUL; Unatego Central HS; Otego, NY; (Y); Hon Roll; Prfct Atten Awd; Air Frc.

JONES, PETER; Foxlane HS; Pound Ridge, NY; (Y); 96/282; AFS; Intnl Clb; Ski Clb; Lit Mag; Off Frsh Cls; Off Soph Cls; Off Jr Cls; Off Sr Cls; Stu Cncl; JV Var Bsktbl; J Alfieri Meml Awd 85-86; U Of S CA; Bus Mgmt.

JONES, RUFUS; Manlius Pebble Hill Schl; Syracuse, NY; (Y); Church Yth Grp; Exploring; Model UN; Quiz Bowl; Acpl Chr; Chorus; Church Choir; Madrigals; Orch; School Musical; Mst Imprvd Vrsty Tnns Plyr 83-84; David & Lauffer Music Awd 82-85; Med.

JONES, SANDI MARIE; Newfane Central HS; Lockport, NY; (Y); VICA; Y-Teens; Acadmc Achve Ltr Bio 85; Acadmc Achvt Ltr Math 84; US Navy; LPN.

JONES, SANDY; Waterville Central Schl; Waterville, NY; (Y); 5/95; GAA; Mathletes; Yrbk Ed-Chief; Socr; Vllybl; High Hon Roll; NHS; Htl Mgmt.

JONES, SCOTT; W C Mepham HS; Bellmore, NY; (Y); Art Clb; Debate Tm; Math Clb; Pres Science Clb; Chorus; Var Trk; JV Wrstlng; Hon Roll; NHS; Prfct Atten Awd; Sci Cngrss Merit Awd 3rd 85; Wrstlng Tournmnt Awd 86.

JONES, SHANNON; John C Birdlebough HS; Phoenix, NY; (Y); 12/175; 4-H; French Clb; Band; Concert Band; Drm Mjr(t); Mrchg Band; School Musical; Cheerleading; Socr; 4-H Awd; Drm Majrtt 86; Chrldg 87; 4-H Awd 83-84; Pre-Dntstry.

JONES, SHERYL; Queens Vocational HS; Brooklyn, NY; (Y); Cmnty Wkr; FHA; Office Aide; OEA; Science Clb; SADD; Church Choir; Yrbk Stf; Stu Cncl; Hon Roll.

JONES, SUSAN; Cicero-North Syracuse HS; N Syracuse, NY; (Y); 65/660; Dance Clb; Drama Clb; Acpl Chr; Band; Chorus; Color Guard; Drill Tm; School Musical; Capt Pom Pon; NHS; SUNY Albany ; Bio.

JONES, TERRI; Auburn HS; Auburn, NY; (Y); Trs FBLA; Hon Roll; Moore Coll Of Art; Advrtsng Art.

JONES, TIPHANY; John F Kennedy HS; Bronx, NY; (Y); VP Dance Clb; Debate Tm; Science Clb; Nwsp Rptr; Var Tennis; Prfct Atten Awd; Rgnts Schlrshp Wnnr 86; Pre-Med.

JONES, TORRENCE; Lackawanna HS; Lackawanna, NY; (Y); Am Leg Boys St; Drama Clb; Quiz Bowl; Varsity Clb; Band; School Play; Stage Crew; Yrbk Stf; VP Stu Cncl; JV L Ftbl; Gntcs.

JONES, WAYNE; Amityville Memorial HS; Massapequa, NY; (Y); 20/300; Chorus; Bsktbl; Crs Cntry; Trk; High Hon Roll; Hon Roll; Prfct Atten Awd; Math Awd 85-86; Hghst Acad Avg For Athlt Sci Awd; NY Tech; Sys Analyst.

JONGEN, AMIE J; Naples Central HS; Naples, NY; (Y); Spanish Clb; Yrbk Stf; Sec Sr Cls; Stu Cncl; Bsktbl; Socr; Sftbl; Vllybl; High Hon Roll; NHS; Keuka Coll; Occptnl Thrpy.

JOO, HYUN J; Commack HS North; East Northport, NY; (Y); Church Yth Grp; English Clb; Church Choir; High Hon Roll; NHS; Mary Alessio Mem Awd, Salomon Bros Inc Schlrshp, French Natl Hnr Soc 86; SUNY Binghamton; Math.

JOOST, INGER; Saranac Lake HS; Paul Smiths, NY; (Y); Church Yth Grp; GAA; Varsity Clb; Church Choir; Var Capt Cheerleading; Im Tennis; Var Timer; Var JV Trk; Im Vllybl; Hon Roll; Acctng.

JORDAN, AMY; Candor HS; Candor, NY; (Y); 1/79; Varsity Clb; Var Capt Bsktbl; Var L Sftbl; Var L Vllybl; High Hon Roll; NHS; Prfct Atten Awd; Val; Quiz Bowl; Scholastic Bowl; Outstndg SR Ath 86; MVP IAC Small Schl Lg Bsktbl 86; SUNY Alfred; Comp Sci.

JORDAN, CHARLES; Eden SR HS; Eden, NY; (Y); Trs VP AFS; Varsity Clb; Nwsp Rptr; Nwsp Stf; Stu Cncl; Ftbl; Psych.

JORDAN, CHRISTOPHER; Amsterdam HS; Amsterdam, NY; (Y); #13 In Class; Cmnty Wkr; Band; Concert Band; Jazz Band; Mrchg Band; High Hon Roll; Hon Roll; Engrng.

JORDAN, CORRIN A; Massapequa HS; Massapequa, NY; (Y); 125/440; Cmnty Wkr; Debate Tm; Drama Clb; Intnl Clb; Key Clb; Political Wkr; School Musical; School Play; Lit Mag; Hon Roll; Cert Of Merit-Stu Author Awd 84; Rgstrnt For Arts Wrtng & Theatre 85-86; SUNY Ctr-Binghamton; Psych.

JORDAN, JAMES; St John The Baptist HS; N Babylon, NY; (S); 6/512; Cit Awd; High Hon Roll; NHS; Spanish NHS; Knghts Of Columbus Schlrshp 84; Hndcppd Vlntr Aid 84-86; Geo Tutor 84.

JORDAN, JOHN H; Pleasantville HS; Pleasantville, NY; (Y); 2/111; Boy Scts; Var Church Yth Grp; Pres Model UN; Var L Socr; Var High Hon Roll; NHS; Ntl Merit SF; Sal; French Clb; Science Clb; Eagle Sct; Newspr Carrier 85.

JORDAN, MARSHA; Belmont Central Schl; Belmont, NY; (Y); 1/21; Church Yth Grp; Spanish Clb; Band; Chorus; Concert Band; Mrchg Band; Bausch & Lomb Sci Awd; High Hon Roll; NHS; Christine Lewis Awd 84-85; Nrsng Schl; Rn.

JORDAN, NANCY L; Auburn HS; Auburn, NY; (Y); 132/424; L Fld Hcky; L Sftbl; High Hon Roll; Hon Roll; Regents Schlrshp Awd 86; St Josephs Schl Nrsng; Nrs.

JORDAN, SONYA; Benjamin Franklin HS; Rochester, NY; (Y); JA; Model UN; Pep Clb; Teachers Aide; Color Guard; Rep Frsh Cls; Var JV Bsktbl; JV Vllybl; Hon Roll; Cmmnctns.

JORDAN, URITH; St Francis Prep; Rego Pk, NY; (Y); Art Clb; Drama Clb; German Clb; Retreat Pgm Ldr 85-86; Pltcs.

JORDAN, VERONICA M; Nortre Dame HS; New York Mills, NY; (Y); 42/158; ROTC; Spanish Clb; Color Guard; Drill Tm; Var Bowling; JV Sftbl; Var Capt Vllybl; Hon Roll; NY ST Rgnts Schlrshp 86; FL Inst Of Tech; Space Sci.

JORDAN, YVETTE; A Philip Randolph HS; Brooklyn, NY; (Y); Church Yth Grp; Civic Clb; Cmnty Wkr; Library Aide; Math Tm; Office Aide; Pep Clb; Political Wkr; Teachers Aide; Church Choir; James J Hackett Awd Oratry 86; Coop Govt Awd 86; U Buffalo; Dntstry.

JORIF, DARLENE; William Floyd HS; Moriches, NY; (Y); 22/459; French Clb; GAA; ROTC; Bsktbl; Trk; Hon Roll; NYS Rgnts Schlrshp 86; St Johns U Annual Schlrshp Awd 86; St Johns U; Toxclgy.

JOSAPHAT, LISA C; Central Islip HS; Central Islip, NY; (Y); Office Aide; Teachers Aide; School Musical; Benedict Coll; Law.

JOSEPH, CINDY; Lehman HS; Bronx, NY; (Y); Cmnty Wkr; Dance Clb; Varsity Clb; Chorus; Orch; School Musical; Variety Show; Rep Jr Cls; Capt Cheerleading; SR Cls VP 86-87; Bsktbl & Sftbll 86-87; Hmn Srvcs.

JOSEPH, CINDY; Olean HS; Olean, NY; (Y); Orch; Church Yth Grp; Nrsng.

JOSEPH, GARY; Adlai E Stevenson HS; Bronx, NY; (Y); Teachers Aide; Nwsp Stf; Rptr Yrbk Stf; Rep Frsh Cls; Pres Stu Cncl; Hon Roll; NHS; Prfct Atten Awd; Acad All-Amer 86; Rgntss Schlrshp 86; Acad Olympic Tm 85-86; Engrng.

JOSEPH, GINA; John F Kennedy HS; Utica, NY; (Y); 18/120; Law.

JOSEPH, GUERSCHOM; Nyack HS; Nyack, NY; (Y); Church Yth Grp; SADD; Rep Jr Cls; Rep Sr Cls; Peace Prize 85-86; Jimmy Swaggart Bible C; Theolgy.

JOSEPH, JULIO; George W Wingate HS; Brooklyn, NY; (Y); 32/332; French Clb; Teachers Aide; School Play; Nwsp Stf; Off Jr Cls; Off Sr Cls; Trk; Wt Lftg; Hon Roll; Prfct Atten Awd; Cnslrs Aide Awd 84-85; Best Weight Lifters Awd 85; Math Tm Awd 83-85; NY U; Elec Engrng.

JOSEPH, MICHELLE A; August Martin HS; Brooklyn, NY; (Y); 108/433; Church Choir; School Musical; Ntl Merit Schol; Wagner Coll; Gynclgst.

JOSEPH, SHAUNDA; Harry S Truman HS; Bronx, NY; (Y); JA; Library Aide; Teachers Aide; Chorus; School Musical; Yrbk Stf; Hon Roll; NHS; Natl JR Hon Soc 84; Arista Natl Hon Soc 86; Pre-Med.

JOSEY, ANTHONY; Aviation HS; Brooklyn, NY; (Y); Computer Clb; Drama Clb; Service Clb; School Play; Yrbk Stf; Rep Stu Cncl; Var Bsktbl; Var L Trk; Cit Awd; NHS; Ntl Mrt For Atten 84-86; Air Frc; Aeronauticl Engr.

JOSHI, SANJAY S; Shaker HS; Latham, NY; (Y); Science Clb; Ski Clb; Nwsp Stf; Ntl Merit Ltr; St Schlr; Temple Yth Grp; High Hon Roll; Am Assoc Physics Tchrs Awd 85; Am Assoc Tchrs Lang Awd 85; 1st Pl Shaker Sci Fair 85; Cornell U; Engrng.

JOSHI, SUNITA A; Greece Athena HS; Rochester, NY; (Y); 7/280; Civic Clb; Cmnty Wkr; DECA; Exploring; Hosp Aide; Math Clb; Science Clb; Ski Clb; Spanish Clb; Yrbk Ed-Chief; U Of R Alumni Schlrshp 86; Acad Lttr & Bar 82-86; Rgnts Schlrshp 86; SUNY Binghamton; Bio.

JOU, PETER; St Agnes HS; New York, NY; (Y); 10/98; Chess Clb; Church Yth Grp; Model UN; Science Clb; Hon Roll; NHS; Math Hons 86; Vol Children Assoc 84-85; Physics.

JOVAN, GREGORY; Fabius-Pompey HS; Lafayette, NY; (Y); Church Yth Grp; Band; Jazz Band; Symp Band; JV Bsbl; JV Bsktbl; Var L Socr; Hon Roll; 1st Tm All Lg Socr Tm 86; Jrnlsm.

JOVENE, KAREN; John H Glenn HS; E Northport, NY; (Y); Am Leg Aux Girls St; Hosp Aide; Varsity Clb; Yrbk Phtg; Yrbk Stf; Pres Stu Cncl; Var Socr; CC Awd; NHS; Spanish NHS.

JOWDY, AMEL; Wilson Central HS; Lockport, NY; (Y); 17/125.

JOWDY, LYNNE; Wilson Central HS; Lockport, NY; (Y); 12/111; Office Aide; Chorus; Yrbk Stf; NHS; Prfct Atten Awd; Bus Clb 86; FSA 86; Niagara County CC; Sec.

JOWERS, ROGER B; Park West HS; Brooklyn, NY; (Y); JA; Wt Lftg; Span Awd 86; Acad Of Aeron; Aviation Elecrnc.

JOY, JENNIFER; St Mayrs HS; Lancaster, NY; (S); 2/166; SADD; Yrbk Stf; Rep Frsh Cls; Rep Soph Cls; Rep Jr Cls; Rep Sr Cls; High Hon Roll; VP NHS; St Bonaventure U; Accntng.

JOY III, ROBERT A; Morris Central HS; Morris, NY; (Y); #1 In Class; Am Leg Boys St; Band; Yrbk Sprt Ed; Stu Cncl; Capt Bsktbl; Bausch & Lomb Sci Awd; 4-H Awd; High Hon Roll; NHS; Val; Comptr Technlgy.

JOYANNE, PAYNE; George Washington HS; New York, NY; (Y); Teachers Aide; Orch; Trk.

JOYCE, AMY; Mercy HS; Albany, NY; (Y); Church Yth Grp; Cmnty Wkr; Drama Clb; Political Wkr; Chorus; School Play; Yrbk Rptr; Yrbk Stf; Rep Frsh Cls; Rep Soph Cls; HS Schlrshp 83-86; Geom Sci, Engl Excllnc 84; Socl Stud Excllnc Trig Achvt, Bio Excllnc 85; Medcn.

JOYCE, CHRISTOPHER P; Plattsburgh HS; Plattsburgh, NY; (Y); 20/155; Cmnty Wkr; Ski Clb; Trs Concert Band; Jazz Band; Mrchg Band; Trs Orch; Hon Roll; NHS; Var L Golf; Acad Awd Mth 83; NYSMA Area All-ST Cncrt Band 83-84; NYSMA Hnrs Rctl 84; PA ST; Elctrcl Engrng.

JOYCE, COLLEEN; Mount Saint Mary Acad; Tonawanda, NY; (Y); Computer Clb; Library Aide; Office Aide; Yrbk Phtg; High Hon Roll; Hon Roll; NHS; NEDT Awd; 1st Prize Photo In Schl Art Shw 86; Sci.

JOYCE, ELIZABETH; Brewster HS; Brewster, NY; (Y); Drama Clb; Hosp Aide; Library Aide; ROTC; Chorus; Drill Tm; School Musical; Lit Mag; Mount ST Mary; Elem Ed.

JOYCE, PATRICK; Lackawanna SR HS; Lackawanna, NY; (Y); Spanish Clb; Varsity Clb; JV Bsbl; Var L Swmmng; Var Capt Vllybl; Accntnt.

JOYCE, STEVEN; Patchogue Medford HS; Patchogue, NY; (S); 71/653; Drama Clb; Pres Band; Concert Band; Mrchg Band; School Musical; School Play; Nwsp Stf; Lion Awd; VP NHS; St Bonaventure U; Mass Comm.

JOYCE, SUSAN; Lackawanna SR HS; Lackawanna, NY; (Y); GAA; Hosp Aide; Church Choir; Yrbk Stf; Rep Frsh Cls; Hon Roll; Chrch-Renew & Lecture; Cazenovia Coll; Bus Admin.

JOYNER, ROBIN; Altmar-Parish-Williamstown HS; Williamstown, NY; (Y); Art Clb; Pep Clb; Scholastic Bowl; Ski Clb; Varsity Clb; Band; Concert Band; Drm Mjr(t); Mrchg Band; Pep Band; Bus.

JUAN, KATHLEEN; Tuckahoe HS; Bronxville, NY; (Y); Drama Clb; Leo Clb; Service Clb; Ski Clb; Concert Band; Mrchg Band; Yrbk Stf; Lit Mag; Tennis; High Hon Roll; High Hnr Awd In Chem, Pre-Calculus & Amer Studies 86.

JUDD, ANDREA; Indian River Central HS; Theresa, NY; (Y); 8/120; Cmnty Wkr; Dance Clb; French Clb; Hosp Aide; Key Clb; Library Aide; Yrbk Stf; Gym; JV Trk; High Hon Roll; Jffrsn CC; Prsnl Nrsng.

JUDD, ERIC J; Roy C Ketcham HS; Poughkeepsie, NY; (Y); 40/500; Church Yth Grp; Stu Cncl; Crs Cntry; Tennis; Trk; High Hon Roll; NHS; Rgnts Schlrshp 86; Clarkson U; Engr.

JUDD, KIMBERLY A; Riverhead HS; Riverhead, NY; (Y); 60/220; Cmnty Wkr; ROTC; Color Guard; Drill Tm; Flag Corp; Gym; DAR Awd; Kiwanis Awd; Lion Awd; Loyal Ordr Moose Ldrshp Awd 86; NJ ROTC Merit Achvt Awd 86; Siena Coll; Crmnl Sci.

JUDGE, KAREN; De Sales Catholic HS; Lockport, NY; (S); 2/30; Ski Clb; Nwsp Rptr; Var Bsktbl; Var Tennis; Var Capt Vllybl; High Hon Roll; NHS; NEDT Awd.

JUDGE, SHERYL; Dominican Commercial HS; Far Rockaway, NY; (Y); Princpls List 85-86; St Johns U; Comp Analyst.

JUDSON, KATHRYN; Ichabod Crane HS; Niverville, NY; (Y); 11/181; Church Yth Grp; Pres 4-H; SADD; Color Guard; Yrbk Stf; 4-H Awd; High Hon Roll; Sec NHS; Outstndng In 4-H 85; Spch Pthlgy.

JUHASZ, MICHAEL; St Francis Prep; Astoria, NY; (Y); Boys Clb Am; Camera Clb; Red Cross Aide; Yrbk Phtg; JV Bsktbl; JV Ftbl; JV Sftbl; Im Vllybl; Cinmtgrphy.

JULES, IVA; George W Wingate HS; Brooklyn, NY; (Y); Church Yth Grp; Dance Clb; Teachers Aide; Church Choir; Bsktbl; Vllybl; High Hon Roll; Prfct Atten Awd; Hunter Coll; Nrsng.

JULES, MICHELE; St Edmund HS; Brooklyn, NY; (S); 7/185; French Clb; Hosp Aide; Service Clb; Church Choir; Ed Yrbk Ed-Chief; Var Cheerleading; High Hon Roll; NHS; Ntl Merit Ltr; NY U; Pedtrcn.

JULIAN, MICHAEL J; Christian Brothers Acad; Fayetteville, NY; (Y); 24/95; Pres FCA; Key Clb; Band; Concert Band; Pep Band; Yrbk Stf; Bsbl; Crs Cntry; Ice Hcky; Socr; Recipient Of 4-Yr Air Force ROCT Schlrshp 86; Recipient NY St Regents Schlrshp; Villanova U; Elect Engrng.

JULIAN, STEPHANIE; Holy Trinity HS; Hicksville, NY; (S); #3 In Class; Math Clb; Math Tm; Sftbl; High Hon Roll; Hon Roll; NEDT Awd; SUNY; Med.

JULIANO, DOREEN; Port Richmond HS; Staten Island, NY; (Y); Office Aide; Trs Jr Cls; Gym; Hon Roll; Wmn Hstry Mnth Cont Awd 86; Wmn Hstry Awd 86; Kingsborough CC; Word Proc Sec.

JULIANO, MARGARET M; St Anthonys HS; Huntington Sta, NY; (Y); 16/225; Drama Clb; JV Var Cheerleading; Lcrss; High Hon Roll; Jr NHS; NHS; Ntl Merit Ltr; Spanish NHS; NY ST Rgnts Schlrshp; U Of Notre Dame; Bio Sci.

JULIANO, MELISSA; Nardin Acad; Orchard Pk, NY; (Y); 13/79; Library Aide; Office Aide; Ski Clb; Stage Crew; Lit Mag; Mgr Bsktbl; Mgr(s); Mgr Sftbl; Hon Roll; Med.

JULIAS, KELLY; Wilson Central Schl; Ransomville, NY; (Y); 4/111; Pres Church Yth Grp; Chorus; School Musical; Yrbk Bus Mgr; VP Jr Cls; Var Capt Bsktbl; Var Capt Fld Hcky; Var Capt Trk; Var Capt Vllybl; NHS; Rgnts Schlrshp Acadmcs 85-86; Moving-Up Day Duchss 84; Hmcmng Prncs 84; Fhsn Merchndsng.

JUNE, CASANDRA; East New York Vo-Tech HS; Brooklyn, NY; (Y); Chorus; Church Choir; Gym; Vllybl; Hon Roll; NY Schl Tech; Engrng.

JUNG, GERALD; Monticello HS; Monticello, NY; (Y); 6/195; SADD; Orch; Nwsp Sprt Ed; VP Stu Cncl; Var Crs Cntry; Bausch & Lomb Sci Awd; NHS; RPI Medl 85; NYS Regnts Schlrshp 86; NYS Stu-Sen Forum 86; U Of Buffalo; Aero Engr.

JUNIOUS JR, ROOSEVELT; Charles H Roth HS; Rochester, NY; (Y); Am Leg Boys St; Boy Scts; Chess Clb; JA; Math Tm; Chorus; Ftbl; High Hon Roll; Hon Roll; Spanish NHS; Cert Merit Achvt Math 83-84; RPI; Electrncs.

JURAS, CHRISTINE; Oceanside HS; Oceanside, NY; (Y); Dance Clb; Chorus; Elem Ed.

JURASICH, SUSAN; Brooklyn HS; Brooklyn, NY; (Y); French Clb; 2nd,3rd Hnrs.

JURASITS, PETER; H Frank Carey HS; Franklin Square, NY; (Y); Ski Clb; Varsity Clb; JV Ftbl; Bus.

JURGENS, BRUCE W; Cairo-Durham JR SR HS; Cairo, NY; (Y); 13/88; Boy Scts; Church Yth Grp; Red Cross Aide; School Musical; School Play; Stage Crew; Sr Cls; Rep Stu Cncl; Vllybl; Hon Roll; Regents Schlrshp Wnnr 86; Plattsburgh ST.

JURIN, JANINNE; Cathedral HS; Astoria, NY; (Y); 92/272; Intnl Clb; Variety Show; Itln Hnr Cert 81; Alge Hnr Cert 83; Awd Partcpn Intl Fest 84-85; Prdcr.

JURKOWSKI, ELIZABETH ANN; Villa Maria Acad; Buffalo, NY; (Y); Art Clb; Yrbk Stf; Hon Roll; Cert Apprec Polis Armor Div Assn 85; Top Awd Pres Prize Art Cont 85; 1st Pl Loyalty Day Poster Cont 86; Advrtsg.

JURON, JASON R; Niagara Catholic HS; Niagara Falls, NY; (Y); 4/90; Spanish Clb; Rep Stu Cncl; JV Bsbl; Var Capt Golf; High Hon Roll; NHS; Med.

JUSKIEWICZ, DIANE; Mt Mercy Acad; W Seneca, NY; (Y); 37/196; Church Yth Grp; French Clb; Science Clb; SADD; Lit Mag; Stu Cncl; Im Bowling; Stat Socr; Hon Roll; Hon Mntn Schlrshp To Mt Mercy 83.

KABAN, RENEE; Lowville Academy And Central Schl; Lowville, NY; (Y); 53/125; 4-H; Pep Clb; Nwsp Rptr; Var L Swmmng; 4-H Awd; Prfct Atten Awd; Lewis Cnty Dairy Princss 86-87; ATC Schl; Vet Asst.

KABASINSKAS, MARISA; Herricks SR HS; Williston Park, NY; (Y); Church Yth Grp; Trs Sec DECA; Key Clb; PAVAS; Concert Band; Mrchg Band; Stage Crew; Hon Roll; NHS; Voice Dem Awd; NYSSMA Solost Medal 86; Apprl Accessrs Mrktng Wttn 1st Pl 86; Schrlshp 86; Bus Adm.

KABISCH, DIANE; Chatham HS; Austerlitz, NY; (Y); 4-H; Library Aide; Spanish Clb; 4-H Awd; Hon Roll; Bus.

KABITZKE, BERNHARD; New Rochelle HS; New Rochelle, NY; (Y); 107/510; Hon Roll; NHS; Fairleigh Dickinson U; Dntstry.

KABOT, MICHAEL C; Liverpool HS; Liverpool, NY; (Y); 132/850; Computer Clb; JA; Latin Clb; Ski Clb; JV Lcrss; Jr NHS; NHS; Regnts Schlrshp 86; Clarkson U; Comp Engrng.

KACH, DAWN; Port Chester SR HS; Port Chester, NY; (Y); VP Church Yth Grp; Spanish Clb; SADD; Band; Concert Band; Mrchg Band; School Musical; L Var Sftbl; Hon Roll; Jr NHS; All ST All Cnty Muscn 83 & 86; Young Athrs Conf At Marymount 85; Gold Key Awd; Acctng.

KACHAYLO, ANDY M; Rome Free Acad; Rome, NY; (Y); Pres Ski Clb; SADD; ATC Canton; Acctg.

KACHIANOS, ANDREW; Wheatley HS; Mineola, NY; (Y); Mathletes; Var Capt Crs Cntry; Var Trk; Cert Hnrary Ment AATSP 86; Wheatley.

KACPRZAK, TERESA; John Marshall HS; Rochester, NY; (Y); Exploring; FBLA; Girl Scts; Mathletes; Math Tm; Teachers Aide; Band; Co-Capt Color Guard; Mrchg Band; Yrbk Stf; Acctg.

KACZKOWSKI, KATHLEEN T; Draper HS; Schenectady, NY; (Y); VP Service Clb; Yrbk Stf; VP Sr Cls; Stu Cncl; Capt Bsktbl; Trk; High Hon Roll; NHS; VP Frsh Cls; VP Soph Cls; Rgnts Schlrshp; Athltc Schlrshp Bsktbl; Siena Coll.

KACZMAREK, CRYSTAL L; Honeoye Falls Lima HS; Honeoye Falls, NY; (Y); Intnl Clb; Sec Band; Concert Band; Jazz Band; School Musical; Nwsp Rptr; JV Socr; High Hon Roll; NHS; St Schlr; U Of Rochester.

KACZOROWSKI, KEVIN; West Seneca East SR HS; Buffalo, NY; (Y); 12/377; Trs Varsity Clb; Nwsp Stf; Var Capt Bsktbl; Var Capt Trk; Var Capt Vllybl; High Hon Roll; Trs NHS; Alfred U Pres Schlr 86; West Seneca Jaycee Awd Recip 86; Track & Field Champ 86; Alfred U; Acctg.

KADELL, NADINE; Maryvale SR HS; Cheektowaga, NY; (Y); 4/300; Pres French Clb; GAA; SADD; Varsity Clb; Nwsp Rptr; Var Trk; High Hon Roll; NHS; Voice Dem Awd; Camera Clb; Pres Acadmc Ftns Awd 85-86; Schltc Excllnc Awd 85-86; Stu Fac Gvmt Awd Outstndng SR Hist Awd 85-86; Geneseo ST; Math.

KADER, NADIA; John Jay HS; Brooklyn, NY; (Y); Teachers Aide; Nwsp Rptr; Nwsp Stf; Yrbk Stf; Prfct Atten Awd; Poem Pblshd NYC Coll Bound Nwsltr 85; Delegtn Ldr For Sch & Senator City-Wd Model Cngrss 86; Indstrl Psychol.

KAESTNER, LISA; Huntington HS; Huntington, NY; (Y); Band; Chorus; Mrchg Band; School Musical; Symp Band; Ed Nwsp Stf; High Hon Roll; NHS; Ntl Merit SF; AFS; A All ST Voice Solo 87.

KAHLER, JAMES C; Crown Point Central HS; Crown Point, NY; (Y); 7/32; Drama Clb; Varsity Clb; VP Frsh Cls; Bsbl; Bsktbl; Sftbl; Swmmng; Wt Lftg; NHS; ACT & SAT Regncy Scholar 85-86; Canton; Mech Engrng.

KAHLER, MARIAN; Bayport-Bluepoint HS; Bayport, NY; (Y); 60/210; Art Clb; Church Yth Grp; Cmnty Wkr; Office Aide; Chorus; School Musical; Nwsp Rptr; Var Score Keeper; Hon Roll; Masonic Awd.

KAHN, CYNTHIA J; La Guardia HS; Riverdale, NY; (Y); 65/437; Art Clb; Yrbk Stf; High Hon Roll; Hon Roll; NHS; Awd Excllnc Ceramcs, Advrtsng 86; Art Hnr Leag; Philadelphia Coll Art; Graphcs.

KAHN, GERALD; New Rochelle HS; Scarsdale, NY; (Y); 169/550; Chess Clb; Computer Clb; Math Tm; Variety Show; Rep Sr Cls; Stat Bsbl; Var Score Keeper; Prfct Atten Awd; Temple Yth Grp; Varsity Clb; Byclng Clb 85-86; Awd For Mrchng In Parade 83, 84 & 85; Rgnts Schlrshp 85-86; SUNY Albny; Writer.

KAHN, MICHAEL; Lakeland HS; Yorktown Hts, NY; (Y); Boy Scts; Orch; Nwsp Stf; Rep Frsh Cls; Rep Soph Cls; Swmmng; Hon Roll; Jr NHS; Eagle Scout 85; Comp Sci.

KAHN, RICK; Mahopac HS; Mahopac, NY; (Y); 36/409; Nwsp Sprt Ed; Nwsp Stf; Yrbk Stf; Trs Jr Cls; Var L Bsbl; Var L Bsktbl; Var L Ftbl; High Hon Roll; Hon Roll; NHS.

KAIER, CAROL L; Rome Catholic HS; Rome, NY; (Y); 1/68; Cmnty Wkr; Drama Clb; School Musical; Yrbk Ed-Chief; Rep Jr Cls; High Hon Roll; Pres NHS; NEDT Awd; Val; Rgnts Schlrshp; Century III Ldrs Cert Of Merit; Pres Acad Ftnss Awd; U Of Rochester; Pre-Med.

KAINE, RON; Clymer Central Schl; Clymer, NY; (Y); Church Yth Grp; Band; Chorus; Church Choir; Mrchg Band; Var Bsbl; JV Var Bsktbl; High Hon Roll; NHS; Trk; Nomntd Mc Donalds All Amer Mrchng Bnd 86; NY ST Grade 5 Vocal Music 86; NY ST All St Chorus 85-86; Mt Vernon Nazarene Coll; Engrng.

KAISER, CHRIS; Kenmore East HS; Buffalo, NY; (Y); Capt Var Bsbl; Capt Var Ice Hcky; High Hon Roll; Hon Roll; Bus Admin.

KAISER, CHRISTINE E; Scio Central Schl; Scio, NY; (Y); 11/46; Color Guard; School Play; Score Keeper; Socr; Vllybl; High Hon Roll; Hon Roll; Jr NHS; NHS; Regnts Schlrshp 86; Genesee CC; Math Sci.

KAISER, ROBERT; St Peters Boys HS; Staten Isld, NY; (Y); 36/163; Library Aide; Political Wkr; Service Clb; Hon Roll; Rep Frsh Cls; Rep Stu Cncl; Amer Lgn Schlrshp Awd; Hstry Awd; NY Inst Of Tech; Htl Mgmt.

KAKAREKA, SHERI; Gloversville HS; Gloversville, NY; (Y); Intnl Clb; Math Clb; Office Aide; Teachers Aide; Chorus; Yrbk Stf; L Gym; Powder Puff Ftbl; High Hon Roll; Hon Roll; U Of MA Amherst; Law.

KALAFARSKI, CAROL; G Ray Bodley HS; Fulton, NY; (Y); 90/236; Hosp Aide; Latin Clb; Variety Show; Yrbk Stf; Sec Jr Cls; Sec Sr Cls; Var Socr; Var Capt Sftbl; Var Capt Vllybl; Kiwanis Awd; Polish Hm Schlrshp Awd 86; Mst Imprvd Athlete 86; Volley Ball Achvt 85; Mst Valuble Plyr 86; Morrisville Coll; Med Lab Tech.

KALAMANKA, SALLY; Salamanca Central HS; Salamanca, NY; (Y); 12/150; Spanish Clb; Stu Cncl; Cheerleading; Mgr(s); Score Keeper; High Hon Roll; Hon Roll; NHS; Spanish NHS.

KALAMENT, THOMAS; Amsterdam HS; Amsterdam, NY; (Y); 73/310; Church Yth Grp; Teachers Aide; Mrchg Band; Orch; Symp Band; Rep Frsh Cls; Rep Stu Cncl; Var Socr; Var Tennis; Hon Roll; Comp Sci.

KALAYJIAN JR, GERALD M; Johnson City HS; Johnson City, NY; (Y); Am Leg Boys St; Boy Scts; Band; Concert Band; Jazz Band; Mrchg Band; Orch; Symp Band; NHS; Prfct Atten Awd; Area-All ST Bnd 85; Histry.

KALBERER, JOAN; Sachem HS; Lk Ronkonkoma, NY; (Y); 352/1559; German Clb; GAA; Girl Scts; Ski Clb; Band; JV Socr; Im Sftbl; Im Vllybl; 1st Cls-Girl Scouts 81; Slvr Awd-Girl Scouts 82; Oneonta; Tchr.

KALBFLEISCH, KATHRYN; James E Sperry HS; Rochester, NY; (Y); 17/270; Church Yth Grp; German Clb; Sec Chorus; Church Choir; Hon Roll; Jr NHS; NHS; Ger Hnr Soc 84; Awd High Grads Germ II 84; Wheaton Clg; Ger Wrtr.

KALETA, NANCY; Kenmore East SR HS; Tonawanda, NY; (Y); Church Yth Grp; GAA; Girl Scts; Pep Clb; JV Bsktbl; JV Sftbl; Achvmnt Awd Perf In Bryant & Stratton Typng Cntst 86; Engl Lit.

KALINOWSKI, ANN; Archbishop Walsh HS; Olean, NY; (Y); Art Clb; Latin Clb; Pep Clb; Swmmng; Hon Roll; Vrsty Ltr W/Swm Tm 85; 400 Rely Awd/Swm Tm 84; Marine Bio.

KALISH, JENNIFER E; Spring Valley SR HS; Monsey, NY; (Y); 19/441; Yrbk Stf; Var Capt Tennis; French Hon Soc; Mu Alp Tht; NHS; WA U St Louis MO; Math.

KALLE, LYNNE; Shenendehowa HS; Clifton Park, NY; (Y); Key Clb; Spanish Clb; Varsity Clb; Band; Concert Band; Mrchg Band; Pep Band; Tennis; Trk; High Hon Roll; OH ST U; Bus.

KALLFELZ, KRISTEN; Bishop Ludden HS; Syracuse, NY; (Y); Church Yth Grp; Cmnty Wkr; Hosp Aide; Yrbk Stf; Stat Bsbl; Var Capt Cheerleading; Coach Actv; Pom Pon; Sftbl; High Hon Roll; Hm Ecnmcs Awd 84&86; Oswego ST Coll; Physcl Thrpy.

KALLFELZ, SUSAN E; Lansing Central HS; Ithaca, NY; (Y); 2/85; Am Leg Aux Girls St; VP French Clb; Pres SADD; Band; Jazz Band; School Musical; Diving; Capt Sftbl; Capt Swmmng; Pres NHS; Rgnts Schlrshp NYS 86; Diving Sctn IV 2nd Pl 85; Cornell U; Bio Sci.

KALME, ANNA; Greenwich Central HS; Greenwich, NY; (Y); Am Leg Aux Girls St; Church Yth Grp; FFA; Sr Cls; Cit Awd; DAR Awd; High Hon Roll; Hon Roll; 2nd Pl Amer Legn Aux Cntst Oratrcl 86; 2nd Pl FFA Public Spkg 86; Bus.

KALMUS, JACKIE; Acad Of St Joseph; Centereach, NY; (Y); Drama Clb; Spanish Clb; School Musical; School Play; Variety Show; VP Stu Cncl; Var Socr; Var Sftbl; Catholic U Of A; Bus Admin.

KALOSKI, RACHEL; Westhampton Beach HS; Westhampton Bch, NY; (Y); 34/250; Band; Mrchg Band; Sec Soph Cls; JV Var Fld Hcky; Var Trk; JV Capt Vllybl; Fld Hcky MVP 84; Fld Hcky Bst Sprtsmnshp 85; Bus Mgmt.

KALPA, LISA; St Marys HS; Depew, NY; (Y); SADD; Stu Cncl; JV Sftbl; Sec Frsh Cls; Sec Soph Cls; Sec Jr Cls; Ferdonia; Bus Mgmt.

KALRA, GITA; Newtown HS; Corona, NY; (Y); 9/781; Pres Debate Tm; Pres French Clb; Library Aide; Math Clb; Office Aide; Nwsp Rptr; Nwsp Stf; Lit Mag; High Hon Roll; Acdmc Olympics 86; Law.

KALSTEIN, MICHELE H; Midwood HS; Brooklyn, NY; (Y); 2/554; Math Tm; Ed Nwsp Stf; Yrbk Stf; Yrbk Stf; Cit Awd; Gov Hon Prg Awd; NHS; Sal; Val; Model UN; Yale U.

KALVERT, SETH; Clarkstown HS North; New City, NY; (Y); SADD; Nwsp Stf; Rep Stu Cncl; JV Socr; High Hon Roll; Mu Alp Tht; NCTE Awd; NHS; DECA; Temple Yth Grp; Columbia U Sci Hnrs Pgm; Amer Chemcl Soc.

KAMALI, MARYAM D; Hillcrest HS; Forest Hills, NY; (Y); 5/800; Cmnty Wkr; Hosp Aide; Library Aide; Office Aide; Y-Teens; Yrbk Stf; Lit Mag; Hon Roll; NHS; Queens Coll Pres Awd 84; NY Library Centennl Wrtng Awd 85; Natl Engl Merit Awd 86; SUNY Binghampton.

KAMAN, SUSAN; Kenmore East HS; Buffalo, NY; (Y); Cmnty Wkr; Drama Clb; German Clb; Math Clb; Pep Clb; Red Cross Aide; Band; Concert Band; Mrchg Band; Orch; Engl.

KAMEL, JAY; Lindenhurst SR HS; Lindenhurst, NY; (Y); 22/550; Art Clb; Service Clb; Ski Clb; SADD; Socr; Hon Roll; NHS; Chess Clb; NY ST Regents Schlrshp 86; Prncpls List 86; Natl Art Hnr Scty 85-86; SUNY-STNY Brk; Elec Engr.

KAMEN, DAVID; Hillcrest HS; Forest Hills, NY; (Y); 270/873; Boys Clb Am; Boy Scts; Office Aide; Band; Culinary Inst Amer; Chef Traing.

KAMINSKI, MICHAEL; Amsterdam HS; Amsterdam, NY; (Y); 55/316; Latin Clb; Varsity Clb; Ftbl; Var JV Trk; Hon Roll; Prfct Atten Awd.

KAMINSKY, ANDREW; Syosset HS; Plainview, NY; (Y); 87/492; AFS; Model UN; SADD; Yrbk Phtg; Yrbk Rptr; Ed Yrbk Stf; Rep Stu Cncl; Tennis; Hon Roll; Regnts Schlrshp; U Of MI; Bus.

KAMINSKY, MATTHEW; Commack HS; Dix Hills, NY; (Y); Aud/Vis; Drama Clb; PAVAS; School Musical; School Play; Stage Crew; Variety Show; Thtr Art.

KAMMEL, CHRISTINE L; Valley Stream Central HS; Valley Stream, NY; (Y); Art Clb; Ski Clb; SADD; JV Sftbl; NHS.

KAMMER, MELISSA; Liverpool HS; Liverpool, NY; (Y); 30/850; Ski Clb; Teachers Aide; NHS; Regnts Schlrshp 86; Hotchks Found Schlrshp 86; SUNY; Vet Sci.

KAMMERER, PATRICIA A; Taconic Hills HS; Hillsdale, NY; (Y); 5/116; Chorus; Concert Band; Jazz Band; Yrbk Phtg; Var Bsktbl; Var Socr; Var Trk; Hon Roll; NHS; NY ST Rgnts Schlrshp 86; Crnl U; Cmnctns Art.

KAMMERER, TRACY; Grand Island HS; Gr Island, NY; (Y); 38/290; French Clb; Girl Scts; JA; Band; Concert Band; Stage Crew; Stu Cncl; Psych.

KANALEY, TIMOTHY; Thomas J Corcoran HS; Syracuse, NY; (Y); Drama Clb; Latin Clb; Quiz Bowl; Science Clb; Band; Church Choir; Concert Band; Mrchg Band; Pep Band; School Musical; All Amer Hall Fame Band Hnrs 85 & 86; Magna Cum Laude Natl Lat Exm 84 & 86; Prfct Scr Geom Regents 85; Biochem.

KANAS, JENNIFER; Connetquot HS; Ronkonkoma, NY; (Y); SADD; Pres Band; Yrbk Stf; Rep Frsh Cls; Rep Soph Cls; Rep Stu Cncl; Var Cheerleading; Var Swmmng; Hon Roll; Sec Jr NHS; Empr ST Gms Synchnzd Swmmng 84-86; James Madison U; Bus.

KANAS, SYLVIA D; William C Bryant HS; Woodside, NY; (Y); 1/625; Latin Clb; Office Aide; Science Clb; Lit Mag; NHS; Prfct Atten Awd; Val; Untd Fed Tchrs Schlrshp 86; Regents Schlrshp 86; Barnard Coll.

KANAS, WILLIAM S; Walt Whitman HS; Huntington Stn, NY; (Y); 48/533; Camera Clb; Church Yth Grp; Cmnty Wkr; Debate Tm; Library Aide; Political Wkr; Spanish Clb; Nwsp Rptr; Nwsp Stf; Yrbk Stf; Stu Rep NYS Cngrsnl Dist 85-86; Rep Pres Clsrm 86; Top Eng Stu Awd, Hnbl Mntn Span 83; Catholic U America; Pol Sci.

KANCHES, DARCY; Galway Central HS; Amsterdam, NY; (Y); 18/83; Pres French Clb; Pres SADD; VP Chorus; School Play; Pres Jr Cls; Pres Sr Cls; Rep Stu Cncl; Capt Cheerleading; High Hon Roll; NHS; Knghts Of Clumbs Awd 86; Awd-Sci For Mst Dtrmntn 86; Cortland; Bio Educ.

KANCZAK, MAUREEN; Cheektowaga Central HS; Cheektowaga, NY; (Y); 88/199; Library Aide; Spanish Clb; Band; Hon Roll; Villa Maria Coll; Erly Chldhd.

KANE, AMY; Mt Mercy Acad; Hamburg, NY; (Y); Church Yth Grp; Cmnty Wkr; French Clb; Hosp Aide; Ski Clb; Im Tennis; Var Trk; Im Vllybl.

KANE, AMY; Ravena-Coeymans-Selkirk HS; Ravena, NY; (Y); Var Socr; Var Sftbl; Med.

KANE, BRUCE A; Oyster Bay HS; E Norwich, NY; (Y); 40/125; Chess Clb; VP Computer Clb; Q&S; Nwsp Rptr; Nwsp Stf; Hon Roll; Ntl Merit Schol; Northeastern U; Comp Sci.

KANE, DAVID; Corning-Painted Post West HS; Corning, NY; (Y); 5/249; JA; Key Clb; Varsity Clb; Stat Bsktbl; JV Ftbl; Capt Lcrss; Socr; High Hon Roll; NHS; St Schlr; NROTC Schlrshp 86; U Of Notre Dame; Elec Engr.

KANE, ELIZABETH; Elmira Free Acad; Elmira, NY; (Y); 24/240; Sec Latin Clb; Red Cross Aide; Band; School Play; Yrbk Sprt Ed; Rep Soph Cls; JV Var Bsktbl; JV Var Tennis; Hon Roll; Kiwanis Awd; March Of Dimes Schlrshp 86; Presdntl Fitns Awd 86; MVP Awd Tennis 85; SUNY-BUFFALO; Phys Therpy.

KANE, GEORGE; Whitestone Acad; Whitestone, NY; (S); 1/35.

KANE, GERALD; Seton Catholic Central HS; Johnson City, NY; (Y); Church Yth Grp; Drama Clb; Chorus; School Musical; School Play; JV Var Crs Cntry; Var Trk; CYO Bsktbll JV 85-86; CYO Vllybll 84-86; Elec Engnrng.

KANE, JENNIFER E; St Francis Prep Schl; Elmhurst, NY; (S); 108/744; Art Clb; Cmnty Wkr; Dance Clb; Nwsp Rptr; Rep Soph Cls; Rep Jr Cls; Hon Roll; Optimate Soc; Cmmnctns.

KANE, JOHN; Bishop Ludden HS; Syracuse, NY; (S); 4/125; SADD; Lit Mag; Pres Soph Cls; Var JV Bsktbl; Ftbl; Var Capt Lcrss; High Hon Roll; NHS; Merit Achvt Awd; Polit Sci.

KANE, JONATHAN L; Jamaica HS; Flushing, NY; (Y); 44/507; Computer Clb; School Musical; Var Capt Golf; NHS; NY ST Rgnts Coll Schlrshp 86; Crtve Arts Soc 86; Queens Coll.

KANE, KATIE; Batavia HS; Batavia, NY; (Y); 3/200; Church Yth Grp; Ski Clb; Var Socr; JV Trk; Hon Roll; NHS; Spn Merit Awd 84 & 86; Hnr Awds & Acad Ltr 84-86; Marine Bio.

KANE, KEVIN; Gates-Chili SR HS; Rochester, NY; (S); 25/446; Boy Scts; Exploring; JV Bsbl; Var JV Swmmng; High Hon Roll; Hon Roll; NHS; Penn ST; Htl Mgmt.

KANE, LAURIE A; Bay Shore HS; Brightwaters, NY; (Y); 7/412; Exploring; Color Guard; Mrchg Band; Orch; High Hon Roll; Hon Roll; NCTE Awd; NHS; Regents Schlrshp 86; Schl Rep Japn Amer Stdnt Schlrshp Fund 85; Fornsc Path.

KANE, RICHARD; Bishop Grimes HS; Syracuse, NY; (Y); 35/200; Trs Stu Cncl; Var L Bsbl; Var L Bsktbl; Var L Socr; Hon Roll; Acadmc All-Am 86.

KANFOUSH, SHARON; Sauquoit Valley Central HS; Sauquoit, NY; (Y); 1/98; Am Leg Aux Girls St; Pres SADD; Trs Jr Cls; Sec Sr Cls; Fld Hcky; High Hon Roll; NHS; NEDT Awd; Opt Clb Awd; Val; LIU Sthmptn U Schlrs Fll Tuitn Awd 86; NYS Rgnts Schlrshp 86; LIU Southampton; Mrn Geolgy.

KANG, CHIA; Oakwood Schl; Elmhurst, NY; (Y); Intnl Clb; Chorus; School Musical; Yrbk Ed-Chief; Yrbk Stf; Rep Stu Cncl; Var Mgr Bsktbl; Var Socr; Var Sftbl; Mgr Wt Lftg; Soc Psych.

KANG, EMIL J; Valley Stream South HS; Valley Stream, NY; (Y); 21/187; Church Yth Grp; Computer Clb; Hosp Aide; Ski Clb; Varsity Clb; Orch; JV Var Socr; Var Tennis; Hon Roll; NHS; NY ST Rgnts Schlrshp & Ntl Orchestra Awd 86; All ST String Orchstra 85; Doctor.

KANG, PETER; Elizabeth Irwin HS; Cliffside Park, NJ; (Y); Church Yth Grp; FBLA; Ski Clb; Chorus; School Play; Yrbk Ed-Chief; Im Bsbl; Im Golf; Var Lcrss; JV Socr; Acad All Amer 84-85; Natl Bus Awd 84-85; Boston Coll; Bus Mgt.

KANG, SAMUEL; Walt Whitman HS; Melville, NY; (Y); 86/479; Boy Scts; Pres Church Yth Grp; Hosp Aide; Key Clb; Pres SADD; Concert Band; Nwsp Bus Mgr; Nwsp Ed-Chief; Jr NHS; Spanish NHS; Pre-Law.

KANITZ, CARON; Herman-Dekalb Central HS; De Kalb Jct, NY; (Y); Church Yth Grp; 4-H; French Clb; Concert Band; Jazz Band; Nwsp Stf; Ed Yrbk Stf; Vllybl; Hon Roll; NHS; The Kings Coll; Bus Adm.

KANKOLENSKI, PAUL; Niagara Wheatfield SR HS; Ransomville, NY; (Y); Ski Clb; JV Var Bsbl; Bowling; Var Capt Ftbl; JV Var Wrstlng; Hon Roll; Comp.

KANSCO, KRIS; Victor SR HS; Victor, NY; (Y); GAA; Quiz Bowl; Spanish Clb; Band; Mrchg Band; Nwsp Rptr; Trs Sr Cls; Stu Cncl; Im Badmtn; JV Var Socr; Pre-Law.

KANTOR, AMY; Port Richmond HS; Staten Island, NY; (Y); Intnl Clb; Service Clb; Spanish Clb; Teachers Aide; Temple Yth Grp; School Musical; Yrbk Stf; Capt Pom Pon; Hon Roll; NHS; Spch Thrpy.

KAO, JULIA; Newton HS; Elmhurst, NY; (Y); 27/781; Pres Debate Tm; VP French Clb; Math Tm; Chorus; Nwsp Stf; Tennis; Hon Roll; Jr NHS; NHS; Prfct Atten Awd; Prncpls Lst 86; Smith; Med.

KAPAL, KARLEEN; Sacred Heart Acad; North Tonawanda, NY; (Y); Cmnty Wkr; JCL; Latin Clb; Chorus; School Musical; Service Clb; Stage Crew; Film Ind.

KAPALA, MARY; Little Falls JR SR HS; Fort Plain, NY; (Y); 1/98; Band; School Musical; Pres Soph Cls; Var Badmtn; JC Awd; VP NHS; Drama Clb; Spanish Clb; SADD; Mrchg Band; Cvc Clb Schlrshp 86; Yrkr Achvmnt Prz 86; Gvrnrs Trphy 2nd Yr 86; Hamilton Coll; Pblc Plcy.

KAPELL, KATHY; Bishop Grimes HS; S Manluis, NY; (S); Computer Clb; Girl Scts; Speech Tm; Var Co-Capt Bsktbl; Crs Cntry; Trk; Vllybl; High Hon Roll; Hon Roll; Cornell; Vet Sci.

KAPETANAKES, BARBARA; Fontbonne Hall HS; Brooklyn, NY; (Y); Teachers Aide; Brnz Medl Art Cont 85; Math Awd 85; Art Wrk Exhbt 85; Polytech Inst Of NY; Elec Engr.

KAPKA, TANYA; Bellport HS; E Patchogue, NY; (Y); 9/395; Sec French Clb; Chorus; Orch; High Hon Roll; Jr NHS; NHS; Ntl Merit Ltr; Computer Clb; Drama Clb; SADD; All-ST Orch 86; All-Cnty Orch 85-86; Ny ST Schl Of Orch Studies Saratoga 86; Engrng.

KAPLAN, DANNY; Jamesville-Dewitt HS; Syracuse, NY; (Y); French Clb; Key Clb; Varsity Clb; Yrbk Phtg; Yrbk Stf; Diving; Golf; Socr; Swmmng; Hon Roll; Marine Bio.

KAPLAN, ERIC; Smithtown HS East; Nesconset, NY; (Y); 1/515; Political Wkr; Pres SADD; Pres Sr Cls; Var Bsktbl; French Hon Soc; High Hon Roll; NHS; Ntl Merit Schol; Jr NHS; Scholastic Bowl; Dctrs Tmrrw Schlrshp 86; Empr ST Schlrshp Excllnc 86; Pres Acad Ftns Awd 86; Princeton U; Med.

KAPLAN, JONATHAN; Wantagh HS; Wantagh, NY; (Y); 21/281; Pres FBLA; Capt Math Tm; Yrbk Phtg; Sr Cls; Swmmng; High Hon Roll; Carnegie Mellon Schrlshp 86; Rgnts Schlrshsp 86; Pres At Ben Franklin Clb 86; Carnegie Mellon; Fin.

KAPLAN, MICHAEL; Bronx HS Science; Bronx, NY; (Y); Boy Scts; Pres Exploring; Teachers Aide; Lng Islnd Natrl Lif Physq & Pwr Champnshp 86; Phys Fitns Comptn 86; Cvl Engr.

KAPLO, VALERIE; Our Lady Of Mercy HS; Pittsford, NY; (Y); Church Yth Grp; Yrbk Stf; Rep Stu Cncl; Var L Tennis; Hon Roll; Earth Sci Awd 84; Amer Studies Awd 86; Engl Regnets Awd 86; Intrnl Bus.

KAPOOR, RAJIV; Bronxville HS; Bronxville, NY; (Y); Ski Clb; JV Socr; Var Tennis; High Hon Roll; Hon Roll; Vanderbilt; Bus.

KAPOOR, RITU; Sacred Heart Acad; New Hyde Park, NY; (S); 46/182; FTA; Chorus; School Musical; Stu Cncl; Hon Roll; NHS; Pres Glee Clb 85-86; Prod Team Schl Musical 85-86; Finance.

KAPPS, SUSAN; St John The Baptist Diocesan HS; Babylon, NY; (S); 24/546; Model UN; SADD; Church Choir; Nwsp Stf; Lit Mag; Stu Cncl; French Hon Soc; Spanish NHS; 2nd Pl Trphy In After Dinner Spking At Hofstra Forensics Tournmnt 86; Fordham U; Pre-Law.

KAPSHO, LYNDA; VVS Central HS; Sherrill, NY; (Y); Yrbk Phtg; Yrbk Stf; Var L Cheerleading; Var L Fld Hcky; Var Score Keeper; Var L Trk; TVL Chmpns, Bst Tm Plyr Fld Hcky 84; TVL 2nd Pl Fld Hcky 85; Art Inst Pittsburgh; Fshn Dsgn.

KAPUS, SUSAN; Grand Island SR HS; Grand Isl, NY; (Y); 33/295; Sec Drama Clb; Hosp Aide; Varsity Clb; Concert Band; School Musical; JV Socr; JV Var Vllybl; Hon Roll; NHS; Art Clb; Cert Senstvty, Aesthtc Awrnss, Cretv Ablty And Art Concpts 86; 1st All Sch Vllybl Trnmnt 86; ST U NY Buffalo; Nrsg.

KAPUSCINSKI, CHRISTINE; Solvay HS; Syracuse, NY; (Y); JA; Band; Concert Band; School Musical; School Play; Yrbk Stf; Off Jr Cls; Var Cheerleading; 3 NYSSMA Solo Awds Music 84-86; Fash Merch.

KARAGHEUZOFF, CHRISTOPHER G; St Francis Prep; Jamaica Estates, NY; (S); 14/744; Art Clb; Hosp Aide; Math Tm; NFL; Speech Tm; SADD; Nwsp Ed-Chief; NHS; Pres Awd Achvt 84-85; Prncpls List 84-85; Forensc Leag ST Qlfr 86.

KARALUS, PETER J; St Marys HS; Buffalo, NY; (Y); 19/150; Trs Church Yth Grp; Drama Clb; Service Clb; Chorus; School Musical; School Play; Hon Roll; NHS; H S Grant 86-87; Aerosp Engrng.

KARAM, JEFFREY M; Pembroke Central HS; Corfu, NY; (Y); 40/115; Boy Scts; Church Yth Grp; Drama Clb; VP Exploring; Ski Clb; Varsity Clb; School Musical; Trs Variety Show; Yrbk Stf; Hon Roll; NY ST Regnts Schlrshp 86; SUNY; Law Enf.

KARANJA, KAMAU E; Fieldston HS; Bronx, NY; (Y); Orch; Nwsp Stf; Var Capt Crs Cntry; Var Capt Swmmng; Var L Trk; Ntl Merit Ltr; Natl Achvt Schlrshp Semi-Fnlst; Bio.

KARASIEWICZ, KAREN; Letchworth Central Schl; Pike, NY; (Y); FFA; VICA; Color Guard; Yrbk Stf; Socr; Sftbl; High Hon Roll; Hon Roll; Ornamntl Horticltr.

KARASZEWSKI, JANET; Maryvale HS; Cheektowaga, NY; (Y); Sec Chrmn Church Yth Grp; SADD; Varsity Clb; Coach Actv; Stat Mgr(s); Var Swmmng; High Hon Roll; Hon Roll; Jr NHS; NHS; Ed Argy Awd 86; Mst Imprvd Swmmr 83-84; Schlr-Athlete Ltr 86; Nrsng.

KARAZIM, KATARZYNA; Windham-Ashland-Jewett HS; Jewett, NY; (S); 2/26; Drama Clb; Science Clb; Ski Clb; Concert Band; Jazz Band; School Play; Yrbk Stf; Pres Stu Cncl; Var Tennis; High Hon Roll; Dartmouth; Aerontcl Engrg.

KARB, MICHAEL; St Marys HS; Lancaster, NY; (S); 4/170; Boys Clb Am; VP Science Clb; Nwsp Rptr; Var Crs Cntry; Var Trk; Hon Roll; NHS; Knights Columbus Upstate NY Regnl Free Throw Champ 84; Buffalo News Subrbn Div Carrier Mnth 85; Bio Sci.

KARCHER, JOANN S; Tonawanda SR HS; Tonawanda, NY; (Y); Trs French Clb; FNA; Pres JA; Sec Ski Clb; Concert Band; Rep Stu Cncl; Hon Roll; Rgnts Nrsng Schlrshp 86; Nrsng.

KARCHESKY, JANET; Bishop Scully HS; Amsterdam, NY; (Y); Var Capt Cheerleading; Hon Roll; Vrsty Lttr Chrldng 84-85 & 85-86; Military Service; Bus Sec.

KARCHNER, KEITH; Monticello HS; Monticello, NY; (Y); 34/195; Debate Tm; Speech Tm; Nwsp Rptr; Yrbk Stf; Cit Awd; NHS; Pres Schlr; Regents Schrlshp Awd 85-86; Hinckley Awd Engl 85-86; Bd Ed Awd Soc Studies 85-86; SUNY; Psychlgy.

KARDASZ, TED; Bishop Ford C C HS; Brooklyn, NY; (S); 6/462; Church Yth Grp; Computer Clb; Science Clb; Im Bowling; Hon Roll; HS Enrchmnt Pgm 86; Pace; Bus.

KAREFF, SCOTT M; Nichols Schl; Williamsville, NY; (Y); Nwsp Rptr; Yrbk Ed-Chief; Var Tennis; Var Wrstlng; DAR Awd; High Hon Roll; NHS; Ntl Merit Ltr; HOBY Fndtn Intl Ldrshp Smnr Ambssdr 84; Cornell Coll; Arts.

KARELIS, VIOLET; Newburgh Free Acad; New Windsor, NY; (Y); Shrthnd Awd 84-85; Typg Awd 85-86; Coop Pgm Certs 85-86; Berkeley Schl; Pro Sec.

KARIM, NASIR; Erasmus Hall HS; Brooklyn, NY; (Y); Science Clb; Badmtn; Socr; Vllybl; Med.

KARIM, SHUJA; Earl L Vandermeulen HS; Mt Sinai, NY; (Y); 60/315; FBLA; Letterman Clb; SADD; Varsity Clb; Nwsp Rptr; Nwsp Stf; JV Bsbl; Var L Trk; High Hon Roll; Hon Roll; Bstn U; Ecnmcs.

KARIMI, ALI; Mahopac HS; Mahopac Falls, NY; (Y); Aud/Vis; Camera Clb; Chess Clb; Radio Clb; Science Clb; Stage Crew; Nwsp Rptr; Nwsp Stf; Capt Bsktbl; JV Ftbl; Ftbl League Chmps 84; Reading Merit Awd 83; Syracuse U; Cmmnctns.

KARIUS, KENNETH C; Deposit Central HS; Deposit, NY; (Y); 1/80; Church Yth Grp; School Play; Pres Jr Cls; Pres Sr Cls; Var Capt Crs Cntry; Var Capt Trk; High Hon Roll; NHS; Ntl Merit Ltr; Val; Cornell U Ntl Schlr; Cornell; Engr.

KARL, DEANNA; Allegany Central HS; Allegany, NY; (Y); FFA; Concert Band; Jazz Band; School Musical; Crs Cntry; Trk; High Hon Roll; Hon Roll; Prfct Atten Awd; Band; Ntl FFA Fndtn Awd Recgnzng Achvt 84; Ag.

KARL, SUSAN; Chester HS; Chester, NY; (Y); #2 In Class; High Hon Roll; Hon Roll; NHS; NEDT Awd; Prfct Atten Awd; Voice Dem Awd; Marshl SR Grad Clss 86; 1st Water Clr Pntng Orng Cnty Fair 84; Cert Outstndg Perfmnc Sos Stud III 86; Psychlgy.

KARLSON, STEFAN; Mahopac HS; Mahopac, NY; (Y); 138/409; Varsity Clb; Nwsp Rptr; Var JV Wrstlng; Hon Roll; Ftbl; JV Var Lcrss; West Point; Prelaw.

KARP, DEBORAH; Cicero-N Syracuse HS; Brewerton, NY; (S); 25/667; Ski Clb; Sftbl; Hon Roll; NHS; Ntl Govt & Hist Awd 85; Syracuse U; Law.

KARPENKO, AIMEE; Royalton-Hartland Central HS; Middleport, NY; (Y); Pres Drama Clb; Pres Girl Scts; Spanish Clb; Teachers Aide; School Play; Stage Crew; Gld Ldrshp Awd, Gold Awd 86; Slvr Awd 84; Niagara Cnty Comm; Jrnlsm.

KARPF, STEPHEN; New Rochelle HS; New Rochelle, NY; (Y); Chess Clb; Library Aide; Ed Lit Mag; High Hon Roll; NHS; Columbia U Book Awd 86; Law.

KARPIUS, PETE; Port Chester SR HS; Port Chester, NY; (Y); Ski Clb; Lit Mag; Var L Golf; US Naval Acad; Aerospc Engnrng.

KARPOWICZ, LYNDA; St John The Baptist DHS; Kings Pk, NY; (Y); FNA; Girl Scts; Hosp Aide; Color Guard; Hon Roll; Bus Mgmt.

KARR, STEVEN V; Arkport Central Schl; Arkport, NY; (Y); 21/60; Ski Clb; School Play; Rep Stu Cncl; Crs Cntry; Mgr(s); Socr; Trk; High Hon Roll; Hon Roll; Regents Schlrshp 88; U Of Buffalo.

KASAPOGLOU, VASILIA; William Cullen Bryant HS; Long Island City, NY; (S); 43/623; Concert Band; Jazz Band; Pep Band; Nwsp Stf; Yrbk Stf; Hon Roll; NHS; Spanish NHS; Htl-Rest Mgmt.

KASHEFSKY, HOWARD; East Meadow HS; East Meadow, NY; (Y); Ed Art Clb; Nwsp Rptr; Var Tennis; Hon Roll; NHS; Sci.

KASINSKI, DARLENE; Hamburg SR HS; Hamburg, NY; (Y); Service Clb; Yrbk Stf; Var Sftbl; Var Vllybl; Cornell U; Vet Med.

KASINSKI, SANDRA; Frontier Central SR HS; Blasdell, NY; (Y); 72/434; French Clb; Intnl Clb; Chorus; JV Socr; Var Mgr Tennis; Hon Roll; NHS; Frgn Lang Mntr 85-86; Frgn Lang.

KASKEL, PAMELA; Syosset HS; Jericho, NY; (Y); Pres Latin Clb; Radio Clb; Nwsp Rptr; Rep Stu Cncl; JV Bsktbl; JV Sftbl; Capt Vllybl; High Hon Roll; NHS; Regents Schlrshp 86; Columbia Schlstc Press Assoc Awd 83; Latin Hnr Scty 86; NW U.

KASKOUN, MEGHAN P; Rome Free Acad; Rome, NY; (Y); 61/462; VP JA; Ski Clb; Nwsp Phtg; Nwsp Rptr; Lit Mag; Rep Stu Cncl; Capt Var Bsktbl; JV Var Fld Hcky; JV Var Sftbl; NHS; NY ST Regents Schlrshp Awd 86; Miami U Of Ohio.

KASONIC, BRIAN; Horseheads HS; Horseheads, NY; (Y); JCL; Latin Clb; Model UN; Spanish Clb; Chorus; JV Im Bsktbl; JV Crs Cntry; Trk; Hon Roll; Finance.

KASPER, PAMELA L; Niskayuna HS; Schenectady, NY; (Y); Cmnty Wkr; French Clb; Capt Hosp Aide; Siena Coll; Acctg.

KASPRYK, JAMES; Johnson City SR HS; Johnson City, NY; (Y); Pres Church Yth Grp; Pres French Clb; Ski Clb; High Hon Roll; Hon Roll; NHS.

KASPRZYK, MARY E; Eden Central HS; Hamburg, NY; (Y); AFS; GAA; School Musical; Yrbk Ed-Chief; Yrbk Phtg; Stu Cncl; Stat Bsbl; Score Keeper; Vllybl; Hon Roll; Regnts Schlrshp 85-86; Art Awd 84; U Of Buffalo; Bus Mgt.

KASPRZYK, THERESA; Holland Central HS; Holland, NY; (Y); Trs AFS; JA; Trs Band; Concert Band; Jazz Band; Mrchg Band; Scrkpr Bsktbl; Scrkpr Fld Hcky; Score Keeper; Scrkpr Vllybl; Amrcn Fld Srvc Schl Prgm Grc 86-87; Fld Hcky Ded Awd Scrkpr 85; Phtgrphy.

KASS, MITCHELL; Flushing HS; Flushing, NY; (Y); 30/410; Cmnty Wkr; Computer Clb; Math Tm; Science Clb; School Musical; Symp Band; Yrbk Phtg; High Hon Roll; Jr NHS; NHS; Stevens Schlrshp 86; Stevesn Inst Of Tech; Elec Engr.

KASS, PENNY; North Babylon HS; N Babylon, NY; (Y); Camera Clb; Church Yth Grp; Computer Clb; Dance Clb; Drama Clb; Girl Scts; Library Aide; Office Aide; Spanish Clb; Chorus; Med.

KASS, SCOTT; Mepham HS; N Bellmore, NY; (Y); Debate Tm; Math Tm; Political Wkr; Science Clb; Acpl Chr; Chorus; Madrigals; Nwsp Rptr; Nwsp Stf; Off Frsh Cls; NYSSMA Trials 85-86; Intrmrl Hcky 84.

KASSEBAUM, JUDE; Bishop Ford C C HS; Brooklyn, NY; (Y); Church Yth Grp; Im Bowling; Coach Actv; Im Ice Hcky; CPA.

KASSEBAUM, PATRICIA; St Edmund HS; Brooklyn, NY; (S); 5/185; Pres Church Yth Grp; English Clb; Pres French Clb; Service Clb; School Play; Yrbk Stf; Lit Mag; Rep Jr Cls; Rep Sr Cls; Capt Bowling.

KASSELAKIS, JOHN; Manhasset HS; Manhasset, NY; (Y); Am Leg Boys St; Boy Scts; Church Yth Grp; Nwsp Rptr; Pres Jr Cls; Pres Sr Cls; Var Ftbl; Var Trk; Var Wrstlng; High Hon Roll.

KASSON, MARY L; Mercy HS; Albany, NY; (Y); 10/80; Am Leg Aux Girls St; Drama Clb; Ski Clb; School Play; Yrbk Stf; Cheerleading; High Hon Roll; Hon Roll; NHS; Pom Pon; Mock Trial Tm 86; Lawyer.

KASSOVER, CRAIG; Sachem North HS; Holbrook, NY; (Y); 383/1500; Ski Clb; Physcl Thrpy.

KAST, MELISSA A; Martin Van Buren HS; Bellerose, NY; (Y); 28/565; Math Tm; School Play; Symp Band; Variety Show; Yrbk Ed-Chief; Gym; Hon Roll; NHS; St Schlr; Svc Hnr Scty 83-85; NY U; Bus.

KASTER, MICHAEL; Portville Central HS; Portville, NY; (Y); Band; Mrchg Band; JV Var Ftbl; JV Ice Hcky; JV Trk; Hon Roll; COMPTR Sci.

KASZUBA, PATTY; Notre Dame Bishop Gibbons HS; Schenectady, NY; (Y); Cmnty Wkr; 4-H; French Clb; Hosp Aide; Variety Show; Yrbk Stf; JV Cheerleading; Hon Roll; Ntl Merit SF; Mktng.

KATES, JULIE; Bronx H S Of Science; New York City, NY; (Y); Dance Clb; Teachers Aide; Yrbk Phtg; Rep Jr Cls; Hnrs Blgy 83-84; Hnrs Trm Papr Englsh 85-86; Hnrs A P Amer Hstry 85-86; Lbrl Arts.

KATS, IRINA; Fox Lane HS; Mount Kisco, NY; (Y); 1/280; Intnl Clb; Chorus; Jazz Band; Yrbk Ed-Chief; High Hon Roll; NHS; Ntl Merit SF; Val; Ballet Cls & Perf, RPI Awd Math & Sci 85; Westchester Smith Clb Bk Awd 85; Princeton U; Applied Math.

KATSOGRIDAKIS, YIANNIS; Holy Cross HS; Flushing, NY; (Y); 2/318; Art Clb; Chess Clb; Debate Tm; Library Aide; Speech Tm; Varsity Clb; Lit Mag; Trk; High Hon Roll; Pres NHS; Frank Galizia Memrl Schlrshp 85-86; Frank Galizia Memrl Schlrshp 84-85; NY U; Mdcl Dr.

KATTMAN, BRADY; Kenmore East HS; Buffalo, NY; (Y); Boy Scts; Church Yth Grp; Exploring; Varsity Clb; Church Choir; Concert Band; Mrchg Band; Capt Crs Cntry; Swmmng; Trk; Engrng.

KATZ, AARON; Jamesville De Witt HS; Jamesville, NY; (Y); 2/215; SADD; Stu Cncl; JV Capt Bsktbl; Var Ftbl; NHS; Ntl Merit Ltr; Ldrshp Svc Awd 86; Med.

KATZ, BETH; Canarsie HS; Brooklyn, NY; (Y); 51/600; Political Wkr; Service Clb; Ski Clb; Temple Yth Grp; Band; Concert Band; School Musical; High Hon Roll; Prfct Atten Awd; Fnlst All Brooklyn H S Essay On Beverly Sills 86; Monroe Cohen Mem Awd & Outstndng Comm Svc 86; CUNY; Hotel Mgmnt.

KATZ, BRIAN; East Meadow HS; East Meadow, NY; (Y); FBLA; Var Lcrss; Var Socr; Bus.

KATZ, BRIAN; Mamaroneck HS; Larchmont, NY; (Y); Trs German Clb; VP Latin Clb; Math Tm; Spanish Clb; Yrbk Phtg; Yrbk Stf; Lit Mag; Var Score Keeper; Var L Socr; Spanish NHS; Latin I Slvr Mdlst 86; Engr.

KATZ, DAVID; J F Kennedy HS; Merrick, NY; (Y); Computer Clb; Mathletes; Math Clb; Math Tm; SADD; Nwsp Rptr; Stu Cncl; Hon Roll; NHS; Ntl Merit Ltr.

KATZ, ELIZABETH; Clarkstown South HS; New City, NY; (Y); Cmnty Wkr; Spanish Clb; SADD; Yrbk Sprt Ed; Yrbk Stf; JV Var Bsktbl; JV Var Socr; Var Sftbl; Hon Roll; NHS.

KATZ, ERIC; Clarkstown South HS; W Nyack, NY; (Y); 1/500; Chess Clb; French Clb; Pres Math Clb; Capt Quiz Bowl; Speech Tm; VP SADD; Jazz Band; Mrchg Band; School Play; Yrbk Stf; Empire ST Schlrshp 86; Rgnts Schlrshp 86; PTA 86; Wlms; Med.

KATZ, GAIL A; Oceanside HS; Oceanside, NY; (Y); 39/520; Drama Clb; Thesps; VP Chorus; Madrigals; School Musical; School Play; Stage Crew; Hon Roll; Jr NHS; NHS; NY ST Regnts Schlrshp 86; All Cnty Chorus 85-86; All ST Womns Chorus 85; Lehigh U; Finc.

KATZ, JAMIE L; Eastchester HS; Eastchester, NY; (Y); Leo Clb; Sec Spanish Clb; Band; Yrbk Stf; Ed Lit Mag; Hon Roll; Trs NHS; Ntl Merit Ltr; Latin Clb; Tufts U; Psych.

KATZ, JENNIFER; John F Kennedy HS; Riverdale, NY; (Y); 58/873; Cmnty Wkr; Debate Tm; Drama Clb; JA; School Musical; School Play; Hon Roll; NHS; Pres Acdmc Ftns Awd 86; Natl Hnr Rl 84-85; Math Awd 84-85; SUNY Porchase; Drama.

KATZ, KENNETH T; Bronx HS Of Sci; Bronx, NY; (Y); Teachers Aide; Y-Teens; Sr Cls; Emery.

KATZ, RACHEL; Rocky Point JR SR HS; Shoreham, NY; (S); 5/210; Computer Clb; Math Tm; Science Clb; Spanish Clb; Jazz Band; Mrchg Band; Orch; School Musical; Symp Band; Hon Roll; Columbia U; Mellrgcl Engnrng.

KATZ, ROSANNE; Herbert H Lehman HS; Bronx, NY; (Y); 21/563; Band; Nwsp Ed-Chief; Hon Roll; NHS; 1st Pl Typing Comp 85; Acadmc Olympics Team 86; Accntng.

KATZ, SHAWN; Lindenhurst SR HS; Lindenhurst, NY; (Y); 35/550; Ski Clb; Spanish Clb; Band; Concert Band; Hon Roll; NHS.

KATZMAN, GAYLE B; Malverne HS; Malverne, NY; (Y); 7/147; Pres Temple Yth Grp; Jazz Band; Mrchg Band; Rep Stu Cncl; Hon Roll; VP NHS; St Schlr; Yth Partcptn Prjct Chairmn 85-86; U Of Rochester; Gentcs.

KATZMAN, MARNIE; South Side HS; Rockville Ctr, NY; (Y); Latin Clb; Sec VP Mathletes; Office Aide; Orch; School Musical; High Hon Roll; NHS; NYSSMA; Natl Latn Hnr Soc 85-86.

KAUFFMAN, LOUISE A; William Nottingham HS; Syracuse, NY; (Y); 32/220; Red Cross Aide; Ski Clb; Spanish Clb; Yrbk Phtg; JV Capt Socr; High Hon Roll; Trs NHS; Spanish NHS; Regents Schlrshp 86; Syracuse U; Pol Sci.

KAUFFMAN, NICHOLAS; Nottingham HS; Syracuse, NY; (Y); Red Cross Aide; Ski Clb; Spanish Clb; JV Ftbl; Var L Lcrss; Hon Roll; Spanish NHS; Pre-Med.

KAUFINGER, GREGORY G; Horseheads HS; Elmira, NY; (Y); Am Leg Boys St; VP Chess Clb; VP Church Yth Grp; VP JA; JCL; Latin Clb; Spanish Clb; Hon Roll; NHS; Latin Awd 84; Aviatn Mgt.

KAUFMAN, BARBARA; Villa Maria Acad; Buffalo, NY; (Y); 11/98; Pres Church Yth Grp; French Clb; Church Choir; Hon Roll; Sec NHS; Friars Scholar St Bonaventure 86; Deans Scholar Cansius Coll 86; Svc Awd 86; St Bonaventure; Mth.

KAUFMAN, CHRISTINE; West Islip HS; W Islip, NY; (Y); Drama Clb; Mathletes; Acpl Chr; Chorus; Madrigals; Swing Chorus; Rep Frsh Cls; Sec Soph Cls; Sec Jr Cls; Var L Pom Pon; Lib Arts.

KAUFMAN, ERIC; East Hampton HS; E Hampton, NY; (Y); 7/170; Am Leg Boys St; Varsity Clb; Socr; JV Trk; Capt Var Wrstlng; DAR Awd; High Hon Roll; Jr NHS; Lion Awd; NHS; Lions Clb Stu Of Mnth March 86; Wrstlg Cnty Rnnr-Up, Leag Champ 86; Physcs Achvt Awd 86; Cornell U; Bus Admin.

KAUFMAN, ERIC A; Horseheads SR HS; Horseheads, NY; (S); 7/380; German Clb; Sec Science Clb; Ski Clb; Chorus; Concert Band; Mrchg Band; Orch; School Musical; High Hon Roll; NHS; Engrng.

KAUFMAN, JOANNE; Horseheads HS; Horseheads, NY; (Y); 3/326; Debate Tm; Drama Clb; Model UN; Spanish Clb; Temple Yth Grp; Chorus; School Musical; Swing Chorus; Variety Show; Stu Cncl; Lib Arts.

KAUFMAN, JODY L; Ward Melville HS; Stony Brook, NY; (Y); 86/711; Hosp Aide; Var Bsbl; Ice Hcky; Socr; High Hon Roll; Rgnts Schlrshp 86; Trvl Tm St Louis & Lng Isl Ice Hockey, Top Dfnsmn LI; All Star Bsbl; Hosp Vol; SUNY Binhamton; Bio Pre-Med.

KAUFMAN, KRISTINE; Newark SR HS; Newark, NY; (Y); 20/289; Pres Drama Clb; Latin Clb; Pres SADD; Band; School Musical; School Play; Yrbk Stf; High Hon Roll; NHS; Ntl Merit SF; JR Hnr Grl 86.

KAUFMAN, RACHEL; James Madison HS; Brooklyn, NY; (Y); 6/756; Hosp Aide; Teachers Aide; Jazz Band; School Musical; Symp Band; Nwsp Rptr; Yrbk Stf; High Hon Roll; NHS; Mathletes; Russn Clb 85-87; Frgn Lang.

KAUFMANN, KIMBERLY; New Rochelle HS; New Rochelle, NY; (Y); Varsity Clb; Var Socr; French Hon Soc; Hon Roll; NHS; 2nd All Arnd Clss 2 Regn 6 Gymstcs Champ 85; Rep USA 3 Man Tm 85; CT ST Champ Gymnstcs 86.

KAUP, MELISSA; Potsdam Central HS; Potsdam, NY; (Y); 13/153; AFS; French Clb; Acpl Chr; Chorus; Rep Soph Cls; DAR Awd; Hon Roll; NHS; Var Trk; Talented JRS 86; Clarkson Schl 86; Clarkson U; Biochem.

KAUPER, RICHARD; Olean HS; Olean, NY; (Y); 13/210; Ski Clb; Varsity Clb; Var Crs Cntry; Var JV Trk; Hon Roll; NHS; NYS Regents Schrlshp 86; Ithaca Coll; Physcl Thrpy.

KAUPPILA, CRAIG; Walton Central Schl; Walton, NY; (Y); 11/102; Am Leg Boys St; Computer Clb; Key Clb; Model UN; Varsity Clb; Var Bsbl; Var Capt Bsktbl; Var Crs Cntry; High Hon Roll; Hon Roll; Indstrl Arts Stu Of Yr 85; Sidneyb Sktbl All-Star Tm 85-86; Waltn Vrsty Basebll Battng Champ 84-85; Communicatns.

KAUS, ROBERT; Mahopac HS; Lagrangeville, NY; (Y); 17/383; Capt Crs Cntry; Var Trk; High Hon Roll; NHS; Pres Schlr; St Schlr; SUNY Buffalo; Engr.

KAUSCH, KURT; Bishop Kearney HS; Rochester, NY; (Y); 10/142; Model UN; Band; Mrchg Band; School Musical; Yrbk Stf; Im Bowling; High Hon Roll; Hon Roll; NHS; Pres Acad Ftnss Awd Acad Achvt 86; Bio Excel 86; Rochester Inst Of Tech; Biotech.

KAUTZ, DAN; Amherst Central HS; Amherst, NY; (Y); Band; Ftbl; YES Vlntr Pgm Outstndng Vlntr Awd 82-85; Chrmn Yth Invlvmnt Cmmtte 86; Entrprnr.

KAVANAGH, BRIAN; Henninger HS; Syracuse, NY; (Y); 2/400; Am Leg Boys St; Boy Scts; Rep Stu Cncl; Var JV Bsktbl; JV Var Crs Cntry; JV Var Lcrss; Hon Roll; Sr Patrl Ldr Boy Scts 82-84; Tchng Hstry.

KAVANAGH, CHRISTOPHER; South Side HS; Rockville Centre, NY; (Y); Latin Clb; Office Aide; Varsity Clb; Var Bsbl; Hon Roll; Ad Promovendum Studium Latinum Natl Latin Hnr Soc 85 & 86; Law.

KAVANAGH, DEBBIE; Seaford HS; Seaford, NY; (Y); SADD; Yrbk Stf; Lit Mag; Lcrss; Mgr(s); High Hon Roll; Hon Roll; Sec NHS; Chem Awd 84-85; Fash Dsgnr.

KAVANAGH, THOMAS; Xavier HS; Jackson Hgts, NY; (Y); 15/240; Church Yth Grp; Computer Clb; ROTC; Yrbk Stf; Rep Frsh Cls; JV Var Tennis; Hon Roll; Ntl Merit Ltr; NEDT Awd.

KAY, BONNIE; William Floyd HS; Mastic Beach, NY; (Y); 1/460; GAA; Key Clb; Trs Spanish Clb; Yrbk Sprt Ed; Trs Stu Cncl; Var Capt Fld Hcky; Bausch & Lomb Sci Awd; NHS; St Schlr; Val; SUNY Albany; Intl Banking.

KAY, GEORGIA; Clarkstown South HS; New City, NY; (Y); Dance Clb; Chorus; JV Vllybl.

KAY, ROSEMARY; Bflo Acad Of The Sacred Heart; Buffalo, NY; (Y); Pres Church Yth Grp; JCL; Latin Clb; Chorus; Im Bowling; Vllybl; Hon Roll; Psych.

KAY IV, WILLIAM H; Arlington HS; Pleasant Valley, NY; (Y); Ski Clb; Yrbk Phtg; Var L Golf; Var L Tennis; Rotary Awd; Spanish NHS; Cornell U; Bus.

KAYMAKCIAN, MARI; St Francis Prep; Rego Park, NY; (S); 115/746; Opt Clb Awd; Acad All Amer 86; 7th Pl Amer Assn Tchrs German 85; Pre-Med.

KAYSER, BUDDY; Salhem HS North; Holbrook, NY; (Y); 211/1600; Art Clb; Church Yth Grp; German Clb; Varsity Clb; Im Socr; Var Capt Wrstlng; Archtctr.

KAYSER, MARK; Brockport HS; Brockport, NY; (Y); 56/340; Latin Clb; Model UN; Radio Clb; Im Badmtn; Im Bsktbl; Var Crs Cntry; Var L Trk; Im Vllybl; High Hon Roll; Hon Roll; Pol Sci.

KAYSER, NICOLE A; Brockport HS; Brockport, NY; (Y); 3/325; Trs Church Yth Grp; German Clb; Chorus; Sec Stage Crew; Stat Ftbl; Var L Trk; High Hon Roll; NHS; Cngrs-Bundestag Schlrshp 84-85; St Lwrnc Trstee Schlrshp 86-90; St Lawrence U; Sci.

KAYTON, BARBARA ANN; Wheatley HS; Mineola, NY; (Y); Camera Clb; Pep Clb; Trs Varsity Clb; School Play; Variety Show; Yrbk Phtg; Yrbk Sprt Ed; Stu Cncl; Var Fld Hcky; Var Lcrss; All Conf, All Cnty, Excptnl SR, Capt Vrsty Fld Hcky 83-85; Northeastern U; Phy Thrpy.

KAZACOS, CHRIS; Charles H Roth HS; W Henrietta, NY; (Y); Thesps; Chorus; School Musical; Stage Crew; Yrbk Stf; VP Jr Cls; JV Bsbl; Hon Roll; Jr NHS; Drama Clb; NYSSMA Solo Awd 86.

KAZENOFF, SUZANNE; Rocky Point HS; Rocky Point, NY; (S); 10/204; Pres French Clb; Math Tm; Thesps; Pres Chorus; Pres Madrigals; School Musical; Lit Mag; High Hon Roll; NHS; Voice Dem Awd; Law.

KAZEROID, SIBYLLE; St Anns Schl; Brooklyn, NY; (Y); Office Aide; PAVAS; Band; Chorus; Church Choir; Madrigals; Orch; School Musical; Crtfct Mrt In Msc 83; Mbr NYC All-Cty HS Bnd & Chrs 83-84; Opera.

KAZLO, LAURI; Crown Point Central HS; Crown Point, NY; (S); 2/35; Varsity Clb; Nwsp Stf; Yrbk Stf; VP Sr Cls; Var Capt Bsktbl; Var L Cheerleading; Var L Socr; Var L Sftbl; NHS; Sal; Prfct Attndnc 82-86; St Lawrence; Bus Adm.

KAZMIERCZAK, JACQUELIN; Hamburg Central HS; Hamburg, NY; (Y); Var Capt Crs Cntry; Var Capt Trk; Hon Roll; NHS; Mst Valuable Persn Trck 83-84; Mst Imprvd Crs Cntry 84; Bus.

KAZMIERCZAK, MICHAEL A; Hutchinson Central Tech HS; Buffalo, NY; (Y); 46/268; VP JA; Mathletes; Math Clb; Math Tm; Nwsp Ed-Chief; Nwsp Rptr; Nwsp Sprt Ed; Nwsp Stf; Var Tennis; Hon Roll; Regents Schlrshp 86; Geneseo ST U; Geophysics.

KAZMIERCZAK III, THOMAS T; St Josephs Collegiate Inst; Cheektowaga, NY; (Y); 40/201; Cmnty Wkr; Drama Clb; Sec German Clb; Concert Band; Orch; Lit Mag; God Cntry Awd; Hon Roll; Boy Scts; Church Yth Grp; Grtr Buffalo Yth Orch-Chmbr Orch-Viola 82-86; NYS Area All ST, Erie Cnty, Niagara Cnty Music 82-86; SUNY Buffalo; Pre Med.

KAZUKIEWICZ, MONICA L; Hutchinson Central Tech HS; Buffalo, NY; (Y); Church Yth Grp; Var Bowling; Var Sftbl; Hon Roll; Jr NHS; Comp Sci.

KEACH, CHRIS; Bay Shore HS; Bay Shore, NY; (Y); 38/406; Am Leg Boys St; Church Yth Grp; Computer Clb; Intnl Clb; Pres Sr Cls; Rep Stu Cncl; Capt JV Socr; Var Tennis; Var Trk; Ntl Merit Ltr.

KEACH, MARGARET; Cicero North Syracuse HS; Clay, NY; (S); Church Yth Grp; Cmnty Wkr; Girl Scts; SADD; Chorus; Mrchg Band; NHS; Teenage Vlntr Yr Awd 85; Onondaga Cmmnty Coll Schlr 85; Natl Hstry & Govt Awds 84; Engl H S Engl Tchr.

KEAGLE, JEFFREY S; Horseheads SR HS; Horseheads, NY; (S); 19/380; German Clb; Variety Show; Nwsp Stf; Var JV Bsbl; Im Bsktbl; Im Vllybl; High Hon Roll; Hon Roll; NHS.

KEANE, DEBRA; St Edmund HS; Brooklyn, NY; (S); 9/200; Girl Scts; Spanish Clb; Church Choir; Hon Roll; NHS; Columbia U.

KEARNEY, BARBARA P; Tonawanda HS; Tonawanda, NY; (Y); 9/220; Am Leg Aux Girls St; SADD; Varsity Clb; Stu Cncl; Var Sftbl; Var Vllybl; High Hon Roll; NHS; Pres Schlr; St Schlr; Regents Schlrshp 86; Pan-Hellenic Awd 86; Tonawanda Yth Brd Schlrshp 86; SUNY Buffalo; Med.

KEARNEY, BRIAN; Lindenhurst HS; Lindenhurst, NY; (Y); Ski Clb; Spanish Clb; Varsity Clb; JV Bsbl; Var L Bsktbl; Im Vllybl; High Hon Roll; Hon Roll; VFW Awd; Tchrs Assn Englsh Achvt Awd 83; Bus Mngmt.

KEARNEY, JEFFERY; Jamestown HS; Jamestown, NY; (Y); Trs Concert Band; Mrchg Band; Ed.

KEARNEY, PAUL; Half Hollow Hills High School East; Dix Hills, NY; (Y); Computer Clb; Trs Drama Clb; Intnl Clb; School Play; JV Trk; Hon Roll; Awd-Crtv Wrtng Cntst-Estrn Sfflk 86; Trck Awd-H S Leag II Chmpns 85-86; Bio-Chem.

KEARNS, MICHAEL P; Bishop Timon HS; Buffalo, NY; (Y); Am Leg Boys St; Church Yth Grp; Chorus; Rep Jr Cls; Rep Sr Cls; Stu Cncl; Bsbl; Bsktbl; Socr; Hon Roll; Comm Svc Awd 86; Political Science.

KEARNS, PATRICK; Port Jervis HS; Port Jervis, NY; (Y); 2/184; Math Tm; Scholastic Bowl; Ski Clb; Var Tennis; High Hon Roll; Pres NHS; Ntl Merit SF; Rotary Awd; Sal; DAR Good Ctzn Awd 86; U Notre Dame; Mech Engrng.

KEARSE, BRADLEY; Long Island Lutheran HS; Hempstead, NY; (S); 37/92; Boy Scts; Camera Clb; Teachers Aide; Var Bowling; Var L Ftbl; Cit Awd; High Hon Roll; Hon Roll; NHS; Spanish NHS; Acad Schlrshp 83; George Mason U; Comp Engrng.

KEARSE, ROBIN; Norman Thomas HS; Brooklyn, NY; (S); 73/597; Computer Clb; Drama Clb; Band; Concert Band; School Musical; Nwsp Rptr; Yrbk Stf; Rep Jr Cls; Pres Sr Cls; Sec Stu Cncl; Hnrd Mayor Koch NYCS Super Yth 85; Norman Thomas HJ Awd Theatre Prod 86; Principals Commdtn Awd Svc; Comp Progrmng.

KEARY, KATHLEEN; Lansingburgh HS; Troy, NY; (Y); French Clb; Hon Roll; Chld Psych.

KEATING, DANIELLE; Bishop Grimes HS; Bridgeport, NY; (S); SADD; School Play; Var Trk; Var Vllybl; High Hon Roll; Hon Roll.

KEATING, JAMES; Niskayuna HS; Schenectady, NY; (Y); AFS; Key Clb; Jazz Band; Orch; Trs Frsh Cls; Trs Soph Cls; Pres Jr Cls; Pres Sr Cls; Var Swmmng; JV Trk.

KEATING, KERI; Walter Panas HS; Peekskill, NY; (Y); Ski Clb; SADD; Varsity Clb; Off Frsh Cls; Off Soph Cls; Off Jr Cls; Off Sr Cls; Stu Cncl; Bowling; Socr; New Paltz SUNY; Psych.

KEAVENY, PATRICK; Williamsville North HS; W Amherst, NY; (Y); Cmnty Wkr; DECA; Political Wkr; Ski Clb; Im Ftbl; JV Wrstlng; Hon Roll; Hnr Roll 85-87; Boston Coll; Comm.

KEBA, PAUL; Moravia Central HS; Locke, NY; (Y); Church Yth Grp; Var Bowling; Var Crs Cntry; Var Trk; Hon Roll; Yorkers 85-86; FL Inst Of Tech; Pilot.

KEEBLER, SUSAN; Waterloo SR HS; Waterloo, NY; (Y); Pres FHA; FTA; Office Aide; Band; Concert Band; Mrchg Band; Yrbk Phtg; Daisy Chain 85; JR Rotarian 86; Float & Ball Prom Comm 82-86; Rochester Dentl Schl; Dentl.

KEEFE, JENNIFER; Cairo-Durham HS; Cairo, NY; (Y); Church Yth Grp; Cmnty Wkr; Band; Concert Band; Pep Band; JV Var Bsktbl; JV L Socr; JV L Sftbl; JV L Vllybl; High Hon Roll; Engl.

KEEFE, MICHAEL; Lansingburgh HS; Troy, NY; (S); 4/186; French Clb; Math Tm; Yrbk Stf; Stu Cncl; Var JV Tennis; High Hon Roll; NHS; Computer Clb; Im Bsktbl; Im Lcrss; Howard E Vergow Salutatrn Awd 83; RPI Medl Mth & Sci 85; Stu Art Awd 83; Hudson Vly CC; Aerontcl.

KEEFE, RICHARD T; Greenport HS; Greeport, NY; (Y); 1/47; Am Leg Boys St; Variety Show; Nwsp Bus Mgr; Yrbk Sprt Ed; Pres Frsh Cls; Pres Soph Cls; Pres Stu Cncl; High Hon Roll; NHS; Ntl Merit Ltr; Flm Wrtng.

KEEFER, JEFF; Middletown HS; Middletown, NY; (Y); Sec Church Yth Grp; French Clb; Sec Political Wkr; Teachers Aide; Hon Roll; NHS; My Quote Reprsnted HS In NY Imagination Celebration 83-84; Psych.

KEEGAN, CHRISTINE; Earl L Vandermeulen HS; Mt Sinai, NY; (Y); 90/310; Art Clb; Drama Clb; FBLA; Leo Clb; Pep Clb; Spanish Clb; SADD; Band; School Musical; Nwsp Stf; Kiwanis Club Awd/Schlrshp 86; SUNY Oswego; Bus.

KEEGAN, MARK; Xavier HS; Brooklyn, NY; (Y); Office Aide; Varsity Clb; Yrbk Stf; Lit Mag; Stu Cncl; Wrstlng; Hon Roll.

KEEGAN, PATRICK; Iowa Preparatory Schl; Eastchester, NY; (Y); 37/204; JV Crs Cntry; JV Golf; Hon Roll; Knigts Of Colmbs Schlrshp 83.

KEEHAN, DAWN; Bishop Scully HS; Fonda, NY; (S); 1/55; 4-H; Sec Math Clb; Red Cross Aide; School Play; Yrbk Stf; Vllybl; 4-H Awd; High Hon Roll; NHS; Ntl Ldrshp Merit Awd 85; Schl Rep Hugh O Brien Yth Found 84; Physics.

KEELEHER, SUSAN A; Frontier Central HS; Hamburg, NY; (Y); 28/430; Exploring; Latin Clb; Stu Cncl; Capt Crs Cntry; Trk; High Hon Roll; Hon Roll; NHS; Pres Schlr; Alfred U Presdntl Schlrshp & Prfrmng Arts Schlrshp 86; Regnts Schlrshp 86; Alfred U; Vet.

KEELEN, MICHAEL R; Troy HS; Wynantskill, NY; (Y); 85/425; German Clb; Bsktbl; Im Socr; SUNY Buffalo; Blgcl Sci.

KEELER, RUSTY; Skaneateles HS; Skaneateles, NY; (S); Ski Clb; Jazz Band; Variety Show; Off Frsh Cls; Off Soph Cls; Ice Hcky; Socr; High Hon Roll; NHS; Hnrbl Mntn Schlstc Art Awds 84; Arch.

KEELEY, JUDITH; Huntington HS; Huntington, NY; (Y); Mathletes; Orch; Nwsp Stf; L Trk; Bausch & Lomb Sci Awd; NHS; Bronze Mdl In Long Island Math Fair; Comp Sci.

KEEN, COLIN; Walt Whitman HS; Huntington, NY; (Y); 21/479; French Clb; Key Clb; Mathletes; Jazz Band; Mrchg Band; Capt Crs Cntry; Var Trk; French Hon Soc; High Hon Roll; Jr NHS; Math.

KEENAN, CAROLYN; Lewiston Porter SR HS; Lewiston, NY; (Y); 47/236; JA; Nwsp Rptr; Hon Roll; St Schlr; Bus Adm.

KEENAN, JOHN; Albertus Magnus HS; Stony Point, NY; (Y); 34/197; Latin Clb; Service Clb; Stage Crew; Capt Bsktbl; Capt Socr; Trk; VP Soph Cls; Pres Jr Cls; Pres Sr Cls; Soccer All Section-2nd Team 85-86; Basketball PSAL Section Honorable Mention 85-86; Law.

KEENAN, KEVIN; Carmel HS; Carmel, NY; (Y); Cmnty Wkr; FBLA; ROTC; SADD; Ftbl; High Hon Roll; Hon Roll; Jr NHS; NHS; Prfct Atten Awd; Political Sci.

KEENAN JR, PAUL J; Jamesville-De Witt HS; Dewitt, NY; (Y); 21/250; JCL; Off Stu Cncl; Var L Crs Cntry; Var L Trk; NHS; Navy ROTC 4 Yr Schlrshp 86; Air Force 4 Yr Schlrshp 86; Tufts U; Naval Aviatr.

KEENE, BECKY; Gilbertsville Central HS; Gilbertsville, NY; (Y); 1/17; Am Leg Aux Girls St; Church Yth Grp; Drama Clb; 4-H; SADD; Band; Chorus; Church Choir; Color Guard; Concert Band; JH Mathmtcs Tchr.

KEENE, DENNIS B; John F Kennedy HS; Mahopac, NY; (Y); 40/194; SADD; Teachers Aide; JV Bsbl; Var Ftbl; JV Trk; Hon Roll; All Lg 2nd Tm Ftbl 85; NYS Rgnts Schlrshp 86; Army ROTC Schlrshp 86; Syracuse U.

KEENE, MEGAN E; Waterloo HS; Waterloo, NY; (Y); 14/168; Ski Clb; Varsity Clb; Yrbk Ed-Chief; Rep Stu Cncl; L Cheerleading; L Trk; Hon Roll; NHS; Regents Schlrshp 86; Syracuse; Chemstry.

KEENEY, BRIAN; G Ray Bodley HS; Fulton, NY; (Y); Science Clb; Band; Concert Band; Jazz Band; Mrchg Band; Symp Band; High Hon Roll; NHS; Prfct Atten Awd; Sci Olypiad Tm 86-87; Math Awd 84-86; Social Stds Awd 84-86; Fin Invstmnt.

KEENEY, CAMI; Batavia HS; Batavia, NY; (Y); 63/218; Church Yth Grp; Band; Concert Band; Mrchg Band; Variety Show; Yrbk Rptr; Yrbk Stf; Genesee CC; Trvl.

KEENLY, ERIC J; Port Byron HS; Port Bryon, NY; (Y); 8/164; Am Leg Boys St; Hosp Aide; Speech Tm; Band; Chorus; Concert Band; Drm Mjr(t); Jazz Band; Mrchg Band; School Musical; Hugh O Brian Yth Fndtn Awd 85; Med.

KEESLER, KELLY; Archbishop Walsh HS; Belmont, NY; (Y); Church Yth Grp; Drama Clb; Pep Clb; Spanish Clb; School Musical; Jr Cls; Stu Cncl; High Hon Roll; Ed.

KEESLER, SEAN; Sauquoit Valley Central HS; Frankfort, NY; (Y); Band; Jazz Band; Hon Roll; NHS; Comp Sci.

KEFER, DEBORAH; Amityville Memorial HS; Massapequa, NY; (Y); 10/200; Drama Clb; FBLA; Math Tm; Temple Yth Grp; Band; Orch; School Play; Nwsp Stf; Yrbk Stf; Stu Cncl; Law.

KEFER, JODI M; Amityville Memorial HS; Massapequa, NY; (Y); 2/215; Drama Clb; Math Tm; Office Aide; Pres Temple Yth Grp; Band; Jazz Band; Mrchg Band; Orch; School Play; Nwsp Stf; Rgnts Schlrshp Wnnr 86; Johns Hopkins U; Pre-Med.

KEGEBEIN, BOB; Vernon Verona Sherrill HS; Verona, NY; (Y); JV Var Ftbl; Im Lcrss; Im Wt Lftg; Hon Roll; Crmnl Just.

KEHL, JENNIFER L; Shoreham-Wading River HS; Shoreham, NY; (Y); Sec VP Church Yth Grp; Computer Clb; Math Tm; Orch; Yrbk Ed-Chief; Yrbk Stf; NHS; Ntl Merit Ltr; Mathletes; Math Clb; Rgnl Rep Amrcn Rgnl Math Lg Cmptn 86; Sfflk Cnty Math Tchrs Assoc Awds 85&86; NY ST Schl Music Awds; Engnrng.

KEHRLE, KARL; Ossining HS; Ossining, NY; (Y); Pres Band; Concert Band; Jazz Band; Mrchg Band; School Musical; Symp Band; Var Tennis; High Hon Roll.

KEIB, JOHN; Jamesville-De Witt HS; Syracuse, NY; (Y); 15/240; Varsity Clb; Nwsp Phtg; Soph Cls; Bsbl; Socr; Wt Lftg; Wrstlng; High Hon Roll; Jr NHS; NHS; MVP Varsity Bsbl, Wrstlng & Scr 85-86; Pltcl Sci.

KEILITZ, KATHLEEN; Lindenhurst SR HS; Lindenhurst, NY; (Y); 17/500; French Clb; Concert Band; Mrchg Band; School Musical; Nwsp Rptr; Rep Soph Cls; French Hon Soc; High Hon Roll; NHS; Recog Awd Hofstra U 85-86; Hofstra U; Intl Bus.

KEINGARSKY, KEITH W; Syosset SR HS; Syosset, NY; (Y); 87/492; Computer Clb; 4-H; Office Aide; Ski Clb; Temple Yth Grp; Hon Roll; NHS; St Schlr; Rgnts Schlrshp 86; Spnsh Awd 83; Nassua Cnty Dpt Cnsmr Affrs Awd 83; SUNY Albany; Acctg.

KEITEL, CRAIG; Earl L Vandermeulen HS; Pt Jefferson, NY; (Y); Nwsp Stf; JV Ftbl; JV Wrstlng; Med.

KEKOLER, NANCY; Abraham Lincoln HS; Brooklyn, NY; (Y); Nwsp Ed-Chief; Nwsp Stf; Yrbk Stf; Ed Lit Mag; High Hon Roll; Trs NHS; Prncpls Awd 84; Golden Recrd Achvt Awd 81; BASIS Publictns Cert Awd 86; Jrnlsm.

KELCH, RICHARD; Half Hollow Hills HS West; Dix Hills, NY; (Y); Boy Scts; Nwsp Phtg; Yrbk Phtg; High Hon Roll; Zoolgy.

KELCHLIN, NANCY; Mt Mercy Acad; Buffalo, NY; (S); 9/208; Debate Tm; JCL; NFL; SADD; Chorus; Variety Show; Nwsp Stf; Off Jr Cls; High Hon Roll; Church Yth Grp; Natl Wnnr-Natl Lang Arts Olympiad 83-84; U Of Buffalo; Physcl Thrpy.

KELEHER, EVELYN JEAN; Pioneer Central HS; Arcade, NY; (Y); Church Yth Grp; Sec French Clb; Chorus; Church Choir; Madrigals; School Musical; Swing Chorus; Cheerleading; Crs Cntry; Fld Hcky; Gold Music Awd 84-85; Music Ther.

KELEKIAN, JIRAIR; Roy C Ketcham HS; Wappingers Falls, NY; (Y); Varsity Clb; High Hon Roll; Hon Roll; Mgr(s); Var Socr; Var Tennis; Pre-Med.

KELIHER, JOHN; Sachem North HS; Holbrook, NY; (Y); 112/1500; Service Clb; Ski Clb; Spanish Clb; Chorus; JV Socr; Zenith Clb Hnr Soc 84-85; Teams USA Soccer Tm Rep USA In Europe 86; Soc Stud Tech.

KELIN, LISA; Lindenhurst HS; Lindenhurst, NY; (Y); 30/550; Am Leg Aux Girls St; Spanish Clb; Varsity Clb; Stat Bsbl; Stat Bsktbl; Var L Socr; JV L Vllybl; Jr NHS; NHS; Polit Sci.

KELLEHER, HELEN C; Stella Maris HS; Rockaway Beach, NY; (Y); 7/213; Cmnty Wkr; Var Math Tm; Pep Clb; Teachers Aide; Band; Chorus; Church Choir; Drm & Bgl; Mrchg Band; Var Bsktbl; Natl Bus Hnr Soc; Rockaway Cath-Jewsh Cmmnty Essy Wnr; Rgnts Schlrshp; Alfred U; Engrng.

KELLEHER, SUSAN; Frontier Central HS; Hamburg, NY; (S); 31/500; Latin Clb; Red Cross Aide; Band; Concert Band; Mrchg Band; School Musical; Symp Band; Stu Cncl; Crs Cntry; Trk; NEDT Cert; Blodmble Chrmn; Vet.

KELLER III, CHARLES W; Addison Central HS; Addison, NY; (Y); Boy Scts; Yrbk Stf; Var L Socr; Var L Swmmng; High Hon Roll; NHS; Engrng.

KELLER, JIM; Henninger HS; Syracuse, NY; (Y); Var Bsbl; Var Ftbl; Hon Roll.

KELLER, KIM; Gowanda Central HS; Dayton, NY; (Y); 26/128; 4-H; Girl Scts; Library Aide; Spanish Clb; Band; Chorus; Yrbk Stf; 4-H Awd; High Hon Roll; Hon Roll; U NC; Accntg.

KELLER, KIMBERLY; Hugh C Williams HS; Canton, NY; (Y); SADD; Thesps; Chorus; School Musical; School Play; Stu Cncl; Socr; Sftbl; High Hon Roll; Hon Roll; Capt-Precsn Fgur Sktng Tm 84-86; Rookie Of Yr-Sccr & Sftbl 85-86; Hlth.

KELLER, LORIE; Athena HS; Rochester, NY; (Y); 83/308; Church Yth Grp; Dance Clb; Letterman Clb; SADD; Orch; VP Frsh Cls; Sec Soph Cls; Sec Jr Cls; JV Var Cheerleading; Hon Roll; Jazz Dance Awd 86; NYSSMA Suprior Rtng Violin Lvl 6 84-85; Fshn Mrchndzng.

KELLER, MATTHEW; Cornwall Central HS; Salisbury Mills, NY; (Y); Boys Clb Am; JV Bsbl; JV Var Ftbl; JV Var Wrstlng; Hon Roll; NHS; Treas Of NHS 86; Ldrshp Camp 85; Air Force; Aeronautics.

KELLETT, KIM; St John The Baptist D HS; Amityville, NY; (Y); 155/497; Art Clb; Church Yth Grp; Ski Clb; SADD; Chorus; Yrbk Stf; Vllybl; Fnlst Chnnl 13 Stu Art Fstvl 86; Wn NY Stck Exchng Awd 86; Art.

KELLEY, CHERYL; Cicero-North Sycacuse HS; Brewerton, NY; (S); 42/667; Girl Scts; Library Aide; Scholastic Bowl; SADD; Mrchg Band; Rep Frsh Cls; Rep Soph Cls; Rep Jr Cls; Rep Sr Cls; Rep Stu Cncl; Vlntr Of Yr 84; U S Navl Sea Cadt.

KELLEY, DEBORAH; Paul V Moore HS; Constantia, NY; (Y); Sec Band; Concert Band; Drm Mjr(t); Jazz Band; Mrchg Band; Symp Band; JV Socr; Hon Roll; MVP Soccer 83; Most Improved Freshman Bank 84; Child Psych.

KELLEY, JAMES A; Sayville HS; Sayville, NY; (Y); 22/330; French Clb; Pres Key Clb; Ski Clb; School Play; JV Ice Hcky; Im Vllybl; High Hon Roll; Kiwanis Awd; NHS; Rgnts Scshlrshp 85-86; Islip Towns Ldrshp Awd 84-85; Mbr Bd Deacons Sayville UCC 84-86; U VT; Econ.

KELLEY, JOSEPH; Burnt Hills Ballston Lake HS; Ballston Lake, NY; (Y); 70/341; Band; Concert Band; Jazz Band; Mrchg Band; Pep Band; JV Socr; Hon Roll; Engnrng.

KELLEY, JULIANNE; Ravena-Corywans-Selkirk SR HS; Coeymans Hollow, NY; (Y); Debate Tm; Drama Clb; French Clb; Orch; School Musical; Nwsp Rptr; Nwsp Stf; Lit Mag; Var Trk; Hon Roll; Cert Commendtn Orch 85; Awd Vol Wrk Histrc Mansion 84; Music.

KELLEY, KAREN; Camden Central HS; Camden, NY; (Y); 22/211; Sec AFS; Am Leg Aux Girls St; Drama Clb; Varsity Clb; Yrbk Stf; Golf; High Hon Roll; NHS; SUNY Coll Cobleskill; Comp Sci.

KELLEY, KERRI; Naples Central Schl; Naples, NY; (Y); 34/64; Church Yth Grp; Cmnty Wkr; Chorus; Yrbk Phtg; Yrbk Stf; Lit Mag; JV Var Sftbl; JV Vllybl; Hon Roll; CC Of The Finger Lakes; Cnslr.

KELLEY, KRISTINE ANN; Wheatland-Chili HS; Scottsville, NY; (Y); Church Yth Grp; Girl Scts; Spanish Clb; Nwsp Bus Mgr; Nwsp Sprt Ed; Hon Roll; Lion Awd; Prfct Atten Awd; Library Aide; Nwsp Rptr; Terry Coots Srv Awd 86; 10 Yr Awd Grl Scts 85; Roberts Wesleyan Coll; Crmnl Js.

KELLEY, LISA; Clifton-Fine Central HS; Oswegatchie, NY; (S); 2/42; French Clb; Yrbk Ed-Chief; Yrbk Phtg; Yrbk Stf; Sec Frsh Cls; JV Bsktbl; High Hon Roll; NHS; Tlntd Jr Pgm 84; St Lawrence U.

KELLEY, MICHAEL; Newark SR HS; Newark, NY; (Y); 40/200; Service Clb; Varsity Clb; Rep Jr Cls; Var L Bsktbl; Stat Score Keeper; Stat Socr; Var L Tennis; NHS; Colgate; Finance.

KELLEY, PATRICIA; Le Roy Central HS; Leroy, NY; (Y); AFS; Library Aide; Spanish Clb; Im Bsktbl; DAR Awd; Math.

KELLEY, ROBIN; C E Gorton HS; Yonkers, NY; (Y); Spanish Clb; Rep Frsh Cls; Rep Soph Cls; Rep Jr Cls; Rep Stu Cncl; Mgr(s); Score Keeper; Var Trk; JV Var Vllybl; Gen Foods Oper Opprtnty Pro Escrow Acct 86; Geom.

KELLEY, TERESA; Pulaski JR SR HS; Pulaski, NY; (Y); 54/98; Drama Clb; 4-H; FFA; Girl Scts; SADD; VICA; Band; Mrchg Band; School Musical; GAA; NY Rep Ntl Ctr West 83; Cntnry Coll Grnt 86; Centenary Coll; Hndcp Educ.

KELLIHER, KYLE A; Ballston Spa HS; Ballston Spa, NY; (Y); 29/244; Boy Scts; Computer Clb; Debate Tm; Drama Clb; 4-H; Math Tm; Science Clb; Stage Crew; High Hon Roll; Ntl Merit Ltr; Worcester Polytech Inst; Med.

KELLMAN, KARL; South Side HS; Rockville Centre, NY; (Y); Chess Clb; Drama Clb; Acpl Chr; Chorus; Church Choir; Madrigals; School Musical; High Hon Roll; Hon Roll; Cmmnty Svc Awd Music 85 & 86; Accptnc All Cntry Chorus 86; Comp Engrng.

KELLMANSON, LYNN; Pittsford Sutherland HS; Pittsford, NY; (Y); Art Clb; Sec Exploring; Hosp Aide; Yrbk Ed-Chief; Yrbk Stf; Cit Awd; High Hon Roll; Hon Roll; NHS; Spanish NHS; Frgn Exch Japan 86; Internshp Rochester Eye Inst 86; Pre-Med.

KELLNER, LAURA; Riverhead HS; Calverton, NY; (Y); 7/190; Drama Clb; Latin Clb; Science Clb; Ski Clb; Concert Band; Mrchg Band; Yrbk Stf; Var Pom Pon; Var Tennis; NHS; Yng Schlrs Pgm Stonybrk U 86; Aspirng Toward Exc Wrtng Awd 86; Magna Cum Laude Ntl Latin Ex 84.

KELLOGG, MICHELLE; E J Wilson HS; Rochester, NY; (Y); 19/320; Sec Church Yth Grp; French Clb; Jazz Band; Mrchg Band; Symp Band; Hon Roll; NHS; Symphnc Bnd Achvt Awd 84-85; Pre-Law.

KELLOGG, SUSAN A; Byron-Bergen HS; Batavia, NY; (Y); 15/100; 4-H; SADD; Band; Concert Band; Mrchg Band; Yrbk Stf; Hon Roll; Stage Crew; Merit Tutn Schlrshp Genesee CC 86; NY ST Rgnts Schlrshp 86; Peer Cnslr 86; Genesee CC; Bus Adm.

KELLY, ALTHEA; Delaware Acad; Hamden, NY; (Y); Intnl Clb; Spanish Clb; Off VICA; Lit Mag; Hon Roll; Prsdntl Acdmc Ftnss Awd 86; Hnr Grad 86; Rgnts Schlrshp 86; Air Force; Elctrncs.

KELLY, AMY; Perry Central HS; Perry, NY; (Y); 10/100; Band; Chorus; Concert Band; Jazz Band; Mrchg Band; School Musical; Cit Awd; High Hon Roll; Hon Roll; NHS.

KELLY, BETH; Sweet Home HS; Williamsville, NY; (Y); Library Aide; Chorus; MI St U; Psychol.

KELLY, BRENDA; Bay Shore HS; Bay Shore, NY; (Y); Chorus; JV Crs Cntry; JV Socr; Var JV Trk; Comp Mgmt.

KELLY, BRIAN A; John S Burke Catholic HS; Pine Bush, NY; (Y); School Musical; Rep Jr Cls; Rep Stu Cncl; Var L Bsbl; High Hon Roll; NHS; Ntl Merit Ltr; NEDT Awd; Pres Schlr; St Schlr; Amer Studies Awd; Bryant Coll; Bus Acctg.

KELLY, BRONWYN; Sacred Heart Acad; Malverne, NY; (Y); SADD; Nwsp Stf; Ed Yrbk Phtg; Yrbk Stf; Stu Cncl; Tennis.

KELLY, CATHERINE; The Mary Louis Acad; Jackson Heights, NY; (Y); Intnl Clb; Office Aide; Coach Actv; Var Crs Cntry; Var Trk; High Hon Roll; Hon Roll; Jr NHS; 1st Pl Daily News Essy Cont 84; Bus Mgmt.

KELLY, CHARMAINE LYNN; Naples Central HS; Naples, NY; (Y); Aud/Vis; Library Aide; Trs Sec Band; Chorus; Concert Band; Mrchg Band; School Musical; Nwsp Ed-Chief; Nwsp Rptr; Nwsp Stf; Regnts Schlrshp Tchr Of Yr 85-86; Pres Acadmc Ftnss Awd; U Of Rochester; Pre Law.

KELLY, CHRIS; Valley Central HS; Montgomery, NY; (Y); Chess Clb; Drama Clb; School Musical; School Play; Stu Cncl; Jrnlsm.

KELLY, CHRISTINE; Madrid-Waddington Central HS; Madrid, NY; (Y); 8/64; AFS; Drama Clb; NFL; Spanish Clb; School Musical; School Play; Yrbk Ed-Chief; Cheerleading; Socr; High Hon Roll; SUNY; Secndry Educ.

KELLY, CHRISTINE RUTH; The Mary Louis Acad; Forest Hills, NY; (Y); 137/262; Cmnty Wkr; Library Aide; Office Aide; Service Clb; Teachers Aide; Yrbk Rptr; Yrbk Stf; Math Hnrs 85; Manhattan Coll; Engrng.

KELLY, CHRISTOPHER P; South Glens Falls HS; S Glens Falls, NY; (Y); 2/225; Am Leg Boys St; Drama Clb; SADD; School Musical; School Play; Trs Soph Cls; Trs Jr Cls; Trs Sr Cls; Rep Stu Cncl; High Hon Roll.

KELLY, CINDY; Solvay HS; Solvay, NY; (Y); Church Yth Grp; Chorus; Hon Roll; Bryant & Stratton; Bus.

KELLY, COLLEEN; Greenville Central HS; Westerloo, NY; (Y); Church Yth Grp; Cmnty Wkr; 4-H; Teachers Aide; Church Choir; Var Sftbl; Hon Roll; Gregg Typng Awd 86; Potsdam NY; Math.

KELLY, DAVID; Dewitt Clinton HS; Bronx, NY; (Y); Art Clb; Key Clb; Office Aide; Science Clb; Speech Tm; Capt Varsity Clb; Band; Color Guard; School Musical; Capt Bsktbl; Syracuse; Med.

KELLY, DAWN M; East HS; Corning, NY; (Y); 117/222; SADD; Varsity Clb; Drill Tm; Stage Crew; Yrbk Stf; High Hon Roll; Hon Roll; Ingenue Modlg Awd Barbizn Nov 84; Fashn Merch Schlrshp 86; SF Teen Magzn Great Modl Srch 85; Bryant & Stratton; Fshn Mrch Mg.

KELLY, DAWN MARIE; Mt St Mary Acad; Buffalo, NY; (Y); Church Yth Grp; Spanish Clb; Teachers Aide; Church Choir; Swing Chorus; Yrbk Stf; Rep Jr Cls; Sec Stu Cncl; Swmmng; Hon Roll; Cnslr For Chldrn.

KELLY, DEIRDRE; North Babylon HS; North Babylon, NY; (Y); 100/464; Cmnty Wkr; Hosp Aide; SADD; Varsity Clb; Yrbk Sprt Ed; Fld Hcky; Mat Maids; Sftbl; High Hon Roll; WNEW Schlrshp 86; Al-Leag Fld Hcky Plyr 86; Al-Cnty Fld Hcky Plyr 86; Mt St Vincents; Spcl Ed.

KELLY, DIANE A; F D Roosevelt HS; Hyde Park, NY; (Y); 10/326; Chorus; School Musical; Stage Crew; Nwsp Stf; Hon Roll; NHS; Ntl Merit Ltr; Drama Clb; English Clb; Math Tm; Smmr Sci Inst 84; Sci Fair 2nd Pl 84-85; Dir Asst-Schl Play 86; U Of Chicago; Bio Sci.

KELLY, EILEEN A; Sacred Heart Acad; Freeport, NY; (Y); 46/186; Math Clb; Math Tm; Stage Crew; Yrbk Rptr; Yrbk Stf; JV Fld Hcky; JV Swmmng; NHS; NY ST Rgnts Schlrshp 86; Hnrs Pgm Schlrshp-Adlphi U 86; Biolgst.

KELLY, HEATHER; Vernon-Verona-Sherrill HS; Vernon, NY; (Y); 64/209; Church Yth Grp; Chorus; JV Vllybl; Hon Roll; Artist.

KELLY, JAMES; Cairo-Durham HS; Purling, NY; (Y); 4-H; School Musical; School Play; Yrbk Stf; Crs Cntry; Mgr(s); Var L Trk; High Hon Roll; Jr NHS; NHS; Eng.

KELLY, JENINE M; St Francis Preparatory Schl; Whitestone, NY; (S); 148/693; Teachers Aide; Im Sftbl; Im Vllybl; Optimate Scty 82-83; Emrld Scty Schlrshp Awd 82; Bus.

KELLY, JUDITH; St Joseph HS; Brooklyn, NY; (Y); French Clb; Girl Scts; Office Aide; Stage Crew; Hon Roll; NHS; Prfct Atten Awd; Hunter; Pre-Med.

KELLY, KATHLEEN; Wallkill SR HS; Wallkill, NY; (Y); Hosp Aide; Var Gym; Var Capt Socr; Var Capt Trk; Hon Roll; Rgnts Nrsng Schlrshp 86; U Of CT; Nrsng.

KELLY, KEVIN; Miller Place HS; Miller Pl, NY; (Y); 28/180; Pres SADD; Pres Frsh Cls; Pres Soph Cls; Var Capt Bsktbl; Var Socr; Var Trk; Vllybl; CC Awd; Lion Awd; Bus Awd 86; Jrnlsm Awd 86; Cmmnty Svc Awd 86; Hofstra U; Bus.

KELLY, KIM; Wellsville HS; Genesee, PA; (Y); 15/124; Art Clb; French Clb; Ski Clb; Varsity Clb; Nwsp Stf; Var L Cheerleading; Var L Sftbl; High Hon Roll; NHS; SUNY-OSWEGO; Zlgy.

KELLY, LEANNE; Lansingburgh HS; Troy, NY; (Y); 26/180; French Clb; Band; Chorus; Bsktbl; High Hon Roll; Hon Roll; NHS; Hudson Valley CC; Bus Adm.

KELLY, LOUISE; Schroon Lake Central HS; Schroon Lake, NY; (S); 2/26; French Clb; VP SADD; Varsity Clb; Pres Frsh Cls; Pres Soph Cls; Sec Stu Cncl; Sftbl; High Hon Roll; NHS; Val; Intl Bus.

KELLY, LYNN; Hamburg SR HS; Hamburg, NY; (Y); 50/375; Quiz Bowl; School Musical; Rep Frsh Cls; Rep Soph Cls; Rep Jr Cls; Rep Sr Cls; Rep Stu Cncl; JV Stat Bsbl; JV Cheerleading; Var Gym.

KELLY, MARY E; Bladwin HS; Baldwin, NY; (Y); 13/476; Boy Scts; Church Yth Grp; Key Clb; Trs Mathletes; Sec SADD; JV Capt Socr; NHS; Ntl Merit Ltr; Steamfitters Indus Schlrshp 86; NYS Rgnts Schlrshp 86; Lehigh U; Engrng.

KELLY, MARY E; Liverpool HS; Liverpool, NY; (Y); 68/823; Varsity Clb; Band; Stage Crew; Yrbk Phtg; Rep Stu Cncl; Var Capt Diving; Var Capt Swmmng; Hon Roll; Jr NHS; NHS; Union Coll Schlrshp; NYS Rgnts Schlrshp; Union Coll; Bio Sci.

KELLY, MATTHEW; Catholic Central HS; Latham, NY; (Y); Pres Latin Clb; Math Clb; SADD; School Musical; School Play; VP Frsh Cls; Var Trk; Hon Roll; NHS; Ntl Merit Ltr; Peer Ldrshp 85-86; Pres Ntl Hnr Soc 86-87; Math.

KELLY, MATTHEW; Ward Melville HS; E Setauket, NY; (Y); Church Yth Grp; Cmnty Wkr; Exploring; French Clb; Library Aide; Red Cross Aide; Stage Crew; Swmmng; Prfct Atten Awd; Ltr Recgntn Supprtng Spec Olympcs 84; Artcl Contrbtr Soc Studs Publctn 84; Var Ath Awd Swmmng 86; Sci.

KELLY, MAURA E; Maria Regina HS; Yonkers, NY; (Y); 2/125; VP Church Yth Grp; Yrbk Bus Mgr; Lit Mag; Bausch & Lomb Sci Awd; High Hon Roll; Pres NHS; Ntl Merit Ltr; Pres Schlr; Sal; Iona Coll Spnsh Cntst 1st Hnrs Spnsh IV 86; NY ST Rgnts Schlrshp 86; Manhattan Coll NY; Arts/Scincs.

KELLY, MELISSA; Plattsburgh SR HS; Plattsburgh, NY; (Y); Chorus; Church Choir; School Musical; Stage Crew; Yrbk Stf; Hon Roll; NHS; Acad Awd Englsh & Chem 86; Dedication To Cls Awd 86; Perf Arts.

KELLY, MICHAEL J; Lindenhurst SR HS; Lindenhurst, NY; (Y); Thesps; Band; Chorus; Concert Band; Drm & Bgl; Mrchg Band; School Musical; School Play; Swing Chorus; Golf; Mus.

KELLY, MICHELE P; Kingston HS; Kingston, NY; (Y); 8/573; VP JA; Library Aide; School Play; High Hon Roll; Jr NHS; NHS; Spanish NHS; Western CT Jr Achvt Conf 86; Marist Pres Schlrshp 86; Regents Coll Schlrshp 86; Marist Coll; Biology.

KELLY, MORAIMA; Cardinal Spellman HS; Bronx, NY; (Y); Church Yth Grp; Cmnty Wkr; Capt Color Guard; Flag Corp; Mrchg Band; School Musical; School Play; Swing Chorus; Variety Show; Latin Clb; Hnr Rl, Vrty Shw Host 85-86; Color Guard Cptn 85; Spelman Coll; Med.

KELLY, NATASHA; Greenwood Central Schl; Rexville, NY; (S); 2/23; Pres 4-H; FFA; Varsity Clb; Pres Chorus; Swing Chorus; Var JV Cheerleading; Var JV Pom Pon; 4-H Awd; VP JETS Awd; NHS.

KELLY, RAMSES T; Cardinal Hayes HS; New York, NY; (Y); 62/258; Rep Sr Cls; Rep Stu Cncl; Var Capt Bsktbl; JV Score Keeper; Pst HS All Star Bsktbl 85-86; Daily News HS All Star Bsktbl 85-86.

KELLY, REGINA; Notre Dame Acad; Staten Island, NY; (Y); Yrbk Stf; Rep Soph Cls; Rep Jr Cls; Trs Sr Cls; Trs Rep Stu Cncl; JV Capt Bsktbl; NHS; PHYSICAL Thrpy.

KELLY, ROBERT M; Amsterdam HS; Amsterdam, NY; (Y); 10/310; Varsity Clb; JV Ftbl; Var Trk; JV Wrstlng; Hon Roll; NHS; Ntl Merit Ltr; Prfct Atten Awd; Athltc Awd Ftbl 83-84; Math.

KELLY, ROBIN ANN LEANICE; St Joseph HS; Brooklyn, NY; (Y); Rep Stu Cncl; Hon Roll; Athlt Yr-Holy Rosry Trck Tm 84; 3 Yrs Prfct Attndnc 83-86; Asst Coach Rosry Trck Tm 85; Pre-Law.

KELLY, SHANNON; Buffalo Acad Of The Sacred Heart; Clarence, NY; (Y); VP French Clb; Red Cross Aide; Chorus; School Musical; School Play; Stage Crew; Nwsp Rptr; Nwsp Stf; Hon Roll; 1st Pl-Tap Dnc Comptn 86; 3rd Pl-Tap Dnc Comptn 85.

KELLY, SHARON; Nazareth Acad; Rochester, NY; (Y); Boy Scts; Office Aide; Spanish Clb; Acpl Chr; Chorus; Italian Awd 85-86; Rgnts Diplma 86; Long Island U; Film.

KELLY, SHAWN; Ripley Central HS; Ripley, NY; (S); Boy Scts; Drama Clb; Quiz Bowl; School Musical; School Play; Yrbk Ed-Chief; Var Tennis; Hon Roll; NHS; Voice Dem Awd; Law.

KELLY, SHERENE; Evander Childs HS; Bronx, NY; (S); Cmnty Wkr; Drama Clb; Office Aide; PAVAS; Red Cross Aide; Acpl Chr; Band; Chorus; Church Choir; Concert Band; Daily Nws Prd Of Ynke Awd 85; Cert Of Merit Awd 85; Big E Awd 84; Crdlgy.

KELLY, STEPHEN; Archbishob Stepanic HS; Yonkers, NY; (Y); Boy Scts; JV Trk; Elec.

KELLY, TAMARA; Camden HS; Camden, NY; (Y); AFS; Drama Clb; Pep Clb; Chorus; Orch; School Play; JV Var Cheerleading; Tennis; High Hon Roll; Hon Roll; Central City Bus Inst; Ex Sec.

KELLY, TAMI; Auburn HS; Auburn, NY; (Y); 31/429; Drama Clb; Sec Intnl Clb; Ski Clb; School Musical; School Play; VP L Fld Hcky; Stat Lcrss; High Hon Roll; NHS; Prfct Atten Awd; Joseph Malvaso Schrshp 86; Presdntl Acadmc Ftns Awd 86; Hnrbl Mntn-Leag Al-Stars Fld Hcky 85; U Of Rochester; Bio.

KELLY, TARA; Herbert H Lehman HS; New York, NY; (Y); #43 In Class; NHS; Prfct Atten Awd; Schlrshp Pace Bus Schl 86; 1st Pl Mdl Duet 84; St Johns U; Cmmnctns.

KELLY, THERESA; Bishop Ford Central Catholic HS; Brooklyn, NY; (S); 25/439; Church Yth Grp; Cmnty Wkr; Computer Clb; Science Clb; Lit Mag; Off Frsh Cls; High Hon Roll; Pres Phy Fit Awd; Acctg.

KELLY, TRACI; Moriah Central HS; Mineville, NY; (Y); 4-H; GAA; Ski Clb; Band; Off Jr Cls; Stu Cncl; Cheerleading; Socr; 4-H Awd; Hon Roll; MVP Chrldng 86; Ithaca; Soc Svcs.

KELLY, VERONICA; Clarkstown North HS; New City, NY; (Y); Capt Debate Tm; Capt NFL; Political Wkr; Service Clb; Capt Speech Tm; Varsity Clb; Var Crs Cntry; Var Socr; Var Trk; Church Yth Grp; 5th Cnty Discus & Shotput 84; Chrprsn Specl Olympcs 86; Binghamton; Law.

KELNER, MICHAEL J; Arlington HS; Poughkeepsie, NY; (Y); 86/566; Drama Clb; Ski Clb; Band; Chorus; Concert Band; Jazz Band; Madrigals; Mrchg Band; School Musical; Symp Band; Hotchkiss Smmr Theater Pgm Schlrshp 85; U MA; Indstrl Engrng.

KELSEY, DAWN; Tottenville HS; Staten Island, NY; (Y); Concert Band; School Musical.

KELSEY, KENNETH LEE; Wayne Central HS; Ontario, NY; (Y); Cmnty Wkr; Socr; Trk; Wrstlng; High Hon Roll; Hon Roll; NHS; Am Chemical Soc Awd For Excllnc In Chem 86; Natl Sci Olympiad Awd For Chem 86; Natl Sci Olympiad Awd; RIT; Electrical Engineer.

KELSEY, KRISTIN; Lansingburgh HS; Troy, NY; (Y); 32/186; Art Clb; 4-H; JA; Key Clb; SADD; Teachers Aide; Chorus; School Musical; School Play; Yrbk Stf; Sr Prdctn Typng Awd 86; Sr Trnscrptn Awd 86; Russell Sage Coll; Psych.

KELSO, KELLY; Allegany Central HS; Allegany, NY; (Y); 5/99; Art Clb; Computer Clb; Drama Clb; Latin Clb; Library Aide; Q&S; Ski Clb; Spanish Clb; Thesps; Chorus; Drssr Fndtn 86-90; Schlrshp Soc 83-85; Drssr Clrk 86-88; Penn ST U.

KELTON, JOHN; Sachem North HS; Holtsville, NY; (Y); 240/1600; Var L Ftbl; Var L Trk; Var Wt Lftg; Hon Roll; NY Inst Of Tech; Orthodntst.

KELTY, DAVID; East Syracuse-Minoa HS; Minoa, NY; (Y); JV Var Bsbl; JV Var Bsktbl; Comm.

KEMMERER, RICHARD; Victor SR HS; Farmington, NY; (Y); 23/228; Church Yth Grp; Varsity Clb; School Play; Stu Cncl; Crs Cntry; Capt Swmmng; Trk; Hon Roll; VP NHS; NY ST Rgnts Schlrshp 86; Syracuse U; Bio Engrng.

KEMP, TONYA; Belmont Central HS; Belmont, NY; (Y); VP GAA; VICA; Color Guard; Rep Frsh Cls; Pres Soph Cls; Pres Jr Cls; Rep Stu Cncl; Cheerleading; Pom Pon; Socr; Alfred U; Law.

KEMPF, NORMA; Miller Place HS; Sound Beach, NY; (Y); Church Yth Grp; FBLA; Varsity Clb; Capt Var Bsktbl; JV Var Tennis; Var Capt Vllybl; All League All Cnfrnce Vllybl 84-86; U Of MD-COLL Pk Vllybl Schlrshp 86; U Of MD-COLL Pk.

KENCIK, AMY; Mount St Mary Acad; Williamsville, NY; (Y); Teachers Aide; Chorus; School Musical; Variety Show; Art Awd St Marys Schl 85; YES Commnty Svc Awd 85 & 86; Medialle Coll; Nrsg.

KENDRA, KEVIN; Vestal SR HS; Apalachin, NY; (Y); Boy Scts; Church Yth Grp; Trs Spanish Clb; Varsity Clb; Yrbk Stf; JV Bsktbl; Var L Socr; Var L Trk; High Hon Roll; Prfct Atten Awd; 3rd Pl Trajectry Cntst Ntl Sci 86; US Naval Acad.

KENDRICK, MARY M; Cazenovia HS; Cazenovia, NY; (Y); Church Yth Grp; Cmnty Wkr; Teachers Aide; Chorus; Stage Crew; Off Frsh Cls; Off Soph Cls; Off Jr Cls; Stu Cncl; Fld Hcky; Trvl.

KENDZIA, CLIFF; Niagara Catholic HS; Niagara Fls, NY; (Y); Boy Scts; Hon Roll; NHS; U Of Buffalo; Phrmcy.

KENG, ALICE; New Rochelle HS; New Rochelle, NY; (Y); Mathletes; Math Clb; Math Tm; Band; Concert Band; Mrchg Band; Symp Band; Nwsp Phtg; Yrbk Phtg; Lit Mag; Outstndng Scl Stds Stu 84; Excllnc-Lang Arts; U Of Puerto Rico; Arctc Ecolgy.

KENNA, JENNIFER; Colonie Central HS; Albany, NY; (Y); Church Yth Grp; Cmnty Wkr; Band; Stu Cncl; Socr; High Hon Roll; Hon Roll; NHS; Plttsbrgh Fndtn Schlrshp, Rgnts Schlrshp 86; Plattsburgh ST U; Nrsng.

KENNEALLY, DESMOND; Archbishop Molloy HS; Woodside, NY; (Y); 77/383; Cmnty Wkr; Crs Cntry; Trk; Hon Roll; Prfct Atten Awd; Acctng.

KENNEDY, ANDREW S; La Fayette Central HS; Jamesville, NY; (Y); 24/96; Band; Mrchg Band; Variety Show; Trs Frsh Cls; Sec Soph Cls; VP Jr Cls; Rep Stu Cncl; Var Crs Cntry; JV Im Lcrss; Hon Roll; MONY Regl Schlstc Art Awds 86; 4 Yr Schlrshp To Cooper Union 86; Schlstc Achvt 84; The Cooper Union; Fine Art.

KENNEDY, CHRIS; Hutchinson Technical HS; Buffalo, NY; (Y); Hon Roll; Mech Engrng.

KENNEDY, CHRIS; Waterville Central HS; Waterville, NY; (Y); 17/90; GAA; Pep Clb; Varsity Clb; VP Jr Cls; Cheerleading; Fld Hcky; Trk; Hon Roll; NHS; Fshn Mrchndsng.

KENNEDY, CHRISTINE; Warsaw Central HS; Warsaw, NY; (S); 8/87; Ski Clb; Trs Spanish Clb; Yrbk Phtg; Sec Soph Cls; Trs Jr Cls; Trs Stu Cncl; Capt Cheerleading; Capt Sftbl; Vllybl; NHS; Comp Awd 85; Rochester Inst Tech; Persnnl.

KENNEDY, DEBORAH D; Fort Plain HS; Ft Plain, NY; (Y); 11/53; Teachers Aide; Chorus; Yrbk Ed-Chief; VP Sr Cls; Cit Awd; NHS; Voice Dem Awd; Trs Church Yth Grp; Mgr Drama Clb; Profcncy Bus 86; Outstndng Stu Bus 83-86; Albany Bus Coll; Bus Adm.

KENNEDY, DENNIS E; Tully Central Schl; Tully, NY; (Y); Am Leg Boys St; Varsity Clb; Pres Stu Cncl; Bsktbl; Lcrss; CC Awd; FFA; SADD; Band; Chorus; Mdl Of Merit 86; Ldrshp Stu Govt 86; Buffalo ST U; Bus.

KENNEDY, ERIC; Waterville Central Schl; Waterville, NY; (Y); #2 In Class; Ski Clb; Varsity Clb; Stu Cncl; L Socr; 4-H Awd; High Hon Roll; NHS; Pres Schlr; Sal; Rgnts Schlrshp 86; Oneida Co Gvt Intrn 85; Colgate U Smnrs 84-86; American U; Intl Rltns.

KENNEDY, GLENN; Lindenhurst HS; Lindenhurst, NY; (Y); Band; Concert Band; Bsbl; Swmmng; Vet Med.

KENNEDY, HOLLY; Ravena-Coeymans-Selkirk HS; Selkirk, NY; (Y); French Clb; Yrbk Stf; JV Var Sftbl; JV Tennis; JV Vllybl; High Hon Roll; Hon Roll; Dntstry.

KENNEDY, JAMES; Bishop Ludden HS; Syracuse, NY; (Y); Rep Soph Cls; Rep Jr Cls; Var Bsbl; JV Bsktbl; High Hon Roll; NHS; Bus.

KENNEDY, JENNIFER; Mineola HS; Mineola, NY; (Y); Key Clb; SADD; Thesps; School Musical; School Play; Variety Show; Rep Stu Cncl; Var Cheerleading; Var Gym; Var Trk; Comm.

KENNEDY, JOHN; Babylon Jr Sr HS; Babylon, NY; (Y); Am Leg Boys St; Math Tm; Pres Soph Cls; Pres Sr Cls; Trs Stu Cncl; JV Var Bsktbl; JV Var Ftbl; JV Var Lcrss; High Hon Roll; NHS.

KENNEDY, KEVIN J; South Side HS; Rockville Centre, NY; (Y); 12/285; Camera Clb; Pep Clb; SADD; Varsity Clb; Nwsp Phtg; Yrbk Phtg; JV Var Bsbl; Var Bsktbl; High Hon Roll; NHS; Bus.

KENNEDY, KIMBERLY A; Portville Central Schl; Olean, NY; (Y); 10/109; Ski Clb; Varsity Clb; Pres Concert Band; Mrchg Band; VP Stu Cncl; Capt Cheerleading; Diving; Swmmng; High Hon Roll; NHS; Olean Gnrl Host Axlry Schlrshp 86; Hmcmng Queen 85; Geneseo ST Coll; Bio.

KENNEDY, LYNN; Smithtown HS West; Smithtown, NY; (Y); Art Clb; Drama Clb; Thesps; Variety Show; Off Frsh Cls; Off Soph Cls; Off Jr Cls; Bowling; Trk; Hon Roll; Grmn Hnr Soc 85; BESFI Schlrshp 85-86; Vrsty Lttr Trck 85; Bio.

KENNEDY, MARGARET; Mt Mercy Acad; Buffalo, NY; (Y); 22/196; Badmtn; Drama Clb; French Clb; Quiz Bowl; Chorus; School Musical; School Play; Lit Mag; Hon Roll; NHS.

KENNEDY, MATTHEW; Shenendehowa Central HS; Clifton Park, NY; (Y); High Hon Roll; Hon Roll; Video Connctn Comp Sci Awd 86; Computers.

KENNEDY, MICHAEL R; Pine Bush HS; Middletown, NY; (Y); 54/298; Church Yth Grp; French Clb; Spanish Clb; Yrbk Stf; Stu Cncl; L Swmmng; Tennis; Hon Roll; Jr NHS; NHS; Pres Pine Bush Athl Assn 84-86; NYS Regents Schlrshp Nwmr 85-86; Membr Enrichmt Prg Gftd/Tlntd 85-86; Muhlenberg Coll; Pol Sci.

KENNEDY, MICHELLE; Tonawanda HS; Tonawanda, NY; (Y); VP French Clb; Trs Frsh Cls; VP Soph Cls; Stu Cncl; Bsktbl; Vllybl; Hon Roll; Soc Wrk.

KENNEDY, RICHARD W; Warwick Valley HS; Warwick, NY; (Y); 13/197; Boy Scts; Church Yth Grp; Ski Clb; Var Ftbl; Var Trk; High Hon Roll; Hon Roll; NHS; NYS Regents Schlrshp 86; Coll Holy Cross; Econ Bus.

KENNEDY, RODRICK; Monroe HS; Rochester, NY; (Y); Camera Clb; Computer Clb; Nwsp Stf; Yrbk Stf.

KENNEDY, SABA; Springfield Gardens HS; Springfield Grdns, NY; (S); Debate Tm; Political Wkr; Variety Show; Pres Frsh Cls; Pres Soph Cls; VP Stu Cncl; Hon Roll; Yth Slte Serv & Acad Awd; Law.

KENNEDY, SAMANTHA; Tottenville HS; Staten Island, NY; (Y); Scholastic Bowl; SADD; Mrchg Band; Symp Band; Variety Show; Rep Stu Cncl; Var Sftbl; Var Vllybl; Ntl Merit Ltr; Girl Scts; Yth Cncl Cmnty Affairs Borough Pres 86; Lib Arts.

KENNEDY, SUSAN; Spackenkill HS; Poughkeepsie, NY; (Y); 17/168; Hosp Aide; Band; Mrchg Band; School Musical; School Play; Nwsp Stf; Yrbk Stf; Var Bsktbl; Var Fld Hcky; Var Sftbl; Natl Frnch Cntst Wnnr 4th, 6th, 4th Pl 84-86.

KENNEDY, THOMAS; Valley Stream Central HS; Valley Stream, NY; (Y); 60/390; AFS; Ski Clb; SADD; Pres Jr Cls; Im Bsktbl; JV Trk; Pharm.

KENNEDY, THOMAS; West Islip HS; W Islip, NY; (Y); Aud/Vis; French Clb; Stage Crew; Hofstra; Intl Bus.

KENNEDY, THOMAS M; Mount Saint Michael HS; Bronx, NY; (S); 10/309; Boys Clb Am; Bsktbl; High Hon Roll; Hon Roll; Jr NHS; NHS; Spanish NHS.

KENNESON, AILEEN ANN; Chittenango HS; Kirkville, NY; (Y); 4/172; Drama Clb; French Clb; Science Clb; Chorus; School Play; High Hon Roll; NHS; JV Golf; Jr NHS; Outstdng Mbr Of Mock Trl Tm 86; GE STAR Awd 86; Fred Kirschenheiter Bio Medallian 86; Cornell U; Biolgcl Sci.

KENNEY, ANTHONY; Westhampton Beach HS; E Moriches, NY; (Y); 28/209; Teachers Aide; Varsity Clb; Bsktbl; Socr; Tennis; Trk; Vllybl; High Hon Roll; Hon Roll; NHS; Rgnts Schlrshp 86; MVP In Sccr & Tnns 86; Clarkson Trstees Awd 86; Clarkson U; Elec Engrng.

KENNEY, KATHLEEN; Hoosick Falls Central Schl; Hoosick Falls, NY; (Y); Hosp Aide; Band; Yrbk Ed-Chief; JV Capt Bsktbl; Var Fld Hcky; Var Sftbl; Hon Roll; Kiwanis Awd; Pres NHS; Wnr 4 Yr Fl Army ROTC Schlrshp 86; Cls C ST Chmpns Bsktbl 86; Norwich Military U; Nrsng.

KENNEY, KELLEY; Newburgh Free Acad; Newburgh, NY; (Y); Church Yth Grp; French Clb; Hosp Aide; Acpl Chr; Chorus; Capt Cheerleading; Gym; Hon Roll; NYS Regents Schlrshp 86; Albany ST; Bus Adm.

KENNEY, LISA; Babylon HS; Babylon, NY; (Y); #67 In Class; Drama Clb; Chorus; School Musical; School Play; Stage Crew; Variety Show; Hon Roll; St Schlr; New Paltz Coll; Brdcstng.

KENNEY, MICHAEL; Susan E Wagner HS; Staten Island, NY; (Y); Camp Fr Inc; Office Aide; Yrbk Stf; Hon Roll.

KENNEY JR, WILLIAM A; Lackawanna SR HS; Lackawanna, NY; (Y); Church Yth Grp; Ftbl.

KENNIS, MATTHEW; Roslyn HS; Roslyn, NY; (Y); 2/250; Cmnty Wkr; Service Clb; Bsbl; Coach Actv; Socr; NHS; ST U Of NY; Chem Engnrng.

KENNY, FINOLA; Rye HS; Rye, NY; (Y); Library Aide; Yrbk Stf; Sftbl; High Hon Roll; Hon Roll; Var Letter Sftbll 86; Schlrrs Awd 86; IONA.

KENNY, GEORGE W; Bronx Of Science HS; Sunnyside, NY; (Y); Rep Stu Cncl; Carnegie; Indstrl Mgmt.

KENNY, LINDA; Dominican Commercial HS; Hollis, NY; (S); 13/289; Drama Clb; Hosp Aide; Chorus; Nwsp Rptr; Rep Frsh Cls; Var Swmmng; Hon Roll; WA Semnr Cngrssnl Wrkshp Schlrshp 85; Dominicn Cmmrcls Sienna Clb 83-86; Ldr Song Chrch 83-86; St Johns U; Law.

KENNY, MATTHEW; Holy Trinity HS; N Bellmore L I, NY; (S); 2/320; Math Clb; Quiz Bowl; Yrbk Stf; Hon Roll; Mu Alp Tht; NHS.

KENNY, STEPHEN L; Grand Island HS; Grand Island, NY; (Y); Boy Scts; JA; JV Swmmng; Im Wt Lftg; Hon Roll; Regnts Schlrshp 86; Echo Soc Schlrshp 86; Acadmc Achvt Awd 86; SUNY-STONY Brook; Pre-Med.

KENT, ADAM; E J Wilson HS; Spencerport, NY; (Y); Exploring; French Clb; Hon Roll; NYS Coll Of Env Sci; Wldlf Bio.

KENT, BARBARA A; Beaver River Central Schl; Beaver Falls, NY; (Y); 2/82; French Clb; Ski Clb; SADD; Band; Yrbk Stf; Trs Jr Cls; Trs Sr Cls; Rep Stu Cncl; High Hon Roll; VP NHS; Rgnts Schlrshp 86; Trstees Awd Clrksn 86; Clarkson U; Cvl Engr.

KENT, ERIC; Goshen Central HS; Goshen, NY; (Y); Drama Clb; Chorus; School Musical; School Play; Stage Crew; Socr; VP NHS; Achvt Awd-Engl 85; 2 Yrs Prfct Atten 86; 3 Yrs All Cnty Chrs 84-86; Enrchmnt Pgm 84-86; RPI; Engrng.

KENT, LANITA; Jasper Central Schl; Jasper, NY; (Y); Church Yth Grp; Drama Clb; French Clb; FFA; Varsity Clb; Chorus; Yrbk Phtg; Var Trk; Hon Roll; Teachers Aide; Pres Phys Fit Awd 82-86; TN Temple U; Ag Tchr.

KENT, LYNNE; Waverly SR HS; Waverly, NY; (Y); SADD; Color Guard; School Play; Yrbk Stf; Rep Soph Cls; Rep Jr Cls; Var Cheerleading; Var Twrlr; Peer Tchg Hnrs 84 & 85; Corning CC; Lib Art.

KENT, SEAN; Fairport HS; Fairport, NY; (Y); 7/580; Chorus; Trs Jr Cls; Trs Sr Cls; Rep Stu Cncl; Var Capt Swmmng; NHS; Penn St Frshmn Excllnc Awd 86; Fairport Sr Cup Wnnr 86; Fairport Ed Assn Schlrhsp 86; Penn ST U.

KENVILLE, BRYAN L; Caledonia-Mumford Central HS; Scottsville, NY; (Y); 2/92; Boy Scts; French Clb; Math Clb; Band; Chorus; Jazz Band; Swing Chorus; High Hon Roll; NHS; Sal; Fnlst NROTC Schlrshp 86; Rgnts Schlrshp NYS 86; Eagle Scout 86; U Of Rochester; Physcs.

KENWARD, MICHAEL L; Medina SR HS; Medina, NY; (Y); 19/170; Chess Clb; Exploring; Concert Band; Off Stu Cncl; JV Golf; High Hon Roll; NHS; GMI; Mech Engr.

KENYON, JODY; Canaseraga Central Schl; Canaseraga, NY; (Y); 7/17; Am Leg Boys St; Band; Mrchg Band; Yrbk Stf; VP Stu Cncl; L Bsbl; JV Capt Bsktbl; L Socr; Hon Roll; NHS.

KENYON, KENNY; Onondaga HS; Nedrow, NY; (Y); Art Clb; Varsity Clb; School Play; Stage Crew; Ftbl; Var Capt Ftbl; Var Capt Wrstlng; High Hon Roll; Hon Roll; NHS; Coachs Awd Wrstlg 86.

KENYON, MICHELLE; Canaseraga Central HS; Canaseraga, NY; (Y); 3/27; Chorus; Off Soph Cls; Pres Jr Cls; Pres Sr Cls; Stu Cncl; Co-Capt Cheerleading; Capt Socr; Sftbl; High Hon Roll; NHS.

KEOUGH, DEBRA; Barker Central HS; Appleton, NY; (S); AFS; Church Yth Grp; 4-H; Sec FFA; Speech Tm; Lit Mag; Stu Cncl; 4-H Awd; 2nd Pl NYS FFA Hrse Profcncy Awd 85; 1st Pl Dist FFA Prepard Publ Spkg Extemprneous Publ Spkg 85; Prof Hrse Trainr.

KEOUGH, ELIZABETH; Faith Heritage HS; Syracuse, NY; (Y); Cmnty Wkr; Dance Clb; Nwsp Stf; Yrbk Stf; Sec Frsh Cls; Sec Soph Cls; Sec Jr Cls; Sec Stu Cncl; Cheerleading; Cit Awd; MVP & Imprvd Plyr In Vrsty Chrldng 85-86; Chrstn Chrctr Awd 83-84; Travel.

KEPHART, TIMOTHY; Horseheads HS; Horseheads, NY; (Y); 37/390; Ski Clb; Spanish Clb; Varsity Clb; Rep Frsh Cls; Var L Bsbl; JV L Bsktbl; Var L Golf; High Hon Roll; Hon Roll; Kiwanis Awd; Elmira Star Gztt Carrier Of Yr 85; Kiwanis Athl Of Mnth 86.

KERAMIDAS, NATACHA; John Jay HS; Cross River, NY; (Y); Cmnty Wkr; Girl Scts; Intnl Clb; Latin Clb; Teachers Aide; School Play; Var Trk; Hon Roll; Vrsty Ltr Trk 86; Wrtr.

KERBER, KEVIN A; Vestal HS; Vestal, NY; (Y); Art Clb; Cmnty Wkr; Speech Tm; VICA; Yrbk Stf; Arts Rcgntn & Tlnt Srch 86; 3rd Pl ST Vica Skl Olympcs-Opning/Clsng Tm 86; Schl Of Visual Arts; Tv Prdctn.

KERBS, KEVIN; Hicksville HS; Hicksville, NY; (Y); High Hon Roll; Socl Studies Achvt Awds-Psych & Crmnl Law 86; Outstndng Stu-Ind Arts 86; Comp.

KERECMAN, JAY; Rome Free Acad; Rome, NY; (Y); 5/490; Boy Scts; Church Yth Grp; Hon Roll; Jr NHS; NHS; Ntl Merit Ltr; Eagle Scout 86; AATG PAD Trip To Germany 86; Bio Med.

KEREKES, ALLYSON T; Pine Plains HS; Clinton Corners, NY; (Y); 12/101; AFS; Church Yth Grp; Pep Clb; SADD; Yrbk Stf; Stat Ftbl; Var Tennis; Tutorial Srv Awd 84; Quinnipiac Coll; Occptnl Thrpst.

KERIEVSKY, ROSS; Wellington C Mepham HS; N Bellmore, NY; (Y); Art Clb; Debate Tm; Math Tm; Boys Clb Am; Yrbk Stf; Stu Cncl; Socr; Tennis; Hon Roll; Jr NHS.

KERINS, JOSEPH; Saint Agnes HS; New York, NY; (Y); 25/119; Pres Frsh Cls; Hon Roll; Yth Awd Ldrshp 82-83; Law.

KERKER, BONNIE; Clarkstown North; New City, NY; (Y); 31/425; Spanish Clb; SADD; Temple Yth Grp; Yrbk Stf; Jr Cls; Tennis; High Hon Roll; Mu Alp Tht; NHS; Regnts Schlrshp 86; PTA Schlrshp 86; Tufts U.

KERLAN, JOSHUA; Geneva HS; Geneva, NY; (S); #4 In Class; French Clb; Letterman Clb; Model UN; Ski Clb; Band; Concert Band; Jazz Band; Mrchg Band; Trs Frsh Cls; VP Sr Cls; Medcn.

KERN, JOSEPH; Smithtown HS West; Smithtown, NY; (Y); Var Trk; Hon Roll; Italn Hnr Socty 85; Pres Acadmc Fit Awd 86; Stony Brook.

KERNAGHAN, DONNA; Deer Park HS; Deer Park, NY; (Y); 7/420; Intnl Clb; Math Clb; Math Tm; Service Clb; High Hon Roll; Jr NHS; NHS; Art Clb; Lit Mag; Polytech Schlrp 85-86; Deer Pk PFC & PTA Schlrp 85-86; Polytech U; Cvl Engr.

KERNAN, PATRICK; Chenango Valley HS; Binghamton, NY; (Y); Hosp Aide; Spanish Clb; SADD; Color Guard; Mrchg Band; Ed Nwsp Stf; Ed Yrbk Stf; Var Tennis; High Hon Roll; Jr NHS; Natl Salute To Yth 86; Pre-Med.

KERNER, LAURAINNE; Sacred Heart Acad; Wantagh, NY; (S); 11/182; Art Clb; French Clb; Science Clb; Trs Chorus; School Musical; Hon Roll; NHS; Molby Coll Sci Far 2nd Bio 84-85; Purdue U; Vet.

KERR, BRIAN D; Aviation HS; Astoria, NY; (S); 6/416; Pres Church Yth Grp; Capt Debate Tm; VP JA; Capt Math Tm; Rptr Nwsp Stf; Stu Cncl; High Hon Roll; Hon Roll; VP NHS; Tech Hnr Soc 85-86; Lawyr.

KERR, DEBI; Stamford Central HS; Davenport, NY; (Y); VP Camera Clb; French Clb; Sec FBLA; Band; Chorus; Color Guard; Yrbk Ed-Chief; JV Capt Cheerleading; High Hon Roll; Hon Roll; Chrldr Yr 84; Most Impvd Stu 84; Travel.

KERR, KAREN; Riverdale Country Schl; Roosevelt Is, NY; (Y); Model UN; SADD; Bsktbl; Fld Hcky; Capt Trk; Hon Roll; Ntl Merit Ltr; GAA; Varsity Clb; Yrbk Phtg; 3 Ltr Vrsty Awd 85 & 86; All Ivy Bbl & Trck.

KERR, LAVERN A; Clara Barton HS; Brooklyn, NY; (Y); 19/485; Church Yth Grp; Dance Clb; Church Choir; Hon Roll; NHS; Prfct Atten Awd; Regent Schlrshp Awd 86; SUNY; Biolgy.

KERR, MECHELLE; Edison Vo-Tech; Rochester, NY; (Y); Exploring; Math Tm; Rep Soph Cls; Rep Jr Cls; Stat Bsktbl; JV Mgr(s); JV Var Trk; High Hon Roll; Hon Roll; Prfct Atten Awd; Urban Lg Rochester Fut Blck Schls 86; Cornell U; Acctg.

KERR, TAMMY; Frontier Central HS; Lake View, NY; (S); 3/500; Pres Art Clb; Pep Clb; Ski Clb; SADD; Off Frsh Cls; Off Sr Cls; Var Cheerleading; High Hon Roll; Hon Roll; NHS; Outstndng Sprtsmnshp Awd In Sftbl 83; MVP In Soccer 83; Ad Crft Advrtsng Awd 84 & 85; Syracuse U; Grphc Arts.

KERR, THERES E; Elmira Free Acad; Elmira, NY; (Y); German Clb; Girl Scts; SADD; High Hon Roll; Hon Roll; Schltc Art Awd-Blue Rbbn 82; Elmira Coll; Art.

KERRICK, BLAKE J; Harrison HS; White Plains, NY; (Y); 55/210; Church Yth Grp; Debate Tm; JV Lcrss; Var Trk; Rotary Awd; Mck Trial Tm Regnl Chmps Southrn Dist NY 85; Yth Vlntrs Harrison.

KERSCHBAUMER, LISA; H Frank Carey HS; Garden City S, NY; (Y); 38/227; FBLA; German Clb; Chorus; Sftbl; Vllybl; High Hon Roll; Outstndng Bus Admin Stu 86; Grmn Awd Schlrshp 86; Outstndng Grmn Awd 85; Adlphi U; Acctng.

KERSHNER, NANCY; Candor Central HS; Owego, NY; (Y); 27/83; Am Leg Aux Girls St; Office Aide; SADD; Color Guard; Yrbk Phtg; Yrbk Stf; High Hon Roll; Hon Roll; Prfct Atten Awd; Pres Amer Lgn Jr Axlry 83; V-Pres Amer Lgn Jr Axlry 82; Chpln Amer Lgn Jr Axlry 81; Cazenovia; Scrtrl Sci.

KERSTING, LAURA; Corning-Painted Post West HS; Painted Post, NY; (Y); Am Leg Aux Girls St; Mrchg Band; Nwsp Stf; Yrbk Stf; Var Capt Gym; Var Swmmng; Capt Var Trk; High Hon Roll; VP NHS; Church Yth Grp; Orgnzd Corning Yth Ct 83-86.

KERWIN, MICHELE; Newfane SR HS; Newfane, NY; (Y); VICA; Y-Teens; JV Sftbl; JV Vllybl; Hon Roll; RN.

KESEL, BRIAN; Cicero N Syracuse HS; Cicero, NY; (S); 19/676; Drm Mjr(t); School Play; Pres Soph Cls; Pres Jr Cls; Pres Sr Cls; CC Awd; NHS; Ntl Merit Ltr; N Syracuse Optmst Yth Apprctn Awd 85; Grtr N Syracuse Yth Ctznshp Awd 85; SUNY Albany; Physcs.

KESISIAN, EDWARD; Aviation HS; Staten Island, NY; (Y); Service Clb; Ski Clb; Chorus; Swmmng; Elec Engrng.

KESSENICH, QUINT; Lynbrook HS; Lynbrook, NY; (Y); Var Ftbl; Var Capt Lcrss; Var Capt Socr; Var Wrstlng; Hon Roll; Kiwanis Awd; NHS; All-Amer 2 Yrs La Crosse 85 & 86; Cnty Wrstlng Champ 2 Yrs Wrstlng 85 & 86; Schlrshp Jhns Hpkns U 86; Johns Hipkins U.

KESSLER JR, DAVID; Chruchville-Chili HS; Churchville, NY; (Y); JCL; Latin Clb; Ski Clb; Band; Stage Crew; Symp Band; Crs Cntry; Trk; Hon Roll; NHS; Engrng.

KESSLER, DAWN; Carmel HS; Lake Carmel, NY; (Y); Var L Bsktbl; Var L Tennis; Var Capt Trk; High Hon Roll; MVP Awd Track 84; MIP Awd Bsktbl 85; MVP In Field Events In Track 86.

KESSLER, LINDA R; Lafayette HS; Buffalo, NY; (Y); 17/210; Trs Frsh Cls; Trs Soph Cls; VP Jr Cls; VP Sr Cls; Rgnts Schlrshp Awd 86; U Of Buffalo; Pre-Law.

KESSLER, MARK; Sanford H Calhoun HS; Merrick, NY; (Y); DECA; Nwsp Rptr; Soph Cls; Im Bsktbl; Var Golf; Im Ice Hcky; Im Lcrss; Im Wt Lftg; U MA.

KESSLER, RENEE M; Camden HS; Camden, NY; (Y); 57/211; AFS; SADD; Band; Concert Band; Orch; School Musical; Sec Trs Sr Cls; High Hon Roll; Prfct Atten Awd; Frgn Lang Clb Pres; Fredonia ST; Frnch.

KESSLER, TODD; Port Richmond HS; Staten Isld, NY; (Y); 18/490; Library Aide; Math Tm; Science Clb; Bsbl; Ftbl; Tennis; Trk; Wt Lftg; High Hon Roll; NHS; Princeton U; Pre Med.

KESTER, DANIEL; Christian Central Acad; Akron, NY; (S); 1/25; Church Yth Grp; Chorus; Church Choir; School Musical; School Play; High Hon Roll; NHS; Ntl Merit SF; Prfct Atten Awd; Val; Brains Awd 84-85; Best Chrstin Exmpl Awd; Most Dependable Awd.

KET-YING, LANA; Christ The King R HS; Queens, NY; (Y); 110/451; Art Clb; Service Clb; SADD; Vllybl; 2nd Hnrs 86.

KETCHAM, DENNIS R; Minisink Valley HS; Otisville, NY; (Y); Cmnty Wkr; Nwsp Stf; Trk; High Hon Roll; Hon Roll; Marist; Acctg.

KETCHEN, JONATHAN; Schenectady Christian Schl; Duanesburg, NY; (S); 3/15; Church Yth Grp; Band; Church Choir; Stage Crew; Variety Show; Nwsp Stf; Yrbk Phtg; Yrbk Stf; Var Socr; Mst Indstrs St 82-83; Outstndng Bio Stu 83-84; Musician.

KETCHEN, MICHAEL D; Schenectady Christian Schl; Duanesburg, NY; (Y); 1/16; Band; Church Choir; Jazz Band; Mrchg Band; Yrbk Stf; Socr; Hon Roll; Val; NY ST Rgnts Schlrshp 85-86; Rnslr Poly Tech Inst; Comp Sci.

KETCHIN, NANCY; Dover HS; Wingdale, NY; (Y); Am Leg Aux Girls St; Math Tm; Band; Concert Band; Jazz Band; Mrchg Band; Rep Stu Cncl; Im Badmtn; Im Vllybl; High Hon Roll; Jrnslm.

KETCHNER, LAURIE; Olean HS; Olean, NY; (Y); 44/211; Church Yth Grp; Varsity Clb; Trs Sr Cls; Var Cheerleading; Hon Roll; Hmcmng Attndnt 85; Prm Chrmn 85; Chrch Yth Pstr 85 & 86; Geneseo U; Elem Ed.

KETELHUT, BILLY; Wilson HS; Spencerport, NY; (Y); Pres Church Yth Grp; Cmnty Wkr; Off Latin Clb; Math Tm; Political Wkr; Teachers Aide; JV Bsktbl; Capt Bowling; Vllybl; Hon Roll; Valparaiso; Marine Bio.

KETTLES, KATHLEEN; Moore Catholic HS; Staten Island, NY; (Y); Church Yth Grp; Hosp Aide; School Musical; Drama Clb; Chorus; School Play; Nwsp Rptr; Yrbk Stf; Lit Mag; VP Frsh Cls.

KEY, TONIA; Murry Bergtram HS; Brooklyn, NY; (Y); Drama Clb; Yrbk Stf; Off Frsh Cls; Off Soph Cls; Off Jr Cls; Off Sr Cls; Kingsborough CC; Bus Adm.

KEYES, ANDREW; Ossining HS; Ossining, NY; (Y); Trs Chess Clb; Computer Clb; Math Clb; Math Tm; Stage Crew; JV Lcrss; Var Trk; High Hon Roll; NHS; Natl Merit Cmmndtn; Nuc Engr.

KEYES, BRADLEY; Clarkstown HS; New City, NY; (Y); Cmnty Wkr; Bsktbl; JV Crs Cntry; Var L Trk; Mu Alp Tht; NHS; Ntl Merit Ltr; Empr ST Gms Dclthln Fnlst 86; Comp.

KEYES, LORI; E Syracuse-Minoa HS; E Syracuse, NY; (Y); Spanish Clb; Band; Color Guard; Concert Band; Mrchg Band; School Musical; Nwsp Stf; Yrbk Stf; NHS; Rnsslr Polytchnc Inst Mdl 86; Educ.

KEYES, PATRICIA; Guilderland HS; Guilderland, NY; (Y); 53/360; Orch; School Musical; High Hon Roll; Ntl Merit Ltr; Concerto Comp Wnnr Piano Empire ST Yth Orch 85; Fnlst Littman Music Comp Concordia Coll 86; Piano Performance.

KEYSER, KENNETH M; Franklin Acad; Constable, NY; (Y); 49/250; AFS; French Clb; Intnl Clb; Model UN; Stage Crew; Nwsp Stf; Yrbk Stf; NYS Rgnts Schlrshp 86; Natl Soc Stu Olympiad 84; Plattsburgh ST U; Crmnl Just.

KEYSOR, NEAL; Saranac Central HS; Saranac, NY; (S); Cmnty Wkr; JV Var Bsbl; JV Var Bsktbl; JV Var Ftbl; High Hon Roll; Hon Roll.

KEYWORK, TOM; Albertus Magnus HS; Tappan, NY; (Y); 25/180; Math Tm; Varsity Clb; Var Lcrss; JV Socr; Var Trk; NHS; Ntl Merit Ltr; Vet.

KHADAROO, TAITHRAM; Lafayette HS; Brooklyn, NY; (Y); Cmnty Wkr; Band; Cit Awd; Hon Roll; Cert Of Hnr & Merit Rgnts Physics 84; Comp Engrng.

KHAGHAN, NEDA; Wheatley HS; East Hills, NY; (Y); Hosp Aide; Science Clb; SADD; Temple Yth Grp; Nwsp Stf; VP Soph Cls; Rep Jr Cls; Political Wkr; VP Frsh Cls; Navy Superior Sci Awd 86; Nwsdy Outstndng Sci Awd 86; Hghst Hnr Long Islnd Sci Cngrss 86; Med.

KHALAK, HANIF; Kenmore East HS; Kenmore, NY; (Y); 4/330; Boy Scts; JA; Math Clb; Orch; Nwsp Rptr; Var Crs Cntry; JV Trk; Bausch & Lomb Sci Awd; High Hon Roll; Pres NHS; SUNY Buffalo Hnrs Pres Schlrshp 86; Rnsslr Plythchnc Inst Mdl For Math & Sci 85; NY Empr ST Schlr; SUNY At Buffalo; Engr.

KHALIL, JONAS; Lehman HS; Bronx, NY; (Y); Church Yth Grp; Cmnty Wkr; Hon Roll; Prfct Atten Awd; Chem Math Amercn Hist Awds 86; Dentstry.

KHAN, NISHAT; Fairport HS; Fairport, NY; (Y); French Clb; Intnl Clb; SADD; Chorus; School Musical; School Play; Yrbk Stf; Im Trk; Cert Merit ST Acad Deca 85-86; Fash Design.

KHAN, PARVEEN; Cicero-North Syracuse HS; Clay, NY; (Y); 147/667; Art Clb; French Clb; Library Aide; Chorus; Vllybl; Prfct Atten Awd; Shrthnd Dctn 84; Shrthnd I Thry 84; LA ST U; Bus Admin.

KHAWLY, MARIANNE; The Ursuline Schl; Eastchester, NY; (Y); Political Wkr; Spanish Clb; Swmmng; Hon Roll; Jr NHS; NHS; Church Yth Grp; Cmnty Wkr; JCL; CCD Tchr Catechist 81-87; Natl Latin Hrn Soc Cum Laude Natl Latin Exam 84-85; Peer Cnslr 86-87; Law.

KHEALIE, DARWIN; High School For The Humaniti; New York, NY; (Y); Art Clb; Boys Clb Am; Church Yth Grp; Cmnty Wkr; Office Aide; Speech Tm; Teachers Aide; Engl Hnr & Art Merit Awd 84; Spnsh Achvt Awd & Globl Hstry Hnr 85; Amer Hstry Hnr & Keybrd Hnr 86; Optmtry.

KHERA, ASHISH; Blind Brook HS; Rye Brook, NY; (Y); AFS; Camera Clb; Chess Clb; French Clb; Mathletes; Math Clb; Math Tm; Golf; Hon Roll; Frnch Comptn 2nd Pl Hnrs 85; Bus.

KHERA, FARHANA; Corning-PP West HS; Painted Post, NY; (Y); AFS; JA; Quiz Bowl; Ski Clb; Band; Concert Band; Mrchg Band; School Musical; Nwsp Rptr; Nwsp Stf; Rep To NYS Hugh O Brien Ldrshp Semnr 85; TFU Japan-US Senat E Schlrshop 85; Micro Bio Wnnr 86; Bio.

KHERA, SAMIRA; Corning-Painted Post West HS; Painted Post, NY; (Y); 3/352; JA; Ski Clb; Thesps; Chorus; Nwsp Ed-Chief; Lit Mag; Chrmn Sr Cls; Bsktbl; NHS; Pres Schlr; Gannett Schlrshp 86; Bst Fair Twntrs Rgnl 85; Sgma X1 Awd 86; Wellesley Coll; Med.

KHODADADIAN, DAVID K; J F Kennedy HS; Plainview, NY; (Y); 10/250; Computer Clb; Mathletes; Math Tm; Temple Yth Grp; Nwsp Rptr; Rep Frsh Cls; Socr; Swmmng; Vllybl; High Hon Roll; Math, Comp & Physics Awds 86; Chem Awd 85; Regents Schlrshp-PTA-ADELPHS U 86; CUNY Medical Schl; Med.

KIAFOULIS, LEONIDAS; Herbert H Lehman HS; Bronx, NY; (Y); #2 In Class; Chess Clb; Church Yth Grp; Computer Clb; Key Clb; Math Clb; Math Tm; Quiz Bowl; Science Clb; Lit Mag; Socr; Awds In Crimnolgy, Math, Comp, Socl Stdies, Sci & Prfct Attndnce 84-86; Cooper U; Engrng.

KIBLER JR, NORMAN; Perry HS; Perry, NY; (Y); Acdmc Achvt Awds Sci 86; Kodak.

KIBLIN, TOM; Lafayette HS; Buffalo, NY; (Y); Computer Clb; Var Ftbl; Var Ice Hcky; Var Wt Lftg; Most Imprvd Plyr Hockey 86; Comp Pgmr.

KICK, MARCY; Horseheads SR HS; Horseheads, NY; (Y); Church Yth Grp; FBLA; Hon Roll; Bus.

KICKBUSH, MICHAEL; Royalton Hartland HS; Middleport, NY; (Y); Stu Cncl; Tennis; Wrstlng; Hon Roll; Soc Stud Achvt Awd 84-85; Niagara CC; Brdcstg.

KIDD, SEAN; South Park HS; Buffalo, NY; (Y); 117/378; Boys Clb Am; Chess Clb; French Clb; JA; Library Aide; Chorus; Church Choir; Stage Crew; Nwsp Stf; Yrbk Sprt Ed; MVP-FTBL; US Army; Radio Engr.

KIDDER, CONNIE; Mexico Central Schl; Fulton, NY; (Y); 4-H; Cmptr Sci.

KIDDER, LAURA J; Laura J Kidder HS; Akron, NY; (Y); 9/137; Hosp Aide; Var Capt Cheerleading; Var L Fld Hcky; Var Pom Pon; Im Socr; Var Sftbl; Hon Roll; Pres NHS; Rgnts Nrsng Schlrshp 86; C E & J H Lesser Schlrshp Clarion U Of PA 86; THS To BWC 86; Clarion U Of PA; Engl Ed.

KIDWELL, STACEY; St John The Baptist HS; Wyandanch, NY; (Y); Church Yth Grp; Dance Clb; Church Choir; School Play; Skidmore; Biology.

KIEFFER, JOAN; Jamesville Dewitt HS; Jamesville, NY; (Y); 67/235; Hosp Aide; Band; Concert Band; High Hon Roll; Hon Roll; Cert Apprctn 84-85; Cert Apprctn 85-86; Pscyhlgy.

KIENIKSMAN, ANDREW; Copiague HS; Copiague, NY; (Y); Nwsp Rptr; Lit Mag; Rep Stu Cncl; Im Var Bsktbl; Hon Roll; NHS; Ntl Merit SF; Schl Rep Hugh O Brian Ldrshp Fndtn 86; Elec Engrng.

KIERNAN, LISA; Beacon HS; Beacon, NY; (Y); VP French Clb; German Clb; Office Aide; Teachers Aide; Varsity Clb; Stage Crew; Hon Roll; Ithaca Coll; Bus Admin.

KIERNAN, MARY S; The Ursuline Schl; New Rochelle, NY; (Y); 6/123; French Clb; Service Clb; Ski Clb; School Play; Ed Nwsp Ed-Chief; Yrbk Phtg; Yrbk Stf; Ed Lit Mag; Stu Cncl; JV Vllybl.

KIERNAN, MICHAEL W; Cardinal Spellman HS; New York, NY; (Y); 23/500; Chess Clb; Cmnty Wkr; Pres Computer Clb; German Clb; Pres Bowling; 1st Hnrs All Theway Through 82-86; Fordham U; Pol Sci.

KIERNAN, PATRICIA; Patchogue-Medford HS; Medford, NY; (S); 36/653; Church Yth Grp; Concert Band; Mrchg Band; Lit Mag; Hon Roll; Jr NHS; NHS; Prfct Atten Awd; NYSMA Awd 84; SR All Am Band Hnrs; St Josephs Clg; Chld Study.

KIESEL, LISA; Hicksville HS; Hicksville, NY; (Y); Band; Concert Band; High Hon Roll; Hon Roll; Jr NHS; NHS; Schlrshp/Schlstc Achvt Awd 85; Flrnc Lanzisera Awd 86; Nrsng.

KIESNOSKI, KENNETH S; Saint Anthonys HS; Smithtown, NY; (Y); 70/240; French Clb; VP SADD; Chorus; Nwsp Rptr; Lit Mag; Crs Cntry; French Hon Soc; Hon Roll; NHS; Ntl Merit Ltr; NYS Regnts Schlrshp; Jrnlsm.

KIFFNEY, BOB; Niskayuna HS; Schenectady, NY; (Y); Boy Scts; Exploring; German Clb; VP Key Clb; Science Clb; Nwsp Rptr; JV Socr; Var L Vllybl; Hon Roll; NHS; Dartmth Bk Awd; ST Lgsltv Rsltn; Cornell U; Engrng.

KIFFNEY, CHRISTINA; Niskauyna HS; Schenectady, NY; (Y); Cmnty Wkr; French Clb; FBLA; JA; Key Clb; Var L Fld Hcky; Powder Puff Ftbl; Bus Mngt.

KIJANKA, JOHN; Frontier Central HS; Blasdell, NY; (Y); Var Bowling; Hon Roll; St U Of NY; Math.

KIKIS, ANTOINETTE; Herbert H Lehman HS; New York, NY; (Y); 93/561; Drama Clb; FHA; Hosp Aide; Pep Clb; Yrbk Stf; Hon Roll; NHS; Publc Spkng 84; Natl Soc Autistic Chldrn Vlntr Svcs 84; Phys Thrpy.

KILANOWSKI, CAROLYN; Pembroke JR SR HS; Corfu, NY; (Y); 26/115; VP German Clb; Science Clb; Nwsp Rptr; Yrbk Stf; Score Keeper; Hon Roll; Hgh Germn Avg 99 84-86; Wartburg Coll IA; Germn Educ.

KILBURN, JEFFREY; Queensbury HS; Glens Falls, NY; (Y); Art Clb; Trk; Ntl Merit Ltr; Animation.

KILBURN, KIMBERLY; Dannemora HS; Elizabethtown, NY; (Y); French Clb; Chorus; Nwsp Stf; Yrbk Stf; Cheerleading; Socr; Sftbl; Hon Roll; Sftbll Ofnsv Awd 85; Med.

KILEEN, MOLLY; Buffalo Academy Of The Sacred Heart; Amherst, NY; (Y); 40/120; Science Clb; Service Clb; Ski Clb; Spanish Clb; Varsity Clb; Nwsp Stf; Rep Frsh Cls; Rep Soph Cls; Rep Jr Cls; Pres Stu Cncl; Nrsng.

KILEY, JAMES D; Saint Francis Prep; Bayside, NY; (Y); Am Leg Boys St; Chess Clb; Pep Clb; Var L Bsktbl; Im Sftbl; Var L Swmmng; JV Trk; Im Vllybl; Peer Cnslng 86; 1st Pl Church Sponsored Stu Tlnt Cont For Piano Recital 84; Law.

KILGANNON, KERY F; Alfred G Berner HS; Massapequa, NY; (Y); 46/412; Pep Clb; Variety Show; Pres Soph Cls; Lcrss; Socr; Wrstlng; NHS; Cmnty Wkr; 4-H; French Clb; All Cnty Wrstlr Nassau Cnty 85 & 86; Nassau Cnty Wrstlng Scholar 86; NYS Regnts Scholar 86; Brown U; Law.

KILGORE, CARLA; Gloversville HS; Gloversvl, NY; (Y); Sec Pres Drama Clb; French Clb; Teachers Aide; Chorus; School Musical; School Play; Stage Crew; Nwsp Rptr; Hon Roll; NHS; City Essy Cntst 1st Pl 84.

KILGORE, MITCHELL; Mc Quaid Jesuit HS; Rochester, NY; (Y); Intnl Clb; Varsity Clb; Var Capt Swmmng.

KILIAN, KATHY; Fairport HS; Fairport, NY; (Y); Cmnty Wkr; Hosp Aide; Math Tm; Concert Band; Jazz Band; Mrchg Band; Orch; Co-Capt Swmmng; High Hon Roll; Hon Roll; She-Shark Awd 84 & 85; Hochstein Schlrp 85; Music Thrpy.

KILLEEN, DEBORA; Our Lady Of Mercy HS; Pittsford, NY; (Y); Church Yth Grp; Spanish Clb; Var L Sftbl; Var L Tennis; Hon Roll; Bus.

KILLEEN, KATHLEEN; Linton HS; Schenectady, NY; (Y); VP Exploring; High Hon Roll; Rgnts Schlrshp 86; Prsdntl Acad Ftns Awd 86; William Smith Coll; Chem.

KILLERLANE, JAMES; Clarkstown South HS; W Nyack, NY; (Y); 7/475; Cmnty Wkr; Nwsp Sprt Ed; Yrbk Sprt Ed; Pres Stu Cncl; Var Capt Ftbl; Var Ice Hcky; Mu Alp Tht; NHS; Church Yth Grp; Brown U Book Awd 86; 1st Hnrs Iona Lang Cntst Spnsh 86.

KILLINO, CATHY JO; John F Kennedy HS; Utica, NY; (Y); Cmnty Wkr; Trs Key Clb; Library Aide; Mathletes; Math Tm; Frsh Cls; Score Keeper; Socr; Hon Roll; NHS; Mohawk Valley CC; Math.

KILLOCK, ROB; Pine Valley Central Schl; S Dayton, NY; (Y); 21/60; Am Leg Boys St; FFA; Rep Sr Cls; Stu Cncl; Var L Bsbl; Var L Bsktbl; Var L Ftbl; Boy Scts; 4-H; Band.

KILLOCK, TABATHA; Kenmore West HS; Buffalo, NY; (Y); French Clb; Library Aide; Sec Math Tm; Hon Roll; NHS; NY ST Rgnts Schlrshp 86; Rgnts Dipl 86; Hnr Clb 86; IN U Bloomington; Comp Sci.

KILMER, BRENDA; Walton Central HS; Walton, NY; (Y); Sec 4-H; Sec FFA; High Hon Roll; Hon Roll; Nursry Oprtns Awd 86; Mst Imprvd Stu Awd 86; Prfct Attndnc 85; Hortcltr.

KILMER, RAY; Wilson Central HS; Lockport, NY; (Y); Varsity Clb; Bsbl; Bsktbl; Ftbl; Wt Lftg; Hon Roll.

KILPATRICK, LUCETRA; John Jay HS; Brooklyn, NY; (Y); Dance Clb; Drama Clb; Hosp Aide; Hon Roll; LIU; Comp Pgmr.

KILTHAU, JOANNA; Batavia HS; Batavia, NY; (Y); Dance Clb; Pep Clb; Chorus; School Musical; Var Cheerleading; Bus.

KIM, AARON; Richmond Hill HS; Kew Gardens, NY; (Y); 6/300; Sec Computer Clb; Var Crs Cntry; Var Trk; NHS; Regents Schlrshp; RPI Mdl; RPI Schlrshp; Rensselaer Polytech Inst; Engr.

KIM, CHONG; Churchville Chili SR HS; Rochester, NY; (Y); 12/300; Math Tm; School Musical; Lit Mag; Trs Stu Cncl; Tennis; High Hon Roll; Masonic Awd; NHS; Model UN; Chorus; Cornell U.

KIM, CLARA J; Irvington HS; Searsdale, NY; (Y); Computer Clb; Hosp Aide; Key Clb; Band; Chorus; Church Choir; Concert Band; Orch; School Musical; Yrbk Stf; Wellesley Bk Awd 86; Pre Med.

KIM, DENNIS Y; Irvington HS; Irvington, NY; (Y); 3/108; Chess Clb; Computer Clb; Teachers Aide; Band; Chorus; School Musical; Swing Chorus; Symp Band; Trs Stu Cncl; Var L Golf; USDAN Full Schlrshp 83-84; Kinhaven Music Camp 85; Columbia Sci Hnrs Prog, Baruch Coll Math Smnr 84.

KIM, HONGSOO; Seward Park HS; New York, NY; (Y); Art Clb; Boys Clb Am; Drama Clb; Broker.

KIM, JANE C; Bronx H S Of Sci; Elmhurst, NY; (Y); French Clb; Acpl Chr; Church Choir; Yrbk Stf; NHS; Teachers Aide; School Musical; Tennis; Vllybl; Prfct Atten Awd; Rgns Schlrshp; Crt Mrt Am Tchrs Frnch; Cornell U; Optmtry.

KIM, JASON; Hillcrest HS; Elmhurst, NY; (Y); 89/832; Church Yth Grp; Exploring; Math Tm; Science Clb; Varsity Clb; Gym; Tennis; Sci Fair Medl 85; Hnrbl Mntn Borough Sci Fair 85; Binghampton; Pre-Med.

KIM, JEANHEE; Roslyn HS; East Hills, NY; (Y); GAA; Hosp Aide; Intnl Clb; Varsity Clb; Chorus; School Play; Stage Crew; Var Capt Vllybl; Hon Roll; NHS; Vllybl Mst Valuable Plyr 85-86; Dartmouth Coll.

KIM, JENNIFER; Eastchester HS; Scarsdale, NY; (Y); 1/160; Pres Church Yth Grp; Capt Debate Tm; French Clb; VP Latin Clb; NFL; Ski Clb; Ed Yrbk Rptr; Var Capt Socr; Quiz Bowl; Church Choir; Rensselaer Mdl Excllnc In Math & Sci 86; Concours Natl De Francais 84-85; Amer Clsscl Lgue 85-86; Yale U; Lbrl Arts.

KIM, JI-HYUN; Notre Dame Acad HS; Staten Island, NY; (Y); Church Yth Grp; Cmnty Wkr; Computer Clb; Var Math Tm; Nwsp Stf; Yrbk Phtg; Swmmng; Wt Lftg.

KIM, KEE; John Dewey HS; Brooklyn, NY; (Y); Art Clb; Chess Clb; Science Clb; Gym; Sftbl; Tennis; Vllybl; Prfct Atten Awd; Art Awd From Daily News 84 & 85; Genetic Engrng.

KIM, KELLY Y; Fayetteville-Manius HS; Manlius, NY; (Y); 2/335; Pres Chess Clb; Math Tm; Model UN; Var L Tennis; High Hon Roll; NHS; Ntl Merit SF; Sal; Computer Clb; JA; Summa Cum Laude-Gld Mdl Latin 82-83; Mst Outstndng Latin Stu 82-84; Pre Med.

KIM, MIHYANG; Jamestown HS; Jamestown, NY; (Y); Acpl Chr; Concert Band; Mrchg Band; Sec Soph Cls; Stu Cncl; Tennis; Hon Roll; NHS; Ntl Merit SF; Eunice Amelia Anderson Awd 84; Pre-Med.

KIM, PATRICIA; Bronx High Schl Of Science; Astoria, NY; (Y); Church Yth Grp; Intnl Clb; Lit Mag; Office Aide; Teachers Aide; Haney Medal-Schl Art Leag Of NYC 84; Hnr Eng; U Of PA; Arch.

KIM, SANDRA; The Nichols Schl; Williamsville, NY; (Y); Chorus; Jazz Band; Nwsp Ed-Chief; Rep Sr Cls; Rep Stu Cncl; Hon Roll; Kiwanis Awd; NHS; NYS Regnts Schlrshp 86; U Of Chicago; Pre-Med.

KIM, SANG JOON; Monsignor Farrell HS; Staten Island, NY; (Y); Aud/Vis; Cmnty Wkr; Library Aide; Spanish Clb; Lit Mag; Im Bsktbl; Im Bowling; Im Ftbl; Var Tennis; High Hon Roll; Otto P Burgdorf Awd-Bio Sci 83-84; Med.

KIM, SUZY; Victor Central HS; Victor, NY; (Y); Am Leg Aux Girls St; Yrbk Ed-Chief; Trs Frsh Cls; Trs Soph Cls; Pres Trs Stu Cncl; Var JV Tennis; Cit Awd; High Hon Roll; Sec NHS; Prfct Atten Awd.

KIM, TAEHOON; Benjamin N Cardozo HS; Woodbury, NY; (Y); 25/510; Capt Chess Clb; Capt Debate Tm; Sec FBLA; Math Tm; VP Science Clb; Gold Mdlst NYC Vrsty Fncng Chmpn 85; 1st & 2nd Grtr Metro NY Math Fair 84 & 85; Tbl Tennis Tm 84-86; MIT; Aeronautic Engrng.

KIM, TAMI; Bayside HS; Bayside, NY; (Y); Latin Clb; Math Tm; Office Aide; Teachers Aide; Band; Concert Band; Cit Awd; Hon Roll; Jr NHS; NHS; Arista 82-85; Stony Brook; Pre-Med.

KIM, YONGHO; Newtown HS; Jackson Hts, NY; (Y); Aud/Vis; Math Clb; Varsity Clb; Church Choir; Lit Mag; Tennis; Hon Roll; Binghamton; Engrng.

KIMBALL, DANIELLE; Hugh C Williams HS; Canton, NY; (Y); Church Yth Grp; French Clb; JA; SADD; Yrbk Phtg; Yrbk Stf; Cheerleading; Coach Actv; Mgr(s); Score Keeper; Talented JRS 86; Outstndng Author Awd 86; Psych.

KIMBALL, DONNA-ANN M; Salvay HS; Baldwinsville, NY; (Y); 4/171; Art Clb; Exploring; Nwsp Rptr; Yrbk Stf; Pres Stu Cncl; Bowling; High Hon Roll; NHS; Rep Frsh Cls; Solvy Tgrs Schlrshp 86; Onondga Comm Schlr 85-86; NY ST Emrgncy Med Tech 86; SUNY; Rsprtry Thrpy.

KIMBALL, JEFFREY; Rome Free Acad; Rome, NY; (Y); 10/500; Ski Clb; Var Lcrss; JV Socr; Hon Roll; Pres Jr NHS; NHS; Engrng.

KIMBALL JR, LA MOTT TYMER D; Corning East HS; Corning, NY; (Y); Letterman Clb; SADD; Varsity Clb; Bsbl; Ftbl; Wt Lftg; Hon Roll; Lion Awd; Princpls Awd 86; Stu Recgntn 85-86; Psych.

KIMBALL, STEPHEN; Huntington HS; Huntington, NY; (Y); Boy Scts; Church Yth Grp; Crs Cntry; L JV Ftbl; Var L Trk; All Lge , & All Conf Lge Track 86; 'engr.

KIMBER, KATHLEEN A; Genesco Central HS; Geneseo, NY; (Y); Drama Clb; Spanish Clb; Chorus; School Musical; Variety Show; Capt Diving; Socr; Capt Swmmng; High Hon Roll; Olympcs Mind ST Champs 85.

KIMBERLY, TODD; Lansing HS; Ithaca, NY; (Y); Am Leg Boys St; Church Yth Grp; Spanish Clb; Band; Bsbl; JV Var Bsktbl; JV Ftbl; JV Golf; Var Socr; High Hon Roll; Outstndng Stu Englsh Awd Frosh; Lbrl Arts.

KIMBLE JR, EDWARD LEE; Odessa-Montour HS; Millport, NY; (Y); 15/86; NHS; Odessey Mnds 83-86; Crnng Cmmnty Coll; Cad.

KIMMEL, ERICH; Clarkstown HS North; Congers, NY; (Y); Cmnty Wkr; German Clb; Math Clb; SADD; Jr NHS; Mu Alp Tht; NHS; Westchstr Bus Inst-Outstndng Achvt 86; Recog Awd-Hlpd Spec Olympcs Kids 86; Amblnc Yth Corps-VP 86-87; Acctnt.

KIMMICH, KATHY; Churchville-Chili HS; Rochester, NY; (Y); Church Yth Grp; Ski Clb; Band; Chorus; Crs Cntry; Trk; High Hon Roll; Hon Roll; JP Sousa Awd; NHS; Elem Ed.

KIMMICH, LISA; Churchville-Chili SR HS; Rochester, NY; (Y); Church Yth Grp; FTA; Ski Clb; Chorus; Church Choir; Mrchg Band; Hon Roll; Color Guard; Concert Band; Typng Awd From Bryant & Strtn 86; Rbrts Wslyn Coll; Elem Ed.

KIMPTON, TODD; Canastota HS; Canastota, NY; (Y); 16/150; Aud/Vis; Church Yth Grp; Var Capt Bsktbl; Im Coach Actv; Var JV Golf; High Hon Roll; Hon Roll; Prfct Atten Awd; Outstndng Drvr Educ Stu 86; Bus Awd 86; SUBY; Bus Admin.

KINAHAN, KATRINA; West Genesee SR HS; Camillus, NY; (Y); 8/425; Church Yth Grp; Cmnty Wkr; Exploring; Hosp Aide; Im Bsktbl; Var Cheerleading; Im Vllybl; High Hon Roll; NHS; Gld Mdl Ntl Ltn Exm 86; Ntl Sci Olmpd 3rd Pl 85; Outstndng Stu Awd Frgn Lng & Mthmtcs 86; SUNY At Buffalo; Phrmcy.

KINDBERG, MARK; Jamestown HS; Jamestown, NY; (Y); 19/396; Am Leg Boys St; Church Yth Grp; Spanish Clb; Chorus; Var Capt Bsktbl; Ftbl; Hon Roll; NHS; Pres Schlr; Vkngs Grnd Ldg Schlrshp 86; Cmmns Schlrshp 86; Grove City Coll; Finance.

KINDER, TODD CHARLES; Thomas J Conoran HS; Syracuse, NY; (Y); Drama Clb; PAVAS; Q&S; Spanish Clb; School Musical; School Play; Nwsp Ed-Chief; Nwsp Rptr; Nwsp Stf; Lit Mag; Mny Art Awd 85-86; Lang Fair Awd Skit 85-86; Jrnlsm.

KINDYA, KIMBERLY; Stuyvesant HS; Elmhurst, NY; (Y); Latin Clb; Nwsp Ed-Chief; Lit Mag; Varsity Clb; English Clb; Service Clb; School Musical; Nwsp Stf; Hon Roll; Ntl Merit Ltr; Silvr Medl, Ntl Latn Cont, Amer Clsscl Soc 84; Wrtr.

KINER, JANIENE; Canarsie HS; Brooklyn, NY; (Y); Church Yth Grp; Teachers Aide; Chorus; Yrbk Stf; Cheerleading; Hon Roll; Prfct Atten Awd; Physcl Ed Awd 86; 100 Pct Awd 86; Bus Mgmt.

KING, ALAN; Bishop Ludden HS; Syracuse, NY; (S); Church Yth Grp; High Hon Roll; Pre-Med.

KING, AMY; Moriah Central HS; Port Henry, NY; (Y); GAA; Yrbk Stf; Sec Frsh Cls; Sec Soph Cls; Sec Jr Cls; Stu Cncl; Cheerleading; Gym; High Hon Roll; Hon Roll.

KING, ANNE; Wilson Central HS; Ransomville, NY; (Y); Cmnty Wkr; Trs 4-H; SADD; School Play; Nwsp Stf; Yrbk Stf; Var Fld Hcky; 4-H Awd; High Hon Roll; Hon Roll; Outstndg Achvt Math 83-84; NY ST Fair 4-H Dog Obednc Resv Chmpn 84, Grand Chmpn 85; Engrng.

KING, BOOKER; Clara Barton HS; Brooklyn, NY; (Y); Church Yth Grp; Spanish Clb; Bowling; High Hon Roll; Spanish NHS; City U NY; Physician.

KING, CARRIE A; Franklin Acad; Burke, NY; (Y); 4/260; French Clb; Hon Roll; NHS; Rgnts Schlrshp 86; St Lawrence U; Comp Sci.

KING, CATHERINE M; St Francis Prep; Bayside, NY; (S); 85/653; Dance Clb; Library Aide; Variety Show; Bsktbl; Im Vllybl; Hon Roll; NHS; Opt Clb Awd; Acad All Amer 85; Pre Med.

KING, CHRISTOPHER; Deposit Central HS; Deposit, NY; (Y); 1/85; Church Yth Grp; Model UN; Band; Stu Cncl; JV L Bsktbl; Var L Crs Cntry; Var L Trk; DAR Awd; High Hon Roll; NHS; Lgsltv Intrnshp 85-86; Arch.

KING, JARRID; Kings Park HS; Kings Park, NY; (Y); 23/422; Computer Clb; Library Aide; Pep Clb; Spanish Clb; Varsity Clb; Rep Frsh Cls; Var Bsktbl; Hon Roll; Med.

KING, JEFFREY; Mount Vernon HS; Mt Vernon, NY; (Y); Chess Clb; Key Clb; Science Clb; Var Socr; MA Inst Tech; Elec Engr.

KING, JOHN; Liverpool HS; Liverpool, NY; (Y); Stu Cncl; Im Bsbl; Im Bsktbl; Var L Ftbl; JV Lcrss; Var L Trk; Hon Roll; Var Wt Lftg; Prfct Atten Awd; 7th Pl Trk & Fld Sectnls New Hartford 86; U MA; Arch Engrng.

KING, JOHN; Mynder Se Acad; Seneca Falls, NY; (Y); Boy Scts; Ski Clb; JV Bowling; Var Crs Cntry; JV Golf; JV Trk; High Hon Roll; Hon Roll; Airforce Acad; Transprtn Tech.

KING, KERRY A; Hunter College HS; New York, NY; (Y); Model UN; School Musical; Yrbk Stf; Ntl Merit SF; Natl Achvt Scholar Semi-Fin 85; Polit Sci.

KING, KIMBERLY; New Berlin Central HS; New Berlin, NY; (Y); 20/52; French Clb; Chorus; Concert Band; School Play; Yrbk Stf; Var Sftbl; JV Vllybl; Cit Awd; Hon Roll; Lion Awd; Rgnts Schlrshp NRSNG 85-86; Rotary Intl Schlrshp 86; Dan Meyers Awd, New Berling FD Schlrshp 86; Cazenovia Coll; RN.

KING, KIWESA; New Rochelle HS; New Rochelle, NY; (Y); French Clb; Chorus; Rep Soph Cls; Rep Jr Cls; Rep Sr Cls; Ntl Achvt Schlrshp Prgrm 86; Mech Engr.

KING, LORI; Paul V Moore HS; Central Sq, NY; (Y); VP Concert Band; Drm Mjr(t); Jazz Band; Mrchg Band; Trs Symp Band; Bsktbl; Socr; Hon Roll.

KING, LYNDA L; Red Jacket Central HS; Palmyra, NY; (Y); 6/90; French Clb; Varsity Clb; Chorus; Madrigals; School Play; Nwsp Rptr; Pres Frsh Cls; Pres Jr Cls; Var Capt Bsktbl; JV Cheerleading; Regents Schlrshp 86; Presdntl Phy Ftnss Awd 84-85; Female Athlt Of Yr 85; Cornell U; Anml Sci.

KING, MARY ANNE; George W Fowler SR HS; Syracuse, NY; (S); 2/400; DECA; FBLA; JA; Nwsp Rptr; Yrbk Stf; Lit Mag; Cheerleading; High Hon Roll; NHS; Ntl Ed Clbs Of Amer 85; Med.

KING, MEGAN T; Our Lady Of Mercy Acad; Plandome, NY; (Y); 19/120; Cmnty Wkr; GAA; Stage Crew; Rep Soph Cls; Rep Jr Cls; Var L Bsktbl; Var L Swmmng; Var L Trk; Hon Roll; NY St Rgnts Schrlrhp 86; Williams Coll.

KING, MICHAEL; Mc Quaid Jesuit HS; Webster, NY; (Y); Camera Clb; Exploring; Stage Crew; Engrng.

KING, NAOMI; Nisvayuna HS; Schenectady, NY; (Y); U Of HI; MBA.

KING, PETER; William Nothingham HS; Syracuse, NY; (Y); 47/220; Latin Clb; Yrbk Sprt Ed; Pres Frsh Cls; Socr; Capt L Tennis; Hon Roll; NHS; Pres Spanish NHS; Harold J Anderson Schlrshp 82-83; St Lawrence U.

KING, RANDY; Keveny Memorial Acad; Watervliet, NY; (Y); Art Clb; Aud/Vis; Cmnty Wkr; JA; Library Aide; Church Choir; School Play; Stage Crew; Var Bowling; RPI Model RR Club 86; Indvl Achvt Awd JA 86; PILOT.

KING, ROBERT; Brockport HS; Brockport, NY; (Y); Spanish Clb; Chorus; SADD; SADD 84-86; Meteorlgst.

KING, ROBERT; Niskayuna SR HS; Scotia, NY; (Y); Spanish Clb; Trs Stu Cncl; JV Crs Cntry; Var L Ice Hcky; Socr; Ntl Merit Ltr; Elec Engrng.

KING, SARAH; Auburn HS; Auburn, NY; (Y); 40/427; VP Varsity Clb; Lit Mag; Trs Sr Cls; Var Capt Socr; JV Capt Sftbl; Var Capt Vllybl; High Hon Roll; NHS; Pres Schlr; Rotary Awd; Natl Sccr Coaches Assn Of Am MVP 86; U Center At Binghamton.

KING, SHAUN; White Plains HS; White Plains, NY; (Y); 206/430; Church Yth Grp; Im Badmtn; Var Socr; Var Swmmng; Var Capt Trk; Cit Awd; 70 Prcnt Trk & Fld Scholar Penn ST 86; Achvt Awd Acctg Westchester Bus Inst 86; NYS Phys Fit Wd 86; Penn ST; Acctg.

KING, TERRY ANN; John Jay HS; Brooklyn, NY; (Y); Church Yth Grp; JA; Model UN; Chorus; Cheerleading; Prfct Atten Awd; Photo.

KING, TRACY; St Marys Girls HS; Manhasset, NY; (Y); 30/170; Camera Clb; Drama Clb; Mathletes; Ski Clb; Spanish Clb; Stage Crew; JV Crs Cntry; Var JV Trk; Hon Roll; NHS; Ltn Awd Cum Laude 83-84; Bus.

KING, YVETTE; The Mary Louis Acad; Jamaica, NY; (Y); Church Yth Grp; Hosp Aide; Office Aide; Pres VP Spanish Clb; Teachers Aide; Yrbk Stf; Sec Jr Cls; NYS Regnts Schlrshp 86; Pres Schlrshp 86; U FL; Rn.

KINGSLEY, DAVID; Penn Yan Acad; Penn Yan, NY; (S); 4/174; Am Leg Boys St; Drama Clb; VP Varsity Clb; Jazz Band; School Musical; Variety Show; Rep Stu Cncl; Capt Trk; Wrstlng; NHS; NY ST Rgnts Schlrshp 86; SUNY Fredonia; Snd Recdg Tech.

KINGSTON, RICHARD J; Iroquois HS; S Wales, NY; (Y); Am Leg Boys St; Church Yth Grp; Cmnty Wkr; VP Dance Clb; Spanish Clb; L Socr; L Trk; Hon Roll; NHS; Crimnlgy.

KINKADE, LEE; Hahn American HS; Apo New York, NY; (Y); Art Clb; Drama Clb; Library Aide; Quiz Bowl; School Play; Ed Yrbk Phtg; Rep Stu Cncl; High Hon Roll; Debate Tm; Letterman Clb; Membrshp CA Schlrshp Fed Sem 84-85; Cntrl Hgh Gld Awd-3 80-4 00 1 Yr 84-85; 1st Pl-Sclptr Are Shwng; Fash Dsgn.

KINKELA, KATHERINE A; The Ursuline Schl; Bronxville, NY; (Y); Church Yth Grp; Debate Tm; Chorus; School Musical; High Hon Roll; Jr NHS; Ntl Merit Ltr; Cmnty Wkr; Drama Clb; Girl Scts; Schlrshp To Ursuline Schl 83; Mod Legislature Of Westchester Co 86; Intrnshp 86.

KINLEN, WILLIAM G; Herbert H Lehman HS; Bronx, NY; (Y); 189/368; Y-Teens; Var Capt Tennis; Bronze Mdl Air Con 86; Sons Am Leg 84-86; Farmingdale U; Air Con/Refrig.

KINN, ERIK; Frontier Central HS; Hamburg, NY; (Y); 65/500; Computer Clb; German Clb; Varsity Clb; Band; Var L Bsbl; Var L Ice Hcky; Hon Roll; NHS; Elec Engrng.

KINNAIRD, DAVID; Portville Central HS; Westons Mills, NY; (Y); Intnl Clb; Model UN; Ski Clb; JV Bsktbl; JV Trk; High Hon Roll; Hon Roll; NHS.

KINNE, MICHELE; Vernon-Verona-Sherrill Central HS; Blossvale, NY; (Y); Church Yth Grp; Computer Clb; JCL; Latin Clb; Orch; Rep Frsh Cls; JV Socr; Trk; High Hon Roll; Hon Roll; Mrn Bio.

KINNEY, ALAN; Mc Quaid Jesuit HS; Rochester, NY; (Y); 32/171; German Clb; Latin Clb; Teachers Aide; Chorus; Jazz Band; Lit Mag; High Hon Roll; NHS; St Schlr; Nazareth Coll Acad Schlrshp 86; Acad Lttr & Svc Bar 84 & 86; Nazareth Coll Rochester; Engl.

KINNEY, DARLENE; Midlakes HS; Clifton Springs, NY; (Y); 88/167; Aud/Vis; Chess Clb; VP Cmnty Wkr; Computer Clb; Dance Clb; Debate Tm; SADD; School Musical; Hon Roll; FHA; JR Mst Imprved Boces 84; All ST Awd In Music Excllnt 83; CCFL; Data Prcssng.

KINNEY, JOANNE; Ward Melville HS; S Setauket, NY; (Y); Ski Clb; Hon Roll; Bus Hnr Scty 86; Outdoor Clb 85-86; Med.

KINNEY, KITRINA; Fillmore Central Schl; Hume, NY; (Y); 30/65; SADD; Band; Concert Band; Nwsp Stf; Stat Vllybl; St John Fisher Coll; Acctng.

KINNEY, LISA; John C Birdlebough HS; Clay, NY; (Y); 57/170; Drama Clb; Pres VP Girl Scts; Spanish Clb; SADD; Teachers Aide; Chorus; Color Guard; School Musical; Kindrgrdn Tchr.

KINNEY, REGINA M; St Francis Prep HS; Bayside, NY; (S); 42/695; Dance Clb; Library Aide; Math Clb; SADD; Chorus; Rptr Lit Mag; Vllybl; Hon Roll; NHS; Optimates Socty; Regents Schlrshp; Comptv Schlrshp St Johns U; Queens Coll; Ed.

KINORY, ADAM D; Bronx Science; New York, NY; (Y); Cmnty Wkr; Exploring; Political Wkr; Red Cross Aide; Temple Yth Grp; Y-Teens; St Schlr; NY ST Rgnts Schlrshp; Instrl Rltns.

KINSELLA, CHRIS J; Ballston Spa HS; Ballston Spa, NY; (Y); Math Tm; SADD; Varsity Clb; Var L Bsktbl; Var L Socr; Var L Tennis; High Hon Roll; Sidmore/Saratogian Acad Achvt Awd 84; US Natl Ldrshp Merit Awd 85; NY St Regents Schlrshp 86; RPI; Aerosp Engr.

KINSELLA, MARTIN; Paul V Moore HS; Central Sq, NY; (Y); 60/280; Am Leg Boys St; Church Yth Grp; Cmnty Wkr; Radio Clb; Speech Tm; Nwsp Rptr; Nwsp Stf; Stu Cncl; Im Bsbl; Var Tennis; 2nd Pl Nwsppr Artcl 85; Mst Imprvd Tns Athlt For Cen Sq 86; Amer U; Law.

KINSEY, SHARON; Grace Dodge Vocational HS; Bronx, NY; (Y); Church Yth Grp; Church Choir; Hon Roll; Nrsg.

KINYON, MARY LOU; Sweet Home SR HS; Williamsville, NY; (Y); Latin Clb; Library Aide; Spanish Clb; Church Choir; Orch; High Hon Roll; NHS; Spanish NHS; Natl Hstry Day Cont 1st Pl Cnty & 3rd Pl ST 85-86; Natl Latin Exam Summa Cum Laude 86; Lbrl Arts.

KIPP, KELLY; Saranac Central Schl; Cadyville, NY; (S); 3/120; Drama Clb; French Clb; Trs SADD; Band; Jazz Band; School Musical; Stage Crew; High Hon Roll; NHS; Plattsburgh U; Canadian Stds.

KIPP, TAMARA; Stissing Mountain HS; Stanfordville, NY; (Y); Cmnty Wkr; Dance Clb; Drama Clb; Band; Mrchg Band; Stage Crew; Swmmng; High Hon Roll; Hon Roll; Ntl Merit Ltr; Good Grades Hnr Key 86.

KIRBY, BRIAN M; Kenmore West SR HS; Kenmore, NY; (Y); 13/450; Boy Scts; Chess Clb; Mathletes; Math Clb; Math Tm; Var L Bowling; High Hon Roll; NHS; Ntl Merit SF; Niagara Frontier Math League Tm 85; 10th Ntl Spnsh Exam 83-84; 1st Jr To Score Prfct 6 Math Meet 84-85; ST U Of NY-BUFFALO; Arch.

KIRBY, CHRISTINE; Oceanside HS; Oceanside, NY; (Y); Cmnty Wkr; Dance Clb; Spanish Clb; Chorus; Hon Roll; Art Awd 84; Bus.

KIRBY, JULIE; Lansing HS; Groton, NY; (Y); Drama Clb; Spanish Clb; Chorus; School Musical; Pres Soph Cls; Trs Sr Cls; Var Capt Sftbl; Var L Swmmng; Hon Roll; Spanish NHS; Comm.

KIRBY, RAYNARD; Guilderland Central HS; Albany, NY; (Y); Key Clb; Varsity Clb; Orch; Stu Cncl; Var Bsktbl; Var Trk; Archtctr.

KIRCHENKO, ANTON S; Earl L Vandermeulen HS; Mt Sinai, NY; (Y); Aud/Vis; French Clb; Yrbk Phtg; AF ROTC Fnlst 86; Navy Fnlst 86.

KIRCHER, CATHY; North Babylon SR HS; N Babylon, NY; (Y); 143/449; Chorus; Stage Crew; Score Keeper; Stat Vllybl; Hon Roll; Jr NHS; Spec Ed.

KIRCHGAESSNER, CHRISTIANE; Blind Brook HS; Rye Brook, NY; (Y); Art Clb; German Clb; Ski Clb; SADD; Chorus; Rptr Yrbk Phtg; Var JV Swmmng; Prfct Atten Awd; Natl Ldrshp & Serv Awds 86; Acad All Amer Awd 85.

KIRCHNER, TIMMY; Half Hollow Hills HS West; Dix Hills, NY; (Y); Chorus; JV Bsktbl; Var Capt Crs Cntry; JV Var Mgr(s); Score Keeper; Var Capt Trk; Hon Roll; Wntr Trck All League 1 Mile All Conf, Sprng Trck All League 2 Mile 86; Bus.

KIRESEN, MICHELLE; Our Lady Of Mercy HS; Webster, NY; (Y); Church Yth Grp; Cmnty Wkr; Dance Clb; Debate Tm; Girl Scts; JA; Model UN; Pep Clb; Red Cross Aide; Service Clb; Cmp Cup Awd 84; Tchng Inst Red Cross 85-86; Psych.

KIRISITS, TODD A; Southwestern HS; Lakewood, NY; (Y); French Clb; Letterman Clb; Ski Clb; Varsity Clb; Band; Chorus; Socr; Tennis; French Hon Soc; High Hon Roll; Acad Achvt Soc Studys 85-86; RIT; Engrng.

KIRK, CHRISTOPHER; Corning West HS; Corning, NY; (Y); AFS; JA; SADD; Thesps; Concert Band; Mrchg Band; School Musical; School Play; Socr; Var Tennis; Cortland; Intl Stds.

KIRK, DAVID B; Bishop Timon HS; W Seneca, NY; (Y); Am Leg Boys St; Cmnty Wkr; SADD; Chorus; Nwsp Stf; Rep Stu Cncl; Var Ftbl; Var Swmmng; Var Trk; VP NHS; Federal Acad; Engrng.

KIRK, DAVID F; Arlington HS; Poughkeepsie, NY; (Y); 2/600; Debate Tm; Var Bsbl; Capt Var Bsktbl; Var Golf; Ntl Merit SF; Sal; Watson Schlrshp Semi-Fin 85-86; Hugh O Brien Ldrshp Schl Rep 83-84; Pol Sci.

KIRK, MONIQUE; Smithtown HS East; Nesconset, NY; (Y); GAA; Service Clb; SADD; Yrbk Stf; Badmtn; JV Capt Socr; Hon Roll; Marine Bio.

KIRKBY, JEFFREY; Indian River Central HS; Evans Mills, NY; (Y); 3/120; Capt Quiz Bowl; Stu Cncl; JV Bsktbl; Var Golf; Cit Awd; DAR Awd; Hon Roll; NHS; Ntl Merit SF; Pres Schlr; Albny Coll Phrmcy; Phrmcy.

KIRKBY, KAREN; Liverpool HS; Liverpool, NY; (Y); 98/850; GAA; Ski Clb; Spanish Clb; Rep Jr Cls; JV Var Mgr(s); Im Powder Puff Ftbl; JV Socr; JV Sftbl; JV Swmmng; Stat Timer; SUNY-GENESEO; Bus Adm.

KIRKBY, ROBERT; Liverpool HS; Liverpool, NY; (Y); 56/825; Ski Clb; Rep Frsh Cls; Rep Soph Cls; Rep Jr Cls; Rep Sr Cls; Rep Stu Cncl; Im Coach Actv; Var L Ftbl; Var L Lcrss; Im Sftbl; Schlrshp Dollrs Schlrs 86; SUNY At Geneseo; Phy Thrpy.

KIRKER, BETSEY LYNN; Downsville Central HS; Downsville, NY; (Y); Sec Spanish Clb; Chorus; School Play; Nwsp Stf; Yrbk Stf; Stu Cncl; Cheerleading; Socr; Hon Roll; Prfct Atten Awd; US Bus Ed Awd 84; Hudson Vly CC; Dentl Hyg.

KIRKLAND JR, MICHAEL; South Shore HS; Brooklyn, NY; (Y); Church Choir; Bsktbl; Ftbl; Trk; Prfct Attndnc Awd Delta Sigma Theta Brklyn Chptr 86; NC A & T Coll; Comp Anls.

KIRKPATRICK, LESLEY A; Commack South HS; Dix Hills, NY; (Y); 16/356; Yrbk Phtg; Yrbk Sprt Ed; Vllybl; High Hon Roll; NHS; Regents Schlrshp; Albany U.

KIRPATRICK, ROBERT; Wallkill HS; Walden, NY; (S); 4/190; Concert Band; Jazz Band; Nwsp Ed-Chief; Yrbk Stf; VP Sr Cls; Var Socr; Var Trk; High Hon Roll; NHS; Ntl Merit Ltr; Area All St Band & Orchestra; Rutgers Coll Hnrs Schlrshp; Bard Coll Hnrs Schlrshp.

KIRST, MARY; Villa Maria Acad; Cheektowaga, NY; (S); 29/90; SADD; Pres Frsh Cls; Pres Soph Cls; Rep Stu Cncl; Var Bsktbl; Var Sftbl; Var Vllybl; Hon Roll.

KISH, PAUL; Fillmore Central HS; Fillmore, NY; (Y); 4-H; Pres FFA; Varsity Clb; Stage Crew; JV Bsbl; Var Bsktbl; JV Socr; Dnfth Awd; Dist Farm Bureau Ctznshp Awd 86.

KISS, ANDY; Mahopac HS; Mahopac, NY; (Y); 150/420; Computer Clb; Red Cross Aide; Science Clb; Nwsp Stf; Hon Roll; Achvmnt Rdng 83; Embry-Riddle; Aviation.

KISSANE, MAIREAD; Monticello HS; Monticello, NY; (S); Church Yth Grp; Debate Tm; Drama Clb; 4-H; NFL; Ski Clb; Spanish Clb; Speech Tm; Teachers Aide; School Musical; Crnl Splmn Awd 85; Stu Ldrs Clb Awd 84; Ntl Frnsc League 85; Law.

KISSANE, SHEILA; North Babylon HS; N Babylon, NY; (Y); 33/460; Spanish Clb; SADD; Trs Stu Cncl; Fld Hcky; JV Vllybl; Jr NHS; NHS; Phys Ftns Awds 84 & 85; Hmn Rltns Committee Awd 86.

KISSEL, DAVID N; West Seneca West SR HS; West Seneca, NY; (Y); 11/559; Chess Clb; Key Clb; Math Tm; Trs Spanish Clb; Varsity Clb; JV Ftbl; Wt Lftg; Hon Roll; NHS; NYS Regents Schlrshp 86; Chem Mdl Hnr 84; GMI; Engrng.

KISSEL, JENNIFER; Lake Placid Central HS; Lake Placid, NY; (Y); 1/45; Cmnty Wkr; Sec Key Clb; Varsity Clb; Trs Soph Cls; Trs Jr Cls; Var Socr; Var Tennis; Bausch & Lomb Sci Awd; High Hon Roll; Sec NHS; Rensselaer Polytchnc Inst Math & Sci Awd 86; Pdtrcn.

KISSEL, TRACI; Oneida HS; Canastota, NY; (S); 14/210; Concert Band; Mrchg Band; JV Capt Fld Hcky; High Hon Roll; Hon Roll; NHS; Vet.

KISSI, EVANS; Yonkers HS; Yonkers, NY; (Y); Cmnty Wkr; Hosp Aide; Math Clb; Math Tm; Office Aide; Lit Mag; High Hon Roll; Hon Roll; Jr NHS; VP NHS; Sprntndnts Schl Clb 90 Brnz Pin 85-86; Rcgntn Outstndng Vlntry Svc 86; Cert Awd Natl Cncl Negro Wmn 86; Columbia U; Pre-Med.

KISZKIEL, REBECCA MARY; Mont Pleasant HS; Schenectady, NY; (Y); 28/250; Pep Clb; Service Clb; Color Guard; Ed Yrbk Stf; Sec Soph Cls; Rep Stu Cncl; French Hon Soc; Hon Roll; Mgr(s); Jr Cls Exec Cmmtee 85-86; Cmmnty Svc Awd 84; Grphc Dsgn.

KITCHEN, WILLIAM; Vernon-Verona-Scherrill Centrl Schl; Vernon Ctr, NY; (Y); 4/200; Am Leg Boys St; Math Tm; Thesps; Varsity Clb; Band; Church Choir; Drm & Bgl; Jazz Band; Mrchg Band; School Musical; Silv City Awds Mth & Sci 85 & 86; Pres Acad Fit Awd 86; Ftbl Lg All Star 85; Clarkson Coll; Chem Engrng.

KITSONIDIS, STEVE; St Francis Prep; Flushing North, NY; (Y); Band; Concert Band; Drm & Bgl; Pep Band; Im Bsbl; JV Crs Cntry; Im Fld Hcky; Im Ftbl; Im Socr; Im Sftbl; Aviation.

KITTELBERGER, J MATTHEW; Brighton HS; Rochester, NY; (Y); 1/325; Jazz Band; Symp Band; Var Capt Swmmng; Ntl Merit SF; German Clb; Varsity Clb; Nwsp Stf; Amer Assn Tchrs Germ Scholar 85; Rennsalaer Polytech Inst Medl 85; Sci.

KITTELL, ERIC; Watkins Glen Ctl HS; Valois, NY; (S); Ski Clb; Var Ftbl; Var L Trk; Hon Roll.

KITTLES, VINCENT; Central Islip HS; Central Islip, NY; (Y); Var Crs Cntry; Var Capt Trk; Hon Roll; Tech Comp Awd 85; Photo.

KLABEN, JASON; Bishop Grimes HS; Syracuse, NY; (Y); Var Bsbl; JV Ftbl; High Hon Roll; Hon Roll; NHS; Arntcl Engrng.

KLABEN, MATTHEW; Bishop Ludden HS; Jordan, NY; (S); Church Yth Grp; Intnl Clb; Math Tm; VP L Crs Cntry; VP L Trk; High Hon Roll; Sci & Engl Awds 84; Engl, Math, French, German, Rlgn, & Soc Studies Awds 85.

KLAFEHN, DAVID; Kendall JR SR HS; Kendall, NY; (Y); 12/84; Pres Church Yth Grp; Pres Sec FFA; Yrbk Phtg; Pres Stu Cncl; Hon Roll; NHS; Pep Clb; Variety Show; JV Var Bsbl; JV Var Bsktbl; FFA Empir Deg Awd 85; Citznshp Awd 85; Morrisville Whippl Schlrshp 86; Morrisville College; Farmg.

KLAMKA, JEFF; John Jay HS; Purdys, NY; (Y); Nwsp Ed-Chief; Nwsp Sprt Ed; Bsktbl; JV Crs Cntry; High Hon Roll; NHS; VP Spanish NHS; Debate Tm; Math Tm; JV Trk; French II Awd 85; Frnch III Awd & Ctznshp Awd 86; Law.

KLANG, TINA; Wellsville HS; Wellsville, NY; (Y); Church Yth Grp; Stu Cncl; Capt Tennis; High Hon Roll; Trs NHS; Prfct Atten Awd; Wellsvl Almn Assn & Wellsvl Lions Clb Schlrshp 86; U Of Buffalo; Pharm.

KLAR, MICHELLE; Cohoes HS; Cohoes, NY; (Y); Art Clb; Cmnty Wkr; Exploring; Girl Scts; JA; Spanish Clb; SADD; Varsity Clb; Bowling; Cheerleading; Volunteer Cohoess Sat Mourning 83-87; Enrichment Pgm; Marine Bio.

KLATT, TINA K; Medina SR HS; Medina, NY; (Y); 10/160; SADD; Acpl Chr; Band; Chorus; Concert Band; Mrchg Band; Swing Chorus; Hon Roll; NHS; NY ST Rgnts Schlrshp 86; Honorati 83; SUNY Bfl; Physcl Thrpy.

KLECAN, KATHRYN; St John The Baptist HS; Islip, NY; (S); 5/512; Var Bsktbl; Var L Sftbl; High Hon Roll; Sci Awd 84-85; Hstry Awd 84-85; Engl Awd 84-85.

KLEIN, ALIZA N; E L Vandermeulen HS; Port Jefferson, NY; (Y); 49/300; Leo Clb; SADD; Color Guard; Concert Band; Capt Flag Corp; Mrchg Band; Stat Bsbl; Var Trk; JV Vllybl; French Clb; Regents Schlrshp 86; ST U NY; Psychlgy.

KLEIN, DENISE; Linton HS; Schenectady, NY; (Y); 8/350; Key Clb; Office Aide; Stu Cncl; JV Cheerleading; JV Socr; Hon Roll; NHS; Val; Bio Achvt Awd; Mgt.

KLEIN, ERIK; Berlin Central HS; Berlin, NY; (Y); 9/90; Am Leg Boys St; Ski Clb; School Musical; School Play; Yrbk Phtg; Pres Sr Cls; Var L Bsbl; Var L Bsktbl; Var L Socr; DAR Awd; Geneseo.

KLEIN, IRA A; North Rockland HS; Haverstraw, NY; (Y); Chess Clb; French Clb; JV Trk; JV Wrstlng; High Hon Roll; NHS; Wt Lftg; Acctg.

KLEIN, JASON M; Blind Brook HS; Rye Brook, NY; (Y); Spanish Clb; Temple Yth Grp; Nwsp Rptr; VP Soph Cls; Rep Jr Cls; Stu Cncl; Hon Roll; Ntl Merit SF; St Schlr; Wesleyan U.

KLEIN, KATHRYN T; Cheektowaga Central HS; Cheektowaga, NY; (Y); 1/199; FTA; JA; SADD; Trs Jr Cls; VP Sr Cls; Score Keeper; Timer; High Hon Roll; Jr NHS; Pres NHS; Elmira Key Awd 85; Regnts Schlrshp 86; Rochester Inst Of Tech.

KLEIN, KRISTIN; Frontier Central HS; Blasdell, NY; (Y); 14/430; French Clb; Girl Scts; Pep Clb; Rep Jr Cls; JV Var Cheerleading; High Hon Roll; Hon Roll; NHS; Pre Law.

KLEIN, MELISSA; South Side HS; Rockville Ctr, NY; (Y); 4/300; Key Clb; SADD; Orch; Nwsp Rptr; Yrbk Stf; High Hon Roll; Jr NHS; NHS; Soc Studies Awd 86; NY All ST Orchestra 86; Wnr Martin Luther King Jr Essay Cntst 86; Psych.

KLEIN, MICHAEL; Smithtown East; St James, NY; (Y); Drama Clb; Exploring; Pres Thesps; School Musical; School Play; Jr Cls; Stu Cncl; Hon Roll; NHS; Spanish NHS; Smithtwn Yuth Bur 85-86; Prs Thespians Soc; Tres Spnsh Ntl Hnr Soc.

KLEIN, MITCHELL; The Harvey Schl; Armonk, NY; (S); Model UN; JV Var Ftbl; JV Lcrss; Stat Mgr(s); Trk; High Hon Roll; Hon Roll; Tax Law.

KLEIN, SCOTT; John H Glenn HS; E Northport, NY; (Y); Chess Clb; Computer Clb; Debate Tm; Mathletes; Political Wkr; Science Clb; Speech Tm; Temple Yth Grp; Wrstlng; High Hon Roll; Med.

KLEIN, SHANNON; Rennsselaer HS; Rensselaer, NY; (Y); Cmnty Wkr; Debate Tm; Key Clb; Pep Clb; SADD; Varsity Clb; Nwsp Stf; Yrbk Rptr; Pres Frsh Cls; VP Soph Cls; Bus.

KLEIN, TAMMIE; Lansingburgh HS; Troy, NY; (Y); Chorus; Yrbk Stf; Score Keeper; Hon Roll.

KLEIN, TAMMY; Palmyra Macedon HS; Macedon, NY; (Y); OEA; SADD; Stu Cncl; Bsktbl; Golf; Var Socr; High Hon Roll; Hon Roll; NHS; Bus Mgmt.

KLEINCLAUS, HOLLY ANNE; Lockport SR HS; Lockport, NY; (Y); 111/411; Camera Clb; Cmnty Wkr; Exploring; FHA; German Clb; Math Clb; Science Clb; Hon Roll; Explrs Merit Awd 84-85; ST U NY; Vet Sci.

KLEINER, SONIA; Clarkstown HS North; New City, NY; (Y); 47/405; Exploring; Natl Beta Clb; Office Aide; Spanish Clb; Sec SADD; Temple Yth Grp; Lit Mag; Off Jr Cls; High Hon Roll; Mu Alp Tht; Binghamton U.

KLEINHAUS, KARINE R; Ramaz HS; Scarsdale, NY; (Y); Dance Clb; Political Wkr; Nwsp Ed-Chief; Trs Jr Cls; Ntl Merit SF; Aud/Vis; Debate Tm; Cert Of Excllnc-Isreali Army Yth Corp 85; Ntl Board Mem Of Yth For Democratic Action 85-86.

KLEINKOPF, ADAM MARK; The Bronx High School Of Science; Bronx, NY; (Y); JA; VP Library Aide; Temple Yth Grp; Sgn Lang Is Cool Sch Clb 85; NYS Regnts Schlrshp 86; Queens Clg CUNY; Eng.

KLEINMAN, AMY-BETH; Monticelle HS; Monticello, NY; (Y); Camp Fr Inc; Cmnty Wkr; Office Aide; Political Wkr; Teachers Aide; Stage Crew; Yrbk Stf; Rep Frsh Cls; Rep Jr Cls; Rep Sr Cls; Psych.

KLEINMAN, JON; South Side HS; Rockville Ctr, NY; (Y); 23/280; Debate Tm; Band; Jazz Band; Mrchg Band; Orch; Nwsp Stf; Lit Mag; High Hon Roll; NHS; 1st Triumpet All Cty Band 84.

KLEINMAN, REID; Lynbrook HS; Hewlett Harbor, NY; (S); Co-Capt Debate Tm; NFL; Co-Capt Speech Tm; Varsity Clb; Nwsp Rptr; Nwsp Stf; Tennis; High Hon Roll; Hon Roll; NHS; Natl Forensic Lg Degree Distinction 86; Cert Merit 84-85; Law.

KLEMENS, DANIEL; Kenmore East HS; Kenmore, NY; (Y); Var Stat Swmmng; High Hon Roll; Hon Roll; Pre-Law.

KLEMENS, GREGORY C; Mount St Joseph Acad; Hamburg, NY; (Y); 4/44; Trs Drama Clb; Pres German Clb; Pres JA; Off School Musical; Lit Mag; Capt Lcrss; High Hon Roll; Voice Dem Awd; Sarah Lawrence Coll; Psychlgy.

KLEMMER, THOMAS; Monticello HS; Smallwood, NY; (Y); Drama Clb; Acpl Chr; Band; Chorus; Jazz Band; Orch; Nwsp Stf; 4-H Awd; High Hon Roll; NHS; Treas Of Natl Hon Soc 86; Embry-Riddle U; Aerontcl Sci.

KLEMPNER, GAIL; Hebrew Acad Of The Five Twns & Rockawys; Far Rockaway, NY; (Y); Civic Clb; Debate Tm; English Clb; FHA; Library Aide; Spanish Clb; Temple Yth Grp; Lit Mag; Hon Roll; Queens Coll.

KLEMZ, THERESA; Cardinal Mooney HS; Rochester, NY; (Y); 55/304; Church Yth Grp; SADD; School Play; Var Capt Cheerleading; High Hon Roll; Hon Roll; Hnds Chrst Awd 86; NY ST Rgnts Schlrshp 86; Monroe CC; Math.

KLENOSKY, MATTHEW; West Hempstead HS; Island Park, NY; (Y); Am Leg Boys St; Computer Clb; Mathletes; Socr; Hon Roll; NHS; Ntl Merit SF; Hghst Avg Bio, Math, Elctrncs 84; Engrng.

KLESZCZEWSKI JR, MARK E; Archbishop Molloy HS; Brooklyn, NY; (Y); 65/383; Boy Scts; French Clb; Intnl Clb; Acpl Chr; Yrbk Phtg; Church Yth Grp; Science Clb; Drill Tm; Lit Mag; Im Trk; NY U; Engl.

KLICK, SUSANNE; S Glens Falls SR HS; S Glens Falls, NY; (Y); 37/238; Bryant Coll; Acctng.

KLIMASZEWSKI, MARY; Villa Maria Acad; Buffalo, NY; (Y); Computer Clb; French Clb; Pep Clb; Hon Roll; Med Tech.

KLIMCZYK, PETER; Maryvale HS; Cheektowaga, NY; (Y); French Clb; SADD; Varsity Clb; Chorus; Church Choir; Var JV Bsktbl; Var JV Socr; Hon Roll; NHS; Nuclear Engineering.

KLIMEK, SUE; Skaneateles Central HS; Mottville, NY; (Y); 23/150; Yrbk Stf; Var Capt Crs Cntry; Trk; High Hon Roll; Hon Roll; NHS; Oswego ST; Sclgy.

KLIMOVICH, JOSEPH; Herbert H Lehman HS; New York, NY; (Y); 33/900; Varsity Clb; Orch; Var Capt Bowling; Coach Actv; High Hon Roll; Prfct Atten Awd; Arista Hnr Soc 86; Hnr Soc 84-85; NY Inst Tech; Electrncs.

KLIMOWSKI, KIMBERLY; West Seneca West SR HS; Cheektowaga, NY; (Y); FBLA; Hon Roll; NHS; Pres Schlr; St Bonaventure U; Acctng.

KLIMPEL, ERIC R; Kingston HS; Tillson, NY; (Y); Am Leg Boys St; Boy Scts; Chess Clb; Church Yth Grp; Trs German Clb; Var L Crs Cntry; Var L Trk; High Hon Roll; NHS; Computer Clb; German Hon Soc 85-87; West Poin; Chemical Engineer.

KLINE, E; Broadolbin HS; Broadalbin, NY; (Y); Trs French Clb; Girl Scts; Varsity Clb; Sec Jr Cls; Pres Sr Cls; Rep Stu Cncl; Var Capt Bsktbl; Var Capt Vllybl; Pres NHS; Pres Schlr; Gold Awd Girl Sct 86; Vllybl Ded Awd 85-86; Repub Clb Awd Excllnce Amer Govt 86; SUNY Geneseo; Spec Ed.

KLINE, JESSICA; Auburn HS; Auburn, NY; (Y); Art Clb; Dance Clb; JA; PAVAS; Spanish Clb; Mrchg Band; Rep Sr Cls; Hon Roll; JC Awd; Prfct Atten Awd; Mny Rgnl Schlstc Art Awds 86; Schwnfrth Ct Of Hnr Exhbtr 86; Art.

KLINE, MITCHELL; Minisink Valley HS; Middletown, NY; (Y); 14/227; Math Tm; Pres Band; Concert Band; Jazz Band; Mrchg Band; Orch; Pep Band; Rep Stu Cncl; High Hon Roll; NHS; Schlstc Excllnc Awd 82-83; Outstndng Mscn 83-86; Chrprsn Yth Govt; Cornell U; Med.

KLINEBERG, LAURIE; East Syracuse-Minoa HS; E Syracuse, NY; (Y); Camera Clb; French Clb; Ski Clb; Yrbk Phtg; Var Gym; Im Vllybl; Hon Roll; Jr NHS; NHS; Cmmnctns.

KLINETOB, NADYA; Broadalbin Central HS; Broadalbin, NY; (Y); 1/75; Am Leg Aux Girls St; Computer Clb; Drama Clb; Trs French Clb; Girl Scts; Letterman Clb; Varsity Clb; Chorus; Rep Frsh Cls; Sec Stu Cncl; Middlebury Schlrp 86; Rgnts Schlrp 86; Middlebury Coll; Comptr Sci.

KLINGENBERGER, TIMOTHY; Churchville-Chili HS; Rochester, NY; (Y); 20/310; Chorus; School Musical; Pres Stu Cncl; Var Capt Crs Cntry; Var Trk; Hon Roll; NHS; Pres Schlr; S M Trainor Awd Acadmc/Athltc Excllnc 83-84; US Army Rsrv Schlrshp/Athlt Awd 86; Lee Cup Awd 86; U Of Rochester; Pre-Med.

KLINGENSCHMITT, GORDON J; Clarence Central SR HS; Akron, NY; (Y); 3/270; Scholastic Bowl; Concert Band; Nwsp Stf; Rep Stu Cncl; JV Var Vllybl; High Hon Roll; NHS; Church Yth Grp; Cmnty Wkr; JCL; Rifle Tm Cptn 86; Mock Trl Tm Witness 86; All St Band 85; Cornell U; Aero Sp Engr.

KLINGENSMITH, MICHELE; Union Endicott HS; Endicott, NY; (Y); 91/525; Ski Clb; Stu Cncl; Hon Roll; NYS Regents Schlrshp86; Co-Op IBM Endicott 85-86; Suggestn Awd-IBM Imprvmnt Sggstn 85-86; Broome CC; Accntng.

KLINGER, EDWARD J; St Francis Prep; Howard Beach, NY; (S); 147/743; Band; Concert Band; Drm & Bgl; Mrchg Band; Im Sftbl; Im Wt Lftg; Hon Roll; Cmmnctns.

KLINGER, MICHELLE; Newfane SR HS; Burt, NY; (Y); 23/150; 4-H; Yrbk Ed-Chief; Yrbk Stf; JV Sftbl; 4-H Awd; High Hon Roll; Hon Roll; Hghst Overall Grd In Child Dev 84; Hghst Overall Grd In Foods Cls 85; Villa Maria Coll; Inter Design.

KLINKE, SHARON T; Liverpool HS; Liverpool, NY; (Y); 62/817; Hosp Aide; Ski Clb; Varsity Clb; Nwsp Phtg; Nwsp Rptr; Nwsp Stf; Rep Jr Cls; Trk; High Hon Roll; NHS; NY ST Rgnts Schlrshp 86; Wllm R Tckr Schlrshp Oswego ST U 86; Oswego ST U; Physcl Thrpy.

KLINZMAN, MARYGRACE; Monroe Woodbury SR HS; Monroe, NY; (Y); Hosp Aide; Band; Concert Band; School Musical; Symp Band; Nwsp Rptr; Crs Cntry; Trk; Orange Cnty Cmnty Clg; Jrnlsm.

KLIRONOMOS, ANTONIA; Lindenhurst SR HS; Lindenhurst, NY; (Y); 114/550; Art Clb; VP Church Yth Grp; French Clb; Yrbk Stf; Rep Frsh Cls; Sec Soph Cls; Rep Jr Cls; Rep Sr Cls; Var Tennis; Hon Roll; TAL Awd Hlth 85; Long Isl U C W Post; Financ.

KLISH, MELINDA; Johnson City HS; Johnson City, NY; (Y); Church Yth Grp; Cmnty Wkr; Dance Clb; Key Clb; Chorus; Church Choir; Grls Bsktbl Lge 82-86; JR Ukrnian Othdx Lge USA Outstndng Serv Awd 86.

KLOC, MICHAEL JOHN; Iroquois Central SR HS; Elma, NY; (Y); 13/300; Boys Clb Am; Hon Roll; Kiwanis Awd; Bryant & Stratton; Elec.

KLOC, WILLIAM; Lansingburgh HS; Troy, NY; (Y); 39/180; Var JV Bsbl; Var JV Ftbl; Wt Lftg; Hon Roll; Jr NHS; Siena; Bus Adm.

KLOCK, JENNIFER; Grand Island SR HS; Gr Island, NY; (Y); 40/340; Camera Clb; Cmnty Wkr; Pep Clb; Band; Concert Band; Orch; Pep Band; School Musical; Stat Score Keeper; Hon Roll; Band Pres 85-86; Outstndng Bandsmn 85-86; Cortland Coll; TV.

KLOCKE, DAN; St Josephs Collegiate Inst; Williamsville, NY; (Y); 2/200; School Musical; Swing Chorus; Sec Stu Cncl; Var Tennis; NHS; Cmnty Wkr; Chorus; Yrbk Stf; Rep Soph Cls; Im Bsktbl.

KLOCKE, NANCY; Mt St Mary Acad; Williamsville, NY; (Y); 16/94; Church Yth Grp; Cmnty Wkr; Computer Clb; Library Aide; Model UN; SADD; Teachers Aide; Chorus; Church Choir; School Musical; Psych.

KLOCKLER, ALAN; Saint Francis Prep; Hollis, NY; (Y); SADD; Band; Concert Band; Mrchg Band; Orch; Pep Band; School Musical; Stage Crew; JV Socr; Im Sftbl; Music.

KLOIBER, WENDY; Cicero-North Syracuse HS; North Syracuse, NY; (S); 3/667; Am Leg Aux Girls St; Cmnty Wkr; SADD; Teachers Aide; Pres Stu Cncl; JV Vllybl; CC Awd; DAR Awd; NHS; Opt Clb Awd; Utopia Clb Lit Awd; Marist Coll; Engl.

KLOSNER, MICHAEL; Bayside HS; Bayside, NY; (Y); Teachers Aide; Band; Nwsp Rptr; High Hon Roll; Ntl Merit SF; Bus Editor Math Mag 85-86; Editor Sci Mag 85-86; Columbia U Sci Hnrs Pgm Schlr 85-86; Yale U; Applied Math.

KLOTZ, MATT; Port Jervis HS; Sparrowbush, NY; (Y); 25/200; Church Yth Grp; Math Clb; Math Tm; Ski Clb; Varsity Clb; Ftbl; Trk; High Hon Roll; Hon Roll; :Engrng.

KLUG, KELLY; East Syracuse Minoa HS; Kirkville, NY; (Y); 40/330; Camera Clb; Church Yth Grp; French Clb; Latin Clb; Stu Cncl; Score Keeper; Hon Roll; Jr NHS; NHS; Fr II Awd 85; Computr Awd 84; Niagara U; Pre-Law.

KNAMM, TY; Holladn Patent HS; Barnavald, NY; (Y); 40/200; Pres Frsh Cls; Pres Soph Cls; Pres Jr Cls; Pres Sr Cls; JV Socr; Im Wt Lftg; Var Wrstlng.

KNAPIK, DENNIS; Xavier HS; Rutherford, NJ; (Y); Boy Scts; Chess Clb; Church Yth Grp; Math Tm; Yrbk Stf; Rep Soph Cls; Mgr(s); Var Swmmng; High Hon Roll; Top Schl Scorer In AHSME Math Comp; Med.

KNAPIK, KAREN; Burnt Hills-Ballston Lake HS; Scotia, NY; (Y); Exploring; FBLA; SADD; Var Tennis; High Hon Roll; Bus Admn.

KNAPIK, KLAUDIA; Southampton HS; Southampton, NY; (Y); Art Clb; Dance Clb; Yrbk Phtg; Var Bsktbl; Var Trk; Var Wt Lftg; Cit Awd; Hon Roll; WYU; Nutrition.

KNAPP, ALLEN; Mahopac HS; Mahopac, NY; (Y); 32/390; Pres Sec Church Yth Grp; German Clb; Math Clb; Math Tm; SADD; Trs Orch; JV Socr; JV Wrstlng; NHS; Pres Schlr; USAF Acad; Mchncl Engrng.

KNAPP, ANNAMARIE; Mercy HS; Albany, NY; (Y); Ski Clb; School Play; Stage Crew; Yrbk Stf; High Hon Roll; NHS; Comp Sci.

KNAPP, CHRISTOPHER; Soranac Lake HS; Lake Clear, NY; (Y); AFS; Ftbl; Trk; Wt Lftg; Comp Pgmmr.

KNAPP, COLIN; Potsdam Central HS; Potsdam, NY; (Y); Art Clb; Computer Clb; Letterman Clb; Math Clb; Math Tm; Spanish Clb; Boys Clb Am; Varsity Clb; Band; Concert Band; Duke; Acctg.

KNAPP, KAREN; Romulus Central HS; Romulus, NY; (Y); Sec 4-H; Spanish Clb; Chorus; Yrbk Stf; Sec Soph Cls; Sec Jr Cls; Sec Sr Cls; Sec Stu Cncl; High Hon Roll; NHS.

KNAPP, LARISSA; New Paltz HS; New Paltz, NY; (Y); 26/176; Dance Clb; Debate Tm; Spanish Clb; Prfct Atten Awd; Nwsp Stf; Jr Cls; Var Trk; High Hon Roll; Pre-Med.

KNAPP, MARI; West Irondequoit HS; Rochester, NY; (Y); 50/389; Cmnty Wkr; Latin Clb; Ski Clb; Teachers Aide; Yrbk Stf; Off Sr Cls; Tennis; Trk; Hon Roll; Prfct Atten Awd; HSTRY.

KNAPP, NICOLE; Fabius-Pompey HS; Fabius, NY; (Y); 2/65; Church Yth Grp; Cmnty Wkr; French Clb; Band; Concert Band; Mrchg Band; Orch; JV Var Socr; Var Sftbl; Var JV Vllybl; Piano Schlrshp 84; NYSSMA Medals 84-86; All ST Cty Awds 84-86; Syracuse U; Bus.

KNAPP, YVONNE D; St Marys Girls HS; Port Washington, NY; (Y); 5/171; Drama Clb; 4-H; Hosp Aide; Model UN; Ski Clb; Chorus; School Musical; High Hon Roll; NHS; Ntl Merit Ltr; Regents Scholar 86; Intl Yth Yr Comm UN Mvmnt Better Wrld Rep 85-86; Natl Yng Ldrs Conf Rep 85; Columbia Coll; Econ.

KNAPTON, AMY; New Lebanon Central HS; E Nassau, NY; (Y); Trs VP French Clb; Math Tm; Ski Clb; Band; Chorus; Sec Sr Cls; Var L Socr; High Hon Roll; NHS; Val.

KNASZAK, MICHELLE; South Park HS; Buffalo, NY; (Y); Aud/Vis; Cmnty Wkr; Library Aide; Spanish Clb; Hon Roll; NHS; Archry; Trocaire Coll; Chld Care.

KNAUF, KRISTY; Pelham Memorial HS; Pelham Manor, NY; (Y); AFS; Hosp Aide; Band; School Musical; Trs Rep Stu Cncl; JV Socr; Var JV Sftbl; DAR Awd; High Hon Roll; NHS; Pres Natl Hnr Scty 86-87; Coll New Rochelle Bk Awd 86; Pre-Law.

KNAUS, ANNE; Horseheads HS; Horseheads, NY; (Y); 4-H; Chorus; Stu Cncl; 4-H Awd; Hon Roll; Invt HS Stu Ambssdr Prgrm 85; Pre-Law.

KNAUST, STEPHANIE; Coxsackie-Athens HS; Coxsackie, NY; (Y); 20/120; Band; Drm & Bgl; Stu Cncl; Hon Roll; NHS; Loonbrg Ldg No 1505 Awd 86; ST U Of NY; Bio Sci.

KNEE, ANDREW; Clarkstown High School North; New City, NY; (Y); Spanish Clb; Temple Yth Grp; Y-Teens; Ftbl; Wrstlng; Spec Olympics Vlntr 86; Bus.

KNEIDL, CATHLEEN M; Shoreham Wading River HS; Wading River, NY; (Y); Cmnty Wkr; Computer Clb; Hosp Aide; Yrbk Stf; St Schlr; Stony Brook.

KNELLER, MARC; Bethpage HS; Plainview, NY; (Y); English Clb; Spanish Clb; Teachers Aide; Varsity Clb; JV Bsbl; JV Socr; Cit Awd; High Hon Roll; Hon Roll; Ctznshp Awd; Bsbll Awd; Tchrs Rcgntn Engl & Spnsh.

KNEPLEY, MATT; Tully Central HS; Tully, NY; (Y); Camera Clb; Ski Clb; Spanish Clb; Varsity Clb; Yrbk Phtg; Yrbk Stf; Var Bsbl; Prfct Atten Awd.

KNEPPER, TIMOTHY; Arlington HS; La Grangeville, NY; (Y); 33/550; Church Yth Grp; Band; Concert Band; Jazz Band; Mrchg Band; Symp Band; Trk; High Hon Roll; Hon Roll; Music.

KNIBBS, TRACEY; Beacon HS; Beacon, NY; (Y); Variety Show; Yrbk Stf; JV Sftbl; Var Tennis; High Hon Roll; Hon Roll; Prfct Atten Awd; Spanish Clb; Stage Crew; Math Awd; Stdyng Piano 10 Yrs; Music Thrpy.

KNICKERBOCKER, JANE; York Central HS; Leicester, NY; (Y); 4/84; Trs Key Clb; Teachers Aide; Band; Concert Band; Jazz Band; Mrchg Band; Pep Band; School Play; Nwsp Rptr; Nwsp Sprt Ed; NYS Rgnts 86; St John Fisher Admttance 86; St John Fisher; Cmnctns.

KNICLEY, GREGORY; Cazenovia Central HS; Cazenovia, NY; (Y); Mathletes; Symp Band; Trs Frsh Cls; Pres Soph Cls; Pres Jr Cls; Pres Sr Cls; Rep Stu Cncl; Var Socr; Var Trk; NHS; Chem Engr.

KNIFFIN, ANDREA; Valley Central HS; Montgomery, NY; (Y); 29/288; Debate Tm; Spanish Clb; Yrbk Stf; Frsh Cls; Soph Cls; Jr Cls; Sec Sr Cls; Capt Cheerleading; High Hon Roll; Gym; Regnts Schlrshp 86; Srena; Comp Sci.

KNIFLEY, JOHN; Geneva HS; Geneva, NY; (S); 8/192; French Clb; VP Ski Clb; Pres Varsity Clb; Rep Stu Cncl; Var L Bsbl; Var L Ftbl; Hon Roll; Trs NHS; Lib Arts.

KNIGHT JR, ARTHUR J; Newfane HS; Newfane, NY; (Y); 14/158; Boy Scts; Drama Clb; Math Tm; Science Clb; Varsity Clb; School Play; Stage Crew; Yrbk Bus Mgr; Mgr(s); Hon Roll; Hghst Avg Bus Dynmcs Awd 85; U Rochester; Comp Sci.

KNIGHT, GEORGE D; Aviation HS; Flushing, NY; (S); 12/416; Boy Scts; Cmnty Wkr; JA; Rep Jr Cls; Rep Stu Cncl; Cit Awd; High Hon Roll; NHS; Prfct Atten Awd; Silver Wings Awd 85; Golden Wings Awd 86; NY ST Rgnts Schlrshp Wnnr 86; Engrng.

KNIGHT, JON M; Mc Quaid Jesuit HS; Fairport, NY; (Y); 18/180; VP Church Yth Grp; Exploring; Sec Spanish Clb; Varsity Clb; Nwsp Rptr; JV Var Bsbl; Var Swmmng; Var Capt Vllybl; High Hon Roll; Hon Roll; Holy Cross Book Awd 85; Regents Schlrshp Wnnr 86; Holy Cross; Pre-Med.

KNIGHT, KELLY J; Moravia Central Schl; Locke, NY; (Y); 11/90; French Clb; Girl Scts; Office Aide; Chorus; High Hon Roll; Hon Roll; Russel Sage Coll; Elem Ed.

KNIGHT, KEVIN; Lindenhurst HS; Lindenhurst, NY; (Y); 8/572; Cmnty Wkr; Debate Tm; Ski Clb; Spanish Clb; Band; Crs Cntry; Swmmng; Trk; High Hon Roll; NHS; Lindy Runner Yr 85-86; Intl Bus.

KNIGHT, KIMBERLY; Groton Central HS; Groton, NY; (Y); Hosp Aide; VP Spanish Clb; Chorus; Yrbk Stf; Rep Stu Cncl; JV Var Cheerleading; JV Var Fld Hcky; Var L Socr; High Hon Roll; NY State Publc High Sch Athletc Assn Awd 83; Hmn Svcs.

KNIGHT, MICHELLE; Warwick Valley HS; Warwick, NY; (Y); 2/190; 4-H; French Clb; SADD; Yrbk Ed-Chief; Trs Soph Cls; Trs Sr Cls; Tennis; DAR Awd; Pres Schlr; Sal; Hgh Hnr Rl 82-86; U Of Scranton; Intl Finc.

KNIGHT, SUZANNE; Warwick Valley HS; Warwick, NY; (Y); 14/200; VP Pres 4-H; Pres VP French Clb; SADD; Yrbk Stf; Trs Jr Cls; Trs Sr Cls; Var JV Tennis; 4-H Awd; High Hon Roll; NHS; Bus Admn.

KNIGHTON, SANDRA; Moore Catholic HS; Staten Island, NY; (Y); 11/172; Chorus; School Musical; Bowling; NHS; Regents Schlrshp 86; Ntl Sci Awd 85; Ntl Merit Ldrshp Awd 86; NY U; Psych.

KNIPES JR, JOSEPH F; Granville Central HS; Wells, VT; (Y); 4/134; AFS; Math Tm; Ski Clb; NHS; Pres Schlr; Mst Outstndng Stu 86; Ciba-Geigy Corp Sci Awd 86; Modern Woodmn Amer Awd 86; U VT; Civil Engrng.

KNISLEY, CHRISTOP W; Monsignor Farrell HS; Staten Island, NY; (Y); French Clb; Nwsp Stf; Bsktbl; Trk; NY St Rgnts Schlrshp 86; Natl Frnch Cntst 84-85; Villanova; Law.

KNISLEY, RACHELLE; Hutch Tech HS; Bufflao, NY; (Y); Girl Scts; Office Aide; Drm & Bgl; Guidence Monitor Schl Volunteer 85-86; Enviromental Scientist.

KNISPEL, JEFFREY; Canarsie HS; Brooklyn, NY; (Y); 1/200; Math Tm; Temple Yth Grp; Color Guard; High Hon Roll; Archon-Arista Trea 86-87; Brooklyn Brd Of Rltrs Essay Awd 85-86; 69th Comm Cncl Essay Awd 85-86; Med.

KNOBLOCH, MARIE C; Warwick Valley HS; Warwick, NY; (Y); 6/200; AFS; French Clb; Hosp Aide; Math Tm; Nwsp Stf; Yrbk Bus Mgr; Yrbk Phtg; Soph Cls; Off Jr Cls; Chrmn Sr Cls; Frnch Awd 83-85; Boston U; Accntng.

KNOLL, AMY; Ossining HS; Ossining, NY; (Y); Radio Clb; VP Pres Orch; High Hon Roll; Hon Roll; Sec NHS; Hosp Aide; Mrchg Band; School Musical; Swing Chorus; Lit Mag; Schl Wrtng Cont 1st Pl Poetry 84; Schl Wrtng Cont 1st Pl Short Story 84-85; Librl Arts.

KNOLL, DANIELLE T; Massapequa HS; Massapequa, NY; (Y); Cmnty Wkr; Dance Clb; Drama Clb; PAVAS; Chorus; School Musical; School Play; Rep Sr Cls; Cheerleading; Stage Crew; Dance Schlrshp Hofstra U 86; :Theater.

KNOLL, KATHERINE; Eden Central HS; Eden, NY; (Y); 60/166; GAA; SADD; Concert Band; Mrchg Band; Pep Band; Symp Band; Im Badmtn; JV Stat Bsktbl; Var Tennis; Im Vllybl; Trocaire Coll; Nrs.

KNOP, JACEK; Dundee Central HS; Himrod, NY; (Y); Am Leg Boys St; Varsity Clb; Var Bsbl; Var Bowling; Var Ftbl; Mgr(s); Wt Lftg; Merit Awd In Essay Cntst 86; SUNY Bfl.

KNOTT, SCOTT A; Cassadaga Valley HS; Gerry, NY; (Y); 2/75; Am Leg Boys St; FFA; VP Sr Cls; Rep Stu Cncl; JV Var Bsbl; JV Var Ftbl; Hon Roll; NHS; Ntl Merit SF; Sal; NY ST Rgnts Schlrshp 86; U Of Dayton; Engrng.

KNOTT, TOM; Union Endicott HS; Endicott, NY; (Y); Computer Clb; Key Clb; Hon Roll.

KNOWLES, LINDA A; Copiague HS; Copiague, NY; (Y); 17/306; German Clb; Yrbk Stf; JV Var Fld Hcky; Score Keeper; High Hon Roll; Hon Roll; Spanish NHS; Germn Natl Hnr Socty 83-86; SUNY Stonybrook; Intl Stds.

KNOWLES, PAUL; Valley Heights Christian Acad; Guilford, NY; (S); 2/11; Church Yth Grp; Chorus; Var Capt Bsktbl; Var Socr; High Hon Roll; NHS; Sal; Church Choir; Hon Roll; Speed Typng 85-86; Hghst Avg 84-85; Bsktbl-Outstndng Accmplshmnts 85-86; Engrng.

KNOX, COLLEEN; Onondaga Central HS; Nedrow, NY; (Y); GAA; Hosp Aide; SADD; Teachers Aide; Varsity Clb; Chorus; Var Score Keeper; Var Socr; Var Sftbl; Hon Roll; Bus.

KNOX, HOLLY; John C Birdlebough HS; Pennellville, NY; (Y); 17/176; French Clb; Var L Trk; High Hon Roll; Awd Hghst Avg Accntng I 86; Awd Outstndg Achvmnt Frnch III 86; Bus Mngmnt.

KNUTSEN, KENNETH C; Williamsville North HS; N Tonawanda, NY; (Y); 32/319; Church Yth Grp; CAP; ROTC; Bsbl; Ftbl; Trk; Wt Lftg; Wrstlng; Hon Roll; NHS; Clarkson U Trstees Schlrshp 86; Clarkson U; Mchncl Engnrng.

KNUTSEN, LAURA; Tottenville HS; Staten Island, NY; (Y); Church Yth Grp; Exploring; School Play; Stage Crew; NHS; Hon Typg Awds 85 & 86; Katharine Gibbs Sec Schl; Sec.

KOBA, ANDREW J; Madison Central HS; Oriskany Falls, NY; (Y); 9/52; Am Leg Boys St; French Clb; Varsity Clb; JV Var Bsktbl; Coach Actv; Score Keeper; Hon Roll; Prfct Atten Awd; Fbus Admin.

KOBASA, KAREN; Cohoes HS; Cohoes, NY; (Y); 1/176; Art Clb; GAA; VP Science Clb; Cheerleading; Var Socr; Sftbl; Var Tennis; Bausch & Lomb Sci Awd; High Hon Roll; NHS; RPI Medal 85; Soccer All Star Tm 84 & 85; Union Coll; Chem.

KOBLEROWSKI, PHIL; Ossining HS; Briarcliff, NY; (Y); 18/250; Aud/Vis; Chess Clb; Cmnty Wkr; Computer Clb; Exploring; Library Aide; Model UN; Var Golf; High Hon Roll; NHS; Moose Lodge Schlrshp Awd 86; GA Inst Tech; Engrng.

KOBOR, BRIDGET; Fayetteville-Manlius HS; Fayetteville, NY; (Y); Church Yth Grp; Sec Jr Cls; Sec Sr Cls; Var Bsktbl; Var Crs Cntry; Im Lcrss; Var Trk; Wt Lftg; NHS.

KOBRIN, DANIEL; Fallsburg JR SR HS; Mt Dale, NY; (Y); Library Aide; Rep Frsh Cls; Rep Soph Cls; Cit Awd; High Hon Roll; Hon Roll; Ft Lauderdale Coll; Bus.

KOCH, DARRYL; Attica Central SR HS; Attica, NY; (S); 11/160; Pres Band; Pres Concert Band; Drm Mjr(t); Pres Mrchg Band; Nwsp Rptr; Stu Cncl; Crs Cntry; Var Capt Swmmng; NHS; HS Stu Dstngshd Soc 85.

KOCH, JOHN C; Seton Catholic Central HS; Endwell, NY; (Y); VP Church Yth Grp; JV Bsktbl; Var Tennis; NYS Regnts Schlrshp 86; Sportmanship Award (Cyo Basketball) 86; SUNY Geneseo; Bus/Mktg.

KOCH, STEPHEN; Edgemont HS; Scarsdale, NY; (Y); Boy Scts; Pres Ski Clb; Pres Jr Cls; Sec Sr Cls; Rep Stu Cncl; Var Socr; Im Vllybl; Coachs Awd-V Soccer 85; USN Acad; Aerosp Engrng.

KOCH, TODD; Fairport HS; Fairport, NY; (Y); JV Var Bsbl; JV Bsktbl; JV Var Ftbl; Ftbl All Cnty Tckle 86; Clarkson U; Indstrl Dist.

KOCH, WAYNE; Attica Central Schl; Attica, NY; (S); 7/175; Band; Mrchg Band; Var Bsbl; Var Bsktbl; Var Socr.

KOCHIAN, JEFFREY L; E Syracuse-Minda Central; East Syracuse, NY; (Y); Am Leg Boys St; Pres JA; Ski Clb; Variety Show; Trs Stu Cncl; Var Socr; Bausch & Lomb Sci Awd; Hon Roll; NHS; Ntl Merit Ltr; U Rochester; Genetcs.

KOCSIS, MARK; Massena Central HS; Massena, NY; (Y); 26/246; Key Clb; Spanish Clb; Yrbk Stf; Frsh Cls; Bsktbl; Crs Cntry; Trk; Hon Roll; Pres Schlr; St Schlr; Regnts Schlrshp 86; Geneseo SUNY; Mgmt.

KOCUR, JACQUELINE; Sacred Heart HS; Yonkers, NY; (S); 5/221; Church Yth Grp; Intnl Clb; Chorus; School Musical; Rep Stu Cncl; JV Mgr Bsbl; JV Mgr Bsktbl; JV Var Cheerleading; High Hon Roll; NHS; Prtl Acadmc Schlrshp 84; Hrng Imprd Tchr.

KOE, FRANCESCA; Ossining HS; Ossining, NY; (Y); Yrbk Stf; VP Frsh Cls; VP Soph Cls; Var L Bsktbl; JV Cheerleading; JV Sftbl; DAR Awd; High Hon Roll; Church Yth Grp; Radio Clb; Italian Hnr Soc 84 & 85; Italian Clb 83-86; Intl Law.

KOEDDING, KAREN E; St Francis Prep; Whitestone, NY; (Y); Cmnty Wkr; Math Tm; Ski Clb; Nwsp Stf; Sftbl; Vllybl; Hon Roll; Rgnts Schlrshp 86; Lbrl Arts.

KOEHLER, GERARD J; St Francis HS; Hamburg, NY; (Y); Nwsp Rptr; JV Ftbl; Var Lcrss; JV Trk; Im Wt Lftg; NHS; Alfrd U; Crmc Engrng.

KOEHLER, SUZANNE; Mount Mercy Acad; Buffalo, NY; (Y); Pres Camp Fr Inc; Pres Drama Clb; Sec French Clb; VP NFL; SADD; School Play; Nwsp Stf; Off Frsh Cls; Hon Roll; NHS; Hugh O Brien Yth Fndtn 84-85; 6th Plc Nichols-Canisius Clssc 84; Accntng.

KOEHNKE, ANDREW; L I Lutheran HS; Farmingdale, NY; (S); 14/94; VP German Clb; Jazz Band; Pres Sr Cls; Rep Stu Cncl; Capt Crs Cntry; Capt Trk; High Hon Roll; Sec NHS; Debate Tm; Ind Engr.

KOELSCH, KEVIN; Cicero-North Syracuse HS; N Syracuse, NY; (S); 32/667; Boy Scts; JA; Math Tm; Varsity Clb; Rep Stu Cncl; Var Lcrss; Var Capt Socr; Hon Roll; NHS; U Of Hartford; Accntnt.

KOENIG, CAROLINE; Commack HS North; Commack, NY; (Y); 23/360; Intnl Clb; SADD; Rep Soph Cls; Off Jr Cls; High Hon Roll; NHS; Accntng.

KOENIG, LYLE; Newfield HS; Coram, NY; (Y); 40/576; Fncng, Vrsty Cnty Chmpns 85-86; SUNY Albany; Law.

KOENIG, MICHAEL L; Hudson HS; Hudson, NY; (Y); 3/160; Cmnty Wkr; Model UN; Band; Mrchg Band; Nwsp Rptr; Nwsp Sprt Ed; Yrbk Bus Mgr; Tennis; Elks Awd; High Hon Roll; U Rchster; Pltcl Sci.

KOENIG, MOSHE A; Torah Temima HS; Brooklyn, NY; (Y); Library Aide; Office Aide; Teachers Aide; High Hon Roll; Hon Roll; Ntl Merit Ltr; Ntl Merit Stu Awd 84-85; NYS Regnts Schlrshp 85-86; Talmudc Law.

KOENIG, REBECCA E; Horace Mann HS; New York City, NY; (Y); Pres French Clb; Yrbk Stf; JV Fld Hcky; Var Lcrss; Ntl Merit Ltr; Rgnts Schlrshp 86; Syrcs U; Pltcl Sci.

KOEPPEL, BRENT; St Patricks C C HS; Elizaville, NY; (S); 1/26; Boy Scts; Drama Clb; Yrbk Phtg; Rep Stu Cncl; Var Capt Bowling; Var Socr; Bausch & Lomb Sci Awd; Elks Awd; NHS; Val; MIT; Elec Engrng.

KOERNER, CAROLYN R; Arlington SR HS; Wappingers Falls, NY; (Y); 31/556; Drama Clb; Pres Girl Scts; Intnl Clb; High Hon Roll; Hon Roll; Rotary Awd; Slvr & Gold Grl Sct Ldrshp Awds 86; Natl German Comp Awd 85; Regents Schlrshp 86; Johnson & Wales; Fshn Merch.

KOERNER, KATHERINE E; Stuyresant HS; New York, NY; (Y); Model UN; Political Wkr; Red Cross Aide; School Musical; Nwsp Ed-Chief; Sec Soph Cls; Sec Jr Cls; Ntl Merit Ltr; St Schlr; Theodore Huebener Mem Awd Excellnc German 85; Model UN Exemplry Delegtn Awd 85; Wesleyan U.

KOERPER, KATHLEEN; Churchville-Chili HS; Rochester, NY; (Y); Art Clb; Church Yth Grp; Teachers Aide; Nwsp Stf; Lit Mag; Rep Stu Cncl; Swmmng; Top 3 Bckstroker At Jr Olympcs Swmmng 83; Evangel Coll; Art.

KOESTER, BARBARA; Holland Central HS; Holland, NY; (Y); AFS; Color Guard; Concert Band; Mrchg Band; Yrbk Stf; Hon Roll; Prfct Atten Awd; Elem Ed.

KOESTER, JULIE; Lyndonville Central HS; Waterport, NY; (Y); Church Yth Grp; Computer Clb; Teachers Aide; Varsity Clb; Yrbk Stf; Var Stat Bsktbl; Var JV Socr; Var Trk; Var JV Vllybl; Hon Roll; Prom Commttee Chrmn 86; SUNY Cortland; Mth.

KOGUT, CHRISTINE; Tully Central HS; Tully, NY; (Y); Church Yth Grp; SADD; Church Choir; Trs Concert Band; Jazz Band; Yrbk Ed-Chief; Var Cheerleading; JV Var Vllybl; High Hon Roll; NHS; Acadmc Top 10-4 Mrkng Perds 85-86; Mst Imprvd Skier-Hghst Acadmc Avg 85; ST Fnlst-Miss Ntl Tn-Ager Pg.

KOGUT, GAIL; Bishop Ludden HS; Syracuse, NY; (S); Church Yth Grp; Political Wkr; Nwsp Rptr; Nwsp Stf; Yrbk Stf; JV Var Cheerleading; High Hon Roll; NHS; Ag.

KOGUT, JENNY; Mount Saint Mary Acad; Grand Isld, NY; (Y); Church Yth Grp; Pep Clb; Ski Clb; Varsity Clb; Var Im Gym; Var Im Tennis; Im Vllybl; High Hon Roll; Ntl Merit SF; NEDT Awd; Psych.

KOHL, KEVIN R; Southwestern Central HS; Lakewood, NY; (Y); 12/146; Am Leg Boys St; VP Band; Drm Mjr(t); Jazz Band; Mrchg Band; School Musical; Trk; Var L Vllybl; Hon Roll; NHS; U Of Notre Dame; Arspc Engrng.

KOHLER, GABY; Huntington HS; Huntington, NY; (Y); Nwsp Rptr; Nwsp Stf; Pscych.

KOHLER, MARGARET; Plainedge HS; Bethpage, NY; (Y); DECA; JV Var Sftbl; Var Tennis; Gregg Typing Awd 86; Katharine Gibbs; Sec.

KOHLER-BRITTON, BROOKE; New Utrecht HS; Brooklyn, NY; (Y); Chorus; Lit Mag; Rgnts Schlrshp 86; Intr Dsgn.

KOHN, DAVID; Lynbrook SR HS; E Rockaway, NY; (Y); Cmnty Wkr; JV Var Bsktbl; Var Golf; JV Var Socr; Var Trk.

KOHR, SUSAN; Nottingham HS; Syracuse, NY; (Y); 19/220; French Clb; Latin Clb; Nwsp Stf; Yrbk Stf; JV Var Socr; JV Sftbl; Hon Roll; NHS; 1st Pl Ntl Frnch Cntst 83-84; 2nd Pl Ntl Frnch Cntst 84-85; Cum Laude Ntl Ltn Exam 83-84; Vndrblt U.

KOLACKI, ELIZABETH; Broadalbin Central Schl; Broadalbin, NY; (Y); 4/73; French Clb; Varsity Clb; Band; Chorus; Var L Bowling; Var L Socr; Var L Trk; Var L Vllybl; NHS; Pres Schlr; Gld Awd Grl Scts 86; Army Rsrv ROTC Schlr/Athlt Awd 86; MVP Trck 85-86; Clarkson U; Engr.

KOLASNY, CARL; John F Kennedy HS; Cheektowaga, NY; (Y); 26/150; Art Clb; Church Yth Grp; English Clb; FCA; PAVAS; Varsity Clb; Nwsp Rptr; Im Bsktbl; L Crs Cntry; L Trk; Schl Chess Chmp Rnr-Up 84; MIP Crs Cntry 84; Crs Cntry Co-Capt 85-86; Engr.

KOLB, WENDY; Tonawanda JR SR HS; Tonawanda, NY; (Y); VP Church Yth Grp; French Clb; SADD; Band; Concert Band; Sec Jazz Band; Mrchg Band; Pep Band; School Musical; Var Trk; Buffalo ST Coll; Scl Stds Ed.

KOLB, WILLIAM; Hamburg Central HS; Hamburg, NY; (Y); Am Leg Boys St; Letterman Clb; Ftbl; Capt Lcrss; Petrlm Engrng.

KOLBE, JEFFREY; Barker Central HS; Gasport, NY; (Y); 17/107; AFS; Debate Tm; French Clb; Varsity Clb; Concert Band; Rep Stu Cncl; Bsbl; Var Capt Ftbl; Hon Roll; U Rochester Schlrshp 86-90; U Rochester; Pol Sci.

KOLBERG, JOHN; W C Mepham HS; N Bellmore, NY; (Y); 30/300; Art Clb; Aud/Vis; Science Clb; Symp Band; Nwsp Stf; Yrbk Stf; Golf; Wrstlng; High Hon Roll; NHS; 1st Pl Sci Cntst 84; 3rd Pl Sci Cntst 85; Schl Svcs 82-84.

KOLCESKI IV, JOSEPH P; Jamesville-De Witt HS; Jamesville, NY; (Y); Church Yth Grp; French Clb; Orch; School Play; Var Trk; Var Wrstlng; High Hon Roll; Hon Roll; Mony Schlstc Art Awd Blue Ribbon & Natl Honrbl Mention 84.

KOLCH, KIMBERLY A; Rome Free Acad; Rome, NY; (Y); 34/412; Church Yth Grp; Exploring; Intnl Clb; SADD; Lit Mag; High Hon Roll; Jr NHS; NHS; Pres Acad Ftns Awd 86; Regents Schrlshp 86; Le Moyne Coll.

KOLIAS, NICK; Vestal Central SR HS; Vestal, NY; (Y); 3/433; Am Leg Boys St; Church Yth Grp; Mathletes; Orch; Var Trk; NHS; T J Watson Mem Schlrshp 86; J Mc Mullen Schlrshp 86; Natl Yng Ldrs Confrnc 86; Cornell U; Engrng.

KOLINSKY, JANET; Sacred Heart Acad; Williston Park, NY; (Y); Art Clb; Girl Scts; Service Clb; Teachers Aide.

KOLKER, DOV; The Wheatley Schl; Old Westbury, NY; (Y); Debate Tm; Mathletes; Var Bowling; Var Capt Tennis; Kiwanis Awd; NHS; All Cnty Newsday Ten Awd 84; All Conf Ten Awd 83-86; Spn Merit Awd 83-86; Tufts U; Pre-Med.

KOLLAR, JEFF; Wantagh HS; Wantagh, NY; (Y); 132/271; Boy Scts; Library Aide; Chorus; School Musical; Variety Show; Swmmng; DAR Awd; VFW Awd; Eagle Sct Boy Scts 86; Suny Cortland.

KOLLAR, PATRICIA KATHERINE; Mercy HS; Albany, NY; (Y); 12/43; Drama Clb; Nwsp Rptr; Yrbk Ed-Chief; Var Capt Bsktbl; Sftbl; High Hon Roll; Hon Roll; NHS; Trk; Church Yth Grp; Mrgrt Snw Vndr Veer Trst Fnd Awd 86; Albnys Trcntnnl Cmmtee 85-86; Albany Coll Of Phrmcy; Phrmcy.

KOLLAR, ROBERT; Farmingdale HS; Farmingdale, NY; (Y); Computer Clb; Spanish Clb; Band; Im Bsktbl; Im Sftbl; Prfct Atten Awd; Suny Farmingdale; Arcrft Engrng.

KOLOCK, CASSANDRA; School Of The Arts; Rochester, NY; (Y); Church Yth Grp; Drama Clb; Chorus; School Musical; School Play; Stage Crew; Nwsp Phtg; Nwsp Rptr; Var Socr; Hon Roll; Red Ribbon Sibleys Schlstc Natl Art Exhibit 85-86; 2nd Schl Arts Spring Art Show 86; Music.

KOLODZIEJ, JEFFREY; Bishop Scully HS; Amsterdam, NY; (Y); 8/49; Latin Clb; Math Clb; Var L Bsbl; Stat Bsktbl; Var L Bowling; Var L Crs Cntry; JV Golf; Mgr(s); High Hon Roll; Mu Alp Tht; Acdmc All Am 86; Smmr Excllnc Fulmont CC 86; Stu Against Drunk Driving 86; Engrng.

KOLOZSVARY, LINDA; Henninger HS; Syracuse, NY; (Y); Ski Clb; SADD; Band; Concert Band; Jazz Band; Mrchg Band; Pep Band; High Hon Roll; Hon Roll; Ntl Assoc Jazz Ed; Outstndng Musicanshp 85-86; Hnry Ment All Star Band 86; Outstndng Stu 86; Onondaga CC; Music.

KOLPIEN, LIZ; Ripley Central Schl; Ripley, NY; (Y); Sec Church Yth Grp; Concert Band; Mrchg Band; Trs Jr Cls; Trs Sr Cls; Stat Bsktbl; Stat Vllybl; Hon Roll; NHS; Natl Engl Merit Awd 85-86; Travel.

KOLPIEN, TIM; Westfield Academy And Central; Westfield, NY; (Y); Pres Model UN; Scholastic Bowl; Mrchg Band; School Musical; Nwsp Stf; Var L Bsktbl; Var Ftbl; Var L Golf; High Hon Roll; Pres NHS; Cmmnctns.

KOLTIS, TEDDY J; Harrison HS; Harrison, NY; (Y); Math Tm; School Musical; School Play; Variety Show; Yrbk Stf; Rep Frsh Cls; Rep Soph Cls; Rep Jr Cls; Trs Sr Cls; Capt Lcrss; NY ST Rgnts Schlrshp 85-86; Natl Latn Exm-Cum Laudus 84-85; Cornell U; Hotl Mgmt.

KOMPALLA, SHARON; West Seneca East SR HS; Cheektowaga, NY; (S); Hst DECA; School Musical; School Play; Rep Frsh Cls; Rep Soph Cls; Rep Jr Cls; Rep Stu Cncl; Hon Roll; Jr NHS; Cert Merit Frnch 83-85.

KOMST, CHRISTINE; Commack HS; Commack, NY; (Y); Church Yth Grp; Cmnty Wkr; GAA; Hosp Aide; Teachers Aide; Chorus; Stage Crew; Yrbk Stf; Socr; Hon Roll.

KOMYATHY, JASON; Valley Central HS; Walden, NY; (Y); Drama Clb; Science Clb; School Musical; School Play; Lit Mag; Rep Jr Cls; Trk; Hon Roll; Art Awd 84; Arch.

KONECKY, KAREN; Union-Endicott HS; Endicott, NY; (Y); 53/450; Ski Clb; Chorus; Church Choir; Concert Band; Jazz Band; Mrchg Band; School Play; Symp Band; Hon Roll; Regents Schlrshp 86; Broome CC; Chem Engr.

KONERT, RICHARD; Bishop Ford Central Catholic HS; Brooklyn, NY; (Y); Computer Clb; Rep Soph Cls; Ctr For Media Arts; Recrdg Arts.

KONG, PHILIP; Edward R Murrow HS; Brooklyn, NY; (Y); 75/669; Aud/Vis; Chess Clb; French Clb; Science Clb; French Hon Soc; Hon Roll; Rep Sr Cls; Rep Stu Cncl; Polytechnic U; Aerosp Engr.

KONHEISER, HEIDI; Sachem North HS; Holbrook, NY; (Y); 151/1500; German Clb; Science Clb; Ski Clb; Rep Jr Cls; High Hon Roll; Hon Roll; Stu Govt Awd 86; Adelphi; Nrsg.

KONIDARIS, HELEN; Archbishop Jakoros HS; Richmond Hills, NY; (S); Cmnty Wkr; Girl Scts; Library Aide; Office Aide; Teachers Aide; Church Choir; Pres Frsh Cls; Rep Jr Cls; Rep Stu Cncl; High Hon Roll; Queens Coll Pres Awd-Achvt 84 & 85; Brooklyn Polytechnic; Cvl Engr.

KONIECZNY, JENNIFER S; Fairport HS; Fairport, NY; (Y); Drama Clb; Orch; School Musical; Yrbk Stf; Sr Cls; Stu Cncl; High Hon Roll; Hon Roll; NHS; Spanish NHS; NYS Regents Schlrshp 86; U Of MI Ann Arbor; Psych.

KONING, JEFF; Bishop Kearney HS; Penfield, NY; (Y); Exploring; Ski Clb; Stage Crew; Hon Roll; U Of Buffalo; Scintst.

KONKO, CHRISTINE; Carey HS; Franklin Square, NY; (Y); #119 In Class; 4-H; Band; Secy.

KONLANDE, MARC K; Mac Arthur HS; Wantagh, NY; (Y); 37/321; Chess Clb; Mathletes; Band; Drm Mjr(t); Jazz Band; JV Bsktbl; JV Capt Socr; High Hon Roll; Concert Band; Mrchg Band; Mdl Cngrs Bst Spkr 86; NYSSMA 85; SUNY Stny Brk; Intl Corp Law.

KONOWITZ, MARC; Middletown HS; Middletown, NY; (Y); Math Tm; Scholastic Bowl; Teachers Aide; Temple Yth Grp; Tennis; High Hon Roll; Hon Roll; NHS; Schlrshp Stdy In Isrl 86; Med.

KONVICKA, JANE; Cazenovia Central HS; Cazenovia, NY; (Y); Church Yth Grp; Cmnty Wkr; 4-H; Pres Girl Scts; Office Aide; Red Cross Aide; Teachers Aide; Chorus; Church Choir; School Musical; Ofcr Grange No 1358 84; Bus Admin.

KOOCH, MICHELLE; Greene Central HS; Greene, NY; (Y); 11/112; Band; Chorus; Concert Band; Mrchg Band; Symp Band; Yrbk Stf; JV Var Vllybl; High Hon Roll; Hon Roll; NY ST Regents Schlrshp 86; St Bonaventure U Friars Schlrshp 86; St Bonaventure U; Bus Mgmt.

KOPASKIE, KATYA; New Paltz Central HS; New Paltz, NY; (Y); 4/157; Drama Clb; Ski Clb; Crs Cntry; Trk; High Hon Roll; NHS.

KOPCZYNSKI, MARY E; St Joseph Hill Acad; Staten Island, NY; (Y); 18/107; Sec Computer Clb; FTA; Math Tm; NFL; Pres Service Clb; Orch; Yrbk Stf; Hon Roll; Ntl Merit Ltr; Prfct Atten Awd; Eastern Cup Virtuoso Accordion Champ 85; Regents Schlrshp 86; Amer Legn Essay Cont 84; Bryn Mawr Coll; Math.

KOPF, ANN; Sweet Home SR HS; Tonawanda, NY; (Y); Aud/Vis; Camera Clb; Computer Clb; DECA; FBLA; Intnl Clb; JA; OEA; Political Wkr; SADD; U Of Buffalo; Acctg.

KOPKO, KRISTINA M; Palmyra-Macedon HS; Macedon, NY; (Y); Band; Concert Band; JV Cheerleading; Var Sftbl; JV Var Vllybl; Im Wt Lftg; Hon Roll; Josephine Palmer Awd 83; NY ST Regents Schlrshp; Fredonia; Music Thrpy.

KOPP, KAREN; Bishop Grimes HS; Syracuse, NY; (S); Cmnty Wkr; Yrbk Stf; Bsktbl; Tennis; Trk; High Hon Roll; Acdmc Athltc All-Amer.

KOPREVICH JR, THOMAS J; Depew HS; Grand Island, NY; (Y); 29/272; Computer Clb; Band; Concert Band; Jazz Band; Mrchg Band; Orch; Pep Band; School Musical; NHS; NYS Regnts Schlrshp 86; NYS Buffalo; Comptr Engr.

KOPS, MITCH; Earl L Vandermeulen HS; Pt Jefferson, NY; (Y); 3/300; Spanish Clb; SADD; Varsity Clb; Yrbk Stf; JV Socr; Var Capt Tennis; High Hon Roll; NHS; Regent Schlrshp 86; U VA.

KOPTA JR, CHARLES; Sherman Central HS; Ripley, NY; (S); Church Yth Grp; Trs FFA; Hon Roll; Art Awd 84; Degree Chautauqua Cnty Farmer 85; Indvdl Accmplshmnt Awd 85; Dairy Farmer.

KORAL, DAN; West Senica West HS; Cheektowaga, NY; (Y); Art Clb; Boy Scts; Drama Clb; Latin Clb; Hnrbl Ment Awd Photo 85; Adv Dsgn.

KORBEL, GWENDOLEN; The Fieldston Schl; Forest Hills, NY; (Y); Cmnty Wkr; Dance Clb; Math Tm; Chorus; Concert Band; School Musical; School Play; Lit Mag; Ntl Merit Ltr; Regents Schlrshp 86; Vassar Coll.

KORCHA, DEANNA; Farmingdale HS; Farmingdale, NY; (Y); 4-H; Ski Clb; SADD; Yrbk Phtg; Yrbk Stf; Rep Stu Cncl; Var Badmtn; Jr NHS; Pre-Law.

KORDANA, KEVIN; Roy C Ketcham HS; Poughkeepsie, NY; (Y); Boy Scts; Jazz Band; Nwsp Ed-Chief; Nwsp Stf; Trs Stu Cncl; Bausch & Lomb Sci Awd; High Hon Roll; NHS; Jr NHS; Ntl Merit Ltr; RPI Mdl For Excllnce In Math & Sci 86; IBM Sr Lge Bsbl All Star Team 85.

KORDOLEMIS, HAROULA; Stuyvesant HS; Long Island Cty, NY; (Y); Church Yth Grp; Library Aide; Teachers Aide; Band; Ed Yrbk Ed-Chief; Pres Stu Cncl; Trk; French Hon Soc; Jr NHS; NHS; NYS Rgnts Schlrshp 86; Prnts Assoc Schlrshp 86; Arista Mbr 86; Barnard Ocll; Crmnl Law.

KORDYJAK, MICHELE; Amsterdam HS; Amsterdam, NY; (Y); 8/290; Concert Band; Mrchg Band; Yrbk Stf; Hon Roll; NHS; Regents Schlrshp 86; Rochester Inst Tech; Bio.

KORDZIEL, KEVIN; Liverpool HS; No Syracuse, NY; (Y); 7/800; Am Leg Boys St; Band; Concert Band; Orch; Symp Band; Var L Crs Cntry; Var L Trk; High Hon Roll; Jr NHS; NHS; Engl Awds 85-86.

KORMAN, JAY; Martin Van Buren HS; Qns Vill, NY; (Y); Aud/Vis; Computer Clb; Service Clb; Teachers Aide; Concert Band; Stage Crew; Cit Awd; Hon Roll; City Cncl Citatn Awd 84; Svc Hnr Soc 86.

KORMONDY, KELLY; Thousand Islands HS; Clayton, NY; (Y); Am Leg Aux Girls St; FHA; Library Aide; Band; Chorus; Color Guard; School Musical; School Play; Hon Roll; Lion Awd; SUNY Purchase; Mrktng.

KORNOWICZ, ANN; Holland Central HS; Dunedin, FL; (Y); AFS; Varsity Clb; Band; Color Guard; Jazz Band; Mrchg Band; Rep Stu Cncl; Var Socr; Jr NHS; 3rd Pl Bys Clb Art Shw 86; Grphc Art.

KOROLOV, MARIA; William Nottingham HS; Syracuse, NY; (Y); 12/220; Math Tm; Science Clb; Teachers Aide; Nwsp Rptr; Lit Mag; High Hon Roll; NHS; Ntl Merit SF; Empire ST Schlrshp Cf Excllnc 86; Outstdng Stu Of Yr Central Tech 84-86; John Mc Mullen Deans Prz; Cornell U Ithaca; Comp Engrng.

KORONA, BETH; Amsterdam HS; Amsterdam, NY; (Y); 1/330; Orch; Mgr Bsktbl; Mgr(s); Score Keeper; Mgr Socr; High Hon Roll; NHS; Harvard Bk Awd 86; Dir Awd-Orch 86; Engrng.

KORONA, LISA; Bishop Scully HS; Amsterdam, NY; (Y); 10/46; Math Clb; Yrbk Stf; JV Var Cheerleading; Hon Roll; NHS; Aviation.

KOROTHY, JOHN; Hicksville HS; Hicksville, NY; (Y); Chorus; Ice Hcky; Pre Law.

KORT, MICHELLE; Walt Whitman HS; Huntington Sta, NY; (Y); Key Clb; Band; Chorus; Church Choir; Bsktbl; JV Capt Cheerleading; Mgr(s); Hon Roll; Spanish NHS; Albany Coll; Acctg.

KORTE, PETER G; Tonawanda JR SR HS; Tonawanda, NY; (Y); Am Leg Boys St; Cmnty Wkr; French Clb; JA; SADD; Stage Crew; Rep Stu Cncl; Var L Ftbl; Im Socr.

KORTESKY, ROCHELLE; Mahopac HS; Mahopac, NY; (Y); 122/419; Cmnty Wkr; Drama Clb; Chorus; Color Guard; School Musical; School Play; Yrbk Rptr; Yrbk Stf; Fld Hcky; Mgr(s); Peer Ldrshp 86; Vol Wrk Arts Cncl 84; Bus Mgmnt.

KORTRIGHT, KENNETH; Central Islip Senior HS; Central Islip, NY; (Y); Varsity Clb; Band; Concert Band; School Musical; Var Bsbl; Ftbl; Wt Lftg; All Schlstc Lg III 85; Cptn Ldrshp Prcssn 86; IN Tech; Cmptr Sci.

KORYTKOWSKI, LYLE; Attica SR HS; Attica, NY; (S); 1/175; Math Tm; Band; Concert Band; Jazz Band; Mrchg Band; Rep Stu Cncl; Var Crs Cntry; Var Wrstlng; All Cntry Band 84-85.

KORYTO, MICHELLE; A G Berner HS; Massapequa Park, NY; (Y); 30/450; Drama Clb; Hosp Aide; Mathletes; Red Cross Aide; Spanish Clb; Trs Orch; Stage Crew; High Hon Roll; NHS; Symphony Orchestra-Concert Mistress 86-87; NY U; Law.

KORZELIUS, JOSEPH; Alexander Central HS; Darien, NY; (Y); Spanish Clb; Concert Band; Mrchg Band; Hon Roll; Jr NHS; NHS; Prfct Atten Awd.

KOSARA, CATHY; Warwick Valley HS; Warwick, NY; (Y); Concert Band; Drm & Bgl; Jazz Band; Co-Capt Bsktbl; Co-Capt Socr; Trk; High Hon Roll; Hon Roll; NHS; Hi-Avg Bio 83-84; Hi-Avg Chem 84-85; Princpls Chem Awd 84-85; Clarkson U; Elec Engrng.

KOSCIUK, BERNARD N; Miller Place HS; Miller Place, NY; (Y); 10/200; Aud/Vis; Chess Clb; Hon Roll; NHS; Sullfolk Cnty Math Tchrs Assn Awd 84; Regnts Schlrshp 86; ST U Of NY; Mech Engrng.

KOSHY, JAY; Faith Heritage Schl; Syracuse, NY; (Y); 1/45; Church Yth Grp; Concert Band; VP Frsh Cls; Trs Jr Cls; VP Sr Cls; Trs Stu Cncl; Var L Trk; Hon Roll; Jr NHS; NHS; Dstngshd Chrstn HS Stdnt Awd 86; Syracuse U; Engrng.

KOSIK, SETH; Half Hollow Hills East HS; Dix Hills, NY; (Y); Cmnty Wkr; Computer Clb; Hosp Aide; Spanish Clb; SADD; Temple Yth Grp; Chorus; Nwsp Rptr; High Hon Roll; Hon Roll; Med.

KOSINSKI, HENRY; La Salle Military Acad; Rye, NY; (S); 2/90; ROTC; School Play; Diving; Var Capt Golf; Var Capt Socr; Swmmng; High Hon Roll; NHS; SAR Awd; U AZ; Archit.

KOSINSKI, KIMBERLY; Wheatland-Chili Central School; Scottsville, NY; (Y); Girl Scts; Spanish Clb; Varsity Clb; Band; JV Bsktbl; Var Vllybl; Hon Roll; Prfct Atten Awd; Hghst Avg Typng I, Spnsh III 85-86; Spnsh.

KOSKO, LAURA; Preston HS; Bronx, NY; (S); 19/89; Church Yth Grp; Drm & Bgl; Stu Cncl; Cheerleading; NHS; Pres Frsh Cls; Trs Soph Cls; Socr.

KOSLOV, TARA; John Dewey HS; Brooklyn, NY; (Y); Service Clb; Ed Nwsp Ed-Chief; Nwsp Stf; Lit Mag; Stu Cncl; Ntl Merit Ltr; NY City Spr Yth 85-86; Law Inst Mock Trl Team 85-86; Stu Mntr 85-86.

KOSMETATOS, DENNIS; Herbert H Lehman HS; Bronx, NY; (Y); Art Clb; Boy Scts; Dance Clb; Varsity Clb; Var Gym; Prfct Atten Awd; Hunter; Chld Psych.

KOSMINOFF, LYNN; Fox Lane HS; Bedford Vlg, NY; (Y); 13/286; Key Clb; Latin Clb; VP Spanish Clb; Lcrss; Vllybl; High Hon Roll; NHS; Hnr Soc Awd 86; Cert Merit Rcgntn Outstndng Schlstc Achvt-Sentr Mary Goodhue 85; Latn Hnr Soc 85 & 86; Bucknell U; Intl Law.

KOST, MONIKA; Lindenhurst HS; Lindenhurst, NY; (Y); 6/550; German Clb; Trs Varsity Clb; Yrbk Sprt Ed; Off Sr Cls; Var Capt Bsktbl; Var Capt Fld Hcky; Var Capt Vllybl; High Hon Roll; NHS; Pres Schlr; Bsktbl 8th Tm All Amer, All Long Island; Daily News All Star,Newsday Clssc, All Lg, Empire ST Games; Spts Med.

KOSTAKIS, ALEXANDRA; Cicero-North Syracuse HS; N Syracuse, NY; (S); 28/623; Camera Clb; Church Choir; Bsktbl; Crs Cntry; Var Capt Tennis; Trk; Vllybl; 1st Pl Estrn Tnns Assoc Dist 12 85; Syracuse U; Piano.

KOSTBAR, LYNN R; Notre Dame Acad; Staten Island, NY; (Y); 11/93; Church Yth Grp; Computer Clb; Girl Scts; Hosp Aide; Yrbk Phtg; VP Bsktbl; Score Keeper; Trs NHS; Ttee Schlrshp-Pace U 86; Rgnts Schlrshp-NY ST 86; Metl Lathers Lcl 46 Schlrshp 86; Pace U; CPA.

KOSTNER, CINDY; St Johns Prep; Long Isld Cty, NY; (Y); 15/480; High Hon Roll; Hon Roll; NHS; Ntl Merit Ltr; Queens Coll; Comp Sci.

KOSTUSIAK, AIMEE J; Kenmore West SR HS; Kenmore, NY; (Y); Church Yth Grp; School Musical; Im Vllybl; High Hon Roll; NEDT Awd; Prfct Atten Awd; Achvt Cert-100 Prcnt Math I, III Rgnts Exms 84 & 86; Tp Stu, Outstndng Accmplshmt Spnsh I Achvt Awd; Bus.

KOSTY, CLARE; Bishop Ludden HS; Syracuse, NY; (S); Church Yth Grp; Chorus; Yrbk Stf; Var Trk; Hon Roll; NHS; Geneseo Coll; Spch Pthlgy.

KOSZALKA, ALEX; La Salle Military Acad; Shelter Island Ht, NY; (S); 15/98; ROTC; Ski Clb; Band; Chorus; Drm & Bgl; Yrbk Stf; Socr; Var Capt Tennis; Var Wt Lftg; Hon Roll; George Washington U; Med.

KOSZALKA, JOAN; Copiague HS; Copiague, NY; (Y); German Clb; Pep Clb; Red Cross Aide; Teachers Aide; School Play; Im Sftbl; Lion Awd; Pell Grant 86-87; SUNY Plattsburgh; Ed.

KOSZUTA, DANETTE; St Marys HS; Alden, NY; (S); 8/182; Ski Clb; Var Bsktbl; Var Tennis; Var Capt Vllybl; Hon Roll; NHS; NEDT Awd.

KOT, MIKE; Bitburg American HS; Apo Ny, NY; (Y); Var Capt Crs Cntry; High Hon Roll; Hon Roll; School Musical; Variety Show; Im Badmtn; JV Ftbl; Im Powder Puff Ftbl; Var Socr; Var L Trk; Physcl Ftns Awd 83-84; X-Cntry & Trck Champnshp Awds 84-85; Vrsty Capt Awd X-Cntry 85-86; Syracuse U; Arch.

KOTAS, BARBARA; Christ The King R H S; Brooklyn, NY; (Y); 105/451; Art Clb; 2nd Hnrs 86.

KOTCH, MICHELE; Elmira Free Acad; Elmira, NY; (Y); Cmnty Wkr; French Clb; Sec Latin Clb; SADD; Rep Soph Cls; Rep Jr Cls; Rep Stu Cncl; Var L Cheerleading; High Hon Roll; NHS; Fnlst Miss Teen Of Amer Schlrshp & Rcgntn Pgnt 86; Accntng.

KOTENOGLOU, DEMETRIOS; Lynbrook HS; Lynbrook, NY; (Y); Church Yth Grp; French Clb; Stage Crew; Nwsp Stf; Lit Mag; Hon Roll; Outstndng Wrk-Pblctn Of Schl Lit Magzn 85; Intl Bus.

KOTIK, THOMAS; Art & Design HS; Brooklyn, NY; (Y); Stage Crew; Variety Show; Hon Roll; Tech Theater.

KOTLYAR, MARINA; Midwood HS; Brooklyn, NY; (Y); French Clb; Mathletes; Teachers Aide; Yrbk Stf; Var Swmmng; JV Vllybl; Wt Lftg; Hon Roll; Prfct Atten Awd; Echo Art Awd 83-84; Mth Tutor Hnr 84-85 & 85-86.

KOTOWSKI, JEFFREY; St Marys HS; Lancaster, NY; (Y); Am Leg Boys St; SADD; JV Var Bsbl; Cnslng.

KOUBEK, KAREN; St Agnes Academic HS; Flushing, NY; (Y); Exploring; Girl Scts; Intnl Clb; Yrbk Phtg; Var Bowling; Var Swmmng; Hon Roll; St Johns U; Tchr.

KOUBEK, MICHAEL; Archbishop Molloy HS; Williston Park, NY; (Y); 145/409; Boy Scts; Exploring; Intnl Clb; Pep Clb; SADD; Yrbk Stf; Stat Bsktbl; L Trk; Cit Awd; Hon Roll; Ntl Rep By Scts Amer Lbrty Wkend 86; Egl Sct 85; St Johns U; Law.

KOUKOULAS, DEMETRA; Fontbonne Hall Acad; Brooklyn, NY; (Y); 11/133; Chess Clb; Cmnty Wkr; French Clb; Office Aide; Service Clb; Teachers Aide; Hon Roll; NHS; Prfct Atten Awd.

KOUNADIS, GEORGIA; Central Islip SR HS; Central Islip, NY; (Y); Church Yth Grp; Band; Concert Band; Mrchg Band; Nwsp Rptr; Nwsp Stf; Hon Roll.

KOURIAMPALIS, CATHY; Fontbonne Hall Acad; Brooklyn, NY; (Y); French Clb; Teachers Aide; Hon Roll; First Hnrs 84-86; Hist Awd 85; Hnrs Frnch 84-86; Bus Adm.

KOURNIANOS, KELI; Nazareth Regional HS; Brooklyn, NY; (Y); Chorus; Hon Roll; NHS; Superior Achvmnt Typng I 86; Bus.

KOUTOULAS, ANGIE; Colonie Central HS; Albany, NY; (Y); 12/439; Cmnty Wkr; Dance Clb; Key Clb; Off Sr Cls; High Hon Roll; Hon Roll; NHS; Ahepan Schlrshp Awd; Psych.

KOVAC, ANDREA; Seton Catholic Central HS; Binghamton, NY; (Y); 52/168; Church Yth Grp; Trs French Clb; Ski Clb; Y-Teens; JV Socr; Var L Trk; Hon Roll; Wells Grnt 86-90; Sons Of Italy Schlrshp 86-90; Natl Merit Art Cont 85-86; Wells COLL; Psych.

KOVAC, IVAN J; Glen Cove HS; Glen Cove, NY; (Y); Computer Clb; Science Clb; Stage Crew; Rep Soph Cls; Rep Jr Cls; Rep Sr Cls; Var Bsktbl; JV Ftbl; JV Lcrss; Hon Roll; Regents Schlrshp Wnnr 85-86; Dip Great Distnctn 86; Most Imprvd V Bsktbl 85-86; Engrng.

KOVACS, MARY A; Lancaster Centeral HS; Depew, NY; (S); Art Clb; DECA; Office Aide; Teachers Aide; DECA Competition Rgnls 3rd Pl Radio Adv 86; DECA Competition ST 1st Pl Radio Adv 86; Suny Oswego; Broadcasting.

KOVAL, ANDREA; Catholic Central HS; Cohoes, NY; (Y); 5/32; JA; Math Tm; Color Guard; Bsktbl; High Hon Roll; Hon Roll; Ntl Bus Hnr Scty 86; Prbtnry Mbr Ntl Hnr Scty 85; Psych.

KOVAL, KARLEEN; Keveny Memorial Acad; Waterford, NY; (S); 23/40; Drama Clb; Ski Clb; School Play; Yrbk Stf; Cheerleading; Sftbl; Tennis; Hon Roll; Samaritan; Nrsg.

KOVNER, MELINDA; Brooklyn Acad; Brooklyn, NY; (Y); 1/45; Yrbk Ed-Chief; Yrbk Phtg; Gov Hon Prg Awd; Hon Roll; Val; Soc Of Dstngshd Amer HS Stu 86; St Johns U; Law.

KOWAL, DEANNA M; Southside HS; Elmira, NY; (Y); 17/317; Aud/Vis; Cmnty Wkr; Trs FBLA; JA; Latin Clb; Quiz Bowl; Mgr Radio Clb; Stage Crew; High Hon Roll; Rgnts Schlrshp 86; Crng CC; Lbrl Arts.

KOWAL, STACY; Auburn HS; Auburn, NY; (Y); Dance Clb; Varsity Clb; Var Gym; Var Mgr(s); High Hon Roll; Hon Roll; Phys Ther.

KOWALCHUK, ALICIA ANN; Wilson Central HS; Ransomville, NY; (S); Latin Clb; Political Wkr; Quiz Bowl; Band; Chorus; Church Choir; Jazz Band; Church Yth Grp; FTA; Mrchg Band; Natl Latin I Gold Medal; OH Schlrshp Test Engl II 10th ST; Cnty JR Hnrs Pgm.

KOWALCZYK, BARBARA; Gloversville HS; Gloversville, NY; (Y); 10/247; Church Yth Grp; Trs Band; Chorus; Church Choir; Concert Band; Jazz Band; Mrchg Band; School Musical; Swing Chorus; Symp Band; Alfred N Johnson Memrl Schlrshp 86; Laurel G 86; Alice E Brown Fllwshp Of Music Awd 86; Suny At Potsdam; Chem.

KOWALCZYK, DON; St Marys HS; W Seneca, NY; (S); 2/178; Boy Scts; Church Yth Grp; SADD; High Hon Roll; Jr NHS; NHS; St Mary Acad Schlrshp 85-86; Intl Stdnt Ldrshp Inst 85; Eagle Sct 86; Psych.

KOWALCZYK, RICHARD; Gloversville HS; Gloversville, NY; (Y); Boy Scts; Drama Clb; Key Clb; Band; Chorus; Jazz Band; Mrchg Band; School Musical; Swing Chorus; NHS; Paul Smiths Coll; Frstry.

KOWALCZYK, STEPHANIE; Sacred Heart Acad; East Amherst, NY; (Y); Pres Church Yth Grp; Teachers Aide; Varsity Clb; Var Sftbl; Var Vllybl; Hon Roll; NHS; JA; JCL; Latin Clb; 1st Tm All Cath Vlybl 86; Acctg.

KOWALINSKI, LISA A; St Francis Prep; Maspeth, NY; (Y); 223/694; Girl Scts; Office Aide; Band; Rep Sr Cls; Vllybl; Regents Schlrshp 86; St Johns U; Bus.

KOWALSKI, JENNIFER; Cortland SR HS; Cortland, NY; (Y); 5/209; Cmnty Wkr; Trs French Clb; Orch; School Musical; Yrbk Stf; Stu Cncl; Hon Roll; NHS; Regents Schrlsh P85-86; Emily A De Camp Mem Awd 86; Cornell U; Animal Sci.

KOWALSKI, JOSEPH C; Bethelehem Central HS; Delmar, NY; (Y); Cmnty Wkr; Intnl Clb; Im Lcrss; JV L Swmmng; Ntl Merit Ltr; Mck Trial Team.

KOWALSKI, KATHI; Tonawanda JR SR HS; Tonawanda, NY; (Y); Pres Church Yth Grp; Drama Clb; French Clb; Office Aide; SADD; School Musical; Nwsp Rptr; Yrbk Stf; VP Jr Cls; VP Sr Cls; Daemon; Spcl Ed.

KOWALSKI, MARK A; Lackawanna SR HS; Lackawanna, NY; (Y); 5/200; Boy Scts; Computer Clb; Library Aide; Spanish Clb; High Hon Roll; NHS; Exlnc In Wrld Hist 84; Rgnts Schlrp 86; U NY Buffalo; Elec Engrg.

KOWALSKI, RONALD; Amsterdam HS; Amsterdam, NY; (Y); Bowling; Comp Pgmng.

KOWASKKI, KATHI; Tonawanda SR HS; Tonawanda, NY; (Y); Pres Church Yth Grp; Sec French Clb; SADD; Varsity Clb; School Musical; Nwsp Rptr; Yrbk Stf; VP Jr Cls; VP Sr Cls; Socr; Spcl Educ.

KOZA, CHERYL; West Babylon HS; W Babylon, NY; (Y); 26/460; English Clb; Spanish Clb; Varsity Clb; Pres Orch; Yrbk Phtg; Rep Stu Cncl; Fld Hcky; High Hon Roll; Jr NHS; NHS; Vrsty Awd Fld Hcky 86; CPA.

KOZAK, RICHARD J; Notre Dame HS; Clinton, NY; (Y); 9/159; ROTC; Spanish Clb; Ed Yrbk Phtg; JV Bowling; Var Socr; Vllybl; High Hon Roll; VP NHS; Mgr(s); U Of Rochester; Biochem.

KOZLOWSKI, FRED; Union Endicott HS; Endwell, NY; (Y); Chess Clb; Church Yth Grp; Cmnty Wkr; Exploring; Political Wkr; SADD; Yrbk Stf; Rep Frsh Cls; Rep Soph Cls; Rep Jr Cls; U Scranton; Pre-Med.

KOZLOWSKI, JEANNE; Westmoreland Central HS; Rome, NY; (Y); Debate Tm; Mathletes; Model UN; Ski Clb; SADD; Nwsp Rptr; Yrbk Stf; Pres Jr Cls; Hon Roll; Rotary Awd; ST U Of NY-MARCY; Telecomm.

KOZLOWSKI, KATHLEEN; Saint Marys HS; Cheektowaga, NY; (Y); 26/140; Quiz Bowl; Rep Frsh Cls; Rep Stu Cncl; JV Var Badmtn; JV Score Keeper; Hon Roll; NHS; NYS Rgnts Schlrshp 85-86; Miss Cheektowaga Fire Prev Rnnr Up 85-86; Am Red Cross Adv 1st Aid Cert 85; Canisius Coll; Cmmnctns.

KOZOWER, MAX J; Williamsville North HS; Getzville, NY; (Y); 5/301; Am Leg Boys St; Mathletes; Var L Ftbl; Var Capt Tennis; High Hon Roll; VP NHS; Ntl Merit Ltr; Amercn Lgn Boys Ntn 85; U Of PA.

KRABACHER, SHELLEY; Rome Catholic HS; Rome, NY; (Y); Church Yth Grp; Pres Exploring; Model UN; Nwsp Stf; Yrbk Stf; Var L Trk; High Hon Roll; Hon Roll; NHS; NEDT Awd; Bus Adm.

KRAEBEL, KIMBERLY; Greece Athena SR HS; Rochester, NY; (Y); 24/300; Capt Var Crs Cntry; Var L Trk; High Hon Roll; Hon Roll; NHS; MVP Crss Cntry 85; MVP Indr Trk 85-86; MVP Outdr Trk 86; Eng.

KRAEMER, PATTI; Warwick Valley HS; Warwick, NY; (S); Church Yth Grp; Cmnty Wkr; Drama Clb; SADD; Acpl Chr; Band; Chorus; Church Choir; Concert Band; Jazz Band; All Cnty & All Area Music Fest 82-86; Hartwick Music Hnr Awd 85; Music.

KRAFT, JULIE; Wayland Central Schl; Wayland, NY; (Y); 7/110; Church Yth Grp; German Clb; Math Clb; Teachers Aide; Band; Concert Band; Jazz Band; Mrchg Band; Orch; Stage Crew; Nice Kid Awd 86; Hghst German Avg 86; Fredonia; Rsrch Genetcst.

KRAFT, TARA; Earl L Vandermeulen HS; Mt Sinai, NY; (Y); 24/300; SADD; Yrbk Stf; VP Frsh Cls; Stu Cncl; Bsktbl; Capt Cheerleading; Fld Hcky; Vllybl; High Hon Roll; NHS; March Of Dimes Distngshd Schlr Awd 86; Olympic Chem Awd 84; U Of Richmond; Librl Arts.

KRAKOWSKI, TRACEY; Frontier Central HS; Hamburg, NY; (Y); 23/444; French Clb; JA; Gym; Hon Roll; Jr NHS; NHS; Pep Clb; Stage Crew; Prfct Atten Awd; S Grottanelli Engrng Schlrshp 86; Redonia-Clarkson; Engrng.

KRALJIC, STEPHEN; Earl L Vandermeulen HS; Mt Sinai, NY; (Y); FBLA; Leo Clb; SADD; Varsity Clb; Yrbk Stf; JV Var Socr; High Hon Roll; Hon Roll; Arch.

KRAMER, ANNE; Hamburg SR HS; Hamburg, NY; (Y); 33/374; Church Yth Grp; Girl Scts; JCL; Latin Clb; Mgr(s); Score Keeper; Vllybl; Hon Roll; Bio.

KRAMER, BEN; Riverhead HS; Riverhead, NY; (Y); 20/198; German Clb; Key Clb; Orch; Rep Stu Cncl; Var Crs Cntry; Hon Roll; Asprng Twrd Excllnc Awd Engl Grmn 84.

KRAMER, CHERYL; Blind Brook HS; Rye Brook, NY; (Y); Spanish Clb; SADD; Sec Temple Yth Grp; Band; Chorus; Ed Nwsp Stf; Sec Stu Cncl; Var Capt Cheerleading; Var L Sftbl; School Musical; Acad All Am Schlr 85-86.

KRAMER, KRISTINA A; St Francis Prep; Bayside, NY; (S); 46/744; Library Aide; NFL; Speech Tm; Chorus; Church Choir; NHS; JR Srv Awd St Marys Hosp For Chldrn 85foptimate Lst 83-84; Prncpl Lst 84-85; Med.

KRAMER, RACHEL Z; Huntington HS; Huntington, NY; (Y); 10/383; Library Aide; Political Wkr; Nwsp Bus Mgr; Nwsp Ed-Chief; Lit Mag; Rep Stu Cncl; High Hon Roll; Jr NHS; NHS; Lab Asst Chem Tchr 85-86; Wesleyan; Chem.

KRAMER, TAMMANY M; Sayville HS; Sayville, NY; (Y); 9/325; Key Clb; Rptr Nwsp Rptr; Ed Yrbk Ed-Chief; Sec Soph Cls; Rep Jr Cls; Rep Sr Cls; JV Fld Hcky; Trk; Sec NHS; Ntl Merit Ltr; Psych.

KRAMLICH, PATRICIA; Chatham Central HS; Valatie, NY; (Y); 22/145; Cmnty Wkr; Pres 4-H; Latin Clb; Teachers Aide; Yrbk Stf; 4-H Awd; Psychol.

KRAMPF, DONNA; The Wheatley Schl; Albertson, NY; (Y); Model UN; Variety Show; Nwsp Bus Mgr; Nwsp Stf; Yrbk Stf; Stu Cncl; Var Capt Cheerleading; Supreme Ct Mem Of Schl Within-A Schl 84-85; Recrdr To Modratr Of Schl Within-A Schl 85-86.

KRANBUHL, MICHAEL; Vernon-Verona-Sherill HS; Blossvale, NY; (Y); 26/200; Lit Mag; High Hon Roll; Hon Roll; Regents Schlrshp 86; Pres Acad Ftnss Awd 86; Clarkson U; Civil Engrng.

KRANGLE, DAVID; East Meadow HS; East Meadow, NY; (S); Key Clb; Mathletes; JV Bsbl; Hon Roll; NHS.

KRANZE, KATIE; Hannibal Central HS; Hannibal, NY; (Y); Varsity Clb; Trs Band; Pres Frsh Cls; Pres Soph Cls; Pres Rep Jr Cls; Pres Sr Cls; Var Capt Bsktbl; Var Capt Socr; Var Sftbl; High Hon Roll; Hnrb Mntn All Star Tm-Sccr 85; 2nd Tm All Star-Bsktbl 86.

KRASINSKI, RICHARD V; St Francis Prep; Whitestone, NY; (S); 36/653; Math Clb; Im Bsktbl; Im Bowling; Im Ftbl; Im Sftbl; Im Tennis; Im Vllybl; High Hon Roll; NHS; Elec Engrng.

KRASNIEWICZ, CATHY; Warwick Valley HS; Warwick, NY; (Y); 7/195; Church Yth Grp; Ski Clb; VP SADD; Off Soph Cls; Var Diving; Var Swmmng; Var JV Vllybl; High Hon Roll; Hon Roll; NHS; Ntl Sci Olympd Bio, Chem, Physcs 84-86; Spnsh Awd 85; Mst Imprvd Vllybll Plyr Vrsty 85; U CO Boulder; Bus.

KRASON, JOHN; St Pauls Schl; Wantagh, NY; (Y); 2/30; Boy Scts; Chess Clb; Stage Crew; Yrbk Stf; Hon Roll; Biol.

KRASSAS, NICOLE R; Bronx High School Of Science; Bronx, NY; (Y); Debate Tm; Speech Tm; Ntl Merit Ltr; NY Regnts Schlrshp 86; NY ST U; Polt Sci.

KRASUCKI, JANELLE; North Rose Wolcott HS; Wolcott, NY; (Y); 13/200; French Clb; Trs Soph Cls; Socr; Hon Roll; NHS; Hugh O Brien Ldrshp Awd; Sociology.

KRAUPNER, MARIE C; St Francis Prep; Middle Village, NY; (S); 174/750; Church Yth Grp; Cmnty Wkr; Spanish Clb; Stage Crew; Bsktbl; Gym; High Hon Roll; NHS; Opt Clb Awd; Cmmnty Svc Awd-Creedmor Hosp 84-85; Fshn Inst Tech; Intr Dsgnr.

KRAUS, GREG; Alden Central HS; Alden, NY; (Y); 4/160; Boys Clb Am; Cmnty Wkr; Science Clb; SADD; Nwsp Rptr; Nwsp Stf; JV Var Bsbl; Im Bsktbl; Im Vllybl; High Hon Roll; Pres Sci Clb 87; Rnr-Up Spllng Bee 81; U Of Buffalo; Chem Engr.

KRAUS, MICHELE; South Shore HS; Brooklyn, NY; (Y); Dance Clb; Orch; Yrbk Stf; Lit Mag; Twrlr; Cit Awd; High Hon Roll; Ntl Merit Schol; Govrnrs Cmmtte Schlrshp Awd 84; Spnsh Awd 84; Engl Mdl 84; NYU; Pre-Med.

KRAUSE, KIM M; Liverpool HS; Liverpool, NY; (Y); Church Yth Grp; Chorus; Church Choir; Mrchg Band; Symp Band; High Hon Roll; NHS; Natl Fld Band Champ 86; SUNY Albany; Math.

KRAUSE, LINDA; Fillmore Central HS; Fillmore, NY; (S); 3/63; SADD; Band; Chorus; VP Jr Cls; Trs Stu Cncl; Capt Socr; Capt Sftbl; Capt Vllybl; High Hon Roll; NHS; Sctn V Grls Sccr Chmpshp 84; Cls C Rgnls Sccr Chmpshp 84; Grls All Star Sccr Tm 85; Biomdcl Engrng.

KRAUSE, PAUL; Honeyoe Falls-Lima HS; Mendon, NY; (Y); Pres Church Yth Grp; Band; Stage Crew; Var L Crs Cntry; JV Socr; JV Tennis; Var L Trk; High Hon Roll; NHS.

KRAUSE, ROBERT E; Depew HS; Depew, NY; (Y); 109/272; Boys Clb Am; Chorus; School Musical; JV Ftbl; Im Wrstlng; Regnts Schlrshp 86.

KRAUSE, ROCHELLE; Pleasantville HS; Pleasantville, NY; (Y); 9/111; Sec Art Clb; Concert Band; Mrchg Band; Trs Frsh Cls; VP Soph Cls; VP Jr Cls; Stu Cncl; Var Sftbl; High Hon Roll; Pres NHS; Barnard Coll.

KRAUSS, CAROLYN N; Pine Bush HS; Middletown, NY; (Y); French Clb; Chorus; Concert Band; Mrchg Band; Jr NHS; NYS Rgnts Schlrshp 86; U Of Buffalo; Phd Psychlgy.

KRAUSS, TODD; Smithtown East HS; St James, NY; (Y); 1/650; Math Tm; Jazz Band; Symp Band; Nwsp Rptr; Off Frsh Cls; Off Soph Cls; Off Jr Cls; NHS; Italian Hnr Soc 85; Sci Olympcs 86; Engrng.

KRAUSS, WALTER; Walt Whitman HS; Huntington Statio, NY; (Y); 43/477; Hosp Aide; Spanish Clb; SADD; JV Bsbl; Var Crs Cntry; JV Ftbl; Im Swmmng; High Hon Roll; Jr NHS; Spanish NHS; Hnrb Mntn Bus Dynmcs 84; 2nd Pl Sci Cngrs Ocngrphy 84; Bus Mngmnt.

KRAUT, JULIE; W C Mepham HS; Bellmore, NY; (Y); Debate Tm; SADD; Band; Sec Soph Cls; Sec Jr Cls; VP Sr Cls; Var Socr; NHS; Enginrng.

KRAVITZ, GLADYS; Curtis HS; Staten Island, NY; (Y); 10/300; Math Clb; Math Tm; Hon Roll; NHS; Ntl Merit Ltr; Schoalr Manhattan Ballet Schl; Comp Pgmmg.

KRAWCZYK, J MARK; Liverpool HS; Liverpool, NY; (Y); 7/816; SADD; Stu Cncl; Var Capt Bsbl; Var Capt Bsktbl; Var L Ftbl; High Hon Roll; Jr NHS; NHS; Ntl Merit Schol; Onondaga Cty Math Awd 84; ROTC, Philip Morris & Cornell Schlrshps 86; Duke U; Elec Engr.

KRAWCZYK, TRACY; Eden Central SR HS; Eden, NY; (Y); AFS; Trs GAA; Girl Scts; SADD; Varsity Clb; Band; Orch; School Musical; School Play; Nwsp Stf; Specl Art Achvt 84, 85 & 86; Stu Cncl Recgntn 84, 85 & 86; Art.

KRAWIEC, ELIZABETH; Valley Central HS; Newburgh, NY; (Y); 17/343; Church Yth Grp; Symp Band; Yrbk Stf; Var Capt Socr; Var Capt Trk; Sec NHS; Spanish NHS; Varsity Clb; Band; Concert Band; Walden Wmns Clb Sprng Trk Awd 85; Coach Lou Walters Awd; Joseph M Fowler Awd 86; Walden PTO Wnnr 85; Elem Educ.

KRAWIECKI, ANNE; Amsterdam HS; Ft Johnson, NY; (Y); Varsity Clb; Yrbk Stf; Var Socr; Var Vllybl; Hon Roll.

KRAYNAK, KARA; Solvay HS; Solvay, NY; (Y); Church Yth Grp; Off Jr Cls; High Hon Roll; Hon Roll; Bus Dynmcs Awd Hghst Avg 84; Scl 11 R Awd Hghst Avg 86; UCLA; Bus Adm.

KRAYNIK, ANDREW; St Marys HS; Elma, NY; (Y); Boy Scts; Camera Clb; Church Yth Grp; Cmnty Wkr; Im Bsbl; Im Bsktbl; Im Bowling; Var Crs Cntry; Var Trk; Var Wrstlng; Eagle Sct 86; Philmont Natl Sct Camp 86; Bishops Altar Boy Mdl 83.

KRCHNIAK, KYLE S; Little Falls HS; Little Falls, NY; (Y); 7/83; Am Leg Boys St; Spanish Clb; Var L Bsbl; Var Bsktbl; Score Keeper; Var L Socr; High Hon Roll; Hon Roll; Bsbll All-Star 85-86; Coll; Engrng.

KREBS, CHARITY; Holy Angels Acad; Williamsville, NY; (Y); 2/38; Chorus; Nwsp Rptr; Yrbk Stf; Pres Soph Cls; Rep Sr Cls; VP Stu Cncl; Badmtn; High Hon Roll; NHS; Sal; Canisius Coll Deans Schlrshp 86; Canisius Coll; Jrnlsm.

KREBS, WILLIAM; Msgr Farrell HS; Staten Island, NY; (Y); 153/301; SADD; Sec Sr Cls; Rep Stu Cncl; JV Capt Bsktbl; Manhatten Coll; Civil Engr.

KRECKER, JOSEPH; Centereach HS; Centereach, NY; (Y); Band; Concert Band; Mrchg Band; Hon Roll; Spanish NHS; Comp Sci.

KREINBERG, GOLDA S; Torah Academy For Girls; Far Rockaway, NY; (Y); Cmnty Wkr; Temple Yth Grp; School Play; Yrbk Ed-Chief; Stern Clge Woman; Acctg.

KREIS, JOHN; Churchbille Chili HS; N Chili, NY; (Y); 31/300; JCL; Math Tm; Model UN; Ski Clb; Chorus; School Musical; Swing Chorus; Bsbl; Dnfth Awd; High Hon Roll; Pres Acad Ftnss Awd 86; SUNY Fredonia.

KREISWIRTH, BARRY; Commack High Schl North; E Northport, NY; (Y); 16/365; Off Stu Cncl; Var Trk; High Hon Roll; Pres NHS; Spanish NHS; Frgn Lang Clb.

KREITMAN, KIM; Long Beach HS; Long Beach, NY; (S); 27/260; Pep Clb; Band; Mrchg Band; School Musical; Lit Mag; JV Socr; Var Capt Trk.

KREITMEIER, REBECCA; Coxsackie-Athens HS; Hannacroix, NY; (Y); Camera Clb; German Clb; Ski Clb; Yrbk Phtg; JV Cheerleading; JV Score Keeper; Vllybl; Plattsburgh.

KREMMIN, KLAUS; Churchville-Chili HS; Churchville, NY; (Y); Am Leg Boys St; Math Tm; Ski Clb; Tennis; Wt Lftg; Bausch & Lomb Sci Awd; Hon Roll; NHS; MIT; Comp Engr.

KREMPA, STEVEN M; Niskayuna HS; Schdy, NY; (Y); Drama Clb; German Clb; School Play; Lit Mag; High Hon Roll; NHS; Cert Awd German 85; Cert Awd Frnch 86; Hon Mntn Crtv Wrtng Cntst 85; Coll Of St Rose.

KREMPL, GARY M; Kingston HS; Lake Katrine, NY; (Y); 46/573; VP Art Clb; Boy Scts; Church Yth Grp; Key Clb; SADD; Jr Cls; Stu Cncl; DAR Awd; High Hon Roll; NHS; Grnd Prz Boy Scts Amer Natl Jmbree Art Exhbt 85; Pratt Inst; Comm Dsgn.

KRENITSKY, DARIA; Solvay HS; Syracuse, NY; (Y); 1/171; Band; Yrbk Stf; Bausch & Lomb Sci Awd; High Hon Roll; Pres Mu Alp Tht; Pres NHS; Val; Hi-Quz Cntrl NY Chmpn Tm 86; Karat Clb 86; U Of Rochester; Chem.

KRENZER, DEBORAH; Caledonia-Mumford Central Schl; Caledonia, NY; (Y); 3/90; Sec Church Yth Grp; Pres VP 4-H; Pres French Clb; Math Tm; Band; Stat Socr; 4-H Awd; High Hon Roll; NHS; Drama Clb; Regents Scholar 86; SUNY Geneseo; Elem Ed.

KRENZER, KATHLEEN; Wheatland-Chili HS; Scottsville, NY; (Y); 14/75; SADD; Yrbk Ed-Chief; Sec Stu Cncl; Hon Roll; Cazenovia Coll; Equine Studies.

KREPPEIN, KIMBERLY L; Valley Central HS; Walden, NY; (Y); 41/288; Spanish Clb; Nwsp Stf; Yrbk Stf; Sec Soph Cls; Sec Sr Cls; Stat Bsbl; Capt Cheerleading; Hon Roll; NHS; Spanish NHS; Chrldr Of Yr Awd 85.

KRESEL, TOBEY; Jamesville-Dewitt HS; Dewitt, NY; (Y); Cmnty Wkr; Hosp Aide; Temple Yth Grp; Chorus; Stage Crew; High Hon Roll; Hon Roll; NHS; Cmnty Svc Awd-Jwsh Hm Of Cntrl NY 84; Cmnty Svc Awd-Schl 84; Bd Of Ed-Temple Soc Of Concord 83-85.

KRESOCK, DAVID M; Elba Central Schl; Elba, NY; (Y); 1/45; Am Leg Boys St; French Clb; Math Tm; Science Clb; Var Bsbl; Var Capt Bsktbl; Bausch & Lomb Sci Awd; High Hon Roll; Jr NHS; NHS; Schl Scholar Mdl 84-86; Rensselaer Polytech Inst Awd 86; SUNY Albany; Patent Law.

KRESSE, CLAIRE; Buffalo Seminary HS; Orchard Pk, NY; (Y); AFS; Art Clb; Debate Tm; Pres 4-H; Political Wkr; Ski Clb; Spanish Clb; Stu Cncl; JV Bsktbl; JV Socr; WNY Frgn Lang Educ Cncl Pstr 1st Prz 85; Law.

KRESSE, DAVID C; St Francis HS; West Seneca, NY; (Y); 34/161; Ski Clb; Spanish Clb; Nwsp Rptr; Lit Mag; Im Bsktbl; Im Bowling; Hon Roll; Outstndg Yth Achvt Awds 85; D Youville Coll.

KRETSCHMANN, DAVID; West Genesee SR HS; Camillus, NY; (Y); Key Clb; Ski Clb; High Hon Roll; NHS; Engr.

KRETSER, BRENDA J; Johnstown HS; Ft Plain, NY; (Y); Color Guard; Mrchg Band; Stat Powder Puff Ftbl; Var Capt Vllybl; Hon Roll; Fulton Montgomery CC All Cnty Scholar 86; Fulton-Montgomery; Sec Sci.

KREUTZER, LYNN; West Seneca East SR HS; Cheektowaga, NY; (Y); Rep Stu Cncl; Hon Roll; Nrsg.

KREVER, KAREN; Glen Cove HS; Glen Cove, NY; (Y); Trs DECA; Drama Clb; Office Aide; Flag Corp; School Musical; Rep Stu Cncl; Var Twrlr; Hon Roll; LIBEC Cntst; Type A Thon Wnnr; Eng Comp Cntst; Acctg.

KRIEGER, SHERRY; Fairport HS; Fairport, NY; (Y); Exploring; Pres 4-H; Library Aide; Hon Roll; SR Achvt Awd For Fabbits 4h 85; SR Achvt Awd For Woodworking 4h 85.

KRIER, DIANA; Villa Maria Acad; Williamsville, NY; (Y); Church Yth Grp; Cmnty Wkr; Chorus; Yrbk Stf; Im Bowling; Hon Roll; U Of Buffalo; Nrsg.

KRIM, LISA; Dobbs Ferry HS; Dobbs Ferry, NY; (S); 3/90; AFS; Key Clb; Chorus; Mrchg Band; School Musical; Var JV Vllybl; French Hon Soc; NHS.

KRINSKY, RICHARD M; James Madison HS; Brooklyn, NY; (Y); 50/750; Cmnty Wkr; Debate Tm; JA; Political Wkr; School Play; Nwsp Stf; Lit Mag; High Hon Roll; NCTE Awd; St Schlr; Won Moot Ct Comp 1st Annual 86; Holocaust Ptry & Essy Cntst 83; Schrshps To Cooper Union NYAA 84; Binghamton; Pre-Med.

KRISBURG, WENDY; Sachem North HS; Holbrook, NY; (Y); 65/1579; Dance Clb; German Clb; Service Clb; Ski Clb; Spanish Clb; Chorus; Hon Roll; Jr NHS; Ithaca Coll; Physcl Thrpy.

KRISHER, KIM; Lyndonville Central HS; Medina, NY; (S); 3/65; Am Leg Aux Girls St; Church Yth Grp; Computer Clb; Band; Var Bsktbl; Var Capt Socr; Var Capt Sftbl; Var Capt Vllybl; Cit Awd; NHS; Engrng.

KRISHNAN, HARI P; Arlington HS; Poughkeepsie, NY; (Y); 7/560; Cmnty Wkr; English Clb; Lit Mag; Ntl Merit Ltr; Thms J Wtsn Mem Schlrshp 86; NY ST Rgnts Schlrshp 86; Colgate U; Prfsr.

KRISSEL, KIMBERLY; Union Endicott HS; Endicott, NY; (Y); Church Yth Grp; Mgr Jr Cls; Cheerleading; Miss NY US Tn Pgnt 4th Pl 84; Dncd Jzz & Bllt 12 Yrs 73-85; Miss NY US Tn Pgnt Top 10 85; FIT; Fshn Mrchdsng.

KRISTEL, KRISTINE; Linton HS; Schenectady, NY; (Y); Pres Red Cross Aide; Off Sr Cls; Var Tennis; Cit Awd; Hon Roll; Cmnty Wkr; Dance Clb; Key Clb; Service Clb; Ski Clb; Ctznshp Awd 84-86; Vrsty Lttr In Tnns 83-84; Red Crss Yth Cncl Pres 84-86; Ithaca Coll; Bus.

KRISTENSEN, SANDRA; Lake George HS; Glens Falls, NY; (Y); 3/95; Key Clb; SADD; Varsity Clb; Chorus; School Play; Rep Stu Cncl; Var Cheerleading; Var Fld Hcky; High Hon Roll; NHS.

KROCHTENGEL, BRIAN; South Shore HS; Brooklyn, NY; (Y); Aud/Vis; Computer Clb; Office Aide; Service Clb; SADD; Comp Prgmng.

KROCZYNSKI, ROBERT; Sachem North HS; Lake Ronkonkoma, NY; (Y); 20/1700; Computer Clb; Ntl Merit Ltr; Sci Olympiad Awd In Chem 85.

KROETZ, JOHN; Aquinas Inst; Rochester, NY; (Y); 27/203; Ski Clb; Yrbk Stf; Socr; Swmmng; Tennis; High Hon Roll; Hon Roll; Prfct Atten Awd; Rochester Inst; Engr.

KROEZ, CAROLYN; H Frank Carey HS; Garden City S, NY; (Y); Office Aide; Varsity Clb; Var L Bsktbl; Var L Trk; JV Var Vllybl; High Hon Roll; Hon Roll; Outstndg Achvt Distribution Stu 86; Nassua Comm; Business.

KROGMANN, DAVID; Glens Falls SR HS; Glens Falls, NY; (Y); Church Yth Grp; Rep Frsh Cls; Rep Soph Cls; JV Bsbl; Var L Ftbl; Hon Roll; Vrsty Ski Team Ltr 86.

KROKONDELAS, PETER; Archbishop Molloy HS; Woodside, NY; (Y); 40/400; Church Yth Grp; Pep Clb; Speech Tm; Ed Yrbk Stf; Crs Cntry; Trk; Hon Roll; NHS; Mid-Hudson Vly Camp Hnr 84-86; Law.

KROME, RONALD N; Mac Arthur HS; Levittown, NY; (Y); 61/321; Hofstra.

KROMER, CATHERINE A; East Aurora HS; E Aurora, NY; (Y); 36/184; Pres Church Yth Grp; Letterman Clb; Chorus; Church Choir; School Musical; Yrbk Sprt Ed; L Sftbl; L Vllybl; Hon Roll; Pres Schlr; Regents Schlrshp Nrsng 86; Niagara U; Nrs.

KRONER, JILL; Eastridge HS; Rochester, NY; (Y); 1/215; Varsity Clb; Band; Color Guard; School Musical; Capt Bsktbl; Var Fld Hcky; Capt Vllybl; High Hon Roll; NHS; Sec French Clb; Harvard Bk Awd; Phi Beta Kappa Recgntn Awd; Notre Dame JR Of Yr Finlst; Dartmouth; Math.

KROPP, BRENDA; Depew HS; Depew, NY; (Y); Teachers Aide; Band; Chorus; Flag Corp; Mrchg Band; School Play; Stage Crew; Hon Roll; NHS; Eclgy Clb-Sectry; Engr.

KROPP, THOMAS J; La Salle Inst; Troy, NY; (Y); 11/90; Am Leg Boys St; Church Yth Grp; Drama Clb; Off ROTC; Stage Crew; Nwsp Stf; Var Lcrss; Var Socr; High Hon Roll; Hst NHS; Elec Engrng.

KROSLOW, MICHELE; The Stony Brook Schl; Stony Brook, NY; (Y); 43/80; Church Yth Grp; Office Aide; Teachers Aide; JV Crs Cntry; JV Fld Hcky; Var Mgr(s); Var Sftbl; Hon Roll; Gold Mdl Work Pgm 85-86; Gold Mrt Awd, Shank Awd 85-86; Messiah Coll; Elem Educ.

KROUSE, SERENA; New Paltz Central HS; New Paltz, NY; (Y); 18/182; Art Clb; Ski Clb; Spanish Clb; Pres SADD; Yrbk Ed-Chief; Rep Jr Cls; Rep Stu Cncl; Trk; High Hon Roll; Sec NHS; Hobart William Smith; Publtcns.

KRUGER, ELKE; The Mary Louis Acad; Forest Hills, NY; (Y); Stage Crew; Nwsp Stf; NHS; 1st Pl German II Lona Lang Cntst 85.

KRUMLAUF, KAREN; John Jay HS; Katonah, NY; (Y); Church Yth Grp; Drama Clb; Chorus; Church Choir; School Musical; School Play; Variety Show; Rep Jr Cls; Rep Stu Cncl; Hon Roll; Fshn Mrchndsng.

KRUPA, MICHAEL; Cardinal Mooney HS; Rochester, NY; (Y); 59/304; Variety Show; Lit Mag; Rep Stu Cncl; Capt Var Bowling; Hon Roll; Top Acctng I Stu 85; Niagara U; Acctng.

KRUPKA, RENEE; Bishop Grimes HS; Clay, NY; (Y); Itln Natl Hon Soc 85-86; Syracuse U; Law.

KRUSZKA, PATRICIA; Frontier Central HS; Hamburg, NY; (S); 7/424; French Clb; Chorus; High Hon Roll; Hon Roll; NHS; Fredonia; Psych.

KRUSZKA, TROY; Frontier Central HS; Hamburg, NY; (Y); Church Yth Grp; Computer Clb; Math Clb; Spanish Clb; Band; Off Stu Cncl; Bowling; Hon Roll; Comp Sci.

KRYWE, STEPHANIE; Somers HS; Katonah, NY; (Y); AFS; Model UN; Yrbk Stf; High Hon Roll; NHS; Spanish NHS; Soc Studs Stu Mnth; Cmmnctns.

KRZEMIENSKI, ELLEN; Lindenhurst HS; Lindenhurst, NY; (Y); 75/550; Spanish Clb; Concert Band; Mrchg Band; Nwsp Ed-Chief; Nwsp Rptr; Yrbk Phtg; Hon Roll; NHS; LIU; Bus Mgt.

KRZYMINSKI, JOHN; St John The Baptist HS; Seaford, NY; (Y); 140/546; Boy Scts; Cmnty Wkr; St Johns U; Crim Just.

KRZYWICKI, CHERYL; Turner/Carroll HS; Buffalo, NY; (Y); 2/100; Yrbk Stf; Var Sftbl; High Hon Roll; NHS; Sal; Church Yth Grp; French Clb; Quiz Bowl; Service Clb; Nwsp Rptr; Schrlshp Canisius Coll; Awds Physics,Psychlgy,Pgmmg; Alumnae Panhellenic Awd; Canisius Coll; Pre-Law.

KUBE, BRENDA; Valley Stream Norh HS; Malverne, NY; (Y); Spanish Clb; Chorus; School Play; High Hon Roll; Bst Supptg Actrss 1 Act Ply 85; Hofstra Frnscs Tourn Dual Intrprtn 3rd Pl Troph 86; Bus.

KUBIAK, JAMES; Maryvale SR HS; Cheektowaga, NY; (Y); 85/305; Church Yth Grp; VP French Clb; Varsity Clb; Stage Crew; JV Bsbl; JV L Ftbl; Var Trk; Var Wrstlng; Buffalo Fndtn Grant 86; Sthamptn Acad Schlrhp 86; Rgnts Diplma With Merits 86; Long Island U; Marine Sci.

KUBIAK, JEFF; H C Technical HS; Buffalo, NY; (Y); Hon Roll; Rochester Inst Tech; Elec Engr.

KUBO, RYU; Tottenville HS; Staten Isld, NY; (Y); Chess Clb; Intnl Clb; Band; Jazz Band; Coach Actv; U Of CA Brkly; Pre-Med.

KUCHER, PHILIP; Port Chester HS; Port Chester, NY; (Y); Art Clb; Ski Clb; Stage Crew; Golf; Hon Roll; Jr NHS; US Navy.

KUCHERA, MARK; Oriskany Central HS; Oriskany, NY; (Y); 10/66; Exploring; Pres Varsity Clb; Band; Yrbk Stf; Pres Sr Cls; Capt L Crs Cntry; Var Capt Trk; Trs NHS; Cit Awd; DAR Awd; Genateska Schlrshp; DAR Good Ctzn Awd; Mohawk Vly CC; Engrng Sci.

KUCZA, MICHAEL J; Brentwood Sorderling HS; Brentwood, NY; (Y); 1/500; Trs DECA; Mathletes; Science Clb; Lcrss; Socr; High Hon Roll; NHS; Pres Schlr; Val; Computer Clb; DECA Finlst On Natl Lvl 86; U Of PA; Bio.

KUDLA, ANNE; De Sales HS; N Tonawanda, NY; (S); 3/35; Yrbk Sprt Ed; Yrbk Stf; Var Capt Bsktbl; Hon Roll; NHS; Var Capt Sftbl; Var Capt Vllybl; All Cath Bsktbl 84-85; Rochester Inst Tech; Bus.

KUDO, SHERRYL; Sachen HS; Holbrook, NY; (Y); Orch; Yrbk Phtg; Wt Lftg; Rgnts Schlrshp 86; Boston U; Pre-Med.

KUECH, DEBORAH; Arlington HS; Poughquag, NY; (Y); Drama Clb; Hon Roll; U NY Binghamton; Pre-Med.

KUEHNER, JUDY; Maine-Endwell SR HS; Endwell, NY; (Y); 40/234; Drm Mjr(t); Mrchg Band; School Musical; Pres Symp Band; Hon Roll; Maine Endwell Clrcl Assoc Achvmnt Awd 86; Maine Endwell Music Dprtmnt Awd 86; Slvr H Nr Rll Awd 83-86; Broome Cmmnty Coll; Exctv Sectr.

KUERZDOERFER, BETH; West Seneca East SR HS; Buffalo, NY; (Y); 27/375; Sec Church Yth Grp; German Clb; Nwsp Stf; Hon Roll; JC Awd; Jr NHS; NHS; Natl Grmn Hnr Socty 84; Ingersoll Rand Rupp Bus Schlrshp 86; Erie CC; Bus.

KUGLER, ERIC; Lehman HS; Bronx, NY; (Y); 4/561; Computer Clb; Orch; Lit Mag; High Hon Roll; Jr NHS; NHS; Prfct Atten Awd; Supr Yth 85-86; Pace U; Comp Sci.

KUGLER, ROSEMARY E; Syosset HS; Woodbury, NY; (Y); 35/492; Dance Clb; Drama Clb; Latin Clb; NFL; Chorus; School Play; Cheerleading; Capt Swmmng; Hon Roll; NHS; Outstndng Swmr 85; SUNY Bnghmtn.

KUHEN, KELLI; Tonawanda HS; Tonawanda, NY; (Y); GAA; VP Girl Scts; Concert Band; Orch; Pep Band; Hon Roll; NHS; Med Crrs Clb VP 86-87; Erie Cnty Bnd 84-85; GS Slvr & Gld Ldrshp Awds Slvr Awd 84-85; Med.

KUHLMAN, CLAUDINE P; Maine-Endwell HS; Endwell, NY; (Y); 19/234; VP French Clb; Trs GAA; Pres Service Clb; School Musical; Yrbk Bus Mgr; Rep Stu Cncl; Var L Tennis; High Hon Roll; NHS; Rotary Awd; U Of AZ; Math.

KUHN, ERIC; Elmira Southside HS; Pine City, NY; (Y); 39/335; French Clb; Latin Clb; Chorus; Hon Roll; Pres Schlr; Rgnts Schlrshp Wnr 86; Crng Comm Coll; Lbrl Arts.

KUHN, JAY; Ward Melville HS; Stony Brook, NY; (Y); Ski Clb; Ice Hcky; JV Socr; JV Tennis; Hon Roll; Bus.

KUHN, LISA M; Nardin Acad; Williamsville, NY; (Y); Art Clb; French Clb; Model UN; Office Aide; Service Clb; Stage Crew; Nwsp Bus Mgr; Nwsp Sprt Ed; Lit Mag; Soph Cls; Bus.

KUI, KWOK SUM; John Adasm HS; Rosedale, NY; (Y); 9/494; Art Clb; Computer Clb; Math Clb; Math Tm; Yrbk Stf; Var Tennis; CC Awd; Hon Roll; JETS Awd; Pres Schlr; Assn Computng Mach Awd 86; Columbia U; Elect Engrng.

KUJAN, DENISE; Scotia-Glenville SR HS; Scotia, NY; (Y); 26/251; 4-H; German Clb; Intnl Clb; Church Choir; Stu Cncl; Fld Hcky; 4-H Awd; High Hon Roll; Hon Roll; NHS; Hghst Avg Home Ec Mdl 86; Binghamton SUNY.

KULESA, THOMAS C; Cicero-North Syracuse HS; North Syracuse, NY; (Y); 117/664; Aud/Vis; Chess Clb; High Hon Roll; Hon Roll; NHS; European Hstry Tutr 86; SUNY Buffalo; Elec.

KULIK, KATHLEEN; Turner-Carroll HS; Buffalo, NY; (Y); Hosp Aide; Hon Roll; Sisters Hosp Of Nrsng; Nrs.

KULIK, MICHELLE; Maryvale HS; Cheektowaga, NY; (Y); Sec French Clb; GAA; SADD; Var Crs Cntry; Var Mgr(s); Var Score Keeper; High Hon Roll; Hon Roll; NHS; SUNY Buffalo; Phrmcy.

KULIKOWSKI, ROSE; John Dewey HS; Brooklyn, NY; (Y); Church Yth Grp; Cmnty Wkr; Dance Clb; FFA; Girl Scts; Office Aide; Service Clb; Chorus; Church Choir; Variety Show; Dramtic Arts.

KULL, MOLLY; Mt Mercy Acad; Elma, NY; (Y); 15/220; 4-H; Latin Clb; Quiz Bowl; Ski Clb; Nwsp Rptr; Socr; Hon Roll; VP NHS; Ntl Merit Ltr; 1st Pl Western NY Sci Congress 85; Engl.

KULMALA, NINA; Smithtown HS East; Nesconset, NY; (Y); Fashion Inst Tech; Fshn Merch.

KULP, PATTI; Fillmore Central HS; Fillmore, NY; (Y); FHA; Key Clb; Nwsp Rptr; Nwsp Stf; Rep Stu Cncl; Sftbl; Vllybl; Hon Roll.

KULPA, KAREN; Maple Hill HS; Castleton, NY; (S); 10/100; Ski Clb; Spanish Clb; Band; School Musical; VP Jr Cls; Rep Stu Cncl; Var Cheerleading; Var Fld Hcky; Var Trk; Hon Roll.

KULPA, REBECCA LYNN; South Lewis HS; Boonville, NY; (Y); 2/86; Band; School Musical; Yrbk Ed-Chief; Cit Awd; 4-H Awd; High Hon Roll; NHS; Voice Dem Awd; Pres 4-H; SADD; NY ST Rgnts Schlrshp; Jostens Fndtn Ldr Schlrshp Fnlst; Potsdam ST Coll; Math Educ.

KULSHRESTHA, SUNITA; The Bronx HS Of Sci; Bronx, NY; (Y); French Clb; VP Key Clb; Ed Lit Mag; Rep Soph Cls; Rep Jr Cls; Rep Sr Cls; Rep Stu Cncl; High Hon Roll; NHS; Pres Schlr; Westinghse Sci Tlnt Srch Semifnlst 86; NYC Sci Fair Fnlst 86; Acad Excllnc-Frnch & Engl 86; MA Inst Of Tech; Med.

KUMAR, VASANTH I; West Seneca West SR HS; West Seneca, NY; (Y); Nwsp Rptr; Off Frsh Cls; Var Trk; Opt Clb Awd; Nrsng Schlrshp 86; U Of Buffalo.

KUMPEL, JAMES J; West Hempstead HS; W Hempstead, NY; (Y); 1/320; Am Leg Boys St; Capt Mathletes; Capt Quiz Bowl; Capt Scholastic Bowl; SADD; Variety Show; Nwsp Rptr; Stu Cncl; Var Tennis; Bausch & Lomb Sci Awd; Princeton Bk Awd 85; Natl 1st Prz Natl Scl Stds Olympd 85; Cornell Natl Schlr 86; Cornell U; Indstrl.

KUMRAH, PRAVEEN; Churchville Chiu HS; Rochester, NY; (Y); JA; Math Tm; Model UN; Science Clb; Badmtn; Bsbl; Socr; High Hon Roll; Hon Roll; Prfct Atten Awd; SUNY Buffalo; Pre Med.

KUNEN, JULIE; New Rochelle HS; New Rochelle, NY; (Y); 4/550; Political Wkr; Temple Yth Grp; Orch; Nwsp Rptr; Lit Mag; NHS; Ntl Merit Schol; Spanish NHS; Brain U Prz Engl; Bard Coll Prz Crit Wrtg; European Hstry AP Awd Bst Wrtg Hstry Dept; Yale U.

KUNES, PHIL; Batavia SR HS; Batavia, NY; (Y); 52/205; Band; Concert Band; Jazz Band; Mrchg Band; Orch; Pep Band; School Musical; Symp Band; Var Ftbl; Outstndng Musicn 84-86; Music.

KUNEY, KATHLEEN; Mynderse Acad; Seneca Falls, NY; (S); 2/138; 4-H; French Clb; Model UN; Chorus; School Musical; Swing Chorus; Trs Frsh Cls; DAR Awd; 4-H Awd; High Hon Roll; Cornell U; Mgt.

KUNKEL, MATTHEW W; East Syracuse Minoa Central HS; East Syracuse, NY; (Y); 1/333; Pres Latin Clb; Quiz Bowl; Band; Variety Show; Var L Trk; Im Vllybl; NHS; Ntl Merit Ltr; Val; Frank J Jervey Alumni Schlrshp Clemson U; Clemson U; Elec Engrng.

KUNKEN, JEFFREY; Friends Acad; Upper Brookville, NY; (Y); Thesps; Acpl Chr; Band; School Musical; School Play; Nwsp Stf; Rep Stu Cncl; Var Bsbl; Var Crs Cntry; NCTE Awd; NY ST Rgnt Schlrshp Wnnr 86; Wnnr Of Friends Acad JR Cls Essy Cont 85; Dir & Prod Of Frnds Acad Mus; Cornell U; Cmmnctns.

KUNKLE, CARRIE; Guilderland Central HS; Schenectady, NY; (Y); Cmnty Wkr; Debate Tm; Girl Scts; Speech Tm; Y-Teens; Yrbk Stf.

KUNTZ, DALEEN; St Marys HS; Buffalo, NY; (Y); Church Yth Grp; Cmnty Wkr; Exploring; Office Aide; Political Wkr; SADD; Teachers Aide; Score Keeper; Hon Roll; Acad Commendatn Amer Studies, Adv Keybrdng, Clerk Typst; Bryant & Stratton; Exec Sec.

KUNZ, SAMANTHA; Roy C Ketcham HS; Poughkeepsie, NY; (Y); Ski Clb; Band; Concert Band; JV Bsktbl; JV Crs Cntry; Stat Socr; Var Trk; JV Vllybl; NHS; Cmmrcl Art.

KUO, MARK H; The Bronx HS Of Science; Whitestone, NY; (Y); Cmnty Wkr; Math Tm; Pres Science Clb; Orch; Lit Mag; Off Sr Cls; Stu Cncl; Var Trk; NHS; Ntl Merit SF; Wrld Gratitude Day Honoree 85; Full Schlrshp To 40th Annl Ledrshp Wrkshp Conf 85; Natl Spanish Exam 85; Molecular Bio.

KUO, YUN G; Ellenville HS; Ellenville, NY; (Y); Computer Clb; SADD; Yrbk Phtg; Yrbk Stf; Rep Jr Cls; Rep Sr Cls; Rep Stu Cncl; Var Tennis; Var Trk; Elctrnc Engrng.

KUOCH, CHUN HEANG; Walton HS; Bronx, NY; (Y); Vllybl; NY Chinese Bilingual Educ Comm Achvt Awd 85; NYC HS Peer Tutoring Prgm Cert Of Hnr 85; Engr.

KUPERMAN, AIDA; John Dewey HS; Brooklyn, NY; (Y); Intnl Clb; Math Tm; Science Clb; Nwsp Rptr; Lit Mag; Im Trk; Capt Vllybl; High Hon Roll; Pol Sci.

KUPERSMITH, SCOTT; John H Glenn HS; E Northport, NY; (Y); Temple Yth Grp; Nwsp Rptr; Var Tennis; High Hon Roll; Hon Roll; Jr NHS; NHS; Spanish NHS.

KUPIEC, KAREN; Cambridge Central HS; Cambridge, NY; (Y); GAA; Teachers Aide; Varsity Clb; Band; Concert Band; Drill Tm; Mrchg Band; Yrbk Phtg; Yrbk Stf; JV Cheerleading; Peer Ldr 85-86.

KUPIEC JR, WILLIAM A; La Salle Inst; Troy, NY; (Y); 2/76; ROTC; Trs Service Clb; Drill Tm; Nwsp Stf; Off Soph Cls; High Hon Roll; Pres NHS; Pres Schlr; Sal; Superior Cad Awd 84-86; Hudson Vly CC; Biomed Engrng.

KUPPINGER, JANET LYNNE; West Irondequoit HS; Rochester, NY; (Y); 102/397; Camera Clb; Cmnty Wkr; Hosp Aide; Spanish Clb; Yrbk Ed-Chief; Yrbk Phtg; Rep Sr Cls; Var L Crs Cntry; Trk; Stat Wrstlng; Crs Cntry Mst Prsrvrnt 84; Advncd Plcmnt Physcs & Amer Hstry 85-86; Chrmn Red Crs Blood Drives 85-86; Soc Sci.

KURDZIEL, ANTHONY M; Haldane Central Schl; Cold Spring, NY; (Y); 10/57; Boy Scts; SADD; Rep Stu Cncl; Capt Bsbl; Var L Ftbl; Hon Roll; Gerlad Timmons Awd 85; Natl Hnr Scty 85-86; Regents Schlrshp 86; U Of Buffalo; Engrng.

KUREK, LORI ANN; Saint Marys HS; Lancaster, NY; (S); 4/166; Girl Scts; Hosp Aide; Library Aide; Science Clb; SADD; Church Choir; Lit Mag; High Hon Roll; Sec NHS; Canisius Coll; Intl Rel.

KUREK, YVONNE; Bishop Ford Central HS; Brooklyn, NY; (Y); Church Yth Grp; Girl Scts; SADD; 2 Hons 84-86; SR Ldrshp 86; Medicine.

KURI, LINDA; Bay Shore HS; Bay Shore, NY; (Y); 41/406; Church Yth Grp; Cmnty Wkr; Hosp Aide; High Hon Roll; Hon Roll; NHS; Rutgers; Accntng.

KURLAND, YETTA G; G Ray Bodley HS; Fulton, NY; (Y); Concert Band; Drm Mjr(t); Mrchg Band; School Musical; School Play; Variety Show; Bsktbl; Trk; Hon Roll; Ntl Merit Schol; U Of Buffalo; Psychlgy.

KURLOWICZ, WENDY; Solvay HS; Solvay, NY; (Y); 25/171; Art Clb; Exploring; Ski Clb; Yrbk Stf; Off Soph Cls; Hon Roll; Hon Stu; Kybrdng Awd; Geneseo Coll.

KURTZ, DIANE; Farmingdale HS; Farmingdale, NY; (Y); Church Yth Grp; Library Aide; Stage Crew; Variety Show; Stonybrook; Phy Thrpy.

KURTZ, JACKIE; Commack HS; Commack, NY; (Y); School Musical; Stage Crew; Yrbk Stf; High Hon Roll; NHS; Ntl Merit Ltr; Adv.

KURTZBERG, KIMBERLY; John Jay HS; S Salem, NY; (Y); JCL; Latin Clb; Math Tm; School Play; Nwsp Rptr; Lit Mag; Var L Socr; Cit Awd; High Hon Roll; NHS; Vasser Coll Bk Awd Wnr 86; N Westchester MADD Essay Cont Wnr 84; Natl Fut Prob Slvg Champs Coach 86.

KURTZMAN, NELLIE; Pelham Memorial HS; Pelham, NY; (Y); AFS; Cmnty Wkr; Drama Clb; Radio Clb; Orch; School Musical; School Play; Nwsp Rptr; Lit Mag; High Hon Roll; Engl.

KURWOSKI, LAURA; Miexico Acad Central; Oswego, NY; (Y); Dance Clb; GAA; Political Wkr; Mrchg Band; Off Soph Cls; Trs Stu Cncl; JV Var Socr; JV Var Sftbl; JV Vllybl; Im Wrstlng; 2nd Tm Vrsty Sftbl 85-86; Cathlc Chrstn Awd 84-85; Bus Adm.

KURYLO, NATALIE; Spackenkill HS; Poughkeepsie, NY; (Y); SADD; Sec Thesps; School Musical; School Play; Stage Crew; Nwsp Ed-Chief; Nwsp Stf; Yrbk Stf; Sec Sr Cls; Stu Cncl; Presdntl Acadmc Ftns Awd 86; ANY ST Rgnts Schlrshp 86; Natl Merit Commnd Stu 85; Appalachian ST U; Bus Mgmt.

KURZ, SUSAN; Preston HS; Bronx, NY; (S); 14/89; Nwsp Stf; DAR Awd; Hon Roll; NHS; Envir Schl Forestry; Wildlf Bio.

KURZAWA, KRISTIN; Pioneer Central HS; Arcade, NY; (Y); 14/248; Girl Scts; Pres SADD; School Musical; Ed Lit Mag; Var L Socr; Var Stat Swmmng; Hon Roll; French Clb; Band; Concert Band; Scl Sci.

KURZAWA, SCOTT; West Seneca East HS; Cheektowaga, NY; (Y); Boy Scts; Exploring; French Clb; Intnl Clb; JV Crs Cntry; JV Trk; French Hon Soc; High Hon Roll; JC Awd; NHS; Acad Exc Physics 86; Phrmcy.

KURZMAN, AMY; New Rochelle HS; Scarsdale, NY; (Y); Hosp Aide; SADD; Pres Temple Yth Grp; Chrmn Stu Cncl; JV Sftbl; Var Tennis; French Hon Soc; NHS; Ntl Merit Ltr.

KUSHNER, DEBORAH; Commack H S North; Commack, NY; (Y); 114/390; Temple Yth Grp; Acpl Chr; Chorus; School Musical; Swing Chorus; Variety Show; Lit Mag; High Hon Roll; NHS; Drama Clb; Tri M Modern Music Mastrs Hnr Soc 82-86; Oneonta; Elem Ed.

KUSHNER, SUSAN M; Williamsville East HS; E Amherst, NY; (Y); 50/307; Art Clb; Cmnty Wkr; Latin Clb; Ski Clb; VP Trs Temple Yth Grp; Off Frsh Cls; Off Soph Cls; Off Jr Cls; Off Sr Cls; High Hon Roll; Regents Schlrshp 86; U Of MMI; Lit.

KUSTERER, JENNIFER; Tuckahoe HS; Bronxville, NY; (Y); Drama Clb; Pres FBLA; Ski Clb; Var JV Cheerleading; Trk; Twrlr; Hon Roll; Regnts Schrshp Nrsng 86; Merrimack Coll; Bus Mrktng.

KUTSCHERA, SONDRA; Delaware Valley Central HS; Callicoon, NY; (Y); AFS; Sec Drama Clb; Chorus; Yrbk Stf; Rep Frsh Cls; Rep Jr Cls; VP Sr Cls; VP Stu Cncl; Cheerleading; Trk; Humanitrn Awd 86; ST U NY; Psychlgy.

KUVEIKIS, CAROLYN MARY; Hampton Bays HS; Hampton Bays, NY; (Y); 15/120; Science Clb; Chorus; Mrchg Band; School Musical; School Play; Stu Cncl; Bsktbl; Cheerleading; Fld Hcky; Hon Roll; Intl Fnc.

KUZLER, ROBERT; Archbishop Molloy HS; Maspeth, NY; (Y); 38/383; Yrbk Phtg; High Hon Roll; NHS; Coach Actv; Acctng.

KUZMACK, MICHAEL S; Rome Free Acad; Ava, NY; (Y); 36/435; Boy Scts; Chess Clb; Church Yth Grp; Letterman Clb; ROTC; Var Swmmng; JV Trk; NHS; St Schlr; Purdue U; Engrng.

KUZMIAK, BETH LYNN; Chatham HS; Ghent, NY; (Y); 62/129; Chorus; Yrbk Stf; Rep Stu Cncl; Stat Bsbl; Capt Var Cheerleading; Var Gym; Hon Roll; Bus.

KWAK, JAMES; Horace Greeley HS; Chappaqua, NY; (Y); 1/300; Ntl Merit Schol; Val; Math Tm; Political Wkr; Orch; School Musical; Nwsp Bus Mgr; Nwsp Ed-Chief; Nwsp Phtg; Nwsp Rptr; 2 Pre-Coll Awds Julliard Schl Of Music 86; Prncpl Cellist All-Eastern Orch 85; Math Olympiad Prog 85; Harvard U; Music.

KWAN, CHIN; Cathedral HS; Elmhurst, NY; (Y); 2/272; Library Aide.

KWAN, T; Seward Park HS; New York, NY; (Y); Drama Clb; Chorus; Bsktbl; Vllybl; High Hon Roll; Hon Roll; Acdmc Awds In Soc Stud, Math, Sci Etc 84-86; Consec Attndnc Awds 84-86; Athlc Trphs 84-85; Elec Engr.

KWARTA, ANN MARIE; Commack North HS; Commack, NY; (Y); Exploring; Hosp Aide; Teachers Aide; Band; Mrchg Band; Symp Band; Trk; Hon Roll; Farmingdale; Nrs.

KWAS, KAREN; Buffalo Acad Of The Sacred Heart; Buffalo, NY; (Y); French Clb; Red Cross Aide; Science Clb; Trs Service Clb; Stage Crew; Nwsp Rptr; Yrbk Stf; Rep Jr Cls; Acdmc Exclnc Bus Dnmcs, Kybrdng & Cmmnctns 86; Vlntr Awd 86; Fashn Inst Of Tech; Fshn Jrnlsm.

KWAS, KEITH A; Lake Shore Central HS; Derby, NY; (Y); 12/284; Church Yth Grp; French Clb; JA; Hon Roll; Jr NHS; NHS; Pres Schlr; Natl Sci Olympiad 84-85; NY ST Rgnts Schlrshp 85-86; Syracuse U; Pre Med.

KWASNIEWSKI, LISA; Lackawanna SR HS; Lackawanna, NY; (Y); Cmnty Wkr; GAA; Spanish Clb; Sftbl; Vllybl; Hon Roll; VP NHS.

KWASNIK, JOHN; Sherburne-Earville Central HS; Sherburne, NY; (Y); 30/169; Am Leg Boys St; Ski Clb; Spanish Clb; SADD; Rep Stu Cncl; JV Var Bsktbl; JV Ftbl; Var Trk; Wt Lftg; Hon Roll; Mst Imprvd Vrsty Bsktbl Plyr 85-86; Cnfrnc Ldrshp Smnr 85; Albny Coll Phrmcy; Phrmcy.

KWIECINSKI, JEANNE N; Hauppauge HS; Hauppauge, NY; (Y); 140/498; Var Capt Swmmng; Greg Rogers Mem Awd 86; Mst Vlable Swmmr Pvt Clb Awd 86; Hauppge Athltc Assn Schlrshp 86; E Strdsburg U; Elem Ed.

KWIT, TINA; Churchville Chili HS; Churchville, NY; (Y); Ski Clb; Art.

KWITKIN, MICHELLE; Plainview-Old Bethpage HS; Plainview, NY; (Y); 1/194; Mathletes; Model UN; Temple Yth Grp; Nwsp Ed-Chief; Lit Mag; High Hon Roll; NHS; Ntl Merit Ltr; Val; Simons Fellowship-Stony Brook U 85; NY St Stu Energy Research Comp-Rnd I Wnr 85-86; Columbia U; Med.

KWOK, JULIE; Bay Shore HS; Bay Shore, NY; (Y); Aud/Vis; Hon Roll; NHS.

KWON, HELEN; John Dewey HS; Brooklyn, NY; (Y); Chess Clb; VP Church Yth Grp; Library Aide; Math Tm; Teachers Aide; Church Choir; Nwsp Rptr; Nwsp Stf; Rep Soph Cls; Im Badmtn; Bowdoin Coll; Tchng.

KWONG, DORIS O; Stuyvesant HS; Elmhurst, NY; (Y); Cmnty Wkr; French Clb; Var Capt Crs Cntry; L Var Tennis; Var Capt Trk; French Hon Soc; Prfct Atten Awd; Office Aide; Teachers Aide; Cert Of Merit Math 83; Cert Of Exclinc Frnch 85; 5th Pl Indvdl & 2nd Pl Tm City B Div Crss Cntry 85; Carnegie-Mellon U.

KYLE, DAVID J; Lawrence HS; Inwood, NY; (Y); 86/414; Pres Art Clb; Drama Clb; English Clb; Pres PAVAS; Nwsp Rptr; Nwsp Stf; Yrbk Stf; Lit Mag; Hon Roll; NHS; NY ST Smmr Schl Of Arts 84; Music & Art Fndtn JR Art Awd 85; Rhode Island Sch/Design; Art.

KYLER, ELIZABETH; Oceanside HS; Oceanside, NY; (Y); 133/532; Pres Camera Clb; VP Key Clb; Thesps; Chorus; Madrigals; School Musical; School Play; Yrbk Phtg; Rgnts Schlrshp 86; All ST Wmns Chrs 85; NY U; Tv-Flm Drctr.

KYNER, ALLISON; Eastchester HS; Eastchester, NY; (Y); French Clb; Key Clb; Ski Clb; Band; JV Var Bsktbl; Var Trk; Hon Roll; NHS; Art.

KYRILLIDIS, HELEN C; St Francis Preparatory Schl; Flushing, NY; (S); 93/744; Church Yth Grp; Math Clb; Band; Church Choir; Nwsp Phtg; NHS; Opt Clb Awd; School Musical; School Play; Law.

KYSER, ROBIN; Allegany Centeral HS; Allegany, NY; (Y); Camp Fr Inc; Church Yth Grp; Library Aide; SADD; Chorus; School Play; Stage Crew; Yrbk Stf; Hon Roll; Jamestown Bus Inst; Acctg.

KYUNG-CHAN, KIM; The Stony Brook Schl; Douglaston, NY; (Y); Art Clb; Chess Clb; Church Yth Grp; Math Clb; Science Clb; JV Var Socr; JV Var Trk; High Hon Roll; Rgnts Schlrshp 86; Chmstry 85; Math Fr NY 85; Mchncl Engr.

LA BARBERA, PATTI; Hauppauge HS; Hauppauge, NY; (Y); 61/500; FBLA; Rep Frsh Cls; Rep Soph Cls; Rep Jr Cls; Rep Sr Cls; Rep Stu Cncl; High Hon Roll; Hon Roll; NHS; AZ ST U; Law.

LA BARCA, LAURA; Saint Francis Prep; Ridgewood, NY; (Y); 33/653; Office Aide; Coach Actv; Crs Cntry; JV L Sftbl; Trs Trk; Im Vllybl; Hon Roll; 7th Rnkd Ntn US Fg Sktr 82; Bldg Ind, Rgnts Schlrshps 86; U DE; Sprts Med.

LA BARGE, EDMUND R; Cohoes HS; Cohoes, NY; (Y); 43/183; Art Clb; Varsity Clb; Stage Crew; Socr; Trk; Wrstlng; Hon Roll; WCL Tourn 2nd; Colonial Cncl Champ 82-85; Wrstlng JR & SR 83-86; Sccr 82; Vrsty Sprtsmnshp 85-86; Engrng.

LA BIANCA, VINCENT; Freeport HS; Freeport, NY; (Y); 24/450; Computer Clb; Exploring; Mathletes; Pres Science Clb; Concert Band; Jazz Band; Variety Show; Nwsp Rptr; JP Sousa Awd; NHS; Rgnst Schlrshp, Mrrl Lynch Schlrshp 86; Pres Acdmc Ftns Awd 86; Hofstra U; Aerospc.

LA BORNE, KATHLEEN M; East Islip HS; E Islip, NY; (Y); 4/425; FBLA; Math Tm; SADD; Socr; Tennis; High Hon Roll; Hon Roll; Jr NHS; Frgn Lang Hnr Soc; 2nd Pl Physics Chem Trophy; Coll Mt St Vincent; Bus.

LA BOUNTY, ERIC; Plattsburgh HS; Plattsburgh, NY; (Y); Bsktbl; Golf; High Hon Roll; Colby Coll Awd Outstndng Achvmnt In Engl 86; Bus Adm.

LA BRAKE, TERRI; Colton-Pierrepont Central Schl; Potsdam, NY; (S); Drama Clb; 4-H; VP French Clb; Band; Chorus; Mrchg Band; Stage Crew; Sftbl; Var Capt Vllybl; Hon Roll; Mth.

LA CASCIA, ANNE; St Francis Preparatory Schl; Richmond Hill, NY; (Y); Girl Scts; Church Choir; Hon Roll; NHS; Presdntl Acadmc Fitness Awd 85-86; Girl Scout Silver Awd 85; Hunter Coll Full Schlrshp 86; Hunter Coll; Film & Video.

LA CASSE, DANE E; Shenendehowa HS; Clifton Park, NY; (Y); 332/675; Boy Scts; JCL; Latin Clb; Band; Var Ftbl; JV Vllybl; Hon Roll; Prfct Atten Awd; Natl Latin Exam Magna Cum Laude 84-85; Cert Merit Outstndng Acdmc Achvt 85-86; Hudson Vly CC; Med Lab Tech.

LA CLAIR, MARCIE A; Indian River HS; Antwerp, NY; (Y); 7/127; Pres VP AFS; Rep Hosp Aide; VP Pres Key Clb; Rep Chorus; Color Guard; Yrbk Phtg; Rep Gym; Rep Socr; Rep Trk; Sec NHS; Elmira Key Schlrshp 85; Nrsng.

LA CLAIR, TAMMY; Saranac Central HS; Morrisonville, NY; (S); 19/121; Band; Chorus; Concert Band; Jazz Band; Mrchg Band; School Play; Var Socr; High Hon Roll; Ntl Merit Ltr; Plattsburgh ST U; Pre-Med.

LA CLAIR, VERNE; Vernon-Verona-Sherrill HS; Vernon, NY; (Y); Church Yth Grp; Band; Mrchg Band; Orch; Im Lcrss; Var Capt Socr; High Hon Roll; Hon Roll; Engrng.

LA COMB, SHERRI A; Odgenburg Free Acad; Ogdensburg, NY; (Y); Cmnty Wkr; French Clb; Thesps; Band; Chorus; School Musical; Nwsp Stf; Concert Band; Pep Band; School Play; NY ST Smmr Schl Thtre 85; Rdrs Thtre 85; NYSMA 84.

LA COMBE, KRISTINE; Paul V Moore HS; W Monroe, NY; (Y); Band; Symp Band; Comp Sci.

LA COURCIERE, JACQUELINE; Our Lady Of Lourdes HS; Poughkeepsie, NY; (Y); 9/188; Am Leg Aux Girls St; Red Cross Aide; Nwsp Rptr; VP Soph Cls; Rep Jr Cls; VP Stu Cncl; Var Capt Cheerleading; Hon Roll; Jr NHS; NHS; Hly Crs Bk Prz & Empire Grls ST; Frdhm U; Psychlgy.

LA CROIX, NOELLE C; St Francis Prepartory Schl; Flushing, NY; (S); 123/695; Art Clb; Dance Clb; Drama Clb; Library Aide; Math Clb; PAVAS; Science Clb; Speech Tm; Thesps; Chorus; Vet Med.

LA DUC, KELLY LEE; Pulaski Acad; Pulaski, NY; (Y); Aud/Vis; GAA; Math Clb; SADD; Chorus; School Musical; Yrbk Stf; Hon Roll; Drama Clb; French Clb; Snow Smmr Enrichmnt Schlrshp Engl 85; Musculr Dystrphy Super Dance Coordntr 86; Syracuse U; Comm.

LA DUC, SAMANTHA E; Plattsburgh SR HS; Plattsburgh, NY; (Y); Cmnty Wkr; Debate Tm; Hosp Aide; JA; Model UN; Office Aide; Political Wkr; Drm Mjr(t); JV Score Keeper; Var JV Socr; Ottaway Fndtn Schlrshp 86; Yng Vlntrs Actn Cert 83; Stu Mnth 85; SUNY Plattsburgh; Fshn Merch.

LA DUE, BABETTE; Ticonderoga HS; Ticonderoga, NY; (Y); Band; Chorus; Jazz Band; Mrchg Band; Variety Show; Yrbk Stf; Bsktbl; Cheerleading; Socr; Trk; Intl Studies.

LA DUE, MICHELLE RENEE; Chenango Valley HS; Binghamton, NY; (Y); 3/175; French Clb; Pres FHA; Chorus; Color Guard; Nwsp Ed-Chief; Yrbk Stf; Capt Twrlr; High Hon Roll; NHS; Rotary Awd; Elmira Key Awd 85; Le Moyne Coll; Advrtsg Exec.

LA FACE, MARIA C; Bishop Grimes HS; Syracuse, NY; (Y); 72/144; Exploring; FBLA; School Play; Onondege Comm Coll; Rdio.

LA FARR, MATTHEW CAMERON; Saint Marys Acad; Ft Edward, NY; (S); 10/52; Art Clb; Chess Clb; Sec French Clb; Office Aide; Pep Clb; Teachers Aide; Varsity Clb; Variety Show; Bsbl; Capt Wrstlng.

LA FAVE, MATTHEW; John F Kennedy HS; Utica, NY; (Y); Aud/Vis; Drama Clb; Library Aide; Math Tm; Band; Chorus; Jazz Band; Mrchg Band; Bowling; Tennis; Rgnts Schlrshp 86; Mohawk Valley CC; Acctg.

LA FAVE, THOMAS; Arlington HS; Poughkeepsie, NY; (Y); 141/566; Var L Golf; Var L Trk; NY St Regents Schlrsp; SUNY; Physics.

LA FEVER, RANDY L; Richburg Central HS; Bolivar, NY; (Y); School Play; Nwsp Rptr; High Hon Roll; Hon Roll; Jr NHS; NHS; Ntl Merit Ltr; Wrld Poetry-Goldn Poet Awd, Hnrbl Mntn 86; Natl Jrnlsm Merit Ltr 84-85; Herkimer Cnty CC; Radio Brdcst.

LA FLOWER, CAROL ANN; St Michael Acad; New York, NY; (Y); SADD; Yrbk Stf; Hon Roll; Regnts Schlrshp 86; Coll Of New Rochelle.

LA FOUNTAIN, LISA; Northern Adirondack Central Schl; Altona, NY; (Y); Key Clb; Yrbk Bus Mgr; Pres Frsh Cls; Stu Cncl; Var Capt Cheerleading; Var Score Keeper; JV Socr; JV Var Sftbl; High Hon Roll; Hon Roll; All Amer Chrldr 85; Wrstlng Bstr VP; Bus Admin.

LA GEORGE, PETER; North Spencer Christian Acad; Candor, NY; (S); 2/7; Church Choir; Stage Crew; Yrbk Stf; Pres Stu Cncl; Var L Bsktbl; High Hon Roll; Voice Dem Awd; Chess Clb; Cmnty Wkr; Teachers Aide; Princpls Awd 84; Yth Inagurl 84; Senate Stu Polcy Forum 84-85; Geneva Coll; Pol Sci.

LA GRONE, KRISTIE; Edison Tech; Rochester, NY; (Y); Church Yth Grp; Pep Clb; SADD; Yrbk Phtg; Yrbk Stf; Var Socr; Hon Roll; Soc Work.

LA GROW, CHRIS; Henninger HS; Syracuse, NY; (Y); 13/300; Drama Clb; Trs Intnl Clb; SADD; Trs Soph Cls; Trs Jr Cls; Var Tennis; High Hon Roll; Var NHS; Var Ntl Merit Ltr; Math Clb; Ntl Olympiad Eng Awd 84; Most Imprvd Tennis 86; Frnch.

LA HART, LINDA; Chateaugay Central HS; Chateaugay, NY; (Y); 9/62; Varsity Clb; Pres Sr Cls; Capt Var Socr; NHS; Pres FFA; Jazz Band; VP Frsh Cls; Pres Soph Cls; Pres Jr Cls; Var Bsktbl; All Northern 2nd Tm Sftbl 85; Frnklin Cnty Dairy Princss 86; Cornell; Vet Med.

LA HART, REBECCA; Saranac Lake HS; Lake Placid, NY; (Y); Yrbk Stf; Trk; Rgnts Bus Math Awd Hghst Grd 83-89; N Country CC; Fshn Merch.

LA JOIE, SANDRA; Half Hollow Hills H S East; Dix Hills, NY; (Y); 137/511; Cmnty Wkr; Office Aide; Red Cross Aide; Band; Nwsp Rptr; Yrbk Ed-Chief; Capt Pom Pon; High Hon Roll; Spanish NHS; NYS Regents Schlrshp, NYSSMA Mus Awds, Cert Merit Assemblywoman Toni Rettaliata 86; Swarthmore Coll; Pol Sci.

LA MAINA, THERESA; Sacred Heart Acad; E Meadow, NY; (Y); 11/186; Church Yth Grp; Pres Math Clb; Math Tm; Service Clb; Chorus; School Play; Hon Roll; NHS; NY St Regents Schlrshp 86; Fairfield U Schlrshp 86; Hofstra U Frshmn Recgntn Schlrshp 86; Binghamdon U; Lawyer.

LA MANNA, FREDERICK; Manhasset HS; Manhasset, NY; (Y); Cmnty Wkr; Service Clb; Varsity Clb; Nwsp Rptr; Pres Soph Cls; Rep Jr Cls; Var Lcrss; Capt Var Wrstlng; High Hon Roll; Ntl Merit Schol; Washington & Lee U; Polt Sci.

LA MENDOLA, NICK; Fairport HS; Fairport, NY; (Y); Model UN; Ski Clb; Stu Cncl; Hon Roll; Intl Econ.

LA MENDOLA, SALVATORE; Monsignor Farrell HS; Staten Island, NY; (S); 5/319; Math Tm; Nwsp Rptr; Rep Soph Cls; Im Bsktbl; Im Bowling; Im Ftbl; Pres NHS; Ntl Merit Ltr.

LA MONT, SUZANNE; Albion HS; Albion, NY; (S); 23/181; Aud/Vis; VP Sec Church Yth Grp; Sec 4-H; JCL; Latin Clb; Ski Clb; JV Var Socr; 4-H Awd; Hon Roll.

LA MONTE JR, BENJAMIN C; Cardinal O Hara HS; Tonawanda, NY; (Y); Church Yth Grp; Computer Clb; Bsktbl; Bus.

LA NEVE, BARBARA; Henninger HS; Syracuse, NY; (Y); 6/400; Dance Clb; GAA; Girl Scts; Rep Frsh Cls; Rep Soph Cls; Rep Jr Cls; Rep Sr Cls; Tennis; High Hon Roll; NHS; Regnts Schlrshp 86; Am Legn Schlrshp 86; Skidmore College; Dnc.

LA PAGE, KAROLYN; Henninger HS; Syracuse, NY; (Y); Drama Clb; French Clb; GAA; Hosp Aide; SADD; Band; Concert Band; School Play; Pres Frsh Cls; Gym; Cmnctns.

LA PETER, CHRISTINA; Somers HS; Mahopac, NY; (Y); 6/196; Drama Clb; Chorus; School Musical; School Play; Stage Crew; Bausch & Lomb Sci Awd; High Hon Roll; NHS; Ntl Merit Ltr; AFS; NY St Regents Schlrshp 86; SUNY; Engrng.

LA PLANTE, KIMBERLY; Lansingburgh HS; Troy, NY; (Y); French Clb; Hosp Aide; Political Wkr; Trs SADD; Chorus; Nwsp Rptr; Yrbk Stf; Off Stu Cncl; Var Fld Hcky; Var Tennis; Pol Sci.

LA POLLA, ELIZABETH; Marlboro Central HS; Highland, NY; (Y); Church Yth Grp; Drama Clb; SADD; Varsity Clb; Color Guard; School Play; Var L Cheerleading; Hon Roll; NHS; French Clb; Fnlst Mss NY Ntl Teen 86; Acctg.

LA PORTA, ANNE; Gloversville HS; Gloversville, NY; (Y); 50/200; Cmnty Wkr; Drama Clb; Girl Scts; Key Clb; Latin Clb; SADD; Teachers Aide; Band; Chorus; Concert Band; Psych.

LA PORTE, KENNA; Northeastern Clinton HS; Mooers, NY; (Y); 50/153; Church Yth Grp; Model UN; Chorus; Concert Band; Yrbk Bus Mgr; Trs Soph Cls; Sec Sr Cls; Rep Stu Cncl; Var Bsktbl; Var Sftbl; Plattsburgh ST; Psych.

LA PURKA, DANIELLE; Riverhead SR HS; Riverhead, NY; (Y); 69/207; Trs 4-H; Hosp Aide; Quiz Bowl; Ski Clb; Chorus; Off Jr Cls; Stu Cncl; Im Bowling; JV Fld Hcky; 4-H Awd; Vet-Med.

LA QUAY, LISA; Pine Valley HS; South Dayton, NY; (S); Pres Trs AFS; Pres Church Yth Grp; Drama Clb; Chorus; Madrigals; School Musical; Bsktbl; Hon Roll; Jr NHS; NHS; Roberts Wesleyan Coll; Elem Ed.

LA ROCCA, ANTHONY; Brooklyn Acad; Brooklyn, NY; (Y); Church Yth Grp; Cmnty Wkr; Band; Bsktbl; Bsktbl; Staten Island Coll; Engineering.

LA ROCCA, CHRISTINE; St John Villa Academy HS; Staten Island, NY; (Y); 2/150; Math Tm; Chorus; School Musical; High Hon Roll; NHS; PAL Stry Tllng Cntst 1st Pl 84.

LA ROCCA, LISA; Richmond Hill HS; Richmond Hill, NY; (Y); 2/288; FBLA; Scholastic Bowl; School Musical; Nwsp Rptr; Off Sr Cls; NHS; Pres Schlr; Sal; Voice Dem Awd; Gov Hon Prg Awd; Super Youth/Pride Yankees Hnr Awd 85-86; Pace U; CPA.

LA ROCCA, MARK; Greenville JR/SR HS; Medusa, NY; (Y); 1/80; Boy Scts; Concert Band; Jazz Band; Trs Jr Cls; Var Bsbl; Var Bsktbl; Var Socr; Bausch & Lomb Sci Awd; High Hon Roll; NHS; Rcvd Vrsty Lttr G 85; All Cnty Band Trumpet 84-86.

LA ROCCO, ANGELA; Le Roy Central HS; Leroy, NY; (Y); French Clb; Girl Scts; Ski Clb; Varsity Clb; Chorus; School Musical; Yrbk Phtg; Yrbk Stf; Pres Sr Cls; Var Sftbl.

LA ROSA, JEFFREY T; Columbia HS; Castleton, NY; (Y); 14/417; Am Leg Boys St; Band; Trk; High Hon Roll; VP NHS; Ntl Merit SF; Econ.

LA ROSA, LISA; Bishop Kearney HS; Brooklyn, NY; (Y); 23/386; Band; Hon Roll; Jr NHS; NHS; Chs Awd ST Domnics Grls Sftbl 84; Pres Acad & Ftns Awd 86; Bus Dprtmntl Awd 86; Brooklyn Coll.

LA ROSA, MARIE; Frontier Central HS; Hamburg, NY; (Y); French Clb; Pep Clb; Rep Frsh Cls; Rep Soph Cls; Rep Jr Cls; Rep Sr Cls; Trs Rep Stu Cncl; Var Capt Crs Cntry; Var Capt Trk; Hon Roll; Mst Imprvd Awd Crs Cntry 85; Physcl Thrpy.

LA ROSA, MICHELE; Curtis HS; Staten Island, NY; (Y); Trs Key Clb; Chorus; School Musical; Bowling; NHS; Prfct Atten Awd; Chem.

LA ROSE, NIKKI; Dannemora Union Free HS; Dannemora, NY; (Y); 3/26; French Clb; Library Aide; Chorus; Yrbk Stf; VP Jr Cls; VP Rep Stu Cncl; Var JV Cheerleading; Var Socr; High Hon Roll; NHS; Mtn Vly Atltc Conf MVAC JV Chrng Comp 84-85; MVAC Vrsty Comp 1st Pl Chrldg Comp 85-86; Medical Science.

LA RUE, LISA; Bishop Ludden HS; Syracuse, NY; (S); Hosp Aide; Capt JV Bsktbl; Coach Actv; Socr; Sftbl; Trk; High Hon Roll; Hon Roll; Piano & Recitals 77-85.

LA SALA, ROSANNE M; St Francis Prep; Queens Village, NY; (S); 129/744; Cmnty Wkr; Math Tm; Band; Concert Band; Mrchg Band; Hon Roll; NHS.

LA SALLA, GINA MARIE; Bethpage HS; Bethpage, NY; (Y); Political Wkr; Yrbk Stf; VP Jr Cls; Pres Sr Cls; JV Bsktbl; Capt Cheerleading; Var Pom Pon; JV Sftbl; JV Vllybl; Dnfth Awd; Bus.

LA SALLE, BRIAN; Archbishop Walsh HS; Ellicot City, MD; (Y); Computer Clb; Letterman Clb; Ski Clb; Spanish Clb; Varsity Clb; Socr; Swmmng; Comp Engrng.

LA SALLE, LAURI; John F Kennedy HS; Utica, NY; (Y); Red Cross Aide; Spanish Clb; Capt Cheerleading; Fld Hcky; NHS; Top 3 Cls 84-85.

LA SARSO, MATTHEW G; Ft Edward HS; Fort Edward, NY; (Y); 2/44; Am Leg Boys St; Yrbk Stf; Pres Jr Cls; Pres Sr Cls; Im Bsktbl; JV Var Ftbl; Var Trk; Hon Roll; NHS; Sal; Albany Coll Of Phrmcy; Phrmcy.

LA SCALA, MICHELLE; The Ursuline Schl; City Island, NY; (Y); 44/123; Cmnty Wkr; Hosp Aide; Hon Roll; NHS; Cert Of Exclinc 85; Latinam Honoris Societatem 85; Quinnipiac Coll; Med.

LA TAILLADE, JASLEAN J; Bronx H S Of Sci; New York, NY; (Y); Cmnty Wkr; Office Aide; Teachers Aide; Lit Mag; NHS; Prfct Atten Awd; 2nd Pl Concours Francais Lvl 1 83.

LA VARNWAY, MICHELLE L; Haverling Central HS; Bath, NY; (S); French Clb; FBLA; Color Guard; Pep Band; School Musical; Symp Band; Var Sftbl; Var Tennis; High Hon Roll; NHS; Corning CC; Acctg.

LA VOY, SHARON; Lake George HS; Glens Falls, NY; (Y); 1/80; Drama Clb; Varsity Clb; School Play; Bsktbl; Vllybl; Bausch & Lomb Sci Awd; High Hon Roll; NHS; Ntl Merit Ltr; Chorus; RPI Math & Sci Awd 86.

LAARMANN, ALICE; Narrowsburg Central Schl; Narrowsburg, NY; (Y); Sec Church Yth Grp; Pep Clb; Ski Clb; Band; Chorus; School Play; Var Cheerleading; Var Socr; Var Sftbl; High Hon Roll; Ct Fr Raphael-Mst Imprvd 83-84; Outstndng Svc-Bnd 81-82; Outstndng Svc-Choir 82-84; York Coll Of PA; Bus Mgmt.

LABAN, WENDI; Gilboa-Conesville Central HS; Gilboa, NY; (Y); GAA; Yrbk Bus Mgr; Var Bsktbl; Var Socr; Bausch & Lomb Sci Awd; NHS; Prfct Atten Awd; St Schlr; Hrn Grad 86; Alfred Ag & Tech; Cad-Cam.

LABARRON, KATHLEEN; Hornell HS; Hornell, NY; (Y); AFS; Church Yth Grp; Dance Clb; Latin Clb; Quiz Bowl; Ski Clb; Band; Chorus; Church Choir; School Musical; Ld Schl Musicl 86.

LABASHINSKY, EILEEN F; St Michaels HS; Brooklyn, NY; (Y); 4/131; Church Yth Grp; Church Choir; Yrbk Stf; Rep Frsh Cls; Rep Soph Cls; High Hon Roll; NHS; NEDT Awd; St Schlr; Yth Ftnss Awd 83; Wshngtn & Lee U; Bio.

LABEILLE, CLAUDINE; Skaneateles HS; Skaneateles, NY; (S); Cmnty Wkr; Model UN; Quiz Bowl; Red Cross Aide; SADD; Variety Show; Yrbk Stf; Pres Frsh Cls; Pres Soph Cls; Trs Stu Cncl; NYS Mth Comptn Awd 83; Pre-Law.

LABEN, BRENNA; Churchville-Chili SR HS; Rochester, NY; (Y); GAA; Ski Clb; Var Capt Socr; High Hon Roll; Hon Roll; Travel.

LABOMBARDA, FRANK; Nazareth HS; Brooklyn, NY; (Y); 90/270; Varsity Clb; Var Bsbl; Im Bsktbl; Im Ftbl; Im Sftbl; Hon Roll; NHS; Brooklyn Coll; Math.

LABOSKI, KENNETH; Irondequoit HS; Rochester, NY; (Y); Latin Clb; Hon Roll; Prfct Atten Awd; Rgnts Schlrshp 86; CC Of The Fingerlakes; Lndscpr.

LABOY, ISABEL; North Rockland HS; Haverstraw, NY; (Y); Intnl Clb; Hnr Awd Achv 85-86.

LABRIE III, JOSEPH; Scotia-Glenville HS; Schenectady, NY; (Y); 35/250; Chess Clb; JA; Trs Ski Clb; Pres Spanish Clb; Band; Mrchg Band; High Hon Roll; Hon Roll; Prfct Atten Awd; SUNY Geneseo; Bio.

LACAGNINA, ANGELA; St Joseph By The Sea HS; Staten Island, NY; (Y); Office Aide; JV Cheerleading; Hon Roll; MVP Awd In Chrldng 85; Acdmc Schrshp 83; Bus Adm.

LACARRUBBA, SAL; East Hampton HS; Amagansett, NY; (Y); SADD; Var JV Ftbl; Var Trk; Wt Lftg; Phy Ed Gold Mdl-Hghst Score 86; Tm Awd-Trck-Mst Vlbl Athlt 86; Arch.

LACCHIA, LAURA; Valley Stream North HS; Valley Stream, NY; (Y); 5/130; French Clb; Band; Yrbk Ed-Chief; Rep Jr Cls; Rep Sr Cls; Socr; French Hon Soc; High Hon Roll; NHS; Ntl Merit Ltr; Delta Kappa Gamma Soc Essay Cont Wnr 85; NYS Regents Scholar Wnr 86; Wellesly Coll; Lang.

LACEWELL, TAMMIE V; Erasmus Hall HS; Brooklyn, NY; (Y); 15/667; VP Church Yth Grp; Office Aide; Teachers Aide; Ed Nwsp Ed-Chief; Nwsp Rptr; Lit Mag; Hon Roll; Jr NHS; NHS; Wrtr.

LACH, AMY; Barker Central HS; Barker, NY; (Y); AFS; Church Yth Grp; Drama Clb; Exploring; French Clb; School Musical; Stage Crew; Sec Soph Cls; Sec Jr Cls; Sec Sr Cls; Slvtn Army Awd 86; Tchrs Assoc Schrlshp 86; Almni Assoc Schlrshp 86; Niagara Cnty CC; Elctrncphlgrp.

LACK, JONATHAN M; Hackley Schl; Peekskill, NY; (Y); Chess Clb; Computer Clb; Mathletes; Math Tm; Political Wkr; School Play; Stage Crew; Hon Roll; Ntl Merit Ltr; St Schlr; RPI Albany; Law.

LACKEY, STEPHEN; Glens Falls HS; Glens Falls, NY; (Y); 19/210; Key Clb; Nwsp Rptr; Nwsp Stf; High Hon Roll; Hon Roll; NHS; Pres Schlr; Union Coll; Physcs.

LACKO, SHERI; Lansing HS; Lansing, NY; (Y); Church Yth Grp; 4-H; Spanish Clb; Powder Puff Ftbl; JV Sftbl; Var JV Vllybl; 4-H Awd; Hon Roll; NHS.

LACOMIS, ELLEN; Shenendehowa HS; Clifton Park, NY; (Y); 1/675; Var Bsktbl; JV Tennis; Var Capt Trk; NCTE Awd; NHS; Ntl Merit Ltr; Val; Leo Clb; Varsity Clb; Off Frsh Cls; Dartmouth Clb Bk Awd 85; Spn Bk Awd 86; Coaches Awd 83; Cornell U; Biochem.

LACON, THOMAS S; H Frank Carey HS; Franklin Sq, NY; (Y); 45/228; Boy Scts; Debate Tm; Trs Key Clb; Mathletes; Thesps; School Musical; Nwsp Stf; VP Lit Mag; Hst Soph Cls; Rep Jr Cls; Jwsh War Vtrns Jean R Tint Brthrhd Awd Wnr 86; By Scts Of Am Egl Sct 86; Mnfctrs Hanvr Trst 86; St Johns U; Pre-Med.

LAD, ILAKUMARI; Christopher Columbus HS; Bronx, NY; (Y); Hon Roll; Comp Sci.

LADD, DARLA; Paul V Moore HS; Central Sq, NY; (Y); AFS; Exploring; Pres German Clb; VP Science Clb; Pres Stu Cncl; High Hon Roll; NHS; Gold Key Art Awd 83; Sprtsmnshp Awd CSSL 83; Pre-Med.

LADSON, KENNITH; All Hallows HS; Bronx, NY; (Y); Boy Scts; Church Yth Grp; Church Choir; Bsbl; Bsktbl; Ftbl; Trk; High Hon Roll; Hunter Coll; Bus.

LAFFERTY, CHRIS; Cuba Central HS; Cuba, NY; (Y); 27/55; French Clb; Key Clb; Model UN; Ski Clb; SADD; Varsity Clb; Rep Stu Cncl; JV Bsktbl; JV Var Ftbl; Var Capt Trk; Acad Grnts Fr Crtlnd ST 85-86; Crtlnd ST; Geolgy.

LAFFERTY, PEGGY; Hilton Central HS; Hilton, NY; (Y); 44/300; Church Yth Grp; Girl Scts; Model UN; Ski Clb; SADD; High Hon Roll; Hon Roll; NHS; Pres Acdmc Fit Awd 86; SUNY; Bio.

LAFFEY, DOROTHY; Holland Patent Central HS; Holland Patent, NY; (Y); 76/180; Spanish Clb; SADD; Temple Yth Grp; Nwsp Stf; Im Bowling; Im Powder Puff Ftbl; Hon Roll; Phys Thrpy.

LAFORCE, SHARI; Hilton Central HS; Hilton, NY; (Y); Model UN; Nwsp Rptr; Yrbk Stf; VP Frsh Cls; VP Soph Cls; Rep Jr Cls; Rep Sr Cls; Rep Stu Cncl; Capt Var Cheerleading; Trk; SUNY Fredonia; Educ.

LAFORGE, DANIEL P; Eastport HS; Speonk, NY; (Y); Am Leg Boys St; Var Bsbl; Var Bsktbl; Var Socr; Hon Roll; NHS; Church Yth Grp; Ski Clb; Varsity Clb; Jr NHS; All Lge-Sccr 84-85; All Lge-Bsktbl 85-86.

LAFORTE, ALEX; New Dorp HS; Staten Island, NY; (Y); Intnl Clb; Im Wt Lftg; Hon Roll; Pre-Law.

LAFRANCESCO, JOHN; Copiague HS; Copiague, NY; (Y); SADD; Spanish Clb; Band; Mrchg Band; JV Bsbl; Var Wrstlng; Law.

LAGA, JENNIFER; Holland Central HS; Holland, NY; (Y); AFS; Varsity Clb; Rep Stu Cncl; Var Cheerleading; Capt Socr; JV Vllybl; High Hon Roll; Hon Roll; Jr NHS; NHS; Top 10 Hnr Stu 86; Intl Bus.

LAGASSE, KEN; RFA HS; Lee Center, NY; (Y); Engl 83; Hstry 83; ST U Of NY; Bus.

LAGO, EVA; St John Villa Acad; Staten Island, NY; (Y); 15/132; Dance Clb; Hosp Aide; JA; Office Aide; Spanish Clb; Crs Cntry; Trk; Hon Roll; Ntl Merit SF; Indoor Trk Awd 84-85; Achvt Awds; Finance.

LAGOMARSINI, ALEX; Aviation HS; Bronx, NY; (S); 18/414; JA; Service Clb; High Hon Roll; Hon Roll; NHS; Prfct Atten Awd; Gld Wngs For Exclnc-Aviatn Mntnc Tech 86; Slvr Wngs For Exclnc-Aviatn Mntnc Tech 85; Hnr Soc Of Avtn; Acad Of Aeronautics; Aerosp.

LAGOY, CRAIG; W Genesee HS; Camillus, NY; (Y); French Clb; Varsity Clb; Var JV Bsbl; JV Bsktbl; Bowling; High Hon Roll; Hon Roll; NHS; Clarkson U; Indstrl Distrbtn.

LAGUZZA, LISA; Vernon Verona Sherrill Central HS; Sherrill, NY; (Y); 19/183; Church Yth Grp; Cheerleading; Timer; Trk; Cit Awd; High Hon Roll; Hon Roll; NHS; Pres Schlr; Trs Frsh Cls; VVSTA Awd; Dllrs For Schlrs Schlrshp; Amer Lgn Ctznshp Awd; Syracuse U; Bio Med.

LAHIFF, COLIN J; John S Burke Catholic HS; Goshen, NY; (Y); 4/152; Yrbk Stf; Var Bsktbl; Im Trk; High Hon Roll; NHS; NEDT Awd; St Schlr; Gnrl Exclnc Mdl; Cthlc U Schlrshp 84; Math Mdl; Lemoyne Coll Schlrshp 85; Notre Dame Schlr; NYS Rgnts; U Of Notre Dame; Math.

LAI, DAVID; Jamesville-De Witt HS; Fayetteville, NY; (Y); German Clb; Math Tm; Chorus; Orch; Swing Chorus; Var Crs Cntry; L Var Tennis; High Hon Roll; NHS; Ntl Merit Ltr; Mth Awd 83-84; Srvc Awd 85-86; All ST Strng Orchstr 85-86; Pre-Med.

LAI, YI-SHIN; Mineola HS; Mineola, NY; (Y); 1/235; Pres Key Clb; VP Sec SADD; Orch; School Musical; Rep Frsh Cls; High Hon Roll; Kiwanis Awd; NHS; Val; Harvard Prz Bk 85; Proclamatn Town Of N Hempstead & Mineola 86; Qlty Key Clb Lt Govrnr 86; MI ST U; Pre-Law.

LAI, YISHIN; Mineola HS; Mineola, NY; (Y); 1/235; Key Clb; Mathletes; SADD; Orch; School Musical; High Hon Roll; Kiwanis Awd; NHS; Val; Harvard Prize Bk; Qlty Key Clb Lt Gvnr Awd; Rcgntn Of Achvt & Outstndng Svc; MI ST U; Political Sci.

LAICHTMAN, ARTHUR; Ossining HS; Ossining, NY; (Y); JV Bsbl; Var L Golf; Var Socr; High Hon Roll; NHS; Lang Awd 84-86; Pre Med.

LAIDLOW, DEBRA; Catherine Mcauley HS; Brooklyn, NY; (S); 6/70; Dance Clb; Library Aide; Nwsp Stf; Yrbk Stf; High Hon Roll; Hon Roll; Comp Sci.

LAIDLOW, NIGEL; St John Baptist HS; Central Islip, NY; (Y); Trk; High Hon Roll; Hon Roll; Polytechnic U; Engr.

LAING, ANDREW; Sherburne-Earlville HS; Earlville, NY; (Y); 1/168; Math Tm; School Musical; Pres Sr Cls; Bsktbl; Ftbl; Wt Lftg; Hon Roll; NHS.

LAING, KIM; St Raymond Acad; Bronx, NY; (Y); Girl Scts; Library Aide; Office Aide; SADD; Band; Mrchg Band; Yrbk Phtg; Medicine.

LAINO, DAVID J; Aviation HS; Woodhaven, NY; (S); 9/416; Church Yth Grp; Nwsp Rptr; Ed Nwsp Stf; NHS; Wings Awd Exclnc Shop Courses 85; Rookie Yr Awd Rnnr Up Bst Frshmn Shop Stdnts 83; Engrng.

LAINO, DENISE; Sacred Heart Acad; Hempstead, NY; (Y); Church Yth Grp; Hosp Aide; SADD; Chorus; School Play; Optmtry.

LAIR, KATHY; Gloversville HS; Gloversville, NY; (Y); 63/269; Church Yth Grp; Drama Clb; SADD; Band; Concert Band; Drm & Bgl; Mrchg Band; Var Bowling; Stat Fld Hcky; Var Sftbl.

LAIRD, KAREN; Rye Neck HS; Mamaroneck, NY; (Y); 25/95; AFS; Key Clb; Sec Ski Clb; Band; School Musical; Variety Show; Civic Clb; Socr; Hon Roll; NHS; Rgnts Schlrshp 86; Colgate U; Physcl Thrpy.

LAIRD, SHERRY; Letchworth Central HS; Bliss, NY; (Y); Church Yth Grp; Drama Clb; FNA; Office Aide; Varsity Clb; Chorus; Church Choir; School Musical; Yrbk Stf; Cheerleading; MVP Vrsty Chrldng 85-86; Prfct Atndnc Awd 84-85; Genesee CC; Spec Ed Tchr.

LAIRES, MICHELLE C; Marymount Schl; City Island, NY; (Y); Cmnty Wkr; Intnl Clb; Library Aide; Model UN; Nwsp Rptr; Yrbk Bus Mgr; Hon Roll; NHS; Fordham Coll; Polt Sci.

LAITNER, URSULA; Cicero-North Syracuse HS; Liverpool, NY; (S); 24/667; German Clb; Band; Color Guard; Sec Soph Cls; Sec Jr Cls; Sec Sr Cls; Rep Stu Cncl; NHS; Mngmnt.

LAJEUNESSE, LISA; Catholic Central HS; Green Island, NY; (S); 17/179; French Clb; Math Clb; Band; High Hon Roll; Hon Roll; NHS; Prfct Atten Awd; Prfct Attndnc 83-84; Achv Frnch 84; Comp Sci.

LAKATOS, JOSEPH P; Saint Francis Prep; Flushing, NY; (S); 35/653; Civic Clb; Office Aide; Var Bowling; Hon Roll; NHS; Opt Clb Awd; Princpls List 83-85; Acctng.

LAKE, BERNADETTE E; Minisinic Valley HS; Middletown, NY; (Y); Drama Clb; Manhattan Coll.

LAKE, PATTI; Valley Central HS; Walden, NY; (Y); Girl Scts; Hosp Aide; Chorus; Rep Frsh Cls; Hon Roll; Diet Techncn.

LAKE, RICKI P; Professional Childrens Schl; Hastings/Hudson, NY; (Y); Drama Clb; French Clb; JA; Key Clb; Latin Clb; Model UN; Band; Chorus; Concert Band; School Musical; Music Awd 84; Ithaca Coll; Muscl Theatre.

LAKHAN, GILLIAN; Brooklyn Technical HS; Brooklyn, NY; (Y); 395/1200; Computer Clb; Rep Stu Cncl; Opertn Crssrds Africa Schlrshp 85; Rsrch & Wrtg Skills Awd 84; Spelman Coll; Comp Sci.

LALIK, ELIZABETH A; Liverpool HS; Baldwinsville, NY; (Y); 35/816; Spanish Clb; School Musical; Yrbk Stf; Rep Stu Cncl; JV Crs Cntry; Var Trk; Hon Roll; NHS; NY ST Regents Schlrshp 86; Cornell U; Intl Bus.

LALKA, SUSAN; Lackawanna SR HS; Lackawanna, NY; (Y); French Clb; Lang.

LALLEY, KAREN; Mt Mercy Acad; Buffalo, NY; (S); Cmnty Wkr; Dance Clb; Debate Tm; Girl Scts; JCL; Latin Clb; NFL; Science Clb; Service Clb; Speech Tm; Am Leg Essay Cont 2nd Pl 83; Tchr.

LALLEY, MARY; Hamburg SR HS; Hamburg, NY; (Y); 11/377; VP Frsh Cls; Pres Soph Cls; Rep Jr Cls; Rep Sr Cls; Rep Stu Cncl; Var L Fld Hcky; Var L Socr; NHS; Quiz Bowl; Band; Harvard Bk Awd 86.

LALLY, TAMMY J; Midlakes HS; Clifton Springs, NY; (Y); 3/161; AFS; Am Leg Boys St; Drama Clb; English Clb; Letterman Clb; Model UN; Sec Spanish Clb; Color Guard; Yrbk Stf; Var L Fld Hcky; U Of Rochester Paideja Awd In Humanities 85; Amer Fld Svc Smmr Exchng Stu To Spain 85; Wells Coll; Frgn Lang.

LALOR, MARGARET K; Ravena Coeymans Selkirk SR HS; New Baltimore, NY; (Y); 22/184; Drama Clb; Spanish Clb; Band; Concert Band; Jazz Band; Mrchg Band; Pep Band; School Musical; School Play; Yrbk Stf; Rgnts Nrsng Schlrshp 86; Nrsng.

LAM, ALVIN; Central Islip HS; Central Islip, NY; (Y); 9/500; Am Leg Boys St; Math Clb; Chorus; School Musical; Variety Show; Lit Mag; Stu Cncl; Lcrss; High Hon Roll; NHS; UCLA; Bus.

LAM, CAM; HS Of Fashion Inds; Jackson Heights, NY; (Y); 43/324; AFS; Art Clb; Computer Clb; JA; Office Aide; Service Clb; Teachers Aide; Cit Awd; Hon Roll; Ntl Merit Ltr; Attndnc Awd 84-86; Math & Engl Hnr Awds 84.

LAM, CHUN MAN; L D Brandeis HS; New York, NY; (Y); 25/544; Band; Nwsp Stf; Hon Roll; NHS; Cert Exclnc 86; Acad Olympc 86; SR Arista Leag 86; Stony Brook; Engrng.

LAM, CHUN PONG; Longwood HS; Shirley, NY; (Y); Chess Clb; VP Computer Clb; Mathletes; Math Tm; JV Ftbl; Bausch & Lomb Sci Awd; High Hon Roll; NHS; RPI; Computer Science.

LAM, FRANCES; Canarsie HS; Brooklyn, NY; (S); 1/498; Cmnty Wkr; Math Tm; Var Bowling; Hon Roll; Prfct Atten Awd; Val; 1st Prz Short Story Awd Ntl Lgu Of Am Pen Wmn 85; 2nd Prz Brooklyn Sci Fair 84; Prncpls Yankess Awd; Comp Engr.

LAM, HEUNG W; Queens Aviation HS; New York, NY; (S); 47/413; JA; Jr NHS; Big Buddy Stdnt 84; Natl Vocatnl Hnr Soc 85; Long Island U; Pharmcy.

LAM, JACKELINE; Professional Childrens Schl; New York, NY; (Y); Chorus; Madrigals; School Musical; High Hon Roll; Van Gelder Schlrshp Manhattan Schl Of Music 85; Manhattan Schl Of Music; Music.

LAM, JOHN; St Agnes HS; Brooklyn, NY; (Y); 35/115; JV Trk; Scnd Hnrs Awd 86.

LAM, LILY; Canarsie HS; Brooklyn, NY; (Y); Chorus; Hon Roll; NHS; Med.

LAM, NOAH; St John The Baptist HS; Great Rvr, NY; (Y); Pres Chess Clb; Pres Math Clb; Math Tm; JV Ftbl; Hon Roll; Mu Alp Tht; Chem Olympiad Awd 85-86; Capt Chess Tm 85-86; U Of WA; Aeronautical Engr.

LAM, THAO; Hutchinson Technical Central; Buffalo, NY; (Y); Natl Beta Clb; Concert Band; Mrchg Band; Nwsp Rptr; Hon Roll; Buffalo Area Engrng Awrnss For Minrts-BEAM 83-84; Cornell U; Acctnt.

LAMACCHIA, MICHAEL; Babylon HS; Babylon, NY; (Y); 30/150; Rep Sr Cls; JV Bsbl; JV Wrstlng; Hon Roll; Distnctv Hnrs Earth Sci Plympiad 84; Pilot.

LAMAR, TIMOOTHY; Park East HS; New York, NY; (Y); Pres Jr Cls; Var Bsbl; Capt Var Bsktbl; JV Sftbl; Var Vllybl; Hon Roll; Math.

LAMAZZA, LONNIE M; Monsignor Farrell HS; Staten Island, NY; (Y); 51/289; Frsh Cls; Im Bsktbl; Im JV Ftbl; Hon Roll; Regnts Schlrshp 86; Baruch Clg; Acct.

LAMB, JAMES; Bayside HS; Whitestone, NY; (Y); Am Leg Boys St; Cmnty Wkr; Office Aide; Political Wkr; Chorus; Madrigals; School Play; Rep Frsh Cls; Var Bowling; Hon Roll; Cty Cncl Stu Svc Hon Citn 83; Chrltt G Msryk Gld Music Awd 83-86; Bnai Brith Outstndng Comm Svc Awd 86; SUNY Albany; Pltcl Sci.

LAMB, LYNETTE; Fabius-Pompey HS; Pompey, NY; (Y); Sec Trs Band; Off Frsh Cls; Sec Soph Cls; Sec Jr Cls; Var Capt Socr; JV Var Sftbl; JV Var Vllybl; High Hon Roll; Hon Roll; NHS; NYSMA Solo & Duet Awds; 2nd Tm All-Str Vlybl All Lge Awd; Nrsng.

LAMBERSON, KEVIN; Cooperstown Central Schl; Cooperstown, NY; (Y); Am Leg Boys St; Boy Scts; Varsity Clb; Concert Band; Rep Sr Cls; Stu Cncl; JV Var Crs Cntry; JV Var Trk; God Cntry Awd; High Hon Roll; Eagle Sct 86; Outward Bound Schlrshp 85; Lake Deleware Boys Camp 80-86; Bus Mgmt.

LAMBERT, ANN; St Barnabas HS; Bronx, NY; (S); 2/188; Library Aide; NFL; Office Aide; Teachers Aide; Yrbk Stf; Twrlr; Hon Roll; Jr NHS; NHS; Spanish NHS; Maria Diona Schlrshp 84-86; Med.

LAMBERT II, DAVID F; Aquinas Inst; Rochester, NY; (Y); Ftbl; Wt Lftg; Hon Roll; Prfct Atten Awd; Comm Art.

LAMBERT, JOHN F; Copperstown Central HS; Cooperstown, NY; (Y); FCA; Letterman Clb; VP Sr Cls; Bsktbl; Golf; Hon Roll.

LAMBERT, LARRY; Saranal Central HS; Morrisonville, NY; (S); 47/105; Wrstlng; Hon Roll; Comp Sci.

LAMBERT, PRISCILLA; Holy Child HS; Scarsdale, NY; (Y); Hosp Aide; Yrbk Stf; Diving; High Hon Roll; Hon Roll; Ntl Merit Schol; Pres Schlrshp 86; Trinity U; Bus.

LAMBERT, THOMAS W; John F Kennedy HS; Yorktown Heights, NY; (Y); 54/218; Am Leg Boys St; Boy Scts; VP JA; Variety Show; Yrbk Stf; JV Crs Cntry; Var L Socr; Im Socr; JV Trk; Hon Roll; Archtctr.

LAMBERTUCCI, SILVIO; Lafayette HS; Brooklyn, NY; (Y); Computer Clb; Exploring; Office Aide; Teachers Aide; Ftbl; Cert Hnr & Mrt Drftng, Eng & Busnss Math 86; Bus.

LAMBOGLOU, TERESA; Port Chester HS; Port Chester, NY; (Y); Hosp Aide; Key Clb; Library Aide; SADD; Yrbk Phtg; Yrbk Stf; Tennis; Hon Roll; Voluntr Svc 50 Hrs Awd; Accntnt.

LAMBRECHT, MELISSA; Walton Central HS; Walton, NY; (Y); Key Clb; Varsity Clb; VP Frsh Cls; JV Var Bsktbl; JV Var Fld Hcky; High Hon Roll; Hon Roll; Delphi Tech; Bus.

LAMBRECHT, SCOTT RICHARD; Vestal SR HS; Apalachin, NY; (Y); Church Yth Grp; Band; Concert Band; Jazz Band; Mrchg Band; Orch; Pep Band; Symp Band; Im Vllybl.

LAMBRECHT, TIMOTHY J; Saratoga Springs SR HS; Saratoga Springs, NY; (Y); 73/491; Boy Scts; Key Clb; Lit Mag; Hon Roll; NHS; Prfct Atten Awd; NY ST Math Leag Fin 86; ST U NY Buffalo; Elec Engrng.

LAMDAN, DAVE; Farmingdale HS; Farmingdale, NY; (Y); Key Clb; Ski Clb; SADD; Var L Ice Hcky; JV Lcrss; Bus Finc.

LAMICA, SHAYNE; Glens Falls HS; Colens Falls, NY; (Y); AFS; Pep Clb; SADD; Chorus; Powder Puff Ftbl; High Hon Roll; Hon Roll; Regents Schlrshp For Nrsng 86; Russel Sage Coll; Nrsng.

LAMKIN, SHARI; Byron-Bergun HS; Byron, NY; (Y); 1/95; Debate Tm; Math Tm; Sec Band; VP Stu Cncl; Var Bsktbl; Var Capt Trk; JP Sousa Awd; Ntl Merit Ltr; Pres Schlr; Val; Chrisopher Hiler Awd Music 85; Ralph & Mina Gillette Mem Schlrp 86; Cornell U; Ind & Labor Rltns.

LAMMERS, JENNIFER; Rocky Point JR SR HS; Rocky Point, NY; (S); #18 In Class; 4-H; VP Girl Scts; Spanish Clb; Chorus; Flag Corp; School Musical; 4-H Awd; Hon Roll; Astro.

LAMONICA, LISA; Frankfort Schyler Central Schl; Frankfort, NY; (S); FBLA; Key Clb; Spanish Clb; SADD; Band; Rep Stu Cncl; Cheerleading; High Hon Roll; NHS; Oswego; Elem Ed.

LAMONT, KATHLEEN; St Edmund HS; Brooklyn, NY; (S); 1/190; Art Clb; JV Bsktbl; Hon Roll; NHS; Spnsh Awd 84; Eng, Art Awds 85; Fordham; Med Tech.

LAMONT, LAURIE A; Shenendehowa HS; Clifton Park, NY; (Y); Key Clb; Office Aide; Teachers Aide; Stage Crew; Cheerleading; High Hon Roll; Prfct Atten Awd; Olympc Natl Typng Cntst 86; Mildred Elley Bus Schl; Ex Secy.

LAMORA, LORI; Saranac Central HS; Redford, NY; (S); 11/129; Spanish Clb; Yrbk Stf; JV Var Bsktbl; Var Capt Socr; JV Var Sftbl; Capt Vllybl; High Hon Roll; NHS; Phy Ed.

LAMOREE, MICHELE; Beacon HS; Beacon, NY; (Y); 50/205; Girl Scts; Key Clb; Spanish Clb; Varsity Clb; Band; Pep Band; Nwsp Rptr; Yrbk Stf; Var Capt Cheerleading; Hon Roll; Girl Scout Silver Awd 85; NYSSMA Solo Comp Blue Mdl Exclnt 84; All Cnty Chorus Slct Group 84; Comm.

LAMORTE, GINA; St Catharine Acad; Ny, NY; (Y); #6 In Class; Church Yth Grp; Dance Clb; Teachers Aide; Y-Teens; Var Twrlr; NHS; Rgnts Chem Awd 86; Rgnts Blgy Awd 85; European Stds 85; Fairleigh Dickinson U; Hygnst.

LAMOS, BARBARA; The Stony Brook Schl; Stony Brook, NY; (Y); Acpl Chr; Yrbk Phtg; Yrbk Sprt Ed; Yrbk Stf; Pres Frsh Cls; Rep Soph Cls; Rep Jr Cls; Rep Sr Cls; Var L Fld Hcky; Var L Trk; Hghtn Coll; Elem Ed.

LAMOTHE, DAPHNE; The Mary Louis Acad; Rosedale, NY; (Y); Sec French Clb; Speech Tm; Orch; Sec Soph Cls; Sec Sr Cls; High Hon Roll; Hon Roll; Pres NHS; Ntl Merit Schol; NEDT Awd; L I Music Tchrs Assn Piano Comp Gold Mdls 84-85; Yale U Scholar 86-87; 1st Hnrs Iona Lang Cont 84-86; Yale U; Law.

LAMPACK, STEPHANIE; Allegany Central HS; Allegany, NY; (S); Drama Clb; Library Aide; Pep Clb; Red Cross Aide; VICA; School Musical; School Play; Yrbk Stf; Var JV Cheerleading; Hon Roll; Airln/Trvl.

LAMPHIER, MARCY; Greenwood HS; Canisteo, NY; (S); 2/23; Science Clb; Varsity Clb; School Play; Trs Frsh Cls; Trs Soph Cls; Trs Jr Cls; Var Bsktbl; Hon Roll; NHS; Cmnty Wkr; 3rd Pl Cnty Spkng Cont 85.

LAMPHIER, TAMMY; Moravia Central HS; Locke, NY; (Y); GAA; Ski Clb; Yrbk Phtg; Yrbk Rptr; Yrbk Sprt Ed; Yrbk Stf; Var Capt Bsktbl; Var Capt Fld Hcky; Var Trk; High Hon Roll; MVP Awd Fld Hcky & Track 85-86; Lttr & Pins High Hnr Rll; Lttr Sweeter For 7 Vrsty Sports 86.

LAMPORT, BRETT; Harley Schl; Fairport, NY; (Y); Jazz Band; JV Tennis; Ltrd Crs-Cntry Skng Tm 84-86; Attnd Eastmn Schl Msc 10 Yrs B Avrg 76-86; Bates Coll; Bio.

LAMURAGLIA, JAMES; Bishop Kearney HS; Webster, NY; (Y); Church Yth Grp; Ski Clb; Band; Concert Band; Drill Tm; Jazz Band; Mrchg Band; Stage Crew; Hon Roll; Potsdam Coll; Physcs.

LANA, WILLIAM; The Anglo-American Schl; New York, NY; (S); Art Clb; Chess Clb; Debate Tm; SADD; Chorus; Nwsp Rptr; Yrbk Stf; Pres Sr Cls; Var Capt Socr; Trk; Economics.

LANARO, MICHON; Washingtonville SR HS; Monroe, NY; (Y); Ski Clb; Band; Concert Band; Jazz Band; Orch; Pep Band; School Musical; Symp Band; Var Crs Cntry; Louis Armstrong Jazz Awd 84; Manhattanville Coll; Poltcl Sci.

LANCE, SUSAN E; Nazareth Acad; Rochester, NY; (Y); 4/157; Latin Clb; Library Aide; Ski Clb; SADD; Sec Band; Jazz Band; School Musical; Nwsp Phtg; NHS; St Schlr; Cook Coll Hnrs Prog 86; NY St Rgnts Schlrshp 86; Ntl Latin Exana-Cum Laude 84; Rutgers U; Bio.

LANCE, THERESA; Catholic Central HS; Troy, NY; (Y); Prfct Atten Awd; Excllnc Advnd Typng 86; Hudson Valley CC; Exec Scrtry.

LANCER, LISA; Hicksville SR HS; Hicksville, NY; (Y); Ski Clb; Spanish Clb; Rep Stu Cncl; Var Capt Cheerleading; Var Tennis; High Hon Roll; Hon Roll; Jr NHS; NHS; Spanish NHS; SUNY Stonybrook; Soclgy.

LANCET, DOUGLAS; Irondequoit HS; Rochester, NY; (Y); 30/370; Boy Scts; Drama Clb; Exploring; Hosp Aide; Intnl Clb; Ski Clb; Spanish Clb; Chorus; Concert Band; Mrchg Band.

LANCETTE, REBECCA; Hudson Falls Central SR HS; Hudson Fls, NY; (Y); 30/217; Church Yth Grp; Spanish Clb; SADD; Yrbk Bus Mgr; Yrbk Stf; Hon Roll; Comptrs.

LANCI, VINCENT; St Marys Boys HS; Roslyn, NY; (Y); Nwsp Stf; Tennis; NHS; Regents Schlrshp 86; Hofstra; Bus Mgmt.

LANDAU, CLAUDIA; Colonie Central HS; Albany, NY; (Y); 9/424; Church Yth Grp; Nwsp Rptr; Sec Stu Cncl; Var Capt Trk; Elks Awd; High Hon Roll; NHS; VFW Awd; Voice Dem Awd; A J Gordon Schlrshp, Gordon Coll 86; Harvard Book Prz 85; AAL All Coll Schlrshp 86; Gordon Coll; Psych.

LANDAU, LISA R; Wellington C Mepham HS; N Bellmore, NY; (Y); 1/360; SADD; Ed Nwsp Stf; Chrmn Jr Cls; Chrmn Sr Cls; Sftbl; Vllybl; Varsity Clb; Pres Schlr; Val; Y-Teens; Regnst Schlrshp 86; Ithaca Clg Schlrshp 86; Parents Without Partnrs Schlrshp 86; Ithaca College; Phys Thrpy.

LANDAU, MELISSA B; Mamaroneck HS; Larchmont, NY; (Y); AFS; Dance Clb; Drama Clb; French Clb; Girl Scts; Math Tm; Political Wkr; Spanish Clb; Teachers Aide; Temple Yth Grp; Soc Studs NY :St Cncl 83; Art Mrt Awd 83; Intl Law.

LANDAU, VANESSA; West Hempstead HS; North Hills, NY; (Y); 13/335; Drama Clb; Orch; School Musical; Variety Show; Nwsp Rptr; Lit Mag; High Hon Roll; Jr NHS; NHS; Ntl Merit Ltr; Deans List 85-86; Regents Scholar 86; Hebrew High Scholar 81; U PA.

LANDEO, EVA; Eastchester HS; Eastchester, NY; (Y); Dance Clb; French Clb; Spanish Clb; SADD; School Musical; Socr; NHS; Drama Clb; Key Clb; Latin Clb; Natl Latn Exm-Magna Cm Laud-Latn I 84; Iona Cntst-Frnch-1st Hnrs 86; Mdcn.

LANDERS, KELLY; Auburn HS; Auburn, NY; (Y); Ski Clb; Band; Chorus; Color Guard; Drm Mjr(t); Flag Corp; Mrchg Band; School Musical; School Play; Sftbl.

LANDERS, KIM; Royalton-Hartland HS; Gasport, NY; (Y); 66/130; VICA; JV Var Sftbl; Hon Roll; Prfct Atten Awd; Outstndng Stu Cosmetlgy 86; Rotary Awd Cosmetlgy 86; Cosmetlgst.

LANDERS, TRICIA; Churchville-Chili HS; Rochester, NY; (Y); Model UN; Acpl Chr; Orch; Yrbk Bus Mgr; Lit Mag; Sec Sr Cls; Sec Stu Cncl; Sftbl; Swmmng; Hon Roll; Child Psych.

LANDESS, BRAD; Marcus Whitman HS; Gorham, NY; (Y); Am Leg Boys St; Varsity Clb; Band; Concert Band; Drill Tm; Jazz Band; Mrchg Band; Pep Band; Yrbk Ed-Chief; Yrbk Phtg; John Phillip Sousa Awd 87; Oswego; Bus.

LANDMAN, GERI; Half Hollow Hills West HS; Dix Hills, NY; (Y); Camera Clb; Church Yth Grp; Dance Clb; Debate Tm; Q&S; Temple Yth Grp; Chorus; Stage Crew; Nwsp Stf; Yrbk Stf.

LANDMAN, KAREN E; Vestal SR HS; Vestal, NY; (Y); 29/430; Ski Clb; Temple Yth Grp; Frsh Cls; Soph Cls; Jr Cls; Sr Cls; Stu Cncl; Var Cheerleading; High Hon Roll; Hon Roll; NYSSMA Awd 83-85; Cornell.

LANDMAN, RITA; Vestal Central HS; Vestal, NY; (Y); Pres French Clb; German Clb; SADD; Temple Yth Grp; Varsity Clb; Rep Soph Cls; Rep Stu Cncl; Var Capt Tennis; Var Capt Vllybl; High Hon Roll; Natl Yth Ldrshp Salute To Youth 85-86; Sci.

LANDOLFI, LISA; Preston HS; Bronx, NY; (S); Camera Clb; Trs Frsh Cls; Sec Soph Cls; Sec Jr Cls; Var Bsktbl; Hon Roll; Jr NHS; NHS; Fordham U.

LANDON, VICKIE; Heidelbert American HS; Apo New York, NY; (Y); 27/135; Church Yth Grp; German Clb; Library Aide; Pep Clb; Teachers Aide; Ftbl; JV Mgr(s); Stat Trk; Stat Wrstlng; U Of MD Munich; Psych.

LANDRIGAN, MARY; Rye Country Day Schl; Mamaroneck, NY; (Y); Aud/Vis; Cmnty Wkr; Drama Clb; Hosp Aide; Chorus; Madrigals; School Play; Stage Crew; Yrbk Ed-Chief; Yrbk Stf; Ntl Merit Fnlst 86; Hrvrd Bk Awd 85; Schlrshp-Smmt Cntry Day-Cncnnti OH 82; Haverford Coll; Bio.

LANDRIO, VALERIE; Notre Dame Bishop Gibbons HS; Delanson, NY; (S); 5/89; Art Clb; Var Tennis; High Hon Roll; NHS; Ntl Merit Ltr; Peer Ldrshp Awd 84-85; NDBG Athl Awd 84-85; William & Mary; Law.

LANDRY, TAMARA; Franklin Acad; Malone, NY; (Y); 8/266; 4-H; French Clb; Hosp Aide; Trs Intnl Clb; Math Tm; Model UN; VP Pep Clb; Varsity Clb; Nwsp Stf; Yrbk Stf; Alcoa Ftdn Schlrshp 86; Oswego ST U; Phy Thrpy.

LANDSTROM, SCOTT; Tottenville HS; Staten Island, NY; (Y); Boy Scts; Chess Clb; School Play; Nwsp Ed-Chief; Rep Frsh Cls; Var Crs Cntry; Capt Trk; Pres Magic Clb 86-87; Capt Fncng Tm 86-87; Soc Dstngshd Amrcn HS Stu 86; Wagner Coll; Astrophyscs.

LANE, ALICE; Sacred Heart Acad; Floral Park, NY; (Y); Art Clb; Church Yth Grp; Cmnty Wkr; FBLA; Intnl Clb; Pep Clb; SADD; Hon Roll; Lion Awd; NHS; Bus.

LANE, DINA; Peru Central HS; Schuyler Falls, NY; (Y); Model UN; Band; Chorus; Mrchg Band; School Musical; Yrbk Stf; Rep Jr Cls; Stu Cncl; High Hon Roll; Hon Roll; Plattsburgh SUNY; Math Educ.

LANE, DOUGLAS; St Patricks Central Catholic HS; Catskill, NY; (S); 2/25; Drama Clb; Nwsp Rptr; Yrbk Stf; L Score Keeper; DAR Awd; Jr NHS; Trs NHS; Ntl Merit Ltr; Elks Clb Tngr Of Yr 86; NY ST Bnghmtn; Jrnlsm.

LANE, KARA; Cicero-North Syracuse HS; Clay, NY; (S); 12/638; Camera Clb; Key Clb; Color Guard; Drill Tm; Powder Puff Ftbl; Score Keeper; Swmmng; Twrlr; Hon Roll; Jr NHS; Natl Hstry Awd 86; Boston U.

LANE, RANDALL A; Briarcliff Manor HS; Pleasantville, NY; (Y); Mathletes; Political Wkr; JV Capt Ski Clb; Nwsp Ed-Chief; Lit Mag; Var L Trk; Hon Roll; VP NHS; NY ST Fnlst Olympics Mind 85; Schl Nom Cntry III Ldrshp Schlrshp Compttn 85; U Of PA; Poltcl Sci.

LANE, ROBIN; Hoosick Falls Central HS; Hoosick Falls, NY; (Y); 15/102; Drama Clb; French Clb; Band; School Play; Cheerleading; High Hon Roll; NHS; U Of SC; Acctg.

LANE, SUSAN; Ward Melville HS; E Setauket, NY; (Y); 62/711; Dance Clb; Drama Clb; French Clb; Chorus; Church Choir; Nwsp Stf; Rep Soph Cls; High Hon Roll; Hon Roll; NHS; Barnard Coll; Archtctr.

LANFAIR, JEFFREY; S New Berlin Cntrl Schl; Norwich, NY; (Y); 6/39; VICA; Off Stu Cncl; High Hon Roll; Hon Roll; NHS; Pres Acdmc Fit Awd 86.

LANFEAR, MONICA; Fort Ann Central Schl; Comstock, NY; (Y); 11/52; Drama Clb; Office Aide; SADD; VICA; School Play; Yrbk Stf; Sftbl; High Hon Roll; Hon Roll; NHS; Mst Outstndng Clb Mem 85-86; VICA Schlrshp 86; Natl VICA Delg Phoenix AZ 86; Cosmetogy.

LANG, BRIAN L; Honeoye Central HS; Honeoye, NY; (Y); Ski Clb; Socr; Regents Schlrshp 86; Alfred ST Clg; Engrng Sci.

LANG, CHRISTINE; Frontier Central HS; Hamburg, NY; (S); 59/449; Drama Clb; Math Clb; Red Cross Aide; Ski Clb; Thesps; Chorus; School Musical; Stage Crew; Yrbk Stf; Mgr(s); NEDT Achvt Awd; Worker Of Yr Awd Town Yth Emplymnt 85; Fredonia Coll; Secndry Ed.

LANG, CHRISTINE; Holy Trinity HS; E Meadow, NY; (S); 4/313; Math Clb; Math Tm; High Hon Roll; NHS; Ntl Merit Ltr; Med.

LANG, CHRISTOPHER; Ward Melville HS; Stony Brook, NY; (Y); Red Cross Aide; Ski Clb; JV Var Bsbl; JV Socr; Var L Swmmng; JV Wrstlng; Hon Roll; Meteorlgst.

LANG, CINDY; Frontier Central HS; Blasdell, NY; (Y); Pep Clb; VICA; Yrbk Stf; Im Vllybl; Data Procssng.

LANG, DEBBIE; Long Island Lutheran HS; Amityville, NY; (S); 1/95; Church Yth Grp; Quiz Bowl; Chorus; Church Choir; School Musical; JV Cheerleading; High Hon Roll; NHS; Mth.

LANG, JENNIFER; Mount Mercy Acad; Buffalo, NY; (Y); Camp Fr Inc; Cmnty Wkr; Latin Clb; Model UN; SADD; Nwsp Stf; Lit Mag; Hon Roll; Med.

LANG, JULIE; Byron Bergen Central HS; Batavia, NY; (Y); 15/100; FTA; Hosp Aide; Chorus; Trk; Hon Roll; Regnts Schlrshp 86; Genesee CC; RN.

LANG, LISA A; Amsterdam HS; Amsterdam, NY; (Y); 16/316; Cmnty Wkr; Hosp Aide; Yrbk Stf; High Hon Roll; Hon Roll; NHS; Prfct Atten Awd; Biomed Engrng.

LANG, RICH; Valley Stream N HS; Franklin Sq, NY; (Y); Cmnty Wkr; Computer Clb; SADD; Yrbk Stf; Var L Bsbl; Var Crs Cntry; Mst Vlbl Plyr Awd Vrsty Bsbl 86; Comp Sci.

LANG, STEPHEN; Holy Trinity HS; East Meadow, NY; (S); 26/404; Math Clb; Math Tm; Bsbl; Actg.

LANG, VALERIE; Honeoye Central Schl; Honeoye, NY; (S); 1/86; VP 4-H; Ski Clb; Capt Color Guard; Lib Concert Band; Jazz Band; Pep Band; 4-H Awd; High Hon Roll; Rep Frsh Cls; Rep Soph Cls; Cornell U; Vet Med.

LANGAN, DAN; Farmingdale HS; N Mass, NY; (Y); 31/650; Ftbl; Capt Gym; Trk; NHS; March Of Dimes Schlrshp 86; Kiwanettes Schlrshp 86; Buffalo U; Aerosp Engr.

LANGDON, PAUL; Franklin Acad; Malone, NY; (Y); Ski Clb; Chorus; Ftbl; Golf; Paul Smiths; Htl Mgmt.

LANGE, ANDREA; John Jay SR HS; Katonah, NY; (Y); Intnl Clb; Ski Clb; Yrbk Phtg; Yrbk Stf; Lit Mag; JV Var Socr; Cit Awd; High Hon Roll; Hon Roll; NHS; Excllnc Drawng-Paintng 85; Futr Artsts 86; Acadmc Al-Amer/Natl Scndry Educ Cncl 86; Fine Art.

LANGE, ANDREW; Kenmore West SR HS; Kenmore, NY; (Y); 25/550; Band; Jazz Band; Orch; School Musical; Variety Show; Im Socr; High Hon Roll; Hon Roll; NHS; Awd Band 86; SUNY Buffalo.

LANGE, JOAN L; St Francis Prep; Douglaston, NY; (S); 45/750; Cmnty Wkr; JV Math Tm; Concert Band; Mrchg Band; NHS; Spanish NHS; Retreat Ldr; Optimate Soc; Prncpls List; SUNY Binghamton; Med Rsrch.

LANGE, LEANNE; Grand Island HS; Grand Island, NY; (Y); 75/300; Church Yth Grp; Teachers Aide; Chorus; School Musical; Stage Crew; Variety Show; Nwsp Stf; Var Cheerleading; Var Pom Pon; Hon Roll; Geneseo Coll; Bio.

LANGE, LINDA; Uniondale HS; Uniondale, NY; (Y); Gym; Swmmng; Vllybl; MI U; Srgry.

LANGE, MICHELLE; Smithtown High School East; St James, NY; (Y); DECA; German Clb; Hosp Aide; Symp Band; Tennis; High Hon Roll; Hon Roll; NHS; German Hnr Soc Treas-VP 84; Schl Kickline Indianettes 86-87; NYSSMA Awd 83-85.

LANGER, LORI J; Oceanside HS; Oceanside, NY; (Y); #15 In Class; Art Clb; Aud/Vis; Camera Clb; Cmnty Wkr; English Clb; French Clb; German Clb; Key Clb; Math Tm; PAVAS; Stu Of Yr Awd 83; Spnsh Awd 83-86; Frgn Lang Awd 86; Queens; Frgn Lang.

LANGEVINE, MICHELLE; Prospect Heights HS; Brooklyn, NY; (S); #12 In Class; Dance Clb; Debate Tm; FBLA; Hon Roll; NHS; Merit For Engl & Phy Ed 85; Awd Sci 86; Syracuse U; Lwyr.

LANGFORD, ADAM; Salem Central HS; Salem, NY; (Y); Am Leg Boys St; Var Bsbl; Var Bsktbl; Elks Awd; Hon Roll; Gilchrest Memrl Awd 86; Adirondack Cmnty Coll; Accntnt.

LANGFORD, CATHERINE E; Marcellus HS; Marcellus, NY; (Y); 6/178; Exploring; Red Cross Aide; Chorus; Yrbk Bus Mgr; Sec Frsh Cls; VP Soph Cls; Rep Sr Cls; VP Stu Cncl; NHS; Regents Schlrshp P86; Schlrshp Pgm 85; Dickinson Coll; Eng.

LANGLEY, JODY; Romulus Central Schl; Romulus, NY; (Y); 4/34; Pres Spanish Clb; SADD; Chorus; Capt Color Guard; Mrchg Band; School Musical; School Play; Variety Show; Yrbk Stf; Sec Jr Cls; Regents Schlrshp 86; Romulus Facity Assn Schlrshp 86; Romulus Comm Sport Schlrshp 86; SUNY Albany; Psych.

LANGLIE, HEATHER M; Johnson City HS; Binghamton, NY; (Y); 5/198; Mathletes; Concert Band; Mrchg Band; Yrbk Ed-Chief; Var Cheerleading; High Hon Roll; NHS; French Clb; Key Clb; Pep Clb; NY ST Rgnts Schlrshp 86; Acad Excllnc Awds 83-86; Yth Slt Pgm Awd 85; ST U Of NY-BNGHMTN; Comp.

LANGLOIS, CAROLYN; Greece Athena HS; Rochester, NY; (Y); 45/307; Church Yth Grp; Cmnty Wkr; DECA; Trs JA; Pep Clb; Ski Clb; Church Choir; Concert Band; School Play; Hon Roll; Mst Imprvd Plyr Awd Chrldng 84; Arch.

LANGNER, MIRIAM; John Jay HS; Wappingers Falls, NY; (Y); 80/519; Drama Clb; German Clb; Hosp Aide; Spanish Clb; Orch; Symp Band; Nwsp Stf; Im Vllybl; High Hon Roll; NHS; Phys Ed Tchrs Awd; Pace U; Child Care.

LANGOLIS, SANDRA; Chateaugay Central HS; Burke, NY; (Y); Band; Chorus; Jazz Band; Orch; School Musical; Trs Frsh Cls; VP Soph Cls; Var L Socr; Var L Sftbl; NHS; 1st Art 85-86; Stdnt Mnth 85; 2nd Spch 84-85; Postam U Crane; Music Ed.

LANGONE, SUSAN; Roslyn HS; Roslyn Hts, NY; (Y); Art Clb; Dance Clb; Drama Clb; SADD; Variety Show; Yrbk Stf; Badmtn; Cheerleading; Art.

LANGOWSKI III, JOHN F; James I O Neill HS; West Point, NY; (Y); Boy Scts; Church Yth Grp; Computer Clb; Nwsp Stf; Yrbk Stf; Var Ftbl; Var Capt Trk; Hon Roll; NHS; 4 Yr Army ROTC Schlrshp; Pres Acdmc Fit Awd; NYS Regents Diploma; Norwich U; Cvl Engrng.

LANGOWSKI, PAMELA A; Mount Mercy Acad; Buffalo, NY; (Y); 25/200; Cmnty Wkr; Computer Clb; JCL; Latin Clb; Mathletes; Chorus; Yrbk Rptr; Lit Mag; Rep Frsh Cls; Rep Soph Cls; Anne Cottrell Schlrshp Mt Mercy Acad 83; 2nd Pl WNY Lang Fair 85; 1st Pl Natl Math Intellitest 84.

LANGSAM, ARIANN; Walt Whitman HS; Huntington Stat, NY; (Y); 4/470; Aud/Vis; Computer Clb; German Clb; Hosp Aide; Key Clb; Mathletes; Pep Clb; Nwsp Stf; Yrbk Phtg; Ed Lit Mag; Navy Sci Awd 84; Brwn U Bk Awd 86; Physcn.

LANGSAM, LILI; Burnt Hills-Ballston Lake HS; Schenectady, NY; (Y); Art Clb; Ski Clb; Cheerleading; Socr; Sftbl; Trk; Hon Roll.

LANGSTAFF, RENEE; Ogdensburg Free Acad; Ogdensburg, NY; (Y); 6/186; Band; VP Stu Cncl; Capt Bsktbl; Capt Swmmng; Trk; CC Awd; Hon Roll; VP NHS; Acdmc All Ntrhn Bsktbl 85-86; All NAC 1st Team Swmng 84 & 85; MVP Swmng 83-85; Ithaca Coll; Physcl Thrpy.

LANGTON, MELANIE; De Sales Catholic HS; Lockport, NY; (Y); 11/33; Varsity Clb; Bsktbl; Cheerleading; Pom Pon; Hon Roll; NHS; Dr Fritz Ms Mem Schlrshp 84; Bth Knyn Mem Schlrshp 85; Jhn Msklk Mem Schlrshp 86; Elem Ed.

LANIER, ROBERT; Beacon HS; Beacon, NY; (Y); 50/250; Boy Scts; Church Yth Grp; Key Clb; Band; Rep Frsh Cls; Rep Soph Cls; Sec Sr Cls; JV Im Bsbl; Var Cheerleading; Var Socr; Beacon Tenns Trnmnt Champ 85; Allegheny Coll; Psych.

LANN, VANESSA; Mamaroneck HS; Mamaroneck, NY; (Y); 1/416; Pres French Clb; Math Tm; School Play; Nwsp Ed-Chief; Nwsp Rptr; French Hon Soc; High Hon Roll; Pres NHS; Ntl Merit Schol; Val; Natl Guild Music Teachers Young Composers Awd 86; Westchester Cncl Engl Chrprsns Poetry Awd 85; Harvard U; Musician.

LANNI, KYM; Greece Athena HS; Rochester, NY; (Y); 72/304; DECA; Math Clb; JV Var Cheerleading; Stat Ftbl; JV Pom Pon; Hon Roll; Italian Club; Bus Admin.

LANNING, CATHIE LYNN; Oxford Academy And Central Schl; Oxford, NY; (Y); 11/86; French Clb; Pep Clb; Red Cross Aide; SADD; Varsity Clb; Band; Chorus; Concert Band; Jazz Band; Mrchg Band; Keuka Coll Schlrshp Grant 86; Fire Dept Schlrshp 86; Firemens Assc Schlrshp 86; Hlth Careers Awd 86; Keuka Coll; Occptnl Thrpst.

LANNING, MICHAEL; Odessa-Mantour Central Schl; Alpine, NY; (Y); Am Leg Boys St; Ski Clb; Concert Band; Mrchg Band; Orch; Yrbk Ed-Chief; Yrbk Rptr; Tennis; High Hon Roll; NHS; Sec IV, Cls C Tnns Sngls Chmpn 86; Stu Yr Awd 82-83; Phy Ed.

LANOUE, J R; Hoosick Falls Central HS; Bennington, VT; (Y); Cmnty Wkr; Exploring; FBLA; SADD; Chorus; School Play; Rep Jr Cls; Capt Bsktbl; Vllybl; Cit Awd; Schlstc Merit Awd 86; Tm Mngmnt.

LANPHEAR, MICHELLE; Dundee Central Schl; Dundee, NY; (Y); VP Band; VP Concert Band; Rep Jazz Band; Rep Pep Band; Var L Socr; JV Var Sftbl; JV Var Vllybl; High Hon Roll; Hon Roll; Prfct Atten Awd; DTA Awd Hghst Achvt Band 82; DTA Awd Hghst Achvt SR Band 84-85; Musicn.

LANSKY, ERIC; Hafl Hollow Hills HS East; Dix Hills, NY; (Y); Debate Tm; FBLA; SADD; Varsity Clb; Stu Cncl; JV Socr; Var JV Tennis; Jr NHS; NHS; High Hon Roll; 1st Pl Foreign Culinary Arts Fest; Intrnshp Pgm Financial Anlyst; Financial Anlyst.

LANTHIER, DARCY; Tupper Lake HS; Tupper Lk, NY; (Y); 9/99; Pep Clb; JV Var Bsktbl; Var Capt Socr; Hon Roll; Frgn Lang.

LANTZ, JACQUELINE ANN; Lincoln HS; Yonkers, NY; (Y); 20/350; Drama Clb; School Play; Stage Crew; Nwsp Stf; Lit Mag; Pres Soph Cls; JV Ftbl; High Hon Roll; Voice Dem Awd; Hon Roll; Vlntr Wrk At St Peter & Paul Schl 84-85; Cable Tv Rep For YNR 84-86; Yonkers Mdl Legsltr For Cnty 86; Playwrite.

LANZIONE, LUCIANNE; Thousand Islands HS; Clayton, NY; (Y); Band; Concert Band; Mrchg Band; School Play; Sec Jr Cls; Hon Roll; Jffrsn Cmmnty Coll; Htl Mgmnt.

LANZISERA, DOMINICK; Locust Valley HS; Bayville, NY; (Y); 2/203; Boys Clb Am; Service Clb; Nwsp Ed-Chief; Var Bsktbl; Elks Awd; High Hon Roll; Sec NHS; Ntl Merit Schol; Sal; Harvard Prz Bk 85; Amherst Coll; Psych.

LANZISERA, JOSEPH; Roy C Ketcham HS; Poughkeepsie, NY; (Y); 16/500; Cmnty Wkr; Math Clb; Political Wkr; VP SADD; Cit Awd; High Hon Roll; Hon Roll; Jr NHS; NHS; Pres Schlr; Marist Coll $3000 Schlrshp 86-90; Marist Coll; Comp Sci.

LAO, CHRIS; Riverhead HS; Aquebogue, NY; (Y); 4/250; French Clb; Ski Clb; Band; Jazz Band; Mrchg Band; JV VP Socr; VP Capt Tennis; NHS.

LAO, DANIRA; Our Lady Of Perpetual Help; Brooklyn, NY; (Y); 36/155; Cmnty Wkr; Drama Clb; English Clb; Hosp Aide; School Musical; School Play; Variety Show; Hon Roll; Pres Schlr; St Schlr; Regents Schlrshp Wnnr 85-86; SR Mary Immaculate Awd Stu Shw Grt Lov Litr 85-86; Aspira Certf Mert 86; Brooklyn Coll; Pre Med.

LAOUTARIS, KATHY; Mt Vernon HS; Mt Vernon, NY; (Y); Boys Clb Am; Church Yth Grp; Cmnty Wkr; Dance Clb; FBLA; Intnl Clb; Math Clb; Science Clb; Teachers Aide; Badmtn; Cert Prfcncy Cntry 21 Accntng 85-86; NYU; Med.

LAPAGE, JUDY; Franklin Acad; N Bangor, NY; (Y); Varsity Clb; Var Capt Bsktbl; Var Socr; JV Var Sftbl; JV Var Vllybl; Hon Roll; Spnsh Awd For Full Yr 100 Avg 85.

LAPE JR, ROBERT E; Walter Panas HS; Peekskill, NY; (Y); Church Yth Grp; Band; Chorus; Concert Band; Jazz Band; Mrchg Band; School Musical; Stage Crew; NHS; SUNY; Music Ed.

LAPHAM, AMY; Lansingburgh HS; Troy, NY; (Y); Drama Clb; Hosp Aide; Sec Key Clb; Political Wkr; Varsity Clb; Chorus; School Musical; High Hon Roll; Hon Roll; NHS; Schenectady CC; Paralegal.

LAPINSKI, ANDREA; Warwick Valley HS; Warwick, NY; (Y); Cmnty Wkr; Computer Clb; Yrbk Stf; Var Cheerleading; Var Powder Puff Ftbl; JV Score Keeper; High Hon Roll; Hon Roll; Bus.

LAPINTA, JACK; Archbishop Molloy HS; S Ozone Pk, NY; (Y); 8/383; Ed Yrbk Stf; NHS.

LAPOINTE, GARY; Mineola HS; Mineola, NY; (Y); Computer Clb; Pres 4-H; Key Clb; SADD; Var Bowling; Var Ftbl; Im Wt Lftg; Var Wrstlng; Springfield Coll; Aeronautics.

LAPORTE, MICHELLE; Herkimer HS; Herkimer, NY; (Y); 31/103; Drama Clb; Hosp Aide; Pep Clb; Q&S; Spanish Clb; Chorus; School Musical; School Play; Stage Crew; Swing Chorus; Gainsville Coll; Pre-Law.

LAPP, JEFFREY A; Mohawk Central HS; Mohawk, NY; (Y); 13/105; Concert Band; Mrchg Band; Hon Roll; Jr NHS; Engr Cvl.

LAPP, WENDY; Our Lady Of Mercy HS; Rochester, NY; (Y); Church Yth Grp; Office Aide; SADD; Chorus; Church Choir; Swing Chorus; Hon Roll; Comp.

LAPPANO, KRISTIN; Cicero-North Syracuse HS; N Syracuse, NY; (S); 42/623; Ski Clb; Band; Concert Band; Mrchg Band; Symp Band; Librl Arts.

LARACUENTE, DIANA; Park West HS HS; New York, NY; (Y); Hon Roll; Math & Spnsh Awd 85; Scl Wrk.

LARAGY, MOLLY; Bishop Kearney HS; Rochester, NY; (Y); 6/140; NFL; Co-Capt Speech Tm; Band; School Musical; School Play; Nwsp Rptr; NHS; Ntl Merit Ltr; St Bonaventure U; Mass Comm.

LARAIA, BO; Byram Hills HS; Armonk, NY; (Y); Chess Clb; Cmnty Wkr; Computer Clb; JA; Office Aide; Science Clb; Teachers Aide; Temple Yth Grp; JA Vice Pres Mktg 85-86; Bus.

LARAIA, MICHAEL; Bethpage HS; Bethpage, NY; (Y); 60/300; Am Leg Boys St; Boy Scts; Pres Spanish Clb; SADD; Varsity Clb; Nwsp Sprt Ed; Pres Stu Cncl; Var Lcrss; Var Capt Socr; Var Swmmng; Lwr NY Sst & Lng Islnd Drvng Encllnc Chmpn 86; Pl 2nd NY ST Dvng Chmpshp 86; Pres Stu Snt 85-86; St Johns U.

LARAMIE, MARK; Northeastern Clinton Central HS; Champlain, NY; (Y); 35/153; Cmnty Wkr; Model UN; Ski Clb; JV Var Bsktbl; Var Golf; Var Capt Socr; Hon Roll; St Schlr; NYS Rgnts Schlrshp 86; Chmpln Wmns Bus Assoc Awd 86; Clarkson U; Engrng.

LARATONDA, DARREN; Maryvale HS; Cheektowaga, NY; (Y); JV Ftbl; Var Trk; Hon Roll; U Buffalo; Bus Admn.

LARAWAY, WESLEY D; Middleburgh Central HS; Middleburgh, NY; (Y); 8/74; Am Leg Boys St; VP Band; Pres Chorus; Capt School Musical; School Play; Swing Chorus; Pres Stu Cncl; High Hon Roll; Prfct Atten Awd; Rotary Awd; Ntl Schl Choral Awd 86; Timothy Murphy Amer Legion 248 Schl Awd 86; Elks Schlrie Co-Tnager Of Yrr 86; Oneonta; Educ.

LARGE, PATRICIA; Grace Dodge Voc HS; Bronx, NY; (Y); AFS; Church Yth Grp; Cmnty Wkr; Dance Clb; FHA; Science Clb; Service Clb; Teachers Aide; Band; Chorus; Comp Prcssng.

LARGIE, ANTHONY; Uniondale HS; Uniondale, NY; (Y); FBLA; Office Aide; Stu Cncl; Wrstlng; CW Post Coll; Wrd Prcssng.

LARGO, SUZANNE; Sacred Heart Acad; Lynbrook, NY; (S); Cmnty Wkr; Office Aide; Acpl Chr; Chorus; Church Choir; Hon Roll; NHS.

LARISH, SUSAN; Fairport HS; Fairport, NY; (Y); Pres Drama Clb; Hosp Aide; Math Tm; Model UN; Yrbk Phtg; Lit Mag; Rep Stu Cncl; Camera Clb; Church Yth Grp; Debate Tm; Joyce Crandall Awd Outstndg Dramatic Perf; Pres & Chmn Intl Comm Rotary Awds Clb; Ltr Stdnt Activities; Harvard; Intl Bus.

LARIVIERE, SUSAN; Fayetteville-Manlius SR HS; Chittenango, NY; (Y); JCL; Red Cross Aide; Concert Band; Flag Corp; High Hon Roll; Hon Roll; Cert Of Achvt-Acadmc Excllnc-Latin 85-86; Cum Honore-Latin 86; Radiology.

LARKIN, AMY; Shenendehowa HS; Clifton Park, NY; (Y); Chrmn Key Clb; Chorus; Drill Tm; Variety Show; High Hon Roll; Hon Roll; Trvl Agent.

LARKIN, COLLEEN; Holy Trinity Diocesan HS; Bellmore, NY; (S); Church Yth Grp; Mathletes; Math Clb; Math Tm; Spanish Clb; Sec Soph Cls; Stu Cncl; Var Capt Bsktbl; JV Var Vllybl; U Scranton; Acctng.

LARKIN, JAMES; Lansingburgh HS; Troy, NY; (S); 10/185; Math Tm; Varsity Clb; Var Crs Cntry; JV Socr; Var Trk; High Hon Roll; Jr NHS; NHS.

LARKIN, MARY M; Mechanicville HS; Mechanicville, NY; (S); 17/100; Ski Clb; Band; Mrchg Band; Nwsp Rptr; Yrbk Stf; Var Cheerleading; Hon Roll; Omega Hnr Soc 84-85; Alpha Hnr Soc 85-86; Med.

LARKIN JR, ROBERT M; Greene Central HS; Greene, NY; (Y); 38/112; Pres Varsity Clb; Band; Sec Frsh Cls; VP Sr Cls; Stu Cncl; JV Var Bsbl; Var L Bsktbl; Var Capt Socr; Hon Roll; Regnts Schlrshp 86; Siena Clg; Acctg.

LARMOND, PAULETTE; Evander Childs HS; Bronx, NY; (S); Church Yth Grp; English Clb; Office Aide; Acpl Chr; Chorus; Church Choir; Swmmng; Cit Awd; Hon Roll; Jr NHS; Big E Club 85; Yale U; Med.

LARMONDRA, JAMIE; G Bay Bodley HS; Fulton, NY; (Y); VP Latin Clb; Y-Teens; Pres Frsh Cls; Rep Stu Cncl; Stat Bsbl; JV Var Socr; High Hon Roll; Hon Roll.

LARMONDRA, LISA; Haverling Central HS; Bath, NY; (Y); 23/136; Off Church Yth Grp; French Clb; Math Clb; Ski Clb; Church Choir; School Musical; Yrbk Rptr; Yrbk Stf; Lit Mag; Stu Cncl; JR Prom Royalty 86; Acctng.

LARRABEE, WILLIAM; Mynderse Acad; Seneca Falls, NY; (Y); 29/160; French Clb; Var L Bsbl; JV Bsktbl; Var Golf; High Hon Roll; Hon Roll; NHS; JR Rotarian 86; JR Prom Boys Court 86; Math.

LARRAGUIBEL, JENNIFER; Ardsley HS; Ardsley, NY; (Y); Key Clb; Library Aide; Model UN; Orch; Lit Mag; Socr; Hon Roll; Natl Hispanic Schlr Awd 85-86.

LARRIUZ, RUTH; A E Stevenson HS; Bronx, NY; (Y); 1/34; JA; Library Aide; High Hon Roll; Hon Roll; Prfct Atten Awd; Achievement League 86; Cert Of Merit 85; Minority Busioness Enterprise Project Cert 86; Veterinarian.

LARSEN, ANN; Susan E Wagner HS; Staten Island, NY; (Y); Church Yth Grp; Intnl Clb; JA; Concert Band; Drill Tm; Variety Show; Ed Yrbk Stf; Hon Roll; Jr NHS; Sec NHS; Comp Engrng.

LARSEN, MICHAEL; Westbury Senikor HS; Westbury, NY; (Y); 11/250; Boy Scts; French Clb; Letterman Clb; Science Clb; Band; Jazz Band; Orch; Yrbk Stf; L Var Bsbl; L Var Tennis; 1st Pl In Annl Sci Fair 84; Med.

LARSON, ELIZABETH ANNE; Fairport HS; Fairport, NY; (Y); 1/584; Church Yth Grp; Lib Concert Band; Orch; Ed Lit Mag; JP Sousa Awd; Ntl Merit Schol; Val; Math Tm; Jazz Band; Mrchg Band; Dplma Hnrs Flute 86; 1st Chr Flute All-NYS Conf Wind Ensmbl 85; 2 Tm All-Mnroe Cnty Tm NYS Math Mt; Princeton U; Engr.

LARSON, KAREN; Maple Hill HS; Castleton, NY; (S); 3/80; Aud/Vis; VP Exploring; Pres Key Clb; Stage Crew; JV Fld Hcky; High Hon Roll; Hon Roll; Sci.

LARSON, KERSTIN; Frewsburg Central Scvhl; Frewsburg, NY; (Y); 23/69; Church Yth Grp; Spanish Clb; Chorus; Church Choir; School Musical; Nwsp Stf; Trs Soph Cls; JV Bsktbl; JV Sftbl; JV Vllybl; Houghton Coll; Music Thrpst.

LARSON, KIMBERLY A; Jamestown HS; Jamestown, NY; (Y); 15/396; Ski Clb; Spanish Clb; Chorus; Color Guard; Mrchg Band; Trs Frsh Cls; Rep Stu Cncl; Tennis; Hon Roll; NHS; Jmstwn CC; Cmnctns.

LARSON, MICHELLE; Ralph R Mc Kee Vo Tech; Staten Island, NY; (Y); 52/202; Yrbk Ed-Chief; Ed Lit Mag; Hon Roll; Library Aide; Teachers Aide; Triple C Awd, Richard Welling Cert, NYC Schlstc Press Assoc Jrnlsm B'nai B'rith Citation 86; NY Inst Tech; Arch Tech.

LARSON, TIMOTHY; John A Coleman HS; Ulster Park, NY; (Y); 28/95; Pres Am Leg Boys St; 4-H; Key Clb; JV Var Bsbl; Var Capt Crs Cntry; Var Capt Socr; Hon Roll; Prfct Atten Awd; Computer Clb; Ski Clb; Natl Sci Olympd Chem 86; Pres Pro Temp 86; Engrg.

LASALLE, CHRIS; Johnstown HS; Johnstown, NY; (Y); Var L Bsbl; Var L Bsktbl; Im Ftbl; JV Golf; Hon Roll; Bus.

LASALLE, HECTOR D; Brentwood High Ross Center; Bay Shore, NY; (Y); 35/500; Band; Concert Band; Jazz Band; Mrchg Band; Symp Band; Nwsp Rptr; Yrbk Rptr; Off Sr Cls; Hon Roll; Brnz Mdl Outstndng Soph Musc 84; Regnts Schlrshp Wnnr 86; PA ST U; Polticl Sci.

LASANTA, CHRISTEL; Frontier Central HS; Blasdell, NY; (Y); DECA; 4-H; French Clb; Trs FFA; ECC; Bookkpng.

LASHER, JAMES L; St Johnsville Central HS; Fort Plain, NY; (Y); 5/26; Am Leg Boys St; Trs Yrbk Stf; Trs Frsh Cls; Trs Soph Cls; Trs Jr Cls; Trs Sr Cls; Mgr Bsktbl; Prsdntl Acdmc Ftnss Awd 86; Rochestr Inst Of Tech; Comp Sci.

LASHER, JO ANN; Dover JR SR HS; Dover Plains, NY; (S); Ski Clb; Yrbk Stf; Mgr(s); JV Sftbl; High Hon Roll; NHS.

LASHER, MARIE; Dolgeville Central HS; Dolgeville, NY; (S); Art Clb; Office Aide; SADD; Teachers Aide; Church Choir; Color Guard; Yrbk Stf; Hon Roll; Jr NHS; Church Yth Grp; Utica Coll Of Syracuse U.

LASHOMB, JEFFREY WAYNE; Massena Central HS; Massena, NY; (Y); 41/246; Nwsp Phtg; Wayne T Moses Schlrshp 86; Knghts Of Columbus Schlrshp 86; Pres Acadmc Ftnss Awd 86; Canton; Engrng Sci.

LASHOMB, MARY KATHRYN; Franklin Acad; Malone, NY; (Y); Spanish Clb; Varsity Clb; Yrbk Stf; Bsktbl; Swmmng; High Hon Roll; Hon Roll; NHS; Epsilon; Russel Sage; Phys Ther.

LASHWAY, SCOTT; Northern Adirondack Central HS; Altona, NY; (Y); Boy Scts; Camp Fr Inc; Debate Tm; Drama Clb; FFA; Art Clb; Variety Show; Stu Cncl; Bsktbl; Hon Roll; Nrthrn Adrndck Chptr Of Ffa Treasurer 85-87; Eagle Scout 86; Postdam; Criminal Justice.

LASKER, JOANNE; Alden Central HS; Alden, NY; (Y); 13/203; Cmnty Wkr; Library Aide; Office Aide; SADD; Yrbk Phtg; Yrbk Stf; High Hon Roll; Hon Roll; Acad Awd & Ltr 86; Exec Sec Sci.

LASOTA, JAMES; Bishop Timon HS; Lackawanna, NY; (S); Cmnty Wkr; SADD; Yrbk Stf; High Hon Roll.

LASSELL, SCOTT; Guilderland Central HS; Altamont, NY; (Y); Aud/Vis; German Clb; Symp Band; Rep Jr Cls; JV Socr; JV Vllybl; Hon Roll; NHS; Brd Ed Schltc Awd 85; Physcst.

LASSIS, LORNA; Dominican Commercial HS; Richmond Hill, NY; (S); 48/288; Church Yth Grp; Dance Clb; JA; Busns Hnr Soc; Sienna Clb 83-86; St Johns; Bus Mgmt.

LAST, DAWN; St Peters HS For Girls; Staten Island, NY; (Y); Chorus; Church Choir; School Play; VP Soph Cls; Trs Stu Cncl; Tennis; St Johns U; Crim Jstc.

LASTER, CHARLES E; Walton HS; Bronx, NY; (Y); 5/90; Chess Clb; FBLA; Mathletes; SADD; Varsity Clb; Jazz Band; School Musical; Variety Show; Pres Frsh Cls; Pres Soph Cls.

LASTIQUE, ESTHER; Stuyvesant HS; Flushing, NY; (Y); Office Aide; Red Cross Aide; Teachers Aide; Chorus; Lit Mag; Var Mgr(s); Var Trk; Head Trnr JR Vrsty Ftbl Tm 85-86; ST U NY Stony Brook; Comp Sci.

LATANYSHYN, MARYANNE; Auburn HS; Auburn, NY; (Y); 27/425; French Clb; Model UN; Lit Mag; Var L Fld Hcky; Score Keeper; Timer; High Hon Roll; Hon Roll; NHS; Pres Schlr; NY Rgnts Schlrshp 86; Dept Hnr In Frnch 86; Boston U; Intl Rel.

LATCHA, SHERON; St Francis Prep; Queens Village, NY; (S); 6/653; Church Yth Grp; Cmnty Wkr; Library Aide; Math Tm; Office Aide; Teachers Aide; NHS; Ntl Merit Ltr; Drill Tm; Prncpls Lst 83-85; Psych.

LATENBERGER, KYLE; E J Wilson HS; Rochester, NY; (Y); Boy Scts; Exploring; Church Choir; Swmmng; Cit Awd; God Cntry Awd; Monroe CC; Law Enfrcemnt.

LATHAN, BRIDGET A; Le Roy Central Schl; Leroy, NY; (Y); Varsity Clb; Concert Band; Drm Mjr(t); Mrchg Band; Yrbk Sprt Ed; Sec Stu Cncl; Var L Bsktbl; Var L Socr; Var L Sftbl; Var L Vllybl.

LATHROP, DAWN; Alden Central HS; Alden, NY; (Y); French Clb; Letterman Clb; Pep Clb; SADD; Concert Band; Rep Frsh Cls; Rep Soph Cls; Rep Jr Cls; Var Cheerleading; Capt Var Crs Cntry; Pre Law.

LATHROP, DAWN; Haverling HS; Bath, NY; (Y); Exploring; 4-H; FHA; Library Aide; Temple Yth Grp; VICA; Chorus; Sftbl; Tennis; Trk; Bus.

LATHROP, MONICA; Canisteo Central HS; Hornell, NY; (Y); 19/76; Pres VP Am Leg Aux Girls St; Church Yth Grp; Cmnty Wkr; Chorus; Church Choir; School Musical; Stage Crew; Rep Stu Cncl; JV Stat Bsktbl; JV Var Sftbl; Elem Ed.

LATHROP, TIM; Avoca Central Schl; Bath, NY; (Y); 7/46; Boy Scts; VP Jr Cls; VP Sr Cls; JV Var Bsbl; JV Var Bsktbl; Hon Roll; Prfct Atten Awd.

LATIMER, IVY; Richmond Hill HS; Brooklyn, NY; (Y); Drama Clb; School Musical; Ed Nwsp Rptr; French Hon Soc; Hon Roll; Jr NHS; NHS; Debate Tm; Yrbk Stf; Crs Cntry; Wnnr-H S Shksprean Cntst 86; Lwyr In Law Clb 86; Stu Of Mnth-Engl & Scl Stds 86; Pre-Law.

LATOCHA, MIKE; Fabius-Pompey HS; Pompey, NY; (Y); JV Var Bsbl; JV Var Socr; JV Var Wrstlng; High Hon Roll; Hon Roll; Engrng.

LATONYA, MURPHY; Poughkeepsie HS; Poughkeepsie, NY; (Y); Girl Scts; VICA; Chorus; Church Choir; JV Cheerleading; Merit Attndnc Awd 83-84; Cosmtlgy.

LATTANZI, GENE; John Dewey HS; Brooklyn, NY; (Y); Band; Jazz Band; Brooklyn Clg; Comm.

LATTARULO, PETER; St Peters Boys HS; Staten Island, NY; (Y); 40/163; Varsity Clb; Nwsp Rptr; Nwsp Sprt Ed; Nwsp Stf; Yrbk Phtg; Yrbk Stf; Rep Soph Cls; Var Capt Socr; Var JV Trk; Hon Roll; St Johns U; Bus Admin.

LATTIMER, WANDA; Hempstead HS; Hempstead, NY; (S); 16/212; Dance Clb; FBLA; Hosp Aide; Pep Clb; Church Choir; Yrbk Stf; Sec Jr Cls; Sr Cls; Sftbl; NYS Regnts Schlrshp 86; St Johns U; Bus Adm.

LAU, ANDREW; Monsignor Farrell HS; Staten Island, NY; (Y); Chess Clb; Computer Clb; Math Tm; Spanish Clb; Concert Band; Mrchg Band; Im Bsktbl; Im Bowling; High Hon Roll; NHS; Engrng.

LAU, CHIU; La Salle Acad; New York, NY; (S); Art Clb; Bowling; Hon Roll.

LAU, KIN HUNG; Bronx H S Of Science; New York, NY; (Y); NHS; Vassar Coll; Law.

LAU, LINDA; HS For The Humants; New York, NY; (Y); 22/160; NY U; Bus.

LAU, MARY; Cornwall Central HS; Cornwall, NY; (Y); Cmnty Wkr; Hosp Aide; Cornwall Hosp Awd 85; ST U; Econ.

LAU, POCHUI; Julia Richman HS; Bronx, NY; (Y); 3/429; FBLA; Hosp Aide; Trs Intnl Clb; Science Clb; Teachers Aide; Sr Cls; Stu Cncl; High Hon Roll; Prfct Atten Awd; Rgnts Schlrshp 86; Awd Bkkpng 86; NY U; Chem.

LAU, WAILANG; Seward Park HS; New York, NY; (Y); Cmnty Wkr; FTA; Hosp Aide; Office Aide; Teachers Aide; Band; Concert Band; Prfct Atten Awd; Spnsh,Tutorng Awd 84; Svc Awd Merit 86.

LAUDADIO, DANIELA; Sachem HS; Holbrook, NY; (Y); 141/1400; Ski Clb; Dowling Coll; Pre-Law.

LAUDISIO, ROSEANNE; Glen Cove HS; Glen Cove, NY; (Y); 30/266; Drama Clb; Band; Concert Band; Jazz Band; Mrchg Band; School Play; Socr; Sftbl; Hon Roll; All Cnty Band 83 & 85; Tchr.

LAUENBORG, KIM; Newfield HS; Selden, NY; (Y); Drama Clb; Red Cross Aide; Hon Roll; Dntstry.

LAUFER, LISA; Lockport SR HS; Lockport, NY; (Y); 112/411; Church Yth Grp; VICA; Drm & Bgl; VP Frsh Cls; Rep Soph Cls; Rep Stu Cncl; JV Sftbl; NCCC; Bus Mgmnt.

LAUMENEDE, TARA; Lynbrook HS; Lynbrook, NY; (Y); French Clb; Varsity Clb; Yrbk Stf; Trs Jr Cls; Var L Badmtn; Var L Cheerleading; Hon Roll; NHS; Badminton County Champion 86; Nrsng.

LAUNDREE, JOHN; Ticonderoga HS; Ticonderoga, NY; (Y); 2/106; Am Leg Boys St; Drama Clb; VP French Clb; Key Clb; Lit Mag; Rep Stu Cncl; Var Crs Cntry; High Hon Roll; NHS; Sal; Clarkson U; Comp Engrng.

LAUNDRY, REESE; Charles H Roth HS; W Henrietta, NY; (Y); Exploring; Hon Roll; Jr NHS; Bio.

LAURA, SUZANNE; Smithtown HS East; Nesconset, NY; (Y); Cmnty Wkr; Hosp Aide; Key Clb; Ski Clb; Spanish Clb; SADD; Stu Cncl; Var Gym; High Hon Roll; Hon Roll; Physcl Thrpy.

LAUREN, STORC; Sachem North HS; Lake Ronkonkoma, NY; (Y); 201/1558; Girl Scts; Im Bsktbl; Im Sftbl; Hon Roll; SUNY Stonybrook; Phys Thrpy.

LAURENZANO, LISA; John H Glenn HS; E Northport, NY; (Y); Varsity Clb; Var Bsktbl; Var Gym; Var Socr; Var Vllybl; Bsktbl MIP 85-86; Vllybl MVP 85-86; Italian Hnr Socy 85-86; UCLA; Pre-Med.

LAURIE, CYNTHIA; Stutgart American HS; APO, NY; (Y); 2/317; Drama Clb; Thesps; Acpl Chr; School Musical; Pres Frsh Cls; Stu Cncl; Capt Powder Puff Ftbl; Var Trk; Cit Awd; NHS; Semi-Fnlst Prsdntl Schlr Pgm 86; Prsdntl Acdmc Ftnss Awd 86; Ntl Achvmnt Schlrshp Outstndg Ngro Stu 86; Georgetown; Intl Rltns.

LAURIELLO, JOHN; Amsterdam HS; Amsterdam, NY; (Y); 28/294; JA; Political Wkr; Concert Band; Drm & Bgl; Jazz Band; Mrchg Band; Nwsp Ed-Chief; High Hon Roll; NHS; Buffalo U; Elect Engr.

LAURILLA, SEAN; Bishop Scully HS; Amsterdam, NY; (Y); 17/46; SADD; Var L Bsbl; Var L Bsktbl; Hon Roll; Cmnty Wkr; Score Keeper; J Spencer Good Sprtmnshp Awd 86; Tri Vly All-Stars Bsbl Team 86; MVP Awd Xmas Bsktbl Tournmnt 85; Dnstry.

LAUTNER, ELIZABET M; St Joseph Hill Acad; Staten Island, NY; (Y); Art Clb; Church Yth Grp; Computer Clb; Drama Clb; French Clb; FTA; Library Aide; Teachers Aide; Yrbk Stf; NEDT Ltr Commnedtn 84; Regents Scholar 85; Pratt Inst; Arch.

LAUX, MICHELE; Buffalo Acad Of The Sacred Hrt HS; Buffalo, NY; (Y); Church Yth Grp; Ski Clb; Nwsp Rptr; Rep Jr Cls; Sec Sr Cls; JV Cheerleading; Var Vllybl; Hon Roll.

LAUZON, DEBORAH; Salmon River Central HS; Fort Covington, NY; (S); Var Crs Cntry; Var Diving; Var Swmmng; Trk; Hon Roll; Coll Of Geneseo; Spcl Educ Tchr.

LAVACCA, SUZANNE; Palmyra-Macedon HS; Palmyra, NY; (Y); SADD; Varsity Clb; Band; Chorus; Concert Band; Mrchg Band; School Musical; School Play; Symp Band; Var Sftbl; Secy.

LAVALLEY, RICK; Potsdam SR HS; Potsdam, NY; (Y); 22/136; VP Spanish Clb; Yrbk Stf; Var Trk; High Hon Roll; Hon Roll; Jr NHS; NHS; Arch.

LAVAS, MICHELE; New Dorp HS; Staten Island, NY; (Y); Intnl Clb; Latin Clb; Chorus; Italian Hnr Soc, Engl, Hstry 83-86; Teacher.

LAVELLE, ALICIA; Hutch Tech HS; Buffalo, NY; (Y); Comp Elec.

LAVELLE, CAROLYN A; Liverpool HS; Liverpool, NY; (Y); 87/874; School Play; JV Var Cheerleading; High Hon Roll; Hon Roll; Jr NHS; NHS; NYS Rgnts Schlrshp 86; St Bonaventure; Engl.

LAVELLE, JENNIFER; Mt Mercy Acad; Buffalo, NY; (Y); Cmnty Wkr; French Clb; Girl Scts; Hosp Aide; Stage Crew; Yrbk Stf; NHS; Schlrshp Attnd MMA 83; Canisius; Sci.

LAVERDA, JAMES; Archbishop Molloy HS; S Ozone Park, NY; (Y); 56/383; JV L Crs Cntry; Var L Trk; Hon Roll; NHS; Bus.

LAVERGNE, CARMEN; Westbury SR HS; Westbury, NY; (Y); 54/267; Pres Chess Clb; Trs Drama Clb; VP FBLA; Key Clb; Chorus; School Musical; Rep Stu Cncl; Hon Roll; Kiwanis Awd; Acad Achvt Awd 83; Culinary Inst Am; Culnry Arts.

LAVERY, ELIZABETH; Springville Griffith Inst; Springville, NY; (S); 66/198; Debate Tm; 4-H; Rptr Trs FFA; Nwsp Rptr; Rep Stu Cncl; JV Var Cheerleading; Var L Crs Cntry; Var L Trk; Kiwanis Awd; Dist 9 Star Hortcltrst 85; Empire Frmr Degree FFA 85; Grange Pub Spkng Awd 85; Alfred Ag & Tech; Florist.

LAVIER, LISA; John F Kennedy HS; Utica, NY; (Y); FBLA; Key Clb; Red Cross Aide; SADD; VICA; Yrbk Stf; JV Bsktbl; JV Vllybl; Hon Roll; Jr NHS; Mohawk Vly CC; Csmtlgst.

LAVIGNE, CHRISTOPHER; Plattsburgh HS; Plattsburgh, NY; (Y); 17/135; Church Yth Grp; Model UN; Varsity Clb; Band; Concert Band; Mrchg Band; Orch; Stage Crew; Var Crs Cntry; Var Swmmng; VA Polytechnic Inst; Arspc Eng.

LAVIGNE, JANELLE; Tupper Lake HS; Tupper Lk, NY; (Y); 4/99; VP Pep Clb; VP Frsh Cls; Rep Soph Cls; Rep Jr Cls; Rep Sr Cls; Rep Stu Cncl; Capt Cheerleading; Var JV Vllybl; NHS; Engrg.

LAVIGNE, ROLAND J; Whitehall Central Schl; Whitehall, NY; (Y); 20/79; Camera Clb; SADD; Varsity Clb; School Musical; JV Ftbl; Var Capt Wrstlng; Hon Roll; NY ST Rgnts Schlrshp Awd 86; Sprts Med.

LAVIN, DIANE; Commack North HS; Smithtown, NY; (Y); Sec Church Yth Grp; Key Clb; Teachers Aide; Capt Varsity Clb; Chorus; Church Choir; Yrbk Stf; Var Capt Bsktbl; Var Fld Hcky; Sftbl; Suffolk Zone Awd Phys Fit, Acadmcs, Ctznshp 86; Empire ST Field Hockey Gold Medal 85; U MD; Bus Admin.

LAVINE, STEFANIE; Farmingdale SR HS; Farmingdale, NY; (Y); 73/600; Am Leg Aux Girls St; Drama Clb; SADD; Chorus; School Musical; Variety Show; Yrbk Stf; Hon Roll; Jr NHS; NYS Rgnts Schlrshp 86; Coll Lvl Exam Pgm Rcvd 30 Crdts 86; Plattsburgh; Psych.

LAVINE, WILLIAM R; St Lawrence Central HS; Brasher Falls, NY; (Y); Chess Clb; Drama Clb; 4-H; Nwsp Rptr; Nwsp Stf; Yrbk Rptr; Yrbk Stf; Swmmng; Cit Awd; Rgnts Nrsng Schlrshp 86; 10 R Scl Stdies Hnrbl Mntn 84.

LAVINIO, LISA; Walter Panas HS; Peekskill, NY; (Y); Drama Clb; FBLA; Band; Concert Band; Jazz Band; Mrchg Band; School Musical; Rep Frsh Cls; High Hon Roll; NHS; Bio.

LAVINO, DINA; New Dorp HS; Staten Island, NY; (Y); 35/600; Art Clb; Hosp Aide; Intnl Clb; Library Aide; Yrbk Stf; High Hon Roll; Hon Roll; NHS; Pres Schlr; Pres Acad Ftns Awd 86; Hnr Key 86; Prmnt Hnr Roll 83-86; Fshn Insti Tech; Fshn Byng.

LAVIOLETTE, MARK; Mont Pleasant HS; Schenectady, NY; (Y); Office Aide; Ski Clb; SCCC; Crmnl Jstc.

LAVIS, MICHAEL J; St Francis HS; Buffalo, NY; (Y); 1/160; PAVAS; Scholastic Bowl; Spanish Clb; Nwsp Ed-Chief; Yrbk Stf; High Hon Roll; NHS; Ntl Merit Ltr; Val; Williams Coll Bk Awd 86; Penn ST U; Astrnmy.

LAVITT, SUSAN; Minisink Valley HS; Middletown, NY; (Y); Band; Concert Band; Mrchg Band; High Hon Roll; Hon Roll.

LAW, ALINA; Lafayette HS; Brooklyn, NY; (Y); Intnl Clb; Library Aide; Math Tm; Office Aide; Teachers Aide; Yrbk Stf; Hon Roll; Kiwanis Awd; Prfct Atten Awd.

LAW, DENISE; Bolton Central Schl; Diamond Pt, NY; (Y); Cmnty Wkr; Computer Clb; Drama Clb; French Clb; Quiz Bowl; Chorus; School Play; Yrbk Stf; Trs Soph Cls; JV Bsktbl; Bus Admin.

LAW, GEORGE; George W Fowler HS; Syracuse, NY; (Y); Church Yth Grp; Chorus; High Hon Roll; Hon Roll; NHS; Prfct Atten Awd; Slver Cert 86; NYS Regnts Scholar 86; Blodgett Voc Alumni Assn John C Donohue Scholar 86; Geneseo SUNY; Comp Sci.

LAW, LESLIE; Parishville Hopkinton Central HS; Colton, NY; (Y); 12/42; Spanish Clb; Band; Chorus; Concert Band; Madrigals; School Musical; School Play; Stage Crew; Variety Show; Hon Roll; Outstndng Musician Awd 85-86; Outstndng Music 84-85; Potsdam ST; Spn.

LAW, MARK; Valley Heights Christian Acad; Norwich, NY; (S); 1/5; Church Yth Grp; Chorus; Church Choir; School Play; Yrbk Rptr; Yrbk Stf; Sec Frsh Cls; Cit Awd; Hon Roll; Christian Hnr Soc 85; Baptist Chrstn Schl NY St Fine Arts Festvl 1st Pl Organ 85; Chrst Compttn 85-86; Music Ed.

LAW, MARNI R; Sherburne-Earlville HS; Sherburne, NY; (Y); 12/130; Drama Clb; Band; Chorus; Concert Band; Mrchg Band; School Play; Cheerleading; High Hon Roll; NHS; Rgnts Diploma 86.

LAW, SHARI; Tonawanda JR SR HS; Tonawanda, NY; (Y); Cmnty Wkr; Sec French Clb; Political Wkr; SADD; Variety Show; Sec Jr Cls; Sec Stu Cncl; Var JV Cheerleading; Hon Roll; Buffalo St Coll; Cmmnctns.

LAW, STEPHEN; Hermon-Dekalb-Central HS; De Kalb Jct, NY; (Y); 7/42; Drama Clb; VP Pres French Clb; Band; Concert Band; Jazz Band; Mrchg Band; Var Capt Wrstlng; High Hon Roll; Hon Roll; NHS; Hermon De Kalb Almn Assn Schlrshp 86; Embry-Riddle; Aviatn Tech.

LAWLER, COREEN; Union Springs HS; Auburn, NY; (Y); Church Yth Grp; Dance Clb; Girl Scts; Chorus; School Musical; School Play; Cheerleading; Vllybl; Bus Mgmt.

LAWLER, SEAN; Auburn HS; Auburn, NY; (Y); German Clb; JA; Letterman Clb; Model UN; Ski Clb; Varsity Clb; Var Ftbl; JV Lcrss; Var Wt Lftg; Cit Awd; Cayaga CC; Poli Sci.

LAWLESS, DIANE; Saugerties HS; Saugerties, NY; (Y); Sec SADD; Variety Show; Yrbk Rptr; Yrbk Stf; JV Var Cheerleading; JV Var Pom Pon; JV Var Powder Puff Ftbl; Var Trk; Hst DAR Awd; Hon Roll; Intr Dsgn.

LAWLOR, KEVIN; St Marys Boys HS; Old Bethpage, NY; (S); 6/148; Hosp Aide; Service Clb; Yrbk Stf; Rep Soph Cls; Rep Sr Cls; Capt L Tennis; High Hon Roll; NHS; Siena Coll; Acctng.

LAWRENCE, ANDREA; Commack H S South; Commack, NY; (Y); Jazz Band; Mrchg Band; Orch; Symp Band; Yrbk Stf; Badmtn; High Hon Roll; NHS; Ntl Merit Ltr; Phys Ther.

LAWRENCE, ANDREW J; Huntington HS; Huntington, NY; (Y); AFS; Boy Scts; Mgr Chorus; Var L Bsktbl; Var L Ftbl; Var Capt Trk; Hon Roll; NHS; Exch Stu AFS 85; All Lg, Conf Trk 400 M Intermdt Hurdles 86; Intl Studies.

LAWRENCE, CLAUDINE; Lake Placid HS; Lake Placid, NY; (Y); AFS; Cmnty Wkr; French Clb; Key Clb; Pep Clb; Varsity Clb; Chorus; Stage Crew; Yrbk Rptr; Yrbk Stf; Marine Bio.

LAWRENCE, FRANCINE; Brockport HS; Hamlin, NY; (Y); Spanish Clb; Yrbk Sprt Ed; Yrbk Stf; Var Capt Cheerleading; Im Socr; High Hon Roll; Hon Roll; Outstndg Schlrshp Achvmnt 84-85; Ithaca; Math.

LAWRENCE, JEAN F; Stena Maris HS; Brooklyn, NY; (Y); 33/213; Hosp Aide; Library Aide; Math Clb; Nwsp Rptr; Hon Roll; Rgnts Schlrshp 86; Full Tuition Schlrshp St Josephs Coll 86; St Josephs Coll; Bus Mgt.

LAWRENCE, JENNIFER; Lowville Academy & Central Schl; Lowville, NY; (Y); 1/112; Pres FTA; Spanish Clb; Band; Tennis; High Hon Roll; VP NHS; Spanish Hrtg Summer Hmsty Prgm & Hugh Obrian Uth Ldrshp Sem 85; Presbyteran Chrch Deacon 84-87; Frgn Lang.

LAWRENCE, KRIS E; Amherst Central HS; Amherst, NY; (Y); 82/313; Model UN; Ski Clb; Teachers Aide; Varsity Clb; Nwsp Rptr; JV Capt Socr; Hon Roll; NHS; VFW Boys ST 86; U MI Smmr Hon Pgm 86; Govt.

LAWRENCE, PAUL; Clara Barton HS; Brooklyn, NY; (Y); 3/483; Dance Clb; Drama Clb; Exploring; School Play; Rep Frsh Cls; Rep Soph Cls; Rep Jr Cls; VP Sr Cls; Rep Stu Cncl; Bausch & Lomb Sci Awd; J K Hackett Mdl For Oratory 86; E Kresber Mem Awd 86; Comptrllrs Awd; Brown U; Math.

LAWRENCE, STACEY; John Jay HS; Brooklyn, NY; (Y); 48/519; Math Tm; Chorus; Color Guard; Yrbk Stf; Jr NHS; Rgnts Coll Schlrshp 86; Bernard M Baruch; Mktg Mtg.

LAWRENCE, VALERIE; A E Stevenson HS; Bronx, NY; (Y); English Clb; Library Aide; Office Aide; Band; High Hon Roll; Hon Roll; NHS; Prfct Atten Awd; Soc Stds Mdl, Engl Gld Mdl 84; Hnr Math 86.

LAWSON, CAROL ANN; Wallkill SR HS; Wallkill, NY; (Y); 20/200; Band; Concert Band; Jazz Band; Trs Stu Cncl; Var L Socr; Var L Trk; JV Vllybl; Hon Roll; NHS; Mrchg Band; NY St Regents Schlrshp 86; Bio.

LAWSON, EDWIN; Besne-Knox-Westerlo HS; Westerlo, NY; (Y); Church Yth Grp; Exploring; Red Cross Aide; SADD; Bsbl; Golf; Hon Roll; Nvl Avtn.

LAWSON, LYDIA M; Mt Vernon HS; Mt Vernon, NY; (Y); 9/550; Pres French Clb; Office Aide; Sec Service Clb; Sec Ski Clb; Concert Band; Mrchg Band; School Musical; Off Sr Cls; Var Gym; High Hon Roll; MVP Gymnstcs 85; Msc Stu/Mnth 84; Aerosp Engrng.

LAWTON, BRUCE; Wayland Central HS; Perkinsville, NY; (Y); Varsity Clb; Yrbk Phtg; Var JV Bsbl; Var JV Socr; JV Trk; Var Capt Wrstlng; Comm Art.

LAWTON, GINNY; Schoharie Central HS; Schoharie, NY; (Y); Church Yth Grp; Band; Concert Band; Prfct Atten Awd.

LAWTON, PAULA; Gowanda Central HS; Gowanda, NY; (Y); Drama Clb; French Clb; Hosp Aide; VICA; School Musical; Rep Stu Cncl; Mgr(s); Sftbl; Trk; Trk; Math Tm; 2nd Pl Hlth Svcs-Skll Olympics 86; Jamestown CC; Hlth Svcs.

LAX, ROBT; Heuvelton Central HS; Rensselaer Falls, NY; (Y); Pres 4-H; VP French Clb; ROTC; Varsity Clb; Rep Stu Cncl; L Bsbl; Var Coach Actv; Prfct Atten Awd; Comprhnsv Socl Stds Awd 86; Proj Chllng Comp & Chem Clarkson U 85-86; Cornell U; Engrng.

LAXTON, TAMI; Cato-Meridian HS; Martville, NY; (Y); Church Yth Grp; Drama Clb; Im Badmtn; JV Score Keeper; Im Sftbl; Im Tennis; Im Vllybl; High Hon Roll; Hon Roll; Cayuga CC; Crmnl Jsut.

LAY, DAVID; Mynderse Acad; Seneca Falls, NY; (S); Boy Scts; Church Yth Grp; CAP; Model UN; Stu Cncl; L Lcrss; Wt Lftg; Rotc.

LAY, THERESA; Gowanda Central Schl; Lawtons, NY; (Y); Stat Var Bsktbl; Var Sftbl; Hon Roll; Seneca Ntn Acadmc Achvmnt Awd 82-86.

LAYCOCK, MAURA; Bishop Grimes HS; Syracuse, NY; (Y); Yrbk Phtg; Yrbk Stf; Trs Sr Cls; Stat Score Keeper; Var Tennis; Var Trk; Hon Roll; Archtctr.

LAYMAN, DENNIS A; West Seneca West SR HS; West Seneca, NY; (Y); 33/559; Mathletes; Math Tm; Varsity Clb; Var Bsbl; JV Var Ftbl; Hon Roll; Jr NHS; NHS; Canisius Coll Deans Schlrshp 86; NYS Regents Schlrshp 86; Canisius Coll; Bus Mgt.

LAYTON, ELISABETH; The Brearley Schl; New York, NY; (Y); Debate Tm; Model UN; Political Wkr; Service Clb; School Musical; School Play; Ed Yrbk Stf; Ntl Merit SF; Pol Sci.

LAZAR, CINDY; Herricks HS; Manhasset Hls, NY; (Y); 20/310; VP SADD; Varsity Clb; Yrbk Sprt Ed; Rep Frsh Cls; Rep Soph Cls; Rep Jr Cls; Var Tennis; High Hon Roll; Hon Roll; NHS; Bus.

LAZAR, KAREN; Coxsackie Athens HS; Glenmont, NY; (Y); 7/110; Spanish Clb; SADD; Chorus; Rep Frsh Cls; Rep Soph Cls; Rep Jr Cls; Chrmn Stu Cncl; Capt Cheerleading; High Hon Roll; NHS; Bus Mrktng.

LAZARO, DEBRA; Moore Catholic HS; Staten Island, NY; (Y); Church Yth Grp; Cmnty Wkr; Sec Frsh Cls; 1st Hnrs For Ovral Yr Avg 85-86; 2nd Hnrs Ovrll Yr Avg 84-85; Cert Of Acad Excllnce 84-86; Staten Island Coll; Cmnctns.

LAZARTO, FRANCIS; Xavier HS; New York, NY; (Y); 76/241; Cmnty Wkr; Teachers Aide; Varsity Clb; Im Bsktbl; Im Fld Hcky; Im Ftbl; JV Var Ice Hcky; JV Var Socr; NHS; Frst Hnrs 83; Frst Hnrs 84; Scnd Hnrs 86; Baruch Coll; Bus.

LAZARUS, ASSAD; Uniondale HS; Greenbelt, MD; (Y); Civic Clb; Debate Tm; Math Clb; Teachers Aide; Hon Roll; Coll Credt Chem & Pascal Comp; Hghst Score ST Regnts Trig Exm JR Yr; Georgetown; Mech Engr.

LAZARUS, SELINA B; Bishop Loughlin HS; Brooklyn, NY; (Y); Cmnty Wkr; Teachers Aide; Varsity Clb; Variety Show; Var Crs Cntry; Var Trk; Hnr Roll 84-85; Attnd Awd 84-85; Athltc Achvt 85-86.

LAZZARA, LISA; Westmoreland Central HS; Westmoreland, NY; (Y); Ski Clb; SADD; Chorus; Nwsp Rptr; Yrbk Stf; JV Var Bsktbl; Var L Socr; Var L Trk; High Hon Roll; Hon Roll; MVP Defense Awd Sccr 85-86; SADD Art Awd 85-86.

LAZZARINO, WILLIAM; Cetnral Islip HS; Central Islip, NY; (Y); Swmmng; Accntng.

LE, LONG; Union-Endicott HS; Endwell, NY; (Y); 54/460; Cmnty Wkr; Computer Clb; Hosp Aide; NFL; Var Socr; Var Tennis; Var Vllybl; High Hon Roll; Hon Roll; Jr NHS; NHS; March Dms Schlrshp 86; Cntnnl Prz Schlrshp 86; Pres Acdmc Ftns Awd 86; U Of Rochester; Pre-Med.

LE, THAI; Hempstead HS; Hempstead, NY; (S); #3 In Class; High Hon Roll; Hon Roll; SUNY Stonybrook; Elec Engr.

LE, TRUNG; Chittenango Central HS; Chittenango, NY; (Y); Intnl Clb; Ski Clb; Socr; Tennis; Cit Awd; Hon Roll; Colgate U.

LE BARON, ROBERTA L; Cassadaga Valley Central Schl; Sinclairville, NY; (Y); 7/70; Math Tm; ROTC; Spanish Clb; Chorus; Nwsp Stf; Yrbk Stf; JV Cheerleading; NHS; Early Coll Enrlmnt Pgm Cassadaga Vly & SUNY Fredonia 85-86; NYS Rgnts Schlrshp 86; SUNY Brockport; Spanish.

LE BARRON, BRIAN; Greenwich Central HS; Argyle, NY; (Y); FFA; Im Var Bsktbl; High Hon Roll; Hon Roll; Dairy Prod Awd, 1st Ag Mech 85; Grad Hnrs, Sci Rgnts Dplma 86; Ag.

LE BLANC, DIANE; Cardinal Spellman HS; Bronx, NY; (Y); Computer Clb; Dance Clb; Chorus; Church Choir; Color Guard; Variety Show; Pres Sr Cls; Hon Roll; Accntg.

LE BLANC, JENNIFER L; Ballston Spa HS; Ballston Spa, NY; (Y); 26/244; Trs French Clb; Pres VP FBLA; JV Var Fld Hcky; Elks Awd; High Hon Roll; NHS; Hollis V Chase Memrl Schlrshp 86; SUNY Plattsbrgh Coll Fndtn Schlrshp 86; Acadmc Achvt Awd 84; SUNY Plattsbrgh NY; Acctng.

LE BLANC, RONA A; Cardinal Spellman HS; Bronx, NY; (Y); 23/509; French Clb; Rep Soph Cls; Stu Cncl; Var Capt Cheerleading; Var Capt Pom Pon; High Hon Roll; Hon Roll; NHS; Dance Clb; Color Guard; French Awd; CYO Chrldng Champshp; Micro Bio.

LE BLANC, TODD; Saugerties HS; Saugerties, NY; (S); 13/262; French Clb; Capt Math Tm; Quiz Bowl; Band; L Socr; L Capt Tennis; High Hon Roll; VP NHS; Ntl Merit Ltr; Unltd Parameters; Lafayette; Comp Sci.

LE CLAIR, PAM; Franklin Acad; Burke, NY; (Y); Pep Clb; Cheerleading; Trk; Hon Roll; Tchrs Assn Frnkln Acad Schlrshp 86; SUNY Plattsburgh; Tchng.

LE CLAIR, TRACY; Saranac Lake HS; Saranac Lake, NY; (Y); 4-H; Orch; School Play; JV Bsktbl; JV Var Socr; JV Var Vllybl; Hon Roll; NHS; Math.

LE FEBVRE, DAVID M; John F Kennedy HS; Carmel, NY; (Y); 90/198; Camera Clb; Chess Clb; Drama Clb; Math Tm; Office Aide; SADD; Teachers Aide; School Musical; School Play; JV Crs Cntry; Am Mensa 84; NYS Regnts Schlrshp 86; Boston U; Law.

LE GUILLOU, CLAUDINE; Commack HS North; E Northport, NY; (Y); SADD; Teachers Aide; Band; Concert Band; Flag Corp; Mrchg Band; School Musical; Symp Band; Yrbk Stf; Badmtn; Bus.

LE HANE, ROBERT; Arlington HS; Poughkeepsie, NY; (Y); Concert Band; Jazz Band; Mrchg Band; Symp Band; Var Diving; Var Swmmng; Var Trk; Ntl Merit SF; Sec Church Yth Grp; Admiral Mrchng Band TOB Atlantic Cst Chmpns 1 Of 2 Solsts 85; Area Al-ST Band NYSSMA Zone 10 85; SUNY Albany; Poli Sci.

LE MARK, KARIANN; Canandaigua Acad; Canandaigua, NY; (Y); SADD; Varsity Clb; JV Capt Bsktbl; Coach Actv; JV Capt Socr; Var Sftbl; Var Trk; MVP Awd & MVP Webster Girls Sccr 86; Trnmnt Hon Mntn All Leag Goalie 86; Brockport; Physcn.

LE MAY, LAUREL LYNN; Tri-Valley Central HS; Neversink, NY; (Y); 3/78; Art Clb; Chess Clb; Church Yth Grp; 4-H; FFA; Yrbk Stf; JV Var Sftbl; High Hon Roll; NHS; NY ST Rgnts Schlrshp 86; PA Assoc Frmr Coop Schlr Awd 85; Amer Cooprtn Inst Awd 85; Cornell U; Anml Sci.

LE PAGE, MICHELLE; Massena Central HS; Massena, NY; (Y); 32/246; French Clb; Var Cheerleading; Var Gym; Stat Lcrss; Var JV Mgr(s); Stat Wrstlng; High Hon Roll; Hon Roll; NHS; Hosp Aide; Rochester Inst Of Tech; Engrng.

LE PAGE, TIM; Masena Central HS; Massena, NY; (Y); Camera Clb; Im Bsbl; Im Bowling; JV Var Ftbl; Im Vllybl; Im Wt Lftg; Capt Var Wrstlng; Iron Man Awd/Wrstlng 86; Coaches Awd/Wrstlng 85; Military.

LE PRE, DOUG; Riverhead HS; Huntington, NY; (S); Camera Clb; Church Yth Grp; DECA; Key Clb; Varsity Clb; Ftbl; Trk; Wt Lftg; DECA Awd 3rd Pl ST Entrprnrshp 86; Bus.

LEACH, BARBARA; Delaware Valley Central Schl; Roscoe, NY; (S); 4/42; AFS; Library Aide; Quiz Bowl; Spanish Clb; Chorus; Yrbk Stf; Trs Frsh Cls; Trs Soph Cls; Trs Jr Cls; Trs Sr Cls.

LEACH, KAREN; Jordan-Elbridge JR SR HS; Jordan, NY; (Y); Band; Mrchg Band; School Play; Nwsp Ed-Chief; Yrbk Stf; Var L Bsktbl; Powder Puff Ftbl; Var L Tennis; Var L Trk; Trs NHS; Onondaga Comm Schlr 85; Carnegie Fndtn Tutoral Schlrshp 84-85; Putsdam Merit Schlrshp 86; SUNY Potsdam; Engl.

LEACH, KATHY; Jordan-Elbridge HS; Jordan, NY; (Y); Concert Band; Mrchg Band; JV Var Bsktbl; Mgr(s); Score Keeper; Var Tennis; Var Trk; Ctzns Schlrshp Fndtn Amer Schlrshp 86; Cazenovia Coll Bsktbl Schlrshp 86; Cazenovia Coll; Fshn Dsgnr.

LEACH, MICHAEL; Grand Island HS; Grand Island, NY; (Y); Boy Scts; Church Yth Grp; Cmnty Wkr; Varsity Clb; Band; Stu Cncl; Var Bsktbl; Im Vllybl; High Hon Roll; NHS; NYS Rgnts Schlrshp 86; Eagle Scout 84; Pres Acdmc Fit Awd 84; NY ST U; Aerospace Engrng.

LEACH, MICHELE; George W Hewlett HS; Valley Stream, NY; (Y); 58/262; Cmnty Wkr; Drama Clb; Thesps; Varsity Clb; School Musical; School Play; Stage Crew; JV Coach Actv; Capt L Gym; Var Trk; Robert Robin Mem Schlrshp 86; PTA Schlrshp 86; MVP Awd For Gymnstcs 86; U Of VT; Dietetics.

LEACH, PATRICIA; Sodus Central HS; Alton, NY; (S); Pres Church Yth Grp; Spanish Clb; Church Choir; Concert Band; High Hon Roll; Sec NHS; Regents Scholar 86; NYSSMA Solo Awds.

LEACH, TAMELA; Naples Central Schl; Naples, NY; (Y); 17/83; 4-H; Office Aide; Teachers Aide; Chorus; Stage Crew; Var Capt Cheerleading; High Hon Roll; Hon Roll; NHS; Art Schlrshp 85; E F Gray Schlrshp 86; Alfred ST; Exec Secy Sci.

LEACH, TAMI MARIE; Queens Vocational HS; Long Island City, NY; (Y); Girl Scts; Office Aide; PAVAS; Teachers Aide; Color Guard; School Musical; School Play; Yrbk Stf; Csmtlgst.

LEAHY, MARYE; Greenville JR SR HS; Greenville, NY; (Y); 13/80; Pres VP Key Clb; Pres Frsh Cls; Var Sftbl; Var JV Vllybl; Exploring; SADD; Teachers Aide; Chorus; Var Bsktbl; Score Keeper; Sprtn Excel Awd Schl Svc, Schl Ltr 86; Sec Ed.

LEAK, CATHERINE; Jamesville-De Witt HS; Jamesville, NY; (Y); Church Yth Grp; Rep Model UN; Mgr Stage Crew; High Hon Roll; NHS; Srvce Awd 86; Natl Lang Arts Olympd Awd 84; ASTRNMY.

LEAK, ROBERT; Springfield Gardens HS; Laurelton, NY; (S); 27/443; ROTC; Drill Tm; Im Badmtn; Im Bsktbl; Im Vllybl; High Hon Roll; NHS; Comp Sci.

LEAL, FERNANDO; St Agnes HS; New York, NY; (Y); 9/109; Crs Cntry; Trk; Hon Roll; NHS; Natl Sci Merit Awd 85; 2nd Hnrs 85-86; Columbia U; Lawyer.

LEANZA, ELISA; Our Lady Of Victory Acad; Eastchester, NY; (S); 11/157; French Clb; SADD; Yrbk Stf; Off Jr Cls; Sftbl; Vllybl; French Hon Soc; High Hon Roll; NHS; Alpha Hnr Soc 85-86; Mth.

LEARD, BARBRA; Frontier SR HS; Lackawanna, NY; (Y); Hon Roll; NHS; Internshp Pgm 87; Child Psych.

LEARNED, HEIDI; Sandy Creek Central HS; Lacona, NY; (S); 3/94; French Clb; Ski Clb; Band; Chorus; Mrchg Band; Pres Sr Cls; Sec VP Stu Cncl; Capt Socr; Capt Vllybl; Pres NHS; Mst Prmsng Grl 82; Hmcmng Qun 85; Hghst Mrk Frnch III Rgnts 85; SUNY Potsdam.

LEARNED, SUE; Franklin Acad; Malone, NY; (Y); French Clb; Varsity Clb; Concert Band; VP Soph Cls; VP L Swmmng; Hon Roll; Trs NHS; NYSSMA All ST Band 85; Elsln Hnr Soc 84-86; Pharmctcl Sci.

LEARY, KATHLEEN; Lynbrook HS; Lynbrook, NY; (Y); Vllybl; Hon Roll; Hofstra U.

LEATBERS, SUZANNE; Greece Athena SR HS; Rochester, NY; (Y); 60/286; Church Yth Grp; Drama Clb; Girl Scts; Chorus; School Musical; Symp Band; Var Tennis; Vllybl; Concert Band; Yrbk Stf; Slvr & Gold Awd Girl Scouts 86; Monroe CC; Sec Stds.

LEATHERLAND, TAMMY LEE; Massena Central HS; Massena, NY; (Y); 34/249; VP Spanish Clb; Band; Concert Band; Jazz Band; Pep Band; Var Capt Bsktbl; Var Mgr(s); L Sftbl; Hon Roll; NHS; NY ST Regents Schlrshp 86; Plattsburgh ST U; Pharmacy.

LEAVY, KAREN M; Stella Maris HS; Rosedale, NY; (Y); 1/225; Hosp Aide; Library Aide; Math Tm; Science Clb; Yrbk Stf; High Hon Roll; NHS; Prfct Atten Awd; Voice Dem Awd; Phi Beta Kappa Schlrshp Adelphi U & Molloy Schlr Schlrshp Molloy Coll Full Tuition 86; NY ST Schlrs; Adelphi U; Bio.

LEBISH, CRAIG L; Centereach HS; Lake Grove, NY; (Y); 1/429; Capt Debate Tm; Concert Band; Jazz Band; Rep Sr Cls; Sec NHS; Boy Scts; Band; Mrchg Band; School Musical; All Cnty All ST Orchstra 85; NY ST Rg Nts Schlrshp 86; Mc Dnlds Tri-ST Jazzz 86; IN U.

LEBOVIC, KENNETH; Hebrew Acad Of Nassau County; W Hempstead, NY; (Y); 1/77; Capt Debate Tm; Pres Math Tm; Yrbk Ed-Chief; Pres Sr Cls; JV Tennis; High Hon Roll; NHS; Ntl Merit SF; Val; Cmnty Wkr; Judith Resnick Sc Mem Sci Awd 86; Phscs Awd 86; Mth Tm Ldng Scr Awd 86; Ntl Hon Scty Schlrshp 86; Harvard U; Pre-Law.

LEBRON, LIZETTE; Dodge Vocational HS; Bronx, NY; (Y); 39/379; Dance Clb; Drama Clb; Model UN; Office Aide; Political Wkr; Nwsp Rptr; Yrbk Ed-Chief; Trs Sr Cls; Gym; Cit Awd; Globl Hist Gold Awd 83; Ecnmcs Gold Awd 85; Socl Stu Blue Awd 86; Lehman Clg; Socl Serv.

LECCE, NICOLA; Berlin Central HS; Berlin, NY; (Y); Camp Fr Inc; Cmnty Wkr; GAA; Girl Scts; Nwsp Stf; Bsktbl; Cheerleading; Socr; Sftbl; Hon Roll.

LECCI, JOHN; Longwood HS; Middle Island, NY; (Y); Church Yth Grp; Debate Tm; Band; Concert Band; Mrchg Band; Trs Sr Cls; Trs Stu Cncl; Var Capt Bsbl; Coach Actv; Var Capt Ftbl; All-Leag Ftbl & Bsbl; Outstndng Stud In Physcl Ed; Ithaca Coll; Lbrl Arts.

LECHLITER, LIZ; Oakfield Alabama Central HS; Oakfield, NY; (Y); VP Art Clb; Church Yth Grp; Sec Pres 4-H; Stage Crew; Rep Stu Cncl; Cit Awd; Dnfth Awd; 4-H Awd; Hon Roll; Jr NHS; 4-H Ldrshp Awd 84; Painting Awd 84; Nyc Home Ec Awd Trip 85; English.

LECHMANSKI, DOROTHY; St John The Baptist HS; Melville, NY; (Y); 55/550; Cmnty Wkr; Hosp Aide; Chrmn SADD; Chorus; Rep Jr Cls; Rep Sr Cls; Stu Cncl; Var Im Vllybl; Hon Roll; Miss Polonia Rnnr Up 86; Political Science.

LECHNER, STEVEN E; Saugerties HS; Saugerties, NY; (Y); Key Clb; Bsktbl; Ftbl; Hon Roll; Olympd Soc Stu Schlr 84; Regnts Schlrshp 86; Canisius Clg; Phys Educ.

LECHOWSKI, GARRET; Frontier Central SR HS; Blasdell, NY; (Y); Aud/Vis; Band; Chorus; Concert Band; School Musical; Swing Chorus; Nwsp Rptr; Music.

LECLAIR, LORI; Northern Adirondack Central HS; Churubusco, NY; (Y); French Clb; Variety Show; Bsktbl; Socr; Hon Roll; Prfct Atten Awd; Commrcl Illstrtn.

LECUSAY JR, DARIO A; Elmont Meorial HS; Elmont, NY; (Y); 6/253; Band; Concert Band; Jazz Band; Mrchg Band; Orch; School Musical; Yrbk Stf; Crs Cntry; NHS; Spanish NHS; Rgnts Schlrshp; U Of NY Buffalo; Doctor.

LEDDY, ARLENE; Delaware Acad; Delhi, NY; (Y); 8/80; German Clb; Girl Scts; Ski Clb; Yrbk Stf; Off Frsh Cls; Off Soph Cls; JV Var Fld Hcky; Var Score Keeper; Var L Sftbl; Var L Vllybl; 2 Ntl Schlstc Gld Kys In Art 85-86; Mst Vlbl Fld Hcky Plr Dfns V 85; Rgnts Schlrshp; Vassar Coll; Art Ed.

LEDDY, BRIAN; Nazareth Regional HS; Brooklyn, NY; (Y); Math Tm; Off Stu Cncl; Capt Var Bowling; JV Ftbl; Var Capt Vllybl; Hon Roll; NHS.

LEDINA, DAVID; Monticello HS; Monticello, NY; (S); Debate Tm; Drama Clb; NFL; Ski Clb; Speech Tm; Temple Yth Grp; Band; Concert Band; Orch; School Musical.

LEDKOVSKY, ELIZABETH A; William Floyd HS; Shirley, NY; (Y); 2/430; Aud/Vis; VP Civic Clb; Pres French Clb; Quiz Bowl; Scholastic Bowl; Thesps; Chorus; Church Choir; Orch; School Musical; Natl Le Grand Concours French Exam 85 & 86; Cornell U; Cmmnctns Arts.

LEDYARD, DEBORAH J; Lake Placid Central HS; Upper Jay, NY; (Y); 4/44; Church Yth Grp; Key Clb; Varsity Clb; School Musical; Yrbk Ed-Chief; Yrbk Stf; Cheerleading; Timer; High Hon Roll; NHS; R Bros, B & B Clwn Coll; Clwn.

LEE, ALICE; James Madison HS; Brooklyn, NY; (Y); VP French Clb; FBLA; JA; Office Aide; Variety Show; Badmtn; Vllybl; Prfct Atten Awd; Rgnts Schlrshp 86; Arista Hnrs Soc 83; NY U; Pre-Law.

LEE, ANA; Newton HS; Elmhurst, NY; (Y); 15/781; Key Clb; Math Tm; Band; Concert Band; Orch; Nwsp Stf; Yrbk Stf; Rep Stu Cncl; Cit Awd; Jr NHS; NYC Assoc Eng L Tchrs Awd For Excellence 84.

LEE, ANDREA OAI-MING; Franklin Delano Roosevelt HS; Staatsburg, NY; (Y); 2/350; Band; Mrchg Band; Orch; School Musical; Var Capt Socr; NCTE Awd; Sec NHS; Ntl Merit Ltr; Church Yth Grp; Concert Band; NY ST Schl Music Assn Conf All-ST Band 85; NY ST Regents Schlrshp 86; Cetacian Behvr.

LEE, ANITA; James Madison HS; Brooklyn, NY; (Y); 155/756; Art Clb; Letterman Clb; Math Tm; School Play; Stage Crew; Yrbk Phtg; Yrbk Stf; Var Tennis; Photogrphy Awd; 1st Prz Sci Fair; Syracuse U; Arch.

LEE, AUDREY; Stuyvesant HS; New York, NY; (Y); Church Yth Grp; Office Aide; Teachers Aide; Lit Mag; Var L Bowling; JETS Awd; NHS; Ntl Merit Schol; United Fed Of Teachers Schlrshp 86; Princeton U; Archtctr.

LEE, BENJAMIN; Vestal Senior HS; Apalachin, NY; (Y); Boy Scts; French Clb; Hosp Aide; Mathletes; Ski Clb; Yrbk Sprt Ed; Sec NHS; Salute To Yth Awd 86; Eagle Sct Awd 86; Rotary Yth Ldrshp Awd 86; Pre-Med.

LEE, BENJAMIN Y; Liverpool HS; Liverpool, NY; (Y); 13/816; Var L Socr; Hon Roll; NHS; Cornell U; Dr.

LEE, BETTY F; Jamaica HS; Jamaica, NY; (Y); 14/500; Math Clb; Math Tm; Office Aide; Science Clb; Teachers Aide; Orch; Lit Mag; High Hon Roll; Hon Roll; Jr NHS; U Of Rochester Urbn Leag Schlshp 86; NYS Regnts Schlrshp 86; U Of Rochester; Math.

LEE, BRIAN; Lansing HS; Groton, NY; (Y); Church Yth Grp; Computer Clb; Var Socr; Var Swmmng; Hon Roll; Ind Art Awd 84; FL ST; Comp Sci.

LEE, CARL; John Jay HS; Katonah, NY; (Y); Art Clb; Camp Fr Inc; FHA; Key Clb; Keywanettes; Q&S; Chorus; Orch; Var Socr; Var Trk.

LEE, CHRISTIN A; Bronx HS Of Sci; Bronxville, NY; (Y); Science Clb; Varsity Clb; Band; Chorus; Concert Band; Jazz Band; Orch; Symp Band; Bsktbl; Sftbl; Music Exc 85; U NH; Music.

LEE, DANNY S; Mc Quaid Jesuit HS; Pittsford, NY; (Y); JA; Varsity Clb; JV Bsbl; Hon Roll; Letterman Clb; Model UN; Ski Clb; Var Ski Tm; Regnt Schlrshp 86; Clarkson U; Engrng.

LEE, DAVID; Archbishop Molloy HS; Forest Hl, NY; (Y); 206/405; Chess Clb; Computer Clb; Math Tm; NY U; Pre Med.

LEE, DAVID; Benjamin N Cardozo HS; Bayside, NY; (Y); VP Church Yth Grp; French Clb; VP JA; Math Clb; Science Clb; Service Clb; Nwsp Rptr; Nwsp Stf; Yrbk Phtg; Yrbk Rptr; JR Statesmn Summr Schl Stanford U 85; Young Diplomats Frgn Exch Pgm 86; Stanford U; Bus.

LEE, DAVID; Huntington HS; Metairie, LA; (Y); 2/383; Chess Clb; Computer Clb; Mathletes; Nwsp Stf; Yrbk Stf; Lit Mag; Bausch & Lomb Sci Awd; High Hon Roll; NHS; Sal; Harvard Bk Prz Awd 85; Forum Tech Sci Awd 86; Tulane U; Pre-Med.

LEE, DAVID; Tottenville HS; Staten Island, NY; (Y); French Clb; Model UN; Rep Frsh Cls; Rep Soph Cls; Rep Jr Cls; Trk; French Hon Soc; NHS; Modl Cngrs 85; Engrng.

LEE, DEBORAH; Academy Of Mt St Ursula; Bronx, NY; (Y); Spanish Clb; Stage Crew; Yrbk Stf; Hon Roll; Engl Hnrs Clss; Wesleyan U; Med.

LEE, DEBORAH; Shenendehowa HS; Clifton Park, NY; (Y); Church Yth Grp; School Play; High Hon Roll; Socl Stds Awd 86; Sci.

LEE, EDWARD; Half Hollow Hills HS; Melville, NY; (Y); Computer Clb; Mathletes; Science Clb; Orch; Rep Stu Cncl; Im Bsktbl; Im Tennis; High Hon Roll; Jr NHS; NHS; Med.

LEE, EUGENE; John H Glenn HS; E Northport, NY; (Y); Debate Tm; Chrmn PAVAS; Science Clb; Orch; High Hon Roll; NHS; Spanish NHS; Howard Koch Mem Schlrshp 85fdean Harrington Mem Schlrshp 83; Suffolk Mus Guild Schlrshp 83; Harvard Coll; Econ Law.

LEE, EUNICE W; Saratoga Springs HS; Saratoga Springs, NY; (Y); 44/500; Church Yth Grp; Key Clb; Ski Clb; Chorus; Pres Frsh Cls; Pres Soph Cls; VP Jr Cls; Pres Sr Cls; Rep Stu Cncl; Var L Tennis; Bstn Coll; Bnkng.

LEE, EVA; Brooklyn Tech HS; New York, NY; (Y); 66/1159; Cmnty Wkr; Computer Clb; Office Aide; Yrbk Ed-Chief; Yrbk Stf; Var Vllybl; Hon Roll; NHS; Holy Cross Book Awd 85; Natl Schlr/Ath Awd 86; Cornell U; Engrng.

LEE, FREDERICK S; East Syracuse-Minoa Centrel HS; Minoa, NY; (Y); Church Yth Grp; French Clb; Hosp Aide; Pres JA; Latin Clb; Red Cross Aide; Science Clb; Band; Concert Band; Jazz Band; Natl Latin Exam-Summa Cum Laude 86; Achvt Awd French 85; Achvt Awd Latin 86; Med.

LEE, GABRIEL; Salamanca Central HS; Salamanca, NY; (Y); 6/150; Am Leg Boys St; Drama Clb; French Clb; Nwsp Phtg; Sr Cls; Stu Cncl; Tennis; French Hon Soc; High Hon Roll; NHS; Pre-Law.

LEE, GEORGE; La Salle Acad; New York, NY; (Y); 15/220; Camera Clb; Yrbk Phtg; Yrbk Stf; Pres Acad Fit Awd 85-86; NYU; Chem.

LEE, GIA; Herricks SR HS; Searingtown, NY; (Y); Am Leg Aux Girls St; Quiz Bowl; SADD; Nwsp Ed-Chief; Chrmn Stu Cncl; Var Cheerleading; NHS; Ntl Merit SF; 1st NY St De Public Spking 84; 2nd Amer Chem Soc Chem Cntst 85.

LEE, GINA; St Catherine Acad; Bronx, NY; (Y); Chorus; School Musical; Hon Roll; Acad All Amer Awd 86; Manhattan Coll Riverdale NY.

LEE, IL; New Rochelle HS; New Rochelle, NY; (Y); Boys Clb Am; Church Yth Grp; Math Tm; Church Choir; Wrstlng; Hon Roll; NHS; Pre-Med.

LEE, JAMES; Susan E Wagner HS; Staten Island, NY; (Y); VP Pres Church Yth Grp; Math Tm; Concert Band; Orch; Nwsp Stf; Lit Mag; Var Crs Cntry; Im Sftbl; Hon Roll; Jr NHS; NYU; Philsphy.

LEE, JAMES M; St Francis Prep; Bayside, NY; (S); 145/653; Im Sftbl; Var Im Tennis; Im Vllybl; Arch.

LEE, JEEHIUN; Union-Endicott HS; Endicott, NY; (Y); 1/450; Debate Tm; French Clb; Hosp Aide; Sec Key Clb; Mathletes; Pres Orch; High Hon Roll; NHS; Ntl Merit Ltr; Val; T J Watson Mmrl Schrlshp 86; NY St Rgnts Schlrshp 86; Cornell U.

LEE, JEFFREY C; Hillcrest HS; Hollis Hills, NY; (Y); 6/801; Church Yth Grp; VP JA; Math Tm; Rep Jr Cls; Gov Hon Prg Awd; Pres NHS; Westinghouse-Honors Group 86; Asian Stu Union Pres 86; Arista Pres 86; Cornell; Engrng.

LEE, JENNIFER; Herricks HS; Roslyn, NY; (Y); Sec Church Yth Grp; Key Clb; Church Choir; Orch; Hon Roll; Jr NHS; Arts-Sci.

LEE, JON; Bronx HS Of Science; Woodside, NY; (Y); Psych.

LEE, JORGE; Bronx HS Of Science; Elmhurst, NY; (Y); Art Clb; Trs Computer Clb; Hosp Aide; JA; Office Aide; Teachers Aide; Concert Band; Im Bsktbl; Im Socr; Im Vllybl; Sci.

LEE, JOSEPHINE; Middletown HS; Middletown, NY; (Y); Computer Clb; Stage Crew; Lit Mag; Rep Stu Cncl; Var Trk; Bausch & Lomb Sci Awd; Hon Roll; NHS; Sal; Math Tm Sec B Chmpnshp 84-86.

LEE, JULIA; Bronx High School Of Science; Flushing, NY; (Y); Trs Intnl Clb; Teachers Aide; Varsity Clb; Orch; Yrbk Phtg; L Socr; Vassar Coll; Jrnlsm.

LEE, JULIE; Northport HS; Northport, NY; (Y); 9/605; Sec Science Clb; Acpl Chr; Orch; Var Im Fld Hcky; High Hon Roll; NHS; St Schlr; Hosp Aide; School Musical; Nwsp Stf; All-State Orchestra 84-85; Orchestra Stu Of Yr 83-86; Musician Of Yr 83; Tufts U.

LEE, KAREN; Brooklyn Tech; Flushing, NY; (Y); 349/1159; Church Yth Grp; Sec Church Choir; Sec Frsh Cls; Capt Bowling; Arista 86; MVP Bowlng 86; Syracuse U; Pre Vet.

LEE, KAREN; Guilderland Central HS; Albany, NY; (Y); Key Clb; Varsity Clb; Var L Socr; Var Capt Vllybl; High Hon Roll; Jr NHS; Awd Excllnc Sci Stds 84&85; Awd Effrt & Achvmnt Math 84; Elem Educ.

LEE, LILLIAN; John Dewey HS; Brooklyn, NY; (Y); 62/738; Math Tm; Teachers Aide; Nwsp Rptr; Nwsp Stf; VP Stu Cncl; NY Cty Bd Of Ed Cooprtn In Govt 86; Dly Nws Prncpls Prd Of Ynkees 86; Cert Excllnc Prsnl Cntrbtn 86; Baruch; Bus Admin.

LEE, LINDA; Notre Dame Acad; Staten Island, NY; (Y); Art Clb; Church Yth Grp; Cmnty Wkr; Hosp Aide; Chorus; Nwsp Stf; Cheerleading; Crs Cntry; Socr; Trk.

LEE, LISA; La Guardia High Schl Of The Arts; Brooklyn, NY; (S); 13/437; Hosp Aide; Library Aide; Office Aide; Teachers Aide; Chorus; Hon Roll; Jr NHS; NHS; French & Srvc Awds; Engr.

LEE, LISA; Spackenkill HS; Poughkeepsie, NY; (Y); 20/175; Cmnty Wkr; Pres Debate Tm; Pres Drama Clb; JA; VP Leo Clb; Pres NFL; Pres Speech Tm; SADD; Pres Thesps; Orch; John F Kennedy Inst In Gvt 85; Washington Cngrsnl Smnr 86; All St Orchestra 1st Violin 86; PHD Law Schl; Pltcl Sci.

LEE, MICHAEL S H; Nichols Schl; E Amherst, NY; (Y); 1/100; Math Tm; Nwsp Ed-Chief; Yrbk Phtg; Lcrss; Trk; Wrstlng; High Hon Roll; NHS; Val; Harvard U.

LEE, MITCHELL D; Brighton HS; Rochester, NY; (Y); Varsity Clb; JV Var Ftbl; Wt Lftg; Law.

LEE, MIYOUNG; John L Miller North HS; Great Neck, NY; (Y); Pres Church Yth Grp; Pres Key Clb; Nwsp Sprt Ed; Stu Cncl; Var Badmtn; Var Crs Cntry; Var Trk; Certf Merit From GNSCCISP 86; Brd Of Ed Certf Of Cmmdntn 86.

LEE, PEARL; Richmond Hill HS; New York, NY; (Y); Debate Tm; Teachers Aide; Band; School Musical; Sr Cls; Crs Cntry; Tennis; Hon Roll; Girl Scts; Key Clb; Daily News Prin Pride Of Yankees Outstndng Achvt Acdmc-Extra Curr Actvts 85; Math Hnr; Stony Brook.

LEE, RENATA; Uniondale HS; Hempstead, NY; (Y); Hosp Aide; Math Tm; Yrbk Stf; JV Badmtn; Var Sftbl; Var Swmmng; High Hon Roll; Hon Roll; NHS.

LEE, ROBERT; Midwood HS; Brooklyn, NY; (Y); 7/667; Church Yth Grp; French Clb; Math Tm; Spanish Clb; Chorus; Nwsp Rptr; Lit Mag; Math.

LEE, ROBERT; Seward Park HS; New York, NY; (Y); Computer Clb; Teachers Aide; Orch; Hon Roll; Friends Of Seward Inc 86; Pace U; Mngmnt Info Sys.

LEE, ROSALIND; Benjamin Franklin HS; Rochester, NY; (Y); Church Yth Grp; Drama Clb; Boys Clb Am; Pep Clb; Band; Chorus; Church Choir; Lit Mag; Sec Frsh Cls; Stu Cncl; Wilmot Fndtn Declmtn Comp Awd 85; Daisy Harquis Jones Drm Gala Awd 86; Duo Actng Comp Awd 86.

LEE, ROSANN; Shenendohowa HS; Clifton Park, NY; (Y); Church Yth Grp; SADD; Teachers Aide; Church Choir; JV Var Socr; Hon Roll; Roberts Wesleyan Coll; Elem Edu.

LEE, SERENA O; St Marys Girls HS; W Hempstead, NY; (Y); 5/171; French Clb; Mathletes; Math Tm; Stage Crew; Hon Roll; NHS; Ntl Merit Ltr; Rnnr Up Lng Islnd Chrl Soc Yng Musicn Tlnt Cmptn 85; Hnrbl Mntn Advncd Catgry NY ST Music Tch Assn; Engrng.

LEE, STEPHEN; Archbishop Molby HS; Howard Beach, NY; (Y); French Clb; Letterman Clb; Varsity Clb; Nwsp Rptr; Yrbk Phtg; Rep Sr Cls; Im Bsbl; Im Bsktbl; Im Ftbl; Im Golf; Rgnts Schlrshp 86; NY U Tstes Schlrshp 86; Manhattan Coll Pres Schrlshp 86; SUNY; Pre-Med.

LEE, STEVEN; Lynbrook HS; E Rockaway, NY; (Y); Spanish Clb; Band; Mrchg Band; School Musical; School Play; Symp Band; Var Capt Golf; Var Wrstlng; Hon Roll; Pre-Law.

LEE, STEVEN G; St Francis Prep; Elmhurst, NY; (S); 36/710; Pres Chess Clb; Computer Clb; Debate Tm; Math Clb; Math Tm; Im Vllybl; 3rd Pl NYS Class Chess Chmpnshp 85; Principles List 86; Engrng.

LEE, SUN HWA; Hillcrest HS; Jackson Hts, NY; (Y); 19/800; Church Yth Grp; Math Tm; Teachers Aide; Orch; Yrbk Stf; Bowling; Vllybl; Hon Roll; NHS; Prfct Atten Awd; Pre-Med.

LEE, SZEWING; Seward Park HS; New York, NY; (Y); 32/544; Aud/Vis; Computer Clb; Teachers Aide; Band; Elctrcl Engnrng.

LEE, TIMOTHY T; Liverpool HS; Liverpool, NY; (Y); 3/850; Exploring; ROTC; Rep Jr Cls; High Hon Roll; NHS; Church Yth Grp; Hon Roll; Jr NHS; Cornell Bk Awd 85; Amer Lgn Schlts Excllnc Medl 85; Soc Of Mayflower Dscndnts Awd 85; Ntl Frnch Cont 84; U Of Notre Dame; Aerosp Engrng.

LEE, TSIUHAR; Hunter College HS; Brooklyn, NY; (Y); Cmnty Wkr; Girl Scts; Regents Collschlrshp Awd 86; Untd Hosp Fund Volntr Svc Awd 86; Biochem.

LEE, WESLEY; Mepham HS; Bellmore, NY; (Y); Debate Tm; Mathletes; Math Clb; Math Tm; Science Clb; Wrstlng; Hon Roll; Jr NHS; NHS; Elec Engrng.

LEE, WOO; Hillcrest HS; Woodside, NY; (Y); 197/801; Art Clb; Intnl Clb; Political Wkr; Teachers Aide; High Hon Roll; Hon Roll; Prfct Atten Awd; Baruch College; Acctnt.

LEEDY, JEAN; Munich American HS; Apo New York, NY; (Y); Ski Clb; Nwsp Phtg; Yrbk Phtg; Var Trk; NHS; French Clb; Model UN; Lit Mag; Var Crs Cntry; Var Powder Puff Ftbl; ST Wnnr TX Fture Prblm Slvng 84; Photo.

LEEPER, JONATHAN; Jamestown HS; Jamestown, NY; (Y); 72/380; Church Yth Grp; Ftbl; Trk; Rennslr Polytech Inst; Aero.

LEFEBER, CRAIG; Avon Central HS; Avon, NY; (Y); 5/90; 4-H; Band; Pres Frsh Cls; Sec Soph Cls; Sec Jr Cls; Var Capt Bsktbl; Var Ftbl; Var Trk; High Hon Roll; NHS; JR Athltc Cup 86; Farm Bureau Awd 86; Close Up Wahsington Trip 86; Aerontcl Engrng.

LEFF, BONNIE; Commack HS North HS; Commack, NY; (Y); French Clb; Hosp Aide; Trs Service Clb; Teachers Aide; Trs Frsh Cls; Trs Soph Cls; VP Jr Cls; French Hon Soc; High Hon Roll; NHS; Bus.

LEFFERS, JOHN W; Whitesboro SR HS; Utica, NY; (Y); 5/306; Am Leg Boys St; Church Yth Grp; Model UN; Varsity Clb; Var Socr; Var Trk; High Hon Roll; NHS; Boy Scts; NFL; Intern NY Acad Sci Summer Sci Rsrch 86; Track N Field Cntrl Oneida Training Prog League Allstar 86; Air Force Acad; Earospace Engr.

LEFFHALM, MICHELE; Babylon JR SR HS; Babylon, NY; (Y); High Hon Roll; Hon Roll; Schlstc Awd For Bus 84; Child Psych.

LEFKOWITZ, JULIE; Scarsdale HS; Scarsdale, NY; (Y); Trs French Clb; Math Tm; Mgr Nwsp Bus Mgr; Nwsp Stf; Rep Stu Cncl; NHS; FBLA; 3rd Prize Amer Chem Scty Cntst 85.

LEFKOWITZ, TARA-LEE; Shaker HS; Latham, NY; (Y); Dance Clb; Sec Key Clb; Ski Clb; School Musical; Pres Frsh Cls; Pres Stu Cncl; JV Socr; Var Capt Tennis; JV Var Trk; Hon Roll; Cmnd Stu Natl Mrt Schlrshp Prgrm 86; Mln Nsln Mrl Schlrshp Awd Exclnc Advncd Hbrw 83; Rice U; Biochmstry.

LEFORT, MICHELLE; Holland Central HS; Strykersville, NY; (Y); 2/99; Varsity Clb; Variety Show; Sec Jr Cls; Sec Sr Cls; Capt Cheerleading; DAR Awd; High Hon Roll; Jr NHS; NHS; Prfct Atten Awd; Deans Scholar Daemen Coll 86; Regents Scholar 86; Daemen Coll; Phys Ther.

LEGAS, HELENE P; St Francis Prep; Jackson Heights, NY; (S); 88/653; SADD; Opt Clb Awd; Mgmt.

LEGG, MARJORIE; La Fayette HS; La Fayette, NY; (S); 8/94; Hosp Aide; Band; Jazz Band; Mrchg Band; Yrbk Ed-Chief; Yrbk Stf; Var Cheerleading; Var Swmmng; High Hon Roll; NHS; Hghst Art Avg Schltc Achvt Awd 83-85; Stu Mnth 85.

LEGGETT, MICHAEL; Wilson Central HS; Ransonville, NY; (Y); 22/111; School Play; JV Bsktbl; Var Capt Ftbl; Var Capt Trk; High Hon Roll; Jane B Moxham Atrny At Law Mem Awd 86; Bus Clb Trsr 86; Niagara U; Bus.

LEGRAND, RICHARD L; Chaminade HS; Hempstead, NY; (Y); French Clb; Service Clb; AATF Natl Frnch Cntst 1st Prz 83 & 4th Prz 85; Biol.

LEGRO, ADRIANA; St Agnes Academic HS; Flushing, NY; (Y); 28/375; Drama Clb; Girl Scts; School Musical; School Play; Hon Roll; NHS; Law.

LEHNER, ERIC; E J Wilson HS; Spencerport, NY; (Y); Am Leg Boys St; Church Yth Grp; Cmnty Wkr; Latin Clb; Math Clb; Model UN; Band; Concert Band; Jazz Band; Mrchg Band; Regents Scholar Awd 86; Rochester Aerie No 52 Frat Order Eagles 86; Rochester Inst Tech; Elec Engr.

LEHR, KRISTIN; Marion Central HS; Marion, NY; (Y); 21/100; German Clb; Ski Clb; Band; Color Guard; Mrchg Band; Yrbk Ed-Chief; Cheerleading; Sftbl; Prfct Atten Awd; Natl Sci Merit Awd 84-85; Law.

LEHRER, SCOTT E; Woodmere Acad; Hewlett Harbor, NY; (Y); Computer Clb; Key Clb; Nwsp Stf; Lit Mag; Var Crs Cntry; Var Socr; Var Tennis; Ntl Merit Schol; Columbia U Sci Hnrs Pgm; Authrd Comp Pgms.

LEHRMAN, STACEY LYNN; New Rochelle HS; Scarsdale, NY; (Y); Dance Clb; Drama Clb; Ski Clb; SADD; Chorus; School Play; Yrbk Stf; Cheerleading; Gym; Sftbl; U Of AZ; Drmtc Thry.

LEIBENSPERGER, DALE B; Elmira Christian Acad; Painted Post, NY; (Y); 3/15; Camera Clb; Church Yth Grp; Yrbk Phtg; VP Jr Cls; Rgnts Schlrshp 86; Robt Wesleyan; Mnstry.

LEIBOLD, JAMES; John S Burke HS; Goshen, NY; (Y); 25/159; Bsktbl; Socr; Tennis; Hon Roll; Wittenberg U; East Asian.

LEIBOWITZ, CAROLYN; Masters Schl; Scarsdale, NY; (Y); GAA; Office Aide; Varsity Clb; Nwsp Rptr; Pres Frsh Cls; Var Bsktbl; Var Socr; Var Trk; Sprts Med.

LEIBY, KAREN; Schalmont HS; Schenectady, NY; (Y); Band; Chorus; Concert Band; Drm Mjr(t); Mrchg Band; Swing Chorus; Sftbl; Vllybl; Hon Roll; Prfct Atten Awd; Bus Mgmt.

LEIDERMAN, JONATHAN; West Hepmstead HS; Island Park, NY; (Y); Computer Clb; Key Clb; Nwsp Sprt Ed; Var Capt Tennis; Hon Roll; NHS; Bus Dynmcs Awd Hgh Avg; Comp Math Awd; Lang Dept Cert Awd Exc In Span 3 Yrs.

LEIDICH, RAYMOND; Union Springs Acad; Middletown, NY; (Y); Boys Clb Am; Church Yth Grp; Ski Clb; Band; Jazz Band; Mrchg Band; School Play; Rep Stu Cncl; Cit Awd; Sr All Amer Hall Of Fme Bnd Hnrs 86; Orange Cnty CC.

LEIMKUHLER, AMY K; Franklin Central Schl; Franklin, NY; (Y); 3/25; Drama Clb; Ski Clb; Band; Chorus; Yrbk Stf; Var Trk; Var Vllybl; NHS; Ntl Merit Ltr; Rotary Awd; Colllege William & Mary.

LEINING, CHRISTINE; Hoosie Valley HS; Schagticoke, NY; (Y); Art Clb; 4-H; Yrbk Stf; Hon Roll; Paier Coll Of AR; Grphc Dsgn.

LEIPER, CATHY; Salamanca Central HS; Salamanca, NY; (Y); DECA; Varsity Clb; Church Choir; Var Capt Cheerleading; Crs Cntry; Gym; Trk; High Hon Roll; Hon Roll; NHS; Physcl Thrpy.

LEIREY, JAMES E; Kingston HS; Kingston, NY; (Y); 68/576; Am Leg Boys St; Y-Teens; Var L Bsktbl; High Hon Roll; NHS; Var Golf; Cum-Laude Mrn Crps Leg Schlrshp 86; Bus Educ Awd Data Proc 86; NYSBCA Acadmc Tm; ST U Of NY Albany; Comp Sci.

LEISENRING, EMILY; Brockport HS; Brockport, NY; (Y); VP French Clb; Spanish Clb; JV Var Cheerleading; JV Var Socr; High Hon Roll; Hon Roll; Crmnl Justice.

LEISING JR, HERB; Bishop Turner Carroll HS; Buffalo, NY; (Y); Boys Clb Am; Computer Clb; Stage Crew; Nwsp Stf; Yrbk Stf; Trs Frsh Cls; JV Var Bsbl; Im Vllybl; Eagle Scout 86; Comp Reprs Tech.

LEISTHER, KAREN; West Seneca West SR HS; W Seneca, NY; (Y); Cmnty Wkr; GAA; Girl Scts; Library Aide; Teachers Aide; Chorus; Var L Bowling; JC Awd; Prfct Atten Awd; Erie CC South; Physcl Thrpy.

LEITER, KENNETH D; Yeshiva University HS; New York, NY; (Y); Capt Debate Tm; Math Tm; Quiz Bowl; Science Clb; Ski Clb; Pres Temple Yth Grp; Nwsp Ed-Chief; Yrbk Stf; Wrstlng; Hon Roll; Ansta Hnr Soc 84-86; Princeton; Intl Rltns.

LELIS, AUSRA T; Mooney,Cardinal HS; Rochester, NY; (Y); Am Leg Aux Girls St; Cmnty Wkr; Girl Scts; SADD; Rep Frsh Cls; Rep Soph Cls; Rep Jr Cls; Rep Sr Cls; Var Capt Trk; Spanish NHS; St John Fisher Coll; Bus.

LEMANOWICZ, DANA C; St Francis Prep; Elmhurst, NY; (S); 30/740; Spanish Clb; Chorus; High Hon Roll; Hon Roll; Ntl Merit Ltr; Educ.

LEMBECK, LORI; Smithtown High School West; Smithtown, NY; (Y); SADD; JV Var Sftbl; JV Vllybl; NHS; Spanish NHS; Boston U.

LEMMO, LISA ANN; Cornwall Central HS; Cornwall, NY; (Y); 1/185; Church Yth Grp; Hosp Aide; Math Tm; Yrbk Stf; Var Crs Cntry; Var Trk; High Hon Roll; NHS; Val; 1st Rnnr Up Miss NY Nat Tn Agr Pgnt 86; Attrny.

LEMOLE, MICHAEL; St Dominics HS; Northport, NY; (S); 7/139; Quiz Bowl; SADD; School Play; L Crs Cntry; High Hon Roll; NHS; Exclnc In Eng,Frnch 84-85; Chem Achvt Awd 85; Webb Inst; Navl Arch.

LEMZA, MICHAEL; Moriah Central HS; Port Henry, NY; (Y); #3 In Class; Ski Clb; Varsity Clb; VP Sr Cls; Bsktbl; Crs Cntry; Ftbl; High Hon Roll; Jr NHS; NHS; Engrng.

LEN, MICHAEL J; Skaneatelts Central Schl; Skaneateles, NY; (Y); Var Ice Hcky; Var Lcrss; Var Socr; JETS Awd; Elec Engrng.

LENANE, EDWARD; Mount Pleasant HS; Schenectady, NY; (Y); 40/214; Key Clb; SADD; Stu Cncl; Var Capt Crs Cntry; Var Capt Trk; French Hon Soc; Hon Roll; Crss Cntry Tm 84-85; Most Vlbl Runnr Schl Recd 85-86; All Star Trk Tm 86; Suny Pittsbrgh; Engrg.

LENARD, HELEN ANNE; Frontier Central HS; Hamburg, NY; (S); French Clb; Science Clb; SADD; Sec Varsity Clb; Chorus; Var Stat Bsktbl; L Crs Cntry; Var Mgr(s); JV Var Sftbl; Var L Tennis; MIP JV Bsktbl 83; Gannon U; Accntnt.

LENCZEWSKI, VINCENT; Archbishop Molloy HS; Middle Vlg, NY; (Y); 20/408; Cmnty Wkr; Hosp Aide; Intnl Clb; Im Bsktbl; Im Ftbl; Im Sftbl; Var Tennis; High Hon Roll; Jr NHS; Kiwanis Awd; NYU Trsts Schlrshp 86; Rgnts Schlrshp 86; ST U-Stony Brook; Doc.

LENER, ED; Charles O Dickerson HS; Ithaca, NY; (Y); 6/87; Church Yth Grp; Computer Clb; High Hon Roll; NY ST Rgnts Schlrshp 86; Griswold Tel 86; VA Tech Hnr Schlrshp 86; VA Tech; Geolgst.

LENHARD, BARBARA; Bishop Kearney HS; Rochester, NY; (Y); Band; Concert Band; Mrchg Band; Orch; Pep Band; Var Score Keeper; Hon Roll; Ntl Merit Ltr.

LENHARD, DANIEL; Hannibal HS; Hannibal, NY; (Y); 2/100; Church Yth Grp; Pres Computer Clb; Library Aide; Yrbk Stf; High Hon Roll; Hon Roll; NHS; Ntl Merit Ltr; Roberts Wesleyan Coll; Comp Sci.

LENIHAN, TOM; Smithtown HS East; Nesconset, NY; (Y); Im Bsbl; Var Ftbl; Var Wt Lftg; Hon Roll.

LENKIEWICZ, DEBRA; Livingston Manor Central Schl; Livingston Manor, NY; (S); 1/50; Girl Scts; Quiz Bowl; Band; Chorus; Nwsp Ed-Chief; Pres VP Stu Cncl; Var Socr; NHS; Val; Girl Scts Silver Awd 85; Pltcl Sci.

LENNING, ALISHA; Curchville Chili SR HS; Rochester, NY; (Y); Rep Church Yth Grp; FTA; Library Aide; Chorus; School Musical; Lit Mag; Hon Roll; Muskingum Coll Msc & Pres Schlrshp 86; NY Rgnts Schlr 86; Muskingum Coll; Elem Educ.

LENNON, BRIAN; Bayport-Blue Point HS; Blue Pt, NY; (Y); Bsktbl; Hon Roll; Acdmc All-Str Awd 86.

LENNON, DAVID; Valley Central HS; Walden, NY; (Y); 4/225; Drama Clb; Math Tm; School Musical; Yrbk Stf; Lit Mag; JV Socr; Var Trk; High Hon Roll; NHS; Spanish NHS.

LENNON, LAURA A; Southampton HS; Southampton, NY; (Y); 2/115; Sec Spanish Clb; Nwsp Ed-Chief; Trs Stu Cncl; Var L Trk; High Hon Roll; Jr NHS; Lion Awd; NHS; Sal; Brown Book Awd For Engl 85; Coll Of Wm & Mary; Engl.

LENNON, MARGARET; Cambridge Central HS; Eagle Bridge, NY; (Y); 8/75; Ed Lit Mag; VP Soph Cls; VP Jr Cls; Var Fld Hcky; Var Sftbl; DAR Awd; High Hon Roll; Hon Roll; NHS.

LENNOX, MERRITT; Liverpool HS; Liverpool, NY; (Y); 70/861; Church Yth Grp; Hosp Aide; JA; Stu Cncl; Hon Roll; Jr NHS; NHS; Erth & Envrnmnt Sci Hnr Awd; Hrng Dsblty Educ.

LENO, CHRISTINA; Holy Trinity D HS; Plainview, NY; (Y); Drama Clb; Math Tm; School Play; Nwsp Rptr; Nwsp Stf; Yrbk Stf; Rep Stu Cncl; High Hon Roll; Hon Roll; Jr NHS; Math Schlrshp Awd 81-82; Math Schlrshp Awd 84-85; Adelphi U; Elem Educ.

LENOIRE, WILLIAM C; Cardinal Spellman HS; New York, NY; (Y); Chess Clb; JV Bsbl; Im Bsktbl; JV Ftbl; Im Vllybl; Im Wt Lftg; NEDT Awd; NY U; Bus Admin.

LENT, CHRISTY LYN; Valley Central HS; Montgomery, NY; (Y); Debate Tm; French Clb; Hosp Aide; Natl Beta Clb; Acpl Chr; Chorus; School Musical; French Hon Soc; Hon Roll; JC Awd; Hugh O Brien Yth Ldrshp Awd.

LENTZE, HUGO F; Mount Assumption Inst; Morrisonville, NY; (Y); 4/77; Am Leg Boys St; Drama Clb; Mathletes; Math Tm; Model UN; Quiz Bowl; Ski Clb; Band; Chorus; Church Choir; All-Amer Band; Military Acad; Pltcl Sci.

LENZ, JONATHAN W; Ward Melville HS; East Setauket, NY; (Y); 48/711; High Hon Roll; Hon Roll; Jr NHS; NHS; Ntl Merit SF; JV Bsktbl; JV Ftbl; JV Lcrss; Lutheran Brotherhd Scholar 86; U Chicago; Bio.

LEO, ROBERT J; Ossining HS; Ossining, NY; (Y); Aud/Vis; Church Yth Grp; Cmnty Wkr; VICA; Var Crs Cntry; Var Golf; Var Trk; Delhi; Crpntry.

LEO, SUZANNE; Ossining HS; Ossining, NY; (Y); VP French Clb; SADD; Sec Band; Mrchg Band; Orch; Mgr Stage Crew; Rep Stu Cncl; Var Capt Fld Hcky; High Hon Roll; NHS; Educ.

LEON, JOSE; Midwood HS; New York City, NY; (Y); Church Yth Grp; Spanish Clb; Orch; Im Bsktbl; Var Trk; Im Vllybl; Trphy Trk 84-86; JR Aristo Soc 83; Med.

LEON JR, JOSE S; St Francis Preparatory HS; Queens Village, NY; (S); 20/744; Church Yth Grp; Spanish Clb; Chorus; Opt Clb Awd; Prfct Atten Awd; NYU; Medcn.

LEON, LIZET; St Joseph HS; Brooklyn, NY; (Y); 23/106; Computer Clb; Nwsp Stf; Yrbk Phtg; Yrbk Stf; Gym; Hon Roll; Adelphi U; Med.

LEONARD, COLLEEN M; Catholic Central HS; Troy, NY; (Y); Church Yth Grp; Math Clb; SADD; Variety Show; Yrbk Stf; Off Soph Cls; Off Jr Cls; Hon Roll; St Schlr; Art Clb; Siena Coll; Math.

LEONARD, ERIN P; Shaker HS; Cohoes, NY; (Y); French Clb; Service Clb; Ski Clb; High Hon Roll; Hon Roll; U Of NH; Cvl Engrng.

LEONARD, GARY; Wheatland-Chili HS; Scottsville, NY; (Y); 5/75; Am Leg Boys St; Jazz Band; Mrchg Band; Pep Band; Sec Jr Cls; Sec Sr Cls; Var Bsbl; Var Capt Bsktbl; Var Capt Socr; Hon Roll; Hall Fame Schlr Athlete Schrlshp 86; Regnts Schrlshp 86; Rotry Schrlshp 86; U Notre Dame; Elect Engr.

LEONARD, JOHN; Wetlake HS; Thornwood, NY; (Y); Am Leg Boys St; French Clb; Trs Spanish Clb; Band; Jazz Band; Nwsp Phtg; Nwsp Rptr; Var Socr; Var Tennis; Hon Roll; Byst NY Hawthorne Amer Lgn 86; Lbrl Arts.

LEONARD, KELLY; Mineola HS; Mineola, NY; (Y); Htl/Rest/Trvl.

LEONARD, KELLY; Voorheesville HS; Voorheesville, NY; (Y); 33/114; Ski Clb; Spanish Clb; Chorus; Nwsp Rptr; Nwsp Stf; Yrbk Stf; JV Vllybl; Kiwanis Awd; Hudson Vly Cmnty Coll; Mrktng.

LEONARD, LAURA; Nardin Acad; Kenmore, NY; (Y); 2/82; NFL; Service Clb; Ski Clb; Lit Mag; Trs Frsh Cls; Trs Jr Cls; Sec Sr Cls; Var Sftbl; Var JV Vllybl; Bausch & Lomb Sci Awd; Vllybl All Star Awd 85-86; Hghst 2 Yr Soc Stud Awd 85; 2 Sftbl All Star Awds 84 & 86; Bus.

LEONARD, MARY E; St Francis Prep; Rockaway Beach, NY; (S); Band; Color Guard; Concert Band; Drm & Bgl; Mrchg Band; Pep Band; JV Bsktbl; Im Coach Actv; JV Sftbl; Im Vllybl; Ironman Awd Sftbl 84; Engl & Spanish Hnrs Classes 83-86; Mt St Marys Coll; Pre Law.

LEONARD, MAUREEN; Wheatland-Chili Central HS; Scottsville, NY; (Y); 2/75; SADD; Band; Rep Pres Stu Cncl; JV Var Bsktbl; JV Var Socr; JV Var Sftbl; High Hon Roll; Hon Roll; Prfct Atten Awd; Bus Adm.

LEONARD, TONIA; Watkins Glen Central HS; Watkins Glen, NY; (Y); Yrbk Stf; Hon Roll; Elem Ed.

LEONARDO, CHRISTINE; Colonie Central HS; Loudonville, NY; (Y); 14/480; VP Church Yth Grp; FBLA; Hst Soph Cls; Hst Jr Cls; Hst Sr Cls; VP Stu Cncl; Capt Cheerleading; Sftbl; High Hon Roll; NHS; Prin Ldrshp Awd 86; PTA Schlrshp 86; Clemson U.

LEONARDO, JOSEPH; Beacon HS; Beacon, NY; (Y); 2/168; Cmnty Wkr; Radio Clb; High Hon Roll; NHS; Sal; Pres Physcl Ftns Awd 86; Lions Clb Awd Sldtrn 86; Awds For Mth, Pblc Spkng, Chmstry & Hlth 86; Vassar Coll; Engrng.

LEONE, ANDREW; Alexander Hamilton HS; Elmsford, NY; (S); Pres Aud/Vis; Church Yth Grp; Key Clb; ROTC; Band; Rep Stu Cncl; Var JV Bsbl; Var JV Ftbl; Var Socr; Im Wt Lftg; Acadmc Schlr Awd Ftbl 83; Biolgcl Sci 85; Audio Engr.

LEONE, DEBRA J; Bay Shore SR HS; Bay Shore, NY; (Y); Church Yth Grp; Cmnty Wkr; Library Aide; Science Clb; Yrbk Phtg; Stu Cncl; Cheerleading; Coach Actv; Capt Gym; Hon Roll; Bus Awd 86; Parsons Schl Design; Int Desgnr.

LEONE, JOHN; Proctor HS; Uitca, NY; (Y); FFA; Pep Clb; Badmtn; Bsbl; Bsktbl; Bowling; Crs Cntry; Ftbl; Socr; Sftbl; JV Awd Bsbl 85.

LEONE, JULIE; Mt St Mary Acad; Kenmore, NY; (Y); Pep Clb; School Musical; Chrmn Swing Chorus; Rep Frsh Cls; Rep Soph Cls; Capt Cheerleading; Tennis; Hon Roll; Liberl Arts.

LEONE, MARIA; Bishop Ford Central Catholic HS; Brooklyn, NY; (Y); 186/427; Computer Clb; Ski Clb; Yrbk Stf; Bowling; Crs Cntry; Trk; Bckpkng Clb 84-85, Dnc A Thon 83, 85 & 86; Assc Schls Inc; Trvl & Trsm.

LEONE, MARIA; Our Lady Of Victory Acad; Yonkers, NY; (S); Drama Clb; School Musical; Lit Mag; Stu Cncl; French Hon Soc; Hon Roll; NHS; Socl Studs Awd 84; Math Awd 85.

LEONE, MICHAEL; Niagara Catholic HS; Niagara Fls, NY; (Y); Ski Clb; JV Bsbl; Im Bowling; Ftbl; Var Swmmng; Im Wt Lftg; Engr.

LEONE, STEPHEN; Midwood HS; Brooklyn, NY; (Y); 113/667; Jazz Band; School Play; Nwsp Sprt Ed; Stu Cncl; Var Tennis; Ntl Merit Schol; Bus.

LEONG, ANGELA; Nazareth Regional HS; Belle Harbor, NY; (S); 2/267; Am Leg Aux Girls St; Camera Clb; Chorus; Nwsp Phtg; Nwsp Rptr; Yrbk Phtg; Ed Yrbk Stf; Stu Cncl; High Hon Roll; NHS; Soc Stud Medl 85; Govrs Cmmttee-Schltc Achvt Citatn 86.

LEONG, KWANG W; Newtown HS; Elmhurst, NY; (Y); 3/667; Pres Chess Clb; VP Computer Clb; Math Clb; Math Tm; Chorus; High Hon Roll; Mu Alp Tht; NHS; Prfct Atten Awd; Natl Merit Cmmndtn 85; Queens Coll Presdts Awd 85; NY St Rgnts Schlrshp Awd 86; Cooper Union; Elect Engrng.

LEONOFF, DAVID; Roslyn HS; Roslyn, NY; (Y); Computer Clb; Office Aide; Crs Cntry; Trk; Muhlenberg Coll; Pre-Med.

LEOPOLDI, ROBERT; Bishop Ford C C HS; Brooklyn, NY; (Y); Boy Scts; Cmnty Wkr; Political Wkr; Pres Sr Cls; Im Bowling; Im Fld Hcky; Nwsp Rptr; Nwsp Stf; Bus Law.

LEOTTA JR, FRANK A; E Islip SR HS; East Islip, NY; (Y); 111/425; Letterman Clb; Yrbk Phtg; Yrbk Rptr; Yrbk Stf; Stu Cncl; JV Bsbl; Var L Fld Hcky; Im Wt Lftg; High Hon Roll; Hon Roll; Pres Phys Ftnss Awd 80; Capt JV Ftbl Tm 84; Hnrbl Mntn Ftbl 86; SUNY Stonybrook; Elec Engrg.

LEPARD, RICHARD; Susquehanna Valley HS; Conklin, NY; (Y); Mathletes; Trs Soph Cls; Trs Jr Cls; Trs Sr Cls; Im JV Bsktbl; JV Ftbl; Var Tennis; Var Trk; High Hon Roll; NHS; Engnrng.

LEPKI, TAMMY; Webster High-R L Thomas HS; Webster, NY; (Y); 167/548; Teachers Aide; Color Guard; Hon Roll; Minr Ltr Schlstcs 83-84; Vet Sci.

LEPKOFF, MELANIE; Baldwin HS; Baldwin, NY; (Y); VP JA; Math Clb; Service Clb; Spanish Clb; Temple Yth Grp; Yrbk Stf; Hon Roll; Prfct Atten Awd; Tp 10 Prcnt Cls 83-84; Farmindale/Hofstra; Vet.

LEPORE, JACQUELINE; St Francis Prep; Bayside, NY; (Y); 112/693; Band; Mrchg Band; Yrbk Stf; Rep Stu Cncl; JV Trk; Hon Roll; Jr NHS; Ntl Merit SF; Optimates List 84-85; St Johns U; Sci.

LEPRE, PATRICK; Mercy HS; Cutchogue, NY; (Y); Boy Scts; Camera Clb; Church Yth Grp; Cmnty Wkr; Computer Clb; SADD; Chorus; Stage Crew; Yrbk Phtg; Crs Cntry; Cobleskill; Phrmcst.

LERCH, PAT; Lynbrook HS; E Rockaway, NY; (Y); Sec Exploring; Sec FBLA; Key Clb; Science Clb; AFS; Var Sftbl; Hon Roll; Molloy; Nrsng.

LERNER, DOREEN; Islip HS; Bayshore, NY; (Y); Cmnty Wkr; Girl Scts; Hosp Aide; Mathletes; Chorus; Yrbk Stf; Rep Stu Cncl; JV Var Socr; JV Var Sftbl; High Hon Roll; SUNY.

LERNER, ERIC; Farmingdale HS; S Farmingdale, NY; (Y); 50/590; Pres FBLA; Nwsp Ed-Chief; Yrbk Rptr; Lit Mag; Hon Roll; Ntl Merit Ltr; St Schlr; NYS Regents Scholar 85; U Miami Half Tuition Scholar 86; U Miami; Comm.

LERNER, SHERI; Tottenville HS; Staten Island, NY; (Y); Model UN; Var Capt Crs Cntry; Var Capt Trk; Advnce All Star Crssentry Trk 84-86; Steve Prefontaine Awd Outstndng Crs Cntry Rnnr 86; MVP Trk 86; Engl.

LEROUX, KEVIN F; Ogdensburg Free Acad; Ogdensburg, NY; (Y); 3/196; French Clb; Math Tm; PAVAS; Quiz Bowl; Jazz Band; Nwsp Stf; Rep Stu Cncl; High Hon Roll; NHS; Church Yth Grp; NYS Regnts Schlrshp 86; Amer Legn Ortrcl Cntst Wnnr 85; U Of Buffalo; Comp Grphcs.

LERUM, VICENTE; Hillcrest HS; Holliswood, NY; (Y); 88/834; Math Tm; Lit Mag; Var Tennis; Hillcrest Math Sci Awd Bronze & Silvr Mdl 85-86; Sci.

LESCAULT, DIANNE; Corinth HS; Corinth, NY; (Y); French Clb; Varsity Clb; JV Var Bsktbl; JV Var Socr; JV Var Sftbl; Var Vllybl; Hon Roll; Prom Qn 86; Miss Congeniality 86; Bus.

LESEFSKE, MICHELLE; Gowanda Central HS; Gowanda, NY; (Y); 80/124; SADD; Thesps; Color Guard; Concert Band; Mrchg Band; Stage Crew; Nwsp Stf; Yrbk Stf; Art Incntv Awd 85-86; Bst Grphc Art Westrn NY 84-85; 3rd Pl Ad Crft Comptn 85-86; Nazereth; Art Thrpy.

LESER, STEVEN H; Alfred G Berner HS; Massapequa Park, NY; (Y); 100/430; Computer Clb; German Clb; Chrmn Spanish Clb; Temple Yth Grp; Var Capt Tennis; NY ST Rgnts Schlrshp 86; ST U Of NY-ALBNY; Comp Sci.

LESHAW, ALICE; Central Islip HS; Central Islip, NY; (Y); Stage Crew; Math.

LESIAK, KAREN; Frontier Central HS; Willowick, OH; (Y); DECA; FBLA; Girl Scts; Latin Clb; Pep Clb; Teachers Aide; Rep Soph Cls; Rep Stu Cncl; Hon Roll; NHS; Bus Fld.

LESINSKI, BONNIE; Grand Island HS; Grand Island, NY; (Y); 19/325; Ski Clb; Sftbl; Hon Roll; NHS; Rgnts Schlrshp 86; Lcl Rtry Clb Schlrshp 86; Lcl Jhn Gntz Mem Schlrshp 86; Hmnts Clb 82-86; ST U Of NY Buffalo; Phrmcy.

LESINSKI II, DAVID H; St Francis HS; Boston, NY; (Y); 6/146; French Clb; Lit Mag; Rep Soph Cls; Rep Jr Cls; Hon Roll; NHS; Prtl Yrly Schlrshp Canisius Coll 86; NYS Rgnts Schlrshp 86; 2nd & 3rd Prz Frnch Entries Lng Fr 84-85; Canisius Coll Buffalo; Cmmnctns.

LESLIE, ANITA M; Buffalo Acad Of Sacred Heart; Williamsville, NY; (Y); 7/126; Science Clb; Spanish Clb; Nwsp Rptr; Var Crs Cntry; Trk; High Hon Roll; Hon Roll; NHS; US Ntl Precsn Figr Sktng Tm Champ 84-86; Empire ST Games Slvr Medl Rowng 85; Gold Mdl Sktng 86; St Marys Coll; Comms.

LESLIE, CHRISTOPHER; Fredonia HS; Fredonia, NY; (Y); Am Leg Boys St; Chorus; School Musical; School Play; Nwsp Rptr; Yrbk Rptr; Lit Mag; JV Var Crs Cntry; Var Swmmng; JV Var Trk; Intl Forgn Lang Awd 86; Acadmc All Amer 86; Comp Sci.

LESNIAK, CHRISTINE; North Collins Central HS; N Collins, NY; (Y); 27/69; Girl Scts; Nwsp Stf; JV Swmmng; Hon Roll; Queen Pag Bands 86; Erie CC; Intr Desgn.

LESNIEWSKI, LAURIE; Buffalo Academy Of The Sacred Heart; Buffalo, NY; (Y); Library Aide; School Musical; Nwsp Rptr; Lit Mag; Voice Dem Awd; Political Wkr; Hon Roll; Spnsh Awd 4 Yrs Exclinc Spnsh 86; Church Lector; Acdmc Tm Altr; Engl.

LESPERANCE, EVE; Academy Of St Joseph; Bayshore, NY; (Y); JA; PAVAS; Orch; Variety Show; St Josephs; Music Educ.

LESSEN, JIMMY; Immaculata HS; New York, NY; (Y); Computer Clb; Drama Clb; English Clb; Chorus; Bsbl; Bsktbl; Ftbl; Sftbl; Hon Roll; St Johns U; Bus.

LESSNER, DONNA; Roy C Ketcham HS; Wappinger Falls, NY; (Y); 79/510; Girl Scts; Nwsp Stf; Yrbk Phtg; Var Capt Gym; High Hon Roll; NHS; Drama Clb; Band; Stage Crew; Yrbk Stf; Girl Scout Wider Oprtnty-Sport Spree 83; Conf-A-All Star Team Gymnstcs 86; U Hartford; Bus.

LESSNER, LAURIE; Niskayuna HS; Schenectady, NY; (Y); Cmnty Wkr; Drama Clb; Latin Clb; Spanish Clb; Pres Temple Yth Grp; School Musical; School Play; Stage Crew; Nwsp Bus Mgr; Nwsp Stf; Hotel Mgmt.

LESSO, CRISS; Johnson City SR HS; Johnson City, NY; (Y); Art Clb; Camera Clb; Ski Clb; SADD; FL Inst Of Tech; Arch.

LESTER, GARY; Mechanicville HS; Mechanicville, NY; (S); 19/125; Church Yth Grp; Spanish Clb; SADD; JV Bowling; Var Crs Cntry; Var Wt Lftg; Var Wrstlng; High Hon Roll; NHS; Paul Smiths Coll; Envir Consrvt.

LESTER, PASCHA D; Watertown HS; Watertown, NY; (Y); Church Yth Grp; Cmnty Wkr; Y-Teens; Var Bsktbl; Var Fld Hcky; Var Sftbl; Im Vllybl; Altrnte Goalie NY Empire ST Games; Northeastern Christian JC; Ed.

LESZCZAK, MARK; Grand Island HS; Grand Island, NY; (Y); 72/298; Ski Clb; JV Ftbl; Var Trk; Im Vllybl; Im Wt Lftg; Hon Roll; FL ST U; Investmnts.

LETA, KURT; Lyndonville HS; Waterport, NY; (Y); 8/90; AFS; Church Yth Grp; Computer Clb; Letterman Clb; Math Clb; Math Tm; Science Clb; Varsity Clb; Bsbl; Bsktbl; MIT; Nuclr Engrng.

LETHIN, DOUGLAS O; Babylon JR SR HS; Babylon, NY; (Y); 10/150; Drama Clb; Thesps; Chorus; School Musical; School Play; Stage Crew; Soph Cls; Trs Jr Cls; Sr Cls; NHS; Comp Sci.

LETIZIA, MISSY; Solvay HS; Solvay, NY; (Y); Church Yth Grp; Computer Clb; Frsh Cls; Soph Cls; Jr Cls; Sftbl; Vllybl; High Hon Roll; NHS; Spnsh Awd 84-85; Trig Awd 84-85; Engl Awd 83-85; Syracuse U; CPA.

LETO, PAULA; Mary Louis Acad; Richmond Hill, NY; (Y); Cmnty Wkr; Teachers Aide; Hon Roll; Schl Svc Awd 84 & 86; Hon Sci Itln 86; St Johns U; Phych.

LETONEN, MELISSA; Mexico Academy & Central Schl; Fulton, NY; (Y); VP Spanish Clb; Sec SADD; VP Rep Frsh Cls; Pres Rep Soph Cls; Pres Rep Jr Cls; Pres Stu Cncl; Score Keeper; Hon Roll; Spanish NHS; Yrbk Stf; Spnsh Comp 2nd Pl 83-84.

LETRIZ, EDGAR; Abraham Lincoln HS; Brooklyn, NY; (Y); Debate Tm; Variety Show; Nwsp Ed-Chief; Nwsp Rptr; Nwsp Stf; Lit Mag; Rep Frsh Cls; Rep Soph Cls; Rep Jr Cls; Hon Roll; Princpls Great Bk Clb 85-86; Intl Bus Mgmt.

LETT, SYLVIA J; Shaker HS; Latham, NY; (Y); GAA; Key Clb; Ski Clb; Band; Nwsp Ed-Chief; Trs Frsh Cls; JV Bsktbl; JV Var Socr; JV Var Trk; Ntl Merit SF; Pre Law.

LETT, TERESA; Liverpool HS; Liverpool, NY; (Y); 71/816; Church Yth Grp; Ski Clb; Church Choir; Jazz Band; Mrchg Band; Symp Band; Hon Roll; Jr NHS; NHS; St Schlr; Soc Stds Awd 84; SUNY Binghamton.

LEUNG, CYNTHIA; James Madison HS; Brooklyn, NY; (Y); 57/756; Yrbk Phtg; Ed Yrbk Stf; Gym; Var Tennis; Mock Trial Awd 83; NY U; Bus.

LEUNG, FRANKIE; Newtown HS; Elmhurst, NY; (Y); Aud/Vis; Band; Jazz Band; School Musical; School Play; Stage Crew; Prfct Atten Awd; Regnts Coll Schlrshp 86; Polytech U; Elec Engr.

LEUNG, HANG LEI; Murry Bergtraum HS; New York, NY; (Y); Intnl Clb; Hon Roll; Acad Schlrshp 86-87; NY City Tech Coll; Htl Mgmnt.

LEUNG, JEANIE; Farmingdale Senior HS; Massapequa Park, NY; (Y); 47/600; Am Leg Aux Girls St; Rep French Clb; VP FBLA; Intnl Clb; Library Aide; Pres Sec Service Clb; SADD; Rep Chorus; Flag Corp; Variety Show; Frmngdl Prnt Tchr Assoc Mrt Awd 86; Bus Educ Dpt Susan Vigiano Mrl Awd 86; NYS FBLA Bus 86; Mount Holyoke Coll; Bus.

LEUNG, JUDY; H S Of Art & Design; New York City, NY; (Y); 24/411; Teachers Aide; Hon Roll; NHS; Rhode Isl Schl Of Dsgn Smr Pre-Coll Prgm 84; Art Drctrs Clb Awd 85; Kodak/Schlstc Awd 86; Schl Vsl Arts; Phtgrphy.

LEUNG, MILLIE; HS Of Fashion Ind; New York, NY; (Y); 18/324; Office Aide; Chorus; Nwsp Stf; Yrbk Stf; French Hon Soc; Hon Roll; Comm.

LEUSCHEL, MAIK; Mahopac HS; Mahopac, NY; (Y); Chess Clb; Orch; Vllybl; Hon Roll; Prfct Atten Awd; Engrng.

LEUSCHNER, JACQUELINE; Connetquot HS; Oakdale, NY; (Y); 162/786; Art Clb; Computer Clb; Dance Clb; Drama Clb; French Clb; Intnl Clb; SADD; Teachers Aide; Acpl Chr; Chorus; Frgn Lang.

LEV, LIYA; H S Of Art & Design; Brooklyn, NY; (Y); 3/412; VP Art Clb; FTA; Library Aide; Office Aide; Teachers Aide; Sec Frsh Cls; Hon Roll; Prfct Atten Awd; Rgnts Schlrshp 86; Art Hnr 84-86; Ntl Fdrtn Tchrs Schlrshp 86; Brown U.

LEVANDOWSKI, JULIE; Fowler HS; Syracuse, NY; (Y); Church Yth Grp; Pres Sr Cls; Im Swmmng; Im Trk; High Hon Roll; Hon Roll; NHS; Band; Yrbk Phtg; Var Capt Cheerleading; Rec Awd For Photogrphy 86; Acctpnc Into Giftd Engl Prog 86; Socilgy.

LEVANO, BRENT; Archbishop Molloy HS; Flushing, NY; (Y); Boy Scts; Hosp Aide; Red Cross Aide; Spanish Clb; Band; Crs Cntry; Trk; Flshng Hosp Med Ctr Awd 84; Queens Coll; Marine Bio.

LEVASSEUR, MIRKO; Hillcrest HS; Queens, NY; (Y); Cmnty Wkr; Hosp Aide; Red Cross Aide; Science Clb; Rep Frsh Cls; Trk; Hon Roll; NHS; Ntl Merit Schol; Prfct Atten Awd; St Johns U; Phrmcy.

LEVENE, DANIEL G; Vestal HS; Binghamton, NY; (Y); 14/453; Varsity Clb; Capt Tennis; NHS; St Schlr; Tennis Vrsty Lttr 5 Yrs; MVP 85; Cptn 85-86; ETA Tennis Singles 84-85; U Of PA.

LEVENSOHN, BETSY; Bethlehem Central HS; Delmar, NY; (Y); 21/304; Am Leg Aux Girls St; Pres Drama Clb; Hosp Aide; Temple Yth Grp; Chorus; School Musical; School Play; Rep Frsh Cls; JV Fld Hcky; High Hon Roll; Bryn Mawr Clg.

LEVENSON, MIYAN M; Fieldston Schl; Bronx, NY; (Y); Drama Clb; PAVAS; Pres Temple Yth Grp; School Musical; School Play; Stage Crew; Nwsp Stf; Ntl Merit Schol; David Stein Schlrshp 84; U Of MA Amherst; Actr.

LEVERNOIS, MICKEY; Guilderlan Central HS; Altamont, NY; (Y); 79/375; Chess Clb; Varsity Clb; Var L Socr; Hon Roll; Most Imprvd Jv Sccr 84; Excptnl Sr & Shared Mvp Awd Varsity Sccr 86; Clarkson U; Civil Engrng.

LEVEROCK, JOHN; Mc Kee Tech HS; Staten Island, NY; (Y); 23/306; Church Yth Grp; Cmnty Wkr; JV Bsktbl; Hon Roll; Seagull Soc 85-86; Engrng.

LEVESQUE, SUSAN; Out Lady Of Lourdes HS; Wappingers Fls, NY; (Y); 26/180; Cmnty Wkr; Yrbk Stf; Var Swmmng; High Hon Roll; Hon Roll; NHS; Prfct Atten Awd; Elec Engrng.

LEVEY, SHIRA; Vincent Smith HS; Plainview, NY; (Y); 6/18; Dance Clb; Drama Clb; Rep Temple Yth Grp; VP Y-Teens; Church Choir; Yrbk Stf; Hon Roll; Spec Ed.

LEVIN, LISA A; Newburgh Free Acad; Newburgh, NY; (Y); 7/621; VP Debate Tm; Spanish Clb; Pres Temple Yth Grp; Acpl Chr; Orch; Nwsp Rptr; Rep Soph Cls; Trs Jr Cls; Trs Stu Cncl; Tennis; U PA.

LEVIN, NAOMI; Forest Hills HS; Forest Hills, NY; (Y); 16/886; Dance Clb; Hosp Aide; Model UN; Sec Science Clb; Temple Yth Grp; Band; School Musical; Variety Show; Rep Sr Cls; High Hon Roll; Med Bio Awd With Hghst Hnrs 86; NY City Chnclrs Roll Of Hnr For Arts 86; Sci Sprvsrs Awd For Phycs 86; Hebrew U Of Jerusalem; Med.

LEVINBOOK, HOWARD; John F Kennedy HS; Merrick, NY; (Y); Computer Clb; Debate Tm; Math Tm; Science Clb; Nwsp Ed-Chief; Nwsp Stf; High Hon Roll; Hon Roll; NHS; Superior Math Avg 83-84; Adelphi Chem Sem 85.

LEVINE, BRIAN J; Earl L Vandermeulen HS; Mt Sinai, NY; (Y); 32/300; Varsity Clb; Band; Concert Band; Jazz Band; Stage Crew; Var Capt Bsbl; Ftbl; Hon Roll; NHS; Prfct Atten Awd; Natl Phys Educ Awd 86; Natl Sci Olympiad 2nd Pl Chem 84; Bio.

LEVINE, CRAIG; Earl L Von Der Meulen HS; Mt Sinai, NY; (Y); Band; Var Bsbl; Var Ftbl; Var Gym; Var Wrstlng; Bus.

LEVINE, DOUG; Jamesville-Dewitt HS; Fayetteville, NY; (Y); 10/240; Trs Key Clb; Latin Clb; Math Tm; Trs Spanish Clb; SADD; Trs Temple Yth Grp; Varsity Clb; Yrbk Bus Mgr; Stu Cncl; JV Socr; Med.

LEVINE, EDWARD S; Yorktown HS; Yorktown Hts, NY; (Y); 63/325; Aud/Vis; JA; Teachers Aide; Hon Roll; SUNY Oswego; Cmmnctns.

LEVINE, JAMIE; W C Mepham HS; Merrick, NY; (Y); Hosp Aide; SADD; Nwsp Stf; Yrbk Stf; Soph Cls; Jr Cls; Chrmn Sr Cls; High Hon Roll; Jr NHS; NHS; Jrnlsm.

LEVINE, JENNIFER; Blind Brook HS; Rye Brook, NY; (Y); Spanish Clb; Chorus; School Musical; School Play; Yrbk Ed-Chief; Sftbl; Vllybl; Zoology.

LEVINE, JOAN; John H Glenn HS; E Northport, NY; (Y); Drama Clb; Capt Drill Tm; School Play; Nwsp Rptr; Capt Pom Pon; High Hon Roll; Hon Roll; NHS; Spanish NHS; Spanish Clb; History Ed.

LEVINE, JULIE; Ward Melville HS; Centereach, NY; (Y); Ski Clb; Temple Yth Grp; Hon Roll; Jr NHS; Bwlng Awd 84; Spnsh Awd 84 & 85; Comp.

LEVINE, MINDI; Bethpage HS; Bethpage, NY; (Y); 65/303; Art Clb; Intnl Clb; Spanish Clb; Band; JV Lcrss; JV Capt Pom Pon; Grphc Art.

LEVINE, RANDI; Abraham Lincoln HS; Brooklyn, NY; (Y); JA; Spanish Clb; Chorus; School Musical; Cit Awd; Hnr Card Achvt Spnsh & Hnr Card Achvt Grp Discsn 85; Med.

LEVINE, RHONDA; Hauppauge HS; Smithtown, NY; (Y); Temple Yth Grp; Y-Teens; Rep Soph Cls; JV Var Cheerleading; High Hon Roll; Hon Roll; Psychlgy.

LEVINE, RICHARD A; Valley Stream South HS; Valley Stream, NY; (Y); Capt Mathletes; Concert Band; Jazz Band; Mrchg Band; Orch; Var Trk; VP NHS; Aud/Vis; Chess Clb; Computer Clb; Rensselaer Polytech Inst Medl 86; Lng Isl Sci Cngrss-Blu Rbn 86; Anne Portnoy Music Schlrshp 85; Math.

LEVINE, SHARON; Commack North; Commack, NY; (Y); Cmnty Wkr; Office Aide; Political Wkr; Teachers Aide; Varsity Clb; Drill Tm; Nwsp Stf; High Hon Roll; NHS; Chorus; Lib Arts.

LEVINE, WYNNE; La Guardia HS; New York, NY; (S); Chorus; Hon Roll; Lit.

LEVINS, GERALD; Torrejon American HS; Apo, NY; (Y); Computer Clb; Ski Clb; Bsbl; Capt Var Socr; Hon Roll; All Conf Soccer 86; All Star Bsbl 84.

LEVITAN, EUGENIA; Clarkstown HS North; New City, NY; (Y); Computer Clb; Math Tm; Lit Mag; Vllybl; Mu Alp Tht; NHS; Math.

LEVY, DAVID J; Baldwin SR HS; Baldwin, NY; (Y); 1/475; Pres Key Clb; Capt Mathletes; Var Crs Cntry; Var Trk; High Hon Roll; NHS; Spanish NHS; Drama Clb; Model UN; Science Clb; 1st Pl High Hnrs Sci Congrs 84-86; Gold Medal Math Fair 85; IA U & MI ST Smmr Sci Prog 85-86; Surgeon.

LEVY, DAVID L; Walt Whitman HS; Melville, NY; (Y); 83/550; Boy Scts; Computer Clb; Key Clb; Political Wkr; Radio Clb; Mrchg Band; Trk; French Hon Soc; Hon Roll; NHS; NYS Rgnts Schlrshp 86; Pilot Grnd Schl Schlrshp; SUNY Stony Brook; Pre-Med.

LEVY, DAVIDD; Clarkstwon South HS; Nanuet, NY; (Y); Fld Hcky; 4-H; Math Clb; Science Clb; Temple Yth Grp; Mu Alp Tht; NHS; Debate Tm; Math Tm; Im Bsktbl; Outstndg Achvt In Advncd Plcmnt Biol 86; Biol.

LEVY, JASON; Scarsdale HS; Scarsdale, NY; (Y); Civic Clb; Hosp Aide; Spanish Clb; Varsity Clb; Nwsp Rptr; Bsktbl; Var Crs Cntry; JV Socr; Capt Var Tennis; Ntl Merit Ltr; AP Amer Hstry 85-86; Hnrs Engl 85-86; Hnrs Math 83-86; Psych.

LEVY, MATTHEW; North Babylon SR HS; N Babylon, NY; (Y); 39/975; Cmnty Wkr; Nwsp Ed-Chief; Nwsp Rptr; Nwsp Sprt Ed; JV Var Tennis; Jr NHS; NHS; Scholar N Babylon PTSA Jrnlsm Smmr Pgm Sycamore 86; Jrnlsm.

LEVY, STACEY; Harrison HS; Harrison, NY; (Y); 15/211; AFS; Drama Clb; French Clb; Math Tm; Temple Yth Grp; Y-Teens; Band; School Play; Variety Show; NHS; Ciba-Geigy Sci Awd 86; Bio.

LEVY, STELLA; Mt Vernon HS; Mount Vernon, NY; (Y); Drama Clb; French Clb; FTA; Rep Key Clb; Office Aide; SADD; Teachers Aide; Pres Temple Yth Grp; School Musical; Yrbk Ed-Chief; Edith Kaplan Mem Awd 86; Stella United Nations Awd; Brandeis U; Drama.

LEVY, SUSAN; New Rochelle HS; New Rochelle, NY; (Y); Dance Clb; Drama Clb; School Play; Capt Diving; Mgr(s); Score Keeper; Sftbl; Capt Swmmng; NHS; Sec Spanish NHS; Comp Sci Awd 83-84; MVP Diving 86-86; Best Performance In Cameo Role 84-86; Bus Mngmt.

LEVY, TANYA; Peter Stuyvesant HS; Brooklyn, NY; (Y); Drama Clb; Library Aide; Red Cross Aide; Chorus; Sec Church Choir; Pep Band; School Play; Co-Capt Cheerleading; Trk; Ntl Merit SF; Natl Achvt Schlrshp Pgm For Outstndng Negro Studnts-Commended Studnt 85; Finance.

LEW, LILY; Murry Bergtraum HS; New York, NY; (Y); Office Aide; Yrbk Stf; Vllybl; Teachers Aide; Yrbk Phtg; Var Bsktbl; Bowling; Gym; Wt Lftg; Bus Admin.

LEW, SHIRLEY; Greece Athena HS; Rochester, NY; (Y); Spanish Clb; Yrbk Stf; JV Vllybl; Hon Roll; Bus.

LEWANDOSKI, DONALD J; Red Creek Central Schl; Sterling, NY; (Y); 49/81; Camera Clb; Chess Clb; French Clb; Ski Clb; Var JV Bsktbl; Socr; JV Wrstlng; Comp Engrng.

LEWANDOWSKI, GERALD; St Marys HS; Depew, NY; (S); 7/166; Camera Clb; Pres Chess Clb; Computer Clb; Yrbk Stf; Im Bowling; High Hon Roll; NHS; Robert F Kennedy Mem Awd 84; Suny Fredonia; Comp Sic.

LEWANDOWSKI, KIMBERLY; Turner-Carroll HS; Buffalo, NY; (S); 2/110; Yrbk Stf; VP Soph Cls; VP Jr Cls; Var Bowling; Var Sftbl; Hon Roll; NHS; Prfct Atten Awd; Servc Awd 85; Med Tech.

LEWANDOWSKI, KRISTINA; Oyster Bay HS; Oyster Bay, NY; (Y); Sec Church Yth Grp; Dance Clb; Hosp Aide; SADD; Chorus; School Musical; Ed Nwsp Phtg; Nwsp Rptr; High Hon Roll; NHS; Comm.

LEWANDOWSKI, LISA; Hamburg HS; Hamburg, NY; (Y); Camp Fr Inc; French Clb; Pres Girl Scts; School Musical; Grl Sct Slvr Awd 84.

LEWIN, THOMAS; Vernon-Verona-Sherrill HS; Vernon, NY; (Y); Am Leg Boys St; Boy Scts; Varsity Clb; Band; Var JV Bsbl; Var JV Ftbl; Var Vllybl; Var JV Wt Lftg; God Cntry Awd; High Hon Roll; Nmntd Hmntrn Awd Oneida Cnty 85; Bus Admn.

LEWINSKI, LISA; Lackawanna SR HS; Lackawanna, NY; (Y); Church Yth Grp; Spanish Clb; High Hon Roll; Hon Roll; Rochester Inst Of Tech; Bio.

LEWIS, ANNE E; Newark SR HS; Newark, NY; (Y); 51/201; VP Pres Band; Chorus; Church Choir; Pres Concert Band; Jazz Band; Mrchg Band; School Musical; Swing Chorus; High Hon Roll; Hon Roll; NYSSMA Vcl & Instrmntl Awd 82-85; Arts & Action Awd 82-83; Buffalo ST Coll; Grphc Design.

LEWIS, ARNOLD; Eastern District HS; Brooklyn, NY; (Y); Library Aide; Office Aide; Teachers Aide; Cert Of Awd Schlstc Achvmnt In Engl 84, French 85 & Music 84; Law.

LEWIS, BETHANN; Notre Dame HS; Elmira, NY; (Y); Art Clb; Cmnty Wkr; Trs 4-H; Ski Clb; Yrbk Stf; 4-H Awd; High Hon Roll; 2 Yr Scholar Notre Dame H S 83; Vet.

LEWIS, CAROL; Charles E Gorton HS; Yonkers, NY; (Y); Church Yth Grp; FBLA; Spanish Clb; Band; Chorus; Church Choir; Yrbk Stf; Cheerleading; Trk; Hon Roll; TV Producer.

LEWIS, CHRISTOPHER; Beacon HS; Beacon, NY; (Y); Church Yth Grp; Civic Clb; FCA; Key Clb; Varsity Clb; Yrbk Stf; Var L Bsktbl; Var L Ftbl; Cit Awd; Hon Roll; Dutchess CC; Civil Engrng.

LEWIS, DANA; Erasmus Hall HS; Brooklyn, NY; (Y); 275/586; Art Clb; Exploring; FHA; PAVAS; Spanish Clb; Nwsp Stf; Yrbk Stf; Var Bsbl; Var Ftbl; Artistic Awds; Buffalo U; Arch.

LEWIS, DONNA; Central Islip SR HS; Central Islip, NY; (Y); 13/348; Sec Aud/Vis; Hon Roll; NHS; Ntl Merit Ltr; Mansfield U; Tvl & Trsm.

LEWIS, EDWARD M; Bronxville Public HS; Bronxville, NY; (Y); ROTC; Band; Concert Band; Orch; Ftbl; Wrstlng; High Hon Roll; Hon Roll; St Schlr; NYS Rgnts Schlrshp 85; AF ROTC Schlrshp 86; Hnrbl Mntn All Cnty Wrstlr 86; Lafayette Coll-Easton; Mech Eng.

LEWIS, JACQUELINE A; Bronx H S Of Science; Bronx, NY; (Y); Key Clb; Political Wkr; Nwsp Bus Mgr; VP Stu Cncl; Ntl Merit Ltr; Daily News/NY Yankees Super Yth Awd 83-85.

LEWIS, JEFF; Niagara Wheatfield HS; Niagara Falls, NY; (Y); 42/292; Latin Clb; Varsity Clb; Golf; Ice Hcky; SUNY Buffalo; Law.

LEWIS, JEFFREY S; Longwood HS; Coram, NY; (Y); Chess Clb; Hon Roll; Accntnt.

LEWIS, JENNIFER; Aquinas Inst; Scottsville, NY; (Y); 14/260; Concert Band; Drm Mjr(t); Mrchg Band; High Hon Roll; SADD; Received Partial HS Schlrshp 83-86; 3rd Rnnr Up Miss Western Mohawk Pgnt 86; Food Studies.

LEWIS, JENNIFER A; Scotia Glenville HS; Scotia, NY; (Y); Sec Spanish Clb; Pres SADD; Band; Mrchg Band; Yrbk Stf; High Hon Roll; Hon Roll; Prfct Atten Awd; Bldmble Wrker 86; Frnds Schnctdy Co Pblc Lbry 86; Elem Educ.

LEWIS, JODI; Grand Island HS; Grand Island, NY; (Y); Church Choir; Yrbk Phtg; Yrbk Stf; Gym; Mgr(s); Trk; Buffalo ST Coll; Scl Wrk.

LEWIS, JULIE; Cairo-Durham HS; Cairo, NY; (Y); Band; Chorus; Pep Band; School Musical; Hon Roll; Jr NHS; Cert Merit 86; 1st Pl Greene Cnty Fair Tlnt Shw 85; NYSSMA Comptns 84; SUNY Albany; Tchg.

LEWIS, KRISTIN; Bishop Grimes HS; Syracuse, NY; (S); 2/188; Latin Clb; Science Clb; Ski Clb; Concert Band; Rep Stu Cncl; Var Capt Cheerleading; Var Socr; High Hon Roll; Mth Awd Hghst Avg 83-85; Sci Awd Hghst Avg 83-84; Music Awd 84-85; Sci.

LEWIS, LISA; Bronx H S Of Science; Queens, NY; (Y); Trs Church Yth Grp; Cmnty Wkr; Dance Clb; Office Aide; Teachers Aide; Cheerleading; Bucknell U; Mngmnt.

LEWIS, LORI; Liverpool HS; Liverpool, NY; (Y); Exploring; JA; Lit Mag; Var L Bsktbl; Coach Actv; Powder Puff Ftbl; Var L Sftbl; High Hon Roll; Trs NHS; Engl Awd 84; U Of Rochester; Psych.

LEWIS, MAUREEN ANN; Saint Saviour HS; Brooklyn, NY; (Y); 13/80; Drama Clb; French Clb; Math Tm; Lit Mag; French Hon Soc; High Hon Roll; NHS; Schlrshp Awd 86; Hist Awd 83-85; Nazareth Coll Schlrshp 86.

LEWIS, MICHELE; Avoca Central HS; Avoca, NY; (Y); 38/48; Ski Clb; Varsity Clb; Chorus; School Play; Yrbk Stf; Rep Stu Cncl; Bsktbl; Socr; Sftbl; Alfred ST Coll.

LEWIS, MICHELLE; Mahapac HS; Putnam Valley, NY; (Y); 96/409; 4-H; Girl Scts; Band; Chorus; Twrlr; 4-H Awd; Hon Roll; Accntng.

LEWIS, MICHELLE; Susan E Wagner HS; Staten Island, NY; (Y); 10/550; Cmnty Wkr; Band; Concert Band; Mrchg Band; School Play; Nwsp Rptr; Trs Jr Cls; Pres Stu Cncl; High Hon Roll; Jr NHS; Law.

LEWIS, NOVADA; Hillcrest HS; Queens, NY; (Y); Band; Chorus; Church Choir; Rep Stu Cncl; Hon Roll; Cmmnty Chrctr & Cncrn 84; Natl Gld Pianotorn 85; :Physcl Thrpst.

LEWIS, PATRICIA; Park West HS; New York, NY; (Y); #166 In Class; Church Yth Grp; Vllybl; Hon Roll.

LEWIS, PAUL; Brewster HS; Brewster, NY; (Y); Pres Sr Cls; Var L Bsktbl; Hon Roll; NHS; Ntl Merit Ltr; Spanish NHS; English Achvt.

LEWIS, PAUL; Rensselaer HS; Rensselaer, NY; (Y); Boys Clb Am; Computer Clb; SADD; Varsity Clb; Yrbk Rptr; Yrbk Stf; Rep Frsh Cls; Rep Soph Cls; Stu Cncl; Bsktbl; Law.

LEWIS, RENEE; Arch Bishop Walsh HS; Olean, NY; (Y); Art Clb; Latin Clb; Pep Clb; Var Diving; Var JV Mgr(s); Var Sftbl; Var Swmmng; Var Ltr & Pin; Acctng.

LEWIS, SUSAN; Harpursville HS; Port Crane, NY; (S); 4/86; French Clb; Varsity Clb; Color Guard; Mrchg Band; Yrbk Stf; Var L Fld Hcky; Var Capt Twrlr; JV Vllybl; High Hon Roll; NHS; Salute To Yth 85; Ntl Sci Olympd Cntst 1st Pl 85; Hghst Schlstc Avg Chem, Frnch 85; Ed.

LEWIS, TERRENCE; Oriskany Central HS; Oriskany, NY; (Y); Boy Scts; Church Yth Grp; Varsity Clb; Concert Band; Yrbk Stf; Rep Stu Cncl; Var L Bsktbl; Var L Socr; Hnr & Awd In Stu Cncl 85; Bio.

LEWIS, TERRI; Bishop Grimes HS; E Syracuse, NY; (Y); Cmnty Wkr; JV Var Socr; JV Var Vllybl; Hon Roll; All Star Trny Tm Vllybl 85-86; Ed.

LEWIS, TRACIE; Mt St Joseph Acad; Buffalo, NY; (Y); 14/44; Church Yth Grp; Debate Tm; JA; Library Aide; Office Aide; Spanish Clb; Chorus; Church Choir; School Musical; School Play; Alert Search Progam 85-86; MSJD Music Awd 85-86; ST U NY; Music.

LEWIS, VICTORIA; Fontbonne Hall Acad; Brooklyn, NY; (Y); 6/139; French Clb; SADD; Teachers Aide; Nwsp Stf; Yrbk Stf; Ntl Ltn Cntst Awd 86; Psych.

LEWONKA, STEPHEN; Hauppauge HS; Smithtown, NY; (Y); 80/550; Boy Scts; Computer Clb; Radio Clb; Hon Roll; Aero Sp Engr.

LEWORTHY, WILLIAM; Liverpool HS; Liverpool, NY; (Y); Boy Scts; Var JV Ftbl; Im Wt Lftg; Jr NHS; Ntl Merit Ltr; Comm.

LEYLAND, LINDA; Churchville-Chili HS; Rochester, NY; (Y); Chorus; Concert Band; Yrbk Ed-Chief; Yrbk Stf; Rep Jr Cls; Capt Cheerleading; Capt Gym; Mgr(s); Socr; Sftbl; Rochester Inst Tech; Bus Admn.

LEYMON JR, WAYNE; Vernon-Verona-Sherrill HS; Vernon, NY; (Y); SADD; Yrbk Phtg; Lit Mag; Var L Trk; Hon Roll; Kiwanis Awd; Bike A Thons Multpl Sclrsis & Diabts 85-86; Buddy Helpr Spec Olympcs 86; MVCC; Crmnl Jstc.

LEYSHON, AMY L; Vestal SR HS; Vestal, NY; (Y); Church Yth Grp; Intnl Clb; Library Aide; Varsity Clb; Band; Lib Concert Band; Trs Mrchg Band; Pep Band; Symp Band; JV Var Bsktbl; NYSSMA-A Wind, B Duet 82; Robert Packer Schl Of Nrsg; Nrs.

LEZAJA, DOROTHY; Bethpage HS; Bethpage, NY; (Y); 140/303; Art Clb; Church Yth Grp; Dance Clb; Cit Awd; Hon Roll; Stat Score Keeper; Hnrbl Mntn/Art Poster Assoc Help Retrd Chldn 85; Empire ST Assoc Distngshd Effort Awd 86; NY Inst Of Tech; Fine Art.

LEZAMIZ, JOSEPH A; Bishop Ford Central Catholic HS; Brooklyn, NY; (Y); Computer Clb; Hon Roll.

LEZCANO JR, CONRADO; Msgr Scanlan HS; Bronx, NY; (Y); 85/295; Capt JV Bsbl; Powder Puff Ftbl; Trk; TCI; Comp Tech.

LI, CHERLYNNE; High School Of Art And Design; Jackson Hts, NY; (Y); Computer Clb; FTA; Math Clb; Math Tm; Office Aide; PAVAS; Political Wkr; Teachers Aide; Stu Cncl; Gov Hon Prg Awd; Super Yth 85; Hnr Rl 86; Acad All Am 86; Cooper Union; Graphic Art.

LI, CHUN; Tottenville HS; Staten Island, NY; (Y); Church Yth Grp; Hosp Aide; Library Aide; Math Clb; Church Choir; Tennis; Hon Roll; NHS; Acad Plympics 85-86; Asian Clb 85-86; Engrng.

LI, JOSEPH J; Bronx High School Of Science; Woodside, NY; (Y); Trs Church Yth Grp; Library Aide; Math Tm; Science Clb; Teachers Aide; Chorus; Church Choir; Lit Mag; Hon Roll; NCTE Awd; Cert Rcgntn Math, Sci, SS, Eng 82; SS Schlrshp Fnlst 85; Rgnts Schlrshp 86; NY U; Comp Sci.

LI, MARIA; Seward Park HS; New York, NY; (Y); Nwsp Rptr; Nwsp Stf; Vllybl; Effrt Awd 83.

LI CAUSI, MICHELE; John A Coleman HS; Ulster Park, NY; (S); 9/64; Debate Tm; Key Clb; Ski Clb; School Play; Yrbk Rptr; Rep Jr Cls; Var Capt Cheerleading; High Hon Roll; Hon Roll; NHS; Centry III Ldrshp Awd 86; Swarthmore; Poli Sci.

LIAMBAS, THOMAS; Bronx H S Of Science; New York, NY; (Y); Office Aide; Prfct Atten Awd; Elec Engrng.

LIAMIDO, KEVIN; La Salle Military Acad; Ronkonkoma, NY; (Y); ROTC; Color Guard; Drm & Bgl; School Musical; School Play; Nwsp Stf; Yrbk Phtg; Computer Clb; Drama Clb; Ski Clb; Best Underclsmn & SR Actr 85-86; U Buffalo; Med.

LIANG, MARILYN; Brighton HS; Rochester, NY; (Y); 20/325; French Clb; Ski Clb; SADD; Varsity Clb; Yrbk Bus Mgr; Sr Cls; Cheerleading; MIT.

LIAO, ANGELA; Newtown HS; Elmhurst, NY; (Y); MIT; Comp Sci.

LIAO, STEVE; Commack High School North; Commack, NY; (Y); 11/361; Computer Clb; Drama Clb; Math Tm; Teachers Aide; School Play; Nwsp Stf; Rep Soph Cls; JV Var Tennis; High Hon Roll; NHS.

LIBBEY, LAURI; J C Birdleborugh HS; Fulton, NY; (Y); 4-H; SADD; Chorus; Madrigals; School Musical; Stage Crew; Swing Chorus; 4-H Awd; Phillips Inst; Cosmtlgst.

LIBENSON, ROBIN; Spackenkill HS; Poughkeepsie, NY; (Y); SADD; Teachers Aide; Temple Yth Grp; Thesps; School Musical; School Play; Stage Crew; Nwsp Ed-Chief; Hon Roll; Ntl Merit Ltr; Stu Dir Of Hs Ply 85; Brd Of Dir Of Cmnty Chldrns Thtr 85-87; Lbrl Arts.

LIBERTY, PERRY; East Meadow HS; East Meadow, NY; (Y); Photogrphy Awd 84; Schl Store Aide 85-87; Hofstra; Acctng.

LIBERTY, STRATTON; Seton Catholic Central HS; Binghamton, NY; (Y); Am Leg Boys St; Art Clb; Church Yth Grp; Drama Clb; School Musical; School Play; Eductnl Drama.

LIBMAN, DAVID; Midwood HS; Brooklyn, NY; (Y); Teachers Aide; ARISTA; Bus Admn.

LIBONATI, ANDREW J; Mount St Michael Acad; Bronx, NY; (S); 37/308; Boy Scts; Band; L Ftbl; L Var Sftbl; Var Wt Lftg; Hon Roll; NHS; Math Awd 83; Leadrshp Awd 83; Bsbl-Tournmnt & MVP 82; Columbia; Opthamlgst.

LIBRADER, ERIK A; Valhalla HS; North White Plain, NY; (Y); 1/120; Boy Scts; Math Tm; Teachers Aide; Rptr Nwsp Stf; Rep Sr Cls; Var Crs Cntry; Var Trk; Hon Roll; Pres NHS; Prfct Atten Awd; Commended Stu In PSAT Merit Schlrshp Vinal 85; NY St Regents Schlrshp Recipient 86; Earth Sci Awd 83; Georgetown U; Bus Mgt.

LIBURDI, DENISE; Union Endicott HS; Endwell, NY; (Y); Dance Clb; Key Clb; Drill Tm; Flag Corp; Cheerleading; Pom Pon; Hon Roll; RIT; Elec Engrng.

LICARI, JODEE; Oneonta HS; Oneonta, NY; (Y); Art Clb; French Clb; SUNY; Art Hstry.

LICATA, CHRISTOPHER; Bishop Timon HS; W Seneca, NY; (Y); Letterman Clb; Ski Clb; Capt Ftbl; Ice Hcky; Score Keeper; Capt Trk; L Wt Lftg; All WNY Ftbl, All Cthlc Ftbl, Trck 85-86; MVP Ftbl 84-86; 3rd Team All NY ST Ftbl 85-86; Ithaca Coll.

LICHSTEIN, AMY; Scarsdale HS; Scarsdale, NY; (Y); Intnl Clb; Temple Yth Grp; Cheerleading; Capt Gym; Tennis.

LICHTENSTEIN, STACY L; Rye Neck HS; Rye, NY; (Y); 4/100; Pres AFS; Key Clb; School Musical; Rep Stu Cncl; JV Var Cheerleading; JV Var Fld Hcky; Var Gym; JV Var Socr; High Hon Roll; NHS; Rgnts Schlrshp 86; Colgate U.

LICHTMAN, CHRISTINE BENJAMINA; Hicksville HS; Hicksville, NY; (Y); 196/456; Mgr Drama Clb; VP FBLA; Political Wkr; Art Clb; Orch; Ed Yrbk Ed-Chief; Trs Stu Cncl; Mgr Trk; High Hon Roll; Dance Clb; NYS Rep Miss Amer Coed Pgnt 85; NY Inst Tech; Hotel Mgmt.

LICHTMAN, STEVEN B; Edgemont HS; Scarsdale, NY; (Y); Art Clb; Nwsp Phtg; Nwsp Rptr; Nwsp Stf; Yrbk Phtg; Lit Mag; Mgr(s); Stat Socr; Ntl Merit Ltr; Straight A Awd 83; Iona Coll Lang Cont 3rd & 4th Hnrs 84-85; Natl Spn Cont Awd 83; Brandeis U; Pre-Law.

LICITRA, GINA; Canarsie HS; Brooklyn, NY; (Y); Drama Clb; Chorus; Madrigals; School Musical; Yrbk Phtg; Powder Puff Ftbl; Sftbl; Twrlr; Hosp Aide; Mrchg Band; Itln Hnr Awd 86; ENYC Essy Cntst Awd Aprthd 86; Law.

LICKFELD, KAREN; Mount Mercy Acad; Buffalo, NY; (Y); 32/200; French Clb; Ski Clb; Yrbk Stf; Crs Cntry; Sftbl; Tennis; Trk; Vllybl; Hon Roll; NHS; Sci Fair 84; U Buffl; Engrng.

LICTUS, AMY; Clymer Central HS; Clymer, NY; (Y); 11/45; Church Yth Grp; Library Aide; Office Aide; Teachers Aide; Chorus; Church Choir; School Play; Yrbk Stf; Trs Frsh Cls; Trs Soph Cls; Bus Stu Of Yr 86; Nazareth Coll Rochester; Bus Ed.

LICURSI, TAMMY; St Marys HS; Cheektowaga, NY; (S); 16/170; Cmnty Wkr; Library Aide; Rep Stu Cncl; High Hon Roll; Hon Roll; NHS; NEDT Awd; 2nd Pl Essy Cntst 85; Acadmc Commndtn A Avrg Keybrdg And Acadmc Exclnc Spnsh 85; Elem Schl Tchr.

LIDDINGTON, JACQUELYNN ANNE; Marathon Central HS; Marathon, NY; (Y); 10/68; 4-H; Ski Clb; Sec Frsh Cls; Pres Stu Cncl; Capt Var Fld Hcky; Sftbl; Cit Awd; 4-H Awd; Hon Roll; NHS; HOBY Ldrshp Awd 84; IAC Fld Hcky All Star 85; Excptnl SR Sftbl 86; Findlay Coll; Vet.

LIDDLE, MARK; Grand Island SR HS; Gr Island, NY; (Y); 69/350; Var Golf; Var JV Ice Hcky; JV Lcrss; U Buffalo; Mech Engrng.

LIDDLE, MELANIE A; Naples Central HS; Naples, NY; (Y); JA; Teachers Aide; Chorus; Concert Band; Jazz Band; Mrchg Band; Pep Band; Pres Schlr; St Schlr; Hon Roll; Jazz Band Piano Awds 85-86; Band Awd 85-86; Music Horizons Eastman Schl Music 85; Nazareth; Music Ed.

LIDDLE, ROGER; Naples Central Schl; Naples, NY; (Y); Boy Scts; Var JV Socr; Hon Roll; US Marine Corps.

LIDDY, DONALD; Camden Central Schl; Camden, NY; (Y); Church Yth Grp; Band; Chorus; Concert Band; Drm & Bgl; Mrchg Band; Orch; JV Trk; Wt Lftg; Var Wrstlng; IOOF 86; ST U Of NY; Elec Tech.

LIDESTRI, AMY; Waterloo SR HS; Waterloo, NY; (Y); 21/154; Church Yth Grp; Dance Clb; French Clb; JV Cheerleading; JV Sftbl; Hon Roll; NHS; Daisy Chain; Comp Sci.

LIEBERMAN, GERRI; The Wheatley Schl; Albertson, NY; (Y); Model UN; Temple Yth Grp; Stage Crew; Nwsp Bus Mgr; Yrbk Stf; Rep Jr Cls; JV Var Cheerleading.

LIEBERMAN, MATTHEW; The Wheatley Schl; Albertson, NY; (Y); 7/133; Drama Clb; Hosp Aide; School Musical; School Play; Ed Nwsp Stf; Yrbk Stf; Trs Soph Cls; Trs Jr Cls; Trs Sr Cls; NHS; U Of PA.

LIEBOWITZ, AMY; Edward R Murrow HS; Brooklyn, NY; (Y); Girl Scts; Office Aide; Political Wkr; Service Clb; Temple Yth Grp; School Musical; Stage Crew; Variety Show; Nwsp Rptr; Nwsp Stf; NY ST Rgnts Scholar 86; Brooklyn Coll Schlr 86; Law Awd 86; SUNY-ALBANY; Pol Sci.

LIEBOWITZ, MICHAEL J; Ward Melville HS; Setauket, NY; (Y); 124/725; Drama Clb; Temple Yth Grp; Band; Drm Mjr(t); Jazz Band; Mrchg Band; Pep Band; School Play; Nwsp Rptr; Yrbk Phtg; NY Regents Schlrshp 86; Psych.

LIEBY, ALICIA M; John S Burke C HS; New Windsor, NY; (Y); 1/153; Cmnty Wkr; Drama Clb; Pres VP 4-H; Model UN; Trs Stage Crew; Lit Mag; High Hon Roll; NHS; Pres Schlr; Teachers Aide; Frdhm U Schlrshp; Frdhm U; Accntng.

LIEDKA, CARRIE; CNS HS; Mattydale, NY; (S); 28/669; Teachers Aide; Lit Mag; High Hon Roll; NHS; Acad All Amer 84-85; Engl & Europn Hstry Tutor 85-86; Oswego; Comp Mngmnt.

LIEFFRIG, PETER; Smithtown West HS; Smithtown, NY; (Y); German Clb; Off Soph Cls; Off Jr Cls; JV Bsktbl; Socr; Hon Roll; Chem.

LIEGEY II, MARK I; Archbishop Molloy HS; Far Rockaway, NY; (Y); 80/384; Art Clb; Cmnty Wkr; French Clb; Teachers Aide; Church Choir; Orch; Im Bowling; Im Sftbl; Im Trk; Hon Roll; :Engr.

LIER, KEVIN M; Bennett HS; Buffalo, NY; (Y); 11/220; Math Tm; Hon Roll; NHS; NY ST Rgnts Schlrshp 86; ST U NY Buffalo Phrmcst.

LIER, KRISTINE; Fonda Fultonville Central HS; Fonda, NY; (Y); Drama Clb; Intnl Clb; Spanish Clb; Color Guard; Drill Tm; Yrbk Stf; Var Cheerleading; Im Gym; Var Capt Vllybl; Stat Wrstlng; Rgnts Schlrshp 86; Le Moyne; Intl Bus.

LIEVAL, MICHAEL; Nanuet HS; Nanuet, NY; (Y); Var Capt Socr; Var Trk; Hon Roll; NHS; All Cnfrnc Sccr 85-86; All Lg Trk 85-86; Advrtsg.

LIFSHEY, DEEBORAH L; Arlington HS; Poughkeepsie, NY; (Y); 12/575; French Clb; Ski Clb; SADD; Temple Yth Grp; Yrbk Ed-Chief; Yrbk Stf; Rep Frsh Cls; High Hon Roll; Rgnts Schlrshp 86; Thomas J Watson Mem Schlrshp 86; Arlngton Hnr Key 86; Cornell U; Indstrl/Lbr Rltns.

LIGA, SAL; Westlake HS; Pleasantville, NY; (Y); Computer Clb; Debate Tm; Math Tm; Spanish Clb; Pres Stu Cncl; Var Trk; High Hon Roll; Jr NHS; NHS; Chess Clb; NY St Sci Supv Assn Sci Awd 85; Pre Med.

LIGAMMARE, TINA; Niagara Catholic HS; Niagara Fls, NY; (Y); Cmnty Wkr; Key Clb; Yrbk Stf; Stat Badmtn; Hon Roll; Psych.

LIGAMMARI, ANDREA; Sweet Home SR HS; Holley, NY; (Y); Rep Frsh Cls; Rep Soph Cls; Rep Stu Cncl; Hon Roll; Prfct Atten Awd; Italian Clb Rep 85-86; Italian Hnr Soc Awd 86; Acctng.

LIGHTCAP, CHRISTOPHER; Springville-Griffith Inst; Springville, NY; (Y); 5/190; Church Yth Grp; French Clb; High Hon Roll; NHS; Ntl Merit SF; Prfct Atten Awd; Accntng.

LIGHTER, GWEN; Blind Brook HS; Rye Brook, NY; (Y); Drama Clb; Red Cross Aide; Science Clb; Chrmn Spanish Clb; School Musical; Nwsp Rptr; Rep Stu Cncl; Var Capt Crs Cntry; Var Capt Socr; High Hon Roll; Fnlst Hugh O Brian Yth Fndtn Ldrshp 85; Miss Natl Teenager Acdmc Excllnce & Fnlst 84.

LIGHTFOOT, JOSEPH C; Ogdensburg Free Acad; Ogdensburg, NY; (Y); 18/186; Am Leg Boys St; Key Clb; Var Ftbl; Var Capt Trk; Hon Roll; Pres NHS; All Conf Ftbll Tm 85; Clarkson U; Mechncl Engr.

LIGHTFOOT, RICHELLE; Twin Tiers Baptist HS; Corning, NY; (S); 1/18; Sec Church Yth Grp; Chorus; Church Choir; Stage Crew; Var Socr; High Hon Roll; Bptst Chrstn Schl Assn NY ST Sci Fair 2nd Pl Math 84-85; Houghton Coll; Bio.

LIGHTFOOTE, TOM; Marcus Whitman JR SR HS; Gorham, NY; (Y); 7/120; Var Capt Bsktbl; High Hon Roll; NHS; VP Soph Cls; L Var Bsbl; L Var Socr; Im Vllybl; Finger Lakes West Bsbl 1st Tm All Str 85; NY ST Regnts Schlrshp 86; Robert L Stape Memrl Awd 85; Syracuse U; Pol Sci.

LILAKOS, MARK; Richmond Hill HS; Richmond Hill, NY; (Y); 2/360; Cmnty Wkr; Debate Tm; Pres Key Clb; School Play; Nwsp Ed-Chief; Pres Soph Cls; VP Jr Cls; Sec Stu Cncl; NHS; Math Clb; New Schl Chncllr Awd 86; HOBY ST Ambssdr 85; Mayrs Yth Cert 86; Acctg.

LILLENSTEIN, DAVID J; Pioneer Central HS; Delevan, NY; (Y); Boy Scts; French Clb; Latin Clb; SADD; Nwsp Stf; Lit Mag; Rep Frsh Cls; Rep Soph Cls; Rep Jr Cls; Rep Sr Cls; Big Mac Schlrshp 86; ROTC Schlrshp 86; Olympcs Of Mnd; Gettysburg Coll; Mngmnt.

LILLIS, COLLEEN; Mount Mercy Acad; Buffalo, NY; (Y); Cmnty Wkr; Ski Clb; SADD; Stage Crew; Lit Mag; High Hon Roll; Hon Roll; NHS; Hnrb Mntn WNY Frgn Lang Fair 84-85; WNY Schl Prss Assn-3rd Pl-Bst Photo 85; D Youville Coll; Nrsng.

LILLIS, TIMOTHY J; Bisho Timon HS; Buffalo, NY; (Y); 17/156; Camera Clb; Cmnty Wkr; Ski Clb; Stage Crew; Variety Show; Nwsp Phtg; Yrbk Phtg; Lit Mag; Rep Stu Cncl; Im Var Bowling; PAL Schlrshp 85; Cmnty Svc Awd 83-86; YABA Cert Of Merit 85; Conisius Coll; Acctng.

LILLY, MICHAEL; Midwood Highschool At BK College; Brooklyn, NY; (Y); Art Clb; Boy Scts; Church Yth Grp; Cmnty Wkr; Office Aide; Teachers Aide; Varsity Clb; Church Choir; Var Bsbl; Score Keeper; Arizona ST U; Hstry.

LIM, GEE YOUNG; Flushing HS; Flushing, NY; (Y); Art Clb; Church Yth Grp; Church Choir; Orch; Lit Mag; Hon Roll; Prfct Atten Awd; Trustee Achvt Adelphi U 86; Adelphi U; Applied Art.

LIM, LINDA; Fashion Industries HS; New York, NY; (Y); 49/324; Library Aide; Teachers Aide; Hon Roll; Prfct Atten Awd; Fash Indstries Schlrshp 83-84; Art Hon Soc 85-86; Cmmrcl Art.

LIM, SOYUNG; Jamaica HS; Jamaica, NY; (Y); Church Yth Grp; Cmnty Wkr; Intnl Clb; Service Clb; Teachers Aide; Orch; School Play; NHS; Prfct Atten Awd; Regents Schlrshp 86; Trustee Schlrshp 86; NY U.

LIM, YONG-SIK; Eastchester HS; Scarsdale, NY; (Y); Church Yth Grp; Drama Clb; Latin Clb; PAVAS; Ski Clb; Pres SADD; Varsity Clb; Band; Chorus; Church Choir; SADD Pres 85-86; Bus Adm.

LIMBACH, STEVEN; Northport HS; E Northport, NY; (Y); Church Yth Grp; Radio Clb; School Play; Lit Mag; Hon Roll; Advrtsng.

LIMERICK, MELISSA; Tioga Central HS; Barton, NY; (S); 25/96; Spanish Clb; Varsity Clb; School Musical; Nwsp Sprt Ed; VP Frsh Cls; VP Soph Cls; VP Jr Cls; VP Stu Cncl; Var Capt Fld Hcky; Var Golf; Natl Span Exm Lvl I 9th In Rgn, 1st In Schl & Lvl II 13th Rgn, 2nd Schl 84-85; Mst Outstndg Ctznshp; Lebanon Valley Coll; Intl Bus.

LIMTHONG, NICOLE; Valley Stream Central HS; Valley Stream, NY; (Y); AFS; Aud/Vis; Computer Clb; Ski Clb; SADD; Yrbk Phtg.

LIN, BETTY; Herricks HS; New Hyde Prk, NY; (Y); Cmnty Wkr; Key Clb; Science Clb; VP Trs Orch; School Musical; Nwsp Stf; NHS; Ntl Merit Ltr; NY All ST Strng Orchstr 85; MENC Cnvntn CT 84; Med.

LIN, PAUL C; The Nichols Schl; E Amherst, NY; (Y); Hosp Aide; Ski Clb; Nwsp Rptr; Ed Nwsp Stf; Ed Yrbk Stf; Ed Lit Mag; Var Crs Cntry; Var Tennis; Var Trk; High Hon Roll; Cornell U; Engrng.

LIN, YUANYU; White Plains HS; White Plains, NY; (Y); Camera Clb; Computer Clb; Math Tm; Crs Cntry; Trk; Hon Roll; NHS; Pres Schlr; ST U Of NY; Engrng Sci.

LINARES, DIOGENES; La Salle Acad; Brooklyn, NY; (S); 4/189; Im Bsbl; Im Bowling; JV Crs Cntry; Im Ftbl; Im Sftbl; JV Trk; High Hon Roll; Hon Roll; NHS; Comp Anlyst.

LINARES, NELLY; Uniondale HS; Hempstead, NY; (Y).

LIND, ERIK; East Hampton HS; E Hampton, NY; (Y); Boy Scts; Chess Clb; CAP; Cmnty Wkr; Exploring; Intnl Clb; Pep Clb; Color Guard; Stage Crew; Golf; Mchncl Drwng Schlrshp Awd; Penn ST U; Engrng.

LINDAHL, DAWN AILEEN; James E Sperry/Greece Athena HS; Rochester, NY; (Y); DECA; JA; Office Aide; VP SADD; VP Jr Cls; Socr; Hon Roll; Camp Fr Inc; Bowling; Wt Lftg; Best Sales VO PRO Trade Schl Jewelry Sale 86; JR Achvt Project Bus 86; All Star Sccr Tm 82-85; Data Processing.

LINDBERG, LAURA M; Nottingham HS; Syracuse, NY; (Y); #27 In Class; Pres Church Yth Grp; Yrbk Bus Mgr; Yrbk Stf; Stat Lcrss; Var Capt Vllybl; Trs NHS; Spanish NHS; Spanish Clb; Hon Roll; Regents Schlrshp; St Lawrence U; Bio.

LINDEMAN, NEAL I; Bronx HS Of Science; Fresh Meadows, NY; (Y); Cmnty Wkr; Office Aide; Science Clb; Temple Yth Grp; Concert Band; School Play; Rep Sr Cls; Im Vllybl; Gov Hon Prg Awd; High Hon Roll; Arista Hnr Soc 85-86; Med.

LINDEMANN, SHERRY; Colonie Central HS; Schenectady, NY; (Y); JA; French Hon Soc; High Hon Roll; Gregg Shrthnd Awd 86; Albany Bus Coll; Legal Sec.

LINDEN, JACK; West Hempstead HS; Island Pk, NY; (Y); 119/320; FBLA; Hon Roll; Nassau CC; Business Admin.

LINDH, POLLY; Duanesburg HS; Delanson, NY; (Y); Camera Clb; Band; Chorus; Concert Band; Jazz Band; Nwsp Phtg; Crs Cntry; Trk; High Hon Roll; JP Sousa Awd; Elem Educ.

LINDHOLM, KATHLEEN; Panama Central HS; Ashville, NY; (Y); 1/62; Quiz Bowl; Band; Chorus; Concert Band; Pep Band; Mgr(s); Score Keeper; Hon Roll; NHS; Acad All-Amer 86; Engl.

LINDNER, GEORGETTE; Edison Tech; Rochester, NY; (Y); Aud/Vis; Boy Scts; JV Vllybl; Prfct Atndnc Awd 83-84 & 85-86; Cert Of Merit In Audio Vsl 85-86; Monroe CC; Plc Sci.

LINDNER, JOHN F; South Shore HS; Brooklyn, NY; (Y); Debate Tm; Office Aide; Teachers Aide; Band; Badmtn; High Hon Roll; Hon Roll; Social Studies, Spnsh & Bio 84 & 85; St Johns U; Bus.

LINDNER, MARC; Northport HS; E Northport, NY; (Y); Var L Ftbl; Var L Lcrss.

LINDOR, DONALD J; Riverhead HS; Riverhead, NY; (Y); Chess Clb; Church Yth Grp; Drama Clb; Chorus; Jazz Band; School Play; VP Soph Cls; Socr; French Clb; Spanish Clb; Rep To Ny St Brd Of Rgnts 84; Alt To NYSCAME All St Chorus 85; Potsdam Coll; Pre-Law.

LINDSAY, CHRIS; Niagara Catholic HS; Niagara Fls, NY; (Y); 10/85; French Clb; Hosp Aide; Key Clb; Red Cross Aide; Ski Clb; Var JV Ftbl; Var Swmmng; NHS; Med.

LINDSAY, DAVID; Nazareth Regional HS; Brooklyn, NY; (Y); Church Yth Grp; Science Clb; SADD; Off Jr Cls; JV Capt Bsktbl; Hon Roll; Prfct Atten Awd; Pre Med.

LINDSAY, JEAN E; Centereach HS; Centereach, NY; (Y); 3/429; Math Tm; Chorus; Church Choir; School Musical; Variety Show; Rep Frsh Cls; Rep Soph Cls; Rep Jr Cls; Rep Sr Cls; Vllybl; Mat Awd 85-86; Assn Admn & Sprvsry Prsnl Schlrshp 86; Frfld Schlrs 86; Crnll Acdmc Schlrshp; Fairfield U; Lbrl Arts.

LINDSAY, KIM M; Scotia Glenville HS; Scotia, NY; (Y); Key Clb; SADD; VP Jr Cls; Trs Sr Cls; Rep Stu Cncl; Var Stat Bsktbl; Hon Roll; SUNY Buffalo; Engrng.

LINDSAY, MAKEBA G; A Philip Randolph Campus HS; Brooklyn, NY; (Y); 16/166; Church Yth Grp; Cmnty Wkr; Hosp Aide; Science Clb; Varsity Clb; Church Choir; Stu Cncl; Hon Roll; NHS; Prfct Atten Awd; Chanclrs Hnr Rl 85; Mst Inquistv Bio 85; Acad Excllnce Bio 83; Xavier U; Bio.

LINDSAY, MARY; Sherburn-Earlville C S HS; New Berlin, NY; (Y); 14/123; Ed Yrbk Stf; Stu Cncl; Var Capt Bsktbl; Var Capt Cheerleading; Var Trk; Hon Roll; NHS; Rotary Awd; Girl Scts; Spanish Clb; SR Schlstc Athlete Of Sus Assn 85-86; All Star 1st Tm Westrn Div Bsktbl 85-86; Exchnge Studnt 86-87; SUNY Cortland; Bus.

LINDSTADT, STACEY; Northport HS; E Northport, NY; (Y); 89/590; School Musical; School Play; Hon Roll; Battle Of The Bands 83-84; Stony Brook U; Psych.

LINDYBERG, ROBERT; Notre Dame-Bishop Gibbons HS; Scotia, NY; (Y); Drama Clb; Band; Concert Band; Jazz Band; Mrchg Band; School Musical; Stage Crew; Variety Show; Rep Frsh Cls; Rep Soph Cls; Manhatten Coll; Math.

LINEKIN, MAURENE; Sachem North HS; Holbrook, NY; (Y); Hosp Aide; Band; Concert Band; JV Tennis; York Coll PA Schlrshp 86; Oswego ST U; Comm.

LINENDOLL, KIMBERLY; Lansingburgh HS; Troy, NY; (Y); Chorus; Jazz Band; Mrchg Band; Orch; School Musical; Nwsp Ed-Chief; Var Fld Hcky; High Hon Roll; Jr NHS; NHS; SUNY Geneseo; History.

LINENFELSER, CHRISTINA; Grand Island HS; Grand Island, NY; (Y); Church Yth Grp; Dance Clb; Hosp Aide; School Musical; Nwsp Stf; Trs Stu Cncl; High Hon Roll; Hon Roll; NHS.

LINGER, PATRICK; Coxsackie-Athens Central HS; Coxsackie, NY; (Y); 13/105; Trs Church Yth Grp; Computer Clb; Spanish Clb; Band; Jazz Band; Pep Band; Var L Socr; Var Trk; High Hon Roll; NHS; All-Cnty Band & Jazz Band 83-86; Rchstr Inst Of Tech; Comp Sci.

LINHART, RONALD A; Baldwin SR HS; Baldwin, NY; (Y); Trs Pres Aud/Vis; Boy Scts; Church Yth Grp; Drama Clb; School Musical; School Play; VP Pres Stage Crew; High Hon Roll; Hon Roll; NHS; Cert Achvmnt Auto Tech, Arch Drwng 86; Drftng 84-85; Engr.

LINK, CHRISTINE; Mahopac HS; Mahopac, NY; (Y); 116/409; Chorus; Color Guard; Drill Tm; Flag Corp; Mrchg Band; JV Var Bsktbl; The Berkeley School; Exec Secty.

LINK, GAIL ANN; Bishop Kearney HS; Webster, NY; (Y); 7/140; Church Yth Grp; JA; Ski Clb; School Play; Variety Show; Im Sftbl; High Hon Roll; Lion Awd; NHS; Wegmans Scholar 86; U Rochester; Bio.

LINK, GEORGE S; Geneseo Central HS; Geneseo, NY; (Y); Church Yth Grp; Ski Clb; Nwsp Ed-Chief; Yrbk Stf; Ftbl; Trk; Wt Lftg; High Hon Roll; Hon Roll; NHS; Arch.

LINK, KIMIKO; Arlington HS; Poughquag, NY; (Y); 56/569; French Clb; Intnl Clb; Political Wkr; Red Cross Aide; Lit Mag; Hon Roll; Ntl Merit Ltr; St Schlr; Civic Clb; Debate Tm; Arlington Scholarship Organization-Harold C Storm Scholarship 86; Barnard Coll; Intl Relations.

LINKENHOKER, RICHARD; Amsterdam HS; Amsterdam, NY; (Y); Varsity Clb; Band; Concert Band; Mrchg Band; VP Sr Cls; Rep Stu Cncl; Var Bsktbl; Var Ftbl; Var Trk; Ntl Merit SF.

LINO, JOSETTE MARIE; Margaretville Central HS; Arkville, NY; (Y); 12/40; Hosp Aide; Chorus; Yrbk Stf; Sec Jr Cls; Capt Cheerleading; Socr; Trk; High Hon Roll; Hon Roll; Track Records; Athletics Awd; Herkimer Cmnty Coll; Psychology.

LINSNER, SAMANTHA J; Romulus Central HS; Romulus, NY; (Y); 2/48; Off Am Leg Aux Girls St; Pres Sec Varsity Clb; Var Bsktbl; Var Capt Socr; Var Sftbl; Var Vllybl; High Hon Roll; Pres NHS; Highest Av Chem, Seneca Co Med Assoc Womens Aux Awd, Math Awd, Sprtsmnshp Awd 86; Lib Arts.

LINTHWAITE, LARRY; Walton Central Schl; Walton, NY; (Y); 13/100; Am Leg Boys St; Boy Scts; Computer Clb; Model UN; Varsity Clb; Bsbl; Crs Cntry; Tennis; High Hon Roll; Hon Roll; Mst Imprvd Rnnr Crss Cntry 85-86; FL Inst Tech; Undrwtr Tech.

LIOTA, ANDREA; Fontbonne Hall Acad; Brooklyn, NY; (Y); Art Clb; Pom Pon; Cert Of Hon Mntn Phy Educ 85-86; St Johns U.

LIPINSKI, MICHELLE; Mount Mercy Acad; Buffalo, NY; (Y); Cmnty Wkr; SADD; Chorus; Swing Chorus; Hon Roll; Mth.

LIPINSKY, STEPHANIE; Ogdensburg Free Acad; Ogdensburg, NY; (Y); 12/226; Church Yth Grp; Dance Clb; JV Cheerleading; JV Var Trk; High Hon Roll; Hon Roll; NHS; Magna Cum Laude Cert-Ntl Ltn Exm 86; Acad Bnqt Hgh Achvts 84 & 85; Potsdam ST; Sci.

LIPKA, HILARY B; John F Kennedy HS; Bronx, NY; (Y); 6/873; Yrbk Stf; Lit Mag; NHS; Rgnc Schlrshp 86; Middlwbury Coll; Sci Fi Athrss.

LIPKIND, LYNNE; Earl L Vandermeulen HS; Pt Jefferson, NY; (Y); 1/333; Cmnty Wkr; French Clb; Latin Clb; SADD; Yrbk Stf; Ed Lit Mag; High Hon Roll; NCTE Awd; NHS; Asst Editor 2nd Pl Przwnng Lit Mag Press Cmpttn 86; Princeton Bk Awd Semi Fnlst 86.

LIPP, ALNA S; Midwood HS; Brooklyn, NY; (Y); 5/589; Pres Computer Clb; Capt Math Tm; Capt Quiz Bowl; Lit Mag; Trs Frsh Cls; Jr NHS; Ntl Merit SF; Cmnty Wkr; Math Clb; ARCHON Ldr 85-86; Arista 84-86; Physican.

LIPPA, KELLI; W Irondequoit HS; Rochester, NY; (Y); 42/329; Exploring; 4-H; Ski Clb; Band; Mgr(s); Socr; Hon Roll; U Of Buffalo; Ecnmcs.

LIPPE, WENDY A; Great Neck South SR HS; Great Neck, NY; (Y); 32/234; VP Drama Clb; PAVAS; Thesps; Chorus; School Musical; School Play; Variety Show; Lit Mag; Pom Pon; Prod/Dir Brdwy Rvw Benefit 85-86; Arts Rcgntn & Tlnt Srch 85-86; Var Mscls & Plays 8-85; Comm.

LIPPITT, KAREN; Humanities HS; Bronx, NY; (Y); Cmnty Wkr; Math Tm; Temple Yth Grp; Yrbk Stf; Hon Roll; NHS; Recog Stu Tchg And Relgs Sch 85-86; Psychtrst.

LIPPOLDT, LISA H; Westhill HS; Syracuse, NY; (Y); 23/150; Art Clb; Drama Clb; Ski Clb; School Musical; School Play; Yrbk Stf; Lit Mag; Trk; NHS; AFS; NYS Rgnts Schlrshp 86; Sprtmnshp Awd 84; Ithaca Coll; Physcl Thrpy.

LIPTON, WILLIAM B; Kingston HS; Kingston, NY; (Y); 15/573; Sec Latin Clb; Math Tm; Quiz Bowl; VP Soph Cls; VP Jr Cls; Im Bsktbl; Var Capt Tennis; French Hon Soc; High Hon Roll; NHS; Tabl Tenns Sprtsmn Of Yr 83.

LIQUORI, DENISE; Cardinal Spellman HS; Bronx, NY; (Y); Pep Clb; Variety Show; Rptr Nwsp Rptr; Im Bsktbl; High Hon Roll; NHS; NEDT Awd; Scarangell Awd Schlrshp 83-86; Eddy Awd For ITV 86; Lay Fclty Assn Schlrshp 86; FIT; Fash Buyer.

LIRIO, PAMELA J; Niskayuna HS; Schenectady, NY; (Y); French Clb; Key Clb; Latin Clb; Pep Clb; Sec Service Clb; Variety Show; Hst Frsh Cls; Hst Soph Cls; Hst Sr Cls; Var Capt Cheerleading; Miss Co-Ed Pageant Semi-Fnlst 84; Psych.

LISANBY, JAMIE; Niagara Wheatfield SR HS; Niagara Falls, NY; (Y); 71/292; Girl Scts; JA; Science Clb; Chorus; School Musical; School Play; Stage Crew; Niagara Cnty CC; Commnctns.

LISANTI, RALPH; All Hallows HS; Bronx, NY; (Y); Var Bsbl; Var Bowling; Var Mgr(s); Baruch Coll; Bus Admin.

LISNITZER, PAMELA; Sachem HS North; Holbrook, NY; (Y); Band; Orch; Rep Frsh Cls; Rep Soph Cls; Rep Jr Cls; Mgr(s); Score Keeper; Swmmng; Vllybl; Hon Roll; Bio.

LITKENHAUS, SANDY; St Peters HS For Girls; Staten Island, NY; (Y); Girl Scts; Math Clb; Math Tm; Varsity Clb; Rep Jr Cls; Rep Stu Cncl; Var Bsktbl; Im Coach Actv; High Hon Roll; Hon Roll; Bsktbl All Star.

LITTLE, DONALD; Henninger HS; Syracuse, NY; (Y); 20/493; Am Leg Boys St; Boy Scts; Mathletes; Math Clb; Math Tm; SADD; Rep Frsh Cls; High Hon Roll; NHS; Penn ST; Mth.

LITTLE, JENNIFER; Friendship Central HS; Friendship, NY; (S); 3/32; 4-H; Thesps; Chorus; Drill Tm; School Play; Sec Frsh Cls; VP Jr Cls; Var Sftbl; 4-H Awd; High Hon Roll.

LITTLE, LORNA R; Bitburg American HS; Apo New York, NY; (Y); 4/82; Am Leg Aux Girls St; Pres Sec Model UN; Concert Band; Ed Lit Mag; Rep Sec Stu Cncl; L Mgr(s); Cit Awd; NHS; Hosp Aide; Red Cross Aide; DODDS Outstndg Mdl United Natns Delegate 86; Mdl US Senator 86; Intl Stu Ldrshp Inst 85; TX Luthern Coll; Med.

LITTLE, ROSOLYN; Hahn American HS; Apo New York, NY; (Y); 22/76; Church Choir; Sec Pres Stu Cncl; Var Capt Bsktbl; Mgr(s); Var L Vllybl; High Hon Roll; Hon Roll.

LITTLE, SCOTT; Southside HS; Pine City, NY; (S); Drama Clb; Pep Clb; Spanish Clb; Varsity Clb; Chorus; Jazz Band; Madrigals; Mrchg Band; School Musical; Symp Band.

LITZ, AUDRA; Lockport SR HS; Lockport, NY; (Y); 33/445; Drama Clb; Latin Clb; Library Aide; Yrbk Stf; Rep Stu Cncl; Var Bowling; Var Trk; Hon Roll; NHS; Prfct Atten Awd; Comp Sci.

LITZ, STEPHANIE; De Sales Catholic HS; Lockport, NY; (S); 1/30; Church Yth Grp; French Clb; Library Aide; Nwsp Ed-Chief; Bsktbl; Socr; Sftbl; High Hon Roll; Hon Roll; NHS; Englsh 9, Hstry 9, Frnch, Math 9, Relgn 9 & Phy Sci Awds; De Sales Schlrshp Awd.

LITZEN JR, JOHN D; Jamestown HS; Jamestown, NY; (Y); Am Leg Boys St; Political Wkr; Spanish Clb; Varsity Clb; VP Sr Cls; Rep Stu Cncl; JV Var Trk; Hon Roll; Fredonia; Math.

LIU, ERIC; Roy C Kethcam HS; Wappingers Falls, NY; (Y); 1/500; Orch; Nwsp Ed-Chief; Yrbk Stf; Var Wrstlng; Sec NHS; Ntl Merit Schol; Val; Drama Clb; PAVAS; School Musical; RPI Math & Sci Mdl, Hnrbl Mntn, & Schlstc Ntl Wrtng Awds 84; Specl Awd Wausau Composers Comp 85; Harvard; Polit Sci.

LIU, LISA; Niskayuna HS; Scotia, NY; (Y); Cmnty Wkr; French Clb; Pep Clb; Variety Show; Off Frsh Cls; Off Soph Cls; Off Jr Cls; Off Sr Cls; Wt Lftg; French Hon Soc; Excllnt In Natl Piano Cmptn 82; Cert Of Merit French 85; GA Tech; Math.

LIU, NOEMI; Wheatley Schl; E Williston, NY; (Y); Orch; Var Sftbl; Albany; Bus.

LIU, PAUL; Jamesville De Witt HS; Dewitt, NY; (Y); 5/230; Math Tm; Chorus; Bausch & Lomb Sci Awd; High Hon Roll; NHS; Ntl Merit Ltr; 4th Pl Cnty Mth Tm Awd 86; U IL Urbana; Elec Engrng.

LIUZZO, JOHN P; St Francis Prep; Whitestone, NY; (S); 169/730; Boy Scts; Church Yth Grp; Office Aide; Varsity Clb; JV Var Ftbl; JV Var Trk; JV Var Wt Lftg; NHS; VFW Awd; Civic Clb; Eagle Scout 85; Emire ST Games 85; Fresh NY ST Record-Hammer Throw 84; Hlth.

LIVEO, MARY ANN; New Utrecht HS; Brooklyn, NY; (Y); #49 In Class; Red Cross Aide; Scholastic Bowl; School Play; Stage Crew; Nwsp Sprt Ed; Ed Yrbk Stf; Ed Lit Mag; Var Capt Swmmng; Hon Roll; NHS; NY U; Jrnlsm.

LIVERMORE, CHRISTOPHER; Marcus Whitman Central HS; Hall, NY; (Y); 34/118; 4-H; Yrbk Stf; Bsktbl; Swmmng; 4-H Awd; Hon Roll; Engrng.

LIVERMORE, LANCE; Cincinnatus Central Schl; Cincinnatus, NY; (Y); Boys Clb Am; Computer Clb; PAVAS; Band; Chorus; Mrchg Band; Bsbl; Ftbl; Mgr(s); Comm Artist.

LIVINGSTON, NANCY E; Smithtown HS East; Smithtown, NY; (Y); Church Yth Grp; French Clb; Hosp Aide; SADD; Chorus; Stage Crew; Lit Mag; Frsh Cls; Soph Cls; Trk; Hosp Vlntr 100 Hrs Pin & Patch 86.

LIZOR, DAVID; Gloversville HS; Gloversville, NY; (Y); Key Clb; Latin Clb; Ski Clb; Var JV Bsktbl; Im Ftbl; Poli Sci.

LIZZUL, MARINA; St Johns The Baptist HS; Ronkonkoma, NY; (Y); Drama Clb; Hon Roll; NY Tech; Cmnctns.

LLANO, FRANCES; St Johns Prep; Elmhurst, NY; (Y); 240/480; Art Clb; Dance Clb; French Clb; Yrbk Stf; Bsktbl; Cheerleading; Hon Roll; 2nd Hnrs Awd 85; Regents Diploma 86; Pace U; Pre Law.

LLEWELLYN, PAUL; Auburn HS; Auburn, NY; (Y); 6/450; Trs Drama Clb; Model UN; School Play; High Hon Roll; NHS; Ntl Merit SF; NY Math Leag Cntst Outstndng Stdnt 86; Italn III Awd 86.

LLOYD, RICHARD; Northern Adirondack Central Schl; Plattsburgh, NY; (Y); 1/86; Am Leg Boys St; Drama Clb; VP Key Clb; Var L Bsktbl; Bausch & Lomb Sci Awd; High Hon Roll; Val; Chess Clb; Computer Clb; NYS Regents Schlrshp 86; NROTC Schlrshp 86; Regents Dipl W/Hnrs 86; Renslr Polytech Inst; Engrng.

LLOYD, RICHARD F; Binghamton HS; Binghamton, NY; (Y); Am Leg Boys St; Ski Clb; Nwsp Stf; Lcrss.

LO, ADRIENNE; Spackenhill HS; Poughkeepsie, NY; (Y); Debate Tm; Math Tm; NFL; Teachers Aide; Band; School Musical; Nwsp Rptr; Nwsp Stf; Yrbk Stf; NHS; Dtchss CO Rgnl HS Exclln 86; All ST Band 85-86; Ntl Frnch Cntst Rgnl & ST Lvl Wnr 84-86.

LO, GEORGE; La Salle Acad; New York, NY; (S); 19/207; Camera Clb; Trs Math Clb; Yrbk Stf; Crs Cntry; Sftbl; Hon Roll; Jr NHS; NHS; Prfct Atten Awd; Sci.

LO BIONDO, DEBBIE; John Marshall HS; Rochester, NY; (Y); Office Aide; Ski Clb; Yrbk Stf; High Hon Roll; Hon Roll; Bus Mgmt.

LO CASCIO, KEITH W; Commack HS South; Commack, NY; (Y); 100/360; Aud/Vis; Church Yth Grp; Varsity Clb; Nwsp Rptr; Nwsp Stf; Var L Bsbl; Var L Crs Cntry; Var L Trk; NY ST Regnts Schlrshp 86; All Leag Basebl 86; SUNY Oswego; Acctg.

LO DESTRO, DENEAN; Alexander Central HS; Darien Center, NY; (Y); 10/87; Spanish Clb; Band; Chorus; Nwsp Stf; Var Crs Cntry; Var Capt Trk; Jr NHS; NHS; Prfct Atten Awd; Acad All American 86; St Bonaventure; Bio.

LO FASO, JOANN; St Johns Prep; S Ozone Park, NY; (Y); Chorus; Hon Roll; St Johns U; Acctg.

LO GATTO, JEANNE MARIE; Hicksville HS; Hicksville, NY; (Y); 147/500; Art Clb; German Clb; Intnl Clb; Science Clb; SADD; Stage Crew; Madeline Wicksel Schlrshp 86; Gnrl Von Steuben Awd 86; Achvmnt Awd Soc Stds 86; Adelphi U.

LO GELFO, CHRISTINE; Centereach HS; Centereach, NY; (Y); 61/429; VICA; Hon Roll; NYS Rgnts Schlrshp 86-87; Suffolk County CC; RN.

LO PARCO, MELONY; Dryden HS; Cortland, NY; (Y); Art Clb; Spanish Clb; SADD; Socr; Gym; Wt Lftg; Hon Roll; Purdue U; Vet Med.

LO PICCOLO, ANTOINETTE; St Dominic HS; Glen Cove, NY; (S); 5/139; Church Yth Grp; SADD; Stage Crew; Tennis; High Hon Roll; NHS; NEDT Awd; Comptr Sci.

LO PICCOLO, CARMELO; Nazareth Regional HS; Brooklyn, NY; (S); 33/280; NHS; Art Awd 82-83; High Avg Certs 82-85; Optntry.

LO RUSSO, CARMELA; Rome Free Acad; Rome, NY; (Y); 10/600; Hosp Aide; Var Crs Cntry; Hon Roll; Jr NHS; NHS.

LO VALLO, LISA MARIE; Kenmore East SR HS; Kenmore, NY; (Y); Capt Cheerleading; Comm.

LOACH, MATTHEW W; Plattsburgh SR HS; Plattsburgh, NY; (Y); Exploring; Model UN; School Play; Hon Roll; Rgnts Schlrshp 86; Elec Engrng.

LOAN, DAWN; Central Square-Paul V Moore HS; Cleveland, NY; (Y); Trs Drama Clb; Band; Chorus; Concert Band; Pep Band; School Musical; School Play; Trs Soph Cls; Stu Cncl; Thesps; Hnr Rl 82-86; Bst Overall Actress 85; Drama.

LOBELL, DANNY; Westfield Academy Central Schl; Westfield, NY; (Y); Ski Clb; Band; Chorus; Concert Band; Jazz Band; Mrchg Band; School Musical; Var Bsbl; JV Var Bsktbl; JV Var Ftbl; Presdntl Fitness Awd; WDOE HS Athlete Of The Day Awd 86; FL Inst Tech; Marine Bio.

LOBO, ARLENE D; Fairport HS; Fairport, NY; (Y); Cmnty Wkr; Science Clb; Hon Roll; Rochester Alum Pnhlnc Schlrshp 86; NY ST Regents Coll Schlrshp 86; Cert Part Chem Exam 85; Rochester Inst; Bio.

LOBOS, JACQUELINE; St Johns Prep; Elmhurst, NY; (Y); Church Yth Grp; Dance Clb; Drama Clb; Chorus; Church Choir; School Musical; Sec Stu Cncl; Awd In Peer Cnslng; Hntr Coll; Pblc Rltns.

LOCALIO, GREGORY; Hastings HS; Hastings-On-Hdsn, NY; (Y); 42/109; AFS; Debate Tm; Key Clb; Model UN; Sec SADD; Yrbk Stf; Trs Sr Cls; JV Bsbl; JV Ftbl; Hon Roll; SUNY Albany.

LOCASCIO, ANDREW; John Adams HS; Ozone Park, NY; (Y); High Hon Roll; Hon Roll; Queens Coll; Gntcs.

LOCASCIO, ANGELA; East Hampton HS; Montauk, NY; (Y); JA; Ed Science Clb; Spanish Clb; Chorus; School Musical; JV Trk; Hon Roll; Spanish NHS; Spnsh Hons 85; Math II 85; Hlth 86; Southampton Coll; Bus.

LOCHRANE, JO ANN; Wayne Central HS; Walworth, NY; (Y); 17/184; Church Yth Grp; Yrbk Stf; High Hon Roll; Hon Roll; NHS; Engl Awd 84; Bus Awd 84.

LOCICERO, CHRIS; Saint Joseph-By-The-Sea HS; Staten Island, NY; (Y); Church Yth Grp; Computer Clb; Lit Mag; Rep Soph Cls; JV Bsbl; Hon Roll; NEDT Awd; Finance.

LOCICERO, DAWN; St Johns Prep; Corona, NY; (Y); 70/458; Variety Show; High Hon Roll; Hon Roll; Prfct Atten Awd; 1st Yr Compltn St Johns U 86; St Johns U; Bus.

LOCKE, NICOLE; Dominican Commercial HS; Rochdale, NY; (S); #31 In Class; Drama Clb; Church Choir; Pre-Med.

LOCKWOOD, KELLIE; North Babylon SR HS; N Babylon, NY; (Y); 63/434; Teachers Aide; VICA; Chorus; JV Var Mgr(s); JV Score Keeper; Hon Roll; Jr NHS; NHS; Ed.

LOCKWOOD, MICHAEL; Hilton Central Schl; Rochester, NY; (Y); Var L Swmmng; Hon Roll; Ntl Merit Ltr; NY ST Regnts Schlrshp 86; RIT Acad Schrlshp 86; Pres Acad Ftns Awd 86; Rochester Inst Tech; Engrng.

LOCKWOOD, MILLINGTON; Springville-Griffith Inst; Springville, NY; (Y); Chorus; Concert Band; Jazz Band; Mrchg Band; School Musical; Swing Chorus; Var Crs Cntry; Var Capt Swmmng; Var Trk; NHS; Most Imprvd Plyr Boys Swmmng 86.

LOCKWOOD, WILLIAM; Pulaski JR SR HS; Pulaski, NY; (S); 3/100; Am Leg Boys St; Math Tm; Ski Clb; Varsity Clb; Band; Mrchg Band; Var L Ftbl; Var L Tennis; High Hon Roll; Ntl Merit Ltr; Natl Merit Lttr Of Cmmdtn 86; RIT; Chem Engrng.

LOCONTE, GENE; St John The Baptist D H S; Islip, NY; (Y); Chess Clb; Rep Frsh Cls; Golf; Hnrbl Ment Ntl Sci Olymd Chem 86; Cert Merit Awd Math,Sco Studies 84-85; Pol Sci.

LODATI, ANTONETTE T; St Francis Prep; Bayside, NY; (S); 235/744; Art Clb; Im Vllybl; Fashion Design.

LODERER, KIRSTEN R; St Francis Prep; Middle Village, NY; (Y); 349/698; German Clb; Ski Clb; Var Gym; Jr NHS; NY ST Rgnts Schlrshp 86; Fordham U.

LODGE, JENNIFER J; East Islip HS; Great River, NY; (Y); 33/425; FBLA; Chorus; Church Choir; Concert Band; Jazz Band; School Musical; Swing Chorus; Nwsp Rptr; Lit Mag; Var Stat Sftbl; LI Sci Congrss High Hnrs 84; NYSMMA Commp High Hnrs; Salisbury ST Coll; Accntng.

LOEB, JUDITH R; Cold Spring Harbor HS; Laurel Hollow, NY; (Y); 40/127; Intnl Clb; Pep Band; Yrbk Stf; Var Socr; JV Sftbl; Var Vllybl; High Hon Roll; Hon Roll; Recog For Rsch Ppr Awd 86; Georgetown U; Intl Relat.

LOEB, STEPHEN; Syosset HS; Woodbury, NY; (Y); Aud/Vis; Computer Clb; Drama Clb; Intnl Clb; Model UN; Radio Clb; SADD; Thesps; Chorus; School Musical; Sprts Drctr WKWZ Radio 85-86; Syracuse U; TV/Radio Cmmnctns.

LOEBENBERG, MICHELE Y; Bais Yaaker HS; Monsey, NY; (Y); 3/25; Cmnty Wkr; Drama Clb; Hosp Aide; Band; Chorus; Concert Band; School Musical; School Play; Yrbk Ed-Chief; St Schlr; Dr Wm M Scholl Wrldwd Schlrshp 86; NY U Schlr 86; Hunter Coll Schlr 86; NYU; Phys Thrpy.

LOEFFLER, MICHAEL; Monsingnor Farrell HS; Staten Island, NY; (Y); 83/320; Band; Concert Band; Jazz Band; Mrchg Band; Symp Band; JV Crs Cntry; JV Var Trk; Hon Roll; US Naval Acad; Aero Engrng.

LOEHFELM, WILLIAM; Monsignor Farrell HS; Staten Island, NY; (Y); Lit Mag; JV Var Socr; JV L Key Clb; NHS; Ntl Merit SF; Cmmncts.

LOEHR, ROBERT C; St Anthonys HS; Northport, NY; (Y); 1/240; Civic Clb; Computer Clb; French Clb; Political Wkr; Teachers Aide; Yrbk Rptr; Im Bsktbl; French Hon Soc; High Hon Roll; NHS; Schltc Of Yr 85; Monsgnr Nolan Schlrshps 83-85; Engrng.

LOESCH, CAROL ANN; Deer Park HS; Deer Park, NY; (Y); 3/480; Pres Mathletes; Capt Math Clb; Capt Math Tm; Pres Service Clb; Pres SADD; Jr NHS; NHS; Pres Schlr; Art Clb; Quiz Bowl; Rgnts Schlrshp Wnr 86; Hnr Scty Schlrshp 86; Twn Bbyln Ser Awd 86; Cornell U; Pr-Md.

LOESCH, PETER; Mercy HS; Shoreham, NY; (Y); Cmnty Wkr; Drama Clb; Library Aide; Office Aide; School Musical; Stage Crew; Nwsp Sprt Ed; Yrbk Phtg; Trk.

LOETMAN, SCOTT; Mepham HS; N Bellmore, NY; (Y); 9/360; Chess Clb; Computer Clb; Pres Mathletes; Pres Math Tm; Science Clb; High Hon Roll; Hon Roll; NHS; Grumman Schlrshp 86; Rgnts Schlrshp 86; GA Inst Of Tech; Comp Sci.

LOEW, DAVID H; Fonda-Fultonville Central HS; Fonda, NY; (Y); 4/111; Intnl Clb; School Play; Nwsp Stf; Yrbk Stf; Var L Bsbl; NHS; Ntl Merit Ltr; High Hon Roll; Hon Roll; Grad Spkr 86; Trinity Coll.

LOFASO, GAETANO; New Dorp HS; Staten Island, NY; (Y); VP Key Clb; Ed Yrbk Stf; Var Crs Cntry; Var Trk; Hon Roll; NHS; Womns Hstry Mnth Awd Poetry Ctgry NY City 85; Itln Hnr Socty 83-86; Rdlgst.

LOFGREN, MICHAEL; Chatham Central HS; Chatham, NY; (Y); 35/135; Aud/Vis; Church Yth Grp; Band; Concert Band; Pep Band; Rep Stu Cncl; JV Ftbl; Hon Roll; Daniel Webster Clg; Avtn.

LOFTHOUSE, CATHY; Kendal JR SR HS; Kendall, NY; (Y); 19/86; AFS; Art Clb; Church Yth Grp; 4-H; Pep Clb; Spanish Clb; Teachers Aide; Chorus; Church Choir; Color Guard.

LOFTIN, LARRY; South Shore HS; Brooklyn, NY; (Y); Office Aide; Trk; Buffalo U; Elec Engrng.

LOGAN, BEVERLY; Midwood HS; Brooklyn, NY; (Y); Church Yth Grp; Girl Scts; Church Choir; Trs Yrbk Bus Mgr; Hon Roll; Arista Awd 84; Cmmnctns.

LOGAN, SUSAN; Irvington HS; Tarrytown, NY; (Y); Church Yth Grp; Cmnty Wkr; Drama Clb; Chorus; School Musical; School Play; Stage Crew; Yrbk Stf; Fld Hcky; High Hon Roll; Cmmnctns.

LOGAN, TONNIE S; Bennett HS; Buffalo, NY; (Y); 13/221; Church Yth Grp; Cmnty Wkr; DECA; Key Clb; Church Choir; Off Stu Cncl; Hon Roll; NHS; Sherman F Feyler Awd 86; Canisius Coll; Fshn Merch.

LOGEL, SANDRA; Gates-Chili SR HS; Rochester, NY; (S); 8/445; Church Yth Grp; Service Clb; Teachers Aide; Band; Concert Band; School Musical; Stage Crew; Rep Soph Cls; Rep Jr Cls; Rep Sr Cls; Socl Stds Dept Awd 84; Mst Imprv Gymnst Tm Awd 82-83; Grove City Coll; Psych.

LOGSDON, KAREN; Williamsville East HS; Williamsville, NY; (Y); Church Yth Grp; Cmnty Wkr; Pep Clb; SADD; School Musical; Yrbk Bus Mgr; Rep Stu Cncl; JV Var Fld Hcky; Latin Clb; Service Clb; Amhrst YES Outstndng Vlntr Awd 84-86; Amhrst YES Advsry Brd 85-86; FL ST Coll; Scndry Ed.

LOGUE, CHRIS; Williamsville South HS; Williamsville, NY; (Y); Cmnty Wkr; Capt Swmmng; High Hon Roll; Hon Roll; NY Empire ST Games 83-85; NY Sectn VI H S Swmmng Champshps 3rd Pl 86; NY ST Swim Mt 17th Pl 86.

LOGUERCIO, ANGELA; Saint Francis Prep; Bayside, NY; (S); 134/744; Art Clb; Im Vllybl; Opt Clb Awd.

LOGUIDICE, MICHELE; Acad Of St Joseph; Coram, NY; (Y); Debate Tm; Service Clb; Speech Tm; Yrbk Stf; JV Bsktbl; Var Vllybl; Bus Law.

LOIA, SANDRA; Saunders HS; Yonkers, NY; (S); VICA; Yrbk Phtg; Yrbk Rptr; Yrbk Stf; Lit Mag; JV Bsktbl; Hon Roll; Prntng.

LOIRA, IRIS; Herbert H Lehman HS; Bronx, NY; (Y); Dance Clb; Chorus; Drill Tm; School Musical; Swing Chorus; Variety Show; Nwsp Rptr; Nwsp Stf; Cheerleading; Gym; Bus Mgmt.

LOK, JASON; The Bronx HS Of Science; New York City, NY; (Y); Chess Clb; Computer Clb; Math Tm; Science Clb; Teachers Aide; NHS; Prfct Atten Awd; Rgnts Schlrshp 86; Biochem.

LOKENSKY, WAYNE; Ramapo SR HS; Spring Valley, NY; (Y); Key Clb; Math Clb; SADD; Band; Pres Stu Cncl; Ftbl; Wrstlng; SUNY Binghamton; Corpt Mgr.

LOLIK, RANDY S; Notre Dame Bishop Gibbons HS; Scotia, NY; (Y); Boys Clb Am; Church Yth Grp; Cmnty Wkr; JA; Teachers Aide; French Clb; JV Bsktbl; Var Ftbl; Var Trk; Var Wt Lftg; Religion Awd 85; Siena Coll; Psychlgst.

LOMBARDI, AMY; Oneida HS; Oneida, NY; (S); 4-H; Intnl Clb; SADD; Chorus; Yrbk Stf; High Hon Roll; Hon Roll; Bus Adm.

LOMBARDI, ANNE; Ward Melville HS; Setauket, NY; (Y); 76/725; Exploring; Hosp Aide; Latin Clb; Math Tm; Spanish Clb; SADD; Nwsp Rptr; High Hon Roll; Jr NHS; NHS; Excl Awd Volntr Wrk 83; NYS Regnts Schlrshp 86; SUNY At Stonybrook; Bio.

LOMBARDI, IRENE; St Barnabas HS; Bronx, NY; (S); 1/173; Drama Clb; Teachers Aide; Variety Show; Nwsp Rptr; VP Jr Cls; High Hon Roll; NHS; Prfct Atten Awd; Itln Hnr Soc 85-86; Fordham U; Chem.

LOMBARDI, LISA; Henninger HS; Syracuse, NY; (Y); 20/400; Exploring; Band; Jazz Band; Yrbk Bus Mgr; Yrbk Phtg; Sec Frsh Cls; Sec Soph Cls; Score Keeper; NHS; Art Clb; Outstndg Rythm Sectn Stu 86; ST Yrbk Cnvtn 86; Cmmrcl.

LOMBARDI, MARIA; Lindenhurst HS; Lindenhurst, NY; (Y); Am Leg Aux Girls St; Leo Clb; Ski Clb; Bsktbl; Var Socr; Sftbl; JV Capt Vllybl; Hon Roll; Acad All Am Media 86; Center For Media Arts; Cinemtgr.

LOMBARDO, JOHN; Newfield HS; Selden, NY; (Y); 41/515; Computer Clb; L Var Golf; FL Insti Of Tech; Comp Sci.

LOMBARDONI, TOM; Johnstown HS; Johnstown, NY; (Y); Variety Show; Nwsp Stf; Yrbk Stf; Trs Sr Cls; Var L Ftbl; Var L Trk; Var L Wrstlng; Hon Roll; NHS; Engrng.

LOMBARDOZZI, MELISSA; Commack HS South; Dix Hills, NY; (Y); Computer Clb; Mathletes; Math Tm; School Musical; School Play; Stage Crew; Nwsp Rptr; Yrbk Phtg; Yrbk Stf; Lit Mag; Vet.

LOMONOCO, CHRIS; Colonie Central HS; Albany, NY; (Y); 72/467; Girl Scts; Hosp Aide; Key Clb; Pep Clb; Socr; Hon Roll; Bus Mgmnt.

LONCZAK, KAROLYN; Lansingburgh HS; Troy, NY; (Y); Sec 4-H; Girl Scts; Varsity Clb; Chorus; Rep Sr Cls; JV Cheerleading; Var Socr; Var Trk; High Hon Roll; NHS; Hudson Valley; Engrng.

LONG, ANDREA; Hutchinson Central Tech; Buffalo, NY; (Y); Church Yth Grp; Girl Scts; Chorus; Rep Jr Cls; Rep Stu Cncl; Sftbl; Var Swmmng; High Hon Roll; Hon Roll; Jr NHS; Rensselaer Medl Math & Sci Awd 86; Wellesley Bk Awd 86; Outstndng JR 86; Biomed Tech.

LONG, DEBRA; Johnstown HS; Johnstown, NY; (Y); Drama Clb; 4-H; Latin Clb; Chorus; Swing Chorus; Variety Show; JV Bsktbl; JV Swmmng; 4-H Awd; Prfct Atten Awd; Med.

LONG JR, DOUGLAS; Albion HS; Albion, NY; (S); 4/220; Boy Scts; Latin Clb; Ski Clb; Var Swmmng; Var Trk; High Hon Roll; Hon Roll; NHS; Stu Of Mnth; Engr.

LONG, JASON; Jamestown HS; Jamestown, NY; (Y); Computer Clb; Spanish Clb; Acpl Chr; Band; Concert Band; Mrchg Band; Rep Frsh Cls; Trk; Jr NHS; Comp Sci.

LONG, JEFF; Valley Central HS; Middletown, NY; (Y); Church Yth Grp; FCA; 4-H; FBLA; Quiz Bowl; Red Cross Aide; SADD; Teachers Aide; VICA; Drm Mjr(t); 3rd Pl Mr Brbrn Bdy Bldng Shw 85; Lawyer.

LONG, JENNIFER; Middletown HS; Middletown, NY; (Y); Hosp Aide; Key Clb; SADD; School Play; Stage Crew; Yrbk Rptr; Yrbk Stf; Var Capt Vllybl; Hon Roll; NHS; JV & Vrsty Ltrs; Pre-Med.

LONG, JERI LYNN; Longwood HS; Middle Island, NY; (Y); 102/487; SADD; Varsity Clb; Stage Crew; Variety Show; Yrbk Stf; VP Soph Cls; Rep Jr Cls; VP Sr Cls; Rep Stu Cncl; Capt Cheerleading; NYS JR Miss Schlrshp Awd 86; Lynchbrg Coll; Bus.

LONG, MATTHEW; Chautauqua HS; Mayville, NY; (Y); Quiz Bowl; VP Frsh Cls; Stu Cncl; Var Swmmng; Var Trk; High Hon Roll; Hon Roll; Jr NHS; NHS; Pres Schlr.

LONG, REBECCA; Mt Mercy Acad; W Seneca, NY; (Y); 10/200; French Clb; SADD; Chorus; Nwsp Stf; Ed Lit Mag; High Hon Roll; Hon Roll; Jr NHS; NHS; Schl Scholar 83.

LONG, SUZANNE; St John The Baptist Dist HS; Babylon, NY; (Y); SADD; Rep Frsh Cls; VP Soph Cls; Pres Sr Cls; VP Stu Cncl; High Hon Roll; Ldrshp Awd 86; Achvt Awd 85.

LONG, TAMMY; Kendall HS; Kent, NY; (Y); 40/86; Exploring; 4-H; Pep Clb; Color Guard; Nwsp Stf; Var Capt Cheerleading; 4-H Awd; Sci.

LONG, TIMOTHY; Monsignor Farrell HS; Staten Island, NY; (S); 15/330; Math Tm; Ed Yrbk Stf; Var Bsbl; Im Bsktbl; Crs Cntry; Im Ftbl; High Hon Roll; NHS; Ntl Merit SF; VP Soph Cls; Schlr Ath Awd; Elec Engrng.

LONGARDO, STEPHANIE; Fontbonne Hall Acad; Brooklyn, NY; (Y); 52/132; Chess Clb; Red Cross Aide; Teachers Aide; Chorus; Nwsp Stf; Yrbk Stf; Lit Mag; Hon Roll; Spanish NHS; Hon Ment Math 9 & 11 84-85.

LONGHOUSE, JOHN; Lansing HS; Freeville, NY; (Y); Am Leg Boys St; Spanish Clb; Stu Cncl; Var Capt Bsbl; Var Capt Bsktbl; Var Capt Ftbl; Cit Awd; High Hon Roll; Lion Awd; NHS; Bsbll MVP All ST 86; Ftbll All Str 85.

LONGO, JAMES; Susan E Wagner HS; Staten Island, NY; (Y); Art Clb; Computer Clb; FBLA; GAA; Girl Scts; JA; Science Clb; SADD; Gym; Hon Roll; Pace U; Comp Pgmg.

LONGO, PATRICIA; Hicksville HS; Hicksville, NY; (Y); Trs FBLA; Yrbk Stf; High Hon Roll; Jr NHS; NHS; 3rd Pl Ecnmcs Trphy-FBLA 86.

LONGOBARDO, VINCENT; Saint Patricks CCHS; Hillsdale, NY; (Y); 7/26; Yrbk Phtg; Yrbk Sprt Ed; Var L Bowling; Var L Socr; U Of Lowell; Med.

LONGORIA, JILL; Woodbridge American HS; A P O New York, NY; (Y); 10/50; Model UN; ROTC; Thesps; School Play; Nwsp Stf; Sec Stu Cncl; Var L Cheerleading; Hon Roll; Ntl Merit SF; Drama Clb; Grand Cross Of Color Intl Order Of Rainbow For Girls; HS Teacher.

LONGWAY, JILL; Thousand Islands HS; Clayton, NY; (Y); Pres Church Yth Grp; Chorus; Church Choir; Concert Band; School Musical; School Play; Jr NHS; Lion Awd; NHS; Girl Scts; Nrsng.

LONGWELL, LISA E; Waterloo SR HS; Waterloo, NY; (Y); 10/168; Pres Church Yth Grp; Varsity Clb; Lib Band; Yrbk Sprt Ed; Var Bsktbl; Capt Var Trk; Var Vllybl; NHS; Regents Schlrshp Awd; St Josephs Schl Nrsng; Nrsng.

LONIGAN, JENNIFER; Valley Central HS; Montgomery, NY; (Y); 60/300; Cmnty Wkr; Acpl Chr; Church Choir; School Musical; School Play; Variety Show; Hon Roll; NYSSMA Sining Lvl 5 Exclnt 84; NYSSMA Sining Lvl 16 Grd 94 & 98 85 & 86; Music.

LONIGRO, VINCENT; Monsignor Farrell HS; Staten Island, NY; (Y); Cmnty Wkr; Math Tm; Im Bsktbl; Im Bowling; Im Ftbl; Im Wt Lftg; Hon Roll; Ntl Merit Ltr; 2nd Honors 84-86; NYU; Lawyer.

LOOK, LISA E; Manlius Pebble Hill HS; Erieville, NY; (S); Model UN; Band; Chorus; Church Choir; School Musical; Stage Crew; Swing Chorus; Lit Mag; Pres Jr Cls; Socr; Intr Design.

LOOK, YVONNE K; The Bronx High Schl Of Science; New York, NY; (Y); Math Tm; Orch; Lit Mag; Im Vllybl; Ntl Merit SF; Bus Adm.

LOOMAN, CYNTHIA; Oppenheim Epratah HS; Dolgeville, NY; (S); 3/37; GAA; Band; Mrchg Band; Off Stu Cncl; Cheerleading; Socr; High Hon Roll; Hon Roll; Jr NHS; NHS; All Cnty Band 84; Ntl Band Awds 84-85; Accntng.

LOOMIS, CHRIS; Salem Washington Acad; W Rupert, VT; (Y); French Clb; Math Tm; SADD; Band; Jazz Band; Mrchg Band; Yrbk Phtg; Yrbk Stf; Im Bsktbl; Hon Roll; Engrng.

LOOMIS, EILEEN; Bishop Maginn HS; Albany, NY; (Y); 21/84; Drama Clb; Girl Scts; Red Cross Aide; Band; School Musical; Nwsp Stf; Tennis; Art Clb; French Clb; JA; Zonta Clb Hmntrn Awd Albany 86; Zonta Clbhmntrn Distr Awd 86; ST Rose Coll; Spec Ed.

LOOMIS, KAREN; Hannibal Central HS; Fulton, NY; (Y); VP Key Clb; Pres SADD; Band; Chorus; Capt Color Guard; Capt Flag Corp; Mrchg Band; School Musical; Symp Band; Tennis; Teachng.

LOOMIS, KATHRYN; Liverpool HS; Liverpool, NY; (Y); 54/841; VP AFS; Art Clb; VP Church Yth Grp; Pres JA; Chorus; Rep Stu Cncl; Hon Roll; Jr NHS; Trs NHS; Syracuse U Pre Coll Schlrshp 86; Acadmc Achvt Art 85-86; Visual Arts.

LOOMIS, KRISTIN; Liverpool HS; Liverpool, NY; (Y); 55/841; Off AFS; Pres Church Yth Grp; SADD; Chorus; School Musical; Yrbk Ed-Chief; Hon Roll; Jr NHS; NHS; Cmnty Wkr; 1st Pl Awd Varden Photo 85; Photo.

LOOMIS, SUSAN; Bishop Maginn HS; Albany, NY; (S); 4-H; French Clb; Girl Scts; Yrbk Rptr; Var Crs Cntry; JV Sftbl; JV Trk; Hon Roll.

LOOP, KIRSTIN; Saugerties HS; Saugerties, NY; (S); 4/252; French Clb; Girl Scts; Trs Band; Yrbk Bus Mgr; Cit Awd; High Hon Roll; NHS; Grl Sct Gld Awd; Marine Bio.

LOOS, JENNIFER; Greece Athena HS; Rochester, NY; (Y); 76/320; Office Aide; Nwsp Stf; Yrbk Stf; Stu Cncl; Co-Capt Bsktbl; Capt Tennis; Hon Roll; Score Keeper; Lilac Teen Comp Semi-Fnlst 85-86; Womens Clb Of Rochester Wnnr 1st Pl Mst Creatv Swing Awd 86; Engl.

LOOS, KAREN; Copiague SR HS; Copiague, NY; (Y); Cmnty Wkr; Office Aide; Stu Cncl; JV Var Sftbl; Vrsty Ltr Sftbll 84; Psych.

LOPANE, CATHERINE; Blessed Sacrament-St Gabiels HS; New Rochelle, NY; (Y); 3/137; Girl Scts; Teachers Aide; Yrbk Stf; Hon Roll; NHS; Knghts Colmbs 86; Mnsgnr Ftzgrld Achvmnt Awd 86; Englsh Awd 86; Iona Coll; Tchr.

LOPARDI, SUZANNE; Mt St Mary Acad; Tonawanda, NY; (Y); 24/136; Dance Clb; GAA; Pep Clb; Teachers Aide; Varsity Clb; Yrbk Ed-Chief; Coach Actv; Capt Swmmng; Cit Awd; Hon Roll; OH ST U; Bio.

LOPAT, JOHN; Cardinal O Hara HS; Tonawanda, NY; (S); 20/127; Trs JA; Spanish Clb; L Var Ftbl; L Var Trk; High Hon Roll; Ntl Hnr Roll 84-85; NY ST U; Cvl Engrng.

LOPERENA, MARIA; St Pius V HS; Bronx, NY; (Y); Hosp Aide; Service Clb; Church Choir; Variety Show; Hon Roll; Prfct Atten Awd; Biol Awd 86; Biol.

LOPES, DEBORAH; Cuba Central Schl; Cuba, NY; (Y); Spanish Clb; Varsity Clb; Band; Chorus; Drm Mjr(t); Mrchg Band; Pep Band; Yrbk Stf; Cheerleading; Socr; Genesee CC; Toursm & Trvl.

LOPEZ, ANNETTE; Manhattan Center For Sci & Math; Bronx, NY; (Y); 10/150; Church Yth Grp; Drama Clb; Library Aide; Teachers Aide; Chorus; Nwsp Rptr; Yrbk Rptr; Yrbk Stf; Hon Roll; Rensselaer Polytech Inst; EE.

LOPEZ, CARLOS V; Automotive HS; New York, NY; (Y); 6/251; Cmnty Wkr; VICA; Yrbk Phtg; Yrbk Rptr; Yrbk Stf; Rep Jr Cls; Hon Roll; Regnts Schlrshp 86; Cooper Union; Arch.

LOPEZ, CHRISTINE; Sachem North HS; Holbrook, NY; (Y); 140/1558; Spanish Clb; Ithaca Coll; Physcl Thrpy.

LOPEZ, CHRISTINE; Solvay HS; Solvay, NY; (Y); 21/177; Exploring; 4-H; Math Clb; VP Spanish Clb; Chorus; School Musical; Variety Show; Yrbk Stf; Frsh Cls; Soph Cls; Bus Awd Advanced Keybrdng I & II 85-86; Adv Plcmnt Amer Hist Awd 86; Giftd & Tlntd Math Hon 85; Rochester Inst; Med Tech.

LOPEZ, CINDY; Bay Shore SR HS; Bay Shore, NY; (Y); 76/406; Drama Clb; School Play; Nwsp Stf; Yrbk Stf; Stat Gym; High Hon Roll; Hon Roll; Bio.

LOPEZ, DEBBIE; St Dominic HS; Bayville, NY; (Y); 31/112; Chorus; School Play; Cheerleading; Hon Roll; All Amer Chrldr 85; Fash Inst Of Tech; Fash Merch.

LOPEZ, DIANA; St Agnes Cathedral HS; Far Rockaway, NY; (Y); 34/429; Art Clb; Cmnty Wkr; High Hon Roll; NHS; Mech Drawing Awd 86; Hofstra U; Mech Engrng.

LOPEZ, ELISA; Schoharie Central Schl; Schoharie, NY; (S); 14/108; Band; Chorus; Variety Show; Yrbk Stf; Var Sftbl; Swmmng; Hon Roll.

LOPEZ, GINA; St Edmunds HS; Brooklyn, NY; (S); Pres Frsh Cls; Pres Jr Cls; Rep Stu Cncl; Bowling; Hon Roll; NHS; Spnsh Awd 84 & 85; Englsh Awd 84; Ldrs Clb 85; Frdhm; Lawyer.

LOPEZ, KEVIN; Archbishop Molloy HS; New York, NY; (Y); 59/383; Art Clb; Church Yth Grp; Computer Clb; Hosp Aide; Band; Jazz Band; Im Bsktbl; Im Ftbl; Im Sftbl; CUNY Medical Schl; Med.

LOPEZ, KIM; Monsignor Scanlan HS; Bronx, NY; (Y); Math Clb; Spanish Clb; Acpl Chr; Yrbk Stf; Off Sr Cls; Bowling; Gym; Sftbl; Trk; Prfct Atten Awd; Gym 85; St John U; Med Assist.

LOPEZ, LUCY; Bishop Ford Catholic Central HS; Brooklyn, NY; (S); 34/439; Church Yth Grp; Cmnty Wkr; Computer Clb; Science Clb; Lit Mag; High Hon Roll; Secy.

LOPEZ, MARTHA; Newtown HS; Jackson Heights, NY; (Y); Dance Clb; Girl Scts; Varsity Clb; Band; Chorus; School Play; Variety Show; Gym; Lcrss; Sftbl; SPFA Cert Excllnce 86; Cert Of Merit In Keybrdng 85; Cert Of Merit In French 85; Frgn Lang.

LOPEZ, OLIVIA; Adelphi Acad; Brooklyn, NY; (S); 1/25; Model UN; Science Clb; Band; Jazz Band; Nwsp Rptr; Nwsp Sprt Ed; Yrbk Stf; Lit Mag; VP Stu Cncl; Var Bsktbl; Mth & Sci Awd 84 & 85; Vllybl MVP 85; Pre-Med.

LOPEZ, RITA JAQUELINE; Wheatley HS; Mineola, NY; (Y); Varsity Clb; Chorus; Stage Crew; Bsktbl; Socr; Sftbl; Vllybl; Art Achvt 85; Outstndng Chorus 84; Orthodntst.

LOPEZ, TABATHA; St Johns The Baptist HS; Bayshore, NY; (Y); Girl Scts; Spanish NHS.

LOPEZ, TRINA; Port Richmond HS; Staten Island, NY; (Y); Merit Roll 86; Coll Of Staten Isl; Nrsng.

LOPEZ, VERONICA; Eastern District HS; Brooklyn, NY; (Y); Math Tm; Spnsh & Sci Awds; Clthng Awd; Polytech U; Cvl Engr.

LOPEZ, WANDA; Monsignor Scanlan HS; Bronx, NY; (Y); 26/276; Temple Yth Grp; JV Bsktbl; 2nd Hnrs 83-86; Acadmc Comndntn Wrld Histry 85-86; Acadmc Comndtn Wrld Histry 85-86; Acadmc Comm Sci; St Johns U; Accntnt.

LOPEZ, WILLIAM; Burgard Vocational HS; Buffalo, NY; (Y); Camera Clb; Church Yth Grp; CAP; Exploring; JA; Red Cross Aide; Nwsp Phtg; Yrbk Phtg; Off Frsh Cls; Tennis; U Bufford; Industry.

LOPITZ, AMANDA; Canastota HS; Canastota, NY; (Y); 19/160; Drama Clb; Trs Science Clb; SADD; Band; Chorus; School Musical; Yrbk Stf; High Hon Roll; Hon Roll; St Schlr; SUNY Geneseo; Bio.

LOPOPOLO, ELIZABETH; Maria Regina HS; Yonkers, NY; (Y); 10/167; Chorus; School Musical; Nwsp Phtg; Nwsp Rptr; Nwsp Stf; Yrbk Phtg; Yrbk Stf; Lit Mag; High Hon Roll; NHS; Schlrshp KC 83-87; Hnrs Convocation 83-87; Bus Fin Anal.

LOPS, PETER; Smithtown High School East; Nesconset, NY; (Y); Var L Ftbl; Var Wt Lftg; Hon Roll; Outstndng Jr Ftbl 85.

LORANDINI, BARBARA; Walt Whitman HS; Melville, NY; (Y); 185/479; Church Yth Grp; Key Clb; SADD; Chorus; Nwsp Stf; Im Socr; Hon Roll; Bus Amdin.

LORD, SHERI LEE; Vestal SR HS; Vestal, NY; (Y); Varsity Clb; Capt Color Guard; Mrchg Band; Hon Roll; Vrsty Lttr 3 Yrs Mrchng Band 86; Broome Comm; Scrtrl.

LORD, TAMMY; Saranac Central Schl; Saranac, NY; (S); 44/126; Yrbk Stf; Var JV Socr; Var Trk; JV Vllybl; High Hon Roll; Hon Roll; Acad Perfct Attndnc Awd 80, 83, 84 & 85; RN.

LORENTZEN, RONALD F; St Anthony HS; N Babylon, NY; (Y); Camera Clb; Computer Clb; Hon Roll; JETS Awd; Rgnt Schlrshp; Hofstra; Law.

LORENZ, MARTHA; Germantown Central HS; Germantown, NY; (S); 10/44; Varsity Clb; School Musical; School Play; Yrbk Stf; JV Var Fld Hcky; JV Var Gym; JV Var Sftbl; JV Var Vllybl; High Hon Roll; Hon Roll; Sec Sci.

LORENZ, MARTIN; Bay Shore HS; Islip, NY; (Y); 24/410; Crs Cntry; Trk; High Hon Roll; Hon Roll; NHS; Prfct Atten Awd; Bio, Math & Engl Acad Achvts 85-86.

LORENZEN, CHRISTOPHER; Valley Stream Central HS; Valley Stream, NY; (Y); Aud/Vis; Boy Scts; Computer Clb; Pres Science Clb; SADD; Concert Band; Mrchg Band; Orch; Stage Crew; NHS.

LORENZO, DANIELLE A; Manhasset HS; Manhasset, NY; (Y); 37/175; Aud/Vis; Drama Clb; Thesps; Band; Chorus; Orch; School Musical; School Play; Stage Crew; JV Socr; Rgnts Schlrshp 86; Skidmore Coll; Music.

LORENZO, LARI; George Washington HS; New York, NY; (Y); 27/321; Service Clb; Teachers Aide; Yrbk Stf; Hon Roll; NHS; Prfct Atten Awd; Typewrtg Medl 86; Dr Norman Elliot Awd High Hnrs 86; Sec.

LORENZO, LISETTE; New Utrecht HS; Brooklyn, NY; (Y); Church Yth Grp; Dance Clb; Key Clb; Office Aide; Nwsp Stf; Chorus; Cheerleading; Co-Capt Gym; Swmmng; Arista & Italian Awd 85; Bus Ed Hnr Scty 86; NY Tech Coll.

LORGE, ILYSE; Oceanside HS; Oceanside, NY; (Y); 47/575; Hosp Aide; Band; Mrchg Band; Orch; Nwsp Ed-Chief; Var Badmtn; Hon Roll; NHS; Northwestern U; Engl.

LORIE, KIRK; East Meadow HS; E Meadow, NY; (Y); Key Clb; Mathletes; VP Soph Cls; VP Jr Cls; VP Sr Cls; Var Bsktbl; Var Lcrss; Var Socr; Hon Roll; Jr NHS; Dntstry.

LORKA, JOHN; Turner Carroll HS; Buffalo, NY; (S); 10/124; Quiz Bowl; Stage Crew; Yrbk Sprt Ed; Pres Frsh Cls; Var Bsbl; Var Ftbl; Im Vllybl; Hon Roll; NHS; Frsh Acad Scholar 83; Acctg.

LORRAINE, SEAN; Trott Vocational HS; Niagara Falls, NY; (Y); Boys Clb Am; Church Yth Grp; Dance Clb; JA; Var Capt Ftbl; Im Capt Vllybl; 2nd Tm All Leag & MVP Awd Ftbl 85-86; Coachs Awd JV 84-85.

LOSAPIO, RANDY J; Roosevelt HS; Yonkers, NY; (Y); 6/245; Pres Key Clb; Nwsp Ed-Chief; Yrbk Ed-Chief; Stu Cncl; Bausch & Lomb Sci Awd; High Hon Roll; NHS.

LOSER, LISA M; Bethpage HS; Plainview, NY; (Y); 10/291; Pres German Clb; Var Capt Crs Cntry; Var Capt Trk; Elks Awd; High Hon Roll; VP NHS; Frgn Lang Awd 84; NY Tele Co Schlrshp 86; Ithaca Clg; Phys Thrpy.

LOSEY, LISA; Brasher Falls Central HS; Brasher Falls, NY; (Y); Girl Scts; Yrbk Stf; Var Cheerleading; Hon Roll; Prfct Atten Awd; Cazenovia Coll; Bus Sec.

LOSINGER, LINDA; Vestal Central SR HS; Vestal, NY; (Y); Drama Clb; Intnl Clb; Ski Clb; Spanish Clb; SADD; Yrbk Stf; Var Trk; Hon Roll; Sci.

LOSITO, JOHN; Elmira Free Acad; Elmira, NY; (Y); 10/240; Am Leg Boys St; Scholastic Bowl; Spanish Clb; SADD; Chorus; Rep Frsh Cls; Rep Soph Cls; Trs Jr Cls; Trs Sr Cls; Rep Stu Cncl; Schuyler-Chemung-Tioga Gdnc Cnslrs Assoc Schlrp 86; Betty O Connor Yth Bwlg Schlrp 86; Jr Bwlr Of Yr; Erie CC; Bus.

LOTENBERG, FRAN; Canarsie HS; Brooklyn, NY; (Y); Church Yth Grp; Office Aide; Temple Yth Grp; Varsity Clb; Chorus; Bowling; Psych.

LOTTER, HEIDI; Fredonia HS; Fredonia, NY; (Y); 27/197; Church Yth Grp; Hosp Aide; Key Clb; Ski Clb; Spanish Clb; SADD; Cheerleading; Hon Roll; Sci.

LOTZ, HEATHER; Academy Of Saint Joseph; Sayville, NY; (Y); Art Clb; Church Yth Grp; Dance Clb; Drama Clb; Hosp Aide; SADD; School Musical; Mgr School Play; Stage Crew; Yrbk Stf; SUNY Oneonta; Bus.

LOUBRIEL, EDUARDO; Louis D Brandeis HS; New York, NY; (Y); French Clb; Office Aide; Teachers Aide; Band; Concert Band; Hon Roll; Brnds Awd Outstndng Achvt Acctg 85-86; Comp Pgmng.

LOUCKS, DARLENE; Guilderland Central HS; Albany, NY; (Y); Trs Church Yth Grp; High Hon Roll; Hon Roll; Jr NHS; NHS; Hghst Avg Hme Eco 86; Hgh Acadmc Achvt-Math 12 Acc 86; Excllnc Amercn Stds II 86; Hudson Valley Comm; Bus Adm.

LOUCKS, LEE A; Mynderse Acad; Seneca Falls, NY; (S); 25/141; Am Leg Aux Girls St; Trs GAA; Yrbk Stf; Var JV Bsktbl; Var JV Socr; Var JV Sftbl; Cit Awd; High Hon Roll; Hon Roll; Pat Hurley Memrl Awd 82-83; 1st Tm All Leag Sftbl 85; Bus Mngmnt.

LOUCKS, NORMAN; Amsterdam HS; Amsterdam, NY; (Y); Sec Trs Church Yth Grp; Cit Awd; High Hon Roll; Hon Roll; NHS; Prfct Atten Awd.

LOUCKS, REBECCA; Amsterdam HS; Amsterdam, NY; (Y); Church Yth Grp; JA; Socr; Hon Roll; Pol Sci.

LOUIE, RICHARD N; Bronx High School Of Science; Flushing, NY; (Y); Math Tm; Lit Mag; Im Tennis; Im Vllybl; Ntl Merit SF; NY ST Math League Cont-3rd Pl Tm Mdl 85; Iona Coll Physics Comp 85; Ntl Spnsh Exam 15th Pl 85; Physician.

LOUIS, NANCY A; Croton Harmon HS; Croton On Hudson, NY; (Y); 1/107; Church Yth Grp; Band; VP Orch; School Play; Nwsp Stf; Hon Roll; NHS; Val; Smith Bk Awd Recog Of Outstndng Achvmt 85; Dartmouth Coll.

LOUIS, TINA; Thomas J Corcoran HS; Syracuse, NY; (Y); Spanish Clb; Concert Band; Jazz Band; Yrbk Stf; Var Bsktbl; Var Socr; Var Sftbl; High Hon Roll; Hon Roll; Var Crs Cntry; Am Musical Fdn Bnd Hns 85; NY ST Schl Music Assoc 86.

LOUISOR, MARGARET; Nazareth Regional HS; Brooklyn, NY; (Y); Chorus; VP Sr Cls; Rep Stu Cncl; Var Cheerleading; Var Crs Cntry; Var Trk; High Hon Roll; Hon Roll; NHS; $100 Acad Schlrshp 85; Social Studies & Math Awds 85; Spanish Awd 86.

LOUIT, ANNE; Mamaroneck HS; Larchmont, NY; (Y); 42/406; Pres German Clb; Math Tm; Nwsp Rptr; Nwsp Stf; Var Crs Cntry; Var Trk; NHS; Spanish NHS; Lit Mag; Caprice Adv; MVP Track 85-86; Clb Schrlshp 86; MA Inst Tech; Pre-Med.

LOUNSBERRY, LAURIE; Greenwood Central Schl; Greenwood, NY; (S); 1/22; Chorus; School Musical; Yrbk Stf; VP Frsh Cls; Pres Soph Cls; Pres Jr Cls; Var Bsktbl; Socr; Trk; NHS; Alfred U; Bus.

LOUNSBERRY, RAYANN; Harpursville Central Scshl; Harpursville, NY; (S); 9/82; Band; Chorus; VP Frsh Cls; Trs Jr Cls; VP JV Bsktbl; Fld Hcky; JV VP Sftbl; High Hon Roll; Hon Roll; NHS; Leag Al-Star Vrsty Sftbl 2nd Tm 85.

LOURINIA, ANTHONY; Rensselaer HS; Nassau, NY; (Y); Var L Bsbl; Var L Bsktbl; Var L Ftbl; Drftng.

LOVALLO, RENEE; Brewster HS; Brewster, NY; (Y); Varsity Clb; Band; Mrchg Band; Var Capt Sftbl.

LOVE, DERRICK; Wilson Magnet HS; Rochester, NY; (Y); #23 In Class; Aud/Vis; JV Bsktbl; Cit Awd; High Hon Roll; Cmnty Wkr; Drama Clb; Intnl Clb; Office Aide; Teachers Aide; Chorus; City Rochester Cert Recgntn 85; Athletic Awds 83-85; Comm.

LOVECCHIO, ANNEMARIE; Lindenhurst HS; Lindenhurst, NY; (Y); Cmnty Wkr; French Clb; SADD; Yrbk Stf; Var Trk; Hon Roll; NHS; Acad All-Amer Schlr Awd 86.

LOVEJOY, MARIELENA; Mamaroneck HS; Larchmont, NY; (Y); Church Yth Grp; Service Clb; Spanish Clb; Acpl Chr; Chorus; Yrbk Stf; JV Sftbl; NHS; Spanish NHS; Comm.

LOVELAND, FRANK; Chatham HS; Chatham, NY; (Y); 32/154; Chorus; Bowling; Score Keeper; Hon Roll; Interp Frgn Lang.

LOVELAND, MARK; Faith Heritage HS; Fulton, NY; (Y); Church Yth Grp; Drama Clb; Band; Chorus; Concert Band; Stage Crew; Yrbk Phtg; Trk; NYACK; Pstrl Mnstrs.

LOVELAND, RICHARD; Hudson Falls SR HS; Hudson Falls, NY; (Y); Drama Clb; Key Clb; Library Aide; SADD; Chorus; Rep Stu Cncl; Cit Awd; Hon Roll; Stage Crew; Yrbk Stf; Bus Club 86; RSP 84; Hlth Ofc Aide 86; Adirondack Comm Coll; RE Agnt.

LOVELESS, KELLY; Northville Central HS; Mayfield, NY; (Y); Varsity Clb; Yrbk Stf; JV Bsktbl; JV Var Cheerleading; JV Var Socr; Timer; High Hon Roll; Hon Roll.

LOVELESS, LAURAL; Broadalbin Central HS; Broadalbin, NY; (Y); Sec 4-H; SADD; Band; Concert Band; Mrchg Band; Variety Show; Lit Mag; 4-H Awd; Hon Roll; Perfect Attndnc Awd 85-86; Perfct Attndnc Awd 84-85; Physcl Ther.

LOVELL, NICOLE; Springfield Gardens HS; Jamaica, NY; (Y); 71/440; Church Yth Grp; GAA; Bsktbl; Hon Roll; Ed.

LOVELL, ROBERTA; Watkins Glen Central HS; Watkins Glen, NY; (Y); 52/128; Drama Clb; French Clb; Letterman Clb; Math Clb; Ski Clb; Varsity Clb; Band; Color Guard; Concert Band; Drm & Bgl; Corning CC; Tchr.

LOVELLO, ADRIENNE; The Mary Louis Acad; Maspeth, NY; (Y); 25/270; Office Aide; Ed Yrbk Phtg; High Hon Roll; Hon Roll; Kiwanis Awd; NHS; Mary Louis Acad NHS Schlrshp 86; St Johns U; Lbrl Arts.

LOVELY, ANGELA; Ogdensburg Free Acad; Ogdensburg, NY; (Y); FHA; Girl Scts; Hosp Aide; Office Aide; Chorus; Yrbk Stf; Trk; Hon Roll; St Lawrence U; Accntg.

LOVERDE, NICK; Sweet Home Central HS; Williamsville, NY; (Y); Boy Scts; VP Church Yth Grp; Cmnty Wkr; Ski Clb; SADD; Var Golf; Lcrss; Hockey Lgu 2nd Pl 81-82; Pnthrs Pause Litry Pblctn 84; Select Chorus 7 Mscl 82; Purdue U; Comm.

LOVERRO, FRANK J; Locust Valley HS; Bayville, NY; (Y); Am Leg Boys St; Pres SADD; Ftbl; Capt Wrstlng; High Hon Roll; Jr NHS; Pres Of Drug & Alcohol Comm 86-87; Law.

LOVERRO, IAN; Herricks HS; Carlsbad, CA; (S); Sec DECA; Yrbk Stf; Voice Dem Awd; 2nd Pl NY ST DECA Pepsi-Cola Learn & Earn Proj 86; 1st, 2nd, & 3rd Pl NY ST DECA Restrnt Mrktng; U CA; Business.

LOVETT, MICHELE; John Dewey HS; Brooklyn, NY; (Y); Math Tm; Teachers Aide; Concert Band; Yrbk Stf; Im Bsktbl; Cit Awd; Hon Roll; Jr NHS; NHS.

LOVITT, SHERRI; North Babylon SR HS; No Babylon, NY; (Y); 21/400; Chorus; Orch; Jr NHS; Attndnc Awd 82-86; Med.

LOVRIA, LAURA; Notre Dame HS; Batavia, NY; (S); 2/65; Drama Clb; School Musical; School Play; VP Stu Cncl; JV Cheerleading; Var Socr; JV Tennis; High Hon Roll; Hon Roll; NHS.

LOW, MARTIN E; Glen Cove HS; Glen Cove, NY; (Y); German Clb; Band; Hon Roll; NY Rgnts Schlrshp 85; Band Coll; Pre-Med.

LOWE, BARBARA; Honeoye Central Schl; Honeoye, NY; (S); Cmnty Wkr; French Clb; Office Aide; Band; Concert Band; Mrchg Band; Sec Frsh Cls; Sec Soph Cls; Sec Jr Cls; Rep Stu Cncl; Psychlgy.

LOWE, ERIN; St Peters HS For Girls; Staten Island, NY; (Y); Art Clb; Stage Crew; Rep Frsh Cls; Rep Stu Cncl; JV Var Cheerleading; Hon Roll; Pre-Law.

LOWE, JENNIFER; Tuckahoe HS; Tuckahoe, NY; (Y); Church Yth Grp; Drama Clb; Leo Clb; Science Clb; School Play; Var L Trk; Hon Roll; Sec Jr NHS; Rotary Awd; Girl Scts; MVP Track 85-86; All League Track Tm 85-86; Sports Med.

LOWENGUTH, JEFFREY; Bishop Kearney HS; Ontario, NY; (Y); 25/142; Varsity Clb; Band; Concert Band; Jazz Band; Mrchg Band; Crs Cntry; Trk; Hon Roll; NHS; Fndrs Mdl 86; Outstndg Athlt 86; Rssll Mrjn Schlrsh& 85; Allegheny Coll; Chem.

LOWERY, MICHAEL; Perry Central HS; Perry, NY; (Y); Computer Clb; FBLA; Chorus; Hon Roll; NHS; Oswegatchie Wrld Chng Yth Mission 86; Select Chrs 86; Pres Perry Free Mth Yth 86; Comp Sci.

LOWNE, YVONNE; Huntington Christian HS; Greenlawn, NY; (S); 1/22; Hosp Aide; Chorus; Pres Frsh Cls; Sec Jr Cls; Stu Cncl; Stat Bsktbl; Var L Cheerleading; NHS; Val; 1st Pl Fine Arts Fstvl Flute Duet 82; Bio.

LOY, CHARLES W; West Babylon HS; West Islip, NY; (Y); 14/423; Nwsp Sprt Ed; Nwsp Stf; Yrbk Bus Mgr; Bausch & Lomb Sci Awd; High Hon Roll; Jr NHS; NHS; Ntl Merit Ltr.

LOYAL, ANDREW; Central HS; Valley Stream, NY; (Y); AFS; Computer Clb; Chorus; Var Bowling; Var Trk; Hon Roll; NCTE Awd; NHS.

LOYSEN, KATHLEEN; Our Lady Of Mercy HS; Rochester, NY; (Y); French Clb; Intnl Clb; Model UN; Ski Clb; SADD; Teachers Aide; Nwsp Rptr; Lit Mag; Hon Roll; Church Yth Grp; Prtl Schlrshp HS Tuition 83-87; Foreign Exchng Stu France 86; Foreign Lang.

LOZADA, JOHN; Roslyan HS; Roslyn, NY; (Y); Band; Orch; Ed Nwsp Stf; Rep Stu Cncl; Var Capt Crs Cntry; Var Capt Trk; NHS; Ntl Merit Ltr; Schlr Athlt Awd 86; Cornell U; Chem.

LOZADA, RICARDO; Amsterdam HS; Amsterdam, NY; (Y); Band; Concert Band; Jazz Band; Mrchg Band; Orch; Pep Band; Yrbk Stf; Trk; Prfct Atten Awd; Chmps GA Peach Bowl; Schenetady Cnty Coll; Clnry Art.

LOZANO, TERESA; Freeport HS; Freeport, NY; (Y); 16/450; Cmnty Wkr; DECA; Mgr French Clb; Mgr Spanish Clb; SADD; Teachers Aide; Chorus; Yrbk Stf; Lit Mag; Rep Stu Cncl; FHS Forgn Lang Dept Lilah Cushman Memrl Schlrshp 86; Cushmn Memrl Schlrshp 86; Long Island U; Forgn Lang.

LOZIER, GLEN E; Ross Corners Christian Acad; Vestal, NY; (Y); 3/20; Church Yth Grp; Computer Clb; Ski Clb; VP Soph Cls; Socr; High Hon Roll; Hon Roll; NY Rgnts Schlrshp 86.

LOZIER, LORI; No Babylon SR HS; No Babylon, NY; (Y); 18/450; Dance Clb; Intnl Clb; VP Stu Cncl; Fld Hcky; French Hon Soc; High Hon Roll; NHS; French Clb; Girl Scts; Coach Actv; Amer Natl Red Crss Adv Swmr 84; Newsdy Hnr Cert 84; Cert Apprctn Town Babylon 86; NYU; Danc Thrpy.

LU, KENNETH; Irondequoit HS; Rochester, NY; (Y); 1/366; Computer Clb; Math Tm; Model UN; Radio Clb; Science Clb; SADD; Bausch & Lomb Sci Awd; High Hon Roll; NHS; Ntl Merit Schol; Monroe Prof Engrs Scty Schlrshp 86; MA Inst Tech; Elec Engr.

LUBANSKI, AMY JO; York Central HS; York, NY; (Y); Art Clb; Ski Clb; Var Bsktbl; Var Cheerleading; Var Socr; Var Sftbl; Var Vllybl; Church Yth Grp; 4-H; Varsity Clb; Pres Phys Fit Awds 82-86; 1st All Star Tm Sftbl 85-86; Hnrb Mntn Bsktbl, Vllybl, Soccr 85-86.

LUBER, KATRINA; Bishop Ludden HS; Camillus, NY; (Y); Church Yth Grp; Speech Tm; Church Choir; School Musical; School Play; Tennis; High Hon Roll; Hon Roll; NHS; Accntng Awd 85-86; Bus Mgnt.

LUBER, MARTIN J; Lakeshore HS; Angola, NY; (Y); 1/286; French Clb; Letterman Clb; SADD; Varsity Clb; Stu Cncl; Swmmng; Lion Awd; NHS; Ntl Merit Ltr; Val; Loyola Hnrs Prgrm 86; Ntl Sci Olympd 84-86; Capt Swm Tm 85; Loyola U Chicago; Pre-Med.

LUBEROF, SHELDON W; Ward Melville HS; Centereach, NY; (Y); 19/710; Computer Clb; Mathletes; Math Tm; Scholastic Bowl; Hon Roll; NHS; Ntl Merit Ltr; Comp Tm Capt 86; Outstndng Jr Math 85; NYS Rgnts Schlrshp 86; Cornell U; Elec Engrng.

LUCA, ROSEANNE; West Babylon HS; W Babylon, NY; (Y); Computer Clb; FNA; Chorus; Concert Band; Orch; Symp Band; Cheerleading; Hon Roll; Nrsg.

LUCAS, ANTOINETTE; De Witt Clinton HS; Bronx, NY; (Y); Chorus.

LUCAS, MARSHALL; Commack HS North; Commack, NY; (Y); 53/390; AFS; Computer Clb; FFA; German Clb; SADD; Band; Concert Band; Drm Mjr(t); SUNY Stony Brook; Comp Sci.

LUCAS, PETER; Bradford Central HS; Bradford, NY; (Y); 5/23; Am Leg Boys St; SADD; Yrbk Sprt Ed; VP Jr Cls; Var Capt Trk; Hon Roll; Aviatn.

LUCAS, VICTORIA LYNNE; Watkins Glen HS; Willard, NY; (S); Math Clb; Ski Clb; SADD; Varsity Clb; Nwsp Stf; Rep Stu Cncl; Stat Bsktbl; JV Sftbl; Capt JV Vllybl; Hon Roll; Bio.

LUCCA, JOEY; City Honors HS; Buffalo, NY; (Y); 33/107; Chess Clb; Church Yth Grp; Debate Tm; Drama Clb; FNA; Red Cross Aide; Spanish Clb; Chorus; Off Frsh Cls; Off Soph Cls; Natl Conf Chrstns & Jews Brthrhd Incntv 85; Joseph Manch Crtv Wrtg Awd 85; Hnrd Into Exec Intrnshp 86; D Youville Coll; RN.

LUCCHESE, ANGELA; Hillcrest HS; Flushing, NY; (Y); 90/830; Church Yth Grp; FCA; GAA; Varsity Clb; Chorus; Var Capt Sftbl; Var Vllybl; Kiwanis Awd; Ntl Merit Ltr; Generoso Pope Scholar Awd 86; Louisa Wingate Underhill Cert 86; St Johns U; Phrmcy.

LUCCHESE, LISA; Mahopac HS; Mahopac, NY; (Y); Off Dance Clb; Hon Roll; NHS; Natl Hspnc Schlr Awd SF 86; Putnam Arts Cncl 1st & 3rd Pl Awds Art Wrk 85; Grphc Dsgn.

LUCE, BRETT; Pulaski SR HS; Pulaski, NY; (Y); Drama Clb; Varsity Clb; Chorus; Concert Band; Mrchg Band; School Musical; Trk; Wt Lftg; Snow Incentive* Awd Summr Camp 85-86; Forestry.

LUCE, PAUL M; Gowanda Central HS; Gowanda, NY; (Y); Am Leg Boys St; Rep JA; Library Aide; SADD; Band; Rep Jr Cls; Chrmn Stu Cncl; Var L Wrstlng; Hon Roll; NHS; SUNY; Forensic Pathology.

LUCERO, MONICA; Adlai E Stevenson HS; Bronx, NY; (Y); Dance Clb; JA; Latin Clb; Library Aide; Office Aide; Service Clb; Teachers Aide; Sec Stu Cncl; Hon Roll; NHS; Natl Hnr Soc Of Scndry Schls 85-86; Spnsh Cert 84-86; Svc Of Prfct Atten 85-86; Dance Cert 85; Acad Cert; Forham U; Comp Sci.

LUCERO, ROXANA; Adlai E Stevenson HS; Bronx, NY; (Y); JA; Spanish Clb; Off Jr Cls; High Hon Roll; NHS; Prfct Atten Awd; Sci Awd, Math Awd, Socl Studies Awd 85; Hunter Coll; Phys Thrpst.

LUCHSINGER, THOMAS A; Mattituck HS; Mattituck, NY; (Y); 16/119; Am Leg Boys St; Church Yth Grp; Mathletes; Math Tm; Chorus; Variety Show; Var Socr; Var Trk; High Hon Roll; NHS; Sufflk Cnty Math Cntst 2nd 85; Mattck Expressn 1st 86; Mock Trl Tm 86.

LUCI, MAUREEN; Amsterdam HS; Amsterdam, NY; (Y); 76/294; Cmnty Wkr; Political Wkr; Band; Concert Band; Mrchg Band; Yrbk Stf; Rep Stu Cncl; Hon Roll; Utica Coll; Accntnt.

LUCIA, BRENDA; Dundee Central HS; Dundee, NY; (Y); Chorus; Trs Sr Cls; High Hon Roll; Hon Roll; Gregg Typng 51, 59; Gregg Shrthnd 60, 70 & 80; Accntng I; Bus.

LUCIA, JEFFREY; Onondaga Central HS; Syracuse, NY; (S); 2/84; Art Clb; Spanish Clb; SADD; Pres Soph Cls; Rep Jr Cls; Rep Stu Cncl; Var Ftbl; JV Wrstlng; High Hon Roll; NHS; Hghst Avg Stu Body 83-84; Cert Awd Hnr Roll Hghst Grds 84-85; Achvt Awds Eng Soc Stud Spn Alg 84-85; Sci.

LUCIANO, MICHELLE; Jeffersonville-Youngsville Ctrl Sch; Jeffersonville, NY; (Y); 5/60; Church Yth Grp; Drama Clb; Church Choir; School Musical; Pres Sec Stu Cncl; High Hon Roll; Sec NHS; Thesps; Chorus; Cardinal Spellman Yth Awd 84; Cash Awd-J-Y-C-S Stu Cncl-Outstndng Ablty & Ldrshp 86; U Of Steubenville; Cmnctns.

LUCIDO, ELIZABETH; Amsterdam HS; Amsterdam, NY; (Y); 93/310; Cmnty Wkr; Sec Pres FBLA; JA; Flag Corp; Yrbk Stf; Sec Frsh Cls; Rep Soph Cls; Rep Jr Cls; Rep Stu Cncl; Hon Roll; Cmmnctns.

LUCIO, OSCAR; Mineola HS; Mineola, NY; (Y); Dance Clb; Var Ice Hcky; Var Socr; French Hon Soc; High Hon Roll; NHS; Farmingdale Clg; Commcl Airln.

LUCK, TODD; Rogers HS; New York, NY; (Y); Church Yth Grp; Bsbl; Bsktbl; Ftbl; Socr; Hon Roll; Prfct Atten Awd.

LUCKETTE, MICHAEL A; East Syracuse Minoa HS; Kirkville, NY; (Y); 50/350; Science Clb; Rep Frsh Cls; Var Trk; Hon Roll; Jr NHS; NHS; Prfct Atten Awd; Most Outstndg Soc Stud Stu 85 & 86; Outstndg Engl Stu 85; Outstndg Bio Awd-97 Avg 85; Aerosp Engr.

LUCKEY, JENNIFER; Uniondale HS; Uniondale, NY; (Y); Art Clb; Dance Clb; Pep Clb; Capt Drm Mjr(t); Capt Pom Pon; Powder Puff Ftbl; Score Keeper; Sftbl; Swmmng; Stat Wrstlng; Spnsh & Art Awd 84; FIT; Art.

LUDLAM, MARGOT; Bellport HS; Brookhaven, NY; (Y); 13/395; Cmnty Wkr; Dance Clb; French Clb; Orch; Nwsp Rptr; JV Bsktbl; JV Sftbl; Cit Awd; French Hon Soc; NHS; Music Awd-Violin NYSSMA 83-86; Dance Traupe 85-86; Law.

LUDOVICO, MARK; Saranac Lake HS; Saranac Lk, NY; (Y); 3/140; Am Leg Boys St; Boy Scts; Yrbk Ed-Chief; Yrbk Stf; Pres Jr Cls; Rep Stu Cncl; Socr; Trk; Bausch & Lomb Sci Awd; Hon Roll; Schl Srv Awd; 2nd Amer Legion Lcl Oratory Cntst; US Naval Acad; Aeronatcl Engrn.

LUDWIG, DANA; Nardin Acad; E Amherst, NY; (Y); 11/87; Cmnty Wkr; Dance Clb; Office Aide; School Musical; Stage Crew; Lit Mag; Rep Frsh Cls; Rep Soph Cls; VP Jr Cls; Rep Stu Cncl.

LUDWIG, JONATHON L; Wayne Central HS; Macedon, NY; (Y); 27/193; Var L Bsbl; JV Im Bsktbl; Im Socr; Im Vllybl; Hon Roll; NHS; NYS Rgnts Schlrshp 86; Le Moyne Coll; Elctrcl Engnrng.

LUDWIG, TRACEY; Nardin Acad; East Amherst, NY; (S); 3/84; Cmnty Wkr; Hosp Aide; Ski Clb; School Musical; Ed Nwsp Stf; Lit Mag; Sec Jr Cls; Pres Sr Cls; Hon Roll; NHS; Acadmc All Amer 85; Yamaha Musci Awd 83-84; Accntng.

LUECKS, THOMAS; Haverling Central HS; Bath, NY; (Y); Boy Scts; Exploring; Latin Clb; Math Clb; Ski Clb; Socr; Hon Roll; Engrng.

LUFFMAN, BONNIE J; Naples Central HS; Canandaigua, NY; (Y); 2/85; Church Yth Grp; Chorus; High Hon Roll; Sal; Natl Sschlstc Art Comp Red Rbbn 85; NYS Regents Schlrshp 86.

LUFKIN, CAMILLE A; Cambridge Central Schl; Cambridge, NY; (Y); Drama Clb; 4-H; Chorus; Madrigals; School Musical; School Play; Lit Mag; High Hon Roll; NHS; Church Yth Grp; Organ Scholar Monterey Organ Buffs 1st Pl 83; Granville Lang Arts Fest 1st Pl Creatv Wrtng 86; Creatv Wrtng.

LUFKIN, JENNIFER; Argyle Central HS; Argyle, NY; (Y); 6/60; Off GAA; Math Tm; Band; Chorus; Jazz Band; Yrbk Sprt Ed; Var Bsktbl; Coach Actv; High Hon Roll; NHS; Hlth.

LUGO, CECILIA; Alfred G Berner HS; Massapequa, NY; (Y); 9/375; Hon Roll; NHS; Accounting.

LUGO, DANIEL; Amityville Memorial HS; Amityville, NY; (Y); 23/372; Drama Clb; Acpl Chr; Orch; School Musical; Swing Chorus; JV Capt Bsktbl; Var Capt Ftbl; Var Trk; High Hon Roll; NHS.

LUGO, EDWIN A; Performing Arts HS; Bronx, NY; (Y); 34/121; Drama Clb; Thesps; School Play; Stage Crew; Hon Roll; Orch; Variety Show; Frsh Cls; Ntl Merit Schol; Prfct Atten Awd; Natl Found Advcmnt Arts 85-86; Am Acad Of Arts; Actr.

LUGO, SANDY; Seaford HS; Seaford, NY; (Y); Yrbk Stf; Cit Awd.

LUGO, YOLANDA; Jane Addams V HS; Bronx, NY; (S); 9/260; Church Yth Grp; Chorus; Cit Awd; Hon Roll; Cert Of Merit Assoc Of Tchrs Soc Stdys 83; NY City Coll; Nrsng.

LUI, WAI; Fashion Industries HS; New York, NY; (Y); 31/335; Chorus; NYU; Bus Admnstrtn.

LUIZZI, BETH; Mercy HS; Rensselaer, NY; (Y); Spanish Clb; School Play; Ed Nwsp Stf; High Hon Roll; Hon Roll; Spnsh I II & III Excllnc 84-86; Excllnc In Engl 84-86; Excllnc In Soc Studies 84-86; SUNY Albany; Spnsh.

LUK, NGA MAN; Richmond Hill HS; Richmond, NY; (Y); Chess Clb; Computer Clb; FBLA; Key Clb; Band; Stage Crew; Off Stu Cncl; Tennis; Prfct Atten Awd; Leaders; Baruch Coll; Bus Mgmt.

LUKAS, MEGAN; Hackley HS; Sparkill, NY; (Y); 14/90; Cmnty Wkr; Drama Clb; Chorus; Orch; School Musical; School Play; Sftbl; High Hon Roll; Hon Roll; Service Clb; Rgnts Schlrshp 86; Merit Schlrshp Prm 85; Vassar.

LUKAS, SCOTT; Wellington C Mepham HS; Bellmore, NY; (Y); Art Clb; L Var Bsbl; L Var Ftbl; French Hon Soc; High Hon Roll; NHS; Bellmore/Merrick Cult Art Awd 84.

LUKASZEWICZ, SUSAN; Notre Dame HS; Batavia, NY; (S); 2/63; Yrbk Ed-Chief; JV Vllybl; High Hon Roll; NHS; Phys Ther.

LUKASZEWSKI, ANN M; John A Coleman HS; Kingston, NY; (S); Sec JA; Pres Key Clb; Service Clb; Spanish Clb; Rep Jr Cls; Var Bsktbl; Var Fld Hcky; Hon Roll; NHS; Hugh O Brian Ldrshp Awd 85; John A Coleman Schlrshp 83-87; Math.

LUKE, CAROL; Ripley Central HS; Ripley, NY; (Y); Church Yth Grp; Pep Clb; Teachers Aide; Band; Chorus; Mrchg Band; School Musical; School Play; Sec Frsh Cls; Sec Soph Cls; Jamestown CC; Elem Tchr.

LUKE, MICHELE; J C Birdlebough HS; Phoenix, NY; (Y); 8/156; 4-H; Latin Clb; Concert Band; JV Var Socr; JV Var Vllybl; 4-H Awd; Hon Roll; NHS; Ctrl NY Huntr/Jumper Assc 84; Jumpr Champ 84; Vet Med.

LUKS, JEFF; Union-Endicott HS; Endwell, NY; (Y); Boy Scts; Key Clb; Temple Yth Grp; Yrbk Ed-Chief; Yrbk Phtg; L Capt Swmmng; Ntl Merit SF; Camera Clb; Library Aide; Mathletes; Eagle Sct 86; Salute Yth Natl Cncl Yth Ldrshp 86; Rotary Yth Ldrshp Awds 86; Carnegie Mellon; Comp Sci.

LUKUS, JEFF; Gates-Chili SR HS; Rochester, NY; (Y); Boy Scts; Camera Clb; Chess Clb; Exploring; Library Aide; Chorus; Yrbk Phtg; JV Var Ftbl; JV Var Wt Lftg; Hon Roll; Indstrl Arts Photo Cont 1st Plc 85; Bus.

LUM, KERRY; Nazareth Acad; Rochester, NY; (Y); Rep Church Yth Grp; Ski Clb; Spanish Clb; SADD; Band; Trk; High Hon Roll; Hon Roll; NHS; Yrbk Stf; Exch Stu Hllnd Yth For Undrstndng 86; Psych.

LUM, SUSAN; Tottenville HS; Staten Isld, NY; (Y); Intnl Clb; Key Clb; Pep Clb; Teachers Aide; Yrbk Rptr; Yrbk Stf; High Hon Roll; Hon Roll; NHS.

LUMAN, AMBER JOELL; Lewiston-Porter HS; Lewiston, NY; (Y); 17/243; Pres Chorus; School Play; Nwsp Ed-Chief; Trs Frsh Cls; Trs Soph Cls; Pres Rep Stu Cncl; Capt Cheerleading; Capt Trk; Capt Vllybl; High Hon Roll; Williams Coll Outstndng Stu Awd 85; Cls 86 Most Likely Succeed; Best All Around; Outstndng Schlr Athlet; PA ST U; Nrsng.

LUMB, JEFF; Auburn HS; Auburn, NY; (Y); Computer Clb; ROTC; Ski Clb; JV Bsbl; Auburn CC; Bus Mngmt.

LUMIA, CHRISTOPHER; Jamestown HS; Jamestown, NY; (Y); Chess Clb; Church Yth Grp; Band; Concert Band; Jazz Band; Mrchg Band; Rep Frsh Cls; Ftbl; Jr NHS; NHS; Mth.

LUMLEY, CHRISTINE; Madrid-Waddinton HS; Canton, NY; (Y); AFS; Drama Clb; French Clb; GAA; Band; Chorus; Concert Band; Mrchg Band; School Musical; School Play; Hnr Awds Top 20 Pct Cosmtlgy Cls 85-86; Cosmtlgy.

LUMSBY, GENIEVE N; The Spence Schl; New York, NY; (Y); Dance Clb; Model UN; Acpl Chr; Chorus; School Musical; School Play; Variety Show; Yrbk Bus Mgr; Sec VP Stu Cncl; Var L Gym; Nlt Achvt Semi-Fnlst 85; Perfrmr.

LUNA, CARLOS; Eastern District HS; Brooklyn, NY; (Y); Art Clb; English Clb; Intnl Clb; Latin Clb; Science Clb; Band; School Play; Crs Cntry; Socr; Trk; DR.

LUNA, ZULMA; Manhattan Center/Sci P Math HS; New York, NY; (Y); 23/159; Camera Clb; French Clb; JA; Office Aide; Teachers Aide; Chorus; Yrbk Phtg; French Hon Soc; Hon Roll; City Coll NY; Psychology.

LUND, ANNE-MARIE; Spackenkill HS; Poughkeepsie, NY; (Y); Thesps; Orch; School Musical; School Play; Nwsp Stf; Ed Lit Mag; JV Capt Vllybl; NHS; Camera Clb; Drama Clb; Rgnl HS Of Excllnc 86; 1st Pl Natl Frnch Cntst Hudson Vlly Rgn Lvl 2A 86; 3rd Pl Natl Frnch 857; Lbrl Arts Coll; Mdrn Lang.

LUND, CHRIS; Sherburne-Earlville HS; Earlville, NY; (Y); 2/167; Church Yth Grp; High Hon Roll; Hon Roll; NHS; Prfct Atten Awd; Acctng.

LUNDEN, STEPHANIE; Northstar Christian Acad; Churchville, NY; (S); 3/28; Rep Stu Cncl; Var Cheerleading; Var Socr; High Hon Roll; Hon Roll; Amer Chrstn Hnr Soc; Natl Sci Merit Awd; Natl Ldrshp & Svc Awd; Lwyr.

LUNDGREN, JENNIFER; School Of The Holy Child; Scarsdale, NY; (Y); Hosp Aide; Chorus; Nwsp Ed-Chief; Yrbk Stf; Lit Mag; Var Fld Hcky; Hon Roll.

LUNDQUIST, MONA E; Garden City HS; Garden City, NY; (Y); Church Yth Grp; Hosp Aide; Key Clb; Red Cross Aide; SADD; Band; Nwsp Stf; Cheerleading; High Hon Roll; Hon Roll; Garden City Lay Ecumenical Awd 86; Hartwick Coll; Educ.

LUNDY, SCOTT; New Lebanon JR SR HS; Old Chatham, NY; (Y); 3/59; Pres Spanish Clb; Pres Frsh Cls; Pres Soph Cls; VP Jr Cls; Trs Stu Cncl; L Capt Bsbl; L Capt Bsktbl; Var Socr; High Hon Roll; NHS; Excllnc Boys Phys Ed 86; MVP JV Bsktbl 85; MVP Vrsty Bsbl 86.

LUNG, JENJEN H; William Cullen Bryant HS; Elmhurst, NY; (Y); 9/623; Church Yth Grp; Math Clb; Math Tm; Church Choir; French Hon Soc; High Hon Roll; NHS; Ntl Merit Ltr; Prfct Atten Awd; St Schlr; Rgnt Schlrshp 86; Math & Sci Fair 3d Wnnr 84; Trphs Rcvd Sr Math Team 85; The John Hopkins U; Elec Engr.

LUNGU, JAMES; Dansville Central Schl; Dansville, NY; (Y); 4-H; Radio Clb; Ski Clb; Stu Cncl; Bsktbl; JV Var Ftbl; JV Swmmng; JV Var Trk; Im Vllybl; 4-H Awd; Yth For Understndg; Natl Eng Merit Awd,Eagl Sct,Cnty Champ 200 M Sprnt; Clarkson Schlrshp,Urbn Leag Sc; Clarkson U; Elec Engrng.

LUNKENHEIMER, BECKY; Cato-Meridian HS; Cato, NY; (Y); 21/100; 4-H; GAA; SADD; Pres Stu Cncl; Var Fld Hcky; Var Trk; Var Vllybl; 4-H Awd; Hon Roll; Prfct Atten Awd; Coaches Awd Trk 86; Anne Kllgh Srv Awd 86; Mst Imprvd Grls Vrsty Fld Hcky 86; Cortland; Phys Ed.

LUNKENHEIMER, LORI; Bishop Scully HS; Gloversville, NY; (Y); Art Clb; Math Clb; JV Var Bsktbl; Var Sftbl; NHS; Vet Asst.

LUNTZ, BARBARA; Fredonia Central Schl; Fredonia, NY; (Y); French Clb; GAA; Key Clb; Science Clb; SADD; Orch; Symp Band; Nwsp Rptr; Nwsp Stf; Yrbk Stf; NY ST Regents Schlrshp 86-90; SUNY Buffalo.

LUO, QI MENG; Seward Park HS; New York, NY; (Y); 45/545; Art Clb; Chess Clb; Cmnty Wkr; Computer Clb; Intnl Clb; Math Clb; Teachers Aide; Bsktbl; Diving; Ftbl; Schl Grad Awd 86; CCNY; Comp Sci.

LUONGO, ANDREA; Cardinal Spellman HS; Bronx, NY; (S); 23/510; Church Yth Grp; Computer Clb; Ski Clb; Rep Jr Cls; Pres Sr Cls; High Hon Roll; NHS.

LUPA, STEPHANIE; Shenendehowa HS; Rexford, NY; (Y); 120/675; AFS; Cmnty Wkr; Chorus; Swing Chorus; High Hon Roll; NHS; Ntl Merit Ltr; Church Yth Grp; VP Exploring; 4-H; Allegheny Coll; Comm Arts.

LUPATKIN, CINDY; Smithtown HS; Smithtown, NY; (Y); Hosp Aide; SADD; Thesps; Chorus; Capt JV Tennis; High Hon Roll; NHS; Spanish NHS; Recvd Excllnc NYSSMA 84.

LUPIA, CARMELA M A; Waterville Central HS; Oriskany Falls, NY; (Y); 9/91; Am Leg Aux Girls St; Nwsp Stf; Yrbk Ed-Chief; Pres Frsh Cls; Sec Soph Cls; Socr; High Hon Roll; Hon Roll; NHS; Wtrvl Tchrs Assoc Schlrshp 86; Shoemaker Mrl Schlrshp 86; Yth Rcgntn Awd 86; Real Est Awd 86; SUNY Oswego; Mrktng.

LUPICA, DANIEL; Hamburg HS; Hamburg, NY; (Y); VP Church Yth Grp; SADD; Sec Chorus; School Musical; Rep Frsh Cls; VP Soph Cls; Im Gym; Im Trk; Wrstlng; Im Socr; SUNY Buffalo; Engrng.

LUPINI, LORI M; Whiteboro SR HS; Whitesboro, NY; (Y); 56/342; Church Yth Grp; GAA; Acpl Chr; Chorus; Var L Bsktbl; Var Capt Fld Hcky; Var L Trk; All Star Fld Hocky 85; Al Str Trck 85; Pin Fld Hock Bsktbll Trck; Cortland; Sci.

LUPO, SALVATORE; Monsignor Mc Clancy HS; Woodside, NY; (Y); 12/213; Crs Cntry; Im Ftbl; Trk; Hon Roll; NHS; Pace U Schlrshp 86; Ntl Sci Olympiad Cert Distctn 85; Barach Coll; Finance.

LUSH, ERIN; Newark SR HS; Palmyra, NY; (Y); 23/186; Chorus; Madrigals; School Musical; Stage Crew; Swing Chorus; Lit Mag; Var Trk; JV Wrstlng; High Hon Roll; Cmnty Wkr; 2nd Hnrs Acdmc Stndng 85; 2nd Pl Wrstlng Trnmnt 86; JR Advrs Cncl 86; Surgeon.

LUSSIER, DENISE; Our Lady Of Lourdes HS; Wappingers Fls, NY; (Y); 12/180; Church Yth Grp; Var L Crs Cntry; Var L Swmmng; Var L Trk; NHS.

LUSTER, ANN; Charles Odickerson HS; Trumansburg, NY; (Y); 11/124; Pres VP Drama Clb; French Clb; Pres Model UN; Political Wkr; SADD; Thesps; School Play; Yrbk Ed-Chief; Yrbk Stf; Rep Frsh Cls; Modl UN Awd 85; Poli Sci.

LUSTIG, KIMBERLY; Wheatland-Chili HS; Hamlin, NY; (Y); 5/70; Ski Clb; SADD; Chorus; School Musical; Stu Cncl; JV Var Vllybl; Hon Roll; Hghst Engl Avg Clss; Cmmnctns.

LUSTIG, ROBIN; H A F T R Hebrew Acad; Woodmere, NY; (Y); Computer Clb; Math Tm; Temple Yth Grp; School Play; Nwsp Stf; Yrbk Bus Mgr; Rep Sr Cls; Gym; Tennis; Vllybl; Housewares Clb Schrlshp 86; NYS Regents Schrlshp 86; Barnard Coll; Econ.

LUSTYIK, SARA; Lake George HS; Lk George, NY; (Y); Dance Clb; Chorus; School Musical; School Play; Lit Mag; Prfct Atten Awd; Socl Wrkr.

LUTGEN, GAYLE; Frewsburg Central Schl; Frewsburg, NY; (Y); 2/64; Band; Hon Roll; Jamestown CC; Hmn Svcs.

LUTHART, MELINDA; L A Webber Schl; Medina, NY; (S); 7/82; Exploring; Spanish Clb; Teachers Aide; VICA; Yrbk Stf; JV Var Vllybl; Hon Roll; Jr NHS; NHS; Prof Awd In Nrsng 85-86; Nrsng.

LUTHART, MELISSA; L A Webber Schl; Medina, NY; (S); 2/82; Library Aide; Yrbk Stf; Score Keeper; Hon Roll; Jr NHS; NHS; Proj Adept 84; Math.

LUTHER, DONALD; Letchworth Central HS; Bliss, NY; (Y); Sec 4-H; Rptr FFA; Varsity Clb; Band; Concert Band; Drm & Bgl; Mrchg Band; Var Bsbl; Var Socr; Var Wrstlng; Cornell U; Lrg Anml Vet Med.

LUTHER, KATRINA; Canastota HS; Canastota, NY; (S); 2/140; Science Clb; SADD; Band; Chorus; Yrbk Stf; JV Cheerleading; Var Golf; High Hon Roll; NHS; Sal; Biochem.

LUTHER, LAURA LEE; Frankfort-Schuyler HS; Frankfort, NY; (Y); Church Yth Grp; 4-H; Spanish Clb; Band; Chorus; Concert Band; Jazz Band; Mrchg Band; Yrbk Stf; Pres Frsh Cls; Grad Barbzn Modlg Schl 80; Leysin Amer Schl Coll Prep 86; Intl Lang.

LUTHER, LEGG; Ravena-Coeymans-Selkirk HS; South Bethlehem, NY; (Y); Key Clb; Church Choir; Rep Soph Cls; Var L Socr; Var L Trk; Capt L Wrstlng; Prfct Atten Awd; Boys Clb Am; German Clb; Varsity Clb; Boy Sct Ctn Of Hnr 83; Col Cncl Wrstlng All-Star 85; Mst Outstndng Wrstler In Col Cncl Trnmnt 85; Comp Tech.

LUTSKY, GARRETT; Herricks HS; New Hyde Park, NY; (Y); 110/290; Mathletes; Bsbl; Ftbl; Rgnts Schlrshp 86; SUNY Albany; Acctg.

LUTTENBERG, DANIELLE; Bronx H S Of Science; New Hyde Park, NY; (Y); SADD; Temple Yth Grp; Concert Band; Gold Mdl Orch/Band Awd 84; Bnai Brith Yth Orgnztn; Amnesty Intl; Hudson Rvr Clearwtr Revival Assn; Bio.

LUTZ, BOB; Bishop Grimes HS; Syracuse, NY; (Y); Ski Clb; Wrstlng; Hon Roll; Go Kart Champ 84-86; Accmplshd Race Car Drvr 86; FL ST; Mktg.

LUTZ, JENNIFER M; Bayport-Blue Point HS; Bayport, NY; (Y); Church Yth Grp; FBLA; Key Clb; Mathletes; SADD; Capt Var Cheerleading; Hon Roll; NHS; Psych.

LUTZ, LAURA M; Westhill HS; Syracuse, NY; (Y); 2/145; VP Art Clb; Exploring; Ski Clb; Lit Mag; Sec Jr Cls; Sec Sr Cls; Trk; Hon Roll; NHS; Drama Clb; Regents Schlrshp 86; NY Telephone Co Schlrshp 86; Clarkson Schl Of Engrng Awd 86; Clarkson U; Engrng.

LUTZ, LISA; Springville Griffith HS; West Falls, NY; (Y); GAA; Key Clb; Spanish Clb; Yrbk Stf; Rep Stu Cncl; JV Var Powder Puff Ftbl; Hon Roll; ST U Of NY; Grphc Artst.

LUTZ, REBECCA A; Oneonta SR HS; Oneonta, NY; (Y); 3/174; Church Yth Grp; Q&S; Thesps; Chorus; Pres VP Concert Band; High Hon Roll; NHS; Cmnty Wkr; Drama Clb; Key Clb; Smith Schlrshp, Rgnts Schlrshp, Stvn W Paine Schlrshp 86; Houghton Coll; Psych.

LUYSTER, CARRIE; John H Glenn HS; Huntington, NY; (Y); 7/268; Hosp Aide; Orch; Variety Show; Trs Frsh Cls; Var Cheerleading; Var Capt Tennis; High Hon Roll; NHS; Ntl Merit Schol; VP Spanish NHS; Prm Qn 85; Bus Mgmt.

LUZADIS JR, DAVID A; Gilbertsville Central Schl; Unadilla, NY; (Y); Am Leg Boys St; Varsity Clb; Band; Chorus; School Play; VP Sr Cls; Bsbl; Capt Socr; High Hon Roll; VP NHS.

LUZZI, MICHELE; Geneva HS; Geneva, NY; (S); 36/175; Varsity Clb; Stu Cncl; JV Var Bsktbl; Mgr(s); Score Keeper; Var Capt Socr; JV Var Sftbl; High Hon Roll; Hon Roll; NHS; Cayuga Cnty CC; Comp Sci.

LY, MAI; Walton HS; Bronx, NY; (Y); JA; Teachers Aide; Hon Roll; NHS; Engr.

LYBA, KARIN; Hamburg SR HS; Hamburg, NY; (Y); Trs Service Clb; Yrbk Stf; Rep Soph Cls; Sec Vllybl; High Hon Roll; Hon Roll; Fash Merch.

LYBOULT, LYNN; John C Birdlebough HS; Phoenix, NY; (Y); Drama Clb; Hosp Aide; Chorus; Color Guard; Flag Corp; Mrchg Band; School Musical; School Play; Var Score Keeper; Var Socr; Nursing.

LYDELL, DIANN; Frewsburg Central HS; Frewsburg, NY; (Y); 6/79; Hosp Aide; Pep Clb; Chorus; Church Choir; Stu Cncl; Var Cheerleading; Var Swmmng; Var Trk; High Hon Roll; NHS; Bio.

LYDEN, MIKE; Babylon JR SR HS; Babylon, NY; (Y); Library Aide; Off Soph Cls; Pres Jr Cls; Off Sr Cls; Pres Stu Cncl; Ftbl; Law.

LYDON, DIANA; Dominican Commercial HS; Bellerose, NY; (Y); Comp.

LYDON, REGINA ANNE; St Francis Prep; Flushing, NY; (Y); 20/693; Math Clb; Ski Clb; School Play; JV Tennis; Im Vllybl; High Hon Roll; NHS; Pres Schlr; Rgnts Schlrshp 86; US Ntl Ldrshp Mrt Awd 85; Mnhtn Coll; Engrng.

LYLE, JENNIFER; Haverling Central HS; Bath, NY; (Y); Camera Clb; Exploring; French Clb; Ski Clb; Color Guard; Yrbk Phtg; Yrbk Stf; Rep Stu Cncl; Socr; Nrsng.

LYLE, KEVIN; Tri Valley Central HS; Liberty, NY; (Y); 13/58; Art Clb; Quiz Bowl; Varsity Clb; School Play; Pres Sr Cls; VP Rep Stu Cncl; Var JV Crs Cntry; Var JV Trk; High Hon Roll; Hon Roll; Outstndng Achvt Awd Art, Accntng, & Hm Econmcs; Art.

LYLE, RUTHIE; Roosevelt HS; Roosevelt, NY; (S); 3/200; Church Yth Grp; Drama Clb; Hosp Aide; Office Aide; Church Choir; Rep Jr Cls; High Hon Roll; Hon Roll; NHS; Martin Luther King Awd-Highest Acadmc Achvt 85 & 86; Northeastern U; Elec Engrng.

LYLE, SCOTT; Gates-Chili HS; Rochester, NY; (S); 18/446; Drama Clb; Exploring; Band; School Musical; School Play; Variety Show; Pres Sr Cls; High Hon Roll; Boy Scts; Computer Clb; Engrng.

LYMAN, JOSEPH; Cicero-N Syracuse HS; Liverpool, NY; (S); 5/781; Boy Scts; JA; Mathletes; Math Tm; School Musical; Jr NHS; Prfct Atten Awd; Achltc Art Awd 84-85; NY ST Smmr Schl Vsual Arts 84; Pre-Med.

LYNAM, ELIZABETH; Our Lady Of Mercy HS; Rochester, NY; (Y); Church Yth Grp; Cmnty Wkr; Hosp Aide; Model UN; Science Clb; Service Clb; Ski Clb; Spanish Clb; Yrbk Stf; Lit Mag; Engl Hnr Awd 84; JR Of Yr 86; Notre Dame JR Of Yr Fnlst 86; Cornell U; Bus.

LYNAM, JOHN LUKE; Cicero-North Syracuse HS; N Syracuse, NY; (Y); 70/800; Cmnty Wkr; Exploring; Science Clb; Teachers Aide; Capt Gym; CC Awd; High Hon Roll; Hon Roll; Jr NHS; NHS; NY ST USGF Gymnstc Champ 84; N Syrause Athlt Achvt 83; Empire ST Games Fnlst Gymnstcs 85; Logan Coll Of Chiropractic; Med.

LYNCH, CAROLINE; George Wingate HS; Brooklyn, NY; (Y); Church Yth Grp; Cmnty Wkr; Drama Clb; Girl Scts; School Play; Hon Roll; Coll Of New Rochelle; Spec Educ.

LYNCH, CARRIE ANN; East Islip SR HS; East Islip, NY; (Y); 4/425; Trs FTA; Ed Lit Mag; Gym; Sftbl; Trk; French Hon Soc; High Hon Roll; NHS; Ntl Merit Ltr; Pres Schlr; Mike Durso Schlrshp 86; Rgnts Schrlshp 86; Hofstra U Distgshd Acad Schrlshp 86; Hofstra U; Elem Ed.

LYNCH, DIONNE; North Eastern Acad; Jamaica, NY; (Y); Church Yth Grp; Debate Tm; Drama Clb; French Clb; Library Aide; Quiz Bowl; Red Cross Aide; Ski Clb; Spanish Clb; Church Choir; Atlantic Union Coll; Doctor.

LYNCH, DONNA; Samuel J Tilden HS; Brooklyn, NY; (Y); Hon Roll; Spnsh Hnr Card 86; Explrng Art Hnr Card 86; Law.

LYNCH, ELIZABETH A; St Francis Prep HS; Ozone Park, NY; (S); 164/744; Girl Scts; Math Clb; Chorus; Nwsp Rptr; JV Crs Cntry; Im Sftbl; JV Trk; Im Vllybl; Im Wt Lftg; Hon Roll; Tutoring Pgm 84-85; Bus Mgmnt.

LYNCH, JAIMESON A; St Joseph Hill Acad; Staten Island, NY; (Y); 14/107; Sec Trs French Clb; Hosp Aide; NFL; PAVAS; Teachers Aide; Var Co-Capt Socr; High Hon Roll; Hon Roll; Ntl Merit Ltr; Drama Clb; Regents Schlr 86; U VA; Drama.

LYNCH, JEAN M; Our Lady Of Victory Acad; Bronx, NY; (S); 14/157; Am Leg Aux Girls St; Church Yth Grp; Hosp Aide; Stage Crew; Yrbk Stf; Lit Mag; Rep Stu Cncl; Stat Score Keeper; Hon Roll; NHS; Kerrymans Assn Schlrshp 82-86; Engr.

LYNCH, JEANNE-MARIE; Baldwin SR HS; Rockville Ctr, NY; (Y); 59/478; Science Clb; Concert Band; Mrchg Band; Trs Sr Cls; Fld Hcky; NHS; Pres Acad Fit Awd 86; Outstndng Acad Achvt 86; Var Capt Archery 85; Var Riflry 84-86; Yth Pol Awarnss 85; U RI; Engrng.

LYNCH, JOE; Guilderland Central HS; Schenectady, NY; (Y); Key Clb; JV Var Crs Cntry; Wt Lftg; High Hon Roll; Jr NHS; Fianace.

LYNCH, KATE; H S For Humanities HS; Weehawker, NJ; (Y); Art Clb; Political Wkr; Lit Mag; Hon Roll; Advanced Plcmt Amer Hstry 85-86; Advanced Plcmt Engl & European Hstry 86-87; Rhode Isl Schl Of Des; Fshn Des.

LYNCH, KIERAN; James Madison HS; Brooklyn, NY; (Y); 25/756; Church Yth Grp; Computer Clb; Math Tm; Science Clb; Service Clb; Teachers Aide; Chorus; Hon Roll; Jr NHS; NHS; Rgnts Schlrshp 86; Arista 86.

LYNCH, LORNA; Albion HS; Albion, NY; (S); 18/179; Spanish Clb; Chorus; Sftbl; Hon Roll; Nrthwstn U; Phtgrphy.

LYNCH, MARGARET; Horseheads SR HS; Horseheads, NY; (S); Pres DECA; Sr Cls; JV Vllybl; Stat Wrstlng; Bryantt Stratton; Fshn Merchng.

LYNCH, MARY JO; Roscoe Central HS; N Branch, NY; (Y); 10/22; Art Clb; Computer Clb; Drama Clb; Spanish Clb; Chorus; School Play; Yrbk Stf; JV Cheerleading; Var Sftbl; Hon Roll; Roscoe Dinner Cmmrce Prz 86; Sullivan Cnty Legl Sec Awd 86; Sullivan Cnty CC; Bus Adm.

LYNCH, MICHAEL; Binghamton HS; Binghamton, NY; (Y); 42/456; Church Yth Grp; Cmnty Wkr; Key Clb; Varsity Clb; JV Var Bsbl; High Hon Roll; NHS; Pres Schlr; Jesse Baker Schlrshp Awd 86; Al-Conf STAC Bsbl-Ptchng 85 & 86; MVP Vrsty Bsbl 85; Rollins Coll FL; Jrnlsm.

LYNCH, MICHAEL; St Francis Prep; Flushing, NY; (Y); 121/650; Var L Bsktbl; NHS; Athlt/Schlr Awd 85; Albany ST U; Bus.

LYNCH, MONICA; Burgard Vocational HS; Buffalo, NY; (Y); Boy Scts; Exploring; School Musical; School Play; Off Jr Cls; Stu Cncl; Bsktbl; Mgr(s); Hon Roll; Explrng 84-86; Mrt Rl Schlrshp 83-86; Prfct Atten Awd 83-86.

LYNCH, TOM; Grand Island HS; Grand Island, NY; (Y); Boy Scts; Church Yth Grp; Ski Clb; Concert Band; Hon Roll; NHS; Eagle Scout 85; Spec Olympcs Coach 85-86; Engrng.

LYNDAKER, MARIE; Beaver River Central HS; Croghan, NY; (Y); Am Leg Aux Girls St; French Clb; GAA; Sec Trs Band; Chorus; Jazz Band; Sec Soph Cls; Trs Sr Cls; Hon Roll; Band Svc Awd.

LYNDAKER, TEMPERANCE; Beaver River Central Schl; Croghan, NY; (Y); Church Yth Grp; French Clb; GAA; Band; Mrchg Band; Orch; Var Sftbl; JV Var Vllybl; Hon Roll; Houghton Coll.

LYNDS, MEREDITH; Cambridge Central HS; Buskirk, NY; (Y); Church Yth Grp; Chorus; Madrigals; School Musical; NHS.

LYNN III, HENRY; Westfield Central HS; Westfield, NY; (Y); Pres Key Clb; Stage Crew; Nwsp Rptr; Yrbk Stf; Var L Bsbl; Var L Bowling; Var JV Ftbl; Im Wt Lftg; Var L Wrstlng; High Hon Roll; Engrng.

LYNN, KERRI; Port Jervis HS; Montague, NJ; (Y); Spanish Clb; Band; Concert Band; Yrbk Stf; Rep Frsh Cls; Rep Stu Cncl; High Hon Roll; Hon Roll; NHS.

LYNNE, KORI; Spacenkill HS; Poughkeepsie, NY; (Y); 25/170; Office Aide; SADD; VP Temple Yth Grp; Thesps; School Musical; Ed Yrbk Bus Mgr; Var Tennis; NHS; Pres Schlr; Abraham J Heschel Hnr Soc 84; NY ST Rgnts Schlrshp 86; Stu Cncl Ldrshp Awd 86; Brndeis U; Psychlgst.

LYON, JAY; New Berlin Central HS; New Berlin, NY; (Y); 20/61; Am Leg Boys St; Church Yth Grp; Cmnty Wkr; French Clb; Varsity Clb; Var Bsbl; JV Var Bsktbl; Bowling; Var Ftbl; Prfct Atten Awd.

LYONS, CAROL; Roy C Ketcham HS; Wappingers Fls, NY; (Y); Drama Clb; Church Choir; School Play; Yrbk Stf; Trk; High Hon Roll; Hon Roll; NHS; Cpa.

LYONS, DANNY; John H Glenn HS; Greenlawn, NY; (Y); French Clb; Varsity Clb; Yrbk Rptr; Var Bsbl; JV Capt Bsktbl; Var Socr; French Hon Soc; High Hon Roll; NHS; Ntl Merit Ltr; PTSA Gold Mdl Engl 84; PTSA Hnrb Mntn Cert 84; 8th Cntry AATF Frnch Cont 86.

LYONS, EDWARD G; Shenendehowa HS; Clifton Park, NY; (Y); 146/675; Nwsp Rptr; NCTE Awd; NY ST U Geneseo; Englsh.

LYONS, ELIZABETH; Dunkirk HS; Dunkirk, NY; (Y); 10/198; German Clb; Office Aide; Varsity Clb; Rep Frsh Cls; Rep Soph Cls; Rep Jr Cls; Hst Sr Cls; Swmmng; Hon Roll; NHS; Regents Scholar; U Rochester; Bus.

LYONS, JEANETTE; Buffalo Seminary; Buffalo, NY; (Y); Art Clb; Cmnty Wkr; Hosp Aide; Service Clb; Spanish Clb; Yrbk Stf; Lcrss; Hon Roll; NHS; Art Editor Of Yrbk 86.

LYONS, MARNIE; Williamsville North HS; Williamsville, NY; (Y); Art Clb; Cmnty Wkr; DECA; Pres Drama Clb; Intnl Clb; Ed Temple Yth Grp; School Play; Nwsp Ed-Chief; JV Fld Hcky; Swmmng; Communications.

LYTLE, PAMELA; Sauquoit Valley HS; Sauquoit, NY; (Y); Exploring; VICA; Chorus; Color Guard; JV Cheerleading; Fld Hcky; Trk; 90 Pct Or Hghr Engl & Art Awds; Cosmtlgy.

LYTTLE, MARCIA; New Rochelle HS; New Rochelle, NY; (Y); Church Yth Grp; Hosp Aide; Varsity Clb; Chorus; Church Choir; Crs Cntry; Trk; Elks Awd; Hon Roll; All Co Shot Put Gannett Nwspr 86; Sec Educ.

MA, AUGUSTINE C; HS Of Art & Design; Woodside, NY; (Y); 2/406; VP Art Clb; Math Clb; Math Tm; PAVAS; Hon Roll; NHS; Prfct Atten Awd; Sal; Office Aide; Teachers Aide; Ntl Art Hnr Soc 84-86; Soc Stds, Math & Sci Hnr Awds 83-86; Cornell U; Arch.

MA, KWOK H; Aviation HS; New York, NY; (S); 31/413; NHS; AIAA; Natl Voc Hnr Soc-Pegasus; NY Polytech; Elect Engrng.

MAASS, CHARLES; Manhasset HS; Manhasset, NY; (Y); 15/175; VP Service Clb; Teachers Aide; Band; Concert Band; VP Jazz Band; Mrchg Band; Pep Band; Bsbl; Capt Swmmng; High Hon Roll; Rgnts Schlrshp 86; Cmmnty Clb Schlrshp 86; Tufts U; Engr.

MAC ADAM, HEATHER; Chittenango HS; Brideport, NY; (Y); Church Yth Grp; Ski Clb; SADD; Concert Band; Yrbk Stf; JV Socr; Jr NHS; French Clb; Timer; Hon Roll; PTSA 85-86; Bible Schl Tchrs Asst 83-86; Spnsrr A Child Christian Mission 84-86; Pediatrician.

MAC ADAM, RUSSELL; Sweet Home SR HS; Tonawanda, NY; (Y); Church Yth Grp; Computer Clb; German Clb; Mathletes; High Hon Roll; NHS; Ntl Merit Schol; Germn Hnr Soc 85-86; Sci Hnr Soc 84-86; ST Mth Comptn 86; Engrng.

MAC AVERY, JENNIFER; Stissing Mt JR-SR HS; Pine Plains, NY; (Y); 10/98; Pres VP Church Yth Grp; Drama Clb; VP Sec 4-H; SADD; School Play; Variety Show; VP Sr Cls; Var Cheerleading; Cit Awd; 4-H Awd; Pomona Grange Schlrshp 86; Dairy Fashns Awd SUNY Cobleskill 86; Regents Schlrshp 86; SUNY Cobleskill; Anml Husbndry.

MAC CARTNEY, ALLISON; Nyack HS; Nyack, NY; (Y); Model UN; Off Soph Cls; Off Jr Cls; JV Lcrss; High Hon Roll; Spanish NHS; Spanish Clb; Yrbk Stf; Stu Cncl; JV Cheerleading; UCLA; Corp Law.

MAC DONALD, AMY; Candor Central HS; Candor, NY; (Y); Band; Chorus; Mrchg Band; Nwsp Rptr; Yrbk Stf; Sec Jr Cls; Var L Trk; Var L Vllybl; NHS; All Cnty Chours 86; Local NFSM 84; Dist NFSM 85; Nrsng.

MAC DONALD, BONNIE; Mt Upton Central HS; Mt Upton, NY; (Y); 4/24; Ski Clb; Pres Spanish Clb; Teachers Aide; Pres Stu Cncl; Score Keeper; Socr; Sftbl; High Hon Roll; NHS; Prfct Atten Awd; Bordon Hose Co Schlrshp, Tri-Vly All Str Soccer, Bst Offnsve Plyr Sccr 85-86; Geneseo; Spec Elem Educ.

MAC DONALD, DONNA; Barker Central Schl; Barker, NY; (Y); 1/105; AFS; Church Yth Grp; French Clb; Trs Sr Cls; Cit Awd; High Hon Roll; NHS; Val; Chorus; Lgsltv Intrn Niagara Cnty 85-86; NY ST Snt Intrn 86; SUNY Albany; Bus Acctng.

MAC DONALD, MELISSA A; Liverpool HS; Liverpool, NY; (Y); 108/816; Hon Roll; Jr NHS; NHS; U NY Buffalo; Psychlgy.

MAC DONALD, MICHAEL D; Manlius Pebble Hill Schl; East Syracuse, NY; (Y); School Musical; Yrbk Phtg; Rep Jr Cls; Capt Bsktbl; Capt Socr; L Trk; Cit Awd; NHS; Boston Coll; Accntng.

MAC DONALD, SCOTT; Maple Hill HS; Castleton-On-Hdsn, NY; (S); 9/92; Spanish Clb; School Musical; Bsbl; Bsktbl; Hon Roll; Acctng.

MAC GIBBON, CHERYL; Walton Central HS; Walton, NY; (Y); 1/97; Am Leg Aux Girls St; Key Clb; Model UN; Varsity Clb; Pres Frsh Cls; Var Bsktbl; Var Fld Hcky; High Hon Roll; NHS; Ntl Merit Ltr; Hghst Avg Bio, Soc Stud 85; Constnt Exclnt Wrk In Rgnts Math 85; Intl Relat.

MAC GREGOR, ELISABETH; Northport HS; Northport, NY; (Y); 36/605; Cmnty Wkr; Pep Clb; Trk; DAR Awd; Hon Roll; Italian Awd 83; Boston Coll; Elem Ed.

MAC GREGOR, JENNIFER A; Pine Bush Central HS; Pine Bush, NY; (Y); 8/250; Office Aide; School Play; Stage Crew; JV Var Socr; Stat Wrstlng; Hon Roll; Jr NHS; NHS; VFW Awd; St Lawrence U.

MAC INTYRE, KIMBERLEY; Delaware Academy & Central HS; Delhi, NY; (Y); German Clb; Ski Clb; Yrbk Stf; Pres Stu Cncl; Fld Hcky; High Hon Roll; Hon Roll; NHS; Church Yth Grp; Office Aide; Graduated With Regents Schlrshp & Hons; Balfour Key Awd; Stud Sen & Pres Cncl Awd; Russell Sage Coll; Intl Studies.

MAC LELLAN, BRIAN; Sayville HS; Sayville, NY; (Y); 140/340; Key Clb; SADD; Yrbk Stf; Off Jr Cls; Bsktbl; :Accnt.

MAC MILLAN, STEPHANIE A; Our Lady Of Mercy HS; Fairport, NY; (Y); 29/172; Dance Clb; English Clb; Intnl Clb; SADD; Teachers Aide; Stage Crew; Yrbk Stf; Hon Roll; Hnrbl Mntn Library Poetry Cntst 82; Vill Nova U; Engl.

MAC NEAL, STACEY R; Waterloo HS; Waterloo, NY; (Y); 2/168; Key Clb; Model UN; Political Wkr; Band; Jazz Band; School Play; High Hon Roll; NHS; Ntl Merit Ltr; Sal; Elmira Coll Key Awd; Penn ST; Pol Sci.

MAC PHERSON, KELLY; Cardinal Mooney HS; Rochester, NY; (Y); 70/303; Cmnty Wkr; Library Aide; Office Aide; SADD; Church Choir; Yrbk Stf; Hon Roll; Spanish NHS; Math Awd 83; Cert Apprectn Community Wrk 86; Cobleskill Ag & Tech; Bus Adm.

MAC SWEENEY, REGINA; Somers HS; Purdys, NY; (Y); Church Yth Grp; Varsity Clb; Sec Jr Cls; Sec Sr Cls; Var Capt Bsktbl; Var Capt Fld Hcky; Var Capt Socr; Hon Roll; Trs Spanish NHS; Capt Powder Puff Ftbl; Outstndng Achvt Awd In Athltcs 86; All Lg HM In Fld Hcky & Bktbl 86; All Trnmt Tm In Sccr 86.

MAC WHINNEY, MELISSA; Ramstein Am HS; Apo New York, NY; (Y); Church Yth Grp; Red Cross Aide; Teachers Aide; Varsity Clb; Chorus; Church Choir; Var Bsktbl; Var Cheerleading; Var Trk; Coaches Awd Trck 86; 3rd Pl All Europe Hrdlr 86; UCSB; Phy Ed.

MACADAEG, CELIE ROSE; Academy Of Saint Joseph HS; S Setauket, NY; (Y); Dance Clb; Pep Clb; PAVAS; Chorus; Variety Show; Dnce Ed Of Amer Regnls & Natls 84-86; Prfct Excllnce Bus 85; Fred Astaire Intl Prfrmg Arts Comp 83; Fordam; Bus.

MACALALAG, GENEVIEVE; Stella Maris HS; Howard Beach, NY; (Y); Math Tm; Spanish Clb; Nwsp Rptr; NHS; Math Trphy JV Math Leag Div B 84; St Johns U; Spch Lang.

MACALUSO, CHRISTINA; South Shore HS; Brooklyn, NY; (Y); 226/696; Drama Clb; Kingsborough CC; Brdcstg Mgr.

MACARI, JEANNIE; St Dominic HS; Huntington, NY; (Y); 25/145; Debate Tm; Model UN; Capt Var Cheerleading; High Hon Roll; Hon Roll; Jr NHS; Sec Soph Cls; Trs Jr Cls; Rep Stu Cncl; NEDT Awd; Law.

MACCARN, TRACIE; Mont Pleasant HS; Schenectady, NY; (Y); 10/260; Key Clb; Ski Clb; Spanish Clb; Band; Concert Band; Jazz Band; Mrchg Band; Orch; Off Soph Cls; Off Jr Cls; Spnsh Clssrm Awd Top Stu 85-86; Union Coll; Bus.

MACCARRONE, TERRY L; Hampton Bays HS; Hampton Bays, NY; (Y); 4/85; Am Leg Boys St; Computer Clb; Mathletes; Chorus; Hon Roll; Jr NHS; VP NHS; Ntl Merit Ltr; Principals Hnr List; Rensselaer Poly Inst; Engrng.

MACCARTNEY, JEAN; Christ The King R H S; Rego Park, NY; (Y); 8/451; Drama Clb; School Musical; Rep Stu Cncl; Hon Roll; NHS; Acctng.

MACCHIA, LARRY; Mount St Michael Acad; Bronx, NY; (Y); 34/292; Im Bsktbl; Im Ftbl; Hon Roll; NHS; Fordham Coll; Bus.

MACCHIA, LAWRENCE J; Mount St Michael Acad; Bronx, NY; (Y); 36/292; JV Bsktbl; Hon Roll; NHS; Frdhm; Bus.

MACCHIA, MICHAEL; Iona Preparatory Sch; Scarsdale, NY; (Y); 3/204; Computer Clb; Sftbl; Swmmng; Timer; DAR Awd; High Hon Roll; Hon Roll; NHS; Genl Excllnc Math, Thelgy, Sci, Latn And Spnsh 83-81; Lwyr.

MACCHIAROLA, MICHELE; St John Villa Acad; Staten Island, NY; (Y); Math Clb; JV Co-Capt Sftbl.

MACCHLA, MICHAEL; Archbishop Molloy HS; Glendale, NY; (Y); 72/383; Art Clb; Computer Clb; Var Capt Swmmng; Natl YMCA Swmmng & Dvng Champnshps 16th 86; All Amer Swmmng 200 IM 400 IM 86.

MACCONE, JANET; Sachem HS; Holtsville, NY; (Y); 120/1390; Art Clb; Spanish Clb; Jr NHS; Pres Schlr; Pred Acdmc Fit Awd 86; St Johns U.

MACDONALD, JASON; Uratego HS; Wells Bridge, NY; (Y); 6/106; Am Leg Boys St; Drama Clb; French Clb; Var Badmtn; JV Bsktbl; Var Crs Cntry; Var Ice Hcky; Var Trk; High Hon Roll; NHS.

MACDONALD, LAURA; Southside HS; Rockville Centre, NY; (Y); 41/273; Key Clb; SADD; Teachers Aide; Concert Band; Variety Show; Var Cheerleading; Hon Roll; Educ.

MACDONALD, ROSS; Franklin Acad; Medford, NJ; (Y); Boy Scts; Ski Clb; Chorus; Yrbk Rptr; Var Capt Bsktbl; JV Crs Cntry; JV Ftbl; Im Ice Hcky; Mst Imprvd Bsktbl & X-Cntry 83-84; Bus.

MACDONALD, STACIE; Blind Brook HS; Rye Brook, NY; (Y); Concert Band; Var Cheerleading; JV Fld Hcky; Var Socr; Psych.

MACDONELL, CHRISTA; Midlakes HS; Clifton Spgs, NY; (Y); French Clb; Model UN; VP Sr Cls; Var Trk; High Hon Roll; Hon Roll; Law.

MACE, ALAN; Elmira Free Acad; Elmira, NY; (Y); Boy Scts; Pres German Clb; VP JA; Ski Clb; Var Diving; Var Swmmng; Hon Roll; NHS; Concert Band; Stage Crew; Order Of Arrow BS 84; Outstdng Achvt Germn Level II 86; USAF; Aerontcl Engrng.

MACE, HEATHER; Tupper Lake HS; Tupper Lake, NY; (Y); Church Yth Grp; Pep Clb; Bsktbl; Mgr(s); Socr; Trk; Hudson Vly CC; Cosmtlgst.

MACEDON, PARRIS M; Morris HS; Bronx, NY; (Y); 29/204; Dance Clb; Chorus; Yrbk Stf; Rep Sr Cls; Stu Cncl; Cheerleading; Jr NHS; NHS; Prfct Atten Awd; St Schlr; Merit Awd All Arnd Acadmc Achvt; Arista; Regnts Nrsg Schlrshp; St Louis U; Nrsg.

MACEK, STEVE; Newfane SR HS; Newfane, NY; (Y); 15/155; Letterman Clb; Math Clb; Trs Science Clb; Varsity Clb; Var Golf; Var Tennis; Var Trk; Hon Roll; Engrng.

MACERA, ROCCO; Lansing HS; Groton, NY; (Y); French Clb; Ski Clb; JV Golf; Im Tennis; French Hon Soc; Bus Adm.

MACEY, ANDREW L; Farmingdale HS; Farmingdale, NY; (Y); Band; Concert Band; Drm & Bgl; Mrchg Band; Orch; School Musical; School Play; Symp Band; JV Bsktbl; Ntl Merit Schol; Engrng.

MACFADDEN, KEVIN; Johnson City SR HS; Johnson City, NY; (Y); SADD; Var Mgr(s); High Hon Roll; Hon Roll; Prfct Atten Awd; Acad Achvt Awd 85-86; Bus Mngmnt.

MACH, KIMBERLY ANNE; St Joseph Acad; Lake Grove, NY; (Y); Church Yth Grp; GAA; Hosp Aide; Science Clb; Teachers Aide; Nwsp Stf; Yrbk Stf; Var Capt Socr; NHS; NEDT Awd; Regnts Schlrshp 86; William Smith Coll Acadmc Schlr 86; Hobart & William Smith Coll.

MACHABEE, DAN; Franklin Acad; Malone, NY; (Y); JV Bsktbl; JV Trk; Elctrncs.

MACHADO, ONIEL; Cardinal Hayes HS; New York, NY; (Y); Rep Stu Cncl; Ftbl; Trk; Wt Lftg; NY Cty Bsbl Chmpns 85; Mercy Coll; Tchr.

MACHAN, PATRICK; Rye HS; Rye, NY; (Y); 15/125; Art Clb; Varsity Clb; Var Crs Cntry; Var Ice Hcky; Var Socr; JV Tennis; Var Trk; High Hon Roll; Hon Roll; Prncpls Svc Awd 86; Hamilton Coll; Ecnmcs.

MACHIONE, JOAN; J A Coleman HS; W Hurley, NY; (Y); #11 In Class; Drama Clb; Key Clb; Ski Clb; School Play; Stage Crew; Rep Frsh Cls; Rep Soph Cls; JV Var Fld Hcky; Var Sftbl; Hon Roll; Eng.

MACHNICKI, STEPHEN C; Salhem HS; Farmingville, NY; (Y); 4/1375; Key Clb; Letterman Clb; Ski Clb; Pres Spanish Clb; Varsity Clb; VP Sr Cls; Bsbl; Var L Swmmng; Jr NHS; NHS; Natl Merit Schlrshp 86; Engl Awd Of Merit; Soc Stud Awd Of Merit; Cornell U; Pre-Med.

MACHUCA, DANIEL; De Witt Clinton HS; Bronx, NY; (Y); Art Clb; Key Clb; Nwsp Rptr; Nwsp Stf; Yrbk Rptr; Yrbk Stf; Engrng.

MACHUGA, MELISSA; Bradford Central Sch; Savona, NY; (S); Church Yth Grp; FBLA; Girl Scts; Chorus; Church Choir; School Play; Nwsp Stf; Yrbk Bus Mgr; NHS; Cert Merit Excllnc 84-85; Corning CC; Bus.

MACIAG, ROBERT; Notre Dame-Bishop Gibbons HS; Schenectady, NY; (S); 2/101; Stu Cncl; Bsktbl; Crs Cntry; Golf; Trk; High Hon Roll; NHS; Engl, Hist Awds; RPI Awd; Engr.

MACIAS, LISSETTE; La Guardia HS Of Music And Arts; Elmhurst, NY; (Y); Dance Clb; Drama Clb; JA; Variety Show; Hon Roll; Alvin Ailey Dance Theatr Scholar 84; Martha Graham Dance Studio Scholar 82; Adelphi U; Comm.

MACIBORKA, JULIANNE; William Cullen Bryant HS; Jackson Heights, NY; (S); Drama Clb; English Clb; Letterman Clb; Nwsp Rptr; Lit Mag; High Hon Roll; NHS; Spanish NHS.

MACIEJEWSKI, JULIE; Alden HS; Alden, NY; (Y); French Clb; Rep Frsh Cls; Rep Soph Cls; Sec Jr Cls; Sec Sr Cls; JV Trk; Hon Roll; NHS; Schl Acdmc Lttr Awds 85-86.

MACIOLEK, JUDITH; Villa Maria Acad; Buffalo, NY; (S); Cmnty Wkr; Computer Clb; VP Latin Clb; School Play; Trs Jr Cls; Rep Stu Cncl; Hon Roll; Prfct Atten Awd.

MACIOLEK, KAREN; Kenmore East HS; Tonawanda, NY; (Y); Church Yth Grp; German Clb; Hosp Aide; Hon Roll; ST U NY Coll Buffalo; Foods.

MACK, ANGIE; North Rose-Wolcott HS; N Rose, NY; (Y); Church Yth Grp; FBLA; Pep Clb; Chorus; Church Choir; Yrbk Phtg; Lit Mag; Var L Bsktbl; Mgr(s); Socr; Rocheste Bus Inst; Bus Adm.

MACK, BRIAN; Mc Quaid Jesuit; Rochester, NY; (Y); Chrmn Varsity Clb; School Play; Nwsp Stf; Im Cheerleading; Var Capt Crs Cntry; Im Ftbl; Var Capt Trk; High Hon Roll; Prfct Atten Awd; St Schlr; Acad Letter; St Champ; Hnr Roll; Villanova; Pol Sci.

MACK, KEITH G; Kingston HS; Kingston, NY; (Y); 23/573; Boy Scts; Church Yth Grp; French Clb; Ski Clb; Yrbk Stf; Var Trk; Im Wt Lftg; Sec French Hon Soc; Jr NHS; NHS; NYS Regents Schlrshp 86; VA Polytech Inst; Engrng.

MACK, KRISTINA; West Seneca East SR HS; Cheektowaga, NY; (Y); DECA; Drama Clb; Hosp Aide; Ski Clb; Spanish Clb; School Musical; School Play; Nwsp Stf; Tennis; Roswell Park Mem Inst Summr Rsrch Pgm 86; Marine Bio.

MACK, LYNN; Frontier Central HS; Hamburg, NY; (Y); Spanish Clb; Var Score Keeper; JV Var Socr; Var Timer; Hon Roll; NHS; Pre-Law.

MACK, MARY M; Notre Dame Bishop Gibbons HS; Schenectady, NY; (S); 3/100; Red Cross Aide; School Musical; Nwsp Stf; Lit Mag; Rep Stu Cncl; Socr; Trk; High Hon Roll; NHS; Frnch Awd 83; Engl Awd 84; Hstry & Serv Awd 85; Siena Coll; Pre-Med.

MACK, MICHELLE; Clara Barton HS; Brooklyn, NY; (Y); Drama Clb; Teachers Aide; Color Guard; Concert Band; Orch; Nwsp Phtg; Nwsp Rptr; Hon Roll; NHS; Ntl Merit Ltr; Frnch Awd 84; Music Awd 84; Sci Awd 84; U Of New York; Intrntnl Bus.

MACK, PAMELA D; Thomas A Edison Tech Voc HS; Long Island City, NY; (Y); 36/415; Drama Clb; SADD; Chorus; School Play; Yrbk Stf; Sec Stu Cncl; Capt Cheerleading; Hon Roll; Kiwanis Awd; Mchncl Drwng 85-86; Spnsh 84-85; Hwrd U Wshngtn DC; Arch.

MACK, ROBERT; Notre Dame Bishop Gibbons HS; Schenectady, NY; (S); 4/100; JA; Ski Clb; Stage Crew; Rep Jr Cls; Var Crs Cntry; Var Ftbl; High Hon Roll; NHS; Bio Awd 85; Union; Law.

MACKENZIE, KRISTIN; Bayport Blue Point HS; Bayport, NY; (Y); Church Yth Grp; Drama Clb; GAA; PAVAS; Teachers Aide; Varsity Clb; Chorus; School Musical; Awd Art Perf; Judges Awd Spcl Distnctn Music; Music.

MACKENZIE, LAURA; Earl L Vandermeulen HS; Mt Sinai, NY; (Y); Church Yth Grp; Cmnty Wkr; Computer Clb; Drama Clb; Hosp Aide; Leo Clb; Mathletes; Math Clb; Math Tm; Band; Span Awd Most Outstndg 9th Grd Stud 84; Won 2nd Plc In Physics Olympiad Contst 86; Pre Med.

MACKEY, ALYCE; Plattsburgh HS; Plattsburgh, NY; (Y); Var Capt Bsktbl; Var Capt Tennis; Var Sftbl; JV Vllybl; Cortland; Math.

MACKEY, ANDREW; North Rockland HS; Stony Point, NY; (Y); Cmnty Wkr; Var Lcrss; JV Socr; Hon Roll; Stu Of Mnth; Engr.

MACKEY, MARY ELLEN; St Johns Prep; Middle Vlg, NY; (Y); 83/458; JV Mgr(s); Var JV Socr; Var Capt Sftbl; Coaches Awd-Sftbl 85; Queens Coll; Phys Educ.

MACKIN, JULIETTE; Fox Lane HS; Pound Ridge, NY; (Y); 11/289; Drama Clb; Acpl Chr; Chorus; Madrigals; School Musical; Var Capt Cheerleading; Stat Lcrss; High Hon Roll; NHS; Pres Schlr; U Of CA-SANTA Barbara; Psychlg.

MACKIN, KELLY; Mineola HS; Williston Pk, NY; (Y); SADD; Stat JV Bsktbl; JV Var Cheerleading; Stat Lcrss; Score Keeper; JV Var Vllybl; Jr NHS; Outstndg Stu 84-85; Stu Orgnztn Apprctn Awd 85-86.

MACKNIK, JACQUELINE; West Genesee HS; Warners, NY; (Y); Church Yth Grp; French Clb; Key Clb; Ski Clb; Band; Orch; School Musical; Rep Stu Cncl; High Hon Roll; NHS; Natl Fr Cont Amer Assn Tchrs Fr; Biol Olympd; Bus Adm.

MACKY, ROBERT; Archbishop Molly HS; Middle Vlg, NY; (Y); Queens Coll; Med.

MACLEOD, LISA; Kenmore East SR HS; Kenmore, NY; (Y); Church Yth Grp; Cmnty Wkr; Pep Clb; Hon Roll; Acctng.

MACNEIL, WENDY; Scotia-Glenville HS; Scotia, NY; (Y); Pres German Clb; Red Cross Aide; SADD; Concert Band; Mrchg Band; Mgr(s); Score Keeper; High Hon Roll; NHS; Church Yth Grp; Elmiro Key Awd 86; Biolgy.

MACNEILL, CAROL; Salem Central HS; Salem, NY; (Y); Am Leg Aux Girls St; GAA; Trs Band; Jazz Band; Yrbk Ed-Chief; Lit Mag; Pres Soph Cls; Pres Jr Cls; JV Var Fld Hcky; High Hon Roll; Hugh O Brien Awd 85; Bio.

MACNER, GERALD J; Utica Free Acad; Remsen, NY; (Y); 20/320; Exploring; Key Clb; Model UN; Ski Clb; Rep Stu Cncl; Var L Bsbl; Im Vllybl; Hon Roll; NHS; Navy ROTC Schlrshp 86; US Air Force Acad 85; U CO Boulder; Aerospace Engr.

MACOMBER III, JOHN H; Greenport HS; Greenport, NY; (Y); 20/45; Am Leg Boys St; Boy Scts; French Clb; Jazz Band; School Musical; Nwsp Phtg; Ed Yrbk Phtg; Bsbl; Bowling; Ftbl; Oswego SUNY; Indstrl Arts Ed.

MACONAGHY, JILL; West Seneca West SR HS; Cheektowaga, NY; (Y); Chorus; Mrchg Band; Stage Crew; Rep Soph Cls; Rep Jr Cls; Rep Stu Cncl; Var Diving; Var Swmmng; Var Trk; Prfct Atten Awd; Earth Sci Hnrs 2nd Hghst Avg Achvmnt 84-85; Sprts Med.

MACORT, SHANNON; Monroe Woodbury HS; Monroe, NY; (Y); Church Yth Grp; Girl Scts; Ski Clb; Chorus; Yrbk Phtg; Yrbk Stf; JV Var Cheerleading; Sftbl; Hon Roll; Travel.

MACRAY, DENNIS J; Heidelberg American HS; Apo, NY; (S); 5/149; Boy Scts; Varsity Clb; Pres VP Stu Cncl; Capt Crs Cntry; Socr; Pres NHS; Ntl Merit Ltr; Church Yth Grp; Model UN; Quiz Bowl; Amer Boy Scts Egl Sct Awd 83; Dfns Dept Stu Rep 85; Intl Stu Ldrshp Inst Stu Dean & Rgnts Brd 82-86; Harvard U; Intl Rltns.

MACRINI, ELIZABETH; St Joseph By-The-Sea HS; Staten Island, NY; (Y); 8/285; Cmnty Wkr; Yrbk Stf; Lit Mag; Tennis; Hon Roll; NHS; Hnrbl Mntn Amrcn Lgn Essy Cntst 84; Acdmc All Amrcn By Ntl Scndry Educ Cncl 84; Acctg.

MACRY, JAMES A; James Madison HS; Brooklyn, NY; (Y); 100/754; NYS Rgnts Scshlrshp 86; St Johns U; Comp Anal.

MACUS, HEIDI J; Baldwin SR HS; Baldwin, NY; (Y); 2/476; Computer Clb; Drama Clb; VP Mathletes; Science Clb; Lit Mag; French Hon Soc; High Hon Roll; NHS; Ntl Merit SF; Sal; Lng Islnd Math Fair Slvr Mdl Wnnr 85; Comp Engrng.

MACVIE, TAMMY A; Wilson Central HS; Wilson, NY; (Y); 5/120; Ski Clb; SADD; Band; Yrbk Stf; Pres Jr Cls; Sec Pres Stu Cncl; High Hon Roll; NHS; Rgnts Schlrshp NY ST 86; NY Tele Schlrshp 86; SUNY Fredonia; Music Educ.

MADDALENA, DANIELLE; St Francis Prep; Douglaston, NY; (Y); 209/746; Hosp Aide; Band; Chorus; Color Guard; Concert Band; Drm Mjr(t); Mrchg Band; School Musical; School Play; Drctrs Awd 85-87; Spcl Educ.

MADDALONI, PHILIP T; Centereach HS; Selden, NY; (Y); Math Tm; French Hon Soc; High Hon Roll; Rnsslr Math & Sci Awd 86; Comp Sci.

MADDEN, DONNA; West Lake HS; Valhalla, NY; (Y); Art Clb; Cmnty Wkr; Dance Clb; Drama Clb; FBLA; Hosp Aide; Sec JA; Spanish Clb; Chorus; Church Choir; Saint Agnus Hosp Awds 85; JR Achvt Awd 85-86; Surgeon.

MADDEN, ELIZABETH; Johnstown HS; Johnstown, NY; (Y); Church Yth Grp; Girl Scts; Red Cross Aide; Spanish Clb; Band; Chorus; Concert Band; Mrchg Band; Silv Ldrshp Awd 83; Silv Awd 83; Gold Ldrshp Awd 84; Svc Bars 83-84; Fulton-Montgomery; Med Rcrds.

MADDEN, GLORIA M; St Francis Prep HS; Woodhaven, NY; (S); 159/746; Church Yth Grp; Hosp Aide; JA; Office Aide; Teachers Aide; Chorus; Church Choir; Hon Roll; Opt Clb Awd; Optmt List Awd 84; Retreat Ldr 85-86.

MADDEN, MAUREEN; Academy Of St Joseph; Hauppauge, NY; (Y); CAP; VP French Clb; Girl Scts; Library Aide; Model UN; Pres Jr Cls; Stu Cncl; Civil Air Patrol Suffolk Cadet Yr 85; Soc Christian Courtesy 85; Stu Pilot Solo Wings 85; Math.

MADDEN, MICHELLE; North Salem HS; Brewster, NY; (Y); Drama Clb; School Play; Nwsp Ed-Chief; Nwsp Sprt Ed; Capt Socr; Tennis; Hon Roll; Sec Chess Clb; VP Soph Cls; VP Jr Cls; Awd-Schlrshp 84; Awd-Frnch III 85; Awd-Spnsh I 86; Librl Arts.

MADDEN, SERENA L; Cincinnatus Centeal HS; Pitcher, NY; (Y); 2/39; Sec Trs Art Clb; Pres Drama Clb; Spanish Clb; School Play; Yrbk Stf; VP Soph Cls; Sec Jr Cls; Rep Stu Cncl; JV Var Cheerleading; Stat Socr; Rgnts Schlrshp 86-87; SUNY Binghamton; Archtctr.

MADDIE, THERESA; Sacred Heart Acad; West Hempstead, NY; (Y); Yrbk Stf; High Hon Roll; Hon Roll; NHS.

MADDOCK, TARA L; West Genesee SR HS; Camillus, NY; (Y); French Clb; Hosp Aide; Ski Clb; Orch; Yrbk Ed-Chief; Yrbk Stf; Rep Soph Cls; Rep Jr Cls; High Hon Roll; NHS; Natl Champ Irish Dancing 83-84; MD ST & Estrn Regnl Irish Dance Champ 84-86; All Cnty Orch 84-86; Bio.

MADIGAN, CHERYL; Tioga Central HS; Nichols, NY; (S); Variety Show; Nwsp Rptr; Yrbk Stf; NHS; Accntng.

MADIGAN, DANIEL G; St Anthonys HS; Northport, NY; (Y); Am Leg Boys St; Boy Scts; SADD; Chorus; JV Ftbl; JV Lcrss; JV Trk; Cit Awd; Egl Sct 85; West Point; Intl Rltns.

MADIGAN, EDWARD SEAN; Burgard Vo Tech; Buffalo, NY; (Y); Boy Scts; Varsity Clb; Stage Crew; Crs Cntry; Trk; Prfct Atten Awd; Physcl Ftns Awd 83-84; USAF Acad.

MADIGAN, JONN; Sachem North HS; Holbrook, NY; (Y); 54/1579; Boy Scts; Ski Clb; JV Bsbl; Var Bowling; Wt Lftg; High Hon Roll; NHS; Bus.

MADIGAN, KIMBERLY D; West Irondequoit HS; Rochester, NY; (Y); Debate Tm; Drama Clb; NFL; Speech Tm; School Musical; School Play; High Hon Roll; Hon Roll; Swmmng; Natl Mrt Cmndtn 85; NYS Rgnts Schlrshp 86; U Of CO; Chmcl Engnrng.

MADIGAN, MICHAEL C; Hoosic Valley HS; Valley Falls, NY; (S); Church Yth Grp; Cmnty Wkr; Band; Var L Bsbl; Var L Bsktbl; Var L Socr; High Hon Roll; Hon Roll; Siena Coll; Bus.

MADISON, ANDREA; Corinth Central HS; Corinth, NY; (S); SADD; Varsity Clb; Band; Swing Chorus; Bsktbl; Fld Hcky; Sftbl; Vllybl; High Hon Roll; NHS.

MADISSOO, ANDRES; Jamesville De Witt HS; Fayetteville, NY; (Y); Boy Scts; German Clb; Key Clb; Crs Cntry; Swmmng; Hon Roll; BSA Eagle Scout 85; U Buffalo; Med.

MADOFF, STACEY; Onteora Central HS; Shokan, NY; (Y); 4/201; Math Tm; Chorus; Swing Chorus; Variety Show; Fld Hcky; High Hon Roll; NHS; Cornell Scholar 86; Roswell Pk Mem Inst Summr Rsrch 85; Regents Scholar 86; Cornell U; Biomed Engrng.

MADONIA, ANTONELLA; Canarsie HS; Brooklyn, NY; (Y); Office Aide; Teachers Aide; Band; School Musical; School Play; Yrbk Stf; Cheerleading; High Hon Roll; NHS; Prfct Atten Awd; Poly Sci.

MADONNA, DAVID; Henninger HS; Syracuse, NY; (Y); 130/460; Boy Scts; Im Crs Cntry; Im Gym; Im Vllybl; Im Wrstlng; Coast Guard Acad; Elec.

MADONNA, LAURA; Academy Of St Joseph; Coram, NY; (Y); Drama Clb; Hosp Aide; Orch; School Play; Yrbk Stf; High Hon Roll; Hon Roll; Jr NHS; NHS; Natl Latin Exam Summa Cum Laude 84; Drama Awd 86; English Awd 85; Columbia U; Theatre.

MADRIGAL, ELMA CHERYL SARREAL; Albertus Magnus HS; Orangeburg, NY; (Y); 20/180; Dance Clb; Math Clb; PAVAS; JV Vllybl; High Hon Roll; Mu Alp Tht; NHS; Spanish NHS; Drama Clb; Bwlg 2nd Pl Tm 9 Troph 82-86; Albany SUNY; Pre-Med.

MADRIGAL, LOURDES; Newtown HS; Elmhurst, NY; (Y); 107/781; GAA; Varsity Clb; Chorus; Sec Frsh Cls; Bsktbl; Vllybl; High Hon Roll; Principals List 85; UC Berkeley; Comp Sci.

MAFFUCCI, JAMES VINCENT; Patchogue-Medford HS; Patchogue, NY; (Y); 104/650; Science Clb; Yrbk Phtg; Var Socr; Var Wrstlng; Hon Roll; Regents Schlrshp 86; Rochester Inst Of Tech; Med Tch.

MAGEE, DAVID M; St Joseph By The Sea HS; Staten Island, NY; (Y); Art Clb; Church Yth Grp; Computer Clb; Political Wkr; Spanish Clb; Nwsp Ed-Chief; Lit Mag; Rep Soph Cls; Hon Roll; St Schlr; NYS Regnts Schlrshp 86; Comp Schlrshp St Johns 86; HS Stu Schlrshp 86; St Johns U.

MAGEE, JOHN E; Glen Cove HS; Glen Cove, NY; (Y); DECA; Hosp Aide; Intnl Clb; Radio Clb; Hon Roll; Pres Intl Humn Rel Clb 85-86; Awd DECA 85-86; Awds I Humn Rel Clb 85-86; Bus Adm.

MAGEE, MICHAEL; Glens Falls SR HS; Glens Falls, NY; (Y); 15/217; Church Yth Grp; Math Tm; Stage Crew; JV Ftbl; JV Var Trk; High Hon Roll; Hon Roll; NHS; Ntl Merit Ltr; Phys Sci.

MAGEN, HUGH E; Oceanside HS; Oceanside, NY; (Y); Mathletes; Model UN; SADD; High Hon Roll; Hon Roll; Jr NHS; NHS; Ntl Merit SF; U Of VA; Engrng.

MAGENTA, JOSEPHINE; Franklin Delano Roosevelt HS; Brooklyn, NY; (Y); Cmnty Wkr; Library Aide; Science Clb; Teachers Aide; Chorus; School Musical; School Play; Variety Show; Cit Awd; Hon Roll; Governors Comm Schlstc Achvt Citation 84.

MAGGI, AGATA; Henninger HS; Syracuse, NY; (Y); SADD; Italian Cultural Soc 86; Daughters Colombus Italian Schlrshp; Le Moyne Coll; Spch Ther.

MAGGIO, CHARLES; H Frank Carey HS; W Hempstead, NY; (Y); 90/350; Civic Clb; Bsbl; Ice Hcky; Hon Roll; Prfct Atten Awd.

MAGGIO, FRANK; Sachem HS; Farmingville, NY; (Y); 667/1558; Ski Clb; Band; Concert Band; Jazz Band; Mrchg Band; Pep Band; School Musical; Wt Lftg; Wrstlng; C W Post; Business Admin.

MAGGIO, JAMES; Central HS; Valley Stream, NY; (Y); Cmnty Wkr; JV Var Socr; Nassau CC; Crimnl Justc.

MAGGIO, JULIE; Southside HS; Rockville Centre, NY; (Y); 100/326; Cmnty Wkr; FBLA; Hosp Aide; Key Clb; Office Aide; Pres Frsh Cls; Hon Roll; Clss Pres 83-84; LIU-CW Post; Bus Admin.

MAGISTRALI, KARIN; Northport HS; Northport, NY; (Y); 164/610; Debate Tm; Girl Scts; JV Bsktbl; Var Crs Cntry; Tennis; Trk; Hon Roll; Prfct Atten Awd; Bst Prfrmnc Of Day In Tennis 84; Mst Imprvd In Tennis 84; Physcl Achvt Awd 83; Stnybrk; Lbrl Arts.

MAGLIOCCO, LAURIE; Binghamton HS; Binghamton, NY; (Y); Church Yth Grp; Cmnty Wkr; French Clb; Key Clb; SADD; Off Jr Cls; Sec Stu Cncl; JV Var Cheerleading; Hon Roll; Prfct Atten Awd; Stu Tchr Liason Comm 85; Law.

MAGNOTTI, CHERYL ANGELA; St John Villa Acad; Staten Island, NY; (Y); 19/125; Chorus; School Musical; School Play; Yrbk Phtg; Yrbk Stf; Var Cheerleading; Socr; Hon Roll; Italian Achvt Awd; Chrldr Awd; Soccer Awd; Staten Island; RN.

MAGNUS, KATHERINE; Tioga Central Schl; Nichols, NY; (S); 14/78; GAA; Quiz Bowl; Scholastic Bowl; Varsity Clb; School Musical; Variety Show; Nwsp Rptr; Jr Cls; Var JV Bsktbl; Hon Roll; Accntnt.

MAGRINO, JOHN; St Anthonys HS; Smithtown, NY; (Y); Cmnty Wkr; Wrstlng; NHS; U Of FL-GNSVLE; Pre-Med.

MAGRO, CAROL; Clarkstown South HS; New City, NY; (Y); Cmnty Wkr; Dance Clb; GAA; Political Wkr; Trs Frsh Cls; Trs Soph Cls; Trs Jr Cls; Trs Sr Cls; Rep Stu Cncl; JV Var Fld Hcky; Siena Coll; Law.

MAGRO, JOE; Valley Stream N HS; Malverne, NY; (Y); JV Bsbl; Var Capt Bsktbl; JV Ftbl; Var Golf; Var JV Socr; Var Trk; High Hon Roll; Hon Roll; All Div Bsktbll 86.

MAGUIRE, LISA; Pittsford Mendon HS; Pittsford, NY; (Y); VP Model UN; Political Wkr; Yrbk Stf; Hon Roll; NHS; Ntl Merit Ltr; Hague Intl Mdl Untd Ntns Delg Ambssdr 85; Rochester Rtry & Assn Untd Ntns Schlrshp 85; U Of MI.

MAGUN, ERIC; John F Kennedy HS; Bellmore, NY; (Y); SADD; Lit Mag; Chrmn Sr Cls; Stu Cncl; Var Ftbl; Var Lcrss; Var Trk; Im Wt Lftg; Hon Roll; Creative Wrtng Awds Nassau Cnty 84; Commnctns.

MAHADEO, SHARON; John Adams HS; Richmond Hill, NY; (Y); Hosp Aide; Science Clb; Stat Bsbl; Hon Roll; NHS; Cert Of Achvt 85-86; Cert Of Svc-Bptst Mdcl Ctr 85-86; Harvard U; Med.

MAHADY, DREW; Cicero-North Syracuse HS; Liverpool, NY; (S); 31/650; Trs Orch; School Musical; School Play; Var L Socr; Hon Roll; NHS; Nyssma Violin Solo Blue Rbbn Mdl 85; Natl Sccr Cmp Sccr Trphy 85; Natl Gstry & Govt Awd 85.

MAHAGAN, LISA; Skaneateles HS; Skaneateles, NY; (Y); 20/148; Band; Concert Band; Jazz Band; Orch; School Musical; High Hon Roll; NHS; Dean Lst Onondaga CC 85-86; Berkley Boston; Clarnt.

MAHALIC, CHRISTOPHER; John F Kennedy HS; Cheektawaga, NY; (Y); 5/148; Varsity Clb; Concert Band; Jazz Band; Bsktbl; Bowling; Tennis; High Hon Roll; NHS; Band; Mrchg Band; Rgnts Schlrshp 86; PAL 86; Buffalo ST Coll; Cmmnctns.

MAHAR, DOREEN; Henninger HS; Syracuse, NY; (Y); DECA; GAA; SADD; Hon Roll; NHS; Soc Srvcs.

MAHAR, MAUREEN; Wilson Central HS; Wilson, NY; (Y); Hosp Aide; School Play; Yrbk Stf; Pres Frsh Cls; Var L Sftbl; High Hon Roll; NHS; Cls C ST Sftbl Champs NY 86; Advrtsng.

MAHAR, MICHAEL; Schenectady Christian Schl; Schenectady, NY; (Y); 2/15; Yrbk Stf; Pres Trs Stu Cncl; JV Bsktbl; Var L Socr; High Hon Roll; Sal; SUNY Geneseo; Acctg.

MAHER, DANIEL; Lindenhurst HS; Lindenhurst, NY; (Y); 169/560; Ski Clb; Varsity Clb; Im Coach Actv; L Ftbl; L Lcrss; Im Wrstlng; Voice Dem Awd; Lacrosse 2nd Team All-Leag 86; Fnlst Voice Of Dmcracy 86; Photo All Lindy Art Show 85; Bus.

MAHER, DIANE; Waterloo SR HS; Waterloo, NY; (Y); Sec Girl Scts; Spanish Clb; Chorus; Mgr(s); Timer; Slvr Awd Grl Sctng 85; Bus Admn.

MAHER, JOANNE P; Massapequa HS; Massapequa Park, NY; (Y); 43/440; VP French Clb; Concert Band; Variety Show; Nwsp Phtg; Yrbk Stf; JV Cheerleading; Hon Roll; NHS; Pres Schlr; St Schlr; Loyola Coll; Englsh.

MAHER, JULIE; Skaneateles HS; Skaneateles, NY; (S); GAA; Hosp Aide; Orch; Socr; Sftbl; Vllybl; High Hon Roll; Hon Roll; Jr NHS; NHS; Music Awd 83-86; INT Design.

MAHER, KATHLEEN A; St Francis Prep; Bellerose, NY; (S); 47/746; Cmnty Wkr; SADD; Band; Im Gym; Figure Sktng Slvr & Gold Medals 84-85; Engr.

MAHER, KELLIE; East Islip HS; E Islip, NY; (Y); 23/425; Dance Clb; Band; SADD; JV Sftbl; French Hon Soc; Hon Roll; Jr NHS; NHS; Prfct Atten Awd; Stony Brook U; Secdry Math.

MAHER, MICHELE; Newburgh Free Acad; Newburgh, NY; (Y); Church Yth Grp; Cmnty Wkr; French Clb; Chorus; Orch; Rep Soph Cls; Rep Stu Cncl; High Hon Roll; Hon Roll; Jr NHS; NHS; Suny; Pol Sci.

MAHER, PEGGY; Bellport SR HS; E Patchogue, NY; (Y); 8/395; French Clb; Ski Clb; Nwsp Stf; Trs Sr Cls; Capt Cheerleading; Capt Var Gym; Var Trk; High Hon Roll; NHS; Prfct Atten Awd.

MAHL, JESSE; Sheep Shead Bay HS; Brooklyn, NY; (Y); 4 Certs Schlrp Accntg & Bus Math 85-86; Cert Achvt Bus Math 86; Accntg.

MAHLAB, MINNA A; Bronx HS Of Science; Bronx, NY; (Y); French Clb; Library Aide; Office Aide; Teachers Aide; Chorus; Lit Mag; Off Frsh Cls; Hon Roll; NHS; Prfct Atten Awd; Ed-In-Chief French Lit Mag 85-86.

MAHLER, CHRISTINE; Franklin Acad; Malone, NY; (Y); Sec Intnl Clb; Model UN; NFL; Chorus; Madrigals; School Play; Swing Chorus; Trs Stu Cncl; Sec Church Yth Grp; Hosp Aide; Acad All-Amer/Amer Achvt Acad-Speech & Drama 85 & Ldrshp 86; SUNY; Scndry Lit Educ.

MAHLER, ELIZABETH; Our Lady Of Mercy HS; Fairport, NY; (Y); 65/169; Girl Scts; SADD; Rep Stu Cncl; JV Vllybl; Hon Roll; MVP JV Vllybl 84; Grl Scout Pin 85; Comm Art.

MAHMUD, UROOJ; Xavier HS; New York, NY; (Y); ROTC; Teachers Aide; Color Guard; Yrbk Stf; Im Fld Hcky; Im Ftbl; High Hon Roll; Ntl Merit SF; Computer Clb; Silver Merit Acad JROTC 83-84 & 84-85; Cadet Of Mnth JROTC 83-84; Columbia Coll; Med.

MAHNEN, BARBARA; Eastchester HS; Scardsale, NY; (Y); French Clb; Hosp Aide; Band; Concert Band; Mrchg Band; School Musical; Nwsp Phtg; Yrbk Phtg; Tennis; Hon Roll; Flm.

MAHNKEN, CHARLIE; West Genesee SR HS; Camillus, NY; (Y); Art Clb; Church Yth Grp; Key Clb; JV Bsbl; High Hon Roll; NHS; Hnrb Mntn Schlstc Art Awds 86.

MAHON, DENISE; Commack HS North; Commack, NY; (Y); Dance Clb; Hosp Aide; Chorus; Trk; Hon Roll; Nrsng.

MAHONEY, AMY L; Ogdensburg Free Acad; Ogdensburg, NY; (Y); 9/185; Concert Band; Jazz Band; Mrchg Band; Pep Band; NHS; Ntl Merit Ltr; French Clb; Band; Hon Roll; Regents Schlrshp; Natl Ledrshp & Svc Awd; St Lawrence U; Govt.

MAHONEY, DANIELLE; Harpursville HS; Harpursville, NY; (S); 12/80; Ski Clb; Band; Chorus; Stage Crew; Sec Frsh Cls; Hon Roll; NHS; JV Var Fld Hcky; JV Sftbl; JV Vllybl; Med.

MAHONEY, JENNIFER; Cobleskill Central HS; Dorloo, NY; (Y); Drama Clb; Chorus; Concert Band; Mrchg Band; School Play; Nwsp Stf; Var L Sftbl; Var L Tennis; Hon Roll; Var L Trk; NY ST Smr Schl Arts/Schl Visl Arts 85; Art.

MAHONEY, KATE; Clarence SR HS; Clarence Ctr, NY; (Y); 61/250; GAA; Band; Symp Band; Var Bsktbl; Powder Puff Ftbl; Var Sftbl; Vllybl; High Hon Roll; Hon Roll; Coaches Awd Vllybl 84; Bst Rbndr 84; Math Stud Of The Mnth 85; Geneseo; Engrng.

MAHONEY, KATHLEEN; Sacred Heart Acad; Pt Lookout, NY; (S); 18/182; Church Yth Grp; Cmnty Wkr; Speech Tm; Chorus; School Play; Sftbl; Swmmng; Co-Capt Trk; High Hon Roll; NHS; Ntl Forensic Leag Deg Merit; 2nd Pl Declamatn; Track V Ltr.

MAHONEY, KEVIN P; Regis HS; Brooklyn, NY; (Y); Computer Clb; Service Clb; SADD; Teachers Aide; Nwsp Rptr; Var L Bsbl; Var L Bsktbl; St Schlr; Le Moyne Coll Jesuit Schlrshp 85-86; Boston College Grant 85-86; Boston Coll; Eng.

MAHONEY, MARGARET; Onondaga Central HS; Syracuse, NY; (Y); Sec Art Clb; Hosp Aide; SADD; Chorus; Yrbk Bus Mgr; Yrbk Ed-Chief; Yrbk Phtg; Yrbk Rptr; High Hon Roll; NHS; Awds Cndy Strppg 84-86; Peopl To Peopl H S Stdnt Ambssdr Prog 86; Syracuse U; Jrnlsm.

MAHONEY, MICHELLE; Midlakes HS; Phelps, NY; (Y); 11/150; French Clb; GAA; Varsity Clb; Rep Stu Cncl; Var Cheerleading; Var Fld Hcky; Var Vllybl; High Hon Roll; Hon Roll; NHS; Acctg.

MAHONEY, SHAFER; Guilderland Central HS; Albany, NY; (Y); 5/380; Cmnty Wkr; Computer Clb; Dance Clb; Math Tm; Quiz Bowl; Science Clb; Acpl Chr; Band; Orch; Nwsp Rptr; Altmnt Almni Assn Awd Englsh 85-87; Hrvrd Clb Bk Awd 85-86; Hghst Hon 81-86; Princeton U; Math.

MAHONEY, STACY; Saint Anthonys HS; St James, NY; (Y); 31/199; Church Yth Grp; Dance Clb; French Clb; Drill Tm; Yrbk Rptr; Rep Frsh Cls; Rep Soph Cls; Rep Stu Cncl; JV Cheerleading; Mgr(s); Ltn Hnr Soc 85-86; Fine Arts.

MAHONEY, THERESA; Sacred Heart Acad; Point Lookout, NY; (S); 3/182; Church Yth Grp; Cmnty Wkr; Speech Tm; Chorus; School Musical; Sftbl; JV Swmmng; Co-Capt Var Trk; High Hon Roll; NHS; Nassau Suffolk Cath Essay Cntst 1st Pl; Trck V Ltr; CYP Sportsmnshp Awd; Eng.

MAHONY, MARGARET; Holy Trinity HS; Freeport, NY; (S); JV Var Gym; Gym 1st, 2nd Pl Beam Indvdls Cmptn 84-85.

MAI, WEI XI; Newtown HS; Elmhurst, NY; (Y); 54/667; Camera Clb; Math Clb; Prfct Atten Awd; NYC Brd Educ Stndng Cmmtt Math Awds 86; Crtfct Hnr Excllnc Schlrshp Newtown HS 86; SUNY; Mech Engr.

MAICON, JAMES; Forahay Prep; Bronx, NY; (Y); Aud/Vis; French Clb; Var L Bsbl; Var Capt Ftbl; French Hon Soc; Hon Roll; NEDT Awd; Gen Excllnc 83-84; Excllnc In Geo & Frnch 84-85; Law.

MAIDA, MICHAEL; Herkimer HS; Herkimer, NY; (Y); Yrbk Stf; Pres Soph Cls; Rep Stu Cncl; Hon Roll; Ed.

MAIELLARO, MICHELLE; Middletown HS; Middletown, NY; (Y); 32/315; French Clb; Teachers Aide; Yrbk Stf; Hon Roll; Middletown Tchrs Assn Scholar 86; Nicholas Sylvester Mem Awd 86; Acad Achvt Awd Engl 86; Orange Cnty CC.

MAIER, CHRISTOPHER W; Edmeston Central HS; Edmeston, NY; (Y); 1/38; Am Leg Boys St; Band; Chorus; Var L Bsbl; Var L Bsktbl; Cit Awd; High Hon Roll; NHS; Val; Math Tm; Sports Awd Outstndg Qualities 86; Rensselear Poly Tech; Compu Eng.

MAIER, KELLY; Oyster Bay HS; E Norwich, NY; (Y); German Clb; SADD; Band; Chorus; Concert Band; Mrchg Band; Stage Crew; High Hon Roll; Chem.

MAIER, KRISTIN L; Kenmore West SR HS; Kenmore, NY; (Y); 31/421; Band; School Musical; School Play; Yrbk Stf; Stu Cncl; Pom Pon; High Hon Roll; Hon Roll; NHS; Pres Schlr; NYS Regents Scholar 86; Canisius Coll Deans Scholar 86; Moore Awd Outstndng Schl Svc 86; Canisius Coll; Pre-Med.

MAINDELLE, ROBERT; Liverpool HS; Liverpool, NY; (Y); 71/764; Am Leg Boys St; Pres German Clb; Bsktbl; Im JV Ftbl; Cit Awd; Elks Awd; NHS; Church Yth Grp; Church Choir; Rep Jr Cls; NJ ST Chmps Ftbl 84; Amer Scty Cvl Engrs Awd 86; US Army Awd Exclnc 86; Fsh Biolgst.

MAINE, BONNIE S; Brookfield Central Schl; Waterville, NY; (Y); 2/20; Cmnty Wkr; Pres 4-H; Band; Chorus; Pres Jr Cls; JV Var Vllybl; High Hon Roll; NHS; Regents Schlrshp 86; Cornell Tradition Freshman Fllwshp 86; Cornell U; Anml Sci.

MAINES, MONICA; Buffalo Traditional Schl; Buffalo, NY; (S); 12/116; French Clb; Office Aide; Trs Jr Cls; Trs Sr Cls; High Hon Roll; Hon Roll; VP NHS; Prfct Atten Awd; Psychlgy.

MAINI, DEBORAH; Bethpage HS; Bethpage, NY; (Y); Co-Capt Chess Clb; Hosp Aide; Science Clb; Spanish Clb; SADD; Var Badmtn; Var Socr; NHS; Nwsp Rptr; Natl Socl Studies Olympd,Wrld Hist 85; Natl Socl Studies Olympd Am Hist 86.

MAINS, DEBORAH; Valley Central HS; Montgomery, NY; (Y); 39/315; Concert Band; Mrchg Band; School Musical; Yrbk Stf; Rep Soph Cls; JV Vllybl; Hon Roll; NHS; Lbr Indstrl Rltns.

MAIO, MELISSA; Corning-Painted Post East HS; Corning, NY; (Y); Dance Clb; Drama Clb; JA; Varsity Clb; Drill Tm; School Musical; School Play; Stage Crew; Yrbk Stf; Rep Jr Cls; Elem Ed.

MAIORINO, JOHN E; Hicksville HS; Hicksvl, NY; (Y); 8/456; Boy Scts; Ski Clb; Variety Show; Bowling; Sftbl; Wt Lftg; Wrstlng; High Hon Roll; Jr NHS; NHS; U Delaware; Chem Engr.

MAIRA, MARGO; Wilton Central HS; Hilton, NY; (Y); VP Math Clb; Ski Clb; SADD; Band; Jazz Band; Mrchg Band; Symp Band; Capt Crs Cntry; Capt Trk; Capt Twrlr; Elem Ed.

MAISANO, MICHELE; Moore Catholic HS; Staten Island, NY; (Y); Spanish Clb; Bowling; Hon Roll; Schlrshp Wagner And Pace; St Johns U; Bus.

MAITA, DENISE; St Joseph By The Sea HS; Staten Island, NY; (Y); Aud/Vis; Computer Clb; Math Clb; JV Bsktbl; Bowling; NHS; Prfct Atten Awd; U Miami; Cmmnctns.

MAJDANIK, MICHELLE A; Royalton-Hartland HS; Gasport, NY; (Y); 29/135; Trs French Clb; Girl Scts; Varsity Clb; Var Diving; Var Swmmng; Var Trk; French Hon Soc; Hon Roll; Jr NHS; NHS; Outstndng Frnch Stdnt 85-86; SUNY Geneseo; Ecnmcs.

MAJEWSKY, MARK; Farmingdale HS; Farmingdale, NY; (Y); Boy Scts; Ski Clb; Hon Roll; BUS Mgmt.

MAJKA, DENISE; New York Mills JR SR HS; Marcy, NY; (Y); Am Leg Aux Girls St; Yrbk Bus Mgr; Pres Sr Cls; Var L Tennis; Hon Roll; VP French Clb; GAA; Key Clb; Sec Ski Clb; SADD; Rgnts Schlrshp 86; Colgate U; Eco.

MAJKOWSKI, LYNNE; West Seneca East SR HS; W Seneca, NY; (Y); Hosp Aide; Chorus; Swing Chorus; Hon Roll; JC Awd; Erie CC; Med Tech.

MAJMIN, WILLIAM; John Dewey HS; Brooklyn, NY; (Y); Hosp Aide; Science Clb; Orch; Chess Clb; JA; Teachers Aide; Bowling; Socr; Vllybl; Wt Lftg; Sci Clb 86; Orch 85; Hosp Aide 84; John Dewey; Phrmcst.

MAJOR, KEN; Bishop Grimes HS; Syracuse, NY; (Y); Chorus; School Musical; School Play; Trs Frsh Cls; Rep Stu Cncl; Crs Cntry; Score Keeper; Var Tennis; Var Wrstlng; Hon Roll; Med.

MAJOR, WILLIS; Jefferson JR SR HS; Rochester, NY; (S); #1 In Class; Pres Stu Cncl; Var Capt Bsktbl; Var Capt Ftbl; High Hon Roll; Hon Roll; Jr NHS; Trs NHS; Prfct Atten Awd; St Schlr; Val; Harvard Bk Awd 84-85; Lawrence Klepper Awd 84-85 & 85-86; Outstndng Stu Law Mgnt-Jefferson 83-4 & 84-5; General Motors Inst; Elec Engr.

MAJTYKA, JENNIFER; Hamburg SR HS; Hamburg, NY; (Y); 77/374; JCL; Latin Clb; Orch; Erie Cnty All-ST Orch 85; Erie Cnty Orch 85-86; Law.

MAK, WRINGLE; South Shore HS; Brooklyn, NY; (Y); Off Jr Cls; Bowling; Schrshp For Achvr & Attndnc 83-84; Princeton; Mngmnt.

MAKELY, GEOFFREY SCOTT; Worcester Central Schl; Worcester, NY; (Y); Am Leg Boys St; Band; School Play; VP Jr Cls; VP Stu Cncl; Bsbl; Bsktbl; Capt Socr; High Hon Roll; NHS; Ctznshp Awd By Am Lg 86; Air Force Acad; Pilot.

MAKEY, CAROLYN; Kenmore East SR HS; Tonawanda, NY; (Y); 54/320; Drama Clb; GAA; School Musical; School Play; Sec Jr Cls; Var Capt Bsktbl; Var Capt Sftbl; Hon Roll; NHS; Frank C Densberger Awd 86; JR Class Awd Otstndng SRS 86; Mst Vlbl Grls Bsktbll Plyr 86; U Of NY; Art.

MAKEYENKO, LAUREN; Hamburg SR HS; Hamburg, NY; (Y); 48/382; AFS; Sec Band; Concert Band; Mrchg Band; Symp Band; Swmmng; Trk; Hon Roll; NHS; NYS Rgnts Schlrshp 86; Zonta Clb Schlrshp 86; MI ST U; Telecomm.

MAKHTIN, OLEG; South Shore HS; Brooklyn, NY; (Y); Math Tm; Nwsp Stf; Yrbk Stf; Prfct Atten Awd.

MAKHULI, MARK; Jamesville-Dewitt HS; Fayetteville, NY; (Y); 41/275; Pres Frsh Cls; Var Bsktbl; Var Capt 4-H Awd; Var Tennis; High Hon Roll; Hon Roll; Elmira Key Awd 86; Pre Med.

MAKINAJIAN, MICHAEL; John H Glenn HS; Huntington, NY; (Y); 89/296; French Clb; Stat Bsktbl; Bowling; Regents Diploma 86; St Johns U Queens; Athltc Admn.

MAKOWSKI, CHRISTOPHER; Hutchinson Technical HS; Buffalo, NY; (Y); 17/256; High Hon Roll; Hon Roll; NHS; ST U Buffalo; Med.

MAKOWSKI, JEFF; Chittenango Central Schl; Chittenango, NY; (Y); Church Yth Grp; Cmnty Wkr; French Clb; SADD; Yrbk Stf; Var Bowling; High Hon Roll; Hon Roll; Jr NHS; NHS; Outstndng Achvt In Math 83; Binghamton; Sci.

MAKRIDES, DEENA; Midwood HS At Brooklyn Clg; Brooklyn, NY; (Y); Intnl Clb; Office Aide; Band; Concert Band; Pep Band; School Musical; School Play; Symp Band; Hunter Coll.

MAKSYMIAK, EDWARD; Mc Quaid Jesuit HS; Penfield, NY; (Y); Boy Scts; Cmnty Wkr; German Clb; Model UN; Service Clb; Ski Clb; School Play; Acad Ltr 86; Intl Bus.

MALABANAN, ARIEL O; Cornwall Central HS; Cornwall, NY; (Y); Math Tm; Band; Concert Band; Jazz Band; Symp Band; Im Bsbl; Bowling; Var JV Swmmng; Var JV Tennis; Hon Roll; Elec Engr.

MALACHOWSKI, AMY T; Williamsville East HS; Williamsville, NY; (Y); 26/300; Drama Clb; Hosp Aide; Chorus; School Musical; School Play; Stage Crew; High Hon Roll; NHS; Ntl Merit Ltr; Latin Clb; Rgnts Schlrshp 86; Oberlin.

MALACHOWSKI, ELIZABETH; Shenendehowa HS; Clifton Park, NY; (Y); Cmnty Wkr; Band; Symp Band; Bsktbl; Hon Roll; Psych.

MALADY, BARRY; Monroe HS; Rochester, NY; (Y); Ski Clb; Bsktbl; Crs Cntry; Swmmng.

MALAK, MICHELLE; Brockport HS; Brockport, NY; (Y); Pres Church Yth Grp; Spanish Clb; Trs Band; Jazz Band; Pep Band; School Musical; Stage Crew; Swing Chorus; JV Var Trk; NHS; Spnsh I Awd 84; Spnsh II Awd 85; Outstndng Prfrmr-Band 83-86.

MALARA, CYNTHIA; Northport HS; East Northport, NY; (Y); 30/585; Camera Clb; Orch; LI Rgnl & State Photo Cnst Fnlst 85; Comp Arts Rcgntn & Tlnt Search 85-86; Loyola Coll; Chem.

MALARK, VALERIE; Saranac Central HS; Dannemora, NY; (S); 43/106; Drama Clb; French Clb; Library Aide; SADD; Chorus; School Musical; Yrbk Ed-Chief; Yrbk Stf; Timer; Hon Roll; Plattsburgh ST; Math.

MALAVE, DIANA; St Pius V HS; Bronx, NY; (Y); Computer Clb; Nwsp Stf; Pres Frsh Cls; Off Soph Cls; Trs Jr Cls; Stu Cncl; Hon Roll; NHS; Prfct Atten Awd; Hghst Aver Schlrshp 84-86; Acctg.

MALAXOS, CONSTANTINE; Mineola HS; Mineola, NY; (Y); 4/200; Trs SADD; Pres Stu Cncl; JV Bsbl; JV Bsktbl; Var Socr; High Hon Roll; NHS.

MALAY, BRIAN; Tupper Lake HS; Tupper Lake, NY; (Y); Wt Lftg; Med.

MALCHO, KARYN; Fairport HS; Fairport, NY; (Y); Church Yth Grp; Ski Clb; JV Capt Swmmng; Hon Roll; Cchs Awd 84; Ldrs Clb 84; Daemen Coll; Phys Thrpst.

MALCHOW, DANA; Tonawanda JR SR HS; Tonawanda, NY; (Y); 42/220; Sec Ski Clb; SADD; Pres Jazz Band; School Musical; Swing Chorus; Yrbk Stf; VP Jr Cls; Pres Stu Cncl; JV Var Cheerleading; Hon Roll; Hugh Obrian Yth Fndtn Awd 84; Stu Agnst Drnk Drvng Rdrs Dgst Schlrshp 86; Oswego ST U; Publc Just.

MALDONADO, CAROLINA; Immaculate HS; New York, NY; (Y); Church Choir; Nwsp Rptr; Bowling; Cheerleading; Pom Pon; Sftbl.

MALDONADO, DIANA; Herbert H Lehman HS; Bronx, NY; (Y); 55/561; Hosp Aide; SADD; Nwsp Rptr; Nwsp Stf; Yrbk Phtg; Yrbk Stf; Var Bowling; Var Sftbl; Hon Roll; NHS; Natl Hnr Soc Arista 86; 3 Yrs Hnr Rl 83-86; Sftbl 83-86; Actuary.

MALDONADO, JENNIFER; Cardinal Spellman HS; Bronx, NY; (Y); Camera Clb; Dance Clb; Spanish Clb; Band; School Play; Stage Crew; Yrbk Ed-Chief; Yrbk Phtg; Stu Cncl; Ntl Merit Schol; Regents Scholar 86; Cngrssnl Merit Awd 86; Senatorl Merit Awd 86; PA ST U; Mktg.

MALDONADO, JOSEPH; Christ The King HS; S Ozone Park, NY; (Y); SADD; Teachers Aide; VP Frsh Cls; VP Soph Cls; Bsbl; Bsktbl; Coach Actv; Fld Hcky; Ftbl; Sftbl; St Johns; Med.

MALDONADO, ROBERT; Chaminade HS; Farmingdale, NY; (Y); Camera Clb; Hosp Aide; Math Clb; Science Clb; Spanish Clb; Nwsp Ed-Chief; Nwsp Rptr; Hon Roll; NHS; Ntl Hspnc Schlrs Semi-Fnlst 86; MIT; Mech Engrng.

MALDONADO, ROSA; East New York Transit Tech HS; Brooklyn, NY; (Y); Sec Church Yth Grp; Teachers Aide; Lit Mag; Hon Roll; Sec Sr Cls; Systms Analysts.

MALDONADO, THOMAS; Scarsdale HS; Scarsdale, NY; (Y); Cmnty Wkr; 4-H; Ski Clb; SADD; Varsity Clb; Band; Concert Band; Mrchg Band; School Play; Symp Band; Williams Coll; Med.

MALEADY, THOMAS; Monsignor Farrell HS; Staten Island, NY; (S); Church Yth Grp; Service Clb; Lit Mag; Im Bsktbl; Im Bowling; Im Ftbl; Im Socr; High Hon Roll; Hon Roll; NHS; Engr.

MALEK, ANDREA R; Lyons JR & SR HS; Lyons, NY; (Y); 4/100; Trs French Clb; Ski Clb; Varsity Clb; Band; Chorus; School Musical; Yrbk Stf; Cheerleading; Tennis; High Hon Roll; Rgnts Schlrshp 86; Geneseo SUNY; Psychology.

MALENA, ALFRED A; Bayside HS; Bayside, NY; (Y); 104/700; Aud/Vis; Chorus; Madrigals; Variety Show; Yrbk Stf; Ntl Merit Ltr; SUNY Albany; Law.

MALESKI, CHARLES E; South Seneca HS; Ovid, NY; (Y); Am Leg Boys St; Boy Scts; Drama Clb; Exploring; 4-H; Ski Clb; Varsity Clb; Band; Chorus; School Musical; MIP Bsbl 86; CCFL; Criminal Justice.

MALESKI, DAVID; Clyner Central HS; Clymer, NY; (Y); Church Yth Grp; FFA; VP Frsh Cls; Var Bsbl; Var JV Bsktbl; Var JV Ftbl; Hon Roll; Greenhand Awd FFA 83-84; Cnty Farmr Awd FFA 85-86; Bus.

MALFITANY, KELLY; Longwood HS; Coram, NY; (Y); Key Clb; Chorus; Nwsp Rptr; Nwsp Stf; Var Sftbl; High Hon Roll; Hon Roll; NHS; Hon Mntn Orgnl Spnsh Essay In Long Island Lang Fair 86; Stanford; Comm.

MALGIERI, CATHY; Saugerties HS; Saugerties, NY; (S); 30/252; Spanish Clb; Pres Varsity Clb; Yrbk Stf; High Hon Roll; NHS; Pre-Law.

MALGIOGLIO, JOSEPH T; Mt Saint Michael Acad; Bronx, NY; (S); 8/384; Church Yth Grp; Nwsp Rptr; Im Bsktbl; Hon Roll; Var Spanish NHS; Mt St Michael 4 Yr Schlrshp 83-87; 1st Hnrs & 2nd Hnrs 83-87; Top 10 Stu Mdl 83-87; NY Inst Tech; Archt.

MALHOTRA, SHILPA; Cathedral HS; Elmhurst Corona, NY; (Y); 1/277; Math Tm; VP Chess Clb; Drama Clb; French Clb; Hosp Aide; Intnl Clb; Library Aide; Band; School Musical; Nwsp Ed-Chief; Sci Awd Excll Awd 86; Trstees Schlrshp 86-87; Rgnts Schlrshp 86; NY U; Pre-Med.

MALIN, DEANNA; Saugerties HS; Saugerties, NY; (Y); 28/250; Spanish Clb; Pres Chorus; Im Gym; Im Vllybl; High Hon Roll; NHS; Daemen; Spnsh.

MALIN, SERENA; Commack North HS; Commack, NY; (Y); Var Capt Socr; JV Sftbl; JV Var Vllybl; High Hon Roll; NHS; Girls Ldrs Corps 83-84.

MALINA, GABRIELLE; Bronx High Schl Of Science; New York, NY; (Y); Debate Tm; English Clb; NFL; Temple Yth Grp; Lit Mag; Tennis; Vllybl; Jrnlsm.

MALIZIA, ANNA A; Mont Pleasant HS; Schenectady, NY; (Y); 3/220; Library Aide; Spanish Clb; Yrbk Stf; DAR Awd; High Hon Roll; Spanish NHS; Accntng Awd 85; Rgnts Schlrshp 86; Engrng.

MALKIN, DIANE L; John F Kennedy HS; Bronx, NY; (Y); 117/873; Aud/Vis; Office Aide; Radio Clb; Temple Yth Grp; Stage Crew; Yrbk Stf; Mgr(s); Score Keeper; JV Sftbl; Regnts Schlrshp Awd 85-86; Hofstra U; Flm Dir.

MALLETTE, NICOLE L; Stuttgart American HS; A P O, NY; (Y); 6/132; Hosp Aide; Pep Clb; Red Cross Aide; Ski Clb; Spanish Clb; Chorus; Sec Soph Cls; VP Jr Cls; Rep Stu Cncl; JV Var Cheerleading; Amer Councils Wmns Club Schlrshp; U GA; Bus Admin.

MALLIAGROS, NADIA; William Cullen Bryant HS; Long Island Cty, NY; (Y); 110/700; 4-H; Intnl Clb; JA; Library Aide; Math Tm; Band; Variety Show; 4-H Awd; Hon Roll; NHS; Greek Club; NY U; Cmmnctns.

MALLOW, KAREN L; Horseheads HS; Horseheads, NY; (S); 40/385; Girl Scts; JCL; Latin Clb; Spanish Clb; SADD; Band; Color Guard; Trk; Hon Roll; Bus & Prof Wmns Yth Ldrshp Conf 85; Elizabethtown Coll; Spts Med.

MALLOY, KATHLEEN; East Syracuse-Minoa HS; Minoa, NY; (S); 176/333; VP DECA; Ski Clb; Variety Show; Var JV Fld Hcky; Im Socr; JV Sftbl; Wilks Coll; Bus.

MALLOY, SHARON ANN; Miller Place HS; Sound Beach, NY; (Y); 46/195; Trs Church Yth Grp; Drama Clb; Office Aide; Chorus; Lit Mag; Tennis; Trk; Hon Roll; Suffolk Cnty CC.

MALONE, LINDA ANN; Lansingburgh HS; Troy, NY; (Y); Drama Clb; Key Clb; Chorus; School Musical; JV Cheerleading; High Hon Roll; Hon Roll; Jr NHS; Lansingburgh Music Detp Chr Awd 84; Frshmn Chrldng Cptn 84; Dance.

MALONEY, DENNIS M; Arlington HS; Poughkeepsie, NY; (Y); Am Leg Boys St; Model UN; JV Ftbl; JV Trk; Hon Roll; Ntl Merit Ltr; Scl Stds Stu Of Mnth 84.

MALONEY, ERIN C; Our Lady Of Mercy HS; Pittsford, NY; (Y); 8/172; Cmnty Wkr; JA; Science Clb; Ski Clb; Nwsp Stf; Yrbk Stf; Hon Roll; NHS; NY ST Regents Schlrshp 86; Yth & Govt 84-86; U Of Notre Dame; Bus.

MALONEY, KAREN; Brewster HS; Brewster, NY; (Y); Camera Clb; Church Yth Grp; JV L Sftbl; Achvt Awd Hmn Dvlpmnt Iii 86; Psych.

MALONEY, MATTHEW; Lansingburgh HS; Troy, NY; (Y); Church Yth Grp; Var JV Ftbl; Var Score Keeper; Im Wt Lftg; High Hon Roll; Jr NHS; NHS; Natl Merit Schlrshp Assn-Sci; Engrng.

MALONEY, NICOLE; Lansingburgh HS; Troy, NY; (Y); Church Yth Grp; Office Aide; Hon Roll; Highest Av Bus Arth 85-86; Hudson Vly CC; Bus Admin.

MALONEY, SHAELAH; Keveny Memorial Acad; Cohoes, NY; (S); 2/37; Trs Jr Cls; Var Capt Bsktbl; Var Tennis; JV Var Vllybl; High Hon Roll; Hon Roll; Prfct Atten Awd; Ntl Bus Hnr Soc; Amer HS Athl; US Bus Ed Awds; Acctng.

MALOON, RICHARD; Frankfort-Schuyler Central HS; Frankfort, NY; (Y); Drama Clb; Trs FBLA; Band; Concert Band; Mrchg Band; School Musical; Variety Show; Bsbl; JV Bsktbl; Var Vllybl; SUNY Oneonta; Mrktng Mngmnt.

MALORZO, MELANIE; Frankfort-Schuyler Central Schl; Frankfort, NY; (Y); Spanish Clb; Yrbk Stf; Trvl.

MALOUF, JILL; Beacon HS; Beacon, NY; (Y); German Clb; Latin Clb; Variety Show; Ed Yrbk Ed-Chief; Yrbk Stf; JV Var Sftbl; Hon Roll; Grphc Dsgn.

MALOY, BETHANNE; Notre Dame Acad; Staten Island, NY; (Y); Church Yth Grp; Stage Crew; Nwsp Stf; Yrbk Phtg; Bowling; Parsons Schl Design; Mrktng.

MALOY, SHARON; John Jay HS; Katonah, NY; (Y); Drama Clb; Acpl Chr; Band; Chorus; School Musical; Variety Show; Off Soph Cls; Cit Awd; High Hon Roll; Hon Roll; Awd Excllnc In Soc Studies 86; Tchr Commndtns-Ss10, Ss11, Eng 11, Frnch 111-4 & Oil Pntng 84-86.

MALTESE, EVAN; Syosset HS; Syosset, NY; (Y); 61/483; Cmnty Wkr; Acpl Chr; Nwsp Rptr; Var Bsbl; High Hon Roll; NHS; Rgnts Schlrshp 86.

MALTESE, SALLY; The Ursuline Schl; New Rochelle, NY; (Y); Library Aide; Cheerleading; Hon Roll; Jr NHS; NHS; Mktg.

MALUENDA, ANNETTE V; Dominican Acad; Elmhurst, NY; (Y); 8/42; Latin Clb; Science Clb; Church Choir; Nwsp Rptr; Yrbk Stf; Rep Jr Cls; Hon Roll; NHS; Rckfllr Ctr Schlrshp 86; Latin Cntst-Slvr Mdl Cum Mxma Lauda; Georgetown U; Law.

MALVAROSA, VINCENT M; Port Chester HS; Port Chester, NY; (Y); Jazz Band; Stage Crew; Yrbk Stf; Lit Mag; Rep Jr Cls; Rep Sr Cls; Hon Roll; Law.

MALVINO, DONNA; H H HS West; Melville, NY; (Y); Dance Clb; Drama Clb; Girl Scts; Leo Clb; SADD; Flag Corp; School Musical; School Play; Stage Crew; Variety Show; FIT; Fash Merch.

MALZ, VICTORIA; Herricks SR HS; Manhasset Hls, NY; (Y); Cmnty Wkr; Hosp Aide; Key Clb; Library Aide; Pres Orch; School Musical; Hon Roll; NHS; ALWS Crd Advncd Lfsvng 84; Nyssma Murid Awd & Vln & Pno 84-86; Imprvng Apprnce Of Schl 86; Med.

MAMBERT, MARK C; Shaker HS; Newtonville, NY; (Y); Holson Vlly CC; Lbrl Arts.

MAMMINA, JOSEPH; Miller Place HS; Miller Place, NY; (Y); 51/248; Aud/Vis; Camera Clb; Church Yth Grp; Computer Clb; Drama Clb; Ski Clb; Thesps; School Play; Stage Crew; VP Sr Cls; Bus Dynmcs Awd 86; Indstrl Arts Awd & Ad Vsl Awd 84; Dowling; Bus Mngmnt.

MAMMONE, CARIN; Sacred Heart Acad HS; Merrick, NY; (S); 5/204; Church Yth Grp; FTA; Math Clb; Service Clb; Yrbk Stf; Hon Roll; NHS; Prncpls Lst 84-85; 1st Hnrs 83-84; Finance.

MAMMONE, JILL E; Hudsoln Falls HS; Fort Edward, NY; (Y); 6/210; French Hon Soc; NHS; NYS Rgnts Schlrshp 86; Adirondack CC; Bus.

MANAHER, COLLEEN; Tonawanda HS; Tonawanda, NY; (Y); Church Yth Grp; French Clb; JA; SADD; School Play; Yrbk Stf; Cheerleading; Trk; Hon Roll; Bus Admin.

MANANDHAR, MOHIT; Hewlett HS; Hewlett Harbor, NY; (Y); Camera Clb; French Clb; Key Clb; SADD; Nwsp Rptr; Var L Ftbl; High Hon Roll; Med.

MANASKIE, KATHLEEN; Hicksville SR HS; Hicksville, NY; (Y); Varsity Clb; Pres Soph Cls; Rep Stu Cncl; Bsktbl; JV Capt Cheerleading; Mgr(s); Var Socr; Hon Roll; Adelphi U; Bus Mgmt.

MANASSERI, MICHAEL D; Professional Childrens Schl; Leonia, NJ; (Y); 1/50; VP Tennis; VP High Hon Roll; Pres Schlr; Val; Racoosn Schlr NYU Sch Of Bus 86; Thomas Hunter Schlr 86; Pres Schlr 86; NYU Sch Of Bus; Intl Bus.

MANCHESTER, JOHN I; Springville-Griffith Inst; Springville, NY; (Y); 3/220; Sec Am Leg Boys St; Pres Key Clb; Math Tm; Ski Clb; Chorus; Nwsp Stf; NHS; Political Wkr; Orch; School Musical; Erie Cnty Fnls Am Lgn Ortcl Cnts 86; Part Clrkson U 85; Bio-Med Engnrng.

MANCHESTER, SCOTT; Elmira Southside HS; Wellsburg, NY; (S); Am Leg Boys St; Sec Church Yth Grp; Drama Clb; Intnl Clb; Pep Clb; Lib Chorus; Madrigals; School Musical; Rep Sr Cls; Hon Roll; Annl X-Mas Cncrt Hnr Soloist 85; Acctng.

MANCHIN, ERIC; Paul V Moore HS; W Monroe, NY; (Y); Boy Scts; Math Tm; Ski Clb; Varsity Clb; Var Ftbl; High Hon Roll; NHS; Georgetown U; Lgl Profsn.

MANCINI, CHRISTOPHER; Bishop Scully HS; Amsterdam, NY; (S); 2/60; Pres Math Clb; Yrbk Stf; Pres Soph Cls; Var L Ftbl; High Hon Roll; NHS; RPI Sci, Math Medal 83; Aeron Engrng.

MANCINI, GEMMA; St Vincent Ferrer HS; Astoria, NY; (S); 41/109; Hosp Aide; Teachers Aide; Ed Nwsp Stf; Yrbk Phtg; Yrbk Stf; Hon Roll; St Johns U; Elem Educ.

MANCINI, JEFF; Auburn HS; Auburn, NY; (Y); Church Yth Grp; Hosp Aide; Hon Roll; Cayhga CC; Comp Sci.

MANCINI, MICHELE; Valley Stream North HS; Franklin Square, NY; (Y); Debate Tm; 4-H; French Clb; Mathletes; Chorus; School Musical; Sec Frsh Cls; Trs Soph Cls; Sec Jr Cls; French Hon Soc; Med.

MANCINI, MICHELLE; Seton Catholic Central HS; Endwell, NY; (Y); Art Clb; Church Yth Grp; Dance Clb; Spanish Clb; SADD; Chorus; Church Choir; School Musical; Yrbk Stf; Comm Art.

MANCUSO, CAROLYN; T R Proctor HS; Utica, NY; (Y); Church Yth Grp; GAA; Hosp Aide; Pep Clb; VICA; Stu Cncl; Gym; Sftbl; Wt Lftg; Hon Roll; Cazenovia; Fshn Dsgn.

MANCUSO, ELLEN; Sacred Heart Acad; Buffalo, NY; (Y); Red Cross Aide; Pres Spanish Clb; Stage Crew; Trk; Rochester Inst Tech; Crmnl Just.

MANCUSO, JULIE; Pelham Memorial HS; Pelham, NY; (Y); 24/157; Ski Clb; Nwsp Rptr; Fld Hcky; Lcrss; Trk; Twrlr; High Hon Roll; Hon Roll; NHS; Model UN; Regents Schlrshp Wnnr; Pres Acad Ftnss Awd; All-Leag Lacrosse; Lehigh U; Bus.

MANCUSO, MARIO; St Francis Prep; Howard Beach, NY; (S); 28/747; Church Yth Grp; Debate Tm; NFL; Political Wkr; Science Clb; Speech Tm; Im Ftbl; Im Ice Hcky; Cit Awd; High Hon Roll; Excllnce Volunteer 85; NY ST Frnsc Forn 85; Brooklyn-Queens Forn Awds 84-85; Pre-Med.

MANCUSO, RICHARD; St Joseph By The Sea HS; Staten Island, NY; (S); 25/300; Nwsp Stf; JV Var Bsbl; JV Var Bsktbl; High Hon Roll; Hon Roll; Hstry Awd 85; Seton Hall; Invstmnt Bnkng.

MANDARINO, LUCIA J; St Catharien Acad; Bronx, NY; (Y); 1/198; Office Aide; Teachers Aide; Hon Roll; NHS; Pres Schlr; Pres Schlr NYU 86; Merit Schlr Mnhttn Coll 86; Awds All Sci,Math,Scl Stds,Bus,Engl,Schl Svc 82-86; Fordham U; Law.

MANDAVA, NARESH; Arlington HS; Poughkeepsie, NY; (Y); 5/576; Debate Tm; Math Clb; High Hon Roll; Natl Merit Commended Schlr 86; Cornell U; Pre Med.

MANDEL, DENISE; Mount Vernon HS; Mt Vernon, NY; (Y); 3/650; Debate Tm; Keywanettes; Spanish Clb; Ed Yrbk Rptr; Ed Lit Mag; Off Jr Cls; Off Sr Cls; Stu Cncl; High Hon Roll; VP NHS; Mock Trial Tm 85-86; Wellesley Alumni Awd Eng Excllnc 86; Writer.

MANDELIS, FRANCINE; Jamesville-Dewitt HS; Fayetteville, NY; (Y); Off Church Yth Grp; Cmnty Wkr; Rep Jr Cls; VP Stu Cncl; JV Var Bsktbl; Var L Trk; Dnfth Awd; High Hon Roll; NHS; Amer HS Athlt 85.

MANDIGO, JAMES ROBERT; St Marys Academy Of The North Country; Corinth, NY; (S); Spanish Clb; Band; Yrbk Stf; Im Bsktbl; Hon Roll; Co-Ownr & Chf Cntry Inn Hdly NY 86; Clnry Arts.

MANDY, AMY; Moriah Central HS; Moriah Ctr, NY; (Y); Cmnty Wkr; Hosp Aide; Library Aide; Office Aide; Pep Clb; Ski Clb; Yrbk Stf; Stu Cncl; Cheerleading; Swmmng; Gregg Awd Typing 85-86; Secretarial.

MANDZAK, MELISSA; Our Lady Of Mercy HS; Rochester, NY; (Y); Pres English Clb; Exploring; French Clb; Girl Scts; Science Clb; High Hon Roll; Hon Roll; Pre Vet.

MANDZYK, CHRISTINE; Mount Saint Mary Acad; Buffalo, NY; (Y); 46/113; Church Yth Grp; Cmnty Wkr; Computer Clb; Girl Scts; Hosp Aide; Library Aide; Model UN; Spanish Clb; Church Choir; School Play; Crtfct Mrt Prtcptn 38th Anl 86 Mdl Untd Ntns Assmbly 86; Ithaca Coll; Blgy.

MANEL, JAMES; Longwood HS; Coram, NY; (S); Am Leg Boys St; Computer Clb; Key Clb; Varsity Clb; Ed Nwsp Ed-Chief; Yrbk Stf; VP Mgr(s); VP Socr; Hon Roll; Raquetbl Clb 86; Bus.

MANELSKI, MARYANN T; Newfield HS; Coram, NY; (Y); 26/576; Art Clb; Aud/Vis; Cmnty Wkr; Drama Clb; Hosp Aide; Thesps; Chorus; School Musical; School Play; Yrbk Stf; Natl Art Hnr Soc 85-86; Phlsphy.

MANESS, JOEL R; Wayne Central HS; Macedon, NY; (Y); 3/184; Am Leg Boys St; Math Tm; Jazz Band; Pres Soph Cls; Trs Sr Cls; Var Capt Socr; Cit Awd; High Hon Roll; NHS; Math Clb; Kirsten Mott Memrl Awd 84; Acadmc Excllnc Awd-Math 86; Outstndng Prfrmnc-Band 86; RPI; Elec Engr.

MANEY, PATRICK T; Columbia HS; Rensselaer, NY; (Y); 42/419; JV Var Ftbl; JV Var Lcrss; High Hon Roll; Jr NHS; Ntl Merit SF; Church Yth Grp; Cmnty Wkr; Dance Clb; Ski Clb; Stage Crew; Bus.

MANFREDI, CHRISTIAN; Niagara Catholic HS; Lewiston, NY; (Y); Boys Clb Am; French Clb; Var Crs Cntry; 2nd Hnrs On Hnr Roll 83-86; Suny Buffalo; Bus.

MANFREDI, MELISSA; Christ The King; Elmhurst, NY; (Y); 16/451; JV Cheerleading; Hon Roll; Schlrshp $2000, $500 Per Yr For CKHS 83; Lgl Sec.

MANG, JACOB; Kenmore West HS; Kenmore, NY; (Y); 8/420; Math Tm; Quiz Bowl; Science Clb; JV Im Socr; JV Trk; High Hon Roll; NHS; Ntl Merit Ltr; Prfct Atten Awd; Pres Schlr; U Buffalo Hnrs Pgm Scholar 86; NYS Regents Scholar 86; U Buffalo.

MANGAN, SUSAN J; Midwood HS; Brooklyn, NY; (Y); 26/556; French Clb; Math Tm; Chorus; School Musical; NHS; Ntl Merit SF.

MANGANO, KENNETH; Garden City SR HS; Garden City, NY; (Y); 34/346; Pres Frsh Cls; Rep Soph Cls; Rep Jr Cls; Var Capt Ftbl; Var Lcrss; JV Wrstlng; High Hon Roll; Jr NHS; NHS; Ntl Merit Ltr; Bucknell U.

MANGIARACINA, DENISE A; Fontbonne Hall Acad; Brooklyn, NY; (Y); Cmnty Wkr; Dance Clb; Service Clb; Ski Clb; Chorus; Cheerleading; Pom Pon; Cert Hnrbl Ment Gov Cls,Women Lit Cls,Typng Cls 85-86; Pace U; Bus.

MANGICOTTI, MARIA ELENA; Torrejon HS; Apo, NY; (Y); Model UN; School Play; JV Bsktbl; High Hon Roll; NHS; Spnsh AP Test 85; Top Perfrmnc Eng 86; Excllnt Perf Bus Lab 86; St Louis U MO; Bus Adm.

MANGIONE, JAMES; Roosevelt HS; Yonkers, NY; (Y); Yrbk Sprt Ed; Var Capt Ftbl; Wt Lftg; High Hon Roll; Hon Roll.

MANGIONE, MICHAEL; The Bronx HS Of Science; Bronx, NY; (Y); Boy Scts; Pres Civic Clb; Cmnty Wkr; JA; Teachers Aide; Y-Teens; Im Bsktbl; Im Co-Capt Sftbl; Im Capt Vllybl; Eagle Sct BSA 84; Ad Altare Dei Relig Awd 83; Cert Merit 84; Engrng.

MANGONE, LORI; Mamaroneck HS; Mamaroneck, NY; (Y); Bsktbl; Sftbl; DAR Awd; Hon Roll; All Conf Sftbl 84-86; MVP Pt Chester Sftbp Tourn 86; Adv Keybrdng Awd Of Excllnc 86; Cornell U; Comp Progrmmr.

MANGRA, MANRAJ BIDESH; Richmond Hill HS; Richmond Hill, NY; (Y); Math Clb; Swmmng; Vllybl; Socr; Hon Roll; Prfct Atten Awd; Poly Tech Inst; Aviation.

MANGUS JR, RICHARD; Cicero-North Syracuse HS; Syracuse, NY; (S); 50/623; JA; Band; Concert Band; Mrchg Band; Bowling; Golf; UCLA; Accntng.

MANICCIA, DAYNA M; Linton HS; Schenectady, NY; (Y); 49/287; JCL; Key Clb; Office Aide; Rep Jr Cls; Trs Sr Cls; Rep Stu Cncl; JV Cheerleading; JV Pom Pon; JV Var Tennis; JV Trk; SUNY; Physcl Thrpy.

MANIGAT, CLAUDE; Saint Francis Prep Schl; Jackson Heights, NY; (S); 203/744; Concert Band; Rep Soph Cls; JV Trk; NHS; Band; Mrchg Band; JV Crs Cntry; Optimates List 85-86; Engrng.

MANIKTALA, ANITA; Cicero-North Syracuse HS; North Syracuse, NY; (S); 14/623; Sec Key Clb; Mathletes; Math Tm; Orch; Var Tennis; High Hon Roll; Jr NHS; Syracuse U; Med.

MANION, ANDREA; Bishop Scully HS; Amsterdam, NY; (Y); 14/54; Drama Clb; VP JA; Yrbk Stf; Sec Sr Cls; Rep Stu Cncl; Hon Roll; NHS; Girl Scts; St Agnello Club Schlrshp 86; Irish American Club Schlrshp 86; Le Moyne; Poli Sci.

MANION, TERESA; Saranac Central HS; Cadyville, NY; (S); 14/100; Library Aide; Band; Concert Band; Jazz Band; Variety Show; Timer; High Hon Roll; Hon Roll; NHS; Prfct Atten Awd; Art.

MANLEY, DEBORAH L; Newburgh Free Acad; Newburgh, NY; (Y); 168/500; Drama Clb; Office Aide; SADD; Teachers Aide; School Musical; Stage Crew; Hnr Partcptn Cnsrvtn Day 83-84; Orange Cnty CC; Pedtrc Srgcl.

MANLEY, JAMIE; Albion HS; Albion, NY; (S); 5/196; Church Yth Grp; Latin Clb; Lit Mag; Rep Frsh Cls; JV Var Crs Cntry; Var JV Trk; High Hon Roll; Jr NHS; NHS; Mst Vlbl Crss Cntry Plyr 84; Crss Cntry All Leag Tm 84; Engrng.

MANLEY, JOHN; Schroon Lake Central HS; Severance, NY; (S); 3/28; Boy Scts; French Clb; Model UN; Score Keeper; Tennis; High Hon Roll; Hon Roll; NHS; Prfct Atten Awd; Schl Scholar Awd.

MANLY, HEIDI; Plattsburgh HS; Plattsburgh, NY; (Y); Cmnty Wkr; Model UN; Ski Clb; Varsity Clb; Sec Stu Cncl; JV Cheerleading; JV Sftbl; Var Swmmng; Hon Roll; Cmmnctns.

MANN, DEBORAH; Onondaga HS; Syracuse, NY; (Y); German Clb; Quiz Bowl; Speech Tm; Chorus; Pres Jr Cls; Stu Cncl; Vllybl; High Hon Roll; Hon Roll; NHS; Frgn Exchng Stu Nrwy; Sci.

MANN, MATTHEW J; Commack HS South; Commack, NY; (Y); 24/360; Mrchg Band; Symp Band; Ed Nwsp Ed-Chief; Ed Yrbk Stf; Rep Stu Cncl; High Hon Roll; NHS; St Schlr; Computer Clb; Sec French Clb; VP Long Isl Fed Temple Yth 85-86; NYS Moot Crt Comptn 84-86; Stu Ldrshp Day 83-86; SUNY Albany; Pol Sci.

MANN, NORMA; South Shore HS; Brooklyn, NY; (Y); Hosp Aide; Orch; School Musical; Yrbk Stf; NHS; Ntl Merit Schol; Pre-Med.

MANN, THOMAS K; Smithtown East HS; Smithtown, NY; (Y); Concert Band; Mrchg Band; JV Socr; Hon Roll; Rgnts Schlrshp; US Merchant Marine Acad.

MANNA, LU; Seward Park HS; New York, NY; (Y); Cmnty Wkr; Office Aide; Bsktbl; Coach Actv; Tennis; Vllybl; Prfct Atten Awd; Intrnshp Prog 86; Benhamton; Hlth Sci.

MANNARINO, JOHN P; Sewanhaka HS; Franklin Square, NY; (Y); 13/335; Exploring; Nwsp Rptr; Yrbk Rptr; Var Tennis; NHS; Ntl Merit SF; Prfct Atten Awd; Engrng.

MANNARINO, RICHARD; Monsignor Farrell HS; Staten Island, NY; (Y); Cmnty Wkr; Band; Concert Band; Jazz Band; Mrchg Band; Symp Band; Pres Jr Cls; Im Bsktbl; Im Bowling; Crs Cntry; Iona Coll Frgn Lang Cntst 2nd Hnrs 85; Pgm Committee Asian Amer Clb 86; Capt NYS Chmpn Mrchng Band; Pre-Med.

MANNE, CHERYL; Southside HS; Rockville Centre, NY; (Y); 116/278; Key Clb; Latin Clb; Model UN; SADD; Temple Yth Grp; Band; Rep Jr Cls; Var Trk; JV Var Vllybl; Hon Roll; AZ ST U; Math.

MANNE, KIMBERLY; Pineview Christian Acad; Delmar, NY; (S); Sec Church Yth Grp; Chorus; Off Soph Cls; VP Stu Cncl; Co-Capt Vllybl; Ntl Fifle Assoc Distngushd Expert 85; Art.

MANNHEIMER, MICHAEL; Commack South HS; Commack, NY; (Y); Math Tm; Nwsp Stf; Yrbk Stf; Lit Mag; JV Tennis; High Hon Roll; Pres NHS; Ntl Merit Ltr; Nwsp Rptr; Sntr-For-Day Pgm; Sflk Cnty Mth Cntst; Ntl Sci Olympd; Law.

MANNIELLO, KIMBERLY; Cold Spring Harbor HS; Cold Spng Harbor, NY; (Y); 24/150; Drama Clb; Office Aide; Acpl Chr; Chorus; Madrigals; School Musical; Yrbk Bus Mgr; High Hon Roll; Jr NHS; Rotary Awd; NY Rgnts Schlrshp 85-86; Bus Tchrs Assn Hnr Awd 86; Svc & Music Schl Awds 86; Davidson Coll.

MANNIGAN, MICHAEL M; General Brown HS; Dexter, NY; (Y); 2/119; Am Leg Boys St; JCL; Chorus; Concert Band; Drm Mjr(t); Mrchg Band; Yrbk Ed-Chief; NHS; Ntl Merit Ltr; Latin Clb; Navy ROTC Schlrshp 86-87; Cornell U; Vet Sci.

MANNING, DEXTER; Amityville Memorial HS; Amityville, NY; (Y); School Play; Var Crs Cntry; Var Trk; Var Wrstlng; Hon Roll; Outstndg Athltc Achvmnt 84; All-Cnfrnc Trck & Fld 86; 4th Pl In Lg 86; NC Coll; Bus Mgmt.

MANNING, ERIC B; The Albany Acad; Albany, NY; (Y); 1/42; Boy Scts; Letterman Clb; Varsity Clb; Band; Mrchg Band; Nwsp Ed-Chief; Lit Mag; JV Var Crs Cntry; JV Var Trk; Capt Wrstlng; Vanderveer Prize 83; Natl Latin Contest-Summa Cum Laude 83; Harvard Prize 84; RPI Mdl-Engrng 84; Princeton; Hstry.

MANNING, KATHARINA; Willsboro Central HS; Willsboro, NY; (Y); 1/35; Trs Church Yth Grp; Trs Girl Scts; Quiz Bowl; Jazz Band; Trs Sr Cls; Capt L Golf; Capt L Socr; Cit Awd; NHS; Val; Rgnts Schlrshp 86; JR Ntl Luge Tm 82-86; Grl Sct Gld Awd 86; Middlebury Coll; Lbrl Arts.

MANNING, LIEANN; Massena Central HS; Massena, NY; (Y); French Clb; Key Clb; Band; Yrbk Stf; JV Var Socr; JV Var Sftbl; Var Vllybl; MMHA Grls Hcky Awd 85-86; Nrthstrn; Phys Thrpy.

MANNING, SUSAN; Union-Endicott HS; Endicott, NY; (Y); 69/435; Church Yth Grp; French Clb; Girl Scts; SADD; Concert Band; Mrchg Band; Yrbk Stf; High Hon Roll; Hon Roll; NHS; Penn ST U; Engrng.

MANNING, TODD F; Chenango Valley HS; Binghamton, NY; (Y); Am Leg Boys St; Art Clb; Varsity Clb; Yrbk Sprt Ed; JV Capt Ftbl; Var Capt Tennis; Var Capt Wrstlng; Hon Roll; NY ST Jr Wrstlng Champ Freestyl 85-86; Bys ST Assmblymn Cnty Exec 86; Art Educ.

MANNINO, JEFFREY; Port Richmond HS; Staten Isl, NY; (Y); Art Clb.

MANNINO, KEVIN; Bishop Ford Central Catholic HS; Brooklyn, NY; (Y); Drama Clb; Nwsp Rptr; Swmmng; NYU Drama Schl; Actor.

MANNINO, LORRAINE; Nazareth Reg HS; Brooklyn, NY; (Y); Math Tm; Speech Tm; Hon Roll; NHS.

MANNIX, COLLEEN; Plattsburgh HS; Plattsburgh, NY; (Y); Varsity Clb; Yrbk Stf; JV Cheerleading; JV Var Socr; JV Sftbl; Hon Roll; Bus Mgmt.

MANNO, LAWRENCE L; St Josephs Collegiate Inst; Wmsvl, NY; (Y); 40/193; Band; Concert Band; VP Pres Jazz Band; School Musical; School Play; Nwsp Stf; High Hon Roll; Hon Roll; St Schlr; Outstndng Mus Citation 86; Outstandng Instrumentalist 84 & 85; SUNY Buffalo; Perf Arts.

MANNO, TERESA; North Rockland HS; Pomona, NY; (Y); Church Yth Grp; Var Bsktbl; JV Var Sftbl; JV Vllybl; Hon Roll; NHS; Med.

MANNS, JOHN; Cazenovia Central Schl; Chittenango, NY; (Y); 35/141; Church Yth Grp; SADD; Var L Socr; Var L Trk; NY ST Rgts Schlrshp 86; All Str Tm Trck 86; MMV Offns Sccr 85; Geneseo SUNY; Blgy.

MANOLI III, VICTOR R; Cairo-Durham HS; Acra, NY; (Y); 25/94; Boy Scts; Camera Clb; Church Yth Grp; Computer Clb; Stage Crew; Bsbl; Var Trk; High Hon Roll; Ntl Merit Ltr; Durham Republcn Clb Mst Imprvd Engl 86; SUNY; Comp.

MANOUSOS, MICHAEL A; C E Gorton HS; Yonkers, NY; (Y); Rep Stu Cncl; Var Lcrss; Var Capt Socr; Ecnmcs.

MANSELL, SCOTT; Mynderse Acad; Seneca Falls, NY; (S); JV Var Bsbl; Var Ftbl; JV Var Wrstlng; Hon Roll; Stdnt Mnth 85; Cazenovia Coll; Art.

MANSFIELD, CHARLES; Garden City HS; Garden City, NY; (S); 10/346; Drama Clb; French Clb; Acpl Chr; Madrigals; School Musical; School Play; Yrbk Ed-Chief; Boy Scts; Church Yth Grp; German Clb; ROTC 4 Yr Schlrshp All Svcs 86-87; Math.

MANSLEY, TOM; Connetquot HS; Bohemia, NY; (Y); 9/700; Boy Scts; Capt Chess Clb; Math Tm; Scholastic Bowl; Ski Clb; Chorus; Socr; High Hon Roll; Hon Roll; Jr NHS; Pace U; Mgt.

MANSOURI, RICHARD P; Horseheads HS; Horseheads, NY; (S); 4/380; Am Leg Boys St; Cmnty Wkr; Hosp Aide; VP JCL; Sec Science Clb; School Musical; Pres Stu Cncl; Im Ice Hcky; Trs NHS; Ntl Merit Ltr; Congrssnl Schlr Natl Yng Ldrs Conf 85; Mrchg Band 1st Pl Novice Cls 83; 3rd Pl AA Clss 84; Biomed Engrng.

MANSUETTA, JACQUELINE; Sachem HS; Lk Ronkonkoma, NY; (Y); 180/1600; Ski Clb; Spanish Clb; Chorus; Yrbk Stf; Lit Mag; Stu Cncl; Var Crs Cntry; Var Trk; NHS; Ed.

MANTELLO, JOSEPH; Iskniskayuna HS; Schenectady, NY; (Y); Key Clb; Pep Clb; Im JV Bsbl; Im JV Bsktbl; Im JV Ftbl; Hon Roll; Ntl Merit Ltr; Niskayuna Tchrs Assc Schlrshp 86; VA Tech; Mech Engrng.

MANTHEY, JEFFREY; Peekskill HS; Peekskill, NY; (Y); 3/142; Boy Scts; Yrbk Stf; Capt Ftbl; Cit Awd; High Hon Roll; NHS; Rotary Awd; Pres Stu Cncl; Golf; Capt Swmmng; Natl Schlr & Athlt Awd 86; Pres Acad Ftns Awd 86; Peekskill Alumni Assoc Schlrshp 86; Villonova; Cvl Engr.

MANTIONE, JOHN; Sachem HS; Holbrook, NY; (Y); 47/1579; Computer Clb; Ed Q&S; Science Clb; Orch; Ed Lit Mag; NHS; Ntl Merit Ltr; Jr NHS; Sci Fctn Clb Fndr & Pres 83-85; Contribtr & Edtr Olwells SF Mag 85; Govs Troph Spec Awd NY 85-86; Carnegie-Mellon U; Engrg.

MANUEL, STEPHANIE; Holland Patent Central HS; Hinckley, NY; (Y); 35/197; AFS; Am Leg Aux Girls St; Debate Tm; School Play; Ed Nwsp Stf; Lit Mag; Crs Cntry; Trk; Hon Roll; Recog Acad Achvt 86; Dickinson Coll; Pol Sci.

MANUS, LAURA; Duanesburg Central HS; Delanson, NY; (Y); Church Yth Grp; Drama Clb; Intnl Clb; Letterman Clb; Pep Clb; Ski Clb; Teachers Aide; Varsity Clb; Chorus; School Musical; Athlete Yr Awd Chrldng 86; Keene ST Coll; Ind Tech.

MANUSE, DEANA J; Bishop Kearney HS; Rochester, NY; (Y); Aud/Vis; Church Yth Grp; Girl Scts; Library Aide; Nwsp Bus Mgr; Yrbk Stf; Rep Stu Cncl; Var Capt Bowling; High Hon Roll; Pres NHS; Rochester Yth Amer Bowlng Alliance Scholar 86; Sci.

MANUUD, MARTIN; Archbishop Molloy HS; Flushing, NY; (Y); 49/383; Acpl Chr; Crs Cntry; Trk; Bus.

MANWARING, DEREK W; Oswego HS; Oswego, NY; (Y); 17/380; Am Leg Boys St; German Clb; Pres Jr Cls; Rep Stu Cncl; JV Var Bsbl; Var Capt Ice Hcky; Var Socr; Var Tennis; High Hon Roll; Hon Roll; Arntcl Engnrng.

MANZANERO, PHILIP; Stamford Central Schl; Stamford, NY; (S); 1/30; FBLA; Spanish Clb; Band; Variety Show; Pres Frsh Cls; Pres Sr Cls; Var Socr; Bausch & Lomb Sci Awd; Hon Roll; Chem Engrg.

MANZARI, H JOHN; Mynderse Acad; Seneca Falls, NY; (Y); 3/140; Am Leg Boys St; Church Yth Grp; Drama Clb; Intnl Clb; Model UN; Red Cross Aide; Spanish Clb; SADD; School Musical; Variety Show; Intern Assmblymn 86; WSI 85; JR Kiwnas 85; St John Fisher Coll; Pltcl Sci.

MANZARI, MARIA; Mynderse Acad; Seneca Falls, NY; (S); #21 In Class; Church Yth Grp; Spanish Clb; Rep Frsh Cls; Pres Jr Cls; JV Var Tennis; High Hon Roll; Hon Roll; Psych.

MANZIN, ANNA; H Frank Carey HS; W Hempstead, NY; (Y); #5 In Class; High Hon Roll; Jr NHS; NHS; Foreign Lang Hon Soc 84-86.

MANZIONE, DEBRA; Maria Regina HS; Valhalla, NY; (Y); 3/166; Band; Nwsp Rptr; Yrbk Stf; Lit Mag; High Hon Roll; NHS; IONA Lang Cntst Span II 1st 86; IONA Coll.

MANZO, GINA M; St Francis Prep; W Hempstead, NY; (S); 110/750; Chorus; JV Var Cheerleading; Coach Actv; JV Gym; Trk; Im Vllybl; NHS; Opt Clb Awd; Awd Exclnce Chrldng 85; Corp Law.

MANZO, MICHAEL; Northport HS; E Northport, NY; (Y); DECA; Mrchg Band; Symp Band; JV Socr; JV Tennis; Im Vllybl; Boy Scts; Computer Clb; Band; Concert Band; Sccr Awd Mgr 80; Sccr Awd Plyr 81; DECA Hon & Awd 86; Virginia Tech; Comp Engrng.

MANZOLINA, SANDRA; Longwood HS; Coram, NY; (Y); 77/487; Hosp Aide; SADD; Nwsp Stf; JV Var Cheerleading; Hon Roll; Engl Awd 86; Pace U; Pltcl Sci.

MAPES, LISA; Lansing HS; Groton, NY; (Y); Chorus; Orch; School Musical; Nwsp Ed-Chief; JV Golf; Cit Awd; High Hon Roll; Lion Awd; NHS; Pres Schlr; Ntl Schl Choral Awd 86; Acdmc Awd Engl 85; All-Arnd SR Music Awd 86; SUNY Fredonia; Spcl Stds.

MAPLEY, JODI; Cato-Meridian HS; Cato, NY; (Y); Church Yth Grp; GAA; Ski Clb; Spanish Clb; Yrbk Stf; Pres Frsh Cls; Pres Soph Cls; Var L Bsktbl; Var L Fld Hcky; Var L Sftbl; Gregg Shrthnd Awd 60 WPM 86; Crmnl Justc.

MAPP, VANESSA; Mount Saint Ursula HS; Bronx, NY; (Y); Camera Clb; Church Yth Grp; Computer Clb; Hosp Aide; Band; Church Choir; Nwsp Rptr; Rep Soph Cls; VP Stu Cncl; Hon Roll; NY U; Obstrcn.

MAQRTUSCELLO, RENEE; Amsterdam HS; Amsterdam, NY; (Y); 17/249; Varsity Clb; VP Soph Cls; Rep Jr Cls; Sr Cls; Capt Cheerleading; NHS; St Schlr; R J Mc Nulty Schlrshp Awd 86; Utica Clg; Nrsg.

MAQUEDA, MARIANO; Mansignor Farrell HS; Staten Island, NY; (Y); Church Yth Grp; Hosp Aide; Spanish Clb; Var L Trk; High Hon Roll; Jr NHS; NHS; Ntl Merit Ltr; Med.

MAR, MAUNG; Brooklyn Technical HS; New York, NY; (Y); 150/1150; Office Aide; Science Clb; Hon Roll; Prfct Atten Awd; Polytech U; Elect Engrg.

MAR, PATRICIA; Seward Park HS; Brooklyn, NY; (Y); 81/524; Teachers Aide; Vllybl; Prfct Atten Awd; Hunter Coll; Nrs.

MARAFFI, JOHN A; Performing Arts; Bronx, NY; (Y); School Play; Stage Crew; JA; Chorus; School Musical; Rep Sr Cls; Stu Cncl; Ftbl; Arts Rcgntn & Tlnt Srch 85; NY U; Drama.

MARAN, PATRICIA; Southampton HS; Water Mill, NY; (Y); 4/106; School Musical; Ed Lit Mag; Pres Frsh Cls; Pres Jr Cls; Var Bsktbl; Var Capt Fld Hcky; Var Capt Trk; NHS; Ntl Merit Ltr; Empire St Gms-Fld Hcky 84-86; Jr Olympcs-Fld Hcky 85-86.

MARANI, DAVID; Midwood HS; Brooklyn, NY; (Y); 103/667; Orch; Lit Mag; Prfct Atten Awd; Arista Lge 86; Math.

MARANI, JEFFREY; George W Fowler HS; Syracuse, NY; (Y); Hon Roll; Welding 1st & 2nd Yr Cert 84-86; Technical Career Inst; Welder.

MARANS, MICHELLE C; Scarsdale HS; Katonah, NY; (Y); Pres French Clb; Hosp Aide; Math Tm; Red Cross Aide; NHS; NYS Rgnts Schlrshp 86; U Of MI; Polit Sci.

MARASCA, JO-ANNE; Holy Trinity HS; Westbury, NY; (Y); Math Clb; Yrbk Rptr; Ed Yrbk Stf; Stu Cncl; Hon Roll; Mu Alp Tht; Adelphis Trustees Schlrshp 86; Adelphis Hnrs Prgm Schlrshp 86; Adelphi U; Bus.

MARASCO, LISA; Edison Tech; Rochester, NY; (Y); Ski Clb; Hon Roll; Bryant/Strattn; Bus Mngmnt.

MARASIGAN, VINCENT; St Marys Boys HS; Westbury, NY; (Y); 3/209; High Hon Roll; Hon Roll.

MARATHE, ARATI; Midwood HS; Brooklyn, NY; (Y); 16/540; Intnl Clb; Math Tm; Spanish Clb; School Musical; Lit Mag; Tennis; High Hon Roll; Jr NHS; Sal; Spanish NHS; Archon Svc Soc 86; Math.

MARATOS, NIKI; St Marys HS; Jamaica, NY; (Y); 15/110; Church Yth Grp; Girl Scts; High Hon Roll; Hon Roll; NHS; Law.

MARBLE, WENDY; Auburn HS; Auburn, NY; (Y); Intnl Clb; SADD; Varsity Clb; Concert Band; Jazz Band; Mrchg Band; School Musical; JV Bsktbl; Var Socr; Var Sftbl; Scr-Coaches Awd Of Mrt 83.

MARCANO, BEVERLY; Eastern District HS; Brooklyn, NY; (Y); Church Yth Grp; JA; Math Tm; Service Clb; Teachers Aide; Church Choir; Yrbk Stf; Vllybl; High Hon Roll; Hon Roll; Govs Comm Schlstc Achvt 84; Spnsh Awds 85-86; Math Awds 84-86; Law.

MARCANO, MARCUS; All Hallows HS; Bronx, NY; (S); 4/90; Letterman Clb; Math Clb; Math Tm; Var Bsbl; Var Capt Bowling; Stat High Hon Roll; Hon Roll; NCTE Awd; NHS; Phy Thrpy.

MARCARIO, DANIELLE MARIE; Clarkstown North HS; New City, NY; (Y); 95/405; Band; Yrbk Phtg; VP Frsh Cls; Var Capt Gym; Var Capt Socr; Var Trk; Jr NHS; Mu Alp Tht; Order Sons Italy 86; Italian Clb 86; All Sectn Ym Tm 86; U MA-AMHERST; Pre-Med.

MARCEDA, ROBERT; Tottenville HS; Staten Island, NY; (Y); Boy Scts; High Hon Roll; Hon Roll; NHS; Comp Drftg.

MARCELLUS, AMY; Indian River Central HS; Theresa, NY; (Y); Latin Clb; Trk; Hon Roll; Elmira Coll; Law.

MARCH, DAVID; Rocky Point HS; Rocky Point, NY; (S); 16/205; Chess Clb; Mathletes; Hon Roll; NYS Regents Schlrshp 86; Suffolk Cnty Math Contst 84-85; Case Western Reserve U; Elec En.

MARCHENA, IVIS; Christopher Columbus HS; Bronx, NY; (S); 70/692; Chorus; School Musical; School Play; Nwsp Rptr; Nwsp Stf; High Hon Roll; NHS; NYU; Tchr Ed.

MARCHESE, KERSTEN C; F D Roosevelt HS; Salt Point, NY; (Y); 16/336; Band; Concert Band; Mrchg Band; Var L Crs Cntry; Var L Trk; Hon Roll; NHS; All Cnty 300 M Dash Rnr 86; 2nd Team All Div Cross Cntry 85; Hmcmng Queen 85; Duke U; Sci.

MARCHESI, GIANCARLO; Westbury HS; Westbury, NY; (Y); 1/150; Variety Show; Var Capt Socr; Rep Frsh Cls; Var Tennis; Im Vllybl; High Hon Roll; NHS; Sal; 1st Pl Sci Awd 84; George Washington U Engr Medal 86; Arch.

MARCHETTA, THOMAS; Tottenville HS; Staten Isld, NY; (Y); Hon Roll; Jr NHS; Princeton; Law.

MARCHETTI, MICHAEL; Bishop Ford Central Cath HS; Brooklyn, NY; (Y); 95/441; Goldn Recrd Achvt Awd 82; Regnts Schlrshp 86; Brooklyn Coll; Law.

MARCHIONE, CHAS; Corcoran HS; Syracuse, NY; (Y); French Clb; SADD; Bowling; Swmmng; Tennis; Hgh Hnr Amer Studs 85-86; Soc Studs.

MARCHIONNA, ANNA; Evander Childs HS; Bronx, NY; (S); 2/383; Dance Clb; Office Aide; Teachers Aide; Orch; Variety Show; Yrbk Rptr; Yrbk Stf; Hon Roll; Prfct Atten Awd; Hnr Schl Awd 84; Assemblyman Seabrook Cert Merit 85; Arista Awd 85; Comp Sci.

MARCIANO, JAMES E; Patchogue Medford HS; Medford, NY; (Y); 6/653; Hon Roll; Jr NHS; NHS; Spanish NHS; Regnts & Elks Club Schlrshp 86; Rensselaer Polytechnic Inst.

MARCIANO, KATHY; Dominican Commercial HS; Richmond Hill, NY; (S); 2/288; Pep Clb; Teachers Aide; High Hon Roll; Queens Coll Pres Awd 84-85.

MARCIANO, LAWRENCE JOHN; E J Wilson Spencerport HS; Rochester, NY; (Y); Spanish Clb; Mrchg Band; Symp Band; Yrbk Stf; Jr Cls; Sr Cls; Hon Roll; NHS; Intl Affrs.

MARCIANO, SCOTT; John Marshall HS; Rochester, NY; (Y); Teachers Aide; JV Bsbl; L Var Socr; L Var Trk; MVP Sccr 86; CCFL; Wldlf Mgmt.

MARCILLE, CHRISTOPHER; Amsterdam HS; Amsterdam, NY; (Y); Band; Mrchg Band; Hon Roll; NHS; Med.

MARCINIAK, DEBORAH ANN; Whitesboro SR HS; Marcy, NY; (Y); 73/306; Hosp Aide; Concert Band; Mrchg Band; Orch; Pres Church Yth Grp; JV Var Bsktbl; Var Socr; Var Trk; Cmnty Wkr; Exploring; Pin Bsktbl 86; Ltr Trck, Sccr & Bsktbl 86; Earnd Pts For Swtr 86-87.

MARCO, GINA; St Raymond Acad; Bronx, NY; (S); Library Aide; High Hon Roll; NHS; Columbia U; Para Legal.

MARCOTRIGIANO, DANIELLE; Port Richmond HS; Staten Island, NY; (Y); Fashion Inst Of Tech; Fash Merc.

MARCOTTE, BRIAN; Auburn HS; Auburn, NY; (Y); JA; Hon Roll; MAA Awd Annl HS Math Exm; Comp Engrng.

MARCUCCI, JILL; Riverside HS; Buffalo, NY; (Y); French Clb; Nwsp Rptr; Swmmng; Rep Stu Cncl; Comp Sci.

MARCUCCI, TIMOTHY; Mc Kinley HS; Buffalo, NY; (Y); 86/216; Mach Tool Tech.

MARCZAK, MARIA; Kings Park HS; Kings Park, NY; (Y); Church Yth Grp; Cmnty Wkr; Debate Tm; Sec SADD; Drm & Bgl; Sec Stu Cncl; Var Capt Cheerleading; Hon Roll; 1st Pl Debate Lng Isl Elmntns 85; Pre Law.

MARCZEWSKI, DAENA; Bennett HS; Buffalo, NY; (Y); 1/220; Yrbk Phtg; Yrbk Stf; Sec Stu Cncl; Capt Cheerleading; Hon Roll; NHS; Wellesley Awd 86; ST U; Bus Comp.

MARDENFELD, SANDRA L; Farmingdale HS; Massapequa Park, NY; (Y); 63/600; Girl Scts; SADD; Temple Yth Grp; Band; Concert Band; Mrchg Band; Orch; Pep Band; School Musical; Symp Band; Buffalo ST; Jrnlsm.

MARE, STEPHEN D; Mepham HS; N Bellmore, NY; (Y); Am Leg Boys St; Boy Scts; Science Clb; Off Soph Cls; Off Jr Cls; Off Sr Cls; Var Capt Ftbl; Var Capt Lcrss; Wrstlng; High Hon Roll; JFK Phys Fitness Awd Best Athlete 83; Aerospc Engrng.

MAREK, ANNE MARIE; Ogdensburg Free Acad; Ogdensburg, NY; (Y); 5/225; Church Yth Grp; Cmnty Wkr; Math Clb; Color Guard; Mrchg Band; Crs Cntry; Trk; High Hon Roll; Hon Roll; NHS; Acdmc Banquet 84-86; Engrng.

MAREK, PAUL; Ogdensburg Free Acad; Ogdensburg, NY; (Y); 12/186; Am Leg Boys St; Church Yth Grp; Math Clb; Capt Var Ftbl; Trk; Wt Lftg; High Hon Roll; NHS; Acad Banquet 83-86; Bus Dynamic Schlrshp Awd 83; NY ST Regents Schlrshp Wnnr 86; Clarkson U; Engnrng.

MARENTETTE, DENISE; Our Lady Of Mercy HS; Pittsford, NY; (Y); Dance Clb; Co-Capt Science Clb; Trs SADD; Rep Jr Cls; Rep Sr Cls; Rep Capt Stu Cncl; Im Cheerleading; Var Gym; Var Trk; High Hon Roll; 3rd Yr Math Hnrs Awd Hghst Avg 86; Frnch 1-2 Awd 84; Astrnmy.

MARESCA, DANIELLE; St John The Baptist; Bay Shore, NY; (Y); Dance Clb; Drama Clb; GAA; Ski Clb; Varsity Clb; School Play; Var Fld Hcky; Score Keeper; Capt Sftbl; Sftbl Capt, 2 Yrs Vrsty, Champs 85-86; Fld Hcky MVP, 2 Yrs Vrsty, Undftd 84-86; Drma Clb 81-83; Law.

MARGIASSO, LISA; Greenville Central HS; Hannacroix, NY; (Y); 35/77; Trs FFA; Key Clb; Stat Bsktbl; Var L Socr; Var Sftbl; JV Var Vllybl; Degr Chptr Greenhand FFA 85; Degr Chptr Farmer FFA 86; 2nd NYS Cont Nrsry Landscape FFA 85; Maria Coll; Trvl.

MARGIES, JANINE; St Dominic HS; N Massapequa, NY; (Y); Church Yth Grp; 4-H; SADD; Rep Stu Cncl; JV Var Cheerleading; Hon Roll; Service Clb; Varsity Clb.

MARIANI, JAMES; Union Endicott HS; Endicott, NY; (Y); French Clb; Ski Clb; SADD; Rep Jr Cls; Var Vllybl; High Hon Roll; Hon Roll; Syracus U; Comp Engnrng.

MARIANO, GERALYN; Mahopac SR HS; Mahopac, NY; (Y); 78/409; Chorus; Hon Roll; NHS; Library Aide; U Santo Tomas; Pre-Med.

MARICLE, KATHLEEN K; Union Endicott HS; Endicott, NY; (Y); 12/430; Cmnty Wkr; French Clb; Key Clb; Yrbk Stf; Rep Soph Cls; High Hon Roll; NHS; Var Trk; Marine Bio Study Pgm 85; NYS Regents Scholar 86; Carl Lansing Jones Scholar 86; SUNY Buffalo; Chem Engrng.

MARILYN, ESTREMO; Richmond Hill HS; Richmond Hill, NY; (Y); French Clb; Key Clb; Service Clb; Speech Tm; School Musical; Variety Show; Lit Mag; Bowling; French Hon Soc; Prfct Attndnc; Frnch Hnr Soc; Engl Hnr Soc; Cmmnctns.

MARIN, PATRICIA; Stuyvesant HS; Rego Park, NY; (Y); Cmnty Wkr; Office Aide; Political Wkr; Teachers Aide; Sec School Musical; Yrbk Stf; Mgr DECA; Sec Stu Cncl; Var L Trk; Jr NHS; Natl Hispanic Schlr Awds Prgm 86; Commended Stu By The Natl Merit Schlrshp Prgm 85; Bio.

MARINA, MERCEDES R; Rome Catholic HS; Rome, NY; (Y); Trs Exploring; Trs Frsh Cls; Trs Soph Cls; Trs Jr Cls; Rep Stu Cncl; JV Cheerleading; Var Trk; MIP Trck 84; 100 Pct Awd Trck 86; All Str Trck 86; Psych.

MARINCIC, KATHLEEN; Hudson Falls SR HS; Glens Falls, NY; (Y); 13/220; Church Yth Grp; French Clb; Science Clb; SADD; Acpl Chr; Chorus; School Musical; High Hon Roll; Hon Roll; NHS; Pres Awd; Rapid Recall Foothills Wnr; Potsdam Coll; Math.

MARINELLI, ANDREW; Auburn HS; Auburn, NY; (Y); Band; Concert Band; Art Clb; Mrchg Band; Orch; School Musical; Stage Crew; JV Bsktbl; Jr NHS; NHS; Libl Arts.

MARINELLO, JOHN; Mont Pleasant HS; Schenectady, NY; (Y); Church Yth Grp; Key Clb; Ski Clb; SADD; Yrbk Phtg; Yrbk Stf; Trs Soph Cls; Stu Cncl; Trk; Evngl Coll; Pre-Med.

MARINELLO, MARK J; Beach Channel HS; Belle Harbor, NY; (Y); 6/390; Capt Math Tm; Scholastic Bowl; SADD; Concert Band; Jazz Band; Pres Jr Cls; Pres Sr Cls; Var Tennis; Var Wt Lftg; NHS; Gold Mdl 4 Yrs 86; Queens Coll Awd Achvmnt 85; Math Assn 1 St Pl In Exam 85; Brown U; Engr.

MARING, KERRY; Whitesboro SR HS; Yorkville, NY; (Y); Boy Scts; Pres Church Yth Grp; Exploring; Varsity Clb; Concert Band; Jazz Band; Mrchg Band; Var L Socr; Var L Trk; Hon Roll; Eagle Scout Awd 83; All-Cnty Orch 84; All-Star Jazz Bnd Cls Aa 86; US Army; Elec Engr.

MARINO, ANN M; Johnson City HS; Johnson City, NY; (Y); 23/198; Hosp Aide; Sec SADD; Capt Color Guard; Stu Cncl; Var Stat Bsbl; Var Capt Tennis; Hon Roll; Sec NHS; Pep Clb; Varsity Clb; Rgnts Schlrshp; Acdmc Achvmnt Awd; SUNY; Radiation Thrpy.

MARINO, DAVID; Clarkstown South HS; W Nyack, NY; (Y); Boy Scts; Civic Clb; Computer Clb; Science Clb; Ntl Merit Ltr; NY ST Sci Supv Assc Phy Awd 86; NJ Sci Leag Top 10 Pct 86; Iona Coll Phy Dept 1st Hon Cert 86; Compu Engrng.

MARINO, DEBRA A; The Mary Louis Acad; Richmond Hill, NY; (Y); 12/270; Camera Clb; Cmnty Wkr; Office Aide; Teachers Aide; Hon Roll; Trs NHS; Long Island U Full Tuition Schlrshp, St Johns Comp Schlrshp, Adelphi U Trustee Schlrshp; St Johns U; Bus.

MARINO, DIANNE; St Agnes Acad; Corona, NY; (Y); SADD; Nwsp Sprt Ed; Teachers Aide; Nwsp Rptr; Nwsp Stf; Bowling; Im JV Twrlr; Var Vllybl; Hon Roll; Vllybl Awd 84; Sprtswrtng 1st Pl 86; 1st & 2nd Pl Twrlng Tm 84-85.

MARINO, ELIZABETH; Sacred Heart Acad; Malverne, NY; (Y); Debate Tm; FTA; Math Clb; NFL; Speech Tm; Teachers Aide; Chorus; Cathlc Fornsc Leag Novice Debate 3rd Plc Trophy 84; Cathlc Frnsc Leag Intermdt Lincol-Douglas Trphy86; &pre-Law.

MARINO, LAURA; Fayetteville-Manlius HS; Manlius, NY; (Y); 70/335; Church Yth Grp; Dance Clb; GAA; Pep Clb; Political Wkr; Service Clb; Ski Clb; SADD; Varsity Clb; School Musical; Dollar For Schlrs Citizens Schlrshp Fndtn 86; Pres Acdmc Fit Awd 86; Villanoua U.

MARINO, MARLEEN; St Francis Prep HS; Glendale, NY; (Y); 150/653; Dance Clb; SADD; Optimate Soc 84; St Johns U; Bus.

MARINO, RIKKI; E J Wilson HS; Rochester, NY; (Y); Yrbk Stf; Rep Stu Cncl; High Hon Roll; Hon Roll; NHS; Schlstc Achvt Soc 83-86; Canton ATC; Rtl Bus.

MARINO, ROBERT; Roosevelt HS; Yonkers, NY; (Y); Wrstlng; Bus.

MARINO, TRACY A; A J Berner HS; Massapequa, NY; (Y); 15/412; Office Aide; SADD; Stage Crew; Nwsp Rptr; Nwsp Stf; Yrbk Bus Mgr; Yrbk Stf; High Hon Roll; NHS; Ntl Merit Ltr; NYS Rgnts Schlrshp Awd; Boston Coll; Fin.

MARINO, VIRGINIA C; St Joseph Hill Acad; Staten Island, NY; (Y); 2/106; Drama Clb; FTA; Spanish Clb; School Play; NHS; Ntl Merit Ltr; NEDT Awd; Sal; Sec Trs Spanish NHS; NY ST Regents Schlrshp 86; AATSP Natl Spnsh Exam 2nd Pl & Hon Ment 85; NY U; Pre-Med.

MARION, KRISTA; Newark SR HS; Newark, NY; (Y); 30/205; Cmnty Wkr; Letterman Clb; Service Clb; Spanish Clb; Varsity Clb; Nwsp Stf; Yrbk Stf; Rep Jr Cls; Trs Cmnty Wkr; Socr; Outstndng Fresh Trk 83-84; Actn Clb 83; Most Imprvd Soccr 84-85; Retl Bus.

MARION, MICHAEL; La Fayette HS; La Fayette, NY; (S); 16/96; Boy Scts; Drama Clb; Model UN; Chorus; Concert Band; Swing Chorus; Var Capt Crs Cntry; Var L Lcrss; High Hon Roll; NHS.

MARION, NANCY; St John The Baptist HS; Central Islip, NY; (Y); Dance Clb; Band; Concert Band; Mrchg Band; School Musical; Hon Roll.

MARK, JENNIFER; HS For The Humanit; New York, NY; (Y); Debate Tm; Drama Clb; Chorus; School Musical; Stage Crew; Variety Show; Lit Mag; High Hon Roll; NHS; 2nd Prize Ntl Lge Of APWI Shrt Stry Cntst HS Stu 86; Theatre.

MARK, LAURA; Washingtonville HS; Washngtnvle, NY; (Y); Computer Clb; Sec Spanish Clb; Var Socr; High Hon Roll; NHS; Fash Inst Tech; Fash Merch.

MARK, SONIA; Catherine Mc Auley HS; Brooklyn, NY; (S); 13/70; Church Choir; Hon Roll; Kingsborough CC; Bus Adm.

MARKAJANI, RACHEL; James E Sperry HS; Rochester, NY; (Y); 63/264; Church Yth Grp; Cmnty Wkr; High Hon Roll; Hon Roll; Secrtry.

MARKARIAN, CHRISTIN M; St Francis Prep Schl; Bayside Queens, NY; (Y); 346/693; Dance Clb; SADD; Mat Maids; Regnts Clg Schlrshp 86; St Johns U; Tchr.

MARKELL, TRENT; Friendship Central Schl; Friendship, NY; (S); 1/33; Trs Pres Church Yth Grp; Band; Jazz Band; Mrchg Band; School Play; Pres Frsh Cls; Pres Soph Cls; Var L Bsktbl; Var L Socr; High Hon Roll; Engrng.

MARKELLO, CHERYL; Eden SR HS; Eden, NY; (Y); Pres VP Church Yth Grp; Sec Chorus; Sec Church Choir; VP Sec Orch; Stu Cncl; JV Var Cheerleading; Stat JV Swmmng; NHS; Varsity Clb; School Musical; Erie Cnty Orchstr 80-86; Area All ST Orchstr 85-86; Potsdam Coll; Communctns.

MARKEY, MARY SUSAN; Herkimer SR HS; Herkimer, NY; (Y); 10/120; Rep Frsh Cls; Rep Soph Cls; Rep Jr Cls; High Hon Roll; Russell Sage Coll; Nrsng.

MARKHAIM, STEFANIE; Mercy HS; Albany, NY; (Y); Hosp Aide; School Play; Yrbk Stf; Stu Cncl; Gym; Socr; Swmmng; Hon Roll; NY ST Bar Assoc; NY ST Mock Trl Partcptn; Blck Womns Assoc Albany-Black Hstry Cont Wnr; Howard U; Theater.

MARKHAM, DANIELLE; Harry S Truman HS; St Albans, NY; (Y); 30/494; Church Yth Grp; Service Clb; Acpl Chr; Band; Chorus; Church Choir; Concert Band; Jazz Band; Rep Stu Cncl; Var Cheerleading; Queens College; Psych.

MARKLE, DEIRDRE A; Saint Francis Prep; Whitestone, NY; (S); 86/745; Church Yth Grp; Girl Scts; Nwsp Rptr; Im Ftbl; Im Sftbl; Im Vllybl; Hon Roll; NHS; Educ.

MARKOWITZ, DEBBIE; Hauppauge HS; Hauppauge, NY; (Y); Cmnty Wkr; Debate Tm; Hosp Aide; Library Aide; SADD; Acpl Chr; Chorus.

MARKOWITZ, MELANIE J; E L Vandermeulen HS; Pt Jefferson, NY; (Y); 13/333; Hosp Aide; SADD; Hon Roll; Jr NHS; NHS.

MARKOWSKI, CHRISTOPHER; Regis HS; Maywood, NJ; (Y); Aud/Vis; Boys Clb Am; Ski Clb; Var Bsbl; JV Socr; High Hon Roll; Hon Roll; Ntl Merit Ltr.

MARKOWSKI, KAREN; Cicero North Syracuse HS; N Syracuse, NY; (S); 43/623; Spanish Clb; Socr; Trk; Vllybl; Math.

MARKS, ALISSA J; Kingston HS; Kingston, NY; (Y); 63/573; Spanish Clb; Ed Nwsp Stf; Rep Bowling; Var Sftbl; Var L Vllybl; High Hon Roll; NHS; Spanish NHS; U Of CT; Cmptr Sci.

MARKS, CATHY; Rhuncbeck Central Schl; Rhinebeck, NY; (Y); Teachers Aide; Stu Of Mnth 86; Bus.

MARKS, CHRISTINE; Ossining HS; Ossining, NY; (Y); German Clb; Band; Orch; Yrbk Sprt Ed; Stat Fld Hcky; High Hon Roll; Hon Roll; Brnze Mdl In Grmn 83; Bus.

MARKS, CHRISTINE; Saratoga Central Catholic HS; Gansevoort, NY; (S); French Clb; Office Aide; Yrbk Ed-Chief; Yrbk Stf; Rep Frsh Cls; Bowling; Tennis; Hon Roll; Acdmc All Amer Schlrs 86; Psychlgy.

MARKS, ELIZABETH; Archbishop Walsh HS; Olean, NY; (Y); 3/50; Dance Clb; Drama Clb; Ski Clb; School Musical; Pres Frsh Cls; VP Soph Cls; Rep Stu Cncl; Capt Cheerleading; High Hon Roll; NHS; Elem/Spec Ed.

MARKUS, REBECCA S; Whitesboro SR HS; Utica, NY; (Y); 27/354; GAA; Intnl Clb; Acpl Chr; Trs Orch; Mgr Stage Crew; Lit Mag; Var JV Tennis; High Hon Roll; Jr NHS; Trs NHS; NYS Regents Schlrshp 86; Rensselaer Polytech Inst Schlrshp; Rensselaer Polytech; Geology.

MARKUSEN, TRICIA; Kendall JR SR HS; Kendall, NY; (S); 1/90; AFS; Ski Clb; Spanish Clb; Concert Band; Mrchg Band; Rep Stu Cncl; Var L Bsktbl; Var L Socr; Var Vllybl; High Hon Roll; Genesee Rgn Leag All-Star Hnrbl Mntn Soccr 85; 1st Chr Flute 85.

MARLATT, AMY LOUISE; Falconer Central HS; Kennedy, NY; (Y); 29/121; Computer Clb; Pres French Clb; JA; Quiz Bowl; Band; Pres Mrchg Band; Orch; School Musical; NHS; Prfct Atten Awd; Hly Nm Schlrsp Our Ldy Of Loreto Chrch 86; Ntnl Schl Orchstr Awd 86; Jamestown Cmnty; Cmptr Sci.

MARLI, RONALD; Monsignor Farrell HS; Staten Island, NY; (Y); Church Yth Grp; Rep Pres Political Wkr; Lit Mag; Pres Rep Jr Cls; Rep Stu Cncl; Hon Roll; Film.

MARLIN, MELISSA A; Cultural Arts HS; Westbury, NY; (Y); Art Clb; Dance Clb; Drama Clb; PAVAS; Acpl Chr; Chorus; School Musical; School Play; Stage Crew; Variety Show; Playwrtng Awd 85; U Of Miami; Musical Theatre.

MARLOWE, JANINE; Northport HS; E Northport, NY; (Y); 4/600; Sec Pep Clb; Pres Orch; Off Jr Cls; Off Sr Cls; JV Socr; Var L Trk; High Hon Roll; Jr NHS; VP NHS; Amrcn Lgn Awd; Bus.

MARLOWE, SHELLY; Franklin Acad; Malone, NY; (Y); 52/266; Hon Roll; Spnsh Awd 99 Avg Spnsh 86; Hnr Rll 85-86; Rochester Inst Tech; Crmnl Jstc.

MAROHN, COLLEEN; Tgonawanda HS; Tonawanda, NY; (Y); 18/219; Church Yth Grp; Drama Clb; Girl Scts; Red Cross Aide; Spanish Clb; Chorus; Concert Band; Stage Crew; Hon Roll; NHS; PA ST; Envrnmntl Engrng.

MAROLDA, GEORGE; St Peters Boys HS; Staten Isld, NY; (Y); 4/165; Im Bowling; Im Ftbl; JV Socr; High Hon Roll; Hon Roll; NHS; Schlrshp St Peters BHS 83-87; Accntng.

MAROLI, DOLORES; Catholic Central HS; Troy, NY; (Y); GAA; Math Clb; Varsity Clb; Variety Show; Yrbk Stf; Rep Frsh Cls; Rep Soph Cls; Sec Trs Jr Cls; VP Sr Cls; Socr; Phys Ftns Awd 84-85; Springfield Coll; Phys Thrpy.

MARONEY, WILLIAM; Allegany Central HS; Allegany, NY; (Y); 10/104; Band; Concert Band; Jazz Band; Mrchg Band; School Musical; Yrbk Stf; High Hon Roll; NHS; Ntl Merit Ltr; Pres Schlr; Rgnts Schlrshp 86; St Bonaventure U Pres Schlrshp 86; Spnsh Awd ACS 86; St Bonaventure U; Pre-Engr.

MAROONEY, RICH; Garden City HS; Garden City, NY; (Y); Service Clb; Nwsp Rptr; Var JV Bsbl; High Hon Roll; NHS; Bus Adm.

MAROTTA, MARK A; Riverhead HS; Hampton Bays, NY; (Y); 1/212; Drama Clb; JCL; Latin Clb; Math Tm; Ski Clb; Ed Yrbk Stf; Pres NHS; Ntl Merit SF; Val; RPI Mdl Exclnce Math & Sci 85; Elec Engrng.

MAROTTA, MARY A; St Joseph Hill Acad; Staten Island, NY; (Y); 37/107; Drama Clb; Keywanettes; NFL; Yrbk Stf; Mgr Socr; Rgnts Schlrshp; Villanova; Comm.

MAROTTE, ROSEMARIE; St John Villa Acad; Staten Island, NY; (Y); 6/123; Drama Clb; Hosp Aide; Math Tm; Sec Service Clb; Chorus; Church Choir; School Musical; School Play; Hon Roll; JR Svc Awd 85; Cert Excllnc Englsh, Bio 85; Nrsng.

MARQUES, ANABELLA; Mineola HS; Mineola, NY; (Y); Church Yth Grp; FBLA; FTA; Mathletes; OEA; Political Wkr; SADD; Thesps; VICA; Yrbk Sprt Ed; Bus.

MARQUETTE IV, CHARLES; Walter Panas HS; Peekskill, NY; (Y); 20/210; FBLA; Office Aide; JV Var Socr; Var Swmmng; Var Trk; High Hon Roll; Hon Roll; NHS; Sunday Schl Trch 85-86; US Naval Acad; Aerontcl Engrng.

MARR, BRENDA; De Ruyter Central HS; De Ruyter, NY; (S); Concert Band; Nwsp Ed-Chief; Sec Soph Cls; Trs Jr Cls; Sec Trs Sr Cls; Var Socr; Var Sftbl; Capt Var Vllybl; NHS; Ntl Merit Ltr; Schlrshp Cup Hghst Avg.

MARR, CLAUDIA M; St Marys Girls HS; Manhasset, NY; (Y); 37/171; French Clb; Hosp Aide; NFL; SADD; Chorus; Nwsp Rptr; Hon Roll; NHS; NEDT Awd; CT Coll; Pltcl Sci.

MARR, DIONNE; Mynderse Acad; Seneca Falls, NY; (S); Church Yth Grp; GAA; Spanish Clb; Capt Var Cheerleading; Var Trk; Hon Roll.

MARR, SUSAN; Waterloo SR HS; Waterloo, NY; (Y); FTA; Pep Clb; Varsity Clb; Pres Frsh Cls; Sec Soph Cls; Rep Jr Cls; Stu Cncl; JV Capt Cheerleading; High Hon Roll; Twrlr; Comm.

MARRA, ANNA; St Edmund HS; Brooklyn, NY; (Y); 2/200; Art Clb; Variety Show; Nwsp Rptr; VP Stu Cncl; Hon Roll; NHS; Ntl Merit Schol; Regnts Schlrshp 86; Itln Assoc Tchrs Schlrshp 86; Fash Inst Tech; Fash Dsgnr.

MARRA, GARY; Manhasset HS; Manhasset, NY; (Y); Mathletes; Service Clb; JV Var Bsbl; JV Var Socr; High Hon Roll; Hon Roll; Engrng.

MARRA, JOHN; Berlin Central Schl; Cropseyville, NY; (Y); Var Bsbl; Var Socr; Var L Wrstlng; Hon Roll; SUNY Albany; Arch.

MARRACELLO, JOSEPH; Nazareth Regional HS; Brooklyn, NY; (Y); 1/300; Math Tm; Nwsp Rptr; Rep Sr Cls; Socr; Trk; NHS; Comp Sci.

MARRANO, LYNN MARIE; Saint Mary HS; Rye Brook, NY; (Y); 6/64; Pep Clb; Capt Bsktbl; Crs Cntry; Sftbl; High Hon Roll; Pres NHS; MVP FAA All Str Gm Grls Bktbl 85; Schlr Athlt Awd US Army Rsrv 84-86; Manhattnvl Coll; Elmntry Ed.

MARRANTINO, JOSEPH; Our Lady Of Lourdes HS; Wappingers Fls, NY; (Y); Church Yth Grp; Math Clb; Math Tm; Lit Mag; Var Crs Cntry; Var Trk; High Hon Roll; Hon Roll; NHS; 1st Pl Engl 84; 7th Conf Crs Cntry 85.

MARRAPESE, AMY J; Mynderse Acad; Seneca Falls, NY; (Y); 14/144; SADD; Sec Trs Band; Jazz Band; Mrchg Band; School Musical; Yrbk Stf; Sec Stu Cncl; Cit Awd; High Hon Roll; NHS; Mary Lou Turkett Ctznshp Awd 84; Regents Schlrshp 86; Geneseo College; Elem Educ.

MARRAST, STEPHANIE; Prospect Heights HS; Brooklyn, NY; (Y); Office Aide; Teachers Aide; School Musical; School Play; Variety Show; Hon Roll; Psych.

MARRELLO, TARA; Rome Catholic HS; Rome, NY; (Y); Hosp Aide; Math Achvmnt Awd 86; Bryant; Cmprs.

MARRERO, LIZ B; John Dewey HS; Brooklyn, NY; (Y); Chorus; Hon Roll; Comp Bus.

MARRIOTT, JOHN; Walt Whitman HS; Huntington Sta, NY; (Y); 128/549; High Hon Roll; Hon Roll; Ntl Merit Ltr; Prfct Atten Awd; Pres Physcl Ftns Awd 83-86; Ntl Spnsh Hnr Soc Schlrshp 85; Acctnt.

MARRIS, TIM; Cazenovia HS; Erieville, NY; (Y); 13/155; Church Yth Grp; Mathletes; Chorus; Pres Stu Cncl; Coach Actv; Var L Wrstlng; NHS; Rotary Awd; John Koerner JR Schlrshp 86; Stu Cncl Schlrshp 86; Citznshp Awd 86; Rochester Inst Tech; Elec Engr.

MARRO, ANTHONY M; Ilion JR SR HS; Ilion, NY; (Y); 15/130; Am Leg Boys St; VP Aud/Vis; CAP; French Clb; Varsity Clb; Yrbk Stf; Var L Bsbl; Var L Bsktbl; Var L Ftbl; Hon Roll; VA Military Inst; Engnrng.

MARROCCO, RENEE; Tottenville HS; Staten Island, NY; (Y); Drill Tm; Off Frsh Cls; Real Estate Law.

MARRONE, CARMELA; Bethpage HS; Plainview, NY; (Y); 12/306; FBLA; Mathletes; SADD; Var Badmtn; Var Tennis; JV Vllybl; Hon Roll; Pres NHS; Med.

MARROON, DEBBIE; Valley Central HS; Walden, NY; (Y); 35/285; Hosp Aide; Band; Color Guard; Concert Band; Mrchg Band; Off Frsh Cls; Off Soph Cls; Off Jr Cls; Off Sr Cls; Stu Cncl.

MARSCH, PETER M; Liverpool HS; Liverpool, NY; (Y); 153/816; Am Leg Boys St; Debate Tm; Rep Stu Cncl; High Hon Roll; NHS; Exploring; Hosp Aide; ROTC; School Musical; Stage Crew; ROTC Perf Awd,Acad Achvt Awd 83-86; Pres Acad Achvt Awd 86; USAF Acad.

MARSCHAUSER, DANA; John H Glenn HS; Greenlawn, NY; (Y); 24/268; French Clb; Letterman Clb; Varsity Clb; Pep Band; Variety Show; Nwsp Stf; Rep Frsh Cls; Rep Soph Cls; Rep Jr Cls; VP Sr Cls; Regents Scholar 86; Bio.

MARSDEN, ALEXANDRA; St John The Baptist HS; Deer Park, NY; (S); 2/546; Sec Math Clb; SADD; Band; Ed Nwsp Stf; Rep Soph Cls; French Hon Soc; Mu Alp Tht; NHS; Ntl Merit Ltr; Hugh O Brien Yth Fndtn Ldrshp Smnr Ambssdr; All Cnty HS Bnd; Tri-M Music Hnr Soc Sec; Duke U.

MARSDEN, ROBERT J; St John The Baptist HS; Deer Park, NY; (S); 3/501; Math Tm; Concert Band; Mrchg Band; JV Var Bsbl; JV Var Bsktbl; French Hon Soc; High Hon Roll; Mu Alp Tht; NHS; Tri-M Msc Hnr Scty 84, 85 & 86; Ntl Sci Olympd Chmstry Awd 85; Cert Of Merit Scl Studies.

MARSEILLE, CAROLYN; Baldwin SR HS; Baldwin, NY; (Y); Dance Clb; French Clb; Sec Key Clb; Service Clb; Acpl Chr; Chorus; Church Choir; Med.

MARSH, DEAN; Cornwall HS; Cornwall Hudson, NY; (Y); Boy Scts; Church Yth Grp; Cmnty Wkr; Drama Clb; Library Aide; Math Clb; Math Tm; Science Clb; Spanish Clb; Thesps; Intl Frgn Lang Awd 84; Johnson & Wales; Acctg.

MARSH, JOHN; St Joseph By The Sea HS; Staten Island, NY; (S); Art Clb; Boy Scts; Var JV Bsbl; Hon Roll; Hnrs Cls 84-86; Bus.

MARSH, KELLY; Brockport HS; Adams Basin, NY; (Y); 16/315; VP Church Yth Grp; Ski Clb; Spanish Clb; Church Choir; Concert Band; Mrchg Band; Symp Band; Yrbk Phtg; High Hon Roll; NHS; Cedarville Coll; Elem Educ.

MARSH, ROBIN S; Randolph Central HS; Kennedy, NY; (Y); 10/86; Am Leg Aux Girls St; Drama Clb; French Clb; Band; Yrbk Ed-Chief; JV Var Bsktbl; Var L Crs Cntry; JV Var Trk; NHS; Emphasis Excllnc Prog Jamestown CC 86; Rochester Inst Of Tech; Engrng.

MARSH, STEVE; Massena Central HS; Massena, NY; (Y); Key Clb; Lit Mag; JV Var Bsktbl; Im Vllybl; Hon Roll; NHS; Prfct Atten Awd; Pres Schlr; Acad Banquet 86; SUNY; Engr Sci.

MARSH, TODD A; Hamburg SR HS; Hamburg, NY; (Y); 5/385; Church Yth Grp; Band; Jazz Band; Orch; School Musical; Hon Roll; NHS; Concert Band; Mrchg Band; Symp Band; Top Ten; U Hnrs Prgm Schlrshp; Rgnts Schlrshp; SUNY; Arch.

MARSH, TOM W; Stamford Central Schl; Stamford, NY; (Y); 3/24; Band; Chorus; Concert Band; Mrchg Band; Yrbk Bus Mgr; Hon Roll; Kiwanis Awd; Aud/Vis; FBLA; Regents, Alumni & Engelke Schlrshp 86; Cazenovia Coll; Intr Dsgn.

MARSHALL, ELENA R; Liverpool HS; Liverpool, NY; (Y); 72/814; Drama Clb; Girl Scts; Hosp Aide; Pres VP Library Aide; Temple Yth Grp; Stage Crew; Elks Awd; Hon Roll; NHS; Eng Dept Hnr Awd 85; Brandies U; Biochem.

MARSHALL, MAUREEN; Newburgh Free Acad; New Windsor, NY; (Y); French Clb; GAA; Pep Clb; Spanish Clb; Pres Sr Cls; Var Bsktbl; French Hon Soc; High Hon Roll; Opt Clb Awd; VFW Awd; Grace Clark Mem Sports Awd 84.

MARSHALL, MICHELLE; Cardinal O Hara HS; Buffalo, NY; (Y); Drama Clb; Spanish Clb; School Play; Yrbk Stf; Hon Roll; Canisius Coll; Mgmt.

MARSHALL, RANDY; Mayfield HS; Mayfield, NY; (Y); Drama Clb; VP Sec Varsity Clb; School Musical; Stage Crew; Rep Frsh Cls; Rep Soph Cls; Rep Jr Cls; Capt Var Bsbl; Capt Var Bsktbl; Capt Var Socr; MVP-BSKTBL, Bsbl, Scr, Tri Vly Hi Scorrer Bkstbl, Athl Yr, All St Tm, Schlrshps 4 Sprts 85-86; Le Moyne Coll; Comp Sci.

MARSHALL, SCOTT; North Rose-Wolcott HS; North Rose, NY; (Y); Am Leg Boys St; Church Yth Grp; Chorus; School Musical; VP Frsh Cls; VP Soph Cls; VP Jr Cls; Var Socr; Var Swmmng; Var Tennis; Bus Adm.

MARSHALL, TIMOTHY J; Gates-Chili SR HS; Rochester, NY; (Y); 46/447; Chess Clb; Math Clb; Ski Clb; Spanish Clb; High Hon Roll; NHS; Rgnts Schlrshp 86; Rochester IT; Micr Engr.

MARSHEL, TABATHA; James Madison HS; Brooklyn, NY; (Y); 55/756; Debate Tm; Teachers Aide; School Play; NHS; Prfct Atten Awd; SUNY; Engl.

MARTAKIS, NICK; Commack High Schl North; E Northport, NY; (Y); Church Yth Grp; SADD; Band; Tennis; Pace U; Acctg.

MARTELLO, JOHN T; T R Proctor HS; Utica, NY; (Y); 62/220; Nwsp Stf; Yrbk Sprt Ed; Rep Sr Cls; Rep Stu Cncl; Var Capt Bsbl; Hon Roll; Prfct Atten Awd; Baseball Schlrshp; Utica Coll; Crmnl Just.

MARTELLO, MICHAEL; Holy Trinity DHS; Hicksville, NY; (S); 13/313; Math Clb; Ski Clb; SADD; School Musical; School Play; Variety Show; Stu Cncl; Hon Roll; NHS; Ntl Merit Schol; Bus Mngmnt.

MARTENSEN, ERIK; Centereach HS; Centereach, NY; (Y); Boy Scts; FTA; JV Socr; NHS; German Hnr Soc 85; Steuben Awd 85; Aerosp Engrng.

MARTER, CHRISTINE; Harry S Truman HS; Bronx, NY; (Y); Sftbl; Capt Vllybl; Bus.

MARTHOL, MARIE M; St Francis Prep Schl; Jamaica, NY; (Y); 153/653; Library Aide; Science Clb; Yrbk Stf; L Crs Cntry; Im Ftbl; L Trk; Ntl Merit SF; Optimate Soc 83; Peer Cnslng/Tutoring 85; Ethnic Org 83-84; Cornell U; Bio.

MARTIN, ADAM; Riverhead HS; Riverhead, NY; (Y); 20/300; Chess Clb; Church Yth Grp; Cmnty Wkr; French Clb; Off ROTC; Science Clb; Drill Tm; Stu Cncl; Im Bowling; Var Trk; Dstngshd Cadet NJROTC 85; Cornell U; Vet.

MARTIN, CAROL A; Newfane HS; Newfane, NY; (Y); 10/184; Church Yth Grp; Varsity Clb; Band; Chorus; School Musical; JV Var Sftbl; JV Var Vllybl; Hon Roll; Sec NHS; Extraordnry Christian Stu Of Amer 86; All Cnty Chorus 86; Outstdng Band & Chorus Stu 86; Philadelphia Coll Of Bible.

MARTIN, CAROL A; Patchogue-Medford HS; Patchogue, NY; (S); 2/653; FBLA; VP Band; Orch; Var Badmtn; JV Tennis; Cit Awd; French Hon Soc; Hon Roll; Sec NHS; Acctg.

MARTIN, CATHERINE E; Cooperstown Central HS; New Lisbon, NY; (Y); 1/97; Capt Quiz Bowl; Band; Drm Mjr(t); Pep Band; School Musical; Rep Stu Cncl; Var Cheerleading; NHS; Ntl Merit SF; Averell Schlrshp-Hghst Avg; 2nd Pl Dist Amer Legion Oratorical Cont; Frnch Awd; Harvard; Physics.

MARTIN, CHRIS; Niskayuna HS; Schdy, NY; (Y); French Clb; Key Clb; Pep Clb; Varsity Clb; JV Ftbl; Var L Ice Hcky; Hon Roll; NHS; Cert Of Merit In Frnch 86; Cert Of Merit In Phy Ed 86; NY ST Bnghmtn; Bio Chmstry.

MARTIN, CHRISTIAN; Lasalle Military Acad; Levittown, NY; (Y); 1/87; ROTC; Scholastic Bowl; Nwsp Stf; Yrbk Phtg; Var Bsbl; Jr NHS; NHS; RPI Mdl Outstndng Math & Sci Stu 86; Genl Exclnc Awd 1st Mrt La Salle 85; Med Dctr.

MARTIN, CHRISTINE; Clayton A Bouton HS; Voorheesville, NY; (Y); 4/112; Band; Stage Crew; Rep Stu Cncl; Var Cheerleading; High Hon Roll; Trs NHS; Ntl Merit Ltr; Pres Schlr; Nwsp Rptr; Var Bsktbl; Spec Svc Awd Hnr Soc, NYS Rgnts Schlrshp 86; Ithaca Coll; Phy Thrpy.

MARTIN, CHRISTINE J; Miller Place HS; Miller Place, NY; (Y); 17/195; Art Clb; Drama Clb; French Clb; Political Wkr; Varsity Clb; Lit Mag; Mgr Crs Cntry; Var Trk; High Hon Roll; NHS; SUNY Binghamton; Hist.

MARTIN, COLLEEN; Notre Dame Acad; Staten Island, NY; (Y); Cmnty Wkr; Capt Var Swmmng; Hon Roll; NHS; Sistr Cnciola Awd-Outstndng Athlt & Schlr-Swmmng 85-86; Sistr Kly Awd-Vrstl & Mst Dedctd Swmmr 84-85.

MARTIN, DALE; Webster HS; Webster, NY; (Y); 125/500; Church Yth Grp; Concert Band; Var Golf; Natl Prsbytrn Schlr 86; Wms Clb Cmmnty Srv Schlrshp 86; Wooster Coll OH; Accntng.

MARTIN, DANA; James E Sperry HS; Rochester, NY; (Y); 15/271; Pres Church Yth Grp; SADD; Var L Bsbl; French Hon Soc; Hon Roll; Sec NHS; Ntl Merit Ltr; Pres Acdmc Fit Awd 86; NYS Rgnts Schlrshp 86; Acdmc Ltr 85; Suny At Bflo; Engrng.

MARTIN, DAWN J; Williamsville East HS; Williamsville, NY; (Y); Am Leg Aux Girls St; Drama Clb; Band; Concert Band; Orch; High Hon Roll; NHS; All ST Orch Wind Ensem 85-86; Ntl Tchrs Wrtng Cntst 85.

MARTIN, DAWN R; Hillcrest HS; Jamaica, NY; (Y); 24/801; Intnl Clb; Orch; Yrbk Phtg; Hon Roll; NHS; Spanish NHS; Spnsh Awd Lvl II 83; Martel Cntst Awd 3rd Pl 85; Acadmc Olympcs Tm 84; NY U; Lingstcs.

MARTIN, DEA; Frontier SR HS; Lakeview, NY; (Y); Drama Clb; French Clb; Ski Clb; Chorus; Jazz Band; Stage Crew; Var Tennis; Hon Roll; Lion Awd; X-Ray Tech.

MARTIN, DENA; Sandy Creek Central Schl; Lacona, NY; (S); 9/88; Trs Church Yth Grp; Trs JCL; Library Aide; Nwsp Stf; Yrbk Stf; Var L Cheerleading; Hon Roll; NHS; Prfct Atten Awd; Bio.

MARTIN, DONNA; Commack HS South; Commack, NY; (Y); Office Aide; Church Choir; Lit Mag; Var Bsktbl; JV Mgr(s); Stat Tennis; Var Twrlr; Var Capt Vllybl; Hon Roll; Girls Ldr Corps 83-86; Gldn Quill Awd 85; All Lge All Conf Plyr-Vlybl 86.

MARTIN, GEORGE; Aviation HS; New York, NY; (S); 44/416; Computer Clb; Nwsp Rptr; Nwsp Sprt Ed; Var Bsktbl; Im Ftbl; NHS; Syracuse U; Aerosp Engrng.

MARTIN, GEORGE; Berne Knox Westerlo HS; Altamont, NY; (Y); Yrbk Sprt Ed; Lit Mag; Pres Stu Cncl; Bsbl; Bsktbl; Bowling; Socr; High Hon Roll; Hon Roll; NHS; Comm Art.

MARTIN, HEATHER; Gowanda Central HS; Perrysburg, NY; (Y); 4/130; Dance Clb; Ski Clb; Thesps; Jazz Band; School Musical; Var Bsktbl; Var Trk; Var Vllybl; High Hon Roll; Pres NHS; Mst Outstndng Grl Athltc 86; Amer Lgn Hgh Hnr Awd 85 & 86; Rochester Inst.

MARTIN, JAMES; Saint Marys Boys HS; Mineola, NY; (Y); Cmnty Wkr; Drama Clb; Political Wkr; Ski Clb; School Musical; School Play; Nwsp Rptr; Yrbk Stf; Trk; Hon Roll; Med.

MARTIN, JENNIFER; Villa Maria Acad; Buffalo, NY; (Y); VP Pres Church Yth Grp; Girl Scts; JV Capt Bsktbl; Var Sftbl; Var Vllybl; Cheektowaga YES Yth Awd 83-84 & 84-85; Med Tech.

MARTIN, JOHN; Miller Place HS; Miller Place, NY; (Y); 48/248; Boy Scts; Varsity Clb; Capt Crs Cntry; Mgr(s); Trk; Hon Roll; Acdmc Hon Indstrl Arts 83-84; Winter Trck Tm MVP 85-86; All Leag & All Conf Sprng Trck 85-86; Mech Engrng.

MARTIN, LAURA; Anatego JR SR HS; Otego, NY; (Y); French Clb; Chorus; Im Mgr Socr; Hon Roll; Anml Hsbndry.

MARTIN, LAURA; Clayton A Bouton JR SR HS; Slingerlands, NY; (Y); Church Yth Grp; French Clb; Band; Chorus; Concert Band; Var Bsktbl; Var Swmmng; Var Trk; Cit Awd; DAR Awd; RPI Sci Math Medal Awd 86.

MARTIN, LAURIE A; Susquehanna Valley HS; Binghamton, NY; (Y); 18/183; Cmnty Wkr; Service Clb; Ski Clb; SADD; Chorus; Concert Band; Mrchg Band; Lit Mag; Jr NHS; NY ST Regnts Schlrshp 86; SUNY Plattsburgh; Intprtr.

MARTIN, LISA; Northstar Christian Acad; Rochester, NY; (S); Church Yth Grp; Sec Frsh Cls; Sec Soph Cls; Sec Jr Cls; Var Capt Bsktbl; Var Capt Socr; NHS; MVP Soccer 86; Ntl Phys Ed Awd 86; Ntl Sci Merit Awd 85; Acad All Am Awd 85; Engrng.

MARTIN, MICHELLE L; Pulaski JR/Sr HS; Richland, NY; (S); Church Yth Grp; French Clb; GAA; Girl Scts; Chorus; Church Choir; Vllybl; Cit Awd; Snow Awd 84; Cincinnati Bible Coll; Elem Tch.

MARTIN, PAMELA JEAN; Greenport HS; E Marion, NY; (Y); 7/45; Pres VP Church Yth Grp; Pres VP 4-H; Math Clb; Yrbk Bus Mgr; Stu Cncl; High Hon Roll; Hon Roll; Lion Awd; NHS; Rotary Awd; Stu Agnst Substnc Abuse-Creatr & Pres 85-86; Prncpls Awd-Outstndg Ldrshp & Svc 86; Southern Seminary JC; Equn Sci.

MARTIN, PATRICIA; Sacred Heart HS; Yonkers, NY; (Y); 11/260; Aud/Vis; Church Yth Grp; Dance Clb; Chorus; Capt Cheerleading; Hon Roll; Jr NHS; NHS; NEDT Awd; Art Clb; Fordham; Liberal Arts.

MARTIN, PATRICIA A; Albertus Magnus HS; Spring Valley, NY; (Y); Church Yth Grp; Cmnty Wkr; Drama Clb; GAA; Girl Scts; Service Clb; SADD; School Musical; Socr; Cit Awd; John Jay U; Crmnl Just.

MARTIN, RICK; Waterville Central HS; Waterville, NY; (Y); 15/100; Varsity Clb; JV Bsktbl; Var Bowling; Var Ftbl; Var Trk; High Hon Roll; Hon Roll; NHS; SUNY; Wildlife.

MARTIN, ROBERT; Mynderse Acad; Seneca Falls, NY; (Y); Church Yth Grp; Intnl Clb; Model UN; Spanish Clb; Lcrss; Wt Lftg; Wrstlng; High Hon Roll; Hon Roll; Law.

MARTIN, SUSAN; Mohawk Central Schl; Ilion, NY; (Y); 22/96; Pres Church Yth Grp; Exploring; Hosp Aide; SADD; Varsity Clb; Mrchg Band; Fld Hcky; Powder Puff Ftbl; Trk; NHS; Keuka Merit Awd 86-87; Keuka Coll; Pre-Med.

MARTIN, TAMMY L; Johnson City HS; Johnson City, NY; (Y); 6/198; Trs Church Yth Grp; Cmnty Wkr; Girl Scts; SADD; Nwsp Rptr; NHS; Voice Dem Awd; High Hon Roll; Hon Roll; Grl Sct Gld Awd 86; Acdmc Achvmnt Awds 84-85; Rgnts Schlrshp; Russell Sage; Physcl Thrpy.

MARTIN, TARA; Marlboro HS; Marlboro, NY; (Y); SADD; Yrbk Stf; Sftbl; NHS; Pre-Med.

MARTIN, TOM; Newburgh Free Acad; Newburgh, NY; (Y); Bsbl; Hon Roll; Prfct Atten Awd; Engrng.

MARTIN, TRAVIS L; S New Berlin Central HS; New Berlin, NY; (Y); 18/38; Am Leg Boys St; Boy Scts; Band; Concert Band; Mrchg Band; School Play; Ftbl; Chenango Cnty Frm Bureu Ctznshp Awd 85; Morrisville Ag & Tech; Lab Tech.

MARTIN, VALERIE; Wilson Central HS; Wilson, NY; (Y); Pres Church Yth Grp; Exploring; FCA; Hosp Aide; Chorus; Church Choir; Var L Bsktbl; Var L Trk; Hon Roll.

MARTIN, VICTORIA; Hugh C Williams HS; Canton, NY; (Y); AFS; Off Frsh Cls; Off Soph Cls; Sec Jr Cls; High Hon Roll; NHS; U Of NH; Bus.

MARTIN, WADE A; Downsville Central Schl; Downsville, NY; (Y); Am Leg Boys St; Varsity Clb; Band; VP Frsh Cls; Trs Soph Cls; Rep Jr Cls; VP Stu Cncl; Var Bsktbl; Var Socr; High Hon Roll; Comptr Sci.

MARTINECK, CHRISTOPHER; St Josephs Collegiate Inst; Grand Island, NY; (Y); Boys Clb Am; Church Yth Grp; Model UN; Quiz Bowl; Im Bsktbl; Golf; NHS; Math.

MARTINEZ, ALICE; Walton HS; Bronx, NY; (Y); Church Yth Grp; Yrbk Stf; NHS; Teachers Aide; Yrbk Phtg; Acad Olympcs 85-86; Pre-Tchng Acad 85-86; Tchng.

MARTINEZ, ANNALISA; Cardinal Mooney HS; Rochester, NY; (Y); 22/317; Hosp Aide; School Play; Rep Frsh Cls; VP Soph Cls; Pres Jr Cls; Var L Socr; Var L Trk; French Hon Soc; Hon Roll; Pres NHS; Cornell U; Indstrl Rltns.

MARTINEZ, ANNETTE; Grace Dodge V HS; Bronx, NY; (Y); Dance Clb; Chorus; Acctng.

MARTINEZ, CINDY; Herbert H Uhman HS; Bronx, NY; (Y); Office Aide; Band; Concert Band; Orch; JV Cheerleading; Hon Roll; Prfct Atten Awd; Comp Hnrs 85-86; Math Hnrs 84-86; DP.

MARTINEZ, DEBORAH; St Catharine Acad; Bronx, NY; (Y); 41/198; Hosp Aide; Ski Clb; SADD; Yrbk Stf; St Johns U; Jrnlsm.

MARTINEZ, DIANA; St Johns Prep; Jackson Hts, NY; (Y); Chorus; Gym; Tennis; Arch.

MARTINEZ, GLADYS M; Christopher Columbus HS; Bronx, NY; (Y); 9/691; Key Clb; Teachers Aide; Band; Yrbk Stf; High Hon Roll; Hon Roll; NHS; Cert Outstndng Grades Math,Sci,Eng,Socl Stud And Spnsh 82-86; Peak 83-86; Regnts Schlrshp 86; Cornell U; Pre Med.

MARTINEZ, JASON L; St Francis Prep; Richmond Hill, NY; (S); 190/746; Var Capt Bsbl; Im Ftbl; Im Vllybl; NHS; Wt Lftg; Optimate Awd 84-85; Mst Imprvd Plyr JV Bsbl Capt 84-85; Coaches Awd JV Bsbl 83-84; Bus.

MARTINEZ, JOSE; James Monne HS; New York, NY; (Y); Computer Clb; Library Aide; Office Aide; Teachers Aide; School Play; Hon Roll; Atten 84; NY Inst Tech; Comp Engr.

MARTINEZ, JOSEPH; Oveens Voc HS; Corona, NY; (Y); 84/335; Var Bsbl; John Jay Coll; Crmnl Jstc.

MARTINEZ, JUAN; Eastern District HS; Brooklyn, NY; (Y); Chess Clb; Math Tm; Teachers Aide; Yrbk Stf; Cert Of Awd Eng And Socl Stu 86; Jrnlsm.

MARTINEZ, MELISSA; Droger B Chaffer HS; FPO New York, NY; (Y); 2/21; FBLA; Nwsp Ed-Chief; Nwsp Stf; Lit Mag; Sec Sr Cls; Var Cheerleading; Var Sftbl; VP NHS; Pres Schlr; Sal; Nrotc Schlrshp 86; U Of Rochester; Naval Aviat.

MARTINEZ, MILDRED; De Witt Clinton HS; Bronx, NY; (Y); FNA; Key Clb; Math Tm; Office Aide; Drill Tm; Nwsp Rptr; Jr NHS; Prfct Atten Awd; Cert Merit Engl 84; Handbl Tm 85-86; Acdmc Olympcs Tm 85-86; Bus.

MARTINEZ, ROSA; John Dewey HS; Brooklyn, NY; (Y); Jrnlsm.

MARTINEZ, ROSANNA; Hempstead HS; Hempstead, NY; (S); Library Aide; Spanish Clb; High Hon Roll; Hon Roll; Ntl Merit Schol; Cert Of Excllnc 85; Medls In Excllnc & Relgn 83; Cert Of Prfct Attend 83; Hofstra U; Med.

MARTINEZ, RUEBEN; Bronx HS Of Sci; Laurelton, NY; (Y); Chess Clb; Math Tm; Spanish Clb; Concert Band; Im Bsktbl; Im Ftbl; Im Sftbl.

MARTINEZ, SERGIO; Art & Design HS; New York, NY; (Y); Art Clb; Church Yth Grp; French Clb; Speech Tm; Teachers Aide; Bsktbl; High Hon Roll; Hon Roll; Prfct Atten Awd; Hnr Awd Excllnc Global Hist II 84; NY Inst Of Tech; Arch.

MARTINEZ, VINCENT; Lindenhurst HS; Lindenhurst, NY; (Y); Cmnty Wkr; Exploring; Band; Mrchg Band; JV Lcrss; Law Enfrcmnt.

MARTINI, JUDE T; Newburgh Free Acad; Newburgh, NY; (Y); 5/621; Pres Church Yth Grp; Church Choir; Trs Jazz Band; Trs Soph Cls; God Cntry Awd; Pres Schlr; Spanish NHS; Service Clb; Band; Concert Band; Pres Acdmc Ftnss Awd 86; Top 10 Sci & Mthawd 86; Adv Plcmnt Lit Awd 86; Frdhm U; Pol Sci.

MARTINI, MARIA; New Rochelle HS; New Rochelle, NY; (Y); Dance Clb; Debate Tm; Pres Drama Clb; Hosp Aide; Pep Clb; Chorus; School Musical; School Play; VP Jr Cls; VP Sr Cls; Bst Dncr In Schl Plys 84 & 86; Bstn Coll; Doctor.

MARTINI, RICHARD B; Moore Catholic HS; Staten Island, NY; (Y); 46/178; Computer Clb; Im Bowling; Socr; Im Vllybl; Hon Roll; NY St Regents Schlrshp 86; NYU.

MARTINO, JOSEPH; Archbishop Molloy HS; Middle Vlg, NY; (Y); 125/385; Drama Clb; Bsktbl; Ftbl; Sftbl.

MARTINO, LINDA; Notre Dame Bishop Gibbons HS; Duanesburg, NY; (Y); French Clb; Band; Concert Band; Jazz Band; Mrchg Band; School Musical; School Play; Variety Show; Hon Roll; Accntng.

MARTINO, RICHARD C; Smithtown High School West; Smithtown, NY; (Y); Teachers Aide; High Hon Roll; Hon Roll; NHS; Itln Hnr Soc 84-86; NY ST Regents Sclrp 86; Hofstra U; Pre Med.

MARTINO, RON; Aquinas Inst; Rochester, NY; (Y); Computer Clb; Debate Tm; Nwsp Stf; Rep Soph Cls; Rep Jr Cls; Stu Cncl; High Hon Roll; Clarkson U; Mech Engnrng.

MARTINOLLI JR, ROBERT; Monsignor Farrell HS; Staten Island, NY; (S); 60/350; Aud/Vis; Chess Clb; Dance Clb; English Clb; SADD; Teachers Aide; Varsity Clb; Yrbk Stf; Off Frsh Cls; Off Soph Cls; Recgntn Comm Person Superdance MDA 85-86; Spcl Awd Ftbl 85; West Point; Elec Engrng.

MARTINS, CRISTINE; Sacred Heart Acad; Mineola, NY; (S); Art Clb; French Clb; Speech Tm; VP Chorus; School Musical; Lit Mag; Hon Roll; NHS; Miss Metro NY Natl Teen-Ager Ctznshp & Tlnt Wnnr 85.

MARTINS, LYNN M; Sleepy Hollow HS; N Tarrytown, NY; (Y); 9/189; Sec Exploring; Lit Mag; Var L Sftbl; Var L Tennis; High Hon Roll; NHS; NY ST Sci Supv Asn Chem Awd 85; Semi-Fin In NCTE Wrtng Comptn 85; U Of DE; Nutrtnl Sci.

MARTINUCCI, MICHAEL; Westlake HS; Hawthorne, NY; (Y); Boy Scts; Church Yth Grp; Ski Clb; JV Bsktbl; JV Var Ftbl; Sftbl; Wrstlng; Hon Roll; Itln Hnr Soc; Comp.

MARTIRANO, DAVE; Mahopac HS; Mahopac, NY; (Y); 75/409; Cmnty Wkr; VP Soph Cls; Pres Jr Cls; Pres Stu Cncl; Pres Bsktbl; Var JV Ftbl; Var JV Lcrss; Var JV Wt Lftg; Dnfth Awd; Hon Roll; I Dare You Awd Free Schlrshp Wk Camp; Math.

MARTIZEZ, MARLENE; Cathedral HS; New York, NY; (Y); 66/277; Cmnty Wkr; Girl Scts; Band; Mrchg Band; Regents Diploma 86; John Jay Coll; Prosctng Atty.

MARTONE, CHRISTINA A; Smithtown East; Nesconset, NY; (Y); Gym; High Hon Roll; Jr NHS; NHS; Pres Schlr; Italian Hnr Scty; NY ST Rg Nts Schlrshp; Pre-Med.

MARTORANO, DONNA; Washingtonville HS; Washingtnvle, NY; (Y); Ski Clb; Trk; Orange County CC; Bus Mgmt.

MARTUCCI, DOREEN; Ursuline HS; Larchmont, NY; (Y); Cmnty Wkr; Im Trk; Piano Awd 84; Tobe Colburn; Fshn Dsgn.

MARTUCCI, MICHILINA T; St Joseph By The Sea HS; Staten Island, NY; (Y); 1/241; Am Leg Aux Girls St; Yrbk Stf; Pres Frsh Cls; Pres Soph Cls; VP Sr Cls; Rep Stu Cncl; NHS; Ntl Merit Ltr; NEDT Awd; Rgnts Schlrshp 85-86; Amercn Chemcl Soc Chem Awd 85; Wagner Coll; Chem.

MARTUCCI, PEGGY; St Catharine Acad; Bronx, NY; (Y); Cmnty Wkr; Dance Clb; Ski Clb; Church Choir; Bsbl; Bsktbl; Coach Actv; Sftbl; Trk; Excllnc NYS Physcl Ftns Tst 84-86; Actng.

MARTUSCELLO, KEVIN; Bishop Scully HS; Amsterdam, NY; (Y); Latin Clb; Yrbk Stf; VP Frsh Cls; Im Bsktbl; JV Ftbl; Var Golf; Northeastern U; Phrmcy.

MARTUSCELLO, KIM; Bishop Scully HS; Amsterdam, NY; (Y); Latin Clb; Math Clb; JV Capt Bsktbl; Var Capt Sftbl; Hon Roll; Mu Alp Tht; NHS; Vrsty Ltr In Sftbl 84-86; Marine Bio.

MARTUSCELLO, RENEE; Amsterdam HS; Amsterdam, NY; (Y); 16/294; Varsity Clb; VP Soph Cls; Rep Jr Cls; Off Sr Cls; Capt Cheerleading; NHS; R J Mc Nulty Schlrshp Awd 86; Utica Coll Of Syracuse U; Nrsng.

MARUBASHI, RIKA; The High School Of Art And Design; Forest Hills, NY; (Y); Art Clb; Dance Clb; FTA; Teachers Aide; Cit Awd; French Hon Soc; Hon Roll; Prfct Atten Awd; Cert Of Merit Spark/Peer Cnslng 86; Cert Of Cmpltn Advrtsng Design Course 85; Schl Of Visual Arts; Illstrtr.

MARULLI, ROSEANN; St Edmund HS; Brooklyn, NY; (S); 6/185; Sec Trs French Clb; Hosp Aide; Lit Mag; Rep Frsh Cls; Rep Soph Cls; Hon Roll; NCTE Awd; NHS; NEDT Awd; Natl Ldrshp Orgnztn 82-85; Partl Schlrshp 83-85; JR Svc Awd 83-84.

MARUSARZ, LEANDRA; Dundee Central Schl; Dundee, NY; (Y); 5/90; Church Yth Grp; French Clb; GAA; Teachers Aide; Church Choir; Stage Crew; JV Var Sftbl; High Hon Roll; Hon Roll; Prfct Atten Awd; Ntl Engl Merit Awd NEMA 85-86; SUNY Delhi; Vet Technlgy.

MARVIN, REBECCA; Lake Placid Central HS; Lake Placid, NY; (Y); Am Leg Aux Girls St; Key Clb; Library Aide; SADD; Band; Chorus; Concert Band; Jazz Band; Mrchg Band; Yrbk Stf; Congressnl Sem 86; Bryant & Stratton; Sec Asst.

MARX, STEPHANIE; Tonawanda SR HS; Tonawanda, NY; (Y); 10/220; Trs French Clb; JV Cheerleading; JV Trk; Hon Roll; NHS; Quality Awd 86; Pres Acad Ftns Awd 86; Faculty Hnr Awd 86; NY U; Bus.

MARYJO, INDOVINO; East Meadow HS; East Meadow, NY; (Y); Chorus; Cheerleading; Sftbl; Cit Awd; Hon Roll.

MARZOCHI, MARIA A; Bishop Grimes HS; Syracuse, NY; (Y); 2/146; Yrbk Stf; Var Cheerleading; High Hon Roll; NHS; Sal; NYS Rgnts Schlrshp; Italian Hnr Soc; Holy Cross Bk Prz-Outstndg JR; Natl Sci Olympiad; U Of Rochester; Bio.

MARZOLF, SHANNON; Alexander Central HS; Darien Center, NY; (Y); 15/84; Office Aide; Spanish Clb; Chorus; Capt Color Guard; Jr NHS; NHS; Prfct Atten Awd; Alfred Ag & Tech Coll; Arch.

MARZOLINO, MICHELLE; St Marys HS; Cheektowaga, NY; (Y); 28/187; Pres Camera Clb; Church Yth Grp; Ski Clb; Yrbk Stf; Var Bowling; JV Sftbl; NHS; Rcgntn In Frnch, Kybrdng & Rlgn; U Of Buffalo; Cmmnctn.

MARZULLO, ROSARIA; Mount St Mary Acad; Buffalo, NY; (Y); Chorus; Yrbk Stf; Rep Frsh Cls; Pres Soph Cls; Pres Jr Cls; Rep Stu Cncl; Hon Roll; Won Coll Schlrshp To Ok City U 85; Won Mdlng Schlrshp 85; Crowned Miss Western Ny 85; Bus.

MASARIK, JOSEPH; St Dominic HS; Levittown, NY; (Y); Cmnty Wkr; Drama Clb; 4-H; School Musical; School Play; Bsktbl; Ftbl; 4-H Awd; Hon Roll.

MASCARENHAS, EMILY; New Rochelle HS; New Rochelle, NY; (Y); GAA; Girl Scts; French Clb; Var Trk; Med.

MASCETTA, ROBERT; Carmel HS; Holmes, NY; (Y); Camera Clb; Yrbk Phtg; Yrbk Stf; Var L Ftbl; Var L Trk; JV Vllybl; Trphy Awd Brkng Trck Rcrd 86; Trophy Awd Mst Outstndg Offnsv Lnmn Ftbll 83; Counsel Fllw HS Prssr 86.

MASCIA, CHRISTOPHER; Hamburg SR HS; Hamburg, NY; (Y); 18/384; Cmnty Wkr; Sec Spanish Clb; Band; Jazz Band; Orch; Symp Band; Rep Sr Cls; JV Ftbl; JV Lcrss; Hon Roll.

MASCIANGELO, JOHN; Fairport HS; Fairport, NY; (Y); 10/650; Yrbk Stf; Rep Soph Cls; VP Jr Cls; Rep Sr Cls; Rep Stu Cncl; Var Trk; VP NHS; Spanish NHS; Spanish Achvt Awd 85; Ledrshp Awd 85; U MI Ann Arbor; Med.

MASELLA, DENISE; St Joseph By The Sea; Staten Island, NY; (Y); Art Clb; Rep Soph Cls; Rep Jr Cls; Hon Roll; NEDT Awd; Spnsh Achvt Awd 84; Suny; Bus.

MASERCOLA, TINAMARIE; Niskayuna HS; Schdy, NY; (Y); Teachers Aide; Sec Frsh Cls; Sec Soph Cls; Sec Jr Cls; Sec Sr Cls; Var Capt Cheerleading; Var Capt Pom Pon; Acpl Chr; Chorus; Church Choir; Schl Svc Awd 86; Prcnpls Awd 86; Coll St Rose; Elem Ed.

MASI, SUZANNE; Lindenhurst HS; Lindenhurst, NY; (Y); 88/548; Hosp Aide; Spanish Clb; Drill Tm; Stage Crew; Twrlr; Hon Roll; Jr NHS; Kiwanis Awd; NHS; Candy Strpng Awd-100 Hrs 86; Farmingdale; Nrsng.

MASIELLO, DOUGLAS S; Allendale Columbia Schl; Rochester, NY; (Y); 3/38; VP Sr Cls; Bsbl; Bsktbl; Socr; NY ST Rgnts Schlrshp 86; Bus Mgmt.

MASIELLO, JOHN; Archbishop Molloy HS; Flushing, NY; (Y); 15/400; Chess Clb; Computer Clb; NHS; Ntl Merit SF; Cong James Scheuer Awd 86; Marcellin Champ Awd Svc 86; NY Tele Co Schlrshp 86; NY U; Med.

MASIELLO, ROBERT; All Hallows HS; Bronx, NY; (Y); 36/140; Boys Clb Am; Var L Bsktbl; Concordia Coll; Bus Adm.

MASILLO, CHRIS; Mephann HS; W Bellmore, NY; (Y); Var Lcrss; Tennis; Var Wrstlng; Boston U; Bus.

MASLAK, JOSEPH; Guilderland Central HS; Albany, NY; (Y); Varsity Clb; Crs Cntry; Ftbl; Trk; Wt Lftg; Hon Roll; Prfct Atten Awd; Hnr Awd-Spnsh III 85-86; Hnr Awd-Spnsh II 84-85; Hnr Awd-Math I 82-83; Math.

MASLEN, LISA; Paul V Moore HS; Mallory, NY; (Y); Church Yth Grp; Band; Symp Band; Hon Roll; Brigham Young U; Bus.

MASLONA, SERENA; West Seneca East SR HS; W Seneca, NY; (S); DECA; Hosp Aide; Ski Clb; Capt Sec Cheerleading; Socr; JC Awd; Mst Outstndng Chrldr Awd 85; DECA Outstndng Srv Awd 86; Fash Merch.

MASLOWSKY, CAREN; Berne-Knox-Westerlo HS; Westerlo, NY; (Y); 4/72; Am Leg Aux Girls St; Church Yth Grp; Quiz Bowl; Mrchg Band; School Play; Lit Mag; Var Trk; High Hon Roll; NHS; Band; NYS Sen Stdnt Plcy Frum Com Secy 86; Yuth Chrst Stdnt Stff 83-87; Med Sci.

MASON, BRYAN L; Limestone HS; Limestone, NY; (Y); 2/27; Church Yth Grp; Drama Clb; Var Capt Bsktbl; Bausch & Lomb Sci Awd; NHS; Ntl Merit Ltr; Sal; Boy Scts; Chorus; Color Guard; All Cnty Chrs; Regents Scholar; Abilene Christian U; Minister.

MASON, JON; Plattsburgh HS; Plattsburgh, NY; (Y); Var L Bsktbl; Var L Trk; Plattsburgh ST; Mass Media.

MASON, MATTHEW P; Cinton HS; Schenectady, NY; (Y); 15/296; AFS; Boy Scts; Intnl Clb; JCL; Teachers Aide; Chorus; Yrbk Stf; Hon Roll; Ntl Merit Ltr; Rgnts Schlrshp 86; Pltcl Sci.

MASON, PAMELA; Potsdam Central HS; Potsdam, NY; (Y); 12/136; AFS; Drama Clb; Exploring; Math Clb; Band; Stat Bsktbl; Stat Ftbl; JV Mgr(s); JV Score Keeper; Sftbl; Talentd Stu 86; Ithaca; Physcl Thrpy.

MASSA, DAVID S; Bayside HS; Whitestone, NY; (Y); Teachers Aide; Band; Variety Show; Hon Roll; St Schlr; Foul-Shooting Champ In DAC Bsktbl League 85; MVP In DAC Bsbl Traveling Tm 84; SUNY; Bus Adm.

MASSAC, ALEXANDER D; Cardinal Spellman HS; Bronx, NY; (Y); Aud/Vis; Boy Scts; Dance Clb; Frsh Cls; Stu Cncl; Var Swmmng.

MASSAFRA, PASQUALE F; Mount Saint Michael Acad; Yonkers, NY; (S); 57/306; Hon Roll; NHS; Manhattan Coll; Elect Engr.

MASSARO, AIMEE; Preston HS; New York, NY; (S); Pep Band; Cmnty Wkr; Computer Clb; Dance Clb; Stage Crew; Variety Show; High Hon Roll; Hon Roll; NHS.

MASSE, MARIE-JULINE; Dominican Commercial HS; Queens Village, NY; (Y); Church Yth Grp; Church Choir; School Play; Swing Chorus; Yrbk Stf; Off Frsh Cls; Off Soph Cls; Off Jr Cls; Stu Cncl; Med.

MASSELLI, ROSEANNE R; Monsignor Scanlan HS; Bronx, NY; (Y); 27/276; Acad Keybrdng,Bus Dynmcs,Child Growth Dev 86; Wood Sec; Corp Sec.

MASSETT, JEFFREY; Hannibal Central HS; Hannibal, NY; (S); Aud/Vis; Band; Ftbl; Capt Lcrss; Var Capt Trk; JV Wrstlng; High Hon Roll; NHS; Hmcmng Crt 84; Air Force; Acctng.

MASSEY, KATHY M; Roy C Ketcham HS; Wappinger Fls, NY; (Y); 24/510; Church Yth Grp; Library Aide; Math Clb; SADD; Yrbk Stf; Stu Cncl; Diving; Trk; High Hon Roll; NHS; Outstndng Ctznshp Awd/Chs Mnhtn Bnk 86; John T Sloper Awd For Cmnty Srv 85; Oral Rbrts U; Med.

MASSILLON, JEAN; Midwood HS; Brooklyn, NY; (Y); 200/584; Varsity Clb; Stage Crew; Var Capt Trk; Prfct Atten Awd; NY ST Rgnts Schlrshp 86; Temple U; Civil Engnrng.

MASSINGER, HEIDI; Brewster HS; Patterson, NY; (Y); Pep Clb; Ski Clb; Trk; Vllybl; Cert Of Hon Fd & Nut V 85; Vrsty B Athltc Awd Ski Tm 84-86; Wstrn CT ST U.

MASSO, MARY; Bishop Ludden HS; Syracuse, NY; (Y); Band; Chorus; Church Choir; Lit Mag; Regents Schlrshp 86; Onondaga CC.

MASSOFF, DANIEL A; Smithtown H S West; Smithtown, NY; (Y); Var JV Ftbl; Wt Lftg; Hon Roll; NHS; Math Tm; Trk; Pres Schlr; Rgnts Schlrshp 86; John Hpkns U; Med.

MASSOP, ALYSIA; Westbury HS; Westbury, NY; (Y); 6/250; Orch; School Play; Nwsp Rptr; Var Cheerleading; Var L Trk; High Hon Roll; Sec NHS.

MAST, TAMI; Christian Central Acad; Alden, NY; (S); 1/16; Chorus; Nwsp Rptr; Yrbk Stf; JV L Socr; Cit Awd; French Hon Soc; High Hon Roll; NHS; Val; Mth Ed.

MASTANDREA, PETER; East Meadow HS; East Meadow, NY; (Y); Church Yth Grp; Band; Var Ice Hcky; JV Lcrss.

MASTEROV, MICHAEL; Bronx HS Of Science; Tenafly, NJ; (Y); Computer Clb; Office Aide; Political Wkr; Teachers Aide; Lit Mag; Ntl Merit SF; Regents Schlrshp 86; Empire St Schlrshp 86; Cooper Union; Engr.

MASTERSON, MEGAN; St John The Baptist HS; Central Islip, NY; (Y); 53/546; Pep Clb; Nwsp Rptr; Nwsp Stf; Hon Roll; Bus.

MASTRANGELO, FRANCES ANN; Bishop Grimes HS; Liverpool, NY; (Y); 69/146; School Musical; School Play; JV Var Cheerleading; Var Pom Pon; High Hon Roll; Hon Roll; FBLA; Ski Clb; Variety Show; JV Bowling; Italian Hnr Soc; Bus.

MASTRANGELO, MARIA; Frontier Central HS; Lake View, NY; (Y); 32/450; Drama Clb; German Clb; Hosp Aide; Pep Clb; Teachers Aide; Stage Crew; Hon Roll; NHS; Prfct Atten Awd; Pres Schlr; Ltry Soc Fndtn Slvr Cert 86; Pres Acad Ftnss Awds Pgm 86; Villa Maria Coll; Erly Chldhd.

MASTROCOLA, ANDREW; Msgr Mc Clancy HS; Jackson Hts, NY; (Y); Hon Roll; 1st Hnrs 83-85; 2nd Hnrs 85-86; Baruch College; Fnce.

MASTROGIOVANNI, ANNA; Bishop Grimes HS; Syracuse, NY; (S); 7/149; Hosp Aide; NFL; Speech Tm; Yrbk Stf; Tennis; High Hon Roll; NHS.

MASTROGIOVANNI, CHRIS; Geneva HS; Geneva, NY; (S); Latin Clb; Model UN; Off Stu Cncl; Ftbl; Ice Hcky; Lcrss; Hon Roll; NHS; Rotary Awd; 1st Tm All Leag Lacross 85; Washington And Lee; Bio.

MASTROIANNI, CHRISTINA; Notre Dame-Bishop Gibbons HS; Rotterdam Jct, NY; (Y); Girl Scts; Hosp Aide; Ski Clb; High Hon Roll; Ntl Hnr Scty 86.

MASTROLEO, KRISTIN; Solvay HS; Solvay, NY; (Y); JA; SADD; Off Frsh Cls; Off Soph Cls; Socr; Sftbl; Vllybl; High Hon Roll; Hon Roll; Vllybl Hnbl Mntn 85-86; Law.

MASTROMARINO, MARIA; Bishop Ford Central Catholic HS; Brooklyn, NY; (Y); 3/390; Math Clb; Hon Roll; Crtfct Merit Schlstc Achvmnt 85-86; Med.

MASTRONARDI, CORINNE; Chenango Valley HS; Binghamton, NY; (Y); Sec Trs Church Yth Grp; School Musical; Sec Sr Cls; Sec Stu Cncl; Var Cheerleading; Var L Trk; Hon Roll; Jr NHS; Cmnty Wkr; Drama Clb; Hmmg Qn 86; Mck Trl Bar Assn Awd 85-86; Liberty U; Pre-Lw.

MASTROTOTARO, NANCY; Maple Hill HS; Castleton, NY; (Y); 20/97; Girl Scts; Ski Clb; Spanish Clb; Varsity Clb; Frsh Cls; Soph Cls; Jr Cls; Sr Cls; Stu Cncl; Trk; MVP Field Hcky 85-86; Mst Imprvd Plyr Fld Hcky 83-84; Johnson & Wales; Fash Merch.

MASUCCI, DEIRDRE; Linton HS; Schenectady, NY; (Y); 15/300; Trs Key Clb; Ski Clb; Band; Concert Band; Mrchg Band; Off Frsh Cls; JV Var Sftbl; Var Tennis; JV Vllybl; Hon Roll; Tennis Awds; Vet.

MATARAGAS, KENNETH J; Babylon JR SR HS; W Babylon, NY; (Y); 7/169; Im Bsktbl; JV Ftbl; Im Wrstlng; High Hon Roll; Hon Roll; Acadmc Hnr Schlrshp 86; NY ST Rgnts Schlrshps 86; Schlstc Awd Sci 85; Dowling; Bus.

MATARAZZO, DIANA MARIE; Sacred Heart Acad; Floral Park, NY; (S); 3/182; Chess Clb; Sec Girl Scts; Math Clb; Math Tm; Science Clb; Band; Hon Roll; NHS; Chem Engrng.

MATASSA, MICHAEL; Brentwood Ross HS; Brentwood, NY; (Y); 69/550; Aud/Vis; Radio Clb; Pres Stu Cncl; Lcrss; Hon Roll; Latin Clb; Math Tm; Nwsp Stf; Yrbk Stf; Trk; Radio Station News Dir Awd 86; Alan Zimmerman Memrl Schlrshp 86; Media Cmmnctns Awd 86; SUNY-NEW Paltz; Cmmnctns.

MATER, J CHRISTINE; Newark SR HS; Newark, NY; (Y); 35/181; Drama Clb; German Clb; Chorus; School Musical; School Play; Variety Show; Lit Mag; High Hon Roll; Hon Roll; NHS; Music.

MATERA, DARLEEN; Sachem High School North Campus; Lake Ronkonkoma, NY; (Y); 289/1569; Yrbk Ed-Chief; Yrbk Phtg; Yrbk Rptr; Lit Mag; Crs Cntry; Trk; Meredith Manor; Equestician Std.

MATERAZZO, LISA MARIE; Bainbridge-Guilford HS; Bainbridge, NY; (Y); 6/72; Ski Clb; Color Guard; Yrbk Stf; Sec Stu Cncl; Var Bsktbl; Capt Sftbl; JV Tennis; High Hon Roll; NHS; Shrthn Awd 84-85; Pres Acadmc Ftns Awd 85-86; Broome CC; Engrng Sci.

MATHER, COLETTE M; Lancaster Central HS; Depew, NY; (Y); Dance Clb; Ski Clb; Teachers Aide; Hon Roll; Educ Pgm Schlrshp 86-87; Cthn Dwng Schlrshp 86-87; NY ST Dnce Olympcs Slvr Awd 85; Elem Educ.

MATHES, ANDREW; Albion HS; Holley, NY; (S); 2/189; 4-H; Latin Clb; Ntl Merit SF; Sal; Acdmc Dcthln 86; Lang.

MATHESON, SCOTT J; Trinity Pawling Schl; Red Hook, NY; (Y); 1/80; Quiz Bowl; Nwsp Sprt Ed; Sr Cls; Var Capt Bsbl; Var L Ftbl; Var L Golf; Bausch & Lomb Sci Awd; High Hon Roll; Jr NHS; NHS; IBM Watson Schlrshp 86; Rnslr Mdl 85; RPI Rgnl Alumni Schlrshp 86; RPI; Engrng.

MATHEW, CAMILLE; St Catharine Acad; Bx, NY; (Y); 94/185; Chorus; School Play; Bnai Brth Frndshp Awd 78-79; Achvt In Music 85-86; NYS Phys Ftns Awd 85-86.

MATHEW, JINU; Notre Dame Acad; Staten Island, NY; (Y); Art Clb; Camera Clb; Church Yth Grp; Computer Clb; Dance Clb; Drama Clb; Math Clb; VP Science Clb; Church Choir; Yrbk Stf; Schlrshp Awd 82-83; St Johns U; Bus.

MATHEW, ROY; Sacred Heart HS; Yonkers, NY; (Y); Camera Clb; Chess Clb; Hon Roll; NHS; CIBA-GIEGY Sci Awd 86; Fortune Pope Awd 86; Manhattan Coll Pres Awd 86; Manhattan Coll; Elec Engrg.

MATHEWS, ANDREW; Charles O Dickerson HS; Trumansburg, NY; (Y); 5/130; Band; Concert Band; Jazz Band; Mrchg Band; Var L Bsktbl; Var L Socr; Var L Trk; High Hon Roll; Vrsty Sccr Hstl Awd 84; 1st Tm IAC All Sccr Star 85; Louis Armstrong Jazz Awd 86; Binghamton Center; Acctng.

MATHEWS, ELLEN; Franklin Academy HS; Malone, NY; (Y); Church Yth Grp; French Clb; Hosp Aide; Pres Intnl Clb; Pres Model UN; Ski Clb; Concert Band; Stage Crew; Symp Band; Crs Cntry; Paul Smiths Coll; Chef.

MATHEWS, GARY JASON; Francis Lewis HS; Flushing, NY; (Y); 10/351; JA; Science Clb; Hon Roll; NHS; Jr NHS; Art Clb; Camera Clb; Office Aide; Teachers Aide; Prfct Atten Awd; Comptrllrs Awd Outstndng Achvt Ec 86; Slvr Mdl & Plq Comp Sci Excel 86; Sci Tlnt Srch Semi Fnlst 86; Columbia U; Comp Sci.

MATHIS, MAUREEN; Le Roy Central Schl; Leroy, NY; (Y); 10/125; Band; Yrbk Sprt Ed; VP Stu Cncl; Var Capt Bsktbl; Var Capt Socr; Var L Trk; Var Capt Vllybl; DAR Awd; High Hon Roll; NHS; Regents Schlrshp 86; Xavier Pres Schlrshp 86; Xavier U; Spec Educ.

MATHIS, MELISSA; Dewitt Clinton HS; New York, NY; (Y); Cmnty Wkr; Debate Tm; Girl Scts; Hosp Aide; Chorus; Orch; Yrbk Stf; Sec Stu Cncl; Var Trk; Cit Awd; Nrsng.

MATHIS, MORIENE; Seton Catholic Central HS; Binghamton, NY; (Y); Art Clb; Church Yth Grp; French Clb; SADD; Chorus; School Musical; Yrbk Ed-Chief; Yrbk Stf; CYO All-Star Chrldr 84-85; WSKG TV Art Cntst 1st Pl 86; Syracuse U; Spch Path© lgy.

MATIAS, KURT; Union-Endicott HS; Endicott, NY; (Y); 152/425; Hon Roll; Prfct Atten Awd; Jnne F Snpp Mem Awd 86; Prfct Attnd Awd 86; Broome Tech CC; Engrng Sci.

MATIS, THERESA; St Barnabas HS; Bronx, NY; (S); 17/188; Drama Clb; Library Aide; Office Aide; Service Clb; Teachers Aide; Nwsp Rptr; Yrbk Stf; VP Jr Cls; Bsktbl; High Hon Roll; NY Italn Wk Cert 85; Manhatten Coll; Math.

MATISON, KARENA; Horseheads HS; Horseheads, NY; (Y); 270/380; Drama Clb; Hosp Aide; Latin Clb; Pep Clb; Acpl Chr; Band; Chorus; Church Choir; Madrigals; JV Cheerleading; Pdtrc Nrsng.

MATLOFF, ELLEN; Geneva HS; Geneva, NY; (Y); Ski Clb; Spanish Clb; Varsity Clb; Rep Jr Cls; Var Cheerleading; Var Diving; Var Powder Puff Ftbl; High Hon Roll; Hon Roll; Mst Imprvd Spnsh 84.

MATOS, CRISOL; Fontbonne Hall Acad; Brooklyn, NY; (Y); 42/132; Church Yth Grp; Civic Clb; Cmnty Wkr; Drama Clb; French Clb; Office Aide; Science Clb; SADD; Varsity Clb; Chorus; Cncl Awd Vol Svc 86; Fontbonne Amb Hugh O Brian Sem 85; Hnry Stu Sec Commty Meetngs 85; Bio.

MATOS, HAYDEE; Msgr Scanlan HS; Bronx, NY; (Y); Boys Clb Am; Church Yth Grp; Intnl Clb; Church Choir; School Play; Pres Jr Cls; Rep Stu Cncl; JV Im Gym; Hon Roll; Prfct Atten Awd; Askd To Srv As Ldr For Frshmn Aid Prog 86; Parsons; Comm Illus.

MATOS, LISA; T R Proctor HS; Utica, NY; (Y); Dance Clb; Hosp Aide; PAVAS; SADD.

MATOS, MONIQUE; Erasmus Hall HS; Brooklyn, NY; (Y); 155/452; Cmnty Wkr; Office Aide; Teachers Aide; Chorus; School Play; Prfct Atten Awd; 1st Annul Holocast Schlrshp Essay 86; Tchrs Engl Cert Merit 86; Borough; Word Proc.

MATOS, ZOILA YUDITH; Washington Irving HS; New York, NY; (Y); 3/423; Hosp Aide; Office Aide; Teachers Aide; Lit Mag; Rep Soph Cls; Trk; Hon Roll; NHS; Prfct Atten Awd; Untd Fdrtn Tchrs Coll Schlrshp 86; NY Rotry Fndtn Grnt 86; Citatn Govs Cmmtee Schlstc Achvt 86; Union Coll; Bio.

MATSAS, ILAN; South Shore HS; Brooklyn, NY; (Y); Var Gym; Engl Hnr 84; NYU; Comptr Prgrmmng.

MATSEN, JEAN; Hastings-On-Hudson HS; Hastings-On-Hudso, NY; (Y); 3/111; Hst 4-H; JA; Key Clb; Orch; High Hon Roll; NHS; Pres Acadmc Ftns Awd 86; NYS Sci Sprvsrs Assoc Sci Awd 86; Dept Awd Sci 86; Coll Of Mt St Vincent.

MATSUO, EUGENE; Scarsdale HS; Scarsdale, NY; (Y); Pres Chess Clb; Pres Computer Clb; VP Debate Tm; Band; Jazz Band; Yrbk Stf; Capt Trk; Capt Wrstlng; Harvard U.

MATT, MICHAEL; Rome Free Acad; Lee Center, NY; (Y); Science Clb; Var Swmmng; High Hon Roll; Jr NHS; Pre-Med.

MATT, WAYNE; Rome Free Acad; Lee Center, NY; (Y); Exploring; Science Clb; Bsbl; Ftbl; Wrstlng; Outstndng Athl 84; Ecology.

MATTARO, SHAWN; Mc Quaid Jesuit HS; Rochester, NY; (Y); 73/169; French Clb; Spanish Clb; Varsity Clb; Lit Mag; Var L Ftbl; Var L Swmmng; Var L Trk; Hon Roll; City Cath Trck All Star 86; Mc Quaid Achvt Mdl 83; Aerospace Engr.

MATTAS, LOUIS C; Patchogue-Medford HS; Patchogue, NY; (Y); 19/621; Church Yth Grp; Mathletes; Math Tm; Orch; High Hon Roll; Hon Roll; Jr NHS; NHS; Prfct Atten Awd; Medford Elem Schl PTO Awd 83; St Johns U Schlrshp 85; St Johns Grk Orthdx Chrch Ldng Schlr 83; ST U Of NY-STNYBRK; Bio.

MATTERA, RICHARD; Sachem North HS; Holbrook, NY; (Y); Camera Clb; Computer Clb; Ski Clb; SADD; Var Wt Lftg; MIT; Spcl Effcts.

MATTES, WILLIAM; E L Vandermeulen HS; Mt Sinai, NY; (Y); 42/300; Boy Scts; Leo Clb; VP SADD; Concert Band; Jazz Band; Mrchg Band; Yrbk Stf; Gym; Swmmng; Wrstlng; Lions Club & Regnts Schlrshp 86; VA Tech; Engrng.

MATTESON, JODY; Waterville JRSR HS; Deansboro, NY; (Y); 15/89; Mathletes; Ski Clb; Band; Chorus; Stage Crew; Yrbk Stf; High Hon Roll; Hon Roll; NHS; Rgnts Nrsng Schlrshp 86; St Elizabeth Schl Nrsng; Nrsng.

MATTESON, MARGARET; Gates-Chili HS; Rochester, NY; (Y); Office Aide; Chrmn Red Cross Aide; Teachers Aide; Chorus; Church Choir; Hon Roll; Delg Amer Red Cross Yth Ldrshp Conf 85; Schl Svc Awd Red Crs Blood Drive & TMR 86; Nazareth; Spec Ed.

MATTESON, MELANIE; Franklin Acad; Malone, NY; (Y); 105/280; Spanish Clb; Chorus; Var Capt Cheerleading; Var L Swmmng; Capt Twrlr; Prfct Atten Awd; Tchrs Fdrtn Schlrshp 86; Ldrshp Excllnc Awd Chrldng 83; Ldrshp Awd Twrlng 84; Elmira Coll; Elem Educ.

MATTESSICH, CLAUDE; Holy Trinity HS; Freeport, NY; (S); Ski Clb; Socr; Trk; High Hon Roll; Hon Roll; NHS; Math Awd 84.

MATTHEI, JULIE; Manhasset HS; Manhasset, NY; (Y); 46/185; GAA; Flag Corp; Nwsp Sprt Ed; Soph Cls; Var Badmtn; Var Mgr(s); Var Capt Socr; Sftbl; Swmmng; Fairfield U; Comm.

MATTHEWS, AARON; Greenville JR SR HS; Freehold, NY; (Y); 25/77; Church Yth Grp; 4-H; FFA; Quiz Bowl; Band; Concert Band; Jazz Band; Mrchg Band; Orch; Pep Band; NYS Champ Dairy Shwmn FFA 1st Pl 86; Greene Cnty Outstndg Hrdsmn 83-85; Delhi A&T; Turf Mgmt.

MATTHEWS, ANGELA; Lansingburgh HS; Troy, NY; (Y); 27/195; French Clb; Chorus; Rep Jr Cls; Var Capt Bsktbl; Var Capt Socr; Capt Var Sftbl; Var Trk; Teachers Aide; Varsity Clb; Yrbk Stf; Nancy E Ballet Mem Awd Girls Athl 86; Colonial Concl All Str Tm Sccr 84&85; Typing Prod Awd 84-85&86; Hudson Vly; Phys Educ.

MATTHEWS JR, DONALD A; Cohocton Central HS; Cohocton, NY; (Y); Stage Crew; Yrbk Phtg; Yrbk Rptr; JV Var Socr; High Hon Roll; Regnts Schlrshp 86; US Marine Corps.

MATTHEWS, ERIN; Lansingburgh HS; Troy, NY; (Y); German Clb; Varsity Clb; Nwsp Stf; Var JV Cheerleading; Var Trk; High Hon Roll; Hon Roll; Jr NHS; NHS; Socl Wrk.

MATTHEWS, JEFF; Genesco Central Schl; Geneseo, NY; (Y); 9/88; Boy Scts; Concert Band; Capt JV Bsbl; Ice Hcky; Capt JV Socr; Sftbl; VP Jr NHS; NHS; Pres Acadmc Ftnss Awd 86; Geneseo Bd Of Ed Awd-Top 10 Of Cls 86; SUNY Potsdam; Comp Sci.

MATTHEWS, KAREN GOLDA; H S For The Humanits; New York, NY; (Y); Cmnty Wkr; Computer Clb; Chorus; School Musical; School Play; Variety Show; Nwsp Stf; Stu Cncl; Prfct Atten Awd; Intl Bus Mgmt.

MATTHEWS, NANCY LEE; Grand Island HS; Grand Island, NY; (Y); 52/320; Church Yth Grp; Teachers Aide; Church Choir; Variety Show; Yrbk Phtg; Var L Lcrss; Mgr(s); Hon Roll; Ntl Merit Ltr; Aud/Vis; NY ST Regents Schlrshp 86; Joseph Malfitano Frng Lang Schlrshp 86; Cornell U; Intr Dsgn.

MATTHEWS, SANDRA; Leroy Central Schl; Leroy, NY; (Y); 15/135; 4-H; Sec Chorus; Mrchg Band; School Musical; Sec Stu Cncl; Cheerleading; Socr; Sftbl; High Hon Roll; Mrch Of Dms Schlrshp 86; SUNY Buffalo; Physcl Thrpy.

MATTHEWS, STEPHEN; Franklin Acad; Malone, NY; (Y); Varsity Clb; L Bsbl; Capt L Bsktbl; Capt L Ftbl; L Trk; Engr.

MATTHEWS, WINSTON; James Madison HS; Brooklyn, NY; (Y); 65/756; Library Aide; Science Clb; Teachers Aide; Band; Chorus; Nwsp Stf; Hon Roll; Prfct Atten Awd; Hofstra; Accntng.

MATTHIE, PATRICIA; Madrid-Waddington JR SR HS; Lisbon, NY; (Y); AFS; French Clb; Spanish Clb; Speech Tm; Yrbk Phtg; JV Crs Cntry; NHS; Aud/Vis; Debate Tm; High Hon Roll; St Lawrence U Tlntd Pgm Photo 86; Acad Exc 84-86; Photo.

MATTHYS, JACK; Sodus Central Schl; Sodus, NY; (Y); Church Yth Grp; Cmnty Wkr; Computer Clb; Radio Clb; Science Clb; Y-Teens; Hon Roll; Bowling; Trk; Am Leg Awd 83; Wayne Area Voc Cntr Prfct Atten Awd 86; Meteorlgst.

MATTICE, KELLY; Hugh C Williams HS; Canton, NY; (Y); Church Yth Grp; Cheerleading; Score Keeper; Timer; Hon Roll; Tlntd JR St Lwrnce U 85-86; Awds Figure Sktng Comptn; Corp Law.

MATTIMORE, MAUREEN; Clarkstown South HS; W Nyack, NY; (Y); SADD; Band; Concert Band; Drm Mjr(t); Mrchg Band; Orch; School Musical; Symp Band; JV Socr; 4-H Awd; Goldn Musc Awd Outstndng Achvt 86; Elem Educ.

MATTINSON, HEATHER L; Huntington HS; Huntington, NY; (Y); 15/383; Ed Lit Mag; High Hon Roll; Jr NHS; Kiwanis Awd; NHS; Lab Asstnt For Chmstry Dept 85-86; SUNY Bfl; Bio Rsrch.

MATTISON, SCOTT; Ogdensburg Free Acad; Ogdensburg, NY; (Y); 15/200; Key Clb; Var L Ice Hcky; Var L Socr; L Var Trk; Im Mgr Vllybl; Hon Roll; NHS; 1st Tm All Lg Sccr 85; Hon Mntn All Nrthrn Hcky 86; Mem Of All Nrthrn Acdmc Hcky Tm 86; Hotchkiss Schl; Cvl Engr.

MATTLE, ANDY; Wayland Central HS; Perkinsville, NY; (Y); 4/120; Math Tm; Trs Frsh Cls; VP Soph Cls; JV Bsbl; Var Ftbl; Var Wrstlng; Hon Roll; NHS; Offnsv Linemn Of Yr Ftbl 85; Govtmntl Stud Prog 86; U Of FL; Marine Bio.

MATTOON, REBECCA; Perry Central HS; Perry, NY; (Y); 3/99; Ski Clb; Varsity Clb; Chorus; School Musical; VP Frsh Cls; Pres Soph Cls; Stu Cncl; Socr; Trk; High Hon Roll; Acad Achvt Awd Sci; Schltc Avg Awd.

MATTREY, MICHELLE; Nardin Acad; E Amherst, NY; (Y); 14/86; Hosp Aide; Library Aide; Model UN; Service Clb; Speech Tm; Stage Crew; Lit Mag; Var Socr; High Hon Roll; Ntl Merit Ltr; Bio.

MATTU, EUNICE; St Peters High School For Girls; Staten Isl, NY; (Y); 5/75; Exploring; FNA; Math Clb; Yrbk Stf; Rep Stu Cncl; Tennis; NHS; Prfct Atten Awd; Untd Cerbrl Plsy Grp Ldr 82-86; American U; Cmptr Sci.

MATURI, RAJ; Jamaica HS; Jamaica, NY; (S); 3/540; Math Clb; Capt Math Tm; Chrmn Science Clb; Ed Lit Mag; Rep Jr Cls; Trs Sr Cls; JV Badmtn; NHS; Ntl Merit SF; Westinghse Sci Tlnt Srch Semi-Fnlst 86; NASA/NSTA Sp Shttl Invlmnt Proj Fnlst 85; JR Sci Fnlst 86; Columbia; Physcn.

MATUSZEWSKI, CHRISTINE; St Agnes Academic HS; Maspeth, NY; (Y); Church Yth Grp; Cmnty Wkr; Service Clb; Variety Show; Yrbk Ed-Chief; Bausch & Lomb Sci Awd; High Hon Roll; NHS; Engrng.

MATZAN, CORRY; Massena Central HS; Massena, NY; (Y); 20/248; French Clb; Cheerleading; Score Keeper; Hon Roll; Jr NHS; NHS; Pres Schlr; GMI; Indstrl Engr.

MAU, CHRISTINE; Bishop Ford HS; Brooklyn, NY; (Y); Church Yth Grp; Civic Clb; Cmnty Wkr; Math Clb; Office Aide; Political Wkr; Science Clb; Teachers Aide; Cit Awd; Ulano Corp Cmmnty Serv Awd 86; Polc Prcnct Cncl Cmmnty Serv Awd 86.

MAU, JEFFREY; Frontier Central HS; Hamburg, NY; (Y); German Clb; Hon Roll; Cmptr Sci.

MAUCIERI, CARMELA; John Dewey HS; Brooklyn, NY; (Y); Variety Show; Bowling; Gym; Sftbl; Vllybl; High Hon Roll; Hon Roll; Prfct Atten Awd; Citatn Achvt 84; Kings Borough Cmnty; Accntng.

MAUDE, KELLY; Massapequa HS; Massapequa, NY; (Y); Cmnty Wkr; German Clb; SADD; Nwsp Stf; Ed Lit Mag; Rep Jr Cls; Trs Stu Cncl; Cit Awd; High Hon Roll; Ntl Merit Ltr; Rgnts Schlrshp 86; Boston U; Cmmnctns.

MAUERSBERG, DIANE; Newark Valley HS; Owego, NY; (Y); 1/114; Library Aide; Varsity Clb; Capt Color Guard; Crs Cntry; Trk; Twrlr; High Hon Roll; JETS Awd; NHS; Val; Rgns Schlrshp 86; Yth Salute 85; 1st Team All Stars Cross Cntry 85; Rochester IT; Elec Engr.

MAUGHAN, MITZI; HS For The Humanits; Hampton, VA; (Y); Church Yth Grp; Cmnty Wkr; Band; Rep Jr Cls; Rep Stu Cncl; Var Capt Swmmng; Hon Roll; Mst Dedctd Swmmr Awd 85-86; Chld Psychol.

MAUL, JAY M; Springville Griffith Inst; Springville, NY; (Y); Am Leg Boys St; Boy Scts; Chess Clb; VP Exploring; Trs Key Clb; Ftbl; Hon Roll; Amer Lgn Sct Yr NY ST 85; Eagle Sct 83; Yth Inc Jr Class Rep 86; Bus Mgmt.

MAULUCCI, ROBERT; Canisius HS; Buffalo, NY; (Y); Church Yth Grp; JCL; Latin Clb; Model UN; Lit Mag; JV Bsbl; JV Ftbl; Var Trk; Hon Roll; Natl Latn Exm-Cum Laude 84-85; Engl Lit.

MAURER, HEIDI; Coxsackie-Athens HS; Earlton, NY; (Y); 11/105; German Clb; Band; Chorus; Stu Cncl; Trk; High Hon Roll; Hon Roll.

MAURER, JOHN; Vestal HS; Binghamton, NY; (Y); Boy Scts; Acpl Chr; Chorus; Hon Roll; NHS; Eagle Scout Slvr Palm 85; Rgnts Schlrshp 86; Broome CC; Engr Sci.

MAURER, JOHN E; Hamburg SR HS; Hamburg, NY; (Y); Chess Clb; Pres German Clb; Var L Trk; Var Vllybl; Hon Roll; NY ST Rgnts Schlrshp 86; Mbr NYS Sctn VI 4x200 Sprnt Rly Indr Trck Chmpns 86; Mchncl Engnrng.

MAURER, KATHLEEN; Newark SR HS; Newark, NY; (Y); 8/197; Church Yth Grp; Drama Clb; Concert Band; Jazz Band; School Musical; Swing Chorus; JP Sousa Awd; NHS; Ntl Merit Ltr; Aud/Vis; Jacob Wilson Engl Awd; Rotary Band Prize; Area All-St Band; Ithaca Coll; Music Educ.

MAURER, LARA; Onteora Central Schl; Woodstock, NY; (Y); 26/210; French Clb; Band; Concert Band; Mrchg Band; JV Cheerleading; Mgr(s); Var L Tennis; Hon Roll; NHS; Mst Vlbl Plyr On Grls Tnns Tm 84; Grad Awd Hghst Cmltv Aver In Frnch 86; SUNY Bnghmtn.

MAURIZIO, LORETTA; Tottenville HS; Staten Island, NY; (S); 18/850; Exploring; Office Aide; Teachers Aide; School Play; Frsh Cls; Sec Soph Cls; Capt Bowling; High Hon Roll; NHS; Bus Adm.

MAURNO, JEANNE; Tuckahoe HS; Bronxville, NY; (Y); Cmnty Wkr; Drama Clb; Hosp Aide; Leo Clb; Model UN; Quiz Bowl; Ski Clb; Varsity Clb; Chorus; School Play; Advtsg.

MAURO, GINA; John H Glenn HS; Huntington, NY; (Y); Cmnty Wkr; Political Wkr; Variety Show; Stu Cncl; Hon Roll; Itln Hnr Soc Treas 84-86; Bus.

MAVROMICHALIS, PATTY; H Frank Carey HS; Garden City S, NY; (Y); 14/275; Church Yth Grp; French Clb; SADD; Yrbk Stf; High Hon Roll; Hon Roll; Jr NHS; NHS; Ntl Merit Ltr; Frgn Lang Hnr Soc 86; Frnch Awds 84-85; Greek Awd Acad Achvt 84; Pre-Med.

MAXEY, COLLEEN; Kenmore East HS; Tonawanda, NY; (Y); Orch; Im Bowling; Alfred ST; Vet.

MAXFIELD, DAVE; Wayne Central HS; Ontario, NY; (Y); Mathletes; Math Tm; JV Var Bsbl; NHS; Band; Chorus; JV Socr; Wrstlng; Ldrshp Prog 85-86; All-Cnty 1st Tm Bsbl 85-86; Outstndg Engl Awd 85-86; Schlrp Day At Brockport ST 85; U Of Buffalo; Cvl Engr.

MAXFIELD, DEREK D; Dundee Central HS; Dundee, NY; (Y); 12/74; Pres AFS; Pres Am Leg Boys St; Aud/Vis; Church Yth Grp; Drama Clb; Sec Varsity Clb; Nwsp Ed-Chief; Yrbk Stf; Var Ftbl; Mgr(s); Yates Cnty Tngr Yr 85; PA House, Rotary Clb Schlrshp 86; Cayuga County CC; Brdcstng.

MAXSON, DANIEL; Walton JR SR HS; Walton, NY; (Y); 18/120; Church Yth Grp; Key Clb; Varsity Clb; Chorus; Concert Band; Mrchg Band; Orch; Trs Stu Cncl; JV Var Ftbl; Var Tennis; Stephen J Holstead Mem Awd/Outstndnd Achvt Tnns Dbls 86; Ceaderville UOH; Accntng.

MAXSON, TRACEY; Walton Central HS; Walton, NY; (Y); AFS; Church Yth Grp; Cmnty Wkr; Drama Clb; 4-H; Hosp Aide; Key Clb; Band; Chorus; Church Choir; Voc Solo 83-84; Elem Ed.

MAXWELL, DAVID B; High School Of Music And Art; Brooklyn, NY; (Y); Boys Clb Am; Boy Scts; Chorus; Drm & Bgl; Var Bsktbl; Mgr(s); Swmmng; Var Trk; Im Wt Lftg; Ntl Merit Ltr; Cmmnctns.

MAXWELL, MARK K; Cortland JR SR HS; Cortland, NY; (Y); 47/194; Aud/Vis; Exploring; Quiz Bowl; Jazz Band; Stage Crew; Swing Chorus; Hon Roll; NHS; Wilkes Coll; TV & Cmnctns.

MAY, BRIAN; Notre Dame-Bishop Gibbons HS; Schenectady, NY; (S); 4/98; JV Var Bsbl; JV Var Bsktbl; Mgr(s); High Hon Roll; Jr NHS; NHS; Religs Stds Awd 84-85; Syracuse U; Cmmnctns.

MAY, CHRISTOPHER J; Maryvale HS; Depew, NY; (Y); Am Leg Boys St; Boy Scts; Church Yth Grp; Band; Mrchg Band; JV Ftbl; Var L Swmmng; Hon Roll; NHS; Eagle Scout 85; News Carrier Of The Month Buffalo News 84; Canisius Coll; Bus Admn.

MAY, DAVID; Williamsville North HS; Getzville, NY; (Y); 9/301; Latin Clb; Mathletes; Nwsp Stf; Yrbk Stf; Var Socr; NHS; Clarkson U; Mech Engrng.

MAY III, JAMES H; Lacawanna SR HS; Lackawanna, NY; (Y); Camera Clb; Computer Clb; Library Aide; Ski Clb; Chorus; Nwsp Phtg; Yrbk Phtg; Yrbk Stf; L Crs Cntry; Var L Ftbl; Woodwkng Awd 84; Ftbl-Div 4-1st Tm Dfnsv 86; YPFA 86; Marine Corps; Engrng.

MAY, JENNIFER; De Sales Catholic HS; Lockport, NY; (S); 5/30; Hosp Aide; Ski Clb; Varsity Clb; Nwsp Rptr; JV Bsktbl; Capt Var Socr; JV Sftbl; High Hon Roll; NHS; NEDT Awd; Nrsng.

MAY, JENNIFER; Lansingburgh HS; Troy, NY; (Y); 57/160; Capt Sr Cls; Var Capt Cheerleading; Pom Pon; High Hon Roll; Hon Roll; Cum Laude 86; Hudson Valley CC; Sec Sci.

MAY, PAUL; Lindenhurst HS; Lindenhurst, NY; (Y); Band; Concert Band; Stage Crew; Badmtn; Socr; Trk; Hon Roll; Mst Imprvd Soccer Plyr 85; MVP In Track 86; Mst Imprvd Plyr In Track 86; Gld Key Awd & Phy Ed Awd 86; Frlgh Dcknsn U; Elec Engr.

MAYBERRY, CHERYL; Lake Placid HS; Lake Placid, NY; (Y); 9/54; AFS; Church Yth Grp; Sec Key Clb; Library Aide; Band; Chorus; Trs Yrbk Stf; Hon Roll; Lion Awd; AAUW 85; Potsdam ST; Bio.

MAYER, BETH A; Waterloo SR HS; Waterloo, NY; (Y); 4-H; Pep Clb; Concert Band; 4-H Awd; Hon Roll; Regents Nrsng Schlrshp 86; Nrsng.

MAYER, CASEY; Ward Melville HS; Stony Brook, NY; (Y); Cmnty Wkr; GAA; SADD; Chorus; Yrbk Phtg; Yrbk Stf; Pres Frsh Cls; Rep Soph Cls; Stu Cncl; Im Badmtn; Outstndg Athletic Achvmnt 86; Bus.

MAYER, CHRIS; Rhinebeck HS; Rhinebeck, NY; (Y); 1/105; Computer Clb; Drama Clb; Math Clb; Quiz Bowl; Spanish Clb; Band; Concert Band; Jazz Band; Mrchg Band; School Musical; RPI Mdl 85; MIT.

MAYER, JENNIFER; Berlin Central HS; Stephentown, NY; (Y); GAA; Chorus; School Musical; Stage Crew; Nwsp Stf; Yrbk Phtg; Stu Cncl; Score Keeper; JV Socr; JV Sftbl; Art.

MAYER, SONNY; Cicero North Syracuse HS; N Syracuse, NY; (Y); 184/667; Church Yth Grp; Trs Key Clb; Nwsp Phtg; Nwsp Rptr; Nwsp Sprt Ed; Nwsp Stf; Var L Ftbl; Athl Clubs Outstndng Stdnt Athl 86; Onondaga CC; Acctg.

MAYERHOFF, ADINA; Yeshiva University HS For Girls; Cedarhurst, NY; (Y); Stage Crew; Im Fld Hcky; St Schlr; Queens Coll; Home Ec.

MAYEWSKI, CHRISTINE; Warwick Valley HS; Warwick, NY; (Y); 3/185; French Clb; Science Clb; Ski Clb; SADD; Nwsp Stf; Yrbk Phtg; Off Frsh Cls; VP Soph Cls; Off Sr Cls; Var Trk; GA Pacific Schlrshp 86; WA U Hnry Schlrshp 86; WA U St Louis; Engrng.

MAYHEW, DEBRA; Heuvelton Central HS; Rensselaer Falls, NY; (Y); Church Yth Grp; 4-H; French Clb; Im Vllybl; 4-H Awd.

MAYHEW, STEPHEN; Royalton-Hartland Central HS; Middleport, NY; (Y); 11/126; Rep Stu Cncl; JV Var Bsktbl; JV Var Ftbl; Var L Trk; Pres NHS; Rotc Schlrshp 86; Presdntl Acad Ftns Awrd 86; NY St Rgnts Schlrshp 86; U Of VT; Accntnt.

MAYLIN, ANGELA; Villa Maria Acad; Buffalo, NY; (S); 4/87; Chorus; Church Choir; Nwsp Rptr; High Hon Roll; Hon Roll; NEDT Awd; Prfct Atten Awd; Val; Schlrshp For Hghst Clss Avg 83; Phys Ther.

MAYO, RAY; Hannibal Central HS; Fair Haven, NY; (Y); Aud/Vis; 4-H; Nwsp Phtg; Nwsp Rptr; Yrbk Phtg; Yrbk Rptr; Photo.

MAYOU, DAVID P; Sodus Central HS; Sodus, NY; (Y); 6/130; Am Leg Boys St; French Clb; VP Model UN; Radio Clb; Band; Mrchg Band; NHS; Ntl Merit SF.

MAYS, DEBBIE; Glen Falls HS; Glens Falls, NY; (Y); 6/219; AFS; Hosp Aide; Key Clb; Chorus; Var Trk; High Hon Roll; NHS; Police Benevolent Assoc Schlrshp 86; Regents Schlrshp 86; Pres Acdmc Fit Awd 86; Holy Cross Coll; Bio.

MAYTON, SUSAN; Owen D Young Central HS; Mohawk, NY; (S); 3/21; Cmnty Wkr; Q&S; Yrbk Bus Mgr; Yrbk Stf; Pres Jr Cls; Pres Sr Cls; Var Capt Vllybl; Cit Awd; DAR Awd; Jr NHS; Bio Regents Awd; Pathology.

MAZARAKIS, TRINA; Center Moriches HS; Center Moriches, NY; (Y); 5/104; Debate Tm; Trs Latin Clb; Spanish Clb; Nwsp Ed-Chief; Nwsp Rptr; Lit Mag; High Hon Roll; NHS; Schl Rep-HOBY Fndtn-NYS Sth 85; Schl Rep-Presdntl Clsrm 86; Co-Pres Of Intract 86; Lwyr.

MAZELIS, LORRAINE; Laguardia HS Of Music & The Arts; New York, NY; (S); Nwsp Rptr; NHS; Politicl Awrnss Clb.

MAZIEJKA, JENNIFER; Hudon Falls SR HS; Hudson Fls, NY; (Y); Church Yth Grp; French Clb; SADD; Yrbk Stf; Im Vllybl; Adirondack CC; Sec Sci.

MAZOUREK, ROBERTA; Newfield Central HS; Newfield, NY; (Y); 23/51; 4-H; Pres VP FHA; Chorus; Yrbk Bus Mgr; Yrbk Stf; W Danby Fire Co Awd & Hme Ec 82; L May Savercool Schlrshp Awd 86; SUNY Alfred; Med Lb Tchnlgy.

MAZUR, JULIE E; Nottingham HS; Syracuse, NY; (Y); 8/220; French Clb; Trs Latin Clb; Ski Clb; Chorus; Sftbl; Trk; High Hon Roll; Hon Roll; NHS; Ntl Merit Ltr; NYS Regnts Schlrshp 86; Cornell U; Comms.

MAZUR, LISA A; Kenmore East HS; Tonawanda, NY; (Y); 22/360; Intnl Clb; Pep Clb; High Hon Roll; Jr NHS; NHS; UAW Schlrshp Awd 86; Parsons Schl Dsgn; Cmnctns Art.

MAZUR, SUZANNE; Central Islip SR HS; Central Islip, NY; (Y); 19/344; Cmnty Wkr; Exploring; Hosp Aide; Flag Corp; Mrchg Band; Stage Crew; Variety Show; Pom Pon; Hon Roll; NY ST Regnts Schlrshp Nrsng 86; Grad W/Rgnts Diploma 86; Molloy Coll; Nrsng.

MAZUREK, KATIE; Springville-Griffth Institute Central; Colden, NY; (Y); French Clb; FBLA; Key Clb; Color Guard; High Hon Roll; Hon Roll; NHS; Acctng.

MAZUROWSKI, DEANNA; Sachem HS; Holbrook, NY; (Y); 272/1579; JV Trk; Spch Pthlgy.

MAZUROWSKI, DONNA; Our Lady Of Mercy HS; Rochester, NY; (Y); French Clb; Hosp Aide; Model UN; Science Clb; Nwsp Rptr; Yrbk Ed-Chief; Lit Mag; Rep Stu Cncl; Var Socr; Var Sftbl; Acad Scholar 83-87; Acad Scholar Cathlc Wmns Clb 85-87; Acad Awd Bio & Spn 85; Bio.

MAZZA, JAMES C; Stissing Mountain JR SR HS; Stanfordville, NY; (Y); 1/84; Boy Scts; Nwsp Stf; High Hon Roll; Hnr Key 83-86; Mst Lkly Succd 86; Usher-Grad Exer 86; Jrnlsm.

MAZZA, JENNIFER; Tottenville HS; Staten Island, NY; (Y); Key Clb; Model UN; Teachers Aide; Yrbk Rptr; Yrbk Stf; Rep Frsh Cls; Rep Soph Cls; Rep Jr Cls; Hon Roll; NHS; Boston U; Jrnlsm.

MAZZARA, JOE; Commack HS South; Dix Hills, NY; (Y); JV Var Ftbl; JV Var Ice Hcky; Var Trk; Im Wt Lftg; High Hon Roll; Hon Roll; Ntl Sci Olympd 2nd Pl 86; Bio.

MAZZAROPPI, MATTHEW; Cicero N Orth Syracuse HS; N Syracuse, NY; (S); 9/700; Math Tm; Ski Clb; Band; Chorus; School Musical; Lit Mag; Trk; CC Awd; Pres NHS; Opt Clb Awd.

MAZZARVLLI, PAUL V; John Jay HS; Katonah, NY; (Y); Am Leg Boys St; Aud/Vis; Debate Tm; Stage Crew; Variety Show; Ed Lit Mag; Wt Lftg; Hon Roll; Ctznshp Awd 86.

MAZZEI, LYNN; Alfred G Berner HS; Massapequa, NY; (Y); Church Yth Grp; Office Aide; Pep Clb; Varsity Clb; VP Soph Cls; VP Jr Cls; Rep Stu Cncl; Var JV Cheerleading; Bus.

MAZZELLA, CHRISTINE; Cardinal Spellman HS; Bronx, NY; (Y); 26/483; Church Yth Grp; Computer Clb; Stu Cncl; JV Capt Bsktbl; Var L Sftbl; Var L Vllybl; High Hon Roll; NHS; NYS Rgnts Schlrshp 86; Chmpnshp Trphy 85 & 86; Queens Coll; Acctng.

MAZZELLA, MICHELE; Marlboro HS; Milton, NY; (Y); 11/150; SADD; Band; Concert Band; Mrchg Band; Stat Bsbl; Stat Bsktbl; High Hon Roll; NHS; Bus Adm.

MAZZELLA, STEPHANIE; North Babylon SR HS; N Babylon, NY; (Y); Sec Stu Cncl; Im Gym; Im Sftbl; High Hon Roll; Hon Roll; Jr NHS; Italian Hnr Soc 85; C W Post; Acctng.

MAZZEO, CARLA; Marlboro HS; Newburgh, NY; (Y); Computer Clb; Dance Clb; Teachers Aide; Varsity Clb; Nwsp Phtg; Nwsp Rptr; Var Diving; Var Swmmng; Var Tennis; Var Trk; Photo Plys 85-86; Video Astrnmy Shws 86; Clg Psych 86; New Platz; Psych.

MAZZICA, MARIA; Lincoln HS; Yonkers, NY; (Y); 25/325; Trk; High Hon Roll; NHS; Ninety Clb 85-86; NY Inst Tech; Arch.

MAZZIE, MARIA; Jamestown HS; Jamestown, NY; (Y); 31/389; French Clb; Trs Acpl Chr; Concert Band; Madrigals; Mrchg Band; Hon Roll; Jr NHS; NHS; Natl Viking Schlrsp 86; Jamestown HS SR Class Achvt Awd 86; ST U Of NY Geneseo; Engl.

MAZZIE, THOMAS; Bay Shore HS; Bay Shore, NY; (Y); 14/365; Am Leg Boys St; Church Yth Grp; Cmnty Wkr; Math Tm; SADD; VP Jr Cls; JV Var Socr; High Hon Roll; NHS; Pres Stu Govt Orgnztn 86-87; Holy Cross; Mth.

MAZZONE, ANTONETTE; Hudson HS; Hudson, NY; (Y); 12/160; SADD; Yrbk Ed-Chief; Yrbk Stf; High Hon Roll; Hon Roll; Jr NHS; NHS; Pres Schlr; Pres Acdmc Ftnss Awd 86; Hudson Crrctnl Fclty Awd 86; Italn Amrcn War Vtrns Axlry Pst Awd 86; Columbia Greene Coll; Bus Admst.

MAZZONE, LAWRENCE; Harborfields HS; Greenlawn, NY; (Y); Var Ice Hcky; Delhi; Carpentry.

MAZZONE, NANCY; St Edmund HS; Brooklyn, NY; (S); 18/224; FBLA; JA; Office Aide; Scholastic Bowl; Y-Teens; Off Frsh Cls; High Hon Roll; Hon Roll; Jr NHS; NHS; Brooklyn Coll; Bus Mgmt.

MAZZOTTA, PATRICIA L; St Catharine Acad; Bronx, NY; (Y); Dance Clb; VP Frsh Cls; NHS; NY Regents Schlrshp; Outstndng Achvt In Psych; Pace U; Comp.

MAZZURCO, SALLY; Jamestown HS; Jamestown, NY; (Y); Off Church Yth Grp; Hosp Aide; Spanish Clb; Acpl Chr; School Musical; Stage Crew; Nwsp Stf; Stu Cncl; Hon Roll; NHS; Prjct Yes Cmnty Svc Awd Most Hrs 84; Span Lang Comp 1st 8 6; Art Awds 83; U NC Chapel Hill; Pre-Med.

MC ADAMS-SPINA, STACY; New Dorp HS; Staten Island, NY; (Y); Art Clb; Yrbk Phtg; Lit Mag; Womn Hstry 84; Commnctns.

MC ADOO, KEITH ANTHONY; Half Hollow Hills East HS; Wheatley Heights, NY; (Y); 70/511; Trs Sec Leo Clb; Political Wkr; Chorus; Madrigals; Swing Chorus; Stat Bsktbl; Mgr(s); DAR Awd; High Hon Roll; NHS; Jack & Jill Amer Inc Scholar 86; Tri-M Music Hnr Soc 83-86; Duke U; Corp Lawyer.

MC ALEER, DIANE M; St Francis Prep; Whitestone, NY; (S); 65/650; NHS; Acad All-Amer 85-86; Scty Of Distngshd Amer H S Stu 85; Natl Ldrshp Merit Awd 85; Columbia U; Med.

MC ALISTER, ROSECLAIR; George Wingate HS; Brooklyn, NY; (Y); 18/119; Church Yth Grp; JA; Church Choir; Hon Roll; Brch Cmmnty Coll; Bus.

MC ALLISTER, CHRISTINA; South Colonie Central HS; Albany, NY; (Y); Band; Off Jr Cls; VP Sr Cls; Rep Stu Cncl; JV Cheerleading; High Hon Roll; Hon Roll; NHS; Church Yth Grp; Girl Scts; SUNY Wrld Hunger Pstr Cntst 1st 87; Advrtsng.

MC ALLISTER, KIM YVETTE; Uniondale HS; Uniondale, NY; (Y); Church Yth Grp; FBLA; Girl Scts; Key Clb; Chorus; Yrbk Phtg; Rep Stu Cncl; JV Mgr(s); Hon Roll; Jr NHS; Liberal Arts.

MC ANDREW, MARK F; St Francis Prep; Bayside, NY; (S); 187/750; Am Leg Boys St; Ski Clb; Coach Actv; Im Ftbl; Var Socr; Im Vllybl; Wt Lftg; Var Wrstlng; Hon Roll; Opt Clb Awd; NYU; Dr.

MC ANDREW, THOMAS; Horseheads HS; Horseheads, NY; (Y); 17/420; Am Leg Boys St; VP Drama Clb; JCL; Ski Clb; Chorus; Concert Band; School Musical; Rep Frsh Cls; Rep Stu Cncl; NHS; Drama Clb Special Effects & Lightng Awd 86; Communications.

MC ANDREWS, PATRICIA A; St Francis Prep; Flushing, NY; (S); 90/693; Drama Clb; Pres SADD; School Musical; School Play; Yrbk Phtg; Rep Soph Cls; Rep Jr Cls; Rep Sr Cls; NHS; Natl Merit Leadrshp Awd.

MC ARDLE, ALLISON; Victor Central HS; Farmington, NY; (Y); Cheerleading; Sftbl; Vllybl; High Hon Roll; Hon Roll; Prfct Atten Awd; Gregg Typng Awd 85-86; Comp Pgmmng.

MC ARDLE, THOMAS M; St Marys Boys HS; Floral Park, NY; (Y); Boy Scts; Chess Clb; Quiz Bowl; Rep Stu Cncl; Capt Var Crs Cntry; Capt Var Trk; Ntl Merit Ltr; Rgnts Schlrshp 86.

MC ARTHUR, DEBORAH; Connetquot HS; Ronkonkoma, NY; (S); 4/699; Science Clb; Band; Drill Tm; Mrchg Band; Yrbk Ed-Chief; Diving; Swmmng; NHS; Ntl Merit Ltr; RPI Mdlst 85; Vet.

MC AULEY, THOMAS; Lake George HS; Glens Falls, NY; (Y); Church Yth Grp; Bsbl; Socr; Wt Lftg; French Hon Soc; High Hon Roll; Hon Roll; Vrsty Lttr 85; Med.

MC AULIFFE, COLLEEN; Rome Catholic HS; Rome, NY; (Y); School Musical; Nwsp Rptr; Yrbk Ed-Chief; Yrbk Stf; Sec Jr Cls; Sec Sr Cls; Var Capt Bsktbl; High Hon Roll; NHS; NEDT Awd; US Stu Cncl Awd 86; Acdmc All-Amer 86; Syracuse U; Jrnlsm.

MC AUSLAN, TERRI A; Mexico HS; Mexico, NY; (Y); 6/182; German Clb; Rep Stu Cncl; Crs Cntry; Hon Roll; NHS; Spanish NHS; Rgnts Schlrshp Wnn 86; NE Conf Tchng Offrgn Lang 86; DA NK Essy 2nd Pl Awd 86; SUNY Oswego; German.

MC AVENEY, GEORDIE; Lincoln HS; Yonkers, NY; (S); #2 In Class; Band; Rptr Nwsp Stf; High Hon Roll; Hon Roll; Jr NHS; NHS; Ntl Merit SF; Engrng.

MC AVOY, JENNIFER; Cicero-North Syracuse HS; Liverpool, NY; (S); 30/667; VP Sec JA; Drm & Bgl; Mrchg Band; Cheerleading; Hon Roll; VP Persnl And Corp Sec Of Yr 84-85; Oswego State; Zoo Tech.

MC AVOY, SANDRA J; Newfane SR HS; Olcott, NY; (S); 1/181; AFS; Exploring; Math Clb; Pep Band; School Musical; Symp Band; Yrbk Stf; Hon Roll; Pres NHS; Ntl Merit Ltr; NY ST U-Buffalo; Vet Med.

MC BATH, EILEEN; Lisbon Central HS; Lisbon, NY; (S); 2/37; French Clb; Band; Mrchg Band; Yrbk Stf; Trs Stu Cncl; Var Vllybl; High Hon Roll; Hon Roll; NHS; Prfct Atten Awd; Bio Chem.

MC BRIDE, BONNIE; Mechanicville HS; Mechanicville, NY; (S); 15/100; Concert Band; Yrbk Phtg; Rep Stu Cncl; L Bsktbl; Capt Socr; L Sftbl; Hon Roll; Jr NHS; French Clb.

MC BRIDE, PATRICK; Archbishop Molloy HS; Jackson Hts, NY; (Y); 72/383; Church Yth Grp; Math Tm; Pep Clb; Science Clb; Im Bsktbl; Im Ftbl; Im Sftbl; Im Trk; Dntstry.

MC BRIDE, TIM; Skaneateles Central HS; Skaneateles, NY; (S); Am Leg Boys St; Var JV Bsbl; Var JV Bsktbl; High Hon Roll; NHS; Ntl Merit Ltr; JV Ftbl; High Hnr Roll 80-86; All-League & Rookie Of The Year Awd Vrsty Bsktbl 86; Merit Schlr Awd; Ivy League; Bus Mgt.

MC CABE, CAITLIN; Roy C Ketcham HS; Poughkeepsie, NY; (Y); Church Yth Grp; Drama Clb; Band; School Musical; School Play; Nwsp Stf; Bsktbl; Trk; DAR Awd; High Hon Roll; Pro Model 84-86; U CA; Commnctns.

MC CABE, JOAN; St Barnabas HS; Bronx, NY; (Y); Library Aide; Varsity Clb; Off Jr Cls; Bsktbl; Stu Of Merit Eng 85-86; Stu Of Mnth Eng 85-86.

MC CABE, KELLY; Mount Mercy Acad; Orchard Park, NY; (Y); Church Yth Grp; Drama Clb; Ski Clb; Spanish Clb; SADD; Varsity Clb; Chorus; Var Crs Cntry; JV Fld Hcky; Var Trk; 1st Pl Awd Art Drwng 83-84; Comp Grphcs.

MC CABE, TIMOTHY; Sayville HS; Sayville, NY; (Y); 31/360; Key Clb; Var Tennis; Var Trk; High Hon Roll; Hon Roll; Jr NHS; Stony Brook.

MC CAFFERY, JEANNE; North Salem HS; Brewster, NY; (Y); Math Clb; Teachers Aide; Band; Variety Show; Nwsp Rptr; Yrbk Ed-Chief; Yrbk Stf; JV Var Socr; Im Swmmng; Var Capt Vllybl; Pol Sci.

MC CAFFREY, BRIAN; Mt St Michael HS; Bronx, NY; (Y); 54/292; Rgnts Schlrshp; Buffalo U; Cvl Engrng.

MC CAFFREY, DAVID; Aquinas Inst; Rochester, NY; (Y); Ski Clb; Chorus; Hon Roll; VP JA; Bus Mngmnt.

MC CAFFREY, LAURIE; Geneva HS; Geneva, NY; (S); 4/175; Am Leg Aux Girls St; French Clb; Ski Clb; School Musical; Lit Mag; Stu Cncl; Bausch & Lomb Sci Awd; High Hon Roll; Pres NHS; Paideia Awd-Humanities 85.

MC CAFFREY, SHANNON; Newburgh Free Acad; Newburgh, NY; (Y); Drama Clb; Acpl Chr; VP Chorus; Madrigals; School Musical; Yrbk Stf; Trs Stu Cncl; Var Crs Cntry; Var Trk; High Hon Roll; GTI Graphics Tech Eng II Awd 86; Most Imprvd Cross Cty Rnnr 84; Wm L Zahn Awd Exc Music Perf 84; Pre-Law.

MC CAFFREY, TRACY A; St Francis Prep; Flushing, NY; (S); 150/750; Church Yth Grp; Im JV Tennis; Opt Clb Awd; Law.

MC CAGUE, STEVEN; Monticello HS; Monticello, NY; (Y); Var Socr; Purdue; Comp Sci.

MC CALL, JEFF; Horseheads HS; Horseheads, NY; (Y); Art Clb; Boy Scts; Debate Tm; Quiz Bowl; Chorus; Variety Show; Yrbk Rptr; Yrbk Stf; Rep Frsh Cls; Rep Soph Cls; Oswego; Comp Pgmmr.

MC CALL, RUSSELL J; Cherry Valley Central HS; Cherry Valley, NY; (Y); 2/26; Drama Clb; VP Varsity Clb; VP Stu Cncl; Var L Bsbl; Var L Bsktbl; Var L Socr; NHS; Boy Scts; Band; Concert Band; Regnts Schlrshp 86; Clarks Schlshp 86; Su Mnth Jan 85; Rensselaer Poly Inst.

MC CALL, SHAWN; Wilson Magnet HS; Rochester, NY; (Y); Math Tm; NHS; Nwsp Stf; Yrbk Stf; Rep Frsh Cls; Off Jr Cls; High Hon Roll; Hon Roll; Prfct Atten Awd; Afro Amer Yth Exc Awd 86; Blk Schlrs Erly Rcgntn Hnr 85.

MC CALL, TIMOTHY; Horseheads HS; Horseheads, NY; (Y); Boy Scts; Computer Clb; Spanish Clb; Band; Concert Band; Mrchg Band; Orch; Var Diving; Hon Roll; Variety Show; Comp Progrmmr.

MC CALLEN, JENNY A; Maria Regina HS; Yonkers, NY; (Y); 17/130; Hosp Aide; Capt Var Swmmng; Capt Var Vllybl; High Hon Roll; Hon Roll; NHS; Church Yth Grp; Exploring; Key Clb; Lit Mag; Hnrs Cnvctn 85-86; Rgnts Nrsng Schlrshp 85-86; Jv Vlbl MVP 83-84; SUNY Binghamton; Pre-Med.

MC CALLUM JR, DAVID C; Irondequoit HS; Rochester, NY; (Y); 38/351; Boy Scts; Stage Crew; Pres Stu Cncl; Capt Trk; CC Awd; Cit Awd; NHS; Pres Schlr; SAR Awd; Rep Frsh Cls; Richard Thomson Mem Outstndng Ldrshp 86; Le Moyne Coll Jesuit Acad Awd 86; NY ST Rgnts Schlrshp 86; Le Moyne Coll; Phych.

MC CANE, CHRISTIE; Lake George Central HS; Lake George, NY; (Y); Church Yth Grp; SADD; Chorus; Color Guard; Mrchg Band; High Hon Roll; Hon Roll; Prfct Atten Awd; Bus.

MC CANN, ANTHONY; Columbia HS; East Greenbush, NY; (Y); 33/417; Political Wkr; Nwsp Ed-Chief; Nwsp Rptr; Nwsp Stf; Lit Mag; Im JV Socr; Hon Roll; NHS; Nwspr Bst Edtrl Wrtng; Lake Forest Coll; Psychlgy.

MC CANN, CHRISTINE; Nardin Acad; West Seneca, NY; (S); Speech Tm; School Musical; School Play; Nwsp Rptr; Lit Mag; Rep Frsh Cls; Rep Jr Cls; Trs Stu Cncl; Hon Roll; NHS; Public Rltns.

MC CANN, CLAIRE; Mt St Ursula HS; Bronx, NY; (Y); 1/140; Trk; High Hon Roll; Hon Roll; Spanish NHS; Clb Slf Defns Clb; Bus.

MC CANN, JEFF; Paul V Moore HS; W Monroe, NY; (Y); High Hon Roll; Hon Roll.

MC CANN, JENNIFER; Half Hollow Hills High School West; Dix Hills, NY; (Y); Pres Church Yth Grp; Cmnty Wkr; Service Clb; Capt Flag Corp; Mrchg Band; School Musical; Swing Chorus; Symp Band; Lit Mag; High Hon Roll; Cpt Flg Corp 86-87; NYSMA Music Awds 83-85; Chrch Dist Pres/Rep For Cnfrnc Lvl 85-87; Spec Educ.

MC CANN, SUZANNE B; Elmira Free Acad; Elmira, NY; (Y); French Clb; Key Clb; Ski Clb; Chorus; High Hon Roll; NHS; NYS Rgnts Schlrshp 86; SUNY Binghamton; Bio.

MC CARROLL, RITA; Notre Dame-Bishop Gibbons HS; Schenectady, NY; (S); 9/100; Var Capt Bsktbl; Crs Cntry; Var Trk; High Hon Roll; NHS.

MC CARTAN, KEVIN; Guilderland Central HS; Albany, NY; (Y); Key Clb; JV Bsktbl; JV Crs Cntry; High Hon Roll; Bus.

MC CARTHY, CATHERINE; Gilbertsville Central Schl; Gilbertsville, NY; (Y); 5/18; Girl Scts; School Play; Rep Stu Cncl; Cheerleading; Crs Cntry; Sftbl; Trk; Intr Dsgn.

MC CARTHY, COLLEEN; Villa Maria Acad; Cheektowaga, NY; (S); VP Church Yth Grp; JV Bowling; Var Capt Cheerleading; Var Gym; Var Sftbl; Var Capt Vllybl; Hon Roll; NHS; Rep Frsh Cls; JR Cls VP 84-85; SR Cls Treas 85-86; Educ.

MC CARTHY, DANIEL; Beacon HS; Beacon, NY; (S); 3/169; Am Leg Boys St; Pres Key Clb; Ed Yrbk Rptr; VP Frsh Cls; VP Stu Cncl; Var Bsbl; Im Coach Actv; Capt Var Ftbl; High Hon Roll; NHS; Naval ROTC Schlrshp Wnnr 86; Apptnd USMA West Point 86; All-Conf Ftbl 84-85; USMA West Point; Comp Engr.

MC CARTHY, DANIEL LYNN; Thomas A Edison JR SR HS; Elmira Hts, NY; (Y); 5/74; Am Leg Boys St; Varsity Clb; Nwsp Stf; Yrbk Stf; Stu Cncl; Ftbl; Trk; Elks Awd; High Hon Roll; Regents Scholar 86; Corning CC; Elec Engrng.

MC CARTHY, DENIS J; Xaverian HS; Brooklyn, NY; (Y); 52/340; Computer Clb; NFL; School Musical; Lit Mag; Jr NHS; Ntl Merit SF; St Jhns U Acdmc Exc Schlrshp 86-87; Helena Rbnstn Schlrshp 84-85 & 85-86; St Jhns U Jmca; Fine Arts.

MC CARTHY, EDWARD; Solvay HS; Solvay, NY; (Y); 3/171; Rep Jr Cls; Capt Ice Hcky; High Hon Roll; Mu Alp Tht; Pres NHS; Ntl Merit Ltr; Pres Schlr; Cmnty Wkr; Sec Key Clb; Letterman Clb; Cntrl Ny Hi-Quiz Chmpns 85-86; Rsrv Ntl Chmpn Arbn Judgng Tm 84; Bill Charles Outstndng Hcky Plr Awd; Cornell U; Pre-Med.

MC CARTHY, ELIZABETH; Niagara Catholic HS; Niagara Falls, NY; (Y); 10/80; Spanish Clb; Stat Bsktbl; JV Var Cheerleading; Stat Vllybl; Hon Roll; NHS; Niagara U; Acctng.

MC CARTHY, HEATHER; Bethpage HS; Bethpage, NY; (Y); 60/306.

MC CARTHY, JENNIFER; Cazenovia HS; Erieville, NY; (Y); High Hon Roll; Hon Roll; Hi-Achvmnt Comp Lit 85; Hi-Achvmnt Soc Stud 86; Hi-Avg Advncd Comp 86; Comp Sci.

MC CARTHY, JO ANN; Nardin Acad; Orchard Pk, NY; (Y); French Clb; Hosp Aide; Service Clb; Ski Clb; School Musical; Yrbk Stf; Rep Soph Cls; Var Bsktbl; Golf; JV Tennis; Glf 1st Pl Cnty Tourn 86 & Sm-Fnls St Jr Grls Amatr Tourn 85 & 86; Sci Fairs 3rd Pl Cnty & Schl 84-86.

MC CARTHY, KAREN; Notre Dame HS; Horseheads, NY; (Y); #1 In Class; Key Clb; Nwsp Ed-Chief; Yrbk Stf; Bsktbl; Socr; Vllybl; High Hon Roll; Lion Awd; NHS; Val; NY Rgnts Schlrshp 86; Cntry III Ldrshp Prog Schl Wnnr 85; Syracuse U; Lawyer.

MC CARTHY, KATHERINE; School Of The Holy Child; Pelham, NY; (S); GAA; Hosp Aide; Ski Clb; Stage Crew; Rep Frsh Cls; Pres Soph Cls; Pres Jr Cls; Pres Stu Cncl; Capt Bsktbl; Capt Fld Hcky; 2nd Hnrs; Modern European Hstry Awd; All Lg Field Hockey.

MC CARTHY, KERRY; Our Lady Of Mercy HS; Fairport, NY; (Y); GAA; Hosp Aide; Varsity Clb; Var JV Bsktbl; JV Score Keeper; JV Socr; JV Sftbl; Hon Roll; MVP Bsktbl; Physcl Thrpy.

MC CARTHY, LAURA; Charles C Damico HS; Albion, NY; (S); 1/189; Am Leg Aux Girls St; Hst Latin Clb; Lit Mag; Trk; High Hon Roll; NHS; Rochester Inst Tech; Engrng.

MC CARTHY, PATRICIA; Rensselaer JR SR HS; Rensselaer, NY; (Y); 41/94; Boys Clb Am; JV Var Cheerleading; JV Var Pom Pon; Hon Roll; Girl Yr 86; Fash Show 86.

MC CARTHY, SEAN P; Monsignor Farrell HS; Staten Island, NY; (Y); 33/288; Cmnty Wkr; Band; Concert Band; Jazz Band; Mrchg Band; Nwsp Rptr; Nwsp Stf; Yrbk Stf; Im Capt Bowling; Hon Roll; 2nd Pl Mrchng Bnd Cls I EMBA.85-86.

MC CARTHY, TIMOTHY; Mt St Michael Acad; Bronx, NY; (Y); 78/299; Var JV Crs Cntry; Var JV Trk; Manhattan; Natural Sci.

MC CARTHY, WILLIAM; St Francis Prep HS; Flushing, NY; (Y); 313/726; Church Yth Grp.

MC CARTY, ANGELA; Bitburg American HS; APO, NY; (Y); Church Yth Grp; Drama Clb; French Clb; Band; Church Choir; Concert Band; School Play; High Hon Roll; Hon Roll; NHS; Educational Olympics Slvr Medal 84; Schlrshp Cert Hnr 85; Wright OH ST U; Pre-Law.

MC CARTY, COLLEEN; Rocky Point JR SR HS; Rocky Point, NY; (S); 3/210; Sec Computer Clb; Mathletes; Spanish Clb; Thesps; School Play; Nwsp Rptr; Nwsp Stf; Sec Frsh Cls; Hon Roll; Aerosp Engr.

MC CARTY, KAREN; Waterloo SR HS; Waterloo, NY; (Y); 35/163; FTA; Acpl Chr; Chorus; Swing Chorus; Nwsp Rptr; Nwsp Stf; High Hon Roll; Hon Roll; Elizabeth J Amidon Mem Awd 86; CC Finger Lks; Acctng.

MC CARTY, SHEILA; Aquinas HS; Rochester, NY; (Y); 25/140; 4-H; Ski Clb; Var L Cheerleading; Var L Socr; Sftbl; Hon Roll; SUNY Brockport; Ed.

MC CARTY, SKIP; Odessa-Montour Central HS; Montour Falls, NY; (Y); Am Leg Boys St; Aud/Vis; School Musical; Ed Lit Mag; Rep Stu Cncl; Var L Bsbl; Var L Bsktbl; Var L Ftbl; Prfct Atten Awd; OMCS Athlt Yr 86; SUNY; Radio.

MC CARVILLE, COLLEEN; Clarkstown HS North; New City, NY; (Y); Natl Beta Clb; JV Bsktbl; Mu Alp Tht; SUNY Oswego; Ed.

MC CAULEY, ROBBYN J; Newburgh Free Acad; Newburgh, NY; (Y); 66/700; Hosp Aide; Service Clb; Yrbk Stf; Pom Pon; High Hon Roll; Jr NHS; Rotary Awd; Rgnts Schlrshp 86; Ithaca Coll Schlrshp 86; Ithaca Coll; Bus Adm.

MC CAULEY, THOMAS G; Vestal SR HS; Binghamton, NY; (Y); 39/430; Boy Scts; Church Yth Grp; Service Clb; Varsity Clb; Rep Stu Cncl; JV Bsktbl; Var Crs Cntry; Var Lcrss; Var Wrstlng; High Hon Roll; Russn Clb 83-86; Boy Scts Amer Lf Sct 83; Boy Scts Amer Lf Grd 85-86; Alt Selct Navl ROTC Schlrshp 86; Holy Cross; Physcs.

MC CLAFFERTY, RITA; Central Islip HS; Central Islip, NY; (Y); 16/320; Cmnty Wkr; Nwsp Phtg; Nwsp Stf; Var Mgr(s); Var Capt Sftbl; Var Capt Tennis; Hon Roll; Josephine Queen Mem Schlrshp 86; Mth Awd A Avrg 4 Yrs 86; 100 Clb 100 Mth Rgnts 86; Suny At Binghamton; Actrl Sci.

MC CLAIN, CHARNAYE; Trott Vocational HS; Niagara Falls, NY; (Y); Dance Clb; Hosp Aide; JA; Yrbk Stf; Hon Roll; NHS; Schlrshp Nrsng 85; VP Natl Hon Soc 86-87; Hon Roll 84-86; Med.

MC CLAIN, CHRISTOPHER; Centereach HS; Selden, NY; (Y); Chorus; NHS; C W Post Coll; Acctg.

MC CLAIN, TONJA; Central Islip HS; Central Islip, NY; (Y); Pep Clb; Band; Mrchg Band; Nwsp Rptr; Nwsp Stf; Pres Frsh Cls; Pres Soph Cls; Rep Jr Cls; Var Capt Cheerleading; Var Capt Sftbl; All Lge Awd Suffolk Cnty Sftbll 84-86; Elec Engrng.

MC CLARY, MELISSA; Uniondale HS; Uniondale, NY; (Y); Drama Clb; School Musical; School Play; Stage Crew; Cmnty Wkr; FBLA; Office Aide; Speech Tm; SADD; Sftbl; Broadcasting.

MC CLELLAND, KEVIN; Olean HS; Olean, NY; (Y); 97/220; Boy Scts; VP Church Yth Grp; Varsity Clb; Band; Concert Band; Mrchg Band; Orch; JV Bsktbl; Var Capt Crs Cntry; Var Capt Trk; Comp Sci.

MC CLEMENTS, SHELLEY J; Camden HS; Camden, NY; (Y); 6/189; AFS; French Clb; Pres SADD; Orch; Nwsp Stf; Yrbk Ed-Chief; Var Cheerleading; Var Pom Pon; High Hon Roll; NHS; Rgnts Schlrshp 86; Lamp Of Lrning Awd 84; Wells Coll; Pre-Med.

MC CLOSKEY, KEVIN F; MSGR Mc Clancy HS; Woodside, NY; (Y); Church Yth Grp; Cmnty Wkr; High Hon Roll; Hon Roll; Ntl Merit Schol; Pace U Schlrshp 86; Pace U; Comp Sys.

MC CLOSKY, MARK; Scotia-Glenville HS; Scotia, NY; (Y); Camera Clb; Cmnty Wkr; Key Clb; Hon Roll; Photographer.

MC CLURE, CHRIS; West Lake HS; Hawthorne, NY; (Y); Ski Clb; Var JV Bsbl; Var JV Bsktbl; Var JV Ftbl; Wrstlng; Hon Roll; Bus.

MC CLURE, LAURIE; St Marys HS; E Aurora, NY; (Y); GAA; Pep Clb; Varsity Clb; School Musical; School Play; Rep Frsh Cls; Rep Soph Cls; Tennis; Scrtrl.

MC CLURE, SHERYL; Narrowsburg Central Schl; Narrowsburg, NY; (Y); 5/25; CAP; SADD; Band; Chorus; Mrchg Band; School Musical; Nwsp Rptr; Yrbk Stf; Jr NHS; NHS; 5th Honors Cum Laude 86; ST U Of NY; Atmsphrc Sci.

MC CLURG, TAD; Perry Central HS; Perry, NY; (Y); Computer Clb; Math Tm; Nwsp Phtg; Yrbk Phtg; Yrbk Stf; Coach Actv; Score Keeper; Var JV Socr; Cit Awd; Hon Roll; Achvt Awd Comp 84 & 86; BOCPS Cert Partcptn 85; Comp Fair 85; Physcs.

MC CLUSKEY, JOHN D; Coxsackie-Athens HS; W Coxsackie, NY; (Y); 2/105; Var Ftbl; High Hon Roll; NHS; Ntl Merit Ltr; Law.

MC COLGIN, KRISTAN; Hamburg SR HS; Hamburg, NY; (Y); 62/326; Church Yth Grp; Capt Color Guard; Swmmng; Tennis; Bus Finance.

MC COMB, LAUREN; Hoosic Valley Central Schl; Valley Falls, NY; (Y); SADD; Band; Chorus; JV Var Bsktbl; JV Var Fld Hcky; JV Sftbl; High Hon Roll; NHS; Yorker Treas 83-84; Select Chorus 85-86; Pre-Med.

MC COMISKEY, THOMAS J; Tottenville HS; Staten Island, NY; (Y); 59/890; Ski Clb; Yrbk Phtg; Var Crs Cntry; Var Trk; High Hon Roll; Hon Roll; NHS; Regents Schlrshp; Rutgers U; Engrng.

MC CONLOGUE, WILLIAM J; Holy Trinity HS; Levittown, NY; (Y); JV Wrstlng; Nassau CC; Engrng.

MC CONNAN, KELLY; Midlakes HS; Clifton Spgs, NY; (Y); 50/170; Camera Clb; 4-H; French Clb; Thesps; Varsity Clb; School Play; Yrbk Sprt Ed; Yrbk Stf; Var Cheerleading; Var Powder Puff Ftbl; Fshn Inst Tech; Fshn Mrchndsng.

MC CONNELL, KATHERINE; East Islip HS; East Islip, NY; (Y); 9/425; FBLA; SADD; Nwsp Bus Mgr; Capt L Tennis; L Vllybl; Jr NHS; NHS; Sprt E Islip Awd, Gld Key Awd 86; Williams Coll; Pol Eco.

MC CONNELL, RHONDA; Indian River Central HS; Theresa, NY; (Y); 17/116; Pres French Clb; Sec Trs Key Clb; Stage Crew; Stu Cncl; Trk; Hon Roll; Prfct Atten Awd; Prjct Charlie Prtcpnt Awds 84&85; Air Force; Air Cargo.

MC CONNELL, SCOTT; Indian River Central Schl; Philadelphia, NY; (Y); 1/142; Computer Clb; Key Clb; Quiz Bowl; Stu Cncl; Crs Cntry; Wrstlng; Bausch & Lomb Sci Awd; High Hon Roll; NHS; Pres Schlr; Engr.

MC CONNELL, SHERRI; Falconer Central Schl; Jamestown, NY; (Y); 8/120; Church Yth Grp; Drama Clb; French Clb; OEA; Ski Clb; Band; Chorus; Church Choir; Concert Band; Orch; Outstndng Social Study Awd 84; Outstndng Drmtst Awd 85; Uyssma Music Awd 84; Psych.

MC CONVET, WILLIAM; Frontier Central HS; Blasdell, NY; (Y); 5/500; Am Leg Boys St; Boy Scts; Concert Band; Mrchg Band; Bsktbl; Vllybl; High Hon Roll; NHS; Voice Dem Awd; MIT; Mech Engrng.

MC CONVEY, WILLIAM; Frontier Central HS; Blasdell, NY; (Y); 1/475; Am Leg Boys St; Boy Scts; German Clb; Concert Band; Jazz Band; Mrchg Band; Var Bsktbl; Var Vllybl; High Hon Roll; NHS; Eagle Scout 85; Naval Acad; Mech Engrng.

MC COOEY, CHARLES; Frontier Central HS; Hamburg, NY; (Y); Boy Scts; Drama Clb; SADD; VICA; School Musical; School Play; Stage Crew; Variety Show; Ftbl; Hon Roll; Carpentry.

MC COOEY, MICHAEL; William Nottingham HS; Syracuse, NY; (Y); 1/306; Math Tm; Lit Mag; Var Crs Cntry; Var Trk; High Hon Roll; NHS; Ntl Merit Ltr; Boy Scts; French Clb; Latin Clb; 1st Cnty Math Cntst 84; Summa Cum Laude Natl Latn Exm 84-85; Natl Frnch Cntst 84-862nd Math Leag 85-86.

MC CORD, CHRISTINE; Francis Schl; Staten Island, NY; (Y); Cmnty Wkr; Girl Scts; School Play; Pres Soph Cls; Capt Cheerleading; Powder Puff Ftbl; Stat Sftbl; High Hon Roll; Hon Roll; Bus Mgmt.

MC CORD, JAY; Salmanca Central HS; Salamanca, NY; (Y); Church Yth Grp; Cmnty Wkr; Nwsp Stf; VP Soph Cls; JV Bsktbl; JV Var Ftbl; Mgr(s); Trk; Wt Lftg; Cit Awd; O M Wrld Fnls 8th Pl 86; Alfred ST; Bldg Constr.

MC CORMACK, CARA L; Our Lady Of Mercy HS; Henrietta, NY; (Y); Drama Clb; Ski Clb; Varsity Clb; School Musical; School Play; Var Diving; JV Vllybl; Hon Roll; MVP Vlybl Tm 85-86; Spec Ed.

MC CORMACK, ELIZABETH A; Pleasantville HS; Pleasantville, NY; (Y); Sec PAVAS; Chorus; School Musical; Yrbk Stf; Twrlr; Sec French Clb; JV Socr; Hon Roll.

MC CORMACK, ERIN; Immaculata Acad; Eden, NY; (Y); Quiz Bowl; Trs Soph Cls; Var Cheerleading; Hon Roll; Trs NHS; Natl Sci Merit Awd Chem 86; Acad All-Amer 86; Marywood Coll; Fash Merch.

MC CORMACK, FRANK; Msgr Farrell HS; Staten Island, NY; (Y); 32/356; JV Socr; French Hon Soc; High Hon Roll; Ntl Merit SF; Mgr Aud/Vis; Teachers Aide; U Of S CA; Film Prod.

MC CORMACK, MICHAEL A; Croton-Harmon HS; Croton-On-Hudson, NY; (Y); AFS; Am Leg Boys St; Boy Scts; Drama Clb; Varsity Clb; Band; Concert Band; Mrchg Band; Yrbk Stf; Stu Cncl; Hnr Key 86; Vasser Bk Clb Awd 86; Rensslr Poly Inst Medal Math,Sci 86.

MC CORMACK, PATRICIA; St Marys HS; Roslyn Heights, NY; (Y); 31/170; Chorus; JV Var Bsktbl; JV Var Vllybl; NHS; Regnts Schlrshp 86; Villanova U.

MC CORMICK, CANDY; Spring Valley SR HS; Spring Valley, NY; (Y); 52/441; Key Clb; Spanish Clb; JV Cheerleading; JV Sftbl; High Hon Roll; Hon Roll; Mu Alp Tht; Spanish NHS; Sci Achvt Awd 86; Pres Acad Ftnss Awd 86; St Thomas Aquinas Acad Schlrshp 86; St Thomas Aquinas Coll; Med Tch.

MC CORMICK, KRISTI; James Madison HS; Brooklyn, NY; (Y); 26/756; Cmnty Wkr; Debate Tm; FBLA; Pres JA; Model UN; Office Aide; Political Wkr; Service Clb; Chorus; School Play; NY ST Bar Assn Mck Trial Awd 86; Cert Achvt Law 86; Cornell U; Law.

MC CORMICK, MARY K; St Marys Girls HS; Great Neck, NY; (Y); 53/171; Art Clb; Im Lcrss; Im Tennis; High Hon Roll; Hon Roll; NHS; Ctr For Crtv Perfmng Arts; St Johns Sat Schlrshp Prog Art; Regnts Schlrshp; RI Sch Of Design; Dsgn/Fash.

MC CORMICK, MEGAN; Rye HS; Rye, NY; (Y); Dance Clb; Ski Clb; Var Socr; Var Swmmng; Var Trk; Hon Roll; Bio.

MC CORMICK, MICHELLE; C W Baker HS; Baldwinsville, NY; (Y); 2/376; Yrbk Ed-Chief; Stu Cncl; High Hon Roll; Jr NHS; NHS; Ntl Merit Ltr; Sal; NYS Rgnts Coll Schlrshp 86; Pres Acad Ftns Awd 86; Cornell U; Econ.

MC CORMICK, PAMALA; Clara Barton HS; Brooklyn, NY; (Y); Church Yth Grp; Drama Clb; Girl Scts; Teachers Aide; Church Choir; Nwsp Rptr; Yrbk Stf; Lit Mag; Hon Roll; Spanish NHS; 12th Congrssnl Martin Luthr King Essy Cntst 2nd Pl 86; Prncpls Pride Of Yankees Awd 85; Howard U; Engl.

MC CORMICK, PAT; Ravena-Coeymans-Selkirk Centrl HS; Selkirk, NY; (Y); Ski Clb; Rep Frsh Cls; Rep Soph Cls; Rep Jr Cls; Rep Sr Cls; Sec VP Stu Cncl; Var Capt Ftbl; Hon Roll; French Clb; High Hon Roll; Stu Ldrshp Committee 86; Plattsburgh ST; Ins.

MC CORMICK, PATRICK; Ravena-Coeymans Selkirk Ctrl HS; Glenmont, NY; (Y); Ski Clb; Rep Frsh Cls; Rep Soph Cls; Rep Jr Cls; Rep Sr Cls; Sec VP Stu Cncl; Var Capt Ftbl; High Hon Roll; French Clb; Hon Roll; Stdnt Ldrshp Comm 86; Prom Ct 86; Plattsburgh ST; Intl Bus.

MC CORMICK, SEAN; Saranac Lake HS; Saranac Lk, NY; (Y); Ski Clb; Engrng.

MC CORMICK, THOMSON T; Vestal SR HS; Binghamton, NY; (Y); Am Leg Boys St; Boy Scts; Ski Clb; Spanish Clb; Trs Stu Cncl; Church Yth Grp; Science Clb; SADD; Trs Soph Cls; Im Tennis; Pres Ntl Hnr Soc 86-87; Vgl Hnr Ordr Of Arrw 86; Egl Sct W/3 Plms 81; Schlrshp U Of Madrid.

MC COSKERY, KAREN; John H Glenn HS; E Northport, NY; (Y); Art Clb; Stage Crew; Lit Mag; Bowling; Hon Roll; Jr NHS; NHS; Spanish NHS; Ed.

MC COURT, ELIZABETH; East Hampton HS; E Hampton, NY; (Y); 27/164; VP Intnl Clb; Trs SADD; Madrigals; School Musical; Trs Stu Cncl; VP L Gym; VP Sftbl; L Trk; Hon Roll; Cmnty Wkr; Digate Awd 86; Cntrbtn Schl Envir Awd 84 & 86; Gold Mdl Stu Govt Svc 86; Child Psychlgy.

MC COURTY, PAMELA; Fashion Indust; Bronx, NY; (Y); 33/358; Model UN; School Play; Sr Cls; Cit Awd; High Hon Roll; Hon Roll; Prfct Atten Awd; Biol Sci Awd 86; Acad All Amer 86; Herbert H Lettman Coll; Pre-Med.

MC CRAE, DERRICK; Park West HS; Brooklyn, NY; (Y); Art Clb; Boys Clb Am; Boy Scts; Cmnty Wkr; Computer Clb; Library Aide; Science Clb; Band; Chorus; Drm & Bgl; Diesel Engnrng.

MC CRANN, TRACI A; A G Berner HS; Massapequa, NY; (Y); 25/425; Church Yth Grp; Cmnty Wkr; GAA; Pep Clb; Acpl Chr; Chorus; Variety Show; JV Var Bsktbl; Im Socr; JV Var Sftbl; Regents Schlrshp 86; Daemen Coll Deans Schlrshp 86; Marquette & St Louis Hnr Awds 86; Daemen Coll; Phy Thrpy.

MC CREA, KATHERINE; Cooperstown Central HS; Cooperstown, NY; (Y); 5/98; 4-H; GAA; Math Tm; Band; Concert Band; Mrchg Band; Pep Band; Stage Crew; Var L Crs Cntry; Var L Socr; Amer Legn Gd Ctznshp Awd 86; Bucknell U.

MC CREAR, KIMBERLY; Forest Hills HS; Jamaica, NY; (Y); 238/854; Queens Coll; Psych.

MC CREEDY, KEITH; Buffalo Traditional Schl; Buffalo, NY; (S); 3/111; Church Yth Grp; Debate Tm; Math Clb; Varsity Clb; Swmmng; Trk; Cit Awd; Hon Roll; NHS; SAR Awd; Swim Tm Capt 85; Natl Hnr Soc Pres 85; Cent III Ldrshp Comp 85; Buffalo ST Coll; Engrng.

MC CUE, LYNDA; John Adams HS; Ozone Park, NY; (Y); Pres Key Clb; Teachers Aide; Trs Stu Cncl; Hon Roll; NHS; Buddy Sys Crdntr 85; Bus.

MC CULLOR, DANIEL THOMAS; Waterloo SR HS; Waterloo, NY; (Y); 20/157; Am Leg Boys St; Pres Drama Clb; Band; Drm Mjr(t); School Musical; Nwsp Stf; Yrbk Phtg; Yrbk Rptr; Tennis; NHS; US Air Frc Acad; Air Trffc.

MC CULLOUGH, DAWN; Wayne Central HS; Ontario, NY; (Y); Am Leg Aux Girls St; Chorus; Color Guard; School Musical; Yrbk Stf; Tchr.

MC CULLOUGH, JAMES A; Jamestown HS; Jamestown, NY; (Y); 21/375; Church Yth Grp; French Clb; Political Wkr; Ski Clb; Bsktbl; Sftbl; L Trk; High Hon Roll; Hon Roll; NHS; U CO; Bus Mgmt.

MC CULLOUGH, MARY; Cornwall Central HS; Salisbury Mills, NY; (Y); Math Tm; Nwsp Stf; Yrbk Stf; Hon Roll; NHS; Educ.

MC CULLY, KATHLEEN; Dryden JR SR HS; Dryden, NY; (Y); Church Yth Grp; Ski Clb; SADD; Varsity Clb; Yrbk Stf; Rep Frsh Cls; Pres Soph Cls; Pres Jr Cls; Pres Sr Cls; Rep Stu Cncl; Rochester Inst Tech; Htl Mgmt.

MC CUMBER, NISSA; William Nottingham HS; Syracuse, NY; (Y); Trs Church Yth Grp; Hosp Aide; Latin Clb; Ski Clb; JV Socr; Var Tennis; High Hon Roll; Sec NHS; Natl Ltn Exm-Cm Laud 3rd Pl 85 & 86; Engrng.

MC CUSKER, JOSEPH; Huntington HS; Huntington, NY; (Y); Key Clb; Band; School Play; Nwsp Sprt Ed; Trs Soph Cls; Var Ftbl; Jr NHS; NHS; Robert Mrazeks Stu Cngrss; Huntington Yacht Clb Sail Tm; Fin.

MC CUTCHAN, KAREN; St John Villa Acad; Staten Island, NY; (Y); 4/130; Math Tm; Chorus; School Musical; School Play; Yrbk Rptr; Yrbk Stf; High Hon Roll; NHS; Excllnce In Amer Hist Awd 85-86; Bus Mgmt.

MC DANIEL, KELLI; Tonawanda HS; Tonawanda, NY; (Y); French Clb; SADD; Band; Mrchg Band; Hon Roll; Niagara U; Accountant.

MC DERMOTT, DEBBIE; Waterloo SR HS; Waterloo, NY; (S); 3/157; French Clb; FTA; Band; Concert Band; Drm Mjr(t); Mrchg Band; Yrbk Stf; Stu Cncl; High Hon Roll; NHS; Yth Agnst Cncr; Med.

MC DERMOTT, JANE; Valley Central HS; Newburgh, NY; (Y); Pres Church Yth Grp; Varsity Clb; Rep Stu Cncl; Var Capt Cheerleading; Var L Sftbl; High Hon Roll; NHS; Spanish NHS; Rep Frsh Cls; Rep Soph Cls; Coach Strauss Awd 86; Cls Awd 86; Hobart And William Smith.

MC DERMOTT, KIMBERLY; Catholic Central HS; Cohoes, NY; (Y); Math Clb; SADD; Variety Show; Yrbk Stf; Rep Frsh Cls; Cheerleading; Var Pom Pon; High Hon Roll; Hon Roll; NHS; Bus Adm.

MC DEVITT, LINDA; Queen Of The Rosary Acad; Long Beach, NY; (S); 8/49; Church Yth Grp; Debate Tm; Drama Clb; Library Aide; Political Wkr; Church Choir; School Play; Stage Crew; Variety Show; Yrbk Stf; SUNY Binghamton; Advrtsng.

MC DIARMID, CORINNE; Sayville HS; W Sayville, NY; (Y); 296/320; Art Clb; FBLA; SADD; Band; Chorus; School Play; Yrbk Phtg; Yrbk Stf; JV Sftbl; Hon Roll; Acad Schlrshp 86; Northwood Inst; Htl Rstrnt.

MC DONAGH, ANNE MARIE; Carmel HS; Carmel, NY; (Y); 89/350; Orch; Yrbk Stf; Cheerleading; Crs Cntry; Trk; Hon Roll; NHS; Irish Step Dancing Ntl Champ 85; Marist; Physcl Thrpy.

MC DONAGH, PATRICIA; Scred Heart Acad; Vlg Of Bellerose, NY; (S); 3/182; Nwsp Ed-Chief; Rep Stu Cncl; High Hon Roll; NHS; Acad All Amer; Biol.

MC DONALD, CHRISTOPHER J; Saint Anthonys HS; East Northport, NY; (Y); 46/242; Nwsp Rptr; JV Crs Cntry; JV Trk; Var Wrstlng; Hon Roll; NHS; Spanish NHS; U Hnrs Pgm, $1000 Schlrshp SUNY; U Of Buffalo; Engrng.

MC DONALD, JASON; The Bronx HS Of Science; College Point, NY; (Y); Library Aide; Pres Model UN; Ed Nwsp Stf; Rep Jr Cls; Schl Rep On Grmn Tv 84-85; Albany Conf On Suicide Alumni Assn Schl Rep 84-85.

MC DONALD, KATHLEEN; Sanford H Calhoun HS; Merrick, NY; (Y); Var Badmtn; JV Vllybl; NHS; Physcl Thrpy.

MC DONALD, MARK J; Carthage Central HS; Felts Mill, NY; (Y); 21/177; Am Leg Boys St; Ski Clb; JV Bsktbl; Var Coach Actv; Var L Socr; Im Vllybl; Hon Roll; NHS; Rotary Awd; ROTC Schlrshp 87; All Str Hnbl Mntn 86; Alfred ST; Comp Dsgn.

MC DONALD, MAUREEN; Mt St Mary Acad; Buffalo, NY; (Y); 25/113; Boys Clb Am; Church Yth Grp; French Clb; Chorus; Yrbk Stf; Var Badmtn; Stat Bsktbl; Var Stat Gym; Mgr(s); Score Keeper; ST U Coll At Buffalo; Elem Mth.

MC DONALD, MELISSA; New Covenant Christian HS; Pittsford, NY; (S); 1/14; Church Yth Grp; Drama Clb; Boys Clb Am; Band; Chorus; Yrbk Stf; Var Bsktbl; Var Socr; High Hon Roll; Hon Roll.

MC DONALD, MELODY E; St Barnabas HS; Bronx, NY; (Y); 45/173; Library Aide; SADD; Nwsp Stf; Jr Cls; Sr Cls; JV Sftbl; Capt Vllybl; NYS Regnts Schlrshp 86; Bernard Baruch; Acctg.

MC DONALD, SHELLEY; Northern Adirondack Central; Ellenburg Depot, NY; (Y); Chess Clb; Key Clb; Library Aide; Pep Clb; Scholastic Bowl; Chorus; Nwsp Stf; Yrbk Stf; Mgr(s); Hon Roll; Plattsburgh ST U.

MC DONELL, HEATHER; Bishop Grimes HS; Syracuse, NY; (S); 11/146; Church Yth Grp; Ski Clb; Trs Band; Capt Var Socr; Var Sftbl; Var Trk; High Hon Roll; NHS; Bio.

MC DONNELL, CATHY; Our Lady Of Victory Acad; New York, NY; (S); 12/157; VP French Clb; Yrbk Sprt Ed; Lit Mag; Var Capt Bsktbl; Var Capt Trk; Var Vllybl; French Hon Soc; NHS; NEDT Awd; Alpha Hnr Soc 85; Ntl Scndry Educ Cncls Acadmc All Amrcn Awd 85; Annl Acamdc Schl Awds 84; Crmnl Justc.

MC DONNELL, DAVID; Uniondale HS; Uniondale, NY; (Y); Boy Scts; FBLA; Office Aide; Chorus; Variety Show; Yrbk Stf; Ftbl; Hon Roll; Jr NHS; Prfct Atten Awd; Prncpls Awd 84; Accntnt.

MC DONNELL, KAREN; Guilderland Central HS; Schenectady, NY; (Y); Trs Key Clb; Ski Clb; Orch; Var Diving; Var Swmmng; Var Trk; High Hon Roll; Hon Roll; Jr NHS; NHS; Schlrshp Awd 4th Mrktng Period 85; Sci Fair Prtcpnt 86; Schlrshp Awrds Diff Subjects 84-86; Sports Med.

MC DONOUGH, DENISE; Warwick Valley HS; Warwick, NY; (Y); 65/195; Var Cheerleading; Var Trk; Hon Roll; Most Outstndng Stu Csmtlgy 85-86; Highest Acdmc Awd Hlth-Genl Sci 84-85; Csmtlgy.

MC DONOUGH, GERARD M; Massapequa HS; Massapequa, NY; (Y); 80/440; Drm Mjr(t); Rep Stu Cncl; JV Bsbl; JV Ftbl; Hon Roll; Cert Recgntn Rssn & Advncd Grmn Lang; US Mltry Acad-West Point; Eco.

MC DONOUGH, JOHN E; Salesian HS; Pelham, NY; (Y); 6/86; Computer Clb; Jazz Band; Trs Stu Cncl; Var Bowling; Im Fld Hcky; NHS; Hofstra U; Music.

MC DONOUGH, KATHLEEN A; St Francis Prep HS; Richmond Hill, NY; (S); 120/750; Ski Clb; SADD; Var CAP; Hon Roll; Opt Clb Awd; Psych.

MC DONOUGH, MARY BETH; Newfane Central Schl; Olcott, NY; (Y); 31/148; Varsity Clb; Trk; Hon Roll; Genessee CC; Trvl-Toursm.

MC DONOUGH, MICHELE; Corning-Painted Post West HS; Corning, NY; (Y); 19/252; Letterman Clb; Varsity Clb; School Play; Var Capt Bsktbl; Var Capt Trk; Var L Vllybl; High Hon Roll; NHS; Ntl Merit Ltr; Rotary Awd; Cornell; Pre-Med.

MC DONOUGH, SUSAN; The Ursuline Schl; New Rochelle, NY; (Y); 23/121; Trs Church Yth Grp; Office Aide; PAVAS; School Musical; High Hon Roll; Hon Roll; Jr NHS; NHS; Dance Clb; Drama Clb; Pres Fitness Awd; New Rochelle Coll Schlrshp Noted Ursuline Schlr; Merit Schlrshp Iona Coll; SUNY-BINGHAMTON.

MC DOUGAL, ALEXANDER J; St Josephs Collegiate Inst; Kenmore, NY; (Y); 29/208; Boy Scts; Pres French Clb; Library Aide; NHS; Egl Sct 85; Ldrshp Awd Frnch Clb-Ntl Hnr Soc 86; Sct Of Yr Awd; Bus Adm.

MC DOUGALL, APRIL; Bitburg American HS; Tempe, AZ; (Y); Church Yth Grp; Drama Clb; Pep Clb; Band; Concert Band; Mrchg Band; Pep Band; School Play; Stage Crew; Hon Roll; AZ ST U; Elec Engrng.

MC DOUGALL, KERRI L; Argyle Central HS; Argyle, NY; (Y); 3/58; Sec Art Clb; VP French Clb; Yrbk Ed-Chief; Rep Stu Cncl; High Hon Roll; NHS; Natl Art Hnr Scty 86; Moore Coll Of Art; Grphc Dsgn.

MC DOWELL, MEGAN; Mercy HS; Hampton Bays, NY; (Y); 17/125; Mathletes; Ski Clb; SADD; Yrbk Stf; Mgr Stat Fld Hcky; Mgr(s); JV Var Sftbl; High Hon Roll; Hon Roll; NHS; Wellesley Coll; Bio.

MC DOWELL, REBECCA; Newark HS; Newark, NY; (Y); VP Church Yth Grp; French Clb; Hosp Aide; Band; Stat Gym; Var L Sftbl; Var L Swmmng; French Hon Soc; High Hon Roll; NHS; Engrng.

MC EACHIN, ANDREW; Mount Vernon HS; Mt Vernon, NY; (Y); Computer Clb; Hon Roll; Comp Engrng.

MC EATHRON, JODIE; Gouverneur HS; Gouverneur, NY; (Y); French Clb; Quiz Bowl; Chorus; Stu Cncl; Var Capt Vllybl; High Hon Roll; Hon Roll; Jr NHS; Masonic Awd; NHS; Vllybl Awds 84 & 85; MVP Vlybl 85; Clarkson U; Ind Engrng.

MC ELLIGOTT, DONALD J; Monsignor Farrell HS; Staten Island, NY; (Y); Capt Math Tm; Im Capt Bowling; Im Ftbl; High Hon Roll; Hon Roll; Rensselaer Polytech Inst; Comp.

MC ELROY JR, BRUCE; Newburgh Free Acad; Newburgh, NY; (Y); 86/572; Computer Clb; Key Clb; JV Crs Cntry; Hon Roll; Orange Co CC Alumni Assoc Schlrhsp 86; Orange Co CC; Bus Mgt.

MC ELROY, JENNIFER; North Warrren HS; Chestertown, NY; (Y); 11/49; Dance Clb; SADD; School Play; Yrbk Stf; Var L Tennis; JV Vllybl; Grad Awd Most Outstndng Bus Stu 86; Adirondack CC; Socl Psych.

MC ELVENE, DARYL; Gowanda Central HS; Helmoth, NY; (Y); 13/135; Am Leg Boys St; Spanish Clb; SADD; Band; Jazz Band; Mrchg Band; Rep Soph Cls; Rep Jr Cls; Var L Bsbl; Capt L Bsktbl; Pre-Med.

MC ELWAIN, MEG; Salmon River Central HS; Bombay, NY; (S); 14/88; Pres VP 4-H; Sec French Clb; Trs Stu Cncl; Var Cheerleading; Var Swmmng; Hon Roll; NHS; Cathlc Daughtr Schlrshp 86; Hudson Valley; Librl Arts.

MC ELWAIN, STEVE; Herkimer HS; Herkimer, NY; (Y); Boy Scts; Rep Frsh Cls; Rep Soph Cls; Rep Jr Cls; Var Golf; Im Socr; Trk; Mohawk Valley CC; Elec Engr.

MC ENEANEY, BARBARA; Valley Stream Central HS; Valley Stream, NY; (Y); 79/349; Crs Cntry; Trk; Hon Roll; NHS; Mst Artstc Awd 83; SUNY Cortland.

MC ENROE, ANN; Scio Central HS; Wellsville, NY; (S); 5/49; Spanish Clb; Yrbk Bus Mgr; Bsktbl; Tennis; Trk; Vllybl; High Hon Roll; NHS; VP Frsh Cls; VP Soph Cls; Teenage Republican St Vice Chrmn 84-85; Acad All Amer Engl, Spnsh 84; Soc Dstngshd Amer HS Stu 85; Pre-Law.

MC ERLEAN, GENEVIEVE; Connetquot HS; Ronkonkoma, NY; (S); 1/699; Cmnty Wkr; Color Guard; Concert Band; Mrchg Band; Sec Soph Cls; Sec Jr Cls; Sec Sr Cls; Im Stat Sftbl; Pres NHS; Val; Outstndng Geom Earth Sci & Engl Awds 83; NY ST Schls Music Assn 9 Medls Solo & Ensmbl 83-85; Cornell U; Bio.

MC FADDEN, CHERYL; Mount Mercy Acad; Orchard Park, NY; (Y); Cmnty Wkr; Hosp Aide; Yrbk Stf; Score Keeper; Hon Roll; Sec NHS; VFW Awd; Scholastic Bowl; Teachers Aide; (Y ST Regnts Schlrshp 86; Hofstra U Admsns Schlrshp 86; St John Fischer Schlrshp 86; SUNY; Corp Lawyer.

MC FADDEN, CRAIG B; East HS; Rochester, NY; (Y); Boys Clb Am; Varsity Clb; Hon Roll; Ntl Merit SF; JV Var Bsktbl; Ntl Schlrshp Achvt Awd 85-86; Howard U; Bus Law.

MC FADDEN, KERRY ANN; Southwestern Central HS; Lakewood, NY; (Y); Church Yth Grp; Cmnty Wkr; Drama Clb; Hosp Aide; Spanish Clb; Chorus; School Musical; Hon Roll; Mc Lennan CC; Drama.

MC FADDEN, REGGIE; Rice HS; Brooklyn, NY; (Y); Computer Clb; Crs Cntry; Trk; NY Inst Tech; Industrl Engr.

MC FADDEN, SHARON; Corcoran HS; Syracuse, NY; (Y); Computer Clb; JA; Speech Tm; Yrbk Stf; Cheerleading; Gym; Vllybl; 4-H Awd; Hon Roll; Prfct Atten Awd.

MC FARLAND, JAMES; Valley Central HS; Montgomery, NY; (Y); Boy Scts; Spanish Clb; School Play; Bsktbl; Ftbl; L Golf; Socr; Wrstlng; Hon Roll; Ltrmn Golf Won ST, Ntl Trmnts 84-86; Wake Forest; Bus.

MC FARLAND, JOHN M; Saugerties SR HS; Saugerties, NY; (Y); Am Leg Boys St; Key Clb; Band; Chorus; Church Choir; Concert Band; Mrchg Band; Ftbl; Trk; Hon Roll; NY ST Smmr Schl Of Arts Choral Inst 86; U Of Hartford CT; Music Educ.

MC FARLAND, KAREN L; Manlius Pebble Hill HS; Syracuse, NY; (Y); Yrbk Bus Mgr; Capt Cheerleading; Var Socr; Var Trk; High Hon Roll; NHS; Ntl Merit Ltr; Exploring; Chorus; Dartmouth Awd 84-85; Natl Merit Semi-Fnlst Outstndg Negro Stus 85-86; Ind Engr.

MC FARLANE, BARBARA; Dominican Commercial HS; Jamaica, NY; (Y); 80/275; Church Yth Grp; Cmnty Wkr; Office Aide; Teachers Aide; Rep Stu Cncl; Score Keeper; Var Vllybl; Jr NHS; Comp Sci.

MC FARLANE, CLEVE; Beach Channel HS; Arverne, NY; (Y); Library Aide; Math Tm; Band; Nwsp Stf; Rep Sr Cls; Stu Cncl; Var Capt Crs Cntry; Var Capt Trk; MVP Trck Awd 86; 3 3-Yr Awds Indr & Outdr Trck & X-Cntry 86; Phys Fit Tm Awd 86; Aerospc Engr.

MC FARLANE, DAN; Leroy HS; Pavilion, NY; (Y); Political Wkr; Nwsp Ed-Chief; Pres Stu Cncl; Trk; Hon Roll; Amer Inst Frgn Stdy France & Spain 85; Washngtn Wrkshps Smnr 86; Polt Sci.

MC FARLANE, KEVIN; Regis HS; Brooklyn, NY; (Y); Aud/Vis; Church Yth Grp; Cmnty Wkr; French Clb; Political Wkr; Varsity Clb; Rep Frsh Cls; Rep Soph Cls; Trs Stu Cncl; Var JV Bsbl; Bishops Ldrshp Project 85-87.

MC FAUL, WENDY; Franklin Acad; Constable, NY; (Y); Pres Church Yth Grp; Sec Hst FBLA; Our Lady Of Victory; Ofc Prac.

MC GARRY, KATE; Chenango Valley HS; Binghamton, NY; (Y); 44/170; French Clb; Ski Clb; Varsity Clb; Yrbk Phtg; Var L Cheerleading; JV Tennis; Var L Trk; Prsdntl Acad Ftnss Awd 86; Prsdntl Physcl Ftns Awd 82-86; U Of Scranton.

MC GARVEY, MICHAEL J; Catholic Central HS; Troy, NY; (Y); 17/170; Math Clb; SADD; Yrbk Rptr; Yrbk Sprt Ed; Bowling; Golf; DAR Awd; Elks Awd; High Hon Roll; NHS; Manhattnvll Coll Ldrshp Schlrshp 86; ROTC Schlr Athlete Awd 86; W M Carley Schlr Athlete Awd 86; Le Moyne Coll; Orthodntstry.

MC GAYHEY, SEAN P; Shelter Island Union Free Schl; Shelter Is, NY; (Y); 7/22; Am Leg Boys St; SADD; Nwsp Rptr; Yrbk Sprt Ed; Var Bsbl; Var Capt Bsktbl; Var Capt Socr; All Lg Bsktbl & Socr; Outstndg Ath.

MC GEE, SEAN; Mahopac HS; Carmel, NY; (Y); 12/409; Am Leg Boys St; Math Tm; Pres Science Clb; Concert Band; Capt Mrchg Band; Orch; Nwsp Rptr; Yrbk Stf; Var Trk; NHS; Comp Engrng.

MC GETRICK, MELISSA; Cato-Meridian HS; Jordan, NY; (Y); 14/72; French Clb; Yrbk Stf; Var Bsktbl; Var Sftbl; JV Vllybl; Hon Roll; NHS; Air Force; Comp.

MC GINN, BERNADET; Maine-Endwell HS; Endwell, NY; (Y); 21/254; Church Yth Grp; GAA; Key Clb; Var JV Bsktbl; Var Swmmng; Var Trk; High Hon Roll; Hon Roll; Rgnts Schlrshp 8; Broome CC; Chld Ed.

MC GINN, KATHERINE; Babylon JR SR HS; Babylon, NY; (Y); Cmnty Wkr; Off Frsh Cls; Rep Soph Cls; Rep Jr Cls; Var JV Cheerleading; Swmmng; Var JV Vllybl; Hon Roll; Psych.

MC GINNIS, MELINDA; John Marshall JR SR HS; Rochester, NY; (Y); Exploring; Mathletes; Math Tm; Yrbk Stf; Var Bowling; Var Swmmng; Stat Trk; Hon Roll; NHS; Italian Club Pres 83-85.

MC GINTY, KELLY; Tonawanda JR SR HS; Tonawanda, NY; (Y); Cmnty Wkr; Girl Scts; Office Aide; Ski Clb; Spanish Clb; Teachers Aide; Y-Teens; School Play; Educ.

MC GIRT, EUGENE A; William H Maxwell HS; Brooklyn, NY; (Y); 50/200; Library Aide; Band; Nwsp Sprt Ed; Yrbk Sprt Ed; Sr Cls; Hon Roll; Rgnts Schlrshp 86; Long-Island U; Data Proc.

MC GIVNEY, MEGHAN; G Ray Bodley HS; Fulton, NY; (Y); Hosp Aide; Latin Clb; Red Cross Aide; Ski Clb; Off Jr Cls; VP Sr Cls; Rep Stu Cncl; Im Mat Maids; Swmmng; Cit Awd; Cls Ldrshp & Rspnblty 86; Trvl & Trsm Mgmt.

MC GLARRY, ROBERT; Albany HS; Albany, NY; (Y); VP Aud/Vis; French Clb; Ski Clb; SADD; Yrbk Sprt Ed; Yrbk Stf; L Bsbl; Hon Roll; NHS; Ntl Merit Ltr; Amherst Coll Schlrshp 86-87; NY ST Regents Schlrshp 86; NY Telephone Co Clg Schlrshp 86; Amherst Coll; Poli Sci.

MC GLONE, COLLEEN; Sodus Central HS; Williamson, NY; (Y); Church Yth Grp; French Clb; Girl Scts; Pres Model UN; Radio Clb; Band; Concert Band; Mrchg Band; Trs Stu Cncl; Tennis; Prs Schlr; American U; Intl Studies.

MC GLYNN, KAREN ANN; North Babylon SR HS; N Babylon, NY; (Y); 10/400; Am Leg Aux Girls St; Drama Clb; Intnl Clb; Office Aide; School Musical; School Play; Sftbl; French Hon Soc; High Hon Roll; NHS; Bus Mngmnt.

MC GOFF, THERESA; Moore Catholic HS; Staten Island, NY; (Y); Math Clb; Ski Clb; Spanish Clb; Cheerleading; Hon Roll; NHS; Ntl Merit Ltr; Acad Awd 1st Hnrs 84-85; Bus.

MC GOLDRICK, STEPHEN; Iona Prep; Pelham, NY; (Y); 15/191; Letterman Clb; Service Clb; Crs Cntry; Trk; High Hon Roll; NHS; Jesuit Schlrshp Le Moyne Coll 86; Holy Cross Schlrshp 86; M Vaushn Cronin Awd 86; Le Moyne Coll; Poli Sci.

MC GORRY, AMY; St Francis Prep; Bayside, NY; (Y); 71/763; Church Yth Grp; Cmnty Wkr; Variety Show; Var Capt Cheerleading; Coach Actv; Swmmng; JV Tennis; Hon Roll; NHS; Im Ftbl; Fin.

MC GORRY, JENNIFER; St Francis Prep; Bayside, NY; (Y); Cmnty Wkr; Political Wkr; Capt Var Bsktbl; Coach Actv; Capt Var Sftbl; Hon Roll; NHS; Church Yth Grp; Pres Stu Cncl; Var Tennis; MVP Bsktbl & Sftbl 83-86; CYO Sprtsmnshp Awd 84; Ledrshp & Acad Schlrshp Manhattanville Coll 86; Manhattanville Coll; Bus Fin.

MC GORY, BRIAN M; Honeoye Central Schl; Honeoye, NY; (Y); Office Aide; NYS Rgnts Schlrshp Awd 86; SUNY Cntn Ag-Tech Coll; Crmnl.

MC GOWAN, KELLY; Ogdensburg Free Acad; Ogdensburg, NY; (Y); 10/211; French Clb; Stu Cncl; Cheerleading; Swmmng; Trk; Hon Roll; NHS; Ntl Merit Ltr; Acad Banq 84 & 85; Wrld Hstry Cont Wnnr 85; Bio.

MC GOWAN, KEN; Massena Central HS; Massena, NY; (Y); JV Ftbl; NY ST DABDA Awd 85; Massena Yth Cncl Vp, Pres 85-86; Comp Sci.

MC GRAIL, STEPHEN; Stamford Central Schl; Stamford, NY; (S); Intnl Clb; Band; Yrbk Sprt Ed; Trs Jr Cls; Stu Cncl; Var Bsbl; Var Bsktbl; Var Socr; High Hon Roll; NHS; Abigail Harper Chapter DAR Awd 83-84.

MC GRATH, COLLEEN; New Lebanon HS; W Lebanon, NY; (Y); Church Yth Grp; Ski Clb; Spanish Clb; Chorus; Variety Show; Yrbk Stf; Trs Soph Cls; Socr; Trk; Hon Roll; Bst Dfnsv-Sccr Plyr 85; Central Hudson Vly Lge-All Lge Tm 2 85; Intr Decorator.

MC GRATH, EILEEN; Herricks HS; New Hyde Park, NY; (S); 129/287; DECA; Varsity Clb; Yrbk Stf; Bsktbl; Crs Cntry; Socr; JV Sftbl; Var Trk; VFW Awd; Voice Dem Awd; All Conf Soccer 83 & 85; Adelphi U; Bus.

MC GRATH, ELIZABETH; Our Lady Of Mercy HS; Rochester, NY; (Y); Church Yth Grp; Cmnty Wkr; French Clb; Intnl Clb; Ski Clb; Rep Stu Cncl; JV Bsktbl; JV Var Tennis; JV Trk; Hon Roll; Schlrshp Roll; Hnr Roll.

MC GRATH, KELLY A; Ward Melville HS; E Setauket, NY; (Y); Cmnty Wkr; Flag Corp; Nwsp Stf; Var Bowling; Sftbl; Hon Roll; Jr NHS; NYS Rgnts Schlrshp 86; Nazareth Coll Rochester; Educ.

MC GRATH, MADALYN; Northstar Christian Acad; Rochester, NY; (S); 9/28; Teachers Aide; Rep Frsh Cls; Rep Soph Cls; Rep Jr Cls; Sec Rep Stu Cncl; Var Capt Cheerleading; Var Score Keeper; Hon Roll; NHS; Roberts Wesleyan; Nurse.

MC GRATH, STEFAN; Southampton HS; Southampton, NY; (Y); 1/103; Letterman Clb; Scholastic Bowl; Spanish Clb; Nwsp Ed-Chief; Sec Stu Cncl; Golf; Trk; High Hon Roll; NHS; Ntl Merit SF; Princeton Bk Awd 86; Gftd & Tlntd Bk Awd 85; Harvard; Law.

MC GRATH, TIMOTHY; St Pauls HS; Valley Stream, NY; (Y); Varsity Clb; Yrbk Bus Mgr; Pres Frsh Cls; Pres Jr Cls; Pres Sr Cls; Pres Stu Cncl; Capt Var Bsbl; Capt Var Bsktbl; Var Socr; Hon Roll; Acdmc All Amer Natl Secdry Ed Cncl 86; St Pauls Schl Socl Stds Awd Hghst Avg 86; Bus Adm.

MC GRATH, TIMOTHY C; Fordham Prep HS; Bronxville, NY; (Y); VP Sr Cls; Var Ftbl; Var JV Trk; Church Yth Grp; Varsity Clb; Band; Var Bsktbl.

MC GRATH, WENDI; Sachem HS; Farmingville, NY; (Y); 387/1558; Intnl Clb; JV Fld Hcky; Score Keeper; Hon Roll; Stat Wrstlng; 3rd Pl Indvdul Proj Ntl Hist Day 83-84; Elem Ed.

MC GRAW, KELLY; Bishop Maginn HS; Albany, NY; (Y); 7/84; Var Capt Bsktbl; Var Sftbl; JV Var Vllybl; High Hon Roll; NHS; Prfct Atten Awd; US Army Rsv Ntl Schlr Athlt Awd; Prncpls Awd Outstndng Merit; US Marn Corps Outstndng Athlt Awd; Hartwick Coll.

MC GRAW, TIM; Grand Island SR HS; Grand Island, NY; (Y); 47/320; Pres Chorus; Madrigals; School Musical; School Play; Stage Crew; Var Capt Socr; NHS; Jane Glssmn PTA Schlrshp Awd 86; R C T Omkinson & P M Zoltoski Mem Awd 86; Natl Schl Choral Awd 86; Fredonia Coll; Cmmnctns.

MC GREEVY, KARA; Hoosic Valley Central HS; Schaghticoke, NY; (Y); Pres 4-H; Hosp Aide; Band; Nwsp Ed-Chief; Nwsp Sprt Ed; Var Capt Cheerleading; Var Capt Fld Hcky; Var Trk; 4-H Awd; Prfct Atten Awd; Spts Comm.

MC GREGOR, JENNIFER S; Midwood At Brooklyn College HS; Brooklyn, NY; (Y); 190/536; Camera Clb; Drama Clb; Latin Clb; Math Tm; Office Aide; Chorus; School Musical; School Play; Yrbk Stf; Regnts Schlrshp 86; St Johns U; Pharm.

MC GRORY, KATHLEEN; Sacred Heart Acad; Stewart Manor, NY; (S); French Clb; FNA; Chorus; Stage Crew; Sftbl; Hon Roll; NHS; Patrice Briganti Mem Awd Sftb L Schlrshp 85; Nrsng.

MC GUINN, JENNIFER; Southampton HS; Southampton, NY; (Y); 3/118; French Clb; Band; Nwsp Stf; Var Tennis; JV Capt Vllybl; High Hon Roll; Jr NHS; NHS; Ntl Merit Ltr; Harvard Prz Bk 86; Acdmc All Amer 86; Hstry.

MC GUINNESS, JOHN; Archbishop Molloy HS; Richmond Hill, NY; (Y); Art Clb; Yrbk Stf; Rep Soph Cls; Var L Crs Cntry; Var L Trk; NHS; Irish Am Soc Class Rep 84-86; Stu Actvty Commtte Exc Bd 85-86; Lib Arts.

MC GUINNESS, LAUREN; Mt Vernon HS; Mt Vernon, NY; (Y); French Clb; Latin Clb; Math Clb; Math Tm; Band; Concert Band; Jazz Band; Mrchg Band; Pep Band; Stage Crew; Pres Physcl Ftns Awd; West Point.

MC GUIRE, ANDREW D; John Jay HS; S Salem, NY; (Y); Ski Clb; Ftbl; Wt Lftg; Wrstlng; Aerospc Engrng.

MC GUIRE, DEBORAH; Middletown HS; Middletown, NY; (Y); Acadmc Achvt Awd Hm Ec 85-86; Law.

MC GUIRE, GEORGE; Susquehanna Valley HS; Binghamton, NY; (Y); 25/200; Chess Clb; Varsity Clb; Rep Jr Cls; Var Bsktbl; Var Socr; Var Tennis; High Hon Roll; Hon Roll; Empire ST Cntrl Regn Sccr Tm 86; Northeastern U; Engrng.

MC GUIRE, LISA MARIE; West Seneca West SR HS; West Seneca, NY; (Y); 54/559; Art Clb; GAA; Girl Scts; Color Guard; Orch; School Musical; School Play; Rep Stu Cncl; Hon Roll; NHS; Am Leg Schrlsh Pawd 86; Prfct Atten Awd 82-86; Kent ST U; Graphic Design.

MC GUIRE, SHEALYN; Our Lady Of Mercy HS; Fairport, NY; (Y); Church Yth Grp; Cmnty Wkr; French Clb; Pres Model UN; Science Clb; Sec Service Clb; SADD; Church Choir; Yrbk Stf; High Hon Roll; Schlrshp Out Lady Mercy 83; Am Chem Soc Awd 86; Physcl Ed Awd 86; Pre-Med.

MC GURRIN, SCOTT H; Palmyra-Macedon HS; Macedon, NY; (S); 2/180; Letterman Clb; Pres Math Clb; Hon Roll; NHS; Ntl Merit SF; Sal; Comp Progrmmng.

MC HUGH, MAUREEN; Webster HS; Webster, NY; (Y); 63/496; Math Tm; Trs Sr Cls; Var Capt Fld Hcky; Var Capt Trk; Cit Awd; High Hon Roll; VP NHS; Prfct Atten Awd; St Schlr; Church Yth Grp; Outstndng Frshmn Stu Of The Yr 83; All Cnty All Grtr Rochester 1st Fld Hcky Tms 86; Dfsv Hcky Plyr; PA ST U; Math.

MC INERNEY, LORAINE; Albertus Magnus HS; Pearl River, NY; (Y); 17/190; Spanish Clb; Stage Crew; JV Var Cheerleading; Coach Actv; Socr; Sftbl; Hon Roll; NHS; Falcon Srv Awd 86; Cmnctns.

MC INNIS, MEGAN E; Kingston HS; Kingston, NY; (Y); 33/573; Key Clb; Nwsp Stf; Off Sr Cls; Stu Cncl; Var Capt Gym; Var Trk; High Hon Roll; NHS; NY ST Rgnts Schlrshp 86; PA ST U; Arch.

MC INTOSH, MICHAEL; Cardinal Hayes HS; Bronx, NY; (Y); 57/258; Computer Clb; Var L Bowling; Hon Roll; Prfct Atten Awd; NC U; Comp Prgrmg.

MC INTOSH, VERNON A; Aviation HS; Laurelton, NY; (S); 50/416; Computer Clb; Hon Roll; Prfct Atten Awd; Aerospace Engrng.

MC INTYRE, DAVID; Fairport HS; Fairport, NY; (Y); Aud/Vis; Cmnty Wkr; Library Aide; Johnson & Wales Coll; Clnry Art.

MC INTYRE, DAWN; Frewsburg Central Schl; Jamestown, NY; (Y); 1/75; Church Yth Grp; Spanish Clb; Band; Chorus; Church Choir; School Musical; VP Jr Cls; Var Bsktbl; VP NHS.

MC INTYRE, EILEEN; Carmel HS; Carmel, NY; (Y); Orch; JV Var Cheerleading; High Hon Roll; NHS; Ntl Merit Ltr; Rotary Awd; Le Moyne Coll; Eng.

MC INTYRE, HEATHER; Gowanda Central Schl; Perrysburg, NY; (Y); 3/130; Pres Church Yth Grp; SADD; Nwsp Rptr; Yrbk Ed-Chief; Yrbk Phtg; Yrbk Stf; Rep Soph Cls; Trs Jr Cls; Pres Sr Cls; NHS; Engrng.

MC INTYRE, SUSAN; Eastchester HS; Eastchester, NY; (Y); Ski Clb; Spanish Clb; SADD; Sec Band; Concert Band; Mrchg Band; Pep Band; Rep Stu Cncl; Var L Crs Cntry; Var Capt Trk.

MC INTYRE, WILLIAM; Mynderse Acad; Seneca Falls, NY; (Y); Chess Clb; Office Aide; Teachers Aide; JV Im Bsbl; L Bowling; DAR Awd; Hon Roll; Own Bus.

MC ISAAC, JENNIFER; Lansingburgh HS; Troy, NY; (Y); 4/200; Hosp Aide; Math Tm; Band; Chorus; Drm & Bgl; Nwsp Stf; JV Var Bsktbl; Var Crs Cntry; Var Socr; Var Trk; Ctznshp Awd 84; Crfts Awd 84; Brssmn Yr Noble Callahan Drm & Bugl Corp 85; Duke U; Psych.

MC KAIN, MARI A; Miller Place HS; Miller Pl, NY; (Y); 14/200; FBLA; Nwsp Stf; Hon Roll; NYS Regents Schlrshp 86; U Of Redlands; Pre Med.

MC KAY, BRENDA; Corning-Painted Post West HS; Painted Post, NY; (Y); Varsity Clb; Rep Stu Cncl; JV Var Cheerleading; Var Diving; Var Gym; High Hon Roll; Hon Roll; SADD; School Play; Rep Soph Cls; Section IV Gymnstc Chmp 5 H S Recrds 83-84; Sectn IV Divg Comptn 6th Pl 83-84; All Amer Chrldr 83-86; Syracuse U; Phy Thrpy.

MC KEE, CARA; Brewster HS; Brewster, NY; (Y); Trs 4-H; Quiz Bowl; Ski Clb; Varsity Clb; JV Socr; Var Tennis; High Hon Roll; Hon Roll; Schlrshp In Italian Awd 84-86; Marine Bio.

MC KEE, JEDIDIAH; Watkins Glen HS; Reading Center, NY; (Y); 16/130; Aud/Vis; Letterman Clb; Band; Chorus; Jazz Band; Yrbk Rptr; Capt Crs Cntry; Trk; Elks Awd; Hon Roll; Houghton Coll; Media.

MC KEE, JON; John C Birdlebough HS; Phoenix, NY; (Y); Art Clb; Computer Clb; Teachers Aide; Archtctr.

MC KEE, LISA; Webster Christian Schl; Williamson, NY; (S); 2/17; Church Yth Grp; Teachers Aide; Chorus; Church Choir; School Play; VP Soph Cls; Sec Jr Cls; Capt Cheerleading; Vllybl; High Hon Roll; Elem Eductn.

MC KEE, MICHAEL; Cicero North Syracuse HS; Clay, NY; (S); 29/623; Spanish Clb; JV Var Lcrss; JV Var Socr; Hon Roll; Opt Clb Awd.

MC KEE, TIM; Haverling Central HS; Bath, NY; (Y); 30/127; JCL; Latin Clb; Crs Cntry; Socr; Wrstlng; High Hon Roll; Hon Roll; NYSPHSAA Chmpn Wrstlng 86; Envrmntl Engrng.

MC KEE, TODD; West Seneca West HS; West Seneca, NY; (S); 117/559; Pres DECA; Office Aide; Spanish Clb; Stage Crew; Rep Stu Cncl; Var Swmmng; JV Vllybl; Cert Hnr Bar Assn Mock Trial Atty 84-85; DEC NY Fnls Regnl 1st Pl Gen Mktg, ST Fnlst 2nd Pl 84-85; Bus Adm.

MC KEEVER, THOMAS; Central Islip SR HS; Central Islip, NY; (Y); Art Clb; Church Yth Grp; 4-H; VP FBLA; Rep Frsh Cls; Rep Soph Cls; Rep Jr Cls; Hon Roll; Bus Mgmt.

MC KENDRICK, KERI; Heuvelton Central HS; Ogdensburg, NY; (S); Trs French Clb; GAA; Chorus; Flag Corp; Co-Capt Cheerleading; Socr; Sftbl; NHS.

MC KENERY, CHELSEA; Ripley Central HS; Ripley, NY; (S); Var Church Yth Grp; Girl Scts; Library Aide; Office Aide; School Musical; Pres Stu Cncl; Cheerleading; Hon Roll; NHS; Ntl Merit Schol; Bus Mgt.

MC KENNA, SUSAN A; Dominican Acad; New York, NY; (Y); Nwsp Rptr; Yrbk Ed-Chief; Yrbk Phtg; Sec Frsh Cls; VP Soph Cls; Hon Roll; Ntl Merit SF; NEDT Awd; Jrnlsm.

MC KENNA, TRICIA; Waterloo SR HS; Waterloo, NY; (Y); 22/154; 4-H; Color Guard; Mrchg Band; Trk; High Hon Roll; Hon Roll; Voice Dem Awd; Hghst Avg Sci 84; Bus Adm.

MC KENZIE, AUDREY; James Madison HS; Brooklyn, NY; (Y); Aud/Vis; Teachers Aide; Color Guard; Hon Roll.

MC KENZIE, BARNET; Evanders Childs HS; Bronx, NY; (Y); Nwsp Rptr.

MC KENZIE, CAROL; Springfield Gardens HS; New York, NY; (S); 17/438; JA; Library Aide; Sftbl; Vllybl; Cit Awd; Hon Roll; Hunter Coll; Nrsng.

MC KENZIE, GEORGIA P; Martin Van Buren HS; Cambria Heights, NY; (Y); 108/565; Church Yth Grp; Drama Clb; Key Clb; Library Aide; Chorus; Orch; Stage Crew; Yrbk Phtg; Spnsh Hnr Soc 85; Phtgrphy.

MC KENZIE, KEVIN; Saranac Central Schl; Saranac, NY; (Y); Trk; Wrstlng; Prfct Atten Awd; Prntng.

MC KENZIE, KIRK; Roosevelt SR HS; Roosevelt, NY; (S); Gym; Var Tennis; High Hon Roll; Hon Roll; NHS; Prfct Atten Awd; Martin Luther King Anl Awd 85; Frnch Awd 84; Tennis Awd 85; Elctrnc Engrng.

MC KENZIE, SARAH; The Franciscan Acad; Syracuse, NY; (Y); Sec FBLA; GAA; Temple Yth Grp; Trs Soph Cls; Capt Vllybl; Hon Roll; Ms GAA 83-85; Hnrs Awd-Engl 86; Ms Vllybl Athltc Awd 82-85; Howard U; Lwyr.

MC KENZIE, SAUNDRA; St Pius V HS; New York, NY; (Y); Rep Dance Clb; Rep Girl Scts; Sec Soph Cls; Rep Jr Cls; NHS; Highest Av Eng, Geom & Hlth Educ Awds 85; Elem Tchr.

MC KENZIE, TRACY; Dodge HS; Bronx, NY; (Y); Dance Clb; Exploring; Service Clb; Nwsp Ed-Chief; Bsktbl; Hon Roll; Prfct Atten Awd; Rep Jr Cls; Nrsg.

MC KENZIE, TRACY; West Seneca East SR HS; Cheektowaga, NY; (Y); DECA; Rep Frsh Cls; Rep Soph Cls; VP Jr Cls; VP Sr Cls; Var Capt Cheerleading; 1st Pl Regionls Peca Comp; 4th Pl Decny ST Comp; Criminal Just.

MC KEON, COLLEEN; Ichabod Crane Central HS; Valatie, NY; (Y); 1/182; Computer Clb; French Clb; Concert Band; Mrchg Band; Yrbk Stf; JV Sftbl; Bausch & Lomb Sci Awd; High Hon Roll; Trs NHS; Val; Most Imprvd Plyr-JV Sftbl 84; NYS Regents Coll Schlrshp 86; Russell Sage Coll Fndrs Schlrshp 86; Russel Sage Coll; Comp Sci.

MC KEON, MATTHEW J; Newburgh Free Acad; New Windsor, NY; (Y); Cmnty Wkr; Key Clb; Teachers Aide; Nwsp Rptr; Swmmng; CC Awd; High Hon Roll; Jr NHS; Regnts Schlrshp 86; Pierce Schlrshp 86; Suny Albany; Lawyr.

MC KERNAN, JOHN; Seton Catholic Central HS; Binghamton, NY; (Y); Chess Clb; Church Yth Grp; Nwsp Stf; Achvt Awd Outstndg Newscarrier 85; Business.

MC KINLEY, TAMMI; Catholic Central HS; Cohoes, NY; (Y); French Clb; Math Clb; Rep Jr Cls; Var L Trk; Bausch & Lomb Sci Awd; High Hon Roll; NHS; Rensellaer Model Awd RPI; Natl Latin Awd; Natl Ldrshp Awd; Georgetown; Frnch Lang.

MC KINNON, MARY; Cato-Meridian HS; Cato, NY; (Y); Church Yth Grp; Intnl Clb; School Play; Variety Show; Trs Jr Cls; Var Sftbl; Var Vllybl; Hon Roll; Prfct Atten Awd; Hnrb Mntn All Star Vllybl 85-86; Csmtlgy.

MC KITTY, GERRY; Holy Cross HS; Bayside, NY; (Y); 36/328; Boy Scts; Church Yth Grp; Cmnty Wkr; Political Wkr; Teachers Aide; Im Bsktbl; Var L Ftbl; Cit Awd; Hon Roll; All City Hon Mntn Ftbll Tm 86; Spcl Olympcs Volntr 85; Regents Schlrshp 86; MI Tech U; Wood & Fiber Utlztn.

MC LAUGHLIN, CARLLENE; Susquehanna Valley HS; Kirkwood, NY; (Y); Political Wkr; Trs Spanish Clb; Yrbk Ed-Chief; Rep Soph Cls; Rep Jr Cls; Rep Sr Cls; Rep Sec Stu Cncl; Var Socr; Hon Roll; Spanish NHS; Forgn Svc.

MC LAUGHLIN, GAIL; Emma Willard Schl; Averill Park, NY; (Y); Pres Computer Clb; Ski Clb; Trk; Engrng.

MC LAUGHLIN, HARRY; Eden Central SR HS; Eden, NY; (Y); Aud/Vis; Boy Scts; FFA; Intnl Clb; SADD; Varsity Clb; JV Coach Actv; Var JV Ftbl; Mgr(s); Var JV Wrstlng; Brown Belt 86; Green Belt 86; Hilbert Clg; Crmnl Just.

MC LAUGHLIN, KATHLEEN; Centereach HS; Centereach, NY; (Y); Chorus; Variety Show; Bsktbl; Crs Cntry; Fld Hcky; Sftbl; Tennis; Trk; Vllybl; Presdntl Physical Fitness Awd 83-87; MVP Track 86; Empire ST Games 85; Track I, Field Hcky Champs 86.

MC LAUGHLIN, MATT; Archbishop Molloy HS; New York, NY; (Y); 20/383; French Clb; SADD; Varsity Clb; Church Choir; JV Crs Cntry; L Swmmng; Hon Roll; NHS; Var L Trk; NYS Regents Schlrshp 87.

MC LAUGHLIN, SCOTT; Lake George Central HS; Lake George, NY; (Y); Ski Clb; Band; Chorus; Drm Mjr(t); Mrchg Band; Swing Chorus; Bsbl; Bsktbl; Ftbl; Mgr(s).

MC LELLAN, KENNETH; Archbishop Molloy HS; Astoria, NY; (Y); 66/380; Church Yth Grp; Church Choir; Im Bowling; Hon Roll.

MC LELLAN, LISA M; Camden HS; Camden, NY; (Y); 65/211; AFS; Pep Clb; Ski Clb; Varsity Clb; Nwsp Rptr; Nwsp Stf; JV Var Cheerleading; JV Var Score Keeper; JV Trk; High Hon Roll; Crmnl Just, R A Wilkes Real Est Schlrshps, E Dorrance Engl Awd 86; Mohawk Valley CC; Crmnl Just.

MC LELLAN, MELISSA; Ward Melville HS; Setauket, NY; (Y); Church Yth Grp; GAA; Mathletes; Ski Clb; SADD; Rep Stu Cncl; Sftbl; High Hon Roll; Hon Roll; U Of FL; Psych.

MC LENDON, SANDI; Holy Trinity HS; Roosevelt, NY; (S); 20/322; Cmnty Wkr; Hosp Aide; Math Clb; Chorus; Stage Crew; Nwsp Stf; Yrbk Stf; Rep Soph Cls; Rep Jr Cls; Cheerleading; Hmcmng Queen 85-86; Knox Coll; Acctg.

MC LEOD, KAREN A; Midwood HS; Brooklyn, NY; (Y); 29/556; Church Yth Grp; Mathletes; Math Tm; Teachers Aide; Church Choir; Concert Band; Yrbk Stf; Vllybl; High Hon Roll; Hon Roll; Columbia; Pre-Med.

MC LEOD, PAMELA; Edison Tech HS; Rochester, NY; (Y); 36/276; Art Clb; Camera Clb; Cmnty Wkr; Exploring; Library Aide; OEA; PAVAS; Red Cross Aide; SADD; Tennis; Strs Bttr Blck Comm Schlrshp 86; Kappa Alpha Psi Frtrnty Schlrshpd 86; Otstndng Achvt Grphc Dsgn 86; Nazareth Coll; Grphc Dsgn.

MC LEOD, SUSAN; Northstar Christian Acad; Rochester, NY; (S); 2/25; Church Yth Grp; Band; Chorus; Trs Soph Cls; Trs Jr Cls; Stat Bsktbl; High Hon Roll; Hon Roll; Acad All Amer Schlr Prgm 85.

MC LINTOCK, GLENN R; Somers HS; Granite Springs, NY; (Y); 5/196; Jazz Band; School Musical; Symp Band; Yrbk Bus Mgr; Yrbk Stf; High Hon Roll; NHS; Ntl Merit Ltr; Spanish NHS; St Schlr; Scl Stdies Stu Of Mnth; U Of PA.

MC LIVERTY, KEITH; Archbishop Molloy HS; Forest Hills, NY; (Y); 150/420; Church Yth Grp; Pep Clb; Science Clb; SADD; Y-Teens; Nwsp Rptr; Yrbk Phtg; Bsbl; Bsktbl; Hon Roll; Class Rep 84; Engr.

MC LOONE, LYNNE; Sacred Heart Acad; N Merrick, NY; (S); 11/186; SADD; Var Capt Bsktbl; Var Sftbl; Var Vllybl; Hon Roll; NHS; Natl Phy Educ Awd 85; Bus.

MC LOUGHLIN, PATRICK; St John The Baptist D HS; Central Islip, NY; (S); 15/546; Math Clb; Teachers Aide; Nwsp Stf; Lit Mag; Trk; High Hon Roll; NCTE Awd; Ntl Merit Ltr; Chess Clb; FTA; Mmost Dedicated Track; Chem Olympd Fnlst; Ntrl Sci.

MC LOUGHLIN, SHEILA; The Ursuline Schl; New Rochelle, NY; (Y); French Clb; Yrbk Stf; Hon Roll.

MC LOUGHLIN, WILLIAM; Fordham Prepatory Schl; Bronx, NY; (Y); Var L Bsktbl; High Hon Roll; Hon Roll; U Of MD; Bus.

MC MAHON, DAVID J; Pierson HS; Sag Harbor, NY; (Y); Am Leg Boys St; Drama Clb; Mathletes; Spanish Clb; School Musical; Yrbk Bus Mgr; Bsktbl; Golf; SUNY Maritime; Bus Mgmt.

MC MAHON, KATHLEEN; Bishop Ludden HS; Camillus, NY; (S); VP Sec JA; SADD; Band; Chorus; School Musical; JV Var Socr; JV Capt Sftbl; JV Capt Vllybl; High Hon Roll; Sci Awd 84.

MC MAHON, MARGARET M; Westhill HS; Syracuse, NY; (Y); 1/145; Hosp Aide; Varsity Clb; Concert Band; VP Jr Cls; Var Capt Crs Cntry; Var Trk; High Hon Roll; NHS; Ntl Merit Ltr; NEDT Awd; Notre Damme Schlr 86; Old Engl W 85; Notre Dame U; Hist.

MC MAHON, MAUREEN; Plattsburgh SR HS; Plattsburgh, NY; (Y); Aud/Vis; Drama Clb; GAA; SADD; Stu Cncl; Var Bsktbl; Ftbl; Var L Socr; Var Sftbl; Hon Roll; Cortland U; Phys Ed.

MC MAHON, MICHAEL G; Carthage Central HS; Carthage, NY; (Y); 1/175; Boy Scts; Pres VP Key Clb; Band; Jazz Band; Var Socr; NHS; Ntl Merit SF; Church Yth Grp; Aud/Vis; Rep Stu Cncl; Rensselaer Polytechnic Inst Math & Sci Awd; Pres Clssrm Yng Amer; Area All ST Band; Elctrcl Engrng.

MC MAHON, NANCY; North Rockland HS; West Haverstraw, NY; (Y); Church Yth Grp; Drama Clb; Spanish Clb; Chorus; Concert Band; Mrchg Band; School Musical; School Play; Psych.

MC MAHON, PATRICK; Aquinas Insti; Rochester, NY; (Y); 16/149; Exploring; High Hon Roll; Hon Roll; Prfct Atten Awd; Acad Achvt Awd Analytc Geom & Calc 85; Scholar CUNY Alfred 86; SUNY Brockport; Crim Just.

MC MAHON, PATRICK M; Westfield Acad And Central Schl; Westfield, NY; (Y); 8/60; Y-Teens; Band; Mrchg Band; Trk; Vllybl; High Hon Roll; NHS; SUNY Cortland; Bio.

MC MAHON, SHAUN; Cato-Meridian HS; Cato, NY; (Y); 4-H; French Clb; Red Cross Aide; Chorus; VP Jr Cls; Var Bsktbl; Bausch & Lomb Sci Awd; 4-H Awd; Jr NHS; NHS.

MC MANIS, DEBORAH; E J Wilson HS; Spencerport, NY; (Y); 2/350; French Clb; Varsity Clb; Yrbk Stf; Rep Stu Cncl; Var Capt Crs Cntry; Var L Trk; Cit Awd; High Hon Roll; NHS; Hrvrd Clb Bk Awd 86; Outstndng Achvt Amer Studys 86.

MC MANUS, CINDI; Union Endicott HS; Endicott, NY; (Y); French Clb; SADD; Varsity Clb; Yrbk Stf; JV Var Socr; Capt Var Vllybl; Hon Roll; All Div Soccr Team 1 85; Law.

MC MANUS, KARA T; St Francis Prep; Holliswood, NY; (S); 90/750; Dance Clb; Ski Clb; Concert Band; Var Cheerleading; Im Ftbl; Var Gym; Im Vllybl; Hon Roll; NHS.

MC MANUS, MARGARET HELEN; Eldred Central Schl; Highland Lake, NY; (Y); 3/38; Trs Varsity Clb; Chorus; Madrigals; Yrbk Stf; Trs Sr Cls; Capt Socr; Capt Trk; Cit Awd; High Hon Roll; Trs NHS; Delta Kappa Gamma Scty 86; Orng Plz Mrchnts Assn 86; Crtlnd Alumni Schlrshp 86; SUNY Crtlnd; Elem Ed.

MC MANUS, MELODY; Bishop Grimes HS; Syracuse, NY; (Y); Band; School Musical; Rep Sr Cls; High Hon Roll; NHS; Natl Ldrshp And Serv Awds 85; High Hnrs Bus Awds 86; Le Moyne College; Bus Admn.

MC MANUS, RICHARD; Bishop Ford CC HS; Brooklyn, NY; (S); 2/400; Math Tm; Science Clb; Nwsp Rptr; Pres Jr Cls; JV Bsbl; Im Vllybl; High Hon Roll; NHS; Cvl Engrng.

MC MANUS, SEAN; Fairport HS; Fairport, NY; (Y); Drama Clb; Trs French Clb; Math Tm; Ski Clb; SADD; Chorus; School Musical; Yrbk Stf; Rep Jr Cls; Hon Roll; Newfane Mth Cont Cert Achvt 85; Cert Merit Frnch III 84; Genetic Engrng.

MC MASTER, PHILLIP; Jordan-Elbridge HS; Jordan, NY; (Y); 46/138; Boy Scts; Church Yth Grp; Exploring; Ski Clb; JV Ftbl; Hon Roll; BSA Eagle 86; SUNY Buffalo; Engrng.

MC MIKLE, MICHELLE; F D Roosevelt HS; Brooklyn, NY; (Y); 174/587; Teachers Aide; Tennis; NY Rgnts Schlrshp 86; Accntnt.

MC MILLEN, LISA; Hannibal Central HS; Hannibal, NY; (Y); 1/119; 4-H; Science Clb; Teachers Aide; Yrbk Stf; VP Jr Cls; Dnfth Awd; 4-H Awd; High Hon Roll; NHS; Prfct Atten Awd.

MC MILLIN, DAWN; Flushing HS; College Pt, NY; (Y); Church Yth Grp; Teachers Aide; Hon Roll; Tchr.

MC MILLIN, KELLI; Newark SR HS; Newark, NY; (Y); Band; Jazz Band; Mrchg Band; Pep Band; High Hon Roll; Hon Roll; Bryant & Stratton Comp Pgmng Schlrshp 86; Bryant & Stratton; Comp Pgmng.

MC MONAGLE, GARY; John C Birdlebough HS; Pennellville, NY; (Y); Band; Concert Band; Mrchg Band; Comp Sci.

MC MORRIS, DEBBIE; Chittenango SR HS; Chittenango, NY; (Y); 18/211; Church Yth Grp; SADD; Chorus; Church Choir; Orch; School Musical; Im Cheerleading; Im Vllybl; High Hon Roll; Hon Roll; Ambassador Coll; Elem Tchr.

MC MORROW, MEGAN; Mt Mercy Acad; W Seneca, NY; (Y); French Clb; Hosp Aide; Ski Clb; Rep Jr Cls; JV Badmtn; Score Keeper; Var Tennis; Im Vllybl; Hon Roll; NHS; Phys Thrpst.

MC MULLAN, JEREMY F; Rocky Pt JR SR HS; Rocky Point, NY; (S); 12/210; Crs Cntry; Trk; High Hon Roll; Mathletes; Ski Clb; Varsity Clb; Band; Mrchg Band; Nwsp Sprt Ed; Nwsp Stf; All Cnty & All League Crs Cntry 85-86; Math.

MC MULLEN, ERIN; Hamburg SR HS; Hamburg, NY; (Y); VP Service Clb; Color Guard; Yrbk Stf; Btty Crckr Awd; Hon Roll; ST U-Fredonia; Elem Ed.

MC MULLEN, RICK; Honeoye Falls-Lima HS; Mendon, NY; (S); 1/160; Am Leg Boys St; Church Yth Grp; Math Clb; Model UN; Var Capt Bsktbl; JV Socr; JV Tennis; High Hon Roll; NHS; Ntl Merit Ltr; Phi Beta Kappa Awd For Recgntn Of Excllnc Schlrshp 85-86; Sci Olympcs 83 & 85; Pres Clssrm 84; Engrng.

MC MULLEN, SUSAN N; Baldwin SR HS; Baldwin, NY; (Y); 16/474; Am Leg Aux Girls St; Church Yth Grp; Hosp Aide; Key Clb; Political Wkr; French Hon Soc; High Hon Roll; Hon Roll; NHS; Repb Clb Awd, Soc Stds Achvt Awd 86; Franklin & Marshall Coll; Arch.

MC NALLY, KELLI; Earl L Vandermuelen HS; Pt Jefferson, NY; (Y); 3/297; Latin Clb; SADD; Thesps; School Play; Yrbk Ed-Chief; High Hon Roll; NHS; Ntl Merit Ltr; Pres Schlr; Art Clb; Lati Awd 86; NY ST Rgnts Schlrshp 86; Dstngshd Ctzn Schlr Awd 86; William & Mary Coll; Bus.

MC NAMARA, DENIS; Commack HS South; Commack, NY; (Y); Church Yth Grp; Drama Clb; Acpl Chr; Chorus; School Musical; School Play; Variety Show; Nwsp Stf; Yrbk Rptr; VP Jr Cls; Dstnctn Natl Sci Olympd Bio 85; Rcgntn Gldn Quill Cntst Dscrptv Wrtng 85; Biolgcl Engrng.

MC NAMARA, ELIZABETH; Fairport HS; Fairport, NY; (Y); DECA; Pep Clb; Ski Clb; SADD; Bus Mgmt.

MC NAMARA, JOHN; Monsignor Farrell HS; Staten Island, NY; (Y); Art Clb; Church Yth Grp; Dance Clb; Bsktbl; JV Var Ftbl; Trk; Hon Roll; Naval Aviater.

MC NAMARA, KERRY; Saranac Lake HS; Saranac Lk, NY; (Y); 3/127; Quiz Bowl; JV Bsbl; JV Var Ftbl; JV Var Trk; Var Wt Lftg; High Hon Roll; Jr NHS; NHS; Naval ROTC 4 Yr Schlrshp 86; US Coast Guard Acad; Marine.

MC NAMARA, LIZ; Edison Tech; Williamson, NY; (Y); Science Clb; Capt Var Swmmng; Hon Roll; Cty Splng Bee Wnnr 85; Marine Bio.

MC NAMARA, LORI; Berne Knox Westerlo HS; Altamont, NY; (Y); Church Yth Grp; Var L Crs Cntry; Var L Trk; Hon Roll; Prfct Atten Awd; Mngmnt.

MC NAMARA, MEREDETH; Our Lady Of Mercy HS; Fairport, NY; (Y); 27/169; Exploring; French Clb; Intnl Clb; Ski Clb; SADD; Yrbk Stf; Score Keeper; Stat Socr; Var Swmmng; High Hon Roll; Med Assist.

MC NAMARA, ROBERT C; Pittsford-Meador HS; Pittsford, NY; (Y); Trs Model UN; Band; Nwsp Sprt Ed; Rep Frsh Cls; Trs Jr Cls; Pres Stu Cncl; Var Capt Lcrss; Socr; Hon Roll; Ntl Merit Ltr; U S Senate Schlrshp 86; Regents Schlr 86; Princeton U; Hstry.

MC NAMARA, SAMANTHA; Rome Free Acad; Rome, NY; (Y); 40/450; Band; Orch; Trs Frsh Cls; Capt Var Sftbl; High Hon Roll; Jr NHS; NHS; Pres Schlr; Vrsty Sftbll MIP 2yrs,Vrsty Sftbll MVP 1 Yr 83-86; COL All Str 3yrs Sftbll 83-86; NY Regnt Schlrsh; Hamilton Coll; Pre-Med.

MC NAMARA, SCOTT; Mayfield HS; Glovesville, NY; (Y); 6/79; Varsity Clb; Pres Frsh Cls; Pres Soph Cls; Pres Jr Cls; Rep Sr Cls; Rep Stu Cncl; Var JV Bsktbl; Var Capt Crs Cntry; Var Capt Trk; NHS; Athl Of Yr 85-86; Best Area Trck Performer In Amsterdam Recorder 86; US Army Reserve Natl Schlr 85-86; Albany ST.

MC NAUGHTON, BETH; Northport HS; Northport, NY; (Y); Flag Corp; Spanish Clb; Band; Chorus; Church Choir; Concert Band; Mrchg Band; School Musical; Nwsp Rptr; JV Fld Hcky; Credtbl 84-86; All Cnty Band 84; Wrk Stdy Awd 86; Mt St Mary; Elem Ed.

MC NAUGHTON, ELIZABETH; St Marys Girls HS; Glen Cove, NY; (Y); Sec Camera Clb; Debate Tm; Political Wkr; Red Cross Aide; Service Clb; Ski Clb; Speech Tm; Stage Crew; Variety Show; Socl Psych.

MC NEAR, DIANA LYNN; Acad Of Mt St Ursula; Bronx, NY; (Y); 18/129; Sec Camera Clb; Cmnty Wkr; VP Dance Clb; Drama Clb; Stage Crew; Variety Show; Nwsp Rptr; Trk; Hon Roll; E T Marshall Schlrshp 86; Stonybrook U; Vet.

MC NEICE, KATHY; Sayville HS; Sayville, NY; (Y); 30/343; Key Clb; Var Trk; NHS; Band; Concert Band; Mrchg Band; JV Tennis; High Hon Roll; Hon Roll.

MC NEIL, ALICE; Harry S Truman HS; Bronx, NY; (Y); JA; Band; Concert Band; Jazz Band; Var Crs Cntry; Var Trk; NYC Super Yth Awd 86; NY ST Trck & Fld Chmpnshps Awd 86; Brnx Borgh Wide Music Schlrshp Awd 83; Comm.

MC NEIL, DANIEL; Tottenville HS; Staten Island, NY; (Y); Exploring; Model UN; Yrbk Stf; Bsbl; Bowling; Aerspc Engr; NASA Mgmt.

MC NEIL, HEATHER; Dover JR-SR HS; Dover Plains, NY; (S); Drama Clb; Varsity Clb; Band; Chorus; Church Choir; School Musical; School Play; Var Bsktbl; Var Fld Hcky; Hon Roll; Prfrmng Arts.

MC NEIL, JAMES H; Skaneateles Central HS; Skanteateles, NY; (Y); 60/160; Am Leg Boys St; Church Yth Grp; Civic Clb; SADD; Varsity Clb; Ftbl; Lcrss; Wt Lftg; Hon Roll; NHS; Notre Dame U; Politics.

MC NEIL, JEFF; Greece Athena HS; Rochester, NY; (Y); 56/305; VP FBLA; DECA; JA; Bsbl; Bsktbl; Ftbl; 1st ST FBLA Cmpttn & 5th Natl Entrprnrshp I 83-84; U Of Buffolo; Bus Admin.

MC NEIL, MARK; Alden HS; Alden, NY; (Y); French Clb; Science Clb; Ski Clb; Concert Band; Bsktbl; Ftbl; Swmmng; Trk; Hon Roll; NHS; U S Air Force Acad; Aerontcl.

MC NEIL, MONICA; Northern Adirondack HS; Ellenburg Depot, NY; (Y); FBLA; Office Aide; Yrbk Stf; Score Keeper; Timer; Sec.

MC NEILL, ANDREW; Geneseo Central HS; Geneseo, NY; (Y); 9/87; Drama Clb; SADD; School Musical; Lit Mag; Rep Stu Cncl; Var Tennis; French Hon Soc; NHS; Cls Up Prgm Slctd Rep Schl For 1 Wk In Dc 86; Mansfield Rdy Wrtng Cmptn 85; Cornell U; Psych.

MC NEILL, DINA; Valley Stream Central HS; Valley Stream, NY; (Y); 34/349; Var L Bsktbl; Var Socr; Var L Sftbl; Var L Vllybl; Hon Roll; Jr NHS; NHS; Bentley Grants & Schlrshps 86-87; Bentley Coll-Mass; Accntng.

MC NEILL, LAUREL L; Newfield HS; Selden, NY; (Y); 63/515; VP Camera Clb; Yrbk Stf; Stu Cncl; Jr NHS; NY ST Rgnts Schlrshp 86; SUNY Stonybrook; Psych.

MC NEILL, PATRICIA; Lawrence HS; Inwood, NY; (Y); Yrbk Stf; High Hon Roll; Hon Roll; Jr NHS; NHS; Prfct Atten Awd; Law.

MC NELIS, ELIZABETH A; Our Lady Of Victory Acad; Yonkers, NY; (Y); 30/156; Church Yth Grp; Dance Clb; Variety Show; Yrbk Bus Mgr; Yrbk Stf; NHS; Ny U BPA Schlrshp 86; Arts Hnrbl Ment 86; Mhattan Coll Schlrshp 86; NY U; Finance.

MC NERNEY, MATT; Brewster HS; Brewster, NY; (Y); Boy Scts; Church Yth Grp; ROTC; Drill Tm; Variety Show; Lit Mag; Bowling; JV Trk; Exchng Stu Italy 85; Russn Study Clb, Wk Trp Russia 86; Arch.

MC NICHOLAS, NOREEN; Our Lady Of Victory Acad; Mount Vernon, NY; (S); 15/157; Church Yth Grp; Cmnty Wkr; Hosp Aide; Spanish Clb; Yrbk Stf; Tennis; Trk; High Hon Roll; NHS; Spanish NHS; Physcl Thrpst.

MC NICHOLAS, ROSEMARIE; Sacred Heart Acad; Valley Stream, NY; (S); 10/189; Pres French Clb; FTA; Hosp Aide; Math Clb; Chorus; School Musical; High Hon Roll; NHS.

MC NIEL, MARIAN; Fillmore Central HS; Houghton, NY; (Y); Library Aide; Office Aide; Chorus; Nwsp Stf; Stat Bsbl; Stat Bsktbl; Var Socr; Hon Roll; Alfred Tech Schl; Archit.

MC NIFF, JAMIE; John A Coleman HS; Lake Katrine, NY; (Y); 30/92; JV Bsktbl; Mgr Fld Hcky; Var Mgr(s); Hnrs In English 85-86; Bus Mngmnt.

MC NULTY, CHRIS; Liverpool HS; Liverpool, NY; (Y); 308/816; Hosp Aide; Spanish Clb; School Musical; Frsh Cls; Soph Cls; Jr Cls; Sr Cls; Stu Cncl; Powder Puff Ftbl; Vllybl; Stu Cncl Schlrshp 86; St Jo Schl Nrsng; Nrsng.

MC NULTY, KATHLEEN E; Our Lady Of Victory Acad; Bronx, NY; (Y); Yrbk Stf; Hon Roll; Lit Mag; Rgnts Schlrshp 86; Nrsng.

MC NULTY, MICHELLE; Jasper Central HS; Greenwood, NY; (Y); Drama Clb; French Clb; Band; Chorus; Concert Band; Mrchg Band; School Play; Yrbk Stf; High Hon Roll; Prfct Atten Awd; Acad All Stars 84-86; Alfred ST Coll; Nrsng.

MC NULTY, SHARON M; St Francis Prep; Bayside, NY; (S); 165/744; SADD; School Play; Optimate List; Busnss Admin.

MC PEEK, MIKE; Susquehanna Valley HS; Binghamton, NY; (Y); Chess Clb; Church Yth Grp; Spanish Clb; Rep Frsh Cls; Rep Soph Cls; Rep Jr Cls; Rep Sr Cls; Var L Bsbl; Var L Bsktbl; Var Ftbl.

MC PHEE, CHRIS; Richmond Hill HS; Richmond Hill, NY; (Y); 5/320; Quiz Bowl; Yrbk Stf; Capt Var Bsbl; Var Bowling; Capt Var Crs Cntry; Cit Awd; High Hon Roll; Hon Roll; Jr NHS; Prfct Atten Awd; Sports Med.

MC PHEE, JENNIFER LYNN; Hutchinson Central Technical HS; Buffalo, NY; (Y); Sec Church Yth Grp; Office Aide; Nwsp Rptr; Ed Nwsp Stf; Rep Soph Cls; Rep Jr Cls; Var Cheerleading; Hon Roll; Prfct Atten Awd; Rep Stu Cncl; Diocesan Cthlc Yth Brd 85-86.

MC POLIN, JENNIFER; Academy Of Saint Joseph; Lake Ronkonkoma, NY; (Y); Cmnty Wkr; Dance Clb; French Clb; FHA; Library Aide; Service Clb; Teachers Aide; Chorus; Yrbk Stf; VP Frsh Cls; Hugh O Brien Yth Found Ldrshp Sem 83; ISLI Ldrshp Sem 84; Frnch Exc 85; WA Coll; Intl Studies.

MC QUADE, JENNIFER; John Jay HS; N Salem, NY; (Y); Chess Clb; Computer Clb; Debate Tm; Intnl Clb; Library Aide; Ski Clb; Variety Show; Rep Stu Cncl; JV Socr; Var Score Keeper; Soc Stds Awd Hnrs 86; Ctznshp Awd 86.

MC QUADE, THERESA M; Ursuline Schl; Pelham Manor, NY; (Y); 13/121; Church Yth Grp; Computer Clb; Hosp Aide; Math Clb; Office Aide; Ski Clb; Spanish Clb; Yrbk Stf; Var Capt Fld Hcky; Trk; Math II H Awd 84-85; Ltn Cum Laude Awd 83; U Of Notre Dame; Med.

MC QUAID, JAMES; Arch Bishop Molloy HS; Brooklyn, NY; (Y); 53/383; Boy Scts; Computer Clb; Im Bsktbl; Im Ftbl; Im Sftbl; High Hon Roll.

MC ROBBIE, EMILY; Potsdam Central HS; Potsdam, NY; (Y); 12/120; Varsity Clb; Yrbk Stf; Rep Frsh Cls; Rep Soph Cls; Sec Sr Cls; Stu Cncl; JV Var Cheerleading; JV Vllybl; NHS; High Hon Roll; Talntd JR 84-85; Barbara Hartle Schlrshp Awd 86; Geneseo Clg; Bio.

MC ROBERTS, CHRISTOPHER J; Ogdensburg Free Acad; Ogdensburg, NY; (Y); Var Crs Cntry; JV Ftbl; Var Trk; NYS Regnts Schlrshp 86; Canton Atc; Cvl Engrng.

MC RORIE, DEBI; North Rose-Wolcott HS; Wolcott, NY; (Y); Am Leg Aux Girls St; Sec Frsh Cls; Sec Soph Cls; Sec Jr Cls; Var JV Socr; Var Tennis; High Hon Roll; Hon Roll; NHS; RIT; Bus Mngmnt.

MC SHERRY, GINA; Centereach HS; Lake Grove, NY; (Y); Cmnty Wkr; Variety Show; Trs Stu Cncl; JV Crs Cntry; JV Var Trk; Hon Roll; Earth Sci Achvt Awd 84; Engl Merit Achvt Awd 84; Physcl Ftns Pres Awd 86; Lang Interpretr.

MC STRAVICK, ELLEN; Newfane HS; Newfane, NY; (S); #4 In Class; Drama Clb; Ski Clb; Concert Band; Pep Band; Stage Crew; Nwsp Rptr; Yrbk Stf; Hon Roll; NHS; Variety Show; NYSSMA Solo Awd Flute & Clairinet 84-85; NY St Music Fest Ensemble Awd 84-85; Mech Engrng.

MC VETTY, G SCOTT; St John The Baptist HS; Sayville, NY; (Y); Im Bsbl; Hon Roll; Prfct Atten Awd; Bus.

MC VETY, ROBERT J; Cazenovia Central HS; Cazenovia, NY; (Y); Am Leg Boys St; Church Yth Grp; Drama Clb; Mathletes; School Musical; Symp Band; JV Bsktbl; L Crs Cntry; JV Socr; Hon Roll.

MC VEY, KAREN; Beacon HS; Chelsea, NY; (Y); 11/205; Drama Clb; Chorus; School Musical; School Play; Nwsp Rptr; Trk; High Hon Roll; Jr NHS; NHS.

MC VICAR, KATHRYN A; Manhasset HS; New Hyde Park, NY; (Y); 42/175; Debate Tm; Trs Drama Clb; Thesps; Band; Stage Crew; Nwsp Rptr; Trs Yrbk Bus Mgr; Rep Stu Cncl; JV Cheerleading; Var Trk; Intl Thspn Soc 85; NY ST Rgnts Schlrshp 85; U Of Chicago; Pyscn.

MC WATT, LESLIE; Malvern HS; Rockville Ctr, NY; (Y); 48/120; Girl Scts; Hosp Aide; Acpl Chr; Chorus; Church Choir; Flag Corp; Madrigals; Mrchg Band; Hon Roll; Prfct Atten Awd; NYS Schl Choral Studies 86; NYSMA 85; Choral Studies.

MC WILLIAMS, KIM; Rhinebeck Central HS; Rhinebeck, NY; (Y); AFS; French Clb; Sftbl; High Hon Roll; Hon Roll; Bus.

MC WITHEY, MICHAEL; John C Bridlebough HS; Fulton, NY; (Y); 33/176; Pres French Clb; Teachers Aide; Var Bsktbl; Bowling; Var Stat Ftbl; Var Stat Trk; Hon Roll; Rotary Awd; CSFA Natl Scholar 86; Jim Mc Dougall Mem Awd 86; Upstate Medical Ctr; Resp Thrpy.

MEACHEM, MARK; Notre Dame Bishop Gibbons HS; Schenectady, NY; (S); 4/101; Nwsp Rptr; Rep Stu Cncl; Capt Bsktbl; Capt Crs Cntry; Trk; High Hon Roll; NHS; Ntl Merit Schol; Hstry & Ntl Merit Ldrshp & Rlgn Awds 82 & 84-86; Cmmnctns.

MEAD, CINDY; Falconer Central HS; Falconer, NY; (Y); 13/120; VP Art Clb; GAA; Spanish Clb; Chorus; Var Bsktbl; Var Capt Cheerleading; Coach Actv; Var Sftbl; Var Tennis; Var Hon Roll; Sftbll MVP Awd 84-86; Work At Mc Donalds 85-86; Nursing.

MEAD, JOHN C; Oxford Acad; Oxford, NY; (Y); Letterman Clb; SADD; Varsity Clb; Im Coach Actv; Var L Socr; Boy Scts; Chess Clb; Computer Clb; Library Aide; Chorus; NY Regnts Schlrshp 86; Navy; Electrncs.

MEAD, LORI; Brockport HS; Brockport, NY; (Y); Sec Church Yth Grp; Spanish Clb; Yrbk Stf; Var Capt Diving; Var Capt Gym; Var Capt Swmmng; High Hon Roll; Hon Roll; NY ST Empr Gms 85; Bus.

MEADE, TRICIA; Sleepy Hollow HS; N Tarrytown, NY; (Y); 23/186; Church Yth Grp; Civic Clb; Debate Tm; Exploring; Girl Scts; Science Clb; Spanish Clb; Teachers Aide; Nwsp Stf; Yrbk Stf; All League Hnrbl Mntn Fld Hcky & Sccr 85-86; Cmmnctns.

MEADERS, LEIGH; Notre Dame Acad; Staten Island, NY; (Y); Pres Church Yth Grp; Yrbk Phtg; Yrbk Stf; JV Bsktbl; JV Sftbl; NHS; Most Imprvd Plyr Sftbll 84-85; Lawyer.

MEADOW, ROXANNE; Mamaroneck HS; Larchmont, NY; (Y); AFS; Red Cross Aide; Service Clb; Spanish Clb; SADD; VP Temple Yth Grp; School Play; Var Swmmng; Cit Awd; DAR Awd; NY ST Rgntns Schlrshp 86; Kiwanis Hlth Awd Schlrshp 86; MI Alumni Anl Gvng Schlrshp 86; U MI; Blgcl Sci.

MEADOWCROFT, DEANNA; Stamford Central HS; Stamford, NY; (Y); 15/35; Sec Camera Clb; French Clb; Pres FBLA; Library Aide; Office Aide; Yrbk Phtg; Yrbk Stf; Capt JV Cheerleading; Var Socr; Moore Coll Art; Art.

MEADOWS, JODI; Fayetteville-Manlius HS; De Witt, NY; (Y); Pep Clb; Temple Yth Grp; Hon Roll; Syracuse U; Grphc Illus.

MEADOWS, TRICIA J; Bishop Ford CCHS HS; Brooklyn, NY; (S); 11/439; Art Clb; Computer Clb; Acad Excllnc; 1st Hnrs; Brooklyn Coll; Art.

MEAGHER, KAREN; Fairport HS; Fairport, NY; (Y); Girl Scts; SADD; Chorus; Yrbk Stf; Hon Roll; Bio.

MEANS, ANNE; Mount Saint Mary Acad; Tonawanda, NY; (Y); Camp Fr Inc; Cmnty Wkr; Pep Clb; Service Clb; Chorus; Variety Show; Yrbk Stf; Rep Jr Cls; Rep Stu Cncl; Var Stat Bsktbl; Outstndng Vlntr YES 85; Buddy Pgm YMCA 84; Bus.

MEANS, CYNTHIA; Our Lady Of Victory Acad; Yonkers, NY; (S); #20 In Class; Computer Clb; French Clb; Science Clb; French Hon Soc; High Hon Roll; NHS.

MEANS, KIMBERLY; Brockport HS; Spencerport, NY; (Y); 18/346; Church Yth Grp; Ski Clb; Var JV Socr; JV Sftbl; High Hon Roll; NHS; Ralph J Beaney Sccr Sprtsmnshp Awd 84; Math.

MEASE, RHONDA; Jamestown HS; Jamestown, NY; (Y); French Clb; Band; Concert Band; Mrchg Band; Symp Band; Music Solo Awd 84; Trvl.

MECA, KELLY ANNE; Amsterdam HS; Amsterdam, NY; (Y); JA; Latin Clb; Varsity Clb; Var Bowling; Var Sftbl; Tennis; Hon Roll; NHS; Acctg.

MECCA, SALVATORE S; Rome Free Acad; Rome, NY; (Y); Capt Bsbl; Bsktbl; Jr NHS; Albany ST Coll.

MECH, TERRI; Brockport HS; Spencerport, NY; (Y); French Clb; Mgr Concert Band; Jazz Band; Mgr Mrchg Band; Pep Band; Var Tennis; Var Trk; High Hon Roll; NHS; Coca Cola Bwlng Trnmnt 85; Physical Therapy.

MEDALLA, APOLINARIO; Briarcliff HS; Briarcliff, NY; (Y); AFS; Cmnty Wkr; SADD; Rep Frsh Cls; Rep Jr Cls; Im Bsktbl; JV Var Ftbl; Hon Roll; Boston Coll.

MEDDAUGH, NANCY; Pittsford Sutherland HS; Pittsford, NY; (Y); Church Yth Grp; French Clb; JA; Band; Crs Cntry; Hon Roll; Smr Frgn Exchng To Avignon Frnc 85; PA ST U; Mrktng.

MEDEIROS, GRETCHEN; Smithtown H S East; St James, NY; (Y); Camera Clb; SADD; Stu Cncl; JV Mgr(s); Hon Roll; Bus.

MEDERRICK, MICHAEL; Roslyn HS; Roslyn, NY; (Y); Key Clb; Y-Teens; Im Bsbl.

MEDINA, CYNTHIA; New Utrecht HS; Brooklyn, NY; (Y); 34/635; Sec Church Yth Grp; Key Clb; Math Tm; Band; Chorus; Church Choir; Rep Soph Cls; Hon Roll; Arista 83-86; NY ST Regnts Schlrshp 86; LI U; Phrmcy.

MEDINA, DARLENE; Earl L Vandermulen HS; Pt Jefferson, NY; (Y); Latin Clb; SADD; Varsity Clb; Yrbk Stf; Rep Frsh Cls; Rep Soph Cls; Rep Jr Cls; Trk; Hon Roll; Bus.

MEDINA, ELIEZER; Cardinal Hayes HS; Bronx, NY; (Y); 120/293; Art Clb; Church Yth Grp; Letterman Clb; Chorus; Jazz Band; Yrbk Stf; High Hon Roll; Hon Roll; Comp Sci.

MEDINA, IRENE; Dodge Voc HS; Bronx, NY; (Y); Prfct Atten Awd; Spanish NHS; Comp.

MEDINA, JESSIE; East New York HS; Brooklyn, NY; (Y); Teachers Aide; Nwsp Stf; Bowling; Hon Roll; Comp Sci.

MEDINA, MELISSA; Immaculata HS; New York, NY; (Y); Drama Clb; English Clb; Chorus; Church Choir; School Play; Hon Roll.

MEDINA, NYDIA; Herbert H Lehman HS; Bronx, NY; (Y); 13/561; Orch; School Musical; Yrbk Stf; Lit Mag; High Hon Roll; Hon Roll; Cert Of Achvt Math, Hnrs Eng 85; Arista Hnr Awd 85-86; Bus Admn.

MEDINA, WANDA; Walton HS; Bronx, NY; (Y); Spanish Clb; Chorus; Sec Sr Cls; Cheerleading; Gym; Vllybl; Cit Awd; Hon Roll; Prfct Atten Awd; Spanish NHS; Spnsh Hon Clss; Prfct Attndc; Ctznshp Awd; Brooklyn Technical; Fshn Merch.

MEDLEY, CYNTHIA; Batavia HS; Batavia, NY; (Y); German Clb; SADD; Concert Band; Mrchg Band; Yrbk Stf; Rep Soph Cls; Score Keeper; Socr; Sftbl; Swmmng; Outstndng Stu Cert Hghst Avg Grmn III 85-86; Bus.

MEDLEY, MICHAEL; Weedsport Central Schl; Weedsport, NY; (Y); 3/90; 4-H; French Clb; Intnl Clb; Math Tm; Spanish Clb; Varsity Clb; Var L Bsktbl; High Hon Roll; Jr NHS; Anne B Sholes Mem Awd 81; Natl Merit Awd Frnch 85; Regents Scholar 86; Cayuga CC; Engrng.

MEDNICK, ATARA; Hebrew Acad; Lawrence, NY; (Y); Temple Yth Grp; School Play; Yrbk Stf; Cit Awd; Linda Pinsky Mrl Awd 86; Stein Coll; Psychlgst.

MEEDER, CURT; Sherman Central HS; Sherman, NY; (S); French Clb; Scholastic Bowl; Rep Frsh Cls; Rep Soph Cls; Trs Jr Cls; JV Bsktbl; Var Crs Cntry; JV Var Tennis; NHS; Ag.

MEEGAN, KELLIE; Auburn HS; Auburn, NY; (Y); Var JV Socr; Trk; High Hon Roll; Hon Roll; Jr NHS; NHS; Lang.

MEEGAN, PATRICK; E L Vandermeulen HS; Mt Sinai, NY; (Y); Art Clb; Church Yth Grp; Drama Clb; School Musical; School Play; JV Socr; Hon Roll; Rgnts Schlrp 87; Phys Sci.

MEEHAN, EILEEN K; St Francis Prep; Floral Park, NY; (S); 28/743; Art Clb; Hosp Aide; SADD; JV Capt Tennis; High Hon Roll; NHS; MVP JV Tnns 84-85.

MEEHAN, JAMES; South Side HS; Rockville Ctr, NY; (Y); Computer Clb; Mathletes; Yrbk Phtg; Var Capt Crs Cntry; Var Trk; Hon Roll; Manhatton Coll.

MEEHAN, RICHARD J; Suffern HS; Suffern, NY; (Y); 50/387; Am Leg Boys St; VP Church Yth Grp; Computer Clb; Hosp Aide; Off Jr Cls; JV Crs Cntry; Var Trk; High Hon Roll; Invtnl Acdmc Wrkshp At West Point 86; Engineering.

MEEK, ALANA; Greece Athena HS; Rochester, NY; (Y); Drama Clb; Exploring; Hosp Aide; Thesps; Chorus; Drm & Bgl; School Musical; School Play; Hon Roll; Excllnt Rtg NYSSMA Solo Cmptn 85; Chld Dev.

MEEKER, JULIANNE E; Notre Dame HS; Elmira, NY; (Y); 45/87; Hosp Aide; Library Aide; Chorus; Stage Crew; Nwsp Stf; Yrbk Bus Mgr; Lit Mag; Score Keeper; JV Var Sftbl; Hon Roll; NY ST Rgnts Nrsng Schlrshp 86; Albny Med Ctr Schl Nrsng; Nrs.

MEERS, STEFANIE; Vestal Senior HS; Vestal, NY; (Y); Drama Clb; French Clb; Varsity Clb; Trk; High Hon Roll; Hon Roll; Prfct Atten Awd; Frgn Rltns.

MEERWARTH, TRACEY; Hoosick Falls Central Schl; Eagle Bridge, NY; (Y); Church Yth Grp; Pep Clb; Trs Ski Clb; Teachers Aide; Nwsp Stf; Yrbk Phtg; Yrbk Stf; Stat Wrstlng; Hon Roll; NHS.

MEGARO, MARIA C; Norman Thomas HS; Woodside, NY; (Y); 19/596; DECA; Service Clb; Chorus; Nwsp Ed-Chief; VP Frsh Cls; Hon Roll; NHS; Rgnts Schlrshp; Amhrst Coll; Pltcl Sci.

MEGGISON, SHERRI; Livonia HS; S Lima, NY; (Y); Am Leg Aux Girls St; Science Clb; Varsity Clb; Nwsp Ed-Chief; Yrbk Stf; Sec VP Stu Cncl; Var Cheerleading; Vllybl; High Hon Roll; NHS.

MEGGS, MICHELLE; St Raymond Academy For Girls; Bronx, NY; (Y); Computer Clb; Boston U; Corp Law.

MEGNA, GINA; Lawrence HS; Lawrence, NY; (Y); 28/414; Sec AFS; Art Clb; Church Yth Grp; Drama Clb; Service Clb; Nwsp Rptr; Nwsp Sprt Ed; JV Var Vllybl; NHS; Drama Clb; Italian Club VP; Sci Cngrs Cert Of Recogntn & Hnrbl Mntn; Hmcmng Queen Fnlst; Comm.

MEGNA, ROSALIE; Commack HS South; Commack, NY; (Y); 51/367; Cmnty Wkr; Hosp Aide; Pres Soph Cls; VP Jr Cls; Pres Sr Cls; JV Sftbl; High Hon Roll; NHS; Rep Stu Cncl; Pres Acdmc Fit Awd 86; Regnts Schlrshp 86; Stonybrook; Bio Sci.

MEHL, RICHARD R; W C Mepham HS; N Bellmore, NY; (Y); 86/360; Am Leg Boys St; Boy Scts; Mathletes; Ski Clb; Var L Socr; Var L Wrstlng; Cit Awd; God Cntry Awd; Pres Schlr; ROTC Schlrshp 86; Egl Sct 84; Schl Systm Mgr 86; VA Military Inst; Elec Engnrng.

MEHLENBACHER, CONNIE; Charles O Dickerson HS; Trumansburg, NY; (Y); Varsity Clb; Var L Bsktbl; Var L Socr; JV Sftbl; Var L Trk; Church Yth Grp; 4-H; French Clb; Lab Tech.

MEHLENBACHER, DIANA; Canisteo Central HS; Hornell, NY; (Y); Art Clb; Aud/Vis; Drama Clb; Girl Scts; PAVAS; SADD; Alfred St Coll; Teach/Para-Lgl.

MEHLENBACHER, RANDY C; Wayland Central HS; Wayland, NY; (Y); Am Leg Boys St; Chess Clb; Trs FFA; Letterman Clb; Ski Clb; Varsity Clb; Capt Var Crs Cntry; Capt Var Trk; Suny Brockport; Engr.

MEHLHAFF, KARIN; Elmont Memorial HS; Elmont, NY; (Y); FBLA; Spanish Clb; Yrbk Stf; Off Frsh Cls; Off Soph Cls; Off Jr Cls; Sec Sr Cls; Jr NHS; NHS; Spanish NHS; Bus.

MEHLMAN, TANYA A; Stissing MT JR & SR HS; Ancramdale, NY; (Y); 23/100; Church Yth Grp; Cmnty Wkr; Variety Show; Yrbk Phtg; Yrbk Rptr; Yrbk Stf; VP Frsh Cls; VP Soph Cls; Stat Ftbl; Var Tennis; Natl Englsh Mrt Awd 85; Natl Rgnts Schlrshp 86; Dtchs CC; Nrsng.

MEHR, MICHAEL; Spring Valley SR HS; Spring Vly, NY; (Y); 99/441; Computer Clb; Key Clb; Ski Clb; Temple Yth Grp; Mrchg Band; Symp Band; Hon Roll; NY ST Regnts Schlrshp 86; U Of Buffalo; Arch.

MEHRDAD, HAMID; Barker Central HS; Buffalo, NY; (Y); 14/104; AFS; Drama Clb; 4-H; School Play; Var Bsktbl; 4-H Awd; Hon Roll; ST U NY; Med.

MEHTA, INDIRA; Forest Hills HS; Forest Hills, NY; (Y); Hosp Aide; Office Aide; Science Clb; Teachers Aide; Yrbk Stf; Var Bowling; Var Socr; High Hon Roll; NHS; Prfct Atten Awd; Regents Schlrshp 85-86; Queens Borough Sci Fr 1st Plc Hon Mntn 85; Prin Awd 84; Barnard Coll.

MEHTA, SUJAN; East Chester HS; Scarsdale, NY; (Y); 45/144; Am Leg Boys St; Debate Tm; NFL; Office Aide; Political Wkr; Speech Tm; SADD; Nwsp Rptr; Yrbk Phtg; Yrbk Stf; Baylor U; Law.

MEIER, CHRISTA M; Kingston HS; Ulster Park, NY; (Y); 2/573; Church Yth Grp; Cmnty Wkr; Drama Clb; Church Choir; Orch; Stu Cncl; High Hon Roll; Jr NHS; Ntl Merit Ltr; Rgnts Schlrshp 86; Grmn Hnr Scty 85-86; SUNY New Paltz; Bio.

MEIER, ELISE; Frontier Central HS; Hamburg, NY; (S); 12/500; Hosp Aide; Ski Clb; Off Soph Cls; Off Jr Cls; Off Sr Cls; Stu Cncl; High Hon Roll; Hon Roll; NHS; Prfct Atten Awd; Exec Board-Stdnt Govt 84-86; Buffalo ST; Eductn.

MEIER, MARYANN R; Holy Trinity HS; Westbury, NY; (S); Church Yth Grp; Science Clb; Spanish Clb; SADD; Teachers Aide; Chorus; School Musical; Yrbk Stf; Rep Frsh Cls; Rep Soph Cls; Schlrshp Awd Hghst Grd Pt Avg Algbr 83; Nassau CC; Elem Ed.

MEIGS, BRIAN; Cazenovia Central Schl; Cazenovia, NY; (Y); VP Exploring; Pres FFA; Band; Ftbl; Hon Roll; Dry Frmng.

MEINDL, GREGORY; Holy Trinity HS; Malvern, NY; (Y); Camera Clb; Cmnty Wkr; 4-H; Band; Concert Band; Jazz Band; Mrchg Band; Orch; School Musical; School Play; Consumer Yth Cntst Nassau Co 1st 82 & 83; NYS 4-H Awd Wnnr 85; NYS Fair Blue Rbbn Solar Enrgy 84; Pratt Inst; Arch.

MEINHOLD, PATTY; Tonawanda HS; Tonawanda, NY; (Y); Spanish Clb; SADD; Color Guard; Yrbk Stf; JV Bsktbl; Var Crs Cntry; Var Swmmng; Var Capt Trk; Hon Roll; NHS; Faculty Hnr Awd 84; Pre-Dntstry.

MEININGER, JENNIFER S; Chruchville-Chili HS; Scottsville, NY; (Y); 23/240; VP Church Yth Grp; JA; Math Tm; Ski Clb; Concert Band; School Play; Yrbk Stf; Lit Mag; Tennis; Hon Roll; NYS Rgnts Schlrshp 86; NYSSMA Clrnt Awd 84; St Lawrence U; English.

MEINKE JR, RICHARD; Depew HS; Depew, NY; (Y); 8/272; Boy Scts; Concert Band; Mrchg Band; JV Ftbl; Hon Roll; Jr NHS; Eagle Badge Boy Scouts 85.

MEISENZAHL, JENNIFER E; Our Lady Of Mercy HS; E Rochester, NY; (Y); 1/172; VP Exploring; Pres SADD; School Musical; School Play; Nwsp Rptr; NHS; Ntl Merit SF; Val; Church Yth Grp; Cmnty Wkr; JR Of Yr 85; Notre Dame Clb Rochester JR Of Yr Fnlst 85; Biol.

MEISNER, AMY; Hamburg SR HS; Hamburg, NY; (Y); 19/386; Sec Church Yth Grp; 4-H; Band; Chorus; Concert Band; Mrchg Band; Orch; School Musical; 4-H Awd; NHS; Saratoga Smmr Schl Art 86; Engl.

MEJALLI, NEZAR; Archbishop Stepinac HS; Yonkers, NY; (Y); 75/180; Debate Tm; Bowling; Manhattan Clg; Pharm.

MEJICOVSKY, LEORA; East Meadow HS; E Meadow, NY; (S); Mathletes; Acpl Chr; Orch; Rptr Nwsp Stf; Hon Roll; NHS; Ntl Merit SF; French Clb; Key Clb; Math Tm; Outstndng Engl Stu Awd 83-84; All Cnty Music Awd 85-86; Lng Islnd Sprng Music Fstvl Awd 85-86; Bio-Chem.

MEKLER, SHANI G; Spring Valley SR HS; Monsey, NY; (Y); 47/441; Key Clb; Yrbk Stf; VP Sr Cls; Stu Cncl; Mgr(s); High Hon Roll; Hon Roll; Spanish NHS; Regnts Schlrshp 86; U Of MI; Librl Arts.

MELBIE, LUCY; Bradford Central Schl; Savona, NY; (Y); Yrbk Sprt Ed; Socr; Sftbl; Vllybl; School Play; Yrbk Stf; Socl Wrkr.

MELCHIORRE, CAROLYN; St Francis Prep; Whitestone, NY; (S); 155/746; Band; Concert Band; Mrchg Band; Orch; Tennis; Hon Roll; NHS.

MELDRUM, CHRISTOPHER A; Mahopac HS; Mahopac, NY; (Y); Im JV Ftbl; JV Var Lcrss; Hon Roll; Biol.

MELE, RICHARD; Central Islip HS; Central Islip, NY; (Y); #2 In Class; NHS.

MELECA JR, THOMAS J; Bishop Kearney HS; Walworth, NY; (Y); Boy Scts; Band; Service Clb; Concert Band; Jazz Band; Mrchg Band; Pep Band; Hon Roll; Engr.

MELECO, VINCENT; Catholic Central HS; Waterford, NY; (Y); Boy Scts; French Clb; Math Clb; Variety Show; Yrbk Stf; Var L Tennis; High Hon Roll; Hon Roll; NHS.

MELENDEZ, ANTONIO; Dewitt Clinton HS; Bronx, NY; (Y); 1/257; Cmnty Wkr; Math Tm; Quiz Bowl; JV Bsbl; High Hon Roll; Hon Roll; Jr NHS; NHS; Val; Regents ST Schlrshp 86; Union Fed Of Tchrs 86; Rnsslr Plytch Inst; Aerntcl Eng.

MELENDEZ, CARMEN; James Monroe HS; Bronx, NY; (Y); 4-H; Teachers Aide; Nwsp Rptr; Nwsp Stf; Lit Mag; Hon Roll; Typg Awd 86; Bronx CC; Bus Tchr.

MELENDEZ, JACQUELINE; St Joseph HS; Brooklyn, NY; (Y); Church Yth Grp; Cmnty Wkr; Computer Clb; Dance Clb; Pres Spanish Clb; Teachers Aide; School Play; Nwsp Ed-Chief; Nwsp Rptr; Nwsp Stf; Psychlgy.

MELENDEZ, JOSE; Morris HS; Bronx, NY; (Y); Church Yth Grp; Cmnty Wkr; JA; Office Aide; Church Choir.

MELENDEZ, MATTHEW; St Agens HS; New York, NY; (Y); 34/112; Boys Clb Am; Var Capt Bowling; Hon Roll; NHS; Telecmnctns.

MELENDEZ, SARA LISA; Acad Of Mt St Ursula; New York, NY; (Y); Cmnty Wkr; Trs Spanish Clb; Variety Show; Yrbk Stf; Rep Soph Cls; Stu Cncl; Spanish NHS; Schrlshp Acad Mt ST Ursula 83-87; 1st Hnrs 83; Cert Awd Spnsh 85; Georgetown U; Intl Bus.

MELENDEZ, YOLANDA; Jane Addams V HS; Bronx, NY; (S); 6/260; Yrbk Stf; Hon Roll; Honor Soc 84; RN.

MELFI, JAMES A; Moore Catholic HS; Staten Island, NY; (Y); Bowling; NYC U; Arch.

MELFI, PATRICK; Bishop Cunningham HS; Oswego, NY; (Y); 3/40; Yrbk Ed-Chief; Var Bsbl; Var Stat Bsktbl; Var Ftbl; Var Golf; Im Wt Lftg; Cit Awd; DAR Awd; Hon Roll; NHS; Nazarth Coll Of Rochester; Engl.

MELICK, JULIE; Canastota Central HS; Canastota, NY; (S); Church Yth Grp; SADD; Band; Concert Band; Mrchg Band; Score Keeper; Stat Vllybl; High Hon Roll; NHS.

MELITA, NANCY; Notre Dame Bishop Gibbons HS; Schenectady, NY; (Y); Art Clb; Exploring; Hosp Aide; SADD; Color Guard; Var Mgr(s); Var Tennis; Cert Achvt Peer Ldrshp Proj Playback 86; St George Masons Yth Awd 86; Chldrn.

MELKUN, PHILIP; Oriskany HS; Floyd, NY; (Y); Am Leg Boys St; Boy Scts; Key Clb; Mathletes; Spanish Clb; Varsity Clb; School Play; Stage Crew; JV Var Bsktbl; Var Capt Trk; Trig Awd Mth Ii 85; Physcs.

MELLEN, BRIAN; Binghamton HS; Binghamton, NY; (Y); Exploring; Lit Mag; Regents Schlrp 86; Elect Engrg.

MELLGREN, KIRSTEN; Lakeland HS; Yorktown Hts, NY; (Y); Band; Concert Band; Jazz Band; Mrchg Band; Orch; School Musical; Stage Crew; Stat Socr; Jr Area All St Orch 84; Acctg.

MELLIEON, LISA; Bishop Loughlin MHS; Brooklyn, NY; (Y); 25/233; Cmnty Wkr; Science Clb; Yrbk Stf; Cheerleading; Hon Roll; NHS; Acad Hnrs 1st Hnrs 84; 4 Scnd Hnrs 84; 3rd Hnrs 86; Howard U; Law.

MELLING, STEVEN; Syosset HS; Syosset, NY; (Y); Lit Mag; Im Bsbl; Var Capt Bowling; Hon Roll; NY Regents Schlrshp 86; Eductnl & Cultrl Fund Of Electrcl Indstry Schlrshp 86; Polytechnic U; Aerosp Engr.

MELLOIII, JOSEPH; Fort Plain HS; Fort Plain, NY; (Y); Am Leg Boys St; Pres Computer Clb; Varsity Clb; Band; Jazz Band; Pres Frsh Cls; Co-Capt Crs Cntry; Golf; Co-Capt Trk; VP NHS.

MELLON, RICHARD; Rome Catholic HS; Rome, NY; (Y); Boy Scts; Church Yth Grp; Rep Frsh Cls; Var JV Ftbl; Var JV Wt Lftg; Crimnl Justc.

MELLONE, BRIAN; Liverpool HS; Liverpool, NY; (Y); 14/900; FCA; Math Tm; School Musical; High Hon Roll; Math Leag 3rd Pl Cnty; Law.

MELTZER, MARNA DENISE; Jamesville De Witt HS; Dewitt, NY; (Y); 56/245; Dance Clb; Model UN; Pep Clb; Political Wkr; Spanish Clb; Temple Yth Grp; Chorus; School Play; High Hon Roll; Hon Roll; Syracuse Jewish Fed Ldng Comndtn 85; Syracuse U; Advstng.

MELVILLE, MARY ELLEN; Corinth Central HS; Corinth, NY; (S); Hosp Aide; SADD; Sec Band; Chorus; Variety Show; Sec Yrbk Stf; Score Keeper; Sec Frsh Cls; Herkimer CC; Med Admin Asst.

MELZER, CLAIRE; Emma Willard Schl; North Miami Beach, FL; (Y); Cmnty Wkr; Debate Tm; Math Tm; Acpl Chr; Ed Lit Mag; Rep Stu Cncl; Cit Awd; Union Coll; Arch.

MEMOLE, MAUREEN; Columbia HS; Rensselaer, NY; (Y); Chorus; Church Choir; Hon Roll; Suny; Comp Sci.

MENAGER, FRANTZ; Springfield Gardens HS; Cambria Heights, NY; (S); French Clb; Im Vllybl; French Hon Soc; Hon Roll; NHS; Sci, Hstry & Math Awds 85; Med.

MENCHER, SANFORD; Walt Whitman HS; Melville, NY; (Y); 11/447; Computer Clb; Key Clb; Mathletes; Spanish Clb; Trs Soph Cls; Var L Socr; Var L Tennis; High Hon Roll; Ntl Merit Ltr; Sec Drm Mjr(t); Travel Schlrshp From Amer Assoc Of Tchrs Of Spnsh & Portgse 86; Dartmouth Coll; Econ.

MENDEL, BRETT D; Vestal SR HS; Vestal, NY; (Y); Am Leg Boys St; Trs French Clb; FBLA; SADD; Temple Yth Grp; Capt L Bsktbl; Coach Actv; Var L Trk; Hon Roll; NHS; Outstndng Vol Svc Awd-Jewish Comm Ctr 84-85; Pre-Med.

MENDEL, ROBYN; Sachem HS; Holbrook, NY; (Y).

MENDEL, SUSAN; St Peters HS Girls; Staten Island, NY; (Y); Chorus; School Musical; Lit Mag; Comp Pgmr.

MENDELSOHN, JENNIFER A; John F Kennedy HS; Old Bethpage, NY; (Y); 1/240; Cmnty Wkr; Model UN; Orch; School Play; Yrbk Ed-Chief; Ed Lit Mag; Var Mgr(s); High Hon Roll; NHS; Ntl Merit Ltr; Hnrs Eng Awds 83-85; Newsday Schlrshp Ldng Schlstc Achvr 86; Orch All ST 84-85; U VA; Eng.

MENDEZ, ANA; George Washington HS; New York, NY; (Y); Spanish Clb; Church Choir; Color Guard; Orch; Vllybl; Cit Awd; NHS; Sal; F Goldberg Meml Awd Genl Excllnc 84; Teresa Humaran Meml Awd 85; Physcn.

MENDEZ, CLAUDIA L; Clara Barton HS; Brooklyn, NY; (Y); 14/485; Church Yth Grp; Hosp Aide; Spanish Clb; Teachers Aide; High Hon Roll; Hon Roll; NHS; Prfct Atten Awd; Regents Schlrshp 86; Cert Merit Sen Bartosiewicz 86; Volunteer Svc Awd 85; NY U; Pre Med.

MENDEZ, DAVID; Amsterdam HS; Hagaman, NY; (Y); 71/316; Boy Scts; Varsity Clb; Band; Concert Band; Mrchg Band; Yrbk Stf; Var Ftbl; Im Trk; Var Wt Lftg; Cit Awd; Boston U; Engrng.

MENDEZ, JO ANTOINETTE; Julia Richman HS; Brooklyn, NY; (Y); 1/32; Church Yth Grp; Hosp Aide; Red Cross Aide; School Musical; Variety Show; Gym; Swmmng; High Hon Roll; Hon Roll; Prfct Atten Awd; Martha Graham Dnc Schlrshp 83-85; Ballet De Puerto Rico Dnc Schlrshp 85; Clrk Ctr Dnc Schlrshp 85-86; Dnce.

MENDEZ, MARTHA; Cardinal Spellman HS; Bronx, NY; (Y); 50/507; Dance Clb; Math Clb; Science Clb; Spanish Clb; Nwsp Stf; Yrbk Stf; Hon Roll; NHS; NEDT Awd; Natl Hspnc Schlr Awd; Handicppd Prjct Hnr Cert 84-85; Psychlgst.

MENDEZ, MERCEDES; John F Kennedy HS; New York, NY; (Y); Art Clb; Chorus; Gym; Vllybl; High Hon Roll; Hon Roll; NCTE Awd; Prfct Atten Awd; Spanish NHS; Computer.

MENDEZ, TREVOR; Erasmus Hall HS; Brooklyn, NY; (Y); Computer Clb; Debate Tm; Math Clb; Math Tm; Science Clb; Capt Socr; High Hon Roll; NHS; Hon Roll; Jamaica Math Assn Comptn Merit Awd 85; Lincoln Douglas Debts Cert Of Merit 86; Assoc Of Tchrs Math Awd; MA Inst Of Tech; Comp Sci.

MENDOLA, MARTIN; Mc Quaid Jesuit HS; Pittsford, NY; (Y); 35/180; Cmnty Wkr; Yrbk Bus Mgr; Pres Stu Cncl; Capt Bsktbl; Ftbl; NHS; Accmpnd Flbrght Schlr To England As Asst 86; Gldn Knght Of Yr Awd 85; Union Coll; Lbrl Arts.

MENDOZA, MELLISSA; Cathedral HS; Holliswood, NY; (Y); 29/300; Library Aide; Yrbk Stf; Engl II Hnrs 85-86.

MENDOZA, ORLANDO; Columbus HS; Bronx, NY; (Y); Bsktbl; Bowling; Vllybl; Wood Wrkng Cls Awd 85; TCI; Electrncs.

MENDOZA, ZORAIDA; Eli Whitney Vocational HS; Brooklyn, NY; (Y); 4/186; Office Aide; Nwsp Ed-Chief; Yrbk Stf; VP Soph Cls; VP Sr Cls; VP Stu Cncl; Vllybl; Hon Roll; NHS; Acad All-Amer 85-86; NY ST Regents Schlrshp 85-86; Elec Engr.

MENDY JR, PAUL B; Lackawanna SR HS; Lackawanna, NY; (Y); 2/250; Am Leg Boys St; Capt Scholastic Bowl; Spanish Clb; Varsity Clb; Band; Mrchg Band; Var L Vllybl; Bausch & Lomb Sci Awd; Hon Roll; Pres NHS; World Hist Awd 84-85; Engrng.

MENECH, HOLLY; Broadalbin HS; Broadalbin, NY; (Y); Church Yth Grp; French Clb; Girl Scts; Hosp Aide; Library Aide; Pep Clb; SADD; School Play; Yrbk Stf; JV Bsktbl; Fulton Montgomery CC; Bus.

MENEELY, AMY; Lintoin HS; Schenectedy, NY; (Y); Church Yth Grp; Dance Clb; Drama Clb; Hosp Aide; Acpl Chr; Chorus; Orch; Stu Cncl; Hon Roll.

MENG, ALICE; New Rochelle HS; New Rochelle, NY; (Y); Math Tm; Mrchg Band; Orch; Pep Band; Symp Band; Nwsp Phtg; Yrbk Phtg; Lit Mag; Var L Socr; NHS; Ntl Hnr Soc Pres 86; Trthln Wnnr 85; Engrng.

MENICKELLI, TODD; Liverpool HS; Liverpool, NY; (Y); Exploring; Var Swmmng; Hon Roll; Mst Outstndng Stu 83; Bus Admn.

MENIFEE, KIMBERLY; Corcoran HS; Syracuse, NY; (Y); Boys Clb Am; Church Yth Grp; Chorus; Church Choir; Var Trk; Hon Roll; Full Schlrshp To Cornell U Summer Pgm 86; Cornell U; Business.

MENNA, DAVID; Fairport SR HS; Pittsford, NY; (Y); Capt Var Ftbl; Var JV Lcrss; Im Wt Lftg; Var JV Wrstlng; Hon Roll; Spanish NHS; Villanova U; Bio.

MENSAH, DOREEN; Cardinal Spellman HS; Bronx, NY; (Y); Cmnty Wkr; PAVAS; Service Clb; Teachers Aide; Chorus; School Musical; Cit Awd; Hon Roll; Prfct Atten Awd; Columbia; Pre-Med.

MENSCHING, DONNA; Clayton A Bouton JR/SR HS; Voorheesville, NY; (Y); Am Leg Aux Girls St; Trs Intnl Clb; Math Tm; Ski Clb; Lit Mag; Tennis; Vllybl; Bausch & Lomb Sci Awd; High Hon Roll; VP NHS; Veterinary Medicine.

MENSCHING, SHARON; Roy C Ketcham SR HS; Wappingers Fls, NY; (Y); Yrbk Stf; Stat Trk; High Hon Roll; Hon Roll; NHS; Legal Studies.

MENTING, DIANE; Mercy HS; Shirley, NY; (Y); 44/128; Church Yth Grp; 4-H; Office Aide; Teachers Aide; Chorus; Church Choir; School Musical; Hon Roll; Oneonta Coll; Data Prcssr.

MENTUCK, MICHELLE; Holy Trinity HS; N Massapequa, NY; (S); Math Clb; Stage Crew; Var Bsktbl; Var Sftbl; Hon Roll; NHS; Bus.

MENZEL, BARBARA; Johnjay HS; Purdys, NY; (Y); 5/253; Science Clb; Ski Clb; Swing Chorus; Rep Frsh Cls; Rep Soph Cls; Rep Jr Cls; Rep Sr Cls; Sec Stu Cncl; Fld Hcky; High Hon Roll; Book Awd 85; Hnrs Eng 10 And 11,Socl Stud,Sci,Chem,Physcs And Comptrs; Middlebury; Poltcl Sci.

MENZEL, SUSANNE; John Jay HS; Purdys, NY; (Y); 3/253; Science Clb; Acpl Chr; Rep Stu Cncl; Var Fld Hcky; JV Socr; High Hon Roll; Sec NHS; Band; Chorus; Orch; Awds Eng 10,11,Sci,Chem; Pyscs,Socl Stu 84-85; Oberlin Clg Book Awd 85; Middlebury Clg; Law.

MENZIE, LARRY; Hicksville HS; Hicksville, NY; (Y); Pres Civic Clb; Cmnty Wkr; Drama Clb; Temple Yth Grp; Drm & Bgl; School Musical; School Play; Stage Crew; Variety Show; Psych.

MENZIES, BELEN; Midwood HS; Brooklyn, NY; (Y); Pratt Inst; Archtctr.

MENZIES, MELISSA M; Stella Maris HS; Far Rockaway, NY; (Y); 69/213; Cmnty Wkr; French Clb; Hosp Aide; Service Clb; Chorus; Ntl Merit Schol; St Josephs Clg; Spec Educ.

MERANUS, ELIZABET; La Guardia H S Of The Arts; Bronx, NY; (Y); 2/121; Dance Clb; Pres JA; Ed Nwsp Bus Mgr; Rep Stu Cncl; Gov Hon Prg Awd; NHS; Sal; Hnbl Mntn ARTS Comp Dance 86; Rgnts Schlrshp 86; Bhai Brith Awd 86; Harvard U; Ballet.

MERANUS, ELIZABETH; La Guardia Arts; Bronx, NY; (Y); 2/122; Dance Clb; JA; Library Aide; Nwsp Ed-Chief; Stu Cncl; Gov Hon Prg Awd; NHS; Ntl Merit SF; Sal; Prid Yankees Awd Acadmc/Extcurrclrs 84; Bnai Brith Awd Cmnty Svc 86; Harvard U; Ballet Dancr.

MERCADANTE, LAURA; Warwick Valley HS; Warwick, NY; (Y); 28/200; Church Yth Grp; Chorus; Church Choir; School Play; Stage Crew; Sftbl; Trk; Cit Awd; Hon Roll; NHS; Physcl Thrpy.

MERCADO, ANA MARIA; St Joseph By The Sea HS; Staten Island, NY; (S); Art Clb; Church Yth Grp; Cmnty Wkr; Chorus; Nwsp Ed-Chief; Nwsp Rptr; JV Mgr(s); Ed.

MERCADO, CARLOS; Rice HS; Bronx, NY; (S); Aud/Vis; Church Yth Grp; Drama Clb; Church Choir; Stage Crew; Yrbk Stf; Fld Hcky; Vllybl; Hon Roll; Bus.

MERCADO, EDWARD; Hutchinson Central Technical HS; Buffalo, NY; (Y); Boy Scts; Stage Crew; Bsbl; Fld Hcky; Cit Awd; Hon Roll; Buffalo Tchrs Fed 80; Amer Leg Cert, S F Feyler Awd 83; Elec Engrng.

MERCADO, JENNY; Grover Cleveland HS; Buffalo, NY; (Y); Cmnty Wkr; Spanish Clb; Stage Crew; Variety Show; Prfct Atten Awd; Spanish NHS; Library Aide; Model UN; Yrbk Stf; Off Sr Cls; Fashion Inst/Tech; Fshn Mdse.

MERCADO, TIMOTHY; Liverpool HS; Liverpool, NY; (Y); 126/934; FBLA; Mathletes; Math Tm; Var Tennis; Natl Hon Soc 85-86; Virgil E Tompkin JR Hon Soc 83-85; Vars Ltr Tnns 84-85; Elec Engrg.

MERCER, KIRSTEN M; The Chapin Schl; New York, NY; (Y); Hosp Aide; Latin Clb; Teachers Aide; Varsity Clb; Chorus; Yrbk Ed-Chief; Off Frsh Cls; Off Soph Cls; Sec Jr Cls; Stu Cncl; Math Lg Cntst Awd NY ST 84; Outstndg Phys Ftnss Awd 85; Magna Cum Laude Natl Latin Exm 84; Harvard U; Sport Med.

MERCER, ROSEMARIE; St Pius V HS; Bronx, NY; (Y); Church Yth Grp; 4-H; FBLA; JA; L Bsbl; Sftbl; 4-H Awd; God Cntry Awd; Hon Roll; JC Awd; Clemson U; Bus Mgmt.

MERCIER, CHRISTOPHER; Mount Saint Michael Acad; Bronx, NY; (Y); 120/330; Church Yth Grp; Pres Computer Clb; Camera Clb; Chorus; Church Choir; Off Jr Cls; Im Bsktbl; Im Ftbl; JV Var Trk; ST U Farmingdale; Comp Sci.

MERCURIO, JOSEPH C; Ardlsey HS; Ardsley, NY; (Y); JA; Stage Crew; Variety Show; NYS Rgnts Schlrshp 86; SUNY Buffalo; Engr.

MERCURIO, MARIA; Glen Cove HS; Glen Cove, NY; (Y); Art Clb; Pep Clb; Service Clb; Sec Trs Spanish Clb; School Play; Variety Show; Nwsp Rptr; Sec Soph Cls; Sec Stu Cncl; Var Capt Cheerleading; YMCA Yth Yr 84.

MERCURIO, MARY C; Queen Of The Rosary Acad; Bellmore, NY; (Y); Girl Scts; Math Hrn Soc-Lab Asst 85-86; NYS Rgnts Schlrshp 86; Smmr Pgm-Adv Stud-Southampton Coll 86.

MERCURIO, ROXANNE; Notre Dame Acad; Staten Island, NY; (Y); Civic Clb; Drama Clb; Chorus; School Musical; School Play; Nwsp Stf; Cheerleading; Crs Cntry; Miss Photogenic In Miss Ntl Teenager Pgnt 84; St Semi-Fnlst In Miss Teen All Amer Pgnt 84; Theatre.

MEREAU, MICHELLE G; Fairport HS; Fairport, NY; (Y); Soph Cls; JV Var Bsktbl; JV Var Sftbl; Hon Roll; Vlprso U Schlrshp & NY ST Rgnts Schlrshp 86; Vlprso U; Intl Rltns.

MEREDITH, SARAH E; Amherst Central HS; Amherst, NY; (Y); Church Yth Grp; Chorus; Church Choir; School Musical; High Hon Roll; NHS; Ntl Merit Ltr; Cmnty Wkr; Red Cross Aide; Jazz Band; Brown U Eng Excllnc Awd 85; NY ST Baptist Yth Convntn-Chairprsn 85; Sweet 16 Singng Grp-Dir 86; Baylor U; Music Eductn.

MERGENDAHL, WILLIAM; Saugerties HS; Saugerties, NY; (S); 26/250; Am Leg Boys St; Math Tm; Quiz Bowl; Pres Band; Trs Soph Cls; VP Jr Cls; Pres Sr Cls; VP Stu Cncl; Var Tennis; Pres NHS; DAR Good Citznshp Awd 85; Pres Clsrm 85; Polit Sci.

MERHAI, BRENDA; Richmond Hill HS; Richmond Hill, NY; (Y); 12/285; English Clb; Math Clb; Spanish Clb; Sec Sr Cls; High Hon Roll; NHS; Pres Schlr; Spanish NHS; Socl Stud Hnr Soc 86; Apartied Essay Awd 86; Bus Hnr Soc 86; Adelphi U; Intl Bus.

MERHAI, MADHUMATTI; Richmond Mill HS; Richmond Hill, NY; (Y); 10/300; Debate Tm; Key Clb; Math Clb; Office Aide; SADD; Varsity Clb; Stage Crew; Nwsp Stf; Crs Cntry; Sftbl; Pre-Med.

MERIN, JASON J; Msgr Farrell HS; Staten Island, NY; (S); Pres Frsh Cls; Computer Clb; NFL; Thesps; Pres Frsh Cls; Im Mgr Ftbl; Hon Roll; Ntl Merit Ltr; Im Mgr Bowling; Im Mgr Socr; Mock Trial Awd; Tae-Kwon-Do.

MERINO, ARMANDO; William Howard Taft HS; Bronx, NY; (Y); Computer Clb; English Clb; French Clb; Math Clb; Science Clb; Spanish Clb; Orch; Nwsp Rptr; Nwsp Stf; Frsh Cls.

MERISIER, JEAN; Prospect Heights HS; Brooklyn, NY; (S); Church Yth Grp; FBLA; Office Aide; Chorus; Socr; Hon Roll; NHS; Prfct Atten Awd; Arista 84; Engrng.

MERK, RAYMOND; Tottenville HS; Staten Island, NY; (S); 6/950; Boy Scts; Cmnty Wkr; Exploring; Key Clb; Quiz Bowl; Ski Clb; Symp Band; Capt Socr; NHS; Prfct Atten Awd.

MERKEL, BONNIE E; Somers HS; Purdys, NY; (Y); 40/197; AFS; German Clb; Intnl Clb; Nwsp Rptr; Yrbk Rptr; Var Crs Cntry; Var Fld Hcky; Capt Trk; Grmn Ntl Hnr Soc 84-86; Trck & Fld Crss Cntry All-Lg All Cnty Hm 83-86; Liberty U.

MERKLE, MELISSA; Cardinal O Hara HS; Tonawanda, NY; (Y); Church Yth Grp; Drama Clb; Girl Scts; Chorus; Church Choir; School Musical; Yrbk Stf; Rep Frsh Cls; Rep Stu Cncl; Stat Crs Cntry; Med Lab Tech.

MERKLEN, TERRY; Schoharie Central HS; Central Bridge, NY; (S); 13/85; VP 4-H; FFA; Key Clb; Capt Quiz Bowl; Spanish Clb; Varsity Clb; Concert Band; Mrchg Band; Yrbk Stf; VP Frsh Cls; Booster Clb Awd,Crss Cntry Sect II 83; Edinboro U.

MERLAU, JENNIFER L; Attica SR HS; Cowlesville, NY; (Y); 40/150; AFS; Church Yth Grp; Drama Clb; 4-H; Church Choir; Concert Band; Jazz Band; Mrchg Band; School Musical; 4-H Awd; NYS Regents Scholar 86; Area All ST Bnd 85 & 86; Pace U; Polit Sci.

MERLAU, JOHN; Attica SR HS; Cowlesville, NY; (S); 4/175; Boy Scts; Church Yth Grp; 4-H; Math Tm; Band; Chorus; Church Choir; Jazz Band; School Musical; Nwsp Stf; Al-ST Mxd Chorus NY 85; Hnr Rll 84-86; Wrld Cnsrvtn Awd By Scts Amer 84; Ahrtt Schl Music; Music Cmpstn.

MERLINO, DENISE; St Catherine Acad; Bronx, NY; (Y); 141/198; Ski Clb; Yrbk Stf; JV Fld Hcky; 2nd Hnrs 85; Lehman Coll; Bus Educ.

MERLINO, JEANETTE; Moore Catholic HS; Staten Island, NY; (Y); Cmnty Wkr; Hosp Aide; Math Tm; Spanish Clb; Stage Crew; Yrbk Stf; Hon Roll; Jr NHS; NHS; Physcl Thrpy.

MERLINO II, MICHAEL; Hamburg SR HS; Hamburg, NY; (Y); Am Leg Boys St; JV Var Socr; Outstndng Stu Awd 83-84; U Of Buffalo; Lwyr.

MERLIS, JORDANA B; The Bronx High School Of Science; New York, NY; (Y); Ski Clb; Yrbk Phtg; NHS; NYS Regnts Schlrshp 86; U Of VT.

MERMELSTEIN, DAVID; Rye HS; Ryebrook, NY; (Y); Yrbk Stf; Var Bsbl; Var Socr; Im Tennis; Spnsh Awd 86.

MERMELSTEIN, PAUL; West Hempstead HS; Island Park, NY; (Y); Computer Clb; Hosp Aide; VP Key Clb; Var Capt Tennis; Hon Roll; NHS; Natl Soc Studs Olympd 85; Excllnce Indstrl Art Awd 84.

MERMIN, MELISSA; Earl L Vandermeulen HS; Pt Jefferson, NY; (Y); Art Clb; Lit Mag; Trk; Art Awd 83; Schl Of Visual Arts; Art Thrpst.

MEROLA, LEIGH; New Rochelle HS; New Rochelle, NY; (Y); 1/630; Church Yth Grp; Spanish Clb; Trs Frsh Cls; Trs Soph Cls; Trs Rep Stu Cncl; Var L Swmmng; NHS; Spanish NHS; Pilot.

MERRIAM, MELISSA; Westfield Acad & Central Schl; Westfield, NY; (Y); Band; Chorus; School Musical; Pres Sr Cls; Stat Bsktbl; Hon Roll; NHS; Fine Arts Hnr Soc.

MERRICK, BRIAN; South Shore HS; Brooklyn, NY; (Y); Math Tm; Band; Drm & Bgl.

MERRIFELD, MELISSA; Cooperstown Central HS; Hartwick, NY; (Y); Hosp Aide; Chorus; Yrbk Stf; High Hon Roll; NHS.

MERRIGAN, KATHERINE A; Half Hollow Hills West HS; Melville, NY; (Y); 41/396; Drama Clb; SADD; Chorus; Color Guard; Camera Clb; School Play; Symp Band; Variety Show; Yrbk Stf; NHS; Jr Natl Hnr Scty 83; NYS Rgnst Schlrshp 86; Trstee Schlrshp Pace U 86; Pace U Pleasantvile; Mrktng.

MERRILL, SARA; South Jefferson Central Schl; Rodman, NY; (Y); 5/155; German Clb; Chorus; Concert Band; School Musical; Swing Chorus; Symp Band; Rep Frsh Cls; JV Var Cheerleading; Hon Roll; NHS.

MERRILL, SCOTT; Alexander Central HS; E Bethany, NY; (Y); Pres Church Yth Grp; Cmnty Wkr; Drama Clb; Exploring; French Clb; Acpl Chr; Chorus; Church Choir; School Musical; School Play; SONY Plattsbrgh Smr Musicl Theat Wrkshp 85; Hnrbl Mntn BMI Natl Sci Fctn Shrt Stry Cntst 85; ASU; Actng.

MERRIMAN, JOSEPH; Westmoreland Cntrl Schl; Whitesboro, NY; (Y); Im Bsbl; Im Ftbl; Im Wt Lftg; Im Wrstlng; Engrng.

MERRITT, DARLENE; Wilson Magnet HS; Rochester, NY; (Y); Sec Jr Cls; Var Trk; High Hon Roll; Hon Roll; Bio.

MERRITT, ELLEN; Gouverneur JR SR HS; Gouverneur, NY; (Y); Band; Chorus; Church Choir; Concert Band; Orch; School Musical; Yrbk Stf; Hon Roll; Jr NHS; Masonic Awd; E O Schwelnus Awd Hghst Blgy Rgnts Grd 84-85; Art Awds Lcl & Rgnl Shws 85-86; Frmr.

MERRITT, JESSICA; West Irondequoit HS; Rochester, NY; (Y); 15/389; Church Yth Grp; Girl Scts; Intnl Clb; Sec Stu Cncl; High Hon Roll; Hon Roll; Prfct Atten Awd; Art Clb; Drama Clb; French Clb; Special Report Of Encllc Englsh & Frnch 85-86; Piano Sololist Supr 81 & 82 & 83; Psych.

MERRITT, PAMELA; Jordan-Elbridge HS; Memphis, NY; (Y); Church Yth Grp; Exploring; Ski Clb; Spanish Clb; SADD; Yrbk Stf; Capt Bowling; VP Trk; JV Vllybl; Hon Roll; Merit Awds In Bowling 81-85; Atlantic Coll; Marine Biolgy.

MERRITT, WENITRA C; Buffalo Acad For Visual & Prfg Arts; Buffalo, NY; (Y); 24/109; Dance Clb; Girl Scts; PAVAS; School Musical; School Play; Stage Crew; Variety Show; Yrbk Stf; VP Jr Cls; Rep Stu Cncl; Svngs Bnd Wng Psi Phi Omega Frat Tlnt Srch 85; 2nd Plc NAACP Act-So Cmptn 84; Plq Mrt Brkfst Chmpn As; CA Inst Fn Arts; Dance.

MERRITTS, DANNY; Walter Panas HS; Peekskill, NY; (Y); Drama Clb; Ski Clb; School Play; Ftbl; Swmmng; Hon Roll; US Intl U; Intl Bus Mgr.

MERRYMAN, MOLLY; Curits HS; Staten Island, NY; (Y); Key Clb; Math Clb; Math Tm; Science Clb; Nwsp Rptr; Swmmng; NHS; All Expnse Pd 1 Mnth Trp To Isrl 85; Chrch Pianst 82-86; 4th Pl In Music Cmptn SI Plyd Piano 86; Music.

MERSBERG, LAURA; Mount Saint Mary Acad; Tonawanda, NY; (Y); Cmnty Wkr; Intnl Clb; Chorus; Yrbk Stf; Co-Capt Cheerleading; Capt Vllybl; Hon Roll; U Of TX; Bus.

MERSINGER, SUSAN; Brushton-Moira Central HS; Brushton, NY; (Y); 17/59; French Clb; Hosp Aide; Band; Church Choir; Mrchg Band; School Play; Stage Crew; Variety Show; Yrbk Stf; Rep Stu Cncl; NY St Regents Schlrshp 86; Hugh O Brien Yth Ldrshp Awd 84; St Josephs Schl Nrsng; RN.

MERTZ, KATHRYN; Holy Trinity HS; Wantagh, NY; (S); 19/313; Mathletes; Math Clb; Math Tm; Nwsp Ed-Chief; Ed Yrbk Phtg; Sec Jr Cls; Pres Sr Cls; Pres Stu Cncl; Hon Roll; NHS; NEDT; USNMA; USNLMA; Math.

MERTZ, TRACY; Rhinebeck Central HS; Rhinebeck, NY; (Y); AFS; Ski Clb; Band; Concert Band; Cheerleading; Gym.

MERWIN, EDWARD P; Great Neck South HS; Great Neck, NY; (Y); 7/250; Boy Scts; Nwsp Stf; NCTE Awd; Harvard Bk Prz 85; 1st Pl NY ST Hstry Day Dmptn Rsrch Papr 85; Amherst Coll; Law.

MERWIN, SHAWN; Walton Central Schl; Walton, NY; (Y); 6/100; Pres AFS; Am Leg Boys St; Cmnty Wkr; Sec Model UN; Nwsp Ed-Chief; Rep Stu Cncl; Var L Bsbl; Var L Bsktbl; High Hon Roll; Pres NHS; Oper Enterprise Schlrshp 86; Dennis Awd Interst Am Gov 86; Purdue U; Ed.

MERZ, CHRISTINE A; St Francis Prep; Glendale, NY; (S); 113/653; Im Ftbl; Im Sftbl; Optimates Soc; Theatre Clb; Tutor Clb; CYO Bsktbl & Sftbl-Coach.

MERZA, MARIA; Saint Peters H S For Girls; Staten Isl, NY; (Y); 5/101; Exploring; VP FNA; JV Math Tm; Yrbk Stf; Lit Mag; VP Sr Cls; Rep Stu Cncl; Var Tennis; Var Trk; Hon Roll; Stu Athlete Awd 85-86; Yth Apprectn Brkfst 86; 1st Hnr Eng Awd 86; Catholic U Am; Comp Sci.

MESCALL, JAMES; St Marys HS; Depew, NY; (S); 20/180; Varsity Clb; JV Bsbl; JV Var Bsktbl; Var Crs Cntry; JV Var Ftbl; Var Trk; High Hon Roll; NHS; Opt Clb Awd; MVP Bsktbl 84; MVP Ftbl 85.

MESCHI, NANCY L; St Anthonys HS; Smithtown, NY; (Y); 13/225; Hosp Aide; Orch; Nwsp Rptr; French Hon Soc; High Hon Roll; Hon Roll; NHS; Latin Hnr Soc; NY St Rgnts Schlrshp; Lemoyne Coll Acadmc Schlrshp; Lemoyne Coll; Psych.

MESLER, STACEY; Monroe-Woodbury SR HS; Newburgh, NY; (Y); Cmnty Wkr; Drama Clb; School Musical; School Play; Nwsp Rptr; Nwsp Stf; Cheerleading; Hon Roll; NY Teen Talent Mst Promsng Actrss 85 & 86; Proc Cmmndtn 85; Miss Monroe 84; Miss Dutchss Area Teen 86; Comm.

MESNIK, PETER R; Yorktown HS; Yorktown Hts, NY; (Y); 2/319; Key Clb; Teachers Aide; Nwsp Stf; Ed Lit Mag; Stu Cncl; Tennis; High Hon Roll; NHS; Sal; CIBA-GEIGY H S Sci Awd 86; Princeton U; Engrng.

MESOLELLA, GREGORY A; Greece Athena HS; Rochester, NY; (S); 9/285; DECA; German Clb; Math Tm; Science Clb; Ski Clb; Pres Frsh Cls; Pres Jr Cls; JV Wrstlng; High Hon Roll; NHS; Schlrhp-Clrksn U Trustee Awd 86; VA Tech; Elec Engr.

MESSA, JO ANN; Preston HS; Bronx, NY; (Y); 6/83; Yrbk Stf; Pres Sr Cls; NHS; SUNY Albny; Psychlgy.

MESSA, JO-ANN; Preston HS; Bronx, NY; (Y); 6/83; Yrbk Stf; Pres Sr Cls; NHS; Half Schlrshp HS 82-83; Math Awd At Grad 86; Albany ST; Psych.

MESSANA, LORI C; St Francis Prep; Little Neck, NY; (S); 8/750; Hosp Aide; Math Clb; Model UN; Ski Clb; Chorus; JV Var Mgr(s); Im Vllybl; High Hon Roll; NHS.

MESSE, THOMAS; Attica Central Schl; Attica, NY; (S); 8/154; AFS; Am Leg Boys St; 4-H; French Clb; Letterman Clb; ROTC; Ski Clb; Varsity Clb; Nwsp Stf; Yrbk Stf; Cornell; Engrng.

MESSER, PAUL JEAN; Troy HS; Wynantskill, NY; (Y); 6/425; Church Yth Grp; French Clb; Yrbk Stf; Rep Stu Cncl; Var Ice Hcky; High Hon Roll; NHS; Ntl Merit SF; NY ST Rgnts Schlrshp 86; Rnsslr Plytech Inst; Arntcl Eng.

MESSINEO, ALESSANDRA M; John Jay HS; Hopewell Jct, NY; (Y); 76/519; School Play; Sec Soph Cls; Sec Jr Cls; Sec Sr Cls; Cheerleading; Cit Awd; NHS; Drama Clb; High Hon Roll; Masonic Awd; Ski Clb; Miss Photogenic 85; Miss John Jay 85; 1st, 2nd & 3rd Pl Awds Ballet, Tap, Jazz & Point; FIT; Fash Merch.

MESSINGER, DAVID W; Chittenango HS; Bridgport, NY; (Y); 4/200; Am Leg Boys St; Drama Clb; Chorus; Concert Band; School Musical; Yrbk Stf; Var L Socr; High Hon Roll; NHS; Ntl Merit Ltr; Physcs.

MESSITT, DONALD; Saratoga Central Catholic HS; Ballston Lake, NY; (S); 4/36; Chess Clb; SADD; Co-Capt Yrbk Stf; Bausch & Lomb Sci Awd; Hon Roll; NHS; Ntl Merit Ltr; Engr.

MESTER, SANDOR; Clarkstown South HS; W Nyack, NY; (Y); 11/475; Math Clb; Math Tm; Nwsp Bus Mgr; JV Bsktbl; JV Trk; Jr NHS; Mu Alp Tht; NHS; Ntl Merit Ltr; Pres Schlr; Rutgers Coll Of Engr; Mech Engr.

METCALF, TERRY J; Rome Free Acad; Rome, NY; (Y); 8/446; AFS; Boy Scts; Model UN; Speech Tm; JV Var Wrstlng; Hon Roll; NHS; Ntl Merit SF; Pres Schlr; Chess Clb; Air Force ROTC Schlrshp 86; Empire ST Schlrshp Of Excllnc 86; Regents Coll Schlrshp 86; Rengselaer Polykehnic; Air Forc.

METE, LAURA; Westlake HS; Valhalla, NY; (Y); Church Choir; Orch; High Hon Roll; Hon Roll; Stu Recgntn Awd 84-85; All Cnty Orch 83-84; Area All ST Orch 85-86.

METHAL, SHANE; Lynbrook HS; E Rockaway, NY; (Y); 12/259; Drama Clb; Concert Band; Mrchg Band; Orch; School Play; Hon Roll; Kiwanis Awd; NHS; NYS Regnts Schlrshp 86; PA ST Schlrshp 86; MVP Awd Roller Hockey 85; Cornell U; Bio Sci.

METTLER, STEPANIE; Cato Meridian HS; Meridian, NY; (Y); Cmnty Wkr; 4-H; Girl Scts; Chorus; Yrbk Stf; Score Keeper; Mgr Vllybl; 4-H Awd; Cayuga CC; Polic Offcr.

METZ, LLOYD M; Horace Greeley HS; Chappaqua, NY; (Y); Church Yth Grp; French Clb; Ed Nwsp Stf; VP Stu Cncl; Var Bsktbl; NHS; Ntl Merit SF; Bk Awd Exc Soc Studies 85; Engrng.

METZ, MARCUS R; Deer Park HS; Deer Park, NY; (Y); Am Leg Boys St; Camera Clb; Church Yth Grp; Cmnty Wkr; Office Aide; Chorus; Church Choir; School Musical; Hon Roll; NY All ST Chorus 85; Music.

METZ, MARY; Sacred Heart Acad; Rockville Centre, NY; (S); 3/182; Art Clb; Church Yth Grp; Cmnty Wkr; French Clb; NFL; SADD; Orch; School Musical; Lit Mag; Socr; Natl Fornsc Lg Degree Hon 85; Nassau Music Edctrs Assn Cert Merit 83; Law.

METZGER, DARLENE; York Central Schl; Leicester, NY; (Y); 7/88; Political Wkr; Sec Band; Lib Chorus; High Hon Roll; NHS; Rotary Awd; VFW Awd; Voice Dem Awd; Am Leg Aux Girls St; Church Yth Grp; Cora W Starr Schlrshp 86; Mcdonald Crew Schlrshp 86; Pres Awd Acadmc Ftnss 86; Monroe CC; Music.

METZLER, KURT DOUGLAS; Dover JR SR HS; Dover Plains, NY; (S); 1/80; Am Leg Boys St; Trs Jr Cls; Sec Sr Cls; High Hon Roll; Jr NHS; Sec NHS; Val; Mst Lkly Sccd; Pol Sci.

METZLOFF, KYLE; Tonawanda HS; Tonawanda, NY; (Y); Computer Clb; Band; Concert Band; Mrchg Band; Swmmng; Tennis; Power Boat Clb Racing Awds 85; Amer Red Cross Sr Lifesvng 86; Most Imprvd Awd Swmmng Tm 86; Erie CC; Naval Arch.

METZNER, LAUREN; Newburgh Free Acad; New Windsor, NY; (Y); Church Yth Grp; Key Clb; Ski Clb; Spanish Clb; Temple Yth Grp; Acpl Chr; Chorus; Nwsp Stf; Yrbk Stf; Lit Mag; Advrtsng.

MEURER, JOSEPH PAUL; Archbishop Molloy HS; Cypress Hills, NY; (Y); Boy Scts; Cmnty Wkr; Math Clb; Sec Spanish Clb; Crs Cntry; Trk; Wt Lftg; Hon Roll; NHS; SF Natl Hspnc Schlrshp Awds & Physcs Club Tutrg 86; Polytechnic U; Mech Engrng.

MEYER, CAROLYN C; Buffalo Academy Of The Sacred Heart; Alden, NY; (Y); 4/125; 4-H; Ski Clb; Spanish Clb; Varsity Clb; Trs Soph Cls; Rep Stu Cncl; Var Badmtn; Mgr(s); Capt Vllybl; Bausch & Lomb Sci Awd; St Bonaventure; Sci.

MEYER, DAWN F; Pawling JR SR HS; Pawling, NY; (Y); 2/55; French Clb; Model UN; Spanish Clb; Thesps; Varsity Clb; Nwsp Rptr; Yrbk Bus Mgr; Vllybl; NHS; Sal; NYS Rgnts Schlrshp Wnr 86; Ctznshp Awd Wnr 86; US Achvmnt Acdmy Awd Frgn Lng 86; SUNY Binghamton; Frgn Lng.

MEYER, DIANE; Lafayette HS; Buffalo, NY; (Y); French Clb; Yrbk Rptr; Yrbk Stf; Trs Jr Cls; Var Tennis; High Hon Roll; Hon Roll; Prfct Atten Awd; Schl Ltr, Pin Vrsty Tnns 86; Sundy Schl Tchr, Grp Ldr-Plays 85 & 86; Pre-Med.

MEYER, ERIKA; HS Of Music & Art; Brooklyn, NY; (S); Art Clb; Camera Clb; Cmnty Wkr; Political Wkr; Teachers Aide; Hon Roll; Arista & Art Hnr Leag 83-86; Soc Sci.

MEYER, GLENN; St John The Baptist D H S; Lindenhurst, NY; (Y); Ski Clb; Varsity Clb; JV Ftbl; JV Lcrss; JV Wt Lftg; Var Wrstlng; Ntl Merit Ltr; Aerotncs.

MEYER, GREG PAUL; Benjamin N Cardozo HS; Little Neck, NY; (Y); 58/531; Chess Clb; Chorus; School Musical; Nwsp Rptr; Pres Schlr; Arista Hnr Soc 85-86; Gold Medal Wnnr Math Fair 85; Regents Schrlshp 86; NY U; Film Dir.

MEYER, JAMIE; Naples Central HS; Naples, NY; (Y); 10/60; Hosp Aide; Var Capt Bowling; High Hon Roll; Hon Roll; Prfct Atten Awd; Var L Socr; Pre-Med.

MEYER, JOHN; Webutuck Central HS; Millerton, NY; (Y); 1/40; Drama Clb; Quiz Bowl; Ski Clb; School Play; VP Sr Cls; Var Socr; Var Tennis; Pres NHS; Ntl Merit Ltr; Val; Outstndng Stu Awd 84; Union Coll; Mech Engrng.

MEYER, LAURA; Mount Mercy Acad; Lakeview, NY; (Y); Church Yth Grp; Drama Clb; Latin Clb; Pep Clb; Ski Clb; Spanish Clb; School Play; Im Socr; Im Sftbl; High Hon Roll; Bus Mgmt.

MEYER, LINDA; Walt Whitman HS; Huntington Sta, NY; (Y); Girl Scts; Hosp Aide; Band; Concert Band; Mrchg Band; Var Badmtn; Var Bowling; JV Tennis; High Hon Roll; Hon Roll; SUNY; Nrsng.

MEYER, MATTHEW; St Marys Boys HS; Hicksvile, NY; (Y); Boy Scts; Ski Clb; Varsity Clb; School Play; Yrbk Stf; Golf; Lcrss; Socr; Bus.

MEYER, MICHELLE LEE; Hampton Bays JR-SR HS; Hampton Bays, NY; (Y); Am Leg Aux Girls St; Science Clb; VP SADD; Chorus; School Musical; Sec Soph Cls; Cheerleading; High Hon Roll; NHS; Stu Mnth 83-84 & 85-86; Nrsng.

MEYER, STACEY; Central Islip HS; Central Islip, NY; (Y); GAA; Varsity Clb; Band; Yrbk Stf; Var Swmmng; Top 10 Phys Ed 85; Photo.

MEYER, THERESA; Connetquot HS; Ronkonkoma, NY; (S); 13/699; Yrbk Stf; Rep Frsh Cls; Rep Jr Cls; Rep Sr Cls; Rep Stu Cncl; Sftbl; Vllybl; Jr NHS; NHS; Sal; Hdsn Vly CC; Dntl Hygn.

MEYER, TOBI M; Shula-Mith HS; Brooklyn, NY; (Y); 6/28; Art Clb; Capt Scholastic Bowl; Ed Yrbk Stf; Lit Mag; Gov Hon Prg Awd; High Hon Roll; NHS; NY U.

MEYER, WILLIAM G; East Syracuse-Minoa Central HS; Minoa, NY; (Y); 99/350; Band; Concert Band; Jazz Band; Variety Show; Hon Roll; Jr NHS; St Schlr; SUNY Morrisville; Engrng.

MEYERS, CAROL; Wilson Central HS; Wilson, NY; (Y); Office Aide; Teachers Aide; Social Svcs.

MEYERS, DEBBY; Lynbrook HS; Lynbrook, NY; (Y); Mathletes; Spanish Clb; Church Choir; Nwsp Stf; Yrbk Stf; Stat Ice Hcky; Hon Roll; Bus Mgmt.

MEYERS, ELLEN; Commack South HS; Dix Hills, NY; (Y); Drama Clb; SADD; Concert Band; Mrchg Band; School Musical; School Play; Symp Band; Yrbk Stf; Badmtn; Mgr(s); Ed.

MEYERS, JANET; Williamsville North HS; Amherst, NY; (Y); VP DECA; German Clb; Ski Clb; Stu Cncl; JV Socr; Cls Steering Committee; Mock Trial Assn 84-86; Action Learning Intrnshp Prog-Law 85-86; Canisus Coll; Bus Mgmt.

MEYERS, TONNETTE; Mt Pleasant HS; Schenectady, NY; (Y); 11/206; Key Clb; Office Aide; Sec Pep Clb; JV Var Sftbl; JV Var Vllybl; High Hon Roll; Hon Roll; Jr NHS; NHS; Prfct Atten Awd; Oneonta U.

MEYRING, ROBERT S; Keveny Memorial Acad; Latham, NY; (Y); 19/40; Band; Concert Band; Jazz Band; Mrchg Band; Yrbk Phtg; JV Var Bsktbl; Hon Roll; Pres Schlr; ST Rgnts Schlrshp 86; Mount St Marys; Msc.

MEZA, RUBEN; Rice HS; New York, NY; (S); 1/100; Aud/Vis; Computer Clb; Chorus; Nwsp Rptr; High Hon Roll; Hon Roll; Schlrshp Rice HS 83-87; Gen Exc Awd 85; 2nd Merit Awd 84; NY Inst Tech; Ind Engr.

MEZYNSKI, DAVE; Perry Central HS; Perry, NY; (Y); Computer Clb; Mathletes; Math Tm; Golf; Hon Roll; NHS; Chem.

MIANO, TINA M; Pine Bush HS; Bullville, NY; (Y); 16/298; FFA; Ski Clb; Spanish Clb; Yrbk Stf; Rep Stu Cncl; JV Fld Hcky; Var Socr; Hon Roll; Jr NHS; Prfct Atten Awd; Rgnts Schlrshp 86; Mt St Mary Coll; Nrs.

MICALIZZI, LARRY; Division Ave HS; Levittown, NY; (Y); 175/335; Varsity Clb; Variety Show; Yrbk Stf; JV Ftbl; JV Var Lcrss; JV Var Wrstlng; All Conf Tm Wrstlng 86; Emblm Awd-Lacrosse & Wrstlng 85 & 86; E Meadow Invtnl 3rd Pl Wrstlng 85; ST U Farmingdale; Crmnl Justc.

MICARA, ANNE; Bishop Ford Central Catholic; Brooklyn, NY; (Y); 20/441; GAA; Service Clb; Church Choir; School Musical; Im Bowling; Sftbl; Tennis; Im Vllybl; Hon Roll; Prtl Schlrshp Kingsborough Coll 86; Acad Excel 83-86; 1st Hnrs 82-86; Kingsborough Coll; Travel.

MICCIANTUNO, KAREN; John H Glenn HS; Huntington, NY; (Y); Art Clb; Teachers Aide; VICA; Chorus; Variety Show; Fld Hcky; Hon Roll; Italian Hnr Soc 84-86; Italian Excllnc Awd 85-86; VICA Awds 85-86; Art.

MICELI, MICHAEL; Herricks HS; Williston Park, NY; (Y); SADD; Var Crs Cntry; Var Ftbl; Var Ice Hcky; Var Mgr(s); Prfct Atten Awd; St Johns; Bus.

MICELI, PETER; Archbishop Molloy HS; Astoria, NY; (Y); 120/390; Art Clb; Science Clb; Yrbk Phtg; Yrbk Stf; Im Fld Hcky; Im Ice Hcky; Im Sftbl; Im Wt Lftg; High Hon Roll; Hon Roll; Sprts Med.

MICHAEL, BARTLETT; Liverpool HS; Liverpool, NY; (Y); 117/884; Church Yth Grp; Concert Band; Rep Stu Cncl; Var Crs Cntry; Var Trk; Hon Roll; NHS; Ntl Merit SF; Rochester Inst Of Tech; Physcs.

MICHAEL, JOSEPH; Middletown HS; Middletown, NY; (Y); Debate Tm; Var Bsktbl; Hon Roll; Med.

MICHAEL, NABILA; Middletown HS; Middletown, NY; (Y); 12/350; School Play; Lit Mag; High Hon Roll; Hon Roll; NHS; Bessie Wallace Awd 86; Spn Awd 86; Orange Cnty CC Scholar 86; Orange Cnty CC; Sci.

MICHAEL, PAMELA D; Queensbury HS; Glens Falls, NY; (Y); 11/253; Sec Church Yth Grp; Key Clb; SADD; Band; Chorus; Church Choir; Cheerleading; Swmmng; High Hon Roll; NHS; NYS Rgnts Schlrshp 86; Allegheny Coll; Bio.

MICHAELS, GARY JON; West Genesee SR HS; Reseda, CA; (Y); 111/450; Mrchg Band; School Play; Yrbk Stf; Off Soph Cls; Off Jr Cls; Off Sr Cls; Im Diving; Im Vllybl; Hon Roll; NHS; U CA Santa Barbara Schlrshp 86-87; Natl Sci Bwl 3rd Pl 86; U CA Santa Barbara; Comp Sci.

MICHAELS, REBECCA J; Auburn HS; Auburn, NY; (Y); 8/425; Pres Drama Clb; Ski Clb; Acpl Chr; Chorus; Madrigals; School Musical; School Play; Swing Chorus; High Hon Roll; NHS; Darthmouth Coll; Math.

MICHAELS, STEPHEN; Berlin Central Schl; Berlin, NY; (S); 3/92; French Clb; Spanish Clb; Chorus; School Musical; School Play; Rep Stu Cncl; High Hon Roll; NHS; Steerng Cmmtte 85-86; Nyack Coll; USAF Chpln.

MICHAELS, VALENTINA; Academy Of St Joseph; E Patchogue, NY; (Y); Debate Tm; Drama Clb; French Clb; Model UN; Science Clb; Thesps; Chorus; School Musical; School Play; Variety Show; Regents Scholar 86; Acad Achvt Awd 83-84; Gibbons Hnrs Scholar Catholic U Amer 86; Catholic U Amer; Theatre Arts.

MICHAILOFF, MICHELLE; Pelham Memorial HS; Pelham, NY; (Y); Church Yth Grp; Cmnty Wkr; French Clb; Intnl Clb; JA; Radio Clb; SADD; Varsity Clb; Chorus; School Play; Ntl Hnr Roll 86; Accntnt.

MICHALAK, ROB; Gates Chili SR HS; Rochester, NY; (Y); Computer Clb; Science Clb; Ski Clb; Spanish Clb; Band; Concert Band; Rep Soph Cls; Rep Jr Cls; Im Vllybl; Hnr Awd Acdmc Excllnc 84; Awd Band 84; Optcl Engrng.

MICHALAK JR, WILLIAM N; Babylon HS; Babylon, NY; (Y); Boy Scts; CAP; ROTC; Spanish Clb; Band; Jazz Band; Mrchg Band; Crs Cntry; Trk; DAR Awd; Eagle Sct 86; Dowling; Arntcs.

MICHALAS, CHRISTINE; Warwick HS; Warwick, NY; (Y); 10/200; Var Cheerleading; Var Swmmng; Timer; Var Vllybl; Cit Awd; High Hon Roll; Hon Roll; NHS; Prfct Atten Awd; Powder Puff Ftbl; Ntl Sci Merit Awd; Marist Coll; Sci.

MICHALEAS, ALEXIA; Glen Cove HS; Glen Cove, NY; (S); VP DECA; Drama Clb; Key Clb; Spanish Clb; Chorus; Drm Mjr(t); Nwsp Stf; Yrbk Stf; Bsktbl; Socr; Pre-Law.

MICHALSKI, SYLVIA; HS For The Humanities Ny; New York, NY; (Y); Drama Clb; French Clb; Spanish Clb; Chorus; NHS; Mc Gill U.

MICHEELS, BARBARA; St Marys Girls HS; Bayside, NY; (Y); Ski Clb; Spanish Clb; Chorus; Stage Crew; Spanish NHS; Intl Bnkng.

MICHEL, ERWIN; John Adams HS; Richmond Hill, NY; (Y); Library Aide; Band; Church Choir; Nwsp Rptr; NHS; Sci.

MICHEL, LISA C; Salem Central Schl; Salem, NY; (Y); 3/62; Hosp Aide; Band; Yrbk Stf; Trs Lit Mag; Bsktbl; Var Fld Hcky; Var Trk; French Clb; Pep Clb; Ski Clb; Mt St Mary Coll Pres Schlrshp 86; NYS Rgnts Schlrshp 86; CIBA-GEIGY Sci Awd 86; Mount St Mary Coll; Nrsg.

MICHEL, MARIE PETIT; Newfield HS; Coram, NY; (Y); 20/515; Church Yth Grp; Drama Clb; Q&S; SADD; Chorus; Nwsp Rptr; Lit Mag; Stu Cncl; Trk; Hon Roll; MVP Awd Fncg 84-86; Cnty ST Champs Girls Trk 86; Postl Fncg Schlrshp 86; Temple U; Pre Med.

MICHEL, MARJORIE; John Dewey HS; Brooklyn, NY; (Y); Cmnty Wkr; Dance Clb; French Clb; JA; Library Aide; Chorus; School Musical; Yrbk Stf; Badmtn; Gym.

MICHEL, RONIDE; Clara Barton For Health Proffsns; Brooklyn, NY; (Y); 6/485; Hosp Aide; Church Yth Grp; French Clb; Intnl Clb; Office Aide; Variety Show; Yrbk Stf; Hon Roll; NHS; Prfct Atten Awd; United Fed Of Teachers Schlrshp 85-86; Medcl Sci 1st Awd 86; Catholic Teacher Awd 86; SUNY-ALBANY; Patholgst.

MICHELS, KENT; Mc Quaid Jesuit HS; Henrietta, NY; (Y); 50/160; Church Yth Grp; Teachers Aide; Im Bsktbl; Coach Actv; Im Ice Hcky; JV Socr; JV Trk; Cathlc Yth Bsktbl Sprtsmnshp Awd 85-86; Capt-Cathlc Yth Org-Bsktbl 85-86; St John Fischer; Math.

MICHIELINI, JOHN A; Baldwin SR HS; Baldwin, NY; (Y); 35/476; Var Capt Lcrss; High Hon Roll; Hon Roll; NHS; Ntl Merit Schol; NY ST Rgnts Schlrshp 3 Math Exc Awd 86; Hfstr U; Bus.

MICILCAVAGE, DEBRA; Union Endicott HS; Endicott, NY; (Y); 81/470; Exploring; Hosp Aide; Band; Mrchg Band; Yrbk Stf; JV Cheerleading; Capt JV Vllybl; Hon Roll; Jessie Baker Schlrshp 86; Jennie F Snapp Schlrshp 86; Wmns Clb/Endicott Schlrshp 86; SUNY Oneonta; Phys Ther.

MICILLO, GINA; Hilton Central HS; Hilton, NY; (Y); 44/301; Model UN; Ski Clb; Mrchg Band; Symp Band; Nwsp Phtg; Nwsp Stf; Var Swmmng; High Hon Roll; Trs NHS; Rep Frsh Cls; Ntl Hnr Soc Schlrshp 86; Prsdntl Ftnss Awd 86; Oswego ST; Cmmnctns.

MICKLE, DONNA; John A Coleman HS; Kingston, NY; (Y); Drama Clb; French Clb; Key Clb; Ski Clb; Chorus; School Play; Yrbk Stf; Bsktbl; Trk; Vllybl; Knights Columbus Awd; St Colemans Parish Awd; Mt St Mary Scholar; Mt St Mary; Spec Ed.

MICKOLIGER, TAMMY; Riverhead HS; Riverhead, NY; (Y); Church Yth Grp; Science Clb; Spanish Clb; Nwsp Rptr; Nwsp Stf; JV Bsktbl; Var Fld Hcky; Sftbl; Prfct Atten Awd; Nrsg.

MIDDELAER, WILLIAM S; Mount Assumption Inst; Plattsburgh, NY; (Y); 3/73; Hosp Aide; Math Clb; Model UN; Stage Crew; Yrbk Stf; Golf; Score Keeper; Bausch & Lomb Sci Awd; High Hon Roll; NHS; Engrng.

MIDDENDORF, AMY; Tioga Central Schl; Owego, NY; (Y); 23/82; Library Aide; Office Aide; Spanish Clb; JV Var Vllybl; Sec.

MIDDLEMISS, CAROL; Fayetteville-Manlius HS; Manlius, NY; (Y); Church Yth Grp; Cmnty Wkr; German Clb; Hosp Aide; SADD; Fld Hcky; Socr; Hon Roll; Screen Prntng Awd Indstrl Arts Dept 86; Vrsty Lttr Fld Hock 85; Pre Law.

MIELENS, MELISSA A; Columbia HS; E Greenbush, NY; (Y); 18/416; Art Clb; Exploring; Model UN; Chorus; Jazz Band; Symp Band; Yrbk Stf; JV Var Socr; NHS; Natl H S Honors Orch 86; All ST Orch-Princpl Flute 85-86; Arts Recgntn & Talnt Srch-Hnrbl Mntn 86; Musician.

MIELNICKI, DANIEL; Henninger HS; Syracuse, NY; (Y); 17/400; Am Leg Boys St; Stu Cncl; Ftbl; Lcrss; Capt Swmmng; High Hon Roll; Hon Roll; NHS; Bio.

MIETT, CATHERINE M; Bishop Grimes HS; East Syracuse, NY; (S); 10/156; Model UN; NFL; Quiz Bowl; Science Clb; Thesps; School Musical; Hon Roll; NHS; Ntl Merit SF; St Schlr; Law.

MIGHELL, KATHY L; Professional Childrens Schl; Northampton, PA; (Y); High Hon Roll; Stu Sch Of Am Ballet 83-85; Schlrshp San Fran Ballets 85; Awd Supr Achvt Frnch & Eng 86; Dickinson Clg.

MIGHTY, ROWAN; George Wingate HS; Brooklyn, NY; (Y); 41/332; Capt Varsity Clb; Crs Cntry; Trk; Cit Awd; High Hon Roll; Pres Schlr; Cert Stu Athltc Trnr 85-86; U Of Pittsburgh; Phrmcy.

MIGLIACCIO, MARK; T R Proctor HS; Utica, NY; (Y); High Hon Roll; Hon Roll; Clarkston; Engrng.

MIGLIAZZO, ANTHONY; Niagara Falls HS; Niagara Falls, NY; (S); 12/250; Key Clb; Socr; High Hon Roll; Hon Roll; Jr NHS; NHS; Cert Of Regntn Prfct Attndnc 85; Achvt Cert Ntl Hist Day 85; Finance.

MIGLIETTA, GINA; Geneseo Central Schl; Groveland, NY; (Y); Var Trk; Hon Roll; Law Enfrcmt.

MIGNELLA, GABRIEL; Bayside HS; Bayside, NY; (Y); 16/650; Am Leg Boys St; Church Yth Grp; Cmnty Wkr; Intnl Clb; Math Clb; Math Tm; Political Wkr; Ed Lit Mag; High Hon Roll; NHS; Crnl U; Hstry.

MIHALKO, GREG; Rensselaer HS; Rensselaer, NY; (Y); SADD; Varsity Clb; Rep Frsh Cls; Rep Soph Cls; Pres Jr Cls; Pres Stu Cncl; Var Capt Bsbl; Var Bowling; Var Ftbl; Jrnlsm.

MIKELL, JEFFREY; Owego Free Acad; Owego, NY; (Y); 14/198; Boys Clb Am; Church Yth Grp; Mathletes; Pep Clb; Ski Clb; Spanish Clb; Varsity Clb; Concert Band; Rep Frsh Cls; Rep Jr Cls; Scndry Ed.

MIKKELSON, KERI; Williamsville South HS; Williamsville, NY; (Y); AFS; German Clb; Chorus; Stu Cncl; High Hon Roll; Hon Roll; NHS; NFMC NE Rgnl Schlrp Wnr 84; Yng Perf Artsts Fredonia Comptn 1st Pl 85 & 86; Music Camp Schlrps 86; Music.

MIKLEJN, TOM; Niagara Catholic HS; Niagara Fls, NY; (Y); 2/87; Am Leg Boys St; Spanish Clb; High Hon Roll; NHS; Engrng.

MIKOLAJCZAK, BERNADETTE; Immaculata Acad; Hamburg, NY; (Y); 7/43; JA; Quiz Bowl; Ed Nwsp Sprt Ed; Ed Yrbk Sprt Ed; JV Cheerleading; Hon Roll; NEDT Awd; Deans Schlrshp Cnss Coll; NYS Rgnts Schlrshp; Canisius Coll; Bus.

MIKULA, MATTHEW; Plainedge Public HS; Massapequa, NY; (Y); Am Leg Boys St; FTA; SADD; School Play; Nwsp Sprt Ed; Yrbk Stf; Pres Sr Cls; Pres Stu Cncl; Capt Swmmng; Tennis; Natl Hstry Day Fnlst 85; Polit Sci.

MIKULEC, JENNIFER; Fairport HS; Fairport, NY; (Y); Cmnty Wkr; Var Gym; High Hon Roll; Hon Roll; Outstndng Achvt Awd 86.

MIKUS, JAY; Cicero-North Syracuse HS; Clay, NY; (Y); 56/625; Church Yth Grp; Ski Clb; Chorus; JV Socr; Var Trk; Hon Roll; NHS; Ithaca Coll Schlrshp 86; Ithaca Coll; Sprts Med.

MILANO, JOHN; Elmont Memorial HS; Elmont, NY; (Y); Variety Show; Ftbl; Hon Roll; NHS; Hofstra U; Sci.

MILAVEC, DANIELLE; Oneonta SR HS; Oneonta, NY; (Y); 6/160; Q&S; Varsity Clb; Band; Nwsp Stf; Trs Sr Cls; Trs Stu Cncl; JV Var Cheerleading; High Hon Roll; Hon Roll; NHS; Rgnts Schlrshp 86; Nicholas B Ottaway Schlrshp 86; SUNY Geneseo.

MILAZZO, LISA; Grover Cleveland HS; Buffalo, NY; (Y); 7/153; CAP; Science Clb; Nwsp Rptr; Sec Frsh Cls; Sec Jr Cls; Sec Sr Cls; Cheerleading; Swmmng; NHS; Embry Riddle; Aerontcl Sci.

MILBANK, DANA T; Sanford H Calhoun HS; Merrick, NY; (Y); 4/313; Band; Jazz Band; Nwsp Sprt Ed; Var Bsktbl; Capt Var Crs Cntry; NCTE Awd; NHS; Ntl Merit Ltr; Exploring; Hosp Aide; Wstnghs Sci Tlnt Srch Hnrs Grp 85-86; Yale; Bio.

MILBORROW, MICHELE; Greece Athena HS; Rochester, NY; (Y); 44/265; JA; School Musical; Symp Band; Hon Roll; Symph Band Sec 83-84, VP 84-85; Fund Raising Coord 85-86; SUNY Fredonia; Psych.

MILCAREK, LINDA; Warsaw Central HS; Warsaw, NY; (S); 7/90; Pres Drama Clb; French Clb; Spanish Clb; Band; Chorus; School Play; Yrbk Stf; Stu Cncl; Cit Awd; NHS; Solo-Festvl Outstndng Ratng 84 & 85; Acadmc Achvt Music Vocl 84 & 85; Geneseo; Music Ed.

MILCH, STEWART; Newfield HS; Coram, NY; (S); 8/576; Hosp Aide; Library Aide; SADD; Band; Concert Band; Jazz Band; Mrchg Band; Nwsp Ed-Chief; Nwsp Rptr; Nwsp Stf; German Hnr Soc 85; Steuben Awd For Excllnc In German 85; Intl Rltns.

MILDEN, SONJA R; Riverhead HS; Riverhead, NY; (Y); Church Yth Grp; Cmnty Wkr; DECA; Pres FBLA; Office Aide; ROTC; VICA; Yrbk Stf; Var JV Cheerleading; HUGS Clb 85-86; Tchrs Aide Boces Smmr Schl 84-85; ABC Coll; Comp Pgmr.

MILEHAM, JEFFREY; Tonawanda JR SR HS; Tonawanda, NY; (Y); 5/219; Am Leg Boys St; Var L Swmmng; Var L Trk; Hon Roll; NHS; Aerspc Engr.

MILEO, LISA A; St Francis Prep; Bellerose, NY; (S); 138/744; Church Yth Grp; Dance Clb; Drama Clb; French Clb; School Musical; School Play; Stage Crew; Hon Roll; St Johns U; Math.

MILES, LORI; Mt Vernon HS; Mt Vernon, NY; (Y); Art Clb; AFS; Drama Clb; 4-H; GAA; Spanish Clb; Band; Concert Band; Mrchg Band; School Musical; Parsons Schl Desgn; Fash Desgn.

MILES, LYNN; Maryvale HS; Cheektowaga, NY; (Y); German Clb; Spanish Clb; Varsity Clb; Band; Concert Band; Mrchg Band; Symp Band; Stu Cncl; Crs Cntry; Trk; Canisus; Med Tech.

MILES, RENEE; Jordan-Elbridge Central HS; Skaneateles Fl, NY; (Y); Girl Scts; Color Guard; Mrchg Band; NHS; Lgl Secy.

MILETIC, ESTER; William C Bryant HS; Astoria, NY; (S); 3/623; Cmnty Wkr; Math Tm; Nwsp Rptr; French Clb; Math Clb; Science Clb; Yrbk Stf; Tennis; Hon Roll; Prfct Atten Awd; Daily News Pride Of Yankees Awd; Math Team Trphy; Natl Sci Olympd Awd; Acctg.

MILETIC, KAREN; New Rochelle HS; New Rochelle, NY; (Y); VP Spanish Clb; SADD; Lit Mag; Pres Frsh Cls; Rep Sr Cls; High Hon Roll; Hon Roll; NHS; Prfct Atten Awd; Spanish NHS; Amer Lgn Awd 84; IONA Lang Cntst 2nd Hnrs Span 85; Med.

MILIOTTO, LYNNE; Mount Saint Mary Acad; Tonawanda, NY; (Y); Church Yth Grp; Cmnty Wkr; French Clb; Lit Mag; Cit Awd; Yth Engd Srvc Outstndng Srvc 84-85; Canisius Coll; Psych.

MILITELLO, MARK; Herkimer HS; Herkimer, NY; (Y); 21/130; Pres Model UN; Capt Ski Clb; Band; Chorus; Concert Band; Jazz Band; Mrchg Band; Var Crs Cntry; Var Golf; Hon Roll; Pre-Law.

MILKS, BRIAN; Randolph Central HS; Little Valley, NY; (Y); 9/89; Am Leg Boys St; 4-H; VP FFA; Ski Clb; Band; Concert Band; Jazz Band; Mrchg Band; Im Bsktbl; High Hon Roll; Empire Degree Farming 86; Profcncy Ag Sales & Svc 86; Clarkson U; Chem Engrng.

MILLAN, CARLOS; Northport HS; East Northport, NY; (Y); DAR Awd; Chess Clb; DECA; Math Clb; Acpl Chr; Band; Chorus; Mrchg Band; Symp Band; Var Capt Trk; Geneseo ST Coll; Pltcl Sci.

MILLAN, ROBERT; De Witt Clinton HS; Bronx, NY; (Y); Office Aide; ROTC; Y-Teens; Drill Tm; Off Sr Cls; Wt Lftg; Cit Awd; Air Forc JROTC Crtfctn Of Cmpltn; Lngvty Rbbn; Acdmc Rbbn; Drll Tm Rbbn; Westchester Bus Inst; Bus Adm.

MILLAR, JAMES G; Clinton Central HS; Clinton, NY; (Y); 15/136; Model UN; SADD; Mrchg Band; Rep Stu Cncl; Var Bsbl; Var Bsktbl; Var Socr; Hon Roll; NHS; Church Yth Grp; Schl Bsktbl Recrd-Pts & Assts 82-86; NYS Rgnts Schlrshp 86; Hamilton Coll.

MILLAR, WENDY K; Camden Central Schl; Blossvale, NY; (Y); 10/212; Debate Tm; Pres SADD; School Musical; School Play; Nwsp Ed-Chief; Var Trk; High Hon Roll; NHS; Ntl Merit SF; Drama Clb; Simons Rock; Mth.

MILLARD, JILL M; Fairport HS; Fairport, NY; (Y); Concert Band; Jazz Band; Mrchg Band; School Musical; High Hon Roll; NHS; Ntl Merit SF; PA ST U; Bus.

MILLBYER, L LYNN; North Rose-Wolcott HS; N Rose, NY; (Y); 12/135; Church Yth Grp; FBLA; Ski Clb; Varsity Clb; Stat Bsktbl; Var Bowling; Trk; NHS; High Hon Roll; U Of KY; Pre-Law.

MILLER, ADRIANNE J; Lake Shore HS; Angola, NY; (Y); 16/284; Concert Band; Mrchg Band; Orch; School Musical; Pres Frsh Cls; VP Stu Cncl; Var Socr; Var Tennis; High Hon Roll; Jr NHS; Outstndng Orch Awd 86; Band Achvt Awd 83; Fredonia ST; Acctg.

MILLER, AMY; Niagara Wheatfield SR HS; Niagara Falls, NY; (Y); VP AFS; Am Leg Aux Girls St; VP Pep Clb; Hst PAVAS; Pres Spanish Clb; Band; Stu Cncl; NHS; IFLA 85-86; NLSA 86; All Amer Awd 86; Psychlgy.

MILLER, ANN M; Prospect Heights HS; Brooklyn, NY; (S); 5/270; Church Yth Grp; Debate Tm; FBLA; Engl & Socl Stds Regents Awds 86; Outstndng Awd Bkkpg 86; Albany ST U; Bus Adm.

MILLER, BRIAN; Olympia HS; Rochester, NY; (Y); Exploring; Im Bsktbl; Im Vllybl; Hon Roll; Cnsrvtn.

MILLER, CARLEN A; Westhill HS; Syracuse, NY; (Y); 8/145; Ski Clb; Spanish Clb; JV Bsktbl; Sftbl; Var Capt Tennis; High Hon Roll; Trs NHS; Ntl Merit Schol; NEDT Awd; Spanish NHS; Rgnts Schlrshp 86-87; U Of Binghamton; Bus.

MILLER, CHERYL; Frontier Central HS; Hamburg, NY; (S); 30/444; Pres Capt Church Yth Grp; VP Exploring; Sec German Clb; Pres Sec Girl Scts; Varsity Clb; High Hon Roll; NHS; Aud/Vis; 4-H; JA; Rifle Tm Capt Ltr 85-86; NACEL Exch Stu Germany 85; Intrnshp Erie Co Sherifs Dept 85-86; Crmnl Just.

MILLER, CHRIS; Pittsford Mendon HS; Pittsford, NY; (Y); Boy Scts; Church Yth Grp; Chorus; Var Ftbl; Wt Lftg; Var L Wrstlng; Hon Roll; All-Cnty Chorus 86; All-Cnty Wrstlng 85-86; All-League St Qualifer 86; Eagle Scout BSA 86.

MILLER, CHRISTIAN; Valley Central HS; Montgomery, NY; (Y); 79/430; Boy Scts; Varsity Clb; Band; JV Crs Cntry; Var Trk; JV Wrstlng; Aerobatic Design 1st Pl 86; Jingle Jog Rd Rale 2nd Pl 85; Comm Coll Schlrshp 85; Engrng.

MILLER, CHRISTINA G; Henninger HS; Syracuse, NY; (Y); 4/400; Art Clb; Church Yth Grp; French Clb; Intnl Clb; Key Clb; Math Tm; Quiz Bowl; Science Clb; Ski Clb; SADD; Regents Scholar 86; U PA; Med.

MILLER, CHRISTOPHER J; East Syracuse-Minoa HS; East Syracuse, NY; (Y); 6/333; Quiz Bowl; Var L Trk; High Hon Roll; Jr NHS; NHS; Ntl Merit Ltr; Pres Schlr; St Schlr; Latin Clb; Vllybl; Many Schlstc Art Awds; Achvmnt Awd Bio & Hlth; Most Artstc Male; Williams Coll; Studio Art.

MILLER, CYNTHIA; Nardin Acad; Cheektowaga, NY; (S); 6/85; Chorus; School Musical; Nwsp Ed-Chief; Sec Lit Mag; Sec Soph Cls; Rep Stu Cncl; Var L Sftbl; High Hon Roll; Hon Roll; NHS; Wellsley Book Awd, 2nd Fredona Press 86; Excel Brtsh Lit, Hnrs Jrnlsm 85; Jrnlsm.

MILLER, DAVID; Oneida HS; Oneida, NY; (S); 18/200; Pres Church Yth Grp; Computer Clb; Science Clb; Varsity Clb; Rep Stu Cncl; L Trk; CC Awd; High Hon Roll; NHS; Natl Sci Merit Awd 86; Comptr Sci.

MILLER, DAVID; Tonawanda HS; Tonawanda, NY; (Y); Var Crs Cntry; Var Trk; JV Var Wrstlng; Hon Roll; Navy.

MILLER, DAWN; Lawrence HS; Atlantic Bch, NY; (Y); Spanish Clb; VP Band; Chorus; Concert Band; Mrchg Band; Orch; Pep Band; School Musical; Stage Crew; Yrbk Bus Mgr; Music Hnr Soc 86; Recvd Nyssma Awds 84-86; Music.

MILLER, DEAN; Notre Dame HS; Utica, NY; (Y); 5/160; Pres FBLA; Capt Key Clb; Math Tm; Ski Clb; Nwsp Rptr; Rep Stu Cncl; Var Capt Socr; Cit Awd; High Hon Roll; Pres NHS; FBLA 1st Pl ST Mr FBLA; Cntrl Oneida Lg Socr All ST; Franklin & Marshall; Bus Mgmt.

MILLER II, DENNIS B; Mynderse Acad; Seneca Falls, NY; (S); 37/138; Model UN; SADD; Chorus; Jazz Band; Camera Clb; School Musical; Rep Stu Cncl; JV Trk; French Clb; Intnl Clb; Engrng.

MILLER, DIANA; Notre Dame HS; Le Roy, NY; (S); 2/63; Bsktbl; Cheerleading; High Hon Roll; Hon Roll; NHS; Awd Hgst Avg Math,Earth Sci 83-85; Child Psych.

MILLER, DOUGLAS; Pittsford Mendon HS; Pittsford, NY; (Y); Boy Scts; Church Yth Grp; Chorus; Var JV Ftbl; Wt Lftg; Var Wrstlng; Hon Roll; Eagle Scout 86; All Lg Wrstlr Monroe Cnty 86; All Cnty Chorus Monroe Cnty 86.

MILLER, DOUGLASS; Union-Endicott HS; Endicott, NY; (Y); Drama Clb; Concert Band; Drm Mjr(t); Jazz Band; School Musical; School Play; VP Frsh Cls; Pres Soph Cls; Trs Stu Cncl; JV Ftbl; Cooking.

MILLER, EARL A; Grand Island SR HS; Gr Island, NY; (Y); Band; Concert Band; Mrchg Band; Pep Band; School Musical; NY ST Rgnts Schlrshp Awd 86; SUNY Fredonia; Acctg.

MILLER, EDWARD A; Glen Cove HS; Glen Cove, NY; (Y); 2/270; Cmnty Wkr; Computer Clb; Science Clb; Spanish Clb; Temple Yth Grp; Thesps; Band; Concert Band; Jazz Band; School Musical; Rgnts Schlrshp 86; Sprntndnts Cup 86; MVP Wrstlng 86; Cornell; Sci.

MILLER, ERIC; Corinth Central Schl; Corinth, NY; (S); Trs Church Yth Grp; French Clb; SADD; Band; Jazz Band; JV Var Bsbl; JV Var Ftbl; Var Golf; JV Var Wrstlng; Jr NHS; Modern Msc Msters Scty 84; FBI Acad; Law Infrcmnt.

MILLER, ERIC W; Odessa-Montour C S HS; Cayuta, NY; (Y); 61/86; Computer Clb; JV Bsbl; Var L Ftbl; Var Wt Lftg; Var JV Wrstlng; Natl Hnr Soc Rcgntn Sci 86; NYS Rgnts Schlrshp 86; Natl Hnr Soc Rcgntn Trig 86; US Marine Corp; Electronics.

MILLER, HEATHER; Newark SR HS; Newark, NY; (Y); 28/191; Church Yth Grp; Drama Clb; SADD; Yrbk Stf; French Hon Soc; High Hon Roll; Hon Roll; NHS; Presbtrn Yth Trienium Delgt 86; Secndry Ed.

MILLER, JAMES; Northern Adiron Dack Central HS; Mooers Forks, NY; (Y); Church Yth Grp; Cmnty Wkr; FFA; Library Aide; Concert Band; Frsh Cls; Soph Cls; Jr Cls; Hon Roll; NHS; Alumni Schlrshp Awd 86; Greenhand & Chptr Degrees FFA 84 & 85; Chptr Meeting Cont FFA 83-85; SUNY-PLATTSBURGH; Math.

MILLER, JANET; Rhinebeck Central HS; Rhinebeck, NY; (Y); Church Yth Grp; Chorus; Church Choir; Rep Frsh Cls; Rep Soph Cls; Stu Cncl; Hon Roll; Music.

MILLER, JANICE; Lowville Acad Centrl Schl; Glenfield, NY; (Y); Pres Church Yth Grp; Cmnty Wkr; FCA; FBLA; VP FHA; Hosp Aide; Chorus; Church Choir; Hon Roll; Cazenovia Coll; Scl Wrkr.

MILLER, JEANINE; Bronx H S Of Science; Brooklyn, NY; (Y); Office Aide; Teachers Aide; Chorus; Yrbk Stf; Rgnts Schlrshp 86; Skdmr Coll; Bio.

MILLER, JEANNINE; Newburgh Free Acad; Newburgh, NY; (Y); Cmnty Wkr; Sec Spanish Clb; Sec Jr Cls; Sec Sr Cls; Rep Stu Cncl; Var Sftbl; Var Capt Swmmng; VP Jr NHS; Opt Clb Awd; Yrbk Stf; Law.

MILLER, JEFFREY; Sayville HS; W Sayville, NY; (Y); 9/380; Key Clb; Mathletes; Concert Band; Drm & Bgl; Mrchg Band; Orch; School Musical; High Hon Roll; NHS; Ntl Cyclng Chmpnshps ID 86; Chem Olympd 86.

MILLER, JEFFREY A; West Seneca West SR HS; West Seneca, NY; (Y); 85/559; Nwsp Stf; JV Var Socr; Jr NHS; NHS; Ntl Merit Ltr; NYS Regnts Schlrshp; Soccr Chmpnshp Awd NYS Athl Assn; Buffalo ST Coll; Rad Brdcstg.

MILLER, JENNIFER; Marion Central Schl; Marion, NY; (Y); 7/98; Am Leg Aux Girls St; French Clb; Pres Varsity Clb; VP Soph Cls; VP Jr Cls; VP Sr Cls; Stu Cncl; Bsktbl; Socr; Sftbl; Scl Wrk.

MILLER, JENNIFER; Niagara Falls HS; Niagara Falls, NY; (S); 10/200; SADD; Nwsp Ed-Chief; Yrbk Stf; Hst Jr Cls; Cit Awd; Hon Roll; Jr NHS; NHS; Lewiston Kiwanis Qn Cntst 85; Stu Congrs 85-86; Knoxville U; Nvlst.

MILLER, JENNIFER; Sacred Heart Acad; Rockville Centre, NY; (S); Art Clb; Cmnty Wkr; Pep Clb; School Play; Nwsp Rptr; Frsh Cls; Soph Cls; Stu Cncl; Hon Roll; NHS; Ambssdr HOBY Sem NY ST 85; USSCA Publictn Inclsn 85.

MILLER, JENNIFER; Torreson American HS; Apo, NY; (Y); 1/106; Sec Church Yth Grp; Exploring; School Musical; VP Jr Cls; Sec Stu Cncl; Var L Crs Cntry; Var L Tennis; JV L Vllybl; High Hon Roll; Sec NHS; Ldrshp Semnr 85; Engrg.

MILLER, JILL A; Syosset HS; Jericho, NY; (Y); 180/504; AFS; Latin Clb; Yrbk Sprt Ed; Rep Stu Cncl; Tennis; Pres Schlr; St Schlr; Attrny Gnrls Offc Wrkr 85-86; Engl Hnrs 85-86; Schlrshp Cmmtte; George Washington U; Accntng.

MILLER, JIM; Ballston Spa HS; Ballston Spa, NY; (Y); 45/240; French Clb; Intnl Clb; Letterman Clb; Science Clb; Ski Clb; Varsity Clb; JV Bsbl; JV Bsktbl; Var Socr; Var Tennis; SUNY Geneseo; Bus.

MILLER, JOANNE; Smithtown HS East; Smithtown, NY; (Y); Church Yth Grp; SADD; Teachers Aide; Chorus; Symp Band; Im Coach Actv; Capt Var Socr; NHS; Political Wkr; Stage Crew; Itln Hnr Soc Treas & Pres 85-86; Yth & Govt 85-86; Law.

MILLER, JOE; Centereach HS; Pt Jefferson, NY; (Y); Computer Clb; Varsity Clb; Bsbl; JV Socr; Var Tennis; Hon Roll; Jr NHS; Rgnts Schlrshp 87; Pres Awd For Achvt In Phy Ed 86; UCLA; CPA.

MILLER, JOHN PAUL; Arlington HS; Poughkeepsie, NY; (Y); Chess Clb; Computer Clb; Debate Tm; French Clb; Math Tm; Political Wkr; Radio Clb; Symp Band; Yrbk Stf; JV Var Trk; Duco Math Leag Sec F Champ 86; Regents Schlrshp 86; Law.

MILLER, JOSEPH; Bitburg American HS; Apo, NY; (Y); Drama Clb; Quiz Bowl; Golf; Hon Roll; NHS; Engrng.

MILLER, JOSEPH; Tappan Zee HS; Blauvelt, NY; (Y); 25/245; Boy Scts; JA; Math Clb; Math Tm; Ski Clb; Chorus; Madrigals; Yrbk Bus Mgr; Bsbl; Golf; Eagle Scout 86; Cornell U; Econ.

MILLER II, JOSEPH L; Fillmore Central HS; Fillmore, NY; (Y); Am Leg Boys St; Ski Clb; Varsity Clb; Band; School Play; Stage Crew; Yrbk Phtg; Trs Jr Cls; Rep Stu Cncl; Bsbl; Bus.

MILLER, JUDI; Moore Catholic HS; Staten Island, NY; (Y); 1/190; Hosp Aide; Math Tm; Ed Nwsp Stf; Ed Yrbk Stf; Rep Stu Cncl; Cheerleading; High Hon Roll; Sec NHS; Am Chem Soc Outsndng Chem Stu 85; Ntl Italian Awd 85; Pre-Med.

MILLER, KAREN; Bethpage HS; Plainview, NY; (Y); French Clb; SADD; Nwsp Stf; High Hon Roll; Hon Roll; Arch Engr.

MILLER, KATHLEEN; Paul V Moore HS; Central Sq, NY; (Y); Cmnty Wkr; Exploring; German Clb; Hosp Aide; Yrbk Bus Mgr; Yrbk Stf; Trs Jr Cls; Trs Sr Cls; Rep Stu Cncl; Capt Var Cheerleading; Med Assist.

MILLER, KEITH; Whitesboro SR HS; Whitesboro, NY; (Y); Boys Clb Am; Camera Clb; Letterman Clb; SADD; Varsity Clb; Nwsp Sprt Ed; L Var Bsbl; JV Bsktbl; L Var Ftbl; Wt Lftg; Bus Mgr.

MILLER, KELLI; Wayland Central HS; Wayland, NY; (Y); Girl Scts; Hosp Aide; Ski Clb; Band; Concert Band; Mrchg Band; Var JV Socr; Hon Roll; Gld Key Awd 86; Med Fld.

MILLER, KIMBERLY; Cicero North Syracuse HS; Clay, NY; (Y); 124/667; Girl Scts; SADD; Band; Concert Band; Mrchg Band; Symp Band; Hon Roll; NHS; NY ST Rgnts Nrsng Schlrshp 86; Pres Acdmc Ftns Awd 86; Crouse Irvng Schl Of Nrs; Nrs.

MILLER, KIMBERLY; Portville Central HS; Cuba, NY; (Y); Chorus; Mrchg Band; Trk; Hon Roll; Jr Vrsty Ltr Vrsty Ltr 84-85; Jr Vrsty Pin 84-85; Chorus Cert 84-85; Bus Admin.

MILLER, KRISTEN; Our Lady Of Mercy HS; Penfield, NY; (Y); 2/175; Cmnty Wkr; 4-H; Rep Service Clb; Stage Crew; Lit Mag; Im Trk; Hon Roll; Merit Roll 3 Yrs; Amer Lit Excel Awd; 1st Brighton U Poetry.

MILLER, KURT; Honeoye Falls Lima Central Schl; Honeoye Falls, NY; (S); 5/160; VP Drama Clb; Pres Intnl Clb; Pep Clb; Chorus; School Musical; High Hon Roll; NHS; Outstndng Bus & Span Stu.

MILLER, LAURIE A; Horace Mann Schl; New York, NY; (Y); Service Clb; Ed Nwsp Stf; Lit Mag; Ntl Merit SF; Writer.

MILLER, LEE R; Monroe-Woodbury SR HS; Monroe, NY; (Y); 8/359; Chess Clb; Intnl Clb; NFL; Political Wkr; Service Clb; Nwsp Stf; Lit Mag; Elks Awd; High Hon Roll; Voice Dem Awd; Outstndg Stu-Sci 83; Outstndg Stu-Soc Stud 84; Merit Schlr Brandeis U 86; Brandeis U; Poltcs.

MILLER, LEE STUART; Amsterdam HS; Amsterdam, NY; (Y); 7/300; Letterman Clb; Varsity Clb; Concert Band; Rep Frsh Cls; Off Soph Cls; Pres Jr Cls; Pres Sr Cls; Rep Stu Cncl; Bsbl; Bsktbl; Army Rsrv Outstndng Stu/Athtl 86; Cornell U; Ecnmcs.

MILLER, LESLIE F; Manhasset HS; Manhasset, NY; (Y); 5/175; Pres Sec Intnl Clb; Sec Service Clb; Sec Band; Orch; School Musical; Nwsp Bus Mgr; Ed Lit Mag; High Hon Roll; NHS; Mathletes; Lgn Islnd Math Fair-Slvr Mdl 85; Ntl Sci Olympd Awd-Chem Physc 84, 85; Prnctn U; Math.

MILLER, LISA; Churchville-Chili SR HS; N Chili, NY; (Y); Pres Church Yth Grp; Pres FHA; Band; Chorus; Concert Band; Flag Corp; Yrbk Stf; Lit Mag; Rep Stu Cncl; Hon Roll; Spec Ed.

MILLER, MARK; Bishop Ludden HS; Syracuse, NY; (S); 2/180; JA; Math Tm; Spanish Clb; VP Jr Cls; Var Socr; High Hon Roll; Earth Sci Awd 84; Clarkson; Chem Engnrng.

MILLER, MARK R; Clarence SR HS; Williamsville, NY; (Y); 19/268; Varsity Clb; Stage Crew; Bsbl; Vllybl; Hon Roll; NHS; Rgnts Schlrhsp 86; Mock Trl Tm Mbr 86; ST U NY Buffalo; Engr.

MILLER, MAUREEN; St Peters High School For Girls; Staten Island, NY; (Y); FNA; Band; School Musical; Swing Chorus; Nrsng.

MILLER, MELINDA; Cicero North Syracuse HS; Clay, NY; (S); 3/625; Pres Computer Clb; Sec JA; Mathletes; SADD; Band; Lit Mag; Var Fld Hcky; Hon Roll; Jr NHS; Natl Govt & Hstry Awd 85; Econ.

MILLER, MELISSA M; Batavia HS; Batavia, NY; (Y); #64 In Class; Accntnt.

MILLER, MERLYN; Northeastern Acad; Brooklyn, NY; (S); Quiz Bowl; Scholastic Bowl; Chorus; Church Choir; Im Score Keeper; Im Vllybl; Hon Roll; Ntl Merit Ltr; Ldrshp Awd 84; Natl Sci Merit Awd Wnr 86; Columbia Union Clg; Comp Sci.

MILLER, MICHAEL; Baldwin Senior HS; Baldwin, NY; (S); 63/476; Drama Clb; VP Band; VP Chorus; Concert Band; Drm & Bgl; Jazz Band; Mrchg Band; School Musical; NHS; Bus Admin.

MILLER, MICHELLE; Dominican Commercial HS; St Albans, NY; (Y); Am Leg Aux Girls St; Drama Clb; Hosp Aide; Office Aide; Variety Show; Gym; Hon Roll; Operation Fun Camp Retarded & Disabled Vlntr Awd Merit 85; Utica Coll.

MILLER, MICHELLE; George Wingate HS; Brooklyn, NY; (Y); Boys Clb Am; Girl Scts; Math Clb; Model UN; SADD; Y-Teens; Church Choir; School Play; Vllybl; Awd-Bst Math Stu In Cls 86; Bus Mngmt.

MILLER, MICHELLE; Norwood-Norfolk Central Schl; Norfolk, NY; (Y); Key Clb; Latin Clb; Band; Chorus; Jazz Band; Rep Stu Cncl; JV Bsktbl; JV Sftbl; Var Capt Vllybl; Hon Roll; All-Cnty Jzz Ensbl 86; Area All-ST 85; Tlntd Jrs 85; Med Tech.

MILLER, MIKE; Lyndonville Central HS; Waterport, NY; (Y); Exploring; Varsity Clb; JV Bsktbl; Engrng.

MILLER, NANCY; East Hampton HS; E Hampton, NY; (Y); 8/116; Church Yth Grp; French Clb; Pres Intnl Clb; SADD; Nwsp Ed-Chief; Yrbk Stf; Stu Cncl; Cheerleading; High Hon Roll; NHS; Hghst Avrg In Math Sequntl 84; Hshst Avrg In Math 13 86; Pres Acad Fitns 86; Bucknell U; Engrng.

MILLER, NICOLE L; The Bronx H S Of Science; Bronx, NY; (Y); Church Yth Grp; Computer Clb; Office Aide; Science Clb; Teachers Aide; School Play; Lit Mag; Prfct Atten Awd; Rcpnt Of Mercedes Gilbert Awd 84; Bio-Chem.

MILLER, PAMELA; Attica Central HS; Varysburg, NY; (Y); Chorus; Color Guard; Nwsp Rptr; Nwsp Stf; Frsh Cls; Rep Soph Cls; Sec Jr Cls; JV Bsktbl; JV Capt Socr; Var Swmmng; Nrsng.

MILLER, PAUL; E J Wilson HS; Spencerport, NY; (Y); Spanish Clb; Varsity Clb; Variety Show; Var L Bsktbl; Var L Socr; High Hon Roll; Hon Roll; NHS; Ntl Merit Ltr; NY ST Regents Schlrshp 86; U Of Dayton Pres Schlrshp 86; U Of Dayton; Mgmt Info Sys.

MILLER, RANDI; E Meadow HS; East Meadow, NY; (Y); Key Clb; Temple Yth Grp; Nwsp Rptr; Nwsp Sprt Ed; Nwsp Stf; Yrbk Stf; Jrnlsm.

MILLER, ROBERT; Arlingotn HS; Billings, NY; (Y); 69/565; JV Bsbl; Im Bowling; Var Ftbl; Var Trk; Natl Achvt Schlrshp Pgm-Cmnd Schlr 86; Elec Engrng.

MILLER, ROBIN; Newfield HS; Selden, NY; (Y); 101/515; Church Yth Grp; Dance Clb; Hosp Aide; Pep Clb; Yrbk Stf; Rep Soph Cls; Rep Jr Cls; Rep Sr Cls; Hon Roll; St Schlr; Mdl Cntry Schl Dist RN Schlrshp 86; Rgnts Nrsg Schlrshp 86; Mt St Mary Coll; Nrsg.

MILLER, RODNEY; North Babylon SR HS; N Babylon, NY; (Y); 61/462; DECA; French Clb; Intnl Clb; Pep Clb; Nwsp Stf; Yrbk Stf; Lit Mag; High Hon Roll; Jr NHS; NHS; Suffolk Cnty 1st Pl Awd 86; NYS Awd 86; Advrtsng.

MILLER, RUSSELL S; Warwick Valley HS; Warwick, NY; (Y); 50/200; SADD; Chorus; Nwsp Sprt Ed; Nwsp Stf; Pres French Clb; Rep Jr Cls; Pres Sr Cls; Rep Stu Cncl; Var Capt Bsktbl; Var Capt Ftbl; ROTC Schlrshp 86; Hnrbl Mntn Bsktbl Tm 86; Miltry Stds.

MILLER, RUTH; Half Hollow Hills HS East; Dix Hills, NY; (Y); Debate Tm; Hosp Aide; Intnl Clb; JA; Leo Clb; Science Clb; Mrchg Band; Symp Band; Nwsp Rptr; Lit Mag; Natl Italian Hnr Soc 86; Pre-Med.

MILLER, SARAH; Cazenovia HS; Cazenovia, NY; (Y); AFS; Drama Clb; School Musical; Stage Crew; Swmmng; High Hon Roll; Hon Roll; Lfsvng Cert 85; Dickinson Coll; Lbrl Arts.

MILLER, SCOTT; Alden HS; Lancaster, NY; (Y); French Clb; Trs Science Clb; School Play; Nwsp Rptr; Nwsp Stf; Var L Badmtn; Hon Roll; Prfct Atten Awd; Acdmc Awd 85-86; Journlsm.

MILLER, STACEY; St Raymond Acad; Bronx, NY; (Y); Church Yth Grp; Dance Clb; Girl Scts; Pep Clb; Band; Mrchg Band; Pep Band.

MILLER, STEPHANIE D; Bronx HS Of Science; Bronx, NY; (Y); Office Aide; Red Cross Aide; Temple Yth Grp; Rep Frsh Cls; Rep Soph Cls; Rep Jr Cls; Rep Sr Cls; Rep Sec Stu Cncl; Mgr(s); Swmmng; Vrsty Ltr Boys Swmmng Team 84-85; Rgnts Schlrshp 86; CUNY Queens Coll; Med.

MILLER, SUSAN; Southside SR HS; Rockville Centre, NY; (Y); 128/278; Church Yth Grp; Drama Clb; 4-H; Key Clb; Pep Clb; Science Clb; Chorus; School Play; Stu Cncl; JV Sftbl; Boston U; Adv.

MILLER, TAMARA J; Fillmore Central Schl; Fillmore, NY; (Y); 20/60; Pres 4-H; Ski Clb; Spanish Clb; Trs Jr Cls; Trs Sr Cls; JV Cheerleading; Var Tennis; Timer; Var Trk; JV Var Vllybl; Rgnts Schlrshp Nrsng 86; St Josephs Schl Nrsng; Nrsng.

MILLER, THOMAS; Penn Yan Acad; Penn Yan, NY; (S); 1/175; Am Leg Boys St; Varsity Clb; Pres Frsh Cls; Pres Soph Cls; Rep Jr Cls; Im Badmtn; JV Bsktbl; Var Trk; Im Vllybl; Im Wt Lftg; Elmira Key Awd; Sci Olympcs; Frnch I-II-III Awds; Cornell U; Engrng.

MILLER, WENDY; Unatego JR SR HS; Wells Bridge, NY; (Y); Camera Clb; Computer Clb; English Clb; French Clb; FHA; Ski Clb; SADD; Trk; French Hon Soc; High Hon Roll; Girls Sct Awds; Long Island U; Trvl.

MILLER, WILLIAM B; East Syracuse-Minoa HS; E Syracuse, NY; (Y); 75/333; Variety Show; Var Ftbl; JV Lcrss; Hon Roll; NHS; Drftg Achvt Awd; Most Imprvd Stu Achvt Awd; Cortland ST U; Sprts Med.

MILLER, YVETTE; North Eastern Acad; Queens Village, NY; (Y); Church Yth Grp; Debate Tm; French Clb; Office Aide; Pep Clb; Scholastic Bowl; Science Clb; Teachers Aide; Chorus; Church Choir; Western New England; Hstry.

MILLER, ZACHARY; Malverne HS; Malverne, NY; (Y); 3/137; Cmnty Wkr; Science Clb; Nwsp Rptr; Lit Mag; Var Crs Cntry; High Hon Roll; Hon Roll; NHS; Hnry Ment Sci Cong 85; Fastest Time Cross Cty 86; Martin Luther King Essay Cntst 86; Rochester U; Chem Engr.

MILLEY, MICHELLE L; West Seneca East SR HS; Cheektowaga, NY; (Y); 23/285; French Clb; German Clb; Nwsp Stf; Yrbk Stf; Lit Mag; Mgr(s); JV Var Swmmng; NHS; Stat Vllybl; High Hon Roll; Germn Ntl Hnr Soc; NYS Regnts Schlrshp; Frnch, Germn & Spnsh Awds 85-86; Westminster Coll; Intl Reltns.

MILLIEN, SAADIAH; St Michael HS; Brooklyn, NY; (Y); Dance Clb; Drama Clb; Girl Scts; Hosp Aide; Science Clb; SADD; Temple Yth Grp; Chorus; School Musical; Variety Show; Brown; Dr.

MILLIGAN, TAMMIE L; Pavilion Central HS; Pavilion, NY; (Y); 7/62; Sec AFS; Nwsp Stf; Yrbk Sprt Ed; Sec Sr Cls; Var L Bsktbl; Var L Socr; Var L Sftbl; High Hon Roll; NHS; St Schlr; Monroe CC; Radiological Tech.

MILLINGTON, CHRIS; Lafayette HS; Brooklyn, NY; (Y); Church Yth Grp; Band; School Musical; JV Bsktbl; High Hon Roll; Kiwanis Awd; Brooklyn Coll; TV.

MILLINGTON JR, ROBERT; Stillwater Central HS; Saratoga Spgs, NY; (Y); 5/94; Key Clb; Math Clb; Ski Clb; Yrbk Stf; Var JV Bsbl; Var L Ftbl; Wt Lftg; High Hon Roll; NHS; Stillwater Comm Schlrshp 86; Worchester Polytech; Aero Engrg.

MILLS, BARBARA; Maryvale HS; Cheektowaga, NY; (Y); Church Yth Grp; Pres Drama Clb; French Clb; SADD; Chorus; Church Choir; School Musical; School Play; Hon Roll; NHS; Acdmc Achvt Eng 85-86; Theater.

MILLS, DAVID G; Niagara Wheatfield SR HS; Niagara Falls, NY; (Y); 21/291; Math Clb; Hon Roll; NHS; Regents Schlrshp; Niagara CC; Comp.

MILLS, DAVID T; North Babylon SR HS; North Babylon, NY; (Y); 44/464; Boy Scts; Chess Clb; Computer Clb; Mathletes; Orch; Nwsp Stf; Gym; High Hon Roll; Pres Schlr; Rgnts, Lmks Schlrshps, Alpha Kappa Alpha Incntv Awd 86; SUNY Buffalo; Engrng.

MILLS, GAYON; Erasmus Hall HS; Brooklyn, NY; (Y); Drama Clb; Pep Clb; Service Clb; School Musical; Nwsp Stf; Lit Mag; Excllnc-Camping 86; NY City Tech Fash Inst; Fash.

MILLS, HEATHER; Jamesville-De Witt HS; De Witt, NY; (Y); Church Yth Grp; Cmnty Wkr; Exploring; Pres German Clb; Girl Scts; JA; Pres Trs Pep Clb; SADD; Nwsp Stf; High Hon Roll; Hon Mntn MONY Schltc Awds-Artwrk 84; 2 Gold Keys MONY Schltc Awds Artwrk 86; Frgn Lang.

MILLS, JAMES; John C Birdlebough HS; Pennellville, NY; (Y); Band; Concert Band; Jazz Band; Mrchg Band; JV Var Wrstlng; Hon Roll; Acdmc Achvt In Wrstlng 85-86; Prfct Atndnt 74-86; Mrsvl Eaton; Jrnlsm.

MILLS, JOSEPH; O Neil HS; Walton, NY; (Y); 2/112; Am Leg Boys St; Model UN; Nwsp Phtg; Yrbk Phtg; Pres Soph Cls; Var Tennis; High Hon Roll; NHS; Ntl Merit Ltr; Voice Dem Awd; Binghamton Press Edtrl Cntst 85; Hghst Avg Erth Sci 83-84; Brd Ed Awds 84-86; Optmtry.

MILLS, LAURA; Maria Regina HS; Crestwood, NY; (Y); 19/166; Church Yth Grp; Cmnty Wkr; JA; Political Wkr; Speech Tm; Church Choir; Variety Show; Nwsp Stf; Yrbk Stf; Rep Frsh Cls; Engrng.

MILLS, LIESBETH; Franklin Acad; N Bangor, NY; (Y); High Hon Roll; Hon Roll; Psychlgy.

MILLS, MARY; Heuvelton Central HS; Ogdensburg, NY; (S); 5/38; Latin Clb; Band; Color Guard; Mrchg Band; School Musical; Yrbk Stf; JV Var Cheerleading; NHS; Acadmc All-Amer 85; Natl Hstry-Govt Awd 85; Natl Ldrshp-Svc Awds 86; U Of NH; Psychlgy.

MILLS, MICHELLE; George Wingate HS; Brooklyn, NY; (Y); Church Yth Grp; Church Choir; Prfct Atten Awd; Bronz Cmnty Coll; Dntl Prfsn.

MILLS, NIKELLE; North Babylon SR HS; No Babylon, NY; (Y); 57/451; Camera Clb; Computer Clb; Intnl Clb; Spanish Clb; Chorus; Trk; Hon Roll; Jr NHS; NHS; Prfct Atten Awd; Psych.

MILLS, REBECCA; Jamesville-De Witt HS; Jamesville, NY; (Y); 81/245; Dance Clb; French Clb; Hosp Aide; JA; SADD; High Hon Roll; Hon Roll; Svc Awds 84-85; NYS Schlrshp 86; Boston U; Htl-Fd Adm.

MILLS, RONALD; Midwood HS; Brooklyn, NY; (Y); 293/589; Cmnty Wkr; Math Tm; Office Aide; Spanish Clb; Band; Chorus; Color Guard; Nwsp Stf; Yrbk Stf; Ftbl.

MILLSAPS, DENISE; Valley Central HS; Walden, NY; (Y); 21/319; Rep Jr Cls; Rep Stu Cncl; Hon Roll; NHS.

MILLSPAUGH, JOSHUA; Charles O Dickerson HS; Trumansburg, NY; (Y); 35/115; Cmnty Wkr; JV Bsbl; Var Golf; Hon Roll; Envrmntl Sci.

MILLWARD, KEVIN J; Southwestern Central HS; Jamestown, NY; (Y); Church Yth Grp; German Clb; Band; Church Choir; Mrchg Band; School Musical; Trk; Prfct Atten Awd; Christian Rock Band 86; Jamestown Comm Coll.

MILNER, DENISE; Brockport HS; Brockport, NY; (Y); 7/315; Church Yth Grp; Drama Clb; Band; School Musical; School Play; Crs Cntry; Trk; High Hon Roll; Cmnty Wkr; Concert Band; Amer Std Awd 86; Elmira Coll Key Awd 86; Musical Theatre.

MILONE III, JOSEPH; Bishop Ford CC HS; Brooklyn, NY; (Y); Mathletes; Bsbl; Bowling; Hon Roll; Holy Cathedral Schlrshp HS; Acctg.

MILOSICH, MARY; Lockawanna SR HS; Lackawanna, NY; (Y); French Clb; GAA; Syracuse U; Comm Art.

MILOT, MICHELLE; Saugerties HS; Saugerties, NY; (Y); 6/256; Am Leg Aux Girls St; French Clb; Chorus; High Hon Roll; NHS; Ntl Merit Ltr; Pres Clssrm Pgm 86; Olympcs Of Mnd-Pres Of Schl Grp 84.

MIN, JULIE ELIZABETH; East Islip HS; East Islip, NY; (Y); 1/487; Pres Band; Ed Nwsp Sprt Ed; Pres Soph Cls; Pres Jr Cls; Tennis; Cit Awd; High Hon Roll; Pres Jr NHS; Pres NHS; Spanish NHS; Empire Grls ST Attrny Genrl 86; Hugh O Brien Yth Fndtn NYS S Rep 85; Chrprsn Liaisn Cmmtee 84-87; Yale U.

MINA, TARA; Washingtonville HS; Washingtonville, NY; (Y); Cmnty Wkr; GAA; Spanish Clb; Band; JV Crs Cntry; Im Socr; Var Trk; Hon Roll; NHS; JR Olympcs Trk & Fld 84; NY ST 6th Pl Trk & Fld 85; Boston U; Bus Amdns.

MINCHILLI, ADRIANA; The Academy Of Mt St Ursula; Bronx, NY; (Y); VP Church Yth Grp; Drama Clb; Yrbk Stf; Off Jr Cls; Stu Cncl; Hon Roll; Lbrl Arts.

MINCIO, EILEEN P; Sachem HS; Holbrook, NY; (Y); 2/1376; Drama Clb; German Clb; Orch; School Musical; School Play; Symp Band; Lit Mag; Im Socr; Im Vllybl; NHS; Congress-Bundestag Yth Exchng Schlr 85; Yale U; Intl Persnl Mgmt.

MINE, LILLIENE; Liverpool HS; Liverpool, NY; (Y); AFS; Chorus; Im Vllybl; NYS Regnts Schlrshp 86; NY ST U Stonybrook; Phy Thrpy.

MINEO, MELANIE; Depew HS; Depew, NY; (Y); Cmnty Wkr; Dance Clb; GAA; Im Badmtn; Im Vllybl; Im Wt Lftg; Hon Roll; Jr NHS; NHS; Gymnst Mnth Intl Gymnst Magzn 86; Qualf Natl Rhythmc Gymnstcs 85; Rbbns & Awds Gymnstcs Comptn 83-86; Bio.

MINER, EVIE; Newfield HS; Newfield, NY; (Y); 8/50; Rep Frsh Cls; Rep Soph Cls; Rep Stu Cncl; JV Var Bowling; JV Vllybl; Hon Roll; Math Awd Hghst Avg 84-85; Acctng Awd 85-86; Tompkins Cortland CC; Accntng.

MINER II, MARVIN C; Palmyra-Macedon HS; Macedon, NY; (Y); 17/186; Church Yth Grp; Acpl Chr; Church Choir; Concert Band; Drm & Bgl; Jazz Band; Mrchg Band; Orch; Symp Band; JV Socr; NYS Schl Music Assoc All State Bdn 85; 1st NYSSMA Area All ST Orchstr 85; Rochester Partiots Drum; Juilliard Schl; Performer.

MINER, MICHELE; Liverpool HS; Liverpool, NY; (Y); 108/884; Church Yth Grp; Exploring; Var Bowling; Var Fld Hcky; JV Var Sftbl; JV Trk; Hon Roll; Jr NHS; NHS; Schlstc Achvt Awd 84; Clarkson U; Engrng.

MINER, TINA L; Afton Central Schl; Afton, NY; (Y); 5/56; 4-H; Pres FFA; Girl Scts; Library Aide; Red Cross Aide; Spanish Clb; Chorus; Capt Swmmng; Cit Awd; 4-H Awd; Dist 4 Preprd Pblc Spkng 86; Dist 4 Extmprnus Spkng 86; Cnty Dairy Prncs 86-87; Suny U Morrisville; Ag.

MINERVA, JULIA; Commack South HS; Commack, NY; (Y); Office Aide; Chorus; Stage Crew.

MINERVA, MATTHEW; Paul D Schreiber HS; Pt Washington, NY; (Y); 24/391; Church Yth Grp; Cmnty Wkr; Var Bowling; NHS; Long Isl Socl Stds Cncl Achvt Awd 84-85; Schlstc Achvt Awd Geom, Bio & Socl Stds 83-84; Engrng.

MING, CHRISTINE; St Raymond Acad; Bronx, NY; (S); 10/85; Computer Clb; Library Aide; Pep Clb; Spanish Clb; Band; Yrbk Stf; High Hon Roll; NHS; Acctnt.

MINGO, MICHELLE; Columbia HS; E Greenbush, NY; (Y); 64/417; Key Clb; Sec Sr Cls; JV Cheerleading; JV Crs Cntry; Var JV Socr; NHS; William Smith Coll; Pre Law.

MINICH, VALERIE; Frontier Central HS; Blasdell, NY; (S); 73/433; FBLA; Pep Clb; Spanish Clb; Band; Concert Band; Mrchg Band; School Musical; JV Bsktbl; JV Sftbl; Hon Roll; U Of Buffalo; Bus Mgt.

MINICOZZI, JOSEPH; Rome Catholic HS; Rome, NY; (Y); Var L Ftbl; Im Ice Hcky; Im Lcrss; Archt.

MINIELLO, JOSEPHINE; Mont Pleasant HS; Schenectady, NY; (Y); Cmnty Wkr; Ski Clb; Yrbk Phtg; Jr Cls; Sr Cls; Var Stu Cncl; Mgr(s); French Hon Soc; Hon Roll; JC Awd; Suny Coll; Socialogy.

MINIKES, HOWARD; Canarsie HS; Brooklyn, NY; (Y); Computer Clb; FBLA; Math Tm; Teachers Aide; Ntl Merit SF; Prfct Atten Awd; Bus.

MINNAUGH, ROBERT; Somers HS; Somers, NY; (Y); AFS; Intnl Clb; Var Capt Crs Cntry; JV Socr; Var Capt Trk; High Hon Roll; NHS; Spanish NHS; Safe Rides 85-86; Finance.

MINNIGH, CYNTHIA; Haverling Central HS; Bath, NY; (Y); 2/120; Church Yth Grp; French Clb; JCL; Math Clb; Band; Drm Mjr(t); Yrbk Bus Mgr; Sr Cls; Stu Cncl; Vllybl; U Of Richmond; Ecnmcs.

MINO, LISA LYNNE; Our Lady Of Mercy HS; Walworth, NY; (Y); 38/172; Cmnty Wkr; Exploring; Band; Concert Band; Sec Frsh Cls; Pres Soph Cls; Var Trk; Hon Roll; JC Awd; Kiwanis Awd; NY ST Rgnts Schlrshp Nrsng 86; Hugh Obrien Yth Fndtn Ldrshp Awd 84; SRGCL Nrsng.

MINOR, CHRISTINA L; Cardinal Mooney HS; Rochester, NY; (Y); Ski Clb; Concert Band; School Musical; Yrbk Stf; Hon Roll; NHS; Spanish NHS; Regents Schlrshp 86; Band 85-86; Lehigh U; Englsh.

MINOR, DOUGLAS; Moravia Central HS; Moravia, NY; (Y); 6/89; Am Leg Boys St; French Clb; Ski Clb; Var Trk; Vllybl; High Hon Roll; NHS; Clarkson U; Vet.

MINTZ, GREG; Mohonasen HS; Schenectady, NY; (Y); Boys Clb Am; Key Clb; Ski Clb; Rep Sr Cls; JV Var Ftbl; Ice Hcky; Trk; Stat Cit Awd; Hon Roll; JC Awd; Outstndng Svc NYS Sgt At Arms Chrmn 86; NYS Lt Gov 86; Kiwanis Schlrshp Outstndng Ctznshp 86; Buffalo U; Comp Sci.

MINTZ, KIMBERLY A; Eden SR HS; Eden, NY; (Y); 13/179; Trs AFS; Chorus; School Musical; Nwsp Ed-Chief; Nwsp Rptr; Nwsp Stf; Yrbk Stf; Im Vllybl; Hon Roll; NHS; U Of Rochester; Engl.

MINTZ, LIZ; Fayetteville-Manlius HS; Manlius, NY; (Y); Drama Clb; Spanish Clb; Sec Thesps; Chorus; School Musical; School Play; Stage Crew; Swing Chorus; Variety Show; Hon Roll; MONY Schltc Art Awds; Art Wrk Pblshd Schl Lit & Art Mag; Area All ST Vcl Chr; Bard Coll; Drama.

MINUCCI, SUSAN; Sachem HS; Ronkonkoma, NY; (Y); GAA; Rep Jr Cls; Var Crs Cntry; Var Capt Trk; Jeff Stone Mem Schrlsh P86; U Buffalo; Bio.

MINUTELLO, ROBERT; Poly Prep; Brooklyn, NY; (Y); Chess Clb; Cmnty Wkr; Computer Clb; Math Clb; Math Tm; Nwsp Ed-Chief; Var Tennis; Wt Lftg; High Hon Roll; Hon Roll; MIP Vrsty Sqush, Vrsty Ltr Sqush 86; Engr.

MINUTELLO, STACEY; East Islip HS; East Islip, NY; (Y); DECA; Office Aide; Teachers Aide; Drill Tm; Rep Stu Cncl; Comm Artist.

MIORIN, YVONNE; Keveny Mem Acad; Wynantskill, NY; (Y); 19/40; Var L Bsktbl; Var L Sftbl; Var L Vllybl; High Hon Roll; Hon Roll; Mnsgnr Mlqun Mem Awd 86; Ovrall Excllnc Physcs Awd 86; Maria Coll; Nrsng.

MIR, RASHID A; Yonkers HS; Yonkers, NY; (Y); 1/287; Pres Math Clb; Nwsp Sprt Ed; Rep Jr Cls; Trs Sr Cls; Rep Stu Cncl; JV Var Socr; Bausch & Lomb Sci Awd; High Hon Roll; Trs NHS; Val.

MIRABELLA, LAURA; Our Lady Of Mercy HS; Rochester, NY; (Y); Church Yth Grp; Model UN; Ski Clb; Church Choir; Hon Roll.

MIRABELLI, SANTINO; Hicksville HS; Hicksville, NY; (Y); Band; Chorus; Concert Band; Mrchg Band; Symp Band; Variety Show; Im Socr; Hon Roll; NHS; Prfct Atten Awd; Berkely Boston; Musc Recdg.

MIRABILE, DINA; Christ The King HS; Howard Beach, NY; (Y); 150/454; Drama Clb; Red Cross Aide; Yrbk Stf; NYU; Jrnlsm.

MIRABITO, DAVE; East Syracuse-Minoa HS; E Syracuse, NY; (Y); Cmnty Wkr; JA; JV Bsbl; Hon Roll; NHS.

MIRADOR, JOSE RAMIL P; Central Islip HS; Daly City, CA; (Y); Art Clb; Computer Clb; PAVAS; Band; Lit Mag; JV Bsbl; JV Var Ftbl; Score Keeper; JV Var Wt Lftg; JV Wrstlng; Ftbl Achvt Awd 84-85; Arch.

MIRAGLIA, AMY; Our Lady Of Mercy HS; Webster, NY; (Y); Church Yth Grp; Hosp Aide; Spanish Clb; SADD; Teachers Aide; Trk; High Hon Roll; Hon Roll; NHS; Monroe CC; Dental Hygiene.

MIRANDA, JOELLE; Cleveland Hill HS; Cheektowaga, NY; (Y); 3/110; GAA; JCL; Ski Clb; SADD; Yrbk Stf; Sec Sr Cls; Var Capt Bsktbl; Var Capt Crs Cntry; Var Capt Trk; NHS; Plc Athltc Lg Schlrshp 86; Chktwga Outstndng Yth Awd 86; Excllnc Math & Phys Educ 86; Ithaca Coll; Phys Thrpy.

MIRANDA, MICHELLE; Torrejon American HS; El Paso, TX; (Y); Church Yth Grp; ROTC; Chorus; Pres Frsh Cls; Pres Soph Cls; Pres Jr Cls; Sec Sr Cls; Var Capt Cheerleading; Pom Pon; Sftbl; Pell Grant; U El Paso; Bus Mgmt.

MIRANTE, TOM; Albertus Magnus HS; Garnerville, NY; (Y); Church Yth Grp; Var Bsbl; Var Bsktbl; Math Hon & Hon Roll & All Star Bsbll; All Star Cnty Champs; All Conf Bsbll Var; Bus.

MIRGUET, PETER S; Greece Athena HS; Rochester, NY; (Y); 19/290; VP DECA; Math Tm; Ski Clb; Rep Stu Cncl; JV Var Golf; JV Socr; Im Vllybl; High Hon Roll; Hon Roll; NHS; Dayton & Regents Schlrshp 86; VA Tech; Bus Admin.

MIRJAH, KAREN; Longwood HS; Coram, NY; (Y); Dance Clb; Yrbk Stf; Stu Cncl; Cheerleading; High Hon Roll; Hon Roll; Hotel Mgmt.

MIRLIS, ERIC; Kings Park HS; Kings Park, NY; (Y); 20/422; Mathletes; Math Clb; Math Tm; Scholastic Bowl; Science Clb; Spanish Clb; High Hon Roll; Wnr Schl Sfflk Cnty Math Assoc Cntst 85-86; Bus Adm.

MIRON, LISA J; Jamesville-Dewitt HS; Jamesville, NY; (Y); 25/250; Cmnty Wkr; Model UN; Spanish Clb; Chorus; School Musical; Stage Crew; Swing Chorus; High Hon Roll; Hon Roll; Trs NHS; NY ST Yng Amer Natl Show Choir Comp 86; Bates Coll.

MIRONOFF, YURI; Sheepshead Bay HS; Brooklyn, NY; (Y); 40/439; Chess Clb; Computer Clb; French Clb; Latin Clb; Radio Clb; Bsktbl; Ice Hcky; Socr; Cit Awd; Albany U; Cmptr Prgrmng.

MIROSLAIGA, URAM; Yonkers HS; Yonkers, NY; (Y); High Hon Roll; Hon Roll; West Chester CC; Nrsg.

MIRSKY, MARK; Ossining HS; Ossining, NY; (Y); 13/255; Model UN; Nwsp Stf; Yrbk Stf; Var Bsktbl; Var Lcrss; Var Socr; NHS; High Hon Roll; Rgnts Schlrshp 86; Middlebury Coll.

MIRUCKI, MOLLY T; Fayetteville-Manlius HS; Fayetteville, NY; (Y); Church Yth Grp; JCL; SADD; Chorus; Variety Show; Yrbk Stf; Lit Mag; JV Socr; Cit Awd; High Hon Roll; Pres Acad Ftns Awd 86; Intr Design.

MIRVILLE, FRITZ G; Prospect Heights HS; Brooklyn, NY; (S); Off Sr Cls; Bsktbl; Socr; Vllybl; Wt Lftg; Hon Roll; Arista Stdts Socty 85; Elctrnc Tech Engrng.

MIRZA, SAMIRA; New Rochelle HS; New Rochelle, NY; (Y); Debate Tm; PAVAS; Thesps; School Play; Nwsp Rptr; Yrbk Phtg; Rep Stu Cncl; Var Swmmng; DAR Awd; Hon Roll; Med.

MISENCIK, JOHN C; Owen D Young HS; Mohawk, NY; (Y); 10/21; Ski Clb; VICA; Bsktbl; Bowling; Ftbl; Socr; Hon Roll; Morrisville Ag & Tech; Ag Mech.

MISENO, ANGELINA; Amsterdam HS; Amsterdam, NY; (Y); Band; Concert Band; Jazz Band; Mrchg Band; Symp Band; Rep Frsh Cls; Rep Soph Cls; Bowling; Hon Roll; Fulton-Montgomery CC; Jrnlsm.

MISENO, NICHOLAS; Amsterdam HS; Amsterdam, NY; (Y); Thesps; School Play; Bowling; Golf; Hon Roll; All-Cnty Schlrshp 86; Amsterdm Tchrs Assn Schlrshp 86; William Anninger Schlrshp 86; Tulton; Math.

MISIASZEK, MICHELE; Whitesboro SR HS; Whitesboro, NY; (Y); 49/306; Pres Trs GAA; Acpl Chr; Yrbk Sprt Ed; Yrbk Stf; Rep Jr Cls; Rep Stu Cncl; Fld Hcky; Trk; Vllybl; Hon Roll; Pre-Law.

MISITA JR, ROBERT M; East Islip HS; East Islip, NY; (Y); 8/425; Math Tm; SADD; Im Sftbl; Var Tennis; High Hon Roll; Jr NHS; NHS; Hon Roll; St Schlr; Grumman Schlrshp Wnnr 86-90; Exchng Amblnc Islips Vlntr; Islip Swm Clb 76-85; U Of Rochester; Sci.

MISKA, STEVEN M; Greenport HS; Greenport, NY; (Y); #3 In Class; Ski Clb; Spanish Clb; Nwsp Rptr; Pres Stu Cncl; Var L Golf; High Hon Roll; NHS; Ntl Merit Ltr; St Schlr; USMA West Point.

MISKANIN, MICHELLE; Ballston Spa SR HS; Ballston Spa, NY; (Y); 15/244; Band; Mrchg Band; Yrbk Stf; Stat Socr; High Hon Roll; Merit And Ldrshp Assc Awd 85; Pres Acadmc Ftns Awd 86; Regnts Schlrshp 86; Colgate U; Math.

MISSANA, MARK; Burnt Hills Ballston Lake HS; Scotia, NY; (Y); Computer Clb; Key Clb; Math Tm; High Hon Roll; NHS; Pre Law.

MISSON, JACKIE; Connetquot HS; Ronkonkoma, NY; (Y); 16/690; Boy Scts; Cmnty Wkr; Band; Mrchg Band; Yrbk Stf; High Hon Roll; NHS; Pres Schlr; Schltc Aptitude Schlrshp 86; Harry S Kaloneck Memrl Schlrshp 86; Town Of Islip Ctznshp Ldrshp Awd 83; Dowling Coll; Acctg.

MISSON, JACQUELINE; Connetquot HS; Ronkonkoma, NY; (S); 16/689; Cmnty Wkr; Math Tm; Mrchg Band; Orch; Yrbk Stf; Fld Hcky; Socr; Cit Awd; Jr NHS; NHS; Humanism Awd 82; Acad All-Amer 84; Dowling Coll Oakdale; CPA.

MISTERKIEWICZ, MARK; Trott Voc; Niagara Falls, NY; (Y); Var Socr; Var Swmmng; Im Vllybl; IN Inst Tech; Comp Sys.

MITCHELL, ANNMARIE; St John The Baptist HS; Oakdale, NY; (Y); 24/546; Hosp Aide; Model UN; SADD; Nwsp Stf; Yrbk Stf; Cheerleading; High Hon Roll; NHS; Spanish NHS; Outstndng Achvt Eng & Soc Stud 85; Ldrshp Awd 86; Natl Eng Merit Awd 86; Boston Coll.

MITCHELL, DANIEL; Alfred-Almond Central HS; Almond, NY; (Y); VP JA; Pres Trs JCL; Yrbk Bus Mgr; Trs Soph Cls; Trs Sr Cls; JV Bsbl; Var Socr; Var Trk; Var Wrstlng; High Hon Roll; SCNDRY Educ.

MITCHELL, DAVID; Newburgh Free Acad; Newburgh, NY; (Y); 28/651; Spanish Clb; Yrbk Stf; Var Crs Cntry; Var Capt Trk; Jr NHS; NHS; Ntl Merit SF; Spanish NHS; Schlr Athle Of Yr Male 86; Regents Schlrshp Wnnr; U S Naval Acad.

MITCHELL, HOLLY; Skaneateles HS; Skaneateles, NY; (Y); 23/148; 4-H; 4-H Awd; Model UN; High Hon Roll; Hon Roll; Jr NHS; NHS; NY ST Hereford Qn 84-85; Cobleskill Ag & Tech; Anml Hsbn.

MITCHELL, JENNIFER; Pioneer Central HS; Yorkshire, NY; (Y); Trs Church Yth Grp; 4-H; Latin Clb; Church Choir; Orch; Rep Jr Cls; Rep Stu Cncl; High Hon Roll; Hon Roll; NHS; Roberts Wesleyan Coll; Elem Ed.

MITCHELL, JOANNE; Tottenville HS; Staten Island, NY; (Y); 115/850; Camera Clb; GAA; Keywanettes; Ski Clb; Band; Mrchg Band; School Musical; Nwsp Stf; Yrbk Stf; Lit Mag; NYS Regent Scholar 86; ST U Albany; Phrmcst.

MITCHELL, JOEY; Northern Adirondeck Central Schl; Altona, NY; (Y); Church Yth Grp; Ski Clb; Band; Concert Band; Mrchg Band; Orch; JV Bsbl; Var Bsktbl; Golf; Var Socr; Eastern Nazarene Coll; Music.

MITCHELL, JOY; Ward Melville HS; Stony Brook, NY; (Y); Nwsp Rptr; Nwsp Stf; Yrbk Stf; JV CAP5; Var Trk; Var Vllybl; Hon Roll; Vrsty Achvt Awd 86; Jrnlsm.

MITCHELL, KAREN; Town Of Webb HS; Old Forge, NY; (Y); Sec Trs French Clb; SADD; Varsity Clb; Yrbk Stf; Lit Mag; Bsktbl; Socr; Tennis; Trk; Vllybl; Regents Schlrshp 86; My Holyoke Coll.

MITCHELL, KIAH; Harry S Truman HS; Bronx, NY; (Y); 64/496; Dance Clb; Drama Clb; Service Clb; Chorus; School Play; Var Swmmng; Var Trk; High Hon Roll; NHS; Prfct Atten Awd; Lwyr.

MITCHELL, LORELEI B; Tappan Zee HS; Sparkill, NY; (Y); 4/254; SADD; Ed Nwsp Stf; Yrbk Stf; Lit Mag; NHS; Ntl Merit Spcl Schlrshp 86; Outstndng Stu In Amer Hstry 86; NY ST Rgnts Schlrshp 86; Swrthmr Coll.

MITCHELL, MARSHA; Keshequa Central HS; Nunda, NY; (Y); AFS; Pres Key Clb; Chorus; Stage Crew; Stat Bsktbl; Score Keeper; Prfct Atten Awd; Rotary Awd; Miss Nunda 83-86; Voted Bst Prsnlty 84-85; SUNY Fredonia; Accntng.

MITCHELL, MICHELE; Erasmus Hall HS; Brooklyn, NY; (Y); Church Yth Grp; Chorus; Hon Roll; Baruch Cmnty Coll; Bus.

MITCHELL, PATRICK; Nottingham HS; Syracuse, NY; (Y); 13/330; Latin Clb; Golf; Hon Roll; NHS; Spanish NHS; 1st Pl Gld Natl Latn Exm 84-85; 2nd Pl Slvr Natl Latn Exm 86; Math.

MITCHELL, STEPHANIE; Holy Trinity HS; Westbury, NY; (Y); Computer Clb; Dance Clb; French Clb; Math Clb; Math Tm; Stage Crew; Yrbk Stf; Stu Cncl; Hon Roll; Mu Alp Tht; MI ST U; Acctng.

MITCHELL, STEPHEN M; Mt St Michael Acad; Bronx, NY; (Y); 59/292; Church Yth Grp; Im Bsktbl; JV Crs Cntry; JV Var Trk; High Hon Roll; Hon Roll; Macedonia Baptst Chrch Anie L Nixon Meml Schlrshp 86; PA ST U Block Incntv Grnt 86; PA ST U; Bus Adm.

MITCHELL, WILLIE; Henninger HS; Syracuse, NY; (Y); JV Bsktbl; Var Ftbl; Var Trk; Hon Roll; Crnll Awd Outstndng Male Athlt 85-86; Arch.

MITEK, SCOTT; Walt Whitman HS; Huntington Statio, NY; (Y); Rep Jr Cls; Trs Sr Cls; JV Var Bsktbl; JV Lcrss; JV Var Socr; Pres Phy Ftnss Awd 85; Bus.

MITIL, ROBERTO; Dewitt Clinton HS; Bronx, NY; (Y); 29/287; Key Clb; Ftbl; Trk; Capt Wrstlng; Prfct Atten Awd; Camera Clb; Church Yth Grp; Latin Clb; Varsity Clb; Nwsp Phtg; All-City Wrstlr/Brnx NY City All-City Ftbll/Athlete Of The Yr 86; Kent ST; Bus Mgt.

MITNIK, ALEX; John Dewey HS; Brooklyn, NY; (Y); Art Clb; Chess Clb; Computer Clb; Intnl Clb; JV Bsbl; Bsktbl; Var Bowling; Ftbl; Socr; JV Sftbl; Stony Brook; Comp Engrng.

MITOLA, DANIEL; Islip HS; Islip, NY; (Y); 8/226; Pres Band; Pres Chorus; Nwsp Stf; Yrbk Stf; Trs Jr Cls; Capt Crs Cntry; Capt Trk; High Hon Roll; Jr NHS; Pres NHS; Ray Hackney Schlrshp 86; Regnts Schlrshp 86; NHS Schlrshp 86; SUNY At Albany; Pre-Law.

MITRZYK, FELICIA; Unatego JR SR HS; Unadilla, NY; (Y); Color Guard.

MITTAK, MICHELINE M; Newark SR HS; Newark, NY; (Y); 2/201; Sec 4-H; Ski Clb; VP FTA; Jazz Band; Nwsp Rptr; JV Tennis; French Hon Soc; High Hon Roll; NHS; Sal; Stu Of Yr 84-85; Lions Clb Schlrshp 86; Regnts Schlrshp 85-86; Cornell U; Marn Biol.

MITTLEMAN, MARJORIE; Holy Trinity HS; Hicksville, NY; (S); 26/403; Drama Clb; Math Clb; Band; School Musical; Nwsp Rptr; Gym; Hon Roll; NEDT Awd; Pre-Law.

MITTUCH, MELINDA; Minisink Valley HS; Westtown, NY; (Y); Church Yth Grp; Pres Key Clb; Band; Church Choir; Concert Band; Jazz Band; Mrchg Band; Hon Roll.

MIX, MOLLY; Maryvale HS; Cheektowaga, NY; (Y); 18/310; Church Yth Grp; French Clb; Pres GAA; Chorus; Im Socr; Im Tennis; Im Vllybl; Hon Roll; NHS; Pres Schlr; ST U NY Buffalo; Pharm.

MLYNAR, JOHN P; Luons JR & SR HS; Lyons, NY; (Y); 10/100; Boy Scts; Science Clb; Ski Clb; Band; Jazz Band; Mrchg Band; School Musical; Hon Roll; NHS; Prfct Atten Awd; Regnts Schlrshp 86; NYS Fredonia; Engr.

MOAK, KRIS; Ravena-Coeymans-Selkirk HS; Ravena, NY; (Y); 7/180; Drama Clb; FBLA; Chorus; School Play; Yrbk Stf; Stu Cncl; JV Vllybl; Stat Wrstlng; High Hon Roll; NHS; Mem Radiology Schl; Ultrsound.

MOAKLEY, JOHN; Tottenville HS; Staten Island, NY; (S); 23/850; Scholastic Bowl; Spanish Clb; Teachers Aide; Concert Band; School Musical; High Hon Roll; Jr NHS; Spanish NHS; Sci Fair 85; Phy Sci.

MOCK, DAMON F; Westbury SR HS; Westbury, NY; (Y); 30/250; Camera Clb; Cmnty Wkr; Capt Debate Tm; Library Aide; Speech Tm; SADD; Concert Band; Orch; Nwsp Ed-Chief; Yrbk Bus Mgr; Lng Islnd Rcrtn Prk & Seisure Assoc Yth Achvt Awd 84-85; Van Son Holland Ink Corp Schlrshp 85-86; Columbia Coll; Prnt Jrnlsm.

MOCK, MICHELLE; Galway HS; Amsterdam, NY; (Y); GAA; Office Aide; SADD; Varsity Clb; Color Guard; Yrbk Stf; Var Cheerleading; Hon Roll; Prfct Atten Awd; Bus.

MODAFFERI, MARIA; Albertus Magnus HS; New City, NY; (Y); Exploring; Girl Scts; Service Clb; Varsity Clb; School Play; JV Var Cheerleading; Italian Amrcn Schlrshp, Beaver Coll Schlrshp 86; Beaver Coll; Phys Thrpy.

MODI, LINA; Cicero North Syracuse HS; Clay, NY; (S); 25/640; Exploring; Hosp Aide; Ski Clb; Orch; Hon Roll; Engrng.

MODICA, EDWARD; Christ The King HS; Ozone Park, NY; (Y); 25/454; Art Clb; Boy Scts; Var Capt Bowling; Hon Roll; NHS; Arch.

MODUGNO, ROBERT; Anthony A Henninger HS; Syracuse, NY; (Y); Church Yth Grp; Computer Clb; JA; SADD; School Play; Nwsp Rptr; Nwsp Stf; JV Lcrss; JV Wrstlng; Bio.

MOENS, ANTHONY; Perry Central HS; Pavilion, NY; (Y); VP 4-H; Pres FFA; Cit Awd; Hon Roll; NHS; Schlstc Achvt Awd Ag Bus Sci 86; ST Farmer Degree FFA 86; Acadmc Achvt Awd Comp Literacy 86; Ag.

MOFFETT, ERIC; Cicero-North Syracuse HS; Liverpool, NY; (S); 92/867; Boy Scts; Chess Clb; Exploring; NHS; Ntl Merit Ltr; Chess Tm Awds Cpt 84-85; Elec Engrng.

MOFFITT, CHRIS; Riverhead HS; South Jamesport, NY; (Y); Art Clb; Latin Clb; Band; Yrbk Phtg; Bsktbl; Sftbl; Jr NHS; Cmmrcl Art.

MOFFITT II, THOMAS J; N Babylon SR HS; N Babylon, NY; (Y); 41/467; Yrbk Stf; Im Capt Bowling; Jr NHS; Chess Clb; Teachers Aide; JV Bsbl; High Hon Roll; Hon Roll; Itln Hnr Soc 85; Frnch/Itln Grp 84; St Johns U; Bus Admin.

MOGELEFSKY, SANDY; South Shore HS; Brooklyn, NY; (Y); Concert Band; Pep Band; Pom Pon.

MOGLIA, CRISTINA; St Marys Girls HS; Douglaston, NY; (Y); Pres Camera Clb; Sec Exploring; French Clb; Ski Clb; Ed Nwsp Ed-Chief; Nwsp Phtg; Nwsp Rptr; Nwsp Stf; Off Stu Cncl; Psych.

MOGLIA, ROSE ANGELICA; Christopher Columbus HS; Bronx, NY; (Y); 44/691; Dance Clb; Drama Clb; Office Aide; Service Clb; Chorus; School Musical; School Play; Variety Show; Lit Mag; Spanish Awd Level II; Engl Awd-Speech-Byasst Princpl; Iona Coll; Psych.

MOGRO, PATRICIA; Niskayuna HS; Schenectady, NY; (Y); Pres Church Yth Grp; Pres FBLA; Spanish Clb; Var Gym; JV Trk; Hon Roll; FBLA Comptn 1st Pl-Bus Grphcs 86; 1st Pl-Cptl Dist Ind Arts Assn Of Archtctrl Plns Of House 85; Fairfield U; Mktng.

MOHAN, BERNIE; Frontier HS; Hamburg, NY; (Y); 15/450; German Clb; Math Clb; Quiz Bowl; Scholastic Bowl; SADD; Varsity Clb; JV Capt Badmtn; Var JV Bsbl; Var JV Bowling; Var JV Coach Actv; CPA.

MOHAWK, AMY; Gowanda Central HS; Gowanda, NY; (Y); #6 In Class; French Clb; Nwsp Stf; Trs Stu Cncl; High Hon Roll; Hon Roll; NHS; Seneca Nat Acdmc Excllnc Awd 83-86; Ed Awd In Art 83; Ad-Craft Cmpttn 2nd Pl & Hon Ment Awd 83&86; Syracuse U; Engrng.

MOHR, ANDREW; Hamburg SR HS; Hamburg, NY; (Y); Church Yth Grp; Radio Clb; SADD; Band; Church Choir; Madrigals; Mrchg Band; School Musical; School Play; Free Trip To Grmny Flm Assoc Of Grmn Tchrs 86; 2nd Pl ST Comp Piano 84.

MOHR, BRENDA; South Side HS; Rockville Centre, NY; (Y); JV Var Socr; Hon Roll; JV Sftbl; Var Trk; MVP Sccr 83 & 84; Hstlr Awd 85; Accntng.

MOHR, DAVID J; Arlington HS; Poughkeepsie, NY; (Y); Church Yth Grp; Drama Clb; Band; Church Choir; Concert Band; Orch; Symp Band; Yrbk Phtg; Kings Coll; Psych.

MOHR, VICKI; Lake Placid Central HS; Fort Lauderdale, FL; (Y); High Hon Roll; Hon Roll; Princeton; Advertising.

MOHRMANN, MARK; Commack HS South; Commack, NY; (Y); 18/375; Cmnty Wkr; Mathletes; Math Tm; VP Temple Yth Grp; Nwsp Stf; Yrbk Stf; High Hon Roll; NHS; Ntl Merit SF; Humntrn Svc Awd 84; Vtd Tm MVP 84-85; Deck Hcky Plyoffs 84-85; Psych.

MOIDEEN, YASMINE; The Bronx HS Of Sci; Bayside, NY; (Y); Hosp Aide; Yrbk Stf; U Of MI Ann Arbor; Psych.

MOISE, SANDRA; Northeastern Acad; Brooklyn, NY; (Y); French Clb; Spanish Clb; Color Guard; Sftbl; Hon Roll; Spanish NHS; Phys Ed Awd 86; Geog Awd 85; Engl Awd 84; Nrsngl.

MOJICA, HILDA; St John The Baptist HS; Brentwood, NY; (Y); JA; Spanish Clb; Chorus; Church Choir; Yrbk Stf; Cit Awd; Hon Roll; Spanish NHS; Physcl Ftns Awd 81; Cert Of Awd Sci Fair 81-83; Psych.

MOJICA, LOURDES; John Jay HS; Brooklyn, NY; (Y); Drama Clb; Hosp Aide; School Musical; School Play; Variety Show; Nwsp Rptr; Lit Mag; Cheerleading; Hon Roll; Altrntv Pgm Dist 15 Awd 84; Outstndng Spnsh Awd 85; Hunter; Nrsng.

MOJICA, NANCY P; Stella Maris HS; Far Rockaway, NY; (Y); 18/211; Art Clb; Library Aide; Chorus; Yrbk Stf; Hon Roll; Val; Acad All Amer Schlr Prog 86; St Josephs Coll Medaille Full Schlrshp 86; Milton Silverman Schlrshp 86; St Joseph Coll; Bus Admin.

MOK, ANNE; HS For The Humanits; New York, NY; (Y); JA; Varsity Clb; Var L Trk; Var L Vllybl; Hon Roll; NHS; Vllybll Cty Chmp Mdl 85-86; Cert In Spnsh; Rutgers U; Phrmcy.

MOK, TAK K; Seward Park HS; Brooklyn, NY; (Y); 4/544; Computer Clb; Teachers Aide; Variety Show; Swmmng; NHS; Rgnts Schlrshp 86; Pres Chinese Culture Clb 85-86; Polytechnic U; Elec Engrng.

MOLDENHAUER, SHERYL; Fairport HS; Fairport, NY; (Y); Church Yth Grp; Trs German Clb; Girl Scts; Intnl Clb; SADD; Varsity Clb; Capt Trk; Hon Roll; NHS; Rgnts Schlrshp 86; Prsdntl Schlrshp Wstmnstr Coll 86; Bnghmtn SUNY.

MOLEA, ANTHONY J; Iona Prep; New Rochelle, NY; (Y); 2/204; Math Tm; NFL; Stage Crew; Im Bowling; Im Ftbl; High Hon Roll; Pres NHS; Prfct Atten Awd; Relgs Educ Tr St Pius X Schl Scarsdl 86-87; Cochd Sftbl, Bsktgbl St Pius X 84-85.

MOLENDA, JANICE; Jamesville-Dewitt HS; Dewitt, NY; (Y); Church Yth Grp; Cmnty Wkr; Hosp Aide; Key Clb; High Hon Roll; NHS; :Soc Scis.

MOLESWORTH, KEITH; Onondaga Central HS; Syracuse, NY; (S); Exploring; Quiz Bowl; Spanish Clb; Yrbk Phtg; Yrbk Stf; Capt VP Bsbl; VP Bsktbl; High Hon Roll; NHS; RIT; Photogrphy.

MOLESWORTH, KELLY JEAN; Onondaga Central HS; Syracuse, NY; (S); GAA; Spanish Clb; SADD; Chorus; Concert Band; Jazz Band; Sftbl; Vllybl; High Hon Roll; NHS; SUNY Oswego; Elem Ed.

MOLINARI, LORI; Greece Athena HS; Rochester, NY; (Y); SADD; Hon Roll; Outstndng Clthng Stu Awd 86.

MOLINELLI, KIM; Tottenville HS; Staten Island, NY; (Y); 59/850; Girl Scts; Key Clb; Scholastic Bowl; Ski Clb; School Musical; Yrbk Ed-Chief; Stu Cncl; NHS.

MOLINO, JOHN; Canisius HS; Lancaster, NY; (Y); Ski Clb; Spanish Clb; Var JV Bsbl; Var Diving; Var JV Ftbl; Var Swmmng; Spanish NHS; 1st Pl Open Clsscl Orgn-Kpplr Keybrd Fstvl 84; Bus Adm.

MOLKWYN, ANIWETA; Rice HS; New York, NY; (Y); Boy Scts; Church Yth Grp; Science Clb; School Musical; Nwsp Ed-Chief; Im Mgr Bsktbl; Crs Cntry; Score Keeper; Trk; High Hon Roll; Squire Crcl Chf 86; Howard; Pre-Law.

MOLL, DAVID; Victor Central HS; Victor, NY; (Y); Cmnty Wkr; Red Cross Aide; Ski Clb; Varsity Clb; Stu Cncl; Im JV Bsktbl; Var JV Ftbl; JV Trk; Hon Roll; Bristol Mountain Ntl Ski Patrol 85-86; Civil Engr.

MOLLENKOPF, CRISTINA M; St Francis Prep; Flushing, NY; (S); 13/744; Hosp Aide; Library Aide; Chorus; Church Choir; NHS; Vet Med.

MOLLER, CARYN I; Centereach HS; Selden, NY; (Y); 44/429; Nwsp Rptr; Nwsp Stf; Yrbk Rptr; Yrbk Stf; Hon Roll; Bus Stu Of Mnth 86; NYS Rgnts Schlrshp 86; Stonybrook U; Econ.

MOLLER, PAUL; Whitesboro SR HS; Whitesboro, NY; (Y); 6/306; 4-H; Service Clb; Varsity Clb; L Var Ftbl; Im Trk; High Hon Roll; Hon Roll; NHS.

MOLLO, CATHY; Sayville HS; W Sayville, NY; (Y); 38/350; Key Clb; Band; High Hon Roll; Hon Roll; NHS; Suffolk CC; Elem Educ.

MOLLO, DINA M; St Francis Preparatory HS; Fresh Meadows, NY; (S); 173/653; Drama Clb; School Musical; Stage Crew; Lit Mag; Hon Roll; Creative Wrtng Mdl; Schl Ltr Drama; Theatre.

MOLLOT, STEPHEN; Williamsville South HS; Williamsville, NY; (Y); SADD; Temple Yth Grp; Band; Var Golf; Var Swmmng; Var Tennis; Hon Roll; U Buffalo; Law.

MOLLOY, DEBRA; St Francis Prep; Little Neck, NY; (Y); 236/653; Var JV Sftbl; Retrt Ldr; Fordham U; Lwyr.

MOLLOY, DEIRDRE D; Rye HS; Rye, NY; (Y); 27/183; Hosp Aide; Keywanettes; SADD; High Hon Roll; Hon Roll; NYS Regnts Schlrshp 86; Loyola Coll MD; Bus Econs.

MOLLUSO, LISA; St John The Baptist HS; Patchogue, NY; (Y); School Play; Stage Crew; Var Tennis; Hon Roll.

MOLLY, R DENNIS; T R Proctor HS; Utica, NY; (Y); Am Leg Boys St; Camera Clb; Computer Clb; School Play; Hon Roll; Gftd & Tlntd Stu Smmr Pgm 86; Comp Engrng.

MOLNAR, WENDY; Alden Central HS; Alden, NY; (Y); Aud/Vis; Spanish Clb; SADD; Drill Tm; Erie CC; Crimnl Invstgtn.

MOLNER, NANCY; Holy Trinity HS; Seaford, NY; (S); 9/313; French Clb; Ski Clb; Teachers Aide; Band; Stage Crew; French Hon Soc; High Hon Roll; NHS; Al-Amer Hll Fm Band Awd 85; Long Islnd Music Tchrs Fstvl-Won 3 Gld Mdls 82-84; 1st Pl Sailng Race 83.

MOLONEY, TARA; Westhampton Beach HS; Southampton, NY; (Y); 18/261; Latin Clb; SADD; Chorus; Drill Tm; Variety Show; Lit Mag; High Hon Roll; Hon Roll; NHS; Pltcl Sci.

MOMANO, KRISTIN; Greece Olympia HS; Rochester, NY; (Y); FBLA; Sftbl.

MONACHINO, JENNIFER L; Pelham Memorial HS; Pelham Manor, NY; (Y); Church Yth Grp; French Clb; JA; Model UN; Church Choir; Nwsp Rptr; Tennis; High Hon Roll; Hon Roll; NHS; All Dvsn Hnrs/Tnns 84-86; 85 NY Athltc Clb Tnns Coaches Awd 85; Yng Athrs Conf At Marymount Coll 85; Law.

MONACO, CAROLYN T; St Francis Pre; Floral Park, NY; (S); Band; Nwsp Rptr; Bsktbl; Hon Roll; NHS; Stonybrook Coll; Phy.

MONACO, DAVID; Gouverneur HS; Gouverneur, NY; (Y); Varsity Clb; Im Capt Bowling; Var L Golf; JV Var Socr; High Hon Roll; Hon Roll; Jr NHS; NHS; Outstndng Spnsh Awd 83-84; SUNY Oswego; Phy Thrpy.

MONACO, HELEN; Tappan Zee HS; Blauvelt, NY; (Y); Pres JA; Nwsp Stf; Lit Mag; Wnnr JA Pres Yr Awd 86; Pres Culinary Arts Club 84-86; Econ.

MONACO, KEITH DWIGHT; Hampton Bays HS; Hampton Bays, NY; (Y); Church Yth Grp; Band; Concert Band; Jazz Band; Mrchg Band; Rep Stu Cncl; Hon Roll; NYSMA Awd Band 86; Bus.

MONAGHAN, AMY; Lindenhurst HS; Lindenhurst, NY; (Y); 26/640; Cmnty Wkr; Drama Clb; French Clb; Thesps; Orch; School Musical; School Play; Variety Show; Nwsp Ed-Chief; Rep Frsh Cls; Stu Mth 85; Stu Yr 86; SUNY Binghamton; Intl Crrspndt.

MONAGHAN, MAUREEN E; Nazareth Acad; Rochester, NY; (Y); 22/142; Drama Clb; Library Aide; Chorus; School Musical; Swing Chorus; Hon Roll; NHS; NYS Rgnts Schlrshp Wnr 86; St Lawrnc U Schlrshp 86; St Lawrence U; Math.

MONAGHAN, MICHAEL; Archbishop Molloy HS; Little Neck, NY; (Y); 2/383; Church Yth Grp; Pep Clb; Science Clb; SADD; Acpl Chr; Ed Lit Mag; Score Keeper; NHS; Lttlnck-Dglstn Amblnce Crps 85-86; Mchncl Engnrng.

MONAHAN, DANIEL; Greece Olympia HS; Rochester, NY; (Y); Ski Clb; Varsity Clb; Var Ftbl; JV Trk; Wt Lftg.

MONAHAN, DANIEL; La Salle Military Acad; College Pt, NY; (Y); 25/87; Art Clb; Camera Clb; ROTC; SADD; Drm & Bgl; Stage Crew; JV Ftbl; JV Swmmng; Var Trk; NHS; Slvr Hnrs 84-86; Mech Engrng.

MONAHAN, ELAINE; West Islip HS; W Islip, NY; (Y); Drama Clb; Orch; School Musical; School Play; High Hon Roll; Hon Roll; NHS; Soc Studys & Earl Sci Excel 86; Cert Of Accmplshmnts Soc Studys 84-85; Spcl Accmplshmnts Awd 85 & 86.

MONAHAN, LEANNE; Curtis HS; Staten Island, NY; (Y); 25/350; GAA; Band; Yrbk Rptr; Cheerleading; L Var Gym; Socr; Var L Vllybl; High Hon Roll; Hon Roll; Phys Thrpy.

MONAHAN, RAYMOND; Valley Stream North HS; Franklin Sq, NY; (Y); 10/128; Chess Clb; Computer Clb; Debate Tm; Drama Clb; Mathletes; NFL; Office Aide; Quiz Bowl; Spanish Clb; SADD; Soc Stud Dept Awd 86; PTA Schlrshp 86; Debate Bst Public Spkr Awd 85; Boston U.

MONASSERI, ANTHONY; Monsignor Farrell HS; Staten Island, NY; (Y); Church Yth Grp; Cmnty Wkr; Spanish Clb; Pres Jr Cls; Im Bowling; Im Ftbl; Hon Roll; 2nd Pl Borough Sci Fair Wnr 83; 1st Pl Schl Sci Fair 82 & 83; Elec Engrg.

MONASTERO, KELLYANNE; North Babylon SR HS; N Babylon, NY; (Y); 48/500; Cmnty Wkr; Spanish Clb; SADD; Nwsp Stf; Yrbk Stf; Lit Mag; Stu Cncl; JV Sftbl; Jr NHS; NHS; Journlsm.

MONCRIEFFE, CARLENE; H C Technical HS; Buffalo, NY; (Y); Natl Beta Clb; Band; Concert Band; Jazz Band; Hon Roll; Comp Sci.

MONDRICK, PATTY; Mexico Academy & Central; Oswego, NY; (Y); German Clb; Intnl Clb; Ski Clb; Spanish Clb; Yrbk Stf; Var Trk; Hon Roll; German Ntl Hnr Soc 85-86; Awds German,Spnsh 83-86; Lang.

MONDSCHEIN, ROBERT; Herricks HS; Roslyn, NY; (Y); Band; Bsktbl; Ftbl; Lcrss; NHS; Phys.

MONER, MILAGROS; Adlai E Stevenson HS; Bronx, NY; (Y); Cmnty Wkr; Library Aide; Teachers Aide; Chorus; Lit Mag; Im Bowling; Var Socr; NHS; Prfct Atten Awd; Achvt Leag 86; Bio Sci.

MONETTE, BRENDA; Northeastern Clinton Central HS; Champlain, NY; (Y); Art Clb; Church Yth Grp; Teachers Aide; Band; Church Choir; Yrbk Stf; Bsbl; Bsktbl; Socr; Hon Roll; North County CC; Health Asstn.

MONGIN, MICHAEL; Johnstown HS; Johnstown, NY; (Y); 10/200; Am Leg Boys St; Nwsp Stf; VP Sr Cls; Var L Bsktbl; Var L Trk; High Hon Roll; NHS; Pre-Law.

MONIE JR, WILLIS; Cooperstown Central HS; Cooperstown, NY; (Y); 20/100; Math Tm; Var Capt Bsktbl; Var Coach Actv; Hon Roll; NHS; Church Yth Grp; Debate Tm; Varsity Clb; Im Score Keeper; JV Trk; RPI.

MONISERA, ANDREA; Port Jervis HS; Sparrowbush, NY; (Y); 9/180; Varsity Clb; Var JV Socr; SUNY; Bio-Chem.

MONKS JR, JOSEPH; Elmont Memorial HS; Valley Stream, NY; (Y); 56/245; Cmnty Wkr; Hst FBLA; Pres Science Clb; Orch; School Play; Nwsp Rptr; Socr; NHS; Aud/Vis; DECA; Fordham U; Law.

MONNO, PATRICIA; Dominican Commercial HS; Flushing, NY; (Y); 57/288; Drama Clb; Chorus; School Musical; School Play; Hon Roll; NHS; St Johns U; Acctg.

MONOPOLI, CARL; Fairport HS; Fairport, NY; (Y); Art Clb; Church Yth Grp; Computer Clb; Exploring; Lit Mag; Socr; Trk; Wrstlng; Hon Roll; Schltc Art Awd 86; Dodge Gallery Awd 86.

MONROE, DORIE; Schuylerville Central HS; Gansevoort, NY; (Y); 1/85; VP French Clb; Math Tm; SADD; Band; Bsktbl; High Hon Roll; Hon Roll; NHS; Val; Awd For Highest Avg 84; Seton Hall Acadmc Schlrshp 86; Seton Hall U; Bio.

MONROE, JAMES; Minisink Valley HS; Middletown, NY; (Y); Drama Clb; Varsity Clb; Chorus; School Play; JV Var Ftbl; Var Trk; Sec Frsh Cls; Sec Soph Cls; Rep Jr Cls; Rep Stu Cncl.

MONROE, JASEN; Charlotte JR SR HS; Rochester, NY; (Y); Aud/Vis; Boys Clb Am; Boy Scts; Pres Church Yth Grp; Drama Clb; Chorus; Pres Church Choir; School Musical; School Play; Stage Crew; Hghst Avg Engl 84; Chem Engrng.

MONROE, JEFFERY D; Batavia HS; Batavia, NY; (Y); 18/230; Orch; L Socr; Capt L Swmmng; Hon Roll; St Schlr; Jan Mc Donalds Athlt Mnth 86; MV Swimmer 86; St Lawrence U; Lawyer.

MONROE, JOHN; Highland HS; Highland, NY; (Y); Boy Scts; Varsity Clb; Stage Crew; Im Bsktbl; Capt Coach Actv; Var Ftbl; Var Trk; Hon Roll.

MONROE, KIMBERLY; Adali E Stevenson HS; Bronx, NY; (Y); 43/432; Girl Scts; Orch; Hon Roll; Prfct Atten Awd; NY Bar Assn Mck Trl 85; NY ST Rgnts Schlrshp 86; Baruch Coll; Bus Mngmnt.

MONROE, MICHAEL; Oneida SR HS; Oneida, NY; (S); Debate Tm; Var Crs Cntry; Var Trk; Bausch & Lomb Sci Awd; High Hon Roll; NHS; RPI Mdl 86; Maxima Cum Laude Natl Latin Exam 86; Coll Classics Lg 85.

MONTABANA, MARK; Mendon HS; Pittsford, NY; (Y); Boy Scts; Var Swmmng; Hon Roll; Prnt Tchr Stdnt Assn Awd Sci 86; Oswego; Bus.

MONTAGNA, WANDA; G Ray Bodley HS; Fulton, NY; (Y); French Clb; Hosp Aide; JA; Science Clb; Ski Clb; Rep Stu Cncl; Stat Lcrss; High Hon Roll; Hon Roll; Ntl Merit Ltr; Bus.

MONTAGUE, NATHAN; Lansing HS; Lansing, NY; (Y); #18 In Class; Boy Scts; French Clb; Ski Clb; School Musical; Stage Crew; Yrbk Phtg; Yrbk Rptr; Var Golf; Var Socr; Var Trk; MVP Track 86; Athlete Achvt Awd Soccer 85; Editor Photo Yrbk 84-85; Photo.

MONTAGUE, SUSAN; Williamsville North HS; E Amherst, NY; (Y); Cmnty Wkr; VP Pres DECA; SADD; Yrbk Stf; Sec Soph Cls; Hon Roll; French Clb; Latin Clb; Spanish Clb; Outstndg Cmpr-Dist Ed Clbs NY Smmr L Drshp Cmp 85; Mgmt.

MONTALTO, SUSAN; St Marys Girls HS; Little Neck, NY; (Y); Hon Roll; St Johns U; Phrmcy.

MONTALTO, TERI-ANNE; Lindenhurst HS; Lindenhurst, NY; (Y); Dance Clb; Capt Pep Clb; Ski Clb; Varsity Clb; Variety Show; Var Capt Cheerleading; Jr NHS; Bus.

MONTALVO, JOSE A; Mount Saint Michael Acad; Bronx, NY; (S); 9/309; Boy Scts; Chess Clb; Im Bsktbl; JV Crs Cntry; JV Trk; Hon Roll; Pre-Med.

MONTALVO, ROBERT; HS For The Humants; New York, NY; (Y); Cmnty Wkr; Library Aide; Spanish Clb; Teachers Aide; Chorus; Hon Roll; NHS; Prfct Atten Awd; Ldrshp Awd 86; NYU; Med.

MONTANA, ADOLF; Port Richmond HS; Staten Island, NY; (Y); JV Socr; Ostndng Stu Crtfct 86; Engr.

MONTANINO, MATTHEW J; Lansingburgh HS; Troy, NY; (Y); 26/185; Exploring; Capt Sr Cls; Bsktbl; High Hon Roll; Hon Roll; NHS; Lansingburgh JR SR PTSA Awd Achvt 85-86; Pres Acad Fit Awd 85-86; Hudson Vly CC; Acctg.

MONTANYE, THERESA; Scotia Glenville SR HS; Scotia, NY; (Y); Cmnty Wkr; Math Tm; Hon Roll; St Rose; Accntnt.

MONTEIRO, DIANE; Lakeland HS; Yorktown Hts, NY; (Y); Drama Clb; Chrmn SADD; Stage Crew.

MONTEITH, MICHAEL; Hutchinson Central Technical HS; Buffalo, NY; (Y); Ftbl; Ice Hcky; U Of Buffalo; Arch Design.

MONTELEONE, LAUREEN; Central HS; Valley Stream, NY; (Y); Art Clb; Church Yth Grp; FBLA; Girl Scts; Spanish Clb; School Play; Socr; Hon Roll; English Ed.

MONTEMARANO, ELLEN S; Nazareth Regional HS; Brooklyn, NY; (S); 21/267; Am Leg Aux Girls St; JA; Speech Tm; Nwsp Phtg; Ed Nwsp Stf; Yrbk Phtg; Ed Yrbk Stf; JV Sftbl; NHS; Ntl Frnsc Lgu Merit Dgr 82; Svc Recgntn Dsbld Prsns 84; Supr Achvt SS & Comp Sci 85.

MONTERO, BRIGIDO; Catholic Central HS; Troy, NY; (Y); Church Yth Grp; Math Clb; Spanish Clb; Var Capt Trk; Hon Roll; Archit.

MONTESANO, PAUL; Linton HS; Schenectady, NY; (Y); Church Yth Grp; Exploring; Intnl Clb; Hon Roll.

MONTESANO, VINCENT; Iona Prep; Mamaroneck, NY; (Y); 15/192; Boy Scts; Pres Y-Teens; JV Bsbl; Capt Var Ftbl; Hon Roll; NHS; Prfct Atten Awd; St Anns Schlrshp 86; Villanova Grnt 86; Villanova U; Bus.

MONTGOMERY, BRENDA; Rhinebeck Central HS; Rhinebeck, NY; (Y); 5/105; Trs Drama Clb; School Musical; Nwsp Stf; Yrbk Stf; NHS; Band; High Hon Roll; Hon Roll; JC Awd; HOBY Awd 84; George A Gordon Spkn Frnch Awd; Donald J Closs Mem Awd; Gazette Ad Awd JR; Bard Coll; Archlgy.

MONTGOMERY, CAROL; Lake George HS; Lake George, NY; (Y); Sec SADD; Chorus; Rep Soph Cls; Rep Stu Cncl; Capt Var Cheerleading; JV Var Sftbl; Stu Of Mnth Grmn 86; Mst Sprtd Chrldr 85; Mst Vlbl JV Chrldr 85; Bus.

MONTGOMERY, CHARLES; Turner/Carroll HS; Buffalo, NY; (Y); Camera Clb; Dance Clb; Hosp Aide; JA; Office Aide; SADD; Church Choir; Drill Tm; Variety Show; Var Crs Cntry; Corp Law.

MONTGOMERY, CHER; Churchville-Chili SR HS; Rochester, NY; (Y); 40/300; High Hon Roll; Hon Roll; Bus Hnr Society 85-86; Pres Acad Ftns Awd 86; Rcptnst.

MONTGOMERY, SALLY; Broadalbin Central HS; Broadalbin, NY; (Y); Church Yth Grp; Drama Clb; Bsktbl; Socr; Sftbl; High Hon Roll; Hon Roll; Schnectady County CC; Justice.

MONTIE, JOE; Copiague HS; Copiague, NY; (Y); Boy Scts; German Clb; Math Clb; Math Tm; Var L Bowling; Var L Socr; High Hon Roll; NHS; Grmn Hnr Soc 84-86; MVP Bwlng 86; Arch.

MONTIE, WALTER; Copiague HS; Copiague, NY; (Y); 14/312; Debate Tm; French Clb; Mathletes; Math Tm; Hon Roll; Pres Schlr; Rgnts Schlrshp 86; LI Hstry Awd 86; Rgnts Dplma 86; Clark U.

MONTILLI, T J; Lawrence HS; Cedarhurst, NY; (Y); Var Ftbl; Var Wt Lftg; Var Wrstlng; Trophy Most Dedicated Wrstlr 84; Var Lttr Ftbll 83-84; Plaque Partipation Ftbll 85-86; Plaque Yth Hcky.

MONTOCCHIO, NARISA; Cardinal Spellman HS; Bronx, NY; (Y); Cmnty Wkr; Science Clb; Hon Roll; Manhattan Coll; Chem Engrng.

MONTON, EILEEN; Notre-Dame Bishop Gibbons HS; Schenectady, NY; (Y); Art Clb; Exploring; Stu Cncl; High Hon Roll; Hon Roll; Mrktng.

MONTONEY, MICHELLE; Cicero-North Syracuse HS; Clay, NY; (S); 4/667; Church Yth Grp; Mathletes; Math Clb; Math Tm; Ski Clb; Band; Concert Band; Jazz Band; Mrchg Band; School Musical; Outstndng Yung NY Dist Wnnr, JR Miss Onondaga Cnty 86; 1st Chair All Cnty 85-86; Union Coll; Bio.

MONTONI, ANTHONY; St Marys HS; Elmont, NY; (Y); 19/180; Cmnty Wkr; Ski Clb; JV Trk; High Hon Roll; Hon Roll; Hnr Roll; Polytechnic U; Engr.

MONTREAL, ANNE; Cicero North Syracuse HS; Mattydale, NY; (S); 47/632; Chorus; Var Bsktbl; Var Socr; JV Sftbl; All Cnty Hnrb Mntn-Sccr 85; Elem Schl Tchr.

MONTROSS, WILLIAM; Rhinebeck Central HS; Rhinebeck, NY; (Y); Am Leg Boys St; Nwsp Sprt Ed; Im Socr; Im Sftbl; Im Vllybl; Cit Awd; High Hon Roll; NHS; Ntl Merit Ltr; Im Badmtn; Dutchess Cnty Rgnl H S Of Exc 86.

MONTROY, ALBERT T; Ogdensburg Free Acad; Ogdensburg, NY; (Y); 8/190; Pres Key Clb; Pres Frsh Cls; Pres Soph Cls; Pres Jr Cls; Pres Sr Cls; Rep Stu Cncl; Var Ftbl; Var Wrstlng; CC Awd; NHS; I Love NY Pstr Cntst Wnnr 83; VA Tech; Arch.

MONTROY, KATHRYN A; Ogdensburg Free Acad; Ogdensburg, NY; (Y); Church Yth Grp; Hosp Aide; Chorus; Color Guard; Mrchg Band; Yrbk Stf; Jefferson CC; Hsplty.

MONTUORI, KAREN; Valley Stream North HS; Malverne, NY; (Y); Cmnty Wkr; Debate Tm; Hosp Aide; Spanish Clb; SADD; Band; Chorus; Mrchg Band; Trs Frsh Cls; VP Pres Stu Cncl.

MOODIE, DANIELLE; Newtown HS; Elmhurst, NY; (Y); Debate Tm; Service Clb; Swmmng; LIU C W Post; Bus Adm.

MOODY, CATHERINE; Fayetteville-Manlius HS; Fayetteville, NY; (Y); Church Yth Grp; Swing Chorus; Yrbk Ed-Chief; Sec Stu Cncl; Capt Var Gym; Hon Roll; NHS; Empire ST Gymnstc Tm 82-84; NROTC Schlrshp; Appt To USCG Acad; Appt To USN Acad; USN Acad; Engrng.

MOODY, EMILY; Kingston HS; Rifton, NY; (Y); Church Yth Grp; Cmnty Wkr; German Clb; Church Choir; Orch; Stu Cncl; High Hon Roll.

MOODY, MICHAEL L; W C Mepham HS; Bellmore, NY; (Y); 120/365; Church Yth Grp; Drama Clb; French Clb; SADD; School Play; Nwsp Rptr; Lit Mag; JV Bsbl; Var Wrstlng; Hon Roll; Regents Scholar NYS 86; Purdue U; Engrng.

MOON, DAWNE; Irondequoit HS; Rochester, NY; (Y); 23/378; Drama Clb; French Clb; VP Model UN; Chorus; Concert Band; Orch; School Musical; School Play; Hon Roll; NY ST Schl Music Assn Merits & Awds Solos 84-85; Advrtsg.

MOON, EDWARD; Christopher Columbus HS; Bronx, NY; (Y); Crs Cntry; Swmmng; Trk; Hon Roll; Polytec U; Elctrcl Engnrng.

MOON, JUDY; Half Hollow Hills West HS; Dix Hills, NY; (Y); Key Clb; Service Clb; Trs SADD; Swing Chorus; Variety Show; Var Crs Cntry; Var Diving; Var Trk; Var Vllybl; High Hon Roll; Top Ten In Sci Olympiad 86; Lge Champ Trphy Vrsty Vllybl 86; 3 Awds Cross Cntry Invit Mts 84; Law.

MOON, LISA; Tioga Central HS; Smithboro, NY; (S); Computer Clb; Pres Varsity Clb; Rep Frsh Cls; Rep Sr Cls; Var Co-Capt Bsktbl; Var Co-Capt Fld Hcky; Var Sftbl; Var Trk; NHS; Bsktbl Leag Co-MVP 84-85; All IAC Fld Hockey 83-85; Leag Shotput, Discus Recrds 84-85.

MOON, PAUL; The Wheatley HS; Albertson, NY; (Y); Church Yth Grp; FCA; Orch; JV Bsbl; Var Ftbl; Wrstlng; Var Ltr Awd 84-86; Vice Pres Chrch Yth Grp 84-86; Bus.

MOONA, SHERRIE; St John Villa Acad; Staten Island, NY; (Y); 17/125; Science Clb; Nwsp Stf; Hon Roll; Cornell U; Med.

MOONAY, DANIEL; Williamsville South HS; Williamsville, NY; (Y); Debate Tm; Temple Yth Grp; Acpl Chr; Band; Concert Band; Jazz Band; Var L Swmmng; Var L Tennis; NHS; Mst Imprvd Swmmr 84-85.

MOONEN, JILL; Vernon-Verona-Sherrill HS; Verona, NY; (Y); Church Yth Grp; Var Socr; Var Vllybl; High Hon Roll; Hon Roll; Soccr All Star Tm 85-86; MVP Soccer 85-86; Art.

MOONEN, PETER; Vernon Verona Sherrill Central Schl; Verona, NY; (Y); 78/199; Ski Clb; Varsity Clb; Var Socr; Var Capt Wrstlng; Empire ST Games Open Divsn Wrstlng 86; SUNY; Ski Area Tech.

MOONEY, AARON; Mc Quaid Jesuit HS; Victor, NY; (Y); Ski Clb; Varsity Clb; Yrbk Sprt Ed; Yrbk Stf; Im Mgr Bsktbl; JV Var Golf; Score Keeper; Wt Lftg; Hon Roll; Bus.

MOONEY, DANNIELLE; Pulaski JR SR HS; Pulaski, NY; (Y); French Clb; GAA; Yrbk Stf; Bowling; Sftbl; John Ben Snow Awd 86; RE Agnt.

MOONEY, ERIN E; Limestone Union Free HS; Limestone, NY; (Y); 3/27; Latin Clb; Pep Clb; Ski Clb; School Play; Yrbk Stf; Sec Frsh Cls; Stu Cncl; Var Capt Cheerleading; High Hon Roll; NHS; NYS Regnts Schlrshp 86-87; St Bonaventure U; Biol.

MOONEY, KENT; New Lebanon Central HS; Canaan, NY; (Y); French Clb; Chorus; School Musical; Variety Show; Var Socr; Var Swmmng; Var Trk; Hon Roll; NHS.

MOONEY, PATRICK; Monsignor Farrell HS; Staten Island, NY; (Y); 38/289; Stu Cncl; Crs Cntry; Trk; NYS Regnts Schlrshp 86; Pres Schlrshp Manhattn Coll 86; Siena Coll.

MOORE, ALEC T; Utica Free Acad; Utica, NY; (Y); 25/335; Trs Drama Clb; Trs French Clb; VP German Clb; Rptr Thesps; VP Orch; School Musical; School Play; Nwsp Stf; Hon Roll; Jr NHS; NY St Regents Schlrshp 86; Brown U; Law.

MOORE, AMY; Naples Central Schl; Naples, NY; (Y); 5/63; Church Yth Grp; Drama Clb; French Clb; Band; Chorus; Church Choir; School Musical; Yrbk Bus Mgr; High Hon Roll; NHS; Marshl-Cmmncmnt Exrcses 86; Elem Educ.

MOORE, BETH; Auburn HS; Auburn, NY; (Y); Church Yth Grp; Model UN; Ski Clb; Chorus; Mrchg Band; Orch; School Musical; Swing Chorus; Symp Band; Hon Roll; Area All ST Bnd 85; Scndry Ed.

MOORE, BRENDA; Alden Central HS; Elma, NY; (Y); French Clb; Letterman Clb; Ed Yrbk Stf; JV Var Trk; Hon Roll; Acad Awd; Natl Sci Olympd; Engrng.

MOORE, CHARLES; Uniondale HS; Uniondale, NY; (Y); Key Clb; Letterman Clb; Var L Ftbl; Var L Trk; Im Wrstlng; Sprts Awds; U Of MD Coll Pk; Phys Thrpst.

MOORE, CHRISTINA; Washingtonville HS; New Windsor, NY; (Y); Dance Clb; Hosp Aide; Intnl Clb; Ski Clb; Chorus; JV Gym; High Hon Roll; Hon Roll; Masonic Awd; Med.

MOORE, DANIEL; Schenectady Christian Schl; Alplaus, NY; (S); 1/15; Var L Bsktbl; Var Capt Socr; High Hon Roll; Outstndng Stu-Erth Sci & Algbr 84; Excllnc Spnsh I 84; Nabsc-AAU Physcl Ftns Pgm Awd 84-86.

MOORE, GERALD S; Bishop Ludden HS; Camillus, NY; (Y); Intnl Clb; Model UN; Varsity Clb; Band; Nwsp Stf; Im Capt Ice Hcky; JV Var Socr; High Hon Roll; Hon Roll; Prfct Atten Awd; U Of Buffalo; Elec Engr.

MOORE, JUBILITH; Germantown Central HS; Elizaville, NY; (S); 7/60; Band; Chorus; School Musical; Sec Jr Cls; Bsktbl; Cheerleading; Fld Hcky; Trk; Cit Awd; High Hon Roll.

MOORE, JULIE; Greece Olympia HS; Rochester, NY; (Y); Drama Clb; VP Chorus; Church Choir; Orch; School Musical; School Play; Stage Crew; Symp Band; High Hon Roll; NHS; Excllnc Awd-Spnsh 85-86; A Solo Rtng-Violin/Vcl Comptns 84-86; Pres-Show Choir 85-86; Vcl Prfrmnc.

MOORE, KATHLEEN D; Walton Central Schl; Walton, NY; (Y); 20/111; Key Clb; Model UN; Varsity Clb; Girl Scts; Orch; Var Bsktbl; Var Tennis; High Hon Roll; Hon Roll; SUNY Cortland.

MOORE, KATHRYN; Romulus Central Schl; Romulus, NY; (Y); Church Yth Grp; Cmnty Wkr; 4-H; Spanish Clb; SADD; Color Guard; Yrbk Stf; JV Sftbl; JV Vllybl; Hon Roll; Htl Mngmnt.

MOORE, MADELEINE; Watkins Glen HS; Watkins Glen, NY; (Y); 17/134; Drama Clb; Letterman Clb; Band; Chorus; Church Choir; Jazz Band; School Play; Swmmng; French Hon Soc; St Schlr; Suny Cortland.

MOORE, MAUREEN; Jamesville-De Witt HS; De Witt, NY; (Y); 56/230; Church Yth Grp; Civic Clb; Hosp Aide; Political Wkr; Red Cross Aide; Chorus; Var L Tennis; JV Vllybl; Sci.

MOORE, MICHAEL; Scotia-Glenville HS; Schenectady, NY; (Y); 1/225; Am Leg Boys St; German Clb; Ski Clb; Tennis; Bausch & Lomb Sci Awd; High Hon Roll; NHS; Pres Schlr; Cornell U; Engrng.

MOORE, PATRICIA A; Wellington C Mepham HS; Bellmore, NY; (Y); Aud/Vis; Church Yth Grp; Drama Clb; Acpl Chr; Concert Band; Madrigals; School Play; Stage Crew; Mgr(s); Hon Roll; NYSMEA Voice Cmptn 84-86; Music Tchr.

MOORE, PATTY; Woodlands HS; White Plains, NY; (Y); Church Yth Grp; Office Aide; Church Choir; Im Bowling; JV Trk; Pace U; Bus Adm.

MOORE, RANDALL; Horseheads HS; Horseheads, NY; (Y); Im Var Ftbl; Hon Roll; Carpentry.

MOORE, RANDY; Sauquoit Valley Central HS; Sauquoit, NY; (Y); Boys Clb Am; Boy Scts; Yrbk Phtg; Yrbk Stf; Stat Bsktbl; Stat Ftbl; JV Var Trk; Cit Awd; Wills Prosser Mem Awd 86; SUNY; Comp Sci.

MOORE, RICHARD; Norman Howard Schl; Pittsford, NY; (Y); Camera Clb; Cmnty Wkr; Ski Clb; Nwsp Bus Mgr; Yrbk Bus Mgr; Bsktbl; Golf.

MOORE, S GORDON; Roy C Ketcham HS; Wappingers Falls, NY; (Y); 69/500; Church Yth Grp; Pres Jr Cls; Pres Sr Cls; Cit Awd; DAR Awd; Hon Roll; NHS; Ntl Merit Schol; JV Bsktbl; JV Ftbl; Accptd GA Tech MITE Prg 85; Delta Stu Achvmnt Awd 85-86; Morehouse Coll; Elec Engrng.

MOORE, SANDRA; Academy Of Mount Saint Ursula; Bronx, NY; (Y); Dance Clb; Intnl Clb; Cit Awd; Lbrl Arts.

MOORE, SCOTT; Hutchinson Central Tech HS; Buffalo, NY; (Y); 15/237; Computer Clb; Science Clb; Nwsp Rptr; Nwsp Stf; Hon Roll; Prfct Atten Awd; Jesse Ketchum Medl Wnnr 83; Altrntr Dir Locl Chptr Natl Wld Turkey Fed 86; Cnty Fair 4 1sts Art 84-85; Comp Sci.

MOORE, SUSAN; Charles H Roth HS; Rochester, NY; (Y); Drama Clb; Library Aide; Spanish Clb; Stage Crew; High Hon Roll; Jr NHS; NHS; Spanish NHS; Spn.

MOORE, TERESA; North Rose-Wolcott HS; N Rose, NY; (Y); Church Yth Grp; Ski Clb; SADD; School Play; Stage Crew; Yrbk Phtg; Cit Awd; High Hon Roll; NHS; Rochester Inst Of Tech; Htl Mtl.

MOORE, TRA VELLA; Riverside HS; Buffalo, NY; (Y); Cmnty Wkr; Drama Clb; FHA; JA; Office Aide; Pep Clb; PAVAS; Chorus; Drill Tm; Variety Show; Modeling Schlrshp 85; Math Awd 83; Secy Awd 83; Bus Mgt.

MOORE, TRICIA; Tottenville HS; Staten Island, NY; (Y); Cmnty Wkr; Band; Mrchg Band; Orch; School Musical; School Play; Symp Band; Hon Roll; NHS; Phrmcy.

MOORES, KENNETH S; Cheektowaga Central HS; Cheektowaga, NY; (Y); JV Ftbl; JV Socr; Var L Trk; JV Wrstlng; Erie CC; Crmnl Jstc.

MOORHEAD, TODD; T J Corcoran HS; Syracuse, NY; (Y); Church Yth Grp; French Clb; Latin Clb; Yrbk Phtg; Hon Roll; NHS; Ntl Latn Exm Slvr Mdl Maxima Cum Laude 85; Ntl Latin Exm Mgna Cum Laude 86; Math.

MOOT, WILLIAM; Letchworth Central HS; Castile, NY; (Y); 1/87; Church Yth Grp; French Clb; Math Clb; Math Tm; Spanish Clb; High Hon Roll; NHS; Alfred ST; Chem Engr.

MORA, JAMES; Cardinal Hayes HS; New York, NY; (Y); 100/270; Camera Clb; Chess Clb; Dance Clb; Pres Spanish Clb; School Musical; School Play; Mgr Stage Crew; Rep Stu Cncl; Var Wt Lftg; Prfct Atten Awd; Coll Of Mt St Vincent; Psych.

MORA, MONICA; Commack HS North; Commack, NY; (Y); 149/390; Varsity Clb; Chorus; VP Soph Cls; VP Jr Cls; Rep Stu Cncl; Var Badmtn; Var Bowling; Var Sftbl; JV Vllybl; Hon Roll; Spec Awd Schl & Extra Corrclr Actv 85; Suffolk CC; Lib Arts.

MORABITO, THOMAS C; Lewis C Obourn HS; East Rochester, NY; (Y); 6/140; Am Leg Boys St; Math Tm; Model UN; Varsity Clb; Soph Cls; Stu Cncl; Bsktbl; NHS; Ftbl; Golf; Pres Rochester Soc Children Of Am Revolution 83-85; Elected NY ST Custodian Of The CAR 85-86; Business.

MORACI, JENNIFER; Centereach HS; Centereach, NY; (Y); Cmnty Wkr; Political Wkr; SADD; Band; Var L Cheerleading; French Hon Soc; High Hon Roll; Jr NHS; NHS; Prfct Atten Awd; Awd Mddl CO Cntrl Schl Dist 86; Mrch Dms Wlk A Thn 85-86; Outstndng Vol, Lk Gr Schl Deaf & Atsto 86; Math.

MORALES, ALBERT; Regis HS; Englewood Cliff, NJ; (Y); Computer Clb; Model UN; Pres Ski Clb; Speech Tm; VP Jr Cls; Pres Sr Cls; Rep Stu Cncl; Ntl Merit SF; Natl Hspnc Schl Awd-Semi Fnlst 86; Pre Med.

MORALES, BEATRICE; Murry Bergtraum HS Of Busines Careers; Brooklyn, NY; (Y); Church Yth Grp; Stage Crew; Rep Frsh Cls; Rep Soph Cls; Rep Jr Cls; Awd Wnnr Peace Corps Awrnss Prgm Essy Cmptn 86; NY U; Jrnlsm.

MORALES, EUNICE; Dodge Vocational HS; New York, NY; (Y); School Musical; School Play; Nwsp Rptr; Nwsp Stf; Sec Frsh Cls; Hon Roll; Hnr Brdg Arts 85; Hnr Partcptn Modl Congrs 86; Exec Secy.

MORALES, JOMALI IVANA; Immaculata HS; New York, NY; (Y); Church Choir; VP Frsh Cls; VP Stu Cncl; Cheerleading; John Jay Coll; Govt Adm.

MORALES, LUZ; George Washington HS; New York, NY; (Y); Drama Clb; Office Aide; Teachers Aide; Band; Concert Band; Orch; Bsktbl; High Hon Roll; Manhattan CC; Exec Sec.

MORALES, MILAGROS; St Raymond Acad; Bronx, NY; (S); 6/84; VP Jr Cls; High Hon Roll; NHS; VP Frsh Cls; Stu Cncl; Hon Roll; Fordham U; Hosp Admin.

MORALES, MISSY; Mahopac HS; Mahopac, NY; (Y); 158/400; Church Yth Grp; Crs Cntry; Sftbl; Trk; Hon Roll; Spanish Clb; Chorus; Bowling; Sci.

MORALES, PATRICIA; Brewster HS; Brewster, NY; (Y); 5/190; Yrbk Ed-Chief; Yrbk Sprt Ed; Sec Stu Cncl; DAR Awd; High Hon Roll; Hon Roll; JC Awd; NHS; Pres Schlr; Spanish NHS; Renesselaer Poly Insti Schlrshp 86-87; Putnam Jaycee Schlrshp 86; Brewster Hg Schl Strr Schlrshp 86-90; Rennsseber Poly Insti; Engrng.

MORALES, VERONICA; Nazareth Regional HS; Brooklyn, NY; (Y); Church Choir; Yrbk Stf; Photogrphy 86; NYU; Nrsng.

MORAN, BRIAN; Monsingnor Farrell HS; Staten Island, NY; (Y); Cmnty Wkr; Computer Clb; Debate Tm; French Clb; Ski Clb; Stage Crew; Im Bsktbl; Im JV Bowling; Im Ftbl; Var L Tennis; Penn ST U Excell Awd 86; Merrill Lynch Schlrshp 86; Teen Action Grp VP 85-86; Penn ST; Engr.

MORAN, CHERYL; Kenmore East SR HS; Kenmore, NY; (Y); Hosp Aide; Concert Band; Jazz Band; Nwsp Ed-Chief; VP Frsh Cls; Rep Sr Cls; Rep Stu Cncl; Var Vllybl; High Hon Roll; Bsktbl; Awd In Flute 84-85; New Mscn Of Yr For Jazz Bnd 84-85; Psychlgy.

MORAN, COLLEEN; Pioneer Central HS; Java Center, NY; (Y); 26/269; 4-H; Pres French Clb; Chorus; School Musical; Sec Swing Chorus; Nwsp Rptr; Lit Mag; Var Fld Hcky; Music Hnr Awd Chrl 86; St Bonaventure U; Comm.

MORAN, COLLEEN; Saquoit Valley Central Schl; Chadwicks, NY; (Y); 4/100; GAA; Yrbk Stf; Var Bsktbl; JV Cheerleading; Var Socr; High Hon Roll; Jr NHS; NHS; Regents Schlrshp 86; MONY Schltc Art Awd-Hrbl Mntn 83 & 86; Syracuse U; Pre Med.

MORAN, DONNA; St Peters HS For Girls; Staten Island, NY; (Y); Girl Scts; Library Aide; Math Tm; Church Choir; School Musical; Lit Mag; High Hon Roll; Hon Roll; Sec NHS; Prfct Atten Awd; Comp Sci.

MORAN, JEAN; Warwick Valley HS; Warwick, NY; (Y); 1/200; Math Tm; Science Clb; SADD; Sftbl; Swmmng; Bausch & Lomb Sci Awd; Cit Awd; High Hon Roll; NHS; Ntl Merit SF; Muc Med.

MORAN, JOSEPH D; Sidney Central HS; Sidney, NY; (Y); 6/110; Am Leg Boys St; Boy Scts; VP FBLA; Trs Varsity Clb; VP Trs Stu Cncl; High Hon Roll; NHS; Prfct Atten Awd; Church Yth Grp; Trs French Clb; Amer Mgmt Assns Oper Entrprs 86; JR Prom Ct Kng 86; Colgate; Pre-Med.

MORAN, KIERAN; Rocky Point HS; Rocky Point, NY; (S); 17/185; French Clb; Varsity Clb; School Musical; Nwsp Rptr; Nwsp Sprt Ed; Var Capt Crs Cntry; Var Capt Trk; Hon Roll; Engrng.

MORAN, LESLIE; Fairport HS; Fairport, NY; (Y); German Clb; Hosp Aide; Key Clb; Chorus; Stu Cncl; JV Fld Hcky; Score Keeper; Var Trk; Hon Roll; Awds Hrsbck Ridng Comptns 84; Ltr Trk 85; U Of Rochester.

MORAN, LORIE; Wall Kill SR HS; Gardiner, NY; (Y); 50/200; Band; Concert Band; Crs Cntry; Gym; Socr; Tennis; Trk; Hon Roll; GAA; Hosp Aide; SUNY Oneonta; Elem Tchr.

MORAN, MARIA M; Our Lady Of Mercy Acad; Massapequa Park, NY; (Y); Cmnty Wkr; Computer Clb; SADD; Cheerleading; Hon Roll; St Schlr; NYS Regents Schlrshp; Catholic U America.

MORAN, MARY; Walter Panas HS; Peekskill, NY; (Y); Var Capt Gym; JV Var Socr; NHS; Vncnt Zeoli Memrl Awd 86; All-Cnty All-Sctn Gymnst 83-86; Prsdntl Acdmc Ftns Awd 86; Ithaca Coll; Cmmrcl Art.

MORAN, MATTHEW; Vernon-Verona-Sherrill Central HS; Vernon, NY; (Y); Cmnty Wkr; Stu Cncl; JV Bsbl; JV Capt Bsktbl; High Hon Roll; Hon Roll; Prfct Atten Awd; 1st Tm Tri-Vlly Lg All-Str Bsbll 86; Bus Mgmt.

MORAN, MICHAEL; Victor Central HS; Victor, NY; (Y); 45/230; Aud/Vis; Model UN; Quiz Bowl; Science Clb; SADD; Varsity Clb; Band; Concert Band; Mrchg Band; Im Badmtn; Mc Donalds Acad Awd Scholar 86; Pres Fit Awd Cert 86; U Rochester Sci Awd 86; Monroe CC; Engrng.

MORAN, MICHELLE N; Mamaroneck HS; Larchmont, NY; (Y); Church Yth Grp; Drama Clb; SADD; School Musical; School Play; Variety Show; Hon Roll; Boston Coll; Psych.

MORAN, MIKE; Walter Panas HS; Peekskill, NY; (Y); Computer Clb; German Clb; High Hon Roll; Jr NHS; NHS; Aerontcl Engrng.

MORAN, RAYMOND; Amsterdam HS; Amsterdam, NY; (Y); 49/288; Library Aide; Varsity Clb; Pres Frsh Cls; Bsbl; Ftbl; Wt Lftg; Wrstlng; Cpa.

MORAN, ROXANA E; Lynbrook HS; Lynbrook, NY; (Y); Leo Clb; Hon Roll; AP Spnsh Test Maximum Grd Of 5 85; Med.

MORAN, THOMAS; Archbishop Molloy HS; Long Island, NY; (Y); SADD; Law.

MORANDI, ALICE; Hoosick Falls Central HS; Hoosick Falls, NY; (Y); Chorus; JV Var Bsktbl; JV Var Fld Hcky; JV Var Trk; Bus Mngmnt.

MORANDI, MARIA; Moore Catholic HS; Staten Island, NY; (Y); Mathletes; Math Tm; High Hon Roll; Hon Roll; Jr NHS; NHS; Var Bsktbl; JV Sftbl.

MORANTE, GUSTAVO; Christ The King Regional HS; Richmond Hill, NY; (Y); Art Clb; Varsity Clb; Var Capt Ftbl; Lineman Of Yr Awd 83-84; Athlt Of Yr Awd 84-85; Art.

MORATH, TRICIA; Fredonia HS; Fredonia, NY; (Y); Pres Church Yth Grp; GAA; Key Clb; Sec SADD; Trs Chorus; Rep Frsh Cls; Trs Jr Cls; Stu Cncl; Var Swmmng; Var Trk; Scndry Educ.

MORDSFELD, RENE; Brittonkill HS; Troy, NY; (Y); FBLA; VICA; JV Socr; JV Var Sftbl; Var Vllybl; Hon Roll; Hnr Roll Vo-Tech Data Prcssng Prgrm 84-86; Albany Bus Coll; Data Procssng.

MOREAU, DAVE; Roy C Ketcham HS; Wappingers Falls, NY; (Y); AFS; Church Yth Grp; Pres 4-H; Band; Stage Crew; JV Bsktbl; L Crs Cntry; Var Trk; Hon Roll; NHS; Soc Stds Achvmnt Awd 85; NYS Rgnts Schlrshp 86; Alfred U; Crmc Engnrng.

MOREAU, MICHELLE; Brasher Falls Central HS; Bombay, NY; (Y); 4-H; Spanish Clb; Socr; 4-H Awd; Hon Roll; NHS; Englsh Awd 83; Physcl Achvt Awd 85.

MOREHOUSE, MICHAEL D; Massena Central HS; Massena, NY; (Y); 20/260; Am Leg Boys St; Church Yth Grp; Key Clb; ROTC; Band; Mrchg Band; Rep Frsh Cls; Rep Soph Cls; Rep Jr Cls; Var Capt Bsktbl; Pre Dntstry.

MOREHOUSE, WENDY; Sacamanca Central HS; Sacamanca, NY; (Y); Church Yth Grp; Exploring; French Clb; Varsity Clb; Sec Stu Cncl; Capt Trk; High Hon Roll; NHS; Olymics Of The Mind Natl Comp 86; Radiologic Tech.

MOREL, JOHN J; Monsignor Farrell HS; Staten Island, NY; (Y); 24/295; French Clb; Bowling; Golf; High Hon Roll; Hon Roll; NHS; SR Hln Flyn Awd, Schlstc Exc Schlrshp & Cmtv Schlrshp 86; St Jhns U; Finance.

MOREL, RAFAEL; De Witt Clinton HS; Bronx, NY; (Y); Hon Roll; Prfct Atten Awd; Bronx CC; Comp Sci.

MORELAND, MICHAEL R; Owego Free Acad; Owego, NY; (Y); Boys Clb Am; SADD; Varsity Clb; Bsbl; Var Capt Bowling; Golf; Hon Roll; All-Conf Bwlng 86; SUNY Buffalo; Cmptr Sci.

MORELL, JOHN; Pal-Mac HS; Palmyra, NY; (Y); Boy Scts; Church Yth Grp; Trs 4-H; Ski Clb; SADD; Rep Frsh Cls; Rep Soph Cls; Stu Cncl; JV Ftbl; Bus.

MORELLI, JOSEPH PETER; Bishop Grimes HS; Syracuse, NY; (Y); Church Yth Grp; Hosp Aide; Math Clb; Ski Clb; Ftbl; Socr; Engrng.

MORELLI, JUSTINE; Brewster HS; Patterson, NY; (Y); Church Yth Grp; Girl Scts; Color Guard; Suny-AL; Pre Med.

MORELLI, MARIANNE I; Franciscan HS; Putnam Valley, NY; (Y); 2/52; School Musical; Variety Show; Nwsp Rptr; Yrbk Ed-Chief; Trs Jr Cls; Trs Sr Cls; High Hon Roll; Trs NHS; Sal; Trs Spanish NHS; Fairfield U; Bio.

MORELLO, MAURIZIO; Anglo-American Schl; New York, NY; (S); Computer Clb; Yrbk Phtg; Var L Bsktbl; Var L Socr; Var L Tennis; High Hon Roll; Hon Roll; NHS; Prfct Atten Awd; Law.

MORELO, MONICA; Newtown HS; Elmhurst, NY; (Y); 39/781; Computer Clb; French Clb; School Musical; Tennis; Hon Roll; Law.

MORENCY, MICHAEL; Mc Quaid Jesuit HS; Rochester, NY; (Y); 83/160; Cmnty Wkr; French Clb; Im Bsktbl; Im Ftbl; Im Ice Hcky; Im Vllybl; Hon Roll.

MORENO, OLGAMILCA; Benjamin Franklin HS; Rochester, NY; (Y); Exploring; ROTC; Pres Spanish Clb; Rep Stu Cncl; High Hon Roll; Hon Roll; SUNY Brockport; Chem.

MORENO, RUBEN; Bx High School Of Science; New York, NY; (Y); Boy Scts; Church Yth Grp; Nwsp Stf; Lit Mag; Rep Soph Cls; Stu Cncl; Var Gym; Frgn Lang Awd 86; Holocaust Studs Mem Awd 86; Indstrl Arts Awd 86; NY U; Pol Sci.

MORET, DWIGHT; All Hallows HS; Bronx, NY; (Y); JA; Office Aide; Var Bsbl; Hon Roll; Ntl Merit Schol; Prfct Atten Awd; Pre-Med.

MORETTA, PAUL; Iroquois Central HS; Elma, NY; (Y); 17/302; Boys Clb Am; Church Yth Grp; Ski Clb; Trs Spanish Clb; Var Capt Bsbl; Var Capt Socr; High Hon Roll; Pres NHS; Prfct Atten Awd; Regents Schlrshp 86; Harvard Bk Awd 85; Elma Kiwanis Bell 86; Northwestern; Biomed.

MORETTI, MICHAEL; Liverpool HS; Liverpool, NY; (Y); 69/816; Art Clb; Spanish Clb; Hon Roll; NHS; School Musical; Jr NHS; St Rose Schlrshp 86; Regents Schlrshp 86; Excell Drwng & Ptng 85-86; St Rose Coll; Spec Ed.

MOREY, DANIEL; Peekskill HS; Peekskill, NY; (Y); 4/146; Cmnty Wkr; Drama Clb; Teachers Aide; Yrbk Phtg; Rep Frsh Cls; Pres Soph Cls; Rep Stu Cncl; Cit Awd; High Hon Roll; NHS; Ithaca Coll; Bus Adm.

MOREY, LAURA; Avon JR SR HS; Avon, NY; (Y); 24/89; Trs Church Yth Grp; Spanish Clb; Chorus; Church Choir; Score Keeper; Stat Wrstlng; Hon Roll.

MORGAN, AMY; Maple Hill HS; Castleton On H, NY; (Y); VP Key Clb; Yrbk Ed-Chief; High Hon Roll; NHS; Chorus; School Play; Nwsp Rptr; Yrbk Stf; Bsktbl; Hon Roll; Elmira Coll Key Awd 86; Phys Thrpy.

MORGAN, BRENDA; John Dewey HS; Brooklyn, NY; (Y); Dance Clb; Teachers Aide; Chorus; School Musical; Nwsp Stf; Capt Badmtn; JV Sftbl; Var Vllybl; Prfct Atten Awd; Dplma Acad Of Finance 86; Outstndng Achvt Bus Awd 86; Bus Assoc Awd Mst Outstndng Stenographer 86; Finance.

MORGAN, CECILE; Copaque SR HS; Amityville, NY; (Y); Church Yth Grp; French Clb; Lit Mag; Sec Soph Cls; Rep Stu Cncl; Hon Roll; Eagle Commended Studnt Awd 85-86; Parson Sch Of Design; Fashn Ill.

MORGAN, CHERYL; Norwood-Norfolk Central HS; Norwood, NY; (Y); 11/130; Chorus; Concert Band; Jazz Band; Yrbk Ed-Chief; VP Jr Cls; Stat Bsktbl; Cit Awd; DAR Awd; Jr NHS; Masonic Awd; Crane Schl Of Music; Music.

MORGAN, CHRISTINE; Nazareth Acad; Rochester, NY; (Y); Chorus; School Musical; School Play; Swing Chorus; Variety Show; Rep Soph Cls; Var Crs Cntry; Var Vllybl; Hon Roll; Ldrshp Awd For Cndctng WNAZ 86; Mst Imprvd Plyr In Vlybl 85.

MORGAN, ELIZABETH; Saranac Central HS; Cadyville, NY; (S); 3/120; French Clb; High Hon Roll; NHS; Bus.

MORGAN, ELIZABETH; York Central HS; Linwood, NY; (Y); Sec 4-H; Office Aide; JV Var Socr; JV Var Sftbl; JV Var Vllybl; Cit Awd; High Hon Roll; Hon Roll; NHS; Ski Clb; Career Mntrshp Prgm 85-86.

MORGAN, KATHLEEN; De Sales HS; Waterloo, NY; (Y); #3 In Class; Am Leg Aux Girls St; Varsity Clb; Chorus; Mrchg Band; School Musical; Var Socr; JV Var Sftbl; High Hon Roll; NHS; JV Bsktbl.

MORGAN, KATHLEEN M; Frontier Central HS; Blasdell, NY; (Y); DECA; FBLA; Hosp Aide; Pep Clb; Chorus; Bsktbl; Erie CC; Bus Admn.

MORGAN, KELLY; The Mary Louis Acad; Maspeth, NY; (Y); 26/262; French Clb; Yrbk Sprt Ed; NEDT Awd; Englsh Achvmnt Awd 86; Frnch Achvmnt Awd 86; Adelphi U; Bus Mgmt.

MORGAN, MICHELLE; Greece Athena SR HS; Rochester, NY; (Y); Church Yth Grp; Cmnty Wkr; Hosp Aide; Thesps; Chorus; School Play; Stage Crew; Yrbk Phtg; Hon Roll; Drama Clb; Greater Rochester Rose Soc Logo Cont Awd Wnnr 85; Elem Ed.

MORGAN, MIKE; Tamarac HS; Troy, NY; (Y); 9/107; Computer Clb; Intnl Clb; Math Tm; Band; Chorus; Pep Band; School Musical; Stage Crew; Yrbk Stf; Hon Roll; Clarkson U; Elec Engrng.

MORGAN, PAUL; Holy Trinity HS; W Hempstead, NY; (S); 13/313; Math Clb; Office Aide; Varsity Clb; Im Bsbl; Var Bsktbl; High Hon Roll; NHS; Chem.

MORGAN, PHILIP; Mahopac HS; Mahopac, NY; (Y); 3/409; Aud/Vis; Sec Computer Clb; VP Science Clb; SADD; Chorus; Rep Frsh Cls; Rep Stu Cncl; Elctrcl Engr.

MORGAN, TERESA; Colton-Pierrepont Central HS; Colton, NY; (S); 1/29; Speech Tm; School Musical; Nwsp Ed-Chief; High Hon Roll; Pres Jr NHS; NHS; High Average Awd 82-85; Outstndng Sci Stu Recgntn Cert 85; Pol Sci.

MORGAN JR, THOMAS; West Seneca East SR HS; Cheektowaga, NY; (Y); Boys Clb Am; Im Socr; Jr NHS; Bio.

MORGAN, TIMOTHY; Chateaugay Central HS; Chateaugay, NY; (Y); 15/58; French Clb; Ski Clb; Varsity Clb.

MORGANS, SHAWN; Liberty HS; Liberty, NY; (Y); Boy Scts; Spanish Clb; Stage Crew; Var JV Ftbl; Hon Roll; NHS; Engrng.

MORGANTE, PAT; Frontier SR HS; Hamburg, NY; (Y); Trs Latin Clb; Varsity Clb; Stu Cncl; JV Ftbl; JV Swmmng; Var Trk; Var Capt Vllybl; High Hon Roll; Hon Roll; Exmptn Frm Fnl Exm Scl Stds 82-84; Vllybll Ldng Spkr & Srvng Rcd 85; Cornell; Vet.

MORIARTY, ANDREW; Ten Broeck Acadd; Franklinville, NY; (Y); 1/60; Am Leg Boys St; Band; School Musical; Stu Cncl; Bsbl; Crs Cntry; Golf; Swmmng; NHS; Ntl Merit Ltr; US Nvl Acad; Engrng.

MORIARTY, BRENDEN S; Millbrook Prep Schl; Millbrook, NY; (Y); Cmnty Wkr; Nwsp Phtg; Yrbk Phtg; Var Bsbl; Var Capt Bsktbl; Var Ice Hcky; Cit Awd; Hon Roll; Rollins Coll Scholar 86; Headmasters Cmmnty Svc Awd 86; HVAL Bstkbl All Star Tm 86; Rollins Coll; Law.

MORIARTY, MARY; Cicero North Syracuse HS; N Syracuse, NY; (Y); 13/667; Church Yth Grp; Trs Hst Stu Cncl; JV Bsktbl; JV Var Socr; Sftbl; High Hon Roll; NHS; Opt Clb Awd; Syracuse Fire Dept Schlrshp 86; Treas Hon Soc 86; CNS Phy Ed Awd 85-86; Siena; Pharmacy.

MORIARTY, SEAN; Cardinal Spellman HS; New Windsor, NY; (Y); 15/509; Trs Intnl Clb; Chorus; School Musical; Nwsp Ed-Chief; Stu Cncl; Mgr Swmmng; High Hon Roll; Pres NHS; Cardinal Spellman Trphy 86; Boston U; Jrnlsm.

MORIN, MANUELA; Hicksville HS; Hicksville, NY; (Y); Dance Clb; Model UN; Capt Varsity Clb; Mrchg Band; Variety Show; Rep Stu Cncl; High Hon Roll; Hon Roll; NHS; Itln Clb 85-87itln Hnr Scty 84-87; Kickln Capt 84-87; Comm.

MORISSET, BERNARD; Bishop Loughlin Memorial HS; Brooklyn, NY; (Y); Radio Clb; Yrbk Stf; Trk; Hon Roll; Psych.

MORLANDO, ANTHONY; Christ The King HS; Ozone Park, NY; (Y); JV L Bsbl; Var Capt Ftbl; St Johns; Sports Info.

MORLEY, SARAH; Emma Willard Schl; Sand Lake, NY; (Y); Orch; Nwsp Phtg; Yrbk Phtg; Rep Trs Stu Cncl; Var Capt Bsktbl; Var L Socr; Var L Sftbl; Var L Vllybl; Church Yth Grp; GAA; Peer Cnslr 85-86; Independent Study As A Stu Athltc Trainer 84-86; Chem.

MORLOCK-WHITNER, CARMALEHA K; Ellicottville Central Schl; Ellicottville, NY; (Y); 15/46; AFS; Am Leg Aux Girls St; Computer Clb; Spanish Clb; Band; Chorus; Color Guard; Concert Band; Mrchg Band; Var Capt Sftbl; Outstndng Instrmntlst 86; Amrcn Lgn Axlry 86; Jean Fitzpatrick Mem Awd 86; Jamestown Cmnty Coll; Cmptr Sci.

MORNING, ANN; Unitd Nations International Schl; New Rochelle, NY; (Y); Concert Band; Orch; School Musical; Lit Mag; Stu Cncl; Ntl Merit Schol; Pres Acad Fit Awd 86; Natl Achvt Scholar 86; Yale U; Pol Sci.

MORONEY, AILEEN; Albertus Magnus HS; Nanuet, NY; (Y); 7/180; Church Yth Grp; Library Aide; Math Clb; Nwsp Rptr; High Hon Roll; Hon Roll; Mu Alp Tht; NHS; Ntl Merit Ltr; Cmmnctns.

MORREALE, JOHN; Lafayette HS; Brooklyn, NY; (Y); Boy Scts; Cmnty Wkr; Yrbk Stf; Hon Roll; Engl Achvt Awds 84; Hotel Mngmnt.

MORREALE, KELLY; Amsterdam HS; Amsterdam, NY; (Y); Office Aide; Chorus; Drm Mjr(t); Gym; Swmmng; Art Cont Collective Cover 86; Cobleskill; Bus.

MORREALE, MATTHEW G; Garden City SR HS; Garden City, NY; (Y); 26/346; Band; Jazz Band; Var Capt Socr; Im Sftbl; Var Tennis; Im Vllybl; High Hon Roll; NHS; Soc Italian Cu Hure Cert Exc 83; Empire ST Soccer Tm 85; Long Isl Select Soccer Tm 85; U PA; Engr.

MORRELLA, JANICE; Alexander Hamilton HS; White Plains, NY; (S); 4/53; French Clb; Key Clb; Yrbk Bus Mgr; Bowling; Trk; High Hon Roll; Jr NHS; NHS; Ntl Merit Schol; Rotary Awd; Mdl Womens Chamber Of Commerce; Rep Stu Govt; U At Albany.

MORRILL, EMMA-KATE; Jamestown HS; Jamestown, NY; (Y); French Clb; SADD; Chorus; Color Guard; Drill Tm; Flag Corp; School Musical; Nwsp Ed-Chief; Nwsp Rptr; 2nd Pl Schlrshp Wstrn NY Schl Press Assn 86; Smmr Jrnlsm Pgm Syrcs U 86; Jrnlsm.

MORRIN, RENEE; Romulus Central HS; Waterloo, NY; (Y); 7/34; Cmnty Wkr; Girl Scts; Red Cross Aide; Teachers Aide; Band; Concert Band; Mrchg Band; Yrbk Stf; High Hon Roll; Hon Roll; CC Finger Lakes; Graphic Art.

MORRIN, RICHARD; North Babylon SR HS; N Babylon, NY; (Y); 9/473; Cmnty Wkr; Var L Socr; Jr NHS; NHS; Finance.

MORRIS, APRIL; Valley Central HS; Montgomery, NY; (Y); 22/315; Band; Variety Show; Hon Roll; NHS; Spanish NHS; Bus Admn.

MORRIS, BRIAN; West Hempstead HS; West Hempstead, NY; (Y); Band; Mrchg Band; JV Bsbl; Var Bsktbl; Var Trk; LI Rec, Park, & Lesiure Svc Assn 86; Nossao Cnty ANCHOR Pgms Vol Yth Achvt Awd 85; Adelphi U; Spec Ed.

MORRIS, CAROL; Minisink Valley HS; Middletown, NY; (Y); Church Yth Grp; Band; Church Choir; Concert Band; Mrchg Band; Nwsp Stf; Trk; Cit Awd; High Hon Roll; NHS; Oneonta ST; Engl Ed.

MORRIS, CHRISTINE; St John The Baptist D HS; W Islip, NY; (Y); Hosp Aide; Flag Corp; Stage Crew; JV Trk; JV Vllybl; Hon Roll; Vet Med.

MORRIS, DANIEL; William E Grady TV HS; Brooklyn, NY; (Y); Aud/Vis; Dance Clb; Math Tm; Office Aide; Service Clb; Nwsp Rptr; Hon Roll; Pride Yankees Awd 86; Engrng.

MORRIS, HOLLY; Churchville-Chili SR HS; Chrchville, NY; (Y); Church Yth Grp; Cmnty Wkr; Spanish Clb; Varsity Clb; Var Tennis; High Hon Roll; Engrng.

MORRIS, JONATHAN; New Rochelle HS; New Rochelle, NY; (Y); French Clb; Ski Clb; Varsity Clb; Band; Nwsp Stf; Lit Mag; Rep Sr Cls; Bsktbl; Coach Actv; Ice Hcky; Cosmo Jr Sccr Lge Slct Tm Prsn 84-86; Advrtsng.

MORRIS, KEVIN; Shenendehowe Central Schls; Clifton Pk, NY; (Y); Aud/Vis; Computer Clb; English Clb; VP Leo Clb; Radio Clb; SADD; Trk; High Hon Roll; Hon Roll; Rep Frsh Cls; Pres Physcl Ftnss Awd; Le Banon Vlly C; Biomed Engr.

MORRIS, LAURIE; Martin Van Buren HS; Queens Village, NY; (Y); 56/565; English Clb; Yrbk Stf; Hon Roll; Superlative Achvt In Creatv Wrtng Mdl 86; Stoney Brook; Humanities.

MORRIS, LOREN W; Mount St Michael Acad; Mt Vernon, NY; (S); 1/309; Ski Clb; Stu Cncl; Var Capt Socr; Hon Roll; NHS.

MORRIS, LYSSA MICHELLE; Hillcrest HS; Jamaica, NY; (Y); 231/801; Dance Clb; Stu Cncl; Girl Scts; Nwsp Stf; Badmtn; Spelmans Hnrs Pgm & Scholar 86; Regents Scholar 86; Spelman Coll; Econ.

MORRIS, MARSEDEAN; Evander Childs HS; Bronx, NY; (S); Dance Clb; Drama Clb; Library Aide; Band; Concert Band; School Play; Nwsp Rptr; Nwsp Stf; Cit Awd; Hon Roll; Band Awd 84; Comp Pgmr.

MORRIS, MATTHEW; Hebrew Acad Of Nasson Cnty; Woodbury, NY; (Y); 12/77; Cmnty Wkr; Office Aide; Service Clb; Temple Yth Grp; Yrbk Ed-Chief; Capt Socr; Hon Roll; NHS; Brandeis U; Law.

MORRIS, MICHAEL; Babylon JR SR HS; Babylon, NY; (Y); 4/150; Am Leg Boys St; Boy Scts; Trs Jr Cls; Trs Sr Cls; Var Crs Cntry; Var Trk; Bausch & Lomb Sci Awd; High Hon Roll; NHS; Ntl Merit Ltr; God & Cntry Awd.

MORRIS, RACHEL; Bishop Loughlin Memorial HS; Brooklyn, NY; (Y); 34/232; Church Yth Grp; Cmnty Wkr; Office Aide; Band; Church Choir; Tennis; Hon Roll; NHS; Prfct Atten Awd; Savings Bond 86; Bishop Loughlin Cert 86; Fordham U; Pre-Med.

MORRIS, SHAWN; Churchville Chili HS; Rochester, NY; (Y); Aud/Vis; Cmnty Wkr; Pep Clb; Radio Clb; Teachers Aide; Stage Crew; JV Im Bsktbl; Coach Actv; Hon Roll; Score Keeper; Awd Bst Drssd 83-84; Hon Awd Defns Bsktbl 83-84; Cmmnctns Dir.

MORRIS, STEPHANIE; Midwood HS; Brooklyn, NY; (Y); 1/5; Band; Chorus; Church Choir; Lit Mag; Socr; U NC; Bus.

MORRIS, STEPHEN; Far Rockaway HS; Arverne, NY; (Y); Key Clb; Office Aide; School Play; Swmmng; Hon Roll; Prfct Atten Awd; Teachers Aide; Yrbk Stf; Mgr Vllybl; Sci & Spnsh Hnr Pin 82-86; Phy Ftnss Awd 85-86; Barlich Coll; Accntnt.

MORRISON, ANITA; Dewitt Clinton HS; Bronx, NY; (Y); Office Aide; Teachers Aide; Chorus; Color Guard; School Musical; Stage Crew; Yrbk Stf; Tennis; Wt Lftg; High Hon Roll; Cornell U; Doctor.

MORRISON, JENNIFER; Albertus Magnus HS; Thiells, NY; (Y); 1/192; Math Tm; Teachers Aide; French Hon Soc; Hon Roll; NHS; Val; Sci Hnr Soc; Math Hnr Soc; Hist Soc Awd; Manhattan Coll; Spec Ed Tchr.

MORRISON, JUDITH; Prospect Heights HS; Brooklyn, NY; (S); Dance Clb; Drama Clb; FBLA; Girl Scts; Math Clb; Natl Beta Clb; Hon Roll; Prfct Atten Awd; Pace U; Bus Admin.

MORRISON, ROSS; Walt Whitman HS; Huntington Sta, NY; (Y); 10/479; French Clb; Key Clb; Concert Band; Nwsp Sprt Ed; Lit Mag; Var Trk; French Hon Soc; High Hon Roll; Jr NHS; Scl Stud Awd 84; Math Cntst Awd 86; Amer Hstry Olympd 86; Law.

MORRISON, STACEY M; Morrisville-Eaton Central HS; Cazenovia, NY; (Y); 3/51; Church Yth Grp; Chorus; Concert Band; Mrchg Band; Var Capt Cheerleading; JV Vllybl; High Hon Roll; Hon Roll; Trs NHS; Rgnts Schlrshp 86; Hope Coll Schlrshp 86; Hope Coll MI; Nrsg.

MORRISSEY, DANIEL; Liverpool HS; Liverpool, NY; (Y); Church Yth Grp; Cmnty Wkr; JA; Hon Roll; Bus Mgmnt.

MORROW, MATT; Long Island Lutheran HS; Huntington, NY; (S); Computer Clb; Band; Concert Band; Bsktbl; Socr; Tennis; High Hon Roll; Hon Roll; NHS.

MORROW, ROBERT; J C Birdlebough HS; Penelvle, NY; (Y); Computer Clb; Library Aide; Ski Clb; Hon Roll; Prfct Atten Awd; Comp Pgmmng.

MORROW, TOM; L I Lutheran HS; Huntington, NY; (Y); 3/95; Mathletes; Chorus; Jazz Band; School Musical; Nwsp Rptr; Yrbk Stf; Socr; Tennis; High Hon Roll; Pres NHS; NROTC; U Virginia; Engrng.

MORROW, VANGIE JILL; Churchville-Chili SR HS; Rochester, NY; (Y); 82/294; FTA; Model UN; Yrbk Ed-Chief; Rep Frsh Cls; Sec Soph Cls; Trs Jr Cls; Rep Sr Cls; Pres Stu Cncl; DAR Awd; Chorus; YFU Exchng Stu Denmark 85; Buffalo ST COLL; Soc Studies.

MORSE, ADRIENNE; Alexander Central HS; Alexander, NY; (Y); Drama Clb; FTA; Chorus; Variety Show; JV Sftbl; Hon Roll; NHS; Acad All-Amer 86; U Of Rchstr; Ed.

MORSE, CHRISTOPHER T; Arlington HS; Poughkeepsie, NY; (Y); 45/560; Aud/Vis; Debate Tm; Ski Clb; Chorus; Hon Roll; NY ST Rgnts Schlrshp 86; Hnrs Key 86; RPI; Mechncl Engrng.

MORSE, DAVID M; La Fargeville Central HS; Lafargeville, NY; (Y); 5/32; Am Leg Boys St; Science Clb; Yrbk Stf; Pres Frsh Cls; Pres Soph Cls; Pres Jr Cls; Pres Stu Cncl; Var Bsbl; JV Var Bsktbl; Hon Roll; Postdam ST; Law.

MORSE, KRISTIN; Schoharie Central HS; Esperance, NY; (S); Key Clb; Ski Clb; Varsity Clb; Band; Chorus; Rep Stu Cncl; JV L Bsktbl; Var L Crs Cntry; Var L Mgr(s); Var L Trk; Recrds Hld 3000 M Trck 82-83; MIP Crss Cntry 83-84; MVP Crss Cntry 84-85; Pre-Dntl.

MORSE, LAURA; Cicero N Syracuse HS; Clay, NY; (S); 9/627; Camera Clb; German Clb; Yrbk Ed-Chief; Yrbk Phtg; Yrbk Rptr; Tennis; Hon Roll; Jr NHS; Oceangrphy.

MORSE, LISA MARIE; Moravia Central HS; Morvavia, NY; (Y); #3 In Class; Am Leg Aux Girls St; School Musical; Swing Chorus; Yrbk Bus Mgr; Sec Stu Cncl; JV Var Vllybl; High Hon Roll; Voice Dem Awd; Debate Tm; Drama Clb; Atwood Spllng Schlrshp 84; Pace U; Intl Mrktng.

MORSE, RICHARD; Groton JR SR HS; Groton, NY; (Y); 5/90; Am Leg Boys St; Church Yth Grp; Computer Clb; Ski Clb; Spanish Clb; Var L Bsbl; Var L Bsktbl; JV Var Ftbl; High Hon Roll; Hon Roll; SUNY-BINGHAMTON; Bus.

MORSE, RICHARD; Schoharie HS; Esperance, NY; (Y); 5/100; Boy Scts; Trs Sr Cls; Capt Crs Cntry; Capt Trk; Capt Wrstlng; NHS; Ntl Merit SF; Am Leg Boys St; Letterman Clb; Elks Awd; Schlr-Athlt Of Yr 86; US Naval Acad Apptmt; NROTC & ROTC Schlrshps; Cornell U; Med.

MORSELLINO, STEVEN; Malverne HS; Malverne, NY; (Y); 3/123; JV Bowling; Var Capt Socr; High Hon Roll; Jr NHS; NHS; Acctg.

MORTENSEN, LANCE; Sachem H S North Campus; Holbrook, NY; (Y); Computer Clb; German Clb; Science Clb; Off Service Clb; Ski Clb; Lit Mag; NHS; Ntl Merit Ltr; Hnrb Mntrn Natl Schtc Wrtng Cont 85; Natl Sci Olympiad Chem 85; Science.

MORTILLARO, DENISE; Clarkstown Nroth HS; Congers, NY; (Y); SADD; Orch; School Musical; Capt Diving; Var L Swmmng; Jr NHS; Mu Alp Tht; Baroque Chamber Orch 83-86; Area All ST Orch 84-85; Coaches Awd Swimmng/Diving 85; Psych.

MORTLOCK, DOUG; Lansing HS; Lansing, NY; (Y); 1/70; Yrbk Phtg; Yrbk Stf; Lit Mag; Socr; Bausch & Lomb Sci Awd; NHS; Ntl Merit SF; Val; NYSAFLT Scholar Awd 86; Cornell U.

MORTLOCK, INGA; Lehman HS; Bronx, NY; (Y); Concert Band; Orch; School Musical; Hon Roll; Awd Eng 85.

MORTON, ANTHONY; Hanau American HS; Apo Ny, NY; (Y); 20/110; Letterman Clb; Spanish Clb; Varsity Clb; Y-Teens; Var Capt Ftbl; Var Trk; Im Wt Lftg; Hon Roll; All-Eurpn Ftbl 86; Mrt Acdmc Achvmnt & Ldrshp 86; Mst Vlbp Plyr Ftbl 86; Bus.

MORTON, JEFFERY T; Brocton Central HS; Fredonia, NY; (Y); 13/52; Am Leg Boys St; Church Yth Grp; Computer Clb; Letterman Clb; Stage Crew; Nwsp Stf; VP Jr Cls; Var Ftbl; Var Mgr(s); Var L Trk; Pltcs.

MORTON, PATRICK H; Hudson Falls SR HS; Hudson Falls, NY; (Y); 23/220; 4-H; Science Clb; Ftbl; Trk; Wt Lftg; NY Beef Ambsdr Alt 85-86; Cnty Horse Bowl; Adironback CC; Mth.

MORTON, SUSAN E; Columbia HS; Rensselaer, NY; (Y); Pres Debate Tm; Pep Band; School Musical; Symp Band; Nwsp Phtg; Ed Yrbk Phtg; Var Tennis; NHS; Ntl Merit Ltr; Smmr Sci Semnr At U S Air Force Acad In Colorago Sprngs 85; U Of Rochester; Bio.

MOSACK, PHILIP; Pine Valley Central Schl; S Dayton, NY; (Y); Ski Clb; Concert Band; Jazz Band; Mrchg Band; Var Capt Ftbl; Var Capt Trk; NY ST Rgnts Schlrshp 86; Grad Frm Pine Vly Wth Hnrs 86; Rochester Inst Tech; Comp Engrn.

MOSBACHER, MARC; Commack HS North; Smithtown, NY; (Y); 1/400; Math Tm; Science Clb; Varsity Clb; Var Capt Tennis; French Hon Soc; High Hon Roll; NHS; Ntl Merit Ltr; Val; 1st Pl Wnnr Sci Fair 84; Long Islnd Sci Cngrss JR Div Hgh Hnr 84; Smithtwn W Invtnl Tnns Sngl 1st Pl; Biochmstry.

MOSCATO, JOHN; Hamburg SR HS; Hamburg, NY; (Y); Church Yth Grp; Cmnty Wkr; Political Wkr; Im JV Bsbl; JV Var Bsktbl; Im Ftbl; Cit Awd; Schl Ltrs Bsktbl,Bsbl,Ftbl 83-86; Bus Mgmt.

MOSCATO, MARGARET; Maria Regina HS; Yonkers, NY; (Y); 6/166; Church Yth Grp; Chorus; School Musical; Nwsp Rptr; Lit Mag; High Hon Roll; NHS; Srv Awd; Ntl Sci Plympd Chem Hon Mntn; Dncr.

MOSCATO, SALVATORE; Archbishop Molloy HS; Ridgewood, NY; (Y); 45/378; Art Clb; Chess Clb; Church Yth Grp; Computer Clb; Intnl Clb; Pep Clb; High Hon Roll; Hon Roll; NHS; SAT Score 1220 87; Psych Major.

MOSCHAK, LISA; Union-Endicott HS; Endwell, NY; (Y); 44/432; French Clb; Key Clb; Ski Clb; Hon Roll; NHS; Most Dedctd Chrldr 84; Regnts Schlrshp 86; Jenny F Snapp Schlrshp 86; PA ST U; Elec Engrng.

MOSCHETTA, SUSAN; Yonkers HS; Yonkers, NY; (Y); 11/287; High Hon Roll; Hon Roll; Berkeley Schls Almni Assn Tuitn Schlrshp 86; Berkeley Schl; Prof Secrtrl.

MOSCOVIC, DINA RENEE; Kenmore East HS; Kenmore, NY; (Y); 5/335; Dance Clb; SADD; Band; Nwsp Rptr; Yrbk Stf; Var Pom Pon; Var Tennis; High Hon Roll; NHS; Intnl Clb; Presdntl Acadmc Ftnss Awd 86; PA ST U; Bus.

MOSELEY, SHARMAINE; Adlai E Stevenson HS; Bronx, NY; (Y); JA; Office Aide; Band; Concert Band; Mrchg Band; Nwsp Stf; Tennis; Hon Roll; Music Awd 84; St Johns U; Bus Admin.

MOSENTHIN, SANDRA R; Oppeqheim Ephratah HS; Johnstown, NY; (Y); 2/29; Trs Church Yth Grp; Sec Girl Scts; Hosp Aide; Rptr Spanish Clb; Nwsp Phtg; Nwsp Rptr; Yrbk Phtg; NHS; Sal; Nwsp Stf; Am Lgn Oratorical Cntst 83-85; Penn View Bible Inst; Mnstry.

MOSER, PAULA; Hilton Central HS; Brockport, NY; (Y); 4/325; Exploring; Math Clb; Aud/Vis; Office Aide; Mrchg Band; Symp Band; Yrbk Stf; Jr Cls; High Hon Roll; NHS; Pre-Law.

MOSES, JOHN; Tinconderoga HS; Ticonderoga, NY; (Y); French Clb; Yrbk Rptr; Bsktbl; Socr; Trk; Bowling Green U; Law.

MOSES, MICHELE; John F Kennedy HS; Plainview, NY; (Y); 8/250; Cmnty Wkr; Sec Debate Tm; Intnl Clb; Model UN; Service Clb; SADD; School Musical; Variety Show; Nwsp Stf; Yrbk Ed-Chief; Natl Hspnc Schlr Fnlst 85-86; U Of VA; Intl Studs.

MOSHER, AMY; Cicero-North Syracuse HS; Clay, NY; (Y); Dance Clb; Rep Frsh Cls; Twrlr; NHS; Fash Inst Tech.

MOSHER, JASON L; Elmira Southside HS; Pine City, NY; (S); 5/400; Boy Scts; Church Yth Grp; Ski Clb; Acpl Chr; Madrigals; School Musical; Rep Jr Cls; JV Socr; JV Tennis; High Hon Roll; NYS Schl Music Assoc 85; Bio Sci.

MOSHER, TOM; Archbishop Walsh HS; Olean, NY; (Y); High Hon Roll; Hon Roll; Pharm.

MOSHOYANNIS, PHILLIP; Oyster Bay HS; East Norwich, NY; (Y); 14/123; Boy Scts; Political Wkr; Thesps; Band; Pres Chorus; Concert Band; Mrchg Band; School Musical; School Play; Yrbk Stf; Cornell U; Law.

MOSIER, CARMEN; La Salle SR HS; Niagara Falls, NY; (Y); 23/250; Am Leg Aux Girls St; Church Choir; Concert Band; Jazz Band; Mrchg Band; Pres Jr NHS; Pres Schlr; AFS; Church Yth Grp; Debate Tm; Louis Armstrong Jazz Awd 86; NY ST Senate Intern Ldr 86; SUNY; Bio Med.

MOSIER, WENDY; Brushton-Moira Central HS; Moira, NY; (Y); Girl Scts; Var Sftbl; JV Var Vllybl; Hon Roll; Intr Dsgn.

MOSKAL, PAULA A; Palmyra-Macedon Central HS; Palmyra, NY; (S); 3/185; Math Tm; Rep Frsh Cls; Rep Soph Cls; Jr Cls; Rep Sr Cls; High Hon Roll; VP NHS; Girls ST 1st Rnnr-Up 85; Harvard Awd 85; Le Moyne; Math.

MOSKALA, ROBIN L; Thomas R Proctor HS; Utica, NY; (Y); 31/200; Cmnty Wkr; Spanish Clb; Hon Roll; NHS; St Schlr; Hartwick Coll; Chld Psychlgy.

MOSKOWITZ, DAVID H; Valley Stream South HS; North Woodmere, NY; (Y); 4/168; Mathletes; Temple Yth Grp; Yrbk Phtg; Bowling; Socr; Bausch & Lomb Sci Awd; High Hon Roll; NHS; Ntl Merit Ltr; Prfct Atten Awd; Rensselaer Polytech Inst Mdl Sci/Math; Rgnts Scshlrshp; Chem Awd.

MOSKOWITZ, LARISSA NOELLE; Gorton HS; Yonkers, NY; (Y); 2/191; Nwsp Ed-Chief; Yrbk Stf; Lit Mag; VP Sr Cls; Var Capt Cheerleading; Var L Tennis; Gov Hon Prg Awd; NHS; Ntl Merit Ltr; Sal; Mcrcs Salute Youth Awd 86; Westchester Cnty Chrldng Scholar 85; Iona Lang Cont 2nd Hnrs Spn II 83; Pace U; Pre-Vet Med.

MOSKOWITZ, SUSAN C; Yeshiva University High Schl For Girl; Forest Hills, NY; (Y); Capt Debate Tm; Temple Yth Grp; Nwsp Bus Mgr; Ntl Merit Ltr; Max Strn Schlrshp 85-89; NYS Rgnts Schlrshp; Stern Coll Fr Wmn; Biolgy.

MOSMEN, JENNIFER; Bethlehem Central HS; Delmar, NY; (Y); 15/304; Hosp Aide; Office Aide; Ski Clb; Rep Frsh Cls; Rep Soph Cls; Rep Jr Cls; Rep Sr Cls; High Hon Roll; NHS; Ntl Merit Ltr; Pres Acadmc Fit Awd 86; Middlebury Coll; Bio.

MOSOVICH, JONATHAN D; The Park School Of Buffalo HS; Buffalo, NY; (Y); Chess Clb; Lit Mag; Trs Jr Cls; Var Socr; Var Tennis; Ntl Merit Ltr; NY Regnts Schlrshp 86; Bio.

MOSS, APRIL; Elmira Southside HS; Elmira, NY; (Y); French Clb; Pep Clb; Chorus; Rep Sr Cls; JV Capt Cheerleading; Trk; High Hon Roll; Masonic Awd; All Cty Chr 82 & 83; All Cnty Chr 82; Natl Achvt Schlrshp Prgm 85; Data Procssng.

MOSS, BRIAN F; Thomas A Edison HS; Elmira, NY; (Y); 6/80; Chrmn Am Leg Boys St; Varsity Clb; Band; Concert Band; Mrchg Band; VP Sr Cls; Var Capt Ice Hcky; Var Capt Tennis; High Hon Roll; Pres Schlr; Rotary Intl Schlrshp, Elks Sullivan Trail Hockey Sprtsmnshp Awd 86; WENY Tennis Awd 85; Union Coll; Bio.

MOSS, DANIELLE; The Mc Burney Schl; New York, NY; (Y); Church Choir; Lit Mag; Stat Crs Cntry; Hon Roll; Jr NHS; NHS; Cmnty Wkr; Dance Clb; Nwsp Stf; YMCA Benihana Schlrshp Japan 84; LEAD Pgm U MD Bus 85; YMCA Yth & Govt 85 & 86; Swarthmore Coll; Econ.

MOSS, JOHN A; Marcellus SR HS; Marcellus, NY; (Y); 19/167; Jazz Band; Symp Band; Var Capt Bsbl; Var Socr; High Hon Roll; Hon Roll; NHS; NYS Rgnts Schlrshp 86; Rollins Coll; Pre Med.

MOSS, KAREN; Lindenhurst SR HS; Lindenhurst, NY; (Y); 51/868; Pres French Clb; German Clb; SADD; Hon Roll; VP NHS; Intl Bus.

MOSS, KATHERINE; Gorton HS; Yonkers, NY; (Y); Band; Bus Schl; Bus.

MOSS, MAGGIE; Mamaroneck HS; Larchmont, NY; (Y); Dance Clb; French Clb; Math Tm; Service Clb; SADD; Stage Crew; Var Vllybl; DAR Awd; The NY ST Cncl For Soc Studies 85; Cert Of Hon; NY ST Sci Superisors Assn Chem Awd 85; History.

MOSSALLAM, SAMER; Fort Hamilton HS; Brooklyn, NY; (Y); 8/586; Cmnty Wkr; French Clb; Hosp Aide; Math Tm; Service Clb; Varsity Clb; JV Swmmng; Wt Lftg; French Hon Soc; 4-H Awd; Frnch Awd 84; Pre-Med.

MOSSING, ANN; Gouverneur Central HS; Gouverneur, NY; (Y); Chorus; Orch; Pres Jr Cls; Sec Stu Cncl; Var Cheerleading; Var Trk; Hon Roll; Jr NHS; NHS; Bus Adm.

MOSSLER, KURT; Westmoreland Central HS; Rome, NY; (Y); #3 In Class; Mathletes; Ski Clb; Concert Band; Drm & Bgl; Mrchg Band; Nwsp Stf; Crs Cntry; Tennis; High Hon Roll; NHS; NYS Rgnts Schlrshp 86; NYS Smmr Schl Of Arts; Illust.

MOST, GLENN; Scarsdale HS; Scarsdale, NY; (Y); Debate Tm; Model UN; Trk; Franklin & Marshall Coll; Psych.

MOSTERT, MICHELE; Delawar Academy & Central HS; Delhi, NY; (Y); Sec Church Yth Grp; Pres Girl Scts; Ski Clb; Spanish Clb; Color Guard; Mrchg Band; Yrbk Stf; Off Sr Cls; VP Stu Cncl; Capt Cheerleading; 3rd Pl Wnr Natl Hstry Cmptn 81; SUNY Cortland NY; Psych.

MOSUNIC, LISA; Lakeland HS; Yorktown Hts, NY; (Y); FBLA; JV Bsktbl; Var Swmmng; Jr NHS; Bus.

MOSURE, TERESA; Oakfield-Alabama Central Schl; Oakfield, NY; (Y); 3/90; French Clb; Math Tm; Ski Clb; Var Crs Cntry; JV Tennis; Var Trk; Var Vllybl; High Hon Roll; NHS; Grls Athltc Assoc Awd Gd Sprtsmnshpo 86; Rgnts Schlrshp 86; Frnch Slc Hghst Avg Awd 85-86; ST U Of NY; Archtctr.

MOTH, LORI; Bishop Ludden HS; Camillus, NY; (S); Exploring; JV Bsktbl; Var Mgr(s); Sftbl; High Hon Roll; NHS; Spnsh Awd, Physcl Sci Awd, & Spnsh Cert; High Hnr Roll & Ntl Hnr Scty; Bryant&stratton; Accntng.

MOTH, LYNN; Bishop Ludden HS; Camillus, NY; (S); Exploring; Bsktbl; Sftbl; High Hon Roll; NHS; Spn, Phys Sci, Bio Awds; Spn Cert; Bryant & Stratton; Acctng.

MOTHERSELL, MICKY; Sandy Creek Central HS; Redfield, NY; (Y); JV Var Bsbl; JV Var Bsktbl; Var Wt Lftg; All Str Awd Var Ftbl, All North All Star Awd; Small Engine Mech.

MOTKOWSKI, JENNIFER; Fairport HS; Fairport, NY; (Y); Cmnty Wkr; Computer Clb; Exploring; Library Aide; Math Tm; JV Stat Bsktbl; Hon Roll; Spanish NHS; Monroe Cnty Math Tm Chmpns 83-84; Law.

MOTLEY, ROHANA; The Stonybrook Schl; Bronx, NY; (Y); 17/84; Art Clb; Dance Clb; Yrbk Phtg; JV Bsktbl; Im Fld Hcky; Mgr(s); JV Sftbl; Var Vllybl; High Hon Roll; Hon Roll; Clark Fndtn Awd 83-85; Ped.

MOTT, ANDREA; Harpursville JR-SR HS; Port Crane, NY; (S); 2/96; Band; Pres Frsh Cls; Pres Soph Cls; Pres Jr Cls; VP Stu Cncl; Var Cheerleading; JV Sftbl; High Hon Roll; NHS; Area All ST Band 85; All Cnty Orchstra 83; Music.

MOTT, ELIZABETH; Jordan-Elbridge HS; Elbdidge, NY; (Y); 11/142; Church Choir; Drm Mjr(t); Mrchg Band; Yrbk Ed-Chief; Yrbk Stf; Var Capt Bsktbl; L Capt Trk; High Hon Roll; Hon Roll; Pres Church Yth Grp; Mst Outstndng Female Ath 86; Alfred U; Ceramc Engrng.

MOTT, LYNETTE; Twin Tiers Baptist HS; Elmira, NY; (S); 2/19; Hosp Aide; Chorus; Orch; Var Socr; DAR Awd; High Hon Roll; Hon Roll; Sal; Cederville Coll; Secndry Ed.

MOTT, TIMOTHY F; Queensbury HS; Glens Falls, NY; (Y); 7/263; Rep Am Leg Boys St; Math Clb; Rep Varsity Clb; School Play; Pres Soph Cls; Pres Jr Cls; Pres Sr Cls; Var L Bsktbl; Var L Tennis; Pres NHS; Hugh Obrian Yth Fndtn Ldrshp Awd 85; Mtrls Sci.

MOTTLE, CHRISTINE; Sacred Heart Acad; E Williston, NY; (S); 4/193; Computer Clb; French Clb; Hosp Aide; Office Aide; Teachers Aide; Variety Show; Tennis; High Hon Roll; NHS; Queen Of Miss Polonia Cntst 85; Med.

MOTWANI, MANOJ; Syosset HS; Syosset, NY; (Y); Cmnty Wkr; Exploring; JV Bsbl; JV Trk; Hon Roll; Regnts Schlrshp 86; Rensselaer Polytech Inst; Med.

MOTYKA, MARY; Oxford Acad HS; Oxford, NY; (Y); 20/86; Am Leg Aux Girls St; Church Yth Grp; French Clb; Red Cross Aide; Color Guard; Mrchg Band; Yrbk Phtg; Yrbk Stf; Rep Frsh Cls; Rep Stu Cncl; Matt Boname Schlrshp; Acad O Hnr; Attndnce Awd; Corland ST; Elem Ed.

MOUCHA, CHRISTINE MARIE; Central Islip SR HS; Central Islip, NY; (Y); Am Leg Aux Girls St; Art Clb; Nwsp Phtg; Nwsp Stf; Var Capt Tennis; Bus.

MOUILLESSEAUX, HEIDI; Spencer-Van Elten HS; Spencer, NY; (Y); Am Leg Aux Girls St; Cmnty Wkr; SADD; Varsity Clb; Yrbk Stf; Pres Soph Cls; Pres Stu Cncl; Capt Fld Hcky; Var Capt Trk; NHS; Eng Schlrshp; Frnch Awds; Am Legn Essy Cntst Wnnr; Nrsg.

MOULIN, ANDREA; Moore Catholic HS; Staten Island, NY; (Y); Swmmng.

MOULTON, JEANNE; Oneonta HS; Oneonta, NY; (Y); 1/174; Girl Scts; Q&S; Ski Clb; Sec Trs Thesps; Nwsp Stf; JV Capt Socr; NHS; Ntl Merit SF; Val; Cornell U.

MOULTON, SANDRA; Avon Central HS; Avon, NY; (Y); 11/91; Girl Scts; Library Aide; Spanish Clb; High Hon Roll; Scholastic Bowl; Ntl Ed Dev Tests Recgntn Superior Perf 84; Perf Aten Awds 82-86; Soc Wrk.

MOULTON, STEVEN B; Sachem HS; Lk Ronkonkoma, NY; (Y); Computer Clb; Ski Clb; Nwsp Rptr; Stu Cncl; JV Socr; JV Tennis; NHS; Regents Schlrshp; Hofstra; Bus Comp Info Syst.

MOULTRIE, MERCEDES Y; Wilson Magnet HS; Rochester, NY; (Y); JV Socr; High Hon Roll; NHS; Spanish Clb; Band; Chorus; Concert Band; Rep Stu Cncl; Urban League Erly Rec 86; Exclnc In Spnsh 83-85; Exclnc In Soc Studies 86; Elec.

MOUNTFORD, ROGER; Scotia-Glenville HS; Scotia, NY; (Y); Key Clb; Spanish Clb; Varsity Clb; Variety Show; Coach Actv; Im JV Socr; Var Swmmng; JV Var Vllybl; Hon Roll; Hartwick.

MOUNTZOUROS, VAS; Newfield HS; Terryville, NY; (S); 89/574; Art Clb; Camera Clb; Church Yth Grp; Q&S; SADD; Nwsp Ed-Chief; Nwsp Rptr; Yrbk Stf; Lit Mag; Fld Hcky; MI Begnnr Fencg 86; VP Art Hnr Socty 86; Hofstra U; Comm Lang.

MOUNTZOUROS, VASILIKY; Newfield HS; Pt Jeff Sta, NY; (Y); 89/515; Art Clb; Q&S; Nwsp Ed-Chief; Nwsp Phtg; Nwsp Rptr; Yrbk Stf; Lit Mag; Fld Hcky; Hon Roll; Jr NHS; NYS Art Tchrs Assoc, Mst Imprvd Beginner Fencing, Nswpr Outstndng Svc 86; Hofstra U; Cmmnctns.

MOUSSIGNAC, SHEILA; Nyack SR HS; Nyack, NY; (Y); Trs Church Yth Grp; Sec Exploring; French Clb; Hon Roll; NHS; Office Aide; Church Choir; Yrbk Stf; Rep Jr Cls; Syracuse U; Med.

MOUSSIGNAC, SPELLMAN; New Rochelle HS; New Rochelle, NY; (Y); Crs Cntry; Var Trk; Var Wrstlng; WV; Bus Adm.

MOUSTAKOS, PETER; Long Island City HS; Astoria, NY; (Y); 11/600; Library Aide; Math Clb; Math Tm; Teachers Aide; Band; Concert Band; Cit Awd; Hon Roll; Jr NHS; NHS; Stonybrook; Bio Engr.

MOUTSIAKIS, DEMETRIUS L; Lindenhurst HS; Lindenhurst, NY; (Y); 3/550; Pres Debate Tm; Trs German Clb; Trs Thesps; Concert Band; Trs Mrchg Band; School Musical; School Play; Var L Trk; Bausch & Lomb Sci Awd; Ntl Merit SF; Natl Sci Olympiad Brnz Medlst 85; Rensselaer Polytech; Physcn.

MOWERS, JACKI; Kendall JR SR HS; Kendall, NY; (Y); 21/90; Ski Clb; Spanish Clb; Concert Band; Jazz Band; Mrchg Band; Rep Stu Cncl; Capt Cheerleading; Socr; High Hon Roll; NHS; Sci.

MOWERS, LINETTE; De Ruyter Central HS; De Ruyter, NY; (Y); 3/37; SADD; Yrbk Stf; VP Jr Cls; Pres Sr Cls; VP Stu Cncl; Capt Cheerleading; Mgr(s); Sftbl; High Hon Roll; Hon Roll; SUNY Brockport; Bus Admn.

MOXLEY, BONNIE; Sherburne-Earlville HS; Eaton, NY; (Y); 18/161; Church Yth Grp; 4-H; French Clb; Office Aide; SADD; Mrchg Band; Trs Stu Cncl; JV Vllybl; 4-H Awd; Hon Roll.

MOY, EDWARD; Seward Park HS; New York, NY; (Y); Art Clb; Chorus; Cooper Union; Arch.

MOY, HELEN; Wagner HS; Staten Island, NY; (Y); 115/498; Math Tm; Office Aide; Band; Chorus; Variety Show; Nwsp Stf; Yrbk Stf; Vllybl; Hon Roll; 5th Yr Spnsh Awd 86; Mt St Mary Coll; Nrsng.

MOY, LINDA; Herbert H Lehman HS; New York, NY; (Y); 1/561; Teachers Aide; School Musical; Tennis; NHS; Prfct Atten Awd; Val.

MOY, ROBERT J; South Shore HS; Brooklyn, NY; (Y); Am Leg Boys St; Boy Scts; Church Yth Grp; FCA; Band; Concert Band; Var L Crs Cntry; Var L Trk; Hon Roll; Prfct Atten Awd; Eagle Scout Awd 86; Crss Cntry Ms Vlbl Plyr Awd 85.

MOY, SANDRA; Fashion Industries HS; New York, NY; (Y); Hosp Aide; Office Aide; Chorus; School Musical; Windw Displ Desgn.

MOY, STEVE; Sheepshead Bay HS; Brooklyn, NY; (Y); 5/429; Library Aide; Math Tm; Science Clb; DAR Awd; Gov Hon Prg Awd; High Hon Roll; Spanish NHS; Acad Olympcs Clb 86; Columbia U; Engrng.

MOYE, DEMETRIA; Center Moriches HS; Ctr Moriches, NY; (Y); DECA; FTA; Var L Bsktbl; Var Socr; Var Trk; JV Vllybl; Hon Roll; Bsktbl Cmp Schlrshp 86; Excel & Ldrshp Hm Ec 86; Mrktng.

MOYE, MONIQUE; Dominican Commercial HS; St Albans, NY; (Y); Drama Clb; PAVAS; Spanish Clb; School Play; Im Gym; High Hon Roll; NHS; Natl Bus Hnr Soc 86; Pres Acad Fit Awd 86; Alpha Kappa Alpha Epsilon Pi Omega Chptr Scholar 86; NYU; Intl Bus.

MOYER, JENNIFER; H Frank Carey HS; Garden City S, NY; (Y); 19/276; VP SADD; Nwsp Rptr; Yrbk Stf; Lit Mag; Var L Bsktbl; Var Capt Trk; High Hon Roll; Hon Roll; Pres Jr NHS; Pres NHS; English.

MOYER, JENNIFER P; Emma Willard Schl; Troy, NY; (Y); Church Yth Grp; Red Cross Aide; Stage Crew; Diving; Swmmng; St Schlr; Drew U.

MOYER, STEFAN J; Newark Valley HS; Owego, NY; (Y); 7/114; 4-H; Ski Clb; Varsity Clb; Socr; 4-H Awd; High Hon Roll; NHS; Rgnts Schlrshp 86; Arch.

MOYNIHAN, COLLEEN; Mexico Academy & Central Schl; Central Square, NY; (Y); Spanish Clb; Yrbk Bus Mgr; Yrbk Rptr; Yrbk Stf; Hon Roll; NHS; Spanish NHS; Schlrshp SPI Cnvntn Syracuse 85; Acctg.

MOYNIHAN, SHAWN; MSGN Farreu HS; Staten Island, NY; (Y); Band; Drill Tm; Mrchg Band; Stage Crew; Im Bsktbl; Im Bowling; JV Socr.

MOZEJKO, CAROL A; The Mary Louis Acad; Brooklyn, NY; (Y); 118/270; Spanish Clb; Hon Roll; NY Regnts Schlrshp 86; St Vincents Schl Nursing; Nrs.

MROZ, TURIA; Depew HS; Depew, NY; (Y); GAA; Variety Show; Yrbk Phtg; Yrbk Rptr; Yrbk Sprt Ed; Debate Tm; Crs Cntry; Capt Trk; Hon Roll; NHS; Pres Phys Ft Awd 84-86; ST Champ Gymn Bars 84; 10th Pl Natl Tumblng 85.

MRZYGLOD, ROBERT; Burgard Vocational HS; Buffalo, NY; (Y); 1/114; High Hon Roll; Hon Roll; Kiwanis Awd; Val; Full Tuition Schlrshp Vale Tech Campus 86; Amer Lgn Schl Awd 86; Vale Tech; Auto Tech.

MUCCINI, LAURA L; St Marys HS; Douglaston, NY; (Y); French Clb; Off Soph Cls; Capt Tennis; NHS; Villanova U.

MUELLER, DENNIS; Southern Cayuga Central Schl; Aurora, NY; (Y); Church Yth Grp; Red Cross Aide; Wrstlng; FFA; Socr; Wrstlng Tm Capt 85-86; Ag.

MUELLER, KLAUS; Saratoga Central Catholic HS; Ballston Lake, NY; (Y); 5/35; Drama Clb; Ski Clb; Teachers Aide; Band; School Play; Yrbk Stf; Tennis; High Hon Roll; NHS; NY ST Regnts Schlrshp 85-86; Acclrtd Stu Skidmore Coll Pgm 85; U Notre Dame; Engrng.

MUELLER, KURT; Aviation HS; Glendale, NY; (Y); Boy Scts; Ski Clb; Nwsp Stf; Wings Awd; Pegasus Soc; Embry Riddle; Aviatn.

MUELLER, MARK; Garden City HS; Garden City, NY; (S); 68/345; Pres Drama Clb; German Clb; Ski Clb; Madrigals; School Musical; School Play; Stage Crew; Swing Chorus; Variety Show; Nwsp Rptr; Regents Scholar 86; Trustees Scholar NYU 86; NYU; Drama.

MUELLER, ROB; Baldwin HS; Baldwin, NY; (Y); Var Bsbl; Office Aide; SADD; JV Bsktbl; JV Ftbl; Im Wt Lftg; JV Wrstlng; High Hon Roll; Hon Roll; NYS Regnts Schlrshp 85-86; NY Inst Of Tech Schlrshp 85-86; Engr.

MUELLER, ROBERT O; Smithtown High School West; Smithtown, NY; (Y); German Clb; Ice Hcky; Hon Roll; Alt Air Force ROTC Schlrshp 86; Rensselaer Polytech Inst; Comp.

MUELLER, ROBT; Niagara Wheatfield HS; N Tonawanda, NY; (Y); Am Leg Boys St; NHS; Elec.

MUERMANN, AMY; Warrensburg Central HS; Warrensburg, NY; (Y); 2/60; 4-H; French Clb; Ski Clb; Yrbk Stf; Bausch & Lomb Sci Awd; Hon Roll; NHS; Pres Clsrm; Elec Engrng.

MUFALLI, NANCY; Sweet Home SR HS; N Tonawanda, NY; (Y); Cmnty Wkr; Concert Band; Orch; Symp Band; Soph Cls; Stu Cncl; Hon Roll; Prfct Atten Awd; Itln Hnr Soc 85-86; Music Cnty & ST Music Awds 83-85; Psych.

MUGLESTON, KENRI; G Ray Bodley HS; Bay City, TX; (Y); 28/266; Boy Scts; Church Yth Grp; Science Clb; Spanish Clb; Varsity Clb; Var Swmmng; Var Tennis; Hon Roll; NY Rgnts Schlrshp 86; Duty To God 86; FL ST U; Dntstry.

MUGNO, ANTHONY; St Marys Boys HS; Roslyn Hts, NY; (S); 10/148; Cmnty Wkr; Ski Clb; Nwsp Rptr; Yrbk Rptr; Yrbk Stf; Var Capt Swmmng; NHS; Spanish NHS; Ntl Rnkng Swmmr Top 16 In Cntry 82-83; Empire ST Games Water Polo Co-Cptn 2nd Pl 85; Fordham U; Finance.

MUGNO, MIKE; Mineola HS; Albertson, NY; (Y); 87/275; Boy Scts; Chorus; Church Choir; Swing Chorus; Bsbl; Bsktbl; Bowling; Socr; Swmmng; Trk; Hnrs Soc Stds; Amer Assoc Coll Lvl Crs; Law.

MUI, MANYI; William C Bryant HS; New York, NY; (Y); 39/623; Math Tm; Teachers Aide; Hon Roll; Regents Coll Schlrshp 86; Arista 85; Foreign Lang Hnr Soc 85; NY UHEALTH Sci.

MUIR, SCOTT A; Pembroke JR & SR HS; Corfu, NY; (Y); 24/109; Boy Scts; Trs Computer Clb; Science Clb; Nwsp Sprt Ed; Bsktbl; Trk; Hon Roll; US Air ForceELCTRNCS.

MULCAHY, DANIEL; Seton Catholic Central HS; Vestal, NY; (Y); Boy Scts; Key Clb; Ski Clb; Varsity Clb; JV Var Socr; Var Trk; NHS; Engrng.

MULCAHY, GREG; Eden SR HS; Eden, NY; (Y); Am Leg Boys St; Cmnty Wkr; Letterman Clb; Political Wkr; SADD; Varsity Clb; Var JV Bsbl; JV Bsktbl; JV Var Ftbl; Hon Roll; Elec Engrg.

MULCAHY, MICHELE; Kendall Central HS; Hamlin, NY; (Y); Pep Clb; Ski Clb; Pres Color Guard; Mrchg Band; Nwsp Stf; JV Var Cheerleading; Var L Pom Pon; High Hon Roll; Hon Roll; Stat Bsbl; Acctng.

MULE, COLETTE; Preston HS; Bronx, NY; (S); Pep Clb; Var Bsktbl; High Hon Roll; NHS; Psych.

MULET JR, LUIS; Garden Schl; Flushing, NY; (S); 6/32; Pres Computer Clb; ROTC; Spanish Clb; Nwsp Stf; Bsktbl; Sftbl; Hon Roll; NHS; Prfct Atten Awd; US Naval Acad; Aerospace.

MULFORD, TODD; Windham-Ashland Jewett Central HS; Windham, NY; (S); 4/28; VP Frsh Cls; VP Soph Cls; Pres Jr Cls; Rep Stu Cncl; Var Bsbl; Var Bsktbl; High Hon Roll; Hon Roll; COMP Sci.

MULHALL, JOHN; Odessa Montour Cntrl HS; Montour Falls, NY; (Y); 1/100; VP Soph Cls; JV Var Bsbl; JV Var Bsktbl; Bausch & Lomb Sci Awd; High Hon Roll; NHS; Val; Quiz Bowl; Rep Stu Cncl; Elmira Coll Key Awd 86; Duke U; Pre-Med.

MULHERN, CHARLES; Sachem North HS; Holtsville, NY; (Y); 35/1579; Ski Clb; Crs Cntry; JV Lcrss; JV Trk; NHS; Amer Lgn Cert Schl Awd 81; Engr.

MULHOLLAND, DANIEL; Bishop Ford Central Catholic HS; Brooklyn, NY; (S); 26/439; Computer Clb; French Clb; Math Clb; Math Tm; Science Clb; Cit Awd; High Hon Roll; NHS; Acctg.

MULL, ANTOINE; Uniondale HS; Hempstead, NY; (Y); Camera Clb; Key Clb; Band; Concert Band; Orch; Nwsp Rptr; Sec Soph Cls; Sec Jr Cls; Sec Sr Cls; Acctg Mgmt.

MULLA, KENNY; Hutch-Tech HS; Buffalo, NY; (Y); Boys Clb Am; Boy Scts; JA; Library Aide; Math Tm; SADD; Yrbk Phtg; VP Jr Cls; Var Bsbl; JV Ice Hcky; U Buffalo; Lwyr.

MULLANE, PATRICIA; Clarkstown HS North; New City, NY; (Y); Cmnty Wkr; Exploring; SADD; Teachers Aide; Ed Lit Mag; JV Capt Cheerleading; Jr NHS; Mu Alp Tht; Peer Helpers Counseling Group 85-87; Psych.

MULLANE, PATRICIA; De Sales Catholic HS; Lockport, NY; (S); 4/30; JV Capt Bsktbl; Var Sftbl; Var Vllybl; Hon Roll; NHS; NEDT Awd; Bus.

MULLARKEY, MARK; Amsterdam HS; Amsterdam, NY; (Y); 11/314; Pres Church Yth Grp; ROTC; Yrbk Stf; Var JV Ftbl; Var JV Trk; High Hon Roll; Hon Roll; NHS; Ntl Merit Ltr; Prfct Atten Awd; Mth.

MULLEN, DAVID C; Xavier HS; Brooklyn, NY; (Y); Cmnty Wkr; Drama Clb; Library Aide; School Play; Stage Crew; Trk; Rgnts Schlrshp 86; Bus Mgmt.

MULLEN, JOY A; Saint Francis Prep; Flushing, NY; (S); 218/653; Church Yth Grp; NFL; Office Aide; Speech Tm; Teachers Aide; Lit Mag; Rep Frsh Cls; Trs Bowling; Spanish NHS; St Johns U; Tchr Engl Ed.

MULLEN, NANCY; Pembroke HS; Corfu, NY; (Y); Pres VP Church Yth Grp; VP 4-H; Band; Jazz Band; Sec Sr Cls; JV Var Bsktbl; Stat Socr; JV Sftbl; JV Vllybl; 4-H Awd; All-Cnty Band Music Awd 84; Music.

MULLEN, PATRICIA; Notre Dame Academy HS; Staten Island, NY; (Y); 2/93; Hosp Aide; Varsity Clb; Pres Stu Cncl; Var Bsktbl; Var Sftbl; NHS; Ntl Merit Ltr; Sal; Bob Lowney Awd Outstndng Stud Athltc; Stud Schlr Athltc Schl & Vrsty Bsktbl/Sftbl:Tm Sprt Awd Sftbl; Johns Hopkins U; Pre-Med.

MULLER, CHANTAL; Emma Willard Schl; Sundown, NY; (Y); Model UN; Teachers Aide; Varsity Clb; Symp Band; Lit Mag; Var Bsktbl; Var Crs Cntry; Var Sftbl; Var Trk; Ntl Sci Awd 84; Yale; Intl Rel.

MULLER, JOHN F; Saratoga Springs SR HS; Saratoga Sprgs, NY; (Y); 17/500; Rep Stu Cncl; High Hon Roll; NHS; Dgtl Eqpt Schlrshp Awd 84; ST Rgnts Schlrshp Awd 86; Union Coll; Lwyr.

MULLER, JOSEPH; Monsignor Farrell HS; Staten Island, NY; (Y); 25/319; Yrbk Stf; Im Bsktbl; Im Ftbl; Hon Roll; Comp Sci.

MULLER, MARK; Greece Athena HS; Rochester, NY; (Y); 26/307; Church Yth Grp; Cmnty Wkr; JA; Science Clb; JV Var Bsktbl; JV Ftbl; Var L Trk; Hon Roll; VP NHS; Prfct Atten Awd; 2nd Tm All Co Bsktbl 85-86; JV MVP 84-85; Engrng.

MULLER, MATT; Guilderland Central HS; Guilderland, NY; (Y); Boy Scts; Church Yth Grp; Letterman Clb; Varsity Clb; Symp Band; Yrbk Rptr; Im JV Bsbl; JV Vllybl; High Hon Roll; Hon Roll; Sci.

MULLER, RICHARD; Port Richmond HS; Staten Island, NY; (Y); 18/800; Math Tm; Band; Orch; Hon Roll; Spanish NHS; Chem.

MULLIGAN, CATHERINE; Bethpage HS; Bethpage, NY; (Y); French Clb; Trs FBLA; Girl Scts; JV Var Pom Pon; High Hon Roll; Hon Roll; Natl Ldrshp Merit Awd 86; Ldrshp Trophy 84; Bus Achvt Awd 86; Bus Mgmt.

MULLIGAN, KATHLEEN MARIE; West Hempstead HS; Island Park, NY; (Y); Am Leg Aux Girls St; VP Art Clb; Spanish Clb; Yrbk Stf; Off Soph Cls; Rep Jr Cls; Off Sr Cls; Var Trk; Hon Roll; NHS; Awd Achvmnt Eng 86; Otstndng Achvmnt Soc Stds 85; Otstndng Achvmnt Soc Stds 86.

MULLIN, CARRIE; Newark SR HS; Marion, NY; (Y); 2/180; Church Yth Grp; Band; Concert Band; Mrchg Band; High Hon Roll; Prfct Atten Awd; NYSSMA Solo Comptn Exc 84 & 86 & Outstndg 85; Elem Tchr.

MULLINS, ROBERT E; St Anthonys HS; Nelville, NY; (Y); 10/389; Am Leg Boys St; Orch; Symp Band; Capt Ftbl; Var Lcrss; NHS; Spanish NHS; Princpls List 84-86; All Lg Ftbl Plyr 85; USAF Acad; Bio.

MULLOY, KELLY; Sauquoit V Alley Central HS; Sauquoit, NY; (Y); 23/99; GAA; Service Clb; SADD; VICA; Chorus; Yrbk Stf; Jr Cls; Stu Cncl; Bowling; Cheerleading; VICA ST Awd Off Practice 2nd Pl 85; VICA ST & Rgnl Data Entry 1st & 2ndpl 86; Mohawk Valley CC; Sec Sci.

MULROY, JOHN; V V S HS; Sherrill, NY; (Y); Church Yth Grp; Mathletes; Bowling; Socr; Vllybl; Brevard Coll FL; Bus Mgmt.

MULVEHILL, ANN M; St Joseph Hill Acad; Brooklyn, NY; (Y); 33/106; Church Yth Grp; Trs Pres FTA; Library Aide; SADD; Trs Sr Cls; JV Var Bsktbl; Var Socr; JV Var Sftbl; Hon Roll; NEDT Awd; NYS Rgnts Schlrshp 86; Pace U Ttees Schlrshp 86; MVP Awd Sftbl Tm 85; Le Moyne Coll.

MULVEY, JOHN; Monsignor Farrell HS; Staten Island, NY; (Y); Boy Scts; Church Yth Grp; Exploring; Rep Frsh Cls; Rep Stu Cncl; JV Bsbl; Im Bsktbl; Im Ftbl; JV Mgr(s); Var L Socr; Phys Thrpst.

MULVIHILL, ARLENE; Saugerties JR SR HS; Saugerties, NY; (S); Pres Spanish Clb; Sec.

MUNCH JR, DONALD J; Lake Shore Central HS; Irving, NY; (Y); 1/320; Am Leg Boys St; Church Yth Grp; 4-H; Ski Clb; Capt Crs Cntry; Trk; God Cntry Awd; High Hon Roll; Jr NHS; NHS; Germ Lang Awd 86.

MUNDT, DENYSE; Mynderse Acad; Seneca Falls, NY; (Y); Church Yth Grp; Drama Clb; Pres French Clb; Off FHA; Chorus; Church Choir; Color Guard; School Musical; School Play; Stage Crew; Finger Lakes CC; Soc Wrk.

MUNDY, KATHLEEN; Holy Trinity HS; Wantagh, NY; (S); 4/313; Capt Math Tm; Band; Nwsp Phtg; Rep Stu Cncl; Im JV Gym; JV Var Sftbl; High Hon Roll; NHS; Ntl Merit Ltr; NEDT Awd; JV Sftbl MVP 84; Acad All Amer 84-85; Phy Educ.

MUNESHWAR, BIBI; Stella Maris HS; Richmond Hill, NY; (Y); Library Aide; Spanish Clb; Hon Roll; Prfct Atten Awd; 1st Hnrs 85; 2nd Hnrs 86; St Johns U; Bio.

MUNGEER, THOMAS; Liberty Central HS; Parksville, NY; (Y); Stage Crew; Capt Bsktbl; Capt Ftbl; Capt Trk; High Hon Roll; Hon Roll; Prfct Atten Awd; AAA Drvr Educ Awd 86; Spcl Rcgntn & Hnr Awd Arch 85&86; Sfty Ptrl 84-86; Arch.

MUNGER, JEWELL; John C Birdlebough HS; Penelvle, NY; (Y); Exploring; French Clb; SADD; Nwsp Stf; JV Socr; JV Trk; JV Vllybl; Hon Roll; NHS; Natl Hstry & Govt Awd 86; Oswego.

MUNGIN, MELVIN; Mount Vernon HS; Mount Vernon, NY; (Y); 13/550; Boy Scts; Computer Clb; Library Aide; Math Tm; Church Choir; JV Ftbl; High Hon Roll; Jr NHS; Stu Mnth In Math 84-85; Tau Epsilon Pi 86; Hgh Scorer In Schl Math Cntsts 84-85; U Of PA; Math.

MUNIZ, ALICE; Catherine Mcauley HS; Brooklyn, NY; (S); 4/70; Cmnty Wkr; Chorus; Rep Stu Cncl; Badmtn; Gym; JV Sftbl; High Hon Roll; Hon Roll; NHS; Dntstry.

MUNIZ, CARMEN; Frontier Central HS; Hamburg, NY; (Y); Church Yth Grp; Spanish Clb; Concert Band; U Of Buffalo; Trnsltr.

MUNIZ, LINDA; Christopher Columbus HS; Bronx, NY; (Y); 13/671; Math Tm; Band; Hon Roll; NHS; Prfct Atten Awd; Arista 82-86; Regnts Schlrshp 86; NY City Coll; Pre-Dntstry.

MUNIZ, YOLANDA; Maria Regina HS; Yorktown Hghts, NY; (Y); Hosp Aide; JA; Key Clb; Library Aide; Trk; Wstchstr Bus Inst Schlrshp 86; Wstchstr Bus Inst; Scrtrl Sci.

MUNLEY, JOHN; Union Endicott HS; Endwell, NY; (Y); Am Leg Boys St; Key Clb; Mathletes; Varsity Clb; JV Bsktbl; Var L Tennis; Bausch & Lomb Sci Awd; High Hon Roll; NHS; Div I All Star Tennis 85.

MUNLEY JR, PAUL; Union Endicott HS; Endwell, NY; (S); 18/450; Church Yth Grp; Key Clb; Mathletes; Nwsp Stf; Yrbk Stf; Rep Stu Cncl; Var L Ftbl; High Hon Roll; Hon Roll; Pres NHS; ROTC Schlrshp 86; Acdmc All-Amer 84-85.

MUNN, JOHN F; La Salle SR HS; Niagara Falls, NY; (S); 6/250; Library Aide; Hon Roll; NHS; GMI; Ind Admn.

MUNOZ, GLORIMAR; Midwood HS; Brooklyn, NY; (Y); Cmnty Wkr; Office Aide; Hlth Prof.

MUNOZ, IVETTE; Beacon HS; Beacon, NY; (Y); Robert Fiance Bty Inst; Csmtlgy.

MUNOZ, LUZ A; Perfomring Arts At La Guardia HS; Jackson Heights, NY; (Y); 43/565; Church Yth Grp; Drama Clb; Service Clb; Teachers Aide; Church Choir; School Musical; School Play; Stage Crew; Variety Show; Rep Sr Cls; Natl Fndtn Advncmnt In Arts 86; Bnai Brith Awd Acting 86; Brigham Young U; Actng.

MUNOZ, MAGALI; Eastern District HS; Brooklyn, NY; (Y); Church Yth Grp; Drama Clb; Spanish Clb; Gym; Guaridia CC; Comp Sci.

MUNOZ, ROBERT; St Agnes HS For Boys; New York, NY; (Y).

MUNOZ, WANDA; Dewitt Clinton HS; Bronx, NY; (Y); Key Clb; Keywanettes; Radio Clb; Varsity Clb; Y-Teens; Chorus; Concert Band; School Musical; School Play; Nwsp Rptr; Comp Lit.

MUNRO, MICHAEL; Bishop Maginn HS; Albany, NY; (S); French Clb; Red Cross Aide; Band; Mrchg Band; Var Bsbl; Var Bsktbl; High Hon Roll; NHS; Ntl Merit Ltr; Geom Awd 84; Schlrp To Bishop Maginn 83-87; Presdntl Outstndg Acad Achvt Awd 84-85; Engrg.

MUNROE II, JAMES; Marcus Whitman HS; Canandaigua, NY; (Y); 1/125; Pres Model UN; Varsity Clb; Rep Jr Cls; Pres Stu Cncl; Var Bsbl; Var Bsktbl; Var Capt Ftbl; High Hon Roll; NHS; Val; NROTC Schlrshp 86; NYS Regnts Schlrshp 86; Cornell U; Biogntl Engr.

MUNSON, JAMES N; Hicksville HS; Hicksville, NY; (Y); Cmnty Wkr; Spanish Clb; Orch; Lit Mag; Rep Stu Cncl; High Hon Roll; Sec Jr NHS; NHS; Ntl Merit Ltr; Spanish NHS; Norbert M Nagler Memrl Schlrhsp Spnsh 84; Natl Schl Orch Awd 84; Coll Engl Profssr.

MUNSON, TAMMY; Sandy Creek Central Schl; Lacona, NY; (S); French Clb; VP Frsh Cls; VP Jr Cls; VP Stu Cncl; Var Capt Cheerleading; Hon Roll; NHS; VFW Awd; Cmnty Wkr; Mst Prmsng Frshmn Grl 84.

MUNYAK, JOHN; Smithtown High School East; Nesconset, NY; (Y); Boy Scts; Key Clb; Orch; JV Var Bsktbl; High Hon Roll; NHS; Pres Schlr; Church Yth Grp; God Cntry Awd; Hon Roll; Italian Natl Hnr Soc 84-86; NYS Regents Schlrshp 86; Newsday Hnr Carrier 86; City Coll NY; Bio-Med.

MUNZ, TRACEY; Blind Brook HS; Rye Brook, NY; (Y); Spanish Clb; Band; JV Fld Hcky; Var JV Socr; Ntl Merit Ltr; Art.

MUNZE, BILL; East Syracuse-Minda HS; E Syracuse, NY; (Y); French Clb; Science Clb; Ski Clb; Band; Concert Band; Im Vllybl; High Hon Roll; Hon Roll; Jr NHS; NHS; Cornell; Attrny At Law.

MUNZER, JOSEPH; St John The Baptist Diocesan HS; Hauppauge, NY; (S); 14/501; Var Capt Bsktbl; Var Golf; High Hon Roll; Ntl Bus Hnr Soc Awd 86; Accntng.

MURA JR, JOHN; Paul V Moore HS; Brewerton, NY; (Y); 3/275; Boy Scts; Varsity Clb; School Play; Yrbk Stf; Crs Cntry; JV Lcrss; JV Var Socr; JV Trk; JV Var Wrstlng; Var High Hon Roll; Engnrng.

MURAIDEKH, ELI; Benjamin N Cardozo HS; Little Neck, NY; (Y); 1/510; Hosp Aide; Science Clb; School Play; Lit Mag; Trs Sr Cls; NHS; Scholastic Bowl; Spanish Clb; School Musical; Yrbk Stf; Westinghouse Sci Talent Srch Fnlst 86; Intl Sci & Engrng Fair Fnlst 86; Govnrs Comm Schltc Achvt 86; Yale U.

MURAIDEKH, ELIE; Benjamin N Cardozo HS; Little Neck, NY; (Y); 1/510; Hosp Aide; Scholastic Bowl; School Play; Trs Sr Cls; Gov Hon Prg Awd; NHS; Val; Drama Clb; Math Tm; Science Clb; 45th Annl Westinghs Sci Tlnt Srch Fnlst 86; ISEF Fnlst 86; Qun Coll Pres Awd Achvt 86; Yale.

MURALT, GINA; Ramstein HS; Apo New York, NY; (Y); Dance Clb; Library Aide; Spanish Clb; Cheerleading; Mgr(s); Powder Puff Ftbl; Socr; Hon Roll; Outstndg Stu Achvt 85-86; St Cloud ST MN; Med.

MURARKA, AMAL; Shenendehowa SR HS; Clifton Pk, NY; (Y); 7/675; English Clb; Intnl Clb; Model UN; SADD; Jazz Band; Symp Band; Stu Cncl; High Hon Roll; NHS; Ntl Merit Ltr; Georgetown U; Pre-Med.

MURASKI, MICHELLE; Guilderland Central HS; Schenectady, NY; (Y); #72 In Class; Key Clb; Trs Varsity Clb; Stu Cncl; Var L Socr; Var L Sftbl; Var L Tennis; High Hon Roll; Hon Roll; Jr NHS; NHS; Elmer C Schacht Scholar Awd 86; NYS Regents Scholar 86; Town Govt Day Awd 86; U VT; Lib Arts.

MURCH, PAT; Odessa-Montour HS; Odessa, NY; (Y); Boy Scts; Varsity Clb; Var L Bsbl; Var L Bsktbl; Hon Roll; Life Scout; Ithaca Coll; Phys Ed.

MURCHIE, CANDY; Tonawanda JR SR HS; Tonawanda, NY; (Y); Church Yth Grp; Cmnty Wkr; French Clb; Hosp Aide; Political Wkr; Church Choir; Jazz Band; School Musical; Hon Roll; Kiwanis Awd; Niagara Cnty CC; Nrsg.

MURDEN, GARFIELD; Aviation HS; Brooklyn, NY; (Y); 209/415; Sec Pres Boy Scts; Pres Church Yth Grp; CAP; Exploring; Science Clb; VICA; Chorus; Var Ftbl; Prfct Atten Awd; Stanford U; Civil Engr.

MURDICK, MICHELLE; Skaneateles Central HS; Skaneateles, NY; (Y); 65/153; Teachers Aide; Chorus; Church Choir; Symp Band; Hon Roll; Cayuga CC; Spec Educ.

MURDOCK, MICHELLE; Victor Central SR HS; Victor, NY; (Y); 13/230; French Clb; ROTC; Varsity Clb; Yrbk Rptr; Rep Stu Cncl; L Swmmng; L Trk; Pres NHS; Rgnts Schlrshp 86; Aquatic Ldrs V-P 83-86; Prsdntl Acdmc Ftns Awd 86; U Of FL; Aerntcl Engr.

MURDOCK, RONDA; Mynderse Acad; Seneca Falls, NY; (Y); 6/144; Am Leg Aux Girls St; Chorus; Jazz Band; Mrchg Band; Yrbk Bus Mgr; Rep Stu Cncl; High Hon Roll; NHS; Pres Schlr; Regnts Schlrshp & Goulds Pumps Inc Schlrshps 86; ST U Of NY Coll Oswego; Math.

MURDOCK, SUZANNE; Oneonta HS; Maryland, NY; (Y); FBLA; Ski Clb; Spanish Clb; Trk; Cobleskill ST; Bus Adm.

MURE, JOSEPH V; Monticello HS; Monticello, NY; (Y); 41/195; Boy Scts; Drama Clb; Capt Math Tm; Band; Jazz Band; School Musical; School Play; Mgr Stage Crew; Nwsp Phtg; Yrbk Phtg; SUNY At Buffalo; Engr.

MURNANE, LISA; Hoosick Falls Central Schl HS; Hoosick Falls, NY; (Y); Church Yth Grp; Drama Clb; Red Cross Aide; Ski Clb; SADD; Band; Chorus; Church Choir; School Musical; School Play; Hudson Valley CC; Crmnl Justc.

MURNEY, JOELL; Waterloo SR HS; Clyde, NY; (S); 12/174; Pres French Clb; Chrmn SADD; Varsity Clb; Nwsp Ed-Chief; Yrbk Ed-Chief; Stu Cncl; Tennis; NHS; Rotary Awd; Voice Dem Awd; Regents Scholar; Engl.

MURPHY, BRIAN; V S Central HS; Valley Stream, NY; (Y); AFS; Computer Clb; German Clb; Science Clb; Spanish Clb; Chorus; Socr; Jr NHS; NHS; Spanish NHS; Germn Hnr Soc; SADD.

MURPHY, BRIAN H; St Francis Prep; Fresh Meadows, NY; (S); 233/746; Drm & Bgl; Mrchg Band; School Play; Ftbl; Wt Lftg; Intnl Clb; MVP Ftbl 84; John Zeek Marchassalla Schlrshp,Ldrshp And Chrctr 85; Penn ST; Aerontcs.

MURPHY, CELESTE MICHELE; Freeport HS; Freeport, NY; (Y); 71/450; Cmnty Wkr; Computer Clb; Pep Clb; Mrchg Band; Yrbk Phtg; Rep Soph Cls; Rep Jr Cls; Rep Sr Cls; Rep Stu Cncl; Var Vllybl; Natl Assn Advncd Colord People 86; Syracuse U; Elec Engr.

MURPHY, CHRISTINE; Roosevelt HS; Yonkers, NY; (Y); Cmnty Wkr; Drama Clb; SADD; Capt Flag Corp; School Musical; School Play; Rep Frsh Cls; Rep Soph Cls; Rep Jr Cls; Mgr(s).

MURPHY, CHRISTOPHER; Spackenkill HS; Poughkeepsie, NY; (Y); 63/176; Computer Clb; Drama Clb; Thesps; School Musical; Camp Fr Inc; Stage Crew; Ftbl; Ntl Merit SF; Comp Sci.

MURPHY, CINDY; The Bronx HS Of Science; Bronx, NY; (Y); Cmnty Wkr; Key Clb; Library Aide; Office Aide; Concert Band; Nwsp Rptr; Nwsp Stf; Prfct Atten Awd; Brdcstng.

MURPHY, COLLEEN; Chenango Valley HS; Binghamton, NY; (Y); Cmnty Wkr; Varsity Clb; Concert Band; Jazz Band; Mrchg Band; Trs Sr Cls; Var Capt Cheerleading; Var JV Sftbl; High Hon Roll; NHS; Salute To Yth Pgm 86; Tchr Rcmmdtn Achvmnt Awd 84; Ithaca Coll; Physcl Thrpy.

MURPHY, DANIEL J; Smithtown West HS; Hawppauge, NY; (Y); 38/430; Boy Scts; School Musical; Pres Sr Cls; Var L Trk; L Capt Wrstlng; High Hon Roll; NHS; Exploring; ROTC; Band; Drcl Natl Cmptn 4th Plc 86; NYS Rsrch Cmptn Fnlst 85; Lng Islnd Yth Of Yr 86; Drexel U; Mtrlgy.

MURPHY, DAVID; Archbishop Malloy HS; Bayside, NY; (Y); 40/400; Nwsp Rptr; Swmmng; Rutgers U; Bio Sci.

MURPHY, DIANE; Patchogue-Medford HS; Medford, NY; (S); 3/658; Band; Concert Band; Mrchg Band; Orch; Symp Band; Jr NHS; NHS; Ntl Merit Ltr; Spanish NHS; Rochester U; Music.

MURPHY, DONNA; Fredonia HS; Fredonia, NY; (Y); Church Yth Grp; Nwsp Stf; Cheerleading; Sftbl; Trk; Vllybl; Ntl Chrldrs Assn Awd Of Excllnc 85; Art.

MURPHY, EDWARD; Sacred Heart HS; Yonkers, NY; (Y); 40/215; Boy Scts; Computer Clb; Science Clb; Band; Bsktbl; Var Bowling; Im Vllybl; Hon Roll; Westchester; Elec Engr.

MURPHY, EDWARD D; Newfare SR HS; Burt, NY; (S); 3/182; Math Clb; Quiz Bowl; Trs Ski Clb; Varsity Clb; Stage Crew; Yrbk Phtg; Pres Stu Cncl; Capt Wrstlng; Cit Awd; Trs NHS; 3rd Pl William Nevins HS Math Cmptn 85; Frnch II & III Acad Awds 84-85; Harvard; Law.

MURPHY, ELIZABETH; Academy Of St Joseph; Hauppauge, NY; (Y); Church Yth Grp; Cmnty Wkr; Debate Tm; Service Clb; Teachers Aide; Yrbk Rptr; Hon Roll; Cathlc Dghtrs Schlr 83; Bus.

MURPHY, ERIN; Skaneateles Central HS; Skaneateles, NY; (S); French Clb; Yrbk Stf; JV Var Bsktbl; Var Crs Cntry; JV Socr; Capt Var Sftbl; Var Tennis; High Hon Roll; Hon Roll; NHS; Comp Sci.

MURPHY, FRANCINE; East Islip HS; Great River, NY; (Y); 24/425; FTA; Chorus; Flag Corp; School Musical; High Hon Roll; Hon Roll; Jr NHS; NHS; Spanish NHS; Adelphi U Trstee Schlrshp 86; Pres Acad Fitness Awd 86; Adelphi U; Math.

MURPHY, JAMES P; Hauppauge HS; Hauppauge, NY; (S); DECA; Office Aide; Teachers Aide; Prfct Atten Awd; 1st Pl Rgnl & 3rd Pl ST DECA-RESTRNT Mrktng & Mgmt 86; Suffolk CC.

MURPHY, JEFF; Maryvale SR HS; Cheektowaga, NY; (Y); DECA; Varsity Clb; Variety Show; JV Im Bsbl; Var JV Bsktbl; JV Im Ftbl; Var L Trk; High Hon Roll; Hon Roll; Prfct Atten Awd; Ftbl All Star 1st Team 85; Bsktbll MIP 86; Best Dfnsv Lineman Ftbl 85; SUNY; Phys Ed.

MURPHY, JEFFREY L; Westbury HS; Westbury, NY; (Y); Boy Scts; Teachers Aide; Varsity Clb; School Play; Stage Crew; Var L Bsbl; Im Bsktbl; L Var Ftbl; L Mgr Gym; Swmmng; Cert Awd Prtcptn BSU & UNICEF 86; Cert Awd Prtcptn Mgr Gymnstcs 85; Cert Awd Prtcptn JV Bsbll 85; Comp Engnrng.

MURPHY, JIM R J; Fairport HS; Fairport, NY; (Y); Cmnty Wkr; Y-Teens; Trk; Wrstlng; Hon Roll; Outdr Trck Red Raider Awd 86; Indoor Trck Red Raider Awd 85-86; Road Runner Club Amer-1500 Mi Club 83; Monroe CC; Early Chldhd Rcrtn.

MURPHY, JOHN; Catholic Central HS; Menands, NY; (Y); Computer Clb; Math Clb; Ski Clb; SADD; Varsity Clb; Bsbl; Bsktbl; Ftbl; Tennis; Hon Roll.

MURPHY JR, JOHN; Susquehanna-Valley HS; Conklin, NY; (Y); Church Yth Grp; CAP; JV Im Ftbl; JV Var Trk; Im Wt Lftg; Capt Var Wrstlng; Hon Roll; Jessie Baker Schlrshp 85-86; SR Wrstlg Schlrshp & Awds 85-86; Rochester Inst; Comp Engrng.

MURPHY, JULIA; Kenmore East SR HS; Kenmore, NY; (Y); Quiz Bowl; Nwsp Rptr; Yrbk Ed-Chief; Yrbk Stf; Lit Mag; JV Tennis; Hon Roll; Potsdam U; Arch.

MURPHY, KATHLEEN; Sacred Heart Acad; Rockville Centre, NY; (Y); Dance Clb; Pres FHA; Hosp Aide; Office Aide; Pep Clb; Political Wkr; Chorus; Madrigals; Yrbk Bus Mgr; Yrbk Phtg; Fnlst Natl Heritg Essy Cntst 85; Acctg.

MURPHY, KELLY; Mercy HS; Albany, NY; (Y); Art Clb; Church Yth Grp; Cmnty Wkr; Dance Clb; Drama Clb; JA; Spanish Clb; Chorus; School Play; Stage Crew; Cazenovia Coll; Fashn Merch.

MURPHY, KERRY; Our Lady Of Victory HS; New York, NY; (S); 10/138; Hosp Aide; Office Aide; SADD; Lit Mag; Rep Stu Cncl; Hon Roll; Rep NHS; Spanish NHS; Bio Awd 84; Stu Recog Awd 84-85; Hugh O Brien Yth Fndtn Schl Wnnr 85; Bus.

MURPHY, LINDA; West Babylon SR HS; W Babylon, NY; (Y); 92/413; Drama Clb; Leo Clb; School Play; Acctg.

MURPHY, LORI; Peekskill HS; Peekskill, NY; (S); 3/156; Band; Trs Stu Cncl; Stat Bsktbl; Stat Ftbl; JV Capt Socr; Var L Sftbl; Var L Swmmng; High Hon Roll; NHS; Ntl Merit Ltr; Schlrshp Awds Hgh Hnr Rll Every Qtr 84-86; Hlth.

MURPHY, LORINDA; Cicero-North Syracuse HS; Clay, NY; (S); 7/650; Mathletes; Math Clb; Math Tm; Band; Color Guard; Mrchg Band; Hon Roll; Jr NHS; Psych.

MURPHY, MANON; Msgr Scanlan HS; College Point, NY; (Y); 26/276; Dance Clb; Yrbk Stf; Crs Cntry; Trk; Hon Roll; Prfct Atten Awd; Airlines.

MURPHY, MARY; Brewster HS; Patterson, NY; (Y); 30/190; Top Career Stdnt Grad Clss 86; Outstndng Awd Hlth Asstg Geriatrcs 85; Comp Awarnss Schlrshp 83; Tchg.

MURPHY, MATHEW J; Town Of Webb HS; Big Moose, NY; (Y); 2/34; Am Leg Boys St; Aud/Vis; Cmnty Wkr; Debate Tm; Math Clb; Math Tm; Pep Clb; Spanish Clb; Varsity Clb; School Play; Outsndng Achvt Math 80; Army ROTC 4 Yr Schlrshp & Nvl ROTC 4 Yr Schlrshp 86; W Pnt Schlrshp Prp 86; Clarkson U; Chem Engrng.

MURPHY, MAUREEN; Lawrence HS; Cedarhurst, NY; (Y); 19/414; Sec AFS; Pres Key Clb; Yrbk Bus Mgr; Rep Stu Cncl; Socr; Sftbl; Trk; Vllybl; NHS; Ntl Merit Ltr; PTA Awd 86; Untd Way Ctznshp Awd 86; U Of Notre Dame; Intl Bus.

MURPHY, MELISA; Somers HS; Granite Spgs, NY; (Y); AFS; SADD; Band; Chorus; Yrbk Stf; Rep Frsh Cls; Mgr(s); Swmmng; JV Capt Tennis; JV Vllybl; Music Awd; Vrs Swmmng Awds; Intl Frgn Affrs.

MURPHY, MICHAEL; Southampton HS; Southampton, NY; (Y); French Clb; Letterman Clb; Varsity Clb; Band; Concert Band; Jazz Band; Mrchg Band; Pep Band; Trs Frsh Cls; Var Capt Ftbl; Elec Engnrng.

MURPHY, MICHAEL S; Don Bosco Prep; Monsey, NY; (Y); 18/186; Model UN; Band; Concert Band; Jazz Band; Mrchg Band; Orch; Nwsp Phtg; Yrbk Phtg; Yrbk Stf; Var Golf; All League Bergen Cty Golf Tm 86; Music Awd Hgst Avg 86; Villanova U; Pol Sci.

MURPHY, MICHELE P; Saint Joseph Hill Acad; Staten Island, NY; (Y); 11/106; Math Tm; Concert Band; Orch; School Musical; Trs Frsh Cls; Hon Roll; NHS; Ntl Merit SF; NEDT Awd; Spanish NHS; Fordham U.

MURPHY, MICHELLE; Brockport HS; Hamlin, NY; (Y); Latin Clb; Score Keeper; Socr; Trk; High Hon Roll; Hon Roll; Ntl Merit Schol; Paul Smiths Coll; Htl/Bus Mgmt.

MURPHY, NANCY; Salamanca Central HS; Little Valley, NY; (Y); 29/143; Spanish Clb; Color Guard; Mrchg Band; High Hon Roll; Hon Roll; Jamestown CC; Nrsng.

MURPHY, PAMELA J; St Francis Prep; Flushing, NY; (S); 64/746; Nwsp Rptr; JV Crs Cntry; Im Powder Puff Ftbl; Var JV Sftbl; JV Trk; NHS.

MURPHY, PETER T; Charles H Roth HS; Rush, NY; (Y); 25/230; Am Leg Boys St; Boy Scts; Exploring; Science Clb; Ski Clb; Spanish Clb; Tennis; Hon Roll; NHS; Btty Bsktbll 84-85; Pilot.

MURPHY, ROSE; St Edmund HS; Brooklyn, NY; (Y); Church Yth Grp; Dance Clb; Var Capt Bsktbl; Im Coach Actv; Hon Roll; Eng Awd 84; Span Awd 84; Rel Awd 86; Emotionally Disturbed.

MURPHY, SEAN; Aquinas Inst; Rochester, NY; (Y); Ski Clb; SADD; JV Var Golf; Im Vllybl; High Hon Roll; Hon Roll; Achvt Awd Thlgy & Englsh; Accptd Boston Coll Smmr Blgy; Cornell; Vet.

MURPHY, STEPHEN C; Fordham Prep; Pelham, NY; (Y); Computer Clb; Debate Tm; Hosp Aide; Cmnty Wkr; NEDT Awd; Stock Market.

MURPHY, SUZANNE; Sacred Heart Acad; Rockville Centre, NY; (Y); SADD; School Play; Stage Crew; Mgr(s).

MURPHY, TARA; St Edmund HS; Brooklyn, NY; (Y); Cheerleading; Hon Roll; Frnsc Med.

MURPHY, THOMAS; West Seneca West SR HS; W Seneca, NY; (Y); Debate Tm; French Clb; Red Cross Aide; SADD; School Musical; Nwsp Ed-Chief; Stu Cncl; Cit Awd; French Hon Soc; NHS; Grad Regents W/Hnrs 86; Canisius Coll; Bus.

MURPHY, TINA; Greece Olympia HS; Rochester, NY; (S); 17/277; Pres DECA; FBLA; Ski Clb; Varsity Clb; JV Socr; Var Swmmng; Im Vllybl; High Hon Roll; Hon Roll; NHS; Outstndng DECA Stu 86; SUNY Genesco; Mgmt Sci.

MURRAY, BETHANY; Mount Mercy Acad; Orchard Park, NY; (Y); 1/215; Cmnty Wkr; Computer Clb; French Clb; Hosp Aide; Quiz Bowl; Swing Chorus; Lit Mag; Stu Cncl; High Hon Roll; NHS; Wstrn NY Acad All Star 86; Hgst Acad Achvt Soph Jr Cls 84-86; Mnhtn Musc Fest Slvr Mdl 85.

MURRAY, BONNIE; West Irondequoit HS; Rochester, NY; (Y); Church Yth Grp; French Clb; SADD; School Musical; Yrbk Phtg; Yrbk Stf; Rep Soph Cls; Rep Jr Cls; Rep Sr Cls; Coach Actv; Geneseo; Elem Spcl Ed.

MURRAY, BRIAN; Waterford-Halfmoon HS; Waterford, NY; (Y); 5/86; Math Clb; Math Tm; Rep Stu Cncl; JV Var Socr; Elks Awd; High Hon Roll; Siera Coll; Bio.

MURRAY, CHRISTOPHER; Fayetteville-Mawlius HS; Manlius, NY; (Y); 140/335; Badmtn; Bsktbl; Suny Plattsburgh; Cvl Engrng.

MURRAY, CYNTHIA; Ramstein American HS; Apo New York, NY; (Y); Church Yth Grp; Church Choir; Drill Tm; Variety Show; Nwsp Rptr; Yrbk Stf; Rep Trs Stu Cncl; Var L Gym; Var L Socr; Hon Roll; Mst Outstndg Vrsty Gymnstcs 85-86; Outstndng Achvt Awd U S Hstry & Engl II 85-86.

MURRAY, DAVE; Smithtown High School East; Nesconset, NY; (Y); Ski Clb; Avncs.

MURRAY, FARRELL; Burgard Vocational HS; Buffalo, NY; (Y); 8/125; JA; Library Aide; Varsity Clb; Stage Crew; Var Ftbl; Var Mgr(s); Var Score Keeper; U Buffalo; Astrnmy.

MURRAY, KAREN; Sacred Heart Acad; Mineola, NY; (S); 3/187; Math Tm; Science Clb; Spanish Clb; High Hon Roll; NHS; Catholic HS Math Lg Jr Vrsty Div Outstndng Achvt 85; Acad All-Amer 85; Vet Med.

MURRAY, LINDA; Cardinal O Hara HS; Buffalo, NY; (Y); 12/120; Church Yth Grp; Drama Clb; Church Choir; Cheerleading; Hon Roll; Acdmc Var Lttr 86; Chrldng Mdl 84; NCCC; Chld Psychlgy.

MURRAY, LISA; Newfane SR HS; Burt, NY; (Y); Girl Scts; Varsity Clb; Band; Symp Band; JV Var Bsktbl; Var Trk; Acctg.

MURRAY, MARYANNE; School Of The Holy Child; Pelham, NY; (S); Art Clb; GAA; Ski Clb; Chorus; School Musical; Nwsp Phtg; Nwsp Stf; Yrbk Phtg; Rep Frsh Cls; Pres Jr Cls; 1/2 Tutn Schlrshp 83-87; Hnrs Excllnc Engl 84-85; Georgetown U; Photo.

MURRAY, PATRICIA; St Francis Prep; Flushing, NY; (Y); 338/750; Var JV Cheerleading; Im Ftbl; Var JV Sftbl; Im Vllybl; Irish Dncg 12th & 18th Pl Regnl & 19th Pl Natl Champ 83-84; Wrld Champ Ireland 84-85; Phys Ther.

MURRAY, PATRICK; Plattsburgh HS; Rouses Point, NY; (Y); Boy Scts; CAP; Model UN; Ski Clb; Var Golf; Var Ice Hcky; Var Socr; Hon Roll; Cpa.

MURRAY, ROBERT; South Shore HS; Brooklyn, NY; (Y); St Johns U; Sports Adm.

MURRAY, ROBERT W; Guilderland Central HS; Guilderland, NY; (Y); 3/375; Debate Tm; Pres Varsity Clb; Rep Stu Cncl; Var L Bsktbl; Var Capt Crs Cntry; Capt L Trk; Bausch & Lomb Sci Awd; Ntl Merit Ltr; Pres Schlr; Hosp Aide; US Army Rsrv Ntl Schlstc Athlt 86; Dartmouth Coll; Bio.

MURRAY, RON; Franklinville Central HS; Franklinville, NY; (Y); Spanish Clb; Varsity Clb; Rep Stu Cncl; JV Bsbl; Var Capt Crs Cntry; Var Capt Trk; Hon Roll; U Rochester; Aero-Space Sci.

MURRAY, SHARLENE; Riverhead HS; Riverhead, NY; (Y); Camera Clb; German Clb; Yrbk Phtg; Off Jr Cls; Vllybl; Mryvl Coll; Psychlgy.

MURRAY, SHARON; Huntington HS; Huntington, NY; (Y); Key Clb; Varsity Clb; Rep Frsh Cls; Rep Soph Cls; Rep Jr Cls; Swmmng; Capt Trk; High Hon Roll; Hon Roll; NHS.

MURRAY JR, THOMAS N; Eastchester HS; Scarsdale, NY; (Y); Drama Clb; Hosp Aide; SADD; Jazz Band; Yrbk Stf; Rep Stu Cncl; Var Capt Crs Cntry; Wrstlng; High Hon Roll; NHS; Hugh O Brien Yth Fndtn NYS S Ldrshp Smnr 86; Nwspapr Carrier Mnth 86; Pre-Med.

MURRAY, TIMOTHY; Cardinal O Hara HS; Buffalo, NY; (S); French Clb; Ski Clb; Stage Crew; JV Ftbl; Var L Trk; High Hon Roll; Hon Roll; Ithaca Coll; Comm.

MURRAY, TRACY; Edison Technical & Industrial HS; Rochester, NY; (Y); Boy Scts; Church Yth Grp; Cmnty Wkr; Exploring; Band; Color Guard; Mrchg Band; School Musical; Bsbl; Swmmng; Grphc Dsgn.

MURRAY, UWADA; Midwood Atbrooklyn College HS; Brooklyn, NY; (Y); Sec Church Yth Grp; Cmnty Wkr; French Clb; Model UN; Office Aide; Drill Tm; Variety Show; Hon Roll; Prfct Atten Awd; Arista Hnr Soc 86; Chem.

MURRELL, ERIC; Alexander Hamilton HS; Elmsford, NY; (Y); NC A&t ST U; Elec Engr.

MURTAUGH, JEFF; Holland Patent Central HS; Holland Patent, NY; (Y); Boy Scts; Church Yth Grp; Varsity Clb; Bsbl; Bsktbl; Coach Actv; Ftbl; Tennis; All Dvsn Awd Tri Vly Dfnsve Ftbl Offnsve 85; Athlete Of Wk Tri Vly Ftbl 85; Tri Vly Chmpn Tnns 85.

MURTHA, JILL; The Acad Of St Joseph HS; Lake Ronkonkoma, NY; (Y); Hosp Aide; Ski Clb; SADD; Variety Show; Yrbk Stf; VP Sr Cls; Stu Cncl; JV Bsktbl; Var Socr; Var Sftbl.

MURTHA, KIM; Mt Mercy Acad; W Seneca, NY; (Y); Pres Church Yth Grp; SADD; Sftbl; FHA; JCL; Latin Clb; Bowling; Coach Actv; Im Fld Hcky; Hon Roll; Med.

MURTHA, LYNN M; Our Lady Of Mercy Acad; Glen Head, NY; (Y); 22/122; Church Yth Grp; Cmnty Wkr; Computer Clb; Drama Clb; Political Wkr; Church Choir; Swmmng; Hon Roll; Ntl Merit Ltr; NYS Regents Scholar; Rutgers U; Mktng.

MUSA, RHAJKUMAR; Amityville Memorial HS; Amityville, NY; (Y); Debate Tm; English Clb; Amityville HS Acadmc Awd 85-86; Stony Brook U; MD.

MUSALL, TRICIA; Cattaraugus Central HS; Cattaraugus, NY; (Y); Pep Clb; Color Guard; Yrbk Stf; Rep Sr Cls; Rep Stu Cncl; Var Bsktbl; Var Capt Cheerleading; Var Trk; JV Vllybl; Hon Roll; Spcl Ed.

MUSANTE, SUSAN A; Garden City HS; Garden City, NY; (Y); 21/346; French Clb; Girl Scts; Hosp Aide; Pep Clb; Bowling; Hon Roll; Jr NHS; NHS; Ntl Merit Ltr; Pres Schlr; NY ST Rgnts Schlrshp 86; Girl Scout Silvr Awd 85; Girl Scout Gold Awd 86; Hofstra U; Bio.

MUSCARELLA, DONNA MARIE; Bishop Kearney HS; Brooklyn, NY; (Y); 90/350; Church Yth Grp; Cmnty Wkr; VP Dance Clb; Drama Clb; Office Aide; Spanish Clb; School Play; Variety Show; Hon Roll; NHS; Pace U & NY ST Regnts Schlrshps 86; Drexel Burnham Emplyees Schlrshp Fund Inc Schlrshp 86; Pace U; Comp Sci.

MUSCARELLA, PAT; Hicksville SR HS; Hicksville, NY; (Y); Bsbl; Bsktbl; Ftbl; Hon Roll; Jr NHS; NHS; Ath Schlr Awd 84-85; Bus Financing.

MUSCATELLO, JOSEPH; Catholic Central HS; Cohoes, NY; (Y); VP JA; Math Clb; SADD; Stage Crew; VP Jr Cls; Pres Stu Cncl; Var Golf; Rgn 1 JR Achvmnt Cnfrnc Awd 84; Aerospc Engnrng.

MUSCENTE, JOE; Sacred Heart HS; Yonkers, NY; (S); 15/223; Church Yth Grp; Yrbk Stf; Bowling; High Hon Roll; Hon Roll; NHS; Manhattan Clg; Bio.

MUSENGO, ERRIN; W Genesee HS; Camillus, NY; (Y); Cmnty Wkr; GAA; Key Clb; Varsity Clb; Band; Chorus; Concert Band; Jazz Band; Mrchg Band; Orch.

MUSHTARE, JOHN; Umtego Central HS; Unadilla, NY; (Y); 3/95; Am Leg Boys St; Ski Clb; Varsity Clb; Band; Jazz Band; VP Soph Cls; Pres VP Stu Cncl; Var L Bsbl; Var L Ftbl; NHS; Aerontcl Engr.

MUSICA, JASON; Upper Room Christian HS; Dix Hills, NY; (S); Church Yth Grp; Computer Clb; Bsktbl; Hon Roll; Agri.

MUSIKAR, LEA D; George W Hewlett HS; Hewlett, NY; (Y); 19/262; French Clb; VP Temple Yth Grp; Chorus; Ed Lit Mag; Hon Roll; NHS; Ntl Merit Ltr; Asst Mgr Vrsty Fncng Tm 85&86; U Of Chicago.

MUSILLO, ANNE; Saugerties HS; Saugerties, NY; (Y); 13/256; French Clb; Church Choir; High Hon Roll; NHS.

MUSSARI, ANTONIO; Victor Central HS; Victor, NY; (Y); Key Clb; VP Frsh Cls; Bsbl; Bsktbl; Coach Actv; Ftbl; High Hon Roll; Hon Roll; U Of WI; Accntng.

MUSSEHL, TRACY; West Seneca West HS; Cheektowaga, NY; (Y); 44/560; Key Clb; SADD; Rep Jr Cls; Hon Roll; Pres Schlr; Pres Acadmc Fitnss Awd 85-86; Schl Sci Dept Awds Erth Sci 83-84/Bio 84-85/Microbio 85-86; ST U Coll Buffalo; Broadcstng.

MUSSER, CORINNE; Binghamton HS; Binghamton, NY; (Y); 10/456; Cmnty Wkr; VP French Clb; Hosp Aide; Key Clb; Sec SADD; Varsity Clb; Rep Stu Cncl; Sftbl; Cit Awd; High Hon Roll; Am Educ Fndtn Natl Hnr Rl 86; Prof Fred E Williams Schlrhsp Awd 86; Pace U; Acctg.

MUSTAFA, BEKIR S; T A Edison Voc Tech HS; Beechhurst, NY; (Y); 2/387; Capt Computer Clb; Math Tm; Scholastic Bowl; School Play; Nwsp Rptr; Hon Roll; NHS; Prfct Atten Awd; Pres Schlr; Sal; Rgnts Schlrshp; Polytech U; Elec-Comp Engr.

MUSTICO, CHRISTEN ANNE; Notre Dame HS; Elmira, NY; (Y); Cmnty Wkr; Hosp Aide; Thesps; Acpl Chr; Pres Chorus; School Musical; School Play; Stage Crew; Nwsp Stf; Yrbk Stf; Area All ST Chr; Crntn Slvr Bwl Awd Outstndng Vlntr Wrk; Daemen; Elem Educ.

MUSTICO, J STEPHEN; Hannibal Central HS; Sterling, NY; (Y); 4/119; Am Leg Boys St; VP 4-H; Key Clb; Band; School Musical; Yrbk Stf; Var Crs Cntry; JV Var Trk; High Hon Roll; NHS; NYS Rgnts Schlrshp 86; Fredonia; Engrng.

MUSTY, DANIEL J; Holland HS; S Wales, NY; (Y); Am Leg Boys St; Church Yth Grp; Hon Roll; Prfct Atten Awd; St Schlr; NYS Regents Scholar 86; Parks Coll St Louis; Aero Engrg.

MUSZYNSKI, GRACEANN; Monsignor Scanlan HS; Flushing, NY; (Y); 4/277; Yrbk Stf; Twrlr; French Hon Soc; High Hon Roll; Hon Roll; NHS; Prfct Atten Awd; Frnch II & III Awds; 3rd Plc Sci Fr; Sr Frshmn Aid; St Johns U; Bus.

MUTH, ERIC R; Binghamton HS; Binghamton, NY; (Y); Am Leg Boys St; Boy Scts; German Clb; Concert Band; Var L Crs Cntry; Var L Swmmng; High Hon Roll; NHS; Band; 150th Annvrsry Cmmrtv Essy Cntst Wnr; Clarkson U; Bio-Engrng.

MUTH, TAMARA; Windham-Ashland-Jewett Central HS; E Jewett, NY; (S); 1/27; Church Yth Grp; Spanish Clb; Chorus; School Play; Var L Cheerleading; 4-H Awd; High Hon Roll; NHS; Drama Clb; Pres 4-H; Mst Imprvd Chrldr 85; All-Cnty Chorus 85; Med.

MUTHIG, SUSAN; Fairport HS; Fairport, NY; (Y); Church Yth Grp; Cmnty Wkr; SADD; Chorus; Swing Chorus; Rep Frsh Cls; Rep Jr Cls; Rep Stu Cncl; Hon Roll; NHS; St John Fisher Coll; Bio.

MUURSEPP, PEETER; John Jay HS; S Salem, NY; (Y); Aud/Vis; Drama Clb; JA; School Musical; School Play; Stage Crew; Variety Show; Cit Awd; High Hon Roll; Hon Roll; Theatr Art.

MYER, DARREN; Sargerties HS; Saugerties, NY; (Y); Symp Band; Ftbl; Hon Roll; NHS; Biotech.

MYERS, ALLAN; New Rochelle HS; Scarsdale, NY; (Y); Computer Clb; Political Wkr; Trs Temple Yth Grp; Rep Soph Cls; Chrmn Jr Cls; NHS.

MYERS, AMY; Kenmore East SR HS; Tonawanda, NY; (Y); Church Yth Grp; 4-H; Intnl Clb; Pep Clb; Ski Clb; Chorus; Church Choir; Drill Tm; Variety Show; Sec Frsh Cls; 4-H Grnd Chmpn 4-H Engl Rdng 83; Rotry Exch Stu Fnlnd 85-86; Lang.

MYERS, DANIEL; St Agnes HS; Long Island City, NY; (Y); 12/111; Im Ftbl; JV Ice Hcky; NHS; Hofstra U; Accntng.

MYERS, JOHN; Falconer Central HS; Kennedy, NY; (Y); 5/120; Am Leg Boys St; Art Clb; Ski Clb; Yrbk Ed-Chief; Yrbk Stf; Rep Stu Cncl; Dnfth Awd; Hon Roll; NHS; Quill & Scroll Awd Jrnlsm; Jamestown Cmnty Coll.

MYERS, KAREN; Canton Central HS; Canton, NY; (Y); French Clb; Chorus; School Musical; School Play; Yrbk Stf; Lit Mag; Var Bsktbl; Var Diving; Var Gym; Sftbl; NY ST Musc Assoc Awd 84; Wells College; Libl Arts.

MYERS, KAREN; Falconer Central Schl; Randolph, NY; (Y); 4/125; Ski Clb; Band; Drm Mjr(t); Jazz Band; Orch; Yrbk Stf; Trs Stu Cncl; JP Sousa Awd; VP NHS; Rgnts Schlrshp-NYS 85-90; Untd Schltc Asstnc-2 Yr Free Tutn 86-88; Grdcki Band Awd 86; Jamestown CC; Bus Adm.

MYERS, KENNETH; Richfield Springs Central HS; Schuyler Lake, NY; (Y); Church Yth Grp; Debate Tm; Chorus; Church Choir; Hon Roll; Outstndng Stu Hlth Svcs Mrkmr Cnty Bcs 86; Nrsng.

MYERS, KRISTA; Manlius Pebble HS; Oneida, NY; (S); Model UN; SADD; Band; Concert Band; Yrbk Ed-Chief; Rep Frsh Cls; Stu Cncl; Cheerleading; Fld Hcky; Golf; Lib Arts.

MYERS, KRISTEN; Clarkstown HS North; Congers, NY; (Y); AFS; SADD; Stage Crew; Off Jr Cls; Capt Vllybl; MVP Vllybll; All Cnty All Dvsn; Dellwood Cntry Clb Schlrshp; U Of VT; Elem Ed.

MYERS, KRISTIN; Owego Free Acad; Owego, NY; (Y); Art Clb; Key Clb; Varsity Clb; Mrchg Band; School Musical; Yrbk Stf; JV Var Cheerleading; Twrlr; Hon Roll; Pres Schlr; NY ST Rgnts Schlrshp 86; Marywood; Teachg.

MYERS, LAURA CHRISTINE; Mercy HS; Selkirk, NY; (Y); Church Yth Grp; Cmnty Wkr; School Play; Stage Crew; Nwsp Rptr; Lit Mag; High Hon Roll; Regents Chlrshp Acad Schlrshp To St Rose; Excell Awds In All Subjcts; Probtnry Mbr Natl Hnr Scty; Coll Of St Rose; Bio.

MYERS, SHAWNIQUE; Park West HS; New York, NY; (Y); Art Clb; Dance Clb; Drama Clb; FNA; Hosp Aide; Office Aide; Teachers Aide; Band; Church Choir; Yrbk Phtg; Doctor.

MYKEL, MILES; Utica Free Acad; Utica, NY; (Y); 27/320; Model UN; Hon Roll; Jr NHS; NHS; Ntl Merit Ltr; NY ST Rgnts Schlrshp 86; US Army.

MYLAND, CATHY; Erasmus Hall HS; Brooklyn, NY; (Y); Church Yth Grp; Cmnty Wkr; FBLA; Hosp Aide; Library Aide; Office Aide; Church Choir; Sftbl; Var Vllybl.

MYLES, LANCE; Rice HS; New York, NY; (Y); JV Var Bsktbl; Hon Roll; Bus.

MYLOD, DEIRDRE; Sacred Heart Acad; Bellerose Village, NY; (S); Dance Clb; Acpl Chr; Band; Chorus; Orch; School Musical; Hon Roll; NHS; All Cnty Orch 85.

MYREE, TROY; Buffalo Tradional HS; Buffalo, NY; (S); 9/110; Band; Church Choir; Jazz Band; Orch; Symp Band; Rep Stu Cncl; Var Bsbl; Var Capt Ftbl; Var Trk; Hon Roll; Brockport; Comp Sci.

MYRON, ROBERT; H Frank Carey HS; Garden City S, NY; (Y); 56/270; Rep Jr Cls; VP Sr Cls; JV Ftbl; Capt Trk; JV Var Wrstlng; Hon Roll; Jr NHS.

MYSLIWIEC, ANITA; Mount Mercy Acad; Orchard Pk, NY; (Y); Church Yth Grp; Dance Clb; Hosp Aide; Science Clb; Orch; Rep Frsh Cls; Im Fld Hcky; High Hon Roll; Cmnty Wkr; Acpl Chr; 2nd Pl Mt Mercy Sci Fair Physics Div 85-86; Slvr Medal NYC Mt Mercy Melodears Comp 84-85.

MYSLIWIEC, TINA; Lansingburgh HS; Troy, NY; (Y); Camp Fr Inc; Hosp Aide; Red Cross Aide; Varsity Clb; Chorus; Yrbk Stf; Var Bowling; Var Socr; High Hon Roll; NHS; HVCC; Chld Care.

MYSLLWIEC, TINA; Lansingburgh HS; Troy, NY; (Y); Camp Fr Inc; Hosp Aide; JA; Red Cross Aide; Varsity Clb; Chorus; Yrbk Stf; Var Bowling; High Hon Roll; NHS; Hudson Valley CC; Chld Care.

MYTKO, DODIE; Sachem North HS; Lake Ronkonkoma, NY; (Y); 40/1558; Orch; JV Var Sftbl; Church Yth Grp; German Clb; Science Clb; Stage Crew; MVP Sftbl 84 & 85; Rookie Yr Vrsty Sftbl 86; Phy Thrpy.

MYZAL, ELISA; Gloversville HS; Gloversville, NY; (Y); SADD; Yrbk Stf; Cheerleading; Fld Hcky; Trk; High Hon Roll; Hon Roll; Prfct Atten Awd; Comm.

NAAR, SYLVIE; New Rochelle HS; Scarsdale, NY; (Y); 42/550; Cmnty Wkr; Computer Clb; French Clb; Intnl Clb; Model UN; SADD; Temple Yth Grp; Y-Teens; Nwsp Rptr; Yrbk Rptr; Academic Fitness Awd; Regents Scholarship; U Of MI; Med.

NABINGER, KATHY; Whitney Point HS; Whitney Point, NY; (S); Sec Church Yth Grp; Sec Latin Clb; Science Clb; Spanish Clb; Concert Band; Jazz Band; School Musical; Band; High Hon Roll; Prfct Atten Awd; Area All ST Bnd 84-86; Marine Studs Enrchmnt Pgm 85; Nyssma Solo & Ensmbl Fstvl 85.

NABORRE, JOSEPH; Huntington HS; Huntington, NY; (Y); JV Lcrss.

NAC LERIO, GREGORY P; Walt Whitman HS; Huntington Sta, NY; (Y); 50/500; Mathletes; SADD; High Hon Roll; Jr NHS; Sfflk Cnty Mth Cntst Hon Mntn 84; CW Pst Campus; Bus.

NACCARATO, DIANE M; Kingston HS; Kingston, NY; (Y); 181/573; 4-H; Hosp Aide; SADD; Chorus; Stage Crew; Yrbk Stf; Capt L Cheerleading; 4-H Awd; Hon Roll; St Schlr; Hartwick Coll; Nrsng BSN.

NACHBAR, STUART M; Farmingdale HS; N Massapequa, NY; (Y); 121/600; VP Aud/Vis; Band; Madrigals; Stage Crew; Stu Cncl; High Hon Roll; Regnts Schlrshp 86; NYSSMA Grp & Solo 82-86; Heschel Hnr Soc 85; Albany; Pol Sci.

NACK JR, JAMES F; Clarkstown South HS; Nanuet, NY; (Y); Boy Scts; Church Yth Grp; Computer Clb; Exploring; German Clb; Im Bowling; JV L Ftbl; Var Trk; Mu Alp Tht; Wrld Conservation Awd 83; Prodea Patria Lutheran Awd BSA 83; Order Of Arrow BSA 83; US Naval Acad; Oceanography.

NACK, WENDY E; Germantown Central HS; Hudson, NY; (S); 1/53; Cmnty Wkr; Chorus; Pres Frsh Cls; Pres Soph Cls; Pres Jr Cls; JV Fld Hcky; Cit Awd; High Hon Roll; NHS; Voice Dem Awd; Grnd Ofcr Intl Ordr Rnbw Grls 85-86; Law.

NACY, KAROLYN; Hudson Falls HS; Hudson Falls, NY; (Y); 1/224; Spanish Clb; Varsity Clb; Band; Var Capt Crs Cntry; Var Capt Trk; NHS; Val; GAA; High Hon Roll; Spanish NHS; Am Legion Hist Prz 86; Intl Sports Exc Cross Cty Tm 86; Pres Acad Ftns Awd 86; Springfield Coll; Athleic Trng.

NADJADI, CLIFFORD; Haverling Central Schl; Bath, NY; (Y); French Clb; Band; Concert Band; Symp Band; Socr; Wrstlng; Recdg Engr.

NADLER, HEATHER; South Shore HS; Brooklyn, NY; (Y); 4-H; Math Tm; Teachers Aide; Chorus; School Play; Yrbk Stf; 4-H Awd; Hon Roll; NHS.

NADLER, RACHELLE; Commack HS South; Commack, NY; (Y); 53/367; Church Yth Grp; Cmnty Wkr; Varsity Clb; Band; Concert Band; Drm Mjr(t); Jazz Band; Mrchg Band; School Musical; Symp Band; Spartan Band & Kickline Assoc Rcgntn Awd 86; CHSS Actv Ctzn Schl & Cmnty Awd 85-86; Drum Mjr Awd 86; Siena Coll.

NAEF, CHRISTIAN; Brewster HS; Brewster, NY; (Y); Church Yth Grp; Ski Clb; Stage Crew; Nwsp Stf; Socr; High Hon Roll; Hon Roll; Nyack Coll; Missions.

NAEKEL, MICHEL-LEE; Sachem HS; Farmingville, NY; (Y); Hon Roll.

NAFZ, ALEX; Roosevelt HS; Yonkers, NY; (Y); Boy Scts; Band; Socr; Schlrshp Otwrd Bnd Schl 86; NY Tech; Arct.

NAGEL, MICHELE A; Stella Maris HS; Rockawaypoint, NY; (Y); Art Clb; AFS; Math Clb; Math Tm; School Play; Sr Cls; Stu Cncl; High Hon Roll; NHS; Rotory Clb Awd For Excllnc In Acctng 86; Parsons Schl Of Design; Graphic.

NAGEL, MINDY; Romulus Central HS; Romulus, NY; (Y); Ski Clb; Color Guard; School Play; Yrbk Bus Mgr; Yrbk Ed-Chief; Yrbk Phtg; Yrbk Stf; Rep Stu Cncl; JV Vllybl; High Hon Roll; Bus Admn.

NAGEL, WENDY; Potsdam SR HS; Potsdam, NY; (Y); 3/134; AFS; Band; Jazz Band; Orch; School Musical; Stu Cncl; Trk; High Hon Roll; NHS; All ST Orch 85; Music Perf.

NAGELSCHMIDT, HEIDI; G Ray Bodley HS; Fulton, NY; (Y); French Clb; German Clb; Yrbk Stf; Swmmng; High Hon Roll; Hon Roll.

NAGENGAST, JOHN; Centereach HS; Centereach, NY; (Y); Bsbl; Hon Roll; Attendance Awd 84-85; Pres Phys Ftnss Awd 86; All League Awd 86; Law.

NAGLE, KELLY ANN; Lakeland HS; Yorktown Hts, NY; (Y); Church Yth Grp; FBLA; Nwsp Stf; Yrbk Bus Mgr; Stat Bsktbl; Var Trk; High Hon Roll; Jr NHS; NHS; Ntl Merit Ltr; Olympic Champ 3rd Pl 83-84; Regnl Olympics 4th Pl 84-85; Ed.

NAGRATH, VIPUL; White Plains HS; White Plains, NY; (Y); 30/421; Boy Scts; Pep Clb; Spanish Clb; Ed Lit Mag; Rep Soph Cls; Rep Jr Cls; Rep Sr Cls; Rep Stu Cncl; JV Bsktbl; Comp Sci.

NAGY, KRISTOPHER S; Horseheads HS; Horseheads, NY; (Y); 66/360; Am Leg Boys St; Art Clb; Nwsp Phtg; Hst Sr Cls; Var Swmmng; Hon Roll; NY ST Summr Schl Of Arts 84; Schltc Art Awd 84-86; Ad Dsgn.

NAGY, STEPHEN; Cooperstown JR SR HS; Cooperstown, NY; (Y); 8/96; Letterman Clb; Math Tm; Ski Clb; Jazz Band; Stu Cncl; Socr; Trk; Bausch & Lomb Sci Awd; Hon Roll; NHS; Clrk Fndtn Schlrshp 86; Louis Armstrng Jzz Awd 86; Duke U; Biomed.

NAGY, STPHEN; Cooperstown Central HS; Cooperstown, NY; (Y); 8/96; Math Tm; Ski Clb; Jazz Band; Socr; Trk; Bausch & Lomb Sci Awd; Hon Roll; NHS; Pickens Memrl Prz Physcs; Louis Armstrong Jazz Awd; Leslie Crain Sci Awd; Duke U; Biomed Engrng.

NAHAS, HEATHER; Notre Dame Acad; Brooklyn, NY; (Y); Pres Sec Church Yth Grp; Computer Clb; Drama Clb; Ski Clb; Spanish Clb; Lit Mag; Bus.

NAHAS, MAGID S; Brighton HS; Rochester, NY; (Y); 8/325; Math Tm; Ski Clb; Spanish Clb; JV Tennis; Ntl Merit SF; Engnrng.

NAHMIAS, SHERI; John Dewey HS; Brooklyn, NY; (Y); Service Clb; Teachers Aide; Yrbk Stf; Off Stu Cncl; High Hon Roll; Jr NHS; Stu Of Yr Awd 84; Hnr Cert Art And Spnsh 84; Grphc Dsgn.

NAIDICH, JASON; John F Kennedy HS; Merrick, NY; (Y); VP Capt Debate Tm; Ed Science Clb; Nwsp Ed-Chief; Hon Roll; NHS; Ntl Merit Ltr; Qulfd-St Champ Debate 85-86.

NAIDU, BABLU; Roy C Ketcham HS; Wapp Fls, NY; (Y); 41/500; Trs Drama Clb; Hosp Aide; Temple Yth Grp; Trs Thesps; Chorus; School Musical; Nwsp Rptr; High Hon Roll; NHS; VFW Awd; 1st Pl Mdl Congress Bst Senator 86; Bst Thespian 86; NYS Regents Scholar 86; Vassar Coll; Pol Sci.

NAIME, DWIGHT S; Manhattan Center For Sci & Math; Bronx, NY; (Y); 57/159; Boys Clb Am; Dance Clb; JA; School Play; Variety Show; Nwsp Sprt Ed; Nwsp Stf; Off Frsh Cls; Off Soph Cls; Stu Cncl; Rgnts Schlrshp 86; Weslyn U; Med.

NAJIM, PETER; Lake Placid HS; Jay, NY; (Y); 5/20; Key Clb; Ski Clb; Band; Jazz Band; Tennis; Wt Lftg; High Hon Roll; Hon Roll; Chiroprctc.

NALLI III, ROCCO; Fort Plain HS; Fort Plain, NY; (S); 3/60; Trs Computer Clb; Pres Drama Clb; Pres French Clb; VP Math Clb; Concert Band; Jazz Band; Mrchg Band; Pep Band; School Musical; Yrbk Stf.

NALTY JR, CARLTON; Monsignor Farrell HS; Staten Island, NY; (Y); 91/356; Rep Frsh Cls; Rep Soph Cls; Off Jr Cls; Sec Rep Stu Cncl; Im Stat Bsktbl; JV L Ftbl; Var L Trk; Cit Awd; Hon Roll; Pep Clb; Big Bro 86-87; 12th Man 86-87; Commtte Mem Super Dance For Msclr Dystrophy Assn 86-87; Bus.

NAM, SUNG; James Madison HS; Brooklyn, NY; (Y); 77/756; Church Yth Grp; Office Aide; NW Berkery ST U; Nrsng.

NAND, SUREKHA; Cardinal Spellman HS; Bronx, NY; (S); 42/500; Computer Clb; Key Clb; Math Clb; Pres Science Clb; High Hon Roll; Hon Roll; Jr NHS; NHS; Ntl Merit Ltr; NY St Regents Schlrshp 86-90; Med.

NAPLE, AMY E; Acad Of The Holy Names; Delmar, NY; (Y); Dance Clb; Drama Clb; Hosp Aide; Teachers Aide; School Play; Yrbk Stf; Lit Mag; Cheerleading; Pom Pon; Socr; Awds Art & Frnch II 84; Natl Olympd Biol Awd 84; Fine Arts.

NAPLES, DAWN; Worcester Central HS; Worcester, NY; (Y); 9/34; Exploring; French Clb; Varsity Clb; Band; Yrbk Stf; Stu Cncl; Var Capt Bsktbl; Var Capt Socr; Var Sftbl; NHS; Clrk Schlrshp 86; Sftbll Coachs Awd 86; Hnr Rll 82-86; Ithaca Coll; Bus Mgmt.

NAPOLI, LARAINE; St Edmund HS; Brooklyn, NY; (Y); Yrbk Stf; Sec Frsh Cls; Hon Roll; Italn Awd 85; Bus Law Awd 86; Persnl Key Brdng Awd 86; St Francis Coll.

NAPOLI, NANCY; Alexander Hamilton HS; Elmsford, NY; (Y); Key Clb; Yrbk Bus Mgr; Yrbk Phtg; Yrbk Rptr; Yrbk Stf; Capt Var Sftbl; Outstndg Perf Sftbl 85-86; Vars Ltr Sftbl 85-86; Outstndg Achvt Bus Westchester Bus Inst 85-86; Westchester Bus; Bus.

NAPOLI, THERESA M; St Joseph Hill Acad; Staten Island, NY; (Y); Pres Computer Clb; Library Aide; Capt Bowling; Coach Actv; Cmptv Schlrshp St Johns U & Rgnts Schlrshp 85-86; St Johns U; Bus Adm.

NAPOLITANO, GRACE; Monticello HS; Monticello, NY; (Y); FBLA; Intnl Clb; SADD; High Hon Roll; Pres NHS; Trpl A Auto Clb Drvr Ed Awd 85; Pace Univ; Accntng.

NAPOLITANO, JASON A; Valhalla HS; Valhalla, NY; (Y); 1/120; Aud/Vis; Camera Clb; Band; Var L Crs Cntry; JV Trk; Var L Wrstlng; Hon Roll; Trs NHS; Ntl Merit Ltr; Wrstlng All Sctn-All Cnty-All Leag Wnnr-6 Trnmnts 82-86; NY Acad Sci-Sci Rsrch Trnng Pgm 85; Yale U; Engrng.

NAPOLITANO, LAURA; Sacred Heart Acad; Westbury, NY; (S); 1/182; Math Tm; Pres Spanish Clb; Chorus; School Musical; Stu Cncl; Hon Roll; NHS; Acad All Amer; Comp Sci.

NAPOLITANO, YOLANDA; St Johns Villa Acad; Staten Island, NY; (Y); 13/125; Acpl Chr; School Musical; School Play; Nwsp Rptr; Yrbk Rptr; Hon Roll; Prfct Atten Awd; PAL Plc Cmmsnr For Day 84; PAL Strs My Grnd Prnts Tld Me Cntst 2nd Pl 85; Ntl Sci Olympd Bio Awd 86; Bus Admin.

NAPORA, LISA; Kenmore East HS; Tonawanda, NY; (Y); Pep Clb; School Musical; School Play; Hon Roll; NHS; Cert Achvt Mth II 84; Physics.

NARAINDAT, AHELIYA; Amityville Memorial HS; Amityville, NY; (Y); VP AFS; Drama Clb; FBLA; Key Clb; SADD; High Hon Roll; Hon Roll; Jr NHS; Prfct Atten Awd; St Johns Coll; Cmptr Prgrmng.

NARANG, CHARU; Our Lady Of Mercy HS; Fairport, NY; (Y); Cmnty Wkr; Exploring; French Clb; Model UN; Science Clb; Yrbk Rptr; Yrbk Stf; JV Var Tennis; Hon Roll; Ntl Merit Ltr; Pre-Med.

NARCISO, CAROLYN; Pleasantville HS; Pleasantville, NY; (Y); Yrbk Phtg; Yrbk Stf; Bsktbl; Trk; Vllybl; High Hon Roll; Hon Roll; Cmmnctns.

NARDELLI, TRINA; Grand Island HS; Grand Island, NY; (Y); Ski Clb; Variety Show; Cheerleading; Socr; Sftbl; U Of Buffalo; Bus Mgmt.

NARDONE, EVA; John A Coleman Catholic HS; Kingston, NY; (S); 2/69; French Clb; Key Clb; Latin Clb; Math Clb; Ski Clb; Church Choir; Stage Crew; High Hon Roll; NHS; Ntl Merit Ltr; Rensselear Sci Math Awd 85; Bio Olympd Awd; Chem Olympd Awd; Arch.

NARDONE, LISA J; Smithtown HS East; St James, NY; (Y); Hosp Aide; Chorus; School Musical; Yrbk Stf; Stu Cncl; Var JV Cheerleading; Co-Capt L Pom Pon; High Hon Roll; NHS; Spanish NHS; Pres Acad Fit Awd 86; NYS Regents Scholar 86; Fairfield U; Cmmnctns.

NARDUCCI, ROBERT V; St Francis HS; Littleneck, NY; (S); 116/770; JA; Bowling; Fld Hcky; Ftbl; Socr; Trk; Vllybl; Wt Lftg; Opt Clb Awd.

NARIKUZHY, HELENA; Uniondale HS; Baldwin, NY; (Y); 6/410; Cmnty Wkr; Hosp Aide; Key Clb; SADD; Nwsp Rptr; VP Jr Cls; VP Sr Cls; Trk; High Hon Roll; Pres NHS; Town Hempstead Cmmnty Svc & Acdmc Excllnc 86; Outstndng Spnsh Stdnt 86; PTSA Outstndng Cmmnty Svc 86; Syracuse U; Bus Adm.

NARKIEWICZ, KRISTEN; Cambridge Central HS; Cambridge, NY; (Y); 15/76; Church Yth Grp; French Clb; Teachers Aide; Band; Concert Band; Mrchg Band; School Musical; School Play; Yrbk Phtg; Yrbk Stf; Ed.

NASH, AMYMERYL; Lynbrok HS; E Rockaway, NY; (Y); AFS; Drama Clb; NFL; Political Wkr; Thesps; School Musical; School Play; Var Trk; Psych.

NASH, BILLY; Frontier Central HS; Lake View, NY; (Y); 119/430; 4-H; Band; Concert Band; Jazz Band; Mrchg Band; School Musical; Golf; Ice Hcky; 4-H Awd; Hon Roll; Msc Awd 86; Prsdntl Schlstc Recgntn 83; Erie Allstr Glf 85-86; Canisius; Glf Mgmt.

NASH, JEANINNE; Guilderland Central HS; Schenectady, NY; (Y); Exploring; Pep Clb; High Hon Roll; Hon Roll; Awd Outstndng Achvt Regnts Bio 85; Awds Excllnc Europn Stds, Engl, Spnsh 85; Awd Achvt Amer Hstry 86; Hudson Valley CC; Bio.

NASH, JILL; Frontier HS; Lake View, NY; (Y); 4-H; German Clb; Concert Band; Mrchg Band; Socr; Swmmng; Trk; 4-H Awd; Hon Roll; NHS; Math.

NASH, KAREN; Carmel HS; Carmel, NY; (Y); Art Clb; SADD; Yrbk Rptr; Yrbk Stf; Hon Roll; Music Mgmt.

NASHWINTER II, RICHARD; Royalton-Hartland Central HS; Middleport, NY; (Y); 17/128; Church Yth Grp; Drama Clb; Pres French Clb; School Musical; School Play; Var Crs Cntry; Var Trk; Hon Roll; SUNY Buffalo; Arch.

NASIS, ELBERT; Commack HS South; Commack, NY; (Y); Q&S; Ski Clb; Teachers Aide; Y-Teens; Gym; Lcrss; Wt Lftg; High Hon Roll; Hon Roll; Gldn Quill Awd Engl Wrtng Awd 86; Med.

NASO, MARK W; Highland HS; Highland, NY; (Y); 5/124; Am Leg Boys St; Ed Yrbk Stf; Var Capt Bsbl; Var Capt Socr; Var L Vllybl; Capt Math Tm; Quiz Bowl; Varsity Clb; Band; Chorus; NYS Hgh O Brn Yth Ldrshp Smnr Ambssdr 84; NYS Clss C Sccr Chmpns 84; Tms Hrld Rcd Schlr Athlt 86; U Of Rochester; Elec Engnrng.

NASO, VINCENZA; St Peters HS For Girls HS; Staten Isl, NY; (Y); 10/104; FNA; Math Tm; Yrbk Stf; Rep Stu Cncl; Hon Roll; NHS; Prfct Atten Awd; Schrrshp Eckerd Coll 86; Merit Math 86; Exc Math 86; Eckerd Coll; Pre-Law.

NASOULIS, DEMETRIOS; Flushing HS; College Point, NY; (Y); 18/392; Boy Scts; Debate Tm; Intnl Clb; Quiz Bowl; Scholastic Bowl; School Play; Yrbk Phtg; Cit Awd; Gov Hon Prg Awd; High Hon Roll; Sci Medl 83; Regnts Schlrshp 86; Baruch Coll; Acctg.

NASS, RACHAEL; Lafayette HS; Brooklyn, NY; (Y); 7/363; Debate Tm; Capt Scholastic Bowl; Chorus; Yrbk Phtg; Ed Lit Mag; Rep Sr Cls; Var Sftbl; La Fayette HS Schlrshp Awd 86; Samuel Lief Memrl Medal Hgh Schlrshp Soc Stds 86; J F Kennedy Mem Mdl; SUNY Binghamton.

NASSAUER JR, FREDERICK J; Westhampton Beach HS; Quogue, NY; (Y); Church Yth Grp; Latin Clb; Quiz Bowl; Band; Jazz Band; Orch; Rep Jr Cls; Var L Socr; Var Capt Tennis; Pres Schlr; Adv Frnch Awd Hghst Avg 85-86.

NASSER, ADIL; Lackawanna SR HS; Lackawanna, NY; (Y); 1/26; French Clb; High Hon Roll; Hon Roll; NHS; Bio Awd 84; French Awd 86; NY ST U Buffalo; Med.

NASSO, THERESA; Sachem HS; Lake Ronkonkoma, NY; (Y); Chorus; Ftbl; Swmmng; Prfct Atten Awd; Suffolk CC; Word Proc.

NASTASI, VINCENT; Archbishop Molloy HS; Howard Bch, NY; (Y); 5/383; Church Yth Grp; Math Tm; Science Clb; Service Clb; Im Ftbl; Bausch & Lomb Sci Awd; High Hon Roll; Prfct Atten Awd; Acadmc Excllnc 85-86; Cooper Union; Elctrcl Engrng.

NASTRI, ANNMARIE; Plainedge HS; N Massapequa, NY; (Y); 4/314; Mathletes; SADD; Jazz Band; Orch; Rep Stu Cncl; Var Stat Lcrss; Var L Tennis; Pres NHS; Pres Schlr; Spanish NHS; MVP Orchstra 83-85; 1st Pl Cntntl Math Leag 83-84; Rgnts Schlrshp 86; Lafayette Coll; Math.

NATALE, PETER; Port Chester HS; Port Chester, NY; (Y); Ski Clb; Concert Band; Mrchg Band; Yrbk Stf; Var Crs Cntry; Var Tennis; Hon Roll; Coachs Awd In Tennis-Most Outgoing Plyr 85-84; Accntng.

NATHAN, RONNA; Fayetteville-Manlius HS; Manlius, NY; (Y); JCL; Latin Clb; VP SADD; Socr; Vllybl; Hon Roll; Law.

NATHAN, SHERRY; Commack HS South; Commack, NY; (Y); Cmnty Wkr; Hosp Aide; School Play; Stage Crew; Nwsp Stf; Var Badmtn; JV Tennis; High Hon Roll; NHS; Computer Clb; Moot Crt 86; Mdln Of Spr Ldrshp Quality St Johns Hosp 85-86; Ntl Hstry Day Cert Of Dstnctn 85; Pre-Med.

NATHANSON, JESSICA A; Linton HS; Schenectady, NY; (Y); AFS; Drama Clb; JCL; Trs Service Clb; SADD; Chorus; Concert Band; Mrchg Band; Orch; School Play; Hugh O Brian Yth Fndtn Ldrshp Cnvtn 83-84; NYS Rgnts Schlrshp 86; Fnlst Shakespeare Rctn Cmptn 85; Wesleyan U; Lang.

NATOLI, TINA; North Babylon SR HS; N Babylon, NY; (Y); 98/467; DECA; Spanish Clb; Stat Vllybl; High Hon Roll; Hon Roll; Jr NHS; NHS; 1st Pl Awd Fd Mktg Suprvsry Lvl & 3rd Pl Sfflk Cnty DECA 86; Brnz Merit Awd DECA 86; C W Post; Hstry.

NAU, THERESE ANN; Saugerties HS; Saugerties, NY; (Y); 13/260; French Clb; Stat Bsktbl; Im Vllybl; Hon Roll; NHS; Ntl Merit SF; Bio Awd 84-85; Engrng.

NAUGHTON, LAURIE; Ossining HS; Ossining, NY; (Y); Church Yth Grp; Cmnty Wkr; Thesps; Acpl Chr; VP Chorus; Church Choir; School Musical; Swing Chorus; Off Jr Cls; Chrmn Stu Cncl; Steering Committee NY ST Assoc Of Stu Cncls 86; All-Cnty Chorus 85-86.

NAUM, TAMRA; East Syracuse HS; East Syracuse, NY; (S); 113/333; DECA; Variety Show; Socr; Top 10 Fin DECA Comtn Entrepreneurshp 86; Outstdng Mrktng Stu Of Yr 86; Chrprsn Civic Conscsnss Proj; Oswego ST.

NAUMOFF, BOBBI LYNN; Frontier Central SR HS; Lake View, NY; (Y); DECA; FBLA; School Play; Hon Roll; NHS; Casanova Clg; Bus Adm.

NAUMOVSKI, MARGARITA; Frontier SR HS; Blasdell, NY; (Y); Art Clb; English Clb; Girl Scts; Pep Clb; Color Guard; Yrbk Stf; Vllybl; High Hon Roll; Hon Roll; Comm Artist.

NAVAGH, JOHN; St John The Baptist HS; Amityville, NY; (S); 3/515; Ski Clb; Var Lcrss; High Hon Roll; NHS; Spanish NHS; Prgrm Gftd HS Stus Adelphi IL 85; Natl Sci Olympd Biolgy,Chmstry 84-85; Engnrng.

NAVARRA, CHRISTINA; New Lebanon Central School; E Nassau, NY; (Y); Cmnty Wkr; Girl Scts; Hon Roll; Prfct Atten Awd; Hon Rl In Rensselaer-Columbis-Greene Cntys Vo-Tec Cntr 85-86; Columbia Greene CC; Data Prcss.

NAVARRA, JOAN; Albion HS; Albion, NY; (Y); Pres 4-H; Pres FFA; Teachers Aide; Sftbl; Cit Awd; 4-H Awd; Dekalb Indiv Accomplshmnt Awd 85; Rotary Clb Schlrshp 86; William Conner Mem Schlrshp 86; Alfred ST Coll; Floricultural.

NAVARRO, ALEX; Hunter College HS; New York City, NY; (Y); Cmnty Wkr; Math Tm; Political Wkr; Nwsp Stf; Lit Mag; Ntl Merit SF; Natl Hispanic Schlr Semi-Fin 86; Polit Sci.

NAVARRO, KIM J; Mt St Michael Acad; New York, NY; (Y); 69/308; JV Var Ice Hcky; Hon Roll; Spanish NHS; St Schlr; Semi-Fnlst ITT Schlrshp Prgrm 86; Mbr Knghts Clmbs 82-86; U Of Central FL; Engr.

NAVARRO, LUCY; Christ The King R HS; Brooklyn, NY; (Y); 6/451; Cmnty Wkr; JA; Nwsp Stf; Yrbk Stf; Rep Jr Cls; Rep Sr Cls; Sec Stu Cncl; Hon Roll; NHS.

NAVAS, DAVID; Le Roy Central HS; Le Roy, NY; (Y); 2/120; Computer Clb; Math Tm; Concert Band; Jazz Band; Mrchg Band; High Hon Roll; NHS; Rensselaer Polytechnic Inst Math & Sci Awd 86.

NAVAS III, PAUL; Cardinal Hayes HS; Bronx, NY; (Y); 69/258; Boys Clb Am; Church Yth Grp; FCA; Varsity Clb; Band; Concert Band; Mrchg Band; Var Ftbl; Wt Lftg; Hon Roll; S Eastern Coll; Acctng.

NAVIAUX, WARD; Cazenovia HS; Cazenovia, NY; (Y); Teachers Aide; Crs Cntry; Trk; Marn Bio.

NAVITSKY, RICHARD; Valley Central HS; Maybrook, NY; (Y); 18/286; Cmnty Wkr; Debate Tm; Science Clb; Varsity Clb; School Play; Stage Crew; VP Frsh Cls; Pres Soph Cls; VP Jr Cls; Off Sr Cls; Columbia Sci Hnrs Pgm 86; Mst Likely To Succeed 86; NYS Sci Symp 86; NYU; Psych.

NAYBEEN, NANCY; Lincoln HS; Yonkers, NY; (Y); Art Clb; Debate Tm; JCL; Band; Off Jr Cls; Bowling; Sftbl; Opt Clb Awd; Fordham U; Medicine.

NAYLOR, TRISTAN; Monroe HS; Rochester, NY; (Y); Red Cross Aide; Yrbk Phtg; Var Swmmng; Var Trk; Hon Roll; Wrtng Awd Mnr HS 86; Advtrsng.

NAZARIO, EDWIN; Cardinal Hayes HS; Bronx, NY; (Y); Camp Fr Inc; Cmnty Wkr; Computer Clb; Spanish Clb; Rep Jr Cls; Sec Stu Cncl; Ftbl; Vllybl; St Johns U; Bus.

NAZARIO, MICHELLE; W Hempstead HS; West Hempstead, NY; (Y); Art Clb; JV Vllybl; Hon Roll; NHS; Diploma Of Merit Spn; St Johns U; Pre Law.

NEAD, MICHAEL; Fairport HS; Fairport, NY; (Y); Boy Scts; Church Yth Grp; Trs German Clb; Math Tm; Model UN; Science Clb; Trs SADD; Rep Stu Cncl; High Hon Roll; Hon Roll; Bio Exprmt STANYS Awd, Hgh Hon To Lcl & St Lvls, Kodak Hon Mntn, US Army Mdln, Sea Grnt Awd 84-85; Fgntcs Engrng.

NEAL, KENNETH; Clara Barion HS; Brooklyn, NY; (Y); Cmnty Wkr; Yrbk Rptr; Ftbl; Hon Roll; Jr NHS; NHS; Ntl Merit Schol; Val; Psychlgst.

NEAL, LISA D; Southwestern Central HS; Lakewood, NY; (Y); 9/145; Church Yth Grp; Trs 4-H; Pres JA; Scholastic Bowl; Trs Spanish Clb; Varsity Clb; Nwsp Stf; Yrbk Stf; Stu Cncl; JV Var Bsktbl; Swmmng MVP 82; Bsktbl 1st Tm All Star Awd 85-86; GA Inst Of Tech; Engrg.

NEAL, NICOLE; Dominican Commercial HS; Jamaica, NY; (Y); Art Clb; Church Choir; Siena Clb Awd 84-85; Elem Schl Tchr.

NEAL, SCOTT; Frontier Central HS; Lake View, NY; (Y); Varsity Clb; Rep Soph Cls; Rep Jr Cls; JV Var Crs Cntry; JV Var Socr; Var Swmmng; JV Var Trk; High Hon Roll; NHS; VFW Awd; Arch.

NEAL, SHAUN M-J; Bellport SR HS; Bellport, NY; (Y); 24/299; Chess Clb; Cmnty Wkr; VP Spanish Clb; Variety Show; Yrbk Sprt Ed; Pres Stu Cncl; High Hon Roll; NHS; Ntl Merit Ltr; Rotary Awd; Yth Awd Ntl Assoc Blck Bsnswmn 86; Dlgt 12th Wrld Fstvl Mth Stdnts Moscow 85; NY ST Rgnts Dplma Hnrs; Georgetown U; Lingst.

NEAL, VICTORIA; John C Birdlebough HS; Phoenix, NY; (Y); 23/159; Drama Clb; French Clb; Temple Yth Grp; Rep Sr Cls; Stu Cncl; High Hon Roll; Hon Roll; Engl Sr Key 86; SUNY New Paitz; Lib Arts.

NEALE, CATHLEEN; Haverling Central HS; Bath, NY; (Y); Am Leg Aux Girls St; Drama Clb; Chorus; Csmtlgy.

NEALE, KELLY; Sharon Springs Central Schl; Sharon Springs, NY; (S); 1/30; Church Yth Grp; FHA; Pres Spanish Clb; Sec Trs Band; Sec Trs Chorus; Trs Concert Band; Jazz Band; Mrchg Band; Rep Stu Cncl; Score Keeper; Fire Dept Essay Awd 84; Dr Robert Shelmandine Music Awd 84; Law.

NEALON, DENNY; Vestal HS; Vestal, NY; (Y); Church Yth Grp; Varsity Clb; L Ftbl; L Lcrss; Hon Roll; Rotary Clbs Yth Ldrshp Cncl 86; Yth Cncl Against Smokg 86; Yth Ldrshp Traing Conf 86; Engrg.

NEALY, WENDY; Brentwood Ross HS; Brentwood, NY; (Y); 9/500; Variety Show; Nwsp Rptr; Off Jr Cls; Rep Sr Cls; Rep Stu Cncl; High Hon Roll; Jr NHS; NHS; Law.

NEAMON, RORI; Alexander Central HS; Corfu, NY; (Y); 10/90; Hosp Aide; Math Tm; Chorus; Variety Show; VP Sr Cls; Rep Stu Cncl; Var L Socr; Hon Roll; VP NHS; Drama Clb; Outstndng Stu Of Yr Awd 83-84.

NEARY, TERESA; West Seneca West SR HS; W Seneca, NY; (Y); Band; Chorus; Concert Band; Mrchg Band; Orch; Hon Roll; JC Awd; Yth Engagd In Serv Awd 86; Awd 9 Yrs Of Dancg 86.

NEAUS, ROBERT; Burgard Vocational HS; Buffalo, NY; (Y); Debate Tm; Hon Roll; Jr NHS; SAR Awd; Aviation Mech.

NECKERS, LUCINDA; Clymer Central HS; Clymer, NY; (Y); Church Yth Grp; Chorus; Sec Trs Stu Cncl; Cheerleading; Pres Score Keeper; Bausch & Lomb Sci Awd; High Hon Roll; NHS.

NECKRITZ, SETH; Port Richmond HS; Staten Island, NY; (Y); Math Tm; Ski Clb; Temple Yth Grp; Orch; Var Co-Capt Tennis; High Hon Roll; NHS; Spanish NHS.

NEDDO, TAMMY; Auburn HS; Auburn, NY; (Y); Drama Clb; French Clb; Stage Crew; Score Keeper; Air Force Acad; Pre Law.

NEDIMYER, ROBERTA; Eden Central SR HS; Eden, NY; (Y); Dance Clb; GAA; Girl Scts; SADD; VICA; Chorus; Church Choir; School Musical; School Play; Yrbk Phtg; Csmtlgy.

NEE, SAMANTHA; St Vincent Ferrer HS; Jackson Hts, NY; (S); Library Aide; Math Tm; Q&S; Church Choir; Nwsp Rptr; Nwsp Stf; Hon Roll; Jr NHS; NHS; Outstndng Achvt NEDT 84; Spnsh Achvt Awds 83-86; St Johns U.

NEEDHAM, LISA; Trott Vocational HS; Niagara Falls, NY; (Y); Am Leg Aux Girls St; Library Aide; RN.

NEEDLE, MICHAEL; Liverpool HS; Liverpool, NY; (Y); 27/816; Stage Crew; Lit Mag; Hon Roll; Jr NHS; NHS; Creativ Wrtg Awd 84-85; Advtsg Desgn Awd 85; Tuitn Schlrshp 86; St Thomas Aquinas; Psych.

NEELLY, CAROLYN PAGE; Fairport HS; Fairport, NY; (Y); 125/600; French Clb; Intnl Clb; Pep Clb; Ski Clb; Yrbk Stf; Stu Cncl; Ftbl; Hon Roll.

NEFF, DOUGLAS; Warsaw Central HS; Warsaw, NY; (S); 10/90; Spanish Clb; JV Var Bsbl; Var Capt Bsktbl; Var Capt Socr; Hon Roll; JR Vrsty Awd Sccr MVP 83; Vrsty Awd Sccr MVP 85; Hnbl Mntn All Greatr Rochester Sccr Tm 85; Alfred ST; Elctrcl Engrng.

NEGER, MARYBETH; St John The Baptist HS; Smithtown, NY; (Y); Cmnty Wkr; Hosp Aide; Office Aide; Chorus; Color Guard; English Honors Awd 85; Community Service Awd 85 And 86; Hofstra Univ; Business Admin.

NEGRA, CHRISTIN; Ward Melville HS; E Setauket, NY; (Y); 39/675; Church Yth Grp; French Clb; Chorus; Church Choir; School Play; JV Cheerleading; JV Mgr(s); JV Score Keeper; JV Im Socr; Im Vllybl; Natl Frnch Cntst 86; Wesleyan U; Intl Rel.

NEGRO, ROSEMARIE J; St Francis Prep; New Hyde Park, NY; (S); 136/744; Art Clb; Service Clb; SADD; Im Vllybl; Hon Roll; NHS.

NEGRON, DENISE; St Raymond Acad; Bronx, NY; (Y); Cmnty Wkr; Library Aide; Office Aide; Teachers Aide; Mrchg Band; Yrbk Stf; VP Soph Cls; Stu Cncl; Hon Roll; Prfct Atten Awd; Bus Admin.

NEGRON, RAFAEL; Cardinal Hayes HS; Bronx, NY; (Y); 33/258; Chorus; School Play; Comptr Sci.

NEGUS, DOUGLAS; Westhill HS; Syracuse, NY; (S); 44/126; Var L Bsbl; Var L Bsktbl; Var L Ftbl; NY ST HS Athl Assn Sect 3 All Div Vrsty Ftbl Awd 85; V Ftbl Sprtsmnshp Awd 85; JV Bsktbl Awd 84-85; Bus Adm.

NEICE, JULIE; Oneil HS; Walton, NY; (Y); 5/90; Sec Key Clb; Sec Varsity Clb; Sec Frsh Cls; Var Bsktbl; Var Fld Hcky; Var Sftbl; High Hon Roll; Sec NHS; Voice Dem Awd; Bus.

NEIDIG, SCOTT; Babylon HS; Babylon, NY; (Y); Boy Scts; Nwsp Stf; JV Socr; Hon Roll; Comp Sci.

NEIDRAUER, KAREN; Churchville Chili SR HS; Churchville, NY; (Y); 65/310; Girl Scts; Mrchg Band; School Musical; School Play; Symp Band; Yrbk Phtg; Lit Mag; Tennis; Girl Sct Gold Ldrshp & Gold Awd 86; Rgnts Schlrshp 86; SUNY Fredonia; Elem Ed.

NEILD, CIELLE; G Ray Bodley HS; Oswego, NY; (Y); Latin Clb; Concert Band; School Musical; High Hon Roll; Hon Roll; Science Clb; Band; Orch; Acad Achvt Exclnc Latin 84-86; Acad Exc Trig & Engl 85; Law.

NEIRO, MARK; New Rochelle HS; New Rochelle, NY; (Y); 58/600; Model UN; Var JV Lcrss; NHS; Spanish NHS; Ski Clb; Stage Crew; Rep Jr Cls; Im Ice Hcky; High Hon Roll; Hon Roll; Lehigh U; Intl Rel.

NEISE, DON; Spackenkill HS; Poughkeepsie, NY; (Y); 77/168; Bsbl; Ftbl; Orval A Todd SR Bsbl Awd 86; Sparton MIP Awd Ftbl 85; Rueben Carrion Mem Awd Bsbl 86; U Of NC; Architecture.

NEISS, LIZA; Union-Endicott HS; Endicott, NY; (Y); High Hon Roll; Hon Roll.

NEISS, THERESA; Chenango Valley JR SR HS; Binghamton, NY; (Y); 31/175; French Clb; Key Clb; Stage Crew; Lit Mag; Var Trk; High Hon Roll; Jr NHS; Rgnts Schlrhsp, Pres Acdmc Ftns Awd 86; SUNY Binghamton; Bus Mgt.

NEISSEN, JOHN D; Troy HS; Troy, NY; (Y); Church Yth Grp; Chorus; Bowling; Swmmng; Wt Lftg; Hon Roll; Siena Coll; CPA.

NEJMAN, RACHEL; Clarkstown HS; New City, NY; (Y); Cmnty Wkr; Chrmn Temple Yth Grp; JV Var Cheerleading; Coach Actv; Im Powder Puff Ftbl; Oswego ST Coll; Adv.

NELKIN, JAY P; Yeshivn University HS; Houston, TX; (Y); Capt Debate Tm; Capt Quiz Bowl; Nwsp Stf; Yrbk Ed-Chief; Rep Frsh Cls; Im Capt Ftbl; Var L Trk; Var Wrstlng; NHS; Ntl Merit SF; Law.

NELLIS, KIMBERLY; Fort Plain Central HS; Davenport, NY; (Y); 18/54; Drama Clb; Office Aide; SADD; Varsity Clb; Chorus; Stage Crew; Sec Soph Cls; Sec Sr Cls; Sec Stu Cncl; Harvey L Smith Mem Awd 86; Stu SR Cls Coop Mst Wth Fclty 86; Qrtr Clb Awd; Mst Outstndng Bus Stu 85-86; Niagara U; Trvl/Trsm.

NELLIS, NICOLE; Gloversville HS; Gloversville, NY; (Y); 57/234; Intnl Clb; Fld Hcky; Mgr(s); Powder Puff Ftbl; Score Keeper; High Hon Roll; Hon Roll; SUNY; Psychlgy.

NELLIST, TIMOTHY; Lyndonville Central HS; Lyndonville, NY; (Y); 15/80; Computer Clb; Math Clb; Band; Concert Band; Jazz Band; Mrchg Band; School Musical; Engrng.

NELLS, TARA; Town Of Webb HS; Old Forge, NY; (Y); Varsity Clb; Band; Concert Band; Jazz Band; Var L Crs Cntry; Var L Socr; Var L Trk; Bausch & Lomb Sci Awd; Hon Roll; NHS; Augsbury N Cnty Schlr Awd 86; Jr Olympc Crss Cntry Ski Tm 84-86; ST Cham Crss Cntry Skiing 86.

NELS, BETH; Liverpool HS; N Syracuse, NY; (Y); Church Yth Grp; Hosp Aide; High Hon Roll; Keoka Coll; Soc Wrk.

NELSEN, CHRISTINE; Mercy HS; Mastic Beach, NY; (Y); Art Clb; Service Clb; Ski Clb; SADD; Yrbk Phtg; Yrbk Stf; Trs Sr Cls; Hon Roll; Intr Dsgn.

NELSON, ANN; South Park HS; Buffalo, NY; (Y); NHS; Alfred U; Zoolgy.

NELSON, BENJAMIN B; Owego Free Acad; Owego, NY; (Y); Drama Clb; German Clb; Quiz Bowl; Scholastic Bowl; School Musical; School Play; Nwsp Stf; Socr; Hon Roll; St Schlr; Hamilton Coll.

NELSON, CHARLES A; Lake Shore HS; Angola, NY; (Y); 86/284; Am Leg Boys St; Nwsp Rptr; Dance Clb; Trs Soph Cls; Trs Jr Cls; Trs Sr Cls; Stat Bsktbl; JV Var Socr; Hon Roll; Jr NHS; Regents Scshlrshp 86; MI ST U; Cmmnctns.

NELSON, DENISE A; Sanford H Calhoun HS; N Merrick, NY; (Y); 16/313; Computer Clb; Key Clb; Off Jr Cls; Hst Jr Cls; Off Sr Cls; Sec Stu Cncl; Var Badmtn; Var Tennis; NHS; Cncl Admin Sprvsrs Schlrshp 86; Rensselaer Polytech; Comp Sci.

NELSON, DIANE; Windham Ashland Jewett Central HS; Hensonville, NY; (S); 1/42; Church Yth Grp; Band; Chorus; Jazz Band; Cheerleading; Trk; High Hon Roll; NHS; Mdls For All-Cnty Bnd 83-86; Mdls For Jazz Bnd 84-86; Mdls For Excllnt Rtngs In NYS Msc Assn Solo Cmp; Roberts Wesleyan Coll; Msc Educ.

NELSON, DOUG; Mexico HS; Pulaski, NY; (Y); VP Art Clb; VP DECA; Rep German Clb; VP SADD; Rep Varsity Clb; Rep Yrbk Stf; Rep Frsh Cls; Rep Soph Cls; Rep Jr Cls; Rep Stu Cncl; Chsn Exchng Prgrm Montcerat 86; Pres Stu Cncl 86-87; Prm Crt Prince 86; CCBI; Bus Mgmt.

NELSON, GEORGE; Mt St Michael Acad; Bronx, NY; (S); 15/308; Var Ftbl; Hon Roll; NHS; Spanish NHS; Peer Facltatr; Spnsh Hgh Merit Awd.

NELSON, JESSICA; Rye HS; Stamford, CT; (Y); Teachers Aide; Bsktbl; Sftbl; Trk; Vllybl; Morris Brown Coll; Phy Ed.

NELSON, JOHANNA; Jamestown HS; Jamestown, NY; (Y); Church Yth Grp; Sec French Clb; Hosp Aide; Intnl Clb; Quiz Bowl; Trs Orch; NHS.

NELSON, JULIE; Huntington HS; Huntington, NY; (Y); Capt Math Tm; Nwsp Phtg; Nwsp Stf; Rptr Lit Mag; High Hon Roll; Hon Roll; NCTE Awd; NHS; Ntl Merit Ltr; Cmpltn Adelphi U Chmstry Smnr Prog Gftd Stu 85; Biolgcl Sci.

NELSON, KARIN; Fairport HS; Fairport, NY; (Y); Drama Clb; Hosp Aide; Intnl Clb; Orch; Rep Sr Cls; Stu Cncl; Var Tennis; Hon Roll; NHS; Wittenberg; Psych.

NELSON, KATHLEEN; Sacred Heart Acad; Long Beach, NY; (S); SADD; Yrbk Stf; High Hon Roll; NHS; Church Yth Grp; Cmnty Wkr; Office Aide; Church Choir; Bus Law.

NELSON, KIMBERLY; Linton HS; Schenectady, NY; (Y); 5/344; Art Clb; Church Yth Grp; Church Choir; Lit Mag; Stu Cncl; Hon Roll; Jr NHS; Masonic Awd; NHS; Ntl Merit SF; BYU; Art.

NELSON, KIRK; Jamestown HS; Jamestown, NY; (Y); 23/396; Hon Roll; Jamestown Comm Coll; Arch.

NELSON, LEILANI; Scarsdale HS; Scarsdale, NY; (Y); Art Clb; Debate Tm; Drama Clb; Hosp Aide; Intnl Clb; NFL; Speech Tm; Temple Yth Grp; Var Capt Crs Cntry; Var Capt Trk; Philosophy.

NELSON, MARK J; Lake George SR HS; Kattskill Bay, NY; (Y); 24/72; Am Leg Boys St; Church Yth Grp; SADD; Varsity Clb; Chorus; Jazz Band; School Musical; Rep Stu Cncl; Var Bsbl; Var Capt Socr; NY ST Regents Schlrshp 85-86; Norwich U; Elec Engrng.

NELSON, MARK R; Saint Johns Acad; Cadyville, NY; (Y); 4/36; Drama Clb; Chorus; Yrbk Ed-Chief; Trs Jr Cls; VP Mgr Bowling; NHS; SADD; Yrbk Bus Mgr; Schlrs Of Dllrs Team 86; Mission Clb 83-86; Floristry.

NELSON, NICHELLE J; Columbia Prep Schl; Brooklyn, NY; (Y); Yrbk Stf; Trk; Ntl Merit SF; Bio.

NELSON, RANDI; Amityville Memorial HS; Massapequa, NY; (Y); Church Yth Grp; FBLA; Key Clb; Office Aide; Teachers Aide; Orch; Variety Show; Mgr(s); Score Keeper; High Hon Roll; Amer Lgn Cert & Acad All-American 84; Cert Schlrshp-Bus Law 86; Syracuse; Law.

NELSON, SANDRA; Frewsburg Central HS; Jamestown, NY; (Y); Band; JV Bsktbl; JV Sftbl; JV Swmmng; Merit Roll 83-86; Hotl Mgr.

NELSON, STEVEN E; Central Islip HS; Central Islip, NY; (Y); French Clb; Band; VP Sr Cls; JV L Bsbl; Var L Ftbl; Var L Mgr(s); Stat L Swmmng; Phy Ed.

NELSON, SUSAN; Margaretville Central HS; Margaretville, NY; (Y); 3/43; Band; Yrbk Stf; Trs Frsh Cls; Trs Soph Cls; Trs Jr Cls; Trs Sr Cls; Bsktbl; High Hon Roll; Hon Roll; NHS.

NEMEC, CHRISTINA; Royalton-Hartland Central HS; Gasport, NY; (Y); 31/130; Drama Clb; Chorus; Church Choir; School Musical; School Play; Nwsp Rptr; Hon Roll; Church Yth Grp; Nwsp Stf; Music Hnr Grad 86; Vrsty Ltr & Pin & Grd Music 86; Bryant & Stratton; Exec Secy.

NEMEC, NANCY; Schoharie Central Schl; Central Bridge, NY; (S); Debate Tm; Varsity Clb; Acpl Chr; Chorus; VP Frsh Cls; VP Soph Cls; Cheerleading; Var Socr; Hon Roll; Sadie Hawkins Daisy May 84; All Cty Choir 83-85.

NEMEROFF, ROBIN; John H Glenn HS; Greenlawn, NY; (Y); Drama Clb; Hosp Aide; Chorus; School Musical; Ed Lit Mag; Trs Stu Cncl; DAR Awd; French Hon Soc; High Hon Roll; NHS; Rnkd 4th & 8th In Suffolk Cnty Frnch Exam 84-86; Adelphi Schl For Intl Studies Schlrshp; Tri-M Pres 84.

NEMETH, GARY; Newfield HS; Selden, NY; (Y); Chess Clb; Spanish Clb; Varsity Clb; JV Var Ftbl; 3 Yrs Var Fencg Team 84-86; NYS Regnts Schlrshp; 2nd In State Comptn; St Johns; Law.

NEMI, NEIL; Liverpool HS; Liverpool, NY; (Y); 19/900; Exploring; Sec JA; JCL; Rep Stu Cncl; Im Bsktbl; Var L Trk; Hon Roll; NHS; SUNY Oswego; Comp Sci.

NENDZA, CHERYL; Clayton A Bouton JR SR HS; Voorheesville, NY; (Y); Intnl Clb; Key Clb; Ski Clb; Spanish Clb; Rep Stu Cncl; Cheerleading; High Hon Roll; Hon Roll.

NENDZA, MONICA; Bishop Grimes HS; Syracuse, NY; (S); Yrbk Stf; Var Bsktbl; Var Capt Tennis; Hon Roll; Trk.

NENTWICH, KEVIN M; Sachem HS; Holbrook, NY; (Y); 150/1500; Var L Ftbl; Regents Schlrshp 86; All Lg Ftbl 85; 2WKA Karate Champ 81, 83 & 85; Albany U; Law.

NERI, JOHN; Corinth HS; Corinth, NY; (Y); 7/100; Spanish Clb; Varsity Clb; JV Bsktbl; Var Ftbl; JV Socr; JV Trk; High Hon Roll; Hon Roll; NHS; Prfct Atten Awd; Notre Dame; Computers.

NERI, PHILIP; North Babylon HS; No Babylon, NY; (Y); 2/485; Intnl Clb; Mathletes; Mrchg Band; JV L Socr; Var L Tennis; High Hon Roll; NHS; Prfct Atten Awd; St Schlr; Italian Hnr Scty 85.

NERON, SABITA; Walton HS; Bronx, NY; (Y); Art Clb; Math Clb; Math Tm; Yrbk Phtg; Bsktbl; Trk; Hon Roll; Prfct Atten Awd; Vllybl; Excllnce Seqntl Math 84-86; Excllnce Art 84-86; Excllnce Typg 86; Advrtsg.

NERSES, NORA; Huntington HS; Huntington, NY; (Y); Capt Mathletes; Orch; School Musical; Lit Mag; High Hon Roll; NHS; Bnz Mdl In Long Islnd Math Fair 86; Lng Isldn Strng Fstvl 84 & 85; Area All ST Orchstra 85; Elec Engrng.

NERSESIAN, MICHAEL S; General Douglas Mac Arthur HS; Wantagh, NY; (S); 54/321; Political Wkr; Nwsp Phtg; Nwsp Rptr; Nwsp Stf; Yrbk Phtg; Yrbk Stf; High Hon Roll; Jr NHS; NHS; Nassau CC; Poltcl Sci.

NERZIG, BRUCE; Newfield HS; Selden, NY; (Y); Boy Scts; Drama Clb; School Musical; Stage Crew; Variety Show; JV Bsbl.

NESBITT, LISA; Albion HS; Albion, NY; (S); 19/176; 4-H; Latin Clb; Ski Clb; Chorus; Swing Chorus; 4-H Awd; High Hon Roll; Hon Roll; VP Jr NHS; Acceptance Rotary Intl Yth Exc 85-86; Cornell U; Intr Design.

NESBITT, STEPHANIE R; Moravia Central Schl; Moravia, NY; (Y); 1/92; Concert Band; Jazz Band; Mrchg Band; School Musical; Stage Crew; Pres Stu Cncl; Var Capt Bsktbl; Var Capt Sftbl; High Hon Roll; Val; US Military Acad; Law.

NESBITT, TANYA; Jane Addams HS; Bronx, NY; (S); 19/260; Lit Mag; Trk; Hon Roll; Special Act & Svc Awd 85; Baruch Coll; Bus Adm.

NESBITT, TERRI; Senior HS; Cato, NY; (Y); French Clb; Girl Scts; Chorus; School Musical; Yrbk Stf; Hon Roll; NHS; Prfct Atten Awd.

NESMITH, ROBT; Grace H Dodge Voc HS; Bronx, NY; (Y); 20/250; Church Yth Grp; Cmnty Wkr; FBLA; Science Clb; Chorus; Nwsp Rptr; Var Bsktbl; Hon Roll; NHS; Prfct Atten Awd; Summr Schlrshp Prog 83-85; Prncpls Pride Of Yankees Awd 85-86; Howard U; Lwyr.

NESPOLE, ANNMARIE A; St Francis Prep; Flushing, NY; (S); 2/746; Library Aide; Science Clb; Chorus; High Hon Roll; NHS.

NESTER, GEORGIA; Sauquoit Valley Cntrl HS; Sauquoit, NY; (Y); 11/99; Sec Drama Clb; Pres VP Chorus; School Musical; School Play; Yrbk Ed-Chief; High Hon Roll; Hon Roll; NHS; NY ST Rgnts Schlrshp 85; Oneida Cnty Music Ed Assoc Schlrshp 86; Area All-St Choir 84-85; Berklee Clg Of Music; Prfrmnc.

NESTER, M NOEL; Long Beach HS; Lido Beach, NY; (S); 40/300; CAP; Hosp Aide; Service Clb; Nwsp Rptr; Ftbl; Capt Lcrss; Wrstlng; NHS; SAR Awd; Gftd Bio Steu Smnr 85; Hlth-Mdcl Fld.

NESTOROWICH, SUSAN; Hutchinson Central Technical HS; Buffalo, NY; (Y); Church Yth Grp; SUNY Buffalo; Mgt.

NETTLETON, JODI; Rome Free Acad; Rome, NY; (Y); Church Yth Grp; Civic Clb; Cmnty Wkr; Intnl Clb; Political Wkr; SADD; Color Guard; Mrchg Band; Yrbk Stf; Sec Sr Cls; SCNDRY Ed.

NETTLETON, KAREN A; Bellport HS; Bellport, NY; (Y); 17/395; VP Sec Church Yth Grp; Girl Scts; Hosp Aide; Latin Clb; Chorus; Church Choir; High Hon Roll; Hon Roll; Jr NHS; NHS; Sci.

NEU, DEBORAH J; Nazareth Acad; Rochester, NY; (Y); Red Cross Aide; Spanish Clb; Stage Crew; Yrbk Stf; High Hon Roll; Hon Roll; NHS; Hghst Math Avg 83; Hghst Asian-Afrcn Avg 83; Spnsh Hnrs 83-85; SUNY Oswego; Comp Sci.

NEUBAUER, LILI; Guilderland HS; Albany, NY; (Y); Am Leg Aux Girls St; Ski Clb; Varsity Clb; Band; Rep Soph Cls; Rep Stu Cncl; Var L Crs Cntry; JV Tennis; Var L Trk; High Hon Roll; Awd Hghst Avg French 5 86; Awd Scl Stud 86; Awd Math 86; Med.

NEUBAUER, MARYANN; Villa Maria Acad; Buffalo, NY; (S); 15/105; Dance Clb; Sec Spanish Clb; Stage Crew; Yrbk Stf; Rep Stu Cncl; Im Vllybl; Hon Roll; NHS; D Youville Coll; Nrsng.

NEUFANG, DONNA M; Marcus Whitman HS; Stanley, NY; (Y); 6/115; Varsity Clb; Ed Yrbk Stf; Pres Frsh Cls; Rep Soph Cls; Pres Jr Cls; Stu Cncl; Var Capt Swmmng; High Hon Roll; NHS; Rotary Awd; Sci Olympcs 82-84; Rochester Inst/Htl/Rest Mgmt.

NEUGEBAUER, JULIE A; Ballston Spa HS; Ballston Spa, NY; (Y); 2/244; Am Leg Aux Girls St; Service Clb; Nwsp Rptr; Stat Socr; Var Tennis; Stat Trk; High Hon Roll; VP NHS; Leo Plant Hghst Blgy Rgnts Scr 84; Rgnts Schlrshp 86; GE STAR Schlrshp 86; MA Inst Of Tech; Engnrng.

NEUHOFF, GEORGIA ANNE; Westhampton Beach HS; East Moriches, NY; (Y); 35/260; Spanish Clb; SADD; Band; Chorus; Concert Band; Mrchg Band; Pep Band; School Musical; School Play; Yrbk Stf; Mary Sabasto Chorus Awd 83; Hampton Fest Music Schlrshp 84-85; Pres Clsrm 86; Bus Admin.

NEUMAIER, PAUL; James Madison HS; Brooklyn, NY; (Y); 240/756; Aud/Vis; Boy Scts; Spanish Clb; JV Bsbl; Hon Roll; Prfct Atten Awd.

NEUMAN, MARK; Northport HS; E Northport, NY; (Y); Aud/Vis; Cmnty Wkr; Computer Clb; Var L Trk; Hon Roll; Jr NHS; NHS; Med.

NEUMANN, KIMIKO; Carmel HS; Carmel, NY; (Y); Art Clb; Drama Clb; French Clb; Band; Chorus; Concert Band; School Musical; JV Var Cheerleading; JV Fld Hcky; Hon Roll; Art Shw Awd-1st Pl Blck & Wht Drwng 86; Fshn Dsgn.

NEUMANN, ROBERTA; York Central HS; Leicester, NY; (Y); AFS; Math Tm; School Musical; Nwsp Rptr; Rep Jr Cls; Var JV Sftbl; High Hon Roll; Hon Roll; Jr NHS; NHS; Span Mrt Awd 85; Suny Buffalo; Criminal Law.

NEUMANN, SHARON; St Dominic HS; Bethpage, NY; (S); 2/160; Quiz Bowl; SADD; School Musical; School Play; JV Sftbl; Var Tennis; Im Vllybl; High Hon Roll; NHS; Achvt Awd Hstry-Mdl 83-84; Spnsh Awd 83-84; Hnrbl Mntn Math 84-85.

NEUWIRTH, SAFRIR; Comsewogue HS; Pt Jefferson Sta, NY; (Y); 6/430; Var Tennis; Hon Roll; NHS; Vrsty Tnns MV Awd 85-86; Spnsh Awd 83-84; Med.

NEVATT, SUZANNE; Union Springs Acad; Clifton Park, NY; (S); 2/30; Ski Clb; Varsity Clb; Band; Concert Band; Pres Soph Cls; Var Cheerleading; High Hon Roll; Hon Roll; NHS; Acadmc All Amer 85-86; Pacific Union Coll; Med.

NEVEN, HEIDI; Chatham HS; Chatham, NY; (Y); 14/134; Ski Clb; Yrbk Phtg; Yrbk Stf; Rep Stu Cncl; Coach Actv; Capt Socr; Capt JV Sftbl; High Hon Roll; Hon Roll; NHS; Hotel Mgmt.

NEVERETTE, JULIE; Massena Central HS; Massena, NY; (Y); JV Bsktbl; Powder Puff Ftbl; JV Vllybl; Dental Hygein.

NEVEU, PAMELA; Vernon Vernona Sherrill HS; Sherrill, NY; (Y); Church Yth Grp; Girl Scts; Hosp Aide; Ski Clb; Spanish Clb; Band; Chorus; Yrbk Stf; Stu Cncl; Var Cheerleading; VA Poly Tech Inst; Chem.

NEVINS, DAVID; Haverling Central HS; Bath, NY; (Y); Boy Scts; French Clb; Latin Clb; Math Clb; SADD; Band; Concert Band; Mrchg Band; School Play; Yrbk Stf; Eagle Sct 86; SUNY; Lib Arts.

NEVINS, GRACE; Onteora Central HS; Boiceville, NY; (Y); 13/201; SADD; School Play; Nwsp Rptr; Yrbk Stf; Chrmn Stu Cncl; Capt Bsktbl; Capt Fld Hcky; Capt Trk; High Hon Roll; Sec NHS; Miron Bldng Prodts Schlrshp $1500 86; Empire St Fld Hockey Team Cap 2 Yrs 84-85; Athl Awd 86; Colgate U.

NEVINS, JENNIFER; Susquehanna Valley HS; Conklin, NY; (Y); GAA; Pep Clb; Varsity Clb; Pres Soph Cls; Pres Jr Cls; Pres Sr Cls; Var Trk; High Hon Roll; NHS; Spanish NHS; Pres Physcl Ftns Awd 82-86; Supr Ftns Awd 84-86; Ithaca Coll; Physcl Thrpy.

NEVINS, JENNIFER; Williamsville South HS; Williamsville, NY; (Y); AFS; French Clb; Chorus; School Play; High Hon Roll; NCTE Awd; Erie Cnty Chrs 83-84; Area All ST Chrs 83-84; Psychlgy.

NEVINS, JOHN; Greenville Central JR SR HS; Hannacroix, NY; (Y); Camera Clb; Key Clb; Political Wkr; Band; Concert Band; Jazz Band; Pep Band; Rep Frsh Cls; Rep Jr Cls; Vars Ltr 86; Schenectady CC; Htl Mgmt.

NEVONE, TRACEY; Allegany Central HS; Allegany, NY; (Y); Library Aide; Pep Clb; Chorus; Yrbk Stf; Var Cheerleading; Var Pom Pon; Var Socr; Wrstlng; Hon Roll; Acctg.

NEW, DAVID; Union Springs HS; Auburn, NY; (Y); Boy Scts; Church Yth Grp; Red Cross Aide; Church Choir; Socr; Hon Roll; Prfct Atten Awd; Math.

NEWBURG, BERNADETTE T; St Joseph Hill Acad; Staten Island, NY; (Y); 23/107; Art Clb; NFL; Hon Roll; Ntl Merit Ltr; NEDT Awd; St Schlr; Drama Clb; FTA; Spanish Clb; Bowling; Regents Schlrshp ST NY 86; 1st NYC Drivers Sfty Awrnss Pstr Comp 84; Coll STATEN Island; Bus.

NEWCOMB, NANCY; Riverhead HS; Riverhead, NY; (Y); 26/221; German Clb; Science Clb; Ski Clb; SADD; Band; Chorus; Church Choir; Concert Band; Mrchg Band; Orch.

NEWCOMBE, LESLIE; Madrid-Waddington Central HS; Chase Mills, NY; (Y); FFA; Varsity Clb; Var Bsbl; Var Socr; Var Vllybl; Mst Valuable Off Plyr Soccr 85-86; 1st Tm All Nrthrn Sectn 10 Bsbl 85-86; MVP Bsbl 85-86.

NEWELL III, GEORGE F; Clarence Central HS; S Londonderry, VT; (Y); Drama Clb; Latin Clb; Chorus; School Play.

NEWELL, PATRICIA; Evander Childs HS; Bronx, NY; (Y); Church Yth Grp; Cmnty Wkr; Debate Tm; Girl Scts; Library Aide; Speech Tm; Teachers Aide; Chorus; Concert Band; Jazz Band; John J Ag; Law Enfrcmnt.

NEWHOUSE, JENNIFER; Tioga Central HS; Owego, NY; (Y); Sec Church Yth Grp; Computer Clb; Church Choir; Rep Frsh Cls; Rep Soph Cls; VP Jr Cls; Sec Stu Cncl; JV Bsktbl; JV Fld Hcky; Score Keeper; Phys Therapy.

NEWKIRK, BETH; Mayfield Central HS; Mayfield, NY; (Y); 22/75; Drama Clb; Hosp Aide; Band; Chorus; Church Choir; Concert Band; Drm Mjr(t); Jazz Band; Mrchg Band; School Musical; Nazareth Coll; Soclgy.

NEWKIRK, DENISE; Mayfield HS; Gloversville, NY; (Y); 7/72; Office Aide; Teachers Aide; Varsity Clb; Nwsp Ed-Chief; Var Socr; Var Vllybl; High Hon Roll; NHS; Home Econ Awd 86; Schlrshp & Athl Awd 85; Avionics.

NEWKIRK, NISA; Newburgh Free Acad; Newburgh, NY; (Y); 4-H; FHA; Library Aide; Yrbk Stf; Stu Cncl; Var Bsktbl; Coach Actv; Sftbl; Vllybl; Cit Awd; Bus Adm.

NEWMAN, AMY; Poland Central HS; Cold Brook, NY; (Y); 19/68; Church Yth Grp; Drama Clb; Varsity Clb; Band; Chorus; Church Choir; Concert Band; School Play; JV Var Cheerleading; Prfct Atten Awd; Utica Schl Of Commerce; Med Sec.

NEWMAN, ANDREW; Hancock Central Schl; Hancock, NY; (Y); 7/80; Am Leg Boys St; Church Yth Grp; German Clb; Band; Chorus; Jazz Band; Bsbl; Bsktbl; Ftbl; NHS.

NEWMAN, BARBARA; Frontier Central HS; Hamburg, NY; (Y); French Clb; Pep Clb; Band; Mrchg Band; Stat Bsktbl; JV Socr; JV Var Sftbl; Var Vllybl; Hon Roll; Prfct Atten Awd.

NEWMAN, BETINA ROSE; George W Fowler HS; Syracuse, NY; (Y); Pep Clb; Spanish Clb; SADD; Variety Show; Sec Jr Cls; Sec Sr Cls; Pom Pon; Score Keeper; Trk; Vllybl; Pres Acdmc Fit Awd 86; Spcl Rcgntn Vlybl 85; Spcl Rcgntn Trck 85; Bryant; Exec Sec.

NEWMAN, DINA; Jamesville-De Witt HS; Dewitt, NY; (Y); 7/250; Key Clb; Math Tm; Model UN; Temple Yth Grp; Chorus; Mgr Stage Crew; High Hon Roll; NHS; Ntl Merit Ltr; Svc Awd 86.

NEWMAN, DWIGHT; Massena Central HS; Massena, NY; (Y); Band; Concert Band; Jazz Band; Mrchg Band; Hon Roll; NHS; Prfct Atten Awd; David M Houlihan Percssn Awd 86; Elec Engrng.

NEWMAN, GREGORY; Greece Athena HS; Rochester, NY; (Y); 24/265; Math Clb; Science Clb; Ski Clb; SADD; Varsity Clb; Var Crs Cntry; Var Capt Trk; Hon Roll; NHS; Ntl Merit Schol; USAF Acad Supt Apptmnt 86; ROTC Scholar 86; NYS Regents Scholar 86; MVP Trk 86; Trk Schl Rcrds 86; USAF Acad; Pilot.

NEWMAN, JENNIFER; Poughkeepsie HS; Poughkeepsie, NY; (Y); SADD; Temple Yth Grp; Yrbk Stf; Swmmng; Prfct Atten Awd; Club 17 Blood Group; Policeman.

NEWMAN, KATHE; Carmel HS; Carmel, NY; (Y); Trs SADD; Concert Band; Jazz Band; Mrchg Band; Orch; School Musical; Symp Band; JV Bsktbl; Var Tennis; Hon Roll; U S Hnr Band 85; Rcrdng Engr.

NEWMAN, MARY; New York Mills JR SR HS; New York Mills, NY; (Y); GAA; Pres Sec Key Clb; Ski Clb; Spanish Clb; Varsity Clb; Chorus; School Play; Yrbk Stf; Sec Frsh Cls; Sec Jr Cls; Grtr Utica Brd Of Realtors Svc Awd 86; Rotary Meeting Exchng 86; Mohawk Vly; Bus Admn.

NEWMAN, SEAN; Midwood HS; Brooklyn, NY; (Y); 288/667; Var Ftbl; Outstndng Defensve Plyr JV Capt 84; Psych.

NEWMARK, SCOTT; H Frank Carey HS; W Hempstead, NY; (Y); Aud/Vis; Temple Yth Grp; JV Lcrss; High Hon Roll; Hon Roll; Duquesne U; Pre Law.

NEWSOM, DORIAN; Faith Heritage HS; Dewitt, NY; (Y); Church Yth Grp; Drama Clb; Church Choir; Rep Jr Cls; Sec Sr Cls; Rep Stu Cncl; Var Socr; Var Trk; Key Clb; Band; Roberts Wesleyan; Intr Dsgn.

NEWSOME, ANDREW; Archbishop Stepinac HS; Mt Kisco, NY; (Y); JV Var Ftbl; NC A&T; Aerontcl Engrng.

NEWTON, DEBBIE; Potsdam HS; Potsdam, NY; (Y); AFS; Drama Clb; French Clb; Chorus; VP Soph Cls; VP Sr Cls; Stu Cncl; Var L Cheerleading; Hon Roll; NHS; Sprtsmnshp Chrldng 86; Clarkson Coll; Bio.

NEWTON, GREGORY; Wyandanch HS; Wyandanch, NY; (Y); 56/157; Am Leg Boys St; Church Yth Grp; JA; Trs Stu Cncl; Capt Ftbl; Capt Trk; Bst JR Athlt 86; Rutgers U; Bus Admin.

NEWTON, KEELAN; Akron Central HS; Akron, NY; (Y); 14/137; Church Yth Grp; Drama Clb; Chorus; School Musical; School Play; Nwsp Stf; Yrbk Stf; Fld Hcky; Capt Trk; NHS; NHS Schlrshp 86; Ithaca Coll; Bus Mgmt.

NEWTON, RHONDA R; Ravena Coeymans Selkirk SR HS; W Coxsackie, NY; (Y); 3/186; Drama Clb; Trs Spanish Clb; School Musical; Ed Lit Mag; Capt Var Tennis; DAR Awd; God Cntry Awd; NHS; Ntl Merit Ltr; Debate Tm; Peter Francisco Awd Amer Hstrn; Pol Sci.

NEWTON, STEVEN R; South Jefferson HS; Adams, NY; (Y); 6/131; Church Yth Grp; Trs German Clb; School Musical; Trs Soph Cls; Trs Jr Cls; Trs Sr Cls; Var Capt Bsktbl; Var L Golf; Hon Roll; NHS; Math Rgnts Awd 83, 84 & 85; NY ST Rgnts Schlrshp 85-86; Jfrsn CC; Engrng Sci.

NEWTON, TIM; Onondaga Central HS; Syracuse, NY; (Y); Exploring; Band; Trk; Hon Roll; NHS; Stu Of Mnth In Elctrcy Boces 86; Onondaga Cntrl; Elctrcn.

NG, DEBBIE; James Madison HS; Brooklyn, NY; (Y); 55/756; Dance Clb; Drama Clb; JA; Math Clb; Service Clb; SADD; Off Jr Cls; Gym; Swmmng; Tennis; NYU.

NG, JIMMY; Brooklyn Academy Prep Schl; Brooklyn, NY; (Y); Computer Clb; Math Clb.

NG, KATHALEEN; Forest Hills HS; Middle Village, NY; (Y); 108/821; Church Yth Grp; Cmnty Wkr; Office Aide; Science Clb; Service Clb; Chorus; Hon Roll; Kiwanis Awd; Prfct Atten Awd; 2nd Pl Queensborough Sci Fair 84; Hon Mem Queensborough Sci Fair 85; NYU; Pre-Med.

NG, KATRINA H; St Francis Prep; Jackson Heights, NY; (S); 27/744; Service Clb; Chorus; Church Choir; NHS; Socl Svc.

NG, LILY; William Cullen Bryant HS; Woodside, NY; (S); Hosp Aide; Library Aide; Orch; Nwsp Rptr; Yrbk Phtg; Rep Jr Cls; Cit Awd; Hon Roll; NHS; Spanish NHS; Ntl Hnr Soc; Ctznshp Awd; Candy Striper; Spnsh Ntl Hnr Soc; Bus.

NG, MARLAND; Stuyvesant HS; New York, NY; (Y); Chorus; Madrigals; School Musical; Stage Crew; VP Frsh Cls; French Hon Soc; Regents Scholar 86; Parsons Schl Desgn; Mktng.

NG, ROBERT; Springfield Gardens HS; S Rosedale, NY; (Y); 25/450; Teachers Aide; Nwsp Rptr; Nwsp Sprt Ed; Nwsp Stf; Lit Mag; Cit Awd; High Hon Roll; Rgnts Dplma, Dplma Merit 86; Hofstra U; Jrnlsm.

NG, TERI; Seward Park HS; New York, NY; (Y); 25/544; Library Aide; Office Aide; Band; Concert Band; Orch; NHS; Regents Schlrshps 86; Cornell U.

NG, VELMA; New Utrecht HS; Brooklyn, NY; (Y); 1/535; Mathletes; Nwsp Rptr; Tennis; Cit Awd; NHS; Ntl Merit Ltr; Val; Cornell U; Biomed Engr.

NGO, HUNG; Binghamton HS; Binghamton, NY; (Y); Chess Clb; Computer Clb; Intnl Clb; Var Badmtn; JV Bowling; High Hon Roll; Hon Roll; RPI; Mech Engr.

NGUYEN, HOANG; Cicero/North Syracuse HS; N Syracuse, NY; (Y); JV Im Socr; Var Vllybl; JV Im Wrstlng; SUNY Morrisville; Elec.

NGUYEN, HOANG JOHN; Margaretville C S HS; Fleischmans, NY; (Y); Cmnty Wkr; English Clb; Radio Clb; Variety Show; Lit Mag; Off Jr Cls; Bowling; Crs Cntry; Socr; Trk; Language Clb 85-86; Acctng.

NGUYEN, HUNG; Bishop Ludden HS; Syracuse, NY; (Y); Art Clb; Var Socr; Upwrd Bnd Pgm Stu Of Yr 85; Syracuse U; Engrng.

NGUYEN, HUNG; Dover JR SR HS; Wingdale, NY; (S); Math Tm; Socr; Hon Roll; NHS; New Paltz.

NGUYEN, HUY; Dover JR-SR HS; Dover Plains, NY; (S); Socr; High Hon Roll; New Paltz; Comp Sci.

NGUYEN, JEANNE DIEP; Roy C Ketcham HS; Wappingers Fls, NY; (Y); Hon Roll; FIT; Fshn Desgn.

NGUYEN, MARY; Seton Catholic Central HS; Johnson City, NY; (Y); 23/162; Church Yth Grp; French Clb; Ski Clb; Yrbk Stf; Jessie Baker Schlrshp 86; H C & C C Burns Schlrshp 86; SUNY Stony Brook; Comp Sci.

NGUYEN, QUOC; Tottenville HS; Staten Island, NY; (Y); Socr; Vllybl; Hon Roll; Jr NHS; MVP-BST Dfns Awd In Soccer 83-84; MVP Awds-All Star, Bst Dfns, & Coaches-Soccer 84-86; Robert Wesleyan Coll; Engr.

NGUYEN, SON; George Ray Bodley HS; Fulton, NY; (Y); 4/220; Science Clb; Varsity Clb; Bsktbl; Ftbl; Tennis; Trk; High Hon Roll; Hon Roll; NHS; Church Yth Grp; Sci Olympia Awd 86; West Point; Aeronutcl Engr.

NGUYEN, THANH; G Ray Bodley HS; Fulton, NY; (Y); Im Bsktbl; Im Socr; Mech Engrng.

NGUYEN, THERESA T H; The Mary Louis Acad; Mineola, NY; (Y); 1/270; Hosp Aide; Math Tm; Service Clb; Teachers Aide; Im Ftbl; High Hon Roll; NHS; NEDT Awd; Art Clb; Office Aide; Deans Hnry Schlrshp 86; Newsday Ldng Schlstc Achvr 86; Schlrshp Summer Schl 85; Johns Hopkins U; Med.

NGUYEN, TRINH; Curtis HS; Staten Island, NY; (Y); Intnl Clb; Teachers Aide; Mrchg Band; Cit Awd.

NGUYEN, VIET; Ossining HS; Ossining, NY; (Y); Computer Clb; Rep French Clb; SADD; Rep Soph Cls; Rep Jr Cls; Rep Stu Cncl; Im Bsktbl; Var Crs Cntry; Var Trk; Hon Roll; Var Boys Spring & Winter Trck Coaches Awd 85-86; Psych.

NGUYEN, YUN; Roy C Ketcham HS; Wappinger Fls, NY; (Y); Ann Zodikoff Mem Awd 86.

NICASTRO, JOANNE; Waterloo SR HS; Waterloo, NY; (Y); 29/180; FTA; Model UN; Political Wkr; Nwsp Ed-Chief; Yrbk Stf; French Hon Soc; Prfct Atten Awd; Air Force; Nrsng.

NICE, CYNTHIA; Huthinson Central Technical HS; Buffalo, NY; (Y); Computer Clb; Yrbk Ed-Chief; Bowling; Hon Roll; :Compu Sci.

NICE, RICHARD D; Horseheads HS; Big Flats, NY; (S); Boy Scts; Latin Clb; Science Clb; Variety Show; Nwsp Rptr; JV Bsktbl; JV Socr; Var Tennis; High Hon Roll; NHS; Engr.

NICHOLAS, PATRICIA; Amsterdam HS; Hagaman, NY; (Y); Var Socr; Var Vllybl; Hon Roll; NHS; Cntry Clb Art Awd 85; Var A Awd 85-86; Art.

NICHOLAS, TARA J; St Francis Prep; College Point, NY; (S); Cmnty Wkr; Chorus; Var Crs Cntry; Im Ftbl; Im Sftbl; Var Trk; Jr NHS; NHS; Tyrone Schlrshp 85; Regnts Nrsg Schlrshp 86; St Johns U; Fnce.

NICHOLLS, TODD; Beacon HS; Beacon, NY; (Y); 2/217; High Hon Roll; NHS; Math, Bio, Chem & Spnsh; Med Doc.

NICHOLS, AMY; Canaseraga Central Schl; Swain, NY; (Y); 2/25; Ski Clb; Varsity Clb; Band; Chorus; Concert Band; Mrchg Band; Cheerleading; Socr; Sftbl; High Hon Roll; All Trnmnt Sftbl Tm 86; MVP Sccr 85; Law.

NICHOLS, ANGELA; Cornith Central HS; Corinth, NY; (Y); French Clb; Varsity Clb; Sec Jr Cls; Sec Sr Cls; Var L Bsktbl; Var L Sftbl; Var L Vllybl; French Hon Soc; Jr NHS; NHS; High Hnr Roll Hnr Rl; Orchestra Miss Congeniality 86; Psych.

NICHOLS, BETH; Corcoran HS; Syracuse, NY; (Y); 1/250; Pres Church Yth Grp; Ski Clb; Trs Spanish Clb; Nwsp Ed-Chief; High Hon Roll; Jr NHS; NHS; Europe Stu Ambsdr 86; Cornell Bk Awd 86; Cornell U; Vet.

NICHOLS, CHRISTOPHER; South Jefferson Central HS; Watertown, NY; (Y); Art Clb; 4-H; French Clb; Stage Crew; Yrbk Ed-Chief; Yrbk Stf; JV Var Ftbl; Hon Roll; NHS; Comp Sci.

NICHOLS, ELLEN; Oppenheim-Ephratah Central HS; Johnstown, NY; (S); Drama Clb; GAA; Spanish Clb; Yrbk Stf; Var Socr; Stat Sftbl; High Hon Roll; VP Jr NHS; NHS.

NICHOLS, LAURA M; Cazenovia Central HS; Cazenovia, NY; (Y); AFS; Girl Scts; Acpl Chr; Band; Pep Band; Yrbk Phtg; JV Fld Hcky; Var L Sftbl; JV Vllybl; Hon Roll; Schltc Money Awd Photo 86.

NICHOLS, LORRAINE; Midwood HS; Brooklyn, NY; (Y); Dance Clb; GAA; Girl Scts; Color Guard; Drm Mjr(t); Kingsboro Coll; Bus.

NICHOLS, MARK; Madrd Waddigton HS; Waddington, NY; (Y); Debate Tm; Drama Clb; French Clb; Speech Tm; Varsity Clb; School Musical; School Play; JV Var Bsbl; Var Ice Hcky; JV Var Socr; Clarson Coll Of Tech Gftd Studnt Prog 84; MVP & All Nrthrn In Soccer 86; Prom Kng; SUNY Canton; Engrng.

NICHOLS, PAUL; Voorheesville HS; Voorheesville, NY; (Y); 43/112; Key Clb; Ski Clb; Band; Concert Band; Nwsp Rptr; Ed Nwsp Stf; Trs Soph Cls; Pres Jr Cls; Pres Stu Cncl; Ftbl; Envrnmtl Chem & Equip Schlrshp 86; Plattsburgh ST Coll; Bus Adm.

NICHOLS, PETER; Mont Pleasant HS; Schenectady, NY; (Y); Boys Clb Am; Boy Scts; Church Yth Grp; JA; Office Aide; JV Bsbl; Timer; God Cntry Awd; High Hon Roll; Hon Roll; Hudson Vly CC; Auto Mech.

NICHOLS, SCOTT; Southside HS; Elmira, NY; (S); 22/300; Drama Clb; Intnl Clb; Spanish Clb; Chorus; School Musical; School Play; Variety Show; JV Socr; High Hon Roll.

NICHOLS, SUSAN; Cazenovia HS; Cazenovia, NY; (Y); 33/150; Exploring; Girl Scts; Jazz Band; Symp Band; Var L Fld Hcky; Var Capt Sftbl; Cit Awd; Hon Roll; Am Leg Aux Girls St; Orch; Juniata Coll; Sci.

NICHOLS, TRACY; Royalton Hartland Central HS; Gasport, NY; (Y); 24/125; Church Yth Grp; 4-H; Var Cheerleading; 4-H Awd; High Hon Roll; Hon Roll.

NICHOLSON, JASON; Penn Yan Acad; Bluff Point, NY; (S); 11/176; Ski Clb; Varsity Clb; Rep Sr Cls; Rep Stu Cncl; Var Capt Bsktbl; Var L Lcrss; High Hon Roll; Hon Roll; NHS; Ntl Merit SF; Math Assn Amer Awd 83-84; Bus Admn.

NICHOLSON, LAURIE; Westfield Academy; Westfield, NY; (Y); AFS; Sec Church Yth Grp; Cmnty Wkr; VP Key Clb; Model UN; Radio Clb; Ski Clb; Varsity Clb; Chorus; Nwsp Stf; Trck Mst Cnstnt Awd 85; Lang.

NICKEL, JEFFREY; Bethlehem Central HS; Delmar, NY; (Y); 32/309; Church Yth Grp; Model UN; Political Wkr; Band; Church Choir; Jazz Band; Nwsp Ed-Chief; High Hon Roll; Hon Roll; NHS; Louis Armstrong Jazz Awd 86; Boston U; Mech Engrng.

NICKEL, STEVEN; Clarkstown HS North; New City, NY; (Y); Pres German Clb; Band; Jazz Band; Mrchg Band; Nwsp Stf; Sec Mgr Lit Mag; Socr; NHS; Bus.

NICKERSON, MICHAEL; Dover JR SR HS; Wingdale, NY; (S); Band; Concert Band; Jazz Band; Mrchg Band; JV Bsktbl; Var Socr; High Hon Roll; NHS; VFW Awd; Voice Dem Awd; Jrnlsm.

NICKLAS, PATRICIA J; The Academy Of St Joseph; Islip, NY; (Y); Drama Clb; Library Aide; Science Clb; Stage Crew; Variety Show; Yrbk Stf; Pres Soph Cls; VP Stu Cncl; Var Capt Badmtn; Var Capt Vllybl; NY ST Rgnts Schlrshp Wnnr 86; Army ROTC Advnce Dsgnee Schlrshp Wnnr 86; Mount Holyoke Coll; Econ.

NICKLAUS, JAMES J; Southern Cayuga Central Schl; Genoa, NY; (Y); 1/72; Pres Drama Clb; Chorus; Church Choir; School Musical; School Play; Pres Frsh Cls; VP Stu Cncl; High Hon Roll; Pres NHS; Ntl Merit SF.

NICKLES, TIMOTHY C; Jamestown HS; Jamestown, NY; (Y); Nwsp Rptr; Nwsp Sprt Ed; Stat Bsktbl; L Ftbl; Var Trk; Hon Roll; St Schlr; Jamestown Cmnty Coll; Engrng.

NICKLIN, REBECCA; Oswego HS; Oswego, NY; (Y); Pres 4-H; Pres JA; Band; Chorus; School Musical; School Play; Variety Show; 4-H Awd; SUNY Canton; Elec Engr.

NICKPEE, CRYSTAL; Walton HS; Bronx, NY; (Y); Girl Scts; Sftbl; Cit Awd; Prfct Atten Awd; Cert Of Merit-Schltc Achvt-Engl 86; Med.

NICLAS, TANIA; Mohonasen SR HS; Schenectady, NY; (Y); 3/172; Art Clb; Church Yth Grp; Cmnty Wkr; SADD; Var Bsktbl; Var Sftbl; Var Vllybl; High Hon Roll; Hon Roll; St Georges Lodg Yth Awd 85; Pres Acdmc Fitness Awd 86; Hudson Vly CC; Lib Arts.

NICOLAIDES, NESTOR A; Port Richmond HS; Staten Is, NY; (Y); Am Leg Boys St; Boy Scts; Church Yth Grp; Cmnty Wkr; Dance Clb; Drama Clb; FCA; Office Aide; SADD; Teachers Aide; Dr Rchrd Don Diego Awd 85.

NICOLAS, DANIELLE; Academy Of Saint Joseph; Centereach, NY; (Y); Exploring; Service Clb; Chorus; Yrbk Ed-Chief; Yrbk Stf; JV Vllybl; NHS; Chrstn Crtsy 85; Supr Acad Achvt Sci 86; Acad Achvt Awd 84.

NICOLELLA JR, ROBERT; Niskayuna HS; Scotia, NY; (Y); Key Clb; Socr; Psychlgy.

NICOLELLIS, KEVIN J; Longwood HS; Yaphank, NY; (Y); Boy Scts; VP Computer Clb; Pres Exploring; Band; Concert Band; Jazz Band; Mrchg Band; Orch; Pep Band; St Schlr; SUNY Buffalo; Elec Engrng.

NICOLICH, CYNTHIA A; St Francis Prep; Flushing, NY; (S); 124/744; Art Clb; Service Clb; Teachers Aide; Stage Crew; Opt Clb Awd; Cmrcl Dsgn.

NICOLL, HOWARD; W C Mepham HS; N Bellmore, NY; (Y); 17/365; Pres VP Drama Clb; Chorus; School Musical; School Play; Nwsp Rptr; VP Stu Cncl; Im Bsktbl; NHS; Acpl Chr; Off Jr Cls; NY ST Regnts Schlrshp 86; NY U Trustee Schlrshp 86; Drama Clb Awd 86; U Of MI; Cmmnctns.

NICOLOSI, DINA; Christ The King Regional HS; Ozone Park, NY; (Y); 129/451; Psych.

NICOLS, JENNIFER; Cooperstown Central Schl; Cooperstown, NY; (Y); Exploring; Library Aide; Quiz Bowl; Chorus; Hon Roll; Ntl Merit Ltr; Cornell; Lawyer.

NICOMEDEZ, WILMA C; Bishop Ford Central Catholic HS; Brooklyn, NY; (Y); 1/441; Math Clb; Math Tm; Science Clb; Lit Mag; High Hon Roll; NHS; Val; Computer Clb; Nwsp Stf; NY ST Rgnts Schlrshp 86; No 1 Rnk Plque 85; Natl Sci Olympd Chem Awd & Mdl 85; Astrnmy.

NICOSIA, JOSEPH; Greenville HS; Climax, NY; (Y); VP Frsh Cls; Bsktbl; JV Socr; Rgnts Schlrshp 86; Engnrng.

NICOSIA, LEEANNE M; Maryvale SR HS; Cheektowaga, NY; (Y); French Clb; Spanish Clb; SADD; Yrbk Stf; Hon Roll; Comm.

NIEDZIELSKI, ROBERT J; Kingston HS; Kingston, NY; (Y); 10/573; AFS; Church Yth Grp; French Clb; Teachers Aide; Band; Church Choir; Concert Band; Mrchg Band; Pep Band; Nwsp Stf; NY ST Regents Scholar 86; Pres Scholar American U 86; American U; Intl Rltns.

NIELI, MARY JANE; Lindenhurst SR HS; Lindenhurst, NY; (Y); 65/549; Chess Clb; Sec Debate Tm; Sec Key Clb; Spanish Clb; Sec Speech Tm; SADD; Band; Yrbk Phtg; Yrbk Stf; Hon Roll; N Lindenhurst Civic Assoc Schlrshp 86; Yrbk Awd 86; Pres Acadmc Fit Awd 86; Geneseo ST U; Med Tech.

NIELSEN, DONNA; Shenendehowa HS; Ballston Lk, NY; (Y); Church Yth Grp; Office Aide; Drill Tm; Im Fld Hcky; Im Socr; Im Sftbl; Hon Roll; Hudson Valley CC; Dentl Hyg.

NIELSEN, ERIK R; Mc Quaid Jesuit HS; Pittsford, NY; (Y); 50/180; Cmnty Wkr; Varsity Clb; Chorus; School Musical; JV Var Socr; JV Trk; JV Var Vllybl; NHS; Regents Schlrshp Awds 86; Acad Lttr Wnnr 85; PA ST U.

NIELSEN, LYNETTE; Le Ray HS; Leroy, NY; (Y); AFS; French Clb; Math Tm; Chorus; Yrbk Stf; Bsktbl; Socr; Trk; High Hon Roll; NHS; Jr Miss Schlrshp Prgrm 87; Mjrt Cptn 86-87; 4 Vrsty Ltrs 85-87; Med.

NIELSEN, NAOMI; Bishop Grimes HS; Syracuse, NY; (Y); French Clb; Yrbk Stf; Rep Soph Cls; Trk; Vllybl; High Hon Roll; Hon Roll; NHS; Ntl Merit Schol; Cert Merit Frnch 85-86; Syracuse U; Frnch.

NIELSON, CHRISTINE; Whitesboro SR HS; Marcy, NY; (Y); VP Orch; School Musical; Yrbk Stf; Hon Roll; Jr NHS; NHS; Pres Acad Ftns Awd 86; Rchstr Inst Tech; Cmptr Engr.

NIEMCZYK, STEPHANIE A; St Francis Prep; Ozone Park, NY; (S); 186/744; Hosp Aide; Library Aide; Im Vllybl.

NIEMCZYK, SUSAN; Amsterdam HS; Amsterdam, NY; (Y); Drm Mjr(t); Trs Jr Cls; Trs Sr Cls; Rep Stu Cncl; Hon Roll; Acctg.

NIENABER, LYNN; Olympia HS; Rochester, NY; (Y); Cmnty Wkr; Girl Scts; Rep Frsh Cls; Rep Soph Cls; Rep Jr Cls; JV Sftbl; High Hon Roll; Hon Roll.

NIENHUIS, LINDA; Rochester Christian HS; Rochester, NY; (S); French Clb; Hosp Aide; Sec Frsh Cls; Sec Soph Cls; Stu Cncl; Var Bsktbl; Var Socr; Var Sftbl; Trk; High Hon Roll; Sprtsmnshp Awd 85; Calvin Coll.

NIENTIMP, THOMAS; Mc Quaid Jesuit HS; Rochester, NY; (Y); 3/175; Boy Scts; Cmnty Wkr; SADD; Varsity Clb; Yrbk Sprt Ed; VP Jr Cls; VP Sr Cls; Im JV Ftbl; Im JV Trk; NHS; Hly Crss Coll Bk Awd 86; MAGIS Pgm; Acdmc Lttr; Ftbll Vrsty Lttr; Lctr St Louis Chrch.

NIERER, CYNTHIA; Dominican Commercial HS; Bellerose, NY; (S); 13/273; Art Clb; Church Yth Grp; Hosp Aide; Spanish Clb; High Hon Roll; Hon Roll; NHS; Natl Bus Hnr Soc 85-86; Regents Scholar 86; Cath Schls Scholar 86; St Johns U; Law.

NIETO, MARIA; The Mary Louis Acad; Flushing, NY; (Y); Spanish Clb; Cert Of Merit-Natl Frnch Cntst 85; Liberal Arts.

NIEVES, AUDREY; St Pius V HS; Bronx, NY; (Y); Church Yth Grp; Exploring; NHS; Mst Prmsng Asprnt-Aspra Of NY 86; Hghst Avg Spnsh II 86; Hghst Avg Lang Arts 85; Pre-Med.

NIEVES, DAVID; Columbus HS; Bronx, NY; (S); Computer Clb; Math Tm; Yrbk Stf; Var Tennis; Ntl Merit Schol; Arch.

NIEVES, JACQUELINE S; Hunter College HS; Brooklyn, NY; (Y); Ntl Merit SF; Maj Bio.

NIEVES, LUZ; De Witt Clinton HS; Bronx, NY; (Y); Art Clb; Drama Clb; School Play; Stage Crew; Lit Mag; Sec Stu Cncl; Hon Roll; Intnl Clb; Office Aide; Nwsp Rptr; Hnr Engl Awd 84-85; Drama Awd Dir 86; Arista Hnr Soc 83-86; Animl Care.

NIGGEMEIER, STEVE; Hicksville SR HS; Hicksville, NY; (Y); Church Yth Grp; 4-H; Yrbk Phtg; 4-H Awd; High Hon Roll; Jr NHS; NHS; Prfct Atten Awd; Mech Engr.

NIGRO, LISA; Lake George Central HS; Lake George, NY; (Y); SADD; Varsity Clb; Chorus; Pres Frsh Cls; Pres Soph Cls; Pres Jr Cls; Stu Cncl; Capt Cheerleading; Hon Roll; NHS; MVP Chrldg; Natl Frnch Awd; Siena Coll; Mktg.

NIKOLAUS, LISA; Sharon Springs Central Schl; Sharon Springs, NY; (S); 4/25; Art Clb; FBLA; Sec FHA; Varsity Clb; Trs Soph Cls; Var Bsktbl; Var Socr; Var Sftbl; Var Vllybl; Hon Roll; Stratford; Trvl.

NIKOLICH, NATALIE; St Francis Prep; Bayside, NY; (S); 77/744; Art Clb; Cmnty Wkr; Library Aide; Speech Tm; Hon Roll; Awd Membrshp Optimate Soc 84; Engrng.

NIKSTENAS, JOSEPH E; Amsterdam HS; Amsterdam, NY; (Y); 21/288; Boy Scts; Pres Church Yth Grp; JA; Church Choir; Mrchg Band; Rep Frsh Cls; Off Soph Cls; Var Tennis; High Hon Roll; Hon Roll; R W Doyle Excl Math 86; Knghts Lithuania Schlrshp 86; Svc Fndrsr Awd 84; Case Western Resv U; Elec Engr.

NIKSTENAS, JUDIANNE; Amsterdam HS; Amsterdam, NY; (Y); 19/310; VP Church Yth Grp; Trs FBLA; Sec Trs JA; Church Choir; Flag Corp; Mrchg Band; Yrbk Stf; High Hon Roll; Hon Roll; NHS; 1st Pl Math Awd Rgnts Lvl 83-84; ROJAC Dlgt 85; 3rd Pl Fund Raiser JR Achvt Bwl-A-Thn 84; Bus.

NILAND, MARIA; Williamsville South HS; Williamsville, NY; (Y); Civic Clb; Cmnty Wkr; GAA; Pep Clb; Political Wkr; Red Cross Aide; Ski Clb; Nwsp Sprt Ed; Nwsp Stf; Rep Frsh Cls; Vrsty Ltrmn Indr Trck Team 84-87; Ltrmn Vrsty Sccr, Swmng Team 84-87; Adv Plcmnt Hstry, Bio, Engl; Law.

NILES, BILL; Port Jervis HS; Port Jervis, NY; (Y); 50/225; Church Yth Grp; Rep Soph Cls; High Hon Roll; Hon Roll; Prfct Atten Awd; TX A&M; Nuclear Engr.

NILES, BROOKE; Hoosick Falls Central Schl; Eagle Bridge, NY; (Y); Sec Frsh Cls; VP Soph Cls; VP Jr Cls; Pres Sr Cls; Capt Stat Bsktbl; Var Capt Fld Hcky; Var Capt Sftbl; Cit Awd; Hon Roll; NHS; Mst Outstndng Stu Clss Of 86; Wmns Sports Fndtn All Star Awd 85; Kosmer Stemper Awd 86; CW Post Coll; Bnkng.

NILES, CHAD K; Brushton-Moira Central HS; Moira, NY; (Y); 33/63; Quiz Bowl; School Play; Rep Stu Cncl; Var Bsbl; NYS Rgnts Schlrshp 86; SUNY; NY ST Trooper.

NILES, ERIC; Sauquiot Valley Central HS; Sauguoit, NY; (Y); Am Leg Boys St; Boys Clb Am; Church Yth Grp; French Clb; Var JV Bsktbl; Var Crs Cntry; Var Trk; Ntl Merit Ltr; Prfct Atten Awd; MIP Trck, X-Cntry 85; Mohawk Valley CC; Sprts Med.

NILSEN, JOANNE; St Anthonys HS; Massapequa, NY; (Y); 9/250; Drama Clb; Girl Scts; Teachers Aide; Church Choir; Orch; Symp Band; Im Socr; French Hon Soc; High Hon Roll; NHS; Fairfield U; Frgn Lang.

NILSEN, SHEILA; Ballston Spa HS; Ballston Spa, NY; (Y); 60/250; SADD; Band; Concert Band; Yrbk Stf; Im Fld Hcky; Im Socr; High Hon Roll; Hon Roll; St Schlr; SUNY Plattsburgh; Humn Svcs.

NIMELY, DOMINIC; Prospect Heights HS; Brooklyn, NY; (S); FCA; Leo Clb; Radio Clb; ROTC; Soph Cls; Bsktbl; Socr; Hon Roll; JETS Awd; Prfct Atten Cert Awd 85; Cert Achvt 85; Cert Merit 85.

NIN, CAROL NOELL; Victor Central HS; Condado, PR; (Y); Girl Scts; JA; Science Clb; School Musical; High Hon Roll; Jr NHS; NHS; Prfct Atten Awd; Library Aide; Office Aide; 1st Pl VP Mktg For PR JR Achvt 85; Outstndg Achvr Of J A Co-Elec Exprnc 84; Notre Dame U; Comp Sci.

NINA, ANTHONY; De Witt Clinton HS; Bronx, NY; (Y); Art Clb; NHS; Socl Stds Awd 84; NY Inst Of Tech; Engrng.

NINA, ELIZABETH; East New York Transit Tech; Brooklyn, NY; (Y); Cmnty Wkr; Computer Clb; English Clb; Office Aide; Teachers Aide; Lit Mag; Rep Frsh Cls; Vllybl; Gov Hon Prg Awd; NCTE Awd; NY City Tech; Htl & Rstrnt Mgr.

NIRENBERG, MELISSA J; Ardsley HS; Dobbs Ferry, NY; (Y); Pres VP JA; Capt Math Tm; Science Clb; School Play; Ed Yrbk Stf; Off Frsh Cls; Ntl Merit Ltr; Debate Tm; Nwsp Stf; High Hon Roll; JA,Pres,Outstndg Yng Buswmn And Publ Spkr Of Yr 85; Twn Of Greenburgh Ptry Cntst 2nd 85; Book Awd 85; Yale U; Med.

NISANIAN, ANAHID JAQUELLINE; Forest Hills HS; Sunnyside, NY; (Y); 83/826; Exploring; Math Clb; Science Clb; Teachers Aide; Orch; Hon Roll; Prfct Atten Awd; Cert Awd Sci Fr & Exbtn 84; Amer Inst Sci & Tech NYC Sci Fr Proj Exbtn 47th Schl Sci Fr 85; Fordham U; Med.

NISKANEN, LISA; Herbert H Lehman HS; New York, NY; (Y); 38/159; Computer Clb; Dance Clb; JA; Spanish Clb; School Musical; Rep Soph Cls; JV Cheerleading; L Gym; JV Pom Pon; High Hon Roll; Co-Op Cert Hnr Roll 83-85; Perfrmng Arts-Dance Prfrmnc 84; Bus Mgmt.

NISSEN, FRANK; Duanesburg Central HS; Delanson, NY; (Y); Chess Clb; 4-H; Chorus; Swing Chorus; Yrbk Stf; Var Trk; Hon Roll; Schl Ltr 85-86; Comp Sci.

NISTICO, GINO; Greenville Central JR SR HS; Greenville, NY; (Y); 50/76; Chess Clb; Church Yth Grp; Pres 4-H; VP FFA; Mgr Radio Clb; Pep Band; School Play; Rep Stu Cncl; Hon Roll; 1st Pl Tlnt Show Solo Drums 85; Svc Awd 86; Extemprns Spkng 3rd Pl FFA 85; Drummer.

NITKIN, ANGELA; Christopher Columbus HS; Bronx, NY; (Y); 15/611; Dance Clb; Drama Clb; Chorus; School Play; Yrbk Stf; Hon Roll; NYU; Pre-Med.

NITKOWSKI, DENISE E; Cheektowaga Central HS; Cheektowaga, NY; (Y); 6/199; FBLA; Ski Clb; Stu Cncl; Swmmng; Hon Roll; Jr NHS; NHS; Church Yth Grp; Girl Scts; Yrbk Stf; Regents Schlrshp 86; Deans Schlrshp 86; 4th Pl In St-Bus 86; Canisius Coll; Comp Sci.

NITTO, MELISSA; Sweet Home SR HS; Tonawanda, NY; (Y); 29/410; Chrmn Church Yth Grp; Sec French Clb; Girl Scts; Pres Pep Clb; SADD; Stat Ftbl; DAR Awd; Sec French Hon Soc; High Hon Roll; Sec NHS; Rgnts Schlrshp Awd 86; Svc Awd 100 Hrs & Over 86; High Achvmnt Awds In Accntng & French 85-86; St Bonaventure U; Bus.

NITTO, PAM; Susquehanna Valley HS; Binghamton, NY; (Y); Mathletes; Pep Clb; Band; Concert Band; Mrchg Band; Lit Mag; Sec Sr Cls; Var L Score Keeper; Hon Roll; Spanish NHS; Sound Am Hnr Band 86.

NITTOLO, FRANCINE E; Bishop Kearney HS; Brooklyn, NY; (Y); 73/337; Church Yth Grp; Cmnty Wkr; Speech Tm; Teachers Aide; JV Cheerleading; Var Capt Twrlr; High Hon Roll; NHS; Pres Schlr; St Schlr.

NIXON, THOMAS; Eastchester HS; Scarsdale, NY; (Y); Boy Scts; Exploring; PAVAS; Spanish Clb; Rep Jr Cls; Rep Stu Cncl; Im Coach Actv; JV Var Socr; Var Trk; Prfct Atten Awd; Baden Powell Scout Spirit Awd 83; East Chester Yth Soccr Tms Awd-Enthusiasm 83; Busnss.

NOAH, ROBERT; Brewster HS; Patterson, NY; (Y); 31/186; Camera Clb; Church Yth Grp; Drama Clb; Chorus; School Musical; Nwsp Phtg; Nwsp Rptr; JV Ftbl; JV Var Wrstlng; NHS; Brewster Starr Schlrshp 86; Albany ST; Lwyr.

NOAILLES, ALEXNDRA; Uniondale HS; Hempstead, NY; (Y); Debate Tm; French Clb; Orch; School Musical; Yrbk Stf; Trs Stu Cncl; Pom Pon; Pblc Spkng Awd 84; Merit Awd In Orchstra 86; Lng Islnd Strng Fstvl Assn Cert 86; Chld Psychlgy.

NOBBS, TOBI; Southwestern Central HS; Jamestown, NY; (Y); 47/155; Pres FCA; Letterman Clb; Office Aide; Scholastic Bowl; Band; Mrchg Band; Capt Bsktbl; Coach Actv; Sftbl; Div 1 Al-Star Bsktbl-Sftbl 84-86; US Marine Corp Distngshd Athlt Awd 84-85; Norwich U; Air Frc Psych.

NOBLE, DENISE; Hugh C Williams HS; Canton, NY; (Y); 24/148; Cmnty Wkr; 4-H; SADD; Sec Thesps; Chorus; Orch; 4-H Awd; High Hon Roll; Hon Roll; Tlntd Srs Prog St Lawrence U 85; Teen Rep St Lawrnc Prog Cmmtee 85; Psych.

NOBLE, JOHN E; Watertown HS; Watertown, NY; (Y); 7/305; Exploring; Quiz Bowl; Varsity Clb; Im Bsktbl; Var Capt Golf; High Hon Roll; NHS; Cmnty Wkr; 2nd Pl Math Cntst 86; Outstndng Athlt Awd Glf 83-86; Natl Army Athlt-Schlr Awd 86; U Of Rochester; Chem Engr.

NOBLE, TAMMY; Watertown HS; Watertown, NY; (Y); 19/305; Church Yth Grp; Trs Exploring; 4-H; Cheerleading; Hon Roll; Trs NHS; Gary Jones Schlrshp 86; Pares Acdmc Ftns Awd 86; U Rochester.

NOBRE, ELIZABETH; Dominican Commercial HS; Jamaica, NY; (S); 15/288; Hosp Aide; Teachers Aide; Yrbk Rptr; Yrbk Stf; NHS; Prfct Atten Awd; Siena Clb; Queens Coll; Educ.

NOBREGA, BEVERLY; Erasmus Hall HS; Brooklyn, NY; (Y); Chess Clb; Computer Clb; Dance Clb; Debate Tm; FBLA; JA; Math Clb; Math Tm; Spanish Clb; Gym; Hunter Coll; Pre-Med.

NOCELLA, STEVE L; Sewanhaka HS; Franklin Square, NY; (Y); 27/350; Am Leg Boys St; Hosp Aide; Rep Sr Cls; VP Stu Cncl; JV Bsbl; JV Ftbl; High Hon Roll; NHS; Pres Schlr; Rotary Awd; Rutgers U; Elec Engrng.

NOCHOWITZ, DENNIS J; St Francis Prep; Woodside, NY; (S); 106/653; Church Yth Grp; JV Var Bowling; Im Ftbl; Im Sftbl; Im Vllybl; 2nd Pl Amer Assn Of Tchrs In German 84; St Johns U; Bus.

NOEL, BRIGITTE; Catholic Central HS; Troy, NY; (S); 25/179; French Clb; Hosp Aide; Pep Clb; School Play; Variety Show; Var Pom Pon; Hon Roll; Prfct Atten Awd; Mth 10 Regents Awd; Albany Coll Phrmcy; Phrmcy.

NOEL, JAMES ADLER; Spring Valley HS; Spring Valley, NY; (Y); #75 In Class; Computer Clb; Debate Tm; French Clb; Math Clb; Math Tm; Band; Lit Mag; Trk; French Hon Soc; Hon Roll; Rgnts Schlrshp 86; Albany; Pol Sci.

NOEVA, KRISTI; Alexander Hamilton HS; White Plains, NY; (Y); Office Aide; Band; Yrbk Stf; Sftbl; Swmmng; High Hon Roll; Hon Roll; Sftbl Awd 86; Westchester CC; Sci.

NOFI, CHRISTINE; Amityville HS; Amityville, NY; (Y); Girl Scts; Key Clb; Ski Clb; Var Tennis; Accntng.

NOFTSIER, JILL; Beaver River Central HS; Castorland, NY; (Y); AFS; Am Leg Aux Girls St; Church Yth Grp; French Clb; Yrbk Bus Mgr; Rep Stu Cncl; High Hon Roll; Hon Roll; VP NHS; Grtst Potntl In Fld Of Bus 86; Frnch.

NOGA IV, JOSEPH L; Mcquiad Jesuit HS; Rochester, NY; (Y); 5/168; German Clb; Teachers Aide; Varsity Clb; Nwsp Stf; Var Capt Trk; High Hon Roll; Ntl Merit Ltr; Amhrst Coll.

NOGAY, JEANNE; Newburgh Free Acad; Newburgh, NY; (Y); Church Yth Grp; JV Bsktbl; High Hon Roll; Hon Roll; Jr NHS; Mt St Mary Coll.

NOISETTE, GREGORY; Nazareth Regional HS; Brooklyn, NY; (Y); Bus.

NOLAN, CATHERINE; Mercy HS; Southold, NY; (Y); GAA; Mathletes; SADD; Yrbk Phtg; Fld Hcky; Golf; High Hon Roll; Hon Roll; NHS; NEDT Awd; Deaf Frnds Cert Of Apprctn 85; Ntl Engl Merit Awd 86.

NOLAN, COURTNEY; Notre Dame HS; New York, NY; (Y); Dance Clb; Drama Clb; VP Soph Cls; VP Jr Cls; Capt Cheerleading; Boston U Schlrshp 86-87; Boston U; Spec Ed.

NOLAN, JAMES; Binghamton HS; Binghamton, NY; (Y); Cmnty Wkr; Key Clb; Political Wkr; Ski Clb; VICA; Nwsp Rptr; Var L Bsktbl; Var L Golf; Hon Roll; ST Champnshp Bsktbl 85-86; U FL; Law.

NOLAN, KATHLEEN K; Sacred Heart Acad; Hempstead, NY; (Y); Dance Clb; Political Wkr; Yrbk Stf; NHS.

NOLAN, KEVIN; E J Wilson HS; Spencerport, NY; (Y); JCL; Latin Clb; Varsity Clb; Var Golf; Var Ice Hcky; JV Socr; JV Var Swmmng; Schlstc Hon Soc Awd Phy Ed 85; Brockport U; Engrng.

NOLAN, MATTHEW G; Heatly HS; Troy, NY; (Y); Chess Clb; CAP; Debate Tm; NFL; Political Wkr; Flag Corp; Symp Band; Trk; High Hon Roll; Hon Roll; Regnts Schlrshp 86.

NOLAN, MICHAEL; Shenendehowa HS; Clifton Park, NY; (Y); AFS; Church Yth Grp; Cmnty Wkr; Computer Clb; German Clb; Ski Clb; JV Lcrss; High Hon Roll; Hon Roll; NHS; Comp Sci.

NOLAN, NANCY L; Allegany Cetnral Schl; Allegany, NY; (Y); 21/101; Nwsp Stf; JV Var Cheerleading; L Pom Pon; JV Trk; High Hon Roll; Hon Roll; Rgnts Coll Schlrshp 86; SUNY; Acctng.

NOLAN, NILS; Garden City SR HS; Garden City, NY; (Y); Boy Scts; German Clb; Hon Roll; Bryant College; Intl Fnces.

NOLAN, ROBERT S; Christian Brothers Acad; Liverpool, NY; (Y); 4/96; Hosp Aide; Ski Clb; Yrbk Stf; JV Golf; JV Socr; High Hon Roll; NHS; Rensselear Math, Sci Medl 85; Holy Cross Bk Awd 85; Skiing Comptn 85-86; U Of Rochester; Biol.

NOLAN, STACEY; Ichabod Crane HS; Stuyvesant, NY; (Y); GAA; Varsity Clb; Yrbk Stf; Rep Stu Cncl; JV Var Cheerleading; Var Mgr(s); Hon Roll; Girl Scts; Var Trk; Srvc Cls Awds 84-86; Awd Schvt Bio; Cobleskill; Hrtcltr.

NOLAN, TERESA; The Mary Louis Acad; Bellerose, NY; (Y); 48/270; Church Yth Grp; 4-H; Office Aide; Church Choir; Variety Show; Bowling; 4-H Awd; NEDT Awd; Regents Scholar 86; Hofstra U Grant 86; Acad Prfrmnce Awd LIU 86; Hofstra U; Bus Mktg.

NOLASCO, MILEDYS; St Catharine Acad; Bronx, NY; (Y); 145/185; Bridgeport U; Intl Bus.

NOLDAN, NANCY; Fayetteville-Manlius HS; Fayetteville, NY; (Y); VP Pres Exploring; Pres Girl Scts; Hosp Aide; JV Var Cheerleading; Gold Awd GSA 85; 200 Hr Svc Awd Candystripping 85; Sci.

NOLDON, JEANE; Park West HS; Bronx, NY; (Y); Computer Clb; Capt Dance Clb; VP English Clb; Math Clb; Math Tm; Office Aide; VP Speech Tm; Teachers Aide; Variety Show; Capt Cheerleading.

NOLES, CHARLES B; City Honors Schl; Buffalo, NY; (Y); 60/108; Church Yth Grp; Cmnty Wkr; Computer Clb; Debate Tm; Library Aide; Math Tm; Red Cross Aide; Teachers Aide; Lit Mag; Bsktbl; Natl Achvt Scholar Black Stu SF 85; ST Mth Tm 84; Bells Tutor Pgm 84; West Point; Aerontcl.

NOLETTE, ALBERT B; Fort Edward HS; Fort Edward, NY; (Y); 1/44; Am Leg Boys St; Boy Scts; Spanish Clb; Yrbk Ed-Chief; Pres Soph Cls; Pres Jr Cls; Ftbl; Golf; Bausch & Lomb Sci Awd; Cit Awd; Acctng.

NOLF, HEATHER; Franklin Central HS; Franklin, NY; (Y); FHA; Girl Scts; Chorus; Color Guard; Mgr(s); Hon Roll.

NOLL, JANINE; Bishop Grimes HS; Syracuse, NY; (S); Exploring; Hosp Aide; Ski Clb; Yrbk Stf; Mgr(s); Var Sftbl; Var Tennis; High Hon Roll; Stu Orgnzd Svc Clb 85-86; Med.

NOLL, NANCY M; Jamesville-Dewitt HS; Fayetteville, NY; (Y); 47/245; Church Yth Grp; Jazz Band; Mrchg Band; School Musical; Swing Chorus; Symp Band; Yrbk Stf; Lit Mag; Var Swmmng; NHS; Natl Merit Commended Schlr 84-85; NY St Regents Schlrshp 86; Superior Rating MI St District 84; Boston Coll; Cmnctns.

NOLL, RICHARD E; Port Richmond HS; Staten Island, NY; (Y); 73/491; Am Leg Boys St; Boy Scts; Drama Clb; Concert Band; Jazz Band; School Play; Pres Sr Cls; Ftbl; Trk; Pres Schlr; Daily News Super Yth 84-86; Mayors Yth Svc Awds-NYC 86; CSI Yng Mscns Comptn-3rdpl 84; SUNY-BINGHAMTON; Poli Sci.

NOLLETTI, NATASHA; Munich American HS; Apo New York, NY; (Y); Church Yth Grp; Yrbk Stf; Off Frsh Cls; Sec Soph Cls; Rep Jr Cls; Sec Sr Cls; Rep Stu Cncl; Powder Puff Ftbl; Hon Roll; NHS; Bus.

NOLTE, LAURA; Lakeland SR HS; Mohegan Lake, NY; (Y); 3/344; Art Clb; Church Yth Grp; Cmnty Wkr; Teachers Aide; Var Capt Bsktbl; Var Capt Sftbl; Var Capt Vllybl; High Hon Roll; VP NHS; Pres Schlr; All Div Vllybl 83-86; Star Of Wk-Evenig Star 83-86; All Sectn Vllbl 86; All Div Hnrb Mntn Bsktbl 86; U Of Hartford; Math Tchr.

NOOCHOOCHAI, MONTAI; Mercy HS; Calverton, NY; (Y); Computer Clb; Model UN; Socr; Engineering Computer.

NOODY, RICHARD L; Lyons JR SR HS; Lyons, NY; (Y); 22/100; French Clb; Ski Clb; Bsbl; Bowling; Ftbl; Wt Lftg; Hon Roll; NYS Rgnts Schlrshp Awd; Clarkson U; Mchncl Engrng.

NOONAN, JAMES R; Mt St Joseph Acad; Buffalo, NY; (Y); 15/42; Boy Scts; Camera Clb; Computer Clb; Drama Clb; Ski Clb; Chorus; Stage Crew; Var Crs Cntry; Var Trk; Ntl Merit Ltr; NYS Regnts Schlrshp 86; Fredonia ST.

NOONAN, JOHN; Brockport HS; Brockport, NY; (Y); Latin Clb; VP Mathletes; Radio Clb; Ski Clb; Band; Crs Cntry; Var Ftbl; Var Trk; Wt Lftg; Pre-Med.

NOONAN, LINDA; Holy Angels HS; Cheektowaga, NY; (Y); 11/36; Chorus; School Musical; Nwsp Rptr; Yrbk Rptr; Rep Frsh Cls; VP Soph Cls; Pres Jr Cls; Pres Stu Cncl; Hon Roll; St Schlr; Excllnce Engl Awd 84; Regents Diploma 86; Mrch Dimes Scholar 86; ST U NY Buffalo; Occ Ther.

NORBERTO, COLON; Lehman HS; Bronx, NY; (Y); Gym; Tennis; Mst Serious Prgmr 85; Excllnc Lgl Rsrch & Mock Trl 85; AP Pascal 86; Frgn Polcy.

NORDEN, PAUL; Msgr Farrell HS; Staten Island, NY; (Y); Boy Scts; Camera Clb; Exploring; Mrchg Band; Soph Cls; Sr Cls; Stu Cncl; CC Awd; Cit Awd; Elks Awd; Eagle Scout 85; John Jay Coll; Law.

NORIEGA, ALICIA; Midwood HS; Brooklyn, NY; (Y); Intnl Clb; Model UN; Chorus; School Musical; Capt Pom Pon; Accntnt.

NORMAN, JOANNE; Sacred Heart Acad; Elmont, NY; (S); School Play; Stage Crew; Var Capt Bsktbl; Mgr Sftbl; Var Capt Vllybl; Hon Roll; NHS; Fairfield; Comp Sci.

NORMAN, MARK J; Mayfield Central HS; Gloversville, NY; (Y); 4/79; Math Tm; Varsity Clb; VP Sr Cls; Var L Bsbl; Var L Bsktbl; Var L Bowling; High Hon Roll; Pres NHS; Prfct Atten Awd; Church Yth Grp; NYS Rgnts Schlrshp 86; Ithaca Coll; Prsnl.

NORMILE, KATHRYN; Spackenkill HS; Poughkeepsie, NY; (Y); Sec Church Yth Grp; Hosp Aide; Sec SADD; Thesps; Band; Church Choir; Pep Band; School Musical; Hon Roll; Regents Schlrshp 86; Pres Acdmc Fit Awd 86; Plattsburgh U; Speech Lang.

NORMILE, WILLIAM; Corinth HS; Corinth, NY; (Y); Am Leg Boys St; SADD; Varsity Clb; Band; Chorus; Concert Band; Jazz Band; Mrchg Band; Bsktbl; Ftbl; Mdrn Music Mstrs Hnr Soc 87; Genetcs.

NORMOYLE, MICHAEL; Sacred Heart HS; Hastings, NY; (Y); Boy Scts; JV Var Bsbl; Capt JV Bsktbl; Im Coach Actv; JV Crs Cntry; JV Var Trk; Hon Roll; NHS; Manhattan; Bus.

NORRIS, JACQUELINE; Connetquot HS; Ronkonkoma, NY; (Y); 186/712; FBLA; Var Cheerleading; Var Sftbl; Var Tennis; JV Vllybl; Hon Roll; Bus Mgmt.

NORRIS, JAMES; Archbishop Molloy HS; Jackson Hts, NY; (Y); Art Clb; Computer Clb; Lit Mag; Swmmng; Ntl Merit SF; 2nd Honors; Eng.

NORRIS, SONDA; Academy Of Mt St Ursula; Bronx, NY; (Y); Science Clb; Yrbk Stf; High Hon Roll; Hon Roll; Hofstra; Acctng.

NORRIS, SUSAN; West Irondequoit HS; Rochester, NY; (Y); 34/389; Church Yth Grp; Church Choir; Var Trk; Hon Roll; Prfct Atten Awd; Urln Leag Roch Outstndng Acdmc Achvt 86; Blck Stu Union Ofcr Rcgntn 86; U Rochester; Chem.

NORTH, EILEEN; Gates-Chili SR HS; Rochester, NY; (S); 2/446; Ski Clb; Band; School Musical; Rep Stu Cncl; Im Crs Cntry; JV Swmmng; High Hon Roll; NHS; Ntl Merit Ltr; Sal; Frgn Lang.

NORTH, MELISSA; Oxford Acad & Central HS; Oxford, NY; (Y); 7/77; Drama Clb; French Clb; Scholastic Bowl; SADD; Chorus; Color Guard; School Play; Stage Crew; Twrlr; Hon Roll; Acdmc Ltr & Bars; Dipolma Of Cmpltn Of Precoll Pgm At Syracuse U; Syracuse U; Marketing Mgmt.

NORTHCRAFT, ANN E; South Kortright Central HS; Hobart, NY; (Y); 4/25; Girl Scts; Pep Clb; Varsity Clb; Chorus; School Play; Stage Crew; High Hon Roll; Hon Roll; Kiwanis Awd; NHS; Nazareth Coll; French.

NORTHROP, AMANDA; Guilderland Central HS; Guilderland, NY; (Y); Dance Clb; Teachers Aide; Fld Hcky; Cit Awd; High Hon Roll; Spec Awd Excllnc Mktg & Outstndng Achvt Socl Prblm 86; Cert Of Merit 86; Northeastern 1; Bus Adm.

NORTHROP, MICHAEL; Corning-Painted Post West HS; Painted Post, NY; (Y); 9/257; Sec Key Clb; Pres Varsity Clb; Var L Crs Cntry; Var Capt Trk; Lion Awd; NHS; Ntl Merit Schol; Frsh Cls; Athlt Mnth 85; Bucknell U; Engr.

NORTHRUP II, KENNETH; John F Kennedy HS; Utica, NY; (Y); 15/150; Am Leg Boys St; Boy Scts; Debate Tm; VP Trs Key Clb; Mathletes; Ski Clb; Pres SADD; JV Bsktbl; Var L Crs Cntry; Var L Vllybl; Penn ST; Hotel/Rest Mgmt.

NORTHRUP, NICOLE; John F Kennedy HS; Utica, NY; (Y); 1/132; Pres Key Clb; Band; Yrbk Ed-Chief; Sec Stu Cncl; Bausch & Lomb Sci Awd; DAR Awd; Hon Roll; JC Awd; Opt Clb Awd; Val; Golub Found Schlrshp 86; Dr Sheehar Schlrshp 86; RPI Medal 85; Cornell U; Bio Sci.

NORTHRUP, SCOTT R; Messana Central HS; Massena, NY; (Y); 6/294; Quiz Bowl; ROTC; Rep Stu Cncl; Var JV Bsbl; Var Crs Cntry; Var JV Ice Hcky; Var JV Socr; Var Trk; High Hon Roll; Hon Roll; Hocky Middl MVP,Outstndng Plyr 85; Nrotc Schlrshp 86; Boston U; Bio Med Eng.

NORTON, CAROLYN; Chester HS; Chester, NY; (Y); 1/65; Band; Jazz Band; Mrchg Band; Var Capt Bsktbl; Var Capt Socr; Var Sftbl; Var Capt Vllybl; High Hon Roll; NHS; Val; MIP Sccr 86; Stu Cncl Awd SR 86; Canisius Coll; Sprts Med.

NORTON, JENNIFER; East Aurora HS; Arcade, NY; (Y); 9/184; Dance Clb; French Clb; JA; Band; School Musical; Nwsp Stf; Hon Roll; NHS; Pres Schlr; Egt Schls85-86; Jr Miss Schlrshp 85-86; Hamilton; Dance.

NORTON, JUDY; Alexander Central HS; Batavia, NY; (Y); VP Church Yth Grp; VP 4-H; Spanish Clb; Varsity Clb; Band; Chorus; Church Choir; Concert Band; Drm Mjr(t); Mrchg Band; JV Sccr Coachs Awd 84-85; Sola Fstvl Good Rtng 84-85; Psychlgy.

NORTON, JULIE D; Alexander Central HS; Batavia, NY; (Y); 5/85; Pres Church Yth Grp; Pres Sec 4-H; Band; Church Choir; Concert Band; Mrchg Band; Capt Socr; Capt Trk; Lion Awd; NHS; Acad All-Amer 86; Regents Schlrshp Awd 86; Ithara Coll; Phys Thrpy.

NORTON, KAREN; Hoosic Valley Central HS; Valley Falls, NY; (S); 8/99; 4-H; Teachers Aide; Band; Concert Band; Mrchg Band; School Musical; Hon Roll; Film Dir.

NORTON, KELLIE; Cicero-North Syracuse HS; North Syracuse, NY; (S); 74/667; Band; Concert Band; Mrchg Band; Orch; Symp Band; Hon Roll; NHS; NY All ST Conf Band 85; All County Orch 86; Onondaga CC; Humanities.

NORTON, KEVIN; Washingtonville HS; Monroe, NY; (Y); Boy Scts; Variety Show; Stu Cncl; Bsbl; Capt Bsktbl; Ftbl; Mgr(s); Score Keeper; Socr; Wt Lftg; Bsktbl Capt; Stu Cncl; Mgr-Ftbl Tm.

NORTON, LAUREL; Greece Athena HS; Rochester, NY; (Y); 129/330; Dance Clb; DECA; Exploring; French Clb; Hosp Aide; SADD; Acpl Chr; Chorus; School Musical; School Play; Smmr Dance Fstvl Grand Champ Tap Grp & Ballet Duet & 3rd Rnnr Up Lyrcl Solo 86; Psychlgy.

NORTON, MARCY; Amsterdam HS; Amesterdam, NY; (Y); Drama Clb; Jazz Band; School Play; Nwsp Stf; Stu Cncl; Cheerleading; High Hon Roll; NHS; Amsterdam Teen Miss 84; Tlnt Am Semi-Fnlst 84; Comm.

NORTON, RAY; Falconer Central HS; Kennedy, NY; (Y); Church Yth Grp; FFA; Varsity Clb; Im Coach Actv; JV Var Ftbl; Var Trk; Var Capt Wrstlng; Pres Schlr; Hazzard Fund Schlrshp, Schl RIT Fund Schlrshp, Brian Overend Awd Wdwrkng, WCTU Spch Awd 86-87; RIT; Chem Engrng.

NORTZ, JULIE; Beaver River Central HS; Beaver Falls, NY; (Y); 4/86; Trs Exploring; Trs French Clb; Pres SADD; Chorus; Drm Mjr(t); School Musical; Yrbk Bus Mgr; Var JV Cheerleading; Pres NHS; Voice Dem Awd; Captain Elizabeth Bush Memrl Schlrshp 86; Greatst Potntl Fld Bus Awd 86; Mst Dedctd Marchng Band Awd; Sieca Coll; Accntng.

NORTZ, PATTI; Beaver River Central HS; Beaver Falls, NY; (Y); Church Yth Grp; Sec Exploring; GAA; Band; Chorus; Ed Yrbk Stf; Sec Sr Cls; JV Cheerleading; Var Tennis; Sec NHS; Tnns All Str; Gd Chrstn Attd Desire Imprv; Spcl Ed.

NORWOOD, CONSUELO; Uniondale HS; Uniondale, NY; (Y); Hosp Aide; Yrbk Stf; Rep Frsh Cls; Var Cheerleading; Var Swmmng; FHA; Band; Mrchg Band; NHS; Svc Activity Awd 84; Nrsg.

NORWOOD, SANDRA; De Witt Clinton HS; Bronx, NY; (Y); Band; Concert Band; Merit Hnrs Awd Readng 85; Jrnlsm.

NOSBISCH, STEVE; Alden Central HS; Alden, NY; (Y); French Clb; Science Clb; SADD; School Musical; Nwsp Stf; Var L Bsbl; Var L Ftbl; Lcrss; Am Leg Boys St; SUNY Albany; Govt.

NOSTRANT, KELLY; Bishop Ludden HS; Syracuse, NY; (Y); Church Yth Grp; Exploring; Variety Show; Lit Mag; Var L Cheerleading; High Hon Roll; NHS; Yrbk Stf; 3rd Pl CYO Chrldng Awd 83 & 85; Cert Of Achvt Hm Ec 84; Cert Of Achvt Sclgy 86; Rgnts Schlrshp 86; Geneseo; Bio-Chem.

NOSTROM, DENISE J; Patchogue-Medford HS; Medford, NY; (Y); 76/621; Dance Clb; Scholastic Bowl; Pres Spanish Clb; Mrchg Band; Stat Bsktbl; Capt Var Cheerleading; Sftbl; Pres Spanish NHS; Stu Mnth 83; Most Dedicated Sftbl 83; Adelphi U; Intl Trade Crspndnt.

NOTARO, RICHARD; Hicksville SR HS; Hicksville, NY; (Y); Var Bsbl; Var Bsktbl; Hon Roll.

NOURSE, DAWN; Pioneer Central HS; Sardinia, NY; (Y); 25/218; Church Yth Grp; French Clb; Pep Clb; Acpl Chr; Chorus; Church Choir; Stage Crew; Swing Chorus; Cheerleading; Dntl Ass.

NOURSE, SHELLY; Warsaw Central HS; Warsaw, NY; (S); 14/90; Drama Clb; French Clb; Spanish Clb; Chorus; School Musical; School Play; Stage Crew; JV Bsktbl; JV Socr; JV Trk; Acad Awd Art II 84-85; Adv Design.

NOVA, JILL; Midwood HS; Brooklyn, NY; (Y); 41/667; Cmnty Wkr; Math Tm; Orch; School Musical; Cit Awd; Hon Roll; Jr NHS; Sal; VP Frsh Cls; Var Bsktbl; Treas Ldrs Clb 85; Pres Ldr Clb 86; NY Super Yth 86; Pre-Med.

NOVAK, KATHY; The Mary Louis Acad; Ridgewood, NY; (Y); Hosp Aide; Intnl Clb; Office Aide; Nwsp Stf; JR Srvc Awd Hosp Vlntr 85; Mary Louis Acad Srvc Awd 86; Bus.

NOVAL, TARA L; Allendale Columbia HS; Pittsford, NY; (Y); Church Yth Grp; French Clb; Yrbk Stf; Lit Mag; French Hon Soc; High Hon Roll; NHS; Juilliard Schl Of Music; Violin.

NOVELL, VICKIE; Vernon-Verona-Sherrill HS; Vernon, NY; (Y); VP Church Yth Grp; Computer Clb; Drama Clb; VP Girl Scts; VP Latin Clb; Math Clb; Thesps; Band; Chorus; Church Choir; Silv Awd Grl Scouts 84; Music Thrpy.

NOVELLE, MONICA; Margaretville Central HS; Arkville, NY; (Y); Cmnty Wkr; Pres SADD; Band; Chorus; Concert Band; Mrchg Band; Yrbk Phtg; JV Capt Cheerleading; Var Socr; Var Sftbl; Rgnl Schlstc Art Awd Photo 86; Cmnctns.

NOVELLI, REBECCA; Trott Vocational HS; Niagara Falls, NY; (Y); 22/180; Hosp Aide; Nwsp Ed-Chief; Trs Stu Cncl; Bowling; Practcl Nrsng Diploma 86; Niagara Canty CC; Surgcl Tech.

NOVETSKY, HILLEL; Yeshivah Flatbush J Braverman HS; Staten Island, NY; (Y); Capt Scholastic Bowl; Chorus; Variety Show; Nwsp Ed-Chief; Nwsp Rptr; Ed Nwsp Stf; Ed Yrbk Stf; Ed Lit Mag; High Hon Roll; Ntl Merit SF; Intl Champ Of Bible Cont 84; Brnz Mdl Amer H S Math Exam 85; Pres Mdl Of Yeshivah Of Flatbush 84; Yeshivah U; Math.

NOVICK, BETH; Commack HS North; Commack, NY; (Y); 40/390; SADD; Pres Temple Yth Grp; Chorus; School Musical; School Play; Stage Crew; High Hon Roll; NHS; Pres Schlr; Spnsh Awd 86; 1st Schl Math Cntst 86; 4th Cnty Natl Spnsh Cntst 86; Brandeis U; Law.

NOVICK, DAVID; Clarkstown North HS; New City, NY; (Y); Political Wkr; Red Cross Aide; SADD; Temple Yth Grp; Law.

NOVOSAT, DEANNA; North Tonawanda SR HS; N Tonawanda, NY; (Y); Camp Fr Inc; Church Yth Grp; Hon Roll; Jr NHS; Architectur.

NOVOSEL, ERICA; Shenendehowa HS; Clifton Park, NY; (Y); St Schlr; Ntl Ltn Exm Hon Merit Smma Cm Ld 84-85; ST Cert Of Mert-Outstndng Schlstc Achvt 85-86; Geolgy.

NOVOTNY, SUSAN; Williamsville East HS; Williamsville, NY; (Y); 55/298; Drama Clb; Intnl Clb; Latin Clb; Sec Pep Clb; VP Chorus; School Musical; Rep Stu Cncl; Var JV Cheerleading; Prncpl Cittn Awd 85-86; Otstndng Srv Awd 85-86; Otstndng Srv Awd 84-85; U Of Buffalo; Phrmcst.

NOWACK, CYNTHIA; Buffalo Seminary; E Aurora, NY; (Y); Cmnty Wkr; Red Cross Aide; VP Science Clb; Nwsp Phtg; Yrbk Phtg; Var Bsktbl; Var Sftbl; Hon Roll; Prfct Atten Awd; AFS; Smmr Pgm Allegheny Coll 86; Court Conduct Rep Buffalo Sem Jr Cls 85-86; Hnbl Mntn Outstndng Art Wrk 85.

NOWACOSKI, CLAUDIA; Tottenville HS; Staten Island, NY; (S); 24/850; Teachers Aide; Concert Band; VP Soph Cls; High Hon Roll; NHS; Church Yth Grp; Comp Sci.

NOWAK, BARBARA; Frontier Central HS; Blasdell, NY; (Y); French Clb; FBLA; Pep Clb; Yrbk Ed-Chief; Yrbk Sprt Ed; Yrbk Stf; Im Bsktbl; Im Vllybl; Hon Roll; ST U NY-BUFFALO; Arch.

NOWAK, CHRISTINE; Grand Island SR HS; Grand Isl, NY; (Y); 46/300; Hosp Aide; Ski Clb; Varsity Clb; Yrbk Phtg; Hst Jr Cls; Hst Sr Cls; VP Stu Cncl; Tennis; Hon Roll; NHS; Bio.

NOWAK, ERIKA; Westmoreland HS; Whitesboro, NY; (Y); 8/100; Trs Ski Clb; Rep SADD; Concert Band; Mrchg Band; Ed Nwsp Phtg; Yrbk Stf; Stu Cncl; High Hon Roll; NHS; Acad Amer All Star, USSCA Awd 86; Pre Vet.

NOWAK, GREGORY; Depew HS; Depew, NY; (Y); Art Clb; Church Yth Grp; Church Choir; Variety Show; Bsktbl; Pres Phys Ftns Awd 83; Career Fair Cmmsnd Cover/Poster Dsgn 86; Rochester IT; Art.

NOWAK, JUDY; St Marys HS; Cheektowaga, NY; (S); 5/170; Church Yth Grp; Exploring; Pres Girl Scts; Ski Clb; Chorus; Lit Mag; Rep Stu Cncl; Hon Roll; NHS; Cmnty Wkr; Girl Scout Silver Awd 84.

NOWAK, JULIE; Albion Central HS; Albion, NY; (S); 28/169; Church Yth Grp; FFA; Trs Rptr VICA; School Musical; Nwsp Stf; Trs Jr Cls; Rptr Sr Cls; Hon Roll; Prfct Atten Awd; Skls Comptn 1st Pl Infrmtn & Procsng Sec 85-86; Alfred ST Coll; Wrd Prosng.

NOWAK, KATHLEEN; Frontier Central HS; Blasdell, NY; (Y); 97/430; French Clb; FBLA; Pep Clb; SADD; School Play; Yrbk Ed-Chief; Yrbk Sprt Ed; Yrbk Stf; Stu Cncl; Hon Roll; NY ST U Bfl; Lawyer.

NOWAK, KENNETH E; Seneca Vocational HS; Buffalo, NY; (Y); 1/195; Trs Sr Cls; Rep Stu Cncl; Hon Roll; NHS; Val; Regents Schlrshp; SUNY Buffalo; Mech Engr.

NOWAK, KRISTINE; Binghamton HS; Binghamton, NY; (Y); Exploring; Key Clb; Model UN; Office Aide; Pep Clb; Red Cross Aide; Off Frsh Cls; Off Soph Cls; Off Jr Cls; Off Sr Cls; Secy Of Cls 85-86; Hmrm Rep For Stu Cncl 84-86; Vrsty Swm Mgr For Grls 84-85; Bus Law.

NOWAK, LAURIE; Alden Central HS; Alden, NY; (Y); Letterman Clb; Spanish Clb; Yrbk Stf; Var Bsktbl; Var Swmmng; Var Capt Trk; Acctng.

NOWAK, LAURIE; Whitesboro SR HS; Whitesboro, NY; (Y); Church Yth Grp; Drama Clb; Acpl Chr; Band; Chorus; Concert Band; School Musical; Swing Chorus; JV Capt Cheerleading; Hon Roll; Music.

NOWAK, MARK; Southside HS; Rockville Ctr, NY; (Y); Boy Scts; Civic Clb; Cmnty Wkr; SADD; Score Keeper; Wrstlng; Hon Roll; St Thomas Aquinas; FBI Spcl Ag.

NOWAK, MARY; Bishop Scully HS; Tribes Hill, NY; (Y); 15/47; Latin Clb; Yrbk Stf; Sec Frsh Cls; VP Soph Cls; Pres Jr Cls; JV Capt Cheerleading; Var Capt Sftbl; Mu Alp Tht; Sec NHS; Mst Dedctd Awd Sftbl 86.

NOWAK, NANCY; Mineola HS; Mineola, NY; (Y); Red Cross Aide; Acpl Chr; Chorus; School Musical; Hon Roll; Cert Apprectn Lunch Bunch 85-86; Awds Concert Singers 83-86; Psychlgy.

NOWAKOWSKI, NICOLE; Grand Island HS; Grand Island, NY; (Y); 55/325; Art Clb; Cmnty Wkr; Drama Clb; Ski Clb; Teachers Aide; School Musical; Yrbk Phtg; Var L Gym; Hon Roll; NHS; ST U Coll; Elem Educ.

NOWHITNEY, LISA; Franklin Central Schl; Franklin, NY; (Y); Drama Clb; Girl Scts; JA; Ski Clb; Spanish Clb; Chorus; Stage Crew; Yrbk Stf; Lit Mag; Pres Frsh Cls; Trvl.

NOWOTARSKI, LUANN; John F Kennedy JR-SR HS; Cheektowaga, NY; (Y); 21/147; Church Yth Grp; Drama Clb; Chorus; School Play; Nwsp Stf; Yrbk Stf; Hst Stu Cncl; Tennis; Girl Scts; Alt Recpnt Of Girls JFK PTA Schlrshp 86; Long Island U Southhampton.

NOWYJ, DONNA M; Westhill HS; Syracuse, NY; (Y); 5/145; Pres Art Clb; Cmnty Wkr; Lit Mag; High Hon Roll; Hon Roll; NHS; NY Smmr Schl Arts Cert Commndtn 84; Schlstc Art Awds Cert Of Merit/Gld Mdl 85; Illstrn.

NOYES, GRETCHEN; G Ray Bodley HS; Fulton, NY; (Y); Ski Clb; Spanish Clb; Band; Mrchg Band; Yrbk Phtg; Off Soph Cls; Crs Cntry; Trk; Hon Roll; Supr Achvt Math 83-84; Acadmcly Hight Span 3 85-86; Awd Hosp Svc 85-86.

NUCHOW, LAUREN R; Tappan Zee HS; Orangeburg, NY; (Y); 11/245; JA; SADD; Sec Stu Cncl; JV Var Cheerleading; Var L Trk; NHS; Outstndng Schlstc & Athlt Achvt 85; Frnkln & Mrshl Coll.

NUFRYK, MARY ANN; Greece Athena HS; Rochester, NY; (Y); FBLA; Hon Roll; Bus.

NUGENT, COLLEEN; Academy Of Saint Joseph; Amityville, NY; (Y); Church Yth Grp; Cmnty Wkr; Drama Clb; Church Choir; School Play; Nwsp Rptr; Hon Roll; CW Post; Comm.

NUGENT, JOHN A; St Francis Prep; Douglaston, NY; (S); 96/744; Computer Clb; Political Wkr; Ice Hcky; Hon Roll; Space Sci.

NUGGET, HOPE; Centereach HS; Centereach, NY; (Y); Pep Clb; Spanish Clb; Temple Yth Grp; Band; Mrchg Band; Orch; Rep Frsh Cls; Rep Soph Cls; Rep Jr Cls; JV Crs Cntry; NY St Soloist Music Assn; Law.

NULMAN, SHMUEL D; Yeshiva Torah Temima HS; Brooklyn, NY; (Y); Rgnts Schlrshp 86.

NUMA, CARLINE; St Joseph HS; Brooklyn, NY; (Y); Office Aide; Chorus; School Musical; School Play; Hon Roll; NHS; Pediatrcs.

NUMSSEN, ERIK; Saugerties HS; Saugerties, NY; (Y); Mrchg Band; Symp Band; JV Ftbl; JV Trk; Cit Awd; Hon Roll; SUNY New Paltz; Bus.

NUNES, PAUL R; Iona Prep; Bronxville, NY; (Y); 18/191; Math Tm; Ed Yrbk Phtg; Crs Cntry; High Hon Roll; Hon Roll; Ntl Merit Ltr; NYS Regnts Schlrshp 86; Rensselaer Schlrshp 86; Rensselaer Polytech Inst; Physc.

NUNEZ, ALISA; East Meadow HS; East Meadow, NY; (Y); Church Yth Grp; 4-H; Mathletes; Band; Mrchg Band; Orch; Pep Band; Cit Awd; 4-H Awd; Hon Roll; Bus Adm.

NUNEZ, MANUEL; Mount St Michael Acad; New York, NY; (Y); Varsity Clb; Lit Mag; Rep Soph Cls; Rep Jr Cls; Rep Stu Cncl; JV Var Crs Cntry; JV Var Trk; Hon Roll; Psych.

NUNEZ, PATRICIA; De Witt Clinton HS; New York, NY; (Y); Nwsp Phtg; Yrbk Phtg; Pre-Schl Educ.

NUNMAKER, JESSICA; Wallkill SR HS; Wallkill, NY; (Y); 34/179; Church Yth Grp; Library Aide; Var Trk; Hon Roll; Mt Saint Marys Coll; Nrsng.

NUNZIATO, MARISA; Ravena-Coeymans-Selkirk HS; Ravena, NY; (Y); French Clb; FBLA; Pres Key Clb; Pep Clb; Trs SADD; Rep Sr Cls; Rep Stu Cncl; Var JV Bsktbl; Var JV Socr; Hon Roll; Coll Of St Rose; Elem Educ.

NUR, PEGGY; The Mary Louis Acad; Sunrise, FL; (Y); Art Clb; GAA; Service Clb; Bowling; Score Keeper; Svc Awd 84-86; Hnr Rll 84-86; Med.

NURENA, KATHLEEN R; Resurrection Acad; Harrison, NY; (Y); GAA; Math Tm; Chorus; Stage Crew; Var L Swmmng; Im Vllybl; Hon Roll; Schlrshp Lng Islnd U 86; Fordham U; Cmnctns.

NUROD, VANESSA; Frankfort Schuyler HS; Frankfort, NY; (S); Art Clb; Church Yth Grp; French Clb; FBLA; Ski Clb; Variety Show; Cheerleading; High Hon Roll; Hon Roll; NHS; NY ST Smr Schl Of Arts 85-86; Advrtsng.

NUSSBAUM, MELISSA; Oceanside HS; Oceanside, NY; (Y); Sec Key Clb; Sec Radio Clb; Spanish Clb; Ed Nwsp Stf; Yrbk Rptr; Hon Roll; NHS; Frgn Lang Awd Span 84-86; Frgn Lang Awd Lat/Greek 86; AATSP Awd Natl Span Cntst 85; Cvl Law Mock Ct 86.

NUSSER, KRYSTLE; Berne-Knox-Westerlo HS; Altamont, NY; (Y); 14/77; FBLA; Mrchg Band; Stu Cncl; Co-Capt Var Cheerleading; Capt Co-Capt Twrlr; 1st Typg Div SUNY Cobleskill Exms 86; 3rd Typg Div Maria Coll Exms 86; Med Secy.

NUWER, JENNIFER; West Seneca East SR HS; Cheektowaga, NY; (Y); Chorus; Awd Effort 80; Awd Best All Around Effrt 81; Merit Roll & Awds Apprectn Chorus 85-86; Bus.

NUZZO, WARREN; Deer Park HS; Deer Park, NY; (Y); French Clb; Polit Sci.

NWANKPA, ONYINYE; Dewitt Clinton HS; Bronx, NY; (Y); Sec Key Clb; Math Tm; Office Aide; Teachers Aide; Acpl Chr; Church Choir; Concert Band; Sec Yrbk Stf; Trk; NHS; Sophie Davis Schl; Medicine.

NYARADY, BARTHOLOMEW; Carmel HS; Carmel, NY; (Y); 20/375; Debate Tm; Model UN; Teachers Aide; School Musical; School Play; Var Capt Bsbl; Var Capt Bsktbl; Var Crs Cntry; Var Trk; Hon Roll; Paris Cup Sccr Trnmnt Hgh Scr Chavenay Frnc 84; Lycee Intl St Germainen Laye Frnc 82-85; West Point; Comp Sci.

O BANNON, JACQUELYN; Cardinal O Hara HS; Tonawanda, NY; (Y); Dance Clb; Drama Clb; French Clb; JA; Im Badmtn; Var Cheerleading; Im Gym; Var Score Keeper; Intl Chrldng Champs 3rd Pl 85, 1st Pl 86; Niagra U; Econ.

O BEIRNE, KATHY; Scotia-Glenville HS; Scotia, NY; (Y); Band; Concert Band; Mrchg Band; Schenectady CC; Chef.

O BRIEN, CASSANDRA; Oneida SR HS; Oneida, NY; (S); Cmnty Wkr; Sec 4-H; Intnl Clb; Service Clb; SADD; Lit Mag; 4-H Awd; High Hon Roll; Jr NHS; NHS; Indep Study Awd 83; Prncpls Recog Awd 83.

O BRIEN, DAVID; Canisius HS; Kenmore, NY; (S); 6/141; Boy Scts; Drama Clb; Pres Latin Clb; Co-Capt Pep Clb; Quiz Bowl; Chorus; School Musical; Stage Crew; Nwsp Stf; Yrbk Stf; Holy Cross Bk Awd 86.

O BRIEN, ERIKA; Monsignor Scanlan HS; Flushing, NY; (Y); 26/277; Intnl Clb; Prfct Atten Awd; 3rd Plc Sci Fr; Nrsng.

O BRIEN, GLENN; East Rockaway HS; East Rockaway, NY; (Y); 15/115; Am Leg Boys St; Computer Clb; Scholastic Bowl; Nwsp Ed-Chief; Yrbk Bus Mgr; Ed Lit Mag; Bsbl; High Hon Roll; Mock Trial; Mdl Cngrss; Law.

O BRIEN JR, JAMES P; Clarkstown North HS; Congers, NY; (Y); Bsktbl; Lcrss; Chrch Awd 84-85; Sndy Schl Tchr 84-85; Bus.

O BRIEN, JAMES PATRICK MICHAEL; Seton Catholic Central HS; Binghamton, NY; (Y); 12/162; Church Yth Grp; Letterman Clb; Ski Clb; SADD; VP Stu Cncl; Bsbl; Bsktbl; Ftbl; High Hon Roll; Hon Roll; Clarkson Pres Trstees Schlrshp 86-87; Peter Witcher & Jessie Baker Schlrshps 86-87; Clarkson U; Elctrcl Engrng.

O BRIEN, JEANNINE; East Hampton HS; Amagansett, NY; (Y); Church Yth Grp; School Play; Variety Show; Yrbk Stf; SADD; Stu Cncl; Var Tennis; Var Trk; Bauder Fashion Coll; Fshn Mrchn.

O BRIEN, JENNIFER; Oneida HS; Oneida, NY; (S); Sec Trs Intnl Clb; Service Clb; Spanish Clb; Sec SADD; Lit Mag; High Hon Roll; Hon Roll; NHS; Bio.

O BRIEN, JENNIFER; Smithtown H S East; Saint James, NY; (Y); Church Yth Grp; DECA; Hosp Aide; Service Clb; SADD; Thesps; School Musical; Stu Cncl; Var L Badmtn; JV Tennis; Thespn Trpe 86; Cndy Strpr Achvt Awd 85.

O BRIEN, JILL; Center Moriches HS; Center Moriches, NY; (Y); 3/104; Cmnty Wkr; Drama Clb; Trs Latin Clb; Math Tm; Ski Clb; School Play; Nwsp Stf; Yrbk Rptr; Lit Mag; Trs Frsh Cls; Comp Sci.

O BRIEN, JOSEPH; Geneseo Central HS; Geneseo, NY; (Y); 2/90; Mathletes; Rep Stu Cncl; Co-Capt Bsbl; Var L Bsktbl; French Hon Soc; High Hon Roll; Jr NHS; NHS; Ntl Merit Ltr; NEDT Awd; SUNY Binghamton.

O BRIEN, KATHLEEN; Rome Free Acad; Rome, NY; (Y); 15/500; Aud/Vis; Intnl Clb; Key Clb; High Hon Roll; Jr NHS; NHS; Math Awd 84; Bio.

O BRIEN, KATHLEEN; Victor Central Schl; Victor, NY; (Y); French Clb; Girl Scts; Stage Crew; Stat Swmmng; Hon Roll; Ruth Mills Mem Schlrshp Spec Ed 86; SUNY-PLATTSBURGH; Spec Ed.

O BRIEN, KELLI; Brewster HS; Brewster, NY; (Y); 15/220; ROTC; Nwsp Rptr; JV Var Fld Hcky; JV Var Sftbl; Hon Roll; NHS; Prfct Atten Awd; Safety Awd; All League Hnrbl Ment Field Hocky; Pub Affairs Officer; Drill Tm Commander 86-87; Annapolis; Frgn Lang.

O BRIEN, KELLY; Chittenango Central HS; Chittenango, NY; (Y); French Clb; GAA; Varsity Clb; Bsktbl; Sftbl; Hon Roll; Jr NHS; Bst Offense Sftbl 84-85; Comp.

O BRIEN, KEVIN; Walter Panas HS; Peekskill, NY; (Y); Variety Show; Coach Actv; Golf; Lcrss; Socr; Capt Swmmng.

O BRIEN, MARSHA D; St Francis Prep; Laurelton, NY; (Y); 164/653; Band; Color Guard; Concert Band; Mrchg Band; Ntl Merit Schol; Opt Clb Awd; Bus Adm.

O BRIEN, MATTHEW; Tamarac HS; Troy, NY; (Y); 15/106; Intnl Clb; Math Tm; Yrbk Stf; Off Stu Cncl; Hon Roll; NHS; Prom King JR SR Prom 86; Troy Rotary Clb Yth Awd 86; PTA Pres Awd 86; Siena Coll; Psych.

O BRIEN, PATRICK; Catholic Central HS; Troy, NY; (Y); 23/189; Math Clb; Variety Show; Var L Crs Cntry; Var L Trk; Hon Roll; NHS; Frshmn 400 Yrd Dsh Rcrd 84; Ithaca; Flm.

O BRIEN, PATRICK MICHAEL; Mynderse Acad; Seneca Falls, NY; (Y); Church Yth Grp; Drama Clb; Ski Clb; Chorus; Swing Chorus; Outstndgn Tenor 86; Treas Yth Grp Assem God 85-86; Houghton Coll; Comp Sci.

O BRIEN, STACEY A; St Francis Prep; Flushing, NY; (S); 111/750; Cmnty Wkr; Opt Clb Awd; Acad All-Amer 86; Bus.

O BRIEN, TYLER; Potsdam HS; W Stockholm, NY; (Y); 46/136; AFS; Boy Scts; CAP; Spanish Clb; Crs Cntry; Trk; 1st Tm All Northern Outdoor Track 110 M Hurdles; Plattsburg ST U; Crmnlgy.

O CALLAGHAN, CHRISTINE; Southhampton HS; Southampton, NY; (Y); 5/120; French Clb; Band; Rptr Nwsp Rptr; Var Vllybl; High Hon Roll; Jr NHS; NHS; Prfct Atten Awd.

O CALLAGHAN, ED; Xavier HS; Breezy Pt, NY; (Y); 1/200; ROTC; Mrchg Band; Off Sr Cls; Stu Cncl; Im L Bsbl; Im Bsktbl; Im Ftbl; High Hon Roll; NEDT Awd; Gold Schltc Awd JROTC; Engrng.

O CALLAGHAN, JOSEPH; South Side HS; Rockville Centre, NY; (Y); 47/250; Computer Clb; SADD; High Hon Roll; Hon Roll; Comp.

O CALLAGHAN, SCOTT; Hicksville HS; Hicksville, NY; (Y); Chess Clb; Church Yth Grp; 4-H; French Clb; Nwsp Stf; Lit Mag; French Hon Soc; 4-H Awd; Jr NHS; Voice Dem Awd; Law.

O CONNELL, EILEEN M; John A Coleman HS; Kingston, NY; (Y); Latin Clb; Stage Crew; Var L Sftbl; Hon Roll; Regents Schlrshp NYS 86; Acad Grant CO St U 86; CO ST U; Pre Vet.

O CONNELL, JOHN; Valley Stream Central HS; Valley Stream, NY; (Y); Var L Bsbl; Dads Clb Outstndng Bsbl 84; Engl Awd 83-85; VS Mail Lg O Neill Awd 85; Elec.

O CONNELL, JOHN J; St Peters Boys HS; Staten Island, NY; (Y); 21/163; Aud/Vis; Boy Scts; Exploring; VP SADD; Stage Crew; Yrbk Phtg; Rep Soph Cls; Rep Jr Cls; JV Crs Cntry; JV Trk; Arspc Engrng.

O CONNELL, KATHRYN R; Rome Catholic HS; Rome, NY; (Y); 19/67; SADD; School Musical; Nwsp Rptr; Yrbk Stf; Mgr(s); High Hon Roll; Hon Roll; Pres Schlr; Hstry Awd 83 & 86; Kybrdng Awd 84 & 86; Physcl Educ Awd 85; Lemoyne Coll; Eng.

O CONNELL, TIMOTHY; Bishop Ludden HS; Syracuse, NY; (S); Math Clb; Math Tm; SADD; Var Bsbl; Var Ftbl; Mgr(s); High Hon Roll; JA; Trk; Achvt Merit Math, JR Clb Chmpshp Golf, Sprtsmnshp Awd Bsbll 85.

O CONNOR, AMY; Liverpool HS; Liverpool, NY; (Y); 279/860; Church Yth Grp; Var Fld Hcky; Hon Roll.

O CONNOR, ANN N; Massapequa HS; Massapequa, NY; (Y); 4/440; Teachers Aide; Yrbk Sprt Ed; Sec Soph Cls; Sec Sr Cls; Var L Socr; Var Trk; NHS; Ntl Merit Ltr; NEDT Awd; French Clb; Nassau Cnty Excptnl Sr Grls Scr 85; All-Lge All-Str Tm 85; All-Div 83; Boston Coll; Math.

O CONNOR, APRIL L; Lakeland HS; Yorktown Heights, NY; (Y); 62/344; Trs Church Yth Grp; FBLA; Hon Roll; Jr NHS; NY ST Regnts Schlrshp 86; NY ST Cert Of Merit 86; Penn ST U; Engrng.

O CONNOR, BOB; Waterloo SR HS; Waterloo, NY; (S); Trs Frsh Cls; Pres Soph Cls; VP Stu Cncl; JV Bsktbl; Var Capt Lcrss; Cit Awd; DAR Awd; Cmmnctns.

O CONNOR, BRENNA; Haldane HS; Cold Spring, NY; (S); 5/55; Am Leg Aux Girls St; Yrbk Stf; Trs Soph Cls; VP Sec Stu Cncl; Var Capt Bsktbl; Var Capt Sftbl; Var L Trk; Var Capt Vllybl; Hon Roll; Pres Jr NHS; Hnbl Mntn All Amer Trck 85; Poughkeepsie Jrnl Athl Yr Vllybl 85; NY ST Discus Champ 85; Phy Ed.

O CONNOR, CHRISTINE; Moore Catholic HS; Staten Island, NY; (Y); 1/200; Debate Tm; Capt NFL; Spanish Clb; Yrbk Stf; Stu Cncl; NHS; Church Yth Grp; Model UN; SADD; Rep Soph Cls; Actvts Ed Of Yrbk 86-87; Acad All Amer Awd 85-86; Ntl Sci Merit Awd 85-86; Prelaw.

O CONNOR, CHRISTOPHER JOSEPH; Bishop Kearney HS; Rochester, NY; (Y); 25/110; Camera Clb; Camp Fr Inc; Chess Clb; Church Yth Grp; Cmnty Wkr; Dance Clb; Drama Clb; English Clb; FTA; JA; Hugh O Brien Ldrshp Awd 84; Intl Rotary Awd 86; Fr Dunn Schlrp 86; Iona Coll; Engl Tchr.

O CONNOR, DANIEL D; Cantis HS; Staten Island, NY; (Y); Office Aide; Orch; Stage Crew; Var Golf; Swmmng; Prncpls Pride Awd 86; Invstmnt.

O CONNOR, DENIS J; Copiague HS; Copiague, NY; (Y); #1 In Class; Am Leg Boys St; Intnl Clb; Service Clb; Nwsp Rptr; Nwsp Sprt Ed; Pres Stu Cncl; Socr; Trk; High Hon Roll; Natl Socl Studies Olympd 85-86; US Senate Yth Pgm 86-87.

O CONNOR JR, EDMUND A; Mount Saint Michael Acad; Bronx, NY; (S); 10/309; JV Crs Cntry; JV Trk; High Hon Roll; Hon Roll; NHS; Schlrshp Mt St Michael 83-86; Schlrshp Grammar Schl 83; Psych.

O CONNOR, EMER; Jamesville-Dewitt HS; Jamesville, NY; (Y); 13/240; Chorus; School Musical; Nwsp Stf; Yrbk Ed-Chief; Lit Mag; JV Crs Cntry; High Hon Roll; NHS; Im Vllybl; St Louis Schlrshp, Rgnts Schlrshp, Bristol Myers Schlrshp, IN U Hnrs Div Schlrshp 85-86; IN U Bloomington; Pre-Med.

O CONNOR, JASON; Kenmore West SR HS; Kenmore, NY; (Y); 31/500; Band; Jazz Band; Mrchg Band; Orch; Capt Swmmng; High Hon Roll; Hon Roll; NHS; Ntl Merit Ltr; Pres Schlr; Outstndg SR Awd Bnd 86; NY ST Rgnts Schlrp 86; ST U Of Buffalo; Lib Arts.

O CONNOR, JIM; L A Webber HS; Lyndonville, NY; (S); 1/95; AFS; Church Yth Grp; Computer Clb; Math Clb; Science Clb; Varsity Clb; Concert Band; Jazz Band; Mrchg Band; Trs School Musical; Proj ADEPT Gftd & Talntd; Mth.

O CONNOR, KATIE; Scotia-Glenville HS; Scotia, NY; (Y); Pres Church Yth Grp; Exploring; Key Clb; Ski Clb; Band; Mrchg Band; Var Diving; JV Var Sftbl; Var Swmmng; Cit Awd; Peer Ldrshp 86; Cazenovia College; Elem Ed.

O CONNOR, KEILA; Wilson Central HS; Wilson, NY; (Y); SADD; Sec Band; Pep Band; Stu Cncl; JV Var Fld Hcky; Var L Trk; High Hon Roll; VP NHS; Fld Hcky MVP Offnsv Trphy 84; Elem Educ.

O CONNOR, KELLY; Mt St Marys Acad; Kenmore, NY; (Y); Girl Scts; Pep Clb; Varsity Clb; Church Choir; Rep Soph Cls; Jr Cls; Rep Stu Cncl; Var Bsktbl; JV Score Keeper; Var Socr; Scr-All Star Team 2yrs Mvp 85-86; Incentive Schlrshp 83.

O CONNOR, KELLY; Newfane HS; Newfane, NY; (Y); Drama Clb; Math Clb; Science Clb; Stage Crew; Yrbk Stf; JV Trk; Stat Vllybl; Hon Roll; Engr.

O CONNOR, KELLY L; St Francis Prep; Fresh Meadows, NY; (S); 41/744; Girl Scts; Library Aide; Band; Chorus; Color Guard; Concert Band; High Hon Roll; Hon Roll; NHS; Opt Clb Awd; Psych.

O CONNOR, LYNNE M; Mohonasen SR HS; Rotterdam, NY; (Y); 20/170; Church Yth Grp; VP Pres French Clb; Key Clb; Nwsp Rptr; Yrbk Sprt Ed; Stu Cncl; Var L Socr; Capt L Sftbl; Hon Roll; Sec NHS; Intl Sftbl Tm 84-85; Oneonta.

O CONNOR, PATRICE B; Sacred Heart Acad; Lynbrook, NY; (Y); 18/182; Office Aide; Spanish Clb; Church Choir; Yrbk Stf; Im Tennis; Hon Roll; NHS; Pres Schlr; DECA; James Madison U; Gen.

O CONNOR, PEG; F D Roosevelt HS; Staatsburg, NY; (Y); 37/200; Varsity Clb; Chorus; Nwsp Bus Mgr; Nwsp Rptr; Var Bsktbl; JV Golf; Var Socr; JV Trk; Hon Roll; NHS; Engrng.

O CONNOR, SCOTT; Union-Endicott HS; Endicott, NY; (Y); Boys Clb Am; Boy Scts; Computer Clb; Var Capt Bowling; JV Trk; Hon Roll; FL Inst Tech; Genetics.

O CONNOR, SEAN P; St Francis Prepartatory Schl; New York, NY; (S); 79/744; JV Var Bsbl; Capt JV Bowling; High Hon Roll; Hon Roll; Prfct Atten Awd; Bsbl Stdnt Athl Awd Hghst Acadmc Avg; Math.

O CONNOR, WILLIAM J; Averill Park HS; Averill Park, NY; (Y); 10/225; Am Leg Boys St; Ski Clb; Varsity Clb; Band; Concert Band; Jazz Band; Mrchg Band; Yrbk Bus Mgr; Var Crs Cntry; Var Socr; Pre-Med.

O CONNOR LITTLE, ROBERT; St Marys Acad; Glens Falls, NY; (S); 3/65; Cmnty Wkr; Drama Clb; 4-H; ROTC; Spanish Clb; Varsity Clb; Band; Color Guard; School Play; VP Pres Stu Cncl; Fan Day Essay Cntst Winner 86; Holy Cross; Officer.

O DEA, CATHERINE M; St Francis Prep; Middle Village, NY; (Y); Drama Clb; Stage Crew; Nwsp Stf; ST Regnts Schlrshp 86; Siena Clg.

O DELL, DENISE; Avoca Central HS; Avoca, NY; (Y); 6/43; Cmnty Wkr; FBLA; Chorus; Mgr School Play; Ed Yrbk Stf; Score Keeper; Trk; High Hon Roll; Hon Roll; NHS; Spec Svc Awd Cmmnty & Stu Cncl 86; Alfred Ag & Tech; Accntg.

O DELL, KEVIN JON; Ogdensburg Free Acad; Ogdensburg, NY; (Y); JV Var Crs Cntry; JV Var Trk; Im Vllybl; Regnts Schlrshp; Clarkson U Canton NY; Sci.

O DELL, SUSAN; Cortland JR SR HS; Cortland, NY; (Y); Office Aide; Band; Concert Band; Mrchg Band; Orch; Pep Band; Hon Roll; NHS; Mrchnd Band Awds 85; Bus.

O DONNELL, AMY C; Eden Central SR HS; Eden, NY; (Y); 18/163; Sec AFS; Band; Mrchg Band; School Musical; Nwsp Phtg; Nwsp Rptr; Yrbk Phtg; Stat Crs Cntry; NHS; Computer Clb; Regnts Schlrshp; Boston U; Intl Rltns.

O DONNELL, BRIDGET; Pulaski JR SR HS; Richland, NY; (Y); Church Yth Grp; Chorus; Color Guard; Csmtlgy.

O DONNELL, CAROL; Tonawanda JR SR HS; Tonawanda, NY; (Y); 6/195; French Clb; Red Cross Aide; Science Clb; Teachers Aide; Chorus; School Musical; High Hon Roll; NHS; Pres Schlr; Zonta Clb Schlrshp 86-88; Bio Stu Of Yr 84; Qlty SR 86; Delhi Agr & Tech U; Vet.

O DONNELL, DANIEL M; St Anthonys HS; East Northport, NY; (Y); 67/240; Nwsp Rptr; Yrbk Phtg; Im Bsktbl; Im Ftbl; JV Im Ice Hcky; Im Wt Lftg; High Hon Roll; NHS; Spanish NHS; Church Yth Grp; Brown Belt Jiu Jitsu 84-86; NY Regents Schlrshp Marron Military Inst; Kings Pt; Engrng.

O DONNELL, GERARD; Monsignor Farrell HS; Staten Island, NY; (Y); 151/291; Sec Soph Cls; Sec Jr Cls; Var Bsbl; JV Bsktbl; Im Bowling; Crs Cntry; Im Ftbl; Hon Roll; John Jay Coll Of Criminl Justc.

O DONNELL, JOHN; Ossining HS; Ossining, NY; (Y); 6/255; Church Yth Grp; JV Var Bsbl; Im Var Ftbl; High Hon Roll; Top 10 Schl Awd Mdl 85-86; Bus Stu Of Month/Slvr Mdl Latin I Ntl Cntst 85; Susquehanna U; Bus Admin.

O DONNELL, KATHLEEN; Franciscan HS; Peekskill, NY; (Y); 12/52; Church Yth Grp; Pep Clb; Spanish Clb; Varsity Clb; Nwsp Bus Mgr; Yrbk Stf; Var Cheerleading; Vllybl; Spanish NHS; Hopwood Schlrshp Lynchburg Coll 86; US Achvt Acadmy 85-86; Lynchburg Coll; Intrntnl Bus.

O DONNELL, KATHLEEN; St Catharine Acad; Bronx, NY; (Y); 38/198; Weschester Bus Inst Scholar; Weschester Bus Inst; Acctng.

O DONNELL, KATHLEEN; Susquehanna Valley HS; Binghamton, NY; (Y); Am Leg Aux Girls St; Mathletes; Trs Service Clb; VP Spanish Clb; Orch; Var L Crs Cntry; Var L Trk; High Hon Roll; Jr NHS; NHS; Pre-Med.

O DONNELL, KEN; Southampton HS; Southampton, NY; (Y); 24/110; VP Frsh Cls; Trs Soph Cls; VP Jr Cls; Var Bsbl; Var Ftbl.

O DONNELL, KERRY; Sacred Heart Acad; East Meadow, NY; (Y); Church Yth Grp; FTA; Office Aide; Service Clb; Spanish Clb; SADD; Chorus; Church Choir; Hon Roll; Psych.

O DONNELL, MARY ELLEN; St John The Baptist DHS; Oakdale, NY; (Y); Pres Ski Clb; Rep Soph Cls; Cheerleading; Powder Puff Ftbl; Socr; Hon Roll; Child Psych.

O DONNELL, MARY T; Floral Park Memorial HS; Floral Park, NY; (Y); 1/150; FBLA; Hst GAA; Nwsp Sprt Ed; Var Bsktbl; Co-Capt Pom Pon; JV Socr; Kiwanis Awd; NHS; Ntl Merit Ltr; Val; MA Inst Tech; Bio-Med Engrng.

O DONNELL, PHYLLIS MARIE; St Joseph By-The-Sea HS; Staten Island, NY; (Y); 2/239; Color Guard; Mrchg Band; Twrlr; High Hon Roll; Hon Roll; NHS; NEDT Awd; Sal; Stony Brook U; Med Technlgy.

O DONNELL, SHELLY; Hugh C William SR HS; Rensselaer Fls, NY; (Y); 56/145; Library Aide; Office Aide; Teachers Aide; Hon Roll; North County; Tchng.

O DONNELL, TARA; Yonkers HS; Yonkers, NY; (Y); Drama Clb; Excllnce Achvt Awds 84 & 85; Bus Awd 86; Writer.

O DRISCOLL, CLARE; St Barnabas HS; Bronx, NY; (S); 11/188; Church Yth Grp; Cmnty Wkr; Office Aide; Teachers Aide; Nwsp Stf; Hon Roll; NHS; Prfct Atten Awd; Spanish NHS; Subjct Reward Relgn 83; Hnrbl Mntn Relgn 85; Natl Sci Olympd-Distnctn Chem 85; Nrsng.

O DRISCOLL, ERIN; Westlake HS; Thornwood, NY; (Y); JA; Latin Clb; Color Guard; Spanish NHS; Saferides 85-86; Bus.

O FARRELL, JOHN J; Cardinal Spellman HS; Bronx, NY; (Y); Church Yth Grp; JV Bsbl; Var Capt Socr; JV Trk; NEDT Awd.

O GARA, PATRICK J; St Francis Prep; Douglaston, NY; (S); 100/755; Concert Band; Hon Roll; Bus.

O GORMAN, CONNIE; J C Birdlebough HS; Phoenix, NY; (Y); 5/180; Hosp Aide; Concert Band; Drm Mjr(t); Mrchg Band; Stat Bsktbl; High Hon Roll; Sr Key Bus Educ, Instrmntlst Mag Merit Awd 86; Sec.

O GORMAN, DENISE; Sacred Heart HS; Yonkers, NY; (S); 8/300; Church Yth Grp; Chorus; Church Choir; JV Var Bsktbl; Var Sftbl; Swmmng; JV Var Vllybl; Hon Roll; Sec NHS; Outstndg 1st Yr CYO 85; Outstndg Vllybl 84; Manhattan; Biochem.

O GRADY, DEBORAH; Catholic Central HS; Troy, NY; (Y); French Clb; Math Clb; Chorus; Yrbk Stf; Off Soph Cls; Off Jr Cls; Off Sr Cls; Off Stu Cncl; Socr; Sftbl; St Rose; Elem Ed.

O HAGAN, MAURA; Walt Whitman HS; Huntington, NY; (Y); 64/549; French Clb; Stage Crew; Stat Bsktbl; Score Keeper; French Hon Soc; High Hon Roll; NHS; Am And Wrld Hist Olympd Cert 84-85; Schlrshp Mt St Vincent 86; Mt St Vincent; Eng.

O HANLON, DENISE; New Dorp HS; Staten Island, NY; (Y); 2/597; Am Leg Aux Girls St; Hosp Aide; Intnl Clb; Pres Key Clb; Math Tm; Political Wkr; Service Clb; Spanish Clb; Stage Crew; Variety Show; Daily News Super Yth Awd 83-84 & 85-86; Regents Schlrshp Wnnr 85-86; Presdntl Acadmc Fitness Awd 85-86; SUNY At Albany; Bus.

O HARA, JOAN; Sacred Heart Acad; Massapequa, NY; (Y); Stage Crew; Nwsp Ed-Chief; Nwsp Rptr; Rep Stu Cncl; Bsktbl; Fld Hcky; Socr; Sftbl; Hon Roll; NHS; Artstc Merit Awd 85; Engl.

O HARA, KATE; Albertus Magnus HS; Pearl River, NY; (Y); Church Yth Grp; Varsity Clb; Stage Crew; Nwsp Rptr; Var Socr; NHS; Rotary Awd; Nanuet Rotary Schlrshp $800 86; U Of New Hampshire; Comm.

O HARA, KATHLEEN; Saint Barnabas HS; Bronx, NY; (Y); 72/189.

O HARA, MEGHAN; Bishop Grimes HS; Jamesville, NY; (S); NFL; Speech Tm; Yrbk Phtg; Yrbk Stf; Rep Soph Cls; Rep Jr Cls; Var Trk; High Hon Roll; Hmcmg Ct; Hmcmg Qn.

O HARA JR, PETER W; F D Roosevelt HS; Hyde Park, NY; (Y); 18/336; Boy Scts; Drama Clb; Exploring; Math Tm; Stage Crew; Hon Roll; NHS; Ntl Merit Ltr; Math Clb; Office Aide; US NROTC 4-Yr Schlrshp 86; NYS Regents Schlrshp 86; Engrng.

O HARE, PATRICK; Abraham Lincoln HS; Brooklyn, NY; (Y); Boy Scts; Office Aide; Yrbk Phtg; Yrbk Rptr.

O HEARN, BRENDAN; Northport HS; Northport, NY; (Y); Model UN; Political Wkr; Ed Nwsp Phtg; Ed Yrbk Phtg; Rep Soph Cls; Rep Jr Cls; Stu Cncl; Cit Awd; Hd Stu Exchng Dlgtn In Japan 85; Vtrns Admin Vlntr 83-86; Intl Affrs.

O HERIEN, JAMES; Stockbridge Valley HS; Munnsville, NY; (S); Cmnty Wkr; Pres Sec 4-H; Co-Capt Pep Clb; Science Clb; SADD; Nwsp Stf; Jr Cls; Stu Cncl; Timer; Cit Awd; M G Adams Awd 84; 4-H Veg Wnnr 85; Nrsg.

O KANE, ANN; Williamsville North HS; North Tonawanda, NY; (Y); 150/301; Sec Trs Church Yth Grp; JA; Chorus; School Musical; Score Keeper; JV Socr; Im Vllybl; Outstndng Yth Awd 86; Comm.

O KEEFE, DARCY; East Islip HS; East Islip, NY; (Y); Church Yth Grp; Band; Concert Band; Var Gym; Var Trk; Astronomer.

O KEEFE, DAVID; Bishop Ludden HS; Camillus, NY; (S); Boys Clb Am; Church Yth Grp; Cmnty Wkr; Lit Mag; Var L Bsktbl; High Hon Roll; Hon Roll; VP NHS; Bus Adm.

O KEEFE, JOHN M; Bishop Timon HS; Buffalo, NY; (Y); 3/150; Computer Clb; Quiz Bowl; Scholastic Bowl; Ed Yrbk Stf; Lit Mag; Var Capt Socr; High Hon Roll; NHS; Prfct Atten Awd; NY ST Rgnts Awd With Hnr 86; Sci Awd For Chem 85; ST U Of NY Bflo; Engrng.

O KEEFE, MICHAEL C; Franklin Acad; Malone, NY; (Y); 157/266; French Clb; Pep Clb; Ski Clb; Varsity Clb; JV Var Bsbl; JV Bsktbl; JV Var Ftbl; NY ST Regnts Schlrshp Wnnr 86; Niagara U; Hist.

O KEEFFE, SEAN; Lawrence HS; Cedarhurst, NY; (Y); Band; Var L Trk; JV Wrstlng; Hon Roll; MVP Vrsty Track Awd 84; Cabinetry Clb Trea 85-86; Bus.

O KELLY, SEAN; Saint Dominic HS; Oyster Bay, NY; (S); 12/119; Pres Church Yth Grp; Model UN; SADD; Nwsp Stf; Var Crs Cntry; Var Golf; NHS; Quiz Bowl; Scholastic Bowl; Little Leag Bsbl Coach; Amer Histry Awd-Hnrbl Mentn; St Johns U; Attrny.

O LEARLY, MIKE; Beacon HS; Beacon, NY; (S); 5/120; Sec Stu Cncl; Var Bsbl; Capt Ftbl; High Hon Roll; NHS; Comp Sci.

O LEARY, BARBARA; Buffalo Traditional HS; Buffalo, NY; (S); 1/111; Math Tm; Political Wkr; Spanish Clb; Varsity Clb; Yrbk Ed-Chief; Yrbk Phtg; Var Socr; Var Capt Sftbl; High Hon Roll; Val; Mech Engrng.

O LEARY, DAVID; St Francis Prep; Bayside, NY; (S); 56/736; Math Tm; Varsity Clb; Capt Socr; Hon Roll; Optimate Soc.

O LEARY, JOHN C; Beach Channel HS; Rockaway Park, NY; (Y); Computer Clb; Debate Tm.

O LEARY, KELLY; Whitesboro SR HS; Whitesboro, NY; (Y); Church Yth Grp; Hosp Aide; Library Aide; SADD; Church Choir; Variety Show; Rep Stu Cncl; Cheerleading; Powder Puff Ftbl; Trk; Geneseo; Speech Pthlgst.

O LEARY, MICHAEL S; Williamsville East HS; Williamsville, NY; (Y); 3/250; Am Leg Boys St; Pres FBLA; Hosp Aide; Math Clb; Science Clb; Ski Clb; Var L Socr; Var L Tennis; Bausch & Lomb Sci Awd; High Hon Roll; The Harvard/Radcliffe Club Bk Awd 86; 1st Pl St FBLA Bus Dynmcs Comp 85; 3rd Pl St FBLA 86; Duke; Engr.

O LEYAR, STEPHEN C; Irondequoit HS; Rochester, NY; (Y); 11/345; Boy Scts; Science Clb; Rep Sr Cls; Var Capt Tennis; Hon Roll; NHS; Ntl Merit Ltr; Prfct Atten Awd; Buffalo U; Engr.

O MALLEY, THERESA LEE; Troy HS; Troy, NY; (Y); 26/477; Drama Clb; Chorus; Concert Band; Drm & Bgl; Mrchg Band; School Musical; Sec Jr Cls; Sec Sr Cls; High Hon Roll; NHS; LIU; Brdcstng.

O MARA, MARY; Sweet Home SR HS; Amherst, NY; (Y); GAA; Ski Clb; Rep Soph Cls; Rep Jr Cls; Var L Swmmng; High Hon Roll; Hon Roll; NHS; NY ST U; Arch.

O MEALIA, KEVIN; Edison Tech HS; Rochester, NY; (Y); Church Yth Grp; Var Bsbl; Var Wrstlng; Hon Roll; Bus Mgmt.

O MELIA, TAMMY SUE; Lansingburgh HS; Troy, NY; (Y); Hosp Aide; Band; Concert Band; Jazz Band; Mrchg Band; School Musical; High Hon Roll; Jr NHS; NHS; Phrmcy.

O NEIL, BRENDA; Madrid-Waddington HS; Madrid, NY; (Y); Drama Clb; GAA; Spanish Clb; Stage Crew; Yrbk Ed-Chief; Pres Jr Cls; Var JV Bsktbl; Var JV Socr; Var JV Trk; Var JV Vllybl; Cazenovia; Child Devlpmnt.

O NEIL, JOHN; Moriah Central Schl; Port Henry, NY; (Y); 2/76; Church Yth Grp; French Clb; Drm & Bgl; Rep Stu Cncl; JV Var Bsktbl; High Hon Roll; Pres NHS; Awd Hghstg Frnch Regnts Mark 86; Math.

O NEIL, KIM; Copiague HS; Amityville, NY; (Y); 11/312; Yrbk Stf; Trs Stu Cncl; Bsktbl; Trk; Vllybl; Cit Awd; High Hon Roll; Sec NHS; Pres Schlr; Howard U Academic Schlrshp 85-86; Army Rotc Schlrshp 85-86; Howard U; Accntng.

O NEIL, LAMONT; Phillips Exeter Acad; Brooklyn, NY; (S); Church Yth Grp; Library Aide; Spanish Clb; Acpl Chr; Church Choir; School Musical; Stu Cncl; Trk; Dollar Awd 84; Stanford U; Pre-Law.

O NEIL, MIKE; Niagara Wheatfield HS; Niagara Falls, NY; (Y); French Clb; Ski Clb; Varsity Clb; VP L Bsbl; VP L Golf; Var Trk; Hon Roll; Law.

O NEIL, PATRICK T; Weedsport JR SR HS; Weedsport, NY; (Y); 6/81; Am Leg Boys St; French Clb; Math Tm; Spanish Clb; Var L Civic Clb; Var L Trk; High Hon Roll; Hon Roll; NHS; Church Yth Grp; Hi Quiz Tm.

O NEIL, SEAN MICHAEL; Our Lady Of Lourdes HS; Newburgh, NY; (Y); Drama Clb; Rep Frsh Cls; Rep Soph Cls; Var Bsktbl; Var Crs Cntry; Var Tennis; NHS; Hly Crss; Bus.

O NEIL, TIMOTHY B; North Tonawanda HS; N Tonawanda, NY; (Y); 26/407; Cmnty Wkr; Exploring; Concert Band; Jazz Band; Mrchg Band; Stu Cncl; Hon Roll; Computer Clb; Debate Tm; French Clb; Sweeney Hose Mem Schlrshp 86; Outstndng Musician Awd 86; Regnl Rollersktng Champ 83-84; RIT; Comp Engr.

O NEILL, ALICIA; Mt Saint Ursula HS; New York, NY; (Y); Girl Scts; Var JV Cheerleading; NEDT Awd; Librl Arts.

O NEILL, BRIAN; Brentwood HS; Great River, NY; (Y); 29/550; Science Clb; Var L Ftbl; Im Wt Lftg; Im Wrstlng; Hon Roll; St Schlr; Rcgntn Physcs Awd 85; Stoneybrook; Biolgcl Sci.

O NEILL, BRIDGET E; Williamsville North HS; Williamsville, NY; (Y); 26/301; Am Leg Aux Girls St; Sec Church Yth Grp; Pep Clb; Church Choir; Concert Band; School Musical; Yrbk Stf; JV Socr; High Hon Roll; NHS; Grove City Coll; Cmnctns.

O NEILL, CATHERINE; Our Lady Of Victory Acad; New York, NY; (S); 2/135; Church Yth Grp; Office Aide; SADD; Chorus; School Musical; Lit Mag; Rep Frsh Cls; Rep Soph Cls; Trs Jr Cls; Rep Stu Cncl; Math Awd 84; Stu Rcgntn Awd 84-85; Math.

O NEILL, CHRISTA; West Babylon SR HS; West Babylon, NY; (Y); 38/400; Pres Sec English Clb; Pres VP Chorus; School Musical; Yrbk Stf; Lit Mag; Var Capt Tennis; High Hon Roll; NHS; NY ST Rgnts Schlrshp 86; Outstndng Music Stu Awd 84-85; U Of MD; Erly Chldhd Educ.

O NEILL, GENEVIEVE; Palmyra-Macedon Central HS; Palmyra, NY; (S); 5/180; Am Leg Aux Girls St; Church Yth Grp; Math Clb; Concert Band; Jazz Band; Mrchg Band; Capt Var Tennis; Hon Roll; NHS; Ntl Merit Ltr; Envrnmntl Studies.

O NEILL, JEROME; Monroe JR SR HS; Rochester, NY; (Y); 1/152; Math Tm; Model UN; Jazz Band; Lit Mag; High Hon Roll; NHS; Awrns Theatr 86; Rochester Pblc Lbry Litry Cntst Wnr 1st Pl 86; Amer HS Math Exam Hnr Rl 86; Wrtng.

O NEILL, KAREN A; St Francis Prep; Flushing, NY; (S); 72/744; Cmnty Wkr; GAA; Band; Nwsp Stf; Var Capt Crs Cntry; Im Ftbl; Im Sftbl; Var Capt Trk; NHS; Optimate Soc 84-85.

O NEILL, KELLIE; The Ursuline Schl; Bronxville, NY; (Y); Hosp Aide; Ski Clb; Yrbk Stf; Rep Sr Cls; Sec Stu Cncl; Swmmng; Tennis; Trk; NEDT Awd; U Of DE; Sprts Med.

O NEILL, LOUIS F; Hunter College HS; Middle Village, NY; (Y); Pres CAP; FHA; Pres NFL; School Musical; School Play; Nwsp Ed-Chief; Nwsp Rptr; Yrbk Stf; VP Frsh Cls; Capt Bsbl; Mus Schlrshp Mannes Coll 84-85; Foundr Schl Nwspapr 82-85; Torpdo Dsmtlng.

O NEILL, PHILIP; Mc Kee Voc & Tech HS; Staten Island, NY; (Y); 2/306; Drama Clb; Band; School Musical; Nwsp Rptr; NCTE Awd; NHS; Ntl Merit Ltr; Amrcn Chem Soc Outstndng Studnt Awd 85; Natl Frgn Pol Assn Essay Wnr 86; Erly Schlastc Admsn To Coll; ST U At Buffalo; Arch.

O NEILL, SHEILA C; Rye HS; Rye, NY; (Y); 13/168; AFS; Cmnty Wkr; Hosp Aide; Nwsp Rptr; Var L Lcrss; High Hon Roll; Hon Roll; NHS; Rye HS Schlrshp Awd 86; U Of TX Austin; Cmmnctns.

O NEILL, TERRI A; Port Jervis HS; Westbrookville, NY; (Y); 17/189; 4-H; Co-Capt Math Tm; Spanish Clb; Varsity Clb; Yrbk Stf; L Mat Maids; High Hon Roll; NHS; Ntl Merit Schol; Pace U.

O NEILL, THOMAS B; Stissing Mountain JR SR HS; Red Hook, NY; (Y); 6/90; Church Yth Grp; Cmnty Wkr; Yrbk Stf; Bsktbl; Ftbl; Mgr(s); Cit Awd; DAR Awd; Gov Hon Prg Awd; High Hon Roll; Marist Coll; Envrnmntl Sci.

O REILLY, JAMES W; Miller Place HS; Sound Beach, NY; (Y); 7/195; Chess Clb; Drama Clb; Stage Crew; Lit Mag; JV Crs Cntry; Intl Thespian Soc 85; Young Schlrs Pgm SUNY Stoney Brook 84 & 85; Suffolk Zone Phys Educ Awd 85; SUNY Stony Brook; Mech Engrng.

O RILEY, MICHAEL F; Gouverneur Central Schl; Gouverneur, NY; (Y); Drama Clb; Speech Tm; School Musical; Var L Crs Cntry; Var Capt Trk; God Cntry Awd; VP NHS; Boy Scts; French Clb; Varsity Clb; St Lawrence Augsbury North Co Schlr 85; Regents Schlrshp 86; Eagle BSA 86; St Lawrence U; Lib Arts.

O SHAUGHNESSY, THOMAS; Xavier HS; Brooklyn, NY; (Y); Pres Camera Clb; French Clb; FFA; Hosp Aide; VP JA; ROTC; Nwsp Phtg; Yrbk Stf; SUNY.

O SHEA, DANIEL; Holy Trinity HS; Massapequa, NY; (S); Math Clb; Ski Clb; Spanish Clb; Var Ftbl; Var Lcrss; NEDT Awd; Engrng.

O SHEA, JANET M; Yorktown HS; Yorktown Height, NY; (Y); 11/319; Sec Dance Clb; French Clb; Sec German Clb; Key Clb; Political Wkr; School Musical; School Play; High Hon Roll; NHS; Band; Ntl Merit Fnlst 86.

O SHEA, JOHN F; Mount Saint Michael Acad; Yonkers, NY; (S); 40/103; Computer Clb; Hon Roll.

O SHEA, KAREN; Moore Catholic HS; Staten Island, NY; (Y); Art Clb; Church Yth Grp; Cmnty Wkr; Hosp Aide; Yrbk Stf; Stu Cncl; Sftbl; Hon Roll; NHS; Gnrl Exclnc 83; Cancr Crsd Citn 84; Captn JR Vrsty Sftbl 85; Englsh.

O SHEA, KATHY; Christ The King HS; Ridgewood, NY; (Y); 30/465; SADD; Frsh Cls; Soph Cls; Bsktbl; High Hon Roll; Hon Roll; Dsgn.

O SHEA, MAURA; Le Roy Central HS; Leroy, NY; (Y); 1/130; Math Tm; Varsity Clb; Yrbk Ed-Chief; JV Stu Cncl; Var Bsktbl; Var Socr; Var Trk; Var Vllybl; NHS; Ntl Merit Ltr; Ntl Ltn Exmntns Slvr Mdl Awd, Cum Laude Awd 85-86; Amer HS Math Exm Schl Wnnr 86; Med.

O SHEA, MICHELE; Sacred Heart Acad; Rockville Centre, NY; (Y); Church Yth Grp; Dance Clb; Hosp Aide; Library Aide; Math Clb; Chorus; Yrbk Bus Mgr; Tennis; Hon Roll; Ntl Hon Soc 85-86; Boston Coll; Engl.

O SHELL, KEVIN; Horseheads HS; Horseheads, NY; (Y); Church Yth Grp; Var Socr; Math.

O SULLIVAN, BRIAN; New Rochelle HS; New Rochelle, NY; (Y); Boy Scts; Camera Clb; High Hon Roll; Hon Roll; NHS; Aerospace Engrng.

O SULLIVAN, GRACE; St John The Baptist HS; Massapequa Pk, NY; (Y); 29/556; Church Yth Grp; Cmnty Wkr; Math Clb; Office Aide; Speech Tm; Teachers Aide; Mrchg Band; Nwsp Rptr; High Hon Roll; Scranton U Schlstc Achvt & Loyola Coll Pres Schlrshp 86; U Of Scranton; Law.

O SULLIVAN, KELLY; Riverhead HS; Riverhead, NY; (Y); DECA; Trs GAA; Pres Science Clb; Trs Frsh Cls; Var Fld Hcky; Im Vllybl; Hon Roll; Jr NHS; Aspiring Toward Excllnce In Math 86; Bus.

O-KANE, NEIL T; Mount St Michael HS; Bronx, NY; (S); 2/309; Chess Clb; Church Yth Grp; Rep Stu Cncl; Crs Cntry; Trk; High Hon Roll; NHS; Prfct Atten Awd; Mt St Michael Acad Schlrshp 83-86.

OAKDEN, LAURIE; Hilton Central HS; Hilton, NY; (Y); Church Yth Grp; Cmnty Wkr; Pres VP 4-H; Sec Sr Cls; Var Cheerleading; Coach Actv; Mgr(s); Capt Swmmng; 4-H Awd; High Hon Roll; Bus Adm.

OAKES, JULIE A; Massena Central HS; Massena, NY; (Y); Red Cross Aide; Powder Puff Ftbl; Stat Socr; Var Vllybl; NHS; Regnts Schlrshp 86; U Of Rochester; Optcl Engrg.

OAKES, PAM; Shenendehowa HS; Clifton Park, NY; (Y); AFS; Aud/Vis; Church Yth Grp; DECA; Intnl Clb; SADD; Off Jr Cls; High Hon Roll; Hon Roll; Drew U; Pol Sci.

OBEL, KENNETH; Hunter College HS; Bronx, NY; (Y); Pres Radio Clb; Nwsp Ed-Chief; Rep Jr Cls; Var Tennis; Ntl Merit SF.

OBERER, JAMIE; Byron-Bergen Central HS; Byron, NY; (Y); Hon Roll; Prfct Atten Awd; Cosmetlgy.

OBERHUBER, LUKAS C; Green Meadow Waldorf Schl; Cambridge, MA; (Y); Chorus; School Musical; Yrbk Phtg; Yrbk Stf; Lit Mag; Rep Frsh Cls; Rep Sr Cls; Bsktbl; Socr; Elec Engrng.

OBERMAN, STACY; Eastchester HS; Scarsdale, NY; (Y); Office Aide; Spanish Clb; SADD; Y-Teens; Nwsp Stf; Spnsh Awd 83; Pre-Law.

OBREZA, CATHERINE; Herkimer HS; Herkimer, NY; (Y); 2/120; Am Leg Aux Girls St; Art Clb; Pres French Clb; JA; Model UN; Chorus; Stage Crew; Nwsp Rptr; Yrbk Stf; Rep Stu Cncl; Engrng.

OBRIEN, MARK; Newark HS; Newark, NY; (Y); Am Leg Boys St; Church Yth Grp; Drama Clb; Spanish Clb; Thesps; Acpl Chr; Band; Chorus; Church Choir; Concert Band; Mark Sherman Awd 85-86; Calvin Coll; Ed.

OBRIST, MICHAEL; C-N-S HS; Clay, NY; (S); 1/623; Mathletes; Math Tm; Ski Clb; JV Ftbl; Wt Lftg; Bausch & Lomb Sci Awd; High Hon Roll; Jr NHS; NHS; Physcs.

OBSTARCZYK, CHERYL; Mount Saint Joseph Acad; Buffalo, NY; (Y); 1/44; VP Drama Clb; School Musical; Yrbk Ed-Chief; Var Badmtn; Var Sftbl; Var Vllybl; High Hon Roll; NHS; Val; Panhellenic Assoc Awd 86; Verna Zimmerman Awd 86; Sportsmnshp Assoc 86; Canisius Coll; Bus Mgmt.

OCALLAGHAN, SHEILA; Saint Marys Girls HS; Mineola, NY; (Y); Dance Clb; Girl Scts; Rep Frsh Cls; Rep Soph Cls; Rep Jr Cls; Pres Sr Cls; Rep Stu Cncl.

OCASIO, WILFREDO; Murry Bergtraum HS; Brooklyn, NY; (Y); 5/28; Boy Scts; Debate Tm; Library Aide; Teachers Aide; Stage Crew; Yrbk Rptr; Yrbk Stf; Rep Jr Cls; Crs Cntry; Gym; Model Congress-Sen 86; Columbia; Biochem Sci.

OCCHIUZZO, MICHAEL; St Anthonys HS; Brentwood, NY; (Y); Art Clb; Chess Clb; Computer Clb; Drama Clb; School Musical; School Play; Variety Show; Nwsp Rptr; Nwsp Stf; Yrbk Rptr; Dun Scotus; Fordham U; Cmmnctns.

OCHSENFELD, TINA; Clarkstown HS South; Bardonia, NY; (Y); Pres Sec Band; Mrchg Band; Var Bsktbl; VP NHS; German Clb; Rep Stu Cncl; JV Sftbl; JV Vllybl; Pre-Med.

OCHSNER, VICKI; Onodaga HS; Lafayette, NY; (Y); Art Clb; GAA; Spanish Clb; SADD; Varsity Clb; Chorus; Variety Show; JV Bsktbl; Var Score Keeper; JV Socr; Morrisville; Rstrnt Mngmnt.

OCKER, KAREN; Ramstein American HS; Apo New York, NY; (Y); Library Aide; Teachers Aide; Yrbk Stf; JV Bsktbl; JV Vllybl; High Hon Roll.

OCONNELL, HOLLY; Burnt Hills Bauston Lake HS; Burnt Hills, NY; (Y); AFS; Drama Clb; Intnl Clb; Chorus; Orch; School Musical; School Play; Fld Hcky; Hon Roll; Intl Relations.

OCONNELL, KERRY; Frontier Central HS; Buffalo, NY; (Y); Church Yth Grp; FBLA; Pep Clb; Ski Clb; Band; Concert Band; Mrchg Band; Yrbk Stf; Hon Roll; Bus.

OCONNELL, LORAINE; Deposit Central Schl; Deposit, NY; (Y); 18/85; Sec Pres Church Yth Grp; Cmnty Wkr; Office Aide; Teachers Aide; Mrchg Band; Fld Hcky; Aud/Vis; GAA; SADD; Varsity Clb; Fll Schlrshp C Olympc Cmp-Fld Hcky 85; Jhn Rssll Awd-Outstndng Stu-Cmnty Affrs 86; Cobleskill; Scrtrl Sci.

OCONNELL, PATTIE; Commack HS North; Commack, NY; (Y); 30/340; Drama Clb; Math Clb; Math Tm; Q&S; Spanish Clb; Teachers Aide; Thesps; Chorus; School Play; Frsh Cls; Bryant Coll; Actuarial Math.

OCONNOR, BERNADETTE; Shenendehowa HS; Clifton Park, NY; (Y); Drama Clb; Chorus; School Musical; School Play; Im Cheerleading; JV Sftbl; High Hon Roll; Hon Roll; Old Dominion U; Crim Jstc.

OCONNOR, CATHY; Monroe Woodbury HS; Highland Mills, NY; (Y); Computer Clb; Drama Clb; Office Aide; Teachers Aide; Chorus; School Musical; Yrbk Stf; Socr; Vllybl; Sectrl Study.

OCONNOR, DAVE; Bethpage HS; Bethpage, NY; (Y); 53/303; Church Yth Grp; Band; Mrchg Band; School Musical; Variety Show; Var Socr; High Hon Roll; Hon Roll; NYSSMA Drum Solo Lvl 6 Rtng A 85; Music.

OCONNOR, DAVID; Weedsport Central HS; Weedsport, NY; (Y); Church Yth Grp; French Clb; School Play; Trs Frsh Cls; Trs Soph Cls; Trs Jr Cls; Bsbl; Ftbl; Swmmng; NY ST Rgnst Schlrshp 86; Ntl Prsbytrn Schlrshp 86; Coll Wooseter; Lbrl Arts.

OCONNOR, ERIN; Lansingburgh HS; Troy, NY; (Y); Varsity Clb; School Play; Pres Frsh Cls; Pres Soph Cls; Pres Jr Cls; Capt JV Bsktbl; Capt JV Sftbl; Var Trk; Pres Jr NHS; NHS; Bus.

OCONNOR, JEFF; Mohonasen HS; Schenectady, NY; (Y); Ski Clb; Bsktbl; Ftbl; Trk; Hon Roll; Vetrinary Medicine.

OCONNOR, JEFFREY L; Cobleskill Central Schl; Cobleskill, NY; (Y); Bsbl; Bsktbl; NY ST Regents 86; ST U Of NY; Pol Sci.

OCONNOR, JOHN; St John The Baptist HS; Selden, NY; (Y); 60/551; Im Bsbl; Var Capt Ftbl; Var Capt Lcrss; Hon Roll; NY Daily News Ath Wk Awd 85; CHSFA Plyr Wk Ftbl 85; Nassau-Suffolk Cath HS Lacross All Lg Awd 86; Bus.

OCONNOR, LOREN; Smithtown HS East; Nesconset, NY; (Y); Hosp Aide; Sec Service Clb; SADD; Mrchg Band; Symp Band; Yrbk Stf; Var Socr; JV Var Vllybl; Hon Roll; Cmnty Wkr; Physcl Therapy.

OCONNOR, MICHELLE; Mahopac HS; Carmel, NY; (Y); 72/409; Red Cross Aide; Ski Clb; SADD; Var Gym; Stat Socr; Im Swmmng; Im Trk; High Hon Roll; Hon Roll; NHS; Chem.

OCULIAN, JOSEPH; James Monroe HS; Bronx, NY; (Y).

ODDE, RONALD; Hutchinson Central Technical HS; Buffalo, NY; (Y); Computer Clb; Capt Debate Tm; Drama Clb; Math Tm; NFL; Scholastic Bowl; Science Clb; Speech Tm; Hon Roll; Ntl Merit Ltr; Comp Engrng.

ODDO, JOANNE; Herbert H Lehman HS; Bronx, NY; (Y); JA; Band; Orch; Hon Roll; NHS; Legal Sec.

ODDO, SAMANTHA LYNNE; Lake George Central HS; Lake George, NY; (Y); 4/72; Girl Scts; Chorus; Yrbk Stf; High Hon Roll; Hon Roll; Jr NHS; NHS; Rotary Yuth Exch Stdnt Brazil 85-86; Bus-Prof Wmns Awd, Outstndng Acad Achvt Awd Schl Bd 86; Siena Coll; Intl Bus.

ODE, DAWN; Mount Mercy Acad; Buffalo, NY; (Y); FHA; Office Aide; Chorus; Church Choir; JV Badmtn; JV Bowling; Var Cheerleading; Hilbert; Acctnt.

ODIAN, MICHAEL; Polytechnic Preparatory Countr Day Schl; Staten Island, NY; (Y); Band; Chorus; Bsbl; Socr; Crdts 83-85; Schlrshp Glkpr Cmp 83; Natl Chmstry Exm 85; Vet Med.

ODLE, SARAH; James E Sperry HS; Henrietta, NY; (Y); 50/271; Cmnty Wkr; Office Aide; G J Jacobson Mem Awd 86; Monroe CC; Sec Math Ed.

ODOM, KELSEY; Bishop Loughlin HS; Brooklyn, NY; (Y); Boy Scts; Church Yth Grp; Computer Clb; Church Choir; Drm & Bgl; Yrbk Stf; Ntl Merit Ltr; Prfct Atten Awd; VFW Awd; Yth Ldrshp Pgm Awd 84; Archtr.

ODONNELL, PATRICK; Linton HS; Schenectady, NY; (Y); Church Yth Grp; JA; JCL; Latin Clb; Swmmng Tm; YMCA Athletic Clb; Awd For Latin Poetry; Niagra; Advertising.

ODRZYWOLSKI, JODYLINN; Union Springs Central HS; Auburn, NY; (Y); Drama Clb; Sec 4-H; Chorus; Color Guard; School Musical; School Play; JV Sftbl; Pre-Law.

OEHLER, LORI; Byron-Bergen HS; Bergen, NY; (Y); Am Leg Aux Girls St; Cmnty Wkr; Sec French Clb; VP FTA; Nwsp Ed-Chief; Var Capt Cheerleading; 4-H Awd; NHS; Amer Lgn Ortrcl Cnst Schl & Cnty Wnnr 86; Stu Cmnty Ctr Bd Dir 84-86; Stu Mck Trls Grp 86; Pltcl Sci.

OEHLSCHLAGER, KRISTINE; Carmel HS; Carmel, NY; (Y); Church Yth Grp; French Clb; Leo Clb; Church Choir; Orch; School Musical; Var Socr; Hon Roll; Prfct Atten Awd; Most Outstndng Stu Typing, Cncrt Mistress Orch 85-86; Chem.

OELCHER, SHANNON; Smithtown HS East; Saint James, NY; (Y); Church Yth Grp; DECA; SADD; Thesps; VP Chorus; Church Choir; School Musical; Symp Band; Jr NHS; NHS; NY St Schls Music Assn Singing & French Horn Solo Comp 83-86; Hotel/Rsrt Mgmnt.

OFFER, ORNA; Yeshiva University HS For Girls; New York, NY; (Y); Temple Yth Grp; Yrbk Phtg; Var Bsktbl; NY ST Regents Scholar 86; NYU; Law.

OFFHAUS, MINDY; Gowanda Central HS; Gowanda, NY; (Y); 19/125; Cmnty Wkr; Ski Clb; Spanish Clb; SADD; Band; Chorus; Color Guard; Concert Band; Flag Corp; Mrchg Band; Millard Fillmore Schl Nrsng.

OGDEN, ELEANOR; Centereach HS; Selden, NY; (Y); Rep Jr Cls; Var Cheerleading; JV Vllybl; High Hon Roll; Hon Roll; NHS; Kickline 84-86.

OGDEN, LINDA; Rocky Point JR-SR HS; Rocky Point, NY; (S); 2/204; Var Sec German Clb; Thesps; Concert Band; Madrigals; School Musical; Yrbk Stf; Lit Mag; NHS; Sal; Drama Clb; Congrss-Bundestag Yth Exchng Pgm 84-85; Intl Reltns.

OGDEN, SUSANNE; Living Word Acad; Fayetteville, NY; (S); Church Yth Grp; Ski Clb; L Var Trk; Var L Vllybl; High Hon Roll; Hon Roll; Bible Quizzing 83-85.

OGI, AMY; Fairport HS; Fairport, NY; (Y); 37/600; Drama Clb; French Clb; Sec Trs Model UN; SADD; Rep Sr Cls; Rep Stu Cncl; Hon Roll; NHS; School Musical; School Play; Lthrn Brthd Schlrshp 86; Rgnts Schlrshp 86; Grove City Coll; Bio.

OGNIBENE, VINCENT; Christ The King Regional HS; Brooklyn, NY; (Y); 4/400; Art Clb; Church Yth Grp; Cmnty Wkr; Computer Clb; Exploring; Science Clb; Y-Teens; Ftbl; Wt Lftg; Wrstlng; Genorosso Pope Schlrshp, Rgnts Schlrshp, 5 Pct Awd 86; St Johns U; Law.

OGOZALEK, JENNIFER; Kings Park SR HS; Kings Park, NY; (Y); 66/485; Church Yth Grp; Band; Concert Band; Mrchg Band; Pep Band; Rep Frsh Cls; Rep Soph Cls; Rep Stu Cncl; Tennis; NHS; NYSSMA Flute Duet & Solo 84; Lawyer.

OGRODNIK, MARNI; Plainedge HS; N Massapequa, NY; (Y); Nwsp Ed-Chief; Lit Mag; Cmnty Wkr; Library Aide; SADD; Temple Yth Grp; 2nd Nassau Cnty Yung Authrs, Dsgnd Promo Pstr HS Muscl, Yrbk Art Ed 86; Fash Inst Tech; Fash Dsgn.

OH, ELAINE; Roosevelt HS; Scarsdale, NY; (Y); Church Yth Grp; Chorus; Nwsp Rptr; Yrbk Rptr; Rep Frsh Cls; Var Swmmng; Mgr Var Tennis; High Hon Roll; Sec NHS; Ntl Merit Ltr; Hnrs In Piano 84-86; Bk Awd 86; Natl Hnr Rl Bk Awd 86; Cornell U.

OHALLORAN, PATRICIA M; St Barnabas HS; Bronx, NY; (Y); 43/173; Sec Trs French Clb; Red Cross Aide; JV Twrlr; Prfct Atten Awd; NYS Rgnts Schlrshp 86; Manhattan Coll; Econ.

OHANIAN, JOHN; Christ The King R HS; Forest Hills, NY; (Y); 194/447; Boy Scts; Var Bsbl; Mst Imprvd Plyr Awd Bsbll 86; Hon Awd Attng Avg 80% Bronze Awd 84; St Johns U; Comp.

OHARA, EILEEN; Nanuet SR HS; Nanuet, NY; (Y); Church Yth Grp; Stat Bsbl; Var JV Cheerleading; Var Capt Fld Hcky; JV Lcrss; Score Keeper; JV Sftbl; Hon Roll; NHS.

OHERN, KELLY; Westhill HS; Syracuse, NY; (Y); Pep Clb; Ski Clb; Chorus; School Musical; Swing Chorus; Variety Show; Var Capt Cheerleading; All Cnty Chorus 86; MVP Chrldng 86; People To People HS Stu Ambssdr Prg 85-86; Onondaga CC; Tchng.

OHLAND, MARK; Liverpool HS; Liverpool, NY; (Y); 67/861; Church Yth Grp; Acpl Chr; Concert Band; Jazz Band; Variety Show; Lit Mag; Hon Roll; Jr NHS; NHS; Spanish Clb; Engrng.

OHLANDT, DARIN; John Jay SR HS; S Salem, NY; (Y); Boy Scts; Church Yth Grp; Latin Clb; Chorus; Rep Stu Cncl; Var Swmmng; JV Trk; High Hon Roll; VP Jr NHS; NHS.

OHMAN, PETER; Franklin Acad; Malone, NY; (Y); Church Yth Grp; French Clb; Hosp Aide; Intnl Clb; Model UN; Ski Clb; Band; Jazz Band; Rep Soph Cls; JV Bsbl; Local Ski Tm No 1 84-85; Amnesty Intl; Boston Coll; Bus.

OHMANN, KYLE; Saranac Lake HS; Saranac Lk, NY; (Y); Boy Scts; Church Yth Grp; Computer Clb; Ftbl; Prfct Atten Awd; Elzbth Mrcn Mem Cmptr Sci Schlrshp 86; Potsdm ST Coll; Cmptr Sci.

OHMSTEDT, MARGUERITE; Saratoga Springs HS; Saratoga Springs, NY; (Y); 32/465; FBLA; Key Clb; Radio Clb; SADD; High Hon Roll; NHS; Ntl Merit Ltr; Semi Fnlst Ntl Hspnc Schlr Awd 86; Spanish Achvt Awd 84; Acadmc Achvt Awd 84; Northeastern U; Civil Engr.

OHSTROM, KELLY G; Hornell HS; Hornell, NY; (Y); 17/204; Art Clb; Latin Clb; Ski Clb; SADD; Band; Chorus; Church Choir; Yrbk Phtg; Yrbk Rptr; Yrbk Sprt Ed; 86 Regents Schlrshp 86; Awd Merit Art 86; Buffalo ST; Dsgn.

OKAL, CHERYL; Alden Central HS; Alden, NY; (Y); Girl Scts; Spanish Clb; SADD; Teachers Aide; Chorus; Church Choir; Yrbk Stf; Prfct Atten Awd; Mth.

OKEEFE, PAMELA; New Rochelle HS; New Rochelle, NY; (Y); 218/550; Boys Clb Am; Church Yth Grp; Library Aide; Service Clb; Sftbl; Westchester CC; Accntng.

OKOLIE, CORDELIA; Murry Bergtraum HS; Brooklyn, NY; (Y); Library Aide; Math Tm; Office Aide; Quiz Bowl; NHS; Cmmnty Ovrrch Pgmg Achvmnt Awd 86; Awd Dly Nws Acdmc Olympc Tm 86; Cert Excllnc Engl 86; Law.

OKONCZAK, KIM; John F Kennedy HS; Cheektowaga, NY; (Y); Drama Clb; Office Aide; PAVAS; Band; School Musical; Yrbk Bus Mgr; Yrbk Stf; Var Crs Cntry; Bryant; Trvl.

OKOYE, AMOGECHUKWU; Amityville Memorial HS; Massapequa, NY; (Y); Church Yth Grp; Key Clb; Office Aide; Band; Mrchg Band; Hon Roll; NHS; Outstndng Negro Stu Schlrshp Fund; Psychlgy.

OLA, UCHE O; Bronx H S Of Science; Bronx, NY; (Y); Library Aide; Teachers Aide; Bsktbl; Wt Lftg; Elec Engrng.

OLACIREGUI, INGRID; St Peters H S For Girls; Rutherford, NJ; (Y); Chorus; Engrng.

OLADAPO, DELE; Mc Kee Technical HS; Staten Island, NY; (Y); 33/306; Trk; Hon Roll; Prfct Atten Awd; Buffalo ST U; Elec Engrng.

OLAFSON, STEVEN; East Islip HS; E Islip, NY; (S); 1/425; Aud/Vis; Computer Clb; Capt Math Tm; Nwsp Rptr; High Hon Roll; Pres Chess Clb; Ntl Merit Ltr; Val; Stu Agnst Drvng Drnk Pres 84-86; Natl Hnr Soc Chrmn 85-86; Engrng.

OLCOTT, DOUG; West Hempstead HS; West Hempstead, NY; (Y); Yrbk Phtg; Yrbk Sprt Ed; Yrbk Stf; Var Capt Socr; Hon Roll; MVP Vrsty Sccr 84-85; Capt Vrsty Sccr 85-86.

OLDS, ELIZABETH M; The Fieldston Schl; New York, NY; (Y); Cmnty Wkr; Orch; Var L Crs Cntry; Ntl Merit SF; Physcs.

OLEA, JOHN; Thomas Alva Edison HS; Flushing, NY; (Y); 25/400; Boy Scts; CAP; SADD; Bowling; Hon Roll; SUNY; Comp Sci.

OLEARY, JENNIFER; Hauppauge HS; Smithtown, NY; (Y); Cmnty Wkr; German Clb; Var Gym; JV Trk; High Hon Roll; Hon Roll; NHS; Prfct Atten Awd; NY ST Summer Schl Arts 85; Boces 2 InstGATE Yth Summr Sessn 86; Art Wrk 85-86; Art.

OLEARY, SUE; Albany HS; Albany, NY; (Y); 44/600; Exploring; 4-H; French Clb; Ski Clb; Stu Cncl; JV Var Cheerleading; Hon Roll; Cert Of Merit In Frnch 84; NY ST U Bfl; Bio Chmstry.

OLECHNA, SHELLEY; Chatham HS; Chatham, NY; (Y); 116/165; Dance Clb; Hosp Aide; Ski Clb; SADD; Chorus; Drill Tm; Im Gym; Im Sftbl; Im Vllybl; Hudson Valley NY; Soc Wrkr.

OLECHOWSKI, KRISTIN; Bishop Scully HS; Amsterdam, NY; (Y); Spanish Clb; SADD; Church Choir; Yrbk Stf; High Hon Roll; Awds In Span, Outstndng Bus 86; Snts Const Co Mem Awd 86; Chldrns Aid Soc Grnt 86; Herkimer Community Coll; Travel.

OLENAHAN, KERRI; Holy Trinity HS; Hicksville, NY; (Y); Service Clb; Bio.

OLENDER, JEFFREY J; Msgr Farrell HS; Staten Island, NY; (Y); 122/305; Cmnty Wkr; Computer Clb; Spanish Clb; Im Bsktbl; JV Im Ftbl; Im Sftbl; Cit Awd; High Hon Roll; Hon Roll; Rgnts Schlrshp 86; 1st Pl Essay Cntst 82; CUNY; Med.

OLENDER, PATTY; Cardinal O Hara HS; Tonawanda, NY; (Y); Drama Clb; Quiz Bowl; Pres Service Clb; Sec Church Choir; Lit Mag; Im Badmtn; High Hon Roll; Hon Roll; NHS; Ntl Merit Ltr; NYS Regents Schlrshp 86; Diocesan Manus Christ Awd 86; Vrsty Letter For Acad 86; St Bonaventure; Brdcstng.

OLEVNIK, CATHERINE A; Brockport Central HS; Hamlin, NY; (Y); 30/330; French Clb; Cheerleading; High Hon Roll; Hon Roll; NHS; Regents Schlrshp 86; Albany ST U; Psych.

OLEWNICKI, JOSEPH; Archbishop Molloy HS; Maspeth, NY; (Y); SADD; Im Ftbl.

OLIN, LISA; Carmel HS; Carmel, NY; (Y); Varsity Clb; Orch; Bsktbl; Sftbl; Vllybl; High Hon Roll; Hon Roll; NHS.

OLINTO, LUIGI T; Mount St Michael HS; Bronx, NY; (Y); 7/291; Church Yth Grp; Y-Teens; Var Capt Ice Hcky; Hon Roll; Rgnt Schlrshp 86; Ice Hcky CHSHL League 85; Clarkson U.

OLIS, JACQUELINE; Queens Vo-Tech HS; Astoria, NY; (Y); 74/335; Library Aide; Teachers Aide; Band; Nwsp Rptr; Yrbk Stf; Coach Actv; Sftbl; Prfct Atten Awd; Admn Asst 86; Nrsry Schl Volunteer 86; Rn.

OLIVA, ANTHONY; Queensbury HS; Glens Falls, NY; (Y); Concert Band; Mrchg Band; Pep Band; JV Ftbl; JV Wrstlng; High Hon Roll; Hon Roll; Bio Sci.

OLIVARI, SUSAN; Rocky Point JR SR HS; Rocky Point, NY; (S); 8/167; English Clb; Concert Band; Mrchg Band; Im Bowling; JV L Fld Hcky; Score Keeper; Stat Sftbl; Hon Roll; Band; Jmp Rop Hrt-Amer Hrt Assn Awd 84; JV Fld Hcky Awd-Mst Imprvd Plyr 85; U Of Denver; Hotl-Restrnt Mgmt.

OLIVELLA, SUZANNE M; Notre Dame HS; Utica, NY; (Y); Cmnty Wkr; Model UN; ROTC; Drill Tm; Nwsp Rptr; Yrbk Stf; Lit Mag; Var Vllybl; High Hon Roll; Rgnts Schlrshp 86; Chem Engrng.

OLIVER, DENISE; Saugerties HS; Saugerties, NY; (S); 24/268; Sec Church Yth Grp; Pres French Clb; Girl Scts; Math Tm; Ski Clb; Varsity Clb; Band; JV Bsktbl; Hon Roll; NHS; Nyssma Flte & Pno 84-85; Girl Scts Slvr Awd 83; Frgn Lng.

OLIVER, JAMAL; Jamal Oliver HS; Bronx, NY; (Y); Art Clb; Science Clb; Var Bsktbl; JV Ftbl; Trk; Cit Awd; All ST Bsktbl 86; Duke U; Engrng.

OLIVER, JASON R; Livonia HS; Lakeville, NY; (Y); 17/131; Am Leg Boys St; Church Yth Grp; Computer Clb; Math Clb; Math Tm; Ski Clb; Teachers Aide; Mrchg Band; High Hon Roll; Hon Roll; Clakrson U; Elec Engrng.

OLIVER, KAREN D; Canaseraga Central HS; Canaseraga, NY; (Y); 1/17; Chorus; Church Choir; Color Guard; Yrbk Ed-Chief; Sec Stu Cncl; Sftbl; Vllybl; High Hon Roll; Pres NHS; Val; Regnts Schlrshp 86; Amercn Lgn Aux Awd 86; George Pratt Memrl Awd 86; Robert C Burgess Memrl Mth Awd 86; Hamilton Coll; Art.

OLIVER, KEITH; Valley Central HS; Ridgewood, NY; (Y); Rep Stu Cncl; Beta Tal Soc Stds Hon Soc 86; Army; Comp.

OLIVER, TAD; Turner/Carroll HS; Buffalo, NY; (Y); 10/97; Dance Clb; FBLA; SADD; Yrbk Stf; Bowling; Var Socr; Cit Awd; Hon Roll; Prfct Atten Awd; Bus Clb Awd 86; Econ Cls Awd 86; Cenisus Coll; Bus Mgmt.

OLIVERI, MICHELLE; Onondaga Central Schl; Nedrow, NY; (Y); Church Yth Grp; Spanish Clb; Hon Roll; NHS.

OLIVERI, PETER; Mount Saint Michael Acad; Bronx, NY; (S); 31/309; Var Socr; Hon Roll; NHS; Youth Fit Achvt Awd 80.

OLIVETO, ANTHONY J; The Bronx Science; New York, NY; (Y); Nwsp Ed-Chief; Lit Mag; Rep Stu Cncl; Capt Socr; NHS; Band; Capt Vllybl; Arista Hnr Soc 85; Semi Fnlst NCTE 85; Cmptr Soc Resdnt; Columbia U; Bus.

OLIVIER, MICHELE; Jericho SR HS; Jericho, NY; (Y); 2/200; Art Clb; VP Key Clb; VP Service Clb; SADD; Teachers Aide; Varsity Clb; Stage Crew; Nwsp Ed-Chief; Nwsp Stf; Yrbk Ed-Chief; Princeton Book Awd 85; Geo WA Schl Engrng Excllnce Awd 85; Columbia U Schltc Press Assn 1st Prize 83; Law.

OLIVIERI, AMY; Alden SR HS; Alden, NY; (Y); French Clb; SADD; Band; Yrbk Stf; Sec Frsh Cls; VP Soph Cls; Sec VP Stu Cncl; Var Tennis; Hon Roll; VP NHS; Pre-Law.

OLIVIERI, STEVEN R; West Seneca West SR HS; West Seneca, NY; (Y); 114/559; Spanish Clb; Rgnts Schlrshp Awd 86; Erie CC; Bus Adm.

OLIVIERO, ANTHONY J; Lawrence HS; Cedarhurst, NY; (Y); 44/414; CAP; Band; Drm & Bgl; Jazz Band; Mrchg Band; Orch; School Musical; Nwsp Rptr; Var Bowling; Mgr(s); NY ST Rgnts Schlrshp 86; Archon Svc Clb VP 85-86; ST U Of NY-STNYBRK; Bio Sci.

OLIVO, CRAIG L; Monroe Woodbury HS; Central Val, NY; (Y); 9/385; Am Leg Boys St; Model UN; Ski Clb; SADD; Varsity Clb; Band; Drm Mjr(t); Mrchg Band; Symp Band; Nwsp Rptr; Pursuit Excllnce Awd Arsa All ST Band 85-86; Law.

OLIVO, KIM; Gates Chili SR HS; Rochester, NY; (Y); Church Yth Grp; Service Clb; Band; Yrbk Stf; Rep Jr Cls; Var Sftbl; Var Tennis; Hon Roll; NHS; Office Aide; Socl Studs Awd 86; Mst Imprvd Ten 85; Mst Imprvd Sftbl 86; Elem Ed.

OLNEY, MELISSA; Rome Free Acad; Westernville, NY; (Y); 141/430; Church Yth Grp; Intnl Clb; Concert Band; Mrchg Band; Yrbk Stf; Hon Roll; Prfct Atten Awd; St Jhn Fshr Coll; Bus Mgmt.

OLOUGHLIN, CONSTANCE; Acad Of Mt St Ursula HS; New York, NY; (Y); Var Bsktbl; Im Trk; Acdmc All Amer Awd 85-86; Duke U; Comp.

OLP, WILL; Waterloo SR HS; Waterloo, NY; (Y); Intnl Clb; Var Ftbl; Var L Lcrss; Engrng.

OLSEN, GARRICK; John Jay SR HS; Goldens Bridge, NY; (Y); Cmnty Wkr; Math Tm; Service Clb; Spanish Clb; School Play; Variety Show; Lit Mag; JV Golf; High Hon Roll; Spanish NHS; Span III Awd 84-85; Natl Hon Soc 86; Bio Awd 84-85; Haverford; Pre Med.

OLSEN, LORI; Bayport-Blue Point HS; Bayport, NY; (Y); Church Yth Grp; Dance Clb; FBLA; Office Aide; Chorus; Flag Corp; Yrbk Stf; Capt Pom Pon; JV Trk; Jr NHS; Katherine Gibbs Ldrshp Awd 86; Katherine Gibbs; Sec.

OLSEVSKIS, KRISTINE; Liverpool HS; Liverpool, NY; (Y); 10/900; Dance Clb; Church Clb; Concert Band; Orch; School Musical; Stage Crew; Symp Band; Hon Roll; Jr NHS; NHS; Cert Of Hnr For Excptnl Acdmc Achvmt 85; Cert Of Merit 86; Math.

OLSON, BRIAN; Mechanicville HS; Mechanicville, NY; (S); 6/105; French Clb; Math Tm; Band; Concert Band; Pep Band; Yrbk Stf; Sec Sr Cls; Socr; High Hon Roll; NHS; U NV Pltsbrg; Jrnlsm.

OLSON, ELIZABETH; De Sales Catholic HS; Lockport, NY; (Y); 7/40; Church Yth Grp; Dance Clb; French Clb; Girl Scts; Nwsp Stf; Yrbk Stf; Cheerleading; Pom Pon; High Hon Roll; NHS.

OLSON, JOHN; Archbishop Molloy HS; Bellerose, NY; (Y); Church Yth Grp; Cmnty Wkr; Drama Clb; French Clb; Pep Clb; Service Clb; SADD; Chorus; JV Var Crs Cntry; JV Var Trk; Knghts Columbus Schlrshp 84.

OLSON, SCOTT; Randolph Central Schl; Conewango Valley, NY; (Y); 4-H; FFA; Var L Bsbl; Var L Bsktbl; JV Ftbl; Pltry Tm Rep NY ST FFA Natl Cnvntn 84-85; Phys Ed.

OLSON, STEPHANIE; Niagara Falls HS; Niagara Falls, NY; (Y); 17/250; Debate Tm; Drama Clb; French Clb; Model UN; Red Cross Aide; Rep Jr Cls; Hon Roll; Lion Awd; Ntl Merit Schol; NYS Rgnts Schlrshp 86-90; Whrlpl Mthrs Clb Schlrshp 86; SUNY At Buffalo; Aerspc Engnr.

OLSON, TRACY A; Earl L Vandermeulen HS; Mt Sinai, NY; (Y); Band; Concert Band; Mrchg Band; Yrbk Stf; Jr Cls; Stat Vllybl; Regents Schlrshp Wnnr 86; SUNY Albany; Law.

OLSZEWSKI, ROBERT T; Liverpool HS; Liverpool, NY; (Y); 5/816; Computer Clb; Exploring; VP JA; Ski Clb; School Musical; High Hon Roll; Jr NHS; NHS; Ntl Merit Ltr; Rochester Inst Of Tech; Comp Sc.

OLSZOWY, CHERYL R; Shenendehowa HS; Clifton Park, NY; (Y); 54/675; Trs Intnl Clb; SADD; High Hon Roll; NHS; NY Enrgy Comptn 3rd Pl 86; Rgnst Schlrshp 86-90; 4 Yr Air Frc ROTC Schlrshp 86-90; Rensslaer Polytech; Engrng.

OLVANY, BRIAN; Smithtown HS East; St James, NY; (Y); Church Yth Grp; SADD; Chorus; Stu Cncl; L Bsktbl; L Socr; Hon Roll; NHS; Poli Sci.

OLVER, TAMMY; Port Jervis HS; Sparrowbush, NY; (Y); 58/159; Church Yth Grp; Varsity Clb; VP Sr Cls; Var Socr; Var Sftbl; Hon Roll; Prfct Atten Awd; Rotary Awd; Girl Scts; Yrbk Stf; NYSPHAA Sftbl ST Champs 85; Mid Area Yth Bwlg Tourn 1st Pl 85; Elctrcl Engrng.

OLWELL, RUSS; Sachem HS; Holtsville, NY; (Y); 23/1500; German Clb; Pres Science Clb; Service Clb; Nwsp Stf; Ed Lit Mag; Off Frsh Cls; NHS; Ntl Merit Ltr; NY Bar Assoc Cert 86; Tollerton-Hood Essy Cntst Hon Mntn 85; Jrnlsm.

OMEARA, TOM; Perry Central HS; Perry, NY; (Y); 24/100; Varsity Clb; Bsktbl; Ftbl; Gym; Socr; Trk; Wrstlng; Hon Roll.

OMURA, GERALDINE; Bronx Science HS; New York, NY; (Y); Girl Scts; Math Tm; Office Aide; Teachers Aide; Off Jr Cls; Rep Sr Cls; NHS; Bowlng Tm Cptn 83-85; Medic Corona Vlntr Amblnc Corp 83-86; Ntl Hispnc Schlr Awd 86; Bio Med.

ONCIOIU, RALUKA; Forest Hills HS; Glendale, NY; (Y); Math Clb; Office Aide; Science Clb; School Musical; Var Socr; High Hon Roll; 1st Prize NYC Ptry Rctl Cntst 84-85-86; Tufts U; Int Rltns.

ONGJOCO, ROXANNE C S; Perry Central HS; Perry, NY; (Y); 2/87; French Clb; Math Tm; Varsity Clb; Concert Band; Jazz Band; Cheerleading; Bausch & Lomb Sci Awd; Hon Roll; NHS; Sal; Perry Vets Mem Schlrshp 86; Almn Assn Awd 86; Math, Lang, Sci, Comp Awds 86; Natl Sci Olympiad Cert; SUNY; Cmptr Sci.

ONGLEY, DENISE; Hamburg SR HS; Hamburg, NY; (Y); Church Yth Grp; High Hon Roll; Hon Roll; Jr NHS; Ambassador Coll; Spanish.

ONISK, TRACY; Coxsackie Athens Central HS; W Coxsackie, NY; (Y); Spanish Clb; Stu Cncl; Trk; High Hon Roll; Hon Roll.

ONORATO, DAWN; John H Glenn HS; E Northport, NY; (Y); Spanish Clb; Varsity Clb; L Var Bsktbl; Capt L Socr; L Var Vllybl; Hon Roll; Spanish NHS; All Lg 1st Tm Sccr 85; Bus Admin.

ONTKUSH, MARK; Niskayuna HS; Schdy, NY; (Y); German Clb; Ski Clb; Yrbk Stf; JV Crs Cntry; Var Wrstlng; Hon Roll; NHS; Pres Schlr; Germn Hnr Socty 86; Colby Coll; Secdry Ed.

ONYEIJE, IHEOMA U; Liverpool HS; Liverpool, NY; (Y); Church Yth Grp; Cmnty Wkr; Hosp Aide; Nwsp Rptr; Nwsp Stf; Var L Trk; Hon Roll; Jr NHS; NHS; 100 Hr & Achvt Awd Volnteer Vet Hosp 83; Outstdng Blck Stu Awd 85; Howard U; Pre-Med.

OOMMEN, SUSY; Sacred Heart Acad; Elmont, NY; (Y); 29/182; Red Cross Aide; SADD; Church Choir; School Musical; Yrbk Stf; Rep Stu Cncl; Var Trk; Hon Roll; NHS; Natl Ldrshp Orgnztn/Hnr Roll 83-86; NY St Regents Schlrshp 86; Jostens Ctzns Ldrsp Fndtn 86; U Of Scranton; Comp Sci.

OPALKA, THOMAS A; Perth Central Sch; Amsterdam, NY; (Y); 4/45; Debate Tm; School Play; Yrbk Stf; VP Sr Cls; Stu Cncl; Var Bsbl; Var Capt Bsktbl; High Hon Roll; NHS; NYS Rgnts Schlrshp 86; Army ROTC Schlrshp 3 Yr 86; Siena Coll; Intl Rltns.

OPETT, ROBERT O; Bloomfield Central HS; Honeoye Falls, NY; (Y); 26/106; Am Leg Boys St; Boy Scts; Latin Clb; Model UN; Rep Stu Cncl; JV Lcrss; JV Var Socr; Var L Trk; Var L Wrstlng; Scientfc Awd Outstndg JR 86; Bus.

OPLADEN, CATHERINE; Attica SR HS; Attica, NY; (Y); 74/172; AFS; Chorus; Color Guard; Swing Chorus; Nwsp Stf; Var L Bsktbl; Var L Score Keeper; Var L Socr; Var L Sftbl; Stat Vllybl; Triple Letter Athletic Awd 86; Nrsng.

OPPEDISANO, SANDRA A; Roosevelt HS; Yonkers, NY; (Y); 48/245; Office Aide; Flag Corp; Mrchg Band; Lit Mag; Capt Twrlr; High Hon Roll; Hon Roll; Ntl Merit Ltr; Rgnts Schlrshp Nrsng 86; Awd Schlstc Excllnc 85; Ntl Band Awd 85-86; Manhattan Coll; Comp Sci.

ORANGE, JOANN; Roy C Ketcham HS; Hughsonville, NY; (Y); 90/520; Girl Scts; Band; Cit Awd; High Hon Roll; NHS; Grl Scout Gold Awd 85; Phrmcy.

ORBACZ, BRIAN; Saugerties HS; Saugerties, NY; (S); 19/249; Math Tm; Spanish Clb; Band; Symp Band; JV Bsktbl; Mgr(s); JV Var Socr; Sftbl; Vllybl; High Hon Roll.

ORBE, LYDIA; Islip HS; Islip, NY; (Y); 36/257; Band; Concert Band; Mrchg Band; Stat Tennis; Trk; Hon Roll; Pres Schlr; Band Achvt Awd 84; SUNY.

ORCHARD, JULIE; Byron Bergen Central HS; Bergen, NY; (Y); French Clb; Pres FTA; Teachers Aide; Yrbk Sprt Ed; Yrbk Stf; Rep Stu Cncl; JV Ice Hcky; JV Vllybl; High Hon Roll; Hon Roll; Achvt Awd 84 & 85; Bus.

ORCUTT, CHERYL; Canisteo Central HS; Canisteo, NY; (Y); 34/78; Hosp Aide; Pep Clb; Chorus; Color Guard; Swing Chorus; Yrbk Stf; Rep Frsh Cls; Rep Soph Cls; Rep Jr Cls; Stu Cncl; Villa Maria; Nursing.

ORDON, DARLENE; Schalmont HS; Schenectady, NY; (Y); 23/150; Art Clb; Drama Clb; Trs French Clb; SADD; Yrbk Phtg; Ed Yrbk Sprt Ed; Lit Mag; Stu Cncl; Hon Roll; School Play; Pres Ftns Awd 86; ST U NY Oneonta.

OREILLY, DEIRDRE; Maria Regina HS; Hartsdale, NY; (Y); 2/166; Church Yth Grp; Key Clb; Nwsp Stf; Co-Capt Yrbk Ed-Chief; Lit Mag; Stu Cncl; High Hon Roll; Sec NHS; Sal; Rep Frsh Cls; 1st Pl Ntl Sci Olympd Chem 85; Police Essy Cntst 3rd Pl Wnnr 86; Engrng.

OREN, PHILLIP; Spackenkill HS; Poughkeepsie, NY; (Y); 3/167; Aud/Vis; Temple Yth Grp; Orch; School Musical; Stage Crew; Socr; NHS; Ntl Merit SF; Pres Schlr; Thomas J Watson Schlrshp 86; Ntl Merit Fnlst 86; Cornell U; Bio.

ORENBUCH, BARUCH; Hebrew Academy-Five Towns & Rockaway; W Hempstead, NY; (Y); #1 In Class; Debate Tm; Math Clb; Capt Math Tm; Capt Quiz Bowl; Ed Yrbk Stf; Rep Frsh Cls; Rep Soph Cls; Rep Jr Cls; Stu Cncl; NHS; Pre-Med.

ORFANIDES, KEITH; Haverling Cental Schl; Kanona, NY; (Y); 17/120; French Clb; Math Clb; VP Band; School Musical; Ed Nwsp Ed-Chief; Yrbk Stf; Stu Cncl; High Hon Roll; NY Math Lg Cert Merit, Pres Acdmc Ftns Awd 86; Natl Soc Stud Olymp 86; Math Educ.

ORGANISCIAK, MARK; Frankfort - Schuyler HS; Frankfort, NY; (S); 5/100; French Clb; Sec Key Clb; Varsity Clb; Trs Band; Concert Band; Jazz Band; Rep Stu Cncl; Var Crs Cntry; Var Ftbl; Var L Trk; Rensselaer Poly Inst; Elect Eng.

ORGANISCIAK, TRACY; Frankfort-Schuyler HS; Frankfort, NY; (S); Trs French Clb; Sec Key Clb; SADD; Band; Trs Frsh Cls; Trs Soph Cls; Trs Jr Cls; Rep Stu Cncl; JV Var Tennis; NHS; Nrsng.

ORGEK, MARK; Williamsville South HS; Buffalo, NY; (Y); Boy Scts; Church Yth Grp; Concert Band; Bowling; Socr; French Clb; Pep Clb; SADD; Band; Mrchg Band; Eagle Scout 86.

ORICCHIO, JANICE; Saunder Trades & Technical HS; Yonkers, NY; (S); 3/204; Nwsp Ed-Chief; Yrbk Bus Mgr; Sec Sr Cls; High Hon Roll; NHS; Suprntndnts Awd 84-86; Svc Mdl Stu Cncl 82; Excllnc Mdls Englh & Spnsh 82; All-A-Rnd Excllnc Awd 79.

ORLANDO, GAIL; Albertus Magnus HS; Haverstraw, NY; (Y); 41/175; Cmnty Wkr; Sec Sr Cls; JV Sftbl; Hon Roll; Pace U; Accntng.

ORLANDO, JOSEPH A; Harrison HS; Purchase, NY; (Y); Am Leg Boys St; Bsbl; Var Golf; JV Socr; Engineering.

ORLANDO, NICKY; Tottenville HS; Staten Isld, NY; (Y); Computer Clb; English Clb; Ski Clb; Varsity Clb; Yrbk Sprt Ed; Capt Ice Hcky; St Johns; Bus Admin.

ORLANDO, RICH; Roy C Ketcham HS; Poughkeepsie, NY; (Y); Im Bsktbl; High Hon Roll; Hon Roll; Jr NHS; Cmptr Sci.

ORLIAN, ETAN; Yeshiva Univ High School For Boys; Brooklyn, NY; (Y); Math Tm; Temple Yth Grp; Yrbk Stf; Gov Hon Prg Awd; High Hon Roll; Ntl Merit SF; 1st Ntl Bible Cont 84; 1st Ntl Cncl Yth Israel Essay Cont 85; Max Stern Schlr To Yeshiva U 85; Comp Sci.

ORMAN, WHITNEY; Williamsville East HS; E Amherst, NY; (Y); FBLA; Ski Clb; High Hon Roll; Hon Roll.

ORMOND, CYNTHIA; Solvay HS; Syracuse, NY; (Y); Art Clb; Pres Church Yth Grp; Cmnty Wkr; Hosp Aide; VP Intnl Clb; Sec Key Clb; Sec Spanish Clb; Trs SADD; Chorus; Church Choir; NYSSMA Solo Medal 86; Achvt Soc Studies 86; Hnrs Pgm 85; Soc Wrk.

ORMSBY, JENNIFER; Niagara Wheatfield HS; Niagara Falls, NY; (Y); Sec Pep Clb; Sec PAVAS; Sec Spanish Clb; Sec Band; Mrchg Band; School Musical; Swmmng; High Hon Roll; NHS; Tri M Music Hnr Soc 86.

ORMSBY, MICHELLE; Alfred-Almond Central Schl; Almond, NY; (Y); Church Yth Grp; Drama Clb; French Clb; Pres Sec FHA; Office Aide; Var JV Sftbl; JV Vllybl; High Hon Roll; Hon Roll; Chorus; Allegany Cnty Fair Ambssdr 85-86; Allegany Cnty Govt Intrnshp Pgm-2nd On Prjct 86; Law.

ORMSTEN, AUDREY; Mepham HS; Merrick, NY; (Y); Drama Clb; Model UN; Orch; Nwsp Stf; Tennis; Trk; Hon Roll; Comm.

ORNER, SCOTT B; Martin Van Buren HS; Bayside, NY; (Y); JA; Pres Temple Yth Grp; School Play; Stage Crew; Nwsp Sprt Ed; Capt Bowling; NYS Regnts Schlrshp 86; Queens; Libl Arts.

ORNSTEIN, SHARI L; Midwood HS; Brooklyn, NY; (Y); 64/632; French Clb; Intnl Clb; PAVAS; Teachers Aide; Chorus; School Musical; Yrbk Phtg; Hon Roll; Untd Fed Tchrs & Regnts Schlrshps 86; Hofstra U; Intl Buyr.

OROURKE, ANNE C; South Lewis Central HS; Constableville, NY; (Y); 7/87; GAA; Chorus; Yrbk Stf; Sec Soph Cls; Rep Stu Cncl; JV Var Socr; High Hon Roll; Hon Roll; St Schlr; Ski Tm; Sienna Grant 86; U Of VT Grant 86; U Of VT; Libl Arts.

ORR, DAVID H; Pulaski JR-SR HS; Pulaski, NY; (S); French Clb; Varsity Clb; Band; Mrchg Band; Var Bsbl; Var Bsktbl; Var Tennis; Snow Incntve Awd; James Madison U; Bus.

ORR, JAMES; Alexander Central HS; Alexander, NY; (Y); 2/82; Bausch & Lomb Sci Awd; High Hon Roll; Lion Awd; NHS; Ntl Merit Ltr; Sal; Ithaca Coll; Film.

ORR, KEREN; Evander Childs HS; Bronx, NY; (Y); 71/383; Church Yth Grp; Computer Clb; Debate Tm; 4-H; Key Clb; Service Clb; Speech Tm; School Play; Tennis; Vllybl; Hunter Coll; Liberal Arts.

ORRACA, MARIE; HS For The Hmnities; New York, NY; (Y); Drama Clb; School Musical; Variety Show; Nwsp Rptr; Nwsp Stf; :Drama.

ORRINGER, SCOTT; Union Endicott HS; Endwell, NY; (Y); Mathletes; VP Temple Yth Grp; Varsity Clb; Band; Rep Soph Cls; Rep Jr Cls; Var Crs Cntry; Var Tennis; Hon Roll; SUNY Buffalo; Bio.

ORSER, SHARON; Skaneateles Central Schl; Skaneateles Falls, NY; (S); Band; Lit Mag; High Hon Roll; NHS; Green Hunter Res Champ Cornell Open Horse Shw 86; Jordan Elbridge Horse Show Hgh Point 84; Resrch Bio.

ORSI, HEATHER; Sacred Heart Acad; Rockville Center, NY; (S); Debate Tm; Math Clb; Yrbk Stf; High Hon Roll; NHS.

ORSZAGH, THOMAS O; Aquinas Inst; Rochester, NY; (Y); Debate Tm; Exploring; NFL; SADD; Yrbk Bus Mgr; Var Swmmng; JV Trk; Tri ST U; Mech Engr.

ORSZULAK, DENISE; Attica SR HS; Cowlesville, NY; (S); 4/150; Sec Band; Concert Band; Mrchg Band; Trs Frsh Cls; Var Capt Bsktbl; Var Sftbl; Var Vllybl; Lion Awd; Sec NHS; All Cnty Bnd 83 & 84; Canisuis Coll; Bio.

ORTEGA JR, JOSE; Bishop Ford Central Catholic HS; Brooklyn, NY; (Y); Cmnty Wkr; Political Wkr; Nwsp Stf; Yrbk Stf; Pres Sr Cls; Rep Stu Cncl; JV Bsbl; Im Ftbl; Var Swmmng; Cit Awd; Hwrd Gldn Achvt Awd 86; Wshngtn Wrkshp Compltn Awd 85; Brklyn Diocese Cthlc Chrts REACH Awd 86; New Schl Social Research; Econ.

ORTEGA, LUIS F; August Martin HS; Brooklyn, NY; (Y); 16/433; Pres Church Yth Grp; CAP; Lit Mag; Hon Roll; NHS; St Schlr; NY ST Regnts Schlrshp 86; Embry Riddle Aerontcl U; Sci.

ORTELL, MARYROSE; Elmira Free Acad; Elmira, NY; (Y); Latin Clb; Spanish Clb; Yrbk Stf; Hon Roll; Engr.

ORTIZ, BENJAMIN; John Dewey HS; Brooklyn, NY; (Y); Science Clb; Band; School Musical; School Play; Sec Frsh Cls; Gov Hon Prg Awd; Jr NHS; Prfct Atten Awd; Vllybl; Natl Hspnc Schlr Awds Fnlst 85-86; NY Cty Cncl Schl & Cmnty Svc Ctatn 82-83; Phrmcy.

ORTIZ, CARMEN; William Howard Taft HS; Bronx, NY; (Y); Camera Clb; Church Yth Grp; Cmnty Wkr; Computer Clb; Dance Clb; Drama Clb; Hosp Aide; Library Aide; Office Aide; Teachers Aide; Lgl Sec.

ORTIZ, CARMEN A; Bushwick HS; New York, NY; (S); Church Yth Grp; Computer Clb; Teachers Aide; Off Jr Cls; Hon Roll.

ORTIZ, CHRISTINE; The Acad Of St Joseph; Pt Jeff Sta, NY; (Y); Art Clb; Library Aide; Pres Service Clb; VP Spanish Clb; Teachers Aide; Nwsp Stf; Im Var Socr; Hon Roll; Outstndng Contrbutn Stu Svc Clb 85-86; Modern Lang.

ORTIZ, DIANE; South Park HS; Buffalo, NY; (Y); Computer Clb; Color Guard; Stu Cncl; Hon Roll; NHS; UCLA; Comp Prog.

ORTIZ, GLORIA I; Cardinal Spellman HS; Bronx, NY; (Y); Computer Clb; Science Clb; Nwsp Rptr; Hon Roll; Bio.

ORTIZ, JEANETTE; Murry Bergtraum HS; Brooklyn, NY; (Y); Office Aide; Teachers Aide; Baruch Coll; CPA.

ORTIZ, MARILYN; Adlai E Stevenson HS; Bronx, NY; (Y); 100/683; Church Yth Grp; Band; Church Choir; Concert Band; Orch; School Play; Tennis; Hon Roll; JP Sousa Awd; Prfct Atten Awd; John Jay Coll; Crmnl Justc.

ORTIZ, MICHAEL; South Shore HS; Brooklyn, NY; (Y); 46/650; Chess Clb; CAP; Drill Tm; NHS; Boys Clb Am; Debate Tm; Exploring; Hspnc Alliance Schlrshp 86; Martin Luther King Schlrshp 86; NY Inst Of Tech; Elec Engr.

ORTIZ, NANCY; South Shore HS; Brooklyn, NY; (Y); PTA Awd For Prog & Chrtr 84; Comp Sci.

ORTIZ, ROSEANNE; Cardinal Spellman HS; Bronx, NY; (Y); Latin Clb; PAVAS; Chorus; School Play; Bsktbl; Hon Roll; Arch.

ORTIZ, SANTIAGO; All Hallows HS; New York, NY; (Y); 17/90; Boy Scts; Computer Clb; Drama Clb; Math Tm; Yrbk Phtg; Yrbk Stf; Var Bsbl; Im Bsktbl; Var JV Bowling; Mgr(s).

ORTIZ, TAMARA; Catherine Mc Auley HS; Brooklyn, NY; (S); 10/67; Dance Clb; Church Choir; Variety Show; Yrbk Phtg; Yrbk Stf; Pres Soph Cls; Rep Jr Cls; VP Sr Cls; VP Stu Cncl; Im Sftbl; Booster Clb Capt 85-86; Manhattan CC-BOROUGH; Bus Admi.

ORTIZ, WILSON; Holy Trinity Diocesan HS; Copiague, NY; (S); 2/403; French Clb; Math Tm; Rep Frsh Cls; Rep Soph Cls; Rep Jr Cls; Off Stu Cncl; Trk; High Hon Roll; NEDT Awd; IA Lang Cont Frnch Awd 84-85; Med Doc Cardlgst.

ORTON, DAVID W; South Glens Falls HS; Wilton, NY; (Y); 15/237; Boy Scts; Computer Clb; Hon Roll; NHS; Pres Schlr; Rensselaer Polytech; Nuclr Engr.

ORWAT, LYNETTE; Saint Marys HS; Cheektowaga, NY; (Y); 35/180; Yrbk Stf; Lit Mag; Rep Soph Cls; Rep Jr Cls; Sec Sr Cls; JV Var Cheerleading; JV Sftbl; Lion Awd; R F Kennedy Art Awd 2 Awds Jr 85-86; ST U Of NY Buffalo; Chld Ed.

ORYSZAK, LISA; Mt Mercy Acad; Buffalo, NY; (Y); French Clb; Hosp Aide; Speech Tm; SADD; Awd Prtcptn Ntl Frnch Tst 83; Vlntr Bfflo Gen Hosp 84 & 85; Canisius; Med.

OSA-YANDE, CADISA; Sweet Home SR HS; North Tonawanda, NY; (Y); Church Yth Grp; Latin Clb; Library Aide; Model UN; Church Choir; Nwsp Rptr; Ed Nwsp Stf; Yrbk Rptr; Yrbk Sprt Ed; Yrbk Stf; Sci Hnr Soc, Rgnl Frgn Lang Fair Frnch/Latin Transltn 85-86; Arch.

OSBORN, DEANNA L; Horseheads SR HS; Horseheads, NY; (Y); 108/380; Art Clb; Church Yth Grp; JV Sftbl; 4-H Awd; Hon Roll; Ntl Merit Ltr; Regnts Schlrshp 86-87; Martime; Marine Engrng.

OSBORN, KIMBERLY; Oneonta HS; Oneonta, NY; (Y); 13/176; Church Yth Grp; Pres FBLA; Key Clb; Yrbk Stf; Off Stu Cncl; Im Bsktbl; Hon Roll; NHS; Outstndg Achvmnt Math 83-84; Bus Wmns Schlrshp 85-86; Smth-Bssll Schlrshp 85-86; Cansius Coll; Acctg.

OSBORN, KYLE; Fayetteville-Manlius HS; Manlius, NY; (Y); 59/335; Model UN; Political Wkr; Variety Show; JV Bsbl; Var Socr; NHS; VP Frsh Cls; VP Soph Cls; Trs Pres Stu Cncl; Colgate U; Lbrl Arts.

OSBORNE, AMY G; Romulus Central HS; Seneca Falls, NY; (Y); Varsity Clb; Chorus; JV Bsktbl; Var Crs Cntry; Var Socr; JV Var Sftbl; Vllybl; Spanish Clb; Mst Imprvd Plyr Sftbll 86; Cayuga CC; Phy Ed.

OSBORNE, AUDREY; East Syracuse Minoa HS; Severen, MD; (Y); Church Yth Grp; Drama Clb; Ski Clb; Spanish Clb; Concert Band; Mrchg Band; Nwsp Stf; Jrnlsm.

OSBORNE, CATHERINE; Liverpool HS; Liverpool, NY; (Y); Church Yth Grp; FBLA; Girl Scts; JA; Yrbk Bus Mgr; Yrbk Stf; Liverpool HS Joint Stu Actvts Schlrshp 86; Onondaga CC; Accntng.

OSBORNE, CONNIE; New Covenant Christian Schl; Fairport, NY; (S); 2/12; Church Yth Grp; Spanish Clb; Band; Chorus; Yrbk Ed-Chief; Var Capt Socr; Var Sftbl; Var Vllybl; Hon Roll; Math.

OSBORNE, DAVID P; East Hampton HS; East Hampton, NY; (Y); Chess Clb; Computer Clb; Teachers Aide; Nwsp Rptr; Lit Mag; NY ST Regents Schlrhp 85-86; VA Wesleyan; Law.

OSBORNE, DEBORAH; Union-Endicott HS; Endwell, NY; (Y); Church Yth Grp; Orch; School Musical; Hon Roll; Church Choir; Prfrm Tehaikouskys Vln Sympy Cncrt 85; Cncrtmstr Area All-St Orchestra NY & Schubert Massing 84-85; New England Cnsrvtry; Music.

OSBORNE, GEORGE B; New Covenant Christian Schl; Walworth, NY; (Y); 1/15; Trs Computer Clb; Band; Capt L Bsktbl; Capt L Socr; Var Sftbl; Im Trk; Im Vllybl; High Hon Roll; Ntl Merit SF; Val; Houghton Coll Ldrshp Training Course Schlrshp 85; St John Fisher Smmr Schlr 85; Male Quartet 83-85; Physics.

OSBORNE, JASON W; Horseheads HS; Horseheads, NY; (S); 27/390; Am Leg Boys St; Latin Clb; Band; Mrchg Band; Nwsp Rptr; Nwsp Stf; VP L Crs Cntry; VP L Trk; NHS; Ntl Merit Ltr; Eagle Sct Gold Palm 82; All Sectn Crs-Cntry 84 & 85; All Sectn Trk 85; Engrng.

OSBOURNE, ALETHIA; Bishop Laughlin Memorial HS; Brooklyn, NY; (Y); Girl Scts; Teachers Aide; Varsity Clb; Var Bsktbl; Im Crs Cntry; Im Trk; Im Vllybl; Hon Roll; Church Yth Grp; Cmnty Wkr; Engl, Mth, & Rdng Cert 83; Cert A Slvr L For Aver 84; Cert Of Prpl L For Aver 85; Med Tech.

OSER, KIMBERLY A; Pleasantville HS; Pleasantville, NY; (Y); Drama Clb; Hosp Aide; PAVAS; Science Clb; SADD; Chorus; School Play; Stage Crew; Lit Mag; Cheerleading; Med Tech.

OSHEA, KEVIN; Archbishop Molloy HS; Bellerose, NY; (Y); Off Church Yth Grp; Chorus; NHS; NY U; Math.

OSHINS, DAVID K; New Dorp HS; Staten Island, NY; (Y); 1/750; Am Leg Boys St; Art Clb; Boy Scts; Math Tm; Office Aide; Lit Mag; Wt Lftg; French Hon Soc; Hon Roll; NHS; Brown Bk Awd 86; Boy Ldr New Dorp Chptr Arista 85-86; Engrng.

OSINSKI, JAMES; Cicero-North Syracuse HS; N Syracuse, NY; (S); 100/667; Mrchg Band; Hon Roll; NHS; Grphc Art.

OSINSKI, MARY; Eden Central HS; Eden, NY; (Y); VP GAA; Var L Bsktbl; Var L Fld Hcky; Var L Sftbl; Var L Vllybl; Hon Roll; NHS; Rep Soph Cls; Rep Jr Cls; Prfct Atten Awd; 1st Tm Divsnl All-Str Fld Hcky, Vllybl & Bsktbl 85-86; Athltc Trng.

OSIT, SUSAN; Hillcrest HS; Jamaica, NY; (Y); 23/832; Office Aide; Teachers Aide; Yrbk Stf; Lit Mag; Hon Roll; Jr NHS; NHS; UFT Shclrshp 4 Yr 86; Cert For Schlstc Excell 86; Excell In Hm Ec 86; NY U; Bus.

OSKOWSKI, DEBBIE; Fontbonne Hall Acad; Brooklyn, NY; (Y); 8/133; Cmnty Wkr; Service Clb; Sec SADD; Chorus; Color Guard; Nwsp Sprt Ed; Yrbk Stf; Coach Actv; Jr NHS; NHS; 1st Pl Ntl Red Cross Adv Comptn 86; Resolutn City Cncl 86; Med.

OSMOND, THOMAS A; East Aurora HS; E Aurora, NY; (Y); 15/184; School Musical; Variety Show; Ed Yrbk Phtg; Pres Sr Cls; Pres Stu Cncl; Swmmng; Var Tennis; NHS; Pres Boys Clb Am; Varsity Clb; Rgnts NY ST Schlrshp 86; Coll Of The Holy Cross.

OSORIO, MARTHA; Hillcrest HS; Flushing, NY; (Y); Office Aide; Coop Educ Pgm; Prsnl Grwth Lb; Bus.

OSORIO, OMAR; De Witt Clinton HS; Bronx, NY; (Y); ROTC; Spanish Clb; Teachers Aide; Off Jr Cls; Coach Actv; Ftbl; JV Gym; JV Socr; Cit Awd; Prfct Atten Awd; AFA Awd; Aviation.

OSPINA, DIANE P; La Guarda - Performing Arts HS; Brooklyn, NY; (Y); 54/186; Band; Madrigals; School Musical; School Play; Swing Chorus; Variety Show; SUNY Purchase.

OSTERHOUDT, KYLE; Sharon Springs Central Schl; Sharon Springs, NY; (S); Spanish Clb; Band; Concert Band; Jazz Band; Mrchg Band; Pep Band; Radio Brdcstng.

OSTERHOUDT, ROBERT W; Marlboro HS; Newburgh, NY; (Y); High Hon Roll; Hon Roll; Jr NHS; NHS; Ntl Assoc Women Constructn Awd 86-87; SUNY; Arch Tech.

OSTERHOUDT, TINA; Saugerties JR SR HS; Saugerties, NY; (Y); 23/250; Sftbl; Vllybl; High Hon Roll; NHS; Acdmc All Amer 86; Ithica; Sprts Med.

OSTERMAN, BILLY; Half Hollow Hills Schl West; Wheatley Heights, NY; (Y); Chess Clb; Library Aide; Mathletes; Bsktbl; High Hon Roll; Hon Roll; Jr NHS; NHS; Ntl Merit Ltr; Dartmouth; Engrng.

OSTERMAN, JEFF; Archbishop Stepinac HS; White Plains, NY; (Y); 70/190; Church Yth Grp; Cmnty Wkr; Key Clb; Pep Clb; VICA; Nwsp Stf; Yrbk Stf; Stu Cncl; Var L Bsktbl; Im Coach Actv; WBC All Star; Siena Coll; Bus Adm.

OSTERWALD, ANNE MARIE; Dominican Commercial HS; Queens Village, NY; (S); 3/273; Church Yth Grp; Teachers Aide; High Hon Roll; Prfct Atten Awd; Sal; Spanish NHS; Maria Regina Clb 82-86; Lang Cntst Iona Coll Mar 1st 86; Peer Grp Ldr 85-86; Molloy Coll; Spanish Tchr.

OSTERWALD, JEANNINE; Dominican Commercial HS; Queens Village, NY; (S); 40/280; Hon Roll; NHS; Sierra Clb; Spnsh.

OSTRANDER, BRENT; Paul V Moore HS; Central Sq, NY; (Y); Church Yth Grp; Radio Clb; Varsity Clb; School Play; Variety Show; Nwsp Rptr; Var Capt Socr; Var Trk; German Clb; Ski Clb; MVP Vrsty Sccr 85; 1st Team All League Sccr 85; Brdcstng.

OSTRANDER, JOANNE; Onteora Central HS; Willow, NY; (S); 62/201; VP DECA; JA; Office Aide; SADD; Color Guard; Mrchg Band; Var Capt Gym; Trk; Hon Roll; Voice Dem Awd; Bus Ed Excllnc Awd 84; ST DECA Comptn-3rd Pl & Hnrbl Mntn 85-86; Regnl DECA Comptn-1st & 2nd 85-86; Johnson Wales Coll; Busnss.

OSTRANDER, JODI; Hancock Central HS; Fishs Eddy, NY; (Y); Band; Chorus; Concert Band; Var Bsktbl; Var Hon Roll; GAA; Spanish Clb; Mrchg Band; Pep Band; Symp Band.

OSTROW, ALEX; West Hempstead HS; Island Park, NY; (Y); Am Leg Boys St; Cmnty Wkr; Computer Clb; Hosp Aide; Mathletes; Temple Yth Grp; Orch; Hon Roll; NHS; Cert Achvt Chem 85; Cert Achvt Comp Mth 86; Spn I Awd 84; Pedtrcn.

OSTROWSKI, DAVID; Greece Atheca HS; Rochester, NY; (Y); 12/332; Boy Scts; Church Yth Grp; Drama Clb; JA; Math Tm; Acpl Chr; Band; Chorus; Concert Band; Jazz Band; Natl Pianists Gld Cup Awd 86; Natl Piano Aud Awd 84-86; Aerosp Engrng.

OSULLIVAN, MICHAEL J; Mount Saint Michael Acad; New York, NY; (S); 20/300; Church Yth Grp; Hon Roll; NHS; Bus.

OSVATH, STEVE; Niagara-Wheatfield HS; North Tonawanda, NY; (Y); 6/296; Ftbl; Cit Awd; High Hon Roll; Trs NHS; NYS Regents Scholar 86; Karr-Parker Scholar 86; SUNY Buffalo; Elec Engrng.

OSWALD, ALLISON; Berlin Central HS; Cherry Plain, NY; (Y); 13/90; GAA; Stage Crew; Pres Stu Cncl; Score Keeper; Socr; Timer; Hon Roll; NHS; NY ST U; Crmnl Jstc.

OSWALT, MARSHA; Royalton Hartland HS; Lockport, NY; (Y); 17/144; French Clb; Spanish Clb; Nwsp Stf; Yrbk Stf; Soph Cls; Stu Cncl; Trk; High Hon Roll; Hon Roll; Niagara U Pres Acad Scholar 86; Mth Awd MFC Corp 86; Regents Nrsg Scholar 86; Nrsg Awd 86; Niagara U; Nrsg.

OSZUST, SHARON; Frontier Central HS; Blasdell, NY; (Y); Drama Clb; French Clb; Latin Clb; Pep Clb; Yrbk Stf; Stu Cncl; JV Var Socr; Hon Roll; NHS.

OTANO, JOHNNY F; Richmond Hill HS; Richmond Hl, NY; (Y); 80/245; Cmnty Wkr; English Clb; Library Aide; Radio Clb; Spanish Clb; Teachers Aide; Band; School Musical; Stage Crew; Variety Show; Physics Physic Advncmnt 86; Queens Coll; Media Engr.

OTERO, FELIX; Herbert H Lehman HS; Bronx, NY; (Y); Chorus; School Musical; School Play; Hon Roll; Indctn Arsta Hon Soc ,6; Lmmy Awd Schl Ply 86; Actor.

OTERO, FERNANDO; United Nations International Schl; Fresh Meadows, NY; (Y); School Play; Yrbk Ed-Chief; JV Socr; Spanish NHS; St Schlr.

OTREMBA, CHRIS; Lackawanna SR HS; Lackawanna, NY; (Y); Office Aide; Spanish Clb; Varsity Clb; Yrbk Stf; Rep Stu Cncl; JV Bsbl; JV Ftbl; JV Var Ice Hcky; High Hon Roll; Brockport.

OTT, GREGORY; East Syracuse-Minoa HS; E Syracuse, NY; (Y); 6/348; Cmnty Wkr; Math Tm; Quiz Bowl; Var Capt Bowling; Cit Awd; High Hon Roll; Jr NHS; NHS; Pres Schlr; NY ST Regents Schlrshp 86; ESM Cls 1966 Schlrshp 86; Walter Bazgollo Schlrshp 86; Clarkson U; Engrng.

OTT, JENNIFER; Saranac Central HS; Cadyville, NY; (S); 11/105; Cmnty Wkr; French Clb; Var Capt Socr; Var Sftbl; Var Capt Vllybl; Hon Roll; NHS; Sftbl-CVAC All Star-Shrtstp & Offnsv Plyr Of Yr 84; Sftbl-CAVC All Star Shrtstp-MVP 85; Psych.

OTT, KATHLEEN; Springville Griffith Inst; East Concord, NY; (Y); Math Clb; Spanish Clb; Trs Sr Cls; High Hon Roll; NHS; Church Yth Grp; Model UN; Concert Band; Trs Jr Cls; Stu Cncl; Mth.

OTT, MARK; Frontier Central HS; Buffalo, NY; (Y); 109/444; Varsity Clb; Capt Swmmng; Industrl Arts Awd 82-83; Most Imprvd Swimmer Awd 84-85; Alfred ST Coll; Comp.

OTTAVIANO, MARK; Martin Van Buren HS; New York, NY; (Y); 176/350; Drama Clb; PAVAS; SADD; Teachers Aide; Jazz Band; School Musical; School Play; Symp Band; Variety Show; Var L Socr; Cert Cmmndtn Fire Dept Cty Of Ny 84; Achvt Rcgntn James Schuerer Cngrssmn 84; Cngrssmns Mdl Hnr 84.

OTTENHEIMER, DEBRAH; Long Beach HS; Long Beach, NY; (S); 14/265; Band; Mrchg Band; School Musical; Yrbk Stf.

OTTLEY, NERISSA; Clara Barton HS; Brooklyn, NY; (Y); Hon Roll; Cert Recgntn Comprehnsv Mth & Sci Pgm 86; Compltn Law Awd 84; Sci Awd 84; Cornell U; Lawyer.

OTTMAN, KRISTEN A; G Ray Bodley HS; Fulton, NY; (Y); Variety Show; Yrbk Stf; High Hon Roll; Hon Roll; NYS Rgnts Schlrshp Awd 86; Clemson U; Pre-Law.

OTTUSO, MARIA; Preston HS; Bronx, NY; (S); 15/89; VP Frsh Cls; VP Soph Cls; Sec Stu Cncl; High Hon Roll; Hon Roll; NHS; Medcl Technlgy.

OUDOM, SIRIVANH; Poughkeepsie HS; Poughkeepsie, NY; (Y); Yrbk Stf; Var Cheerleading; Var Socr; Var Tennis; Hon Roll; NHS; Prfct Atten Awd.

OUGHTERSON, ANTHONY; Auburn HS; Auburn, NY; (Y); Boy Scts; Crs Cntry; Socr; Trk; Boy Scout Eagle Badge 86.

OUGHTON, TERESA; Johnstown HS; St Johnsville, NY; (Y); 26/170; VP Frsh Cls; Crs Cntry; Socr; Sftbl; Trk; Hon Roll; NHS; Ski Clb; Stu Cncl; Bsktbl; Mid Atlantic JR Olympc Tm Crs Cntry Ski 86; Silv Mdl Empire ST Games Crs Cntry Ski 86; 2nd Tm Sftbl; Keene ST Coll; Mth.

OURSLER, TERI; Tully JR SR HS; Marietta, NY; (Y); Drama Clb; SADD; Chorus; Yrbk Stf; Poughkeepsie Culunary Arts.

OUTERBRIDGE, CRYSTAL R; George Washington HS; New York, NY; (Y); Nwsp Stf; Ntl Merit SF; Mass Comms.

OUTHOUSE, DAVID; Roy C Ketcham HS; Poughkeepsie, NY; (Y); Boy Scts; Church Yth Grp; Ski Clb; Var Bsktbl; Var Trk; Cit Awd; Hon Roll; Arch.

OUTLAW, TERESA P; Cardinal Spellman HS; Bronx, NY; (Y); 109/509; NFL; Science Clb; Speech Tm; Stage Crew; Hon Roll; Rgnts Schlrshp 86-87; Fordham U; Psychlgy.

OVADY, ELIZABETH; Stamford Central HS; S Kortright, NY; (S); 2/29; Art Clb; Quiz Bowl; Spanish Clb; Teachers Aide; Varsity Clb; Band; Concert Band; Mrchg Band; Score Keeper; Var Socr; New Paltz ST U; Graphic Dsgn.

OVERBAUGH, JOHN; Charles O Dickerson HS; Trumansburg, NY; (Y); Am Leg Boys St; Thesps; Varsity Clb; Concert Band; Jazz Band; School Play; Stage Crew; Yrbk Phtg; Var L Socr; Var L Tennis; Rotary Intl Exchng Stu 86-87; Long Island U; Brdcst Comm.

OVERHOLT, ANTOINETTE; H C Technical HS; Buffalo, NY; (Y); Library Aide; Office Aide; SADD; Rep Stu Cncl; Capt Bowling; DAR Awd.

OVERMOHLE, SANDRA; Bishop Luddin HS; Liverpool, NY; (Y); Cmnty Wkr; Varsity Clb; Rep Jr Cls; Var L Bsktbl; JV Socr; Hon Roll; All-Lge Awd 2nd Tm Bsktbl 85-86; All Trny Tm Knghts Of Clmbs Chrstn Trny 85-86; Bus Man.

OVERSLAUGH, SUE; Pittsford Mendon HS; Pittsford, NY; (Y); Orch; Ed Yrbk Stf; Capt Var Fld Hcky; Stat Ice Hcky; Hon Roll; Church Yth Grp; Cmnty Wkr; SADD; School Musical; Yrbk Rptr; Union Coll; Lbrl Arts.

OVERTON, JOSEPH; Alfred E Smith HS; New York, NY; (S); 1/217; VICA; Im Ftbl; Sftbl; Hon Roll; NHS; Prfct Atten Awd; Arch.

OWEN, KATERI M; Lewiston Porter SR HS; Youngstown, NY; (Y); 14/236; Drama Clb; French Clb; Orch; Hon Roll; NHS; St Schlr; Lmp Lrng Awds 84-85; Prsdntl Schlrshp Niagara U 86; Niagara U; Nursing.

OWENS, ANGELA; Torreson American HS; Apo, NY; (Y); Church Yth Grp; English Clb; Pep Clb; Science Clb; Teachers Aide; Band; Concert Band; Mrchg Band; Pep Band; Symp Band; Auburn U; Vet Med.

OWENS, CHARLES; St Josephs Regional HS; Tappan, NY; (Y); 27/167; Spanish NHS.

OWENS, EDWARD V; Xavier HS; New York, NY; (Y); Pres Church Yth Grp; Cmnty Wkr; JA; ROTC; Church Choir; Concert Band; Wrstlng; Elks Awd; Hon Roll; Yth Of Yr-Afrcn Meth Episcpl Chrchs 85-86; North Eastern U; Law.

OWENS, KRISTIN; West Seneca East SR HS; W Seneca, NY; (Y); Pres Drama Clb; Chorus; School Musical; School Play; Pres Stu Cncl; Var Swmmng; Hon Roll; Jr NHS; NHS; Ger Natl Hnr Soc 84; Alt For Congress-Bundestag Yth Exchng Prog 86-87; 4 Outstdng Ger Stu Awds; U Of MA Amherst ; Educ.

OWENS, MARK C; La Salle Inst; Cahoes, NY; (Y); Civic Clb; Office Aide; Band; Concert Band; Drill Tm; Drm Mjr(t); Mrchg Band; Nwsp Stf; Yrbk Stf; Socr; NY ST Rgnts Schlrshp; Rensselaer Poly Inst; Engrng.

OWENS, PAULETTE; Academy Of Mt St Ursula; Mt Vernon, NY; (Y); Sec Church Yth Grp; Chorus; Church Choir; Hon Roll.

OWENS, STACY; Holland Patent HS; Holland Patent, NY; (Y); French Clb; Chorus; Concert Band; School Play; Symp Band; Rep Soph Cls; Rep Jr Cls; JV Var Cheerleading; High Hon Roll; Hon Roll; Drama.

OWENS, TIMOTHY; Lansingburgh HS; Troy, NY; (Y); 6/160; Church Yth Grp; Math Tm; Bsktbl; Golf; Cit Awd; High Hon Roll; Jr NHS; NHS; Pres Schlr; Rgnts Schlrshp NYS 86; Siena Coll; Bus.

OWLETT, KRISTY; Charles O Dickerson HS; Trumansburg, NY; (Y); Church Yth Grp; Spanish Clb; Varsity Clb; Bsktbl; Socr; Var Sftbl; JV Var Vllybl; Comm.

OWUSU, EMMA; Springfield Gardens HS; Rosedale, NY; (Y); Drama Clb; GAA; Math Clb; Red Cross Aide; Science Clb; Vllybl; Hon Roll; Prfct Atten Awd; Wt Lftg; High Hon Roll; Nrsng Admnstrtr.

OYEDEJI, ADEOLA; High School For The Hmnts; New York, NY; (Y); Church Yth Grp; Cmnty Wkr; Service Clb; Chorus; Church Choir; Off Sr Cls; Rep Stu Cncl; L Trk; Prfct Atten Awd; New York St Bar Awd; Corporate Lawyer.

PAAR, SEAN; Olean HS; Olean, NY; (Y); 86/200; Varsity Clb; JV Var Ftbl; JV Var Trk; Gld Key Blu Rbbn Awd Jamestown CC Intrschlstc Art Comptn 86; 20 Pt Awd 86; Art.

PACANOWSKI, KATHRYN MARIE; Westfield Acad; Westfield, NY; (Y); 3/65; Quiz Bowl; Teachers Aide; Nwsp Rptr; Rep Stu Cncl; Co-Capt Cheerleading; Elks Awd; High Hon Roll; NHS; Voice Dem Awd; Regnts Schlrshp 86; Stdnt Wk Locl Papr 86; Stdnt Mnth Aprl 85; Syracuse U; Psych.

PACE, TONY; New Dorp HS; Staten Island, NY; (Y); Office Aide; Hon Roll; Italn Hon Soc 84-86; Acad Aeronautics.

PACELLA, DANTE J; Canisius HS; Strykersville, NY; (Y); 65/163; Church Yth Grp; Pres VP 4-H; Lit Mag; NYS Rgnts Schlrshp 86; Mrs Louis M Jacobs Schlrshp Awd 85; Canisius Coll Awd 86; Canisius Coll.

PACER, ROSANNE; Lackawanna SR HS; Lackawanna, NY; (Y); Church Yth Grp; Spanish Clb; Bowling; Sftbl; Hon Roll; NHS; Comp Sci.

PACHECO, ANA; Hillcrest HS; Jamaica, NY; (Y); Badmtn; Gym; Wt Lftg; Hon Roll; Prfct Atten Awd; Cmpsttn Cls Eng RCT Wrtng 86; Std Yr Squntl Math III 86; 1 Yr Sequentl Math I & II Rgnts 85-86; Queens Coll; Soc Wrkr.

PACHECO, KEVIN; Eastern District HS; Brooklyn, NY; (Y).

PACHECO, MIGUEL; Seward Park HS; New York, NY; (Y); Capt Swmmng.

PACHNOS, HELENE; St Edmund HS; Brooklyn, NY; (S); 2/185; English Clb; Spanish Clb; Nwsp Stf; Yrbk Stf; Lit Mag; High Hon Roll; Jr NHS; NHS; NEDT Awd; Sal; Schlrshp Awd; Corp Lawyer.

PACHUCKI, DOROTHY; Guilderland HS; Altamont, NY; (Y); 4-H; JV Bsbl; 4-H Awd; SUNY Cobleskill; Wrd Proc.

PACIFICO, FRANCESCA; Westlake HS; Valhalla, NY; (Y); SADD; Yrbk Stf; Var Sftbl; Hon Roll; NHS; Ntl Merit Ltr; Itln Natl Hnr Socty; All Leag Hnbl Mntn Vrsty Sftbl; Itln Natl Achvt Awd; Bus.

PACIFICO, LAURA; Hamburg SR HS; Hamburg, NY; (Y); 32/382; French Clb; Latin Clb; Hon Roll; NHS; Rgnts Schlrshp 86; Coll Bus & Pblc Admnstrtn Schlrshp 86; NY U; Bnkng.

PACIFICO, LOUIS; Hamburg SR HS; Hamburg, NY; (Y); Ski Clb; Trs Frsh Cls; Dentstry.

PACIFICO, OLIVER; Clarkstown North HS; Congers, NY; (Y); Mu Alp Tht; Med.

PACIOREK, STEVEN; Southside HS; Elmira, NY; (Y); Am Leg Boys St; Pres Church Yth Grp; Spanish Clb; Varsity Clb; Var Crs Cntry; Var Golf; Var Trk; Engrng.

PACK, BOB; Seton Catholic Central HS; Endwell, NY; (Y); Am Leg Boys St; Chess Clb; Church Yth Grp; Mathletes; Ski Clb; Var Socr; Var Trk; Hon Roll; NHS; Ntl Merit Ltr; Seton Schlr Awd 84-85; Elect Engr.

PACKARD, MICHAEL G; Hudson Falls SR HS; Hudson Falls, NY; (Y); 45/230; Boy Scts; French Clb; NYS Regnts Schlrshp 86; Clarkson U; Mech/Chem Engr.

PACKMAN, JON; Wilson Magnet HS; Rochester, NY; (Y); Boy Scts; Church Yth Grp; Ski Clb; Yrbk Stf; Ftbl; NHS.

PADGETT, SANDRA; Port Jervis HS; Pt Jervis, NY; (Y); 13/184; Drama Clb; Math Tm; Band; Concert Band; Mrchg Band; School Musical; Off Jr Cls; High Hon Roll; NHS; Prfct Atten Awd; Var Ltr Band 86; Bio.

PADILLA, JONATHAN; Fordham Preparatory HS; New York, NY; (Y); Camera Clb; Off French Clb; Nwsp Phtg; Ed Yrbk Phtg; Yrbk Stf; Pres Acdmc Fit Awd 86; Commrcl Art.

PADLOVSKY, ESTHER M; Newtown HS; Jackson Hts, NY; (Y); 8/667; Orch; Rep Frsh Cls; Rep Soph Cls; Rep Jr Cls; Rep Sr Cls; Rep Stu Cncl; High Hon Roll; Mu Alp Tht; VP NHS; Myrs Spr Yth 84; Sci Prjct Awd Spnsrd Pfizer Inc Indstries 84; Rgnts Schlrshp 86; Math.

PADOVANO, LINDA; St John The Baptist HS; Bay Shore, NY; (S); 36/546; Church Yth Grp; JCL; Rep Frsh Cls; Rep Soph Cls; Stat Lcrss; Sftbl; High Hon Roll; NHS; Physcl Thrpy.

PADUA, JOSEPH M; Franklin Acad; Malone, NY; (Y); 6/256; French Clb; Band; Crs Cntry; Hon Roll; NHS; Epsilon Hnr Scty 83-86; Rnslr Poly Tech Inst; Engrng.

PADULA, LORRI; St John Villa Acad; Staten Island, NY; (Y); 2/123; Math Clb; Spanish Clb; Yrbk Stf; Capt Cheerleading; Hon Roll; Sec NHS; 2nd General Excllnce 86; 2nd Hnrs Chem, Latin, Pre-Calcls 86; Engrng.

PADULA, SUSAN; Solvay HS; Syracuse, NY; (Y); JA; Key Clb; SADD; Chorus; School Musical; School Play; Variety Show; Yrbk Stf; Stu Cncl; Nrsng.

PAEZ, HAROLD; Brooklyn Tech HS; Brooklyn, NY; (Y); 172/1159; Computer Clb; Science Clb; Service Clb; Yrbk Stf; Hon Roll; NHS; Ntl Hisp Schlrs Prog 86; 3rd Pl Wnnr PAL Lit Cntst 85; Cert Dstnctn Ntl Sci Olympd 83; Bio.

PAGAN, ANGEL; Alfred E Smith HS; New York, NY; (S); 3/120; Debate Tm; VICA; Yrbk Stf; Im Bsbl; Im Bsktbl; Im Ftbl; Im Sftbl; Hon Roll; NHS; Prfct Atten Awd; Pace U; Jrnlsm.

PAGAN, ELSA IRIS; Thomas R Proctor HS; Utica, NY; (Y); 14/202; French Clb; Spanish Clb; Capt Vllybl; DAR Awd; High Hon Roll; NHS; Mayors SR Achvt Awd, Metro Bus & Prof Wmns Club Schlrshp & Proctr Forgn Lang Dept Awd For Exc 86; Utica Coll; Law.

PAGAN, FELIX; Far Rockaway HS; New York, NY; (Y); 136/338; Key Clb; Varsity Clb; Chorus; Var Bsbl; Capt Ftbl; Var Swmmng; Var Wrstlng; Pres Schlr; Art Awd 84; Ftbl Awd 83; Northern AZ U; Engrng.

PAGAN, MICHAEL; Cardinal Spellman HS; Bronx, NY; (Y); 88/483; Boy Scts; Pres Church Yth Grp; Debate Tm; Latin Clb; VP NFL; Pres Science Clb; Speech Tm; Stage Crew; Nwsp Rptr; Nwsp Stf; Ad Altare Dei Awd 83; Pope Pius XII Awd 84; SUNY; Pre Law.

PAGAN, RALPH; Dewitt Clinton HS; New York, NY; (Y); ROTC.

PAGANELLI, FRANK V; St Marys Acad; Glens Falls, NY; (S); 7/62; Am Leg Boys St; French Clb; Stage Crew; Var L Bsktbl; Var Capt Ftbl; High Hon Roll; Chess Clb; Drama Clb; SADD; Varsity Clb; Bus.

PAGANO, KIMBERLY ANN; Charles E Groton HS; Yonkers, NY; (Y); Intnl Clb; Spanish Clb; Nwsp Rptr; Nwsp Stf; Yrbk Ed-Chief; Yrbk Stf; Lit Mag; Sprntndts Awd Acdmc Excllnc; Wstchstr Vssr Clb Bk Awd 86; Cmptv Fgr Sktr 83-86; Pre-Med.

PAGANO, MARCO; Midwood HS; Brooklyn, NY; (Y); 44/677; Boy Scts; Hosp Aide; Teachers Aide; Nwsp Rptr; Bsbl; High Hon Roll; Hon Roll; SEER Hrnbl Mntn; Med.

PAGANUZZI, ENEZ; Resurrection HS; Eastchester, NY; (Y); Girl Scts; NFL; Speech Tm; Chorus; Stage Crew; Variety Show; Pres Stu Cncl; Cit Awd; Hon Roll; NHS; CBS Schlrshp 86; Chase NBW Good Ctznshp Awd 86; CYO Art Awd 86; Fordham U.

PAGE, EILEEN; Nottingham HS; Syracuse, NY; (Y); Drama Clb; Latin Clb; Var Diving; Var Trk; High Hon Roll; NHS; Magna Cum Laude.

PAGE, JUDY; Bishop Maginn HS; Albany, NY; (S); Cmnty Wkr; Latin Clb; Math Clb; School Play; Nwsp Rptr; Yrbk Stf; Trk; High Hon Roll; NHS; Nrsg.

PAGE, MICHAEL; E J Wilson HS; Spencerport, NY; (Y); 111/368; Boy Scts; Church Yth Grp; Varsity Clb; JV Swmmng; God Cntry Awd; Cmnty Wkr; Ski Clb; Stage Crew; Rep Frsh Cls; Stu Cncl; Egl Sct Awd 84; Mst Imprvd Swmr; Trvl.

PAGEN, DIANE R; The High School Of Art And Design; Elmhurst, NY; (Y); 26/400; Hon Roll; NHS; Regents Schlrshp 86; Long Isl U Brooklyn Full Schlrshp; Nat Assoc Tchrs French Awd 82 & 84.

PAGLIAROLI, ETHEL; John C Birdlebough HS; Phoenix, NY; (Y); Cmnty Wkr; Drama Clb; Pres Girl Scts; Office Aide; Chorus; Color Guard; School Musical; Swing Chorus; Hon Roll; JV Var Sftbl; Johnson & Wales; Culinary Arts.

PAGNOTTA, PAUL; Marlboro HS; Marlboro, NY; (Y); 35/150; Church Yth Grp; Varsity Clb; School Play; Trs Soph Cls; Trs Jr Cls; Trs Sr Cls; Var Ftbl; High Hon Roll; NHS.

PAHL JR, DONALD E; Newfane SR HS; Lockport, NY; (S); 6/158; Drama Clb; Library Aide; Hon Roll; NHS; Hghst Math Course II Ave 84-85; Math Tchr.

PAHMER, ALLYSON; Sanford H Calhoun HS; Merrick, NY; (Y); 15/313; VP DECA; Key Clb; Nwsp Rptr; Nwsp Stf; Yrbk Sprt Ed; Yrbk Stf; Off Soph Cls; Pres Jr Cls; Off Sr Cls; Stat Bsbl; SR Otstndng Srv Awd 86; DECA Otstndng Indvul Achvmnt 85-86; DECA Otstndng Srv Awd 85-86; Georgetown U.

PAICE, KARRI; G Ray Bodley HS; Fulton, NY; (Y); 105/261; Church Yth Grp; French Clb; Variety Show; Yrbk Stf; Var L Crs Cntry; Var L Trk; Hon Roll; Johnson Wales Coll; Culnry Arts.

PAIK, JULIANA S; Amherst Central HS; Amherst, NY; (Y); 2/298; Yrbk Stf; Im Badmtn; Var Capt Gym; High Hon Roll; NHS; Prfct Atten Awd; Outstndg Art Stu Awd 83; Ntl Sci Olympd 84 & 86; Pres Phys Ftnss Awd 84 & 85; Pre-Med.

PAINO, CYNTHIA L; Norwich HS; Norwich, NY; (Y); 2/216; Sec Chorus; Sec Mrchg Band; School Play; Yrbk Stf; Sec Stu Cncl; Bsktbl; Socr; Capt Sftbl; NHS; Sal; NYS Rgnts Schlrshp 86; Oper Enterprise Wnnr 85; St Bonaventure Frairs Schlrshp 86; St Bonaventure U; Acctg.

PAINTER, JAMES; Jamestown HS; Jamestown, NY; (Y); Capt Ftbl; Var Wrstlng; Jr NHS; Law.

PAIS, SALVATORE; Brooklyn Technical HS; Jackson Heights, NY; (Y); 65/1159; Debate Tm; Math Clb; VP Math Tm; Teachers Aide; Ed Lit Mag; High Hon Roll; Hon Roll; NHS; Ntl Merit Ltr; NY Rgnts Schlrp 86; Citatn Merit 86; Talent Srch Cntst 86; MIT; Aerontcl Engrg.

PAJION, JONATHAN; Roslyn HS; Roslyn Est, NY; (Y); Computer Clb; French Clb; Lit Mag; JV Crs Cntry; Var Trk; Ntl Merit Ltr; Cert Merit Magna Cum Laude Outstndng Perf Latin Ex 86; Cert Hnr Annual Nassau Clscl Soc 86.

PAJONK, STEPHANIE MARIE; Valley Central HS; Montgomery, NY; (Y); 47/286; Debate Tm; Spanish Clb; Band; Yrbk Stf; Var Capt Bsktbl; JV Capt Cheerleading; Var Tennis; Capt Var Vllybl; NHS; Spanish NHS; Vlly Cntrl Tchrs Assoc Awd 86; Laforge Mann Schlrshp Awd 86; SUNY Buffalo; Spcl Educ.

PAK, JEANNY; Bay Shore HS; Bay Shore, NY; (Y); 7/241; Orch; Trs Soph Cls; Rep Jr Cls; Rep Stu Cncl; JV Tennis; High Hon Roll; VP NHS; Soc Studies Orchestra Achvt Awd 86; Math.

PAK, PETER TONGPIL; Susan E Wagner HS; Staten Island, NY; (Y); German Clb; JV Crs Cntry; Var Trk; JV Wrstlng; Kiwanis Awd; Hnrb Mntn ST Of OH Math Cntst 84-85; Csmtlgst.

PALADINO, ANN MARIE; East Islip HS; East Islip, NY; (Y); 49/425; Cmnty Wkr; FBLA; Hosp Aide; Flag Corp; Mrchg Band; Rep Sr Cls; Cit Awd; High Hon Roll; NHS; VFW Awd; E Islip Sectrl Assn Schlrshp 86; Alfred U; Bus Admn.

PALASCIANO, STEPHEN; Lincoln HS; Yonkers, NY; (S); 53/330; Aud/Vis; Key Clb; Political Wkr; Stage Crew; Nwsp Phtg; Nwsp Rptr; Nwsp Stf; Yrbk Phtg; Yrbk Rptr; Yrbk Stf; Cross Cntry Trk Cty Champs 84; Outward Bound Rcpnt 85; Engr.

PALASKI, RICH; Whitesboro SR HS; Marcy, NY; (Y); 36/304; Computer Clb; Science Clb; Speech Tm; Lit Mag; High Hon Roll; Opt Clb Awd; Vet Med.

PALATNIK, ERIC; John H Glenn HS; Long Island, NY; (Y); Cmnty Wkr; Science Clb; Ski Clb; Spanish Clb; Temple Yth Grp; Nwsp Rptr; Nwsp Stf; Rep Stu Cncl; Bowling; Trk; Film On Suicide Prvntn 85-86; Psychlgy.

PALAWASTA, CAROL; Sacred Heart Acad; Lattingtown, NY; (Y); Cmnty Wkr; Dance Clb; Library Aide; Math Clb; PAVAS; SADD; Teachers Aide; Variety Show; DAR Awd; Hon Roll.

PALAZZO, GRACE E; Christopher Columbus HS; Bronx, NY; (Y); 10/672; Math Tm; Hon Roll; Rgnts Schlrshp 86; Baruch Coll Schlrshp 86; Baruch Coll; Acctg.

PALAZZO, JERIANNE; Nazareth Regional HS; Brooklyn, NY; (Y); Band; Nwsp Sprt Ed; Nwsp Stf; Rep Jr Cls; Off Sr Cls; Var Bsktbl; Sftbl; Var Vllybl; JA; PAVAS; HOBY Sem 85; Eqstrn.

PALAZZO, LOUIS; Mount St Michael Acad; Bronx, NY; (Y); 6/290; Chess Clb; Computer Clb; Spanish Clb; Stu Cncl; Crs Cntry; JV Trk; Hon Roll; NHS; Spanish NHS; Med.

PALAZZO, STACI; Sacred Heart Acad; Merrick, NY; (Y); Spanish Clb; Church Choir; Accntng.

PALAZZOTTO, MARIA B; Deer Park HS; Deer Park, NY; (Y); 9/436; German Clb; Math Clb; Variety Show; Rep Stu Cncl; High Hon Roll; NHS; JA; Chorus; School Musical; Yrbk Phtg; Deer Pk PFC & PTA Schlrshp Fund 86; C W Post Acad & Cooperative Educ Schlrshps 86; C W Post Greenvale; Math.

PALERMO, HEATHER; Avon HS; E Avon, NY; (Y); Computer Clb; FBLA; JA; Library Aide; Chorus; JV Bsktbl; Hon Roll; NYS FBLA Cert-ST Ldrshp Cnfrnc 86; Rochester Inst Tech; Comp Pgmng.

PALERMO, RONALD; Ben Franklin HS; Rochester, NY; (Y); Boys Clb Am; Boy Scts; Church Yth Grp; Exploring; Red Cross Aide; Chorus; School Musical; Variety Show; Var Bsbl; JV Var Crs Cntry; Law.

PALESTRANT, CHRISTOPHER W; Newtown HS; Elmhurst, NY; (Y); 31/667; Chorus; School Musical; Yrbk Stf; Lit Mag; Rep Stu Cncl; High Hon Roll; Prfct Atten Awd; Stu Ldr Arista Hnr Soc 86; NY City Fin Engl Spkng Union Skspr Ortrcl Cont 84 & 86; NY All Cty Chrs; Coll Wooster; Ed.

PALEY, MICHAEL J; Walt Whitman HS; Huntington Sta, NY; (Y); 110/540; Computer Clb; Key Clb; Im Bsktbl; Var JV Lcrss; JV Socr; NY ST Rgnts Schlrshp 85-86; U Rchstr; Bio Med Engrng.

PALICKI, TRACY A; Depew HS; Depew, NY; (Y); 18/272; Library Aide; Hon Roll; NY ST Rgnts Schlrshp 86; Deans Schlrshp Canisius Coll 86; Canisius Coll; Accntng.

PALISANO, JAMES F; Canisius HS; Cheektowaga, NY; (Y); 10/169; Stat Bsktbl; Stat Crs Cntry; Mgr(s); Score Keeper; NHS; Rnsslr Mdl Excllnc Sci & Math 85; Mu Aplha Theta 86; Canisius Coll; Comp Sci.

PALIWODA, RICHARD; Archbishop Molloy HS; Ridgewood, NY; (Y); French Clb; VP Intnl Clb; Pres SADD; Ed Yrbk Stf; Im Bsktbl; L Trk; VP NHS; NY ST Rgnts Schlrshp 86; NYU Trst Schlrshp 86; Lcl 32 B-J Thms Shrtmn Schlrshp 86; NY U; Intl Bus.

PALJUSEVIC, KATHY; Christopher Columbus HS; New York, NY; (S); Office Aide; Political Wkr; Teachers Aide; Hon Roll; Ntl Merit Ltr; Prfct Atten Awd; Accntng.

PALLADINO, DANA; Notre Dame Academy HS; Staten Island, NY; (Y); Cmnty Wkr; Drama Clb; Political Wkr; Stu Cncl; Cheerleading; Tennis; Trk; Pre-Med.

PALLESCHI, PATRICK; Fairport HS; Fairport, NY; (Y); Key Clb; Model UN; Red Cross Aide; Ski Clb; Nwsp Stf; Merit Rll 84-86.

PALLINI, ROSANNE; St Catharines Acad; Bronx, NY; (Y); 2/203; Teachers Aide; High Hon Roll; NHS; Full Schlrshp 85-86; Iona College; Educ.

PALLONE, KEVIN; Niagara Wheat Field SR HS; Niagara Falls, NY; (Y); Latin Clb; PAVAS; Chorus; Stage Crew; Swing Chorus; Bsbl; Golf; Hon Roll; Jr NHS; NHS; Dstngshd Acmmplshmnt Bio 85; Awd Acadmc Excllnc 85-86; Tri M Musc Hnr Soc 86; U Of SC; Bio.

PALLOTTA, SCOTT; Amsterdam HS; Amsterdam, NY; (Y); 12/296; Varsity Clb; Concert Band; Mrchg Band; Socr; Trk; Hon Roll; JP Sousa Awd; NHS; Ntl Merit Schol; Kazimer Nevulis Sci Schlrsp 86; Clarkson U; Engrng.

PALMA, DANIEL; Saratoga Springs SR HS; Saratoga Springs, NY; (Y); 89/473; Trs Church Yth Grp; Letterman Clb; SADD; Varsity Clb; Orch; Yrbk Sprt Ed; Yrbk Stf; Bsbl; Socr; Jr NHS; Northeastern Coll; Comp Sci.

PALMA, PAOLA A; Bishop Kearney HS; Brooklyn, NY; (Y); 1/338; Cmnty Wkr; Library Aide; Math Tm; Office Aide; Political Wkr; Nwsp Ed-Chief; Nwsp Rptr; Nwsp Stf; Lit Mag; High Hon Roll; Iona Lang Cntst Wnnr 84-85; NYU; Pre-Med.

PALMER, ALTHEA; Midwood HS; Brooklyn, NY; (Y); Camera Clb; Church Yth Grp; Cmnty Wkr; Office Aide; Teachers Aide; Orch; Btty Crckr Awd; Hon Roll; Prfct Atten Awd; Stage Crew; Indstrl Arts Awd 85; Schl Vlntr Prog Awd 85; Blue Hnr Rll 85; NY U; Bus Adm.

PALMER, ANDREA R; The Mary Louis Acad; Brooklyn, NY; (Y); Church Yth Grp; Office Aide; Church Choir; School Play; Pres Sr Cls; Stu Cncl; NY ST Regnts Schlrshp; Howard U; Med Doc.

PALMER, DAVID J; Alfed G Berner HS; Massapequa Pk, NY; (Y); 11/365; Am Leg Boys St; Rep Church Yth Grp; Drama Clb; Mathletes; Spanish Clb; Nwsp Bus Mgr; Nwsp Rptr; Yrbk Stf; Pres Sr Cls; Jr NHS.

PALMER, DAVID J; Scarsdale HS; Scarsdale, NY; (Y); Camera Clb; Spanish Clb; Temple Yth Grp; Nwsp Phtg; Nwsp Rptr; Ed Lit Mag; St Schlr; Spnsh Clb Lit Cntst 1st Prz 84-85; NY U; Bus.

PALMER, DOUGLAS D; Hartford Central Schl; Granville, NY; (Y); Computer Clb; Drama Clb; French Clb; Mathletes; Science Clb; Ski Clb; School Play; JV Bsbl; JV Socr; High Hon Roll; Empire ST Schlrshp Exc 86; Hartwick Coll; Math.

PALMER, ELAINE; Schoharie Central HS; Sloansville, NY; (Y); VP Key Clb; Pres SADD; Acctg.

PALMER, GAYLAN; Mount Markham HS; W Winfield, NY; (Y); 4/130; Church Yth Grp; Drama Clb; Acpl Chr; Chorus; Church Choir; Concert Band; Jazz Band; School Musical; NHS; Opt Clb Awd; Top Stu In Drmtcs 85-86; Cnfrnc All-ST Choir 84-85; Area All-ST Orchstra 1st Chair 85; Eastman Schl Of Music; Music Ed.

PALMER, JAMES; Uork Central School; Piffard, NY; (Y); Cmnty Wkr; L Var Bsbl; L Var Bsktbl; Crs Cntry; Im Vllybl; Jr NHS; Livingston Cnty All Star Bsbl 85 & 86; Frnch Merit Hons 84-86; Pres Phys Ftnss Awd 85 & 86; Pol Sci.

PALMER, JOSEPH PATRICK; Canajoharie HS; Canajoharie, NY; (Y); 14/88; Am Leg Boys St; Trs FCA; Yrbk Sprt Ed; Capt Bsktbl; Capt Ftbl; L Trk; Elks Awd; Pres Jr NHS; Trs NHS; Pres Schlr; NYS Regnts Schrlshp 86; Pit Crew 86; Rensselaer Poly Tech; Dentst.

PALMER, JOSEPH W; Depew HS; Depew, NY; (Y); 2/272; Computer Clb; Chorus; Concert Band; Jazz Band; Mrchg Band; Bausch & Lomb Sci Awd; Hon Roll; NHS; Prfct Atten Awd; Hnrs Prgm To SUNY Bfl 86; NY ST U Bfl; Comp Engrng.

PALMER, KRISTEN M; Saratoga Springs HS; Saratoga Springs, NY; (Y); 10/491; Am Leg Aux Girls St; SADD; Orch; Trs Soph Cls; JV Var Bsktbl; High Hon Roll; Trs NHS; Rgnts Schlrshp; Tchrs Assoc Schlrshp; Albany Coll Of Phrmcy Of Union.

PALMER, KRISTINA; Bishop Cunningham HS; Fulton, NY; (Y); Hosp Aide; High Hon Roll; Hon Roll; Soc Wrkr.

PALMER, LISA; Coxsackie Athens JR SR HS; W Coxsackie, NY; (Y); 16/110; SADD; Chorus; Off Frsh Cls; Off Soph Cls; Off Jr Cls; Off Stu Cncl; Sftbl; High Hon Roll; Hon Roll.

PALMER, NICHOLAS; Monsignor Farrell HS; Staten Island, NY; (Y); Chess Clb; Math Tm; High Hon Roll; NHS.

PALMER, STEPHEN F; Whitehall JRSR HS; Whitehall, NY; (Y); 18/79; Computer Clb; Letterman Clb; Varsity Clb; Var L Crs Cntry; Var Capt Ftbl; JV Tennis; Var Capt Trk; Var Capt Wrstlng; Regents Schlrshp Awd 85-86; U Of CT-CENTRAL; Phys Ed.

PALMER, WENDY; Hornell HS; Hornell, NY; (Y); 20/180; VP AFS; Library Aide; PAVAS; Sec SADD; Color Guard; Symp Band; High Hon Roll; Hon Roll; Ntl Merit Ltr; Elmntry Ed.

PALMERI, JOY A; St Francis Prep; Bayside, NY; (S); 124/746; Acpl Chr; Band; Chorus; Concert Band; Mrchg Band; Pep Band; NHS; Opt Clb Awd; Bus Adm.

PALMERINI, MARCO; Sachem North HS; Lake Ronkonkoma, NY; (Y); Var JV Socr; NHS; Aerosp Engr.

PALMERO, JENNIFER; East Meadow HS; East Meadow, NY; (Y); Hosp Aide; Lit Mag; Wrd Prcssr.

PALMESANO, PHIL; Hornell HS; Hornell, NY; (Y); Am Leg Boys St; Var Bsbl; High Hon Roll; Hon Roll; Bus Admn.

PALMIERI, CHRISTINE; High Schl Of The Performing Arts; Brooklyn, NY; (S); 3/121; Service Clb; Band; Concert Band; Orch; Rep Sr Cls; Rep Stu Cncl; Hon Roll; NHS; Val; Office Aide; Music Hnr Leag; SR Lounge Commtt; Entertnmnt.

PALMIERI, FRANCINE; Marlboro HS; Marlboro, NY; (Y); Girl Scts; Band; Chorus; Im Gym; Im Score Keeper; Hon Roll; Bus Adm.

PALMIERI, KATHIE L; Maine Endwell SR HS; Endwell, NY; (Y); 14/234; Hosp Aide; Key Clb; Pep Clb; Service Clb; Varsity Clb; Yrbk Stf; Var Swmmng; JV Capt Vllybl; Hon Roll; NHS; Worcester Polytech Inst; Biotec.

PALMIERI, MICHELLE; Hoosic Valley Central HS; Schaghticoke, NY; (Y); Hon Roll; Hdsn Vly CC; Accntng.

PALMIERI, MISSY; Marlboro HS; Newburgh, NY; (Y); Spanish Clb; SADD; Varsity Clb; Socr; Sftbl; Vllybl; Btty Crckr Awd; High Hon Roll; Boces Food Svc I 85-86; Culinary Inst Amer; Chef.

PALMINTERI, ANTONETTA; Lindenhurst SR HS; Lindenhurst, NY; (Y); Cmnty Wkr; French Clb; SADD; Teachers Aide; Varsity Clb; Ed Yrbk Stf; Socr; Trk; Hon Roll; NHS; Hofstra U; Eng.

PALMIOTTI, ANDREW; Highland HS; W Park, NY; (Y); 34/124; Band; Concert Band; Jazz Band; Mrchg Band; JV Socr; Hon Roll; Etrscn Ldg 2238 Ordr Sns Itly Awd 86; ST U NY New Paltz; Elec Engr.

PALUCH, GLEN; Orchard Park HS; Blasdell, NY; (Y); 4-H; Varsity Clb; Drm & Bgl; Mrchg Band; 4-H Awd; Trs Band; Concert Band; Pep Band; Trs Symp Band; Physcs.

PALUMBO, ANTHONY; Notre Dame-Bishop Gibbons HS; Amsterdam, NY; (S); 25/101; Var Bsbl; Var Bowling; JV Crs Cntry; Spanish Awd; Frgn Study Prog; Civil Engrng.

PALUMBO, CHRISTINE A; St Francis Prep; Flushing, NY; (S); 190/746; Art Clb; Dance Clb; Yrbk Stf; Rep Jr Cls; Tennis; Trk; Im Vllybl; NHS; Opt Clb Awd.

PALUMBO, DAVID; East Meadow HS; East Meadow, NY; (Y); 16/350; Dance Clb; FBLA; Math Tm; Science Clb; Nwsp Rptr; Lit Mag; Var Capt Crs Cntry; Var Socr; Var Capt Trk; Vllybl; PROBE Sci Mag Awd 86; Peter Kostynick Schlrshp 86; Franklin; Pre-Med.

PALUMBO, FRANK; Mineola HS; Mineola, NY; (Y); SADD; Varsity Clb; Coach Actv; Socr; Wrstlng; Pace U; Real Est.

PALUMBO, MARIA; Marlboro Central HS; Marlboro, NY; (Y); 17/150; Varsity Clb; Rep Jr Cls; Bsktbl; Score Keeper; Sftbl; Vllybl; High Hon Roll; Hon Roll; NHS; Math II Regnts Awd 86; Math.

PALUMBO, TAMARA; Frankfort Schuyler Central HS; Frankfort, NY; (Y); FBLA; Key Clb; Spanish Clb; Yrbk Stf; Trk; Mohawk Vly Cmnty; Bus.

PANAGAKIS, ANDREA; Cicero-North Syracuse HS; Clay, NY; (S); 8/667; Dance Clb; Math Clb; Math Tm; Pep Clb; SADD; Band; Drill Tm; Flag Corp; Mrchg Band; Orch; Cornell U; Vet.

PANAGAKOS, NICHOLAS; Port Richmond HS; Staten Island, NY; (Y); Boy Scts; Church Yth Grp; Dance Clb; School Play; Variety Show; Rep Stu Cncl; Capt Var Ftbl; U Of Syracuse; Comp.

PANAGAKOS, PETER; Arch Bishop Iakajos HS; Jamaica, NY; (S); 1/12; Church Yth Grp; Math Clb; Yrbk Ed-Chief; VP Stu Cncl; Capt Bsktbl; High Hon Roll; NHS; Val; Queens Coll Pres Awd 82-86; Queens Dist Atty Stu Advsry Comm 84-85; St Johns U; Mktg.

PANARIELLO, JO ANN; Bishop Kearney HS; Brooklyn, NY; (Y); Office Aide; Teachers Aide; Brooklyn College; Tchr Spch.

PANARO, STEPHEN V; The Nichols Schl; Snyder, NY; (Y); Ski Clb; Chorus; Madrigals; Yrbk Phtg; Lit Mag; Var Trk; Ntl Merit SF; Pre-Med.

PANCZYSZYN III, FRANK T; Mc Quaid Jesuit HS; Rochester, NY; (Y); 94/172; Church Yth Grp; Varsity Clb; Chorus; School Musical; Var Ice Hcky; JV Mgr(s); Hon Roll; Hands Christ Awd 86; Regents Scholar; Clarkson U; Comp Sci.

PANDOLFI, MICHAEL; W C Mepham HS; N Bellmore, NY; (Y); JV Bsbl; Hon Roll; NHS; Engrng.

PANDOLFINO, GLEN; Monsignor Farrell HS; Staten Island, NY; (Y); French Clb; Sec Frsh Cls; VP Jr Cls; Rep Stu Cncl; Im Bsktbl; JV Ftbl; Hon Roll.

PANDOLFO, JOHN; Roosevelt HS; Yonkers, NY; (Y); Drama Clb; Chorus; Soph Cls; Jr Cls; Stu Cncl; Capt Bowling; High Hon Roll; Hon Roll; St Johns U; Phrmcy.

PANDOZY, CAROLYN F; Chazy Central Rural Schl; Chazy, NY; (Y); 5/35; 4-H; Band; Concert Band; Nwsp Stf; Yrbk Stf; Sec Sr Cls; L Var Cheerleading; High Hon Roll; NHS; Chorus; Rgnts Schlrshp 86; Skidmore; Bus Adm.

PANEK, DAVID; Eden SR HS; Hamburg, NY; (Y); 20/170; AFS; 4-H; Ski Clb; JV Ftbl; Var Swmmng; Var Trk; Hon Roll; Church Yth Grp; ROTC; Varsity Clb; Engr.

PANEK, LEA ANN; Lockport SR HS; Lockport, NY; (Y); 46/411; Trs AFS; Church Yth Grp; Girl Scts; Concert Band; Flag Corp; Mrchg Band; Symp Band; Rep Stu Cncl; Var JV Swmmng; God Cntry Awd; ROTC Schrlshp; Distngushd Stu Merit Schlrshp; NYS Regnts Schlrshp; Niagara County CC; Pre-Engrng.

PANEK, REGINA C; Fowler HS; Syracuse, NY; (Y); 7/250; Quiz Bowl; Lit Mag; Var Bsktbl; Bowling; Cheerleading; Sftbl; Tennis; High Hon Roll; Hon Roll; NHS; Bio, Chem & Eng Awds; Vol Awd Helping Hndcpd; Miss Polonia Heritage 86; Upstate Medical Ctr; Resp Ther.

PANELLA, ELIZABETH; Saugerties HS; Saugerties, NY; (Y); NYU Manhattan; Psych.

PANETTA, JOSEPH R; Notre Dame HS; Oriskany, NY; (Y); 7/156; Am Leg Boys St; Drama Clb; Spanish Clb; Thesps; Chorus; Nwsp Rptr; Yrbk Ed-Chief; Lit Mag; NYS Stu Advsry Comm 84-86; Colgate U; Intl Reltns.

PANG, CHU; John Dewey HS; Brooklyn, NY; (Y); Chess Clb; Computer Clb; Debate Tm; English Clb; Exploring; FBLA; FFA; JA; Math Tm; Science Clb; T Roosevelt Pstr Wnng Awd, C Columbus Pster 3rd; Bst Chss Plyr NJ; Cornell; Tchng.

PANNETTA, KERRY; St Peters HS For Girls; Staten Isl, NY; (Y); Boy Scts; Church Yth Grp; Exploring; VP FNA; Church Choir; Lit Mag; Sec Jr Cls; Sec Sr Cls; Prfct Atten Awd; Mrt Rl 86; St Johns U; Bus.

PANNONE, ANTHONY; St Joseph By The Sea HS; Staten Island, NY; (Y); Am Leg Boys St; Church Yth Grp; Rep SADD; Stage Crew; Pres Stu Cncl; Bsbl; Hon Roll; NLSA 86; Acad All Amer 85; USAA 85-86; Stony Brook; Dentl.

PANNU, HARPREET KAUR; Albany Academy For Girls; Cohoes, NY; (Y); 1/18; Cmnty Wkr; Hosp Aide; Library Aide; Model UN; Office Aide; Chorus; Nwsp Rptr; Lit Mag; Pres Frsh Cls; Trs Sr Cls; Recipient Dora Lott Donahue Schlrshp 86; Math & Sci Awd 86; RPI Albany Med Coll; Bio Med.

PANTANO, MICHAEL; Gates-Chili HS; Rochester, NY; (Y); Aud/Vis; Church Yth Grp; Cmnty Wkr; JV Var Ftbl; Wt Lftg; High Hon Roll; NHS; Outstndng Achvmnts In Math, Sci, & Social Studies 86; Engr.

PANTELIADIS, PHYLLIS; St Francis Prep; Corona, NY; (S); 66/744; Art Clb; Political Wkr; Service Clb; Im Ftbl; Im Sftbl; JV Wrstlng; Opt Clb Awd; Retreat Ldr; Stain Glass, Scultprng, Pntng & Fbrc Dsgn Art Clb; Arch.

PANTING, HILDA; Cathedral HS; Ny, NY; (Y); 74/272; Hon Roll; Bus Mgnt.

PANTOJA, JOSEPH; Archbishop Molloy HS; Long Isl City, NY; (Y); Computer Clb; JA; Science Clb; Church Choir; Nwsp Stf; High Hon Roll; Jr NHS; NHS; Ntl Merit Ltr; Queens Coll Pres Awd Achvt 85; Columbia U; Engrng.

PANTON, JAMES; Niagara Wheatfield HS; Niagara Falls, NY; (Y); VICA; JV Swmmng; Prfct Atten Awd; JV Ltr Swim 85; Prfct Atten 83-86; Rochester Inst Tech; Inds Engr.

PANTORNO, SUSAN; Seaford HS; Seaford, NY; (Y); Dance Clb; Drama Clb; Political Wkr; SADD; Chorus; School Musical; School Play; Swing Chorus; High Hon Roll; NHS; Chorus Achvmnt Awd 84; Chorale Svc Awd 85 & Prfmnce Awd 86; Bio Engr.

PANUS, STEPHEN; Victor HS; Farmington, NY; (Y); 90/230; AFS; Letterman Clb; Model UN; Spanish Clb; Varsity Clb; Var L Ftbl; Var L Trk; VP Frsh Cls; Stu Cncl; AFS Lang Study Prog 86.

PANZARELLA, VICTORIA; Herbert H Lehman HS; Bronx, NY; (Y); Church Yth Grp; PAVAS; Church Choir; Lit Mag; Englsh.

PANZELLA, CHRIS; Walt Whitman HS; Huntington, NY; (Y); 126/476; Church Yth Grp; Mathletes; Chorus; Hon Roll; NHS; Arch.

PANZER, BRIAN; E J Wilson HS; Rochester, NY; (Y); 26/350; VP Cmnty Wkr; Spanish Clb; VP Jr Cls; JV Socr; Var Trk; Dayton U; Mech Engr.

PANZER, LEONARD B; Hackley Schl; Purchase, NY; (Y); 8/89; Chess Clb; Model UN; Yrbk Stf; Im Ice Hcky; JV Lcrss; High Hon Roll; Silvr Medl NY ST Olympd Spokn Russn 86; Cert Merit Recpnt NY ST Regnts Schlrshp 86; Bucknell U; Bus Adm.

PANZONE, THOMAS V; St Francis Prep; Jackson Hgts, NY; (Y); 321/746; Am Leg Boys St; Chess Clb; Band; Concert Band; Jazz Band; Mrchg Band; Im Bowling; Crs Cntry; Im Sftbl; Trk; Law.

PAOLANTONIO, JO ANN; Sewanhaka HS; Stewart Manor, NY; (Y); Drama Clb; Girl Scts; Thesps; Chorus; School Musical; School Play; Swing Chorus; Variety Show; Yrbk Phtg; JV Cheerleading; Bst Thespn Troupe No 3846 86; Most Drmtc 86; City Coll Of NY; Prfmg Arts.

PAOLONE, ELIZABETH A; Shaker HS; Latham, NY; (Y); JA; Service Clb; Orch; Yrbk Stf; Mgr Sftbl; Vllybl; Hon Roll; NHS; Rgnts Schlrshp 85-86; George Wshngtn U; Intl Bus.

PAOLOZZI, MARYROSE; Whitesboro SR HS; Utica, NY; (Y); Church Yth Grp; Dance Clb; Library Aide; Ski Clb; Nwsp Rptr; Capt Cheerleading; Utica Coll; Bus Adm.

PAONESSA, ANN; Our Lady Of Mercy HS; Rochester, NY; (Y); English Clb; Varsity Clb; Nwsp Sprt Ed; Lit Mag; Rep Stu Cncl; JV Var Bsktbl; Var Crs Cntry; JV Var Socr; Var Trk; High Hon Roll; 1st Prz Brighton Libry Poetry Cntst SR Div 86.

PAP, CHRISTINA; Hamburg SR HS; Hamburg, NY; (Y); 7/379; Hosp Aide; Quiz Bowl; Band; Capt Color Guard; Orch; Rep Stu Cncl; Var L Fld Hcky; JV Socr; Hon Roll; NHS; Pres Catalina Clb 86-87; Northeastern U; Engrng.

PAPA, DEBORAH; Fonda-Fultonville Central HS; Fonda, NY; (Y); 28/114; Band; Yrbk Sprt Ed; Trs Frsh Cls; Trs Soph Cls; Trs Jr Cls; Trs Sr Cls; Stu Cncl; Cheerleading; Capt Socr; Trk; Cortland; Math.

PAPA, PETER; Frankfort Schuyler HS; Frankfort, NY; (Y); Spanish Clb; Wt Lftg; Var Wrstlng; Cit Awd; Hon Roll; Good Ctznshp Awd 86; Mohawk Valley CC; Crmnl Just.

PAPA, REGINA; Johnstown HS; Johnstown, NY; (Y); Intnl Clb; Band; JV Var Bsktbl; JV Sftbl; Var Timer; Hon Roll; Bus Mgmt.

PAPA, THERESA; Cathedral HS; Long Island Cty, NY; (Y); 20/277; Church Yth Grp; Cmnty Wkr; French Clb; FNA; Hosp Aide; Intnl Clb; Library Aide; Chorus; Church Choir; School Play; NYS Regents Scholar 86; Acad All Amer 86; SUNY Stony Brook; Phys Ther.

PAPAGEORGE, ANNA; F D Roosevelt HS; Brooklyn, NY; (Y); 57/587; Ed Lit Mag; NHS; Pres Schlr; Library Aide; Teachers Aide; Band; Arista 83; Lioness Clb Awd 83; Brooklyn Coll; Tchr.

PAPAGNI, DINA M; St Francis Prep; Bayside, NY; (S); 129/742; Math Clb; SADD; Rep Soph Cls; Rep Jr Cls; Rep Stu Cncl; Hon Roll; Stanford U; Law.

PAPAILLER, MYRTHO C; Nazareth Regional HS; Brooklyn, NY; (S); 29/267; Camera Clb; Debate Tm; Speech Tm; Band; Yrbk Phtg; Chrmn Sr Cls; Cheerleading; Crs Cntry; Trk; Hon Roll; JR Actvty, Soc Stu & Phys Ftnss Awds; Hoftra; Bus Adm.

PAPASTRATIS, MARY; Binghamton HS; Binghamton, NY; (Y); High Hon Roll; NHS; ST U NY; Acctng.

PAPATSOS, CAROL; West Hempstead HS; Island Park, NY; (Y); Pres Soph Cls; Pres Jr Cls; Hon Roll; Sec NHS; Art Clb; Lit Mag; Rep Frsh Cls; Var Sftbl; Var Swmmng; Mth Achvt Awd 86; Spn III Achvt Awd 86; Natl Art Hnr Soc Pres 86; Mth.

PAPE, CYNTHIA L; Liverpool HS; Liverpool, NY; (Y); 46/816; Church Yth Grp; Hosp Aide; JA; Concert Band; Jazz Band; Mrchg Band; Trk; Jr NHS; NHS; Opt Clb Awd; Ntl Merit Cmnd Schlr 85; Ithaca Coll; Physcl Thrpy.

PAPE, LISA; Onteora HS; Boiceville, NY; (Y); 5/201; Hosp Aide; Math Tm; SADD; Yrbk Ed-Chief; Capt Cheerleading; Stat Trk; Bausch & Lomb Sci Awd; High Hon Roll; NHS; Roswell Park Mem Inst Summr Pgm 85; U Rochester; Biochem.

PAPELE, ILANA; Dover HS; Millbrook, NY; (S); 5/75; Drama Clb; Ski Clb; Chorus; School Musical; JV Var Cheerleading; Fld Hcky; Score Keeper; Jr NHS; NHS; Outstndng Dtchss Stu 86.

PAPELINO, JEANNINE M; Notre Dame HS; Utica, NY; (Y); 64/158; Art Clb; FBLA; School Musical; School Play; Yrbk Phtg; Yrbk Stf; Lit Mag; Hon Roll; Ntl Merit Ltr; Hosp Aide; Schlstc Art Awds 86; NY ST Fair Poster Cntst; MUCC; Commrcl Adver.

PAPERTSIAN, MARK; Archbishop Stepinac HS; Hastings On Hudso, NY; (Y); 47/174; Church Yth Grp; High Hon Roll; Hon Roll; Cornell; Botany.

PAPINI, BARBARA; Moore Catholic HS; Staten Island, NY; (Y); Math Clb; Spanish Clb; SADD; Bowling; Tennis; Arch.

PAPP, MARY; West Genesee SR HS; Camillus, NY; (Y); French Clb; Ski Clb; High Hon Roll; Hon Roll; Hnr Roll 85-86; High Hnr Roll 85-86; SUNY; Systms Anlyst.

PAPPALARDO, FABIO; Bishop Ford C C HS; Brooklyn, NY; (Y); Im Bowling; JV Tennis; Hon Roll; St Francis Coll; Avtn.

PAPPAS, DEMITRA M; St Francis Prep; Bayside, NY; (S); 4/653; Debate Tm; Library Aide; Model UN; Nwsp Ed-Chief; Nwsp Rptr; High Hon Roll; NHS; Ntl Merit Ltr; Church Yth Grp; Politcs.

PAPPAS, KALI; Saint Francis Prep; Whitestone, NY; (Y); 220/750; Church Yth Grp; Cmnty Wkr; Dance Clb; Hosp Aide; Intnl Clb; Library Aide; Math Clb; Office Aide; SADD; Teachers Aide.

PAPPAS, KATINA; Pelham Memorial HS; Pelham, NY; (Y); AFS; Church Yth Grp; Exploring; Model UN; Concert Band; School Musical; School Play; Stage Crew; Nwsp Bus Mgr; Yrbk Stf; Peer Counselling 86.

PAPROCKI, KRISTA; Fairport HS; Fairport, NY; (Y); Sec French Clb; Girl Scts; Library Aide; Model UN; SADD; Chorus; Yrbk Stf; Rep Stu Cncl; Hon Roll; Prfct Atten Awd; Intl Bus.

PAPUCCI, NELSON; Seton Catholic Central HS; Huntsville, AL; (Y); 9/162; Nwsp Rptr; Var Wrstlng; DAR Awd; Hon Roll; NHS; Ntl Merit SF; U Of San Diego Trstee Awd 86; Burns Schlrshp 86-87; U Of San Diego; Elctrcl Engrng.

PARADIS, JOSEPH M; Thomas Edison HS; Elmira Hgts, NY; (Y); 2/86; Am Leg Boys St; JCL; Latin Clb; Model UN; Varsity Clb; School Musical; Var Bsbl; Var Ftbl; Var Wrstlng; High Hon Roll; Rensselaer Ply Tech Inst Math & Sci 86; Arch.

PARADISE, KATHY; Mt Mercy Acad; Orchard Park, NY; (Y); FHA; Pep Clb; SADD; Teachers Aide; Trs Frsh Cls; Im JV Badmtn; JV Bsktbl; JV Trk; Hon Roll; Geneseo; Educ.

PARADISE, STEVEN; Myndersz Acad; Seneca Falls, NY; (Y); Art Clb; Library Aide; Science Clb; JV Bsbl; Golf; High Hon Roll; Hon Roll; Spartan Schl Of Aero; Aviation.

PARADISO, STEPHEN J; Monsignor Farrell HS; Staten Island, NY; (Y); 123/305; Chess Clb; Capt Wrstlng; NYS Regnts Schlrshp 86; Wrstlng 86; St Johns U Staten Isl; Fince.

PARALEMOS, PARASKEVI; St Francis Prep; Bayside, NY; (S); 9/653; Church Yth Grp; Cmnty Wkr; Math Clb; Im Sftbl; Im Vllybl; High Hon Roll; NHS; Ntl Merit Ltr; Bus.

PARANGELO, VICTOR; Commack H S North; Smithtown, NY; (Y); 25/360; Spanish Clb; Var Crs Cntry; Sftbl; Capt Var Trk; High Hon Roll; NHS; Spanish NHS; Long Island Sci Cong 83-84; Pres Schlr Athlete Soc 86-87; Spcl Olympics; Engrng.

PARASCANDOLA, PATRICIA; St Agnes Cathedral HS; Rosedale, NY; (Y); Nwsp Stf; Yrbk Stf; NHS; St Johns U; Elem Ed.

PARASCH, MICHAEL; Seton Catholic Central HS; Endwell, NY; (Y); Art Clb; Boy Scts; French Clb; Key Clb; Ski Clb; SADD; JV Bsbl; Bsktbl; Var Tennis; Sctng Eagle Awd; Engrng.

PARASHAR, MEETA; Spackenkill HS; Poughkeepsie, NY; (Y); 17/167; Hosp Aide; School Play; Nwsp Stf; Yrbk Stf; Trk; High Hon Roll; Rgnts Schlrshp 86; RPI; Med.

PARASKEVA, HELEN; Center Moriches HS; Ctr Moriches, NY; (Y); 22/92; Art Clb; Computer Clb; Library Aide; Ski Clb; Spanish Clb; Drill Tm; Stage Crew; Yrbk Stf; Im Vllybl; Hon Roll; Cert Of Merit-Peer Ldr Cnslr 84-86; 3rd Pl Poster-Drg Abuse Cntst Awd 83; Denotes Rgnts Dploma 86; SUNY Brockport; Bus Admin.

PARATORE, CHRISTINE; St John The Baptist HS; Kings Park, NY; (Y); Church Yth Grp; Pep Clb; VP Frsh Cls; JV Im Cheerleading; Var Pom Pon; Im Wt Lftg; Hon Roll; Acdmc Achvt Math 84-85; Elem Educ.

PARATORE, CLAUDIA; Sanford H Calhoun HS; Merrick, NY; (Y); 47/313; SADD; Nwsp Stf; Yrbk Stf; Off Soph Cls; Off Jr Cls; Off Sr Cls; Stu Cncl; Mgr Wrstlng; Hon Roll; Computer Clb; SUNY Albany; Bus Admin.

PARAVATI, MICHELLE; Albertus Magnus HS; W Nyack, NY; (Y); 5/175; Church Yth Grp; Sec Stu Cncl; Var Capt Cheerleading; Coach Actv; JV Var Sftbl; Hon Roll; Mu Alp Tht; NHS; Spanish NHS; Math.

PARCHMENT, MICHELLE; Dewitt Clinton HS; Bronx, NY; (Y); Aud/Vis; Cmnty Wkr; Hosp Aide; Office Aide; Hon Roll; Stu Mnth 86; Arista Hnr Soc 85; Meritrs Perfrmnce Awd Off Aide 84; Nrsng.

PARCO, LISA; Lindenhurst SR HS; Lindenhurst, NY; (Y); School Play; Stage Crew; Hon Roll.

PARDES, HILARY; South Shore HS; Brooklyn, NY; (Y); Gym; Brooklyn Coll; Ed.

PARDI, KAREN; Christ The King HS; Rego Park, NY; (Y); 1/350; Art Clb; Cmnty Wkr; Computer Clb; Math Clb; Office Aide; DAR Awd; Ntl Merit SF; Val; Pres Awd Achvt 83-86; Govnrs Comm Schltc Achvt Schlrshp 86; Dean Schlrshp 86; Cornell U; Eng.

PARDO, MARY; Canarsie HS; Brooklyn, NY; (Y); 34/498; Yrbk Stf; Rep Sr Cls; Hon Roll; Prfct Atten Awd; Cmnty Wkr; Office Aide; Teachers Aide; Arista 82; 1st Pl Ind Arts Technlgy Exhbt 85; NYC Engl Excl & Achvt Awds 83; Brookyn Coll; Elem Ed.

PARDO, WALTER; New York Military Acad; Ridgewood, NJ; (Y); 10/86; Church Yth Grp; Drama Clb; Model UN; ROTC; Varsity Clb; Chorus; School Musical; School Play; Variety Show; Nwsp Rptr; Pres Phys Ftnss Awd; Amer Hstry Olympd; Bst Actr Awd; US Mltry Acad; Aerosp Engrng.

PARDUE, JAYMES; Walter Panas HS; Peekskill, NY; (Y); 4-H; Var Diving; JV Ftbl; Bio.

PAREDES, LEIDY; Eastern District HS; Brooklyn, NY; (Y); Tennis; Vllybl; Hon Roll; Hnr Rll 85; Math.

PARENTE, CARMELLA; Mercy HS; Albany, NY; (Y); Church Yth Grp; Chorus; School Play; Yrbk Stf; VP Soph Cls; Rep Stu Cncl; Var Cheerleading; High Hon Roll; Hon Roll; Exclnc-Soc Stu 84-85; Exclnc-Eng 85; Exclnc-Frnch Math Rlgn Sci 84.

PARENTE, JOHN; Monsignor Farrell HS; Staten Island, NY; (Y); Am Leg Boys St; Boy Scts; Lit Mag; Mgr(s); Var L Swmmng; Hon Roll; NHS; Swmmng Schlstc Awd 84; CCD Tchr 85-87; Ad Altare Dei Cathlc Relgs Awd 85; Engrng.

PARENTE, MICHELE; Dominican Commercial HS; Richmond Hill, NY; (S); 1/288; Hosp Aide; Teachers Aide; Church Choir; Swmmng; High Hon Roll; NHS; Prfct Atten Awd; Siena Club Awd 84-85; Law.

PARENTI, CHRISTINE; Farmingdale SR HS; Farmingdale, NY; (Y); SADD; Flag Corp; Yrbk Rptr; Cheerleading; Hon Roll; NHS; Theatre Clb Sec 86-87; Yrbk Circltn Edtr & Treas 85-87; Peer Cnslng 86-87.

PARENTIS, MICHAEL A; Nichols Schl; Buffalo, NY; (Y); Nwsp Rptr; Yrbk Stf; VP Jr Cls; Pres Stu Cncl; Var Bsktbl; Var Capt Ftbl; Var Capt Lcrss; High Hon Roll; NHS; Ntl Merit Ltr; II Frm Mrt Awd 84; Yale Awd 85; Irwin Awd 86; Yale U; Bio.

PARES, NAYDA; John Dewey HS; Brooklyn, NY; (Y); Aud/Vis; Dance Clb; School Musical; School Play; Ed Yrbk Ed-Chief; Rep Stu Cncl; Vllybl; High Hon Roll; Jr NHS; Hackett Mdl Perfmg Arts 86; Binghamton U; Psych.

PARFITT, CANDACE E; La Salle SR HS; Niagara Falls, NY; (S); 44/260; Off Drama Clb; School Play; Yrbk Stf; Lit Mag; VP Soph Cls; Pres Jr Cls; Pres Sr Cls; Stu Cncl; Crs Cntry; Trk; Yrbk Art Edtr 86; Potsdam Coll; Art.

PARGETER, RACHEL S; Warwick Valley HS; Warwick, NY; (Y); 7/195; AFS; Cmnty Wkr; Drama Clb; French Clb; Library Aide; Band; Orch; School Play; Nwsp Stf; Yrbk Stf; NYS Regnts Schlrshp 86; 1st Pl Natl Sci Olympd Tst Bio 83; Cornell U; Anml Sci.

PARHAM, SHEILA; Of Fashion Industries HS; Brooklyn, NY; (Y); Art Clb; Cmnty Wkr; Teachers Aide; Stage Crew; Variety Show; Fshn Inst Tech.

PARIBELLI, MARY LENORE; Wallkill SR HS; Clintondale, NY; (Y); 24/194; Girl Scts; Hosp Aide; Chorus; Mrchg Band; Nwsp Rptr; Lit Mag; Bausch & Lomb Sci Awd; Hon Roll; NHS; Girl Scout Catholic Awd Marian Medal 83; Girl Scout Silver Awd 83; Suny Oneonta Coll; Elem Educ.

PARIKH, DHAVAL K; Plainedge HS; Seaford, NY; (Y); 6/314; Library Aide; Mathletes; Quiz Bowl; Scholastic Bowl; High Hon Roll; NHS; Ntl Merit Ltr; Spanish NHS; Rennsellaer Mdl 85; PA ST; Med.

PARILLO, BRIAN; Fairport HS; Fairport, NY; (Y); Boy Scts; Model UN; Ski Clb; Yrbk Bus Mgr; Yrbk Stf; Rep Stu Cncl; High Hon Roll; NHS; Ntl Merit Ltr; Spanish NHS; Eagel Scout 84; Finance.

PARINI, FRANK; Smithtown HS East; Smithtown, NY; (Y); Key Clb; JV Var Ftbl; Hnr Rll 84-86; JV Ftbl Tm; Vrsty Ftbl & Let Wnr.

PARIS, CYDNEY; Mount St Mary Acad; Buffalo, NY; (Y); Hosp Aide; Pep Clb; Ski Clb; Yrbk Phtg; Socr; Med.

PARIS, JOHN; Walt Whitman HS; Huntington Stat, NY; (Y); 37/540; Key Clb; Var Trk; High Hon Roll; Jr NHS; NHS; Spanish NHS; S Huntington Tchrs Assoc Schlrshp 86; Prsdntl Physcl Ftns Awd 86; Villanova U; Mech Engrng.

PARIS, KAREN L; L C O Bourn HS; Pittsford, NY; (Y); 15/123; Sec Varsity Clb; Rep Frsh Cls; VP Jr Cls; Pres Sr Cls; Rep Stu Cncl; Var JV Fld Hcky; Var JV Vllybl; NHS; FCA; JR Rotarian 85-86; Babcock-Emerson Awd 85-86; E Rochester H S SR Clss Schlrp 85-86; U MA Amherst.

PARIS, PATRICIA; Rome Catholic HS; Rome, NY; (Y); Red Cross Aide; SADD; School Musical; Yrbk Stf; Var Capt Cheerleading; JV Socr; Var Sftbl; NHS; Rotary Awd; Acad All Ame Schlr 83-86; Achvt Kybrdng, Bus Comm 86; Achvt Home Ec 83; Upstate Med Ctr; Sci.

PARISI, DAVID; H C Technical HS; Buffalo, NY; (Y); Chess Clb; Math Tm; Band; Concert Band; Jazz Band; Hon Roll; All Hgh 1st Brd Chess 85.

PARISI, IRENE; Port Richmond HS; Staten Island, NY; (Y); 73/560; Hosp Aide; Pep Clb; Ski Clb; School Musical; School Play; Pedtrcn.

PARISI, JENNIFER A; Notre Dame Acad; Staten Island, NY; (Y); 8/93; Cmnty Wkr; Computer Clb; Science Clb; Chorus; Crs Cntry; Trk; NHS; Ntl Merit SF; Mst Imprvd Plyr Trk-Fld 85; Stevens Inst Tech; Comp Engr.

PARISI, LINDA; Lafayette HS; Brooklyn, NY; (Y); JA; Math Tm; Office Aide; Service Clb; Teachers Aide; Ed Yrbk Phtg; High Hon Roll; NHS; Prfct Atten Awd; Val.

PARISI, MELINDA; Franciscan HS; Peekskill, NY; (Y); 1/50; Political Wkr; School Musical; Nwsp Stf; Yrbk Stf; Pres Jr Cls; Stat Vllybl; Bausch & Lomb Sci Awd; NHS; Ntl Merit Ltr; Val; Pres Acad Ftns Awd 86; Regnts Schlrshp 86; Gen Exc Ads 86; Villanova U; Psychlgy.

PARISI, VIRGINIA; John Dewey HS; Brooklyn, NY; (Y); Debate Tm; Office Aide; Spanish Clb; Teachers Aide; Hon Roll; Political Sci.

PARISIAN, NICOLE; Massena Central HS; Massena, NY; (Y); Am Leg Aux Girls St; SADD; Rep Frsh Cls; Rep Soph Cls; Stu Cncl; JV L Cheerleading; Var L Socr; Var L Trk; Hon Roll; NHS; Rotary Internatl Stu Abrd Exchng Pgm Frnc 85; Tlntd JR Pgm St Lrnce U 86; Girl Vars Scert Awd 85-86.

PARK, CHUL-IN; The Mcburney Schl; New York, NY; (Y); 1/70; Orch; Yrbk Stf; High Hon Roll; Hon Roll; Jr NHS; NHS; Val; VP French Clb.

PARK, CHUN SAE; New Town HS; Elmhurst, NY; (Y); 1/35; Library Aide; Math Tm; Office Aide; Teachers Aide; Prfct Atten Awd; Nclr Physcs.

PARK, HENRY; Bronx HS Of Science; Woodside, NY; (Y); Church Yth Grp; Key Clb; Yrbk Phtg; Sr Cls; Bsbl; Bsktbl; Var Trk; Im Vllybl; NHS; Pres Acad Ftns Awd 86; Cornell U; Microbio.

PARK, JENNIFER; G Ray Bodley HS; Fulton, NY; (Y); Exploring; French Clb; Science Clb; Concert Band; Orch; High Hon Roll; Hon Roll; Compu Sci.

PARK, JENNY; Herricks SR HS; Roslyn, NY; (Y); DECA; Hosp Aide; Yrbk Sprt Ed; Rep Soph Cls; Off Jr Cls; Cheerleading; VFW Awd; Voice Dem Awd; DECA Trvl Toursm Rgn 83 & 84; DECA Apparel Accssrs ST 85; Lbrl Art.

PARK, KRISTINA; Haverling Central HS; Bath, NY; (Y); 15/120; French Clb; Latin Clb; Math Clb; School Musical; Yrbk Stf; Trs Stu Cncl; Var Capt Vllybl; Pres NHS; JCL; Spanish Clb; Canon Donald C Means Ctzn Schlrp 86; Hobart & Wm Smith Coll; Econ.

PARK, LISA A; East Syracuse-Minoa HS; East Syracuse, NY; (Y); 66/333; Pres Church Yth Grp; JA; Variety Show; Stat Ftbl; Var Tennis; Var Stat Trk; Hon Roll; Jr NHS; NHS; Prfct Atten Awd; SUNY U At Buffalo, NY.

PARK, MARIA; The Mary Louis Acad; Bayside, NY; (Y); 87/270; Aud/Vis; Cmnty Wkr; Hosp Aide; Mathletes; NFL; Church Choir; Nwsp Rptr; Im Bowling; NEDT Awd; St Schlr; Piano Gold Medal 84-85; N ST Bar Assoc Mock Trial 86; U Of MA-AMHERST; Econ.

PARK, SUJIN; Bayside HS; Flushing, NY; (Y); 59/650; Art Clb; Sec Church Yth Grp; Math Tm; Orch; Nwsp Rptr; Ed Yrbk Stf; Lit Mag; High Hon Roll; Hon Roll; St Schlr; St Gaudens Awds 86; NY ST Regnts Schlrshp 86; Parsons Schl Of Design.

PARKER, ALFRED; Burgard HS; Buffalo, NY; (Y); Library Aide; Math Clb; SADD; Teachers Aide; Variety Show; Bsbl; Bsktbl; Crs Cntry; Ftbl; Trk; Vrsty Bsktbl Awd 85-86; X-Cntry Awd 85-86; Avtn.

PARKER, CORNELLA; Gorton HS; Yonkers, NY; (Y); Church Yth Grp; Library Aide; Church Choir; Bsktbl; Crs Cntry; Vllybl; Bus Mngmnt.

PARKER, DAVID A; Mc Quaid Jesuit HS; Batavia, NY; (Y); Hosp Aide; Ski Clb; Stage Crew; Ed Yrbk Stf; Sec Frsh Cls; VP Soph Cls; Ice Hcky; High Hon Roll; NHS; Var Socr; Aws Hst Sci Rsrch Smnr 84-85; Outstndng Chinese Schlrshp Awd 84-85; Prnts Aws Outstndng 84-8; Harvard.

PARKER, DONOVAN; W H Taft HS; Bronx, NY; (Y); 4-H; Socr; Law.

PARKER, GEORGE; Bronx High School Of Science; New York, NY; (Y); NY Rgnts Coll Schlrshp 86; Baruch Schlr Awd 86; Baruch Coll.

PARKER, JIM; New Hartford HS; New Hartford, NY; (Y); Boy Scts; Church Yth Grp; SADD; Concert Band; Jazz Band; Mrchg Band; Symp Band; Capt Var Lcrss; Law.

PARKER, JO ANNE; Sherburne-Earlville Cntrl Schl; Smyrna, NY; (Y); 33/167; VP Sr Cls; Var JV Cheerleading; Stat Lcrss; Bus.

PARKER, JULIE; Akron HS; Akron, NY; (Y); 8/130; Drama Clb; French Clb; Girl Scts; Chorus; Nwsp Stf; Sec Stu Cncl; Var Swmmng; Var Trk; Hon Roll; NHS; Stu Union Awd 86; Baldwin-Wallace Coll; Mth.

PARKER, KELLY; Tonawanda JR SR HS; Tonawanda, NY; (Y); Church Yth Grp; Cmnty Wkr; VP Spanish Clb; Var Cheerleading; Bus.

PARKER, LISA; Hoosick Falls Central Schl; Hoosick Falls, NY; (Y); Pep Clb; Band; Rep Stu Cncl; Business.

PARKER, LISA; Letchworth Central HS; Warsaw, NY; (Y); Drama Clb; School Play; Stage Crew; Yrbk Stf; High Hon Roll; NHS; BUS Mgmnt.

PARKER, LUANN; Clara Barton HS; Brooklyn, NY; (Y); Exploring; Hosp Aide; Office Aide; Science Clb; Spanish Clb; JV Cheerleading; High Hon Roll; Prfct Atten Awd; Spanish NHS; Awd From Magnolia Tree Earth Ctr 86; CMSP Semnrs On Careers In Engrng Tech & Comp Sci 86; UCLA; Gynecology.

PARKER, MARK; Caledonia-Mumford HS; Scottsville, NY; (Y); 35/90; Varsity Clb; Var L Bsbl; Var L Ftbl; Var Wt Lftg; Hon Roll; Prfct Atten Awd; Urban Leag Black Schlr 85-86; Natl Hon Roll 84-85; Widener U; Bus Mgmt.

PARKER, MICHELE; St Marys HS; Depew, NY; (S); 24/200; JA; Sec Office Aide; Nwsp Rptr; Lit Mag; Rep Frsh Cls; Rep Soph Cls; Rep Jr Cls; Hon Roll; Jr NHS; NHS; Tuition To Villa Maria Coll Bflo NY 86; Villa Maria Coll; Intr Dsgn.

PARKER, SANDRA; East Syracuse Minoa HS; E Syracuse, NY; (Y); Exploring; Science Clb; Ski Clb; Concert Band; Jazz Band; Hon Roll; Paul Smith; Trvl.

PARKER, SCOTT G; Gananda Central HS; Walworth, NY; (Y); Am Leg Boys St; Socr; U Of Miami; Mrn Bio.

PARKER, SHARON; Queen Of The Rosary Acad; Roosevelt, NY; (S); Cit Awd; Hon Roll; Advnc Plcmnt Pin 80; Hgh Acdmcs 81; Fshn Merch & Rtlng.

PARKER, STACY; Sachem HS; Lake Ronkonkoma, NY; (Y); 135/1685; Cmnty Wkr; Dance Clb; Drama Clb; Hosp Aide; PAVAS; Lit Mag; Coach Actv; George Farce Acad Scholar 86; Dancing Schl Awd 83; Film.

PARKER, STEFAN J; Cohoes HS; Cohoes, NY; (Y); 27/200; Exploring; French Clb; FTA; Varsity Clb; Nwsp Ed-Chief; Stu Cncl; Capt Var Score Keeper; Var Tennis; Hon Roll; Prfct Atten Awd; MVP Soccer Team 84; Siena Coll; Intl Fnc.

PARKER, TODD; Corning-Painted Post West HS; Painted Post, NY; (Y); Church Yth Grp; Key Clb; Letterman Clb; Ski Clb; Varsity Clb; Band; Mrchg Band; Var L Lcrss; Var L Socr; JV Tennis; Bio.

PARKHURST, LORETTA; Hannibal Central HS; Fulton, NY; (S); 1/119; VP Sec 4-H; French Clb; SADD; Yrbk Stf; Capt Bowling; 4-H Awd; High Hon Roll; Kiwanis Awd; NHS; Val; SUNY Oswego; Secndry Ed.

PARKS, BONNIE S; Nardin Acad; Buffalo, NY; (Y); Model UN; Service Clb; Ski Clb; Yrbk Phtg; Yrbk Rptr; Yrbk Stf; Lit Mag; Im Badmtn; Im Crs Cntry; Var Sftbl; Pres Hnr Awd Frm John Carroll U 86; John Carroll U; Mass Cmmnctns.

PARKS, CURTIS; Auburn HS; Auburn, NY; (Y); Boy Scts; Chess Clb; Math Clb; Science Clb; SADD; Bsktbl; Ftbl; Golf; Trk; Wt Lftg; Outstndg Staff Stu Of Wk BSA 84; Cayuga CC.

PARKS, JOHN; Amsterdam HS; Amsterdam, NY; (Y); Am Leg Boys St; Band; Concert Band; Jazz Band; Mrchg Band; Nwsp Ed-Chief; Yrbk Stf; Im Bsbl; Var Golf; Var Trk; MA.

PARKS, STACY; Wayland Central Schl; N Cohocton, NY; (Y); Cmnty Wkr; Pres Sec 4-H; Ski Clb; Varsity Clb; Mrchg Band; Rep Jr Cls; JV Var Bsktbl; JV Var Vllybl; Cit Awd; God Cntry Awd; Schl Merit Roll Hgh Avg 84-86; Alfred ST; Bus Admin.

PARLATO, ANTHONY; Center Moriches HS; Center Moriches, NY; (Y); 2/90; VP Pres Stu Cncl; Var Capt Bsktbl; Var Capt Socr; High Hon Roll; NHS; Sal; Art Clb; Church Yth Grp; French Clb; Latin Clb.

PARLITSIS, MARIA; Roosevelt HS; Yonkers, NY; (Y); 81/247; Pres Drama Clb; Hosp Aide; Concert Band; Mrchg Band; School Play; Variety Show; Yrbk Phtg; Stu Cncl; Var Capt Cheerleading; High Hon Roll; Akp Schlrshp 86; Pace U; Nrsng.

PARMAR, HENRY; Trott Vo Tech; Niagara Falls, NY; (Y); Boy Scts; Church Yth Grp; 4-H; Office Aide; Church Choir; Hon Roll; Prfct Atten Awd; Cmpltn Of Job Trng Course 84; Yellow Belt In Karate 85; Niagara U.

PARMELEE, SHARON L; Arlington HS; La Grangeville, NY; (Y); 13/576; French Clb; Intnl Clb; Math Tm; Service Clb; Ski Clb; High Hon Roll; St Schlr; Hnr Key 86; Cornell Trad 86; Cornell U; Operations Rsrch.

PARMER, TRACEY; Westlake HS; Thornwood, NY; (Y); Pep Clb; Spanish Clb; Yrbk Stf; Hon Roll; Spanish NHS; Fordham U; Acctng.

PARMERTER, MARK R; Andrew S Draper Central HS; Schenevus, NY; (Y); Am Leg Boys St; Aud/Vis; Drama Clb; Spanish Clb; Teachers Aide; Nwsp Rptr; Yrbk Sprt Ed; VP Bsbl; High Hon Roll; NHS; Bus Math Regents Awd 85; Principals List 85-86; Mountain Update Schl Spnsrd Tv Show 86; Hartwick Clg; Radio Prdctn.

PARMET, ANDREA K; Ward Melville HS; E Setauket, NY; (Y); Drama Clb; Hosp Aide; Service Clb; Temple Yth Grp; Rgnts Schlrshp 86; Untd Syngage Yth Exec Brd 86; Comm Yth Srvcs Yth Brd 85; SUNY Buffalo; Psych.

PARODI, MELISSA; Sachem High Schl North; Ronkonkoma, NY; (Y); 29/1579; Drama Clb; French Clb; JA; Acpl Chr; Chorus; Madrigals; School Musical; School Play; Swing Chorus; Variety Show; Bst Actrss Awd 84; Schl Choral Stds 85; Mst Imprvd Musician 85; Pre-Law.

PARR, SCOTT KENNETH; Kenmore East SR HS; Tonawanda, NY; (Y); 12/330; Church Yth Grp; VP Varsity Clb; Variety Show; Nwsp Rptr; JV Var Bsbl; JV Var Bsktbl; High Hon Roll; Trs NHS; Hon Roll; Hans H Schambach Schlrshp Wnnr 86; Hamilton Coll; Compu Sci.

PARRA, FLAMINIA; Immaculata HS; New York, NY; (Y); Church Yth Grp; Hon Roll; Awd Acad Excllnc 86; Hnrb Mntn Acad Avg 85-86; Baruch Coll; Fin.

PARRA, GLADYS; Louis D Brandeis HS; New York, NY; (Y); Art Clb; Capt Bowling; Srv Awd 84-86; Long Island U; Comm.

PARRILLO, SARA; Cooperstown Central HS; Cooperstown, NY; (Y); 28/100; Red Cross Aide; Chorus; Ed Yrbk Stf; Lion Awd; Schlstc Art Awds Hnbl Mntn 85-86; Art Awd 86; Clark Schlrshp 86; Advrtsg Dsgn.

PARRIS, JAMES; HS Of Art And Design; Hollis, NY; (Y); Art Clb; Church Yth Grp; Debate Tm; FTA; JA; Office Aide; Service Clb; Teachers Aide; Church Choir; School Musical; Outstndng Vlntr Young Artst 83-86; Schlstc Apt Tst 86; Hnrd In Dly News Under Super Youth 86; Art.

PARRISH, LAURA; Cicero-North Syracuse HS; Clay, NY; (S); 71/676; Drama Clb; Teachers Aide; Thesps; Chorus; School Musical; Stage Crew; Var Bowling; JV Vllybl; High Hon Roll; NHS; ST U Of NY; Bio Sci.

PARRISH, PENNY; Sachem North HS; Farmingville, NY; (Y); Library Aide; Chorus; Wt Lftg.

PARROTT, JODI; Salamanca HS; Salamanca, NY; (Y); 10/164; Art Clb; GAA; Varsity Clb; Band; Concert Band; Mrchg Band; Pep Band; Sec Frsh Cls; Sec Soph Cls; Sec Jr Cls; Syracuse; Advrtsng.

PARROTTA, NICHOLAS; Frankfort Schuyler HS; Frankfort, NY; (Y); FBLA; Pep Clb; Spanish Clb; Varsity Clb; Band; Yrbk Sprt Ed; Stu Cncl; Bsbl; Hon Roll; NHS; Pre Med.

PARRY, KAREN; Thomas J Corcoran HS; Syracuse, NY; (Y); Church Yth Grp; GAA; Spanish Clb; Yrbk Phtg; Var Cheerleading; Engl 11 Most Outstndng Stu 86; Outstndg Achvt Spnsh Regents 86; Outstndng Achvt Onalg Regents 83; Phy Thrpst.

PARSNICK, TODD; Union Springs Central Schl; Union Spgs, NY; (Y); 14/120; Boy Scts; Church Yth Grp; Ski Clb; Spanish Clb; Y-Teens; Yrbk Stf; JV Var Socr; JV Var Tennis; JV Wrstlng; High Hon Roll; Chemical Engineer.

PARSONS, BRAD T; Oneida HS; Oneida, NY; (Y); Am Leg Boys St; Church Yth Grp; Drama Clb; Spanish Clb; Varsity Clb; Chorus; School Musical; School Play; Yrbk Phtg; Yrbk Rptr; Thtrcl Arts.

PARSONS, JILL; Guilderland Central HS; Albany, NY; (Y).

PARSONS, MATT; Falconer Central HS; Falconer, NY; (Y); Chorus; JV Bsbl.

PARSONS, MICHAEL; Naples Central HS; Naples, NY; (Y); 6/62; VP Jr Cls; JV L Bsbl; Var Capt Socr; JV L Swmmng; High Hon Roll; Rensaeleer; Engrng.

PARSONS, TODD T; Sidney HS; Sidney Center, NY; (Y); Am Leg Boys St; Church Yth Grp; Drama Clb; 4-H; French Clb; Band; Chorus; Concert Band; Jazz Band; Mrchg Band; Sci Fld.

PARTANNA, LENNY; South Shore HS; Brooklyn, NY; (Y); Office Aide; SADD; Band; Jazz Band; Orch; School Musical; Variety Show; Pharmcy.

PARTHEMORE, CHERYL; Ossining HS; Ossining, NY; (Y); Sec Church Yth Grp; Dance Clb; Acpl Chr; Sec Chorus; Church Choir; Hon Roll; Busnss.

PARTON, BRENDA; Le Roy Central HS; Le Roy, NY; (Y); 5/138; Varsity Clb; Var L Bsktbl; Var L Sftbl; Var L Vllybl; High Hon Roll; Jr NHS; NHS; Church Yth Grp; Spanish Clb; Band; Sec V All Tournmnt Tm Sftbll 85-86; Schl Lab Asst Sci Dept 85-86; Ingham U Schlrshp, Legion Awd 86; Monroe CC; Dntl Hygn.

PARTRIDGE, EDWARD; Fabius-Pompey HS; Lafayette, NY; (Y); Church Yth Grp; Band; Concert Band; Nwsp Rptr; Nwsp Sprt Ed; Nwsp Stf; NYSSMA Music Awd 86; All-Cnty Music Awd 86; Rnsslr Ply-Tech Inst; Mech Engr.

PARTRIDGE, MARGARET; Mt Mercy Acad; Blasdell, NY; (Y); VP Church Yth Grp; Varsity Clb; Chorus; Church Choir; School Musical; Stat Bsktbl; Var Vllybl; High Hon Roll; Hon Roll; Sec NHS; Liberal Arts Canis; Vet Med.

PARYZ, LEONARD; Lackawanna SR HS; Lackawanna, NY; (Y); JV Var Ftbl; Construction.

PARZYCH, MELISSA A; Horseheads HS; Horseheads, NY; (Y); JA; Library Aide; Spanish Clb; SADD; Hon Roll; Ntl Merit Ltr; NYS Regnts Schlrshp 86; Corning CC; Elem Educ.

PASCAL, ROUANDY; South Shore HS; Brooklyn, NY; (Y); French Clb; Hosp Aide; Intnl Clb; Math Clb; Radio Clb; Science Clb; Nwsp Ed-Chief; Nwsp Stf; Vllybl; DAR Awd; Med Schl.

PASCALE, CATHY; Lindenhurst SR HS; Lindenhurst, NY; (Y); Girl Scts; Key Clb; School Play; Hon Roll; 3rd Pl Intl Foods-Long Island Lang Fair 83; St John Fisher Coll; Accntng.

PASCALE, DEIRDRE; Newfield HS; Selden, NY; (Y); Girl Scts; Hosp Aide; Spanish Clb; High Hon Roll; Hon Roll; Jr NHS; Spanish NHS.

PASCALE, PETER; Port Chester HS; Port Chester, NY; (Y); Band; Concert Band; Mrchg Band; School Musical; JV Var Bsbl; Im JV Bsktbl; Hon Roll; Mu Alp Tht; Sci Hnr Soc 85-86; Pres Of Pt Chester HS Band 86-87.

PASCHKE, MICHAEL D; Patchogue-Medford HS; Medford, NY; (Y); 123/653; Off Sr Cls; Im Bsktbl; Im Tennis; Im Vllybl; Ntl Merit Schol; Regents Schlrshp 86; SUNY; Psych.

PASCOE, JAMES W; Gates Chin HS; Rochester, NY; (Y); Am Leg Boys St; Trs German Clb; Mathletes; Stage Crew; Rep Soph Cls; Var L Crs Cntry; Var L Swmmng; Bausch & Lomb Sci Awd; NHS; Aud/Vis; Chem Achivement Awd From American Chemical Society 86.

PASCUAL, VERONICA; Sacred Heart Acad; Uniondale, NY; (S); Church Yth Grp; Civic Clb; Office Aide; Chorus; Orch; School Musical; Yrbk Stf; Hon Roll; NHS; Med.

PASCUCCI, LYNN; Catholic Central HS; Waterford, NY; (Y); Church Yth Grp; French Clb; VP JA; Math Clb; Math Tm; Red Cross Aide; Pres Spanish Clb; SADD; Chorus; Color Guard; Acctg.

PASEV, DIANE; Herbert H Lehman HS; Bronx, NY; (Y); JA; Office Aide; Teachers Aide; Band; Concert Band; Jazz Band; Cit Awd; High Hon Roll; Hon Roll; Jr NHS; Law.

PASH, TIM; Chenango Valley HS; Binghamton, NY; (Y); 7/174; Concert Band; Jazz Band; Mrchg Band; Symp Band; Yrbk Rptr; Var L Socr; Var L Trk; High Hon Roll; Jr NHS; NHS; Syracuse U; Aerosp Engrng.

PASHA, NOSHEEN; Midwood HS; Brooklyn, NY; (Y); 32/600; Math Tm; Chorus; Hon Roll; Bus Adm.

PASHOUKOS, CHRISTOPHER M; Bellport HS; Medford, NY; (Y); 7/250; Drm Mjr(t); Jazz Band; Orch; Nwsp Stf; Yrbk Stf; Trs Jr NHS; VP NHS; Ntl Merit SF; Pres Clsrm Yng Amers 85; NY ST Smmr Schl Arts Schl Orch Stds 85; Hugh O Brien Yth Fndtn 83; Music.

PASHTOON, FARID; E L Vandermeulen HS; Pt Jefferson, NY; (Y); 1/294; Computer Clb; French Clb; Mathletes; Nwsp Stf; Yrbk Stf; Lit Mag; High Hon Roll; NHS; Pres Schlr; Val; RPI-MATH/Sci Awd 85; Bst Math Stu 86; Bst Sci Stu 86; Cornell U; Engrng.

PASI, SUNIL; Herkimer SR HS; Herkimer, NY; (Y); 13/120; Pres Aud/Vis; Computer Clb; Trs Soph Cls; Rep Stu Cncl; Var L Trk; Hon Roll; VP NHS; Ntl Merit Ltr; Vrsty H Acad Awds 84-85; Empire ST Schlrshp Of Excel 86; Darmouth Coll; Psych.

PASIECZNY, WILLIAM; Hahn American HS; Apo New York, NY; (Y); 4/76; Nwsp Ed-Chief; Var L Bsbl; Var L Ftbl; JV L Socr; Var L Wrstlng; Hon Roll; NHS; Exploring; ROTC; Drill Tm; Schlr Atlt Of Yr 85-86; Wrstlng Won 4th Pl In Western Regnls & 9th In Cetral Eur Opeans; Air Force Acad; Pilot.

PASINSKI, SUE; Pembroke Central HS; Akron, NY; (Y); Computer Clb; English Clb; Pep Clb; Ski Clb; Spanish Clb; Teachers Aide; Drill Tm; Yrbk Phtg; Yrbk Stf; JV Cheerleading; Trvl.

PASKORZ, GRACE E; Valley Stream North HS; Valley Stream, NY; (Y); 25/128; Church Yth Grp; Debate Tm; Band; Chorus; Church Choir; Jazz Band; Swing Chorus; L Badmtn; French Hon Soc; Hon Roll; NY ST Rgnts Schlrshp 86; All-Div Rfl Tm 85; All-Cnty Chorus 86; Adelphi; Optmtry.

PASKOWSKI, JOSEPH; Charlestown HS North; New City, NY; (Y); Cmnty Wkr; Computer Clb; Teachers Aide; Variety Show; Ed Yrbk Stf; Im Bsbl; Hon Roll; Mu Alp Tht; NHS; Ntl Merit Schol; MD Prog.

PASQUANTOIVO, CAROLYN; Pelham Memorial HS; Pelham, NY; (Y); Drama Clb; FCA; PAVAS; SADD; School Musical; School Play; Rep Jr Cls; French Hon Soc; Hon Roll; NHS; Thtre-Dnce.

PASQUARELLA, MICHAEL V; Schalmont HS; Schenectady, NY; (Y); 41/168; Church Yth Grp; Ski Clb; Bsbl; Bsktbl; Socr; Hon Roll; U Of MN; Aero Engr.

PASSALACQUA, COLLEEN; Sauquoit Vly Central Scl; Sauquoit, NY; (S); 2/100; Service Clb; SADD; Band; Chorus; Concert Band; Mrchg Band; School Musical; School Play; Yrbk Stf; Fld Hcky; Bus & Mgmt.

PASSALARIS, TINA; Herricks SR HS; New Hyde Park, NY; (Y); 4/250; Hosp Aide; Variety Show; Nwsp Ed-Chief; Nwsp Stf; Rep Soph Cls; Rep Jr Cls; Rep Sr Cls; Hon Roll; NCTE Awd; Ntl Merit Ltr; Ntl Hnr Scty Of Scndry Schls 85; Rcgnzd Lcl Cmnty Srv 86; NY ST Clmba Coll; Jrnlsm.

PASSANITI, LISA MARIE E; Hancock Central HS; Lakewood, PA; (Y); Band; Chorus; Drm Mjr(t); Jazz Band; Mrchg Band; Pep Band; Swing Chorus; Symp Band; Rotary Awd; All Co Band, Chorus, Jazz Band, Swing Choir; Hartwick Jazz Ensemble; NYSSMA Excllnt Rtng; Music Perf.

PASSANTINO, STEVEN; Mc Kee Tech HS; Staten Island, NY; (Y); 25/306; Art Clb; Stage Crew; Hon Roll; Attndnc 84-85; Engrng.

PASSARETTI, CHRIS; St John The Baptist HS; N Babylon, NY; (Y); 33/567; Boy Scts; Church Yth Grp; Bsbl; Hon Roll; Rep Yth At Cnfrnc Rome Italy 83; SUNY Stnybrk; Comp Sci.

PASSARO, ANTHONY; Greenville Central HS; Greenville, NY; (Y); 15/81; Sec Boy Scts; Trs FFA; Key Clb; Spanish Clb; School Musical; VP Frsh Cls; Var Bsbl; Var Capt Bsktbl; JV Socr; DAR Awd; Schl Letter 86; Schlr Cnty Leag MVP Bsktbll 86; Engrng.

PASSARO, SUSETTE; Maria Regina HS; Yonkers, NY; (Y); Dance Clb; NFL; Radio Clb; Speech Tm; Church Choir; Nwsp Stf; Yrbk Rptr; Lit Mag; NHS; Frdhm Lang Cntst 2nd Pl 86; Health.

PASSERO, MICHELLE; Saranack Lake HS; Saranac Lk, NY; (Y); AFS; Yrbk Stf; Var L Diving; Var Golf; JV L Socr; Var L Swmmng; Var L Trk; High Hon Roll; NHS; Miss Frankllin Cty Teen Ager 85; Prom Comm Chairmn 86; U VT; Bus.

PASSMORE, KATHLEEN; Ellenville Central HS; Ellenville, NY; (Y); Pres Church Yth Grp; German Clb; Pep Clb; Band; Chorus; Yrbk Phtg; Yrbk Stf; Rep Frsh Cls; Rep Soph Cls; Cheerleading; Marist Coll; Bus Adm.

PASTAKIA, NEPA; Richmond Hill HS; Woodhaven, NY; (Y); 11/288; Art Clb; English Clb; Math Clb; Math Tm; Service Clb; Spanish Clb; Rep Jr Cls; High Hon Roll; Prfct Atten Awd; Schlrshp From Adelphi U 86; Arista Awd 85-86; Knghts Of Columbus Math Awd 86; Adelphi U; Pre-Med.

PASTEL, DAVID A; Liverpool HS; Liverpool, NY; (Y); 3/850; Pres Latin Clb; Math Tm; Trs NFL; Ski Clb; VP Socr; Vllybl; High Hon Roll; Trs NHS; Ntl Merit SF; Acad Excllnce Earth Sci, Trig, Latin III, Pre-Calcls.

PASTERNAK, CARY; Lansing HS; Ithaca, NY; (Y); 7/90; Am Leg Aux Girls St; Pres Spanish Clb; Speech Tm; Orch; Swmmng; High Hon Roll; NHS; Acadmc Awd Engl 85-86; Acamdc Awd Spnsh 84-85; Cornell Schl; Hotel/Rest Mgmt.

PASTORE, JOHN V; Patchogue-Medford HS; Hampton Bays, NY; (Y); 69/769; Am Leg Boys St; Chorus; Rep Nwsp Stf; JV Ftbl; Var L Wrstlng; Hon Roll; Jr NHS; NHS; 3rd Pl All Lg Wrstlng 86; 6th Pl Suffolk County Wrstlng 86; 9th Grade Stu Of Mo 84; Science.

PATCHEN, JASON; Bethlehem Central HS; Delmar, NY; (Y); 112/315; Boy Scts; Church Yth Grp; Key Clb; Varsity Clb; Nwsp Stf; Yrbk Bus Mgr; Yrbk Ed-Chief; Rep Frsh Cls; Rep Soph Cls; Rep Jr Cls; Sccr Schlrshp 84; Eagle Scout Awd 85; Bsbl Awd 83; Princeton; Astronaut Engrng.

PATEL, ALPA; Union-Endicott HS; Endicott, NY; (Y); Drama Clb; French Clb; Key Clb; Orch; School Musical; School Play; High Hon Roll; Hon Roll; NHS; Mathletes; Engrng.

PATEL, ANITA G; Fairport HS; Fairport, NY; (Y); 40/600; Debate Tm; Hosp Aide; Math Tm; Sec Science Clb; Stu Cncl; Var Trk; Hon Roll; NHS; Assn Indians In Amer Stu Awd 85; U Of Rochester.

PATEL, BHARAT; Potsdam HS; Potsdam, NY; (Y); Computer Clb; Math Clb; Math Tm; Model UN; Quiz Bowl; Varsity Clb; Var Bsktbl; JV Sftbl; Hon Roll; NHS; Elctrcl Engrng.

PATEL, BHARTI; Franklin Acad; Malone, NY; (Y); Intnl Clb; Model UN; Yrbk Stf; Trk; North Country CC.

PATEL, HARSHITA; Kingston HS; Lake Katrine, NY; (Y); 50/573; French Clb; Latin Clb; Yrbk Phtg; Yrbk Stf; French Hon Soc; High Hon Roll; NHS; SUNY Stny Brk; Engnrng.

PATEL, MANISHA; W Tresper Clarke HS; Westbury, NY; (Y); 9/193; French Clb; Model UN; Chorus; Sec Lit Mag; Rep Frsh Cls; Bowling; Lcrss; Socr; Tennis; Bausch & Lomb Sci Awd; Rgnts Schlrshp 86; U Of Rochester.

PATELLIS, SOPHIA; Herricks SR HS; New Hyde Park, NY; (Y); Church Yth Grp; Cmnty Wkr; DECA; Stage Crew; Hon Roll; Pre Med.

PATELLO, MICHAEL; Archbishop Walsh HS; Belmont, NY; (Y); Computer Clb; 4-H; JCL; Latin Clb; Band; Bowling; High Hon Roll; Hon Roll; SUNY At Buffalo; Sci.

PATENAUDE, PAULA; Madrid-Waddington HS; Madrid, NY; (Y); Drama Clb; French Clb; Varsity Clb; Band; Concert Band; Mrchg Band; School Play; JV Var Cheerleading; Var Socr; JV Twrlr; Plattsburgh; Bus.

PATEREK, JENNIFER; Hauppauge HS; Commack, NY; (Y); Church Yth Grp; DECA; FBLA; Hosp Aide; Rep Jr Cls; Sr Cls; Var L Pom Pon; High Hon Roll; NHS; FBLA 1st Plc Bus Dynmcs Cntyh Lvl 85; DECA 11th Plc Finance Crdt Cnty Lvl 86.

PATERNITT, DAWN R; Jamestown HS; Jamestown, NY; (Y); 21/396; VP Debate Tm; Intnl Clb; Ski Clb; Capt Color Guard; Capt Flag Corp; Nwsp Rptr; Yrbk Stf; Rep Stu Cncl; Swmmng; NHS; Wnnr Cnty Amercn Legn Ortrcl 85 & 86; Jnr Miss Schlrshp Pgnt 86; Jamestown CC; Med.

PATERNOSTER, CHRISTOPHER L; East Islip HS; E Islip, NY; (Y); Am Leg Boys St; Pres SADD; Band; Nwsp Ed-Chief; JV Var Socr; Var L Tennis; Cit Awd; High Hon Roll; Jr NHS; NHS; U Of VA; Aerospc Engr.

PATERNOSTER, FRANK; Mt St Michael HS; Bronx, NY; (Y); 29/309; Spanish Clb; Im Bsktbl; Im Fld Hcky; Im Ftbl; NHS.

PATHARE, SHAILESH S; Bronx HS Of Science; New York, NY; (Y); Art Clb; Cmnty Wkr; Hosp Aide; Science Clb; Service Clb; Teachers Aide; ARISTA 86; Rgnts Schlrshp 86; SUNY Binghamton.

PATINO, CARLOS A; Aviation HS; Woodside, NY; (S); 25/416; Math Tm; Sec NHS; Silver Wings Of Pegasus Soc 85-86; Mech Engrg.

PATINO, OSCAR; La Salle Military Acad; Uniondale, NY; (Y); Math Clb; ROTC; Varsity Clb; Band; Crs Cntry; Trk; Wt Lftg; Wrstlng; Acad All Amer Natl Secndry Ed Cncl 85-86; Norwich U; Engrng.

PATMOS, MARCIA; Linton HS; Schenectady, NY; (Y); 31/340; Church Yth Grp; JCL; Key Clb; Service Clb; Church Choir; Yrbk Bus Mgr; Yrbk Phtg; Soph Cls; Jr Cls; Trs Sr Cls.

PATNODE, COREY; Unionville HS; W Chester, PA; (Y); 80/300; Nwsp Stf; Swmmng; Hon Roll; Acad Engl Awd 85; Most Dedictd Smim Tm Awd 85; Coaches Awd For Swim Tm 84; Bus.

PATRENICOLA, CELESTE; Cardinal Spellman HS; Bronx, NY; (Y); Cmnty Wkr; Dance Clb; Stage Crew; Nwsp Rptr; Nwsp Stf; Lit Mag; Hon Roll; Crdnl Spllmn Yth Awd 86.

PATRICIA, KRISTI; V V S Central HS; Sherrill, NY; (Y); 6/280; Church Yth Grp; Rep Frsh Cls; JV Cheerleading; High Hon Roll; NHS; Rotary Awd; Eglsky Blt Schlrshp; Etude-Bshrp Schlrshp; Suny Purchase; Dance.

PATRICK, BRIAN RICARDO; Sachem North HS; Holbrook, NY; (Y); Art Clb; Computer Clb; Pres Spanish Clb; Ed Lit Mag; NHS; Nmbr 1 Stu In Karate Schl 83; 3rd Pl Drwng In I Love NY Cntst 84; 1st Pl Karate Trnmnt 83; U Of PA; Ec.

PATRICK, CHARLES; Lansingburgh HS; Troy, NY; (Y); Hon Roll; HVCC.

PATRICK, GAIL; John Dewey HS; Brooklyn, NY; (Y); Aud/Vis; VP JA.

PATRICK, WILLIAM; Frankfurt American HS; Apo, NY; (Y); 4/290; Art Clb; Boy Scts; Cmnty Wkr; Computer Clb; German Clb; Temple Yth Grp; Cit Awd; High Hon Roll; Jr NHS; NHS; Delta Epsilon Phi 86; Gldn Eagle Awd & Hochste Leistung 85; Ntl Art Hnr Scty 85; Cornell U; Grphc Dsgn.

PATRIE, STEPHEN; Franklin Acad; Brushton, NY; (Y); Concert Band; Jazz Band; School Play; Hon Roll; Drama Clb; French Clb; Mathletes; PAVAS; Band; Symp Band; NY ST Hist Day Wnr 84; Perf Arts.

PATRIGNANI, ANTHONY; Waterford Halfmon HS; Waterford, NY; (Y); Boy Scts; Cmnty Wkr; French Clb; Letterman Clb; Math Clb; Political Wkr; Red Cross Aide; SADD; Band; Chorus; Natl Soc Studies Awd; Eagle Scout With Palm; Natl Eagle Scout Soc; Order Of Wrstlg & Track Sprtsmnshp; Hudson Valley; Criminal Justice.

PATRONAGGIO, NANCY; Mt Mercy Acad; W Seneca, NY; (Y); FHA; Girl Scts; JA; Chorus; School Musical; School Play; Stage Crew; Rep Frsh Cls; Cheerleading; Sftbl; Canisus Coll; Bus Mgmt.

PATRUNO, FRANK; Sachem High School North; Holtsville, NY; (Y); 445/1700; Ski Clb; Concert Band; Mrchg Band.

PATSOURAKIS, EVDOXIA; Hillcrest HS; Jamaica, NY; (Y); Art Clb; Computer Clb; French Clb; German Clb; Teachers Aide; Chorus; Variety Show; Off Jr Cls; Badmtn; Bsbl; Comp Prgmr.

PATTEN, DIANE; Albertus Magnus HS; Bardonia, NY; (Y); Church Yth Grp; Var Crs Cntry; Var Trk; Hon Roll; NHS; Clarkstown Yth Ct.

PATTEN, JENNIFER; Jane Addams Vo-Tech; Bronx, NY; (S); 3/260; Variety Show; Rep Sr Cls; Hon Roll; NHS; Prfct Atten Awd; Engrng.

PATTENGILL, VIKKI; South New Berlin Central HS; S New Berlin, NY; (Y); 2/40; Yrbk Ed-Chief; Rep Stu Cncl; High Hon Roll; Lion Awd; NHS; Sal; Prfct Scores Bio & Geomtry Rgnts 84; US Coast Gurard; Consvrtn.

PATTERER, WILLIAM J; Liverpool HS; Liverpool, NY; (Y); 43/884; Am Leg Boys St; VP FBLA; German Clb; VP JA; Band; JV Lcrss; Var Trk; High Hon Roll; Jr NHS; NHS; Engrng.

PATTERSON, ALICE-ANN; Argyle Central HS; Argyle, NY; (Y); Art Clb; Ski Clb; Band; Chorus; Mrchg Band; Yrbk Stf; VP Soph Cls; JV Cheerleading; Var Fld Hcky; Var Tennis; Bio.

PATTERSON, DAVID K; New Hartford HS; New Hartford, NY; (Y); 57/260; Pep Clb; Ski Clb; Concert Band; Jazz Band; Mrchg Band; Pep Band; Var Tennis; Hon Roll; JETS Awd; NHS; Top 10 Pct Natl Engrng Apt Search 84; Le High U; Elec Engrng.

PATTERSON, JANET A; Lake Shore Central SR HS; Derby, NY; (Y); 20/284; Church Yth Grp; Spanish Clb; Teachers Aide; Band; Chorus; Orch; School Musical; Stu Cncl; Var L Tennis; NHS; Bryant & Stratton; Trvl.

PATTERSON, JENNIFER; Notre Dame Bishop Gibbons HS; Schenectady, NY; (Y); Key Clb; Spanish Clb; Band; Var Cheerleading; Var Crs Cntry; Var Trk; Chmcl Engrng.

PATTERSON, LEANORA J; Horace Mann Schl; Bronx, NY; (Y); Dance Clb; Spanish Clb; VP Chorus; School Musical; School Play; Hnrs Spnsh III 84; Hnrs For Hstry Of Cntmpry Art 85; U PA; Sclgy.

PATTERSON, MICHAEL A; Edison Tech; Rochester, NY; (Y); 19/276; Ftbl.

PATTERSON, RACHAEL; New Berlin Central HS; New Berlin, NY; (Y); 2/65; Church Yth Grp; Spanish Clb; Band; Color Guard; Drm Mjr(t); Mrchg Band; Yrbk Stf; Rep Stu Cncl; Bsktbl; Socr; AZ ST U; Biotechncl Engr.

PATTERSON, SCOTT; South Lewis Central HS; Greig, NY; (Y); 8/87; Band; Pres Stu Cncl; Bsbl; Bsktbl; Trk; High Hon Roll; Hon Roll; NHS; Prfct Atten Awd; Mohawk Valley CC; Surveyng Tec.

PATTERSON, THOMAS; Minisink Valley HS; Middletown, NY; (Y); 9/250; Pres Church Yth Grp; Drama Clb; School Play; VP Jr Cls; Sec Sr Cls; Sec Stu Cncl; JV Bsktbl; Var L Ftbl; NHS; Prfct Atten Awd; Engrng.

PATTERSON, TINA M; Ravena Coeymans Selkirk HS; Ravena, NY; (Y); #6 In Class; Art Clb; Church Yth Grp; 4-H; Spanish Clb; Yrbk Stf; Sec Jr Cls; Trs Sr Cls; Socr; High Hon Roll; NHS; Rgnts Schlrshp; SUNY Binghamton.

PATTI, DENISE R; Kenmore West SR HS; Kenmore, NY; (Y); 34/420; Band; Concert Band; Mrchg Band; School Musical; Ed Yrbk Stf; JV Trk; Hon Roll; Sec NHS; Human Rel Peer Tm; Plasmapheresis Donar Rgm.

PATTI, MICHELE LEE; Averill Park HS; Troy, NY; (Y); 5/240; Hosp Aide; VP Soph Cls; Var Capt Bsktbl; Var Capt Socr; Capt Var Sftbl; High Hon Roll; Sec NHS; St Rose Acdmc Schlrshp, Rev James I Borden Mem Awd, Edith Grace Craig Reynolds Schrshp 86; Coll ST Rose; Bio.

PATTISON, JAMES S; Paul V Moore HS; Central Square, NY; (Y); Band; Concert Band; Mrchg Band; Pep Band; Symp Band; Hon Roll; Morrisville Coll; Conservation.

PATTON, KENNETH A; Hamilton Central Schl; Earlville, NY; (Y); 12/56; Nwsp Ed-Chief; Var L Crs Cntry; Ntl Merit Ltr; SUNY Morrisville; Engrng.

PATURZO, ELIZABETH; Uniondale HS; Uniondale, NY; (Y); Church Yth Grp; Yrbk Stf; JV Var Sftbl; High Hon Roll; Hon Roll; Jr NHS; NHS; Sci Fair-Hon Mntn 84; Psych.

PAUGH, CHRISTINA M; Pawling HS; Pawling, NY; (Y); 1/55; Cmnty Wkr; Model UN; Chorus; Color Guard; Yrbk Sprt Ed; VP Jr Cls; Sftbl; Vllybl; High Hon Roll; Val; Bucknell U; Accntng.

PAUL, AMY; Troupsburg Central Schl; Woodhull, NY; (Y); 3/14; Scholastic Bowl; Speech Tm; Pres Chorus; Yrbk Sprt Ed; Sec Sr Cls; Var L Bsktbl; Var L Socr; DAR Awd; High Hon Roll; NHS; MIP Bsktbl 84; SR Grl Outstndng Athlt 86; ST U Of NY; Jrnlsm.

PAUL, DEANNA ELAINE; Saint Francis Prep; Jackson Heights, NY; (S); 23/744; Cmnty Wkr; SADD; Im Ftbl; Im Gym; Twrlr; High Hon Roll; NHS; Cert Appr Cath Charities Oper Fun 85; 8 Ice Sktg Achvt Patches & 3rd Pl Trphy 83-86; Twrlg Awds 83-86; Bus.

PAUL II, FREDERICK E; Mayfield HS; Gloversville, NY; (Y); Capt Var Bowling; Trk; Amstrdm Rcrdr Nwspapr Mst Outstndng Athlt Bowling 86.

PAUL, GRETCHEN; Fairport HS; Fairport, NY; (Y); VP Church Yth Grp; German Clb; SADD; Teachers Aide; Band; Church Choir; Hon Roll; Yrbk Stf; Lit Mag; Stbn Soc Awd Grmn 86; ASSE Exchng Stu Grmny 84; Choir Accmpnst 81-86; Grmn Trnsltr.

PAUL, HEATHER; Jamesville-De Witt HS; Jamesville, NY; (Y); 73/234; SADD; Church Yth Grp; Key Clb; Im Bsktbl; High Hon Roll; Hon Roll; Bio Chem.

PAUL, JOHN H; Paul V Moore HS; Hastings, NY; (Y); 27/310; Am Leg Boys St; Trs Church Yth Grp; Exploring; Var Crs Cntry; JV Var Socr; Hon Roll; Masonic Awd; NHS; Pres Schlr; Rifle Tm Captain 85-86; Boston U; Bio-Med.

PAUL, JOSEPH WESLEY; Nazareth Regional HS; Brooklyn, NY; (Y); Church Yth Grp; Cmnty Wkr; Math Tm; Science Clb; Im Bsktbl; Hon Roll; Natl Hnr Socty 86; 2nd & 3rd Hnrs 84-85; Polytechnic Inst Of NY; Engrng.

PAUL, MARTINE; Prospect Heights HS; Brooklyn, NY; (S); Hosp Aide; Chorus; Church Yth Grp; Cmnty Wkr; Math Clb; Speech Tm; Yrbk Stf; Off Sr Cls; Vllybl; Nrsng.

PAULEY, BRIAN; Royalton Hartland HS; Gasport, NY; (Y); 20/131; French Clb; Varsity Clb; Stu Cncl; Capt Var Socr; Var Swmmng; Capt Var Tennis; NY ST Rgnts Schlrshp 86; 1st Bptst Chrch Lckprt Schlrshp 86; Prsdntl Acdmc Ftnss Awd 86; SUNY Geneseo; Mgmt Sci.

PAULEY, MICHELLE; Randolph Central HS; Randolph, NY; (Y); 47/85; 4-H; Girl Scts; Ski Clb; Spanish Clb; Acpl Chr; Yrbk Stf; Rep Stu Cncl; JV Crs Cntry; Score Keeper; Var JV Sftbl; Jamestown CC; Math.

PAULIN, JOHN; Northville HS; Northville, NY; (Y); 5/60; Church Yth Grp; SADD; Varsity Clb; Yrbk Sprt Ed; Trs Stu Cncl; Var L Bsktbl; Var L Crs Cntry; Var Capt Trk; Hon Roll; NHS; Math 10 Prz; Clarkson U; Engrng.

PAULK, KIM; Cathedral HS; Bronx, NY; (Y); Intnl Clb; Stage Crew; Variety Show; Bsktbl; Mgr(s); Sftbl; Vllybl; Hon Roll; Val; Merit Awds Bsktbl 82-86; Vlbl Plyr Awd Bsktbl 85-86; Most Achvd Plyr Awd Bsktbl 84-85; Law.

PAULO, DWAYNE; Corning East HS; Beaver Dams, NY; (Y); VICA; Corning CC; Auto Bdy.

PAULSON, LORETTA; Carmel HS; Carmel, NY; (Y); Trs French Clb; St U Of NY; Accntng.

PAVELKA, MISHELLE; Oneida SR HS; Durhamville, NY; (Y); FNA; Hosp Aide; Band; Color Guard; Concert Band; Drm & Bgl; Mrchg Band; Hon Roll; Prfct Atten Awd; Nrs.

PAVLIDES, ANNA C; St Francis Prep; Elmhurst, NY; (S); 79/744; Cmnty Wkr; Computer Clb; Dance Clb; School Musical; Opt Clb Awd; NY U; Nutrition.

PAVLIK, TONY J; Corning East HS; Corning, NY; (Y); Cmnty Wkr; FCA; Letterman Clb; Pep Clb; SADD; Varsity Clb; Yrbk Stf; Bsbl; Bsktbl; Coach Actv; All ST Coll Leg Ftbl Ldng Rusher In Area 84 & 85; Set All Time Schl Record Rushing Yard 84-85; Loyola Coll; Business.

PAVLIN, JORDAN M; Wheatley Schl; Albertson, NY; (Y); Debate Tm; Drama Clb; School Play; Stage Crew; Nwsp Bus Mgr; Stu Cncl; Var Stat Bsktbl; NCTE Awd; Vassar Coll; Engl.

PAWELA, MARK; Frontier Central HS; Hamburg, NY; (Y); 7/450; Ski Clb; JV Var Ice Hcky; Hon Roll; NHS; NEDT Awd; Regents Schlrshp; Fredonia ST; Engrng.

PAWELCZAK, BARBARA; West Seneca East SR HS; Cheektowaga, NY; (Y); 22/410; DECA; JA; Lit Mag; Rep Frsh Cls; Trs Soph Cls; Rep Jr Cls; VP Sr Cls; Cheerleading; Pom Pon; Hon Roll; Rgnts Schlrshp 86; Hnrbl Mntn ST Lvl Cmptn DECA 85-86; 1st Plc Wnr Rgn Cmptn 86; Geneseo; Econ.

PAWLAK, DOUG; Fredonia HS; Fredonia, NY; (Y); German Clb; Var L Crs Cntry; JV Socr; Var L Trk.

PAWLICZEK, JAMIE; Minisink Valley HS; Goshen, NY; (Y); Ski Clb; Varsity Clb; Yrbk Stf; Pres Jr Cls; VP Sr Cls; Rep Stu Cncl; Var Socr; Capt Trk; High Hon Roll; NHS.

PAWLIK, TOM; L A Webber HS; Waterport, NY; (S); 6/70; AFS; Church Yth Grp; Computer Clb; Exploring; 4-H; Math Clb; Varsity Clb; Chorus; School Musical; School Play; Schlr Athl 84; Coaches Trphy 85; Engr.

PAWLIKOWSKI, DENNIS T; Mexico HS; Parish, NY; (Y); 1/182; Spanish Clb; JV Var Ftbl; Var Trk; Hon Roll; NHS; Spanish NHS; Val; Mayflower Compct Wnnr 82 & 85; Acad All Amer 85; Schlr-Athlt Mdls 84-85; U Of AZ; Engr.

PAWLIKOWSKI, RUSTY; Mexico Acad; Parish, NY; (Y); 2/200; Boy Scts; Variety Show; Var Ftbl; Var Trk; Var Wt Lftg; High Hon Roll; NHS; US Army Res Natl Schlr Ath 86; MACS Schlr Ath Gold Mdl 85-86; U TX; Applied Mth.

PAWLIKOWSKI, SUZANNE; Vernon Verona Sherrill HS; Vernon, NY; (Y); Girl Scts; Chorus; Drm & Bgl; Lit Mag; Hon Roll; Vet Med.

PAWLIKOWSKY, KATHLEEN; Dominican Commercial HS; Ozone Park, NY; (Y); Rep Frsh Cls; Rep Soph Cls; Rep Jr Cls; Prfct Atten Awd; Nrsng.

PAWLOSKI, CHRISTOPHER; Southampton HS; Southampton, NY; (Y); 10/113; Art Clb; Boy Scts; Drama Clb; French Clb; Letterman Clb; Math Tm; Varsity Clb; School Musical; School Play; Stage Crew.

PAWLOSKI, MARK; Canisins HS; Elma, NY; (S); 5/161; Church Yth Grp; Capt Crs Cntry; Var Trk; Hon Roll; Mu Alp Tht; NHS; John Garrity Memrl Awd 85; Engrng.

PAWLOWSKI, ELIZABETH A; West Seneca East HS; Cheektowaga, NY; (Y); 35/375; Church Yth Grp; DECA; JA; Key Clb; Yrbk Rptr; Stu Cncl; Hon Roll; NY ST Rgnts Schlrshp 86; Forgn Lang Awd Frnch 83 & 84; Buffalo ST Coll; Cmmnctns.

PAWLOWSKI, JULIE; Lansing HS; Ithaca, NY; (Y); Church Yth Grp; French Clb; Girl Scts; Ski Clb; Chorus; Orch; Symp Band; Diving; Swmmng; High Hon Roll; Rotary Yth Ldrshp Awd 86; Cornell Hotel SchlHTL Mngmnt.

PAWLOWYCH, ARKADIUS; Martin Van Buren HS; Bellerose, NY; (Y); 34/576; JA; Office Aide; Service Clb; Teachers Aide; Var Tennis; Hon Roll; Prfct Atten Awd; Phys Fit Achvt Awd 84; Sci Fair 2nd Pl 86; Credit Roll 83-85; Mech Engr.

PAXSON, WHITNEY; York Central Schl; Retsof, NY; (Y); AFS; Library Aide; Band; Chorus; Concert Band; Mrchg Band; Pep Band; School Musical; School Play; Swing Chorus; Solo Fsetvl Band Chorus 84-86; All Cty Chorus 84-86; MUSIC.

PAYNE, ALEX; De Witt Clinton HS; New York, NY; (Y); Art Clb; Nwsp Stf; Capt Bowling; Hon Roll; PRIDE Yankees 86; Boston U; Pub Rel.

PAYNE, CHRIS; Bishop Ludden HS; Syracuse, NY; (Y); Boy Scts; Chorus; Yrbk Phtg; Pres Sr Cls; Trk; NHS; MONY Schlstc Art Awds 86; Art.

PAYNE, DAVID; Warsaw Central HS; Warsaw, NY; (S); 10/88; Drama Clb; Chorus; School Musical; School Play; Variety Show; Cit Awd; High Hon Roll; NHS; Spanish Clb; Teachers Aide; Hnr Bearer Alt 85; Spnsh Awd Acadmc Sucss 84; Fredonia ST Coll; Engl.

PAYNE, ERIN; Lakenheath American HS; APO New York, NY; (Y); Church Yth Grp; Cmnty Wkr; Library Aide; Prfct Atten Awd; Elem Educ.

PAYNE, LA TONYA; St Francis Preparatory Schl; Jamaica, NY; (Y); 174/653; Church Yth Grp; VP Cmnty Wkr; Dance Clb; Hosp Aide; Church Choir; Yrbk Phtg; NHS; Ntl Merit Ltr; Med.

PAYNE, MICHAEL; Penn Yan Acad; Penn Yan, NY; (S); 1/174; Am Leg Boys St; Intnl Clb; Varsity Clb; Lit Mag; VP Frsh Cls; VP Soph Cls; Rep Stu Cncl; Capt L Ftbl; JV Lcrss; Var L Trk; Sectn V Cls B Wrstlng Champ 86; Scott Trainor Mem Awd 86; Excllnce Frnch 83-85; Cornell U; Elec Engrng.

PAYNE, RODNEY; Altmar-Parish-Williamstown HS; Altmar, NY; (Y); Ski Clb; Varsity Clb; L Bowling; Var L Trk; High Hon Roll; Hon Roll; NY ST Rgnts Schlrshp 86; Dollrs Schlrs Schlrshp 86; Amer Lgn Ctznshp Awd 86; SUNY Oswego; Pblc Acctnt.

PAYNE, SABRINA; Bishop Kearney HS; Brooklyn, NY; (Y); Dance Clb; Library Aide; St Schlr; Black Achvt Awd PA ST 86; NYS Regents Scholar 86; Howard U; Elec Engrng.

PAYNE, SUSAN M; Linton HS; Schenectady, NY; (Y); 15/300; Pres Key Clb; Ski Clb; Yrbk Rptr; Lit Mag; Off Frsh Cls; Off Soph Cls; Off Jr Cls; Stat Bsbl; Stat Ftbl; Stat Ice Hcky; RPI; Bio Med Engrng.

PAYNE, TRACY M; Bad Kreuznach HS; APO New York, NY; (Y); Pres Exploring; Hosp Aide; Library Aide; ROTC; Teachers Aide; Band; Drill Tm; Sec Sr Cls; Var JV Cheerleading; Cit Awd; ROTC Ldrshp Devlpmnt Awd I,II,III 82-86; Psych.

PAYTON, LANCE; Cardinal Hayes Memorial HS; New York, NY; (Y); 19/258; Art Clb; Camera Clb; French Clb; Math Tm; Yrbk Stf; Off Jr Cls; JV Var Bsbl; Ice Hcky; JV Socr; Jerome Holland Memrl Cornell Summer Coll Schlrshp 86; Cornell U; Pltcl Sci.

PAZDA, KIMBERLY J; Lancaster HS; Depew, NY; (Y); 60/470; Church Yth Grp; Ski Clb; Chorus; School Musical; Nwsp Stf; Trk; Hon Roll; NHS; Ntl Merit Ltr; OEL; Gordon Coll; Elem Ed.

PAZO, MARISOL; St Vincent Ferrer HS; Elmhurst, NY; (Y); 1/110; Cmnty Wkr; Dance Clb; Library Aide; Math Tm; Spanish Clb; High Hon Roll; NHS; Pres Schlr; Val; Math, Hist And Eng 85-86; Fordham U; Arch.

PAZOGA, VICTORIA A; Minisink Valley HS; Middletown, NY; (Y); Key Clb; Band; Concert Band; Mrchg Band; Yrbk Stf; JV Cheerleading; High Hon Roll; Hon Roll; Yth In Govrnmnt; Bus.

PEABODY, SHANNON MARIE; Pulaski JR SR HS; Pulaski, NY; (Y); Drama Clb; GAA; Ski Clb; Mrchg Band; School Play; Yrbk Stf; Sec Jr Cls; Stu Cncl; Capt Ftbl; Tennis; NY ST U Oswego; Lib Arts.

PEACOCK, DARIUS; John Dewey HS; Brooklyn, NY; (Y); Chess Clb; Computer Clb; Culinary Arts.

PEAKE, MAKI; Unatego JR-SR HS; Franklin, NY; (Y); FHA; SADD; JV Var Fld Hcky; Score Keeper; Timer; Var Vllybl; Prfct Atten Awd; Phy Ed.

PEARCE, LORNA; Delaware Academy & Central HS; Delhi, NY; (Y); 4-H; Pres FHA; Intnl Clb; Band; Concert Band; Mrchg Band; Nwsp Stf; 4-H Awd.

PEARLMAN, DAVID; Farmingdale HS; N Massapequa, NY; (Y); Var L Bsktbl; Var L Ftbl; Im Wt Lftg; Bus.

PEARSON, EILEEN REBECCA; Amsterdam HS; Amsterdam, NY; (Y); Rep Stu Cncl; Im Wt Lftg; Hon Roll; Ukrairian Am Citizens Clb Ladies Aux 86; William Aninger Schlrshp 86; SUNY At Cobleskill Comp Awd 86; SUNY At Albany; Acctg.

PEARSON, JANE; New Dorp HS; Staten Island, NY; (Y); Girl Scts; Intnl Clb; Co-Capt Math Tm; Teachers Aide; Hon Roll; NHS.

PECK, GEORGE W; Taronic Hills Central Schl; Copake Falls, NY; (Y); 8/140; Am Leg Boys St; Band; Concert Band; Jazz Band; Mrchg Band; Trk; Hon Roll; NHS; Outstndng Achvt Frnch III 86; Engrng.

PECK, KATRINA; Webster HS; Webster, NY; (Y); 73/548; Church Yth Grp; Pres 4-H; VP JA; Ski Clb; Swing Chorus; Fld Hcky; French Hon Soc; High Hon Roll; Jr NHS; NHS; Acad Dcthln B Tm 86; NY Prncss Natl Cmprs & Trlrs 80; ST Fnlst Mss Amrcn Co-Ed Pgnt 86; Cornell U; Vet Med.

PECK, KEVIN; Schuylerville Central Schl; Schuylerville, NY; (S); 4-H; FFA; Var Bsktbl; Var Ftbl; 4-H Awd; Hon Roll; Jr NHS; NHS; Church Yth Grp; Math Clb; 1st Holstein Jdgng Awd 85; 1st Milk & Fat 2 Yr Old NYS 83; All Star Wasaren Lg Ftbl 85; Cornell U; Anml Sci.

PECK, KIMBERLY; Johnstown HS; Johnstown, NY; (Y); Crs Cntry; Trk; High Hon Roll; Hon Roll; NHS; Crs Cntry Skiing 82-86; Mst Dedicated Latin I Stu 84-85; Fltn Cnty CC; Chld Psychlgy.

PECK, LARA; Fairport HS; Fairport, NY; (Y); Drama Clb; Exploring; Ski Clb; SADD; Yrbk Stf; Trk; Lbrl Arts.

PECK, MARY; Scotia-Glenville HS; Scotia, NY; (Y); Church Yth Grp; Girl Scts; Spanish Clb; SADD; Teachers Aide; Yrbk Stf; Hon Roll; Ntl Merit SF; Comp Sci.

PECK, RENEE; Fairport HS; Fairport, NY; (Y); Boy Scts; Church Yth Grp; Drama Clb; Library Aide; Y-Teens; Chorus; Church Choir; School Musical; Yrbk Stf.

PECK, ROBIN; Chateaugay Central HS; Chateaugay, NY; (Y); 4-H; Library Aide; Teachers Aide; Nwsp Rptr; Var Socr; Var Sftbl; 4-H Awd; Hon Roll; Prfct Atten Awd; Tchr.

PECK, WILLARD; Schuylerville Central HS; Schuylerville, NY; (S); 4-H; FFA; Math Tm; SADD; Pres Jr Cls; Var L Bsktbl; Var Ftbl; 4-H Awd; Hon Roll; NHS; Ag Econs.

PECKHAM, HEATHER; Watertown HS; Watertown, NY; (Y); Church Yth Grp; VP Key Clb; Mrchg Band; School Musical; Swing Chorus; Symp Band; High Hon Roll; NHS; Voice Dem Awd; Brown U Bk Awd 86; Natural Sci.

PECKMAN, LINDA; Roy C Ketcham HS; Poughkeepsie, NY; (Y); 88/560; Drama Clb; French Clb; Yrbk Phtg; Yrbk Stf; High Hon Roll; Hon Roll; Pres Acad Ftnss Awd 86; Live Oak HS Acad Crtfct 84; Crtfct Achvmnt Mst Otstndng Stu Algbr 84; Fshn Inst Of Tech; Phtgrphy.

PECORARO, JEFF; Hutch Tech; Buffalo, NY; (Y); Ice Hcky; Hon Roll; Rit; Comp Sci.

PEDALINO, PETER; Monsignor Farrell HS; Staten Island, NY; (Y); Aud/Vis; Camera Clb; Library Aide; Yrbk Phtg; Bsktbl; Bowling; Ftbl; Jr NHS; NHS; 1st Hnr Rll 83-86; Columbia U; Engrng.

PEDERSEN, ARTHUR; Munich American HS; Apo New York, NY; (Y); Boy Scts; Model UN; ROTC; Ski Clb; Var Ftbl; Var Trk; NHS; Rep Soph Cls; Rep Jr Cls; Engrng.

PEDONE, MATTHEW; Huntington HS; Huntington, NY; (Y); Band; Concert Band; Jazz Band; Mrchg Band; Hon Roll.

PEDUZZI, AUDREY; Msgr Scanlan HS; Queens Vlg, NY; (Y); 5/257; Cmnty Wkr; Hosp Aide; Red Cross Aide; Sftbl; Vllybl; Hon Roll; NHS; Le Blond Mem Schlrshp 86; Pres Acad Ftns Awd 86; Brony Dist Attrny Citatn 86; Adelphi U; Soc Wrk.

PEEBLES, STEVE; Vestal HS; Apalachin, NY; (Y); 15/430; Mathletes; Sec Varsity Clb; Pres Chorus; Pres Jr Cls; Capt Crs Cntry; Capt Trk; High Hon Roll; NHS; Rgnts Schlrshp 86; Robert Heath Schlrshp 86; Don Osborne Awd 85-86; Cornell U; Pre-Med.

PEED, JIM; Auburn HS; Auburn, NY; (Y); Art Clb; Camera Clb; Cmnty Wkr; JA; Radio Clb; Ski Clb; SADD; Chorus; Bsbl; Bsktbl; RIT; Bus.

PEEK, CHAD EVAN; Brockport HS; Brockport, NY; (Y); Varsity Clb; Var Ftbl; Im Wt Lftg; High Hon Roll; Hon Roll; SUNY; Comm Art.

PEEPLES, SHELTON; Art & Design HS; Bronx, NY; (Y); Art Clb; Bsktbl; Norfolk ST U; Bus Admin.

PEETS, CARLENE; Port Jervis HS; Port Jervis, NY; (Y); Cmnty Wkr; Chorus; Church Choir; Rep Stu Cncl; Var Tennis; High Hon Roll; Hon Roll; NHS; Prfct Atten Awd; Karate Dmstrtn Awd 84; Vrsty Tnns Awd 84 & 85; Sci.

PEGANOFF, MATTHEW; Jamestown HS; Jamestown, NY; (Y); Hosp Aide; Ski Clb; Spanish Clb; Yrbk Phtg; Golf; Wt Lftg; Wrstlng; Golf Letter 84-85; Phrmcy.

PEIMER, LAURA; Ossining HS; Ossining, NY; (Y); Sec French Clb; Spanish Clb; Chorus; Sec Orch; School Musical; High Hon Roll; Hon Roll; NHS; Englsh Awd Ptry 2nd Pl 85; Frnch Awd 86; Hstry.

PEINKOFER, BRIAN; Saint Josephs Collegiate Inst; Eggertsville, NY; (Y); 15/199; Church Yth Grp; Office Aide; Science Clb; Ski Clb; Teachers Aide; Chorus; Im Bowling; Trk; High Hon Roll; Sec NHS.

PEIRICK, DEBRA; Holland Central HS; East Aurora, NY; (Y); 9/107; Am Leg Aux Girls St; Cmnty Wkr; Rep Stu Cncl; JV Capt Cheerleading; JV Socr; High Hon Roll; Hon Roll; Jr NHS; Ed.

PEITA, DOUGLAS S; Kenmore East SR HS; Buffalo, NY; (Y); 9/430; German Clb; Intnl Clb; Rep Frsh Cls; Im Bsktbl; Var Mgr(s); Var Tennis; Im Vllybl; High Hon Roll; Jr NHS; NHS; Rgnts Schlrshp Wnnr 86-87; Cornell; Bio.

PEJO, SAMUEL; Seton Catholic Central HS; Binghamton, NY; (Y); Key Clb; Ski Clb; Varsity Clb; Trs Sr Cls; Var Socr; Var Tennis; Gld & Slvr Mdlst Ntl & JR Olympcs 84 & 86; SUNY Binghamton.

PEKAR, MELANIE; Corinth Central Schl; Corinth, NY; (Y); Pres Aud/Vis; Boys Clb Am; Drama Clb; SADD; Varsity Clb; VICA; Off Stu Cncl; Stat Bsktbl; Score Keeper; Hon Roll; Audio-Vsl Awd VP & Pres 85-86; Lbry Awd V-Pres 85; Scrtrl Fld.

PELCZYNSKI, DARLEEN; Villa Maria Acad; Buffalo, NY; (Y); Church Yth Grp; Computer Clb; VP Hst FBLA; Pep Clb; Teachers Aide; Stu Cncl; Vllybl; Hon Roll; Trocaire Coll; Med Asst.

PELCZYNSKI, SABRINA; E Meadow HS; E Meadow, NY; (S); Drama Clb; Hosp Aide; Key Clb; Mathletes; Math Tm; Band; Orch; School Musical; School Play; Nwsp Rptr; All ST Symph Orch 85; All Cnty Nassau Strng Orch 83-86; Long Island Strngs 83-86; Penn ST; Psychtrst.

PELISH, TOM; Spackenkill HS; Poughkeepsie, NY; (Y); Debate Tm; Thesps; School Musical; School Play; Trs Frsh Cls; VP Jr Cls; Tennis; Hon Roll; NHS; Rotry Ldrshp Camp 85; Econ.

PELLEGRINI, CHRISTINE; Half Hollow Hills HS East; Dix Hills, NY; (Y); 36/514; Cmnty Wkr; SADD; Band; Chorus; Concert Band; Mrchg Band; Orch; Symp Band; Yrbk Stf; High Hon Roll; NY ST Regnts Schlrshp 86; Band Hnrs Awd 86; Franklin & Marshall Coll; Med.

PELLEGRINO, CRYSTI; Gloversville HS; Gloversville, NY; (Y); 70/234; DECA; Pep Clb; SADD; Teachers Aide; Yrbk Stf; JV Fld Hcky; Trk; Vllybl; Mry Bachnr Ury Awd 86.

PELLEGRINO, LISA; Sauquoit Valley Central HS; Frankfort, NY; (Y); 2/102; Cmnty Wkr; GAA; Girl Scts; Spanish Clb; Stage Crew; Yrbk Phtg; Yrbk Rptr; Pres Frsh Cls; Trs Soph Cls; Trs Jr Cls; Utica Coll; CPA.

PELLEGRINO, MICHELLE; Lindenhurst HS; Lindenhurst, NY; (Y); 88/550; Church Yth Grp; Spanish Clb; JV Vllybl; Hon Roll; NHS; Hofstra U; Acctng.

PELLEGRINO, SAMANTHA Y; Gorton HS; Yonkers, NY; (Y); 3/191; Church Yth Grp; Cmnty Wkr; Drama Clb; Intnl Clb; JA; Office Aide; Q&S; Red Cross Aide; Spanish Clb; Band; SUNY-ALBANY; Jrnlsm.

PELLETT, ANNE; Sacred Heart Acad; Stewart Manor, NY; (S); Library Aide; SADD; Chorus; Yrbk Stf; High Hon Roll; NHS; Regina Cordium Fll Schlrshp Achvng Hghst Acadmc Avg 84 & 85.

PELLICANO, LAURIE K; East HS; Corning, NY; (Y); 52/222; Dance Clb; Pres VP JA; Ski Clb; Band; Color Guard; Concert Band; Drill Tm; Mrchg Band; Var Pom Pon; Trk; St John Fisher Coll; Bus Admin.

PELLICCI, LISA P; St Francis Prep; College Point, NY; (S); 91/750; Church Yth Grp; Cmnty Wkr; Dance Clb; Math Tm; Church Choir; JV Capt Cheerleading; Cit Awd; Hon Roll; NHS; Spanish NHS; Boston U; Med.

PELLICCIO, VICTORIA; St Barnabas HS; Bronx, NY; (S); 5/188; Church Yth Grp; Pep Clb; Stu Cncl; Score Keeper; Hon Roll; NHS; Itln Ntl Hnr Soc; Psych.

PELORO, CONCETTINA M; Bishop Kearney HS; Brooklyn, NY; (Y); 6/338; Cmnty Wkr; Hosp Aide; Math Tm; Lit Mag; Rep Soph Cls; High Hon Roll; NHS; St John U Schltc Exclnc Schlrshp 86; NY U Trustee Schlrshp 86; Medl Recog Outstndng Serv 86; St Johns U; Law.

PELOSI, ELIZABETH; Sacred Heart Acad; Williamsville, NY; (Y); 6/140; Cmnty Wkr; French Clb; Model UN; Science Clb; School Musical; Nwsp Ed-Chief; Lit Mag; High Hon Roll; NHS; Holy Cross Coll Bk Awd; Canisius Coll; Cmmnctns.

PELOSI, JOLISA; Broadalbin Central Schl; Broadalbin, NY; (Y); Drama Clb; 4-H; Girl Scts; Library Aide; Spanish Clb; Band; Color Guard; Mrchg Band; JV Bsktbl; Var Bowling; Dellti; Vet Asst.

PELTIER, PATRICK M; Roy C Ketcham HS; Wappingers Falls, NY; (Y); #118 In Class; Art Clb; Library Aide; Political Wkr; Teachers Aide; Nwsp Rptr; Nwsp Stf; Yrbk Stf; Lit Mag; High Hon Roll; Hon Roll; SUNY New Paltz; Gentc Engrng.

PELTON, KARI A; Nardin Acad; Buffalo, NY; (Y); 38/85; Cmnty Wkr; JA; Model UN; Ski Clb; Stage Crew; Hon Roll; ST Rgnts Schlrshp 86; ST Assmblymn & Sntr Mrt Certs 86; Boston U; Econ.

PELUSO, ANTHONY; Archbishop Molloy HS; S Ozone Pk, NY; (Y); 175/350; Art Clb; Intnl Clb; Chorus; Yrbk Stf; Trk; Hon Roll; Dentstry.

PELUSO, BARBARA; New Utrecht HS; Brooklyn, NY; (Y); Trs Key Clb; Yrbk Stf; Hon Roll; NHS; Guardians Hydrcphls Awd 84; Columbia Asso Bklyn ST Island PO Inc 86; Brooklyn Coll.

PELUSO, STEPHANIE; John Dewey HS; Brooklyn, NY; (Y); Library Aide; Band; High Hon Roll; Prfct Atten Awd; Val; Achvt Awd Mth 83; Golden Recrd Achvt Awd 83; Comptrllrs Awd 83; Baruch Coll; Mgmt.

PELZAR, JENNIFER; Clarkstown HS North; Congers, NY; (Y); Hon Roll; Mu Alp Tht; NHS.

PEMPEL, AARON K; Ithaca HS; Ithaca, NY; (Y); Am Leg Boys St; Boy Scts; Drama Clb; School Musical; Nwsp Stf; Pres Stu Cncl; Capt Crs Cntry; Capt Trk; Jr NHS; NHS; Cornell U; Govt.

PENA, ELBERT; Central Islip SR HS; Central Islip, NY; (Y); 8/380; Math Clb; Math Tm; JV Tennis; NHS; Med.

PENA, FRANCIS; Archbishop Molloy HS; Elmhurst, NY; (Y); #383 In Class; Math Clb; Math Tm; Chorus; Hon Roll; Music Clb 83-86; NYU; Med.

PENDER, MELODY; Nazareth Regional HS; Brooklyn, NY; (Y); 46/276; Church Yth Grp; Cmnty Wkr; FCA; FHA; Hosp Aide; SADD; Y-Teens; High Hon Roll; Hon Roll; Bronze S Awd For Grades Above 85 Pct 83-86; Lincoln U; Psych.

PENDERGAST, JAMES; Farmingdale HS; Massapequa, NY; (Y); Church Yth Grp; Band; Church Choir; Hon Roll.

PENDERGAST, MICHELLE; Cicero-North Syracuse HS; N Syracuse, NY; (S); 38/667; Mathletes; Math Tm; Chorus; Color Guard; Hon Roll; NHS; Comp Sci.

PENDLETON, EVA; Bellport HS; Bellport, NY; (Y); 5/395; Trs French Clb; Leo Clb; Math Tm; SADD; Orch; Ed Nwsp Stf; French Hon Soc; High Hon Roll; NHS; Ntl Merit Ltr; Mbrshp NY Yth Symphny Carnegie Hll 83-86; Schl Of Orchstrl Studies 83-86; NY All-ST Orchstra 85; Law.

PENDLETON, LISA; Plattsburgh SR HS; Plattsburgh, NY; (Y); Teachers Aide; JV Var Gym; Score Keeper; Mgr Stat Sftbl.

PENELTON, CAL; Mc Kinley HS; Buffalo, NY; (Y); 39/216; Boys Clb Am; English Clb; Model UN; Concert Band; Variety Show; Rep Jr Cls; Off Stu Cncl; Crs Cntry; Buffalo ST Coll; Bus.

PENESIS, GEORGE; St Francis Prep; Fresh Meadows, NY; (S); 86/746; Am Leg Boys St; Boy Scts; Bsktbl; JV Var Socr; Vllybl; Hon Roll; Cooper Union; Mech Engrng.

PENG, TIMOTHY R; Smithtown High Schl East; St James, NY; (Y); Trs Camera Clb; Chess Clb; Key Clb; Radio Clb; Teachers Aide; Thesps; Nwsp Stf; Yrbk Phtg; Mgr Crs Cntry; Mgr(s); NY ST Rgnts Schrlshp 86-90; NY ST Empire Schrlshp Of Excllc 86-90; Yale U.

PENK, TIMOTHY; Ravena-Coeymans-Selkirk HS; Selkirk, NY; (Y); Boy Scts; Pres French Clb; Spanish Clb; Band; Jazz Band; Yrbk Stf; Stu Cncl; JV Var Bsbl; JV Var Ftbl; High Hon Roll.

PENNA, DAVID; Central HS; Valley Stream, NY; (Y); Computer Clb; Band; Concert Band; Mrchg Band; Orch; School Musical; Hon Roll; Tempo Music Hnr Soc 86; Music.

PENNA, THOMAS G; Niagara Wheatfield SR HS; Niagara Falls, NY; (Y); 7/291; Math Clb; Model UN; Lcrss; High Hon Roll; NHS; Rensselaer Plytch; Physics.

PENNA, TOM; Niagara Wheatfield HS; Niagara Falls, NY; (Y); 7/292; Math Clb; Model UN; Lcrss; High Hon Roll; NHS; RPI; Physcs.

PENNACHIO, ROBERT; St Marys Boys HS; Douglaston, NY; (S); 7/146; Yrbk Ed-Chief; Hon Roll; NHS; Offcr Schl Svc Orgnztn 85; St Johns U.

PENNANT, STEPHANIE; James Madison HS; Brooklyn, NY; (Y); 43/756; Color Guard; Nwsp Ed-Chief; Sec Frsh Cls; Hon Roll; Frgn Lng Tchr Awd 86; Cmnty Srvc ST Sntr 84; U Of PA; Bnkng Bus.

PENNELL, DEENA; Mohonasen HS; Schenectady, NY; (Y); Key Clb; SADD; Nwsp Stf; Rep Jr Cls; Cheerleading; High Hon Roll; Psychlgy.

PENNER, DEANNA; Midlakes HS; Seneca Castle, NY; (Y); 6/130; GAA; Spanish Clb; SADD; Var Fld Hcky; Var L Sftbl; Twrlr; Var Vllybl; High Hon Roll; Rochester Inst Tech; Comp Sci.

PENNEY, KEITH; Smithtown East HS; Saint James, NY; (Y); German Clb; SADD; Stu Cncl; Var L Ftbl; Capt Var Lcrss; Capt Var Wrstlng; High Hon Roll; NHS; Grmn Natl Hnr Soc; Cornell; Pre-Med.

PENNEY, LOREN; Roy C Ketcham HS; Poughkeepsie, NY; (Y); Socr; Dutchess Comm; Engrg.

PENNICK, LAMONT; South Park HS; Buffalo, NY; (Y); Var Capt Bsktbl; Var Ftbl; John Henry Newman Chapter Awd 85.

PENNIL, ERIKA; A E Stevenson HS; Bronx, NY; (Y); Church Yth Grp; Chorus; Yrbk Stf; Var Bowling; Var Socr; Hon Roll; NHS; Silv Mdl Awd Spn 84; Psych.

PENNING, CHRISTOPHER; South Glens Falls Central Schl; S Glens Falls, NY; (Y); 27/237; Hon Roll; Green Belt Tadashii-Do Karate 86; Boston U; Aerospc Engrng.

PENNON, BETTINA VITA; Center Moriches HS; Ctr Moriches, NY; (Y); Church Yth Grp; Drama Clb; FTA; Girl Scts; Library Aide; Radio Clb; Band; Chorus; Church Choir; School Musical; Hmcmng Queen & Prom Queen 85-86; Prom Princess 84-85; Hofstra U; Spec Educ.

PENROSE, DINA A; Academy Of St Joseph; Coram, NY; (Y); VP Trs Church Yth Grp; Drama Clb; Hosp Aide; Math Tm; Service Clb; Ski Clb; Teachers Aide; Church Choir; Stage Crew; Hon Roll; St Michaels Coll VT; Math.

PENSA, GINA; Commack HS North; East Northport, NY; (Y); 96/362; Cmnty Wkr; Office Aide; Spanish Clb; Off Frsh Cls; Off Soph Cls; Off Jr Cls; Hon Roll.

PENSKI, SARAH; Colton-Pierrepont HS; Colton, NY; (S); 3/25; Pres Rptr 4-H; French Clb; Yrbk Stf; Sec Frsh Cls; JV Bsktbl; Cheerleading; JV Var Socr; Cit Awd; 4-H Awd; Plattsburgh; Nrsng.

PENVOSE, JAN; Tonawanda SR HS; Tonawanda, NY; (Y); 1/220; Nwsp Ed-Chief; Yrbk Stf; Rep Stu Cncl; Var Socr; Var Trk; Bausch & Lomb Sci Awd; Cit Awd; High Hon Roll; NHS; French Clb; Rensselaer Medfal Math Sci Awd 86; Math.

PENZA, CHRISTINE A; Huntington HS; Huntington, NY; (Y); 70/383; AFS; Church Yth Grp; Cmnty Wkr; Hosp Aide; Political Wkr; Scholastic Bowl; Var Bsktbl; Var Fld Hcky; Var Vllybl; NHS; Engrng.

PEPE, PAMELA; Mayfield HS; Gloversville, NY; (Y); Drama Clb; Chorus; School Musical; Nwsp Rptr; Yrbk Ed-Chief; High Hon Roll; Sec Jr NHS; Sec NHS; Church Yth Grp; School Play; Dram Clb Awd Dedctn, Smmr Coll Schlrshp 86; Comm.

PEPITONE, DYANNA; Sacred Heart Acad; Malverne, NY; (S); 2/189; Service Clb; SADD; Nwsp Stf; Yrbk Stf; JV Bsktbl; Var Trk; High Hon Roll; Sec NHS; Amer Chem Soc NY Sectn Awd 85.

PEPPER, MELISSA; Addison Central Schl; Woodhull, NY; (S); 7/104; Ski Clb; Varsity Clb; Sec Concert Band; Sec Mrchg Band; Yrbk Stf; Trs Sr Cls; Var Capt Cheerleading; Var Sftbl; High Hon Roll; NHS; Mst Imprvd Plyr Vrsty Sftbl 85; Houghton NY; Bus Adm.

PEQUEEN, SALLY; Kenmore West SR HS; Buffalo, NY; (Y); French Clb; Band; Concert Band; Mrchg Band; School Musical; JV Swmmng; Var Trk; High Hon Roll.

PERAGINE, ANDREW; Archbishop Molloy HS; Wood Haven, NY; (Y); 70/383; Boy Scts; Church Yth Grp; Cmnty Wkr; Math Tm; Service Clb; Varsity Clb; Variety Show; Var Bsbl; JV Trk; Hon Roll; Eagle Scout 86; City Champs JV Bsbl 85; Cert Math Tm 86.

PERAGINE, LYNN; The Acad Of St Josep; Ronkonkoma, NY; (Y); Hosp Aide; Library Aide; Chorus; Nwsp Rptr; Nwsp Stf; Crs Cntry; Trk; Hon Roll; Praisewrthy Lst.

PERALTA, IVELISSE; Dominican Commercial HS; Ozone Park, NY; (Y); 67/288; Dance Clb; High Hon Roll; Hon Roll; NHS; Princpls List 84-86; Siena Clb 85-86; Loyola Marymount U; Comm Arts.

PERCELY, ADAM; Minisink Valley HS; Westtown, NY; (Y); Drama Clb; SADD; Chorus; School Play; Psych.

PERCHIKOFF, LISA; Seaford HS; Seaford, NY; (S); Service Clb; Teachers Aide; Orch; Yrbk Stf; Lit Mag; Vllybl; Hon Roll; Jr NHS; NHS; Engl Achvt Awd.

PERCY, JACQUELINE; John H Glenn HS; Huntington, NY; (Y); Cmnty Wkr; Drama Clb; School Musical; School Play; Lit Mag; High Hon Roll; Hon Roll; Jr NHS; NHS; Spanish NHS.

PEREIRA, ALICIA; St John The Baptist HS; Deer Pk, NY; (Y); Art Clb; Hon Roll; Bus Law.

PEREIRA, DOUGLAS; Cornwall Central HS; Cornwall-On-Hdsn, NY; (Y); Church Yth Grp; Band; Jazz Band; Symp Band; Ftbl; Trk; Wrstlng.

PEREIRA, MARYANN; St Francis Prep; Corona, NY; (Y); 300/720; Spanish Clb; SADD; Rep Jr Cls; Im Sftbl; Im Tennis.

PERERA, HYACINTH; Central Islip HS; Central Islip, NY; (Y); 56/348; Math Clb; Stage Crew; Socr; High Hon Roll; Hon Roll; Prfct Atten Awd; Computer Clb; FBLA; FTA; Band; Boces II Comp Repair Technlgy 85; Hnr Soc & Prfct Atten 86; SUNY Farmingdale; Elec Engrng.

PERESS, HARRY; Rye Country Day HS; Harrison, NY; (Y); 10/81; AFS; Cmnty Wkr; Hosp Aide; Temple Yth Grp; Nwsp Stf; Yrbk Stf; Lit Mag; Tennis; Ntl Merit Schol; Ntl Frnch Cntst 4th Pl Cnty 83; Boston U; Bus.

PERETSON, ROBERT; South Shore HS; Brooklyn, NY; (Y); Drama Clb; Gym; Real Est.

PEREZ, BLANCA; John Dewey HS; Brooklyn, NY; (Y); Sec Church Yth Grp; Pres JA; Library Aide; Math Tm; Chorus; Color Guard; School Musical; School Play; Prfct Atten Awd; NY ST Regents Schlrshp 86; Manhattanville Ldrshp Schlrshp 86; NY City Brd Of Educ Hnr Frgn Lang 86; Manhattanville Coll; Spec Educ.

PEREZ, CHRISTOPHER; Monsignor Farrell HS; Staten Island, NY; (S); Chess Clb; Hosp Aide; Spanish Clb; Im Bsktbl; Im Bowling; Im Ftbl; Hon Roll; Med.

PEREZ, DANIEL; Jefferson HS; Rochester, NY; (Y); Chorus; High Hon Roll; Hon Roll; Prfct Atten Awd; Eastmn Schl Music Schlrshp 86-87; Arch.

PEREZ, EDGAR; Bay Shore HS; Bay Shore, NY; (Y); 84/406; Camera Clb; Computer Clb; Var Capt Gym; High Hon Roll; Hon Roll; Comp Sci.

PEREZ, EDWIN; Saint Agnes HS; New York, NY; (Y); 41/110; Church Yth Grp; Cmnty Wkr; Debate Tm; Mrchg Band; JV Ftbl; JV Trk; Hon Roll; Boys Clb Am; Boy Scts; Camera Clb; NY ST Yth Cncl Yth Advct 86; Syracuse U; Bus Admin.

PEREZ, HIEDE; High School Of Fashion Industr; Brooklyn, NY; (Y); 208/324; Dance Clb; Girl Scts; Chorus; School Musical; Stage Crew; Rep Jr Cls; Pres Sr Cls; Im Gym; Engl Awd 85; Atten Cert 84-86; Yale U; Crmnl Law.

PEREZ, ILIANA; Lafayette HS; Buffalo, NY; (Y); Spanish Clb; Hon Roll; Med Sec.

PEREZ, LAURA; St Agnes HS; Kew Gardens, NY; (Y); Hosp Aide; SADD; Teachers Aide; Chorus; Rep Soph Cls; High Hon Roll; Med.

PEREZ, MARA; Msgr Scanlan HS; Bronx, NY; (Y); Intnl Clb; JV Bsktbl; Var JV Score Keeper; High Hon Roll; Prfct Atten Awd; B Con Edsn Schlrshp Awd 86; Top 10% Frshmn Yr 84.

PEREZ, MARGARET; James Madison HS; Brooklyn, NY; (Y); 38/756; Teachers Aide; Band; Concert Band; Hon Roll; Prfct Atten Awd; Acctg.

PEREZ, MARIA; High Schl Of Fashion Industy; Bronx, NY; (Y); 37/324; Office Aide; Chorus; Yrbk Stf; Arista Socty 83-84; Fshn Dsgn.

PEREZ, MARIBEL; Long Island City HS; Ny Cty, NY; (Y); Pres Church Yth Grp; Hosp Aide; Teachers Aide; Chorus; Yrbk Rptr; Lit Mag; Sftbl; Cit Awd; Hon Roll; Prfct Atten Awd; Pre-Me.

PEREZ, MARTHA; Cardinal Spellman HS; New York, NY; (Y); Flag Corp; NY U Schlrshp ,L; 2nd Hnrs 85-86; NY U; Comp Sci.

PEREZ, NANCY; The Mary Louis Acad; Jackson Heights, NY; (Y); Var Cmnty Wkr; Spanish Clb; Yrbk Stf; Pace U; Comp Sci.

PEREZ, ROSALYN; St Raymond Acad; Bronx, NY; (S); 12/69; Science Clb; Spanish Clb; Nwsp Stf; Yrbk Stf; Timer; High Hon Roll.

PEREZ, TIMOTHY M; Bishop Grimes HS; Syracuse, NY; (Y); Ski Clb; Socr; Highest Avrg Math Ii 85-86; Busi.

PEREZ, VINCENT; Louise D Brandies HS; New York, NY; (Y); Stu Cncl; BMCC; Pol Sci.

PEREZ, WILLIAM; Eastern District HS; Brooklyn, NY; (Y); Church Yth Grp; JA; Library Aide; Science Clb; Teachers Aide; Rep Frsh Cls; Hon Roll; Jr NHS; Hnrb Mntn 47th Brklyn Sci Fair, Natl Sci Olympd Awd 85; GTA Essay Cont 86; Cornell U; Adlscnt Psych.

PERFETTI, COLLEEN; Catholic Central HS; Troy, NY; (Y); Church Yth Grp; French Clb; Math Clb; Math Tm; SADD; Teachers Aide; Variety Show; Yrbk Stf; Cheerleading; French Hon Soc; Frnch Awd 84-85; Chrldng Awd JV Cmptn 85; Georgetown U; Intl Bus.

PERFETTO, LOUIS; Nazareth Regional HS; Brooklyn, NY; (Y); 45/267; Cmnty Wkr; Ski Clb; Varsity Clb; Var Capt Bsbl; Var Capt Bowling; Im Ftbl; High Hon Roll; Hon Roll; NHS; St Schlr; Athl Schlrshp U Chrlstn 86; Acadmc Schlrshp Wagner Coll 86; All Star, MVP Daily News HS All Star 86; U Of Charleston; Pre-Med.

PERHAM, MARIA; Gloversville HS; Gloversville, NY; (Y); 15/235; Aud/Vis; French Clb; Key Clb; Color Guard; High Hon Roll; Lion Awd; Church Yth Grp; Intnl Clb; Yrbk Stf; A Johnson Mem Schlrp 86; Laurel G Awd 86; Pres Acad Fit Awd 86; Stu Govt Tchrs Mem Awd 86; Frank Awd 86; Clarkson U; Cvl Engrg.

PERI, CHRISTINE; Seaford HS; Seaford, NY; (Y); 15/269; Band; Lit Mag; Cheerleading; Vllybl; High Hon Roll; Hon Roll; Acad All Amer 86; Fairfield U; Acctng.

PERICONI, PRISCILLA; Acad Of St Joseph; Brightwaters, NY; (Y); Dance Clb; Chorus; Yrbk Stf; High Hon Roll; Natl Frnch Cont Laureate 84; Stu Trimester 85; Acad Achvt Awd 85.

PERINE, JESSICA; Sanford H Calhoun HS; Merrick, NY; (Y); 30/313; Drama Clb; Key Clb; Quiz Bowl; Band; Yrbk Stf; Var Badmtn; Var Tennis; Var Trk; High Hon Roll; NHS; Soc Studies Fair & Sci Fair 83; Suny Binghamton; Psych.

PERIS, ELIZABETH ANNE; James E Sperry HS; Pittsford, NY; (Y); GAA; SADD; Concert Band; Jazz Band; School Musical; JV Var Cheerleading; French Hon Soc; High Hon Roll; Jr NHS; NHS; Scndry Ed Sci.

PERITORE, DEBORAH LYNN; Ward Melville HS; E Setauket, NY; (Y); Cmnty Wkr; DECA; Band; Yrbk Stf; Jr NHS; Bus Adm.

PERKINS, CHRISTOPHER J; Wayland Central HS; Dansville, NY; (Y); 19/110; Hon Roll; Hnrs Clb 83-84; Rochester Inst Of Tech; Cmptr.

PERKINS, JAMES; G Ray Bodley HS; Fulton, NY; (Y); French Clb; JV Bsbl; JV Var Bsktbl; JV Var Socr; Engl Yr Acad Achvnt 84; FL ST; Bus Mgmt.

PERKINS, JULIE M; Camden Central HS; N Bay, NY; (Y); 12/186; AFS; Church Yth Grp; Ski Clb; Yrbk Stf; High Hon Roll; NHS; Houghton Coll; Math.

PERKINS, PAMELA; South Shore HS; Brooklyn, NY; (Y); 306/600; Church Yth Grp; Dance Clb; Church Choir; Bsktbl; Trk; Wt Lftg; Prfct Atten Awd; Cert Of Sci Dept Of Correctns 85; Cert Of Proficncy-Bus 85; Perfect Attndnc Awd 86; York Coll; Med Lab Technlgy.

PERKINS, RODERICK D; Interlaken Christian Schl; Ithaca, NY; (Y); 1/3; Church Yth Grp; Chorus; Yrbk Stf; Var Capt Bsktbl; Score Keeper; Ntl Merit SF; Prfct Atten Awd; Val; 1st Spllng Christian Ed ST 84-85, 1st Intl 85.

PERKINS, ROSS; Camden SR HS; Camden, NY; (Y); AFS; Am Leg Boys St; Church Yth Grp; Drama Clb; Intnl Clb; Sec Science Clb; Ski Clb; SADD; Varsity Clb; School Musical; Bio.

PERKINS, WALTER; Addison Central HS; Addison, NY; (Y); Church Yth Grp; Pres Computer Clb; Library Aide; Chorus; School Play; Bowling; Real Est.

PERL, ANDREA; York Preparatory Schl; New York, NY; (Y); 1/90; Hosp Aide; Temple Yth Grp; School Play; Nwsp Stf; Yrbk Phtg; Yrbk Stf; Rep Frsh Cls; Rep Soph Cls; Hon Roll.

PERLMAN, DENISE; Spackenkill HS; Poughkeepsie, NY; (Y); 24/176; Leo Clb; SADD; Temple Yth Grp; Yrbk Stf; Bsktbl; Fld Hcky; Ftbl; Sftbl; Mu Alp Tht; Hon Roll.

PERNA JR, ANTHONY J; Middletown HS; Middletown, NY; (Y); Debate Tm; Math Tm; Yrbk Stf; Lit Mag; JV L Ftbl; High Hon Roll; Hon Roll; NHS; Ntl Merit SF; Top Mth Stu 86; Top Hstry Stu 84; Pre-Law.

PERNAT, BRANDON; Whitesboro Central Schl; Whitesboro, NY; (Y); 28/304; Pres Church Yth Grp; Mathletes; Model UN; Science Clb; Var L Crs Cntry; Var L Trk; NHS; Varsity Clb; Hon Roll; Elec Engrng.

PERNICK JR, JAMES A; St Josephs Collegiate Inst; Kenmore, NY; (Y); 79/180; Letterman Clb; Varsity Clb; Nwsp Sprt Ed; Var L Bsbl; Im JV Bsktbl; Im JV Ftbl; Var L Socr; Im Wt Lftg; Hon Roll; Prfct Atten Awd; Capt-Vrsty Bsbl Tm 86; All Cthlc Hnrs-Vrsty Bsbl 86; Schlrshp-Bsbl-U Of Chrlstn & Mnsfld U 86; Mansfield U; Bus.

PERNINI, BRUNA; Yonkers HS; Yonkers, NY; (Y); Cmnty Wkr; Hosp Aide; SADD; Nwsp Stf; Yrbk Stf; Lit Mag; High Hon Roll; Hon Roll; Prfct Atten Awd; Sprntndnts Awd 84-86; Accntng.

PERO, CARA MARIA; Half Hollow Hills HS West; Dix Hills, NY; (Y); Church Yth Grp; Science Clb; SADD; Chorus; Yrbk Stf; JV Var Cheerleading; JV Mgr(s); Score Keeper; Hon Roll; Sprno Slst NYSSMA Mdl 85 & 86; Acctg.

PEROTTI, JEFF; Solvay HS; Syracuse, NY; (Y); 28/171; Math Clb; Spanish Clb; Yrbk Bus Mgr; Off Soph Cls; Off Jr Cls; Off Sr Cls; Stu Cncl; Cit Awd; Hon Roll; Gradtd With Hnrs 86; Mdl Of Merit 86; Onondaga Cmnty Coll; Htl Mgmt.

PERPIGNAN, RALPH; South Shore HS; Brooklyn, NY; (Y); Teachers Aide; Prfct Atten Awd; Indstrl Art Awds 86; Brooklyn Clg NY; Paramedic.

PERRETTA, DOUGLAS; Canarsie HS; Brooklyn, NY; (Y); Library Aide; Office Aide; Band; School Play; High Hon Roll; Hon Roll; FL Atlantic U; Sys Anylst.

PERRICONE, SCOTT T; Sachem North HS; Holbrook, NY; (Y); 238/1385; Computer Clb; French Clb; Science Clb; Ski Clb; Rep Sr Cls; Hon Roll; NY ST Regents 86; LI Sci Cngrss 84; Earth Sci Achvt Awd 83; SUNY-STNY Brk.

PERRIGO, MARTIN; Tupper Lake Central Schl; Tupper Lk, NY; (Y); 2/103; Drama Clb; 4-H; School Musical; School Play; Stage Crew; Bausch & Lomb Sci Awd; 4-H Awd; Hon Roll; NHS; Sal; Clarkson U; Elec Engnrng.

PERRIN, LAURA L; Liverpool HS; Liverpool, NY; (Y); 11/800; Church Yth Grp; Exploring; Church Choir; Mrchg Band; School Musical; School Play; Yrbk Stf; Jr NHS; NHS; Ntl Merit Ltr; NY ST Regents Schlrshp 86; Cornell U; Bio.

PERRIN, MICHELLE; Alexander Central Schl; Alexander, NY; (Y); 23/83; Dance Clb; Drama Clb; 4-H; Ski Clb; Spanish Clb; Yrbk Ed-Chief; Yrbk Phtg; Yrbk Stf; Socr; Sftbl; Bryant & Stratton Acctg Schlrshp 86; WY Cnty Bnk Awd 86; Frank Innes Schlrshp 86; Bryant & Stratton; Acctg.

PERRONE, JOHN; Half Hollow Hills HS East; Dix Hills, NY; (Y); Church Yth Grp; Drama Clb; Acpl Chr; Band; Chorus; Church Choir; Concert Band; Jazz Band; Mrchg Band; School Musical; Stu Of Mnth 83; NYSSMA 86; Engrng.

PERRONE, LILLA; Curtis HS; Staten Island, NY; (Y); 2/30; Computer Clb; Key Clb; Math Tm; Science Clb; Orch; Hon Roll.

PERROTTE, SARAH; Maple Hill HS; Castleton, NY; (Y); Library Aide; Math Tm; Band; Concert Band; Mrchg Band; School Musical; Nwsp Stf; Yrbk Stf; Bsktbl; Fld Hcky; Bus.

PERROTTI, ANGELA; Queen Of The Rosary Acad; Long Beach, NY; (S); 1/50; Drama Clb; Library Aide; Church Choir; School Play; Sftbl; High Hon Roll; Hon Roll; NHS; Bus Hnr Socty 84-86; Nassau CC; Lang.

PERROTTI, MICHAEL; Lansingburgh HS; Troy, NY; (Y); Scholastic Bowl; Varsity Clb; Ftbl; Wrstlng; High Hon Roll; Hon Roll; Jr NHS; NHS; Engr.

PERRY, ANN; Grand Island SR HS; Grand Isl, NY; (Y); Art Clb; Church Yth Grp; Girl Scts; Ski Clb; Variety Show; Stu Cncl; Hon Roll.

PERRY, ANNA; Watkins Glen HS; Watkins Glen, NY; (S); 5/135; Letterman Clb; Math Clb; Scholastic Bowl; Spanish Clb; Nwsp Stf; Var Tennis; DAR Awd; High Hon Roll; NHS; Spanish NHS; Amer H S Math Exam 2nd Pl 85; Suny Geneseo; Educ.

PERRY, DAVID; Spencerport HS; Spencerport, NY; (Y); French Clb; Red Cross Aide; Var Vllybl; High Hon Roll; Hon Roll; NHS; Pre-Med.

PERRY, DENISE; Uniondale HS; Uniondale, NY; (Y); 7/410; Hosp Aide; Red Cross Aide; Yrbk Stf; Pom Pon; High Hon Roll; Hon Roll; Jr NHS; Var NHS; Outstndng Serv Vlntr 84; Lawrence Road J H PTA Schlrshp 86; Washngton Sq U And Clg Schlrshp 86; NY U; Poltc Sci.

PERRY, JAMES M; Maine-Endwell SR HS; Endwell, NY; (Y); 27/236; Church Yth Grp; Ski Clb; SADD; School Play; Var Tennis; Hon Roll; NHS; NYS Rgnts Schlrshp 86; SUNY Albany; Bio.

PERRY, K MICHELLE; Plattsburgh SR HS; Plattsburgh, NY; (Y); Cmnty Wkr; SADD; Varsity Clb; Band; Rep Stu Cncl; JV Var Socr; Capt JV Vllybl; Hon Roll; NHS; Acad Achvmt Awd Social Stds 86; Surgeon.

PERRY, KARLA M; Franklin Acad; Malone, NY; (Y); 50/272; Trs Spanish Clb; Rep Yrbk Stf; Rep Stu Cncl; Spanish NHS; Merit Diploma For Spnsh Five 86; Cert Of Merit Fr Assmbly Of NY 86; US Mrn Corps; Cryptlgc Trnsltr.

PERRY, KRISTEN; Parishville-Hopkinton Central HS; Potsdam, NY; (S); 2/44; Sec Trs Church Yth Grp; Math Tm; Church Choir; School Musical; Stage Crew; Var Capt Cheerleading; High Hon Roll; Hon Roll; Trs NHS; Prfct Atten Awd; Talnted JR Awd 85; Excllnce Fr III 85; Excllnce Course III 85; SUNY Potsdam; Sec Mth.

PERRY, LORI J; Geneva HS; Geneva, NY; (S); 28/175; Church Yth Grp; French Clb; Library Aide; Office Aide; Var Cheerleading; Im Vllybl; High Hon Roll; Frnch Composition Awd 83; Lebanon Vly Coll; Act Sci.

PERRY, MARY C; Rome Catholic HS; Rome, NY; (Y); 13/68; Sec Drama Clb; Nwsp Sprt Ed; Nwsp Stf; Yrbk Sprt Ed; High Hon Roll; Hon Roll; NEDT Awd; Rgnts Schlr 85-86; Nwspr Layout Editor; Syracuse U; Pre-Med.

PERRY, NATASCHA; Walter Parlas HS; Peekskill, NY; (Y); Church Yth Grp; Dance Clb; Girl Scts; Intnl Clb; Library Aide; Office Aide; Radio Clb; SADD; Y-Teens; Variety Show; Hnr Awds 85 Pct Avr 83-86; Bst Stdnt Awd 84-85.

PERRY, RENARD; Rice HS; New York, NY; (S); #6 In Class; Nwsp Rptr; Crs Cntry; High Hon Roll; Hon Roll; Law.

PERRY, RHONDA; John Dewey HS; Brooklyn, NY; (Y); Dance Clb; Math Tm; Band; School Play; Nwsp Rptr; Vllybl; Wt Lftg; Prd Ynks Awd 85-86; Grkr Chptr Lnks Shlrshp 86; UFT Schlrshp 86; Barnard Coll; Intrl Rltns.

PERRY, RICH; Massena Central HS; Massena, NY; (Y); 14/235; Cmnty Wkr; Yrbk Stf; Pres Frsh Cls; Pres Soph Cls; Pres Jr Cls; Pres Sr Cls; Pres Stu Cncl; JV L Bsbl; Var L Ftbl; Var L Trk; Ftbl All Northern, All Up ST Tm, Acadmc Alla M 85-86; Wrstlng Coaches Awd 86; H Clar, Rtry, Stu Cncl; Rochester Inst; Grphc Dsgn.

PERRY, ROBERT J; Fort Plain Central HS; Fort Plain, NY; (Y); Am Leg Boys St; Aud/Vis; Boy Scts; Computer Clb; Drama Clb; Jazz Band; Mrchg Band; Yrbk Phtg; Elks Awd; Pres NHS; Audio-Vsl Serv Awd 85-86; Hugh O Brian Yth Fndtn 84-85; Drm Clb Awd 85-86; Berklee Coll; Prfssnl Prfmng.

PERRY, RON; Franklin Acad; Malone, NY; (Y); Computer Clb; FBLA; SADD; Swing Chorus; Sftbl; Tennis; Wt Lftg; Hon Roll; Pres Schlr; Plattsburg ST; Data Proc.

PERRY, RUBY ELLEN MORGAN; Portville Central HS; Portville, NY; (Y); GAA; Pep Clb; Chorus; Church Choir; Cheerleading; Pom Pon; Swmmng; Timer; Trk; High Hon Roll; Math.

PERRY, TINA M; East Syracuse Minoa HS; Kirkville, NY; (Y); 17/333; Trs Church Yth Grp; Pres Spanish Clb; Variety Show; Stat Socr; JV Var Sftbl; Twrlr; JV Var Vllybl; High Hon Roll; Jr NHS; NHS; Rgnts Schlrshp 86; SUNY Binghamton.

PERRY III, ZOLLIE THOMAS; Smauel Gompers HS; Bronx, NY; (Y); Art Clb; Computer Clb; Mathletes; Ski Clb; Band; Gym; Hon Roll.

PERSCHBACH, PENNY; Newfield HS; Selden, NY; (Y); 59/535; Hosp Aide; Teachers Aide; Spanish NHS; Rgnts Dplma 86; Middle Cntry Scrtrl Assoc Schlrshp 86; Berkeley; Accntng.

PERSELL, JULIE; Jamestown HS; Jamestown, NY; (Y); Spanish Clb; Band; Chorus; Concert Band; Mrchg Band; Nwsp Stf; Stu Cncl; Hon Roll; U Of NC; Medical.

PERSICO, PHILIP; Cardinal Spellman HS; Bronx, NY; (Y); 30/450; Chorus; School Musical; Yrbk Phtg; Yrbk Stf; Off Frsh Cls; Stu Cncl; Hon Roll; NHS; Acctncy.

PERSON, ANTHONY EARL; Bishp Ford Central Catholic HS; Brooklyn, NY; (Y); Church Yth Grp; Cmnty Wkr; JA; Varsity Clb; Nwsp Stf; Stu Cncl; Im Bsktbl; Trk; Hon Roll; Prfct Atten Awd; Corp Law.

PERSONTE, SHARON; Edison Tech & Occupational Ed Cntr; Rochester, NY; (Y); JV Var Mgr(s); Cit Awd; Hon Roll; NHS; Prfct Atten Awd; Preschl Chldrn Tchr.

PERSONTE, TRACY L; Naples Central Schl; Naples, NY; (Y); Church Yth Grp; English Clb; Chorus; Church Choir; Cheerleading; High Hon Roll; Hon Roll; Duane Schultz Mem Rotary Awd 86; Alfred ST Coll; Exec Sec.

PERTAK, JILL; Crown Point Central Schl; Crown Point, NY; (S); Varsity Clb; Sec Jr Cls; Var Bsktbl; Var Socr; Var Sftbl; Elks Awd; Hon Roll; NHS; Prfct Atten Awd; Canton U New York; Lab Tech.

PERYEA, DEBORAH A; Ausable Valley Central HS; Keeseville, NY; (Y); 9/130; Cmnty Wkr; Key Clb; Model UN; Scholastic Bowl; Rep Stu Cncl; Var L Socr; High Hon Roll; NHS; Ntl Merit Ltr; St Schlr; St Lawrence U; Gov.

PESA, SANDY; St Francis Preparatory Schl; Bayside, NY; (S); 114/744; Library Aide; Band; Concert Band; Drm & Bgl; Mrchg Band; School Musical; Yrbk Stf; Hon Roll; Jr NHS; NHS; Top Honor Music; Boston Coll; Frnch.

PESCE, LYNN; St Barnabas HS; Bronx, NY; (Y); 20/189; Pres Frsh Cls; Var Sftbl; Var Swmmng; Var Twrlr; Acad Hnrs 84-86.

PESIRI, BARBARA; St John The Baptist HS; Amityville, NY; (Y); 9/500; High Hon Roll; Hon Roll; Jr NHS; NHS; Spanish NHS; Bus Hnr Soc 85-86; Cert Merit Math, Sci & Socl Studies 85-86; Acctng.

PESKOWITZ, PENINA; Yeshiva Univ HS For Girls; Flushing, NY; (Y); 52/110; Cmnty Wkr; Nwsp Ed-Chief; NYS Regnts Schlrshp 87; Queens Coll; Comp Sci.

PESQUERA, ANTHONY; All Hallows HS; Bronx, NY; (Y); JV Bsbl; Bsktbl; Hon Roll; John Jay Coll; Engl.

PETCHPRAPA, CATHERINE; Tottenville HS; Staten Island, NY; (S); 14/850; Scholastic Bowl; Orch; School Musical; School Play; Symp Band; Lit Mag; High Hon Roll; Jr NHS; Spanish NHS; Mdl Cngrs 86; Doctor.

PETENDREE, LYNETTE; St Catharine Acad; Bronx, NY; (Y); #17 In Class; Debate Tm; Rep Frsh Cls; High Hon Roll; NHS; Fordham U; Cmmnctns.

PETER, ANILA; Blessed Sacrement/St Gabriel HS; Pelham, NY; (Y); 1/138; Cmnty Wkr; Pres Sr Cls; Pres Stu Cncl; Bausch & Lomb Sci Awd; High Hon Roll; JC Awd; Jr NHS; Ntl Merit Ltr; Pres Schlr; Hugh O Brian Ldrshp Ambssdr Awd 84; Pres Fittness Awd 86; NY Regents Schlrshp 86; Albany/Siena Med Schl; Bio.

PETER, GEORGINA E; Sleepy Hollow HS; N Tarrytown, NY; (Y); 24/180; Cmnty Wkr; Sec Drama Clb; School Play; Nwsp Ed-Chief; Nwsp Phtg; Nwsp Rptr; Lit Mag; High Hon Roll; NHS; NY Regents Schlrshp 86; Syracuse U; Pblc Comm.

PETER, JOSEPH; St Marys HS; Depew, NY; (S); 1/160; Quiz Bowl; Trs Science Clb; SADD; Nwsp Rptr; High Hon Roll; NHS; NEDT Awd; Outstndng Acadm Achvmnt Awd In Eurpn Cltrs Hnrs 85 & In Afro, Adian Cltrs 84.

PETER, LAURA; St Marys HS; Depew, NY; (S); 22/166; Camera Clb; SADD; Yrbk Ed-Chief; Yrbk Stf; Hon Roll; NHS; Canisius Coll; Comm.

PETERKIN, TANYA; Cardinal Spellman HS; Bronx, NY; (Y); Dance Clb; JA; Science Clb; Teachers Aide; Chorus; Swing Chorus; High Hon Roll; Hon Roll; Christn Actn Corps 85-86; Sign Lang Clb 85-86; Crew Of Mnth 86; Columbia U; Comptrs.

PETERMAN, RENEE; Valley Stream Central HS; Valley Stream, NY; (Y); 47/349; SADD; Concert Band; Mrchg Band; Orch; Lit Mag; Socr; JP Sousa Awd; NHS; Pres Schlr; Church Yth Grp; Tempo-Music Hon Soc 83-86; Rcqtgbl 82-86; Oswego; Elem Educ.

PETERMAN, TARA A; Carmel HS; Carmel, NY; (Y); 63/375; Church Yth Grp; Intnl Clb; Nwsp Rptr; Nwsp Stf; Yrbk Stf; Lit Mag; Bsktbl; Trk; Vllybl; Hon Roll; VP Natl Hnr Scty; Capt JV Bsktbl; Intl Rltns.

PETERS, BRIAN M; Newburgh Free Acad; Newburgh, NY; (Y); Art Clb; 4-H; Hon Roll; Var Swmmng; NYS Regnts Schlrshp 86; 3rd Pl NYS Visl Art Olympcs 86; FIT; Advtsg.

PETERS, CYNTHIA; Charles O Dickerson HS; Trumansburg, NY; (Y); 12/120; Am Leg Aux Girls St; Church Yth Grp; French Clb; Ski Clb; SADD; Varsity Clb; Socr; Tennis; Trk; High Hon Roll; Hnr Rl; French.

PETERS, DAVID; London Central HS; APO, NY; (Y); 17/126; Boy Scts; Church Yth Grp; Drama Clb; Letterman Clb; Quiz Bowl; Spanish Clb; Nwsp Rptr; Bsktbl; Crs Cntry; Trk; Mrn Sci.

PETERS, DEANNE L; Wells Central HS; Northville, NY; (Y); French Clb; Library Aide; Radio Clb; Band; Chorus; School Musical; Yrbk Stf; VP Frsh Cls; Vllybl; Hon Roll; Rgnts Schlrshp In Nrsng 85-86; Fltn Mntgmry CC; Nrsng.

PETERS, DEBBIE; Wellsville HS; Wellsville, NY; (Y); 22/121; Cmnty Wkr; Key Clb; Pep Clb; SADD; Stage Crew; Nwsp Bus Mgr; Nwsp Rptr; Nwsp Stf; Pres Stu Cncl; High Hon Roll; NY ST Regnts Schlrshp 85-86; U Of Buffalo; Commctns.

PETERS, DENISE; Ticonderoga HS; Hague, NY; (Y); Hosp Aide; Yrbk Stf; JV Bsktbl; Var Trk; Hon Roll; Specl Eductn Teachr.

PETERS, JAN M; Bethelem Central HS; Delmar, NY; (Y); Church Yth Grp; Cmnty Wkr; Key Clb; Office Aide; Red Cross Aide; SADD; Teachers Aide; Stage Crew; Yrbk Stf; Var Fld Hcky; Ntl Hnr Soc 86-87; Hgh Hnr Roll; Spnsh.

PETERS, JANICE; John Dewey HS; Brooklyn, NY; (Y); Dance Clb; Drama Clb; Library Aide; Chorus; Yrbk Stf; Vllybl; Drama.

PETERS, JOSEPH; Northport SR HS; Northport, NY; (Y); Boy Scts; Church Yth Grp; Cmnty Wkr; Exploring; Science Clb; Band; Var Crs Cntry; Var Trk; Im Wt Lftg; Hon Roll; BSA Order Arrow Brthrhd 84; Rnng & Hg Jmp Awds 84-86; Pre Med.

PETERS, KEITH; Remson Central JR SR HS; Remsen, NY; (Y); FFA; Band; Concert Band; Mrchg Band; JV Bsktbl; Var Socr; Var Trk; High Hon Roll; Hon Roll; Eng Jr Yr Ctznshp Awd 85; USAF Acad; Elctrnc Tech.

PETERS, KRISTIN; Williamsville East HS; Williamsville, NY; (Y); Church Yth Grp; French Clb; FBLA; Ski Clb; Stu Cncl; Fld Hcky; High Hon Roll; Hon Roll; Psych.

PETERS, LAWRENCE; Liverpool HS; Liverpool, NY; (Y); Hon Roll; Acadmc Achvt Awd 85-86; Comp Electncs.

PETERS, MELISSA; Saugerties HS; Saugerties, NY; (Y); Church Yth Grp; Mrchg Band; Powder Puff Ftbl; Tennis; Trk; Twrlr; NHS; Math.

PETERS, MICHELLE; Linton HS; Schenectady, NY; (Y); 1/322; Pres Intnl Clb; Office Aide; Lit Mag; Off Stu Cncl; Var L Tennis; French Hon Soc; High Hon Roll; Sec NHS; Treas Of Lintonians 86-87; Slvr Poet Awd From Wrld Of Poetry 86; Cmptd In NCTE Wrtg Cmptn 86; Law.

PETERS, SCOTT; Aquinas Inst; Rochester, NY; (Y); 30/163; Church Yth Grp; Drama Clb; Letterman Clb; Spanish Clb; SADD; Varsity Clb; Stage Crew; Var L Bsbl; Var L Ice Hcky; JV Trk; Physcl Sci Achvt Awd 82; Mechcl Drwng Achvt Awd 86; Rochester Inst; Elec Engr.

PETERS, SHARON; Pembroke HS; Corfu, NY; (Y); 1/120; Pres VP Stu Cncl; High Hon Roll; NHS; Ntl Merit Ltr; Val; AFS; Art Clb; 4-H; Band; Concert Band; Soph Clss Outstndg Stu & Stu Choice 84-85; 1st Chr All Cnty Bnd 85-86.

PETERS, SHEILINE R; Chautauqua Central HS; Mayville, NY; (Y); Drama Clb; Library Aide; Ski Clb; Varsity Clb; Acpl Chr; Band; Concert Band; School Play; Yrbk Stf; Bsktbl; Geneseo ST Coll.

PETERSDORF, LISA; South Park HS; Buffalo, NY; (Y); Church Yth Grp; Cmnty Wkr; Debate Tm; Library Aide; Mathletes; Red Cross Aide; Nwsp Stf; Yrbk Stf; High Hon Roll; NHS; Tchng.

PETERSEN, DANA; Sherburne-Earlville Central HS; Poolville, NY; (Y); 4/169; Art Clb; Intnl Clb; Ski Clb; Fld Hcky; Score Keeper; Swmmng; Hon Roll; NHS; Natl Sci Merit Awd 86; Oprtn Entrprs Schlrshp Wnr 86; Librl Arts.

PETERSEN, DAVID; Pioneer Central HS; Java Village, NY; (Y); 9/258; CAP; Band; Jazz Band; School Musical; Lit Mag; Var Golf; Var Tennis; NHS; Ntl Merit SF; French Clb; Prpsfl Lfe Clb 86; Engr.

PETERSEN, JOSEPH; Cornwall Central HS; Highland Mills, NY; (Y); Boy Scts; Ski Clb; Var Ftbl; Wt Lftg; Trk; Albany; Law.

PETERSEN, JULIA; Mynderse Acad; Seneca Falls, NY; (Y); Church Yth Grp; Cmnty Wkr; FHA; Girl Scts; Spanish Clb; Band; Chorus; Color Guard; Concert Band; School Musical; Nrsg.

PETERSEN, LISA; Sacred Heart Acad; Malverne, NY; (Y); Church Yth Grp; Hosp Aide; Chorus; Church Choir; Nwsp Ed-Chief; Bowling; Hon Roll; NHS; Adelphi U Trustee Schlrshp 86; NYS Rgnts Schlrshp Nrsng 86; March Dimes Awd Wnnr 86; Adelphi U; Nrsng.

PETERSON, ANN; Churchville Chili SR HS; N Chili, NY; (Y); Church Yth Grp; Hosp Aide; Band; Chorus; Church Choir; Concert Band; Jazz Band; Mrchg Band; School Musical; Swing Chorus; Music Ed.

PETERSON, APRIL; Watkins Glen HS; Watkins Glen, NY; (S); 13/111; French Clb; Letterman Clb; Stu Cncl; Cheerleading; Hon Roll; Bus.

PETERSON, BARBARA; Washingtonville HS; Campbell Hall, NY; (Y); 1/260; Pres Church Yth Grp; Spanish Clb; Color Guard; Flag Corp; Mrchg Band; Yrbk Stf; Hon Roll; NHS; Regents Schlrshp 86; Trsts Schlr 86; BYU.

PETERSON, CAROLE; Westfield Central Schl; Westfield, NY; (Y); Yrbk Stf; Sec Jr Cls; Rep Stu Cncl; L Trk; High Hon Roll; Hon Roll; Chld Psch.

PETERSON, DAN; Jamestown HS; Jamestown, NY; (Y); Pres German Clb; Stage Crew; Rep Frsh Cls; Rep Soph Cls; Rep Jr Cls; Rep Stu Cncl; 1st Pl Chautauqua Cnty Sci Fair 83; Spartan Aero; Aerontcs.

PETERSON, DON; Norwood-Norfolk Central Schl; Norwood, NY; (Y); JCL; Key Clb; Latin Clb; Office Aide; Rep Soph Cls; Trs Jr Cls; JV Bsbl; Var Ice Hcky; JV Var Socr; High Hon Roll; Math.

PETERSON, KAREN; Centereach HS; Selden, NY; (Y); Nwsp Rptr; Yrbk Stf; Pom Pon; Vllybl; Jr NHS; Syracuse; Law.

PETERSON, KIM; Hornell SR HS; Hornell, NY; (Y); 4/179; Latin Clb; Ski Clb; Concert Band; Yrbk Stf; Cheerleading; High Hon Roll; Hon Roll; NHS; NY St Rgnts Schlrshp 86; U Of Buffalo.

PETERSON, LISA; Horseheads HS; Horseheads, NY; (S); Pres Church Yth Grp; Pres JCL; Model UN; SADD; Color Guard; Concert Band; Orch; Rep Stu Cncl; NHS; Ntl Merit SF.

PETERSON, NOELLE; Cicero-North Syracuse HS; Clay, NY; (S); 21/623; Church Yth Grp; 4-H; Band; Concert Band; Mrchg Band; Symp Band; 4-H Awd; High Hon Roll; Hon Roll; Jr NHS; Kings Coll; Bus.

PETERSON, SHARON L; Vestal SR HS; Endicott, NY; (Y); 27/430; Church Yth Grp; French Clb; Rep Sr Cls; Hon Roll; Rgnts Schlrshp 86; Baptist Bible Coll.

PETERSON, ZANE; Paul V Moore HS; Central Sq, NY; (Y); Church Yth Grp; Computer Clb; German Clb; Im JV Bsbl; JV Crs Cntry; Im Var Socr; High Hon Roll; Hon Roll; SAT Schlrshp 86; Ambassador Coll; Comp Opertn.

PETFIELD, STEVEN; Westlake HS; Hawthorne, NY; (Y); 48/171; Am Leg Boys St; Cmnty Wkr; Yrbk Sprt Ed; Yrbk Stf; Bsktbl; Ftbl; Trk; Hon Roll; Rotary Awd; Athlt Schlr Awd; Stu Rcgntn Awd; Pace U; Accntng.

PETION, HERVAY; Prospect Heights HS; Brooklyn, NY; (S); Band; Swmmng; City Coll Of NY; Mech Engrng.

PETIT, CHERIE; Alden Central HS; Alden, NY; (Y); Hon Roll; Prfct Atten Awd.

PETIT MICHEL, MARIE; Newfield HS; Coram, NY; (S); 20/546; Art Clb; Church Yth Grp; Drama Clb; SADD; Chorus; Church Choir; Nwsp Rptr; Lit Mag; Trk; Hon Roll; All Sst Trk Rnnr 85-86; MVP Fencing 83-85.

PETRAGANANI, AMY; Liverpool HS; Liverpool, NY; (Y); 9/850; JA; JCL; Ski Clb; Rep Jr Cls; High Hon Roll; Jr NHS; NHS; Math,Bk Awd 85-86; Bus.

PETRAGLIA, LAURA; Lincoln HS; Yonkers, NY; (S); 10/350; Art Clb; Drama Clb; School Play; Stage Crew; Nwsp Rptr; High Hon Roll; Hon Roll; Ntl Merit Ltr.

PETRAGLIA, SCOTT; North Babylon HS; N Babylon, NY; (Y); 81/450; English Clb; Chorus; Bowling; Socr; St Johns; Jrnlsm.

PETRAITIS, BONNIE; John H Glenn HS; E Northport, NY; (Y); Hon Roll; Spanish NHS; CW Post; Spnsh Educ.

PETRALIA, FRANCES; Marlboro Central HS; Marlboro, NY; (Y); 8/150; VP Church Yth Grp; SADD; Varsity Clb; JV Var Cheerleading; JV Sftbl; Stat Trk; High Hon Roll; NHS; Spnsh Rgnts Awd 84; Ltn Cum Laude Awd Ntl Tst 86; SUNY Albany.

PETRALIA, MARK; Lindenhurst HS; Lindenhurst, NY; (Y); Varsity Clb; JV Bsbl; Bsktbl; Var Tennis; Hon Roll; Furman; Bus Adm.

PETRAMALE, FRANCIS R; St Patricks CC HS; Catskill, NY; (Y); 1/35; Am Leg Boys St; Drama Clb; French Clb; Political Wkr; Nwsp Stf; Yrbk Stf; Pres Jr Cls; Bausch & Lomb Sci Awd; Elks Awd; Pres NHS.

PETRAMALE, PATRICIA; Saugerties HS; Saugerties, NY; (S); 6/252; French Clb; Math Tm; Ski Clb; Chorus; Yrbk Stf; Soph Cls; JV Var Bsktbl; JV Sftbl; Hon Roll; NHS.

PETRASK, TRACY; Schalmont HS; Schenectady, NY; (Y); Cmnty Wkr; Crs Cntry; Score Keeper; Socr; Tennis; Vllybl; High Hon Roll; Hon Roll; Prfct Atten Awd; Proud Amrcn Wnnr 80; Gftd Pgm 80-83; Sci, Wngl, Math Soc Stds Awds 81-83; Med Asst.

PETRAUSKAS, BARBARA ANN; Corcoran HS; Syracuse, NY; (Y); 3/232; Am Leg Aux Girls St; Drama Clb; GAA; Key Clb; Math Tm; Pep Clb; Spanish Clb; SADD; Band; Chorus; Orondaga CC Cmnty Schlr 86; Syracuse Heald Jrnl Paper Carrier Of Yr 83; Htl Mgmt.

PETRIE, PATRICK; Amsterdam HS; Amsterdam, NY; (Y); Concert Band; Mrchg Band; Hon Roll; Graph Art.

PETRILLO, THOMAS R; Mount Vernon HS; Scarsdale, NY; (Y); Am Leg Boys St; Aud/Vis; Church Yth Grp; Hosp Aide; Pres Key Clb; Ski Clb; Nwsp Sprt Ed; Yrbk Sprt Ed; Var Capt Bsbl; JV Bsktbl; All Cnty All Lgu Bsbl 85; Cnty Leg Cnty Rectn Head Boys ST 86.

PETRIZZO, CATHY; West Hempstead HS; Charlestown, WV; (Y); 87/320; Drama Clb; Ski Clb; School Play; Rep Frsh Cls; Badmtn; Swmmng; Hon Roll; Outstndg Perf Sci 82-83, Bus Math 83-84 & Accntg 84-85; Shepherd Coll; Accntg.

PETRIZZO, MICHAEL; Monsignor Farrell HS; Staten Island, NY; (Y); 35/335; Debate Tm; Im Mgr Bsktbl; Var JV Ftbl; Trk; JV Var Wt Lftg; JV Wrstlng; Hon Roll; Boston U; Aerosp Engr.

PETROCONE, ROBERT; Mineola HS; Mineola, NY; (Y); 25/235; Trs English Clb; Key Clb; Lit Mag; High Hon Roll; Hon Roll; NHS; Pres Schlr; Cmptr Sci Awd 86; Rgnts Schlrshp 86; Resselear Plythchn; Aero Engr.

PETRONE, JAY; Broadalbin Central HS; Johnstown, NY; (Y); 4-H; French Clb; JV Bsbl; High Hon Roll; Hon Roll; AAHPERD Yth Ftnss Proj-SR Div Yth Fitnss Achvt Awd.

PETROSKY, ANDREW J; Arlington HS; La Grangeville, NY; (Y); 41/560; JV Bsbl; Hon Roll; Ntl Merit Ltr; Acdmc Hnr Key 86; Rensselaer Polytech Inst; Arch.

PETROZAK, BRENDA; Middletown HS; Middletown, NY; (Y); 13/388; Drama Clb; Acpl Chr; Chorus; School Musical; Swing Chorus; Nwsp Stf; Yrbk Ed-Chief; Cheerleading; High Hon Roll; Hon Roll; Hmcmg Qn-Spch Awd; Hstry Chrldr; Orng Plaza Schlrshp & Hffmn Ldg Schlrshp; Syracuse U; Brdcst Jrnlsm.

PETRUCCELLI, SUSAN; Liverpool HS; Liverpool, NY; (Y); Art Clb; Ski Clb; Yrbk Phtg; JV Trk; Hon Roll; Chorus; Stage Crew; Im Powder Puff Ftbl; Merit Cert Adv 86; Design.

PETRUCCO, CLAUDIA; Sacred Heart Acad; Westbury, NY; (S); 18/182; AFS; Cmnty Wkr; Girl Scts; Hosp Aide; Sec Intnl Clb; Model UN; NFL; Service Clb; Speech Tm; School Musical; Soc St Awd 82; Biomed Engrg.

PETRULLO, MICHAEL A; Mount Saint Michael Acad; Bronx, NY; (Y); 20/291; JV Bsbl; JV Bsktbl; JV Var Ftbl; JV Socr; JV Var Wt Lftg; Hon Roll; NHS; Spanish NHS; Pace U; Acctg.

PETRUNICH, KEVIN G; Maine Endwell SR HS; Endwell, NY; (Y); 24/240; Boys Clb Am; Boy Scts; Cmnty Wkr; Key Clb; Ski Clb; Var Tennis; Hon Roll; NHS; NY St Regnts Schlrshp Wnnr 86; Silver Merit Awd Hnr Rl; Ltr Tennis 85-86; Broome CC; Elect Engr.

PETRUSH, CHRISTOPHER A; Vestal SR HS; Vestal, NY; (Y); 49/430; French Clb; Varsity Clb; School Musical; Stu Cncl; Im Bsktbl; Var L Ftbl; JV Lcrss; High Hon Roll; NHS; Prfct Atten Awd; Rgnts Schlrshp & Rnslr Schlrshp 86; Rnslr Poly Tech Inst; Med.

PETRUZZELLO, MICHAEL; Port Chester HS; Port Chester, NY; (Y).

PETRY, CRAIG J; Patchogue-Medford HS; Patchogue, NY; (Y); 44/621; Hon Roll; NHS; Trs Mdcl Explrs Pst 623 86; Rgnts Schlrshp 86; SUNY Stonybrk; Bio.

PETRY, NANCY; Jamestown HS; Jamestwon, NY; (Y); 2/400; Intnl Clb; Sec Trs Latin Clb; Political Wkr; Chorus; Stu Cncl; High Hon Roll; Jr NHS; Sec NHS; Ntl Merit Ltr; Rotary Awd; Nrmn Tnkhm Awd-Amer Hstry 85; Dvs Schlrshp-Sltatrn 86; Rndlph-Mcn Wmns Coll Distngsh Schlr; Randolph Macon Wmns Coll; Psych.

PETSCHKE, CHRISTINE; Kenmore East SR HS; Kenmore, NY; (Y); 1/330; Dance Clb; Math Clb; Concert Band; School Musical; Pom Pon; VP NHS; Val; Band; Color Guard; Mrchg Band; Educ Awd Of Soc Of Mayflower Descndts 86; Commndtn In Natl Merit Schlrp 85; Rensselaer Schlrp 86; Rensselaer Polytech Inst; Engrg.

PETTA, RICHARD J; Merchanicville HS; Mechanicville, NY; (Y); 17/105; Spanish Clb; Var Crs Cntry; Hon Roll; NHS; Regents Schlrshp 86; Syracuse U Schlrshp 86; Syracuse U; Aerosp Engrg.

PETTEYS, SARA; Greenwich Central HS; Greenwich, NY; (Y); Sec FFA; SADD; Chorus; Yrbk Stf; JV Sftbl; Trk; Hon Roll; Vrsty Lttr Trck 86.

PETTIE, JENNIFER; Holy Trinity HS; Hempstead, NY; (Y); AFS; Math Clb; Ski Clb; SADD; Nwsp Ed-Chief; Nwsp Rptr; Hon Roll; NHS; Acdmc All-Amrcn 86; Stanford; Med.

PETTIGRASS, JOE; Auburn HS; Auburn, NY; (Y); 30/500; Model UN; High Hon Roll; Hon Roll; Jr NHS; NHS; Prfct Atten Awd; Acad All Amer 86.

PETTINELLI, NEAL; P V Moore HS; Brewerton, NY; (Y); Varsity Clb; JV Var Bsktbl; JV Var Ftbl; Lcrss; JV Wrstlng; High Hon Roll; Hon Roll; Rotary Awd.

PETTIT, DAPHNE; Gloversville HS; Gloversville, NY; (Y); Teachers Aide; Band; Concert Band; Jazz Band; Mrchg Band; Orch; Pep Band; Symp Band; Mgr(s); Mgr Vllybl; All Cnty Band 83-85; All Cnty Jazz Band 85-86; Bus Mgmnt.

PETTIT, ELIZABETH; West Islip HS; W Islip, NY; (Y); Hosp Aide; Chorus; Im Badmtn; Var Swmmng; Im Vllybl; Hon Roll; Jr NHS; NHS; Elem Schl Tutor 85-86; Med.

PETTIT, JOEL D; La Fargeville Central Schl; Clayton, NY; (Y); Am Leg Boys St; School Play; Pres Stu Cncl; Var Bsbl; JV Var Bsktbl; Var Socr; Hon Roll; NHS; Chorus; Clayton Rtry Schlstc Awd 86; US Army Reserve Ntl Schlr/Athlete Awd & Athltc Achvmnts 86; Jefferson CC; Compu.

PETTIT, LARA; Huntington HS; Huntington, NY; (Y); Cmnty Wkr; Key Clb; Capt Drill Tm; School Play; Variety Show; Sec Sr Cls; Stu Cncl; Var Socr; Hon Roll; Vet Med.

PETZ, JOANN M; St Francis Prep; Whitestone, NY; (S); 141/750; Hon Roll; Ntl Merit Ltr; Mrktng.

PETZOLD, KEITH; Farmingdale HS; Farmingdale, NY; (Y); Var L Bsktbl; JV Ftbl; JV Lcrss; Hon Roll; Jr NHS; U Of DE; Bus.

PEYKAR, MICHELLE; Commack South HS; Dix Hills, NY; (S); Chorus; Madrigals; Variety Show; Hon Roll; Early Childhd Eductn.

PFAFF, KRISTEN; Clarkstown High School North; New City, NY; (Y); 36/450; Church Yth Grp; Ski Clb; SADD; Band; Stu Cncl; High Hon Roll; Hon Roll; Vrsty Ltr-Ski Team; Vrsty Ltr-Twrlng; Rgnts Schlrshp; Coll Of Holy Cross; Pre-Law.

PFAFFENBACH, KURT; Shenendehowa HS; Clifton Park, NY; (Y); Drama Clb; Intnl Clb; Ski Clb; School Play; JV Ftbl; Socr; Var JV Trk; High Hon Roll; Hon Roll.

PFARNER, JAMES D; Eden Central HS; Eden, NY; (Y); VP Varsity Clb; Var Capt Ftbl; Im Vllybl; JV Var Wrstlng; Hon Roll; NHS; Sr Cls; Stu Cncl; 1st Plc Wstrn NY Indstrl Arts Exbt 84; Rcpnt NY ST Rgnts Schlrshp 86; Le Moyne Coll; Lbrl Arts.

PFEIFER, LORI; Fontbonne Hall Acad; Brooklyn, NY; (Y); 2/130; Hosp Aide; Teachers Aide; Variety Show; Tennis; High Hon Roll; NHS; Sal; Senators Awd 86; Pres Acad Ftnss Awd 86; Fordham U; Bus Adm.

PFEIFFER, DENNIS; Olean HS; Olean, NY; (Y); Spanish Clb; Im Bsktbl; Im Golf; Im Wrstlng; Hon Roll.

PFIESTER, CHRISTINE; Tully Central HS; Tully, NY; (Y); 11/69; Drama Clb; Spanish Clb; SADD; Varsity Clb; Chorus; School Musical; Swing Chorus; Yrbk Phtg; Sec Sr Cls; Cheerleading; Sprtsmnshp Awd, Elzbth V Wd Awd, Drvrs Ed Awd, Vrsty Plq PTO Awd 86; Hnr Grad 86; SUNY; Psych.

PFIFFER, DAVID W; Thomas Edison HS; Elmira, NY; (Y); Am Leg Boys St; Mathletes; Rep Stu Cncl; Var Capt Bsbl; Var L Bsktbl; Var L Ftbl; High Hon Roll.

PFLANZ, STEVEN E; Greece Athena HS; Rochester, NY; (Y); 1/267; Boy Scts; German Clb; Sec Pres JA; Ski Clb; Var L Crs Cntry; Var L Trk; High Hon Roll; NHS; Ntl Merit SF; Val; Frgn Lang Stu Of Yr 83-84; Med.

PFUELB, SALLY; Nardin Acad; West Falls, NY; (Y); 18/79; Debate Tm; Office Aide; Yrbk Phtg; Trs Frsh Cls; VP Soph Cls; Pres Jr Cls; Pres Stu Cncl; Vllybl; Hon Roll; NHS.

PFUHLER, ROBERT; St Peters Boys HS; Staten Isld, NY; (Y); 1/165; Band; Bsbl; Bsktbl; NHS; Doctor.

PFUNDSTEIN, KEVIN J; Nazareth Regional HS; Brooklyn, NY; (S); 37/267; Rep Frsh Cls; Var L Bsbl; JV Crs Cntry; Im Ftbl; Im Sftbl; JV Trk; Hon Roll; NHS; Prfct Atten Awd; Princpls List; NY Inst Tech; Elec Engrng.

PHAM, PHILIP V; Clarkstown HS South; West Nyack, NY; (Y); 7/475; Math Tm; Science Clb; SADD; Orch; Stage Crew; Nwsp Stf; Jr NHS; Mu Alp Tht; Pres NHS; Ntl Merit SF; Biochem.

PHAN, DUC; Smithtown East; St James, NY; (Y); JV Trk; Im Wt Lftg; JV Wrstlng; High Hon Roll; Jr NHS; NHS; Binghamton; Pre-Med.

PHAN, TAM; Troti Vocational HS; Niagara Falls, NY; (Y); VICA; Stage Crew; Off Soph Cls; Stu Cncl; Powder Puff Ftbl; Socr; Trk; Vllybl; Hon Roll; Buffalo ST U; Elect Engr.

PHAT, CHUCK; Medwood HS; Brooklyn, NY; (Y); 207/667; Office Aide; Service Clb; Spanish Clb; SADD; Orch; Bsktbl; Ftbl; Lcrss; Vllybl; Wt Lftg.

PHELAN, DANA; Ursuline Schl; Ardsley, NY; (Y); Ski Clb; Nwsp Rptr; Trk; Hon Roll; Jr NHS.

PHELAN, FRANCES A; St Francis Prep; Maspeth, NY; (S); 103/740; Nwsp Rptr; Im Ftbl; JV Capt Sftbl; JV Trk; JV Vllybl; Opt Clb Awd; Holy Name FDNY Scholar 83.

PHELAN, MARYBETH; Mechanicville HS; Mechanicville, NY; (S); 10/100; Spanish Clb; Band; Sec Soph Cls; Var Cheerleading; Var Sftbl; Var Trk; Cit Awd; High Hon Roll; NHS; Kybrdng/Comm Awd 84-85; Psych.

PHELPS, DENISE L; Alexander Central Schl; Darien Center, NY; (Y); 4/85; Trs Spanish Clb; Band; Trs Chorus; Yrbk Sprt Ed; Var Capt Bsktbl; Var Capt Socr; Var Capt Sftbl; Var Capt Vllybl; NHS; Math Tm; Acad All Amer 86; Suny Geneseo; Scndry Math Educ.

PHELPS, KITTY L; John C Birdlebough HS; Fulton, NY; (Y); 12/160; Cmnty Wkr; Var L Trk; Var Stat Vllybl; High Hon Roll; NHS; Prfct Atten Awd.

PHELPS, PATRICIA; Ilion HS; Ilion, NY; (Y); Girl Scts; Hosp Aide; Office Aide; Chorus; Church Choir; Color Guard; Orch; HCCC; Paralegan Asst.

PHELPS, TONIA; Mt Vernon HS; Mt Vernon, NY; (Y); Dance Clb; Hosp Aide; Latin Clb; Library Aide; Band; Concert Band; Orch; Var Trk; Hon Roll; NHS; NYU; Medcn.

PHETTEPLACE, DAPHNE; Skaneateles Central Schl; Auburn, NY; (S); Band; Orch; Symp Band; Co-Capt Cheerleading; Powder Puff Ftbl; High Hon Roll; Hon Roll; NHS; Telecmmnctns.

PHIFER, LISA; Ossining HS; Ossining, NY; (Y); 58/260; Church Yth Grp; Cmnty Wkr; Acpl Chr; Band; Chorus; Church Choir; Concert Band; Mrchg Band; Orch; Symp Band; H S Schlrshp Pin 85 & 86; Ntl Hnr Soc 86; Howard U; Bus Adm.

PHILIP, NERISSA; Westbury SR HS; Westbury, NY; (Y); Chorus; Stage Crew; Stat Bsktbl; Acdmc Achvt Awd In Chmstry & Spnsh 86; Pre-Med.

PHILIP, SNEHA; Emma Willard Schl; Hopewell Jct, NY; (Y); Nwsp Phtg; German Clb; Ski Clb; Stage Crew; Ed Yrbk Stf; Rep Stu Cncl; Im Socr; Im Sftbl; Im Tennis; Var Trk; Gold Medl Olympd Russn 86; Med.

PHILIPPE, LILIANE; Pine Bush HS; Middletown, NY; (Y); Church Yth Grp; 4-H; Hosp Aide; Library Aide; Office Aide; Pep Clb; Yrbk Stf; Var Trk; 4-H Awd; Hon Roll; Norfolk U-VA; Med.

PHILIPSBERG, GLENN A; Ward Melville HS; Stony Brook, NY; (Y); Church Yth Grp; Debate Tm; Hosp Aide; Hon Roll; Stony Brook U; Bus.

PHILLIP, DI ANN G; Nazareth Regional HS; Brooklyn, NY; (S); 23/267; FHA; Spanish Clb; Teachers Aide; Chorus; Nwsp Rptr; JV Mgr(s); JV Sftbl; High Hon Roll; Hon Roll; NHS.

PHILLIP, FRANCIS; Nazareth Regional HS; Brooklyn, NY; (S); 1/267; Capt Debate Tm; VP JA; NFL; Sec Speech Tm; Nwsp Stf; High Hon Roll; NHS; Ntl Merit Ltr; Natl Achvt SF; Natl Quarter Fin Extemprns Spkng 84-85; Med.

PHILLIP, NITA; South Side HS; Wyandanch, NY; (Y); Church Choir; Variety Show; Var Trk; Vrsty S Ltr Trck 86; 4th Pl Medl Trck-Trpl Jmp 86; Modlng Trophy 84; AL A&M; Bus Mgmt.

PHILLIPS, ANDRE W; Mount St Michael Acad; Bronx, NY; (Y); Computer Clb; Trs Key Clb; Rep Stu Cncl; Var L Socr; Hofstra U; Med.

PHILLIPS, ANGELA; Cattaraugus Central HS; Cattaraugus, NY; (Y); 23/58; Church Yth Grp; Computer Clb; Trs FBLA; Spanish Clb; VICA; Y-Teens; Band; Chorus; Color Guard; Concert Band; Alfred ST; Data Prcssng.

PHILLIPS, BILL; Mont Pleasant HS; Schanectady, NY; (Y); 2/210; Am Leg Boys St; Aud/Vis; Boy Scts; Church Yth Grp; Spanish Clb; Band; Concert Band; Jazz Band; Orch; Wrstlng; Knights Phythias 86; Pres Acadmc Ftns 86; Tech Svc Excllnc 86; Union Coll; Elec Engr.

PHILLIPS, BOB; Salem Central HS; Salem, NY; (Y); French Clb; SADD; Yrbk Stf; Trs Frsh Cls; Trs Soph Cls; Var Bsbl; Var Bsktbl; Var Crs Cntry; JV Ftbl; Var Trk; Peer Cnslr 85-86; All Star Tm-Bsktbl Cls D Sctn II 85-86; Jnr Prm Crt; Sprts.

PHILLIPS, CHRIS; Clarkstown H S North; Congers, NY; (Y); SADD; Band; Concert Band; Mrchg Band; JV Bsbl; Coach Actv; Var Score Keeper; Spcl Olympcs 86; Springfield Coll; Phy Thrpy.

PHILLIPS, JAMES; Rochester Christian HS; Rochester, NY; (S); 1/13; Drama Clb; Spanish Clb; Chorus; Orch; Yrbk Stf; Trs Stu Cncl; Var Capt Bsktbl; Var Capt Socr; Trk; High Hon Roll; Assoc Christian Schls Intl Distngushd Stu Awd 84; Sportsmnshp Awd 84-85.

PHILLIPS, KENT; Queensbury HS; Glens Falls, NY; (Y); JV Trk; JV Var Wt Lftg; Hon Roll; Mech Engrng.

PHILLIPS, KIMBERLY; Sachem HS North; Lake Ronkonkoma, NY; (Y); 7/1389; Spanish Clb; Band; Mrchg Band; Var Bowling; Hon Roll; NHS; Hofstra U; Math Tchr.

PHILLIPS, KRISTINE M; Amsterdam HS; Amsterdam, NY; (Y); 51/294; Sec Trs 4-H; Band; Concert Band; Mrchg Band; Nwsp Stf; Yrbk Stf; 4-H Awd; Hon Roll; SUNY Oneonta; Spch Cmnctns.

PHILLIPS, LAUREEN; Madrid Waddington HS; Waddington, NY; (Y); Drama Clb; Spanish Clb; SADD; Teachers Aide; Acpl Chr; Band; Chorus; Concert Band; Mrchg Band; School Musical; Potsdam ST U; Span Tchr.

PHILLIPS, LORENE; West Genesee SR HS; Syracuse, NY; (Y); Cmnty Wkr; Drama Clb; Acpl Chr; Chorus; Church Choir; Orch; School Musical; Im Sftbl; High Hon Roll; NHS; NYSSMA Conf All ST Womens Chorus 85; Most Outstndg Underclssmn Chorus Awd 85-86; Schlrshp Summerfame; Voice Performance.

PHILLIPS, MARK; Mt Vernon HS; Mt Vernon, NY; (Y); Boy Scts; Computer Clb; Dance Clb; Socr; Swmmng.

PHILLIPS, OCTOBER M; Norwood Norfolk Central HS; Norwood, NY; (Y); 21/130; Art Clb; Pres Church Yth Grp; Drama Clb; Hosp Aide; Spanish Clb; SADD; Band; Chorus; Church Choir; Concert Band; Bixlor Memrl Schlrshp 86; NY ST U; Ed.

PHILLIPS, PAMELA; Park W HS; Manhattanville, NY; (Y); Girl Scts; Hosp Aide; Office Aide; Drm Mjr(t); School Play; Stage Crew; Bsktbl; Cheerleading; Gym; Swmmng; Yale; Lawyr.

PHILLIPS, ROBERT; Biship Scully HS; Amsterdam, NY; (Y); 18/56; Church Yth Grp; Varsity Clb; Rep Frsh Cls; Rep Soph Cls; Var Bsbl; Var Bsktbl; Hon Roll; NHS; St Johns Soc Schlrshp 86; David Masto Awd 86; Hartwick Coll; Bus Mang.

PHILLIPS, ROBERT; Johnson City SR HS; Johnson City, NY; (Y); 15/200; Band; Concert Band; Mrchg Band; Orch; Symp Band; Ftbl; Wt Lftg; Hon Roll; Prfct Atten Awd; Bys ST Spnsrd By VFW; Lions Clb ST Bnd; US Mltry Acad; Comp Pgmg.

PHILLIPS, RUSSELL; Salmon River HS; Hogansburg, NY; (Y); Exploring; Var Bsbl; Sftbl; Army; MP.

PHILLIPS, SHANDA; The Harley HS; Rochester, NY; (Y); French Clb; SADD; Acpl Chr; School Play; Yrbk Ed-Chief; Lit Mag; Rep Soph Cls; Rep Jr Cls; JV Var Socr; Cmnty Wkr; Schlstc Art Awd 84.

PHILLIPS, TERESA; Avon Central HS; Honeoye Falls, NY; (Y); 4-H; Spanish Clb; Chorus; Var Trk; Cornell U; Vet-Sci.

PHILLIPS, TODD; Faith Heritage HS; Syracuse, NY; (Y); Boy Scts; Church Yth Grp; JV Var Bsktbl; Var Socr; Var Trk; Brigham Young U; Eng.

PHILLIPS, WILLIAM A; Whitney Point Central Schl; Binghamton, NY; (S); Latin Clb; Science Clb; Yrbk Stf; Rep Frsh Cls; Var JV Bsbl; Var JV Bsktbl; Var JV Socr; Hon Roll; Ntl Merit Ltr; Pre-Law.

PHILLS, DARRYL; St Francis Prep; St Albans, NY; (Y); Bsktbl; Bowling; Ftbl; Sftbl; Vllybl; Bus Adm.

PHILO, KIMBERLY; Scotia Glenville HS; Scotia, NY; (Y); Pres DECA; Yrbk Stf; Pres Stu Cncl; Var Capt Cheerleading; Cit Awd; Hon Roll.

PHINNEY, LEANNE; Lake George HS; Lake George, NY; (Y); 23/87; JA; Ski Clb; SADD; Yrbk Stf; Trs Jr Cls; JV Var Bsktbl; Var L Fld Hcky; Var Powder Puff Ftbl; Stat Vllybl; Hon Roll; Ithaca Coll; Phys Ther.

PHOUDAD, RUNGSINEE; Charles H Roth HS; Rochester, NY; (Y); French Clb; GAA; Latin Clb; Rep Stu Cncl; Cheerleading; Var Tennis; Hon Roll; Jr NHS; VP NHS; Ntl Merit Ltr; U Of Rochester; Life Sci.

PHUNG, THUY; Walton HS; Brooklyn, NY; (Y); 1/600; Math Tm; Office Aide; Science Clb; Band; NHS; Prfct Atten Awd; Val; Full Tuition Schrlshp 85; Pregents Schrlshp 85; Acad Olympic Awd 85; U Rochester; Bio.

PIACITELLI, FRANK; Cazenovia Central HS; Cazenovia, NY; (Y); 4/150; Drama Clb; Chorus; Concert Band; School Musical; JV Crs Cntry; JV Tennis; Ntl Merit Ltr; School Play; Symp Band; Hon Roll; RIT Alumni Schrlshp 86; NY ST Rgnts Schlrshp 86; Pres Acad Ftns Awd 86; Rchstr Inst Of Tech; Grphc Dsgn.

PIAMPIANO, CHRISTINE; Goshew Central HS; Goshen, NY; (Y); Cmnty Wkr; Drama Clb; Math Tm; SADD; Stage Crew; Gym; Score Keeper; Socr; Capt Var Sftbl; VP Tennis; Hnr Awd Spnsh; Hnr Awd Cllge Sklls; Maritime; Sci.

PIANA, JOHN A; Little Falls JR SR HS; Little Falls, NY; (Y); 12/90; Am Leg Boys St; Service Clb; Spanish Clb; Yrbk Stf; JV Var Bsktbl; Var Golf; High Hon Roll; Rotary Awd; Bus.

PIANKA, JOSEPH; St John The Baptist; W Islip, NY; (S); Science Clb; High Hon Roll; Hon Roll; No 1 Ltn Hnrs Awd 85; Math & Soc Studs Mrt Awds 85; Stoney Brook U; Med.

PIASCIK, MARIA; St Georges Acad; New York, NY; (Y); Bsktbl; Vllybl; 2nd Hnr 85-86; Baruch Coll; Bus.

PIATEK, ZEN; Poughkeepsie HS; Poughkeepsie, NY; (Y); Drama Clb; Ski Clb; School Musical; School Play; Stage Crew; Variety Show; Hon Roll; Prfct Atten Awd; Dutchess Comm Coll; Elctrncs.

PIATT, REBEKAH; Riverhead HS; Jamesport, NY; (Y); Church Yth Grp; Latin Clb; Ski Clb; Trs Concert Band; Mrchg Band; Pres Frsh Cls; Prfct Atten Awd; Cmmnctns.

PIAZZA, LAURA; Jamestown HS; Jamestown, NY; (Y); Spanish Clb; Yrbk Phtg; Rptr Yrbk Stf; Bus Htl Mgmt.

PIAZZA, LISA; Lansingburgh HS; Troy, NY; (Y); Varsity Clb; Yrbk Stf; Var Score Keeper; Var Socr; High Hon Roll; Jr NHS; NHS; Prfncy In Acctng Awd 86; Bus Awd In Typng 85; Siena Coll; Bus & Cmmrc.

PIAZZA, MARIA; Franklin Delano Roosevelt HS; Brooklyn, NY; (Y); Band; Hon Roll; NYU Brooklyn; Bus Mngmnt.

PICARD, AMY; Catholic Central HS; Clifton Pk, NY; (Y); Cmnty Wkr; Drama Clb; Leo Clb; Chorus; Church Choir; School Play; Variety Show; Yrbk Stf; Hon Roll; Maria U; Erly Chldhd Dvlpmnt.

PICARD, NANCY; Dominican Commercial HS; Queens Vlge, NY; (Y); Church Yth Grp; Cmnty Wkr; Hosp Aide; Intnl Clb; Chorus; School Musical; Yrbk Stf; High Hon Roll; Hon Roll; Pres Schlr; Outstndng Achvt Chrstn Invlvmnt 86; Presdntl Acad Fitness Avw Pgm 85-86; Hnrb Mntn Comm Vlntr Wrk 86; Pace U; Bio.

PICARDI, CHRISTINA MARY; Paul D Schreiber HS; Port Washington, NY; (Y); 171/369; Cmnty Wkr; SADD; Band; Concert Band; Mrchg Band; Yrbk Stf; Rep Frsh Cls; Rep Soph Cls; Rep Jr Cls; Rep Sr Cls; Harvey Lewis Schlrshp 86; SUNY Albany.

PICARDO, WANDA; Louis D Brandeis HS; New York, NY; (Y); Boys Clb Am; Camera Clb; Computer Clb; Dance Clb; Hosp Aide; Intnl Clb; JA; Chorus; School Musical; Stage Crew; BMCC; Nrsg.

PICARIELLO, ANTHONY; Port Richmond HS; Staten Island, NY; (Y); Aud/Vis; Im Bsbl; Im Bsktbl; Im Coach Actv; Im JV Ftbl; Im Sftbl; Cmmnctns.

PICCIANO, JODIE ANN; The Mary Louis Acad; Fresh Meadows, NY; (Y); 120/263; Cmnty Wkr; Drama Clb; Office Aide; Chorus; School Musical; School Play; NEDT Awd; Excllnc Religious Studies 86; U Steubenville; Soclgy.

PICCIONE, RACHEL ASTARTE; Brockport HS; Brockport, NY; (Y); Pres Drama Clb; Radio Clb; Chorus; Madrigals; School Play; Stage Crew; Swing Chorus; High Hon Roll; Conf All ST 85; Acting.

PICCIOTTO, JOE; West Hempstead HS; Island Park, NY; (Y); Art Clb; Chess Clb; Computer Clb; Exploring; FBLA; Math Clb; Ski Clb; Yrbk Phtg; Pres Jr Cls; Bsbl; Appld Arts Awd; MVP Awd Soccer; St Johns; Med Tech.

PICCIRILLO, KAREN; Mohonasen HS; Schenectady, NY; (Y); 4/172; Key Clb; Pep Clb; Red Cross Aide; Ski Clb; Pres Spanish Clb; Trs Band; Chorus; Concert Band; Trs Mrchg Band; Orch; STAR Schlrshp GE Co 86; NY ST Regents Schlrshp 86; Pres Schlrshp Siena Coll 86ROTC Schlrshp 85-86; Siena Coll Loudonville NY.

PICCO, LORI; Waverly JR SR HS; Waverly, NY; (Y); Church Yth Grp; Ski Clb; Band; Concert Band; Mrchg Band; School Musical; School Play; JV Frsh Cls; Cheerleading; Swmmng; Phy Ftnss Awd 84-85; All Cnty Swmmr 85; Psychtry.

PICCOLI, DONNA; Warwick Valley HS; Warwick, NY; (Y); FBLA; Hon Roll; Berkeley Schl; Bus.

PICCOLO, JULIE; Hoosic Valley Central HS; Johnsonville, NY; (Y); French Clb; Band; Concert Band; School Musical; Nwsp Stf; Var Mgr(s); JV Sftbl; Var Trk; High Hon Roll; Hon Roll.

PICHETTE, ERNIE R; Oneida HS; Canastota, NY; (Y); 52/200; Concert Band; Drm & Bgl; Jazz Band; Orch; School Musical; School Play; Symp Band; Var L Bowling; JV Ftbl; Hon Roll; Oswego ST U; Bus.

PICHEY, ANNETTE; Lockport SR HS; Lockport, NY; (Y); Camera Clb; Church Yth Grp; Office Aide; Teachers Aide; Yng Vlntrs Amer 83-84.

PICINIC, FIDES; St Franics Prep; Bayside, NY; (Y); Hosp Aide; Chorus; High Hon Roll; Hofstra; Acctng.

PICKETT, DANIEL; Mechanicville HS; Mechanicville, NY; (S); 5/120; Math Tm; Varsity Clb; Yrbk Sprt Ed; Rep Frsh Cls; Rep Soph Cls; Rep Jr Cls; Rep Sr Cls; Rep Stu Cncl; Var Co-Capt Bsbl; Var Co-Capt Bsktbl; RPI Mdl For Math & Sci 85; Math Awd 85-86; Chem Awd 86; Engrng.

PICKETT, KRISTEN; Mechanicville HS; Mechanicville, NY; (S); 7/100; Sec French Clb; Math Tm; Ski Clb; SADD; Band; Mrchg Band; Nwsp Rptr; Nwsp Stf; Yrbk Phtg; Yrbk Stf; Math Awd 85; Omega Hnr Soc 84; Alpha Hnr Soc 85; Engrng.

PICKETT, MICHELLE; Schoharie Central Schl; Central Bridge, NY; (Y); Teachers Aide; Varsity Clb; Chorus; Trs Soph Cls; JV Var Cheerleading; JV Var Socr; Hon Roll; Bus.

PICKUP, SHANNON; Olean HS; Olean, NY; (Y); 48/200; French Clb; Ski Clb; Varsity Clb; Chorus; Concert Band; Mrchg Band; Sec Stu Cncl; JV Var Cheerleading; Var Trk; Hon Roll; Intr Desgnr.

PICO, KARINA; Grace Dodge Vocational HS; Bronx, NY; (Y); Library Aide; Math Tm; Office Aide; Teachers Aide; Hon Roll; Prfct Atten Awd; Prd Of Ynk Awd 85 & 86; Accntng.

PICOLLA, JOHN A; Oneonta SR HS; Oneonta, NY; (Y); 21/180; Am Leg Boys St; Thesps; Concert Band; Drm Mjr(t); Jazz Band; Pep Band; Symp Band; Rep Stu Cncl; Hon Roll; NHS; Instrmntl Excel Awd, Stdnt Mnth Awd 86; NYS Sci Awd 83; Coll Oneonta; Bus Mgmnt.

PICOZZI, JANETTE; Walt Whitman HS; Huntington Sta, NY; (Y); 76/549; Sec Sr Cls; Var JV Cheerleading; Jr NHS; NHS; Church Yth Grp; Band; Yrbk Stf; Stat Lcrss; Trk; High Hon Roll; Awd Merit Spnsh 83; Hmcmng Qun 85; Siena; Ed.

PIECH, KARI ANN; Whitney Point HS; Richford, NY; (Y); 15/124; Trs French Clb; Ski Clb; Chorus; Yrbk Stf; Cheerleading; High Hon Roll; Hon Roll; Pres NHS; Clute Mem Scholar 86; Bryant & Stratton; Acctng.

PIECH, KRISTEN; Lockport SR HS; Lockport, NY; (Y); 11/411; AFS; Drama Clb; Band; Drm Mjr(t); School Musical; Rep Stu Cncl; JV Cheerleading; High Hon Roll; JP Sousa Awd; NHS; All Am Hall Fame Band Awd 85-86; Gannon U; Elect Engr.

PIECHALAK, KAREN; Villa Maria Acad; Cheektowaga, NY; (S); Trs Church Yth Grp; French Clb; Girl Scts; Pep Clb; Chorus; Hon Roll; Prfct Atten Awd; Comptrs.

PIECZYNSKI, TERESA M; West Seneca HS; W Seneca, NY; (Y); 53/559; GAA; Spanish Clb; Yrbk Stf; Var L Socr; Var L Vllybl; Hon Roll; JC Awd; NHS; Rgnts Schlrshp 86; Canisius Coll; Math.

PIEERNO, LISA; Port Richmond HS; Staten Island, NY; (Y); Church Yth Grp; French Clb; Teachers Aide; School Play; Variety Show; Hon Roll; Elem Italn Teachr 86-87; New York U; Mgmt.

PIEKUNKA, MELISSA; Fairport HS; Fairport, NY; (Y); Exploring; Intnl Clb; Model UN; Rep Frsh Cls; Rep Soph Cls; Var Sftbl; Hon Roll; Pres Schlr; Rgnts Nrsng Schlrshp 86; Pres Schlrshp; Knt ST U; Nrsng.

PIEN, GRACE; Elmira Southside HS; Pine City, NY; (Y); 2/436; Sec Key Clb; Pres Latin Clb; Varsity Clb; Ed Yrbk Ed-Chief; Var L Trk; Sec NHS; Ntl Merit SF; Sal; Chorus; Orch; All ST Strng Orch 85; Corning Philhrmnc Yth Orch Assoc Concrtmstr 84-85; Stu Curric Cncl Comm Chrprsn; Physcn.

PIERCE, CHUCK; Pittsford Mendon HS; Pittsford, NY; (Y); 6/280; JV Tennis; Hon Roll; Syracuse U; Pre Dentl.

PIERCE, JOSEPH; Hornell HS; Hornell, NY; (Y); Boy Scts; Ski Clb; JV Var Socr; Alfred Tech Schl; Arch.

PIERCE, JULIE; Canisteo Central HS; Canisteo, NY; (Y); 17/80; FBLA; Office Aide; Orch; Yrbk Stf; Sec Stds.

PIERCE, KATHY; Glvoersville HS; Gloversvl, NY; (Y); AFS; Drama Clb; SADD; Band; Mrchg Band; School Musical; Yrbk Ed-Chief; Var Trk; High Hon Roll; AFS Summer Exc Stu Brazil 86.

PIERCE, LAURA; Lowville Acad; Lowville, NY; (Y); SADD; Rep Frsh Cls; Rep Soph Cls; Sec Jr Cls; Sec Sr Cls; Stu Cncl; JV Var Bsktbl; JV Var Socr; JV Var Sftbl; NHS; Math.

PIERCE, LISA; Commack North HS; Commack, NY; (Y); Pres Church Yth Grp; Cmnty Wkr; GAA; Trs Soph Cls; Rep Stu Cncl; Capt L Fld Hcky; Var L Vllybl; High Hon Roll; Hon Roll; Field Hockey NY Empire ST Tm 86.

PIERCE, NEIL J; Carthage Central Schl; Carthage, NY; (Y); 9/200; Am Leg Boys St; Church Yth Grp; Band; Concert Band; Jazz Band; Swing Chorus; JV Var Socr; Elks Awd; High Hon Roll; NHS; Fredonia ST; Music.

PIERCE, PAULA; Minisink Valley HS; New Hampton, NY; (Y); 87/250; Dance Clb; Yrbk Phtg; Yrbk Sprt Ed; Yrbk Stf; High Hon Roll; Hon Roll; Mr & Mrs Hrbrt Gldsmth Awd 86; Air Force; Bus.

PIERCE, SCOTT; Churchville-Chili HS; N Chili, NY; (Y); Ski Clb; JV Var Wrstlng; Geneseo ST Coll; Comp Sci.

PIERCE, STEPHANIE; Sandy Creek Central HS; Lacona, NY; (S); 1/92; Pres Drama Clb; Band; Chorus; Church Choir; Drm Mjr(t); Jazz Band; School Musical; L Socr; Sec NHS; Ntl Merit Ltr; NYS Regents Schlrshp 86; Owseg Cty Music Educators Assn Schlrshp 86; All-ST Band 85; Eastman Schl Of Music; Music Ed.

PIERCE, TIMOTHY; Onondaga HS; Syracuse, NY; (S); 4/80; German Clb; Varsity Clb; Band; Jazz Band; VP Jr Cls; Var L Bsbl; Var L Bsktbl; Var L Ftbl; High Hon Roll; NHS; Engrng.

PIERCYNSKI, KRISTIN; Earl L Vandermeulen HS; Mt Sinai, NY; (Y); Trs Frsh Cls; Rep Jr Cls; Trs Stu Cncl; Capt Cheerleading; Var Vllybl; Cit Awd; High Hon Roll; Hon Roll; Stu Cncl Ldrshp Awd; Hlth Awd; Vllybl Trnmnt All Trnmnt Tm Awd; Bus.

PIERPOINT IV, GEORGE W; Ardesley Sleeping HS; White Plains, NY; (Y); Am Leg Boys St; Boy Scts; Church Yth Grp; Exploring; SADD; Varsity Clb; Yrbk Phtg; Crs Cntry; Golf; Trk; West Point Mltry Acad; Arch.

PIERRE JR, CLAUDE JEAN; Nazareth Regional HS; Brooklyn, NY; (S); 10/267; Cmnty Wkr; Math Tm; Nwsp Sprt Ed; Im Bsktbl; JV Im Ftbl; Var L Socr; Var L Trk; Jr NHS; NHS; Nrthwstrn U; Pdtrcn.

PIERRE, JUDITH; Clara Barton HS; Brooklyn, NY; (Y); Hon Roll; Comp.

PIERRE, MARVIN; Bishop Cunningham HS; Oswego, NY; (S); 1/30; Church Yth Grp; English Clb; French Clb; Yrbk Stf; Jr Cls; Var Bsbl; JV Bsktbl; High Hon Roll; Pres NHS; Acdmc All Amer 86; Chem Engrng.

PIERSON, MICHELLE; Corning-Painted Post West HS; Painted Post, NY; (Y); Ski Clb; Varsity Clb; Var Capt Cheerleading; Var JV Sftbl; High Hon Roll; Jr NHS; NHS; Ntl Chrldrs Assn Awd Of Exc 84; UCA Rgnl Chrldng Chmpnshp Awd Of Exc 85fMVP Erwwin Vly Sftbl 84.

PIERSON, PAUL A; Newfield HS; Coram, NY; (Y); 6/576; Cmnty Wkr; Q&S; Concert Band; Ed Lit Mag; VP Frsh Cls; JV L Ftbl; NHS; Ntl Merit Ltr; Chess Clb; Jazz Band; Fencing; NY Regnts Schlrshp; Boston U; Math.

PIETERS, KEVIN; Amherst Central SR HS; Snyder, NY; (Y); 115/292; Church Yth Grp; Jazz Band; Orch; School Musical; Symp Band; Var Bowling; Var Golf; Hon Roll; NHS; Band; Diocesan CYO Brd Mbr; Christ The King CYO Pres & Advsry Brd Mbr 85-86; Drummr In Dixielnd Bnd 84-86; Bus Mgmt.

PIETRASZEWSKI, DENISE M; Cheektowaga Central HS; Cheektowaga, NY; (Y); 4/199; Color Guard; Hon Roll; Jr NHS; NHS; Ntl Merit Schol; NY ST Schlrshp Rgnts 86-87; Canisius Coll Deans Schlrshp 86-87; Canisius Coll; Comp Sci.

PIETROGALLO, TOM; Beacon HS; Beacon, NY; (Y); 50/217; Drama Clb; Science Clb; Spanish Clb; Varsity Clb; School Play; Stage Crew; Trs Sr Cls; JV Var Ftbl; Hon Roll; Peggy Wood Awd & Bst Bck Stage Wrkr & Scnc Crew Hd 86; Finc.

PIETROPAOLO, MICHAEL; Somers HS; Yorktown, NY; (Y); AFS; Church Yth Grp; VP Intnl Clb; Yrbk Stf; Var Crs Cntry; Var Trk; Hon Roll; NHS.

PIETRZAK, TINA; Coxsackie-Athens HS; Athens, NY; (Y); 17/105; Art Clb; Band; Chorus; Nwsp Ed-Chief; Nwsp Stf; Yrbk Stf; Rep Stu Cncl; Gym; Socr; High Hon Roll; Bus.

PIETRZYKOWSKI, LORI; Byron-Bergen Central HS; Bergen, NY; (Y); 17/104; Var Capt Bsktbl; Var Capt Socr; Var L Sftbl; Hon Roll; NHS; Prfct Atten Awd; 4-H; 4-H Awd; Jr NHS; Bsktbl 86; Feml Athlt Of Yr 86; Sprts Excllnc Tm 86; U Of Rochester; Bus Mgmt.

PIGNATARO, ROSE MARIE; The Mary Louis Acad; Maspeth, NY; (Y); 34/270; Am Leg Aux Girls St; Library Aide; Office Aide; Political Wkr; Chorus; Nwsp Stf; Lit Mag; Girl Scts; Nwsp Rptr; Hon Roll; Full Schlrshp-Hunter Coll 86; Regents Schlrsp 86; Hunter Coll; Phys Thrpst.

PIGNONE, FRANK; South Park HS; Buffalo, NY; (Y); Boys Clb Am; Cmnty Wkr; Office Aide; Political Wkr; Stage Crew; Im Ftbl; Im Wt Lftg; High Hon Roll; NHS; Math Tutr 85-86; Cert Honor Mock Trl 85-86; West Pt; Crmnl Justc.

PIGOTT, GREGSON H; Elmont Memorial HS; Valley Stream, NY; (Y); 2/239; VP Computer Clb; Spanish Clb; Band; Jazz Band; Mrchg Band; Ftbl; Trk; Jr NHS; NHS; Sal; Commndtn Scorg Amng Top 7 Pct Blck Stdnts Takg PSAT 85; All Dist Band 85-86; All Cnty Band 86; Med.

PIGOTT, MELISSA; Churchville-Chili HS; Churchville, NY; (Y); 17/294; GAA; JA; VP Sr Cls; Capt Cheerleading; Capt Socr; Trk; High Hon Roll; Hon Roll; NHS; Pres Schlr; Natl Latin Exam Cum Laude 83; US Marine Corps Distgshd Athlt Awd 86; All Lgue Awd Sccr 85; Air Force; Elec.

PIJANOWSKI, LISA; Sprinville Griffith Inst; Colden, NY; (Y); Church Yth Grp; 4-H; FFA; Key Clb; Var Bsktbl; Var Tennis; JV Trk; Var Vllybl; Hon Roll; Alfred ST; Floricltr Prod.

PIKAS, IHOR; Grand Island HS; Gr Island, NY; (Y); Computer Clb; Library Aide; Chorus; Hon Roll; Med.

PIKE, AMEIGH; Cicero-North Syracuse HS; Clay, NY; (S); 64/667; Ski Clb; Hon Roll; NHS; Potsdame Coll; Comp Info Sci.

PIKE, CHRISTOPHER; Onteora HS; Woodstock, NY; (Y); 32/210; German Clb; Math Tm; Concert Band; Jazz Band; Mrchg Band; Nwsp Rptr; Var Socr; Var Trk; JP Sousa Awd; NHS; Rgnts Schlrshp 86; Chryl Vrendenburg Mem Awd 86; Smpr Fdls Awd 86; Union.

PIKE, ROBERT; Hugh C Williams HS; Canton, NY; (Y); 12/145; Nwsp Rptr; Nwsp Stf; Pres Frsh Cls; VP Jr Cls; Var JV Bsbl; Var JV Bsktbl; High Hon Roll; Hon Roll; NHS; Ntl Merit Ltr; Math.

PIKE, ROBERT A; Rome Free Acad; Rome, NY; (Y); 32/550; Ski Clb; Concert Band; Mrchg Band; JV Socr; Var Tennis; Hon Roll; Jr NHS; NHS; Aud/Vis; Band; Clarkson U; Engrng.

PIKE, TRACEY; Cicero North Syracuse HS; N Syracuse, NY; (S); 35/623; SADD; Teachers Aide; Chorus; Nwsp Stf; Trs Stu Cncl; JV Cheerleading; Im Powder Puff Ftbl; Hon Roll; Boy Scts; CNS Soc; Wmns Vcl Ensmbl; Irsh Stp Dncr-Btlr Acad Trdtnl Irsh Stp Dncng; St John Fisher Coll; Scl Wrk.

PIKULA, NANCY; Villa Maria Acad; Cheektowaga, NY; (S); 18/90; JCL; Latin Clb; Trs Pep Clb; Chorus; Nwsp Stf; Rep Stu Cncl; Stat Bsktbl; High Hon Roll.

PILARINOS, GEORGIA; St Johns Prep; Astoria, NY; (Y); 41/480; Intnl Clb; JA; Service Clb; Chorus; School Musical; Hon Roll; Hunter Coll; Med.

PILCHER, BARBARA; Fabius-Pompey HS; Fabius, NY; (Y); Pres Church Yth Grp; Varsity Clb; Band; Concert Band; Sec Frsh Cls; Bsktbl; Socr; Sftbl; Cit Awd; Hon Roll; 1st Tm Al-Cnty-Sftbl; Vrsty; Cortland; Educ.

PILCHER, TAMMY; Fabius-Pompey HS; Fabius, NY; (Y); Varsity Clb; Bsktbl; Socr; Capt Trk; High Hon Roll; Hon Roll; NHS; MVP Trck 84-86; Cmmnctns.

PILGER, RHONDA; Frontier SR HS; Hamburg, NY; (Y); DECA; Drama Clb; French Clb; FBLA; Girl Scts; School Play; JV Crs Cntry; Var JV Trk; Var Hon Roll; NHS; U GA; Bus Admn.

PILIERO, CLAIRE MICHELLE; Hampton Bays HS; Hampton Bays, NY; (Y); 5/90; Band; Concert Band; Jazz Band; Mrchg Band; School Musical; Crs Cntry; Sftbl; High Hon Roll; NHS; Cross Country Hustler Awd 84-85; NY ST Schl Music Assn Solo Fest Awd 85-86; Mock Trial Tm Awd 85-86; Music.

PILKINGTON, LAURA; Rocky Point JR SR HS; Rocky Point, NY; (Y); 25/200; Church Yth Grp; Drama Clb; Band; Concert Band; Mrchg Band; Fld Hcky; Trk; Hon Roll; NHS; Hm Extnsn Awd Schlrshp 86; Tchrs Bnvlnt Fnd Of Long Island 86; Rcky Pt Tchrs Assoc Schlrshp; ONEONTA U; Dietician.

PILLAR, MATTHEW; Long Beach HS; Long Beach, NY; (S); 2/265; Band; Jazz Band; Nwsp Rptr; Yrbk Stf; Var L Crs Cntry; CC Awd; NHS; Ntl Merit SF; Sal; Wstnghs Sci Tlnt Srsh 86; Schlstc Achvt Awd 86fcngrsnl Schlr Yth Ldrshp Cncl 86; Law.

PILLER, CHRISTOPHER P; Cobleskill Central Schl; Cobleskill, NY; (Y); 2/116; School Musical; Stage Crew; Socr; Tennis; Trk; Bausch & Lomb Sci Awd; High Hon Roll; Masonic Awd; Trs NHS; Sal; NY ST Rgnts Schlrshp Awd 86; Bio Awd 84; Math Awd 84; Hobart Coll; Bio.

PILLITTERI, JOSEPHINE; Sacred Heart Acad; West Hempstead, NY; (S); 18/182; FTA; Library Aide; SADD; Hon Roll; NHS; St Johns U Cmptv Schlrshp 86; St Johns U; Ed.

PILPEL, PATRICIA; Sacred Heart Acad; New Hyde Park, NY; (Y); Computer Clb; Service Clb; SADD; Chorus; Hon Roll; Bus.

PIMENTEL, CELINES; Emma Willard Schl; Troy, NY; (Y); Dance Clb; Debate Tm; Drama Clb; FBLA; Intnl Clb; Key Clb; Latin Clb; Library Aide; Model UN; Q&S; NY ST Rgnts Schlrshp 85-86; Tufts U.

PIMENTEL, SARITA; John F Kennedy HS; Bronx, NY; (Y); 47/870; Church Yth Grp; Pres JA; Rep Science Clb; Church Choir; Var Bowling; Hon Roll; NHS; Pres Schlr; Regents Coll Schlrshp 86-87; Coll Of Bus & Public Admin Schlrshp From NY U 86-87; NY U; Finance.

PIMM, COLLEEN; Byron-Bergen HS; Bergen, NY; (Y); Band; Color Guard; Concert Band; Flag Corp; Mrchg Band; Nwsp Stf; Yrbk Stf; Sftbl; Swmmng; Hon Roll; Sec.

PINA, ANNETTE; Randolph Central HS; Conewango Valley, NY; (Y); 1/86; Drama Clb; Pep Clb; Spanish Clb; School Play; Stage Crew; Yrbk Phtg; Yrbk Stf; Lit Mag; Hon Roll; VP NHS; Comp Sci.

PINA, BETTY; Msgr Scanlan HS; Jackson Heights, NY; (Y); 129/276; Dance Clb; Drama Clb; Intnl Clb; Spanish Clb; School Play; Hon Roll; Prfct Atten Awd.

PINARD, MICHAEL; Uniondale HS; Uniondale, NY; (Y); FBLA; SADD; Band; Nwsp Stf; C W Post; Commnctns.

PINCHEVSKY, POLINA; High Schl Of Art And Design; Brooklyn, NY; (Y); 17/300; Art Clb; Office Aide; PAVAS; Quiz Bowl; Teachers Aide; Yrbk Stf; Rep Sr Cls; Rep Stu Cncl; Hon Roll; NHS; Art Drctrs Clb Awd 85; Natl Art Hnr Scty 85; Parson Schl Of Dsgn; Grphc Arts.

PINCKNEY, JOEL; Dundee Central HS; Lakemont, NY; (Y); Am Leg Boys St; Varsity Clb; Nwsp Stf; Trs Frsh Cls; VP Soph Cls; Trs Jr Cls; Var L Bsbl; Var L Bsktbl; High Hon Roll; 1st Tm All Star Bsbl 86.

PINE, JEFF; Auburn HS; Auburn, NY; (Y); Boy Scts; Church Yth Grp; High Hon Roll; Hon Roll; Comp Tech.

PINE, ROBERT; Hoosick Falls Central Schl; Hoosick Falls, NY; (Y); Varsity Clb; Wrstlng; Bus.

PINEDA, DARLENE; Sacred Heart Acad; Valley Stream, NY; (Y); Art Clb; Capt Debate Tm; NFL; Capt Speech Tm; Lit Mag; 1st Natl Debate Elims-Var Tm 86; 1st Intermed Tm Debate 85; 3rd St Debate Elims Novice Tm 84; Bio.

PINEDA, DOMINGO; Cutris HS; Bronx, NY; (Y); Boys Clb Am; Cmnty Wkr; FTA; Latin Clb; SADD; Band; School Musical; School Play; Yrbk Stf; JV Bsbl; Phys Ed.

PINEDA, FREDDY; Alfred E Smith HS; Bronx New York, NY; (S); 8/217; Hon Roll; NHS; Prfct Atten Awd; Tchr.

PINEDO, PEGGY; John Dewey HS; Brooklyn, NY; (Y); Bus.

PINEIRO, IRENE; New Rochelle HS; New Rochelle, NY; (Y); Church Yth Grp; Girl Scts; Library Aide; Acpl Chr; Chorus; Church Choir; Comp Engrng.

PINEIRO, NANCY; Beach Channel HS; Rockaway Beach, NY; (Y); Office Aide; Chorus; Nwsp Rptr; Cit Awd; Hon Roll; Prfct Atten Awd; Spanish NHS; Principls List 85; Coll Mt St Vincent; Psych.

PINGITORE, ANDREW F; Cassadaga Valley Central HS; Sinclairville, NY; (Y); 5/76; Pres Frsh Cls; Pres Soph Cls; VP Jr Cls; Stu Cncl; Var JV Ftbl; Var JV Vllybl; Var Wrstlng; Hon Roll; NHS; Natl Thspn Scty 83-86; Natl Art Hnr Scty 84-86; Jamestown CC; Elec Engr.

PINGITORE, MICHAEL; Scotia-Glenville HS; Scotia, NY; (Y); Varsity Clb; JV Bsbl; Var Bsktbl; Var Ftbl; Hon Roll; Babe Ruth Al-Star Amsterdam 84; Comps.

PINGRYN, MICHAEL; Auburn HS; Auburn, NY; (Y); 47/492; Varsity Clb; Bsbl; Bowling; High Hon Roll; Hon Roll; Auburn Yng Am Bwlng Allnc Schlrshp 86; Brockport ST; Math.

PINHO, TARA; Hauppauge HS; Hauppauge, NY; (Y); Church Yth Grp; PAVAS; Ski Clb; SADD; Thesps; Chorus; School Musical; School Play; Stage Crew; Cheerleading; HS Music Awd; Theatre Awd; Vrsty Sport Awd.

PINILLA, LESLIE; Evander Childs HS; Bronx, NY; (Y); Church Yth Grp; Drama Clb; School Musical; Variety Show; Lit Mag; Stu Cncl; Diving; Swmmng; Chncllrs Roll Hnr Poet Cont 86; Actg.

PINNER, MIRIAM; Whitney Point HS; Whitney Point, NY; (Y); 3/124; Trs Church Yth Grp; JCL; Teachers Aide; Chorus; High Hon Roll; NHS; Pres Acdmc Ftns Awd 86; Highest Ability Sr Sci Amigo Lodge IOOF 86; Broome CC; Chld Care.

PINNICK, SHANNON; Hillcrest HS; Hollis, NY; (Y); 290/850; Church Yth Grp; Cmnty Wkr; Drama Clb; Church Choir; School Musical; Rep Frsh Cls; Rep Jr Cls; VP Stu Cncl; Var Gym; Prfct Atten Awd; Spnsh Honors Awd 84; Socl Studies Honors Awd 84; Schl Svc Awd 86; Howard U; Busnss Admin.

PINNOCK, BLONDEL; La Guardra H S Of Music & Art; Bronx, NY; (S); 33/437; Church Yth Grp; Office Aide; Political Wkr; Service Clb; Teachers Aide; Church Choir; Orch; Swing Chorus; Nwsp Bus Mgr; Yrbk Stf; Regents Schlrshp 86; Columbia U; Corporate Law.

PINO, TRACY; Upper Room Christian HS; Smithtown, NY; (S); Church Yth Grp; Nwsp Stf; Yrbk Stf; Stat Cheerleading; Sftbl; Cit Awd; Hon Roll.

PINTO, STEVEN; Monticello HS; Rock Hill, NY; (Y); VP Church Yth Grp; French Clb; Yrbk Stf; VP Sr Cls; Rep Pres Stu Cncl; Var Capt Bsbl; High Hon Roll; Hon Roll; NHS; Pres Ftns Awd; Siena Coll Grnt; Siena Coll.

PINTO, VILMA; Dominican Commercial HS; New York, NY; (S); 24/288; Hosp Aide; Teachers Aide; Yrbk Rptr; Yrbk Stf; NHS; Prfct Atten Awd; Siena Clb Awd 83-85; Arch.

PINZONE, VINCENT JOHN; Valley Stream North HS; Valley Stream, NY; (Y); Church Yth Grp; Cmnty Wkr; Office Aide; Teachers Aide; Varsity Clb; Variety Show; Bsbl; Ftbl; Wt Lftg; Wrstlng; Law.

PIOCHE, ROBERT A; St Francis Prep; Queens Village, NY; (Y); Church Yth Grp; Dance Clb; Tennis; Wt Lftg; Ntl Merit SF; Med.

PIORKOWSKI, RICHARD; Cicero-North Syracuse HS; Mattydale, NY; (S); 21/623; Church Yth Grp; Civic Clb; FCA; Mathletes; Political Wkr; Red Cross Aide; Spanish Clb; Sierra Coll; Med.

PIOTROWSKI, MICHELLE; East Islip HS; Islip Terrace, NY; (Y); Church Yth Grp; Dance Clb; Drama Clb; Hosp Aide; Stage Crew; High Hon Roll; Hon Roll; Suffolk CC; Phy Thrpst.

PIOTROWSKI, PAULA; Mont Pleasant HS; Schenectady, NY; (Y); 22/210; Hosp Aide; Key Clb; Pep Clb; Ski Clb; Chorus; Rep Frsh Cls; Frnch Embssy Cert Excllnce 85; Frnch Hon Soc Schlrshp 86; Lemoyne Coll Jesuit Schlrshp 86; Le Moyne Coll; Engl.

PIPARO, JOSEPH; Cardinal O Hara HS; Tonawanda, NY; (Y); Bsbl; Bsktbl; Hon Roll; Mech Engrng.

PIPER, CANDACE; St Josephs HS; Amityville, NY; (S); 5/107; Nwsp Rptr; Yrbk Stf; NHS; Hnr Rll 82-86; Prtl Schlrshp 84-86; Penn ST; Jrnslsm.

PIPER, CHERYL; Oneida HS; Oneida, NY; (S); 7/210; Church Yth Grp; Var Trk; High Hon Roll; NHS; Pres Schlr; Goshen Coll; History.

PIPER, JAY; Elmira Southside HS; Elmira, NY; (Y); 14/320; Am Leg Boys St; Drama Clb; Intnl Clb; Key Clb; Pep Clb; SADD; Chorus; Swing Chorus; Pres Stu Cncl; NHS; Soroptimist Schlrshp 86; Hobart Acad Schlrshp 86; Zonta Clb Schlrshp 86; Hobart Coll; Intl Bus.

PIPER, SCOTT; Mohawk Central HS; Franfort, NY; (Y); 25/95; Art Clb; Church Yth Grp; JA; Red Cross Aide; Chorus; Stage Crew; Stu Cncl; Tennis; Vllybl; Wm C Schrader Awd 86; Buffalo U; Elec Engrng.

PIPER, SUSAN; Union Endicott HS; Endicott, NY; (Y); Sec Church Yth Grp; Cmnty Wkr; Dance Clb; Hon Roll; Educ.

PIPMAN, MOR; Curtis HS; Staten Island, NY; (Y); 13/225; Art Clb; Hosp Aide; Key Clb; Math Tm; Political Wkr; Nwsp Stf; Lit Mag; Crs Cntry; Trk; NHS; Ntl Hspnc Achvrs Schlrshp 86; SUNY; Cmnctns.

PIQUERO, ANA ISABEL; The Ursuline Schl; Mamaroneck, NY; (Y); Cmnty Wkr; French Clb; Pres Spanish Clb; Teachers Aide; Hon Roll; Jr NHS; NHS; 1st Hnrs Spnsh III 85; 1st Pl Spnsh IV, Hnr Cmmnty Svc Prj 86; Engl.

PIRAINO, BRIAN; Bishop Grimes HS; Syracuse, NY; (S); Var L Bsbl; Var L Ftbl; Hon Roll.

PIRAINO, NANCY; Dominican Commercial HS; Jamaica, NY; (S); Church Yth Grp; Hosp Aide; Hon Roll; Jr NHS; St Johns U; Comp Sci.

PIRGER, BRUCE E; Sauquoit Valley HS; Sauquoit, NY; (Y); 1/100; Church Yth Grp; Computer Clb; Rep Stu Cncl; Im Bsktbl; JV Trk; Bausch & Lomb Sci Awd; High Hon Roll; Hon Roll; NHS; Opt Clb Awd; 3rd In NY ST Optmst Wrtng Cntst 86; NY Acad Of Sci Prgm 86; Outstndng Schlr Wad 84-86; RIT; Comp Sci.

PIRKO, KEVIN; Dyrden HS; Dryden, NY; (Y); French Clb; SADD; School Musical; School Play; Pres Stu Cncl; Capt Var Bsbl; Capt Var Bsktbl; Var L Ftbl; High Hon Roll; NHS; Communctn.

PIRONE, CHRISTINE; Mineola HS; Mineola, NY; (Y); 13/235; Church Yth Grp; Key Clb; SADD; Orch; School Musical; Nwsp Rptr; Ed Yrbk Stf; Trs Sr Cls; Kiwanis Awd; NHS; Rdrs Dgst Sadd Schrlshp 86; Hfstra Frshmn Rcgntn Awd 86; Hfstra U.

PISANI, WILLIAM; Iona Prep Schl; Ardsley, NY; (Y); 24/204; Computer Clb; JA; Im Fld Hcky; Im Ftbl; JV Socr; High Hon Roll; Prfct Atten Awd; 1st Nnr Rl 86; Soccer Awd 84-85; 2nd Hnr Rl 84; Fairfield U; Bus.

PISANO, CRAIG; Smithtown High School East; Smithtown, NY; (Y); Key Clb; Crs Cntry; Tennis; Trk; Italian Hnr Soc 85; Fordham U; Bus.

PISANO, MICHAEL; Valley Central HS; Montgomery, NY; (Y); 15/315; Spanish Clb; High Hon Roll; NHS; Spanish NHS; IBM Co Op Pgm 86-87; SYS Anlyst.

PISAPIA, DENISE; Holy Trinity HS; Levittown, NY; (S); 13/313; Math Clb; Capt Math Tm; Office Aide; Nwsp Rptr; JV Var Cheerleading; Capt Gym; Var Trk; High Hon Roll; NHS; 2nd Pl-CHSAA Mile Walk 85; 3rd Pl-CHSGAA JV Beam 85; Sprtsmnshp Awd-JV Gymnstcs 85; Accntng.

PISCIOTTA, JOYCE; John Jay HS; Brooklyn, NY; (Y); Hon Roll; Brooklyn Coll; Law.

PISCITELLO, MARY; Hicksville HS; Hicksville, NY; (Y); Church Yth Grp; Dance Clb; Hosp Aide; JA; Science Clb; Band; Concert Band; Drm & Bgl; Capt Mrchg Band; Pep Band; Nrsng.

PISCONTI, SYLVIA; Cathedral HS; Astoria, NY; (Y); 33/272; Variety Show; Im Bsktbl; Var Gym; Im Vllybl; Hon Roll; All Amercn Acdm Awd 85-86; Comp Engr.

PISELLA, GIOACCHINO; High School Of Art Of Design; Astoria, NY; (Y); Art Clb; Computer Clb; Hon Roll; Jr NHS; Pres-Kenny Art Gllry 86; Arch.

PISKOROWSKI, DARCY; La Webber HS; Lyndonville, NY; (Y); Chorus; JV Cheerleading; Nrsng.

PISKUNOWICZ, THERESA; Turner Carroll HS; Buffalo, NY; (S); Church Yth Grp; Church Choir; Yrbk Stf; Hon Roll; NHS; Scholar Awad 83; Sci.

PISTILLI, VALERIE; Moore Catholic HS; Staten Island, NY; (Y); Hosp Aide; Math Clb; NFL; SADD; Yrbk Stf.

PISTONE, LISA ANN; Dominican Commercial HS; Brooklyn, NY; (Y); Cmnty Wkr; FHA; Siena Clb 82-86; Pres Acdmc Fit Awds 86; Hnbl Awd Relgn 86; Prncpls Lst Vlntr Wrk 85-86; St Johns U; Schl Tchr.

PITA, AGUSTIN J; St John Prep; Queens, NY; (Y); Spanish Clb; Yrbk Rptr; Yrbk Stf; Hon Roll; Hnr Anml Behavior, Yrbk Stf Awd 85; Hunter Coll; Neuro Sci.

PITCHER, SHAWN; Franklin Acad; Malone, NY; (Y); Hon Roll; Prfct Atten Awd; Frnkln Acad Schlrshp 85-86; Psych.

PITKANEN, DARLENE; Smithtown West HS; Hauppauge, NY; (Y); Flag Corp; Yrbk Phtg; Yrbk Stf; Mgr(s); French Hon Soc; Hon Roll; NHS; Hewlett Pakcard Employee Schlrshp 86; Burger King Career Ed Pgm 85-86; SUNY.

PITNEY, BIZZIT; Lansing HS; Ithaca, NY; (Y); 12/80; French Clb; SADD; Ed Lit Mag; VP Soph Cls; VP Jr Cls; Stu Cncl; Var Bsktbl; Var Trk; High Hon Roll; ST Sen Stu Forum 86; Biochem.

PITSCHI, JOHN P; Patchogue Medford HS; Patchogue, NY; (Y); Boy Scts; Science Clb; School Play; Stage Crew; Rep Frsh Cls; Rep Soph Cls; Hon Roll; Jr NHS; NYS Regnts Schlrshp 85-86; Cornell U Smmr Coll 85; Brookhaven Natl Lab Sci Intrnshp 84; Temple U; Bus.

PITTARI, PAUL; Archbishop Molloy HS; Middle Village, NY; (Y); 1/401; Math Clb; Math Tm; Crs Cntry; Trk; Bausch & Lomb Sci Awd; Gov Hon Prg Awd; NHS; Ntl Merit Ltr; Val; Cit Awd; RPI Medal Exc Math,Sci 85; Pres Awd Achvt 83-86; Schlrshp Penn ST; SUNY; Engrng.

PITTELLI, LAUREN; St John Villa Acad; Staten Island, NY; (Y); Hon Roll; Area Studies Awd 84; Signs Of Life Awd Integrated Math II 84-85; Eng 10 Awd 85; Eng 11 Awd 86.

PITTERS, DOUGLAS; Bronx HS Of Science; Bronx, NY; (Y); Camera Clb; Church Yth Grp; VP JA; Acpl Chr; Church Choir; NHS; Bonus For Extra Wrk VP Of Mrktng; Achvts Stu Co 86; Sci.

PITTMAN, ALAN; Niskayuma HS; Schenectady, NY; (Y); Trs Drama Clb; Chorus; Jazz Band; Orch; School Musical; School Play; Swing Chorus; Symp Band; Lit Mag; NHS; Prfrmng Arts.

PITTMAN, CAROLINE J; E J Wilson HS; Rochester, NY; (Y); French Clb; JCL; Latin Clb; Math Tm; Jazz Band; Symp Band; High Hon Roll; Hon Roll; NHS; Harvard Bk Awd 85; Rgnts Schlrshp 86; Amer Frgn Lang Awd 84; SUNY Geneseo; Frnch Educ.

PITTNER, CINDY; Bishop Grimes HS; Syracuse, NY; (S); Cmnty Wkr; Variety Show; Yrbk Phtg; Yrbk Sprt Ed; Bsktbl; Socr; Sftbl; High Hon Roll; Algb Awd 84; Phys Ther.

PITTNER, JULIE; Bishop Grimes HS; Syracuse, NY; (S); 16/146; Cmnty Wkr; Variety Show; Capt Bsktbl; Crs Cntry; Socr; Sftbl; VP NHS; High Hon Roll; Hon Roll; Acadmc All Amer 84-85; Ed.

PITTS, CHARLENE; Indian River Central HS; Antwerp, NY; (Y); Church Yth Grp; Dance Clb; Chorus; Church Choir; School Play; Stage Crew; Variety Show; Score Keeper; Hon Roll; Game Wrdn.

PITURA, ROBT; Woodlands HS; Hartsdale, NY; (Y); Aud/Vis; Church Yth Grp; Computer Clb; Stage Crew; Yrbk Stf; Comp Pgmmng.

PIXLEY, DAWN; Rush-Henrietta Sperry HS; Pittsford, NY; (Y); 9/280; Pres Church Yth Grp; SADD; Chorus; Church Choir; Jazz Band; School Musical; French Hon Soc; High Hon Roll; NHS; Genesee Vly HS Chem Achvt 86; Psych.

PIXTON, MORNA S; Vestal HS; Vestal, NY; (Y); 4/435; Church Yth Grp; Drama Clb; French Clb; Mathletes; Ski Clb; SADD; School Play; Stage Crew; Socr; High Hon Roll; Art Competitions Awds 82; Yale U.

PIZARRO, EVELYN; John Jay HS; Brooklyn, NY; (Y); Dance Clb; Drama Clb; Hosp Aide; JA; Office Aide; Teachers Aide; Band; School Musical; School Play; Eng Achievement Awd 86; College Bound Awd 84; Hunter Coll; Nrsng.

PIZON, LISA; Sandy Creek Central HS; Richland, NY; (S); 27/95; Office Aide; SADD; Teachers Aide; JV Bsktbl; Hon Roll; NHS; Council 82 Schlrshp Awd 86; Bryant & Stratton; Med Asst Sec.

PIZZI, ANN MARIE DELLI; St Catharine Acad; Bronx, NY; (Y); 3/200; Dance Clb; Hosp Aide; Office Aide; Teachers Aide; Nwsp Ed-Chief; Rep Soph Cls; Stu Cncl; NCTE Awd; NHS; Manhattan Coll Schlrship, Fordham U Schlrshp & Regnts Schlrshp 86; Manhattan Coll; Bio.

PIZZI, JOLIE A; Cardinal Mooney HS; Rochester, NY; (Y); 57/304; Chorus; School Musical; Nwsp Ed-Chief; Nwsp Rptr; Lit Mag; Trk; Hon Roll; Peer Mnstry; Flk Grp; Regnts Schlrshp Awd; St Bonaventures.

PIZZICHEMI, DOMINICK; Archbishop Stepinac HS; Yonkers, NY; (Y); 90/174; Im Bsktbl; Hon Roll; Iona Coll; Acctg.

PIZZITOLA, MARIANNE; Longwood HS; Coram, NY; (Y); Trs Key Clb; VP Concert Band; VP Mrchg Band; School Musical; Yrbk Bus Mgr; Yrbk Phtg; High Hon Roll; Fredonia ST Coll Music Pgm Scholar 85; Schl Cultural Arts Music 84.

PJONTEK, ELLEN; Bishop Maginn HS; Albany, NY; (S); Latin Clb; Yrbk Stf; Cheerleading; High Hon Roll; Hon Roll; NHS.

PLACE, JENNIFER; Oxford Acad; Oxford, NY; (Y); French Clb; Ski Clb; Varsity Clb; JV Var Bsktbl; Var Fld Hcky; Powder Puff Ftbl; JV Sftbl; Hon Roll; Empire ST Games 85; Best Dfnsv Plyr/Bsktbl 86; Sus-E All Star Tm/Fld Hcky 85.

PLACE, KAREN; Oxford Academy Central Schl; Oxford, NY; (Y); 19/85; FFA; Varsity Clb; JV Bsktbl; JV Fld Hcky; Powder Puff Ftbl; JV Sftbl; Cit Awd; Hon Roll; Prfct Atten Awd; Sus-East All Star Fld Hcky 84; Bst Def Pyr Fld Hcky 85; Regents Schlrshp 85; SUNY; Envir Bio.

PLAISTED, DONNA; Waverly JR SR HS; Chemung, NY; (Y); Pres Church Yth Grp; VP 4-H; Pres FHA; Ski Clb; SADD; 4-H Awd; Cazanovia; Fshn Mrchndsg.

PLAKUS, MELINDA; Victor Central HS; Victor, NY; (Y); Art Clb; Color Guard; School Musical; School Play; Stage Crew; Yrbk Stf; Hon Roll; Mth.

PLAMBECK, SUSAN; Roy C Ketcham HS; Poughkeepsie, NY; (Y); Boy Scts; Church Yth Grp; Drama Clb; High Hon Roll; Hon Roll; Jr NHS; NHS; Natl Assoc Bio Tchrs Hnrs Awd 86; US Army Sci & Engrng Mld/Cert Supr Achvt 86; 1s Sci Fair, 2nd Rgnl; Animal Sci.

PLANTY, MICHAEL; Cicero-North Syracuse HS; N Syracuse, NY; (S); 24/623; Church Yth Grp; Exploring; Capt FCA; Art Clb; Bsktbl; Hon Roll; Art Awd 85; Crmnl Sci.

PLATT, JASON; Rhinebeck Central HS; Rhinebeck, NY; (Y); Exploring; Spanish Clb; Varsity Clb; Var Capt Socr; Var Tennis; Hon Roll; Spanish NHS; All Leag & All Sectn Sccr 85-86; All Leag & All Sectn Tennis 84-86; Oceangrphy.

PLATZ, MARCIE; Truopsburg Central HS; Knoxville, PA; (Y); 5/13; Aud/Vis; Computer Clb; Teachers Aide; Yrbk Rptr; Hon Roll; NHS; Ntl Merit Ltr; Pres Schlr; 4-H; French Clb; Unsung Hero Awd 85; Otstndng Bus Stu 86; King Coll; Bus Admin.

PLATZMAN, ANDREA; Midwood HS; Brooklyn, NY; (Y); Band; Chorus; School Play; Nwsp Phtg; Lit Mag; Var Tennis; Hon Roll; I Love NY Art Awd 84; Intl Law.

PLAWNER, LAUREN; Edward R Murrow HS; Brooklyn, NY; (Y); 1/669; Hosp Aide; School Play; Nwsp Rptr; Yrbk Phtg; Gov Hon Prg Awd; Pres Schlr; Val; Renssalear Polytech Awd Math, Sci 85; 1st Pl Awd Amer Inst Sci Fair 85; T Roosevlt Oratry Cntst Wnr 85; Cornell U; Bio.

PLAYER, SUZANNE C; Sacred Heart Acad; Lynbrook, NY; (Y); 29/181; Cmnty Wkr; Debate Tm; FTA; NFL; Spanish Clb; School Musical; Nwsp Stf; Hon Roll; NHS; Regnts Schlrshp; Iona Clg Lang Cmptn 1st Hnrs; St Johns U Cmptn Schlrshp; Intl Stds.

PLAZA, DAGMAR; Cardinal Spellman HS; Bronx, NY; (Y); Church Yth Grp; Dance Clb; Science Clb; Spanish Clb; Drill Tm; Flag Corp; Off Jr Cls; Sec Sr Cls; French Hon Soc; Hon Roll; Natl Cert Educ Dev-Natl Educ Dev Tests 84; Legal Stu.

PLESSAS, JUDE; Bishop Grimes HS; Syracuse, NY; (S); 1/146; SADD; Band; School Play; Stu Cncl; Bsktbl; Capt Tennis; Bausch & Lomb Sci Awd; High Hon Roll; NCTE Awd; NHS; Bio Awd; RPI Math & Sci Awd; Trig Awd; Cornell.

PLETTER, MELISSA D; Binghamton HS; Binghamton, NY; (Y); Hosp Aide; Temple Yth Grp; Nwsp Ed-Chief; Rep Frsh Cls; High Hon Roll; NHS; Pres Schlr; Ntl Cncl Yth Ldrshp 85; Rgnts Schlrshp 85-86; Ntl Conf Of Synagogue Yth Ntl Good Name Citation 85; Stern Coll; Phys Therapy.

PLEVA, DAVID; East Meadow HS; East Meadow, NY; (Y); 35/340; FBLA; Science Clb; JV Bsbl; JV Var Ftbl; Hon Roll; NHS; Meadowbrook Schlrshp 86; St Jons U; Law.

PLIMI, TONIA C; Long Beach HS; Long Beach, NY; (Y); 4-H; Full Schlrshp To Adelphi U 86-87; Adelphi U; Dance.

PLIMLEY, MARK; Beacon HS; Beacon, NY; (Y); 72/217; Ski Clb; Varsity Clb; JV Badmtn; Var Bsbl; Var JV Ftbl; Var JV Ice Hcky; Engrng.

PLISZAK, STEVEN; Patchogue-Medford HS; Patchogue, NY; (S); Band; Concert Band; Jazz Band; Mrchg Band; Orch; School Musical; Symp Band; Kiwanis Awd; Church Yth Grp; Wrstlng; Mgmt Inf Systms.

PLITNICK, LISA; Coxsackie-Athens HS; Hannacroix, NY; (Y); Church Yth Grp; Spanish Clb; Band; Chorus; Church Choir; Gym; Socr; Trk; High Hon Roll; Hon Roll; Elem Ed.

PLITT, MICHAEL; Stagerties HS; Malden Hudson, NY; (Y); French Clb; Ski Clb; Im Bsktbl; Hon Roll; Ntl Scl Stds Olypd 1st, 4th 85, 86.

PLOCHOCKI, SUSAN; Cicero-North Syracuse HS; N Syracuse, NY; (S); 8/623; Computer Clb; Office Aide; Nwsp Rptr; Var Tennis; Hon Roll; Dstngshd Amer HS Stu Awd 86.

PLONKA, CARIANNE; Mount Mercy Acad; Buffalo, NY; (Y); Drama Clb; SADD; Chorus; Tennis; Hon Roll; 2nd Pl Awd Frgn Lang Fair Spn 85; Niagara U; Nrsng.

PLOTNICKI, LOUIS; Depew HS; Buffalo, NY; (Y); Varsity Clb; Var Bsktbl; Hon Roll; Comp Sci.

PLOTSKER, MICHAEL; Haftr HS; Far Rockaway, NY; (Y); Math Clb; Science Clb; Temple Yth Grp; Yrbk Stf; Lit Mag; Rep Stu Cncl; Var L Bsktbl; Im Bowling; Im Fld Hcky; Im Ftbl; Rgnts Schlrshp 86; Queens Coll; Med.

PLOUFFE, DANIELLE; Susquehanna Valley HS; Conklin, NY; (Y); Church Yth Grp; Pep Clb; Trs Band; Chorus; Jazz Band; Mrchg Band; Orch; School Musical; Hon Roll; Spanish NHS; Cornell U Smr Coll-Arch 86; NYSSMA Awds 83-86; Arch.

PLOWE, LARRY; Albion HS; Albion, NY; (S); JV Bsbl; Hon Roll; Math.

PLOWE, TARA; Sweethome SR HS; Tonawanda, NY; (Y); Art Clb; Church Yth Grp; Dance Clb; Girl Scts; Ski Clb; SADD; Varsity Clb; Chorus; Church Choir; School Musical; Prfct Atttndnce 84-86; Bst All Round Chrldr 86; Sci Fair Merit Awd 84; Oswego ST; Med Tech.

PLOWS, LISA B; Brookfield Central HS; W Edmeston, NY; (Y); 1/20; Band; Concert Band; Mrchg Band; Trs Yrbk Stf; Bausch & Lomb Sci Awd; High Hon Roll; NHS; Val; NYS Regents Schlrshp 86; Rochester Inst Of Tech Alumni Schlrshp 86; Rochester Inst Of Tech; Comp Sc.

PLUAS, ROXANA; Washington Irving HS; New York, NY; (Y); 9/423; Church Yth Grp; Teachers Aide; Yrbk Ed-Chief; Dnfth Awd; High Hon Roll; NHS; Prfct Atten Awd; Arista 85; Bus Hnr Soc 85; Wrd Proc Awd 86; Pace U.

PLUFF, MICHAEL; Altmar-Parish-Williamstown HS; Parish, NY; (Y); French Clb; Varsity Clb; Capt Bsbl; Capt Bsktbl; Capt Ftbl; High Hon Roll; US Army Res Schlr/Ath Awd 86; Dollors For Schlrs Scholar Fuller Bus Scholar 86; Le Moyne Coll; Law.

PLUMMER, KATRINA MARI; Tupper Lake HS; Tupper Lk, NY; (Y); Camera Clb; Letterman Clb; Pres Pep Clb; Yrbk Phtg; Yrbk Rptr; Stu Cncl; L Cheerleading; JV Var Socr; Stat Vllybl; Spec Ed Tchr.

PLUMMER, STEPHANIE; Springfield Gardens HS; Laurelton, NY; (S); Band; Bsktbl; Vllybl; Hon Roll; Psych.

PLURETTI, SUSANNE; Mynderse Acad; Seneca Falls, NY; (Y); GAA; JV Bsktbl; JV Var Sftbl; Var Capt Vllybl; Hon Roll; Sctn 5 Sftbl Cls B All Star Tm 86; Cayuga Cnty CC; Crmnsl Jstc.

PLUSCHAU, LYNDA M; Greenport HS; Orient, NY; (Y); 4/38; French Clb; Nwsp Sprt Ed; Yrbk Ed-Chief; Pres Jr Cls; Cheerleading; Fld Hcky; Vllybl; High Hon Roll; NHS; Rotary Stu Mnth 86; Wilkes Coll Achvt Schlrsp 86; Regents Schlrshp 85-86; Wilkes Coll; Nrsng.

PLYTER, LISA; Newark SR HS; Newark, NY; (Y); 5/201; Am Leg Aux Girls St; Nwsp Stf; Yrbk Stf; Capt Var Swmmng; NHS; Spanish NHS; Rochester Alumni Scholar Wittenberg U 86; Wittenberg Alumni Scholar 86; Wittenberg U; Bus Adm.

POCHATKO, GARY M; La Salle SR HS; Niagara Falls, NY; (S); 7/250; Library Aide; VP Stu Cncl; JV Var Ftbl; NHS; Hnr Soc Treas 85-86; Niagara U; Bus.

POCHUNOW, ANN-MARIE; Bishop Kearney HS; Rochester, NY; (Y); Cmnty Wkr; JA; Office Aide; Teachers Aide; Band; Yrbk Stf; Bowling; Coach Actv; Sftbl; Hon Roll.

PODADERA, JOSE LUIS; St Agnes HS; Jackson Hts, NY; (Y); 5/99; Boy Scts; Church Yth Grp; Spanish Clb; Im Bsktbl; Capt Vllybl; NHS; Rensselaer Polytech Inst; Engr.

PODLESSKI, NICOLE; Oyster Bay HS; Oyster Bay, NY; (Y); German Clb; Girl Scts; Yrbk Phtg; Yrbk Stf; Bsktbl; Sftbl; Vllybl; Fshn Merch.

PODOLAK, KELLIE; Central Islip SR HS; Central Islip, NY; (Y); Trs Girl Scts; Concert Band; Mrchg Band; Pep Band; Yrbk Stf; Off Soph Cls; Rep Jr Cls; Trs Sr Cls; Hon Roll; Grl Sct Gld Awd 87; St Joseph Acad; Educ.

PODOLEC, TIFFANI; Johnstown HS; Johnstown, NY; (Y); Intnl Clb; Var Ski Clb; Stu Cncl; JV Var Bsktbl; Var Crs Cntry; JV Var Fld Hcky; Var Trk; High Hon Roll; Hon Roll; NHS; Mech Drwg Awd 85; Engl II Awd 86; Arch.

PODRAZA, VINCENT A; St Francis Prep; Middle Village, NY; (S); 60/744; Cmnty Wkr; German Clb; Science Clb; Service Clb; Pres Spanish Clb; Chorus; Jr NHS; NHS; Opt Clb Awd; St Johns U; Bus.

PODRAZIK, MARK; Niskayuna HS; Schenectady, NY; (Y); Cmnty Wkr; Trs Pres Drama Clb; VP Trs Exploring; Latin Clb; Chorus; School Musical; School Play; Nwsp Bus Mgr; Nwsp Rptr; NHS; Jrnlsm.

POE, DARRELL D; Julia Richman HS; Flushing, NY; (Y); #27 In Class; Boy Scts; Church Yth Grp; JA; Quiz Bowl; Chorus; Church Choir; Hon Roll; Regents Schlrshp 86; All Boro Choir Ltr Rcgntn 84; Hofstra U; Bnkng.

POECKING, KEVIN; Hamburg SR HS; Hamburg, NY; (Y); 23/390; French Clb; Model UN; Concert Band; Jazz Band; Mrchg Band; Orch; Symp Band; Hon Roll; NHS; Egl Sct; Case Western Reserve U; Math.

POERSCHKE, SUSAN; Niagara Wheatfied HS; N Tonawanda, NY; (Y); 41/296; Am Leg Aux Girls St; Trs Church Yth Grp; Teachers Aide; NHS; SUNY Geneseo; Acctng.

POHLMAN, JENNIFER; St Marys HS; Depew, NY; (S); 4/182; GAA; Ski Clb; SADD; Varsity Clb; VP Frsh Cls; Rep Soph Cls; Trs Jr Cls; Stu Cncl; Cheerleading; Tennis; Engl Achvt Awd 83-84; Mst Imprvd Plyr Var Ten 84-85; Oral Roberts U; Psych.

POHLMAN, RENAYE; West Seneca West SR HS; W Seneca, NY; (Y); Hosp Aide; JV Cheerleading; Hon Roll; Shorthand Awd 86; Buffalo ST Coll; Phys Thrpy.

POHLY, MICHAEL; The Wheatley Schl; Old Westbury, NY; (Y); Trs Model UN; Varsity Clb; Capt Stage Crew; Ed Nwsp Stf; L Crs Cntry; Capt Tennis; NHS; Bronze Mdlst Long Island Math Fair 83-84; Rnd 1 Wnnr NY ST Energy Rsrch Cmptn 84-85.

POHORILLE, CECILIA; New Rochelle HS; New Rochelle, NY; (Y); French Clb; SADD; Nwsp Stf; Yrbk Stf; Sec Soph Cls; Var Crs Cntry; Var Trk; French Hon Soc; High Hon Roll; NHS.

POINTER, RACHEL; Fairport HS; Fairport, NY; (Y); Cmnty Wkr; French Clb; Chorus; Stage Crew; Rep Sr Cls; Rep Stu Cncl; Hon Roll; NHS; Prfct Atten Awd; Pres Schlr; Regnts Scholar 86; Boston U.

POISS, ISLEEN SUSAN; Waldorf HS; New Hyde Park, NY; (Y); Acpl Chr; Madrigals; Orch; School Musical; School Play; Yrbk Ed-Chief; Fld Hcky; German Clb; Lstd Outstndg Nassau Schlr Newsday 86; Cert Mrt Germ-Amer Sch Ass 84; Grd A Lvl 6 ST Msc Assc Eval 85; Wellesley Coll; Art Hist.

POISSANT, JULIE; Franklin Acad; Malone, NY; (Y); 103/262; Church Yth Grp; Cmnty Wkr; Drama Clb; French Clb; Ski Clb; School Play; Stage Crew; Marist Coll; Acctng.

POISSANT, STEVE; Williamsville North HS; Williamsville, NY; (Y); Church Yth Grp; SADD; Teachers Aide; Band; Pep Band; School Musical; Symp Band; Amhrst Outstndng Vlntr 84-86; Spec Educ.

POKALSKY, LAURA; Webster SR HS; Webster, NY; (Y); 32/495; Church Yth Grp; Girl Scts; Math Tm; Concert Band; JV Var Fld Hcky; NHS; Spanish NHS; JA; Office Aide; Ski Clb; Rgnts Schlrshp 86; Hmltn Coll Schlrshp 86; Jr Achvmnt Area 1st Rnr-Up Co Yr 84; Hamilton Coll; Biolgy.

POKLINKOWSKI, VALERIE; Honeoye Central HS; Hemlock, NY; (S); 11/71; Band; Concert Band; Jazz Band; Mrchg Band; Pep Band; JV Var Bsktbl; JV Var Socr; JV Var Sftbl; JV Vllybl; Hon Roll; Accntng.

POKORNOWSKI, KEVIN A; Depew HS; Cheektowaga, NY; (Y); Am Leg Boys St; Varsity Clb; Trs Band; Concert Band; Jazz Band; Mrchg Band; Variety Show; Var Bowling; Var Vllybl; Hon Roll; Canisius Coll; Pre-Med.

POKORNY, CAROLYN; Half Hollow Hills HS East; Melville, NY; (Y); Drama Clb; NFL; Political Wkr; Capt Speech Tm; School Musical; School Play; Hon Roll; Awd Achvmnt Ntl & ST Dbt & Spch Cmptn 86; 1st Pl Cthlc Frnsc Lg Drmtc Prfrmnc 85; Law.

POKOWITZ, CHRISTINE; John A Coleman HS; Rosendale, NY; (Y); 9/92; Off 4-H; Pres French Clb; Off Key Clb; School Play; Stage Crew; 4-H Awd; High Hon Roll; Hon Roll; NHS.

POLAK, GREG; Riverhead HS; Aquebogue, NY; (Y); 87/200; Key Clb; Latin Clb; Ski Clb; VICA; Var Capt Bsbl; Var Capt Ftbl; Wt Lftg; Prfct Atten Awd; MVP In Bsbl 84-85; All-Lg & All-Cnty In Bsbl 86; All-Lg & All-Cnty In Ftbl 85.

POLAKIEWICZ, ANNE MARIE; Frontier Central HS; Blasdell, NY; (Y); Pres French Clb; JV Var Bsktbl; JV Var Sftbl; JV Var Vllybl; High Hon Roll; Hon Roll; NHS; Mentor 85-86; Acctg.

POLANCO, DENNIS; HS Of Art & Design; Bronx, NY; (Y); 71/420; Art Clb; Band; School Musical; Stu Cncl; Var Bsbl; Vllybl; Hon Roll; Fordham U Rose Hill; Bio.

POLANCO, MARY; Adlar E Stevenson HS; Bronx, NY; (Y); Debate Tm; English Clb; Teachers Aide; Band; Chorus; Concert Band; School Play; Soph Cls; Stu Cncl; High Hon Roll; Excllnc-Creatv Wrtg 84; Achvt Leag Medl 86; Lawyr.

POLAND, GREGORY A; Spackenkill HS; Poughkeepsie, NY; (Y); Thesps; L Band; Chorus; Jazz Band; Pep Band; School Musical; Variety Show; Var L Socr; Var L Trk; NY ST Smmr Schl Of Arts 85; NYSSMA Area AllST & AllST Altrnt Bnd 84 & 85; 1st Prz Tlnt Cntst 85; Point Park Coll; Musical Theat.

POLANSKI, MIROSLAW A; Seward Park HS; New York, NY; (Y); 38/544; Debate Tm; Math Tm; Nwsp Stf; Regents Schlrsp 86; Hunter Coll Mrt Awd 86; Hunter Coll; Medicine.

POLAROLO, DAVID J; New Hartford Central HS; New Hartford, NY; (Y); Boy Scts; Exploring; Band; Chorus; Concert Band; Mrchg Band; Mohawk Valley CC; Aerontcl Eng.

POLESHUCK, ELLEN; Brighton HS; Rochester, NY; (Y); 45/325; Cmnty Wkr; Latin Clb; Spanish Clb; SADD; Thesps; School Play; Stage Crew; Nwsp Rptr; Yrbk Stf; Ntl Merit Ltr; Wegmans Schlrshp $2200 Yr 86; Dartmouth Coll; Psych.

POLETO, DONALD; Hutch Tech; Buffalo, NY; (Y); Rep Frsh Cls; Elect Clb 85-86; U Of Buffalo; Electronics Engr.

POLETO, LINDA; Catholic Central HS; Green Island, NY; (Y); Drama Clb; German Clb; Math Clb; Pep Clb; Sec SADD; Varsity Clb; Stage Crew; Yrbk Stf; High Hon Roll; NHS; Bio.

POLETTO, VALENTINA K; Saugerties HS; Saugerties, NY; (S); 1/253; Am Leg Aux Girls St; French Clb; Ski Clb; Band; Nwsp Stf; JV Var Cheerleading; Im Socr; High Hon Roll; NHS; Val; Intl Yth Day 85; Intl Rltns.

POLI JR, DAVID R; Torrejon HS; APO, NY; (Y); Church Yth Grp; CAP; Cmnty Wkr; ROTC; SADD; Color Guard; Drill Tm; VP Stu Cncl; High Hon Roll; NHS; Daedln Awd Outstndng Ldrshp 86; 3rd Yr JRROTC Cadets 85-86; All Conf & Rgnl Chmp Wrestling 85-86; Military Pilot.

POLICANO JR, ALBERT; East Meadow HS; E Meadow, NY; (Y); 52/340; FBLA; Concert Band; Mrchg Band; Var Bsbl; Im Bsktbl; Im Ftbl; Im Ice Hcky; Hon Roll; NHS; Pres Schlr; Hofstra U; Elec Engr.

POLINSKY, ROBERT; Lanassie HS; Brooklyn, NY; (Y); Aud/Vis; Debate Tm; Drama Clb; PAVAS; Quiz Bowl; Service Clb; School Musical; School Play; Variety Show; Cit Awd; Ecnmcs.

POLISANO, NADINE; Hamburg SR HS; Hamburg, NY; (Y); AFS; Cmnty Wkr; Sec French Clb; Girl Scts; Chorus; School Musical; Nwsp Rptr; Nwsp Stf; Mgr(s); Mgr Vllybl; Journ.

POLISOTO, DEBBIE; Hamburg Central HS; Hamburg, NY; (Y); 5/380; Aud/Vis; Band; Chorus; Jazz Band; Madrigals; Mrchg Band; School Musical; Symp Band; Hon Roll; SUNY Buffalo; Engrng.

POLIZZI, CAROL; Mary Louis Acad; Flushing, NY; (Y); Hosp Aide; Teachers Aide; High Hon Roll; NHS; Ntl Merit Schol; Qns Coll Pres Awd Achvmnt 84; Schlrshp Soph Yr 83; Trstee Schlrshp NYU 85; NY U; Music.

POLIZZI, MATTHEW; York Central HS; Restof, NY; (Y); Art Clb; Ski Clb; Band; Concert Band; Jazz Band; Mrchg Band; Pep Band; Bsbl; U Of Rochester; Bus Mgmt.

POLK, KEN; Williamsville East HS; Williamsvl, NY; (Y); Am Leg Boys St; Cmnty Wkr; Pres Temple Yth Grp; Capt Varsity Clb; Trs Soph Cls; Trs Jr Cls; Pres Stu Cncl; JV Capt Bsktbl; Powder Puff Ftbl; Var L Socr; Area Pres Of Yth Grp 85.

POLLACK, DANI; Tottenville HS; Staten Island, NY; (S); 25/800; High Hon Roll; Hon Roll; NHS; NY U.

POLLACK, DAVID; Midwood HS; New York, NY; (Y); 148/607; Band; Orch; School Musical.

POLLACK, WILLIAM A; Valley Heights Christian Acad; Sherburne, NY; (S); 2/11; Church Yth Grp; Computer Clb; Stage Crew; Nwsp Ed-Chief; Var Bsktbl; Var Socr; 1st Co Intl Comp Prob Slvng Cntst 85; Supervisors Awd 83; Elec Engrng.

POLLAK, ARTHUR; General Douglas Mac Arthur HS; Levittown, NY; (S); 3/321; Cmnty Wkr; Debate Tm; Pres Mathletes; Capt Quiz Bowl; Nwsp Ed-Chief; Ed Yrbk Stf; High Hon Roll; NHS; Ntl Merit Ltr; Opt Clb Awd; Untd Cerbrl Plsy Tag Dy 1st Pl Trphy-Slvr Div 84-85; Untd Cerbrl Plsy Tag Dy Chrmn Levittwn 84-86; Bus.

POLLITT, MAUREEN; Albertus Magnus HS; Stony Pt, NY; (Y); 18/180; Church Yth Grp; Drama Clb; Math Clb; Varsity Clb; Mrchg Band; Bsktbl; Tennis; Timer; Pres Acad Fit Awd; Natl Mth & Sci Hnr Soc; Holy Cross; Econ.

POLLOCK, DEBRA A; Norwood-Norfolk Central HS; Norwood, NY; (Y); JCL; Key Clb; Latin Clb; Chorus; Church Choir; Rep Frsh Cls; Rep Soph Cls; Var Cheerleading; High Hon Roll; Hon Roll; Diploma From Barbizon Mdlng Schl 84; Tlntd JRS Awd 85; Canton AIC; Nrsng.

POLNAK, DONALD; Lansingburgh HS; Troy, NY; (Y); Drama Clb; SADD; Band; Chorus; School Musical; School Play; High Hon Roll; Boys Clb Am; Boy Scts; Hon Roll; Music Ed.

POLNER, RICH; Smithtown HS East; Nesconset, NY; (Y); Debate Tm; Radio Clb; Rep Stu Cncl; Var L Ftbl; Var Wrstlng; Rep Spanish NHS; Cornell; Law.

POLONCARZ, LISA; St Marys HS; E Aurora, NY; (Y); 15/170; Church Yth Grp; Ski Clb; JV Sftbl; Hon Roll; NHS; Acadmc All Amer Schlr Awd 86; Pre Med.

POLSINELLI, VITO; Mont Pleasant HS; Schenectady, NY; (Y); 8/208; Ski Clb; Spanish Clb; Ftbl; Wt Lftg; Wrstlng; NHS; Spanish NHS; Pres Acadmc Fitns Awd 86; Clarkson; Mech Engr.

POLTRAS, KAREN; Centereach HS; Selden, NY; (Y); Office Aide; Chorus; Socr; French Hon Soc; Hon Roll; NHS; Bus.

POLVINO, JAMES M; Gates Chili SR HS; Rochester, NY; (Y); 57/455; Radio Clb; Band; Concert Band; Jazz Band; Mrchg Band; Stage Crew; High Hon Roll; Ntl Merit Ltr; Regnts Schlrshp 86; SUNY Genespo; Biochem.

POLVINO JR, JAMES R; Charles H Roth HS; W Henrietta, NY; (Y); Ski Clb; Varsity Clb; Var Lcrss; Var Capt Socr; Wt Lftg; High Hon Roll; Jr NHS; NHS; Spanish NHS; Ski Team Rcng V Capt; 10th In St In Nastar Skng 85; Athltc & Schlstc Lttrs 85-86; Engr.

POLY, CHRISTOPHER; Ramstein American HS; Apo New York, NY; (Y); ROTC; SADD; Teachers Aide; Variety Show; JV Stu Cncl; Hon Roll.

POLZINETTI, MARK; De Sales HS; Seneca Falls, NY; (Y); 15/54; Am Leg Boys St; JV Bsktbl; Var Golf; Hon Roll; NHS; Econ.

POMA, MIREILLE; Mamaroneck HS; Larchmont, NY; (Y); French Clb; Varsity Clb; Var Fld Hcky; JV Lcrss; Hon Roll; Soc Studies Hon Awd 84; Frnch Contst 84 & 85 & 86; Bus.

POMERANZ, LARRY; Niskayuna HS; Niskayuna, NY; (Y); Cmnty Wkr; Key Clb; Pres Trs Temple Yth Grp; Var JV Golf; High Hon Roll; NHS; Pres Schlr; Rgnts, Gen Elec Schlrshps; Yeshiva U; Ntrl Sci.

POMEROY, ANTHONY C; Newfane SR HS; Newfane, NY; (S); 10/149; Boy Scts; VP Church Yth Grp; Drama Clb; Math Clb; Math Tm; Band; Church Choir; Concert Band; School Musical; School Play; Boy Scts God/Cntry Awd 84; Egl Sct 85; Brnz & Slvr Plm 85-86; Accntng.

POMICTER, JOHN; Sandy Creek Central HS; Lacona, NY; (Y); VICA; Var L Ftbl; Var L Wrstlng; Technol Coll; Ar Condtng.

POMILIO, JULIANN; Dominican Commercial HS; Brooklyn, NY; (S); 21/273; Cmnty Wkr; Hon Roll; NHS; Siena Clb 83-86; Prncpls List 83-86; Natl Bus Hnr Soc 85; Bus Sec.

POMM, ROBERT; Wayland Central HS; N Cohocton, NY; (Y); 4-H; Math Clb; Band; Jazz Band; Bsbl; Bowling; Diving; Ftbl; Socr; Swmmng; Paul Smiths Coll; Culnry Arts.

PONCE, ALYSSA; Yonkers-Lincoln HS; Yonkers, NY; (Y); Church Yth Grp; Office Aide; Hon Roll; Achvmnt Awd 83-84; Journlst.

POND, HEATHER; Fairport HS; Fairport, NY; (Y); Drama Clb; Stage Crew; Yrbk Stf; Hon Roll; Pres Of Chrch Orntd Grp 86; Yng Wmn Prsnl Prog Awd 85-86; Elem Ed.

POND, SHERRI; Mexico Acad & Central; Mexico, NY; (Y); 15/160; Church Yth Grp; Pres Trs Spanish Clb; Varsity Clb; Color Guard; Yrbk Rptr; Yrbk Stf; Jr Cls; Crs Cntry; Hon Roll; NHS; Bryant U; Ctrl Sci.

PONG, CINDY R; Norwich HS; Norwich, NY; (Y); 9/200; French Clb; Spanish Clb; School Musical; Stu Cncl; Var Tennis; High Hon Roll; NHS; Prfct Atten Awd; Rotary Awd; Spanish NHS; Rgnts Schlrshp 86; Hnr Stu 86; SUNY Buffalo; Pre-Med.

PONSOLLE, MICHELLE R; Pine Bush HS; Pine Bush, NY; (Y); Concert Band; Drm Mjr(t); Mrchg Band; School Musical; Var Swmmng; JV Vllybl; Hon Roll; Jr NHS; NHS.

PONTERIO, LAUREN; Blind Brook HS; Rye Brook, NY; (Y); Spanish Clb; Acpl Chr; Chorus; School Musical; Yrbk Bus Mgr; Var JV Sftbl; Var Capt Vllybl.

PONTICELLO, ANGELO; Mc Quaid Jesuit HS; Pittsford, NY; (Y); 43/175; Church Yth Grp; Cmnty Wkr; Hosp Aide; Ski Clb; SADD; Varsity Clb; Var L Bsbl; Var L Socr; Var Trk; High Hon Roll; Acad Ltr Wnr 85; Pittsford Brighton Pst Sccr Tm 85; SADD Offcr 86; U Of Stds; Law.

PONTILLO, CHRISTINE; Westlake HS; Thornwood, NY; (Y); Pep Clb; Spanish Clb; Yrbk Stf; High Hon Roll; Hon Roll; Spanish NHS; Fashion Inst Tech; Intr Desgn.

PONTON, STEVE; Grand Island HS; Grand Island, NY; (Y); 10/290; Boy Scts; Church Yth Grp; Church Choir; Im Bsbl; Var Tennis; Im Vllybl; High Hon Roll; French Clb; Ski Clb; Spanish Clb; Eagle Scout 83; Law Enfrcmnt.

POOLE, DORRETTA; Gilbertsv Ille Central HS; S New Berlin, NY; (Y); Band; Concert Band; Mrchg Band; Drill Tm; Frsh Cls; Soph Cls; Jr Cls; Sr Cls; Cheerleading; Crs Cntry; Fash Adm.

POOLE, TONYA; James E Sperry HS; Rochester, NY; (Y); Sec Church Yth Grp; DECA; SADD; VICA; Chorus; Church Choir; Yrbk Stf; Rep Jr Cls; Var JV Bsktbl; Hon Roll; Vopros Bst 84-85; Johnson & Wales MCC; Rstrnt Mg.

POON, ANITA; Fontbonne Hall HS; Brooklyn, NY; (Y); 1/133; Cmnty Wkr; Math Tm; Teachers Aide; Nwsp Rptr; Nwsp Stf; Yrbk Stf; Chrmn Sr Cls; Cheerleading; High Hon Roll; NHS; Ranking 2nd Schlrshp 83-84; Ranking 1st Schlrshp 84-86; Boston Coll; Commercial Art.

POON, MELINDA; Midwood HS; Brooklyn, NY; (Y); Art Clb; Cmnty Wkr; Hosp Aide; Library Aide; Office Aide; Spanish Clb; Teachers Aide; Band; Lit Mag; Cit Awd; Howard J Golden Cert Of Apprctn 84; Ldrshp Awd 84; Comm Schltc Achvt 84; Ed.

POON, POKWAN; Seward Park HS; New York, NY; (Y); Office Aide; Teachers Aide; Prfct Atten Awd; Med.

POORAN, NAKECHAN; F D Roosevelt HS; Brooklyn, NY; (Y); 21/587; Math Tm; Quiz Bowl; Hon Roll; JETS Awd; NHS; Prfct Atten Awd; Plytech U; Comp Engnrng.

POPE, EDWARD P; West Babylon HS; W Babylon, NY; (Y); Boy Scts; Cmnty Wkr; Red Cross Aide; SADD; Varsity Clb; Variety Show; Var L Crs Cntry; Var L Trk; Var L Wrstlng; Cit Awd; NYU; Physcl Thrpy.

POPE, PATRICIA; Attica SR HS; Attica, NY; (Y); 11/150; Drama Clb; Band; Concert Band; Mrchg Band; School Musical; School Play; Rep Stu Cncl; Var Tennis; NHS; Buffalo ST U; Crmnl Justice.

POPE, TYANN; Cathedral HS; Ny, NY; (Y); 12/272; FNA; Cert Atten 85-86; 2nd Hnrs Acad 83-86; Math.

POPIEL, AMY; Potsdam Central HS; Potsdam, NY; (Y); Church Yth Grp; Hosp Aide; Ski Clb; Sec Spanish Clb; Varsity Clb; Yrbk Stf; JV Var Cheerleading; JV Var Pom Pon; Phys Thrpy.

POPKIN, DEBBY; Midwood HS; Brooklyn, NY; (Y); 133/667; Yrbk Stf; Lit Mag; Hon Roll; Ntl Merit SF; Psych.

POPLAWSKI, THOMAS J; Middletown HS; Middletown, NY; (Y); Camera Clb; Key Clb; High Hon Roll; NYS Regnts Schlrshp & Achvt Awds 86; NYU Buffalo; Elec Engr.

POPOVICH, PHILLIP; Corning-Painted Post West HS; Ft Washington, PA; (Y); 31/252; JA; Letterman Clb; Bsbl; Bsktbl; Golf; Soccer Keeper; High Hon Roll; Hon Roll; NHS; Pres Schlr; PA ST U; Med Rsrch.

POPOWSKI, CHRIS; Rome Free Acad; Rome, NY; (Y); JV Bsktbl; JV Socr; JV Vllybl; Pilot.

POPPITI, KIMBERLY D; New Field HS; Lelden, NY; (Y); SADD; Variety Show; Jr NHS; Natl Medl-Horsmnshp 84-86; ASPCA Maclay Hrsmnshp Fnls NY 84-86; Top 10 Natl PHA 85-86; SUNY Stony Brook.

POPPLETON, MICHELLE L; Williamsville North HS; E Amherst, NY; (Y); 16/301; Chorus; Madrigals; Nwsp Stf; Trs Stu Cncl; Var Capt Socr; High Hon Roll; NHS; Am Leg Aux Girls St; Chorus 84-86; NY All State Chors 85-86; NYSSMA Cmptn Prfct Rtng Mixd Chors 82-86; Boston U; Comms.

PORCELLI, JEFFREY; Cardinal Mooney HS; Rochester, NY; (Y); 12/304; Exploring; Hosp Aide; Ski Clb; JV Ftbl; Bausch & Lomb Sci Awd; High Hon Roll; Hon Roll; Ntl Merit Ltr; U Buffalo Hnr Pgm Schlrshp 86; Weymans Fd Mkts Schlrshp 86; SUNY Buffalo; Elec Engrng.

PORES, JOSEPH; Hicksville HS; Hicksville, NY; (Y); Science Clb; Band; Mrchg Band; Stu Cncl; Im Lcrss; NHS; Hnrbl Mntn Sci Congrs 86; NY Schl Chiropractic.

PORN, MARY; Bishop Grimes HS; Clay, NY; (Y); Church Yth Grp; Cmnty Wkr; Yrbk Stf; JV Capt Bsktbl; Var Tennis; High Hon Roll; NHS; Vrsty Ltr For Tnns 86; Rcgntn For Cmndbl Wrk In Engl 86; Le Moyne; Bio-Chem.

POROSKY, CHRIS; Notre Dame HS; Elmira, NY; (Y); 16/88; Chess Clb; Math Clb; School Play; Crs Cntry; Trk; French Hon Soc; St Schlr; Clarkson U; Compu Engrng.

PORPORA, TRACEY ANN; Tohenville HS; Staten Isld, NY; (Y); Latin Clb; Yrbk Rptr; Yrbk Stf; Cheerleading; Prfct Atten Awd; Classics Inst; Lbrl Arts.

PORRAS, CAROLYN; Fashion Industri; Brooklyn, NY; (Y); Dance Clb; English Clb; Service Clb; Teachers Aide; Sftbl; Vllybl; Hon Roll; Prfct Atten Awd; Lawyer.

PORTALES, KAREN; George Hewlett HS; Hewlett, NY; (Y); 5/262; Church Yth Grp; Cmnty Wkr; Pres French Clb; Nwsp Rptr; Lit Mag; Rep Stu Cncl; Hon Roll; Rep Frsh Cls; Rep Soph Cls; Rep Jr Cls; Natl Frnch Cont 3rd Pl Nassau Cnty 86; Natl Hspnc Schlr 86; Natl Frnch Cont 5th Pl Nassau Cnty 85; U Of PA.

PORTELLE, SARA; Tottenville HS; Staten Island, NY; (Y); FNA; Hosp Aide; Pom Pon; Cert & Pin Nrsg Asst 86; Coll Staten Island; Tchg.

PORTEOUS, LEIGH; Albion HS; Albion, NY; (Y); 20/176; JA; Trs Spanish Clb; Band; Pres Frsh Cls; Rep Jr Cls; Var Capt Cheerleading; JV Var Sftbl; Cngrssnl Schlr Of Natl Yng Ldrs Conf 86; ST U Of NY; Ecnmcs.

PORTER, AMY; Poland Central Schl; Cold Brook, NY; (Y); 3/62; Drama Clb; French Clb; SADD; Concert Band; Yrbk Ed-Chief; Frsh Cls; Soph Cls; Stu Cncl; JV Cheerleading; JV Socr; Utica Schl Cmmrce; Admn Secy.

PORTER, CANDACE; Grand Island HS; Grand Island, NY; (Y); 27/300; Cmnty Wkr; Dance Clb; French Clb; Library Aide; SADD; Band; Church Choir; Concert Band; Mrchg Band; Pep Band; Engrng.

PORTER, CHRIS; Fabius-Pompey HS; Apulia Station, NY; (Y); Var L Bsktbl; Hon Roll; Letterman Clb; Varsity Clb; All Star Team Lafayette Bsktbl 85; JR Prom Ct 86; Conservation.

PORTER, DAWN; Grand Island HS; Gr Island, NY; (Y); 12/297; Hosp Aide; Yrbk Sprt Ed; Hst Jr Cls; Hst Sr Cls; Stu Cncl; Var Capt Socr; Var L Vllybl; Hon Roll; NHS; Acadmc Achvt Awd; Apprectn Wrk Specl Olympcs; Ithaca Coll; Physcl Therpy.

PORTER, ELIZABETH; Oakwood Schl; Poughkeepsie, NY; (Y); AFS; Pres French Clb; Varsity Clb; Chorus; Yrbk Bus Mgr; VP Jr Cls; VP Sr Cls; Var Capt Cheerleading; Var Socr; Var Sftbl; Paul Pfetze Merit Schlrshp Oakwood 83-87; Disarmament Committee 83-85; Cornell.

PORTER, JACQUELINE; Saugerties HS; Saugerties, NY; (Y); Tuitn Schlrshp Brkly Coll 86; Berkely; Bus.

PORTER, KATHY; Bishop Grimes HS; N Syracuse, NY; (S); Exploring; Var Bsktbl; Var Socr; JV Sftbl; High Hon Roll; Hon Roll; NHS; Vet Med.

PORTER, LAURA; Oakfield-Alabama Central HS; Oakfield, NY; (Y); Yrbk Stf; Var L Socr; JV Var Sftbl; Genesee CC.

PORTER, SHAWN; G Ray Bodley HS; Fulton, NY; (Y); Church Yth Grp; Var Tennis; Var Trk; High Hon Roll; NHS; Chess Clb; Science Clb; Chorus; Stu Cncl; Var Crs Cntry; Acad Achvt Awd Soc Stds 84; Bus Admn.

PORTER, TIFFANY; West Seneca East SR HS; W Seneca, NY; (Y); Church Yth Grp; Library Aide; Ski Clb; Church Choir; Nwsp Phtg; Hon Roll; Oral Roberts U; Nsrg.

PORTERFIELD, CHARLES A; Vestal Central HS; Apalachin, NY; (Y); 77/435; Boy Scts; Pres Intnl Clb; Band; Off Mrchg Band; Orch; Lcrss; NHS; Ntl Merit Ltr; Exclnce Awd 86; Regnts Schlrshp 86; PA ST; Elec Engrg.

PORTIS, KERI L; Roosevelt JR SR HS; Roosevelt, NY; (S); Church Yth Grp; Pres SADD; Band; Church Choir; Concert Band; Mrchg Band; School Play; Yrbk Stf; Hon Roll; NY ST Miss Black Teen 84; Chrch Schl Asst Sprintndnt 85-86; Hampton Inst; Pblc Rltns.

PORTO, MARYANNE; Holland Central HS; South Wales, NY; (Y); 5/100; Varsity Clb; Fld Hcky; High Hon Roll; Hon Roll; Jr NHS; NHS; Regents Schlrshp 86; Suny At Buffalo; Pharmacy.

PORTORREAL, LEYNA; William Howard Tait HS; Bronx, NY; (Y); Office Aide; Teachers Aide; NHS; Prfct Atten Awd; ST U New Paltz; Compu Dsgn.

POSANKA, ELAINE; Ward Melville HS; E Setauket, NY; (Y); 175/675; Drama Clb; German Clb; Library Aide; SADD; Mrchg Band; School Play; Nwsp Rptr; Nwsp Stf; Yrbk Stf; Hon Roll; German Awd-Plcmt; Slvr Cert-Hnr Roll; Rgnts Schlrshp Awd; Regis Coll; Eng.

POSELUZNY, ANNETTE B; W C Bryant HS; Woodside, NY; (Y); 18/623; Hosp Aide; Sec Key Clb; Science Clb; Church Choir; Orch; Nwsp Rptr; Lit Mag; Capt Swmmng; NHS; Westinghouse Sci Tlnt Srch SF 85-86; Equitable Schlr Ath Awd 86; Otto Burgdorf Sci Comptn Wnnr 86; U Buffalo; Phys Thrpy.

POSILLICO, DOROTHEA; Westbury SR HS; Westbury, NY; (Y); 28/275; Church Yth Grp; Cmnty Wkr; Var Bowling; JV Cheerleading; Hon Roll; NCTE Awd; Finance.

POSKOSH, SCOTT; Midwood HS; Brooklyn, NY; (Y); 291/559; Chess Clb; Computer Clb; Color Guard; Orch; School Musical; School Play; Lit Mag; Prfct Atten Awd; Rgnts Schlrshp 86; SUNY Coll; Comp Sci.

POSNER, FELICIA; John F Kennedy HS; Merrick, NY; (Y); Trs Band; Concert Band; Var Sftbl; Hon Roll; Jr NHS; Math Clb; Math Tm; SADD; Temple Yth Grp; Yrbk Stf; Psych.

POSSER, JOCELYN; Academy Of St Joseph; Nesconset, NY; (Y); Hosp Aide; Library Aide; Spanish Clb; Orch; Nwsp Rptr; Nwsp Stf; Stu Cncl; NEDT Awd; NY ST Regnts & NY Telephn Acadmc Schlrshps 86; SUNY Stony Brook; Atty.

POST, JESSE; Coxsackie-Athens HS; Coxsackie, NY; (Y); 28/105; Am Leg Boys St; Band; Chorus; Bsbl; Bsktbl; Ftbl; Gym; Socr; High Hon Roll; Hon Roll; Hudson Vly CC; Engrng.

POST, ROBERT; Alexander Central Schl; Alexander, NY; (Y); JV Bsbl; Jr NHS; Comp Sci.

POSTAL, GREGORY J; Amityville Memorial HS; Amityville, NY; (Y); 5/210; Drama Clb; Temple Yth Grp; Nwsp Ed-Chief; NHS; Ntl Merit Ltr; Cmnty Wkr; School Play; Nwsp Stf; Rgnl Wnnr Ntl Hist Day 86; ; Fndr & Chrmn HSIC 85-86; Chair LIF Tmpl Yth Scl Actcon Comm 84-86; Brandeis U; Pre-Med.

POSTEL, NANCY; Hendrick Hudson HS; Montrose, NY; (Y); Church Yth Grp; SADD; Variety Show; Yrbk Sprt Ed; Var Capt Cheerleading; Var Fld Hcky; Var Capt Socr; High Hon Roll; Hon Roll; Sec NHS; Intl Bus.

POSTELL, WILLIAM; Cicero N Syracuse HS; Brewerton, NY; (S); 34/623; Var JV Bsktbl; Var JV Lcrss; Elec Engrng.

POTENZA, DAMON F; Archbishop Stepinac HS; Yorktown Hts, NY; (Y); 3/195; Church Yth Grp; Civic Clb; Cmnty Wkr; Computer Clb; Debate Tm; Intnl Clb; JA; Radio Clb; Science Clb; Yrbk Stf; Holy Cross Bk Awd 85; I TV Anchorman Awd, Sons Italy Schlrhsp 86; Vassar Coll; Med.

POTENZA, PATRICIA L; Queensbury HS; Queensbury, NY; (Y); 26/253; Drama Clb; Trs French Clb; Red Cross Aide; SADD; School Musical; Sec Stu Cncl; High Hon Roll; NHS; Teachers Aide; Church Choir; Pres Clssrm Grad 86; Regents Schlrshp Wnnr 86; ST Lawrence U; Psychology.

POTENZA, PHIL; Clarkstown North HS; New City, NY; (Y); Var Ftbl; Var Trk; Hon Roll; NHS; Coachs Awd-Sprg Trck 86; Law.

POTOWSKI, KIMBERLY; Commack HS; Commack, NY; (Y); Spanish Clb; Drm Mjr(t); Jazz Band; Symp Band; Yrbk Phtg; Var L Crs Cntry; Var L Trk; High Hon Roll; NHS; Ntl Merit Ltr; Wlgdn Quill Awd 84; NY ST Music Assn Awd Excllnc Flute 84-86; Cornell U; Frgn Lang.

POTTER, ANNA; Cazenovia HS; Cazenovia, NY; (Y); Drama Clb; Chorus; School Musical; Yrbk Stf; VP Soph Cls; Pres Stu Cncl; JV Cheerleading; Var Socr; Hon Roll; NHS; Bus.

POTTER, ELIZABETH S; Chapin Schl; New York City, NY; (Y); Cmnty Wkr; Hosp Aide; JCL; Latin Clb; Red Cross Aide; Teachers Aide; Chorus; Yrbk Stf; Frsh Cls; Jr Cls; Untd Hsptl Fnd Vlntr Srv Awd; Hrvrd U; Hedonist.

POTTER, JON C; Skaneateles HS; Skaneateles, NY; (Y); 27/154; Yrbk Ed-Chief; Yrbk Stf; Lit Mag; High Hon Roll; Hon Roll; NHS; 1st Prz Natl Lgue Of Pen Womens Poetry Cntst 86; Rgnts Schlrshp 86; Natl Merit Schlrshp Prog 86; Genespo ST U; Psych.

POTTER, MARY ANNE; James E Sperry HS; Rochester, NY; (Y); 37/275; Church Yth Grp; French Clb; GAA; SADD; Teachers Aide; Coach Actv; Score Keeper; Sftbl; French Hon Soc; High Hon Roll; Monroe Comm Coll; Elem Ed Tchr.

POTTER, REBECCA J; Schalmont HS; Duanesburg, NY; (Y); Pres VP 4-H; Chorus; Concert Band; Yrbk Stf; JV Capt Bsktbl; Var Capt Socr; Cit Awd; 4-H Awd; High Hon Roll; Sec NHS; The Stephen Mazzarella Mem Awd 84; AAHPERD Achvt Awd 86; Grand Champ Pon Of Saratoga Cnty Fair 85.

POTTER, ROBYN; Vestal SR HS; Vestal, NY; (Y); SADD; Hon Roll; AZ ST U; Bus.

POTTINGER, PAUL S; Riverdale Country Schl; New York, NY; (Y); Model UN; Nwsp Rptr; Ed Nwsp Stf; Lit Mag; Hon Roll; NCTE Awd; Ntl Merit SF; Vrsty Fncng Tm Capt & MVP 84-85; Outstndng Engl Stu 85; Engl.

POTTS, KATRINA; Clarkstown South HS; Bardonia, NY; (Y); Drama Clb; German Clb; Band; Jazz Band; Nwsp Stf; Off Frsh Cls; Off Soph Cls; Rep Jr Cls; High Hon Roll; Jr NHS; Acad All-Amer; Crdlgst.

POTTS, SUSAN; Cardinal Ohara HS; North Tonawanda, NY; (S); 1/128; Camp Fr Inc; Church Yth Grp; Ski Clb; VP Spanish Clb; Stage Crew; Rep Frsh Cls; Stat Bsktbl; JV Bowling; Var Crs Cntry; Stat Socr; Natl Hnr Soc Schlrp 85-86; Chem.

POUCHER, MICHELLE; Allegany Central HS; Allegany, NY; (Y); Church Yth Grp; Pep Clb; Concert Band; Mrchg Band; JV Var Cheerleading; JV Swmmng; JV Trk; High Hon Roll; NHS; Hmcmng Attendant; Med.

POULIN, AMANDA; Berlin Central HS; Cropseyville, NY; (S); 6/72; Church Yth Grp; 4-H; Science Clb; Chorus; Drill Tm; JV Cheerleading; JV Var Socr; 4-H Awd; High Hon Roll; NHS; Cobleskill; Vet.

POULIOT, LINDA; Corcoran HS; Syracuse, NY; (Y); Hosp Aide; SADD; Var Capt Crs Cntry; Var Capt Trk; High Hon Roll; Hon Roll; Jr NHS; MVP Indoor Trck 86; C Irving Mem Hosp Schl; Nrsng.

POULIOT, MICHELLE; Kendall JR SR HS; Kendall, NY; (Y); Sec Art Clb; Aud/Vis; Pres Sec Church Yth Grp; Drama Clb; Girl Scts; Pep Clb; Band; Chorus; Concert Band; Jazz Band; Music Tchng.

POULIS, ATHENA; Hillcrest HS; Jamaica, NY; (Y); Church Yth Grp; Cmnty Wkr; Dance Clb; Intnl Clb; Office Aide; Nwsp Rptr; Yrbk Stf; Lit Mag; Hon Roll; Schl Intl Stds 84-86; Paintng Indstry Schlrshp Awd 86-87; Stonybrook; Clncl Psychlgy.

POULOUTIDES, JOHN; Ossinging HS; Ossining, NY; (Y); Band; Concert Band; Mrchg Band; Symp Band; Var Capt Ice Hcky; High Hon Roll; Hon Roll.

POULSEN, CYNTHIA; Pulaski JR SR HS; Pulaski, NY; (Y); Math Clb; Chorus; Color Guard; Hon Roll.

POUND, LAURA; Frontier Central HS; Hamburg, NY; (S); 24/440; Church Yth Grp; Red Cross Aide; Ski Clb; Band; Rep Soph Cls; Socr; High Hon Roll; Hon Roll; NHS; NEDT Awd; Ntl Frnch Contst Awd 84-85; Ntl Hstry & Govt Awd 85; U Of Buffalo; Intl Reltns.

POUPORE, LAURIE; Northern Adirondack Central HS; Churubusco, NY; (Y); Church Yth Grp; Drama Clb; Sec FFA; Pep Clb; Nwsp Ed-Chief; Nwsp Rptr; Yrbk Stf; Sec Frsh Cls; JV Var Score Keeper; Sftbl; FFA Empire Deg 86; Cnty Dairy Maid 86; Comm.

POURIA, DANIELLE C; Sewanhaka HS; New Hyde Pk, NY; (Y); DECA; Chorus; Variety Show; Cheerleading; Bus Hon Soc 86; Bus Admin.

POVOL, JILL; Spackenill HS; Poughkeepsie, NY; (Y); 50/174; VP Leo Clb; Ski Clb; SADD; Temple Yth Grp; Thesps; Band; Pep Band; School Musical; School Play; Yrbk Phtg; Accntng.

POWALOWSKI, BRIAN; St Marys HS; Cheektowaga, NY; (Y); 32/184; Boy Scts; Red Cross Aide; Ski Clb; SADD; Varsity Clb; Church Choir; Stage Crew; JV Crs Cntry; Var Socr; Var Trk; Naval Acad; Aviation Pilot.

POWELL, JAMES; Lake George HS; Lk George, NY; (Y); 2/73; Am Leg Boys St; Pres German Clb; SADD; School Play; Pres Jr Cls; Pres Sr Cls; JV Var Bsktbl; Im Vllybl; DAR Awd; VP NHS; Williams Clg Bk Awd 85; AFROTC Full Tuin Schlrshp 86; Adirondack Balln Fest Aerontc Schlrshp 86; Boston U; Metrlgy.

POWELL, JENNIFER; Harpursville JR SR HS; Binghamton, NY; (Y); 4/85; Band; Trs Stu Cncl; Var L Sftbl; High Hon Roll; NHS; Prfct Atten Awd; Pres Schlr; Ski Clb; Spanish Clb; Chorus; Babe Rth Awd; US Army Rsvr Ntl Schlr Athle Awd; Outstndng Fml Athlt Awd; Broome CC; Engrng Sci.

POWELL, KI; Lake George HS; Lake George, NY; (Y); 26/74; German Clb; Band; Chorus; Color Guard; Mrchg Band; School Musical; School Play; Bsktbl; Bowling; Vllybl; Acctg.

POWELL, SHANNON; Stamford Central Schl; Stamford, NY; (Y); 7/37; Cmnty Wkr; French Clb; Teachers Aide; Acpl Chr; Band; School Musical; Swing Chorus; Yrbk Stf; Cit Awd; Church Yth Grp; NYSMA Vocal Music 85 & 86; NY Spec Olympcs Vlntr 83-86; Catskill Cmmnty Chorale Soc Awd 85; Music Thrpy.

POWELL, SHARON; Greenville Central Schl; Earlton, NY; (Y); 16/70; Key Clb; Yrbk Stf; Bus Admin.

POWELL, TERESA; Westbury HS; Westbury, NY; (Y); Intnl Clb; Key Clb; JV Bowling; Var Sftbl; Var Im Vllybl; Hon Roll; Kiwanis Awd; Accntnt.

POWER, ANNE; St Vincent Ferrer HS; Astoria, NY; (Y); 20/115; Church Yth Grp; Service Clb; Variety Show; Rep Frsh Cls; Pres Soph Cls; Rep Jr Cls; Stu Cncl; Cheerleading; Hon Roll; Philips Beth Israel Nrsng Schshp 86-87; Nrsng Regents Schlrshp 86-87; Beth Israel Schl Nrsng; RN.

POWER, BRIAN; Mahopac HS; Mahopac, NY; (Y); 91/309; Aud/Vis; Radio Clb; Stage Crew; Rep Frsh Cls; L Var Lcrss; Hon Roll; Commnctns.

POWER, KERRY; St Vincent Ferrer HS; Sunnyside, NY; (Y); 45/109; Church Yth Grp; Church Choir; St Jhns U; Bus.

POWERS, AMY E; Shenendehowa HS; Clifton Park, NY; (Y); 33/675; Drama Clb; Key Clb; Ski Clb; Stage Crew; Yrbk Phtg; Yrbk Stf; Mgr Bsktbl; JV Cheerleading; High Hon Roll; NHS; Rgnts Schlrshp; U Of VT; Bus.

POWERS, CHRISTOPHER; E J Wilson HS; Rochester, NY; (Y); Am Leg Boys St; French Clb; Band; Concert Band; Mrchg Band; Bsbl; Socr; High Hon Roll; Engrng.

POWERS, CLARE; Mercy HS; Riverhead, NY; (Y); Church Yth Grp; Drama Clb; Ski Clb; Varsity Clb; Church Choir; Color Guard; Drill Tm; Drm & Bgl; Drm Mjr(t); Flag Corp.

POWERS, DONALD; Hilton Central HS; Hilton, NY; (Y); Letterman Clb; Varsity Clb; Nwsp Sprt Ed; Var Capt Crs Cntry; Ftbl; Var Capt Trk; Art Clb; Cmnty Wkr; High Hon Roll; Mst Outstndng Trk Undrclsmn 86; All Cnty, Div Chmps, 2nd Sect Trk 85; Chmpshp Tm 84; LIU; Art.

POWERS II, GERALD J; Le Roy HS; Leroy, NY; (Y); Camera Clb; Church Yth Grp; Letterman Clb; Varsity Clb; Var Ftbl; JV Golf; Im Ice Hcky; Im Lcrss; Im Wt Lftg; Engrng.

POWERS, JOSEPH E; Babylon HS; Babylon, NY; (Y); 6/179; Cmnty Wkr; Dance Clb; Church Choir; Rep Jr Cls; Rep Sr Cls; Rep Stu Cncl; JV Var Bsbl; JV Var Socr; High Hon Roll; NHS; Babylon Comm Schlrshp 86; NYS Regnts Schlrshp 86; Clarkson U; Engrng.

POWERS, KATHRYN; Babylon HS; Babylon, NY; (Y); Am Leg Aux Girls St; Cmnty Wkr; Dance Clb; Church Choir; Rep Sr Cls; Var JV Fld Hcky; High Hon Roll; NHS; Varsity Clb; Variety Show; Natl Sci Olympd 84-85; Babylon Tchrs Assn Bus Awd 85-86; All Lg Fld Hcky Awd 84-85; Bus.

POWERS, KIM; Maria Regina HS; Yonkers, NY; (Y); Varsity Clb; Var Capt Bsktbl; Var Sftbl; Rk Of Yr Bsktbll 83-84; Otstndng Plyr Bstkbll 84-85; Bus.

POWERS, LAURA; New Rochelle HS; New Rochelle, NY; (Y); Church Yth Grp; Civic Clb; Math Tm; Chrmn Model UN; Symp Band; Lit Mag; Im Var Sftbl; NHS; Spanish NHS; Chrstn Actn Awd Nw Rochll HS Rlgn 86; Isaac E Young JHS 9th Grd Bnd & Phys Ed Awd 84.

POWERS, LYNN; The Franciscan Acad; Baldwinsville, NY; (Y); Art Clb; Drama Clb; GAA; JA; Nwsp Rptr; Var L Bsktbl; Hon Roll; NHS; Chess Clb; Conf Upstate Schls All Leag Awd MVP Bsktbl 86; Georgetown U; Bus.

POWERS, MICHAEL; Center Moriches HS; Center Moriches, NY; (Y); 6/91; Drama Clb; French Clb; VP Service Clb; Band; Chorus; School Musical; Sec Soph Cls; L Var Crs Cntry; NHS; Nwsp Stf; Piano 9 Yrs; Theatre.

POWERS, STEPHANIE; Brushton-Moira Central HS; Moira, NY; (Y); French Clb; SADD; Band; Chorus; Rep Stu Cncl; Hon Roll; Stoney Brook U; Physcl Thrpy.

POWERS, STEPHEN J; West Seneca West SR HS; West Seneca, NY; (Y); 26/559; Chorus; Church Choir; School Musical; CC Awd; Hon Roll; JC Awd; NHS; Westminster Choir Coll; Mus.

POWERS, TAMMY; Moravia HS; Moravia, NY; (Y); French Clb; JV Var Vllybl; Bus.

POWLESS, BRADLEY; Lafayette HS; Nedrow, NY; (Y); JV Bsktbl; Var L Ftbl; Var L Lcrss; Hon Roll; Bwmn Indn Schlrshp 86; Rdny Greene Mem Sprtsmnshp Awd 86; Nzrth Coll; Elem Ed.

POWLESS, DAWN M; Lockport SR HS; Lockport, NY; (Y); 59/412; Latin Clb; Yrbk Stf; Pres Frsh Cls; Rep Soph Cls; Rep Jr Cls; Rep Sr Cls; Rep Stu Cncl; Var Capt Cheerleading; Hon Roll; Jr NHS; New York St Rgnts Schlrshp; U Of FL; Psych.

POWLEY, JOHN FRANCIS; Lyndonville Central/L A Webber HS; Lyndonville, NY; (S); 3/90; Church Yth Grp; Computer Clb; Math Clb; Science Clb; Varsity Clb; Band; Concert Band; Mrchg Band; Stage Crew; JV Mgr(s); Stdnt Mnth 84; Schlr Athl 85; Sci.

POYNEER, RACHAEL; Elmira Free Acad; Elmira, NY; (Y); Church Yth Grp; Acpl Chr; Chorus; High Hon Roll; Perf Atten 84-85; Corning CC; Sec.

POYNTON, MISSY; Silver Creek Central HS; Silver Creek, NY; (Y); Girl Scts; Hosp Aide; Ski Clb; Spanish Clb; Chorus; School Musical; Cheerleading; Sftbl; Trk; Nazareth Coll Rochester; Mus.

POZIN, DINA; Valley Stream North HS; Malverne, NY; (Y); Debate Tm; Pres 4-H; FTA; Spanish Clb; Temple Yth Grp; Nwsp Stf; 4-H Awd; High Hon Roll; Hon Roll; NHS; Spnsh II Awd Hghst Avg 84-85; Acctg.

POZO, HUMBERTO; Bushwick HS; Brooklyn, NY; (S); JA; Jr NHS; Columbia U; Astrnmy.

POZZA, KARI; Arlington HS; Pleasant Vly, NY; (Y); 149/565; NY ST Rgnts Schlrsh& 85-86; Certs Of Merit 86; SUNY A&t Cobleskill; Hrs Hsbnd.

POZZA, KARINA L; Arlington HS; Pleasant Valley, NY; (Y); 149/565; NYS Regnts Schlrshp 86; SUNY Cobleskill; Horse Hsbndry.

POZZI, JOHN; Seton Chatholic HS; Endwell, NY; (Y); Varsity Clb; Bsktbl; L Ftbl; L Trk; Wrstlng; Alfred ST; Bus.

PRADO, JAVIER; The Nichols Schl; Williamsville, NY; (Y); Chess Clb; Ski Clb; Var L Bsbl; Var L Golf; Bus.

PRAGMAN, CHRISTOPHER; Franklin Delano Roosevelt HS; Hyde Park, NY; (Y); 29/200; Library Aide; Math Tm; Acpl Chr; Band; Chorus; Concert Band; Jazz Band; Mrchg Band; Orch; School Musical; Cooper Union Schl Engrng Schlrshp, Schl Play Lead 86; Cooper Union; Aerontcl Engrng.

PRAINITO, ANN M; Ossining HS; Ossining, NY; (Y); Boy Scts; Exploring; French Clb; Red Cross Aide; Chorus; Gym; Var Mgr(s); Trk; Hon Roll; Westchester CC; Nrsng.

PRAIRIE, LISA; Centereach HS; Centereach, NY; (Y); JV Fld Hcky; Capt Var Sftbl; Hon Roll; All ST MARYA Sftbl 85; Centereach Vrsty Coachs Awd 86; MI ST; Criml Justice.

PRASAD, ANJANA; Huntington HS; Huntington, NY; (Y); AFS; Hosp Aide; Socr; Elec Engnrng.

PRASAD, SANJIV; Vestal HS; Binghamton, NY; (Y); 16/430; Mathletes; Varsity Clb; Var Capt Socr; Tennis; Var L Trk; Wt Lftg; Hon Roll; NHS; All Stac All Star Soccer Midfielder 84-85; Vestal Soccer Acad Awd 85; Intl French Language Awd 83; Cornell U; Pre-Med.

PRASHAW, LISA; Massena Central HS; Massena, NY; (Y); Church Yth Grp; Teachers Aide; Band; Mrchg Band; JV Cheerleading; Powder Puff Ftbl; Var Trk; JV Var Vllybl; Hon Roll; NHS; U VT; Engrng.

PRASS, MICHELLE; George Wingate HS; Brooklyn, NY; (Y); Bsbl.

PRATER, LONNIE; Bishop Loughlin HS; Brooklyn, NY; (Y); Wt Lftg.

PRATT, DANIEL; Mechanicville HS; Mechanicville, NY; (S); Math Tm; Spanish Clb; SADD; Varsity Clb; Band; Trs Stu Cncl; JV Var Socr; Var Wrstlng; Cit Awd; DAR Awd; Vrsty Wrstlg Mst Imprvd 84-85; Omega & Alpha Hnr Socty 84-86.

PRATT, JENNIFER; Roy C Ketcham HS; Wappingers Fls, NY; (Y); Church Yth Grp; Cmnty Wkr; Var Capt Gym; High Hon Roll; Hon Roll; NHS.

PRATT, JOSEPH C; Dundee HS; Dundee, NY; (Y); 22/83; Am Leg Boys St; Varsity Clb; Band; Chorus; Concert Band; Jazz Band; Mrchg Band; Var L Bsktbl; Var L Tennis; Tennis MVP 85-86; :Sports Med.

PRATT, JULIANNE E; Medina SR HS; Medina, NY; (Y); 11/160; Church Yth Grp; Hosp Aide; Band; Socr; Var Capt Swmmng; Var Trk; Hon Roll; NHS; Rgnts Schlrshp 86; Daisy Chain 85; Ithaca Coll; Bio.

PRATT, MELISSA M; Granville Central HS; Middle Granville, NY; (Y); 13/134; Church Yth Grp; Spanish Clb; SADD; Church Choir; Var L Bsktbl; Var L Fld Hcky; Var L Sftbl; Var L Vllybl; Hon Roll; Regnts Schlrshp 86; Cortland ST U; Phys Educ.

PRATT, STEVEN B; Holland Patent HS; Holland Patent, NY; (Y); 6/145; Am Leg Boys St; Boy Scts; Church Yth Grp; FTA; Varsity Clb; Chorus; Variety Show; Yrbk Stf; Var Bsbl; Capt Socr; Colagate U; Phys Tchr.

PRAUL, DARRYL S; Mynderse Academy; Seneca Falls, NY; (Y); 3/150; Am Leg Boys St; Church Yth Grp; French Clb; SADD; Varsity Clb; School Musical; School Play; Stage Crew; Yrbk Sprt Ed; Rep Stu Cncl; Sprtsmmnshp Awd; Cornell U; Med.

PRAY, EMILY; Newburgh Free Acad; New Windsor, NY; (Y); Pres VP 4-H; French Clb; Library Aide; SADD; Yrbk Stf; 4-H Awd; Hon Roll.

PRAY, MICHAEL T; Newburgh Free Acad; New Windsor, NY; (Y); Aud/Vis; Computer Clb; Drama Clb; 4-H; Scholastic Bowl; Science Clb; School Play; Stage Crew; Var L Vllybl; Hon Roll; Geneseo ST; Vet Med.

PRAY, VICKI; Wayne Central HS; Ontario, NY; (Y); Church Yth Grp; Trs Exploring; Girl Scts; SADD; Yrbk Stf; JV Socr; Hon Roll; NHS; Acad Achvt Frnch III 84-85; Grl Scout Silv Awd 83-84; Nazareth Coll; Spec Ed.

PREAU, EDNA; Murry Bergtraum HS; Brooklyn, NY; (Y); Church Yth Grp; Church Choir; Variety Show; Yrbk Stf; Dly Nws Ynkees Hnr Pgm 85; NY Cnty Tricntnnl Cmmemrtn Cntst 84; Law.

PRECHTL, RUSSELL F; Ithaca HS; Pine Valley, NY; (Y); Am Leg Boys St; Boy Scts; Cmnty Wkr; Exploring; Service Clb; Chorus; Jr NHS; Phys Asst.

PREFER, KATHLEEN A; Susan E Wagner HS; Staten Island, NY; (Y); 75/466; Girl Scts; Hosp Aide; Office Aide; Chorus; Ed Yrbk Stf; Lit Mag; Var Crs Cntry; Hon Roll; NHS; Rotary Awd; Grl Sct Gold Awd 85; Spch And Hearng Essy Cntst Wnnr 85; NYS Regnts Nrsg Schlrshp 86; St Vincents Sch Nrsg; Nrsg.

PREIS, PAMELA A; Longwood SR HS; Middle Island, NY; (S); 12/487; Church Yth Grp; SADD; Chorus; Drm & Bgl; Var Bowling; Coach Actv; High Hon Roll; Jr NHS; NHS; Prfct Atten Awd; Elem Ed.

PREISCHE, SCOTT; Herkimer SR HS; Herkimer, NY; (Y); 13/100; Spanish Clb; Band; Concert Band; Mrchg Band; Var L Bsbl; Var L Bsktbl; Var L Ftbl; Im Vllybl; Im Wt Lftg; Im Wrstlng; Al-Conf Plyr Bsbl/Ptchr 86; Radiolgy.

PREISCHEL, JEFFREY SCOTT; Eden SR HS; Eden, NY; (Y); AFS; Band; Chorus; Jazz Band; Orch; L Swmmng; All ST Zone Orch,Chorus 82-86; SUNY; Sound Recordng.

PREISCHEL, MARK; Eden SR HS; Eden, NY; (Y); 7/163; AFS; Aud/Vis; 4-H; Varsity Clb; JV Socr; Var Swmmng; 4-H Awd; High Hon Roll; NHS; Pres Schlr; Gen U Scholar U Cincinnati 86-87; NYS Regents Scholar 86-87; U Cincinnati; Aerospc Engrng.

PREISSLER, MICHAEL F; Tuxedo HS; Tuxedo Park, NY; (Y); 12/98; Math Tm; Ski Clb; Spanish Clb; Rep Stu Cncl; Var Capt Bsbl; Var Socr; Trk; High Hon Roll; Hon Roll; Jr NHS; Rensselaer Plytech Inst; Engr.

PREMOCK, BRIAN P; Owego Free Acad; Apalachin, NY; (Y); 5/220; Trs Church Yth Grp; Pres Exploring; Key Clb; Off Stu Cncl; Var Vllybl; High Hon Roll; Pres NHS; Rotary Awd; JV Bowling; Var Tennis; IBM Thomas J Watson Mem Schlrshp 86; Rotary Yth Ldrshp Awd 85; Gannett Nwspr Carrier Schlrshp 86; Penn ST U; Elec Engrng.

PREMUS, JENNIFER M; Goshen Central HS; Goshen, NY; (Y); Cmnty Wkr; Band; Concert Band; NHS; NY ST Regents Schlrshp 86; Art Achvt Awd 82; ST U Of NY Binghampton; Bio.

PRENEVAU, WILLIAM; Williamsville North HS; E Amherst, NY; (Y); DECA; Ski Clb; Spanish Clb; SADD; Yrbk Stf; JV Bsbl; Capt Var Ftbl; Var Tennis; Wt Lftg; Bus Adm.

PRENO, CHRISTOPHER A; Ogdensburg Free Acad; Odgdensburg, NY; (Y); 42/200; Am Leg Boys St; Sec Church Yth Grp; Key Clb; Pep Clb; Hon Roll; Var JV Ftbl; JV Ice Hcky; JV Socr; Var JV Trk; Im Vllybl; Wrld Hstry Cntst Wnnr 85; Envrnmntl Engrng.

PRENTICE, TODD; Oakfield-Alabama Central HS; Oakfield, NY; (Y); Church Yth Grp; Drama Clb; Church Choir; Ftbl; Trk; Cert Hnr Scl Stud 83-84; MP Army.

PRESCOTT, DEBORAH; Mercy HS; Albany, NY; (Y); School Play; Stage Crew; High Hon Roll; Hon Roll; Psychl Sci & Socl Stds Achvt Awds 83; Art Awd & Cert For Being Art Shw 86; ST U Albany; Psych.

PRESCOTT, MARIA; M Bergraum H S For Business Careers; Brooklyn, NY; (Y); Dance Clb; Teachers Aide; Chorus; School Play; Nwsp Rptr; Yrbk Ed-Chief; Yrbk Rptr; Hon Roll; NHS; Sal; Mck Trl Trnmnt Lwyr 86.

PRESLEY, SANDRA; Trott Vocational HS; Niagara Falls, NY; (Y); Air Force; Comp.

PRESS, ALAN L; Ardsley HS; Ardsley, NY; (Y); VP French Clb; VP JA; Math Tm; Band; Jazz Band; Pres Orch; Yrbk Ed-Chief; Rep Stu Cncl; JV Var Socr; Hon Roll; NY All ST Strng Orch 85-86; NY Regnts Schlrshp 86; Tufts U; Law.

PRESS, DAVID L; Ardsley HS; Ardsley, NY; (Y); Drama Clb; French Clb; Pres JA; Math Tm; Chorus; Pres Orch; Yrbk Ed-Chief; Rep Stu Cncl; Var Trk; High Hon Roll; NY ST Orch 84-86; NY Regnts Schlrshp; Stanford U; Law.

PRESS, JOEL; Amityville Memorial HS; Massapequa, NY; (Y); FBLA; Math Tm; Band; Jazz Band; Orch; Nwsp Ed-Chief; Yrbk Phtg; High Hon Roll; NHS; Ntl Merit Ltr; Jane Bean Mem Awd 84; NYSSMA All Cnty 85; Natl Merit Schlrp Sm-Fnlst 86.

PRESSER, ROBBY; John F Kennedy HS; Merrick, NY; (Y); SADD; Temple Yth Grp; Band; Nwsp Rptr; Hon Roll; NHS; Awd Wrk Untd Crbrl Plsy Ctr 86; Bus.

PRESSIMONE, DARIO A; Mount Saint Michael Acad; Bronx, NY; (Y); 12/294; Var Ice Hcky; High Hon Roll; NHS; 2nd Pl-Rbrt Frst Ptry Cntst 86; 4 Yr Schlrshp Awd-Brnrd Brch Coll 86; Prfct Atten 85-86; Bernard Baruch.

PRESTEGAARD, RICH; Clarkstown South HS; New City, NY; (Y); Boy Scts; Pres Church Yth Grp; German Clb; Yrbk Sprt Ed; Var L Bsktbl; Capt L Ftbl; Jr NHS; Coaches Awd Ftbl 85; Chrprsn Athletes Agnst Drug Abuse 85-86; Sports Med.

PRESTON, CAROLINE A; Maria Regina HS; Mt Vernon, NY; (Y); Dance Clb; Political Wkr; Chorus; Yrbk Phtg; Hon Roll; NHS.

PRESTON, DARIANN; Ossining HS; Ossining, NY; (Y); Var JV Sftbl; Westchester Bus Inst Achvmnt Awd 85-86; Achvmnt Awd Itln 85-86; Dstngshd Accmplshmnt 86.

PRESTON, DEBI; Perry Central HS; Perry, NY; (Y); 18/100; AFS; 4-H; Spanish Clb; Chorus; Yrbk Stf; Cit Awd; High Hon Roll; Hon Roll; NHS; Acdmc Achvt Awd In Bus 86; Accntng.

PRESTON, KAREN; Our Lady Of Mercy HS; Rochester, NY; (Y); Church Yth Grp; JA; Library Aide; School Play; Variety Show; Hon Roll; JR Achvt Awd 86; Scl Wrk.

PRESTON, SANDRA; Academy Of The Holy Names; Albany, NY; (Y); Cmnty Wkr; Drama Clb; Hosp Aide; School Play; Nwsp Bus Mgr; Lit Mag; Tennis; NYS Rgnts Nrsng Schlrshp 86.

PRESUTTI, PATRICIA; Archbishop Walsh HS; Olean, NY; (Y); Church Yth Grp; Cmnty Wkr; Dance Clb; Girl Scts; Capt Varsity Clb; School Musical; Sec Trs Jr Cls; Pres Sr Cls; Capt Cheerleading; Hon Roll; Sprt Of Coop Awd; Schl Bk Store Kpr.

PRETTITORE, GINA; St Francis Prep; Flushing, NY; (Y); 125/653; Art Clb; Church Yth Grp; Dance Clb; Spanish Clb; Yrbk Stf; Sftbl; Wt Lftg; Wrstlng; NHS; Opt Clb Awd; NYS Rgnts Nrsng Schlrshp 86; Bernard Baruch Incntv Awd 86; Angcdmc Grnt St Johns 86; St Johns U; Mrktng.

PREVOST, DEBBIE; Dominican Commercial HS; Rosedale, NY; (Y); Church Choir; Swmmng; Gld Mdl Lng Isl Tchrs Music Assoc 83; Prncpls Lst 84-86; Pre-Law.

PREZEAU, RODNEY; Regis HS; Jamaica Estates, NY; (Y); Computer Clb; SADD; Var Bsbl; Im Bowling; Im Wt Lftg; High Hon Roll; Im Socr; Im Bsktbl; Teachers Aide; Ntl Hspnc Schlr Awds Prog Semfnlst 86; Ntl Achvt Schlrsp Awd Outstndng Negro Stu 86; Rgnts Schlrshp 86; Yale U; Ecnmcs.

PRICE, ALLEN C; American Renaissance Schl; Memphis, TN; (Y); 1/17; Chess Clb; JA; Math Clb; Math Tm; Jazz Band; Stage Crew; Symp Band; High Hon Roll; Hon Roll; Jr NHS; Stanford; Physcs.

PRICE, ANGELA; Julia Richman HS; New York, NY; (Y); Dance Clb; Girl Scts; Office Aide; Teachers Aide; School Musical; School Play; Variety Show.

PRICE, CAROLYN E; Poland Central Schl; Barneveld, NY; (Y); 2/59; Concert Band; Stu Cncl; Crs Cntry; DAR Awd; 4-H Awd; High Hon Roll; Sal; Cmnty Wkr; 4-H; French Clb; Pres NHS Schl Chptr 85-86; Rep Schl Dist Plcy Cmmtees 85-86; Schlrshp Rgnts Pratt Inst 86; Pratt Inst Brklyn; Cvl Engngrng.

PRICE, JACQUELINE M; Monroe JR SR HS; Rochester, NY; (Y); #5 In Class; Computer Clb; Exploring; Library Aide; Math Tm; Varsity Clb; Lit Mag; Rep Jr Cls; Pres Sr Cls; JV Bsktbl; Var L Trk; Prism Awd For Acad Excllnce; Outdr Track Clss B City Champs; Awd For Excllnce In Engl.

PRICE, JEFFREY; Cardinal Hayes HS; New York, NY; (Y); 101/254; French Clb; Off Soph Cls; Off Jr Cls; JV Bsbl; Prfct Atten Awd; Accntnt.

PRICE, JULIE; Fairport HS; Fairport, NY; (Y); DECA; Intnl Clb; Yrbk Stf; Hon Roll; Ithaca Coll; Bus Admnstrtn.

PRICE, JUSTINE; La Guardia High Schl Of Music And Art; New York, NY; (S); Art Clb; Cmnty Wkr; Nwsp Phtg; Nwsp Rptr; Nwsp Stf; Yrbk Phtg; Yrbk Stf; Hon Roll; NHS; Schl Club SOS Rascism 86; Political Awareness Clb 85-86; Oberlin; Vis Art.

PRICE, KIERA; St Francis Prep; College Pt, NY; (Y); 364/700; Cmnty Wkr; Drama Clb; Hosp Aide; Service Clb; School Musical; JV Gym; JV Trk; Nrsng.

PRICE, SHARI; Westbury SR HS; Westbury, NY; (Y).

PRICE, SUSAN S; Brooklyn Friends Schl; Brooklyn, NY; (Y); Cmnty Wkr; Dance Clb; Library Aide; Service Clb; Stage Crew; Nwsp Rptr; Lit Mag; Ntl Merit Ltr; Prfct Atten Awd; St Schlr; Ntl Arts & Tlnt Rcgntn 85-86; ATIS Fstvl Arts 85.

PRIEBE, ALESHA; De Sales HS; Lyons, NY; (Y); 2/54; Am Leg Aux Girls St; Varsity Clb; VP Stu Cncl; Var Capt Bsktbl; Var Capt Cheerleading; Var L Crs Cntry; JV Var Sftbl; High Hon Roll; NHS; Sal; Sctn 5 Clss D Grls Bsktbl Trnmnt MVP 85-86; Wllsly Bk Awd 86; Pre-Med.

PRIEBE, PAULA J; Clarence Central HS; Clarence, NY; (Y); Am Leg Aux Girls St; Drama Clb; Model UN; Varsity Clb; Church Choir; Stage Crew; Var Crs Cntry; Var Trk; High Hon Roll; NHS; Biochem.

PRIES, CATHERINE; The Wheatley HS; E Williston, NY; (Y); Church Yth Grp; Computer Clb; Mathletes; Math Clb; Chorus; Church Choir; Nwsp Stf; Rep Frsh Cls; Rep Soph Cls; Rep Jr Cls; Besr Archer 85; Bronze Math League 86; Girls St 86; Lehigh-Buchnell; Math.

PRIETO, CESAR; Immaculata HS; New York, NY; (Y); Computer Clb; School Play; Pres Jr Cls; Pres Sr Cls; Pres Stu Cncl; Capt Bowling; Im Swmmng; Hon Roll; Pace U Trustie Schlrshp 86; Rgnts Schlrshp & Dplma 86; Pace U; Finance.

PRIETO, KRIS-ANNE; Janesville-Dewitt HS; Dewitt, NY; (Y); Boy Scts; Cmnty Wkr; Exploring; JA; Pep Clb; Nwsp Rptr; Nwsp Stf; Comp Sci.

PRIKAZSKY, THERESA; Union Endicott HS; Endwell, NY; (Y); Key Clb; Varsity Clb; Nwsp Stf; Yrbk Stf; Rep Jr Cls; JV Crs Cntry; Var L Gym; Var Trk; Hon Roll; Ucla; Elect Engr.

PRIMACK, JONATHAN; Comamck H S South; Commack, NY; (Y); Cmnty Wkr; Spanish Clb; Swing Chorus; Nwsp Ed-Chief; High Hon Roll; Sec NHS; Vrsty Fncng Cap 86-87; Engl Awd For Dscrptn 84-85; Doc.

PRIMACK, LISA; Our Lady Of Lourdes HS; Poughkeepsie, NY; (Y); 5/200; Hosp Aide; JA; JV Sftbl; High Hon Roll; Hon Roll; Jr NHS; NHS; Ntl Merit SF; Rgnts Schlrshp 86; Vassar Coll; Bus.

PRIME, AMY; Ft Plain HS; Ft Plain, NY; (Y); 30/50; Cheerleading; Score Keeper; Sftbl; Timer; Trk; Schenectady CC; Htl Tchnlgy.

PRIME, PAM; Huntington HS; Huntington, NY; (Y); Hosp Aide; Chorus; Stage Crew; Var Fld Hcky; Swmmng; Hon Roll; Jr NHS; NHS; Physical Therapy.

PRIMEAU, JOHN; Cobleskill Central Schl; Howe Cave, NY; (Y); VP 4-H; Band; Concert Band; Mrchg Band; High Hon Roll; Hon Roll; Vet Med.

PRIMERANO, GINA; Cicero-North Syracuse HS; North Syracuse, NY; (S); 18/667; Art Clb; JA; High Hon Roll; Hon Roll; Ntl Merit SF; Hnr Soc 84-85; Pace U.

PRIMICERIO, LAURIE; Sachem HS; Farmingville, NY; (Y); 128/1597; German Clb; GAA; Ski Clb; Bsktbl; Mgr(s); Sftbl; Vllybl; Hon Roll; NHS; Psychlgy.

PRIMIS, CRAIG; East Meadow HS; East Meadow, NY; (S); Hosp Aide; Key Clb; Mathletes; Math Clb; Math Tm; Spanish Clb; Nwsp Ed-Chief; Nwsp Rptr; Nwsp Sprt Ed; Nwsp Stf.

PRINCE, CHRIS; Colonie Central HS; Loudonville, NY; (Y); Var Ftbl; Lcrss; Wt Lftg; Hon Roll; Schenectady Cnty CC; Engrng.

PRINCE, GRANT; Midwood HS; Brooklyn, NY; (Y); Variety Show; Var Ftbl; Var Wt Lftg.

PRINZI, MARK; Avon Central HS; Avon, NY; (Y); 10/100; Am Leg Boys St; French Clb; Chorus; Var Socr; Var Swmmng; Var Capt Tennis; High Hon Roll; NHS; Rgnt Schlrshp; Cornell U; Vet Sci.

PRINZO, DOMINICK; Sachem North HS; Lake Ronkonkoma, NY; (Y); 251/1200; Boy Scts; Church Yth Grp; Ski Clb; SADD; Chorus; Yrbk Stf; Rep Jr Cls; Bsbl; Bowling; Fld Hcky; Sqntl I Mth 83-84; Sqntl II Math 84-85; Sqntl III Mth 85-86; Advrtsng.

PRIOLO, PAULA; Bishop Luddan HS; Liverpool, NY; (Y); 4-H; JA; Co-Capt Math Tm; 4-H Awd; High Hon Roll; NHS; Church Yth Grp; Nwsp Rptr; JV Socr; Le Moyne Summr Schlr 86; Clb Congrss Trip Cornell 84; Comp.

PRIOLO, PETER; Monsignor Farrell HS; Staten Island, NY; (Y); Varsity Clb; Swmmng; Comp Engrng.

PRIORE, LORRAINE; St Agnes Academic Schl; College Point, NY; (Y); 3/271; Cmnty Wkr; Library Aide; Chorus; Hon Roll; NHS; Queens Coll; Elem Educ.

PRITCHARD, DENISE; Frankfort-Schuyler Schl; Frankfort, NY; (S); 17/110; Computer Clb; GAA; Math Clb; Yrbk Sprt Ed; Yrbk Stf; Rep Soph Cls; Capt Var Bsktbl; Capt Var Fld Hcky; Var Socr; Capt Var Trk; VP Natl Hnr Soc 85-86; All Star Fld Hcky 85-86; Comp Sci.

PRITCHARD, SETH; Greenwood Central HS; Rexville, NY; (S); 4/25; Science Clb; Rep Frsh Cls; Rep Soph Cls; Rep Jr Cls; Stu Cncl; Var Bsbl; JV Bsktbl; Socr; Hon Roll; Black Burn; Bus.

PRITCHETT, DANIELLE D; The Bronx H S Of Science; Brooklyn, NY; (Y); Girl Scts; Model UN; Yrbk Stf; Lit Mag; Crs Cntry; Jr NHS; NCTE Awd; Ntl Merit Ltr; Church Yth Grp; Cmnty Wkr; NY Libry Soc Outstndng Yng Writer Awd 85; Achvmnt Schlrshp Negro Stu SF 85; Chem.

PRITCHETTE, PATRICIA; Riverside HS; Buffalo, NY; (Y); Church Yth Grp; Office Aide; Teachers Aide; Chorus; Hon Roll; Prfct Attndnc Awd 83; Outstndg Sci Effrts 83; 4-H 80-83; Accntnt.

PRITTY, PENNY; Gouverneur HS; Gouverneur, NY; (Y); Art Clb; Band; Concert Band; Jazz Band; Mrchg Band; Pep Band; Sec Jr Cls; Sec Sr Cls; Cheerleading; Crt Rprtng.

PRIVETT, CHRISTIAN L; Mc Quaid Jesuit HS; Rochester, NY; (Y); 39/176; NFL; Thesps; Band; Jazz Band; Nwsp Stf; Bsktbl; JV Ftbl; Var Score Keeper; Var Trk; High Hon Roll; Regnts Schlrshp 86; SJFC Schlrshp 86; St John Fisher Clg; Mass Comm.

PRIVITERA, DAVID M; City Honors Schl; Buffalo, NY; (Y); 27/105; Spanish Clb; Acpl Chr; Trs Chorus; School Musical; Stage Crew; Var L Bsbl; Stat Bsktbl; Wt Lftg; Hon Roll; NY ST Rgnts Schlrshp 86; ST U Of NY Buffalo; Archtctr.

PRIVITERA, KIMBERLY; Buffalo Acad Of The Sacred Heart; Buffalo, NY; (Y); French Clb; Ski Clb; Yrbk Phtg; Hon Roll; Engrng.

PRIVITERA, MARY JO; Cardinal O Hara HS; N Tonawanda, NY; (Y); Art Clb; VP JA; Pep Clb; Church Choir; Nwsp Rptr; Im Badmtn; Mgr(s); Score Keeper; VP Socr; High Hon Roll; Marie Moutnain Mem Awd Loyal Ded Svc 86; Bus.

PROBST, CHRISTINE; Central Islip HS; Central Islip, NY; (Y); Nwsp Stf; 3rd Pl Essay Cntst Blck Hist Mnth 85; Dowling; Elem Ed.

PROBST, JAMES; Frontier Central HS; Buffalo, NY; (Y); Church Yth Grp; Cmnty Wkr; French Clb; Varsity Clb; JV Var Ftbl; Elec Engr.

PROBST, SHARI; Cobleskill HS; Cobleskill, NY; (Y); Cmnty Wkr; 4-H; FBLA; FHA; Girl Scts; Hosp Aide; Library Aide; Band; JV Bsktbl; Im Mgr Gym; Math.

PROCOPIO, JOSEPH; Cazenovia Central Schl; Cazenovia, NY; (Y); Jazz Band; School Musical; Symp Band; NHS; Ntl Merit Ltr; Band; Concert Band; Mrchg Band; Rep Stu Cncl; Bsbl.

PROCOPIO, MARIA LYNNE; Bishop Grimes HS; Syracuse, NY; (S); NFL; Chorus; School Musical; Pres Rep Frsh Cls; Sec Soph Cls; Pres Jr Cls; JV Var Cheerleading; High Hon Roll; Hon Roll; Music Awd 85; Music.

PROCOPIO, MARY J; Sauquoit Valley Central Schl; Chadwicks, NY; (Y); 21/100; GAA; VP Concert Band; Mrchg Band; Stu Cncl; Crs Cntry; Socr; Tennis; Hon Roll; NEDT Awd; MONY Rgnl Schlstc Art Awd 82-85; Dir Accptnc Schl Of Visual Arts 85; SUNY; Spec Educ.

PROCOPIO, NICHOLAS; Fayetteville-Manlius HS; Manlius, NY; (Y); Stu Cncl; Im Bsktbl; JV Ftbl; JV Lcrss; Score Keeper; Hon Roll.

PROCOPS, TONI; Springfield Gardens HS; Rosedale, NY; (S); 1/438; Office Aide; Mgr(s); Var Sftbl; Capt Vllybl; Cit Awd; Hon Roll; Jr NHS; NHS; Salute Yth Awd 84-85; Arista Soc 84-85; Queens Coll Pres Awd Achvtmnt 84-85.

PROEFROCK, CHRISTINE; Pine Valley Central Schl; Cherry Creek, NY; (Y); 8/68; VP AFS; Drama Clb; Band; VP Chorus; Concert Band; Mrchg Band; School Musical; School Play; Hon Roll; Pres Jr NHS; CCMTA Cnty Music Scholar 85; SUNY Fredonia; Music.

PROEFROCK, KRISTEN D; Niagara Wheatfield SR HS; N Tonawanda, NY; (Y); 51/291; Church Yth Grp; Pep Clb; Spanish Clb; Yrbk Ed-Chief; Hon Roll; Prfct Atten Awd; NY ST Rgnts Schlrshp 86; Fulton-Montgomery CC; Vsl Comm.

PROFETA, ADRIANNE; Maria Regina HS; Yonkers, NY; (Y); Cornell U; Vet Sci.

PROFETA, DENISE; Mahopac HS; Mahopac, NY; (Y); 47/409; Science Clb; Nwsp Stf; Yrbk Stf; Lit Mag; JV Vllybl; NHS.

PROFETA, JOHN J; St Francis Prep; Whitestone, NY; (S); 276/744; Am Leg Boys St; Im Ftbl; Im Sftbl; Hon Roll; Cmmnctns.

PROKOP, SCOTT; Valley Stream South HS; Valley Stream, NY; (Y); Nwsp Rptr; Nwsp Sprt Ed; Nwsp Stf; Yrbk Stf; Var Bsbl; Var Capt Ftbl; Var Capt Wrstlng.

PROKUP, LEE ANN; St John Villa Acad; Staten Island, NY; (Y); Church Yth Grp; SADD; Stage Crew; Yrbk Stf; Pres Soph Cls; Pres Jr Cls; Pres Sr Cls; Bowling; Cit Awd.

PRONESTI, SCOTT; Anthony A Henninger HS; Syracuse, NY; (Y); 12/400; Band; Jazz Band; Mrchg Band; Pep Band; Symp Band; Yrbk Ed-Chief; Yrbk Phtg; Yrbk Sprt Ed; Swmmng; High Hon Roll; Suny Binghamton.

PROOF, SHELLEY; Rochester Christian Acad; Rochester, NY; (S); 2/4; Art Clb; Church Yth Grp; Teachers Aide; Chorus; School Play; Soph Cls; Stu Cncl; Bsbl; Vllybl; Hon Roll; Christian Conduct 83-84; Monroe CC; Comp Sci.

PROPER, JACKIE; Johnson City HS; Johnson City, NY; (Y); Cmnty Wkr; Hosp Aide; Pres Temple Yth Grp; Nwsp Stf; Hon Roll; Ntl Merit Ltr; JR Leag Salute Yth Awd 86; Amer Clsscl Leag & Nat JR Clsscl Leag Magna Cum Laude Cert 86; Arch.

PROPER, ROBIN; Perry Central HS; Perry, NY; (Y); 14/127; Hst FHA; Sec Spanish Clb; Chorus; Yrbk Stf; Score Keeper; Var Socr; JV Vllybl; High Hon Roll; Hon Roll; NHS; Govt Intrshp Pgm 85-86; JR Prom Queen 86; Acctnt.

PROPHETE, DANIELLE; Christ The King Rhs; Rosedale, NY; (Y); 17/380; Computer Clb; Speech Tm; School Play; Nwsp Stf; Yrbk Stf; High Hon Roll; Hon Roll; NHS; Ntl Merit Ltr; SUNY Stony Brook; Comp Sci.

PROPHETE, DOMINIC; Uniondale HS; Hempstead, NY; (Y); Chess Clb; Debate Tm; FBLA; Off NFL; SADD; Tennis; Timer; Trk; Frnch Stu; Binghamton; Politc Sci.

PROSCHER, LINDA; Ossining HS; Ossining, NY; (Y); 54/248; 4-H; 4-H Awd; Hon Roll; Westchester Bus Inst; Sec.

PROSCIA, JENNIFER L; St Marys Girls HS; Manhasset, NY; (Y); 15/169; Math Clb; Ski Clb; Chorus; Stage Crew; Nwsp Phtg; Im JV Tennis; JV Trk; High Hon Roll; Hon Roll; NHS; Fordham; Bus.

PROSEUS, HEATHER; Sodus HS; Sodus Pt, NY; (Y); Sec AFS; Drama Clb; Sec Intnl Clb; Sec Model UN; Radio Clb; Science Clb; SADD; Yrbk Sprt Ed; Pres Stu Cncl; JV Socr; Schlr Art Awd 86; UN Conf Cert 84; Soc Sci.

PROSPER, LISA; Half Hollow Hills HS East; Dix Hills, NY; (Y); Capt Color Guard; Mrchg Band; Stage Crew; Mgr(s); Score Keeper; Trk; Music.

PROSPERINO, SANDRO; Valhalla HS; N White Plains, NY; (Y); Am Leg Boys St; Drama Clb; Teachers Aide; School Play; JV Capt Socr; Trk; Hon Roll; Itln Clb; Sccr Clb MIP 85-86; Acctg.

PROSSEDA, KELLY; Fontebonne Hall Acad; Brooklyn, NY; (Y); Cmnty Wkr; Drama Clb; Political Wkr; SADD; Chorus; School Musical; School Play; Rep Frsh Cls; Coach Actv; Var Sftbl; Bus.

PROSSER, KIM; Clyde-Savannah Central HS; Clyde, NY; (Y); Political Wkr; Band; Jazz Band; Var L Bsktbl; Var L Sftbl; Var L Tennis; Var L Vllybl; High Hon Roll; Cayuga Cnty CC; Erly Chldhd Ed.

PROSSER, MARK; Auburn HS; Auburn, NY; (Y); Intnl Clb; Ski Clb; Band; Jazz Band; Mrchg Band; Symp Band; High Hon Roll; NHS; Architecture.

PROTASS, JOSH M; Rye Country Day Schl; New Rochelle, NY; (Y); Nwsp Ed-Chief; VP Soph Cls; VP Jr Cls; VP Sr Cls; Tennis; Ntl Merit Ltr; Northwestern Div.

PROULX, DONNA; Brasher Falls Central HS; N Lawrence, NY; (Y); Church Yth Grp; Exploring; Band; Concert Band; Pep Band; Hon Roll; NHS; Prfct Atten Awd; Chorus; Mrchg Band; Outstdng Achvt SR Hgh Art 85; Art.

PROUT, MAUREEN; Herbert H Lehman HS; New York, NY; (Y); 58/521; Church Yth Grp; Hosp Aide; Stage Crew; Nwsp Rptr; Nwsp Stf; Yrbk Rptr; Yrbk Stf; Jr NHS; NHS; Prfct Atten Awd; Politc Yth Org 86.

PROUT, SARA A; North Salem HS; Brewster, NY; (Y); 4/96; SADD; Chorus; School Musical; School Play; Variety Show; Yrbk Ed-Chief; Stu Cncl; Var Socr; NHS; Wellesley Coll; Intl Rltns.

PROUTY, ROBIN; Rochester Christian Acad; Byron, NY; (S); 1/3; Trs Church Yth Grp; VP French Clb; Band; Church Choir; Yrbk Stf; Cheerleading; Socr; Trk; High Hon Roll; NHS; Roberts Weslyan Coll; Psych.

PROVENZANO, MARK; Blind Brook HS; Rye Brook, NY; (Y); Aud/Vis; Camera Clb; Office Aide; Teachers Aide; Band; Nwsp Stf; Yrbk Stf; JV Bsbl; Var Bowling; Var Ftbl; Villanova; Bus Mktg.

PROVICK, JENNIFER; Hamburg SR HS; Hamburg, NY; (Y); 76/384; Camp Fr Inc; Church Yth Grp; Band; Symp Band; D Youville Coll; Nrsng.

PROVNZANO, DONNA; Smithtown HS East; Saint James, NY; (Y); Art Clb; Camera Clb; Drama Clb; PAVAS; Ski Clb; Spanish Clb; Thesps; School Play; Variety Show; Lit Mag; 1st Pl St James 5 Mile Run 86; Commercl Art.

PROVOOST, JONATHAN; Farmingdale HS; Farmingdale, NY; (Y); Jazz Band; Forest Rangery.

PROVOST, DAWN; Prospect Heights HS; Brooklyn, NY; (Y); FBLA; JA; Library Aide; Mathletes; Math Clb; Math Tm; Office Aide; Teachers Aide; High Hon Roll; Hon Roll; RN.

PROVOST, ERIC; East Meadow HS; E Meadow, NY; (Y); Comp Sci.

PROWTEN, PAMELA L; Hamburg SR HS; Hamburg, NY; (Y); 69/382; Trs Church Yth Grp; Chorus; Var JV Mgr(s); JV Socr; Hon Roll; NHS; Rgnts Schlrshp 86; SUNY Geneso; Intl Bus.

PRUCHNOWSKI, DONNA; Cardinal O Hara HS; Tonawanda, NY; (Y); Trs Spanish Clb; Teachers Aide; Yrbk Stf; Badmtn; Stat Bsbl; Capt Cheerleading; Trk; Hon Roll; Chrldr Of Yr 86; Niagara U; Math.

PRUDEN, JOSEF; Far Rockaway HS; Jamaica, NY; (Y); Key Clb; Law Cert 86; Regents Endorsed Diploma 86; Law Clb 82-86; Engrng Cert 86; News Day Awd HS Yr 86; C W Post; Bus Mgmt.

PRUDHOMME, FERNANDO; George Washington HS; New York, NY; (Y); Cmnty Wkr; Latin Clb; PAVAS; Orch; School Play; Stage Crew; Nwsp Rptr; Nwsp Stf; Yrbk Rptr; Yrbk Stf; Comm Awd Diploma 86; Drama/Spch Gold Mdl Awd 86; Mayor Koch Recog Awd 85; U Of Bridgeport; Jrnlsm.

PRUIKSMA, JANICE; Coxsackie-Athens HS; Coxsackie, NY; (Y); 50/102; Church Yth Grp; Cmnty Wkr; SADD; Rep Frsh Cls; Rep Soph Cls; VP Jr Cls; Rep Stu Cncl; Var L Socr; Var L Sftbl; Var L Vllybl; All Cnty Sr Hgh Chrs; Elem Educ.

PRUSCHKI, AMY; Valley Central HS; Walden, NY; (Y); Color Guard; Yrbk Stf; VP Soph Cls; VP Jr Cls; Pres Sr Cls; Stat Ftbl; JV Vllybl; Bus Mgt.

PRUSINOWSKI, DANIEL P; Moravia Central Schl; Locke, NY; (Y); 4/94; Mathletes; Quiz Bowl; Var L Crs Cntry; Var Tennis; Im Vllybl; Var L Wrstlng; High Hon Roll; St Schlr; N Cntry CC; Resrce Mgmt.

PRUSS, ERIC; Arlington North HS; Poughkeepsie, NY; (Y); 4/567; Math Tm; Im Bsktbl; Im Socr; Im Swmmng; High Hon Roll; NHS; Ntl Merit Ltr; Ntl Russian Essay Wrtng & Spkng Gold Mdls 84 & 86; Swmmng Awds 84; Cornell U; Physcs.

PRUTSMAN, JENNIFER JILL; Cattaraugus Central Schl; Cattaraugus, NY; (Y); Spanish Clb; Chorus; Pres Soph Cls; VP Stu Cncl; Stat Bsktbl; Capt Var Cheerleading; Var Sftbl; Var Vllybl; Bausch & Lomb Sci Awd; Hon Roll; Bio.

PRUTSMAN, KATHLEEN; Jasper Central HS; Jasper, NY; (Y); Drama Clb; French Clb; Teachers Aide; Chorus; Color Guard; Yrbk Stf; JV Sftbl; High Hon Roll; Hon Roll; NHS; Major Ltr Awd Actvts 85-86; Engl.

PRYLUCK, TRACEY; Patchogue-Meford HS; Medford, NY; (Y); 3/800; Scholastic Bowl; Sec Temple Yth Grp; Trs Band; Nwsp Ed-Chief; Rptr Stu Cncl; High Hon Roll; NHS; Ntl Merit Ltr; Debate Tm; Drama Clb; Schl Rep NYS Stuy Senate Forum 86; NYSSMA Solo Fstvl 84-86; Natl Sci Olympd Prtcpnt 84; Lbrl Arts.

PRYOR, LEONARD; Tottenville HS; Staten Isld, NY; (Y); Var Bsktbl.

PRZEDWIECKI, STEPHANIE; Sachem HS; Farmingville, NY; (Y); 138/1385; GAA; Var JV Socr; Var Vllybl; Hofstra Recog Schlrshp 86; Pace Recog Schlrshp 86; Amer Recog Schlrshp 86; Hofstra U; Acctng.

PRZEPASNIAK, MARY JO; Mount Mercy Acad; Buffalo, NY; (Y); Girl Scts; Intnl Clb; JCL; Model UN; Science Clb; Church Choir; Hon Roll; Jr NHS; 3rd Pl WNYS Lang Fair 84-85; Hon Mntn WNYS Lang Fair 86; Ind Engrng.

PRZETAKIEWICZ, WENDY; Carmel HS; Carmel, NY; (Y); High Hon Roll; Bst Typist Typng II 85; Bst Stenogrphr Steno I 86; Comp Pgmmr Comp RPG I 86; :Bus.

PRZEZDZIECKI, STEVE; Scotia-Glenville HS; Scotia, NY; (Y); JV Bsbl; Im Ftbl; High Hon Roll; Hon Roll; Pre Med.

PRZYBYSZ, KENNETH P; Hutchison Central Technical HS; Buffalo, NY; (Y); 4/266; Camp Fr Inc; Color Guard; Yrbk Phtg; Hon Roll; VP NHS; Lawrence Inst Of Tech; Arch.

PSAROUDIS, LAURA; St Joseph Hill Acad; Staten Island, NY; (Y); 49/106; Computer Clb; Drama Clb; Pres VP French Clb; FTA; Library Aide; Trk; NEDT Awd; 2nd Pl Cntntl Math Leag Awd; Regnts Comptv Schlrshp; Lehigh U.

PSOTA, AMY B; Ward Melville HS; Stony Brook, NY; (Y); DECA; Ski Clb; Spanish Clb; Stu Cncl; Var Capt Swmmng; Hon Roll; Regnts Schlrshp Wnnr 86; Regnl Fnlst DECA Comptn 86; Big Sistr Voluntr 86; Clemson U; Bus.

PTAK, THOMAS R; North Collins Central Schl; North Collins, NY; (Y); FFA; VICA; Hon Roll; Prfct Atten Awd; Empire Farmer Degree Awd 86; Dairy Prodctn Awd 86; Merit Roll 86; Agri.

PUCCI, TERESA; Christ The King R HS; Maspeth, NY; (Y); Capt Cheerleading.

PUCCIA, CHRISTINA; Thomas J Corcoran HS; Syracuse, NY; (Y); French Clb; SADD; Yrbk Stf; Hon Roll; Coll; Psychlgy.

PUCCIO, GERARD; Manhasset HS; Manhasset, NY; (Y); Cmnty Wkr; Spanish Clb; Var Tennis; High Hon Roll; Hon Roll; Var Ten Nassau Cnty Champnshp Awd 86; Hgh Scorng Perfrmnce Natl Spn Exam Awd 86; Bus.

PUCCIO, JOSEPH; Archbishop Molloy HS; Rosedale, NY; (Y); 38/383; SADD; Chorus; Rep Soph Cls; Hon Roll; Sec NHS; Church Yth Grp; Dance Clb; Science Clb; Yrbk Stf; Stnnr Sprt Awd 85; Yr Pres Tutrng Clb 86; Ldr Of Tutrng Clb 86; Nrblgy.

PUCELLO, MARGARETHA; Solvay HS; Solvay, NY; (Y); 29/170; Church Yth Grp; Ski Clb; Stage Crew; Rep Sr Cls; Stu Cncl; Hon Roll; Grad With Hnrs 86; Presdntl Acamc Ftns Awd 86; Rgnts Schlrshp 86; OCC; Mrn Bio.

PUCHALSKI, CHRISTOPHER J; North Tonawanda SR HS; North Tonawanda, NY; (Y); Am Leg Boys St; Boy Scts; Pres 4-H; Model UN; Ski Clb; Pres SADD; Drm & Bgl; Rptr Yrbk Stf; Rep Stu Cncl; 4-H Awd; Ad Altare Dei 85; Law.

PUCHEBNER, RON; Greece Olympia HS; Rochester, NY; (Y); 18/390; Ski Clb; Teachers Aide; Socr; Tennis; Hon Roll; NHS; Sblys Art Awd 86; MI ST; Mech Engr.

PUCKETT, SCOTT AUSTIN; Greece Arcadia HS; Rochester, NY; (Y); 3/285; Boy Scts; Math Tm; Band; Var Ftbl; Var Capt Trk; Bausch & Lomb Sci Awd; High Hon Roll; Hon Roll; NHS; Pres Schlr; Rgnts Schlrshp #250 Yr 86; Edward Watson Schlrshp $700 86; Amer Legion Schlrshp $250 86; U Of Buffalo; Pre Med.

PUDA, FRANK; Olean HS; Olean, NY; (Y); 57/210; ROTC; Science Clb; Varsity Clb; Trs Frsh Cls; Rep Stu Cncl; Var Bsbl; Var Bsktbl; Im Ftbl; Im Vllybl; Hon Roll; ST John FisherCOMP Math.

PUDELL, STEVEN; East Meadow HS; East Meadow, NY; (S); Nwsp Ed-Chief; Nwsp Sprt Ed; JV Socr; Var Tennis; Mathletes; Math Clb; Spanish Clb; VP Sec Temple Yth Grp; Orch; Nwsp Rptr.

PUETZER, JENNIFER; St Marys Girls HS; Glen Cove, NY; (Y); Dance Clb; Ski Clb; JV Cheerleading; Acctg.

PUFPAFF, SUE; St Marys HS; Sloan, NY; (S); Am Leg Aux Girls St; Hon Roll; NHS; Canisius Coll; Pre-Med.

PUFPAFF, SUSAN; St Marys HS; Sloan, NY; (Y); 14/162; Am Leg Aux Girls St; High Hon Roll; NHS; Canisius Coll; Pre Med.

PUGH, KELLY; Lindenhurst HS; Lindenhurst, NY; (Y); Church Yth Grp; French Clb; Key Clb; Varsity Clb; Im JV Bsktbl; Var JV Fld Hcky; Var JV Sftbl; Im JV Vllybl; Hmkrs Chllngr Awd Outstndng Achvmnt 86; York Coll PA; Elem Educ.

PUHLE, JEFFREY; West Hempstead HS; West Hempstead, NY; (Y); Computer Clb; German Clb; Radio Clb; Ski Clb; Band; Concert Band; Jazz Band; Orch; School Play; Bowling; Outstndg Achvt Ger 85-86; Outstndg Achvt Music 83-86; Comp Pgmmg.

PULEO, JOSEPHINE; Dominican Commercial HS; Ozone Park, NY; (S); 30/288; Teachers Aide; Yrbk Stf; High Hon Roll; NHS; Intrntl Cookg Chinese 84-85; Siena Clb Tour Guide 84-85; Peer Ldr JR Rng Danc Comm 86; Adelphi; Law.

PULEO, PATRICIA; Hamburg Central HS; Hamburg, NY; (Y); 4-H; Girl Scts; SADD; Band; Chorus; Mrchg Band; Im Stat Bsktbl; 4-H Awd; Concert Band; Symp Band; Olympcs Mind 83-84; Acctng.

PULEO, PATRISE; Seaford HS; Seaford, NY; (Y); Art Clb; Math Clb; Math Tm; SADD; Concert Band; Flag Corp; Mgr(s); High Hon Roll; NHS; Ntl Merit Ltr.

PULLARO, RAYMOND G; F D Roosevelt HS; Poughkeepsie, NY; (Y); Am Leg Boys St; Band; Chorus; School Musical; VP Stu Cncl; Crs Cntry; Golf; Trk; Hon Roll; Pres NHS; Masters; Engrng.

PULLEN, STEVEN; Fairport HS; Fairport, NY; (Y); 10/605; Computer Clb; Science Clb; SADD; Wrstlng; High Hon Roll; Hon Roll; NHS; Mst Imprvd Ath 83; Regents Scholar 86; PA ST U; Sci.

PULLIAM, CHRISTINA; Evandeo Childs HS; Bronx, NY; (S); Chorus; School Play; Rep Stu Cncl; Sftbl; Jr NHS; Prfct Atten Awd; Governors Comm Schlstc Achvt Citation 83; Kingsboro Coll; Travel.

PULLIAM, SAMANTHA; The Stony Brook Schl; Beckley, WV; (Y); 2/84; Art Clb; Church Yth Grp; Teachers Aide; Orch; Stage Crew; Stu Cncl; Var Capt Bsktbl; Var Capt Fld Hcky; High Hon Roll; Cum Laude Soc Hnrs 83-86; Best All Around Athlete Schlrs Schl 86; Duke U.

PULLIN, KIRSTEN; Wallkill SR HS; Wallkill, NY; (S); Concert Band; JV Var Bsktbl; High Hon Roll; NHS; Ntl Merit Ltr; Band; Mrchg Band; Var Socr; JV Sftbl; Var Trk; Frnch Awd 82-85; Engl Awd 82-85; Soc Studs Awd 85; U Of VA; Intl Law.

PULLINS, PAIGE ALLISON; Fayetteville-Manlius HS; Fayetteville, NY; (Y); 140/325; Church Yth Grp; Exploring; Trs German Clb; Ski Clb; SADD; Orch; Coach Actv; Socr; Swmmng; Hon Roll; Exchnge Stud Grmny ASSE 84; Cllrs For Schrs Schlrshp 86; Pre-Coll Arch Syracuse U 85; Catholic U Of Amer; Arch.

PULTZ, DIANNA; Marlboro HS; Marlboro, NY; (Y); 8/150; Church Yth Grp; SADD; Varsity Clb; Band; Chorus; Church Choir; Color Guard; Concert Band; Drm Mjr(t); Mrchg Band; Elem Ed.

PULVER, DARYL T; Webutuck Central Schl; Millerton, NY; (Y); 2/52; Am Leg Boys St; Trs French Clb; Quiz Bowl; Spanish Clb; Yrbk Stf; Crs Cntry; Socr; Trk; NHS; Ntl Merit Ltr; Regnl HS Exclnc Bard Coll 86; Chem & Physcs Awd 85 & 86; Chem Resrch.

PULVIRENTI, PATRICIA; St Joseph-By-The-Sea HS; Staten Island, NY; (Y); 3/240; Red Cross Aide; Crs Cntry; Gym; Socr; Trk; High Hon Roll; NHS; Ntl Merit Schol; Gov Comm Schlstc Achvt Schlrshp 85-86; NY U; Ind Psychlgy.

PUMA, MARIA; Catholic Central HS; Rensselaer, NY; (S); 8/179; Math Clb; Spanish Clb; Band; School Play; Variety Show; Rep Soph Cls; Pom Pon; High Hon Roll; VP NHS; NY ST Math Lgu 84-85; Cert Of Achvt Vlntry Prtcptn 84-85; Excllnc In Spnsh 83-84; Clarkson U; Chem Engr.

PUMFORD, VAL; Falconer Central Schl; Jamestown, NY; (Y); 3/120; Church Yth Grp; Soroptimist; Band; Jazz Band; Mrchg Band; Rep Stu Cncl; Var Crs Cntry; Var Trk; Hon Roll; NHS; Gerntlgy.

PUMILIA, VICKI L; Marlboro Central HS; Milton, NY; (Y); 10/168; Camera Clb; 4-H; Nwsp Stf; Yrbk Stf; Var Vllybl; High Hon Roll; Hon Roll; Jr NHS; NHS; Pres Schlr; Rgnts Schlrshp 86; Hotel Mgmt.

PUNN, JASON; North Babylon SR HS; N Babylon, NY; (Y); 4/460; Am Leg Boys St; Intnl Clb; Trs Temple Yth Grp; School Play; Nwsp Stf; Yrbk Stf; JV Tennis; NHS; Drama Clb; High Hon Roll; Most Likely To Succeed 84; Chem Olympiad 86; Spec Olympics Volun 86; Aero Engrng.

PUNTUNIERO, FRED; St Marys HS; Sloan, NY; (Y); Bsktbl; U Of Buffalo; Archtct.

PUOPOLO, KRISTINE A; Liverpool HS; Liverpool, NY; (Y); 1/816; Math Tm; VP Speech Tm; Pres Speech Tm; NCTE Awd; NHS; Ntl Merit SF; Val; Exploring; Hosp Aide; High Hon Roll; Rensselaer Polytech Inst Sci-Math Mdl 85; Mayflower Cmpct Awd Amer Hstry 85; Dartmouth Bk Awd 85.

PUPO, ROBERT; Churchville Chili HS; Churchville, NY; (Y); Chess Clb; Var JV Bsbl; Im Bsktbl; Im Vllybl; Im Wt Lftg; High Hon Roll; Ntl Merit Ltr; Math Tm; AHSME 85-86; AIME 86; Mth Lg All Star 85-86; Comp Sci.

PURCELL, BRIDGET; Henninger HS; Syracuse, NY; (Y); Boys Clb Am; GAA; JA; Key Clb; SADD; Band; Trs Frsh Cls; VP Soph Cls; Pres Jr Cls; NHS; Pre Law.

PURCELL, ERIN; Lansingburgh HS; Troy, NY; (Y); JA; Key Clb; Ski Clb; Chorus; Color Guard; High Hon Roll; Hon Roll; Gregg Shrthnd Awd 85-86; Typwrtng Awd 86; Cazenovia Coll; Exec Sec.

PURCELL, GERALDINE; Renss Middle- HS; Rensselaer, NY; (S); SADD; Varsity Clb; Yrbk Stf; Sec Soph Cls; Trs Jr Cls; Rep Stu Cncl; JV Bsktbl; Var Score Keeper; Hon Roll; Coll St Rose; Acctg.

PURCELL, JIM; Frontier Central HS; Blasdell, NY; (Y); Art Clb; Yrbk Ed-Chief; Yrbk Stf; Hon Roll; NHS; Hon Mntn Hmbrg Sun Ad Crft Cntst Drwng Advrtzmnts 86; Erie Comm Coll; Arch.

PURCELL, MICHAEL; Xavier HS; Brooklyn, NY; (Y); Church Yth Grp; Math Clb; ROTC; Rep Soph Cls; Hon Roll; NY ST Regents & St Johns U Schlrshp 86; Holy Name Scty Schlrshp 86; St Johns U; Accntng.

PURCELL, SHARON; Catholic Central HS; Troy, NY; (Y); Drama Clb; German Clb; Math Clb; SADD; School Musical; School Play; Stage Crew; Yrbk Rptr; Yrbk Stf; Rep Stu Cncl; Peer Ldrshp Recgntn Awd 86; Lang Arts Olympcs Hon Mntn 4th Plc 85; Creative Wrtng.

PURCELL, TODD; Pittsford Mandon HS; Pittsford, NY; (Y); DECA; French Clb; Lit Mag; Var Crs Cntry; JV Trk; Hon Roll; NHS; Mrktng Stu Of Yr 86; Bus Mgmt.

PURGAR, MARY; Smithtown HS East; Nesconset, NY; (Y); Camera Clb; Cmnty Wkr; 4-H; Office Aide; Chorus; 4-H Awd; Hon Roll; Rgnts Depcomia 86; SUNY Stony Brook; Pre-Med.

PURVES, TODD; Fairport HS; Fairport, NY; (Y); VP Sr Cls; JV Var Golf; JV Var Swmmng; Hon Roll; Ntl Merit Ltr; Spanish NHS; Tm Sprkplg 86; JV Mst Vlbl Smwm 85; Pre-Med.

PURVIS, JENNIFER; Sachem HS; Farmingville, NY; (Y); 85/1385; French Clb; GAA; Concert Band; JV Var Socr; Var L Trk; Vllybl; Jr NHS; NHS; NYSSMA Mdls Clarinet 83; Capt Of Trvl Tm Sccr 83-84; Regents Schlrshp Wnnr 85; Mahattonville Coll; Psych.

PUSATERE, KIMBERLY; Ballston Spa HS; Ballston Spa, NY; (Y); 12/244; Hosp Aide; Math Tm; Nwsp Stf; Yrbk Bus Mgr; Yrbk Ed-Chief; Yrbk Sprt Ed; Rep Stu Cncl; High Hon Roll; NHS; Latn Hnr Scty 86; William Smith Coll; Bus Econ.

PUSHKARSH, VANESSA; St Patricks Central Catholic HS; Durham, NY; (S); 5/30; Cmnty Wkr; Drama Clb; School Play; Nwsp Rptr; Nwsp Stf; Yrbk Stf; Sec Trs Jr Cls; Rep Stu Cncl; Score Keeper; Hon Roll; Amer Cncr Soc Daffodil Queen 84-85; Siena Coll; Jrnlsm.

PUSKARZ, JACQUELINE CAROL; Gloversville HS; Gloversville, NY; (Y); 4/233; Yrbk Ed-Chief; Trs Frsh Cls; Trs Soph Cls; Trs Jr Cls; Trs Sr Cls; Stu Cncl; Am Leg Aux Girls St; Service Clb; Nwsp Ed-Chief; Yrbk Phtg; Stu Yr Laurel G Princ Awd 85; Stu Mnth 85; DAR Ctznshp Awd 85-86; Coll St Rose; Advrtsng.

PUSLOSKIE, MATTHEW; Avon HS; Avon, NY; (Y); 13/100; Church Yth Grp; Trs Frsh Cls; Trs Soph Cls; Trs Jr Cls; Pres Stu Cncl; Var JV Bsbl; Var Capt Bsktbl; Var Capt Ftbl; Var Wt Lftg; High Hon Roll; Livingston Cnty All Star Ftbl 85; Greg Strothers Awd 85; Acctg.

PUSTELNIK, CHARLES; Bishop Timon HS; Buffalo, NY; (S); 17/160; SADD; Nwsp Rptr; Nwsp Stf; Yrbk Rptr; Yrbk Stf; Im Vllybl; Hon Roll; Bio Awd 83; Canisius Coll; Engl.

PUTIGNADO, KRISTINA M; N Babylon HS; N Babylon, NY; (Y); 17/500; Spanish Clb; Nwsp Rptr; VP Frsh Cls; VP Stu Cncl; Socr; Sftbl; High Hon Roll; NHS; Bus Admin.

PUTIGNANO, SUSAN; Ursuline Schl; Bronxville, NY; (Y); Sec VP Church Yth Grp; Ski Clb; Rep Frsh Cls; Rep Soph Cls; Pres Jr Cls; Pres Stu Cncl; NY ST Summer Sch Visual Arts 86; Peer Counselor-Ursuline 85-87; Public Relations Committee-Ursuline; Appalachia Dickonson Coll; Psyc.

PUTKOWSKI, KAREN; Amsterdam HS; Amsterdam, NY; (Y); 70/201; Varsity Clb; Yrbk Bus Mgr; Rep Stu Cncl; Var Capt Vllybl; Schlrshp NY ST Regnts Nrsg Schlrshp 86; Fulton Montgomery Coll; RN.

PUTMAN, ANN; Heuvelton Central HS; Heuvelton, NY; (S); 4/40; Latin Clb; Band; Church Choir; Concert Band; Mrchg Band; Yrbk Stf; Trs Jr Cls; Pres Sr Cls; NHS; Jostens Hnr Mdl; Latin Achvt Awd; Phys Ed Awd; Potsdam Coll; Mth.

PUTNAM, APRIL; Richfield Springs Central HS; Richfield Springs, NY; (Y); Chorus; Color Guard; Mrchg Band; School Musical; Yrbk Stf; Hon Roll; Capt Colorguard 86; Prom Queen 86; Bryant & Stratton; Bus Mgmt.

PUTNAM, TODD; Queensbury HS; Glens Falls, NY; (Y); Art Clb; Ftbl; Trk; Hon Roll; Comp Sci.

PUTNEY, ANGELA; Mamaroneck HS; Larchmont, NY; (Y); Computer Clb; Pres Trs Girl Scts; Math Tm; Spanish Clb; Chorus; NHS; Spanish NHS; 1st Pl-Ntl Comp Slvng Cntst 86; 2nd Pl-Intl Comp Slvng Cntst 84; John Gnreux Awd-Math 86; MIT.

PUTNEY, J MICHAEL; Elmira Southside HS; Elmira, NY; (Y); Varsity Clb; Chorus; Var JV Bsktbl; Var JV Ftbl; Var JV Wt Lftg; Finger Lakes CC; Envrnmntl Con.

PUTORTI, FREDDY; Whitehall JR SR HS; Whitehall, NY; (Y); #5 In Class; Pres French Clb; Science Clb; Trs SADD; Pres Band; Yrbk Bus Mgr; Pres Sr Cls; Hon Roll; NHS; NY ST Regnts Schlrshp 86; SUNY Plattsburgh; Bus Mgmt.

PUTRE, ERIKA; Baldwin SR HS; Baldwin, NY; (Y); Political Wkr; Teachers Aide; Nwsp Rptr; Var Badmtn; Var Fld Hcky; High Hon Roll; Hon Roll; NHS; Spanish NHS; Achvt Awds In Span, Eng, Histry 84-86; Bus.

PUTRINO, DONALD; Union Endicott HS; Endicott, NY; (Y); Im JV Bsktbl; High Hon Roll; Prfct Atten Awd; Acctng.

PUTTEN, RICHARD VANDER; St John The Baptist HS; Bohemia, NY; (Y); Art Clb; Church Yth Grp; Cmnty Wkr; Band; Chorus; Orch; NY Inst Tech; Hotel Adm.

PUTTHARUKSA, KULRAVEE; Eastchester HS; Eastchester, NY; (Y); French Clb; Key Clb; Pres Latin Clb; SADD; Chorus; Nwsp Ed-Chief; Capt Ed Yrbk Stf; High Hon Roll; NHS; Prfct Atten Awd; Algebra Regnts 84; Slvr Maxima Cum Laude 86; Iona Coll Lang Cntst 1st Hnrs 85.

PYKE, JAMES M; G Ray Bodley HS; Fulton, NY; (Y); Boy Scts; Drama Clb; Science Clb; Chorus; School Musical; School Play; Stage Crew; Var Socr; High Hon Roll; NHS; Chem.

PYLYSHENKO, KATJA; Brockport HS; Brockport, NY; (Y); Ski Clb; Yrbk Ed-Chief; Var Cheerleading; DECA; Hon Roll; Pres Schlr; Rgnts Schlrshp 86; 3-1-3 Coll Study Pgm 86; 11 Yrs Ukranian Saturday Schl 85; American U; Intl Relat.

PYNADATH, DAVID V; Johnstown HS; Johnstown, NY; (Y); 1/203; Boy Scts; Math Tm; Quiz Bowl; Band; Nwsp Sprt Ed; Bausch & Lomb Sci Awd; NHS; Outstndng Rsrch Awd STANYS Sci Fair 85; Rensselaer Mdl Of RPI Troy 86; Balfour Awd 86; Elec Engr.

PYSKADLO, MICHELE; Keveny Memorial Acad; Cohoes, NY; (Y); 10/40; Concert Band; Jazz Band; Sec Soph Cls; Capt Var Cheerleading; High Hon Roll; NHS; Ntl Ldrshp Merit Awd 84-86; NY ST Rgnts Nrsng Schlrshp 86; Peer Ldrshp 84-86; Russell Sage Coll; Nrsng.

PYSKATY, JEFFREY; Barker Central HS; Barker, NY; (Y); 3/110; Pres AFS; French Clb; VP Jr Cls; Pres Stu Cncl; JV Bsktbl; Capt L Tennis; Bausch & Lomb Sci Awd; Hon Roll; Sec NHS; 4-H; Potsdam Merit & NY ST Regnts & Marion S Pike Schlrshps 86; SUNY Potsdam; Math Ed.

PYTKO, MARY LOURDES; John F Kennedy HS; Utica, NY; (Y); 23/120; Pres Church Yth Grp; Key Clb; SADD; Rep Jr Cls; Sec Sr Cls; Pres NHS; Albany Coll Pharmacy; Phrmcy.

PYTLUK, SCOTT; John Dewey HS; Brooklyn, NY; (Y); Capt Scholastic Bowl; Science Clb; Orch; Symp Band; Nwsp Rptr; NCTE Awd; Spanish NHS; Val; Steven J & Peggy V Kumble Schlr Gov Comm Schl Achvt 86; NY Pub Libr Awd 86; Amer Assn Physcs Tchrs 86; Brown U; Psych.

PYZDROWSKI, ADAM; Phoenix Central HS; Fulton, NY; (Y); 1/25; Accounting.

QUACKENBUSH, CRAIG M; Waterloo SR HS; Waterloo, NY; (Y); 75/170; Am Leg Boys St; Boy Scts; Camera Clb; Var JV Lcrss; Cit Awd; Prfct Atten Awd; Eagle Scout 84; Cayuga CC; Jrnlsm.

QUACKENBUSH, JANE; Hugh C Williams HS; Canton, NY; (Y); Thesps; Varsity Clb; Chorus; School Musical; School Play; Yrbk Stf; Sftbl; Vllybl; Elem Educ.

QUAGLIA, JEANINE M; Pine Bush HS; Middletown, NY; (Y); 25/278; Band; Chorus; Concert Band; Yrbk Stf; Rep Soph Cls; Rep Jr Cls; Hon Roll; Jr NHS; NHS; Pres Schlr; Lone Island U.

QUAGLIN, GREG R; Walt Whitman HS; Huntington, NY; (Y); 9/560; Computer Clb; Debate Tm; German Clb; Latin Clb; Mathletes; SADD; Stage Crew; Nwsp Rptr; High Hon Roll; NHS; German Hnr Soc Pres JR Rep 84-86; Mathletes Capt & Sec 82-86; Stu Against Drunk Driving 84-86; U Of PA; Elec Engrng.

QUAINTANCE, ELIZABETH; Alexander Central HS; Alexander, NY; (Y); Ski Clb; Chorus; Color Guard; Variety Show; Yrbk Ed-Chief; Trs Jr Cls; Var Cheerleading; JV Var Socr; Prfct Atten Awd; Bus.

QUALLS, NEILL; Moore Catholic HS; Staten Island, NY; (Y); Boy Scts; Drama Clb; English Clb; Chorus; School Play; Stage Crew; Rep Frsh Cls; Rep Soph Cls; Rep Jr Cls; JV Bowling; Rght To Life Ortrcl Cntst 86; Engl.

QUAN, DIANNA; William Nottingham HS; Syracuse, NY; (Y); 1/220; Hosp Aide; Spanish Clb; Orch; Nwsp Ed-Chief; Ed Lit Mag; Cit Awd; High Hon Roll; Jr NHS; NHS; Ntl Merit SF; Val; Bio Chem.

QUAN, HOANG; Richmond Hill HS; Richmond Hill, NY; (Y); Math Clb; Lit Mag; Rep Soph Cls; Trs Sr Cls; Var Tennis; NHS; Arista.

QUARANTILLO, NATALIE; Grand Island HS; Gr Island, NY; (Y); Church Yth Grp; Sec Chorus; School Musical; School Play; Stage Crew; Variety Show; Sec Sr Cls; Var Capt Swmmng; Hon Roll; NHS; Med.

QUARM, JEANNE; Honeoye Central HS; Holcomb, NY; (S); 9/67; Sec Pres Band; Nwsp Rptr; Trs Sr Cls; Rep Stu Cncl; Var Capt Socr; JV Capt Sftbl; Var Vllybl; Hon Roll; NHS; Altrnt Grls ST 84-85; Math.

QUARRIE III, EUGENE A; Byram Hills HS; Armonk, NY; (Y); 22/150; Am Leg Boys St; Chess Clb; Church Yth Grp; Intnl Clb; Math Clb; Math Tm; SADD; Rep Sr Cls; Capt Crs Cntry; Trk; Hmnts Fstvl; Hmn Rltns Clb; SUNY Bnghmtn; Pltcl Sci.

QUARTERMAN, LESLIE A; Notre Dame Schl; New York City, NY; (Y); Drama Clb; Model UN; Yrbk Stf; Pres Jr Cls; Mgr(s); Jr NHS; Natl Mrt Cmmnd Schlr 85; Carneige-Mellon U Awd 85; Intl Rltns.

QUATRINI, DAN; Amsterdam HS; Amesterdam, NY; (Y); Varsity Clb; Pres Frsh Cls; Rep Soph Cls; Rep Jr Cls; Rep Sr Cls; Trs Stu Cncl; Var Bsbl; JV Bsktbl; Capt Ftbl; Prfct Atten Awd; Bus.

QUATTROCIOCCHI, AMY; Union-Endicott HS; Endicott, NY; (Y); Church Yth Grp; Computer Clb; Drama Clb; French Clb; Key Clb; Mathletes; Orch; Yrbk Stf; High Hon Roll; NHS.

QUATTRONE, TRACY; Olean HS; Olean, NY; (Y); 15/250; Science Clb; Varsity Clb; Bsktbl; Mgr(s); Score Keeper; Trk; High Hon Roll; Hon Roll; Jr NHS; NHS; Bio.

QUCSADA, RUDY; Herbert H Lehman HS; Bronx, NY; (Y); Art Clb; Drm & Bgl; Stage Crew; Bsbl; Socr; Wt Lftg; Hunter Coll; Sci.

QUELLER, TIFFANY; Riverdale Country Schl; New York, NY; (Y); School Musical; School Play; Off Stu Cncl; SADD; Thesps; Art Awd 85-86; Shakespeare Comptn 84-86; Theater.

QUETELL, JENNIFER; Msgr Scanlan HS; Bronx, NY; (Y); French Clb; Intnl Clb; Temple Yth Grp; Church Choir; Yrbk Stf; Chld Psychlgy.

QUIBELL, MATTHEW D; Dansville SR HS; Dansville, NY; (Y); 12/147; Am Leg Boys St; Varsity Clb; Yrbk Sprt Ed; Stu Cncl; Var L Bsbl; Var L Bsktbl; Hon Roll; Band; Var L Crs Cntry; Var JV Socr; Career Mentorship Pgm 85-86; Script-D Awd ; Ldrshp Retreat 85-86; Rochester Inst; Biomedical Comp.

QUICK, CLIFTON J; Kingston HS; Port Ewen, NY; (Y); 48/573; Ski Clb; Spanish Clb; Teachers Aide; Yrbk Phtg; Yrbk Stf; Rep Stu Cncl; Crs Cntry; Var Trk; NHS; Spanish NHS; 4 Yr ROTC Army Scholar 85; NYS Regnts Scholar 86; Clarkson U; Civl Engrng.

QUICK, KELLY; Amsterdam HS; Amsterdam, NY; (Y); Varsity Clb; Var Cheerleading; Stat Mgr(s); Stat Score Keeper; Hon Roll; Accntng.

QUICK, PATTY; Addison Central HS; Addison, NY; (Y); Exploring; Rep Frsh Cls; Score Keeper; Socr; Trk.

QUICKENTON, LAURA; Schoharie Central HS; Schoharie, NY; (Y); Key Clb; Varsity Clb; Chorus; School Musical; School Play; Yrbk Stf; JV Cheerleading; Var Socr; Var Sftbl; JV Capt Vllybl; Art.

QUIETT, D ERIC; Barker Central HS; Barker, NY; (Y); 10/107; AFS; Boy Scts; Church Yth Grp; Varsity Clb; Var Capt Crs Cntry; Var Capt Trk; God Cntry Awd; Hon Roll; NY ST Rgnts Schlrshp 86; U S Army Schlr Athlt Awd 86; Sci Achvmnt Awd; U S Air Force; Math.

QUIG, TREVOR; Pulaski Academy Central School; Parish, NY; (Y); Aud/Vis; Math Clb; Varsity Clb; Wt Lftg; JV Var Wrstlng; Comp Pgmmng.

QUIGG, MICHAEL; Patchogue Medford HS; Medford, NY; (S); VP Band; Concert Band; Drm Mjr(t); Jazz Band; Mrchg Band; Orch; School Musical; Cit Awd; NHS; Spanish NHS; All Cnty Concert Band-1st Chair Alto Sax 85; All Cnty Jazz Ensmbl-1st Chair Alto Sax 85 & 86; Music Perfmnc.

QUIGLEY, CHRISTINE H; Dansville SR HS; Dansville, NY; (Y); 5/160; Am Leg Aux Girls St; Band; Concert Band; Mrchg Band; Yrbk Stf; Stu Cncl; Var Socr; Var Trk; NHS; Mrktng.

QUIGLEY, KATE; Bishop Ludden HS; Syracuse, NY; (Y); JV Capt Bsktbl; Var Trk; Hon Roll; Intro To Chem.

QUIGLEY, KELLY; Mt Mercy Acad; W Seneca, NY; (Y); Camp Fr Inc; Drama Clb; Ski Clb; Spanish Clb; SADD; Chorus; Stage Crew; Im Badmtn; Im Fld Hcky; Latin Clb; Merit Hnr 85-86; Mock Trl 85-86; Schl Sci Fair 83-84; U Of Buffalo; Intl Study.

QUIJANO, AIMEE; The Wheatley HS; Roslyn Hts, NY; (Y); Cmnty Wkr; Sec Mathletes; Model UN; Band; Yrbk Ed-Chief; Yrbk Stf; VP Jr Cls; Stu Cncl; Gym; NHS; 2nd Pl Spnsh Poetry Cntst 85; Oustndng Rtng NUSMA Comptn Piano 86; Aeronautic Engr.

QUIMBY, ELIZABETH; Le Roy Central HS; Le Roy, NY; (Y); 2/135; Pres AFS; French Clb; Math Tm; Spanish Clb; VP Sr Cls; L Tennis; High Hon Roll; Jr NHS; NHS; Sal; Olmstead Engl Prze 86; Pulsafeeder Schlrshp Awd 86; NY U.

QUIMBY, SHARON; Le Roy Central Schl; Le Roy, NY; (Y); 1/135; AFS; Math Tm; Spanish Clb; JV Sftbl; Bausch & Lomb Sci Awd; High Hon Roll; NHS; Ntl Merit Ltr; Pres Schlr; Val; Olmstead Engl Prze 86; Pulsafeeder Schlrshp 86; William Smith Clg; Clscs.

QUINN, CARL; Chatham HS; Austerlitz, NY; (Y); 45/135; 4-H; Library Aide; Chrmn SADD; Ed Lit Mag; Hon Roll; Photogrphr.

QUINN, CHARLES; Valley Central HS; Montgomery, NY; (Y); 15/343; Church Yth Grp; Debate Tm; Math Tm; Science Clb; Spanish Clb; School Musical; Var Ftbl; Hon Roll; NHS; Ntl Merit Ltr; Sci Hnrs Pgm 86-87; Physician.

QUINN, CHRISTINE; White Plains HS; White Plains, NY; (Y); 34/440; Church Yth Grp; Hosp Aide; Spanish Clb; Chorus; Yrbk Stf; Ed Lit Mag; High Hon Roll; Hon Roll; NHS; Regnts Schlrshp 86; Gannette Wstchstr Nwspr Ptry Awd 84-86; RICH Awd 85; SUNY Binghampton; Mgmt.

QUINN, DAVID L; Westhampton Beach HS; East Moriches, NY; (Y); 101/221; Aud/Vis; Boy Scts; Stage Crew; Var Mgr(s); NYS Rgnts Schlrshp 86; Maritime Coll; Marine Bio.

QUINN, ELAINE; Albertus Magnus HS; Valley Ctg, NY; (Y); 1/178; Var Cheerleading; Var Tennis; High Hon Roll; NHS; Ntl Math Hnr Soc 85-86; Sci Hnr Soc 86; Spnsh Clb 83-85.

QUINN, KATHLEEN; Saratoga Central Catholic HS; Ballston Spa, NY; (S); 4/35; Drama Clb; Ski Clb; Varsity Clb; School Play; Stage Crew; Pres Jr Cls; Stu Cncl; Var Capt Bsktbl; Capt Crs Cntry; High Hon Roll; Cmnctns.

QUINN, KATHRYN; Ealr L Vandermeulen HS; Mt Sinai, NY; (Y); Cmnty Wkr; Trs Leo Clb; Color Guard; Concert Band; Mrchg Band; School Musical; School Play; Stage Crew; Nwsp Rptr; High Hon Roll; Extraordnry Svc Mrch Band 85-86; MIP Trk 84; SUNY Binghampton; Intl Rel.

QUINN, KATHY; Tioga Central HS; Barton, NY; (Y); Church Yth Grp; Drama Clb; Girl Scts; SADD; Varsity Clb; Church Choir; Variety Show; Rep Stu Cncl; JV Var Cheerleading; Hon Roll; Miss NYS Natl Teen Fin 86; Reading Excllnce 83; Hghst Soc Studs Avg 83; Ridley Lowell; Exec Sec.

QUINN, KELLY; Villa Maria Acad; Buffalo, NY; (S); 4/98; Church Yth Grp; Computer Clb; French Clb; Math Clb; Pep Clb; Rep Jr Cls; Hon Roll; NHS; Erie CC; Medcl Lab Tech.

QUINN, MAE; Tottenville HS; Staten Island, NY; (Y); 75/870; Drama Clb; School Musical; School Play; Yrbk Rptr; VP Jr Cls; VP Sr Cls; Capt Twrlr; NHS; Magic Clb 85-87; Princpls Pride Yankees Awd 86; Teaching.

QUINN, SUZANNE; St Marys Girls HS; Glen Head, NY; (Y); 7/185; Drama Clb; Math Clb; Ski Clb; School Musical; School Play; Yrbk Stf; VP Stu Cncl; Var Tennis; High Hon Roll; NHS.

QUINN, TRACY L; The Nichols Schl; Orchard Park, NY; (Y); Cmnty Wkr; Mgr(s); JV Tennis; High Hon Roll; Hon Roll; Regnt Schlrshp 86; Schlstc Art Awds Regnl Photogrph Wnnr 86; St Marys Coll.

QUINONES, ARLENE; Christopher Columbus HS; New York, NY; (Y); 164/792; Cmnty Wkr; JA; Office Aide; Political Wkr; Red Cross Aide; Teachers Aide; Band; Typwrtng Awd 86; John Jay Coll; Crmnl Justice.

QUINONES, FELIX; St Agnes HS For Boys; New York, NY; (Y); 7/110; JV L Crs Cntry; JV L Trk; Hon Roll; NHS; Bus Adm.

QUINONES, SANDY; Herbert H Lehman HS; Bronx, NY; (Y); 36/89; Cmnty Wkr; Band; Concert Band; Jazz Band; School Musical; Im Gym; Im Socr; Im Vllybl; Im Wt Lftg; High Hon Roll; Math Merit Awd 84; Achvt Awd 86; Lehman Coll; Pre Med.

QUINTANO, STEVEN; St Marys Boys HS; N Merrick, NY; (S); 12/151; Varsity Clb; Var Capt Bsbl; Var Capt Ice Hcky; High Hon Roll; Hon Roll; NHS; Bst Defns Hcky 85; Empire ST Gms Hcky 86; Sprtsmnshp Awd Hcky 84; Bus.

QUINTERO, ALISSA; Adlai E Stevenson HS; Bronx, NY; (Y); Church Yth Grp; Dance Clb; JA; Science Clb; Concert Band; Mrchg Band; School Play; Yrbk Ed-Chief; JP Sousa Awd; NHS; Medicine.

QUINTERO, SOFIA; James Monroe HS; Bronx, NY; (Y); 1/240; Drama Clb; Nwsp Rptr; Lit Mag; Pres Sr Cls; Trk; Pres NHS; Val; Library Aide; School Musical; School Play; NYS Regents Scholar 86; Dist Atty Citatn Hnr 86; Rensselaer Mdl Excllnce Mth & Sci 86; Columbia U; Law.

QUIRK, DENISE; Centereach HS; Centereach, NY; (Y); Hosp Aide; VFW Awd; Engl.

QUIRKE, DEIRDRE; Cardinal Spellman HS; Bronx, NY; (Y); Art Clb; Church Yth Grp; Pep Clb; Hon Roll; Rgnts Schlrp Nrsng 86; 2nd Hnrs 84-86; Mount St Vincent; Biol.

QUIROLGICO, ANA-LIZA R; St Vincent Ferrer HS; Woodside, NY; (S); 24/76; Science Clb; Chorus; Nwsp Rptr; Ed Nwsp Stf; Rep Stu Cncl; Hon Roll; Jrnlsm.

QUIROS, ANTONIO; De Witt Clinton HS; Bronx Nyc, NY; (Y); JA; Math Clb; Math Tm; Quiz Bowl; Radio Clb; Nwsp Rptr; Nwsp Sprt Ed; Nwsp Stf; Bsbl; Trk; Cornell; Pre Med.

QUONCE, SANDRA; Sandy Creek Central HS; Pulaski, NY; (S); French Clb; Teachers Aide; Band; Mrchg Band; Yrbk Stf; Trs Soph Cls; Trs Jr Cls; Bsktbl; Sftbl; NHS; Travel.

RAB, FAZLE; Long Island City HS; Astoria, NY; (Y); Cit Awd; Hon Roll; Comp Engr.

RABASCO, SAVERIO; Nazareth Regional HS; Brooklyn, NY; (S); 31/267; Varsity Clb; Var Ftbl; Capt Socr; Hon Roll; Coachs Awd Sccr 84.

RABB, JACQUELINE; Laguardia Music & Art HS; Sunnyside, NY; (S); 19/500; Library Aide; Teachers Aide; Hon Roll; NHS.

RABBIA, MARK; John F Kennedy HS; Utica, NY; (Y); Debate Tm; Key Clb; Ski Clb; Spanish Clb; SADD; Stu Cncl; Golf; High Hon Roll; Hon Roll; NHS; Syracuse U; Aerospc Engrng.

RABE, THOMAS E; Maraathon Central HS; Marathon, NY; (Y); 3/68; Am Leg Boys St; Band; School Play; Trk; High Hon Roll; NHS; Pres Schlr; Cmnty Wkr; Drama Clb; French Clb; 4th Am Legs Oratrcl Cntst 86; Clarkson U; Engrg.

RABEL, JULYN; Midwood HS; Brooklyn, NY; (Y); 178/667; Church Yth Grp; Hosp Aide; Office Aide; Service Clb; Teachers Aide; Chorus; Church Choir; School Musical; Pedtrcn.

RABIDEAU, DEATA; Dover JR SR HS; Dover Plains, NY; (Y); 1/130; Am Leg Aux Girls St; Math Clb; Science Clb; Spanish Clb; Band; Chorus; Concert Band; Jazz Band; Mrchg Band; Pep Band; Math, Sci Awd 85-86; Band Awd 84-86; Engrng.

RABIDEAU, TODD; Saranac Central HS; Morrisonville, NY; (S); 38/105; Band; Concert Band; Jazz Band; Hon Roll; Trck Drvng.

RACANELLI, DOMINIQUE; Freeport HS; Freeport, NY; (Y); Girl Scts; Leo Clb; Teachers Aide; Mrchg Band; School Musical; Capt Twrlr; High Hon Roll; NHS; Prfct Atten Awd; Mdrn Lang.

RACANO, ANTHONY; Cardinal Spellman HS; Bronx, NY; (Y); Aud/Vis; Camera Clb; Church Yth Grp; Drama Clb; PAVAS; School Play; Stage Crew; Yrbk Stf; Lit Mag; Coach Actv; Rgnts Schlrshp 86; St Johns U; Cmnctn.

RACE, JOLENE; Hudson HS; Hudson, NY; (Y); Cmnty Wkr; Dance Clb; Band; Church Choir; Concert Band; Mrchg Band; Variety Show; Nwsp Stf; Yrbk Stf; Pom Pon; Herkimer Comm Coll; Ocptnl Thrp.

RACHLINSKI, SCOTT; Frontier SR HS; Hamburg, NY; (Y); Art Clb; Sec Chess Clb; Church Yth Grp; Ski Clb; Spanish Clb; Chorus; Church Choir; Ed Yrbk Phtg; Hon Roll; NHS; Cornell U; Htl Admin.

RACHOW, KIMBERLY; Hilton HS; Hilton, NY; (Y); SADD; Nwsp Rptr; Rep Soph Cls; Rep Jr Cls; Var Capt Cheerleading; Hon Roll; NY ST Regents Schlrshp 86; Syracuse U; Jrnlsm.

RACHT, ANDREA; Anthony A Henninger HS; Syracuse, NY; (Y); Church Yth Grp; Rptr DECA; Intnl Clb; JA; Key Clb; Spanish Clb; SADD; Stage Crew; NHS; Pub Spkng 1st Pl Trophy DECA Comptn 85-86; Ed.

RACHUN, DORTHEA; Coxsackie-Athens JR-SR HS; West Coxsackie, NY; (Y); 34/110; Q&S; Spanish Clb; Ed Nwsp Stf; Mgr Yrbk Stf; High Hon Roll; Hon Roll; NHS; SUNY; Eng.

RACINE, NICOLE; Northeastern Clinton Central Schl; Rouses Point, NY; (Y); 4/153; Band; Church Choir; Jazz Band; School Musical; Bausch & Lomb Sci Awd; High Hon Roll; Hon Roll; NHS; Ntl Merit Ltr; Rgnts Schlrshp 86; Outstndg Chmstry & Spnsh Stu 85; St Lwrnc U; Chem.

RACITI, MELISSA Y; St Marys Girls HS; Little Neck, NY; (Y); #2 In Class; Art Clb; Math Clb; Pres Spanish Clb; Cit Awd; High Hon Roll; Hon Roll; Jr NHS; NHS; Regnts Schlrshp 86; Locl Union 3 William A Hogan Memrl Schlrshp 86; Natl Hispnc Schlr Awds 86; Columbia U; Pol Sci.

RACKMALES, LAURA A; Sleepy Hollow HS; Tarrytown, NY; (Y); 2/178; German Clb; Hosp Aide; Latin Clb; Chorus; School Musical; School Play; Yrbk Stf; Lit Mag; Capt Tennis; High Hon Roll; NY ST Supvrs Awd Bio 85; U Of MI; Lang.

RACKMYRE, CHRISTINA; Gloversville HS; Gloversville, NY; (Y); Rep Frsh Cls; Rep Soph Cls; Bsktbl; Powder Puff Ftbl; Sftbl; Trk; Vllybl; Hon Roll; Dora Louden Schlrsh& 86; Debi Schmtt Mem Schlrshp 86; Mrgrt E Hmm Sprtsmnshp Awd 86; Cobleskill.

RADBELL, NICOLE; Lawrence HS; Lawrence, NY; (Y); French Clb; Office Aide; School Musical; Cheerleading; Sftbl; Hon Roll.

RADEKER, SCOTT; Unatego Central HS; Unadilla, NY; (Y); 7/97; Spanish Clb; Band; Concert Band; Mrchg Band; JV Var Bsbl; Var Capt Bsktbl; JV Var Ftbl; High Hon Roll; NHS; Rotary Awd; Sprts Med.

RADER, ERIC; Susquehanna Valley HS; Binghamton, NY; (Y); Art Clb; Var L Ftbl; Var L Trk; Im Bsktbl; Im Sftbl; Im Vllybl; Im Wt Lftg; Hon Roll; Hamilton; Cvl Engnrng.

RADESI JR, FELIX J; York Central HS; Lercester, NY; (Y); 2/88; Var L Bsbl; Var Bsktbl; Var Capt Ftbl; Bausch & Lomb Sci Awd; High Hon Roll; NHS; Sal; Math Tm; VP Frsh Cls; VP Soph Cls; NY ST Rgnts Schlrshp 86; Clsrm Hnrs In Math 83-85; U Rchstr; Engrng.

RADIC, RUDOLF; Mc Kee Technical HS; Staten Island, NY; (Y); 8/306; Exploring; ST U Of NY Buffalo; Engr.

RADLEY, SHARON; De Ruyter Central HS; Deruyter, NY; (S); Church Yth Grp; Band; Chorus; Concert Band; Jazz Band; Mrchg Band; School Musical; Yrbk Stf; Vllybl; Hon Roll; MIP Vlybl 85.

RADLIFF, BRYAN; Shenendehowa HS; Clifton Park, NY; (Y); 355/675; Cmnty Wkr; Orch; Var Capt Ftbl; Var Lcrss; JV Socr; Var Capt Wrstlng; High Hon Roll; NYS Sect II Wrstlng Champ 86; HS Ms Hnrd Plyr Wrstlng 86; HS Coaches Awd 85-86; Norwich U; Crmnl Law.

RADMAN, DANNY; St Francis Prep; Jackson Heights, NY; (S); 174/744; Computer Clb; Band; Nwsp Stf; Im Sftbl; Im Vllybl; Wt Lftg; Hon Roll; NHS; RI Sch Design; Arch.

RADMAND, ROSHANAK; Lynbrook SR HS; Armonk, NY; (Y); 58/239; French Clb; Spanish Clb; Yrbk Stf; Trk; Hon Roll; Ntl Merit Ltr; Mount St Marys Coll; Bio.

RADMORE, DAVID M; Cortland JR SR HS; Cortland, NY; (Y); 18/188; Var Am Leg Boys St; Chorus; Church Choir; Hon Roll; NHS; Drama Clb; Latin Clb; Thesps; School Musical; School Play; Bass II Sctn Ldr Conf All ST Chorus 85; Stu & Prtcpnt Prodigy Inc Schlrshp Prg & $2000 Ldshp Awd 86; Manhattanville; Psychlgy.

RADOMSKI, THOMAS B; Niagara Catholic HS; Niagara Falls, NY; (Y); 18/87; Church Yth Grp; Debate Tm; French Clb; Intnl Clb; Varsity Clb; High Hon Roll; Hon Roll; Lion Awd; Prfct Atten Awd; Var Capt Bsbl; NY ST Regents Schlrshp 86; U Of Buffalo; Elec Engrng.

RADONIS, RICHARD; East Meadow HS; East Meadow, NY; (Y); Boy Scts; Camera Clb; Rep Cmnty Wkr; Rep FBLA; Key Clb; Pres SADD; Yrbk Phtg; Stu Cncl; Var Ice Hcky; Var Lcrss; NYC Empr ST Gms 86; Vrsty Lttr Awd Lacrss 86; Outstndg Effrt Awd 86; U S Military Acad.

RADU, BOGDANA; Newburgh Free Acad; Newburgh, NY; (Y); Spanish Clb; Chorus; School Play; Stage Crew; Lit Mag; High Hon Roll; Hon Roll; Jr NHS; Syracuse; Law.

RADUNS, STEVEN T; Akron Central HS; Akron, NY; (Y); Boy Scts; Niagara Cnty CC; Cmptr.

RADZIEJEWSKI, CHRISTINE; Plainedge HS; N Massapequa, NY; (Y); 16/303; School Musical; Ed Nwsp Stf; Yrbk Ed-Chief; High Hon Roll; Hon Roll; NHS; Ntl Merit Ltr; Mathletes; Spanish Clb; SADD; Wesleyan Schlr 86; NYS Rgnts Schlrshp 86; U Of Richmond Schlrshp 86; U Of Richmond; Engl.

RADZIEWICZ, ALISA; Sacred Heart Acad; Garden City, NY; (Y); 10/300; Dance Clb; Debate Tm; FNA; Hosp Aide; Pep Clb; Ed Lit Mag; SADD; JV Var Trk; Hon Roll; NHS; Slctd IA Spnsh Cmptn 85; Hsptl Vlntr Srv Awd 85; Hlth Rltd Fld.

RADZVILLA, JESSICA; St Marys Girls HS; Pt Washington, NY; (Y); 28/177; Political Wkr; Ski Clb; SADD; Chorus; Stage Crew; Yrbk Stf; Crs Cntry; Trk; High Hon Roll; NHS; Pol Sci.

RAE, RON; Tonawanda SR HS; Tonawanda, NY; (Y); Church Yth Grp; Computer Clb; Stu Cncl; JV Var Ftbl; Var L Trk; Hon Roll; Arntcl Engrng.

RAEDER, LISA; Horseheads HS; Horseheads, NY; (Y); 62/367; DECA; French Clb; Girl Scts; Band; Chorus; Concert Band; Mrchg Band; High Hon Roll; Hon Roll; Im Bsktbl; Piano Awards 83-86; Bus Mktng.

RAEMORE, MICHAEL C; Corning East HS; Corning, NY; (Y); 17/222; Varsity Clb; Yrbk Bus Mgr; Capt Bsbl; JV Ftbl; Ice Hcky; High Hon Roll; NHS; NY ST Regnts Schlrshp 86; Columbia U; Bus.

RAEZ, RICHARD; Seward Park HS; New York, NY; (Y); Computer Clb; Science Clb; Concert Band; Rep Jr Cls; Cert Of Merit Meritorious Srv 86; Arista Hon Soc 85; Cert Of Merit Bio 85; Bio.

RAFF, KENNETH; Scarsdale HS; Scarsdale, NY; (Y); Office Aide; Spanish Clb; Temple Yth Grp; Varsity Clb; Off Sr Cls; Var Bsbl; Coach Actv; JV Trk; Hon Roll; AP Bio 86; Law.

RAFFAELE, DONNA; Manhasset HS; Manhasset, NY; (Y); Cmnty Wkr; Drama Clb; Library Aide; Sec Spanish Clb; School Play; Stage Crew; Yrbk Stf; Im Bsktbl; Hon Roll; St Johns; Bus.

RAFFE, MELINDA J; Riverhead HS; Riverhead, NY; (Y); 12/196; JCL; Latin Clb; Ski Clb; Yrbk Stf; VP Sr Cls; Var Capt Cheerleading; Var Capt Tennis; Jr NHS; Rgnts Schlrshp 86; Inter Act Clb 84-86; Grls Ldrs Clb VP 83-86; Clarkson U; Bus Admin.

RAFFERTY, DENISE; The Academy Of St Josephs; Commack, NY; (Y); FHA; Am Leg Aux Girls St; Library Aide; Hon Roll; NEDT Awd; NY ST Regents Schlrshp 85-86; Marist Coll; Lbrl Arts.

RAFTERY, BRIAN; Msgr Farrell HS; Staten Island, NY; (Y); Boy Scts; Computer Clb; Spanish Clb; Lit Mag; Im Bsktbl; Im Bowling; JV Crs Cntry; Im Ftbl; High Hon Roll; NHS; Scouting World Cnsrvtn Awd 84; 50 Mile A Foot- A Float Awd 84; Philmont Exp In NM 84; Mech Engr.

RAGNI, FRANK; Mt St Michael Acad; Bronx, NY; (Y); 58/291; Im Bsbl; Im Ftbl; High Hon Roll; Hon Roll; Im Sftbl; Manhattan Clg; Mech Engrg.

RAGONE, ANTHONY P; Salesian HS; Bronx, NY; (Y); 18/86; Boy Scts; Church Choir; Stu Cncl; Bsbl; NHS; Rgnts Schlrshp 86; Iona Coll; Bus.

RAGONE, PATRICIA; John Dewey HS; Brooklyn, NY; (Y); 29/680; Intnl Clb; Spanish Clb; Teachers Aide; Chorus; School Play; Nwsp Rptr; Nwsp Stf; VP Stu Cncl; Cit Awd; High Hon Roll; NY Tokyo Sister City Exc Stu 85; Chancellors Roll Hnr 85; NYS Regnts Schlrshp 86; SUNY.

RAGONESE, SHAWN; Cicero-North Syracuse HS; North Syracuse, NY; (S); 75/667; Church Yth Grp; Im Badmtn; Var L Trk; Hon Roll; NHS; Theolgy.

RAGUSO, LAURA; Aquinas HS; Bronx, NY; (Y); 4/178; Cmnty Wkr; Variety Show; VP Soph Cls; Pres Jr Cls; Stu Cncl; High Hon Roll; Hon Roll; Itln Ntl Hnr Soc 85; Prsdntl Awd Acdmc Ftnss 86; Clmbs Allnc Awd 86; Inoa Coll; Cmmnctns.

RAHILLY, CHRISTINE; Cardinal Spellman HS; Bronx, NY; (Y); 44/509; Intnl Clb; Pep Clb; Ski Clb; Nwsp Stf; Var Capt Swmmng; Hon Roll; NHS; NEDT Awd; Fairfield U; Bus.

RAI, SUBHAS; Mohonasen SR HS; Schenectady, NY; (Y); Computer Clb; ROTC; Varsity Clb; Nwsp Rptr; Yrbk Stf; Capt Im Bsktbl; Var L Ftbl; Var L Trk; Hon Roll; NHS; Mst Valuable Rnnr Awd Var Trk Lg 85; Engrng.

RAICHLIN, ANDREW; Jordan-Elbridge JR SR HS; Memphis, NY; (Y); Boy Scts; Chess Clb; Computer Clb; Concert Band; Mrchg Band; Nwsp Stf; Golf; Jr NHS; Rochester Inst Of Tech; Cmpter.

RAIMOND, JOHANNA J; Bishop Kearney HS; Scottsville, NY; (Y); 10/140; Ski Clb; Var L Bsktbl; Var L Socr; Var L Sftbl; Var L Vllybl; High Hon Roll; NHS; Ntl Merit Ltr; Var Club Treas 85-86; Hamilton Coll; Law.

RAIMY, CATHERINE; Sherburne Earlville Central HS; Smyrna, NY; (Y); 19/158; Church Yth Grp; Band; Hon Roll; NHS; Prfct Atten Awd.

RAJGURU, MANISH; James E Sperry HS; Rochester, NY; (Y); 12/280; Boy Scts; SADD; Varsity Clb; Var Crs Cntry; JV Var Trk; NHS; Spanish NHS; Acdmc Letters 86; Clss Numbers 85; Bus Mgmt.

RAKE, JENNIFER; Johnson City SR HS; Johnson City, NY; (Y); Pep Clb; Ski Clb; Yrbk Ed-Chief; Yrbk Stf; Pres Frsh Cls; Pres Soph Cls; Pres Jr Cls; Pres Sr Cls; Stu Cncl; Var Cheerleading; Schlstc Excllnce Awd 84-86; Salute Yth Rcgntn 86; William & Mary; Math.

RAKOCE, RICHARD C; Massena Central HS; Massena, NY; (Y); Varsity Clb; Rep Frsh Cls; Rep Soph Cls; Rep Jr Cls; JV Bsktbl; Var L Ftbl; Var L Lcrss; Im Vllybl; Im Wrstlng; 1st & Ind Team All Nrthrn La Crosse 85-86; Mst Imprvd Ftbl Awd 85; Empire ST Games 86; SUNY Cntn; Crmnl Jstc.

RAKOSKE, ERIC; Cobleskill Central Schl; Cobleskill, NY; (Y); Aud/Vis; Boy Scts; Church Yth Grp; Cmnty Wkr; Computer Clb; Red Cross Aide; Varsity Clb; Stage Crew; JV Bsktbl; Var L Ftbl; MVP Field Events 86; Engr.

RAKOWSKI, SANDRA; Charles O Dickerson HS; Ithaca, NY; (Y); 11/86; Sec Spanish Clb; Yrbk Stf; Rep Sr Cls; Stu Cncl; Model UN; SADD; L Stat Bsktbl; L Mgr(s); JV L Sftbl; NHS; Spnsh Awd Hgst Avc Psnsh 86; Geneseo ST U; Mgmt Sci.

RALLIFORD, NADIA; Mt Vernon HS; Mt Vernon, NY; (Y); Hosp Aide; Red Cross Aide; VICA; Crs Cntry; Trk; Hon Roll; Dctr.

RALPH, JACQUELINE S; Northeastern Acad; Bronx, NY; (S); School Play; Nwsp Phtg; Nwsp Rptr; Nwsp Stf; Jr Cls; Cheerleading; Sftbl; Vllybl; Hon Roll; Med.

RALSTON, LARRAINE; Massena Central HS; Massena, NY; (Y); 150/300; Church Yth Grp; Sec Key Clb; Radio Clb; Sec Trs Band; Sec Trs Concert Band; Jazz Band; Mrchg Band; Pep Band; Yrbk Bus Mgr; Yrbk Stf; Key Clb Schlrshp-Mst Actvts 86; Lavine Awd-Music Schlrshp, Ldrshp 86; ATC Canton; Retl Bus Mgmt.

RAMAIAH, SUNITHA; The Wheatley Schl; Old Westbury, NY; (Y); Hosp Aide; Model UN; Ed Lit Mag; Stu Cncl; Socr; NHS; Ntl Merit Ltr; Summa Cum Laude Natl Lat Exm 85; 1st Pl Hofstra U Certmen De Poesia Espanola 82-85; Yale Mod U N Awd; Intl Rel.

RAMBACH, MARK; Hamburg SR HS; Hamburg, NY; (Y); 113/230; Church Yth Grp; JV Bsktbl; Var Capt Ftbl; Hon Roll; Arch.

RAMBARAN, MICHEAL; Cardinal Spellman HS; New York, NY; (Y); Boy Scts; French Clb; Ftbl; High Hon Roll; MA Inst Tech; Arch.

RAMBAUD, VERONICA; New Lebanon Central HS; Williamstown, MA; (Y); French Clb; Yrbk Stf; Trs Frsh Cls; Hon Roll; Hudson Vly Auto Clb Awd 85; Excllnt Proctn Frnch 86; Gordon B Drowne Memrl Awd 86; Becker JC; Trvl-Toursm.

RAMBERT, DARNELL; Long Island Lutheran HS; Roslyn Heights, NY; (S); 30/90; Drama Clb; Thesps; Concert Band; Jazz Band; Madrigals; School Musical; Nwsp Bus Mgr; Yrbk Phtg; Trs Stu Cncl; NHS; Music.

RAMDASS, SEAN; De Witt Clinton HS; New York, NY; (Y); ROTC; Band; Cit Awd; Acad Aeronautics; Comp Sci.

RAMER, STEVEN; Brockport HS; Hamlin, NY; (Y); 7/345; Boy Scts; Trs 4-H; Model UN; Concert Band; Mrchg Band; Stat Bsktbl; High Hon Roll; NHS; Eagle Scout 86; Pres Schlrshp At SUNY Plattsburg 86; NY ST Rgnts Schlrshp 86; SUNY Plattsburgh; Biochem.

RAMIEZ, EMPERATRIZ; Cathedral HS; Brooklyn, NY; (Y); 29/281; Chorus; Hon Roll; Borough Manhattan CC; Psych.

RAMIREZ, BRENDA; Eastern District HS; Brooklyn, NY; (Y); 1/34; Cmnty Wkr; Service Clb; Teachers Aide; Stu Cncl; High Hon Roll; Hon Roll; NHS; Prd Of Th Ynks Awd 86; Pdtrcn.

RAMIREZ, DAVID; Beach Channel HS; Flushing, NY; (Y); Varsity Clb; Var Ftbl; Wt Lftg; Prfct Atten Awd; Vrsty Ftbl 84-86; Wght Lftg 84-86; Vrsty Clbs 84-86; Engrng.

RAMIREZ, JOSE; Lindenurt SR HS; Lindenhurst, NY; (Y); 5/450; Debate Tm; German Clb; Spanish Clb; Band; Concert Band; Mrchg Band; School Musical; School Play; Stage Crew; VP NHS; Med.

RAMIREZ, LISSETTE M; Evander Childs HS; Bronx, NY; (Y); 53/383; FHA; Office Aide; Science Clb; VP Frsh Cls; Vllybl; 4th Pl Sci Fr 83; Suny; Psych.

RAMIREZ, LORENA; Hillcrest HS; Elmhurst, NY; (Y); 87/800; Hosp Aide; Sr Cls; Stu Cncl; Trk; Wt Lftg; Med Tech.

RAMIREZ, MAGDA; John Jay HS; Brooklyn, NY; (Y); Hosp Aide; Model UN; Hon Roll; Prfct Atten Awd; Achvt 85; Commdtn Intermdt Alge 86; Pass All Subjts 86; Occup Thrpst.

RAMIREZ, MARGARET; Bronx High School Of Sci; New York, NY; (Y); Sec Church Yth Grp; Cmnty Wkr; Office Aide; Pep Clb; Sec Spanish Clb; Church Choir; Yrbk Rptr; Cheerleading; Natl Hispnc Schlr Awds 86; Commctns.

RAMIREZ, MIGUEL; Richmond Hill HS; Richmond Hill, NY; (Y); Boys Clb Am; Boy Scts; Church Yth Grp; Key Clb; Office Aide; Service Clb; Pres Spanish Clb; Teachers Aide; Band; Lit Mag; Pol Sci.

RAMIS, CRISTOBAL; Hampstead HS; Hempstead, NY; (Y); 52/373; Band; Mrchg Band; Ftbl; Lcrss; Wrstlng; High Hon Roll; Hon Roll; NHS; Comp Sci.

RAMNARINE, ROBERT; Hillcrest HS; New York, NY; (Y); 16/801; Chess Clb; Computer Clb; Hosp Aide; Math Clb; Math Tm; Band; Concert Band; School Musical; High Hon Roll; Ntl Hisp Schlrs Awds Prog Semi-Fnlst 86; Pre-Med.

RAMOND, NICHOLAS; Trinity Schl; New York City, NY; (Y); Cmnty Wkr; Letterman Clb; Math Clb; Trs Spanish Clb; Teachers Aide; Coach Actv; Var Swmmng; Var Trk; St Schlr; Hamilton Coll; Biochem.

RAMOS, ARLENE F; James Monroe HS; Bronx, NY; (Y); 10/239; Drama Clb; Gym; Hon Roll; NHS; Prfct Atten Awd; NY U; Accntng.

RAMOS, CARRIE; John Dewey HS; Brooklyn, NY; (Y); Drama Clb; FNA; FTA; Hosp Aide; Latin Clb; Office Aide; Spanish Clb; SADD; Teachers Aide; Y-Teens.

RAMOS, ELAINE; Acad Of Mt St Ursula; Bronx, NY; (Y); Drama Clb; Spanish Clb; Band; Concert Band; Variety Show; Vllybl; Cit Awd; Hon Roll; Prfct Atten Awd; Crmnl Jstc.

RAMOS, JEANET; Christ The King R HS; Ozone Park, NY; (Y); 72/451; Var Cheerleading; 2nd Hons 85-86; Archtctr.

RAMOS, JOHANNA; Smithtown High School East; Hauppauge, NY; (Y); Rptr Aud/Vis; Hosp Aide; Office Aide; Thesps; Color Guard; Stage Crew; Variety Show; Lit Mag; Stu Cncl; JV Badmtn; Pol Sci.

RAMOS, LIZ; Catherine Mc Auley HS; Brooklyn, NY; (S); 2/68; Dance Clb; Chorus; Yrbk Stf; Pres Jr Cls; Pres Stu Cncl; Var Sftbl; Capt Vllybl; Hon Roll; NHS; Chem.

RAMOS, MANUEL; Dewitt Clinton HS; New York, NY; (Y); Drm Mjr(t); Var Ftbl; Cit Awd; Pres Phys Ftnss Awd; Art Awd; Elec.

RAMOS, MICHELLE; Midwood H S At B K College; Brooklyn, NY; (Y); Art Clb; Cmnty Wkr; Chorus; School Musical; Yrbk Stf; Lit Mag; Swmmng; Arista 83-84; Psych.

RAMOS, ROSE; Riverside HS; Buffalo, NY; (Y); Cheerleading; Art.

RAMOS, SONIA M; St Johns Prep; Jackson Hts, NY; (Y); Art Clb; Dance Clb; Latin Clb; Yrbk Phtg; Yrbk Stf; JV Cheerleading; NY U; Med.

RAMOS, YVONNE; T Raymond Acad; Bronx, NY; (S); Church Yth Grp; Drama Clb; Office Aide; Spanish Clb; Band; Pres Frsh Cls; Pres Jr Cls; Stu Cncl; JV Cheerleading; Hon Roll; John Jay Of Crmnl Jstc; Lawyer.

RAMOTAR, VALMIKI; Brentwood HS; Brentwood, NY; (Y); 2/500; Math Tm; Hon Roll; Jr NHS; NHS; Sal; 1st Pl NY ST Math Cntst 85-86; Amer & European Studs Awds 83-85; Accntng Dept Awd 84-85; Polytechnic U; Elec Engrng.

RAMPASAUD, CONWAY; Amityville Memorial HS; Massapequa, NY; (Y); Nwsp Rptr; Var Socr; Hon Roll; Jr NHS; U Of Miami; Pre-Med.

RAMPERSAUD, SHAKTI; William Howard Taft HS; Bronx, NY; (Y); #1 In Class; Office Aide; Hon Roll; NHS; Prfct Atten Awd; Cert Prog Partcptn Close Up Fndtn 86; Cert Hnr NYC H S Peer Tutrg 86; Engl Lit.

RAMPULLA, ANDREW; St John The Baptist HS; Massapequa, NY; (Y); 159/501; Debate Tm; SADD; Yrbk Stf; Rep Frsh Cls; Rep Soph Cls; Rep Jr Cls; Ftbl; Lcrss; Trk; Wt Lftg; Offnsve MVP Tailback 83 & 84; NYS Wnnr 200 M Trk 83; Dntstry.

RAMSAY, JAMES; L I Luthern HS; Huntington, NY; (S); 41/100; Spanish Clb; Nwsp Rptr; Nwsp Sprt Ed; Yrbk Rptr; Yrbk Sprt Ed; JV Bsktbl; JV Ftbl; Var Golf; Var Capt Tennis; Hon Roll; Brdcstng.

RAMSDEN, TOM; Sachem H S North; Ronkonkoma, NY; (Y); 115/1558; Drama Clb; German Clb; Science Clb; Acpl Chr; School Musical; Variety Show; Bsktbl; Socr; Im Vllybl; Jr NHS; All NY ST Chr 85-86; Nvl Arch.

RAMSEY, ANGELA; Saranac Central HS; Cadyville, NY; (S); Chorus; Csmtlgy.

RAMSTEDT, FREDERIC; Pelham Memorial HS; Pelham, NY; (Y); 17/178; Am Leg Boys St; Boy Scts; Thesps; Lit Mag; Rep Jr Cls; Hon Roll; NHS.

RAMSUNDAR, ARLENE; Evander Childs HS; Bronx, NY; (S); 18/383; Yrbk Stf; Lit Mag; Rep Sr Cls; Hon Roll; Prfct Atten Awd; Math Awd 85; Physcs Cert Merit 85; Chem Cert Of Merit 86; Baruch Coll; Comp Sci.

RANALLO, PAMELA J; Medina HS; Medina, NY; (Y); 17/156; Bsktbl; Fld Hcky; Sftbl; Vllybl; Hon Roll; NHS; Pres Soph Cls; Pres Jr Cls; Pres Stu Cncl; Orleans Cnty JR Miss 86; ST U Of NY Buffalo; Spnsh.

RANCK, TIM; Wayne Central HS; Walworth, NY; (Y); Boy Scts; Math Tm; Band; Concert Band; Pep Band; School Musical; Var Crs Cntry; Var Wrstlng; Hon Roll; NHS; Eagle Scout 85; Acad Achvt Spnsh III 86; Mst Impvd Crss Cntry 85; Biotech.

RANDALL, BARBARA; North Rose Wolcott HS; North Rose, NY; (S); Trs Spanish Clb; Sec Band; Sec Chorus; Pres Soph Cls; Sec Sr Cls; Sec Stu Cncl; Var Sftbl; Mgr Swmmng; Cit Awd; DAR Awd; Hugh O Brien Ldrshp Awd 83; Altrnte To Girls St 84; U Of Rochester Paideia Awd 85; Med.

RANDALL, JEAN; Auburn HS; Auburn, NY; (Y); Church Yth Grp; ROTC; Acpl Chr; Band; Chorus; Church Choir; Color Guard; Concert Band; Mrchg Band; Hon Roll; NYS Rgnts Schlrp 86; USAF JROTC Cert Compltn 86; Cayuga CCC; Sci.

RANDALL, JENNIFER; Manlius-Pebble Hill Schl; Manlius, NY; (S); Library Aide; Model UN; Teachers Aide; Chorus; Madrigals; School Musical; Swing Chorus; Yrbk Phtg; Var Soph Cls; Stu Cncl; Prm Cmmtte Treas 84-85; Prm Cmmtte 85-86; Orthpdc Srgn.

RANDALL, KIM MARIE; Tonawanda HS; Tonawanda, NY; (Y); 56/200; Church Yth Grp; Ski Clb; TEA Schlrshp Tnwnda Educ Assoc 86; Riverview PTA Schlrshp 86; Buffalo St Schlrshp 86; Buffalo St Coll; Spec Educ.

RANDALL, KWAFI J; High School Of Art And Design; Bronx, NY; (Y); FTA; Girl Scts; Office Aide; Variety Show; Cheerleading; High Hon Roll; Hon Roll; Fashion Inst Of Tech; Fshn Merc.

RANDALL, ROBERT; Letchworth Central HS; Castile, NY; (Y); 5/86; Spanish Clb; Varsity Clb; Chorus; Yrbk Phtg; Yrbk Stf; Swmmng; Tennis; Cit Awd; High Hon Roll; NHS; SUNY Oswego; Metrlgy.

RANDALL, SONJA; Glens Falls HS; Glens Falls, NY; (Y); 90/217; French Clb; Pep Clb; Nwsp Stf; High Hon Roll; Hon Roll; Mildred Elley Bus Schl; Ct Repr.

RANDALL, STEPHANIE D; Arkport Central Schl; Arkport, NY; (Y); 3/60; Am Leg Aux Girls St; Ski Clb; Sec Frsh Cls; JV Var Socr; JV Var Vllybl; High Hon Roll; Ntl Merit Ltr; Office Aide; Yrbk Stf; Off Stu Cncl; Bryant & Stratton Schlrshp; Regnts Clg Schlrshp; Arkport Acadmc Soc Membr; Bryant & Stratton; Exec Sec.

RANDALL, TRINA; Long Island City HS; Long Is Cty, NY; (Y); Teachers Aide; Band; School Musical; School Play; Stage Crew; Yrbk Phtg; Yrbk Rptr; Yrbk Stf; Cit Awd; Prfct Atten Awd; U Of SC; Law.

RANDAZZO, CAROLINE; Nazareth HS; Brooklyn, NY; (Y); NHS.

RANDERIA, SONAL; Bronx HS; Sunnyside, NY; (Y); Teachers Aide; Ntl Merit Ltr; Cert For Spnsh Paper 86; Barnard Coll.

RANDOLPH, DAVINA; Monroe Schl Of The Arts; Rochester, NY; (Y); 39/179; Church Yth Grp; Office Aide; Teachers Aide; Chorus; Church Choir; Madrigals; School Musical; School Play; Variety Show; Yrbk Stf; Urbn Lg 86; Debtnt Clb 86; Rlph Bnch 86; Bethune Cook-Man; Music.

RANDOLPH, MARCELLUS; Alfred E Smith HS; New York City, NY; (S); 7/31; Boys Clb Am; Debate Tm; FCA; JA; SADD; Varsity Clb; Bsktbl; High Hon Roll; Hon Roll; Prfct Atten Awd; Cert Of Awd 82; Hnr Roll 84; US Navy; Firemen Apprntshp.

RANEY, BARBARA; Babylon SR HS; Babylon, NY; (Y); Varsity Clb; Band; Yrbk Stf; Var Cheerleading; Var Capt Gym; JV Var Vllybl; High Hon Roll; Hon Roll; NHS; Schlstc Awd Physcl Ed 85-86; Prncpl List Plaque 84-85; Boston Coll; Law.

RANGAIAH, THEJOMANI; Scarsdale HS; Scarsdale, NY; (Y); Cmnty Wkr; Hosp Aide; Spanish Clb; Jr Cls; Sr Cls; Lehigh U; Bio.

RANIERI, PAUL K; Nazareth Regional HS; Brooklyn, NY; (S); 28/267; Var Capt Ftbl; High Hon Roll; Hon Roll; CHSFL Div A Plyr Of Wk Rnnr-Up 84; Prncpls Lst 85; Stu Athlt 84; Acctng.

RANKA, JINENDRA; Roy C Ketcham HS; Poughkeepsie, NY; (Y); Chess Clb; Computer Clb; Math Clb; Jazz Band; Symp Band; Yrbk Stf; Stu Cncl; High Hon Roll; NHS; Ntl Merit Ltr; Intl Sci & Engrng Fair Fnlst 86; 2nd Pl US Patnt Off ISEF 86; Grn Prz Dutchess Cnty Sci Fair 86; Engrng.

RANKIN, DENISE K; Hamburg SR HS; Hamburg, NY; (Y); 79/374; Cmnty Wkr; French Clb; Chorus; High Hon Roll; Hon Roll; Natl Sci Olympd Awd Earth Sci 84; Cert Merit Frnch Cls 84; Comp Sci.

RANKIN, DONNA; Tioga Central HS; Nichols, NY; (Y); 3/96; Variety Show; Rep Frsh Cls; Sec Soph Cls; Trs Jr Cls; Sec Stu Cncl; Var Capt Bsktbl; Var Capt Vllybl; High Hon Roll; NHS; Ntl Merit Ltr; Rochester Inst Tech; Engrng.

RANKIN, KAUNITA DIAHANN; Niagara Falls HS; Niagara Falls, NY; (Y); 116/250; Church Yth Grp; JA; Acpl Chr; Church Choir; Yrbk Stf; Rep Jr Cls; Rep Sr Cls; Rep Stu Cncl; IN Inst Of Tech; Indstrl Engr.

RANKINS, RANDY; Richfield Springs Central Schl; Richfield Spgs, NY; (Y); 3/56; Yrbk Ed-Chief; Yrbk Rptr; Yrbk Stf; Tennis; High Hon Roll; Hon Roll; Jr NHS; NHS; Clark Schlrshp 86; Griffen Jones Awd 86; Utica Coll; Crmnl Justc.

RANSOM, JASON; Frewsburg Central HS; Frewsburg, NY; (Y); 12/85; Church Yth Grp; Pres Frsh Cls; Pres Soph Cls; Var L Bsktbl; Var Crs Cntry; Var Ftbl; Var Trk; Wt Lftg; Hon Roll; Presdntl Physcl Ftnc Awd 82; Merit-Physcl Ftns Awd 81; Rochester Inst Of Tech; Accntng.

RANSOM, LINDA; Fairport HS; Fairport, NY; (Y); Chorus; Nwsp Stf; Yrbk Phtg; Yrbk Stf; Inter Decorator.

RAO, ANJALI; Jericho HS; Syosset, NY; (Y); 25/200; Cmnty Wkr; Drama Clb; SADD; Chorus; School Play; Nwsp Stf; Lit Mag; Hon Roll; NHS; St Schlr; Jericho Cider Mill Schlrshp 86; Comm Arts Ctr Awd 86; Cathloic Leag Relgious Civil Rights Awd 86; Harvard U; Gov.

RAO, SHOBA; Emma Willard Schl; Loudonville, NY; (Y); Computer Clb; Intnl Clb; Temple Yth Grp; Comp Sci.

RAPACIOLI, NADINE; Academy Of Mount St Ursula; Pelham Bay, NY; (Y); 4/137; Drama Clb; Chorus; School Play; Nwsp Bus Mgr; Yrbk Ed-Chief; Rep Frsh Cls; Rep Soph Cls; High Hon Roll; NEDT Awd; Science Clb; 1st Pl Iona Lang Cntst Frnch II & III 83&84; Intl Rltns.

RAPASADI, ROBERT; Canastota HS; Canastota, NY; (S); 6/160; Boy Scts; Church Yth Grp; VP Intnl Clb; Sec Leo Clb; Science Clb; SADD; Nwsp Stf; Rep Frsh Cls; Rep Soph Cls; Rep Jr Cls; Hghst Avg Soc Studs 84; Hnrb Mntn Ftbl All Stars 85; Colgate.

RAPOPORT, ROSTISLAV; Franklin D Roosevelt HS; Brooklyn, NY; (Y); Cmnty Wkr; Library Aide; Office Aide; Orch; School Play; Nwsp Stf; VP Frsh Cls; Var Bsktbl; Var Trk; Hon Roll; Regents Scholar 85; Long Island U; Phrmcy.

RAPOSH, BOHUMIL; Mount St Michael Academy; Bronx, NY; (Y); 31/329; Computer Clb; French Clb; Letterman Clb; Office Aide; Hon Roll; Im Bsktbl; Im Ice Hcky; Var L Socr; Im Hcky Chmpns 85; Bskbl Chmps 84; Var Sccr City Chmps 85; Wrk Prt Tm Mcdnlds; Cmptrs.

RAPP, JILL; Jamesville-De Witt HS; Dewitt, NY; (Y); Church Yth Grp; French Clb; Key Clb; SADD; Cheerleading; Diving; Pom Pon; Swmmng; High Hon Roll; Hon Roll.

RAPPAPORT, EVAN; Clarkston SR HS South; New City, NY; (Y); Chess Clb; Drama Clb; Scholastic Bowl; Band; Mrchg Band; School Musical; School Play; Stage Crew; Lit Mag; Bowling.

RAPPAPORT, GAIL B; Trinity HS; New York, NY; (Y); Cmnty Wkr; Yrbk Phtg; Yrbk Stf; Rep Stu Cncl; Var L Lcrss; Var L Swmmng; Capt L Vllybl; NY ST Regnts Schlrshp 86; Foundr Santas Helprs; Chaplain's Awrd For Comm Serv 86; U Of PA; Psych.

RAPPAPORT, MARCI; Glen Cove HS; Glen Cove, NY; (Y); Sec French Clb; Key Clb; Pep Clb; SADD; Stat Bsktbl; Stat Lcrss; Score Keeper; Var Vllybl; Hon Roll; NHS.

RAPPAZZO, ROSANNA; Albany HS; Albany, NY; (Y); 7/600; Hon Roll; NHS; Art Schlrshp NY Brd Ed Comprhnsv Schlrshp Fund 86; ST U Of NY Albany; Math.

RAPPL, MARY; Buffalo Academy Of Sacred Heart; Williamsville, NY; (Y); Pres German Clb; Acpl Chr; School Musical; Pres Soph Cls; Pres Stu Cncl; Crs Cntry; Trk; Hon Roll; NHS; Pres Schlr; NYS Regents Schlrshp, Pres Acdmc Ftns Awd 86; Canisius Coll; Chem.

RAPPOLE, BERT W; Jamestown HS; Jamestown, NY; (Y); 4/390; Pres Church Yth Grp; Quiz Bowl; School Musical; Trs Frsh Cls; Pres Soph Cls; Rep Jr Cls; Rep Sr Cls; Var L Socr; Jr NHS; NHS; Stanford U.

RAQUEL, SANCHEZ; Monroe HS; Rochester, NY; (Y); Varsity Clb; Im Coach Actv; Im Socr; Var Trk; JV Vllybl; Hon Roll; NCTE Awd; Prfct Atten Awd; Spanish NHS; Phy Educ 86; Rcrd Kpng 86; Gd Effrt & Excelnt Behvr 85; U Of Rochester; Doc.

RASCHIATORE, HOLLY L; L C Obourn HS; E Rochester, NY; (Y); 1/120; Sec Exploring; Capt Math Tm; Yrbk Bus Mgr; Yrbk Ed-Chief; Bausch & Lomb Sci Awd; High Hon Roll; NHS; Pres Schlr; Val; Veronica Maher Scholar Rochester Chptr Red Crs 86; Regents Scholar 86; E Rochester Amblnce Scholar 86; Nazareth Coll Rochstr; Biochem.

RASHA, KYLE W; Rome Free Acad; Lee Center, NY; (Y); Am Leg Boys St; Boy Scts; Church Yth Grp; Variety Show; Soph Cls; Jr Cls; Sr Cls; Trk; JR Statesmn Amer Summer Schl Stanford U 86; Co-Ord MC & Talent Show JR Statesmn 86KC Awds 81-86; Cal Tech; Bio.

RASHFORD, SONDRA; Vernon Verona Sherrill Central HS; Verona, NY; (Y); Pres Var Church Yth Grp; GAA; Spanish Clb; Rep Frsh Cls; Rep Soph Cls; Rep Jr Cls; JV Var Socr; JV Var Vllybl; High Hon Roll; NHS; Chld Psych.

RASK, KURT; Shaker HS; Latham, NY; (Y); School Musical; JV Diving; Var Capt Gym; Var Swmmng; Ntl Merit Schol; Schlrshp Syracuse U; All Am Status Gym 84-86; V Ltr Gym; Syracuse U; Bus Mgmt.

RASMUSSEN, BONNIE A; Ross SR HS; Brentwood, NY; (Y); 2/500; Pres Computer Clb; Radio Clb; Yrbk Stf; VP Stu Cncl; Mgr Wrstlng; High Hon Roll; Pres Jr NHS; Sec NHS; Ntl Merit Ltr; Sal; Hghst Acdmc Avg 83; Ldrshp Awd Hnr Clb 84; Adlephi U.

RASMUSSEN, KARI; Hugh C Williams HS; Canton, NY; (Y); 3/150; Model UN; School Play; Stage Crew; Nwsp Rptr; Yrbk Ed-Chief; Lit Mag; Trk; High Hon Roll; NHS; Voice Dem Awd.

RASMUSSEN, MELISSA; Narrowsburg Central HS; Narrowsburg, NY; (Y); 3/25; Ski Clb; Band; Chorus; School Musical; Yrbk Ed-Chief; Rep Sr Cls; Trs Stu Cncl; Cit Awd; High Hon Roll; NHS; Girl Of Yr 86; Hosp Schlrshp 86; Svc To Music Awd 86; Alfred ST; Med Rcrd Tech.

RATAJCZAK, CINDY; St Marys HS; Cheektowaga, NY; (S); 16/166; Cmnty Wkr; Ski Clb; Nwsp Rptr; Lit Mag; Hon Roll; NHS; NY St Rgnts Schlrshp 86; European Cltrs Hnrs Awd 84; Soc Studies.

RATELLE, TERESA; Hoosic Valley HS; Schaghticoke, NY; (Y); French Clb; Spanish Clb; SADD; JV Bsktbl; JV Sftbl; Hudson Valley; Elem Ed.

RATER, MARTY; Clymer Central Schl; Findley Lake, NY; (Y); 9/54; Pres FFA; Pres Jr Cls; Pres Stu Cncl; Var Bsktbl; Var Capt Ftbl; Capt Trk; High Hon Roll; Alfred ST Coll; Ag Tchr.

RATH, RANDALL G; Glens Falls HS; Glens Falls, NY; (Y); 19/204; Am Leg Boys St; SADD; Pres Jr Cls; Pres Sr Cls; JV Var Bsbl; JV Var Bsktbl; JV Var Ftbl; Wt Lftg; NHS.

RATHBONE, TABETHA A; Edmeston Central HS; Burlington Flats, NY; (Y); 6/37; Pres 4-H; GAA; Math Tm; Red Cross Aide; Band; Chorus; Socr; Vllybl; High Hon Roll; Hon Roll; 1st Am Essy 85; Schlrshp Red Cross Sem 85; Talbot Awd High Hist Avrg & Regnts 85; Geneseo ST; Bus Mgmt.

RATHJE, JERILYNN; Roscoe Central Schl; Cooks Falls, NY; (Y); 11/23; Cmnty Wkr; Sec 4-H; SADD; Teachers Aide; Varsity Clb; Chorus; School Play; Stage Crew; Ed Yrbk Stf; Trs Frsh Cls; Natl Hairdrssrs Assn Cnty Awd 86; Fash Inst Tech NYC; Cosmtc.

RATKA, LISA; Frontier Central HS; Hamburg, NY; (Y); French Clb; FBLA; SADD; Rep Jr Cls; Rep Stu Cncl; High Hon Roll; Hon Roll; NHS; SUNY Buffalo; Bus.

RATNARATHORN, MONDHIPA; Notre Dame Acad HS; Staten Island, NY; (Y); Math Tm; Science Clb; Stu Cncl; Var Capt Swmmng; Cit Awd; High Hon Roll; Jr NHS; NHS; Sal; Stdnt Athl Awd, Hnry Ment Sci Fair 86; Outstndng Chem Awd 85.

RATNER, DAVID; P D Schreiber HS; Port Washington, NY; (Y); 69/391; AFS; Hosp Aide; Latin Clb; Quiz Bowl; Yrbk Stf; Stu Cncl; Stat Bsbl; Stat Bsktbl; Var Socr; Long Island Cncl Soc Studs Awd 85; Cum Laude Awd Natl Latin Exam 85; Med.

RATOWSKI, TRACI; Hugh C Williams HS; Canton, NY; (Y); SADD; Stage Crew; Stat Lcrss; Comm.

RATTO, ANDY; North Warren Central HS; Chestertown, NY; (Y); 4/49; Math Clb; VP Pres SADD; Concert Band; Jazz Band; Mrchg Band; School Play; Yrbk Phtg; Rep Frsh Cls; Rep Stu Cncl; Tennis; Adirondack CC; Bus.

RATTOBALLI, RICHARD; St Marys Manhasset HS; West Hempstead, NY; (Y); 5/148; Ski Clb; Var JV Lcrss; High Hon Roll; Hon Roll; NHS; Hghst Hnrs 83-85; Hofstra U; Bus Adm.

RATUNIL, LUDEMO; Mc Quaid Jesuit HS; Mt Morris, NY; (Y); 16/163; Camera Clb; Orch; Yrbk Phtg; Im Ice Hcky; High Hon Roll; Hon Roll; 2 Time Acad Ltr Recip 85 & 86.

RAUCH, LARRY; New Rochelle HS; Scarsdale, NY; (Y); Trs FBLA; Hon Roll; NHS; Outstndng Achvmnt Spnsh 85; Hnry Heilbrn Awd & Sinai Hnr Scty Temple Israel 85; Mltpl Hnrs Attndnc; Bus Adm.

RAUCH, LEN; Bishop Ludden HS; Liverpool, NY; (Y); Boys Clb Am; Cmnty Wkr; Political Wkr; Variety Show; Off Frsh Cls; Off Soph Cls; Off Jr Cls; Stu Cncl; JV Var Bsbl; Capt Var Bsktbl.

RAUCHENBERGER, CATHERINE; St Marys Girls HS; Douglaston, NY; (Y); 20/200; French Clb; Stage Crew; Nwsp Stf; NHS; Lang.

RAUS, KIM; Onondaga HS; Syracuse, NY; (S); 8/67; Exploring; Spanish Clb; SADD; Varsity Clb; Rep Frsh Cls; Rep Soph Cls; Rep Jr Cls; Trs Stu Cncl; Cheerleading; High Hon Roll; Le Moyne; Accntng.

RAUSCH, ERIK; Long Island Lutheran HS; Hicksville, NY; (S); 7/93; Band; Jazz Band; JV Var Bsbl; Var Capt Bsktbl; Var JV Ftbl; Cit Awd; High Hon Roll; NHS; Bsbl MVP 85; Engrng.

RAUSCH, JULIE; L I Lutheran HS; Hicksville, NY; (S); Church Yth Grp; Band; Bsktbl; Vllybl; High Hon Roll.

RAUSCH, ROBERT; Guilderland Central HS; Albany, NY; (Y); Nwsp Rptr; Nwsp Stf; JV Crs Cntry; Im Golf; Hon Roll; NHS; Prfct Atten Awd; Law.

RAUSCHER, DAVID G; The Harley Schl; Pittsford, NY; (Y); Model UN; Varsity Clb; Nwsp Rptr; Nwsp Stf; JV Var Socr; JV Tennis; Var Vllybl; Boston U; Bus.

RAUSCHER, KIM; Seaford HS; Seaford, NY; (Y); Civic Clb; FBLA; Political Wkr; NY U; Pre-Law.

RAUSHI, DEBORAH; Scotia-Glenville HS; Scotia, NY; (Y); 3/250; Sec Trs Church Yth Grp; Trs SADD; Band; Orch; High Hon Roll; NHS; Prfct Atten Awd; Pres Schlr; Intnl Clb; Key Clb; Am Assoc Tchrs Spnsh Medal 86; Schrlshp Cert Merit 86; Hist Found Essay Cntst Merit Wnnr 85; St Lawrence U.

RAUTENSTRAUCH, SANDRA; Attica SR HS; Strykersville, NY; (Y); 26/176; AFS; Sec VP Church Yth Grp; Drama Clb; Pres Girl Scts; Band; Church Choir; Concert Band; Var Crs Cntry; Var Trk; Slvr Awd 2nd Hghst Awd In Grl Scts 84; Hmn Srvs.

RAUTENSTRAUCH, SUSAN; Chalres H Roth HS; West Henrietta, NY; (Y); 30/200; Cmnty Wkr; Pres Red Cross Aide; SADD; Pres Red Cross Aide; SADD; Yrbk Ed-Chief; Rep Stu Cncl; Stat Mgr(s); Var Capt Swmmng; Var Capt Wrstlng; NY ST Rgnts Schlrshp 85-86; Amer Red Cross Wrkshp 85; Slippery Rock U; Sprts Med.

RAVENEL, LAYSALLE; Roosevelt JR SR HS; Roosevelt, NY; (S); JA; High Hon Roll; Hon Roll; NHS; Ntl Merit SF; Prfct Atten Awd; MIT; Engrng.

RAVERT JR, W JOHN; Southside HS; Elmira, NY; (Y); 10/319; Church Yth Grp; Pep Clb; Spanish Clb; Varsity Clb; Var Crs Cntry; Var L Trk; Hon Roll; NHS; Yth County 85; Elmira Star Gazette Carrier Mnth Awd 83; Regents Schlrshp 86; SUNY-BUFFALO; Aero Sp Engr.

RAVO, ADRIENNE L; Walt Whitman HS; Huntington, NY; (Y); 11/550; Computer Clb; Dance Clb; Teachers Aide; Lit Mag; Capt Cheerleading; Mgr(s); High Hon Roll; Jr NHS; NHS; Spanish NHS; Treas Amer Heritg Clb 85-86; Prncpls Lst 85-86; Top Wnnr Natl Spnsh Exm Lvl 5 86; Adelphi U; Elem Ed.

RAWLEIGH, ANGEL; Perry Central HS; Perry, NY; (Y); 7/100; Varsity Clb; Frsh Cls; Trs Church Yth Grp2; Trs Sr Cls; Cheerleading; High Hon Roll; Hon Roll; NHS; Natl Sci Olympd 86; SUNY Geneseo; Ed.

RAWNER, REGINA; Stuyvesant HS; Brooklyn, NY; (Y); Temple Yth Grp; Yrbk Stf; Var L Crs Cntry; Var L Trk; NHS; Ntl Merit Ltr; Spanish NHS; Library Aide; Math Tm; Spanish Clb; Hbrw Cltr Clb-Treas 85; Bnai Brith 86; Empr ST Schlrshp 86; Tulane U; Chem.

RAY, ARLANNA L; Roosevelt HS; Yonkers, NY; (Y); Art Clb; Church Yth Grp; Cmnty Wkr; FCA; Hosp Aide; JA; Library Aide; Office Aide; OEA; Red Cross Aide; Cert Of Excllnc & Achvt In The Bible 84-86; Adolescents Voc Explrtn Excllnc Cmptn 84; Crmnlgy Achvt 86; Crmnl Law.

RAY, CINDY R; Hancock Central HS; Hancock, NY; (Y); Hst Chorus; Concert Band; Jazz Band; School Play; Pres Sr Cls; Trs Stu Cncl; DAR Awd; High Hon Roll; Hon Roll; Trs NHS; NYS Rgnts Schlrshp 86; SUNY Cortland; Psych.

RAY, DAVID; Tully Central HS; Apulia Station, NY; (Y); 17/65; Art Clb; Boy Scts; Cmnty Wkr; Drama Clb; 4-H; Hosp Aide; Library Aide; Mathletes; PAVAS; Science Clb; Morrisville Coll; Ag Sci.

RAY, DIANE PATRICIA; Monsignor Scanlan HS; Flushing, NY; (Y); 3/278; Church Yth Grp; Math Clb; Yrbk Stf; Var Vllybl; High Hon Roll; NHS; Prfct Atten Awd; 1st & 2nd Hnrs; Acdmc Achvmnt Math, Engl, Hstry, Spnsh & Acctg; Bus.

RAY, JON; Fox Lane HS; Mt Kisco, NY; (Y); Intnl Clb; Spanish Clb; Lit Mag; Var Ftbl; Var Capt Trk; Hon Roll; Columbia Schlstc Press Assoc Awd 84; Cmmnctns.

RAYBURN, DAVID; Beacon HS; Beacon, NY; (S); 5/210; VP Key Clb; Pres Varsity Clb; Yrbk Stf; Rep Stu Cncl; Var Ftbl; JV Socr; Var Wrstlng; High Hon Roll; NHS; Elec Engr.

RAYBURN, JODIE; Beacon HS; Beacon, NY; (S); 1/216; Sec Key Clb; Band; Yrbk Stf; Sec Jr Cls; Rep Stu Cncl; Stat Ftbl; Sftbl; High Hon Roll; NHS; Vet.

RAYCHAUDHURI, RENEE; Ossining HS; Ossining, NY; (Y); Chorus; Yrbk Stf; Soph Cls; Rep Stu Cncl; Tennis; Pro Tennis Plyr.

RAYDEN, LISA D; Sheepshead Bay HS; Brooklyn, NY; (Y); Art Clb; Camera Clb; Bowling; Hon Roll; Regnts Schlrshp 86; Alexander Medl For Art 86; Brooklyn Coll; Art.

RAYESKI, ELIZABETH A; Corning-Painted Post West HS; Corning, NY; (Y); Letterman Clb; Thesps; Varsity Clb; Chorus; Church Choir; School Musical; Rep Frsh Cls; Rep Soph Cls; Rep Jr Cls; Rep Sr Cls; Grad W/Hnrs-Math & Spnsh 85-86; Rgnts Schlrshp 85-86; Corning CC; Physcl Thrpy.

RAYMO, JIM; Henninger HS; Syracuse, NY; (Y); JV Ftbl; Var JV Lcrss.

RAYMO, STEVE; Whitesboro Central HS; Utica, NY; (Y); Trs Church Yth Grp.

RAYMON, ROMA; Indian River JR-SR HS; Theresa, NY; (Y); Church Yth Grp; Sec Latin Clb; Band; Yrbk Stf; Stu Cncl; Bsktbl; Swmmng; Trk; High Hon Roll; Dance Clb; Sci Fld.

RAYMOND, JOSIE; Bishop Kearney HS; Scottsville, NY; (Y); 10/140; Ski Clb; Trs Varsity Clb; L Bsktbl; L Socr; Capt L Sftbl; L Vllybl; High Hon Roll; NHS; Ntl Merit Ltr; Regents Scholarshp; Hamilton Coll; Law.

RAYMOND, PIERRE R; Prospect Heights HS; Brooklyn, NY; (Y); French Clb; Intnl Clb; Stage Crew; Nwsp Stf; Off Frsh Cls; Vllybl; High Hon Roll; Hon Roll; Spanish NHS; Cathlc Tchrs Assoc Diocs Bklyn Inc 86; Assoc Blck Ed NY 86; Pan Amer Soc US 86; Hunter Coll; Bilinqual Ed.

RAYMOND, SCOTT; Deposit Central HS; Deposit, NY; (Y); Boy Scts; Bsbl; JV Capt Ftbl; JV Capt Wrstlng; High Hon Roll; Hon Roll; Natl Sci Olympiad 84-85; Culinary Inst Of Amer; Fd Serv.

RAYMOND, STACEY; Moriah Central HS; Mineville, NY; (Y); 1/89; AFS; Hosp Aide; Red Cross Aide; Rptr Yrbk Stf; High Hon Roll; Pres NHS; Pres Schlr; St Schlr; Val; French Clb; Ntl Hon Soc Awd 86; John Mulholland Awd Almni Assn 86; Regnts Diplma W/Hons 86; Niagara U; Psych.

RAYNOR, GINA; Mepham HS; Bellmore, NY; (Y); Debate Tm; Sec Orch; Yrbk Stf; Off Frsh Cls; Bsktbl; Lcrss; Mgr(s); Capt Socr; High Hon Roll; Prfct Atten Awd; Med.

RAYNOR, MICHELLE; Southampton HS; Southampton, NY; (Y); 16/100; French Clb; Yrbk Phtg; Yrbk Stf; Powder Puff Ftbl; Hon Roll; NHS; Art.

RAYOS, LEANDRO; Thomas A Edison HS; Jamaica, NY; (Y); Office Aide; Service Clb; Varsity Clb; Rep Soph Cls; Im JV Bowling; Vllybl; Wt Lftg; Hon Roll; Prfct Atten Awd; J Henry Holloway Cert Intl Grphc Arts 84.

RAZEY, CHRISTINE; Portville Central HS; Olean, NY; (Y); 27/109; Pres Church Yth Grp; Pep Clb; Church Choir; Concert Band; Mrchg Band; Yrbk Stf; High Hon Roll; Hon Roll; All-Cnty Msc Awd 83-86; Bethany Bible Coll; Chrstn Educ.

RAZUKAS, CHRISTIAN; Bishop Ford C C HS; New York, NY; (Y); 22/420; Hosp Aide; Math Tm; Science Clb; Teachers Aide; Nwsp Ed-Chief; Pres Soph Cls; Ntl Merit SF; Mathletes; Nwsp Rptr; Yrbk Stf; U Of MI Giving Schlrshp 86; U Of MI; Chem.

RAZULIS, JOHN; Ceentral Islip HS; Central Islip, NY; (Y); Math Clb; Math Tm; Ftbl; Trk; Wrstlng; Coll Calc 10th & 11th Grd Fr Coll Crdts 85-86; 98% Natl HS; Engr.

RAZZANO, MARY; Johnstown HS; Johnstown, NY; (Y); Stu Cncl; JV Bsktbl; JV Cheerleading; JV Var Sftbl; Timer; Bryant & Straton; Stwrdss.

REA, DONNA A; Churchville Chili HS; Churchville, NY; (Y); 1/320; Aud/Vis; Math Tm; Chorus; School Musical; Val; FTA; School Play; High Hon Roll; Ntl Merit Ltr; VFW Awd; Rbrts Wesleyan Coll; Music Educ.

REA, ROBERT K; Saugerties Central HS; Saugerties, NY; (S); 94/252; German Clb; Quiz Bowl; Trk; Hon Roll; Social Studies Olympiod Wnnr 84-85; Ulster Cnty CC; Pre-Law.

READ, THERESA; Byron-Bergen Central Schl; Byron, NY; (Y); Hosp Aide; Teachers Aide; Score Keeper; Cayuga Cnty CC; Rtl Bus Mgmt.

REAGAN, JAMES M; Waterloo SR HS; Waterloo, NY; (Y); 16/161; FTA; Ski Clb; Spanish Clb; Teachers Aide; JV Ftbl; Hon Roll; Rgnts Schlrshp 86; SUNY At Oswego; Math.

REAGAN, MARK; Henninger HS; Syracuse, NY; (Y); 3/400; Lbrl Arts.

REAGAN, MICHELLE D; Bethlehem Central HS; Delmar, NY; (Y); 121/304; Cmnty Wkr; Drama Clb; Girl Scts; Key Clb; Chorus; School Musical; School Play; Yrbk Stf; Rep Stu Cncl; Var Civic Clb0; Jacobs Pllw 85; TX Chrstn U; Bllt.

REALMUTO, ATHENA; Williamsville North HS; Getzville, NY; (Y); DECA; Bus Mgt.

REALMUTO, JENNIFER; Smithtown HS East; Smithtown, NY; (Y); Church Yth Grp; Drama Clb; Thesps; Acpl Chr; Chorus; Church Choir; School Musical; School Play; Variety Show; Hon Roll; NYSSMA Perf Score 86-87, All Cnty Mxd Chrus 85-86; Music.

REALS, STACEY; East Syracuse-Minoa HS; E Syracuse, NY; (Y); Exploring; Office Aide; Ski Clb; Chorus; Church Choir; School Musical; Stage Crew; Jr NHS; Merit Roll; Prncpls Cabinet; Bus.

REARDON, EILEEN; School Of The Holy Child; White Plains, NY; (S); Hosp Aide; School Play; Nwsp Sprt Ed; Rep Jr Cls; Swmmng; Vllybl; Hon Roll.

REARDON, JOANN; Saint Barnabas HS; Bronx, NY; (S); 23/188; Cmnty Wkr; Math Clb; Hon Roll; Prfct Atten Awd; Fire Safty Awd 80; Coburn; Buyer.

REARDON, KEITH P; Iona Preparatory HS; Yonkers, NY; (Y); Am Leg Boys St; Church Yth Grp; Cmnty Wkr; Political Wkr; Ski Clb; Nwsp Stf; Yrbk Stf; Diving; Lcrss; Swmmng; Vet.

REARDON, MATT; Spackenkill HS; Poughkeepsie, NY; (Y); 11/169; School Musical; Yrbk Ed-Chief; Var L Ftbl; Var L Trk; Var L Wrstlng; Hon Roll; VP NHS; Thesps; School Play; Stage Crew; Mid Hudson Wrstlng Offcls Assn Outstndg Stu Athl 86; NYS Rgnts Schlr 86; Army Rsrv Ntl Schl/Athl 86; West Point; Intl Affrs.

REARDON, MICHAEL; Port Jervis HS; Port Jervis, NY; (Y); 68/200; Chess Clb; Church Yth Grp; Computer Clb; Scholastic Bowl; School Musical; Stage Crew; Hon Roll; Squire Mnth 86; Cmptrs.

REARDON, SHARON; Salmon River Central HS; Bombay, NY; (S); 10/88; Church Yth Grp; French Clb; Teachers Aide; Band; Concert Band; Yrbk Stf; Hon Roll; NHS; Prfct Atten Awd; Plattsburgh ST U; Elem Educ.

REAVES, ANGELA; Nottingham SR HS; Syracuse, NY; (Y); 93/220; Church Yth Grp; Civic Clb; Scholastic Bowl; Spanish Clb; Church Choir; Var 4-H Awd; Dance Clb; Exploring; 4-H; SADD; Acad Excell Awds Urban Leag Spnsrd Cntsts 84 & 85; Acad Awds Gvn By Chrch & Lmyne Coll 84 & 85; Suny Albany; Comp Sci Fld.

REAVES, ANITA DAWN; Elsworth J Wilson HS; Rochester, NY; (Y); Concert Band; Nwsp Stf; Rep Sr Cls; Bsktbl; High Hon Roll; Sec NHS; Ntl Merit SF; Art Edtr Yrbk 85-86; Stu Brd Ed Pres 85-86; MI ST U; Mktng.

REBEOR, DANIEL; G Ray Bodley HS; Fulton, NY; (Y); 46/261; Aud/Vis; Civic Clb; Drama Clb; German Clb; Library Aide; School Musical; School Play; Stage Crew; Nwsp Sprt Ed; Bsktbl; Press Clb Scholar 86; Audio-Visual Awd 86; Yth Crt Apprctn Plaque 86; SUNY Fredonia; Cmmnctns.

REBL, LESLIE; Griffith Inst & Central Schl; Glenwood, NY; (Y); Drama Clb; School Play; Stage Crew; SADD; Color Guard; Flag Corp; Psych.

REBUCK, PAUL S; Liverpool HS; Liverpool, NY; (Y); 49/830; Var Capt Ftbl; Var L Trk; High Hon Roll; Hon Roll; NHS; NY St Regents Schlrshp 86; Amherst Coll; Pre-Med.

RECALDE, CONSUELO; Division Avenue HS; Levittown, NY; (Y); 2/335; Band; Lit Mag; Pom Pon; Bausch & Lomb Sci Awd; Hon Roll; Jr NHS; VP NHS; Sal; VFW Awd; U Schlr Awd Frm C W Post 86-87; Carin Finch Awd Frm Ntl Hon Soc 86; C W Post U; Math.

RECALL, LESLIE A; Cathedral Preparatory Seminary; Bronx, NY; (Y); 16/22; Church Yth Grp; NFL; Speech Tm; School Musical; School Play; Pres Sr Cls; VFW Awd; Voice Dem Awd; Drama Clb; Library Aide; Cathedral Prep Sem Cert Merit Forensics 84; Pol Sci.

RECAME, ERIC J; East Islip HS; East Islip, NY; (Y); Varsity Clb; Band; Concert Band; Drm & Bgl; Jazz Band; Mrchg Band; School Musical; JV Var Socr; NYSSMA Awd Solo 85 & 86; Snyssma Awd Bank Comp 85-86; Engrng.

RECESSO, ART; Johnstown HS; Johnstown, NY; (Y); Boy Scts; Computer Clb; Teachers Aide; Var Ftbl; Var L Wrstlng; Comp Sci.

RECHEN, EILEEN; New Paultz HS; Highland, NY; (Y); 27/120; Var Fld Hcky; Var Sftbl; Hon Roll; NHS; Sr Athltc Awd; SUNY Oswego; Phys Thrpy.

RECHER, TIM; Byram Hills HS; Armonk, NY; (Y); 70/150; Am Leg Boys St; VP JA; Letterman Clb; Political Wkr; SADD; Stu Cncl; Var L Ftbl; High Hon Roll; Hon Roll; Awd Achvt 85; Awd Determntn 86; ST Regnts Awd 86; U Of IA; Bus.

RECINE, ANNA; St Barnabas HS; Yonkers, NY; (S); 2/188; Drama Clb; Library Aide; Office Aide; Nwsp Rptr; Pres Frsh Cls; Rep Stu Cncl; High Hon Roll; NHS; Prfct Atten Awd; Spanish NHS; Maria Diona Scholar 82 & 83; St Johns U Scholar 85; Natl Sci Awd Enrgy Cnsrvtn Cont 84; Mahattan Coll; Biol.

RECORD, JENNIFER; Irondequoit HS; Rochester, NY; (Y); 2/343; Pres Church Yth Grp; Ski Clb; Chorus; School Musical; Var Swmmng; Kiwanis Awd; NHS; Pres Schlr; Sal; NY ST Rgnts Schlrshp 86; U NY Bfl; Elec Engr.

RECORE, MICHELLE; Franklin Acad; Malone, NY; (Y); FBLA; Hosp Aide; Office Aide; Church Choir; North Country CC; Bus.

RECTOR, JILL; Fairport HS; Fairport, NY; (Y); VP Church Yth Grp; Sec FBLA; Key Clb; Chorus; Yrbk Stf; Rep Stu Cncl; JV Cheerleading; JV Tennis; Hon Roll; K-Mart Employee Mnth, 2nd Shrthnd Cntst 86; Mktg.

REDING, JUDITH; Gates Chili SR HS; Rochester, NY; (S); 44/446; FBLA; Stu Cncl; Mgr(s); JV Socr; Stat Swmmng; Gov Hon Prg Awd; High Hon Roll; Jr NHS; NHS; St John Fisher Coll; Cmmnctns.

REDING, LAURENE; Alexander Central HS; Attica, NY; (Y); Varsity Clb; Chorus; Church Choir; VP Soph Cls; Crs Cntry; Trk; Vllybl; Hon Roll; Pres Jr NHS; NHS; Comp Sci.

REDING, MATTHEW E; Byron-Bergen Central Schl; S Byron, NY; (Y); Am Leg Boys St; Var JV Bsbl; Var JV Socr; Bus.

REDMAN, MIKE; Hicksville HS; Hicksville, NY; (Y); Variety Show; Rep Stu Cncl; Var Bsbl; Var Ice Hcky; Im Wt Lftg; Achvt Awd Amer Hstry Rgnts 86.

REDMOND, ANNMARIE; Academy Of St Joseph; Smithtown, NY; (Y); Art Clb; Cmnty Wkr; Hosp Aide; Nwsp Stf; Yrbk Stf; Sec Stu Cncl; Cheerleading; Var JV Score Keeper; Chrstn Courtsy Awd; Supr Acadmc Achvt Awd Art; Law.

REDMOND, DALE; Oriskany Central HS; Oriskany, NY; (Y); Boy Scts; Trs Key Clb; Model UN; Varsity Clb; School Play; Nwsp Rptr; Yrbk Rptr; JV Crs Cntry; Var Trk; NHS; Bus.

REDMOND, KATHLEEN; Minisink Valley HS; Unionville, NY; (Y); Church Yth Grp; Ski Clb; Varsity Clb; Band; Rep Stu Cncl; JV Socr; Var Trk; High Hon Roll; NHS; Rotary Awd; Blue Mdl NY ST Schl Music Assn 84; 1st Pl Sec IX 1500m Wlk 85; Math Awd 86; Acctg.

REDMOND, PAMELA; North Rockland HS; Tomkins Cove, NY; (Y); NFL; Band; Mrchg Band; Yrbk Phtg; Co-Capt Tennis; Arch.

REDMOND, TIFFANY; Bishop Scully HS; Amsterdam, NY; (S); 4/56; Math Clb; Political Wkr; JV Cheerleading; High Hon Roll; NHS; Sec-Natl Hnr Soc 86; Coll Of St Rose; Bio.

REED, ANALISE; Valley Central HS; Montgomery, NY; (Y); Hosp Aide; French Clb; Science Clb; Acpl Chr; Band; Concert Band; Mrchg Band; Orch; School Musical; Symp Band; Music.

REED, ANDY; James I O Neill HS; West Point, NY; (Y); 9/140; Church Choir; Church Yth Grp; Drama Clb; Scholastic Bowl; School Musical; School Play; Var Ftbl; Var Capt Swmmng; NHS; Ntl Merit Ltr; Bst Hist Stu In Jr Clss 85; Worcester Polytech; Biomed Engr.

REED, BRENT; Broadalbin HS; Broadalbin, NY; (Y); 4-H; Letterman Clb; Pep Clb; Spanish Clb; Varsity Clb; Band; Var JV Bsktbl; Var L Trk; 4-H Awd; Hon Roll; Outstndng Vrsty Trck Athlt MVP 85-86; Schl Trck & Fld Recrd Hldr 85-86; Ithaca Coll; Physcl Thrpy.

REED, DANNY; Saratoga Springs SR HS; Saratoga Sprgs, NY; (Y); 2/491; Trs FBLA; Orch; Lit Mag; High Hon Roll; Trs NHS; NYS Rgnts Schlrshp 86; Harvard Bk Awd 85; Saratoga Cnty Yth Ctznshp Awd 86; Colby Coll; Ec.

REED, JOHN; Hendrick Hudson HS; Croton On Hudson, NY; (S); 15/187; Debate Tm; NFL; VP Science Clb; VP Speech Tm; Im Vllybl; High Hon Roll; NHS; Drama Clb; Lit Mag; Rotary Intl Yth Exchng Stu To Italy 86-87; Mt Carmel Soc Awd For Excell In Italian 84; Bio Rsrch.

REED, KARNA; Roxbury Central HS; Roxbury, NY; (Y); Church Yth Grp; Cmnty Wkr; Girl Scts; Hosp Aide; Library Aide; Red Cross Aide; Teachers Aide; VICA; Band; Chorus; Volntr/Candystripr Of Yr Awd 84; 2nd Volntr Of Yr Awd 85; Cazenovia Coll; Hmn Svcs.

REED, MATTHEW W; Fairport HS; Fairport, NY; (Y); Math Tm; Pres Model UN; Political Wkr; Lit Mag; Stu Cncl; Hon Roll; NHS; Ntl Merit SF; Natl Hstry & Govt Awd; Pol Sci.

REED, MICHELE; Linton HS; Schenectady, NY; (Y); 12/286; Vllybl; Hon Roll; NHS; Acctng.

REED, RYAN; Sherman Central Schl; Sherman, NY; (Y); 8/42; FFA; Chorus; Pres Frsh Cls; Pres Church Yth Grp; Pres Jr Cls; Pres Sr Cls; Pres VP Stu Cncl; Var L Bsbl; Var Capt Bsktbl; Var Capt Ftbl; Vet.

REED, SCOTT A; Gouverneur JR SR HS; Gouverneur, NY; (Y); Church Yth Grp; Computer Clb; German Clb; Speech Tm; Chorus; Gov Hon Prg Awd; NHS; Camera Clb; Library Aide; NFL; Clarkson U Outstndg Yng Sci Awd 84; Amer Assoc HS Physcs Tchrs Outstndg Stu 85; Amer Comp Sci Leag 85; Astrophysics.

REED, SEAN A; Bishop Loughlin Memorial HS; Brooklyn, NY; (Y); 1/233; Chess Clb; Pres Computer Clb; VP Radio Clb; Science Clb; Trs Jr Cls; Trs Sr Cls; Im Tennis; Im Wt Lftg; High Hon Roll; NHS; Yale; Math.

REED, STACEY; Cambridge Central HS; Cambridge, NY; (Y); Church Yth Grp; Drama Clb; Band; Concert Band; Mrchg Band; School Musical; Yrbk Stf; Trs Jr Cls; Var Fld Hcky; Hon Roll; Math.

REED, THOMAS; Frontier Central HS; Blasdell, NY; (Y); Latin Clb; Varsity Clb; Band; Var Bowling; Hon Roll; NHS; Prfct Atten Awd; Polc Dept.

REEDHEAD, TERESA; Churchville-Chili HS; Churchville, NY; (Y); VP AFS; GAA; Band; Chorus; Color Guard; Var Capt Cheerleading; Var Socr; JV Sftbl; High Hon Roll; Hon Roll; Travel Tourism.

REEDY, JOHN; Sweet Home SR HS; Amherst, NY; (Y); Latin Clb; Chorus; School Musical; Off Soph Cls; Var Bsktbl; JV Vllybl; Hon Roll; Ntl Merit Ltr; Bst Ltn Stu 84; Awd Acad Achvt 85 & 86.

REEP, DEBORAH R; Corning-Painted Post East HS; Corning, NY; (Y); 44/222; Dance Clb; Pres SADD; Chorus; Rep Stu Cncl; JV Cheerleading; High Hon Roll; NHS; Pres Schlr; Corning Painted Pst Eductnl Scrtry Assoc Schlrshp 86; Cazenovia Coll; Bus Mngmnt.

REESE, JONATHAN P; West Babylon HS; W Babylon, NY; (Y); 9/420; Am Leg Boys St; Variety Show; Stu Cncl; Bsktbl; Ftbl; Lcrss; NHS; Yale U; Econ.

REESE, KAREN; Nazareth Acad; Rochester, NY; (Y); VP Church Yth Grp; Drama Clb; Exploring; Hosp Aide; Math Clb; Church Choir; School Musical; Rep Frsh Cls; VP Church Yth Grp; Rep Stu Cncl; Outstndng Ldrshp 86; VA ST; Elec Engr.

REESE, PAMELA; Broadalbin Central HS; Gloversville, NY; (Y); Drama Clb; Letterman Clb; Band; Chorus; School Play; Yrbk Stf; JV Cheerleading; Var L Socr; Jr NHS; VFW Awd; Adirondock CC; Jrnlsm.

REEVE, CARIN; Penn Yan Acad; Keuka Park, NY; (Y); 9/175; Pres Church Yth Grp; Model UN; Pep Clb; Pres Band; Drm Mjr(t); Jazz Band; Cheerleading; NHS; Amer Musical Foundtn Awd 83; Cert Of Merit-French I, II & III 84 & 85; Intl Busnss.

REEVE, MARY P; Bishop Grimes HS; Cazenovia, NY; (S); 1/150; Church Yth Grp; Hosp Aide; Latin Clb; Math Clb; DAR Awd; High Hon Roll; Math Tm; Science Clb; Rsrv Champ Cntrl NY Drssage 85; WNY Ntl Pony Clb; Pres Limestone Pony Clb 84-85; Harvard; Chem.

REEVES, CHRISTINE; Saugerties HS; Saugerties, NY; (S); French Clb; Acpl Chr; Chorus; Powder Puff Ftbl; VP Tennis; Var Capt Vllybl; Hon Roll; Barbizon Modlng Schl Grad 84-85; All Cnty Chorus 83-85; Deaman; Phys Thrpy.

REEVES, DANIEL; Valley Stream HS; Valley Stream, NY; (Y); Aud/Vis; Stage Crew; Cit Awd; Mst Outstndng Stdnt Tech Arch 86; SUNY; Arch.

REEVES, DOMINIC; South Shore HS; Brooklyn, NY; (Y); Y-Teens; Medl Schlrshp Spec Ed 86; Long Island U; Law.

REEVES, MELISSA; Niskayuna HS; Schenectady, NY; (Y); Sec Cmnty Wkr; Sec VP Drama Clb; French Clb; SADD; Chorus; School Musical; School Play; Stage Crew; Swing Chorus; Pep Clb; Cert Merit Frnch 85-86; OH U; Drama.

REEVES, SANDY; Park West HS; New York, NY; (Y); Cmnty Wkr; Computer Clb; English Clb; Hosp Aide; PAVAS; Spanish Clb; Speech Tm; Jr Cls; Bsbl; Sftbl; Cmprhnsv Math & Sci Prog I & II; Nrsng.

REFERMAT, JOHN; Mcquaid Jesuit HS; Rochester, NY; (Y); 39/165; Boy Scts; Drama Clb; Exploring; French Clb; Nwsp Bus Mgr; Nwsp Stf; Ftbl; Tennis; High Hon Roll; NHS; Ntl Frnch Cntst Awd 84; Eagle Scout 84; Poli Sci.

REGAN, BRIAN M; Hamburg HS; Hamburg, NY; (Y); Boy Scts; Dance Clb; Drama Clb; German Clb; Ski Clb; Acpl Chr; Band; Chorus; Concert Band; Jazz Band; SUNY; Sound Tech.

REGAN, CATHY; Sachem HS; Lake Ronkonkoma, NY; (Y); 180/1558; Church Yth Grp; Cmnty Wkr; DECA; Band; 4th Pl Finance & Crdt DECA Rgnl 86; Para-Lgl.

REGAN, JENNIFER; Delaware Academy And Central; Delhi, NY; (Y); Spanish Clb; Chorus; Color Guard; Variety Show; Sec Sr Cls; Bsktbl; Cheerleading; Crs Cntry; Trk; High Hon Roll; MIP Bsktbl 84-85; Schl Rbndng Rcrd 85-86; Union Coll; Psych.

REGAN, JOHN G; Kenmore West HS; Kenmore, NY; (Y); Am Leg Boys St; Church Yth Grp; SADD; Varsity Clb; Variety Show; Sec Frsh Cls; Pres Soph Cls; VP Jr Cls; Pres Stu Cncl; Var Capt Ftbl; Hnrb Mntn All Star Tm Ftbl 85; Sen Am Leg Boys ST 86; U Buffalo.

REGAN, MARY; Smithtown HS West; Smithtown, NY; (Y); GAA; Ski Clb; Rep Jr Cls; Stu Cncl; JV Var Bsktbl; JV Var Socr; JV Var Sftbl; Hon Roll; Spanish NHS; Bus.

REGAN, MATT; Cazenovia Central HS; Cazenovia, NY; (Y); Debate Tm; Exploring; Stage Crew; Ftbl; Trk; High Hon Roll; Hon Roll; Hghst Achvmnt Bio Awd 85; Pre-Med.

REGAN, NOREEN M; John Jay HS; Katonah, NY; (Y); 6/253; Church Yth Grp; Variety Show; VP Sr Cls; Rep Stu Cncl; Var L Bowling; Var Capt Fld Hcky; Var Capt Socr; High Hon Roll; Pres NHS; Willms Coll Bk Awd 85; U Of Rochester; Chem.

REGAN, PAMELA; Acad Of Mount St Ursula; Bronx, NY; (Y); Drama Clb; Pep Clb; Science Clb; SADD; Stage Crew; Nwsp Rptr; Stu Cncl; High Hon Roll; NEDT Awd.

REGAN, ROBERT F; Garden City SR HS; Garden City, NY; (Y); 20/346; German Clb; Band; Lit Mag; JV L Socr; Im Sftbl; L Var Swmmng; High Hon Roll; Jr NHS; NHS; Ntl Merit Ltr; Pres Acad Ftns Awd 85-86; SUNY Binghamton; Bio Sci.

REGAN, TAWNA; Avon JR SR HS; Avon, NY; (Y); Church Yth Grp; GAA; Spanish Clb; Yrbk Stf; Coach Actv; Diving; Gym; Socr; Sftbl; Vllybl; Desire Awd Vlybl 86; Coachs Awd Chrldg 84.

REGENHARD, CHRISTINA; Bronx High School Of Science; Bronx, NY; (Y); School Play; Lit Mag; Pres Of Leag Envrmntl & Anml Protectn 85-86; NY Regnts Schlrshp Awd; Mc Gill U Montreal; Zoolgy.

REGER, MICHELE; Union Endicott HS; Endicott, NY; (Y); 44/430; Ski Clb; Varsity Clb; Concert Band; Var Gym; Var Trk; Hon Roll; Rgnts Schlrshp 86; NYSPHSAA Awd Gymnstcs 2nd Plc Bm 6th Plc Vlt 86; Union Endicott Vsty Gymnstcs MVP; PA ST U; Engr.

REGIS, TIM; Frontier HS; Blasdell, NY; (Y); Varsity Clb; JV Var Bsktbl; Var Golf; Var Vllybl; Church Yth Grp; Bus.

REGULSKI, PETER A; Binghamton HS; Binghamton, NY; (Y); 65/456; VP SADD; VP Varsity Clb; Ftbl; Wt Lftg; High Hon Roll; Hon Roll; Prfct Atten Awd; Elliott Schlrshp Best Math-Athlete 86; Plice Athlete Lge Awd 86; U S Marine Awd Outstdng Athlete 86; U Of ME Orono; Civil Engr.

REH, NANCY; Martin Van Buren HS; Bellerose, NY; (Y); 57/576; Church Yth Grp; GAA; Girl Scts; JA; Office Aide; Service Clb; Teachers Aide; School Musical; Var Sftbl; Super Yth Daily Nes 85; Credit Rl 84-8l; Hlth Svc.

REHAC, LORI; West Seneca West SR HS; Buffalo, NY; (Y); 163/572; Teachers Aide; Church Choir; Color Guard; School Musical; School Play; Stage Crew; Cert Merit Peer Cnslng 84-85; SUNY Fredonia; Spch Path.

REHBEIN, JESSICA; Johnstown HS; Johnstown, NY; (Y); CAP; Drama Clb; FCA; French Clb; GAA; Intnl Clb; Letterman Clb; Q&S; Varsity Clb; Nwsp Rptr; Sctn II Chmpns Fld Hockey 85-86; Rgnl Chpns Fld Hockey/St Fnlsts 85-86; Ny St Schlstc Qlfr Fld Hockey; Jrnlsm.

REHL, PETER; Woodlands HS; Hartsdale, NY; (Y); Key Clb; JV Var Socr; Hon Roll; NHS; 5th Annual Young Authors Conf For Excellence In Writing 85.

REHLER, KRISTIN; Allegany Central HS; Allegany, NY; (Y); Am Leg Aux Girls St; Band; School Play; Nwsp Rptr; Yrbk Bus Mgr; Trs Stu Cncl; Capt Cheerleading; Swmmng; High Hon Roll; NHS; Cnty Intrnshp Pgm 86-87; Schlrshp Soc 83-86; Pre-Law.

REHLER, LOUISE; Friendship Central HS; Friendship, NY; (Y); Chorus; School Play; Bsktbl; Socr; Sftbl; Hon Roll; Bus.

REHM, DONNA L; Whitehall JR SR HS; Whitehall, NY; (Y); 1/75; Spanish Clb; Band; Mrchg Band; Yrbk Ed-Chief; Yrbk Stf; High Hon Roll; Hon Roll; NHS; Pres Schlr; Val; Renselear Polytechnic Inst Mdl 85; Prsdntl Schlrshp Plattsburgh ST; Plattsburgh ST; Accntng.

REICH, DAVID M; Smithtown H Schl West; Smithtown, NY; (Y); German Clb; School Musical; Im Vllybl; High Hon Roll; NHS; Ttee Schlrshp NYU 86; SUNY Binghamton; Med.

REICH, WENDY; Kennedy HS; Bellmore, NY; (Y); Art Clb; Key Clb; Cheerleading; High Hon Roll; Bus.

REICHERT, MICHELLE; Washingtonville HS; Monroe, NY; (Y); Band; Chorus; Concert Band; School Musical; Dancing Schl Awds 73-84; Med.

REICHERT, PAUL; Hamburg SR HS; Hamburg, NY; (Y); 10/380; Am Leg Boys St; Model UN; Madrigals; Mrchg Band; School Musical; School Play; Symp Band; Nwsp Stf; NHS; Ntl Merit Ltr; Hamilton Clg; Pre Law.

REICHERT, STEVEN; Hamburg SR HS; Hamburg, NY; (Y); Boy Scts; Church Yth Grp; Concert Band; Jazz Band; Mrchg Band; Symp Band; Hon Roll; NHS; JV Var Lcrss.

REICHERT, THOMAS; Brockport HS; Spencerport, NY; (Y); 12/335; Church Yth Grp; Exploring; Pres German Clb; Mathletes; Var Mgr(s); Im JV Socr; NHS; Ntl Merit Ltr; Math Exam Awd 84; Elec Engrg.

REICHGOTT, SETH A; Mamaroneck HS; Larchmont, NY; (Y); SADD; Temple Yth Grp; Thesps; Jazz Band; School Play; Stage Crew; High Hon Roll; Jr NHS; NHS; Ntl Merit Schol; Wesleyan U; Theater.

REID, DONNA; Albion Central HS; Eagle Harbor, NY; (Y); Church Yth Grp; Pres Sec 4-H; Teachers Aide; Ed Lit Mag; 4-H Awd; Prfct Atten Awd; Genessee CC; Humn Svcs.

REID, KATHLEEN; Dominican Commercial HS; Hollis, NY; (Y); Drama Clb; FHA; Varsity Clb; Mrchg Band; School Musical; Var L Swmmng; Siena Clb 84-86.

REID, KRISTIN L; Argyle Central HS; Argyle, NY; (Y); 3/65; Cmnty Wkr; French Clb; Math Clb; Band; Jazz Band; Yrbk Stf; Stu Cncl; Var JV Vllybl; DAR Awd; NHS; Rep Cnty Yth Cncl 85; Apptd Yth Org 85; Wnnr Of Am Legns Natl Oratcl Cntst 86; Cornell U; Bus Adm.

REID, MARK; G Ray Bodley HS; Fulton, NY; (Y); Boy Scts; Church Yth Grp; Varsity Clb; Var Swmmng; God Cntry Awd; Hon Roll; Prfct Atten Awd; Aerosp Engr.

REID, MICHAEL J; E J Wilson SR HS; Spencerport, NY; (Y); 11/300; Church Yth Grp; Cmnty Wkr; Ski Clb; Varsity Clb; JV Var Bsbl; JV Var Bsktbl; Coach Actv; High Hon Roll; Hon Roll; NHS; Earth Sci Ahvt Awd 83; Chem Achvt Awd 85; GMI; Elec Engrng.

REID, NICOLE; John Jay HS; Brooklym, NY; (Y); English Clb; FBLA; Library Aide; Yrbk Stf; Rep Frsh Cls; Rep Soph Cls; Hon Roll; Outstndng Bus Schlrshp 84; Pre-Law.

REID, ONEIL; Monroe JR SR HS; Rochester, NY; (Y); Boy Scts; Im Coach Actv; Var L Socr; Var Tennis; High Hon Roll; Hon Roll; Arch.

REID, TAMI; St Peters HS For Girls; Staten Isl, NY; (Y); Red Cross Aide; Chorus; School Musical; School Play; Stage Crew; Trs Sr Cls; Rep Stu Cncl; Coach Actv; Mgr(s); JV Sftbl; SUNY At Stonybrook.

REID, TRICIA; Our Lady Of Mercy HS; Fairport, NY; (Y); Pres Debate Tm; Yrbk Stf; VP Soph Cls; Var Socr; Var Trk; Var Vllybl; High Hon Roll; Span Awds Lvls 2-4 Ex Span 2-3 84-86; MVP Vrsty Vllybll Tm 85; Genesee Vlly Chem Awd Hon Mntn 86; Spanish.

REIDLICH, PATRICIA; Sachem HS; Lk Ronkonkoma, NY; (Y); 93/1385; Ski Clb; Spanish Clb; JV Var Cheerleading; Hon Roll; NHS; Pres Acad Fit Awd 86; Acad Schlrshp To Alfred U 86; Emory U.

REIDY, JILL; Pittsford Mendon HS; Pittsford, NY; (Y); AFS; French Clb; Hosp Aide; Ski Clb; Band; Var L Crs Cntry; JV Socr; Var L Trk; High Hon Roll; NHS; Teen Amer Dplmt To Frnc Drng Smr 86; Med Prfsn.

REIF, RICHARD P; Lakeland HS; Mohegan Lake, NY; (Y); 9/360; Ski Clb; Spanish Clb; Temple Yth Grp; Stu Cncl; JV Lcrss; High Hon Roll; Jr NHS; NHS; St Schlr; Lafayette Coll; Engrng.

REIG, MERRIE; New Dorp HS; Staten Isl, NY; (Y); #18 In Class; Dance Clb; Debate Tm; Intnl Clb; Political Wkr; Science Clb; Spanish Clb; Band; Nwsp Ed-Chief; Rptr Lit Mag; Stu Cncl.

REILLER, EDWARD; Lackawanna SR HS; Lackawann, NY; (Y); Political Wkr; High Hon Roll; Hon Roll; Atlantic Coll; Oceangrphy.

REILLEY, STEPHEN P; St John The Baptist HS; Massapequa Pk, NY; (Y); Hon Roll; Mth Awd 85; Nassau CC; Paralegal.

REILLY, CHRISTOPHER H; Jamestown HS; Jamestown, NY; (Y); 41/396; Spanish Clb; Var Bsbl; Var Bsktbl; JV Ftbl; Jr NHS; NHS; Canisius Coll; Mktg.

REILLY, ELIZABETH; Newburgh Free Acad; New Windsor, NY; (Y); Key Clb; Ski Clb; Spanish Clb; Varsity Clb; Trs Soph Cls; Trs Jr Cls; Tennis; High Hon Roll; Jr NHS; Spanish NHS; Engrng.

REILLY, ELLEN T; St Francis Prep; Middle Village, NY; (S); 19/653; Art Clb; Cmnty Wkr; Dance Clb; Hosp Aide; Library Aide; Gym; NHS; Prncpls Lst 83-85; Erly Chlhd Educ.

REILLY, JEAN; Miller Place HS; Miller Place, NY; (Y); 17/203; Church Yth Grp; Varsity Clb; Lit Mag; Var Bsktbl; Var Capt Crs Cntry; JV Fld Hcky; Var Capt Trk; High Hon Roll; NHS; Prfct Atten Awd; Schl Wide Speech Cont-Bronze Mdl 83; All-St Cross Cntry 84; Middle Cntry Tchrs Assn Schlrshp 86; Psych.

REILLY, KATHY; Seuisnhaka HS; Bellerose, NY; (Y); 110/346; Art Clb; FBLA; Off Frsh Cls; Off Soph Cls; Hon Roll; Mst Imprvd Stu 83-86; Fshn Inst Of Tech; Fshn Dsgnng.

REILLY, LYNN; St Joseph Hill Acad; Staten Island, NY; (Y); 24/109; FTA; Service Clb; Teachers Aide; Rep Soph Cls; Rep Jr Cls; Capt Swmmng; High Hon Roll; NHS; SADD; Stage Crew; Rep Stu Cncl; Hnry Mntn Schlrshp To Siena Coll 86; NY ST Rgnts Schlrsp 86; Advnc All Star Swmr 85; Albny Med Coll; Doctor.

REILLY, PATRICIA ANNE; Roslyn HS; Roslyn Heights, NY; (Y); 51/250; Sec Computer Clb; Science Clb; Swmmng; Semi-Fnlst Wstnghse Sci Tlnt Srch 85-86; Hgh Hnrs 84; Spkr Mtrpltn JR Sci & Hmnts Sympsm 86; U Of VA; Mech Engrng.

REILLY III, PAUL V; Herkimer SR HS; Herkimer, NY; (Y); 22/110; Drama Clb; SADD; Chorus; School Musical; School Play; Pres Jr Cls; Rep Stu Cncl; Var L Bsktbl; Var L Ftbl; Hon Roll; Stu Of Month HS Slctd Supt 86; Pre Law.

REILLY, RENEE; Rome Free Acad; Rome, NY; (Y); 66/420; Intnl Clb; Key Clb; SADD; Chorus; Yrbk Phtg; Trs Stu Cncl; Var Bowling; Score Keeper; Hon Roll; Jr NHS; Ithaca Coll; Fin.

REILLY, RUTH; La Fayette Central HS; Manlius, NY; (Y); Art Clb; Spanish Clb; Color Guard; Concert Band; Mrchg Band; Yrbk Stf; Trs Sr Cls; JV Sftbl; High Hon Roll; Hon Roll; Art Awds 83-86; Summr Sch Of Arts Prgm 84; Blue Ribbn Regl Schltc Art Awds 84; Schlrshp Savannah Sch; Buffalo ST Clg; Art.

REILLY, SHARON; Rome Catholic HS; Rome, NY; (Y); Am Leg Aux Girls St; VP Service Clb; Pres SADD; Nwsp Rptr; Yrbk Rptr; Pres Frsh Cls; Rep Jr Cls; Var Capt Socr; Sftbl; NEDT Awd; All Star Soccer & MVP 85-86; All Star Softball Coaches Awd 85-86; Boston Coll; Pre-Med.

REIMAN, PATRICK; Fredonia HS; Fredonia, NY; (Y); JV Ftbl; Var Trk; Bausch & Lomb Sci Awd; Medicine.

REIMANN, AMY; Smithtown High School West; Smithtown, NY; (Y); Church Yth Grp; SADD; Acpl Chr; Chorus; Church Choir; School Musical; School Play; French Hon Soc; NHS; German Hnry Scty.

REIMANN, RICK; Rensselaer Middle HS; Rensselaer, NY; (Y); Aud/Vis; Boys Clb Am; Computer Clb; SADD; Varsity Clb; Yrbk Stf; Trs Frsh Cls; Rep Soph Cls; Rep Jr Cls; JV Var Ftbl; HVCC; Engrng.

REIMER, JOANNA; Bishop Mc Mahon HS; Buffalo, NY; (Y); Yrbk Stf; Hon Roll; Prfct Atten Awd; Mngmt.

REINES, JEFF; Longwood HS; Ridge, NY; (Y); Math Clb; Math Tm; Ski Clb; SADD; High Hon Roll; NHS; Ntl Merit Schol; Prfct Atten Awd; Pre-Med.

REINHARDT, CHARLES; John Jay SR HS; Fishkill, NY; (Y); 115/520; Nwsp Bus Mgr; Nwsp Rptr; Nwsp Stf; Stat Bsktbl; Stu Of Wk-Math & Socl Studies 83-84; Admin Awd-Outstndng Stu 85-86; Oswego ST U; Cmnctns.

REINHARDT, DANA; Westlake HS; Pleasantville, NY; (Y); Trs AFS; Hosp Aide; Pres Rep Intnl Clb; Pres JA; Church Choir; Color Guard; School Musical; Var Tennis; Var Trk; Art Clb; ST Fnlsts Mss Amrcn Coed Pgnt 84; Crtv Achvt Art 86; Marriott Fd Svc Waitrss Trng86; Psych.

REINHARDT, EDITH; Flushing HS; Flushing, NY; (Y); Dance Clb; Math Tm; Office Aide; Teachers Aide; Concert Band; Nwsp Rptr; Nwsp Stf; Lit Mag; High Hon Roll; Hon Roll; Law.

REINHARDT, ELINOR; Garden Schl; Elmhurst, NY; (S); 3/34; Aud/Vis; Computer Clb; Pres Spanish Clb; Nwsp Rptr; Nwsp Stf; Ed Yrbk Stf; Var Bsktbl; Var Sftbl; Hon Roll; Jr NHS; Jrnlsm.

REINHARDT, HAL D; W Trespar Clarke HS; Westbury, NY; (Y); 7/193; FBLA; School Musical; Ed Yrbk Stf; VP Soph Cls; Pres Jr Cls; VP Sr Cls; VP Stu Cncl; Im Var Socr; Var L Trk; Hon Roll; Rgnts Schlrshp 86; SUNY Binghamton; Bus.

REINHART, GARRY; Rensselaer JR SR HS; Rensselaer, NY; (Y); 4/63; DECA; Nwsp Rptr; High Hon Roll; Hon Roll; Hnrbl Ment Comptn Region 86; NY Inst Tech; Acctng.

REINSDORF, ANDREW; Coxgakie-Athens Centra Schl; Athens, NY; (Y); 31/105; German Clb; Ski Clb; Mrchg Band; Yrbk Stf; JV Var Socr; Im Tennis; High Hon Roll; Hon Roll; U Of Rochester; Law.

REIPOLD, CRAIG; Sweet Home SR HS; Tonawanda, NY; (Y); Science Clb; High Hon Roll; Hon Roll; Prfct Atten Awd; Med.

REIS, MARIA; North Babylon SR HS; N Babylon, NY; (Y); Chorus; Var Socr; JV Vllybl; Hon Roll; Jr NHS; Accntng.

REISDORF, SANDRA; Holland Central HS; Strykersville, NY; (Y); Church Yth Grp; GAA; AFS; Trs 4-H; JA; Church Choir; JV Capt Bsktbl; Var Fld Hcky; High Hon Roll; Hon Roll; Erie Cmnty Coll; Acctg.

REISER, JESSICA; Fairport HS; Fairport, NY; (Y); Church Yth Grp; 4-H; Girl Scts; Y-Teens; Band; Cit Awd; 4-H Awd; High Hon Roll; Hon Roll; NHS; 4-H Harper Scholar 86; Regents Scholar 86; U Pittsburgh; Econ.

REISER, LYNN; Kenmore East HS; Kenmore, NY; (Y); Color Guard; Mrchg Band; Orch; School Musical; Swing Chorus; Var Vllybl; High Hon Roll; NHS; Prfct Atten Awd; Lbrl Arts.

REISKE, STACEY; Brewster HS; Brewster, NY; (Y); Intnl Clb; Spanish Clb; Nwsp Rptr; French Hon Soc; NHS; Spanish NHS; Span Cert Merit 84 & 86; Fren Cert Merit 85; Intl Reltns.

REISMAN, CHARLES; Commack High School North; E Northport, NY; (Y); Chess Clb; Computer Clb; Math Tm; Spanish Clb; Jazz Band; Mrchg Band; School Musical; Symp Band; High Hon Roll; NHS; Perfrmnc Awd Perfrmng Solo Band; 1st Plc Suffolk Cnty Math Cntst; Nassau/Suffolk All Str Mth Tm; Comp Sci.

REISNER, KIMBERLY; Notre Dame-Bishop Gibbons HS; Schenectady, NY; (S); Girl Scts; Cheerleading; Powder Puff Ftbl; Tennis; High Hon Roll; NHS; Ntl Merit Ltr.

REISTROM, CATHERINE; Henninger HS; Syracuse, NY; (Y); Sec Art Clb; Intnl Clb; Key Clb; Nwsp Rptr; Nwsp Stf; Off Jr Cls; Off Sr Cls; JV Socr; JV Sftbl; JV Vllybl.

REITER, SCOTT W; Clinton Central HS; Clinton, NY; (Y); 15/146; Am Leg Boys St; Boy Scts; Debate Tm; Drama Clb; Key Clb; Model UN; NFL; Political Wkr; Spanish Clb; Speech Tm; Bronze Palm Eagle Scout 83; Kiwanis Boy Yr 86; Wake Forest U; Poli Sci.

REITZ, JOSEPH; Tioga Central HS; Barton, NY; (S); 1/100; Camera Clb; Computer Clb; Library Aide; School Musical; Variety Show; Var Crs Cntry; Var Golf; High Hon Roll; Hon Roll; NHS; Electrcl Engrng.

REITZ, KRISTEN A; Clarence Central HS; Williamsville, NY; (Y); 13/268; Band; Concert Band; Mrchg Band; Orch; Pep Band; School Musical; School Play; Symp Band; Hon Roll; NHS; Mbr Of Best Sectn Of Band 85; All-ST Bnd Mbr 84-85; All-Cnty Band Or Orch 81-86; Engrg.

REKERS, WENDI L; Irondequoit HS; Rochester, NY; (Y); 7/393; Church Yth Grp; Exploring; Latin Clb; Ski Clb; Varsity Clb; Chorus; Coach Actv; Var Diving; Var Capt Gym; Var L Swmmng; Bio.

REKOSH, JENNIFER E; George W Hewlett HS; Hewlett, NY; (Y); 25/260; Teachers Aide; Chorus; School Musical; School Play; Lit Mag; NHS; Ntl Merit SF; Drama Clb; French Clb; Hon Roll; Vrsty Letter & Mgr-Fencing 84-85; Best Poem Awd 84-85 Anthrplgy Awd 84-85; All Cnty Chorus 85-86.

RELYEA, SCOTT; Colonie Central HS; Albany, NY; (Y); JV Lcrss; Var Capt Socr; Hon Roll; NHS; Ntl Merit Ltr; Chas Di Pietro Mem Grphc Art Awd, Rgnts Schlrshp, Crst Litho/Capital Bindery Awd 86; RIT; Grphc Dsgn.

RELYEA, TIMOTHY J; Whitesboro SR HS; Whitesboro, NY; (Y); 9/354; Pres Church Yth Grp; Science Clb; Church Choir; Jazz Band; Pres Orch; Rep Stu Cncl; VP Crs Cntry; VP Trk; NHS; Ntl Merit Ltr; Rgnts Schlrshp 86; Colgate U.

REMBOULIS, EMMANUEL M; Aviation HS; Floral Park, NY; (S); 13/417; Boy Scts; Office Aide; Ski Clb; Drill Tm; Hon Roll; NHS; Aviatn Tech.

REMEZA, RIMAS; St Francis Prep; Ozone Pk, NY; (Y); 379/756; Computer Clb; Band; Im Mgr Ftbl; Cmptr Sci.

REMILLARD, MICHELE; East Syracuse-Minoa HS; E Syracuse, NY; (Y); 33/333; Exploring; French Clb; Political Wkr; Color Guard; Jazz Band; Nwsp Ed-Chief; Yrbk Stf; Sftbl; Hon Roll; NHS; Hnrs Eng Awd 86; Jrnlsm Awd 86; Frnch Awd 85; George WA U; Pol Sci.

REMINGTON, DANIELLE; Newark HS; Newark, NY; (Y); 15/201; Cmnty Wkr; Ski Clb; Concert Band; Mrchg Band; Nwsp Stf; Yrbk Ed-Chief; Rep Stu Cncl; Pres French Hon Soc; High Hon Roll; NHS; NYSSMA Awds 83-85; NCHA Natl Schlrshp 86; NCHA NYS Schlrshp 86; SUNY Oswego; Zoology.

REMIS, DAVID; Spackenkill HS; Poughkeepsie, NY; (Y); Debate Tm; Leo Clb; NFL; Temple Yth Grp; Nwsp Stf; Yrbk Stf; Stu Cncl; Forensic Psychlgst.

REMSEN, ANTHONY; Williamsville East HS; Williamsville, NY; (Y); Church Yth Grp; FBLA; Band; Gym; Var Capt Wrstlng; Hon Roll; Regnts Schlrshp 86; Engr.

RENALDO, DAVID; Veronon-Verona-Sherrill HS; Oneida, NY; (Y); Boy Scts; Church Yth Grp; Ski Clb; Yrbk Stf; Pres Soph Cls; Rep Stu Cncl; Capt JV Socr; Var Trk; High Hon Roll; NHS.

RENALDO, JOHN; Glen Cove HS; Glen Cove, NY; (Y); 53/273; Aud/Vis; Socr; Trk; U Of NY Buffalo; Phrmcy.

RENAULD, MARK; Schuylerville Central Schl; Greenwich, NY; (Y); 1/130; 4-H; FFA; Math Clb; Wrstlng; High Hon Roll; NHS; FFA Awds 84; Teen Ldrs ST Fair; Clb Congrss; Mth Tchrs Awd Hghst Combined Avg Mth I II III 85; Ag.

RENCH, ADAM; John Adams HS; Howard Beach, NY; (Y); Cmnty Wkr; Office Aide; Teachers Aide; Temple Yth Grp; Y-Teens; Cit Awd; Hon Roll; Prfct Atten Awd; Acctng.

RENCHER, KATHRYN; North Babylon SR HS; North Babylon, NY; (Y); 74/460; DECA; Red Cross Aide; Var Capt Fld Hcky; Var Capt Vllybl; Hon Roll; NHS; Athlt Of Yr 86; Prmom Queen 86; MVP In Vlybl 86; SUC Pltsbrgh; Bus Adm.

RENDA, JULIE; Nardin Acad; Williamsville, NY; (S); Cmnty Wkr; Service Clb; Ski Clb; School Musical; Yrbk Phtg; Sec Lit Mag; Rep Stu Cncl; Cheerleading; Trk; NHS.

RENDINO, CHRISTINE; Bishop Ludden HS; Baldwinsville, NY; (Y); 1/186; Debate Tm; Model UN; Political Wkr; Speech Tm; Variety Show; Nwsp Phtg; Nwsp Rptr; Rep Sr Cls; Var Trk; High Hon Roll; Onondaga Comm Coll Schlr 86; Le Moyne Coll Sumr Schlr 85; Syracuse U Schlrshp 84; Cornell U; Indstrl Reltns.

RENEE, GAUCI; Tottenville HS; Staten Island, NY; (Y); School Musical; Yrbk Stf; Var Capt Cheerleading; NHS; Sci Inst; NYU; Med.

RENFRO, JULIA; John A Coleman HS; Rhinebeck, NY; (Y); 1/90; AFS; Cmnty Wkr; French Clb; Key Clb; Ski Clb; Band; School Musical; Yrbk Ed-Chief; Yrbk Phtg; Yrbk Sprt Ed; RPI-MATH/Sci Awd 86; Hghst GPA In Cls Of 87 85-86; Schlrshp Awd-Memory Of JA Coleman 86; Intl Bus.

RENK, ANNE; Bishop Grimes HS; Mattydale, NY; (Y); Church Yth Grp; Girl Scts; Hosp Aide; Latin Clb; Speech Tm; Chorus; School Musical; School Play; Yrbk Stf; Hon Roll; Holy Cross Bk Awd 86; Grl Sct Gld Pin 83; Outstndg Vlntr 85; Nrsng.

RENNER, JAMES W; Honeoye Central Schl; Honeoye, NY; (Y); 13/66; Church Yth Grp; Computer Clb; Spanish Clb; Rep Stu Cncl; JV Socr; Im Vllybl; High Hon Roll; Hon Roll; St Schlr; NYS Regnts Schlrshp 86; Rochester Inst Of Tech; Comp En.

RENNIE, ANNE; Holy Angels Acad; Kenmore, NY; (Y); 3/36; Ski Clb; Yrbk Stf; VP Frsh Cls; Rep Soph Cls; Rep Jr Cls; VP Sr Cls; Pres NHS; Part Acad Scholar Canisius Coll 86; 4th Bal Bm & 7th Flr NYS Cls I Gym Champs 86; Outstndg Stu/Ath; Canisius Coll; Psych.

RENODIN, JOHN L; Poland Central Schl; Coldbrook, NY; (Y); Church Yth Grp; Bausch & Lomb Sci Awd; NHS; Rgnts Schlrshp 86; Clarkson U; Comp Sci.

RENTZ, STEPHEN W; Columbia HS; Castleton, NY; (Y); 114/432; Computer Clb; Ski Clb; Jazz Band; Mrchg Band; Orch; Pep Band; Symp Band; Var Capt Golf; Hon Roll; Rgnts Schlrshp; Data Prcsng.

RENZ, THEODORE; Christ The King Regional HS; Middle Village, NY; (Y); 80/451; Computer Clb; FHA; Ski Clb; Stage Crew; Bsbl; Bsktbl; Bowling; Ftbl; Sftbl; Arch.

RENZI, DAVID A; Watertown HS; Watertown, NY; (Y); Am Leg Boys St; Latin Clb; Var Bsktbl; Capt Ftbl; Capt Trk.

REOME, TERRY; Franklin Acad; Malone, NY; (Y); Hosp Aide; Prfct Atten Awd; Spnsh Cert Excel 86; Air Force.

REPICCI, CARMEN; Gowada Central HS; Gowanda, NY; (Y); JV Var Bsktbl; Var Sftbl; Var Trk; Hon Roll; Hmecmg Qn 85-86; Erie Comm; Mech Drwng.

REPICE, CHRISTOPHER G; Linton HS; Schenectady, NY; (Y); 19/310; Church Yth Grp; Cmnty Wkr; Computer Clb; JCL; Latin Clb; Rep Frsh Cls; Var L Bsbl; Golf; Hon Roll; Comp Sci.

REPOLE, MARIA; Sacred Heart Acad; Garden City, NY; (Y); Cmnty Wkr; Math Clb; Chorus; Hon Roll; NHS; Tchr.

REPP, CAROLYN D; St Anthonys HS; Massapequa Park, NY; (Y); 4/225; Church Yth Grp; Chorus; Drm & Bgl; Madrigals; School Musical; Variety Show; Yrbk Rptr; High Hon Roll; NHS; NEDT Awd; Italian Natl Hnr Soc; All Cnty Choir; Williams Coll; Frgn Lang.

REPPI, CARMEN; Sodus Central HS; Sodus Pt, NY; (Y); Boy Scts; Church Yth Grp; French Clb; Var Golf; JV Var Wrstlng; High Hon Roll; Hon Roll; Bio Fld.

RESETARITS, JEFFREY; Canisius HS; Buffalo, NY; (S); 8/160; English Clb; Math Clb; Ski Clb; Band; Rep Stu Cncl; High Hon Roll; Sr Ltwght 8 Am & Canadian Schlstc Rowing Natls 86; 1st Sr Ltwght 4 Canadian Schlstc Rowing Natl 86; Med.

RESKO, JODY; Bronx High School Of Science; Glendale, NY; (Y); Rep Jr Cls; Med.

RESSLER, DEENA; Westfield Acad; Westfield, NY; (Y); Girl Scts; Letterman Clb; Varsity Clb; Chorus; Cheerleading; Score Keeper; Swmmng; High Hon Roll; Hon Roll; NHS; Wjtn Essay Contst Winnr 83-84; Awd Great Imprvmnt Music 83-85; U Of SC; Math.

RESTIVO, VINNY; Lincoln HS; Yonkers, NY; (Y); Camera Clb; Engrng.

RETAN, MARK; Cazenovia Central HS; Manlius, NY; (Y); JV Bsktbl; Var Golf; Hon Roll; Prfct Atten Awd; Intl Bus.

REUTER, BENJAMIN H; Jefferson Central Shcl; Worcester, NY; (Y); 2/18; Am Leg Boys St; Varsity Clb; Band; Concert Band; Jazz Band; School Musical; School Play; Lit Mag; VP Frsh Cls; Trs Sr Cls; NYS Rgnts Schlrshp, Stamford Rotary Schlrshp, Cngrsnl Medal Merit 86; Gettysburg Coll; Allied Hlth.

REUTER, KAREN L; Poland Central Schl; Cold Brook, NY; (Y); French Clb; SADD; Varsity Clb; Band; Yrbk Stf; JV Var Bsktbl; Var JV Socr; Stat Sftbl; High Hon Roll; Hon Roll; Girls Vrsty Bsktbll MVP 85-86; Engrng.

REUTER, SHANNON; Johnstown HS; Johnstown, NY; (Y); Sec Frsh Cls; Sec Soph Cls; Sec Jr Cls; Rep Stu Cncl; Im JV Cheerleading; Var Diving; Var Swmmng; High Hon Roll; Frnch II Awd 84; Frnch III Awd 85; Mth.

REYDA, JOE; Sherman Central HS; Sherman, NY; (S); 3/42; Chorus; JV Var Ftbl; Hon Roll; NHS; Church Yth Grp; Cmnty Wkr; French Clb; Letterman Clb; Quiz Bowl; SADD; Adm.

REYES, ANGEL; St Agnes HS; Manhattanville, NY; (Y); 20/106; Boy Scts; Church Yth Grp; Orch; School Musical; Bsktbl; Crs Cntry; Trk; NYTEC; Elctrcl Engrng.

REYES, CHRISTINA; Hancock Central HS; Preston Park, PA; (Y); 4/70; Church Yth Grp; Pep Clb; VP Spanish Clb; Chorus; VP Jr Cls; Rep Stu Cncl; Stat Bsktbl; Capt Cheerleading; VP NHS; Yrbk Phtg; Acdmc Achvmnt Awd 84-85; 2 Blue Lttr Awds 85&86; Oprtn Entrprs Fll Schlrshp 86; Bus.

REYES, DEYANIRA; George Washington HS; New York, NY; (Y); 61/321; Art Clb; Scholastic Bowl; Spanish Clb; Color Guard; Cit Awd; Hon Roll; NHS; Ntl Merit Ltr; Prfct Atten Awd; Spanish NHS; Lehman Coll; Bus Admin.

REYES, DORIAN LINDA; Adlai Stevenson HS; Bronx, NY; (Y); Band; Hon Roll; Prfct Atten Awd.

REYES, GEORGE; Peru Central HS; Plattsburgh, NY; (Y); 2/156; Church Yth Grp; Debate Tm; Math Tm; JV Bsbl; JV Bowling; JV Golf; High Hon Roll; NHS; Prfct Atten Awd; Clemson U; Engrng.

REYES, ISABEL; Dominican Commercial HS; Brooklyn, NY; (Y); Spanish Clb; Teachers Aide; Nwsp Rptr; Stat Bsktbl; Capt Cheerleading; Hon Roll; Jr NHS; NHS; Spanish NHS; Siena Club 83; Principals List 83; NY U; Psych.

REYES, JOSE; William Howard Taft HS; Bronx, NY; (Y); 4/22; Bausch & Lomb Sci Awd; NHS; Acdmc Olympcs Cert & Trphy Prtcptn 86; Cnflct Mgmt Rsrcs Inc Cert Of Awd 85; Arista Ntl Hnr Soc Cert; U Of Rochester; Comp Sci.

REYES, LAUREEN; St Pius V HS; Bronx, NY; (Y); NHS; Hghst Aver Bio, Exeptnl Effrt Frnch III, Hnrbl Ment Engl II Awds 86; Spec Ed.

REYES, MANUEL; All Hallows Inst; New York City, NY; (Y); Cmnty Wkr; Hosp Aide; Ski Clb; Rep Stu Cncl; Swmmng; Frnch, Rdng, Hstry Hon 83-86; Buffalo U; Nclr Med.

REYES, MYRNA; Aquinas HS; Bronx, NY; (Y); 21/170; Cmnty Wkr; Service Clb; Spanish Clb; Chorus; School Musical; Pres Soph Cls; VP Sr Cls; Capt Var Twrlr; High Hon Roll; NHS; Ldrshp Wrkshp; Soph Acdmc Hnrs; Offc Svc; Fordham U; Elem Educ.

REYES, ROBERT; Grace Dodge VHS; Bronx, NY; (Y); Model UN; JV Ftbl; St Johns U; Bus Mgmt.

REYES, ROLAND; St Hildas & St Hughs Schl; Elmhurst, NY; (Y); Chorus; Var Bsktbl; Cit Awd; Comp Awd 84.

REYES, VICTOR; Beach Channel HS; Edgemere, NY; (Y); Spanish Clb; SADD; Band; Orch; Off Jr Cls; Bsbl.

REYMERS, KURT E; Sherburne-Earlville Central Schl; Earlville, NY; (Y); 2/127; Pres Drama Clb; Math Tm; VP Ski Clb; Pres Band; Concert Band; Jazz Band; Mrchg Band; NHS; Ntl Merit Ltr; Putsdam Coll; Prcsn Prfrmnc.

REYNOLDS, BARB; Nazareth Acad; Rochester, NY; (Y); 22/115; Drama Clb; Chorus; School Musical; Var Socr; Hon Roll; Arch.

REYNOLDS, CHRISTINE; Lindenhurst SR HS; Lindenhurst, NY; (Y); 5/500; Church Yth Grp; French Clb; Quiz Bowl; Band; School Play; Variety Show; Nwsp Stf; High Hon Roll; NHS; Voice Dem Awd; Engrng.

REYNOLDS, CHRISTINE; Marlboro Central HS; Marlboro, NY; (Y); Sec Church Yth Grp; Sec French Clb; Varsity Clb; Concert Band; Jazz Band; Var Mgr(s); Var Score Keeper; Var JV Trk; High Hon Roll; Hon Roll; All St Band 86; All County Band; Music Prfrmnc.

REYNOLDS, EDITH; Churchville-Chili SR HS; Rochester, NY; (Y); Band; Chorus; Concert Band; Jazz Band; Mrchg Band; Pep Band; Nwsp Rptr; Nwsp Stf; Bsktbl; Trk; International Exchange Student To Israel 85; IA ST U; Fisheries Mgnt.

REYNOLDS, ELISABETH; Villa Maria Acad; Cheektowaga, NY; (S); 10/90; Church Yth Grp; JCL; Latin Clb; Pep Clb; Nwsp Stf; Trs Soph Cls; Trs Jr Cls; Rep Stu Cncl; Var Cheerleading; NEDT Awd; Boston; Pre-Law.

REYNOLDS, ERIC; Portville Central HS; Portville, NY; (Y); Am Leg Boys St; Pres Drama Clb; Band; Concert Band; Drm Mjr(t); Jazz Band; VP Mrchg Band; Pep Band; School Play; Stage Crew; Gifted & Tlntd Prgm Mntrshp At Local Radio Sta 86; Syracuse U; Comm.

REYNOLDS, JANE A; Onteora Central HS; Bearsville, NY; (Y); 1/201; Capt Math Tm; Quiz Bowl; SADD; Var L Bsktbl; Var L Tennis; Var L Trk; Dnfth Awd; NHS; Ntl Merit SF; Val; Century III Ldrshp Awd 85; Physcs.

REYNOLDS, JILL; Gouverneur HS; Richville, NY; (Y); 1/140; Quiz Bowl; Concert Band; Orch; Stat Socr; Bausch & Lomb Sci Awd; DAR Awd; NHS; Math Tm; Acpl Chr; Mrchg Band; Yorker Hist Clb 85; Schlrshp Of Excllnc 86; Dean Oratcls 1st 86; Paul Smiths Clg; Envrnmntl Sci.

REYNOLDS, JOHN; East Meadow HS; East Meadow, NY; (Y); Cmnty Wkr; FBLA; Key Clb; Office Aide; SADD; Stage Crew; Variety Show; Pres Frsh Cls; VP Soph Cls; VP Jr Cls; Bus.

REYNOLDS, MARK; Newark Central HS; Newark, NY; (Y); FFA; High Hon Roll; Hon Roll; Prfct Atten Awd; Stu Mth Awd 86; Prncpls Awd 86; NY ST Senate Hnr 86; Army; Ag.

REYNOLDS, MARK D; Hamburg SR HS; Hamburg, NY; (Y); 13/396; Boy Scts; VP Church Yth Grp; Yrbk Rptr; Yrbk Stf; Lit Mag; High Hon Roll; Hon Roll; NHS; JA; Spanish Clb; NY ST Rgnts Schlrshp 86; U Schlr Hnrs Prgm U Of Bfl 86; U NY Bfl; Bus Adm.

REYNOLDS, MATTHEW; Archbishop Molloy HS; Lic, NY; (Y); 187/383; Am Leg Boys St; Library Aide; SADD; Chorus; Church Choir; Rep Jr Cls; JV L Trk; John J Santuccis Stu Advisry Cmtee 85-86; US Coast Grd Acad; Crmnl Justc.

REYNOLDS, PAUL; Clarkstown S HS; W Nyack, NY; (Y); Church Yth Grp; JV Bsbl; JV Ftbl; Ftbl Tm Chmps 83; Babe Ruth Leag Bsbl Tm Chmps & All Star 83-85; Bus.

REYNOLDS, RACHAEL; Bainbridge-Guilford HS; Bainbridge, NY; (Y); 12/72; Pres Church Yth Grp; Drama Clb; French Clb; Band; Jazz Band; Orch; School Play; Yrbk Stf; High Hon Roll; Hon Roll; Fndtn Schlrshp Frm SUNY Plattsburgh 86; SUNY Plattsburgh; Accntng.

REYNOLDS, RICHARD; Chatham HS; Austerlitz, NY; (Y); Aud/Vis; Church Yth Grp; Cmnty Wkr; Library Aide; Red Cross Aide; Columbia Greene CC; Mgmt.

REYNOLDS, SCOTT; Mahopac HS; Mahopac, NY; (Y); Boys Clb Am; Church Yth Grp; Cmnty Wkr; Im JV Ftbl; Hon Roll; Coll; Envrnmtl Cnsrvtn.

REYNOLDS, STACY; The Masters Schl; Wyoming, NY; (Y); Church Yth Grp; Cmnty Wkr; 4-H; Hosp Aide; Teachers Aide; Stage Crew; Stu Cncl; Cheerleading; Vllybl; Cit Awd; 2 Comm Svc Awds For Cndy Strpng 85-86; Awds For Hndlng Dogs In Dog Show 83-84; Bus.

REYNOLDS, SUZAN; Palmyra-Macedon HS; Palmyra, NY; (Y); Sec Church Yth Grp; Cmnty Wkr; Color Guard; Symp Band; Yrbk Stf; Tennis; Vllybl; Prfct Atten Awd; Climara Coll; Socl Sci.

REYNOLDS, TAMERA; Monticello HS; Monticello, NY; (Y); 26/192; Intnl Clb; Spanish Clb; Nwsp Phtg; Yrbk Phtg; Rep Stu Cncl; Var Capt Gym; Var Trk; Im Vllybl; Hon Roll; Pres NHS; Regnts Schlrshp; Block Achvt Awd 86; Penn ST; Law.

REYNOLDS, THOMAS; Salmanca Central Schl; Salamanca, NY; (Y); Boy Scts; Drama Clb; Exploring; French Clb; SADD; Concert Band; Pep Band; School Musical; High Hon Roll; Hon Roll; Aero Engrng.

REYNOLDS, TRACY; Saugerties HS; Saugerties, NY; (Y); French Clb; Office Aide; Chorus; School Musical; School Play.

REYNOLDS, VALERIE; Colonie Central HS; Albany, NY; (Y); Intnl Clb; Spanish Clb; Band; Chorus; Concert Band; Pep Band; Symp Band; High Hon Roll; Hon Roll; Volunteer Wrk Villa Mary Nrsng Hm 84-85; Maria Coll; Nrsng.

REYNOSO, CYNTHIA; Long Island City HS; Queens Vil, NY; (Y); Church Yth Grp; Office Aide; Teachers Aide; Church Choir; School Play; Yrbk Stf; Rep Jr Cls; Hon Roll; Pan Amer Essy Cntst Awd 86; Outstndng Ctznshp Awd 85 & 86; Lbrl Arts.

REYNOSO, SILVANO; Park West HS; New York, NY; (Y); Im Swmmng; High Hon Roll; Hon Roll; Prfct Atten Awd; NY Rgnts Schlrshp 86; Genl Excllnc Medl-Rnkg 3 Out Of 500-83; 2 Diamond H Pins 83; Embry Riddle Aero U; Aero Sci.

REZNIK, JACK; John Dewey HS; Brooklyn, NY; (Y); Camera Clb; Chess Clb; Archit.

RHEE, DAE-SUNG; Half Hollow Hills HS East; Melville, NY; (Y); Capt Chess Clb; Church Yth Grp; Computer Clb; Mathletes; Church Choir; JV Bsbl; JV Socr; High Hon Roll; Hon Roll; GA Tech; Nclr Engrng.

RHEE, JONG; Flushing HS; Flushing, NY; (Y); Mrchg Band; Pep Band; Symp Band; Capt Vllybl; Prfct Atten Awd; Rgnts Dplm 86.

RHIND, KIRSTEN; Chatham Central HS; Chatham, NY; (Y); 29/117; Cit Awd; Elks Awd; High Hon Roll; Church Yth Grp; Chorus; Orch; Schl Citznshp Prz 86; Cty Citznshp Awd Svc Commuty 86; Choir Orch Svc Awds 86; Becker JC; Physcl Thrpy.

RHINEHART, THERESA; Penn Yan Acad; Penn Yan, NY; (S); 17/175; Church Yth Grp; GAA; Pep Clb; Rep Sr Cls; Var Capt Cheerleading; Sec NHS; Rgnts Schlrshp Wnnr 86; Acad Schlrshp-Gannon U 86; Ecllnc Frnch I & III Awds 83 & 85; Gannon U; Physn Asstnt.

RHODEHAMEL, MARI; Newark SR HS; Hiram, OH; (Y); 20/210; Drama Clb; Acpl Chr; Chorus; Church Choir; Concert Band; School Play; Swing Chorus; Ed Lit Mag; NHS; Church Choir; Garfield Schlrshp Hiram Coll 86; United Methodist Cntrl NY Conf Schlrshp 86; Hiram Coll In OH; Bio.

RHODES, DEBBIE; Mont Pleasant HS; Schenectady, NY; (Y); 19/142; Key Clb; Pep Clb; Spanish Clb; SADD; Orch; Nwsp Stf; JV Cheerleading; Var Trk; NHS; Spanish NHS; Scl Wrk.

RHODES, DESMOND; Hutchinson Central Technical HS; Buffalo, NY; (Y); Boy Scts; Camp Fr Inc; Church Yth Grp; Cmnty Wkr; Computer Clb; Nwsp Stf; JV Bsktbl; Var Mgr(s); Socr; Ntl Ldrshp Awd 84-85; Bus Admn.

RHODES, LIESL C; Lewiston-Porter HS; Lewiston, NY; (Y); 1/236; French Clb; Ski Clb; Pres Band; Orch; Trk; Capt Vllybl; Hon Roll; NHS; 2 Time All Leag 1st Tm Vllybl 85-86; Lncr Cncl 86; Marine Bio.

RHODES JR, RONALD; Henninger HS; Syracuse, NY; (Y); French Clb; Spanish Clb; Crs Cntry; Ftbl; Lcrss; Trk; High Hon Roll; NHS; Prfct Atten Awd; Transltr UN.

RHODES III, STEPHEN; Monsignor Farrell HS; Staten Island, NY; (Y); 3/300; Am Leg Boys St; Teachers Aide; Nwsp Ed-Chief; Ed Yrbk Stf; Ed Lit Mag; JV Bsbl; Im Bsktbl; High Hon Roll; NHS; Ntl Merit Ltr; Amer Schlstc Press Assoc Awd 1st Pl 86; MVP CYO Bsktbl 85-86; Schlr Athl Awd 85; Bus Adm.

RHODES, WENDY; Horseheads HS; Horseheads, NY; (Y); 117/360; 4-H; German Clb; Chorus; Color Guard; 4-H Awd; Hon Roll; Prfct Atten Awd; Grt Amer Smkout Hnr Recog 83; SUNY Cobleskill; Erly Chldhd.

RIANNA, SILVANA; Bayshore HS; Bay Shore, NY; (Y); Band; Concert Band; Mrchg Band; Orch; School Musical; High Hon Roll; Hon Roll; Outstndng Band Stu 84-85; Outstndng Scl Stds & Sci Stu 83-84; RN.

RIBACK, VALERIE; North Babylon S HS; N Babylon, NY; (Y); Girl Scts; Teachers Aide; Chorus; Yrbk Stf; JV Var Sftbl; High Hon Roll; Hon Roll; Jr NHS; Prfct Atten Awd; Pres Ftnss Awd 84; Babysttng Awd 80; Crmnl Jstc.

RIBBY, NATALIE; Churchville-Chili SR HS; Churchville, NY; (Y); 6/320; Exploring; Ski Clb; Band; Mrchg Band; Sftbl; Swmmng; High Hon Roll; NHS; Pres Schlr; Pres Acad Ftnss Awd 86; Pol Sci.

RIBEIRO, MARCELO; Middletown HS; Middletown, NY; (Y); Boy Scts; Key Clb; Red Cross Aide; SADD; Varsity Clb; Band; Drm & Bgl; Pres Frsh Cls; VP Soph Cls; Var Socr; 3rd Plc King Sr Cls 86; Awd Englsh 2nd Lang 86; Chnc To Cm USA Exchng Stu 85; Dctr.

RIBEIRO, SERGIO; Oyster Bay HS; Mill Neck, NY; (Y); Var Bowling; Var Socr; French Hon Soc; Hon Roll; Frnch Achvmnt Awd 83; Outstndng Stu Athletic Achvt Awd 86; NY U; Bus Adm.

RIBLE, JUDITH; Dannemora HS; Dannemora, NY; (Y); 2/24; Pres French Clb; Library Aide; Band; Chorus; Mrchg Band; High Hon Roll; Sec NHS; Hghst Hnr Roll 86; Natl Frnch Cntst Awd 86; Lbrl Arts.

RICATTI, MARIA; Lafayette HS; Brooklyn, NY; (Y); Cmnty Wkr; Ski Clb; Spec Ed.

RICCARDELLA, DAMIAN; St Peters Boys HS; Staten Island, NY; (Y); 13/163; Bsbl; Bowling; Trk; High Hon Roll; Hon Roll; Jhnsn Wls Coll; Clmry Arts.

RICCELLI, SHARI; West Genesee HS; Camillus, NY; (Y); Camp Fr Inc; Cmnty Wkr; Hosp Aide; Office Aide; Variety Show; High Hon Roll; Prfct Atten Awd; Daemn Coll Physcl Thrpy Schlrshp 86-87; Hgh Hnr Roll 6 Smstrs 83-86; Daemen Coll; Phycsl Thrpy.

RICCHETTI, PATRICK; Northport HS; Northport, NY; (Y); Cmnty Wkr; Intnl Clb; Pep Clb; Im Vllybl; SAR Awd; NYS Rgnts Schlrshp; Ntl Assoc Wmn Cnstrctn Schlrshp 86; MS ST U Schlrshp 86; MS ST U; Arch.

RICCHIUTI, MICHAEL; West Islip HS; W Islip, NY; (Y); 34/525; Drama Clb; Chorus; Jazz Band; School Musical; Swing Chorus; Variety Show; JV Bsbl; Lou Armstrong Jazz Awd 86; Music Spnsrs Schlrshp 86; Frederic Chopin Piano Awd 86; Berkeley Coll; Music.

RICCI, JOSEPH; Auburn HS; Auburn, NY; (Y); Church Yth Grp; Acpl Chr; Chorus; School Musical; Swing Chorus; Bsktbl; Crs Cntry; Trk; High Hon Roll; NHS; 11th Grd Chorus Awd & Music Awds 86; Awd Excptnl Prfrmnc Physcs 86; Chem.

RICCI, TRACY; Waterford-Halfmoon HS; Waterford, NY; (Y); 2/80; Math Tm; Stu Cncl; Var JV Fld Hcky; Score Keeper; JV Sftbl; Cit Awd; DAR Awd; High Hon Roll; Sec NHS; Sal; Boston Coll; Erly Chldhd Ed.

RICCIARDI, ANN; Moore Catholic HS; Staten Island, NY; (Y); Art Clb; Yrbk Stf; Stu Cncl; Mgr Var Sftbl; Hon Roll; NHS; Acadmc All Am 86; Pre Pfo Med.

RICCIARDI, JOSEPH; Christ The King Regional HS; Kew Gardens, NY; (Y); Boy Scts; JV Var Ftbl; Mandl Schl; Med Lab Tech.

RICCIARDI, MICHAEL; Monsignor Farrell HS; Staten Island, NY; (S); 19/320; Aud/Vis; VP Rep Jr Cls; Rep Stu Cncl; Im Bsktbl; Var L Ftbl; Wt Lftg; High Hon Roll; NHS; Cllgt Sprts Am Blue Chp Awd 86; Mst Cnsstnt Dfnsv Bck Awd 84-85.

RICCIO, KIM; William E Grady HS; Brooklyn, NY; (Y); 85/318; Aud/Vis; Cmnty Wkr; Service Clb; Teachers Aide; VICA; Yrbk Ed-Chief; Off Soph Cls; Chancellors Roll Hnr Citatns 86; Kingsborough CC Found Awd 86; Bureau Eng Achvt Awd Jrnlsm 86; Brooklyn Coll; Elem Ed.

RICCOBONO, THERESA; H Frank Carey HS; Franklin Sq, NY; (Y); 25/228; Drama Clb; Thesps; Varsity Clb; Chorus; Nwsp Stf; Yrbk Stf; Var L Sftbl; Var L Vllybl; High Hon Roll; Hon Roll; Ron Lane Mem Schlrshp 86; Donald E Kelly Spcl Achvt Awd 86; Cls 74 Svc Awd 86; 6 Yr Svc Awd Chorus 86; Adelphi U; Fine Arts.

RICE, CHERYL; Haverling Central Schl; Bath, NY; (Y); French Clb; FBLA; Sftbl; Swmmng; Vllybl; High Hon Roll.

RICE, DAVID; Alden Central HS; Alden, NY; (Y); Church Yth Grp; French Clb; Science Clb; School Musical; Nwsp Stf; JV Var Bsbl; Hon Roll; Prfct Atten Awd; Comp Sci.

RICE, ERIN; Ward Melville HS; Setauket, NY; (Y); 9/700; Trs GAA; Yrbk Rptr; Yrbk Stf; Cheerleading; High Hon Roll; Jr NHS; NHS; Ntl Merit Ltr; Var L Crs Cntry; Var L Trk; Pre Med.

RICE, HEATHER; Hamburg SR HS; Hamburg, NY; (Y); 140/374; VP French Clb; Hosp Aide; School Musical; Stu Cncl; Capt Gym; Sci.

RICE, JULIE W; Eden SR HS; Eden, NY; (Y); 10/166; GAA; Model UN; Trs Band; VP Sr Cls; Rep Stu Cncl; Stat Bsktbl; Var Capt Crs Cntry; Var Trk; NHS; AFS; MENC All Estrn Chrs 85; Conf All ST Chrs 84-85; U Of TX-AUSTIN; Govt.

RICE, KIMBERLY S; Skaneateles HS; Auburn, NY; (Y); 37/154; Pres VP Church Yth Grp; Dance Clb; Girl Scts; Var Capt Cheerleading; High Hon Roll; Hon Roll; NHS; SUNY Geneseo; Accntg.

RICE, MICHELE L; Patchogue-Medford HS; Patchogue, NY; (Y); 43/653; German Clb; Girl Scts; Library Aide; SADD; Orch; School Musical; Hon Roll; Jr NHS; NHS; Prfct Atten Awd; GS Slvr Ldrshp Awd 83; Regnts Schlrshp 86; Tisch Schl Of Arts NYU; Flmkng.

RICE, NICOLE A; Brentwood Sonderling HS; Bay Shore, NY; (Y); GAA; Varsity Clb; JV Bsktbl; Var Socr; Var Capt Sftbl; High Hon Roll; Hon Roll; Trstee Grnt 86; Albrght Coll; Pre-Med.

RICE, SHARLET; Sachem HS; Holbrook, NY; (Y); 250/1385; Computer Clb; Dance Clb; Spanish Clb; Acpl Chr; Chorus; Madrigals; Nwsp Stf; Pres Acadmc Ftnss Awd 86; Choir Grp Comptn-A Rtng 83 & 86; NYSSMA Solo Comptn-Excllnt Rtng 83; SUNY New Paltz.

RICH, HILLARY; Half Hollow Hills H S East; Dix Hills, NY; (Y); Drama Clb; Office Aide; SADD; Acpl Chr; Chorus; School Musical; Swing Chorus; Yrbk Stf; High Hon Roll; Hon Roll; Teen Tlnt Showcase Awd 84; Theater.

RICH, JON; Clarkstown North HS; New City, NY; (Y); Spanish Clb; Temple Yth Grp; Varsity Clb; Nwsp Rptr; Var Capt Tennis; All Conf Hnrbl Mentn Tnns 85; UCLA; Pre Med.

RICH, KERRY; Frontier Central HS; Hamburg, NY; (S); Computer Clb; Math Clb; Science Clb; Teachers Aide; Rep Stu Cncl; Var Capt Bsktbl; Var Capt Socr; Var Capt Swmmng; Vllybl; NHS; Natl Hstry & Govt Awd 84-85; Stu Of Mnth 85-86; Grove City Coll; Comp.

RICH, KIAWANA; St Peters High Schl For Girls; Staten Isl, NY; (Y); 12/102; Chorus; Yrbk Stf; Lit Mag; NHS; Hnr Untd Crbrl Plsy 83-85; Gvrnrs Ctn Chrctr, Ctznshp, Schlrshp & Srvc 86; Wagner Coll; Mcrbio.

RICH, MARTIN; Clarence HS; Clarence Ctr, NY; (Y); Aud/Vis; Orch; School Musical; JV Bsktbl; JV Ftbl; Var Tennis; Hon Roll.

RICHAR, PATRICK; Charles O Dickerson HS; Mecklenburg, NY; (Y); 7/115; Spanish Clb; Nwsp Ed-Chief; Nwsp Rptr; Nwsp Stf; Rep Stu Cncl; High Hon Roll; NHS; 3rd Pl Am Legion Oratrcl Cntst 86; 1st Pl Short Story Div 86; Awd Exc Writng 85; Tech.

RICHARD, GINA M; Henninger HS; Syracuse, NY; (Y); 75/500; Church Yth Grp; Spanish Clb; Ldrs Of Tommorrow 86; Baylor U; Lawyer.

RICHARD, HIBBERT; West Babylon SR HS; W Babylon, NY; (Y); Church Yth Grp; Library Aide; Chorus; Church Choir; School Play; Var JV Bsktbl; JV Ftbl; Capt Var Trk; Hon Roll; Prfct Atten Awd; Air Force Acad; Aero.

RICHARD, SANDRA M; St John Baptist HS; Bayshore, NY; (Y); 15/546; Boys Clb Am; Hosp Aide; Math Clb; Chorus; School Musical; French Hon Soc; High Hon Roll; NHS; Ntl Merit Ltr; Modern Music Hnr Soc 82-86; Commended Negro Awd 86; Hofsha; Bioengnrng.

RICHARDS, BEN; Gilbertsville Central HS; Gilbertsville, NY; (Y); 4-H; Rep Stu Cncl; Var Bsktbl; JV Crs Cntry; Socr; Hon Roll; ST U Oreonta; Crmnl Jstc.

RICHARDS, CRAIG; Salmon River Central HS; Constable, NY; (Y); 10/110; Var Capt Bsktbl; Var Capt Ice Hcky; Var Socr; Hon Roll; NHS; Acad All-Northern For Hcky 85; Many All-Trny Tms 85-86; MVP Rome Trny 85; Bio.

RICHARDS, ELLA JEAN L; Midwood At Brooklyn Coll; Brooklyn, NY; (Y); 135/589; Church Yth Grp; Library Aide; Math Tm; Science Clb; Band; Church Choir; Concert Band; Ntl Merit SF; Med.

RICHARDS, GERALD M; Columbia Grammar And Prep; New York, NY; (Y); Teachers Aide; School Play; Stage Crew; Nwsp Rptr; Yrbk Stf; VP Soph Cls; Asked By Mayor To Wrk In His Press Ofc 83-84; Comp Prog.

RICHARDS, JEANNINE; Cairo-Durham HS; Freehold, NY; (Y); Church Yth Grp; Office Aide; Concert Band; Stage Crew; Sec Rep Stu Cncl; Bsktbl; Socr; Vllybl; High Hon Roll; NHS; Cert For Outstndng Schlstc Achvt 84-86; Soccer Team Chmpns 85; Amer Red Crs Advncd Swmr 83-85; Marine Bio.

RICHARDS, KIRA; Hilton Central HS; Hilton, NY; (Y); 80/310; Exploring; JA; Model UN; Chorus; Color Guard; School Musical; School Play; Stage Crew; Valparaiso U; Accntng.

RICHARDS, LAVERDA; Springfield Gardens HS; Rosedale, NY; (Y); Church Yth Grp; Cmnty Wkr; Debate Tm; Math Tm; Office Aide; Church Choir; Cheerleading; Vllybl; Med.

RICHARDS, TODD; Salmon River Central Schl; Ft Covington, NY; (Y); 15/94; French Clb; Mgr(s); Socr; Hon Roll; NHS; Prfct Atten Awd; Regents Schlrshp 85-89; Clarkson U; Accounting.

RICHARDS, YVETTE; Nazareth Regional HS; Brooklyn, NY; (Y); Dance Clb; Chorus; School Play; Hon Roll; NHS; Awd Math 83.

RICHARDSON, CINDEE; Oakfield-Alabama JR & SR HS; Oakfield, NY; (Y); Trs Church Yth Grp; French Clb; Chorus; Church Choir; Trs Rep Stu Cncl; JV Capt Bsktbl; JV Var Socr; Stat JV Sftbl; Hon Roll; Oswego U; Crmnl Jstc.

RICHARDSON, COLETTE; Murry Bergtraum HS; Brooklyn, NY; (Y); Nwsp Ed-Chief; Pres Frsh Cls; Rep Soph Cls; VP Jr Cls; Rep Stu Cncl; Capt Cheerleading; Im JV Crs Cntry; JV Tennis; Im JV Trk; Hon Roll; Irwintobin Physcl Educ Awd 84; CSA Prnt Ldrshp Awd 84; Chancellors Nw Schl Fllwshp 86; Cornell; Ecnmcs.

RICHARDSON, DAWN; Auburn HS; Auburn, NY; (Y); Drama Clb; Girl Scts; Intnl Clb; SADD; Varsity Clb; School Play; Variety Show; Yrbk Stf; Var Socr; Hon Roll; Med.

RICHARDSON, DESMOND S; Laquardia High School Of The Arts; Laureltonqueens, NY; (Y); Dance Clb; Church Choir; Variety Show; Julliard Prfrmng Arts; Chrgrphy.

RICHARDSON, FELECIA A; Grace H Dodge V HS; Bronx, NY; (Y); FBLA; Color Guard; Drm & Bgl; Bsktbl; Hon Roll; Acctng.

RICHARDSON, KEYZA; Roosevelt JR-SR HS; Roosevelt, NY; (S); 5/180; Drill Tm; Mrchg Band; Yrbk Sprt Ed; Yrbk Stf; Rep Frsh Cls; Rep Soph Cls; Sr Cls; High Hon Roll; Hon Roll; NHS; Dr Martin Luther King Jr Highest Acadmc Achvt 84-85; Dr Martin Luther King Jr Achvt Awd 85-86; U Of VA; Accntng.

RICHARDSON, LORI; Canton HS; Canton, NY; (Y); 13/114; Chorus; Trs Jr Cls; Trs Sr Cls; Var Capt Socr; Var L Sftbl; Var L Trk; High Hon Roll; Hon Roll; VP NHS; Frederick S Wilder Awd All Arnd Bst Stu 86; Allegheny Coll.

RICHARDSON, NICOLE; N Babylon S HS; N Babylon, NY; (Y); Intnl Clb; Model UN; Office Aide; Teachers Aide; Band; Church Choir; Color Guard; Mrchg Band; Bsktbl; Cheerleading; Columbia U; Med.

RICHARDSON, YVETTE A; Eli Whitney Vocational HS; Brooklyn, NY; (Y); 2/186; Math Clb; Nwsp Ed-Chief; NHS; Sal; Debate Tm; Office Aide; Yrbk Phtg; Pres Soph Cls; Hon Roll; 1st New York City VICA Elec Cntst 86; Regents Schlrshp 86; CUNY; Elec Engrng.

RICHER, FRANCESCA; Beach Channel HS; Belle Harbor, NY; (Y); 4/360; Concert Band; Nwsp Phtg; Yrbk Stf; Var Tennis; High Hon Roll; Pres Acadmc Fit Awd 86; Gld Medl Excllnc Wrtg 86; Slvr Medl Excllnc Bio 86; WA U; Art.

RICHLIN, RENEE M; New York Mills JR & SR HS; Utica, NY; (Y); 8/64; Church Yth Grp; Key Clb; Ski Clb; Spanish Clb; Band; Chorus; School Musical; Var Cheerleading; Hon Roll; Regnts Schlrshp 86; Rochester Inst Tech; Med Tech.

RICHMOND, ANDREA; Mahopac HS; Mahopac, NY; (Y); 132/340; Yrbk Phtg; Cheerleading; Bus.

RICHMOND, MARIETTA; Notre Dame Academy HS; Staten Island, NY; (Y); 9/93; Sec Church Yth Grp; Drama Clb; Library Aide; Office Aide; Pres Science Clb; Stage Crew; Im Coach Actv; Var Socr; JV Var Sftbl; NHS; Rgnts Schlrshp 86; Coaches Awd In Sftbl 84; Dedication/Team Sprt Awd In Soccer 86; Stnybrk; Physcl Thrpst.

RICHMOND, MARJORIE; Spring Valley SR HS; Monsey, NY; (Y); 41/441; Orch; Nwsp Stf; Lit Mag; High Hon Roll; Hon Roll; NHS; Spanish NHS; Regnts Schlrshp 86; SUNY; Jrnlsm.

RICHMOND, MEAGHAN; Jamestown HS; Jamestown, NY; (Y); 31/389; Church Yth Grp; Hosp Aide; Spanish Clb; Acpl Chr; Chorus; Mrchg Band; Symp Band; Rep Frsh Cls; Jr NHS; NHS; USA Schlrshp 86; Hon JR Rtrn 86; Pres Acdmc Ftns Awd 86; Jamestown CC; Lang.

RICHO, FRANK; Ramstein HS; Apo New York, NY; (Y); 68/270; 4-H; Scholastic Bowl; Jazz Band; Orch; Capt Var Bsktbl; High Hon Roll; Ntl Merit Ltr; Drama Clb; Library Aide; Math Clb; Mst Outstndng Awd Math 84-86; Mst Outstndng Awd Sci 84-85; All Conf Plyr Bsktbl 85-86; Pre-Med.

RICHTER, BRENDA; Tioga Central HS; Owego, NY; (S); 10/96; SADD; Sec Frsh Cls; Sec Soph Cls; Rep Jr Cls; Sec Sr Cls; Co-Capt Bsktbl; Co-Capt Vllybl; High Hon Roll; VP NHS; NY ST Schl Music Assn Awd-100 Perfct Scr 85.

RICKARD, ERIC G; Poland Central Schl; Boonville, NY; (Y); Pres Am Leg Boys St; Pres Cmnty Wkr; Pres Varsity Clb; Trs Sr Cls; Pres Stu Cncl; Var Bsktbl; Var Mgr(s); Boys Clb Am; Drama Clb; SADD; NYS Senate Stu Policy Forum 86; Coll St Rose Ldrshp Wrkshp 85; Treas Schl Store 85-86; Bus.

RICKARD, MICHELE; Notre Dame Bishop Gibbons HS; Schenectady, NY; (S); Art Clb; Church Yth Grp; French Clb; Hosp Aide; Var Capt Tennis; Var Trk; High Hon Roll; Hon Roll; Eastern Nazarene Coll; Med.

RICKEN, JILL; Onteora Central HS; Woodstock, NY; (Y); 18/201; PAVAS; Ski Clb; Chorus; School Play; Yrbk Phtg; JV Cheerleading; Var Capt Tennis; High Hon Roll; Hon Roll; NHS; Mid-Hudson Athltc Lg 1st Sngles Ten Champ 84-86; All MHAL 1st Sngles Ten 85-86; Ten Sec 9 Fnlst 85-86; Le High U; Law.

RICKENBACH, NANCY; Greene Central HS; Chenango Forks, NY; (Y); 4/130; GAA; Ski Clb; Spanish Clb; Band; Chorus; Mrchg Band; Yrbk Ed-Chief; Cit Awd; Sec NHS; Church Yth Grp; Fac Key Awd Band; Empire ST Games Archry84; Roberts Wesleyan Clg; Med Tech.

RICKETTS, LOAIANN; Nazareth Regional HS; Brooklyn, NY; (Y); Dance Clb; Office Aide; Chorus; Stage Crew; Variety Show; Yrbk Stf; Rep Stu Cncl; Var Cheerleading; Var JV Sftbl; Hon Roll; Recgntn Superior Achvt Soc Studies,Gov 84-86; Bus.

RICKETTS, LORIANN; Narareth Regional HS; Brooklyn, NY; (Y); Dance Clb; Office Aide; Speech Tm; Chorus; Stage Crew; Variety Show; Yrbk Stf; Rep Stu Cncl; Var Cheerleading; Mgr(s); Rec Supr Achvt Soc Studies 84-85; Rec Supr Achvt Stud Gov 85-86; Awd Bronze N Studies Achv 85-86; Bus Adm.

RICKETTS, RAQUEL; Uniondale HS; Uniondale, NY; (Y); Church Yth Grp; Library Aide; Church Choir; Trk; Hon Roll; Doctor.

RICKS, JUANITA M; North Rockland HS; Pomona, NY; (Y); 71/574; Cmnty Wkr; DECA; Drama Clb; Office Aide; Scholastic Bowl; Chorus; Flag Corp; School Musical; Yrbk Rptr; Rep Stu Cncl; Natl Merit Schlrshp Lttr Of Achvt 85.

RICO, DANIEL; Central Islip HS; Central Islip, NY; (Y); 9/368; Chess Clb; Debate Tm; Mathletes; Spanish Clb; School Play; Bsktbl; Var Capt Socr; Wt Lftg; Hon Roll; Spanish NHS; Spnsh Awd 2nd Pl Suffolk Cnty 86; Suny At Albany; Bnkng.

RICOTTA, MARIA; Trott Vocational HS; Niagara Falls, NY; (Y); 4/131; Hosp Aide; Nwsp Stf; High Hon Roll; Top Schlr Awd 83; ARGY Schlrshp 86; Niagara CC; Reg Nrsng.

RICUPERO, VANESSA; Abraham Lincoln HS; Brooklyn, NY; (Y); Dance Clb; Drama Clb; GAA; Girl Scts; Office Aide; Teachers Aide; Chorus; School Play; Yrbk Stf; Rep Jr Cls; Itln Awd Lang 85; St Francis Clg.

RIDDELL, LORIE; Frankfort-Schuyler HS; Frankfort, NY; (Y); Church Yth Grp; Exploring; FBLA; Key Clb; Spanish Clb; SADD; School Musical; Yrbk Stf; High Hon Roll; Hon Roll; Svngs Bnd Wng Cntst Kwldg 86; Pn Hnr Typng Ovr 30 WPM 85; Pn Hnr Schl Ldrshp 85; Utica Schl Commerce; Lgl Sec.

RIDDELL, ROSEMARIE; Brockport HS; Brockport, NY; (Y); 9/335; Nwsp Sprt Ed; Yrbk Stf; Sec Frsh Cls; Sec Soph Cls; Sec Jr Cls; Pres Sr Cls; Rep Stu Cncl; Var Capt Swmmng; High Hon Roll; NHS; Most Likely To Succeed 86; Regents Schlrshp Wnr 86; Rep BHS Monroe Cnty Chem Exam; Cornell U; Bio Sci.

RIDER, BILLY JO; Dundee Central HS; Dundee, NY; (Y); Am Leg Aux Girls St; FHA; FNA; Ski Clb; Yrbk Stf; Sftbl; Hon Roll; NHS; Stu Of Mnth 86; Elem Educ.

RIDER, TAMMY; Coxsackie Athens JR SR HS; W Coxsackie, NY; (Y); Rep Spanish Clb; Rep SADD; Rep Frsh Cls; Rep Soph Cls; Rep Jr Cls; Rep Stu Cncl; Var L Bsktbl; Var L Score Keeper; Var L Trk; Hon Roll; Phy Ed Tchr.

RIDGE, MELANIE; Marlius Pebble Hill HS; Liverpool, NY; (S); Debate Tm; Exploring; Model UN; Office Aide; Stage Crew; Yrbk Ed-Chief; Vllybl; Hon Roll; NHS; Lawyer.

RIDGES, TAMMIE; Clara Barton HS For Health Profsns; Brooklyn, NY; (Y); Hosp Aide; Quiz Bowl; Scholastic Bowl; Spanish Clb; Teachers Aide; Nwsp Rptr; Hon Roll; Spanish NHS; Med.

RIDGEWAY, ANDY; Sandy Creek Central HS; Lacona, NY; (Y); Exploring; Wrstlng; Hon Roll; Mst Imprvd Wrstlr 85; Phys Ed Mst Imprvd 84; Bus.

RIDGEWAY, MATT; Sandy Crek Central Schl; Orwell, NY; (S); 12/98; French Clb; Intnl Clb; Band; Concert Band; Jazz Band; Mrchg Band; School Musical; Bsktbl; Hon Roll; NHS; NY ST Regents Scholar 86; Plattsburgh ST Coll; Mth Ed.

RIEDEL, DAWN; Carmel HS; Carmel, NY; (Y); Yrbk Stf; Sec Jr Cls; Sec Sr Cls; Cheerleading; High Hon Roll; Hon Roll; Ed.

RIEDERER, HEIDI A; Frontier Central HS; Lake View, NY; (Y); 45/500; Church Yth Grp; Cmnty Wkr; French Clb; Pep Clb; SADD; Thesps; Band; Chorus; Concert Band; Mrchg Band; Arion Awd Music 86; All Cnty Bnds & Orch 83 & 85; Area All ST Band 86; Buffalo ST Coll; Spec Ed.

RIEDL, IRENE; Lake Placid HS; Lake Placid, NY; (Y); Debate Tm; Key Clb; School Play; Stage Crew; Rep Jr Cls; Cheerleading; Pom Pon; Trk; Wt Lftg; Hon Roll; Psych.

RIEGER, CHRISTINE; Schuylerville HS; Greenwich, NY; (Y); 4-H; French Clb; Math Clb; Band; Nwsp Ed-Chief; Yrbk Stf; Var Mgr(s); Var Score Keeper; 4-H Awd; Hon Roll; Vice Chrmn NYS Teenage Republicans 85-86; News Reptr Cnty 4-H Teen Cncl 84-86; Syracuse; Intr Dsgn.

RIEHL, KRISTA; St Edmund HS; Brooklyn, NY; (S); 11/193; English Clb; Library Aide; Spanish Clb; Hon Roll; NHS; Ntl Lang Arts Olympiad 84; 1st Hnrs Awd 84-85; Engl Awd 85.

RIENZO, ELIZABETH; Commack HS South; Commack, NY; (Y); Drama Clb; Off Chorus; School Musical; School Play; Stage Crew; Yrbk Stf; Lit Mag; Hon Roll; Teachers Aide; Y-Teens; Girls Ldrshp Corps; All Cnty Chrs; Comm Art.

RIESEL, CHAD; Herkimer HS; Herkimer, NY; (Y); JV Var Ftbl.

RIESTERER, DONNA; Sacred Heart Acad; West Hempstead, NY; (Y); Aud/Vis; PAVAS; SADD; School Play; Stage Crew; VP Soph Cls; Rep Jr Cls; Rep Stu Cncl; Coach Actv; Var Socr; Culinary Inst; Chef.

RIEZ, MATTHEW; Newfield HS; Coram, NY; (Y); Scholastic Bowl; VP Science Clb; Concert Band; Mrchg Band; Var Bowling; JV Trk; High Hon Roll; Jr NHS; NHS; Computer Clb; LONG Island Sci Cngrss Merit Awd 86; Bio-Med Engrng.

RIFENBURGH, CONNIE; Beacon HS; Poughkeepsie, NY; (Y); Key Clb; Varsity Clb; Nwsp Stf; Var Trk; High Hon Roll; Jr NHS; NHS; Library Aide; Jr Socl Lge Awd 86; Dutchess CC; Rcrtn Ldrshp.

RIFENBURGH, MELISSA; Hoosic Valley Central HS; Schaghticoke, NY; (Y); 35/96; Drama Clb; 4-H; Chorus; School Musical; School Play; Nwsp Rptr; Yrbk Ed-Chief; Hon Roll; Art Awd Outstndng Creative Ablty Art 85-86; Mohawk Vly CC; Advrtsng Dsgn.

RIFFLARD, TAMMY; Washingtonville HS; Washingtonville, NY; (Y); Church Yth Grp; Girl Scts; Rep Stu Cncl; Var Capt Cheerleading; Fld Hcky; Var Score Keeper; Var Vllybl; Hon Roll; Mst Imprvd Chrldr 85; Mst Vlbl Wntr Chrldr 86; Geneseo; Spec Educ.

RIGATTI, AMY L; Amsterdam HS; Amsterdam, NY; (Y); 1/246; Yrbk Stf; Var Crs Cntry; Capt Var Trk; High Hon Roll; Sec NHS; Val; NYS Regnts Schlrshp 86; NY Telephn Clg Schlrshp 86; U Of Rochester; Biomed Engrng.

RIGG, CAROLIE; De Witt Clinton HS; Bronx, NY; (Y); Pres 4-H; Girl Scts; Rep Stu Cncl; Trk; Vllybl; Cit Awd; Hon Roll; Health Careers Outstndng Acad Achvt 86; Psych.

RIGGINS III, DORKIN; Central Islip HS; Central Islip, NY; (Y); Acpl Chr; Band; Concert Band; Drm & Bgl; Mrchg Band; School Musical; School Play; Pace; Psych.

RIGGIO, LOUIS; Lafayette HS; Buffalo, NY; (Y); Boys Clb Am; French Clb; Letterman Clb; Var Bsbl; Var Ice Hcky; JV Wt Lftg; All Star & Super All Star Tm Explr Hockey League; Merit Roll; U Of Buffalo Coll; Bus.

RIGGS, JOHN MATTHEW; Mexico Acad; Mexico, NY; (Y); JV Bsbl; JV Capt Ftbl; Wt Lftg; Elec Engr.

RIINA, ANDREA; Midwood HS; Brooklyn, NY; (Y); 43/556; Cmnty Wkr; Intnl Clb; Library Aide; Office Aide; Service Clb; Chorus; Church Choir; Lit Mag; NHS; Mdcl Sci Inst 83-86; Arsta Hnr Soc 85-86; 1st Prz Wnnr Ctywd Essy Cntst 84; NY U; Pre Law.

RIKER, MATTHEW D; Saratoga Springs HS; Gansevoort, NY; (Y); 94/495; Pres Church Yth Grp; Varsity Clb; Pres Acpl Chr; Pres Chorus; Church Choir; Swing Chorus; Variety Show; L Ftbl; Wrstlng; NYS Regents Schlrshp 86; Ftbl MVP 85; Ftbl Best Defsive Lineman 83-85; Pace U; Pre-Law.

RILEY, CLEOPATRA; Dominican Commercial HS; Laurelton, NY; (S); Hosp Aide; Rep Soph Cls; Rep Sr Cls; Rep Stu Cncl; Hon Roll; NHS; Girl Scts; Sierra Clb 82-86; Stony Brook; Doc.

RILEY, DEBORAH A; South Side HS; Rockville Center, NY; (Y); 62/284; Thesps; School Musical; School Play; Stage Crew; Variety Show; Socr; Trk; High Hon Roll; Hon Roll; Jr NHS; Track Mdl For Discus 84; Rgnts Schlrshp 86; Lehigh U; Engr.

RILEY, DENNAY; John Dewey HS; Brooklyn, NY; (Y); Dance Clb; Drama Clb; Band; Church Choir; Concert Band; School Musical; Variety Show; Nwsp Phtg; Cit Awd; Prfct Atten Awd; Hunter Coll.

RILEY, ERIN; Chittenango HS; Chittenango, NY; (Y); 2/200; Am Leg Aux Girls St; SADD; School Musical; Pres Sec Stu Cncl; JV Capt Tennis; High Hon Roll; NHS; Ntl Merit Ltr; Church Yth Grp; Cmnty Wkr; Jr Hnr Scty Outstndng Mbr Awd 84; Jr Hnr Scty Svc Awd 85; Mock Trl Semifnlst 86.

RILEY, JOANNE; Dodge V HS; Bronx, NY; (Y); Nwsp Rptr; Rep Frsh Cls; Rep Soph Cls; Rep Jr Cls; Hon Roll; Prfct Atten Awd; Voice Dem Awd; Political Wkr; NYSBA Prtcptn Awd 85-86; Closeup Pgm Wash DC 86; Upwrd Bnd Pgm BCC 85; Howard U; Bus Admin.

RILEY, JOSEPH; Salamanca Central HS; Salamanca, NY; (Y); Am Leg Boys St; French Clb; Band; Concert Band; Jazz Band; Mrchg Band; Pep Band; French Hon Soc; High Hon Roll; NHS; Chem Engrng.

RILEY, JUDY; Fairport HS; Fairport, NY; (Y); Cmnty Wkr; Exploring; Library Aide; Ski Clb; Yrbk Stf; Page Yr Awd 86; Edinboro U; Erly Chldhd Ed.

RILEY, KAREN L; E J Wilson HS; Rochester, NY; (Y); 1/290; JCL; Red Cross Aide; Thesps; Var L Bsktbl; Var L Mgr(s); Var L Socr; High Hon Roll; NHS; Val; Drama Clb; Rgnts Schlrsh 86; Intl Frgn Lang Awd 85; Exchng Stu France 85; Kenyon Coll; Intl Rltns.

RILEY, KIM; Mepham HS; Bellmore, NY; (Y); Acpl Chr; Chorus; Yrbk Stf; Off Jr Cls; Cheerleading; Hon Roll; Bus Admin.

RILEY, MICHAEL; Lansingburgh HS; Troy, NY; (Y); 3/200; Boys Clb Am; French Clb; JA; JV L Bsktbl; Var L Socr; Var L Trk; High Hon Roll; Jr NHS; NHS; Cert Merit 86; RPI; Engrng.

RILEY, VICKI; Baldwin SR HS; Baldwin, NY; (Y); Church Yth Grp; Dance Clb; Office Aide; Church Choir; Orch; High Hon Roll; Hon Roll; Vet.

RINALDI, CAROLYN; Washingtonvle Central HS; Washingtnvle, NY; (Y); Cmnty Wkr; French Clb; Ski Clb; Stage Crew; Variety Show; Nwsp Stf; Yrbk Stf; Stat Socr; Stat Vllybl; Hon Roll; Law.

RINALDI, ELLEN N; Maine-Endwell SR HS; Endwell, NY; (Y); 31/234; Key Clb; Pep Clb; Spanish Clb; SADD; Nwsp Ed-Chief; Nwsp Rptr; Hon Roll; Regnts Schlrshp 86; Coll Of St Rose; Advrtsng Dsgn.

RINALDI, JOHN; St John The Baptist HS; Deer Park, NY; (Y); Off Band; Concert Band; Mrchg Band; Var Bowling; Var Socr; Hon Roll; Dwlng Coll; Law.

RINALDI, OLIMPIA T; St Catharine Acad; Bronx, NY; (Y); 23/200; Nwsp Rptr; Hist Clb; Hunter Coll; Computer.

RINALDO, CLAUDINE; De Sales HS; Waterloo, NY; (Y); Varsity Clb; Band; Mrchg Band; School Musical; JV Var Bsktbl; Var Capt Cheerleading; JV Var Socr; Concert Band; JV Var Score Keeper; Outstndng Chrldr 85-86; Cazenovia; Merch.

RINALDO, FRANK C; Oneida SR HS; Oneida, NY; (Y); 26/200; Am Leg Boys St; Letterman Clb; Varsity Clb; Symp Band; Yrbk Stf; Pres Soph Cls; L Capt Ftbl; Pres Schlr; Church Yth Grp; Ski Clb; All League Cornerback Ftbl 85; Most Outstndng Ftbl 85; Mayors Yth Advsry Cncl 83-86; Rochester Inst Tech; Mech Eng.

RINAS, AMY; Northport SR HS; Northport, NY; (Y); Cmnty Wkr; French Clb; Hosp Aide; Office Aide; Pep Clb; Teachers Aide; Varsity Clb; Band; Concert Band; Mrchg Band; Intl Bus.

RINDFLEISCH, JULIE; Union Springs Central Schl; Cayuga, NY; (Y); Church Yth Grp; Rptr 4-H; Color Guard; JV Fld Hcky; 4-H Awd; Mltry Polc.

RING, HOLLY; Indian River Central HS; Evans Mills, NY; (Y); Church Yth Grp; JV Var Bsktbl; JV Var Socr; JV Var Sftbl; NHS; Band; Mrchg Band; Stu Cncl; Hon Roll; Prfct Atten Awd; Math.

RING, LAURA; Sweet Home SR HS; Amherst, NY; (Y); GAA; Chorus; School Musical; Swmmng; Trk; Eng Awd 85; Geneseo; Physcl Thrpy.

RINGELHEIM, STEPHANIE; Port Richmond HS; Staten Island, NY; (Y); SADD; Teachers Aide; Temple Yth Grp; School Play; Stage Crew; Variety Show; Yrbk Stf.

RINGLE, LESLIE; Nardin Acad; Buffalo, NY; (Y); Model UN; Spanish Clb; Yrbk Ed-Chief; Trs Soph Cls; Rep Jr Cls; High Hon Roll; Denison U Acad Scholar 86; Canisius Coll Acad Scholar 86; NYS Regents Scholar 86; Denison U; Intl Rltns.

RINGO, STACY; South Side HS; Hempstead, NY; (Y); Church Yth Grp; Church Choir; Badmtn; Hon Roll; Howard U; Law.

RINGO, TIMOTHY; Hugh C Williams HS; Canton, NY; (Y); 7/120; Math Tm; Yrbk Stf; Lit Mag; Golf; High Hon Roll; Hon Roll; Pres Schlr; St Lawrence U Pt/Time Schlrshp 85-86; Clarkson U Proj Chllng 85-86; NY ST Rgnts Schlrshp 86; Cornell U; Mtrlgy.

RINN, LYSSA; Commack North HS; Commack, NY; (Y); Teachers Aide; Temple Yth Grp; Band; Concert Band; Nwsp Rptr; Nwsp Stf; Lit Mag; Var JV Tennis; High Hon Roll; Hon Roll; Law.

RIOBO, CARLOS; St Francis Prep; Fresh Meadows, NY; (S); 23/653; Debate Tm; Trs Science Clb; Band; Orch; Pep Band; Nwsp Rptr; Var Trk; Im Vllybl; Trs NHS; Ntl Hspnc Schlr Awds Smfnlst 85-86; Bio.

RION JR, FREDERICK J; Kingston HS; Kingston, NY; (Y); 94/574; Boys Clb Am; Cmnty Wkr; Ski Clb; SADD; Chorus; Variety Show; Yrbk Stf; Stu Cncl; Bsbl; Bsktbl; Kingston Colmts Schlrshp; NY ST U; Bus.

RIORDAN, CHRISTOPHER; Archbishop Molloy HS; Maspeth, NY; (Y); 110/400; Church Yth Grp; Intnl Clb; Im Bsktbl; JV Var Crs Cntry; Im Ftbl; JV Var Trk; Prfct Atten Awd.

RIORDAN, JOHN; West Islip HS; W Islip, NY; (Y); Art Clb; Scholastic Bowl; School Musical; Im Badmtn; Var Bowling; Lcrss; JV Var Socr; Im Vllybl; Elon Christon Coll; Txtl Mrktng.

RIORDAN, MIKE; John H Glenn HS; E Northport, NY; (Y); Boy Scts; Swmmng; Trk; Wt Lftg.

RIOS, ALLAN; Clarkstown South HS; Nanuet, NY; (Y); Aud/Vis; Cmnty Wkr; Biol.

RIOS, CARMENCITA; Midwood HS; Brooklyn, NY; (Y); 318/667; Cmnty Wkr; Hosp Aide; Med.

RIOS, CELIA; Sachem North HS; Farmingville, NY; (Y).

RIOS, ELIZABETH; Amsterdam HS; Amesterdam, NY; (Y); Church Yth Grp; FBLA; FNA; Hosp Aide; Spanish Clb; Church Choir; Spencer; Crt Rprtr.

RIOS, GLORIA; St Francis Prep; Astoria, NY; (Y); Church Yth Grp; Debate Tm; Speech Tm; Hon Roll; NHS; Frdhm U; Law.

RIOS, JOSE; John Dewey HS; Brooklyn, NY; (Y); Chess Clb; Teachers Aide; Orch; Nwsp Stf; Rep Soph Cls; Rep Sr Cls; Cit Awd; Rep Frsh Cls; Regents Schlrshp Awd 86-87; Acad Olympic Tm 84-86; Samuel A Welcome Awd Legal Studies 86; Baruch Coll CUNY; Acctg.

RIOUX, SHEILA; Cicero-North Syracuse HS; Mattydale, NY; (S); 2/667; Math Tm; Ski Clb; Capt Drill Tm; Mrchg Band; Sec Stu Cncl; Powder Puff Ftbl; High Hon Roll; NHS; Opt Clb Awd; Sal; Rensselaer Mth & Sci Awd; Wellesey Bk Awd; Utopia Lit Awd 85; Bio.

RIPKE, KAREN; Bethpage HS; Bethpage, NY; (Y); 32/306; French Clb; GAA; Sec Frsh Cls; Sec Soph Cls; VP Jr Cls; Var Bsktbl; Var Sftbl; Var Capt Vllybl; High Hon Roll; Jr NHS; Var Vllybl Capt All Cnty 85; Var Sftbl All Cnty 86; Var Bsktbl All Div 86.

RIPPS, ANDREW S; Baldwin SR HS; Baldwin, NY; (Y); 41/476; Q&S; SADD; Temple Yth Grp; Nwsp Ed-Chief; Nwsp Sprt Ed; Stu Cncl; High Hon Roll; Pres Schlr; Spanish NHS; St Schlr; Dstngshd Acdmc Schlrshp Hofstra U 86; Cert Excllnce Soc Stud 83-84; Hofstra U; Jrnlsm.

RISEWICK, MOLLY; Nazareth Acad; Rochester, NY; (Y); Exploring; Ski Clb; Band; Chorus; Rep Frsh Cls; Rep Soph Cls; JV Bsktbl; Var Socr; Var Trk; Hon Roll; Math.

RISINIT, MICHAEL; Archbishop Stepinac HS; Rye, NY; (Y); 55/199; Boy Scts; Cmnty Wkr; Pep Clb; Mary Friese Lowell Mem Schlrp 86; U ME Orono; Wldlf Biol.

RISOLO, JOHN; Bishop Kearney HS; Rochester, NY; (Y); 4/247; JA; Varsity Clb; Var Capt Ftbl; Wt Lftg; Var Wrstlng; High Hon Roll; NHS; Ntl Merit Ltr; Pres Schlr; NY ST Rgnts Schlrshp 86; U Rchstr; Med.

RISPOLI, GABRELLE; Mc Kee Voc & Tech HS; Staten Island, NY; (Y); 52/317; Office Aide; Nwsp Rptr; Nwsp Sprt Ed; Bsbl; Bsktbl; Cheerleading; Ftbl; Hon Roll; Chiropractic.

RISSBERGER, ALAN; Churchville Chili HS; Rochester, NY; (Y); Math Tm; Lit Mag; High Hon Roll; Hon Roll; Ntl Merit Ltr.

RIST, DAVID; Greece Olympia HS; Rochester, NY; (Y); Ski Clb; Im Bsktbl; Im Vllybl; Engrng.

RIST, MARK M; Hadley-Luzerne Central Schl; Lake Luzerne, NY; (Y); 4/65; Pres Church Yth Grp; Band; Jazz Band; Mrchg Band; Symp Band; Hon Roll; NHS; NY Scty Dcndnts Myflwr Awd Hstry 85; Hghst Grd Englsh 85; Rgnts Schlrshp; Adirondack CC; Chmst.

RISTICH, TOMMY; Gates Chili HS; Rochester, NY; (Y); 1/446; Exploring; Spanish Clb; JV Socr; High Hon Roll; Val; Rgnts Schlrshp 86; Math Awd 85; Spnsh Awd 85; U Of Rochester; Engrng.

RITA, ROSA; Preston HS; Bronx, NY; (S); Science Clb; Teachers Aide; Var Twrlr; High Hon Roll; Hon Roll; NHS; Cert Of Achvt For Acdmc Exc 83-85; Ntl Ed Dvlpmnt Tst Cert Of Achvt 85; NY U; Bus Adm.

RITACCIO, VALERIE; Long Beach HS; Long Beach, NY; (S); 28/265; School Musical; Rep Stu Cncl; Hon Roll; NHS; NY ST Regents Schlrshp 86; Itln-Frnch.

RITTENBERG, SUZANNE; New Rochelle HS; New Rochelle, NY; (Y); 44/550; Hosp Aide; Band; Concert Band; Mrchg Band; Yrbk Phtg; Rep Jr Cls; Var Swmmng; Hon Roll; NHS; Spanish NHS; WA U.

RITTENHOUSE, MICHELLE; Union-Endicott HS; Endicott, NY; (Y); Debate Tm; VP Key Clb; High Hon Roll; Hon Roll; NHS; Optimist Ortrcl Awd 85; Accntrng.

RITTER, ANA J; Bas Torah Acad; Monsey, NY; (Y); Dance Clb; Drama Clb; Hosp Aide; Math Clb; Quiz Bowl; Pres Temple Yth Grp; Yrbk Bus Mgr; Pres Stu Cncl; Hon Roll; Rgnts Schlrshp Awd 86; Stern Coll For Women; Comp Anly.

RITTER, CHUCK; Williamsville East HS; East Amherst, NY; (Y); 19/302; Cmnty Wkr; Computer Clb; French Clb; Math Clb; Ski Clb; Rep Jr Cls; Rep Sr Cls; Rep Stu Cncl; JV Bsktbl; Var Trk; Ldrshp Awd Yth Vlntr Grp 85; Vrsty Ltr Rifle Tm 84-86; JR Golf Champ Local Clb 85; Cornell U; Bio.

RITTER, DANAH; Spackenkill HS; Poughkeepsie, NY; (Y); 31/167; Leo Clb; Temple Yth Grp; Thesps; Band; School Musical; School Play; Trk; Hon Roll; NHS; Pres Acdmc Ftns Awd 86; Union Coll.

RITTER, JAMES; Ravena-Coeymans-Selkick Centrl HS; Coeymans, NY; (Y); French Clb; Key Clb; Math Tm; Lit Mag; Var Crs Cntry; Capt Var Tennis; High Hon Roll; NHS; Tennis Achvt Awd 86; Ind Engr.

RITTER, JENNIFER; Albertus Magnus HS; Tuxedo, NY; (Y); Drama Clb; Yrbk Sprt Ed; Vllybl; Mu Alp Tht; NHS; Regents Scholar 86; Rensselaer Scholar 86; Rensselaer Polytech; Civil Engr.

RITTER, WILLIAM T; Thomas A Edison HS; Elmira, NY; (Y); Am Leg Boys St; French Clb; Model UN; Ski Clb; Varsity Clb; Chorus; School Play; Nwsp Stf; Rep Soph Cls; Rep Jr Cls; Intl Realtions.

RITTINGER, BARBARA; Seton Catholic Central HS; Vestal, NY; (Y); French Clb; Key Clb; Ski Clb; SADD; Varsity Clb; Yrbk Stf; Rep Stu Cncl; Var L Socr; Trk; Hon Roll; English.

RITTLER, LESLIE; Hilton Central HS; Rochester, NY; (Y); #44 In Class; Exploring; 4-H; Office Aide; Ski Clb; 4-H Awd; Hon Roll; SUNY; Bio Tech.

RITUNO, RANDI; Masters Schl; Rye, NY; (Y); Cmnty Wkr; GAA; VP Frsh Cls; Pres Jr Cls; Pres Sr Cls; Off Stu Cncl; Stat Bsktbl; Var Fld Hcky; Var Lcrss; Nwsp Rptr; All Lg Lacrosse 86; Amer HS Ath 85; Head Fund Raiser Lacross Tm England 86; Lib Arts.

RITVANEN, SEPPO; Saugerties HS; Saugerties, NY; (S); Boy Scts; Church Yth Grp; German Clb; Varsity Clb; Band; Concert Band; Socr; High Hon Roll; NHS; FIT; Engrng.

RITZENTHALER, SUE; Royalton-Hartland HS; Gasport, NY; (Y); Church Yth Grp; Dance Clb; Girl Scts; PAVAS; Ski Clb; Chorus; Nwsp Stf; Niagra CC; Bus Adm.

RIVAS, MONICA; Torrejon American HS; Apo, NY; (Y); Cmnty Wkr; Debate Tm; French Clb; Red Cross Aide; Band; Jr Cls; Sr Cls; Stu Cncl; Crs Cntry; High Hon Roll; Georgetown U; Intl Rltns.

RIVENBURG, DAVID B; Hudson HS; Hudson, NY; (Y); 25/150; Camera Clb; Computer Clb; Band; Concert Band; Jazz Band; Mrchg Band; Orch; Pep Band; School Musical; School Play; Regents Schlrshp 86; Comp Sci.

RIVERA, ALBERTO; Herbert H Lehman HS; New York, NY; (Y); Orch; JV Var Ftbl; Var Wrstlng; Hon Roll; Slvr Pin Woodcraft 86; Arista 85; Cert Of Achvt Pysch-Human Sexuality 85; Elevtr Constr.

RIVERA, ANA; Yonker HS; Yonkers, NY; (Y); Church Yth Grp; Latin Clb; Office Aide; Spanish Clb; Achvmnt Awd Accntng 86; Achvmnt Awd Shrt Hnd 86; Achvmnt Awd Typng 85; Berkleys; Exec Sec.

RIVERA, ANTHONY; Beach Channel HS; Far Rockaway, NY; (Y); Var Crs Cntry; Var Ftbl; Var Trk; Hon Roll; Prfct Atten Awd.

RIVERA, AVIANCA; John Dewey HS; Brooklyn, NY; (Y); Aud/Vis; Drama Clb; School Play; Stonybrook; Stewardess.

RIVERA, BERNADETTE; Adlai E Stevenson HS; Bronx, NY; (Y); 17/303; French Clb; Latin Clb; Service Clb; SADD; VP Frsh Cls; Pres Soph Cls; Rep Stu Cncl; French Hon Soc; Hon Roll; NHS; Geom; Keyboardg; Pre-Law.

RIVERA, CARLOS A; St Francis Prep; Ridgewood, NY; (Y); Med.

RIVERA, DAVID; St John The Baptist HS; Central Islip, NY; (Y); 36/501; Band; Concert Band; Hon Roll; Ntl Schl Trffc Sfty Pstr Prog 84; Cert Of Merit Soc Studys 85; Arch.

RIVERA, ELIZABETH; Jane Addams Vocational HS; Bronx, NY; (S); 16/250; Office Aide; Yrbk Stf; Hon Roll; Pol Sci.

RIVERA, EVELYN; Dominican Commercial HS; Brooklyn, NY; (Y); 98/210; Drama Clb; Capt Color Guard; Pep Band; Rep Jr Cls; Pres Stu Cncl; Swmmng; Pace; Educ.

RIVERA, GRACE; Wm Taft HS; Bronx, NY; (Y); Church Yth Grp; Computer Clb; Dance Clb; Drama Clb; 4-H; School Play; Off Jr Cls; Bsbl; Bsktbl; Cheerleading; Comptrs.

RIVERA, IVONNE; Babylon JR SR HS; Babylon, NY; (Y); Flag Corp; Var Trk; High Hon Roll; Schlstc Awd Art 83; 1st Pl Sci Fair 83; Chld Psychlgy.

RIVERA, JEANETTE; Norman Thomas HS; Bronx, NY; (Y); 2/596; Ed English Clb; FBLA; Political Wkr; Service Clb; Ed Lit Mag; Stu Cncl; Cit Awd; High Hon Roll; Jr NHS; NHS; Geo Regnts Awd 84; Regnts Schlrshp 86; Pace; CPA.

RIVERA, JENNIFER; Adlai E Stevenson HS; Bronx, NY; (Y); Boys Clb Am; Hosp Aide; JA; Nwsp Rptr; Swmmng; NHS; MS Pgm Scholar Phillips Acad 84-86; Mth & Sci Minority Stu; Mktng.

RIVERA, JOHANNA; St Raymond Acad; Bronx, NY; (S); 1/84; Capt Band; JV Stu Cncl; High Hon Roll; Hon Roll; NHS; Fordham U; Med.

RIVERA, JOHN; Frontier Central HS; Hamburg, NY; (Y); 108/435; Drama Clb; SADD; Thesps; Varsity Clb; Band; Chorus; Concert Band; Jazz Band; Mrchg Band; School Musical; Loyal Order Of Moose Ldg Schlrshp 86; Dirctrs Awd In Music 86; Outstndng Contrbtn Actor 86; Oswego ST; Commnctns.

RIVERA, KEVIN C; Brentwood H Schl Ross Center; Brentwood, NY; (Y); 46/550; Church Yth Grp; Cmnty Wkr; Computer Clb; Teachers Aide; High Hon Roll; Hon Roll; Prfct Atten Awd; Schlrshp-Eastrn NM 86; Schlrshp Tampa U 86; Semifnlst/Milw Schl Of Engrng Schlrshp 86; FL Inst Of Tech; Comp Engrng.

RIVERA, LILY; Cardinald Spellman HS; Bronx, NY; (Y); Dance Clb; Drama Clb; Pres Spanish Clb; Drm Mjr(t); School Play; Gym; Sftbl; Twrlr; Vllybl; Span Hnrs 86; Cornell U; Psychol.

RIVERA, LIZA; Ursuline HS; Stamford, CT; (Y); 51/121; Church Yth Grp; Cmnty Wkr; Computer Clb; Spanish Clb; Hon Roll; Iona Awd 86; Frdhm; Comp Sci.

RIVERA, MARCOS; Mount St Michael Acad; Bronx, NY; (S); 25/309; Boy Scts; NHS; Govt Job.

RIVERA, MARISEL; Peekskill HS; Peekskill, NY; (Y); 17/147; Stat Ftbl; Church Yth Grp; Debate Tm; Yrbk Bus Mgr; Yrbk Stf; VP Jr Cls; High Hon Roll; Hon Roll; NHS; Oral Roberts U; Bus Mgr.

RIVERA, MARISOL; Central Islip HS; Central Islip, NY; (Y); Spanish Clb; SADD; Chorus; Flag Corp; School Musical; School Play; Stage Crew; Nwsp Stf; Lit Mag; Pres Stu Cncl; Charles Mulligan PTA Schlrshp 86; Am Intl COLL Pres Schlrshp 86; Intl Bus.

RIVERA, MARISOL; Murry Bergtraum HS; Brooklyn, NY; (Y); Church Yth Grp; Teachers Aide; Church Choir; Variety Show; Swmmng; Trvl.

RIVERA, MARITZA; Bronx HS Of Science; Bronx, NY; (Y); Cmnty Wkr; Office Aide; Service Clb; Spanish Clb; Teachers Aide; Lit Mag; Cheerleading; Prfct Atten Awd; 1st Plc Spnsh Natl Exm 4th Yr III Ctgry 86; Rdgntn Pstr Cmpgn Beautfy Sbwys & Buses NYC; Bio.

RIVERA, MICHAEL; Erasmus Hall HS; Brooklyn, NY; (Y); Art Clb; Ntnl Hnr Scty Crtfct Mbrshp 86; Achvmnt Awd Attndnc 86; Crtfct Achvmnt Soc Stds 86.

RIVERA, MICHELE; Newburgh Free Acad; Newburgh, NY; (Y); Band; Concert Band; Jazz Band; Mrchg Band; Trs Orch; Pep Band; School Musical; Symp Band; JV L Mgr(s); JV Var Vllybl; Fuente Scholar 86 N; Oneonta ST Coll; CPA.

RIVERA, MICHELLE; St Vincent Ferrer HS; New York City, NY; (Y); 30/135; Dance Clb; Math Clb; Rgnts Nrsng Schlrshp 85; Math Lge Awd 85; Hunter; CPA.

RIVERA JR, MIGUEL A; Nazareth Regional HS; Brooklyn, NY; (Y); Var Bsbl; JV Var Bsktbl; Hon Roll; FBI.

RIVERA, RAFAEL; Msgr Scanlan HS; Bronx, NY; (Y); 76/296; Boys Clb Am; Church Yth Grp; Dance Clb; Intnl Clb; JA; Radio Clb; Spanish Clb; Teachers Aide; Varsity Clb; Stage Crew; Baruch Coll; Bus Adm.

RIVERA, RAQUEL; Dominican Commercial HS; Richmond Hill, NY; (Y); Dance Clb; Spanish Clb; Rep Frsh Cls; 4 Yr Partl Schlrshp 83; Pre-Law.

RIVERA, RAUL; Msgr Scanlan HS; Bronx, NY; (Y); Am Leg Boys St; Boys Clb Am; Boy Scts; Cmnty Wkr; Math Clb; Red Cross Aide; Swmmng; Trk; Prfct Atten Awd; Medical.

RIVERA, RUBEN; Christ The King RHS; Flushing, NY; (Y); 50/451; SADD; JV Var Bsbl; Hon Roll; Civil Engr.

RIVERA, RUBEN; Morris HS; Bronx, NY; (Y); VP Pres Cmnty Wkr; JA; School Musical; Stage Crew; Yrbk Stf; NHS; Prfct Atten Awd; $400 Schlrshp Coro Fndtn Pblc Afrs Prog 85-86; Engrng.

RIVERA, SANDRA; Saint Pius V HS; Bronx, NY; (Y); Chess Clb; Library Aide; Service Clb; Church Choir; Nwsp Stf; Sec Soph Cls; Hon Roll.

RIVERA, STEPHANIE; John Jay HS; Brooklyn, NY; (Y); Commndtn Italian 85-86; Lawyer.

RIVERA, WILFREDO; Eastern District HS; Brooklyn, NY; (Y).

RIVERE, LAINIE; J F Kennedy HS; Merrick, NY; (Y); Drama Clb; School Play; Yrbk Stf; Rep Frsh Cls; Hon Roll; NHS.

RIVERO, CARMELITA; Smithtown High Schl East; Smithtown, NY; (Y); Chess Clb; Girl Scts; Capt Color Guard; Drm & Bgl; Mrchg Band; Symp Band; Sftbl; Hon Roll; NHS; Spanish NHS; Hspnc Schlr Awds Pgm 85-86; SUNY Buffalo; Med Tech.

RIVERS, BRADLEY R; Liverpool HS; Liverpool, NY; (Y); 158/816; Cmnty Wkr; JA; JV Trk; Hon Roll; St Schlr; Onondaga CC; CPA.

RIVERS, KEN; Clayton R Bouton JR SR HS; Altamont, NY; (Y); Church Yth Grp; Im Bsktbl; Hon Roll; Prfct Atten Awd; Accntng.

RIVERS, MELISSA; Charles H Roth HS; W Henrietta, NY; (Y); Church Yth Grp; French Clb; GAA; Rep Soph Cls; JV Cheerleading; JV Sftbl; Var Tennis; JV Vllybl; Hon Roll; Pres Cltrl Exch 86; Scl Studies Hnrs 85; Sec Of Cltrl Exch 85; Pre-Med.

RIVET, CRAIG; Mechanicville HS; Mechanicville, NY; (S); Math Tm; Spanish Clb; Yrbk Stf; JV Bsbl; Var Crs Cntry; Var Wrstlng; High Hon Roll; Jr NHS; NHS; Prfct Atten Awd.

RIVLIN, TERI; Fayetteville-Manlius HS; Manlius, NY; (Y); Cmnty Wkr; Hosp Aide; Office Aide; Teachers Aide; Temple Yth Grp; Nwsp Rptr; Nwsp Stf; Stu Cncl; Hon Roll; NHS; Vlntr Awd Cndystrpng; Schlrshp Israel Smmr 85; Nwspaper Certf.

RIVOLI, JULIA; Gates Chili SR HS; Rochester, NY; (Y); 70/446; Drama Clb; VP Science Clb; Ski Clb; School Musical; Rep Frsh Cls; Rep Soph Cls; Rep Jr Cls; Rep Sr Cls; Rep Stu Cncl; JV Var Socr; Rgnts Schlrshp 86; Potsdam Coll; Ntrl Sci.

RIZZA, LORRENA M; T R Proctor HS; Utica, NY; (Y); 73/201; GAA; Pep Clb; Nwsp Ed-Chief; Bsktbl; Mgr(s); Score Keeper; Sftbl; Timer; Prfct Atten Awd; Cazenovia Coll; Bus Mgmt.

RIZZI, ANTOINETTE; St Edmund HS; Brooklyn, NY; (S); 2/200; Pres Soph Cls; Pres Jr Cls; Rep Stu Cncl; Pres Jr NHS; Prfct Atten Awd; Val; Art Clb; Church Yth Grp; Tuitn Scholar 85-86; Sci Fair Awd 83-84; NEDT Awd 84-85; St Johns U; Phrmcy.

RIZZI, TOM; St Francis Prep HS; Maspeth, NY; (Y); JV Var Bsbl; JV Var Bsktbl; JV Var Ftbl; Hlf Schlrp 4 Yrs HS; Syracuse U; Math.

RIZZO, CHRISTINA; Moore Catholic HS; Staten Island, NY; (Y); Drama Clb; Hosp Aide; Library Aide; Political Wkr; Chorus; School Musical; School Play; Stage Crew; Yrbk Stf; Pres Frsh Cls; Pace; Bus.

RIZZO, JAMES; Frontier HS; Hamburg, NY; (S); 50/440; Chess Clb; Cmnty Wkr; Varsity Clb; JV Var Bsktbl; Var Mgr(s); Var Score Keeper; Hon Roll; NHS; Prfct Atten Awd; Var Vllybl.

RIZZO, JOHN; St Francis Prep; Ozone Park, NY; (S); Hosp Aide; Science Clb; Band; Hon Roll.

RIZZO, VICTOR P; Pelham Memorial HS; Pelham, NY; (Y); Aud/Vis; Computer Clb; School Play; Stage Crew; Socr; Trk; Wt Lftg; Excllnce Bsc Comp 83-84; Excllnce In Wrtng 85-86; Excllnce In SS 85-86; Renssalear Poly Inst; Aero Engr.

RIZZUTO, DINA; South Shore HS; Brooklyn, NY; (Y); Art Clb; Church Yth Grp; Dance Clb; Service Clb; Teachers Aide; Orch; Yrbk Stf; Pom Pon; Fash Inst Tech; Fash Merch.

ROACH, CYNTHIA; Lake George HS; Lake George, NY; (Y); 22/86; Concert Band; Mrchg Band; School Play; Var Fld Hcky; Gym; French Hon Soc; Hon Roll; Church Yth Grp; 4-H; Band; Excllg Peer Ldr Awd 85; Acdmc Achvt Frnch Awd 85; Plcd 7th Concrs Natl De Francais 85; Psych.

ROACH, DANIEL JOSEPH; O Neil HS; Walton, NY; (Y); Computer Clb; Varsity Clb; Chorus; Orch; Rep Stu Cncl; JV Var Bsktbl; JV Crs Cntry; Var L Tennis; NYS Music Assn Ratng 86NYS Youth Orch 86; Music Ed.

ROACH, JENNIFER; Bishop Ludden HS; Syracuse, NY; (S); French Clb; German Clb; Trs Soph Cls; JV Cheerleading; Var Crs Cntry; Var Trk; High Hon Roll; Lang.

ROACH, MICHELLE; Auburn HS; Auburn, NY; (Y); Hon Roll; Emerson Hi-Y Prom 84; B & S Bus Inst; Lgl Secy.

ROACHE, ERNEST; Sherman Central Schl; Ripley, NY; (Y); Boy Scts; 4-H; FFA; Keywanettes; Chorus; Bsbl; Bsktbl; Ftbl; Wrstlng; 4-H Awd; PPA Awd Lvstck Prod 85-86; Home Imprvmnt Awd 85-86; Constr Tech.

ROAN, HOPE; Huntington HS; Huntington Sta, NY; (Y); Var Sftbl; Hon Roll; Var Bsktbl; Fairleigh Dickerson U; Hist.

ROARK, LISA KATHLENE; Plattsburgh City HS; Plattsburgh, NY; (Y); 7/159; Cmnty Wkr; Model UN; SADD; Sec Jr Cls; Sec Stu Cncl; Vllybl; High Hon Roll; NHS; Hmcmgn Queen 85; U Of Vermont; Psych.

ROARK, TRACY; Bishop Ludden HS; Syracuse, NY; (S); Church Yth Grp; French Clb; Sec Frsh Cls; Sec Soph Cls; Sec Jr Cls; Var L Socr; Var L Swmmng; Var L Trk; Var Capt Vllybl; Hon Roll.

ROBARGE, MARY; Franklin Acad; Malone, NY; (Y); French Clb; Chorus; Swing Chorus; Hon Roll; Russell Sage Coll; Acctg.

ROBAYO, ALEX; Newfield HS; Selden, NY; (Y); Boy Scts; Computer Clb; German Clb; Spanish Clb; JV Crs Cntry; Var Trk; High Hon Roll; Hon Roll; Jr NHS; NHS; Excllnc In Frgn Lang 84; Spnsh Awd 86; Grmn Awd 85; Comp Sci.

ROBBEN, DAWN; The Ursuline Schl; Rye, NY; (Y); Art Clb; Ski Clb; Rep Jr Cls; Rep Sr Cls; Stu Cncl; Swmmng; Trk; DAR Awd; MVP Swmmng 85; Gen Excel Svc JR Cls 86; Providence; Advtsng.

ROBBINS, ALICIA; Gowanda Central HS; Gowanda, NY; (Y); 6/127; VP Church Yth Grp; Drama Clb; French Clb; Girl Scts; Thesps; Chorus; School Musical; School Play; Stage Crew; Nwsp Rptr.

ROBBINS, BRIAN D; Prattsburg Central HS; Prattsburg, NY; (Y); 3/30; Am Leg Boys St; Varsity Clb; Yrbk Stf; Bsbl; Capt Bsktbl; High Hon Roll; NHS; Wstrn NY All Star 86; Comp Sci.

ROBBINS, DENISE M; Islip HS; Islip, NY; (Y); 50/250; Art Clb; Hosp Aide; Key Clb; Letterman Clb; Mathletes; Q&S; Nwsp Ed-Chief; Jr Cls; Sr Cls; Bsktbl; The American U; Comm.

ROBBINS, GENE B; August Martin HS; Jamaica, NY; (Y); 1/433; Church Yth Grp; Lit Mag; Trk; Gov Hon Prg Awd; Ntl Merit Ltr; Prfct Atten Awd; Val; Acdmc Olympics 84-86; Queens Coll Pres Awd Achvmnt Jr & Sr 83-85; Police Comm Essay Cntst 82-83; MA Inst Tech; Elec Engr.

ROBBINS, RHONDA; Gowanda Central HS; Perrysburg, NY; (Y); 17/127; AFS; Pres Church Yth Grp; Drama Clb; Girl Scts; Library Aide; Spanish Clb; SADD; Thesps; Band; Concert Band; Hugh O Brian Ldrshp Sem 85; Bus Adm.

ROBBLE, KAREN; Colonie Central HS; Loudonville, NY; (Y); 15/467; Cmnty Wkr; Hosp Aide; Intnl Clb; Key Clb; Library Aide; Pep Clb; SADD; JV Cheerleading; High Hon Roll; NHS; Pediatrcn.

ROBEN, DEBRA R; Island Trees HS; Levittown, NY; (Y); 9/215; SADD; Band; Jazz Band; Sec Soph Cls; Sec Jr Cls; Pres Stu Cncl; Var Badmtn; Var Capt Vllybl; NHS; Drama Clb; NYS Regnts Schlrshp 86; St Johns U; Bus.

ROBERSON, KARON MARIE; Jamaica HS; E Elmhurst, NY; (Y); 85/455; Dance Clb; PAVAS; Science Clb; Service Clb; Spanish Clb; Chorus; School Musical; Variety Show; Rep Stu Cncl; Hon Roll; Alpla Kappa Alpha Srrty Cert Honrry HS Achvmnts 86; Dollar For Schlr Schlrshp 86; Brandeis U; Pre Law.

ROBERSON, LISA; Wilson Magnet HS; Rochester, NY; (Y); Chorus; Church Choir; Variety Show; Mgr(s); Score Keeper; Sftbl; Vllybl; Cit Awd; High Hon Roll; Hon Roll; Urban Lge Black Schlr 86; Roberts Wesleyan Coll; Med Tech.

ROBERSON, PATRINA; Central Islip HS; Central Islip, NY; (Y); FBLA; Girl Scts; SADD; Chorus; Yrbk Stf; Capt Cheerleading; Mgr(s); Score Keeper; Swmmng; Hon Roll; Pre-Law.

ROBERSON, TYRONE; Rice HS; New York, NY; (Y); Nwsp Rptr; Yrbk Stf; Var Crs Cntry; Var Trk; Hon Roll; Iona Coll; Bus Adm.

ROBERT, LUI; Bishop Ford C C HS; Brooklyn, NY; (Y); 44/441; Computer Clb; Math Tm; Hon Roll; Prfct Atten Awd; NYS Regents Schlrshp 86; Polytechnic U; Comp Sci.

ROBERT, TAMMI; Massena Central HS; Massena, NY; (Y); Church Yth Grp; Cmnty Wkr; Office Aide; Band; Concert Band; Mrchg Band; Variety Show; Stu Cncl; Powder Puff Ftbl; Hon Roll; Med Secy.

ROBERT, WADE; Skaneateles HS; Skaneateles, NY; (Y); 56/148; Church Yth Grp; Chorus; Concert Band; Jazz Band; Stage Crew; Symp Band; Trk; Hon Roll; NHS; U Of ND.

ROBERTO, DONNA; Union Endicott HS; Endicott, NY; (Y); 98/425; Cmnty Wkr; Key Clb; Band; Mrchg Band; Symp Band; Stu Cncl; Hon Roll; Prfct Atten Awd; Grand Lodge NY Order Sons Of Italy In Amer Schlrshp 86; NY U Binghamton; Lib Arts.

ROBERTS, AMY; John Jay HS; Katonah, NY; (Y); Office Aide; Chorus; Variety Show; JV Capt Cheerleading; Cit Awd; Hon Roll; Pre-Law.

ROBERTS, AMY; North Warren Central HS; Chestertown, NY; (Y); 3/49; 4-H; Math Tm; Band; Chorus; Concert Band; Yrbk Stf; Cit Awd; 4-H Awd; Hon Roll; NHS; Co 4-H Mdl For Hrsmnshp & Ldrship 82 & 84; SUNY; Ag.

ROBERTS, ARTHUR; Bayport-Blue Point HS; Blue Point, NY; (Y); 41/249; Boy Scts; Voice Dem Awd; Comp Engr.

ROBERTS, CHERI LA RAE; Sacred Heart Acad; West Hempstead, NY; (Y); 18/180; Cmnty Wkr; Math Clb; SADD; Yrbk Stf; Rep Stu Cncl; High Hon Roll; NHS; Ntl Merit Ltr; FHA; Ntl Achvt Commd Stu 86; Clncl Psychlgy.

ROBERTS, DAVE; Cohoes HS; Waterford, NY; (Y); 50/175; Varsity Clb; JV Bsbl; Var Golf; Var Trk; Var Wrstlng; US Air Force; Navigation.

ROBERTS, DAVID P; Baldwin SR HS; Baldwin, NY; (Y); 23/490; Am Leg Boys St; Cmnty Wkr; High Hon Roll; Hon Roll; Kiwanis Awd; Pres Schlr; Soc Studies Awd 86; Achvt Physics 86; SUNY.

ROBERTS, DAWN; Martin Van Buren HS; Cambria, NY; (Y); Var Vllybl; JA; Service Clb; Varsity Clb; School Play; Stage Crew; Var Bsktbl; Var Score Keeper; Hon Roll.

ROBERTS, DAWN; W C Bryant HS; Astoria, NY; (S); 86/623; VP Key Clb; Library Aide; Science Clb; Chorus; Nwsp Rptr; Nwsp Stf; Sr Cls; Cit Awd; Hon Roll; Prfct Atten Awd; Excllnc Engl Acad Lttr & Pin 84-85; GPA Hnr Certs 84-85; Baruch Coll; Jrnlsm.

ROBERTS, DIANA; Shoreham Wading River HS; Shoreham, NY; (Y); Mathletes; School Musical; Yrbk Ed-Chief; Yrbk Phtg; Rep Sr Cls; JV Gym; NCTE Awd; NHS; Oustndng Scl Stds Stu 86; Prsdntl Acdmc Ftnss Awd 86; Shrhm Wdng Rvr Tchrs Assoc Schrlshp 86; Start U NY; Hstry.

ROBERTS, DIANE M; Hammondsport Central Schl; Hammondsport, NY; (Y); 5/68; Am Leg Aux Girls St; Church Yth Grp; Girl Scts; Band; Church Choir; Jazz Band; Pres Soph Cls; Stu Cncl; High Hon Roll; NHS; ROTC Schlrshp 86; Cornell U; Ind Engr.

ROBERTS, GEMMA; Marlboro HS; Marlboro, NY; (Y); Varsity Clb; Rep Jr Cls; Crs Cntry; Trk; Hon Roll; NHS; Fshn Coordntn.

ROBERTS, HEATHER; Westmoreland Cntrl HS; Westmoreland, NY; (Y); 40/86; 4-H; GAA; Varsity Clb; Band; Chorus; Nwsp Stf; Bsktbl; Score Keeper; Socr; Sftbl; Capt Bsktbl Tm 85-86; High Hnr Roll 85-86; Data Proc.

ROBERTS, KENNETH A; Yonkers HS; Yonkers, NY; (Y); 5/287; FBLA; Nwsp Stf; Yrbk Stf; Pres Stu Cncl; Capt Var Bowling; DAR Awd; High Hon Roll; NHS; Regents Schlrshp 86; Natl Cncl Of Negro Wmn 86; Suprt Clb 90 Acad Awd 85; ST U Of NY Albany; Accntng.

ROBERTS, LAURA; Carmel HS; Carmel, NY; (Y); Camera Clb; Cmnty Wkr; 4-H; GAA; Spanish Clb; SADD; Chorus; Church Choir; Drill Tm; Mrchg Band; Travel.

ROBERTS, LISA; Sharon Springs Central Schl; Sharon Springs, NY; (S); 2/28; Sec Girl Scts; VP Spanish Clb; Trs Frsh Cls; Var Bsktbl; Hon Roll; Sec NHS; NEDT Awd; Secndry Engl Ed.

ROBERTS, MAUREEN; Mercy HS; Riverhead, NY; (Y); Church Yth Grp; Cmnty Wkr; GAA; Mathletes; Ski Clb; SADD; Yrbk Stf; Rep Jr Cls; Var Bowling; Var Sftbl; Principls Lst 84-86.

ROBERTS, MELISSA; Chenango Forks Central HS; Chenango Forks, NY; (Y); 1/200; Exploring; Ski Clb; VP Trs Band; Rep Stu Cncl; JV Socr; High Hon Roll; NHS; Val; Hosp Aide; Quiz Bowl; Salute To Yth 85; Apprntc Brdg Pgm 84-85; Membr All-Cnty Band 83; Wshngtn & Lee U; Jrnlsm.

ROBERTS, MELISSA; Oneida SR HS; Oneida Castle, NY; (S); 19/200; Sec Church Yth Grp; VP SADD; Band; Chorus; Var L Crs Cntry; Var L Trk; Hon Roll; NHS; Houghton Coll; Bio.

ROBERTS, PATRICIA; Scotia-Glenvill HS; Scotia, NY; (Y); AFS; SADD; Varsity Clb; Im Socr; L Vllybl; High Hon Roll.

ROBERTS, PAUL; The Stony Brook Schl; Wenham, MA; (Y); 32/87; Chorus; Madrigals; Orch; School Musical; School Play; Stu Cncl; Coach Actv; Crs Cntry; Trk; Hon Roll; Swanson Trphy Sprior Athltc Prfmnce 85-86; Kresge Christian Ldrshp Schlrshp 84-85; Engl Spkng 86-87; Dartmouth Coll; Law.

ROBERTS, SCOTT; Frontier HS; Blasdell, NY; (Y); Mgr(s); Var Wrstlng; Hon Roll.

ROBERTS, SEAN; Franklin K Lane HS; Woodhaven, NY; (Y); Var Bsktbl; NYS Rgnts Schlrshp; The Hunter Coll Merit Awd; Hunter Coll; Bus.

ROBERTS, SHARON; Colonie Central HS; Loudonville, NY; (Y); Art Clb; Church Yth Grp; Drama Clb; FBLA; Intnl Clb; SADD; Pres Church Choir; Concert Band; Rep Jr Cls; Var Cheerleading; Chem Engrng.

ROBERTS, SOPHIA; John H Glenn HS; Greenlawn, NY; (Y); Sec Church Yth Grp; Drama Clb; Church Choir; JV Bsktbl; Var Tennis; Vrsty Awd Most Imprvd Tennis Plyr 86; Med.

ROBERTS, TANYA; Alden Central HS; Alden, NY; (Y); Church Yth Grp; Library Aide; Spanish Clb; Speech Tm; Yrbk Stf; Rep Stu Cncl; Stu Cncl Schlrshp 86; Library Aide Awd 85-86; Alden Chptr No 401-Ordr Of Estrn Star Schlrshp 86; Daemen Coll; Psych.

ROBERTSON, AMY; Charles O Dickerson HS; Trumansburg, NY; (Y); 17/114; 4-H; Spanish Clb; Band; Concert Band; Mrchg Band; Trs Frsh Cls; Trs Soph Cls; Trs Jr Cls; Cit Awd; 4-H Awd; Retailng.

ROBERTSON, CYNTHIA A; Ilion Central HS; Ilion, NY; (Y); 31/141; Sec Church Yth Grp; Hosp Aide; Chorus; Var Badmtn; Hon Roll; NHS; St Schlr; Offcl Block I Awd Badminton 83-84; Herkimer Cnty CC; Occptnl Thry.

ROBERTSON, DIANE; Knox Memorial Central HS; Russell, NY; (S); 5/28; Varsity Clb; Chorus; Yrbk Stf; Rep Jr Cls; Rep Stu Cncl; Var Capt Bsktbl; Coach Actv; Var Sftbl; High Hon Roll; Hon Roll; Hstry Tchr.

ROBERTSON, JEFFREY; Caledonia-Mumford Central Schl; Caledonia, NY; (Y); 7/95; Math Tm; Trs Spanish Clb; Band; Swing Chorus; Yrbk Stf; Var L Golf; High Hon Roll; Pres NHS; Area All State Chorus; Livingston Co All State Math Tm; U Notre Dame; Acctg.

ROBERTSON, MANDUME; Mount Vernon HS; Mt Vernon, NY; (Y); Cmnty Wkr; Office Aide; High Hon Roll; Howard U; Audio Engr.

ROBERTSON, MARGARET; Mount Saint Mary Acad; Kenmore, NY; (Y); Pres Church Yth Grp; Trs Girl Scts; Hosp Aide; Var Capt Bsktbl; Var Gym; Var Capt Sftbl; Var Capt Vllybl; Hon Roll; NHS; Wellesley Coll Bk Awd 86; Grl Scout Slvr Awd 83; Grls Sftbll All Catholic 86; Phys Therapy.

ROBERTSON, MARK; St Dominic HS; Oyster Bay, NY; (Y); 36/119; Quiz Bowl; Nwsp Phtg; Yrbk Phtg; Yrbk Stf; Pres Sr Cls; Stu Cncl; JV Ftbl; Hon Roll; Camera Clb; Pep Clb; NYS ST Rgnts Schlrshp 86; St Johns U.

ROBERTSON, MICHAEL; Bishop Timon HS; W Seneca, NY; (Y); Letterman Clb; SADD; Chorus; Capt Bsbl; JV Bsktbl; Var Ftbl; Var Ice Hcky; MVP Bsbl; Athlt Of Wk Ftbl; Athlt Of Yr; 1st Tm Ftbl; 2nd Bsbl; 3rd Tm Ftbl; Canisius College; Bus.

ROBEY, ETHAN; Hunter College HS; New York, NY; (Y); Pres Art Clb; Lit Mag; Mu Alp Tht; Ntl Merit SF; Acad Excllnc Awd Hebrew HS 84; Bronze Medal Natl Socl Studies Olympiad 85; Art Hist.

ROBICHAUD, TIMOTHY; Stillwater Central HS; Stillwater, NY; (Y); 2/100; Pres Key Clb; Varsity Clb; JV Bsbl; JV Bsktbl; JV Var Ftbl; L Var Wt Lftg; High Hon Roll; NHS; Ntl Merit Ltr; Sal; Rgnts Schlrshp, Key Clb Schlrshp 86; Ntl Hst Awd Ftbl 86; Union Coll; Physcs.

ROBIDOUX, LISA; John F Kennedy HS; Utica, NY; (Y); FBLA; GAA; SADD; Bsktbl; Sftbl; Vllybl; Bus.

ROBILOTTO, MARLENE; Poland Central Schl; Poland, NY; (Y); French Clb; Ski Clb; Trs Spanish Clb; SADD; Chorus; Jazz Band; Orch; Symp Band; Yrbk Stf; Rep Stu Cncl; NYSSMA Solo Rtng 86; Nw Englnd Music Cmp Hnr Cmpr Awd & Wrkng Schlrshp 83; Johnson & Wales; Clnry Arts.

ROBIN, BETH; Ward Melville HS; S Setauket, NY; (Y); Wt Lftg; Hon Roll; Outstndng Achvt Frnch Awd 84; Comm.

ROBIN, MARNI R; Edgemont HS; Scarsdale, NY; (Y); Art Clb; Dance Clb; Exploring; French Clb; Ski Clb; Var Capt Bsktbl; JV Var Sftbl; JV Vllybl; Rgnts Schlrshp 86; SUNY Binghamton.

ROBINS, DAVID; Clarkstown HS North; New City, NY; (Y); Boy Scts; Church Yth Grp; German Clb; Stu Cncl; Var Capt Ice Hcky; Var Lcrss; Wt Lftg; High Hon Roll; Hon Roll; Jr NHS; Empr ST-HCKY Tm 86; Lbrty Wkend-Bnjo 86; NJ Lttl Dvls Mdgt AA Tm 84-86; Queens U-Ontario; Chmcl Engrng.

ROBINSON, ALICE; Corinth Central HS; Corinth, NY; (S); 4/80; Drama Clb; Hosp Aide; SADD; Band; Var Cheerleading; Var Fld Hcky; High Hon Roll; NHS; Spanish NHS; Pep Clb; Modern Music Masters Hnr Soc 85; Coast Guard.

ROBINSON, ALICIA; Corinth Central HS; Corinth, NY; (Y); Sec Trs Church Yth Grp; Hosp Aide; SADD; Varsity Clb; Band; Var Cheerleading; Var Fld Hcky; High Hon Roll; Sec NHS; Spanish NHS; Med.

ROBINSON, ANDREW; Hamburg SR HS; Hamburg, NY; (Y); 62/374; AFS; Boy Scts; Chess Clb; Church Yth Grp; Concert Band; Mrchg Band; Hon Roll; Band; Dir Hamburg Inst Tv 85-86; Ad Craft Art Awd 85-86; Musicl Poster Desgn Comptn Wnnr 85-86; Inf Systms Mgmt.

ROBINSON, ANGELA; Churchville-Chili HS; Rochester, NY; (Y); Chorus; Stage Crew; Variety Show; High Hon Roll; Hon Roll; Prfct Atten Awd; 2nd Pl Awd Vocal Solo 84; Vet Med.

ROBINSON, ARTHUR M; Bronx High School Of Science; Bronx, NY; (Y); Cmnty Wkr; Y-Teens; Var L Swmmng; Library Aide; Chorus; NHS; Engrg.

ROBINSON, CHERYL; Riverhead HS; Riverhead, NY; (Y); NYU Dental Coll; Dntst.

ROBINSON, CHRIS; Pittsford Mendon HS; Pittsford, NY; (Y); School Play; Yrbk Phtg; Yrbk Stf; Var Golf; Hon Roll; Schltc Art Awd 84; Ptlnd Sch Art Hnrb Mntn Awd 86; Soph Art Awd PTSA 85; Art Edtr Yrbk.

ROBINSON, COLBY; Bitburg American HS; Apo Ny, NY; (Y); 11/141; Math Tm; Natl Beta Clb; Rep Jr Cls; JV Var Ftbl; NHS; Embry-Riddle U; Aviation Tech.

ROBINSON, DIANE; Midwood HS; Brooklyn, NY; (Y); 49/667; Library Aide; Model UN; Scholastic Bowl; Teachers Aide; School Musical; Rptr Nwsp Rptr; Rptr Yrbk Rptr; High Hon Roll; Prfct Atten Awd; Recitation Awd 84; Engl Hnr Awd 84; Spn Hnr Awd 84; Arista Hnr Soc 86; Cornell U; Pre-Law.

ROBINSON, DONNA; Lindenhurst HS; Encinitas, CA; (Y); 96/583; Church Yth Grp; Dance Clb; Spanish Clb; Chorus; School Musical; School Play; Variety Show; Hon Roll; Dancing Awds; Bus Mgmnt.

ROBINSON, FRANK; Oyster Bay HS; Oyster Bay, NY; (Y); 19/122; Hon Roll; NHS; Var Capt Socr; Var Trk; Mst Imprvd Plyr Sccr, Fncng 84; Al-Leag Sccr, Fncng, MIP Fncng 85; MVP Sccr, Al-Conf Sccr 86; Cornell U; Engr.

ROBINSON, GORDON; Troupsburg Central Schl; Woodhull, NY; (Y); Aud/Vis; Rep Stu Cncl; JV Var Bsktbl; Hon Roll.

ROBINSON, HOLLY M; Canastota HS; Canastota, NY; (Y); 7/150; Science Clb; SADD; Band; Chorus; Mrchg Band; School Musical; Score Keeper; High Hon Roll; Rgnts Schlrshp 85-86; Geneseo Coll.

ROBINSON, ISAAC; Dewitt Clinton HS; New York, NY; (Y); Key Clb; Bsktbl; Hon Roll; Acctng.

ROBINSON, JENNIFER; Frontier HS; Hamburg, NY; (Y); 12/500; Church Yth Grp; VP Drama Clb; French Clb; Latin Clb; Off Soph Cls; Off Jr Cls; JV Socr; High Hon Roll; NHS; Ntl Merit SF; Fashion Mrchndsng.

ROBINSON, JOY; Canastota HS; Canastota, NY; (S); 2/155; Pres Church Yth Grp; Chorus; School Musical; Stage Crew; Variety Show; Bausch & Lomb Sci Awd; DAR Awd; High Hon Roll; Pres NHS; Ntl Merit Ltr; Alfred U; Lib Arts.

ROBINSON, L T; Farmingdale SR HS; S Farmingdale, NY; (Y); Boy Scts; Church Yth Grp; 4-H; Intnl Clb; Library Aide; Church Choir; Bsbl; Bsktbl; Bowling; Ftbl; Public Spkng Merit Roll 84-86; Moorehouse; Spnsh.

ROBINSON, LEISEL; Rome Free Acad; Rome, NY; (Y); 19/550; Pres VP Church Yth Grp; Jazz Band; Rep Frsh Cls; L Im Fld Hcky; Var L Trk; Cit Awd; DAR Awd; High Hon Roll; Jr NHS; NHS; 5 Yr Natl Guild Of Piano Stu Natl Awd 86; Area All-St All-Cnty All-Cty Part 84-86; Bus Admin.

ROBINSON, LLOYD; Alfred E Smith HS; Bronx, NY; (S); 15/217; Church Choir; NHS; Voc Schl Tchr.

ROBINSON, MICHAEL; Lisbon Central HS; Lisbon, NY; (S); 2/50; Pres Church Yth Grp; Computer Clb; Spanish Clb; Trs Frsh Cls; Trs Soph Cls; Trs Jr Cls; Pres Stu Cncl; JV Var Bsktbl; High Hon Roll; Hon Roll.

ROBINSON, MURIEL; P V Moore HS; Brewerton, NY; (Y); AFS; Drama Clb; Radio Clb; Chorus; Color Guard; School Musical; Stage Crew; SUNY Potsdam; Elem Tchr.

ROBINSON, NADINE; Cardinal Spellman HS; New York, NY; (Y); Church Choir; Lit Mag; Trk; High Hon Roll; Hon Roll; Art Awd 84-86; Illstrtn.

ROBINSON, PATRICIA; Waterloo SR HS; Waterloo, NY; (Y); 22/145; FTA; Pep Clb; Spanish Clb; Band; Concert Band; Mrchg Band; Nwsp Stf; Yrbk Phtg; Hon Roll; NHS; Advrtsng.

ROBINSON, PAULA; Eastridge HS; Rochester, NY; (Y); 12/250; Cmnty Wkr; GAA; Spanish Clb; Varsity Clb; School Musical; Yrbk Bus Mgr; Fld Hcky; Capt Sftbl; High Hon Roll; Pres NHS; Bethany Rgnl Ldrs Schlrshp 86; PTSA Tchrs Schlrshp 86; Bethany Coll WV.

ROBINSON, PETER; Schenectady Christian Schl; Schenectady, NY; (S); Off Jr Cls; Stu Cncl; Bsktbl; Socr; Trk.

ROBINSON, RICHARD; Stissing Mt JR SR HS; Stanfordville, NY; (Y); 2/100; AFS; Boy Scts; Drama Clb; Band; Nwsp Rptr; Yrbk Phtg; Socr; Trk; High Hon Roll; Temple Yth Grp; Dntstry.

ROBINSON, ROSLYN; Pierson HS; Sag Harbor, NY; (Y); 15/45; Dance Clb; Drama Clb; Radio Clb; Band; Church Choir; School Musical; School Play; Yrbk Stf; Spanish Clb; Pres Frsh Cls; Acadmc Hgh Hnrs 86; Svc Awd 86; Prncpls Awd 86; Berkeley; Fshn Mrchndsng.

ROBINSON, SCOTT; North Tonawanda SR HS; N Tonawanda, NY; (Y); 157/398; Computer Clb; Chorus; Swing Chorus; JV Bsbl; Bsktbl; Var Bowling; Sftbl; Vllybl; Prfct Atten Awd; Comps.

ROBINSON, SEAN H; Hempstead HS; Hempstead, NY; (Y); 37/237; Church Yth Grp; Computer Clb; Math Clb; Science Clb; Crs Cntry; Ftbl; Trk; High Hon Roll; Hon Roll; Rgnts Schlrshp 86; Lng Islnd Sci Cngrss 84; 2nd Pl Stnybrk Engrng Cntst 86; Rutgers U; Elec Engrng.

ROBINSON, SHELLI M; Walton Central Schl; Walton, NY; (Y); 29/110; 4-H; Hosp Aide; Nwsp Stf; JV Var Sftbl; Var Trk; High Hon Roll; Prfct Atten Awd; Rgnts Schlrshp Wnnr; Cazenovia Coll; Nrsng.

ROBINSON, SHERRY; Kensington HS; Buffalo, NY; (Y); Computer Clb; Girl Scts; Hosp Aide; Church Choir; Yrbk Stf; Ntl Merit Ltr; JA Awd; U Buffalo; Socl Wrkr.

ROBINSON, TAUNYA; Uniondale HS; Hempstead, NY; (Y); Mgr(s); Score Keeper; Var Swmmng; Pace U; Comp Sci.

ROBINSON, THOMAS; Grand Island HS; Gr Island, NY; (Y); 14/297; VP Model UN; Band; Jazz Band; Pres Frsh Cls; Pres Soph Cls; Pres Jr Cls; Pres Sr Cls; Var Golf; Var Lcrss; VP NHS; Acdmc Ltr; Outstndng Bio Stu; Bst Bassist Schl; Aerntcl Engr.

ROBINSON, TIA; Valley Central HS; Middletown, NY; (Y); 29/315; Spanish Clb; Band; Capt Color Guard; Concert Band; Mrchg Band; Yrbk Stf; Stu Cncl; Stat Bsktbl; Capt Bowling; Var L Socr; Comp Sci.

ROBISHAW, JENIFER J; Arlington HS; Pleasant Vly, NY; (Y); Trs VICA; Var JV Cheerleading; Chld Psychlgst.

ROBISON, DEAN E; Norwich SR HS; Norwich, NY; (Y); 7/200; Am Leg Boys St; School Musical; Rep Frsh Cls; Rep Soph Cls; Rep Jr Cls; Rep Sr Cls; VP Pres Stu Cncl; Var Bsbl; Var L Diving; High Hon Roll; Finlst Empire ST Gams Diving 85-86; Annapolis; Bus Admin.

ROBLEDO, PILAR; HS For The Hmnties; New York, NY; (Y); Political Wkr; Mgr(s).

ROBLES, ANNA; Norman Thomas HS; New York, NY; (S); Pres DECA; Office Aide; Band; Church Choir; Yth Ldrshp Devlpmnt Proj 86; Berkeley Schl; Bus Adm Mngmnt.

ROBLES, ANTHONY; All Hallows HS; Bronx, NY; (Y); JV Bsbl; Im Bsktbl; Hon Roll.

ROBLES, NAIDA; Seward Park HS; New York, NY; (Y); Office Aide; Teachers Aide; Band; Concert Band; Yrbk Stf; Prfct Atten Awd; Acctng.

ROBLES, RUDOLPH GILBERT; Mc Quaid Jesuit HS; Pittsford, NY; (Y); Boy Scts; Camera Clb; Computer Clb; Drama Clb; Ski Clb; School Play; Stage Crew; Nwsp Rptr; Lit Mag; Hon Roll; Mc Quaid Mck Trial 85-86; Ld Schl Ply 85; Engl.

ROBLYER, WENDY; Odessa-Montour Central School; Montour Falls, NY; (Y); 1/86; Trs SADD; Trs Band; Trs Frsh Cls; Trs Soph Cls; Rep Stu Cncl; L Var Bsktbl; L Var Trk; Capt L Vllybl; Trs NHS; Val; Chancellors Prz U Of MD 86; Watkins Glen Mentour Flls Rtry Schlrshp 86; U Of MD; Physcl Thrpy.

ROBOLOTTO, KEELY; Bishop Maginn HS; Albany, NY; (S); Math Clb; JV Bsktbl; Var Cheerleading; Var Pom Pon; JV Var Sftbl; High Hon Roll; NHS; Prfct Atten Awd; Accntng.

ROCA, FRANCISCO; South Shore HS; Brooklyn, NY; (Y); 99/696; Math Tm; Nwsp Stf; Strrtt Cty Hspnc Allnc Soc Schlrshp 86; Awd Merit In Bkpng 86; Fordham U; Accntng.

ROCA, GUS; Plainedge HS; N Massapequa, NY; (Y); Varsity Clb; Var Socr.

ROCCA, MICHELE; Port Richmond HS; Staten Island, NY; (Y); Computer Clb; Radio Clb; Teachers Aide; Band; Trk; Cit Awd; Merit Rl 84-85; St Johns-Staten Isl; Comp Prgmg.

ROCCANOVA, ANN; Tottenville HS; Staten Isld, NY; (Y); Church Yth Grp; Teachers Aide; SUNY; Engrng.

ROCCO, GARY R; Flushing HS; College Point, NY; (Y); 59/392; Math Tm; Nwsp Rptr; Nwsp Stf; Hon Roll; NY ST Regents Coll Schlrshp 86; Queens Coll; Engr.

ROCCOMBLI, TERESA; Flushing HS; Flushing, NY; (Y); Library Aide; Office Aide; Teachers Aide; School Play; Bsktbl; Gym; Sftbl; Swmmng; Vllybl; Most Imprvd Plyr Awd Bsktbl 86; Laguardia CC; Polc Offcr.

ROCHA, CANDIDO G; Hunter College HS; Brooklyn, NY; (Y); Rep Sr Cls; Var Trk; Mu Alp Tht; Ntl Merit Ltr; 4th & 6th Frnch Cntst Ntl 82 & 84; NYU; Comp Engr.

ROCHE, BRIDGET; Thomas J Corcoran HS; Syracuse, NY; (Y); Hosp Aide; Ski Clb; Socr; Trk; Sclgy.

ROCHE, EUGENE J; St Francis Prep; Queens Village, NY; (S); 218/744; Church Yth Grp; JV Bsktbl; Im Socr; Im Socr; Hon Roll; Stu Athl Awd 85; Math.

ROCHE, JASON J; Union Springs Central Schl; Auburn, NY; (Y); 20/100; Drama Clb; Sec German Clb; School Play; Var Bsbl; Var Socr; High Hon Roll; Hon Roll; NY ST Regents Schlrshp 86; Cayuga Cnty CC; Lbrl Arts.

ROCHE, MATTHEW L; Union Springs Central HS; Auburn, NY; (Y); NY ST Regents Schlrshp 86; Cayuga CC; Data Proc.

ROCHE, MICHAEL; Regis HS; New York, NY; (Y); SADD; Var L Bsktbl; Im Bowling; Im Socr; Im Tennis; Rand Mc Nally Achvt Schlrshp 86; Boston College; Bus.

ROCHE, ROSA; William Howard Taft HS; Bronx, NY; (Y); Church Yth Grp; Girl Scts; Office Aide; Church Choir.

ROCK, KAREN; Ticonderoga HS; Putnam Station, NY; (Y); 18/96; Church Yth Grp; Drama Clb; SADD; Acpl Chr; Pres Chorus; Church Choir; School Musical; Swing Chorus; Yrbk Stf; NHS; Art Potter Memrl Schlrshp Music 86; Uptown Dancrs Awd Excllnc Vocl Music 86; Wrld Of Bible Inst; Socl Wrk.

ROCKHILL, KEITH J; Brusthon-Moira Central HS; Moira, NY; (Y); French Clb; Yrbk Sprt Ed; Yrbk Stf; Stage Crew; NHS; Comptr Sci St Lawrence U 84-85; NYS Regnts Schlrshp 86; Le Moyne Coll; Comp Sci.

ROCKHILL, SHERRI; Whitesboro SR HS; Whitesboro, NY; (Y); Hosp Aide; Band; Concert Band; Mrchg Band; Pep Band; Mohawk Valley CC; Humn Serv.

ROCKHILL, STEPHEN; Ticonderoga Central HS; Ticonderoga, NY; (Y); Rep Frsh Cls; Rep Soph Cls; Rep Jr Cls; L Bsktbl; L Socr; L Trk; Hon Roll; JR Prom Ct 86; Elec Engrng.

ROCKOW, BOBBI L; Wheatland Chili Central Schl; Scottsville, NY; (Y); 5/76; SADD; School Musical; Yrbk Bus Mgr; Yrbk Stf; Rep Trs Stu Cncl; Hon Roll; Lion Awd; NHS; Prfct Atten Awd; Cazenovia; Equine Stud.

ROCKWELL, LISA; Dolgeville Central Schl; Stratford, NY; (Y); Drama Clb; GAA; SADD; Varsity Clb; Chorus; School Play; Stage Crew; Rep Frsh Cls; Sec Soph Cls; JV Var Cheerleading; Laura F Helterline Mem Awd, Home Econ Awd; Herkimer CC; Nrsry Educ.

ROCKWELL, LISA; Whitesboro SR HS; Marcy, NY; (Y); Natl Beta Clb; Sec Science Clb; Chorus; Stu Cncl; JV Trk; Hon Roll; Rcrdng Scrtry Alfa Beta Gama 86; Socl Wrkr.

ROCKWELL, ROBERT GREGORY; Salamanca HS; Killbuck, NY; (Y); 27/138; Debate Tm; French Clb; Ski Clb; Im Bsbl; Im Bsktbl; Im Ftbl; Wt Lftg; High Hon Roll; Hon Roll; Bus Scholar 86 & 87; Flagler Coll; Acctng.

ROCQUE, MARSHALL G; Whitehall Central HS; Whitehall, NY; (Y); 11/80; Am Leg Boys St; Church Yth Grp; French Clb; SADD; Varsity Clb; Y-Teens; Pres Frsh Cls; Pres Soph Cls; Pres Jr Cls; Bsktbl; Lbrl Arts.

RODAK, NICK; Attica SR HS; Warsaw, NY; (S); 9/160; AFS; Am Leg Boys St; JA; Math Tm; Band; Jazz Band; Crs Cntry; Trk; NHS; Cornell; Vet Med.

RODAS, CONNIE; Kendall JR SR HS; Kendall, NY; (Y); 21/75; Spanish Clb; Band; Concert Band; Jazz Band; Mrchg Band; Socr; Sftbl; High Hon Roll; Hon Roll; NHS.

RODDA, CARL; New Lebanon Central HS; Hancock, MA; (Y); Yrbk Ed-Chief; Cmnty Wkr; Drama Clb; Math Tm; Spanish Clb; School Play; Variety Show; Yrbk Rptr; Yrbk Stf; Rep Stu Cncl; Grad Usher; Law.

RODDEN, CHRISTINE; St Vincent Ferrer HS; New York, NY; (Y); Hosp Aide; Q&S; Chorus; Madrigals; School Musical; Variety Show; Nwsp Rptr; Yrbk Stf; Church Yth Grp; Thesps; Manhattan Coll Schrlshp; Regnts Nrsng Schlrshp; Manhattan Coll; Psychlgy.

RODE, DAVID W; Half Hollow Hills East HS; Dix Hills, NY; (S); DECA; School Play; Var Crs Cntry; JV Socr; Var Trk; MVP Trck 86; Conf Champ 400 Mtr 86; Hnbl Mntn ST Comp DECA; SUNY Farmingdale; Bus.

RODEN, ALAN J; Scarsdale HS; Armonk, NY; (Y); Computer Clb; SADD; Chorus; Stage Crew; Nwsp Rptr; Nwsp Stf; Rep Soph Cls; Im Bsktbl; Im Tennis; Im Wt Lftg; Lafayette Coll; Pre-Med.

RODENAS, ALMA; Springfield Gardens HS; Queens Village, NY; (S); 2/473; JA; Sftbl; Trk; Vllybl; Hon Roll; Jr NHS; NHS; Sal; Adelphi; Pre-Med.

RODERICK, DENISE; North Salem HS; N Salem, NY; (Y); 5/94; Variety Show; Var L Bsktbl; Var Mgr(s); Var Score Keeper; JV Var Socr; Var L Sftbl; High Hon Roll; NHS; Natnl Hnr Scty Schlrshp 86; All Leg Hnrbl Mentn Softbl 86; All Str Softbl 83; Villanova U; Sci.

RODGERS, ANDREW T; F D Roosevelt HS; Hyde Park, NY; (Y); 32/336; Cmnty Wkr; Concert Band; JV Var Bsktbl; Var Tennis; Ntl Merit Ltr; NYS Regents Schlrshp 86; VA Tech; Engrng.

RODIER, STEVEN; Ward Melville HS; Stony Brook, NY; (Y); Aud/Vis; Library Aide; Stu Cncl; JV Bsktbl; Hon Roll; Jr NHS; Library Svc Outstndng Svc 84; Sport Awd Ftbl,Bsbl,Bsktbl,Vlybl 84; 1st Lt Vol Fire Dept 84-85.

RODMAN, THOMAS; Hauppauge HS; Hauppauge, NY; (Y); DECA; FBLA; SADD; Varsity Clb; Rep Sr Cls; Var JV Socr; Var Capt Trk; Hon Roll; Ski Clb; Nwsp Phtg; All Leag, Conf, Cnty Trk 85-86; Cnty Wnr DECA Comp 86; Colgate; Bus Admin.

RODRIGO, RACHAEL; Saugerties HS; Glasco, NY; (Y); 24/250; French Clb; Math Tm; Varsity Clb; Mrchg Band; Yrbk Phtg; High Hon Roll; NHS; Art Awds Coach Hs Plyrs, Art Clb & Arts Cncl 86; Art Schlrshp Wdstck Schl Of Art 85&86; Art.

RODRIGUE, NANCY; Acad Of Mt St Ursula; Bronxville, NY; (Y); 7/147; Drama Clb; VP GAA; School Musical; School Play; Mgr Stage Crew; Rep Frsh Cls; Pres Jr Cls; Sec Stu Cncl; Var Capt Bsktbl; Intl Reltns.

RODRIGUEZ, AIDA; Cardinal Spellman HS; New York, NY; (Y); Spanish Clb; 1st/2nd Hnrs; Baruch Coll; Bus.

RODRIGUEZ, ARLENE; St Catherine Acad; Bronx, NY; (Y); School Musical; School Play; Swmmng; Music Awd 1986; Drama,Actress.

RODRIGUEZ, BRENDA; John Dewey HS; Brooklyn, NY; (Y); Church Yth Grp; Library Aide; Office Aide; Spanish Clb; Chorus; Tennis; Wt Lftg; High Hon Roll; Hon Roll; Prfct Atten Awd; Arch.

RODRIGUEZ, CARLOS; Canarsie HS; New York, NY; (Y); Drmtlgst.

RODRIGUEZ, CLAUDIA E; Hillcrest HS; Flushing, NY; (Y); 206/801; Hosp Aide; Stage Crew; NYS Regnts Schlrshp 86; Polytech U; Aero Engr.

RODRIGUEZ, DENISE MARIE; St Catharine Acad; Bronx, NY; (Y); 6/198; Dance Clb; Teachers Aide; Yrbk Bus Mgr; Yrbk Ed-Chief; Yrbk Rptr; Yrbk Stf; Hon Roll; Jr NHS; NHS; Prfct Atten Awd; Pres Scholar Iona Coll 86; Scholar Coll New Rochelle 86; Outstndg Acad Achvt 86; Bus Ed Awd 86; St Johns U; Paralgl Stud.

RODRIGUEZ, DENNIS; Bishop Grimes HS; Clay, NY; (Y); Cmnty Wkr; Var Bsbl; Var Ftbl.

RODRIGUEZ, ELIZABETH; Queens Vocational HS; Astoria, NY; (Y); 53/335; Drama Clb; Office Aide; Cheerleading; Hon Roll; Scholar Awd 84; Bus Adm.

RODRIGUEZ, ERICA; Eastchester HS; Scarsdale, NY; (Y); Church Yth Grp; Key Clb; Latin Clb; SADD; Chorus; Yrbk Phtg; Rep Sr Cls; Cheerleading; Sftbl; Vllybl; Ms Westchester Cnty Teen Fin 85; Yth Fit Achvt Awd 86; SUNY Cortland.

RODRIGUEZ, ERROL; Cardinal Hayes HS; New York, NY; (Y); 53/256; Boy Scts; 4-H; Hosp Aide; Pre-Med.

RODRIGUEZ, EVA; Bishop Ford C C HS; Brooklyn, NY; (Y); Chorus; Dentstry.

RODRIGUEZ, IRENE; Mount Vernon HS; Mount Vernon, NY; (Y); 20/550; Keywanettes; Office Aide; Spanish Clb; Capt Drill Tm; Ed Yrbk Stf; Lit Mag; Capt Pom Pon; High Hon Roll; NHS; U Of S FL; Comp Sci.

RODRIGUEZ, IRIS; Park West HS; New York, NY; (Y); 352/505; Dance Clb; Ski Clb; Bowling; Cheerleading; Gym; Sftbl; Swmmng; Tennis; Wrstlng; JETS Awd; Svc Awd,Schlrhp,Atten Awd 81; Vllybl Mdl,Chrldng Trphy 80; APT Awd,Math Hnrs,Splling Hnrs 80; Law.

RODRIGUEZ, ISMAEL; Aviation HS; New York, NY; (Y); 62/415; Church Yth Grp; Cmnty Wkr; Red Cross Aide; Band; Concert Band; Mrchg Band; Nwsp Rptr; Nwsp Sprt Ed; Nwsp Stf; Cit Awd; Cert Hghst Grd Atmtv Cls, Englsh Cls; Cert Achvt Typwrtng; Academy Of Aeronautics; Arcrft.

RODRIGUEZ, ISRAEL; Park West HS; Brooklyn, NY; (Y); 19/270; Aud/Vis; Band; Off Frsh Cls; Swmmng; High Hon Roll; Hon Roll; Pratt Inst; Elec Engrng.

RODRIGUEZ, JAMES; High School Of Art & Design; Bronx, NY; (Y); Advrtsng.

RODRIGUEZ, LILLIAN; Union Springs Acad; Utica, NY; (Y); 5/27; Church Yth Grp; Ski Clb; Band; Yrbk Stf; Hon Roll; NHS; Trs Soph Cls; VP Jr Cls; Stat Bsktbl; US Airforce Acad; Piloting.

RODRIGUEZ, MARILYN; Murry Bergtraum HS; Woodside, NY; (Y); French Clb; Intnl Clb; Latin Clb; Pep Clb; Band; Sr Cls; Cheerleading; NHS; VP Frsh Cls; Trk; Awd Excel Phys Educ 84; Hall Of Fame Awd 84; Johnson & Wales; Mgmt.

RODRIGUEZ, MARITZA; Cathedral HS; Ny, NY; (Y); 36/272; FNA; Band; Chorus; Band Awd 84-86; Atten Awd 86; Marymount Manhattan Coll; Ed.

RODRIGUEZ, MARY; James Madison HS; Brooklyn, NY; (Y); Dance Clb; Drama Clb; French Clb; FBLA; Intnl Clb; PAVAS; Radio Clb; Chorus; School Musical; Lit Mag.

RODRIGUEZ, MAYLEN; Newtown HS; Elmhurst, NY; (Y); 37/781; Office Aide; Teachers Aide; Orch; Yrbk Stf; Sr Cls; Hon Roll; Jr NHS; NHS; Prfct Atten Awd; Cert Awd Music 84; Cert Awd Svc 86.

RODRIGUEZ, MICHELLE; Hicksville SR HS; Hicksville, NY; (Y); Cmnty Wkr; Political Wkr; Varsity Clb; Band; Church Choir; Concert Band; Mrchg Band; Orch; Pep Band; Symp Band; Soc Studies Amer Hist Achvt Awd 86; Soc Studies Cnsmr Studies Achvt Awd 86; Sec Of Ldrs Clb 84; Bus Mgmt.

RODRIGUEZ, NANCY; Queen Of The Rosary Acad; Roosevelt, NY; (Y); 23/50; Girl Scts; SADD; Stage Crew; Variety Show; Yrbk Stf; Hon Roll; Nassau Comm Coll; Bus Admin.

RODRIGUEZ, NANETTE; St John The Baptist HS; Central Islip, NY; (Y); Church Yth Grp; Chorus; Color Guard; Nrsng.

RODRIGUEZ, NELLY I; John Jay HS; Brooklyn, NY; (Y); Science Clb; Ski Clb; Church Choir; School Play; High Hon Roll; Hon Roll; Prfct Atten Awd; Spanish NHS; Intrmdrt Albgra Schlrshp Cert 86; Ntl Spnsh Exmntns Cert Prtcptn 86; Kybrdng Cert Achvt 85; Law.

RODRIGUEZ, NORA; Grover Cleveland HS; Buffalo, NY; (Y); 4/153; Church Yth Grp; Rep Jr Cls; Rep Sr Cls; Rep Stu Cncl; Hon Roll; Jr NHS; NHS; Rgnts Schlrshp 86; FIC Schlrshp 86; Fordham U; Bus Admin.

RODRIGUEZ, NORMA; William Howard Taft HS; Bronx, NY; (Y); JA; Office Aide; Teachers Aide; Cit Awd; Hon Roll; Jr NHS; NHS; Natl Aritsa Soc 86-87; Arista Sec 86-87; Spn Awds Excllnce 84-86; Travel/Trsm.

RODRIGUEZ, OSCAR; White Plains HS; Beacon, NY; (Y); Chess Clb; Socr; Tennis; High Hon Roll; Hon Roll; Jr NHS; NHS; Centro Hispano Fo Wht Plns Awd 86; Syracuse U; Arch.

RODRIGUEZ, PHILLIP; All Hallows HS; Bronx, NY; (Y); OK U; Bus Adm.

RODRIGUEZ, RANDY; All Hallows Inst; Bronx, NY; (Y); Drama Clb; Off Jr Cls; Var Wt Lftg; Hon Roll; John Jay; Acctng.

RODRIGUEZ, ROBERT; Woodlands HS; Elmsford, NY; (Y); Key Clb; Band; Nwsp Phtg; Yrbk Phtg; Rep Frsh Cls; Rep Soph Cls; JV Bsbl; JV Var Crs Cntry; JV Var Trk; NHS; Bus Adm.

RODRIGUEZ, RUTH; Yonkers HS; Yonkers, NY; (Y); Art Clb; FCA; FBLA; JA; Capt Sftbl; Bus Awd 86; Cert Conduct 84; Cert Punctuality 85; Exec Sec.

RODRIGUEZ, SANDRA; Eastern District HS; Brooklyn, NY; (Y); Dance Clb; Chorus; Capt Vllybl; Hon Roll; BASIS Pblctns Awd/Editor 86; Paralegal.

RODRIGUEZ, TERRY A; Bronx HS Of Science; Bronx, NY; (Y); Camera Clb; Latin Clb; SADD; Chorus; Swmmng; Regents Scholar 86; Schl Vis Art; Fshn Photo.

RODRIGUEZ, VILMA; St Raymond Acad HS; Bronx, NY; (Y); 63/85; Spanish Clb; Band; Mrchg Band; Yrbk Stf; L Cheerleading; L Pom Pon; Acctg.

RODRIQUEZ, WILLIAM; Uniondale HS; Hempstead, NY; (Y); Cmnty Wkr; Band; Concert Band; Jazz Band; Mrchg Band; Orch; VP Stu Cncl; Var Bsbl; Var JV Wrstlng; High Hon Roll; Hnr Mntn Sci Fair; Acctng.

ROE, CHANTAL; Jamesville-Dewitt HS; Dewitt, NY; (Y); Exploring; Band; High Hon Roll; Hon Roll; Law.

ROE, JULIE; Rome Free Acad; Rome, NY; (Y); Church Yth Grp; Cmnty Wkr; Hosp Aide; Library Aide; Y-Teens; Hon Roll; Wagner Coll; Psychlgy.

ROEBACK, SHIRELL; James Madison HS; Brooklyn, NY; (Y); 103/750; Dance Clb; Girl Scts; JA; Pep Clb; Political Wkr; Varsity Clb; Church Choir; Drill Tm; School Play; Off Stu Cncl; Stony Brook; Real Est Lwyr.

ROEDEL, CHRIS; Smithtown West HS; Smithtown, NY; (Y); Computer Clb; Ski Clb; Golf; Wt Lftg; Wrstlng; Comp Sci.

ROEDER, GERARD; Washingtonville SR HS; Campbell Hall, NY; (Y); 4-H; JV Bsbl; Var Crs Cntry; Trk; NHS; Schlr Ath; Indr & Outdr ST Champ 3200m Relay 86; Natl Champ Indr 3200m Relay 86; Syracuse U; Comm.

ROELOFS, KEVIN; Geneva HS; Geneva, NY; (S); 7/175; Trs Latin Clb; Ski Clb; Varsity Clb; Band; VP Frsh Cls; VP Soph Cls; VP Jr Cls; Var L Ftbl; Capt Ice Hcky; Capt Lcrss.

ROEMER, KIMBERLY A; Mayville Central Schl; Dewittville, NY; (Y); 4/36; Ski Clb; Nwsp Stf; Pres Sr Cls; Rep Stu Cncl; Capt L Bsktbl; Stat Score Keeper; Var L Vllybl; High Hon Roll; Hon Roll; VP NHS; Pres Schlrshp Amer U 86; U Schrshp Amer U 86; NY ST Rgnts Schlrshp 86; The Amer U; Cmnctns.

ROEMER, SUSAN; St Edmund HS; Brooklyn, NY; (Y); Library Aide; Model UN; Yrbk Stf; Pres Frsh Cls; Sec Jr Cls; Brnrd M Brch Coll; Comp Sci.

ROEMMELT, MARNEY; West Genesee HS; Syracuse, NY; (Y); French Clb; JA; Orch; School Play; Off Jr Cls; Rep Sr Cls; High Hon Roll; Jr NHS; NHS; Yth Orch 85-87; Eastern Music Camp 83-84; Psychlgy.

ROENER, ROBERT; Monsignor Farrell HS; Staten Island, NY; (Y); French Clb; Lit Mag; Im Bowling; Im Ftbl; Hon Roll; 1st Pl Natl French Cont Level 2 85; 3rd Pl Natl French Cont Level 3 86; 1st Hnrs Cert Iona Lang Frn 85; Law.

ROENTHAL, MICHAEL L; Ward Melville HS; S Setauket, NY; (Y); 4/711; Pres Debate Tm; Nwsp Phtg; Nwsp Rptr; Yrbk Phtg; Stu Cncl; High Hon Roll; NHS; Ntl Merit Schol; Simons Resrch Fellowship 85; Cornell U Schl Of ILR; Ind Rel.

ROESSLER, BARBARA; Bolton Central HS; Bolton Landing, NY; (Y); 4/20; Computer Clb; French Clb; Yrbk Ed-Chief; Pres Frsh Cls; Bsktbl; Socr; Sftbl; Pres NHS; JV Bsktbl Mst Imprvd Plyr 83-84 & Mst Valbl 84-85; Siena Coll; Accntg.

ROETTGERS, AUDREY H; Nanuet SR HS; Pearl River, NY; (Y); 5/164; Cmnty Wkr; Debate Tm; Exploring; Hosp Aide; Math Tm; Model UN; Quiz Bowl; SADD; Orch; School Musical; Bryn Mawr Coll; Pre Med.

ROETZER, SHANNON; Alden SR HS; Alden, NY; (Y); French Clb; FTA; Girl Scts; SADD; Teachers Aide; Yrbk Stf; Rep Frsh Cls; Rep Soph Cls; JV Bsktbl; Im Socr; Law.

ROGACKI, LAURA; Connetquot HS; Ronkonkoma, NY; (Y); 20/743; Church Yth Grp; Sec SADD; Orch; Lit Mag; Fld Hcky; Tennis; Trk; Vllybl; Jr NHS; NHS; NYSSMA Awds 84-86; Outstndng Achvt Awd Keybrdng/ Cmmnctns 85; Spec Ed.

ROGALA, ERIC; Hilton Cetral HS; Hilton, NY; (Y); 1/300; Computer Clb; Exploring; Math Clb; Model UN; Tennis; High Hon Roll; NHS; Val; Joseph C Wilson Scholar; Honorary Phi Beta Kappa; U Rochester Paideia Awd; U Rochester; Laser Engrng.

ROGALSKI, JOANNA; Mt St Mary Acad; Buffalo, NY; (Y); Computer Clb; French Clb; Pep Clb; Chorus; Nwsp Ed-Chief; Yrbk Phtg; Im Badmtn; High Hon Roll; Ntl Merit Ltr.

ROGAN, NOREEN; Marlboro Central HS; Marlboro, NY; (Y); Dutchess Co CC; Bus Admin.

ROGENTHIEN, STEPHEN B; Clarence Central SR HS; Clarence, NY; (Y); 7/268; Drama Clb; JCL; Latin Clb; Varsity Clb; Nwsp Stf; Var L Socr; Hon Roll; NHS; St Schlr; NY ST Rgnts Schlrshp 86; Buffalo Nws Carrier Of Mnth 83; Nrth Amer Scr Cmps Shtout Cmpn 82; SUNY Buffalo; Biochmcl Phrmclg.

ROGERS, CAROL; Springville-Griffith Inst; Glenwood, NY; (Y); VP AFS; Cmnty Wkr; 4-H; Spanish Clb; Color Guard; JV Var Bsktbl; Gregg Typing Awd 86; Crmnl Just.

ROGERS, CHRISTINE E; Sayville HS; Sayville, NY; (Y); 13/334; Church Yth Grp; 4-H; Key Clb; Concert Band; School Musical; Nwsp Stf; Bausch & Lomb Sci Awd; High Hon Roll; NHS; Ntl Merit Ltr; Colgate U; Chem.

ROGERS, CLAUDETTE H; Mexico Academy Central Schl; Mexico, NY; (Y); Church Yth Grp; French Clb; Band; Chorus; Church Choir; Concert Band; Mrchg Band; JV Vllybl; Dnfth Awd; 4-H Awd.

ROGERS, COLLEEN; East Islip HS; E Islip, NY; (S); 21/425; Am Leg Aux Girls St; SADD; Ed Lit Mag; Off Stu Cncl; Im Vllybl; NHS; Ntl Merit Ltr; Art Clb; Math Tm; Stage Crew; Long Islnd Socl Stds Cncl Achmnt Awd 84; Long Islnd Bnk Amer Hstry Awd 85; Outstdng Englsh Stu 83; Doc.

ROGERS, CRAIG BRIAN; Perth Central HS; Amsterdam, NY; (Y); Rep Spanish Clb; Band; School Play; Nwsp Ed-Chief; Rep Stu Cncl; Var Bowling; NHS; Answrs Pls Drl Tm 83-84; Canton Ag & Tech; Accntng.

ROGERS, CRYSTAL; Niagara Catholic HS; Niagara Fls, NY; (Y); 4/85; French Clb; JA; Pres Key Clb; Hon Roll; NHS; Schl Scholar 84; Chrprsn Hmcmng Comm 85.

ROGERS, DARCY; Keveny Memorial Acad; Waterviet, NY; (Y); 24/40; French Clb; GAA; Band; Badmtn; Bsbl; Capt Bsktbl; Tennis; Trk; Twrlr; Capt Vllybl; Gardon Walk Schlrshp 86; Patroon Conf 1st Bsktbl 85-86; SUNY; Bus Adm.

ROGERS, DONNA; Dundee Central HS; Himrod, NY; (Y); AFS; Band; Chorus; Concert Band; Mrchg Band; School Musical; Symp Band; Yrbk Stf; Trk; High Hon Roll; Bus Mgmt.

ROGERS, JENNIFER; Kamburg HS; Hamburg, NY; (Y); Hon Roll; SUNY Purchase; Engl.

ROGERS, KAREN; Salem Central Schl; Salem, NY; (Y); 2/62; Church Yth Grp; VP Pep Clb; Pres Band; Jazz Band; Yrbk Stf; Ed Lit Mag; JV Var Fld Hcky; NHS; Sal; French Clb; WA Cnty Repblcn Womns Clb Awd 86; SR Band MV Membr 86; Gordon Coll; Ed.

ROGERS, KELLY; Bradford Central Schl; Bradford, NY; (S); 2/29; Hst FBLA; Yrbk Ed-Chief; Pres Sr Cls; Capt Cheerleading; Capt Socr; Capt Sftbl; High Hon Roll; Pres NHS; Prfct Atten Awd; Ntl Phys Ed Awd 85.

ROGERS, LAURA L; Mt Markham SR HS; W Winfield, NY; (Y); 60/115; Drama Clb; FHA; Library Aide; Speech Tm; Chorus; School Play; Nwsp Rptr; Yrbk Stf; Hon Roll; Silvr Dllr Perfct Effrt Cls 85; Utica Sch Of Comm; Legl Sec.

ROGERS, LAUREN; Connetquot HS; Ronkonkoma, NY; (Y); 7/712; Concert Band; Jazz Band; Mrchg Band; School Musical; Stage Crew; Ed Lit Mag; JV Socr; High Hon Roll; Jr NHS; NHS.

ROGERS, MARIA; Westhampton Beach HS; Manorville, NY; (Y); 43/220; Church Yth Grp; Drama Clb; Band; Concert Band; Mrchg Band; School Play; Lit Mag; VP Stu Cncl; Hon Roll; Jr NHS; Outstndng Achvt Instrmntl Music 84; NYSSSA Schl Thtre Stu 84; Jrnlsm.

ROGERS, MARY; G Ray Bodley HS; Fulton, NY; (Y); French Clb; Acpl Chr; Chorus; Hon Roll.

ROGERS, MICHAEL; Mynderse Acad; Seneca Falls, NY; (Y); 14/140; Am Leg Boys St; French Clb; Ski Clb; Yrbk Phtg; Yrbk Stf; JV Bsktbl; L Crs Cntry; L Trk; High Hon Roll; NHS; Mt Union; Sprts Med.

ROGERS, PAUL D; Vernon HS; Sherrill, NY; (Y); 72/199; Church Yth Grp; Cmnty Wkr; FCA; Letterman Clb; Varsity Clb; Y-Teens; Var L Ftbl; JV Var Trk; JV Var Wrstlng; Cit Awd; Dakota-Weslyan U; Bus Mngmnt.

ROGERS, SHELLEY; Valley Central HS; Walden, NY; (Y); Church Yth Grp; FBLA; Service Clb; Chorus; Hon Roll; Wmn Repblcn Clb Awd For Hstry 86; Law.

ROGERS, STEVE; Islip HS; Islip, NY; (Y); Mathletes; Red Cross Aide; Band; Concert Band; Jazz Band; Mrchg Band; Orch; School Musical; Crs Cntry; Socr; NYSCAME Music Fstvl 85-86.

ROGERS, SUE; Grand Island HS; Grand Island, NY; (Y); Chrmn Church Yth Grp; Drama Clb; Girl Scts; Chorus; Church Choir; Madrigals; School Musical; School Play; Stage Crew; Stu Cncl; Slvr Awd Grl Scts 84; Madrgl Of Yr 86; FL ST U; Spec Ed.

ROGERS, TODD; East Islip HS; East Islip, NY; (Y); JV Bsbl; JV Bsktbl; Var L Tennis; High Hon Roll; Hon Roll; Jr NHS; Spanish NHS; Bus.

ROGERS JR, WILLIAM; Cardinal Hayes HS; New York, NY; (Y); Boy Scts; Church Yth Grp; Cmnty Wkr; Library Aide; Trk; Engr.

ROGGE, ANTOINETTE; Norman Thomas HS; Bronx, NY; (Y); 68/597; JA; Chorus; Hon Roll; NHS; Ftr Scrtries Assoc 84-86; NY U; Physcl Thrpy.

ROGOWSKI, JULIE G; West Seneca West SR HS; S Cheektowaga, NY; (Y); 6/559; Spanish Clb; Nwsp Rptr; Yrbk Stf; Sec Jr Cls; Stu Cncl; JV Socr; High Hon Roll; JC Awd; NHS; Yth Svc-Outstndg Vlntr Svc Cmnty 83 & 84.

ROGOWSKI, RENEE; Catholic Central HS; Cohoes, NY; (Y); Math Clb; Ski Clb; Orch; School Play; Variety Show; JV Crs Cntry; JV Trk; Hon Roll; Dowling; Airln Pilot.

ROHADFOX, KIM MARIE; Nottingham HS; Syracuse, NY; (Y); 31/230; Pres Church Yth Grp; Pres Exploring; SADD; Church Choir; Nwsp Stf; Sec Frsh Cls; Rep Soph Cls; Trs Jr Cls; Var Capt Cheerleading; JV Vllybl; NC Cntrl; Pre-Med.

ROHAN, PATRICK T; E Meadow HS; E Meadow, NY; (S); 15/340; Science Clb; Jazz Band; Mrchg Band; Symp Band; Pres Soph Cls; Pres Jr Cls; Pres Sr Cls; Var JV Ftbl; Var JV Lcrss; Hon Roll.

ROHDE, BRET; Babylon HS; W Babylon, NY; (Y); Drama Clb; School Musical; French Clb; Math Clb; Chorus; School Play; Stage Crew; Nwsp Rptr; Yrbk Stf; Gold Mdl Wnnr Long Island Mth Fair 85; Cet Merit Babylon Schl Lit Cont; Dickenson; Bus.

ROHE, LINDA; Saint Johns Prep HS; Astoria, NY; (Y); 17/480; Computer Clb; Bsktbl; High Hon Roll; Hon Roll; Jr NHS; NHS; Prfct Atten Awd; Regents Schlrshp 86; Queens Coll; Comm.

ROHER, MICHAEL A; Madison Central HS; Bouckville, NY; (Y); Am Leg Boys St; FFA; High Hon Roll; Hon Roll; NHS; Prfct Atten Awd; Bronze Medal Outstndng Work In Math 86; Achvt Awd In Physics 86; Hinman Schlrshp $1000 86; Pres Acad 86; Suny Morrisville NY; Elect Eng.

ROJANASOMSITH, KAESARIN; Seward Park HS; New York, NY; (Y); AFS; Co-Capt Girl Scts; Ski Clb; Capt CAP; NHS; Prfct Atten Awd.

ROJAS, CLARA I; Academy Of St Joseph; Brentwood, NY; (Y); Art Clb; Aud/Vis; Drama Clb; Hosp Aide; Math Tm; Chorus; School Musical; Var Socr; High Hon Roll; NHS; Natl Art Honor Soc 85; Natl Hispanic Schlr Awd Semi-Fnlst 86; Pre-Med.

ROJAS, NORMA ALICIA; Mount Saint Joseph Acad; Amherst, NY; (S); Drama Clb; French Clb; Spanish Clb; School Play; Sftbl; Tennis; French Hon Soc; Hon Roll; NHS; Spanish NHS; Bus Adm.

ROLF, MIRIAM; Springville GI HS; Springville, NY; (Y); 3/192; French Clb; Spanish Clb; Chorus; Orch; Trs Sr Cls; Mgr Tennis; Vllybl; Hon Roll; NHS; Soc Of Myflwr Dscndnts Awd 86; U S Army Rsrv Ntl Schlr/Athlt Awd 86; Altn J Beasr Schlrshp 86; SUNY Coll Of Fredonia; Pre-Med.

ROLFE, LAURIE M; West Seneca West SR HS; Cheektowaga, NY; (Y); Aud/Vis; Q&S; Spanish Clb; Chorus; Yrbk Ed-Chief; Stu Cncl; Score Keeper; High Hon Roll; Prfct Atten Awd; Yrbk Bus Mgr; Cert Recgntn Vlntrs W Seneca Develpmnt Ctr; Peer Cnslng; Canisius Coll; Bus.

ROLINCE, MARY; Solvay HS; Syracuse, NY; (Y); Band; Concert Band; Off Frsh Cls; Off Soph Cls; Off Jr Cls; Off Sr Cls; Hon Roll; Onondaga CC; Dntl Hygn.

ROLITA, DAWN; Westlake HS; Hawthorne, NY; (Y); Church Yth Grp; Cmnty Wkr; French Clb; Quiz Bowl; Spanish Clb; Stage Crew; Yrbk Stf; High Hon Roll; Hon Roll; Spanish NHS; Acctng.

ROLLA, CHRISTINE; Carmel HS; Carmel, NY; (Y); Girl Scts; Leo Clb; Orch; Hon Roll; Simmins Bus Schl; Steno.

ROLLER, MICHELE; Garden City HS; Garden City, NY; (Y); 78/346; Hosp Aide; Office Aide; SADD; Sr Cls; JV Fld Hcky; Hon Roll; Jr NHS; Kiwanis Awd; Rep Frsh Cls; Rep Soph Cls; Rgnts Schlrshp 86; Pres Acad Ftns Awd 86; U Of MA Amherst; Fin.

ROLLINS, DENNIS; De Witt Clinton HS; Bronx, NY; (Y); Key Clb; Teachers Aide; Color Guard; Hon Roll; Prfct Atten Awd; Law.

ROLLO, HEATHER; Riverhead HS; Calverton, NY; (Y); 3/250; Spanish Clb; Chorus; Swing Chorus; Yrbk Stf; Im Fld Hcky; NHS; Rgnts Schlrshp 85-86; Ldrs Clb Pres 84-85; Cornell U; Pre-Vet.

ROLLS, BETH A; Buffalo Seminary; Buffalo, NY; (Y); AFS; Art Clb; Pep Clb; Science Clb; Rep Frsh Cls; Im Badmtn; Im Bowling; JV Fld Hcky; Var L Lcrss; Im Score Keeper; Var Sccr, Bea Massmary Lg All St 85-86; Var La Crosse Coaches Awd 86; Prfct Attndnce 85-86; Law.

ROLON, JACKIE; Taft HS; Bronx, NY; (Y); Dance Clb; Teachers Aide; Vllybl; Secy.

ROLOSON, EDWARD J; South Seneca HS; Interlaken, NY; (Y); 7/88; Am Leg Boys St; Church Yth Grp; French Clb; Varsity Clb; Coach Actv; Var Crs Cntry; Var Wrstlng; NHS; Cornell; Aerospce Engnrng.

ROLSTON, LEON; All Hallows Inst; Bronx, NY; (S); 3/38; Math Tm; Nwsp Rptr; Hon Roll; History Clb-Sec; Harvard Medical Schl; Pre-Med.

ROM, INGRID; Christ The King R H S; Ridgewood, NY; (Y); 1/450; Intnl Clb; Math Tm; VP SADD; Rep Frsh Cls; Rep Soph Cls; Rep Jr Cls; Pres Sr Cls; Pres Stu Cncl; Hon Roll; NHS; Queens Coll Acadmc Achvt Awd 84-86.

ROMAGNOLO, STEPHEN; Port Richmond HS; Staten Island, NY; (Y); 7/685; Art Clb; Camera Clb; Math Clb; Math Tm; Tennis; High Hon Roll; Hon Roll; Jr NHS; NHS; Psychtry.

ROMAIN, JULIE; Mount Mercy Acad; Buffalo, NY; (Y); 30/198; French Clb; Model UN; SADD; Variety Show; Rep Frsh Cls; Im Badmtn; Im Fld Hcky; Im Vllybl; Hon Roll; U Of NY; Pre-Law.

ROMAIN, PIERRE; Nyack HS; Nyack, NY; (Y); Chorus; Ftbl; Trk; Wt Lftg; Wrstlng; Hon Roll; Prfct Atten Awd; Outstndg Effort Hlth Awd 86; Comm Svc Awd 86; Honrbl Mention All Conf Wrstlng 86; Whestchester CC; Chiropractor.

ROMAINE, JOAN; Valley Central HS; Walden, NY; (Y); Service Clb; Varsity Clb; Color Guard; Lit Mag; Sec Jr Cls; Rep Stu Cncl; JV Sftbl; Var Capt Tennis; Sec NHS; Spanish NHS; Ida A Ruscitti Awd-Tnns 84; Coach Crisci Awd-Tnns 86; Syracuse U; Psych.

ROMAN, BRIAN; Whitesboro SR HS; Whitesboro, NY; (Y); 8/306; Model UN; Ski Clb; Varsity Clb; Band; Concert Band; Jazz Band; Mrchg Band; Orch; School Musical; JV Crs Cntry; Law.

ROMAN JR, HECTOR; Brewster HS; Brewster, NY; (Y); Ski Clb; Sec Varsity Clb; Trs Sr Cls; Var Capt Bsbl; Var Socr; Wrstlng; Prfct Atten Awd; All-Lg Hon Mntn Wrstlng; Ski Tm; Cmmnctns.

ROMAN, KIM; Dominican Commercial HS; Richmond Hill, NY; (Y); Chorus; Queensborough CC; Fbr Optics.

ROMAN, MARILYN; Newburgh Free Acad; Newburgh, NY; (Y); Pres Church Yth Grp; Church Choir; High Hon Roll; NHS; Prfct Atten Awd; Sundy Schl Tchr Yr 84.

ROMAN, MATILDE; Domincon Commercial HS; Brooklyn, NY; (Y); 110/270; Variety Show; Capt Cheerleading; Sftbl; Hon Roll; Law.

ROMAN, RAYMOND; William Howard Taft HS; Bronx, NY; (Y); Var Bsbl; Capt Bowling; Plc Offcr.

ROMAN, REGINA M; West Hempstead HS; West Hempstead, NY; (Y); 91/320; Drama Clb; Band; Chorus; Church Choir; Concert Band; Mrchg Band; School Musical; School Play; VP Soph Cls; Hon Roll; Ldng Role Actng Awds; Music Awd; CW Post; Music.

ROMAN, RUTH; Trinity Schl; New York, NY; (Y); Model UN; Pres Spanish Clb; Var Capt Bsktbl; Lcrss; Socr; Ntl Merit SF; Delta Sigma Theta Sor Schlrshp 84-86; Mst Outstndng Cntrbtn Sccr & Bsktbl 85-86; Pltcs.

ROMAN, STEVE; Kings Park HS; Kings Park, NY; (Y); 48/388; Art Clb; DECA; Math Clb; Science Clb; Spanish Clb; Varsity Clb; Lit Mag; Trs Jr Cls; Wrstlng; Hon Roll; 2nd Pl Leag Wrstlng Tourn 83 & 86; ST Champ DECA Travl & Toursm 85; Auburn U; Indstrl Dsgn.

ROMAN, VICTOR; Bishop Ford Central Catholic HS; Brooklyn, NY; (Y); Boy Scts; CAP; Color Guard; Drill Tm; JV Swmmng; Embry Riddle Aero U; Aeronatcs.

ROMANCHIK, JOS; Brewster HS; Brewster, NY; (Y); Church Yth Grp; Sec Sr Cls; Var Coach Actv; Var JV Ftbl; Var JV Lcrss; Wt Lftg; Hon Roll; La Crosse All-Lg Hon Mntn 86; Capt Vars Smmr Lg Lacrosse 86; Archtctr.

ROMANELLO, MELISSA; Nardin Acad; Orchard Pk, NY; (Y); Church Yth Grp; Office Aide; Swing Chorus; Lit Mag; Bsktbl; Sftbl; 1st Tm All Star Sftbl; Bsktbl Hnrbl Ment; Psychlgst.

ROMANI, WILLIAM A; Ithaca HS; Ithaca, NY; (Y); Off Am Leg Boys St; VP Stu Cncl; Capt Var Bsbl; JV Ftbl; Var Golf; Var Ice Hcky; NHS; Ntl Merit Ltr; Stu Rep-Cty Schl Brd 85-86; :VFW Vtrns Cmmtte-Yth Of Yr 85; U Of DE; Phys Thrpy.

ROMANO, DANIEL; Fort Hamilton HS; Brooklyn, NY; (Y); 37/553; Boy Scts; Church Yth Grp; NHS; NYC Acctng & Comp Awd 85; Dr Norman W Elliott Acctng Awd 86; Baruch Coll; Pblc Acct.

ROMANO, MARIA T; Marymount Schl; Bronx, NY; (Y); Cmnty Wkr; Intnl Clb; Model UN; Political Wkr; Nwsp Ed-Chief; Yrbk Phtg; Lit Mag; Hon Roll; NHS; Ntl Merit Ltr; Yale U; Lawyr.

ROMANO, PAMELA; Hampton Bays JR SR HS; Hampton Bays, NY; (Y); Am Leg Aux Girls St; Mathletes; Sec SADD; Varsity Clb; Jazz Band; School Musical; Rep Frsh Cls; VP Soph Cls; Rep Jr Cls; Sec Stu Cncl.

ROMANO, TERRI; Spackenkill HS; Poughkeepsie, NY; (Y); 14/168; Church Yth Grp; Cmnty Wkr; Drama Clb; Hosp Aide; Teachers Aide; Sec Band; School Musical; Yrbk Stf; Capt Vllybl; High Hon Roll; Providence Coll; Fin.

ROMANZO, DANIEL; Shenendohowa HS; Ballston Lake, NY; (Y); Boy Scts; Cmnty Wkr; SADD; Stu Cncl; Var Crs Cntry; Var Trk; NHS; Pres Computer Clb; Ski Clb; Rep Soph Cls; 1st Annl Upstate NY JR Sci & Hmnts Sympsm 86; Subrbn Schlstc Cncl Allstr Awd X-Cntry All-Str Tm 85; U S Air Force Acad; Pilot.

ROMEO, BARBARA; Msgr Scanlan HS; Bronx, NY; (Y); 18/257; Intnl Clb; Vllybl; NHS; Nora O Keeffe Memorial Schlrshp 86; Socl Studies Gold Mdl 86; St Johns U; Pharmcy.

ROMER, ELLEN R; Williamsville East HS; Williamsville, NY; (Y); FBLA; Yrbk Stf; Stu Cncl; Var Fld Hcky; L Trk; High Hon Roll; NHS; Rgnt Schlrshp 86; Pres B Nal B Rith Yth Grp 85; Invlvd Cmmnty & Ldrshp Pgms 83-86; U Of MI; Pltcl Sci.

ROMER, RANDALL J; Columbia HS; East Greenbush, NY; (Y); 25/400; Ski Clb; JV Bsbl; Capt JV Bsktbl; Var Ftbl; JV Trk; High Hon Roll; NHS; Rensselaer Polytech; Engrng.

ROMERO, DENISE; John Dewey HS; Brooklyn, NY; (Y); Brooklyn College; Elem Tchr.

ROMERO, GINGER; The Dalton Schl; Brooklyn, NY; (Y); Aud/Vis; Cmnty Wkr; Yrbk Phtg; Yrbk Stf; Rep Stu Cncl; Var Trk.

ROMERO, LISA; Park West HS; New York, NY; (Y); Dance Clb; Office Aide; Hon Roll; HS Awareness Prg Pilot Awd 86; Amer Hist, Ec & Engl Awds 86; Yth Fit Achvmnt Awd 85; Intl Bus.

ROMERO, MANUEL ALEX; Commack North HS; Commack, NY; (Y); Art Clb; French Clb; Nwsp Rptr; Nwsp Stf; Rep Jr Cls; JV Socr; French Hon Soc; Hon Roll; Ntl Art Hnr Soc 86; Pre-Med.

ROMERO, MARGARITA; Fashion Industries HS; Bronx, NY; (Y); Art Clb; Church Yth Grp; Cmnty Wkr; Computer Clb; FBLA; FNA; Hosp Aide; Red Cross Aide; SADD; Hon Roll; Scholar 84; Fash Illstrtn.

ROMERO, NANCY; New Dorp HS; Staten Island, NY; (Y); Latin Clb; Pres Frsh Cls; Gym; Italian Hnr Sco VP 83-87; Med.

ROMERO, VICTORIA; Oneonta SR HS; Oneonta, NY; (Y); 17/174; Church Yth Grp; French Clb; JA; Model UN; Spanish Clb; Chorus; Church Choir; Hon Roll; NHS; Natl Hspnc Awds Pgm Fnlst 85-86.

ROMITO, DENISE MARIE; Comsewogue HS; Pt Jefferson Sta, NY; (Y); Hosp Aide; Nwsp Phtg; Yrbk Stf; Var Crs Cntry; Hon Roll; NHS; Prfct Atten Awd; Awd Hgst Avg Engl,Studio Photo 85-86; March Dimes Walk A Thon Rep 83-86; Phrmcy.

ROMONOW, LAURIE; Guilderland Central HS; Schenectady, NY; (Y); Dance Clb; Off Jr Cls; Sec Pres Stu Cncl; High Hon Roll; NHS; Dartmouth Bk Clb Awd 86; Awd Exc Physlgy,Spnsh 86; Pre-Med.

ROMULUS, ROUDY; Nazareth Regional HS; Brooklyn, NY; (Y); SADD; Bsktbl; Mgr(s); Score Keeper; Hon Roll; NHS; Hofsta U; Finc.

ROMYN, C RACHEL; Corning-Painted Post East HS; Corning, NY; (Y); Ski Clb; Varsity Clb; Yrbk Ed-Chief; Ed Yrbk Stf; Rep Stu Cncl; JV Socr; Var Trk; High Hon Roll; Hon Roll; NHS; NYS Regents Schlrshp Awd 86; NC ST U; Bus.

RON, S ZVI; Yeshivah Of Flatbush HS; Brooklyn, NY; (Y); Nwsp Stf; Yrbk Stf; VP Soph Cls; VP Jr Cls; Mgr(s); Score Keeper; Timer; High Hon Roll; Hon Roll; NHS; Dentstry.

RONACHER, MICHAEL; Paul V Moore HS; Central Sq, NY; (Y); SADD; JV Bsktbl; Coach Actv; Var Socr; Var Capt Tennis; Im Vllybl; Hon Roll; Cobl Skill; Env Sci.

RONAN, REGINA; Northport HS; Northport, NY; (Y); Var Bsktbl; Var Socr; Var Trk; Var Vllybl; Sccr All Lg 85; Bsktbl All Lg, All Cnty & All Trnmnt Tm Sufflok Cnty Plyoffs 85-86.

RONCONE, PAUL; South Park HS; Buffalo, NY; (Y); Boy Scts; Im Bsbl; JV Ftbl; Var Socr; Var Trk; Hon Roll; NHS; Bar Assn Mock Trail Prtcpnt 85-86; Hgst Math Avg Entire Schl 83; Math Tutor 85-86; U Of Buffalo; Accntnt.

RONCSKA, ROBERT A; Dunkirk HS; Dunkirk, NY; (Y); Am Leg Boys St; Church Yth Grp; Key Clb; Letterman Clb; Pep Clb; Ski Clb; Varsity Clb; Yrbk Stf; Pres Stu Cncl; Ftbl; Al-Star Ftbl Obsrvr Plyr Wk 85; Capt Ftbl 86; Aerontcs.

RONDA, KAREN; St Barnabas HS; Bronx, NY; (Y); Chess Clb; Drama Clb; Spanish Clb; Chorus; Yrbk Phtg; Prfct Atten Awd; Spcl Serv Awd 84-85; Reg Nrs.

RONDON, CHERRIE ANN MARIE; Franklin D Roosevelt HS; Brooklyn, NY; (Y); Church Yth Grp; FBLA; Math Tm; Rep Jr Cls; Cit Awd; Hon Roll; Regents Schlrshp 86; Stu Of The Month 84; Natl Arista Socy 86; Long Island U; Comp Sci.

RONEY, LISA; Hancock Central HS; Lakewood, PA; (Y); Church Yth Grp; Library Aide; Office Aide; Spanish Clb; Chorus; School Play; Rep Stu Cncl; JV Var Bsktbl; Hon Roll; Sec NHS; Natl Cncl Yth Ldrshp Rep 86; Lgl Asst.

RONZONI, ANNE C; Manhasset HS; Manhasset, NY; (Y); 32/175; Spanish Clb; Chorus; Yrbk Stf; Rep Jr Cls; Rep Sr Cls; Capt Var Cheerleading; Capt Var Gym; Var L Socr; High Hon Roll; Hon Roll; Fairfield U; Bus.

ROODE, STEVE; Roy C Ketcham HS; Poughkeepsie, NY; (Y); Computer Clb; Math Tm; JV Trk; High Hon Roll; Hon Roll; Cmptr Sci.

ROONEY, JEANNE; Hamburg HS; Hamburg, NY; (Y); Spanish Clb; Var Bsktbl; Cheerleading; Hon Roll; NHS; Acctng.

ROONEY, JEFF; Mahopac HS; Mahopac, NY; (Y); 130/409; Science Clb; Ski Clb; Engrng.

ROONEY, LAUREN; New Paltz HS; New Paltz, NY; (Y); #35 In Class; Cmnty Wkr; Sec Jr Cls; Stu Cncl; Var Bsktbl; Var Fld Hcky; Im Swmmng; Var Trk; Hon Roll; NHS; MV Swimmer 85; Hmcmng Attndnt 84; Bus Admin.

ROONEY, MELISSA; Linton HS; Schenectady, NY; (Y); Dance Clb; French Clb; Hosp Aide; JA; Key Clb; Off Jr Cls; Im Mgr Bsktbl; Im Mgr Sftbl; U Of SC; Psychology.

ROONPRAPUNT, CHAN; Alfred G Berner HS; Massapequa, NY; (Y); 4/365; Chess Clb; Mathletes; Ed Nwsp Stf; JV Var Bowling; Bausch & Lomb Sci Awd; Hon Roll; NHS; U PA; Pre Med.

ROOSA, LEIGH; Marlboro Central HS; Newburgh, NY; (Y); 8/159; Am Leg Boys St; Sec Computer Clb; Yrbk Stf; High Hon Roll; Jr NHS; NHS; Acdmc All Amer 86; Dutches CC; Elec Engrng.

ROOT, JULIANNE M; Jordan-Elbridge Central HS; Jordan, NY; (Y); Church Yth Grp; Spanish Clb; Band; Chorus; Church Choir; Color Guard; Concert Band; Var Tennis.

ROOT, KIMBERLY; Brockport HS; Brockport, NY; (Y); Pres Sec 4-H; Sec Trs French Clb; Concert Band; Jazz Band; Mrchg Band; Symp Band; 4-H Awd; High Hon Roll; Hon Roll; NHS; Repr CO NYS Fair 83-84; Elem Educ.

ROOTENBERG, SHARYN; Midwood HS At Brooklyn Clg; Brooklyn, NY; (Y); 324/667; Temple Yth Grp; Chorus; Nwsp Ed-Chief; VP Frsh Cls; VP Soph Cls; VP Stu Cncl; NHS; Prfct Atten Awd; Cmnty Wkr; Daily News Principals Pride Awd 85.

ROPER, JOHN; Newburgh Free Acad; Newburgh, NY; (Y); 98/621; Church Yth Grp; High Hon Roll; Hon Roll; St Schlr; NY ST Rgnts Schlrshp; Susquehanna U; Languages.

RORECH, DOUGLAS; Babylon JR SR HS; Babylon, NY; (Y); Civic Clb; Math Clb; Varsity Clb; Band; Rep Sr Cls; Ftbl; Lcrss; Socr; Wrstlng; NHS; Mrktng.

ROSADO, BRENDA; Walton HS; Bronx, NY; (Y); Dance Clb; Office Aide; Teachers Aide; Nwsp Stf; Cheerleading; NHS; Cert Of Merit Math 84; Global Hist 85; Yankees Awd Outstndng Acadmc & Extra Curriclr Actvty 85; Baruch Coll; Accntng.

ROSADO, CONNIE; Adlai E Stevenson HS; Bronx, NY; (Y); Church Yth Grp; Cmnty Wkr; JA; Office Aide; Teachers Aide; Orch; Spanish NHS; B Nai Brith Awds 84; Med.

ROSADO, DAVID; Rice HS; New York, NY; (Y); Chess Clb; Hon Roll; Prfct Atten Awd; Gen Excllnc Awd JR Yr 85, SR Yr 86; Div Arts & Sci Schlrshp Poly Tech U 86; Poly Tech U; Physcst.

ROSADO, JOSUE J; Fiorello H La Guardia HS; New York, NY; (Y); 165/554; Art Clb; Church Yth Grp; Cmnty Wkr; PAVAS; Spanish Clb; Church Choir; Yrbk Stf; Sr Rep & Ldr Pstr Clb & Crtn Clb 85-86; Hnrs Art Hstry 85-86; Yrbk Cvr Dsgnr; Cal Coll Arts & Crfts; Film.

ROSADO, TABETHA; Herbert H Lehman HS; Bronx, NY; (Y); Yrbk Stf; Lit Mag; Frsh Cls; Soph Cls; Trs Jr Cls; Pres Sr Cls; Stu Cncl; Hon Roll; NHS; Prfct Atten Awd; Fshn Inst Tech; Instr Dsgn.

ROSADO, VICTOR; Midwood HS; Brooklyn, NY; (Y); Boy Scts; Teachers Aide; Var Ftbl; Engrng.

ROSALIA SR, ANTHONY; Sheepshead Bay HS; Brooklyn, NY; (Y); 9/439; VP Computer Clb; Math Clb; Science Clb; Teachers Aide; Ed Yrbk Phtg; Hon Roll; NHS; Acad All Amer 84-85; Brooklyn Coll; Med.

ROSARIO, ANGELICA; Seward Park HS; New York, NY; (Y); Camera Clb; Chess Clb; Debate Tm; Drama Clb; Library Aide; Service Clb; Teachers Aide; Chorus; School Play; Nwsp Ed-Chief; NYS Senate Achvt Awd & Meritrs Svc Cert; Martin Luther King Mdl; Cornell Coop Ext Awd; Acad Awds.

ROSARIO, BELINDA ANN; De Witt Clinton HS; Bronx, NY; (Y); Art Clb; Drama Clb; School Musical; School Play; Variety Show; Hon Roll; Cert Grad Of Lab Anml Care, Awd Guidance Cnslr & Awd Pssng Al Clss Soc Studies Dept 85-86; Zoology.

ROSARIO, ELIZABETH; Adlai E Stevenson HS; Bronx, NY; (Y); FBLA; GAA; JA; Teachers Aide; Stage Crew; Capt Vllybl; Hon Roll; Jr NHS; NHS; Ntl Merit Schol; All Amer Math Schlrshp 85-86; UNFO; Bus Mgt.

ROSARIO, ERIC; John Dewey HS; Brooklyn, NY; (Y); Latin Clb; Rep Office Aide; Quiz Bowl; Science Clb; Rptr Teachers Aide; Nwsp Rptr; Ed Nwsp Stf; Im Bowling; Im Ftbl; Im Golf; S A Welcome Awd Excel Lgl Stds, Gldn Rcrd Achvt Awd, Frnch Tchrs Assn Awd 86; Cornell U; Pol Sci.

ROSARIO, FRANCISCO; All Hallows HS; Bronx, NY; (Y); Computer Clb; Hon Roll; Iona Coll; Comp Prog.

ROSATI, GLORIA; Kenmore East HS; Kenmore, NY; (Y); Drama Clb; PAVAS; Chorus; Church Choir; School Musical; School Play; Stage Crew; Swing Chorus; Nwsp Stf; Hon Roll.

ROSATI, STEPHAINE; Shoreham Wading River HS; Shoreham, NY; (Y); SADD; Yrbk Stf; JV Bsktbl; Var Tennis; JV Var Vllybl; NHS; Nexus 85-86.

ROSBROOK, WAYNE; Indian River Central HS; Philadelphia, NY; (Y); Rep Stu Cncl; Var L Ftbl; Var L Tennis; Im Vllybl; Var L Wrstlng; NEDT Awd; Frntgr League Hnrb Mntn All Star Ftbl 84; Watertwon Dailey Temes All North All Star Ftbl 84; Jefferson CC.

ROSCELLO, WALTER; Dryden Central HS; Dryden, NY; (Y); 1/140; VP French Clb; Yrbk Stf; Ntl Merit Schol; Val; Boy Scts; Church Yth Grp; Ski Clb; SADD; Chorus; Rep Stu Cncl; Amer Chem Soc Chemcl Olympd; JETS Cmptn-Math; Regnts Schlrshp; Carnegie; Math.

ROSCINI, ROBYN; Fayetteville Manlius HS; Fayetteville, NY; (Y); 217/335; Cmnty Wkr; JA; Swmmng; Hon Roll; Mock Trial; Jr Guild; Savannah Coll Art/Dsgn; Arch.

ROSCOE, MICHELLE; Tappan Zee HS; Piermont, NY; (Y); 85/245; Church Yth Grp; Band; Chorus; Church Choir; Drm & Bgl; Drm Mjr(t); Off Frsh Cls; Sftbl; Rockland Negro Schlrp 86; Howard U; Bus Mgmt.

ROSE, ALBERT; Parkwest HS; Bronx, NY; (Y); 88/483; Aud/Vis; CAP; JA; Band; Church Choir; Cit Awd; Telecmmnctns.

ROSE, ANGEL; Uniondale HS; Uniondale, NY; (Y); Church Yth Grp; Cmnty Wkr; Hosp Aide; Temple Yth Grp; Band; Church Choir; Hon Roll; Concert Band; Off Jr Cls; Air Force; Pedtrcn.

ROSE, DAVID S; Walt Whitman HS; Huntington Sta, NY; (Y); Computer Clb; Latin Clb; Mathletes; Nwsp Stf; Lit Mag; Cit Awd; High Hon Roll; Jr NHS; NHS; English Clb; Piano, Sci & Math Gld Mdls 83; Itln Hnr Soc 86; Stony Brook U; Law.

ROSE, DEBBIE; South Shore HS; Brooklyn, NY; (Y); Orch; School Musical; Hon Roll; NHS; Bnai Brth Yth Org 85-87; Medcn.

ROSE, DWAINE; Park West HS; Brooklyn, NY; (Y); Boy Scts; Church Yth Grp; JA; Church Choir; Rep Frsh Cls; Hon Roll; Elec Engrng.

ROSE, DWIGHT; Evander Childs HS; Bronx, NY; (Y); Chorus; School Musical; Stage Crew; Cit Awd; Mth.

ROSE, ELIZABETH; Herkimer SR HS; Herkimer, NY; (Y); 11/130; Drama Clb; School Musical; School Play; Yrbk Stf; Sec Jr Cls; Rep Stu Cncl; Var Cheerleading; Var Gym; Var Trk; High Hon Roll; Pre Vet Sci.

ROSE, GEORGIA; Mt Vernon HS; Mt Vernon, NY; (Y); Debate Tm; School Musical; School Play; Stu Cncl; Gym; Trk; Hon Roll; Jr NHS; Soph Cls; Jr Cls; Mock Trl Tm 86; Prs Girl Mrshls 86-87; Cmmnctns.

ROSE, JODY; Dominican Commercial HS; New York, NY; (Y); 29/288; Church Yth Grp; Teachers Aide; Chorus; Church Choir; Rep Frsh Cls; Rep Soph Cls; Rep Jr Cls; Pres Stu Cncl; Var Swmmng; NHS; Bus.

ROSE, KRISTIN; Hilton HS; Hilton, NY; (Y); 34/275; Chorus; Concert Band; Mrchg Band; High Hon Roll; Hon Roll; Princpls Lst 83-84; AM Chem Soc 84-85; Pres Acdmc Fitns Awd 85-86; SUNY; CPA.

ROSE, LINDA; Bethpage HS; Bethpage, NY; (Y); 108/303; Spanish Clb; Yrbk Stf; Hon Roll; Nassau Cmnty Coll; Bus Adm.

ROSE, MARK; Scotia-Glenville HS; Scotia, NY; (Y); Spanish Clb; Varsity Clb; Yrbk Stf; Coach Actv; Socr; Vllybl; Jr NHS.

ROSE, NANCY; Cazenovia Central HS; New Woodstock, NY; (Y); 4-H; 4-H Awd; Hon Roll; Bus.

ROSE, OVETA; Saint Barnabas HS; Freeport, NY; (Y); Drama Clb; Library Aide; Office Aide; SADD; Band; Chorus; School Musical; Nwsp Ed-Chief; Pres Frsh Cls; Rep Soph Cls; Soc Stud Hon Awd 84-85; Engl Hon Awd 84-85; Avg Awd 84-85; St Johns U; Law.

ROSE, RONAELE N; Spence Schl; Rosedale, NY; (Y); Dance Clb; Spanish Clb; Nwsp Phtg; Nwsp Stf; Yrbk Phtg; Badmtn; Stat Bsktbl; Sftbl; Trk; NHS; Ntl Merit SF 85; Ntl Hnr Soc 85; Lawyer.

ROSE, SALOME; Poughkeepsie HS; Poughkeepsie, NY; (Y); SADD; Teachers Aide; SUNY Stoneybrook; Med.

ROSE, WENDY; Mechanicville HS; Mechanicville, NY; (Y); 50/106; Church Yth Grp; Debate Tm; SADD; Teachers Aide; VICA; JV Var Mat Maids; Score Keeper; Hon Roll; Ntl Merit Ltr; Hudston Valley CC; Soc Wrkr.

ROSEKRANS, CHRISTINE; Catholic Central HS; Troy, NY; (S); 23/172; Cmnty Wkr; Math Clb; High Hon Roll; Hon Roll; NHS; Spnsh III 85; Spnsh I, Soc Stud 83; Mount St Mary Coll; Nrsg.

ROSELLI, KATHERINE; Pine Bush HS; Middletown, NY; (Y); Pres 4-H; Band; Chorus; Concert Band; Drm & Bgl; Mrchg Band; JV Bsktbl; JV Crs Cntry; Wt Lftg; 4-H Awd; Band Trophy 84; 4-H Mdl Of Achvmnt 85; Cornell; Vet.

ROSELLI, MITCH; Hornell HS; Hornell, NY; (Y); Am Leg Boys St; Boys Clb Am; Boy Scts; FCA; Chorus; JV Bsbl; JV Var Bsktbl; JV Var Ftbl; Im Wt Lftg; Hon Roll; RIT; Bus Adm.

ROSELLI, TIA; Hornell HS; Hornell, NY; (Y); Library Aide; Spanish Clb; Cert Of Merit Achvt Keybrdg 85-86; Alfred ST Clg; Exec Sec.

ROSEMAN, LESLIE; Masters Schl; Chappaqua, NY; (Y); Cmnty Wkr; French Clb; Hosp Aide; Library Aide; Nwsp Rptr; Nwsp Stf; Lit Mag; Off Jr Cls; Hon Roll; Awd Libr Aide 86; Horace Greeley.

ROSEN, BRIAN M; Clarkstown South HS; West Nyack, NY; (Y); Am Leg Boys St; Cmnty Wkr; Red Cross Aide; Service Clb; SADD; Varsity Clb; Band; Concert Band; Jazz Band; Mrchg Band; Coaches Awd Tennis 85; Am Lg Boys ST Rep 86; Psychology.

ROSEN, COREY D; Jamestown HS; Jamestown, NY; (Y); French Clb; Political Wkr; Ski Clb; SADD; Temple Yth Grp; Rep Jr Cls; Ftbl; Wt Lftg; Hon Roll; NHS; Phrmcy.

ROSEN, KENNETH; Lynbrook HS; Hewlett, NY; (S); Debate Tm; Mathletes; Math Tm; NFL; VP Science Clb; Speech Tm; Chorus; NHS; Newsppr News Edtr 85-86; H S All Cnty Chorus Qualf 85-86.

ROSEN, ROBIN; Sachem HS North; Bayside, NY; (Y); 94/1396; Drama Clb; Ski Clb; SADD; Chorus; Madrigals; School Musical; Var JV Tennis; Jr NHS; NHS; Pres Schlr; NYSSMA Mdl Vcl Per 85; Long Island Sci Cngrs Mrt Awd 84; NYSSMA Mdl Piano Perf Excel Rtng 83; George Washington U; Intl Law.

ROSEN, SARA; South Side HS; Rockville Centre, NY; (Y); Drama Clb; Latin Clb; Mathletes; Thesps; Band; Chorus; Sec Madrigals; School Musical; NHS; Cornell U.

ROSENBACH, VIRGINIA ANNE; Franciscan Acad; Parish, NY; (Y); Art Clb; FBLA; GAA; Girl Scts; Teachers Aide; Stage Crew; Variety Show; Bsktbl; Socr; Vllybl; NY ST Rgnts Dplmt 86; U Of TN; Lbrl Arts.

ROSENBERG, ALISON; La Guardia H S Of The Arts; Howard Beach, NY; (S); 20/660; Art Clb; Rep Jr Cls; Hon Roll; Pres Jr NHS; RI Schl Dsgn; Cmmrcl Arts.

ROSENBERG, HELENE; Somers HS; Yorktown, NY; (Y); Teachers Aide; Nwsp Rptr; Nwsp Stf; Yrbk Bus Mgr; Yrbk Stf; High Hon Roll; Hon Roll; Schlstc Achvt Exc Math 86; Cert Awd Outstndng Accomplshmnt Math 84; Bus.

ROSENBERG, LAURA; South Shore HS; Brooklyn, NY; (Y); Teachers Aide; Temple Yth Grp; Chorus; School Play; Stage Crew; Arista Hnr Soc 84-86.

ROSENBERGEN, CHARLES J; Pawling JR SR HS; Pawling, NY; (Y); 8/54; Church Yth Grp; Latin Clb; Math Tm; Band; Mrchg Band; Nwsp Sprt Ed; Yrbk Stf; JV Bsktbl; JV Score Keeper; Hon Roll; NYS Regents Schlrshp 86; SUNY-STONY Brook; Engr.

ROSENBLATT, PAULETTE D; Art & Design HS; New York, NY; (Y); 12/406; Gov Hon Prg Awd; Pres NHS; Debate Tm; Variety Show; Hon Roll; Natl Hon Soc Mdl 86; Sci Awd 86; Arch Cert Of Excllnc 86; Cornell U; Plnt Sci.

ROSENBLUM, CINDY; Mineola HS; Roslyn Heights, NY; (Y); 10/200; Debate Tm; Trs French Clb; Math Tm; Service Clb; Pres Temple Yth Grp; Nwsp Stf; Bowling; High Hon Roll; Jr NHS; NHS; Math.

ROSENBLUM, DARREN; John F Kennedy HS; Merrick, NY; (Y); Debate Tm; Hosp Aide; Political Wkr; Spanish Clb; Hon Roll; NHS; Ntl Merit SF; Debate Trnmnt 1st Pl 85; Debate Trnmnt 4th & 5th Pl 86; Law.

ROSENBLUM, NANCY; G W Hewlett HS; Woodmere, NY; (Y); Spanish Clb; SADD; Temple Yth Grp; Nwsp Stf; JV Bsktbl; Mgr(s); Hon Roll; NHS; Achvt Awd Spnsh Clb 86; Amer Assn Tchrs Spnsh-Portugs 83 & 85; Bus.

ROSENFELD, STEVEN M; Flushing HS; College Point, NY; (Y); 9/400; Computer Clb; Debate Tm; Scholastic Bowl; Color Guard; School Musical; Yrbk Rptr; Prfct Atten Awd; Chess Clb; Drama Clb; Teachers Aide; Rgnts Schlrshp; ARISTA Boy Ldr; Stnybrk; Comp Sci Systm Anlyst.

ROSENGOLD, BRIAN S; Walt Whitman HS; Huntington Sta, NY; (Y); 43/550; Teachers Aide; SADD; Var JV Bsbl; JV Ftbl; High Hon Roll; Hon Roll; Jr NHS; NYS Rgnts Schlrshp 86; ST U Of NY Albany; Bus.

ROSENHAHN, WENDY; Kenmore East HS; Kenmore, NY; (Y); Dance Clb; Girl Scts; Hosp Aide; Trs Band; Church Choir; Color Guard; Orch; Yrbk Phtg; High Hon Roll; NHS; SUNYAB; Phrmcy.

ROSENOW, RACQUEL; South Park HS; Buffalo, NY; (Y); Boys Clb Am; Camera Clb; Yrbk Stf; Cit Awd; High Hon Roll; Hon Roll; NHS; Boys Clb Am; Camera Clb; Yrbk Stf; Art Achvt Awds; Wlrd Prc.

ROSENSAFT, MOSHE; Shaarei Torah Of Rockland HS; Monsey, NY; (S); Temple Yth Grp; Nwsp Stf; Yrbk Stf; Lit Mag; Bsbl; Bsktbl; Ftbl; High Hon Roll; Hon Roll; NHS; Deans List 85-86; Columbia U; Dentistry.

ROSENSTEIN, MARK; Middletown HS; Middletown, NY; (Y); Bsktbl; Trk; Hon Roll; Key Clb; Ski Clb; Yrbk Stf.

ROSENTHAL, CHERYL; Kings Park HS; Kings Pk, NY; (Y); 46/382; Political Wkr; Pres Temple Yth Grp; Nwsp Ed-Chief; Lit Mag; Stu Cncl; Socr; Capt Vllybl; High Hon Roll; NHS; St Schlr; Syracuse U; Law.

ROSENTHAL, EILEEN; Acad Of St Joseph; Sayville, NY; (Y); Service Clb; SADD; Teachers Aide; Church Choir; Yrbk Stf; Engl.

ROSENTHAL, JEROME P; Williamsville East HS; Williamsville, NY; (Y); 22/294; Drama Clb; Math Tm; VP Temple Yth Grp; School Play; Var Tennis; Var Wrstlng; High Hon Roll; Hon Roll; 1st Pl New Fane Math Cntst/Gemtry 84; Top Hnr Math Stu 83; Engr.

ROSENTHAL, JOSEPH A; Bayshore HS; Bayshore, NY; (Y); 21/412; Chess Clb; Drama Clb; Math Tm; Thesps; School Musical; School Play; Stage Crew; Var Socr; Hon Roll; NHS; Regents Schrlshp 86; SUNY-BINGHAMTON; Physics.

ROSENTHAL, MARC; Glen Cove HS; Glen Cove, NY; (Y); 75/256; Computer Clb; Drama Clb; FBLA; Model UN; Thesps; Stage Crew; Trk; Hon Roll; Law.

ROSENTHAL, RICHARD H; Fayetteville-Manlius HS; Manlius, NY; (Y); 96/335; JCL; SADD; Acpl Chr; Chorus; Nwsp Phtg; High Hon Roll; Hon Roll; Camera Clb; Computer Clb; Drama Clb; Cnty Mck Trl Tm Champ 86; Law.

ROSENTHAL, YITZCHAK S; Yeshiva University High Schl For Boys; Brooklyn, NY; (Y); St Schlr; Yeshiva Univ Belkin Schlrshp 85-86; Yeshiva U.

ROSENWASSER, CHRISTINE K; St Joseph Hill Acad; Staten Island, NY; (Y); 15/110; Pres Church Yth Grp; Hosp Aide; Math Tm; Service Clb; Stage Crew; Yrbk Stf; Var Crs Cntry; Var Trk; Hon Roll; Ntl Merit SF.

ROSENZWEIG, TODD; White Plains HS; White Plns, NY; (Y); Art Clb; Boy Scts; Quiz Bowl; Temple Yth Grp; Stat Bsbl; JV Bsktbl; Stat Score Keeper; Escnmcs.

ROSEO, RICHARD J; Syosset HS; Syosset, NY; (Y); Band; Mrchg Band; Pep Band; Symp Band; Yrbk Phtg; Yrbk Stf; Crs Cntry; Trk; Ntl Merit Ltr; St Schlr; Engl Hnrs 86; Soc Studs Hnrs 86; SUNY Stony Brook.

ROSER, SANDRA; Valley Central HS; Walden, NY; (Y); Church Yth Grp; Drama Clb; Acpl Chr; Church Choir; School Musical; Off Jr Cls; Stu Cncl; French Hon Soc; Spanish NHS; French Clb; All Co Chorus 84-85; Fshn Inst Techlgy; Mrchndsng.

ROSEWATER, KAREN; Bethlehem Central HS; Delmar, NY; (Y); 1/304; VP Temple Yth Grp; Chorus; Orch; Ed Yrbk Stf; DAR Awd; VP NHS; Empire ST Schlrshp Of Excllnc 86; Harvard Bk 85; RPI Medl 85; Yale U; Med.

ROSHDO, ELIZABETH; De Witt Clinton HS; Bronx, NY; (Y); Off Soph Cls; Var Sftbl; Mchncl Engr.

ROSKO, SUE; Shenendehowa HS; Ballston Lake, NY; (Y); Church Yth Grp; Cmnty Wkr; Intnl Clb; Ski Clb; SADD; Concert Band; Nwsp Rptr; Yrbk Rptr; Var L Cheerleading; High Hon Roll; Consistnt Hnr Roll Achvt Gold Pin 84; Var Certs 84-85; Cmndtn For Hlp Grad 86; Socl Sci.

ROSMARINO, BETTINA; Cazenovia Central HS; Cazenovia, NY; (Y); 6/140; Var Trk; High Hon Roll; Hon Roll; NHS; Syracuse U; Nutrtnst.

ROSOF, ELANA; Huntington HS; Huntington, NY; (Y); AFS; Key Clb; SADD; Temple Yth Grp; High Hon Roll; NHS; VFW Awd; Drtmth Bk Awd 86; Sufflk Co Math Tst 86.

ROSS, ALFRED; Our Savior Lutheran HS; New York, NY; (Y); 3/32; Bsktbl; Socr; Hon Roll; Ntl Merit Ltr; IA; Pre-Med.

ROSS, ALLISON; Rivedale Country Schl; New York, NY; (Y); French Clb; Off Soph Cls; Off Jr Cls; Off Sr Cls; Sec Stu Cncl; Tennis; Stat Vllybl; Hon Roll.

ROSS, BARBARA; Clarence SR HS; Clarence Ctr, NY; (Y); 50/252; Latin Clb; Chorus; Var Fld Hcky; JV Vllybl; Med Dr.

ROSS, BRIAN K; Hudson Falls HS; Hudson Falls, NY; (Y); 4/214; Drama Clb; French Clb; Key Clb; Acpl Chr; Band; Chorus; Concert Band; Jazz Band; Mrchg Band; Orch; Jostens Fndtn Scholar 86; Sandy Hill Scholar 86; CIBA Geigy Sci Awd 86; Coll Of Holy Cross; Acturl Sci.

ROSS, DEBORAH L; Dunkirk HS; Dunkirk, NY; (Y); 27/210; VP Camera Clb; Church Yth Grp; Computer Clb; French Clb; Pep Clb; Science Clb; School Play; Stage Crew; Yrbk Phtg; Rep Soph Cls; NY ST Rgnts Schlrshp 86; BASF Wyandotte Corp Schlrshp 86; Cert Of Merit Awd 96 Pct Avg 85; Chatham Coll; Vet Med.

ROSS, DIANNE M M; Christopher Columbus HS; Bronx, NY; (Y); 97/690; Church Yth Grp; Dance Clb; Drama Clb; Chorus; Church Choir; School Play; Hon Roll.

ROSS, DONNA; James E Sperry HS; Henrietta, NY; (Y); 25/300; Exploring; GAA; VP Spanish Clb; VP Jr Cls; Pres Stu Cncl; Cheerleading; Trk; High Hon Roll; Jr NHS; VP Spanish NHS; Vrsty Lttr 86; Vrsty Nmbrs 85; Merit Awd Spnsh 85; Pre-Med.

ROSS, ELIZABETH; Nazareth Regional HS; Brooklyn, NY; (Y); Chorus; Var Bsktbl; Hon Roll; Earth Sci Mdl 85-86; Math.

ROSS, JAMES D; Nottingham HS; Syracuse, NY; (Y); Boy Scts; Church Yth Grp; Im JV Bsktbl; Im JV Ftbl; Im JV Mgr(s); Im JV Socr; NY Regnts Diplm 86; Acctnt.

ROSS, JEFFREY; Lackawanna SR HS; Lackawanna, NY; (Y); French Clb; Varsity Clb; JV Var Bsbl; JV Var Ftbl; Hon Roll; NHS; JV Ftbl Mst Val Lineman Awd 85; JR Prom King 86; Econ.

ROSS, KATHRYNE; Ichabod Crane HS; Valatie, NY; (Y); 4/188; Drama Clb; Rep German Clb; SADD; Flag Corp; School Play; Var Crs Cntry; Var Trk; High Hon Roll; NHS; Rotary Awd; Vrsty Ltr Trck/Crss Cntry 82-83; Soph Of Yr, Hugh O Brian Yth Fndtn 84; Schl Svc Awd 85; Lafayette Coll; Intl Rel.

ROSS, KEVIN; Heuvelton Central Schl; Ogdensburg, NY; (S); Latin Clb; Varsity Clb; Band; Concert Band; Mrchg Band; VP Soph Cls; Bsbl; Bsktbl; Socr; NHS; MVP Of Christmas Tourn Bstbl 85; Jostens Hnr Mdl For Acad Achvt 85; Phrmcst.

ROSS, KRISTEN; La Salle SR HS; Niagara Falls, NY; (S); 11/250; Girl Scts; Library Aide; Hon Roll; Jr NHS; Lion Awd; NHS; Psych.

ROSS, LANA; Ticonderoga HS; Hague, NY; (Y); 10/105; Rep Jr Cls; VP Sr Cls; Stu Cncl; Cheerleading; Golf; Gym; Vllybl; High Hon Roll; Hon Roll; NHS; Presdntl Acadmc Ftns Awd 86; Moses Schlrshp 86; Coll Of Saint Rose; Elem Educ.

ROSS, LAURA; Pineview Christian Acad; Averill Park, NY; (S); Church Yth Grp; Drama Clb; School Play; Rep Frsh Cls; Sec Soph Cls; Pres Jr Cls; Pres Stu Cncl; Capt Cheerleading; Vllybl; High Hon Roll; Valley Forge Chrstn Clg; Msntry.

ROSS, LESLIE; Ossining HS; Ossining, NY; (Y); VP Temple Yth Grp; Pres Sr Cls; JV Var Socr; Var Capt Tennis; NHS; Ski Clb; Nwsp Stf; Yrbk Stf; Sec Frsh Cls; Sec Soph Cls; Coachs Awd Vrsty Tennis 84-85; 2 Tm Wnnr 1st Pl Poetry & 2nd Pl Shrtstry Cntst 85-86; Clncl Psych.

ROSS, LISA; Niagara Falls HS; Niagara Falls, NY; (Y); 70/250; Chess Clb; Hosp Aide; Nwsp Rptr; Yrbk Stf; NHS; Kelley Bus Inst Schlrshp 86; Kelleys Bus Inst; Bus.

ROSS, LISA; Turner/Carroll HS; Buffalo, NY; (S); Drama Clb; Girl Scts; School Play; Stat Bsktbl; Mgr(s); Capt Var Sftbl; Var Vllybl; Hon Roll; NHS; Eric CC; Psych.

ROSS, MELANIE K; Pittsford Mendon HS; Pittsford, NY; (Y); 3/250; Church Yth Grp; Drama Clb; Chorus; Church Choir; Madrigals; School Musical; Stage Crew; Variety Show; Hon Roll; Cheerleading; Mst Musicl 86; Snd Of Amerc Hnr Chrs 86; NYS Schl Music Assn Conf All ST 86; Liberty U; Musicl Prfrmnc.

ROSS, MICHELLE; Edison Tech; Rochester, NY; (Y); 30/276; Exploring; Teachers Aide; Varsity Clb; Var Capt Bsktbl; Var Socr; Var Trk; Var Capt Vllybl; NHS; Blck Schlr Awd 86; Schlr-Athlt By US Army Rsrv 86; Wmns Sprts Fndtn All Star Awd 86; Lehigh U; Elec Engrng.

ROSS, PETER; Frontier Central HS; Lake View, NY; (Y); Boy Scts; Stage Crew; West Point; Ofcr.

ROSS, RICHARD; Mt Vernon HS; Mt Vernon, NY; (Y); 39/440; Camera Clb; Political Wkr; Science Clb; High Hon Roll; Hon Roll; 3 Cert Of Achvmnt NSBA 85-86; 2 Cert For Excllnc Bus WBI 85-86; Cert Apprctn IRS 86; Accntng.

ROSS, ROBERT; Franklin Acad; Malone, NY; (Y); 52/262; Cmnty Wkr; Chorus; Swing Chorus; Var L Crs Cntry; Var L Trk; Hon Roll; Prfct Atten Awd; Acdmc All-Amrcn 86; Vrsty SR 3-Lttrmn Seasn Awd 85-86; Paul Smiths; Chef Trng.

ROSS, SUSAN; St Joseph By-The-Sea HS; Staten Island, NY; (Y); Art Clb; Dance Clb; Lit Mag; Hon Roll; NHS; Cert Awd Spnsh; Cert Mert Prfrmnc NEDT; Cert Excllnc Ballet; NY Inst Of Tech; Htl Adm.

ROSS, TONI; Morris HS; Bronx, NY; (Y); JA; Cit Awd; Hon Roll; Prfct Atten Awd; Pres Soph Cls; VP Jr Cls; Rep Stu Cncl; Capt Bsktbl; Var Crs Cntry; Var Vllybl; Bus Admin.

ROSS, TRACY; West Seneca West SR HS; Buffalo, NY; (Y); Church Yth Grp; GAA; Spanish Clb; Rep Frsh Cls; Rep Soph Cls; Rep Jr Cls; Im Cheerleading; JV Trk; Hon Roll; Alfred U; Acctng.

ROSSBACH, SUSAN; Gloversville HS; Gloversville, NY; (Y); Trs Exploring; French Clb; Chorus; Swing Chorus; Yrbk Ed-Chief; Yrbk Stf; Rep Sr Cls; High Hon Roll; Hon Roll; Elem Ed.

ROSSER, ROBERT; Lake Placid HS; Lake Placid, NY; (Y); 4/44; Boys Clb Am; Key Clb; Ski Clb; Stu Cncl; Crs Cntry; High Hon Roll; NHS; Varsity Clb; Yrbk Sprt Ed; Yrbk Stf; Bud Colby Ski Jumping Schlrshp, 9th Nordic Cmbnd Yth Natls Ski 86; 1st Plattsburgh Y Triathlon 85; U VT; Psych.

ROSSI, ALEXANDER R; Collegiate Schl; New York, NY; (Y); Pres Ski Clb; Pres Spanish Clb; Nwsp Bus Mgr; Yrbk Bus Mgr; VP Stu Cncl; Var Socr; Var Trk; Var Capt Wrstlng; Ntl Merit SF; Ecnmcs.

ROSSI, ANTHONY; Archbishop Molloy HS; Long Isl City, NY; (Y); 107/383; German Clb; Chorus; 10 Yrs Brooklyn Bys & Grls Chrs 86; Cmmnctns.

ROSSI, DEREK; Fox Lane HS; Mt Kisco, NY; (Y); 153/277; Cmnty Wkr; Bsbl; JV Bsktbl; Score Keeper; Pace U; Bus.

ROSSI, ERIC S; Commack H S North; Commack, NY; (Y); 56/390; Am Leg Aux Girls St; School Musical; Nwsp Rptr; NHS; Ntl Merit Ltr; Empire ST Scholar Excllnce 86; Modern Music Masters 86; Mst Outstndng Scholar SUNY Oswego 86; SUNY Oswego; Pol Sci.

ROSSI, GREGORY; North Babylon SR HS; No Babylon, NY; (Y); 87/425; Intnl Clb; JV Socr; JV Tennis; Cmrcl Airln Pilot.

ROSSI, JOANNE; Blind Brook HS; Rye Brook, NY; (Y); Cmnty Wkr; French Clb; Hosp Aide; Model UN; Spanish Clb; Chorus; School Musical; School Play; Nwsp Stf; Fld Hcky.

ROSSI, VICTORIA; St John The Baptist HS; Smithtown, NY; (Y); Church Yth Grp; Cmnty Wkr; Dance Clb; Hosp Aide; Nwsp Stf; Var Tennis; JC Awd; Dancing Awd 85; Lasell; Htl Admin.

ROSSILLO, MARIA; Bishop Ford Central Catholic HS; Brooklyn, NY; (Y); 2nd Hnrs.

ROSSINI, ANTHONY DAVID; St Francis Prep Schl; Beechhurst, NY; (Y); 198/653; Im Bsbl; Im Bsktbl; Im Vllybl; High Hon Roll; Hon Roll; Rgnts Schlrshp SAT 86; Cmmndtn Dscplnry Excllnc 82-86; Fresh Optimist Soc 82; Manhattan COLL; Micro Bio.

ROTBARD, ERIC J; Clarkstown North HS; New City, NY; (Y); Band; Concert Band; Jazz Band; Mrchg Band; Symp Band; Lit Mag; Hon Roll; Jr NHS; NHS; NY ST Rgnts Schlrshp 86; SUNY Bnghmtn; Pre-Med.

ROTELLA, JEFF; Shoreham-Wading River HS; Shoreham, NY; (Y); Art Clb; Intnl Clb; Band; Var L Socr; JV L Tennis; Var L Trk; JV L Wrstlng; NHS; NYS Summr Schl Arts 86; Mth Fair Gold Mdlst & Silv Mdlst 84-85; Summr Inst Gifted & Tlntd 85; Arch.

ROTENBERG, MIRIAM; Hebrew Acad O Fth Five Towns Rockaway; Cedarhurst, NY; (Y); 2/57; Temple Yth Grp; Yrbk Ed-Chief; NHS; Ntl Merit Ltr; Sal; Michlalah.

ROTERT, MELISSA A; Cardinal Mooney HS; Rochester, NY; (Y); 20/304; Library Aide; School Musical; Nwsp Rptr; Score Keeper; French Hon Soc; Hon Roll; NY ST Regents Scholar 86; Geneseo Coll; Elem Ed.

ROTGIN, MICHAEL; John F Kennedy HS; Merrick, NY; (Y); Debate Tm; Key Clb; Science Clb; Nwsp Rptr; Socr; Hon Roll; NHS.

ROTH, ALLEN; Mohonasen HS; Schenectady, NY; (Y); Ski Clb; JV Bsbl; JV Var Ftbl; Trk; Wrstlng; NHS; Engrng.

ROTH, BARBARA A; Huntington HS; Huntington Sta, NY; (Y); 109/385; Trs Computer Clb; Capt Mathletes; Quiz Bowl; School Play; Stage Crew; Nwsp Rptr; Yrbk Stf; Sftbl; Tennis; Hon Roll; Rgnts Schlrshp 86; Brkhvn Ntl Lab Brdge Cntst Hnrb Mntn 86; Sflk Cnty Math Fair 85; Comp Sci.

ROTH, BETSY; Tonawanda SR & JR HS; Tonawanda, NY; (Y); Church Yth Grp; SADD; Band; Chorus; Church Choir; Concert Band; Orch; School Musical; JV Var Cheerleading; Trk; Bus.

ROTH, CARROL ADRIENNE; Shulamith High Schl For Girls; Brooklyn, NY; (Y); Art Clb; Stage Crew; Yrbk Bus Mgr; Lit Mag; Hon Roll; NEDT Awd; NY St Rgnt Schlrshp Awd 86; NYC Cmptrllrs Awd-Excllnc In Comp Sci 86; Exemp Chrtcr & Schl Svc Awd 86; Brooklyn Coll.

ROTH, CHEDVA; Shulamith H S For Girls; Brooklyn, NY; (S); 2/30; Art Clb; Nwsp Stf; Yrbk Stf; High Hon Roll; Lgl Profsn.

ROTH, DAVID; Manlius Pebble Hill HS; Fayetteville, NY; (S); Temple Yth Grp; Tennis; Hon Roll; Barilan U-Israel; Lang.

ROTH, JANICE M; Elba Central Schl; Elba, NY; (Y); 5/71; 4-H; FHA; FNA; FTA; Science Clb; Teachers Aide; Yrbk Stf; High Hon Roll; Jr NHS; NHS; Regnts Coll Schlrshp 86-91; Merit Tuitin Awd 86-88; Regnts Diplma 86; Genesee CC; Tchr.

ROTH, JOHN M; Whitesboro SR HS; Utica, NY; (Y); 114/364; Boy Scts; Church Yth Grp; Science Clb; Chorus; School Musical; Rep Soph Cls; Rep Stu Cncl; Var JV Wrstlng; Hon Roll; Rgnts Schlrshp 86; Utica Coll Sci Fair 2nd Pl Sr Div 84; Cert Merit MVCP Cntst 86; Mohawk Valley CC; Data Proc.

ROTH, KATHY; Holland HS; Holland, NY; (Y); Co-Capt Bsktbl; Vllybl; Hon Roll; MIP Bsktbl 84; St John Fisher Coll; Comptr Sci.

ROTH, KIMBERLY; Ichabod Crane Central HS; Valatie, NY; (Y); 13/181; Drama Clb; Math Clb; Trs SADD; Color Guard; School Play; Yrbk Stf; Lit Mag; JV Fld Hcky; High Hon Roll; Hon Roll; NYS Nrsg Regnts Schlrshp; Pres Acadmc Fit Awd; USAF; Electrncs.

ROTH, KRISTEN; G Ray Bodley HS; Fulton, NY; (Y); 2/261; Pres Church Yth Grp; Science Clb; Band; Jazz Band; Mrchg Band; School Musical; Var L Crs Cntry; Dnfth Awd; JC Awd; Sal; Janet H Griswold Schlrshp PEO Sistrhd 86; Houghton Coll.

ROTH, MICHELE; Middletown HS; Middletown, NY; (Y); VP Art Clb; Drama Clb; Scholastic Bowl; Teachers Aide; Acpl Chr; School Musical; Swing Chorus; Ed Lit Mag; Art Edtr Yrbk; Art Hon Soc Pres; Cmmrcl Art.

ROTH, ROBERT I; Bronx High School Of Science; Bayside Queens, NY; (Y); Art Clb; JA; Library Aide; Nwsp Ed-Chief; Nwsp Rptr; Nwsp Stf; Yrbk Stf; Lit Mag; NY ST Regnts Clg Schlrshp 86; Arista 86; NY U; Flmmkg.

ROTH JR, RONALD M; Greenville Central Schl; Greenville, NY; (Y); 10/80; Am Leg Boys St; Boy Scts; Sec Spanish Clb; Nwsp Ed-Chief; Yrbk Stf; VP Stu Cncl; Bsktbl; L Socr; Var L Trk; NHS; Schl Rcrd 600 Meter Relay 86; St Lwrnc U.

ROTHENBERG, SANDRA L; Jamesville-Dewitt HS; Dewitt, NY; (Y); 29/245; VP German Clb; VP Pep Clb; Nwsp Ed-Chief; Nwsp Rptr; Swmmng; High Hon Roll; NHS; Syracuse U; Bio-Engrng.

ROTHENBERGER, JENNIFER; Frontier Central HS; Hamburg, NY; (Y); 37/498; Sec Church Yth Grp; Pep Clb; Spanish Clb; Chorus; Church Choir; Color Guard; Yrbk Stf; High Hon Roll; Hon Roll; NHS; Secy Sci.

ROTHKOPF, ROBERT A; Massapequa HS; Massapequa, NY; (Y); 114/440; Computer Clb; Quiz Bowl; VP Spanish Clb; Teachers Aide; Mrchg Band; Symp Band; High Hon Roll; St Schlr; Hebrew Clb 86; NY ST U Bfl; Comp Prgmr.

ROTHMAN, ALAN E; Yeshiva Univ H S For Boys; New York, NY; (Y); Math Tm; Temple Yth Grp; Nwsp Ed-Chief; Jr NHS; NHS; St Schlr; Max Stern Schlr Yeshiva U 85; Yeshiva Coll; Pol Sci.

ROTHMAN, ELLYN; Mc Kee Technical HS; Staten Island, NY; (Y); 31/209; Girl Scts; Library Aide; School Play; Yrbk Stf; Rep Soph Cls; VP Sr Cls; Var JV Cheerleading; Seagull Sec 85; Super Yth 85; Stevens Inst Of Tech; Comp Pgmr.

ROTHMAN, ILYSSA; James Madison HS; Brooklyn, NY; (Y); 4/859; Debate Tm; French Clb; Pres JA; Math Tm; Quiz Bowl; School Musical; Nwsp Rptr; Yrbk Ed-Chief; High Hon Roll; NHS; Charles Robertson Awd 86; NY City Spcl Stu Awd 84-86; Ldrshp Awd 86; Cornell U; Psych.

ROTHMAN, JACY; Central Islip SR HS; Central Islip, NY; (Y); Library Aide; Sec VP Math Clb; Sec VP Math Tm; Hon Roll; Comp Awd 86; Lbry Awd 86; Comp Sci.

ROTHMAN, PHILIP; Smithtown H S East; Nesconset, NY; (Y); Nwsp Rptr; Chrmn Frsh Cls; Off Soph Cls; Off Jr Cls; Var Trk; Var L Wrstlng; NHS; Italian Hnr Soc 84-86; Ldrshp Conf 85; Cornell ILR; Finance.

ROTHSTEIN, DEBRA M; Bronx Schl Of Sci; Flushing, NY; (Y); Science Clb; Service Clb; Teachers Aide; Var Frsh Cls; Var Soph Cls; Var Jr Cls; Var Sr Cls; Wstnghse Sci Tlnt Srch Cmptn Hnrs Awd 85-86; Cornell U; Med.

ROTHSTEIN, RUSSELL I; Rawaz Upper Schl; Bronx, NY; (Y); Capt Math Tm; Trs Temple Yth Grp; School Play; Nwsp Stf; Yrbk Stf; Var Capt Bsktbl; Var L Sftbl; Ntl Merit Ltr; St Schlr; Govnrs Committee Schltc Achvt Citation & Schlrshp 86; Harvard.

ROTHSTEIN, TRACY; Commack South; Dix Hills, NY; (Y); Girl Scts; Office Aide; Teachers Aide; Temple Yth Grp; Color Guard; Symp Band; Trs Frsh Cls; VP Soph Cls; Socr; Trk; Lwyr.

ROTOLI, CHRISTA; Nazareth Acad; Rochester, NY; (Y); Latin Clb; Yrbk Stf; Bowling; Hon Roll; St John Fisher; Vet.

ROTTENBERG, JASON; Valley Central HS; Walden, NY; (Y); 16/300; Boys Clb Am; Boy Scts; Letterman Clb; Varsity Clb; Band; Concert Band; Lit Mag; Var Ftbl; Var Trk; Hon Roll.

ROTTER, SHARON; Shulamith HS; Brooklyn, NY; (S); 1/28; Chorus; School Musical; Nwsp Ed-Chief; Yrbk Ed-Chief; Pres Jr Cls; NHS; NEDT Awd.

ROULAND, SUZANNE; Waterloo SR HS; Waterloo, NY; (Y); VP Church Yth Grp; French Clb; Spanish Clb; Temple Yth Grp; Chorus; Church Choir; Ricks Coll; Comp Engr.

ROUNDS, BRYAN; Seton Catholic Central HS; Binghamton, NY; (Y); Art Clb; Drama Clb; Ski Clb; School Musical; School Play; Tennis; High Hon Roll; Hon Roll; Cert Hnr Mck Trial NYS Bar Assoc 85-86; Seton Cathlc Cntrl Awd Excllnc Theatr Arts 85; 1st Pl WSKG; Pre-Law.

ROURKE, COLLEEN; Skaneateles Central HS; Skaneateles, NY; (S); Cmnty Wkr; Red Cross Aide; Yrbk Stf; High Hon Roll; Hon Roll; NHS; Ntl Gold Mdl Art Awd 2 Blu Rbbns & Gold Key 84; Art Gold Key & Hnrbl Mntn Rgnl Schlstc Awd 85.

ROURKE, ELIZABETH A; Voorheesville HS; Voorheesville, NY; (Y); 4/112; Am Leg Aux Girls St; 4-H; Intnl Clb; Band; Chorus; School Play; Trk; Cit Awd; High Hon Roll; NHS; SUNY Binghamton; Bio.

ROUX, ALEX; Westmoreland Central HS; Westmoreland, NY; (Y); 20/80; Concert Band; Jazz Band; Mrchg Band; Nwsp Sprt Ed; Var Capt Bsbl; Var Ftbl; High Hon Roll; Am Leg Schl Awd 86; Pres Acad Fit Awd 86; Spts Boosters Scholar 86; Mohawk Vly; Bus Adm.

ROUX II, GERARD; Broadalbin Central HS; Broadalbin, NY; (Y); 3/96; Boy Scts; Exploring; French Clb; Letterman Clb; Varsity Clb; JV L Bsktbl; Var L Socr; JV L Trk; Cit Awd; High Hon Roll; Eagle Awd 83; Ntl Mdl Of Merit For Lfsvng 84; Union Law Schl; Lwyr.

ROVIN, MARC R; Valley Stream South HS; Valley Stream, NY; (Y); 33/168; Pres AFS; Mathletes; Ski Clb; Varsity Clb; Band; Jazz Band; Mrchg Band; Orch; Rep Frsh Cls; Rep Soph Cls; Music Achvt Awd 84-86; 1st Seat Dstrct Bnd Alto Sax 85-86; WA U St Louis; Intl Bus.

ROWAN, KELLY; Smithtown H S West; Smithtown, NY; (Y); Church Yth Grp; Hosp Aide; Teachers Aide; Stu Cncl; Mgr(s); Socr; Hon Roll; LAWYR.

ROWAN, KERRY; Commack North HS; Commack, NY; (Y); Pres Church Yth Grp; Cmnty Wkr; Hosp Aide; Teachers Aide; Orch; School Musical; Fld Hcky; Trk; Hon Roll; Hsptl Svc Awd 85-86; Tchr Aide Awd 86; NYSMA Mus Awd 86; Nrs.

ROWAN, WILLIAM M; Briarcliff HS; Briarcliff, NY; (Y); SADD; Nwsp Phtg; Yrbk Bus Mgr; Yrbk Phtg; Im Badmtn; High Hon Roll; Hon Roll; NHS; Ntl Merit Ltr; LIBA-GEIGY Sci Awd 86; 1st Pl Olympcs Mind Rgnl-Capt 85; 2nd Pl Olympcs Mind Rgnl-Capt 86; U Of VA; Pre Med.

ROWE, FRANCIS; Boys & Girls HS; Brooklyn, NY; (Y); 68/385; Boy Scts; Hon Roll.

ROWE, GORDON; Fairport HS; Fairport, NY; (Y); Art Clb; Computer Clb; Yrbk Stf; Hon Roll; Congrssnl Art Exhibit 85; Grphic Art.

ROWE, HEATHER; Wheatland Chili Central HS; Rochester, NY; (Y); Chrmn Pep Clb; Chrmn SADD; VICA; Yrbk Phtg; Yrbk Rptr; Yrbk Stf; Rep Frsh Cls; Rep Soph Cls; Rep Jr Cls; Rep Stu Cncl; Stu Yr For Wemoco Occu Schl 86.

ROWE, JEFFREY ALLEN; Elmira Free Acad; Elmira, NY; (Y); 15/240; Boy Scts; Pres Church Yth Grp; French Clb; VP Ski Clb; Concert Band; Tennis; High Hon Roll; Trs NHS; Pres Schlr; NY ST Regnts Schlrshp 86; Pres Acdmc Fit Awd 86; Corning CC; Engrng.

ROWE, JENNIFER; Smithtown H S East; Smithtown, NY; (Y); French Clb; Hosp Aide; Ski Clb; SADD; Stu Cncl; Badmtn; Bsktbl; Sftbl; Hon Roll; Off Frsh Cls; NYSSMA Piano; SUNY; Bus Adm.

ROWE, JULIANNE; Anthony A Henninger HS; Syracuse, NY; (Y); JA; Band; Concert Band; Jazz Band; Mrchg Band; Pep Band; Symp Band; Im Sftbl; High Hon Roll; Real Est Brkr.

ROWE, TAMMY; Schoharie Central Schl; Schoharie, NY; (S); Key Clb; Varsity Clb; VICA; JV Var Bsktbl; JV Var Sftbl.

ROWELL, DAVID; Onondaga Central HS; Marietta, NY; (S); 5/70; Art Clb; Computer Clb; Spanish Clb; Varsity Clb; Yrbk Bus Mgr; Crs Cntry; Trk; High Hon Roll; NHS; Ntl Merit Ltr; Rochester Inst Of Tech; Comptr.

ROWEN, NANCY; John Jay HS; Cross River, NY; (Y); Drama Clb; Teachers Aide; School Musical; School Play; Variety Show; Lit Mag; JV Var Vllybl; Cit Awd; Hon Roll; John Jy Vllybll Sprtsmnshp Awd 84; Educ.

ROWINSKI, JEFF; Notre Dame-Bishop Gibbons HS; Schenectady, NY; (Y); Ski Clb; School Musical; Stage Crew; JV Var Ftbl; JV Var Trk; Hon Roll; JV Bsktbl; Religion Awd 83-84; Order Of Lance 85-86; Bus Mgmt.

ROWLAND, KERRI; Smithtown HS East; Smithtown, NY; (Y); French Clb; Office Aide; Political Wkr; SADD; Teachers Aide; Hon Roll; Paralgl.

ROWLAND, MICHAEL; Corinth Central Schl; Porter Corners, NY; (S); 3/80; Church Yth Grp; French Clb; Chorus; Church Choir; School Musical; Bsktbl; High Hon Roll; NHS; Acad Achvt Awd 85; Minister.

ROWLES, KAREN; Hamburg SR HS; Boston, NY; (Y); Band; Concert Band; Mrchg Band; JV Bsktbl; Var Trk; Var Vllybl; Hon Roll.

ROWLEY, CHRIS; Auburn HS; Auburn, NY; (Y); Speech Tm; Varsity Clb; Lcrss; Socr; Swmmng; High Hon Roll; NHS; Soc Stds Dept Amer Hstry Awd 86; Achvt Awd Typng Prsnl Use 86.

ROWLEY, DAVID A; Honeoye Central HS; Livonia, NY; (Y); 5/64; Am Leg Boys St; French Clb; Science Clb; Rep Stu Cncl; JV Bsbl; Bausch & Lomb Sci Awd; High Hon Roll; NHS; Ntl Merit SF; NYS Rgnts Schlrshp 86; Ntl Hnr Soc Schlrshp Semifnlst 86; Eductnl Comm Schlrshp Fndtns Semifnlst 86; U Of Rochester; Optcs.

ROWLEY, VICTORIA; Falconer Central HS; Kennedy, NY; (Y); Church Yth Grp; French Clb; FBLA; Girl Scts; Hosp Aide; Spanish Clb; Hon Roll; Voice Dem Awd; Miss Kennedy Fire Queen 86-87; Dist Yth Grp Sec 83; Jamestown CC; Frgn Bus Mgmnt.

ROWSER, DEANNA; H C Technical HS; Buffalo, NY; (Y); Library Aide; Drill Tm; Hon Roll; Var Cheerleading; Var Vllybl; Beam Engrng Clb 83-86; Beta Sigma Phi Hon Srty 84-86; Syracuse U; Bus Mgmt.

ROXBURY, BERNARD; Regis HS; New York, NY; (Y); Boy Scts; Church Yth Grp; Nwsp Rptr; Im Bsbl; Im Bsktbl; Im Bowling; Im Socr; Ntl Merit Schol; Fld Hcky; Ftbl; Resig Cert Of Merit 83; NY U Schlrshp 86; NY U; Accntng.

ROXBURY, SHARON; Shenendehowa HS; Ballston Lk, NY; (Y); Camera Clb; Church Yth Grp; Intnl Clb; Chorus; Church Choir; Drill Tm; Variety Show; High Hon Roll; Top 10 Pcnt Cls 85; Superstar Natl Drill Tm 85; Bus Adm.

ROY, MICHEAL; Waterville Central HS; Waterville, NY; (Y); 9/95; Debate Tm; Mathletes; NFL; Nwsp Rptr; Yrbk Stf; Rep Stu Cncl; High Hon Roll; Jr NHS; Booster Clb Sec 85-86; Pol Sci.

ROY, PATRICIA L; Perth Central Schl; Ft Johnson, NY; (Y); 3/50; Debate Tm; DECA; School Play; Yrbk Ed-Chief; Yrbk Phtg; Vllybl; DAR Awd; High Hon Roll; Rgnts Schlrshp Wnr 86; Rnslr Plytchnc Inst; Cvl Engr.

ROYCE, JOHN; Gouverneur JR SR HS; Gouverneur, NY; (Y); Im JV Ftbl; US Army; Machnst.

ROYCE, JOLENE LENORE; Mount Markham HS; W Winfield, NY; (Y); 11/118; Aud/Vis; Church Yth Grp; Drama Clb; Exploring; GAA; Girl Scts; SADD; Acpl Chr; Chorus; Church Choir; Optmst Of Mnth 86; Rgnts Schlrshp 86; Clark Schlrshp 86; Rochester Inst; Ultrasound Tech.

ROYER, CATHIE LEE; S H Calhoun HS; N Merrick, NY; (Y); 17/313; Drama Clb; Key Clb; Nwsp Stf; Yrbk Stf; Rep Soph Cls; Rep Jr Cls; Stat Score Keeper; NHS; Ntl Merit SF; Fnlst Miss Long Island Pagnt 86; Regents Schlrshp 86; Villanova U; Finance.

ROYS, MELISSA ANNE; Waterville Central HS; Waterville, NY; (Y); Aud/Vis; Church Yth Grp; Ski Clb; Nwsp Bus Mgr; Nwsp Ed-Chief; Nwsp Phtg; Nwsp Rptr; Stat Bsktbl; Mgr(s); Score Keeper; Film Video Dsgn.

ROZANSKI, JOLENE; Frontier Central HS; Lake View, NY; (Y); Pres Spanish Clb; Band; Concert Band; Mrchg Band; Stu Cncl; Var JV Socr; Stat Sftbl; Var JV Vllybl; Hon Roll; Pre-Law.

ROZENBERG, LANA; Midwood HS; Brooklyn, NY; (Y); 28/680; Hon Roll; Ntl Merit Schol; Prfct Atten Awd; Columbia U; Med.

ROZENFELD, YURI; The Anglo-American Schl; Brooklyn, NY; (S); Chess Clb; Nwsp Sprt Ed; Yrbk Sprt Ed; Var Socr; Var Trk; High Hon Roll; Hon Roll; NHS; Won Sci Fair Comptn 84; Economics.

ROZINES, GWEN H; Monroe HS; Rochester, NY; (Y); 3/154; Cmnty Wkr; Math Tm; Sec VP Temple Yth Grp; Ed Yrbk Stf; Rep Jr Cls; Rep Sr Cls; High Hon Roll; Jr NHS; Pres NHS; Harvard Bk Awd 85; Boston U; Occ Ther.

ROZSAS, SHARON; Acad Of Mount St Ursula; Bronx, NY; (Y); 2/150; Drama Clb; Science Clb; SADD; Nwsp Ed-Chief; Stu Cncl; Hon Roll; Engrng.

ROZYCZKO, VINCENT; Cicero-N Syracuse HS; N Syracuse, NY; (S); 3/623; Exploring; Mathletes; Var Bsktbl; L Socr; Im Wt Lftg; Hon Roll; Jr NHS; Bio.

RUANE, JENNIFER; Rome Catholic HS; Rome, NY; (Y); Civic Clb; Library Aide; School Musical; Sec Soph Cls; JV Var Bsktbl; Stat Mgr(s); Im Powder Puff Ftbl; Var Score Keeper; Spch Ther.

RUBAR, KATHY; Lowville Acad; Lowville, NY; (Y); Art Clb; FHA; Math Clb; Varsity Clb; Chorus; School Play; Stage Crew; Stat Bsktbl; Score Keeper; Tennis; Howard B Sackett Cert Achvmnt Dpnbl Stu 85-86; NNYSAS Art Awd 86; MONY Rgnl Schlstc Art Awd 86; Bus Mag.

RUBECK, CHRISTOPHER; Hamburg SR HS; Hamburg, NY; (Y); 21/390; Ski Clb; Teachers Aide; Lit Mag; JV Bsbl; JV Crs Cntry; Var L Ice Hcky; Var L Lcrss; Capt Socr; High Hon Roll; NHS; Soph, Jr & Sr Of The Yr 84-86; Tchrs Awssoc Schlrshp Awd 86; Regents Schlrshp 86; Geneseo ST U; Journlsm.

RUBEL, KAREN A; St Francis Prep Schl; Douglaston, NY; (S); 14/744; Hosp Aide; Science Clb; Principals List 83-85; Med.

RUBENDALL, DENISE; St John The Baptist HS; N Massapequa, NY; (S); Chorus; Orch; Cheerleading; Powder Puff Ftbl; High Hon Roll; Spanish NHS; Hofstra; Fshn Mrchndsg.

RUBENSTEIN, KENNETH; Yeshira University HS; Suffern, NY; (Y); 30/120; Math Tm; Temple Yth Grp; Nwsp Rptr; Yrbk Rptr; Yrbk Sprt Ed; JV Var Bsktbl; Sftbl; NY ST Rgnts Schlrshp 86; All Star Vrsty Bsktbl 86; MVP Chmpnshp Game 86; ST U Of NY; Law.

RUBENSTEIN, MICHAEL; West Genesee SR HS; Syracuse, NY; (Y); 132/531; Computer Clb; Key Clb; Rep Stu Cncl; JV Var Bsbl; Im Bsktbl; JV Var Socr; High Hon Roll; Hon Roll; Prfct Atten Awd; Im Golf.

RUBILOTTA, JAMES; Cazenovia HS; Manlius, NY; (Y); Var L Bsbl; JV Var Bsktbl; JV Var Golf; High Hon Roll; Hon Roll; Trophy Best Offnsv Plyr Bsktbl 85-86; Commtte Athletc Code 86; Bus.

RUBIN, ANDREW; Blind Brook HS; Tuckahoe, NY; (Y); Boy Scts; Variety Show; Var JV Bsbl; Var JV Bsktbl; Var JV Score Keeper; Var JV Socr; Engrng.

RUBIN, ANNE; Scarsdale HS; Scarsdale, NY; (Y); AFS; French Clb; Hosp Aide; Teachers Aide; Temple Yth Grp; School Musical; Yrbk Stf; Var Mgr Swmmng; NHS; Ntl Merit SF; Natl Endwmnt Humanities Bicentennial Yngr Schlr 86.

RUBIN, GLENN S; Tottenville HS; Staten Island, NY; (Y); 60/870; Model UN; NHS; Regents Schlrshp 86; Hnr Key 86; Binghamton; Mgt.

RUBIN, HEIDI; Uniondale HS; Uniondale, NY; (Y); Mathletes; SADD; Band; Jazz Band; Mrchg Band; Crs Cntry; Trk; Jr NHS; NHS; Svc Awd 84.

RUBIN, JASON; W C Mepham HS; N Bellmore, NY; (Y); 3/360; Computer Clb; Mathletes; VP Math Clb; VP Math Tm; VP Scholastic Bowl; Chorus; Gov Hon Prg Awd; NHS; Ntl Merit SF; St Schlr; Genrl Elec Star 86; Cornell U; Ecnmcs.

RUBIN, JESSICA; Sachom HS; Ronkonkoma, NY; (Y); 71/1558; German Clb; Science Clb; Service Clb; Chorus; Yrbk Rptr; Ed Yrbk Stf; Lit Mag; Hon Roll; Jr NHS; NHS; 1st Sci Fair 85; Jrnlsm.

RUBIN, JESSICA S; Oceanside HS; Oceanside, NY; (Y); 50/600; Chrmn Debate Tm; Hst Key Clb; Temple Yth Grp; Varsity Clb; Sec Band; Lit Mag; Var L Cheerleading; Var Capt Gym; High Hon Roll; NY ST Rgnts Schlrshp 86; Envrnmntl Law.

RUBIN, SHARON M; Ward Melville HS; S Setauket, NY; (Y); 2/725; Computer Clb; Hosp Aide; Latin Clb; Library Aide; Math Tm; Teachers Aide; High Hon Roll; Jr NHS; NHS; Ntl Merit Ltr; U PA.

RUBIN, STACY; W C Mepham HS; N Bellmore, NY; (Y); Debate Tm; Mathletes; Math Tm; Political Wkr; Science Clb; Teachers Aide; Temple Yth Grp; Y-Teens; Stu Cncl; Hon Roll.

RUBIN, SYDELLE; Commack HS North; Smithtown, NY; (Y); 1/390; Am Leg Aux Girls St; Hosp Aide; Orch; Nwsp Rptr; Stu Cncl; NCTE Awd; Val; Simons Fllwshp 84; Intrdsplnry Sci Rsrch Pgm 85; Newsday Ldng Schlstc Achvr 86; Harvard U; Intl Law.

RUBIN, THOMAS; Holy Trinity HS; Hicksville, NY; (S); 3/403; Computer Clb; Math Clb; Ski Clb; Spanish Clb; Hon Roll; NEDT Awd; Bio-Chem.

RUBINO, ANN; Johnstown HS; Johnstown, NY; (Y); Band; Concert Band; Orch; Pep Band; Symp Band; Nwsp Rptr; High Hon Roll; Hon Roll.

RUBINO, GEORGENE; Fontbonne Acad; Brooklyn, NY; (Y); Cmnty Wkr; Dance Clb; Hosp Aide; Office Aide; Teachers Aide; Yrbk Stf; High Hon Roll; Cert Hnrbl Mntn Lang Arts I, Italian I & Western Cvlztn I 83-84; Cert Hnrbl Mntn Amer Stds 85-86; Boston U; Newscaster.

RUBINO, LISA; Notre Dame Acad HS; Staten Island, NY; (Y); Dance Clb; SADD; Cmnty Wkr; Yrbk Stf; JV Trk; Rnr-Up Borogh Sci Fr 86; AATSP Natl Spnsh Exam Prtcpnt 86; Berry Schl Perf Arts Schlrshp Awd Wnr 84; Pre-Med.

RUBINOV, JULIA; John Dewey HS; Brooklyn, NY; (Y); Library Aide; Science Clb; Teachers Aide; NY U; Corp Lawyer.

RUBINSTEIN, DIANE; Patchogue-Medford HS; Medford, NY; (S); Trs Band; Trs Concert Band; Trs Mrchg Band; Orch; School Musical; Music Perf.

RUBINSTEIN, JONATHAN; Shenendehowa HS; Clifton Park, NY; (Y); 233/650; Computer Clb; Pres Temple Yth Grp; Jazz Band; High Hon Roll; Comm.

RUCHLIN, STEPHEN L; Williamsville South HS; Williamsville, NY; (Y); Bowling; Golf; Ivy League; Law.

RUCKDESCHEL, GORDON; Liverpool HS; Liverpool, NY; (Y); 4/860; Trs JA; Math Tm; Chorus; School Musical; High Hon Roll; Jr NHS; Trs NHS; Ivy Leag U; Intl Rltns.

RUCKEL, DIANNE; Clarkstown North; Congers, NY; (Y); Dance Clb; Varsity Clb; Variety Show; Var Bsktbl; JV Var Socr; JV Var Trk; Trck Coaches Awd 85; Rockland Cnty Keybdng Cont 86; Bus.

RUDDY, JULIA; Madrid-Waddington HS; Madrid, NY; (Y); GAA; Chorus; School Musical; Pres Soph Cls; JV Cheerleading; Var Capt Socr; Var L Trk; Var L Vllybl; High Hon Roll; Hon Roll; Vrsty Vllybll 1st Tm All Northern 85; Physcl Ther.

RUDICH, NIKKI; Tottenville HS; Staten Isld, NY; (Y); Key Clb; Natl Beta Clb; VP Temple Yth Grp; NHS; Law.

RUDINSKI, JULIE; Warwick Valley HS; Pine Isld, NY; (Y); Sec VP FFA; Math Tm; Sftbl; Hon Roll; Jeff Morgan, Chris Fotey & Samuel Paffenroth Mems 86; Orange Cnty Comm Coll; Math.

RUDKOWSKI, CHRISSI; Connetquot HS; Bohemia, NY; (Y); Cmnty Wkr; Girl Scts; Chorus; Rep Soph Cls; Crs Cntry; Hon Roll; Ntl Sci Awd Bio 83-84; Leigh; Bus Mngmt.

RUDOLPH, DANIELLE; Rye HS; Rye, NY; (Y); AFS; Drama Clb; Hosp Aide; Model UN; Thesps; Chorus; School Musical; Stage Crew; Variety Show; Rep Frsh Cls; Musical Dir Rye HS Musical Revue 86; Dir & Musical Dir Musical Revue 87; Iona Lang Cntst 84-85.

RUDOLPH, JOHN-PAUL; Sodus Central HS; Sodus, NY; (Y); 1/120; Am Leg Boys St; VP Trs Church Yth Grp; Varsity Clb; Var L Crs Cntry; Var L Wrstlng; Cit Awd; Lion Awd; Pres NHS; Rotary Awd; Model UN; Elmira Key Awd 86; Math Cntst Awd 86; Acad Ltr Awd 84-86; Acctng.

RUDOLPH, MICHAEL; Mercy HS; Coram, NY; (Y); 60/123; Ski Clb; Varsity Clb; Rep Frsh Cls; Var Bsbl; JV Bsktbl; Var Capt Ftbl; Wt Lftg; Engrng.

RUDOLPH, SCOTT; Ravena-Coeymans-Selkirk HS; Selkirk, NY; (Y); SADD; Off Frsh Cls; Off Soph Cls; Off Jr Cls; Off Sr Cls; Bsktbl; Ftbl; Platsburgh ST U; Bus Adm.

RUEB, ERIKA A; St Francis Prep HS; Whitestone, NY; (S); 80/653; Dance Clb; Hosp Aide; Math Clb; SADD; Im Sftbl; JV Trk; Im Vllybl; NHS; Opt Clb Awd; Acad All Amer; Achvt, Ldrshp Merit Awds; Bus Mgt.

RUEBEL, THERESA M; Hoosick Falls Central HS; Petersburg, NY; (Y); Ski Clb; Sec Soph Cls; Sec Jr Cls; Sec Sr Cls; JV Cheerleading; JV Var Fld Hcky; Hon Roll; NHS; NYS Rgnts Schrshp 86; Plattsburgh.

RUECKHER, NIAMH; Christ The King Regional HS; Ridgewood, NY; (Y); 6/374; Aud/Vis; German Clb; Intnl Clb; Math Tm; Office Aide; Service Clb; Chorus; Swmmng; CC Awd; Hon Roll; Pace Trustes Schlrshp 86; Baron Von Steuben Schlrshp 86; Regens Schlrshp 86; Pace U; CPA.

RUFF, SHERRY; Holy Angels Acad; Buffalo, NY; (Y); Church Yth Grp; JA; Science Clb; Spanish Clb; Stage Crew; Nwsp Rptr; Lit Mag; Rep Jr Cls; Rep Sr Cls; JV Bsktbl; SUNY Coll; Excptnl Chld Educ.

RUFFILLO, PAUL; Archbishop Molloy HS; Jackson Hgts, NY; (Y); Im Bsktbl; Im Ftbl; Im Sftbl; Hon Roll; Bus.

RUFFING, ELIZABETH; Rondout Valley Central HS; Bloomington, NY; (Y); 1/250; Cmnty Wkr; French Clb; Yrbk Stf; High Hon Roll; Jr NHS; NHS; Val; NYS Rgnts Schlrshp 86; Dan Holleran Memrl Awd 86; Essy Cntst Wnnr Cnty CC 86; Yale U; Engl.

RUFO, JOAN; Roosevelt HS; Yonkers, NY; (Y); Church Yth Grp; Yrbk Stf; Off Jr Cls; Mgr(s); Score Keeper; Sftbl; Timer; Accounting.

RUFOLO, JENNIFER N; Fontbonne Hall Acad; Brooklyn, NY; (Y); 5/133; Hosp Aide; High Hon Roll; Hon Roll; NHS; Drama Clb; Library Aide; Office Aide; School Play; Stage Crew; NEDT Awd; Adelphi U; Biolgy.

RUGANI, LAMBERT; Newtown HS; Elmhurst, NY; (Y); Chorus; Nwsp Stf; Yrbk Stf; Stu Cncl; Bsktbl; Hon Roll; NHS; NYS Regnts Schlrshp; Bus.

RUGGERI, KATHLEEN; Smithtown High School East; Smithtown, NY; (Y); Hosp Aide; Letterman Clb; Ski Clb; Band; Concert Band; Mrchg Band; JV Bsktbl; High Hon Roll; NHS; Spanish NHS; Fairfield U; Math.

RUGGIERO, KRISTIE; West Seneca West SR HS; Orchard Park, NY; (Y); Hosp Aide; Chorus; Color Guard; Drm & Bgl; Flag Corp; School Musical; Capt Twrlr; JC Awd; Library Aide; Office Aide; Color Guard Co-Capt Prncpls Awd 86; Sci Achvt Awd 85; Bus.

RUGGIERO, MARIA; Valley Stream Central HS; Valley Stream, NY; (Y); Ski Clb; Variety Show; Lit Mag; High Hon Roll; Hon Roll; Jr NHS; Italian Natl Hnr Soc; Hofstra U; Chld Psych.

RUGGIERO, PATRICIA A; Sachem North HS; Holbrook, NY; (Y); 47/1362; Service Clb; Spanish Clb; Band; Concert Band; NHS; NY Regents Schlrshp 86; Acad Schlrshp Hofstra U 86; Hofstra U; Pre-Law.

RUGGIERO, PETER; Greenville Central HS; Earlton, NY; (Y); 24/76; Ad.

RUGGIERO, VICTORIA; Pine Bush Central HS; Circleville, NY; (Y); Aud/Vis; DECA; Office Aide; Drm & Bgl; School Play; JV Bsktbl; Gym; Im Score Keeper; Bus.

RUIZ, EMILY; Performing Arts At Laguardia HS; Bronx, NY; (Y); 27/122; Drama Clb; Rep Soph Cls; Hon Roll; Prfct Atten Awd; NY U; Drama.

RUIZ, EVELYN; John Dewey HS; Brooklyn, NY; (Y); Teachers Aide; Hon Roll; Attys Gen Triple C Awd Charctr Courage & Community Concern 82; Baruch Coll; Law.

RUIZ, HUGO; Saint Anthonys HS; Long Beach, NY; (Y); JV Ftbl; NEDT Awd; Natl Hspnc Schlr Awd Smi-Fnlst 86; Acdmc All-Amrcn; US Achvmnt Acad Awd 84-85; Med.

RUIZ, LAURIE; Central Islip SR HS; Central Islip, NY; (Y); 24/383; Band; Nwsp Rptr; Nwsp Stf; VP Sr Cls; Hon Roll; Music Hnr Socty Tempo 86; Psych.

RUIZ, RALPH; Central Islip HS; Central Islip, NY; (Y); Art Clb; Aud/Vis; Camera Clb; Drama Clb; PAVAS; Band; Concert Band; School Musical; School Play; Stage Crew; Phys Top Ten 79-80; Outstndng Sculpture & Crmcs Awd 85-86; Top 5 Actors 86; Five Town Coll; Music.

RUKEYSER, PETER L; Mamaroneck HS; Larchmont, NY; (Y); Pres Ski Clb; Band; Nwsp Bus Mgr; Nwsp Ed-Chief; Trs Frsh Cls; VP Soph Cls; JV Socr; Spec Natl Merit Schlrp 86; Harvard U; Econ.

RULIS, LEIGH ANN; Union Springs Central HS; Auburn, NY; (Y); 10/110; Ski Clb; Yrbk Phtg; Yrbk Stf; VP Soph Cls; VP Jr Cls; Var JV Cheerleading; JV Golf; JV Var Socr; High Hon Roll; NHS; Math.

RULLI, JEANETTE; Brewster HS; Brewster, NY; (Y); Varsity Clb; Concert Band; Pres Stu Cncl; Var Capt Cheerleading; Var Tennis; French Hon Soc; High Hon Roll; NHS; Spanish NHS; Chrldng-MVP 85.

RUMMEL, ANNETTE; Newburgh Free Acad; Newburgh, NY; (Y); Church Yth Grp; Church Choir; Concert Band; Symp Band; High Hon Roll; Hon Roll; Bus.

RUMMO, VALERIE; Glen Cove HS; Glen Cove, NY; (Y); 14/264; French Clb; Key Clb; Service Clb; Yrbk Sprt Ed; JV Var Sftbl; Var Tennis; Hon Roll; NHS; Vrsty Lttr Tnns 83; 3yr Spcl Tnns Regntn Awd Plaque 85; Vrsty Lttr Vrsty Sftbll 85; Med.

RUMPF, SCOTT; Gouverneur Central HS; Gouverneur, NY; (Y); 17/140; 4-H; FFA; Varsity Clb; Var L Crs Cntry; Var L Trk; Hon Roll; Navy; Nuclr Power Pgm.

RUMPH, LATONYA; William E Grady HS; Brooklyn, NY; (Y); Girl Scts; Math Tm; Service Clb; Band; Chorus; Rep Soph Cls; Rep Jr Cls; Stat Bsktbl; Stat Gym; Stat Score Keeper; Baruch Coll; Bus Adm.

RUMSEY, SCOTT; Valley Central HS; Middletown, NY; (Y); Spanish Clb; Varsity Clb; Variety Show; Var Capt Ftbl; Var Trk; Hon Roll.

RUNALDUE, MICHAEL; Hahn American HS; Apo New York, NY; (Y); Boy Scts; German Clb; Ski Clb; JV Socr; Hon Roll; Cvl Engrng.

RUNCO, DENISE; Mercy HS; Sag Harbor, NY; (Y); 4/125; Math Clb; Ski Clb; Spanish Clb; Yrbk Stf; Sftbl; Tennis; High Hon Roll; NHS; Ntl Merit Ltr; Acad All Amer 86; Princpls List 84-86; Bus.

RUNFOLA, DAVID; Canisius HS; Orchard Park, NY; (S); Boys Clb Am; Drama Clb; Varsity Clb; School Musical; Rep Frsh Cls; Rep Soph Cls; Ftbl; Trk; Wrstlng; Hon Roll; Bus.

RUNFOLA, RANDALL PHILIP; Jamestown HS; Jamestown, NY; (Y); 25/400; Church Yth Grp; Letterman Clb; SADD; Concert Band; Rep Sr Cls; Capt L Bsktbl; Capt L Trk; High Hon Roll; NHS; Opt Clb Awd; Tutoring Achvt Awd 85; 3rd Pl Natl JR Olympcs Trk Mt 84; U Dayton; Pre-Law.

RUNIONS, KEVIN D; Mexico HS; Fulton, NY; (Y); Science Clb; Spanish Clb; Pres Band; Concert Band; Jazz Band; Mrchg Band; School Play; L Var Socr; Var Capt Trk; Var L Wrstlng; NY Rgnts Schlrshp Awd 86; 1st Upstate NY JR Sci & Hmnts Sympsm 3rd Plc 86; Cornell U; Navy.

RUNKLE, JENNIFER; Aubunr HS; Auburn, NY; (Y); 10/500; Am Leg Aux Girls St; Pres Church Yth Grp; Trs German Clb; Math Clb; Chrmn Model UN; Jazz Band; School Musical; Stage Crew; High Hon Roll; NHS; Red Cross Swim Acoss Trphy 84-86; Psych.

RUNO, JOCELYN M; John F Kennedy HS; Cheektowaga, NY; (Y); 12/135; Drama Clb; Varsity Clb; Color Guard; School Play; Yrbk Stf; Stu Cncl; Cheerleading; Hon Roll; Jr NHS; NHS.

RUOCCO, ERIKA; Amsterdam HS; Amsterdam, NY; (Y); Trs Art Clb; Pres Church Yth Grp; Varsity Clb; School Play; Yrbk Stf; Mgr(s); Mat Maids; Score Keeper; Hon Roll; Phys Therapy.

RUOCCO, JOSEPHINE; Hauppauge HS; Smithtown, NY; (Y); DECA; Mgr Ftbl; Trk; Vllybl; High Hon Roll; Art Clb; Cmnty Wkr; Rep Frsh Cls; Mgr(s); Hon Roll; ACE Awd Wrd Frndlies 86; Wrk Art Shws Schl 85-86; Grphc Dsgn.

RUOFF, ELIZABETH; Sacred Heart Acad; Garden City, NY; (Y); Math Tm; SADD; School Play; Stage Crew; Hon Roll; NHS; Engrng.

RUOSO, OTELLO G; Huntingston HS; Huntington Statn, NY; (Y); Church Yth Grp; Stage Crew; JV Ftbl; NYS Rgnts Schlrshp 86; SUNY Albany; Acctg.

RUPERT, KAREN D; Morristown Central Schl; Ogdensburg, NY; (Y); 1/35; Am Leg Aux Girls St; Band; Chorus; Var Capt Bsktbl; Var Capt Socr; Var Capt Sftbl; Var Capt Vllybl; Bausch & Lomb Sci Awd; NHS; Spanish NHS; NYS Regnts Schlrshp 86; Plattsburgh ST U; Phys Thrpy.

RUPERTI, YVONNE; Our Lady Of Lourdes HS; Hopewell Jct, NY; (Y); Church Yth Grp; Sec Stu Cncl; Im Sftbl; JV Trk.

RUPP, JEFF; Hugh C Williams HS; Canton, NY; (Y); Boy Scts; Thesps; Chorus; Church Choir; Jazz Band; Orch; Swmmng; Hon Roll; NHS; Marine Bio.

RUPP, KELLY; Fredonia HS; Fredonia, NY; (Y); 4-H; Hosp Aide; Sec Key Clb; Spanish Clb; Band; Chorus; Stage Crew; Sec Symp Band; Var JV Cheerleading; 4-H Awd; Selctd Smmr Enrchmnt Prog 86; Math.

RUSAK, JAMES P; Haverling Central Schl; Bath, NY; (S); Church Yth Grp; Exploring; French Clb; Math Clb; Ski Clb; Band; Jazz Band; Orch; High Hon Roll; NHS; Engrng.

RUSH, JEFFREY; Lindenhurst SR HS; Lindenhurst, NY; (Y); 63/550; ROTC; Ski Clb; Var L Trk; Hon Roll; Marine Corps.

RUSH, STEVEN; New Amsterdam HS; Amsterdam, NY; (Y); High Hon Roll; NHS; St Schlr; NYS Rgnts Scshlrshp, M Lurie Schlrshp 86; Fulton Montgomery CC; Comp Sci.

RUSHLOW, LAURIE A; Hilton Central HS; Hamlin, NY; (Y); 15/305; Cmnty Wkr; Drama Clb; Exploring; French Clb; Sec Math Clb; SADD; Var Civic Clb; Var Tennis; High Hon Roll; NHS; Rgnst Schlrshp 86; SUNY Oswego; Zoolgy.

RUSHTON, DEREK; Bishop Ford Central Catholic HS; Brooklyn, NY; (Y); Computer Clb; Comp Sci.

RUSIN, BILL; Eden Central SR HS; Eden, NY; (Y); Varsity Clb; Band; Drm & Bgl; Jazz Band; Mrchg Band; School Musical; Var Trk; Var Vllybl; Hon Roll; NHS; All Cnty Band 84-86; All ST Band 84 & 86.

RUSIN, LEAH; West Seneca West SR HS; Cheektowaga, NY; (Y); German Clb; GAA; Office Aide; SADD; Varsity Clb; Chorus; Color Guard; School Musical; School Play; Rep Frsh Cls; NY ST Schl Music Assoc Lvl 6 Solo & Duet Mdl Grd Of Excllnc 86; Hgst Hnrs In Eurpn Cltr 85; U Of Buffalo; Psych.

RUSK, DANIEL; Marlboro Central HS; Milton, NY; (Y); 7/150; Varsity Clb; VP Frsh Cls; VP Soph Cls; VP Jr Cls; Var Capt Bsktbl; High Hon Roll; Jr NHS; NHS.

RUSKOUSKI, JODY; Dover JR SR HS; Wingdale, NY; (S); 10/80; Art Clb; Church Yth Grp; Stage Crew; Trs Frsh Cls; Stu Cncl; High Hon Roll; NHS; Voice Dem Awd; Advrstng Dsgn.

RUSS, DEL; Mexico HS; Mexico, NY; (Y); Church Yth Grp; German Clb; Concert Band; Jazz Band; Mrchg Band; Variety Show; JV Capt Bsbl; Prfct Atten Awd; Schlr Ath Gold & Bronze Mdlst 84 & 86; Geneseo; Comp Sci.

RUSS, GLENN A; Unatego Central Schl; Otego, NY; (Y); Am Leg Boys St; Boy Scts; Drama Clb; Varsity Clb; Stage Crew; Yrbk Phtg; Yrbk Stf; Var Bsktbl; Var Ftbl; Hon Roll; Navy; Data Proc.

RUSSELL, AMY B; Whitesboro SR HS; Whitesboro, NY; (Y); 21/354; Church Yth Grp; Mathletes; Intnl Clb; High Hon Roll; Hon Roll; Jr NHS; NHS; Engrng.

RUSSELL, ANDY; Ticonderoga HS; Ticonderoga, NY; (Y); 2/110; Trs Latin Clb; Rep Stu Cncl; Var L Bsktbl; Var L Crs Cntry; JV Ftbl; Var L Trk; High Hon Roll; NHS; Ntl Merit Ltr; US Military Acad; Engrng.

RUSSELL, BONNIE S; Westbury SR HS; Westbury, NY; (Y); 9/210; Pres Red Cross Aide; SADD; Orch; Yrbk Ed-Chief; Sec Frsh Cls; Var Badmtn; Var Tennis; High Hon Roll; Kiwanis Awd; NHS; Sci.

RUSSELL, BRIAN; Westmoreland Central HS; Westmoreland, NY; (Y); Debate Tm; Math Clb; Model UN; Var Ftbl; High Hon Roll; Hon Roll; CPA.

RUSSELL, CHRISTINE H; Mohonasen SR HS; Schenectady, NY; (Y); Art Clb; Drama Clb; Pres JA; Spanish Clb; School Play; Nwsp Rptr; Hon Roll; NHS; Prfct Atten JA 83-84 & 84-85.

RUSSELL, D TODD; Frontier Central HS; Lakeview, NY; (Y); 49/450; Pres German Clb; Pres Science Clb; Varsity Clb; Rep Sr Cls; Rep Stu Cncl; Var L Socr; Hon Roll; NHS; Germn Clb Scholar 86; Mt Union Coll; Pre-Med.

RUSSELL, DAVID L; Walton Central Schl; Walton, NY; (Y); 3/120; Am Leg Boys St; Pres Church Yth Grp; Pres Sec 4-H; Pres FFA; Concert Band; Jazz Band; Mrchg Band; 4-H Awd; High Hon Roll; NHS; FFA Awds 82-86; Dr A F Peck Schlrshp 86; Cornell U; Anml Sci.

RUSSELL, DIANNA; Mynderse Acad; Seneca Falls, NY; (S); 11/141; Church Yth Grp; Drama Clb; FHA; Pep Clb; Band; Chorus; Church Choir; Color Guard; Concert Band; Jazz Band; English.

RUSSELL, DONNA; Parishville-Hopkinton Central HS; Parishville, NY; (S); 4/45; Chorus; Variety Show; Hon Roll; NHS; Potsdam ST; Lib Arts.

RUSSELL III, GEORGE J; Shenendehowa Central HS; Clifton Park, NY; (Y); 199/650; Hon Roll; Outstndng Schlstc Achvt Yr 83-84; Schlstc Achvt Outstdng Avg Yr 84-85; Vet.

RUSSELL, HENRY J; St Anthonys HS; Pt Jeff Stat, NY; (Y); 99/240; Nwsp Rptr; Yrbk Stf; JV Var Crs Cntry; Var Trk; French Hon Soc; NHS; Track League Cty Champ 86; Henry Russell Awd Cross Cty 83; St Bunaventure U; Mass Comm.

RUSSELL, HOPE; Dominican Commercial HS; Cambria Hts, NY; (S); Church Yth Grp; Girl Scts; Teachers Aide; Hon Roll; Kiwanis Awd.

RUSSELL, JANE; Brushton-Moira Central HS; Brushton, NY; (Y); 1/66; 4-H; Hosp Aide; SADD; Band; Yrbk Ed-Chief; Rep Stu Cncl; 4-H Awd; NHS; Church Choir; Ntl Hnr Soc Awd 84; Radiolgc Technlgst.

RUSSELL, JESSICA; Salmon River Central HS; Ft Covington, NY; (Y); 4/96; Church Yth Grp; French Clb; Band; Concert Band; Yrbk Stf; Trs Stu Cncl; Ice Hcky; Socr; Trk; Hon Roll; Am Musical Ambsdr 84; Natl Prsbytrn Yth Triennium 83; Millikin U Schlrshp 86; Natl Presbyterian Schlr; Millikin U; Physcl Thrpy.

RUSSELL, JODI; Mechanicville HS; Mechanicville, NY; (S); 11/92; Church Yth Grp; Ski Clb; Spanish Clb; SADD; Varsity Clb; Concert Band; Yrbk Sprt Ed; Trs Frsh Cls; Trs Soph Cls; Var Socr; Omega Hnr Soc 84-85; Alpha Hnr Soc 85-86; Engrng.

RUSSELL, JOHN; Tottenville HS; Staten Island, NY; (Y); 29/700; Model UN; Science Clb; Teachers Aide; School Musical; Stage Crew; Lit Mag; Pres Jr Cls; Trs Sr Cls; Stu Cncl; Jr NHS; U Buffalo; Arch Engrng.

RUSSELL, JOHN B; Vestal Central Schl; Vestal, NY; (Y); 196/430; Varsity Clb; Var Socr; Var Trk; Var Wrstlng; Hon Roll; NYS Rgnts Schlrshp 86; Broome CC; Comp Sci.

RUSSELL, KELLEY SUZANNE; Eden SR HS; Eden, NY; (Y); 22/160; Pres Band; School Musical; Trs Frsh Cls; Sec Jr Cls; Pres Sr Cls; Sec Stu Cncl; Var L Cheerleading; Hon Roll; JP Sousa Awd; NHS; NY ST Regnts Schlrshp 86; EDEN Tchrs Assn Schlrshp 86; Stu Council Svc Awd 86; SYC Potsdam; Engl.

RUSSELL, LAURA; St Joseph By-The-Sea HS; Staten Island, NY; (Y); 6/285; Church Yth Grp; Dance Clb; Hosp Aide; Co-Capt Color Guard; Mrchg Band; Yrbk Phtg; Co-Capt Twrlr; High Hon Roll; NHS; 150 Hrs Svc St Vincents Hosp 86; Ushr Mass 85; Dncng Hgh Achvmnt Awd 86; Columbia U; Hstry.

RUSSELL, MICHAEL; Dewitt Clinton HS; Bronx, NY; (Y); Hon Roll; 100 Pct Atten Awd 85.

RUSSELL, MICHELLE A; Salmon River Central HS; Brushton, NY; (Y); Sec French Clb; Chorus; Trs Concert Band; Trs Frsh Cls; Trs Soph Cls; Trs Jr Cls; Trs Sr Cls; VP Stu Cncl; JV Var Cheerleading; French Hon Soc; Biochem.

RUSSELL II, REB; Seton Catholic Central HS; Endwell, NY; (Y); 34/164; Boy Scts; Varsity Clb; Var Capt Ftbl; Var L Wrstlng; All Star Ftbl Offnsv & Defnsv Tackl Vrsty 85; Eagle Scout 83; Military.

RUSSELL, STEVEN; Oxford Academy And Central Schl; Oxford, NY; (Y); FFA; VICA; Bsktbl; Hon Roll; Auto Mech.

RUSSEN, TOM; Horseheads HS; Horseheads, NY; (Y); 4-H; FFA; Nwsp Rptr; 4-H Awd; Cert Of Achvt NY ST Coll/Eclgy 84-85; FFA Forest Awd Tree ID 85-86; Frst Mgmt Awd Weyerhause Co; Consrvtn.

RUSSI, KIMBERLY; Penfield HS; Rochester, NY; (Y); Art Clb; Church Yth Grp; Cmnty Wkr; JA; Chorus; Stage Crew; Off Frsh Cls; Hon Roll; Hnrb Mntn Sibelys Schltc Art Show 86; CC Of Finger Lks; Graphic Art.

RUSSILLO, ANTHONY; Westhampton Beach HS; Westhampton Beach, NY; (Y); Church Yth Grp; French Clb; Spanish Clb; Band; Mrchg Band; School Musical; Ntl Merit Ltr; Var Ftbl; Var Trk; Boy Scts; Ntl Hstry & Govt Awd 86; Brnz Mdl Mth Acad Dcthln 86; Military Acad; Mltry.

RUSSIN, MICHAEL T; Marlboro Central HS; Milton, NY; (Y); 10/150; Church Yth Grp; Varsity Clb; Band; Chorus; Concert Band; Jazz Band; Var Trk; High Hon Roll; Hon Roll; NHS; Sullivan Cnty Comp Cntst 2nd Pl 86; Drexel U; Comp.

RUSSO, ANTHONY E; Mount Saint Michael Acad; Bronx, NY; (Y); 46/292; Art Clb; Computer Clb; Hon Roll; Westchester Bus Inst; Comp Mgmt.

RUSSO, ANTHONY J; Newfield HS; Newfield, NY; (Y); 2/46; Am Leg Boys St; Ski Clb; Varsity Clb; Jazz Band; Rep Stu Cncl; Var Capt Trk; High Hon Roll; Jr NHS; Ntl Merit Ltr; Sal; Slctd Repr HS Albany ST Snt Pol Frm 86; RPI; Engnrng.

RUSSO, CHRISTINA M; St Francis Prep; Jackson Heights, NY; (S); Drama Clb; Library Aide; School Musical; School Play; Stage Crew; Hon Roll; NHS; St Johns U; Chld Psych.

RUSSO, CHRISTINE; The Mary Louis Acad; Flushing, NY; (Y); GAA; Hosp Aide; Office Aide; Varsity Clb; Im Bsktbl; Im Gym; Var L Swmmng; Im Vllybl; Hon Roll; Mdl For Swmng 84.

RUSSO, DEAN; Savgerties JR SR HS; W Camp, NY; (Y); 13/250; Am Leg Boys St; VP German Clb; Math Tm; Ski Clb; Symp Band; JV Var Socr; High Hon Roll; NHS; Rep Frsh Cls; Rotary Clb Intl Scholar Camp; Engrng.

RUSSO, DONNA; St Edmund HS; Brooklyn, NY; (Y); 30/145; Art Clb; Hosp Aide; Office Aide; Yrbk Stf; Trs Frsh Cls; JV Bsktbl; JV Sftbl; High Hon Roll; NYS Rgnts Schlrshp 86-91; Presdntl Acadmc Ftns Awd 86; Lond Island U; Pdtrc Physcl Thr.

RUSSO, FRANK; Maryvale HS; Cheektowaga, NY; (Y); 10/300; Church Yth Grp; Im Bsktbl; Im Fld Hcky; JV Ftbl; Var Tennis; Var Trk; Hon Roll; Jr NHS; Acctng.

RUSSO, GABRIELLE; Irongequoit HS; Rochester, NY; (Y); Girl Scts; Latin Clb; Teachers Aide; Score Keeper; Vllybl; Intl Bus.

RUSSO, JON; Romulus Central HS; Romulus, NY; (S); 1/70; Soroptimist; Band; Concert Band; Jazz Band; Var L Ftbl; Bausch & Lomb Sci Awd; High Hon Roll; Trs NHS; Am Leg Boys St; Cmnty Wkr; Cornell Smmr Coll $1500 Schlrshp 86; Hghst Clss Achvmnt Awd 84-86; Math Awd 86; Cornell; Chem Engr.

RUSSO, JOSEPHINE; Port Richmond HS; Staten Island, NY; (Y); Chorus; Cit Awd; Hon Roll; St Johns U; Insurance.

RUSSO, JOSEPHINE S; White Plains HS; White Plns, NY; (Y); 4-H; Math Tm; Pep Clb; VP Stu Cncl; Capt Cheerleading; High Hon Roll; NHS; French Clb; Varsity Clb; Var L Gym; Med.

RUSSO, KIMBERLY M; Immaculata Acad; Lake View, NY; (Y); Church Yth Grp; Dance Clb; FNA; Girl Scts; JA; Latin Clb; Spanish Clb; Varsity Clb; Nwsp Rptr; Cheerleading; U Buffalo; Sci.

RUSSO, KRISTIN; St Marys Girls HS; Pt Washington, NY; (Y); 6/180; Dance Clb; Math Clb; Ski Clb; Spanish Clb; School Musical; Nwsp Rptr; Nwsp Stf; High Hon Roll; NHS; Ntl Merit SF; Iona ST Lang Contst-1st Hnrs 85 & 86; Latin Contst-Cum Laude 85; HS Bowl Rep-C W Post 86; Accntng.

RUSSO, LAURA; Hauppauge HS; Hauppage, NY; (S); 13/491; Church Yth Grp; DECA; Varsity Clb; Orch; Var Bsktbl; Var Capt Sftbl; Var Capt Tennis; Var Trk; High Hon Roll; NHS; HS Schlr Athlete Awd 86; Suffolk Cnty Gold Key Awd 86; Presdntl Schlrshp 86; Villanova U; Clinical Psych.

RUSSO, LOUIS P; Ft Edward Union Free HS; Ft Edward, NY; (Y); 1/44; Yrbk Bus Mgr; VP Frsh Cls; Trs Jr Cls; Im Bsktbl; Var Capt Ftbl; Var Trk; Im Wt Lftg; Bausch & Lomb Sci Awd; Cit Awd; Hon Roll; Moot Ct Tm Capt 85-86; Varsty Clb Pres 85-86; Stu Senate 85; U Of Rochester; Comp Sci.

RUSSO, MARTIN; Regis HS; Middle Village, NY; (Y); Computer Clb; Ski Clb; Capt Var Socr; Ntl Merit Schol; 4 Yr Schlrshp; Ordr Of The Owl; Natl Hispnc Schlr Awds; Corp Law.

RUSSO, NANCY; Academy Of The Resurrection HS; Port Chester, NY; (Y); 1/82; Dance Clb; Math Clb; Chorus; School Musical; Yrbk Stf; High Hon Roll; Ntl Merit Ltr; NYS Regents Schlrshp 86; Tuland U Schlrshp 86; Tulane U; Languages.

RUSSO, PAM; Pelham Memorial HS; Pelham, NY; (Y); AFS; 4-H; JA; SADD; Fshn Inst; Mrchndsng.

RUSSO, RON; G Ray Bodley HS; Fulton, NY; (Y); Church Yth Grp; Mrchg Band; JV Var Bsbl; JV Bsktbl; Hon Roll; Music.

RUSSO, ROSA; West Hempstead HS; West Hempstead, NY; (Y); Hon Roll; Bus.

RUSSO, SALVATORE; Greater New York Acad; Brooklyn, NY; (S); Church Yth Grp; Nwsp Rptr; Nwsp Sprt Ed; Yrbk Sprt Ed; Trs Jr Cls; Im Bowling; Var Sftbl; Im Vllybl; Hon Roll; NHS; Cooper Union Coll; Comp Engr.

RUSSO, SEAN P; Johnstown HS; Johnstown, NY; (Y); Political Wkr; Band; Var L Crs Cntry; Var L Swmmng; High Hon Roll; NHS; Ntl Merit Ltr; Quiz Bowl; Concert Band; Jazz Band; Englsh & Soc Stds Awds, Sci Awd, 1st Yr Comp Prz 84-86; Mst Imprvd Swmmr, Mst Dedctd Swmmr 84-86; Finc.

RUSSO, STEPHEN; Monsignor Farrell HS; Staten Island, NY; (Y); 2/319; Church Yth Grp; Spanish Clb; Concert Band; Jazz Band; Yrbk Stf; Rep Frsh Cls; Stu Cncl; Hon Roll; NHS; Hugh O Brien Yth Fndtn 85; Law.

RUSSO, SUSAN A; St Catharine Acad; Bronx, NY; (Y); Cmnty Wkr; Teachers Aide; Nwsp Ed-Chief; NHS; Regents Schlrshp 86; Hugh O Brian Yth Fndtn 84; Mt St Vincent Coll; Scndry Ed.

RUSSO, THOMAS P; Arlington HS; Poughkeepsie, NY; (Y); 17/570; VP French Clb; Math Tm; SADD; Nwsp Rptr; Yrbk Stf; Lit Mag; Ntl Merit Ltr; NY ST Regents Schlrp 86; Arlington H S Hnr Key 86; Boston U; Jrnlsm.

RUSSOM, JEFFREY; Mechanicville HS; Mechanicville, NY; (S); 14/105; VP Band; Concert Band; Mrchg Band; Symp Band; Yrbk Phtg; Yrbk Stf; Bsbl; High Hon Roll; Hon Roll; NHS; Skidmore Coll Awd; Alfa, Omega & Aristoi Hnr Soc; NE Music Festvl; Rochester Inst Tech; Photogrphy.

RUTH, KAREN A; Liverpool HS; Liverpool, NY; (Y); 96/816; Church Yth Grp; JA; SADD; Chorus; Church Choir; School Musical; Im Bowling; High Hon Roll; Hon Roll; NHS; NYS Regnts Schlrshp 86; ST U Of NY Oswego; Chem.

RUTH, TIM; Oakfield-Alabama Central Schl; Basom, NY; (Y); Var L Bsbl; Var L Bsktbl; Var L Ftbl; MVP Sectnl Bsbll Gm 84; MVP Sectnl Bsbll Game 86.

RUTIGLIANO, JAMES; Sachem North HS; Holtsville, NY; (Y); 112/1330; Art Clb; Science Clb; Ski Clb; Spanish Clb; Wt Lftg; NY Rgnts Schlrshp 86; ST U At Stny Brk.

RUTIGLIANO, TOM; Smithtown HS West; St James, NY; (Y); Computer Clb; German Clb; Mathletes; Math Tm; Ntl Merit SF; Cooper Union; Engrng.

RUTKOSKE, THERESE; St John The Baptist HS; E Islip, NY; (Y); Church Yth Grp; GAA; Political Wkr; Church Choir; Bsktbl; Sftbl; Hon Roll; St Josephs Patchogue; Chld Stdy.

RUTKOWSKI, COLLEEN A; St Anthonys HS; Huntington, NY; (Y); Church Yth Grp; Ftbl; Trk; Hon Roll; NEDT Awd; NY ST Rgnts Schlrshp; SUNY Stnybrk; Vtrnrn.

RUTKOWSKI, MARIA; Ticonderoga HS; Ticonderoga, NY; (Y); 4/112; Church Yth Grp; FCA; Pres VP 4-H; Key Clb; Sec SADD; Chorus; VP Stu Cncl; Var Crs Cntry; Var Trk; NHS; Chem Engrng.

RUTKOWSKI, RICHARD; Springville Griffith Institute HS; West Falls, NY; (Y); 14/196; 4-H; Chorus; School Musical; Symp Band; Var Crs Cntry; Var Trk; 4-H Awd; NHS; SADD; Hugh O Brian Yth Ldrshp Rep 84; St Bonaventure; Math.

RUTLAND, CHERYL; Jamestown HS; Jamestown, NY; (Y); Nwsp Stf; SADD; Chorus; Bsktbl; Geneva Coll; Elem Educ.

RUTLEDGE, PATTY; Hugh C Williams HS; Canton, NY; (Y); Sec 4-H; FNA; Library Aide; Teachers Aide; Mgr(s); Var JV Socr; JV Vllybl; 4-H Awd; CCBI; Bus.

RUTSCH, ALEXANDRA; Pelham Memorial HS; Pelham, NY; (Y); Art Clb; Hosp Aide; Yrbk Stf; Trs Frsh Cls; Sec Soph Cls; Chrmn Jr Cls; Stu Cncl; JV Bsktbl; JV Lcrss; JV Vllybl; Schl Vis Arts NYC; Comm Art.

RUTTER, MARIE; Bishop Ford C C HS; Brooklyn, NY; (Y); Cmnty Wkr; Drama Clb; School Play; Stage Crew; Bowling; Sftbl; Swmmng; Trk; Vllybl; Hon Roll; 1st & 2nd Hnrs 85-86; Brkln Coll.

RUTZ, DAVID; Mynderse Acad; Seneca Falls, NY; (S); 22/138; Church Yth Grp; JV Bsbl; JV Var Bsktbl; Var Golf; High Hon Roll; Hon Roll; Block M Sports Clb 85-86.

RUVOLO, KRISTINA MARIE; Our Lady Of Perpetual Help; Brooklyn, NY; (Y); 15/155; Drama Clb; Pres Intnl Clb; Chorus; School Musical; School Play; Nwsp Stf; Yrbk Ed-Chief; Pres Soph Cls; Sec Sr Cls; High Hon Roll; Dist Atty Elizabeth Holtzman Citatn Hnr 86; Religion Awd Excllnce 86; Brooklyn Coll; Theatre.

RUWET, DIANE; Auburn HS; Auburn, NY; (Y); Var L Golf; Var L Swmmng; JV Var Vllybl; High Hon Roll; Hon Roll; CPA.

RUZEWSKI, ROBERT M; Cheektowaga Central HS; Cheektowaga, NY; (Y); 29/199; Church Yth Grp; Cmnty Wkr; Var L Ftbl; Wt Lftg; Regents Coll Schlrshp; Merit Roll; Erie CC; Elec Engr.

RUZZIER, GINA; Farmingdale HS; Farmingdale, NY; (Y); Dance Clb; Drama Clb; Chorus; School Musical; School Play; Stage Crew; Swing Chorus; Hon Roll; NHS; NYSSNA Ensmbl Awd 86; Drm.

RYAN, ALICIA; Mount Vernon HS; Mt Vernon, NY; (Y); 34/600; Dance Clb; Girl Scts; Library Aide; Nwsp Stf; Bucknell U; Med Tech.

RYAN, AMY O; Corning-Painted Post East HS; Corning, NY; (Y); 8/221; Chrmn Am Leg Aux Girls St; Letterman Clb; School Play; Ed Yrbk Rptr; Pres Sr Cls; Capt Bsktbl; High Hon Roll; NHS; Ntl Merit Ltr; Rotary Awd; Full Tuition Scholar George WA U 86; Regents Scholar 86; George WA U; Jrnlsm.

RYAN, DANIEL J; Batavia HS; Batavia, NY; (Y); 14/205; AFS; Am Leg Boys St; Ftbl; Hon Roll.

RYAN, DEIRDRE; Our Lady Of Victory Acad; Yonkers, NY; (S); 9/128; French Clb; SADD; Lit Mag; Tennis; French Hon Soc; NHS; Rlgn Awd 83-84; Social Stud Awd 84-85.

RYAN, DIANE; Johnstown HS; Johnstown, NY; (Y); Church Yth Grp; Band; Concert Band; Mrchg Band; Variety Show; Stat Bsktbl; Var Crs Cntry; JV Var Trk; Physch.

RYAN, GARY; Hoosic Valley Central HS; Johnsonville, NY; (Y); Church Yth Grp; Band; Mrchg Band; JV Var Bsbl; Stat Church Yth Grp; Var Golf; Engrng.

RYAN, JAMES A; Babylon HS; Babylon, NY; (Y); 25/175; Sr Cls; Var JV Bsktbl; Var L Ftbl; Hon Roll; NYS Rgnts Schlrshp Awd 86; Fairfield U; Stk Brkr.

RYAN, JAMES J; Bellport SR HS; Bellport, NY; (Y); Church Yth Grp; French Clb; Ski Clb; Band; Jazz Band; Pep Band; Yrbk Phtg; JV Socr; JV Tennis; Var Trk; NTS Sch Musc Assn 85; NYS Regnts Schlrshp 86; Niagara U; Intl Stu.

RYAN, JULIE; Onondaga Central HS; Nedrow, NY; (S); 3/69; Trs Church Yth Grp; Spanish Clb; Band; Chorus; Rep Stu Cncl; Capt L Crs Cntry; Capt L Trk; High Hon Roll; NHS; Outstndng Spnsh I Stu 82-83; Mst Outstndng Crs Cntry 85-86; Le Moyne Coll; Engrng.

RYAN, KATIE; Saranac Central HS; Saranac, NY; (S); Variety Show; Yrbk Stf; Capt Var Bsktbl; Var L Socr; Var JV Sftbl; Var L Trk; Var JV Vllybl.

RYAN, KELLY; Jordan-Edbridge HS; Weedsport, NY; (Y); 11/130; French Clb; Band; Chorus; Mrchg Band; Yrbk Stf; Im JV Bsktbl; JV Var Computer Clb; Im JV Sftbl; Im JV Vllybl; Hon Roll; All-Leag Slctn-Sccr 84-85; Cayuga Cnty Lgsltr Stu Govt Day 85; Schltc Sci Fair-Hnrb Mntn 82; Physcl Thrpy.

RYAN, KELLY; Lindenhurst SR HS; Lindenhurst, NY; (Y); Spanish Clb; Thesps; School Play; Nwsp Stf; Badmtn; Cmmnctns Arts.

RYAN, LAURA; The Mary Louis Acad; Flushing, NY; (Y); 19/270; Office Aide; Service Clb; Orch; Nwsp Ed-Chief; Vllybl; High Hon Roll; Jr NHS; NHS; St Schlr; 1st Pl Engl Medal 83; Essay Wnnr 83; NY ST Regnts Schlrshp 86; Cornell U; Microbio.

RYAN, MARGARET M; St Johns Acad; Plattsburgh, NY; (Y); 9/38; Am Leg Aux Girls St; Drama Clb; French Clb; Latin Clb; Model UN; Chorus; Yrbk Stf; Socr; High Hon Roll; NHS; Helen Judge Lewis Schlrshp Awd 86-87; AFS Intl & Intercltrl Pgm In Italy 86-87; Intl Rltns.

RYAN, MARY ANNE; Hugh C Williams HS; Canton, NY; (Y); 6/135; Sec Pres Church Yth Grp; Pres Sec 4-H; Capt Var Cheerleading; 4-H Awd; High Hon Roll; NHS; Rotary Awd; Math Tm; SADD; Varsity Clb; Hugh O Brian Yth Ldrshp Awd 85; Congress Dbundestag Frgn Exch Pgm SF, St Lawrence U Part-Time Schlr; Sci.

RYAN, MICHAEL; Spackenkill HS; Poughkeepsie, NY; (Y); 75/200; Var Bsbl; Var Bsktbl; Football All-Cntry 85; Comp Engrnr.

RYAN, MICHELE; Mohonasen HS; Schenectady, NY; (Y); Band; Concert Band; Mrchg Band; Stu Cncl; JV Cheerleading; Pom Pon; Hon Roll; Actvy Prldr Orgnztn 85-86; Cmptv Rllr Sktg In NE Rgn; Bus Mgmt.

RYAN, MICHELLE D; Brockport HS; Hamlin, NY; (Y); Cmnty Wkr; Ski Clb; High Hon Roll; St Schlr; Buffalo ST U; Psychlgy.

RYAN, MITCH; Marlboro HS; Newburgh, NY; (Y); Wt Lftg; Hon Roll; Math.

RYAN, PATRICIA A; St Joseph Hill Acad; Staten Island, NY; (Y); 1/106; Dance Clb; Trs Drama Clb; NFL; Capt Speech Tm; Yrbk Rptr; French Hon Soc; Pres NHS; Ntl Merit SF; Val; Church Yth Grp; Cntry III NY ST Fnlst 85-86; NY Regents Schlrshp 86; Concours I Frnch Awd 8 4-85.

RYAN, ROBERT W; Mount St Michael Acad; Bronx, NY; (Y); Boys Clb Am; Church Yth Grp; Var JV Bsktbl; Cit Awd; Regents Schlrshp 86; Cardinal Spellman Yth Awd 85; Baruch Coll; Bus.

RYAN, SALLY; Nardin Acad; Orchard Park, NY; (Y); French Clb; Ski Clb; School Play; Stage Crew; Lit Mag; Rep Stu Cncl; High Hon Roll; NHS; Trk; Hon Roll; Exch Stu Denmark Wth Schlrp 85; Schlrp To Nardin Acad 83; Intl Rltns.

RYAN, STEVEN; Kenmore East SR HS; Tonawanda, NY; (Y); Cmnty Wkr; Hosp Aide; Pep Clb; Varsity Clb; Nwsp Rptr; Socr; Tennis; High Hon Roll; NHS; Ntl Merit Schol; West Point Military Acad.

RYAN III, THOMAS VINCENT; Walter Panas HS; Peekskill, NY; (Y); 2/240; Exploring; FBLA; SADD; Rep Frsh Cls; Trs Jr Cls; Var Golf; Var Swmmng; High Hon Roll; NHS; Ntl Merit Ltr; Var Swmmng All Div II Hnrb Mntn 86; Engrng.

RYAN, TIMOTHY J; Canajoharie HS; Canajoharie, NY; (Y); Am Leg Boys St; Band; Mrchg Band; Yrbk Ed-Chief; Bsktbl; Ftbl; Trk; Hon Roll; Jr NHS; NHS; Engrg.

RYAN, WALTER; Scotia-Glenville HS; Scotia, NY; (Y); Camera Clb; Drama Clb; Key Clb; Ski Clb; Yrbk Phtg; JV Crs Cntry; Var L Trk; Ltr Trk 85-86; Blk Blt 85; Brnz Mdl Judo 86; Hofstray; Cmmrcl Art.

RYBITSKI, JOHN; Colonie Central HS; Albany, NY; (Y); Band; Concert Band; Jazz Band; Symp Band; Im Bsbl; JV Lcrss; JV Var Wrstlng; Wilkes Coll; Med Tech.

RYDER, LINDA; Lynbrook HS; Lynbrook, NY; (Y); Lit Mag; Hon Roll; SUNY Buffalo; Arch.

RYDER, MAUREEN ELIZABETH; Newfield HS; Selden, NY; (Y); 169/515; Cmnty Wkr; VP SADD; Chorus; School Musical; Coach Actv; Fld Hcky; Mgr(s); T M Laudicina Awd 82; SUNY; Eco.

RYDZEWSKI, JOHN; Massena Central HS; Massena, NY; (Y); 25/230; Aud/Vis; Hon Roll; Clarkson Coll; Chmcl Engrng.

RYLANCE, JENNY; Kingston HS; Kingston, NY; (Y); Pres Key Clb; Ski Clb; Chorus; Stu Cncl; JV Cheerleading; Elmira Coll.

RYMARCHYK, GRETCHEN; La Fayette Central HS; Jamesville, NY; (Y); 7/93; Art Clb; Ski Clb; Spanish Clb; Varsity Clb; Chorus; School Musical; Yrbk Stf; Socr; High Hon Roll; St Schlr; Pres Acad Fit Awd 86; John P Mc Daniel Awd & Princpls Awd 86; Natl MONY Art Cont Hnrb Mntn 83 & 86; Hofstra U; Biochem.

RYNER JR, STEPHEN; Paul D Schreiber HS; Port Washington, NY; (Y); Art Clb; Latin Clb; Mathletes; NHS; Ntl Merit Ltr; Comp Sci.

RYNGWALSKI, ANDREA; Villa Maria Acad HS; Buffalo, NY; (S); 6/105; Computer Clb; SADD; Pres Sr Cls; Rep Stu Cncl; Bowling; Gym; High Hon Roll; VP NHS; Prfct Atten Awd; Spec Mnstr Eucharst 86; Lector 85-86; Chrch Yth Grp 85; Canisius Coll; Pre-Med.

RYS, AUDRA; Catholic Central HS; Latham, NY; (Y); German Clb; Math Clb; Trs SADD; Chorus; School Musical; School Play; Yrbk Stf; High Hon Roll; Hon Roll; NHS; Accptnc Into The NY St Smmr Schl Of Arts 86; Excllnc In Art 85; Excllnc In Engl 86; Art Edu.

RYS, NANCY; West Seneca West SR HS; West Seneca, NY; (S); 13/559; DECA; Yrbk Stf; JC Awd; Jr NHS; Asst Principals Awd 83; Accntng.

RYSEDORPH, TROY T; Columbia HS; Nassau, NY; (Y); Am Leg Boys St; Sec Church Yth Grp; Debate Tm; Scholastic Bowl; Nwsp Rptr; Nwsp Stf; JV Socr; JV Trk; Var Vllybl; High Hon Roll; Rnslr Poly Tech Inst Math & Sci Awd 85-86; Grmn Slvr Awd 85-86; Engrng.

RYSZKA, LISA; Mount Mercy Acad; W Seneca, NY; (Y); 28/168; Computer Clb; Quiz Bowl; Spanish Clb; SADD; Nwsp Rptr; Nwsp Stf; Im Bowling; Hon Roll; NY ST Regnts Schlrshp Awd 85-86; Presdntl Acadmc Ftns Awd 86; ST U Of NY; Phrmcy.

RZEPKA, JENNIFER; Whitesboro SR HS; Whitesboro, NY; (Y); 26/306; GAA; Ski Clb; Chorus; Stage Crew; Yrbk Stf; Stu Cncl; Fld Hcky; Sftbl; Jr NHS; NHS.

RZESZOT, DAWN; Villa Maria Acad; Buffalo, NY; (Y); Dance Clb; Girl Scts; Chorus; Church Choir; Gym; Trvl Trsm.

RZESZOT, RANDI; Vestal SR HS; Apalachin, NY; (Y); Boys Clb Am; Varsity Clb; Var Crs Cntry; Score Keeper; Var Trk; Wrstlng; High Hon Roll; Hon Roll; Prfct Atten Awd; Mech Engrg.

RZEZNIK, LAWRENCE; Amsterdam HS; Hagaman, NY; (Y); 45/350; Varsity Clb; Yrbk Stf; Trs Frsh Cls; Sec Sr Cls; Bsbl; Bsktbl; Crs Cntry; Trk; Hon Roll; SUNY Geneseo; Bio.

RZUCIDLO, KEVIN; Mc Kee Tech HS; Staten Island, NY; (Y); Off Stu Cncl; Mech Engrng.

SAAR, CHRISTINE; E Hampton HS; E Hampton, NY; (Y); SADD; Stu Cncl; Var Tennis; Var Trk; Hon Roll; Ntl Merit Ltr; Psych.

SAAR, JAMES; Susquehanna Valley HS; Conklin, NY; (Y); Church Yth Grp; Drama Clb; Quiz Bowl; Stage Crew; Var Capt Bowling; Var Ftbl; Hon Roll; All Star Sftbll Team 85; NYS Athletic Assn Awd 86; English.

SABADOS, PETER; Msgr Farrell HS; Staten Island, NY; (S); Aud/Vis; Service Clb; Im Bsbl; Im Bsktbl; Im Bowling; Im Ftbl; Im Sftbl; High Hon Roll; NHS; Pharm.

SABATINE, MARC S; The Dalton Schl; New York, NY; (Y); Chess Clb; Debate Tm; Model UN; Nwsp Ed-Chief; Rep Stu Cncl; Im Fld Hcky; Ntl Merit SF; Bst Dely Harvard Mod U N 84; Sci.

SABATINE, MARNIE; Bloomfield Central Schl; Victor, NY; (Y); 4/104; Concert Band; Jazz Band; Mrchg Band; JV Var Trk; Bausch & Lomb Sci Awd; NHS; 4-H; Latin Clb; School Musical; Yrbk Stf; Mth.

SABATINO, JOSEPH; Babylon HS; Babylon, NY; (Y); Math Tm; Bsbl; Bsktbl; Lcrss; Var Capt Socr; Var Tennis; Hon Roll; Spnsh Awd 83-84; All League 2nd Team In Soccer 84 & 85; Smr Pltcl Sci Crs 84.

SABETT, SARA; Niagara Catholic HS; Niagara Fls, NY; (Y); Church Yth Grp; Civic Clb; Drama Clb; Chorus; Yrbk Stf; Feder Schl Clsscl Ballet Full Schlrshp 85; Central PA Ballet; Prof Stage.

SABIN, TODD A; Southside HS; Elmira, NY; (Y); 1/325; Chess Clb; Latin Clb; Ski Clb; NHS; Val; Boy Scts; Church Yth Grp; Band; High Hon Roll; Rgnts Coll Schlrshp, Empire St Schlrsh Exclnce, U Hnr Schlr SUNY Buffalo 86; Alpha Sigma Hnr Soc; SUNY Buffalo; Elec Engrng.

SABINO, REGINA; Malverne HS; Lynbrook, NY; (Y); 22/121; Key Clb; Varsity Clb; Nwsp Rptr; Nwsp Stf; JV Var Cheerleading; Cit Awd; Hon Roll; Jr NHS; Kiwanis Awd; Cmmnctns.

SABIO, IVAN; John Dewey HS; Brooklyn, NY; (Y); Boy Scts; Computer Clb; Science Clb; Pre-Med.

SABLICH, CARMELA; St Johns Prep; Astoria, NY; (Y); Hon Roll; NHS; Prfct Atten Awd; St Jhns U; Bus.

SABO, CHRISTIE; Mount Mercy Acad; W Seneca, NY; (Y); Computer Clb; French Clb; Science Clb; SADD; Nwsp Rptr; Nwsp Stf; High Hon Roll; Hon Roll; VP NHS; Sci Fair Awd Hnr Mntn 85; Bst Nws Stry Schl Ppr 86; Hofstra U; Intl Bus.

SABO, JOSHUA A; Columbia HS; Troy, NY; (Y); 36/417; Math Tm; Model UN; Political Wkr; Temple Yth Grp; Var Capt Socr; Var Trk; Hon Roll; NHS; Ntl Merit SF.

SABOL, ANDREW B; Waterville Central Schl; Waterville, NY; (Y); 3/90; Mathletes; Pep Clb; Ski Clb; Nwsp Stf; Yrbk Stf; VP Sr Cls; Socr; High Hon Roll; NHS; Ntl Merit SF; Physcn.

SABOL, JEFF; Waterville Central Schl; Waterville, NY; (Y); Mathletes; Pep Clb; Ski Clb; Varsity Clb; Chorus; School Musical; Rep Stu Cncl; Socr; Tennis; High Hon Roll; Altrnt Boys ST 86; Physcl Sci.

SABOL, JOSEPH E; Baldwin HS; Baldwin, NY; (Y); Mathletes; Varsity Clb; Var Capt Wrstlng; St Schlr; NYS Regnts Schlrshp 86; Outstndng Wrstlr 86; E Regnl Greco Wrstlng Champ 86; Bus.

SABOL, MICAH; Pine View Christian Acad; Gansevoort, NY; (S); #1 In Class; Chess Clb; Church Yth Grp; Ski Clb; Band; Chorus; Yrbk Bus Mgr; Yrbk Ed-Chief; Socr; Trk; Cert Cmpltn Bng Teen Mssnry Astria 84; Gordon Coll; Psychlhy.

SABON, SUZANNE; Christ The King R HS; Brooklyn, NY; (Y); Yrbk Stf.

SACCARO, JACQUELINE; Whitestone Acad; Bayside, NY; (S); 2/30; Nwsp Stf; Yrbk Stf; Slvr Mdl Algbr II, Chem, Typng, Calculus, Engl 12 85-86; Clss Slttrn 86; St Johns U; Bus.

SACCO, DEANNA; John F Kennedy HS; Utica, NY; (Y); Key Clb; Rep Stu Cncl; JV Sftbl; Hon Roll; SUNY Oswego; Bus Mgmt.

SACCOMANNO, JOHN J; West Seneca HS; West Seneca, NY; (Y); 53/375; Chess Clb; Jazz Band; School Musical; Im Bsktbl; Im JV Ftbl; JV Var Trk; Hon Roll; St Schlr; NYS Regnts Schlrshp 86; U Of Buffalo; Arch.

SACCOMANNO, KRISTA; Sacred Heart Acad; Floral Park, NY; (Y); Cmnty Wkr; FNA; Hosp Aide; Office Aide; SADD; Chorus; Tennis; Nrsng.

SACHER, ANDY; Saugerties HS; Saugerties, NY; (S); Church Yth Grp; FCA; German Clb; Latin Clb; Math Tm; School Play; JV Var Socr; Marine Bio.

SACHS, LAURA; Waterville Central HS; Waterville, NY; (Y); French Clb; Mathletes; Band; Sec Chorus; Concert Band; Jazz Band; Mrchg Band; School Musical; Swing Chorus; Yrbk Stf; Prmry Educ.

SACKETT, KAREN; Honeoye-Falls Lima HS; Lima, NY; (S); 11/160; VP Sec 4-H; Sec Pep Clb; Trs Band; Concert Band; Mrchg Band; School Musical; Nwsp Stf; 4-H Awd; High Hon Roll; NHS; All-Cnty & Area All-State Bands; Band Lttr; All-Amer Hall Of Fame Band Hnrs; GMI; Bus.

SACKEY, ALLYSON M; Louis D Brandeis HS; Bronx, NY; (Y); 1/544; Nwsp Rptr; Nwsp Stf; High Hon Roll; NHS; Ntl Merit SF; Val; Arista 85; Bus.

SACKS, STEVEN; Spring Valley SR HS; Spring Vly, NY; (Y); 88/441; Key Clb; Ski Clb; SADD; Sec Temple Yth Grp; Chorus; School Play; Stage Crew; JV Tennis; Hon Roll; Regents Schlrshp 85-86; U Of Buffalo; Engrng.

SACZYNSKI, MICHELLE; North Rose-Wolcott HS; Wolcott, NY; (Y); Red Cross Aide; Varsity Clb; Yrbk Stf; Trs Frsh Cls; Rep Frsh Cls; Mgr(s); JV Var Socr; High Hon Roll; NHS; Syracuse U; Cvl Engrng.

SADDLEMIRE, WILLIAM; Roy C Ketcham HS; Poughkeepsie, NY; (Y); Var Bsbl; Var Ftbl; VA Wesleyan Coll; Bus.

SADDLIER, PAIGE; Cardinal Spellman HS; Bronx, NY; (Y); Cmnty Wkr; Dance Clb; French Clb; Hosp Aide; Pep Clb; Swmmng; Dictaphone Corp Schlrshp 86; Regents Schlrshp 86; SUNY Stonybrook; Med.

SADLER, CHRISTOPHER B; Hamburg SR HS; Hamburg, NY; (Y); 12/390; Model UN; Madrigals; Orch; School Musical; Symp Band; Yrbk Ed-Chief; Yrbk Stf; High Hon Roll; NHS; Pres Schlr; NY ST Rgnts Schlrshp 86; Ithaca Coll; Orchstrl Mngmnt.

SADLER, TRACY; Msgr Scanlan HS; New York, NY; (Y); 13/257; Church Yth Grp; Cmnty Wkr; Intnl Clb; Spanish Clb; Hon Roll; NHS; Brnx Dist Attrnys Awd 86; Antmy & Physlgy 86; Acctg 86; Binghamton-SUNY; Psychlgy.

SADLON, BARBARA; Little Falls JR SR HS; Little Falls, NY; (Y); 14/96; Pres Church Yth Grp; FTA; GAA; Band; Concert Band; Mrchg Band; Orch; High Hon Roll; NHS; SUNY Coll Oneonta; Elem Educ.

SADOFSKY, ALYSON J; Walter Panas HS; Peekskill, NY; (Y); 3/220; Drama Clb; French Clb; Pres Hst FBLA; Political Wkr; Sec SADD; School Play; Yrbk Stf; Sec Frsh Cls; Sec Soph Cls; Sec Jr Cls; Fnlst Otstndng Yng Nw Yrkr 85; U Of PA; Fin.

SAEZ, MICHELE; Port Richmond HS; Staten Island, NY; (Y); SADD; Temple Yth Grp; School Musical; Yrbk Stf; Pres Stu Cncl; Cheerleading; Hon Roll.

SAFARIK, IRENE M; Academy Of St Joseph; Huntington, NY; (Y); Church Yth Grp; Cmnty Wkr; Girl Scts; Hosp Aide; Red Cross Aide; Trs Frsh Cls; JV Capt Bsktbl; Coach Actv; Var Mgr(s); Socr; Spnsh Achvt Awd; Mst Imprvd Vrsty Socr Plyr; George Mason U; Intl Stds.

SAFEER, SANDI G; Hawthorne Cedar Knolls HS; Brooklyn, NY; (Y); 1/47; Yrbk Stf; Stu Cncl; Bsktbl; Sftbl; Swmmng; Vllybl; Pres Schlr; Unit Dir Awd 85; Renee Hessel Mem Awd Math 85; SF Ntl Hispnc Schlr Awd 86; Buffalo U; Acctng.

SAGE, KELLY; Salamanca JR SR HS; Salamanca, NY; (Y); Office Aide; Capt Color Guard; Mrchg Band; Yrbk Stf; Twrlr; Olean Business Inst; Secy.

SAGE, MARK; Huntington HS; Huntington, NY; (Y); Key Clb; Mathletes; SADD; Ftbl; Golf; Hon Roll; Engr.

SAGER, TRINA; Valley Central HS; Newburgh, NY; (Y); Variety Show; Vllybl; Jr NHS; NHS; VP Spanish NHS; Spanish.

SAGESSER, MARY; Lindenhurst SR HS; Lindenhurst, NY; (Y); Spanish Clb; JV Bsktbl; JV Var Sftbl; Hon Roll; NHS; 2nd Prz Fire Dept Easy Cntst 85.

SAHA, JOLLY; Clarkstown North HS; Congers, NY; (Y); Cmnty Wkr; Hon Roll; Bst Fgr 86; SUNY Albany; Crmnl Law.

SAHM, PETER; Onondaga HS; Syracuse, NY; (S); Trs German Clb; Band; Jazz Band; Rep Stu Cncl; Var Trk; High Hon Roll; Hon Roll; NHS; RIT; Elec Engrng.

SAIKKONEN, CAROLYN; Spencer-Van Etten JR SR HS; Spencer, NY; (Y); 8/87; Art Clb; Pep Clb; SADD; Chorus; Rep Sr Cls; Rep Stu Cncl; JV Var Cheerleading; High Hon Roll; NHS; Alfred ST Clg; Acctg.

SAINT, TANIA; Evander Childs HS; Bronx, NY; (Y); Chorus; Symp Band; Big E Clb Prfct Attndnc For Sem 85-86; Symphnc Band; Syracuse U; Music.

SAINT JUSTE, DOMINIQUE; Catherine Mc Avley Hs; Brooklyn, NY; (S); 7/70; French Clb; Pres Sr Cls; Hon Roll; Jr NHS; NHS; Ldrshp 84-85; Yth Ftns Achvt Awd 83-84; Long Island U.

SAISON, TANIA M; Friends Acad; Sea Cliff, NY; (Y); Var Score Keeper; NY St Regents Schlrshp 86; Merit Schlrshp At Alvin Ailey Amer Dance Center 85; Columbia Coll; Sports Med.

SAJDA, JENNIFER; Commack HS South; Commack, NY; (Y); Church Yth Grp; Orch; School Musical; School Play; Symp Band; Nwsp Ed-Chief; Nwsp Rptr; Nwsp Stf; Yrbk Stf; High Hon Roll; Accntng.

SAJKOWKSI, MARTA; Midwood HS; Brooklyn, NY; (Y); Computer Clb; Math Tm; Band; School Musical; School Play; Yrbk Stf; Off Frsh Cls; Stu Cncl; Swmmng; Hon Roll; Boston U; Pysch.

SAKSENBERG, CHERYL R; Midwood HS; Brooklyn, NY; (Y); 178/556; Drama Clb; Office Aide; Variety Show; Lit Mag; Archr Schl Svc Scty 85-86; Hofstra U.

SALA, SUZETTE; Mechanicville HS; Mechanicville, NY; (S); 9/105; French Clb; SADD; Varsity Clb; Yrbk Stf; Trk; High Hon Roll; Hon Roll; NHS; Skidmore Coll Awd; Alfpha Omega Aristori Hnr Soc; Russell Sage; Bio.

SALADINO, MARIE; Villa Maria Acad; Cheektowaga, NY; (S); 5/90; JCL; Pep Clb; Acpl Chr; Sec Stu Cncl; Swmmng; High Hon Roll; NEDT Awd; Prfct Atten Awd; Spec Ed.

SALADYGA, TAMMY; Depew HS; Depew, NY; (Y); 20/300; Office Aide; Socr; Hon Roll; Bus.

SALAMACK, TONI MARIE; Sacred Heart HS; Yonkers, NY; (Y); Church Yth Grp; Drama Clb; 4-H; Hosp Aide; School Play; Hon Roll; Mercy College; Comm.

SALAMINO, JOSEPH; Bishop Grimes HS; Syracuse, NY; (Y); Church Yth Grp; Dance Clb; SADD; Var Bsbl; Im Bsktbl; Hon Roll; Prfct Atten Awd; Onondaga CC; Bus Mgmt.

SALAMONE, BILL; Frankfort-Schuyler HS; Frankfort, NY; (Y); Key Clb; Varsity Clb; Capt Bsktbl; Capt Ftbl; High Hon Roll; Mohawk Valley Comm; Mech Engr.

SALAS, GABBAL; De Witt Clinton HS; New York, NY; (Y); JV Bsbl; Var Gym; Phy Ed Awd 84; Compu Elec.

SALBEGO, ANDREA; Watkins Glen HS; Watkins Glen, NY; (Y); 15/110; Church Yth Grp; Dance Clb; Hosp Aide; Yrbk Stf; Hon Roll; Med.

SALCE, STACEY; East Syracuse-Minoa HS; Orlando, FL; (Y); 32/333; JA; High Hon Roll; Hon Roll; Jr NHS; NHS; Pres Schlr; U Of Cntrl FL.

SALEEM, ASMA; St Agnes Acad; Flushing, NY; (Y); Library Aide; Office Aide; Teachers Aide; Sec Frsh Cls; Stat Badmtn; Stat Gym; Stat Tennis; Hon Roll; Sci.

SALERNO, AMY; East-Syracuse-Minoa HS; East Syracuse, NY; (S); Pres DECA; French Clb; Science Clb; Concert Band; Rep Soph Cls; Rep Jr Cls; Rep Sr Cls; JV Var Bsktbl; JV Var Fld Hcky; JV L Sftbl; Outstndng Cmmnty Svc Awd 85-86; Schl Svc Awd 86; Cnty Pblc Spkng Awd 1st Plc 86; Syracuse U; Advrtsng.

SALERNO, ANNE; Camden HS; Camden, NY; (Y); AFS; Drama Clb; Girl Scts; Varsity Clb; Sec Y-Teens; School Musical; School Play; Nwsp Ed-Chief; Yrbk Ed-Chief; Sec Stu Cncl; Military; Aviation.

SALERNO, BETH ANN; North Babylon SR HS; N Babylon, NY; (Y); 2/460; Cmnty Wkr; School Musical; Nwsp Stf; Mgr(s); Exploring; Intnl Clb; Library Aide; Office Aide; Pep Clb; Spanish Clb; Ambssdr To H O Brien Yth Fndtn; Yng Schlr Ldrshp Smnr; TACT; Pre-Med.

SALERNO, TRACEY; North Rose Wolcott HS; N Rose, NY; (Y); 9/135; Church Yth Grp; Ski Clb; Varsity Clb; Var Swmmng; Var Trk; High Hon Roll; NHS; FFA; Var Diving; SUNY Oswego.

SALES, BARRY; Midwood HS; Brooklyn, NY; (Y); School Musical; School Play; JV Var Ftbl; Hon Roll; Cert Of Otstndng Schvt 86; Cert Encllnc Srvc Chrctr Schlrshp 85; Awd 1st Yr Vrsty Ftbll Tm 85; Hampton U; Law.

SALES, CRISTINA; Acad Of St Joseph; Hauppauge, NY; (Y); Aud/Vis; Drama Clb; Hosp Aide; Chorus; School Musical; Yrbk Phtg; Pres Jr Cls; Ntl Merit Schol; Val; Christian Courtesy Mdl 83; Brown U; Law.

SALGADO, MANUEL; St Agnes HS; Richmond Hill, NY; (Y); Letterman Clb; Spanish Clb; Lit Mag; Im Bsktbl; JV Var Crs Cntry; Im Ftbl; JV Var Trk; Im Vllybl; Im Wrstlng; Pre-Med.

SALICE, WILLIAM C; Sachem North HS; Ronkonkoma, NY; (Y); 226/1385; Church Yth Grp; Radio Clb; Ski Clb; SADD; NY ST Regents Schlrshp 86; Suffolk CC; Accntng.

SALICRUP, MADELINE; Jane Addams Vocational HS; Bronx, NY; (S); 1/266; Church Yth Grp; High Hon Roll; Hon Roll; Prfct Atten Awd; Val; Honor Soc 85; Highest Honor 80-82; Nursng.

SALIERNO, JOSEPH; St Anthonys HS; Centereach, NY; (Y); Teachers Aide; Concert Band; Symp Band; Yrbk Rptr; Im Bowling; French Hon Soc; Hon Roll; Jr NHS; NHS; SAT Merit Schlrshp & NY ST Rgnts Schlrshp 86; Dowling Coll; Accntnt.

SALIM, SARWAT; Franklin Delano Roosevelt HS; New York, NY; (Y); 2/791; Cmnty Wkr; Math Tm; Spanish Clb; Lit Mag; Bsktbl; Cit Awd; Gov Hon Prg Awd; High Hon Roll; Prfct Atten Awd; Arista Hnr Soc Pres 86.

SALINAS, EDWIN; Evander Childs HS; Bronx, NY; (Y); Cmnty Wkr; Debate Tm; Color Guard; Yrbk Sprt Ed; Stu Cncl; Bsktbl; Socr; Swmmng; Wt Lftg; High Hon Roll.

SALISBURY, EDITH N; Cardinal Spellman HS; Bronx, NY; (Y); 182/508; Dance Clb; French Clb; Pep Clb; Rep Frsh Cls; Rep Soph Cls; Stu Cncl; Var Swmmng; 1st Hnrs 85; 2nd Hnrs 83 & 86; Rgnts Schlrshp NYS 86; Stony Brook U; Psych.

SALISBURY, JILL; Union-Endicott HS; Endwell, NY; (Y); Drama Clb; Key Clb; Band; Chorus; Color Guard; Mrchg Band; School Musical; Rep Jr Cls; Rep Stu Cncl; Hon Roll; Psych.

SALISBURY, MICHELLE; Marion Central Schl; Marion, NY; (Y); 19/96; French Clb; Band; Chorus; Capt Color Guard; Concert Band; Mrchg Band; School Musical; Yrbk Stf; Hon Roll; Solo Comp Frnch Horn Rtng Exclnt 83-84; Monroe CC; Comp Sci.

SALKOFF, JONATHAN L; The Bronx High School Of Science; Roosevelt Island, NY; (Y); Band; Mrchg Band; Stage Crew; Yrbk Stf; L Mgr(s); Capt Swmmng; Jr NHS; NHS; Ntl Merit SF.

SALLEY, DANIELLE; C- PP West HS; Corning, NY; (Y); Chorus; School Musical; School Play; Co-Capt Yrbk Stf; JV Stat Trk; High Hon Roll; Hon Roll.

SALMAN, AMY; New Rochelle HS; New Rochelle, NY; (Y); Cmnty Wkr; Model UN; Political Wkr; VP SADD; Chorus; Stu Cncl; Sftbl; Var Vllybl; High Hon Roll; Natl Hnr Soc, Spanish Hnr Soc, Music Hnr 86; Music Hnr Soc Tri-M 85; Vet Med.

SALMON, BETH; Solvay HS; Syracuse, NY; (Y); Church Yth Grp; Exploring; Political Wkr; Chorus; Church Choir; Var Bsktbl; Var Trk; Capt Vllybl; High Hon Roll; Hon Roll; Crtv Wrtng Awd 86; All-Cnty 2nd Tm Vlybl 86; Vars Onondaga Lg Champs 83-86; Writer.

SALOB, LARRY; Commack North HS; Commack, NY; (Y); 10/360; Computer Clb; Ed Nwsp Ed-Chief; Nwsp Rptr; JV Socr; French Hon Soc; High Hon Roll; NHS; Wnnr Suffolk Readng Cncl Annual Art Cover Cont 85 & 86; Wnnr Long Isl Opthlmlgcl Soc Poster Cont 86; Art.

SALOMON, EDWIN; Nazareth Regional HS; Brooklyn, NY; (Y); JV Trk; Hon Roll; Jr NHS; NHS; Prfct Atten Awd; Polytechnic; Elec Engrng.

SALSBURY, JACQUELINE R; Notre Dame HS; Utica, NY; (Y); 17/168; Cmnty Wkr; 4-H; Yrbk Stf; Rep Frsh Cls; Rep Soph Cls; Stu Cncl; Powder Puff Ftbl; High Hon Roll; NHS; Regents Scholar 86; Utica Coll; Pre-Law.

SALTER, JOSEPH; H C Technical HS; Buffalo, NY; (Y); Aud/Vis; Boys Clb Am; Church Yth Grp; French Clb; Wrstlng; Sherman F Feyler Awd 83; Blck Enrchmt Socty 85-86.

SALTON, GILLIAN G; Horace Mann Schl; New York, NY; (Y); Exploring; SADD; Var Capt Swmmng; Ntl Merit SF; German Clb; Math Tm; Radio Clb; Lit Mag; V Water Polo Capt 85; Big Bro/Sistr Head 85; Asphalt Green Vol Yth Awd 84.

SALTS, BERNADETTE; John F Kennedy HS; Somers, NY; (Y); Chess Clb; Church Yth Grp; SADD; Chorus; Church Choir; Serve-Awd 82-86; Mount Saint Mary; Nrsng.

SALUATO, LINDA; H Frank Carey HS; Franklin Square, NY; (Y); 44/215; Pres Leo Clb; Hon Roll; FIT; Intr Dsgn.

SALUBAYBA, MARIA; Academy Of Mt St Ursula; Bronx, NY; (Y); Church Yth Grp; Chorus; Variety Show; Yrbk Stf; 1st Hon Awd 84; Berkley Coll Of Music; Voice.

SALUS, EMILY W; Fox Lane HS; Mt Kisco, NY; (Y); 43/275; Drama Clb; French Clb; Teachers Aide; Chorus; School Musical; Stage Crew; Lit Mag; High Hon Roll; Aud/Vis; Computer Clb; NY St Rgnts Schlrshp 86; German Awd 85; U Of CA Berkeley.

SALVA, THOMAS J; Rome Free Acad; Rome, NY; (Y); Cmnty Wkr; Intnl Clb; Red Cross Aide; JV Bowling; JV Golf; JV Trk; High Hon Roll; Hon Roll; Jr NHS; Prfct Atten Awd; Sectnl Bowl Tourn 86; Engrng.

SALVAGE, KRISTAN; Auburn HS; Auburn, NY; (Y); JA; Varsity Clb; Cheerleading; Coach Actv; Sftbl; Bausch & Lomb Sci Awd; High Hon Roll; NHS; Ithaca Coll; Lbrl Arts.

SALVAGNI, MARY ANN; Solvay HS; Solvzy, NY; (Y); Cmnty Wkr; French Clb; Hosp Aide; JA; JCL; Key Clb; Band; Concert Band; School Musical; Stage Crew; Engrng.

SALVATI, AMY; Auburn HS; Auburn, NY; (Y); 3/425; Library Aide; Nwsp Stf; Lit Mag; High Hon Roll; NHS; Rgnts Schlrshp 86; Ntl Merit Ltr Of Cmndtn 86; SUNY Coll Geneseo; Optmtry.

SALVATO, LINDA; H Frank Carey HS; Franklin Square, NY; (Y); 44/222; Pres Leo Clb; Hon Roll; Fash Inst Tech; Intr Desgn.

SALVATORE, DAVID; Eastridge HS; Rochester, NY; (Y); 39/200; Aud/Vis; Exploring; JA; JV Crs Cntry; Var Swmmng; Var Tennis; CC Awd; High Hon Roll; Hon Roll; NHS; Cert Recgntn Safety Cncl 86; Plaque Fire Dpet Rescue Elderly Citzn 86; Rochester Inst Tech; Mgmt.

SALVATORE, GARY H; Niagara Wheatfield HS; Sanborn, NY; (Y); 18/292; Church Yth Grp; Latin Clb; PAVAS; Ski Clb; Varsity Clb; JV Ftbl; Var Capt Socr; Var Capt Tennis; Cit Awd; Hon Roll; Bys St Fnlst 84-85; Houghton Coll; Dnstry.

SALVATORE, JOSEPH; Linton HS; Schenectady, NY; (Y); 22/300; Boy Scts; Church Yth Grp; Key Clb; Office Aide; Teachers Aide; Band; Chorus; Church Choir; Concert Band; Jazz Band; All ST Area Band 83-86; US Navy Band Concrt 86; Union Coll Jazz Ensmble 82-86.

SALVATORE, LUCILLE; Pelham Memorial HS; Pelham, NY; (Y); Church Yth Grp; SADD; Chorus; Church Choir; Orch; Capt JV Cheerleading; Hon Roll; AFS Stu Exchng Svc 85-86; Mock Trial 86.

SALVATORE, PRAINITO; Dew Utrecht HS; Brooklyn, NY; (Y); 4/635; Hosp Aide; VP Key Clb; Math Tm; Chorus; Ed Yrbk Phtg; Rep Frsh Cls; Rep Sr Cls; Hon Roll; NHS; Generoso Pope Mem Scholar 86; Dist Atty Citation Awd 86; NYU; Med.

SALYER, BETH L; Shoreham-Wading River HS; Shoreham, NY; (Y); Church Choir; Yrbk Stf; Lit Mag; Rep Soph Cls; Rep Jr Cls; JV Gym; Var Trk; Psych.

SALZER, CHRISTINE; Freeport HS; Freeport, NY; (Y); Key Clb; SADD; Concert Band; Nwsp Stf; Yrbk Sprt Ed; Stu Cncl; JV Lcrss; Var Socr; High Hon Roll; NHS; LI Math Fair Bronze Mdl 86; Prfct Attndnce Awd 85-86; Psych.

SALZER, STACEY; Berne-Knox Westerlo HS; Berne, NY; (Y); 10/77; Church Yth Grp; Cmnty Wkr; Teachers Aide; Band; Chorus; Church Choir; Concert Band; Jazz Band; Mrchg Band; Orch; Band Awd Grad 86; 2 Music Schlrshps Berne Knox & Schoharie Cnty 86; Musicn Yr Troph 84-86; SUNY Potsdam Crane Schl; Music.

SALZMAN, GREGG; John Dewey HS; Brooklyn, NY; (Y); School Musical; Nwsp Ed-Chief; Nwsp Rptr; Capt Swmmng; Vllybl; Jr NHS; Econ.

SALZMAN, RANDI; Commack H S South; Dix Hills, NY; (S); Drama Clb; PAVAS; School Musical; School Play; Nwsp Phtg; Rep Stu Cncl; Var JV Vllybl; Hon Roll; Cmnty Wkr; Dance Clb; Boces Scholar Gifted & Talntd 84; Tri M Hnr Soc 85; Bus Adm.

SAM, SUSAN; Academy Of Mt St Ursula; Bronx, NY; (Y); Computer Clb; Library Aide; Nwsp Rptr; 1st Hnrs 83-85; 2nd Hnrs 85-86; Jrnlsm.

SAMADI, ALBERT; Roslyn HS; Roslyn Hts, NY; (Y); Science Clb; Band; Chorus; Bsktbl; Socr; Natl Sci Olympd Awd Excllnc 85-86; SUNY Stony Brook; Biochem.

SAMANLEGO, CLAUDIA; Longwood HS; Coram, NY; (Y); 4-H; Chorus; School Play; Variety Show; Sftbl; 4-H Awd; Hon Roll.

SAMAREL, PAUL; Amityville Memorial HS; Massapequa, NY; (Y); Mgr Drama Clb; FBLA; Capt Math Tm; Orch; Var Tennis; High Hon Roll; NHS; Chess Clb; School Musical; School Play; Comp Sci.

SAMAROO, DENISE; Mt St Ursula HS; Yonkers, NY; (Y); Science Clb; SADD; Trk; Fordham U; Sci.

SAMBOLIN, JOSEPH; All Hallows HS; Bronx, NY; (Y); Aud/Vis; Church Choir; Yrbk Rptr; Trk; Monroe Bus Inst.

SAMDANI, AMER; Midwood HS; Brooklyn, NY; (Y); 9/650; Aud/Vis; VP Intnl Clb; Library Aide; Math Tm; Quiz Bowl; Pres Spanish Clb; Band; Hon Roll; Newsletter Wrtr; Cardlgst.

SAMELOFF, KIM; Coxsackie Athens Central HS; Coxsackie, NY; (Y); Girl Scts; Spanish Clb; SADD; Sec Soph Cls; Sec Jr Cls; Stu Cncl; Score Keeper; Trk; Bus.

SAMET, SCOTT; Commack H S South; Dix Hills, NY; (Y); 9/354; Computer Clb; Exploring; Mathletes; Math Tm; Spanish Clb; Temple Yth Grp; Nwsp Rptr; Ed Nwsp Stf; Var Tennis; High Hon Roll; Natl Sci Merit Awd 83-84; Wnnr Sci Olympiad For Chem 84-85; Wnnr NY ST Rgnts Schlrshp 85-86; U Of PA; Corp Law.

SAMIOU, EVELYN; Long Island City HS; Long Island Cty, NY; (Y); 32/549; Computer Clb; FBLA; Math Tm; Office Aide; Teachers Aide; Rep Sr Cls; Cit Awd; Hon Roll; Scty Of Dstngshd Amer HS Stu 86; NYU Schlrshp 86; NY U; Cmmrcl Advrtsng.

SAMLAND, SUSAN; Grand Island HS; Grand Island, NY; (Y); 5/320; Church Yth Grp; GAA; Varsity Clb; Concert Band; Var L Swmmng; High Hon Roll; Hon Roll; NHS; Engrng Schlrs Prgrm At NC ST U; NC ST U; Engrng.

SAMMLER, MICHAEL T; Mc Quaid Jesuit HS; Rochester, NY; (Y); Boy Scts; Church Yth Grp; Political Wkr; Ski Clb; Teachers Aide; JV Crs Cntry; JV Swmmng; Hon Roll; U NV Reno; ROTC.

SAMMONS, STEPHANIE; York Central Schl; Leicester, NY; (Y); 12/92; Rptr Church Yth Grp; 4-H; Key Clb; Service Clb; Ski Clb; Band; Chorus; Church Choir; Concert Band; Pep Band; Ivan H Hilficker Awd 86; SUNY; Med Tech.

SAMOKAR, SCOTT; Dover JR SR HS; Dover Plains, NY; (S); #3 In Class; Math Clb; Wrstlng; High Hon Roll; Hon Roll; NHS; Civil Svc.

SAMPAIO, OLINDA; Our Lady Of Victory HS; Tarrytown, NY; (S); 11/128; Art Clb; French Clb; Service Clb; SADD; Lit Mag; Var Trk; French Hon Soc; High Hon Roll; NHS; Boston U; Polt Sci.

SAMPERI, SHARON; Nazareth Acad; Rochester, NY; (Y); SADD; Stage Crew; Nwsp Rptr; Yrbk Stf; Var Socr; Var JV Sftbl; High Hon Roll; Hon Roll; NHS; Dentistr.

SAMPLES JR, JOHN W; Perth Bible Christian Acad; Amsterdam, NY; (Y); 3/7; Band; Chorus; Church Choir; Concert Band; Mrchg Band; Pep Band; School Musical; School Play; Pres Stu Cncl; Bsbl; Christn Athlete Yr 86; Schlrshp Act Score 27 86; Pensacola Christian Coll; Bus.

SAMPOGNA, MARIA; Fabius Pompey HS; Jamesville, NY; (Y); Drama Clb; SADD; Band; Church Choir; School Play; Ed Nwsp Rptr; Nwsp Stf; Yrbk Stf; Var Trk; Cit Awd; Math.

SAMPSON, CAROL LYNN; Mahopac HS; Mahopac, NY; (Y); 20/409; Church Yth Grp; French Clb; Chorus; High Hon Roll; Hon Roll; NHS; Educ.

SAMPSON, JENNIFER A; Valley Stream North HS; Elmont, NY; (Y); 2/128; Chrmn Debate Tm; Mathletes; Nwsp Rptr; Var Badmtn; Var Trk; NHS; Sal; Vrsty Rfl Capt; NY ST Rgnts Schlrshp; Rensselaer Polytechnic Inst.

SAMPSON, LISA; Smithtown East HS; Smithtown, NY; (Y); Ski Clb; SADD; Yrbk Phtg; Yrbk Stf; Frsh Cls; Soph Cls; Jr Cls; Sr Cls; Stu Cncl; Socr; Phys Thrpy.

SAMSON, ROSANNE M; Emma Willars Schl; Loudonville, NY; (Y); 7/96; Ski Clb; School Play; Stage Crew; Nwsp Stf; Trs Jr Cls; Rep Stu Cncl; Im Sftbl; Ntl Merit Ltr; Im Cheerleading; Im Socr; NY Regents Schlrshp 86; Emma Willard Bstrs Awd 85; Day Stu Proctor 85-86; EW Awd; Cum Laude Scty; Siena Coll; Bio.

SAMUEL, ALLYSON; Cathedral HS; Bx, NY; (Y); 144/277; Drama Clb; Intnl Clb; Band; Mrchg Band; Nwsp Rptr; Nwsp Stf; Rep Sr Cls; Var Sftbl; VFW Awd; Rgnts Schlrshp Of NY 86; LIU CW Pst; Cmnctns.

SAMUEL, SHERLY; Hillcrest HS; Richmond Hills, NY; (Y); Computer Clb; English Clb; FCA; FNA; Hosp Aide; Math Tm; Science Clb; Speech Tm; Badmtn; God Cntry Awd; Med.

SAMUEL, TONYA; Cardinal Spellman HS; Bronx, NY; (Y); Computer Clb; Science Clb; Chorus; Hon Roll; U MI; Bio.

SAMUELS, DIONNE; Groton HS; Yonkers, NY; (Y); 32/191; Hosp Aide; Spanish Clb; Mary Mount Schlrshp 86-87; Marymount Coll Tarrytown; Med.

SAMUELS, SHERRY L; Scarsdale HS; Scarsdale, NY; (Y); Spanish Clb; Teachers Aide; Temple Yth Grp; Var Bsktbl; Var Socr; Var Capt Trk; NHS; Ntl Merit Ltr; Varsity Clb; Brown U.

SAMUELS, SIOBHAN; Adad Of Mount St Ursula; Bronx, NY; (Y); Art Clb; Yrbk Stf; JV Var Bsktbl; Parsons Art Schl; Art.

SAMULAK, KAROLINA; Watertown HS; Watertown, NY; (Y); Drama Clb; Var Tennis; Var Trk; Hon Roll; Mbr Of Natl Hnr Soc 86; Med Schl.

SAN ANGELO, AUDRA; Newark SR HS; Newark, NY; (Y); Drama Clb; Office Aide; Teachers Aide; Chorus; Capt Color Guard; School Musical; School Play; Stage Crew; Swing Chorus; Yrbk Stf; Clr Gd Lttr 84; CCFL; Bus Admin.

SAN DIEGO, JO-ANNE; Fontbonne Hall Acad; Brooklyn, NY; (Y); 33/136; Art Clb; Computer Clb; French Clb; Library Aide; Nwsp Stf; Cheerleading; Hon Roll.

SAN LUCAS, PAUL; All Hallows Inst; Yonkers, NY; (S); 1/40; High Hon Roll; NHS; Med.

SAN MIGUEL, ALEJANDRO; The Browning Schl; Tenafly, NJ; (Y); 3/31; Cmnty Wkr; Nwsp Rptr; Pres Stu Cncl; Var L Bsbl; Var Capt Socr; Ntl Merit Ltr; Natl Hspnc Schlr Fnls 86; ISAL All Star-Sccr 85-86; Bliss All Star-Bsbl 85-86; U Of PA; Corporate Law.

SAN MIGUEL, VICTOR E; Holy Cross HS; Woodside, NY; (Y); 9/362; Cmnty Wkr; Mgr(s); NHS; Ntl Merit SF; 4 Yr Schlrshp 81-86; Natl Mrt Schlrshp Semi-Fin 85; Duke U; Engrng.

SAN SOUCIE, BRENDA; Plattsburgh HS; Plattsburgh, NY; (Y); 30/180; Camera Clb; Church Yth Grp; Drama Clb; Radio Clb; Spanish Clb; SADD; Varsity Clb; Chorus; Church Choir; School Musical; Treas Vrsty Clb 84-86; Producer Schl Play 83-84; Evangel Coll; Law.

SANCHEZ, ANGEL; John Jay HS; Brooklyn, NY; (Y); Cmnty Wkr; Off Jr Cls; Swmmng; Hon Roll; Outstndng Schlrshp In SMQ 3x 86; NYC Tech Coll; Elec Engrng.

SANCHEZ, ERICK; Bronx HS Of Science; Elmhurst, NY; (Y); Aerontcl Engrng.

SANCHEZ, GLENN; Smithtown HS West; Smithtown, NY; (Y); Ski Clb; Bsktbl; L Crs Cntry; L Capt Lcrss; L Socr; JV Wrstlng; Hon Roll; VP NHS; Pres Schlr; Church Yth Grp; Brkhvn Natl Lab Brdg-Bldg Cntst 17th Pl 85; Rgnts Schlrshp 86; Yale U; Chem Engrng.

SANCHEZ, HERMES; Eastern District HS; Brooklyn, NY; (Y); Science Clb; Nwsp Sprt Ed; Var Stat Bsbl; Var Trk; Hon Roll; Prfct Atten Awd; Comp Pgrmg.

SANCHEZ, JOHNNY; William Howard Taft HS; Bronx, NY; (Y); Boy Scts; Camera Clb; Dance Clb; Red Cross Aide; Band; Color Guard; School Play; Nwsp Stf; Lit Mag; Prfct Atten Awd; Mentorng Hnr Awd 85; SR Bnd Awd 84; Math & Physcl Ed Awds 83 & 85; Med.

SANCHEZ, KATHLEEN; Dominican Commercial HS; Jamaica, NY; (Y); 37/288; Church Yth Grp; Cmnty Wkr; Sftbl; Swmmng; Hon Roll; Jr NHS; Prfct Atten Awd; John Jay Coll; Lawyer.

SANCHEZ, MANUEL; Hillcrest HS; Flushing, NY; (Y); Concert Band; Rep Soph Cls.

SANCHEZ, MARIA R; Earl L Vandermeulen HS; Mt Sinai, NY; (Y); Camp Fr Inc; Civic Clb; Cheerleading; Trk; Vllybl; High Hon Roll; NHS; Regents Schlrshp 86; Stony Brook U; Comp.

SANCHEZ, MARYANN; Brewster HS; Brewster, NY; (Y); 23/190; VP Band; Mrchg Band; Yrbk Stf; Rep Stu Cncl; Capt Gym; Trk; Cit Awd; French Hon Soc; Hon Roll; Sec NHS; Cert Of Honor Engl II Adv 85; MVP Var Gymnstcs 86; Boston U; Bus Mrkttng.

SANCHEZ, PHILIP A; Scarsdale HS; Scarsdale, NY; (Y); Debate Tm; NFL; Swmmng; Mst Imprvd Mn Swm Tm 85-86; Law.

SANCHEZ, TERESA; Freeport HS; Freeport, NY; (Y); Var Bsktbl; Coach Actv; Var Socr; Var Capt Sftbl; High Hon Roll; NHS; All-Cnty Sftbll Grls 86; All-Div Bsktbll Grls 86; Irnwmn Clb 86; Poly Sci.

SANCHEZ, XAVIER M; Hillcrest HS; Woodside, NY; (Y); 2/832; Chess Clb; Hosp Aide; Math Tm; Science Clb; Band; Vllybl; Hon Roll; NCTE Awd; Ntl Merit Ltr; Sal; Gld Mdl Math & Sci 84; Qns Clg Pres Jr Awd Achvt 85; Untd Found Tchrs Schlrshp 86; NY U; Pre Med.

SANCHEZ, YVETTE; The Mary Louis Acad; Floral Park, NY; (Y); 152/300; Aud/Vis; Church Yth Grp; Spanish Clb; Variety Show; Stat Score Keeper; St Johns U; Pharm.

SAND, TOM; Colonie Central HS; Albany, NY; (Y); 18/457; JV Var Bsktbl; Var Golf; High Hon Roll; Scholastic Bowl; NHS; Qualified NY ST PHSAA Golf Tourn 86; Bus Adm.

SANDBERG, STEVEN; John H Glenn HS; E Northport, NY; (Y); Computer Clb; Nwsp Stf; Bowling; High Hon Roll; Hon Roll; Jr NHS; Spanish NHS.

SANDBROOK, DOUGLAS; Saugerties HS; Saugerties, NY; (Y); Ski Clb; SADD; Thesps; Nwsp Phtg; Nwsp Rptr; Yrbk Phtg; Yrbk Rptr; Var L Ftbl; Var Tennis; Var L Trk; Athltc Trng.

SANDELLA, GINA; Dominican Acad; New York, NY; (Y); Church Yth Grp; Drama Clb; Q&S; School Musical; School Play; Nwsp Phtg; Nwsp Rptr; Ed Nwsp Stf; Ed Lit Mag; Stu Cncl; Schlrshp Fr My Schl 86; Outstndng Phtgrphy & Comm Affrs Rprtr Awd 85.

SANDER, HENRY; Delaware Academy And Central HS; Delhi, NY; (Y); Band; Mrchg Band; Var L Ftbl; Var L Trk; Im Wt Lftg; Hon Roll; Schlrshp From Delaware County Superintendants 86; SUNNY Ag & Tech Delhi; Civil.

SANDERLIN, JOSEPH; Mac Arthur HS; Levittown, NY; (Y); Cmnty Wkr; 4-H; Band; Trk; Cit Awd; 4-H Awd; Hon Roll; 4-H Awds; Sci.

SANDERS, LABRON; South Shore HS; Brooklyn, NY; (Y); Capt Crs Cntry; Capt Trk; 3 Yr Vrsty Awd 86.

SANDERS, ROBIN; Weedsport JR SR HS; Weedsport, NY; (Y); 20/88; French Clb; Office Aide; Yrbk Stf; JV Cheerleading; JV Sftbl; Var Trk; Hon Roll; Prfct Atten Awd; Cayuga CC; Cmmnctns.

SANDERS, RUSSELL; East Hampton HS; Montauk, NY; (Y); Boy Scts; Var Ftbl; Var Trk; Im Wt Lftg; High Hon Roll; Hon Roll; L V I S Book Awd 84; Penn ST; Aeron Engrng.

SANDERS, TINA; Abgyle Central HS; Argyle, NY; (Y); 14/56; Hosp Aide; Yrbk Phtg; Yrbk Stf; High Hon Roll; Hon Roll; FHA; BOCES Nrs Aid High Hnrs 86; Co-Op Prog At Plsnt Vly Inf 86-87; Adirondack CC; Reg Nrs.

SANDERS, TRACIE; Kenmore East SR HS; Tonawanda, NY; (Y); Church Yth Grp; SADD; Church Choir; Bsktbl; Score Keeper; Vllybl; Hon Roll; Adrian Coll; Psychology.

SANDERSON, BRYAN; Oceanside HS; Oceanside, NY; (Y); Var Capt Bsbl; Hon Roll; NASSAU Cnty Bsbll Coaches Assoc Plyr Wk 85-86; Plyrs Plyr Awd 86; Ellon Coll; Bus.

SANDERSON, DENISE; Westfield Central HS; Westfield, NY; (Y); 13/54; Am Leg Aux Girls St; Trs Church Yth Grp; Nwsp Sprt Ed; Yrbk Stf; Sec Soph Cls; Trs Stu Cncl; Var JV Bsktbl; Var Sftbl; Var JV Vllybl; High Hon Roll; Pres Phys Ftnss Awd; Natl Sci Merit Awd 84; Accntng.

SANDHU, PAPU; Eastport HS; Speonk, NY; (Y); 3/60; Mathletes; Quiz Bowl; Bsbl; Bsktbl; Bausch & Lomb Sci Awd; High Hon Roll; Hon Roll; Jr NHS; NHS; Prfct Atten Awd; Spnsh, Chem, Math; ST Regnts Schlrshp; Hofstra; Pre-Law.

SANDKLEV, JENNIFER; Susan E Wagner HS; Staten Island, NY; (Y); Capt Drill Tm; Capt Bowling; Hon Roll; VP Sons Norwya 83; Staten Island; Acctng.

SANDLER, MARLO; Huntington HS; Huntington, NY; (Y); Key Clb; Varsity Clb; Trs Frsh Cls; VP Soph Cls; JV Pres Stu Cncl; Stat Bsktbl; Var Sftbl; Var Tennis; High Hon Roll; NHS; VFW Wrtng Awd 86.

SANDLER, MELISSA; Wheatley HS; Old Westbury, NY; (Y); Drama Clb; JV Var Cheerleading; Var Tennis; Dance Clb; Model UN; School Play; Yrbk Stf; Lit Mag; Stu Cncl; Grphcs Edtr In Schl Nwspr 86-87; Grphc Arts.

SANDLER, MICHAEL; Herricks HS; Williston Park, NY; (Y); 2/235; Band; Concert Band; Mrchg Band; Var Bowling; Hon Roll; NHS; Hofstra U; Bus Mngmnt.

SANDOVAL, DIANA; Hillcrest HS; Hollis, NY; (Y); 32/801; Church Choir; Orch; Rgnts Schlrshp 86; Prnts Assn Awd-Acad Achvt Music 86; NYU; Nrsg.

SANDOW, WENDI; Dobbs Ferry HS; Dobbs Ferry, NY; (S); AFS; Key Clb; Chorus; Concert Band; Jazz Band; Mrchg Band; School Musical; Yrbk Stf; Stu Cncl; Var Capt Tennis; Music Ed.

SANDS, JILL R; Sanford H Calhoun HS; Merrick, NY; (Y); 1/313; VP Exploring; Key Clb; Pres Math Tm; Bausch & Lomb Sci Awd; NHS; Ntl Merit SF; Val; Computer Clb; Dance Clb; Variety Show; Rensselaer Polytec Inst Mth/Sci Awd & NY Sci Spvs Assc Awd All-Arnd Sci Achv 85; Intl Sm-Fnlst Piano; Med.

SANELLI, PINA C; St Francis Prep HS; Maspeth, NY; (S); Hosp Aide; Science Clb; Speech Tm; Yrbk Stf; Trk; High Hon Roll; NHS; Wt Lftg; Outstndng Svc Awd 83-84.

SANELLI, TINA R; Gates-Chili SR HS; Rochester, NY; (S); 17/446; Church Yth Grp; Cmnty Wkr; Math Tm; Service Clb; Stu Cncl; High Hon Roll; NHS; Proj Accptnce NYS Engry Cons Cmptn 85; Indstrl Engr.

SANFILIPPO, ROBERT F; Orchard Park HS; Orchard Park, NY; (Y); 7/465; Am Leg Boys St; Aud/Vis; Church Yth Grp; Computer Clb; Debate Tm; JA; Math Tm; Science Clb; Spanish Clb; Band; 1st Clrnt In All ST Conf Bnd 85; 1st Pl In Sci Fair 84-85; Its Acad Team 84-86; Harvard U; Engrng.

SANFORD, DANIEL; Charlotte Valley Central Schl; Davenport, NY; (S); 5/34; Am Leg Boys St; Spanish Clb; Pres Varsity Clb; VP Stu Cncl; Var Bsbl; JV Var Bsktbl; Var Socr; Pres NHS; High Hon Roll; Cvl Engrng.

SANFRATELLO, THOMAS A; Alexander Central HS; Batavia, NY; (Y); Boy Scts; Cmnty Wkr; Ski Clb; Varsity Clb; Band; Concert Band; Drm & Bgl; Mrchg Band; Var Socr; Var Tennis; Perdu U Merit Of Hon 86; Pre Law.

SANGER, CHERYL; Mohonasen HS; Schenectady, NY; (Y); High Hon Roll; Hon Roll; Phtgrphy.

SANGES, MARK; Gloversville HS; Gloversville, NY; (Y); 26/219; Aud/Vis; Computer Clb; Library Aide; Office Aide; SADD; Nwsp Stf; Yrbk Stf; Rep Frsh Cls; Rep Soph Cls; Comp Engrng.

SANGI, DANIELLE; Saugerties HS; Saugerties, NY; (Y); Ski Clb; Band; Concert Band; Mrchg Band; Symp Band; JV Var Bsktbl; Var Sftbl; JV Vllybl; Hon Roll; NHS; Albany ST; Psychology.

SANGURIMA, JESSICA E; Fontbonne Hall Acad; Brooklyn, NY; (Y); 3/130; Drama Clb; French Clb; Hosp Aide; Chorus; Church Choir; High Hon Roll; NHS; NEDT Awd; NY ST Rgnts Schlrshp & NY U Trustees Schlrshp 86-87; NY U; Med.

SANGVIC, HARRIET; Lindenhurst HS; Lindenhurst, NY; (Y); 15/594; Art Clb; Ski Clb; School Musical; Nwsp Stf; VP Soph Cls; Tennis; Trk; Kiwanis Awd; NHS; Voice Dem Awd; MVP Tennis 85-86; Gold Key Awd 86; Acad Hlth,Physcl Ftns Awd 86; Boston U; Bus.

SANIAGO, PETER; Monsignor Scanlan HS; Bronx, NY; (Y); 65/278; Boys Clb Am; School Play; Stu Cncl; Bsktbl; Powder Puff Ftbl; Score Keeper; Swmmng; Vllybl; NY CC; Arch.

SANON, EDISON; Nazareth Regional HS; Brooklyn, NY; (Y); 64/267; Cmnty Wkr; JA; Math Tm; Sec NFL; Trs Speech Tm; School Play; Nwsp Bus Mgr; Nwsp Rptr; Nwsp Stf; Hon Roll; Distngushd Svc Awd 86; Tablet Spch Deb Awd 3rd Pl 86; Fnlst Ntl SF Fornscs 86; NY U; Lib Art.

SANPIETRO III, JOHN; Holy Cross HS; College Point, NY; (S); 54/307; Pres Debate Tm; Drama Clb; Office Aide; Speech Tm; School Musical; Nwsp Rptr; Nwsp Stf; Yrbk Phtg; Ed Lit Mag; Hon Roll; Law.

SANSARICQ, PATRICIA; Mary Louis HS; Flushing, NY; (Y); 47/270; Art Clb; Hosp Aide; Rep Soph Cls; Rep Sr Cls; Rep Stu Cncl; Crs Cntry; Im Ftbl; NEDT Awd; Cncrs Ntl De Frncs Awd 83-85; New York U.

SANSEVERINO, RENEE; Our Lady Of Victory; Yonkers, NY; (S); 21/122; Nwsp Rptr; Rep Frsh Cls; High Hon Roll; NHS; Polic Ofcr Crmnlgy.

SANSIVIERO, WAYNE; Huntington HS; Huntington, NY; (Y); Key Clb; Letterman Clb; Variety Show; Ftbl; Lcrss; JV MVP Lacrosse 85; All Leag Slctn & Hon Mntn 86; Vrsty Lacrosse Leag I; Bus.

SANSONE, JENNIFER; St John Villa Acad; Staten Island, NY; (Y); 16/127; Hosp Aide; JA; Stage Crew; Tennis; Hnr Awd Relig & Eng 86; Merit Awd 85 & 86; Pace U; Bus.

SANSOTTA, NICKY; James Madison HS; Brooklyn, NY; (Y); 119/756; Elec Engr.

SANTABARBARA, ANTHONY; Scotia-Glenville HS; Scotia, NY; (Y); Key Clb; Varsity Clb; Yrbk Stf; Ftbl; Trk; Wrstlng; Hon Roll; Acctg.

SANTACESARIA, NANCY; Greece Olympia HS; Rochester, NY; (Y); 11/277; FBLA; Math Tm; Varsity Clb; Tennis; High Hon Roll; Masonic Awd; NHS; Pres Schlr; St John Fisher Adm Schrlshp 85-86; Regents Schrlshp 85-86; Outstndng Bus Stu 85-86; St John Fisher Coll; Mgmt.

SANTAGATA, FABIO; Archbishop Molloy HS; Astoria, NY; (Y); Computer Clb; Math Tm; Science Clb; High Hon Roll; NHS; IONA Lang Cntst, Italian II 1st Hnrs 84; Bus Admin.

SANTALESA, DEBBIE; St Francis Prep; Flushing, NY; (Y); 100/750; JV Var Cheerleading; Var Socr; NHS; Opt Clb Awd; Dance Clb; Office Aide; Rep Frsh Cls; Wt Lftg; Hon Roll.

SANTALESA, DEBORAH L; St Francis Prep; Flushing, NY; (S); 100/750; Dance Clb; Office Aide; Rep Frsh Cls; JV Var Cheerleading; Var Socr; Vllybl; Wt Lftg; NHS; Opt Clb Awd; Psych.

SANTANA, JENNIFER; Frontier HS; Blasdell, NY; (Y); 4-H; FBLA; Hosp Aide; Pep Clb; Chorus; Yrbk Stf; JV Bsktbl; JV Sftbl; Im Swmmng; Hon Roll; Med Tech.

SANTANGELO, MARIA; St Johns Preparatory Schl; Brooklyn, NY; (Y); 92/497; Art Clb; Hon Roll; Fashion Insti Tech; Fshn Dsgn.

SANTANIELLO, NINA; Our Lady Of Victory Acad; Mt Vernon, NY; (S); 8/157; Art Clb; Natl Beta Clb; PAVAS; Political Wkr; Teachers Aide; Lit Mag; High Hon Roll; NHS; Spanish NHS; Spnsh Medal 83-85.

SANTARSIERO, ANDREW; West Hempstead HS; West Hempstead, NY; (Y); Ski Clb; Jazz Band; Trk; Hon Roll; Jr NHS; Hofstra U; Bus.

SANTASIERI, CHRISTINA; Midlakes HS; Phelps, NY; (Y); 7/143; French Clb; Letterman Clb; Varsity Clb; Pres Frsh Cls; Pres Stu Cncl; Fld Hcky; Vllybl; High Hon Roll; NHS; Prfct Atten Awd; Pres Ftns Awd 84; Bus Adm.

SANTIAGO, ABEL; Hempstead HS; Hempstead, NY; (Y); Church Yth Grp; Cmnty Wkr; Dance Clb; Cit Awd; Prfct Atten Awd; Engl Achvt 84; Comp.

SANTIAGO, ANNETTE; Mt St Ursula HS; Bronx, NY; (Y); Sec Camera Clb; Drama Clb; Yrbk Stf; Off Stu Cncl; Hon Roll; Nrsng.

SANTIAGO, CHRISTINA; Center Moriches HS; Mastic, NY; (Y); Computer Clb; FBLA; Key Clb; Spanish Clb; Color Guard; Mrchg Band; Yrbk Stf; Lit Mag; Score Keeper; Hon Roll; Suffolk CC; Bus Mgmt.

SANTIAGO, DAPHINE; Eastern District HS; Brooklyn, NY; (Y); #80 In Class; Art Clb; Dance Clb; Library Aide; Spanish Clb; Teachers Aide; Nwsp Stf; Gym; Vllybl; Cert Merit Spnsh 83; Cert Awd Achvt Physcl Ed,Engl 84; Kingsboro CC; Sec.

SANTIAGO, EDDIE; Queens Vocational HS; Brooklyn, NY; (Y); Capt Bsbl; Capt Ftbl; Capt Sftbl; Wt Lftg.

SANTIAGO, EDDIE; Xavier HS; Ridgewood, NY; (Y); Chess Clb; Computer Clb; Debate Tm; Red Cross Aide; Hon Roll; NEDT Awd; St Peters Frnch Cntst 1st Hnrs 85; Columbia U; Med.

SANTIAGO, ESTHER; Grace H Dodge Voc HS; Bronx, NY; (Y); Art Clb; Church Yth Grp; Cmnty Wkr; Drama Clb; Spanish Clb; School Play; Cheerleading; Vllybl; Cit Awd; Hon Roll; Tp 10 Gregg Stu Awd 86; Engl Achvt Medl 84; Outstndng Achvt Rgnts Bio 85; Fordham U; Bus Adm.

SANTIAGO, LIZETTE; Adlai E Stevenson HS; Bronx, NY; (Y); Dance Clb; Hosp Aide; Vllybl; NY Chaptr Assoc Tchrs Spnsh Awd 85; Law.

SANTIAGO, MARCELINA; West Hempstead HS; Island Park, NY; (Y); Spanish Clb; Hon Roll; AATSP 1st Pl Spnsh III 84, Spnsh IV 86; Elem Educ.

SANTIAGO, RITA M; St Francis Prep; Corona, NY; (S); 215/750; Cmnty Wkr; Dance Clb; Spanish Clb; Spec Ed.

SANTINI, PATRICIA; Sacred Heart HS; Yonkers, NY; (S); 2/210; Nwsp Rptr; Nwsp Stf; Yrbk Phtg; Yrbk Stf; High Hon Roll; Hon Roll; Trs NHS; Scared Heart Schlrshp 82-85; Italian Cntst 1st Hnr Awd 84; Comp.

SANTMAN, DARA; Commack H S South; Commack, NY; (Y); 50/400; Band; Jazz Band; Orch; School Musical; Symp Band; JV Var Tennis; High Hon Roll; NHS; Concert Band; JV Sftbl; Golden Quill Awd 84; Tri M Music Hnr Soc 86; Psych.

SANTO, DAWN MARIE; Herbert H Lehman HS; Bronx, NY; (Y); Cmnty Wkr; Hosp Aide; Office Aide; Science Clb; Nwsp Rptr; Yrbk Stf; Trs Sr Cls; NHS; Prfct Atten Awd; Med.

SANTOMASSINO, KENNETH T; Wm Floyd HS; Shirley, NY; (Y); Chess Clb; Computer Clb; Ski Clb; School Play; NY ST Rgnts Schlrshp 86; Tae Kwon Do Karate Hgh Brn Blt 85; Clarkson U; Comp Engrng.

SANTOMERO, STEVEN P; Floral Park Memorial HS; Floral Park, NY; (Y); 14/150; Aud/Vis; VP Computer Clb; Stage Crew; JV Socr; Hon Roll; NHS; Rgnts Schlrshp & Merit Schlrshp From NY Tech; NY Inst Of Tech; Comp Sci.

SANTON, DOUGLAS; Bishop Scully HS; Amsterdam, NY; (S); 7/56; Math Clb; Red Cross Aide; Yrbk Stf; JV Ftbl; High Hon Roll; Mu Alp Tht; NHS.

SANTORA, JASON M; Watervliet HS; Watervliet, NY; (Y); 2/105; Sec Teachers Aide; School Play; VP Stu Cncl; DAR Awd; Elks Awd; High Hon Roll; Pres NHS; Pres Schlr; Sal; Art Clb; Rennselaer Polytech Inst Awd Exclnce Math & Sci 85; Alt TV Quiz Pgm Answers Please 85; Siena Coll; Cmmnctns.

SANTORE, GINA; Moore Catholic HS; Manalapan, NJ; (Y); Spanish Clb; Yrbk Stf; Pres Frsh Cls; Pres Soph Cls; Pres Jr Cls; Rep Stu Cncl; JV Cheerleading; Rutgers U; Hlth Care Admin.

SANTORO, LINDA; Wantagh HS; Wantagh, NY; (Y); 35/270; Key Clb; Office Aide; Nwsp Stf; Yrbk Stf; Capt Pom Pon; High Hon Roll; Hon Roll; NHS; Hofstra U; Accctng.

SANTORO, MICHAEL; Hudson Falls SR HS; Hudson Fls, NY; (Y); Key Clb; SADD; Jr Cls; Ftbl; Socr; Wrstlng.

SANTOS, ARACELIS; Grace Dodge V HS; Bronx, NY; (Y); Computer Clb; Spanish Clb; Band; Chorus; School Play; Off Frsh Cls; Off Jr Cls; Vllybl; Cit Awd; Hon Roll; Lehman Coll; Sec.

SANTOS, DIANE; Mineola HS; Mineola, NY; (Y); Pres FBLA; Hosp Aide; Key Clb; SADD; Hon Roll.

SANTOS, FERNANDO; Bishop Ford Catholic HS; Brooklyn, NY; (Y); Tennis; Elect Engrg.

SANTOS, GRACELYN FERNANDEZ; Curtis HS; Staten Island, NY; (Y); 1/262; Church Yth Grp; Civic Clb; Cmnty Wkr; FNA; Sec Intnl Clb; Library Aide; Math Tm; Soroptimist; Stage Crew; Lit Mag; City Coll Of NY Schlr Prog Awd 86; Miss NY 85; 1st Rnr Up Miss Natl Teen Pgnt 86; Miss Manila-USA 85; Pre-Med.

SANTOS, MARK; Solvay HS; Solvay, NY; (Y); 18/171; Church Yth Grp; Math Clb; Pres Concert Band; Stage Crew; Off Jr Cls; Off Sr Cls; Bsktbl; Ftbl; NHS; Le Moyne Coll; Acctg.

SANTOSTEFANO, FRANK; Maple Hill HS; Nassau, NY; (Y); Aud/Vis; Drama Clb; Exploring; Key Clb; Ski Clb; Spanish Clb; Stage Crew; Yrbk Phtg; Yrbk Stf; Hon Roll; Comp Engrng.

SANTOSUS, PATRICIA L; Mineola HS; Mineola, NY; (Y); 50/235; Key Clb; SADD; Band; Concert Band; Mrchg Band; JV Var Cheerleading; Var Socr; JV Var Sftbl; Hon Roll; Pep Clb; Suny-Albany; CPA.

SANTOWSKI, BECKY; St Marys HS; Depew, NY; (S); 12/175; Science Clb; Varsity Clb; Yrbk Stf; Lit Mag; Capt Bsktbl; Var Crs Cntry; Capt Vllybl; High Hon Roll; NHS; NY St Rgnts Schlrshp 86; Cornell U; Botany.

SANTWANI, KISHORE M; Fairport HS; Fairport, NY; (Y); Computer Clb; Leo Clb; VICA; High Hon Roll; Hon Roll; St Schlr; RIT; Elctcl Engnrng.

SANTY, DARYLE; Bishop Grimes HS; Syracuse, NY; (Y); Ski Clb; JV Bsbl; Hon Roll; AZ ST; Accntnt.

SANTY, JOEL; Franklin Acad; Malone, NY; (Y); Ski Clb; Varsity Clb; Var L Diving; Var L Ftbl; Var Trk; High Hon Roll; Hon Roll; NHS; Marshall E Howard Schlrshp; Earth Sci Merit 84; Bio Merit 85; J O Ballard Mem Schlrshp 86; Sports Med.

SAPERSTEIN, CARIN; Port Richmond HS; Staten Island, NY; (Y); Nwsp Rptr; Tennis; High Hon Roll; NHS; Arch.

SAPINSKI, RYSZARD; Brooklyn Technical HS; Brooklyn, NY; (Y); 24/1159; Capt Quiz Bowl; VP Science Clb; Rep Sr Cls; Rep Stu Cncl; Im Vllybl; High Hon Roll; Rep NHS; Prfct Atten Awd; Trstee Schlrshp 86; NY U; Biolgy.

SAPIRMAN, LOUIS; Tottenville HS; Staten Island, NY; (S); 22/850; Exploring; Scholastic Bowl; School Musical; School Play; Stage Crew; Trs Jr Cls; Swmmng; High Hon Roll; NHS; Bst Spkr-Livingston Mdl Congrss 86; Pre-Law.

SAPONARA, NICHOLAS R; St Francis Prep; Whitestone, NY; (S); 190/653; Rep Jr Cls; Rep Sr Cls; JV Bsbl; Ftbl; Vllybl; Ntl Merit SF; Schlrshp To NY Inst Of Tech 86; NY Inst Of Tech; Aero Sp Engr.

SAPONE, CAROL; Scotia Glenville HS; Scotia, NY; (Y); French Clb; JA; Key Clb; Concert Band; Jazz Band; Yrbk Stf; Bsktbl; Tennis; High Hon Roll; NHS; Awds For Comm Svc 84-85; Lib Arts.

SAPORITA, CHRISTOPHER; St Marys Boys HS; Williston Pk, NY; (S); 9/157; Boy Scts; Drama Clb; Exploring; Ski Clb; School Play; Var Crs Cntry; Var Lcrss; Score Keeper; JV Trk; Hon Roll; Eagle Scout 85; Educ.

SAPORITO, ANNA MARIA; St Joseph-By-The Sea HS; Staten Island, NY; (Y); 7/265; Var Drama Clb; Chorus; School Play; Hon Roll; NHS; Italian Mdl; 1st In Psychology; St Johns U.

SARAMA, MARK; West Seneca East HS; Cheektowaga, NY; (Y); Merit Rl 85-86.

SARATELLA, JACQUELINE; Martin Van Buren HS; Bayside, NY; (Y); 114/1000; GAA; Teachers Aide; Band; Concert Band; School Musical; Symp Band; Yrbk Stf; Hon Roll; St Johns U; Bus.

SARAVIA, MARY; Roy C Ketcham HS; Wappingers Falls, NY; (Y); Cmnty Wkr; Drama Clb; Thesps; Chorus; School Musical; School Play; Stage Crew; Ed Yrbk Stf; Stu Cncl; Lttr Roy C Ketcham Drm Clb 84-85; 3 Strs Thespian Soc 85-86; NY ST Music Assoc 2 Yrs 84-86; Jrnlsm.

SARDARO, DANIELLE; Stissing Mountain JR SR HS; Red Hook, NY; (Y); 28/101; AFS; Chorus; Yrbk Stf; Var Cheerleading; JV Var Fld Hcky; Var Trk; Hon Roll; Greene CC Columbia; Crmnl Jstc.

SARDINA, HEATHER; Fillmore Central HS; Freedom, NY; (Y); 10/60; Church Yth Grp; Band; Chorus; Church Choir; Mrchg Band; Bsktbl; Hon Roll; NHS; Houghton Coll; Mus Educ.

SARFATI, PETER; Newtown HS; Elmhurst, NY; (Y); 41/781; Chess Clb; French Clb; Band; Jazz Band; Orch; Lit Mag; Prfct Atten Awd; Cert Of Merit For Outstndg Schlrshp In Alg 84; Cert Of Awd For Schlrshp 84; Qns HS Fest Music Awd 85; Engineering.

SARGENT, MARC; Rayalton-Hartland SR HS; Middleport, NY; (Y); VICA; Var Socr; Hon Roll; Prfct Atten Awd; Stu Of Mnth 85-86; Comp Prog.

SARLES, KIMBERLY M; Roscoe Central HS; Roscoe, NY; (Y); 4/21; Drama Clb; Ski Clb; Chorus; School Play; Ed Yrbk Stf; Lit Mag; Rep Sr Cls; Hon Roll; Jr NHS; NHS; L K Fndtn Schlrshp 86-87; Dr & Mrs C H Rynlds Sci Awd 82-83; One Act Plys 83; Syracuse University.

SARNACKI, ALEXANDER C; J F Kennedy HS; Utica, NY; (Y); 53/130; Boy Scts; Pres Exploring; Ski Clb; Nwsp Rptr; Tennis; Ntl Merit Ltr; NYS Regnts Schlrshp 86; Utica Clg; Comp Sci.

SARNOWSKI, PATRICIA; Notre Dame Bishop Gibbons HS; Scotia, NY; (S); 7/100; Rep Soph Cls; Rep Jr Cls; Rep Sr Cls; Mgr(s); Dnfth Awd; High Hon Roll; NHS; Pres Schlr; Mt St Mry Coll; Pblc Rltns.

SARRA, JAMIE; Mount Mercy Acad; W Seneca, NY; (Y); Spanish Clb; School Play; Var Im Bowling; Var Sftbl; JV Var Vllybl; Vlybl MVP 85-86; NY U; Drama.

SARRETT, JEFFREY; Oceanside HS; Oceanside, NY; (Y); 31/515; Computer Clb; Key Clb; Ski Clb; Spanish Clb; Nwsp Stf; High Hon Roll; Jr NHS; NHS; Gld Medl Long Island Mth Fair 83; Excllnt Recog Long Islnd Sci Fair 83; U Of MI; Finc.

SARRIS, ARCHIE; V S Central HS; Valley Stream, NY; (Y); Camera Clb; Chess Clb; Computer Clb; Science Clb; Varsity Clb; Yrbk Phtg; HOFSTRA; Aerospc Engrng.

SARUBBI, ANNA; Bishop Kearney HS; Brooklyn, NY; (Y); 5/365; Cmnty Wkr; Math Tm; Chorus; Mgr Stage Crew; Nwsp Bus Mgr; Yrbk Stf; Ed Lit Mag; High Hon Roll; NHS; Prfct Atten Awd; LFA Awd Lcl 1261 86; Kngsbrgh CC Fndtn Awd 86; Prsdntl Acdmc Ftnss Awds Pgm 86; Hunter Coll; Pre-Med.

SARVAIYA, NASIM; Sherman Central Schl; Sherman, NY; (Y); French Clb; Cheerleading; Tennis; Fredonia U.

SASS, CYNTHIA; Lackawanna SR HS; Lackawanna, NY; (Y); Church Yth Grp; Girl Scts; Chorus; Church Choir; Erie Comm Coll; Sec.

SASSE, ROBERT J; Fiarport HS; Fairport, NY; (Y); Church Yth Grp; Drama Clb; German Clb; Ski Clb; JV Trk; Hon Roll; NY ST Rgnts Schlrshp 86; Monroe CC; Engrng Sci.

SASSI, REBEKAH; Gloversville HS; Gloversvl, NY; (Y); Drama Clb; Chorus; School Musical; School Play; Stage Crew; Swing Chorus; Yrbk Stf; Trs Stu Cncl; NHS; Foster Prnts Pln Schlrshp; Fine Arts.

SASSO, SISTO; Amsterdam HS; Amsterdam, NY; (Y); Air Force.

SATELL, EVA; Grover Cleveland HS; Brooklyn, NY; (Y); 1/612; Am Leg Aux Girls St; Math Clb; Capt Math Tm; Scholastic Bowl; Science Clb; Var Tennis; Gov Hon Prg Awd; NCTE Awd; NHS; Pres Schlr; Untd Fdrtn Of Tchrs Schlrshp Fnd 86-87; Gvnrs Cmt Of Schlstc Achvt Awd 86; Queens Coll Achvt Awd 85-86; Cornell U; Med.

SATELMAJER, HEIDI; Union Springs Acad; Union Springs, NY; (Y); 20/48; Ski Clb; Band; Concert Band; Sec Sr Cls; Hon Roll; Natl Music Prfrmnce Trust Funds Awd 86; Atlantic Union Coll; Phys Ther.

SATO, AMY F; Lake Placid HS; Lake Placid, NY; (Y); 1/41; CAP; Drama Clb; Chorus; School Musical; Yrbk Stf; Bausch & Lomb Sci Awd; High Hon Roll; NHS; Ntl Merit SF; Rensselaer Medal-Math & Sci 85.

SATRYANO, MARIKAY; Our Lady Of Lourdes HS; Hopewell Jct, NY; (Y); 28/180; AFS; Church Yth Grp; Drama Clb; Political Wkr; SADD; Varsity Clb; Drm & Bgl; Nwsp Stf; Yrbk Stf; Rep Soph Cls; Pol Sci.

SATTERLY, BARBARA; Groton Central HS; Groton, NY; (Y); Church Yth Grp; Ski Clb; Spanish Clb; Sec Stu Cncl; Stat Bsbl; Var Cheerleading; JV Sftbl; High Hon Roll; Hon Roll; Math.

SAUCHUK, MYRIAM; F K Lane HS; Wood Haven, NY; (Y); 25/688; Nwsp Stf; Hon Roll; NHS; Hackett Medal Spch 86; Houghton Coll; Comm.

SAUDNERS, IAN G; Newark Valley HS; Newark Valley, NY; (Y); 1/120; Am Leg Boys St; Boy Scts; Drama Clb; French Clb; Quiz Bowl; Ski Clb; Varsity Clb; School Musical; School Play; Stage Crew; Amherst MA; Neurosci.

SAUER, ARTHUR; Bay Shore HS; West Islip, NY; (Y); 49/377; Church Yth Grp; Cmnty Wkr; Yrbk Ed-Chief; Yrbk Sprt Ed; Off Frsh Cls; Off Soph Cls; Off Jr Cls; Off Sr Cls; Off Stu Cncl; Crs Cntry; Siena Grant 86; Bay Shore Cmnty Stu Aid Grant 86; Outstndng Acad Achvt Awd 85-86; Siena; Attrny.

SAUL, CHRISTINE; Roy C Ketcham HS; Poughkeepsie, NY; (Y); Church Yth Grp; High Hon Roll; Jr NHS; Arts Awd Ceramics 86; Art Inst Of Philadelphia; Art.

SAULLO, DANIEL; Amsterdam HS; Amsterdam, NY; (Y); 15/316; Red Cross Aide; Scholastic Bowl; Spanish Clb; Varsity Clb; Var L Bsbl; JV Bsktbl; Var L Ftbl; Im Score Keeper; Im Wt Lftg; High Hon Roll; Ntl Hnr Soc 84-86; Ltrs-Ftbl & Bsbl 84-86; Hgh Hnr Rll-Hnr Rll 83-86; Accntng.

SAULYS, VYTAS; Shoreham-Wading River HS; Shoreham, NY; (Y); Computer Clb; Teachers Aide; Chorus; Orch.

SAUMIER, JOEL; Franklin Acad; Malone, NY; (Y); Pres Church Yth Grp; Var Swmmng; Prfct Atten Awd; Criminal Just.

SAUNDERS, RENEE; Westfield Academy & Central HS; Westfield, NY; (Y); 5/65; Am Leg Aux Girls St; Scholastic Bowl; Ski Clb; Nwsp Rptr; VP Frsh Cls; VP Jr Cls; Rep Stu Cncl; JV Var Cheerleading; High Hon Roll; NHS; U Rochester.

SAUNDERS, SUSAN; Romulus Central HS; Geneva, NY; (S); Office Aide; Sec SADD; Band; Concert Band; Jazz Band; Mrchg Band; Orch; Pep Band; School Musical; Yrbk Ed-Chief; Rochester Bus Inst; Lgl Scrtry.

SAUNDERS, TRACY; Northeastern Acad; New York, NY; (S); Church Yth Grp; Cmnty Wkr; Library Aide; Science Clb; Variety Show; Nwsp Rptr; Nwsp Stf; Rep Sr Cls; Badmtn; Swmmng; Bus Mgmnt.

SAUNDERS, WENDY; Janesville De Witt HS; Jamesville, NY; (Y); 34/264; French Clb; Latin Clb; Ski Clb; Var Socr; Var Trk; High Hon Roll; NHS; Opt Clb Awd; Socl Stds Acad Awd 86; Mst Promising Rookie Trkc 86.

SAURI, ANGEL; H S For The Humanits; New York, NY; (Y); High Hon Roll; Hon Roll; Bus.

SAURMAN, JOHN R; Walt Whitman HS; Melville, NY; (Y); 104/540; Key Clb; JV Golf; JV Lcrss; Hon Roll; JV Ftbl; U DE; Bus Adm.

SAUVE, JOCIANA; Cathedral HS; Ny, NY; (Y); Art Clb; Cmnty Wkr; Band; Mrchg Band; Pres Frsh Cls; VP Sr Cls; Hon Roll; Sullivan Cnty CC; Cmnctns.

SAUVE, SHERRY; Tupper Lake HS; Tupper Lake, NY; (Y); Art Clb; Computer Clb; Badmtn; Crs Cntry; Fld Hcky; Gym; Lcrss; Tennis; Vllybl; Pep Clb; Outstndng Sewing Studnt; 6 Gregg Typng Achvt Awds; Excllnt Typng Commendtn; Exec Sec.

SAVAGE, ANNE; Yorkwotn HS; Yorktown Hts, NY; (Y); 19/319; Cmnty Wkr; Key Clb; SADD; Chorus; Jazz Band; Symp Band; VP Stu Cncl; High Hon Roll; NHS; IBM Sci Awd 86; Smth Coll Bk Awd 85; Prk 52 Blty Awd Invlvmt Comm Affrs 86; Cornell U; Math.

SAVAGE, COLLEEN; Dominican Acad; Elmhurst, NY; (Y); Computer Clb; Variety Show; Sec Frsh Cls; Im Sftbl; Hon Roll; Co-Pres Gaelic Soc 85-87; Cert Merit Excllnc NEDT ,J; Acctg.

SAVAGE, DAVID; Nazareth Regional HS; Rockaway Point, NY; (Y); 83/250; Math Tm; Bnkng.

SAVANA JR, PHILIP A; Miller Place HS; Miller Place, NY; (Y); 29/220; JV Ftbl; Im Ice Hcky; Var L Wrstlng; Hon Roll; Jr NHS; Pres NHS; Math Sequential Course I & II 83-85; Pres Natl Hnr Scty 85-87; Hofstra U; Bus Mgt.

SAVANNAH, DEBORAH; West Seneca West SR HS; West Seneca, NY; (Y); 35/559; GAA; Hosp Aide; Chorus; Nwsp Rptr; Mgr Bsktbl; Mgr Sftbl; Swmmng; Hon Roll; Jr NHS; NHS; Volunteer Of Yr Buffalo Cath Diocese Yth Orgnztn 84; SUNY Birmingham; Nrsg.

SAVANNAH, DENISE; West Seneca West SR HS; W Seneca, NY; (Y); 4/565; GAA; Key Clb; Mathletes; Red Cross Aide; Ski Clb; Spanish Clb; Socr; Swmmng; JC Awd; Trs Jr NHS; Lions Clb Awd 86; Tchrs Assoc Schlrshp 86; Natl Hnr Soc Schlrshp 86; U Of NY Buffalo; Spch Pathlgy.

SAVARI, SERAP A; Benjamin N Cardozo HS; Bayside, NY; (Y); 2/531; Mathletes; Capt Math Tm; Scholastic Bowl; Lit Mag; Gov Hon Prg Awd; Jr NHS; NHS; Ntl Merit SF; Pres Schlr; Sal; Wstnghse Sci Tlnt Srch Fnlst 86; Mobil Fndtn Schlrshp Awd 86; Wnnr Empire ST Schlrshp 86; MA Inst Tech; Elec Engrng.

SAVASTANO, MICHAEL; North Babylon HS; N Babylon, NY; (Y); Intnl Clb; Drm Mjr(t); Jazz Band; Orch; JV Var Bsbl; Bsktbl; High Hon Roll; NHS; Office Aide; Band; Coaches Awd 84; Italian Hnr Soc 85; Intl Baccalaureate Pgm 85-86; Chld Psych.

SAVASTINO, ANDREW; Liverpool HS; Liverpool, NY; (Y); 150/850; Church Yth Grp; Computer Clb; VP JA; Var L Tennis; MIP-VRSTY Tnns Tm 86.

SAVILLE, RUSSELL; Hudson Falls HS; Hudson Falls, NY; (Y); 37/214; 4-H; Ski Clb; SADD; Acpl Chr; Chorus; Church Choir; School Musical; Stage Crew; Off Frsh Cls; Off Church Yth Grp; Kingsbury Volntr Fire Co 86; Van Bishop Music Awd 86; Drama Clb Awd 86; SUNY Cobleskill; Ag.

SAVINO, DIANE; Moore Catholic HS; Staten Island, NY; (Y); Stage Crew; Nwsp Stf; Yrbk Stf; Hon Roll; St Johns U; Acctg.

SAVINO, TRACEY A; East Islip HS; Islip Terrace, NY; (Y); 5/425; Band; Concert Band; Mrchg Band; Orch; School Musical; Mat Maids; High Hon Roll; Jr NHS; NHS; Prsdntl Acad Ftns Awd 86; Amrcnsm Awd 86; Outstndng Achvt In Italian 86; Coll Of Nore Dame; Lawyer.

SAVIO, CHRISTINA; Farmingdale SR HS; Farmingdale, NY; (Y); Art Clb; Dance Clb; Key Clb; Ski Clb; Rep Frsh Cls; Hon Roll; Merit Roll; Karate Prmtns; Art Cert For Art Shws; Buffalo; Engl.

SAVKA, TRACY LYNN; Vestal SR HS; Vestal, NY; (Y); VP German Clb; Intnl Clb; SADD; Band; Chorus; Church Choir; Concert Band; Rep Frsh Cls; Rep Sr Cls; Rep Stu Cncl; Yth Cncl Agnst Smkng 84-86; Prfct Atten 84-85; Broome CC.

SAVKAR, SONYA; Niskayuna HS; Schenectady, NY; (Y); AFS; Trs German Clb; Latin Clb; Political Wkr; Lit Mag; Mgr Tennis; NHS; Ntl Merit Ltr; Frgn Lang Hnr Scty 86-87; Cornell U; Bus.

SAVONA, ANTHONY W; Sachem North HS; Centereach, NY; (Y); 53/1365; Art Clb; Radio Clb; NHS; Regents Schlrshp 86; St Johns U.

SAVONE, DINO; Lincoln HS; Yonkers, NY; (Y); Camera Clb; Computer Clb; Hon Roll; Fordham U; Law.

SAVORY, KEVIN; Grand Island HS; Grand Island, NY; (Y); 32/325; Trs Church Yth Grp; Ski Clb; VP Band; Jazz Band; Var Diving; Im Vllybl; Hon Roll; NHS; Boy Scts; Varsity Clb; Egl Sct 84; Rtry Ctzn Of Mnth 85; Clarkson U; Engnrng.

SAWDEY, ROBIN; York Central HS; Piffard, NY; (Y); Trk; Cls Rm Hnr Awd Home Ec 85-86; AFS & Library Clb 84-86; MCC; Human Svcs.

SAWHNEY, SARA; John Dewey HS; Brooklyn, NY; (Y); Dance Clb; Hosp Aide; VP JA; Science Clb; Service Clb; Nwsp Rptr.

SAWICKI, ERIC; Susquehanna Valley SR HS; Binghamton, NY; (Y); Chess Clb; Computer Clb; Mathletes; Pep Clb; VP Spanish Clb; SADD; Variety Show; Nwsp Bus Mgr; Nwsp Rptr; Rep Soph Cls; Natl Spnsh Cntst 1st Pl 85; SUNY Binghamton; Entrprnr.

SAWKIW JR, MICHAEL; Cohoes HS; Cohoes, NY; (Y); 4/184; Church Yth Grp; Political Wkr; Science Clb; Stu Cncl; High Hon Roll; NHS; Ntl Merit Schol; Spnsh Merit Awd 83-85; Union Coll; Comp Engrng.

SAWN, DALE; Queensbury HS; Glens Falls, NY; (Y); 44/262; Chorus; Trk; Hon Roll; Prfct Atten Awd.

SAWTELL, SEAN E; Roy C Ketcham HS; Wappinger Fls, NY; (Y); 24/500; 4-H; Math Clb; High Hon Roll; Hon Roll; NHS; Regents Scholar.

SAWYER, MELONY R; Akron Central JR SR HS; Lockport, NY; (Y); 26/137; Church Yth Grp; Library Aide; Nwsp Rptr; Yrbk Ed-Chief; Yrbk Phtg; Bsktbl; Sftbl; Vllybl; NYS Regents Schlrshp 86; Nazareth; Eng Tchr.

SAXE, HEATHER; Gates-Chili SR HS; Rochester, NY; (S); 3/446; VP French Clb; Hosp Aide; Mathletes; Band; Jazz Band; School Play; Stage Crew; High Hon Roll; NHS; Ntl Merit Ltr; Geology.

SAXE, MAUREEN E; Waverly HS; Waverly, NY; (Y); 3/150; Hosp Aide; Chorus; Church Choir; School Play; NHS; St Schlr; Beaver Coll; Sci Illustrtn.

SAXENA, MANU; Beach Channel HS; Rockaway, NY; (Y); 3/350; Computer Clb; Math Clb; Math Tm; Science Clb; SADD; Nwsp Ed-Chief; Diving; Bausch & Lomb Sci Awd; Gov Hon Prg Awd; High Hon Roll; Westinghouse Sci Tlnt Srch 86; Rensselaer Mdl Math 85; Steven Specter Humntrn Awd 86; Cornell; Physics.

SAXON, CLARISSIE L; South Park HS; Buffalo, NY; (Y); Teachers Aide; Hon Roll; Hnr Achvt In Sci Awd 83; Natl JR Greats Bks Prog Clb 86; U Of Buffalo; Writer.

SAXTON, CHRIS; Southwestern Central HS; Jamestown, NY; (Y); Spanish Clb; High Hon Roll; Hon Roll; Dept Achvt Awds-Sci & Scl Stds 83-84; Engl Dept Achvt Awd 84-86; Med.

SAYA, RUTH; The Franciscan Acad; Syracuse, NY; (Y); 8/26; VP Debate Tm; GAA; Ski Clb; Yrbk Stf; Sec Stu Cncl; Capt Cheerleading; Tennis; Hon Roll; St Josephs Hosp; Nrsng.

SAYER, SYLVIA; Saint Vincent Ferrer HS; Jackson Hts, NY; (Y); 9/119; High Hon Roll; Hon Roll; Recipnt Medaille Schlrshp 86; Hnr Medal GPA 90 Pct 86; Saint Joseph Coll; Child Psych.

SAYERS, FAWN; Connetquot HS; Oakdale, NY; (Y); 283/700; Art Clb; Church Yth Grp; Drama Clb; Var Cheerleading; Var Capt Gym; Cit Awd; Hon Roll; MVP Gymnstcs 83 & 85; Coach Awd 84-85; Al-Cnty Tm Gymnstcs 85-86; W Sayvl Fire Dept Schlrshp 86; Springfield Coll MA; Sprts Bio.

SAYLES, LISA; Oneida HS; Oneida, NY; (S); 1/215; Sec Civic Clb; Mathletes; Sec Sr Cls; CC Awd; Dnfth Awd; Pres NHS; Val; RPI Math & Sci Awd 85; JR Achvt Awd 85; Med.

SBUTTONI, KERI-LYN; Meray HS; Albany, NY; (Y); Chorus; Var Capt Cheerleading; JV Coach Actv; Var Capt Pom Pon; High Hon Roll; Hon Roll; NHS; 4 Yr Schlrshp Mercy HC 83; Acadmc Awds 84-86; Pre-Law.

SCACCIA, JENNIFER; York Central HS; Mt Morris, NY; (Y); Art Clb; 4-H; Band; Swmmng; Wt Lftg; 4-H Awd; Hon Roll; Parsons LA; Fshn Dsgn.

SCACCIA, MICAHEL; Rome Catholic HS; Utica, NY; (Y); Cmnty Wkr; Letterman Clb; Spanish Clb; SADD; Varsity Clb; Stage Crew; Off Frsh Cls; Stu Cncl; Bsbl; Golf; Schl Engl Awd Ishmn Yr 84; Hist & Gvt Awd NHGA 86; Typng Awd 86; VT Acad; Lwyr.

SCADUTO, MATTHEW; Smithtown HS West; Smithtown, NY; (Y); JV Bsbl; JV Ftbl; JV Trk; JV Wrstlng; Hon Roll 80-83; Manhattan Coll; Hstry.

SCAFIDE, LISA; Smithtown HS; Hauppauge, NY; (Y); Dance Clb; Drama Clb; French Clb; Spanish Clb; Cheerleading; Mgr(s); Itln Clb 83-86; Itln Hnr Soc 83-86; Kickln 85-86; Tobe Coburn; Intl Buyr.

SCAIFE, JENNIFER; Linton HS; Schenectady, NY; (Y); 5/296; Acpl Chr; Band; Church Choir; Var Socr; Var Trk; Kiwanis Awd; NHS; Pres Schlr; Church Yth Grp; 4-H; AAL All-Coll Schlrshp 86; Amherst Coll Schlrshp 86; Amherst Coll; Neurosci.

SCALES, SHAYNE; Thousand Islands Central HS; Clayton, NY; (Y); JA; Mathletes; School Play; Hon Roll; Jr NHS; Lion Awd; NHS; Lgl Secy.

SCALI, MARY ANN; John A Coleman HS; Tillson, NY; (S); 5/65; Drama Clb; VP Sec French Clb; Pres Soph Cls; Pres Jr Cls; Rep Sr Cls; Var L Crs Cntry; Var L Fld Hcky; Var L Trk; Church Yth Grp; Ski Clb; Clss Sprt Awd; Parents Assc Ldrshp & Dpndblty Awd.

SCALIA, MARCELLA A; St Francis Prep; Whitestone, NY; (S); 138/749; Hosp Aide; Church Choir; Nwsp Stf; Var JV Cheerleading; Trk; NHS; Optimate Sccty; Intrml Prgm In Ftbl & Vlybl.

SCALISE, DON; Grand Island HS; Grand Island, NY; (Y); Boy Scts; Church Yth Grp; Cmnty Wkr; FCA; Hosp Aide; Red Cross Aide; Band; Concert Band; Jazz Band; Pep Band; Canisus Coll; Chem.

SCALISE, PETER; Connetquot HS; Oakdale, NY; (Y); 144/712; Aud/Vis; Camera Clb; Computer Clb; Radio Clb; SADD; Ftbl; Ice Hcky; Wt Lftg; Wrstlng; Hon Roll; Stoneybrook; Med.

SCALLAN, GREGORY; Msgr Farrell HS; Staten Island, NY; (Y); 43/319; Cmnty Wkr; Service Clb; Spanish Clb; Rep Soph Cls; Im Bsktbl; Var Crs Cntry; Var Trk; High Hon Roll; Jr NHS; NHS; NYC CHSAA Soph All Str X-Cntry 84; NY St Empr St Games Fnlst Trck 85; Tchr Of Christn Message 86; Elec Engr.

SCALLY, DONNA; Hudson Falls SR HS; Hudson Fls, NY; (Y); 2/275; Am Leg Aux Girls St; Church Yth Grp; Drama Clb; Key Clb; SADD; High Hon Roll; NHS; Ntl Merit SF; Westminster; Psych.

SCALZA, LISA; N Babylon HS; No Babylon, NY; (Y); 67/450; Drama Clb; Hosp Aide; Intnl Clb; Thesps; School Musical; School Play; Bsktbl; Socr; Tennis; High Hon Roll; Phys Ther.

SCALZI, LISA; New Paltz HS; New Paltz, NY; (Y); 16/176; Debate Tm; Radio Clb; Spanish Clb; Chorus; Flag Corp; Nwsp Stf; Trk; Vllybl; High Hon Roll; NHS; Spkng Awd Arlngtn Mdl Cngrss 85; SUNY Albany; Chem.

SCALZO, DAVID; Jamesville-De Witt HS; Dewitt, NY; (Y); 10/245; Church Yth Grp; Exploring; VP Pres Model UN; Variety Show; Rptr Nwsp Stf; Var L Crs Cntry; Var L Trk; High Hon Roll; VP NHS; Ntl Merit Schol; Ondga Cnty Med Soc Axlry Schlrshp 86; Acdmc Achvt Hlth Awd 86; Dlgt Awd Mdl UN Cnfrnc 86; Lehigh U; Med.

SCAMPOLI, JOSEPH; Germantown Central HS; Elizaville, NY; (S); 5/53; Yrbk Stf; Vllybl; High Hon Roll; Hon Roll; NHS.

SCANLAN, KELLY; West Irondequoit HS; Rochester, NY; (Y); Model UN; Mgr Radio Clb; School Musical; Yrbk Phtg; Yrbk Stf; Photo.

SCANLON, KELLEY; Henninger HS; Syracuse, NY; (Y); Faith Cntr 83-86; Phi Sigma Delt Sorority 85-86; Part Time Job 86; Jrnlsm.

SCANLON, MAUREEN; Glen Cove HS; Glen Cove, NY; (Y); 20/266; Sec Civic Clb; French Clb; Pep Clb; Yrbk Stf; Var Score Keeper; JV Sftbl; Var Trk; Var Vllybl; Hon Roll; NHS; Bio.

SCANLON JR, THOMAS J; Our Lady Of Lourdes; Poughkeepsie, NY; (Y); 70/180; Church Yth Grp; Drama Clb; Ski Clb; School Play; Yrbk Stf; Var Capt Socr; Pre Law.

SCANLON, VERA M; Marymount Schl; Brooklyn, NY; (Y); Church Yth Grp; Pres Intnl Clb; Pres Speech Tm; Rep Jr Cls; Rep Sr Cls; Bsktbl; Hon Roll; NHS; Ntl Merit Ltr; Pol Sci.

SCANNAPIECO, THOMAS; Hicksville HS; Hicksville, NY; (Y); 12/456; Boy Scts; Science Clb; Ski Clb; Var Bowling; JV Golf; Im Ice Hcky; High Hon Roll; Jr NHS; NHS; VFW Awd; U DE; Chem Eng.

SCANNELL, PATRICK S; Lake Placid Central Schl; Lake Placid, NY; (Y); 4/44; Church Yth Grp; Key Clb; Varsity Clb; Yrbk Stf; Var Capt Crs Cntry; Var Capt Trk; NHS; Ntl Merit SF; CAP; Yrbk Rptr; 2 Schl Rcrds Trck 84-85; 23rd ST Chmpshp X Crss Sking 84-85; Colgate U; Lib Arts.

SCANO, NICOLE; F D Roosevelt HS; Poughkeepsie, NY; (Y); SADD; Lit Mag; Cheerleading; Sftbl; Hon Roll; Rgnts Schlrshp 86; Rutgers; Engrng.

SCARABELLI, PETER; John H Glenn HS; E Northport, NY; (Y); Chess Clb; Chorus; Ftbl; Trk; Wrstlng; High Hon Roll; Hon Roll; Jr NHS; Corp Law.

SCARANTINO, STEPHEN; Garden City SR HS; Garden City, NY; (Y); 90/360; Exploring; Intnl Clb; Mrchg Band; Yrbk Rptr; Yrbk Stf; Trs Jr Cls; Rep Stu Cncl; Socr; High Hon Roll; Jr NHS; Exploring Citation; Distnghsd Svc Awd Med Exporer Conf BSA 86.

SCARBOROUGH, JANEL; Freeport HS; Freeport, NY; (S); Cmnty Wkr; VP DECA; Radio Clb; Teachers Aide; Rep Frsh Cls; Rep Soph Cls; Rep Jr Cls; Rep Stu Cncl; Var Capt Cheerleading; Cit Awd; 1st Pl Nassau DECA Elmntns 86; Brdcstng.

SCARBOROUGH, RALPH; Richmond Hill HS; Richmond Hill, NY; (Y); 20/308; Office Aide; Hon Roll; Jr NHS; NHS; Mth Hnr Soc 85-86; Eng Hnr Soc 86; Soc Stud Hnr Soc 86; Bus Admin.

SCARBOROUGH, THOMAS M; Millbrook Schl; Poughkeepsie, NY; (Y); Nwsp Stf; Ice Hcky; Lcrss; Socr; High Hon Roll; Hon Roll; St Schlr; Hd Of Arts Cmnty Svc-Commended Twice; Cornell U; Natural Rsrcs.

SCARDINA, MARY BETH; Bayport Blue Point HS; Bayport, NY; (Y); 27/210; Orch; Score Keeper; Hon Roll.

SCARDINO JR, RICHARD J; St Francis Prep; Ozone Park, NY; (S); 13/653; Math Tm; High Hon Roll; NHS; Ntl Merit Ltr; Acadmc Al-Amer 85; Medcl Dr.

SCARDINO, TRICIA; Fairport HS; Fairport, NY; (Y); Drama Clb; Chorus; School Musical; Stage Crew; Yrbk Sprt Ed; Yrbk Stf; High Hon Roll; Hwlt-Pckrd Schlrshp 86; NY ST Rgnts Schlrshp 86; Drama.

SCARFONE, PAULA; Hilton Central HS; Hilton, NY; (Y); 27/299; Drama Clb; Model UN; School Play; Nwsp Stf; Ed Yrbk Stf; High Hon Roll; Hon Roll; NHS; Geneseo ST U; Bus.

SCARIATI, FRANK A; Mt St Michaels Acad; Bronx, NY; (Y); Chess Clb; Computer Clb; Church Choir; Bsktbl; Fld Hcky; Ftbl; Sftbl; Hon Roll; Ntl Merit Ltr.

SCARINGE, DELYNN; Colonie Central HS; Albany, NY; (Y); 40/482; Drama Clb; Pres Sec Key Clb; Pres Pep Clb; Orch; Off Stu Cncl; Cheerleading; Score Keeper; High Hon Roll; Kiwanis Awd; NHS; Princpls Leadrshp Awd 86; ST U-Albany NY; Eductn.

SCARINGE, MICHELLE; Bishop Maginn HS; Albany, NY; (S); Math Clb; VP Jr Cls; JV Var Cheerleading; JV Var Pom Pon; High Hon Roll; Hon Roll.

SCARINGELLA, MICHELE; Sacred Heart Acad; New Hyde Park, NY; (S); 3/182; Intnl Clb; Math Clb; Var Math Tm; School Play; Nwsp Ed-Chief; Var Socr; NHS; Cthlc Dghtrs Amer Essy Cntst 84; Engl.

SCARPELLI, ELIZABETH; Albertus Magnus HS; Pearl River, NY; (Y); 88/175; Ski Clb; JV Sftbl; Tennis; Manhattan Coll; Bus.

SCARPELLO, RACHEL; Hamburg SR HS; Hamburg, NY; (Y); AFS; Church Yth Grp; Library Aide; SADD; Chorus; Nwsp Stf; Cazenovia Clg; Socl Wrk.

SCARSELLA, DAVID J; Binghamton HS; Binghamton, NY; (Y); 56/500; Var Wrstlng; High Hon Roll; Hon Roll; Rgncy Schlrshp 85-86; SUNY Binghamton.

SCARTON, H JAMES; Troy HS; Troy, NY; (Y); 8/490; Boy Scts; Pres Drama Clb; Red Cross Aide; Chorus; Jazz Band; School Musical; School Play; Nwsp Rptr; NHS; Ntl Merit Ltr; Rensselaer Polytech; Engr.

SCATENATO, ANTHONY V; Harrison HS; Harrison, NY; (Y); 37/200; Boy Scts; Church Yth Grp; Computer Clb; Math Tm; Band; Concert Band; Jazz Band; Mrchg Band; Pep Band; Symp Band; SUNY-BUFFALO; Engr.

SCATTAGLIA, CHRISTINA; St John Villa Acad; Staten Island, NY; (Y); 23/103; Art Clb; Dance Clb; Math Tm; Stage Crew; Yrbk Stf; Rep Jr Cls; VP Stu Cncl; Diligence & Efrt Awd 86; Lang Study Exclnc Awd 86; Natl Sci Olympiad 83-84; Fshn Inst Of Tech; Fshn Buying.

SCATURRO, ANGELO; Marlboro Central HS; Marlboro, NY; (Y); 4/160; Am Leg Boys St; Church Yth Grp; SADD; Varsity Clb; Yrbk Stf; Rep Soph Cls; Tennis; High Hon Roll; Jr NHS; NHS; Albany ST U; Law.

SCAVO, SUSAN; Hicksville SR HS; Hicksville, NY; (Y); Church Yth Grp; Dance Clb; French Clb; Hosp Aide; SADD; Flag Corp; Orch; Stage Crew; Rep Stu Cncl; Swmmng; Med.

SCAVONE, PETER; St John The Baptist HS; Massapequa, NY; (S); 13/501; Ftbl; Lcrss; Hon Roll; Ftbl Dfnsv Capt 84; Vrsty Lcrss All Leag Hon Ment 85; Vrsty Ftbl 1st Tm All Leag Dfns Athl/Acad Awd 85.

SCAZZERO, JAMES D; Pelham Memorial HS; Bronxville, NY; (Y); 16/160; Teachers Aide; Variety Show; Pres Jr Cls; Rep Stu Cncl; JV Var Bsbl; JV Bsktbl; Var Capt Ftbl; Wt Lftg; Hon Roll; NHS; Ntl Ftbl Fndtn Schlr Athlete Awd 86; 2 Vrsty Lttrs; Notre Dame U; Engr.

SCERBO, DEBBIE; Dominican Commercial HS; Richmond Hill, NY; (Y); Drama Clb; Pep Clb; Y-Teens; Chorus; Wt Lftg; St Johns U; Psych.

SCERBO, ED; G Ray Bodley HS; Fulton, NY; (Y); 19/250; Exploring; Ski Clb; Variety Show; Lcrss; Capt Socr; Wt Lftg; Wrstlng; Hon Roll; St Schlr; Fulton Polish Hm Schlrshp 86; FL Inst Of Tech; Aircrft Sys.

SCHAAF, DENISE M; Keshegua HS; Hunt, NY; (Y); 7/68; Sec Church Yth Grp; Pep Clb; Sec Ski Clb; Band; Chorus; Nwsp Stf; Yrbk Stf; Trs Frsh Cls; Soph Cls; Jr Cls; U Of Buffalo; Pharm.

SCHAAL, TODD; Camden Central HS; Camden, NY; (Y); Mathletes; Varsity Clb; Rep Soph Cls; Bsbl; Ftbl; Wt Lftg; Wrstlng; High Hon Roll; NHS; Engrng.

SCHABER, BETHANN; Alden Central HS; Lancaster, NY; (Y); Am Leg Aux Girls St; Letterman Clb; VP SADD; School Musical; Swing Chorus; Yrbk Ed-Chief; Rep Stu Cncl; Var Cheerleading; Var Tennis; Trs NHS; Bio.

SCHABER, REBA; Mount Assumption Inst; Plattsburgh, NY; (Y); Drama Clb; 4-H; Nwsp Ed-Chief; Im Powder Puff Ftbl; High Hon Roll; Rgnts Schlrshp 86; High Hnrs Grad 86; US Air Force.

SCHACHENMAYR, VOLKER; Northwood Schl; Lake Placid, NY; (Y); 2/35; Trs Drama Clb; Pres Key Clb; Ski Clb; Concert Band; Jazz Band; Mrchg Band; School Play; Var Crs Cntry; Var Golf; JV Socr; Lib Arts.

SCHADE, KATHY; Avon Central HS; Rush, NY; (Y); 4-H; Ski Clb; Band; Yrbk Stf; JV Socr; Var Trk; Vllybl; Hon Roll; Jr NHS; Bus.

SCHAEFER, CATHERINE M; Villa Maria Acad; Sloan, NY; (Y); Church Yth Grp; French Clb; Girl Scts; School Play; Variety Show; Var Cheerleading; Hon Roll; Erie CC; Resprtry Thrpy.

SCHAEFER, FRANK; John Jay SR HS; Goldens Bridge, NY; (Y); Science Clb; Cit Awd; Exclince Math; Comp Dsgn.

SCHAEFER, KAREN JEANETTE; Linton HS; Schenectady, NY; (Y); JCL; Key Clb; Pres Service Clb; Chorus; Nwsp Stf; Rep Frsh Cls; Off Soph Cls; VP Jr Cls; Pres Sr Cls; Rep Stu Cncl; NYU; Econ.

SCHAEFER, NANCY; Ward Melville HS; Centereach, NY; (Y); 64/665; VP Pres GAA; Hosp Aide; Ski Clb; Spanish Clb; SADD; Nwsp Stf; Yrbk Stf; Var Capt Fld Hcky; Var VP Trk; High Hon Roll; Outstndng Acad Achvt 84-86.

SCHAEFER, SANDY; Walt Whitman HS; Huntington, NY; (Y); 30/487; Church Yth Grp; 4-H; GAA; Key Clb; Mathletes; Chorus; Co-Capt Gym; Mgr(s); Var L Trk; Mst Dtrmnd Bst Attitutde Gym Awd 85; Physcl Thrpy.

SCHAEFER, TERRY; Bethpage HS; Bethpage, NY; (Y); Cmnty Wkr; Exploring; German Clb; Hosp Aide; Red Cross Aide; Pres SADD; Stu Cncl; Score Keeper; Capt Swmmng; Timer; Nrsng.

SCHAEFER, THOMAS; Msgr Farrell HS; Staten Island, NY; (S); 68/292; Bsbl; Bsktbl; Ftbl; Trk; Wt Lftg; Columbia U; Bus.

SCHAEFFER, CHRIS; Mc Quaid Jesuit HS; Penfield, NY; (Y); Church Yth Grp; Letterman Clb; Ski Clb; Im Ftbl; Var Golf; Rswl Pk Mem Inst Rsrch Prtcptn Pgm 86; Pre-Med.

SCHAEFFER, CHRISTOPHER P; City Honors Schl; Buffalo, NY; (Y); 1/105; Drama Clb; Latin Clb; Mathletes; Quiz Bowl; Science Clb; VP Soph Cls; Pres Jr Cls; Pres Sr Cls; Chrmn Stu Cncl; Co-Capt Socr; Havard Bk Awd 85; Engr.

SCHAEFFER, MATTHEW; Mc Quaid Jesuit HS; Rochester, NY; (Y); Cmnty Wkr; Varsity Clb; Ed Yrbk Ed-Chief; Var L Trk; NHS; Prfct Atten Awd; U Of Rochester; Bus.

SCHAEFFLER, LISA; Corcoran HS; Syracuse, NY; (Y); Church Yth Grp; Computer Clb; Office Aide; Ski Clb; Spanish Clb; Band; School Play; Capt Bowling; Im Sftbl; Im Swmmng; Bryant & Stratton Business.

SCHAFER, SUZANNE; Fairport HS; Fairport, NY; (Y); Pres Trs Church Yth Grp; Trs German Clb; Ski Clb; Chorus; Swing Chorus; Rep Jr Cls; Rep Stu Cncl; JV Fld Hcky; Hon Roll; NHS.

SCHAFER, TONIA; Ramstein American HS; Apo New York, NY; (Y); FBLA; JA; Socr; JV Vllybl; Outstndng Achvt-Eng & Busnss 86; Soccer Mgr Let & Plaque 86; Sec.

SCHAFFER, BETH; Ravena-Coeymans-Selkirk HS; Ravena, NY; (Y); Art Clb; Drama Clb; FTA; Pres German Clb; Girl Scts; Capt Pep Clb; SADD; School Musical; School Play; Yrbk Ed-Chief; Owns-Crng Fbrgls Art Cntst 85; JCA; Cmrcl Art.

SCHAFFER, JACKIE; Haverling Central HS; Bath, NY; (Y); Art Clb; Church Yth Grp; French Clb; FTA; JCL; Latin Clb; Yrbk Stf; Score Keeper; DAR Awd; Hon Roll; Psych.

SCHAFFER, JODIE; Herricks HS; Roslyn, NY; (Y); Hosp Aide; PAVAS; SADD; Stage Crew; Variety Show; Rep Frsh Cls; Rep Soph Cls; Off Sr Cls; Rep Stu Cncl; JV Var Tennis; Lib Arts.

SCHAFFER, KIRSTIN; E J Wilson HS; Spencerport, NY; (Y); French Clb; Ski Clb; Band; Hon Roll; ASPCA Fnls 85; Horse Awds; Kent ST; Arch.

SCHAFFNER, MICHAEL; Watkins Glen HS; Watkins Glen, NY; (Y); Boy Scts; Math Clb; VICA; JV Ftbl; Hon Roll; 3rd VICA Cmptn Elec 86; Eagle Scout Awd 85; Rochestor Inst/Tech; Elec Engr.

SCHAFRICK, STACY; Sewanhaka HS; Floral Pk, NY; (Y); Church Yth Grp; FBLA; Hon Roll; Law.

SCHAGREN, ELISSA; Lafayette HS; Brooklyn, NY; (Y); 10/300; Scholastic Bowl; Service Clb; Yrbk Bus Mgr; Lit Mag; Jr NHS; NCTE Awd; NHS; PTA Schltc Awd 83; Brooklyn Coll; Jrnlsm.

SCHAJER, ROBERT W; Professional Childrens Schl; New York, NY; (Y); Camera Clb; Drama Clb; Thesps; Chorus; School Musical; School Play; Stage Crew; Variety Show; Yrbk Ed-Chief; Rep Sr Cls; Regnts Schlrshp 86; Vassar Coll; Actr.

SCHALK, NADINE; Royalton-Harhand Central HS; Middleport, NY; (Y); 35/130; Church Yth Grp; Spanish Clb; Hst SADD; Chorus; Pres Orch; School Musical; Yrbk Bus Mgr; Yrbk Phtg; Score Keeper; NHS; Concordia Msc Schlrshp Awd 86; Lckprt Rtry Evelyn Bayliss Msc Awd Schlrsh& 86; Concordia; Msc Educ.

SCHALK, RICHARD; Cardinal Ohara HS; Tonawanda, NY; (Y); French Clb; Capt Ftbl; Var Trk; High Hon Roll; Hon Roll; Vrsty Ftbl All Cath & Mst Dedctd Plyr 85-86; Vrsty Trck All Cath & MVP 86; Canisius Coll; Bus.

SCHALLER, KATHLEEN; Spring Valley SR HS; Monsey, NY; (Y); 10/441; Church Yth Grp; Spanish Clb; Church Choir; Yrbk Stf; High Hon Roll; Jr NHS; Mu Alp Tht; NHS; Ntl Merit Ltr; Spanish NHS; U Michigan; Comp Sci.

SCHALLERT, DANIEL; Cooperstown Centeral HS; Hartwick, NY; (Y); Var JV Bsbl; Var Capt Ftbl; All Star Ftbl & Bsbl 85 & 86; Cooperstown Friends Bsbl Awd 86; MVP Bsbl 86; Walter Eggleston Ftbl Awd; Cortland ST; Phys Ed.

SCHANG, TIM; Hahn American HS; Apo New York, NY; (Y); Exploring; Model UN; Yrbk Stf; Off Jr Cls; Stu Cncl; Var L Crs Cntry; Var L Socr; Var L Wrstlng; Hon Roll; NHS.

SCHANZ, RODNEY; Middleburgh Central Schl; Middleburgh, NY; (S); Church Yth Grp; Trk; Cit Awd; High Hon Roll; Hon Roll; NHS; Prfct Atten Awd; Cert Meritrous Awd Ltr 84-85; Hghst Avg Elctrcl Trades I At Vo Tech 84-85; Elctrcn.

SCHANZENBACHER, LISA; Williamsville North HS; W Amherst, NY; (Y); Spanish Clb; SADD; JV Im Socr; Hon Roll; Mst Imprvd Sccr Plyr Schl Tm 85; Med Rcrd Adm.

SCHAPIRO, ALLISON; Port Richmond HS; Staten Island, NY; (Y); Math Tm; Temple Yth Grp; Chorus; Variety Show; Yrbk Stf; VP Stu Cncl; Var Tennis; High Hon Roll; Hon Roll; Spanish NHS; Psych.

SCHARF, CHRISTOPHER; Franklin Acad; Malone, NY; (Y); Boy Scts; Church Yth Grp; 4-H; French Clb; NFL; Ski Clb; Spanish Clb; Speech Tm; Varsity Clb; Off Frsh Cls; Paul Smiths Coll; Htl Mgmt.

SCHARRETT, JOHN; Cornwall Central HS; Cornwall Hudson, NY; (Y); Ski Clb; Jazz Band; School Play; Rep Frsh Cls; Rep Soph Cls; Rep Jr Cls; Rep Stu Cncl; Var L Socr; Var L Tennis; Hon Roll; Mech Engr.

SCHATZ, JEFFREY; Malverne HS; Long Beach, NY; (Y); Cmnty Wkr; Computer Clb; Mathletes; Math Tm; Var Bsbl; Var Tennis; Wt Lftg; Hon Roll; Prfct Atten Awd; Crss-Cntry Awd & Hrns 84-85; Math.

SCHATZLE, BARBARA K; Roy C Ketcham HS; Wappingers Falls, NY; (Y); Drama Clb; Ski Clb; Stage Crew; Yrbk Phtg; Ed Yrbk Stf; Rep Stu Cncl; Stat Bsktbl; Stat Ftbl; Hon Roll; Psych.

SCHAUB, CHRISTINE; Moore Catholic HS; Staten Island, NY; (S); 21/173; Church Yth Grp; Drama Clb; Chorus; Church Choir; School Musical; Nwsp Stf; Im Bowling; Var Socr; Hon Roll; NHS; St Johns U 85; Tchr.

SCHAUER, BETH; East Islip HS; Islip Terrace, NY; (Y); Cmnty Wkr; Hosp Aide; Intnl Clb; SADD; Band; Orch; Soph Cls; Bsktbl; Fld Hcky; Score Keeper; Sci Fair Bio 1st Pl 86.

SCHAUER, LYNN; Altmar Parish Willmstwn Cntrl HS; Parish, NY; (Y); 13/102; French Clb; Varsity Clb; Yrbk Stf; Off Stu Cncl; Stat Bsktbl; Var L Socr; Var Capt Var Trk; High Hon Roll; Hon Roll; Rptr NHS; NYS Regnts Schlrshp 86; SUNNY Buffalo; Art Ed.

SCHECHNER, SANDRA; Midwood HS At Brooklyn College; Brooklyn, NY; (Y); 20/667; Math Tm; Concert Band; Lit Mag; Var Trk; Im Wt Lftg; Hon Roll; Arista 86; Sci.

SCHECHTER, BASYA; Shulamith HS For Girls; Brooklyn, NY; (S); Dance Clb; Scholastic Bowl; School Musical; High Hon Roll; Pres NHS; Schl Svc Awd 86.

SCHECHTER, LISA; Mahopac HS; Mahopac, NY; (Y); 127/409; Spanish Clb; Bowling; Crs Cntry; Score Keeper; Trk; High Hon Roll; Hon Roll; Bus.

SCHECK, JENNIFER; Commack HS South; Commack, NY; (Y); Yrbk Stf; Stat Wrstlng; High Hon Roll; Trs NHS; Commack HS S Ldrshp Awd 86; Ntl Sci Olympiad-Bio 84-85; Suffolk Cnty Math Contest 3rd Pl 86; Law.

SCHEER, LAURIE; Mepham HS; N Bellmore, NY; (Y); Cmnty Wkr; Temple Yth Grp; Band; Off Jr Cls; Lcrss; Pom Pon; Hon Roll; NHS; Concert Band; Mrchg Band; U FL; Phy Thrpy.

SCHEFFLER, ERIC; Fox Lane HS; Bedford, NY; (Y); 52/270; Chess Clb; Scholastic Bowl; Ski Clb; Spanish Clb; School Musical; Socr; Trk; High Hon Roll; Ntl Merit Ltr; Spnsh Diplma Merit 84-86; Prfrmd 10 Classcl Guitar Cncrts; Awd Achvt Physcs Bwl 86.

SCHEFFLER, RONALD; Frontier Central HS; Blasdell, NY; (S); 38/444; Im Bsktbl; High Hon Roll; Hon Roll; NHS; NEDT Awd.

SCHEFFLER, TOM; St John The Baptist HS; Massapequa, NY; (Y); Boy Scts; Exploring; Band; Concert Band; Jazz Band; Mrchg Band; Stage Crew; Symp Band; LIMTA 85-86; Five Towns; Rcrdng Studio Engr.

SCHEFIELD, LYNN; Thousand Islands HS; Clayton, NY; (Y); 10/100; Varsity Clb; Chorus; Bsktbl; Socr; Vllybl; High Hon Roll; Hon Roll; NHS; Intl Essay Cont Wnnr 85; Ithaca Coll; Bio.

SCHEIMAN, KARA; Newfield HS; Selden, NY; (Y); Intnl Clb; Science Clb; Service Clb; Frsh Cls; Soph Cls; Jr Cls; Sr Cls; Stu Cncl; Hon Roll; Spanish NHS; Sci.

SCHEINA, MARTHA J; Sachem HS; Farmingville, NY; (Y); 183/1385; Church Yth Grp; German Clb; GAA; Var Capt Trk; Hon Roll; NY ST Rgnts Schlrshp 86; St Josephs Coll Acad Schlrshp 86; St Josephs Coll.

SCHELL, DAVID M; Carthage Central HS; Carthage, NY; (Y); 1/200; Pres Church Yth Grp; Math Clb; Nwsp Stf; Tennis; High Hon Roll; NHS; Ntl Merit SF; Bus Mgt.

SCHELL, GEORGE A; Mc Quaid Jesuit HS; Fairport, NY; (Y); Model UN; Chorus; School Musical; VP Capt Crs Cntry; VP L Trk; Hon Roll; NHS; Royden Smith Mem Schlrshp 85; Regents Schlrshp 86; Eagle Sct 84; U Of Rochester.

SCHELL, JAMES M; St Francis Prep; Middle Village, NY; (S); 8/653; VP Computer Clb; Math Tm; Vllybl; NHS; Prncpls List 83-85; Queens Coll Prsdntl Awd 83-85; Stu Actv Awd 85; Elec Engr.

SCHELL, KELLY; Lawrence HS; Inwood, NY; (Y); AFS; Dance Clb; Orch; Sftbl; Hon Roll; Arizona; Pltcl Sci.

SCHELLBERG, LAURA; Sachem HS; Holbrook, NY; (Y); 144/1600; German Clb; Ski Clb; Band; Yrbk Stf; JV Bsktbl; JV Socr; Sftbl; Var Tennis; Var Vllybl; NHS.

SCHEMINGER, HOLLY; Archbishop Walsh HS; Olean, NY; (Y); Math Clb; Spanish Clb; Yrbk Phtg; Sec Trs Frsh Cls; VP Stu Cncl; Var Capt Bsktbl; Score Keeper; High Hon Roll; Mu Alp Tht; NHS.

SCHEMITSCH, RICHARD; Msgr Mc Clancy Memorial HS; Glendale, NY; (Y); 68/251; Computer Clb; Hosp Aide; Church Choir; Trk; Hon Roll; Schl Sci Fr 2nd & 3rd Pl 83 & 85; St Johns U; Elec Engrng.

SCHEMPF, JUDY; Fabius Pompey HS; Pompey, NY; (Y); 4/150; Girl Scts; Pres SADD; Nwsp Ed-Chief; Rep Frsh Cls; Var L Cheerleading; Var L Pom Pon; High Hon Roll; Jr NHS; NHS; Exploring; Cortland Schlr Pgm, Oper Enterprise Schlr 86; Bio.

SCHENKMAN, MARK; E L Vandermuelen HS; Mt Sinai, NY; (Y); FBLA; Temple Yth Grp; Band; Concert Band; Jazz Band; Mrchg Band; Orch; Symp Band; St Schlr; NYS Rgnts Schlrshp 86; SUNY Albany; Pre-Med.

SCHEPER, JEANNE; John Adams HS; Howard Bch, NY; (Y); Church Yth Grp; Office Aide; Teachers Aide; Church Choir; High Hon Roll; Hon Roll; NHS; Prfct Atten Awd; 2 Italian Awds 86; Educ.

SCHEPISI, MICHELE; James E Sperry HS; Rochester, NY; (Y); 15/300; French Clb; Latin Clb; Rep Frsh Cls; Rep Soph Cls; Rep Jr Cls; Rep Stu Cncl; JV Var Sftbl; JV Vllybl; French Hon Soc; Hon Roll; Law.

SCHER, ALEX; Shenea Schawa HS; Clifton Park, NY; (Y); 67/680; SADD; Pres Temple Yth Grp; JV Bowling; High Hon Roll; Hon Roll; NHS; Elec Engrng.

SCHER, CARA F; Wantagh HS; Wantagh, NY; (Y); 30/275; Pres Drama Clb; SADD; Temple Yth Grp; Acpl Chr; Chorus; Orch; School Musical; School Play; Variety Show; Hon Roll; Arts Recogntn Talent Search 86; Syracuse U; Musical Theatre.

SCHER, MATTHEW; South Side HS; Rockville Centre, NY; (Y); 3/278; Boy Scts; VP Latin Clb; Mathletes; Pres Science Clb; JV Var Tennis; JV Var Wrstlng; Bausch & Lomb Sci Awd; JETS Awd; NHS; Ntl Merit Ltr; Engrng.

SCHEREK, ROXANE J; Sanford H Calhoun HS; Merrick, NY; (Y); 17/313; Hst DECA; Scholastic Bowl; Rptr Nwsp Rptr; Yrbk Bus Mgr; Yrbk Phtg; Yrbk Stf; Off Soph Cls; Hon Roll; St Schlr; Bus.

SCHERER, MICHELLE; Susquehanna Valley HS; Conklin, NY; (Y); VP SADD; Nwsp Rptr; Nwsp Stf; VP Sr Cls; Pres Stu Cncl; Stat Trk; Var JV Vllybl; Hon Roll; Spanish NHS; Scl Wrk.

SCHERHAUFER, SCOTT; Chenago Forks HS; Castle Creek, NY; (Y); 24/174; Var Bsbl; Var Capt Wrstlng; Hon Roll; NHS; NY ST Wrstlg Fnlst 85 & 86; Oswego ST; Environmental.

SCHERMERHORN, CARRIE; Whitney Point HS; Whitney Pt, NY; (Y); Church Yth Grp; French Clb; Ski Clb; Concert Band; Jazz Band; Mrchg Band; Var Cheerleading; High Hon Roll; Band; Widener U; Fshn Merch.

SCHETTINE, KATRINA; York Central HS; Linwood, NY; (Y); Pres Art Clb; 4-H; Ski Clb; Teachers Aide; School Play; Ed Nwsp Ed-Chief; Nwsp Stf; Socr; Tennis; Trk; 1st Rnnr Up Miss Livingston Cnty 85; Phys Fit Awds 84-86; Fash Desgn.

SCHIAVI, CHRISTINE; Batavia HS; Batavia, NY; (Y); GAA; Ski Clb; Varsity Clb; Chorus; School Musical; Swing Chorus; Capt Var Tennis; High Hon Roll; Rotary Awd; Outstndng Chorus Stu 86; Brockport; Bus.

SCHIAVONE, DANIEL W; Holley JR SR HS; Holley, NY; (Y); 4/102; Pres Frsh Cls; Pres Soph Cls; Pres Jr Cls; Sec Sr Cls; Pres Stu Cncl; JV Tennis; Bausch & Lomb Sci Awd; High Hon Roll; NHS; Acadmc All Amercn 86; Rgnts Schlrshp-NY ST 86; U Of Buffalo; Med.

SCHIAVONE, LYNN; Mahopac HS; Mahopac, NY; (Y); 69/409; Church Yth Grp; Dance Clb; Ski Clb; Im Crs Cntry; Im Trk; High Hon Roll; Hon Roll; NHS; Rutgers U.

SCHIAVONE, SHANNON; Marlboro HS; Marlboro, NY; (Y); Pres Chorus; Yrbk Stf; Hon Roll; Ntl Hnr Roll 86; Marist Coll; Bus Mgmt.

SCHIAVONI, CHARLES; Cold Spring Harbor HS; Cold Spring Har, NY; (Y); 8/140; Intnl Clb; Letterman Clb; Mathletes; Lcrss; Swmmng; High Hon Roll; Hon Roll; Jr NHS; NHS; Georgetown U; Econ.

SCHICK, CURTIS; W C Mepham HS; N Bellmore, NY; (Y); Boy Scts; JV Crs Cntry; Var Trk; Hon Roll; Jr NHS.

SCHICKEL II, HUBERT C; Franklin Acad; Malone, NY; (Y); 21/266; AFS; Am Leg Boys St; Boy Scts; Church Yth Grp; French Clb; Math Tm; Model UN; ROTC; Ski Clb; Speech Tm; Cornell; Pre Med.

SCHICKEL, MICHELLE; Franklin Acad; Malone, NY; (Y); Sec 4-H; French Clb; Band; Concert Band; JV Crs Cntry; Hon Roll.

SCHICKLER, DAVID; Mc Quaid Jesuit HS; Rochester, NY; (Y); 4/175; German Clb; Letterman Clb; Ski Clb; Pres SADD; Varsity Clb; School Musical; Yrbk Stf; Crs Cntry; High Hon Roll; Boy Scts; Tp Frshmn Trck-Fld 84; Outstndng Stdnt Athl Crss Cntry 84-86; Intl Bus.

SCHIEBEL, LIZABETH J; Moore Catholic HS; Staten Island, NY; (Y); 50/172; Math Tm; VP Sr Cls; Stu Cncl; Im Bowling; Var Tennis; Hon Roll; NHS; U S Natl Ldrshp Merit Awd 86; St Johns U Comptv Schlrshp Wnnr 86; NY ST Regents Schlrshp Wnnr 86; Bus.

SCHIEMANN, SONIA A; Tuxedo HS; Greenwood Lake, NY; (Y); 4/97; Church Yth Grp; Drama Clb; Math Tm; Spanish Clb; SADD; Chorus; Stage Crew; Yrbk Ed-Chief; NHS; Stu Cncl Rep 82-86; Mullentey Coll; Bio.

SCHIERMAN, REBECCA; Blind Brook HS; Rye Brook, NY; (Y); AFS; Drama Clb; French Clb; Chorus; School Musical; School Play; Variety Show; Nwsp Stf; Var Socr.

SCHIFF, MARK; E L Vandermeulen HS; Mt Sinai, NY; (Y); 9/333; French Clb; Band; Mrchg Band; Symp Band; VP Jr Cls; High Hon Roll; Drama Clb; Leo Clb; SADD; Temple Yth Grp; Bus Dynmcs Awd 83-84.

SCHIFF, SUSAN; Christopher Columbus HS; Bronx, NY; (S); Computer Clb; Office Aide; Teachers Aide; Chorus; School Musical; Trs Jr Cls; Hon Roll; Ntl Merit Schol; Nema Natl Engl Merit Awd 85; Suny Binghamton; Teaching.

SCHIFFER, CHRIS; Iona Prep Schl; Valhalla, NY; (Y); 33/207; Computer Clb; Science Clb; Stage Crew; Lit Mag; Var L Swmmng; Hon Roll; Iona Coll; Mgmt Info Sys.

SCHIFFERT, MONICA; De Sales Catholic HS; Lockport, NY; (S); 1/33; Church Yth Grp; Yrbk Stf; Bausch & Lomb Sci Awd; NHS; NEDT Awd; Val; Pre-Law.

SCHIFFHAUER, DAVE; Grand Island HS; Grand Island, NY; (Y); 9/320; Ski Clb; Concert Band; Jazz Band; School Musical; JV Ice Hcky; Var Tennis; Im Vllybl; Hon Roll; NHS; Mst Outstndng Musician 86; Cornell U; Elec Engrng.

SCHIFFHAUER, JILL; Grand Island HS; Gr Island, NY; (Y); 4/325; Hst Sec Art Clb; Dance Clb; Hosp Aide; Ski Clb; Church Choir; Trs Pres Concert Band; School Musical; High Hon Roll; Trs NHS; Ntl Merit Ltr; Biolgcl Sci.

SCHIFLA, KELLY L; Lancaster HS; Lancaster, NY; (Y); AFS; Art Clb; Church Yth Grp; DECA; JA; Office Aide; Pep Clb; Color Guard; Drill Tm; Mrchg Band; SUNY Fredona; Tech.

SCHIHL, DAWN; Cardinal O Hara HS; Buffalo, NY; (Y); French Clb; Variety Show; Yrbk Stf; Rep Soph Cls; Pres Jr Cls; Sec Sr Cls; Rep Stu Cncl; Capt Var Cheerleading; Var Capt Pom Pon; Hon Roll; Schlrshps To Cardnl O Hara HS 84; Danc Schlrshp NYC 84; Brdcstg.

SCHILLAWSKI, DAVID; Holland Patent HS; Holland Patent, NY; (Y); Pres 4-H; French Clb; FFA; Varsity Clb; Var Capt Wrstlng; 4-H Awd; FFA Grnhnd, Dry Cttl Jdng Awds & Agri Awds 86; HS & Rgnts Dplms 86; SUNY Morrisville; Agri Bus.

SCHILLER, CARRIE; Mynderse Acad; Seneca Falls, NY; (Y); Pres Church Yth Grp; Ski Clb; Yrbk Stf; JV Var Tennis; JV Var Vllybl; Parish Cncl Hnr Elec 86-87.

SCHILLER, CHRISTOPHER; Baldwin HS; Baldwin, NY; (Y); Science Clb; Hofstra U; Brdcstng.

SCHILLING, LAURA; Schreiber HS; Sands Point, NY; (Y); 50/408; Cmnty Wkr; Latin Clb; SADD; Teachers Aide; Varsity Clb; Nwsp Rptr; Nwsp Stf; Yrbk Stf; Stu Cncl; Bsktbl; Regent Schrlsh P86; Poetry Awds 84-86; Emory U.

SCHILLOFF, ANDY; Union-Erdicott HS; Endicott, NY; (Y); Chem Engrng.

SCHIMEL, RICHARD; Half Hollow Hills HS East; Dix Hills, NY; (Y); 174/520; Cmnty Wkr; SADD; Temple Yth Grp; Varsity Clb; Chorus; Variety Show; Trs Frsh Cls; VP Jr Cls; Stu Cncl; L Ftbl; Capt All Lg Lacrosse 86.

SCHINDLER, JULIE; Irondequoit HS; Rochester, NY; (Y); 32/328; Aud/Vis; Church Yth Grp; Hosp Aide; Radio Clb; Ski Clb; Chorus; Church Choir; School Musical; School Play; Stage Crew; Ntl Merit Cmmnded Stdnt 85; Cmptr Engrng.

SCHINZING, RUSSELL; Faith Heritage HS; Syracuse, NY; (Y); Church Yth Grp; Band; Orch; Trs Soph Cls; Pres Jr Cls; Var L Bsktbl; Var L Socr; Var L Trk; Jr NHS; NHS; Lemoyne Coll; Microprocssng.

SCHIZER, DAVID M; Midwood HS; Brooklyn, NY; (Y); 1/539; Pres Chess Clb; Capt Debate Tm; Math Tm; Concert Band; Orch; Nwsp Ed-Chief; Tennis; Gov Hon Prg Awd; Spanish NHS; Val; History.

SCHLACTUS, PETER M; Scarsdale HS; Scarsdale, NY; (Y); 1/380; Pres Model UN; Orch; School Musical; Nwsp Rptr; Stu Cncl; NHS; Ntl Merit SF; Debate Tm; Drama Clb; VP Intnl Clb; NY ST All ST Orch 85; NY ST Area All ST Orch 83-86; Ellen Burstein Memrl Awd Excllnc Jew Ed 85; Intl Rel.

SCHLAGENHAUF, JOHN; Oakfield-Alabama Central HS; Basom, NY; (Y); 23/93; Am Leg Boys St; French Clb; Office Aide; Var Bsbl; Var Bsktbl; JV Ftbl; Golf; Hon Roll; St Schlr; NYS Rgnts Schlrshp 86; AFL-CIO Schlrshp 86; Eric CC; Crmnal Justc.

SCHLAGER, CATHERINE; West Seneca West SR HS; W Seneca, NY; (Y); Cmnty Wkr; GAA; Library Aide; Chorus; Var Bowling; High Hon Roll; Awd Super Achvmnt & Excllnc Prfrmnc Bio 84-85; RN.

SCHLAGER, DIANE; Mount Mercy Acad; Buffalo, NY; (Y); French Clb; JA; Yrbk Stf; JV Stat Score Keeper; JV Sftbl; Var JV Vllybl; Hon Roll; NHS; Sci.

SCHLANSKY, EMILY; Commack HS North; E Northport, NY; (Y); Y-Teens; Off Jr Cls; Bus.

SCHLATNER, ADAM J; Valley Stream South HS; Valley Stream, NY; (Y); 10/168; AFS; Mathletes; SADD; Yrbk Stf; Jr Cls; Stu Cncl; JV Bsbl; JV Socr; High Hon Roll; SUNY Binghamton; Law.

SCHLEE, KARIN; Connetquot HS; Ronkonkoma, NY; (S); 8/696; Yrbk Phtg; JV Crs Cntry; JV Var Sftbl; Jr NHS; Trs NHS.

SCHLEGEL, ERIC C; Columbia HS; Castleton, NY; (Y); 2/417; Mrchg Band; Orch; Pep Band; Symp Band; Var Tennis; Hon Roll; NHS; Ntl Merit SF; Sal; Sem Fnlst Intl Chem Olympd 85; Renslr Mdl 85; NY Math Lgu 84; Dartmouth U; Physics.

SCHLEIGH, MOLLY; Brockport HS; Brockport, NY; (Y); Mathletes; JV Var Bsktbl; JV Swmmng; JV Var Vllybl; High Hon Roll; Hon Roll; Crmnl Jstce & Psych.

SCHLEIN, JENNIFER; Blind Brook HS; Rye Brook, NY; (Y); Cmnty Wkr; Pres Temple Yth Grp; Acpl Chr; Var Capt Bsktbl; Varsity Clb; Chorus; School Musical; JV Sftbl; JV Tennis; Occptl Thrpy.

SCHLENKER, SHERRY; St Patricks C C HS; Catskill, NY; (Y); Drama Clb; School Play; Off Frsh Cls; Stu Cncl; Socr; Rgnts Nrsng Schlrshp 86; Columbia-Greene CC; Nrsng.

SCHLENKER, STEVEN J; Gloversville HS; Mayfield, NY; (Y); 3/238; Pres AFS; French Clb; Math Tm; Mrchg Band; Nwsp Rptr; Ed Yrbk Stf; Rep Jr Cls; Var Golf; High Hon Roll; Ntl Merit SF; Stanford; Ec.

SCHLESINGER, WENDY; Hauppauge HS; Hauppauge, NY; (Y); Cmnty Wkr; Temple Yth Grp; Orch; Var Capt Gym; Hon Roll; Amer Studies.

SCHLEYER, GLEN; H Frank Carey HS; Garden City, NY; (Y); 17/287; Cmnty Wkr; German Clb; Mathletes; JV Var Crs Cntry; Trk; High Hon Roll; NCTE Awd; NHS; Ntl Merit SF; Frgn Lang Hnr Soc 85-86.

SCHLOSSER, DAVID W; Tenbroeck Acad; Franklinville, NY; (Y); 5/60; Boy Scts; Church Yth Grp; Varsity Clb; Var L Ftbl; Var L Trk; Hon Roll; Wt Lftg; BSA Eagle Scout 85; Ad Altare Dei Awd 84; SUNY Syracuse; Envrnmntl Bio.

SCHLOSSER, SARAH; Olean HS; Olean, NY; (Y); 38/200; Cmnty Wkr; Varsity Clb; Bsktbl; Sftbl; Var Trk; Natl Sci Olympd Awd 84 & 86; Cnty Govt 86-87; Law.

SCHMELLER, JESSE; Glen Cove HS; Glen Cove, NY; (Y); 36/265; Boy Scts; Science Clb; Varsity Clb; Nwsp Bus Mgr; Var Crs Cntry; Var Trk; Hon Roll; NHS; Ordr Of Arrw Sctng 84; US Mrchnt Marine Acad; Dk Ofcr.

SCHMERSAL, DENISE; Roy C Ketcham HS; Poughkeepsie, NY; (Y); 75/525; AFS; Cmnty Wkr; Hosp Aide; Trk; Hon Roll; Wtr Sfty Instrctr 86; SR Lfgrd/Red Cross 85; Lbrl Arts.

SCHMIDLI, DOREEN; Niagara Wheatfield SR HS; Niagara Falls, NY; (Y); Church Yth Grp; FCA; FBLA; Pep Clb; Chorus; High Hon Roll; Hon Roll; NHS; Prfct Atten Awd; Crmnl Jstc.

SCHMIDT, ALLEN; Eden SR HS; Eden, NY; (Y); Church Yth Grp; Ski Clb; Var Bsbl; Prfct Atten Awd; Three Qtr Schlrshp 85; Drafting.

SCHMIDT, BRENDA; Keveny Memorial Acad; Cohoes, NY; (S); 3/33; Math Clb; Band; Chorus; School Play; JV Cheerleading; JV Capt Vllybl; High Hon Roll; Computer Clb; Natl Bus Hon Soc 84-86; RPI; Comp Sci.

SCHMIDT, CHRISTINE; Gouverneur JR & SR HS; Gouverneur, NY; (Y); Office Aide; Hon Roll; Tp Achvrs S W Tech 84-86.

SCHMIDT, CONNIE; Hancock Central School; Lakewood, PA; (Y); Church Yth Grp; Hosp Aide; Spanish Clb; Chorus; Im Socr; Vllybl; Hon Roll; Hgh Lit Awd 84; Secy.

SCHMIDT, CYNTHIA A; Kingston HS; Bloomington, NY; (Y); Acpl Chr; Yrbk Stf; Var Stu Cncl; Trk; French Hon Soc; High Hon Roll; Jr NHS; NHS; Ntl Merit Ltr; French Clb; NY ST Rgnts Schlrshp 86; Rensselaer Polytech Inst.

SCHMIDT, DAVID; St Marys HS; Cheektowaga, NY; (S); 10/165; Church Yth Grp; Cmnty Wkr; Var Bsktbl; Var Crs Cntry; Var Trk; NHS; Canisius Coll; Econ.

SCHMIDT, DOUGLAS; Tonawanda JR SR HS; Tonawanda, NY; (Y); 7/220; JV Bsbl; Hon Roll; NHS; Pres Schlr; Canisius Coll Acad Merit Scholar 86; Tonawandas Qlty Stu 86; Faclty 4 Yr Hnr Awd 86; Canisius Coll; Mth.

SCHMIDT III, FREDERICK S; Northport HS; New York, NY; (Y); Boy Scts; SADD; Var L Ftbl; Var L Lcrss; Var L Wrstlng; Comp Sci.

SCHMIDT, KAREN G; Argyle Central HS; Argyle, NY; (Y); 4/54; 4-H; French Clb; Math Tm; SADD; Chorus; Yrbk Phtg; Stu Cncl; Var Sftbl; High Hon Roll; NHS; Info Systms Mngmnt.

SCHMIDT, MARY BETH; Fowler HS; Syracuse, NY; (Y); SADD; Nwsp Rptr; Nwsp Stf; Pres Frsh Cls; Pres Soph Cls; Pres Jr Cls; Var Diving; Var Capt Sftbl; Var Swmmng; Ntl Merit Schol; Nrsng.

SCHMIDT, MICHAEL; Honeoye Central HS; Honeoye, NY; (S); 7/67; Church Yth Grp; French Clb; Ski Clb; JV Bsktbl; Var JV Socr; High Hon Roll; Hon Roll; NHS; Rep Sci Olympics Comp & Sci 83 & 85; Comp Team Olympics Mind 86; Comp Engr.

SCHMIDT, STEVEN; Mc Quaid Jesuit HS; Pittsford, NY; (Y); 1/165; Boy Scts; Camera Clb; Model UN; Ed Yrbk Phtg; Sec Soph Cls; Pres Jr Cls; Pres Sr Cls; Im JV Bsbl; Var L Bsktbl; Cmnty Wkr; Harvard Alumni Awd 86; Eagle Scout Awd 86; Hnr Awd Bst Avg 85; Engrng.

SCHMIDT, SUSAN L; Half Hollow Hills HS East; Dix Hills, NY; (Y); 62/514; German Clb; Hosp Aide; SADD; Band; Co-Capt Color Guard; Orch; JV Mgr Bsktbl; High Hon Roll; Jr NHS; NHS; Mrch Dms Hlth Career Awd 86; Stony Brook U; Phy Thrpy.

SCHMIDTKA, GAYLE; Vernon-Verona-Sherrill HS; Verona, NY; (Y); Computer Clb; SADD; Varsity Clb; JV Var Socr; JV Vllybl; Hon Roll.

SCHMIED, ALISON; Geneseo Central HS; Geneseo, NY; (Y); Am Leg Aux Girls St; Church Yth Grp; Drama Clb; Girl Scts; Math Tm; SADD; Chorus; Church Choir; School Musical; School Play; Cornell U; Ind Rltns.

SCHMIEDER, LINDA; Mercy HS; Southampton, NY; (Y); Drama Clb; Pep Clb; Varsity Clb; Chorus; Yrbk Stf; Rep Soph Cls; Gym; Tennis; Trk; Mst Imprvd Plyr 84; MVP Tennis 85; Marist Coll; French.

SCHMITT, EUGENE; Eden Central SR HS; Boston, NY; (Y); Computer Clb; Sec Band; Drm & Bgl; Jazz Band; Orch; Pep Band; School Musical; Im Vllybl; Hon Roll; NHS.

SCHMITT, JENNIFER; Mahopac HS; Mahopac, NY; (Y); 53/383; Dance Clb; Chorus; Hon Roll; NHS; ST U Of NY Albany; Frnch.

SCHMITT, LAUREN; Arlington HS; Lagrangeville, NY; (Y); German Clb; Girl Scts; Color Guard; Natl Ger Hnr Soc 86; Girl Scout Slvr Awd 85.

SCHMITT, LORELLIE; Greenwood Central Schl; Rexville, NY; (S); 5/30; Cmnty Wkr; Spanish Clb; Varsity Clb; Chorus; Color Guard; School Play; Yrbk Ed-Chief; Yrbk Stf; Sec Frsh Cls; Sec Soph Cls; Coaches Awd 85; Chrldg Awd-Most Spirited 84, MVP 85; Binghamton; Psych.

SCHMITT, PHILIP; Central Islip HS; Central Islip, NY; (Y); 7/300; Computer Clb; Math Clb; Nwsp Rptr; Nwsp Stf; Lit Mag; JV Lcrss; NHS; Ntl Merit SF; Elec Engrng.

SCHMITZ, EDWARD; Eden SR HS; Eden, NY; (Y); 1/172; AFS; JV Bsbl; Im Bowling; JV Golf; Var L Tennis; Im Vllybl; High Hon Roll; NHS; Prfct Atten Awd; Outstndng Bkkpg/Acctg I Stu 85; Mst Prof Bkkpng/Acctg II Stu, Cert De Merite 86; CPA.

SCHMITZ, JOSEPH; Bainbridge-Guilford HS; Bainbridge, NY; (Y); Boy Scts; Church Yth Grp; Spanish Clb; Band; Chorus; Church Choir; Concert Band; Mrchg Band; Orch; Hon Roll; Bus Adm.

SCHMITZ, STEFAN; Archbishop Molloy HS; Glendale, NY; (Y); 89/383; Boys Clb Am; Church Yth Grp; Cmnty Wkr; SADD; Acpl Chr; Chorus; Church Choir; Bowling; Tennis; Hon Roll; Stonybrook; Psych.

SCHMOLKA, ANDREW; Scarsdale HS; Scarsdale, NY; (Y); 2/423; Cmnty Wkr; French Clb; Intnl Clb; School Play; Nwsp Ed-Chief; Capt Bsbl; Capt Bsktbl; High Hon Roll; NCTE Awd; Pres NHS; Yale U.

SCHMULSON, LOUIS J; Christopher Columbus HS; Bronx, NY; (Y); 40/670; Library Aide; Band; Bowling; Capt L Tennis; Cit Awd; Hon Roll; Prfct Atten Awd; Rgnts Schlrshp 86; Prncpls Ynks Pride Awd 85; Arista Awd 85-86; ST U Of NY-ALBANY; Accntng.

SCHNABEL, DEBORAH; Mineola HS; Mineola, NY; (Y); 25/200; Key Clb; Sec SADD; Concert Band; Drill Tm; High Hon Roll; NHS; Church Yth Grp; French Clb; Band; Trs Frsh Cls; Pol Sci.

SCHNABEL, DEIDREA M; West Babylon HS; W Babylon, NY; (Y); 46/400; Church Yth Grp; Cmnty Wkr; DECA; Hosp Aide; SADD; Chorus; Variety Show; Var Tennis; High Hon Roll; Hon Roll; West Babylon High Sch Ldrs Clb 85-86; Varsity Tnns Ltte 82-83; Berkshire Nrsng Hm Recgnztn Awd 82; Catholic U Of Amer; Bus Mgmt.

SCHNACKENBERG, JURGEN E; Taconic Hills HS; Hudson, NY; (Y); 10/185; Am Leg Boys St; Church Yth Grp; Var Bsktbl; Var Socr; Var Tennis; NHS; Prfct Atten Awd; Span Achvt Awd 86.

SCHNAKENBERG, ROBT; John H Glenn HS; E Northport, NY; (Y); FFA; Quiz Bowl; Nwsp Rptr; Nwsp Stf; Pres Soph Cls; High Hon Roll; Hon Roll; Ntl Merit SF; US Acdmc Dcthln 85-86; Ping Pong Clb C-Pres 84-8l.

SCHNALL, SCOTT; Bay Shore HS; Bay Shore, NY; (Y); Cmnty Wkr; Temple Yth Grp; Nwsp Phtg; Nwsp Rptr; Nwsp Stf; Bus.

SCHNAUBER, DEBBIE; Churchville Chili HS; Rochester, NY; (Y); Ski Clb; Socr; Sftbl; Genesee CC; Travel.

SCHNAUBER, GLENN; Churchville Chili SR HS; Rochester, NY; (Y); 9/319; Pres Latin Clb; Math Tm; Pres Model UN; Chorus; Madrigals; School Musical; Nwsp Ed-Chief; Pres Stu Cncl; Aud/Vis; Church Yth Grp; Bst Debatr-Mdl UN 85-86; Bst Debatr-Yth Govt ST Cnvntn Albany 86; Awd Excllnc Sci 83; U Of Buffalo; Aerospc Engrng.

SCHNAUBER, LISA; Thousand Island HS; Depauville, NY; (Y); Band; School Play; Variety Show; Stat Ftbl; Hon Roll; Jefferson CC; Legl Secy.

SCHNAUDIGEL, KEVIN; Carmel HS; Carmel, NY; (Y); Var L Bsktbl; Var L Ftbl; Var L Tennis; Hon Roll; Carmel Police Dept Outstndg Yth Awd 86; Chem.

SCHNEID, MEGAN; Commack HS North; Commack, NY; (Y); 48/366; Drama Clb; PAVAS; Service Clb; Orch; School Musical; School Play; High Hon Roll; NHS; Off Soph Cls; Off Jr Cls; ICA Art Awd 84 & 85; NVSSMA 6a 84 & 86; Lng Islnd Strng Fstvl & All Cnty 84 & 86; Theatre Arts.

SCHNEIDER, ALAN; Lindenhurst HS; Lindenhurst, NY; (Y); Computer Clb; Band; Socr; Comp Pgmmr.

SCHNEIDER, ELIZABETH; Acad Of St Joseph; Smithtown, NY; (Y); Library Aide.

SCHNEIDER, EMILIE; Mount Saint Mary Acad; Buffalo, NY; (Y); Church Yth Grp; Dance Clb; Sec Girl Scts; Church Choir; School Musical; Variety Show; High Hon Roll; Hon Roll; NHS; NEDT Awd; 1st & 3rd Pl Awd Track & Fld Prog Meet 85; U Of Buffalo; Psych.

SCHNEIDER, ERIC; Hamburg HS; Hamburg, NY; (Y); Church Yth Grp; Cmnty Wkr; German Clb; Im Bsbl; JV Var Ice Hcky; JV Lcrss; JV Var Socr; Defiance Coll; Busnss Admin.

SCHNEIDER, ERIKA; Coxsackie-Athens HS; W Coxsackie, NY; (Y); #22 In Class; German Clb; Girl Scts; Chorus; Sftbl; Trk; Vllybl; High Hon Roll; Hon Roll; Vllybl Awd 84; Trck Awd 86; JC Of Albany; Med Scrtry.

SCHNEIDER, LAURENCE S; Commack HS; Commack, NY; (Y); Aud/Vis; Office Aide; Service Clb; Ski Clb; Teachers Aide; Temple Yth Grp; Y-Teens; Nwsp Stf; Stu Cncl; Bsbl; NYS Rgnst Schlrsh Wnnr 85-86; U MD College Park; Bus Acctg.

SCHNEIDER, LAWRENCE; Tottenville HS; Staten Island, NY; (Y); 42/871; Model UN; Stage Crew; Nwsp Stf; Wrstlng; High Hon Roll; NHS; SUNY Binghamton; Bus Admn.

SCHNEIDER, PATRICIA; Cairo-Durham HS; Purling, NY; (Y); Red Cross Aide; Teachers Aide; School Musical; School Play; Yrbk Stf; Rep Jr Cls; Vllybl; High Hon Roll; NHS; St Rose; Educ.

SCHNEIDER, STEVE; West Genesee SR HS; Camillus, NY; (Y); Boy Scts; Hst Key Clb; Jazz Band; Orch; Symp Band; Bsktbl; JV Crs Cntry; Var Trk; High Hon Roll; Hon Roll; Bus Lawyer.

SCHNEIDER, SUSAN; Wellington C Mepham HS; Merrick, NY; (Y); Band; Concert Band; Mrchg Band; Yrbk Rptr; Yrbk Stf; Jr Cls; Tennis; Trk; High Hon Roll; NHS; Bus Admnstn.

SCHNEIR, WILLIAM; Archbishop Molly HS; S Ozone Park, NY; (Y); 38/383; Cmnty Wkr; Pep Clb; NHS; Spanish Tutor; Coach Boys Sprts Prgm; Comm.

SCHNELL, BARRY; Babylon HS; Babylon, NY; (Y); Math Clb; Math Tm; Soph Cls; JV Bsbl; Bsktbl; Ftbl; Hon Roll; Boces Tlntd & Gftd Smmr Prog 83-85; Med.

SCHNELL, BRIAN; Grand Island SR HS; Grand Island, NY; (Y); 6/300; Hosp Aide; Mathletes; Ski Clb; Bausch & Lomb Sci Awd; High Hon Roll; Hon Roll; NHS; Best Regnts Bio Stu 83; Regnts Chem Stu 84; Exchng Stu 84-85; Cert Mastry Gamma 85; Math.

SCHNELL, IRA; Huntington HS; Huntington, NY; (Y); Im Capt Bsktbl; Im Coach Actv; Var Capt Ftbl; Im Wt Lftg; Hon Roll; Psychlgy.

SCHNELL, RAYMOND; Mercy HS; Shoreham, NY; (Y); 10/140; Boy Scts; Mathletes; Math Clb; Varsity Clb; Church Choir; Bsbl; Bsktbl; Ftbl; High Hon Roll; NHS; Ntl Music Hnr Soc 85-86; Lwyr.

SCHNELL, TYSON; Gloversville HS; Gloversvl, NY; (Y); Boy Scts; Band; Concert Band; Jazz Band; Mrchg Band; Pep Band; Symp Band; Lit Mag; Hon Roll; Prfct Atten Awd.

SCHNIPPER, ERIC; Roslyn HS; Roslyn, NY; (Y); Debate Tm; NFL; Quiz Bowl; Scholastic Bowl; Capt Band; Capt Jazz Band; JV L Bsbl; Var L Trk; NHS; Ntl Merit Schol; Empr ST Schlrshp Excllnc 86; Naer Trmd Soc NY Fire Dept Schlrshp 86; U PA; Med.

SCHNURBUSCH, TAMIE; James E Sperry HS; Rochester, NY; (Y); 69/271; JA; Spanish Clb; School Play; Lit Mag; Var Gym; Var Mgr(s); Hon Roll; Jr NHS; Potsdam College Merit Scholarship 86; Editor Of Poetry Magazines 86; SUNY Potsdam; Elem Educ.

SCHOELERMAN, ROBIN M; Tonawanda JR/SR HS; Tonawanda, NY; (Y); 16/220; Trs Church Yth Grp; Cmnty Wkr; Drama Clb; Political Wkr; Chorus; Church Choir; School Musical; School Play; NHS; Pres Schlr; (Y ST Regents Schlrshp 86; SUNY; Archlgy.

SCHOEMAKER, LISA; George W Fowler HS; Syracuse, NY; (Y); 5/199; Drama Clb; Band; Concert Band; School Play; Rep Frsh Cls; Pres Soph Cls; VP Jr Cls; Rep Stu Cncl; Var Bsktbl; Var Capt Socr; U S Army Rsrv Ntl Schlr Athlt Awd 86fonadaga Cmnty Schlrshp 86; Athlt Of Yr 86; SUNY Oswego; Bus Adm.

SCHOEN, JENNIFER; Commack South HS; Commack, NY; (Y); Acpl Chr; Chorus; School Musical; Variety Show; High Hon Roll; Hon Roll; Gldn Quill Awd 85; Plyd Oliver In Schl Musical 86; Penn ST; Bus Mgmt.

SCHOEN, MARY E; Patchogue-Medford HS; Patchogue, NY; (Y); 26/621; Drama Clb; Hosp Aide; Radio Clb; Band; Chorus; Jazz Band; Orch; School Musical; Nwsp Stf; Yrbk Bus Mgr; Regents Schlrshp 86; NY Telephone Schlrshp 86; SUNY Binghamton; Eng.

SCHOENBERG, ALAN; Commack South HS; Dix Hills, NY; (Y); Mathletes; Math Tm; Teachers Aide; Temple Yth Grp; JV Tennis; High Hon Roll; Ntl Sci Olympd Awd/Chem 86; Pre-Med.

SCHOENBORN, WILLIAM C; Hamburg SR HS; Hamburg, NY; (Y); 19/392; Var JV Bsbl; Var JV Ftbl; Hon Roll; NHS; Rgnts Schlrshp-NYS 86; Fratrnl Lodge Schlrshp 86; Grange Schlrshp 86; Cornell U; Anim Sci.

SCHOENDORF, SUSAN; Brentwood Ross HS; Brentwood, NY; (Y); 11/500; Rptr Nwsp Rptr; Ed Yrbk Ed-Chief; Rep Frsh Cls; Rep Sr Cls; Pres Stu Cncl; High Hon Roll; Sec Jr NHS; NHS; Teachers Aide; Chorus; Ldrshp Awd 84; Regents Schrlshp 86; Distngushd Schlrshp 86; Hofstra U; Corp Law.

SCHOENING, ANGELA; Smithtown High School West; Smithtown, NY; (Y); Church Yth Grp; SADD; Concert Band; Mrchg Band; Var Crs Cntry; Var L Trk; High Hon Roll; NHS; Itln Hnr Soc 84; Vet.

SCHOENTHAL, JULIE; Corning-Painted Post West HS; Painted Post, NY; (Y); 13/253; VP Church Yth Grp; SADD; Thesps; Band; Chorus; Church Choir; Concert Band; Jazz Band; Mrchg Band; School Musical; PTSA Jenkins Mem Schlrshp 86; Patty Perry Mem Shlrshp 86; Regents Schlrshp-NY St 86; Geneseo SUNY; Elem Educ.

SCHOFF, ROBERT W; St Johnsville Central HS; St Johnsville, NY; (Y); Am Leg Boys St; French Clb; Band; Chorus; Concert Band; Yrbk Stf; Var L Bsbl; Var L Bsktbl; Var L Socr; Dnfth Awd; Outstndg Amer Ctznshp 86; Outstndg Sprtsmnshp Bsbl 86; Dedctn In Sprts 85; Comp Sci.

SCHOFFEL, HILARY; Sheepshead Bay HS; Brooklyn, NY; (Y); Library Aide; PAVAS; Spanish Clb; Band; Concert Band; School Musical; Archon Soc Svc Pin, Cert 86; Psych.

SCHOFIELD, SAMANTHA A; Churchville-Chili HS; Churchville, NY; (Y); Church Yth Grp; Exploring; Girl Scts; Symp Band; Var Diving; Mgr(s); JV Socr; Var Trk; Band Cncl Sec 85-87; Shadowng Career Explrtn Athletic Training 86; Outstndng Svc Awd Band 84-86; Sports Med.

SCHOFIELD, STEPHEN J; Chester HS; Chester, NY; (Y); 1/85; Am Leg Boys St; Band; Concert Band; Jazz Band; Mrchg Band; Yrbk Bus Mgr; Yrbk Stf; VP Jr Cls; NHS; Voice Dem Awd; Rnr-Up Tim Ed Pgm Stu Essy Cntst 84; Hugh O Brn Yth Ldrshp Smnr 85; Arion Awd Outstndng Mscl Achvt 86; Ec.

SCHOLL, REBECCA; Westfield Academy And Cntrl; Westfield, NY; (Y); Ski Clb; Y-Teens; Acpl Chr; Chorus; Concert Band; Mrchg Band; School Musical; Rep Stu Cncl; Cheerleading; High Hon Roll; Sci Merit Awd 84-85.

SCHOLNICOFF, NATHANIEL; Curtis HS; Staten Island, NY; (Y); Nwsp Ed-Chief; Var Ftbl; JV Coachs Awd 84; DTC Comp Sci Awd 84.

SCHOLPP, SONDRA; Chatham HS; Canaan, NY; (Y); 27/125; Cmnty Wkr; VP 4-H; Library Aide; Teachers Aide; Chorus; Capt Bsktbl; Elks Awd; High Hon Roll; Hon Roll; Prfct Atten Awd; Human Srvcs.

SCHOLZ, ERIKA; Victor Central Schl; Victor, NY; (Y); Acpl Chr; Chorus; Color Guard; Madrigals; School Musical; School Play; Yrbk Phtg; Hon Roll; Pres Schlr; Sibleys Art Show 84; Simpson Coll; Grphc Art.

SCHONER, THERESA; Groton Central HS; Cortland, NY; (Y); 2/60; Library Aide; Office Aide; Chorus; Lit Mag; Stat Crs Cntry; High Hon Roll; NHS; Sal; Swmmng; Acctg Awds 84 & 86; Shrthd Awds 85-86; Clrcl.

SCHOOLEY, TAMMIE; Mynderse Acad; Seneca Falls, NY; (Y); 10/144; Intnl Clb; Jazz Band; School Musical; Swing Chorus; Yrbk Stf; Sec Jr Cls; Rep Stu Cncl; High Hon Roll; NHS; Grls ST Altrnt 85; Elizabethtwn Coll; Occupn Thrpy.

SCHOPPE, KAREN; Wayne Central HS; Ontario, NY; (S); 160/195; Var Capt Bsktbl; JV Var Socr; Var L Sftbl; Var Capt Vllybl; All Greater Rochester Hnrble Mntn 85.

SCHORR, DANIEL P; Briarcliff HS; Braircliff Manor, NY; (Y); Trs AFS; Am Leg Boys St; Band; Nwsp Ed-Chief; Var Bsbl; JV Bsktbl; Var Socr; High Hon Roll; NHS; Renssealer Polytchnc Inst Mdl Achvt Math & Sci 86.

SCHRADER, BERT A; Amsterdam HS; Amsterdam, NY; (Y); Computer Clb; ROTC; Band; Mrchg Band; Symp Band; Var Bowling; Var Capt Sftbl; Hon Roll; NHS; Prfct Atten Awd; NY ST Rgnts Schlrshp 86; Army ROTC Shclrshp 86; Clemson U; Ceramic Engnrng.

SCHRADER, CORINNE; Walt Whitman HS; So Hunt, NY; (Y); 156/540; Dance Clb; Spanish Clb; Variety Show; Yrbk Stf; JV Capt Cheerleading; Stat Ftbl; Mgr(s); Hon Roll; Spanish NHS; ST Johns U; Elem Educ.

SCHRADER, JILL; Wayland Central HS; Wayland, NY; (Y); French Clb; Pres FBLA; Math Tm; Varsity Clb; JV Var Cheerleading; JV Var Socr; Var Trk; JV Vllybl; High Hon Roll; Sec Church Yth Grp; Nice Kid Awd 85; Alfred Tech; Bus Adm.

SCHRADER, KAREN; Kings Park SR HS; Kings Park, NY; (Y); Pres Art Clb; Church Yth Grp; Hosp Aide; Chorus; JV Bsktbl; JV Var Tennis; High Hon Roll; Hon Roll; Jr NHS; NHS; Natl Trffc Safty Postr Pgm Cmndtn 85; Smr Isnt Gftd-Tlntd Stu Schlrshp 84; Math Tutrng Apprctn Ltr 85; Art.

SCHRADER, SCOTT; Attica SR HS; Strykersville, NY; (Y); 25/156; 4-H; Band; Mrchg Band; Rep Stu Cncl; Var Golf; JV Var Socr; Hon Roll; Rgnts Schlrshp Wnr 86; Bhmn-Ashe Schlrshp 86; Miami U; Bio.

SCHRADER, SCOTT; Batavia HS; Batavia, NY; (Y); 19/210; Ski Clb; Yrbk Stf; Bsbl; Ice Hcky; Sftbl; Hon Roll.

SCHRAER, LYNANN; Minisink Valley HS; Middletown, NY; (Y); Church Yth Grp; Girl Scts; Band; Chorus; Church Choir; Concert Band; Mrchg Band; Symp Band; Yrbk Stf; Swmmng; Outstndng Soloist Awds Flute 82-86; All Cnty Band 84-85; Interlochen Ntl Music Camp Smmr 86; Syracuse U; Sec Schl Music Dir.

SCHRAGER, LARA S; Vincent Smith HS; Lattingtown, NY; (Y); #4 In Class; Yrbk Stf; Hon Roll; Syracuse; Fash Cnsltnt.

SCHRAML, MARK F; Mc Quaid Jesuit HS; W Henrietta, NY; (Y); 33/185; Camera Clb; Science Clb; Teachers Aide; Varsity Clb; Crs Cntry; Var L Trk; High Hon Roll; Mst Imprvd Rnnr Indoor Trk 85; Regents Scholar; St Lawrence.

SCHRANK, CAREY; Brockport HS; Brockport, NY; (Y); 143/350; Camp Fr Inc; Dance Clb; Drama Clb; Exploring; Spanish Clb; School Musical; Yrbk Stf; Rep Soph Cls; Rep Jr Cls; High Hon Roll; 1st Pl In Dnc Cmptn 85; SUNY Brckprt; Bus.

SCHRANK, PHILIP; Tottenville HS; Staten Island, NY; (S); 3/850; French Clb; Concert Band; School Musical; JV Var Ftbl; Im Wt Lftg; Bausch & Lomb Sci Awd; French Hon Soc; High Hon Roll; Jr NHS; Ntl Merit SF; Concours Ntl Frnch Cntst Awd Excl; Bio Engr.

SCHRAVEN, KRISTIN; Albion HS; Albion, NY; (S); 1/169; JA; Ski Clb; Spanish Clb; Sec Sr Cls; Rep Stu Cncl; Cheerleading; Socr; Trk; Dnfth Awd; Hon Roll; JR Achvmnt Schlrshp Dale Carnegie Crse 86; Rgnts Schlrshp Wnr 86; Cornell U; Biology.

SCHREIBER, BRUCE H; Red Hook Central HS; Red Hook, NY; (Y); 5/134; JV Var Bsbl; Var Ftbl; High Hon Roll; Hon Roll; NHS; Pres Schlr; NYS Rgnts Schlrshp 85; Smr Ocnlgy Crs Occdntl Coll 85; Empr ST Gms Hdsn Vly Rgn Swmng 83-84; Bucknell U; Blgy.

SCHREIBER, DORIS; North Babylon SR HS; N Babylon, NY; (Y); 63/450; Chorus; Mgr(s); Hon Roll; Jr NHS; NHS; Vctnl Indl Clbs Of Amer Job Interview 1st Pl Awd 86; Dcmnt Of Cmptncy Med Asstng/Clncl 86; Bus Adm.

SCHREIBER, DOUGLAS C; Willsboro Central HS; Whallonsburg, NY; (Y); 3/90; Pres 4-H; Scholastic Bowl; Ski Clb; Yrbk Stf; Golf; Socr; 4-H Awd; High Hon Roll; Pres NHS; Natl 4-H Conf 56th Annl 86; Ithaca Coll; Polit Sci.

SCHREIBER, JOHN; H S Of The Humanits; New York, NY; (Y); Computer Clb; JA; Stage Crew; Rep Frsh Cls; Var Bsbl; Var Socr.

SCHREINER, LISA ANN; Hamburg Central SR HS; Hamburg, NY; (Y); 60/384; Cmnty Wkr; Rep 4-H; Girl Scts; JCL; SADD; Lit Mag; Im Vllybl; Hon Roll; Ntl Merit SF; Latin Clb; GSA USA Gold Awd 86; Natl Sci Olympiad Bio 84; Bio-Chem.

SCHREMMER, TOBIAS; Manhasset HS; Manhasset, NY; (Y); 26/185; Var Bsbl; JV Socr; Pres Schlr; St Schlr; VP-ANKANS 85-86; NY U; Fin.

SCHRENK, MICHAEL R; Burgard Vocational HS; Buffalo, NY; (Y); Boy Scts; CAP; Exploring; Radio Clb; Red Cross Aide; Teachers Aide; Nwsp Rptr; Rep Frsh Cls; VP Sr Cls; Rep Stu Cncl; Erie CC; Crmnl Justc.

SCHRILLA, SCOTT; Cicero-North Syracuse HS; Clay, NY; (S); Var Golf; NHS; Wood Prod Engrng.

SCHRIMPE, KRISTEN; Long Island Lutheran HS; Farmingdale, NY; (S); Drama Clb; Chorus; Church Choir; School Musical; School Play; Rep Soph Cls; High Hon Roll; Hon Roll; Jr NHS; NHS; Acadmc All-Amer At Large Div Schlr Pgm 86; Prom Qn 85; NEMA Awd 85; Paralgl Sectry.

SCHRODER, ELIZABETH A; Charles H Roth HS; Rochester, NY; (Y); 1/195; Church Yth Grp; GAA; Pres Spanish Clb; Band; Pres Concert Band; Jazz Band; School Musical; Socr; High Hon Roll; JETS Awd; Harvard Book Awd 85; Phi Beta Kappa Schlr 86; NYSMA Hi Achvt Spanish & Grt Cntrbtn Span Pgm 83-86; St Bonaventure U; Biophysics.

SCHRODER, KATHLEEN A; Sanford H Calhoun HS; Merrick, NY; (Y); 6/313; Church Yth Grp; DECA; Nwsp Stf; VP Jr Cls; Capt Cheerleading; Capt Trk; Cit Awd; Hon Roll; NHS; Pres Schlr.

SCHRODER, MARILYN; Hoosic Valley HS; Valley Falls, NY; (Y); Band; Chorus; School Musical; Stu Cncl; JV Var Cheerleading; JV Var Fld Hcky; Hon Roll; VP NHS; Math Assn Amer Awd; Natl Merit Schlrshp Candidate.

SCHROEDER, INGRID; Clarkstown South HS; New City, NY; (Y); Church Yth Grp; 4-H; German Clb; SADD; Band; Church Choir; Concert Band; School Musical; Twrlr; 4-H Awd; US House Of Repr Page 85-86; U Of VA; Pltcs.

SCHROEDER, JAMES H; Jamestown HS; Jamestown, NY; (Y); Boy Scts; Nwsp Rptr; Nwsp Sprt Ed; Capt Var Diving; Hon Roll; Opt Clb Awd; BSA Order Of Arrw 84-86; NY St Maritime Acad; Sci.

SCHROEDER, SCOTT A; Floral Park Memorial HS; Floral Park, NY; (Y); Pres Computer Clb; Mathletes; Chorus; High Hon Roll; NHS; Empire ST Gms Gld Mdl Wnnr Archry 84-85; NY ST Archry Chmpn 85; (4 ST Indr Archry Chmpn 85; Hofstra U; Engrng.

SCHROEDER, THOMAS J; Wantagh HS; Wantagh, NY; (Y); Church Yth Grp; Cmnty Wkr; Band; Concert Band; Jazz Band; Mrchg Band; Orch; Var Capt Bsktbl; Coach Actv; Hon Roll; Regents Scholar 85-86; SUNY Buffalo; Auto Engrng.

SCHROM, VENUS; Duanesburg Central Schl; Esperance, NY; (Y); Drama Clb; Chorus; Yrbk Stf; Sec Frsh Cls; Sec Soph Cls; Sec Jr Cls; JV Var Cheerleading; Gym; Hon Roll; NHS; Cert Hnr Bkkpng/Accntng 85; Mst Vlble Chrldr 86; Accntng.

SCHRON, MICHAEL; Columbia Prep; New York, NY; (Y); Pres Spanish Clb; Lit Mag; Rep Soph Cls; Ntl Merit SF.

SCHROT, RUDOLPH; Olean HS; Olean, NY; (Y); 2/211; Am Leg Boys St; Pres Drama Clb; Ski Clb; Pres Thesps; Acpl Chr; Pres Chorus; Orch; School Musical; School Play; Hon Roll; Outstndgn Thesbian Awd, Natl Schl Chrl Awd, Natl Schl Orch Awd 86; Yale U; Physics.

SCHRUFER, LINDA; Kingston HS; Kingston, NY; (Y); 70/573; French Clb; French Hon Soc; High Hon Roll; Hon Roll; Jr NHS; Bio.

SCHRYVER, JILL; Tupper Lake HS; Tupper Lk, NY; (Y); Church Yth Grp; Yrbk Stf; Rep Frsh Cls; Rep Soph Cls; Rep Jr Cls; Rep Stu Cncl; Cheerleading; High Hon Roll; NHS; Regents Schlrshp 86; Lion Sclb Awd Most Promsng Stu Eng 86; Utica Coll; Pre-Med.

SCHRYVER, JIM; Churchville Chili HS; N Chili, NY; (Y); Var Bsktbl; Coach Actv; Ftbl; Wt Lftg; Hon Roll.

SCHTIERMAN, IRWIN; East Meadow HS; East Meadow, NY; (Y); Cmnty Wkr; FBLA; Key Clb; Temple Yth Grp; Yrbk Rptr; JV Capt Bsbl; Var Capt Bsktbl; Var Ftbl; Nat Tessler Memrl Awd/Svc, Charctr 84 & 85.

SCHUBACH, STEPHANIE; Lowville Academy Central Schl; Lowville, NY; (Y); French Clb; SADD; Swing Chorus; Yrbk Phtg; VP Jr Cls; Var Capt Bsktbl; Var Swmmng; Bausch & Lomb Sci Awd; High Hon Roll; NHS; Biolgy.

SCHUBERT, ELIZABETH; Southampton HS; Southampton, NY; (Y); Pep Clb; Ski Clb; Mrchg Band; School Play; Swing Chorus; Yrbk Stf; JV Var Cheerleading; Bus.

SCHUBERT, ROBIN; Caledonia-Mumford HS; Churchville, NY; (Y); 33/89; Ski Clb; Pres Spanish Clb; Chorus; Swing Chorus; Rep Stu Cncl; Stat Bsbl; Capt Cheerleading; MVP Bsktbl Chrldng 85 & 86; MVP Ftbl Chrldng 84; Rotary Exchng-Sweden 86.

SCHUBMEHL, BARRY; Wayland Central Schl; Dansville, NY; (Y); French Clb; Varsity Clb; Var Bsbl; Var JV Bsktbl; JV Socr; NHS; Engr.

SCHUCK, DIANE; Holy Trinity HS; Bethpage, NY; (S); Church Yth Grp; Math Clb; Ski Clb; Band; Stage Crew; Trk; NEDT Awd.

SCHUCK IV, JOHN; Archbishop Walsh HS; Hinsdale, NY; (Y); Ski Clb; Varsity Clb; Rep Frsh Cls; Rep Stu Cncl; JV Var Bsbl; JV Var Ftbl; JV Var Ice Hcky; Var Wt Lftg; Hon Roll; Boy Scts; Penn ST; Elec Engr.

SCHUDER, KIRSTEN G; Hackley Schl; Eastchester, NY; (Y); 22/89; Art Clb; Church Yth Grp; Debate Tm; Drama Clb; Key Clb; Model UN; Band; Chorus; Church Choir; Concert Band; U Of WI; Econmcs.

SCHUESSLER JR, DONALD; Attica HS; N Java, NY; (S); 6/175; Boy Scts; Ski Clb; Band; JV Var Bsbl; JV Var Socr; Var Swmmng; Var Tennis; Hon Roll; Ntl Merit Ltr; US Naval Acad.

SCHUHL, SUE; Burnt Hills Ballston Lake HS; Ballston Lake, NY; (Y); Church Yth Grp; Dance Clb; 4-H; Var Sftbl; Var Vllybl; High Hon Roll; Hon Roll.

SCHULMAN, DEBRA M; Smithtown West HS; Smithtown, NY; (Y); Ski Clb; Mrchg Band; Orch; Symp Band; Var L Socr; Var L Vllybl; High Hon Roll; Hon Roll; NHS; Spanish NHS; NY ST Regents Schlrshp 85-86; Pres Acad Ftnss Awd 86; ST U Of NY Binghamton; Bio.

SCHULMAN, STEPHANIE; Scarsdale HS; Scarsdale, NY; (Y); Cmnty Wkr; Hosp Aide; Sec Intnl Clb; Spanish Clb; Varsity Clb; Nwsp Ed-Chief; Off Jr Cls; JV Socr; Capt Var Tennis; Hon Roll.

SCHULT, HEIDI; Clarkstown North HS; New City, NY; (Y); 77/405; Church Yth Grp; Sec Spanish Clb; SADD; Rep Stu Cncl; Capt L Fld Hcky; Capt L Trk; NHS; Exploring; Trs GAA; Rep Jr Cls; Coachs Awd Fld Hcky 83-85; Selctd All Sec T, Cnty And Div Tm 85; Homecmng Qn 85; Siena Clg; Poltcl Sci.

SCHULTE, DONNA; Charlotte Valley Central HS; Oneonta, NY; (S); 1/35; Pres Spanish Clb; Jazz Band; School Musical; Pres Swing Chorus; Pres Jr Cls; Var Cheerleading; Var Trk; VP NHS; Rotary Yth Ldrshp Awd; MVP JV Chrldr; Area All-State Jazz Choir; Albany ST; Math.

SCHULTHEIS, DAVID F; W T Clarke HS; Westbury, NY; (Y); 1/196; Yrbk Sprt Ed; VP Frsh Cls; VP Jr Cls; Pres Sr Cls; JV Crs Cntry; JV Var Ftbl; Capt Var Trk; Hon Roll; NHS; Val; Al-Conf MVP Trck; Jewsh War Vet Ctznshp Awd; Athltc Ldrs Clb-Offcr; Engrng.

SCHULTZ, AMY; Oriskany Central HS; Rome, NY; (Y); 26/66; Church Yth Grp; Pres VP Key Clb; Sec SADD; Church Choir; School Play; Yrbk Phtg; Var Capt Sftbl; Kiwanis Awd; Rotary Awd; Greater Utica Bd Realtrs Inc 86; Valley Forge Christian; Comm.

SCHULTZ, CINDY; Coxsackie Athens JR SR HS; W Coxsackie, NY; (Y); 5/115; German Clb; Ski Clb; Chorus; High Hon Roll; Hon Roll; NHS; NYS Regents Schlrshp 86; Schlrshp From St Rose For 4 Yrs; Coll Of St Rose; Acctng.

SCHULTZ, DERRICK M; Newfane Central HS; Lockport, NY; (S); 1/159; Band; Concert Band; Jazz Band; Pep Band; School Musical; Symp Band; Crs Cntry; Trk; Hon Roll; NHS; Ntl Assoc Jazz Ed Muiscnshp Citatn 84; Mu Alpha Theta 85; Cross Cty MVP 85; Med.

SCHULTZ, DORIANNE; Wilson Central HS; Ransomville, NY; (Y); 8/111; VP Church Yth Grp; Hosp Aide; Chorus; School Musical; Sec Soph Cls; Sec Jr Cls; Sec Sr Cls; Var Capt Bsktbl; JV L Sftbl; High Hon Roll; NY ST Rgnts Nrsng Schlrshp 86; Russell Sage Coll; Physcl Thrpy.

SCHULTZ, ELIZABETH; St Johns Preparatory Schl; Astoria, NY; (Y); 38/458; Church Yth Grp; Cmnty Wkr; 4-H; High Hon Roll; NHS; Prfct Atten Awd; NYS Regents Schlrshp 86; Coll Engl Mdl 86; NY U; Engl.

SCHULTZ, ERIC W; Lewiston-Porter HS; Lewiston, NY; (Y); 5/236; Church Yth Grp; Computer Clb; French Clb; Orch; Nwsp Sprt Ed; Im Bowling; Im Tennis; High Hon Roll; Hon Roll; NHS; Lamp Of Lrng Awd 84-85; Mst Outstnding In Scl Studies 85; NY ST Rgnts Schlrshp 86; Canisius Coll; Law.

SCHULTZ, JEFFREY E; James A Beneway SR HS; Ontario, NY; (Y); 17/187; Church Yth Grp; French Clb; Band; Concert Band; Jazz Band; Mrchg Band; Pep Band; School Musical; Rep Stu Cncl; JV Socr; Outstndg Perf Tuba Solo/All Cntry Band 83 & 84 & 86; Bio Achvt 85; Am Stud, Band Achvt 86; St John Fisher; Biochem.

SCHULTZ, MARYANNE P; Lewiston-Porter HS; Lewiston, NY; (Y); 15/236; Pres Church Yth Grp; Trs Sec French Clb; Church Choir; Trs Orch; Stage Crew; Im Stat Bowling; Var Capt Pom Pon; Im Vllybl; High Hon Roll; NHS; Mst Outstndng In Orchstra 84; Mst Imprvd In Frgn Language 85; NY ST Rgnts Schlrshp 86; Canisius Coll NY; Phrmcy.

SCHULTZ, MICHAEL J; Bronxville HS; Bronxville, NY; (Y); Letterman Clb; Varsity Clb; Variety Show; Nwsp Stf; Yrbk Stf; Var Capt Bsbl; Var Capt Bsktbl; Coach Actv; JV Ftbl; Var L Socr; Oscar Dey Williams Awd Math 84; All Leag Bsbl 85-86; SUNY Buffalo; Grphc.

SCHULTZ, MINDY; Longwood HS; Coram, NY; (Y); 17/600; Math Clb; Math Tm; Science Clb; Chorus; Stat Wrstlng; High Hon Roll; Psychlgy.

SCHULZ, CATHLEEN M; Mount Mercy Acad; W Seneca, NY; (Y); 27/220; Exploring; Girl Scts; JCL; SADD; JV Sftbl; Var JV Vllybl; NHS.

SCHULZ, EDWARD; Albion HS; Albion, NY; (S); 30/179; Sec Exploring; Spanish Clb; Sci.

SCHULZ, JOHN; Lake George Central Schl; Glens Fls, NY; (Y); Varsity Clb; Band; Jazz Band; Mrchg Band; Var Bsbl; Bsktbl; Var Ftbl; Socr; Hon Roll; Jr NHS; Outstndng Sr Sports Awd 86; Hartwick Coll; Bus Mgt.

SCHUMACHER, BETSY; Tioga Central HS; Nichols, NY; (Y); Computer Clb; Red Cross Aide; Ski Clb; Spanish Clb; Varsity Clb; Variety Show; Nwsp Rptr; Nwsp Stf; Rep Frsh Cls; VP Soph Cls; Retail Mgmt.

SCHUMACHER, ELISA ANN; Uniondale HS; Hempstead, NY; (Y); 8/300; Pres Sec Drama Clb; NFL; Acpl Chr; Orch; School Musical; School Play; Nwsp Stf; Yrbk Stf; JV L Cheerleading; St Schlr; Outstndng Achvt Music 86; Messiah Coll Schlrshp 86; Outstndng Contribution To Drama 86; Messiah Coll; Politcl Sci.

SCHUMACHER, LAURA; Cicero North Syracuse HS; N Syracuse, NY; (Y); 37/667; Trs Church Yth Grp; Debate Tm; Exploring; Ski Clb; Teachers Aide; Color Guard; Stu Cncl; Stat Score Keeper; NHS; MONY Schlstc Art Awd Hnrbl Ment 85; Georgetown U; Intl Rel.

SCHUMACHER, MICHAEL; Mc Quaid Jesuit HS; Rochester, NY; (Y); Boy Scts; Letterman Clb; Office Aide; Varsity Clb; Var Crs Cntry; JV Var Trk; Hon Roll; Roy Smith Mem Awd To Mst Imprvd Rnnr 85; City Catholic All Star Awd Crss Cntry 85.

SCHUMACHER, TODD; Bay Shore HS; Brightwaters, NY; (Y); 7/406; Art Clb; Math Clb; Math Tm; Varsity Clb; Lit Mag; Gym; Im Ice Hcky; Var Lcrss; Var Socr; High Hon Roll; Outstndng Sci Stu Of Yr 83-84; Outstndng Achvt Socl Stud 85-86; 3rd Cnty Math Cntst 85-86; 1st Sci Fair; Pre Med.

SCHUMAKER, MICHAEL; Bishop Maginn HS; West Coxsackie, NY; (S); 14/86; CAP; Math Clb; Ski Clb; Spanish Clb; Nwsp Rptr; Frsh Cls; JV Ftbl; High Hon Roll; Hon Roll; Embry Riddle Aero U; Aero Engrg.

SCHUMAKER, SHERRY; Hannibal HS; Hannibal, NY; (S); Varsity Clb; VICA; Band; Yrbk Stf; Rep Frsh Cls; Rep Soph Cls; Rep Jr Cls; Rep Sr Cls; Stu Cncl; Capt Vllybl; Jr Prom Queen 85; Graphic Arts.

SCHUMAN, MICHAEL; Niagara Wheatfield SR HS; Niagara Falls, NY; (Y); 47/292; Jazz Band; Hon Roll; Rgnts Schlrshp 86; NCCC; Snd Rcrdg Tech.

SCHUMAN, STACY; Bethpage HS; Plainview, NY; (Y); 7/291; Spanish Clb; Temple Yth Grp; Yrbk Ed-Chief; Cit Awd; Elks Awd; High Hon Roll; Jr NHS; NHS; Sprngfld Coll Hmnc Awd 85; BHS Hmnc Awd 85; Adelphi Pres Schlrshp 86; Rgnts Schlrshp 86; Adelphi U.

SCHUMANN, ELIZABETH; North Salem HS; Brewster, NY; (Y); Hosp Aide; Math Clb; Nwsp Stf; Var Tennis; High Hon Roll; NHS; Ntl Merit Ltr.

SCHUMCHYK, THOMAS; Westhampton Beach HS; East Moriches, NY; (Y); VICA; Hon Roll; Harry B Ward Tech Ctr Electrcl Installation 86; Inquiry USA Soc Studies 86; Electrician.

SCHUMM, LISA; Prt Jervis HS; W Brookville, NY; (Y); Cmnty Wkr; Math Tm; Scholastic Bowl; Yrbk Stf; High Hon Roll; VP NHS.

SCHUMM, MARIANNE; North Babylon SR HS; North Babylon, NY; (Y); 79/464; Art Clb; French Clb; Intnl Clb; Office Aide; Nwsp Stf; Lit Mag; Var Cheerleading; Capt Var Gym; French Hon Soc; High Hon Roll; Pres Acad Fit Awd 86; Boston U Scholar 86; Boston U; Advrtsng.

SCHUNER, JACQUI; L A Webber HS Lyndonville Central; Lyndonville, NY; (Y); 11/75; Varsity Clb; VICA; School Musical; High Hon Roll; NHS; Prfct Atten Awd; JV Bsktbl; JV L Socr; JV L Sftbl; Orleans Cnty Yth Recgntn Awd 86; Regnt Schlrshp Nrsg 86; Monroe CC; Radlgy.

SCHUNKE, BARBARA; Buffalo Acad Of The Sacred Heart; Buffalo, NY; (Y); 8/142; Hosp Aide; JCL; Trs Latin Clb; Science Clb; Ski Clb; Chorus; School Musical; Swing Chorus; High Hon Roll; NHS; Latn Mrt Awd 85; Notre Daem U; Nclr Engr.

SCHUR, DAVID; Cardinal Mooney HS; Livonia, NY; (Y); 25/317; Boy Scts; Ski Clb; Nwsp Rptr; High Hon Roll; Hon Roll; Ntl Merit Ltr; Latin Natl Hnr Soc 82-84; Purdue U; Elec Engrng.

SCHURAVETSKY, YAROSLAV B; Newtown HS; Jackson-Heights, NY; (Y); Church Yth Grp; Debate Tm; German Clb; Service Clb; Prfct Atten Awd; Office Aide; Politecnic U NY.

SCHUREK, KEVIN GERARD; Hampton Bays HS; Hampton Bays, NY; (Y); 1/83; Boy Scts; Bsktbl; Trk; DAR Awd; Elks Awd; Hon Roll; Lion Awd; NHS; Ntl Merit Ltr; Prfct Atten Awd; Amer Lgn Schl Awd 82-85; Natl Sci Olympiad Mdl 83; Newsday Schlrtc Achvr 86; Prncpls Hnr List 82; Penn ST; Aerospc Engrng.

SCHUSTER, CAROLYN; Johnson City HS; Binghamton, NY; (Y); Ski Clb; Band; Chorus; Mrchg Band; Orch; Hon Roll; Acad Excllnc Awd 84-85; 3 Nyssma Awds 83-84; Ithaca Coll; Socl Sci.

SCHUTZ, JULIE; Naples Central HS; Canisteo, NY; (Y); Church Yth Grp; 4-H; Girl Scts; Chorus; Color Guard; JV Bsbl; JV Bsktbl; JV Socr; 4-H Awd; Hon Roll; Engl Imprvmnt 86; Nrsng.

SCHUYLER, MICHAEL; St Joseph By The Sea HS; Staten Island, NY; (Y); Church Yth Grp; Dance Clb; Ed Lit Mag; Var Crs Cntry; Var Trk; NEDT Awd; Schls Awd Hon Englsh 85; Phrmcst.

SCHWAB, MELISSA; Falconer Central Schl; Kennedy, NY; (Y); Pres 4-H; Hst FBLA; GAA; Rep Stu Cncl; Capt Cheerleading; Vllybl; 4-H Awd; Bus.

SCHWAB, MICHAEL; Hamburg SR HS; Boston, NY; (Y); 26/374; JV Bsktbl; Im Ftbl; Var Capt Vllybl; Hon Roll; NHS.

SCHWAB, PAMELA; Mount Mercy Acad; Orchard Park, NY; (Y); Camera Clb; L 4-H; French Clb; Ski Clb; Nwsp Phtg; Yrbk Phtg; Yrbk Stf; Trk.

SCHWABL, CRAIG; Bishop Timon HS; W Seneca, NY; (Y); Boy Scts; Ski Clb; Var Tennis; High Hon Roll; Hon Roll; NHS; MVP Var Ten 86; Engrng.

SCHWABL, JILL; Mt Mercy Acad; Buffalo, NY; (Y); 6/165; Dance Clb; Model UN; Ski Clb; Rep Jr Cls; Rep Sr Cls; Var Cheerleading; Im Tennis; JV Vllybl; High Hon Roll; Hon Roll; Fairfield U Schlrshp 86-87; Fairfield U; Math.

SCHWALB, STACEY; Lindenhurst HS; Lindenhurst, NY; (Y); GAA; Key Clb; Leo Clb; SADD; Orch; Yrbk Stf; Socr; Hon Roll; Kiwanis Awd; Soccr Awd 83-84; Hofstra; Elem Ed Tchr.

SCHWARTZ, BARBRA; Clarkstown North HS; Atlanta, GA; (Y); Pep Clb; Spanish Clb; SADD; Temple Yth Grp; Psych.

SCHWARTZ, BRIAN P; Camden HS; Blossvale, NY; (Y); 10/186; AFS; Am Leg Boys St; Spanish Clb; SADD; Church Choir; Yrbk Stf; High Hon Roll; NHS; Le Moyne Coll; Chem.

SCHWARTZ, CINDY; Clarkstown HS South; Spring Valley, NY; (Y); Cmnty Wkr; Temple Yth Grp; Orch; School Musical; Ed Nwsp Stf; Yrbk Rptr; NHS; Vncnt Fsta Trng Awd Schlrshp 86; SUNY Binghampton.

SCHWARTZ, DAVID I; Jamesville-Dewitt HS; Jamesville, NY; (Y); 9/246; Math Tm; Band; Concert Band; Jazz Band; High Hon Roll; NHS; Ntl Merit Ltr; Chess Clb; Mathletes; Model UN; Earth Sci 83; Eng Humanities 84; Mechncl Drwng 85; SUNY Binghamton; Cvl Engrng.

SCHWARTZ, DEBORAH; New Rochelle HS; Scarsdale, NY; (Y); 6/550; Teachers Aide; Mrchg Band; Symp Band; Nwsp Ed-Chief; Yrbk Rptr; High Hon Roll; NHS; Spanish NHS; 1st Hnrs Iona Coll Lg Cntst Span Lvl 4 85; PTSA Awd Outstndg Schlrp Physcs 86; Prin Awd For Schlrp 86; U PA.

SCHWARTZ, EDEN; Clarkstown North HS; New City, NY; (Y); DECA; Drama Clb; FTA; SADD; Teachers Aide; VP Temple Yth Grp; Chorus; Stage Crew; Elem Ed.

SCHWARTZ, GREGG R; Bayside HS; New York, NY; (Y); 127/684; Aud/Vis; Chorus; Madrigals; School Play; Yrbk Stf; Capt Tennis; Hon Roll; Regents Schlrshp ST Of NY 86; SUNY; Bus.

SCHWARTZ, GREGORY; Scarsdale HS; Scarsdale, NY; (Y); Intnl Clb; Model UN; Stage Crew; Jr Cls; Acctng.

SCHWARTZ, JOAN; Commack HS South; Little Neck, NY; (Y); 42/367; Nwsp Ed-Chief; Pres Frsh Cls; Stu Cncl; High Hon Roll; Hon Roll; NCTE Awd; NHS; JV Bsktbl; JV Cheerleading; JV Sftbl; Regents Schlrshp 85-86; SUNY Binghmton; Eng.

SCHWARTZ, JODI; South Shore HS; Brooklyn, NY; (Y); 42/726; Drama Clb; JA; Math Tm; Service Clb; Chorus; School Musical; School Play; Stage Crew; Variety Show; Cheerleading; Rgnts Schlrshp 86; NYU; Pre-Law.

SCHWARTZ, MARK; Churchville-Chili HS; Churchville, NY; (Y); Model UN; Pep Clb; Ski Clb; Chorus; Stage Crew; Nwsp Phtg; Yrbk Phtg; Im Bowling; Var L Trk; Hon Roll; U Of Rochester; Engrng.

SCHWARTZ, MARK; Sachem High Schl North; Holbrook, NY; (Y); 151/1700; Cmnty Wkr; Drama Clb; PAVAS; Thesps; Chorus; School Musical; School Play; JV Socr; Im Vllybl; Hon Roll; Ithaca Coll; Bus.

SCHWARTZ, MICHAEL; Lawrence HS; Woodmere, NY; (Y); 30/414; Chess Clb; JCL; Trs Latin Clb; Math Tm; Spanish Clb; Rep Stu Cncl; Var Socr; Im Sftbl; High Hon Roll; NHS; Regents Schlrp 86; PTA Schlrp SR Boy Awd 86; SR Athl Awd Accr 86; Binghamton; Med.

SCHWARTZ, MICHAEL; Sweet Home SR HS; Tonawanda, NY; (Y); German Clb; Nwsp Rptr; Nwsp Stf; Rep Frsh Cls; Rep Soph Cls; Rep Jr Cls; Var Socr; High Hon Roll; Ntl Merit Ltr; Prfct Atten Awd; Engrng.

SCHWARTZ, ORIT; Shulamith HS; Staten Island, NY; (S); 1/45; Art Clb; Yrbk Rptr; Pres Stu Cncl; High Hon Roll; Hon Roll; Val; Hgh Schl Bwl; Amer Chmcl Soc Awd; Bus.

SCHWARTZ, RENEE; Hamburg SR HS; Hamburg, NY; (Y); 41/374; Church Yth Grp; Cmnty Wkr; 4-H; French Clb; Hon Roll; Sec Studies.

SCHWARTZ, STEVEN R; Fairport HS; Fairport, NY; (Y); 20/600; Ski Clb; Concert Band; Jazz Band; Mrchg Band; Orch; Rep Stu Cncl; Var Capt Socr; NHS; VFW Awd; Bucknell U; Mech Engrg.

SCHWARZ, JENNIFER; Riverhead HS; Riverhead, NY; (Y); Cmnty Wkr; Hosp Aide; Key Clb; Ski Clb; Spanish Clb; Band; Drm & Bgl; Trk; Psych.

SCHWARZ, KRISTEN; School Of The Holy Child; Rye, NY; (Y); 3/37; School Play; Yrbk Ed-Chief; Var Fld Hcky; French Hon Soc; High Hon Roll; NHS; Ntl Merit Ltr; Boston Coll; Pol Sci.

SCHWARZ, NANCY J; Kings Park HS; Kings Park, NY; (Y); 40/393; Spanish Clb; SADD; Twrlr; Hon Roll; Jr NHS; NHS; DECA Rstrnt Mngmnt Awd 86; Manhattan Coll Prsdntl Schlrshp 86; Rgnts Schlrshp Awd; Manhattan Coll; Intl Bus.

SCHWARZ, VERA; Hicksville HS; Hicksvl, NY; (Y); 5/380; German Clb; Spanish Clb; Chorus; Nwsp Stf; High Hon Roll; Hon Roll; Jr NHS; NHS; Germ Natl Hon Soc Pres; PA ST U; Vet Med.

SCHWARZENBERG, LORI; H Frank Carey HS; Franklin Square, NY; (Y); 25/279; 4-H; Hosp Aide; VICA; Orch; High Hon Roll; VP NHS; Molloy Coll; Nrsng.

SCHWARZROCK, STEPHEN; Monsignor Farrell HS; Staten Island, NY; (Y); Math Clb; JV Var Bsbl; Im Ftbl; High Hon Roll; Hon Roll; Prfct Atten Awd.

SCHWEINBERGER, DONNA M; Fairport HS; Fairport, NY; (Y); 23/600; Church Yth Grp; Drama Clb; French Clb; Chorus; Church Choir; School Musical; Rep Sr Cls; Rep Stu Cncl; Hon Roll; NHS; Holy Cross Schlrshp; Coll Of The Holy Cross.

SCHWEITZER, JILL D; Woodmere Acad; North Woodmere, NY; (Y); Drama Clb; French Clb; SADD; School Play; Stage Crew; Nwsp Rptr; Nwsp Stf; Yrbk Stf; Lit Mag; Regents Schrlshyp 86; Bus.

SCHWEITZER, JOHN W; Babylon HS; Babylon, NY; (Y); Band; Rep Soph Cls; JV Var Bsbl; JV Var Bsktbl; Var Ftbl; Comp Sci.

SCHWEITZER, MICHAEL; Horseheads HS; Elmira, NY; (Y); 22/426; Am Leg Boys St; Science Clb; Concert Band; Mrchg Band; Nwsp Phtg; Sec Stu Cncl; Var L Swmmng; High Hon Roll; NHS; JCL.

SCHWEIZER, DONALD; Holland Central HS; Holland, NY; (Y); Am Leg Boys St; FFA; Var Bsbl; Hon Roll; Regents Schlrshp 86; Pres Acad Ftns Awd 86; Alfred ST; Mech Tech.

SCHWEIZER, LISA; Moore Catholic HS; Staten Island, NY; (Y); 20/172; Pres French Clb; Ski Clb; School Musical; School Play; Nwsp Stf; Cheerleading; Mgr(s); Sftbl; NHS; Ntl Merit Ltr; Schl Sci Fr Ovrll Wnnr 85; Fairfield U; French.

SCHWENDER, SUSAN; Smithtown High School East; St James, NY; (Y); Sec Church Yth Grp; Cmnty Wkr; Acctg.

SCHWENDY, KENT M; Beaver River Central Schl; Carthage, NY; (Y); 3/83; Am Leg Boys St; Pres Exploring; Church Choir; School Musical; Ed Yrbk Ed-Chief; Ed Lit Mag; Var Swmmng; Var Trk; High Hon Roll; NHS; North Country Schlr 86; USAF ROTC Schlrshp 86; Rensselaer Polytech; Elec Engrn.

SCHWENK, GREGG; Skaneateles Central HS; Skaneateles, NY; (S); High Hon Roll; NHS; Writing.

SCHWENKER, QUINN; Mc Quaid Jesuite HS; Rochester, NY; (Y); Ski Clb; Nwsp Rptr; Navl Arch.

SCHWENKLER, MARY; Notre Dame HS; Elmira, NY; (Y); 9/88; Pres Service Clb; Ski Clb; Band; Jazz Band; Yrbk Stf; Var Sftbl; Var Tennis; JP Sousa Awd; NHS; Varsity Clb; Rgnts Schlrshp 85; Rlgn.

SCHWITZ, GWEN; John A Coleman HS; Kingston, NY; (S); French Clb; Key Clb; School Play; Fld Hcky; Trk; Hon Roll.

SCIALLA, PATRICIA J; Floral Park Memorial HS; Floral Park, NY; (Y); 7/150; GAA; Varsity Clb; Band; Concert Band; Mrchg Band; Nwsp Sprt Ed; Yrbk Stf; Capt Crs Cntry; Var Trk; High Hon Roll; Italian Clb Pres; Jr Womens Clb Floral Pk Schlrshp 86; Union Coll; Chem.

SCIAME, EMILIA; St Francis Prep; Springfield Garde, NY; (Y); Library Aide; Teachers Aide; Chorus; Color Guard; Mrchg Band; Prfct Atten Awd; Math.

SCIANCALEPORE, JAMES G; Glens Falls HS; Glens Falls, NY; (Y); 27/220; Boy Scts; Key Clb; Nwsp Ed-Chief; Yrbk Stf; Var Trk; High Hon Roll; NHS; Regents Schlrshp 86; Le Moyne Coll; Eng.

SCIARRA, APRIL; Herkimer Senior HS; E Herkimer, NY; (Y); 9/126; Rep Stu Cncl; Var Capt Cheerleading; Trk; Elks Awd; High Hon Roll; NHS; Sisterhd Temple Beth Joseph Awd 86; Francis Schermer Prz 86; Prncpls Awd 86; Russell Sage Col; Psych.

SCIBILIA, REGINA; Niagara Catholic HS; Niagara Fls, NY; (Y); Cmnty Wkr; Cheerleading; Fld Hcky; Mgr(s); Swmmng; WA Wrkshp Rep Congrssnl Smnr WA 86; Donna Brace Ogilvie Crtv Wrtng Awd Poetry 86; Cert Merit Vlntr.

SCIERA, CHRISSY; Wheatland-Chili HS; Scottsville, NY; (Y); 19/78; Church Yth Grp; Var Cheerleading; JV Socr; Var Sftbl; Hilbert Coll; Paralegal.

SCIOLINO, MARIE A; West Seneca West SR HS; Cheektowaga, NY; (Y); 43/559; VP Church Yth Grp; Key Clb; Spanish Clb; Trs Band; Mrchg Band; Hon Roll; Jr NHS; Kiwanis Awd; NHS; Symp Band; Rgnts Nrsng Schlrshp 8; Canisius Coll; Pre-Med.

SCIORTINO, DANIEL; Cicero-North Syracuse HS; N Syracuse, NY; (S); 20/680; German Clb; Im Bsbl; Im Bsktbl; Im Bowling; Var Ftbl; Hon Roll; Mech Engr.

SCIORTINO, JEFFREY J; Honeoye Falls-Lima HS; Honeoye Falls, NY; (Y); Aud/Vis; Debate Tm; Math Tm; Pres Model UN; Ski Clb; School Musical; Hon Roll; NYS Rgnts Schlrshp 86; Gld Key Mrt Awd Wd Artwrk 85; ST U Of NY Fredonia; Physcs.

SCIORTINO, MARIA G; St Francis Prep; Bayside, NY; (S); 103/746; Dance Clb; Chorus; Stage Crew; Yrbk Stf; JV Cheerleading; Optimates Hnr List 84-85; Stonybrook U; Psychlgy.

SCIOTTI, GERRI; Watervliet HS; Watervliet, NY; (Y); JA; Math Tm; Varsity Clb; Rep Stu Cncl; Var Bowling; JV Sftbl; Var Vllybl; High Hon Roll; Hon Roll; NHS; Govnrs Cncl Alchl & Trffc Sfty Stu 86; Slvr Mdl NYS Olympd Spkn Rssn 86; Schlrshp Wnnr Ntl Endwmnt 86; Acctng.

SCISM II, JAMES H; Rondout Valley HS; Kingston, NY; (Y); 9/154; Am Leg Boys St; JA; Band; Chorus; Stage Crew; JV Var Ftbl; Bausch & Lomb Sci Awd; NHS; Pres Schlr; Math Clb; Regents Schlrshp 86; Rgnts Dplma Hnrs 86; SUNY; Engr.

SCITUTTO, PATRICIA A; Marymount Of Ny HS; New York, NY; (Y); Sec NFL; School Play; Nwsp Stf; Yrbk Stf; Rep Frsh Cls; Rep Sr Cls; Var Capt Bsktbl; Sftbl; Hon Roll; NHS; Ortr NYCFL Natl Frnsc Trnmnt 86; Mst Vlbl Plyr Bsktbl Tm 83-86; Washington & Lee U; Psychtry.

SCLAFANI, THOMAS; Archbishop Molloy HS; Flushing, NY; (Y); 30/383; French Clb; Pep Clb; Nwsp Stf; Crs Cntry; Trk; Hon Roll; NHS; Brdcst Jrnlsm.

SCOBELL, KIMBERLY A; George W Fowler HS; Syracuse, NY; (Y); JV Cheerleading; JV Sftbl; Hon Roll; Merit Rll; Bus.

SCOBELL, SUSAN; West Genesee SR HS; Camillus, NY; (Y); Key Clb; Ski Clb; Yrbk Stf; Rep Soph Cls; Rep Jr Cls; Var Trk; High Hon Roll; Hon Roll; NHS; Rensselear Polytech Inst; Cmptr.

SCOCCA, MICHAEL A; St John The Baptist HS; Copiayne, NY; (Y); 44/492; Chess Clb; Model UN; Science Clb; School Play; Hon Roll; Law.

SCOLA, LINDA; Bishop Kearney HS; Brooklyn, NY; (Y); 19/365; Computer Clb; Key Clb; Library Aide; Math Clb; Math Tm; Capt Bowling; Hon Roll; NHS; Hofstra U; Engnrng.

SCOLNIK, MERYL; Earl L Vandermeulen HS; Port Jefferson, NY; (Y); Art Clb; French Clb; Pep Clb; Spanish Clb; SADD; Chorus; School Musical; Var Capt Cheerleading; Hon Roll; NYSSMA 84; Natl Span Ex 85; SADD Conv SUNY Stony Brook 85; Syracuse U.

SCOPELLITE, MICHAEL; Christ The King Regional HS; Middle Village, NY; (Y); Ski Clb; SADD; Yrbk Stf.

SCORDARAS, MARIA; Saint Edmund HS; Brooklyn, NY; (S); NY U; Frgn Lang.

SCOTT, ALBERT; Mount St Micheal HS; Bronx, NY; (Y); 125/297; Chess Clb; Computer Clb; School Play; Pres Frsh Cls; Socr; Hon Roll; Humanties.

SCOTT, ANDREA; Rome Catholic HS; Rome, NY; (Y); 10/68; Ski Clb; School Musical; Rep Frsh Cls; Sec Soph Cls; Sec Jr Cls; Sec Stu Cncl; Var Capt Cheerleading; Capt Ice Hcky; High Hon Roll; Hon Roll; Latn Awd 86; Polish Indepndt Schlrshp 86; Niagara U Pres Schlrshp 86; Clemson U; Comp Sci.

SCOTT, ANGELA; Midwood HS; Brooklyn, NY; (Y); Art Clb; Drama Clb; Service Clb; Varsity Clb; Chorus; School Play; JV Bsktbl; Var Cheerleading; Var Score Keeper; Ntl Merit Ltr; NY U; Nrs Admin.

SCOTT, ANNA LISA; High Schl Of Fashion Indust; Brooklyn, NY; (Y); 42/324; Church Yth Grp; Computer Clb; Library Aide; Teachers Aide; Yrbk Stf; Pom Pon; Hon Roll; Prfct Atten Awd; Designer.

SCOTT, ANNETTE; Franklin Acad; Malone, NY; (Y); Varsity Clb; Pres Sr Cls; Rep Stu Cncl; Swmmng; Trk; Hon Roll; Prfct Atten Awd; Econ.

SCOTT, CHRIS; Grand Island SR HS; Grand Isl, NY; (Y); Latin Clb; Band; Concert Band; Mrchg Band; Pep Band; School Musical; Var Golf; Var L Ice Hcky; Var L Lcrss; Im Vllybl; Schltc Achvt 86; U Of MI; Orthpdcs.

SCOTT, CHRISTIAN A; Windsor Central HS; Windsor, NY; (Y); Drama Clb; Mathletes; Band; Concert Band; School Musical; School Play; Yrbk Stf; High Hon Roll; NHS; Musc Assoc Awd 83-84; Natl Cncl Yth Ldrshp 86; Math.

SCOTT, CORY; Heuvelton Central Schl; Depeyster, NY; (Y); 30/80; Latin Clb; Varsity Clb; Concert Band; Drm & Bgl; Jazz Band; Orch; Variety Show; Im Bsbl; JV Bsktbl; Var Socr; John Lennon Awd 85; Hghst Grade Achvd On N4SSMA Solo 82; Canton ATC; Crmnl Jstc.

SCOTT, DANESSIA MARIE; Mount Saint Joseph Acad; Buffalo, NY; (Y); Church Yth Grp; Library Aide; Quiz Bowl; Yrbk Stf; Pres Jr Cls; VP Sr Cls; Rep Stu Cncl; Hon Roll; NHS; Cnsius Coll Mrtn Lthr Kng Grnt 86; Lnhrdt Sclrshp 86; Outstndg Achvmnt Strt Lw 86; Canisius Coll; Poly Sci.

SCOTT, DANIEL C; Franklin Acad; Constable, NY; (Y); 18/266; Spanish Clb; Bowling; Trk; Vllybl; Hon Roll; NHS; Prfct Atten Awd; Sci Awds Phys & Earth Sci 83-84; SUNY Morrisville; Ag.

SCOTT, DAWN; Liverpool HS; Liverpool, NY; (Y); JA; Chorus; Var Trk; Hon Roll; Howard U; Bus Adm.

SCOTT, DAWN; Ossining HS; Ossining, NY; (Y); Girl Scts; JA; Var Crs Cntry; Capt Var Trk; High Hon Roll; Bus.

SCOTT, DAWN MARIE; Hannibal Central Schl; Hannibal, NY; (Y); Trs French Clb; Band; Drill Tm; School Musical; Yrbk Ed-Chief; Yrbk Phtg; Ed Yrbk Rptr; Trs Yrbk Stf; High Hon Roll; Sec NHS; Med.

SCOTT, DWAYNE; George W Wingate HS; Brooklyn, NY; (Y); Boys Clb Am; Church Yth Grp; Stage Crew; Wt Lftg; Hon Roll; Ntl Merit Ltr; York Coll; Accntng.

SCOTT, EDDIE; Niagara Catholic HS; Niagara Falls, NY; (Y); 30/105; Church Yth Grp; Computer Clb; FBLA; JA; SADD; JV Bsktbl; Var Ftbl; 4-H Awd; Hon Roll; Church Ythgrp Wrttn Essy King 84; Bus Admn.

SCOTT, ELEANOR; Baldwin SR HS; Baldwin, NY; (Y); #38 In Class; Drama Clb; Girl Scts; Thesps; Chorus; Orch; School Musical; School Play; Var Badmtn; Hon Roll; VFW Awd; Orchestra Arion Awd 86; Long Island U.

SCOTT, ELIZABETH; Hampton Bays JR SR HS; Hampton Bays, NY; (Y); SADD; Varsity Clb; Chorus; Yrbk Bus Mgr; Sec Jr Cls; JV Bsktbl; Capt Var Fld Hcky; JV Var Sftbl; Hon Roll; Prfct Atten Awd; Field Hockey All Leag 84-85; Sftbll All Tournmnt 84-85; Katherine Gibbs Sec Schl; Sec.

SCOTT, GARY; Pelham Memorial HS; Pelham, NY; (Y); 23/160; Church Yth Grp; Cmnty Wkr; Var Capt Bsbl; Var Capt Bsktbl; Var Capt Ftbl; Wt Lftg; Hon Roll; NHS; Conedison Sports Awd 85; NY Daily News All Star Bsbl 86; NY Daily News MVP Bsktbl 86; Villanova U.

SCOTT, JEAN-PAUL; Edison Tech; Rochester, NY; (Y); Var Crs Cntry; JV Ftbl; Var Trk; Var Wrstlng; Hon Roll; NHS; William C Bnz Awd Crss Co 85-86; Wrbt Wrtng Awd 84-85.

SCOTT, JEFFREY W; Savona Central HS; Savona, NY; (Y); 6/45; Am Leg Boys St; Chorus; School Play; Yrbk Phtg; Yrbk Stf; Bsbl; JV Capt Bsktbl; L Socr; Trk; Nclr Engnrng.

SCOTT, KEVIN; Mc Quaid Jesuit HS; Webster, NY; (Y); 20/158; Jazz Band; School Musical; JV Bsbl; Im Bsktbl; Im Ftbl; JV Trk; Hon Roll; Acad Ltr Achvt Awd 85; Fr II Hnrs Cls 85; Cont Prgrss Mth 83-85; U Notre Dame; Engrng.

SCOTT, LINDA; Caledonia Mumford Central Schl; Caledonia, NY; (Y); 10/87; Drama Clb; French Clb; Math Tm; High Hon Roll; Hon Roll; NHS; Salvtn Army Awd 86; Rgnts Schlrp 86; Geneseo St Coll; Spch Path.

SCOTT, MARK; Knox Memorial HS; Russell, NY; (S); 1/30; Mrchg Band; Yrbk Stf; Pres Stu Cncl; Bsbl; Capt Bsktbl; Socr; Bausch & Lomb Sci Awd; DAR Awd; High Hon Roll; Pres NHS; Alfred U; Ceramc Engrng.

SCOTT, NEAL; Franklin Acad; Constable, NY; (Y); JA; High Hon Roll; Hon Roll; NHS; Cert Merit Basic Pgmmg 85-86; Natl Sci Olympd 84; Astronaut.

SCOTT, PATRICIA; Roosevelt JR SR HS; Roosevelt, NY; (Y); 27/192; FBLA; Office Aide; Yrbk Stf; Sftbl; Vllybl; Ntl Merit Ltr; Martin Lthr King Jr Awd 83-84; Winston Salem ST U; Bus Admin.

SCOTT, PATRICK; Christopher Columbus HS; Bronx, NY; (S); Boy Scts; Church Yth Grp; Cmnty Wkr; Computer Clb; Key Clb; Teachers Aide; Band; Church Choir; Jazz Band; Off Jr Cls; Comp Applctns.

SCOTT, RAYMOND; Uniondale HS; Hempstead, NY; (Y); Am Leg Boys St; Church Yth Grp; SADD; Acpl Chr; Chorus; Church Choir; Var L Ftbl; Var L Trk; Jr NHS; All-Nassau Cnty Chr 85-86; Hnrb Mntn All Cnty Ftbl Team 86; Westpoint; Engrng.

SCOTT, SHANNON; Academy Of St Joseph; Coram, NY; (Y); Art Clb; Dance Clb; French Clb; Hosp Aide; Service Clb; SADD; Hon Roll; Prfrmnc Awd Ntl Assn Dnce & Afflitd Artst 84; Rlgs Stds Awd; Ctchst Cert 86; 2nd Hon Lst 85-86; Soc Sci.

SCOTT, SHERYL; Charles O Dickerson HS; Trumansburg, NY; (Y); 27/120; French Clb; SADD; JV Capt Bsktbl; Score Keeper; Hon Roll; Bus.

SCOTT, TOM; Northern Adirondack Central HS; Ellenburg, NY; (Y); 1/80; Am Leg Boys St; Boy Scts; French Clb; Pres Key Clb; Rep Stu Cncl; L Var Bsbl; L Var Bsktbl; L Var Socr; High Hon Roll; Pres NHS; MVP Bsbl 85; Prncpls Awd Math 86; Creatv Wrtg Cntst Hnbl Mntn 86; St Lawrence; Engrng.

SCOTTO, JOAN; Bishop Ford Central Catholic HS; Brooklyn, NY; (S); 4/360; Yrbk Stf; Tennis; NHS; Activities Cncl Ldr 85.

SCOTTO, MICHELE; St Joseph By The Sea HS; Staten Island, NY; (S); Art Clb; Computer Clb; Color Guard; Mrchg Band; Nwsp Ed-Chief; Nwsp Stf; Yrbk Stf; VP Jr Cls; Hon Roll; St Johns U; Lib Art.

SCOTTO, VICTORIA L; Saint Francis Prep; Douglaston, NY; (S); 11/744; Math Tm; School Play; Rep Stu Cncl; JV Crs Cntry; JV Var Tennis; NHS; Pres Schlr; Spanish NHS.

SCOVILLE, JENNIFER; Geneseo Central HS; Geneseo, NY; (Y); 10/90; Spanish Clb; Yrbk Phtg; Yrbk Stf; Rep Stu Cncl; JV Var Socr; JV Var Sftbl; High Hon Roll; NHS; Pres Schlr; Spanish NHS; Regents Schlrshp 85-86; NY U; Photo.

SCOZZAFAVA, THOMAS; Gouverneur HS; Gouverneur, NY; (Y); Church Yth Grp; Teachers Aide; Band; Concert Band; Mrchg Band; Pep Band; Variety Show; Off Stu Cncl; JV Bsbl; JV Var Bsktbl; Bsktbl Tm Empire Games 85-86; Taft Schl; Dntstry.

SCOZZARO, DEANA; Sweet Home SR HS; N Tonawanda, NY; (Y); Chorus; Stu Cncl; Cheerleading; Hon Roll; Italian Hnr Scty 85-86; Buffalo ST; Spec Educ.

SCRAGG, SANDRA; St Joseph By-The-Sea HS; Staten Island, NY; (Y); 15/270; Drama Clb; Chorus; School Musical; School Play; Nwsp Rptr; Nwsp Stf; High Hon Roll; Hon Roll; NHS; Dance Clb; First Hon Roll 84; Sec Hon Roll 85; Jrnlsm.

SCRIBNER, ANDREW W; Horace Mann Schl; Bronx, NY; (Y); Band; JV Crs Cntry; JV Ftbl; Ntl Merit Ltr; Latin & Precalcls Hnrs; Biochem.

SCRIBNER, STEVE; Gloversville HS; Gloversville, NY; (Y); Band; Mrchg Band; Nwsp Stf; High Hon Roll; Hon Roll; Prfct Atten Awd; Concert Band; Acctg.

SCRIMALE, RICHARD; Solvoy HS; Solvay, NY; (Y); 7/171; Pres Math Clb; Off Frsh Cls; Off Soph Cls; Off Jr Cls; Off Sr Cls; Var Capt Bsktbl; Capt Ftbl; Var Capt Golf; Var High Hon Roll; Regents Schlrshp; Solvay Bank Schlrshp; Cayuga County Coll; Accntnt.

SCRIVANI, ANDREW; St Peters Boys HS; Staten Isld, NY; (Y); 45/163; English Clb; SADD; Var Bsbl; L Ice Hcky; L Trk; Hon Roll; Acadmc All Am 86; Comm.

SCRONIC, TRACEY; John Jay HS; Katonah, NY; (Y); Girl Scts; Acpl Chr; Yrbk Ed-Chief; Trs Soph Cls; VP Jr Cls; Off Sr Cls; Rep Stu Cncl; Cheerleading; Sftbl; Cit Awd; Wnnr Of Mt Holyoke Awd For Excllnc In Eng 86; Wnnr Of United Way Essy Cntst 85; English.

SCUDERI, ANTHONY; New Dorp HS; Staten Island, NY; (Y); Drama Clb; School Play; Lit Mag; Wt Lftg; Spectrum Awd Excllnc Creative Wrtng 86; Chancellors Roll Of Hon Poet Rep Awd 86; NYS Rgnt Schlrshp 86; Plattsburgh; Engl.

SCUDERI, CARYN; Bishop Grimes HS; Fayetteville, NY; (S); 4/146; Ski Clb; Sec Frsh Cls; JV Socr; High Hon Roll; NHS; Hmcmng Queen 85; Bus Adm.

SCUDERI, JOANNE L; James Madison HS; Brooklyn, NY; (Y); 30/745; Church Yth Grp; Girl Scts; Off JA; Office Aide; Chorus; School Play; Hon Roll; Prfct Atten Awd; Pace U; CPA.

SCULLY, ELIZABETH; John F Kennedy HS; Utica, NY; (Y); 9/117; Church Yth Grp; Key Clb; Spanish Clb; Jr NHS; Sec Trs NHS; Bus Mngmt.

SCULLY, KEVIN; Cicero-North Syracuse HS; N Syracuse, NY; (S); 35/623; Band; Concert Band; Jazz Band; Mrchg Band; Orch; Symp Band; JV Crs Cntry; Soloist Awd 85.

SCULLY, LIZ; Bay Shore HS; Bayshore, NY; (Y); Aud/Vis; Office Aide; Speech Tm; Nwsp Stf; Yrbk Stf; Stu Cncl; Var L Sftbl; Var Vllybl; Hon Roll; Crmnl Law.

SCURIA, CAMILLE M; Patchogue-Medford HS; Medford, NY; (Y); 52/621; Lit Mag; High Hon Roll; Hon Roll; Jr NHS; NHS; Spanish NHS; SUNY; Psych.

SCUTT, CHRISTOPHER M; Troupsburg Central Schl; Troupsburg, NY; (Y); 2/14; Capt Scholastic Bowl; Band; Church Choir; Symp Band; Var L Socr; Var L Trk; High Hon Roll; NHS; Ntl Merit Ltr; Prfct Atten Awd; Al-Amer Acadmc Natl Scndry Ed Cncl 86; MIP Awd Sccr 84; Hnrbl Mntn Al-Star Sccr Tm 85; Grove City Coll PA; Elec Engr.

SCZUPAK, ROBERT; G Ray Bodley HS; Fulton, NY; (Y); 3/260; Scholastic Bowl; Science Clb; Ski Clb; Spanish Clb; Concert Band; Orch; Var Capt Swmmng; NHS; Ntl Merit SF; Polc Benevlt Awd 84.

SEABON, VICKIE; Benjamin Franklin HS; Rochester, NY; (Y); VP JA; Model UN; Pep Clb; Concert Band; Mrchg Band; Pep Band; School Musical; School Play; Rep Stu Cncl; Hon Roll; Blck Schlr Hnr 84-86.

SEALY, CAMILLE; Murry Bergtraum HS; Brooklyn, NY; (Y); Church Yth Grp; Band; Church Choir; U Of Bridgeport; Corp Atty.

SEAMAN, ELWOOD; Glen Cove HS; Glen Cove, NY; (S); Boys Clb Am; Cmnty Wkr; DECA; SADD; Socr; Norrisville Coll; Bus Admin.

SEAMAN, JENNIFER; The Masters Schl; Bedford, NY; (Y); Cmnty Wkr; Pres French Clb; Hosp Aide; Chorus; Church Choir; L Stat Bsktbl; Im Crs Cntry; Var L Fld Hcky; Im Golf; Mgr(s); Proctor 86-87.

SEAMAN, STACEY; Beacon HS; Beacon, NY; (Y); 18/160; Varsity Clb; Capt Var Crs Cntry; Capt Socr; Var Capt Trk; Hon Roll; NHS; Crs Cntry Trophy 84; Trk Trophy 86; 2nd Pl Mem Day Lions Clb Essay Cont 86; NY Inst Tech; Arch.

SEAMANS, JONATHAN D; Chittenango HS; Chittenango, NY; (Y); Am Leg Boys St; Band; Off Jr Cls; JV Bsbl; Var L Bsktbl; Var L Crs Cntry; Var L Trk; High Hon Roll; Jr NHS; Pres NHS; Stu Of Wk 84-85; Most Imprvd Cross Country Rnnr At Sprts Bnqt 85-86; Civil Engineering.

SEAMON, WENDY; G Ray Bodley HS; Fulton, NY; (Y); Drama Clb; Library Aide; Science Clb; Chorus; School Musical; School Play; Yrbk Phtg; Yrbk Stf; Cheerleading; Hon Roll; Prfct Att 84-86; Sci Olmpd ST At Wst Pt 86; Phtgrphy Awd 85; Frstry.

SEAR, MARY; Archbishop Walsh HS; Olean, NY; (Y); Spanish Clb; School Musical; Yrbk Stf; Pres Soph Cls; VP Sr Cls; Rep Stu Cncl; Cheerleading; High Hon Roll; NHS; Fndtn Of Intrntn Cooprtn Schlrshp 85; Elem Ed.

SEARLE, JO ANNE LOUISE; Shenendehowa HS; Ballston Lake, NY; (Y); 10/675; Key Clb; Off Sr Cls; JV Socr; Cit Awd; Elks Awd; Hon Roll; NHS; Sprtsmnshp Awd 83; Outstndng Achvt Bio 84; Marshall Hall Awd Outstndng Bldrs Clb Part Of Key Clb 83; SUNY Buffalo; Socl Sci.

SEARLS, KAREN; Hilton Central HS; Hilton, NY; (Y); 3/319; VP Church Yth Grp; Swing Chorus; Rep Stu Cncl; JV Cheerleading; JV Var Swmmng; High Hon Roll; NHS; Ntl Merit Ltr; Harvard Prize Bk 86; Mst Vlbl Swmmr 85.

SEARS, JEFF; Cazenovia Central HS; Cazenovia, NY; (Y); Aud/Vis; Band; Stage Crew; JV Var Bsktbl; JV Var Ftbl; JV Var Trk; NHS; Elec Engr.

SEAY, DONAVAN; Wah Whitman HS; Huntington, NY; (Y); 131/540; Aud/Vis; Computer Clb; Office Aide; Spanish Clb; Chorus; High Hon Roll; Hon Roll; Jr NHS; Spanish NHS; Northeastern U; Crmnl Just.

SEBAK, KAMLA; James Addams U HS; Brooklyn, NY; (S); 21/266; Chorus; Hon Roll; Hnr Soc 86; NY U; Nrsg.

SEBAYAN, ELIZABETH; Tottenville HS; Staten Isld, NY; (Y); Church Yth Grp; Teachers Aide; Socr; Cit Awd; Hon Roll; NHS; Schlr Athl Awd Trphy 86; Tpng Accuracy Speed Awds 85-86; IN Bus Inst 86; Law.

SEBESTA, LIA; Solvay HS; Solvay, NY; (Y); Church Yth Grp; Hosp Aide; Spanish Clb; Yrbk Stf; Jr Cls; High Hon Roll; NHS; Awds Bio,Engl,Geo 84-85; Awds Engl,Trig,Soc Studies 85-86.

SEBLANO, PAUL; Franklin Delano Roosevelt HS; Brooklyn, NY; (Y); Computer Clb; English Clb; Service Clb; Nwsp Rptr; Pres Stu Cncl; Wt Lftg; Hon Roll; Physcl Ftns Bdy Dvlpmnt Awd 84-85; Bio Awd 85; Hnrs Inst Awd 85; Brooklyn Coll; Comp Prog.

SECAUR, MARK; Auburn HS; Auburn, NY; (Y); Church Yth Grp; JA; Varsity Clb; Var Bsktbl; Im JV Ftbl; High Hon Roll; Hon Roll; NHS; Bio.

SECOND, ROBIN; Cazenovia Central HS; New Woodstock, NY; (Y); Hon Roll; Pre-Med.

SECONDO, ANDREA; Hornell HS; Hornell, NY; (Y); Dance Clb; Band; Color Guard; Concert Band; Mrchg Band; Sec Jr Cls; Trs Stu Cncl; Var Socr; Var Trk; High Hon Roll; Span Awd Merit 84-85&85-86; Exec Sec.

SECOR, DAVID E; Clyde Savannah HS; Savannah, NY; (Y); Am Leg Boys St; Band; Jazz Band; VP Frsh Cls; VP Jr Cls; VP Sr Cls; Rep Stu Cncl; Capt Bsbl; Bsktbl; NHS; U Of Buffalo; Cvl Engrng.

SEDA, CRISTINA; Sachem HS; Holbrook, NY; (Y); 607/1558; School Musical; Sftbl; Hon Roll; Prlgl Stds.

SEDA, ERIN; Valley Stream Central HS; Valley Stream, NY; (Y); Spanish Clb; SADD; Chorus; Spanish NHS.

SEDDON, SUSAN; Northport HS; E Northport, NY; (Y); 29/590; Computer Clb; Mathletes; SADD; High Hon Roll; Psychlgy.

SEDER, TODD; Hillcrest HS; Flushing, NY; (Y); Chorus; Hon Roll; Arista, B Chancy Awd 84; St Johns; Acctg.

SEDITA, PAUL A; E J Wilson HS; Rochester, NY; (Y); Math Clb; Spanish Clb; Varsity Clb; Im Bsktbl; Im Socr; Var L Trk; High Hon Roll; Hon Roll; NHS; Ntl Merit Ltr; Phi Beta Kappa Awd For Exc 86; Rgnts Schlrshp 86; Astrophyscs.

SEDORE, ELAINE ROSE; Owego Free Acad; Owego, NY; (Y); AFS; Camera Clb; Drama Clb; Hosp Aide; Chorus; Concert Band; Mrchg Band; Stage Crew; Nwsp Stf; Var Trk; Tioga Cnty Yth Cncl 85-86; Cert Sgn Lang For Deaf 86; Tompkins Cnty CC; Trvl.

SEEFELDT, HILARY; Tottenville HS; Staten Isld, NY; (Y); Pres Sec Exploring; Key Clb; Ski Clb; Teachers Aide; Yrbk Stf; Var Capt Swmmng; High Hon Roll; Hon Roll; Kiwanis Awd; NHS; Pride Of Yankees Outstndng Achvmnt Acdmc & Extr Acrrclr Actvties 86; Athlt Schlr Awd 86.

SEEGMULLER, SUZANNE; Mahopac HS; Mahopac, NY; (Y); 4/409; Cmnty Wkr; Science Clb; Rptr Yrbk Stf; Capt Vllybl; Stat Wrstlng; High Hon Roll; NHS; Amer Lgn Girls ST Cmptn Rnnr Up 86; Olympcs Of Mind Rgnl Cmptn-Judg 86; Engrng.

SEEKINGS, CARRIE; Cassadaga Valley HS; Cassadaga, NY; (Y); 16/75; Church Yth Grp; Math Clb; Spanish Clb; Varsity Clb; Trs Band; Chorus; Church Choir; Concert Band; Sec Sr Cls; Var Capt Cheerleading; NY ST Girls ST 85; PA ST; Acctg.

SEEKINS, LAURI; Jamestown HS; Jamestown, NY; (Y); Ski Clb; Color Guard; Mrchg Band; Off Jr Cls; Stu Cncl; Cit Awd; Jamestown CC; Psych.

SEELBACH, CHRISTINA; Mt St Mary Acad; Buffalo, NY; (Y); Church Yth Grp; Cmnty Wkr; Chorus; Stage Crew; Variety Show; Gym; Hon Roll; Prfct Mth Regents Exam 84-86; Bus.

SEELEY, AMY; Amsterdam HS; Amsterdam, NY; (Y); Trs FBLA; Hon Roll; Fulton Montgomery CC Typing Cmptn 1st Pl 86; Bus.

SEELEY, ELIZABETH; Mexico Acad; Mexico, NY; (Y); Pres Church Yth Grp; Spanish Clb; Chorus; Church Choir; Color Guard; Mrchg Band; Trk; Hon Roll; Prfct Atten Awd; Spanish NHS; Lee Coll; Comp.

SEELEY, HEATHER; Churchville Chili HS; North Chili, NY; (Y); Key Clb; Pep Clb; Ski Clb; Chorus; Off Stu Cncl; Wt Lftg; High Hon Roll; Hon Roll; VP Jr NHS; NHS; U Of NY Albany; Art.

SEELEY, JOHN M; Midlakes HS; Phelps, NY; (Y); 2/153; Am Leg Boys St; French Clb; Letterman Clb; Varsity Clb; Var L Bsbl; Var L Bsktbl; Var L Vllybl; High Hon Roll; NHS; Slctd Schl Repr Schl Sci Olympds 86; Comm.

SEELEY, MARYALYCE; Mercy HS; Manorville, NY; (Y); Yrbk Stf; VP Frsh Cls; VP Jr Cls; VP Stu Cncl; Cheerleading; Golf; Trk; High Hon Roll; Jr NHS; Ntl Eng Merit Awd 86; Hnrs Princpls List 83-86; Acad All Am Awd 86; Med.

SEELOW, DONALD; Broadalbin HS; Broadalbin, NY; (Y); Drama Clb; Library Aide; ROTC; Nwsp Stf; Yrbk Stf; Off Sr Cls; Var Capt Bsbl; Cit Awd; Hon Roll; Coaches Awd Bsbll 86; Bill Stillman Awd Mst Athltc 86; Air Force; Avtn Mechncs.

SEEPAUL, MANESHWAR; William Howard Taft HS; New York City, NY; (Y); Office Aide; Teachers Aide; Off Sr Cls; Vllybl; Prfct Atten Awd; Cert Outstndng Achvt Frnch 85; Hunter Coll; Engrng.

SEERAM, LLOYD; De Witt Clinton HS; Bronx, NY; (Y); 54/257; Aud/Vis; Church Yth Grp; FNA; JA; Office Aide; Chorus; Church Choir; Pres Frsh Cls; Gym; Wt Lftg; Awd In Engl 84; Awd For Svc In Coll Blind Prog 86; U At Buffalo; Bus Adm.

SEERY, JOHN; Holy Trinity HS; West Hempstead, NY; (Y); JV Crs Cntry; Var Trk; Var Wrstlng; IA Coll; Bus.

SEETAL, JOYCELYN; Sacred Heart Acad; Hempstead, NY; (Y); Debate Tm; NFL; Chorus.

SEEWALDT, VIRGINIA; The Wheatley Schl; E Williston, NY; (Y); Am Leg Aux Girls St; VP Church Yth Grp; Rep Frsh Cls; Rep Soph Cls; Sec Jr Cls; Rep Stu Cncl; JV Bsktbl; Var Trk; NHS; Psych.

SEGAL, MICHELLE; The Masters HS; Beaverton, OR; (Y); French Clb; Hosp Aide; JA; School Play; VP Frsh Cls; JV Socr; JV Trk; Hon Roll; Mu Alp Tht; NHS; Engl Achvmnt Awd 84; Math Achvmnt Awd 84; Volntr Spec Olympics Vol 86; UC Berkeley; Pre Law.

SEGALL, KEVIN; Baldwin SR HS; Baldwin, NY; (S); Chorus; JV L Ftbl; Comp Sci.

SEGALOWITZ, SUSAN; Port Richmond HS; Staten Island, NY; (Y); Math Tm; Office Aide; SADD; Teachers Aide; Chorus; School Musical; School Play; Stage Crew; Yrbk Stf; High Hon Roll; Bus.

SEGAR, KAREN; James E Sperry HS; Henrietta, NY; (Y); 3/270; Drama Clb; Thesps; Chorus; Jazz Band; Madrigals; School Musical; French Hon Soc; NHS; Ntl Merit Schol; Wegmans Schlrshp 86; Godfrey Jacobsen Schlrshp 86; Math Dept Awd 86; Oberlin Coll; Rssn Study.

SEGINA, CHRIS B; Laurens Central HS; Mt Vision, NY; (Y); Varsity Clb; Band; Concert Band; Jazz Band; Mrchg Band; Var L Ftbl; Var L Wrstlng; Hon Roll; Ftbl All Stars 85 & 86.

SEGUIN, JENNIFER; Catholic Central HS; Troy, NY; (Y); Drama Clb; Girl Scts; Math Clb; Trs Pep Clb; VP Spanish Clb; Chorus; School Musical; School Play; Uncle Sam Toastmastrs Moe Kelly Mem Schlrshp 84; Psychlgy.

SEGUINOT, MADELINE; Humanities HS; New York, NY; (Y); Lit Mag; Hon Roll; Prfct Atten Awd; Med.

SEHWANI, DAVE; Moore Catholic HS; Staten Island, NY; (Y); Sec Computer Clb; Math Clb; Math Tm; Spanish Clb; Im Bsktbl; Im Bowling; Im Ftbl; JV Trk; Hon Roll; Elec Engr.

SEIBERT, MARK; Cardinal O Hara HS; Buffalo, NY; (Y); Boys Clb Am; Var Bsbl; Var Bsktbl; Var Capt Ftbl; Hon Roll; Jr NHS; Elct Into US Achvt Acad For Ftbl 85; Erie Cnty Athltc All Star Awd 86; Accnt.

SEIDBERG, DANIEL R; Fayetteville-Manlius HS; Jamesville, NY; (Y); 29/335; Camera Clb; Var L Crs Cntry; Var Capt Trk; High Hon Roll; Hon Roll; NHS; 7 Time Vrsty Lttr Wnnr-Crss Cntry & Trk 82-86; Colgate U; Pre-Med.

SEIDEL, SUZANNE; Salmon River Central HS; Fort Covington, NY; (S); 3/88; Church Yth Grp; French Clb; Band; Chorus; Concert Band; Jazz Band; French Hon Soc; Hon Roll; NHS; Hartwick Coll; Intl Hotel Mgmt.

SEIDES, DAVID H; Edgemont HS; Hartsdale, NY; (Y); Computer Clb; Mathletes; Ski Clb; Temple Yth Grp; Off Soph Cls; Stat Bsktbl; Stat Ftbl; JV Socr; Earth Sci Awd 83; NY St Regents Schlrshp 86; U Of Rochester; Comp Sci.

SEIFERTH, FRED; Attica SR HS; Cowlesville, NY; (S); 5/167; French Clb; Ski Clb; Band; Jazz Band; Trs Stu Cncl; JV Bsbl; JV Crs Cntry; Var JV Socr; Var Wt Lftg; Hon Roll; VP Band 85-86; Buffalo ST; Cmmnctns.

SEIFRIED, CHRISTINE; Delaware Valley Central Schl; Cochecton, NY; (S); 1/42; High Hon Roll; NHS; Ntl Merit SF; Pres Schlr; Val; Regents Scholar 86; BOCES Gifted & Talntd Satllt Pgm 86; Catskill Art Soc Hnrb Mntn 85; Delhi Coll; Acctng.

SEIGEL, DONNA; Cuba Central Schl; Cuba, NY; (Y); 15/55; Hosp Aide; Model UN; Spanish Clb; VP SADD; Teachers Aide; Varsity Clb; Chorus; Var Co-Capt Cheerleading; Tennis; Trk; Hnrbl Mntn At Arts Festvl; Alfred Ag Tech; Accntng.

SEIKEN, ERIC; Half Hollow Hills Hs East; Dix Hills, NY; (Y); Cmnty Wkr; SADD; Varsity Clb; Stage Crew; Yrbk Phtg; Var Golf; Var Swmmng; Var Tennis; Im Wt Lftg; High Hon Roll.

SEINFELD, MARA; HS Of Art & Design; Brooklyn, NY; (Y); Library Aide; Nwsp Rptr; Nwsp Stf; Lit Mag; Sftbl; Hon Roll; NHS; Natl Art Hnr Soc 86; Illustrator.

SEITZ, JULIE ANN; Our Lady Of Mercy HS; Penfield, NY; (Y); Aud/Vis; Intnl Clb; Spanish Clb; Variety Show; Rep Soph Cls; Rep Stu Cncl; JV Var Bsktbl; Capt Var Sftbl; Hon Roll; GAA; NY ST Pblc Athltc Assn Bsktbll Chmpnshp 85.

SEKELSKY, TERRI; West Seneca East SR HS; Depew, NY; (Y); 38/375; DECA; Ski Clb; SADD; Hon Roll; Jr NHS; U Buffalo; Bus Acctnt.

SEKUL, STACEY; Pelham Memorial HS; Pelham Manor, NY; (Y); Church Yth Grp; Cmnty Wkr; Exploring; Spanish Clb; Band; Flag Corp; High Hon Roll; Jr NHS; NHS; Spanish NHS; Spnsh IV Merit Awd 85; NY U; Pltcl Sci.

SELASSIE, SENGAL M; Collegiate Schl; New York, NY; (Y); Church Yth Grp; Latin Clb; Math Tm; Model UN; Chorus; Stage Crew; Nwsp Sprt Ed; JV Bsktbl; Var Crs Cntry; Trk; Cum Laude 85; Hilson Schlrshp Hnr Awd 85; X-Cntry Var Awd Ltr, Track Var Awd Ltr 83, 84 & 85; Harvard.

SELBY, LETITIA; John-Jay HS; Brooklyn, NY; (Y); Dance Clb; FBLA; Office Aide; Teachers Aide; Jr Cls; Cheerleading; Vllybl; Hunter Coll.

SELDEN, JO LYNNE; Panama Central Schl; Ashville, NY; (Y); 2/62; Quiz Bowl; Diving; Swmmng; Trk; Hon Roll; NHS; Vet.

SELDES, RICHARD; South HS; Valley Stream, NY; (Y); 15/168; Drama Clb; School Play; Yrbk Stf; Stu Cncl; Bsktbl; Capt Ftbl; Trk; High Hon Roll; NHS; All Cnty Ftbl 85; All Cnty Trck 85 & 86; Regents Schlrshp Awd 86; Johns Hopkins U; Pre-Med.

SELG, CHRISTINE; Bellport HS; E Patchogue, NY; (Y); 31/395; Hosp Aide; School Play; Variety Show; Rep Stu Cncl; High Hon Roll; Hon Roll; Jr NHS; NHS; Outstndng Accomplshmnt Mth Achvt Awd 84-85, Frnch III & IV 85-86; Ed.

SELICATO, GRACE; Bishop Grimes HS; Syracuse, NY; (S); Science Clb; Ski Clb; Concert Band; School Musical; Yrbk Stf; Sec Soph Cls; Sec Jr Cls; Var Cheerleading; High Hon Roll; Cert Hgh Achvt Mth Dept Awd 84; Music Awd 85; Cert Cmmndtn Itln 84; Phrmcy.

SELIG, JULIE; J F Kennedy HS; Merrick, NY; (Y); Key Clb; Tennis; Hon Roll; NHS.

SELIGMAN, CATHERINE R; New Rochelle HS; New Rochelle, NY; (Y); SADD; Temple Yth Grp; Mrchg Band; Symp Band; Yrbk Stf; JV Socr; JV Swmmng; JV Vllybl; NHS.

SELIGMAN, LYDIA E; Syosset HS; Syosset, NY; (Y); 158/481; Art Clb; Camera Clb; Varsity Clb; Band; Mrchg Band; Nwsp Phtg; Nwsp Stf; Bsktbl; Sftbl; FIT; Advtg.

SELINSKY, SCOTT T; St Anthonys HS; Pt Jefferson Sta, NY; (Y); French Clb; SADD; Lit Mag; L Crs Cntry; Trk; Hon Roll; Ntl Merit Ltr; NYS Rgnts Schlrshp 85-86; Frnch Natl Hnr Scty; Duns Scotus; Siena Coll; Marines.

SELLARS, LA TANYA; Hauppauge HS; Hauppauge, NY; (Y); Camera Clb; Cmnty Wkr; Office Aide; Varsity Clb; VICA; Chorus; Nwsp Phtg; Nwsp Stf; Yrbk Phtg; Yrbk Stf; TAP 86; Suffolk Cmnty Coll; Rtl Bus Mgm.

SELLERS, LESLIE; James E Sperry SR HS; Henrietta, NY; (Y); 49/264; JA; JV Bsktbl; Hon Roll; Jr NHS; Achvt/Chmstry Ntl Sci Olympd 86; Prtcptn NY ST Acdmc Dcthln 86; Urbn League Erly Rcgntn 86; Hampton Inst; Chem.

SELLERS, TIMOTHY C; Sidney HS; Unadilla, NY; (Y); 3/102; Pres Art Clb; Pres French Clb; Rep Stu Cncl; Var L Socr; Var Tennis; High Hon Roll; NHS; Ntl Merit SF; Math Clb; Math Tm; NY ST Smmr Schl Visual Arts 83; Stdnt Enrgy Resrch Comptn Proj 85-86; Olympc Mind ST Chmp NY Tm 83; Astrophyscs.

SELLICK, JENNIFER; Midlakes HS; Phelphs, NY; (Y); French Clb; Letterman Clb; Ski Clb; Trs Soph Cls; Trs Jr Cls; Var Bsktbl; Var Capt Socr; Var L Sftbl; Var L Trk; Hon Roll; Parlgl Asst.

SELLICK, RICH; Schoharie Central Schl; Schoharie, NY; (Y); Pres Trs Key Clb; JV Bowling; Hon Roll; Crtfct Of #1 Cmnty Svc 85-86; Hudson Valley CC; Archtctr.

SELTZER, ROBERT M; Depew HS; Lancaster, NY; (Y); Computer Clb; Math Clb; Science Clb; Band; Mrchg Band; Variety Show; Golf; Swmmng; Vllybl; Ntl Merit Schol; Rgnts 86; APA Educ Fndtn 86; RIT; Qntm Physcs.

SELYUTIN, VALERIE; John Dewey HS; Brooklyn, NY; (Y); Art Clb; Chorus; Color Guard; School Musical; School Play; French Hon Soc; Fash Dsgn.

SEMIAN, STEPHEN; Monsignor Farrell HS; Staten Island, NY; (Y); 45/300; Yrbk Stf; Im Bsktbl; Im Bowling; Im Ftbl; Hon Roll; Ntl Merit Ltr; NY U; Bnkng.

SEMIDEY, PASCUAL; De Witt Clinton HS; Bronx, NY; (Y); 25/259; Nwsp Rptr; Nwsp Stf; Hon Roll; NHS; Prfct Atten Awd; Gvrnrs Cmmtee Schlstc Achvmnt Citatn 86; Mdl Fr Svc 86; Asst Edtr The Hstry Jrnl 86; Real Est.

SEMINSKI, AMY; Union Endicott HS; Endwell, NY; (Y); Key Clb; Band; Color Guard; Mrchg Band; Symp Band; Hon Roll; Mktg.

SEMMLER, KIMBERLY; Hilton Central HS; Hilton, NY; (Y); Church Yth Grp; Dance Clb; Sec FBLA; Ski Clb; Teachers Aide; Variety Show; Stu Cncl; Var Trk; JV Var Vllybl; 4-H; Hgh Hnr & Hnr Roll 83-87; Top 15 Fnlsts Of Miss Amer Coed Pgnt 86; JR Prm Qn 86; Bus Mgmt.

SEMONCHIK, ROBERT; Watervliet JR SR HS; Watervliet, NY; (Y); Boy Scts; Pres Camera Clb; Pres Exploring; Pres JA; Science Clb; Pres Concert Band; Jazz Band; Mrchg Band; School Play; High Hon Roll; Rnslr Cnty All Star Band 84; U S Airforce Acad; Arspc.

SEMPLE, CHRISTINE BOBB; John Dewey HS; Brooklyn, NY; (Y); Teachers Aide; Band; Hon Roll; Baruch Coll; Acctg.

SENA, JENNY; New Dorp HS; Staten Island, NY; (Y); 17/600; Intnl Clb; Pres Latin Clb; Library Aide; Chorus; Nwsp Stf; Lit Mag; Cit Awd; Hon Roll; NHS; 2nd Pl Wnr In Cty-Wd Itln Ptry Cntst-Slvr Mdl 85-86; Gld Hnr Key For Schlstc Achvt 86; Wagner Coll; Dntst.

SENDROVITZ, HOWARD M; Plainview-Old Bethpage HS; Plainview, NY; (Y); 35/195; Cmnty Wkr; Model UN; Temple Yth Grp; Band; Mrchg Band; School Play; Nwsp Rptr; Hon Roll; NHS; Ntl Merit Ltr; Pres Poltcl Issues Clb; Earth Sci Olympd 1st Pl; Outstndg Bus Stu Awd; SUNY Binghampton; Law.

SENECA, CANDACE; Wallkill SR HS; Wallkill, NY; (Y); Science Clb; Band; Concert Band; Rep Frsh Cls; Rep Jr Cls; Rep Stu Cncl; Sftbl; Hon Roll; Prfct Atten Awd; Pres Phy Fit Awd 85-86; Bio.

SENECAL, JULIE; Paul V Moore HS; Parish, NY; (Y); GAA; Nwsp Phtg; Nwsp Rptr; Nwsp Stf; Yrbk Phtg; Yrbk Rptr; Yrbk Stf; Sec Jr Cls; Rep Stu Cncl; JV Var Cheerleading; Cmnctns.

SENFT, ANNE; Auburn HS; Auburn, NY; (Y); 7/500; Am Leg Aux Girls St; Drama Clb; Chorus; School Musical; School Play; Nwsp Ed-Chief; Nwsp Stf; High Hon Roll; NHS; Coyuga CC & Lemoyne; Bus Mngmt.

SENG, JEFFREY M; Center Moriches HS; Center Moriches, NY; (Y); 4/92; Boy Scts; Ski Clb; Spanish Clb; JV Bsbl; Var Socr; Im Sftbl; Im Vllybl; Sec NHS; Comm Schlrshp 86; Newsday High Hon Semi-Fnlst 86; Rgnts Schlrshp Ny St 86; SUNY Albany; Bus Adm.

SENGER, LORRAINE; Vestal Central HS; Vestal, NY; (Y); Church Yth Grp; Hosp Aide; Color Guard; Mrchg Band; Prfct Atten Awd; Nrsng.

SENGLAUB, MARCY; Naples Central Schl; Naples, NY; (Y); 7/64; Band; Chorus; Concert Band; Mrchg Band; School Musical; School Play; Sec Soph Cls; High Hon Roll; Hon Roll; Ski Clb; All Cnty Chorus 84-85; All St Choir 83-86; Frnch Ed.

SENGLE, GARY; West Ironoequoit HS; Rochester, NY; (Y); 36/396; Var Ice Hcky; Var Lcrss; Hon Roll; NHS; Prfct Atten Awd; Pres Schlr; 3rd Pl Natl Lat Exam 85; NY ST Regnts Schlrshp 86; Clarkson U; Engrng.

SENIOR, LYNDELL; Uniondale HS; Uniondale, NY; (Y); Debate Tm; Band; Concert Band; Jazz Band; Orch; School Musical.

SENITZER, ILENE; New Rochelle HS; New Rochelle, NY; (Y); Cmnty Wkr; Girl Scts; Pep Clb; Spanish Clb; VP Temple Yth Grp; Chorus; School Play; High Hon Roll; Hon Roll; Oneanta; Psych.

SENKOWSKY, SONYA K; Spencer-Van Etten Central HS; Van Etten, NY; (Y); 4/86; Am Leg Aux Girls St; School Play; Nwsp Ed-Chief; Yrbk Stf; Ed Lit Mag; NHS; Pres Schlr; Rep Art Clb; Trs Aud/Vis; Drama Clb; S Ve Tchrs Assoc Schlrshp 86; La Salle Full Tuition U Schlrshp 86; JR Miss Aacad Achvt Awd & Schlr 86; La Salle U; Commun.

SENS, BRIAN; Fairport HS; Fairport, NY; (Y); Church Yth Grp; Cmnty Wkr; SADD; Lcrss; JV Var Socr; Hon Roll; Htl Mgmt.

SENUS, KEN; John F Kennedy HS; Utica, NY; (Y); Aud/Vis; Spanish Clb; Bsktbl; Ftbl; Band; Mrchg Band; Orch; Symp Band; Utica Coll; Bus Mgmt.

SENUS, PETER; West Genesee Sr HS; Camillus, NY; (Y); Am Leg Boys St; Church Yth Grp; Cmnty Wkr; Exploring; Rep Jr Cls; JV Var Bsktbl; High Hon Roll; Hon Roll; Jr NHS; NHS; West Point; Engrng.

SENZER, ADRIENNE I; Tappan Zee HS; Tappan, NY; (Y); 16/245; Science Clb; VP SADD; Concert Band; School Musical; Nwsp Stf; Var Tennis; NHS; Outstndg Achvmt Math Awd 83-84; Cert Apprctn Hlpng Spcl Ed Stdnts 84-85; NY ST Rgnts Schlrshp 85-86; SUNY Binghamton; Psych.

SENZON, SHARI L; Massapequa HS; Massapequa, NY; (Y); 4/445; Yrbk Stf; VP Frsh Cls; Pres Soph Cls; Pres Jr Cls; Pres Sr Cls; Var Capt Gym; NHS; Ntl Merit Ltr; Hosp Aide; Acad All Amer 86; NYS Regents Scholar 86; U PA; Pre-Med.

SEOBARRAT, REJENDRA; Midwood H S At Brooklyn College; Richmond Hill, NY; (Y); Intnl Clb; Spanish Clb; Attorny Genrl Triple C Awd 83; TV Comm & Arts 83; Jr Arista 83; Med.

SEPANIC, TOM; Buffalo Traditio; Buffalo, NY; (S); 11/115; Church Yth Grp; VP Jr Cls; VP Sr Cls; Rep Stu Cncl; Var Bsbl; Capt Var Ice Hcky; Var Socr; Hon Roll; Prfct Atten Awd; Cmnty Wkr; MVP Hockey & Bsbl 85.

SEPHTON, AMY; Westhampton Bch HS; Mastic, NY; (Y); 60/212; FBLA; Band; Mrchg Band; Pep Band; Yrbk Stf; Lit Mag; Trk; Hon Roll; Rgnts Schlrshp 86; Comm Awd Mst Outstndng Bus Stu 86.

SEPP, JEANNA; East Hampton HS; Montauk, NY; (Y); Church Yth Grp; Cmnty Wkr; Computer Clb; Red Cross Aide; SADD; Varsity Clb; Yrbk Sprt Ed; Yrbk Stf; JV Sftbl; Var Tennis; Springfield MA; Sport Med.

SEPULVEDA, EILEEN; Grace Dodge HS; Bronx, NY; (Y); Cmnty Wkr; Teachers Aide; Chorus; Color Guard; Bsktbl; Swmmng; Vllybl; Fordham U; Bkkpr.

SEPULVEDA, HIRAN; Lafayette HS; Brooklyn, NY; (Y); Cmnty Wkr; Church Choir; Stage Crew; Cert Of Exelence Intrmdt Alg/Amer Hstry/Envrmntl Sci; Commnctn.

SEQUEIRA, JANICE; Greater New York Acad; Brooklyn, NY; (S); 1/34; Chorus; Nwsp Ed-Chief; Yrbk Ed-Chief; Pres Soph Cls; Var Capt Vllybl; Dnfth Awd; NHS; Val; Natl Ldrshp & Svc Awd 86; Dstngshd Ctznshp Awd 86; Atlantic Union Coll; Med.

SERAFINI, LISA M; Mohonasen SR HS; Schenectady, NY; (Y); 19/176; Church Yth Grp; Pres SADD; Mrchg Band; Nwsp Ed-Chief; Yrbk Sprt Ed; VP Jr Cls; Capt L Trk; DAR Awd; NHS; St Schlr; Mst Imprvd Grls Outdr Trck 85; Outstndng Amer Stdnt 86; Penn ST; Arch Engrng.

SERAPHIN, ARUN; The Stony Brook Schl; Po Jefferson St, NY; (Y); 1/99; Chess Clb; Cmnty Wkr; Math Tm; Var JV Crs Cntry; Var Mgr(s); Stat Tennis; JV Trk; Bausch & Lomb Sci Awd; High Hon Roll; Jr NHS; Brwn U Bk Awd Wrtng 85-86; Rnsslr Math & Sci Awd 85-86; Twrs Memrl Awd Gld Mdl 85-86; MIT; Engrng.

SERAYDARIAN, ROSINE; Cathedral HS; Jackson Hgt, NY; (Y); 9/277; French Clb; School Musical; Hon Roll; Gold Mdls Math 84-86; Gold Mdl Atten 82-86; Soc Wmn Engrs Cert Of Merit 86; Cardinal Gracias Awd 86; Polytechnic U; Elec Engr.

SERBALIK, JOYCE; Mcehanicville HS; Mechanicville, NY; (S); 3/110; French Clb; SADD; Yrbk Stf; Rep Stu Cncl; JV Cheerleading; High Hon Roll; NHS; Frnch Awd; Engl Awd; Skidmore Coll Awd; Sunny Geneseo; Law.

SERBINOWSKI, CELESTE; Eden Central SR HS; Hamburg, NY; (Y); FFA; GAA; Concert Band; Jazz Band; JV Bsktbl; Sftbl; Var Swmmng; JV Var Vllybl; Hon Roll; NHS; Chemist.

SERGEL, JULIE A; Ellicottville Central HS; Ellicottville, NY; (Y); 2/47; Art Clb; GAA; Ski Clb; Varsity Clb; Yrbk Ed-Chief; Yrbk Stf; Stu Cncl; JV Cheerleading; Mgr Mgr(s); Trk; Hmcmng Queen 85; Rgnts Schlrshp 86; Fashn Inst Of Tech; Pttrnmkng.

SERGIO, CHRISTOPHER; MSGR Farrell HS; Staten Island, NY; (Y); Ski Clb; Varsity Clb; Im Bowling; Im Ftbl; Score Keeper; Var Trk; JV Wrstlng; Hon Roll; Ntl Merit SF; NY Empire St Games 85; Bst Athlete In Fld Events 85; Bus Mgt.

SERIANNI, DENISE; T R Proctor HS; Utica, NY; (Y); Hosp Aide; Chorus; Rep Stu Cncl; Cheerleading; Italian Clb 84-86; Bus Mgmt.

SERINO, CARMINE; North Babylon SR HS; N Babylon, NY; (Y); 12/450; Computer Clb; Mathletes; Chorus; JV Var Bsbl; High Hon Roll; Jr NHS; NHS; Suffolk Cnty Math Cntst 12 Lvl 2nd Pl 86; Math.

SERIO, JIM; Silver Creek HS; Silver Creek, NY; (Y); Boy Scts; French Clb; Library Aide; Var Crs Cntry; Bus Mgmt.

SERPER, KEITH; North Babylon SR HS; N Babylon, NY; (Y); 110/450; DECA; Chorus; JV Gym; JV Socr; Jr NHS.

SERRA, ROBERT F; Canisius HS; Elma, NY; (Y); 34/169; Am Leg Boys St; Computer Clb; Ski Clb; Varsity Clb; Stage Crew; Yrbk Stf; Var Bsbl; JV Bsktbl; Var Ftbl; Var Trk; NY St Rgnts Schlrshp 86; All Cathlc Ftbl & Wrstlg Tms 86; AZ ST; Engrng.

SERRANO, IRIS; Morris HS; Bronx, NY; (Y); Hosp Aide; Office Aide; Chorus; Hon Roll; Prfct Atten Awd; Hnr Comp Math 86; Hnrs Scl Stds & Chorus 85.

SERRANO, JENNIFER; Minisink Valley HS; Westtown, NY; (Y); VP Key Clb; Varsity Clb; Band; Concert Band; Mrchg Band; Capt Tennis; High Hon Roll; Hon Roll; NHS; NYSSMA Solo & Ensmbl Mdls Flute 83-85; Math.

SERRANO, NEYDA; Cathedral HS; Ny, NY; (Y); 76/277; Church Yth Grp; Drama Clb; Library Aide; Office Aide; Church Choir; Variety Show; Boston Coll; Law.

SERRANO, TERESITA; West Hempstead JR SR HS; Island Pk, NY; (Y); 69/320; Capt Color Guard; Drm & Bgl; Hon Roll; Joan Sweeny Fnd Awd Mst Imprvd Sec Stu 86; Am Assc Tchrs Spn Mdl Awds Excl Spn 4 Yrs 86; Drctrs Awd 86; Nassau Comm Coll; Music.

SERRETTE, ANDREW; Newburgh Free Acad; Newburgh, NY; (Y); French Clb; Chorus; Im JV Bsktbl; JV Var Crs Cntry; Im Ftbl; JV Var Trk; High Hon Roll; Hon Roll; Pickd Tchrs Stu Govt Prgm 82-83; Chem.

SERRITELLA, MIA A; Fairport HS; Fairport, NY; (Y); 30/585; Drama Clb; Key Clb; Sec Pres Pep Clb; Lit Mag; Rep Stu Cncl; High Hon Roll; Hon Roll; Sec NHS; Natl Latin Exam-Magna Cum Laude 85; DAV Schlrshp Semi-Fnlst 86; Ithaca Coll; Law.

SESNIE, CATHRYN; Mt Mercy Acad; W Seneca, NY; (Y); 16/190; Church Yth Grp; Ski Clb; Spanish Clb; Stage Crew; Nwsp Stf; Crs Cntry; Trk; Hon Roll; Jr NHS; NHS; Sci-Math.

SESSLER, CATHERINE; Bishop Grimes HS; Syracuse, NY; (S); Church Yth Grp; Cmnty Wkr; Bsktbl; High Hon Roll; Hon Roll; Syracuse U; Law.

SESSLER, CHERYL A; Honeoye Falls-Lima HS; Honeoye Falls, NY; (Y); 22/160; SADD; VP Band; Trs Chorus; Concert Band; Drm Mjr(t); Jazz Band; Mrchg Band; Orch; School Musical; Nwsp Ed-Chief; Rusk Griffes Schlrshp 86; JR All Amer Hall Fame Band Hnrs 85; Amer Mscl Fndtn Band Hnrs 83; Baldwin Wallace Cnsrvtry; Music.

SESZTAK, LUCY B; Christopher Columbus HS; Bronx, NY; (Y); 28/671; Teachers Aide; Chorus; Nwsp Stf; Yrbk Stf; Hon Roll; Prfct Atten Awd; Merit Awd Ecnmcs; Regnts Clg Schlrshp Awd.

SETARI, MARIA; St Catharine Acad HS; Bronx, NY; (Y); Fordham U.

SETH, ROBERT H; Depew HS; Depew, NY; (Y); 47/275; Pres Church Yth Grp; Drama Clb; Chorus; Mrchg Band; School Musical; Swing Chorus; Variety Show; Var Crs Cntry; Var Capt Trk; NYS Regnts Schlrshp 86; Paul Smiths Coll; Hotl Rest Mgt.

SETO, JANICE; Hgh Schl Of The Humaniti; New York, NY; (Y); Church Yth Grp; Service Clb; Teachers Aide; Church Choir; Rep Frsh Cls.

SETTEMBRINI, ELIZABETH; Mahopac HS; Mahopac, NY; (S); Church Yth Grp; French Clb; Hosp Aide; SADD; Var Bowling; JV Var Cheerleading; Var Crs Cntry; Stat Lcrss; Var Trk; High Hon Roll; Law.

SETZER, ERIC; Aquinas Inst; Rochester, NY; (Y); 20/200; Varsity Clb; Nwsp Rptr; Nwsp Stf; Rep Soph Cls; Trs Sr Cls; Stu Cncl; Var L Crs Cntry; Var L Trk; Aquinas Trck & Crss Cntry Mst Imprvd 85-86; Bus Adm.

SEUL, MICHAEL; St Anthonys HS; Centereach, NY; (Y); Church Yth Grp; Nwsp Sprt Ed; Hon Roll; NHS; Parish Cncl, St Johns U Acdmc Schlrshp, Usher Soc 85-86; Duns Scotus Hnr Rl 82-86; St Johns U; Pharm.

SEVERANCE, HEIDI; Chatham Central HS; Canaan, NY; (Y); Church Yth Grp; Cmnty Wkr; Pep Clb; Ski Clb; Teachers Aide; Band; Concert Band; Mrchg Band; Pep Band; Yrbk Stf; 1st Pl SUNY Cobleskill Coll HS Day Early Chldhd Devlpmnt 85; Prom Comm 86; Cortland; Psych.

SEVERANCE, STEVE; West Seneca Christian Schl; Orchard Park, NY; (Y); 2/11; Church Yth Grp; Ski Clb; School Play; Pres Jr Cls; Pres Sr Cls; Var Bsbl; Var Bsktbl; Var Capt Socr; Sal; Regents Schlrshp 86; Cedarville Coll.

SEVERIN, CHERYL; White Plains HS; White Plains, NY; (Y); Art Clb; Hosp Aide; Library Aide; Chorus; Vllybl; Nrsng.

SEVERSON, KENNETH; Saint Marys Acad; Schenectady, NY; (Y); Chess Clb; ROTC; Bsktbl; Var Ftbl; Var Trk; High Hon Roll; NHS; Hist Awd 84; Engr.

SEVIER, BRYAN; Fabius-Pompey HS; Jamesville, NY; (Y); Varsity Clb; Stage Crew; Var L Bsktbl; Var L Socr; Hon Roll; SUNY Alfred; Elec Engrng Tech.

SEVILLA, ARMI; Stuyvesant HS; Elmhurst, NY; (Y); Hosp Aide; Office Aide; School Musical; Lit Mag; Var Sec Cheerleading; Var L Sftbl; JETS Awd; Corp Awd Wnnr Seer Comptn Natl Enrgy Foundtn 85; JR Svc Awd Untd Hosp Fund NY 85; SUNY Binghamton; Engrng.

SEVITS, RICHARD; Valley Central HS; Walden, NY; (Y); Boy Scts; Montgomerys Wmns Repblcn Clb Mst Imprvd JR Bay Soc Studies 86.

SEWGOBIND, SHEAHAN; Eastern District HS; Brooklyn, NY; (Y); Church Yth Grp; Comp Sci.

SEWING, MICHELLE; Syosset HS; Syosset, NY; (Y); 63/485; Art Clb; English Clb; Band; Chorus; Nwsp Rptr; Lit Mag; JV Swmmng; NCTE Awd; NHS; VFW Awd; 1st Pl NYS Wrtg Cont From Libertys View PTA 86; Gen Hnrs Eng SS & Mth 86; 1st Pl Wrtg Cont 85; Bowdoin; Engl.

SEWKUMAR, AMANDA I; St Catharine Acad; Bronx, NY; (Y); Dance Clb; Library Aide; Office Aide; School Musical; Nwsp Stf; Yrbk Stf; Rep Jr Cls; VP Sr Cls; Stu Cncl; Hon Roll; Herbert H Lehman; Accntng.

SEXTON, DEIDRA; Letchworth Central HS; Bliss, NY; (Y); Art Clb; Aud/Vis; Church Yth Grp; Spanish Clb; Church Choir; Yrbk Stf; High Hon Roll; Hon Roll; Cnslng.

SEXTON, JOAN; Earl L Vandermeulen HS; Mt Sinai, NY; (Y); Art Clb; Church Yth Grp; 4-H; Pres FHA; Library Aide; VP Pep Clb; Spanish Clb; SADD; Chorus; Rep Frsh Cls; Hsptl Pstr Contst Wnr 85; MBSC Swmng Awd 84; Mt St Vncnt Coll; Psychtry.

SEYCHEW, KRISTIN K; Holy Angels Acad; Kenmore, NY; (Y); 3/36; Drama Clb; Acpl Chr; Nwsp Stf; Yrbk Bus Mgr; Yrbk Ed-Chief; Stu Cncl; High Hon Roll; NHS; Ntl Merit SF; Voice Dem Awd; Cnsius Coll Acadmc Merit Schlrshp 86; NYS Rgnts Schlr 86; Canisius Coll; Bus.

SEYMOUR, ANGELA; Northstar Christian Acad; Spencerport, NY; (S); 1/27; Ski Clb; High Hon Roll; Amer Chrstn Hnr Scty 85-86; Comp Prgmr.

SEYMOUR, FRED; Binghamton HS; Binghamton, NY; (Y); Am Leg Boys St; SADD; Varsity Clb; Var Capt Bsbl; JV Im Ftbl; Hon Roll; Prfct Atten Awd; Suprm Crt Appls Jstc NYS Amer Lgn Boys ST 86; All Div, 1st Bsbl Team 86; Brme Cnty Amer Lgn Stln Bse; Sprts Med.

SEYMOUR, LISA; Berlin Central HS; Petersburg, NY; (S); #4 In Class; Band; Nwsp Stf; Yrbk Stf; High Hon Roll; NHS; Hnr Stu Clb 84-86; Answers Please TV Quz Shw 85; Biotech.

SFORZA, ADRIENNE; St Edmund HS; Brooklyn, NY; (Y); Church Yth Grp; English Clb; Yrbk Stf; Hon Roll; Relgn Hnr Awd Excllnce; Brooklyn Coll; Pre-Law.

SFORZA, SHARON; Huntington HS; Huntington, NY; (Y); Hosp Aide; Key Clb; Varsity Clb; Drill Tm; School Play; Variety Show; Cheerleading; Score Keeper; Hon Roll; Statue Of Liberty Drll Tm-Closing Ceremony 86; Cmmnctns.

SGRO, MARIA; Churchville Chili HS; Rochester, NY; (Y); Yrbk Phtg; Yrbk Rptr; Yrbk Sprt Ed; Yrbk Stf; Lit Mag; Trs Sr Cls; Bowling; Hon Roll; NHS; Pres Schlr; Pres Schlrshp Niagara, Fac Awd, John C Malloch Schlrshp 86; Niagara U; Eng Tchr.

SGROI, PATRICK; West Seneca East SR HS; West Seneca, NY; (S); 18/375; Pres DECA; Pres Varsity Clb; Nwsp Stf; Yrbk Bus Mgr; Var Bsktbl; Var Crs Cntry; Var Capt Trk; JC Awd; NHS; 1st Pl NY ST DECNY Comptn General Mktg 85; Bus Mngmnt.

SHADE, DENISE M; Kendall JR SR HS; Morton, NY; (S); #7 In Class; Chorus; Concert Band; Mrchg Band; JV Cheerleading; High Hon Roll; Jr NHS; NHS; AFS; Sec Art Clb; Stu Mnth 85; All-St Sr High Chorus 85; Acdmc Ltr 83-84; Phys Ther.

SHADLE, ELLEN; Buffalo Seminary; Eden, NY; (Y); Art Clb; Church Yth Grp; Service Clb; Chorus; Church Choir; School Musical; Variety Show; Yrbk Ed-Chief; Willow Bend Club MIP Swmmr 84; Prtcptr Nyssma Music Cmpttns 85.

SHADRICK, CHRISS; Hgh Schl For The Humantie; Staten Island, NY; (Y); Church Yth Grp; Cmnty Wkr; Chorus; School Musical; Stage Crew; Yrbk Stf; Cert Excllnc Relgs Stds 83; Cert Excllnc Engl 83; Zoolgy.

SHAFER, JEREMY; Churchville Chili SR HS; N Chili, NY; (Y); Am Leg Boys St; Church Yth Grp; High Hon Roll; Exploring; Nwsp Rptr; Hon Roll; Genesee Vly HS Chem Rcgntn 86; Clarkson; Chem Engr.

SHAFER, MICHAEL; Schoharie Central HS; W Berne, NY; (S); 7/85; Computer Clb; Ski Clb; Band; Mrchg Band; Yrbk Stf; High Hon Roll; Hon Roll; NHS; Math Awd 81; NYSSMA Solo Awd 84; Indstrl Art Wdwrkng Awds 81; Comp Sci.

SHAFER, MICHAEL; Shaharie Central HS; West Berne, NY; (Y); 5/73; Computer Clb; Ski Clb; Band; Mrchg Band; Yrbk Stf; Hon Roll; NHS; Pres Acad Ftns Awd 86; Hon Awd 86; Most Intrst In Math Awd 86; Clarkson U; Comp Engrng.

SHAFER, MICHELE; Amsterdam HS; Amsterdam, NY; (S); Hosp Aide; JA; Latin Clb; Rep Stu Cncl; JV Var Cheerleading; High Hon Roll; Hon Roll; NHS; Clsscl Studies.

SHAFFER, SCOTT; Union Endicott HS; Endicott, NY; (Y); 261/450; Boys Clb Am; Church Yth Grp; Pep Clb; Varsity Clb; Band; Stu Cncl; JV Bsbl; JV Var Ftbl; U Of Buffalo; Cvl Engr.

SHAFFSTALL, CAROL; Sewanhaka HS; Floral Pk, NY; (Y); 61/431; Church Yth Grp; Math Clb; Teachers Aide; Church Choir; Hon Roll; Math Hnr Scty 86; Advncd Thlgcl Stdy 86; Bible Stdy Instrctr 83; Asbury Coll; Nrs.

SHAGNER, KATHRYN; Northville Central HS; Northville, NY; (Y); Art Clb; 4-H; Chorus; Nwsp Phtg; Nwsp Rptr; Yrbk Stf; Var Crs Cntry; Var Trk; 4-H Awd; NY Army Natl Grd 85; Conrad H Annabelle Gillen Schlrshp & Byron Schuyte Fndtn Schlrshp 86; Morrisville Ag & Tech; Hrse Mng.

SHAH, HIMANSHU; Newtown HS; Elmhurst, NY; (Y); Art Clb; Chess Clb; Math Clb; Math Tm; Vllybl; Hon Roll; Mu Alp Tht; Prfct Atten Awd; Mrchnt Mrn Essy Cntst Wnr 85; 3rd Anl Cndn Essy Cntst Wnr 85; St Johns U; Phrmcy.

SHAH, MEERA; Mynderse Acad; Seneca Falls, NY; (Y); Pres Spanish Clb; SADD; Chorus; Concert Band; Swing Chorus; Rep Stu Cncl; Cit Awd; Hon Roll; NHS; Ed.

SHAH, RUTA; John Adams HS; S Ozone Pk, NY; (Y); Drama Clb; Q&S; Spanish Clb; Stage Crew; Yrbk Phtg; Ed Yrbk Rptr; NHS; SUNY Stony Brook; Med.

SHAH, SEJAL; W C Bryant HS; New York, NY; (S); 78/623; Art Clb; FTA; Hosp Aide; Key Clb; Library Aide; Math Clb; Office Aide; Science Clb; Service Clb; Nwsp Rptr; Cty Cncl Awd 83; Lbrl Arts.

SHAJI, THOMAS; Long Island City HS; Long Island City, NY; (Y); Church Yth Grp; Library Aide; Office Aide; ROTC; Church Choir; Yrbk Stf; Bsktbl; Sftbl; Tennis; Outstndng Merit Ltr 85; Vlntr Wrk Hosp, Chrch, Schl 85-86; Med.

SHALLO, SCOTT; Hudson HS; Hudson, NY; (Y); Church Yth Grp; Intnl Clb; Model UN; SADD; Band; Jazz Band; Var Tennis; U Of VT; Accntng.

SHAMASH, DANNY; Sachen HS North Campus; Holtsville, NY; (Y); 70/1579; Cmnty Wkr; Computer Clb; Science Clb; Service Clb; Ski Clb; Temple Yth Grp; JV Crs Cntry; JV Trk; Jr NHS; NHS; 1st Mdl Sci Congress 84; Rbbn Merit Long Island Sci Congress 84; Cert Achvt Smmr Enrichment 84; Law.

SHAMI, VANESSA; Huntington HS; Huntington, NY; (Y); Cmnty Wkr; Hosp Aide; Science Clb; Teachers Aide; Sec Orch; Sec Symp Band; Var Crs Cntry; Var Fld Hcky; JV Socr; High Hon Roll; Hnr Stu Cert Of Rec From Adelphi U Dept Of Chem 86.

SHAMPANIER, JUDY; Commack H S North; Commack, NY; (Y); 10/390; SADD; Temple Yth Grp; Yrbk Stf; Rep Stu Cncl; Var Badmtn; VP French Hon Soc; NHS; Ntl Merit SF; Simons Fellowship For Research 85; Chrstn Strich Mem Schlrshp 86; Columbia U.

SHANAHAN, ELLEN J; Nardin Acad; Kenmore, NY; (Y); 9/80; JA; Ski Clb; Spanish Clb; Nwsp Stf; Yrbk Phtg; JV Badmtn; Var L Socr; Var L Tennis; High Hon Roll; Ntl Merit SF; NY ST Regents Schlrshp 86; Canisius Coll Deans Schlrshp 86; Pol Sci.

SHANAHAN, JENNIFER; Fairport HS; Fairport, NY; (S); Church Yth Grp; DECA; French Clb; Library Aide; Office Aide; Pep Clb; SADD; Off Jr Cls; Rep Stu Cncl; Natl Fin DECA 86; 3rd Pl Wnnr Sci Fair 84; Mrktng.

SHAND, CHRISTINE; Herbert H Lehman HS; Bronx, NY; (Y); Engl Cert Achvt 86; Psychology Cert Achvt 85; IOWNA.

SHAND, URSULA; George W Wingate HS; Brooklyn, NY; (Y); Math Tm; Science Clb; Nwsp Rptr; Nwsp Stf; Lit Mag; Bausch & Lomb Sci Awd; Hon Roll; Prfct Atten Awd; Indctd SR Arista 85; 1st Sci Fair 86; Psych.

SHANG, TOM; Oyster Bay HS; E Norwich, NY; (Y); Boy Scts; Computer Clb; Mathletes; Band; Stage Crew; Ed Yrbk Phtg; Yrbk Stf; Lit Mag; JV Capt Socr; Var Tennis; Bus.

SHANKAR, SUSAN; Jamaica HS; Queens Village, NY; (Y); 14/450; Cmnty Wkr; Hosp Aide; Math Clb; Service Clb; Teachers Aide; Orch; School Musical; Variety Show; Yrbk Stf; High Hon Roll; Ntl Art Awd Of Amer 85.

SHANKS, KATHLEEN; Fillmore Central HS; Freedom, NY; (S); 2/63; Pres Church Yth Grp; Pres Spanish Clb; Trs SADD; Band; Jazz Band; School Play; Nwsp Stf; High Hon Roll; NHS; All County Band; County Govt Intern; Engrng.

SHANKS, KATHRYN L; Hamburg SR HS; Hamburg, NY; (Y); 6/391; AFS; Band; Orch; Pres Jr Cls; Pres Sr Cls; Var Swmmng; Var Capt Trk; Hon Roll; NHS; Cheerleading; Wllsly Book Awd 85; NYS Rgnts Schlrshp 86; Premed.

SHANKS, LAUREN; Hamburg SR HS; Hamburg, NY; (Y); 36/380; JCL; Spanish Clb; Rep Frsh Cls; Rep Soph Cls; Rep Jr Cls; Rep Sr Cls; Sec Stu Cncl; JV VP Cheerleading; JV Var Socr; Hon Roll; Wms Bk Awd 85-86; Chem.

SHAPIRO, ABIGAIL; The Chapin Schl; New York, NY; (S); NFL; Political Wkr; Speech Tm; Teachers Aide; Nwsp Rptr; Yrbk Stf; Lit Mag; Frsh Cls; Ntl Merit SF; Ocot Fin CFL Natl Forn Trnmnt 84; Amer Hstry Olympd Mdl 85; 3rd Pl Fictn Cont; NFAA Hnrb Mntn 86; Harvard U.

SHAPIRO, ALLEN M; Bayside HS; Flushing, NY; (Y); 217/686; JA; Office Aide; Temple Yth Grp; Stage Crew; Cit Awd; Hon Roll; Cert Of Merit Acctg 84-85; Buffalo U; Bus Admin.

SHAPIRO, JEFFREY; West Irondequoit HS; Rochester, NY; (Y); 30/389; Lib Boy Scts; Math Tm; Model UN; Chrmn SADD; Temple Yth Grp; Var Crs Cntry; Hon Roll; Eagl Sct 86; Spec Reprts Excllnc 86; BSEE; Intl Rep Multntl Corp.

SHAPIRO, JUSTINE; Rye HS; Rye, NY; (Y); Spanish Clb; Socr; Hon Roll; Photogrphy.

SHAPIRO, LEAH SUE; Monticello HS; Kauneonga Lake, NY; (Y); Sec FBLA; SADD; VP Jr Cls; VP Sr Cls; Var L Crs Cntry; Var L Tennis; Var L Trk; NHS; Prfct Atten Awd; Stage Crew.

SHAPIRO, LUYDMILA; Midwood HS; Brooklyn, NY; (Y); 261/667; Cmnty Wkr; English Clb; Library Aide; Teachers Aide; Hon Roll; Prfct Atten Awd; Cert Ed Excllnce; Baruch Coll; Bus Mgmt.

SHAPIRO, MARNI; Herricks HS; Manhasset Hls, NY; (Y); Quiz Bowl; Temple Yth Grp; Nwsp Stf; Yrbk Stf; Hon Roll; Jr NHS; NHS.

SHAPIRO, MATHEW J; Oakwood Schl; Cincinnati, OH; (Y); German Clb; School Musical; Yrbk Stf; Music.

SHAPIRO, MICHAEL; Monticello HS; Kauneonga Lake, NY; (Y); 10/195; Boy Scts; Math Tm; Quiz Bowl; Stage Crew; JV Var Bsbl; Var JV Wrstlng; Hon Roll; Jr NHS; NHS; Ntl Merit Ltr; Fran De Fazio Mem Schlrshp 86; NY ST Regnts Schlrshp 86; SR Hnr Soc Schlrshp 86; Syracuse U; Engrng.

SHAPIRO, NATASHA E E; The Chapin Schl; New York, NY; (Y); Drama Clb; Rep Latin Clb; Model UN; NFL; School Play; Yrbk Phtg; Yrbk Stf; Ntl Merit SF; French Clb; JCL; Natl Latn Exm Summa & Maxima Cum Laudes 84 & 85.

SHAPIRO, PETER; Mamaroneck HS; Larchmont, NY; (Y); French Clb; Nwsp Sprt Ed; Nwsp Stf; Yrbk Rptr; Yrbk Stf; JV Bsktbl; Hon Roll; Ntl Merit Ltr.

SHAPIRO, ROBIN; John Dewey HS; Brooklyn, NY; (Y); Cmnty Wkr; School Play; Rep Jr Cls; Rep Stu Cncl; Vllybl; Loyola U; Theatr.

SHAPIRO, SCOTT; Honeoye Falls-Lima HS; Honeoye Falls, NY; (S); 2/160; Pres Math Clb; Model UN; SADD; Variety Show; Pres Sr Cls; JV Bsktbl; High Hon Roll; NHS; Sal; USNLMA Wnnr; Pol Sci.

SHARER, SUZANNE; Mamaroneck HS; Larchmont, NY; (Y); Service Clb; Spanish Clb; Nwsp Stf; JV Sftbl; Safe Rds Act Secy, SR Advsr 86-87; Pre Law.

SHARLOW, BETTY; Madrid-Waddington HS; Waddington, NY; (Y); Cmnty Wkr; French Clb; Math Clb; SADD; Color Guard; Mrchg Band; JV Var Cheerleading; Var Mgr(s); Honor Frm Boces Top 20 Pct In Cls Of Csmtlgy 85-86; Csmtlgy.

SHARLOW, STEPHEN; Potsdam Central HS; Potsdam, NY; (Y); 11/130; AFS; Boy Scts; Church Yth Grp; Drama Clb; Math Clb; Math Tm; Pres Spanish Clb; Varsity Clb; Band; Chorus; St Lawrence Cnty Talented Jr 85-86; 2 Spanish Merit Notices; Plattsburgh ST; Crmnlgy.

SHARMA, DEVINDRA; John Adams HS; S Ozone Park, NY; (Y); Yrbk Stf; Var Socr; NHS; Prfct Atten Awd.

SHARP, KAREN B; Immaculata Acad; W Seneca, NY; (Y); French Clb; Nwsp Rptr; Nwsp Stf; Yrbk Phtg; Yrbk Stf; Rep Soph Cls; VP Jr Cls; VP Sr Cls; Hon Roll; Dept Schlrshp At Daemen Coll 86; Daemen Coll.

SHARPE, CHRISTINA; Germantown Central HS; Germantown, NY; (S); 13/48; VP Church Yth Grp; GAA; Varsity Clb; Var Bsktbl; Stat Fld Hcky; Mgr(s); Score Keeper; Springfield; Math Educ.

SHARPE, KELLY; Schoharie Central Schl; Schoharie, NY; (S); 8/120; Key Clb; Sec Varsity Clb; Chorus; VP Jr Cls; Var L Bsktbl; Var L Socr; Var L Sftbl; Var L Vllybl; High Hon Roll; Hon Roll; Mth Awd 84-85; Teaching.

SHARROTT, JULIE; Jackets Harbor Central HS; Sackets Harbor, NY; (Y); 3/28; Pres Church Yth Grp; Spanish Clb; Yrbk Stf; VP Jr Cls; Rep Stu Cncl; High Hon Roll; NHS; Cmnty Wkr; Red Cross Aide; Y-Teens; Outstndng Amer HS Stu 85; Rochester Inst Tech; Travel Mgm.

SHARSKY, MARIANNE; John H Glenn HS; East Northport, NY; (Y); Yrbk Stf; Rep Frsh Cls; Cheerleading; Trk; Vllybl; High Hon Roll; Hon Roll; Jr NHS; NHS; Spanish NHS; Bus.

SHATARA, CHRISTINA; Uniondale HS; Uniondale, NY; (Y); Church Yth Grp; Office Aide; SADD; Yrbk Stf; Sec Rep Frsh Cls; High Hon Roll; Hon Roll; Jr NHS; NHS; Major Awd 83-84; Hofstra U; Bus.

SHATRAU, TRACY; G Ray Bodley HS; Oswego, NY; (Y); 27/241; Drama Clb; Acpl Chr; Chorus; Church Choir; Madrigals; Orch; School Musical; School Play; High Hon Roll; Syracuse Symphny Yth Orch 85-86; Ithaca COLL; Violin Tchr.

SHAUGER, JEFF; Cooperstown Central HS; Fly Creek, NY; (Y); Boy Scts; 4-H; French Clb; Ski Clb; Varsity Clb; Band; Jazz Band; Mrchg Band; Orch; Pep Band; Fnlst Ruggles Esasy Cntst 86; Schlrshp Outward Bound 86; Cornell U; Bio.

SHAUL, MATTHEW; Jamestown HS; Jamestown, NY; (Y); Church Yth Grp; Ski Clb; Spanish Clb; Band; Concert Band; Jazz Band; Mrchg Band; Tennis; NHS; N Tinkham Awd Hist 86; Pre Med.

SHAULINSKI, SHELLY; Fairport HS; Fairport, NY; (Y); SADD; Chorus; Jazz Band; School Musical; Secy.

SHAVER, RENEE; Delaware Acad; Delhi, NY; (Y); Church Yth Grp; Spanish Clb; Band; Chorus; Church Choir; Concert Band; Jazz Band; Mrchg Band; School Musical; Yrbk Stf; H W Cannon Awd For Vocal Music 86; Clarke Sampson Awd 86; Rotary Clb Citznshp Awd 86; Hartwick Coll; Nrsng.

SHAW, BRIAN; Cicero-North Syracuse HS; North Syracuse, NY; (S); 31/623; Capt FCA; Key Clb; Spanish Clb; Hon Roll.

SHAW, CHARLES; Carthage Central HS; Carthage, NY; (Y); 76/187; School Play; Stu Cncl; Jefferson CC; Lib Arts.

SHAW, COLEEN; St Marys Girls HS; Westbury, NY; (Y); Chorus; JV Bsktbl; Var Sftbl; Sunny U Stonybrook; Nrs.

SHAW, DAVID D; Fairport HS; Fairport, NY; (Y); Boy Scts; Computer Clb; Band; Chorus; Pres Jazz Band; Mrchg Band; Hon Roll; Berklee; Cmpstn.

SHAW, HEATHER; Paul V Moore HS; W Monroe, NY; (Y); Trs FBLA; Teachers Aide; Chorus; Yrbk Stf; Stat Score Keeper; Var Sftbl; Hon Roll; Pre Law.

SHAW, IDA; St Raymond Acad; New York, NY; (Y); 15/68; Cmnty Wkr; Library Aide; Office Aide; Mrchg Band; Nwsp Rptr; Nwsp Sprt Ed; Rep Jr Cls; Pom Pon; Hon Roll; Computer Clb; Lib Aide Merit Awd 86; Scnd Hnrs 82-86; Hunter Coll; Jrnlsm.

SHAW, JAMES S; Clarkstown SR HS North; New City, NY; (Y); 3/450; SADD; Yrbk Sprt Ed; JV Var Bsbl; High Hon Roll; Mu Alp Tht; NHS; Trs Spanish Clb; JV Ftbl; Im Vllybl; Rensselaer Poly-Tech Inst Mdl Math & Sci, NY Acad Sci Rsrch Trn Pgm, Admin Assoc Awd; Natl Sci Olym; Duke U.

SHAW, JOHN; C P P West HS; Corning, NY; (Y); Rep Frsh Cls; Bus Mgnmt.

SHAW, JOSEPH; Mynderse Acad; Seneca Falls, NY; (S); 5/138; Stu Cncl; High Hon Roll; Comp Sci.

SHAW, KELLY; Romulus Central Schl; Romulus, NY; (Y); VP Church Yth Grp; Sec Spanish Clb; Band; Mrchg Band; Orch; Sec Soph Cls; Rep Stu Cncl; Var Capt Socr; JV Capt Sftbl; Hon Roll.

SHAW, LESLIE; West Seneca East SR HS; W Seneca, NY; (Y); 15/375; Church Yth Grp; French Clb; Nwsp Stf; Rep Stu Cncl; French Hon Soc; High Hon Roll; NHS; Rgnts Schlrshp 86-87; Aamco Trnsmsns Schlrshp 86-87; Amer Lgn Schlrshp 86-87; SUNY At Buffalo; Psych.

SHAW, NICOLE; Corcoran HS; Syracuse, NY; (Y); Church Yth Grp; French Clb; JA; Chorus; Church Choir; Bsktbl; Prfct Atten Awd; High Hnr Roll 83; Perfect Attend Awd 83; Syracuse U; Lawyer.

SHAW, PAT; Dryden HS; Brooktondale, NY; (Y); Art Clb; Cmnty Wkr; Office Aide; Lit Mag; Var Trk; High Hon Roll; Hon Roll; Prfct Atten Awd; Cornell U; Arch.

SHAW, RICHARD; Bay Shore SR HS; Bay Shore, NY; (Y); 65/404; Computer Clb; Science Clb; Band; Chorus; Mrchg Band; JV Socr; Var Trk; Achvt Merit Chem,Soc Studies 86; Pre-Med.

SHAW, TAMI L; Granville Central HS; North Granville, NY; (Y); AFS; French Clb; GAA; Yrbk Rptr; Stat Bsbl; L Crs Cntry; Fld Hcky; Hon Roll; NHS; Rensselaer Polytech Inst; Biol.

SHAW, TRACY; Grand Island HS; Grand Island, NY; (Y); Sec Art Clb; Sec Church Yth Grp; Drama Clb; French Clb; Red Cross Aide; School Musical; School Play; Yrbk Stf; Rep Stu Cncl; Hon Roll; 2nd Pl Enrgy Cnsrvtn Sci Cntst 86; Erie CC; Dntl Hygn.

SHAW, TRIXINE; Portville Central HS; Portville, NY; (Y); AFS; Teachers Aide; Capt Color Guard; Capt Mrchg Band; JV Var Cheerleading; High Hon Roll; Hon Roll; Church Yth Grp; Cmnty Wkr; Letterman Clb; Chrldng Cptn Ftbl 84; Awd Bst Chrldng Squad Bsktbl 85; Ex Secr.

SHAWL, HEIDI; Friendship Central Schl; Friendship, NY; (S); 5/27; Church Yth Grp; 4-H; Band; Chorus; Jazz Band; Mrchg Band; School Play; VP Stu Cncl; Capt Bsktbl; High Hon Roll; 4-H Hardmand Awd 85; Natl Honor Soc 85-86; NY Grand Champn 4-H Drill Tm-Capt 81-85; Alfred ST Coll; Lab Tech.

SHAY, SUSAN; F D Roosevelt HS; Poughkeepsie, NY; (Y); 57/360; Art Clb; Rgnts Dplma 86; Vassor; Elem Teachng.

SHAY, THOMAS P; St Anthonys HS; Islip, NY; (Y); Church Yth Grp; Science Clb; Crs Cntry; Trk; Ntl Merit Schol; Trstee Schlrshp 86; Hofstra U; Bus Admin.

SHEA, CHRISTOPHER M; Oyster Bay HS; Oyster Bay, NY; (Y); Cmnty Wkr; Computer Clb; German Clb; Library Aide; Nwsp Stf; Lit Mag; High Hon Roll; Hon Roll; Gallaudet Coll; Crtve Wrtng.

SHEA, CYNTHIA; Mont Pleasant HS; Schenectady, NY; (Y); 5/142; Key Clb; Spanish Clb; Color Guard; Mrchg Band; Yrbk Stf; High Hon Roll; Trs Spanish NHS; Hon Roll; Math Assn Amer Math Awd 85-86; Rensselaer Medl 85-86; Rensselaer Polytechnic Inst.

SHEA, JACQUELYN; Mount Mercy Acad; Buffalo, NY; (Y); #12 In Class; Computer Clb; JA; JCL; SADD; JV Bsktbl; JV Vllybl; Hon Roll; VP Jr NHS; VP NHS; Latin Clb; 1st Pl Regnl Latin Comptn 84.

SHEA, LORI-LYN; Franklin Acad; Constable, NY; (Y); Pres 4-H; Band; VP Jr Cls; 4-H Awd; NHS; Epsilon 85-87; Phi Sigma Pres 85-87; Plattsburg ST U; Educ.

SHEA, PATRICK; West Hempstead HS; West Hempstead, NY; (Y); Hon Roll; Cert Of Acctng 86; Acctng.

SHEAHAN, MALACHI; Roy C Ketcham HS; Poughkeepsie, NY; (Y); Drama Clb; Thesps; Stage Crew; Rep Stu Cncl; High Hon Roll; Jr NHS; NHS; Hudsn Vly Photo Cntst 1st Pl 85; Johns Hopkins; Med.

SHEAN, TERRY; Churchville Chili SR HS; Rochester, NY; (Y); Church Yth Grp; Cmnty Wkr; Drama Clb; Library Aide; Office Aide; Ski Clb; VICA; Hon Roll; May Stu Mo Bocess II Voc Schl 86; 2nd Pl NYS VICA Dntl Asstng Cntst 86; Air Force; Dntl.

SHEARER, LAURA; Clayton A Bouton HS; Voorheesville, NY; (Y); Drama Clb; Girl Scts; Intnl Clb; Ski Clb; Varsity Clb; Chorus; Stage Crew; Fld Hcky; Trk; Hon Roll; Knigts Lf Pyths 86; PTSA Schlrshp 86; 10 Yr Awd Girl Scts 86; Champlain Clg; Fash Merch.

SHEARING, CYNTHIA; Perry Central HS; Perry, NY; (Y); 5/85; 4-H; FFA; Band; Chorus; Mrchg Band; School Musical; Cit Awd; 4-H Awd; High Hon Roll; NHS; NYS Regents Scholar 85-86; US Collegiate Wind Bands Europn Tour 86; Natl FFA Band 85; Cornell U; Pre-Vet Med.

SHEEDY, KAREN A; Walter Panas HS; Peekskill, NY; (Y); 6/243; SADD; Sec Soph Cls; Sec Sr Cls; Stu Cncl; Var Capt Tennis; High Hon Roll; NHS; Girl Scts; Rep Frsh Cls; Hon Roll; NY St Regents Schlrshp 86; Chase/Nbw Citizenship Awd 86; Hugh O Brien Yth Ldrshp Fndtn 84; U Of Delaware; Intl Bus.

SHEEHAN, JOSEPH R; Wheatland-Chili HS; Scottsville, NY; (Y); 8/70; Chorus; Concert Band; Jazz Band; Mrchg Band; School Musical; Var Crs Cntry; Hon Roll; NHS; Regents Schlrshp 86.

SHEEHAN, LAURA; Kenmore East HS; Kenmore, NY; (Y); Drama Clb; Math Clb; PAVAS; Concert Band; Orch; School Musical; School Play; Yrbk Phtg; High Hon Roll; Hon Roll; ST U Of NY Buffalo; Educ.

SHEEHAR, MEGHAR; Westhampton Beach HS; Westhampton Beach, NY; (Y); Drama Clb; English Clb; Ski Clb; Teachers Aide; Temple Yth Grp; Yrbk Stf; Lit Mag; Gym; Pom Pon; Trk; Fairfield; Psychlgy.

SHEELEY, SUSETTE; Ellenville Central HS; Phillipsport, NY; (Y); 4/106; Drama Clb; Band; School Musical; School Play; Yrbk Stf; Cheerleading; High Hon Roll; NCTE Awd; NHS; Binghamton T; Bio.

SHEERAN, MICHAEL; Niskayuna HS; Schenectady, NY; (Y); German Clb; Renseller Polytech; Comp Sci.

SHEETS, CHRISTINE M; Red Jacket Central Schl; Shortsville, NY; (Y); 2/90; Pres Varsity Clb; Chorus; Madrigals; School Musical; Yrbk Ed-Chief; Sec Frsh Cls; Sec Soph Cls; Sec Jr Cls; Capt Socr; NHS; Bausch Lomb Sci Awd 86; Natl Elks Schlrshp 86; Class Saltrn 86; U Of Rochester; Pre Med.

SHEFF, BRIAN; Frontier Central HS; Hamburg, NY; (Y); Boy Scts; Socr; Swmmng; High Hon Roll; Hon Roll; NHS.

SHEFF, DANIEL; Frontier Central HS; Hamburg, NY; (S); 4/444; Am Leg Boys St; Boy Scts; Church Yth Grp; Pres Exploring; JV L Socr; High Hon Roll; Hon Roll; NHS; NEDT Awd; Eagl Sct Awd 83; Bus Adm.

SHEFFER, MELISSA; Hoosick Falls Central Schl; Hoosick Falls, NY; (Y); 4-H; French Clb; Pep Clb; Ski Clb; Band; Chorus; Church Choir; JV Mgr(s); JV Score Keeper; 1st Altrnt Dairy Prncss/Rensslr Co 86; Early Chldhd Ed.

SHEFFIELD, AMY; Brockport HS; Brockport, NY; (Y); 130/330; 4-H; Teachers Aide; Yrbk Stf; High Hon Roll; Computer Clb; Hnr Carrier For My Times-Union Paper Rt 83; CCFL CC; Crmnl Jstc.

SHEFFIELD, DARRELL; Williamsville South HS; Williamsville, NY; (Y); Var Golf; Bus.

SHEIKH, AAMIR; Franklin D Roosevelt HS; New York, NY; (Y); Aud/Vis; Debate Tm; Math Tm; Band; Rptr Lit Mag; VP Stu Cncl; Cit Awd; NHS; Cornell; Med.

SHEIL, CARYN; Valley Stream Central HS; Valley Stream, NY; (Y); AFS; Church Yth Grp; Girl Scts; SADD; Chorus; Orch; Variety Show; Var Badmtn; JV Capt Bsktbl; Var Socr; Tchr To Deaf.

SHEIL, JAMES M; La Salle Acad; Brooklyn, NY; (Y); Boy Scts; St Schlr; Iona Clg; Libl Arts.

SHEILS, KIMBERLY; Romulus Central HS; Willard, NY; (S); Spanish Clb; Varsity Clb; VP Band; Concert Band; Mrchg Band; Var Bsktbl; Var Sftbl; Var Vllybl; High Hon Roll; NHS; Pre-Law.

SHEINHEIT, MICHAEL B; HS Of The Humantie; New York, NY; (Y); AFS; Camera Clb; Cmnty Wkr; Drama Clb; School Musical; School Play; Stage Crew; Nwsp Ed-Chief; Bsbl; Ice Hcky; Communications.

SHEINTUL, MILENA; Midwood HS; Brooklyn, NY; (Y); Office Aide; French Hon Soc; Hon Roll; Prtcptn Gateway Voyagers 84; Cornell; Psychlgy.

SHELANSKEY, TAMI; Corning-Painted Post West HS; Painted Post, NY; (Y); Church Yth Grp; Sec FBLA; Hosp Aide; Spanish Clb; Drm & Bgl; Stage Crew; Bowling; Trk; High Hon Roll; Hon Roll; Hghst Spnsh Avg Awd 81-82; Cert Of Merit-Assmbly Of NY 86; Corning CC; Bus Admin.

SHELAT, CHANDRESH; Liverpool HS; Liverpool, NY; (Y); French Clb; JA; Yrbk Stf; Im Mgr Bsbl; Bsktbl; Var Tennis; JV Trk; Hon Roll; Jr NHS; NHS; Bio Awd Volun Disc Ct 85; Human Phys Awd 86; Lttr Trck Volun At Crouse Irving Hosp 85; Cornell; Med.

SHELDON, AMY; Sweet Home SR HS; Tonawanda, NY; (Y); SADD; Orch; School Musical; Off Frsh Cls; Off Soph Cls; Off Jr Cls; Var Trk; NHS; Zoolgy.

SHELDON, THOMAS; Pine Valley Central HS; Cherry Creek, NY; (Y); Band; Chorus; Concert Band; Mrchg Band; Boy Scts; 4-H; Bsbl; Bsktbl.

SHELEY, JULIE; South Jefferson Central HS; Adams, NY; (Y); 3/155; Hosp Aide; Varsity Clb; Concert Band; Yrbk Sprt Ed; Sec Frsh Cls; Pres Sr Cls; Var Capt Socr; Hon Roll; NHS; Church Yth Grp; Clss Rep Stu Govt Day 85; Var Soccr Leag 85; Ithaca; Phys Thrpy.

SHELFORD, THOMAS J; St Anthonys HS; Huntington, NY; (Y); 15/420; Chrmn Am Leg Boys St; Art Clb; Church Yth Grp; Varsity Clb; Nwsp Stf; Yrbk Stf; Lit Mag; Capt Var Crs Cntry; Capt Var Trk; NHS; U S Naval Acad.

SHELTON, GEORGIANA; Paul D Schreiber HS; Port Washington, NY; (Y); 32/414; Drama Clb; Spanish Clb; Chorus; Nwsp Rptr; Nwsp Stf; High Hon Roll; NCTE Awd; NHS; SUNY Bnghmtn; Englsh.

SHELTON, JEFFREY M; Carthage Central HS; Black River, NY; (Y); Am Leg Boys St; Var JV Bsktbl; Var L Ftbl; Var L Trk; High Hon Roll; NHS; All Str Trck; 2nd Tm All Str Ftbl.

SHELTON, ROBERT; Irondequoit HS; Rochester, NY; (Y); 13/380; Boy Scts; Orch; School Musical; Var Ftbl; Im Wt Lftg; Var Capt Wrstlng; Hon Roll; NHS; Pres Schlr; Rgnts Schlrshp 86; Dartmouth Bk Clb Awd 85; NYS Schl Music Assoc Solo Comptn 83; Carleton Coll; Engl.

SHELTON, SHAWN; Frontier Central HS; Hamburg, NY; (Y); Boy Scts; French Clb; Math Clb; Concert Band; Jazz Band; Bsktbl; French Hon Soc; Hon Roll; NHS; NY ST Rssn Olympd Hnr Mntn Awd 86; Ntl Frnch Cont Awd 85; U Buffl; Premed.

SHEN, JOYCE; Bethlehem Central HS; Delmar, NY; (Y); 1/304; DAR Awd; Elks Awd; NHS; Ntl Merit Ltr; Wnr Muc Tchrs Assoc Compt; Brckprt Yng Art Compt; Gst Solost; Yale U; Law.

SHENE, HEATHER M; Riverhead HS; Riverhead, NY; (Y); 32/200; Drama Clb; Acpl Chr; Band; Chorus; Concert Band; Jazz Band; Mrchg Band; Orch; School Musical; School Play; Yrbk Awd 86; Fredonia ST; Cmmnctns.

SHEPARD, ERIK S; New Hartford SR HS; New Hartford, NY; (Y); Var L Diving; Jr NHS; NHS; Ntl Merit Schol.

SHEPARD, KAREN; Fox Lane HS; Pound Ridge, NY; (Y); 8/277; French Clb; Ski Clb; Y-Teens; Nwsp Stf; Swmmng; High Hon Roll; NHS; Coaches Awd 84-85; High Pt Awd 84.

SHEPARD, KEVIN; Frewsburg Central HS; Frewsburg, NY; (Y); Aud/Vis; Church Yth Grp; Computer Clb; Quiz Bowl; Nwsp Stf; Stat Swmmng; Cit Awd; NHS; Pres Schlrshp Jdsn Coll Elgin IL 86-87; Judson Coll Elgin IL; Comp.

SHEPARD, LAURIE; Lackawanna SR HS; Lackawanna, NY; (Y); Hon Roll; Scholar Summr Schl Art Inst Chatava VA 86.

SHEPARD, LORI A; Earl L Vandermeulen HS; Mt Sinai, NY; (Y); 25/280; Hosp Aide; Latin Clb; Yrbk Stf; Rep Jr Cls; Rep Sr Cls; Stat Bsbl; Var Bowling; Vllybl; Hon Roll; NHS; NY ST Mdrn Miss 85-86; Citatn Frm NYS Assmbly 86; U Of Buffalo; Med Technlgy.

SHEPARD, LYNDA; Mohawk Central Schl; Mohawk, NY; (Y); 2/95; French Clb; JA; Pep Clb; Spanish Clb; Yrbk Stf; Stu Cncl; Im Powder Puff Ftbl; Var Tennis; Bausch & Lomb Sci Awd; Elks Awd; Bousch & Lomb Sci Schlrshp-U Of Rochester 86-90; 1st Pl-Bus Eng Bus Comptn-84; Rgnts Schlrshp 86; U Of Rochester; Bio.

SHEPARDSON, J A; Chatham HS; Chatham, NY; (Y); 18/135; Ski Clb; Band; Chorus; Orch; School Musical; Yrbk Stf; Crs Cntry; High Hon Roll; NHS; Voice Dem Awd; St Michael Winooski; Bio.

SHEPARDSON, NANCY ELIZABETH; Auburn HS; Auburn, NY; (Y); 35/500; JA; Office Aide; Typwrtng Prfcncy Cert 84-86; Cayuga CC; Soc Wrkr.

SHEPHARD, SHANNON; Akron Central HS; Akron, NY; (Y); 1/135; Drama Clb; School Musical; Nwsp Rptr; Var Cheerleading; DAR Awd; High Hon Roll; Pres NHS; Pres Schlr; Val; Westminster Coll; Pre-Law.

SHER, MICHAEL L; New Dorp HS; Staten Island, NY; (Y); Boy Scts; Trs Computer Clb; Key Clb; Tennis; Elks Awd; NHS; Rotary Awd; 3rd Awd Borough Wide Sci Fair 84; 1st Pl Borough Wive Soc Studies Fair 86; Amherst Coll; Pre-Med.

SHER, ROBERT C; Scarsdale HS; Scarsdale, NY; (Y); Cmnty Wkr; Spanish Clb; Nwsp Stf; Rep Stu Cncl; Socr; Trk; Ntl Merit SF.

SHERER, BRIAN A; Lawrence HS; Cedarhurst, NY; (Y); Key Clb; Spanish Clb; SADD; Temple Yth Grp; Band; JV Capt Bsbl; Var L Socr; High Hon Roll; Jr NHS; NHS; Cert Merit Spn Awd 86; Pre-Med.

SHERIDAN, CECILIA; Hauppauge HS; Hauppauge, NY; (Y); DECA; Office Aide; Spanish Clb; SADD; Teachers Aide; Varsity Clb; Orch; Rep Soph Cls; Rep Jr Cls; Rep Stu Cncl; Merch.

SHERIDAN, CHRIS; Brewster HS; Brewster, NY; (Y); Ski Clb; Band; Concert Band; Bsbl; Bsktbl; Bowling; Golf; Hon Roll; Accntng.

SHERIDAN, LAURIE; Anthony A Henninger HS; Syracuse, NY; (Y); Cmnty Wkr; Pres SADD; Frsh Cls; Soph Cls; Jr Cls; Sr Cls; Tennis; Cit Awd; High Hon Roll; NHS; Dale Carnegie Achvmnt Awd 86; Stop DWI Prtcptn Awd 86; Engl Awd 84; Elem Educ.

SHERIDAN, MICHELLE; Cornwall Central HS; Cornwall, NY; (Y); Math Tm; Spanish Clb; Concert Band; Hon Roll; Sci.

SHERIDAN, TIM; Copenhagen Central Schl; Watertown, NY; (S); 3/45; 4-H; French Clb; SADD; Rep Stu Cncl; Capt Var Bsktbl; Var Golf; Capt Var Socr; High Hon Roll; NHS; Bio.

SHERIFF, ALENA; New Rochelle HS; New Rochelle, NY; (Y); Drama Clb; Phy Thrpy.

SHERIFF, DARIN; New Rochelle HS; New Rochelle, NY; (Y); Cmnty Wkr; Computer Clb; U Of Bridgeport; Comp Sci.

SHERLINE, DAVID; John F Kennedy HS; Utica, NY; (Y); Ski Clb; School Play; Crs Cntry; Ftbl; Socr; Vllybl; Wt Lftg; Wrstlng; Bus.

SHERMAN, BECKY; Perry Central HS; Perry, NY; (Y); Band; Chorus; Concert Band; Jazz Band; Mrchg Band; JV Var Socr; JV Var Sftbl; Var Trk; High Hon Roll; Church Yth Grp; Bus.

SHERMAN, DAVID; Christopher Columbus HS; Bronx, NY; (Y); Key Clb; Office Aide; Tennis; Hon Roll; Chancellors Roll Of Hnr 86; Awd Outstndg Awchvmnt Acadmc & Extra Actvts 86; Cert Of Merit Psychlgy 85; Philosophy.

SHERMAN, JILL; Commack HS; Dix Hills, NY; (Y); Computer Clb; Mathletes; Math Tm; Yrbk Stf; Badmtn; Socr; NHS; 9th Comp Sci League 86; Treas Comp Hnr Soc 85-86; Syst Anlyst.

SHERMAN, JOHN; Newburgh Free Acad; Newburgh, NY; (Y); 55/786; Boy Scts; Church Yth Grp; Cmnty Wkr; Drama Clb; Political Wkr; Ski Clb; SADD; Teachers Aide; Acpl Chr; Chorus; CSEA Scholar Awd 86; Poetry Awd 85; Bus Mgmt.

SHERMAN, KEVIN; Auburn HS; Auburn, NY; (Y); Hon Roll; Sci Awd 86; Acctng.

SHERMAN, KRISTINE; Plattsburgh HS; Plattsburgh, NY; (Y); Service Clb; Varsity Clb; VP Frsh Cls; VP Jr Cls; VP Stu Cncl; Var Gym; JV Var Sftbl; High Hon Roll; Hon Roll; NHS; Mth Acad Awd 86; Home Ec Acad Awd 86; Elem Ed.

SHERMAN, LISA; Notre Dame-Bishop Gibbons HS; Schenectady, NY; (S); 11/100; Church Yth Grp; Exploring; Red Cross Aide; Capt Flag Corp; Stage Crew; Var JV Vllybl; High Hon Roll; Hon Roll; NHS; Acad All Am; Geneseo; Ed.

SHERMAN, ROBERT J; Miller Place HS; Miller Place, NY; (Y); Trs VP Drama Clb; Quiz Bowl; School Musical; School Play; Stage Crew; Lit Mag; Var L Tennis; High Hon Roll; Trs NHS; Regents Schlrshp 86; Rensselaer Polytechnic Inst.

SHERMAN, THEODORE J; G Ray Bodley HS; Fulton, NY; (Y); German Clb; Coach Actv; Var Ice Hcky; Var Socr; Var Trk; Prfct Atten Awd; U Rochester; Psych.

SHERNOWITZ, KIM; Hauppauge HS; Commack, NY; (Y); Cmnty Wkr; Hosp Aide; SADD; Rep Stu Cncl; High Hon Roll; NHS; Ntl Merit Ltr; Prfct Atten Awd.

SHERONY, MELANIE J; Bishop Kearney HS; Fairport, NY; (Y); 1/140; Math Clb; Sec Drill Tm; Mrchg Band; Nwsp Stf; Yrbk Stf; Lit Mag; Twrlr; High Hon Roll; NHS; Val; PHI Beta Kappa Schlr Rcgntn; Nys Rgnts Schlrshp; Northwestern U; Elec Engrng.

SHERRY, KAREN; Sweet Home SR HS; Tonawanda, NY; (Y); 5/410; Cmnty Wkr; GAA; SADD; Nwsp Stf; Stu Cncl; Capt Fld Hcky; Socr; NHS; Prfct Atten Awd; Spanish NHS; Hon Men Feat Schl Paper 85; All Star Vassar Summer Fld Hcky Cmp 84; La Sertoma Yth Svc Awd 86; Bus Adm.

SHERRY, LILLIAN; Southampton HS; Southampton, NY; (Y); Chorus; High Hon Roll; Hon Roll; NHS; Nrsg.

SHERWIN, CAROL S; Manhasset HS; Floral Park, NY; (Y); 4/200; Sec Cmnty Wkr; Sec French Clb; Office Aide; Teachers Aide; Temple Yth Grp; Yrbk Ed-Chief; Lit Mag; High Hon Roll; NHS; Ntl Merit Ltr; Dakin Mem Chem Awd 86; Wesleyan U; Chem.

SHERWIN, JACLYN; Franklin Acad HS; Malone, NY; (Y); French Clb; Hosp Aide; Varsity Clb; Concert Band; Pres Soph Cls; Var L Swmmng; Hon Roll; NHS; Secndry Ed.

SHERWIN, THOMAS; Cicero North Syracuse HS; N Syracuse, NY; (S); 42/667; Pres German Clb; Yrbk Phtg; NHS; ST Media Art Comp Fnlst Comp Div 85; Comp Sci.

SHERWINTER, TOVA; Yeshiva University HS For Girls; Monsey, NY; (Y); 5/150; Cmnty Wkr; English Clb; Hosp Aide; Quiz Bowl; Rep Stu Cncl; Ntl Merit Schol; St Schlr; Scholastic Bowl; Rep Jr Cls; Watson-IBM Schlrshp Awd Wnnr 86; Max Stern Schlr At Yeshiva U 85; Coord Cmnty Svcs Prgm 83-85; Yeshiva U; Pre-Med.

SHERWOOD, DAVID; Southampton HS; Southampton, NY; (Y); 15/115; Sec Soph Cls; Rep Stu Cncl; Socr; High Hon Roll; Hon Roll; Jr NHS; NHS; NYS Rgnts Schlrshp; PTO Awd For Drftng; Southampton HS Mem Schlrshp; Syracuse U; Arch.

SHERWOOD, JENNY; Lansing HS; Lansing, NY; (Y); Band; School Musical; Swmmng; High Hon Roll; Lion Awd; NHS; Ntl Merit Ltr; Rotary Awd; MVP Swmmng; Outstndng Math Stu.

SHERWOOD, JULIE ANNE; Lakenheath American HS; A P O New York, NY; (Y); Letterman Clb; Service Clb; Teachers Aide; Stage Crew; Trs Frsh Cls; Sec Stu Cncl; Var L Tennis; Cit Awd; Hon Roll; Masonic Awd; Pst Hnrd Qn Intl Ordr Jbs Dghtrs 85; Vrsty Lttr Stu Cncl 85-86; Poly Sci.

SHERWOOD, KELLY; Dover JR-SR HS; Dover Plains, NY; (S); 4/70; Yrbk Phtg; Yrbk Stf; Stu Cncl; Bowling; Fld Hcky; High Hon Roll; Hon Roll; Jr NHS; NHS; Ntl Hnr Soc 83-85.

SHERWOOD, KRIS; Victor Central Schl; Victor, NY; (Y); 210/220; Church Yth Grp; French Clb; GAA; Quiz Bowl; SADD; Orch; Yrbk Ed-Chief; Rep Frsh Cls; Rep Soph Cls; Rep Jr Cls; Section 5 Diving Title 84; Aquatic Ldr Awd; Young Woman In Excllnc 86; AZ ST U; Accntng.

SHERWOOD, LEANNA; Addison Central HS; Cameron Mills, NY; (Y); Science Clb; Yrbk Ed-Chief; NHS.

SHERWOOD, MICHELLE; Cardinal Spellman HS; Bronx, NY; (Y); Art Clb; Cmnty Wkr; Dance Clb; Color Guard; Mrchg Band; Stage Crew; Fashion Inst; Fshn Illstrtr.

SHERWOOD, SHELLY; Cato-Meridian HS; Cato, NY; (Y); Im Badmtn; Hon Roll; Coyuga CC; Bus Mgmt.

SHEVLIN, DEBRA; Cornwall Central HS; Cornwall Hudson, NY; (Y); VP Church Yth Grp; Band; Church Choir; Concert Band; Yrbk Phtg; Yrbk Rptr; Yrbk Stf; Stat Crs Cntry; JV Trk; Acctng.

SHEWELI, WILLIAM; Aquinas Inst; Rochester, NY; (Y); 50/150; Church Yth Grp; Civic Clb; SADD; Bsbl; Wt Lftg; CC Awd; Hon Roll; English Clb; Political Wkr; Church Choir; Ukrainian Natl Assn Scholar 86; Scotti-Aguinas Awd 85; Bus Law & Typg Awds 86; SUNY Albany; Jrnlsm.

SHICKLUNA, BILL; Grand Island HS; Grand Island, NY; (Y); Mathletes; Model UN; Ski Clb; Im Mgr Vllybl; Canisius Coll; Mrktg.

SHIELDS, DEBRA ANNE; Northport HS; Northport, NY; (Y); 54/605; Acpl Chr; Mrchg Band; Symp Band; Yrbk Stf; Rep Sr Cls; Var Crs Cntry; Var Capt Trk; Elks Awd; High Hon Roll; NHS; NY ST Cvl Law Moot Ct Chmpn 85; Nrthprt Lgl Hall Fm 85-86; Coll Holy Cross; Attrny.

SHIELDS, G ZACHARY; Hoosick Falls Central Schl; Petersburg, NY; (Y); Cmnty Wkr; Computer Clb; French Clb; Ski Clb; JV Bsbl; JV Var Ftbl; Bus Adm.

SHIELDS, KELLIE; Schoharie Central HS; Delanson, NY; (S); 2/102; Key Clb; VP Varsity Clb; Concert Band; Jazz Band; Pres Frsh Cls; Pres Jr Cls; Var L Socr; Var L Sftbl; L JV Vllybl; Ntl Merit Ltr; JR All Amer Hall Fame Bnd Hnrs 85; NY Area All ST Bnd 83-85; Sci.

SHIELDS, STACEY A; The Chapin Schl; Bronx, NY; (Y); Cmnty Wkr; Dance Clb; Nwsp Rptr; Rep Stu Cncl; Sec Bsktbl; Prfct Atten Awd; Better Chance Inc Schlr 82; Leopold-Scheep Fndtn Scholar 83; Natl Merit Commndtn 85; Bio Engrng.

SHIELDS II, THOMAS R; Vernon Verona Sherrill HS; Vernon, NY; (Y); 1/200; Mathletes; Rep Stu Cncl; Var L Bsbl; JV Bsktbl; Im Lcrss; Var L Socr; Bausch & Lomb Sci Awd; High Hon Roll; Pres NHS; Ntl Merit SF; Rensselaer Plythech Inst Mdl 85; Slvr Cty Clb Awd 86; AHSME Schl Wnr 86; Clarkson U; Engr.

SHILLINGFORD, CLINTON K; Hunter College HS; Brooklyn, NY; (Y); Teachers Aide; Band; Chorus; Variety Show; Ntl Merit SF; U PA; Law.

SHILOH, DARLENE; Herbert Lehman HS; Bronx, NY; (Y); Sec FHA; Chorus; Yrbk Stf; Stu Cncl; Tennis; Hon Roll; NHS; Prfct Atten Awd; Bus Hnr Awd 85-86; Photo Awd 86; Engl Hnr Awd 83-86; Katherine Gibbs Coll; Bus.

SHIM, JESSE; Huntington HS; Huntington, NY; (Y); AFS; Pres Chess Clb; Key Clb; Orch; High Hon Roll; Hon Roll; Jr NHS; NHS.

SHINBEIN, ILENE; Port Richmond HS; Staten Island, NY; (Y); Dance Clb; Drama Clb; Library Aide; Math Tm; Chorus; School Musical; Cheerleading; High Hon Roll; NHS; Spanish NHS; Pre-Law.

SHINGLER, NANCY; Pioneer Central HS; Freedom, NY; (Y); 4/258; Trs French Clb; SADD; Chorus; School Musical; School Play; Lit Mag; Hon Roll; NHS; Elem Educ.

SHINSATO, LILLIAN T; St Francis Prep; S Ozone Pk, NY; (S); 92/746; Dance Clb; Girl Scts; Service Clb; Im Ftbl; Im Sftbl; Trk; Im Vllybl; Wt Lftg; NHS; Opt Clb Awd; Empir ST Karate Championshpd 1st Pl Trophy 85; Binns NYS Tourn 2nd Pl 85; Girl Mile 11t Pl Medal 84; Stanford U; Psychlgy.

SHIPPEE, LISA; Cairo-Durham HS; E Durham, NY; (Y); Chorus; School Musical; Yrbk Stf; Cheerleading; Socr; Sftbl; Trk; High Hon Roll; Jr NHS; NHS; Stu All Cnty Chrs 84; CHVL All Leag Sccr Team 84-85; Sccr All Star Team 85-86; Actng.

SHIRES, BRENT; Fairport HS; Fairport, NY; (Y); Church Yth Grp; Concert Band; Jazz Band; Mrchg Band; Orch; Yrbk Phtg; Yrbk Stf; Hon Roll; Ntl Merit Ltr; Prfct Atten Awd; Wegmans Food Mkts Schlrshp 86-88; Auburn Jazz Fstvl-All Star Jazz Awd 86; Hochstn Schl/Music Schlrshp; SUNY Potsdam; Music.

SHIRHALL, SCOTT C; Whitney Point Central Schl; Richford, NY; (Y); 11/123; Science Clb; Ski Clb; Rep Stu Cncl; JV L Ftbl; Var L Golf; High Hon Roll; Hon Roll; Natl Cncl Yth Ldrshp Salute Yth 86; Sci.

SHIRK, LORI A; Southside HS; Pine City, NY; (Y); 3/319; Pres Sec Church Yth Grp; Sec Rep Latin Clb; Chorus; Concert Band; Drm Mjr(t); Mrchg Band; Symp Band; VP Jr Cls; Trs Sr Cls; Var L Tennis; Army ROTC 4 Yr Schlrshp; Bucknell U; Math.

SHIRLEY, SHARON; Hermon-Dekalb Central HS; De Kalb Jct, NY; (Y); 2/40; Drama Clb; Nwsp Stf; Yrbk Ed-Chief; Yrbk Stf; Wrstlng; High Hon Roll; Sec NHS; Sal; French Clb; Pep Clb; Rgnts Schlrshp 86; 1st Awd Ctznshp Essay 85; Whiz Quiz Tm 85-86; Houghton Coll; Engl.

SHIRLEY, THOMAS EDWARD MICHAEL; Massena Central Schl; Massena, NY; (Y); Boy Scts; Exploring; Leo Clb.

SHIRTZ, JOHN; Jamesville-Dewitt HS; Dewitt, NY; (Y); 23/230; Pres Church Yth Grp; Exploring; Rep SADD; Var Capt Socr; High Hon Roll; NHS; French Clb; JA; Political Wkr; Ski Clb; Mony Art Awd, SADD Svc Awd 86; Gld Star Emplye Awd 85; Dntstry.

SHISHIK, SERENE; Keveny Memorial Acad; Waterford, NY; (S); 8/42; Debate Tm; Drama Clb; Q&S; Ski Clb; Color Guard; Orch; Camp Fr Inc; Yrbk Stf; Cheerleading; Sftbl; Natl Bus Hnr Socty 85; Albany Coll Of Pharmacy; Pharm.

SHISHMANIAN, LORETTA; W C Bryant HS; New York, NY; (S); Debate Tm; Library Aide; Teachers Aide; Chorus; Variety Show; Nwsp Rptr; Cit Awd; Hon Roll; NHS; Prfct Atten Awd; Acad Ltrs & Pins Germ 85; Acad Ltr Engl 85.

SHIVERS, ERIC; Mercy HS; Middle Island, NY; (Y); SADD; Varsity Clb; Church Choir; Nwsp Phtg; Yrbk Phtg; Rep Frsh Cls; Var JV Bsbl; Var Ftbl; Var Mgr(s); Var Score Keeper; Var Clb 85-86; Ron Darlings All Amer Bsbl Camp 84-86; MVP Bsbl 83-84; John Jay Coll; Crimnl Law.

SHIVERS, SHEREE; Dominican Commercial HS; Jamaica, NY; (Y); 57/273; Art Clb; Cmnty Wkr; Computer Clb; Dance Clb; Hosp Aide; Ski Clb; Spanish Clb; Tennis; Timer; Vllybl; Siena Clb 82-86; Outstndng Acad Achvt Ftns Awd 86; Stony Brook; Nrsng.

SHIVERY, ALISA; Niagara Catholic HS; Niagara Fls, NY; (Y); Spanish Clb; Hon Roll; Niagara Cnty CC; Artist.

SHLEFSTEIN, DEBBIE L; Midwood HS; Brooklyn, NY; (Y); #53 In Class; Math Tm; Model UN; Office Aide; Temple Yth Grp; Chorus; Hon Roll; Arista & Archon 85; Hebrew Hnr Soc 83; U MI Ann Arbor; Pre-Med.

SHOEMAKER, JEFF; Midlakes HS; Newark, NY; (Y); 25/125; Am Leg Boys St; Letterman Clb; Varsity Clb; High Hon Roll; Hon Roll; NHS; JV Var Bsktbl; JV Var Socr; JV Var Vllybl; Alfred U; Engrng.

SHOEMAKER, KELLY SUE; Cazenovia HS; Chittenango, NY; (Y); 21/150; FBLA; Girl Scts; JA; Mrchg Band; Symp Band; Cit Awd; High Hon Roll; Hon Roll; Madison Cnty Scholar 86; SUNY Morrisville; Acctng.

SHOEMAKER, THOMAS; St Dominics HS; E Norwich, NY; (S); 1/130; Trs Church Yth Grp; Cmnty Wkr; Quiz Bowl; SADD; JV Co-Capt Ftbl; High Hon Roll; Prfct Atten Awd; Im Bsktbl; Im Vllybl; Hon Roll; Cert Of Acad Excel Spnsh II & Bio 84-85; Supr Prfrmnce NEDTS 83-84; Math.

SHOEN, DUANE R; Norwood-Norfolk Central HS; Norwood, NY; (Y); 2/130; Band; Chorus; Concert Band; Jazz Band; VP Stu Cncl; JV Socr; High Hon Roll; NHS; Ntl Merit Ltr; Sal; Clarkson U; Acctg.

SHOLL, DONNIE; Jamestown HS; Jamestown, NY; (Y); Computer Clb; Spanish Clb; Im Ice Hcky; Comp Pgmng.

SHOOTS, DAVID W; Penn Yan Acad; Penn Yan, NY; (Y); 2/150; Am Leg Boys St; Orch; Pres Sr Cls; Var L Crs Cntry; Var L Tennis; Var L Wrstlng; High Hon Roll; NHS; Frsh Cls; American Mathematics Competition School Winner 85-86; Elec Engrng.

SHOPLAND, VIRGINIA; Paul V Moore HS; Brewerton, NY; (Y); Church Yth Grp; JA; Band; Chorus; Concert Band; Mrchg Band; School Musical; Swing Chorus; Nwsp Stf; Hon Roll; Band Secy 84-85; Area All-State Band & Orchstra 83-86; MUSIC.

SHORE, FELICE S; Walt Whitman HS; Huntington Sta, NY; (Y); 19/549; Key Clb; Spanish Clb; Nwsp Bus Mgr; Lit Mag; High Hon Roll; NHS; Cornell U; Math.

SHORTINO, KRISTEN; E J Wilson HS; Spencerport, NY; (Y); Cmnty Wkr; French Clb; Ski Clb; Var Capt Socr; Var Capt Trk; Var L Vllybl; Hon Roll; Yrbk Stf; St Select Soccer Tm 86; 1st Tm All League Indoor Track, 2nd Tm All Cnty Soccer 85-86; European Fund.

SHORTT, LAURIE; Nardin Acad; Buffalo, NY; (S); 11/85; Ski Clb; Lit Mag; Capt Sftbl; Capt Vllybl; High Hon Roll; Hon Roll; Potsdam Coll; Chemcl Engrng.

SHOVA, SCOTT; Franklin Academy; Malone, NY; (Y); Trk; Elec.

SHOWA, MARY BETH; Frankfort Schuyler HS; Utica, NY; (Y); Cmnty Wkr; FBLA; Hosp Aide; Key Clb; Pep Clb; Spanish Clb; Chorus; Yrbk Stf; Stu Cncl; Fld Hcky; Rose Torchia Med Awd 86; Maria Regina Clg; Occup Thrpy.

SHOWELL, MONICA A; St Saviour HS; Brooklyn, NY; (Y); Dance Clb; Drama Clb; French Clb; Science Clb; Concert Band; Orch; Variety Show; French Hon Soc; NHS; St Johns U Jamaica.

SHRADER, PAMELA C; Vestal SR HS; Apalachin, NY; (Y); 71/436; Ski Clb; Spanish Clb; SADD; Varsity Clb; Mrchg Band; Cheerleading; Mgr(s); Twrlr; Hon Roll; NHS; Nazareth Schlrshp 86; Fairfield U; Spnsh.

SHTROMBERG, IRENE; Midwood HS; Brooklyn, NY; (Y); 125/625; French Clb; Intnl Clb; Im Chorus; Bowling; Swmmng; Wt Lftg; Hon Roll; Lib Arts.

SHUBA, TERESA; Cato-Meridian HS; Cato, NY; (Y); Trs FFA; JA; Leo Clb; Yrbk Stf; High Hon Roll; Hon Roll; 2nd Pl-Mrrsvll Emplymnt Intrview Cntst 85; Morrisville Ag & Tech; Hrtcltur.

SHUBACK, SUSAN J; John S Burke Catholic HS; Florida, NY; (Y); Rep Jr Cls; Pres Sr Cls; Var L Cheerleading; High Hon Roll; NEDT Awd; Social Stds Olympd 85; Rgnts Schlrshp 86; Chem Awd 85; Genrl Excllnc 84; Trinity Coll WA DC; Poltcl Sc.

SHUBERT, JENNIFER; Grand Island HS; Grand Island, NY; (Y); Drama Clb; Ski Clb; Chorus; Madrigals; School Musical; School Play; Stage Crew; Swing Chorus; Hon Roll; Mst Imprvd Spotlightr 85 & 86; Pres Spotlighters 86-87; Sec Choir 86-87; Cmmnctns.

SHUBERT, TRACI; Grand Island HS; Grand Island, NY; (Y); 11/317; Hosp Aide; Mathletes; Ski Clb; Chorus; Madrigals; School Musical; Var JV Socr; NHS; Ntl Merit SF; Rotary Awd; Boston U; Intl Rel.

SHUEMAKER, JENNIFER; Sacred Heart Acad; East Amherst, NY; (Y); Cmnty Wkr; French Clb; Science Clb; Ski Clb; Stage Crew; Yrbk Stf; Stat Bsktbl.

SHUEY, DAVID; Webster Christian Schl; Webster, NY; (S); 2/10; Church Yth Grp; Chorus; School Play; Yrbk Stf; Off Sr Cls; Var Capt Bsktbl; Var Capt Socr; High Hon Roll; Stage Crew; Nwsp Stf; Chrstn Chrctr Awd 83-85; Chrstn Sprtsmnshp Awd 83-85; Clemson U; Elec Engr.

SHUFELT, LYNN; Alexander Central HS; Darien, NY; (Y); Var Bsktbl; Var Capt Crs Cntry; Var Sftbl; Var Trk; Var Vllybl; Hon Roll; Jr NHS; Fre Dept Sprtsmnshp Awd 84-85; Sectnl All-Str Crss Cntry 83-85; Phy Ed.

SHUKHAT, BEATA; Brooklyn Academy Prep Schl; Brooklyn, NY; (Y); GAA; Math Tm; High Hon Roll; Child Psych.

SHULER, TINA; Dodge HS; Bronx, NY; (Y); Long Island U.

SHULLA, MICHELE; Newark HS; Newark, NY; (Y); 54/197; Camp Fr Inc; Church Yth Grp; Cmnty Wkr; French Clb; Girl Scts; Hosp Aide; Teachers Aide; Chorus; Church Choir; Mrchg Band; Cmnty Volntr Awd 86; Cayuga CC; Elem Ed.

SHULMAN, JAY; Herricks HS; Roslyn, NY; (Y); JV Var Bowling; NHS; Med.

SHULTES, TRICIA; Bethlehem Central HS; Delmar, NY; (Y); 27/300; Church Yth Grp; GAA; Var Crs Cntry; Var Trk; High Hon Roll; Hon Roll; NHS; Poem Publshd In Schl Lit Magzn 86; Hnrb Mntn-African Essay Cntst 84; Yth Minister.

SHULTS, DALE; Canajoharie Central HS; Canajoharie, NY; (Y); 39/86; 4-H; Ski Clb; Varsity Clb; Var Ftbl; Var Wt Lftg; Var Wrstlng; 4-H Awd; Hon Roll; Teen Cncl Pres 84-86; SUNY Alfed; Comp Drftng.

SHULTZ, JAMES; Lowville Central HS; Lowville, NY; (Y); 3/120; Pres 4-H; VP FFA; Scholastic Bowl; Spanish Clb; Im Bsktbl; Cit Awd; Dnfth Awd; 4-H Awd; High Hon Roll; Hon Roll; Whipple Schlrshp 86; Capt Elizabeth Bush Mem Schlrshp 86; Morrisville; Engrng.

SHULTZ, NELLIE; Alexandria Bay Central HS; La Fargeville, NY; (Y); Church Yth Grp; Cmnty Wkr; FFA; Church Choir; Yrbk Phtg; Yrbk Stf; Bowling; Cheerleading; Jefferson CC; Bus Admn.

SHUM, ANNIE; James Madison HS; Brooklyn, NY; (Y); 44/754; Regnts Schlrshp 86; Asian Stu Unions Offcr, Secy 86; Ansta 85-86; NY U; Stockbrkr.

SHUM, MARY; Norman Thomas HS; Corona, NY; (S); 13/597; Church Yth Grp; Pres FBLA; JA; Trs NHS; Prfct Atten Awd; NY U; Acctng.

SHUMSKY, DAVID; Bethpage HS; Plainview, NY; (Y); 4-H; Golf; Hon Roll; Farmingdale U; Engr.

SHUST, PAUL; Warwick Valley HS; Warwick, NY; (Y); Computer Clb; JV Bsbl; Var Bsktbl; Capt Bowling; Var Socr; Bausch & Lomb Sci Awd; High Hon Roll; Lion Awd; Natl Sci Olympd Chmstry; Amer Assoc Physcs Tchrs Awd; Natl Frnch Cntst Rgnl Wnr; Northeastern; Bus Financ.

SHUSTER, TINA; St Johnsville Central Schl; St Johnsville, NY; (S); 3/25; Church Yth Grp; Sec 4-H; Sec French Clb; Pres Band; Chorus; Church Choir; DAR Awd; 4-H Awd; NHS.

SHUSTRIN, JARRETT; South Shore HS; Brooklyn, NY; (Y); Science Clb; Service Clb; Yrbk Ed-Chief; Rptr Lit Mag; Var Trk; Hon Roll; Pres NHS; Office Aide; Variety Show; Brooklyn Borough Sci Fair 1st Pl 84-85; NYC Sci Fair Fin 84-85; Pride Fo NY Yankees Awd 86; Pre-Med.

SHUTES, EDWARD; Hornell HS; Hornell, NY; (Y); Stu Cncl; Tennis; Bsktbl; Babe Ruth League Bsbl; Journlsm.

SHWOM, MATTHEW; Lynbrook HS; Ny, NY; (Y); Temple Yth Grp; Varsity Clb; Variety Show; Wrstlng; Hon Roll; Gentc Engrng.

SHYMKIW, CHRISTINE A; Union Springs HS; Auburn, NY; (Y); #17 In Class; Spanish Clb; Chorus; School Musical; JV Cheerleading; Coach Actv; High Hon Roll; Philip Morris Scholar 86; NY ST Regents Scholar 86; St John Fisher; Cmmnctns.

SIANO JR, ANTHONY P; Midwood HS; Brooklyn, NY; (Y); Boy Scts; Chess Clb; Teachers Aide; Concert Band; School Play; Yrbk Stf; Stu Cncl; Mgr(s); Socr; Cit Awd; Eagle Scout 86; Doctor Of Chiropractic.

SIBLEY, NORMAN; Ticonderoga HS; Ticonderoga, NY; (Y); Boy Scts; Pres Church Yth Grp; Latin Clb; Church Choir; Lit Mag; Mgr Bsbl; Mgr Ftbl; Hon Roll; Mgr(s); Score Keeper; De Vry; Elec Tech.

SICH, NATALY; Alfred-Almond Central HS; Alfred Sta, NY; (Y); French Clb; SADD; Band; Yrbk Stf; Sec Jr Cls; Rep Sr Cls; JV Var Cheerleading; Var Crs Cntry; Score Keeper; JV Socr; Alfred U; Lib Arts.

SICIGNANO III, HENRY; Williamsville East HS; Williamsville, NY; (Y); 4/302; Model UN; Nwsp Ed-Chief; Pres Stu Cncl; Capt L Crs Cntry; Capt L Trk; Cit Awd; DAR Awd; High Hon Roll; NHS; Sal; Ntl Hnr Socty Natl Schlrshp 86; Mst Actv & Mst Schl Spirt 86; Harvard U.

SICILIANO, JAMES; Sachem High Schl North Campus; Lake Ronkonkoma, NY; (Y); 325/1452; Ski Clb; Band; Concert Band; Jazz Band; Symp Band; Coach Actv; Co-Capt Gym; JV Trk; JV Wrstlng; Ntl Merit Schol; Fordham U.

SICILIANO, JOSEPH; Iona Preparatory Schl; Yonkers, NY; (Y); 10/204; Chess Clb; Library Aide; Math Tm; Lit Mag; Im Bowling; JV Socr; High Hon Roll; Ntl Merit Ltr; Accntng.

SICINA, CHRISTINE; Newburgh Free Acad; Newburgh, NY; (Y); Spanish Clb; Chorus; JV Bsktbl; Var Sftbl; Hlth Care Admnstr.

SICK, MICHELE; Cohocton Central HS; Cohocton, NY; (S); 1/25; French Clb; Band; Chorus; Pres Frsh Cls; Pres Soph Cls; Pres Jr Cls; Var Socr; Sftbl; High Hon Roll; NHS; Frgn Exch Stu France 85; Nice Kid Awd 84; Hghst Cls Avg 85.

SICKLER, DANIELLE; Stissing Mt JR SR HS; Stanfordville, NY; (Y); AFS; Art Clb; Library Aide; Chorus; Variety Show; Cheerleading; Hon Roll; Bus.

SICKLES, KIM; York Central HS; Linwood, NY; (Y); AFS; 4-H; Library Aide; Capt Color Guard; School Musical; Stage Crew; Hon Roll; Giftd 79-80; Mentrshp Pgm BOEES 85-86; Spnsh.

SICKMEN, ELISA; Ward Melville HS; Stony Brook, NY; (Y); Art Clb; Drama Clb; SADD; Chorus; School Musical; Variety Show; Lit Mag; JV Tennis; Capt JV Vllybl; High Hon Roll.

SICKO, HEATHER; Berlin Central HS; Petersburg, NY; (Y); GAA; Chorus; Yrbk Stf; Lit Mag; Sec Soph Cls; VP Jr Cls; Rep Sr Cls; Sec Stu Cncl; Capt Cheerleading; Var Score Keeper; SUNY Cobleskill; Htl Tech.

SIDARI, PHILLIP; Albion HS; Albion, NY; (S); 9/189; Off Boy Scts; Pres Computer Clb; Latin Clb; Math Tm; Golf; Swmmng; Hon Roll; Ntl Merit SF; Acdmc Dcthln ST Cmptn 86; MA Inst Of Tech; Elctrnc Engr.

SIDE, SUZANNE M; Newark SR HS; Newark, NY; (Y); 66/201; Pres Church Yth Grp; Cmnty Wkr; Library Aide; Office Aide; Band; Pres Ed Lit Mag; Cit Awd; Rotary Awd; Girl Scts; Hosp Aide; NY ST Am Lgn Aux Schlrshp 86; Grl Sct Gold Awd 84; W Indies Rep Grl Scts 85; SUNY Oswego; Psychlgst.

SIDEL, HENRY C; The New Lincoln Schl; New York, NY; (Y); Debate Tm; Model UN; Nwsp Rptr; Stu Cncl; Socr; Tennis; St Schlr; Band; School Play; Ed Lit Mag; Edtr Lit Mag 83-84; Stu Rep Bd Of Trustees 85-86; Intrn Harpers Mag 86; Crtv Wrtg.

SIDER, JOHNNY F; Edison Technical Occup Ctr; Rochester, NY; (Y); 3/276; Chess Clb; VP Church Yth Grp; Pres Church Choir; Var L Ftbl; JV Wrstlng; Hon Roll; NHS; Klepper Awd 84; Harvard Bk Awd 85; Elec Engr.

SIDERATOS, PEGGY; Fontbonne Hall Acad; Brooklyn, NY; (Y); SADD; Teachers Aide; School Play; Variety Show; Lit Mag; High Hon Roll; NHS; Prfct Atten Awd; Var Awds Phy Ed, Bio Chem 84-86; Spnsh Awds 84-86; Brooklyn Coll; Psych.

SIDERIS, PANTELIS; Long Island City HS; Astroia, NY; (Y); Boy Scts; Capt Bowling; Cit Awd; Hon Roll; Prfct Atten Awd; Bus.

SIDES, LAURA; Scotia-Glenville HS; Scotia, NY; (Y); Sec Drama Clb; Key Clb; Spanish Clb; Thesps; Acpl Chr; School Musical; Stage Crew; Yrbk Stf; High Hon Roll; NHS; Music Ltr; Theater.

SIDHU, JAGJEET S; Anglo American HS; New York, NY; (Y); VP Chess Clb; Science Clb; Nwsp Rptr; Var Fld Hcky; Var Socr; Var Trk; Stat Vllybl; Hon Roll; NYS Rgnts Schlrshp 86; NY U; Engr.

SIDLE, DAVID; Odessa-Montour HS; Alpine, NY; (Y); 25/86; Am Leg Boys St; Boy Scts; Varsity Clb; Chorus; School Musical; Lit Mag; Pres Sr Cls; Pres Pres Stu Cncl; Var L Ftbl; Var Capt Trk; Most Outstndg Competator For Trck & Field 85 & 86; 1st Pl Creative Word Prcssng Stud Media Fest 86; Business.

SIDONI, LAURA; Niagara Falls HS; Niagara Falls, NY; (S); 19/250; Office Aide; Yrbk Stf; High Hon Roll; Hon Roll; Jr NHS; NHS; Top 10 Awd 83; Top 25 83; Buffalo ST Coll; Dietetics.

SIDOTI, ANGELA; Moore Catholic HS; Staten Island, NY; (Y); 13/177; Cmnty Wkr; Intnl Clb; Teachers Aide; Chorus; Yrbk Stf; Bowling; High Hon Roll; NHS; Pres Schlr; Wrkd Down Syndrm Childrn 84-86; Eddy Awd Edtrl 86; Shakespeare Fnlst 86; Rutgers Clg; Phrmcy.

SIDOTI, MARYBETH; Tuckahoe HS; Eastchester, NY; (Y); 11/54; Art Clb; Church Yth Grp; Cmnty Wkr; Nwsp Stf; Yrbk Stf; Lit Mag; Hon Roll; NHS; Outstndng Achvt 11 Hnrs Engl 86; Outstndng Achvt 12 AP Engl 86; Prsdntl Acad Ftnss Awd 86; U Of RI; Psych.

SIEBELS, CHRIS; Gouverneur Central HS; Gouverneur, NY; (Y); VP 4-H; Chorus; School Musical; Rep Stu Cncl; JV Bsktbl; JV Var Socr; Var Trk; Hon Roll; Jr NHS; NHS; Natl Scl Stds Olympd Awd Wnnr 86; Acdmc Let Awd 85; Math.

SIEBERT, CHRIS; Lyndonville Central HS; Lyndonville, NY; (S); 10/95; Aud/Vis; Varsity Clb; JV Var Bsbl; Var Capt Socr; Var Capt Wrstlng; Hon Roll; Jr NHS; NHS; Chairman JR Cls Float 85; Giftd Talntd Pgm 85; Tchr.

SIEBERT, JULIE; Pembroke JR SR HS; Batavia, NY; (Y); Art Clb; VP 4-H; Spanish Clb; Varsity Clb; Chorus; Yrbk Phtg; Trs Stu Cncl; Var L Trk; Hon Roll; NHS; Spnsh Hgh Avg Awd 84-86; Genesee CC; Bus.

SIEBERT, KATHRYN; Batavia HS; Batavia, NY; (Y); Cmnty Wkr; 4-H; Political Wkr; Band; Yrbk Stf; Rep Jr Cls; Rep Stu Cncl; VP Cheerleading; VP Stat Swmmng; Hon Roll; Lang Arts Awd 84; Genesee Cnty Essay Cntst Wnr 84; Swmng Awds 85.

SIEBS, MICHELE; George Wingate HS; New York, NY; (Y); Elctrcl Engr.

SIEG, KELLIE; South Park HS; Buffalo, NY; (Y); Nwsp Stf; Hon Roll; Jr NHS; NHS; Crtfct Achvmnt Math, English & Social Studies 83; Pre-Med.

SIEGA, STEVEN J; Bronx H S Of Science; Middle Village, NY; (Y); Debate Tm; Library Aide; NFL; JV Crs Cntry; JV Trk; Ntl Merit SF; Prfct Atten Awd; 2nd Bio Sci Proj; 2nd Italian Essay Cont; NYU; Real Est.

SIEGEL, AUDRA; Commack South HS; Commack, NY; (S); Drama Clb; Chorus; Madrigals; School Musical; School Play; High Hon Roll; Hon Roll; NHS; Office Aide; PAVAS; All Cnty Msc Awds 84-85; NYSSMA Solo Awds 83-85; Music.

SIEGEL, CLIFFORD; Saunders Trade & Tech HS; Yonkers, NY; (Y); 6/204; Chess Clb; Cmnty Wkr; Computer Clb; JA; Political Wkr; Ski Clb; Varsity Clb; Yrbk Stf; Off Soph Cls; Bsktbl; Lcl 1500 Schlrshp 86; Sprntndnt Awd 83-86; 90 Clb; SUNY Binghamton; Bus.

SIEGEL, DEBBIE; Middletown HS; Middletown, NY; (Y); Drama Clb; Teachers Aide; Band; Chorus; Drm Mjr(t); Mrchg Band; School Musical; Swing Chorus; Symp Band; Im Vllybl; Bus.

SIEGEL, JILL; Commack North HS; E Northport, NY; (Y); 25/390; French Clb; Latin Clb; Temple Yth Grp; Var Badmtn; Var Mgr(s); Pres French Hon Soc; High Hon Roll; NHS; Pres Schlr; Cornell; Pre-Med.

SIEGEL, JILL; James Sperry HS; Henrietta, NY; (Y); 25/271; Drama Clb; French Clb; Latin Clb; SADD; Thesps; Chorus; Madrigals; School Musical; French Hon Soc; NHS; Pres Acad Ftnss Awd 86; Rochester Inst; Scl Wrk.

SIEGEL, KAREN SARAH; James E Sperry HS; Henrietta, NY; (Y); 21/300; SADD; Thesps; School Play; Stage Crew; French Hon Soc; Jr NHS; NHS.

SIEGEL, MERYL; Commack HS South; Commack, NY; (Y); #160 In Class; Office Aide; SADD; Teachers Aide; Temple Yth Grp; Hon Roll; Delhi; Htl Tech.

SIEGEL, SHARRI; Lawrence HS; North Woodmere, NY; (S); AFS; Trs DECA; Spanish Clb; Temple Yth Grp; Mgr Ed Yrbk Stf; Stu Cncl; 3rd Pl DECA NY ST Ldrshp Conf 86; DE Ca Ntl Conf Cert Of Excllnc 86; Hon Soc 84-87; Bus.

SIEGEL, TINA; Mepham HS; N Bellmore, NY; (Y); SADD; Band; Nwsp Stf; Yrbk Stf; Rep Soph Cls; Rep Jr Cls; Rep Sr Cls; Hon Roll; NHS.

SIEGWARTH, KIRK; Somers HS; Somers, NY; (Y); Church Yth Grp; Chorus; Jazz Band; School Musical; Var Capt Crs Cntry; Var Capt Trk; Bausch & Lomb Sci Awd; High Hon Roll; NHS; Drama Clb; All-Cnty Hnrbl Mntn X-Cntry 85; Schl Rcrd 800 Mtrs 86; NYSSMA Trmbn Slo At Lvl 6 86; Aerspc Engr.

SIERACKI, MICHAEL; Hutchinson Central Technical HS; Buffalo, NY; (Y); Band; Concert Band; Jazz Band; Mrchg Band; Orch; Mgr(s); Swmmng; Hon Roll; SAR Awd; U Of NY Buffalo; Elec Engrng.

SIEROSLAWSKI, LYNN; St Marys HS; Depew, NY; (Y); Office Aide; Ski Clb; SADD; JV Sftbl; JV Vllybl; Hon Roll; Med.

SIESTO, PAUL; Greece Olympia HS; Rochester, NY; (Y); JV Trk; High Hon Roll; Hon Roll.

SIEUPERSAD, IAN S; Aviation HS; Bronx, NY; (S); 34/415; JA; Nwsp Sprt Ed; Rep Soph Cls; Rep Jr Cls; Capt Ftbl; Aviatn Hnr Soc 84-86; Pegasus Soc-Tech Hnr Soc-84-86; Bus Mgmt.

SIEVERS, MARIA; Commack HS North; E Northport, NY; (Y); 59/390; Cmnty Wkr; French Clb; Nwsp Stf; Off Frsh Cls; Off Soph Cls; Off Jr Cls; Off Sr Cls; High Hon Roll; Hon Roll; NHS; Regents Schlrshp; Siena Coll; Bus.

SIFERT, ERIC; Saratoga Central Catholic HS; Schuylerville, NY; (S); Stage Crew; JV Ftbl; High Hon Roll; NHS; Engrng.

SIFF, MARNIE; Roslyn HS; Roslyn Est, NY; (Y); AFS; Trs Exploring; Hosp Aide; Chorus; Yrbk Stf; Lit Mag; Var Sftbl; Psych.

SIINO, VINCENT J; St Francis Prep; Sunnyside, NY; (S); Church Yth Grp.

SIKORA, CAREN; Longwood HS; Coram, NY; (S); 6/450; SADD; Band; Concert Band; Mrchg Band; Stage Crew; High Hon Roll; NHS; SUNY Binghamton.

SIKORSKI, JULIE; Cardinal Mooney HS; Rochester, NY; (Y); 10/315; Cmnty Wkr; Hosp Aide; Chorus; Church Choir; VP Stu Cncl; Coach Actv; French Hon Soc; High Hon Roll; Hugh O Brien Yth Fndtn Ldrshp Svc Awd 83-84; Amer Chem Socty Chem Cntst 2nd Pl 85; Cornell U; Pre-Law.

SIKORSKI, LYNN; Frontier Central HS; Blasdell, NY; (Y); Art Clb; SADD; Hon Roll; Prfct Atten Awd; Sec.

SIKORSKI, RAYMOND; Manhasset HS; Manhasset, NY; (Y); 23/185; Nwsp Ed-Chief; Lit Mag; NHS; Pres Schlr; St Schlr; Debate Tm; Drama Clb; Mathletes; Political Wkr; Service Clb; Tufts U; Libl Arts.

SILBER, NANCY E; Plainview-Old Bethpage HS; Plainview, NY; (Y); 7/194; Exploring; Key Clb; Sec Model UN; SADD; Trs Acpl Chr; Chorus; Madrigals; School Musical; Swing Chorus; Ed Lit Mag; NYS Rgnts Schlrshp 86; Natl Merit Stu 85; Svc To HS Awd 84 & 85; Cornell U; Indstrl Relat.

SILBER, STEVE; Clarkstown HS North; New City, NY; (Y); Boy Scts; Cmnty Wkr; Spanish Clb; Trk; Bus.

SILBERMAN, STACY; Newfield HS; Coram, NY; (Y); Girl Scts; Chorus; Yrbk Phtg; Cit Awd; High Hon Roll; Jr NHS; NHS; Spanish NHS.

SILBERMAN, STEVEN; Blind Brook HS; Rye Brook, NY; (Y); AFS; Drama Clb; Spanish Clb; School Play; Nwsp Stf; JV Var Bsktbl; Var Golf; JV Var Socr; Cit Awd; Wstchstr Arts Pgm 86-87; Comm.

SILIVESTRO, MICHAEL; Gates-Chili HS; Rochester, NY; (S); Aud/Vis; Computer Clb; Exploring; Off VICA; Stage Crew; Lit Mag; High Hon Roll; Prfct Atten Awd; Acadmc Achvt Awd 84-85; US Air Frc; Electrcl Engrng.

SILKEY, SHANNON; Jamesville-Dewitt HS; Fayetteville, NY; (Y); French Clb; Girl Scts; Hosp Aide; Key Clb; Ski Clb; VP Pres SADD; Chorus; School Play; Stage Crew; Sec Jr Cls; Jamesville-De Witt Svc Awd 86; SUNY Geneso; Lib Arts.

SILL, SHERRI M; Paul V Moore HS; Parish, NY; (Y); Church Yth Grp; Chorus; Church Choir; School Musical; Swing Chorus; Var Trk; High Hon Roll; NHS; Tchr Of Msc.

SILLIMAN, BRUCE; Victor Central HS; Macedon, NY; (Y); Jazz Band; Socr; Hon Roll; CC Finger Lakes; Engrng.

SILVA, ISABEL; New Rochelle HS; New Rochelle, NY; (Y); 55/550; French Clb; French Hon Soc; Hon Roll; NHS; Computer Clb; Math Clb; SADD; Chorus; Lit Mag; Bertha F Smith Awd 86; Natl Cncl Jewish Wmn Hghr Incntv Awd 86; Zonta Intl Awd 86; Manhattan Coll; Acctng.

SILVA, MICHAEL; New Dorp HS; Staten Island, NY; (Y); Temple Yth Grp; Pep Band; School Musical; Symp Band; Rep Jr Cls; Capt Crs Cntry; Capt Trk; High Hon Roll; Spanish NHS; Trphy PSAL X-Cntry Chmpshps 85; Arntcl Engrng.

SILVANIC, THERESA M; Sidney HS; Sidney, NY; (Y); 1/98; French Clb; Math Clb; Varsity Clb; Chorus; VP Pres Stu Cncl; Var L Sftbl; High Hon Roll; NHS; Drama Clb; Office Aide; Achvmnt Awd 84-86; Clrk Awds Hghst & 2nd Hghst Avg 83-84; Colgate U; Bus.

SILVER, BARBARA; Nottingham HS; Syracuse, NY; (Y); 2/300; Hosp Aide; Latin Clb; Spanish Clb; Nwsp Rptr; Nwsp Stf; Yrbk Stf; High Hon Roll; NHS; Spanish NHS; 3rd Pl Spnsh III Oswego Lang Fair 85; Silvr Medl Ntl Latn Exm 85; CPA.

SILVER, BRIAN M; Smithtown High School East; Smithtown, NY; (Y); Camera Clb; Nwsp Ed-Chief; Nwsp Phtg; Lit Mag; Off Jr Cls; Off Sr Cls; French Hon Soc; NHS; Ntl Merit SF; Med.

SILVER, EDWARD; Yeshira University HS; New York, NY; (Y); St Schlr; Yeshiva U.

SILVER, RINA; Newfield HS; Selden, NY; (Y); 21/517; Quiz Bowl; Nwsp Stf; Yrbk Stf; Hon Roll; Jr NHS; SUNY Albany; Crprt Lwyr.

SILVERBERG, MARK; Smithtown HS East; Nesconset, NY; (Y); NYS U Binghamton; Opthlmlgst.

SILVERIO, CYNTHIA; Franklin Delano Roosevlet HS; Poughkeepsie, NY; (Y); Church Yth Grp; Ski Clb; Ed Yrbk Stf; Rep Frsh Cls; Var Cheerleading; Hon Roll; NHS; Pre-Law.

SILVERMAN, CINDY; Seaford HS; Seaford, NY; (Y); 44/260; Dance Clb; Teachers Aide; Band; Flag Corp; Mrchg Band; Symp Band; Hon Roll; Millersville U; Elem.

SILVERMAN, DOUG; Commack HS North; Commack, NY; (Y); 153/373; Aud/Vis; SADD; Im Bsktbl; Im Wt Lftg; UCLA; Law.

SILVERMAN, KIM; Bellport HS; E Patchogue, NY; (Y); Stage Crew; Var Socr; Hon Roll; Math Tm; Stat Ftbl; High Hon Roll; Prfct Atten Awd; Shorthand I 86; Office Procdurs I 86; Keyboardng Ii 85; Briarcliffe; Secretary.

SILVERMAN, MARJORIE S; Horace Mann HS; White Plains, NY; (Y); Cmnty Wkr; German Clb; Orch; Nwsp Rptr; JV Var Bsktbl; JV Var Vllybl; Duke U; Psychlgy.

SILVERMAN, MARK S; Scarsdale HS; Scarsdale, NY; (Y); JV Tennis; JV Trk; Hon Roll; Ntl Merit Ltr; VP Of Pltfrm Ten Clb; NYS Rgnts Schlrshp; Trinity Coll Hartford CT.

SILVERMAN, SANDOR; Monticello HS; Monticello, NY; (Y); Debate Tm; FBLA; NFL; Quiz Bowl; Scholastic Bowl; School Play; Stage Crew; Lit Mag; NHS; Ntl Merit Schol; Co-Fndr Garmers Gld 85; Ed & Fndr Monticello H Litrcy Mgz 86; SR St Ct Syst & Fndr 86; Kings Point Acad; Sci Fctn Athr.

SILVERS, TAMMY; Southside HS; Elmira, NY; (Y); Ski Clb; Spanish Clb; SADD; Varsity Clb; Concert Band; Mrchg Band; School Musical; Symp Band; Var Tennis; Hon Roll; Math.

SILVERSTEIN, CAROL; Tottenville HS; Staten Isld, NY; (Y); Office Aide; Band; Concert Band; JV Crs Cntry; JV Var Trk; Var Vllybl; NHS; Ntl Merit Ltr; NY Spr Yth 86.

SILVERSTEIN, CARYN S; Abraham Lincoln HS; Brooklyn, NY; (Y); 10/416; Cmnty Wkr; Computer Clb; Hosp Aide; Office Aide; Political Wkr; Nwsp Stf; Rptr Lit Mag; Hon Roll; Jr NHS; NHS; SUNY; Biolgcl Sci.

SILVESTRI JR, PEDRO; Bay Shore HS; Bay Shore, NY; (Y); 82/406; Computer Clb; Hon Roll; Bio Course Std Sea Shore & Anmls 85; Comp Awd Pascal 86; Aerontcl.

SIMAITIS, ANDREA; Waverly HS; Waverly, NY; (Y); Aud/Vis; Church Yth Grp; Girl Scts; Hosp Aide; Ski Clb; Band; School Play; Nwsp Rptr; Cheerleading; Swmmng; Oratorcl Cont 85 & 86; Tioga Cnty All-Star Swmmg 85; Arch.

SIMAO, ROSEANNE; Solvay HS; Syracuse, NY; (Y); Church Yth Grp; Spanish Clb; Variety Show; Jr Cls; Bsktbl; High Hon Roll; Hon Roll.

SIMCOX, DAWN; Niagara Wheatfield S HS; Niagara Falls, NY; (Y); Girl Scts; Latin Clb; Pres Varsity Clb; Pres Frsh Cls; Pres Soph Cls; Var Capt Bsktbl; Var Capt Socr; Var Capt Sftbl; Vllybl; High Hon Roll; NY ST Indoor Sccr Champ 85; Wendys Plyr Of Wk Bsktbl 86; Var Bsktbl Rookier Of Yr 86; Army ROTC; Phy Thrpy.

SIMEONE, CAROL ANNE M; St Agnes Academic HS; Flushing, NY; (Y).

SIMEONE, PAUL T; Tottenville HS; Staten Island, NY; (Y); 36/871; Im Bsktbl; Var Bowling; Hon Roll; NHS; Ntl Merit Ltr; St Schlr; Bucknell U; Bio.

SIMES, JEFFREY A; The Fieldston Schl; Bronxville, NY; (Y); Orch; School Musical; School Play; Off Sr Cls; Pres Sec Stu Cncl; Capt L Crs Cntry; L Var Trk; Ntl Merit SF; Pres Schlr; Columbia Sci Hnrs Prog 84.

SIMICLE, MICHAEL; Bishop Ludden HS; Syracuse, NY; (Y); Letterman Clb; Ski Clb; Yrbk Stf; Var JV Ftbl; Var JV Lcrss; Wt Lftg; Hon Roll; St Michaels VT; Accntg.

SIMIELE, JO ANNE; Solvay HS; Solvay, NY; (Y); Church Yth Grp; Girl Scts; Math Clb; Chorus; Variety Show; Off Soph Cls; Off Jr Cls; High Hon Roll; Awd Outstndng Achvt Chem 85-86; Math.

SIMIELE, MARY BETH; Solvay HS; Solvay, NY; (Y); 14/175; Yrbk Ed-Chief; Rep Sr Cls; JV Var Vllybl; High Hon Roll; NHS; Solvay Geddes Vetrns Schlrshp 86; ST U Coll Arts & Sci; Biochem.

SIMION, PAUL I; Mt St Michael Acad; Bronx, NY; (S); 25/306; Art Clb; Camera Clb; Computer Clb; Ski Clb; Stage Crew; Nwsp Rptr; Yrbk Stf; Rep Stu Cncl; Socr; NHS; Fordham U; Law.

SIMIONESCU, ADRIANA; Benjamin N Cardozo HS; Bayside, NY; (Y); Drama Clb; PAVAS; School Play; Stage Crew; French Hon Soc; High Hon Roll; Hon Roll; NCTE Awd; Ntl Merit Schol; Prfct Atten Awd; Regents Schlrshp 86; St Johns Natl Merit Schlrshp 86; St Johns Coll; Psychlgy.

SIMITIAN, CARL; Archbishop Molloy HS; Queens, NY; (Y); Cmnty Wkr; FBLA; Political Wkr; Red Cross Aide; Service Clb; SADD; Ice Hcky; Lcrss; Sftbl; Swmmng; Bus.

SIMKOVSKY, DANA MARIE; Utica Free Acad; Utica, NY; (Y); Trs Church Yth Grp; Drama Clb; Hst Key Clb; School Play; Stage Crew; Hon Roll; NHS; Amer Diabetes Assn Citation 86; Occ Thrpy.

SIMKULET, JAMES M; Johnson City SR HS; Binghamton, NY; (Y); 1/198; Capt Mathletes; Varsity Clb; VP Jr Cls; VP Sr Cls; Var L Bsktbl; Var L Tennis; VP NHS; Ntl Merit SF; Pep Clb; JV Bsbl; Scottish Rite Masons Outstndng Stdnt 85.

SIMMERMACHER, TODD W; Vestal HS; Apalachin, NY; (Y); Boy Scts; Exploring; Natl Beta Clb; Varsity Clb; Band; Concert Band; Jazz Band; Mrchg Band; Pep Band; School Musical; Regent Schlrshp 86; SUNY Buffalo; Aerontcl Engrng.

SIMMONDS, YOLANDA; Catherdral HS; Ny, NY; (Y); 100/355; Chorus; Pace U; Acctng.

SIMMONS, AMANDA; G Ray Bodley HS; Fulton, NY; (Y); 29/241; Chorus; Color Guard; Mrchg Band; School Musical; High Hon Roll; Hon Roll; Prfct Atten 83-84; Paul Smiths Coll; Chef Training.

SIMMONS, CHRISTOPHER; Northstar Christian Acad; Canandaigua, NY; (S); Church Yth Grp; Church Choir; VP Frsh Cls; Pres Soph Cls; Rep Jr Cls; Var Capt Bsbl; Bsktbl; Var Capt Socr; NHS; Rep Sr Cls; Acctg.

SIMMONS, DAWN; Norht Babylon SR HS; No Babylon, NY; (Y); Intnl Clb; Sec Spanish Clb; Band; Concert Band; Mrchg Band; School Musical; Nwsp Stf; High Hon Roll; Hon Roll; Jr NHS.

SIMMONS, ERICA; William Nottingham HS; Syracuse, NY; (Y); Church Yth Grp; Cmnty Wkr; Hosp Aide; Chorus; Church Choir; School Musical; Variety Show; Nwsp Rptr; VP Soph Cls; Capt Sftbl; Crossrdr In Crossroads To The Caribbean Prgm 86; Stu Of Upward Bound Prgm Lemoyne COLL 84-86.

SIMMONS, KEVIN; Dundee Central HS; Dundee, NY; (Y); SADD; Chorus; Concert Band; Mrchg Band; Var L Bsktbl; Var L Ftbl; Var L Trk; Boy Scts; Church Yth Grp; Crpntry.

SIMMONS, KIM; Ripley Central HS; Ripley, NY; (S); Band; Chorus; Mrchg Band; Yrbk Stf; Stu Cncl; Cheerleading; Sftbl; Tennis; Hon Roll; Art.

SIMMONS, KRISTINA; Canton Central HS; Canton, NY; (Y); 2/150; Sec Church Yth Grp; Q&S; Pres Thesps; Chorus; School Musical; School Play; Lit Mag; High Hon Roll; NHS; Congrs-Bundestag Alt 86.

SIMMONS, MARTHA; Sacred Heart Acad; Seaford, NY; (S); 11/182; Math Clb; Math Tm; Band; Chorus; Rep Stu Cncl; Hon Roll; NHS; Ntl Merit Ltr; Ntl Hnr Roll 83-84; Lwyr.

SIMMONS, MICHAEL D; Red Jacket Central HS; Shortsville, NY; (Y); Am Leg Boys St; JV Bsbl; JV Var Wrstlng; Chess Clb; 4-H; Spanish Clb; 4-H Awd; Cert Achvt Comp 84; Pal Bsbl 2nd Pl City Trnmnt 84; Pal Bsbl 1st Pl Trophy 84; SUNY Albany; Acctng.

SIMMONS, ROBERT R; Edmeston Central Schl; Edmeston, NY; (Y); 5/33; Am Leg Boys St; Computer Clb; Math Clb; Varsity Clb; Yrbk Stf; Var Socr; Var L Trk; High Hon Roll; Hon Roll; Cobleskill; Comp Sci.

SIMMONS, SHIRLEY; Queens Vocational HS; Brooklyn, NY; (Y); 106/365.

SIMMS, CARL; St Francis Xavier HS; New York, NY; (Y); ROTC; Var Bsktbl; Var Score Keeper; Hon Roll; NEDT Awd; Fordham U; Psychtrst.

SIMMS, ICEMA; George W Wingate HS; Brooklyn, NY; (Y); Church Yth Grp; Teachers Aide; Church Choir; Score Keeper; Vllybl; High Hon Roll; Hon Roll; Prfct Atten Awd; Comp Prog.

SIMOLO, HENRY; Mynderse Acad; Seneca Falls, NY; (S); 39/140; Yrbk Stf; Hon Roll; Cazenovia Coll; Comm Illus.

SIMON, DAVID; Auburn HS; Auburn, NY; (Y); 275/500; Church Yth Grp; SADD; Varsity Clb; Var L Ftbl; Var L Lcrss; Var L Swmmng; Hon Roll; SUNY Geneseo; Ed.

SIMON, DONNA; Evander Childs HS; Bronx, NY; (S); #3 In Class; Var Tennis; Capt Vllybl; Cit Awd; Gov Hon Prg Awd; Prfct Atten Awd; Pediatrtn.

SIMON, HOWARD; Sheepshead Bay HS; Brooklyn, NY; (Y); 32/429; Library Aide; Office Aide; Service Clb; Temple Yth Grp; School Musical; School Play; Tennis; Hon Roll; NHS; Prfct Atten Awd; CW Post; Flm.

SIMON, JEREMY; Yeshiva U HS For Boys; New York, NY; (Y); 3/108; Math Tm; Temple Yth Grp; Nwsp Stf; Hst Lit Mag; Rep Frsh Cls; Rep Jr Cls; Ntl Merit SF; St Schlr; Arista 84-86; Max Stern Scholar Yeshiva U 85; JR Acad NY Acad Sci 84-86; Med.

SIMON, MATTHEW; John Dewey HS; Brooklyn, NY; (Y); School Play; Variety Show; Bsktbl; Tennis; Regents Schlrshp 86; SUNY Albany; Law.

SIMON, NEAL J; George W Hewlett HS; N Woodmere, NY; (Y); 4/260; Math Tm; Pres Frsh Cls; Pres Soph Cls; Pres Jr Cls; VP Stu Cncl; Socr; Tennis; NHS; Ntl Merit SF; AATF Natl Frnch Cntst Levl II 6th Isld Wide & Levl III 3rd Isld Wide; AATSP Natl Spnsh Cntst; Frnch.

SIMON, PAMELA B; Bayside HS; Whitestone, NY; (Y); 10/658; Cmnty Wkr; Debate Tm; Temple Yth Grp; Band; Yrbk Stf; Rep Soph Cls; Trs Jr Cls; Rep Sr Cls; NHS; Ntl Merit SF; Prd Of Ynks Awd 85; Boston U; Econ.

SIMON, RICHARD; Roy C Ketcham HS; Fishkill, NY; (Y); 112/500; Temple Yth Grp; Band; High Hon Roll; Hon Roll; Prfct Atten Awd; Pres Schlr; Excllnc Amer Stds 85; 2nd Yr Awd 86; Whittier Coll.

SIMON, ROBERT P; Lackawanna SR HS; Lackawanna, NY; (Y); Art Clb; Capt Chess Clb; Pres JA; Spanish Clb; Crs Cntry; High Hon Roll; Hon Roll; VFW Awd; NY ST Regents Schrlshp 86; Math.

SIMON, TAMMY; Susquehanna Valley HS; Binghamton, NY; (Y); 32/187; Art Clb; Key Clb; Yrbk Stf; Stu Cncl; Trk; Hon Roll; Merchdsng.

SIMONCINI, TINAMARIE; St John Villa Acad; Staten Island, NY; (Y); 44/140; Cheerleading; St Johns U; Bus Mgmt.

SIMONDS, TIMMIE; Binghamton HS; Binghamton, NY; (Y); 34/450; Boy Scts; Pres Church Yth Grp; Debate Tm; English Clb; Hosp Aide; Key Clb; Band; Chorus; Church Choir; Jazz Band; Med.

SIMONE, HOLLY; Bay Shore HS; Brightwaters, NY; (Y); SADD; Yrbk Stf; Lit Mag; JV Fld Hcky; Gym; JV Capt Vllybl; High Hon Roll; Hon Roll; Outstndg Achvt Soc Sci 86; Soc Sci.

SIMONE, MICHAEL; Gates-Chili HS; Rochester, NY; (Y); Computer Clb; Ski Clb; Rep Frsh Cls; Var JV Swmmng; High Hon Roll; Syracues U; Comp Sci.

SIMONELLI, MARK; Aquinas Inst; Rochester, NY; (Y); 2/207; Pres VP Drama Clb; Math Clb; SADD; School Musical; School Play; Stage Crew; Nwsp Ed-Chief; Nwsp Stf; Yrbk Stf; Pres Stu Cncl; U Of Miami; Med.

SIMONS, DAN; Holland Central HS; Strykersville, NY; (Y); 1/128; AFS; Am Leg Boys St; Boy Scts; Band; Jazz Band; Stat Bsktbl; Var Trk; High Hon Roll; Trs NHS; Prfct Atten Awd; RIT; Nuclr Med Tech.

SIMONS, JAIME; Marlboro HS; Marlboro, NY; (Y); Boy Scts; Exploring; FFA; Radio Clb; Science Clb; Bsktbl; Tennis; Wt Lftg; Forestry.

SIMONS, KATHLEEN; Sacred Heart Acad; Westbury, NY; (S); 18/200; Church Yth Grp; Cmnty Wkr; Library Aide; Math Tm; SADD; Chorus; School Musical; Var Socr; NHS.

SIMPKINS, DEIRTRE; Dominican Commercial HS; Jamaica, NY; (Y); 87/265; Church Yth Grp; Drama Clb; Girl Scts; Church Choir; School Play; Cheerleading; Pres Acadmc Ftnss Awd 86; Natl Spch And Drama Awd 86; The City Clg; Law.

SIMPSON, DAWN; Greenville Central HS; Freehold, NY; (Y); 8/80; Church Yth Grp; Drama Clb; Trs Exploring; Pres Key Clb; Pres Latin Clb; Pres SADD; Sec Frsh Cls; Stat Score Keeper; Hon Roll; NHS; Bio.

SIMPSON, GAELLYN; Newark SR HS; Newark, NY; (Y); 37/200; German Clb; Letterman Clb; Spanish Clb; VP Varsity Clb; Var Capt Socr; Var L Trk; High Hon Roll; Hon Roll; Spanish NHS; Wegmans Schlrshp 86; Cazenovia Coll; Fshn Merch.

SIMPSON, HEATHER; Newark SR HS; Newark, NY; (Y); 4/200; Am Leg Aux Girls St; Church Yth Grp; Pres German Clb; Service Clb; Nwsp Stf; Yrbk Stf; Sec Trs Frsh Cls; Sec Trs Soph Cls; Var L Socr; Var Trk; Harvard Model Congress 86; German Hon Soc 85-86; Bio.

SIMPSON, JACQUELINE; Notre Dame Acad; Staten Island, NY; (Y); Dance Clb; Drama Clb; Teachers Aide; School Musical; School Play; Variety Show; Nwsp Stf; Yrbk Phtg; Yrbk Rptr; Yrbk Stf; Villanova; Brdcst Jrnlsm.

SIMPSON, JOAN; New Rochelle HS; New Rochelle, NY; (Y); Political Wkr; SADD; Teachers Aide; Chorus; Church Choir; School Musical; School Play; Stu Cncl; Bsktbl; Sftbl; Alpha Kappa Alpha Awd 85; PK; Nrsng.

SIMPSON, LISA MARIE; Cicero N Syracuse HS; Clay, NY; (S); 53/667; Hosp Aide; Color Guard; Mrchg Band; Powder Puff Ftbl; Hon Roll; NHS; 50 Hr Awd Volntr Wrk Syracuse VA Hosp 85; Maria Regina Coll; Bus Mgmt.

SIMPSON, MATTHEW; La Salle Military Acad; Stony Brook, NY; (S); 15/100; ROTC; Drm & Bgl; Nwsp Rptr; Rep Stu Cncl; Var L Ftbl; JV Lcrss; Var Capt Swmmng; Var L Trk; Hon Roll; All Leag Ftbl 85; Polit Sci.

SIMPSON, STACY; Oakfield-Alabama HS; Oakfield, NY; (Y); Art Clb; GAA; Library Aide; Ski Clb; Chorus; Capt Color Guard; Sec Soph Cls; Sec Rep Stu Cncl; Stat Bsktbl; Socr; Genesee CC; Frshn Merch.

SIMS, MELISSA DENISE; Grand Island HS; Gr Island, NY; (Y); Church Yth Grp; Cmnty Wkr; Hosp Aide; JA; Red Cross Aide; Teachers Aide; Church Choir; School Play; Stage Crew; Rep Stu Cncl; U Buffalo; Pediatrician.

SIMS, SCOTT; Avoca Central HS; Hornell, NY; (Y); 8/60; Computer Clb; French Clb; FBLA; Varsity Clb; Yrbk Bus Mgr; Yrbk Stf; Var Capt Bsktbl; Var L Trk; Cit Awd; Hon Roll; Pol Sci.

SINACORE, SUSANNE; Sacred Heart Acad; Stroudsburg, PA; (Y); Cmnty Wkr; Dance Clb; FNA; Hosp Aide; Library Aide; Math Clb; SADD; Chorus; Hon Roll; Jr NHS; E Stroudsburg U; Engrng.

SINAGUGLIA, STEPHEN; Bishop Kearney HS; Rochester, NY; (Y); 16/141; Church Yth Grp; Teachers Aide; Hon Roll; NHS; Pres Acdmc Ftns Awd 86; Monroe CC; Bus Adm.

SINCAVAGE, MARLA; Union-Endicott HS; Endicott, NY; (Y); Computer Clb; Drama Clb; French Clb; Key Clb; Mathletes; Color Guard; Drill Tm; Flag Corp; Mrchg Band; Orch.

SINCLAIR, ALYSON; Lawrence HS; Lawrence, NY; (Y); 20/414; Cmnty Wkr; Dance Clb; SADD; Temple Yth Grp; Sec Jr Cls; VP Sr Cls; Stu Cncl; Var Tennis; High Hon Roll; Jr NHS; Cornell Ntl Schlr Awd 86; Archon Hnr Soc Cert 86; Century III Ldrshp Cntst 2nd Pl 86; Cornell U; Comm.

SINDACO, SANDRA; Kings Park SR HS; Northport, NY; (Y); 108/393; Science Clb; Teachers Aide; Chorus; Sec Frsh Cls; Sec Soph Cls; Var Capt Jr Cls; Var Capt Trk; Cit Awd; Gld Key 86; Mrch Dimes Hlth Career Awd 86; U S Army Rsrv Natl Schlr Athl 86; Quinnipiac Coll; Phy Thrpy.

SINDONE, JENNIFER; Cicero-North Syracuse HS; N Syracuse, NY; (S); 58/667; Key Clb; Ski Clb; Var Capt Fld Hcky; JV Sftbl; Hon Roll; NHS.

SINDONI, LORI; Waverly JR-SR HS; Waverly, NY; (Y); 9/160; Pep Clb; Yrbk Phtg; Yrbk Stf; Rep Sr Cls; Rep Stu Cncl; Var Capt Cheerleading; Var L Sftbl; Hon Roll; NHS; Rotary Awd; Ithaca; Physcl Thrpy.

SINES, ROGER; Bainbridge-Guilford HS; Bainbridge, NY; (Y); Spanish Clb; Band; Mrchg Band; Orch; Trs Soph Cls; VP Jr Cls; Stu Cncl; Bsbl; Bsktbl; Ftbl; MVP JV Ftbl 84; Engineer.

SINFIELD, JOY; Warwick Valley HS; Warwick, NY; (Y); Drama Clb; 4-H; Band; Chorus; Concert Band; Mrchg Band; School Musical; School Play; Stage Crew; Symp Band; 4-H Capitol Day 86; 4-H NYC Home Ec Trip; LIU Southampton; Mar Sci.

SINGAL, AJAY; Newtown HS; Elmhurst, NY; (Y); 1/45; Chess Clb; Library Aide; Math Clb; High Hon Roll; Mu Alp Tht; Prfct Atten Awd; Bus Inst Awd 85 & 86; St Johns U; Elec Engrng.

SINGER, JONATHAN B; Ramaz Schl; Stamford, CT; (Y); Aud/Vis; Boy Scts; Computer Clb; Political Wkr; Temple Yth Grp; Stage Crew; Ed Yrbk Stf; Capt Trk.

SINGER, RACHEL; Paul D Schreiber HS; Pt Washington, NY; (Y); 5/408; SADD; Pres Temple Yth Grp; Chorus; Orch; School Musical; School Play; Var Trk; NHS; NYS Rgnts Schlrshp 86; Englsh Awd 86; Duke U; Bus Adm.

SINGH, LAJWANTI; Richmond Hill HS; Richmond Hill, NY; (Y); 29/316; Hon Roll; Prfct Atten Awd; Frgn Lang Hon Soc 85-86; Scl Stu Hon Rll 85-86; Engl Hon Roll 86; NY U; Ec.

SINGH, LEONARD; Erasmus Hall HS & The Acad Of The Arts; Brooklyn, NY; (Y); Intnl Clb; Math Tm; Science Clb; Yrbk Ed-Chief; Lit Mag; Bausch & Lomb Sci Awd; NHS; Prfct Atten Awd; Computer Clb; Library Aide; Erasmus Hl Sci Cont 1st Pl 85 & 86; 3rd Pl Cty Math Tm 86; MIT; Elec Engrng.

SINGH, NAVIN; Stuyvesant HS; Woodside, NY; (Y); Chess Clb; Pres Computer Clb; Math Tm; Political Wkr; Nwsp Rptr; NHS; St Schlr; Temple Yth Grp; School Musical; Cit Awd; Untd Fed Tchrs Schlrshp 86; Tp Prgrmmr Awd 84; Amer Lgn Awd 83; Brown U; Physcn.

SINGH, RAJANEE; Walton HS; Bronx, NY; (Y); Office Aide; Teachers Aide; Nwsp Stf; Yrbk Ed-Chief; Hon Roll; Jr NHS; NHS; Prfct Atten Awd; Spnsh I 84; Spnsh II 85; Typng 84; Mdl.

SINGH, SUBASH; Mount Vernon HS; Mount Vernon, NY; (Y); 13/550; FBLA; Library Aide; Math Clb; Office Aide; Teachers Aide; Yrbk Stf; Im Bsbl; Im Bsktbl; Cit Awd; High Hon Roll; Manhattan Coll Pres Awd 86; Manhattan Coll; Engrng.

SINGLE, RICHARD M; Massapequa HS; Massapequa, NY; (Y); 3/440; Mathletes; Band; JV Bsktbl; Var L Lcrss; JV Socr; High Hon Roll; Pres NHS; Ntl Merit Ltr; St Schlr; Church Yth Grp; NYS Regnts Schlrshp 86; H J Reilly & ROTC Schlrshps 86-87; Rensselaer Polytech Inst; M Eng.

SINGLETON, BELINDA; New Rochelle HS; New Rochelle, NY; (Y); Church Yth Grp; Cmnty Wkr; Dance Clb; FCA; Library Aide; PAVAS; SADD; Church Choir; School Musical; Btty Crckr Awd; Spcl Achvmnt Awd Engl 84; Awd Sci 84; Awd Cookng 84; Lehman Coll; Nrsng.

SINGLETON, TARA; HS Fashion Industrs; New York, NY; (Y); Dance Clb; Hosp Aide; Intnl Clb; Office Aide; Service Clb; Variety Show; Cheerleading; Coach Actv; Vllybl; Fashion Merchandising.

SINHA, SHILPI; Mercy HS; Center Moriches, NY; (Y); Cmnty Wkr; Math Tm; Yrbk Stf; Hon Roll; Mdl Rcgntn Prtcptng NYSSMA Sng Solo 83; Stony Brook; Med.

SINHA, VINCETA; The Harley Schl; Pittsford, NY; (Y); French Clb; Hosp Aide; Chorus; Nwsp Rptr; Var Cheerleading; French Hon Soc; High Hon Roll; Cncrs Nationale De Frncs 84-85; Ntl Ltn Exm Cum Laude, Magna Cum Laude 84-85; Chmpn Smmr Dnce Fstvl 86; Med.

SINICROPI, JOE; Amsterdam HS; Amsterdam, NY; (Y); 6th Pl-Bkkpg Cmptn Cobleskill 86; FMCC; Acctg.

SINICROPI, MICHAEL; Amsterdam HS; Amsterdam, NY; (S); 1/294; Varsity Clb; Yrbk Bus Mgr; Rep Frsh Cls; Rep Soph Cls; VP Jr Cls; VP Sr Cls; Bsbl; Bsktbl; Capt Ftbl; High Hon Roll; R P I Math, Sci & Engl Awds 83-84; Math.

SINIGAGLIA, NICHOLAS; Archbishop Molloy HS; Flushing, NY; (Y); Computer Clb; Intnl Clb; Pep Clb; Science Clb; Service Clb; Nwsp Stf; Im Bsktbl; Im Fld Hcky; Im Capt Sftbl; NHS; Acadmc Achvt Awd 84; Acctg.

SINK, JENNIFER; Royalton Hartland Central HS; Sumpter, SC; (Y); 46/131; Church Yth Grp; Cmnty Wkr; Drama Clb; Girl Scts; Hosp Aide; Office Aide; Teachers Aide; Hon Roll; Gregg Typng Awd 85; Bryant & Stratton Typng Cntst Awd 86; SC U; Bus Adm.

SINKO, A LAURA; The Harvey Schl; Irvington, NY; (Y); Church Yth Grp; Library Aide; Chorus; Church Choir; JV Var Bsktbl; JV Stat Socr; JV Var Sftbl; Hon Roll; St Schlr; Tchng Music In Schl; Carnegie-Mellon U; Music Compst.

SINNONA, JOSEPH; La Salle Acad; Brooklyn, NY; (S); Church Yth Grp; Library Aide; Office Aide; Band; Color Guard; School Play; Nwsp Phtg; Nwsp Rptr; Nwsp Stf; Lit Mag; Cmps Mnstry-Ltrgcl Spkr 84-86; NY U; Bus Adm.

SINNOTT, PAUL; Saugerties HS; Glasco, NY; (Y); Trs Soph Cls; Bsbl; Bsktbl; Bowling; Golf; Hon Roll; Ulster County CC; Acctg.

SINOPOLI, STEVEN; Nottingham HS; Syracuse, NY; (Y); 42/275; Exploring; Latin Clb; Hon Roll; NHS; Syracuse U; Accntnt.

SINRAM, SUZANNE; Bay Shore HS; Brightwaters, NY; (Y); Office Aide; JV Bsktbl; JV Sftbl; Hon Roll; Stony Brook U; Psych.

SINROD, ALYSIA L; Massapequa HS; Massapequa, NY; (Y); 18/440; French Clb; Key Clb; SADD; Acpl Chr; Variety Show; Var Trk; Hon Roll; NHS; Ntl Merit Ltr; Spanish Clb; Rgnts Schlrshp 86; Cornell U; Vet Med.

SINYAVICH, IGOR; Archibishop Molloy HS; Astoria, NY; (Y); 76/383; Chess Club 84-87.

SIPKINS, DOROTHY A; Carmel HS; Carmel, NY; (Y); 1/350; VP Leo Clb; Math Tm; Spanish Clb; Orch; Nwsp Rptr; Ed Lit Mag; High Hon Roll; NHS; Ntl Merit SF; Val; Pre-Med.

SIPLEY, DAVE; Jamesvilee Dewitt HS; Syracuse, NY; (Y); 18/244; Boy Scts; Pres German Clb; Hosp Aide; Model UN; Chorus; Swing Chorus; Yrbk Phtg; Var L Socr; High Hon Roll; NHS; Eagle Sct 84; Cornell U Book Awd Outstndng JR 86.

SIPOS, ZOE P; Frontier SR HS; Hamburg, NY; (Y); Pres Latin Clb; Office Aide; Pres Ski Clb; Trs Band; Mrchg Band; Trs Jr Cls; JV Var Cheerleading; Hon Roll; Math Hnrs 84-87; Actn Intrnshp Prog 86; Lwyr.

SIPPERLY, AMY; Academy Of The Holy Names; Loudonville, NY; (Y); Hosp Aide; Ski Clb; Stage Crew; Yrbk Stf; Rep Soph Cls; Rep Sr Cls; Rep Stu Cncl; Rossell Sage Clg; Ed.

SIPPLE, AUDRA; Delaware Valley Central HS; Mileses, NY; (S); 5/45; Quiz Bowl; Teachers Aide; Chorus; Pres Frsh Cls; Rep Soph Cls; Pres Jr Cls; Pres Sr Cls; Trs Stu Cncl; Cit Awd; High Hon Roll; SUNY; Elem Educ.

SIRICO, MICHAEL; Warwick Valley HS; Warwick, NY; (Y); Band; Concert Band; Mrchg Band; Var Capt Bsktbl; Var Capt Ftbl; Var Golf; Powder Puff Ftbl; JV Socr; Var Trk; JV Wrstlng.

SIRIGNANO, AMY; Hamson HS; Mamaroneck, NY; (Y); 58/215; Church Yth Grp; Debate Tm; VP French Clb; Intnl Clb; Ski Clb; Band; Concert Band; Jazz Band; Mrchg Band; School Play; Chase NBW Stu Ctznshp Awd 86; Mck Trl ST Fnlsts 85; Rtry Intl Stu Of Yr 86; U Of Miami; Music Indstry.

SIRIGNANO, JACQUELINE; The Mary Louis Acad; Richmond Hill, NY; (Y); Church Yth Grp; Cmnty Wkr; Dance Clb; Drama Clb; Exploring; GAA; Political Wkr; Pres Sr Cls; JV Vllybl; Hon Roll; Jewish Fndtn Ed Womn Schlrshp; St Johns U; Mktg.

SIRMANS, FRANKLIN; New Rochelle HS; New Rochelle, NY; (Y); Cmnty Wkr; Stu Cncl; Var Ice Hcky; Var Socr; Var Capt Tennis; Vrsty Tnns-Mst Prmsng Plyr 84-85; JV MVP Tnns 83-84; Georgetown.

SISK, STEVEN H; Greece Athena HS; Rochester, NY; (Y); 57/250; Chess Clb; Church Yth Grp; Drama Clb; Math Tm; Thesps; School Play; Stage Crew; Hon Roll; Regents Schlrshp 86; SUNY; Media.

SISKIND, MARNI J; Baldwin SR HS; Baldwin, NY; (Y); 27/476; Hosp Aide; Key Clb; High Hon Roll; Hon Roll; Cndy Strpr 100 Hr Pin 86; NY St Rgnts Schlrshp 86; Scl Stds Achvmnt Awd 83-85; U Of Rochester.

SISLEY, COLLEEN; Whitesboro SR HS; Whitesboro, NY; (Y); 12/354; SADD; Chorus; Yrbk Stf; High Hon Roll; Hon Roll; Trs Jr NHS; NHS; Variety Show; Stu Cncl; NYS Regents Schlrshp 86; AP Engl 86; Hnrs Engl, Scl Stds, Acclrtd Sci Awds 83-86; SUNY-STONY Brk.

SISON, MARIA L; St Francis Prep; Rosedale, NY; (S); 144/746; Ski Clb; Rep Soph Cls; Rep Jr Cls; Rep Stu Cncl; Var Trk; Var Wrstlng; Hon Roll; NHS; Ftbl; Im Sftbl; Optimate Soc 84-85; 8 Judo Comptn Awds.

SISSON, CHRISTIE; Victor Central HS; Macedon, NY; (Y); 4/228; Church Yth Grp; Varsity Clb; Rep Stu Cncl; JV Capt Bsktbl; JV Var Socr; JV Var Vllybl; High Hon Roll; NHS; Am Chem Soc Chem Achvt Awd 86; Sch Letter 85; Stu Bk Store Awd 86; Elec Engrng.

SISSON, KEN; Cassadaga Valley HS; Sinclairville, NY; (Y); 15/110; Pres Church Yth Grp; 4-H; Letterman Clb; Varsity Clb; Pres Frsh Cls; Bsktbl; Tennis; Vllybl; Hon Roll; Math & Sci.

SISSON, MICHAEL; Bainbridge-Guilford HS; Bainbridge, NY; (Y); 19/72; VP Church Yth Grp; French Clb; Band; Church Choir; Concert Band; Mrchg Band; Orch; High Hon Roll; Intrmdt Algbr Awd 86; Accntnt.

SISTO, LORRAINE; Carmel HS; Carmel, NY; (Y); Yrbk Stf; Trs Stu Cncl; Var Cheerleading; High Hon Roll; NHS; MVP Var Ftbl Chrldr 85-86; Bus Mgt.

SITTS, TRACY; Corinth Central HS; Corinth, NY; (Y); Drama Clb; Spanish Clb; SADD; Varsity Clb; School Play; Sec Soph Cls; Sec Jr Cls; Var Cheerleading; Var JV Sftbl; Spanish NHS.

SIU, LAI-MEI; Murry Bergtraum HS; New York, NY; (Y); Art Clb; Drama Clb; Girl Scts; Office Aide; Teachers Aide; Bsktbl; Gym; Vllybl; Wt Lftg; NHS; Hon Soc Awd/Schlrp 85; Hon Soc Awd 86; Cert Exc Accntg 85; Accntg.

SIU, SUK YEE; Norman Thomas HS; New York, NY; (S); 31/600; FBLA; Prfct Atten Awd; Fash Inst Tech; Fash Merch.

SIVERTSEN, JOSEPH; Hornell HS; N Hornell, NY; (Y); JV Socr; UCSB; Comp Engrng.

SIXT, CHERYL E; Horseheads HS; Horseheads, NY; (S); 10/380; Spanish Clb; SADD; Color Guard; Hon Roll; NHS; Ntl Merit SF; Mth.

SKEELS, CATILIN; John F Kennedy HS; Brewster, NY; (Y); 21/200; Church Yth Grp; Math Tm; Teachers Aide; Drm & Bgl; Drm Mjr(t); Mrchg Band; Nwsp Rptr; Crs Cntry; Stat Lcrss; Score Keeper; Acdmc Awd For Hgh Hnrs 82-86; Frnch Awd 85; Nrthestrn U; Comp Sci.

SKEEN, VALERIE; George W Wingate HS; Brooklyn, NY; (Y); Jr Arista 85 Avg 85; Coll Bnd Hnrs Scty 86; Sr Arista 89.54 Avg/Prncpls Lst 86; Cmptr Tech.

SKELLIE, TAMMY; Salem Washington Acad; E Greenwich, NY; (Y); Hosp Aide; Math Tm; SADD; Chorus; Yrbk Bus Mgr; Yrbk Phtg; Capt Bowling; Fld Hcky; Hon Roll; Rptr 4-H; WA Cnty Dairy Prncss 86-87; 3 Tm Hgh Avg Bwlg Clb 84-86; Rochester Isnt Of Tech; Spch.

SKELTON, KIRSTINA; Aquinas Inst; Webster, NY; (Y); 17/215; Drama Clb; VP French Clb; SADD; Chorus; School Musical; School Play; Nwsp Rptr; Nwsp Stf; High Hon Roll; Hon Roll; Marlow Schlrshp 83-84; Law.

SKERRITT, STEFANIE Y; Adlai Ewing Stevenson HS; Bronx, NY; (Y); 40/467; Church Yth Grp; Cmnty Wkr; JA; Teachers Aide; Church Choir; NHS; Prfct Atten Awd; Prtstnt Tchrs Assoc Schlrshp 86; Engl Awd 82-83; Regents Schlrshp 86; Hunter Coll; Elem Ed.

SKERRY, MAURA K; St Johns Acad; Plattsburgh, NY; (Y); 7/38; Cmnty Wkr; Latin Clb; SADD; Var JV Cheerleading; Co-Capt Swmmng; High Hon Roll; NYS Regents Scholar 86; Offcrs Clb Scholar 86; SUNY Plattsburgh; Bus Adm.

SKINKIS, INTA A; Bayside HS; Bayside, NY; (Y); 2/658; Church Yth Grp; Math Tm; Yrbk Ed-Chief; Capt Var Vllybl; High Hon Roll; NHS; Sal; NY ST Regents Schlrshp 86; Georgetown U; Intl Rltns.

SKINNER, KARI ANNE E; Our Lady Of Mercy HS; Rochester, NY; (Y); 59/172; Church Yth Grp; Ski Clb; SADD; Teachers Aide; Y-Teens; Stage Crew; Yrbk Stf; Tch 3rd Grd Relgn Ed 84-86; Intl Food Clb 84-85; Mktg.

SKINNER, KERRY; Dominican Commercial HS; Woodhaven, NY; (S); Dance Clb; NHS; St Johns.

SKINNER, STACEY; Minisink Valley HS; Slate Hill, NY; (Y); Drama Clb; Acpl Chr; Band; Chorus; Concert Band; Jazz Band; Mrchg Band; Orch; School Play; High Hon Roll; NYS Schl Music Assn-Duet-Lvl 4-Outstndng 84-85; NYSSMA-SOLO Lvl 5-Mdl 85-86.

SKINNER, WENDY; Mynderse Acad; Seneca Falls, NY; (S); 30/141; Var L Socr; High Hon Roll; Hon Roll; Math.

SKLENAR, JOHN A; N Rose-Wolcott Central Schl; N Rose, NY; (Y); Am Leg Boys St; VP Ski Clb; Varsity Clb; Lcrss; Var L Socr; High Hon Roll; Pres Schlr; NY ST Rgnst Schlrshp 85-86; US Presdntl Acadmc Ftns 85-86; Tnns MVP, Ltr 84-86; RIT Rochester NY; Comp Engrng.

SKOBEL, SHARI; Walter Paras HS; Peekskill, NY; (Y); Cmnty Wkr; Hosp Aide; Ski Clb; SADD; Rep Jr Cls; Rep Stu Cncl; Var L Cheerleading; Hon Roll; 1st Pl In Hosp Pstr Cntst 86; Art Wrk Shwn In Lcl Exibit 85-86; Grphc Desgn.

SKOLNIK, URSULA N; Plainedge HS; Massapequa, NY; (Y); 17/304; Hosp Aide; Latin Clb; Mathletes; VP Temple Yth Grp; School Musical; Ed Lit Mag; High Hon Roll; NHS; Spanish NHS; 1st Pl Winner Schl, Cnty, & ST Level & Natl 3rd Pl Winner Natl Hist Day Comptn 84; Medcl Club Pres; Adelphi U; Pre-Med.

SKOP, ELISA; Frontier Central HS; Hamburg, NY; (Y); 25/500; Art Clb; French Clb; Latin Clb; Pep Clb; Band; School Play; Off Stu Cncl; High Hon Roll; Hon Roll; NHS; Mensa Mbrshp Pin 85; Sci Fair-Gold Rbbn Cnty Cmptn 84; RIT; Bio.

SKORA, THOMAS; Frontier Central HS; Blasdell, NY; (Y); Latin Clb; Var L Bowling; Var L Golf; High Hon Roll; Hon Roll; NHS; Prfct Atten Awd; 2nd Pl Golf Trnmnt 84; Clarkson Coll; Engr.

SKOUNTZOS, EMMANUEL; Fort Hamilton HS; Brooklyn, NY; (Y); 85/536; Civil Engrng.

SKOWRONEK, TERRY; Amsterdam HS; Amsterdam, NY; (Y); Swmmng; Timer; Trk; High Hon Roll; Recorder Carrier Of Yr 84; Bio.

SKOWRONSKI, ELIZABETH; Mt Mercy Acad; Blasdell, NY; (Y); JCL; Science Clb; Ski Clb; Hon Roll; Canisius Coll; Bio.

SKRETNY, AMY; Nardin Acad; S Cheektowaga, NY; (S); Ski Clb; Chorus; Orch; School Musical; Lit Mag; Var Tennis; NHS; Church Yth Grp; Office Aide; Church Choir; 2nd Pl Dbls Team In Tennis 84, 1st Pl 85; U Of Buffalo Hnrs Choir 85; Music.

SKROCKI, ROBIN; Onondaga Central HS; Syracuse, NY; (S); 7/72; FBLA; Spanish Clb; Varsity Clb; School Play; Yrbk Ed-Chief; VP Sr Cls; Rep Stu Cncl; JV Bsktbl; Var Capt Cheerleading; Var Tennis; St John Fisher Coll; Law.

SKULICZ, SHARON; Mt St Marys Acad; Amherst, NY; (Y); Dance Clb; Hosp Aide; Pep Clb; PAVAS; Red Cross Aide; School Musical; Swing Chorus; Yrbk Stf; Rep Frsh Cls; Rep Soph Cls; Dance Awd St Joes Swng Chrs 86; Psych.

SKUPINSKY, GREG; Hicksville HS; Hicksville, NY; (Y); Bsbl; Bsktbl; Ftbl.

SKURCENSKI, KRISTEN; Pine Valley Central HS; Cherry Creek, NY; (S); Am Leg Aux Girls St; Sec Pres 4-H; Ski Clb; Chorus; Sec Stu Cncl; Trk; 4-H Awd; Hon Roll; Pres NHS; Ntl Merit Ltr; Math.

SLADER, RICH; Archbishop Stepinac HS; Ossining, NY; (Y); 70/180; Ski Clb; VICA; Bsbl; Bsktbl; Hon Roll; Syracuse; Bus.

SLAGER, LISA KIM; Naples Central HS; Naples, NY; (Y); 4-H; French Clb; GAA; Spanish Clb; Chorus; Nwsp Rptr; Bsktbl; Socr; Sftbl; Vllybl; Grls All Star Bsktbl 86; Grls All Star Soccr 85-86; St Bonaventure U; Cmmnctns.

SLAGLE, JENNIFER; Williamsville South HS; Williamsville, NY; (Y); AFS; Chorus; Var L Trk; Hon Roll; Bus.

SLAKA, KATHY; Sewanhaka HS; Franklin Sq, NY; (Y); 14/300; French Clb; GAA; Service Clb; Varsity Clb; Variety Show; Var Bsktbl; Var Capt Socr; Var Capt Sftbl; French Hon Soc; Hon Roll; All Cnty Sftbl 84-86; Boston U; Pre-Med.

SLANE, ROBIN; Northport HS; E Northport, NY; (Y); 240/605; Church Yth Grp; Cmnty Wkr; Debate Tm; Political Wkr; Band; Chorus; Church Choir; Concert Band; Mrchg Band; NHS; Debt Rnnr Up Law Day At Happaugue Ct 85; Natl Hnr Socty 85; CW Post Schlrshp 85; SUNY Stonybrook; Engl Lit Jrnl.

SLAPELIS, LINDA; Bishop Kearney HS; Webster, NY; (Y); JA; Letterman Clb; Var JV Cheerleading; High Hon Roll; Hon Roll; ST U Of Fredonia; Chmstry.

SLASKI, ANNE-CHRISTINE; Scotia-Glenville HS; Scotia, NY; (Y); Church Yth Grp; Cmnty Wkr; Key Clb; Red Cross Aide; Spanish Clb; Gym; Cit Awd; High Hon Roll; Hon Roll; Pltcl Sci.

SLATER, JOHN; Lindenhurst HS; Lindenhurst, NY; (Y); 6/578; Ski Clb; Varsity Clb; JV Bsbl; Var Crs Cntry; Var Trk; Bausch & Lomb Sci Awd; High Hon Roll; Jr NHS; Surgn.

SLATER, KRISTEN; Frontier HS; Hamburg, NY; (Y); 4-H; Girl Scts; Ski Clb; Chorus; Im Sftbl; Im Swmmng; Im Vllybl; 4-H Awd; Hon Roll; NHS; Vet.

SLATER, TAMI; Greece Olympia HS; Rochester, NY; (Y); Sec DECA; Yrbk Stf; Rep Frsh Cls; Rep Soph Cls; Rep Jr Cls; Rep Sr Cls; Rep Stu Cncl; Im Vllybl; Hon Roll; Local Comptns Distrbtv Educ Clbs Of Amer; Oswego ST; Mrktn.

SLATER, TAMMY; Sandy Creek Central HS; Sandy Creek, NY; (S); 5/98; Sec Drama Clb; JCL; Band; Chorus; Mrchg Band; School Musical; Var Socr; JV Var Vllybl; Hon Roll; Trs NHS; Regents Schlrshp 86; Cum Laude Latin Awd 83; Utica Coll Of Syracuse U; Med.

SLATTER, MARK; Park West HS; Atlanta, GA; (Y); Cmnty Wkr; Office Aide; Band; Concert Band; School Play; Stu Cncl; Hon Roll; Atten Awd, Excel Pwr Mech Awd, Small Engine Tech 83; GA ST U; Law.

SLATTERY, CAROL A; S H Calhoun HS; Merrick, NY; (Y); 12/313; Hst Key Clb; Sec Mathletes; Sec Soph Cls; Hon Roll; NHS; Vlntr Of Mnth 83; Regnts Schlrshp 86; U Of Rochester; Math.

SLAVKIN, DEBORAH; Bay Shore HS; Bay Shore, NY; (Y); 17/376; Sec Intnl Clb; Pres Temple Yth Grp; Band; Ed Nwsp Sprt Ed; Rep Stu Cncl; Var L Tennis; High Hon Roll; NHS; Concert Band; Mrchg Band; Ribbn Excllnce Sci Proj Long Isl Congrss 84; E VP LIFTY 86-87; NYSSMA ST; Confirmtn Awd 85.

SLAWINSKI, JENNIFER; Hutchinson Central Technical HS; Buffalo, NY; (Y); Nwsp Rptr; Nwsp Stf; Rep Jr Cls; Sec Stu Cncl; Socr; Hon Roll; SUNY; Bus.

SLEEZER, LUCINDA; James-Dewitt HS; Dewitt, NY; (Y); 39/206; Church Yth Grp; Cmnty Wkr; Key Clb; Model UN; Ski Clb; Chorus; Stage Crew; High Hon Roll; Hon Roll; NHS; Archtctr.

SLEPACK, MAYA; La Guardia HS Of Music And Art; Brooklyn, NY; (Y); Dance Clb; JA; Yrbk Phtg; Yrbk Stf; Hon Roll; NHS; Martha Graham Dance Ctr Teen-Age Schlrshp 85-86; Regents Schlrshp 86; NYU; Neuro Sci.

SLEVIN, UNA; Sacred Heart Acad; Garden City, NY; (S); 60/182; Pep Clb; School Play; Stage Crew; Yrbk Phtg; Rep Jr Cls; VP Stu Cncl; Cheerleading; Capt Swmmng; Hon Roll; NHS; Hstry.

SLEZAK, REBECCA A; Amsterdam HS; Amsterdam, NY; (Y); 8/300; Church Yth Grp; Varsity Clb; Yrbk Ed-Chief; Socr; High Hon Roll; NHS; Rensslr Polytech Inst; Pre-Med.

SLIKER, LAURA; York Central HS; Leicester, NY; (Y); 15/96; Art Clb; Sec 4-H; Sec Key Clb; Office Aide; Scholastic Bowl; Sec Band; Concert Band; Mrchg Band; School Play; Pres Stage Crew; Morrisville Ag; Equst Scsi.

SLILATY, ANN-MARIE; Binghamton HS; Binghamton, NY; (Y); 60/456; Church Yth Grp; Hon Roll; Prfct Atten Awd; Broome CC; Trvl.

SLILATY, ELVEER; Binghamton HS; Binghamton, NY; (Y); Church Yth Grp; Band; Concert Band; Jazz Band; Mrchg Band; Rep Stu Cncl; Timer; JV Vllybl; Hon Roll.

SLINGERLAND, JANET; Earl L Vandermeulen HS; Pt Jefferson, NY; (Y); 1/333; Leo Clb; Acpl Chr; Jazz Band; Yrbk Stf; Hon Roll; NHS; Drama Clb; Mathletes; Band; Outstndng 9th Grd Stu Awd 84; 3rd Pl Sfflk Cnty AATSP Spnsh Cntst 85acdmc All Amer Schlr Prog 86; Engr.

SLIVA, KAREN ANN; Fairport HS; Victor, NY; (Y); Intnl Clb; Varsity Clb; Nwsp Phtg; Nwsp Rptr; Nwsp Stf; JV Capt Fld Hcky; Ftr Edtr Of Nwspr 85-86; News Edtr JR Edtn Of Nwspr 85; Merit Roll 85-86; ST U Of NY Frdnia; Comm.

SLIVA, RENEE; Nyack HS; Valley Cottage, NY; (Y); 10/287; Math Tm; Spanish Clb; Band; Variety Show; Rep Frsh Cls; JV Var Socr; JV Var Trk; High Hon Roll; NHS; Spanish NHS; Natl Sci Olympd Chem 85; Hnrary Sci Cert Spn Hnr Soc 86; U VA; Sci.

SLOAN, TRACY; Depew HS; Depew, NY; (Y); French Clb; GAA; Girl Scts; Hon Roll; Jr NHS; Buffalo ST; Elem Ed.

SLOANE, CAROLANN; Bishop Kearney HS; Brooklyn, NY; (Y); 22/338; Hon Roll; NYS Rgnts Schlrshp 86-87; Trstee Schlrshp NY U 86-87; NY U; Educ.

SLOBOD, MICHELE; Middletown HS; Middletown, NY; (Y); Math Tm; Political Wkr; SADD; Trs Temple Yth Grp; Yrbk Stf; Rep Jr Cls; Sec Stu Cncl; JV Socr; High Hon Roll; Hon Roll; Law.

SLOCUM, CHRISTY; G Ray Bodley HS; Fulton, NY; (Y); German Clb; Capt Color Guard; Capt Flag Corp; Mrchg Band; Rep Stu Cncl; Capt Twrlr; Hon Roll; Prfct Atten Awd; Bst Mrchr Mrchg Band 85; Colrgrd Awd Bst Plyr 85; Perf Attndnc Awd Colrgrd 84-85; Elem Ed.

SLOCUM, KATHRYN ANN; Cazenovia HS; New Woodstock, NY; (Y); 10/150; Am Leg Aux Girls St; Church Yth Grp; Capt Var Sftbl; Hon Roll; NHS; Regents Schlrshp 86; Ithaca Coll; Phys Ther.

SLOCUM, RANDY; Bishop Scully HS; Amsterdam, NY; (Y); Var Ftbl; Hon Roll; Bst Offnsv Plyr-Vrsty Ftbl 85-86; SUNY Brockport; Bus Adm.

SLOMOVITZ, LAUREL; Bethpage HS; Plainview, NY; (Y); 45/306; Drama Clb; FBLA; PAVAS; Spanish Clb; Thesps; School Musical; School Play; Cheerleading; High Hon Roll; Masquers Guild 83-86; Italian Soc 83-86; Dance Capt Showstoppers 83-86; Actng.

SLOWIK, PAUL THOMAS; Lancaster Central HS; Lancaster, NY; (S); Boy Scts; Trs DECA; VP JA; Pep Clb; JV Ftbl; Hon Roll; Eagle Scout Awd 82; Boy Scout Of Yr Awd 84; Ad Altari Dei 85; Air Force; Police Offcr.

SLUCE, SALLY; Alden HS; Alden, NY; (Y); 44/206; French Clb; JA; SADD; Varsity Clb; Ed Yrbk Stf; Var JV Bsktbl; L Var Trk; Var L Vllybl; Kiwanis Awd; Pres Schlr; Alden Tchrs Assoc Awd 86; U Of Buffalo; Math.

SLUCHAN, ANDREA B; The Chapin Schl; New York, NY; (Y); Sec Art Clb; JCL; Latin Clb; NFL; Speech Tm; SADD; Im Bsktbl; Var Sftbl; Comm.

SLUSSER, RICHARD; Odessa-Montour Central Schl; Montour Falls, NY; (Y); Varsity Clb; Var Bsktbl; Var Ftbl; Var Trk; Hon Roll; Engrng.

SLUTZ, DENISE; Canarsie HS; Brooklyn, NY; (Y); St Johns U; Sci.

SLY, CHRISTINE; Cicero-North Syracuse HS; Clay, NY; (S); 12/667; Math Tm; Ski Clb; Band; Concert Band; Mrchg Band; Orch; Symp Band; Hon Roll; NHS; Bio.

SLY, SEAN; Mc Graw Central JR SR HS; Mcgraw, NY; (Y); 3/39; Ski Clb; VP Varsity Clb; Rep Stu Cncl; Var L Bsbl; Var L Socr; High Hon Roll; Kiwanis Awd; NHS; Boy Scts; Church Yth Grp; Schlr Athlete Awd 86; Stu Of Mnth 85-86; Rensslr Plytchnc Inst; Engrg.

SMALKIN, ERIC N; Patchogue-Medford HS; Patchogue, NY; (Y); Debate Tm; Latin Clb; Library Aide; Lit Mag; High Hon Roll; Hon Roll; NHS; NY ST Rgnts Schlrshp 86; Washington Sq U Coll Schlrshp 86; NY U; Phlsphy.

SMALL, CURTIS; Central Islip SR HS; Central Islip, NY; (Y); SADD; Band; Concert Band; Var Ftbl; TEMPO Music Awd 86; Hofstra; Acctng.

SMALL, IRMA; John Jay HS; Brooklyn, NY; (Y); Library Aide; PAVAS; Variety Show; Hon Roll; Fshn Clb Awd 85-86; Physcl Thrpy.

SMALL, LORALEE; Massena Central HS; Massena, NY; (Y); Hosp Aide; Mgr(s); Var Capt Socr; Var Sftbl; Var Trk; High Hon Roll; Hon Roll; Var Vllybl; St Elizabeths; Nrsg.

SMALL, MAXINE MARGARET; Grace Dodge Voc HS; Bronx, NY; (Y); Pres Church Yth Grp; Cmnty Wkr; Trs FBLA; Girl Scts; Chorus; Church Choir; Var Sftbl; Hon Roll; Prfct Atten Awd; Art Awd Ntl Art Museum 84; SC U; Law.

SMALLS, DARIAN; De Witt Clinton HS; New York, NY; (Y); Boys Clb Am; Cmnty Wkr; Teachers Aide; Varsity Clb; Chorus; School Musical; School Play; Bsktbl; Diving; Gym; Good Attndc 83; Engrg.

SMALLS, SHEILA; Fashion Industries HS; Bronx, NY; (Y); 9/324; Band; Chorus; High Hon Roll; Prfct Atten Awd; Bus Admin.

SMALLWOOD, THERESA; Walton HS; Bronx, NY; (Y); Trs Church Yth Grp; Debate Tm; Office Aide; Pres SADD; Chorus; Church Choir; Rep Frsh Cls; Rep Stu Cncl; Cit Awd; Prfct Atten Awd; Penn ST U; Mrktng Dir.

SMARSCH, SANDRA; Port Richmond HS; Staten Island, NY; (Y); Var Bsktbl; Var Sftbl.

SMART, TRACEY; Newark Valley HS; Berkshire, NY; (Y); 6/114; Sec Church Yth Grp; Mgr Drama Clb; Ski Clb; Varsity Clb; Yrbk Stf; VP Stu Cncl; Capt Fld Hcky; Var Sftbl; High Hon Roll; VP NHS; Schlrshp Wnnr Salute Yth 85; 1st Tm IAC Leag & Tioga Co Fldhcky All Stars 85; Hmcmng Queen 85; Princeton; Comp Sci.

SMEAL, TROY A; Lewiston Porter HS; Lewiston, NY; (Y); 1/238; Am Leg Boys St; French Clb; JA; Pres Sr Cls; VP NHS; Ntl Merit SF; Val; Wash Crossing Fndtn-Hon Mntn 86; Senate Yth Pgm; Princeton U; Pol Sci.

SMEDLEY, PAMELA; Bainbridge-Guilford HS; Bainbridge, NY; (Y); 21/70; 4-H; Spanish Clb; Band; Cheerleading; Vllybl; 4-H Awd; High Hon Roll; Hon Roll; Church Yth Grp; Hosp Aide; Sherwood Boehlert Mdl Merit Awd 86; Pres Acadmc Ftnss Awd 86; Delhi Ag & Tech Clg; Bus Adm.

SMEETS, SYNNOVE; Emma HS; The Netherlands, NY; (Y); Sr Cls; Tennis; U Utrecht Neatherlands; Vet Med.

SMELTER, STACEY; Haldane Central Schl; Cold Spring, NY; (S); 2/55; Pres AFS; Drama Clb; Ski Clb; SADD; School Play; Nwsp Ed-Chief; Lit Mag; Rep Stu Cncl; High Hon Roll; RPI Math & Sci 85; Genetic Rsrch.

SMERKA, SUSAN; Lackawanna SR HS; Lackawanna, NY; (Y); GAA; Political Wkr; Spanish Clb; Sec Jr Cls; VP Sr Cls; Rep Stu Cncl; Var JV Sftbl; High Hon Roll; NHS; Boys Assn Sftbl Awd 85; SUNY Buffalo; Elec Engrng.

SMESTER, RUBEN; Greater New York Acad; Mt Sinia, NY; (S); 2/34; Im Bsktbl; Im Vllybl; Dnfth Awd; Hon Roll; NHS; Prfct Atten Awd; Stny Brk U; Bus Mngmnt.

SMITH, AINSWORTH; Hempstead HS; Hempstead, NY; (S); Boy Scts; FBLA; High Hon Roll; Hon Roll; NHS; Martin Luther King Awd; Hempsted H S Cert Of Awd; Emry Riddle Aero U; Aircrft Eng.

SMITH, ALISON; Our Lady Of Mercy HS; Rocchester, NY; (Y); School Musical; School Play; Yrbk Phtg; Lit Mag; Hon Roll; Roch Pub Lib JR Lit Awds Lttr Of Cmmndtn 85; HS May Court 86; Outstndg Awd European Culture Hnrs 85; Engl.

SMITH, AMANDA M; Richfield Springs Central HS; Richfield Springs, NY; (Y); Am Leg Aux Girls St; GAA; Chorus; Concert Band; Jazz Band; Mrchg Band; Swing Chorus; Rep Stu Cncl; High Hon Roll; NHS.

SMITH, ANDREW; St Marys HS; Lancaster, NY; (Y); Science Clb; JV Ftbl; JV Socr; Im Trk; Hon Roll; U Of Buffalo; Chem.

SMITH, ANGELA; Newburgh Free Acad; Newburgh, NY; (Y); Church Yth Grp; Library Aide; Pep Clb; SADD; Varsity Clb; Chorus; Pep Band; Capt Bsktbl; Cheerleading; JC Awd; Wrd Proc.

SMITH, BETH A; Letchworth Central Schl; Portageville, NY; (Y); Varsity Clb; Yrbk Ed-Chief; Yrbk Rptr; Sec Soph Cls; Sec Jr Cls; Pres Sr Cls; Pres Stu Cncl; Var Bsktbl; Var Socr; Hon Roll; NYS Rgnts Schlrshp 86; Houghton Coll; Sci Tchr.

SMITH, BETH ANN; Grand Island HS; Grand Island, NY; (Y); Drama Clb; Chorus; School Musical; Hon Roll; Broadcasting.

SMITH, BRENDA; Arkport Central Schl; Arkport, NY; (Y); 10/48; Ski Clb; Drill Tm; School Musical; School Play; Yrbk Rptr; Yrbk Sprt Ed; Yrbk Stf; Rep Soph Cls; Sec Stu Cncl; Cheerleading; Lgl Scrtrl.

SMITH, BRENDA; Guilderland HS; Schenectady, NY; (Y); 116/370; Letterman Clb; Varsity Clb; JV Bsktbl; Coach Actv; Score Keeper; Var L Sftbl; Hon Roll; U S FL; Marine Bio.

SMITH, CAROLINE WOODBRIDGE; Seton Catholic Central HS; Binghamton, NY; (Y); Hosp Aide; Key Clb; Ed Yrbk Ed-Chief; Rep Stu Cncl; Var Tennis; Hon Roll; Cmnty Wkr; French Clb; Ski Clb; Varsity Clb; Seton Schlr Awd 85; Rgnts Schlrshp 86; Irish Essay Cntst 2nd Pl 86; Emory U; Engl.

SMITH, CAROLYN; Hempstead HS; Hempstead, NY; (S); Cmnty Wkr; Pres FBLA; Var Badmtn; Im Tennis; High Hon Roll; NHS; Risg Star Awd Tupprwr 85; Cet Of Exclnc 85; Berkeley Schl Awd 86; Columbia; Comp Sci.

SMITH, CAROLYN; Roy C Ketcham HS; Poughkeepsie, NY; (Y); 176/500; Church Yth Grp; Office Aide; High Hon Roll; Hon Roll; Ntl Merit Ltr; SUNY New Paltz.

SMITH, CASSANDRA; Clara Barton HS; Brooklyn, NY; (Y); Church Yth Grp; Church Choir; Hon Roll; Sec Jr NHS; Josiah Macy Pre-Medcn Hnr Pgm 83-86; Cty Coll Bridge-To-Mdcn Pgm 86; Pre-Med.

SMITH, CHARLES E; Sachem HS; Holtsville, NY; (Y); 83/1351; Boy Scts; Math Tm; Radio Clb; Cit Awd; German Clb; Science Clb; SADD; Lit Mag; Rep Stu Cncl; Im Vllybl; Pope Piux XII Boy Sct Awd 83; Extra Ord Mnstr 86; Space Sci.

SMITH, CHERIE L; Greece Athena HS; Rochester, NY; (Y); 3/264; VP Pres DECA; Ski Clb; Rep Varsity Clb; Symp Band; Sec Frsh Cls; VP Soph Cls; VP Pres Stu Cncl; JV Var Socr; Var Capt Vllybl; NHS; Prncpls Awd Athl Schlr 86; Acad All Amer 83-84; Cornell U; Engr.

SMITH, CHERYL; High Schl Of Art & Design; Bronx, NY; (Y); 61/406; FTA; Pres Intnl Clb; Office Aide; Hon Roll; NCTE Awd; NHS; Prfct Atten Awd; Natl Art Hnr Soc Pres 85-86; U Of S CA; Motn Pict Prod.

SMITH, CHRISTINE; Rivearhead HS; Riverhead, NY; (Y); 49/223; Sec Key Clb; Aspring Toward Excllnt 85; Key Clubber Of Yr 84; Majoretts Catp 85-86; Gruman Data Systems Inst.

SMITH, CHRISTINE; Seton Catholic Central HS; Binghamton, NY; (Y); Church Yth Grp; Key Clb; Stu Cncl; Cheerleading; Paralgl.

SMITH, CHRISTINE M; Newfane SR HS; Lockport, NY; (Y); AFS; Drama Clb; Girl Scts; Band; Church Choir; School Musical; Stage Crew; NYS Regnts Schlrshp 86-87; Engl.

SMITH, CHRISTOPHER F; New Hyde Park Memorial HS; New Hyde Pk, NY; (Y); Am Leg Boys St; Boy Scts; Church Yth Grp; Drama Clb; Acpl Chr; Chorus; Church Choir; School Musical; School Play; Variety Show; Fordman U; Law.

SMITH, CHRISTOPHER S; Pine Plains Central HS; Ancram, NY; (Y); 5/98; Church Yth Grp; Honor Key 86; Acad Excllnc 86; Spnsh Awd 86; St John Fisher Coll.

SMITH, COLIN KEITH; HS For The Humaniti; Burnsville, NC; (Y); Aud/Vis; Dance Clb; Chorus; School Musical; Stage Crew; Rep Stu Cncl; Var L Socr; L Vllybl; Hon Roll; Lit Mag; Clerk, Stu Activities Comm 84-85; 4th Pl Dist ST OH Chem Exam, 11th ST 85; Midwstrn Assn Frnch 84; UNC Charlotte.

SMITH, CYNTHIA; Jamestown HS; Jamestown, NY; (Y); 57/396; Trs Church Yth Grp; Spanish Clb; Stu Cncl; JV Var Bsktbl; Var Crs Cntry; Var Capt High Hon Roll; Hon Roll; Jr NHS; Prfct Atten Awd; Donna Mick Incntv Awd 86; Ntl Schlr Athltc Awd 86; Grl Athlt Of Yr 86; SUNY Bnghmptn; Acctng.

SMITH, CYNTHIA; Onteora Central HS; Olivebridge, NY; (Y); 28/175; Trk; Hon Roll; 1st Pl OCS Sci Olympics 83 & 84.

SMITH, DAMIAN; Monticello HS; Monticello, NY; (Y); Trs Key Clb; Chorus; Yrbk Stf; Trs Frsh Cls; Trs Soph Cls; Trs Jr Cls; Trs Sr Cls; Stu Cncl; Vllybl; High Hon Roll; Ithaca; Photogrphy.

SMITH, DANIEL; Eden Central HS; Eden, NY; (Y); FFA; High Hon Roll; Hon Roll; Prfct Atten Awd.

SMITH, DANIELLE; St Marys Girls HS; Bayside, NY; (Y); Civic Clb; Ski Clb; Stage Crew; Hnrs Frnch & Engl; Bus Mgmt.

SMITH, DARCY; Berlin Central HS; Berlin, NY; (Y); 16/82; GAA; Chorus; Nwsp Stf; Yrbk Phtg; Lit Mag; VP Stu Cncl; Var Socr; Var Sftbl; High Hon Roll; Hon Roll; Cert Merit 86; Cntrl Hudson Vly Leag-Hnrbl Mntn 84-85; US Army; Phy Thrpy.

SMITH, DARLENE M; Oneill JR SR HS; Walton, NY; (Y); 2/108; Drama Clb; Model UN; Varsity Clb; Chorus; Mrchg Band; Nwsp Stf; Yrbk Stf; Jr NHS; Sal; AFS; Rgnts Schlrshp; Keuka Coll; Elem Ed.

SMITH, DAVID; New Berlin Central HS; New Berlin, NY; (Y); Boy Scts; French Clb; Varsity Clb; School Play; Stu Cncl; Bsbl; Bsktbl; Ftbl; Jr NHS.

SMITH, DAVID; Pelham Memorial HS; Pelham, NY; (Y); Aud/Vis; Chess Clb; Math Tm; Radio Clb; SADD; Hon Roll; NHS; Spanish NHS; Vlntr Svcs Audo Vsul Dpt 83; Wstchstr Intrschlstc Math Leag 86.

SMITH, DAVID M; Whitesboro HS; Marcy, NY; (Y); 30/365; Pres Church Yth Grp; Model UN; SADD; Varsity Clb; Orch; Ed Lit Mag; Var Golf; Hon Roll; Opt Clb Awd; Suny At Albany; Russian Lang.

SMITH, DEAN; Argyle Central HS; Argyle, NY; (Y); Ski Clb; Varsity Clb; Yrbk Stf; JV Var Bsbl; JV Bsktbl; JV Var Socr; Bus Admin.

SMITH, DEBORAH; Hutchenson Central Technical HS; Buffalo, NY; (Y); Band; Variety Show; Rep Frsh Cls; Sftbl; Hon Roll; Jr NHS; Buffalo ST.

SMITH, DEBRA; Hugh C Williams HS; Canton, NY; (Y); Sec Spanish Clb; Yrbk Stf; Trk; 2nd Tm All Nrthrn Indoor Trk 85; 1st Pl Adirondack Regn Empire ST Games 84; 7th Pl NY ST Empire 84; Plattsburge ST U; Acctng.

SMITH, DENISE; Midlakes HS; Seneca Castle, NY; (Y); 10/145; Am Leg Aux Girls St; VP Drama Clb; Model UN; Spanish Clb; Stage Crew; Yrbk Ed-Chief; Yrbk Stf; Im Powder Puff Ftbl; High Hon Roll; Hon Roll; Indstrl Engr.

SMITH, DENNIS; Smithtown East HS; Nesconset, NY; (Y); Letterman Clb; Ski Clb; Hon Roll; JV Bsbl; JV Var Ftbl; Bus Adm.

SMITH, DIANNE; Stockbridge Valley Central Schl; Munnsville, NY; (S); 1/45; GAA; Mathletes; Math Clb; Science Clb; Spanish Clb; SADD; Nwsp Rptr; Yrbk Stf; JV Var Socr; Var Sftbl; MIP Soccr 84-85.

SMITH, DINA; Stissing Mtn JR SR HS; Red Nook, NY; (Y); 17/101; Church Choir; School Play; Yrbk Stf; V Ltr & Pin-Bsktbl Chrldng 86; Dutchess CC; Accntng.

SMITH, DOREEN M; E J Wilson HS; Spencerport, NY; (Y); French Clb; JCL; Latin Clb; Mathletes; Pres Math Clb; Math Tm; Symp Band; Hon Roll; NHS; NY ST Regents Schlrshp 86; SUNY-OSWEGO; Math.

SMITH, DOUG; Marlboro Central HS; Milton, NY; (Y); 39/160; Boy Scts; SADD; JV Ftbl; Im Wt Lftg; Hon Roll; NHS; Engrng.

SMITH, DOUGLAS; Bishop Kearney HS; Webster, NY; (Y); 1/142; Teachers Aide; JV Ftbl; High Hon Roll; JETS Awd; NHS; Prfct Atten Awd; Sal; St Schlr; UR Alum Schlrshp 86; St John Fisher Pres Schlrshp 86; SUNY Geneseo Schlrshp 86; U Of Rochester.

SMITH, DOUGLAS; Monsignor Farrell HS; Staten Island, NY; (Y); 16/350; Am Leg Boys St; Service Clb; Pres Spanish Clb; Ed Yrbk Stf; Hon Roll; NHS; Rep Monsignor Farrell At U N Conf For The Homeless 86.

SMITH, DOUGLAS D; Clarence Central SR HS; Akron, NY; (Y); 18/269; Sec Computer Clb; JCL; Latin Clb; School Musical; School Play; Tennis; Vllybl; NHS; Mck Trial Tm WNY Champs Tm Capt 85-86; Its Acadmc Brdcst Qz Prog 84-85; Qrtrly Math Awds 84-86; Elctrcl Engrng.

SMITH, EDNA; Susquehanna Valley HS; Harpursville, NY; (Y); Aud/Vis; Church Yth Grp; FCA; GAA; Varsity Clb; Var JV Bsktbl; Var Socr; Var Sftbl; Var Trk; High Hon Roll; MVP & Bst Def Sccr 84-85; Mst Imprvd Plyr Trck 86; Cazenovia Coll; Acctg.

SMITH III, EDWARD E; Archbishop Molloy HS; Brooklyn, NY; (Y); 180/383; Im Ftbl; Trk; Comp Sci.

SMITH, ELIZABETH H; Pulaski JR SR HS; Pulaski, NY; (S); GAA; Math Clb; Var Bsktbl; Var Socr; Var Trk; High Hon Roll; NHS; Snow Enrchmnt Awd 84; Sci Awd 85; Wrld Hist Awd 85.

SMITH, ELLEN; Hornell HS; Hornell, NY; (Y); High Hon Roll; NHS; Acctg.

SMITH, ERIC; Southern Cayuga Central Schl; Auroroa, NY; (Y); 3/80; Boy Scts; 4-H; French Clb; Quiz Bowl; Im Vllybl; Var Wrstlng; 4-H Awd; High Hon Roll; NHS; Ntl Merit SF; Poli Sci.

SMITH, ERIN; Franklin Acad; Bangor, NY; (Y); Hosp Aide; Canton ATC; Bus.

SMITH, FELICE KELLY; Erasmus Hall HS; Brooklyn, NY; (Y); Chorus; Bowling; Cheerleading; Score Keeper; Swmmng; Hon Roll; Typg Awds 85; Globl Stu Awd 85; Word Proc Awd 86; John Jay Clg; Lwyr.

SMITH, FRANCISCO; Stuyvesant HS; Brooklyn, NY; (Y); Exploring; Gym; Ntl Merit SF; Stu Natl Negr Schlrshp; NY Regnts Schlrshp Awd; Med.

SMITH, FRED; Binghamton HS; Binghamton, NY; (Y); Rep Frsh Cls; Broome CC; Aero Engrng.

SMITH, FRED; Potsdam Central HS; Potsdam, NY; (Y); AFS; Drama Clb; Math Tm; Quiz Bowl; Spanish Clb; SADD; School Musical; Hon Roll; Ntl Merit Ltr; Brown U Book Awd 86; Film Studies.

SMITH, GARY; New Rochelle HS; New Rochelle, NY; (Y); Aud/Vis; Temple Yth Grp; Hon Roll; NHS; Iona; Bus Mgmt.

SMITH, GINA; Alden Central HS; Alden, NY; (Y); Church Yth Grp; Cmnty Wkr; FTA; Science Clb; VP Spanish Clb; Teachers Aide; Church Choir; School Musical; School Play; Yrbk Stf; Liberty U; Bus.

SMITH, GREGORY C; Huntington HS; Huntington Bay, NY; (Y); 105/383; Church Yth Grp; Drama Clb; VP Key Clb; SADD; Acpl Chr; Chorus; Pres Frsh Cls; Rep Stu Cncl; Var Capt Lcrss; Hon Roll; Hugh O Brien Yth Fndtn 84; NY ST Rgnts Schlrshp 86; St Lwrnc U.

SMITH, HEATHER L; Newfane Central Schl; Newfane, NY; (Y); 13/181; Sec Church Yth Grp; Pres Drama Clb; Varsity Clb; Church Choir; School Play; Symp Band; Nwsp Stf; Var L Cheerleading; Mu Alp Tht; St Schlr; Albany HS Intern 85-86; SUNY Geneseo; Bus Admin.

SMITH, JAMIE; Perry Central HS; Perry, NY; (Y); Boy Scts; NHS; Mt Morris Amblnc Stu 86; Lackland; Plc Sci.

SMITH, JANET YOLANDA; Saint Pius V HS; Bronx, NY; (Y); Library Aide; Service Clb; Church Choir; Hon Roll; NHS; Prfct Atten Awd; Rgnts Schlrshp 86; Manhattan Coll; Pre-Med.

SMITH, JASON; Corning-Painted Post West HS; Painted Post, NY; (Y); Pres VP JA; Scholastic Bowl; Thesps; School Musical; Nwsp Rptr; Yrbk Stf; Trs Sr Cls; Rep Stu Cncl; High Hon Roll; NHS; NY ST Yth Senate Forum Dlgt 85; Commntcns.

SMITH, JEFF; Eden SR HS; Eden, NY; (Y); Boy Scts; Church Yth Grp; Varsity Clb; Band; Symp Band; Rep Soph Cls; Rep Stu Cncl; Bowling; Coach Actv; Mgr(s); Morrisville; Engnrng.

SMITH, JENNIFER; Camden Central HS; Camden, NY; (Y); 3/178; Cmnty Wkr; Debate Tm; Drama Clb; Nwsp Stf; Yrbk Stf; High Hon Roll; NHS; Intnl Clb; Ntl Merit Ltr; Rgnts Schlrp 86; Seeds Of Selflessnss Awd & Schlrp 86; Harden Schlrp 86; Colgate U; Intl Rltns.

SMITH, JENNIFER A; Salamanca Central HS; Kill Buck, NY; (Y); 5/136; Am Leg Aux Girls St; DECA; Model UN; Band; Yrbk Stf; VP Pres Stu Cncl; Capt Swmmng; French Hon Soc; NHS; Ntl Merit Ltr; Hiram Coll; Phrmcy.

SMITH, JENNIFER L; Upton Lake Christian Schl; Millbrook, NY; (Y); Church Yth Grp; Chorus; Church Choir; Nwsp Ed-Chief; Nwsp Rptr; Nwsp Stf; Var Cheerleading; Var Socr; High Hon Roll; Hon Roll; Psych.

SMITH, JENNIFER M; Owego Free Acad; Owego, NY; (Y); Church Yth Grp; Ski Clb; Varsity Clb; Band; Var Capt Socr; Hon Roll; Elmira Key Awd 85; All Conf All Stars 85; County Band; SUNY-ALBANY; Pre-Chiro.

SMITH, JEROME; New Rochelle HS; New Rochelle, NY; (Y); 205/550; Chess Clb; Var Socr; Tennis; Hnrd JR Yr MUP Scr Tm 83-84; Cptn New Rchll All Str Sccr 85-86; Wrkstdy Grant NY Med Coll 84; U MA; Dntstry.

SMITH, JILL; Bay Shore HS; Brightwaters, NY; (Y); Cmnty Wkr; GAA; SADD; Rep Soph Cls; Rep Jr Cls; Rep Stu Cncl; Gym; Var L Socr; Trk; JV Vllybl; Outstndg Achvt Hnr Bus 86; Bus.

SMITH, JODI; Bronx HS Of Science; Bronx, NY; (Y); Spanish Clb; Teachers Aide; Chorus; Prfct Atten Awd; Pre-Law.

SMITH JR, JOSEPH G L; Bitburg American HS; Apo Ny, NY; (Y); 4/130; Boy Scts; Church Yth Grp; Drama Clb; Orch; L Crs Cntry; JV Socr; High Hon Roll; Hon Roll; NHS; Msc Schlrshp U Of TX 84; Bst Gmtry Stu 85; Bst Analytc Gmtry Stu 86; FL ST U; Math.

SMITH, JOSETTE; Our Saviour Lutheran HS; Bronx, NY; (Y); Church Yth Grp; Church Choir; Bowling; Art Awd 84.

SMITH, JOSIE A M; Ogdensburg Free Acad; Ogdensburg, NY; (Y); Hosp Aide; Chorus; Color Guard; Nwsp Stf; Yrbk Stf; Cheerleading; Trk; High Hon Roll; Hon Roll; Nrs Asst.

SMITH, JOSLYN; Midwood HS; Brooklyn, NY; (Y); 39/556; Service Clb; Band; Concert Band; Variety Show; High Hon Roll; Hon Roll; United Fed Tchrs Schlrshp Awd 86; Rgnts Schlrshp Awd 86; Syracuse U; Med.

SMITH, JULIE; Geneseo Central HS; Geneseo, NY; (Y); Cmnty Wkr; Spanish Clb; SADD; Yrbk Stf; JV Sftbl; High Hon Roll; Hon Roll; Jr NHS; Bio.

SMITH, KARA; Port Jervis HS; Cuddebackville, NY; (Y); 4-H; Yrbk Stf; Hon Roll; Spnsh.

SMITH, KAREN; Union Springs Central Schl; Cayuga, NY; (Y); 15/97; Ski Clb; Band; Chorus; School Musical; Yrbk Stf; Trs Jr Cls; Trs Sr Cls; Cheerleading; Socr; Tennis.

SMITH, KAREN E; Queensbury HS; Glens Falls, NY; (Y); 31/253; Chorus; Hon Roll; Ntl Merit SF; Regents Schlrshp 86; Adirondack CC; Elem Educ.

SMITH, KATHI; Elmire Free Acad; Elmira, NY; (Y); 19/246; Mgr JA; SADD; VICA; High Hon Roll; NHS; Church Yth Grp; Bryant & Stratton Bus Inst Scholar 86; Mark Twain Cntry Schltc Achvr 86; Pres Acad Fit Awd 86; Bryant & Stratton; Comp Pgmmg.

SMITH, KATHLEEN; New Drop HS; Staten Isl, NY; (Y); Debate Tm; Girl Scts; Spanish Clb; NY Univ; Sclgy.

SMITH, KELLY; Broadalbin Central HS; Broadalbin, NY; (Y); Girl Scts; Hosp Aide; Varsity Clb; Pres VP Band; Concert Band; Mrchg Band; School Play; Var L Socr; Var L Trk; Var L Vllybl; Nazareth Coll; Psych.

SMITH, KELLY; East Syracuse-Minoa HS; E Syracuse, NY; (Y); Dance Clb; Science Clb; Ski Clb; Fld Hcky; Sftbl; Trk; Vllybl; Hon Roll; Jr NHS; NHS; Achvt Awd Art Hstry 84-85; Math.

SMITH, KELLY; Glens Falls HS; Glens Falls, NY; (Y); 39/201; High Hon Roll; Hon Roll; Art Thrpy.

SMITH, KELLY; North Rose-Wolcott HS; Savannah, NY; (Y); FBLA; Spanish Clb; Cit Awd; Rochester Bus Inst; Acctg.

SMITH, KELLY; Oppenheim-Ephratah Central Schl; St Johnsville, NY; (S); 4/28; GAA; VP Spanish Clb; Yrbk Sprt Ed; Sec Stu Cncl; Var L Cheerleading; Var L Socr; Var L Vllybl; Hon Roll; Jr NHS; VP NHS.

SMITH, KELLY A; Cheektowaga Central HS; Cheektowaga, NY; (Y); #3 In Class; Band; Concert Band; Mrchg Band; Fld Hcky; Hon Roll; Jr NHS; NHS; Voice Dem Awd; NYS SMA Flute Solo 6a 86; Deans Schlrshp Canisius Coll 86; NYS Rgnts Schlrshp 86; Canisius Coll; Law.

SMITH, KEN; Cornwall Central HS; Cornwall, NY; (Y); Band; Concert Band; Jazz Band; Symp Band; Bowling; Ftbl; Tennis; Trk; Wt Lftg; Hon Roll; Metrlgy.

SMITH, KENSALA A; Buffalo Acad Fo V S & Perf Arts; Cheektowaga, NY; (Y); 22/109; Church Yth Grp; Chorus; Church Choir; School Musical; School Play; Rep Frsh Cls; NY St Schl Music Assn Citation 84-85; Awd Of Excellence 85; Arts Recgntn And Talent Search Prgm 85-86; Fredonia ST; Music Educ.

SMITH, KENT; Mercy HS; Shoreham, NY; (Y); Boy Scts; Chess Clb; Cmnty Wkr; Letterman Clb; Ski Clb; Varsity Clb; Var Ftbl; Var Tennis; Var Wt Lftg; NEDT Awd; U Of S FL; Bus Adm.

SMITH, KERRI; Harborfields HS; Centerport, NY; (Y); 28/290; Dance Clb; Drama Clb; Hosp Aide; Drm & Bgl; Yrbk Stf; Lit Mag; Hon Roll; NHS; Adelphi U; Bio.

SMITH, KIM; Mahopac HS; Mahopac, NY; (Y); 108/409; GAA; Red Cross Aide; Science Clb; SADD; Nwsp Stf; Yrbk Stf; Im Bsktbl; Var JV Sftbl; Hon Roll; Marine Bio.

SMITH, KIMBERLY; Mercy HS; Loudonville, NY; (Y); Cmnty Wkr; Debate Tm; Pep Clb; Stage Crew; Yrbk Stf; Var Capt Cheerleading; Var Capt Pom Pon; High Hon Roll; NHS; Hgh Hnr Awd-Every Sbjct 84-85; Pre Med.

SMITH, KIMBERLY; The Franciscan Acad; Syracuse, NY; (Y); 5/24; Trs FBLA; Sec GAA; NFL; SADD; Yrbk Stf; Trs Stu Cncl; Capt Sftbl; NHS; Bus Dynmcs Awd 85; Schlrshp Alumni Francisan Acad 83-84.

SMITH, KRAIG; Dryden HS; Dryden, NY; (Y); Church Yth Grp; Spanish Clb; JV Var Bsbl; JV Bsktbl; JV L Ftbl; Wrstlng; Hon Roll; Punt,Pass,Kick 2nd Pl Awd 79; Pitch Hit Run 1st Pl Awd 80; Engrng.

SMITH, KYLE D; Little Falls JR SR HS; St Johnsville, NY; (Y); 20/84; Am Leg Boys St; Trs Church Yth Grp; Drama Clb; Exploring; Trs VP 4-H; Band; Mrchg Band; Yrbk Stf; Trk; Dgnstc Ultrasnd.

SMITH, KYLE V; Campbell Central HS; Campbell, NY; (Y); #1 In Class; Am Leg Boys St; Boy Scts; French Clb; Pep Clb; Ski Clb; Chorus; School Musical; Trs Frsh Cls; Trs Soph Cls; Trs Jr Cls; Comp.

SMITH, LAUREN; Rome Free Acad; Rome, NY; (Y); Intnl Clb; SADD; Yrbk Bus Mgr; Yrbk Phtg; Yrbk Rptr; Yrbk Stf; Im Fld Hcky; Im Sftbl; JV Vllybl; Crmnl Just.

SMITH, LAURIE; Batavia SR HS; Batavia, NY; (Y); 20/218; Sec Drama Clb; Service Clb; SADD; Color Guard; School Musical; Variety Show; Hon Roll; Merit Tuitn Aws Schlrshp; Lang Arts Awd; Outstndng Achvt Sr Lit; Genesee CC; Pltcl Sci.

SMITH, LAWRENCE M; Newfield HS; Selden, NY; (Y); 68/576; Boy Scts; Chess Clb; Church Yth Grp; Spanish Clb; Varsity Clb; JV Var Ftbl; Hon Roll; Sci Excllnc Awd 83; Bsbl MVP & All Str 84; Attndnc Awd 97 Pct 83-86; PA ST U; Aerosp Engrng.

SMITH, LILLIAN; Academy Of St Joseph; Brightwaters, NY; (Y); Drama Clb; Library Aide; School Play; Variety Show; Yrbk Stf; Trs Soph Cls; Pres Stu Cncl; NHS; Sal; Pres Schlrshp U Tampa 86; Comtv Schlrshp U Dallas 86; Almne Awd 86; Indiana U; Telecmnctns.

SMITH, LINDA; Irondequoit HS; Rochester, NY; (Y); 14/370; Aud/Vis; Trs Church Yth Grp; Ski Clb; Pres SADD; Orch; Symp Band; Stu Cncl; JV Sftbl; Hon Roll; Prfct Atten Awd; Intl Rltns.

SMITH, LINDA S; Newburgh Free Acad; New Windsor, NY; (Y); 21/572; Girl Scts; Library Aide; Radio Clb; Acpl Chr; Chorus; Madrigals; High Hon Roll; Jr NHS; NHS; Prfct Atten Awd; Girl Scout Gold Awd 86; Pres Schlrshp 86; Regents Schlrshp 86; Coll New Rochelle; Math.

SMITH, LISA; Hicksville HS; Hicksville, NY; (Y); 72/456; FBLA; Hosp Aide; Ski Clb; Yrbk Stf; Hon Roll; NHS; Clara E Mellusa Schlrshp 86; Nassau CC; Bus Adm.

SMITH, LISA; New Rochelle HS; New Rochelle, NY; (Y); 100/600; Hon Roll; NHS; Bkkpng & Accntng Awd 86; Law Day Mock Trail Comp Cert 86; Rgnts Endrsd HS Dplma 86; New Rochelle.

SMITH, LISA M; Marcus Whitman JR-SR HS; Middlesex, NY; (Y); 7/112; Am Leg Aux Girls St; Sec Trs Varsity Clb; Sec Band; Concert Band; Mrchg Band; Yrbk Ed-Chief; Sec Frsh Cls; Sec Soph Cls; Sec Jr Cls; JV Var Bsktbl; Wstrn NY All-Star Acad Achvt 86; Yates Cnty Yth Band 86.

SMITH, LIZA; Cleveland Hill HS; Cheektowaga, NY; (Y); Church Yth Grp; French Clb; JCL; Latin Clb; Speech Tm; SADD; Orch; Hon Roll; Opt Clb Awd.

SMITH, LYMAN; Dannemora HS; Dannemora, NY; (Y); 1/25; French Clb; Band; Drm Mjr(t); Yrbk Phtg; Bsktbl; High Hon Roll; Sec Trs NHS; Top 6 Natl Frnch Cntst 83-86.

SMITH, LYNN B; Pulaski Acad; Pulaski, NY; (S); 5/100; Boys Clb Am; Boy Scts; Exploring; Trk; Pres NHS; Pgm Dir Schl TV Sta 85-86; Hist.

SMITH, MARCUS LE RONE; Midwood HS; Brooklyn, NY; (Y); 377/645; Cmnty Wkr; Computer Clb; Band; Var Ftbl; Bus Mngmt.

SMITH, MARK W; Honeoye Falls-Lima HS; Lima, NY; (Y); 9/160; Am Leg Boys St; Church Yth Grp; Model UN; Chorus; School Musical; High Hon Roll; NHS; Ntl Merit Schol; Voice Dem Awd; Dplma Orgn Eastmn Schl Msc Prep Dept 86; Empr ST Schlrshp Exclnc 86; Prsdntl Acdmc Ftns Awd 86; Oberlin Coll.

SMITH, MARLON; George W Wingate HS; Brooklyn, NY; (Y); Computer Clb; Library Aide; Concert Band; School Play; Variety Show; Var Crs Cntry; Var Trk; Hon Roll; Prfct Atten Awd; Boys Trck League Champ; Stony Brook; Comp Tech.

SMITH, MARY; Geneseo Central Schl; Geneseo, NY; (Y); 5/90; Trs Drama Clb; French Clb; Math Tm; Ski Clb; SADD; Chorus; School Musical; Yrbk Stf; Rep Stu Cncl; Var L Tennis; Olympics Of The Mind 2nd & 5th Pl Tms Natl Comptn 85; Rgnl Soc Stds Olympiad 85-86; Mentorshp Prog 86; Psych.

SMITH, MATTHEW; Grand Island HS; Grand Island, NY; (Y); Bsbl; Bsktbl; Atl Year 83-84.

SMITH, MATTHEW B; Walton Central JR SR HS; Walton, NY; (Y); 5/85; Boy Scts; Key Clb; Model UN; Varsity Clb; God Cntry Awd; High Hon Roll; Voice Dem Awd; Pres Sr Cls; JV Ftbl; Var L Trk; Vrsty Frbl 85-86; Vrsty Wrstlng 83-86; Boy Sct; Engr.

SMITH, MATTHEW P; Kings Park HS; Kings Park, NY; (Y); 31/383; Church Yth Grp; Cmnty Wkr; Teachers Aide; Church Choir; High Hon Roll; Hon Roll; Jr NHS; NHS; Ntl Merit Ltr; NYS Regents Schlrshp 86; Film.

SMITH, MAUREEN; Notre Dame Bishop Gibbons HS; Ballston Lk, NY; (Y); Letterman Clb; Pep Clb; SADD; Varsity Clb; Nwsp Sprt Ed; Off Frsh Cls; Off Soph Cls; Rep Jr Cls; Rep Sr Cls; Rep Stu Cncl; Am Athelte 84-85; MVP Track 84-86; NDBG Order Lance Sprng Track 85-86; Morrisville Coll; Fash Merch.

SMITH, MELISSA; Morrisville-Eaton HS; Morrisville, NY; (Y); 6/60; GAA; Mathletes; VP Soph Cls; Rep Stu Cncl; Var Bsktbl; JV Cheerleading; Var Fld Hcky; Var Score Keeper; Var Trk; DAR Awd; DAR Good Citzn Awd 86; Ath Of Yr 86; Clarkson U; Comp Mgmt.

SMITH, MICHAEL; Westbury HS; Westbury, NY; (Y); 21/250; Dance Clb; Mathletes; Band; Concert Band; Jazz Band; Orch; School Play; High Hon Roll; Hon Roll; Prfct Atten Awd; 3rd Pl Wstbry Sci Fair 84; F Arden Burd Mem Awd 84; Mst Cngnl Stu Awd 84; Bentley Coll; Acctng.

SMITH, MICHELLE; Brooklyn Technical HS; Brooklyn, NY; (Y); 499/1159; Dance Clb; Yrbk Stf; Off Sr Cls; Capt Cheerleading; Vllybl; Hon Roll; NHS; Office Aide; Teachers Aide; Prfct Atten Awd; Chllngr 511 Crew Schlrshp Of NYIT 86; 369 Vet Assn Schlrhsp Awd 86; NY Inst Tech; Graphic Dsgn.

SMITH, MICHELLE; Guilderland HS; Albany, NY; (Y); Varsity Clb; Symp Band; Var Bsktbl; Var Socr; Var Sftbl; Prfct Atten Awd; GAA; Band; Im Ftbl; Im Tennis; Comp Oper.

SMITH, MIKE; Coxsackie-Athens HS; West Coxsackie, NY; (Y); JV Bsktbl; JV L Ftbl; Var L Socr; Var L Trk; Hon Roll; Comp Pgmng.

SMITH, MISSY; Pioneer HS; Arcade, NY; (Y); 12/250; Latin Clb; Band; Concert Band; Mrchg Band; Orch; Symp Band; Hon Roll; Jr NHS; NHS; U Of Miami; Music.

SMITH, MONICA; Sarah J Hale HS; Brooklyn, NY; (Y); Church Yth Grp; FBLA; Teachers Aide; Church Choir; Capt Sftbl; Capt Vllybl; High Hon Roll; Hon Roll; NHS; Prfct Atten Awd; Bus Mgmt.

SMITH, NICOLE; Franklin Acad; Constable, NY; (Y); Girl Scts; Cheerleading; Pom Pon; Psych.

SMITH, ODETTE MARSINAY; Northport HS; Northport, NY; (Y); Art Clb; Aud/Vis; Church Yth Grp; PAVAS; Chorus; Nwsp Ed-Chief; Nwsp Rptr; Yrbk Ed-Chief; Yrbk Rptr; Lit Mag; Bst Engl Stu 83; Rgnts Schlrshp 86; Prtl Schlrshp NY U 86; NY U.

SMITH, PATRICIA; New Dorp HS; Staten Island, NY; (Y); 250/600; Drama Clb; Intnl Clb; Library Aide; Teachers Aide; Band; Chorus; Orch; Rep Sr Cls; Rep Stu Cncl; Tennis; Itln Hon Soc 82-86; Wagner Coll; Ped.

SMITH, PEGGY; Tioga Central Schl; Barton, NY; (S); 13/78; Camera Clb; Cmnty Wkr; Dance Clb; 4-H; GAA; Hosp Aide; Library Aide; Varsity Clb; Stage Crew; Variety Show; Vrsty Sftbl-Tm Bttng Ldr 85; Equine Sci.

SMITH, PENNY; Tri-Valley Central HS; Claryville, NY; (Y); 18/75; Pres Band; Chorus; Jazz Band; High Hon Roll; JP Sousa Awd; Sec NHS; Drama Clb; Girl Scts; Political Wkr; Spanish Clb; Band Schlrshp 86; Schlrshp Lcl Fr Dept 86; Tp 10 SR Awd 86; US Snt Pg 84; U Of MA; Cmmnctns.

SMITH, PETER; Clarkstown North HS; New City, NY; (Y); Letterman Clb; SADD; Varsity Clb; L Ftbl; L Lcrss; Bus.

SMITH, R WADE; Owen D Young C S HS; Fort Plain, NY; (S); 3/23; Concert Band; Yrbk Stf; Trs Jr Cls; Var L Bsktbl; Var L Socr; NHS; 4-H; Varsity Clb; Nwsp Stf; Colgate U Semnr Prgm 85-86; 2 Time Cnty Wnnr-Best In Show-Wdwrkg 4-H 83 & 85; 1st Tm All Leag Soccr 85.

SMITH, RACHEL; Forestville Central HS; Forestville, NY; (Y); Mathletes; Spanish Clb; Varsity Clb; Color Guard; Mrchg Band; Yrbk Stf; Var Capt Bsktbl; Var Sftbl; Var Capt Vllybl; Hon Roll; Sckt Schlrshp 86; Dnkrk Clb Awd 86; Brockport ST; Soc Wrk.

SMITH JR, RANSON; Hunter College HS; Brooklyn, NY; (Y); Boy Scts; Church Yth Grp; Computer Clb; Church Choir; Yrbk Stf; Im Wrstlng; Ntl Merit Ltr.

SMITH, REBECCA; Mohonasen HS; Schenectady, NY; (Y); 24/172; Trs Key Clb; Spanish Clb; Nwsp Phtg; Yrbk Stf; Var JV Bsktbl; JV Vllybl; High Hon Roll; Hon Roll; NHS; Union Coll.

SMITH JR, ROBERT JOSEPH; Hutchinson Central Technical HS; Buffalo, NY; (Y); Chess Clb; Quiz Bowl; Scholastic Bowl; Nwsp Stf; Hon Roll; Jrnlsm.

SMITH, SABRINA; Cardinal Spellman HS; Bronx, NY; (Y); French Clb; Flag Corp; Trk; French Hon Soc; Hon Roll; Rgnst Schlrshp In Nrsng 86; Baruch Coll; Bus Mngmnt.

SMITH, SAMANTHA; Our Lady Of Lourdes HS; Poughkeepsie, NY; (Y); Nwsp Stf; JV Stat Crs Cntry; JV L Trk; NHS; SUNY; Acctg.

SMITH, SARAH; Shenendehowa HS; Clifton Park, NY; (Y); Girl Scts; Chorus; Var Score Keeper; JV Var Trk; Hon Roll; Novice Ladies Figure Skating 84-86; Empire ST Games Novice 84-86.

SMITH, SCOTT; Union Endicott HS; Endicott, NY; (Y); Boys Clb Am; Boy Scts; Hon Roll; SUNY Oswego; Comp Sci.

SMITH, SCOTT A; Immaculate Heart Central HS; Watertown, NY; (Y); 15/78; Pres Church Yth Grp; Cmnty Wkr; Trs FBLA; Yrbk Phtg; JV Ftbl; Regnts Schlrshp 86; Potsdam SUNY Clg; Math.

SMITH, SCOTT G; Owego Free Acad; Apalachin, NY; (Y); 6/220; Boy Scts; Drama Clb; Key Clb; Concert Band; Jazz Band; Mrchg Band; School Musical; Nwsp Stf; Stu Cncl; NHS; Gannett Newscarrier Schlrshp 86; Penn ST U Schlr 86; Yth Salute 85; PA ST U; Chem Engrng.

SMITH, SEAN L; Bellport HS; Brookhaven, NY; (Y); Aud/Vis; Variety Show; Boy Scts; Nwsp Phtg; Nwsp Stf; Rep Stu Cncl; Crs Cntry; Hon Roll; Cert Merit Hofstra U Forensics Tour 86; Comm.

SMITH, SHANE R; Baldwin SR HS; Baldwin, NY; (Y); 51/476; Am Leg Boys St; Key Clb; SADD; Band; Concert Band; Drill Tm; Drm Mjr(t); Jazz Band; Mrchg Band; Lcrss; Ntl Arion Awd Band 86; Jewish Am War Vet Awd 86; All Div Awd Riflery 86; USAF Acad; Engr.

SMITH, SHARMAINE; Immaculata HS; New York, NY; (Y); Church Choir; Nwsp Rptr; Var Bsbl; 2nd Honors 83-85; Intramural Bsktbl 85-86; Intramural Swmng 83-86; St Johns U; Juvnl Crimnlgy.

SMITH, SHERRIE; Addison Central HS; Addison, NY; (Y); Art Clb; Dance Clb; Drama Clb; Mrchg Band; School Play; Variety Show; Yrbk Stf; Twrlr; High Hon Roll; NHS; Actrss.

SMITH, SONJA E C; St John The Bapt DHS; Wyandanch, NY; (Y); 109/516; Church Yth Grp; Dance Clb; Hosp Aide; Model UN; Speech Tm; SADD; Church Choir; Yrbk Stf; Lit Mag; Sec Sr Cls; Venettes Cltrl Wrkshp Excllnc Dnc Awd 84; Georgetown U; Phrmcy.

SMITH, STEPHANIE; Mercy HS; Albany, NY; (Y); Church Yth Grp; Exploring; Hon Roll; Math 9 Excllnc 83-84; Math 10 Excllnc 84-85; Art II Excllnc 85-86; Math Tchr.

SMITH, STEPHANIE A; Sachem HS; Farmingville, NY; (Y); 89/1395; Ski Clb; Rgnts Schlrshp 86; U Of S FL; Bus.

SMITH, STEPHEN; Brewster HS; Brewster, NY; (Y); 7/220; French Clb; Library Aide; Spanish Clb; Church Choir; Concert Band; Mrchg Band; School Musical; Nwsp Bus Mgr; Rep Stu Cncl; French Hon Soc; Bus Adm.

SMITH, STEPHEN; HS For The Humaniti; New York, NY; (Y); Computer Clb; Library Aide; Teachers Aide; Pres Soph Cls; Bsbl; Var Coach Actv; Var Mgr(s); Var L Socr; Var L Swmmng; High Hon Roll; NYU Swimming Scholar 85-86; Govt Agent.

SMITH, STEVE; Warwick Valley HS; Warwick, NY; (Y); 40/180; Ski Clb; JV Var Bsbl; JV Bsktbl; JV Var Ftbl; Var Capt Vllybl; Hon Roll; Temple U; Bus Admin.

SMITH, STEVEN; Gloversville HS; Gloversville, NY; (Y); Boy Scts; French Clb; Intnl Clb; Key Clb; SADD; Yrbk Stf; Rep Jr Cls; JV Ftbl; Var Golf; Hon Roll; Bus Mgnt.

SMITH, SUSAN; Hoosick Falls Central HS; Hoosick Falls, NY; (Y); Pres Exploring; Red Cross Aide; Pres SADD; Mgr(s); Mgr Sftbl; Merit Awd 84-86; PTA Ldrshpawd 86; Arcrft Frfghtrs.

SMITH, SUSAN EL-LYNN; Upper Room Christian Schl; Central Islip, NY; (S); Church Yth Grp; Church Choir; High Hon Roll; Prfct Atten Awd; Pastors Awd 81-86; Apollos Awd; Isiah.

SMITH, SUSAN M; Arlington HS; Pleasant Valley, NY; (Y); 102/535; Cmnty Wkr; Girl Scts; School Play; Stage Crew; Lit Mag; Hon Roll; Ntl Merit Ltr; Rgnts Schlrshp 86; Gld Mdl Spkn Rssian Olympda 86; Brnz Mdl Wrtn Rssian Olympda 86; Buffalo SUNY; Vsl Art.

SMITH, SUZANNE; Bishop Kearney HS; Brooklyn, NY; (Y); 15/337; Hosp Aide; Key Clb; Math Tm; Ski Clb; Rep Jr Cls; Rep Sr Cls; Hon Roll; NHS; Pres Schlr; Natl Achvt Awd Bio 83; Manhattan Coll Presdntl Schlrshp 86; Pratt Inst Srch-Future Engrs Schlrshp 86; Manhattan Coll; Engrng.

SMITH, SUZANNE; Dryden Central HS; Dryden, NY; (Y); Am Leg Aux Girls St; SADD; Sec Sr Cls; Sec Stu Cncl; JV Var Bsktbl; JV Var Fld Hcky; High Hon Roll; NHS; Spanish Clb; Sec Jr Cls; Part In Big Brthr Big Sstr Prgm; Phy & Scl Sci.

SMITH, SUZANNE; Sacred Heart Acad; Manhasset, NY; (S); French Clb; Hosp Aide; Library Aide; SADD; Chorus; School Musical; Nwsp Rptr; Rep Stu Cncl; Hon Roll; NHS; Bus.

SMITH, SYLVIA; Gates-Chili SR HS; Rochester, NY; (Y); Pres Church Yth Grp; French Clb; Chorus; Pres Church Choir; Stu Cncl; JV Co-Capt Bsktbl; JV Trk; JV Vllybl; High Hon Roll; Urban League Blck Schlrs Awd 85; Rec For Acad Achvt 85; Bus Admin.

SMITH, TARA; Guilderland Central HS; Albany, NY; (Y); 4-H; Red Cross Aide; Service Clb; SADD; Varsity Clb; Stat Bsktbl; Var L Sftbl; Var L Swmmng; Var L Trk; Var L Vllybl; MVP Vrsty Vllybll 85; IA ST U; Vet.

SMITH, TERESA; Keveny Memorial Acad; Cohoes, NY; (Y); 11/34; Dance Clb; Variety Show; Sec Soph Cls; Sec Jr Cls; Bsktbl; Crs Cntry; Score Keeper; Sftbl; Tennis; Vllybl; William Moylan Schlrshp Awd 83; Natl Bus Hnr Scty 86; Ldrshp Cnslr Acad All-Amer 86; Phy Thrpy.

SMITH, TERESA; Lyons HS; Lyons, NY; (Y); Ski Clb; SADD; Color Guard; Cheerleading; Merit Lst 84-86; CCFL; Acctg.

SMITH, TERESA A; Half Hollow Hills High Schl East; Melville, NY; (Y); 7/511; Church Yth Grp; Mathletes; Science Clb; Teachers Aide; Yrbk Ed-Chief; Lit Mag; Stu Cncl; High Hon Roll; Jr NHS; NHS; Stony Brook U Simons Rsrch Fllwshp Awd 85; MA Inst Tech; Engrng.

SMITH, THERESA; Clarence SR HS; Clarence Ctr, NY; (Y); Church Yth Grp; VP FBLA; SADD; Church Choir; 2nd Pl FBLA Conts Off Procdrs 86; SUC Cobleskill; Hosp Mgmt.

SMITH, THOMAS FRANCIS; George F Baker HS; Greenwood Lake, NY; (Y); 24/88; Am Leg Boys St; Spanish Clb; Yrbk Stf; VP Jr Cls; Var Bsbl; Bowling; Var Socr; Jr NHS; Arch.

SMITH, TODD; Pembroke Central HS; Corfu, NY; (Y); 7/100; Band; Concert Band; Mrchg Band; Bsktbl; Socr; Tennis; High Hon Roll; Hon Roll; Engrng.

SMITH, TOM; Middletown HS; Middletown, NY; (Y); Boston Coll; Bus.

SMITH, TRACY; Our Saviour Lutheran HS; Bronx, NY; (Y); 2/27; Church Choir; Bsktbl; Score Keeper; Sftbl; Trk; Vllybl; Cit Awd; High Hon Roll; Hon Roll; NHS; Natl Merit Ldrshp.

SMITH, VERONICA ROSE; Ichabod Crane HS; Valatie, NY; (Y); Civic Clb; Drama Clb; German Clb; Ski Clb; Band; Color Guard; Mrchg Band; School Musical; School Play; Hon Roll; Long Island U; Comm Pilot.

SMITH, VIOLA; Midwood HS; New York, NY; (Y); Exploring; Library Aide; Service Clb; Orch; Var Crs Cntry; Trk; High Hon Roll; Hon Roll; Honorary Svc Awd 86; Engrng.

SMITH, WENDY; Corcosan HS; Syracuse, NY; (Y); Art Clb; Pres Church Yth Grp; French Clb; Ski Clb; SADD; Y-Teens; Church Choir; Yrbk Stf; High Hon Roll; Hon Roll; Roberts Wesleyan; Art Educ.

SMITH, WILLIAM; Sachem HS; Farmingville, NY; (Y); 182/1580; Church Yth Grp; Cmnty Wkr; Computer Clb; German Clb; Library Aide; Ski Clb; Drm & Bgl; Im Bowling; Jr NHS; Zenith Clb 83-85; Comp Engr.

SMOKOWSKI, JAMES N; Bshop Timon HS; Lackawanna, NY; (Y); Pres Art Clb; Drama Clb; Yrbk Rptr; Yrbk Stf; Lit Mag; Hon Roll; NHS; NY ST Rgnts Schlrp, Full Tuitn Schlrp To Cooper Union, Acad Ex Awd, Ex In Tech Drwng Awd 86; The Cooper Union; Arch.

SMOLEN, MICHELLE; The Franciscan Acad; Syracuse, NY; (S); 2/27; Church Yth Grp; Trs GAA; Pres Speech Tm; Yrbk Stf; Pres Stu Cncl; Capt Sftbl; Capt Vllybl; DAR Awd; High Hon Roll; NHS; Law.

SMOLENSKI, KARL; Penn Yan Acad; Penn Yan, NY; (Y); 2/180; Am Leg Boys St; Bausch & Lomb Sci Awd; French Hon Soc; High Hon Roll; NHS; Ntl Merit Ltr; Arch Engr.

SMOROL, JASON; Bishop Grimes HS; N Syracuse, NY; (Y); Cmnty Wkr; SADD; Chorus; School Play; Pres Sr Cls; JV Var Ftbl; Var Capt Wrstlng; Ski Clb; Variety Show; Rep Frsh Cls; Mass Cmnctns.

SMOTHERS, CHRISTY; Camden HS; Taberg, NY; (Y); FBLA; Chorus; Orch; High Hon Roll; Hon Roll; Bus Admin.

SMRTIC, MATTHEW J; Gloversville HS; Gloversville, NY; (Y); SADD; Variety Show; VP Frsh Cls; Var Capt Socr; Hon Roll; St Schlr; Rgnts Schlrshp; Clarkson U; Engrng.

SMULOWITZ, JACK M; Yeshiva Shaar Hatorah HS; Flushing, NY; (Y); High Hon Roll; Ntl Merit Ltr; Ny St Rgnts Coll Schlrshp 86; Queens Coll Schlrshp 86; Empire St Scholarship Of Excellence.

SMULSKI, CEZARY; Curtis HS; Staten Island, NY; (Y); Var Socr; Hny Mdl Awd Schl Art Lg Of NYC 85; CSI; Bus Admin.

SMYTH, KELLY ANN; Hicksville HS; Hicksville, NY; (Y); 51/456; Math Clb; SADD; Chorus; Socr; Trk; High Hon Roll; NHS; MVP Winter Track 84-85; Cptn 85-86; Mfg Trust Schlrshp 86; Pres Acad Ftns Awd 86; Stony Brook; Mech Engr.

SNAPE, STEPHEN; John Jay HS; Brooklyn, NY; (Y); Aud/Vis; Boys Clb Am; Boy Scts; Church Yth Grp; Computer Clb; FCA; JA; Varsity Clb; Band; Concert Band; Rochester Inst Tech; Elec Engr.

SNEAD, DAWN; Belport HS; Bellp Ort, NY; (Y); Church Yth Grp; Ski Clb; Chorus; Church Choir; Madrigals; School Musical; Var Cheerleading; JV Coach Actv; Capt Var Gym; Pom Pon; Regents Dplm 87; Wake Forest U; Educ.

SNEDAKER, VALERIE; Susquehanna Valley HS; Binghamton, NY; (Y); Church Yth Grp; Cmnty Wkr; Office Aide; Spanish Clb; SADD; Teachers Aide; Htl Mngmnt.

SNELL, BONNIE; Wyandanch Memorial HS; Wyandanch, NY; (Y); 9/140; French Clb; Pres Key Clb; Teachers Aide; Nwsp Rptr; Nwsp Stf; Yrbk Ed-Chief; Stu Cncl; High Hon Roll; Hon Roll; Ntl Merit Ltr; Regents Schlrshp 85-86; Bus Dynmcs Awd 82-83; NY Inst Of Tech; Bus Admn Info.

SNELL, JULIE; Potsdam HS; Potsdam, NY; (Y); French Clb; JV Cheerleading; Hon Roll; UCLA; Bio.

SNELL, VICTORIA; Red Jacket Central HS; Manchester, NY; (Y); 13/89; French Clb; Varsity Clb; Band; Chorus; Madrigals; School Musical; VP Soph Cls; Pres Sr Cls; Var Cheerleading; Hon Roll; NYS Regnts Nrs Schlrshp 86; Alfred U; Nrs.

SNELLINGER, ANDREA; Port Jervis HS; Pt Jervis, NY; (Y); 5/170; Thesps; Acpl Chr; Chorus; School Musical; Yrbk Stf; Rep Var Stu Cncl; Var JV Socr; Var JV Trk; High Hon Roll; VFW Awd; French Awd All Cnty Chours 83-85; NYSSMA Solo A Olympcs Of Mind, All Cnty Chorus 85-86; Engr.

SNELLINGER, LUCY; Port Jervis HS; Port Jervis, NY; (Y); 1/182; Scholastic Bowl; Trs SADD; Varsity Clb; Yrbk Ed-Chief; Trs Stu Cncl; Socr; Capt Trk; Bausch & Lomb Sci Awd; Elks Awd; High Hon Roll; Natl Hon Soc Schlrshp 86; Rotary Clb Schlrshp 86; Natl Elks Schlrshp 86; Manhattan Coll; Bio Chem.

SNIDER, JILL D; Carthage Central HS; Carthage, NY; (Y); 8/235; Pres Spanish Clb; Band; Mrchg Band; Nwsp Rptr; Sec Soph Cls; Var Tennis; Stat Vllybl; High Hon Roll; NHS; Rotary Awd; Good Sprtsmnshp Awd 84-85; NY ST Rgnts Schlrshp 85-86; U Of Buffalo; Aerospc Engnrng.

SNITIKER, LEIGH; The Wheatley Schl; E Williston, NY; (Y); Dance Clb; Lit Mag; Trs Frsh Cls; Trs Soph Cls; Trs Jr Cls; NHS; AATF Natimae Frnch Cntst Fnlst 85; Hon Mntn Ntl Itln Cntst 85; Econ.

SNOW, CINDY; Union Endicott HS; Endicott, NY; (Y); 8/430; Key Clb; Concert Band; Orch; Cit Awd; High Hon Roll; NHS; Presdntl Acadmc Ftns Awd 86; Outstndng Achvt-Scl Stds Awd 86; Ida E Strkv Awd-Latin 86; Broome CC; Chmcl Engrng.

SNOW, JEFFREY; Greenville Central HS; Greenville, NY; (Y); 10/67; Pres Aud/Vis; Camera Clb; Computer Clb; Key Clb; Pres Science Clb; School Musical; Stage Crew; Nwsp Phtg; Yrbk Phtg; Rep Stu Cncl; Spartn Clb Schlrshp & Art Achvmnt Recgntn Awd; RPI; Engrng.

SNOW, JOHN; Auburn HS; Auburn, NY; (Y); Letterman Clb; Model UN; SADD; Varsity Clb; Trs Frsh Cls; Var JV Bsktbl; Var Capt Lcrss; High Hon Roll; Hon Roll; All Star Div I Schls Onondaga Lg Var Lacrosse 86-87.

SNOWDEN, KEISHA; East Ridge HS; Rochester, NY; (Y); Art Asstnt Awd 81; Awd Of Merit 85-86; Distrb Ed Clbs Of NY Rgnl Fnls 86; John & Wales Coll; Fash Mdsg.

SNYDER, CHERI; Cicero-N Syracuse HS; Clay, NY; (Y); 253/667; Art Clb; Computer Clb; Office Aide; Stage Crew; Stu Cncl; Im Vllybl; Hon Roll; Rgnl Schltc Art Awd 83; Art Achvt Awd 83; Herkimer; Psych.

SNYDER JR, CLAIR; Hornell HS; Hornell, NY; (Y); 33/185; Capt L Wrstlng; High Hon Roll; Prfct Atten Awd; Letterman Clb; Cert Of Merit Elec Constrctn 86; Svc & Oprtn Hvy Equip Dplm 84-86; Williamsport CC.

SNYDER, CRISTAL; Rensselaer HS; Rensselaer, NY; (Y); Key Clb; Math Tm; SADD; Yrbk Stf; Vllybl; High Hon Roll; Hon Roll; Sci.

SNYDER, DANIEL; Albion HS; Albion, NY; (S); 8/171; VP Church Yth Grp; Drama Clb; Band; Chorus; Church Choir; Mrchg Band; School Musical; School Play; High Hon Roll; VP NHS; 2nd Pl Teen Tlnt Music Comptn 84; U Buffalo; Mech Engrng.

SNYDER, DEBORAH; Batavia HS; Batavia, NY; (Y); 45/205; Sec Exploring; 4-H; Girl Scts; Stage Crew; Yrbk Stf; Var JV Bsktbl; Hon Roll; Paper Carrier Yr 85; Barbizon Schl Mdlng Grad 86; Genesee CC; Crmnl Just.

SNYDER, ERIC; St Francis HS; Elma, NY; (Y); Ski Clb; Nwsp Rptr; Lit Mag; Rep Frsh Cls; Rep Stu Cncl; Var Golf; Im Wt Lftg; Hon Roll; NHS; Super 7 Athlts Of Wk-Lcl TV Sta; Golfer Of Yr MVP; Centinneal Prize Schlrshp & BDGA Schlrshp; U Of Rochester; Englsh.

SNYDER, JAMMATHON J P; Milford Central HS; Maryland, NY; (Y); Am Leg Boys St; Varsity Clb; Stage Crew; Nwsp Stf; Bsktbl; Crs Cntry; Socr; Trk; Astrocom Athltc Awd 86; Gradtn Mrshll 86; Bus Admin.

SNYDER, KELLY; Camden Central HS; Camden, NY; (Y); FBLA; Red Cross Aide; Varsity Clb; Bsktbl; Sftbl; Hon Roll; Rotary Awd 50 Pts Scholar 84-85; AZ ST; Bus.

SNYDER, MAE; Tioga Center HS; Owego, NY; (Y); Dance Clb; JV Var Sftbl; Prfct Atten Awd; Natl Sci Olympd Bio 84; Yth Ftns Achvt Awd 84 & 85; Nrsng.

SNYDER, MICHAEL S; Brockport HS; Brockport, NY; (Y); 70/350; Exploring; Pres Frsh Cls; Stu Cncl; JV Var Bsbl; JV Bsktbl; Ftbl; High Hon Roll; Hon Roll; Rgnts Schlrshp; Brckprt Ldrshp Rep; U Of Buffalo; Indstrl Engrng.

SNYDER, MOLLY; Candor Central HS; Candor, NY; (Y); Church Yth Grp; Scholastic Bowl; SADD; Band; School Play; Yrbk Bus Mgr; Yrbk Ed-Chief; JV Trk; Hon Roll; NHS; Hlth.

SNYDER, PATRICIA; Center Moriches HS; Ctr Moriches, NY; (Y); Art Clb; Drama Clb; French Clb; Ski Clb; School Play; Stage Crew; Yrbk Stf; Cheerleading; Crs Cntry; Sftbl; Johynson & Wales; Clnry Arts.

SNYDER, PEGGY; South Jefferson Central HS; Mannsville, NY; (Y); 18/153; Church Yth Grp; French Clb; Chorus; Yrbk Stf; Stu Cncl; Hon Roll; Schl Press Inst 86; NYSSMA Solo Awd 85; Herkimer CC; Paralgl.

SNYDER, ROBERT; Riverside HS; Buffalo, NY; (Y); 10/161; JA; Yrbk Stf; High Hon Roll; Jr NHS; NHS; Regents Diploma; Musicn.

SNYDER, SHELLY; Ravena Coeymans Selkirk HS; Selkirk, NY; (Y); Church Yth Grp; Pres FBLA; Trs Key Clb; SADD; Rep Frsh Cls; Rep Soph Cls; Rep Jr Cls; Stat Bsbl; JV Var Socr; Im Vllybl; Bryant; Acctng.

SNYDER, STACY; Chatham HS; Ghent, NY; (Y); Ski Clb; Band; Jazz Band; Yrbk Stf; Rep Frsh Cls; Var Capt Crs Cntry; Var Capt Trk; X-Cntry Went To ST MIP 85-86; Athletic Training.

SNYDER, SUSAN; Baldwin SR HS; Baldwin, NY; (Y); Nwsp Rptr; Var Bsktbl; Var Sftbl; JV Vllybl; Athletic Clb Sftbl Achvt 84.

SNYDER, WENDY; Brighton HS; Rochester, NY; (Y); 1/325; Temple Yth Grp; Sec Thesps; Chorus; School Musical; School Play; Stage Crew; Variety Show; Ntl Merit Ltr; Womns Wstrn Glf Fndtn Schlrshp 86; NY ST Rgnts Schlrshp 86; Outstndng Spnsh Stu Awd 85; Cornell U; Pre Med.

SNYDER JR, WILLIAM A; Saratoga Springs HS; Gansevoort, NY; (Y); 1/460; Am Leg Boys St; JA; JV Bsbl; Var Bowling; Var Golf; Cit Awd; Jr NHS; NHS; Pres Schlr; Val; Pres Schlrshp 86; Regnts Schlrshp 86; Harriet W Sharp Meml Math Awd 86; Siena College; Bus.

SO, PATRICK-HENRIE; Archbishop Molloy HS; Kew Gardens, NY; (Y); Hosp Aide; Chorus; Var L Trk; High Hon Roll; NHS; Ntl Merit Ltr.

SOANES, ELIZABETH; The Harley Schl; Fairport, NY; (Y); Cmnty Wkr; VP Sec Varsity Clb; Chorus; Yrbk Stf; Sec Sr Cls; Capt Bsktbl; Socr; Capt Trk; Ntl Merit Ltr; Church Yth Grp; Wms Coll Bk Awd 85; Rgnts Schlrshp 86; Middlebury Coll; Biochem.

SOBEL, JASON; Kennedy HS; Merrick, NY; (Y); FBLA; Bsbl; Ftbl; Hon Roll; NHS; Bus.

SOBEL, LAUREN A; Clarkstown North HS; New City, NY; (Y); 24/410; Math Tm; Nwsp Stf; Yrbk Stf; High Hon Roll; Mu Alp Tht; NHS; NY Acad Of Sci Internship 85; Westinghouse Semi-Fnlst 86; Yth For Understanding Schlrshp To Japan 85; Cornell U; Orgnztnl Behavior.

SOBIERAJ, CHERYL; Palmyra-Macedon Central HS; Macedon, NY; (S); 8/180; Math Clb; Ski Clb; Concert Band; Mrchg Band; School Play; Symp Band; Yrbk Ed-Chief; Yrbk Rptr; Sec NHS; Acclrtd Math 83-86; Union Coll; Chem.

SOBOCINSKI, ERIC; Hauppauge HS; Smithtown, NY; (Y); Varsity Clb; JV Var Bsbl; Var Bsktbl; High Hon Roll; Hon Roll; NHS; Prfct Atten Awd; All Leag Bsktbl 86; Med.

SOBOLESKI, DANA; Springville Griffith Inst; Springville, NY; (Y); Pres French Clb; GAA; Rep Frsh Cls; Rep Soph Cls; Rep Jr Cls; Rep Stu Cncl; JV Bsktbl; Trk; High Hon Roll; NHS; Psych.

SOCHI, KEI; Harborfields HS; Centerport, NY; (Y); 1/290; Orch; Lit Mag; Stu Cncl; Var L Badmtn; Var L Fld Hcky; NHS; Val; Mathletes; Service Clb; Mgr(s); Yth Gov NY ST 86; Phi Beta Kappa Alumni Citatn 86; Hugh O Brian Yth Ldrshp Sem 84; Princeton U; Phlsphy.

SOCIE, DAVID; Niagara Wheatfield SR HS; Niagara Fls, NY; (Y); 27/292; German Clb; Varsity Clb; Var Capt Socr; Hon Roll; NHS; Rgnts Schlrshp 86; MVP In Soccer 84 & 85; Boys ST 85; U Bflo; Elec Engrng.

SOCOLOW, PAUL; Webutuck Central Schl; Wassaic, NY; (Y); 1/60; Am Leg Boys St; Pres French Clb; Math Tm; Spanish Clb; Sec Jr Cls; Var Crs Cntry; Var Trk; High Hon Roll; NHS; Ntl Merit Ltr; Bio.

SODANO, TOM; Lynbrook SR HS; Lynbrook, NY; (Y); Aud/Vis; Pres Key Clb; Service Clb; Variety Show; Vllybl; JV Wrstlng; Englsh.

SODEN, JULIEANN; Our Lady Of Mercy Acad; Huntington, NY; (Y); 8/120; Computer Clb; Debate Tm; Hosp Aide; Nwsp Sprt Ed; Var Swmmng; High Hon Roll; Sec NHS; Ntl Merit Ltr; NEDT Awd; Frfld U; Finance.

SODEN, KATHLEEN E; Albany HS; Albany, NY; (Y); 153/600; Cmnty Wkr; Girl Scts; Latin Clb; Science Clb; Var Crs Cntry; Var Trk; Hon Roll; JC Of Albany; Fine Arts.

SODIKOFF, KARIN; Oceanside HS; Oceanside, NY; (Y); 72/536; Debate Tm; Key Clb; Mathletes; Service Clb; Nwsp Stf; Yrbk Stf; Hon Roll; Jr NHS; NHS; Bst Spkr-New Rchll Mdl Cngrss 85; NY Rgnts Schlrshp 86; SUNY Binghamton.

SODOS, NADJA S; Hunter College HS; Flushing, NY; (Y); Hosp Aide; Stage Crew; Nwsp Rptr; Nwsp Stf; Yrbk Stf; Regents Schlrshp 86; Starr Fndtn Schlrshp 86; Comm.

SOFIA, FRANK; Cicero North Syracuse HS; N Syracuse, NY; (S); 86/667; Church Yth Grp; Hst Pres Key Clb; Ed Nwsp Ed-Chief; Nwsp Rptr; Nwsp Stf; Rep Frsh Cls; Rep Soph Cls; Rep Jr Cls; Rep Sr Cls; CC Awd; Geneseo College; Commctns.

SOFRONAS, CYNTHIA; Fox Lane HS; Pound Ridge, NY; (Y); 61/312; French Clb; Ski Clb; VP Pres SADD; Chorus; Yrbk Phtg; Yrbk Stf; Rep Stu Cncl; Capt Var Fld Hcky; Var Lcrss; Hon Roll; Engl.

SOGER, WARREN; Warwick Valley Central HS; Warwick, NY; (Y); 13/200; AFS; Computer Clb; FFA; Science Clb; Ski Clb; SADD; Temple Yth Grp; Pres Jr Cls; Rep Stu Cncl; Im Bowling; US Air Frc Acad.

SOHAN, CHANDRAWATTIE; John Jay HS; Brooklyn, NY; (Y); 49/549; Computer Clb; Library Aide; Math Clb; Teachers Aide; Gym; Socr; High Hon Roll; Hon Roll; Drop Out Prevention 85; Mock Trial 85; Bus Skills 84; John Jay Coll; Pre-Law.

SOHAN, YUDESH; Bronx High School Of Science; Brooklyn, NY; (Y); Office Aide; Teachers Aide; Chorus; Var Bsktbl; Prfct Atten Awd; Fr Awd 85; Brooklyn Coll; Chem.

SOHMER, SHIRLEY; Wayne Central HS; Ontario, NY; (Y); 7/200; SADD; Concert Band; Mrchg Band; School Musical; Yrbk Stf; Lit Mag; Rep Stu Cncl; JV Crs Cntry; Score Keeper; NHS; Acadmc Excllnc Europn Cultr Stud 85; Phy Ed Svc 86; Band Dilignc 86; ST U Of NY; Poli Sci.

SOHN, CATHERINE; Mamaroneck HS; Larchmont, NY; (Y); FBLA; Service Clb; Pre-Med.

SOHN, EUNCHU; Tottenville HS; Staten Isld, NY; (Y); Key Clb; High Hon Roll; Prfct Atten Awd; Fndmntls Of Art-Merit Awd, Jenks H S 83-84; Indstrl Art-Hnrs, Jenks H S 83-84; Engrng.

SOHN, JOONG; Tottenville HS; Staten Isld, NY; (Y); Intnl Clb; Math Tm; JV Bsktbl; Var Ftbl; Wt Lftg; NHS; MIT; Engrng.

SOHNG, HEIDI U; Our Lady Of Lourdes HS; Wappingers Falls, NY; (Y); 7/189; Hosp Aide; Teachers Aide; Church Choir; Nwsp Rptr; Nwsp Stf; Yrbk Stf; Sec Stu Cncl; Hon Roll; Jr NHS; NHS; Cornell U; Bus.

SOHOSKI, THAD; G Ray Bodley HS; Fulton, NY; (Y); 1/241; French Clb; Science Clb; Y-Teens; Tennis; Bausch & Lomb Sci Awd; High Hon Roll; NHS; Hnrs Awd Calculus 86; Hnrs Awd A P Chem 86; Bausch Lomb Awd 86; Med.

SOHRAB, SHAHRAM; West Genesee SR HS; Camillus, NY; (Y); Exploring; VP Mathletes; Off Jr Cls; Off Sr Cls; Stu Cncl; Socr; Tennis; Hon Roll; NHS; Onondaga Cnty Math Awd 85; Clrksn U; Comp Engrng.

SOJDA, ANN; Alexander Central HS; Alexander, NY; (Y); FTA; Teachers Aide; Varsity Clb; Chorus; Var Capt Trk; Var Vllybl; NHS; Ms Teen NY Pagnt 86; NY ST Indr Outdr Trck Meet 85-86; Empire ST Games 85-86; Elem Educ.

SOKALSKI, LINDA; Gayfield Central HS; Gloversville, NY; (Y); 4-H; SADD; Color Guard; 4-H Awd.

SOKOL, ELYSE; Tottenville HS; Staten Island, NY; (S); 9/850; Teachers Aide; Temple Yth Grp; High Hon Roll; NHS; Prfct Atten Awd; NY ST Coll; Lbrl Arts.

SOKOLOWSKI, TERESA A; Horseheads SR HS; Horseheads, NY; (S); 14/382; Church Yth Grp; Varsity Clb; Var L Trk; High Hon Roll; NHS; Ntl Merit Ltr; Science Clb; Spanish Clb; JV Bsktbl; MVP Crss Cntry, Trck 85; ST Qual Cross Cntry & Indr Trck 85-86; Hmcmng Ct 85; People To People 84.

SOLA, SAMUEL; Mt St Michael Acad; Yonkers, NY; (Y); Am Leg Boys St; Boy Scts; Chess Clb; Cmnty Wkr; Drama Clb; Office Aide; Science Clb; Church Choir; Color Guard; Drill Tm; Comm Svc Awd 82-83; MT St Michael Schlrshp 82-83; Brother Jude Schlrhsp 83-84; Arspc Engr.

SOLAK, DAVE; Kenmore East HS; Converse, TX; (Y); Trs Exploring; Varsity Clb; Orch; JV Trk; JV Var Vllybl; High Hon Roll; Hon Roll; Navel Acad.

SOLAK, SCOTT; Ossining HS; Ossining, NY; (Y); Church Yth Grp; JV Bsbl; High Hon Roll; Hon Roll; Schlrshps Awd Pgm 84-86; Italn Hgh Achvt Awds 84-86; Math Cntst 5th Pl 84-85; FL Inst Of Tech; Marine Bio.

SOLAN, KELLY; Gates-Chili HS; Rochester, NY; (Y); Church Yth Grp; Drama Clb; Service Clb; Teachers Aide; School Play; Swmmng; Paul Smiths Coll; Htl Mgmt.

SOLANO, LOUIS; Mount Vernon HS; Mt Vernon, NY; (Y); Church Yth Grp; Cmnty Wkr; Varsity Clb; VICA; Concert Band; Socr; NHS; William Roger Coll; Arch.

SOLARI, FABIANA; Sacred Heart Acad; Huntington, NY; (Y); Church Yth Grp; Pres Computer Clb; Hosp Aide; Var Swmmng; Hon Roll; NHS; Bio.

SOLAUN, LOURDES; Nazareth Acad; Rochester, NY; (Y); Intnl Clb; Math Clb; Spanish Clb; Band; Chorus; Concert Band; High Hon Roll; Hon Roll; NHS; Music Lessons Flute 83-87; Engr.

SOLBERG, ROBERT S; Queensburg HS; Glens Falls, NY; (Y); 36/253; Key Clb; Teachers Aide; Stage Crew; VP Frsh Cls; Stu Cncl; Var L Ftbl; L Trk; L Wrstlng; High Hon Roll; Hon Roll; NY ST Rgnts Schlrshp 86; Comp Math Awd 83; Ftbl Dfnsv Plyr/Yr Awd 85; U Of Buffalo; Comp Sci.

SOLES, KELLY; Alexander Central HS; Alexander, NY; (Y); Pres Spanish Clb; Band; Chorus; Color Guard; Yrbk Ed-Chief; Yrbk Phtg; Yrbk Stf; Cheerleading; NHS.

SOLES, PAMELA; De Sales Catholic HS; Lockport, NY; (Y); Aud/Vis; Exploring; 4-H; Ski Clb; Yrbk Stf; JV Capt Cheerleading; JV Vllybl; 4-H Awd; Sllng Awd 4-H & Schl 84-86; Niagara County CC.

SOLIMENE, VITO J; Bronx High School Of Science; Bronx, NY; (Y); Var Golf; Var Gym; Ntl Merit Schol; Comp Assisted Drftng Clb Pres 85-86; Columbia U; Comp Sci.

SOLIS, ROBERT; St John The Baptist HS; Brentwood, NY; (Y); Chess Clb; Cmnty Wkr; Computer Clb; Spanish NHS; Hotel & Rest Mgmt.

SOLIZ, SYDNEY; Blind Brook HS; Rye Brook, NY; (Y); Drama Clb; Model UN; Spanish Clb; SADD; School Play; Lit Mag; JV Socr; JV Tennis; Boston Coll; Comm.

SOLLER, ELISABET V; Brockport HS; Brockport, NY; (Y); 14/323; JV Var Cheerleading; Var Pom Pon; High Hon Roll; Hon Roll; NHS; MIP Var Chrldng 84; MVP Var Chrldng 85; Rgnts Schlrshp 86; Hobart & Wm Smith Coll; Econ.

SOLOMON, ANTHONY; Samuel Gompers V T HS; Bronx, NY; (Y); 5/32; Art Clb; FBLA; JA; PAVAS; Bsbl; Bsktbl; Vllybl; Hon Roll; Prfct Atten Awd; Phys Ftns Awd 86; Math Cert 85; Eng Cert 85; Arch.

SOLOMON, BARBRA; St Agnes Acad; Flushing, NY; (Y); 4/245; Yrbk Phtg; Rep Stu Cncl; VP NHS; Iona Coll Lang Cntst Scnds Hnrs Frnch II 85; Engrng.

SOLOMON, CHERYL; Walton HS; Bronx, NY; (Y); Hosp Aide; Chorus; Prfct Atten Awd; Cert Achvt 86; Accntg.

SOLOMON, RONALDO; Whitney Point HS; Castle Creek, NY; (Y); 2/124; Boy Scts; French Clb; Science Clb; Yrbk Bus Mgr; Trs Jr Cls; Trs Sr Cls; Capt Socr; Trk; Trs NHS; Ntl Merit SF; Intl Studies Assn Schlrshp To Study In France 85; Ntl Cncl On Yth Ldrshp Salute To Yth 85; US Naval Acad; Elec Engrng.

SOLOSKI, SHANE D; Catholic Central HS; Schaghticoke, NY; (Y); Spanish Clb; Varsity Clb; Band; Chorus; School Musical; Variety Show; Lit Mag; Ftbl; Socr; NY ST Rgnts Schlrshp; Coll Of St Rose; Music.

SOLOWSKY, ANN MARIE; H Frank Carey HS; Franklin Square, NY; (Y); 54/280; Cmnty Wkr; FBLA; Intnl Clb; Orch; Yrbk Stf; Off Frsh Cls; Pres Soph Cls; Pres Jr Cls; Pres Sr Cls; Stu Cncl; St Johns U; Mgmt.

SOMAI, NATASHA; Evander Childs HS; Bronx, NY; (Y); Church Yth Grp; Cmnty Wkr; Spanish Clb; Off Soph Cls; Off Jr Cls; Bowling; Golf; Vllybl; Hon Roll; Prfct Atten Awd; Rgnts Schlrshp 85-86; Awd-Mst Imprvd-Golf 84-85; Cert Of Merit-Sntr & Assmblymn 85-86; SUNY-ONEONTA.

SOMAN, MICHELLE; Tappan Zee HS; Blauvelt, NY; (Y); Yrbk Phtg; L Diving; L Trk; FL; Fshn Mrcndsng.

SOMERS, LAUREL; Smithtown HS East; St James, NY; (Y); Band; Orch; Symp Band; Crs Cntry; Hon Roll; NYSSMA All-Cnty & All-ST Bnd 85; NYS Rgnts Schlrshp 86; SUNY Stonybrook; Psych.

SOMERS, ROBIN; Copiague HS; Copiague, NY; (Y); Var Vllybl; Prlgl.

SOMERVILLE, BRIAN; Mynderse Acad; Seneca Falls, NY; (Y); 19/148; Am Leg Boys St; Church Yth Grp; Ski Clb; Acpl Chr; Band; Chorus; Church Choir; Swing Chorus; Sftbl; High Hon Roll; Chaplain Yth Fellowship; Liberty U; Hotel Mngmnt.

SOMIN, LYNN; Huntington HS; Huntington, NY; (Y); Teachers Aide; Band; Sec Chorus; Concert Band; Mrchg Band; Orch; Pep Band; School Musical; School Play; Symp Band; Ltr Band 85; A Rtng All ST 85-86; Elem Ed.

SOMMA, GREGG; Moore Catholic HS; Staten Island, NY; (Y); 67/172; Stage Crew; Bsbl; Bowling; Tennis; Hon Roll; St Johns U SI; Math.

SOMMER, JESSICA; Indian River Central HS; Theresa, NY; (Y); 5/145; AFS; Latin Clb; Stage Crew; Yrbk Stf; Var Tennis; Hon Roll; Spllng Bee Wnnr 2nd Pl 83; Jefferson CC; Engrg.

SOMMER, NANCY; Hauppauge HS; Hauppauge, NY; (Y); Ski Clb; Chorus; High Hon Roll; Hon Roll; Atty.

SOMMER, SHEILA; Fredonia HS; Fredonia, NY; (Y); 3/180; Key Clb; Science Clb; Ski Clb; Spanish Clb; Orch; Nwsp Rptr; Yrbk Phtg; Tennis; Trk; Church Yth Grp; Order Of Eastern Star Englsh Awd 86; ESSPA Jrnlsm Comptn 1st Rnnr-Up 85; ST U Of NY Buffalo; Engrng.

SOMMERS, JULIE; Domiknican Commercial HS; Glendale, NY; (S); Church Yth Grp; Rep Stu Cncl; Swmmng; High Hon Roll; Jr NHS; Sec.

SOMMERS, MARY; Bishop Grimes HS; Syracuse, NY; (Y); Exploring; Band; Concert Band; Jazz Band; Nwsp Ed-Chief; Nwsp Rptr; Nwsp Sprt Ed; Nwsp Stf; Hon Roll; NHS; Cmnctns.

SOMMERS, MICHELLE; Dominican Commercial HS; Glendale, NY; (S); Church Yth Grp; Rep Stu Cncl; Var Swmmng; High Hon Roll; Jr NHS; Kiwanis Awd; Sec.

SON, SRANE; Edison Tech HS; Rochester, NY; (Y); Math Clb; Hon Roll; Prfct Atten Awd; Cert Of Merit Achvt Math 85; Cert Of Merit Math Clb 86; MCC; Elect Tech.

SONI, ABDON; All Hallows HS; New Yhork, NY; (Y); 2nd Hnrs 83-84; 1st Hnrs 84-85; IONA; Cmptr Sci.

SOŃKIN, MICHAEL; East Islip HS; East Islip, NY; (Y); 37/450; Bsktbl; Ftbl; High Hon Roll; Hon Roll; Jr NHS; NHS; Prfct Atten Awd; Pres Schlr; Spanish NHS; Spanish Clb; Tchrs Fed Crdt Union Schlrshp 86; NYSAHPE RD Awd Outstndng Physcl Prfrmnc Schlrshp & Ctznshp 86; SUNY; Soc Sci.

SONNAK, SAMANTHA; Beacon HS; Beacon, NY; (S); 5/206; Am Leg Aux Girls St; Drama Clb; Girl Scts; Key Clb; Latin Clb; School Musical; School Play; Nwsp Ed-Chief; DAR Awd; High Hon Roll; Peggy Wood Awd Best Suprtng Actress 85; Harvard Model Congress 86; Smmr Sci Inst SUNY 85; Med.

SONNENSTEIN, MICHAEL; E Meadow HS; E Meadow, NY; (S); 3/340; FBLA; Pres Key Clb; Sec Temple Yth Grp; Band; Orch; Nwsp Ed-Chief; Var Crs Cntry; Var Trk; VP NHS; Columbia U Sci Hnrs Prog 84.

SONNTAG, DANIEL; Huntington HS; Huntington, NY; (Y); Art Clb; Aud/Vis; Computer Clb; Drama Clb; Library Aide; Band; Color Guard; Stage Crew; Yrbk Stf; Rep Jr Cls; SUNY; Psychlgst.

SONNY, MARYA; Syosset HS; Syosset, NY; (Y); 3/490; Hosp Aide; Trs Leo Clb; Ed Nwsp Rptr; Var Bsktbl; Var Socr; Trs NHS; Ntl Merit Ltr; Clmba U Schltc Prss Assn Awd-Jrnlsm 83, 86; Newsdy Hgh Hnrs Schlrshp Rnnr-Up 86; MA Inst Of Technlgy; Premed.

SOOHOO, JAMES; New Rochelle HS; New Rochelle, NY; (Y); Church Yth Grp; Nwsp Rptr; Nwsp Stf; Yrbk Rptr; Yrbk Stf; Lit Mag; JV Lcrss.

SOONG, SUSAN; Williamsville East HS; East Amherst, NY; (Y); 3/301; Pres French Clb; Sec VP Math Clb; Model UN; Ski Clb; Pres Orch; Pres NHS; Ntl Merit Ltr; Wellesley Bk Awd 85; NY All ST String Orch Concrtmistrss 85; Natl Hnrs H S Orch 86.

SOOTHCAGE, TERRY ANN; Whitehall JR SR HS; Whitehall, NY; (Y); 12/76; French Clb; Trs Ski Clb; SADD; Varsity Clb; Yrbk Stf; Pres Frsh Cls; Pres Stu Cncl; Var Crs Cntry; Score Keeper; Computer Clb; NY ST Rgnts Schlrshp 86; CIBA Sci Awd 86; Plattsburgh ST U; Engrng.

SOPICKI, LAURA; Immaculate Academy HS; Lackawanna, NY; (Y); French Clb; Orch; Nwsp Stf; Yrbk Ed-Chief; Stu Cncl; Trk; Hon Roll; Canisius Coll; Lang.

SORBELLO, ELIZABETH; Rome Catholic HS; Rome, NY; (Y); 5/68; Chorus; School Musical; Nwsp Stf; Yrbk Stf; Capt Var Trk; Hon Roll; Sec NHS; Pres Acdmc Fit Awd 86; Le Moyne Carson Schlrshp & Grant 86; Le Moyne Coll; Psychlgy.

SORBERO, MARK; Amsterdam HS; Amsterdam, NY; (Y); Latin Clb; Varsity Clb; Rep Frsh Cls; Rep Jr Cls; Rep Stu Cncl; Var JV Ftbl; High Hon Roll; NHS; Boy Scts; 4-H.

SORCE, MARIA F; Niagara Wheatfield HS; Niagara Falls, NY; (Y); 32/300; VP Pep Clb; Hon Roll; NHS; Cert Of Merit And Achvt 83-86; Brynt And Stratton Sec Sci Schlrshp 86; NYS Regnts Schlrshp 86; Bryant & Stratton; Info Procssg.

SORECA, LORI A; Baldwin SR HS; Baldwin, NY; (Y); 48/476; GAA; VP Key Clb; SADD; Bsktbl; Lcrss; Mgr(s); Score Keeper; Hon Roll; NHS; Pres Schlr; Regents Scholar 86; SUNY Binghampton; Bio.

SORENSEN, LINDA; L I Lutheran HS; Malverne, NY; (S); 10/94; French Clb; Ski Clb; SADD; Yrbk Stf; Var Socr; Cit Awd; High Hon Roll; Hon Roll; Jr NHS; NHS; Nutrition.

SORGIE JR, JOSEPH G; William Floyd HS; Mastic Beach, NY; (Y); 179/454; Var Trk; Navy; Aviatn Elec.

SORIANO, ELIZABETH T; St Francis Prep; Flushing, NY; (S); 15/653; Cmnty Wkr; Drm & Bgl; High Hon Roll; VP NHS; Most Dedctd Judo Plyr 84; Bio.

SORKIN, DIANA; F D R HS; Brooklyn, NY; (Y); 18/637; Art Clb; Cmnty Wkr; Variety Show; Lit Mag; High Hon Roll; NHS; Pres Schlr; St Gaudins Mdl 86; 8th Annl Statue Of Lbrty Pstr Cntst 86; Anmls Of Frdm Sclptr Cntst 85; Pratt Inst; Grphc Dsgn.

SORRELL, SHELLEY; Northern Adirondack Central Schl; Ellenburg Depot, NY; (Y); Girl Scts; Teachers Aide; Band; JV Bsktbl; JV Var Socr; JV Sftbl; JV Var Vllybl; High Hon Roll; Hon Roll; VFW Awd; Plattsburagh ST; Psych.

SORRENTINO II, GERALD; St Francis HS; West Seneca, NY; (Y); Var Ice Hcky; Hon Roll; NY ST Rgnts Schlrshp 86; St Bonaventure; Comp Engr.

SORRENTINO, MARIA; Mohonasen HS; Schenectady, NY; (Y); Cmnty Wkr; SADD; Flag Corp; Nwsp Stf; Bsktbl; Vllybl; Maria Coll; Physcl Thrpy.

SOSA, EVA; Bronx H S Of Science; Far Rockaway, NY; (Y); Latin Clb; Red Cross Aide; Spanish Clb; Acpl Chr; Orch; Stage Crew; Lit Mag; Var Cheerleading; Im Vllybl; Gov Hon Prg Awd; Engr Womn Hnr Math & Sci 86; Soc Of Wmn Ad Awd/Peer Sprt & Acadmc Excllnc & Actv 86; Cornell U; Engr.

SOSA, MARIBEL; Hutchinson Central Technical HS; Buffalo, NY; (Y); ROTC; ROTC; Concert Band; Jazz Band; Nwsp Rptr; Hon Roll; Cmnty Wkr; Mrchg Band; Nwsp Stf; Yrbk Stf; Boston U; Engrng.

SOSA, TARA; Monroe HS; Rochester, NY; (Y); Hosp Aide; Math Tm; Model UN; Jazz Band; Stu Cncl; Crs Cntry; High Hon Roll; NHS; Trk; Prfct Atten Awd; Harvard Bk Awd 86; Lawrence Klepper Schlr Ath Awd 83 & 84; Rochester Pub Libr JR Lit Awd 86; Physician.

SOSKIND, PAMELA; Bronx HS Of Science; Flushing, NY; (Y); Political Wkr; Varsity Clb; Orch; Socr; Vet Med.

SOSNE, PAMELA; Kings Park SR HS; Kings Park, NY; (Y); 5/422; Pres Debate Tm; NFL; Science Clb; Sec Speech Tm; Symp Band; Nwsp Ed-Chief; Tennis; NHS; Temple Yth Grp; Concert Band; Stu Cngrs Albny NY 86; Tchrs Awd Physcs 86; Fnlst Bausch & Lomb Awd 86; Law.

SOSNICKI, DARLENE; Center Mohches HS; Ctr Moriches, NY; (Y); 24/91; Sec Spanish Clb; Band; Church Choir; Hon Roll; NYSSMA Awds Fluet Solo 84-86; Optmetry.

SOTO, AIMEE; Grace Dodge Voc HS; Bronx, NY; (Y); Yrbk Ed-Chief.

SOTO, ALEXANDER; Benjamin Franklin HS; Rochester, NY; (Y); Trs Church Yth Grp; Exploring; Quiz Bowl; Scholastic Bowl; Var Tennis; Bausch & Lomb Sci Awd; High Hon Roll; Hon Roll; NHS; Samuel Jorres Schlrshp Awd 86; Cert Outstndng Schltc Achvt 86; Cert Partcptn HS Prog Cnts 86; NY Inst Of Tech; Comp Sci.

SOTO, BIGDALIA; John Jay HS; Brooklyn, NY; (Y); Hosp Aide; Office Aide; Science Clb; Teachers Aide; Chorus; Color Guard; School Musical; School Play; Cit Awd; Hon Roll; Won Tckts To Washington Dc 84; Mdl Swng, Awd In Spnsh & Cookng 84; Awd Mth & Art 85; Hunter Coll; RN.

SOTO, CAROLYN; Yonkers HS; Yonkers, NY; (Y); Girl Scts; Prfct Atten Awd; Bkpng & Accntng Awd FBLA 86; Pace U; Accntng.

SOTO, CINDY; St Agnes Academic Schl; Flushing, NY; (Y); 26/296; Cmnty Wkr; Dance Clb; School Play; Variety Show; Yrbk Phtg; Cheerleading; Twrlr; Hon Roll; NHS; St Johns; Optmtry.

SOTO, LIZETTE; Alfred E Smith HS; Bronx, NY; (Y); Library Aide; Varsity Clb; VICA; Color Guard; Yrbk Stf; Wrstlng; High Hon Roll; Hon Roll; NHS; Prfct Atten Awd; US Army Resrv Natl Schlr Awd 84 & 85; Bronx Bourough Rpes Achvt Awd 84; Intl Papr Co Schlrshp 85; Maritime Coll; Mecnhcl Engr.

SOTO, MYRA; George Wingate HS; Brooklyn, NY; (Y); Sec Church Yth Grp; Office Aide; Teachers Aide; Church Choir; Stage Crew; High Hon Roll; JR Arista 84; Law Bus.

SOTO, STEVE; Park West HS; Brooklyn, NY; (Y); Boys Clb Am; Exploring; Key Clb; Math Clb; Radio Clb; Ski Clb; Nwsp Phtg; Bsbl; Bsktbl; Wt Lftg.

SOTOMAYOR, JAMES; Bronx HS; Yonkers, NY; (Y); Aud/Vis; Boy Scts; Library Aide; Red Cross Aide; Var Trk; Med.

SOTTUNG, ROBERT; Hicksville HS; Hicksville, NY; (Y); Band; Concert Band; Var Ice Hcky; JV Lcrss; High Hon Roll; Arch.

SOUCHECK, BLANCHE E; Smithtown H S West; Kings Park, NY; (Y); VP Thesps; Mrchg Band; Orch; Pep Band; Symp Band; Socr; Trk; Pres Schlr; Spanish NHS; St Schlr; Bst Thespian Awd 86; Band Awd Grad SR 86; Rutgers U; Doctor.

SOULE, DEBBIE; W C Mepham HS; N Bellmore, NY; (Y); Pres Acpl Chr; Dance Clb; Drama Clb; Math Tm; Madrigals; School Musical; High Hon Roll; NHS; All ST Chorus NYSSMA 85-86; All Cnty Chorus NMEA 84-86; Suny Albany; Psych.

SOULE, KIM; Hilton HS; Brockport, NY; (Y); 4-H; Ski Clb; Lit Mag; JV Trk; High Hon Roll; Hon Roll; Sury Brockport Coll; Bus Adm.

SOULOPULOS, ELIZABETH; St Francis Prep; Whitestone, NY; (S); Church Yth Grp; School Play; Nwsp Rptr; Nwsp Stf; Rep Jr Cls; Im Sftbl; Im Vllybl; Hon Roll; Spanish NHS; Georgetown U; Intl Law.

SOURBES, MAGALI; Mamaroneck HS; Larchmont, NY; (Y); German Clb; Spanish Clb; Spanish NHS; 2nd Pl Iona Coll Lang Cntst Frnch 85; Lycee Renoir; Film.

SOUTHALL, DIANA E; Newfane HS; Lockport, NY; (S); 5/181; Aud/Vis; Drama Clb; Sec Math Clb; Ski Clb; Nwsp Stf; Ed Yrbk Ed-Chief; Hon Roll; NHS; Ntl Merit Ltr; Acdmc Lttr Math & Engl 85; Bus.

SOUTHARD, GAIL; Cato-Meridian HS; Cato, NY; (Y); 4-H; French Clb; Trs GAA; Concert Band; Var Crs Cntry; Var Trk; Var Vllybl; Hon Roll; NHS; Prfct Attndnc Awd 6 Yrs 86; Bus.

SOUTHARD, JOAN; Academy Of St Josephs; Massapequa Pk, NY; (Y); SADD; Yrbk Phtg; Yrbk Stf; Sec Frsh Cls; Sec Stu Cncl; Var Bsktbl; Var Crs Cntry; Var Tennis; Var Trk; Hon Roll; Vrsty Tnns-Mst Imprvd Plyr 84; Boston Coll; Pre-Med.

SOUTHARD II, JOHN L; Thomas A Edison HS; Elmira, NY; (Y); 1/74; Am Leg Boys St; Model UN; Quiz Bowl; Pres Stu Cncl; Trk; Bausch & Lomb Sci Awd; Cit Awd; Lion Awd; Val; Chess Clb; RPI Math & Sci Awd 85; Elmira Coll Key Awd 85; Clarkson U; Chem.

SOUTHARD, TERRI; Emira Southside HS; Elmira, NY; (Y); 50/330; Dance Clb; Pep Clb; Ski Clb; Spanish Clb; Varsity Clb; Chorus; Mrchg Band; Nwsp Stf; Yrbk Stf; Tennis; SUNY Oswego.

SOUTHWICK, CATHY; Williamsville South HS; Williamsville, NY; (Y); AFS; Church Yth Grp; Cmnty Wkr; Dance Clb; Library Aide; SADD; Hon Roll; Outstndng YES 85; Art.

SOUZA, BETH; Roy C Ketcham HS; Poughkeepsie, NY; (Y); Art Clb; Church Yth Grp; Dance Clb; Pep Clb; Varsity Clb; School Musical; Rep Stu Cncl; Var Capt Cheerleading; Hon Roll; Hotel Mgnt.

SOWINSKI, ALEXANDRA; St Marys Girls HS; Glen Head, NY; (Y); 26/170; Church Yth Grp; Math Clb; JV Crs Cntry; Var JV Trk; High Hon Roll; Hon Roll; NHS; Aerosp Engr.

SPACE, CAROL A; Fairport HS; Fairport, NY; (Y); VP Pres SADD; Chorus; Yrbk Bus Mgr; Rep Sr Cls; Capt Cheerleading; Hon Roll; NHS; St Lawrence U; Bio.

SPACK, MELISA; Grover Cleveland HS; Buffalo, NY; (Y); Art Clb; Spanish Clb; Ski Clb; Score Keeper; Sftbl; Trk; Vllybl; Hon Roll.

SPADAFORA, ADRIANA; St Catharine Acad; Bronx, NY; (Y); 4/185; Teachers Aide; Variety Show; Hon Roll; NHS; Ntl Merit Ltr; 1st Hnr Frnch Ii & Iii Iona Lng Cntst 85 & 86; Englsh Awd 85; Psych.

SPADARO, JOHN; Nazareth Regional HS; Brooklyn, NY; (Y); SADD; Nwsp Rptr; Bus.

SPADO, GINA; Frankfort-Schuyler HS; Frankfort, NY; (S); French Clb; FBLA; GAA; Key Clb; SADD; Concert Band; Rep Stu Cncl; Vllybl; High Hon Roll; NHS; Bus Adm.

SPAGNOLA, BRIAN; Amsterdam HS; Amsterdam, NY; (Y); 40/316; Cmnty Wkr; Rep Stu Cncl; JV Var Bsbl; JV Var Bsktbl; Hon Roll; Jr NHS; NHS; Frshmn Bsktbll Capt 83-84; Bus Admin.

SPAGNOLI, CHRISTIAN; Onondaga Central HS; Syracuse, NY; (S); 1/71; Trs Science Clb; Spanish Clb; High Hon Roll; NHS; Physcs.

SPAGNOLO, ANTHONY; Spring Valley HS; Spring Vly, NY; (Y); 5/441; High Hon Roll; Hon Roll; Jr NHS; Mu Alp Tht; NHS; Spanish NHS; Church Yth Grp; Computer Clb; Math Clb; Spanish Clb; NY ST Regnt Schlrshp 86; Fll Schlrshp Manhattan Coll Schl Of Engrng 86; Manhattan Coll NY; Elctrcl Eng.

SPAID, BRIAN M; Charles H Roth HS; Henrietta, NY; (Y); 6/195; Boy Scts; Crs Cntry; Ftbl; Capt Trk; French Hon Soc; Hon Roll; Jr NHS; NHS; Rgnts Schlrshp Awd 86; St John Fisher Coll; Bus.

SPANAKOS, HELEN; Garden City SR HS; Garden City, NY; (Y); Art Clb; Camera Clb; Dance Clb; French Clb; GAA; Hosp Aide; Intnl Clb; Key Clb; Letterman Clb; Office Aide; Financg.

SPANBURGH, JOHN; Fayetteville-Manlius HS; Manlius, NY; (Y); Im Bsktbl; JV Ftbl; Wt Lftg; Hon Roll; Pre Phrmcy.

SPANER, DOUGLAS; New Rochelle HS; New Rochelle, NY; (Y); Ski Clb; Stage Crew; Yrbk Phtg; Var Capt Lcrss; Var L Socr; NHS; Multi-Media Awd 84.

SPANGENBURG, CHRIS; Kendall JR SR HS; Kendall, NY; (Y); 29/84; FTA; Pres Pep Clb; Capt Color Guard; School Musical; Rep Stu Cncl; Capt Var Cheerleading; JV Var Socr; High Hon Roll; Hon Roll; Prfct Atten Awd; Jone Awd Schl Awd 86; SUNY Oswego; Elem Educ.

SPANNHAKE, PAUL; Spackenkill HS; Poughkeepsie, NY; (Y); Rep Frsh Cls; Rep Soph Cls; Rep Jr Cls; Capt L Golf; High Hon Roll; Arch Engrng.

SPARKS, PAMELA; Acad Of St Joseph; Ft Salonga, NY; (Y); Library Aide; Pep Clb; Service Clb; SADD; Teachers Aide; High Hon Roll; Social Work.

SPARKS, SONELL; De Witt Clinton HS; Bronx, NY; (Y); Cmnty Wkr; Debate Tm; Key Clb; Library Aide; Office Aide; Teachers Aide; Cit Awd; Hon Roll; NHS; Prfct Atten Awd; Stanley Simons Crtfct Achvmnt 84; Exclnc Sci Mth Frnch & SS 85; Brnx Spr Yth 85; Prd Ynks 85; PRE-MED Nrsrgn.

SPARKS, YARVETTA; Corcoran HS; Syracuse, NY; (Y); Church Yth Grp; Band; Chorus; COMP.

SPARLING, JANICE; Ripley Central HS; Ripley, NY; (S); 6/26; Pep Clb; Trs Rep Frsh Cls; Trs Pres Jr Cls; Pres Sr Cls; Rep Stu Cncl; Var Bsktbl; Var Sftbl; Var Capt Vllybl; Hon Roll; NHS; Outstndng Sportsmnshp, Loyalty, Spirit, Dedication; Vllybll, Sftbll; Vllybll Sherman Tournmnt All Star; Villa Maria Coll; Nrsng.

SPARLING, MARGARET; Elmira Southside HS; Elmira, NY; (Y); 37/305; Aud/Vis; Cmnty Wkr; FBLA; JA; Radio Clb; Spanish Clb; Chorus; Stage Crew; Nwsp Rptr; Nwsp Stf; Achvt Awd; JR Exec Awd; Exec Awd; Corning CC; Exec Sec.

SPARR, PAUL; St Francis Prep; Bellerose, NY; (Y); Im Bsktbl; Im Bowling; Aerontcs.

SPARRER, JENNIFER; Lyndonville Central HS; Lyndonville, NY; (Y); Church Yth Grp; Cmnty Wkr; Chorus; Church Choir; School Play; Yrbk Stf; Cheerleading; Cntrl City Bus Inst; Rtl Mrktg.

SPAS, LISA; Dundee Central Schl; Dundee, NY; (Y); Drama Clb; Girl Scts; Acpl Chr; Band; Chorus; School Musical; School Play; Var L Bsktbl; Var L Socr; JV Sftbl; Dundee Symphnc Steel Drum Bnd; Music Teacher.

SPATAFORA, NICOLETTE; Huntington HS; Huntington, NY; (Y); Hon Roll; Linguistcs.

SPATARO, JOHN C; Forest Hills HS; Middle Village, NY; (Y); 29/840; Library Aide; Office Aide; Yrbk Bus Mgr; Rep Sr Cls; NHS; Regents Scholar 86; Queens Coll Pres Merit Awd 83; NY U; Attrny.

SPATH, MARGARET ELLEN; Mercy HS; Rensselaer, NY; (Y); 2/46; Pep Clb; Var Capt Bsktbl; Var Sftbl; High Hon Roll; Jr NHS; NHS; Ntl Merit Ltr; Sal; Siena Coll-Pres Schlrshp 86-87; NY St Regents Schlrshp 86-87; Siena Coll; Comp Sci.

SPAULDING, JENNIFER J; East Syracuse-Minoa HS; E Syracuse, NY; (Y); 5/333; Ski Clb; Concert Band; Mrchg Band; Variety Show; Yrbk Stf; Var Fld Hcky; High Hon Roll; Jr NHS; NHS; NY ST Regents Scholar 86; Ithaca Coll; Cmmnctns.

SPEAKER, ANNE; Brockport HS; Brockport, NY; (Y); Church Yth Grp; Cmnty Wkr; Latin Clb; Mathletes; Mgr Radio Clb; Ski Clb; Stage Crew; High Hon Roll; NHS.

SPEAR, NOEL; Clarkstown HS; New City, NY; (Y); Ski Clb; Jazz Band; Orch; School Musical; Pres Jr Cls; JV Crs Cntry; JV Trk; High Hon Roll; Mu Alp Tht; NHS.

SPEARMAN, MELANIE; Dryden JR & SR HS; Dryden, NY; (Y); Church Yth Grp; Ski Clb; Lit Mag; JV Var Fld Hcky; Stat Ftbl; Im Vllybl; High Hon Roll; Hon Roll; NHS.

SPECHT, MICHAEL J; Ward Melville HS; Setauket, NY; (Y); 114/711; JV Bsbl; Var L Bsktbl; Var L Socr; High Hon Roll; Jr NHS; NHS; NHS; NY ST Regnts Schlrshp Wnnr; Al-Leag I 1st Tm Sccr; 3-Vlg Schls 4-Sport Awd; SUNY Binghamton; Bus.

SPEEDLING, THOMAS J; Tottenville HS; Staten Island, NY; (Y); 33/871; Boy Scts; Var Crs Cntry; Var Trk; High Hon Roll; Hon Roll; Jr NHS; NHS; St Schlr; Med.

SPENCE, CAPLE; Smithtown HS West; Smithtown, NY; (Y); Boy Scts; Cmnty Wkr; Hosp Aide; Rep Jr Cls; Rep Stu Cncl; Crs Cntry; High Hon Roll; Hon Roll; Spanish NHS; Runner-Up Stu Congress Cntst 85; Enrichmnt Brookhaven Natl Lab 85; Enrichmnt Cornell U Of Engnrg 86; Med.

SPENCE, HOWARD; Nazareth Regional HS; Brooklyn, NY; (Y); Boy Scts; Church Yth Grp; Cmnty Wkr; Computer Clb; Library Aide; PAVAS; Chorus; School Play; Gym; Hon Roll; 2nd Hnrs B Av; Sci & Rlgn Awd; St John U; Entrtnr.

SPENCE, RUTH; Pelham Memorial HS; Pelham, NY; (Y); Political Wkr; SADD; Yrbk Phtg; Yrbk Sprt Ed; Yrbk Stf; Lit Mag; Pres Frsh Cls; Trs Soph Cls; VP Jr Cls; Pres Stu Cncl; Hubh O Brian Ldrshp Smnr 85; Ldrshps Smnrs 84-86; Artst.

SPENCER, CATHI; Central Islip HS; Central Islip, NY; (Y); 19/382; Exploring; FNA; Girl Scts; Hosp Aide; Band; Stage Crew; Lit Mag; Trs Frsh Cls; Trs Soph Cls; Trs Jr Cls; SUNY; Spch Pathlgy.

SPENCER, CONNIE; Lowville Academy Central Schl; Lowville, NY; (Y); FHA; Off Frsh Cls; Bsktbl; Bus Adm.

SPENCER, DANIEL R; Maple Grove JR Sr HS; Bemus Point, NY; (Y); 12/88; Church Yth Grp; Spanish Clb; Yrbk Stf; Pres Frsh Cls; Rep Soph Cls; Rep Sr Cls; Stu Cncl; Var L Bsktbl; Var L Trk; High Hon Roll; Awds Scorng 90 Pct NYS Regnts Ex 84-86; Acad Ltr 3.5 86; Chem.

SPENCER, DONNA; New Rochelle HS; New Rochelle, NY; (Y); Church Yth Grp; Cmnty Wkr; Church Choir; Yrbk Ed-Chief; Var Sftbl; Law.

SPENCER, FAYE; Addison Central HS; Addison, NY; (Y); GAA; VP Score Keeper; Var Socr; Var L Sftbl; Hon Roll; Cntrl Cty Bus Inst; Bus.

SPENCER, JAMES; John Jay HS; Wappingers Falls, NY; (Y); 1/519; Pres Debate Tm; Pres Orch; Trs Jr Cls; Trs Sr Cls; Bausch & Lomb Sci Awd; Ntl Merit SF; Val; 3rd Pl Awd In Math At Intl Sci & Engrng Fair 85; Thomas J Watson Mem Schlrshp 86; Stnfrd U; Math.

SPENCER, MARK D; Dansville SR HS; Dansville, NY; (Y); 14/147; Am Leg Boys St; Church Yth Grp; Cmnty Wkr; Drama Clb; Letterman Clb; Math Clb; Ski Clb; Varsity Clb; Band; Chorus; Cls Up Prgm 86; Stu Ldrshp Retreat 85 & 86; All Cnty Bnd 84 & 85; Pltcl Sci.

SPENCER, ROBERT; J C Birdlebough HS; Phoenix, NY; (Y); 1/180; Concert Band; Drm Mjr(t); Jazz Band; Pres Stu Cncl; Bausch & Lomb Sci Awd; VP NHS; Ntl Merit Ltr; Val; Mrchg Band; Off Frsh Cls; Area All ST Band 86, All Cnty 86.

SPENCER, ROBYN; Canarsie HS; Brooklyn, NY; (Y); Cmnty Wkr; Cornll Skidmore Bates; Psychlgy.

SPENCER, SURAYA; Uniondale HS; Baldwin, NY; (Y); Mathletes; Band; Mrchg Band; Rep Sr Cls; Rep Stu Cncl; Cheerleading; Gym; Trk; High Hon Roll; Jr NHS; Engrng HS Pgm Manhattan Coll 86; Indstrl Engrng.

SPENGLER, ANDREA M; Franklin K Lane HS; Woodhaven, NY; (Y); 2/659; Scholastic Bowl; Chorus; Rep Sr Cls; Tennis; High Hon Roll; Jr NHS; NHS; Sal; St Schlr; Cmptv Schlrshp St Johns U 86; Schltc Excllnc Schlrshp St Johns U 86; St Johns U; Elem Tchr.

SPENGLER, SARAH; Hamburg SR HS; Hamburg, NY; (Y); Pres AFS; Library Aide; SADD; Acpl Chr; Chorus; Church Choir; Madrigals; School Musical; Stage Crew; Nwsp Stf; Psychlgy.

SPENSIERI, ANNA C; St Francis Prep; Flushing, NY; (S); 120/750; Dance Clb; Intnl Clb; Chorus; Hon Roll; Bus.

SPERA, MARIA; St Marys Girls HS; Garden City, NY; (Y); 8/160; Hosp Aide; Trs Service Clb; Stage Crew; High Hon Roll; NHS.

SPERA, PATRICIA; Port Richmond HS; Staten Island, NY; (Y); Cmnty Wkr; French Clb; Math Tm; Band; School Musical; French Hon Soc; Hon Roll; NHS; Alt NY Tokyo Exch Pgm 85; Awd Soc Of Prof Frnch Amer 86; Biol Med.

SPERANZA, CARLA; De Sales Catholic HS; Lockport, NY; (Y); 13/28; Hosp Aide; Varsity Clb; Nwsp Phtg; Yrbk Phtg; JV Var Bsktbl; Var Capt Socr; Var Sftbl; Prfct Attndnc Awd 82-83; Lcl Hosp Awd 50 Hrs-More Svc 85; Physcl Thrpy.

SPERBER, DE ANN K; Wayne Central HS; Walworth, NY; (Y); 16/193; Girl Scts; Hosp Aide; Mathletes; Color Guard; Mgr Stage Crew; Yrbk Ed-Chief; Yrbk Stf; Var L Tennis; Hon Roll; NHS; NYS Rgnts Schlrshp 86; Math Exclnce Awd 84; 100 Hr Vol Pin Highland Hosp Rochester 85; Hofstra U; Pre-Med.

SPERICO, LORI A; Eastport HS; Eastport, NY; (Y); 4/45; French Clb; Scholastic Bowl; Varsity Clb; Yrbk Ed-Chief; VP Stu Cncl; Capt Var Bsktbl; Capt Var Socr; Capt Var Sftbl; Hon Roll; NHS; All Suffik Cnty Girls Soccr And Sftbl 83-84; Outstndng Achvt Eng 85; U Of Buffalo; Chem Engrg.

SPERLING, APRIL; East Meadow HS; Farmingdale, NY; (S); 37/340; Aud/Vis; Computer Clb; Drama Clb; Science Clb; Thesps; Mrchg Band; Stage Crew; Lit Mag; Regents Schlrp 86; Xavier U Pres Schlrp; Xavier U; Filmmaking.

SPERRY, JOHN; Lake George Central HS; Lake George, NY; (Y); 10/84; Varsity Clb; School Play; VP Jr Cls; Rep Stu Cncl; Var Bsbl; Var Bsktbl; Var Socr; High Hon Roll; Hon Roll; NHS; Adirondack Lg All St Soccer 85-86; Pblc Rltns.

SPETER, ANDREW; Walt Whitman HS; Huntington Sta, NY; (Y); 45/497; Key Clb; Mathletes; Nwsp Phtg; JV Var Tennis; High Hon Roll; Hon Roll; Jr NHS; Spanish NHS; 1st Pl Sci Fair 83; Honarary Mntn Sci Fair 84; Johns Hopkins; Pre-Med.

SPEZIALE, LANCE; Dunkirk HS; Dunkirk, NY; (Y); Am Leg Boys St; Computer Clb; Key Clb; Letterman Clb; Ski Clb; Varsity Clb; Var L Ftbl; Var Swmmng; Var Trk; Hon Roll; West Point.

SPICCI, ANTHONY A; Greece Olympia HS; Rochester, NY; (Y); 24/287; Am Leg Boys St; Pres Drama Clb; Off Ski Clb; School Play; Yrbk Ed-Chief; Crs Cntry; Trk; Cit Awd; High Hon Roll; NHS; NYS Rgnts 86; Monroe Cnty Assmbly Awd 86; U Of Rochester Schlrshp 86; SUNY Genesco; Blgy.

SPICHAL, VOLKER; Sachem HS; Farmingville, NY; (Y); 10/1400; Math Tm; Pres Ski Clb; JV Tennis; Jr NHS; NHS; NY Rgnts Schlrshp 85-86; U Of Vermont; Bus.

SPIEGEL, JENNI; Mineola HS; Williston Pk, NY; (Y); Pres Sec Church Yth Grp; Sec SADD; Scrkpr Bsktbl; Scrkpr Ftbl; Scrkpr Lcrss; Scrkpr Socr; Trk; Scrkpr Vllybl; Cmnty Wkr; Hon Roll; Nrsng.

SPIEGEL, KATHERINE; Academy Of St Joseph; Sayville, NY; (Y); Church Yth Grp; Hosp Aide; Pep Clb; Service Clb; SADD; Teachers Aide; Variety Show; JV Vllybl; AATF Ntl Frnch Awd 84; ASJ Ltn Excllnc Awd 86; Mrktg.

SPIEGELGLASS, JOY; Patchogve-Medford HS; Medford, NY; (Y); 15/620; Pres Var Temple Yth Grp; Chrmn Jr Cls; Off Sr Cls; Jr NHS; NHS; Pres Schlr; Spanish NHS; Drama Clb; Library Aide; Spanish Clb; Knghts Of Pyths Schlrshp 86; Margaret Hinkel Memrl Incntv Awd 86; U Of MA; Cmmnctns.

SPIEGLER, MARC A; Hawthorne Valley HS; Philmont, NY; (Y); 1/9; Cmnty Wkr; Yrbk Stf; Rep Frsh Cls; Rep Soph Cls; Rep Jr Cls; Rep Sr Cls; Rep Stu Cncl; JV Var Bsktbl; JV Var Vllybl; Ntl Merit SF; Rgnts Schlrshp 85; Hstry.

SPIELMAN, GEORGE LESLIE; Roxbury Central HS; New York, NY; (S); Church Yth Grp; Cmnty Wkr; Drama Clb; Library Aide; Ski Clb; Spanish Clb; Band; Chorus; Church Choir; Concert Band; Mst Imprvd Athlt 82; Cert On Bio Regnts Scr 85; MVP Sccr 83; Suny Of Delli; Accntnt.

SPILLANE, DAWN MARIE; H Frank Carey HS; Franklin Square, NY; (Y); Cmnty Wkr; VP Leo Clb; Hon Roll; Nassau CC; Physcl Therapy.

SPILLANE, KATHY; Moore Catholic HS; Staten Island, NY; (Y); Co-Capt NFL; School Musical; School Play; Im Swmmng; Var Tennis; NHS; Church Yth Grp; Spanish Clb; Yrbk Stf; Rep Frsh Cls.

SPILLANE, KRISTIN; Jamesville Dewitt HS; Syracuse, NY; (Y); French Clb; SADD; Band; Concert Band; Yrbk Stf; L Var Swmmng; High Hon Roll; Hon Roll; Ntl Merit Ltr.

SPILLMAN, CHRISTOPHER E; Livonia Central HS; Conesus, NY; (Y); 17/142; Am Leg Boys St; Ski Clb; Band; Mrchg Band; Var Capt Socr; High Hon Roll; Hon Roll; Pep Band; Im Bsktbl; Pres Acad Ftnss Awd 86; Acad Achvmnt Awd 86; NYS Regnts Schlrshp 85-86; Monroe Comm Coll; Eng.

SPINA, JANE; Frankfort-Schuyler Central Schl; Frankfort, NY; (S); 24/113; FBLA; Key Clb; Spanish Clb; Yrbk Stf; Var JV Vllybl; High Hon Roll; Suny At Oswego; Bus Adm.

SPINAK, ROBERT; Clarkstown North HS; New City, NY; (Y); JV Var Tennis; Jr NHS; Srv Spcl Olympcs 86; Med.

SPINK, RACHEL; Letchworth Central HS; Castile, NY; (Y); Cmnty Wkr; Color Guard; Yrbk Stf; VP Soph Cls; Rep Sr Cls; Cheerleading; Sftbl; High Hon Roll; Mst Outstndng Plyr In Sftbl 86; Med Asstnt.

SPINK, TAMATHA; Pioneer Central HS; Sardinia, NY; (Y); Aud/Vis; French Clb; JCL; Latin Clb; Chorus; Psych.

SPINKS, PHILIP; Sherman Central HS; Sherman, NY; (S); 2/37; Church Yth Grp; Drama Clb; French Clb; Chorus; Church Choir; School Play; Stage Crew; Stat Ftbl; High Hon Roll; NHS; Acadmc Al-Amer 84-85; Comp Repair.

SPINNER, JILL; Nardin Acad; E Amherst, NY; (Y); Ski Clb; School Musical; Stage Crew; Lit Mag; VP Frsh Cls; Sec Stu Cncl; Bsktbl; Merit Rll 84-86; Act Stdnt Bdy Ldr 84-86; Optmtry.

SPINOSA, SUSAN; Haverling Central Schl; Bath, NY; (Y); Library Aide; Boces Career Ctr-Bus Mach 85-86; Rochester Inst Of Tech; Psych.

SPIRO, JENNIFER L; Port Chester HS; Port Chester, NY; (Y); 9/240; Chess Clb; Computer Clb; VP Drama Clb; FTA; Key Clb; Ski Clb; VP Thesps; Pres Band; Pres Orch; Yrbk Stf; Regnts Schlrshp 86; Fairfield U; Law.

SPITERI, SAL; Archbishop Molloy HS; Rego Pk, NY; (Y); 88/383; Art Clb; Computer Clb; Ski Clb; Im Bsktbl; Crs Cntry; Im Ftbl; Im Sftbl; Trk; Hon Roll; Lcrss; Engrng.

SPITHOGIANIS, DESPINA; Whitestone Acad; Whitestone, NY; (S); 1/30; Nwsp Rptr; Yrbk Ed-Chief; Gold Medls All Subjects 83-86; Valdictrn 86; NYU Trustee Schlrshp 86; Fordham U; Pol Sci.

SPITZ, DONNA; Bishop Maginn HS; Ravena, NY; (Y); Art Clb; Dance Clb; Debate Tm; Drama Clb; English Clb; Ski Clb; SADD; Teachers Aide; Chorus; Nwsp Phtg; Tnns Awd 84-86; Ftbl Awd 86; Suny Coll Cableskill; Elem Ed.

SPITZ, STEVEN; Pierson HS; Sag Harbor, NY; (Y); 1/45; Am Leg Boys St; Spanish Clb; Nwsp Rptr; Yrbk Stf; VP Soph Cls; Pres Jr Cls; Pres Sr Cls; Rep Stu Cncl; Var Capt Bsbl; Var Capt Socr; U S Marine Corps Distngshd Ath Awd 85; NYS Regents Scholar 86; A Newsday Leadng Schlr 86; Brown U; Hstry.

SPODARYK, KAREN; Bishop Scully HS; Broadalbin, NY; (Y); Sec Art Clb; Hosp Aide; PAVAS; JV Capt Bsktbl; Cheerleading; Hon Roll; Natl Art Hnr Soc 83-86; 2nd Pl Century Clb Art Cont 84; Olympics Of Visual Arts 2nd Pl 85; Cazenovia Coll; Grphc Arts.

SPODARYK, KRISTEN; Bishop Scully HS; Broadalbin, NY; (Y); Drama Clb; French Clb; Pep Clb; Varsity Clb; School Play; Yrbk Stf; Var Capt Cheerleading; Var Pom Pon; Hon Roll; Maria Coll; Occptnl Thrpy.

SPONZA, LAURIE A; Sachem HSN HS; Holtsville, NY; (Y); 3/1579; Math Clb; Sec Math Tm; Scholastic Bowl; Orch; Bausch & Lomb Sci Awd; High Hon Roll; NHS; Ntl Merit Ltr; Schlr Yr 84; SCMTA Cnty Wnnr 1st Pl Lev II 85; Vet.

SPOOR, KEVIN; Mc Quaid Jesuit HS; Rochester, NY; (Y); Pres Debate Tm; Letterman Clb; Model UN; Science Clb; Ed Nwsp Stf; Yrbk Bus Mgr; Sec Stu Cncl; Stat Ftbl; High Hon Roll; NHS; Acad Lttr 85; U Of Notre Dame; Pre-Med.

SPOOR, SHERRY; Marlboro HS; Marlboro, NY; (Y); Cmnty Wkr; Library Aide; Office Aide; SADD; Teachers Aide; Var Vllybl; Hon Roll; Vrsty Ltr Vlybl 86; Nrs Aide Spec Achvt Awd 85; Libry Aide Spec Achvt Awd 85; Secy.

SPOSATO, CAREN M; Saint Dominic HS; Huntington Sta, NY; (Y); 17/119; Cmnty Wkr; Quiz Bowl; Ed Nwsp Rptr; Sec Stu Cncl; Cheerleading; Score Keeper; Hon Roll; Mdrn Art Awd 85; Vsul Arts.

SPOSATO, SARA; St Dominic HS; Huntington Stat, NY; (Y); 2/141; Library Aide; Model UN; Quiz Bowl; SADD; Nwsp Stf; Sec Stu Cncl; Cheerleading; High Hon Roll; NHS; Frnch, Eng, Math, Soc Studs, Theolgy, & Chem Awds; Biochem.

SPOTILA, JENNIFER; Cardinal OHARA HS; Tonawanda, NY; (S); 3/145; Drama Clb; French Clb; Political Wkr; Quiz Bowl; School Musical; Nwsp Ed-Chief; Nwsp Rptr; High Hon Roll; NHS; Brnz Mdl W NY Sci Congress 83; Three Scholar 83; Polit Sci.

SPOTO, MARK D; Southwestern Central HS; Jamestown, NY; (Y); 1/150; Am Leg Boys St; Scholastic Bowl; Concert Band; Jazz Band; Madrigals; Mrchg Band; Var Capt Vllybl; Dnfth Awd; NHS; Ntl Merit Ltr; Empire St Schlrshp Excllnce, Joseph M Golando Mem Awd Band Excllnce, Darwin C Perkins Math Awd 86; Boston U; Aerospace Engrng.

SPRAGUE, CHRIS; Whitesboro SR HS; Utica, NY; (Y); Library Aide; Band; Pep Band; Hon Roll.

SPRAGUE, ROBERT; Griffith Inst; Colden, NY; (Y); Pres Church Yth Grp; French Clb; JV Var Ftbl; High Hon Roll; NHS; Gold Medl-Buffalo Museum Of Sci Fair 82 & 86; Amere Lgn Awd 85; Aerosp Engrng.

SPRAKER, MELISSA; Richfield Springs Central HS; Richfield Spgs, NY; (Y); GAA; Var Fld Hcky; JV Var Vllybl; Hon Roll.

SPRENZ, VALERIE M; Alfred G Berner HS; Massapequa, NY; (Y); 7/412; Concert Band; Orch; Variety Show; Nwsp Rptr; Yrbk Stf; Cheerleading; NHS; Ntl Merit Ltr; Dance Clb; Drama Clb; NYS Regents Schlrshp 86; Deans Schlrshp Cornell U 86; Cornell U; Pre-Med.

SPRING, JEFF; Frontier Central HS; Athol Springs, NY; (Y); FBLA.

SPRING JR, SHAWN; Maple Hill HS; Castleton, NY; (S); 20/92; Radio Clb; Tennis; Hon Roll; Im Wrstlng; Regents Alg Final Exam High Grade 84; Arch.

SPRINGER, BERNICE; George W Wingate HS; Brooklyn, NY; (Y); Band; Chorus; Concert Band; SUNY; Psych.

SPRINGER, LAUREN; Stuyvesant HS; Brooklyn, NY; (Y); Library Aide; Science Clb; Lit Mag; Natl Achvt Schlrshp Pgm-Commended Studnt 85; Natl Hispanic Schlr Awds Pgm-Semi Fnlst 85.

SPRINGER, PAMELA; Attica Central HS; Attica, NY; (S); 12/150; Yrbk Stf.

SPRINGER, ROBERT M; Bronx HS Of Science; Fresh Meadows, NY; (Y); Aud/Vis; Civic Clb; Cmnty Wkr; Political Wkr; Pres Temple Yth Grp; Nwsp Rptr; Rep Stu Cncl; Hon Roll; St Schlr; Camera Clb; Molly Leffler Mem Schlrshp-Study & Trvl In Israel 85; SUNY-ALBANY; Attorney.

SPRINGER, SCOTT; Midwood At Brooklyn College; Brooklyn, NY; (Y); 151/667; Hosp Aide; Service Clb; Temple Yth Grp; Capt Lcrss; Albany; Pre-Med.

SPRINGER, SEAN; Hudson HS; Hudson, NY; (Y); 20/160; AFS; Chess Clb; Hon Roll; NHS; Dutchess CC; Comm Art.

SPRINGSTEEN, JEFFREY; Union-Endicott HS; Endicott, NY; (Y); Church Yth Grp; Drama Clb; Im Bsbl; Im Socr; Air Force.

SPROLE, LILA; Lansing Central HS; Ithaca, NY; (Y); Cmnty Wkr; Drama Clb; Spanish Clb; SADD; Chorus; School Musical; School Play; Stage Crew; Hon Roll; NHS; Awd For Taking Jets Eng Exam 86; Awd For Taking Jets Bio Exam 86; Psychology.

SPROUL, LISA E; Cohocton Central HS; Cohocton, NY; (Y); 2/27; French Clb; Scholastic Bowl; Band; Yrbk Phtg; VP Stu Cncl; Scrkpr Socr; Capt Trk; Vllybl; Cit Awd; High Hon Roll; Hghst Avg Hstry 83 & 85; Hghst Score NYS Hstry Regents 85; Regents Scholar 86; St Bonaventure U; Biol.

SPRUILL, YOLONDA; Fashion Industries HS; Brooklyn, NY; (Y); Dance Clb; Office Aide; Teachers Aide; Badmtn; Vllybl; Hon Roll; Prfct Atten Awd; Hon Cert Engl/Lang Arts 85; Cheyney U; Merchndsng.

SQUEO, MARYANN; St Joseph By The Sea HS; Staten Island, NY; (Y); Hon Roll; 2nd Highst Avg In Econ 86; Dante Mdl For Italian Studies 86; Coll Of Staten Isl; Tchr.

SQUERI, JOHN M; Nazareth Regional HS; Brooklyn, NY; (S); 6/276; French Clb; Math Tm; Varsity Clb; Crs Cntry; Trk; Wt Lftg; High Hon Roll; NHS; Calcls, Chem Awds 83 & 85; Sprt Awds Trck, X Cntry Tms 83-85; Aero Engr.

SQUIER, DENISE; Lakeland SR HS; Mahopac, NY; (Y); 20/344; Church Yth Grp; Drama Clb; SADD; Teachers Aide; Band; Chorus; School Musical; NHS; Debate Tm; 4-H; Presdntl Acadmc Ftns Awd 86; Mdrn Miss Schlrshp Pgnt Fnlst 85; Stetson U; Music Educ.

SQUIERS, KEVIN; Hoosick Falls Central HS; Eagle Bridge, NY; (Y); Boy Scts; Cmnty Wkr; French Clb; Chorus; Var Bsbl; Var Bsktbl; Prfct Atten Awd; Egl Sct 85; Asst Sctmstr 85 & 86; Ordr Of ArrwBSA 84-86.

SQUILLACE, LINDA; Linton HS; Schenectady, NY; (Y); 1/296; Lit Mag; DAR Awd; French Hon Soc; High Hon Roll; JC Awd; VP NHS; Ntl Merit Ltr; Val; Elks Ntl Schlrshp 86; Kiwanis Schlrshp 86; Mt Holyoke Coll; Med.

SQUIRE, KIM; John Dewey HS; Brooklyn, NY; (Y); Art Clb; Band; Chorus; LIU; Data Procssg.

SRIVASTAVA, MONISHA; E L Vandermeolen HS; Port Jeff, NY; (Y); 30/287; Cmnty Wkr; Variety Show; Nwsp Stf; Yrbk Stf; Lit Mag; Var L Tennis; High Hon Roll; Hon Roll; Plcd 3rd Tnns Conf; Hgh Hon Roll 85; SUNY Stony Brook; Pre-Med.

SRODA, JANET; Penfield HS; Penfield, NY; (Y); 194/351; Church Yth Grp; Drama Clb; SADD; Chorus; Church Choir; Stage Crew; Hon Roll; Monroe CC; Soc Wrk.

ST ANDREWS, JOHN; Ticonderoga HS; Ticonderoga, NY; (Y); 5/112; Aud/Vis; Boy Scts; Rep Frsh Cls; L Ftbl; L Trk; High Hon Roll; NHS; Prfct Atten Awd; Clarkson U; Engr.

ST CLAIR, ANGELA T; Saranac Central HS; Plattsburgh, NY; (S); 2/107; Church Yth Grp; Q&S; Yrbk Stf; Rep Stu Cncl; JV Cheerleading; High Hon Roll; Trs NHS; Ntl Merit Ltr; JV Cheerleading Ldrshp Awd 84; Century III Ldrs Pgm Cert Of Merit 85; Long Island U; Phrmcy.

ST CYR, PATRICIA; Huntington HS; Huntington, NY; (Y); Church Yth Grp; Pres Civic Clb; Cmnty Wkr; DECA; Sec Political Wkr; Service Clb; Chorus; Church Choir; Mrchg Band; Orch; Comm Svc Awd 84-86; Smmr Music Schrlshp Orch 81-82; Am Inst Frgn Study 81; Cornell U; Pre-Med.

ST GEORGE, JENNIFER; Schoharie Central HS; Schoharie, NY; (S); 10/80; Drama Clb; French Clb; Hosp Aide; Key Clb; SADD; Yrbk Stf; VP Stu Cncl; Tennis; High Hon Roll; Schl Fr Awd 85; Acad All Amer; Cndystriper 50 Hr Pin; Russell Sage Coll; Psych.

ST GERMAIN, ALISON; Our Lady Of Lourdes HS; Verbank, NY; (Y); Cmnty Wkr; Varsity Clb; Nwsp Rptr; Rep Frsh Cls; Trs Stu Cncl; Var JV Sftbl; JV Trk; High Hon Roll; Hon Roll; NHS; Recgntn Vlntr Svcs 85; Acad Awd 84-86; Yahama Music Fest 84-85; Med.

ST GERMAIN, KATHERINE A; Our Lady Of Lourdes HS; Verbank, NY; (Y); 18/180; Hosp Aide; Ski Clb; Varsity Clb; School Play; Nwsp Stf; Stu Cncl; Coach Actv; Capt Var Sftbl; High Hon Roll; NHS; Regntn Vlntr Svcs 85; HS Acdmc Awd 84-86; ST Frnch Tst Prtcptn Awd 84&86; Indstrl Engnrng.

ST GERMAINE, CYNTHIA; Mynderse Acad; Seneca Falls, NY; (S); Intnl Clb; Band; Color Guard; Concert Band; Jazz Band; Mrchg Band; School Musical; Rep Stu Cncl; Twrlr.

ST JOHN, KATHLEEN M; Remsen Central Schl; Forestport, NY; (Y); 3/44; Sec Trs Church Yth Grp; 4-H; Yrbk Stf; High Hon Roll; Hst NHS; Voice Dem Awd; Acad All-Amer 86; NYS Regents Schlrshp 86; Deans Schlrshp 86-87; Canisius Coll; Mrkt Rsrch.

ST JOHN, MARK L; Canajoharie Central HS; Palatine Bridge, NY; (Y); 5/90; Am Leg Boys St; Church Yth Grp; Cmnty Wkr; FCA; Red Cross Aide; SADD; Varsity Clb; Chorus; Ftbl; Trk; Ftbl Outstndng Lnmn Plaq Tri-Vly Leaque Champs & NYS PHS AA Sec II Chmps 85-86, 2nd Effort D Awd; Math.

ST JOHN, MELISSA; Catholic Central HS; Troy, NY; (S); 12/179; Drama Clb; French Clb; Mathletes; Math Clb; Nwsp Ed-Chief; Pom Pon; French Hon Soc; High Hon Roll; NHS; Vlntr Bureau Awd 83; Piano Rectl Awd 83; Babson Clg; Fince.

ST JOHN, OKARI; Gates-Chili SR HS; Rochester, NY; (Y); Bsktbl; Ftbl; Trk; Vllybl; Wt Lftg; Hon Roll; Sci Engrng.

ST LOUIS, JULIE A; Carthage Central HS; Deer River, NY; (Y); Chorus; Yrbk Ed-Chief; Yrbk Stf; Stu Cncl; Cheerleading; JCL; High Hon Roll; NHS; Prfct Atten Awd; Homecomg Prncss 84-85; Prom Prncss 85-86; Syracuse U; Comm.

ST MARY, JEFF; Franklin Acad; Malone, NY; (Y); French Clb; Ski Clb; Ed Nwsp Phtg; Ed Yrbk Phtg; VP Frsh Cls; Pres Jr Cls; Bsbl; Bsktbl; High Hon Roll; NHS; Franklin Acad Schlrshp Awd 85 & 86; Pre-Med.

ST ONGE, COLLEEN; G Ray Bodley HS; Fulton, NY; (Y); French Clb; JV Var Cheerleading; Dance.

ST ONGE, SCOTT; Hoosic Valley Central HS; Schagticoke, NY; (Y); Camera Clb; Yrbk Phtg; Yrbk Stf; Var Bsbl; USMC; Airprt Crsh Crw.

ST PETER, MATTHEW; Sherburne-Earlville HS; Sherburne, NY; (Y); Am Leg Boys St; French Clb; Yrbk Stf; JV Bsbl; Var L Ftbl; Var L Lcrss; Var Trk; Im Wt Lftg; Prfct Atten Awd; Lib Arts.

ST PIERRE, CHRISTIAN; Cohoes HS; Cohoes, NY; (Y); 6/171; High Hon Roll; NHS; Visual Arts Awd; Frances Lerg Koretz Mem Scholar Visl Arts; Exclince Frnch; SUNY Purchase; Visual Arts.

ST PIERRE, DANIELLE; Morian Central Schl; Port Henry, NY; (Y); Sec French Clb; GAA; Sec Trs Concert Band; Yrbk Stf; Pres Frsh Cls; Pres Soph Cls; Rep Stu Cncl; Capt Cheerleading; High Hon Roll; NHS; SUNY Potsdam; Pre Law.

ST PIERRE, RICHARD; Schalmont HS; Schenectady, NY; (Y); Boys Clb Am; Boy Scts; Science Clb; Ski Clb; Teachers Aide; Concert Band; Mrchg Band; Hon Roll; Prfct Atten Awd; Boys Clb Most Imprvd Swimmer 83; Comp Sci.

ST ROC, WOLFF RALPH; Lafayette HS; Brooklyn, NY; (Y); Girl Scts; Health Careers Awd 85-86; Stu Of The Month 77-78; Comp Bus.

ST ROSE, VALERIE; Bishop Ford HS; Brooklyn, NY; (Y); JV Cheerleading; Var Vllybl; Hon Roll.

STABILE, THOMAS J; Ardsley HS; Ardsley, NY; (Y); Model UN; Spanish Clb; Nwsp Sprt Ed; Spanish NHS; 1st Hnr IONA Prep Schl 83 & 84; Hnr Roll 85-86.

STACEY, KAREN; Frontier Central HS; Hamburg, NY; (Y); Cmnty Wkr; FBLA; Latin Clb; Sftbl; High Hon Roll; Hon Roll; Prfct Atten Awd; U Buffalo; Banking.

STACHINA, KATHY; Morris Central HS; Morris, NY; (Y); Band; Concert Band; Jazz Band; Mrchg Band; Var L Bsktbl; Var L Socr; Var L Sftbl; NHS; Sal; Schlrshp Hghst GPA 83-86; MVP Vrsty Sftbl 83 & 86; MVP JV Bsktbl 83; Coll Of St Rose; Bus.

STACHOWIAK, MARCIA A; West Seneca SR HS; West Seneca, NY; (Y); 25/559; Key Clb; Mathletes; Rep Stu Cncl; Im Bowling; French Hon Soc; High Hon Roll; Jr NHS; Pres NHS; Prfct Atten Awd; Regnts Clg Schlrshp Wnnr 85-86; Natl Hnr Soc Bkstre 85-86; UB; Engrng.

STACHOWIAK, MICHELLE; Villa Maria Acad; Buffalo, NY; (S); 1/106; Art Clb; Hosp Aide; JCL; Quiz Bowl; Service Clb; High Hon Roll; Pres NHS; NEDT Awd; Debate Tm; Latin Clb; Prncpls Schlrshp 83-85; Afro-Asian Essy Cntst 84; Outstndg Svc 85; St Bonaventure U; Bio.

STACK, LILLIAN; Dewitt Clinton HS; Bronx, NY; (Y); Hosp Aide; Key Clb; Office Aide; Color Guard; School Musical; Cit Awd; Hon Roll; NHS; Val; Sci Awd 84; Math Awd 84; Outstndg Voluntr Awd Pharmcy Dept 86; Cornell U; Pre Med.

STACKEWICZ, STACIE; Schalmont HS; Schenectady, NY; (Y); JV Capt Bsktbl; JV Capt Socr; JV Capt Sftbl; High Hon Roll; Hon Roll; NHS; Sister Of Lima Lang Awd 86; NYU; Cmmnctns.

STACKONIS, KRISTI; Union-Endicott HS; Endicott, NY; (Y); Church Yth Grp; Band; Chorus; Church Choir; Jazz Band; Mrchg Band; School Musical; School Play; Drama Clb; All-Star Band Awd In Jazz 85-86; Music.

STACY, RON; North Tonawanda SR HS; N Tonawanda, NY; (Y); Church Yth Grp; Varsity Clb; Var Capt Bowling; Yth Bwlrs Tour Schlrp 86; NFL Indivdls Champ Awd Bwlng 86; U Buffalo; Ag.

STADEL, CHERYL L; Holland Central HS; Holland, NY; (Y); 5/99; Sec AFS; Sec Trs JA; Red Cross Aide; Capt Color Guard; Stat Vllybl; High Hon Roll; Sec NHS; Rep Stu Cncl; Prfct Atten Awd; Library Aide; Dale Carnegie Schlrshp 84; Amer Lgn Axlry 83-86; NY ST Rgnts Schlrshp 86; Smith Coll.

STADELMAN, KAREN; De Sales Catholic HS; Lockport, NY; (S); 2/33; Hosp Aide; Yrbk Stf; High Hon Roll; Pres NHS; Ntl Merit Ltr; Sal; Ortho Surgry.

STADLER, JOHANNA; St Hildas & St Hughs HS; New York, NY; (Y); Cmnty Wkr; Teachers Aide; Chorus; Cit Awd; Hon Roll; NHS; Ntl Merit SF; Psych.

STADTLANDER, SHEILA; Lansingburgh HS; Troy, NY; (Y); Sec German Clb; SADD; Varsity Clb; Var Capt Crs Cntry; Var Socr; Var Trk; High Hon Roll; Jr NHS; NHS; Sftbl Vnsngburgh Miss Sftbl Lge 84-85; Marie Clg Utica; Occptnl Thrpy.

STAEBLER, LAURA; Alfred G Berner HS; Massapequa, NY; (Y); 52/396; Cmnty Wkr; Drama Clb; Hosp Aide; Library Aide; Red Cross Aide; Acpl Chr; Fld Hcky; Swmmng; Hon Roll; Villanova; Nrsg.

STAEHR, DIANE; Union Springs HS; Cayuga, NY; (Y); 10/105; Church Yth Grp; VP German Clb; Ski Clb; Band; Chorus; School Musical; Var Cheerleading; High Hon Roll; Hon Roll; NHS; NYSSMA Outstndng Music Awd Clrnt 87; 4-H Fd & Ntrtn Ctznshp 86; Grmn Awd 87; Psych.

STAFFA, JAMES A; Eden SR HS; Eden, NY; (Y); Math Tm; Orch; School Musical; Im Vllybl; Bausch & Lomb Sci Awd; Hon Roll; NHS; Ntl Merit SF; Prfct Atten Awd; Erie Cty Solo Festvl Awd 85-86; Chem Engr.

STAFFORD, DENISE; Sharon Springs Central Schl; Sharon Springs, NY; (S); 5/26; FBLA; FHA; Varsity Clb; Yrbk Bus Mgr; Sec Frsh Cls; Pres Soph Cls; Pres Jr Cls; Var Capt Bsktbl; JV Capt Cheerleading; Sftbl; Robert L Fitch Ldrshp Awd 84-85; Sharonsprngs Fire Qn 86; Spencer Bus Inst; Acctg.

STAFFORD, JENNIFER C; Maple Grove JR SR HS; Jamestown, NY; (Y); 7/86; Church Yth Grp; French Clb; Ski Clb; Band; Yrbk Stf; Sftbl; Jr NHS; NHS; Grove City Coll; Educ.

STAFFORD, NELSON; Sherburne-Earlville HS; Earlville, NY; (Y); Church Yth Grp; Ski Clb; School Play; Stage Crew; JV Ftbl; Mock Trial 86; 9th Comp Lit Exam NYS Dept Educ 85; Frgn Lang.

STAFFORD, SIOBHAN; St Vincent Ferrer HS; New York, NY; (Y); Church Yth Grp; Drama Clb; Political Wkr; Chorus; School Play; SF Miss NYS Teen Am 84; Miss NY Coleen Queen SF 85; Berkley Secretarial; Bus.

STAGICH, CHRIS; Saugerties HS; Saugerties, NY; (S); Acpl Chr; Sec Band; Chorus; Mrchg Band; Yrbk Stf; Sec Frsh Cls; Var Bsktbl; JV Sftbl; JV Vllybl; Hon Roll; Ed.

STAGLIANO, LORI ANN; E J Wilson HS; Rochester, NY; (Y); 7/300; JCL; Pres Latin Clb; Math Clb; Ski Clb; Chorus; Nwsp Stf; Sftbl; High Hon Roll; Hon Roll; NHS; Wgmns Schlrshp 86; Yng Amer Bwlng Allnc Schlrshp 86; Syrcse U Schlrshp 86; Syracuse U; Acctg.

STAGNER, MARY B; Camden Central HS; Blossvale, NY; (Y); 19/211; AFS; Ski Clb; Golf; High Hon Roll; Hon Roll; Morrisville A&T Coll; Acctg.

STAGNITTA, SALVATORE; Bishop Ford Central Catholic HS; Brooklyn, NY; (Y); Dance Clb; Intnl Clb; Ski Clb; Varsity Clb; Rep Frsh Cls; Rep Soph Cls; Stu Cncl; JV Var Swmmng; Hon Roll; St Johns U; Law.

STAGNITTA, TRACI L; Bishop Grumes HS; Liverpool, NY; (Y); Church Yth Grp; Intnl Clb; High Hon Roll; Jr NHS; Itln Hnr Soc 85-87; Outstndg Math Ablty Awd 84-86; JR Schlr Day SUNY Cortland 86; SUNY Cortland; Crmnl Jstc.

STAHL, SHERYL; Bronx H Schl Of Science; Bronx, NY; (Y); Office Aide; Political Wkr; Teachers Aide; Yrbk Stf; Lit Mag; Ntl Merit Ltr.

STAHLER, ESTHER D; Yeshiva Univ H S For Girls; Flushing, NY; (Y); Art Clb; Cmnty Wkr; Math Clb; Math Tm; Y-Teens; Swmmng; Hon Roll; Ntl Merit Ltr; Sal; Qns Schl Awd; CUNY Queens Coll; Math.

STAHLIN, BRUCE; Fayetteville-Manlius HS; Manlius, NY; (Y); Church Yth Grp; Jazz Band; Orch; School Musical; Swing Chorus; Symp Band; Drama Clb; Thesps; Sec Band; Smmr Fame Pgm 86; 1s Tpl Awd Talnt Comptn 85; Schlrshp Roberts Wesleyan Coll 86; Music.

STAHLMAN, JASON; Jamestown HS; Jamestown, NY; (Y); 1/396; Am Leg Boys St; Latin Clb; Quiz Bowl; Capt Camp Fr Inc; Orch; Rep Sr Cls; NHS; Val; Ski Clb; Spanish Clb; Empr ST Schlrshp Of Excellnc 86; Rnld L Sthlmn Sci Awd 86; Cornell U; Arspc Engrng.

STAHURA, MARY; Frontier SR HS; Blasdell, NY; (S); 55/500; Hosp Aide; Spanish Clb; Teachers Aide; Chorus; Color Guard; Concert Band; Yrbk Stf; Hon Roll; NHS; Girl Scts; MVP Sftbl Awd 84; Med Tech.

STAIMAN, ARI; Bronx Science HS; New York, NY; (Y); Cmnty Wkr; Yrbk Phtg; Ed Lit Mag; JV Var Score Keeper; Manage BX Sci Vllybl 85-87; 2nd Pl NYC Wood Wrkng Cont 86; All-Star Tm Vllybl 84-86.

STALEY, JEANNETTE E; Dewitt Clinton HS; Bronx, NY; (Y); Hosp Aide; Church Choir; School Musical; School Play; High Hon Roll; Hon Roll; Ralph Freyer Mem Awd 84.

STALEY, LYNN; Saranac Central HS; Saranac, NY; (S); 18/105; Drama Clb; French Clb; SADD; Chorus; Stage Crew; Yrbk Stf; Hon Roll; Nrsng.

STALICA, KEVIN; Pembroke Central HS; Corfu, NY; (Y); 4-H; Trk; 4-H Awd; Hon Roll; Excllnce Spn 86.

STALKER, MARK D; Chatham HS; East Chatham, NY; (Y); Cmnty Wkr; Dance Clb; Ski Clb; Chorus; School Musical; School Play; Swing Chorus; Crs Cntry; Trk; Hon Roll; Hudson Vly CC; Crim Justice.

STAMATEDES, CHRIS; Wallkill HS; Wallkill, NY; (S); 1/168; JV Var Bsbl; High Hon Roll; NHS; Ntl Merit Schol; Prfct Atten Awd; Acad Awd Bus, Math, Engl, Spnsh, Soc Stds 84; Acad Awds Math, Engl Spnsh 85; Math Sci.

STAMM, ANNA; Vestal SR HS; Denmark 2100; (Y); 5/410; German Clb; Chorus; Orch; Rptr Yrbk Ed-Chief; Yrbk Rptr; High Hon Roll; NHS; Ntl Merit Ltr; Yrbk Stf; Hon Roll; Watson Schlrshp SF, Early Grad, NY ST Rgnts Schlrshp Fnlst 86; U Copenhagen.

STAMM, SUSAN; Groton Central HS; Groton, NY; (Y); 11/86; Church Yth Grp; Dance Clb; Hosp Aide; Spanish Clb; VP Jr Cls; Rep Stu Cncl; Stat Bsbl; JV Var Cheerleading; High Hon Roll; Hon Roll; Prs Gamma Aplha Pimu Chap; Bus Admin.

STAMP, MICHAEL; Canisius HS; Amherst, NY; (Y); JV Var Bsbl; JV Bsktbl; JV Var Ftbl; Im Vllybl; Wt Lftg; Hon Roll; Golf Amhrst Audbn; Cntry Clb Trnmnts Awds & Hnrs; Jesuit Coll; Bus.

STAMPFER, BRIAN; South Park HS; Buffalo, NY; (Y); Cmnty Wkr; Hon Roll.

STANARD, BRYAN; G Ray Bodley HS; Fulton, NY; (Y); Boy Scts; Var L Golf; High Hon Roll; Hon Roll; Elect Engr.

STANCIL, SHIRLENE; Far Rockaway HS; Far Rockaway, NY; (Y); 45/338; Teachers Aide; Chorus; Church Choir; Cit Awd; Hon Roll; Prfct Atten Awd; Coop Awd 86; Fiorello H Laguardia CC; Bus.

STANCO, TRACEY; Commack HS South; Commack, NY; (Y); Church Yth Grp; SADD; Band; Concert Band; Mrchg Band; Mgr(s); Score Keeper; Timer; Hon Roll; Plattsburg ST; Acctng.

STANEK, ELAINE; Union Endicott HS; Endicott, NY; (Y); Drama Clb; French Clb; Key Clb; School Play; Yrbk Stf; High Hon Roll; NHS; Bio.

STANEK, JENNIFER; West Seneca West SR HS; W Seneca, NY; (Y); French Clb; GAA; Var Trk; French Hon Soc; Hon Roll; Pres Schlr; Art Achvt Awd 84; Sci Hnr Awd 86; Bio.

STANEK, MICHAEL; Alden Central HS; Alden, NY; (Y); 36/203; Computer Clb; French Clb; Science Clb; Ski Clb; SADD; Band; Concert Band; Jazz Band; Mrchg Band; Pep Band; NYS Regents Scholar 86; St Bonaventure U; Fin.

STANFORD, DERRICK; Uniondale HS; Uniondale, NY; (Y); Boy Scts; Spanish Clb; Bsbl; Bsktbl; Crs Cntry; Ftbl; Trk; Wrstlng; High Hon Roll; Hon Roll; Penn ST; Math.

STANFORD, KAREN; George Wood Wingate HS; Brooklyn, NY; (Y); Math Tm; Yrbk Stf; Hon Roll; Prfct Atten Awd; Principls List 85; SR Arista 85; Hnr Svc Awd 84; Cuny; Pediatrician.

STANFORD, MARCIA; Buffalo Traditional HS; Buffalo, NY; (S); 8/115; Library Aide; Band; Concert Band; Mrchg Band; Nwsp Stf; Cit Awd; High Hon Roll; Hon Roll; NHS; Prfct Atten Awd; Data Proc.

STANGL, BRUCE; Pioneer Central HS; Arcade, NY; (Y); Boy Scts; Church Yth Grp; Latin Clb; Nwsp Rptr; Nwsp Stf; Ed Lit Mag; Rep Stu Cncl; Swmmng; Psych.

STANGLE, KATHY; Perth Central HS; Amsterdam, NY; (Y); 20/44; Pres 4-H; Quiz Bowl; SADD; Teachers Aide; 4-H Awd; Scl Wrk.

STANGLE, MICHELE; Broadalbin Central Schl; Amsterdam, NY; (Y); Spanish Clb; Color Guard; Mrchg Band; Rep Stu Cncl; Hon Roll; Hvcc; Soclgy.

STANIA, JENNIFER; John C Birdlebough HS; Pennellville, NY; (Y); French Clb; ROTC; Socr; Trk; Vllybl; NHS; MVP Offense-Scr 85; Hopwood Schlr Exclnt Rating 86; Hs Prtcptn-US Nalav Sea Cdt Corps 83; Electrncs.

STANIASZEK, KAREN; Turner/Carroll HS; Buffalo, NY; (S); Yrbk Stf; JV Bowling; Hon Roll; NHS; Schlrshp Awd 83; Nrsg.

STANISZEWSKI, AUDREY; Villa Maria Acad; Lancaster, NY; (S); 8/98; Pres VP JCL; Pres Orch; Pres Trs Stu Cncl; High Hon Roll; Trs NHS; Ntl Merit Ltr; Voice Dem Awd; NY Brd Of Regnts Cert Of Recgntn 84; Optomtry.

STANISZEWSKI, RAELYNN; Lackawanna SR HS; Lackawanna, NY; (Y); 3/256; Var Capt Bsktbl; Var Capt Sftbl; Var Capt Swmmng; Var Capt Vllybl; High Hon Roll; Hon Roll; Hgst Schlstc Achvt 85; MVP Swmmng,Vlybl,Bsktbl 86; Regents Schrlshp 86; Canisius Coll; Engr.

STANKEWICZ, MONICA M; Westhill SR HS; Syracuse, NY; (Y); 19/147; Church Yth Grp; Drama Clb; Spanish Clb; SADD; Chorus; Church Choir; Jazz Band; School Musical; School Play; Nwsp Stf; Natl Educ Dev Awd 83-84; NY St Regents Schlrshp 86; ST U Of NY; Music Thrpy.

STANKO, STACEY; Longwood HS; Coram, NY; (Y); 67/399; School Musical; Variety Show; Rep Soph Cls; Rep Jr Cls; Rep Sr Cls; Stu Cncl; Co-Capt Cheerleading; Gym; High Hon Roll; Hon Roll; Suffolk CC; Crmnl Justice.

STANKUNAS, RICHARD; Schalmont HS; Schenectady, NY; (Y); 19/170; Computer Clb; Math Clb; Chorus; Im Bsktbl; Var Capt Bowling; Var Capt Golf; JV Socr; Var Capt Tennis; High Hon Roll; Hon Roll; Sectn II Golfng Qual 85; Sect II All Star Golfng Tm 85; NYS Mth Awd Outstndng Achvt 83; Clarkson U; Chem Engrng.

STANLEY, JENNIFER; Shaker HS; Latham, NY; (Y); Cmnty Wkr; Dance Clb; Trs French Clb; Latin Clb; SADD; Chorus; School Musical; Co-Capt Var Cheerleading; Hon Roll; NHS; Natl Hon Soc Earth Sci Awd 86; Judge Guy Delollo Mem Schlrshp Awd 86; Hartwick Coll; Lbrl Arts.

STANLEY, KISHA; Hempstead HS; Hempstead, NY; (Y); 11/250; Hon Roll; NHS; Syracuse U; Bio.

STANLEY, NOREEN E; East Syracuse-Minoa HS; Minoa, NY; (Y); Dance Clb; PAVAS; Y-Teens.

STANLEY II, WILLIAM; Valley Central HS; Walden, NY; (Y); 140/323; Boy Scts; Church Yth Grp; Varsity Clb; Church Choir; Var L Ftbl; Var L Trk; Im Wt Lftg; Ftbll Offnsv Lnmn Of Yr 86; Outstndg Yth Of Yr 86; Fnlst Hmmr Empire ST Games 86; St John Fisher Coll; Bus Admin.

STANOJEVIC, JOHN; Rocky Point JR SR HS; Rocky Pt, NY; (S); 4/175; FBLA; Spanish Clb; Varsity Clb; JV Var Bsktbl; JV Socr; High Hon Roll.

STANTON, DAVID; Fairport HS; Fairport, NY; (Y); NYS Regnts Shlrshp 86; Rochester Inst/Tech; Elec Engr.

STANTON, JILL; Frewsburg Central HS; Frewsburg, NY; (Y); 8/79; Church Yth Grp; Drama Clb; FCA; Pep Clb; Ski Clb; Spanish Clb; SADD; Chorus; School Play; Trs Frsh Cls; Jamestown CC; RN.

STANTON, KEVIN P; Chenango Valley HS; Binghamtlon, NY; (Y); Am Leg Boys St; VP Church Yth Grp; Ski Clb; Trs Band; Trs Mrchg Band; Yrbk Stf; Var JV Socr; Var L Trk; High Hon Roll; NHS; Engrng.

STANTON, KIM M; Bryon-Bergen HS; Bergen, NY; (Y); AFS; Church Yth Grp; FTA; Library Aide; Office Aide; Teachers Aide; Chorus; Yrbk Stf; Hon Roll; Genesee Cmnty Coll; Gnrl Stdies.

STANZIANI, NICOLA; Newtown HS; Elmhurst, NY; (Y); 44/781; Math Tm; Scholastic Bowl; Band; Concert Band; Jazz Band; Hon Roll; Prfct Atten Awd; Jr Engrng Tech Soc 84-85; Italian Clb 84-85.

STAP, JOYCE; Valley Central HS; Montgomery, NY; (Y); 33/286; Church Yth Grp; Band; Yrbk Stf; Var Vllybl; Hon Roll; NHS; Spanish NHS; Rgnts Schlrshp 86; SUNY Delhi; Vet Tech.

STAPELFELDT, KARIN L; Pittsford Mendon HS; Pittsford, NY; (Y); Pep Clb; SADD; Varsity Clb; Nwsp Stf; Yrbk Stf; JV Capt Tennis; Var Vllybl; Hon Roll; NHS; Ntl Merit Ltr; Colgate U; Intl Rltns.

STAPLES, RONALD; Riverside HS; Buffalo, NY; (Y); Am Leg Boys St; Boy Scts; Bsbl; Ftbl; Bus.

STAPLES, SHANIQUA; Newburgh Free Acad; Newburgh, NY; (Y); Var JV Cheerleading.

STAPLETON, MICHAEL; Mc Quaid Jesuit HS; Fairport, NY; (Y); 85/180; Camera Clb; Cmnty Wkr; Letterman Clb; Ski Clb; Teachers Aide; Varsity Clb; Nwsp Rptr; Var L Mgr(s); Var Capt Swmmng; Hon Roll; St Joes; Slsmn.

STAPLETON, SHANNON M; Auburn HS; Auburn, NY; (Y); 9/428; Church Yth Grp; Orch; Symp Band; High Hon Roll; NHS; St Schlr; Prsdntl Natl Hnr Scty 84-86; Pro Msca Schlrshp Awd Wnr 86; Dstrct Wnr Natl Fdrtn Msc Clbs 85; Boston Coll; Msc.

STARACE, MARGARET; Martin Van Buren HS; Qns Vill, NY; (Y); 25/576; Church Yth Grp; French Clb; School Play; Trs Stu Cncl; Swmmng; French Hon Soc; Hon Roll; NHS; Svc Hnr Soc, Pride Yankees Super Yth Awd 86; Nrsng.

STARK, ANDREW; Maple Hill HS; Castleton, NY; (Y); Pres Key Clb; NHS; Smmr Sci Sem 85; USAFA; Elect Engr.

STARK, BRIAN A; Ardsley HS; Hartsdale, NY; (Y); Civic Clb; JA; Political Wkr; Temple Yth Grp; Band; Jazz Band; Mrchg Band; Bsktbl; Socr; JV Wrstlng; Regents Schlrshp 86; Charmn Westchestr Model Leg 85-86; Finance.

STARK, KATHIE; Ramstein American HS; Apo New Yok, NY; (Y); Pep Clb; Sec Stu Cncl; JV Var Vllybl; Hon Roll; Jr NHS; Outstndng Achvt Cosmtlgy II 85-86; Cosmtlgy.

STARK, LEONARD; John Glenn HS; Greenlawn, NY; (Y); Quiz Bowl; Scholastic Bowl; Spanish Clb; Temple Yth Grp; School Play; Nwsp Sprt Ed; Yrbk Sprt Ed; VP Sr Cls; JV L Ftbl; Var L Tennis; Lt Gov Ny St Yth & Gov 86-87; Pol Sci.

STARK, RACHEL; Susan Wagner HS; Staten Island, NY; (Y); Cmnty Wkr; School Musical; Lit Mag; Stu Cncl; Cheerleading; Gym; Socr; NHS.

STARK, SUSAN ALLISON; Roy C Ketcham HS; Poughkeepsie, NY; (S); Chrmn Drama Clb; Sec Thesps; Jazz Band; School Musical; School Play; Pres Stu Cncl; Var L Tennis; High Hon Roll; VP Jr NHS; NHS; Lynn Davis Mem Awd Exclnc 84; Tnns 2nd Pl Eastern Tnns Assoc Dist 85; Dutchss Cnty Rgnl HS Of Exc 86.

STARKMAN, ELISABETH KERR; Half Hollow Hills High School West; Dix Hills, NY; (Y); Church Yth Grp; Art Clb; Key Clb; Leo Clb; SADD; Varsity Clb; Bsktbl; Hon Roll; Jr NHS; NHS.

STARKMAN, SCOTT D; Alfred G Berner HS; Massapequa, NY; (Y); 2/412; Library Aide; Mathletes; Spanish Clb; SADD; Teachers Aide; Nwsp Stf; Rep Frsh Cls; Rep Soph Cls; Hon Roll; NHS; Ltr Exclnce Span & Drftng 83; NY U; Lib Arts.

STARKS, CHRISTOPHER; Schoharic Central HS; Sloansville, NY; (Y); Boys Clb Am; Chess Clb; Church Yth Grp; Computer Clb; Chorus; Stage Crew; Yrbk Stf; Rep Cmnty Wkr; Crs Cntry; Wrstlng; Illstrtn.

STARKS, DANA; Massena Central HS; Massena, NY; (Y); 101/256; Church Yth Grp; Band; Concert Band; Mrchg Band; Pep Band; Var L Cheerleading; JV Gym; JV Ice Hcky; Im Powder Puff Ftbl; Hon Roll; Cazenovia Coll; Chld Care.

STAROPOLI, LYNNE; Nazareth Acad; Rochester, NY; (Y); 2/162; SADD; Varsity Clb; VP Frsh Cls; Var Bsktbl; Var Capt Socr; Var Sftbl; Cit Awd; DAR Awd; High Hon Roll; VP NHS; Rochester Yng Amer Awd 86; Fairfield U; Psychology.

STAROWITZ JR, LEO; Byron-Bergen HS; Elba, NY; (Y); Camera Clb; Computer Clb; 4-H; Science Clb; Band; Concert Band; Mrchg Band; Stage Crew; Stu Cncl; Var Golf; 4-H Agri Bus Awd Trip; GCC; CPA.

STARR, LINDA J; Newburgh Free Acad; New Windsor, NY; (Y); 31/621; Church Yth Grp; Spanish Clb; JV Socr; High Hon Roll; Hon Roll; Jr NHS; Rotary Awd; Rtry Excng Stu Brazil 84-85; Rgnts Schlrshp 86; SUNY New Paltz; Intl Rltns.

STARR, MICHAEL; Clarkstown HS South; Spring Valley, NY; (Y); Mu Alp Tht.

STARRS, LAURA; Canastota JR SR HS; Canastota, NY; (S); 1/200; Drama Clb; Concert Band; Mrchg Band; School Musical; School Play; Variety Show; Nwsp Rptr; JV Tennis; NHS; Pres 4-H; Area All ST Chorus 85; Mst Outstndng Vocal Musc 84; Hghst Avg Chem 84.

STASHKO, LAURETTE M; Johnson City HS; Johnson City, NY; (Y); 4/198; Key Clb; Latin Clb; Pep Clb; Band; Concert Band; Mrchg Band; Yrbk Stf; Stu Cncl; High Hon Roll; NHS; NY ST Regents Schlrshp; Music Svc Bar; Music Var Lttr; SUNY Buffalo; Pharm.

STASINSKI, DAVID; Kenmore East HS; Tonawanda, NY; (Y); 42/330; Pep Clb; Varsity Clb; Stu Cncl; JV Var Vllybl; High Hon Roll; Hon Roll; NHS.

STASIO, LISA; Connetquot HS; Oakdale, NY; (Y); 160/763; Dance Clb; Hosp Aide; Yrbk Phtg; Yrbk Stf; Trs Frsh Cls; Trs Soph Cls; Trs Jr Cls; Trs Sr Cls; Trs Stu Cncl; JV Cheerleading; Nrsng.

STASIO, LISA; Mount Mercy Acad; Buffalo, NY; (Y); Computer Clb; JA; Math Clb; Spanish Clb; Nwsp Stf; Hon Roll; U Of NY Buffalo; Math.

STASIUK, TANIA J; Bethlehem Central HS; Delmar, NY; (Y); 32/304; Cmnty Wkr; Drama Clb; English Clb; Nwsp Rptr; Var Capt Crs Cntry; High Hon Roll; NHS; Ntl Merit SF; GAA; Intnl Clb; NY Prs Assns Btr Nwspr Cntst Hnrb Mntn Sprts Cvrg 84; Librl Arts.

STASZAK, CHRIS; Scotia-Glenville HS; Scotia, NY; (Y); 74/240; Cmnty Wkr; Pres DECA; Key Clb; Var L Bsbl; Var L Bsbl; Var L Ftbl; NY ST 1st Pl In Mngmnt Dcsn Mkng 86; Law.

STATEN, MICHELE; Hendrick Hudson HS; Verplanck, NY; (Y); 5/187; Hosp Aide; Church Choir; VP Jr Cls; VP Sr Cls; Capt Bsktbl; Capt Sftbl; Capt Tennis; NHS; Pres Schlr; Church Yth Grp; Smith Bk Awd 85; Jr & Sr Clss Svc Awd 85-86; Most All-Arnd In Sr Clss 86; Providence Coll; Bio.

STATES, NANCY; Odessa-Montour HS; Odessa, NY; (Y); Church Yth Grp; FHA; Lit Mag; Capt Bsktbl; High Hon Roll; Hon Roll; Elmira Coll Key Awd 86; Bus.

STATLER, TRACI A; Hillcrest HS; Kew Gardens, NY; (Y); Radio Clb; Ski Clb; Thesps; Nwsp Phtg; Nwsp Sprt Ed; Yrbk Phtg; Var Sftbl; Var Capt Vllybl; NCTE Awd; Sta Mgr Of Schl Radio 84-86; U NC Chapel Hill; Brdcst Jrnls.

STATOFF, MICHELLE; Mineola HS; Albertson, NY; (Y); Hosp Aide; Key Clb; Service Clb; Spanish Clb; Hon Roll; Med.

STATT, LISA; E J Wilson HS; Rochester, NY; (Y); VP Exploring; French Clb; Girl Scts; Math Tm; Symp Band; Yrbk Stf; St Schlr; NYS Rgnts Schlrshp 86; Monroe CC; Pharm.

STATTLER, RIC; Longwood SR HS; Shirley, NY; (S); 1/411; Art Clb; Intnl Clb; School Play; Ed Nwsp Bus Mgr; Lit Mag; NHS; VFW Awd; Fndr & Co-Pres CRC Rcrtn; Peer Ldrshp Cmmnty Svc; Fshn Advsr Stu Cncl; Art.

STAUB, DEREK; Grand Island SR HS; Grand Island, NY; (Y); Boys Clb Am; Boy Scts; Church Yth Grp; Exploring; Ski Clb; Band; Concert Band; Drill Tm; Mrchg Band; Im Bsktbl; Law.

STAVISH, MARIA; Clarkstown HS South; New City, NY; (Y); Church Yth Grp; Latin Clb; SADD; Orch; School Musical; Yrbk Stf; JV Var Twrlr; JV Vllybl; JV Bsktbl; Score Keeper; Scranton U; Physcl Thrpy.

STAVISKY, KATHERINE; Fairport HS; Fairport, NY; (Y); French Clb; Sec Girl Scts; Library Aide; Model UN; Science Clb; SADD; Nwsp Stf; Lit Mag; Girl Scot Silvr Awd 84; Natl Fed Music Clbs 2nd 3 Time Supr Winr 85.

STAVRIS, DEANNA; St Edmund HS; Brooklyn, NY; (S); 10/200; Hon Roll; NHS; Hnr Cert-Math, Engl, Histry, Relgn, Gym 84-85; Natl Lang Arts Olympd 84; Cmmndtn Sci, Hstry 84; Psychlgy.

STAWITZKY, ERIC; Forestville Central Schl; S Dayton, NY; (Y); Var L Bsbl; Var Co-Capt Bsktbl; Var L Ftbl; Var L Vllybl; High Hon Roll; NHS; Coachs Awd Vrsty Bsbll 86; Cmptr Sci.

STAYER, ROSE; Allegany Central HS; Allegany, NY; (Y); 4-H; Stat Bsktbl; Hon Roll; :Spcl Ed.

STEA, NELLA; Yonkers HS; Yonkers, NY; (Y); Intnl Clb; Nwsp Stf; Yrbk Stf; Off Sr Cls; Outstndng Stu Certf 86; Elizabeth Seton Coll; Sec Sci.

STEAR, JENNIFER; Irondequoit HS; Rochester, NY; (Y); 63/375; French Clb; Sec Model UN; Radio Clb; Band; Chorus; School Musical; School Play; Hon Roll; Ntl Merit Ltr; Smmr Schlr Prg St John Fishers 86; Pychlgy.

STEARNS, KIMBERLY ANN; Johnstown HS; Johnstown, NY; (Y); Ski Clb; Varsity Clb; Yrbk Stf; Capt Var Cheerleading; Powder Puff Ftbl; Hon Roll; Fshn Mrchndsng.

STEARNS, LISA; Solvay HS; Syracuse, NY; (Y); Hosp Aide; Spanish Clb; Psych.

STEARNS, PATRICIA; Mont Pleasant HS; Schenectady, NY; (Y); 13/241; Pres French Clb; Mgr(s); JV Sftbl; Pres French Hon Soc; Hon Roll; NHS; Bkkpg Awd 86; Genevieve Brooke Meml Awd Frnch 86; Coll Of Saint Rose; Acctg.

STEARNS, SARAH DICKEY; South Glens Falls SR HS; Gansevoort, NY; (Y); 2/228; Am Leg Aux Girls St; Varsity Clb; Band; Yrbk Stf; Rep Stu Cncl; Var Capt Fld Hcky; Var Tennis; Var Capt Vllybl; NHS; Ntl Merit Schol; DAR Regnl Gd Ctzns Awd 86; Armd Frcs Schlr Athlt Awd 86; Empire St Gms Schlstc Vllybll Tm 84-85; Dartmouth Coll; Lbrl Arts.

STEBBINS, MARK; West Genesee SR HS; Camillus, NY; (Y); 36/426; Church Yth Grp; Exploring; French Clb; Ski Clb; Church Choir; High Hon Roll; Hon Roll; NHS; U Buffalo; Elec Engrng.

STEBBINS, MARK W; Skaneateles HS; Skaneateles, NY; (Y); Boy Scts; Church Yth Grp; Eagle Awd.

STEC, CHERYL; Roy C Ketcham HS; Poughkeepsie, NY; (Y); Letterman Clb; Varsity Clb; Band; Jazz Band; Symp Band; Var L Swmmng; High Hon Roll; Hon Roll; Pghkps Soccer Clb 1st Pl Team; Wdsn Trphy Swm Meet 1st Pl Trphy; Empire ST Gms In Swmng; Chmstry.

STECK, LORI ANNE M; Buff Acad For Visual & Perfmng Arts; Buffalo, NY; (Y); 15/104; Cmnty Wkr; Chorus; Var Capt Ice Hcky; Var Capt Sftbl; Var Capt Vllybl; Hon Roll; NHS; RITF Schlrp 86-87; MVP Hockey, Sftbl & Vlybl 83-86; All Hgh Tm Vlybl, Sftbl & Hcky 85-86; Rochester Inst Of Tech; Accntg.

STECKEL, CHERYL A; Sacred Heart Acad; Long Beach, NY; (Y); Art Clb; French Clb; FTA; Service Clb; SADD; Teachers Aide; Chorus; Lit Mag; St Johns U; Fine Arts.

STEDMAN, STEVEN C; Attica Central HS; Attica, NY; (Y); 18/160; Band; Concert Band; Jazz Band; Mrchg Band; Frsh Cls; Stu Cncl; Bsktbl; Hon Roll; NHS; Prfct Atten Awd; Geneseo; Sci.

STEEGE, KURT; Archbishop Molloy HS; Jackson Heights, NY; (Y); 47/380; Church Yth Grp; Church Choir; Rep Soph Cls; Rep Jr Cls; L JV Crs Cntry; L JV Trk; High Hon Roll; NHS; All Star Frshmn Crss Cntry A Tm 83; Educ.

STEELE, DENISE; Frontier SR HS; Blasdell, NY; (Y); Pep Clb; Ski Clb; Spanish Clb; Chorus; Sec Frsh Cls; Stu Cncl; Var Co-Capt Cheerleading; Powder Puff Ftbl; Ntl Merit Ltr; Canisius Coll; Lawyer.

STEELE, ELAINE; Connetquot HS; Oakdale, NY; (S); 32/750; Civic Clb; Intnl Clb; Band; Concert Band; Mrchg Band; Pep Band; Symp Band; High Hon Roll; Jr NHS; NHS; Smmr Gftd & Tlntd Prog; Mrktng.

STEELE, JACQUELINE; Poughkeepsie HS; Poughkeepsie, NY; (Y); 34/160; Band; School Play; Cheerleading; Socr; High Hon Roll; Hon Roll; Suny New Paltz; Secndry Ed.

STEELE, JULIE; Washingtonville HS; Washingtonville, NY; (Y); FCA; Natl Beta Clb; Spanish Clb; Chorus; Yrbk Stf; Hon Roll; NHS; Ntl Merit Ltr; Voice Dem Awd; Applalchian ST U; Scndry Educ.

STEELE, TODD; Pittsford-Menden HS; Fairport, NY; (Y); DECA; Ski Clb; JV Tennis; Marketing Awd 85-86; Cooperative Wrk 85-86; Correll; Psychlgy.

STEENROD, GEORGE; Newark Valley HS; Berkshire, NY; (Y); #5 In Class; High Hon Roll; Rgnts Schlrshp & Art Awds 86; Elmira Coll; Archlgy.

STEFANI, LAWRENCE; Ward Melville SR HS; East Setauket, NY; (Y); 96/725; Boy Scts; Church Yth Grp; Pres Computer Clb; Latin Clb; Capt Math Tm; Mrchg Band; Yrbk Stf; High Hon Roll; NHS; Prfct Atten Awd; Ntl HS Cntst Hnrbl Mntn Level II 85; Ntl Rfl Assn Shrpshtr 83; Gld Cert For Outstndng Acdmv Acnvt 84; Rchster Inst Of Tech; Comp Engr.

STEFANKO, JACQUELINE; Columbia HS; E Greenbush, NY; (Y); 7/417; Crs Cntry; Fld Hcky; Trk; High Hon Roll; NHS; Ntl Merit Ltr; Regents Schlrshp; Syracuse U; Med.

STEFANSKI, SHEILA; Salamanca Central HS; Salamanca, NY; (Y); #2 In Class; French Clb; Red Cross Aide; Ski Clb; Yrbk Stf; Sec Jr Cls; JV Var Sftbl; VP French Hon Soc; High Hon Roll; NHS; 1st Prize Cattaraugus Cnty Consrvtn Essay Cont 83; Rochester Inst Tech; Microelec.

STEFF JR, JAMES L; Hutch-Tech HS; Buffalo, NY; (Y); 15/266; Exploring; JA; Science Clb; Nwsp Stf; High Hon Roll; Hon Roll; NHS; NYS Regents Sclrp 86; Air Force.

STEFFAN, SHERRY; Frontier Central HS; Blasdell, NY; (Y); Hon Roll; Church Yth Grp; French Clb; Math Clb; Yrbk Stf; Var Crs Cntry; Var Trk; JV Vllybl; NHS; Prfct Atten Awd; Yth Brd Trck & Fld Awd 86; Prtcptd ST Mt Trck 85; Sprtsmnshp Awd Bsbl 84; SUNY Buffaloi; Math.

STEFFENS, BARBARA; Newtown HS; Elmhurst, NY; (Y); Aud/Vis; Cmnty Wkr; Hosp Aide; Office Aide; Service Clb; Teachers Aide; Hon Roll; NCTE Awd; NHS; Sal; Queensboro; Eng Lit.

STEFL, KIM; Union Springs Acad; Salamanca, NY; (Y); Ski Clb; Chorus; Church Choir; Concert Band; Hon Roll; NHS; Andrews U; Med Sec.

STEFURA, JOHN; Coxsackie Athens HS; Coxsackie, NY; (Y); German Clb; Band; Concert Band; Jazz Band; Rep Frsh Cls; Socr; FIT; Fash Dsgnr.

STEGEMAN, ANN MARGARET; Uniondale HS; Uniondale, NY; (Y); 40/500; Camera Clb; Church Yth Grp; Dance Clb; Drama Clb; Chorus; School Play; Yrbk Ed-Chief; Sftbl; High Hon Roll; Hon Roll; Sci Fair 3rd Pl Wnnr 83-84; Julliard; Theatre.

STEGER, DANIEL; Lackawanna SR HS; Lackawanna, NY; (Y); Computer Clb; French Clb; JA; L Ftbl; Ice Hcky; Wrstlng; Hon Roll; UB; Comp Sci.

STEGMAIER, KIMBERLY; Malverne HS; Malverne, NY; (Y); #1 In Class; Dance Clb; Pres Key Clb; Band; Concert Band; Mrchg Band; Pep Band; Nwsp Stf; Yrbk Stf; Lit Mag; Trs Soph Cls; Malverne HS Deptmntl Awds 85-87; 1st Prz Essay Cntst By Chap 2 Of Amer Acad Of Pediatrics 87.

STEGMEIER, ROBERT; St Marys HS; Alden, NY; (S); Socr; Var Capt Wrstlng; Hon Roll; NHS; All Star Lg Goalie 86; MIP Wrstlr 84 & 86; St Bonaventure; Fin.

STEGMEIER, WILLIAM; St Marys HS; Alden, NY; (S); 3/176; Varsity Clb; JV Bsktbl; Var Crs Cntry; Var Trk; Hon Roll; NHS; Cert Merit Awd Phy Ed 84-85; Cert Merit Awd Spnsh II 84-85; Cahisius; Accntng.

STEIGER, MAUREEN; Sweet Home SR HS; N Tonawanda, NY; (Y); Soc Studies Awd 85.

STEIN, ANDREW; Lynbrook HS; Lynbrook, NY; (Y); 7/239; AFS; Quiz Bowl; Scholastic Bowl; Nwsp Ed-Chief; Nwsp Sprt Ed; JV Bsktbl; L Socr; L Trk; High Hon Roll; NHS; NY ST Regnts Schlrshp 86; Cornell U; Pre-Law.

STEIN, BETH S; Fairport HS; Fairport, NY; (Y); French Clb; SADD; Nwsp Stf; Yrbk Stf; Lit Mag; Hon Roll; Frgn Lang.

STEIN, CARA; Tottenville HS; Staten Island, NY; (S); GAA; Temple Yth Grp; Varsity Clb; Band; Chorus; Yrbk Stf; Lit Mag; Off Frsh Cls; Off Soph Cls; Off Jr Cls; Empire State Grls 86; Ntl Frnch Cntst 86; Forgn Lang.

STEIN, CARYN; Oceanside SR HS; Oceanside, NY; (Y); Hosp Aide; Chorus; Var Capt Badmtn; Trk; Hon Roll; Nassau CC; Elem Ed.

STEIN, DAVID; Rockland Country Day HS; New City, NY; (S); Pres Sr Cls; Rep Stu Cncl; Var Capt Bsbl; Var Socr; Var Tennis; Drama Clb; Ski Clb; Hon Roll; Athlete Of The Yr Awd 83-84; Tri Cnty League All Star MVP Offense 85; Babe Ruth Bsbl All-Star 84; Bates Coll.

STEIN, JEFFREY; Gates Chili HS; Rochester, NY; (Y); Boy Scts; Church Yth Grp; Ski Clb; Rep Frsh Cls; Rep Sr Cls; Var Crs Cntry; Var Trk; High Hon Roll; Hon Roll; Prfct Atten Awd.

STEIN, JENNIFER; Clarkstown South HS; New City, NY; (Y); SADD; JV Twrlr; Journlsm.

STEIN, JEREMY; Curtis HS; Staten Island, NY; (Y); Computer Clb; Office Aide; Band; Concert Band; Mrchg Band; Nwsp Stf; JV Ice Hcky; Var Tennis; Hon Roll; All Cty Mrchg Band 86; Law.

STEIN, MIA; Christopher Columbus HS; Bronx, NY; (Y); Drama Clb; Chorus; School Musical; Nwsp Rptr; Lit Mag; Hon Roll; Pres Schlr; Rgnts Schlrshp 86; SUNY Stonybrook.

STEIN, STACEY; Greece Athena SR HS; Rochester, NY; (Y); 46/264; Cmnty Wkr; DECA; Hosp Aide; Ski Clb; School Musical; Symp Band; Yrbk Stf; Sec Stu Cncl; Var Cheerleading; Hon Roll; NY ST Rgnts Nrsng Schlrp 86-87; Ithaca Coll Schlrp 86-87; Ithaca Coll.

STEIN, THOMAS; Elmira Southside HS; Elmira, NY; (Y); 68/450; VP Pres Church Yth Grp; Letterman Clb; Pep Clb; Spanish Clb; Varsity Clb; Im Bsbl; JV Bsktbl; Var Golf; Hon Roll; Armed Srvcs; Elec Engr.

STEINBACH, KATRINA; Paul V Moore HS; Constantia, NY; (Y); Radio Clb; Concert Band; Nwsp Rptr; Hon Roll; 1st Pl Stu Authr Cntst 86; Advncd Math Pgm 83-85; Engl Educ.

STEINBAUM, SARAH; The Wheatley Schl; Old Westbury, NY; (Y); Model UN; Yrbk Stf; Rep Frsh Cls; Rep Soph Cls; Rep Jr Cls; Elctd Stu Rep Brd Educ 85-86; Wheatly Mck Trl Tm 85-86; 1st Plc Hofstra U Spnsh Poetry Cntst 86.

STEINBERG, DIMITRI; Hunter College HS; New York, NY; (Y); Chess Clb; Math Clb; Math Tm; Model UN; Lit Mag; Hon Roll; Mu Alp Tht; Ntl Merit SF; Scl Studies Olympiad Amer Hist 84 & Wrld & Amer Hist 85; Harvard; Soviet Studies.

STEINBERG JR, JOSEPH F; Henninger HS; Syracuse, NY; (Y); 29/400; Var Ftbl; Capt Var Lcrss; High Hon Roll; Nazareth Coll Rochester; Hstry.

STEINBERG, MELISSA; Commack HS South; E Northport, NY; (Y); 128/357; Office Aide; Teachers Aide; Chorus; School Musical; School Play; Stage Crew; Variety Show; Hon Roll; Sun New Paltz; Bus Mgmt.

STEINBERG, NOAH; Friends Acad; Oyster Bay Cv, NY; (Y); Debate Tm; French Clb; German Clb; Nwsp Ed-Chief; Lit Mag; JV Bsbl; Var Ftbl; Var Ice Hcky; JV Lcrss; High Hon Roll; Princeton U; U S Pres.

STEINBERGER, BETH A; Washingtonville SR HS; Blooming Grove, NY; (Y); VP Trs Church Yth Grp; Cmnty Wkr; French Clb; Rep Sr Cls; Pres Stu Cncl; Bsktbl; Var Vllybl; Hon Roll; NHS; Variety Show; Orange Cnty Enrchmnt 85-86; Indoor Flr Hockey 83-86; Coll Of Holy Cross.

STEINER, DANA; Perry Central HS; Perry, NY; (Y); 44/88; Art Clb; Library Aide; Stu Cncl; Hon Roll; Olympcs Mind 1st, 2nd, 3rd Pl 82-86; Mech Engrng.

STEINER, JASON; Victor Central HS; Victor, NY; (Y); Quiz Bowl; Scholastic Bowl; JV Var Bsbl; JV Var Bsktbl; Cit Awd; Hon Roll; Rochester Inst-Perdue; Engrng.

STEINER, MATTHEW; Alden Central HS; Alden, NY; (Y); 40/204; Church Yth Grp; FTA; Teachers Aide; Nwsp Stf; Var Crs Cntry; Var Capt Wrstlng; John R Duncan Mem 86; Geneseo SUNY; Psych.

STEINER, PATRICK; Msgr Mc Lancy HS; Astoria, NY; (Y); 17/215; Pres Chess Clb; Drama Clb; School Play; Stage Crew; High Hon Roll; Hon Roll; Jr NHS; NHS; Pres Schlr; Miss Hmmrth Schlrshp Mem Msgr J V Mcclancy 86; Mnhttn Coll Pres Schlrshp 86; Mnhttn Coll; Engrng.

STEINER, SUSAN CAROL; Alden Central HS; Alden, NY; (Y); 1/203; SADD; Yrbk Ed-Chief; Stat Bsktbl; Bausch & Lomb Sci Awd; NHS; Pres Schlr; Val; GAA; School Musical; School Play; Bus Career Dvlpmnt Prg Intl Schlrshp 86; Fnlst Nat Wide Ms Teenage Amer 85; Westinghouse Schlrshp 86; SUNY; Bus Admin.

STEINFELD, ROBIN; York Prep; New York City, NY; (Y); Dance Clb; Drama Clb; Office Aide; Scholastic Bowl; Spanish Clb; SADD; Teachers Aide; School Musical; School Play; Variety Show; George Washington U; Bio.

STEINFORT, KELLY J; Johnson City HS; Binghamton, NY; (Y); 17/198; Dance Clb; FHA; Spanish Clb; Drill Tm; Variety Show; Yrbk Stf; High Hon Roll; Hon Roll; Regents Schlrshp; Perfrmng Arts.

STEINKE, STEVEN; Sea Ford HS; Seaford, NY; (Y); 81/270; Church Yth Grp; Cmnty Wkr; Exploring; BOSTON U; Bus Mgmt.

STEINMARK, STEVEN; Hicksville SR HS; Hicksville, NY; (Y); Bsbl; Ice Hcky; Wt Lftg; Hon Roll; MVP Var Bsbl 86; All Conf Bsbl 86; Nassau Cnty Coaches Assoc Plyr Wk 86; AZ ST U; Bsbl Plyr.

STEINMETZ, WILLIAM C; E J Wilson HS; Spencerport, NY; (Y); 8/296; Varsity Clb; Pres Stu Cncl; JV Bsbl; JV Bsktbl; Var Crs Cntry; Cit Awd; High Hon Roll; NHS; VFW Awd; St John Fisher Coll; Fin Mgmt.

STEINS, DANIEL; Hutch Tech; Buffalo, NY; (Y); Pres Trs Church Yth Grp; Cmnty Wkr; Hon Roll; Thomas J Lipton Awd Sprtsmnshp Boys Clb 86.

STELL, MIKE; Faith Baptist Acad; Baldwinsville, NY; (S); Chorus; Church Choir; Nwsp Rptr; VP Stu Cncl; Var L Bsktbl; Var L Socr; Var L Trk; Var L Vllybl; High Hon Roll; Arch.

STELLA, AMANDA; Corcoran HS; Syracuse, NY; (Y); Ski Clb; Band; Concert Band; Jazz Band; Mrchg Band; Pep Band; School Musical; Socr; Flght Atten.

STELLER, TRACEY; Owego Free Acad; Apalachin, NY; (Y); 11/205; Church Yth Grp; Trs Key Clb; Rep Stu Cncl; Crs Cntry; Var Fld Hcky; Var Sftbl; High Hon Roll; Hon Roll; NHS; Pres Schlr; March Of Dimes 86; Tioga Cnty Courier All Star Tm Fld Hcky 85; U Scranton; Biol.

STELLING, NICOLE; East Meadow HS; East Meadow, NY; (Y); Trs Soph Cls; JV Var Socr; Var Vllybl; Scl Wrk.

STEMLEY, TINA; Roosevlet HS; Roosevelt, NY; (Y); 25/166; Pres Church Yth Grp; VP FBLA; Hosp Aide; Pres Spanish Clb; Sec SADD; Capt Color Guard; Yrbk Rptr; Prfct Atten Awd; Spanish NHS; Roosevelt HS Math Engrng Sci Achvt; US Achvt Acad Ldrshp Awd; Frgn Lang Clb Awd; Nassau CC; Comp Sci.

STENBERG, TAMARA; Romulus Central Schl; Fayette, NY; (S); Office Aide; Band; Concert Band; Mrchg Band; Orch; School Musical; Variety Show; Cheerleading; Socr; Hon Roll; CCBI-SYRACUSE; Bus Admin.

STENHOUSE, LAURA; Skaneateles Central HS; Skaneateles, NY; (S); Socr; High Hon Roll; Hon Roll; NHS; Peer Sharing 85-86; Vet.

STENOS, MARINA; Newtown HS; Corona, NY; (Y); 116/781; German Clb; Chorus; School Play; Yrbk Stf; Crtfct Hnr Eng 84; Crtfct Hnr Spnsh 84; Crtfct Hnr Sci 84; Ctfct Hnr Sci 84; Litr.

STENSHORN, VICKY; Letchworth Central HS; Gainesville, NY; (Y); 2/84; Math Tm; Pres Ski Clb; Color Guard; Pres Concert Band; Yrbk Stf; Socr; Vllybl; VP Sec NHS; Pres Schlr; Sal; Sci Awd 86; Emhart Corp Schlrshp 86; High Hnr; Alfred U; Cermc Engr.

STENSTROM, ANDREA; Falconer Central HS; Falconer, NY; (Y); 30/122; Pres Church Yth Grp; JA; VP Band; Pres Frsh Cls; Pres Soph Cls; Pres Sr Cls; Rep Stu Cncl; JV Capt Bsktbl; Capt Sftbl; Hon Roll; Fredonia; Acctg.

STENTO, PAUL; Seton Catholic Central HS; Binghamton, NY; (Y); 75/165; Pres Church Yth Grp; Varsity Clb; Band; Jazz Band; Rep Stu Cncl; Capt Var Bsktbl; Capt Var Socr; Capt Var Trk; Cit Awd; Prfct Atten Awd; James C Carlin Memrl Awd 86; Earl Rogers Memrl Awd 86; US Marin Corps Dstngshd Athlt Awd 86; Marist Coll; Bus.

STEPANIAN, BRYAN; Blind Brook HS; Rye Brook, NY; (Y); Boy Scts; Pres Church Yth Grp; JA; Math Tm; Ski Clb; Spanish Clb; Yrbk Stf; Bsbl; Var Golf; Finance.

STEPHAN, CATHY; St Marys Diocesan HS; Lancaster, NY; (Y); Varsity Clb; VP Soph Cls; Rep Soph Cls; Rep Jr Cls; Pres Sr Cls; JV Badmtn; Var Tennis; Var Trk; High Hon Roll; NHS; ISLI Notre Dame U 84; SUNY Buffalo; Bio Sci.

STEPHAN, DINA; Mynderse Acad; Seneca Falls, NY; (Y); Hgh Hnr Rll; Natl Hnr Soc; Soc Dstngshd Amer HS Stu; SUNY-OSWEGO.

STEPHAN, JENNIFER M; Tappan Zee HS; Piermont, NY; (Y); 10/245; Yrbk Sprt Ed; Yrbk Stf; Pres Frsh Cls; Pres Jr Cls; Pres CAP; Stu Cncl; Var Capt Swmmng; NHS; Ntl Merit Ltr; Pres Schlr; All Section Swimming 86; Columbia Univ Sci Hnrs Prgrm 85; Comp Sci.

STEPHAN, LISA; Cardinal O-Hara HS; Amherst, NY; (S); Church Yth Grp; Drama Clb; Girl Scts; Quiz Bowl; Sec Spanish Clb; Teachers Aide; School Musical; Nwsp Ed-Chief; High Hon Roll; NHS; Law.

STEPHANI, ANDREW; Valley Central HS; Montgomery, NY; (Y); 3/288; Church Yth Grp; French Clb; Capt Math Clb; Science Clb; Band; Concert Band; Jazz Band; Mrchg Band; School Musical; Variety Show; Police Fdrtn Schlrhsp 86; Yale U; Pre-Law.

STEPHANS, STACY ELIZABETH; Chenango Forks HS; Binghamton, NY; (Y); 3/180; Am Leg Aux Girls St; Key Clb; Spanish Clb; Var Bsktbl; High Hon Roll; Hon Roll; NHS; Yth Salute Pgm 86; Bio.

STEPHEN, LYNNEA Y; Convent Of The Sacred Heart HS; New York, NY; (Y); Camera Clb; Church Yth Grp; Cmnty Wkr; Dance Clb; Drama Clb; Library Aide; Teachers Aide; Chorus; Church Choir; School Musical; Schl Scholar 82-86; LEAD Bus Pgm Northwestern U; Outstndng Negro Stu Commended Stu 85; News Commentr.

STEPHENS, AMY; Living Word Acad; Syracuse, NY; (S); SADD; Chorus; Socr; Sftbl; Vllybl; High Hon Roll; Hon Roll; Typng Awds 83-85; Alg Awd 83-84; Onondaga CC; Bus.

STEPHENS, LAURA L; Depew HS; Depew, NY; (Y); School Musical; JV Var Cheerleading; Hon Roll; Jr NHS; Pres Schlr; St Schlr; Church Yth Grp; Pep Clb; Chorus; Church Choir; NYS Regents Scholar 86; NY Regents Diploma With Hnrs Grad 86; Erie CC; Bus Adm.

STEPHENS, TIMOTHY; Iona Preparatory Schl; New Rochelle, NY; (Y); 15/207; English Clb; Teachers Aide; Lit Mag; JV Ftbl; NHS; Ntl Merit Ltr; Headmasters List 86; Finance.

STEPNOWSKI, DAWN; East Meadow HS; East Meadow, NY; (Y); 11/340; FBLA; Key Clb; Chorus; Hon Roll; NHS; SUNY Binghamton; Psych.

STEPNOWSKY JR, CARL J; Southold HS; Southold, NY; (Y); 1/71; Am Leg Boys St; Capt Math Tm; Ed Lit Mag; Rep Stu Cncl; Var Capt Bsktbl; Var Capt Socr; Var Capt Tennis; High Hon Roll; NHS; Natl Stu Ldrshp Serv Awd US Achvt Acad 84; Stu Advsry Comm Cnty Exectve Traff Sfty 86-87.

STEPOWSKI, RICHARD; Hamburg Central HS; Hamburg, NY; (Y); 21/389; Church Yth Grp; Spanish Clb; Var Capt Bsktbl; Var Trk; Var JV Vllybl; Hon Roll; NHS; Prfct Atten Awd.

STERBENZ, KRISTEN M; Smithtown East HS; Smithtown, NY; (Y); Trs French Clb; Chorus; Orch; School Play; Symp Band; French Hon Soc; Hon Roll; Lng Island Flute Clb 2nd Plc 85; Saratoga Summer Schl Arts Altrnt 85; NYSSMA All-St Bnd 85-86; Ithaca Coll; Cmnctns.

STERCKX, RACHEL; Commack HS North; E Northport, NY; (Y); 57/361; Cmnty Wkr; Dance Clb; French Clb; SADD; Stage Crew; French Hon Soc; NHS; Yamaha Electn Kybrd Fstvl 86; Lang.

STERGAS, BRETT A; Johnstown HS; Johnstown, NY; (Y); Capt Ski Clb; Frsh Cls; Soph Cls; JV Crs Cntry; JV Tennis; Hon Roll; NHS; NYS Rgnts Schlrshp 86; Clarkson U; Mchncl Engnr.

STERGAS, ROXANNE; Johnstown HS; Johnstown, NY; (Y); Color Guard; NHS; Cert 5th Pl Wrd Procssng Comptn 86; Law.

STERLACCI, LINDA; Moore Catholic HS; Staten Island, NY; (Y); Math Tm; Sec Frsh Cls; Sec Soph Cls; Sec Jr Cls; JV Cheerleading; Math.

STERLING, MATTHEW T; Heatly HS; Greenisland, NY; (Y); 3/23; Am Leg Boys St; Boy Scts; Key Clb; Teachers Aide; Sec Frsh Cls; Var Bsbl; Score Keeper; Elks Awd; High Hon Roll; NHS; NYS Rgnts Dplm 86; Hdsn Vlly Comm Coll; Bus Admin.

STERLING, SCOTT; Midwood HS; Brooklyn, NY; (Y); 1/667; Math Tm; Spanish Clb; Band; Nwsp Stf; Var Bowling; Ntl Merit SF.

STERN, PAUL; Manlius Pebble Hill HS; Fayetteville, NY; (S); Chorus; School Musical; School Play; L Var Socr; Var L Trk; Hon Roll; Pres Phys Ftnss Awds 81-85; Miltry Offcr.

STERN, SCOTT; Commack South HS; Commack, NY; (Y); Exploring; Office Aide; Teachers Aide; Temple Yth Grp; Var Capt Bsktbl; High Hon Roll; NHS; Ldrhsp Awd Stu Cncl.

STERNMAN, MARK S; Scarsdale HS; Scarsdale, NY; (Y); Chess Clb; Trs Debate Tm; Trs Intnl Clb; School Play; Lit Mag; Im Bsktbl; Im Sftbl; High Hon Roll; NHS; Ntl Merit Ltr.

STETHERS, JOHN; Henninger HS; Syracuse, NY; (Y); Computer Clb; FCA; Yrbk Sprt Ed; JV Var Ftbl; JV Var Lcrss; Wt Lftg; High Hon Roll; Hon Roll; Ntl Merit Schol; Prfct Atten Awd; Ithaca Coll; Sprts Med.

STETZ, KIM; Plattsburgh HS; Plattsburgh, NY; (Y); 12/200; Ski Clb; Yrbk Phtg; Yrbk Stf; Trs Stu Cncl; Vllybl; High Hon Roll; Jr NHS; NHS; Hghst Hnrs For Avg Above 95 86; Albany ST U.

STEUERNAGEL, KELLY; Cardinal O Hara HS; Kenmore, NY; (S); Drm Mjr(t); Stage Crew; Bowling; Mgr(s); Mat Maids; Score Keeper; Vllybl; High Hon Roll; Bus.

STEVENS, BEVERLY; Indian River Central HS; Antwerp, NY; (Y); 73/115; AFS; Chorus; Color Guard; Mrchg Band; School Musical; Rep Frsh Cls; Rep Soph Cls; Rep Jr Cls; Rep Sr Cls; Cheerleading; All Star Chrldng Awd 85-86; Var Ltrs & Pins 83-86.

STEVENS, BRIAN; John Marshall HS; Rochester, NY; (Y); Bsbl; Ftbl; Trk; Cit Awd; Turner Awd 81; Key To City Awd 83; Pensacola JC; Engr.

STEVENS, COLEEN P; Richmond Hill HS; Rosedale, NY; (Y); 31/296; Cmnty Wkr; English Clb; Key Clb; Math Clb; Office Aide; Spanish Clb; Chorus; School Musical; Variety Show; Nwsp Rptr; Ntl Achvmnt Schlrshp Outstndng Stu 85; Med.

STEVENS, DENISE; Trott Vocational HS; Niagara Falls, NY; (Y); 5/140; Am Leg Aux Girls St; Hosp Aide; Yrbk Stf; Hon Roll; Harmon L Gregory Mem Awd 86; Rgnts Schlrp 86; Wiagara CC; Engrg.

STEVENS, EDWARD T; Liverpool HS; Liverpool, NY; (Y); 82/816; Church Yth Grp; Exploring; JA; ROTC; Variety Show; Yrbk Phtg; Yrbk Stf; Rep Stu Cncl; L Wrstlng; Hon Roll; USAF ROTC Schlrshp 86; Natl JA Talent Show 2nd 85; Union Coll; Pre-Med.

STEVENS, HEATHER; Batavia HS; Batavia, NY; (Y); 55/211; Color Guard; Var Sftbl; Var Swmmng; Var Vllybl; Hon Roll; Acctng.

STEVENS, JENNIFER A; Shenendehowa SR HS; Clifton Park, NY; (Y); 172/675; Orch; Nwsp Rptr; Cheerleading; Sftbl; High Hon Roll; Hon Roll; GAA; Ski Clb; Nwsp Stf; Swmmng; Pres Acdmc Ftns Awd 86; NY ST Rgnts Schlrshp 86; Siena Coll; Mktg.

STEVENS, KATHLEEN; Hoosick Falls Central Schl; Hoosick Falls, NY; (Y); Exploring; FBLA; Band; Frsh Cls; Ntl Merit Ltr; Hudson Valley CC; Acctg.

STEVENS, LOUIS; Midwood HS; Brooklyn, NY; (Y); Boy Scts; Orch; Capt Diving; Mgr(s); Var Capt Socr; Var Capt Swmmng; Timer; Brockport SUNY.

STEVENS, MICHAEL J; Hamburg HS; Hamburg, NY; (Y); 14/382; Band; Concert Band; Mrchg Band; Symp Band; Bsktbl; JV Tennis; Hon Roll; NHS; Recngtn Schlstc Awd IA ST U 86; NYS Regnts Schlrshp 86; Ntl Band Awd 86; IA ST U; Comp Engr.

STEVENS, MIKE; Dryden HS; Harford, NY; (Y); Am Leg Boys St; Church Yth Grp; Quiz Bowl; Lit Mag; JV Var Bsbl; JV Var Ftbl; High Hon Roll; NHS; Ntl Merit Ltr; Wt Lftg; Mansfield U Ready Writing Cntst 1st 85 & 86; Baptist Bible Coll; Theology.

STEVENS, SANDRA E; Owego Free Acad; Endicott, NY; (Y); 13/224; Key Clb; Pres SADD; Stu Cncl; High Hon Roll; NHS; Ntl Merit Ltr; French Clb; Quiz Bowl; Band; Concert Band; NYS Regents Schlrshp 86; Empire St Games Gld Tm Medals Rifle, Bronze Indvdl Mdl 84; US Military Acad; Engrng.

STEVENS, VICTORIA; Rome Free Acad; Rome, NY; (Y); 9/450; Intnl Clb; Key Clb; Ski Clb; SADD; Band; Pres Frsh Cls; Pres Jr Cls; Pres Sr Cls; Var Capt Tennis; Im Vllybl; Rgnts Schlrshp 86; Prsdntl Ftns Awd 86; Colgate Smnr 86; Dartmouth Coll; Lbrl Arts.

STEVENSON, JOHN; Wayland Central HS; Wayland, NY; (Y); Sec FFA; Hon Roll; Lion Awd; 1st Pl-FFA Trctr Drvng Comptn-Rgn 85; 5th Pl-ST Fair Trctr Drvng Comptn 85; Nice Kid Awd 85; Alfred Ag Tech; Ag Engrng.

STEVENSON, MARGARET; Watkins Glen HS; Burdett, NY; (Y); 27/100; Church Yth Grp; Trs 4-H; FHA; Library Aide; VP SADD; Band; Mrchg Band; Sftbl; Vllybl; 4-H Awd; Med Ofc Asst.

STEVES, AMY J; Glen Falls HS; Glen Falls, NY; (Y); 15/225; Sec Frsh Cls; Sec Soph Cls; JV Var Cheerleading; High Hon Roll; Hon Roll; NHS; Ntl Govt & Hstry Awd 85; Ntl Ldrshp & Srvc Awd 86; NY Rgnts Schlrshp Nrsng 86; SUNY Plattsbrgh; Nrsng.

STEWARD, DAN; Randolph Central Schl; Kennedy, NY; (Y); 6/83; Am Leg Boys St; Drama Clb; FFA; VP Soph Cls; Var Capt Bsbl; Var Capt Bsktbl; Var Capt Ftbl; Hon Roll; NHS; Pres Schlr; Vars Ftbl MVP Troph 85; Vars Bsbl MVP Troph 86; US Army Rsrv Natl Schlr Athl Awd 86; Cornell U; Engrg.

STEWARD, DANIEL; Randolph Central Schl; Kennedy, NY; (Y); 6/85; Am Leg Boys St; Drama Clb; FFA; VP Soph Cls; Var Capt Bsbl; Var Capt Bsktbl; Var Capt Ftbl; Hon Roll; NHS; Pres Schlr; MVP Ftbl 85; MVP Bsbl 86; Cornell U; Engrg.

STEWART, CHERYL; Malverne HS; W Hempstead, NY; (Y); GAA; Varsity Clb; JV Sftbl; Vllybl; Hon Roll; Syracuse; Engnrng.

STEWART, CINDY; Richfield Springs Central Schl; Richfield Springs, NY; (Y); GAA; Girl Scts; VICA; Band; Chorus; Concert Band; Mrchg Band; School Musical; Rep Stu Cncl; Var L Cheerleading; Cosmtlgy.

STEWART, DARA; The Masters Schl; New York, NY; (Y); Cmnty Wkr; French Clb; GAA; Hosp Aide; Varsity Clb; School Play; Socr; Sftbl; Fencng 2nd Pl Invtnl 86; Ltr Commndtn Recgntn Comnty Serv 86.

STEWART, DAWN; La Guardia HS; Jamaica Queens, NY; (Y); Variety Show; Yrbk Stf; Rep Sr Cls; Arts Rcgntn & Tlnt Srch Hnrbl Mntn 86; Alvn Aly Amer Dnc Cntr Mrt Schlrshp 84-85; Dnc Schlrshp 83-85; U Of MD; Dance.

STEWART, DIANA; Jamesville-De Witt HS; Fayetteville, NY; (Y); 50/250; SADD; Yrbk Stf; Im Sftbl; Var Swmmng; High Hon Roll; Hon Roll; Pres French Clb 85-86; Vrsty Swmg Ltrs 83-85; Med.

STEWART, DWIGHT; John Dewey HS; Brooklyn, NY; (Y); Am Leg Aux Girls St; Chorus; Color Guard; Concert Band; Jazz Band; School Musical; School Play; Stage Crew; Variety Show; Bsbl; Won Sci Fair Awd Dist 17 84; Music Awds Plyng Trombone 84; Lawyer.

STEWART, KIM; Charles H Roth HS; Rush, NY; (Y); VP Church Yth Grp; GAA; Spanish Clb; Yrbk Stf; Rep Stu Cncl; JV Var Vllybl; High Hon Roll; Hon Roll; Jr NHS; Spanish NHS; Commnctns.

STEWART, MATTHEW; South Shore HS; Brooklyn, NY; (Y); Math Tm; Hon Roll; Prfct Atten Awd; Cert Merit In Math 84-85; Arista/Archon Scty 84.

STEWART, MILTON; Pulaski JR-SR HS; Richland, NY; (S); 2/90; Math Clb; VP Jr Cls; Im Wt Lftg; High Hon Roll; NHS.

STEWART, NANCY; New Dorp HS; Staten Island, NY; (Y); Drama Clb; French Clb; Intnl Clb; Concert Band; Mrchg Band; School Musical; Variety Show; French Hon Soc; Hon Roll; Jr NHS.

STEWART, PAUL; Cairo-Durham HS; E Durham, NY; (Y); Hon Roll; Acad Prfrmnce Awd LIU 86; LIU; Chem.

STEWART, RUBYANN; Marlboro HS; Marlboro, NY; (Y); 21/150; Church Yth Grp; Girl Scts; Library Aide; Chorus; Color Guard; Drm & Bgl; NHS; Girl Scout Gold Ldrshp 84; Girl Scout Slvr Awd 83; Psych.

STEWART, TIMOTHY; Catholic Central HS; Troy, NY; (Y); Boys Clb Am; Ski Clb; High Hon Roll.

STIEF, NEAL; N Babylon SR HS; No Babylon, NY; (Y); 30/478; Var Bsbl; Var Coach Actv; Var Ftbl; Var Socr; Var Trk; VP Jr NHS; NHS; Var Wrstlng; St Johns U & Jackie Robinson Fndtn Sports Mgmt Awd 85.

STIFFEY, HEATHER; Northville Central HS; Hadley, NY; (Y); Band; Chorus; Church Choir; Drm Mjr(t); School Musical; Yrbk Stf; Var Cheerleading; JV Socr.

STIFFLEAR, LUKE; Avon JR SR HS; Avon, NY; (Y); Ski Clb; Sec Sr Cls; Var L Ftbl; Var L Wrstlng; Hon Roll; NEDT Awd; Engnrng.

STIKELEATHER, MARIA; Cornwall Central HS; New Windsor, NY; (Y); Spanish Clb; High Hon Roll; Hon Roll; NHS; U Cncnti; Engrng.

STILES, DICK; Greenwich Central HS; Greenwich, NY; (Y); Boy Scts; Varsity Clb; Band; Concert Band; Jazz Band; Mrchg Band; School Musical; VP Jr Cls; Stu Cncl; Var Bsbl.

STILES, KAREN; Bishop Maginn HS; Rensselaer, NY; (Y); 42/84; Ski Clb; Spanish Clb; SADD; Chorus; School Musical; School Play; Stage Crew; Yrbk Stf; Cheerleading; Pom Pon; Plattsbgrh ST; Comp Sci.

STILES, LISA; Iroquois Central HS; East Aurora, NY; (Y); 67/267; Dance Clb; Girl Scts; Sec Key Clb; SADD; Capt Color Guard; Concert Band; Orch; School Musical; Capt Bowling; Cheerleading; U Of NY; Med.

STILLMAN, SUSAN; Sachem H S North; Centereach, NY; (Y); 231/1558; Church Yth Grp; Dance Clb; GAA; Ski Clb; Spanish Clb; Bsktbl; Fld Hcky; Sftbl; Vllybl; Long Island Bus Inst; Bus.

STILLWAGGON, MARY E; Old Westbury School Of The Hly Child; Point Lookout, NY; (Y); Dance Clb; Debate Tm; Drama Clb; Service Clb; Chorus; Nwsp Rptr; Lit Mag; Pres Sr Cls; VP Stu Cncl; High Hon Roll; Wnnr-NYS Rgnts Schlrshp 86; Svc Awd-Svc To Eldrly 84; Coll Of Wllm & Mary; Thtr Arts.

STILLWELL, DOREEN; Tully JR-SR HS; Tully, NY; (Y); Red Cross Aide; SADD; Varsity Clb; Chorus; Concert Band; Jazz Band; Pep Band; School Musical; Var Cheerleading; NHS; Altrnt-Frntrs Of Sci Pgm-Hgh Ablty Stu 86; Medcl Tech.

STILLWELL, LAURIE; Shenendehowa HS; Clifton Park, NY; (Y); 58/675; Science Clb; SADD; Symp Band; Nwsp Ed-Chief; JV Sftbl; JV Trk; Voice Dem Awd; English Clb; Band; Concert Band; 1st Pl GE Hall Of Hstry Essay Cont 85; Fin In Golub Fndtn Schlrshp Cont 86; Cobleskill Schlrshp 86; Cobleskill; Bio Tech.

STILSON, LORI; East HS; Corning, NY; (Y); 83/202; Church Yth Grp; Dance Clb; Drama Clb; Exploring; JA; Pep Clb; Drill Tm; School Play; Stage Crew; Cheerleading; Achvt Awd Drill Tm Cmp 85; Maui CC-HAWAII; Bus Mngmnt.

STIMERS, SANDRA; Liverpool HS; Liverpool, NY; (Y); 148/816; Church Yth Grp; Exploring; Hosp Aide; Chorus; Orch; School Musical; School Play; Stage Crew; Jr NHS; NHS; Pres Acad Ftnss Awd 86; Natl Hnr Soc 85; U Of Buffalo; Commnctns.

STIMIK, JULIE R; Binghamton HS; Binghamton, NY; (Y); Am Leg Aux Girls St; Cmnty Wkr; 4-H; Varsity Clb; Rep Stu Cncl; Var Capt Bsktbl; High Hon Roll; Hon Roll; NHS; Prfct Atten Awd; Natl Salute Yth 86-87; ST U Of NY; Yth Agncy Admin.

STIMPFL, VICTORIA; Dominican Commercial HS; Glendale, NY; (S); Hon Roll; Jr NHS; Dentistry.

STIMPHIL, GREGOR; Springfield Gardens HS; Springfield Grdns, NY; (Y); 5/440; Chess Clb; Math Clb; Math Tm; Off Soph Cls; Chrmn Jr Cls; Capt Tennis; Hon Roll.

STINGONE, WILLIAM; Archbishop Molloy HS; Jamaica, NY; (Y); Hosp Aide; Yrbk Stf; Im Bsktbl; L JV Crs Cntry; Im Sftbl; Var L Tennis; Var L Trk; High Hon Roll; NHS; Ntl Merit Ltr; Acad Excllnce Awd 84-86; Jrnlsm.

STINSON, FRANK; Rice HS; Bronx, NY; (Y); Art Clb; Computer Clb; Church Choir; Yrbk Stf; Hon Roll; NHS; NYU; Cmptr Sci.

STINSON, T ANDREW; Hahn American HS; Apo New York, NY; (Y); Boy Scts; Pres Drama Clb; Band; Mrchg Band; Pep Band; School Play; Stage Crew; Ftbl; Wrstlng; Hon Roll; Prof Stag Actr.

STINTON, DANIEL; John H Glenn HS; Huntington, NY; (Y); Computer Clb; School Musical; School Play; JV Crs Cntry; JV Ftbl; Wt Lftg; High Hon Roll; Hon Roll; Ntl Merit Schol; U Of Notre Dame; Accntnt.

STINTON, KEITH J; Commack HS South; Commack, NY; (Y); 60/367; Church Yth Grp; Office Aide; Bsbl; Im Ftbl; Im Ice Hcky; NY ST Rgnts Schlrshp Wnnr 86; Pl Wnnr Intra-Schl Erth Sci Olympd 85; C W Pst Scl Engl Pgm 85-86; Siena Coll; Accntng.

STIO, VINNY; Commack HS South; Dix Hills, NY; (Y); 159/328; Aud/Vis; Church Yth Grp; Varsity Clb; Rep Stu Cncl; Var Capt Bsbl; Var Capt Bsktbl; Im JV Ftbl; Cortland ST; Athl Trnng.

STIRLEN, W CHRISTOPHER; Sutherland HS; Rochester, NY; (Y); JV Ski Clb; Acpl Chr; Chorus; Church Choir; JV Socr; Hon Roll; Ntl Merit Schol; U CO; Mech Aerospc Engrng.

STITT, ANDY; Bay Port-Blue Point HS; Blue Pt, NY; (Y); Boy Scts; Mathletes; Hon Roll; Bus Admin.

STITT, DOUGLAS F; Ogdensburg Free Acad; Odgensburg, NY; (Y); 28/186; Am Leg Boys St; Key Clb; Quiz Bowl; Var L Ice Hcky; Var Capt Socr; Var Capt Trk; St Schlr; Army ROTC 4 Yr Schlrshp 85-86; Air Force ROTC 3 Yr Schlrshp 85-86; Norwich U Schlrshp 85-86; Norwich U; Hist.

STITT, MARCY W; Lycee Francais De N Y; New York City, NY; (Y); Yrbk Stf; Rep Frsh Cls; Rep Jr Cls; Rep Sr Cls; U Of CA-LA; Actng.

STIVERSON, SHELLI; Fairport HS; Fairport, NY; (Y); German Clb; Girl Scts; Orch; Lit Mag; Rep Stu Cncl; Var L Swmmng; Hon Roll; SUNY; Psychlgy.

STJOHN, STEPHEN; Bronx HS Of Science; Rosedale, NY; (Y); Camera Clb; Church Yth Grp; Cmnty Wkr; Cornell; Engrng.

STOCK, CHRIS; Newark SR HS; Newark, NY; (Y); 16/181; Math Tm; Red Cross Aide; Swing Chorus; Lit Mag; JV L Tennis; High Hon Roll; NHS; Cmnty Wkr; Teachers Aide; Variety Show; Dartmouth Bk Awd 86; Schl Hnr Boy 86; All Cty Choir 84-86; Engrng.

STOCK, ERIC; Mc Quaid Jesuit HS; Rochester, NY; (Y); Cmnty Wkr; School Musical; Yrbk Phtg; Stu Cncl; Socr; Camera Clb; Varsity Clb; Yrbk Stf; Hon Roll; City Cath Lg 2nd Tm Soccr 85; Brighton-Pittsford Post 2nd Tm All Star Soccr 85; Berklee Coll Music; Drums.

STOCK, JASON; Newark SR HS; Newark, NY; (Y); 31/181; Red Cross Aide; Chorus; Swing Chorus; Var Swmmng; L Var Tennis; Hon Roll; NHS; School Musical; Yrbk Stf; Lit Mag; All Lg Selectn Vars Tnns 85; All-ST Choir 85; Physcs.

STOCK, PAMELA; Cleveland Hill HS; Cheektowaga, NY; (Y); GAA; Band; Chorus; Yrbk Stf; JV Bsktbl; Hon Roll; Cert Credt Century 21 Acctg 84; Cert Prfcncy Century 21 Acctg 85; Erie CC; Bus Adm.

STOCKMAN, DAVID JOHN; Fort Ann Central Schl; Fort Ann, NY; (Y); 8/56; Am Leg Boys St; French Clb; Ski Clb; Ed Yrbk Stf; Pres Frsh Cls; Pres Soph Cls; Pres Jr Cls; Var Capt Bsktbl; Socr; NHS; Cotland; Physcl Ed.

STOCKMAN, MARK; Friendship Central HS; Friendship, NY; (S); Aud/Vis; Boy Scts; Cmnty Wkr; Computer Clb; Political Wkr; Spanish Clb; Chorus; School Play; Yrbk Stf; Stu Cncl; NY ST Rgnts Schlrshp Wnr 86; All Cnty Msc 85-86; Alfred U; Navy.

STOCKTON, JEFFREY C; Cortland JR SR HS; Cortland, NY; (Y); VP Frsh Cls; VP Soph Cls; Pres Jr Cls; Pres Sr Cls; Ftbl; Lcrss; Cit Awd; Hon Mntn-Ftbl 85; Crmnl Justc.

STOCKWELL, KIMBERLY; Frewsburg Central HS; Frewsburg, NY; (Y); 10/60; Church Yth Grp; FCA; Ski Clb; Spanish Clb; SADD; Chorus; School Musical; Rep Stu Cncl; Stat Bsbl; JV Bsktbl; Allegheny Coll; Elem Ed.

STOCUM, EMILY; Whitney Point HS; Castle Creek, NY; (Y); 7/123; Church Yth Grp; Civic Clb; Cmnty Wkr; 4-H; French Clb; Girl Scts; Science Clb; Teachers Aide; Chorus; Church Choir; Rotry Mst Outstndng Feml Ldrshp 85; Mst Outstndng Feml SR Cls 86; Pres Acdmc Fitns Awds 86; Coll Of New Rochelle; Bio.

STOCUM, LINDA; Tupper Lake HS; Tupper Lake, NY; (Y); 24/99; Camera Clb; Church Yth Grp; Debate Tm; 4-H; Hosp Aide; Pep Clb; Political Wkr; Yrbk Stf; Stu Cncl; JV Bsktbl; Cmnctns.

STOCUM, SUE; Watkins Glen HS; Watkins Glen, NY; (S); 13/139; French Clb; Letterman Clb; Yrbk Stf; Var Capt Bsktbl; Stat Ftbl; Var L Swmmng; Var Capt Trk; Var Capt Vllybl; French Hon Soc; High Hon Roll; Bus Adm.

STODDARD, AMY; Elmira Southside HS; Pine City, NY; (S); Sec Church Yth Grp; German Clb; Intnl Clb; Church Choir; Madrigals; Mrchg Band; Orch; Symp Band; Hon Roll; Al-ST Wind Ensmbl 85; Music Prfrmnc.

STODDARD, CHERRI; Mople Hil HS; Castleton On H, NY; (Y); Drama Clb; Spanish Clb; Score Keeper; Sftbl; Hon Roll; Journalism.

STOECKER, AMY; Cazenovia Central HS; Cazenovia, NY; (Y); 2/141; Am Leg Aux Girls St; Church Yth Grp; SADD; Band; Chorus; Sec Stu Cncl; Var Swmmng; Var Trk; High Hon Roll; NHS; Eng And Spnsh Achvt Awds 85; Bk Awd 86; Am Mgmt Assoc Semnr Schlrshp 86; Bio.

STOECKL, LISA; Tonawanda SR HS; Tonawanda, NY; (Y); Church Yth Grp; Trs Sec Girl Scts; Office Aide; Sec Chorus; Church Choir; School Musical; School Play; Stage Crew; Swing Chorus; Bowling; Occ Ther.

STOEHR, MICHELLE; Babylon HS; Babylon, NY; (Y); 1/200; Art Clb; Cmnty Wkr; Drama Clb; Church Choir; Jazz Band; Nwsp Ed-Chief; Lit Mag; Var Gym; High Hon Roll; NHS; Sm-Fnlst Yng Miss Mag JR Miss Pgnt 84; Gld Mdl LI Math Fair 86; Top Stu In Cls Awd 84; Writer.

STOFF, MATTHEW; Oceanside HS; Oceanside, NY; (Y); 93/540; Boy Scts; Thesps; Chorus; Jazz Band; Trs Mrchg Band; School Musical; Trk; Cit Awd; JP Sousa Awd; Var Rifle Capt 83-86; MVP/Plyrs Plyr Var Rifle 84-86; NYS Rgnts Schlrshp 86; Orch, Cncrt Bnd, Var Shw; U MI; Med.

STOFFERS, CAROL; St Peters HS For Girls; Staten Isl, NY; (Y); 8/101; School Play; Yrbk Stf; High Hon Roll; NHS; Church Yth Grp; Exploring; Library Aide; Spanish Clb; Chorus; Church Choir; NY ST Nrsng Schlrshp 86; SUNY; Chrprctr.

STOIO, ANGELA MARIE; Whitesboro SR HS; Whitesboro, NY; (Y); 82/354; Church Yth Grp; Exploring; Hosp Aide; Cheerleading; Fld Hcky; Powder Puff Ftbl; Sftbl; Hon Roll; Cmnty Wkr; SADD; Genetaska Clb Ctznshp Awd 86; Beta Sgma Phi Incntv Awd 86; Utica Coll; Bio.

STOKER, JAMES; Huntington HS; Huntington, NY; (Y); Drama Clb; VP Chorus; Concert Band; Jazz Band; Mrchg Band; Pep Band; Stage Crew; Swmmng; High Hon Roll; Trs NHS; Telluride Assoc Smmr Pgm Schlrshp 86.

STOKER, MARY; Stockbridge Valley Central Schl; Munnsville, NY; (S); 1/45; GAA; Concert Band; Mrchg Band; Nwsp Sprt Ed; Yrbk Ed-Chief; Var L Socr; Capt L Sftbl; Capt L Vllybl; NHS; Val; Most Imprvd Plyr Sftbl 84-85; Athltc Trainer.

STOKER, SUSAN; Clarkstown South HS; New City, NY; (Y); Church Yth Grp; Debate Tm; SADD; Nwsp Stf; Yrbk Stf; Var Cheerleading; Var Fld Hcky; Var Gym; Var Lcrss; Athletes Agnst Substance Abuse; Law.

STOKES, SHELDON; Newark SR HS; Newark, NY; (Y); Church Yth Grp; Library Aide; Swmmng; Olympcs Of Th Mind 86; Vrsty Ltrs In Swmng 85-86; Engrng.

STOKLOSA, PAMELA; St Marys HS; Cheektowaga, NY; (Y); NHS; GMI; Engrng.

STOLAR, BRIAN; Berner HS; Massapequa Park, NY; (Y); 3/412; Cmnty Wkr; Mathletes; Nwsp Rptr; Var L Bsbl; JV L Socr; Hon Roll; NHS; Ntl Merit Ltr; Pres Schlr; George Washington U Medl Excllnc Math & Sci; SUNY Binghamton Schl Of Mgmt.

STOLL, REBECCA; Cheektowaga Central HS; Cheektowaga, NY; (Y); 117/190; Camp Fr Inc; French Clb; Office Aide; SADD; Color Guard; Drill Tm; Flag Corp; Mrchg Band; Yrbk Stf; Trs Stu Cncl; Outstndg Treas Stu Cncl 86; Merit Roll 85-86.

STOLLER, STACY; Roy C Ketcham HS; Wappingers, NY; (Y); 8/550; Political Wkr; Thesps; Nwsp Rptr; Socr; Swmmng; Trk; High Hon Roll; NCTE Awd; NHS; Ntl Merit SF.

STOLTIE, DAVID; Potsdam Central HS; Potsdam, NY; (Y); 1/150; Computer Clb; French Clb; Math Clb; Ski Clb; Orch; Symp Band; JV Var Socr; High Hon Roll; NHS; Clrksn U; Bio.

STONE, BENJAMIN; Midwood HS; Brooklyn, NY; (Y); 81/667; Orch; Nwsp Rptr; Nwsp Stf; Stu Cncl; Lcrss; Socr; Wrstlng; Jrnlsm.

STONE, CARMELLA; Mohawk Central Schl; Frankfort, NY; (Y); 13/95; Art Clb; Sec French Clb; Band; Concert Band; Mrchg Band; Sec Jr Cls; Sec Sr Cls; Pres Stu Cncl; Var Capt Vllybl; Hon Roll; Vllybl MVP 85-86; Art Schlrshp; Vllybl Schlrshp; Cazenovia College; Intr Dsgn.

STONE, ERIC R; Horseheads SR HS; Big Flats, NY; (S); Am Leg Boys St; Pres Debate Tm; JCL; Pres Sec Latin Clb; Science Clb; Trs SADD; Off Stu Cncl; NHS; Church Yth Grp; Rep Soph Cls; Amer Lgn Yth Cnty 85; Pres Clssrm Yng Amer 85; Chembowl 85; Law.

STONE, GREGORY; Minisink Valley HS; Pt Jervis, NY; (Y); Computer Clb; Ski Clb; JV Trk; High Hon Roll; NHS; Prfct Atten Awd; Rotary Awd; Olympics Of The Mind & Sci Olympiad 85-86; Elec Engrng.

STONE, JANET; Fayetteville-Manlius HS; Manlius, NY; (Y); 3/335; German Clb; JCL; Chorus; Nwsp Stf; NHS; Ntl Merit Ltr; Empire ST Schlrshp 86; Dartmouth Clb Bk Awd 85; Cornell U; Engrng.

STONE, JEFF; Mc Quaid Jesuit HS; Webster, NY; (Y); Cmnty Wkr; Ski Clb; Varsity Clb; JV Crs Cntry; Var L Trk.

STONE, JEFFREY; Bishop Grime HS; Syracuse, NY; (Y); Var JV Bsbl; Var JV Bsktbl; JV Crs Cntry; Hon Roll; Bus.

STONE, LESLEY A; Hoosic Valley Central HS; Valley Falls, NY; (S); 6/99; Band; Chorus; School Musical; School Play; Sec Soph Cls; Rep Stu Cncl; Mgr Crs Cntry; Var Fld Hcky; Mgr(s); Mgr Trk; NY ST Smmr Schl Of Arts 85; Graphic Dsgn.

STONE, MARK; Jamesville-De Witt HS; Fayetteville, NY; (Y); 1/234; Math Tm; Stage Crew; Score Keeper; High Hon Roll; NHS; Val; Rensselaer Poly-Tech Inst Math/Sci, Math Lg Awd 86; Chem Lab Maintenance Job 85 & 86; Phys Sci.

STONE, MATTHEW; Brighton HS; Rochester, NY; (Y); Var Capt Golf; Ntl Merit Ltr; Pres Schlr; Rgnts Schlrshp 86; Hobart Coll.

STONE, MATTHEW; Horseheads HS; Horseheads, NY; (Y); JCL; Latin Clb; Ski Clb; Crs Cntry; Trk; Hon Roll; Arntcl Engrng.

STONE, MICHELLE M; Lansing HS; Ithaca, NY; (Y); 29/75; VP Computer Clb; Trs French Clb; Ski Clb; Nwsp Phtg; Yrbk Phtg; Powder Puff Ftbl; Sftbl; Trk; Capt Vllybl; Hon Roll; JR Art Awd 85; Most Invlvd Racr-Ski Tm 84; Bowling Green ST U; Rest Mgmt.

STONE, NELSON; Jamesville-Dewitt HS; Jamesville, NY; (Y); Church Yth Grp; CAP; Exploring; Ski Clb; Im Bsktbl; Im Socr; Hon Roll; Econ.

STONE, PAUL F; Whitney Point Central Schl; Whitney Point, NY; (Y); Am Leg Boys St; French Clb; Science Clb; Var L Bsbl; Var L Bsktbl; Var L Socr; High Hon Roll; Hon Roll; NHS; Broome CC; Conservation.

STONE, STACEY; Maple Hill HS; Castleton, NY; (S); 8/97; Exploring; French Clb; Fld Hcky; Socr; Sftbl; High Hon Roll; Hon Roll; Vet.

STONECIPHER, ALLAN; Skaneateles Central Schl; Skaneateles, NY; (Y); Aud/Vis; Computer Clb; Office Aide; Ski Clb; Stage Crew; Hon Roll; Cayyga County CC; Comp Technlg.

STONER, KELLY; Wayne Central HS; Ontario, NY; (Y); Var Crs Cntry; Var Mgr(s); Var Socr; Var L Sftbl; JV Var Vllybl; Hon Roll; NHS; Prfct Atten Awd; Ldrshp Sem 85-86; VP NHS 87; Tihaca; Commun.

STORCH, ROBERT; Saugerties HS; Mount Marion, NY; (S); Exploring; JA; High Hon Roll; Hon Roll; Prfct Atten Awd.

STORCHEVOY, PATRICIA; Valley Stream Central HS; Valley Stream, NY; (Y); 179/349; Teachers Aide; Stage Crew; Sftbl; Hon Roll; Nassau CC; Mrktng.

STORDY, MATHEW; Ramstein American HS; Apo New York, NY; (Y); Boy Scts; Chess Clb; Exploring; Ski Clb; Var Crs Cntry; JV Trk; Pres Acad Fit Awd 86; AFROTC 4 Yr Schlrshp 86; Officer Wives Clb Schlrshp 86; U Of CT; Math.

STOREN, KEN; Mahopac HS; Mahopac, NY; (Y); 14/435; AFS; Aud/Vis; Church Yth Grp; Cmnty Wkr; Drama Clb; Political Wkr; Science Clb; SADD; Band; Chorus; Engnrng.

STORES, JACQUELINE; Attica HS; Attica, NY; (S); 2/175; French Clb; Pres Frsh Cls; Sec Stu Cncl; DECA; Fld Hcky; Socr; Sftbl; Vllybl; High Hon Roll; Hon Roll; Soc Of Dstngshd Amer HS Stu 85-86; High Avg Awds 81-84; Psych.

STOREY, DOLORES; Holy Trinity Dioc HS; W Hempstead, NY; (S); Church Yth Grp; Girl Scts; Math Clb; Hon Roll; NEDT Awd.

STOREY, LAURA L; Notre Dame HS; Westmoreland, NY; (Y); ROTC; Sftbl; High Hon Roll; NHS; Rgnts Schlrshp 86; Geneseo; Mgt Sci.

STORINO, DANIELLE C; South Jefferson Central HS; Adams, NY; (Y); Church Yth Grp; French Clb; Pres Girl Scts; Ski Clb; Band; Concert Band; Mrchg Band; Yrbk Stf; Rep Stu Cncl; Tennis; Silv Awd Grl Scouts 84; Var Ltr Ten 86; Band Mdl 86; Sci.

STORNELLI, MARCUS A; Red Creek Central HS; Martville, NY; (Y); 1/80; Chess Clb; French Clb; Ski Clb; SADD; Trs Yrbk Stf; Trs Soph Cls; Trs Jr Cls; Trs Sr Cls; Trs Stu Cncl; Im Bsktbl; Empire St Schlrshp 86; Pres Schlrshp 86; Regents Schlrshp 86; Alfred U; Bus.

STORNES, SALLY; Falconer Central HS; Falconer, NY; (Y); 9/120; Pres Church Yth Grp; 4-H; Ski Clb; Spanish Clb; Mrchg Band; Orch; Rep Stu Cncl; Vllybl; High Hon Roll; NHS; 2nd Dog ST Fair 4-H 84; VFW Awd 86; Blue St Fair Dog Brace 85; Jamestown CC; Math Tchr.

STORY, PAULA; Gowanda Central Schl; Gowanda, NY; (Y); 28/124; AFS; Drama Clb; Spanish Clb; Color Guard; School Musical; Mgr Trk; Stat Wrstlng; VP Theta Rho Assmbly 86; Amvets Schlrshp 86; Central Cty Bus Inst; Crt Rptr.

STORY, ROBIN; Tioga Central Schl; Owego, NY; (Y); 48/86; Church Yth Grp; Dance Clb; FCA; Varsity Clb; Church Choir; Variety Show; Rep Stu Cncl; Coach Actv; Var JV Score Keeper; Var JV Sftbl; Csmtlst.

STOTT, ROBIN; Kingston HS; Kingston, NY; (Y); 40/573; Church Yth Grp; Church Choir; Yrbk Stf; French Hon Soc; High Hon Roll; Jr NHS; NHS; Pres Schlr; Ulster Cnty CC.

STOUT, MIKE; Union Endicott HS; Endicott, NY; (S); JV Var Bsbl; Bsktbl; JV Var Ftbl; JV Var Wt Lftg; Ftbl Div 1 All Star Tm Offns Grd 85.

STOUT, TAMARA; Churchville-Chili SR HS; Rochester, NY; (Y); Church Yth Grp; Pep Clb; Ski Clb; SADD; Nwsp Stf; VP Frsh Cls; Stu Cncl; Var Cheerleading; Var Trk; Hon Roll; Brdcst Jrnlsm.

STOUTENBURG, JEFFREY; Onteora JR SR HS; West Hurley, NY; (S); 3/195; VP DECA; Chorus; Concert Band; Drm Mjr(t); Mrchg Band; Orch; High Hon Roll; Hon Roll; NHS; Voice Dem Awd.

STOWE, RICHARD K; Newark SR HS; Newark, NY; (Y); 14/186; Am Leg Boys St; Math Tm; Acpl Chr; Chorus; School Musical; Elks Awd; High Hon Roll; NHS; Ntl Merit Ltr; Rotary Awd; Latin Hnr Soc; Genetics.

STOY, JOANN; Unatego JR SR HS; Otego, NY; (Y); 7/98; Drama Clb; Ski Clb; Spanish Clb; VP SADD; Rep Stu Cncl; JV Var Fld Hcky; JV Var Sftbl; High Hon Roll; NHS; Op Entrps Schlrshp 86; Spnsh Hertg Summr Prog Schlrshp 86; Pre Vet Svc.

STOYLE, SHAWN J; Dunkirk SR HS; Dunkirk, NY; (Y); Am Leg Boys St; Cmnty Wkr; Computer Clb; Letterman Clb; Ski Clb; Varsity Clb; Rep Frsh Cls; Off Sr Cls; Var JV Bsbl; Var Socr; Excllnc Engl Ii, Soc Studies Ii, Physics 86; Excllnc Comp, Soc Studies 10, Engl 10 85.

STRACHAN, TRACY; Far Rockaway HS; Jamaica, NY; (Y); 20/338; Key Clb; Office Aide; Scholastic Bowl; Teachers Aide; Band; School Play; Yrbk Stf; Hon Roll; NHS; Pres Acad Fit Awd 86; Cert Excllnce Natl Assn U Wmn 86; Cert Excllnce Sci 86; William & Mary; Obstrcn.

STRACQUALURSI, MARIE; Corcoran HS; Syracuse, NY; (Y); Art Clb; GAA; Ski Clb; Socr; Sftbl; Hon Roll; Prfct Atten Awd; Mktg.

STRADAR, ANN D; Newburgh Free Acad; Newburgh, NY; (Y); 9/621; French Clb; Key Clb; Chorus; Nwsp Stf; Rep Soph Cls; Rep Sr Cls; Var Sftbl; Var Tennis; French Hon Soc; Jr NHS; Georgetown U; Liberal Arts.

STRAHM, DIANE; New Dorp HS; Staten Island, NY; (Y); 132/698; Drama Clb; Intnl Clb; Key Clb; Office Aide; PAVAS; Teachers Aide; School Play; Variety Show; Nwsp Rptr; Nwsp Stf; 1st Pl In SING & Ldng Role; Comm.

STRAIN, SHEILA; Keshequa Central HS; Mt Morris, NY; (Y); 8/66; Pres AFS; Am Leg Aux Girls St; Church Yth Grp; VP French Clb; VP Spanish Clb; Sec Band; Trs Chorus; Nwsp Rptr; Nwsp Stf; Pres Stu Cncl; Haughton Coll; History.

STRAND, LOREN C; Hamilton Central HS; Hamilton, NY; (Y); Pres Art Clb; School Musical; Nwsp Ed-Chief; Yrbk Stf; Stu Cncl; Bsktbl; Crs Cntry; Trk; High Hon Roll; St Schlr; Natl Hnr Soc 84-86; Dr Melbourne S Reed Mem Frnch Prz 86; Art Schlrshp 86; Trinity Coll Hartford; Comp Sci.

STRANDBERG, DAVID C; Brockport SR HS; Brockport, NY; (Y); 12/335; Mathletes; Radio Clb; Ski Clb; Sec Concert Band; Jazz Band; Mrchg Band; Pep Band; JV Trk; High Hon Roll; Ntl Merit SF; Regents Schlrshp 86; Rensselaer Alumni Schlrshp 86; Mc Donalds All Am Band 85; Rensselaer Polytech Inst; Comp.

STRANGE, RODNEY J; Southside HS; Elmira, NY; (Y); French Clb; Hosp Aide; Pep Clb; Political Wkr; Varsity Clb; Nwsp Rptr; Sec Soph Cls; Sec Jr Cls; Pres Sr Cls; Rep Stu Cncl; Broadway JR HS Schlrshp 86; Yth Cnty Rep Mock Govt 85; Hosp Vlntr Awd 84; Poli Sci.

STRANGIS, FRANCO; La Salle SR HS; Niagara Falls, NY; (S); #4 In Class; Drama Clb; Socr; Trk; Hon Roll; NHS; Itln.

STRANZL, STEVEN E; Cardinal Spellman HS; Bronx, NY; (Y); German Clb; Concert Band; Jazz Band; Mrchg Band; Orch; School Musical; School Play; Hon Roll; Acadmc All Am 86; St Johns U; Phrmcy.

STRASSBERG, ADAM FRANKLIN; Ramapo SR HS; Monsey, NY; (Y); 1/529; Bausch & Lomb Sci Awd; French Hon Soc; High Hon Roll; Jr NHS; Mu Alp Tht; NHS; Ntl Merit Ltr; Val; Computer Clb; Intnl Clb; Grg Washngtn U Engrng Mdl 85; Rnsslr Plytchnc Inst Math & Sci Mdl 85; Peter Sills Schlrshp Awd 83; Harvard U; Elctrcl Eng.

STRASSBURG, JILL; Tonawanda JR SR HS; Tonawanda, NY; (Y); Trs Church Yth Grp; SADD; Varsity Clb; Yrbk Stf; Stu Cncl; L Socr; Capt Sftbl; L Swmmng; L Vllybl; 2nd Tm All Str Sftbl 85; 1st Tm All Leag Bsktbl 86; Nrsg.

STRASSER, ALISON; Suffern HS; Suffern, NY; (Y); 2/393; Cmnty Wkr; Teachers Aide; Mrchg Band; Orch; School Musical; Symp Band; Yrbk Bus Mgr; NHS; Ntl Merit Ltr; Sal; Area All-ST Soloist 84-85; Regents Schlrshp 86; AATF Frnch Comptn 2nd Pl Hdsn Vly Regn 83-84; PA U.

STRASSER, PATRICIA; Lehman HS; Bronx, NY; (Y); 20/541; Aud/Vis; Band; Hon Roll; NHS; Prfct Atten Awd; Keyboardng Awd 86; Comp Awd 85; Italian Clb 84; Pace U; Acctng.

STRASSER, SHERREE R; Sanford H Calhoun HS; N Merrick, NY; (Y); 52/313; SADD; Pres Temple Yth Grp; Nwsp Ed-Chief; Var Bsktbl; Var Socr; JV Sftbl; JV Vllybl; Hon Roll; Rgnts Schlrshp 86; Meritious Svc Citatn-Natl Conf Of Synagogue Yth 84; Svc Citatn-Schl SADD 85; Yeshiva U; Ed.

STRASSNER, CHRISTINE; Victor SR HS; Farmington, NY; (Y); Church Yth Grp; SADD; Teachers Aide; Varsity Clb; Church Choir; Stage Crew; Rep Stu Cncl; Var Swmmng; Bowling-2nd St Tm, 1st Dbls & Tm, 2nd Sngls-City 84; Schl Bkstr Mgr; Asst Cnslr Camp Phys Handicap 84; Spec Ed.

STRATTON, CYNTHIA L; E J Wilson HS; Spencerport, NY; (Y); Church Yth Grp; Drama Clb; Exploring; French Clb; Spanish Clb; VP Band; Mrchg Band; School Musical; School Play; Stage Crew; Regents Schlrshp Wnnr, Monroe All-Cnty Bnd, Rotary Intl Essy Cntst Local Wnnr 86; PA ST U; Pltcl Sci.

STRATTON, MICHELE; Westfield Central HS; Westfield, NY; (Y); Teachers Aide; Sec Sr Cls; Stat Bsktbl; Var L Trk; Hon Roll; George S Kent Memrl Math Schlrshp 85.

STRAUS, RACHEL; Blind Brook HS; Purchase, NY; (Y); DECA; Drama Clb; French Clb; PAVAS; Band; Concert Band; Orch; School Play; High Hon Roll; Hon Roll; Ltrtr Cls Suny Coll 86; 6th Annl Yng Athrs 86; Jacobs Pillow Cnfrnc 86.

STRAUS, SHERRY; Jamaica HS; Jamaica, NY; (Y); 9/507; Chess Clb; Math Clb; Temple Yth Grp; Var Trk; High Hon Roll; Hon Roll; Jr NHS; NHS; Prfct Atten Awd; NY ST Rgnts Schlrshp 85; Brnz Mtl Excel Math 86; Prncpls Prd Ynks Awd 85; U PA; Nrsng.

STRAUSS, ALEX; Oyster Bay HS; Oyster Bay, NY; (Y); Yrbk Stf; Rep Frsh Cls; Rep Soph Cls; Rep Jr Cls; Cheerleading; Sftbl; Vllybl; High Hon Roll; Hon Roll; Law.

STRAUSS, EVAN; Commack HS South; Dix Hills, NY; (Y); Teachers Aide; Temple Yth Grp; Nwsp Stf; VP Frsh Cls; VP Soph Cls; VP Jr Cls; Off Stu Cncl; Tennis; High Hon Roll; NHS; Gldn Quill Awd-Descrptv Essay 85; Actv Ctzn Of Schl & Cmmnty Awd 84-86; Sci Olympiad 85; Bio.

STRAWS, LYNEESE; Grace Dodge Vocational HS; Bronx, NY; (Y); Computer Clb; FBLA; Office Aide; Church Choir; Rep Stu Cncl; Bsktbl; Bowling; Socr; Vllybl; Art Clb; Gold Awd Stenogrphy & Sci 85 & 86; Blue Awd Engl & Sci 84; Gold Awd Hstry 86; Comp Anlys.

STRAZZA, CLAUDINE MICHELE; Cardinal Spellman HS; Bronx, NY; (Y); Church Yth Grp; Cmnty Wkr; Dance Clb; French Clb; Science Clb; Nwsp Rptr; Hon Roll; Law.

STRCICH, FRANK; Commack North HS; Commack, NY; (Y); Var Bsbl; Var Ftbl; Hon Roll; Im Wt Lftg; Capt Wrstlng; U Of MD; Engr.

STREATER, LINDA; Walton HS; Bronx, NY; (Y); Computer Clb; Debate Tm; Girl Scts; Hosp Aide; Teachers Aide; Chorus; Capt Vllybl; Hon Roll; Prfct Atten Awd; NAACP Awd Chrus 84; Emory U; Prof Nrsg.

STREET, NANCY; Honeoye Central HS; Honeoye, NY; (S); 3/68; Am Leg Aux Girls St; French Clb; Band; Jazz Band; Mrchg Band; Pres Jr Cls; Pres Sr Cls; Var Capt Bsktbl; Var Capt Socr; VP Pres NHS; Natl Merit Commnd Stu 85; Cornell U; Bio Chem.

STREETER, KIMMARIE; Frankfort-Schuyler HS; Frankfort, NY; (Y); Sec Church Yth Grp; FBLA; Yrbk Stf; French Clb; Library Aide; SADD; Chorus; Color Guard; High Hon Roll; Hon Roll; CCBI; Crt Rptr.

STREIT, ALISON; Bronx HS Of Science; New York City, NY; (Y); Cmnty Wkr; Drama Clb; JA; Teachers Aide; Temple Yth Grp; Chorus; School Play; Ed Lit Mag; Wesleyan U.

STRENZWILK, HEATHER A; Fairport HS; Fairport, NY; (Y); Church Yth Grp; Drama Clb; Math Tm; School Play; Stage Crew; Nwsp Rptr; Nwsp Stf; Yrbk Stf; Rep Stu Cncl; St Schlr; Stu Dir Charleys Aunt; St John Fisher Coll; Cmmnctns.

STRESING, JOHN L; West Seneca West SR HS; West Seneca, NY; (Y); 52/559; Rptr Nwsp Stf; Var Bowling; Im Ftbl; Capt Golf; Ice Hcky; Hon Roll; NHS; Rgnts Schlrshp 85-86; U Of Buffalo; Engrng.

STRIBICK, DANIEL; West Seneca East SR HS; W Seneca, NY; (Y); Church Yth Grp; Var Tennis; High Hon Roll; JC Awd; Jr NHS; NHS; Prfct Atten Awd; Magna Cum Laude Latin Awd 83-85diploma De Merito Spnsh Awd 85-86.

STRICKLAND, BRENT; Webster HS; Webster, NY; (Y); 65/500; Boy Scts; Church Yth Grp; Exploring; Ski Clb; Orch; Var Crs Cntry; JV Trk; Cit Awd; Hon Roll; Jr NHS; Eagle Scout 85; Regents Schlrshp 86; Suny Buffalo; Mechncl Engrng.

STRICKLAND, TRACEY ANN V; W C Mepham HS; N Bellmore, NY; (Y); Art Clb; Debate Tm; Drama Clb; Orch; School Play; Nwsp Rptr; Vllybl; CC Awd; Hon Roll; Jr NHS; Lehigh U; Med.

STRICKNER, BRYAN T; Wheatland Chili Central Schl; Scottsville, NY; (Y); Boy Scts; Library Aide; Pres Model UN; Chorus; Bsbl; Score Keeper; Trk; Poli Sci.

STRIEGLER, SUSAN; Frankfort Schuyler Central HS; Frankfort, NY; (S); 23/101; Spanish Clb; Band; Concert Band; Mrchg Band; Bowling; Fld Hcky; Trk; High Hon Roll; Utica Coll; Pre-Med.

STRIGLER, LEAH Z; Ramaz Schl; New York, NY; (Y); English Clb; Ed Lit Mag; Ntl Merit SF; Awds Of Merit; Piano Prfmnc-Hebrew Arts Schl; Wrtng.

STROBER, BENNA F; Lawrence HS; Woodmere, NY; (Y); 42/414; Sec DECA; Pres Key Clb; School Play; Cheerleading; High Hon Roll; NHS; Ntl Merit Schol; AFS; Drama Clb; Govt In Actn-Hsptlty Chrmn 84-86; Archon-Natl Merit Hnr Soc 83-86; Peer Grp 84-86; SUNY Albany; Bus.

STRODE, HEATHER; Torrejon American HS; APO, NY; (Y); Church Yth Grp; Drama Clb; Pep Clb; Chorus; School Play; L Cheerleading; L Swmmng; L Trk; High Hon Roll; Prfct Atten Awd; Schlstc Achvt Awd 85; Outstndng Achvt U S Hstry Awd 86; Brigham Young U; Educ.

STROEBEL, KAREN; Colonie Central HS; Albany, NY; (Y); Church Yth Grp; CAP; Girl Scts; Ski Clb.

STROM, CHRISTOPHER; West Seneca West HS; W Seneca, NY; (Y); Debate Tm; DECA; French Clb; Red Cross Aide; SADD; JV Crs Cntry; Var Swmmng; 4th Pl Hon Ment DECA ST Conf 85; 2nd Pl DECA Cmpttv Event Concord 86; Superior Achvmnt/Excllnc 85; Elec Engrng.

STRONG, LISA; Union Springs Acad; Kansas City, MO; (Y); Library Aide; Ski Clb; Teachers Aide; Varsity Clb; Church Choir; Variety Show; Yrbk Stf; Cheerleading; Cit Awd; Witnssg Tm 84-86; Dorm Rep 85-86; Bus Adm.

STROUD, RHONDA; J C Wilson Magnet HS; Rochester, NY; (Y); Math Tm; Science Clb; Band; Yrbk Stf; Tennis; Bausch & Lomb Sci Awd; High Hon Roll; JETS Awd; NHS; Physcs.

STROUP, BONNIE; Riverhead HS; Aquebogue, NY; (Y); 9/229; Ski Clb; Acpl Chr; Chorus; Yrbk Stf; VP Frsh Cls; VP Soph Cls; VP Jr Cls; Var Tennis; Jr NHS; NHS; Intl Bus.

STROZYK, SCOTT; Maryvale HS; Cheektowaga, NY; (Y); Cmnty Wkr; Hosp Aide; Spanish Clb; SADD; School Musical; Rep Stu Cncl; Var JV Bsktbl; Var Capt Ftbl; Im Trk; High Hon Roll; Comp Sci.

STRUBLE, BONNIE; Albion HS; Albion, NY; (S); 2/178; Sec Girl Scts; Spanish Clb; Teachers Aide; Color Guard; High Hon Roll; Jr NHS; NHS; Ntl Merit Ltr; Sal; NY ST Regnts Schlrshp 86; Chemcl Engrng.

STRUMER, NANCY; The Masters Schl; Braircliff Mnr, NY; (Y); Mgr Radio Clb; Acpl Chr; Orch; Nwsp Phtg; Ed Yrbk Phtg; Coach Actv; Diving; Mgr(s); Var Vllybl; Hon Roll; Music Schlrshp Intrlochn Ctr For Arts 83-85; BDA Photo Exhbtn 86; Frgn Ec.

STRUNK, KATHY; Malverne HS; Lynmbrook, NY; (Y); 38/121; Sftbl; Trk; Vllybl; Math Excllnc; Computers.

STRUSS, DANIELLE; Lawrence HS; Atlantic Bch, NY; (Y); Art Clb; French Clb; Science Clb; School Musical; Yrbk Sprt Ed; Yrbk Stf; Off Soph Cls; Off Jr Cls; Off Sr Cls; JV Var Cheerleading; High Hnr Rll 84-86.

STRUSS, DEBRA; Hauppauge HS; Hauppauge, NY; (Y); Orch; Lit Mag; Off Stu Cncl; Bowling; Cheerleading; High Hon Roll; Hon Roll; Jr NHS; Phy Educ Awd 84; Bus.

STUART, REBECCA J; Addison Central HS; Cameron, NY; (Y); 4/104; Sr Cls; Stu Cncl; Var Capt Socr; Var Sftbl; Vllybl; DAR Awd; High Hon Roll; NHS; Leag All Star Soccr Tm 85-86; U Of Buffalo; Psychlgy.

STUART, SEAN; Fayetteville-Manlius HS; Manlius, NY; (Y); Boy Scts; Church Yth Grp; Varsity Clb; Bsktbl; Var Ftbl; Var L Trk.

STUART, STEVEN; Germantown Central HS; Germantown, NY; (Y); 17/48; Boy Scts; Concert Band; Jazz Band; Mrchg Band; School Musical; School Play; JV Bsbl; JV Var Bsktbl; Var L Socr; Hon Roll; Maratine Coll; Engrng.

STUART, THOMAS R; Scotia Glenville HS; Scotia, NY; (Y); 11/250; Church Yth Grp; Band; Mrchg Band; JV Bsbl; Ntl Merit Ltr; Clarkson; Engrng.

STUBA, BETH; Hugh C Williams HS; Canton, NY; (Y); 3/150; VP Church Yth Grp; JA; Stat Bsktbl; Cheerleading; JV Var Socr; Var Trk; Elks Awd; High Hon Roll; NHS; Clarkson; Txclgy.

STUBER, TAMMY; G Ray Bodley HS; Fulton, NY; (Y); German Clb; Science Clb; Band; Drm Mjr(t); Orch; Yrbk Phtg; Var Bsktbl; Var Sftbl; NHS; Exploring; Roswell Pk Mem Prog 86; Bio.

STUCIN, LAURA A; Tottenville HS; Staten Island, NY; (Y); 32/871; Pres Church Yth Grp; Key Clb; SADD; Teachers Aide; Yrbk Stf; Co-Capt Tennis; Var Capt Vllybl; NHS; Ntl Merit Ltr; Staten Isl Advnc All-Star Vlybl 85; SUNY Albany; Art Dirctr.

STUCKY, RENEE; Whitesboro HS; Whitesboro, NY; (Y); Art Clb; Camera Clb; Church Yth Grp; Cmnty Wkr; Dance Clb; PAVAS; SADD; School Musical; School Play; Im Tennis; Intr Dsgn.

STUCZYNSKI, KEN; St Marys HS; Depew, NY; (S); 10/170; Pres Science Clb; Flag Corp; Nwsp Rptr; Yrbk Stf; VP Jr Cls; Hon Roll; NHS; Hgh Schl Chapl Sacristen 86; Sci.

STUDIER, LISA A; Brockport HS; Brockport, NY; (Y); 6/340; Band; Concert Band; Jazz Band; School Musical; Nwsp Stf; Score Keeper; Trk; High Hon Roll; NHS; Ntl Merit Ltr; Hstry & Ltn Awds 82-83 & 85-86; Oberlin Coll.

STUERT, RALPH; Frontier SR HS; Lakeview, NY; (S); 2/444; Math Clb; Varsity Clb; Concert Band; Mrchg Band; School Musical; Var Bsbl; High Hon Roll; Jr NHS; NHS; 2nd Rgnl Sci Fair Engrng 83; NYS Rgnts Schlrshp 86; Engrng.

STUHLER, MICHAEL; Cicero North Syracuse HS; Mattydale, NY; (S); 97/667; Exploring; NHS; Elec Engrng.

STUHR, GREGORY; Eden Central HS; Eden, NY; (Y); Chorus; Concert Band; School Musical; Nwsp Rptr; Pres Stu Cncl; Var JV Ftbl; NHS; AFS; Church Yth Grp; Drm & Bgl; Am Legn Essy Awd 86; Solo Musc Awd 86; Spirit Of Yth 86; Permg Arts.

STULGIS, CHRISTINE; Franciscan Acad; Liverpool, NY; (Y); Nwsp Phtg; Nwsp Rptr; Nwsp Stf; Yrbk Stf; Trs Frsh Cls; Hon Roll; MI Intrschlstc Press Assoc Hon Men Sprts Photgrphy 85; Achvt Awd Alg II 86.

STULMAKER, JEFFREY M; Herkimer HS; Herkimer, NY; (Y); 13/130; Aud/Vis; Model UN; SADD; Trs Temple Yth Grp; Band; Chorus; Mrchg Band; School Musical; Variety Show; Nwsp Rptr; All-ST Chorus 85; SUNY Geneseo; Math.

STUMBAUGH, BRIAN; Ravena-Coeymans-Selkirk HS; Ravena, NY; (Y); 8/184; Yrbk Ed-Chief; Lit Mag; Rep Frsh Cls; Rep Soph Cls; Rep Jr Cls; Rep Sr Cls; Rep Stu Cncl; Var Capt Bsbl; JV Bsktbl; Var JV Ftbl; Stu Of Mnth 86; Colonial Cncl Ftbl All-Star 86; RPI; Biotech.

STUMM, BRIAN; W C Mepham HS; N Bellmore, NY; (Y); Boy Scts; Computer Clb; Mathletes; Math Clb; Math Tm; Scholastic Bowl; VP Science Clb; Hon Roll; NHS; 3rd Pl Sci Bwl At Ntl Sci Olympiad 86; Slvr Pin Nassau Cnty Math Cmptn 86; Vrsty Ltr Acdmc Quiz 86; Engrng.

STUMPF, FRANZ; Batavia HS; Batavia, NY; (Y); Chess Clb; Math Tm; Band; Concert Band; Mrchg Band; JV Crs Cntry; JV Trk; Ntl Merit Ltr; Comp Sci.

STUMPF, SUSAN; Bishop Ford Central Catholic HS; Brooklyn, NY; (S); #4 In Class; Art Clb; French Clb; Science Clb; Acad Excllnc 84-86; Pace U; Bus.

STUNDTNER, ELIZABETH A; East HS; Corning, NY; (Y); 10/222; Drama Clb; Model UN; Spanish Clb; Frsh Cls; Soph Cls; Jr Cls; Sr Cls; Stu Cncl; Tennis; High Hon Roll; Chemung Canal Scholar 86; Alpha Kappa Delta Scholar 86; Amer Assn U Wmn 86; St Lawrence U; Pre-Law.

STUPPI, CHRIS; Walt Whitman HS; Huntington, NY; (Y); 139/477; Trk; Hon Roll; Grmn Spkng Awd 83-84; Hofstra U; Acctg.

STURDEVANT, LISA; Tioga Central HS; Nichols, NY; (Y); Computer Clb; Office Aide; Ski Clb; SADD; Nwsp Stf; Rep Frsh Cls; Rep Soph Cls; Stu Cncl; Capt Cheerleading; Fld Hcky; Comm.

STURGES, KEVIN; Mc Kee Technical HS; Staten Island, NY; (Y); 66/306; Boy Scts; Ski Clb; Ftbl; Wt Lftg; :Engr.

STURGESS, KELLEY; Unatego JR SR HS; Unadilla, NY; (S); 3/88; Am Leg Aux Girls St; Drama Clb; Band; Jazz Band; School Musical; Vllybl; NHS.

STURIANO, CHRIS; Francis Xavier HS; New York, NY; (Y); 9/250; Rep Soph Cls; Var L Ftbl; Var L Socr; Vrsty Ltr Rugby 86; Strght Hnrs Acadmc Pgm 83-86; Hnr Rll 83-86; Pre-Med.

STURIANO, SHARON; Malverne HS; Malverne, NY; (Y); Office Aide; Spanish Clb; School Play; Stage Crew; Soph Cls; Bsktbl; Socr; Sftbl; Trk; NCTE Awd; Phys Thrpy.

STURM, LINDA; Eden Central HS; Eden, NY; (Y); GAA; Chorus; School Musical; Var JV Bsktbl; Var L Fld Hcky; Var L Trk; NHS; Ntl Merit SF; Art Awd High Achvt 85-86; Spnsh Awd 86; Physcl Thrpy.

STURM, MICHELLE; Union Springs Acad; Union Springs, NY; (Y); Leo Clb; Ski Clb; Teachers Aide; Band; Concert Band; Trs Frsh Cls; Trs Sr Cls; Bsktbl; Sftbl; Swmmng; Atlantic Union; Htl/Mtl Mgmt.

STURMAN, DANIEL; Niskayuna HS; Schenectady, NY; (S); 19/425; Aud/Vis; Boy Scts; Pres Computer Clb; VP JA; Math Tm; Mrchg Band; Symp Band; Nwsp Stf; High Hon Roll; NHS; Comptr Sci.

STURNIOLO, KAREN; Nardin Acad; Buffalo, NY; (S); Church Yth Grp; Ski Clb; Variety Show; Nwsp Stf; Pres Soph Cls; Pres Sec Stu Cncl; Var Crs Cntry; Var Trk; Peer Outrch Cnslng Prgm Agnst Alchlsm 85-86; St Josephs U; Pre-Med.

STURZ, JEANNE; Hicksville HS; Hicksville, NY; (Y); Art Clb; Drama Clb; SADD; Teachers Aide; Thesps; Stage Crew; Yrbk Stf; NHS; Art Ther.

STUTZ, DAVE; Bonn American HS; Billings, MT; (Y); Church Yth Grp; Letterman Clb; Pres Band; VP Soph Cls; Var Capt Ftbl; Var Capt Wrstlng; High Hon Roll; Ntl Merit SF; Aud/Vis; Boy Scts; Mst Outstndng Wrstler 85-86; Math.

STUZIN, MICHELLE NANCY; Bethpage HS; Plainview, NY; (Y); 40/293; VP French Clb; FBLA; Spanish Clb; Stu Cncl; Var Capt Bsktbl; Var Capt Fld Hcky; Var Gym; Capt Lcrss; JV Sftbl; 4 Yr Prgrss Awd 86; MVP Fld Hcky 86; MVP Lcrss 86; Cornell U; Intl Bus.

STYCZYNSKI, MARK; Catholic Central HS; Clifton Pk, NY; (Y); Math Clb; Nwsp Rptr; Nwsp Stf; Yrbk Rptr; Var L Tennis; High Hon Roll; Hon Roll; NHS.

STYLES, DIANA; Olean HS; Olean, NY; (Y); Camp Fr Inc; Church Yth Grp; Drama Clb; French Clb; PAVAS; Teachers Aide; Thesps; Acpl Chr; Chorus; Church Choir; (Y ST Smr Schl Arts 86; Chatauqua Inst 85; Musicl Theatr NYC.

STYNES, WENDY; Moore Catholic HS; Staten Island, NY; (Y); Cmnty Wkr; VP French Clb; Math Clb; Ski Clb; Stage Crew; Nwsp Rptr; Yrbk Ed-Chief; Im Cheerleading; High Hon Roll; Pres NHS.

SU, VICKI; Forest Hills HS; New York City, NY; (Y); Church Yth Grp; Debate Tm; Pres Service Clb; Band; Church Choir; Ed Yrbk Stf; Pres Frsh Cls; Capt Vllybl; High Hon Roll; Trs NHS; NY Rgnts Schlrshp 86; Queensb Orough Sci Fair-1st Pl 84; Wheaton Coll IL; Mssnry Doc.

SUAKUN, YURY; Midwood HS; Brooklyn, NY; (Y); Chess Clb; Cmnty Wkr; Varsity Clb; Y-Teens; Concert Band; NY U.

SUAREZ, ELIZABETH; St Pius V HS; Bronx, NY; (Y); NHS; Hghst Avg Sequential Math II 85-86; Architect.

SUAREZ, JOSE; Eastern District HS; New York, NY; (Y); Camera Clb; English Clb; FBLA; JA; Off Sr Cls; Wt Lftg; High Hon Roll; Hon Roll; Comp.

SUAREZ, JOSE H; Regis HS; Queens Village, NY; (Y); Computer Clb; Yrbk Rptr; Yrbk Stf; Lit Mag; Bowling; Hon Roll; NHS; Spanish NHS; Schlrshp 82-86; Natl Hispanic Schlrs Awd Schlrshp 86-87; Building Industries Schlrshp 86; Duke U.

SUAREZ, LISA; Tottenville HS; Staten Island, NY; (Y); 65/871; Chorus; Oneonta; Psychlgy.

SUAREZ, RAFAEL; All Hallows HS; Bronx, NY; (Y); Boy Scts; Crs Cntry; Trk; John Jay Coll; Law Enforcement.

SUAREZ, ROBERT; Xavier HS; Brooklyn, NY; (Y); Computer Clb; French Clb; Hosp Aide; Varsity Clb; Band; Drill Tm; Mrchg Band; Bsbl; Swmmng; Wt Lftg; Natl Hspnc Schlr Awds Pgm Fnlst 86; Frgn Exchnge Pgm 85; NY U; Dr.

SUBA, WENDY; Whitesboro SR HS; Utica, NY; (Y); Church Yth Grp; GAA; Acpl Chr; Band; Chorus; Church Choir; Concert Band; Mrchg Band; Orch; School Musical; Cortland U; Mngr Of Physcl Educ.

SUBACH, RUTH; Smithtown HS East; Smithtown, NY; (Y); Camera Clb; Chess Clb; Church Yth Grp; French Clb; Teachers Aide; Chorus; Church Choir; French Hon Soc; High Hon Roll; Hon Roll; SUNY; Math.

SUCATO, ANTHONY R; West Seneca West SR HS; West Seneca, NY; (Y); 18/559; Band; Concert Band; Jazz Band; Mrchg Band; Orch; Variety Show; Capt Bsktbl; Vllybl; Hon Roll; NHS; NY St Lgnts Schlrshp 86; Dir Awd Music 83; ST U Of NY; Indstrl Engrng.

SUCHIN, ELLIOT; John F Kennedy HS; Merrick, NY; (Y); Capt Debate Tm; Science Clb; Concert Band; Yrbk Ed-Chief; High Hon Roll; VP NHS; Wnnr Grvnrs Trphy Essy Cntst 85; Med.

SUCHMAN, DEBBIE; Dominican Acad; New York, NY; (Y); Science Clb; SADD; School Musical; Stage Crew; Nwsp Stf; Rep Stu Cncl; Sftbl; High Hon Roll; Hon Roll; NEDT Awd; HS 1/2 Schlrshp 84-87; Natl Latin Exam Cum Laude 83-84; Natl Sci Merit Awd 86; Intl Frgn Lang Awd 85; NY U; Acctg.

SUDA, MAUREEN L; Archbishop Walsh HS; Olean, NY; (Y); Drama Clb; Sec French Clb; Latin Clb; Church Choir; School Musical; Nwsp Rptr; Yrbk Phtg; Stat Bsktbl; High Hon Roll; Pres NHS; Bus Admin.

SUDAC, IVAN; Cardinal O Hara HS; Buffalo, NY; (S); Boys Clb Am; Boy Scts; JA; Trs Pres Stu Cncl; Im Badmtn; Bsktbl; Var Capt Golf; Var Timer; High Hon Roll; Hon Roll; Rochester Inst; Elec Engr.

SUDUL, CYNTHIA; Moore Catholic HS; Staten Island, NY; (Y); Spanish Clb; Yrbk Stf; Hon Roll; Early Chldhd Ed.

SUESS, ALEX; Saugerties HS; Saugerties, NY; (S); 7/256; Pres Church Yth Grp; Math Tm; Chorus; Rep Stu Cncl; Bsktbl; Ftbl; High Hon Roll; NHS; Comp Cntst Wnnr 85; Social Stds Olympd 85; Hope Coll; Comp Sci.

SUGAR, MARNI; Beach Channel HS; Rockaway, NY; (Y); 45/450; Yrbk Sprt Ed; Rep Stu Cncl; Var Socr; Var Vllybl; NYC Assn Frgn Lang Chrmn; Boston U.

SUGARMAN, DIANE JUDITH; Jamesville-Dewitt HS; Fayetteville, NY; (Y); Intnl Clb; Model UN; Political Wkr; Chorus; School Musical; Stage Crew; Nwsp Stf; Sftbl; Var Swmmng; Camdian Amer Model United Ntn Corrd 86-87; Intl Rltns.

SUGG, NICOLE; Victor HS; Macedon, NY; (Y); 5/302; Am Leg Aux Girls St; Trs GAA; VP Varsity Clb; Pres Jr Cls; Pres Sr Cls; Rep Stu Cncl; Capt L Bsktbl; Capt L Socr; Cit Awd; Trs NHS; Ideal Teammate Awd Var Bsktbll 85-86; Lbrl Arts.

SUGGS, EDMENSON; Lafayette HS; Brooklyn, NY; (Y); Var Ftbl; L Trk; Arista Soc 86; Arkon Soc 85; Bus Mgmt.

SUGLIA, DONNA; Mt Mercy Acad; W Seneca, NY; (Y); Drama Clb; Ski Clb; Pres Spanish Clb; Im Fld Hcky; High Hon Roll; NHS; Mock Trl Cert 86; Chem.

SUGRUE, PATTY; Lynbrook HS; Lynbrook, NY; (Y); Trvl.

SUHR, AMY; Kendall Centall Schl; Kendall, NY; (Y); 35/93; Sec Church Yth Grp; Pep Clb; Church Choir; VP Color Guard; Rep Stu Cncl; Var Capt Cheerleading; Hon Roll; Prfct Atten Awd; Outstndg Bsktbl Chrldr 85-86; Acad Ltr 85-86; Geneseo; Acctnt.

SUKHDEO, ALICIA; Newtown HS; Elmhurst, NY; (Y); Church Yth Grp; Dance Clb; Political Wkr; Speech Tm; Chorus; Church Choir; School Play; Nwsp Rptr; Rep Soph Cls; Var Gym; Ornstein Humntrian Hnr, Engl Awd, Vcl Music Awd & Gymnstcs Awd; Communications.

SULEM, NANCY; Broadalbin Central Schl; Gloversville, NY; (Y); Drama Clb; Library Aide; Sec Spanish Clb; Color Guard; Mrchg Band; School Play; Yrbk Ed-Chief; Cheerleading; High Hon Roll; Jr NHS; Bus Adm.

SULLI, MIKE; Farmingdale HS; Farmingdale, NY; (Y); Computer Clb; Math Clb; Stage Crew; Jr Cls; Ftbl; Ice Hcky; Sftbl; Trk; Wt Lftg; Ntl Merit Ltr.

SULLIVAN, ANN MARIE; Vicenza American HS; APO New York, NY; (Y); 14/55; Drama Clb; Model UN; Spanish Clb; SADD; Chorus; School Musical; School Play; High Hon Roll; Hon Roll; NHS; Air Force; Public Affairs.

SULLIVAN, BRIAN; Carmel HS; Carmel, NY; (Y); Church Yth Grp; Im Var Bsktbl; Var JV Ftbl; Var Golf; High Hon Roll; Hon Roll; Prfct Atten Awd; St Johns U; Cmptr Sci.

SULLIVAN, CARRIE; Glens Falls HS; Glen Falls, NY; (Y); AFS; Camera Clb; Cmnty Wkr; Girl Scts; Letterman Clb; Varsity Clb; Yrbk Phtg; Yrbk Sprt Ed; Yrbk Stf; JV Bsktbl; Glens Falls Hosp; Rdlgy Tech.

SULLIVAN, CLAIRE; Mamaroneck HS; Mamaroneck, NY; (Y); Spanish Clb; Badmtn; Var JV Sftbl; JV Vllybl; Hist.

SULLIVAN, COLLEEN; Liverpool HS; Liverpool, NY; (Y); 166/835; DECA; Stu Cncl; Powder Puff Ftbl; Sftbl; High Hon Roll; Untd Lcrpl Fctly Assoc Mem Schlrshp Prsntd Annly Hnr All Dcsd Fclty 86; SUNY Oswego; Elem Educ.

SULLIVAN, DARIN; Portledge Schl; Locust Valley, NY; (Y); 1/12; Model UN; School Musical; School Play; Nwsp Rptr; VP Frsh Cls; VP Jr Cls; VP Stu Cncl; L Ice Hcky; Capt Lcrss; Var Socr; Ayers Acdmc Awd 86; US Amry Schlr/Athlt Schlr 85-86; Prtldge Schl Of Physcs Awd 85-86; U Of Richmond; Bus.

SULLIVAN, EILEEN M; Carmel HS; Carmel, NY; (Y); 39/350; Art Clb; High Hon Roll; Hon Roll; NHS; Ntl Merit Ltr; Svrl Awds In Poster Cntsts 83-85; SUNY Alfred Schlrshp 86; SUNY Alfred; Cmrcl Art.

SULLIVAN, ERIK; Bayport-Blue Pt HS; Bayport, NY; (Y); Cmnty Wkr; JV Var Bsktbl; JV Var Socr; Ulrich Bsktbl Awd 86; Presdntl Schlr 86; USC; Mrktng.

SULLIVAN, HEATHER; Guilderland Central HS; Albany, NY; (Y); Drama Clb; Chorus; School Musical; Stage Crew; Swing Chorus; Rep Stu Cncl; Im JV Score Keeper; High Hon Roll; Hon Roll; Jr NHS; Outstndng Achvt Soc Stds, Cmnty Svc 85-86; Law.

SULLIVAN, JAMES; Frontier Central HS; Lakeview, NY; (Y); Latin Clb; Spanish Clb; Varsity Clb; Band; Jazz Band; Stu Cncl; JV Ice Hcky; Var Socr; Im Var Swmmng; NHS.

SULLIVAN, JEAN; Sacred Heart Acad; Mineola, NY; (Y); Pep Clb; SADD; School Musical; School Play; Pres Stage Crew; Yrbk Rptr; Hotel/Rest Mgmt.

SULLIVAN, JEFFREY; Webster HS; Webster, NY; (Y); Ntl Merit Ltr; U Of NC.

SULLIVAN, JOHN L; Malverne HS; Lynbrook, NY; (Y); 3/143; Exploring; Quiz Bowl; Ski Clb; Lit Mag; Sec Stu Cncl; High Hon Roll; Hon Roll; NHS; Ntl Merit SF; Woodman Of The Wrld Life Ins Scty Amer Hstry Awd 85; Socl Stds Awd 83-85; Pre-Med.

SULLIVAN, JOHN W; East Islip HS; Islip Terrace, NY; (Y); #20 In Class; Cmnty Wkr; Hosp Aide; Math Clb; Stu Cncl; Var L Crs Cntry; Var JV Socr; Im Sftbl; Var Trk; High Hon Roll; Hon Roll; Rgnts Schlrshp 85-86; ROTC 86-87; Binghamton; Chem.

SULLIVAN, KAROLYN R; Clymer Central Schl; Clymer, NY; (Y); 4/47; Pres AFS; VP Band; Chorus; Yrbk Stf; VP Sr Cls; JV Var Bsktbl; Var L Sftbl; JV Var Vllybl; Pres NHS; Schlrshp Ldrshp Svc Awd 84-86; Bst Def Plyr Girls Var Bsktbl 84-86; Var Sftbl Div III All Star Tm 86; Slippery Rock U; Phy Ed.

SULLIVAN, KERRY; St John The Baptist HS; Bethpage, NY; (Y); Exploring; Hosp Aide; Red Cross Aide; Chorus; School Musical; 4-H Awd; Volntr Wrk Svc Red Crss 86; Nrs.

SULLIVAN, KEVIN; Fordham Prep; Bronx, NY; (Y); Var L Bsbl; Hon Roll; Frshmn Yr 2nd Hnrs 83-84; JR Yr 2nd Hnrs 85-86.

SULLIVAN, KIM; Shoreham-Wading River HS; Shoreham, NY; (Y); Mathletes; Ski Clb; Nwsp Rptr; Yrbk Stf; Soph Cls; Jr Cls; Sr Cls; Trs Stu Cncl; Fld Hcky; Vllybl; Blgy.

SULLIVAN, LESLEY; Roy C Ketcham HS; Poughkeepsie, NY; (Y); Yrbk Bus Mgr; Var L Socr; Var Timer; Var Trk; Cit Awd; High Hon Roll; Hon Roll; Physcl Thrpy.

SULLIVAN, LISA; Jamesville De Witt HS; Fayetteville, NY; (Y); Church Yth Grp; Cmnty Wkr; French Clb; Key Clb; Pep Clb; SADD; Stage Crew; Hon Roll; Im Diving; JV Gym; Gymnastic Awd Local Comp Private Schl 81; Cortland Coll; Bio.

SULLIVAN, LORY; Vestal SR HS; Vestal, NY; (Y); Church Yth Grp; Cmnty Wkr; Dance Clb; Exploring; French Clb; SADD; Yrbk Ed-Chief; Yrbk Stf; Capt Sftbl; 1st Pl Sftbll Tm Vstl Lg 85; All-Str ME Sftbll 86; IBM Coop Pstn 86-87; VA U; Bus Mgmt.

SULLIVAN, MARY; Our Lady Of Mercy HS; Pittsford, NY; (Y); Church Yth Grp; Cmnty Wkr; Spanish Clb; Capt Cheerleading; Var Gym; Hon Roll; Nrsg.

SULLIVAN, MARYANN; Catholic Central HS; Troy, NY; (Y); French Clb; Math Clb; Math Tm; Pep Clb; SADD; Varsity Clb; Yrbk Stf; JV Capt Cheerleading; Var L Pom Pon; Ed.

SULLIVAN, NANCY; New Dorp HS; Staten Island, NY; (Y); 70/597; Cmnty Wkr; Latin Clb; Var Bsktbl; Var Mgr(s); Var Score Keeper; JV Sftbl; Hon Roll; Pres Scholar Concordia Coll 86; Patrlmn Thomas Schimenti Mem Awd 86; Outstndg Achvt Steno 86; Concordia Coll; Elem Ed.

SULLIVAN, ROBERT; Cardinal Spellman HS; Bronx, NY; (Y); Cmnty Wkr; Intnl Clb; Im Bsktbl; Im Ftbl; Hon Roll; Manhattan Coll; Fgn Svc Ofcr.

SULLIVAN, SEAN; Monsignor Farrell HS; Staten Island, NY; (S); Mrchg Band; Stage Crew; JV Socr; Hon Roll; Bus.

SULLIVAN, SHANNON; Sacred Heart Acad; Lynbrook, NY; (Y); JV Sftbl; Var Vllybl; Hon Roll; Bus.

SULLIVAN, SHANNON M; Stissing Mt JR SR HS; Red Hook, NY; (Y); 15/100; AFS; Yrbk Rptr; Yrbk Stf; JV Bsktbl; Var Capt Fld Hcky; Trk; Hon Roll; Regents Schlrshp Awd 86; SUNY-ALBANY.

SULLIVAN, WILLIAM; Johnstown HS; Johnstown, NY; (Y); Church Yth Grp; Intnl Clb; Var Bsktbl; Var Golf; Var Capt Tennis; Hon Roll; Regents Scshlrshp Awd 85-86; Tennis MVP; Le Moyne Coll Syracuse; Bus.

SULLIVAN III, WILLIAM F; Wilson Magnet HS; Rochester, NY; (Y); 9/70; Cmnty Wkr; Math Tm; Chrmn Model UN; Yrbk Phtg; Var Swmmng; High Hon Roll; Ntl Merit Ltr; Delg Intl Model UN 86; NY ST Regents Scholar 86; Natl Sci Olympd Awd Bio 84; MI ST U.

SULTAN, CYNTHIA; Briarcliff HS; Briarcliff Mnr, NY; (Y); Drama Clb; French Clb; Temple Yth Grp; Y-Teens; Chorus; School Musical; School Play; Swing Chorus; Yrbk Stf; Lit Mag; B Nai Brith Awd 86; Natl Ha Dassah Israel Scholar 86; Amer Zionist Yth Fndtn Scholar 86; SUNY Albany; Psych.

SULTAN, HEENA; Midwood HS; Brooklyn, NY; (Y); 58/667; Cmnty Wkr; Debate Tm; Hosp Aide; Intnl Clb; Math Tm; Science Clb; Service Clb; Yrbk Stf; Lit Mag; NHS; Doctor.

SUMME, KELLY M; Akron Central HS; Akron, NY; (Y); 2/137; Church Yth Grp; French Clb; Ed Lit Mag; Var L Fld Hcky; Hon Roll; Sec NHS; Ntl Merit SF; Pres Schlr; Sal; NY ST Rgnts Schlrshp; St Bonaventure U; Frnch.

SUMMERVILLE, DARCIE; G Ray Bodley HS; Fulton, NY; (Y); 48/261; Church Yth Grp; 4-H; Latin Clb; Spanish Clb; Church Choir; Orch; School Musical; Variety Show; JV Socr; Hon Roll; Syracuse Symphny Yth Orchstr 84-86; Otstndng Awd Orchestra Schl 86; Ithaca Coll; Music Ed.

SUMMERVILLE, DOUGLAS; Tottenville HS; New York, NY; (S); #10 In Class; Concert Band; JV Crs Cntry; JV Trk; High Hon Roll; Jr NHS; NHS; Stn Islnd Scl Stds Fair 1st Pl 86; Crss Cntry Trck MVP 83; Indr/Otdr Trck & Fld MVP 84.

SUMMERVILLE, JODY; Letchworth Central HS; Castile, NY; (Y); Rptr FBLA; High Hon Roll; Hon Roll; ST U Coll At Buffalo; Scl Wrk.

SUMNER, KIMBERLY L; East Syracuse Minoa Central HS; E Syracuse, NY; (Y); 6/333; Trs Drama Clb; Sec Exploring; VP JA; Pres NFL; Trs Thesps; Mgr Concert Band; Jazz Band; NHS; Ntl Merit Ltr; Voice Dem Awd; Natl Yng Ldrs Conf 85; All ST Frnscs Trnmnt 85-86; All ST Concrt Band 86; Cornell U; Psych.

SUMNER, LEE; Amsterdam HS; Amsterdam, NY; (Y); Boys Clb Am; Church Yth Grp; Civic Clb; Wt Lftg; Wrstlng; Hon Roll; Prfct Atten Awd; Syracuse U; Lawyer.

SUMNER, STEPHEN; Northport HS; East Northport, NY; (Y); 84/579; Acpl Chr; Chorus; Orch; Nwsp Stf; Yrbk Stf; Hon Roll; Jr NHS; NHS; Long Island String Fest 84; All Cnty Music Fest 84; GATE 83-84; Tchrs Fedrl Credit Union 3r Pl 85.

SUMOWICZ, ALESSANDRA M; Convent Of The Sacred Heart HS; Jackson Heights, NY; (Y); Cmnty Wkr; Debate Tm; Math Tm; Service Clb; Chorus; Nwsp Ed-Chief; Im Lcrss; Jr NHS; NEDT Awd; JR Acad Of NY Acad & Sci 85-86; Rgnts Schlrshp 86; Acdmc Awd 83 & 84; Tufts U.

SUMTER, WINEFRED; Freeport HS; Freeport, NY; (Y); 63/450; Church Yth Grp; Cmnty Wkr; Pep Clb; Church Choir; Nwsp Sprt Ed; Rep Frsh Cls; Rep Soph Cls; Rep Jr Cls; Rep Sr Cls; Pres Sec Stu Cncl; Oper Get Ahd SR Schlrshp, Mrtn Lthr King Jr Schlrshp, Wm C Rhds Ins Agncy Schlrshp 86; Pace U; Acctg.

SUN, CHYI; Scarsdale HS; Scarsdale, NY; (Y); French Clb; VP Girl Scts; Hosp Aide; Yrbk Rptr; Ed Yrbk Stf; JV Trk; Im Vllybl; Ntl Merit Ltr.

SUNDERLAND, REBECCA; Peru Central HS; Peru, NY; (Y); Lit Mag; Art.

SUNDSTROM, STEVE; Alden Central HS; Alden, NY; (Y); Letterman Clb; Science Clb; Spanish Clb; SADD; Bsbl; Bsktbl; Var Ftbl.

SUNG, RHEE HO; Half Hollow Hills HS East; Melville, NY; (Y); Chess Clb; Church Yth Grp; French Clb; Mathletes; Chorus; Lit Mag; JV Bowling; JV Socr; JV Tennis; French Hon Soc.

SUNG, SUE H; Bronx H S Of Science; New York, NY; (Y); VP Church Yth Grp; Intnl Clb; Library Aide; Church Choir; Rptr Yrbk Stf; Rep Stu Cncl; Trk; Im Vllybl; Sec NHS; UFT Schlrshp 86; Cooprtn Govt Awd 86; NYU.

SUNSHINE, ROB; Roosevelt HS; Yonkers, NY; (Y); 21/586; Aud/Vis; Camera Clb; Computer Clb; FBLA; Leo Clb; Office Aide; Radio Clb; ROTC; Scholastic Bowl; Ski Clb; Oxford; Dctr.

SUOZZI, FRAN; St Marys HS; Cheektowaga, NY; (Y); 18/186; Computer Clb; 4-H; SADD; Var Bsktbl; Im Bowling; Var Crs Cntry; Im Ice Hcky; Var Socr; Var Trk; Cit Awd; Buffalo Nws Carrier Mnth 86; Phy Fit Achvt Awds 84-86; RIT; Elctrcl Engrng.

SUOZZI, JOSEPH P; Batavia HS; Batavia, NY; (Y); Ski Clb; Yrbk Stf; Pres Jr Cls; Pres Sr Cls; Rep Stu Cncl; JV Bsbl; Var L Ftbl; JV Var Wt Lftg; U Of Dayton; Crmnl Jstc.

SUOZZO, CHRISTINA; Harborfields HS; Greenlawn, NY; (Y); French Clb; Yrbk Stf; Outstndng Svc Bus Ed Dept 86; Banking.

SUPINSKI, NICOLE; Plattsburgh HS; Plattsburgh, NY; (Y); Ski Clb; Sec Stu Cncl; Trk; Hon Roll; Phys Thrpy.

SUPLEY, LUCINDA L; Tully Central HS; Tully, NY; (Y); French Clb; High Hon Roll; NHS; Radio/TV Brdcstng.

SURACE, FRANK; Clarkstown SR High School South; Bardonia, NY; (Y); Var Bsbl; Var Bsktbl; Capt Var Ftbl; Outstndng Stu Awd 83-85; Bus.

SURDICH, ANTHONY J; St Francis Prep; College Point, NY; (S); Baruch Coll; Mktg.

SURENTO, TIMOTHY J; Amsterdam HS; Amsterdam, NY; (Y); Church Yth Grp; JA; Political Wkr; Band; Concert Band; Jazz Band; Mrchg Band; Symp Band; Hon Roll; St Schlr.

SURI, MADHU; Half Hollow Hills HS West; Dix Hills, NY; (Y); 55/396; Pres French Clb; Key Clb; Political Wkr; SADD; Nwsp Rptr; JV Trk; DAR Awd; High Hon Roll; Sec NHS; NY U Schlr; Excllnc Bkkpng & Acctg 86; NY ST Rgnts Schrlshp 86; NY U; Finance.

SURI, NIRJA; Cicero North Syracuse HS; North Syracuse, NY; (S); 13/743; Debate Tm; Ski Clb; SADD; Nwsp Rptr; Nwsp Stf; Lit Mag; Stu Cncl; JV Badmtn; Hon Roll; Jr NHS; Spn Awd 84; Law.

SURIANI, SUSAN F; Hornell HS; N Hornell, NY; (Y); Camp Fr Inc; Latin Clb; Ski Clb; Drm Mjr(t); Yrbk Stf; Pres Jr Cls; Rep Stu Cncl; JV Cheerleading; Var Vllybl; Hon Roll; All-Cnty Music Festvl Awd 86; Bus.

SURMAN, STEPHANIE R; Pembroke JR & SR HS; Corfu, NY; (Y); 1/115; Math Tm; Pres Science Clb; Stu Cncl; Score Keeper; Trk; Bausch & Lomb Sci Awd; High Hon Roll; Pres NHS; Ntl Merit Ltr; Val; Rochester Inst Of Tech; Ind Eng.

SUROWIEC, CHUCK; Wayne Central HS; Ontario, NY; (Y); 7/190; Ski Clb; VP Soph Cls; JV Bsktbl; L Var Ftbl; L Var Trk; High Hon Roll; Hon Roll; Pres NHS.

SURPRENANT, TRACY; Poland Central Schl; Poland, NY; (Y); 10/78; Drama Clb; SADD; Varsity Clb; Chorus; School Play; Off Jr Cls; Stu Cncl; Cheerleading; Hon Roll; NHS; Schlrshp Awd-Hnr Roll All Yr 85; Chmpn Bio & Shrthnd 85; Chmpn In Chrs 84; Mohawk CC; Lgl Sec.

SURRANO, PATRICIA; Ravena Coeymans Selkirk HS; Selkirk, NY; (Y); 10/200; FBLA; Key Clb; SADD; DAR Awd; NHS; Rep Frsh Cls; Rep Soph Cls; Rep Jr Cls; Rep Sr Cls; Rep Stu Cncl; Syracuse U; Bus Adm.

SUSICE, CHRISTINE; St Regis Falls Central Schl; St Regis Falls, NY; (Y); Band; Chorus; Sec Frsh Cls; Trs Sr Cls; JV Var Cheerleading; High Hon Roll; NHS; Acad All Amer 86; Cntrl City Bus Inst Merit Scholar 86; Natl Chrldg Achvt Awd 86; Central City Bus Inst; Exec Sec.

SUSLIK, MICHELLE; Auburn HS; Tabb, VA; (Y); Church Yth Grp; VP German Clb; JV Var Vllybl; Hon Roll.

SUSSMAN, ERIC; Manhasset HS; Manhasset, NY; (Y); 44/175; Band; Concert Band; Jazz Band; Mrchg Band; Rep Frsh Cls; Var Ftbl; Var Lcrss; Var Capt Socr; Var Capt Wrstlng; High Hon Roll; Outstndng Attd And Perfrmnc 85; All Div Wrstlng 84-85; All Leag And Conf Soccr 85-86; Cornell; Engrg.

SUSSMAN, RANDI B; John F Kennedy HS; Riverdale, NY; (Y); 37/873; Cmnty Wkr; JA; Math Tm; Yrbk Ed-Chief; VP Stu Cncl; Var Vllybl; NHS; Regents Schlrshp 86; Acad All Amer 86; U Of Rochester; Econ.

SUSZCZYNSKI, JEAN E; Commack HS South; Commack, NY; (Y); 94/367; Pres Church Yth Grp; Cmnty Wkr; Hosp Aide; Chorus; Var Bsktbl; JV Socr; Capt Var Vllybl; High Hon Roll; Pres Schlr; Y-Teens; Gld Key Awd For Sprts NY ST 86; Pred Acdmc Ftns Awd 86; SUNY Geneseo.

SUSZKA, LYNN; St Marys HS; Alden, NY; (S); 17/166; Hosp Aide; Teachers Aide; NHS; 4-H; Science Clb; Im Bowling; 4-H Awd; NY ST Regnts Schlrshp 86; Ithaca Coll; Phy Thrpy.

SUTFIN, MIKE; East Syracuse Minoa HS; Kirkville, NY; (Y); 130/333; Latin Clb; Ski Clb; Variety Show; Var JV Ftbl; Var JV Lcrss; Var JV Wrstlng; Canisius Coll; Envr Engr.

SUTHERLAND, JULI; Union-Endicott HS; Endicott, NY; (Y); Church Yth Grp; Key Clb; Orch; School Musical; Hon Roll; Physical Thrpy.

SUTHERLAND, MELODY; Pulaski JR SR HS; Pulaski, NY; (Y); GAA; Color Guard; Yrbk Stf; Socr; Timer; Law.

SUTHERLAND, MOIRA; Huntington HS; Huntington, NY; (Y); Art Clb; French Clb; School Play; Lit Mag; Rep Frsh Cls; Rep Soph Cls; Rep Jr Cls; JV Crs Cntry; High Hon Roll; Hon Roll; Bryn Mawr; Lang.

SUTHERLAND, THOMAS; West Hempstead HS; West Hempstead, NY; (Y); 1/335; Ski Clb; Rep Band; Rep Concert Band; Jazz Band; Mrchg Band; Pep Band; School Musical; Hon Roll; Jr NHS; NHS; Italian Clb Sec/Treas 85; St Johns U; Phrmcy.

SUTIN, MITCHEL; John Dewey HS; Brooklyn, NY; (Y); Computer Clb; Office Aide; Scholastic Bowl; Rep Soph Cls; Rep Jr Cls; Trs Tennis; Hon Roll; Math Clb; Quiz Bowl; Teachers Aide; Hnr Roll 83-84; Stu Math Tchr Prg 85-86; Acadmc Olympic Tm 85-86; Poli Sci.

SUTLIFF, TODD H; Hadley-Luzerne Central HS; Corinth, NY; (Y); Am Leg Boys St; Band; Concert Band; Jazz Band; Mrchg Band; JV Var Bsbl; JV Var Bsktbl; Var Ftbl; Var Socr; Hon Roll; Stu Spectrum 86.

SUTTER, JENNIFER; Grand Island HS; Grand Island, NY; (Y); 29/300; Church Yth Grp; Girl Scts; Quiz Bowl; Band; Var Bsktbl; Var L Cheerleading; High Hon Roll; NHS; Chorus; Church Choir; 1st Pl Awd Sci Fair Lectr/Demo 84; Awd Compltn Boot Cmp Australn Mssnry Endvr 85; Typg I Awd 85; Cornell U; Indstrl Psychol.

SUTTON, BEVERLY; Sauquoit Valley Central HS; Sauquoit, NY; (Y); 7/99; SADD; Yrbk Stf; High Hon Roll; Hon Roll; Masonic Awd; NEDT Awd; Prfct Atten Awd; Intl Ordr Rainbw Grls Schlrshp; Barbara Walden Memrl Awd; Regnts Schlrshp; Potsdam SUNY; Comp Sci.

SUTTON, JUDITH L; Dansville SR HS; Dansville, NY; (Y); 36/160; Drama Clb; Chorus; Concert Band; Mrchg Band; School Play; Yrbk Stf; Church Yth Grp; Hosp Aide; Library Aide; NY ST Rgnts Schlrshp 86; Top Awd Vcl Solo Cmptn 84, 85 & 86; Cmptn Choir 86; U NY Bfl; Law.

SUTTON, MARY; St John The Baptist HS; W Islip, NY; (Y); Trk; Hon Roll; Nassau CC; Liberal Arts.

SUTTON, PATRICK; Alden Central HS; Lancaster, NY; (Y); Pres Science Clb; Pres Spanish Clb; School Musical; Nwsp Rptr; Nwsp Stf; Yrbk Phtg; JV L Bsbl; Im Bsktbl; Var L Tennis; Hon Roll; Natl Sci Olympiad Earth Sci 84.

SUWCZINSKY, JULIE; Herricks HS; New Hyde Park, NY; (Y); Dance Clb; Girl Scts; Hosp Aide; Key Clb; Library Aide; Band; Chorus; Concert Band; Mrchg Band; Co-Capt Pom Pon; 100 Hr Svc Awds For Hosp Aide 85; Grl Scouts Silver Ldrshp Awds 85; Liberal Arts.

SVARZKOPF, AMY; St Marys HS; E Aurora, NY; (S); JV Bsktbl; Hon Roll; NHS; ST U NY-BUFFALO; Engrng.

SVEC, MICHAEL; Shenendehowa HS; Waterford, NY; (Y); 312/650; Church Yth Grp; Scholastic Bowl; Ski Clb; Spanish Clb; SADD; Teachers Aide; JV JV Bsbl; JV JV Bowling; Hon Roll; Criminal Jstc.

SVIRIDA, MATTHEW; Valley Stream Central HS; Valley Stream, NY; (Y); Computer Clb; Science Clb; Spanish Clb; JV Bsktbl; Var JV Socr; Hon Roll; NHS; Spanish NHS.

SVITAVSKY, DANIEL E; Hilton HS; Hamlin, NY; (Y); 2/315; Math Clb; Model UN; Chorus; Jazz Band; Mrchg Band; School Musical; School Play; Symp Band; High Hon Roll; NHS; HOBY Ldrshp Fndtn 84; Notre Dame Clb Rochester Scholar Fin 86.

SVOBODA, SUSAN; Commack HS South; Commack, NY; (S); Church Yth Grp; Cmnty Wkr; Hosp Aide; Teachers Aide; Chorus; Church Choir; School Musical; Trs Soph Cls; Trs Jr Cls; High Hon Roll; Stdnt Recgntn Awd 85; NYSSMA Excel Rtng 84; 100 Hrs Svcs 85; Cornell U; Nutrition.

SWABY, LAUREL; Mt Vernon HS; Mt Vernon, NY; (Y); JV Var Ftbl; High Hon Roll; Cmmnctns.

SWAHLON, ROBERT; Frontier Central HS; Hamburg, NY; (Y); 50/500; SADD; Hon Roll; NHS; Engrng.

SWALD, MELISSA; Whitesboro SR HS; Whitesboro, NY; (Y); 46/300; Church Yth Grp; GAA; Model UN; Science Clb; Orch; School Musical; JV Fld Hcky; JV Sftbl; Hon Roll; 3rd Pl Whitesboro SADD Essay Cntst 86; Jrnlsm.

SWALWELL, STACEY; Trott Voc HS; Niagara Falls, NY; (Y).

SWAN, JEFF; Newfane SR HS; Newfane, NY; (Y); 19/180; Varsity Clb; Band; Trs Frsh Cls; Trs Soph Cls; Capt JV Bsbl; Var JV Bsktbl; Var JV Ftbl; All-League Baseball; Math.

SWAN, THOMAS; Warrensburg Central Schl; Warrensburg, NY; (Y); 5/60; 4-H; Trs SADD; Sec Band; School Musical; School Play; Yrbk Ed-Chief; Dnfth Awd; 4-H Awd; High Hon Roll; VP NHS; CA ST Polytech U; Civil Engr.

SWANSON, ELIZABETH; Avon Central HS; Avon, NY; (Y); 3/95; Sec AFS; Rep Church Yth Grp; Drama Clb; Pres Band; Pres Soph Cls; VP Sec Stu Cncl; JV Var Socr; High Hon Roll; Ski Clb; Spanish Clb; Close-Up Pgm WA D C 86; Bnd Solo NYSSMA All Cnty All ST 83-86; Olympcs Of Mind Schl Rep Comp 84; Psych.

SWANSON, KURT A; Jamesville De Witt HS; Jamesville, NY; (Y); 40/245; Var L Crs Cntry; Var L Trk; High Hon Roll; Hon Roll; Ntl Merit Ltr; NY ST Rgnts Schlrshp; Syracuse U; Comp Sci.

SWANSON, LISA; Panama Central HS; Ashville, NY; (Y); 2/65; Pres Church Yth Grp; Pres Band; Chorus; School Musical; Capt Bsktbl; Capt Sftbl; Capt Swmmng; JP Sousa Awd; NHS; St Schlr; Chautauqua Lk Region Schlrshp $700 86; Cummins Engine Co Schlrshp $500 86; Brigham Young U; Physcl Thrpy.

SWANSON, MICHELLE; Frewsburg Central HS; Frewsburg, NY; (Y); 12/85; Soph Cls; Exploring; Pep Clb; Spanish Clb; Chorus; Var Crs Cntry; Var Trk; JV Vllybl; Hon Roll; Hmcmng Attendent 84 & 86; Prom Queen Attendent 86; Jamestown CC; Legal Sec.

SWANSTON, TIMOTHY; Yonkers HS; Yonkers, NY; (Y); TCI; Elec.

SWARTWOOD, MELISSA; Dundee Central HS; Rock Stream, NY; (Y); FHA; Chorus; Color Guard; Sftbl; Twrlr; Prfct Atten Awd; FHA Awd Outstndng Wrk; Cazenovia; Acctg.

SWARTZ, BRAD; Falconer Central HS; Falconer, NY; (Y); 4/125; Am Leg Boys St; Quiz Bowl; Concert Band; Jazz Band; Mrchg Band; School Musical; Yrbk Phtg; Tennis; Timer; NHS; Gld Key Awd Rgnl Art Show 86; 2 Yr Schlrshp Jmstwn Comm Coll 86; Blue Rbn FCS Art Show 86; Jmstwn Comm Coll; Elctrcl Engr.

SWARTZ, STEPHANIE; Bishop Ludden HS; Syracuse, NY; (S); Church Yth Grp; Exploring; Ski Clb; Speech Tm; Yrbk Stf; Var JV Socr; Var JV Sftbl; Var Trk; Var JV Vllybl; High Hon Roll; 2nd Pl Forensic Trophy 84; Earth Sci Awd 84; Home Ec Awd 84; Hnrb Mntn Frnch Awd 85; Pre-Med.

SWEDISH, KRISTEN; Harborfields HS; Centerport, NY; (Y); Office Aide; Drill Tm; VP Frsh Cls; Rep Stu Cncl; Stat Lcrss; Capt Pom Pon; Vllybl.

SWEENEY, BRIAN; Iona Prep; Scarsdale, NY; (Y); 67/204; Cmnty Wkr; Hosp Aide; Ski Clb; Rep Soph Cls; Rep Jr Cls; Rep Stu Cncl; Bsktbl; Capt Ftbl; Trk; Wt Lftg; Ldrshp Awd; Big Brother Capt Awd; Publc Rltns.

SWEENEY, DOUGLAS; Monsignor Farrell HS; New York, NY; (Y); 55/319; Aud/Vis; Church Yth Grp; Letterman Clb; Spanish Clb; Varsity Clb; JV Var Bsktbl; Capt Im Ftbl; High Hon Roll; Jr NHS; NHS; Pre Med.

SWEENEY, JOHN; St Joseph By The Sea HS; Staten Island, NY; (S); Am Leg Boys St; SADD; Lit Mag; Frsh Cls; Trs Stu Cncl; Var Bsktbl; NEDT Awd; Schlrshp & Hnr Prog 83-87; US Mltry Acad.

SWEENEY, KATHLEEN; Holy Angels Acad; Grand Island, NY; (Y); 4/37; Art Clb; French Clb; Hosp Aide; Latin Clb; Quiz Bowl; Ski Clb; Varsity Clb; Nwsp Stf; Yrbk Stf; High Hon Roll; Pres Schlr Awd St Laurence U 86; Chem Awd Hnr 84; Hgh Schltc Achvt Awd 86; Case Western Res U; Chem.

SWEENEY, KIM; Thousand Island HS; Clayton, NY; (Y); 1/85; School Play; Sec Sr Cls; Stat Score Keeper; JV Socr; JV Vllybl; High Hon Roll; Jr NHS; Lion Awd; NHS; Val; Regnts Schlrshp 86; SUNY Oswego; Accntng.

SWEENEY, MARIE B; St Francis Prep; Whitestone, NY; (S); 136/653; Cmnty Wkr; Ski Clb; Chorus; Crs Cntry; Mgr Timer; Mgr Trk; Hon Roll; Opt Clb Awd; Psych.

SWEENEY, MARK T; Kingston HS; Kingston, NY; (Y); Am Leg Boys St; Debate Tm; French Clb; Key Clb; Model UN; Pep Clb; Ski Clb; SADD; JV Bsbl; JV Var Ftbl; Chrmn Of Winter Carnival 85-87; Pres Of Harvard Model UN; Selected Hugh O Brien Youth Fndtn 85.

SWEENEY, ORVILLE R; Uniondale HS; Uniondale, NY; (Y); Library Aide; Varsity Clb; JV L Crs Cntry; JV L Ftbl; Score Keeper; Var Capt Trk; JV L Wrstlng; Prfct Atten Awd; Soph Triple Jump Record 85; U Of TN; Business.

SWEENEY, STEVE; Gloversville HS; Gloversville, NY; (Y); Am Leg Boys St; French Clb; Key Clb; ROTC; Band; Chorus; Drill Tm; Mrchg Band; Crs Cntry; Ftbl; Bst Fld Perf Track 85-86; Mst Outstndng Fld Perf Track 86; Engrng.

SWEENEY, TAMMY; Parishville Hopkinton Central HS; Potsdam, NY; (Y); JV Var Socr; JV Sftbl; JV Var Vllybl; Hon Roll; NHS; Mater Dei Clg; Legl Sec.

SWEENEY, TERENCE W; St Anthonys HS; Smithtown, NY; (Y); 34/240; Chorus; Im Bsktbl; Var L Crs Cntry; Im Ftbl; Var L Trk; French Hon Soc; High Hon Roll; Hon Roll; NHS; Ntl Merit SF; Bus Adm.

SWEENEY JR, WILLIAM R; Amsterdam HS; Hagaman, NY; (Y); NHS; Band; Concert Band; Jazz Band; Mrchg Band; Orch; Hon Roll; Rgnt Schlrshp 86; Geneseo Coll; Bio.

SWEET, CHANDY; Alden Central HS; Alden, NY; (Y); Sec Letterman Clb; Science Clb; Spanish Clb; SADD; School Musical; School Play; Rep Stu Cncl; Var JV Cheerleading; Var Sftbl; Hon Roll; U Of Buffalo; Corp Law.

SWEET, DIANNA; Canton Central HS; Canton, NY; (Y).

SWEET, JEFF; Smithtown HS West; Smithtown, NY; (Y); Art Clb; Math Tm; Spanish Clb; Varsity Clb; L Crs Cntry; L Trk; High Hon Roll; NHS; Ntl Merit Ltr; Spanish NHS; Med.

SWEET, KEVIN; Linton HS; Schenectady, NY; (Y); Spanish Clb; Band; Ftbl; Hudson Valley CC; Real Est.

SWEET, THOMAS P; Lowville Acad & Central Schl; Lowville, NY; (Y); Golf; JV Wrstlng; Hon Roll; Regents Schlrshp 86; Sons & Daughters Alumni Schlrshp SUNY Canton ATC 86-87; SUNY Canton ATC; Cvl Tech.

SWEETING, DAVID; Archbishop Molloy HS; Brooklyn, NY; (Y); 202/385; Art Clb; Church Yth Grp; Computer Clb; Im Bsktbl; Im Ftbl; Fine Arts.

SWENDER, JENNIFER; Jamesville-De Witt HS; Dewitt, NY; (Y); 6/250; German Clb; Chorus; School Musical; Swing Chorus; Variety Show; Yrbk Stf; High Hon Roll; NHS; Wellesley Book Awd 86; Schltc MONY Art Awd 83 & 85; Engl, Vocal Music Awds 86; Muscl Theatr.

SWENDSEN, LOUISE; Narrowsburg Central HS; Narrowsburg, NY; (Y); Yrbk Phtg; Hon Roll; NHS; 1st Yr Home Ec Awd 84; Schl Hlpr Awd 85-86; Sec.

SWENSON, LINDA; Falconer Central HS; Falconer, NY; (Y); 21/127; Trs Ski Clb; Varsity Clb; Capt Color Guard; Rep Stu Cncl; Crs Cntry; Trk; Capt Vllybl; Cit Awd; NHS; Pres Schlr; JR Miss Schlrshp Prgrm 86; Optmst Clb Ctznshp Yr 86; Union Coll; Md.

SWENSON, SCOTT; Mynderes Acad; Seneca Falls, NY; (S); 17/136; Chess Clb; Trs Model UN; School Musical; School Play; Rep Stu Cncl; JV Var Ftbl; JV Lcrss; Var Trk; Var Capt Wrstlng; DAR Awd; Mst Imprvd Wrestler 84-85; Lbrl Arts.

SWENTON JR, WILLIAM F; Smithtown West HS; Hauppauge, NY; (Y); VP DECA; Symp Band; Off Stu Cncl; Var L Lcrss; JV Capt Socr; Im Vllybl; French Hon Soc; High Hon Roll; VP Jr NHS; NHS; Econ.

SWEREDIUK, DAVE; Vernon Verona Sherrill HS; Verona, NY; (Y); Church Yth Grp; Computer Clb; Cit Awd; High Hon Roll; Hon Roll; Comp.

SWEREDIUK, DAVID; Vernon Verona Sherrill HS; Verona, NY; (Y); Trs Church Yth Grp; Computer Clb; Cit Awd; High Hon Roll; Hon Roll; Comp Tech.

SWETLAND, KIMBERLY; Allegany Central HS; Allegany, NY; (Y); 16/104; Art Clb; Cmnty Wkr; Debate Tm; Drama Clb; Girl Scts; Hosp Aide; Political Wkr; Red Cross Aide; Speech Tm; Band; Natl Hist Govrn Awd 86; Olean Exchng Clb Schlrshp 86; AVX Schlrshp 86; St John Fisher Coll; Poltcl Sci.

SWICK JR, SIGRID; Jamaica HS; New York, NY; (Y); 96/507; Science Clb; Var L Swmmng; Regents Schlrshp 86; U Buffalo; Civil Engrng.

SWIERAT, MICHELE; Lancaster HS; Lancaster, NY; (S); 84/461; Hst DECA; Office Aide; Teachers Aide; Chorus; Stu Cncl; Hon Roll; Jrnlsm.

SWIERAT, MIKE; New York Mills JR SR HS; Yorkville, NY; (Y); 7/62; Trs Key Clb; Pres Ski Clb; Pres Spanish Clb; Varsity Clb; Trs Sr Cls; Var L Bsktbl; Capt L Crs Cntry; Capt L Trk; NHS; Athl Schlrshp Crs Cntry 86; Utica Coll; Math.

SWIMLEY, CAROL; Midlakes HS; Clifton Spgs, NY; (Y); Pres Trs Church Yth Grp; Cmnty Wkr; Drama Clb; Spanish Clb; Band; Church Choir; Concert Band; Mrchg Band; Hon Roll; Nrsg.

SWINARSKI, NIKI; Frontier Central HS; Blasdell, NY; (Y); Boys Clb Am; Science Clb; Ski Clb; Ftbl; Med.

SWIRIDUK, DANIEL; West Seneca East HS; Buffalo, NY; (Y); 37/375; Church Yth Grp; Varsity Clb; Var Crs Cntry; JV Var Ftbl; Var Trk; Hon Roll; Jr NHS; NHS; Im Vllybl; Frshmn Hnrs Schlrshp Edinboro U 86; Ger NHS 84-86; Edinboro U; Pre-Med.

SWISS, CARISSA LEIGH; Huntington HS; Huntington, NY; (Y); 11/383; Key Clb; Drill Tm; Stu Cncl; Bsktbl; Elks Awd; High Hon Roll; Trs Jr NHS; Trs NHS; Pres Acad Fit Awd 86; J Taylor Finley Stu Govt Awd 86; Carnegie Mellon U; Archit.

SWITALA, TAMMY; Newfane Central HS; Olcott, NY; (Y); Diving; Yrbk Stf; Fld Hcky; Niagara CC; Frnch Tchr.

SWITZER, JENNIFER; Frontier Central SR HS; Hamburg, NY; (Y); Camp Fr Inc; 4-H; German Clb; Orch; Hon Roll; Bus Adm.

SWITZER, LINDA; West Feneca East SR HS; W Seneca, NY; (Y); 142/420; DECA; GAA; VP JA; Rep Frsh Cls; Rep Soph Cls; Trs Jr Cls; Sec Sr Cls; Bsktbl; Var Capt Tennis; JV Var Vllybl; 2nd Pl Job Interview Deca ST Comptn 86; Jayncee Awd Tennis 85; 1st Pl Job Interview 86; Geneseo Coll; Ed.

SWITZER, MARY VICTORIA; Bethlehem Central HS; Glenmont, NY; (Y); 11/304; GAA; Girl Scts; Concert Band; Rep Stu Cncl; JV Capt Fld Hcky; High Hon Roll; NHS; Pres Schlr; St Schlr; Grl Sct Gld Awd 86; Fairfield U.

SWITZER, MICHELE; Rome Free Acad; Rome, NY; (Y); 30/448; Chorus; School Play; Yrbk Stf; L Var Bowling; Hon Roll; Jr NHS; NHS; Ntl Merit Schol; Pres Schlr; Bwlng Schlrshp 86; Ptsdm ST U; Math.

SWOBODA, VALERIE; Hamburg SR HS; Hamburg, NY; (Y); 10/400; Drama Clb; French Clb; Ski Clb; Chorus; Yrbk Ed-Chief; Yrbk Rptr; Lit Mag; High Hon Roll; NHS; Awd Exc Interprtv Readng 86; Jrnlsm.

SWOPE, TRACEY M; Haverling Central Schl; Bath, NY; (S); 4/116; Church Yth Grp; French Clb; Math Clb; School Musical; Yrbk Stf; Rep Stu Cncl; NHS; Cmnty Wkr; FHA; Robert Wesleyan Coll Hnr Schlrshp 86; Chrch Tlnt Awd-Ventriloquism 84-86; Robert Wesleyan Coll; Psych.

SYDNOR, VALARIE; The Tuckahoe HS; Tuckahoe, NY; (Y); Dance Clb; FBLA; GAA; Leo Clb; Band; Chorus; Church Choir; Sec Ed Jr Cls; Cheerleading; Cazenovia Coll; Bus Adm.

SYKES, DEBBIE; Smithtown East HS; Nesconset, NY; (Y); Pres German Clb; Hosp Aide; Stu Cncl; Nesconset Txpyrs Awd Schlrshp 86; German Hnr Soc 85; Elem Educ.

SYKES, MONICA; St Joseph HS; Brooklyn, NY; (Y); 5/103; Speech Tm; School Play; Yrbk Stf; Capt Cheerleading; Hon Roll; NHS; Spec Math Awd 86; Cmptrllrs Awd 86; Hunter Coll; Psych.

SYLKA, WENDY; Villa Maria Acad; Buffalo, NY; (S); 3/106; Computer Clb; JCL; Chorus; Rep Jr Cls; Swmmng; NHS; NEDT Awd; ASHME Awd 85; U Of Buffalo; Aerpsc Engrng.

SYLLA, JEAN M; St Francis Prep; Queens Village, NY; (Y); Computer Clb; JA; Im Bsktbl; JV Crs Cntry; Im Ftbl; Var Score Keeper; Im Socr; Im Sftbl; JV Trk; Im Vllybl.

SYLVANDER, JENNIFER; St John The Baptist HS; Lindenhurst, NY; (S); 23/512; Hon Roll; St Johns Schlrshp 83; Hofstra; Accntnt.

SYLVESTER, LAURA; Bethpage HS; Bethpage, NY; (Y); 10/306; Church Yth Grp; Spanish Clb; Soph Cls; Jr Cls; Var Badmtn; JV Var Vllybl; High Hon Roll; NHS; Intl Rel.

SYLVESTER, RAYE ANN; Cicero-North Syracuse HS; N Syracuse, NY; (Y); German Clb; Office Aide; Varsity Clb; Color Guard; Flag Corp; Mrchg Band; Stat Bsktbl; Twrlr; Grmn Clb Schlrshp 86; Outstndg Prfrmnc & Dedctn CNS Band 82-86; Awd Excllnc CNS Color Gd 86; Onondaga CC; Rl Estate.

SYMANSKY, SERENA; Lake George HS; Lake George, NY; (Y); 5/84; Chorus; Stage Crew; Yrbk Ed-Chief; High Hon Roll; NHS; Engrng.

SYMES, CHERYL; Centor Moriches HS; Center Moriches, NY; (Y); 1/92; Spanish Clb; Chorus; Drill Tm; School Musical; Yrbk Stf; Trs Soph Cls; Sec Sr Cls; High Hon Roll; Pres NHS; Val; Stu Mnth C M Rotary Club 86; Peer Ldrshp Chert 85.

SYMONDS, DELEA; Indian River HS; Evans Mills, NY; (Y); 30/142; Sec Trs FFA; Key Clb; Latin Clb; Im Coach Actv; JV Var Sftbl; Hon Roll; PA Assoc Of Farmrs Co Op 86; Gobleskill Clg; Vet Tech.

SYMONDS, MICHELLE; Troupsburg Central Schl; Troupsburg, NY; (Y); 1/14; Chorus; Yrbk Ed-Chief; Pres Sr Cls; Sec Stu Cncl; Var L Socr; Var L Trk; Mu Alp Tht; NHS; Val; Aud/Vis; Acad All Stars; Regnts Schrlshp; SUNY; Acctng.

SYPOSS, RACHEL; Mount Saint Mary Acad; Sanborn, NY; (Y); 7/112; 4-H; French Clb; Chorus; Lcrss; Mgr(s); Score Keeper; 4-H Awd; High Hon Roll; Hon Roll; NHS; Cblskll Coll Fndtn Schlrshp 86; SUNY Agri & Tech Coll Dairy Fshn Schlrshp 86; SUNY Ag & Tech; Agri Sci.

SYREK, JEFFREY; Conisius HS; Orchard Pk, NY; (Y); 25/145; Exploring; Model UN; Varsity Clb; School Play; Stage Crew; Nwsp Phtg; Yrbk Phtg; Yrbk Stf; Im Bsktbl; Im Ftbl; All Cath 500 Freestyle Chmpn 84-86; Duke; Pre-Med.

SYRKETT, SHARI; Uniondale HS; Hempstead, NY; (Y); Band; Concert Band; Mrchg Band; Orch; School Musical; Yrbk Stf; VP Jr Cls; Bsktbl; Crs Cntry; Trk; Lawrence Road JHS Outstndng French Stu Awd 84.

SYSAK, IRENE; St George Acad; New York, NY; (Y); 4/32; Drama Clb; School Musical; Nwsp Stf; Yrbk Stf; Lit Mag; Rep Frsh Cls; NHS; Art Clb; Dance Clb; Ski Clb; Rgnts Nrsg Schlrshp 86; Awd For Excllnc 86; NY U; Med.

SZABLINSKI, JOANNE; Saugherties HS; Saugerties, NY; (S); French Clb; Yrbk Stf; Im Socr; Im Vllybl; High Hon Roll; Hon Roll; Prfct Atten Awd; Rice U; Math.

SZACHACZ, SHERI; Commack HS South; Commack, NY; (Y); Office Aide; Teachers Aide; Chorus; JV Sftbl; French Hon Soc; High Hon Roll; Golden Quill Awd 84-85; Ntl Sci Olympiad 85; Vol Wildlife 84-86; Cornell; Vet-Med.

SZALASNY, DENISE; John F Kennedy JR SR HS; Cheektowaga, NY; (Y); 24/146; Church Yth Grp; GAA; Yrbk Stf; Stu Cncl; Bsktbl; Crs Cntry; Socr; Tennis; Hon Roll; NHS; Regents Schlrshp 86; ST U; Physcl Thrpy.

SZALKOWSKI, KELLEY; Whitesboro SR HS; Utica, NY; (Y); 2/306; Model UN; Ski Clb; Stage Crew; Yrbk Bus Mgr; Yrbk Ed-Chief; Yrbk Stf; Sec Sr Cls; Rep Stu Cncl; High Hon Roll; Hon Roll; Mt Holyoke Awd 86; Harvard; Intl Bus.

SZANTOR, KIRSTEN; Wilson Central HS; Wilson, NY; (Y); 15/115; Church Yth Grp; Computer Clb; Model UN; SADD; Church Choir; School Musical; Yrbk Stf; Stu Cncl; Hon Roll; NHS; Jenkins Memrl Schlrshp NYS PTA Teachng Schlrshp 86; Buffalo ST Coll; Elem Eductn.

SZCZEPANKIEWICZ, BRUCE; St Josephs Collegiate Inst; Buffalo, NY; (Y); 7/193; Church Choir; Im Crs Cntry; Var Capt Swmmng; Hon Roll; NHS; Ntl Merit Ltr; St Schlr; Cornell U Deans Schlrshp 86-87; Excllnc Sci Awd 86; Cornell U; Medcl Dr.

SZCZEPANSKI, CHERYL; Nardin Acad; W Seneca, NY; (Y); Dance Clb; French Clb; School Musical; Lit Mag; Hon Roll; Jr NHS; High Achvt In French IV 86; 1st Pl In Schl Sci Fair

SZCZYGIELSKI, ANNE; Villa Maria Acad; Buffalo, NY; (Y); Service Clb; Bryant & Stratton Acctg Schlrshp 86-87; Bryant & Stratton; Acctg.

SZEGNER, JOHN; Sachem HS North; Lk Ronkonkoma, NY; (Y); German Clb; Var Ftbl; Var Wt Lftg; Engrng.

SZEMATOWICZ, CAMILLE; Hamburg SR HS; Hamburg, NY; (Y); 3/370; AFS; French Clb; Band; Concert Band; Mrchg Band; Soph Cls; Cheerleading; NHS; Ntl Merit Ltr; Cornell U; Engrng.

SZENEITAS, BERNARD; John Jay HS; Brooklyn, NY; (Y); Art Clb; Boy Scts; FBLA; JA; ROTC; Hon Roll; Brklyn Coll; Bus.

SZETO, JENNIE M; St Francis Preparatory HS; Woodside, NY; (Y); 204/653; Library Aide; Band; Chorus; Concert Band; Im Vllybl; Opt Clb Awd; Polytech U; Aerosp Engr.

SZINGER, MARTIN; Kenmore East SR HS; Kenmore, NY; (Y); 3/325; Computer Clb; Math Tm; Concert Band; Jazz Band; Orch; School Musical; High Hon Roll; NHS; Rensselaer Polyt Inst Awd Top Math Stu 86; 2nd Pl Canisius Comp Cntst 86; RPI; Comp Engr.

SZKODZINSKI, RICHARD; Bishop Ford CCHS HS; Brooklyn, NY; (S); Computer Clb; Ski Clb; Stage Crew; Nwsp Ed-Chief; Nwsp Rptr; Yrbk Phtg; Mgr Bsktbl; Tennis; Pres Phys Fit Awd 85; NYU; Med.

SZMAL, PAUL M; Paul V Moore HS; W Monroe, NY; (Y); Pres FBLA; Pres Radio Clb; High Hon Roll; Hon Roll; NHS; Drama Clb; School Play; Nwsp Stf; Rep Frsh Cls; Rep Soph Cls; Newhouse Schl Brdcstng; Radio.

SZOKOLI, JOHN; John Glenn HS; Greenlawn, NY; (Y); Church Yth Grp; Bsbl; Ftbl; Wrstlng; Hon Roll; Sprts Med.

SZOZDA, LISA; Keveny Memorial Acad; Waterford, NY; (S); Cmnty Wkr; Dance Clb; Red Cross Aide; Church Choir; Bowling; Swmmng; High Hon Roll; Prfct Atten Awd; Psychlgy.

SZPARA, KRISTIN; Lackawanna SR HS; Lackawanna, NY; (Y); GAA; Spanish Clb; Concert Band; Mrchg Band; Hon Roll; NHS; Acadmc Tm 85-86.

SZUCS, MONIKA; St Johns Prep; Astoria, NY; (Y); 38/548; Hosp Aide; Yrbk Stf; Jr Cls; Sr Cls; JV Var Tennis; Hon Roll; NHS; Prfct Atten Awd; Rgnts Schlrshp 86; Music Awd 83; MVP Awd 85; Stonybrook U; Dntst.

SZULEWSKI, TRACY; Miller Place HS; Miller Place, NY; (Y); Church Yth Grp; FBLA; Ski Clb; Varsity Clb; Concert Band; Sec Soph Cls; VP Jr Cls; JV Golf; Var Stat Socr; JV Trk; Spnsh Awd 84; Kybrdng Awd 85; Bus.

SZWED, ANNA; Villa Maria Acad; Cheektowaga, NY; (S); French Clb; Girl Scts; Hon Roll; Pre-Med.

SZYMANSKI, CHARLES S; Lewiston Porter HS; Youngstown, NY; (Y); 1/220; Am Leg Boys St; Cmnty Wkr; Key Clb; Model UN; Rep Frsh Cls; Rep Soph Cls; VP Jr Cls; Rep Sr Cls; VP Stu Cncl; Var Socr; INTL Rltns.

SZYMANSKI, KERRY; Victor SR HS; Victor, NY; (Y); 27/228; Varsity Clb; Rep Stu Cncl; Badmtn; Bsktbl; Sftbl; Tennis; High Hon Roll; Hon Roll; NHS; MIP Grls Vrsty Tennis 86; Vrsty Ltr 85; 1T Bar 86.

SZYMKO, SHELLEY ANN; Whitesboro SR HS; Marcy, NY; (Y); 20/341; VP Pres 4-H; GAA; Science Clb; Orch; Nwsp Rptr; Yrbk Rptr; Ed Lit Mag; Var Cheerleading; Var Socr; NHS; Polish Leg Am Vet Ntl Schlrshp 86; NY ST Regents Schlrshp 86; Pres Acad Ftns Awd 86; Union Coll; Bio.

TABB, LORI; Corning-Painted Post West HS; Corning, NY; (Y); Political Wkr; Quiz Bowl; SADD; Chorus; Madrigals; School Musical; High Hon Roll; Hon Roll; Cmnty Wkr; SOAR Giftd Cretv Stu 83-86; Pre-Law.

TABB, STEPHEN; Tottenville HS; Staten Island, NY; (Y); Rep Stu Cncl; Hon Roll; Mdl Cngrss Chrmn 86; Bus.

TABER, GINNY; Guilderland Central HS; Altamont, NY; (Y); 50/365; Cmnty Wkr; SADD; Teachers Aide; Cit Awd; High Hon Roll; Hon Roll; Outstndng Cmmnty Svc 86; Supr Svc Musicl 86; Acdmc Excllnc Engl 85; SUNY Albany; Spec Ed.

TABON, FREDDIE; Mohawk Heights HS; Bronx, NY; (Y); English Clb; JA; Library Aide; Office Aide; Teachers Aide; Variety Show; Vllybl; High Hon Roll; Hon Roll; Fulton Mtgmry CC 84-85; Awd Psng Rgnts Rdng 85; Accnt.

TABONI, MARY; West Seneca West SR HS; W Seneca, NY; (Y); 9/559; Key Clb; Spanish Clb; Rep Sr Cls; Rep Stu Cncl; High Hon Roll; JC Awd; Jr NHS; NHS; Prfct Atten Awd; Pres Schlr; James Stillwell Scholar 86; Spn Clb Scholar 86; Excllnce Sci 85; Canisius Coll; Mth.

TABOR, JEFF; Cooperstown Central HS; Cooperstown, NY; (Y); Varsity Clb; Band; Color Guard; Concert Band; Mrchg Band; Pep Band; Bsbl; Ftbl; Swmmng; Wt Lftg.

TABUTEAU, HERRIOT; Xavier HS; New York, NY; (Y); Church Yth Grp; Computer Clb; Science Clb; Chorus; Lit Mag; Hon Roll; Ntl Merit SF; Author How To Get A's In Schl; Founder Ed Chief Comp Mag; Wesleyan U; Physcn.

TACHMAN, LEE; Susan Wagner HS; Staten Island, NY; (Y); JA; Capt Bowling; Var Ftbl; Wt Lftg; Hon Roll; NY U.

TACZANOWSKI, EVA M; Commack HS South; Commack, NY; (Y); GAA; Intnl Clb; Teachers Aide; Pres Sr Cls; JV Bsktbl; JV Capt Socr; JV Sftbl; High Hon Roll; Hon Roll; Vrsty Athltc Awd 85-86; JV Mst Imprvd Plyr Sftbll & Soccr 84-85; Pre-Med.

TADDEO, ANNALISA N; Sachem HS North; Farmingville, NY; (Y); 270/1385; Cmnty Wkr; Drama Clb; French Clb; Hosp Aide; Teachers Aide; Orch; School Musical; Hon Roll; Library Aide; School Play; Dwlngs Hnr Acdmc Schlrshp 86; Dowling Coll; Psych.

TADDEO, CHRIS; St Marys Boys HS; Plainview, NY; (Y); 149/179; JV Bsbl; Var Crs Cntry; Trk; St Johns U; Bus.

TADDEO, LORI A; Our Lady Of Mercy Acad; Plainview, NY; (Y); 5/130; Church Yth Grp; Computer Clb; Dance Clb; Hosp Aide; Pep Clb; Service Clb; SADD; Teachers Aide; Nwsp Ed-Chief; Nwsp Rptr; Prtl Acdmc Schlrshp St Johns U,U Of Scranton,Boston U & Qunnipiac Coll 86-90; U Of Scranton; Physcl Thrpy.

TAGGART, JANET L; Vestal SR HS; Vestal, NY; (Y); Drama Clb; Girl Scts; Ski Clb; Acpl Chr; Chorus; Church Choir; Orch; School Musical; School Play; Stage Crew; Binghamton Yth Symphny 86; NYS Regnts

TAGLIENTI, ANGELA; W Seneca E SR HS; W Seneca, NY; (S); 26/375; Sec Drama Clb; Pres Concert Band; School Musical; Yrbk Ed-Chief; NHS; Jazz Band; Mrchg Band; JV Sftbl; Hon Roll; JC Awd; All Cnty Bnd 85; Dequesne U; Jrnlsm.

TAGLIONE, MICHAEL A; Stillwater Central HS; Stillwater, NY; (Y); 3/90; Drama Clb; French Clb; Key Clb; Math Tm; SADD; Yrbk Stf; Jr Cls; Sr Cls; High Hon Roll; Hon Roll; Stillwater Comm Schlrshp Awd 86; SR Citizens Awd Highest Avg French 86; J Edward Mc Clements Awd 86; SUNY Oswego; Communications.

TAHER, ISMAHAN; Lackawanna SR HS; Lackawanna, NY; (Y); Library Aide; Spanish Clb; Hon Roll; Chorus; NY ST U; Med.

TAIT, HEATHER; Walton HS; Bronx, NY; (Y); Office Aide; Teachers Aide; Nwsp Rptr; JV Socr; Prfct Atten Awd; LIU Cw Post; Bus Mngmnt.

TAKEISHI, CHRISTINE Y; Laguardia HS Of Music & The Arts; New York, NY; (Y); Art Clb; Church Yth Grp; Intnl Clb; Office Aide; OEA; PAVAS; JV Bsktbl; JV Gym; Off Coopertv Ed 85; Pratt Inst; Graphic Desgnr.

TAKEMOTO, KOMEY; Franklyn K Lane HS; Brooklyn, NY; (Y); Trs Band; Trs Concert Band; Trs Jazz Band; Trs Mrchg Band; Nwsp Phtg; Nwsp Rptr; Nwsp Stf; NY U; Law.

TALAMO, TERESA; Lafayette HS; Brooklyn, NY; (Y); 18/366; Church Yth Grp; Girl Scts; Intnl Clb; Stage Crew; Nwsp Rptr; Yrbk Stf; Stu Cncl; Bowling; High Hon Roll; NHS; John F Kennedy Awd Character & Svc 86; Kiwanis Medal Excllnce French 86; Pace U; Business Mgmt.

TALARICO, GINA; Frankfort-Schuyler HS; Frankfort, NY; (Y); GAA; Spanish Clb; SADD; Variety Show; Yrbk Stf; Var Badmtn; High Hon Roll; Hon Roll; Herkimer Cnty CC; Trvl.

TALBOT, GERALDINE; Saint Francis Prep; Bayside, NY; (Y); Pep Clb; Chorus; Pom Pon; Spnsh Hnr 84-86; Eng Hnrs 85-86; Advncd Plcmnt Eng 86; Law.

TALDONE, LYNDA; Cardinal Spellman HS; Bronx, NY; (Y); Rep Sr Cls; Hon Roll; Pace U; Accntg.

TALIO, ROSEMARIE; Westlake HS; Pleasantville, NY; (Y); Hosp Aide; Chorus; Nwsp Rptr; Pres Frsh Cls; Rep Stu Cncl; Var Socr; High Hon Roll; NHS; Spanish NHS; Stu Rcgntn Outstndng Ldrshp 85; Hsptl Awd Vlntr Srvcs 83; Thspn Soc 86; Med.

TALLANT, STEPHEN; Liverpool HS; Liverpool, NY; (Y); Church Yth Grp; Pres JA; Nwsp Stf; Rep Stu Cncl; Im Bsktbl; Var L Golf; High Hon Roll; Hon Roll; Opt Clb Awd; Bus.

TALLARIHI JR, THOMAS D; New Rochelle HS; New Rochelle, NY; (Y); 2/550; Capt Math Tm; Model UN; Band; Concert Band; Jazz Band; Symp Band; JV Socr; JP Sousa Awd; NHS; Ntl Merit Schol; Geo Washington U Engrng Mdl 85; Westchester Golf Assoc Caddie Schlrshp, Bk NY Schlrshp 86; U PA; Econ.

TALLEUR, DENISE; St Agnes Academic HS; Whitestone, NY; (Y); Trk; Hon Roll; Queens Coll.

TALLINI, REUCCIO; Sweanhara HS; S Floral Pk, NY; (Y); 20/365; Art Clb; Computer Clb; Math Clb; Office Aide; High Hon Roll; Hon Roll; Jr NHS; NHS; Doctor.

TALVY, LOURDES D; Lynbrook HS; East Rockaway L I, NY; (S); 1/300; Chess Clb; Computer Clb; Debate Tm; Mathletes; Math Clb; Math Tm; NFL; Political Wkr; Quiz Bowl; Spanish Clb; Long Island Yth Orch 81-86; St Vincent De Paul Essay Cntst Hnbl Mntn 86; Lead Singer/Pianist Rck Bnd; Med.

TAM, ALICE; La Guardia High Schl Of Music And Art; New York, NY; (S); 7/437; Camera Clb; Church Yth Grp; Computer Clb; Hosp Aide; Library Aide; Office Aide; Chorus; Church Choir; Stage Crew; Yrbk Stf; Sci Awd 83; Cert Merit Assmblymn Paul Viggio Vocl Perfrmnc 83; Svc Awd From Stdnt Govt 83; Biochem.

TAM, ED; John Glenn HS; E Northport, NY; (Y); Church Yth Grp; Mathletes; Science Clb; Rep Frsh Cls; JV Capt Ftbl; Lcrss; High Hon Roll; Jr NHS; NHS; Spanish NHS; Slvr Mdl In Math 83-84; Engrng.

TAMARAZO, FRANK; Mckee Technical HS; Staten Island, NY; (Y); 5/306; Aud/Vis; Drama Clb; Math Tm; Band; Church Choir; School Musical; Hon Roll; NHS; MA Inst Of Tech; Comp Sci.

TAMAYO, AMY E; Our Lady Of Mercy HS; Pittsford, NY; (Y); 20/175; Science Clb; SADD; School Musical; School Play; Nwsp Stf; Trk; NHS; Boston Coll; Bio.

TAMAYO, MAYVELYN G; St Francis Prep; Jamaica, NY; (S); 31/746; Hosp Aide; Ski Clb; Im Powder Puff Ftbl; Im Sftbl; Im Vllybl; High Hon Roll; NHS; Prncpls Lst 84-85.

TAMBACAS, ELAINE M; Williamsville East HS; Williamsville, NY; (Y); 49/300; Cmnty Wkr; Drama Clb; French Clb; Sec Latin Clb; Pep Clb; Ski Clb; Yrbk Stf; Fld Hcky; Sftbl; High Hon Roll; Amhrst YES-OUTSTNDNG 85; NY ST Rgnts Schlrshp 86; Mgncm Laude-Tl ACL Test 84; U Of Buffalo; Psychlgy.

TAMBURRI JR, ROBERT; Lynbrook HS; Lynbrook, NY; (Y); 36/240; Exploring; FBLA; VP Trs Spanish Clb; Ed Lit Mag; Trs Sr Cls; NHS; Peter Kostynik Schlrshp Awd 86; SUNY Albany; Commodity.

TAMBURRINO, SHARON; Herkimer HS; E Herkimer, NY; (Y); 22/107; Drama Clb; Pres Sec FHA; JA; Pep Clb; SADD; Band; Chorus; Concert Band; Mrchg Band; Pep Band; All Cnty Bnd Chr 82-86; Central City Bus Inst; Para Lgl.

TAMER, BONNIE L; Utica Free Acad; Utica, NY; (Y); 12/300; Dance Clb; Drama Clb; Hosp Aide; Key Clb; Spanish Clb; Thesps; Band; Chorus; Concert Band; Mrchg Band; Oyaron Schlr 86; Hrtwck Coll; Comp Sci.

TAMISO, MARY-MARGARET; Cazenovia Central HS; Cazenovia, NY; (Y); Church Yth Grp; Teachers Aide; Chorus; Color Guard; Orch; Yrbk Phtg; Yrbk Stf; Var Sftbl; Hon Roll; Recognition In Aiding Teacher.

TAMMARO, MICHAEL; Port Chester SR HS; Port Chester, NY; (Y); 10/280; Am Leg Boys St; Key Clb; Ski Clb; Pres Frsh Cls; Pres Jr Cls; Var Bsbl; Capt Ftbl; Hon Roll; Jr NHS; NHS; Natl Mth Hnr Soc 86; Natl Italian Hnr Soc 85; Engrng.

TAMPAKIS, SOPHIA; Bishop Ford CC HS; Brooklyn, NY; (S); Yrbk Stf.

TAMPONE, FRANK; John A Coleman HS; Kingston, NY; (S); 2/90;

TANG, ANDREW R; Garden City SR HS; Garden City, NY; (Y); 8/346; French Clb; German Clb; Stage Crew; Yrbk Bus Mgr; Tennis; Jr NHS; NHS; Ntl Merit Ltr; Pres Acad Ftnss Awd 86; Wesleyan U; Pre-Med.

TANG, DINH; Jefferson HS; Rochester, NY; (S); 2/78; Church Yth Grp; Intnl Clb; Office Aide; SADD; Teachers Aide; Yrbk Stf; Rep Jr Cls; Rep Sr Cls; Sec Stu Cncl; Co-Capt Cheerleading; U Of R 85 Paideia Awd 85-6; Pris 2m Tm Mem Of Yr Awd 84-5; Alpha Phia Alpha Frtrnty Inc Cert Awd 85-6; U Of Buffalo; Comp Sci.

TANG, JACK; Bronx HS Of Science; Holliswood, NY; (Y); Hosp Aide; Math Tm; Teachers Aide; Ntl Merit Ltr; Prfct Atten Awd; Boston U; Dr.

TANGORRA, JENNIFER; Frankfort-Schuyler HS; Frankfort, NY; (S); 39/100; FBLA; Spanish Clb; Yrbk Stf; Rep Frsh Cls; Sec Sr Cls; Rep Stu Cncl; Var Capt Cheerleading; Var Vllybl; High Hon Roll; NHS; MVCC; Word Proc.

TANGREDI, TERESSA; Catholic Central HS; Loudonville, NY; (Y); Yrbk Stf; Var JV Cheerleading; Var Tennis; Var JV Trk; High Hon Roll; Trs NHS; Spnch Awd 84-86; Chem.

TANGUMA, LONNIE; Pulaski JR SR HS; Pulaski, NY; (Y); FBLA; GAA; Math Tm; Sec Soph Cls; Var Socr; Acad All Amrcn 85; Bryant & Stratton; Exec Sec.

TANGUMA, YOLANDA; Pulaski JR SR HS; Pulaski, NY; (Y); FBLA; GAA; Math Clb; Sec Soph Cls; Bsktbl; Socr; Trk; Bryant & Stratton; Exec Sec.

TANNA, KAUSHIKA; Riverside HS; Buffalo, NY; (Y); Math Tm; Varsity Clb; Nwsp Stf; Var Sftbl; Var Vllybl; Hon Roll; NHS; Acctng.

TANNAR, AUDREY; Warwick Valley HS; Warwick, NY; (Y); 63/186; Aud/Vis; Church Yth Grp; Radio Clb; Church Choir; Swing Chorus; Variety Show; Cheerleading; Trk; Hon Roll; JA; Hghst Fin Avg Health Sci Awd 85; Orange Cnty CC; Cmmnctns.

TANNER, CINDY; Clayton A Bouton JR SR HS; Voorheesville, NY; (Y); Spanish Clb; Band; Ed Yrbk Stf; Im Bsktbl; Var Fld Hcky; Vllybl; High Hon Roll; Hon Roll; NHS; Prfct Atten Awd; Intl Stds.

TANNER, DAVID; Sandy Creek Central Schl; Lacona, NY; (S); 8/101; Am Leg Boys St; Computer Clb; JCL; Varsity Clb; Chorus; Var Bsktbl; Vllybl; Hon Roll; NHS; Prfct Atten Awd; Regents Scholar NYS 86; Clarkson U; Elec Engrng.

TANNER, DAVID C; Madison Central Schl; Madison, NY; (Y); 4/56; Am Leg Boys St; Chess Clb; Varsity Clb; Concert Band; Mrchg Band; Stu Cncl; Socr; Hon Roll; NHS; Engrng.

TANNER, JEANNIE; West Hampstead HS; Charles Town, WV; (Y); 62/320; Ski Clb; Lit Mag; Badmtn; Hon Roll; Outstdng Achvt Astronomy 85; Sheppard Coll; Accntng.

TANNER, JULIE; Berlin Central HS; Petersburg, NY; (Y); 10/82; GAA; Ski Clb; Chorus; Yrbk Stf; Var Cheerleading; Var Socr; Hon Roll; NHS; Mgr(s); High Hon Roll; Ntl Chrldng Assn Merit Ltr 85; SUNY Of Plattsburgh.

TANON, ROBERT; St Francis Prep HS; Flushing, NY; (Y); Church Yth Grp; Cmnty Wkr; Hosp Aide; JA; Political Wkr; Nwsp Ed-Chief; Nwsp Rptr; VFW Awd; Polc Civln Citn Cert Of Horism 86; Hunter Clg CUNY; Comm.

TANTILLO, ROSARIO; Hicksville HS; Hicksville, NY; (Y); Cmnty Wkr; FBLA; ROTC; Ski Clb; SADD; Teachers Aide; Var Tennis; High Hon Roll; Jr NHS; NHS; Italian Hnr Soc 86; ROTC Model Rocketry Awd 85; Pre-Law.

TAO, BETTY; Ft Hamilton HS; Brooklyn, NY; (Y); 27/509; Office Aide; Chorus; Stu Cncl; High Hon Roll; Hon Roll; NHS; Prfct Atten Awd; Ft Hamilton HS Hnr Acad 83-86; Bus Educ Advsry Commision 86; NYU CBPA Schlrshp 86; NY U; Tax Atty.

TAO, TING; H S For The Humanits; New York, NY; (Y); Boys Clb Am; Chess Clb; Math Tm; Spnsh 85; Merit Roll 85; Math Gio 85; Polytechnic; Engrng.

TAPLIN, FRANK; Lindenhurst HS; Lindenhurst, NY; (Y); 8/600; French Clb; Varsity Clb; Bsktbl; Tennis; Hon Roll; NHS.

TAPLIN JR, WAYNE; Pulaski JR SR HS; Richland, NY; (Y); 56/100; Boy Scts; Varsity Clb; Var Bsbl; Var Bsktbl; Capt Var Ftbl; VP Frsh Cls; Pres Soph Cls; Pres Jr Cls; Stu Cncl; Im Vllybl; John Ben Snw Awd 83; SUNY Brckprt; Physcl Educ.

TAPOLOW, STEFANIE M; Abraham Lincoln HS; Brooklyn, NY; (Y); 18/431; Camera Clb; Key Clb; Science Clb; Yrbk Phtg; Yrbk Stf; Rep Stu Cncl; High Hon Roll; Jr NHS; NY ST Regnts Schlrshp 86; Svc Awd 86; Arista Awd 82-86; U MD.

TARACIDO, JAMES; New Rochelle HS; New Rochelle, NY; (Y); Var Lcrss; Var Socr; NHS; Sccr Tm Wn Dana Cup Denmark 85; Bus.

TARALLO, BETHANY A; Schalmont HS; Schenectady, NY; (Y); 8/160; French Clb; Concert Band; Jazz Band; Mrchg Band; Yrbk Stf; Rep Soph Cls; Score Keeper; High Hon Roll; Hon Roll; NHS; Boston U.

TARANTINO, LYNDA; Canisteo Central Schl; Canisteo, NY; (Y); 4/78; Am Leg Aux Girls St; Ski Clb; Band; School Play; Yrbk Ed-Chief; VP Jr Cls; Pres Stu Cncl; JV Golf; Var Socr; Cit Awd; St Bonaventure U; Bus Mgmt.

TARANTINO, MARIA LUISA; St Catharine Acad; Bronx, NY; (Y); 5/185; Church Yth Grp; Dance Clb; Teachers Aide; Yrbk Stf; High Hon Roll; Hon Roll; NHS; Iona Lang Cont 86; Fordham U; Psych.

TARANTO, ANNE C; Lynbrook SR HS; Lynbrook, NY; (Y); 4/239; Sec Drama Clb; NFL; Scholastic Bowl; Chorus; Nwsp Stf; Yrbk Ed-Chief; Pres Sr Cls; Pres Stu Cncl; VP NHS; Ntl Merit SF; Lawyer.

TARANTO, LYNDA; Central HS; Valley Stream, NY; (Y); Art Clb; Church Yth Grp; Girl Scts; Office Aide; Spanish Clb; Teachers Aide; Church Choir; School Musical; School Play; Stage Crew; Nassau CC; Early Chldhd Educ.

TARASOFF, SANDRA; Clarkstown High School North; Congers, NY; (Y); 6/450; NFL; Pep Clb; Rep Frsh Cls; JV Vllybl; High Hon Roll; Hon Roll; Jr NHS; Mu Alp Tht; NHS; USMA West Point.

TARIGO, JOE; Clarkstown HS North; New City, NY; (Y); Church Yth Grp; Cmnty Wkr; SADD; JV Lcrss; Prfct Atten Awd; Italian Club.

TARKOWSKI, KIM; Frankfort Schuyler HS; Frankfort, NY; (Y); Cmnty Wkr; Spanish Clb; Trk; High Hon Roll; NHS; Utica Coll Syracuse U; Pre-Vet.

TARMINO, JAY; Gates-Chili HS; Rochester, NY; (Y); JV L Bsbl; Var L Ice Hcky; Brochport ST; Phys Ed.

TARVER, PHYLLIS; Bishop Grimes HS; Syracuse, NY; (Y); Cmnty Wkr; Debate Tm; Hosp Aide; Library Aide; Teachers Aide; French Hon Soc; Hon Roll; Cmmnty Vlntr Svc 81-82; NAACP Awd Prtcptn Ntl Cnvnts & ACT-SO Pgm 86; Med Rsrch.

TARVER III, WALTER L; Henninger HS; Syracuse, NY; (Y); 56/354; Political Wkr; Ftbl; Lcrss; Trk; High Hon Roll; Hon Roll; Prfct Atten Awd; Comp Sci.

TARZIA, MICHELE; Liverpool HS; Clay, NY; (Y); 223/785; Church Yth Grp; Concert Band; School Musical; Potsdam; Pol Sci.

TASCILLO, MARK; Mayfield Central Schl; Gloversville, NY; (Y); 5/72; Church Yth Grp; Drama Clb; Stage Crew; Nwsp Phtg; High Hon Roll; Hon Roll; Ntl Merit Ltr; Prfct Atten Awd; NY ST Rgnts Schlrshp 86; Presdntl Acadmc Ftns Awd 86; Fulton-Montgmry Trstees Schlrshp 86; Fulton-Montgmry CC; Elec Engr.

TASIKAS, DAN; Penfield HS; Rochester, NY; (Y); Chess Clb; Church Yth Grp; Cmnty Wkr; Speech Tm; Golf; Socr; Spch Tm 83-84; Church Yth Grp 81-86; Cmmnty Wrkr 80-86; Engrng.

TASSEFF, ALEXANDRA; West Seneca West SR HS; W Seneca, NY; (Y); Trs Church Yth Grp; Spanish Clb; Orch; Rep Stu Cncl; Hon Roll; Jr NHS; NHS; Math.

TASSIELLO, MARIA; St Joseph Hill Acad; Staten Island, NY; (Y); VP Church Yth Grp; FTA; VP Frsh Cls; VP Soph Cls; VP Jr Cls; VP Sr Cls; Rep Stu Cncl; Var Socr; Var Trk; Itln Clb Pres-2 Yrs; Thrsns Of Amer-Pres 1 Yr, Treas 1 Yr; HOBY Fndtn Ambssdr 84; Pace U.

TATE, LUCINDA; Clifton-Fine Central Schl; Star Lake, NY; (S); 3/43; French Clb; Band; Chorus; School Play; Var Score Keeper; Var L Socr; Var L Trk; High Hon Roll; NHS; AFS; St Lawrence U Tlntd Jrs Pgm; Alma Coll; Music Ed.

TATE, VALERIE; Park West HS; New York, NY; (Y); Church Yth Grp; Girl Scts; Office Aide; Speech Tm; Chorus; Pres Soph Cls; SVP 86; UNCC; Hotel Mgmt.

TATIS, JULIE; Martin Van Buren HS; Bayside, NY; (Y); 43/576; Dance Clb; JA; Teachers Aide; Chorus; School Musical; Off Jr Cls; Hon Roll; Excllnc Cobol Comp Prog 85.

TAUBMAN, PAM; Roy C Ketcham HS; Poughkeepsie, NY; (Y); Pres AFS; Cmnty Wkr; Trs Intnl Clb; Key Clb; Nwsp Rptr; Yrbk Phtg; Yrbk Stf; High Hon Roll; NHS; Ski Clb; Exc Recogntn Am Studies 85; OH Tests Schlstc Achvt Frnch 84; Comm.

TAVEL, JASON; East Meadow HS; East Meadow, NY; (Y); FBLA; Temple Yth Grp; Varsity Clb; Band; Mrchg Band; Score Keeper; Socr; Tennis; Trk; Wrstlng; Prostetics.

TAVERAS, RICHARD; John Jay HS; Brooklyn, NY; (Y); 41/575; Computer Clb; Science Clb; Spanish Clb; Embry Riddle Aero U; Aero Sci.

TAVERNESE, TRACY; Oyster Bay HS; East Norwich, NY; (Y); Cmnty Wkr; Trs Spanish Clb; SADD; Chorus; Yrbk Phtg; Yrbk Stf; Var Fld Hcky; High Hon Roll; Hon Roll; NHS; Hnr Roll 85-86; Spn.

TAVERNIA, LEE; Franklin Acad; Malone, NY; (Y); VP 4-H; Ftbl; Wrstlng; 4-H Awd; Hon Roll; NHS; Epsilon 84-86; Mst Imprvd Wrstlr 84-85; Elctrcl Engrng.

TAVERNIA, TAMMY; Franklin Acad; Malone, NY; (Y); Pres VP 4-H; Chorus; Madrigals; Swing Chorus; 4-H Awd; Hon Roll; NHS; Epsilon 85-86; Spnsh Awd 85-86; Nazareth Coll Rochester; Music.

TAVERNIER, MAUREEN; Fillmore Central HS; Fillmore, NY; (S); 10/60; SADD; Chorus; Orch; Variety Show; Rep Stu Cncl; JV Cheerleading; Var Tennis; Var Trk; Hon Roll; NHS; Nazareth Coll; Acctng.

TAWIL, KHOULOUD; Yonkers HS; Yonkers, NY; (Y); Art Clb; Cmnty Wkr; FBLA; Girl Scts; Office Aide; ROTC; SADD; Band; Chorus; School Play; Bus Mgmt.

TAYLOR, D JAY; North Rose-Wolcott HS; Wolcott, NY; (Y); JV Swmmng; Eagle Scout 85; Order Arrow; Regnl ST Comptn Sci Olymp 86; Vet.

TAYLOR, DAIVERY; Freeport HS; Freeport, NY; (Y); 46/500; Computer Clb; 4-H; Hosp Aide; Mathletes; School Musical; School Play; Variety Show; Yrbk Stf; Stu Cncl; Bsbl; Georgetown U; Law.

TAYLOR, DAVID; Archbishop Molloy HS; Flushing, NY; (Y); 34/383; Cmnty Wkr; French Clb; Hosp Aide; Pep Clb; Science Clb; SADD; Pre Med.

TAYLOR, DAVID; Pinecrest Christian HS; Salisbury Ctr, NY; (Y); 1/3; Chess Clb; Debate Tm; Pres Natl Beta Clb; Pres Stu Cncl; Var Bsktbl; Var Trk; High Hon Roll; Extraord Chrstn Stu Of Amer 85-86; MA Inst Tech; Elctrnc Engrng.

TAYLOR, DEBBIE; Saranac Central HS; Cadyville, NY; (S); Rptr FBLA; Hosp Aide; Hon Roll; Me Sec.

TAYLOR, DOUGLAS C; Christian Brothers Acad; Liverpool, NY; (Y); 14/86; Var JV Socr; Hon Roll; FCA; Letterman Clb; Im Lcrss; Im Vllybl; 1st Team All League Sccr Team 84 & 85; Rchster Inst Tech; Comp Engrng.

TAYLOR, GARRY; Fillmore Central Schl; Houghton, NY; (Y); Boys Clb Am; FFA; Band; JV Socr; JV Wrstlng; Hon Roll.

TAYLOR, GEOFFREY; Huntington HS; Huntington, NY; (Y); Key Clb; Orch; Var Capt Tennis; High Hon Roll; Hon Roll; NHS.

TAYLOR, GRIEBE; Fort Ann Central HS; Ft Ann, NY; (Y); 20/60; Am Leg Aux Girls St; Chess Clb; Cmnty Wkr; Exploring; Ski Clb; SADD; Pep Band; Swmmng; Trk; Voice Dem Awd; Natl Oretoricl Cont 1st Pl; Ft Anne Resc Sqd; Outstndng Soprano Penncrest Chmbr Sngrs; Penn ST; Pre Law.

TAYLOR, JAMES; Hutchinson Central Tech HS; Buffalo, NY; (Y); Pres Church Yth Grp; Pres Church Choir; Var Bsktbl; Var Capt Ftbl; Stat Mgr(s); Var Capt Trk; Syracuse U; Phy Ed.

TAYLOR, JASON W; Thomas A Edison HS; Elmira Hgts, NY; (Y); Pres Am Leg Boys St; VP Chess Clb; French Clb; Varsity Clb; School Musical; VP Frsh Cls; VP Soph Cls; VP Jr Cls; Var L Tennis; Var L Wrstlng; Chem Engr.

TAYLOR, JENNIFER; Glen Cove HS; Glen Cove, NY; (Y); Church Yth Grp; Cmnty Wkr; Hosp Aide; Latin Clb; Science Clb; Ed Yrbk Stf; JV Crs Cntry; Var JV Mgr(s); JV Socr; Var JV Timer; Schl Awd Human Rel Clb 86.

TAYLOR, JILL; Hilton Central Schl; Rochester, NY; (Y); 15/305; Ski Clb; Drill Tm; JV Socr; Hon Roll; Intrprtr.

TAYLOR, JIM; Frontier Central HS; Hamburg, NY; (Y); Boy Scts; Ski Clb; Varsity Clb; VICA; Var Bsbl; JV Bsktbl; Coach Actv; JV Capt Ftbl; Wt Lftg; Hon Roll; MVP Vrsty Ftbl 85; Cortland U; Tech Elect.

TAYLOR, JOHN; Attica Central Schl; Cowlesville, NY; (S); Var Ftbl; Arch.

TAYLOR, KAREN; Sauquoit Valley Central HS; Cassville, NY; (Y); 5/102; VP Sec 4-H; VP Soph Cls; Rep Stu Cncl; Var JV Fld Hcky; 4-H Awd; High Hon Roll; Masonic Awd; NHS; NEDT Awd; SADD; Dstngshd JR Stu Cnty Hlstn Clb 85-86; Cornell Trdtn Hnry Fllw 86-87; Cornell U; Ag Ec.

TAYLOR, KARLA M; Marathon Central HS; Cortland, NY; (Y); 3/68; SADD; Teachers Aide; Chorus; Pres Sr Cls; Rep Stu Cncl; Var Capt Bsktbl; Var Capt Fld Hcky; Hon Roll; NHS; St Schlr; SUNY Potsdam; Biol.

TAYLOR, KELDA; Hutch Tech HS; Buffalo, NY; (Y); Church Yth Grp; JA; Pres Church Choir; Drill Tm; Trk; Outstndng Achvt Awd 83; Mrt Yth In Art Awd 83; Ctznshp Awd 83; Air Frc; Psych.

TAYLOR, KEVIN; Kaiserslautern American HS; Apo, NY; (Y); Rep JA; ROTC; Rep Varsity Clb; Color Guard; Rep Drill Tm; Rep Jr Cls; L Bsktbl; Var L Ftbl; L Gym; L Trk; Air Force; Elec Engnr.

TAYLOR, KEVIN A; New Fane SR HS; New Fane, NY; (Y); 22/181; Boy Scts; Church Yth Grp; Varsity Clb; Church Choir; Pres Concert Band; Pep Band; Trs Symp Band; JV Var Bsktbl; Score Keeper; Var L Trk; NY ST Regents Schlrshp 86; Army; Prsnl Mgmt.

TAYLOR, LAURIE; Bishop Grimes HS; N Syracuse, NY; (Y); Church Yth Grp; Cmnty Wkr; 4-H Awd; Stratford Schl; Travl/Toursm.

TAYLOR, LISA; Falconer Central HS; Falconer, NY; (Y); 1/120; Am Leg Aux Girls St; Pres Concert Band; Pres Jr Cls; Pres VP Stu Cncl; Sftbl; Tennis; Dnfth Awd; High Hon Roll; NHS; Opt Clb Awd; MVP Sftbl Awd; NYSSMA Awds; Doc.

TAYLOR, LYNORE; N Babylon SR HS; N Babylon, NY; (Y); 2/464; VP Trs Intnl Clb; Pres VP Spanish Clb; Madrigals; Ed Yrbk Stf; High Hon Roll; Kiwanis Awd; Lion Awd; NHS; Pres Schlr; Sal; Alpha Kappa Alpha Schlrshp 86; Jack & Jill Amer 86; Delta Sigma Theta Sorty 86; MA Inst Of Tech; Elctrcl Engr.

TAYLOR, MARCI JAN; Salem Central HS; Pawlet, VT; (Y); 5/58; GAA; Fld Hcky; Sftbl; Trk; High Hon Roll; Hon Roll; Sthrn UT Coll; Acctng.

TAYLOR, MICHELLE; Vestal HS; Binghamton, NY; (Y); 92/430; Church Yth Grp; French Clb; Ski Clb; Chorus; Church Choir; School Musical; Sec Jr Cls; Rep Stu Cncl; NHS; SUNY Geneseo; Publ Rel.

TAYLOR, OCTAVIA TRINETTE; The Garden Schl; Laurelton, NY; (S); Cmnty Wkr; Debate Tm; Library Aide; Office Aide; Service Clb; Nwsp Rptr; Lit Mag; Frsh Cls; Sec Soph Cls; Cheerleading; Srv Orgnztn 85; Schl Ltr For Chrldng 84 & 85; Brdcst Cmnctns.

TAYLOR, OPAL; Bishop Loughlin HS; Brooklyn, NY; (Y); 29/233; Library Aide; School Play; Gym; High Hon Roll; Hon Roll; Trk; Cert Of Merit 82-86; Hunter Coll; Nrsg.

TAYLOR, RICHARD; Avon JR SR HS; Avon, NY; (Y); 29/98; Spanish Clb; Trk; Hon Roll; Jr NHS; Prfct Atten Awd; Bus Admin.

TAYLOR, ROBERT; Half Hollow Hills HS East; Wheatly Hts, NY; (S); Boy Scts; DECA; Auto Sales.

TAYLOR III, ROBERT; Honeoye Central HS; Honeoye, NY; (S); 4-H; French Clb; Ski Clb; Jazz Band; Rep Frsh Cls; Rep Soph Cls; Pres Jr Cls; Rep Stu Cncl; JV Var Socr; Aerontcl Engrng.

TAYLOR, SCOTT; Wyoming Central Schl; Wyoming, NY; (S); 1/23; French Clb; Red Cross Aide; Lit Mag; Bsbl; Hon Roll; NHS; Med.

TAYLOR, SHUNDA M; St Anthonys HS; Deer Park, NY; (Y); Church Yth Grp; JA; Varsity Clb; Stu Cncl; Bsktbl; Cheerleading; Trk; High Hon Roll; Hon Roll; Prfct Atten Awd; 5yr Vrsty Awd 85-86; Dun Scotees 82-86; Marist Coll; Math.

TAYLOR, STEPHANIE; Walton Central HS; Walton, NY; (Y); 3/120; AFS; Cmnty Wkr; Key Clb; Acpl Chr; Chorus; VP Soph Cls; Sec Sr Cls; Var Cheerleading; High Hon Roll; Bus.

TAYLOR, STEPHEN; St John The Baptist D HS; W Babylon, NY; (Y); Model UN; French Hon Soc; NHS; Engl Hnrs 86; Culnry Art.

TAYLOR, TAMI; Southside HS; Rockville Ctr, NY; (Y); Drama Clb; FBLA; Girl Scts; Key Clb; Mathletes; SADD; Stage Crew; Hon Roll; Long Island U; Physcl Thrpy.

TAYLOR, WENDY; Sodus Central HS; Williamson, NY; (Y); 27/135; French Clb; Science Clb; Varsity Clb; Band; Sec Frsh Cls; Cheerleading; Tennis; Pres Awd 86; Alfred ST Coll; Med.

TAYLOR, WILLIAM; Solvay HS; Syracuse, NY; (Y); High Hon Roll; Hon Roll; Comp Pgmr.

TAYLOR, WILLIAM D; Pinecrest Christian HS; Salisbury Ctr, NY; (S); Chess Clb; Debate Tm; Natl Beta Clb; Yrbk Bus Mgr; Pres Stu Cncl; Bsktbl; Trk; High Hon Roll; Hon Roll; Extrdnry Chrstn Stu Of Amer 86; ACSI Dist Amer HS Stu 86; MA Inst Tech; Elec Engr.

TCHOU, BETTY; Midwood HS; Brooklyn, NY; (Y); 150/556; Drama Clb; Service Clb; Lit Mag; Rep Stu Cncl; Cheerleading; Prfct Atten Awd; Regents Schlrshp 86; Acctg.

TEACHER, WILLIE; Beach Channel HS; Far Rockaway, NY; (Y); Drama Clb; Thesps; School Musical; School Play; Nwsp Rptr; VP Sr Cls; Aud/Vis; Office Aide; Chorus; Lit Mag; Schlrshp Camp Rising Sun 85; Prncpls List 86; Brown U; Bus Mgmt.

TEAGUE, STEPHEN S; Stony Brook Schl; Port Jefferson, NY; (Y); Pres Church Yth Grp; FCA; JA; Spanish Clb; Var Ftbl; Wt Lftg; High Hon Roll; Hon Roll; Ntl Merit Schol; U Of AR.

TEALE, MICHELE; Gloversville HS; Gloversville, NY; (Y); 43/235; Intnl Clb; Color Guard; Capt Bsktbl; Capt Cheerleading; Powder Puff Ftbl; Sftbl; Hon Roll; Rgnts Schlrshp 86; Brbra Gffrd Awd Bsktbll 86; Cmmnctns.

TEARS, NATALIE; Wallkill SR HS; Wallkill, NY; (Y); 19/186; Church Yth Grp; Chorus; School Play; Stage Crew; Yrbk Rptr; Yrbk Stf; Off Jr Cls; High Hon Roll; Hon Roll; NHS; Nrs.

TEATOR, HOLLY; Bensselaer HS; Rensselaer, NY; (Y); DECA; Nwsp Rptr; Nwsp Stf; Yrbk Rptr; Yrbk Stf; Cheerleading; Hon Roll; JR Yr MVP For Ftbl Chrldng 85; SR Yr MVP For Ftbl Chrldng 86; Capt Ftbl & Bsktbl Chrldng 85-86; Mildred Elley Schl; Exec Sec.

TEBANO, ARMANDO; Mont Pleasant HS; Schenectady, NY; (Y); 69/260; German Clb; Key Clb; Pep Clb; Ski Clb; Yrbk Phtg; Var Socr; Var Trk; Hon Roll; Lwyr.

TEBBETTS, NICHOLE; Ramstein American HS; Apo New York, NY; (Y); Church Yth Grp; School Musical; Stage Crew; High Hon Roll; Hon Roll; Cosmetlgy.

TECHMAN, MARC; Auburn HS; Auburn, NY; (Y); Var Bowling; High Hon Roll; Hon Roll; Syracuse U; Cmmnctns.

TEDD, JILL; Lowville Acad; Lowville, NY; (Y); Im Powder Puff Ftbl; Sociolgy.

TEDD II, MICHAEL T; Goshen Central HS; Goshen, NY; (Y); 7/186; Drama Clb; Ski Clb; Spanish Clb; School Musical; School Play; Stage Crew; Socr; High Hon Roll; NHS; Pres Schlr; SUNY Geneseo; Mgmt Sci.

TEDESCO, JULIE; Depew HS; Depew, NY; (Y); 39/272; Art Clb; Cmnty Wkr; Hon Roll; NHS; Prfct Atten Awd; Bryante Stratton Commercial Art Schlrshp 86; Allentown Vlg Art Soc Schlrshp 86; Pres Acad Fitness Awd; Bryante Stratton Bus Inst; Arts.

TEDESCO, KATHLEEN; St Marys Acad; Glens Falls, NY; (Y); 5/45; Drama Clb; French Clb; Key Clb; SADD; Chorus; School Musical; Nwsp Rptr; Yrbk Ed-Chief; Cheerleading; High Hon Roll; Marquette U; Engl.

TEDESCO, LORI; Mont Pleasant HS; Schenectady, NY; (Y); 4/210; Key Clb; Ski Clb; Spanish Clb; Yrbk Bus Mgr; Yrbk Stf; Socr; Hon Roll; NHS; Pres Schlr; Spanish NHS; Hrvrd Book Awd 85; Schntdy Fnctn Of Tchrs Schlrshp 86; Le Moyne Coll; Bus & Cmnctns.

TEDESCO, SAL; Cardinal Spellman HS; Bronx, NY; (Y); Stage Crew; Im Mgr Bsktbl; Hon Roll.

TEDESCO, TARA L; Gloversville HS; Gloversville, NY; (Y); Drama Clb; Sec French Clb; Chorus; Color Guard; Mrchg Band; School Musical; School Play; Yrbk Stf; Sftbl; Hon Roll; NYS Regnts Schlrshp 86; Clg Of ST Rose; Comp Info Syst.

TEDFORD, ERIC; Chittenango HS; Chittenango, NY; (Y); French Clb; Science Clb; Spanish Clb; Im Ftbl; Var JV Socr; JV Tennis; Var JV Wrstlng; 1st Pl Trphy Socr 85-86; Bethany Coll; Math.

TEDQUIST, DAN; Jamestown HS; Jamestown, NY; (Y); L Swmmng; L Trk; Hi Pnt Wnnr Trck 86; Law.

TEED, DENNIS; Clymer Central HS; Clymer, NY; (Y); Outstndng Achvt Awd 86; Bldng Houses.

TEED, TAMARA; Wayland Central HS; Wayland, NY; (Y); 31/101; Girl Scts; Red Cross Aide; Gym; Hon Roll; Bus.

TEEHAN, FRANCIS; St Raymonds For Boys; Bronx, NY; (Y); 7/170; Math Tm; Science Clb; JV Bsbl; JV Bsktbl; Im Bowling; Im Ftbl; Im Sftbl; High Hon Roll; Hon Roll; Manhattan; Compu Sci.

TEEMLEY, BRAD; Ripley Central HS; Ripley, NY; (S); 5/40; Drama Clb; School Play; Pres Soph Cls; Var Capt Bsbl; Var L Bsktbl; Var L Crs Cntry; Score Keeper; Prfct Atten Awd; Ntl Engl Merit Awd 85-86; Military; Biochem.

TEEPS, DAVID; Vernon-Verona-Sherrill Central HS; Vernon, NY; (Y); 21/199; Church Yth Grp; Computer Clb; Band; Mrchg Band; High Hon Roll; Hon Roll; NHS; Mohawk Vly CC; Elect.

TEETER, KIRSTEN; Watkins Glen HS; Valois, NY; (Y); #16 In Class; Aud/Vis; Cmnty Wkr; Drama Clb; 4-H; Quiz Bowl; School Play; Mgr Nwsp Stf; French Hon Soc; 4-H Awd; Hon Roll; Natl Wmns Hl Of Fm Wrtng Cntst 83; Human Svcs.

TEETER, MARCIA; Newark SR HS; Newark, NY; (Y); 23/201; Cmnty Wkr; Ski Clb; Band; Concert Band; Nwsp Stf; Yrbk Stf; Swmmng; French Hon Soc; Lion Awd; NHS; Rtry Intl Schlrshp 86; Mst Imprvd Swmmr; Vlntr Rcgntn Awd 85-86; SUNY Oswego; Physcl Thrpy.

TEETO, DARLENE; Trott Vocational HS; Niagara Falls, NY; (Y); FNA; GAA; SADD; VICA; Stage Crew; Variety Show; Nwsp Sprt Ed; Nwsp Stf; Yrbk Stf; Pres Soph Cls; Pre-Med.

TEETSEL, BARBARA; Somers HS; Yorktown Hts, NY; (Y); 9/202; Pres AFS; Art Clb; Girl Scts; Intnl Clb; Yrbk Rptr; High Hon Roll; Hon Roll; NHS; Spanish NHS; NY ST Rgnts Schlrshp 86; P Rilo Mem Schlrshp 86; Heritage Hills Schlrshp 86; Syracuse U; Envrnmntal Bio.

TEHAN, PATRICIA; Frankfortischuyler HS; Frankfort, NY; (Y); 38/101; Pres Exploring; Pres French Clb; SADD; Mrchg Band; Nwsp Sprt Ed; Yrbk Stf; JV Bsktbl; Var Tennis; Var Trk; NHS; NY ST Regents Nrsng Schlrshp 86; Herkimer Cnty 40 & 8 Nrsng Schlrshp 86; Mohawk Vlly CC; Nrsng.

TEHOKE, DONALD; Williamsville East HS; Williamsville, NY; (Y); Church Yth Grp; Cmnty Wkr; FBLA; Yrbk Stf; Var Bowling; YABA 1st Pl 5 Man Tm & 4 Man Tm 85-86; Gift Cert Mrktng Poster Cntst 86; Bus Mngmnt.

TEICH, JAMES; Bishop Ludden HS; Syracuse, NY; (S); 1/180; Cmnty Wkr; Exploring; Math Tm; Model UN; Nwsp Stf; Yrbk Stf; Var Mgr(s); High Hon Roll; Pres NHS; Val; Holy Crss Bk Awd 85; Le Moyne Coll Smmr Schlr 85; SUNY Coll Cortlnd Schlr 85; Engrng.

TEICHER, STEPHANI G; City Honors HS; Buffalo, NY; (Y); 5/104; VP Church Yth Grp; Ski Clb; School Musical; Yrbk Ed-Chief; Stu Cncl; L Trk; St Schlr; Varsity Clb; Chorus; School Play; NYSAFLT Grnd Prz Wnnr-Art Cmptn 85-86; Hgh Art Cmptn-Daemon Coll 2nd Prz Pntg 86; RI Schl Of Design; Fash Dsgn.

TEICHMAN, MARGARET; Poughkeepsie HS; Poughkeepsie, NY; (Y); Yrbk Stf; Swmmng; Advrtsng Exec.

TEIN, NAOMI LEE; Horace Mann Schl; New Rochelle, NY; (Y); Exploring; Acpl Chr; Chorus; School Musical; Variety Show; Var JV Crs Cntry; Hosp Aide; Service Clb; School Play; Stage Crew; NY ST Regents Scholar 86; Cornell.

TEITLER, JILL; New Dorp HS; Staten Island, NY; (Y); Drama Clb; Concert Band; Jazz Band; Pep Band; School Musical; Lit Mag; Hon Roll; Daily News Music Excllnc Awd 86; Music.

TEJEDA, YIRA; Prospect Heights HS; Brooklyn, NY; (Y); Hon Roll; Arista, Schlrshp Awd Engl, Wmns Govt 85-86; Medgar Evers Coll; Arch.

TEJERA, PETER; Christian Brothers Acad; Syracuse, NY; (Y); 10/95; Pep Clb; Red Cross Aide; High Hon Roll; SF Natl Hispnc Schlrs Awd Pgm 86; Cornell U; Pre-Med.

TEKMITCHOV, SOPHIA; Bolton Central HS; Bolton Landing, NY; (Y); Computer Clb; French Clb; Chorus; Yrbk Ed-Chief; Yrbk Stf; JV Vllybl; Hon Roll; NHS.

TELESCA, PAMELA; Acad Of The Rsrrctn; Rye Brook, NY; (Y); Art Clb; Church Yth Grp; Math Clb; Teachers Aide; Stage Crew; Ed Yrbk Stf; Rep Stu Cncl; Hon Roll; NHS; Marymount U Of VA; Chldhd Educ.

TELLALIAN, SABRINA; Bethpage HS; Plainview, NY; (Y); 1/310; Spanish Clb; Capt Drill Tm; Var Badmtn; High Hon Roll; L Jr NHS; VP NHS; Val; Chem Awd 85; Soc Stds Awd 84; Kybrdng Awd 84; Med.

TELLER, PHILIP; Canisius HS; Amherst, NY; (Y); Cmnty Wkr; Pep Clb; Chorus; Var Bsbl; JV Im Bsktbl; Cheerleading; JV Im Golf; Im Vllybl; Hon Roll; Outstndg Vol Awd 86; Scndry Educ.

TELLIER, KARA; Colonie Central HS; Albany, NY; (Y); Church Yth Grp; DECA; Ski Clb; Chorus; Church Choir; Orch; Variety Show; Cheerleading; High Hon Roll; Hon Roll; Decny 86 Regionl Qualfr Apprl & Accsrs 86.

TELOVSKY, WILLIAM; Albion HS; Albion, NY; (S); 12/174; Church Yth Grp; 4-H; Spanish Clb; Church Choir; Stage Crew; 4-H Awd; God Cntry Awd; NHS; Pres Clssrm Young Amer WA DC 86; Lawyer.

TEMPESTOSO, GABRIELE; Bishop Timon HS; W Seneca, NY; (S); Nwsp Rptr; Socr; High Hon Roll; Hon Roll.

TEMPLE, HERMINA; Roosevelt Jr-Sr HS; Roosevelt, NY; (S); 1/160; 4-H; Drm Mjr(t); Orch; Yrbk Ed-Chief; Mgr Bsbl; High Hon Roll; NHS; Prfct Atten Awd; Val; Northeastern U; Accntng.

TEMPLER, THERESA; Niskayuna HS; Schdy, NY; (Y); Cmnty Wkr; Pep Clb; Varsity Clb; Variety Show; Capt Var Cheerleading; Coach Actv; Powder Puff Ftbl; Sftbl; SUNY Albany.

TEMPONE, DANIEL; Msgr Farrell HS; Staten Island, NY; (Y); Spanish Clb; Yrbk Stf; Im Bsbl; Hon Roll; Pres Schlrshp 86; U Scranton; Acctg.

TEN BROECK, JACQUELINE; Middletown HS; Middletown, NY; (Y); Teachers Aide; Band; Mrchg Band; Bus.

TENACE, MELISSA; Mont Pleasant HS; Schenectady, NY; (Y); 19/206; Pres German Clb; Key Clb; Office Aide; VP Pep Clb; Nwsp Stf; Rep Sr Cls; JV Mgr(s); Hon Roll; NHS; Hudson Valley CC; Acctnt.

TENAGLIA, ELIZABETH A; Oxford Acad; Mc Donough, NY; (Y); #2 In Class; Am Leg Aux Girls St; French Clb; Band; Chorus; Nwsp Ed-Chief; Bausch & Lomb Sci Awd; High Hon Roll; Hon Roll; NHS; Prfct Atten Awd; Opertn Entrprs 85; Hghst Rgnts Avg 85; Acdmc Chllng Tm 86; Rochester Inst Tech; Biotech.

TENEDORIO, MICHAEL; Mineola HS; Mineola, NY; (Y); 31/235; JV Bsktbl; High Hon Roll; Hon Roll; Jr NHS; Hofstra U; Indstrl Engr.

TENG, ERIC; Herricks SR HS; New Hyde Park, NY; (Y); Art Clb; VP DECA; Math Clb; Ed Nwsp Stf; Ed Yrbk Stf; Cit Awd; JC Awd; Jr NHS; NHS; 1st Pl NY ST Deca Stu Of Yr 86; 1st Pl Consumer Affairs Awd 85; Congressional Arts Ward Fine Arts 86; Carnegie Mellon U; Graphic Dsn.

TENNENT, KEILA C; De Witt Clinton HS; Bronx, NY; (Y); 2/257; Church Yth Grp; Cmnty Wkr; Office Aide; Service Clb; Varsity Clb; Nwsp Rptr; Nwsp Stf; Yrbk Rptr; Yrbk Stf; Pres Stu Cncl; Amherst Coll; Pre-Med Obstrcn.

TENNEY, RYAN; Batavia HS; Batavia, NY; (Y); 36/250; Bsbl; Bsktbl; Ftbl; Hon Roll; Monroe Cnty All Star-Bsbl; Accntng.

TENNY, JIM; Elmira Free Acad; Elmira, NY; (Y); Sec Church Yth Grp; Pres JA; Var Diving; Var Golf; Var Capt Swmmng; High Hon Roll; Hon Roll; Embry-Riddle U; Aernautcl Engr.

TEPEDINO, MARIA; North Babylon HS; N Babylon, NY; (Y); Nwsp Stf; Lit Mag; VP Sr Cls; Var Sftbl; Hon Roll; NHS; Jrnlsm.

TEPPER, J MARK; Geneva HS; Geneva, NY; (S); 37/175; French Clb; Latin Clb; Model UN; Nwsp Sprt Ed; Lit Mag; Rep Frsh Cls; Var JV Ice Hcky; Var JV Lcrss; Prfct Atten Awd; Rotary Awd; A J Hammond Hist Essy Cntst 1st Pl; Lit Magzn Poem Cnst 1st Pl; U Of Buffalo; Elec Engr.

TEPPER, JONATHAN D; New Rochelle HS; New Rochelle, NY; (Y); 43/550; Camera Clb; Ski Clb; Nwsp Ed-Chief; JV Bsbl; JV Lcrss; NHS; Ntl Merit SF; Duke U; Bus Adm.

TERAUDS, SANDRA; Connetquot HS; Ronkonkoma, NY; (Y); 1/700; Chess Clb; Math Tm; Quiz Bowl; Science Clb; Band; Mrchg Band; Nwsp Rptr; Lit Mag; High Hon Roll; NHS; Westinghouse Hnr 86; Empire ST Scholar Excllnce 86; Columbia Sci Hnrs Pgm 84-86; MA Inst Tech; Srgn.

TERCHOWITZ, CELIA; John F Kennedy HS; Utica, NY; (Y); 15/130; Band; Concert Band; Nwsp Rptr; Nwsp Stf; Bowling; High Hon Roll; Hon Roll; Jr NHS; Mohawk Vlly CC; Bus Adm.

TERILLI, MARC J; Pelham Memorial HS; Pelham, NY; (Y); 41/158; Im Ftbl; Hon Roll; NY Inst Of Tech; Electro Tech.

TERLECKEY, STEPHEN; Bishop Scully HS; Amsterdam, NY; (Y); 10/55; 4-H; Trs Math Clb; Bsbl; High Hon Roll; Mu Alp Tht; NHS; Ntl Merit Schol; Syracuse U; Indstrl Mgmt.

TERNOSKY, ROBERT L; Solvay HS; Solvay, NY; (Y); 20/171; Computer Clb; FBLA; Math Clb; JV Bsbl; High Hon Roll; Hon Roll; Exclnc Comp Sci 84; Regnts Schlrshp 85-86; Rochester Inst Tech; Comp Sci.

TERRANCE, DENISE; Anthony Henninger HS; Syracuse, NY; (Y); Art Clb; Drama Clb; VP JA; Key Clb; Trs Spanish Clb; SADD; Stage Crew; Hon Roll; Bus Mngmnt.

TERRANOVA, ANN MARIE; The Buffalo Seminary; Buffalo, NY; (Y); Church Yth Grp; Drama Clb; French Clb; Chorus; Orch; School Musical; School Play; Hon Roll; Ntl Merit Schol; Clsscl Perf.

TERRANOVA, LISA; Newfield HS; Coram, NY; (Y); Church Yth Grp; Dance Clb; Concert Band; Mrchg Band; School Play; Nwsp Rptr; Trk; Jr NHS; Spanish NHS; Pres Phys Fit Awd 84 & 85; Econ.

TERRELL, JAMES A; Mc Quaid Jesuit HS; Fairport, NY; (Y); 16/170; Ski Clb; Spanish Clb; Varsity Clb; Var L Ftbl; Var L Trk; High Hon Roll; NHS; St Schlr; Rgnts Schlrshp 86; Semi-Fnlst Pres Schlrshp Villanova U 86; Cornell U; Elec Engr.

TERRITO, JOHN; Southwestern Central HS; Jamestown, NY; (Y); Var Bowling; Var Golf; Comp Engrng.

TERRIZZI, JOSEPH; Bishop Ford HS; Brooklyn, NY; (Y); JV Trk.

TERRY, AMY; The Masters Schl; Dallas, TX; (Y); Church Yth Grp; Cmnty Wkr; Dance Clb; Drama Clb; FCA; GAA; Hosp Aide; Thesps; Acpl Chr; Chorus; UCLA; Drama.

TERRY, CHRISTINE; Chatham HS; Austerlitz, NY; (Y); 4-H; Ski Clb; Hon Roll; Biomedical Tech.

TERRY, DAVID R; Horseheads SR HS; Elmira, NY; (S); 31/380; JCL; Latin Clb; Science Clb; Band; Concert Band; Mrchg Band; School Musical; Rep Soph Cls; Hon Roll; Ntl Merit Ltr.

TERRY, MICHELLE; Nazareth Acad; Rochester, NY; (Y); Cmnty Wkr; FBLA; Teachers Aide; Sec Soph Cls; Hon Roll; Lincoln U; Acctg.

TERRY, TOM; Westhampton Beach SR HS; East Quogue, NY; (Y); 37/243; Church Yth Grp; Computer Clb; Band; Var Socr; Im Wt Lftg; Var Wrstlng; Hon Roll; Vrsty Sccr MIP 85; JV Sccr Sprts 84; JVWRSTLNG MIP 84; Bus Adm.

TERSY, ANGELINA; Dominican Commerical HS; Flushing, NY; (S); 14/288; Dance Clb; Drama Clb; Hosp Aide; Chorus; School Play; High Hon Roll; NHS; Prncpl List 83-86; St Johns U; Med Doctor.

TERWILLIGER, JAMES; Corning-Painted Post West HS; Corning, NY; (Y); Pres Church Yth Grp; JA; Quiz Bowl; Band; Concert Band; Mrchg Band; High Hon Roll; NHS; Ntl Merit Ltr; Weleyan Coll; Christian Ed.

TERWILLIGER, ROBERT W; Saugerties Central Schls; Saugerties, NY; (Y); 26/252; German Clb; Ski Clb; High Hon Roll; Hon Roll; NHS; Rgnts Coll Schlrshp 86; 1st Pl Amer Hstry-Natl Soc Stud Olympiad 85; 3rd Pl Wrld Hstry NSSO 84; Siena Coll; Polit Sci.

TERWILLIGER, TAMMY; Addison Central Schl; Addison, NY; (Y); Ski Clb; Color Guard; Yrbk Sprt Ed; VP Jr Cls; JV Cheerleading; JV Socr; JV Var Sftbl; Var Swmmng; Dnfth Awd; Paul Smith; Tourism.

TESIERO, KELLY M; Columbia HS; Rensselaer, NY; (Y); 24/417; Key Clb; Trs SADD; Orch; Rep Soph Cls; Rep Sr Cls; Im JV Sftbl; Im JV Vllybl; High Hon Roll; NHS; Pres Schlr; All Cnty Music Festival 82-84; All Star & Sprtsmnshp Awds E Greenbush Summer Sftbl 83-84; Ithaca; Physcl Thrpy.

TESORIERO, MARK; Monsignor Farrell HS; Staten Island, NY; (Y); Church Yth Grp; Cmnty Wkr; Ski Clb; Varsity Clb; Im Bsbl; Im Bsktbl; Im Bowling; Im Ftbl; Var Socr; DAR Awd; Pltcl Sci.

TESSEYMAN, MICHELLE; Hamburg HS; Hamburg, NY; (Y); 85/374; JCL; Latin Clb; Sec Service Clb; Chorus; Orch; School Musical; Var Tennis; DAR Awd; Hon Roll.

TESSIER, BARBARA; Niagara Wheatfield SR HS; Sanborn, NY; (Y); Hst Pep Clb; VP PAVAS; Trs Spanish Clb; VP Band; Mrchg Band; School Musical; High Hon Roll; NHS; Mdrn Music Mstrs 85&86; Acdmc All-Amrcn 84-86; Indstrl Engnrng.

TESSIER, TROY A; Brasher Falls Central HS; Nicholville, NY; (Y); 1/101; Concert Band; Pres Frsh Cls; Pres Soph Cls; JV Var Bsktbl; Var L Socr; High Hon Roll; Hon Roll; JETS Awd; NHS; Val; St Lawrence U Schlr Awd 86-87; Outstndng Sci Stu Awd 82-83; St Lawrence U; Ecnmcs.

TESSITORE, RICHARD; Oneonta HS; Oneonta, NY; (Y); 15/174; Art Clb; Hon Roll; Natl Soc Studies Olympiad & 11th Grd Cls Awds 85; Art Awd 85; Air Force; Electncs.

TESTINI, GUY; Levittown Division Avenue HS; Levittown, NY; (Y); 33/335; Math Clb; Pres Spanish Clb; SADD; Varsity Clb; School Play; Stage Crew; Variety Show; Nwsp Rptr; VP Frsh Cls; VP Soph Cls; Acadmc All Amer 86; Tulane U; Pol Sci.

TETER, JULIE E; Horseheads HS; Horseheads, NY; (S); 22/370; Cmnty Wkr; VP Debate Tm; Drama Clb; Exploring; Pres Intnl Clb; Model UN; Scholastic Bowl; Science Clb; SADD; Chorus; Pres Harris Hill Soaring Corp JR Mbrs 85-86; Cornell; Biochem.

TETER, LORIE; Middletown HS; Middletown, NY; (Y); Trs Church Yth Grp; Political Wkr; Church Choir; Yrbk Stf; Hon Roll; Nyrsma Music Grading-Piano Solo B, A, & B 84-86; Bus.

TETRAULT, TAMI J; Owego Free Acad; Owego, NY; (Y); 19/300; Church Yth Grp; Drama Clb; Office Aide; Acpl Chr; Band; Church Choir; Mrchg Band; 4-H Awd; NHS; Cmnty Wkr; Salt Ldrshp Trning-Hghtn Coll 84; NYS Rgnts Schlrshp 86; 4-H Ctznshp Awd Trip Wshngtn DC 83; Houghton Coll; Chrstn Psychlgy.

TETTE, THOMAS; Gates-Chili HS; Rochester, NY; (Y); Stu Cncl; JV Bsbl; L Ftbl; Wt Lftg; High Hon Roll; Hon Roll; Bus.

TETTERIS, BILLY; Mineola HS; Albertson, NY; (Y); 14/235; Yrbk Stf; High Hon Roll; Pres Acdmc Fit Awd 86; Hofstra U; Accntng.

TEUFEL, CHRISTINA I; Shoreham-Wading River HS; Shoreham, NY; (Y); Sec Church Yth Grp; Mathletes; SADD; Sec NHS; St Schlr; NY ST Rgnts Schlrshp 86; Outstndg Stu Clthng & Txtls 85; NYS Sci Olympiad 85-86; Grove Cty Coll; Bus Admin.

TEUTSCHMAN, LAURAYNE; Mineola HS; Mineola, NY; (Y); Key Clb; SADD; Pres Jr Cls; Rep Stu Cncl; Var Gym; Stat Lcrss; Score Keeper.

TEVLIN, MARYANN; Lindenhurst HS; Lindenhurst, NY; (Y); Nwsp Rptr; Hon Roll; Nrsng.

TEW, GERALDINE; Kings Park HS; Kings Park, NY; (Y); Cmnty Wkr; Dance Clb; Hosp Aide; Chorus; Church Choir; Hon Roll; Nrs.

TEWES, ERIC M; Phelham Memorial HS; Pelham, NY; (Y); 26/153; Office Aide; Radio Clb; Ski Clb; Yrbk Phtg; Yrbk Stf; Lcrss; Tennis; Hon Roll; NHS; Pres Acad Fit Awd 86; Fordham U; Pre-Med.

THACHER, JEFFREY T; Potsdam Central HS; Potsdam, NY; (Y); 13/122; SADD; Band; Chorus; Orch; School Musical; Off Stu Cncl; NHS; Ntl Merit Ltr; Voice Dem Awd; AFS Exchng Stu-Yugoslavia 85; NY All ST & Area All ST Chrses 85; Boston U.

THAI, SENH; New Utrecht HS; Brooklyn, NY; (Y); 12/644; Nwsp Rptr; Acad All Am Ntl Hnr Rl 85-86; UFT Schlrshp 86; Brooklyn Coll; Elect Engr.

THAINE, TRACY; Lyndonville Central HS; Medina, NY; (S); 6/90; Sec Trs AFS; Math Clb; Trs Spanish Clb; Band; Trs Jr Cls; Capt Var Cheerleading; Hon Roll; VP Jr NHS; NHS; Psychlgy.

THAKKAR, AMINIDHAN; Valley Stream Central HS; Valley Stream, NY; (Y); Aud/Vis; Computer Clb; Leo Clb; Pres Science Clb; Service Clb; Spanish Clb; SADD; Teachers Aide; Yrbk Stf; High Hon Roll; Pre Med.

THALER, DEREK C; Oriskany Central Schl; Oriskany, NY; (Y); Am Leg Boys St; Letterman Clb; Sec Spanish Clb; Varsity Clb; School Play; Stage Crew; VP Soph Cls; Var Capt Bsbl; Var L Bsktbl; Capt Var Ftbl; Outstndng Frosh 84; Most Imprvd Basebll 86; Bus.

THALMANN, F CHRISTOPHER; Sidney HS; Sidney, NY; (Y); 12/100; Boy Scts; Exploring; Mathletes; Service Clb; Nwsp Rptr; Nwsp Stf; Im JV Bsktbl; Var Socr; Hon Roll; NHS; NYS Rgnts Schlrshp 86; Clrk Awd For Excllnc In Acad 86; Excllnt Atten Awd 86; PA ST; Geo Sci.

THAM, KHAI; Far Rockaway HS; Far Rockaway, NY; (Y); #3 In Class; Key Clb; Math Tm; Office Aide; Scholastic Bowl; Teachers Aide; Stage Crew; Yrbk Stf; Off Sr Cls; Bowling; Capt Tennis; Suft Schlrshp 86; Gvrnrs Comm Schlshp 86; NY U Schlrshp 86; NY U; Pre-Med.

THATCHER, KIMBERLY R; St Francis Prep; Flushing, NY; (S); 81/744; Dance Clb; GAA; Office Aide; NHS; Spanish NHS; Hosp Aide; Teachers Aide; Chorus; Church Choir; Wt Lftg; PA ST; Defns Atty.

THATER, ILENE E; Pavilion Central Schl; Le Roy, NY; (Y); VP FHA; Spanish Clb; Nwsp Stf; Score Keeper; Trk; Jr NHS; NHS; NY ST Rgnts Schlrshp 86; Genesee CC; Human Svcs.

THAYER, TODD W; Pittsford Mendon HS; Pittsford, NY; (Y); Concert Band; Jazz Band; VP Jr Cls; Pres Sr Cls; Var L Ftbl; Var L Lcrss; Var Capt Wrstlng; NHS; Ntl Merit Ltr; Mrchg Band; NYS Regents Schlrshp 86; Gary Dibella Mem Schlrshp 86; Vince Lombardi Schlrshp 86; Dartmouth Coll; Sci.

THEBAUD, SANDRA; The Mary Louis Acad; Richmond Hill, NY; (Y); 91/270; Drama Clb; Hosp Aide; Library Aide; School Play; Pres Sr Cls; Gym; Outstndng Achvt Awd 83; NY ST Regnts Schlrshp 86; Cert Of Hnr NY ST Bar Assoc 86; NY U; Psych.

THELEN, TAMARA; Moriah Central HS; Mineville, NY; (Y); AFS; Spanish Clb; High Hon Roll; Engr.

THEN, LUIS; De Witt Clinton HS; Bronx, NY; (Y); JA; Gym; Trk; Wt Lftg; Cit Awd; High Hon Roll; Hon Roll; NHS; Prfct Atten Awd; Med.

THERIAULT, BRIAN; Gouverneur HS; Gouverneur, NY; (Y); Church Yth Grp; 4-H; Golf; Socr; Hon Roll; Oswego ST U; Bus Admin.

THERO, DANIEL P; La Salle Inst; Latham, NY; (Y); 1/83; Am Leg Boys St; ROTC; Nwsp Ed-Chief; Var Trk; Bausch & Lomb Sci Awd; Elks Awd; High Hon Roll; NHS; Ntl Merit Ltr; Pres Schlr; Rnsslr Mdl Math & Sci 86; NY St Rgnts Schlrshp; Siena Coll; Med.

THIERLING, CURTIS; New Lebanon Central Schl; Canaan, NY; (Y); Am Leg Boys St; French Clb; Chorus; Sec Stu Cncl; Bsbl; Bsktbl; Socr; Cit Awd; Hon Roll; NHS; Bershire Cmnty Coll; Engrng.

THIESSEN, JASON; Linton HS; Schenectady, NY; (Y); 1/355; Exploring; JCL; Stage Crew; Ntl Merit Ltr; Med.

THILL, MELISSA; Eden SR HS; Eden, NY; (Y); AFS; Church Yth Grp; SADD; Varsity Clb; Band; Drm & Bgl; Mrchg Band; Symp Band; Frsh Cls; Fld Hcky; Radlgc Tech.

THILLET, LISA; St Catharine Acad; Bronx, NY; (Y); 54/185; Computer Clb; GAA; Service Clb; Ski Clb; Teachers Aide; Swmmng; Prfct Atten Awd; Bio Cmndtn 84-85; Excllnc Amer Hstry 85-86; Alg II Cmndtn 85-86; St Johns U; Comp Pgmng.

THILLMAN, LORI M; Waterloo SR HS; Waterloo, NY; (Y); 8/176; Drama Clb; French Clb; FTA; Teachers Aide; Varsity Clb; Chorus; Yrbk Stf; Var Trk; High Hon Roll; NHS; SUNY Oneonta; Elem Educ.

THIMSEN, MICHAEL; Hahn American HS; Apo New York, NY; (Y); 13/80; VP Church Yth Grp; Cmnty Wkr; Letterman Clb; Model UN; VP Jr Cls; Sec Stu Cncl; Var L Bsbl; Var L Crs Cntry; Var L Ftbl; Var L Tennis; MVP Tnns Sphmr JR Yrs 85 & 86; Rep Hahn HS Brian Bowl 85; U Of WA; Md Cmmnctns.

THISTLE, MEGAN; Painted Post West HS; Painted Post, NY; (Y); 20/254; Chorus; School Musical; Trk; High Hon Roll; NHS; Rochester Inst Tech; Biotech.

THIVIERGE, KEVIN J; St Marys Boys HS; Floral Park, NY; (Y); JV Capt Socr; St Schlr; Coll Of St Rose; Bus Adm.

THOMANN, DAVID J; Webster HS; Webster, NY; (Y); 100/500; German Clb; Ski Clb; Band; Var L Bsbl; Socr; Hon Roll; Bob Brkhldr Mem Awd 85-86; Outstndg Math Stu 82-83; Cert Hnr Grmn Lang 84-85; U Of Rochester; Mech Engnrng.

THOMAS, ANGELICA L; Richmond Hill HS; Richmond Hill, NY; (Y); 27/288; English Clb; School Play; Nwsp Ed-Chief; Nwsp Rptr; Rep Frsh Cls; Rep Soph Cls; Sec Jr Cls; Trs Stu Cncl; Pres NHS; Voice Dem Awd; Dly Nws Prncpls Pride Of The Ynkees 83-86; Jrnlsm Awd 86; NY Cty Assn Of Tchrs Fo Engl Awd 86; Bard Coll; Inbtl Rltns.

THOMAS, BILL; Shenendehowa HS; Rexford, NY; (Y); 53/675; Var Bsbl; Var Bsktbl; Var Ftbl; NHS; USAFA; Aero Engrng.

THOMAS, BRIAN; Rome Catholic HS; Rome, NY; (Y); Church Yth Grp; Mgr Bsktbl; Var Golf; Mgr(s); High Hon Roll; Kiwanis Awd; NHS; NEDT Awd; Prfct Atten Awd; Arch.

THOMAS, CATHERINE; Franciscan Acad; Liverpool, NY; (S); Church Yth Grp; NFL; Teachers Aide; Acpl Chr; Chorus; Color Guard; School Musical; School Play; Stage Crew; Variety Show; Numrs Music Comptns, 6-Tm Wnnr Yamaha Natl Elctv Fstvl Keybrds, Rgnls 85; Juilliard; Music.

THOMAS, CHRISTINE J; Penfield HS; Penfield, NY; (Y); 4-H; Orch; School Musical; JV Trk; Cit Awd; 4-H Awd; Hon Roll; Wrld Yth Symphny 84; E Mscl Fstvl Cncrt Wnnr 85; Rochester Phil Yth Orch 7 Yrs Prncpl 2 Yrs Soloist 86; Eastman Schl Music; Music Perf.

THOMAS, CRAIG; Hornell HS; Hornell, NY; (Y); Am Leg Boys St; Math Clb; JV Bsbl; Var Bsktbl; Var Capt Socr; High Hon Roll; NHS; Ntl Merit Ltr; Actrl Sci.

THOMAS, CRAIG O; Wellsville HS; Wellsville, NY; (Y); 10/118; Key Clb; Nwsp Stf; Stu Cncl; JV Bsktbl; Var JV Socr; NHS; Alfred U Sthrn Tier Schlrshp 86; Regents Schlrshp 86; Alfred U; Crmc Engr.

THOMAS, DARLENE; Franklin Acad; N Bangor, NY; (Y); Church Yth Grp; Hst FBLA; Hosp Aide; SADD; Epsilon Clb 86; 1st Plc Awds Flng & Bus Englsh 86; Hon Men ST Comptn Flng 86; Hudson Valley CC; Accntng.

THOMAS, DAWN; Greenwich Central Schl; Greenwich, NY; (Y); Trs Girl Scts; Band; Chorus; Var Cheerleading; Var Crs Cntry; Var Sftbl; Var Trk; High Hon Roll; NHS; Masonic Awd Ashlar Lodge 584 85; Mth Ed.

THOMAS, DAYANA; Commack HS South; Dix Hills, NY; (Y); 134/356; Office Aide; Teachers Aide; Stat Bsktbl; Var Mgr(s); Score Keeper; Var Socr; Var L Vllybl; Hon Roll; Gold Key Awd 86; Cedar Crest Coll; Nrsng.

THOMAS, DILIP; Half Hollow Hills High Schl East; Dix Hills, NY; (Y); 12/512; Computer Clb; Hosp Aide; SADD; Var Tennis; French Hon Soc; High Hon Roll; Hon Roll; Jr NHS; NHS; Ntl Merit Ltr; Frgn Lang Achvt Awd 83; Johns Hopkins U; Physician.

THOMAS, GEORGE; Murry Bergtraum HS; Brooklyn, NY; (Y); Boys Clb Am; Church Yth Grp; Computer Clb; Band; Church Choir; Jazz Band; Rep Sr Cls; Hon Roll; NHS; Awd For Excllnc Math Sci & Soc Stud 83-84; Math & Sci Awd 84-85; Math Sci & Comp Awd 85-86; Cornell; Elect Engr.

THOMAS, GEORGETTE; Tamarac HS; Troy, NY; (Y); 48/110; Boy Scts; Varsity Clb; Yrbk Stf; Off Soph Cls; Off Jr Cls; Off Sr Cls; JV Capt Bsktbl; JV Var Socr; Var Capt Sftbl; Outstndng SR Athlt 86; US Mrn Corps Dstngushd Athlt Awd 86; Brttnkl PTA Incntv Awd 86; Exec Secty.

THOMAS, JACALYN; Pulaski JR SR HS; Pulaski, NY; (S); Intnl Clb; Varsity Clb; Var L Bsktbl; Hon Roll; French Clb; Math Tm; Ski Clb; Band; Concert Band; Mrchg Band; Snow Enrchmnt Awd, Sprts Camp Schlrshp 85; Math Stdnt Awd 83.

THOMAS, JERRY; Canton HS; Canton, NY; (Y); Library Aide; Quiz Bowl; Stu Cncl; JV Socr; Stat Vllybl; High Hon Roll; Hon Roll; Law Enfrcmnt.

THOMAS, JOSEPH; Knox Memorial Central Schl; Russell, NY; (S); French Clb; Jazz Band; Mrchg Band; School Play; Yrbk Phtg; VP Stu Cncl; Var Bsbl; Var Socr; High Hon Roll; NHS; Oswego ST U; Meteorology.

THOMAS, JUSTIN; Fonda-Fultonville HS; Fonda, NY; (Y); 3/111; AFS; Nwsp Stf; Crs Cntry; Swmmng; Trk; High Hon Roll; NHS; U MI.

THOMAS, KAREN; Fashion Industries HS; Staten Island, NY; (Y); 124/324; Church Yth Grp; Dance Clb; Drama Clb; Office Aide; Teachers Aide; Concert Band; Variety Show; Yrbk Stf; Rep Stu Cncl; Capt Coach Actv; Cert Of Awd 1st Bb Clrnt 84; Cert Of Awd Sci Fair 84; Phys Ed Merit Awd 1s Tpl Osbstrcl Crse 85; Bus Managemnt.

THOMAS, KAREN; G Ray Bodley HS; Fulton, NY; (Y); Church Yth Grp; Drama Clb; Sec Trs Girl Scts; Latin Clb; Band; Church Choir; Concert Band; Mrchg Band; School Musical; Stage Crew; Acctg.

THOMAS, KATRINA; George Fowler HS; Syracuse, NY; (Y); FBLA; Office Aide; Pep Clb; Variety Show; Gym; Trk; High Hon Roll; Hon Roll; Prfct Atten Awd; Achvt Acad Schlrshp Merit Awd Engl 86; Outstndng Coop Yr Mutual NY 86; Spnsh & Sci Awd 85; Hofstra U; Bus Adm.

THOMAS, KELLI; Rome Free Acad; Rome, NY; (Y); 21/381; Intnl Clb; Trs Sr Cls; Var JV Fld Hcky; Sftbl; JV Vllybl; Hon Roll; Jr NHS; NHS; Pres Schlr; Key Clb; Regents Schlrshp 86; MIP Var Fld Hcky 84; Clarkson U; Engrng.

THOMAS, KELLY M; Whitesboro SR HS; Utica, NY; (Y); 15/350; SADD; Acpl Chr; Madrigals; School Musical; Swing Chorus; High Hon Roll; NHS; Drama Clb; Variety Show; Jr NHS; Sound Of Am Hnr Chrs 84; Drake Pres Founders Schlrshp 86; NYSSMA All St Mixed Chrs 86; Drake U; Pharm.

THOMAS, LEEMA; Martin Van Buren HS; Jamaica, NY; (Y); Church Yth Grp; Math Tm; Office Aide; Science Clb; Service Clb; Spanish Clb; Spanish NHS; Cert Mrt Engl, Spanish 86; Communications.

THOMAS, LEON W; Nazareth Regional HS; Brooklyn, NY; (S); 14/267; Church Yth Grp; JA; Concert Band; Jazz Band; Im Crs Cntry; Var Ftbl; Im Var Trk; High Hon Roll; Scholastic Bowl; Jass Ensmbl, Math & Comptr Certfs; Mech Engr.

THOMAS, LISA; Tully Central HS; Tully, NY; (Y); Church Yth Grp; French Clb; GAA; Girl Scts; Varsity Clb; Yrbk Stf; Off Frsh Cls; Off Soph Cls; Off Jr Cls; Off Sr Cls; Educ.

THOMAS, LISA RENEE; Uniondale HS; Hempstead, NY; (Y); Dance Clb; Girl Scts; Prfrmng Arts.

THOMAS, M; Park West HS; Bronx, NY; (Y); #1 In Class; Hon Roll; Val.

THOMAS, MAURICE P; Claude C Doxtator HS; Waterloo, NY; (Y); 111/155; Im Sftbl; Im Vllybl; Im Wt Lftg; Prfct Atten Awd; Accntng.

THOMAS, MELISSA; Holland Patent HS; Holland Patent, NY; (Y); School Play; Nwsp Ed-Chief; Nwsp Rptr; Nwsp Stf; Lit Mag; Var Powder Puff Ftbl; High Hon Roll; Hon Roll; Outstndng Svc Awd Editor Newspaper 85-86; Jrnlsm.

THOMAS, MERCY; Yonkers HS; Yonkers, NY; (Y); Church Yth Grp; Church Choir; Achcmnt Awd Ynkrs HS 86; Physcn Asst.

THOMAS, MIKE; John F Kennedy HS; Utica, NY; (Y); Church Yth Grp; Cmnty Wkr; Sci Lab Asst 84-86; Mohawk Vly CC; Bio.

THOMAS, OMILANA; Richmond Hill HS; S Ozole Pk, NY; (Y); 35/310; Office Aide; Chorus; Variety Show; Cheerleading; Hon Roll; Prfct Atten Awd; Spanish NHS; Engl Hnr Soc 84-86; Art Cartoonng Awd 85; NY U; TV Comm.

THOMAS, PAMELA; Park West HS; Brooklyn, NY; (Y); 5/483; Church Yth Grp; Cmnty Wkr; Dance Clb; Teachers Aide; Gov Hon Prg Awd; High Hon Roll; Hon Roll; Stonybrook U; Chld Psych.

THOMAS, PATTI; Lyndonville Central HS; Waterport, NY; (Y); 4/75; Computer Clb; Varsity Clb; Band; Color Guard; Cheerleading; High Hon Roll; NHS; Ntl Merit Ltr; NY ST Regents Schlrshp 86; SUNY Brockport; Nursng.

THOMAS, PATTI; Union Springs Acad; Blossvale, NY; (S); 5/45; Church Yth Grp; Library Aide; Teachers Aide; Band; Chorus; Church Choir; Concert Band; School Musical; Yrbk Stf; Off Soph Cls; Deans Awd 86; Atlantic Union Coll; Psych.

THOMAS, PAUL; Prospect Heights HS; Jamaica Queens, NY; (Y); FBLA; Socr; NHS; Natl Hnr Scty 86; Ftr Bus Ldrs Of Amer 85-86; Comp Prog.

THOMAS, RAQUEL-VANESSA; Acad Of Mount Saint Ursula; Bronx, NY; (Y); Cmnty Wkr; Girl Scts; Chorus; JV Var Cheerleading; NEDT Awd; Howard U; Bus Acctnt.

THOMAS, ROBERT; South Park HS; Buffalo, NY; (Y); Am Leg Boys St; Model UN; Yrbk Phtg; Rep Stu Cncl; Var L Swmmng; Bausch & Lomb Sci Awd; Hon Roll; Jr NHS; Pres NHS; SAR Awd.

THOMAS, ROBIN; Franklin Acad; Malone, NY; (Y); Pep Clb; Ski Clb; Varsity Clb; JV Var Cheerleading; Bus.

THOMAS, RUBY; Bushwick HS; Brooklyn, NY; (S); 20/233; Science Clb; Church Choir; School Play; Capt Badmtn; Capt Trk; L Vllybl; Prfct Atten Awd; Phrmcy.

THOMAS, SHARON; Skaneateles HS; Skaneateles, NY; (S); Church Yth Grp; Latin Clb; JV Bsktbl; JV Sftbl; High Hon Roll; NHS; Sunday Schl Tchr 84-85; Comp Sci.

THOMAS, STEVEN; Cicero-North Syracuse HS; North Syracuse, NY; (S); 95/667; Math Tm; Im Socr; JV Trk; Hon Roll; Planetry Sci.

THOMAS, SUJA; Albertus Magnus HS; Spring Valley, NY; (Y); Church Yth Grp; Cmnty Wkr; Debate Tm; Drama Clb; Hosp Aide; Chorus; Stage Crew; Yrbk Stf; Hon Roll; Mth Hnr Rl 86.

THOMAS, SUSAN; Beacon HS; Beacon, NY; (S); 1/150; French Clb; Key Clb; Trs Varsity Clb; Trs Soph Cls; Trs Jr Cls; Capt Cheerleading; Sftbl; High Hon Roll; Pres NHS; Val; Comp Sci.

THOMAS, SUSAN; Berlin Central Schl; Cherry Plain, NY; (Y); Girl Scts; Chorus; Mgr(s); Score Keeper; Cit Awd; Hon Roll; Prfct Atten Awd; Hudson Vly CC; Med Secy.

THOMAS, TAMMY; Dundee Central Schl; Dundee, NY; (Y); Band; Chorus; Church Choir; Color Guard; Concert Band; Mrchg Band; High Hon Roll; Hon Roll; A Avg Spansh II Awd 86; Gregg Shrthnd 60 Wpm 86; Bus.

THOMAS, TRACEY; Sauquoit Valley Central HS; Sauquoit, NY; (Y); 16/102; GAA; SADD; Chorus; Church Choir; Variety Show; Yrbk Stf; JV Bsktbl; Var Bowling; Var Fld Hcky; Var Sftbl; Scott Bennett Mem Awd $50 Awd 86; MSV In Sftbl 86; Highest Rgnts Mark In Bus Math 86; Hudson Vly Comm Clg; Dntl Hygne.

THOMAS, WENDY; Duanesburg Central HS; Delanson, NY; (Y); 4/70; Camera Clb; Band; Chorus; Concert Band; Jazz Band; Mrchg Band; Nwsp Phtg; Yrbk Phtg; Socr; NHS; Archtctr.

THOMAS, YVONDRIA; Edison Technical HS; Rochester, NY; (Y); Pres Church Yth Grp; Sec Church Choir; School Musical; Rep Jr Cls; Cit Awd; High Hon Roll; NHS; Prfct Atten Awd; Urban Lge Recog Of Blck Schlrs 86; Chldrns Mem Schlrshp 85-86; Graphc Dsgn.

THOMAS-SHAHEED, KALENA; Curtis HS; Staten Island, NY; (Y); Girl Scts; Hosp Aide; Library Aide; Gym; Med.

THOMASES, ANDREW N; Clarkstown HS; New City, NY; (Y); 9/450; Camera Clb; Math Clb; Math Tm; Science Clb; Concert Band; Yrbk Phtg; Im Swmmng; Var Trk; Bausch & Lomb Sci Awd; High Hon Roll; Gwu Outstndng JR In Sci 85; NY Acad Of Sci 85; Lederle Labs Schlrsp 86; Pta Schlrshp 86; Amherst Coll; Sci Phy.

THOMASSIAN, JAN; Westbury HS; Westbury, NY; (Y); 4/250; Church Yth Grp; Varsity Clb; Church Choir; Nwsp Stf; Yrbk Bus Mgr; VP Stu Cncl; Tennis; High Hon Roll; Pres NHS; Val; Harvard Bk Awd 86; Wheaton College.

THOMPSON, AMY; York Central Schl; Leicester, NY; (Y); Yrbk Stf; Sec Frsh Cls; Sec Soph Cls; Pres Jr Cls; Pres Sr Cls; Capt Bsktbl; Socr; Trk; Mgr VP Vllybl; Hon Roll; Bus Clss Rm Hnrs, Outstndng Athlte, Prom Chrprsn 85-86; CCFL; Bus.

THOMPSON, ANNE MARIE; Brewster HS; Patterson, NY; (Y); Spanish Clb; JV Var Cheerleading; MIP JV Chrldg; Mst Enthstc Chrldr.

THOMPSON, BRIGITT; Long Island Lutheran HS; Hempstead, NY; (S); Spanish Clb; SADD; Chorus; Church Choir; High Hon Roll; Hon Roll; NHS; Engl.

THOMPSON, CARLA; Wheatland Chili JR SR HS; Scottsville, NY; (Y); 7/75; Chorus; Concert Band; Jazz Band; Mrchg Band; School Musical; School Play; Var Stat Bsktbl; Cit Awd; Hon Roll; NHS; Plaque Outstndng Black Schlrs 86; Awd Outstndng Prfrmnc Engl 86; Rgnts Diploma 86; Brayant & Stratton; AOS.

THOMPSON, CARLTON E; South Side HS; Rockville Centre, NY; (Y); 32/285; Key Clb; JV Var Bsbl; JV Bsktbl; Bowling; High Hon Roll; Hon Roll; NHS; Ntl Merit Ltr; Natl Merit Scholar Pgm Outstdng Negro Stu Semi-Fin 85; Natl Merit Scholar Pgm Cmmnded Stu 85; Lat Awd; Bus.

THOMPSON, CAROL; Maryvale SR HS; Depew, NY; (Y); German Clb; GAA; Girl Scts; Chorus; Accntng.

THOMPSON, COLIN; Lake Lacid Central HS; Laurelton, NY; (Y); Boy Scts; Church Yth Grp; Cmnty Wkr; JA; Varsity Clb; Band; Church Choir; Jazz Band; Crs Cntry; Trk; ST U At Binghamton; Real Est.

THOMPSON, CONNIE; Addison Central Schl; Addison, NY; (Y); 20/110; Pres Church Yth Grp; Church Choir; High Hon Roll; NHS; Prfct Atten Awd; NY ST Regents Schlrshp Nrsng 86; Plattsburgh; Nrsng.

THOMPSON, DENISE; Bishop Loughlin Memorial HS; Brooklyn, NY; (Y); 19/232; Church Yth Grp; Cmnty Wkr; Computer Clb; Hosp Aide; Office Aide; Teachers Aide; Band; Jazz Band; Variety Show; Nwsp Stf; Altrnt Nrsng Rgnts Schlrshp 86; SR All Am Hll Fm Bnd Hnrs 86; Gld L&I Slvr L Awd 83-86; Pre-Med.

THOMPSON, DONNA; Windham-Ashland-Jewett Central HS; Jewett, NY; (S); 8/41; Drama Clb; French Clb; Chorus; Church Choir; School Play; Yrbk Stf; Pres Frsh Cls; Pres Sec Stu Cncl; Var Capt Cheerleading; Hon Roll; Mst Val Chrldr 85; Soclgy.

THOMPSON, EDWARD D; Msgr Farrell HS; Staten Island, NY; (Y); French Clb; Nwsp Sprt Ed; Off Stu Cncl; Im Bsktbl; Im Ftbl; Hon Roll; Rgnts Schlrshp; Villanova U; Lib Arts.

THOMPSON, GLENDA; Walton Central HS; Walton, NY; (Y); 8/96; AFS; Key Clb; Chorus; Yrbk Stf; Var Cheerleading; High Hon Roll; Schlrshp Pin Avg 90; Soc Wrk.

THOMPSON, HAYLEY; Midwood High Schl At Brooklyn Clg; Brooklyn, NY; (Y); 195/667; Model UN; Chorus; Church Choir; School Musical; Variety Show; Nwsp Stf; Cheerleading; Archon 86; Psych.

THOMPSON, JAMES M; Red Jacket HS; Shortsville, NY; (Y); Am Leg Boys St; Drama Clb; PAVAS; Chorus; Concert Band; Jazz Band; Madrigals; School Musical; School Play; Nwsp Ed-Chief; Ithaca Coll; Drama.

THOMPSON, JENNIFER; Schuylerville Central HS; Schuylerville, NY; (Y); French Clb; Math Tm; SADD; Band; Chorus; School Musical; Yrbk Ed-Chief; Fld Hcky; Jr NHS; NHS.

THOMPSON, JOHN; Rye HS; Rye, NY; (Y); Key Clb; Office Aide; Bsktbl; L Ftbl; Lcrss; Hon Roll; SPRTS Med.

THOMPSON II, JOHN R; Calasanctious Schl; Kenmore, NY; (Y); Math Tm; Ski Clb; Chorus; Church Choir; Madrigals; Yrbk Stf; Rennsalaer Poly Inst; Math.

THOMPSON, JOSEPH B; Johnson City HS; Johnson City, NY; (Y); Cmnty Wkr; Political Wkr; VP Ski Clb; Yrbk Phtg; Rep Stu Cncl; JV L Bsbl; Var L Bsktbl; Var L Ftbl; Var L Trk; Prfct Atten Awd; NY ST Regents Scholar 86; St Lawrence U Scholar 86-87; St Lawrence U; Pol Sci.

THOMPSON, KAREN; Kings Park SR HS; Kings Pk, NY; (Y); Art Clb; Church Yth Grp; Drama Clb; VP VICA; Chorus; Church Choir; Rep Frsh Cls; High Hon Roll; Outstndng Stu Awd 86; UICA 1st Pl Awd 86; Natl Lang Arts Olympiad-1st Pl 83; Suffolk Cnty CC; Data Prcsng.

THOMPSON, KARL; Evander Childs HS; Bronx, NY; (S); High Hon Roll; Hon Roll; Princeton U; Engrng.

THOMPSON, KATHY L; Palmyra-Macedon HS; Macedon, NY; (Y); 15/180; Hosp Aide; Hon Roll; Rgnts Schlrshp 86; Gregg Awd Typing 85; Hmcmng Princess 85; SUNY Brockport; Nrsng.

THOMPSON, KATRINA; Oakfield Alabama Central HS; Oakfield, NY; (Y); 5/93; French Clb; Math Clb; Band; Chorus; Church Choir; Jazz Band; Mrchg Band; Pres Frsh Cls; Stu Cncl; Var Crs Cntry; Rgnts Schlrshp; Amrys Schlr/Athlt Awd; Lions Clb Top 5 Schlrshp; Geneseo-SUNY.

THOMPSON, KEVIN; Silver Creek Central HS; Silver Creek, NY; (Y); 21/98; Church Yth Grp; Key Clb; Ski Clb; Varsity Clb; Band; Var Bsbl; Var Crs Cntry; Var Ftbl; Hon Roll; Rgnts Schlrshp 86; ST U Of NY Frdnia; Glgy.

THOMPSON, LORI; Naples HS; Naples, NY; (Y); 19/65; Spanish Clb; Band; Concert Band; Mrchg Band; Pres Soph Cls; Pres Jr Cls; Var Cheerleading; JV Var Socr; Var Sftbl; Hon Roll; Bus Mngmnt.

THOMPSON, MEG; Wilson Central HS; Burt, NY; (Y); SADD; Teachers Aide; JV Var Bsktbl; Var Fld Hcky; JV Var Sftbl; JV Var Vllybl; Hon Roll; Prfct Atten Awd; Office Aide; Band; Bsktbl All Leag, Fld Hocky All Leag, Sftbl All Leag 2nd Tm, 1st Tm; Ed.

THOMPSON, MICHAEL; Curtis HS; Staten Island, NY; (Y); Science Clb; Nwsp Rptr; Rep Jr Cls; VP Sr Cls; Rep Stu Cncl; L Trk; Hon Roll; NHS.

THOMPSON, MICHELE; Northport HS; East Northport, NY; (Y); 275/600; Am Leg Aux Girls St; Computer Clb; Intnl Clb; OEA; PAVAS; Service Clb; Spanish Clb; Acpl Chr; School Musical; School Play; C W Post U; Bus Fncng.

THOMPSON, MITZIE; Franklin HS; Rochester, NY; (Y); JA; Teachers Aide; Badmtn; Bsbl; Bsktbl; Socr; Sftbl; Swmmng; Tennis; Vllybl; Outstndng Achvt Sci Awd 84; Sec.

THOMPSON, PENNY; York Central Schl; Leicester, NY; (Y); 30/94; Yrbk Sprt Ed; Yrbk Stf; Var L Socr; Var L Sftbl; Var Capt Vllybl; Hon Roll; Kiwanis Awd; Sec Frsh Cls; Sec Soph Cls; Sec Jr Cls; MVP-VLLYBL 86; Lawrence H Smith Awd-Athltc Excllnc 86; Pres Awds-Phys Ed 84-86; SUNY Cortland; Phy Ed.

THOMPSON, PETE; Southwestern HS; Lakewood, NY; (Y); Am Leg Boys St; Church Yth Grp; German Clb; Natl Beta Clb; Ski Clb; Varsity Clb; Band; Var L Crs Cntry; Var L Trk; High Hon Roll; Hnr Soc 86; Bus.

THOMPSON, PHILLIP; Burgard Voc; Buffalo, NY; (Y); Aud/Vis; Camp Fr Inc; Debate Tm; Varsity Clb; VICA; Var Bsbl; Var Bsktbl; Var Ftbl; Var Trk; Navy.

THOMPSON, RENEE; Liberty Central HS; Liberty, NY; (Y); Chorus; Swing Chorus; Yrbk Sprt Ed; VP Sr Cls; Rep Stu Cncl; Var L Socr; JV Var Sftbl; High Hon Roll; Hon Roll; NHS; Area All St For Chorus 86; Rcvd Grade Of VA Solo Rtngs Sngng 86; Russel Sage Coll; Sec Ed.

THOMSEN, RICHARD; Wilson Central HS; Lockport, NY; (Y); 19/110; Boy Scts; Church Yth Grp; Cmnty Wkr; Math Clb; Science Clb; Spanish Clb; School Play; Bsktbl; Trk; Wrstlng; Pres Acadmc Ftnss Awd 86.

THOMPSON, SALLYANNE; Hamburg SR HS; Hamburg, NY; (Y); #78 In Class; German Clb; Library Aide; SADD; Chorus; Nwsp Ed-Chief; Lit Mag; Im JV Vllybl; Hon Roll; Zool.

THOMPSON, SHARON; Wilson Central HS; Burt, NY; (Y); Teachers Aide; JV Bsktbl; Hon Roll; Hlth.

THOMPSON, SHAWN; Sachem HS North; Holbrook, NY; (Y); 13/1600; Boy Scts; Math Tm; Ski Clb; Spanish Clb; Band; JV Gym; NHS; Ntl Merit SF; Superior Achvt-Spnsh; Hrbl Mntn-Socl Studies; 2nd Pl-Sachem Hstry Fair Paper; Georgetown; Stock Brkr.

THOMPSON, SUZANNE M; Hugh C Williams HS; Canton, NY; (Y); 9/115; Pres Exploring; French Clb; Teachers Aide; Varsity Clb; Yrbk Stf; Socr; Capt Trk; DAR Awd; High Hon Roll; NHS; Rgnts Schlrshp 86; Ntl Schlr Athlt Awd 86; Ntl Hnr Soc 85 & 86; Ithaca Coll; Physcl Thrpy.

THOMPSON, TAMMI; Midlakes HS; Phelps, NY; (Y); 34/150; VP Church Yth Grp; Dance Clb; French Clb; Library Aide; Church Choir; Stage Crew; Yrbk Stf; Timer; Var Trk; Hon Roll; Psych.

THOMPSON, TERESA; Charles D Amico Albion HS; Albion, NY; (Y); 12/176; Band; Concert Band; Drm & Bgl; Jazz Band; Mrchg Band; Symp Band; Ntl Merit Schol; Church Yth Grp; Computer Clb; Rochester Inst; Comptnl Math.

THOMSEN, BILL; Seaford HS; Seaford, NY; (Y); 105/250; Ice Hcky; Vllybl; Hon Roll; Rcqtbl 1st Pl 84-85; Rcqtbl 1st Pl 85-86; Mech Drwg II 1st Pl Mdl 84; Farmingdale Coll; Arch.

THOMSON, LAURA; Akron Central HS; Akron, NY; (Y); 4-H; FHA; Ski Clb; Band; Concert Band; Mrchg Band; Swmmng; Educ.

THOMSON, MARGUERITE; St Saviour HS; Brooklyn, NY; (Y); French Clb; Science Clb; Lit Mag; Im Vllybl; High Hon Roll; Hon Roll; NEDT Awd; St Schlr; Hofstra U; Intl Bus.

THORNDIKE, PATRICIA A; Emma Willard Schl; Troy, NY; (Y); Art Clb; Drama Clb; French Clb; PAVAS; School Musical; School Play; Stage Crew; Lit Mag; Pres Frsh Cls; Var Fld Hcky; Drama Awd 83; Actor.

THORNE, GARY; Seaford HS; Wantagh, NY; (S); Boy Scts; Exploring; Red Cross Aide; Band; Concert Band; Mrchg Band; Symp Band; Cit Awd; Elks Awd; Lion Awd; Rifle Tm Capt 85-86; Racqtbll Tm 85-86; St Johns; Law Enfrcmnt.

THORNE, MICHELE; Uniondale HS; Uniondale, NY; (Y); Dance Clb; Office Aide; SADD; Orch; Sec Stu Cncl; Var Capt Cheerleading; Schlstc Awd 84; Rsrch.

THORNHILL, TRACEY N; The Dalton Schl; Hollis, NY; (Y); Trs Church Yth Grp; Office Aide; Service Clb; Teachers Aide; Chorus; Church Choir; Yrbk Stf; Mgr(s); Soclgy.

THORNTON, JOCELYN; Chenango Forks HS; Binghamton, NY; (Y); 12/174; FBLA; Yrbk Bus Mgr; Trs Jr Cls; Trs Sr Cls; Rep Stu Cncl; Sftbl; High Hon Roll; NHS; Pres Schlr; Rotary Awd; Stu Of Yr In Hlth 86; Achvt In Englsh Hnrs 86.

THORNTON, KIM; Cazenovia HS; Manlius, NY; (Y); Chorus; Yrbk Stf; Hon Roll; C W Post Campus; Bus.

THORNTON, LISA; Clarkstown North HS; Mahwah, NJ; (Y); Csmtlgy.

THORNTON, NANCY; Mineola HS; Mineola, NY; (Y); FBLA; Mrchg Band; Rep Stu Cncl; Stat Bsktbl; Stat Lcrss; Pom Pon; JV Sftbl; Var Vllybl; High Hon Roll; NHS; Acctng.

THORNTON, TRACY; Hutchinson Technical Ctr; Buffalo, NY; (Y); Model UN; SADD; Drill Tm; Nwsp Stf; Yrbk Phtg; Yrbk Stf; Georgetown U; Med Tech.

THORP, CARINE; Watkins Glen HS; Hector, NY; (S); 11/128; Church Yth Grp; Library Aide; Quiz Bowl; Band; Church Choir; Concert Band; Mrchg Band; School Play; NHS; Equestrn Mgmt.

THORP, LAURA; Twin Tiers Baptist HS; Burdett, NY; (Y); 3/19; Chorus; Church Choir; Sec Frsh Cls; Rep Trs Soph Cls; Rep Trs Jr Cls; Var Bsktbl; JV Var Cheerleading; Var Capt Socr; Var Capt Vllybl; Hon Roll; Engl.

THORP, MARK ANDREW; Gananda HS; Walworth, NY; (Y); 3/36; Trs 4-H; French Clb; Ski Clb; JV Bsbl; High Hon Roll; Lion Awd; Pres NHS; Prfct Atten Awd; Pres Schlr; NY ST Regent Schlrshp 86; Houghton Coll Frshmn Acad Awd Schlrshp 86; Houghton Coll; Sci-Resrch.

THORPE, DASHIA A; John Jay HS; Brooklyn, NY; (Y); Drama Clb; Library Aide; Model UN; Office Aide; Color Guard; Drill Tm; School Musical; Stage Crew; Variety Show; Cheerleading; Deans List, Hnr Rll 82-84; John Jay Coll; Crmnl Jstc.

THORPE, LISA; John Dewey HS; Brooklyn, NY; (Y); Hosp Aide; Library Aide; Office Aide; Schlrshp Awd-Acadmc 83; Grwth & Prsnl Achvt-Co-Oprtv Educ 86; Frello H La Guardia CC; Accntn.

THORPE, STEVE; Jamestown HS; Jamestown, NY; (Y); French Clb; Ski Clb; Var Fld Hcky; Rochester Inst Of Tech; Chem.

THORPE, WILLIAM; G Ray Bodley HS; Fulton, NY; (Y); VP French Clb; Var Ice Hcky; Var Lcrss; Var Socr; High Hon Roll; Hon Roll; NHS; Soph Of The Year 84-85; 2nd Tn All-League In Hockey 85-86; 2nd All-County In Lacrosse 85-86; Engrg.

THRASHER, DAVID C; East Aurora HS; East Aurora, NY; (Y); 33/184; Spanish Clb; Varsity Clb; Bsktbl; Coach Actv; Socr; Tennis; Hon Roll; NHS; NY S Rgnts Schlr 86; Med.

THROM, PETER J; Iroquois HS; Elma, NY; (S); 42/300; Band; Chorus; Church Choir; Concert Band; Jazz Band; Mrchg Band; Pres Orch; Pep Band; School Musical; School Play; Prncpl Bassist Tanglewood Inst Orch 85; Grtr Bufflo Yth Orch Prncpl Bassist 85-86; Mst Musicl 85-86; Julliard Schl; Music.

THRONE, ELIZABETH A; Westhill HS; Syracuse, NY; (Y); Spanish Clb; Chorus; Nwsp Rptr; Nwsp Stf; Yrbk Stf; Lit Mag; Trk; Hon Roll; NHS; Cntrl NY Mdl Arcrft Assn Schlrshp 86; Advrstng.

THRONSEN, WENDY; Valley Central HS; Walden, NY; (Y); Pres Church Yth Grp; Debate Tm; Spanish Clb; Band; Concert Band; Mrchg Band; Orch; School Musical; Symp Band; Frsh Cls; Mus Ther.

THUMAN, JAMES; Islip Public HS; Islip, NY; (Y); 23/247; Jazz Band; Nwsp Phtg; Yrbk Phtg; Pres Schlr; US Army; Arbrn Rngr.

THUMM, WILLIAM T; John H Glenn HS; Greenlawn, NY; (Y); Am Leg Boys St; Boy Scts; ROTC; Band; Jazz Band; Lit Mag; Lcrss; Hon Roll; NHS; Chess Clb; NYSSMA Mtls 84-86; Engnrng.

THUNE, KELLY; Thousand Islands HS; Cape Vincent, NY; (Y); 15/80; AFS; Dance Clb; Band; Chorus; Jazz Band; School Musical; School Play; Swing Chorus; JV Var Cheerleading; JV Var Socr; All ST & Bi Cnty Band & Chorus 83-86; Amer Field Stu Abrd Stu To Finland 86; Music.

THURLOW, DAVID K; Horseheads HS; Horseheads, NY; (S); 14/380; Art Clb; JCL; Nwsp Rptr; Crs Cntry; Trk; High Hon Roll; Hon Roll; NHS; Ntl Merit Ltr; Var Lttrs, Hnrs 84-86; Yale; Biol.

THURSTON, MORGAN R; Newark Valley HS; Richford, NY; (Y); 8/120; Pres Varsity Clb; Pres Sr Cls; Rep Stu Cncl; Var Bsktbl; Var Ftbl; Var Golf; High Hon Roll; NHS; Rgnts Schlrshp 86; Cortland SUNY; Polit Sci.

TIAMSIC, MARY GRACE; St George Acad; Hollis, NY; (Y); 7/31; Computer Clb; Ski Clb; Stage Crew; Nwsp Phtg; Nwsp Rptr; Yrbk Phtg; Yrbk Stf; Pres Sr Cls; Vllybl; Hon Roll; Natl HS Awd Excllnc 86; Scholstc Achvt Awds 86; Fordham U; Comp Sci.

TIBERIA, THERESA; Vestal Central HS; Vestal, NY; (Y); Rep Church Yth Grp; Spanish Clb; SADD; Mrchg Band; Rep Jr Cls; Rep Cmnty Wkr; High Hon Roll; NHS; Drama Clb; Concert Band; Math.

TICHENSKY, DOUGLAS A; Red Creek JR SR HS; Red Creek, NY; (Y); School Play; Yrbk Stf; Var L Bsbl; Im Bsktbl; Im JV Socr; Im Vllybl; Im Wt Lftg; Hon Roll; Prfct Atten Awd; SUNY At Delhi; Constr Engrng.

TIDDICK, MISSY; Dryden JR SR HS; Dryden, NY; (Y); Spanish Clb; VP Frsh Cls; Rep Soph Cls; Rep Jr Cls; Rep Stu Cncl; Bsbl; JV Cheerleading; Mgr(s); High Hon Roll; Hon Roll; Long Island U; Psychlgy.

TIEDE, LYNN; Vilseck American HS; W Germany; (Y); 1/38; Model UN; SADD; Band; Lit Mag; Pres Stu Cncl; Mgr Tennis; Val; Church Yth Grp; Hosp Aide; JCL; JR Sci & Hum Symp Rgnl & Natl Rep 84-86; Intl Stu Ldrshp Inst Rep 85; Stu Of Yr Awd 86; Rhodes Coll; Intl Studies.

TIEDE, MARY; Alexander Central HS; E Bethany, NY; (Y); Sec Drama Clb; Math Tm; Band; Chorus; Variety Show; Trk; God Cntry Awd; Jr NHS; Lion Awd; NHS; Genesee Cnty Jr Miss Rep 86; Acadmc All Amer 86; Pre Law.

TIEDEMANN, KATIE; Skaneatles HS; Skaneateles, NY; (S); Model UN; Yrbk Stf; Rep Stu Cncl; Im Lcrss; Capt Var Socr; Capt Var Trk; High Hon Roll; Hon Roll; NHS; Church Yth Grp; Bus.

TIERNAN, JULIE; Norwood-Norfolk Central HS; Chase Mills, NY; (Y); Hon Roll; Hghst Shrthnd Rgnts Awd 86; Hghst Shrthnd, Hlth Aver Awds 85; Central City Bus Inst; Sectrl.

TIERNAN, STEVE; Potsdam SR HS; Potsdam, NY; (Y); 39/141; French Clb; Math Clb; Varsity Clb; Var L Ftbl; Var L Trk; Im Wt Lftg; Hon Roll; All Northern Conf Ftbl 85; Ntl Ldrshp Awd 85; Ntl Ftbl Achvt Awd 84-85; Forestry.

TIERNEY, ERIN; Nottingham HS; Syracuse, NY; (Y); Church Yth Grp; French Clb; Hosp Aide; Latin Clb; SADD; Chorus; Church Choir; Var Socr; Var L Sftbl; JV Trk; Slvr Mdl Natl Latn Exam Lvl 2 85; Slvr Mdl Natl Latn Exam Lvl 3 86.

TIETGEN, MARGARET; Honeoye Falls-Lima HS; Honeoye Falls, NY; (S); Cmnty Wkr; Hosp Aide; Variety Show; Sec Sr Cls; Rep Stu Cncl; Var JV Bsktbl; Var Capt Socr; Trk; Vllybl; High Hon Roll; Excell Achvt Latin & Sci 85; Chem Exam 85; Rochester Lilac Teen Pgm 85.

TIETJEN JR, HERMAN H; John Coleman HS; Rhinebeck, NY; (Y); Exploring; PAVAS; Stage Crew; Yrbk Stf; Var L Socr; Early Admssns Wister CC 87; Marist Coll; Comp Sci.

TIETJEN JR, JOHN C; Huntington HS; Huntington, NY; (Y); 34/380; Mathletes; Varsity Clb; Acpl Chr; Chorus; School Musical; School Play; Variety Show; Var Capt Socr; Jr NHS; NHS; Regents Scholar 86; SUNY Binghampton.

TIFFANY, LARS; Lafayette HS; Lafayette, NY; (S); 4/96; JA; Model UN; Yrbk Bus Mgr; Pres Jr Cls; Rep Stu Cncl; JV Var Bsktbl; Var Capt Ftbl; JV Var Lcrss; High Hon Roll; NHS; Vrsty Ftbl-2nd Tm All Leag Safty; Vrsty La Crosse-2nd Tm All Leag Defns.

TIFFANY, TERESA; Victor Central HS; Farmington, NY; (Y); 9/223; Sec Model UN; Concert Band; Mrchg Band; Var Crs Cntry; JV Socr; JV Vllybl; High Hon Roll; Lion Awd; NHS; SUNY Buffalo; Biochem.

TIGER, JANET L; Yeshiva University HS; Lawrence, NY; (Y); Temple Yth Grp; School Play; Ed Nwsp Rptr; JETS Awd; St Schlr; Doctor.

TILENIUS, ERIC W; Walt Whitman HS; Huntington Sta, NY; (Y); 3/549; VP Debate Tm; Mathletes; Band; Nwsp Ed-Chief; French Hon Soc; NHS; Ntl Merit SF; Computer Clb; French Clb; Latin Clb; Intl Comp Magzn Artcls Pblshd 84-86; Found Color Venture Comp Sftwr Co 85; VP & Nwsltr Ed Comp Clb 85; Bus.

TILIGADAS, MARGARITA; Bronx HS Of Science; Flushing, NY; (Y); Camera Clb; French Clb; Math Clb; Political Wkr; Chorus; Yrbk Phtg; Im Vllybl; Hon Roll; NHS; Ntl Merit Ltr; UIT Schlrshp 86; Harvard.

TILLIS, MARIA E; Seton Catholic Central HS; Vestal, NY; (Y); Am Leg Aux Girls St; SADD; Varsity Clb; Rep Jr Cls; Rep Sr Cls; Rep Stu Cncl; Cheerleading; Pom Pon; High Hon Roll; NHS.

TILLMAN, JOHN; Corning-Painted Post West HS; Painted Post, NY; (Y); 20/386; JA; Key Clb; Political Wkr; Varsity Clb; Yrbk Bus Mgr; Yrbk Ed-Chief; Pres Frsh Cls; Pres Soph Cls; Pres Jr Cls; Stu Cncl; Bus.

TILLMAN, MARIA; Mount Vernon HS; Mt Vernon, NY; (Y); Church Yth Grp; Church Choir; Soc Sec Adm Spec Act Svc Awd 85.

TILLOTSON, JOHN W; Marathon Central Schl; Marathon, NY; (Y); 1/64; Am Leg Boys St; Quiz Bowl; Pres Jr Cls; Var Bsbl; Var L Bsktbl; Var Capt Socr; Bausch & Lomb Sci Awd; NHS; Rnsslr Polytech Inst Math Sci Awd 86; Intl Allnc Thtrcl Stg Emplyees Lcl No 9 Schlrshp 86; Engnrng.

TILLOTSON, WILLIAM MICHAEL; Fairport HS; Fairport, NY; (Y); Ski Clb; Stu Cncl; JV Bsbl; JV Ftbl; Hon Roll; Corprt Law.

TIMAN, RANDIELLEN; Carmel HS; Carmel, NY; (Y); Band; Orch; Yrbk Stf; Capt Bsktbl; Socr; Vllybl; High Hon Roll; Hon Roll; NHS; Prfct Atten Awd; Scl Wrk.

TIMBERLAKE, SANDRA; Frankfurt American HS; Apo New York, NY; (Y); Sec Trs Art Clb; Drama Clb; Speech Tm; Thesps; School Play; Powder Puff Ftbl; Prfct Atten Awd; Pres Fitness Awd 83-84.

TIMERMAN, DAN; La Fargeville Central Schl; La Fargeville, NY; (Y); 1/38; Quiz Bowl; Chorus; Jazz Band; School Musical; VP Stu Cncl; JV Var Bsktbl; Var Socr; NHS; Val; Church Yth Grp; Pres Clsrm Young Amer; Louis Armstrong Jazz Awd; U Of FL; Ag Sci.

TIMERSON, MICHELLE; C W Baker HS; Baldwinsville, NY; (Y); Drama Clb; Letterman Clb; Teachers Aide; Thesps; Concert Band; Flag Corp; Jazz Band; School Musical; School Play; Var L Swmmng.

TIMM, ELIZABETH; Walter Panas HS; Peekskill, NY; (Y); Teachers Aide; Chorus; Hon Roll; Inter Ethnc Clb 83-84; Intr Dsgn.

TIMMERMAN, WENDY; Little Falls JR SR HS; Little Falls, NY; (Y); 6/96; Church Yth Grp; GAA; Girl Scts; Band; Concert Band; Nwsp Rptr; Badmtn; Fld Hcky; High Hon Roll; NHS; SR Incntv Awd 86; Alfred Pres Schlrshp 86; Alfred U; Psych.

TIMMONS, APRIL; Trott Vocational HS; Croton-On-Hudson, NY; (Y); 9/147; Med Prof.

TIMOFY, CHRISTINA; Solray HS; Solvay, NY; (Y); Ski Clb; Spanish Clb; Chorus; Concert Band; Yrbk Ed-Chief; Frsh Cls; Soph Cls; Jr Cls; Hon Roll; Awd Band & Chorus 86; Stengrphr.

TIMONY, JOHN; Archbishop Molloy HS; Belle Harbor, NY; (Y); 188/383; Computer Clb; Im Bsktbl; Im Ftbl; Var Trk; Mst Imprvd Stdnt Acdmcly 84.

TIMOTHY, KELLY; Avoca Central HS; Bath, NY; (Y); 12/41; Boy Scts; French Clb; Chorus; JV Var Bsbl; JV Ftbl; Hon Roll; Genessee CC; Conservtn.

TINDALE, TOMAS M; Bishop Kearney HS; Rochester, NY; (Y); JV Ftbl; Hon Roll; Rgnts Schlrshp 86; Monroe CC; Indstrl Math.

TINDALL, JENNIFER; Westhill SR HS; Syracuse, NY; (S); 6/126; AFS; Church Yth Grp; Exploring; Pres Spanish Clb; Var JV Bsktbl; Var Crs Cntry; Var Trk; Hon Roll; Prfct Atten Awd; All Cty Hnrbl Mntn Bsktbl 84-85; Ntl Hnr Soc 85-86; Phy Thrpy.

TINGLEY, JIM; Canisteo Central HS; Canisteo, NY; (Y); Am Leg Boys St; Church Yth Grp; Cmnty Wkr; Ski Clb; Im Bsbl; JV L Bsktbl; Var JV Ftbl; Im Tennis; Var L Trk; Bio.

TINNEY, LYNN; John Dewey HS; Brooklyn, NY; (Y); Dance Clb; Debate Tm; PAVAS; Teachers Aide; School Musical; School Play; Stage Crew; Variety Show; Rep Frsh Cls; Bowling; Bwlng Awd 86; Advrtsg.

TINSLEY, MARK; Fairport HS; Fairport, NY; (Y); Ski Clb; SADD; Im Bsbl; Im Bsktbl; Im Ftbl; Im Sftbl; Engr.

TINSLEY, TYWANDA; Mount Vernon HS; Mt Vernon, NY; (Y); Cmnty Wkr; Dance Clb; Spanish Clb; Chorus; School Musical; Cheerleading; Hon Roll; NHS; CPA Clb Sec; Black Unity Clb; Acctg.

TINSLEY, WANDA; Murry Bergtraum HS; Brooklyn, NY; (Y); Teachers Aide; Trk; Prfct Atten Awd; Paralgl.

TINSMON, MICHAEL; Greece Athena SR HS; Rochester, NY; (Y); 16/310; Computer Clb; German Clb; Ski Clb; Var JV Bsbl; High Hon Roll; Hon Roll; Jr NHS; NHS.

TIRADO, DAISY; Grace Dodge Vocational HS; Bronx, NY; (Y); Yrbk Stf; Bkkpng Hnrs Awd 85; Engl Hnrs Awd 86; Jrnlsm Hnrs Awd 85; Acct.

TIRADO, PAUL; St Agnes HS; Manhattan, NY; (Y); 3/97; Cmnty Wkr; Dance Clb; VP JA; Model UN; Yrbk Ed-Chief; Sec Stu Cncl; Wt Lftg; High Hon Roll; VP NHS; Ntl Merit SF; Ntl Hspnc Schlr Awd Pgm Semifnlst 86; Most Lkly To Succeed 86; Ldrshp Trng Awd 84; Harvard U; Bus Adm.

TIRALONGO, FRANK; Bishop Ford CC HS; Brooklyn, NY; (Y); 15/400; Dance Clb; Key Clb; Red Cross Aide; Science Clb; Service Clb; Variety Show; Stu Cncl; Score Keeper; Socr; Schwartz Coll; Phrmcy.

TIRANNO, LISA; Williamsville South HS; Williamsville, NY; (Y); Hosp Aide; Pep Clb; Red Cross Aide; Ski Clb; SADD; Varsity Clb; Rep Frsh Cls; Rep Soph Cls; Rep Jr Cls; Var Gym; Bus Mgmt.

TIRRITO, LOUISE; Farmingdale HS; Farmindale, NY; (Y); 126/600; Trs 4-H; Girl Scts; Hon Roll; Merit Roll; Math Awd; Katherine Gibbs; Accntng.

TISDALE, LORANCE; Edison Technical HS; Rochester, NY; (Y); Boy Scts; Math Tm; Science Clb; Teachers Aide; Variety Show; JV Var Bsktbl; JV Var Ftbl; JV Var Trk; High Hon Roll; Hon Roll; Ftbl,Track John Kiggins Athlete Awd 85-86; Comp Sci.

TISI, ARTIE; Moore Cathlic HS; Staten Island, NY; (Y); 8/183; Library Aide; Math Tm; SADD; Yrbk Stf; Swmmng; High Hon Roll; NHS; Cert Acdmc Excllnc 85-86; ALISI Itln Lvl II Cntst 2nd Pl 86; Acdmc All-Amrcn 85-86; Pre-Med.

TITONE, JILL J; Roy C Ketcham HS; Wapp Fls, NY; (Y); 35/500; Drama Clb; Thesps; School Musical; School Play; Rep Stu Cncl; Stat Var Bsktbl; JV Capt Socr; High Hon Roll; NHS; Church Yth Grp; NYS Rgnts Schlrshp 86; Georgetown U; Nrsng.

TITTEMORE, SHARON; Mahopac HS; Mahopac, NY; (Y); 42/420; Band; Concert Band; Drm Mjr(t); Mrchg Band; Orch; Pep Band; JV Bsktbl; Stat Crs Cntry; Stat Lcrss; Mgr(s); Rtry Intl Ldrshp Cnfrnc Schlrshp 85; Pre-Law.

TITTERTON, JOHN; Cold Spring Harbor HS; Huntington, NY; (Y); 2/127; Concert Band; Jazz Band; Nwsp Rptr; Var Bsktbl; Var Lcrss; Var Capt Socr; High Hon Roll; NHS; Hrvrd Bk Awd 86.

TITUS, LYNELLE; Evander Childs HS; Bronx, NY; (S); 11/383; Variety Show; Lit Mag; Var Vllybl; Prfct Atten Awd; Hnr Schl 83; Apieta-Supr Schlrshp Ctznshp, Svc 85; Big E Clb 85.

TIWARI, JAGDEESH; Newton HS; Hollis, NY; (Y); 11/784; Computer Clb; Math Clb; Science Clb; Orch; Sftbl; Vllybl; High Hon Roll; JETS Awd; Prfct Atten Awd; Outstndng Achvt In Acad Extra Curricular Actvts 85; Cert Of Hnr 85; Cert Of Merit In Soc Studies 84; Engnrng.

TLOCKOWSKI, MICHAEL; Hampton Bays HS; Hampton Bays, NY; (Y); 14/115; Science Clb; Chorus; School Musical; Pres Frsh Cls; Pres Soph Cls; Pres Jr Cls; VP Stu Cncl; Hon Roll; Ecnmcs.

TO, ANGELA; Curtis HS; Staten Island, NY; (Y); Cmnty Wkr; VP Pres Key Clb; Science Clb; Teachers Aide; Varsity Clb; Nwsp Stf; Capt Cheerleading; Var Gym; Pride Of Yankees Outstndg Achvt In Acad 85.

TO, EDWARD HA; Brooklyn Technical HS; Elmhurst, NY; (Y); 40/1159; Chess Clb; Computer Clb; Debate Tm; Exploring; Math Clb; Math Tm; Pres Science Clb; Service Clb; Ed Lit Mag; High Hon Roll; CIT Acad Schrslhp 86; NY Acad Sci 83-86; Case Western Reserve U; Elect.

TOAL, KEVIN; Alexander Central HS; Alexander, NY; (Y); Chorus; Prfct Atten Awd; Air Force.

TOBACK, ALLEGRA; New Rochelle HS; New Rochelle, NY; (Y); Drama Clb; French Clb; Teachers Aide; Temple Yth Grp; Acpl Chr; Band; Chorus; Church Choir; Concert Band; Mrchg Band; Music Honors Soc 85-87; Temple Awd For Achievement & Music; Westchester Co Youth Symphony & Chorus; Liberal Arts.

TOBAR, SILVIA; Freeport HS; Freeport, NY; (Y); 14/450; Art Clb; French Clb; Spanish Clb; Teachers Aide; Chorus; Lit Mag; High Hon Roll; Hon Roll; NHS; Tchr Aid Assn Schlrshp 86; NY U Trste Schlrshp 86; Athena Clb Freeprt Memrl Schlrshp 86; NY U.

TOBIN, BRIAN; St Marys Boys HS; Port Washington, NY; (S); 18/147; Yrbk Stf; Rep Frsh Cls; Stu Cncl; Im Bsktbl; JV Crs Cntry; Im Fld Hcky; JV Var Lcrss; Hon Roll; NHS; Mount Saint Marys; Bus.

TOBIN, DOUGLAS; Long Island Lutheran HS; Woodbury, NY; (S); Aud/Vis; Church Yth Grp; Stage Crew; Var Socr; Var Wrstlng; Hon Roll; Jr NHS; NHS.

TOBIN, KELLY; Eldred Central HS; Pond Eddy, NY; (Y); 5/32; Ski Clb; Varsity Clb; Band; Chorus; Yrbk Stf; Trs Soph Cls; Pres Jr Cls; Pres Sr Cls; Var L Bsktbl; Var L Socr; U Of Scranton; Scndry Educ.

TOBIN, KEVIN; Wm E Grady Vo Tech; Brooklyn, NY; (Y); 30/318; Aud/Vis; Service Clb; Stage Crew; Bowling; High Hon Roll; Donald M Halpern Schl Svc Awd; Dept Awd In Broadcasting Tech; Wm E Grady Archon Soc; Cntr For Media Arts; Video Main.

TOBIN, REGINA; Cicero-North Syracuse HS; N Syracuse, NY; (S); 5/667; Church Yth Grp; Lit Mag; Stu Cncl; Hon Roll; NHS.

TOBIN, TRACEY; Rye HS; Rye, NY; (Y); Cmnty Wkr; Var Socr; Var Vllybl; High Hon Roll; Hon Roll; NHS; B Nai Brith Awd 86.

TOBIN, WILLIAM DAVID; Pelham Memorial HS; Pelham Manor, NY; (Y); Camera Clb; Drama Clb; Radio Clb; Ski Clb; School Play; Rep Frsh Cls; Rep Soph Cls; Rep Jr Cls; JV Var Ftbl; Hon Roll; Latin Natl Exam Magna Cum Laude 84; Eng.

TOBON, LYNN D; Moore Catholic HS; Staten Island, NY; (Y); 5/176; Church Yth Grp; Cmnty Wkr; French Clb; Math Tm; Chorus; Stage Crew; Lit Mag; High Hon Roll; Sec NHS; Ntl Merit Ltr; Drew U.

TOCH, SIPHANNY; Seward Park HS; New York, NY; (Y); Quiz Bowl; Teachers Aide; High Hon Roll; Amelia Ashe Awd 86.

TOCKARSHEWSKY, ROBERT; Saint Francis Prep; Flushing, NY; (Y); 191/653; Am Leg Boys St; Pres Stu Cncl; L Bsktbl; Var L Trk; Im Vllybl; DAR Awd; Prfct Atten Awd; NY ST Rgnst Schlrshp 85-86; Stu Athlt Awd 83; Stu Ldrshp Awd 86; Fairfield U; Finc.

TODARO, JEFFERY J; John F Kennedy HS; Buffalo, NY; (Y); 33/148; Var Boy Scts; Var ROTC; Var Varsity Clb; Var Jazz Band; Yrbk Stf; Var Bsbl; Var Bsktbl; Var Ftbl; St Schlr; Computer Clb; Syracuse U; Mltry Ofcr.

TODARO, KRISTIN L; Eden SR HS; Eden, NY; (Y); 33/166; Computer Clb; Ski Clb; Band; School Play; Rep Sr Cls; L Cheerleading; JV Tennis; JV Trk; NHS; Aud/Vis; Regents Schlrshp Winner; Allegheny Coll; Intl Bus.

TODD, ANDREA L; Haverling Central Schl; Bath, NY; (Y); 17/112; Church Yth Grp; JCL; Latin Clb; Band; Concert Band; Mrchg Band; Orch; School Musical; High Hon Roll; Rgnts Schlrshp 86; Oneonta ST; Engl.

TODD, CATHY; Hornell SR HS; Hornell, NY; (Y); Dance Clb; JCL; Ski Clb; Trs Frsh Cls; Rep Stu Cncl; JV Capt Cheerleading; Coach Actv; JV Var Pom Pon; High Hon Roll; Ntl Merit Ltr; Bus.

TODD, DOUG; Schalmont HS; Schenectady, NY; (Y); Exploring; JV Ftbl; JV Trk; Prfct Atten Awd; Original Compostn 84-85; 5-K-3rd Brnz 83; Elec Engrng.

TODD, MICHAEL; Saranac Lake HS; Saranac Lk, NY; (Y); 42/132; Church Yth Grp; Cmnty Wkr; Letterman Clb; School Musical; Var Capt Ftbl; Var Capt Ftbl; Var Capt Trk; Mst Outstndng Athl Hockey, Ftbl & Track 85-86; Mst All Around Athl SLMS, 5th St Trck, Schl Rylty 86; SUNY Potsdam; Bus Admin.

TODISCO, PAUL; Cicero North Syracuse HS; N Syracuse, NY; (S); 18/623; Computer Clb; Band; Concert Band; Jazz Band; Orch; Lit Mag; Tennis; High Hon Roll; NHS; Mensa 84; Natl Hstry & Govt Awd 86; Prodgy Inc Piano 84-86.

TOELSIN, CHRISTINE; Sweet Home SR HS; Amherst, NY; (Y); Church Yth Grp; GAA; SADD; School Musical; Stu Cncl; Bsktbl; Cheerleading; Socr; Hon Roll; JR All ST Chorus 83; JR Erie County Chorus 84; Sociology.

TOENNIESSEN, AMY; Desales Catholic HS; Lockport, NY; (Y); 4/33; Am Leg Aux Girls St; Ski Clb; Nwsp Stf; Yrbk Stf; Capt Cheerleading; Vllybl; DAR Awd; Hon Roll; Ntl Merit Ltr; Rev Jhn Duggn Awd; Jr Svc Leag Awd; Nazareth; Bus Admn.

TOENNIESSEN, SCOTT P; Newfane SR HS; Newfane, NY; (S); #9 In Class; Camera Clb; Computer Clb; Exploring; 4-H; Band; Concert Band; Jazz Band; Pep Band; School Musical; Symp Band; Outstndng Bnd Hnr 84-85; Comp Sci.

TOEPFER, JENENE; Villa Maria Acad; Buffalo, NY; (Y); Hon Roll; E Clntn Cmmnty Cncl Go For It Clb Pres 83-84; Phy Thrpy.

TOGAMI, TAKAKO; Bayside HS; Bayside, NY; (Y); 18/658; Orch; Hon Roll; Math Tm; Office Aide; PAVAS; Rgnts Schlrshp 86; NYU; Intl Bus.

TOHILL, THOMAS; Sachem North HS; Lk Ronkonkoma, NY; (Y); CAP; Radio Clb; Im Timer; Im Wrstlng; Cmmnctn.

TOIA, PHILIP F; Bishop Grimes HS; Syracuse, NY; (S); Church Yth Grp; Exploring; Math Clb; Math Tm; Science Clb; Rep Frsh Cls; Sec Stu Cncl; High Hon Roll; Aero Engrng.

TOJEIRA, MARIA; New Utrecht HS; Brooklyn, NY; (Y); 3/518; Key Clb; Band; Mrchg Band; Ed Nwsp Ed-Chief; Nwsp Rptr; Yrbk Ed-Chief; Lit Mag; Gov Hon Prg Awd; JP Sousa Awd; NHS; Bay Ridge Fstvl Of Arts 86; Cthlc Tchrs Assoc Schlrshp 86; Rgnts Schlrshp 86; Fordham U; Jrnlsm.

TOKAR, RICHARD S; South Seneca HS; Ovid, NY; (Y); 9/85; Am Leg Boys St; Varsity Clb; Band; Chorus; Jazz Band; School Play; Var L Bsktbl; Var Ftbl; Var L Tennis; Hon Roll.

TOKARCZYK, THERESA A; Frontier Central HS; Hamburg, NY; (Y); 9/500; Cmnty Wkr; Sec Spanish Clb; Stu Cncl; High Hon Roll; Hon Roll; NHS; Prfct Atten Awd; Cert Of Mrt For Sci Fair 84; Wstrn NY Sci Cngrs Cert 84; MBA; Bus Admin.

TOKARSKA, BARBARA; St Johns Prep; Brooklyn, NY; (Y); 1/458; Am Leg Aux Girls St; Rep Soph Cls; Rep Jr Cls; Rep Sr Cls; Rep Stu Cncl; High Hon Roll; VP Jr NHS; VP NHS; NY ST Regents Schlrshp 86; Natl Sci Olympiad In Bio 83; Gov Committee Awd 86; Math.

TOKASH, WILLIAM; Grand Island SR HS; Grand Isl, NY; (Y); Letterman Clb; Ski Clb; Varsity Clb; Swmmng; Hon Roll; Canadian Math Cmptn Top 25% 84; SUNY Buffalo; Med.

TOLEDANO, KEVIN; Mahopac HS; Mahopac, NY; (Y); 2/410; Math Tm; Science Clb; JV Ftbl; Im Wt Lftg; Im Wrstlng; High Hon Roll; NHS; Sci Stu Of Mnth 85; Elec Engrng.

TOLEDO, PATRICIA; Dodge V HS; Bronx, NY; (Y); Nwsp Rptr; Sec Jr Cls.

TOLEDO, REBECCA; Norman Thomas HS; Bronx, NY; (S); DECA; Orch; Jr Cls; DECA Ldrshp Training Camp Public Spkng 3rd Pl 85; DECA Rgnl Comptn Public Spkng 2nd Pl 86; Johnson & Wales Coll; Mgt.

TOLEDO, SYLVIA C; Walton HS; Bronx, NY; (Y); Computer Clb; FTA; Scholastic Bowl; Yrbk Phtg; Yrbk Stf; Tennis; Vllybl; Cit Awd; Jr NHS; NHS.

TOLENTINO, EUGENIA; Academy Of Saint Joseph; Great River, NY; (Y); Hosp Aide; Sec Pep Clb; Stage Crew; Yrbk Stf; Sec Frsh Cls; JV Bsktbl; Var Tennis; Ntl Merit Ltr; NEDT Awd; NY ST Regents Schlrsp 86; Creighton U.

TOLENTO, GINA; Moore Catholic HS; Staten Island, NY; (Y); French Clb; Math Tm; Nwsp Rptr; Yrbk Phtg; Pres Rep Soph Cls; Pres Rep Jr Cls; Sftbl; High Hon Roll; NHS; Ntl Merit Ltr; Bsktbl Coachs Awd 85; Brooklyn Coll; Pre-Med.

TOLESON, MITCHELL C; Paul V Moore HS; Constantia, NY; (Y); 55/286; Am Leg Boys St; Exploring; ROTC; Rep Stu Cncl; Im JV Bsbl; Hon Roll; SUNY Buffalo; Engrng.

TOLKIN, MATT; Xavier HS; New York, NY; (Y); Boys Clb Am; Var Socr; Hon Roll; Advncd Plcmnt Hist; Rugby Tm E Cst Champshp Wnrs Vars.

TOLLIVER, JOEL E; Charles H Roth HS; W Henrietta, NY; (Y); Spanish Clb; Concert Band; Var Ftbl; Var Trk; Var Wt Lftg; High Hon Roll; Hon Roll; NHS; Spanish NHS; Varsity Clb; Acad Ltr 86; Engrng.

TOM, ANNIE; St Francis Prep; Bayside, NY; (S); 181/653; Girl Scts; Library Aide; VP Band; Concert Band; Mrchg Band; Im Sftbl; JV Im Tennis; JV Trk; Im Vllybl; Opt Clb Awd; Preprof Med.

TOMA, MICHAEL; Mechanicville HS; Mechanicville, NY; (S); 25/106; Church Yth Grp; Cmnty Wkr; Ski Clb; Spanish Clb; SADD; Band; Mrchg Band; VP Frsh Cls; Rep Soph Cls; Trs Jr Cls; Siena Coll; Accntng.

TOMAINE, MAUREEN; Union-Endicott HS; Endicott, NY; (Y); Key Clb; Pep Clb; Band; Flag Corp; Mrchg Band; Hon Roll; Rstrnt Mgmt.

TOMAKA, RICH; Hamburg SR HS; Hamburg, NY; (Y); 97/387; DECA; Band; Variety Show; JV Bsbl; 300 Game At Hamburg Legion Lanes Jr Easter Tournament; Vincennes; Bus.

TOMALTY, DEREK; Potsdam Central HS; Potsdam, NY; (Y); 13/130; AFS; Church Yth Grp; Computer Clb; Sec Exploring; Math Clb; Model UN; Hon Roll; NHS; Clarkson U; Mech/Aerospace Eng.

TOMAN, PETER M; Earl C Vandermeulen HS; Port Jefferson, NY; (Y); 43/300; French Clb; Leo Clb; SADD; Nwsp Stf; Yrbk Stf; Im Bsbl; JV Socr; NHS; Rutgers; Engrng.

TOMASELLO, ANGELO; Cardinal O Hara HS; Buffalo, NY; (Y); Capt Ftbl; Canisius Coll; Bus Finance.

TOMASINI, HEATHER; East Islip HS; E Islip, NY; (Y); 81/425; Church Yth Grp; Pep Clb; SADD; Varsity Clb; JV Capt Cheerleading; JV Var Tennis; JV Trk; Var Vllybl; Hon Roll; Hst Jr NHS; PACE U; Intl Bus.

TOMASINI, JENNY; Charles E Gorton HS; Yonkers, NY; (Y); 10/191; Spanish Clb; Band; Stage Crew; Nwsp Stf; Yrbk Stf; Lit Mag; Hon Roll; NHS; Edwn G Mchlln Schlrshp 86; Cntry Hnrs Clb 82-86; Sklly Olympcs 84-85; Westchester CC; Food Svc.

TOMASINO, CARRIE; Wayne Central HS; Macedon, NY; (Y); 44/184; Girl Scts; SADD; Chorus; Concert Band; Mrchg Band; School Musical; Hon Roll; Cheerleading; Vet.

TOMASZEWSKI, CHRISTINE; South Side HS; Rockville Centre, NY; (Y); 25/278; 4-H; French Clb; Key Clb; Mathletes; Science Clb; 4-H Awd; High Hon Roll; Jr NHS; NHS; Bus.

TOMASZEWSKI, REGINA; Alexander Central HS; Alexander, NY; (Y); AFS; 4-H; Teachers Aide; Concert Band; Jazz Band; Mrchg Band; Band-Stu Of Mth 84; Band-Solo Fstvl Awds 85-86; Cncrt Band-Mst Imprvd Sec 83-84; Comp Pgmr.

TOMB, STEPHEN; Notre Dame-Bishop Gibbons HS; Ballston Lk, NY; (Y); Pep Clb; Ski Clb; SADD; Varsity Clb; Stu Cncl; Bsktbl; Ftbl; Trk; Hon Roll; Springfield; Ed.

TOMBLINE, PATRICE; Brewster HS; Brewster, NY; (Y); 1/210; Varsity Clb; Nwsp Ed-Chief; Nwsp Rptr; Lit Mag; Rep Stu Cncl; Tennis; High Hon Roll; NHS; Spanish NHS; Voice Dem Awd.

TOMCZAK, KIM; Nazareth Acad; Rochester, NY; (Y); 13/152; JA; Library Aide; NFL; Stage Crew; Nwsp Rptr; Nwsp Stf; Yrbk Rptr; Yrbk Stf; Lit Mag; Stu Cncl; Ithaca Coll Schlrshp 86; JR Ftr Secr Clb Typng Excllnc Awd 85; St John Fisher Coll; Jrnlsm.

TOMIC, JERRY; Longwood HS; Shirley, NY; (Y); Math Clb; Math Tm; Yrbk Rptr; Yrbk Stf; High Hon Roll; Hon Roll; Suffolk Cnty Acadmc Decathlon 84-86; NY U; Bus.

TOMILO, LAURIE; Lackawanna SR HS; Lackawanna, NY; (Y); French Clb; Band; Concert Band; Mrchg Band; High Hon Roll; NHS; Csmtlgy.

TOMILOWICZ, LYNN; Our Lady Of Victory Acad; Yonkers, NY; (S); 9/157; Drama Clb; Sec Spanish Clb; Nwsp Stf; Off Frsh Cls; Off Soph Cls; Hon Roll; NHS; Spanish NHS; Part Scholar Ou Lady Of Victory; Dietcn.

TOMITA, MASAHIRO; Fox Lane HS; Mt Kisco, NY; (Y); #89 In Class; Boys Clb Am; Golf; Wrstlng; Engrng.

TOMKOSKY, MICHAEL; Charles H Roth HS; Henrietta, NY; (Y); Cmnty Wkr; Varsity Clb; Capt Var Ftbl; JV Lcrss; Wt Lftg; Var Capt Wrstlng; High Hon Roll; Hon Roll; Jr NHS; Ntl Merit Ltr; Outstndng Awd-Monroe Cnty Tech Educ Assn 85; Alfred U; Psych.

TOMLINSON, GREGG G; Broadalbin HS; Broadalbin, NY; (Y); Drama Clb; Letterman Clb; Church Choir; Lit Mag; Socr; Trk; Cit Awd; High Hon Roll; Pres Vrsty Ltrmn Club 86; Mst Dedictd In Soccer 85; FHCC; Criminal Law.

TOMLINSON, HEWAN K; High Schl Of Music & The Arts; New York, NY; (Y); 4/121; Rep Jr Cls; Rep Sr Cls; Rep Stu Cncl; Hon Roll; Prfct Atten Awd; Mayors Hnr Roll 82-85; Princtn U; Dancer.

TOMLINSON, RICHARD W; Pine Valley Central HS; Cherry Creek, NY; (S); 7/62; 4-H; French Clb; Scholastic Bowl; Socr; Var Trk; 4-H Awd; Hon Roll; NHS; SUNY Fredonia; Bio Chem.

TOMMANEY II, MICHAEL; Bishop Maginn HS; Albany, NY; (S); Computer Clb; Debate Tm; Math Clb; Nwsp Ed-Chief; Nwsp Rptr; High Hon Roll; NHS; Russian Clb 84-85; Russian Awd; Mth Awd; Comp Sci.

TOMMASO, RALPH; Moore Catholic HS; Staten Island, NY; (Y); Math Clb; Math Tm; Ski Clb; Concert Band; Jazz Band; Yrbk Stf; Stu Cncl; Finance Mgt.

TOMOSSONIE, ROBIN; Westhampton Beach SR HS; East Moriches, NY; (Y); Church Yth Grp; Pres Latin Clb; Chorus; Drill Tm; Pep Band; Yrbk Stf; JV Score Keeper; NHS; Computer Clb; Hosp Aide; Latin Hnr Soc 86; Cert Of Apprctn Cntrl Suffolk Hosp 85.

TOMPKIN, JOHN P; Newfield Central Schl; Newfield, NY; (Y); 10/51; Computer Clb; Drama Clb; Math Clb; Science Clb; Varsity Clb; School Musical; School Play; Stage Crew; Variety Show; JV Bsktbl; NYS Regnts Schlrshp Awd 86; NY ST Clss D Bsktbl Fnlst Boys 86; Trojn Masquers Drama Awd 86; U Of Southern CA; Tech Theatr.

TOMPKINS, AMY; G Ray Bodley HS; Fulton, NY; (Y); 32/261; French Clb; Color Guard; Mrchg Band; Trs Frsh Cls; Trs Soph Cls; Trs Jr Cls; Trs Sr Cls; Trs Stu Cncl; Score Keeper; Pres Tennis; Clss 53 Awd Ldrshp Unity 86; Nestus Schlrhsp Hmmkng 86; Jr Clss Prom Queen 85; Carenovia Coll; Fshn Dsgn.

TOMPKINS, JODIE; Sandy Creek Central HS; Williamstown, NY; (S); 12/98; Cmnty Wkr; Computer Clb; VP 4-H; Pres Intnl Clb; JV Var Vllybl; High Hon Roll; Hon Roll; Rptr NHS; JCL; Band; Nrs Aid; Yth Vlntrs Of Amer; SUNY Cobleskill; Prof Chef.

TOMPKINS, JOHN; Stamford Central HS; Stamford, NY; (S); 4/39; Band; Concert Band; Mrchg Band; Variety Show; Trs Frsh Cls; Pres Soph Cls; Pres Jr Cls; Var Capt Bsktbl; Var Golf; Var Capt Socr.

TOMPKINS, MICHELLE; Oxford Academy HS; Greene, NY; (Y); 4/71; French Clb; Concert Band; Mrchg Band; Yrbk Stf; JV Var Bsktbl; JV Var Sftbl; High Hon Roll; Hon Roll; NHS; SADD; Natl Chem Socty Lit Awd 3rd Pl 83; Pre-Med.

TOMS, ROBERT; Copiague SR HS; Copiague, NY; (Y); JA; Latin Clb; Ski Clb; Teachers Aide; Band; Concert Band; Jazz Band; Mrchg Band; Orch; School Musical; TV Brdcstng.

TOMSKI, KIMBERLY; Pembroke Central HS; Batavia, NY; (Y); Teachers Aide; Varsity Clb; Rep Stu Cncl; Stat Bsktbl; Mgr(s); Stat Sftbl; Stat Vllybl; Hon Roll; NHS; Elem Ed.

TONER, JENIFER L; John Marshall JR SR HS; Rochester, NY; (Y); 4/158; Pres Church Yth Grp; Cmnty Wkr; Mathletes; Red Cross Aide; Teachers Aide; Pres VP Stu Cncl; Hon Roll; NHS; Sec Soph Cls; Rep Jr Cls; Brghm Yng U Ldrshp Schlrshp 86; Brigham Young U; Elem Educ.

TONER, MICHAEL; St Anthonys HS; Centereach, NY; (Y); JV Wrstlng; Hon Roll; Jr NHS; Sienna; Bus.

TONER II, PHILIP MICHAEL; Sodus Central HS; Sodus, NY; (Y); 12/120; Am Leg Boys St; Church Yth Grp; Drama Clb; Model UN; Political Wkr; Concert Band; School Play; JV Socr; Var Tennis; High Hon Roll; Model.

TONINO, MICHELE; Dominican Commercial HS; Bellerose, NY; (Y); Art Clb; Dance Clb; Intnl Clb; Variety Show; Prncpls List 83-86; Prbtnry Stu Intl Hons Soc; Physcl Thrpst.

TOOKER, DAWN; Corinth Central Schl; Corinth, NY; (S); Church Yth Grp; Cmnty Wkr; Girl Scts; SADD; VICA; Band; Chorus; Cheerleading; Hon Roll; Jr NHS; Air Natl Grds.

TOOL, CYNTHIA G; Saranac Central HS; Morrisonville, NY; (S); 35/103; Church Yth Grp; Teachers Aide; Bsktbl; Score Keeper; Var Sftbl; Var Capt Vllybl; Hon Roll.

TOOLAN, CATHY; Irvington HS; Tarrytown, NY; (Y); Key Clb; Varsity Clb; Concert Band; Mrchg Band; Nwsp Sprt Ed; Yrbk Stf; Var Bsktbl; Var Capt Sftbl; Var Capt Vllybl; Hon Roll; All Leag Bsktbll, Sftbll & Vllybll & All Trnmnt Sftbll 84-86; 2nd Tm NY Dly News All Star Sftbll 86.

TOOLAN, JOHN; Cardinal Spellman HS; Bronx, NY; (Y); Aud/Vis; Stage Crew; Im Bsktbl; Var JV Bowling; NY ST Regents Scholar 86; 2nd Hnrs Awd 86; Estrn CT ST U; Cmmnctns.

TOOLEY, LAURIE A; Liverpool HS; Liverpool, NY; (Y); 55/816; Ski Clb; School Musical; Rep Stu Cncl; Var Golf; JV Var Sftbl; JV Var Vllybl; Wt Lftg; High Hon Roll; NHS; Vllybl Awd 86; Regnts Clg Schlrshp 86; Binghamton ST; Libl Arts.

TOOMB, MATTHEW D; Mount Saint Michael HS; Bronx, NY; (Y); 78/291; Computer Clb; Varsity Clb; Y-Teens; JV Var Bsbl; JV Var Bsktbl; JV Var Coach Actv; JV Var Fld Hcky; JV Var Ftbl; JV Var Golf; Im Sftbl; NY ST Regents Schrlshp 85-86; U Dayton.

TOOMER, SONYA; Middletown HS; Middletown, NY; (Y); Church Yth Grp; Cmnty Wkr; Dance Clb; FBLA; Girl Scts; Key Clb; Church Choir; Flag Corp; Gym; Hon Roll; Soph Of Yr Awd For Band 84-85; Hnrs For Pres Of Yth Grp 85-86; Howard U; Comp Sci.

TOOMEY, CAROL; Sauquoit Vly Cntrl HS; New Hartford, NY; (Y); 14/99; GAA; Drm Mjr(t); VP Soph Cls; Sec Stu Cncl; JV Var Cheerleading; JV Var Socr; Var Tennis; Hon Roll; Jr NHS; NHS; 2nd Hghst Aver; K Roemer Mem Awd Math; Hghst Acctg I Rgnts Mrk; Mohawk Vall CC; Acctg.

TOPAL, LAURA; Bronx High School Of Science; Bronx, NY; (Y); Drama Clb; Orch; School Musical; School Play; Nwsp Rptr; Yrbk Stf; NHS; Hon Mntn Bronx Sci Fair 83; Bronx Day Games 3 Mile Run 85; Comm.

TOPALOVICH, STEFAN; St Pauls Schl; Garden City, NY; (Y); Var Capt Bsbl; Var Capt Ftbl; Var Golf; Var Lcrss; Var Capt Socr; Var Tennis; Ftbl Coaches Awd 85; Bus Admin.

TOPKIN, WAYNE W; Smithtown West HS; Smithtown, NY; (Y); Math Tm; SADD; Yrbk Stf; Pres Jr Cls; Off Sr Cls; Pres Stu Cncl; Bsbl; Ftbl; NHS; Ntl Merit SF; NYS Rgnts Schlrshp 86; Vassar Coll; Law.

TOPPIN, NOLAN; All Hallows Inst; New Yhork, NY; (Y); JV Bowling; Pace U; Comp Tech.

TOPPING, DAVE; Edison HS; Elmira Hts, NY; (Y); Am Leg Boys St; Boy Scts; Computer Clb; French Clb; Ski Clb; Varsity Clb; School Play; Nwsp Ed-Chief; Nwsp Rptr; Nwsp Sprt Ed; Athl Of Yr 85-86; Recrd Hldr Most Pts Scrd Bsktbl 86; Kiwanis Athl Of Yr 85-86; Ithaca Coll; Cmmnctns.

TOQUICA, CLAUDIA; Bellport HS; Bellport, NY; (Y); Capt Dance Clb; Variety Show; Hon Roll; Bio.

TOREBKA, THOMAS; Bolton Central HS; Bolton Landing, NY; (Y); 2/24; Pres Frsh Cls; Pres Soph Cls; Pres Jr Cls; Var Bsbl; Var Capt Bsktbl; Coach Actv; Var Capt Socr; Hon Roll; VP NHS; Amer Lgn Awd 84; Sienna; Opthlmlgst.

TORHAN, EDW; Walter Panas HS; Peekskill, NY; (Y); 38/220; Ski Clb; Variety Show; Vllybl; Hon Roll; Jr NHS; Prsdntl Acad Ftnss Awd 85-86; Suny Buffalo; Engrng.

TORICK, CARLA; Hauppauge HS; York, PA; (Y); Concert Band; Mrchg Band; Capt L Swmmng; JV L Trk; High Hon Roll; NHS; All Cnty & All ST Swmr 84-85; Suffolk Cnty Champ 500 Yd Freestyl 85; Mst Vlbl 84; Med.

TORITTO, MONICA; Mineola HS; Mineola, NY; (Y); SADD; Mrchg Band; Nwsp Rptr; Yrbk Stf; Sec Stu Cncl; Sftbl; High Hon Roll; NHS; Phys Thrpy.

TORMEY, LEANNE; New Rochelle HS; New Rochelle, NY; (Y); 116/600; Model UN; Pres Service Clb; Nwsp Ed-Chief; Pres Frsh Cls; Pres Soph Cls; Pres Jr Cls; Cit Awd; NHS; W Clark Memrl Awd 86; J R Gaddy Jrnlsm Awd 86; Svc Chldrn Awd 86; George WA U.

TORMEY, MEGAN GARRY; Cold Spring Harbor HS; Lloyd Harbor, NY; (Y); 40/135; Drama Clb; Intnl Clb; Acpl Chr; Chorus; School Musical; School Play; Variety Show; Sec Sr Cls; Cheerleading; Hon Roll; Nassau Music Eductrs Assn All Cnty Chorus 84-86; Wake Forest U; Musical Thtr.

TORNATORE, ELENA; Canastota JR SR HS; Canastota, NY; (S); GAA; Intnl Clb; Leo Clb; Science Clb; SADD; Teachers Aide; Rep Stu Cncl; JV Var Fld Hcky; JV Sftbl; JV Vllybl; Mst Ded Fld Hockey 83; MIP Vllybl 83; Co-Capt JV Fld Hockey 84; Math.

TORNATORE, MARIA; John A Coleman HS; Kingston, NY; (Y); Key Clb; Hon Roll; Prfct Atten Awd; Mt St Mary Coll; Elem Ed.

TORO, JUAN J; All Hallows HS; Bronx, NY; (Y); Bowling; Hon Roll; NHS; St Johns; Lwyr.

TORONTO, JOHN D; Ward Melville HS; Stony Brook, NY; (Y); Am Leg Boys St; Debate Tm; Ed Lit Mag; Im Wt Lftg; High Hon Roll; NHS; Math Tm; Nwsp Bus Mgr; Jr NHS; Enlisted In Marine Corps Reserve 86; Attended Teenage Repub Schl Of Politics 86; Chrmsn Of Ward Melvl; Cornell U; Law.

TORRANCE, CRYSTAL; Edison Tech; Rochester, NY; (Y); Church Yth Grp; Cmnty Wkr; Office Aide; Church Choir; Rep Frsh Cls; Trk; Hon Roll; Flexiblty 85; Nrs.

TORRANCE, MICHELLE E; Goshen Central HS; Goshen, NY; (Y); Drama Clb; Chorus; School Musical; School Play; Var L Cheerleading; JV Score Keeper; JV Sftbl; Hon Roll; NEDT Awd; 4-H; Hghst Math Achvt 83; Psych.

TORRES, ANGELA; Cardinal Spellman HS; Bronx, NY; (Y); 48/500; Computer Clb; Dance Clb; Political Wkr; Color Guard; Flag Corp; School Musical; Yrbk Stf; Lit Mag; High Hon Roll; NEDT Awd; RIT Alumni Schltc Scholar 86-87; Rochester Inst Tech; Htl Mgmt.

TORRES, ANTON; Midwood HS; Brooklyn, NY; (Y); Service Clb; Teachers Aide; Lit Mag; Hon Roll; Prfct Atten Awd; Archon Svc League 85-86; Film Dir.

TORRES, CARMEN; Cathedral HS; Long Island, NY; (Y); 50/272; Rep Frsh Cls; VP Jr Cls; Rep Stu Cncl; Hon Roll; NY U; Pre-Med.

TORRES, CHRISTINE; Bay Shore HS; Bay Shore, NY; (Y); Drama Clb; SADD; Color Guard; Mrchg Band; School Musical; Yrbk Stf; Lit Mag; Socr; Hon Roll; Outstndng Achvt Spnsh 85; Nrsng.

TORRES, EILEEN; Cardinal Spellman HS; Ny, NY; (Y); Computer Clb; Pep Clb; Rep Spanish Clb; Color Guard; Rep Jr Cls; High Hon Roll; Cornell U; Law.

TORRES, ELIZABETH; Dodge Vocational HS; Bronx, NY; (Y); Hon Roll; Prfct Atten Awd; Top 10 Secy JR Clss 86; Amer Stds 86; The Wood School; Exec Secy.

TORRES, EUGENE PATRICK; Hutchinson Central Tech; Buffalo, NY; (Y); Boys Clb Am; Office Aide; Rep Jr Cls; Var L Ice Hcky.

TORRES, EVELYN; Cardinal Spellman HS; Bronx, NY; (Y); Computer Clb; Spanish Clb; Yrbk Stf; Hon Roll; Supplemental Educatnl Opportunity Grant 86-87; Pace U Grant In Aid 86-87; Pace U; Business.

TORRES, JANET; Bishop Loughlin MHS; Brooklyn, NY; (Y); 41/232; Spanish Clb; Hon Roll; Prfct Atten Awd; Long Island U; Nrsng.

TORRES, KENNETH; Newfield HS; Selden, NY; (Y); FBLA; Library Aide; Office Aide; Variety Show; JV Crs Cntry; JV Var Score Keeper; JV Trk; Attnd Awd 83-84; US Navy; Avtn Elec.

TORRES, MICHELE; John F Kennedy HS; New York, NY; (Y); 85/873; Cmnty Wkr; Teachers Aide; Chorus; Variety Show; Nwsp Rptr; NHS; Spanish NHS; Law.

TORRES, NANCY A; St Francis Prep; Richmond Hill, NY; (S); 99/744; Service Clb; Rep Soph Cls; Im Ftbl; Hon Roll; NHS; Lwyr.

TORRES, WANDA; George Washington HS; New York, NY; (Y); Church Yth Grp; Chorus; Church Choir; School Musical; Variety Show; Var Bsbl; Tennis; Vllybl; Spanish NHS; Cert Coll Bnd Pgm; Acdmc Ablty & Chrtr Sci Dept 86; Emer Mdcl Tech Dplma 86; Borough Manhattan CC; Secty.

TORRETTA, THOMAS JOHN; St Peters Boys HS; Staten Island, NY; (Y); 18/163; Church Yth Grp; Math Tm; Science Clb; SADD; Im Bsbl; Im Bsktbl; Im Bowling; JV Crs Cntry; Im Ftbl; Var Sftbl; Soc Stdies Awd 2nd Pl 83; Sci Fair Awd 1st Pl 83; Mth Awd 83.

TORTA, JONATHAN; Bainbridge-Guilford HS; Bainbridge, NY; (Y); 13/87; Church Yth Grp; Computer Clb; Drama Clb; VP 4-H; School Play; Hon Roll; 4-H Leadership Conf 86; Boces Meadia Arts 1st Pl Best Of Shaw 86; NY Summer Sch Of Arts 86; RIT; Comp Graphics.

TORTORICI, CHRISTINA; Colonie Central HS; Schenectady, NY; (Y); 3/490; French Clb; High Hon Roll; Siena Coll; CPA.

TORTORICI, MARYANN; Smithtown High School West; Smithtown, NY; (Y); Band; Mrchg Band; School Musical; Symp Band; Yrbk Phtg; Yrbk Rptr; Hon Roll; Office Aide; Yrbk Stf; NY ST Rgnts Schlrshp 86; Italian Hnr Scty Sec 85-86; Hofsha U; Pre-Law.

TORTORIELLO, TRACEY; Moore Catholic HS; Staten Island, NY; (Y); #3 In Class; Cmnty Wkr; Spanish Clb; SADD; Bowling; High Hon Roll; Hon Roll; Jr NHS; NHS; Amer Inst Of Sci & Tech 1st Pl 86; Intl Frgn Lang Awds 85; Acad All-Amer 85.

TORZEWSKI, MICHELLE; Mt Mercy Acad; W Seneca, NY; (S); 8/161; Cmnty Wkr; Hosp Aide; Quiz Bowl; Service Clb; SADD; Nwsp Ed-Chief; Nwsp Rptr; Nwsp Stf; Lit Mag; High Hon Roll; Rgnts Nrsng Schlrshp 86; Natl Hnr Soc; Trocaire; Nrsng.

TOSCANO, ANN MARIE; John Marshall HS; Rochester, NY; (Y); 14/155; Exploring; Office Aide; Red Cross Aide; SADD; Teachers Aide; Yrbk Stf; Lit Mag; Pres Soph Cls; Rep Jr Cls; Pres Sr Cls; Vtrns Of Frgn Wars Lylty Day 86; Otstndng HS Athlts Of Amer 86; HS Acdmc All-Amer 86; St John Fisher; Cmmnctn.

TOSCH, KIM; Fairpot HS; Fairport, NY; (Y); Church Yth Grp; Sec 4-H; Office Aide; Yrbk Stf; 4-H Awd; Hon Roll; Spanish NHS; 4-H Home Ec Awd Trp NY Cty 86; Wmns Clb Rchstr Swng Cntst 2nd Plc Wnr 86; Cnty Mdl Hnr Clthng 85; Fshn Dsgn.

TOSH, GAIL; Jamesville-Dewitt HS; Jamesville, NY; (Y); Cmnty Wkr; Girl Scts; Mrchg Band; School Musical; Symp Band; Bsktbl; Sftbl; High Hon Roll; Susquehanna Vly Band 83-85; Dist Band 84; Schl Video Magzn Reportr 84-85; Smith Coll; Eng.

TOSI, CAROYN; Fox Lane HS; Mt Kisco, NY; (Y); Church Yth Grp; Chorus; Lib Church Choir; Hon Roll; HS Chorus Music Awd 85; St Marks Chrch Choir Music Awd-Mt Kisco NY 84; Music.

TOSTANOSKI, TINA M; Corning Painted Post West HS; Corning, NY; (Y); Band; Chorus; Sftbl; Vllybl; High Hon Roll; Hon Roll; Prfct Atten Awd; Outstndng Stu 84-85; Most Employable 85-86; Mark Twain Cty Schlstc Achvr 86; Corning CC; Nrsng.

TOSTI, CHRISTOPHER D; Morris Central Schl; New Berlin, NY; (Y); Am Leg Boys St; Camera Clb; Cmnty Wkr; Yrbk Phtg; Yrbk Stf; Rep Jr Cls; Bsbl; Bsktbl; Socr; Math Tutor; Phtgrphy.

TOTH, LYNN M; Vestal HS; Vestal, NY; (Y); Sec Church Yth Grp; Key Clb; Ski Clb; SADD; Varsity Clb; Church Choir; Off Soph Cls; Off Jr Cls; Var Cheerleading; Var Fld Hcky; Art Educ.

TOTH, THOMAS; Hicksville SR HS; Hicksville, NY; (Y); Ski Clb; Hon Roll; Bus.

TOTO, MARTIN; Mepham HS; N Bellmore, NY; (Y); Debate Tm; Hosp Aide; SADD; Varsity Clb; Band; Mrchg Band; Symp Band; Yrbk Stf; Bus.

TOUCHET, JAMES P; East Islip SR HS; Islip Terr, NY; (Y); Am Leg Boys St; Boy Scts; JV Var Wrstlng; French Hon Soc; High Hon Roll; Jr NHS; NHS; Prfct Atten Awd; French Clb; Egl Sct 86; Pres Phys Ftns Awds 83-84; NRA Mrksmnshp Awds 81; Rensselaer Polytech; Engnrgn.

TOUHER, BRIAN; Fox Lane HS; Mt Kisco, NY; (Y); 22/277; Ski Clb; Band; Concert Band; Jazz Band; Orch; Rep Frsh Cls; Var Ftbl; JV Lcrss; High Hon Roll; NHS; Sci Supervisors Assoc Awd 85; Cert Merit Awd 86; Outstndng Music Dept Awd 84; Cornell; Chem Engr.

TOUHEY, GERARD; Msgr Farrell HS; Staten Island, NY; (Y); 85/300; Key Clb; Bsktbl; Ftbl; Hon Roll; Secnd Hnrs 84-85-86; Econ.

TOULON, SIMONE E; Bronx HS Of Science; Little Neck, NY; (Y); Art Clb; Drama Clb; Girl Scts; Hosp Aide; Library Aide; Math Tm; Teachers Aide; Nwsp Ed-Chief; Nwsp Stf; Yrbk Stf; UFT Svc Awd 84; 1st Pl Statue Of Lbrty News Essay 84; Hnrb Mntn Wrld Poetry Cntst 86; NYU; Writing.

TOUSSAINT, IVA; Murry Bergtraum HS; Bronx, NY; (Y); Church Yth Grp; FNA; Church Choir; Cert Awd Prfct Attndnc 83-86; Nrsng.

TOUSSAINT, JEAN; De Witt Clinton HS; Bronx, NY; (Y); Business Administration.

TOUSSAINT, MARIO; La Salle Military Acad; Springfield Gdn, NY; (Y); ROTC; Color Guard; Drill Tm; Ftbl; Engrng.

TOUSSAINT, SHARI L; Medina SR HS; Medina, NY; (Y); 6/160; AFS; 4-H; Band; Concert Band; Mrchg Band; Rep Stu Cncl; JV Stat Vllybl; 4-H Awd; Hon Roll; NHS; Rgnts Schlrshp 86; RIT Alumni Schlrshp 86; Jr Miss 1st Rnr Up Orlns Cnty 86; Rochester Inst Of Tech; Photo.

TOVO, KATHIE; Smithtown High School East; Saint James, NY; (Y); Camera Clb; Church Yth Grp; Civic Clb; Cmnty Wkr; Dance Clb; DECA; Drama Clb; GAA; Key Clb; Service Clb; 4th Pl Radio Advrtsng ST Career Conf DECA 86; Cmmnctns.

TOW, MICHAEL H; Great Neck South HS; Great Neck, NY; (Y); 11/234; Capt Model UN; Chorus; Jazz Band; School Musical; Ed Nwsp Stf; Ed Lit Mag; NCTE Awd; Acpl Chr; Madrigals; Orch; Ntl Merit Fnlst 86; Brklyn Music Teachrs Guild Solo Rctl Awd 85; Mdl Cngrss Chrmn 85-86.

TOWER, JAMES; Amsterdam HS; Amsterdam, NY; (Y); 50/320; French Clb; JV Ftbl; Var Trk; Hon Roll; Arch.

TOWERS, MARY F; F D Roosevelt HS; Poughkeepsie, NY; (Y); 75/365; SADD; Band; Concert Band; Mrchg Band; Yrbk Stf; Trk; Assumption Coll.

TOWERS, NELLA; Corinth Central HS; Porter Corners, NY; (Y); French Clb; SADD; Varsity Clb; Var Capt Fld Hcky; Var JV Sftbl; Prfct Atten Awd; Adirondack CC; Comp Progmng.

TOWERS, PAULINE; Our Lady Of Lourdes HS; Poughkeepsie, NY; (Y); 45/180; Ski Clb; Var Diving; Var Swmmng; Hon Roll; NHS; Volunteer Recogntn Awd 84; Exemplry Volunteer Scv Awd 85; Psychlgy.

TOWLES, PETER; South Jefferson Central HS; Mannsville, NY; (Y); 15/150; French Clb; Im Bowling; JV Ftbl; Engrng.

TOWNE, CARRIE; Cato-Meridian Central HS; Cato, NY; (Y); Powder Puff Ftbl; Cheerleading; Fld Hcky; Ski Clb; Wheelock; Cnslng.

TOWNE, SHAWN; Ticonderoga HS; Ticonderoga, NY; (Y); Pres Church Yth Grp; Drama Clb; French Clb; Chorus; School Musical; School Play; Yrbk Stf; Rep Soph Cls; Rep Jr Cls; Rep Sr Cls; Music Achvt Awds 84-86; Cntrl City Bus Inst; Bus Adm.

TOWNSEND, MARY JO; Harpursville JR SR HS; Harpursville, NY; (S); 16/86; Ski Clb; School Play; VP Soph Cls; VP Jr Cls; Var Fld Hcky; Var Sftbl; Var Vllybl; High Hon Roll; Hon Roll; All League Fld Hcky & Vllybl 2nd Tm 84-85; All League Fld Hcky 1st Tm 85-86; Le Moyne Coll; Mgt.

TOWNSEND, PATRICE; Mt Saint Ursula HS; Bronx, NY; (Y); Church Yth Grp; Computer Clb; Red Cross Aide; Church Choir; Drill Tm; Flag Corp; Off Jr Cls; Swmmng; Trk; Vllybl; Med.

TOWNSEND, ROBERT E; Whitehall HS; Whitehall, NY; (Y); 3/78; Drama Clb; Science Clb; Color Guard; Yrbk Sprt Ed; Pres Soph Cls; Var Capt Crs Cntry; Var Capt Trk; Bausch & Lomb Sci Awd; High Hon Roll; NHS; Old Dominion U; Elec Engrng.

TOWNSLEY, LISA; St John Villa Acad; Staten Island, NY; (Y); 1/123; Yrbk Stf; Var Cheerleading; High Hon Roll; Hon Roll; NHS; Math Tm; Spanish Clb; General Excellence 84-86.

TRACEY, CATHERINE; Newburgh Free Acad; Newburgh, NY; (Y); French Clb; Chorus; Stage Crew; French Hon Soc; Hon Roll; Frgn Lang.

TRACEY, DEBRA L; St Francis Prep; Whitestone, NY; (S); Cmnty Wkr; SADD; Tennis; Hon Roll.

TRACEY, SHEILA; Arlington HS; Poughkeepsie, NY; (Y); Hosp Aide; Band; Color Guard; Bsktbl; Bowling; Mgr(s); Sftbl; Swmmng; Vllybl; Awd Mst Prfssnl Prgrss Nrsng 85-86; Dutchess CC; Nrsng.

TRACKEY, DAVID; Hudson Falls Central HS; Hudson Falls, NY; (Y); 27/214; Buffalo ST; Engrg.

TRACY, BETH A; Ogdensburg Free Acad; Ogdensburg, NY; (Y); French Clb; Concert Band; Mrchg Band; Pep Band; Trs Jr Cls; Swmmng; Trk; NHS; Regents Schlrshp 86; Acad Banquet 81-86; Colgate U.

TRACY, MICHELLE; Susquehanna Valley HS; Conklin, NY; (Y); Pep Clb; Rep Frsh Cls; Sec Soph Cls; Sec Jr Cls; Rep Stu Cncl; Var Cheerleading; Var Tennis; Var Trk; JV Vllybl; High Hon Roll; Bus.

TRACY, MILISSA; Cobleskill Central HS; Schoharie, NY; (Y); Aud/Vis; 4-H; FBLA; FHA; Girl Scts; Hosp Aide; Library Aide; Im Gym; SUNY Ag & Tech; Bus Mgmt.

TRAIGER, DEAN; Southside HS; Rockville Centre, NY; (Y); Boy Scts; Pres Computer Clb; SADD; Pres Temple Yth Grp; JV Wrstlng; Hon Roll; Med.

TRAILL, GEORGIA; Springfield Gardens HS; Queens, NY; (Y); 4/440; Math Clb; Math Tm; Teachers Aide; Trk; Vllybl; Hon Roll; Jr NHS; NHS; Nrsng.

TRAMA, STEPHEN; Archbishop Molloy HS; Howard Bch, NY; (Y); Art Clb; Boy Scts; Church Yth Grp; Cmnty Wkr; Hosp Aide; Ftbl; Trk; Ft Troike Ldrshp Pgm 82; Stony Brook Coll; Physcl Thrpy.

TRAMMEL, KEVIN; Chenango Forks HS; Binghamton, NY; (Y); 2/176; Am Leg Boys St; SADD; Pres Frsh Cls; VP Stu Cncl; Golf; Capt Socr; DAR Awd; Kiwanis Awd; NHS; Sal; Broone CC; Mech Engrg.

TRAMONTO, GIA M; Irondequoit HS; Rochester, NY; (Y); 170/350; Pres DECA; Hon Roll; Monroe CC; Fshn Merchndsng.

TRAN, HA; Walton HS; Bronx, NY; (Y); 5/575; Math Tm; Church Choir; Untd Fed Tchr Schlrshp 86; Comptrllr Awd 86; Physcs Awd 86; Polytechnic U; Elctrcl Engr.

TRAN, HAO; Middleton HS; Middletown, NY; (Y); Im L Fld Hcky; JV Var Socr; Im Vllybl; NYS Rgnl Sccr Chmpnshp 85; Rit; Elec Engr.

TRAN, TRU; HS Of Art & Design; Elmhurst, NY; (Y); Computer Clb; Math Tm; Yrbk Stf; Hon Roll; NHS; Prfct Atten Awd; Ntl Art Hnr Soc 86; Arista Soc 84; Marlane Ellen Nussbaum Mem Awd 84; Industrl Design.

TRANCHINA, MARK S; Monsignor Farrell HS; Staten Island, NY; (Y); 6/290; Math Tm; VP Sr Cls; Bsktbl; JV Var Ftbl; Var Wt Lftg; High Hon Roll; NYS Regnts Schlrshp 86; Sclr Athltc Awd 86; Most Consistnt Dfnsv Back 86; Princeton U; Engrng.

TRANI, JOHN J; Sheepshead Bay HS; Brooklyn, NY; (Y); Am Leg Boys St; Math Tm; Var Vllybl; Mck Trl 84-85; Cmp Cnsclr Mntlly Rtrd 85; Syracuse U; Scrn Wrtr.

TRANQUILLO, DONALD; Mamaroneck HS; Larchmont, NY; (Y); Boy Scts; Computer Clb; Var JV Bsbl; Cit Awd; RPI; Comp Engrng.

TRAPANI, JOSEPH; Archbishop Molloy HS; Jackson Hgts, NY; (Y); 12/383; Camera Clb; Science Clb; Variety Show; High Hon Roll; Hon Roll; NHS; Ntl Merit SF.

TRAPINI, ANNETTE; Scotia-Glenville HS; Scotia, NY; (Y); Key Clb; Varsity Clb; Yrbk Stf; VP Soph Cls; Pres Jr Cls; Rep Stu Cncl; Var Socr; High Hon Roll; VP NHS; Sub Cncl Girls All Star 2nd Tm Sccr 85.

TRAPLETTI, LUCY; Mt Vernon HS; Mount Vernon, NY; (Y); 37/550; Sec Trs Library Aide; Trs SADD; Band; Mrchg Band; Yrbk Bus Mgr; Trs Lit Mag; Hon Roll; Fash Inst Of Tech; Aprl Prod Mg.

TRASHER, STEVE; York Central Schl; Leicester, NY; (Y); Church Yth Grp; Ski Clb; Rep Jr Cls; Capt Var Bsbl; Capt Var Bsktbl; Var L Ftbl; High Hon Roll; Hon Roll; All Greater Rochester Bsktbl Tm Hnrb Mntn; Ithaca Coll; Bus.

TRAUGOTT, JENNIFER; E J Wilson HS; Rochester, NY; (Y); 3/325; VP Trs Drama Clb; French Clb; Acpl Chr; VP Chorus; School Musical; Swing Chorus; Yrbk Stf; High Hon Roll; NHS; Ntl Merit SF; Otstndng Achvmnt Chrs 83-86; Englsh.

TRAUMER, BARBARA; New Rochelle HS; New Rochelle, NY; (Y); AFS; Art Clb; Aud/Vis; Boys Clb Am; Dance Clb; FHA; Model UN; Spanish Clb; Yrbk Stf; Powder Puff Ftbl; Acad Diploma 87; Art Achvt Awd 83; Cert Of Achvt In Metric Measure 84; Coll Of St Elizabeth; Pblshr.

TRAUTMANN, JANE; Lindenhurst SR HS; Lindenhurst, NY; (Y); Trs German Clb; Thesps; Sec Concert Band; Mrchg Band; School Musical; Mgr Stage Crew; Variety Show; Nwsp Rptr; Var Trk; Hon Roll; Advrtsg.

TRAUTWEIN, PEGGY; Lancaster HS; Depew, NY; (S); 94/461; DECA; Office Aide; Hon Roll; NHS; Buffalo ST Coll; Elem Ed.

TRAVERSE, KARA; Ballston Spa HS; Ballston Spa, NY; (Y); Nwsp Stf; Rep Frsh Cls; Trs Soph Cls; Trs Jr Cls; Stu Cncl; JV Fld Hcky; High Hon Roll; Hon Roll; Psych.

TRAVIESO, HECTOR; Harry S Truman HS; Bronx, NY; (Y); 37/499; NHS; Acctng.

TRAVIS, CLAUDEEN; Sherburne-Earlville HS; Sherburne, NY; (Y); Cmnty Wkr; Drama Clb; English Clb; Girl Scts; Spanish Clb; SADD; School Musical; School Play; Stage Crew; Bsktbl; Miss Chenange Cnty & Miss Teen Of NY 85; Miss Teen Of U S 85; 2 Schlrshp Acad Of Theatrcl Arts 85; Ithaca; Comm.

TRAVIS, KRIS; Chenango Forks HS; Binghamton, NY; (Y); French Clb; Ski Clb; Stu Cncl; Stat Ftbl; Swmmng; Tennis; Hon Roll; Prfct Atten Awd; Broome CC; Liberal Arts.

TRAVIS, MELISSA; Chatham HS; Chatham, NY; (Y); Church Yth Grp; JA; Teachers Aide; JV Var Vllybl; Hon Roll; JR Hnrs 85-86; Bus.

TRAVIS, MICHAEL; Penn Yan Acad; Penn Yan, NY; (Y); 21/173; Am Leg Boys St; Model UN; Ski Clb; Chorus; Rep Stu Cncl; Var Capt Golf; DAR Awd; High Hon Roll; Voice Dem Awd; Ithaca Coll; Fin.

TRAVIS, TAMMIE; Westfield Academy & Central Schl; Westfield, NY; (Y); AFS; Intnl Clb; Sec VP Key Clb; Teachers Aide; Band; Chorus; School Musical; Cheerleading; High Hon Roll; Hon Roll; Outstndng Stu Awd 86; Cosmtlgy.

TRAVIS, THEODORE; Palyra-Macedon HS; Palmyra, NY; (S); 8/167; Pres Church Yth Grp; Varsity Clb; Trs Frsh Cls; Trs Jr Cls; VP Jr Cls; Var Golf; JV Var Socr; Cit Awd; NHS.

TRAWITZ, KIMBERLY; Fairport HS; Fairport, NY; (Y); Church Yth Grp; Ski Clb; Varsity Clb; Chorus; Church Choir; Yrbk Bus Mgr; Yrbk Stf; Rep Jr Cls; Cheerleading; Var Crs Cntry; 3rd Tm Kinney Ntl Mt/X-Cntry 85; 2nd All ST Tm NY/X-Cntry 85; Slvr Medlst NY Empire ST Gms 85; Pol Sci.

TRAZOFF, SHARI; Tottenville HS; Staten Island, NY; (S); 21/850; Hosp Aide; High Hon Roll; Hon Roll; Jr NHS; NHS; SUNY; Law.

TREIS, JULIE; Fairport HS; Fairport, NY; (Y); Intnl Clb; Spanish Clb; SADD; Yrbk Stf; Rep Jr Cls; Mgr Trk; Hon Roll; Spanish NHS.

TREITEL, MARK; Earl L Vandermeulen HS; Pt Jefferson, NY; (Y); 7/333; Off Aud/Vis; VP Temple Yth Grp; Nwsp Rptr; Yrbk Stf; Ed Lit Mag; JV Trk; NHS; Ntl Merit Ltr; Simmons Rsrch Fllwshp Awd 86; NY Metro Cmmnctns VP United Synagogue 86-87; Hon Roll 84-86.

TREMBLAY, J PAUL; Seton Catholic Central HS; Apalachin, NY; (Y); Art Clb; Chess Clb; Mathletes; Science Clb; Hon Roll; NYS Rgnts Schlrshp 86; VA Polytech Inst; Engrng.

TREMBLAY, PAUL; Seton Catholic Central HS; Apalachin, NY; (S); 12/162; Art Clb; Chess Clb; Mathletes; Science Clb; Service Clb; Hon Roll; NY ST Rgnts Schlrshp 86; VA Polytech Inst; Engrng.

TREMONT, JEFFREY; Watertown HS; Watertown, NY; (Y); 10/305; Ed Yrbk Stf; Trs NHS; Prfct Atten Awd; Walker Family Engr Schrlshp 86; Victor Remorino Sci Awd 86; William P Herring Mem Schlrshp 86; Jefferson CC; Engrng Sci.

TRENTO, THERESA; Minisink Valley HS; Middletown, NY; (Y); Art Clb; Sec 4-H; Hosp Aide; Library Aide; Ski Clb; Variety Show; Var Crs Cntry; Var Trk; Sec 4-H Awd; Hon Roll; Orng Cnty CC; Srgcl Nrs.

TRESTON, LORI; Canarsie HS; Brooklyn, NY; (Y); Am Leg Aux Girls St; Orch; Sftbl; Hon Roll; Afro Am Clb 85-86; Close Up Clb 85-86; SUNY; Acctng.

TRETIAK, SANDI; Frankfort-Schuyler HS; Frankfort, NY; (S); GAA; Key Clb; High Hon Roll; NHS; Contntl Mth Lg 84; Vrsty Ltr Bdmntn 85; Band Booster Awd 84 & 85; Sci.

TREUBERT, ELIZABETH; Acad Of St Joseph; Centereach, NY; (Y); Aud/Vis; Drama Clb; Hosp Aide; Church Choir; School Musical; School Play; Stage Crew; Ntl Merit Ltr; St Schlr; U PA; Nrsng.

TREUTLE, ROSEMARIE; Patchogue Medford HS; Medford, NY; (Y); 80/621; Dance Clb; Leo Clb; SADD; Twrlr; Hon Roll; NHS; Prfct Atten Awd; SUNY Oswego; Merchndsg.

TREVETT, LYNN; Gloversville HS; Gloversville, NY; (Y); Church Yth Grp; Trs Intnl Clb; Jazz Band; Mrchg Band; School Musical; School Play; Stage Crew; Swing Chorus; Nwsp Stf; Yrbk Stf; Rgnts Schlrshp Wnnr 86; SUNY Potsdam; Scndry Ed Englsh.

TREVVETT, PAUL H; Poland Central HS; Poland, NY; (Y); French Clb; Red Cross Aide; Ski Clb; SADD; Band; Concert Band; Var Badmtn; Var Crs Cntry; Var Trk; High Hon Roll; Natl Socl Stds Olympd Awd 84-86; Natl Hnr Socty 84-86.

TREXLER, LAUREL; Fillmore Central HS; Houghton, NY; (S); 1/61; Church Yth Grp; French Clb; Art Clb; Yrbk Ed-Chief; Yrbk Stf; High Hon Roll; NHS; Val; Standard Bearer & JR Cls Marshall 85; Houghton Coll.

TREZZA, MARIE JANIS; Lindenhurst HS; Lindenhurst, NY; (Y); French Clb; Spanish Clb; Orch; School Musical; Stage Crew; High Hon Roll; NHS; Dowling Coll; Acctg.

TRIANDAFILS, RICHARD; Ward Melville HS; Setauket, NY; (Y); Ski Clb; JV Socr; JV Vllybl; Hon Roll; Ski Instrctr Ski Clb 85; SAP Org 85-86; Bus.

TRIEB, PENNY; Irvington HS; Irvington, NY; (Y); 34/109; VP Computer Clb; Key Clb; Pres SADD; Band; Chorus; Mrchg Band; Orch; Lit Mag; Hon Roll; Merit Schlrshp 86; Foreing Lang Club 84-86; Brandeis; Psychlgy.

TRIFOSO, SUSAN J; Horseheads HS; Horseheads, NY; (S); 46/380; Spanish Clb; Band; Mrchg Band; Orch; JV Cheerleading; High Hon Roll; NHS; Sec Soph Cls; Rep Stu Cncl; Chrldg 83; Band Cmptn Flute 84; Elem Educ.

TRIGLIA, FRANCES; St John The Baptist HS; Deer Park, NY; (Y).

TRIM, BRIAN; Bishop Maginn HS; Albany, NY; (S); Latin Clb; Band; School Musical; School Play; Nwsp Ed-Chief; High Hon Roll; Hon Roll; NHS; Frstry.

TRINCELLITO, KAREN; Saugertius JR/SR HS; Saugerties, NY; (Y); Trs Spanish Clb; JV Sftbl; Hon Roll; Suny New Paltz; Bus.

TRINDADE, JOHN; Bishop Ford Central Catholic HS; Brooklyn, NY; (Y); Off Computer Clb; JV Math Tm; Pres Science Clb; Ed Nwsp Rptr; Im Capt Bowling; Vllybl; High Hon Roll; NHS; St Schlr; Pace Trustee Schlrshp 86; NVCTC; Acctg.

TRINGALI, GIANNA; Eastchester HS; Eastchester, NY; (Y); Drama Clb; Leo Clb; Chorus; School Musical; School Play; Variety Show; Art.

TRINGALI, TIFFANY; Liverpool HS; Liverpool, NY; (S); 111/816; DECA; Ski Clb; Stu Cncl; Cheerleading; Powder Puff Ftbl; High Hon Roll; NHS; Pres Schlr; 1st Pl Apparrell & Accessories Regnl & ST DECA Comptn 86; SUNY; Bus Admin.

TRINH, LINH; Aviation HS; Brooklyn, NY; (Y); 50/412; Art Clb; Cit Awd; NYIT; Aero Engr.

TRINIDAD, ADRIANA; Dominican Commercial HS; Jamaica, NY; (Y); Church Yth Grp; Soph Cls; Stu Cncl; Swmmng; Accntng.

TRINIDAD, JUAN; Xavier HS; New York, NY; (Y); Aud/Vis; Chess Clb; Im Bsbl; Im Bsktbl; NEDT Awd; Natl Hispnc Schlr Awds Prog SF 86; Regents Coll Schlrhsp 86; Manhattan Coll; Engrng.

TRIPALDI, DEBBIE; Walt Whitman HS; Huntington, NY; (Y); 7/476; GAA; Band; Mrchg Band; Var Capt Bsktbl; Var Socr; Var Capt Vllybl; High Hon Roll; Hon Roll; Jr NHS; Ntl Merit Ltr; AATSP 1st 85; All Cnty Vlybl, Sccr, Bsktbl 86; Stdnt Mnth, Mst Outstndng Stdnt 84; Pre Law.

TRIPODI, NATALIE; Hampton Bays JR SR HS; Hampton Bays, NY; (Y); 8/106; Science Clb; SADD; Hon Roll; Prfct Atten Awd; SUNY; Physcl Sci.

TRIPP, CRAIG; Bolton Central HS; Bolton Landing, NY; (Y); 7/20; Variety Show; Yrbk Stf; VP Jr Cls; Var L Bsbl; Var L Bsktbl; Var L Socr; Hon Roll; NHS; Aerospace Engrng.

TRIPP, JAMES L; Mc Quaid Jesuit HS; Pittsford, NY; (Y); Boy Scts; Church Yth Grp; Cmnty Wkr; Ski Clb; Varsity Clb; Var L Ftbl; Hon Roll; NHS.

TRIPP, ROBERT; Cooperstown Central Schl; Cooperstown, NY; (Y); Ski Clb; Concert Band; Mrchg Band; Pep Band; Var Crs Cntry; Var Trk; NHS; Ntl Merit Ltr; Intern Rsrch Asst NY Acad Sci 86; U VT; Chem.

TRIPP, STEPHANIE; Harpursville HS; Port Crane, NY; (Y); Drama Clb; Intnl Clb; Varsity Clb; Drm Mjr(t); Jazz Band; Mrchg Band; School Play; Sec Sr Cls; Sec Stu Cncl; Capt Cheerleading; ROTC Schlrshp 86; MVP Ftbl, Bsktbl Chrldng 86; Norwich U; Lang.

TRIVEDI, KAMINI J; Niagara Catholic HS; Grand Island, NY; (Y); Church Yth Grp; Cmnty Wkr; Drama Clb; French Clb; VP Key Clb; Red Cross Aide; Nwsp Rptr; Nwsp Stf; Yrbk Stf; Rep Stu Cncl; SUNY Buffalo Almni Ass Awd 85; Fr Kroupa Otstndng Stu Awd Rnr-Up 85; Rgnts Schlrshp Awd 86; Cornell U.

TRIZZINO, DAPHNA; John Dewey HS; Brooklyn, NY; (Y); Math Tm; Teachers Aide; Nwsp Stf; Yrbk Stf; Rep Frsh Cls; Rep Soph Cls; Rep Jr Cls; HOBY Fndntn For Outstndng Soph 83-84; Cooprtn In Gov 86; Hlcst Mem Essay Cntst Fnlst 86; Saint Johns U; Lawyer.

TROCCIA, KATHY; Elmira Free Acad; Elmira, NY; (Y); 31/255; AFS; French Clb; Yrbk Stf; Sec Frsh Cls; Rep Stu Cncl; Cheerleading; Hon Roll; Pres Ftns Awd; SUNY Stonybrook; Pre Med.

TROCH, RODNEY; Center Moriches HS; Center Moriches, NY; (Y); Computer Clb; Ski Clb; Yrbk Stf; Gerald S Levine Schlrshp Excllnc Sci 86; Excllnc Comp Stds 86; Kean Coll; Comp Sci.

TROCHA, INGRID M; St Francis Prep Schl; Glendale, NY; (S); 144/692; German Clb; Math Clb; Chorus; Stage Crew; Tennis; Trk; Vllybl; Opt Clb Awd; Ridgewood Volntr Ambulance Corps 86; Finc.

TROCHIANO, CHRISTOPHER; Tottenville HS; Staten Island, NY; (Y); 29/850; Art Clb; Boy Scts; Key Clb; Model UN; SADD; Ftbl; Wt Lftg; Pace U Schltc Schlrshp 86; NY Telepne Co Schlrshp 86; Turgers U; Comm.

TROENDLE, REBECCA; Jamesville-Dewitt HS; Syracuse, NY; (Y); Girl Scts; Model UN; Political Wkr; Chorus; School Musical; Yrbk Stf; High Hon Roll; NHS; French Clb; Nwsp Rptr; Intl Rltns.

TROFINOFF, BARBARA J; Beacon HS; Beacon, NY; (Y); Cmnty Wkr; FTA; Office Aide; Varsity Clb; Nwsp Rptr; Yrbk Bus Mgr; Var Tennis; Annual Harvard Model Cngrs 86; Psych.

TROIANI, BEATRICE; West Hampton Beach HS; East Quogue, NY; (Y); 19/261; Spanish Clb; Mrchg Band; Pep Band; Lit Mag; Rep Stu Cncl; Bsbl; Stat Bsktbl; Socr; JV Im Vllybl; Hon Roll.

TROIANO, BARBARA; Ward Melville HS; E Setauket, NY; (Y); 142/675; Varsity Clb; Var Capt Bsktbl; Var Fld Hcky; JV Capt Sftbl; JV Capt Vllybl; High Hon Roll; James Madison U; Bus Mgmt.

TROIANO, TRICIA; John H Glenn HS; E Northport, NY; (Y); Dance Clb; Hosp Aide; Band; Mrchg Band; Yrbk Stf; Stu Cncl; Fld Hcky; Trk; Farmingdale Stony Pk; Spec Ed.

TROISE, FRANK; Moore Catholic HS; Staten Island, NY; (Y); Lit Mag; Rep Stu Cncl; Hon Roll.

TROISI, DAWN; Wantagh HS; Wantagh, NY; (Y); Mathletes; Spanish Clb; Nwsp Rptr; Yrbk Ed-Chief; Yrbk Stf; Sec Frsh Cls; Pres Soph Cls; Pres Jr Cls; Pres Sr Cls; Var Badmtn; Am Leg Awd Ldrshp 86.

TROISI, KIMBERLY; Mynderse Acad; Seneca Falls, NY; (Y); 1/130; Am Leg Aux Girls St; School Musical; Yrbk Sprt Ed; Pres Frsh Cls; Sec Jr Cls; Var L Crs Cntry; High Hon Roll; NHS; Ntl Merit Ltr; Masonic Ldg Awd Engl; Lang Dept Awd Spnsh; Trautman Mem Soc Studies; Hugh O Brian Yth Fndtn Ldrshp Sem; Bio.

TROJANOVIC, SILVIA; Frontier SR HS; Lakeview, NY; (Y); Pres VP German Clb; Pep Clb; Concert Band; Stu Cncl; Stat Bsktbl; Var Score Keeper; Var JV Socr; JV Im Vllybl; Hon Roll; Tght Grmn To Elem Chldrn 86; Cornell; Vet.

TROLLER, NOELLE; Bishop Grimes HS; Syracuse, NY; (Y); Drama Clb; Speech Tm; Band; Concert Band; School Musical; Variety Show; Cheerleading; Pom Pon; Sftbl; Hon Roll; High Achvt Music.

TROMBLY, JOHN J; Immaculate Heart Central HS; Watertown, NY; (Y); 7/80; Church Yth Grp; Cmnty Wkr; Nwsp Stf; Yrbk Bus Mgr; Yrbk Ed-Chief; Ice Hcky; Hon Roll; Spanish Clb; School Play; Variety Show; NYS Regents Schlrp 86; Cum Laude Natl Latin Exam 84; Le Moyne Coll; Comp Sci.

TROMBLY, MICHAEL; Ogdensburg Free Acad; Rensselaer Falls, NY; (Y); 48/190; Church Yth Grp; Nwsp Stf; Yrbk Stf; Stu Cncl; Regnts Schlrshp 86; Keuka Clg; Bus Mgmt.

TRONCOSO, JACQUELINE; Preston HS; Bronx, NY; (S); Computer Clb; Drama Clb; Science Clb; Teachers Aide; Stage Crew; Trs Soph Cls; Pres Jr Cls; Bowling; High Hon Roll; Jr NHS; NEDT Achvt Awd 83; Cert Comp Pgm Part I 84; Cert Merit Comp Pgmmng Part II 85; St Johns; Mktng Mngmnt.

TRONOLONE JR, MICHAEL F; Norwich HS; Norwich, NY; (Y); 6/216; Pres Soph Cls; Pres Jr Cls; Pres Sr Cls; Var L Ftbl; Var L Wrstlng; High Hon Roll; NHS; Boy Scts; Exploring; Leo Clb; Army ROTC Schlrshp 86; Hugh O Brian Yth Ldrshp Awd 84; Ldrshp Awd 85; Physicin.

TROPP, PATA LATREEA; Bronx High School Of Science; New York, NY; (Y); Teachers Aide; Nwsp Rptr; Clmba U; Bio Chmstry.

TROST, JENNIFER; Clarence Central SR HS; Clarence Ctr, NY; (Y); Latin Clb; Pep Clb; Chorus; Hon Roll; Nrs.

TROTMAN, SHAYNE; St Joseph HS; Brooklyn, NY; (Y); Stage Crew; Yrbk Stf; Swmmng; Hon Roll; :Psych.

TROTSKY, JULIE; Villa Maria Acad; Buffalo, NY; (Y); Computer Clb; FBLA; School Play; Gym; Bryant & Stratton; Exec Sec.

TROTTER, ANGELA; Massena Central HS; Massena, NY; (Y); Hosp Aide; Band; Concert Band; Jazz Band; Mrchg Band; JV Var Bsktbl; JV Score Keeper; Var Capt Swmmng; Var Trk; Erly Chldhd Dev.

TROUTMAN, TERI; Churchville-Chili HS; Rochester, NY; (Y); Church Yth Grp; Math Tm; Model UN; Teachers Aide; Stu Cncl; Coach Actv; Var Swmmng; Var Trk; High Hon Roll; NHS; Math.

TROVATO, RICHARD L; Liverpool HS; Liverpool, NY; (Y); Computer Clb; JA; Math Clb; Hon Roll; Jr NHS; NHS; Prfct Atten Awd; NYS Regnts Schlrshp 86; ST U Of NY Buffalo; Aero Engr.

TROWBRIDGE III, PAUL; Alden Central HS; Corfu, NY; (S); 35/205; Aud/Vis; Pres VP 4-H; Trs VP FFA; Stage Crew; 4-H Awd; ST Extemporaneous Spkng Cntst 8486; Outstndng Cty Beef Stu 85; Star Chptr Farmer 85; Aernutcl Engr.

TROWERS, SONIA; New Rochelle HS; New Rochelle, NY; (Y); Church Yth Grp; Cmnty Wkr; GAA; Hosp Aide; SADD; Var L Tennis; Wrstlng; Hon Roll; Jr NHS; NHS; Duke; Pre-Med.

TRUAX, MELISSA D; Lowville Acad & Central HS; Lowville, NY; (Y); Girl Scts; Latin Clb; Spanish Clb; Nwsp Stf; Yrbk Ed-Chief; Score Keeper; JV Var Socr; Hon Roll; Rgnts Schlrshp 86.

TRUAX, RANDY L; Keshoqua Central HS; Dalton, NY; (Y); 3/60; Spanish Clb; High Hon Roll; Hon Roll; U Of NYS Educ Dept Rgnts Schlrshp 86; Bryant & Stratton Bus Inst; Bus.

TRUDEAU, CHRISTOPHER; Amsterdam HS; Amsterdam, NY; (Y); 116/316; Boy Scts; Band; Concert Band; Mrchg Band; Yrbk Stf; Crs Cntry; Trk; Air Force; Engrng.

TRUE, LAURIE; Saranac Central HS; Saranac, NY; (S); Church Yth Grp; Cmnty Wkr; SADD; Yrbk Stf; Trs Stu Cncl; JV Var Socr; JV Sftbl; JV Vllybl; Hon Roll; Soccer Best Dfnse Man 4 Yrs 83-86; Prom Ct 85; Lttr & Pin Sprts 82-86; CUPH Med Central; Radiologic.

TRUEMAN, DANIEL L; Shoreham-Wading River HS; Shoreham, NY; (Y); Science Clb; Acpl Chr; Chorus; Madrigals; Orch; School Musical; School Play; Stage Crew; Im Badmtn; Im Bsktbl; All ST Violinst 85-86; Lng Islnd Sci Cngrss Hghst Hnrs 86; Intl Sci Fair Fnlst 86; Stanford U; Music.

TRUEX, SHELLEY; Susquehanna Valley HS; Binghamton, NY; (Y); 12/180; Drama Clb; Pep Clb; Spanish Clb; Chorus; School Play; Nwsp Rptr; Nwsp Stf; Stu Cncl; Vllybl; NHS; Suny Binghamton; Pre-Law.

TRUEX, VICKI; Susquehanna Valley HS; Binghamton, NY; (Y); 44/173; Drama Clb; Band; Concert Band; Variety Show; Nwsp Rptr; Yrbk Stf; Rep Stu Cncl; Tennis; Vllybl; Hon Roll; Acadmc All Amercn 85-86; Area All ST Chrs; SUNY; Music.

TRUFELLI, MICHELE; St Marys Girls HS; Manhasset, NY; (Y); 3/180; French Clb; Ski Clb; Mgr Stage Crew; Yrbk Ed-Chief; Var Cheerleading; Var Swmmng; High Hon Roll; NHS; Ntl Merit SF.

TRUFFER, LORI E; Ward Melville HS; Setauket, NY; (Y); Hosp Aide; Ski Clb; Mgr(s); JV Socr; Var Trk; High Hon Roll; Hon Roll; Rgnts Schlrshp 86; U Of New Hampshire; Lbrl Arts.

TRUJILLO, MARIBEL; Academy Of St Joseph; Centereach, NY; (Y); Dance Clb; Spanish Clb; Sec SADD; Variety Show; Yrbk Stf; Praise Wrthy Lst; Excllnc Spnsh; Dance.

TRUMAN, TRACY; Afton Central HS; Nineveh, NY; (Y); FBLA; Spanish Clb; SADD; Stu Cncl; Cheerleading; Fld Hcky; High Hon Roll; Hon Roll; NHS; Prfct Atten Awd; Ltr Actvty Points 86; Field Hockey Regnl Champs Medal 85; Oerp Enterprise SF 86; Mohawk Valley; Mrktng.

TRUMBAUER, TAMMY; Herkimer SR HS; Herkimer, NY; (Y); 14/113; Church Yth Grp; ROTC; Acpl Chr; Chorus; Concert Band; Jazz Band; School Musical; Hon Roll; NHS; Robert Wesleyan; Bus Admn.

TRUMPOWSKY, ERIC; James E Sperry HS; Rochester, NY; (Y); 24/273; Drama Clb; Thesps; Chorus; Jazz Band; Madrigals; School Musical; French Hon Soc; Hon Roll; Rgnts Schlrshp, Musicn Yr 85-86; All ST Mxd Choir 85; Potsdam; Music.

TRUONG, MAI; James E Sperry HS; Henrietta, NY; (Y); #6 In Class; French Clb; Church Choir; Trs Stu Cncl; Im Vllybl; French Hon Soc; High Hon Roll; Sec NHS; Prfct Atten Awd; Cert De Merit 85-86; Annl Genesee Vly H S Chem Achvt 86; U Of R; Med.

TRUONG, MYPHUONG; Curtis HS; Staten Island, NY; (Y); 1/304; Intnl Clb; Math Clb; High Hon Roll; Hon Roll; NHS; Prfct Atten Awd; Val; Super Yth 84 & 85; Med.

TRUST, JANE ELLEN; Clarkstown South HS; New City, NY; (Y); Capt Debate Tm; Var GAA; Capt Speech Tm; Band; Concert Band; Mrchg Band; Fld Hcky; Lcrss; Brdcstng.

TRYBALSKI, FRANCINE; Rome Catholic HS; Rome, NY; (Y); 27/68; Hosp Aide; School Musical; Yrbk Bus Mgr; Ed Yrbk Ed-Chief; Yrbk Stf; Sec Frsh Cls; Var Trk; Hon Roll; Nrsg Schlrshp 86; St Josephs Hosp Hlth; RN.

TRYPUC, HEATHER; Patchogue Medford HS; Patchogue, NY; (S); 6/653; Girl Scts; Math Tm; Concert Band; Mrchg Band; Orch; Capt Var Tennis; Jr NHS; NHS; Spanish NHS; Perf Atten Awd 83-85; R A Goodale Acad, Ctznshp Awd, Grl Sct Slvr Ldrshp 83; NYSSMA Music Awds 83-86; Acctng.

TRYT, KRYSTINA; Our Lady Of Mercy HS; Rochester, NY; (Y); Var Church Yth Grp; Cmnty Wkr; Pres Dance Clb; Exploring; French Clb; SADD; Chorus; Church Choir; Ed Yrbk Stf; Hon Roll; French Awd 85; Schlrshp Travel Poland Dance Course 86; Alliance Coll; Accntng.

TRZASKA, ELAINE; Southpark HS; Buffalo, NY; (Y); Boys Clb Am; Nwsp Stf; High Hon Roll; Hon Roll; Jr NHS; NHS; Keystone Club Babcock Boys/Girls Club 83; Psych.

TRZASKOS, TODD; Amsterdam HS; Amesterdam, NY; (Y); 9/326; Yrbk Stf; Pres Sr Cls; Var Capt Socr; Var Capt Wrstlng; High Hon Roll; Pres NHS; Hugh O Brien Yth Ldrshp St Sr 85; Intl Bus.

TRZYBINSKI, MARTIN; Turner Carroll HS; Buffalo, NY; (Y); 10/165; 4-H; Stage Crew; Bsbl; Bsktbl; Ftbl; 4-H Awd; Ntl Merit Ltr.

TSANG, ANNA; Richmand Hill HS; Richmond Hill, NY; (Y); 87/300; Cmnty Wkr; Girl Scts; VP Key Clb; School Musical; Lit Mag; Rep Stu Cncl; Bowling; Hon Roll; Prfct Atten Awd; SADD; Bus Hnr Soc, Soc Stds Hnr Rll 85-86; ST Pstr Awd 85; Bernard M Baruch Coll; Bus Ed.

TSANG, OILING; John Dewey HS; Brooklyn, NY; (Y); Badmtn; Vllybl; Prfct Atten Awd; Pratt Schlrshp 86; Pratt Inst; Arch.

TSANTRIZOS, STACEY; East Meadow HS; E Meadow, NY; (Y); Church Yth Grp; Girl Scts; Key Clb; Chorus; Drm Mjr(t); Yrbk Stf; JV Cheerleading; Cit Awd; Hon Roll; Awd Best Stu Greek 84-86; Pre-Med.

TSATSARONIS, CHRIS; St Francis Prep; Flushing, NY; (S); 208/744; Aud/Vis; Cmnty Wkr; Drama Clb; Teachers Aide; Stage Crew; Yrbk Stf; Im Ftbl; Hon Roll; NHS; Prfct Atten Awd; NY U; Med.

TSEKERIDES, TED E; Sleepy Hollow HS; N Tarrytown, NY; (Y); 4/180; Church Yth Grp; Math Clb; Math Tm; Model UN; Political Wkr; Science Clb; Nwsp Rptr; Nwsp Stf; Yrbk Stf; Pres Frsh Cls; Sci-Engr Fair Awd US Army 86; Ciba Gerby Math-Sci Awd 86; Con-Edison Schlr-Athlt Awd 86; Columbia U; Biochem.

TSIVIN, YURY; Franklin D Roosevelt HS; New York, NY; (Y); Computer Clb; English Clb; JA; Math Tm; Office Aide; Quiz Bowl; Science Clb; Outstndg Achv Sci Research Awd 86; Seers Awd 86; Bourough Fair Awd 86.

TSOLOMYTIS, EVIE; St Catherine Acad; Bronx, NY; (Y); 37/200; Office Aide; Teachers Aide; Chorus; Rep Soph Cls; Rep Stu Cncl; Iona Coll; Journlsm.

TSU, JAMES; John Dewey HS; Brooklyn, NY; (Y); Teachers Aide; Nwsp Ed-Chief; Construction Engr.

TU, CHENG; St Agnes HS; New York, NY; (Y); 27/111; Intnl Clb; Var Capt Bowling; Hon Roll; Stoney Brook U; Comp Sci.

TU, LINGCHIH; Franklin K Lane HS; New York, NY; (Y); 31/659; Math Tm; Rgnt Schlrshp 86; SUNY-STNY Brk; Engrng.

TUBBS, JOY; Saratoga Central Catholic HS; Saratoga Springs, NY; (S); 15/36; Chess Clb; Church Yth Grp; Cmnty Wkr; Debate Tm; French Clb; Office Aide; Ski Clb; Pres Chorus; Church Choir; Nwsp Stf; All Cnty Chorous; Msc Awd 86; Brklee Coll Of Music; Vcl Msc.

TUBBS, LYNN; Chatham Central HS; Chatham, NY; (Y); Pres Church Yth Grp; Band; Chorus; School Musical; Variety Show; Yrbk Stf; Var Capt Cheerleading; High Hon Roll; NHS; Concert Band; Rotary Ldrshp Conf 85; Child Psych.

TUBBS, MICHAEL; Crown Point Central HS; Crown Point, NY; (S); 3/34; Boy Scts; Drama Clb; Scholastic Bowl; Varsity Clb; School Play; Nwsp Stf; Bsbl; Bsktbl; Hon Roll; NHS; Elec Engrng.

TUBLISKY, ILYSE; Smithtown High Schl West; Kings Park, NY; (Y); SADD; Yrbk Sprt Ed; Yrbk Stf; Frsh Cls; Soph Cls; Jr Cls; Sr Cls; Stu Cncl; Mgr Bsbl; Var Capt Cheerleading; Regents Schlrshp Awd 85-86; SUNY Albany; Bus Mgt.

TUCCI, LARRY; Lindenhurst HS; Lindenhurst, NY; (Y); Yrbk Stf; Bsbl; Diving; Swmmng; Hon Roll; Acdmc All-Amer Awd 86; Lndnhrst Natl Lttle Lge Schlrshp 86; Nassau Community; TV Prod.

TUCCILLO, GAIL; Cornwall Central HS; Highland Mills, NY; (Y); Ski Clb; Spanish Clb; Nwsp Rptr; Nwsp Stf; Yrbk Phtg; Yrbk Stf; High Hon Roll; Hon Roll; NHS; Business.

TUCEK, TIMOTHY R; Bainbridge-Guilford Cent Schl; Bainbridge, NY; (Y); Ski Clb; Varsity Clb; Ftbl; Ice Hcky; Trk; Hon Roll; Broome CC; Engrng Sci.

TUCHRELLO, TIMOTHY; Livonia Central HS; Avon, NY; (Y); Art Clb; Camera Clb; Yrbk Phtg; Bsktbl; High Hon Roll; Hon Roll; Jr NHS; Sibleys Art Awd 86; Approval For Schl Of Performing Arts 86; Geneseo Art How Honrbl Mention 85; Rochester Inst Of Tech; Film.

TUCK, MICHAEL; New Rochelle HS; New Rochelle, NY; (Y); Ski Clb; Rep Frsh Cls; Var L Ftbl; Var L Trk; Magna Cum Laude Latin Achvt Tst 86; Law.

TUCKER, DORRIS D; Kenmore West HS; Kenmore, NY; (Y); 37/420; Drama Clb; Pres French Clb; Pres Acpl Chr; School Musical; Variety Show; Yrbk Stf; Stu Cncl; JV Var Cheerleading; Cit Awd; High Hon Roll; Pres Acad Fit Awd 86; US Sec Ed Awd 85; Outstndg Vocl Stu 86; Miami OH; Biol.

TUCKER, ERVENA; George W Wingate HS; New York, NY; (Y); Cmnty Wkr; Teachers Aide; Lawyer.

TUCKER, FAREALE; Poughkeepsie HS; Poughkeepsie, NY; (Y); GAA; Variety Show; Off Jr Cls; Bsktbl; Vllybl; High Hon Roll; Atten Awds 83-86.

TUCKER, JENNIFER; Jamesville Dewitt HS; Dewitt, NY; (Y); 14/234; Math Tm; Model UN; Stage Crew; High Hon Roll; NHS; Acad Awd Soc Studies 86; Bio.

TUCKER, JOY CELESTE; Hempstead HS; Hempstead, NY; (Y); Church Yth Grp; Hosp Aide; Model UN; Tennis; High Hon Roll; Hon Roll; NHS; MESA/STEP Ofc Treas 83-86; Law Clb Nassau Bar Assoc 86; Engl.

TUCKER, JULIE; Auburn HS; Auburn, NY; (Y); Am Leg Aux Girls St; Varsity Clb; Nwsp Sprt Ed; VP Frsh Cls; Pres Soph Cls; Pres Jr Cls; Pres Sr Cls; Var Capt Bsktbl; Var Capt Sftbl; NHS; Dom Gasparo Mem Awd For Bsktbl, Sftbl & Sccr 86; MVP-BSKTBL 84; Most Defensive-Sccr 85; Pre-Med.

TUCKER, KATHY; Warrensburg Central HS; Warrensburg, NY; (Y); 16/52; Yrbk Stf; Sec Sr Cls; Hon Roll; Norstar Bus Awd 86; Unique Plcmnt Awd Mst Prof Stu Awd 86; St Bonaventure U; Acctng.

TUCKER, LANCE; Ravena-Coeymans-Selkirk HS; Ravena, NY; (Y); Boy Scts; German Clb; Yrbk Phtg; VP Jr Cls; L Var Bsktbl; L Var Jr Cls; L Var Trk; Hon Roll; Boy Scts; German Clb; Bus Adm.

TUCKER, MARK; Edmundian Ignatius Rice HS; New York, NY; (Y); 6/96; Chorus; Church Choir; Stage Crew; Rep Soph Cls; Rep Jr Cls; Rep Sr Cls; Rep Stu Cncl; Cit Awd; High Hon Roll; Rice Scholar 83; Pre-Law.

TUCKER, TIMOTHY; St Marys HS; E Aurora, NY; (Y); Boy Scts; Church Yth Grp; SADD; Church Choir; Im Mgr Bsktbl; JV Var Ftbl.

TUE, DEBORAH; John H Glenn HS; E Northport, NY; (Y); Trs Church Yth Grp; Spanish Clb; Yrbk Stf; High Hon Roll; Hon Roll; NHS; Spanish NHS; Bus.

TUFARIELLI, GIA-CYNTHIA; St Edmund HS; Brooklyn, NY; (Y); Rep Frsh Cls; High Hon Roll; Italn Hnr Rl 83-86; Intl Bus.

TUGAW, CURT; Liverpool HS; Liverpool, NY; (Y); 106/850; Trs Church Yth Grp; Sec JA; Library Aide; Acpl Chr; Chorus; Church Choir; Nwsp Ed-Chief; Nwsp Rptr; Stat Bsktbl; Stat Ftbl; Syracuse Post-Standard Carrier Of Yr 85; NY ST Central Rgn Carier Of Yr 85; CNY JA Corp Sec Of Yr; SUNY Albany; Bus.

TULLAR, TERI; Cicero-N Syracuse HS; Clay, NY; (S); 64/626; Pres Church Yth Grp; Drama Clb; Ski Clb; Band; Mrchg Band; School Play; Stu Cncl; Var Golf; Powder Puff Ftbl; NHS; Natl Merit Fndtn 85-86; WV U; Med.

TULLY, WILLIAM T; John S Burke Chs HS; Chester, NY; (Y); Art Clb; Drama Clb; Ski Clb; School Play; Lit Mag; Crs Cntry; Trk; Ntl Merit Ltr; NEDT Awd; NYS Rgnts Schlrshp; SUNY Geneseo; Artst.

TULOWIECKI, LINDA; Liverpool HS; Liverpool, NY; (Y); 230/750; Ski Clb; Golf; Powder Puff Ftbl; Socr; Sftbl; Swmmng; Tennis; Vllybl; Hon Roll; Ntl Merit Ltr; Schlrshp Cnsrmr Crdt Assctn 86; Cert Of Hnr & Merit 84-86; Canton ATC; Accntng.

TUMIA, VINCENT; Northstar Christian Acad; Rochester, NY; (S); Church Yth Grp; Drama Clb; JA; School Play; Yrbk Stf; Var Socr; Hon Roll; NHS; MIP Soccer 85; Word Life Schlrshp 84-86; Word Life Bible Inst; Thlgy.

TUMMONS, SANDRA; Saranac Lk Central HS; Saranac Lk, NY; (Y); 14/150; Computer Clb; Rep Frsh Cls; Rep Stu Cncl; Bsktbl; NHS; Cmmnctns.

TUMMONS, TAMMY; Franklin Acad; Malone, NY; (Y); Hon Roll; Outstndg Adv Clrk Typsts 86; Schltc Awd For Achvt 86; Mater Dei Coll; Med Sec.

TUNCA, DENIZ; F D Roosevelt HS; Brooklyn, NY; (Y); 41/587; Cmnty Wkr; Math Tm; Teachers Aide; Band; Cit Awd; Hon Roll; Pres Schlr; Baruch Coll; Bus.

TUNG, YING; Murry Bergtraum HS Business Careers; New York, NY; (Y); Library Aide; NHS; Acctng.

TUNG, YUKI MIYAMOTO; Edgemont HS; Scarsdale, NY; (Y); L Crs Cntry; L Trk; Brown U Clb Westchester Cnty Reg Schlr 86; SUNY Yng Plywrghts Assc Schlrshp 85; Brown U; Ec.

TUNNICLIFF, JEFFREY; Addison Central HS; Cameron, NY; (Y); Chess Clb; Library Aide; High Hon Roll; Hon Roll; NHS.

TUOHY, DANIELLE M; St Vencent Ferrer HS; Woodside, NY; (Y); Art Clb; Hon Roll; Rgnts Schlrshp Nrsng 86; Wagner Coll Acdmc Schlrshp 86; Adelphi U; Nrsng.

TURANO, KIM; Moore Catholic HS; Staten Island, NY; (Y); Ski Clb; Spanish Clb; School Musical; Cheerleading; Hon Roll; NHS; Physcl Thrpy.

TURANO, MARIANNE; St Catharane Acad; Bronx, NY; (Y); Dance Clb; Math Clb; Ski Clb; Yrbk Ed-Chief; Yrbk Stf; Stu Cncl; Hon Roll; Val; Manhattan Coll; CPA.

TURCO, JON SCOTT; Monsignor Farrell HS; Staten Island, NY; (Y); VP Debate Tm; Hosp Aide; VP Spanish Clb; Varsity Clb; VP Soph Cls; VP Jr Cls; Stu Cncl; Var L Ftbl; Var L Socr; Var L Trk; Exclnce Mock Trial Awd NYS Bar Assoc, Jr Statesmen Am Princeton Conf Best Debator 86; DAR 82-83; Pre-Law.

TURCOTTE, MONICA; Honeoye Central Schl; Hemlock, NY; (S); 7/69; French Clb; Sec Chorus; Madrigals; School Musical; School Play; Swing Chorus; Yrbk Stf; Pres Stu Cncl; Hon Roll; NCTE Awd; Oswego; Lng.

TURER, JOLEEN GEORGI; New Rochelle HS; New Rochelle, NY; (Y); 61/550; Cmnty Wkr; Model UN; Stage Crew; Var L Tennis; Hon Roll; Lion Awd; NHS; US Dept Of Ed Pres Acdmc Fitness Awd 86; Tennis Mag Jr Sportsmnshp Awd 84; Svc Awd 83; NY U.

TURGUT, UMMULHAN; Greece Athena HS; Rochester, NY; (Y); French Clb; Vllybl; High Hon Roll; Hon Roll; Pre-Law.

TURI, LINDA; John F Kennedy HS; Utica, NY; (S); 6/130; Chorus; Church Choir; Nwsp Ed-Chief; Yrbk Ed-Chief; Var Badmtn; High Hon Roll; Jr NHS; NHS; Regnts Schlrshp 86; Cortlnd Coll; Pre-Law.

TURIC, MICHELLE; Thomas A Edison JR SR HS; Elmira Hts, NY; (Y); #22 In Class; Varsity Clb; School Musical; Sec Frsh Cls; Sec Soph Cls; Sec Jr Cls; Sec Sr Cls; Var Capt Bsktbl; Var Capt Sftbl; Var Capt Swmmng; Var L Trk; Athl Of Yr 86; Hmcmng Queen 85; Empire St Games Vllybl 85; Winthrop Coll; Accntng.

TURINO, CARRIE; Catholic Central HS; Troy, NY; (Y); Church Yth Grp; Math Clb; Pep Clb; Science Clb; Spanish Clb; SADD; Varsity Clb; Variety Show; Yrbk Stf; Var JV Cheerleading; Pol Sci.

TURK, KEVIN; Msgr Farrell HS; Staten Island, NY; (Y); 3/300; Aud/Vis; Cmnty Wkr; Lit Mag; Var Crs Cntry; Var Trk; High Hon Roll; NCTE Awd; NHS; Engr.

TURK, ROBYN; Wantagh HS; Wantagh, NY; (Y); 42/279; Pres French Clb; Hosp Aide; Pres SADD; Temple Yth Grp; VP Soph Cls; Rep Stu Cncl; Var Swmmng; NHS; Drama Clb; Mathletes; Abraham Joshua Heschel Hnr Soc 85-86; Amer Lg Cert Schl Awd Comp Elec 84; NY Regents Scholar 86; Lang.

TURKER, BILGIN; HS Of Fashion Industry; Flushing, NY; (Y); 41/350; Drama Clb; Library Aide; Teachers Aide; School Play; Yrbk Stf; Vllybl; Ntl Merit Schol; Hon Mntn Excllnc Plywrtng Cntst 86; Alxndr Outstndng Achvt Awd Art 86; Hcktt Ortry Awd 86; Honter Coll; Media.

TURMEL, DEBORAH; Rensselaer Middle HS; Rensselaer, NY; (Y); DECA; FBLA; Voc Indstrl Clbs Of Amer Reprtr 86; Comp Prog.

TURNBULL, IRENE REBECCA; Murry Bergtraum HS For Busnss Careers; Brooklyn, NY; (Y); Computer Clb; Debate Tm; FHA; Hon Roll; NHS; Prfct Atten Awd; Attrny Gnrls Trpl C Awd 84; Cmptrllrs Awd 84; Afrcn Chrstn Tchrs Assn Mrtn Lthr Kng JR Awd 84; Bus Admn.

TURNBULL, TRACEY; Mahopac HS; Mahopac, NY; (Y); 26/409; SADD; Chorus; Yrbk Stf; VP L Bsktbl; VP L Fld Hcky; VP L Socr; Im Vllybl; High Hon Roll; NHS; Prfct Atten Awd; Al Conf Field Hockey 84-85; Ed.

TURNER, ELLYN; Oceanside HS; Oceanside, NY; (Y); 70/531; Key Clb; Spanish Clb; Hon Roll; Jr NHS; Acctg.

TURNER, GUINEVERE J; O Neill HS; Highland Falls, NY; (Y); 20/150; Debate Tm; Drama Clb; French Clb; Pep Clb; Nwsp Rptr; Ed Lit Mag; High Hon Roll; NHS; Amer Lgn Awd-Spch 85; Vassar Coll; Jrnlsm.

TURNER, JASON; West Hempstead HS; W Hempstead, NY; (Y); Pres Church Yth Grp; Spanish Clb; Variety Show; Nwsp Rptr; Var Capt Ftbl; L Trk; Wt Lftg; High Hon Roll; Jr NHS; NHS; Bus Admin.

TURNER, JILL ELIZABETH; Madrid-Waddington Central HS; Waddington, NY; (Y); 22/56; French Clb; Trs Band; Concert Band; Mrchg Band; School Musical; Stage Crew; Yrbk Rptr; Stat Bsbl; Hon Roll; Excellence Creative Writing Awd 86; St Ptrsbrg JR Coll; Secndry Ed.

TURNER, JOHN; Lansingburgh HS; Troy, NY; (Y); Boys Clb Am; Pres Sr Cls; Bsbl; Bsktbl; Capt Ftbl; Wt Lftg; High Hon Roll; Jr NHS; Pres NHS; Sal; Business Awd 86.

TURNER, JOSEPH; Saranac Lake HS; Bloomingdale, NY; (Y); Boy Scts; Yrbk Stf; Rep Jr Cls; JV Var Ftbl; US Air Frc; Avitn.

TURNER, KEREN; Liverpool HS; Baldwinsville, NY; (Y); 69/884; Radio Clb; Ski Clb; Band; Var Crs Cntry; Var Trk; High Hon Roll; NHS; Rotary Awd; Exploring; Rep Stu Cncl; JV Crew 86; Commtns.

TURNER, LAURA; The Mary Louis Acad; Richmond Hill, NY; (Y); 120/270; Chorus; Mt St Vincent Comptv Schlrshp; NYS Schlrshp; Mt St Vincent; Nrsng.

TURNER, MICHAEL; Fairport HS; Fairport, NY; (Y); Pres Drama Clb; Radio Clb; Acpl Chr; School Musical; School Play; Rep Stu Cncl; Im Vllybl; Hon Roll; NY Smmr Schl Thtre 85; Thtre.

TURNER, RITA; Sherburne Earlville HS; Earlville, NY; (Y); 11/160; 4-H; FBLA; Band; Chorus; Sec Stu Cncl; NHS; Rgnts Schlrshp 86; Geneseo; Elem Tchr.

TURNER, STEPHENIE; Auburn HS; Auburn, NY; (Y); 120/392; Intnl Clb; ROTC; Drill Tm; Nwsp Stf; JV Fld Hcky; DAR Awd; Hon Roll; Mss Hrngtn Awd 86; Mltry Ordr Of Wrld Wrs 84; Ntl Sojourners Awd 85; Memphis ST U; Crmnl Jstc.

TURNER, TISHA L; Notre Dame Schl; New York, NY; (Y); Chess Clb; Dance Clb; Drama Clb; Math Clb; Math Tm; Science Clb; School Play; Yrbk Stf; Cheerleading; Comp Engrng.

TUROK, MICHAEL S; Yeshiva Univ HS; Jamaica Estates, NY; (Y); Mathletes; Math Tm; Band; Nwsp Ed-Chief; Yrbk Stf; Rep Stu Cncl; Im Bsktbl; Var Sftbl; NHS; Ntl Merit SF; Princeton U; Bio Chem.

TURQUE, THEO; H S For The Humaniti; New York, NY; (Y); Chorus; Rep Soph Cls; Var Socr; Var Trk; Law Clb 84.

TURTURRO, DIANE J; W C Mepham HS; Bellmore, NY; (Y); 13/360; Hosp Aide; Math Tm; Sec Science Clb; Band; Nwsp Rptr; Nwsp Stf; Yrbk Stf; Cmnty Wkr; French Hon Soc; Hon Roll; Regents Schlrshp Awd 86; NAFL Awd Frgn Lang 83; Rochester Inst Tech; Bio-Med.

TURTURRO, NANCY; Bellport HS; E Patchogue, NY; (Y); Cmnty Wkr; French Clb; Orch; School Musical; Off Frsh Cls; Off Soph Cls; Stu Cncl; Hon Roll; Jr NHS; Frnch Awd Apprctn 86; Dqncl I Math Awd Apprctn 85; Cert Grad Barbizon 83-84; Fshn Inst Tech; Fshn.

TUTHILL, KATHLEEN; Mercy HS; Riverhead, NY; (Y); 5/125; Math Clb; Church Choir; Var Crs Cntry; Var JV Fld Hcky; Var JV Sftbl; High Hon Roll; Mth Awd; Srv Awd; Mst Vlbl Plyr On JV Fld Hcky.

TUTONE, JENNIFER; South Shore HS; Brooklyn, NY; (Y); Dance Clb; Model UN; Co-Capt Pep Clb; SADD; Chorus; Yrbk Stf; Stu Cncl; Capt Cheerleading; Gym; Sec NHS; Archon 86; Engrng.

TUTTLE, BRIAN D; Waterville Central Schl; Waterville, NY; (Y); 6/89; Am Leg Boys St; Varsity Clb; Jazz Band; Pres Sr Cls; Rep Stu Cncl; L Crs Cntry; Capt L Socr; L Tennis; High Hon Roll; NHS; Air Force ROTC Schrlshp 86; NY ST Regents Schlrshp 86; Clarkson U; Comp Sci.

TUTTLE, DANIEL D; Newfane SR HS; Lockport, NY; (S); Church Yth Grp; Bsbl; Hon Roll; Drftg.

TUTTLE, KEVIN; Waterville Central HS; Waterville, NY; (Y); Camera Clb; Ski Clb; Varsity Clb; Stage Crew; Yrbk Phtg; Sec Frsh Cls; VP Soph Cls; Var Capt Socr; Var Trk; Hon Roll; Elec Engrng.

TUTTLE, MICHAEL; Maple Hill HS; Castleton, NY; (S); French Clb; JV Var Bsbl; JV Var Bsktbl; JV Socr; Hon Roll; Acctng.

TUTTLE, SHANNON MARIE; Corinth Central HS; Corinth, NY; (Y); Cmnty Wkr; Drama Clb; GAA; Speech Tm; SADD; Variety Show; Yrbk Stf; Pres Jr Cls; Fld Hcky; Hon Roll; Hmcmng Princess 85; Spoke Baccaloureate 86; Nrsng Home Volunteer 84-85.

TUXBURY, LARRY D; Shaker HS; Latham, NY; (Y); Chorus; School Musical; School Play; Stage Crew; Swing Chorus; Crs Cntry; NHS; U Of VT; Med.

TVAROHA, JILL; Groton Central HS; Groton, NY; (Y); Art Clb; Dance Clb; Drama Clb; 4-H; FHA; PAVAS; Chorus; Color Guard; Mrchg Band; School Play; Chorus 82-85; Karate 85; Dance 82-85; Dance Instr.

TVAROHA, SUSAN M; Groton HS; Groton, NY; (Y); Am Leg Aux Girls St; Cmnty Wkr; Library Aide; Spanish Clb; Sec Stu Cncl; Var L Crs Cntry; Var L Trk; High Hon Roll; Hon Roll; NHS; Frnds Of Publc Libr Awd 84-85; Math Cont Awd 84-85; Typg Awd 85-86; Math.

TWAROG, PAUL; Saint Marys HS; Elma, NY; (Y); 12/163; Drama Clb; Office Aide; SADD; Varsity Clb; School Musical; School Play; Stage Crew; Nwsp Rptr; Nwsp Stf; Yrbk Stf; Svc Schl 86; Eagles Lancaster Honorary Awd 86; NYU; Cardiac Care.

TWINING, KURT; Newfield HS; Selden, NY; (Y); Variety Show; Ftbl; Wrstlng; French Hon Soc; High Hon Roll; Hon Roll; Jr NHS; NHS; Ntl Merit Ltr; Cmnty Wkr; Cnslr Spec Olymps 86; Jmp Rop Hrt Vlntr 84; Ldrshp Awd Wrstlng 86; Med.

TWOMCY, TRACI; Mercy HS; Jamesport, NY; (Y); 23/106; Mathletes; Math Tm; Ski Clb; Bsktbl; Fld Hcky; Socr; Sftbl; High Hon Roll; NHS; All-Lg & All-Cnfrc Awd Sftbll 85; All-Lg, All-Cnfrnc & All-Cnty Awd Sftbll 86; Fld Hcky All-Lg Awd 86; Vet.

TWOMEY, LEAH; Churchville-Chili HS; North Chili, NY; (Y); GAA; Ski Clb; Crs Cntry; Mgr(s); Score Keeper; Tennis; Hon Roll; 3rd Pl Spn Skit 85; MVP JV Sftbl 85; Mst Imprvd Var Sftbl 86; Socl Wrk.

TWOREK, CINDY A; W Seneca E SR HS; W Seneca, NY; (Y); 1/375; French Clb; Key Clb; Trs Stu Cncl; Bausch & Lomb Sci Awd; High Hon Roll; JC Awd; NHS; Pres Schlr; Val; Canisus Coll Ldrshp Inst Cert 85; Jhns Hpkns U; Pltcl Sci.

TWOREK, JON; St Marys HS; Cheektowaga, NY; (S); 25/171; Exploring; Trs Jr Cls; Rep Stu Cncl; JV Var Ftbl; Socr; Trs NHS; Church Yth Grp; Nwsp Rptr; Var Trk; Peac & Jstc Awd 83; Co-Chrmn SR Prom 86; ST U Of NY Genesee; Accntng.

TYBUSH, CHRISTINE; Ballston Spa SR HS; Ballston Spa, NY; (Y); 9/256; Drama Clb; Red Cross Aide; SADD; School Musical; Stage Crew; Variety Show; Cheerleading; Tennis; High Hon Roll; NHS; Regents Schlrshp 86; Presdntl Schlrshp 86; Skidmore Schlstc Dinner 83; Hartwick Coll; Math.

TYCHO, BEATA; Dominican Commercial HS; Woodhaven, NY; (Y); 37/220; Cheerleading; Gym; Hon Roll; NHS; Comm.

TYLER, ANNA CHRISTINA; Jamesville Dewitt HS; Fayetteville, NY; (Y); 33/225; Church Yth Grp; French Clb; Band; Var L Swmmng; Var L Trk; NHS; Ntl Merit Ltr; High Hon Roll; Bio & Eng Awds 86; Vet Med.

TYLER, SHANNON; Saugerties HS; Saugerties, NY; (Y); 25/250; Cmnty Wkr; French Clb; Library Aide; Office Aide; Chorus; Mrchg Band; Hon Roll; NHS.

TYLUTKI, THOMAS; Bishop Scully HS; Amsterdam, NY; (Y); 9/55; Am Leg Boys St; 4-H; Latin Clb; Math Clb; Quiz Bowl; Science Clb; Rep Stu Cncl; Bsktbl; Var L Crs Cntry; Im Vllybl.

TYNAN, ANN MARIE; The Mary Louis Acad; Flushing, NY; (Y); 72/280; JV Bowling; NEDT Awd; NEDT 84; Peter F Clark Teamsters Union Awd 86; Manhattan Coll; Engineering.

TYNDALL, KIMBERLY; Walt Whitman HS; Hunt Station, NY; (Y); Church Yth Grp; Cmnty Wkr; Girl Scts; Office Aide; Red Cross Aide; Spanish Clb; Band; Concert Band; Stage Crew; Symp Band; Italian Hnr Scty 86-87; Villanova; Frgn Lang.

TYNDELL, JENNIFER; Corning Painted Post West HS; Beaver Dams, NY; (Y); 23/252; Exploring; JA; Political Wkr; Ski Clb; Rep Sr Cls; Var L Trk; High Hon Roll; NHS; Pres Schlr; Rep Frsh Cls; NYS Regents Schlrshp Rcpnt 86; U Of Buffalo; Orthdntst.

TYNER, MELINDA; Avoca Central Schl; Avoca, NY; (Y); Computer Clb; French Clb; FBLA; Varsity Clb; Band; Chorus; Sec Frsh Cls; Sec Soph Cls; Sec Jr Cls; Cheerleading; Mst Imprvd Athlt 84; Cortland Coll; Physcl Ed.

TYO, SUZANNE; Red Jacket Central HS; Shortsville, NY; (Y); 1/91; Am Leg Aux Girls St; VP SADD; VP Chorus; Pres Stu Cncl; Var Capt Cheerleading; Trs NHS; Val; Church Yth Grp; Dance Clb; Drama Clb; NYS Teen Repub Vice Chrmn 84-86; Finger Lakes Life Undrwrtr Outstndg Teen Of Yr Awd 86; St John Fisher Coll; Frgn Lang.

TYRAS, JON; Oyster Bay HS; Oyster Bay, NY; (Y); 7/130; Letterman Clb; SADD; Concert Band; Jazz Band; Stage Crew; Lit Mag; Sec Sr Cls; JV Capt Ftbl; L Socr; High Hon Roll.

TYRRELL, KAREN; James Madison HS; Brooklyn, NY; (Y); Church Yth Grp; Key Clb; Red Cross Aide; Chorus; Hunter Coll; Nrsng.

TZETZIS, SPRIO; Jamesville-De Witt HS; Syracuse, NY; (Y); Church Yth Grp; Computer Clb; High Hon Roll; Schlrshp Smmr Sns Lemoyne Coll Bio & Comp Sci 86; Bio.

UBINA, FREGILA JILL; John Dewey HS; Brooklyn, NY; (Y); Concert Band; Variety Show; Cit Awd; Hon Roll; Baruch Coll; Acctng.

UCHITELLE, JENNIFER; Scarsdale HS; Scarsdale, NY; (Y); Varsity Clb; Var Cheerleading; Var Capt Gym; Div A Chmpnshps Gymstc 85-86.

UDELL, ROBERT; Walt Whitman HS; Huntington Sta, NY; (Y); 35/475; Key Clb; Mathletes; Sec VP Spanish Clb; Varsity Clb; Nwsp Stf; Golf; High Hon Roll; Sec VP Spanish NHS.

UDICIOUS, JOHN R; Roth HS; Rush, NY; (Y); 8/195; Varsity Clb; VP Sr Cls; JV Var Bsbl; JV Var Socr; Hon Roll; Jr NHS; NHS; Spanish NHS; Rgnts Schlrshp 86; U NY Bfl; Engrng.

UH, BENJAMIN S; Newfield HS; Coram, NY; (Y); 1/515; Q&S; Drm Mjr(t); Jazz Band; Lit Mag; Var Trk; French Hon Soc; NHS; Spanish NHS; Val; Taekwondo 1st Degree Black Belt 83; 2nd Degree Black Belt 86; SEAS Columbia U; Blumed Engrng.

UHL, LAWRENCE; Kingston HS; Kingston, NY; (Y); 39/573; Boy Scts; Key Clb; Nwsp Rptr; Nwsp Stf; Socr; Jr NHS; Kiwanis Awd; NHS; Am Leg Boys St; Trs Frsh Cls; James Studley Mem 86; Acad Achvt & Fit Awd 86; All Lg Soccr Tm 85; SUNY Stony Brook; Elec Engr.

UHTEG, MICHELLE; Pioneer Central HS; Chaffee, NY; (Y); 4-H; Swmmng; 4-H Awd; Bus.

ULICKI, ANNE; Mt Mercy Acad; West Seneca, NY; (Y); 19/163; Church Yth Grp; Computer Clb; Girl Scts; SADD; Nwsp Stf; Ed Yrbk Stf; Off Sr Cls; Coach Actv; Score Keeper; JV Sftbl; Slvr Ldrshp Awd; Regents Schlrshp; U Of Buffalo; Sprts Med.

ULLOA, FRANCISCO; Cardinal Hayes HS; New York, NY; (Y); 82/244; Dance Clb; Letterman Clb; Mrchg Band; Rep Stu Cncl; High Hon Roll; Hon Roll; Prfct Atten Awd; Bus Adm.

ULLOA, JUAN C; Louis D Brandeis HS; New York, NY; (Y).

ULMER, KAREN; Cardinal Spellman HS; City Island, NY; (Y); 57/700; Am Leg Aux Girls St; Band; Drm Mjr(t); Mrchg Band; Yrbk Phtg; Yrbk Stf; Stu Cncl; L Vllybl; High Hon Roll; NHS; Notre Dame; Acctnt.

ULRICH, VICTORIA; Westbury SR HS; Westbury, NY; (Y); 10/200; Church Yth Grp; Nwsp Rptr; Nwsp Stf; JV Bowling; Var Tennis; High Hon Roll; Hon Roll; NHS; Pre Engrng Pgm 83-85; Bus.

UMANA, ELIZABETH; Moore Catholic HS; Staten Island, NY; (Y); Intnl Clb; Yrbk Stf; Bowling; Hon Roll; Prfct Atten Awd; Mrn Bio.

UMBARGER, TRINA; Mt Vernon HS; Mt Vernon, NY; (Y); Girl Scts; Hon Roll; Lgl Secy.

UMBRIACO, MELANIE; Trott Vocation & Tech; Niagara Falls, NY; (Y); Var Sftbl; Cosmetlgy.

UMLAND, DENISE; Bitburg American HS; Apo Ny, NY; (Y); Church Yth Grp; Dance Clb; Cheerleading; Gym; Powder Puff Ftbl; Hon Roll; Pres Physcl Ftns Awd 86; U Minnesota; Mktg.

UNDERHILL, CAROLINE; Alexander Central HS; Batavia, NY; (Y); AFS; French Clb; FTA; Ski Clb; Teachers Aide; Band; Concert Band; Mrchg Band; Hon Roll; Prfct Atten Awd; Bst Section Mrchg Bnd 84; Geneseo ST U; Elem Ed.

UNDERHILL, MARY EMILY; Scotia-Glenville HS; Scotia, NY; (Y); 15/244; Sec Key Clb; Var Capt Cheerleading; Var JV Fld Hcky; Var Swmmng; NHS; Darlene Hill Memrl Schlrshp 86; Pres Hnr Awd 86; Vrsty Plq 86; Albany Coll Pharm; Pharm.

UNDERWOOD, RUTH; Addison Central Schl; Addison, NY; (Y); JCL; Chorus; Concert Band; Madrigals; Mrchg Band; Orch; Symp Band; Variety Show; Yrbk Stf; NHS; Corning Yth Philhrmnc Orch 85-86; UW Symphny Schl Music 86; All Conf Band 85-86; All Cnt Bands 84-86; SUNY Binghamton.

UNDERWOOD, WYATT WESLEY; Smithotwn H S East; St James, NY; (Y); VP Church Yth Grp; Civic Clb; VP Cmnty Wkr; Office Aide; SADD; Cit Awd; Hon Roll; Neighborhood Watch Awd; St Jayes Civic Assn Awd; Elec Engrng.

UNG, HOA; Herbert Lehman HS; Bronx, NY; (Y); Math Tm.

UNGARELLI, BELANNE M; Oyster Bay HS; East Norwich, NY; (Y); 1/122; French Clb; SADD; Sec Band; Chorus; Sec Concert Band; Sec Mrchg Band; School Musical; Yrbk Stf; Lit Mag; High Hon Roll; Holy Cross Acad Achvt & Ctznshp Bk Awd 85; NY ST Rgnts Schlrshp Wnnr 86; NY ST Schls Msc Rbbns; U Of PA; Accntng.

UNGARO, DONNA; Tuckahoe HS; Bronxville, NY; (Y); 22/54; FBLA; Sec Varsity Clb; Nwsp Bus Mgr; Nwsp Rptr; Nwsp Stf; Ed Yrbk Stf; Capt Var Cheerleading; Coach Actv; JV Sftbl; CC Awd; Slvrs Gld Schlrshp 86; Grd Irn Clb Schlrshp 86; SR Awd Hghst Av Bus 86; Iona Colle; Bus Admin.

UNITAS, CAROLYN; Patchogue-Medford HS; Medford, NY; (Y); Church Yth Grp; Chorus; Color Guard; Madrigals; Orch; School Musical; School Play; Nwsp Rptr; Cheerleading; NHS; All Co Choir SCMEA Suffolk Co, All St Choir; Frnch Hnr Soc; Perf Arts.

UNSELT, STACY C; Attica Central HS; Alden, NY; (Y); 16/150; AFS; Church Yth Grp; Varsity Clb; Band; Color Guard; Mrchg Band; Nwsp Rptr; Yrbk Stf; Cheerleading; NHS; Genesco; Bus.

UNSWORTH, ADAM; Potsdam HS; Potsdam, NY; (Y); 10/140; Church Yth Grp; French Clb; Concert Band; Jazz Band; Orch; Var Capt Bsktbl; Hon Roll; NHS; Natl H S Hnrs Orch 86; Natl Concerto Comp Oberlin Coll 85; All ST Bnd 85; Music Perf.

UPCRAFT, KIMBERLY; Mexico HS; Lycoming, NY; (Y); Sec German Clb; Chorus; Concert Band; Jazz Band; Mrchg Band; School Musical; Variety Show; Hon Roll; NHS.

UPCRAFT, VICKY; Oswego HS; Oswego, NY; (Y); Ski Clb; Band; Color Guard; Mrchg Band; Sftbl; Twrlr; High Hon Roll; Hon Roll; Byrant & Stratton; Comptrs.

UPDE GRAFF, KAREN M; Horseheads SR HS; Elmira, NY; (Y); Cmnty Wkr; Drama Clb; Hosp Aide; JCL; Latin Clb; Science Clb; SADD; Nwsp Rptr; Yrbk Phtg; Off Jr Cls; JR Clscl Leag 1st Pl Cls 1 Mythlgy Awd NY ST 84; Corning CC; Crmnl Jstcs.

UPDIKE, PAUL; Charles O Dickerson HS; Trumansburg, NY; (Y); 10/120; Am Leg Boys St; Band; Jazz Band; Mrchg Band; JV Var Bsbl; JV Var Ftbl; Im Wt Lftg; Hon Roll; NHS.

UPSON, ROY D JR; Grove St HS; Mohawk, NY; (Y); 6/95; Am Leg Boys St; Church Yth Grp; French Clb; L Bowling; L Ftbl; L Golf; High Hon Roll; Jr NHS; NHS; Schuyler Wargms Clb-VP 81; West Pt Military Acad; Chmstry.

UPTEGROVE, MARY; Letchworth Central HS; Castile, NY; (Y); 12/96; Church Yth Grp; Cmnty Wkr; Library Aide; Mrchg Band; Hon Roll; Prfct Atten Awd; Tchng.

UPTON, PATRICIA; Dominican Commercial HS; Richmond Hill, NY; (Y); 78/280; Church Yth Grp; Drama Clb; Hon Roll; Oper FUN 84; Excptnl Chldrns Religious Educ 84-85&85-86; Spec Educ.

URAM, MICHAEL K; Hastings HS; Hastings On Hud, NY; (Y); 12/128; AFS; Model UN; Ski Clb; Nwsp Rptr; JV Var Socr; High Hon Roll; NHS; French Clb; Intnl Clb; Key Clb; Hugh O Brian Outstndng Soph 83-84; AFS Summer Abroad To Honduras 85; Dartmouth Coll.

URAM, MIROSLAWA; Yonkers HS; Yonkers, NY; (Y); Intnl Clb; High Hon Roll; Hon Roll; Westchester CC; Nrs.

URBAN, MICHAEL W; Longwood HS; Coram, NY; (Y); VICA; JV Ftbl; JV Trk; High Hon Roll; Hon Roll; 1st Pl Trphy NY ST For Crpntry 86; Outstndng Stu Awd In BOCES II 86; Indstrl Art Awd 86; Crpntr.

URBAN, SHERENE; Uniondale HS; Uniondale, NY; (Y); Art Clb; SADD; Chorus; Orch; School Musical; Yrbk Phtg; Yrbk Sprt Ed; Var Gym; Var Swmmng; Jr NHS; All-Cnty String Orchstra; Svc Awd; NY U; Photo Jrnlst.

URBANCZYK, CHERYL; South Jefferson HS; Adams, NY; (Y); AFS; Church Yth Grp; German Clb; Spanish Clb; Yrbk Stf; JV Capt Cheerleading; L Crs Cntry; L Trk; High Hon Roll; NHS; Trophy Outstndg Schlstc Achvmnt 85; Med.

URBANSKI, DENISE; Hutchinson Central Technical HS; Buffalo, NY; (Y); Church Yth Grp; Natl Beta Clb; Rep Frsh Cls; Rep Jr Cls; Rep Stu Cncl; Med.

URDY, BETH; Glens Falls SR HS; Glens Falls, NY; (Y); 9/204; Pres SADD; Yrbk Stf; Rep Frsh Cls; Rep Soph Cls; Rep Jr Cls; Bsktbl; Mgr(s); Powder Puff Ftbl; Var Capt Swmmng; JV Trk; Ntl Hnr Soc 86.

VAN EPPS, AMY; Hugh C Williams HS; Canton, NY; (Y); 14/150; Thesps; Band; Chorus; Church Choir; Jazz Band; School Musical; Stage Crew; Capt Vllybl; High Hon Roll; NHS; Acad Letter Awd 85 86; 2nd Tm All Northern Vllybl 86; Youth Am Choir 86; Engrng.

VAN EPPS, TODD; Colonie Central HS; Albany, NY; (Y); Var Crs Cntry; Var Trk; Hon Roll; NHS; Varsity Let Indoor Trk 85-86.

VAN EVERY, MONICA; Lansing HS; Lansing, NY; (Y); 3/80; Jazz Band; Orch; School Musical; Swmmng; Lion Awd; NHS; Rotary Awd; Church Yth Grp; Spanish Clb; Cit Awd; Rngl Acdmc Awd Span 84; Rngl Awd Mus 86 & 87; Supr Rtng Fest Music 87; Med.

VAN HANDEL, LEIGH; Union-Endicott HS; Johnson City, NY; (Y); Drama Clb; Key Clb; Ski Clb; Concert Band; Jazz Band; Mrchg Band; Orch; Symp Band; Hon Roll; NHS; Oberlin; Msc Prfrmnc.

VAN HANEGEN, WENDEY; Newark SR HS; Newark, NY; (Y); #47 In Class; Drama Clb; Rptr FBLA; Chorus; School Musical; Swing Chorus; Variety Show; CC Finger Lakes; Cmmnctns.

VAN HOESEN, STEVE; Coxsackie-Athens HS; Athens, NY; (Y); 15/135; German Clb; SADD; Varsity Clb; Band; Pres Frsh Cls; Rep Soph Cls; Rep Jr Cls; Rep Stu Cncl; Var L Bsbl; Im Bowling; Bus Admin.

VAN HORN, KARYN; Eastridge HS; Rochester, NY; (Y); 16/214; Hosp Aide; Varsity Clb; Band; Mrchg Band; School Musical; Pres Stu Cncl; JV Fld Hcky; Var Capt Swmmng; High Hon Roll; NHS; Alfred U; Nrsng.

VAN KLEECK, DE ANNA; Albertus Magnus HS; Nanuet, NY; (Y); Drama Clb; Stage Crew; Crs Cntry; Trk; Bus.

VAN LARE, DANIEL; Charles H Roth SR HS; Rush, NY; (Y); Computer Clb; Band; Jazz Band; School Musical; Stage Crew; Var Crs Cntry; Var Golf; High Hon Roll; NHS; Vrsty Sprts Ltr 86; Schlstc Ltr 86.

VAN LARE, TAMMY; Marion Central HS; Marion, NY; (Y); Natl Beta Clb; Var Bsktbl; JV Score Keeper; JV Var Socr; JV Var Vllybl; MIP Athl 84-85; Bill White Awd Vllybl 85-86; 1st St Tm Vllybl, 2(d Tm All Str Bsktbl 85-86; Csmtlgy.

VAN LENT, MICHAEL; Hugh C Williams HS; Dekalb Jct, NY; (Y); 15/150; Math Tm; Model UN; Varsity Clb; Lit Mag; Var L Trk; High Hon Roll; NHS; Ntl Merit Ltr; Letterman Clb; JV Var Socr; Month Switzerland Exprmnt Intl Living 86; Recvd 4.0 Both Clss Taken St Lawrence U 85-86; Math.

VAN LEUVAN, TERI; Watervliet JR SR HS; Watervliet, NY; (Y); 1/134; Math Tm; Band; Stage Crew; Trs Jr Cls; Rep Stu Cncl; Bowling; Var Vllybl; Bausch & Lomb Sci Awd; High Hon Roll; VP NHS; Advncd Russn Colg Credt 85-86; Silvr Mdl Lang Spch Cmptn 86; Rensslr Mdl Excllnc Math & Sci 86; Rsrch Bio.

VAN NATTEN, GREG; Schoharie Central Schl; Howes Cove, NY; (S); Computer Clb; Var Tennis; Hon Roll; Air Force; Math.

VAN NESS, JENNIFER A; St Francis Prep; Whitestone, NY; (S); 12/653; Cmnty Wkr; Math Tm; Ski Clb; Chorus; Crs Cntry; Im Sftbl; Im Vllybl; NHS; Ntl Merit Ltr; Opt Clb Awd; Al-Amer Schlr 84-85; Regnts Schlrshp 84-85; Psychlgst.

VAN NOSTRAND, JUDD; North Babylon SR HS; North Babylon, NY; (Y); 23/600; Camera Clb; FBLA; Intnl Clb; Office Aide; Chorus; Yrbk Phtg; JV Socr; Var Tennis; High Hon Roll; Pres Schlr; Twn Babylon Envrnmntl Cnsrvtn Awd 80; Hnr Bus Dynamics 84; Tact Peer Grp Facilitator 85-86; Drexel Univ; Bus.

VAN NOSTRAND, LARA L; North Babylon HS; North Babylon, NY; (Y); 10/500; Hosp Aide; Intnl Clb; Spanish Clb; Mgr Socr; High Hon Roll; Jr NHS; NHS; Natl Soc Prof Engrs 86; Polytechnic U Scholar 86; Polytechnic U; Chem Engrng.

VAN NOTE, DOUG; Hamburg HS; Hamburg, NY; (Y); AFS; Church Yth Grp; German Clb; Socr; Marine Arch.

VAN ORD, DEREK; Chautauqua Central HS; Sherman, NY; (Y); Church Yth Grp; Band; Chorus; Trs Jr Cls; Rep Stu Cncl; Crs Cntry; Var Capt Swmmng; Hon Roll; Trs NHS; Voice Dem Awd; Pres Acad Ftnss Awd 86.

VAN ORMER, SHARON; Cazenovia Central HS; Cazenovia, NY; (Y); Hon Roll; Awd-Most Imprvd In Bio 85; Awd Most Imprvd Engl 86; Awd Outstndng Achvt Socl Studies 86; Travel.

VAN REMMEN, PATRICK; Lake Shore Central HS; Angola, NY; (S); 11/264; VP Concert Band; Jazz Band; Orch; School Musical; School Play; Yrbk Ed-Chief; Pres Yrbk Stf; Var Capt Tennis; Pres NHS; Drama Clb; Math Champ 85-86; Ntl Hnr Soc 86; NY ST Rgnts Schlrshp 86; MI ST U; Jrnlsm.

VAN RY, KIMBER; York Central Schl; Piffard, NY; (Y); Key Clb; Math Tm; Science Clb; Var Tennis; High Hon Roll; NHS; Eng 11 Clsrm Hnrs 85-86; Chem Engrng.

VAN RYN, CAROLINE; Mahopac HS; Mahopac, NY; (Y); 43/409; Color Guard; Mrchg Band; Orch; Nwsp Stf; JV Sftbl; High Hon Roll; Hon Roll; NHS; Area All-ST Orch 84-85; Part Tm Jb Lcl Twn Hall 84; Law.

VAN SCHAICK, MARK; Thousand Islands HS; Cape Vincent, NY; (Y); 6/80; Band; School Play; Variety Show; Var Socr; Hon Roll; Jr NHS; NHS; Concert Band; Jazz Band; Mrchg Band; Elmira Clg Key Awd Schlrshp 86; Cape Vincent Clayton Lions Clb Schlr 86; Silvr Mtl Whiz Quiz Tm 86; Poltc Sci.

VAN SLYKE, CHIP; Maple Hill HS; Castleton, NY; (S); 8/100; Aud/Vis; Exploring; Ski Clb; Stage Crew; JV Var Socr.

VAN SLYKE, DAVID; Beacon HS; Beacon, NY; (Y); 27/160; Am Leg Boys St; Pres Church Yth Grp; Pres Latin Clb; Capt Letterman Clb; Capt Crs Cntry; Capt Trk; Hon Roll; Jr NHS; Kiwanis Awd; NHS; Natl JR Olympic Racewlkng Champ 84; Kiwan Loan Awd 86; SUNY Plattsburgh; Econ.

VAN SLYKE, JAMES; Groton Central HS; Cortland, NY; (Y); Var L Bsktbl; Var L Ftbl; FL Inst Tech; Aviatn.

VAN SLYKE, JOANNE; Kenmore East HS; Tonawanda, NY; (Y); 112/320; Hosp Aide; Chrmn Pep Clb; Teachers Aide; School Musical; Var L Fld Hcky; Hon Roll; Hall Of Fame Awd-Ldrshp 86; Long Island U SouthamptnLAWYR.

VAN SLYKE, RICHARD; Waterville Central HS; Waterville, NY; (Y); Pres Church Yth Grp; Varsity Clb; Stage Crew; Trs Frsh Cls; VP Stu Cncl; Var L Bsktbl; Var L Trk; Hon Roll; Albany ST; Cmptr Sci.

VAN STRY, SHARON; Frewsburg Central HS; Frewsburg, NY; (Y); 20/86; SADD; Yrbk Ed-Chief; Pres Stu Cncl; Var Capt Bsktbl; Var Capt Sftbl; Var Capt Vllybl; Cit Awd; Hon Roll; Robet O Woodad Athltc Trphy & Schlrshp 86; Wntr Wknd Qun 86; Stu Ctzn Athlt Trphy & Schlrshp 86; Jamestown CC; Med Lab Tech.

VAN VAL KENBURGH, MINDY; Scotia-Glenville HS; Scotia, NY; (Y); 30/240; Drama Clb; Ski Clb; Thesps; Sec Chorus; School Musical; Variety Show; Cheerleading; Vllybl; Hon Roll; NHS; Rgnts Schlrshp 86; Bus Schlrshp 86; West TX ST U; Bus Admin.

VAN VALKENBURGH, DOUG; Schalmont SR HS; Schenectady, NY; (Y); Church Yth Grp; Ski Clb; Hon Roll; Prfct Atten Awd.

VAN VALKENBURGH, MINDY JO; Scotia-Glenville HS; Scotia, NY; (Y); 27/240; Drama Clb; Ski Clb; Thesps; Sec Chorus; School Musical; Variety Show; Cheerleading; Vllybl; Hon Roll; NHS; Rgnts Schlrshp 86; Bus Schlrshp 86; West TX ST U; Bus Admn.

VAN VLIET, RICHARD; Newtown HS; Elmhurst, NY; (Y); 38/667; Band; Nwsp Stf; Var Bsbl; Hon Roll; NHS; Prncpls List 83-84; NY ST Rgnts Schlrshp 86; Hofstra U.

VAN WORMER, GERALD; South Jefferson Central HS; Mannsville, NY; (Y); 5/155; Boy Scts; French Clb; FTA; Band; Chorus; Jazz Band; Mrchg Band; Yrbk Bus Mgr; Stu Cncl; NHS; Roger Macy Mem Awd 85; Jefferson CC; Bus.

VAN WORMER, MICHAEL; South Jefferson Central HS; Mannsville, NY; (Y); 1/155; Boy Scts; German Clb; Jazz Band; Swing Chorus; Yrbk Sprt Ed; Pres Jr Cls; Var L Crs Cntry; Bausch & Lomb Sci Awd; NHS; Ntl Merit Ltr; Engrng.

VANBRUNT, SENTA; Hutchinson Central Technical HS; Buffalo, NY; (Y); Church Choir; Our Best-Poems & Name Printed 83-84; Awd For Effort & Achvt In Art 82-83; Awd For Bst In Chlk Drwngs; Artist.

VANCE, BEAUMONT; Fairport SR HS; Fairport, NY; (Y); Bsktbl; Ftbl; Hon Roll; Ntl Merit Ltr; Spanish NHS; Bst Stu IPS 83.

VANCE, TRACEY; John F Kennedy HS; Utica, NY; (Y); 20/132; Nwsp Stf; Yrbk Stf; Trs Frsh Cls; Trs Soph Cls; Rep Stu Cncl; Capt Cheerleading; High Hon Roll; Hon Roll; Awd Outstndg Attitude Cntrl City Bus Inst 86; SUNY; Accntng.

VANCURA, SHARON M; Ramapo SR HS; Pomona, NY; (Y); 26/529; Church Yth Grp; Cmnty Wkr; Office Aide; Cit Awd; DAR Awd; NHS; Dante Mdl For Excllnc In Itln 86; Itln Hnr Soc 85-86; Mona Lisa Ldg; Natl Hnr Soc; Italian Hnr Soc; Manhattanville Clg; Rmnc Lang.

VANDE WALKER, CYNTHIA; Gloversville HS; Gloversville, NY; (Y); 2/270; Teachers Aide; Yrbk Stf; Rep Sr Cls; JV Crs Cntry; Var Sftbl; JV Trk; NHS; Lang Clb; Prncpls Advsry Cmmttee; USAF Acad; Aeronaut Engrng.

VANDEN OEVER, JOHN; Auburn HS; Auburn, NY; (Y); Church Yth Grp; Drama Clb; Church Choir; School Play; Stage Crew; Variety Show; JV Trk; Hon Roll.

VANDENBOSCH, BRIAN; Niagara Catholic HS; Lewiston, NY; (Y); Spanish Clb; JV Ftbl.

VANDENHEUVEL, MICHELLE; Center Moriches HS; Ctr Moriches, NY; (Y); 9/109; Concert Band; School Musical; Nwsp Bus Mgr; Yrbk Bus Mgr; Sec Frsh Cls; Sec Jr Cls; Var Cheerleading; JV Sftbl; High Hon Roll; NHS; Outstndg Achvmnt Calculus, Engl 11 & Shrthnd 86; Bus.

VANDENTHOORN, JILL E; Riverhead HS; Riverhead, NY; (Y); 6/221; Pres Church Yth Grp; Key Clb; Latin Clb; Ski Clb; Orch; Var L Tennis; NHS; NYS Regnts Schlrshp 86; Stu Bar Assn 85-86; SUNY Geneseo; Elem Ed.

VANDER PUTTEN, MIKE; St John The Baptist; Bohemia, NY; (Y); Boy Scts; Church Yth Grp; Band; Mrchg Band; Stage Crew; Var Trk; Eagle Sct; Engr.

VANDER VEEN, KRISTEN; Paul V Moore HS; Central Sq, NY; (Y); 6/300; Cmnty Wkr; Chorus; Concert Band; Nwsp Ed-Chief; Rep Stu Cncl; Var L Crs Cntry; Var L Trk; High Hon Roll; NHS; AFS; JR Achvt Awd Frgn Lang 85-86; Incntv Plq Partcptn HS Sports 86; Ntl Sci Fndtns Frntrs Sci Prog 86-87; Bio Chem.

VANDERBECK, WENDY; North Rose Wolcott HS; Walcott, NY; (Y); Ski Clb; Band; Chorus; Cheerleading; Socr; Trk; Hon Roll; AZ ST Coll; Elem Ed.

VANDERBILT, KEVIN; Avon Central HS; Avon, NY; (Y); 5/87; Am Leg Boys St; Church Yth Grp; Spanish Clb; Var Golf; JV Var Socr; High Hon Roll; Jr NHS.

VANDERHOEK, MARK; Jamesville Dewitt HS; Jamesville, NY; (Y); 26/205; Hosp Aide; Political Wkr; Spanish Clb; Varsity Clb; Var Capt Crs Cntry; Var Capt Trk; High Hon Roll; NHS; Mtl Of NY Schlstc Art Awd Gld Ky-84 & Hnrbl Mntn 85; Zoolgy.

VANDERLAAN, BRETT; Fort Plain HS; Fort Plain, NY; (S); 1/53; Am Leg Boys St; Computer Clb; Intnl Clb; Concert Band; Jazz Band; Mrchg Band; School Musical; Var Socr; Bausch & Lomb Sci Awd; Ntl Merit Ltr.

VANDERMARK, BRANDI L; Emma Willard Schl; Greene, NY; (Y); Church Yth Grp; Spanish Clb; Band; Concert Band; Mrchg Band; Orch; Rep Frsh Cls; Var Fld Hcky; Im Gym; JV Vllybl; Stu Proctor; Psych.

VANDERMARK, JEFFREY; Bainbridge-Guilford HS; Bainbridge, NY; (Y); Pres 4-H; Sec FFA; Band; Chorus; Stage Crew; Variety Show; 4-H Awd; Prfct Atten Awd; Fire Dpt 86; Tri-Valley Hrsmns Assoc Awds 83-86; Chenango Co Hrsmns Assoc 83-85; Art.

VANDERMARK, LINDA; Monticello HS; White Lake, NY; (Y); Church Yth Grp; Dance Clb; Drama Clb; Girl Scts; Intnl Clb; High Hon Roll; Hon Roll; Sec Sllvn Cnty CYO 86-87; Pres Prsh CYO 86-87; Crdnl Spdlmn Yth Awd Rcgntn Outstndg Svc 86; Scl Wrkr.

VANDERSTEUR, DEREK; Oakfield-Alabama Central HS; Oakfield, NY; (Y); 18/86; Church Yth Grp; Drama Clb; Ski Clb; School Play; Trk; Hon Roll; NHS; U Dayton OH; Ind Engr Tech.

VANDERVEER, HILARY; Spackenkill HS; Poughkeepsie, NY; (Y); SADD; Thesps; School Musical; Swing Chorus; Yrbk Stf; Rep Stu Cncl; JV Capt Fld Hcky; Var Capt Socr; NHS; Leo Clb; Literary Editor-Yrbk 86-87; 10th Pl Natl Frnch Cntst 84-85; Hnr Roll 83-86.

VANDEWAL, JENNIFER; Guilderland Central HS; Schenectady, NY; (Y); Key Clb; Varsity Clb; Var Cheerleading; JV Sftbl; High Hon Roll; Hon Roll; Bus.

VANDUZER, LISA; Warwick Valley HS; Warwick, NY; (Y); 32/195; Aud/Vis; Drama Clb; Radio Clb; Trk; High Hon Roll; Hon Roll; NHS; Lmp Knwldg Awd 2nd Yr Pin 86; Mst Cls Sprt 86; SR Spkr Grad 86; SUNY Oswego; Cmnctns.

VANEPPS, CURTIS; Candor Central HS; Candor, NY; (Y); Am Leg Boys St; Varsity Clb; Band; Chorus; Concert Band; Var JV Bsktbl; Var JV Trk; High Hon Roll; NHS; Church Yth Grp; Engl Hnr; Elec Engrng.

VANEPPS, TERRY; Le Roy Central Schl; Leroy, NY; (Y); Varsity Clb; JV Ftbl; Var Trk; JV Var Wrstlng; High Hon Roll; Hon Roll; Mech Engrng.

VANFLEET, LESLIE; Jasper Central HS; Woodhull, NY; (Y); 2/40; French Clb; Band; Chorus; Concert Band; Mrchg Band; Yrbk Stf; VP Jr Cls; Pres Sr Cls; High Hon Roll; Trs Sec NHS; Acedmc All Star 85-86; Var Ltr Awd 85-86; Cert Merit Jr Clss 85-86; Maria Regina Coll; Libr Sci.

VANHORN, CHARLES; Nottingham HS; Syracuse, NY; (Y); 76/300; Boy Scts; Chess Clb; SADD; Band; Stat JV Mgr(s); Stat JV Score Keeper; Hon Roll.

VANICHPONG, SOMSAK; Clarkstown HS South; New City, NY; (Y); SADD; Band; Concert Band; Jazz Band; Mrchg Band; Cit Awd; Hon Roll; Bio.

VANIER, LISA; Franklin Acad; Malone, NY; (Y); 1/266; AFS; Jazz Band; Symp Band; Trs Sr Cls; Elks Awd; NHS; Pres Schlr; Val; Empire ST Scholar 86; Regents Scholar 86; All ST Bnd NYSSMA 86; Crane Schl Music; Music Ed.

VANLEUVAN, GARY; Onondaga Central HS; Nedrow, NY; (Y); Exploring; German Clb; Hosp Aide; Science Clb; SADD; Var Bsbl; JV Crs Cntry; Var Ftbl; Wt Lftg; Var Wrstlng; FL Inst Of Tech; Sprts Med.

VANLOGEN, EMILY; St Francis Prep; Richmond Hill, NY; (Y); Art Clb; Church Yth Grp; Computer Clb; Girl Scts; Pep Clb; PAVAS; Red Cross Aide; Church Choir; Drm Mjr(t); Yrbk Stf.

VANN, ROBERT; Cammack High School South; Commack, NY; (Y); Pres Computer Clb; Band; Jazz Band; Mrchg Band; School Musical; High Hon Roll; NHS; Ntl Merit Ltr; Cmnty Wkr; Mathletes; Mdls Gold 84-85, Slvr 83-84 Math Fair; NYSSMA Gld Mdl 83-84; Cmptr Sci.

VANORA, JUDI; H Frank Carey HS; Franklin Square, NY; (Y); 51/279; Camera Clb; Cmnty Wkr; Sec French Clb; SADD; Rptr Nwsp Stf; Rptr Yrbk Stf; French Hon Soc; Hon Roll; Frgn Lang Awd Outstndng Srv To Frnch Clb; Cmmndtn Rprt Scl Stds 84; Frgn Lang Hnr Roll Frnch 85; Jrnlsm.

VANSALISBURY, GEORGE; Archbishop Molloy HS; Ridgewood, NY; (Y); Boy Scts; Church Yth Grp; Pep Clb; Chorus; Im Bsktbl; Im Ftbl; Hon Roll.

VANSCHAICK, FRANCIS; South Jefferson Central HS; Adams Center, NY; (Y); Church Yth Grp; Pres FFA; Ski Clb; Varsity Clb; Band; Chorus; Concert Band; Swmmng; 4-H Awd; Hon Roll; Hobart Cornell; Bus Admin.

VANSICKLE, SUSAN; Mynderse Acad; Seneca Falls, NY; (S); #31 In Class; 4-H; Stu Cncl; Trk; High Hon Roll; Hon Roll; SUNY; Vet Sci.

VANTRAN, ANNE; Valley Central HS; Walden, NY; (Y); 20/300; Natl Beta Clb; Spanish Clb; Band; Concert Band; Mrchg Band; Symp Band; Off Jr Cls; High Hon Roll; Hon Roll; NHS; Elem Tchr.

VANWART, KRISTEN; Johnstown HS; Johnstown, NY; (Y); Crs Cntry; Hon Roll; NHS; USAF; Air Space Craft.

VANWOERT, DAVID; Pelham Memorial HS; Pelham, NY; (Y); Aud/Vis; Chess Clb; Drama Clb; Math Tm; Ski Clb; Pep Band; School Musical; School Play; JV Tennis; Hon Roll; Vlntr Ado Vsl Asst Awd; Jrnlsm.

VARA, RUSSELL; West Seneca East SR HS; West Seneca, NY; (S); 19/375; Cmnty Wkr; VP DECA; VP JA; Office Aide; Hon Roll; Jr NHS; NHS; Prfct Atten Awd; 1st Pl-Rgnl DECA Wnr 85-86; DECA Outstndng Svc Awd 85; DECA Top Fund-Rsng Sls Awd 85; U Of Buffalo; Bus Mgmt.

VARANASI, RAVIKANT; Oakwood Schl; Wappingers Falls, NY; (S); Cmnty Wkr; Computer Clb; Math Tm; Office Aide; Teachers Aide; Pres Sr Cls; Rep Stu Cncl; Var Capt Bsktbl; Var L Crs Cntry; Var Capt Tennis; Columbia U Sci Hnrs Progrm 85-87; Paul Pfeutze Mert Schlrshp 83-87; Awd Acad Achvt Delt Sgm Tht 84; Bio-Med.

VARDY, KRISTEN B; St Francis Prep; Bayside, NY; (S); 75/746; Dance Clb; Drama Clb; School Musical; JV Vllybl; Opt Clb Awd; Vet.

VAREAM, CRAIG; Wellington C Mepham HS; N Bellmore, NY; (Y); Cmnty Wkr; Off Jr Cls; Stu Cncl; Var Bsbl; Var Ftbl; Var Capt Socr; Bus Admin.

VARELA, JULIO; Fordham Preparatory Schl; Bronx, NY; (Y); Spanish Clb; School Play; Stage Crew; Nwsp Stf; Yrbk Stf; VP Jr Cls; Pres Stu Cncl; Hon Roll; NHS; Ntl Hspnc Schlr Awds Fnlst 86; Ntl Latn Exm Magna Cum Laude 85; Engl.

VARGAS, GERSON; Evander Childs HS; Bronx, NY; (S); Band; Swmmng; Comptrllrs Awd 83; Hnr Schl 84; Cert Merit 84; Comp Pgmng.

VARGAS, JUAN; Adlai E Stevenson HS; New York, NY; (Y); Cmnty Wkr; Bsbl; Fld Hcky; Sftbl; Swmmng; Wt Lftg; Long Island U; Accntng.

VARGAS, MYRA; Msgr Scanlan HS; New York, NY; (Y); Dance Clb; Cheerleading; Gym.

VARGAS, ROBERTO; James Madison HS; Brooklyn, NY; (Y); 35/756; Science Clb; Band; Jazz Band; Hon Roll; ARISTA 84-86; NY City Engl Tchrs Cont 1st Pl 85; Med.

VARKEY, SHERIN; East Syracuse Minoa HS; Minoa, NY; (Y); Dance Clb; Exploring; Im Tennis; Im Vllybl; High Hon Roll; Hon Roll; Jr NHS; NHS; Prfct Atten Awd; Johns Hopkins; Med.

VARKONYI, MARIA; Christ The King Regional HS; Maspeth, NY; (Y); 12/451; Stu Cncl; Hon Roll; NHS; Comp Sci.

VARLAMOS, CYNTHIA; Harrison HS; Harrison, NY; (Y); Pres Church Yth Grp; VP Latin Clb; Church Choir; Jazz Band; Mrchg Band; Orch; Symp Band; Var Socr; High Hon Roll; NHS.

VARLARO, JOSEPH; Frankfort-Schuyler Central HS; Frankfort, NY; (Y); Am Leg Boys St; School Musical; Variety Show; Rep Frsh Cls; Pres Jr Cls; Pres Sr Cls; Tennis; Cit Awd; High Hon Roll; NHS; Amrcn Lgn Boys ST 86; SR Cls Pres 86-87; Schl Musicl 84 & 86-87; Pre Med.

VARMA, SARITA; Yonkers HS; Yonkers, NY; (Y); Camera Clb; JA; SADD; Band; Mrchg Band; High Hon Roll; Hon Roll; NHS; Supr Awd For Acadmc Excllnce With Above 90 Avg 84; Soc Stud Cert Of Excllnce 86; Columbia; Bus Mgmt.

VARNEY, SCOTT; Hudson Falls HS; Hudson Falls, NY; (Y); 28/226; Boys Clb Am; Camera Clb; Computer Clb; Spanish Clb; Chorus; School Musical; Crs Cntry; Tennis; Non Instrctnl Employees Schlrshp 86; Burgoyne Ave PTA Schlrshp-Sawyer Schlrshp 86; Hstry Essy Prz 86; Morrisville Coll; Eclgy.

VARUGHESE, SHOBHA; Our Lady Of Victory Acad; Yonkers, NY; (S); 1/128; SADD; Rep Stu Cncl; Trk; High Hon Roll; NHS; Spanish NHS; Art Clb; Hosp Aide; Gen Excllnc 84 & 85.

VARUZZO, LISA M; Arlington HS; Lagrangeville, NY; (Y); 30/600; Intnl Clb; Chorus; Concert Band; Jazz Band; Mrchg Band; Orch; School Musical; High Hon Roll; VIP Wnr-Clrnt Solo Hudson Vly Philhrmnc 84; Chautaugua Smr Music Fstvl Schlrshp 85; Al-ST Conf 84-85; Prfrmnc Major Clarinet.

VASILE, PAMELA A; Harrison HS; White Plains, NY; (Y); 6/200; Band; VP Concert Band; Drm Mjr(t); Jazz Band; Mrchg Band; Pep Band; Stage Crew; Nwsp Stf; Hosp Aide; NHS; Coll Of Holy Cross; Bio.

VASSALLO, FRANK; Jamestown HS; Jamestown, NY; (Y); 14/380; French Clb; Chorus; Trs Mrchg Band; Pres Symp Band; Stu Cncl; JV Bsktbl; Var L Golf; High Hon Roll; Jr NHS; NHS; SUNY Geneseo; Bus Adm.

VASSO, JANE; Our Lady Of Victory Acad; Bronx, NY; (S); 6/157; Latin Clb; Math Clb; Science Clb; Spanish Clb; Speech Tm; SADD; Chorus; Yrbk Stf; Lit Mag; Rep Frsh Cls; Alpha Hnr Scty 85; Manhattan Coll; Engr.

VATER, DAVID; St Marys HS; Tonawanda, NY; (S); Yrbk Stf; NHS; Medcl Tech.

VAUGHAN, CRAIG; North Tonawanda SR HS; N Tonawanda, NY; (Y); CAP; Ski Clb; Var Ftbl; Var Trk; Im Wt Lftg; Cit Awd; High Hon Roll; Jr NHS; Prfct Atten Awd; Ctznshp Awd 84; Hnr Ltrs 85-86; Mech Drawng.

VAUGHAN, ERIC D; Kingston HS; Woodstock, NY; (Y); Pres Art Clb; Chorus; Church Choir; Yrbk Stf; Rptr Lit Mag; High Hon Roll; Spanish NHS; Regnts Schlrshp 86; Syracuse; Grphc Arts.

VAUGHAN, THERESA; Eastchester SR HS; Scarsdale, NY; (Y); Ski Clb; Spanish Clb; Timer; Trk; Bus.

VAUGHN, ARTHUR; Uniondale HS; Uniondale, NY; (Y); Church Yth Grp; FBLA; Spanish Clb; SADD; Chorus; Variety Show; JV Bsktbl; Var L Ftbl; Var L Trk; Hon Roll; Awds For Bsktbl & Trck & Fld 84 & 85; Chmpnshp Of Chmpns All Star Trck Meet 86; Accntng.

VAUGHN, ERIKA J; Laguardia High Schl Of Music & Arts; Cambria Heights, NY; (Y); Church Yth Grp; Dance Clb; Drama Clb; GAA; PAVAS; Science Clb; Thesps; School Musical; School Play; Stage Crew; Mst Outstndng Stu Drama 85; Howard U; Pre-Law.

VAUGHN, PAMELA; Horseheads HS; Horseheads, NY; (Y); 75/380; Church Yth Grp; Drama Clb; German Clb; Ski Clb; Band; Chorus; Church Choir; Concert Band; Jazz Band; Mrchg Band; Marywood Coll; Int Dsgn.

VAVONESE, DANIEL; Thomas J Corcoran HS; Syracuse, NY; (Y); Cmnty Wkr; Ski Clb; Spanish Clb; Yrbk Stf; JV Crs Cntry; Var Trk; High Hon Roll; Hon Roll; Jr NHS; NHS; Perfect Score On Bio Exam 85; Magna Cum Laude On Natl Latin Exam 86; Bio Engr.

VAYNSHTEYN, KAREN; John Dewey HS; Brooklyn, NY; (Y); JA; Bus.

VAZQUETELLES, DANIEL; All Hallow Inst; Bronx, NY; (S); 8/40; Exploring; Church Choir; Hon Roll; NHS; Prfct Atten Awd; Comp.

VAZQUEZ, DAVID J; Mount Saint Michael Acad; Bronx, NY; (S); 12/309; Ski Clb; Var Trk; Hon Roll; NHS; Spanish NHS; Manhattan Coll; Chem.

VAZQUEZ, FRANCISCO; Archbishop Molloy HS; Hollis, NY; (Y); 82/383; High Hon Roll; Hon Roll; Im Ftbl; NY Cty Cmptrlrs Awd In Sci & Math 83; Top 11 Pct Of Amer Stu In Rdng Cmprhnsn & Math 83; Lawyer.

VAZQUEZ, GLORIA; William Howard Taft HS; Bronx, NY; (Y); Dance Clb; Nwsp Stf; Yrbk Stf; Trk; Hon Roll; Prfct Atten Awd; Schlrshp Cert Awd 84; Citznshp Cert 85; Dr.

VAZQUEZ, LAURA; Aviano American HS; A P O New York, NY; (Y); 6/25; Model UN; Pep Clb; Chorus; Yrbk Stf; Pres Jr Cls; Pres Sr Cls; Rep Stu Cncl; Hon Roll; NHS; Natl Hispnc Schlr Awd SF 85-86; Intl Affrs.

VAZQUEZ, NANCY; Cardinal Spellman HS; Bronx, NY; (Y); 94/600; Math Clb; Science Clb; Spanish Clb; Stu Cncl; Frdhm U; Bus Adm.

VAZQUEZ, SUSANA; St Raymond Acad; Bronx, NY; (Y); Computer Clb; Drama Clb; Library Aide; Office Aide; Spanish Clb; Band; Yrbk Stf; Hon Roll; Prfct Atten Awd; Pom Pon; Modelng Awd Cert 85.

VAZQUEZ, VICTOR; John Dewey HS; Brooklyn, NY; (Y); Chess Clb; English Clb; JA; Teachers Aide; Band; Color Guard; Concert Band; Orch; School Musical; Stage Crew; Stonybrook; Human Svcs.

VEA, MARIE C; Notre Dame HS; Horseheads, NY; (Y); 7/88; Church Choir; School Play; Nwsp Ed-Chief; Lit Mag; Jr Cls; Off Sr Cls; Var Cheerleading; Var Tennis; Cit Awd; NHS; Dghtrs Amer Rvltn Gd Ctzn Awd 85; Rgnts Schlrshp 86; Awd Rcgntn Cmnty Invlvmt 86; St John Fisher Coll NY; Pre-Md.

VECCHIARELLA, AIMEE; Salamanca JR SR HS; Salamanca, NY; (Y); 17/120; FHA; Ski Clb; NHS; JCC Jamestown; Psych.

VECCHIARELLO, GINA; Pelham Memorial HS; Pelham, NY; (Y); SADD; Band; School Musical; Nwsp Sprt Ed; Yrbk Ed-Chief; Sec Frsh Cls; Pres Soph Cls; Sec Jr Cls; Var JV Cheerleading; NHS; Empire Grls ST Altrnt 86; Smith Coll Bk Awd 86.

VECCHIARIELLO, VICTORIA; Mahopac HS; Mahopac, NY; (Y); 103/409; Hosp Aide; Yrbk Stf; JV Crs Cntry; Stat Socr; Hon Roll; Peer Ldrshp Pgm 86; Medical.

VEEDER, ABBIE; Pineview Acad; Albany, NY; (S); 1/9; Church Yth Grp; Drama Clb; Red Cross Aide; Teachers Aide; Chorus; Church Choir; School Play; Yrbk Phtg; VP Jr Cls; VP Sr Cls; Outstng Achvt Engl, Bible, Bus, Soc St; Russell Sage Coll; Psych.

VEENSTRA, ALEXANDER ALI; Polytechnic Prep Country Day Schl; Brooklyn, NY; (Y); Aud/Vis; Boys Clb Am; Boy Scts; Church Yth Grp; Computer Clb; Dance Clb; JA; Office Aide; Varsity Clb; Band; Eagle Scout 84; Srv Awd Cystic Figrosis Fndtn 84; 6th Pl Wrstlng NY ST Champ 86; Air Force Acad; Engrng.

VEGA, ALICIA; Herbert H Lehman HS; Bronx, NY; (Y); Camera Clb; Bowling; Prfct Atten Awd; NY Inst Of Tech; Architecture.

VEGA, CHRISTINE; The Mary Louis Acad; Flushing, NY; (Y); Church Yth Grp; Girl Scts; Hosp Aide; Pep Clb; Spanish Clb; Teachers Aide; Hon Roll; 2nd Hnrs Math; Bus.

VEGA, IDA; Academy Of Mount Saint Ursula; Bronx, NY; (Y); Drama Clb; Red Cross Aide; Spanish Clb; Stage Crew; Yrbk Stf; Off Stu Cncl; Capt Var Cheerleading; Sftbl; Trk; Nursing.

VEGA, KEVIN; James Monroe HS; Bronx, NY; (Y); Boy Scts; Nwsp Stf; Var Ftbl; Hon Roll; NHS; Financing.

VEGA, LIZETTE; De Witt Clinton HS; Bronx, NY; (Y); Chorus; Vocblry Awd 84; Gld Mdl 84; Ceramic Awd For Outstndng Svc 86; Tchr.

VEGA, ROSEMARIE; Aquinas HS; Bronx, NY; (Y); 31/169; Cmnty Wkr; Computer Clb; Science Clb; Yrbk Stf; NHS; Spanish NHS; Debate Tm; High Hon Roll; Hon Roll; Lehman Coll; Bio.

VEGA, VICTORIA; Adali E Stevenson HS; Bronx, NY; (Y); Cmnty Wkr; FCA; JA; Office Aide; Teachers Aide; Band; Im Tennis; Hon Roll; Prfct Atten Awd; Achvmnt Lge 86; Chld Psych.

VEGA, WANDA; Our Lady Of Perpetual Help; Brooklyn, NY; (Y); 11/155; Bowling; High Hon Roll; Hon Roll; Prfct Atten Awd; Regents Schlrshp 86; Pace U; Erly Chld Ed.

VEGA-LUNA, ALBERT; Tottenville HS; Staten Island, NY; (Y); Model UN; Ski Clb; Hon Roll; Comp Engrng.

VEGLIA, MICHELE; Schaemont HS; Schenectady, NY; (Y); Art Clb; Aud/Vis; Cmnty Wkr; Dance Clb; Drama Clb; PAVAS; Thesps; School Play; Stage Crew; Hon Roll; Tp 10 Drma Awd-Tlnt Amer 85; Orgnl Art Wrk Awd 85; Spkng ST Legsltv Substnc Abus 85; Dean JC; Theatr Arts.

VEITCH, STACY; Fort Plain HS; Fort Plain, NY; (S); Office Aide; Sec Frsh Cls; Sec Soph Cls; Sec Jr Cls; Rep Stu Cncl; Capt Var Cheerleading; JV Var Socr; Stat Sftbl; Var Trk; NHS; Pre-Med.

VELASCO, MARTHA; Ossining HS; Ossining, NY; (Y); 25/260; Church Yth Grp; French Clb; Hosp Aide; Math Tm; Sec Spanish Clb; Yrbk Stf; High Hon Roll; Hon Roll; Mu Alp Tht; Iona Coll Lang Cont-Frnch 2nd Hons 84-85; Ntl Frnch Cont 4th Pl Lcl, 5th Rgn 84-85; Albertus Magnus Coll; Pre-Med.

VELASCO, SONIA; Cardinal Spellman HS; Yonkers, NY; (Y); Church Yth Grp; Trs Key Clb; Science Clb; Nwsp Rptr; Nwsp Stf; Vllybl; High Hon Roll; Hon Roll; Fordham U; Engrng.

VELAZQUEZ, CASSANDRA; Nottingham HS; Syracuse, NY; (Y); Church Yth Grp; Hosp Aide; VP SADD; Cheerleading; Var Vllybl; Dnfth Awd; Hon Roll; Spanish NHS; MVP Vllybl, Rdrs Digest SADD Schlrshp Wnnr 86; Nrsng.

VELAZQUEZ, MARILYN; Park East HS; Manhattan, NY; (Y); Art Clb; Computer Clb; Dance Clb; Chorus; Yrbk Phtg; Yrbk Stf; Off Sr Cls; Vllybl; Hon Roll; Prfct Atten Awd; The Wood Schl; Bus Mang.

VELETANGA, JUAN; St George Acad; New York, NY; (Y); Cmnty Wkr; Spanish Clb; Hon Roll; Hon Roll; Engrng.

VELEY, VICKIE L; Keshequa Central Schl; Dalton, NY; (Y); 1/60; Pres VP 4-H; Math Tm; Band; Cit Awd; 4-H Awd; High Hon Roll; NHS; Prfct Atten Awd; Val; Rochester Bus Inst; Accntng.

VELEZ, DARREN; Kings Park SR HS; Fort Salonga, NY; (Y); Computer Clb; Nwsp Rptr; Nwsp Stf; Lit Mag; Hon Roll; Ntl Merit SF; Ltry Mag Achvmnt Awd 85-86; Jrnlsm.

VELEZ, EDGAR; John Jay HS; Brooklyn, NY; (Y); Wt Lftg; Hon Roll; Delhi ST U; Vet Medicine.

VELEZ, JOSEPH; Herbert H Lehmen HS; Bronx, NY; (Y); Debate Tm; Chorus; School Play; Yrbk Stf; Rep Jr Cls; Var Bsktbl; Var Capt Socr; Var Sftbl; Church Yth Grp; Computer Clb; Athletic Awds Soccer,Bsktbl 83-86; Gold Metal Ind Arts 85-86; Elect Engr.

VELEZ, LOURDES; James Monroe HS; Bronx, NY; (Y); Office Aide; Spanish Clb; Teachers Aide; Chorus; Concert Band; Orch; School Play; JV Sftbl; JV Vllybl; High Hon Roll; Albrt Enstn Coll Of Med; Med.

VELEZ, RENELLE L; St Francis Preparatory HS; New York, NY; (S); 111/744; Cmnty Wkr; Chorus; NHS; Acpl Chr; Optimate Scty 84-85; Chorus Cncl 84-86; St Francis Judo Team 85-86; Med.

VELEZ, ROBERT; Central Islip HS; Central Islip, NY; (Y); Boy Scts; Math Clb; Band; Concert Band; Mrchg Band; NY Tech; Accntng.

VELEZ, ZENA; Bay Shore SR HS; Bay Shore, NY; (Y); 30/400; Yrbk Stf; Lit Mag; Rep Frsh Cls; Sec Soph Cls; Sec Jr Cls; Stu Cncl; Var Socr; MVP Sccr 83-84; Stu Govt Orgnztn VP 86-87.

VELIA, ELIZABETH; Canaseraga Central HS; Canaseraga, NY; (Y); 4/17; Yrbk Stf; Sec Frsh Cls; Trs Soph Cls; Rep Jr Cls; Rep Sr Cls; Stu Cncl; High Hon Roll; Hon Roll; NHS; Prfct Atten Awd; Bus Admin.

VELIA, KEITH; Smithtown High School West; Smithtown, NY; (Y); NYS Regents Schlrshp 86; Achvt Awd Southhampton Coll 86; Dowling; Acctg.

VELILLA, SANDRA; HS Of Fashion Indstrs; Bronx, NY; (Y); 27/324; Dance Clb; Math Tm; Chorus; Variety Show; Yrbk Stf; Hon Roll; Val; Arista Hnr Scty Club; NYU; Comm Arts.

VELLA, ADRIENNE; Dominican Commercial HS; Baldwin, NY; (S); 10/288; Wt Lftg; High Hon Roll; Hon Roll; Jr NHS; Sienna Clb 84-86; Prncpls Lst 84-86; St John U; Comp Prgmr.

VELLIOS, LAMBRINA; Manhasset HS; Manhasset, NY; (Y); Church Yth Grp; Dance Clb; Debate Tm; French Clb; Service Clb; Nwsp Sprt Ed; Yrbk Stf; Kiwanis Awd; NHS; Ntl Merit Ltr; Princeton Bk Awd 85; Ldrshp Merit Awd 86; Acad All Am 86.

VELLUCCI, LYNNE; Fort Hamilton HS; Brooklyn, NY; (Y); 10/509; JA; Office Aide; Science Clb; Chorus; School Musical; Stu Cncl; VP NHS; Pres Schlr; Natnl Hnr Scty 84-86 & Vp 85-86; Ft Hamilton HS Hnr Acadmy Prgrm 83-86; Advancd Placmnt Pgrm; Fordham U.

VELLUTINO, GIAN CARLO; Hackley HS; Thornwood, NY; (Y); 6/90; Drama Clb; Model UN; Band; Chorus; Jazz Band; Orch; School Musical; Crs Cntry; Tennis; JP Sousa Awd; Prncpl Trmpt NY All ST Orchstra 86; Thtre Leag Westchester Cmptn Top Prize Wnnr 85.

VELLUTINO, GIANCARL; Hackley HS; Thornwood, NY; (Y); 5/100; Chess Clb; Model UN; Band; Chorus; Concert Band; Jazz Band; Orch; Lit Mag; Crs Cntry; Tennis; Chaminade Clb Wnnr 86; Fnlst 17 Magazine/GM Concerto Cmptn 86; Theatr Leag/Westchestr Wnnr 85; Princeton U; Med.

VELTEN, DAWN; Oxford Acad & Central HS; Oxford, NY; (Y); Sec Church Yth Grp; French Clb; VP SADD; Varsity Clb; Band; Var L Fld Hcky; Powder Puff Ftbl; Var L Sftbl; Var L Vllybl; Prfct Atten Awd; Amrcn Chem Soc 86; Outstndg Chem Stu 86; Athltc Trng.

VELTZ, TOM; Mc Quaid Jesuit HS; Pittsford, NY; (Y); Varsity Clb; Bsbl; Bsktbl; Golf; Wt Lftg; High Hon Roll; French Clb; Yrbk Phtg; Prfct Atten Awd; Notre Dame; Engrng.

VENDITTI, ANTHONY; Monsignor Farrell HS; Staten Island, NY; (Y); JV Bsbl; Hon Roll; Archt.

VENEGAS-GIRON, RICARDO A; Christian Brothers Acad; Liverpool, NY; (Y); 16/91; Chess Clb; Exploring; Hosp Aide; Pres VP JA; Math Tm; Yrbk Stf; Rep Frsh Cls; Rep Jr Cls; High Hon Roll; Natl Hispn Scholar Awd SF 86; VP JA Mktng Yr 85; 1st Rnnr Up VP Mktng 84; 1st Rnnr Up Achvr Yr 83; Comp Engrng.

VENEY, SHERYLYN; Hauppauge HS; Hauppauge, NY; (Y); 95/530; Camera Clb; Cmnty Wkr; Band; Concert Band; Mrchg Band; School Play; Symp Band; Variety Show; Var Fld Hcky; High Hon Roll; Var Sprts Awd 85; Blck Achvt Awd 86; Penn ST; Cmnctns.

VENEZIA, ALICIA; St Agnes Acad HS; Bayside, NY; (Y); Cmnty Wkr; SADD; Twrlr; Hon Roll; Hofstra U; Comp Pmgmr.

VENEZIA, MIKE; New Dorp HS; Staten Island, NY; (Y); 72/597; Mathletes; JV Var Bsbl; JV Var Bsktbl; High Hon Roll; Italianhnr Soc 84-85; Achvt Awd Exc Woodwrkng II 85-86; Wagner Coll.

VENN, CHARLES; Wheatland-Chili HS; Scottsville, NY; (Y); Boy Scts; Church Yth Grp; Exploring; Ski Clb; JV Bsbl; Var Cheerleading; Natl Eagle Scout Hon In Boy Scouts 84; Awd Intl Art Exhibit 85; Art.

VENNE, ROBIN; Saranac Central HS; Redford, NY; (S); Girl Scts; Band; Concert Band; Jazz Band; Mrchg Band; Pep Band; Stage Crew; Hon Roll; Bst Rookie Yr Awd Band 83-84; Acctnt.

VENNOCHI, LESLIE; New Rochelle HS; New Rochelle, NY; (Y); 89/500; English Clb; Library Aide; NHS; Church Yth Grp; Cmnty Wkr; Hosp Aide; Spanish Clb; Lit Mag; High Hon Roll; Relig Concern & Loyalty For Comm Awd 86; Westchester CC; Bus.

VENTAROLA, ANTHONY; Mount Saint Michael Acad; Bronx, NY; (Y); 6/291; Chess Clb; Computer Clb; Yrbk Stf; Lit Mag; Off Sr Cls; Bowling; Hon Roll; NHS; Cooper Union 86; Cooper Union; Civl Engr.

VENTIMIGLIA, JOSEPH; Uniondale HS; Uniondale, NY; (Y); Am Leg Boys St; Var JV Bsbl; Var JV Socr; High Hon Roll; NHS; Cvl Engnrng.

VENTO, JENNIFER; Carle Place HS; Westbury, NY; (Y); 10/116; Hosp Aide; School Musical; JV Var Cheerleading; Var Capt Gym; High Hon Roll; Hon Roll; Varsity Clb; Spanish NHS; Schlr/Athl Awd 86; Hofstra U.

VENTRICE, JOSEPH; Milwood HS; Brooklyn, NY; (Y); 400/667; JV Ftbl; Ctznshp Awd 82; Arista 82-83; Baruch U; Accnt.

VENTRUDO, MARGARET J; Moore Catholic HS; Staten Island, NY; (Y); 10/180; Off SADD; Nwsp Rptr; Yrbk Bus Mgr; Rep Stu Cncl; JV Bsktbl; Var Co-Capt Socr; Var L Tennis; Hon Roll; NHS; Managng Edtr Yrbk 86-87; H S Corres Lcl Nwspapr 85-87; Spch Pth.

VENTRUELLA, GAIL; Holy Trinity Dioc HS; Hicksville, NY; (Y); Math Clb; Ski Clb; Cheerleading; High Hon Roll; NHS; Hnr Ment Spnsh Cmpttn 86.

VENTURA, RICHARD; Frankfort-Schuler HS; Utica, NY; (S); Math Tm; Pep Clb; Spanish Clb; Band; Concert Band; Bowling; High Hon Roll; NHS; Engrng.

VERA, CESAR; Ossining HS; Ossining, NY; (Y); Art Clb; Office Aide; Hon Roll; Hnrbl Ment Bnk NY 84; FIT; Fash Dsgn.

VERA, FABIAN; Dewitt Clinton HS; Bronx, NY; (Y); Art Clb; Computer Clb; English Clb; Spanish Clb; Band; School Play; Bsbl; Hon Roll; Prfct Atten Awd; Law.

VERA, STEVE LUIS; De Witt Clinton HS; Bronx, NY; (Y); 43/257; Boy Scts; ROTC; Chorus; Drill Tm; VP Jr Cls; Stu Cncl; Cit Awd; Hon Roll; Prfct Atten Awd; Cert Med Asst 86; Comptn Cert Air Force 86; Tchrs Assoc Awds Merit In Art 86; Norwich U.

VERBANOFF, AMY; Frontier Central HS; Hamburg, NY; (Y); Civic Clb; Capt GAA; Ski Clb; Pres Concert Band; Pres Soph Cls; VP Pres Stu Cncl; Capt Sftbl; Capt Vllybl; French Hon Soc; High Hon Roll; Math.

VERBJAR, MICHELLE; Hilton Central HS; Hilton, NY; (Y); Var Cheerleading; Var Trk; High Hon Roll; Hon Roll; 2nd Pl Rbbn Art Shw 85; 1st Pl Rbbn Art Shw 86; Cmmrcl Art.

VERBOCY, JOHN; Buffalo Vocational Technical Center; Buffalo, NY; (Y); Cmnty Wkr; Political Wkr; Slf Pride Grtfctn Achvg Bst Grds Lf 85-86; Bryant & Stratton Bus Inst; Eng.

VERBRIDGE, WENDY; Marion JR-SR HS; Marion, NY; (Y); 11/80; Office Aide; Concert Band; Jazz Band; Mrchg Band; School Musical; JV Var Socr; Var Sftbl; Hon Roll; NHS; Pres Schlr; SUNY Morrisvl; Comp Sci.

VERDE, JOANNE; Carmel HS; Carmel, NY; (Y); Art Clb; Chorus; Yrbk Stf; High Hon Roll; Hon Roll; NHS; Italian Schlrshp 86; Cert Of Merit 86; Wstchstr CC; Acting.

VERDECIA, GISSEL E; St Francis Prep; Ozone Park, NY; (S); 9/744; Dance Clb; High Hon Roll; Chem.

VERDINO, GREGORY T; St Anthonys HS; Fort Salonga, NY; (Y); Drm & Bgl; Jazz Band; Orch; Symp Band; Nwsp Bus Mgr; Nwsp Stf; High Hon Roll; Hon Roll; NHS; Spanish NHS; Rgnts Schlrshp 86; Wesleyan U; Intl Pol.

VERDINO, VICKI; St Edmund HS; Brooklyn, NY; (Y); Art Clb; Infshn Dsgn.

VERDURA, ANDREA; Saint Francisx Preparatory HS; Flushing, NY; (Y); Chorus; Variety Show; Yrbk Phtg; Schl Visual Arts; Art.

VERFENSTEIN, JOSEPH; East Meadow HS; Eastmeadow, NY; (Y); German Clb; Band; Concert Band; Jazz Band; Mrchg Band; Orch; Symp Band; JV Ftbl; JV Lcrss.

VERGA, MELISSA C; St Francis Prep; Flushing, NY; (S); 104/744; Math Clb; Service Clb; Chorus; Hon Roll; Math.

VERHEYLEWEGHEN, CHRIS; Minisink Valley HS; Pt Jervis, NY; (Y); Art Clb; Ski Clb; Stat Bsbl; Sftbl; High Hon Roll; Hon Roll; NHS; Chosen For Ldrshp Conf By Rotary Clb 85; U Of Binghamton; Psychology.

VERINI, CHRISTINE; Cardinal Spellman HS; Bronx, NY; (S); Intnl Clb; Pep Clb; Sec Science Clb; Service Clb; Ski Clb; Yrbk Ed-Chief; Yrbk Phtg; VP Sr Cls; Cheerleading; Hon Roll.

VERKLEIR, KELLEY; Amsterdam HS; Amsterdam, NY; (Y); 4/294; Drill Tm; Flag Corp; Tennis; High Hon Roll; NHS; Ntl Merit Ltr; Outstndg Spn & Eng Stu 86; Marie Curie Scholar & Cls 45 Mem Scholar 86; SUNY Plattsburgh; Envir Engr.

VERMEULEN, DAVID E; Newfane SR HS; Newfane, NY; (Y); Am Leg Boys St; Boy Scts; Varsity Clb; Band; Jazz Band; Symp Band; Capt Var Crs Cntry; Var L Trk; Hon Roll; Eagle Sct 86; Aviation.

VERNA, MICHELE; West Irondequoit HS; Rochester, NY; (Y); 20/388; JA; Spanish Clb; Chorus; Madrigals; School Musical; Swing Chorus; Nwsp Rptr; Crs Cntry; Sftbl; Trk; Rgnts Schlrshp NYS 85-86; Ntl Hnr Soc 84-85; Monroe CC; Psych.

VERNA, SHIRLEY; St Joseph HS; Brooklyn, NY; (Y); French Clb; Office Aide; Stage Crew; Off Sr Cls; Bsbl; Cheerleading; Coach Actv; Good HS Spirt 85-86; Hunter Coll; Pre-Med.

VERNI, DENISE M; West Babylon SR HS; W Babylon, NY; (Y); 3/420; Leo Clb; SADD; Varsity Clb; Concert Band; Mrchg Band; Orch; Yrbk Ed-Chief; Var Socr; High Hon Roll; Ches Clb; NY ST Regnts Schlrshp 86; Nwsday Hgh Hnrs Cmptn/Ldng Suffolk Cnty Schlstc Achvr 86; ST U NY Binghamton; Bus.

VERRILLI, JOHN; Msgr Farrell HS; Staten Island, NY; (Y); 91/350; Chess Clb; Tennis; Trk; Hon Roll; Bus Adm.

VERSACE, NICOLE; James E Sperry HS; Pittsford, NY; (Y); Cmnty Wkr; Sec French Clb; JA; Latin Clb; SADD; Yrbk Phtg; Yrbk Stf; Rep Stu Cncl; Socl Studies Hnr Soc 85-86; Sed Of Frnch Clb Awd 85-86; Soclgy.

VERSO, LAURA; Bishop Mc Mahon HS; Kenmore, NY; (Y); 1/41; JA; Latin Clb; Yrbk Ed-Chief; Pres Jr Cls; Rep Stu Cncl; Im Bowling; Stat Sftbl; Hon Roll; NHS; Val; Hghst Avg Engl, Lat, Relig Study; Bst Cls 86; Niagara U; Crmnlgy.

VERSPOOR, SHERYL; Sayville HS; W Sayville, NY; (Y); 22/350; Church Yth Grp; Key Clb; Band; Church Choir; Concert Band; Mrchg Band; Yrbk Stf; Var Fld Hcky; Stat Ftbl; Var Trk; Acctg.

VERUTES, CHRISTINA; Garden City HS; Garden City, NY; (Y); Church Yth Grp; German Clb; Trs Model UN; Trs Service Clb; SADD; Band; Concert Band; Mrchg Band; Nwsp Rptr.

VERZELLA, LISA LYNN; East Rochester HS; East Rochester, NY; (Y); 1/129; Am Leg Aux Girls St; Pres Exploring; Pres Varsity Clb; Pres Band; Orch; School Play; Nwsp Rptr; Var Fld Hcky; Var Sftbl; MVP Vrsty Fld Hcky, 2nd Tm All Cnty 85; Empire ST Fld Hcky Tm 86; Outstndg Band Musicn 85; Music.

VESCIO, LEANNE; Jamesville Dewitt HS; Fayetteville, NY; (Y); Church Yth Grp; French Clb; Key Clb; SADD; Yrbk Bus Mgr; Var JV Cheerleading; Score Keeper; Cit Awd; Hon Roll; Big Sister Little Sister Awd 86; Bus.

VESELY, LISA; Islip HS; Islip, NY; (Y); Church Yth Grp; SADD; Church Choir; Nwsp Stf; Yrbk Stf; Rep Frsh Cls; Var Mgr(s); Hon Roll; NHS; Rotary Awd; Prsdntl Physcl Fitns Awd 83-85; Intrnl Bus.

VESELY, LIV; Sachem HS; Nesconset, NY; (Y); 173/1558; Church Yth Grp; CAP; Cmnty Wkr; Hosp Aide; Church Choir; Swmmng; Jr NHS; Ski Clb; Stage Crew; Fnlst Miss Teen NY Pagnt 85 & 86; Rnr-Up Miss Loves Baby Soft Cont 85; 3rd Pl Schl Sci Fair 84; Georgetown U; Intl Rel.

VESNESKE, LISA M; Trott Vocational & Technical HS; Niagara Falls, NY; (Y); 32/147; Nwsp Rptr; Nwsp Stf; Yrbk Rptr; Yrbk Stf; Hst Sr Cls; Hon Roll; Popularity Poll Awd Mst Friendlst 86; Cert Nurses Aid Cert 84; RN.

VESSEY, ROBERT C; Spring Valley HS; Spring Valley, NY; (Y); 12/441; CAP; French Clb; Math Tm; Concert Band; Mrchg Band; Church Yth Grp; JV Socr; French Hon Soc; High Hon Roll; NHS; NY Math Leag Cert Of Merit 85; Janice P Hostel Memorial Awd For Excell In Math 83; Bus Mgmt.

VETERE, DONNA; St Vincent Ferrer HS; Elmhurst, NY; (S); 12/110; Library Aide; Nwsp Rptr; Rep Soph Cls; Rep Sr Cls; Hon Roll; NHS.

VETRANO, GINO; Archbishop Molloy HS; Ozone Park, NY; (Y); Rep SADD; Rep Varsity Clb; JV Bsbl; Im Ftbl; Pres Sftbl; Rep Trk; Rep Wt Lftg; Law.

VETTENBURG, KAREN; Sherman Central HS; Clymer, NY; (Y); Drama Clb; VP 4-H; Pres FFA; Sec Trs Girl Scts; Chorus; School Play; Yrbk Stf; Var Sftbl; Var Tennis; JV Var Vllybl; NY ST Empire Frmr Degr 86; Cnty & Chptr Frmr Degr 86; Altrnt Dairy Prncss 86; Alfred; Anml Husbndry.

VETTER, CHRISTINE; Corning-Painted Post West HS; Painted Post, NY; (Y); Varsity Clb; Sec Soph Cls; Sec Jr Cls; Sec Sr Cls; Trs Rep Stu Cncl; Var Capt Cheerleading; Var Gym; Var Capt Sftbl; High Hon Roll; NHS; Natl HS Cheerldng Champ 84; U Of NC; Biochem.

VETTER, MAUREEN; Sewanhaka HS; Floral Park, NY; (Y); 75/361; Church Yth Grp; Drama Clb; Girl Scts; Thesps; Chorus; Church Choir; School Musical; Variety Show; VP Frsh Cls; VP Soph Cls; Stu Exchng MI & OH 83-86; Dist Chorus & Pres 85-86; Mst Poplr & Best Prsnlty 85-86; Nassau CC; Librl Arts.

VETTER, PHILIP A; Hunter College HS; Glendale, NY; (Y); Boy Scts; Pres Church Yth Grp; Math Tm; Pres Service Clb; Church Choir; Swmmng; Ntl Merit SF; Mrchg Band; Math Assn Amer Math Exm Natl Hnr Rll 85; MAA AHSME Natl Merit Rll 84; Sci Rsrch.

VETTORINO, AUGUST; Tuckahoe HS; Tuckahoe, NY; (Y); 26/57; Ski Clb; VP Varsity Clb; Nwsp Rptr; Yrbk Rptr; Rep Stu Cncl; Var Capt Bsbl; Var Capt Bsktbl; Var Capt Ftbl; Wt Lftg; Hon Roll; Italian Civic Assoc Schlrshp Awd 86ftuckahoe Auxlry Police Schlrshp Awd 86; Chchs Awd Bst Male Awd 86; Purdue U.

VIANA, CONNIE GARAY; Mamaroneck HS; Mamaroneck, NY; (Y); Teachers Aide; NHS; Ntl Merit Ltr; Ntl Mrt Fnlst 86; Law.

VIBHUSTIEN, PRAPAN; Aviation HS; New York, NY; (Y); 75/415; Boys Clb Am; U Of CA Berkeley; Comp Engnrng.

VICCHIULLO, DOMINICK; Minisink Valley HS; Port Jervis, NY; (Y); Drama Clb; Chorus; High Hon Roll; Hon Roll; All Cnty Chrs 83-86; Area All ST Chrs 83-86; Hofstra; Pre-Law.

VICENTE, BRIAN T; Hauppauge HS; Hauppauge, NY; (Y); 96/502; Cmnty Wkr; Service Clb; Band; Concert Band; Jazz Band; Mrchg Band; Symp Band; High Hon Roll; Hon Roll; NHS; Naval Acad Prep Schl; Ofcr.

VICENTE, HEATHER; Mynderse Acad; Seneca Falls, NY; (Y); Church Yth Grp; FHA; Band; Chorus; Concert Band; Mrchg Band; Var L Socr; Hon Roll; Stat Var Bsbl; Stat Var Wrstlng; Most Outstndg Soprano-JV Chrs 84; All Cnty Chrs 84; Math Tchr.

VICENTE, PAULA C; Mineola HS; Mineola, NY; (Y); Art Clb; Spanish Clb; Wt Lftg; S O Rep; Farmingdale; Bus Law.

VICINI, LISA; Mahopoc HS; Mahopac, NY; (Y); 87/409; Yrbk Stf; Var Capt Cheerleading; Dnfth Awd; Hon Roll; Hosp Aide; Band; Concert Band; Stat Bsbl; US Chrldng Achvt Awds 86; Acad All-Amer At Large Div 86; Bus.

VICKERD, MELANIE; Hamburg SR HS; Hamburg, NY; (Y); Aud/Vis; Cmnty Wkr; 4-H; JCL; Latin Clb; Library Aide; Var Sftbl; JV Var Vllybl; MVP Awd Vllybl 83 & 84; Consrvtn.

VICKERS, JAMES V; Perth Central Schl; Amsterdam, NY; (Y); French Clb; School Play; VP Frsh Cls; VP Soph Cls; VP Jr Cls; Pres Sr Cls; Capt Bsbl; Socr; VP NHS; NY Regents Schlrshp 86; ROTC Schlrshp 86; U Of Tampa; Telecomm.

VICKERY, SHARON; Lansingburgh HS; Troy, NY; (Y); 3/190; Church Choir; Concert Band; Mrchg Band; School Musical; Ed Nwsp Ed-Chief; Capt Crs Cntry; Capt Trk; Pres NHS; Ntl Merit Ltr; Lois C Smith Chmstry Schlrshp Russell Sage Coll 86; Chem Engrng.

VICTOR, JEFFREY; Sachem High School North; Farmingville, NY; (Y); 525/1500; Hofstra; Comp Sci.

VIDA, PETER; Pulaski JR SR HS; Pulaski, NY; (Y); Chess Clb; Computer Clb; Crs Cntry.

VIEIRA, ELSA M; Sacred Heart Acad; Queens Village, NY; (Y); 27/181; Art Clb; Cmnty Wkr; Drama Clb; French Clb; Chorus; Lit Mag; Hon Roll; NHS; Ntl Merit Schol; Iona Coll Frnch Awd 1st Hnrs 84-85; Pomona Coll; Lang.

VIELE, ANITA; John Marshall HS; Rochester, NY; (Y); Am Leg Aux Girls St; Church Yth Grp; Math Tm; Pres Spanish Clb; Nwsp Stf; Rep Stu Cncl; Socr; High Hon Roll; NHS; Prfct Atten Awd; Lwrnc Klppr Mst Prmsng Stu Awd 85-86.

VIENNEAU, JEAN; Sperry HS; Rochester, NY; (Y); 40/271; Church Yth Grp; French Clb; Bowling; Socr; French Hon Soc; High Hon Roll; Hon Roll; Schlstc Ltrs 85; Ntl Sci Olympiad Cert 86; Cert Of Achvt For Hghst GPA 85 & 86; SUNY Frsno; Chmstry.

VIETRI, SHERRY; Gloversville HS; Gloversville, NY; (Y); 22/250; French Clb; Office Aide; Sec Pep Clb; SADD; Teachers Aide; Rep Frsh Cls; Rep Soph Cls; Rep Jr Cls; Rep Sr Cls; Im Var Cheerleading; Outstndng Bus Awd 86; Acctng.

VIGARS, KEITH A; Arlington HS; Pleasant Valley, NY; (Y); 108/565; Dutchess CC; Vet Med.

VIGENER, NIKLAS H; Clifton Fine Central HS; Cranberry Lake, NY; (Y); 8/44; German Clb; Lit Mag; Var Socr; Var Trk; Var Wrstlng; Hon Roll; NY ST Regents Schlrshp 86; SUNY-POTSDAM; Elec Engr.

VIGGIANO, CHRISTINE; Sacred Heart Acad; W Hempstead, NY; (Y); 16/191; Church Yth Grp; Math Tm; Pep Clb; Stu Cncl; Crs Cntry; Hon Roll; NHS; Adelphi Trustee Schlrshp 86; Acad All Am 86; Nassau CC; Physcl Thrpst.

VIGGIANO, WENDY; Plainedge HS; Massapequa, NY; (Y); FNA; Hosp Aide; Spanish Clb; High Hon Roll; Hon Roll; Spanish NHS; Med.

VIGLIANTE, LISA; Fontbonne Hall Acad; Brooklyn, NY; (Y); 32/140; Dance Clb; Drama Clb; Hon Roll; Lion Awd; Prfct Atten Awd; Awds-Alg, Wrld Cvlztn, Art, Sci & Gym 84; Awds-Trig, Wrld Civ II, Mjr Art I & Itln 85; Pepperdine U; Art.

VIGLIOTTI, ANTHONY; Westbury HS; Westbury, NY; (Y); 2/250; Pres Mathletes; Pres Science Clb; Rep Frsh Cls; JV Ftbl; Im Ice Hcky; High Hon Roll; Trs NHS; Med Prof.

VIGLIOTTI, FRANK; Commack HS South; Commack, NY; (S); Drama Clb; Teachers Aide; Thesps; Chorus; School Musical; School Play; Variety Show; Nwsp Phtg; Nwsp Stf; Yrbk Phtg; NY U; Music Thtre.

VIGLIOTTI, RENEE; Eastchester HS; Scarsdale, NY; (Y); Drama Clb; Pres Chorus; School Musical; School Play; Variety Show; Cheerleading; Prfct Atten Awd; Ntl Amer Music Plaque/Svc Awd 85; Dramatics.

VILCEUS, BERLINE; Samuel J Tilden HS; Brooklyn, NY; (Y); 22/557; FBLA; French Hon Soc; Hon Roll; U Rochester; Bus Adm.

VILLA, MAUREEN; Mercy HS; Peconic, NY; (Y); 1/125; Mathletes; Yrbk Stf; Rep Frsh Cls; Pres Soph Cls; Rep Jr Cls; JV Var Bsktbl; Var Capt Crs Cntry; Var Trk; High Hon Roll; NHS; Top Slsprsn Awd Annl Rffl; MVP Bsktbll.

VILLAFANE, MICHELLE; St John The Baptist HS; Brentwood, NY; (Y); Southern Seminary; Equestrian.

VILLAFANE, TANIA; Greece Athena HS; Rochester, NY; (Y); 95/300; FBLA; Spanish Clb; Rep Frsh Cls; Rep Soph Cls; Rep Jr Cls; Stat Bsbl; Stat Bsktbl; Score Keeper; Stat Socr; Hon Roll; U Of Buffalo; Trvl.

VILLALOBOS, JOSEPHINE; High School Of Fashion Industry; Brooklyn, NY; (Y); 47/324; Library Aide; Scholastic Bowl; Teachers Aide; Chorus; School Musical; Hon Roll; Prfct Atten Awd; Human Svcs.

VILLALOBOS, NATALIE; Fashion Industries HS; Brooklyn, NY; (Y); 52/324; Office Aide; Orch; School Musical; School Play; Prfct Atten Awd.

VILLANI, JAMES J; Mt St Michael Acad; Bronx, NY; (S); 15/299; Computer Clb; English Clb; Letterman Clb; Ski Clb; Varsity Clb; Lit Mag; Rep Stu Cncl; Socr; High Hon Roll; NHS; Dance Comm 84-86; Flor Hockey Intrmurl 83-84; Ftbl Intrmurl 83-84.

VILLANO, JOHN P; Miller Place HS; Miller Plaze, NY; (Y); 27/201; Rep Church Yth Grp; Political Wkr; VP Soph Cls; Var Capt Bsbl; Var JV Socr; Hon Roll; NHS; Rgnts Schlrshp; Amry ROTC Schlrshp; Spnsh Awd; SUNY Stny Brk; Engrng.

VILLANO, MINDI; East Meadow HS; East Meadow, NY; (S); 62/340; FBLA; Key Clb; Science Clb; Band; Yrbk Phtg; JV Cheerleading; JV Lcrss; Var Socr; JV Vllybl; NHS; Cornell U; Med Doctor.

VILLANUEVA, NANCY; Park West HS; New York, NY; (Y); Church Yth Grp; Library Aide; Math Tm; Office Aide; Chorus; Vllybl; Hon Roll; Pride Of Ynkees 85; CMSP Mth Awd In Algebra & Geomtry 85; Bus.

VILLANUEVA, RODNEY; Monsignor Farrell HS; Staten Island, NY; (S); Chess Clb; NFL; Spanish Clb; Hon Roll; NHS; Smifnslt NY ST Frnsc Leag ST Trnmnt 85; Smifnlst Ntl Trnmnt Chtlc Frnsc Leag 85; Med.

VILLARUEL, MERVYN; George Wingate HS; Brooklyn, NY; (Y); Boy Scts; Socr; AL Avtn & Tech Coll; Flght Tch.

VILLAS, TERESITA; John Dewey HS; Brooklyn, NY; (Y); Im Mgr Wt Lftg; BMCC Chld Care Ed Pgm Awd 85; FL Inst Of Tech; Sci.

VILLATORO, ERIC; Eastern Disrict HS; New York, NY; (Y); Church Yth Grp; Spanish Clb; Nwsp Ed-Chief; Yrbk Ed-Chief; Socr; Hon Roll; Caribe Pgm 86; Queens Coll; Bus Admin.

VILLIELM, ROBERT P; Kingston HS; Rifton, NY; (Y); 67/573; Pres Drama Clb; Spanish Clb; Stage Crew; Hon Roll; Jr NHS; Ntl Merit Ltr; NY ST Rgnts Schlrshp 86; Comp Prgmr.

VINCENT, ERIN; Hamburg HS; Hamburg, NY; (Y); 2/374; Church Yth Grp; FCA; Band; Chorus; Church Choir; Mrchg Band; Orch; Symp Band; Hon Roll; NHS; RPI Awd Math, Sci 86; 1st 9th Gr 84.

VINCENT, MICHAEL; Briarcliff HS; Briarcliff, NY; (Y); Art Clb; Church Yth Grp; Cmnty Wkr; Lit Mag; JV Var Ftbl; Greater Ossining Art Cncl Awd 86; Caramoor Art Exhibtn Cert Achvt 86; Colgate U; Graphc Arts.

VINCENT, VERONICA M; Westbury SR HS; Westbury, NY; (Y); 17/250; Church Yth Grp; Mathletes; Chorus; Church Choir; Stage Crew; JV Sftbl; Im Swmmng; Var Tennis; Var Im Vllybl; High Hon Roll; US Bus Educ Awd 83; John Jay CUNY; Crmnl Just.

VINCENZO, MICHAEL; Monsignor Farrell HS; Staten Island, NY; (Y); Band; Concert Band; Mrchg Band; Stage Crew; VP Intnl Clb; JV Crs Cntry; JV Trk; NHS; Ntl Merit SF; Art.

VINCH, BRENT; Cicero-North Syracuse HS; N Syracuse, NY; (S); 39/623; Cmnty Wkr; German Clb; JA; Var Capt Crs Cntry; Var Capt Trk; Hon Roll; Bus Mgmt.

VINCH, DANA; Cicero-North Syracuse HS; North Syracuse, NY; (S); 29/667; VP Exploring; Spanish Clb; Stu Cncl; Capt Crs Cntry; Trk; NHS; Rochester Inst Of Tech; Engrng.

VINCIGUERRA, CHRISTINE; Sachem High School North Campus; Lake Ronkonkoma, NY; (Y); 89/1584; GAA; Hosp Aide; Sec Intnl Clb; Radio Clb; Chorus; Im JV Socr; NHS; Sprtsmnshp Awd Socr Clb 83; Librl Arts.

VINCIGUERRA, SCOTT; Paul V Moore HS; Brewerton, NY; (Y); FCA; SADD; Varsity Clb; Band; Concert Band; Mrchg Band; JV Var Bsktbl; Var Capt Crs Cntry; Var Capt Trk; Most Valuble Player Cross Cntry 85-86; NY ST Cross Cntry Championships 85-86; All Lg Awds Crs Cntry; Cartland ST; Physical Edu Tchr.

VINETTE, KERRI; Victor Central HS; Victor, NY; (Y); #58 In Class; Science Clb; Ski Clb; Color Guard; School Play; Stage Crew; Crs Cntry; Trk; Hon Roll; SUNY Regnts Schlrshp 86; SUNY Coll Oswego.

VINISKI, TOD M; Fairport HS; Fairport, NY; (Y); 25/619; Computer Clb; Math Tm; Pres Science Clb; Ski Clb; JV Capt Socr; Hon Roll; NHS; Spanish NHS; NY ST Rgnts Schlrshp 86; Clrksn Schlrshp; Clksn U; Engrng.

VINOJ, JOHN; Wellsville HS; Wellsville, NY; (Y); 30/120; Nwsp Rptr; Badmtn; Socr; Var Trk; Vllybl; Am Socr Amb 86; Def Socr Plyr Of Yr 86; Mst Imprvd Mn/Socr 85; Steuben Cnty Allst/Hnrb Mntn-Socr 86; E Riddle Arntcl U; Pilotng.

VINYARD, KELLEY; Geneseo Central Schl; New York, NY; (Y); Var JV Cheerleading; Var Pom Pon; Hon Roll; Dependblty Awd Chrldng 85; Law.

VIOLANTE, DAVID A; Wallkill SR HS; Clintondale, NY; (Y); Boy Scts; VP Church Yth Grp; Red Cross Aide; SADD; Band; Concert Band; Jazz Band; Stage Crew; God Cntry Awd; Swdsh Inst; Massage Thrpst.

VIRELLA, MARIBEL; James Monroe HS; Bronx, NY; (Y); Church Yth Grp; Vllybl; Hon Roll; Typg And Spnsh Awds 84; Bus Math Awd 86; John Jay Co; Lwyr.

VIRELLA, ROSARIO; Grace Dodge Vocational HS; Bronx, NY; (Y); 1/18; Math Tm; Nwsp Rptr; Pres Jr Cls; Sftbl; Hon Roll; Daily Nws Princpls Prde Yank Awd 85; Med.

VIRGO, WANDA V; St Barnabas HS; Bronx, NY; (Y); 49/178; Camera Clb; Variety Show; Nwsp Rptr; Pres Stu Cncl; Swmmng; Amer Boys & Mens Clb Awd 86; Lehman Coll; Nrsg.

VIRKLER, JOSEPH; Lowville Central Schl; Lowville, NY; (Y); Debate Tm; Varsity Clb; Yrbk Stf; VP Frsh Cls; VP Soph Cls; Stu Cncl; Var L Bsktbl; Var L Ftbl; Hon Roll; Prfct Atten Awd; Civil Engr.

VIROLA, LISA M; Laguardia HS; New York City, NY; (Y); 242/551; Art Clb; Hosp Aide; Library Aide; PAVAS; Teachers Aide; Chorus; Variety Show; Hon Roll; Awd Merit Illstrtn 86; Parsons; Stg Dsgn.

VIRTUOSO, CHRISTINE; Port Chester HS; Port Chester, NY; (Y); Yrbk Stf; Hon Roll; Italian Hnr Soc 84-85.

VIRZERA, DIANE L; A G Berner HS; Massapequa, NY; (Y); 2/400; Key Clb; Library Aide; Pep Clb; Nwsp Ed-Chief; Nwsp Phtg; Nwsp Rptr; Hon Roll; NHS; Law.

VISCIANO, CAROLYN; Commack HS North; Commack, NY; (Y); Spanish Clb; Lit Mag; Var Cheerleading; High Hon Roll; Hon Roll; US Slvr Poet Awd 86; Spnsh Tutor 84-86; Kickline Gdnc & Gym Aide 82; Hfstra U; Intl Bus.

VISCO JR, DONALD P; Sachem HS; Holtsville, NY; (Y); 32/1580; Jr NHS; NHS; Im Bsktbl; Im Bowling; JV Tennis; Trk; 1st Pl-Crtv Wrtng Cntst 84-85; 3rd Pl-Outstndng Chem Stu 84-85; Chmcl Engrng.

VISCONTI, MARIA; Solvay HS; Syracuse, NY; (Y); Church Yth Grp; Concert Band; Jr Cls; Achvt Awd Band 3 Yrs 86; Htl Rstrnt Mgmt.

VISCONTI, WILLIAM A; Monsignor Farrell HS; Staten Island, NY; (Y); 37/298; Art Clb; Mgr Computer Clb; FBLA; Ski Clb; Yrbk Stf; Im Capt Bsktbl; Im Capt Bowling; Im Capt Ftbl; Hon Roll; Pace U NY City; Mgmt Info Sys.

VISCOSI, JAMES; Oriskany Central HS; Oriskany, NY; (Y); 1/85; Drama Clb; Key Clb; Band; Stu Cncl; High Hon Roll; Jr NHS; NHS; Ntl Merit Ltr; Comp Engr.

VISCOSI, LISA; John F Kennedy HS; Utica, NY; (Y); FBLA; Hosp Aide; Sec Frsh Cls; Sec Soph Cls; Pres Jr Cls; Pres Sr Cls; Rep Stu Cncl; Co-Capt Cheerleading; NHS; Elmira Coll Key Awd 86.

VISCOVICH, EDDIE; Archbishop Molloy HS; Floral Park, NY; (Y); Cit Awd.

VISCUSO, JOSEPH; Monsignor Farrell HS; Staten Island, NY; (Y); Var Bsbl; Im Bsktbl; Ftbl; Var Wt Lftg; NY City Fire Dept Schlrshp 83; Holy Name Schlrshp 83.

VISNESKI, NANCY; Salamanca JR SR HS; Salamanca, NY; (Y); Drama Clb; French Clb; Thesps; Band; Jazz Band; Mrchg Band; School Play; Yrbk Rptr; Trk; Hon Roll; Bus.

VISSLAILLI, TAMMY; Oyster Bay HS; Oyster Bay, NY; (Y); Spanish Clb; Var Fld Hcky; Var Sftbl; Hon Roll; Vet-Med.

VISSUSKUS, CHRIS; Roy C Ketcham HS; Wappingers Falls, NY; (Y); Capt JV Swmmng; Prfct Atten Awd; Engrng.

VITA, PETER; Lindenhurst SR HS; Lindenhurst, NY; (Y); 2/500; French Clb; Math Tm; High Hon Roll; Hon Roll; NHS; Ntl Merit Ltr; Sal; Chess Clb; Math & Sci Awd 86; Soc Wmn Engrs Awd 86; Natl Sci Supv Assoc 86; Stony Brook; Opthlmlgy.

VITAGLIANO, JULIANNE; Trott Vocational HS; Niagara Falls, NY; (Y); Dance Clb; Library Aide; Spanish Clb; Hst Jr Cls; Trs Sr Cls; Pres Stu Cncl; Hon Roll; Erie CC; Diet.

VITALE, TIMOTHY; Unatego JR Ssr HS; Unadilla, NY; (Y); 10/94; Spanish Clb; High Hon Roll; NHS; Prfct Atten Awd; Excllnt Atten Awd Chenango DE Bus Ed Cncl; Law.

VITEK, SUSAN; Notre Dame Bishop Gibbons HS; Schenectady, NY; (Y); French Clb; Red Cross Aide; Ski Clb; Stu Cncl; Tennis; Psych.

VITERE, CYNTHIA LYNN; Pelham Memorial HS; Pelham, NY; (Y); 19/156; French Clb; Political Wkr; School Musical; JV Bsktbl; Var Sftbl; Var Vllybl; High Hon Roll; NHS; Spanish NHS; AFS; Pres Acad Ftnss Awd 86; Most Impvd Stu Engl 86; SUNY Albany; Hstry.

VITO, JAMES; Cardinal Mooney HS; Rochester, NY; (Y); 155/350; Bsbl; Sftbl; St John Fisher; Engrng.

VITOULIS, GREGORY; Germantown Central HS; Elizaville, NY; (S); 6/44; Yrbk Stf; Rep Soph Cls; High Hon Roll; Chorus; School Musical; School Play; Yrbk Bus Mgr; Hon Roll; NHS; Voice Dem Awd; Marist Coll; Englsh.

VITRANO, VICTORIA; Sacred Heart Acad; Rockville Centre, NY; (S); 18/186; Hosp Aide; Pres Intnl Clb; Math Tm; SADD; Nwsp Rptr; Yrbk Ed-Chief; Pres Jr Cls; Rep Sr Cls; NHS; Ntl Merit Ltr; Hist.

VITTI, PATRIZIA E; Saint Francis Preparatory Schl; Elmhurst, NY; (S); 5/744; Art Clb; Cmnty Wkr; Library Aide; Office Aide; Science Clb; Church Choir; NHS; Prncpls List; Law.

VITTORIO, MELODIE; Liverpool HS; Liverpool, NY; (Y); 312/926; DECA; Girl Scts; Band; Mrchg Band; Yrbk Stf; Powder Puff Ftbl; Onondaga Cnty JR Miss 85-86; Wegmans Work Achvt Schlrshp; Maria Regina; Bus Admin.

VIVIAN, DAVID; Plattsburgh HS; Plattsburgh, NY; (Y); Cmnty Wkr; Model UN; Ski Clb; Varsity Clb; Rep Jr Cls; JV Bsbl; L Ice Hcky; L Socr; L Trk; Hon Roll; Comm.

VIVIAN, LESA; Alexander Central HS; Darien Ctr, NY; (Y); Pres AFS; Girl Scts; Chorus; Concert Band; Mrchg Band; Teachers Aide; JV Var Socr; Var Swmmng; Hon Roll; Spec Educ Tchr.

VIVIANI, PETER; Rome Free Acad; Rome, NY; (Y); 39/456; Cmnty Wkr; Intnl Clb; Ski Clb; JV Var Lcrss; High Hon Roll; Jr NHS; Pres Phys Ftnss Awd 86; Schl Single Game Scoring Record In La Crosse 86; Boston Arch Ctr; Arch.

VIVIEN, ALEX; Nazareth Regional HS; Brooklyn, NY; (S); 7/276; Var L Bsktbl; Var Capt Ftbl; High Hon Roll; Hon Roll; Mth Mdls 83-85; Oceanogrphy Mdl 85; Nazareth 4 Yr Scholar 82; Engrng.

VIVO, ANDREW; Bishop Ford Cntrl Catholc HS; Brooklyn, NY; (S); 9/439; Science Clb; Bus.

VIVOLO, CARMELINA; Bethpage HS; Bethpage, NY; (Y); 55/303; FBLA; GAA; SADD; Yrbk Stf; Badmtn; Bsktbl; Fld Hcky; Vllybl; Bus.

VLOCK, ROBERT; Gloversville HS; Gloversvl, NY; (Y); Cmnty Wkr; Drama Clb; Pres Temple Yth Grp; Band; Stage Crew; Symp Band; Tennis; High Hon Roll; Hon Roll; Ntl Merit Ltr; Med.

VLOGIANITIS, ANDREA; Garden City HS; Garden City, NY; (Y); 99/341; VP Church Yth Grp; Spanish Clb; SADD; Var Bsktbl; Var Mgr(s); Var Trk; High Hon Roll; Hon Roll; Jr NHS.

VOCE, CAROLYN A; Holland Patent Central HS; Barneveld, NY; (Y); 55/150; Church Yth Grp; Exploring; GAA; JV Capt Cheerleading; Gym; Powder Puff Ftbl; Hon Roll; Ntl Chrldrs Assoc Awd Of Excllnc 85; South Eastern Acad; Trvl Asst.

VOELKER, DIANE; Eastridge HS; Rochester, NY; (Y); 4/130; Trs FBLA; Math Clb; High Hon Roll; NHS; VFW Awd; 1st Pl-Bus Math-FLBA 86; Evergreen ST Coll; Comp Pgmng.

VOERG, DOROTHY; Saugerties HS; Saugerties, NY; (S); Ski Clb; Variety Show; Off Civic Clb; Powder Puff Ftbl; Stat Socr; Sftbl; Stat Wrstlng; Albany Coll Phrmcy; Phrmcy.

VOGEL, HOLLY; Solvay HS; Syracuse, NY; (Y); Church Yth Grp; Band; Concert Band; Jazz Band; School Musical; Yrbk Stf; Rep Soph Cls; High Hon Roll; Hon Roll; Onondaga All Cnty Cncrt Bnd 84-86; Excllnc Soc Stds 85-86; Excllnc Band 85; Elem Ed.

VOGEL, KERI LYN; Villa Maria Acad; Buffalo, NY; (S); 16/87; Chorus; Church Choir; Hon Roll; Prftc Attndnc 84-85; Psych.

VOGEL, RONALD; Clarkstown High School North; Congers, NY; (Y); French Clb; Math Tm; Co-Capt Scholastic Bowl; Stage Crew; Mu Alp Tht; NHS; Vincent Festa Tutrng Awd 86; Math Magzn Edtr; NY Maith Fair Semi Fnlst 85; Wesleyan U; Bio.

VOGEL, SHOSHANA; Curtis HS; Staten Island, NY; (Y); Key Clb; Band; Concert Band; Camera Clb; L Orch; School Musical; Symp Band; Yrbk Stf; Cheerleading; Hon Roll; Boston U; Cmnctns.

VOGELHUT, MARLENE; Franklin D Roosevelt HS; Brooklyn, NY; (Y); 44/587; Girl Scts; Math Tm; Quiz Bowl; Teachers Aide; Band; Yrbk Stf; Hon Roll; NHS; SUNY Binghamton; Comp Sci.

VOGLER, SCOTT G; Gates-Chili HS; Rochester, NY; (Y); 3/560; Am Leg Boys St; Aud/Vis; French Clb; Math Tm; Ski Clb; Varsity Clb; Stage Crew; JV Var Crs Cntry; JV Var Trk; High Hon Roll; 800 Math Sat Score 86; Concours De Francais Cntst 85; Wnnr Spelling Bee 84; Bucknell U; Engrng.

VOGT, AMY; Lafayette HS; Lafayette, NY; (S); 6/96; Trs Soph Cls; Var Capt Cheerleading; High Hon Roll; NHS; Hghst Avg Geom 82; Hghst Avg Span II 83; Mst Sprtd Chrldr 85.

VOGT, STEPHAN; Green Meadow Waldorf Schl; Spring Valley, NY; (Y); 4/15; Chorus; Concert Band; Orch; School Musical; School Play; Stage Crew; Yrbk Ed-Chief; Yrbk Phtg; Lit Mag; Pres Stu Cncl; Rgnts Schlrshp 86; Sclptr Awd 86; Drftng & Dsgn Awd 85; Fashn Inst Of Tech; Fshn Dsgn.

VOLAN, CHRISTOPHER J; La Fayette Central HS; Jamesville, NY; (S); 18/96; Computer Clb; French Clb; Model UN; Ski Clb; SADD; Varsity Clb; Nwsp Stf; Var Lcrss; JV Var Wrstlng; NHS; Rochester Inst Of Tech; Engr.

VOLEL, CAROLINE; Bronx HS Of Science; Hollis, NY; (Y); Dance Clb; Library Aide; NFL; Spanish Clb; Speech Tm; Teachers Aide; Lit Mag; NHS; Ntl Merit Ltr; Med.

VOLK, CHRISTINE J; Kingston HS; Kingston, NY; (Y); 34/573; French Clb; Girl Scts; Yrbk Stf; JV Vllybl; French Hon Soc; High Hon Roll; Jr NHS; NHS; NYS Regents Scholar 86; Syracuse U; Acctng.

VOLK, JOHN S; St John The Baptist Diocesan HS; Massapequa, NY; (S); 9/600; Boy Scts; Nwsp Rptr; Nwsp Stf; Yrbk Stf; Lit Mag; Crs Cntry; Trk; Hon Roll; NHS; Ntl Merit SF; Hnrs Schlrshp 86; Schlrshp Fairfield Univ 86; Bio.

VOLKERS, NANCY E; Williamson SR HS; Williamson, NY; (Y); 1/86; AFS; Sec Trs Exploring; Science Clb; VP SADD; Band; Concert Band; Mrchg Band; School Musical; Stage Crew; Yrbk Stf; Drew U; Bio Sci.

VOLKERT, CAROL; Christian Central Acad; Tonawanda, NY; (Y); 2/16; VP Church Yth Grp; Chorus; Nwsp Rptr; Ed Yrbk Ed-Chief; Rep Jr Cls; Rep Sr Cls; Socr; Var Sftbl; Var Vllybl; Hon Roll; Sportmnshp Awd Soccer 85-86; Houghton Coll; Bus Adm.

VOLKMAN, PATRICIA LYNN; Clymer Central HS; Findley Lk, NY; (Y); 6/45; Office Aide; Teachers Aide; Chorus; Yrbk Stf; Trs Stu Cncl; Var Cheerleading; Var Capt Sftbl; Capt Var Vllybl; High Hon Roll; NHS; Acctng Awd 85-86; Acctng.

VOLKWEIN, JAMES F; Clayton A Bouton HS; Voorheesville, NY; (Y); 1/120; Am Leg Boys St; Band; Pres Stu Cncl; Capt Tennis; Capt Vllybl; Bausch & Lomb Sci Awd; DAR Awd; Pres NHS; Math Tm; Ski Clb; Century III Ldrshp Schlrshp Fnlst 85; Harvard; Law.

VOLLARO, MICHELE; Fontbonne Hall Acad; Brooklyn, NY; (Y); Art Clb; Camera Clb; Computer Clb; Library Aide; Office Aide; SADD; Teachers Aide; Chorus; School Play; Yrbk Stf; Pace U Brooklyn; Accntng.

VOLLARO, TRACY ANN; Academy Of St Joseph; Islip, NY; (Y); Cmnty Wkr; Hosp Aide; Library Aide; Science Clb; Variety Show; Nwsp Stf; JV Bsktbl; Var Socr; Var Sftbl.

VOLLKOMMER, DAWN; N Babylon SR HS; No Babylon, NY; (Y); Gym; High Hon Roll; Hon Roll; NHS; Prfct Atten Awd; Newspaper Carrier Bus 83-86; Farmingdale; Comm Adv.

VOLLMAR, MIKE; Victor Central HS; Farmington, NY; (Y); 25/200; Boy Scts; Model UN; Pep Clb; Quiz Bowl; Band; Church Choir; Concert Band; Drm & Bgl; Jazz Band; Mrchg Band; Amer Chem Socty Hgh Achvt 86; Schl 1st Sci Olympd 86.

VOLLRATH, EILEEN; Mercy HS; Center Moriches, NY; (Y); Library Aide; SADD; Yrbk Phtg; Yrbk Stf.

VOLO JR, RICHARD; Bellport HS; Medford, NY; (Y); Math Tm; Orch; Ed Nwsp Ed-Chief; High Hon Roll; Pres Jr NHS; NHS; Cmmnctns.

VOLPE, DENISE; Lindenhurst HS; Lindenhurst, NY; (Y); 60/550; German Clb; Sec Science Clb; Color Guard; Drill Tm; Mrchg Band; Yrbk Stf; Hon Roll; NHS; March Dimes Awd 86; St Josephs Coll; Child Psychlgy.

VOLPE, THOMAS; Archbishop Molloy HS; Flushing, NY; (Y); 14/383; Cmnty Wkr; Hosp Aide; Sec Pep Clb; Var L Crs Cntry; Var L Trk; High Hon Roll; NHS; Ntl Merit Ltr; Med.

VOLTMANN, KIMBERLY; Lancaster Central SR HS; Alden, NY; (S); 91/461; Church Yth Grp; Cmnty Wkr; DECA; Girl Scts; Pep Clb; Red Cross Aide; Varsity Clb; Yrbk Stf; Bsktbl; JV Fld Hcky; Awds 1st Pl Rgn 12 DECA 2nd Pl NYS Rstrnt Mrktng Mbr Slct Fture Ldrs Mrktng Crt Of Excllnce 85-86; Graceland Coll; Pre-Law.

VOLZ, MICHAEL; V S Central HS; Valley Stream, NY; (Y); Computer Clb; Yrbk Stf; Var Bowling; Var Crs Cntry; JV Socr; Var Trk; Hon Roll; Mu Alp Tht; NHS; Cert Trky Trot 85; Arch.

VON BARGEN, FREDERICK J; Long Island Lutheran HS; Oyster Bay, NY; (S); Band; VP Soph Cls; Rep Stu Cncl; Var Bsbl; Var Bsktbl; Var Crs Cntry; Cit Awd; Hon Roll; Jr NHS; NHS; Paul Jud Awd 83; MVP Crss Cntry 85-86.

VON BEVERN, MICHAEL; Msgr Farrell HS; Statenisland, NY; (Y); Boy Scts; Varsity Clb; Im Bsktbl; Var L Bowling; JV Diving; Im Ftbl; JV Socr; JV Swmmng; Cit Awd; Hon Roll; Wgnr Coll Schlrshp 86; Amer Lgn Egl Sct Of Yr 84; Wgnr Coll; Ec.

VON BOTHMER, MARIA E; Spence HS; New York, NY; (Y); Art Clb; French Clb; Nwsp Bus Mgr; Nwsp Rptr; Regents Schlrshp 86; Princeton U.

VON BUTTGEREIT, KAREN; Dominican Commercial HS; Rosedale, NY; (Y); 41/288; Sec 4-H; Drm & Bgl; Cheerleading; Swmmng; Sec.

VON DIEZELSKI, MIKE; John H Glenn HS; E Northport, NY; (Y); Church Yth Grp; Var Socr; Hon Roll; NHS; Elwood Nghbrhd Watch Pgm 83-85; Law.

VON ESCHEN, LAURA ANN; Ward Melville HS; Stony Brook, NY; (Y); 78/711; Drama Clb; Chorus; School Play; Nwsp Rptr; Var Trk; High Hon Roll; Jr NHS; NHS; Intnl Clb; PAVAS; Rotary Intl Yth Exchng To Thailand 84-85; Cum Laude In A Latin II Contst 83; Schl Bookstore Mgr 85-86; Vassar Coll; Drama.

VON ESSEN, PAMELA; South Side HS; Rockville Centre, NY; (Y); 5/300; Cmnty Wkr; Key Clb; Yrbk Sprt Ed; Yrbk Stf; VP Frsh Cls; Var Capt Bsktbl; Var Capt Sftbl; Var Capt Vllybl; High Hon Roll; Jr NHS; U Of PA.

VON HASSEL, DOUGLAS; St Johns Diocesion HS; Babylon, NY; (Y); Boys Clb Am; Boy Scts; Cmnty Wkr; Drama Clb; Ski Clb; School Play; Golf; Capt Var Ice Hcky; Tennis.

VON MAUCHER, GARY; Scotia-Glenville HS; Scotia, NY; (Y); Am Leg Boys St; French Clb; JA; JV Bsbl; Bowling; High Hon Roll; Hon Roll; Ntl Merit Ltr; Engrng.

VON SEGGERN, KRISTEN; Bishop Grimes HS; Syracuse, NY; (S); 14/146; Cmnty Wkr; Drama Clb; FBLA; Ski Clb; Band; School Play; Yrbk Stf; Crs Cntry; Trk; High Hon Roll; 1st Pl Essay-Cnty Of Onondaga 85; Amer Collgt Windbands 85; Band Hall Of Fame 85; Bus.

VONA, LINDA; Bishop Maginn HS; Rensselaer, NY; (S); High Hon Roll; Hon Roll; Spnsh Awd.

VONA, SALVATORE; Msgr Farrell HS; Staten Island, NY; (Y); 9/319; Camera Clb; Hosp Aide; Math Tm; Teachers Aide; Stage Crew; Lit Mag; Im Bsktbl; Im Ftbl; High Hon Roll; Hon Roll; Iona Coll Lang Awd Italn 85; Fordham U Italn Poetry Awd 86; Med Engrng.

VONHOENE, TED; Mc Quaid Jesuit HS; Fairport, NY; (Y); 40/200; Varsity Clb; Sec Soph Cls; JV Var Bsktbl; JV Ftbl; Var Score Keeper; JV Socr; Var Tennis; High Hon Roll; Fnc.

VONKRAMER, BRENDA; Pembroke Central HS; Corfu, NY; (Y); Sec Church Yth Grp; German Clb; Chorus; Church Choir; Variety Show; Stat Var Bsktbl; Mgr(s); Var Score Keeper; Mgr Var Sftbl; Hon Roll; Nrsng.

VONSCHILLER, ERIKA; Clinton Central HS; Clinton, NY; (Y); 34/134; Art Clb; Political Wkr; Chorus; School Musical; Var L Socr; Bessie Griffin Schlrshp; Hartwick Coll; Math.

VOORHEES, CASEY; Le Roy Central HS; Leroy, NY; (Y); AFS; Boy Scts; Ski Clb; Spanish Clb; Varsity Clb; JV Var Socr; High Hon Roll; Hon Roll; Purdue U; Phy Thrpy.

VOORHEES, ROBIN; Batavia HS; Batavia, NY; (Y); Y-Teens; Chorus; Swing Chorus; Bsktbl; Sftbl; Tennis; Vllybl; Sportsmnshp Awd Bsktbl 86; Ath Trainer.

VOPARIL, CHRISTOPHER; Walt Whitman HS; Huntington Stat, NY; (Y); #49 In Class; Church Yth Grp; Key Clb; Sec Concert Band; Jazz Band; Mrchg Band; Symp Band; Bowling; Lcrss; High Hon Roll; Jr NHS; Lbrl Arts.

VORA, SHILPA; Forest Hills HS; Rego Park, NY; (Y); 42/826; English Clb; Office Aide; Yrbk Stf; High Hon Roll; Hon Roll; NHS; Prfct Atten Awd; Spec Achvt Awd Art 83; Attdnc Awds 84-85; Regnts Schlrshp 86; Comp Sci.

VORCE, LINDA; Indian River Central HS; Black River, NY; (Y); 12/126; Band; Concert Band; Jazz Band; Mrchg Band; School Musical; School Play; Sftbl; NHS; High Hon Roll; Hon Roll; Nazareth Alumni Schlrshp 86; Nazareth Coll; Bio.

VOREL, MICHAEL J; La Salle SR HS; Niagara Falls, NY; (S); 11/250; Hon Roll; NHS; Prfct Atten Awd; U Of Rochester; Elec Engr.

VOSS, HEIDI; Keene Central Schl; Keene Valley, NY; (Y); 3/16; Drama Clb; French Clb; Scholastic Bowl; Teachers Aide; Chorus; School Musical; Yrbk Stf; Pres Soph Cls; Sec Jr Cls; Pres Sr Cls; Excllnc Algbr & Acctg; Suptndnt Acadmc Awd; Keuka Coll; Nrsg.

VOSSELLER, JOHN; Commack North HS; E Northport, NY; (Y); 98/364; High Hon Roll; Hon Roll; Suffolk Cnty Math Cntst 2nd Pl; Pal Ftbll; Outstndng Achvmnt Awd Math; Coll; Math.

VOTRA, LISA; Parishville Hopkinton HS; Potsdam, NY; (S); 1/45; JA; Office Aide; Teachers Aide; Concert Band; Jazz Band; School Musical; Variety Show; High Hon Roll; NHS; Spanish Excel I II III 83-85; Achvmnt In Phy Ed 85; Mater Dei; Sec.

VOULGARIS, ARIS P; Freeport HS; Freeport, NY; (Y); 10/450; Church Yth Grp; Computer Clb; Mathletes; Science Clb; Nwsp Stf; Bsbl; High Hon Roll; NHS; Pres Schlr; Guidnc Dept Schlrshp & Dr Mervin Livingston Schloss Fndtn Schlrshp 86; SUNY Binghamton; Acctg.

VROMAN, MARYLOU; Sleepy Hollow HS; Tarrytown, NY; (Y); Aud/Vis; Debate Tm; Drama Clb; German Clb; Math Tm; Chorus; School Musical; School Play; Hon Roll; Library Aide; NCTE Schl Semi-Fnlst 86; Math.

VROOMAN, LYNNE; Linton HS; Schenectady, NY; (Y); Drill Tm; Hon Roll; Cheyney U; Child Psychlgy.

VU, VINCE; Port Jervis HS; Port Jervis, NY; (Y); Church Yth Grp; Exploring; Hosp Aide; Church Choir; JV Var Socr; Grnt From Scrd Hrt R C Chrch To Snds Of Smr Mnth At Wittenberg U 85; Med.

VUKSIC, PAULA; St Catharine Acad; Clifton, NJ; (Y); 9/201; Stu Cncl; NHS; Farileigh Dickinson U; Acctg.

VULCANO, MICHAEL; Frankfort-Schuyler Central HS; Frankfort, NY; (Y); 13/100; Drama Clb; Spanish Clb; School Musical; School Play; Stage Crew; Stu Cncl; Ftbl; Trk; High Hon Roll; NHS; Regnts Schlrshp 86; Hamers Trst Schlrshp 86; Mohawk Vly Gen Hosp 86; Siena Coll; Pre Med.

VULIN, CHRISTINE; The Mary Louis Acad; Kew Gardens, NY; (Y); 67/270; Camera Clb; Cmnty Wkr; Girl Scts; Hosp Aide; Intnl Clb; Office Aide; Color Guard; Variety Show; Im Ftbl; Hon Roll; NY ST Regents Schlrshp 85; Fordham U; Jrnlsm.

VURAL, MATTHEW O; Jamesville-Dewitt HS; Dewitt, NY; (Y); 3/247; Debate Tm; Ski Clb; Stage Crew; Nwsp Rptr; Var Crs Cntry; Var Trk; Pres NHS; Bio Awd Schlstc; Chem Awd; Soc Studies Awd; Bio-Chem.

VURCKIO, JAMES; Port Richmond HS; Staten Is, NY; (Y); Art Clb; Cmnty Wkr; Science Clb; Nwsp Rptr; Ftbl; Bus.

WACHMAN, ALLYSON; Clarkstown North HS; New City, NY; (Y); French Clb; Capt Pep Clb; SADD; Temple Yth Grp; Varsity Clb; Band; Yrbk Bus Mgr; VP Frsh Cls; Stu Cncl; Var Capt Cheerleading.

WACHSLER, JANA; Potsdam HS; Potsdam, NY; (Y); AFS; French Clb; JA; Math Tm; Quiz Bowl; SADD; Orch; School Musical; School Play; Stage Crew; SUNY Geneseo; Psych.

WACHSPRESS, JONATHAN; Shaarei Torah Of Rockland Cty HS; New York, NY; (S); Computer Clb; Math Clb; School Play; Lit Mag; Off Soph Cls; Bsktbl; Fld Hcky; High Hon Roll; NHS; 1st Pl Team Bramson Ort Comp Cont 84.

WACHSSTOCK, SUZANNE E; Brandeis Schl; Lido Beach, NY; (Y); Debate Tm; Nwsp Bus Mgr; Yrbk Stf; Pres Stu Cncl; Var Capt Sftbl; Var Capt Vllybl; NHS; Ntl Merit SF; GAA; Yrbk Phtg; Century III Ldr 85; MVP Vllybl & Sftbl 85; Law.

WACHTER, BRET; Churchville-Chili HS; North Chili, NY; (Y); Band; Chorus; School Musical; Yrbk Phtg; Off Stu Cncl; Var Trk; Hon Roll; Rep Sr Cls; Rep Jr Cls; Rep Soph Cls; NYSSMA Band Perf VI A 84; NYSSMA Choir Perf VI A 85; NYSSMA Solo Comp VI A 86; Rochester Inst Tech.

WADAS, LINDA; Curtis HS; Staten Island, NY; (Y); Cmnty Wkr; Quiz Bowl; Science Clb; Teachers Aide; Yrbk Ed-Chief; Lit Mag; Hon Roll; Prfct Atten Awd; Frnch Exchng Pgm 85-86; Arista 86; Sci Mag Stf 85-86.

WADDELL, BRIAN; Schoharie Central HS; Schoharie, NY; (Y); Boy Scts; Stu Cncl; Mchnc.

WADE, CHRYSTAL L; Bronx High School Of Science; Bronx, NY; (Y); Camera Clb; Office Aide; Teachers Aide; Regnts Schlrshp 86; Nrs.

WADE, JEFFREY; Marlboro Central HS; Newburgh, NY; (Y); Aud/Vis; Drama Clb; Library Aide; Stage Crew; Capt Tennis; Hon Roll; Princpls Svc Awd 86; Comm.

WADE, MARY E; F D Roosevelt HS; Hyde Park, NY; (Y); 15/336; Pres Am Leg Aux Girls St; Church Yth Grp; Band; Sec Frsh Cls; Sec Soph Cls; Sec Jr Cls; Sec Sr Cls; JV Capt Bsktbl; Var Capt Sftbl; Var Capt Tennis; Rotry Yth Ldrshp 84; Fairvw Fire Dept Actvty Prz 86; Johns Hopkins U; Rsrch Psych.

WADE, MICHAEL; Union Springs HS; Aubrun, NY; (Y); Letterman Clb; Varsity Clb; Var Ftbl; Capt Var Wrstlng; Went To Empire ST Gms 86; Most Impvd Plyr 86; Gym Tchr.

WADE, PATRICIA; St John Villa Acad; Brooklyn, NY; (Y); 6/122; Church Yth Grp; Math Tm; Ntl Sci Olympd Awd-Bio 85; Spnsh Achvt Awds 84-86; Engl Achvt Awd 84; Hlth.

WADE, TIMOTHY; Tioga Central HS; Owego, NY; (Y); 8/90; Boys Clb Am; Boy Scts; Camera Clb; Computer Clb; Debate Tm; Math Clb; Science Clb; Ski Clb; SADD; Variety Show; Elmira Coll Key Awd Schlrshp 86; US Naval Acad; Math.

WADHWANI, DAN; Victor HS; Victor, NY; (Y); 2/250; Am Leg Boys St; Boy Scts; Model UN; Band; Drm & Bgl; Pep Band; Socr; Tennis; High Hon Roll; NHS; Amer Chem Soc Chem Awd 86; Pre Med.

WADKINS, SAMANTHA; Oakwood HS; Hyde Park, NY; (Y); Drama Clb; Hosp Aide; Intnl Clb; Stu Cncl; Mgr(s); Exmplry Stndg 86-87; Bus.

WADLER, JEFFREY R; Margaretville Central Schl; Fleischmanns, NY; (Y); 9/38; Drama Clb; Chorus; School Musical; Stu Cncl; Socr; Wrstlng; DAR Awd; NY ST Rgnts Schlrshp 86; ST Snte Stu Plcy Frm 85; NY Educ Dept Yth For Yth 85; SUNY-ALBANY; Pltcl Sci.

WADMAN, HOPE; Hanau HS; Apo Ny, NY; (Y); Pres Church Yth Grp; Cmnty Wkr; Library Aide; Church Choir; Hon Roll; Merit Awd Wrld Hstry 85; Cornell U; Htl Admin.

WADSWORTH, MICHELE; Colonie Central HS; Albany, NY; (Y); Art Clb; Intnl Clb; PAVAS; Spanish Clb; SADD; JV Mgr(s); JV Score Keeper; JV Timer; JV Vllybl; Hon Roll; Hnr Roll 83-84; VT ST U Castleton; Art Educ.

WAFF, KIMBERLY; Pembroke JR SR HS; Corfu, NY; (Y); 2/130; Math Tm; Band; Concert Band; Jazz Band; Mrchg Band; School Musical; High Hon Roll; NHS; Sal; SUNY Buffalo; Engrng.

WAFFNER, ANISA; Cazenovia HS; New Woodstock, NY; (Y); Nwsp Stf; Trk; Hon Roll; Bus Schl; Travel & Tourism.

WAGER, JERRY; Gates-Chili SR HS; Rochester, NY; (Y); 55/446; Church Yth Grp; Exploring; German Clb; Band; Concert Band; Jazz Band; Mrchg Band; JV Bsktbl; JV Var Socr; JV Var Tennis; NY ST Regnts Schlrshp Awd; WV U; Aerosp Engrng.

WAGES, STPEHEN; Duanesburg JR SR HS; Delanson, NY; (Y); Art Clb; Camera Clb; Pres 4-H; Intnl Clb; Orch; Variety Show; Nwsp Rptr; Yrbk Phtg; Var Socr.

WAGGESTAD, LAURA; Albertus Magnus HS; New City, NY; (Y); Sec Cmnty Wkr; Math Clb; Pep Clb; Var JV Trk; High Hon Roll; Hon Roll; Jr NHS; Mu Alp Tht; NHS; Natl Sci Hnr Scty 86; Chmcl Engr.

WAGGLE, DARCI; Midlakes HS; Clifton Spgs, NY; (Y); 27/147; Art Clb; VP Cmnty Wkr; French Clb; GAA; Varsity Clb; Fld Hcky; Hon Roll; Sibleys Schlstc Art Awds Cert Of Merit 86; Hon Ment Midlakes Art Show 86; Cazenovia Coll; Cmmrcl Illstrtn.

WAGGONER, JILL; Notre Dame HS; Attica, NY; (S); Library Aide; Ski Clb; Yrbk Stf; JV Var Bsktbl; JV Var Cheerleading; JV Var Pom Pon; Var Sftbl; Hon Roll; NHS; Prfct Atten Awd; FIT; Designer.

WAGLER, JENNIFER; Spackenkill HS; Poughkeepsie, NY; (Y); SADD; Thesps; Band; Stage Crew; Yrbk Stf; High Hon Roll; NHS; Pres Acdmc Ftns Awd, NYS Regents Schlrshp 86; Clarkson U; Engrng.

WAGMAN, TRACEY; Wantagh HS; Wantagh, NY; (Y); 64/276; Mathletes; Pres Spanish Clb; Temple Yth Grp; Nwsp Stf; Yrbk Stf; Rep Frsh Cls; Tennis; Hon Roll; SUNY Albany; Bus.

WAGNER, AMY; Silver Creek Central HS; Silver Creek, NY; (Y); 1/89; Girl Scts; Ski Clb; Spanish Clb; VP Jr Cls; Trs Stu Cncl; Crs Cntry; Trk; Hon Roll; NHS; Engrng.

WAGNER, CHRISTINE; Half Hollow Hills HS West; Melville, NY; (Y); Girl Scts; Band; Concert Band; Mrchg Band; Symp Band; Bsktbl; Coach Actv; Mgr(s); Score Keeper; Socr; Girl Scout Slvr Awd 86; Accntng.

WAGNER, CHRISTINE ANNE; Mexico Central HS; Mexico, NY; (Y); Color Guard; School Musical; Variety Show; Yrbk Ed-Chief; Yrbk Stf; Rep Sr Cls; Hon Roll; Spanish Clb; Rep Jr Cls; Dollars For Schlrs 86; Show Fndtn Schlrshp 85; Phys Educ Awd 83; Canton ATC; Bus Mngmnt.

WAGNER, DAVID M; West Seneca West SR HS; West Seneca, NY; (Y); 2/559; Chess Clb; Mathletes; Cit Awd; High Hon Roll; JC Awd; Jr NHS; NHS; Sal; Natl Mrt Spec Schlrshp 86; Rgnts Schlrshp 86; Outstndng Male 85; Rnsslr Ply-Tch Inst; Nclr Engr.

WAGNER, DONNA A; Cheektowaga Central HS; Cheektowaga, NY; (Y); 2/199; Yrbk Stf; High Hon Roll; Jr NHS; NHS; Sal; St Schlr; Outstndng Bus Stu Cert 85-86; Erie CC; Bus Admin.

WAGNER, ERIC; Niskoyuna HS; Clifton Park, NY; (Y); Pres Aud/Vis; Exploring; Band; Concert Band; Albany ST U; Crmnl Lw.

WAGNER, ERIKA; Monroe HS; Rochester, NY; (Y); Church Yth Grp; Math Tm; Model UN; Office Aide; Band; Concert Band; Mrchg Band; Tennis; High Hon Roll; NHS; Phys Thrpy.

WAGNER, FRANCIS; St Francis HS; Buffalo, NY; (Y); Ntl Merit SF; NYS Regnts Schlrshp 86; SUNY Canton; Frstry Bio.

WAGNER, JENNIFER; N Spencer Christian Acad; Newfield, NY; (S); Sec Pep Clb; Band; Chorus; Church Choir; School Musical; Yrbk Stf; Var Capt Cheerleading; High Hon Roll; Principals Awd 84-85; Natl Fed Music Clbs Supr Wnr 85; Mth.

WAGNER, JENNIFER; Sacred Heart HS; Yonkers, NY; (S); 1/230; Chorus; Nwsp Stf; Rep Soph Cls; Vllybl; High Hon Roll; NHS; Tution Schlrshp 83-85; Physcn.

WAGNER, JOHANNA; Southampton HS; Southampton, NY; (Y); 47/115; SADD; VICA; Wt Lftg; Hon Roll; Outstndng Stu Yr 86; Maureen Hoiftmas Scholar 86; Southampton Lumber Co Outstndng Voctnl Stu 86; Johnson & Wales; Culinary Arts.

WAGNER, KEN; Seaford HS; Seaford, NY; (S); 2/275; School Play; Nwsp Rptr; Stu Cncl; Var Crs Cntry; Var Trk; High Hon Roll; NHS; Sal; St Schlr; Dstngshd Acad Awd-Hofstra U 86; Frnch Svc Awd 85; Acad All Amer 86; Hofstra U Hemp NY; Pre-Med.

WAGNER, LYNN; Remsen HS; Remsen, NY; (Y); 10/45; Mathletes; VP Sec Band; Yrbk Stf; Cheerleading; Socr; Trk; Cit Awd; High Hon Roll; Sec NHS; Mst Congenial Chrldr 85; Suny-Oneonta; Soc.

WAGNER, MARK I; Kings Park HS; Northport, NY; (Y); 14/422; Am Leg Boys St; Debate Tm; Rep Stu Cncl; JV Var Bsbl; JV Var Bsktbl; NHS; Quiz Bowl; Science Clb; Off Jr Cls; Hon Roll; Acceptnc To Cornell & Harvard Smmr Schls86; Mngmnt.

WAGNER, MARYELLEN; Gates-Chili HS; Rochester, NY; (Y); Hon Roll; Hm Econ 85-86; Bryant & Stratton; Bus Mgmt.

WAGNER, MELISSA; Thomas J Corcoran HS; Syracuse, NY; (Y); French Clb; GAA; Hosp Aide; Latin Clb; Nwsp Stf; Yrbk Stf; Var Capt Socr; Cit Awd; Hon Roll; Prfct Atten Awd; Natl Latin Exam Maxima Cum Laude Slvr Mdl 86; Outstndng Achvt In Cmnty Cert 86; Med.

WAGNER, MIMI; Voorheesville Central HS; Voorheesville, NY; (Y); Intnl Clb; Key Clb; Service Clb; Pres SADD; Yrbk Ed-Chief; Yrbk Stf; VP Frsh Cls; VP Soph Cls; Pres Jr Cls; JV Var Sftbl; Outstndng Ldrshp Awds 85-86; Grtst Contbtn Yrbk 86; Intl Bus.

WAGNER, PATRICIA; Queens Vocational HS; Brooklyn, NY; (Y); Drama Clb; Chorus; Socr; Sftbl; Trk; Vllybl; Awd Cosmetology 86; Working With Handicap Childrn.

WAGNER, PAUL; St Hildas Schl; Bronx, NY; (Y); 2/21; Computer Clb; Drama Clb; Latin Clb; Office Aide; Chorus; School Musical; School Play; Stage Crew; Yrbk Ed-Chief; High Hon Roll; Empr ST Schlrshp 86; NY Clscl Clb Trnsltn Cntst 86; Scty Myflwr Dscndts Hstry Achvmnt Awd 85; U Of Rochester; Elec Engr.

WAGNER, STEPHEN; Bishop Kearney HS; Henrietta, NY; (Y); 30/142; L Capt Ftbl; L Capt Trk; Hon Roll; Ntl Merit Ltr; NY St Regents Schlrshp 86; Pres Acad Awd 86; Canisius Coll; Hstry.

WAGNER, TRACI; North Rose-Wolcott HS; Wolcott, NY; (Y); VP FBLA; Capt Cheerleading; Stat Wrstlng; High Hon Roll; NHS; Sci Olympiad Tm 86.

WAGONER, BARBARA S; Schalmont SR HS; Schenectady, NY; (Y); 3/160; Church Yth Grp; Trs 4-H; Concert Band; Flag Corp; Var Trk; High Hon Roll; Sec NHS; Hon Roll; Masonic Awd; Sec Dance Clb; NYS Regents Scholar 86; Pres Acad Fit Awd 86; Schalmont Tchrs Assn Scholar Awd 86; Ithaca Coll; Phys Thrpy.

WAGONER, JENIFER; Pulaski JR SR HS; Pulaski, NY; (Y); Church Yth Grp; FBLA; Sec Frsh Cls; Bus Mgmnt.

WAHL, MIKE; Troy HS; Troy, NY; (Y); 25/500; Ski Clb; Varsity Clb; Wt Lftg; Wrstlng; High Hon Roll; NHS; Arch.

WAHLENMAYER, KIM; Hamburg Central HS; Hamburg, NY; (Y); 1/370; French Clb; Pres Band; Church Choir; Concert Band; Mrchg Band; Orch; School Musical; Symp Band; Var JV Vllybl; High Hon Roll.

WAHLER, JOHN J; Sachem North HS; Farmingville, NY; (Y); 136/1400; German Clb; Science Clb; Varsity Clb; Swmmng; NYS Regents Scholar 86; Swmmng Var Ltr 85; Stonybrook U; Law.

WAHMAN, JESSICA T; Bronx High School Of Science; New York, NY; (Y); Skidmore Coll; Horse Trnr.

WAINIO, MICHAEL D; Liverpool HS; Liverpool, NY; (Y); Am Leg Boys St; Cmnty Wkr; Concert Band; Jazz Band; Mrchg Band; JV Var Swmmng; Hon Roll; NHS; Exploring; Hosp Aide; Cert Of Hnr Acdmc Achvmnt 85; Ntnl Mrchng Bnd Comp 86; Coll; Pre-Med.

WAINWRIGHT, DENISE; Schoharie Central HS; Schoharie, NY; (Y); Exploring; Key Clb; Office Aide; Varsity Clb; Chorus; Bsktbl; Socr; Sftbl; Vllybl; MIP Vrsty Bsktbl 85-86; Albany Bus Coll; Data Wrd Proc.

WAINWRIGHT, LESLIE; Mt Mercy Acad; Buffalo, NY; (Y); 2/183; Church Yth Grp; French Clb; Chorus; Stage Crew; Yrbk Stf; Im Vllybl; French Hon Soc; High Hon Roll.

WAIT, CRYSTAL L; St Regis Falls Central; St Regis Falls, NY; (Y); 3/31; Math Tm; Yrbk Ed-Chief; Vllybl; Hon Roll; NHS; Rgnts Schlrshp 86; Math Cntst Awd 85; Potsdam ST; Lbrl Arts.

WAIT, RUSSELL H; Palmyra-Macedon HS; Macedon, NY; (S); 9/169; Church Yth Grp; Math Clb; Math Tm; Ski Clb; SADD; Chorus; Stu Cncl; JV Ftbl; High Hon Roll; Hst NHS; Math.

WAKEMAN, REBECCA; Oakfield-Alabama Central HS; Basom, NY; (Y); 3/95; AFS; Church Yth Grp; Math Tm; Band; Chorus; Church Choir; Hon Roll; NHS; Nrsng.

WAKIE, FRANCINE; St John Villa Acad; Staten Island, NY; (Y); Letterman Clb; Spanish Clb; Sec Trs Sr Cls; Rep Stu Cncl; Im Socr; JV Var Sftbl; Capt Var Swmmng; Stat Timer; Hon Roll; NHS; MVP Schl Swim Team 84-86; Coaches Awd Swmmng 84-85; Accntng.

WAKLEY, RENEE; Niagara Catholic HS; Lewiston, NY; (Y); French Clb; Yrbk Bus Mgr; Ed Yrbk Ed-Chief; Yrbk Stf; Trs Jr Cls; Trs Sr Cls; Stat Vllybl; Hon Roll; Psych.

WALAG, KATHY; Brewster HS; Patterson, NY; (Y); 16/192; Church Yth Grp; Girl Scts; Varsity Clb; VP Frsh Cls; Rep Stu Cncl; JV Bsktbl; JV Var Fld Hcky; Stat Lcrss; Stat Mgr(s); Var Sftbl; Sez Ftnss Ldr 86; Pres Acdmc Fit Prg 86; 2nd & 3rd Putnam Arts Cncl Annl Stu Art Show 86; Wittenberg U; Cmmrcl Arts.

WALCK, TIMOTHY; Niagara Wheatfield HS; Sanborn, NY; (Y); 1/300; Church Yth Grp; FCA; High Hon Roll; NHS; JR Marshall Awd 86; Engrng.

WALCOTT, MAURICE; Hempstead HS; Hempstead, NY; (S); 3/261; Boy Scts; Yrbk Phtg; Yrbk Stf; Crs Cntry; Trk; High Hon Roll; Hon Roll; NHS; Engr.

WALD, DINA J; H S For The Humanits; New York, NY; (Y); Pres Church Yth Grp; Teachers Aide; Pres Temple Yth Grp; Varsity Clb; School Play; Stage Crew; Nwsp Rptr; Nwsp Stf; Rep Soph Cls; Stat Bsktbl; NYC Div Vlybl Champ 85-86; Outstndng Comm Svc Snyagogue 85-86; OH ST U; Aviation.

WALDMAN, DAVID; East Islip HS; Islip Terrace, NY; (Y); 11/425; Cmnty Wkr; Band; School Play; Nwsp Rptr; Rep Stu Cncl; Var L Socr; NHS; Debate Tm; Political Wkr; NYS Regents Schlrshp 86; Navy Rsrvs Ofcr Trng Corps Schlrshp 86; Lucy Oshea Schlrshp-E Islip Tchrs 86; SUNY Maritime; Marine Transprt.

WALDMAN, OWEN; Clarkstown North HS; West Nyack, NY; (Y); Spanish Clb; Nwsp Rptr; Var Capt Bsktbl; Wt Lftg; AR ST U.

WALDMAN, ROBERT; East Islip HS; Islip Terrace, NY; (Y); 6/425; Math Clb; SADD; School Musical; Nwsp Rptr; Rep Stu Cncl; Var L Socr; NHS; Pres Schlr; Debate Tm; Political Wkr; NYS Rgnts Schlrshp 86; Air Force Rsrvs Offcr Trng Crps Schlrshp 86; Air Force Acad Schlrshp 86; US Air Force Acad; Plt.

WALDMANN, ERIC; Curtis HS; Staten Island, NY; (Y); Key Clb; Nwsp Rptr; Yrbk Phtg; T Heugens Grmn Schlrshp Awd; Fulbright Yung Diplmts Exch Pgm Grmny; UN Usher; Penn ST U; Archlgy.

WALDMILLER, THOMAS; Churchville-Chili SR HS; Rochester, NY; (Y); 60/300; Chorus; School Musical; Rep Stu Cncl; High Hon Roll; Hon Roll; Prfct Atten Awd; Pres Schlr; Father Geiger Schlrshp Awd 82; Dean Herrick Mem Awd 86; Spartan Schl Aeronautics; Mech.

WALDROP, JUNE; Amsterdam HS; Amsterdam, NY; (Y); 27/327; JA; Varsity Clb; VP Frsh Cls; Pres Jr Cls; Rep Stu Cncl; Cheerleading; Tennis; Trk; Vllybl; Hon Roll; Bdcst Jrnlsm.

WALEGIR, GINA; Christ He King Regional HS; S Ozone Park, NY; (Y); 2/454; Church Yth Grp; Cmnty Wkr; Office Aide; Church Choir; Hon Roll.

WALKER, ALETHEIA; Riverside HS; Buffalo, NY; (Y); JA; Pep Clb; Bowling; Awd For Excllnc Spnsh 86; Merit Rll Awd 86; Mst Polite SR Clss Awd 86; Bus Law.

WALKER, ANDREA; Tioga Central HS; Barton, NY; (Y); Computer Clb; Dance Clb; Library Aide; SADD; Varsity Clb; Nwsp Stf; JV Var Mgr(s); Hon Roll.

WALKER, ANGELA MICHELLE; Hutchinson Central Technical HS; Buffalo, NY; (Y); Church Yth Grp; Cmnty Wkr; Library Aide; Natl Beta Clb; Office Aide; Church Choir; Nwsp Bus Mgr; Bowling; DAR Awd; Rochester Inst Tech; Comp Engrn.

WALKER, BRUCE; John Jay HS; Hopewell Jct, NY; (Y); Math Tm; Science Clb; Soph Cls; Rep Jr Cls; Var L Bsbl; Var L Socr; Var L Trk; Hon Roll; Bsbll Vrsty MVP 86; Ldrshp Cnfrnc Sffrn 85; Sccr Vrsty; USMA; Engr.

WALKER, CLARENCE D; Brighton HS; Rochester, NY; (Y); 54/325; Aud/Vis; Church Yth Grp; Ntl Merit SF; Radio Clb; Stat Bsktbl; Im Vllybl; Blck Stu Union Acadmc Awd 83-85; Trea Blck Stu Union 83-86; Urban Lgu Blck Schlr Awd 86; Aerspc Engr.

WALKER, COLLEEN; Hoosic Valley Central HS; Melrose, NY; (S); 3/99; Pres 4-H; OK JR Hon Soc 83-84; Hudson Vly CC; Nrsng.

WALKER, DANIEL; Roy C Ketcham HS; Wappingers Falls, NY; (Y); Boy Scts; Cmnty Wkr; Drama Clb; Stage Crew; Socr.

WALKER, DEIDRE; The Franciscan Acad; Syracuse, NY; (Y); 6/25; FBLA; GAA; Yrbk Stf; Trs Stu Cncl; Var JV Vllybl; High Hon Roll; Hon Roll; Jr NHS; NHS; Ntl Merit Ltr; Prom Commttee 84-86; Hnr Soc Treas 85-86; Clarkson U; Math.

WALKER, DENNIS; Newfield Central HS; Newfield, NY; (Y); 9/54; Am Leg Boys St; Varsity Clb; Band; Jazz Band; Bsktbl; Ftbl; Hon Roll; Masonic Awd; US Army Rsrv Natl Schlr/Athlt Awd 86; NYSPHSAA Chmpnshp Cls D Trnmnt All-Str 86; Outstndng Sr Athlt; Albany ST; Bus.

WALKER, DOUG; Copiague SR HS; Copiague, NY; (Y); Hon Roll; Prfct Atten Awd; Bus.

WALKER, GINEVRA; La Guardia H S Of Music & The Arts; New York, NY; (S); Chorus; School Musical; Nwsp Ed-Chief; JV Lcrss; Hon Roll; Drama Clb; French Clb; Library Aide; Mathletes; Teachers Aide; 1st Pl AATF Natl Frnch Cont 84; Excell Engl 84; Harvard; Mlclr Bio.

WALKER, GREGORY W; Lewiston-Porter SR HS; Lewiston, NY; (Y); 66/236; Church Yth Grp; Computer Clb; German Clb; ST Regents Scholar 85-86; SUNY Buffalo; Engrng.

WALKER, INA B; Lafayette HS; Brooklyn, NY; (Y); Cmnty Wkr; Yrbk Stf; Lit Mag; JV Crs Cntry; JV Trk; Btty Crckr Awd; Hon Roll; Hlth Crs Bureau Crtfct Hlth Asst 86; Crtfct Awd Yth Cmmnctn 86; NY Tech Coll; Dntl Hygnst.

WALKER, JENNIFER; Westmoreland HS; Rome, NY; (Y); 4-H; Model UN; Sec Pres Ski Clb; Ski Clb; Nwsp Phtg; Yrbk Phtg; 4-H Awd; High Hon Roll; NHS; Lbrl Arts.

WALKER, JOAN; Smithtown West HS; Smithtown, NY; (Y); Cmnty Wkr; Dance Clb; Drama Clb; Hosp Aide; Thesps; Chorus; School Play; Variety Show; Yrbk Stf; High Hon Roll; Vlntrg Hnr Awd 84; St Johns U; Pre Law.

WALKER, KAREN; Clarkstown South HS; West Nyack, NY; (Y); Church Yth Grp; Math Tm; Nwsp Stf; Var Bsktbl; Var Crs Cntry; Var Trk; Most Vlbl Fres And Soph Athlt; Jrnl News Carrier Of Yr; MVP Bsktbl Trnmnt.

WALKER, KIM; Acad Mt St Ursula HS; Bronx, NY; (Y); Computer Clb; Dance Clb; Acctg.

WALKER, LAURA; Grace Dodge HS; Bronx, NY; (Y); Grace Dodge; Shrthnd.

WALKER, LEA; E J Wilson HS; Spencerport, NY; (Y); Church Yth Grp; French Clb; JA; Varsity Clb; Swing Chorus; JV Var Tennis; Var Trk; Cmnty Wkr; Drama Clb; Exploring; Vrsty Trck Wstrn Div Champs; Supr Ratg Natl Fed Piano Fest; Natl Hnr For Piano Fed Fest.

WALKER, LOUISE M; Sachem HS; Lake Ronkonkoma, NY; (Y); 154/1385; French Clb; Chorus; Rgnts Schlrshp 86; Schltc Aptd Schlrshp 86; Dowling Coll; CPA.

WALKER, MELISSA; Tioga Central HS; Barton, NY; (S); 13/96; Church Yth Grp; Debate Tm; Latin Clb; Library Aide; High Hon Roll; Hon Roll; NHS; Ltn Slvr Mdl Awd 83; Comp Sci.

WALKER, MICHELLE; Grace H Dodge HS; Bronx, NY; (Y); Model UN; Nwsp Ed-Chief; Nwsp Rptr; Nwsp Sprt Ed; Hon Roll; Mrtn Lthr King Essy Cnst 86; Bkkpng 86; C Nstnl Gvrnmt 86; Jrnlsm.

WALKER, MONIQUE; La Guardia Music & Art Schl; Brooklyn, NY; (Y); Church Yth Grp; Girl Scts; Office Aide; PAVAS; Teachers Aide; Chorus; Church Choir; Madrigals; School Musical; Rep Frsh Cls; Music.

WALKER, NANCY L; Smithtown HS East; Smithtown, NY; (Y); Cmnty Wkr; Hosp Aide; Varsity Clb; Band; Yrbk Stf; Frsh Cls; Soph Cls; Jr Cls; Sr Cls; Stu Cncl; Cls Athlt 86; Vllybl Tm Capt All Leag & All Conf 86; Natl Hnr Soc 85-86; Grls Ldrs Clb VP 86; Lehigh; Bus Admin.

WALKER, RHONDA; Canisteo Central HS; Canisteo, NY; (Y); 2/88; SADD; Band; Orch; School Musical; Yrbk Stf; Stu Cncl; Socr; High Hon Roll; Hon Roll; NHS; Govt Intrn 86; Frgn Exchng Stu 86; Acdmc All-Strs 85-86; Pre-Law.

WALKER, ROBERT; Newburgh Free Acad; Newburgh, NY; (Y); Key Clb; Band; Concert Band; Jazz Band; Mrchg Band; JV Var Ftbl; JV Wrstlng; High Hon Roll; Hon Roll; Chorus; Pol Sci.

WALKER, WANDA; Thomas J Corcoran HS; Syracuse, NY; (Y); Church Yth Grp; GAA; Intnl Clb; JA; Church Choir; School Play; Var Mgr Bsktbl; AAU-JR Olympics Bsktbl 86-87; Empire St Baptist Union & Sndy Sch Cngrs Of Chrstn Edu 81-84; Brockport U; Comp Sci.

WALKIN, GYNENE; Tottenville HS; Staten Island, NY; (S); 1/1000; Cmnty Wkr; Office Aide; Teachers Aide; High Hon Roll; Jr NHS; Ntl Merit Ltr; Awd Frm Spnsh-Prtgse Tchrs Assoc 86; Won Essy Cntst 85; Physcl Thrpy.

WALKLETT, ROBERT A; East Syracuse-Minoa HS; East Syracuse, NY; (Y); Church Yth Grp; JA; Latin Clb; SADD; Band; Concert Band; Drm & Bgl; Mrchg Band; Pep Band; Variety Show; Regents Scholar; Geneseo U; Music.

WALL, JEFFREY; E Syracuse-Mina HS; E Syracuse, NY; (S); VP DECA; VP JA; Pres Science Clb; SADD; Var Tennis; Var Wrstlng; Jr NHS; MVP Tennis 85-86; 2nd ST Deca Comptn 85-86; Colgate U; Bus Adm.

WALLACE, ANDREW; West Irondequoit HS; Rochester, NY; (Y); 23/380; Latin Clb; Band; Jazz Band; Mrchg Band; Orch; Lit Mag; Hon Roll; NHS; Pres Acad Fitnss Awd; Tchrs Assoc Schlrshp 86; Roberts Weleyan Coll; Music.

WALLACE, BONNIE M; Valley Central HS; Montgomery, NY; (Y); Church Yth Grp; Cmnty Wkr; Girl Scts; Color Guard; Concert Band; Mrchg Band; Rep Soph Cls; Hon Roll; Prfct Atten Awd; Slvr Awd Grl Sctng 85; Mtl NY ST Stu Music Assoc 86; Pres Of Adptd Grndprnt Pgm 85-86; Acctng.

WALLACE, CRAIG; All Hallows Inst; Bronx, NY; (Y); High Hon Roll; Hon Roll; Phys Ftnss Achvt Awd 83; Bus.

WALLACE, DEBORAH; Uniondale HS; Uniondale, NY; (Y); FBLA; Key Clb; Chorus; Yrbk Stf; High Hon Roll; Hon Roll; Libry Awd 83-84; St Johns; Psych.

WALLACE, DOUGLAS; Msgr Farrell HS; Staten Island, NY; (Y); 70/315; Boy Scts; Church Yth Grp; Pres Frsh Cls; Bsktbl; Fld Hcky; Ftbl; High Hon Roll; Engrng.

WALLACE, EDDIE W; Lyons Central HS; Lyons, NY; (Y); Am Leg Boys St; Drama Clb; 4-H; Spanish Clb; Chorus; School Musical; Bsbl; Bsktbl; Ftbl; Wrstlng; Mansfield ST PA; Fiber Optics.

WALLACE, JAMES; Bainbridge-Guilford C S HS; Bainbridge, NY; (Y); Band; Orch; Nwsp Sprt Ed; Yrbk Sprt Ed; Var Badmtn; Var Bsbl; Var Bsktbl; Var Ftbl; French Clb; Chorus; Hghst Bttg Avg Bsbll 84&85; Orchstra Outstndg Prfrmnc 86; NY ST Sctn IV Mns Sngls Bdmtn 85&86.

WALLACE, JENNIFER; Rome Catholic HS; Lee Center, NY; (Y); 6/79; 4-H; Service Clb; SADD; Yrbk Stf; High Hon Roll; Hon Roll; NHS; NEDT Awd; Acad All Am Awd SF Schlrshp 85-86; Hm Ec Awd 85-86; Springfield Coll; Physcl Thrpy.

WALLACE, JENNIFER P; Ward Melville HS; Setauket, NY; (Y); 90/720; French Clb; Ski Clb; Jazz Band; Orch; Nwsp Stf; High Hon Roll; Jr NHS; NHS; Ntl Merit Ltr; Art Clb; Regents Schlrshp; Coll Of The Holy Cross.

WALLACE, JOHN; Monsignor Farrell HS; Staten Island, NY; (Y); Aud/Vis; Camera Clb; Chess Clb; Yrbk Phtg; Yrbk Stf; Im Bowling; Im Fld Hcky; Im Ftbl; High Hon Roll; Hon Roll; Pre-Law.

WALLACE, JOHN M; Eldred Central Schl; Eldred, NY; (Y); 1/30; Ski Clb; Varsity Clb; Yrbk Stf; VP Frsh Cls; VP Soph Cls; Crs Cntry; Trk; NHS; Val; NYS Regnts Schlrshp 86; SUNY At Stonybrook; Mech Engr.

WALLACE, LORIE; Camden Central HS; N Bay, NY; (Y); Cmnty Wkr; High Hon Roll; Hon Roll; Cackelberry Castle Schlrshp 86; Madison Oneida Cnty Nrsng Duty Awd 86; Morrisville Coll; RN.

WALLACE, RHONDA JEAN; Geneseo Central HS; Geneseo, NY; (Y); Chess Clb; Pres Church Yth Grp; GAA; PAVAS; Chrmn SADD; Yrbk Phtg; Stat Socr; JV Sftbl; Swmmng; Var Vllybl; VP & Pres Yrkrs 83-85; Sgn Lang Tchr Jr Sndy Schl Stu 84-86; Johnson & Wales Coll; Fshn Merc.

WALLACE, ROBERT; Dewitt Clinton HS; Bronx, NY; (Y); 9/257; Debate Tm; Scholastic Bowl; Trk; Hon Roll; Prfct Atten Awd; Regent Schlrshp Wnnr 86; Edtr Hist Journl 86; Binghampton U; Comp Sci.

WALLACE, STACEY; Earl L Vandermeulen HS; Mt Sinai, NY; (Y); Computer Clb; Debate Tm; GAA; Ski Clb; Sec Sr Cls; Cheerleading; Vllybl; Art Clb; Camp Fr Inc; Dance Clb; Most Athltc Girl Trophy 83; Intl Busnss.

WALLACE, STACEY A; St Joseph Hill Acad; Staten Island, NY; (Y); 5/107; FTA; Library Aide; Math Tm; Service Clb; Teachers Aide; Stage Crew; Hon Roll; NHS; Ntl Merit SF; Spanish NHS; Natl Lang Arts Olympd 84.

WALLACH, PAM H; Scarsdale HS; Scarsdale, NY; (Y); Cmnty Wkr; Band; Var Bsktbl; Var Sftbl; JV Co-Capt Tennis; JV Trk; Hon Roll; Ntl Merit Ltr; Regents Schlrshp 86; Cert Apprctn Vol Svc 86; U MI.

WALLACH, PATRICK; East Meadow HS; East Meadow, NY; (S); 9/340; Computer Clb; FBLA; Math Clb; Math Tm; Nwsp Stf; Fld Hcky; High Hon Roll; Hon Roll; NHS; 1st Pl Cnty Bus Comp Exam 86; 2nd Pl Cnty Accntng Exam 86; 1st Pl HS AHSME 100 Pts 86; Hofstra U; Banking.

WALLER, ELIZABETH; St John The Baptist HS; Ronkonkoma, NY; (Y); 25/526; Boy Scts; Church Yth Grp; Cmnty Wkr; Exploring; Girl Scts; Band; High Hon Roll; Hon Roll; Law.

WALLETT, JODY; Northeastern Clinton Central HS; Champlain, NY; (Y); Cmnty Wkr; French Clb; Sec Pres Key Clb; Model UN; Yrbk Ed-Chief; Yrbk Stf; Hon Roll; Prfct Atten Awd; Best Sci Stu Awd 84; Med.

WALLEY, DAVID; O Neill HS; Walton, NY; (Y); Band; Concert Band; Orch; School Musical; Bowling; Var JV Ftbl; Trk; Wt Lftg; High Hon Roll; Hon Roll.

WALLINGFORD, VICTORIA; Geneseo Central HS; Geneseo, NY; (Y); 12/87; Yrbk Phtg; Sec Frsh Cls; VP Soph Cls; JV Var Socr; Var Capt Swmmng; Var Capt Trk; High Hon Roll; Jr NHS; NHS; Prfct Atten Awd; Syracuse U; Arch.

WALLQUIST, KENNETH M; Rome Free Acad; Rome, NY; (Y); Computer Clb; French Clb; Math Clb; ROTC; Science Clb; Im Tennis; Im Vllybl; NHS; Ntl Merit Ltr; Prfct Atten Awd; MI ST U; Elec Engrng.

WALLSHEIN, NORI E; Ward Melville HS; Selden, NY; (Y); 47/725; Intnl Clb; Office Aide; Spanish Clb; High Hon Roll; Jr NHS; Regents Schlrshp 86; Kickline 84-86; Spnsh Tchr; Tutor 85-86; SUNY-STONY Brook; Tchr.

WALPOLE, GREGORY L; Dannemora HS; Dannemora, NY; (Y); 1/22; French Clb; Trs Frsh Cls; Trs Soph Cls; VP Jr Cls; Pres Stu Cncl; Var Bsbl; Var Bsktbl; Var Socr; High Hon Roll; VP NHS; Nvl ROTC, NYS Regents Schlrshps 86; Appointed US Coast Guard Acad 86; Rochester Inst Tech; Engrng.

WALPOLE, KATIE; Donnemora Union Free HS; Dannemora, NY; (Y); 6/25; French Clb; Chorus; Nwsp Rptr; Nwsp Stf; Yrbk Stf; Rep Stu Cncl; JV Var Cheerleading; Socr; Sftbl; High Hon Roll; Boston U; Sci.

WALPOLE, MARYBETH; Lehman HS; Bronx, NY; (Y); 112/565; Church Yth Grp; Variety Show; Var Cheerleading; Hon Roll; Prfct Atten Awd; Psych Awd Excllnc 85-86; Pace U; Bus Mang.

WALROD, LAURA; Southwestern HS; Lakewood, NY; (Y); 52/170; 4-H; French Clb; Girl Scts; Letterman Clb; Ski Clb; Band; Chorus; School Play; Crs Cntry; Trk; Chautauqua Cnty Conf 3 Miles Tm 2nd Pl 84-85; Chautauqua Cnty Girls Trck Mt Div 1 83-84; SUNY Geneseo; Psych.

WALSH, BRENDEN; Eastchester HS; Eastchester, NY; (Y); Cmnty Wkr; Band; Jazz Band; Var Capt Bsbl; Var Capt Bsktbl; Var Capt Ftbl; Hon Roll; Sec NHS; All Section,League Bsbl 85-86; Hon Mentn All Leag Bsktbl,Ftbl 85-86; Providence Coll; Lib Arts.

WALSH, CHRIS; East Meadow HS; E Meadow, NY; (Y); 132/340; JV Var Bsbl; AIR Force.

WALSH, CHRISTINE E; St Francis Prep; Whitestone, NY; (S); 125/694; Cmnty Wkr; Hosp Aide; Office Aide; Service Clb; SADD; Teachers Aide; Yrbk Phtg; Rep Sr Cls; Rep Stu Cncl; Im Bowling; Pediatrcn.

WALSH, COLLEEN; West Seneca East SR HS; W Seneca, NY; (Y); DECA; Nwsp Stf; Off Jr Cls; Trs Sr Cls; Stu Cncl; Var Tennis; High Hon Roll; JC Awd; Jr NHS; Trs NHS; Niagara U; Bus Mgmt.

WALSH, DEBORAH; Holy Trinity Diocesan HS; Seaford, NY; (S); 28/408; Cmnty Wkr; Hosp Aide; Office Aide; Ski Clb; SADD; Church Choir; Yrbk Stf; Hon Roll; NEDT Awd; Math Cert Supr Achvt 84; Bus.

WALSH, JOHN; Churchville Chili HS; North Chili, NY; (Y); Church Yth Grp; Band; JV Var Bsbl; JV Var Bsktbl; JV Ftbl; Var Vllybl; High Hon Roll; NHS; NY ST Bsktbl Cochs Assoc Acad Tm 85-86; Vrsty Bsebl Cochs Awd Attde 85-86; Roberts Weslyan Coll; Phlsphy.

WALSH, JOHN; Iona Preparatory Schl; Rye, NY; (Y); Boy Scts; Computer Clb; Yrbk Phtg; Bowling; Crs Cntry; Lcrss; Socr; Wt Lftg; Hon Roll; Clarkson U; Mchncl Engr.

WALSH, JULIE; St Marys HS; W Seneca, NY; (Y); Cmnty Wkr; GAA; Pep Clb; Ski Clb; Varsity Clb; Trs Frsh Cls; VP Soph Cls; JV Cheerleading; Var Sftbl; Physcl Thrpst.

WALSH, KATHRYN GAETANA; Freeport HS; Freeport, NY; (Y); 37/450; Church Yth Grp; Key Clb; Ski Clb; Concert Band; Variety Show; Var Capt Gym; JV L Lcrss; Trk; Hon Roll; Rep Soph Cls; LIABEC Awd 85; NYSMA Awd 83-85; Pace U; CPA.

WALSH, KELLY; Babylon JR SR HS; Oak Bch, NY; (Y); Varsity Clb; Chorus; Rep Frsh Cls; Rep Soph Cls; Off Sr Cls; JV Var Bsktbl; JV Crs Cntry; JV Var Tennis; JV Trk; JV Var Vllybl; Schltc Achvt Awd Art; Art.

WALSH, KELLY; E J Wilson HS; Spencerport, NY; (Y); French Clb; Im Sftbl; Hon Roll; Bus Awd 83-84; Soc Stu Awd 83-84; Bus.

WALSH, KELLY F; Averill Park HS; Sand Lake, NY; (Y); 12/210; 4-H; Ski Clb; School Musical; Stage Crew; Nwsp Stf; Im Gym; JV Tennis; 4-H Awd; NHS; Drama Clb; Regents Schlrshp 85-86; ST U; Albany.

WALSH, KERRY E; Bayside HS; Whitestone, NY; (Y); 22/658; Math Tm; Ed Yrbk Stf; Lit Mag; Hon Roll; Kiwanis Awd; NHS; NY Rgnts Schlrsp 86; Hunter Coll; Nrs.

WALSH, KEVIN P; Bronx High School Of Science; Bronx, NY; (Y); 5/900; Cmnty Wkr; Im Bsktbl; Coach Actv; Im Sftbl; Regnts Schlrshp 86; Fordham U.

WALSH, KRISTEN; Fontbonne Hall Acad; Staten Island, NY; (Y); 4/130; French Clb; Library Aide; Teachers Aide; Im Vllybl; High Hon Roll; NHS; NEDT Awd; Chess Clb; Acdmc Schlrshp 82-84; Hon Sci, Math, Eng, Hstry, Lang 82-86; Summa Cum Lude Gld Mdl Ntl Ltn Exm 85; Fordham U; Cmnctns.

WALSH, MICHAEL J; Whitesboro SR HS; Whitesboro, NY; (Y); 1/306; Am Leg Boys St; Church Yth Grp; Model UN; Yrbk Stf; JV Var Bsktbl; JV Var Ftbl; Var L Tennis; Bausch & Lomb Sci Awd; Pres NHS; Ntl Merit Ltr; RPI Math & Sci Awd 86; Aerospc Engrng.

WALSH, MICHELE; Onondago Central HS; Syracuse, NY; (Y); Cmnty Wkr; Spanish Clb; Teachers Aide; Score Keeper; Bus.

WALSH, MONICA; Sacred Heart Acad; Floral Park, NY; (S); 18/204; Pep Clb; SADD; Chorus; Hon Roll; NHS; Spanish II Awd Most Cnstnt Stu 84; Engl Lit Wrtng Cntst 83; Med.

WALSH, ROBERT; New Rochelle HS; New Rochelle, NY; (Y); Nwsp Stf; JV Bsktbl; JV Lcrss; JV Socr; Swmmng; NHS; Engrng.

WALSH, SARAH; Mt St Mary Acad; Tonawanda, NY; (Y); Chorus; Church Choir; Stage Crew; Yrbk Stf; Hon Roll; 1st Pl Awds Cllgrphy & Pntng Mt St Marys Art Shw 85; 3rd Pl Awds Scl Stmnt & Pn Ink Drwng 86; Fshn Inst Tech; Art Fshn Dsgn.

WALSH, SHANNON; Union-Endicott HS; Endicott, NY; (Y); Var Capt Bowling; Coach Actv; Var Capt Sftbl; DAR Awd; High Hon Roll; NHS; Prfct Atten Awd.

WALSH, SHARON; Frontier Central HS; Blasdell, NY; (Y); Cmnty Wkr; French Clb; FBLA; School Play; Var Mgr(s); JV Socr; Hon Roll; NHS; Bus Mgmt.

WALSH, THOMAS; Archbishop Stepinac HS; Bronx, NY; (Y); 34/174; Ski Clb; Nwsp Rptr; Var JV Crs Cntry; JV Ftbl; Var JV Trk; NHS; Schlrshp Full Tuition 83; Engrng.

WALSH, THOMAS; Sandy Creek Central HS; Sandy Creek, NY; (S); Computer Clb; French Clb; Varsity Clb; Yrbk Stf; Bsktbl; Wt Lftg; Hon Roll; NHS; Natl Hnr Scty 86; Physcl Thrpst.

WALSH, TINA; Monticello HS; Wurtsboro, NY; (S); 1/150; VP Debate Tm; NFL; Band; School Musical; Nwsp Bus Mgr; Nwsp Rptr; High Hon Roll; Jr NHS; Ntl Merit Ltr; Law.

WALTER, ANNE; Albion HS; Albion, NY; (S); 6/179; Latin Clb; Teachers Aide; Yrbk Stf; Sec Sr Cls; Stat Bsktbl; Var Socr; Hon Roll; NHS; Sci.

WALTER, BRUCE J; Walt Whitman HS; Huntington, NY; (Y); 1/450; Computer Clb; German Clb; Mathletes; High Hon Roll; Jr NHS; Suffolk Cnty Math Tchrs Assoc Outstndng Jr Awd 86; Simons Fllwshp At Stony Brook U 86; Physcs.

WALTER, CAROLYN; St Marys HS; Lancaster, NY; (Y); Aud/Vis; Varsity Clb; School Musical; School Play; Variety Show; VP Sr Cls; Var Capt Bsktbl; Var Tennis; Var Capt Vllybl; NHS; MVP Var Tnns 86; Most Imprvd Plyr Var Vlybl 85; Lib Arts.

WALTER, CINDY; Albion HS; Albion, NY; (S); 4/169; Color Guard; Sec Frsh Cls; Rep Sr Cls; Rep Sec Stu Cncl; Stat Bsbl; Var JV Cheerleading; JV Socr; Sec Jr NHS; Sec NHS; Roberts Wesleyan Coll; Soc Wrk.

WALTER, KEVIN A; Beekmantown Central Schl; Plattsburgh, NY; (Y); 1/150; Math Tm; Model UN; Quiz Bowl; Trs Varsity Clb; Pres Jr Cls; Crs Cntry; Trk; High Hon Roll; Pres NHS; Ntl Merit SF; Cntry III Ldrshp Schlr 86; Brown U; Med.

WALTER, MARC R; Hackley HS; Scarsdale, NY; (Y); 40/89; Model UN; Acpl Chr; Band; Orch; School Musical; Stu Cncl; L Bsbl; L Bsktbl; L Socr; Hon Roll; NY ST Rgnts Schlrp Awd 86; Colgate U.

WALTER, MARK E; E L Vandermeulen HS; Mt Sinai, NY; (Y); 1/300; Mathletes; Nwsp Ed-Chief; Nwsp Phtg; Nwsp Rptr; Nwsp Stf; Lit Mag; JV Var Socr; Var VP Tennis; High Hon Roll; NHS; Brown U; Engrng.

WALTER, MICHAEL; Fort Plain Central HS; Fort Plain, NY; (S); 6/70; Boy Scts; Varsity Clb; Yrbk Phtg; Var L Crs Cntry; Hon Roll; NHS; Yr End Bio Awd 85; Naval Acad.

WALTER, SETH L; Edward R Murrow HS; Brooklyn, NY; (Y); 132/669; Boy Scts; Chess Clb; VP JA; OEA; VP Temple Yth Grp; Rep Sr Cls; Rep Stu Cncl; Ntl Merit SF; Eagle Scout 84; Genetic Engrng.

WALTER JR, WILLIAM; Archbishop Molloy HS; Jackson Heights, NY; (Y); 219/401; Computer Clb; German Clb; Math Clb; Math Tm; Im Bsktbl; Var Crs Cntry; Var Trk; NHS; Ntl Merit Ltr; Coll Of Insurance; Actuarial.

WALTERS, BRENDA; Baldwin SR HS; Baldwin, NY; (Y); Brown U; Psych.

WALTERS JR, CHARLES A; Rome Catholic HS; Rome, NY; (Y); 6/67; Nwsp Stf; VP Frsh Cls; Pres Soph Cls; Pres Jr Cls; Pres Sr Cls; L Var Ftbl; Bausch & Lomb Sci Awd; High Hon Roll; NHS; Dyett Fdn Schlrshp 86; Anna & Meyer Gardner Schlrshp 86; Hamilton Coll Ftbll Cmp MVP 85; Siena Coll; Bio.

WALTERS, DAVID N; Marcus Whitman HS; Penn Yan, NY; (Y); 36/120; Model UN; Quiz Bowl; Varsity Clb; Church Choir; Var L Bsbl; Var L Ftbl; Hon Roll; Regents Scshlrshp 86; SUNY Brockport; Cmmnctns.

WALTERS, ERIC A; Newfane Central HS; Burt, NY; (Y); Boy Scts; Exploring; Spanish Clb; NYS Rgnts Schlrshp 86; Bryant & Stratton; Accnt.

WALTERS, GEORGE; Copiague HS; Copiague, NY; (Y); Am Leg Boys St; Cmnty Wkr; Mathletes; Math Tm; SADD; Var Bsbl; Var Ftbl; Hon Roll; NHS.

WALTERS, HEATHER; Cazenoria Central HS; Cazenovia, NY; (Y); Church Yth Grp; Church Choir; Var Stat Sftbl; Hon Roll; Hghst Achvmnt Englsh 85-86; Bus.

WALTERS, JOHN S; Pittsford Mendon HS; Pittsford, NY; (Y); Chess Clb; Math Clb; Model UN; Ski Clb; Chorus; Var Crs Cntry; Var JV Trk; Hon Roll; NHS; Natl Hnr Soc 85-86; German Bowl Awd 84-85; Math Clb Awd 83-86; SUNY Buffalo; Engrng.

WALTERS, JON; Curtis HS; New York, NY; (Y); Var Bsbl; High Hon Roll; NHS.

WALTERS, LISA; Moravia Central HS; Moravia, NY; (Y); Pep Clb; Chorus; Yrbk Stf; High Hon Roll; Hon Roll; Prfct Atten Awd.

WALTERS, MARIA; Patchogue Medford HS; Patchogue, NY; (Y); 8/750; Drama Clb; Math Tm; Chorus; School Musical; Variety Show; Hst Soph Cls; Stu Cncl; Tennis; Var Trk; NHS; Grg Wshngtn U Awd Mth & Sci 85; PTA Awd 83; Frnch Awd 85; Sci.

WALTERS, MICHAEL SCOTT; Watkins Glen Central HS; Watkins Glen, NY; (S); 7/130; Am Leg Boys St; Church Yth Grp; Band; Jazz Band; Yrbk Stf; French Hon Soc; High Hon Roll; Hon Roll; NHS; Acadmc All Amer 84-85; Colgate U; Physics.

WALTHER, EVELYN A; Dominican Commercial HS; Glendale, NY; (Y); 110/297; Computer Clb; Drama Clb; GAA; Girl Scts; Yrbk Phtg; Yrbk Rptr; Yrbk Stf; VP Trs Swmmng; Hon Roll; Prfct Atten Awd; St Cthrn Sienna Hon Roll 83-86; Prncpls Lst 83-86; NY City Tech Coll; Htl Mgt.

WALTHER, KELLY; Gloversville HS; Gloversvl, NY; (Y); Pep Clb; SADD; Teachers Aide; Cheerleading; Fld Hcky; Hon Roll; Crmnl Jstc.

WALTON, CURTIS A; St Francis Prep; Cambria Hts, NY; (Y); 154/653; Art Clb; Church Yth Grp; Hon Roll; Ltr Cmndtn Natl Merit Schlrshp 84; Math.

WALTS, TABETHA; Indian River Central HS; Theresa, NY; (Y); 18/130; Hst Key Clb; Latin Clb; Office Aide; Chorus; School Musical; Var Tennis; Var Trk; Hon Roll; NEDT Awd; Thrsa Rtry Clb Schlrshp 86; Pres Acad Ftns Awd 86; Excllnt Schlrshp 85-86; Jfrsn Comm Coll; Med Tech.

WALTZ, JOSEPH M; Hoosick Falls Central HS; Hoosick Falls, NY; (Y); 1/105; Band; Stu Cncl; L Bsbl; Stat Bsktbl; Stat Ftbl; DAR Awd; High Hon Roll; Hon Roll; NHS; Drama Clb; Kiwns & Prncpls Schlrshp Awds 83, 84; Albany Coll Of Phrmcy; Phrmcy.

WALTZER, LESLIE; John Adams HS; Howard Beach, NY; (Y); 2/494; Debate Tm; Math Tm; Nwsp Stf; Yrbk Stf; Sec Sr Cls; Sftbl; Trk; High Hon Roll; NHS; Val; Athltc Leag Awds, Rcgntn Schlrshp 86; NYC Assn Asst Prncpls Sprvsn-Engl 86; Scty Mayflwr Dscndnts Awd; Cornell U; Cnsmr Ecnmcs.

WALTZER, MICHELE; John Adams HS; Howard Beach, NY; (Y); 3/594; Debate Tm; Math Tm; Nwsp Ed-Chief; Yrbk Stf; Var Sftbl; Off NHS; Sal; Mitchell Pruches Mem Awd 86; Asst Principals Soc Studies Awd 86; Cornell U; Business Admin.

WALTZER, TODD; Fonda-Fultonville Central Schl; Fultonville, NY; (Y); 7/110; High Hon Roll; Hon Roll; NHS; Mchncl Drawing Awd 85; Clarkson U; Cvl Engrng.

WALZ, JEANETTE; Villa Maria Acad; Kenmore, NY; (S); 8/105; Computer Clb; Hosp Aide; Pep Clb; Spanish Clb; School Play; Yrbk Stf; Rep Frsh Cls; Rep Jr Cls; Off Stu Cncl; Bowling; USNMLA 85; Bnk Amer Awd 82; Suny Buffalo; Pre Med.

WAMBACH, BETH; Our Lady Of Mercy HS; Pittsford, NY; (Y); English Clb; Pres Varsity Clb; Pres Soph Cls; Rep Stu Cncl; Capt Bsktbl; Var Socr; Capt Sftbl; High Hon Roll; Dartmouth Book Clb Awd 86; MVP Private Parochial Lg Bsktbl 86; Schlr Ath Awd 86; Sci.

WANDA, DIAZ; Eastern District HS; Brooklyn, NY; (Y); Art Clb; CAP; Dance Clb; English Clb; Red Cross Aide; Chorus; Capt Cheerleading; Swmmng; Stat Vllybl; Schlstc Achvt In Sci & Mth 86; Hunter Coll; Psych.

WANDELL, JILL; Keveny Memorial Acad; Cohoes, NY; (Y); 23/40; Q&S; Color Guard; Yrbk Stf; Score Keeper; Vllybl; High Hon Roll; Hon Roll; Jr NHS; NHS; Offc Proc Achvt Awd 86; Hudson Valley CC; Sec Sci.

WANDERSEE, ROBIN; Mexico HS; Mexico, NY; (Y); Art Clb; Trs Spanish Clb; Capt Color Guard; Mrchg Band; Cheerleading; High Hon Roll; Hon Roll; Pres NHS; Spanish NHS; Acdmc Engl Awd; Mst Vlbl Color Gurd Stu 85; Bnnr Capt Awd 85; Arch.

WANDERSLEBEN JR, WERNER G; York Central Schl; Retsof, NY; (Y); Am Leg Boys St; Math Tm; VP Frsh Cls; Rep Soph Cls; JV Var Ftbl; Im Vllybl; Im Wt Lftg; High Hon Roll; Engrng.

WANECSKI, MARY BETH; Vestal SR HS; Vestal, NY; (Y); Var Socr; High Hon Roll; Hon Roll; Social Wrk.

WANG, BOBBY; Ellenville Central HS; Phillipsport, NY; (Y); 5/110; Pres Trs Cmnty Wkr; Computer Clb; Band; Yrbk Stf; Var L Socr; Var L Tennis; High Hon Roll; NHS; NY ST Regents Scholar 86; ST U NY; Bio Sci.

WANG, GRACE E; Bayside HS; Flushing, NY; (Y); 4/658; Math Tm; Teachers Aide; Madrigals; Yrbk Stf; Lit Mag; Gov Hon Prg Awd; Hon Roll; NHS; Qns Coll Pres Awd 85; Untd Fed Tchrs Awd Schlrshp 86; U Of PA; Bus Mgmt.

WANG, MARCY; Farmingdale HS; Farmingdale, NY; (Y); Drama Clb; Thesps; Chorus; School Play; Stage Crew; Nwsp Rptr; Yrbk Stf; The Intl Thespian Socy 85-86; Best Actress & Supporting Actress Awds 85-86; Theatre Arts.

WANG, RICHARD E; John L Miller Great Neck North HS; Great Neck, NY; (Y); 11/236; Art Clb; Ed Lit Mag; Var Trk; NCTE Awd.

WANGELIN, DEANNA; Holland Central HS; Holland, NY; (Y); Boys Clb Am; Speech Tm; Varsity Clb; Nwsp Stf; Yrbk Stf; Sec Frsh Cls; Sec Soph Cls; Sec Jr Cls; Var Capt Cheerleading; Var Capt Socr; Genesee CC; Trvl.

WANGELIN, SANDY; Holland Central HS; Holland, NY; (Y); 13/114; AFS; Church Yth Grp; Pres Band; Chorus; Pres Concert Band; Pres Mrchg Band; Hon Roll; Jr NHS.

WANGENSTEIN, GEORGE; North Rockland HS; West Haverstraw, NY; (Y); JV Var Ftbl; JV Lcrss; Comm.

WANGER, MINTA I; Midwood HS; Brooklyn, NY; (Y); 131/559; School Musical; School Play; Yrbk Stf; Lit Mag; Var Cheerleading; Alxndr Medal 86; Rgnts Schlrshp 86; Illstrtr.

WANGERIN, ANN; Albion HS; Albion, NY; (Y); Church Yth Grp; Cmnty Wkr; Library Aide; Spanish Clb; Teachers Aide; Var Bsktbl; Genesee CC; Trvl.

WANGLER, STEPHEN D; Canisius HS; Williamsville, NY; (Y); 45/169; Spanish Clb; Hon Roll; NHS; Ntl Merit Schol; Spanish NHS; Canisius Coll.

WAPPMAN, ROBERT; Frontier Central HS; Hamburg, NY; (Y); 141/444; French Clb; Political Wkr; Science Clb; VP Varsity Clb; JV Bsbl; JV Bsktbl; L Var Ftbl; L Var Trk; Cit Awd; Prfct Atten Awd; Natl Achvt Acad Ldrshp Awd 86; Intrnshp Cngrssmn Jack Kemp 86; Lake Shore Goalfllws Outstndg SR Awd; Cortland SUNY; Pol Sci.

WARBURTON, KIM; Uniondale HS; Hempstead, NY; (Y); Am Leg Aux Girls St; Ed FBLA; JA; VP Science Clb; Stu Cncl; Cheerleading; Score Keeper; High Hon Roll; Jr NHS; NHS; Spansh Awd 84; PTA Schlrshp Awd 84; Schl Svc Awd Mdlln Awd 75 Points 84; Bus Mgmt.

WARCHOL, LAURA; Saranac Lake HS; Paul Smith, NY; (Y); Yrbk Rptr; Yrbk Stf; Powder Puff Ftbl; Score Keeper; Trk; Hon Roll; Accptd Barbizon Modlg Sch 84; Grad Modlg Sch 85; Hnrbl Mntn Art Shw 85-86; N Country CC; Modl.

WARD, ANASTASIA; Ramstein American HS; APO New York, NY; (Y); Drama Clb; Radio Clb; Speech Tm; Chorus; School Musical; School Play; Variety Show; Church Yth Grp; Debate Tm; FBLA; Exc Awd For Drmtctng Solo 86; Mst Potentl In Ftr Awd/Drama Clb 85-86; Acgtress.

WARD, ANGELA MARIE; Academy Of Mount Saint Ursula; Bronx, NY; (Y); 57/123; Cmnty Wkr; Computer Clb; Drama Clb; SADD; School Musical; Yrbk Stf; Off Stu Cncl; Bowling; ULS Law Prgm 85; Cty Coll NY; Lawyer.

WARD, BARBARA A; Oneida SR HS; Oneida, NY; (Y); 29/200; Spanish Clb; Varsity Clb; Yrbk Phtg; Yrbk Stf; Var L Fld Hcky; Var L Trk; High Hon Roll; Hon Roll; Rgnts Schlrshp 86; Sullivan Cnty CC; Phtogrphy.

WARD, BRENDAN; Mount St Michael Acad; Yonkers, NY; (Y); 78/273.

WARD, BUFFI; H S Of Fashion Indstrs; Kew Gardens, NY; (Y); 24/327; Cmnty Wkr; Teachers Aide; Yrbk Stf; Hon Roll; Ntl Merit Ltr; Hnr Rll 83 & 86; Psych.

WARD, CARA; Bishop Maginn HS; Albany, NY; (Y); 40/84; Cmnty Wkr; Drama Clb; Hosp Aide; PAVAS; Red Cross Aide; School Musical; School Play; Nwsp Rptr; Yrbk Rptr; Hon Roll; Miss NY Natl Teen Pgnt 84-86; Plattsburgh; Mass Med.

WARD, CATHRINE; Sachem HS North; Holbrook, NY; (Y); 49/1558; French Clb; GAA; Chorus; Rep Jr Cls; Im Bsktbl; Var L Socr; Var Trk; Jr NHS; Off NHS; Hstry Prfssr.

WARD, COLEEN; Auburn HS; Auburn, NY; (Y); 177/370; Cmnty Wkr; Rep Jr Cls; JV Cheerleading; Niagra U; Mass Comm.

WARD, DANIELLE; Gloversville HS; Gloversville, NY; (Y); French Clb; SADD; Stat Bsktbl; Hon Roll; Physcl Thrpst.

WARD, DAVID; Trott Vocational HS; Niagara Falls, NY; (Y); Church Yth Grp; JV Bsbl; Var Bowling; Var Golf; Im Wrstlng; Hon Roll; Jr NHS; Crpntry.

WARD, DONALD S; Walter Panas HS; Peekskill, NY; (Y); Pres Church Yth Grp; Concert Band; Mrchg Band; JV Ftbl; JV Var Tennis; Hon Roll; Hampton U; Arch.

WARD, JENNIFER; Ossining HS; Ossining, NY; (Y); 34/260; Church Yth Grp; VP JA; Pres Chorus; Co-Capt Color Guard; Stu Cncl; Var Capt Fld Hcky; Trs NHS; Rotary Awd; SADD; School Musical; Natl Choral Awd; Al-Leag, Al-Sctn Fld Hcky; U Of DE; Athltc Trnng.

WARD, JILL; Brushton Moira Central HS; Moira, NY; (Y); Teachers Aide; School Play; Yrbk Stf; Jr Cls; Bsktbl; Bowling; Sftbl; Hon Roll; NHS; Pre-Law.

WARD, JOHN; Allegany Central Schl; Allegany, NY; (Y); JV Trk; High Hon Roll; Hon Roll; Pres Schlr; Rochester Inst Tech; Tech.

WARD, KARYN; Longwood HS; Middle Isle, NY; (Y); Drama Clb; Key Clb; SADD; Chorus; Yrbk Stf; Hon Roll; Jr NHS; Psych.

WARD, KEITH; Corcoran HS; Syracuse, NY; (Y); PAVAS; Y-Teens; Yrbk Sprt Ed; Var L Ftbl; Var Ice Hcky; Wt Lftg; Mst Outstndng Offnsv Plyr Ftbl 84; JR Olmpc Boxg Champ NY ST 84; U Of ME; Bio.

WARD, KEVIN; Saugerties Central Schls; Saugerties, NY; (Y); Ski Clb; Var Capt Bsbl; Var Capt Bsktbl; Var Golf; Hon Roll.

WARD, KRISTINE; Canastota HS; Canastota, NY; (S); 4/157; VP GAA; Bsktbl; Var Co-Capt Fld Hcky; Var Co-Capt Sftbl; High Hon Roll; Trs NHS; Ust Tm All Str Fld Hcky 85-86; Mst Outstndng Fld Hcky 84-85; PA ST U; Accntng.

WARD, LYNN; Lawrence HS; Cedarhurst, NY; (Y); French Clb; Spanish Clb; Lit Mag; Im Socr; Hon Roll; Regnts Schlrshp 86; SUNY.

WARD, LYNNE; Gloversville HS; Gloversvl, NY; (Y); SADD; JV Fld Hcky; High Hon Roll; Hon Roll; Prfct Atten Awd; Poet.

WARD, MARGARET; Southhampton HS; Southampton, NY; (Y); Church Yth Grp; GAA; Church Choir; Concert Band; Yrbk Stf; Cheerleading; High Hon Roll; Hon Roll; NHS; Brookhaven Minrty Pgm 83; Asstnt Church Clrk 86; Columbia Of NYC; Bus Adm.

WARD, MICHAEL; Connetquot HS; Ronkonkoma, NY; (Y); 43/694; Math Tm; Drama Clb; Band; Drm Mjr(t); Mrchg Band; School Musical; School Play; Yrbk Stf; Hst Soph Cls; JV Trk; Helen B Duffield Mem Schlrshp 86; Sons Italy St Schlrshp 86; Bst Commrcl Art Awd 86; Parsons Schl Design; Fash Dsgn.

WARD, PATRICK; Herkimer HS; Herkimer, NY; (Y); 19/122; Yrbk Stf; Im Ftbl; High Hon Roll; Hon Roll; Prfct Atten Awd.

WARD, SARAH; Corinth Central Schl; Corinth, NY; (S); 1/80; SADD; Band; Chorus; Pres Soph Cls; Var L Fld Hcky; French Hon Soc; High Hon Roll; Trs Jr NHS; NHS; Acad Achvt Awd; Engr.

WARD, SHARON; Ward Melville HS; Setauket, NY; (Y); 205/725; Church Yth Grp; French Clb; Ski Clb; Yrbk Stf; JV Var Vllybl; Rgnts Schlrshp 85-86; SUNY Stony Brook.

WARD, SUZANNE; Salamanca Central HS; Salamanca, NY; (Y); 1/170; VP Jr Cls; VP Sr Cls; Capt Cheerleading; Cit Awd; French Hon Soc; High Hon Roll; NHS; Art Clb; Ski Clb; Amer Lg Awd 84; Mth & Sci Awd 84-85; Rochester Inst Tech; Advrtsng.

WARD, SUZANNE M; R-H Roth HS; Honeoye Falls, NY; (Y); 28/250; Exploring; Radio Clb; Band; Chorus; Concert Band; Jazz Band; Orch; School Musical; Swmmng; Trk; NYS Regnts Schlrshp; Tenr Saxophnst SUNY Geneseo Wind Ensmbl; SUNY Potsdam; Music Ed.

WARD, TARA; St Marys Girls HS; New Hyde Park, NY; (Y); 15/160; Cmnty Wkr; Hosp Aide; Ski Clb; Spanish Clb; School Musical; School Play; Stage Crew; Stu Cncl; Im Gym; Im Pom Pon; Winthrop Hosp Volntr Awd 86; Phy Thrpst.

WARD, THERESA; Minisink Valley HS; Port Jervis, NY; (Y); 48/224; Church Yth Grp; Drama Clb; Library Aide; SADD; Chorus; High Hon Roll; Hon Roll; Ntl Merit Ltr; Pres Schlr; VFW Awd; SR Awd Choir; Mst Imprvd Sr Choir; Advrtsng.

WARD, TIMOTHY; La Salle Military Acad; Southampton, NY; (Y); ROTC; Drill Tm; Nwsp Stf; Ftbl; Sftbl; Silver Hnrs For Average 85 Pct; Dickinson Coll; Lawyer.

WARDROP, MATTHEW; Briarcliff HS; Briarcliff Manor, NY; (Y); Church Yth Grp; Yrbk Stf; Socr; Trk; Hon Roll; St George Assn NYCPD Schlrshp 86; Pres Acadmc Ftnss Awd 86; Widener U; Bus.

WARE JR, KEITH; Alden SR HS; Alden, NY; (Y); Aud/Vis; Church Yth Grp; VP Band; Concert Band; Jazz Band; Pep Band; School Musical; Stage Crew; Symp Band; Sci-Math.

WARE, OBA N; Nazareth Regional HS; Brooklyn, NY; (Y); Boy Scts; Church Yth Grp; Band; Concert Band; Bsktbl; L Crs Cntry; Score Keeper; L Trk; Hon Roll; Comp Pgmr.

WARENCHAK, CAROL; Lansingburgh HS; Troy, NY; (Y); Art Clb; Church Yth Grp; German Clb; Spanish Clb; Varsity Clb; Band; Concert Band; Jazz Band; Mrchg Band; Pep Band; Sienna; Dntl Tech.

WARGULA, JENNIFER C; Hamburg SR HS; Hamburg, NY; (Y); 1/390; Cmnty Wkr; Dance Clb; Chorus; Color Guard; Flag Corp; Mrchg Band; Yrbk Ed-Chief; High Hon Roll; NHS; Val; RPI Medalist For Highest Achvt In Math & Sci 85; Awds In Math, Spnsh, Sci 83-86; Alumni Schlrshp 86; U Of PA; Bio.

WARHOL, NANCY G; Mount Mercy Acad; Buffalo, NY; (Y); 74/163; Cmnty Wkr; Drama Clb; Science Clb; Service Clb; SADD; Chorus; Stage Crew; Yrbk Stf; Coach Actv; Hon Roll; Alfred ST Coll; Secrtrl Sci.

WARING, KEISHA; Fashion Indstrs; New York, NY; (Y); 68/324; Drama Clb; FHA; Girl Scts; Orch; Hon Roll; Prfct Atten Awd; Columbia U; Law.

WARMUTH, ERIC; Whitesboro SR HS; Marcy, NY; (Y); 25/354; Pres Science Clb; Varsity Clb; Var L Socr; L Trk; High Hon Roll; Hon Roll; NHS; NY ST Regnts Schlrshp 85-86; Engrng.

WARMUTH, JENNIFER E; Rome Catholic HS; Bedford, MA; (Y); 2/70; Church Yth Grp; Cmnty Wkr; Drama Clb; Library Aide; Political Wkr; Chrmn Red Cross Aide; School Musical; School Play; Stage Crew; Nwsp Phtg; ROTC Schlrshp, U MA; Engrng.

WARNE, JENNIFER; Wayne Central HS; Ontario, NY; (Y); Church Yth Grp; Intnl Clb; Teachers Aide; Band; Chorus; Bausch & Lomb Sci Awd; High Hon Roll; NHS; Excllnce Spanish & Earth Sci 84; European Hist & Engl Hnrs 85; Math II, Engl Hnrs, Chem 86.

WARNER, ANDREW J; Pelham Memorial HS; Pelham, NY; (Y); PAVAS; Band; Concert Band; Jazz Band; Mrchg Band; Pep Band; Mgr(s); Hon Roll; NHS.

WARNER, ANITA; Perry Central HS; Perry, NY; (Y); 30/100; Pres Trs AFS; Library Aide; Spanish Clb; Chorus; Yrbk Stf; Cit Awd; High Hon Roll; Hon Roll; Bus & Achvt Awds 86; Bus Admin.

WARNER, JENNIFER; Cato-Meridian HS; Cato, NY; (Y); 4-H; Band; Mrchg Band; JV Bsktbl; Var Fld Hcky; 4-H Awd; Hon Roll; NHS; Prfct Atten Awd; Church Yth Grp; Dairy Maid 84; Bus.

WARNER, JOAN; De Witt Clinton HS; Bronx, NY; (Y); Debate Tm; Hon Roll; St Johns U; Accntng.

WARNER, MARNIE; Susquehanna Valley HS; Binghamton, NY; (Y); Pep Clb; Nwsp Rptr; Pres Frsh Cls; VP Soph Cls; Rep Jr Cls; JV Var Bsktbl; Var Mgr(s); VP Trk; Hon Roll; Spanish NHS; Plcd 14th St Meet Track & Long Jmp 86; 5th Yr Awd Pres Physcl Ftnss Awd; Bus.

WARNER, MARY; Alexander Central HS; E Bethany, NY; (Y); Church Yth Grp; Math Tm; Sec Spanish Clb; Varsity Clb; Nwsp Bus Mgr; Var Crs Cntry; Var Trk; Lion Awd; NHS; Prfct Atten Awd; SUNY; Math Edu.

WARNER, SCOTT; Alexander Central HS; Alexander, NY; (Y); Trs Church Yth Grp; Varsity Clb; JV Bsktbl; Var Swmmng; Var Trk; Elec Engr.

WARNER, TIMOTHY J; Notre Dame HS; E Bethany, NY; (Y); Yrbk Stf; Var Wrstlng; Hon Roll; NHS; NY ST Regents Schlrshp & Diploma; Albany Coll Of Pharm; Pharm.

WARNER, VIRGINIA; Caledonia-Mumford Central HS; Caledonia, NY; (Y); Church Yth Grp; Drama Clb; Girl Scts; Library Aide; Pep Clb; Teachers Aide; Band; Chorus; Color Guard; Mrchg Band.

WARNER, WENDY; Riverhead HS; Calverton, NY; (Y); Church Yth Grp; French Clb; Band; Chorus; Rep Stu Cncl; Var L Crs Cntry; Var Gym; Var L Trk; Tchr.

WARNICA, JEFF; Burgard Vocational HS; Buffalo, NY; (Y).

WARNICK, MICHAEL; Kenmore West HS; Kenmore, NY; (Y); Political Wkr; Varsity Clb; Bsbl; Ftbl; Wrstlng; High Hon Roll; Hon Roll; NHS; Ntl Merit Ltr; Pres Schlr; NY ST Regents Schlrshp 85-86; Pres Natl Hnr Socty 85-86; GM Inst; Engrng.

WARNICK, SPENCER K; Comojshane HS; Canajoharie, NY; (Y); 2/88; Aud/Vis; FCA; Pres Ski Clb; Yrbk Ed-Chief; Capt Crs Cntry; Capt Trk; Elks Awd; High Hon Roll; NHS; Sal; Union Coll; Elec Engrng.

WARNOCK, CHRISTOPHER A; Massapequa HS; Massapequa Pk, NY; (Y); Church Yth Grp; Church Choir; Cmnty Wkr; French Clb; Nwsp Stf; Hon Roll; Rgnts Schlrshp Awd 86; Full Schlrshp Cooper Union Schl Art 86-90; The Cooper Union; Graphic Arts.

WARREN, ALLYSON; Amsterdam HS; Amsterdam, NY; (Y); 63/325; Varsity Clb; Capt Bsktbl; Sftbl; Capt Tennis; Hon Roll.

WARREN, BRIDGET; Granville HS; Hampton, NY; (Y); 12/130; Varsity Clb; Frsh Cls; Stu Cncl; Var Bsktbl; Var Capt Fld Hcky; Var Capt Vllybl; Elks Awd; High Hon Roll; Prfct Atten Awd; Pred Ftns Awd For Extr Effrt 86; Grn Mnt Coll; Cert Pblc Acctnt.

WARREN, COLLEEN; Newburgh Free Acad; Newburgh, NY; (Y); 27/550; Spanish Clb; Acpl Chr; Chorus; Yrbk Stf; Swmmng; High Hon Roll; Jr NHS; NHS; Spanish NHS; SR Spirit Awd 85; Lt Archie Stone Lylty Awd 86; Siena Coll; Bus Mgmt.

WARREN, KAREN; Uniondale HS; Hempstead, NY; (Y); Church Yth Grp; Library Aide; Church Choir; Orch; High Hon Roll; Hon Roll; Jr NHS; Oral Roberts U; Elem Educ.

WARREN, KARIN; Minisink Valley HS; Middletown, NY; (Y); 5/250; Sec Key Clb; Band; Concert Band; Mrchg Band; JV Trk; High Hon Roll; JP Sousa Awd; NHS; Ntl Merit Ltr; Regents Schlrshp 86; Tae Kwon Do Blk Blt 86; Cornell U; Meteorolgy.

WARREN, KIM; Binghamton HS; Binghamton, NY; (Y); Church Yth Grp; High Hon Roll; Hon Roll; NHS; Prfct Atten Awd; Med Lab Tech.

WARREN, RONEVE; Uniondale HS; Uniondale, NY; (Y); Church Yth Grp; Hosp Aide; Yrbk Stf; Rep Frsh Cls; Cheerleading; Score Keeper; Am Lgn Awd 83; Awd Acad Achvmnt 83; Awd Schl Srv 84; Psychtry.

WARRINER, DARRYL; Greenwood Central HS; Rexville, NY; (S); 3/30; Aud/Vis; FFA; Yrbk Stf; High Hon Roll; Hon Roll; NHS; Alfred ST Coll; Med Tech.

WARRINER, JENIFER; Greenwood Central HS; Greenwood, NY; (S); Varsity Clb; Chorus; Color Guard; School Musical; School Play; Yrbk Stf; Sec Jr Cls; Cheerleading; Score Keeper; Hon Roll; Schlstc Awd Hnr 85; Bus Adm.

WARRINER, JUDY; Greenwood Central HS; Canisteo, NY; (S); Varsity Clb; Band; Chorus; Color Guard; Flag Corp; Swing Chorus; Yrbk Stf; Rep Soph Cls; Sec Stu Cncl; Hon Roll; Bus.

WART, KATRINA; Cooperstown Central HS; Cooperstown, NY; (Y); French Clb; Color Guard; Oneonta-Utica Schl/Cmmrce; Bus.

WARTELL, BRUCE E; Irondeguoit HS; Rochester, NY; (Y); 17/346; Latin Clb; Science Clb; Ski Clb; Stage Crew; Rep Sr Cls; Var Golf; Var Socr; Var Tennis; High Hon Roll; NHS; Monroe Soc Prof Engrs Schlrshp 86; U TX Engrng Fndtn Schlrshp 86; Army ROTC Schlrshp 86; U TX Austin; Engrng.

WARTER, OREN; Clarkstown South SR HS; Bardonia, NY; (Y); Chess Clb; JA; Math Clb; Math Tm; Quiz Bowl; Science Clb; Temple Yth Grp; Im Bowling; Gov Hon Prg Awd; High Hon Roll; Bowling Schlrshp Tourn 86; Chem Stu Yr 85; Yth Understandng Exch Stu 85; Sci.

WASHBURN, ANN; Le Roy Central HS; Leroy, NY; (Y); High Hon Roll; Bus Adm.

WASHBURN, KEITH G; Letchworth Central HS; Castile, NY; (Y); Varsity Clb; VICA; Im Bsbl; Var Ftbl; Im Sftbl; Capt Trk; Im Vllybl; Var Wt Lftg; Cit Awd; High Hon Roll; Sprtsmnshp Awd 86; Outstndng Stu Awd Voc Ed 86; Elec.

WASHBURN, NEIL; Allegany Central Schl; Allegany, NY; (Y); 15/102; Drama Clb; English Clb; French Clb; ROTC; Ski Clb; School Play; Stage Crew; Yrbk Stf; Hon Roll; Prfct Atten Awd; Law Enfrcmnt.

WASHINGTON, CHARLENE; Fashion Industries HS; Brooklyn, NY; (Y); 39/324; Dance Clb; JA; Teachers Aide; Y-Teens; Chorus; Capt Cheerleading; Hon Roll; NHS; Pnctlty 85; Engl/Lang Arts 85; Ntl Sci Olympd 84; Psychlgy.

WASHINGTON, ELIZABETH; East Islip HS; East Islip, NY; (Y); 39/425; Church Choir; Concert Band; Mrchg Band; Orch; School Musical; Nwsp Stf; Var Trk; Cit Awd; Dnfth Awd; High Hon Roll; PTSA Scholar 86-87; Bst Woodwind Awd All Cnty Music Fstvl 82-83; Music Achvt Awd 85-86; SUNY Potsdam; Psych.

WASHINGTON, KENDRA; Buffalo Traditional HS; Buffalo, NY; (S); 5/130; Church Yth Grp; Dance Clb; Office Aide; Chorus; Church Choir; Drill Tm; Rep Frsh Cls; Rep Soph Cls; Rep Jr Cls; Trk; Faithful Svc Awd 84; Mayors Physcl Fitns Awd 78; Jones Spec Anniversary Awd 78; Med.

WASHINGTON, ROBIN; Clara Barton HS; Brooklyn, NY; (Y); 50/485; Girl Scts; Capt Quiz Bowl; Teachers Aide; Band; Sec Trs Chorus; Variety Show; Lit Mag; Stu Cncl; Hon Roll; Prfct Atten Awd; Pace U; Comp Sci.

WASHINGTON, STEPHANIE; Freeport HS; Freeport, NY; (Y); Key Clb; Bsktbl; Sftbl; Vllybl; Hon Roll; All Dvsn Bstkbll 86.

WASHINGTON, STEPHANIE; Queen Of The Rosary Acad; Wyandanch, NY; (Y); 14/49; Trs Frsh Cls; Pres Jr Cls; VP Sr Cls; Capt Bsktbl; Var Socr; Capt Trk; Hon Roll; Mu Alp Tht; NHS; Schlrshp For Cath Negroes 86; Outstndg Cnslr Awd 85; Excptnl SR Sccr Tm 86; ST U Buffalo; Nuclr Med.

WASHINGTON, TANEDRA LYNN; Farmingdale HS; Amityville, NY; (Y); Girl Scts; Spanish Clb; Variety Show; Badmtn; Cheerleading; Tennis; Vllybl; Wt Lftg; Hon Roll; Ntl Merit Ltr; Berkley Bus Schl; Micro Comp Ac.

WASHINGTON, TANYA; Herbert H Lehman HS; Bronx, NY; (Y); 121/561; Bsktbl; Accntng.

WASHINGTON, THERESA; Fashion Industries HS; Corona, NY; (Y); 40/325; Church Yth Grp; Dance Clb; Church Choir; Prfct Atten Awd; Dnc Awd 86; Engl & Lang Arts Hnr Roll 86; Anna Whitfield Brunson Music Awd 84; Jrnlsm.

WASHINSKI, ANNE MARIE; Bishop Ludden HS; Syracuse, NY; (S); Yrbk Stf; JV Cheerleading; Stat Lcrss; JV Mgr(s); High Hon Roll; MONY Rgnl Schlstc Art Awds Hnrbl Mntn 84; Schlstc Art Awds Cert Merit 84; Dey Bros JR Fshn Brd 85-86.

WASHKO, CHRISTINE; Lake George HS; Lake George, NY; (Y); CC Awd; High Hon Roll; Hon Roll; Non-Cert Emplyees Assoc Awd 86; Stu Of Mo Bus 85-86; Adirondack CC; Bus.

WASILENKO, JOYCE; Sacred Heart HS; Yonkers, NY; (S); 3/250; Rep Stu Cncl; JV Var Cheerleading; High Hon Roll; NHS; NEDT Awd; Tuition Schlrshp 84 & 85; 1 Full Semstr Tuition Schlrshp 85; Psych.

WASLEY, DANIEL J; La Salle SR HS; Niagara Falls, NY; (S); 9/258; Key Clb; Letterman Clb; Library Aide; Lit Mag; Trs Frsh Cls; Var JV Bsktbl; Var JV Trk; Hon Roll; NHS; NYS Rgnts Schlrshp 86; Niagara U; Acctng.

WASNIK, RENEE; Cato Meridian HS; Cato, NY; (Y); Camera Clb; French Clb; Hon Roll; Cayuga Co Auto Clb Drv Ed Awd 86; Eqstrn Awd 3rd PHA Hgh Scr Awd 83-84, 4th 85-86; Equine Stdy.

WASS, STEVEN; John F Kennedy HS; Buffalo, NY; (Y); 39/135; Am Leg Boys St; Church Yth Grp; Varsity Clb; Bsbl; Bsktbl; Crs Cntry; Acctng.

WASSE, VALERIE; Grand Island HS; Grand Island, NY; (Y); Church Yth Grp; Ski Clb; Concert Band; Variety Show; Stu Cncl; Tennis; Hon Roll; Athl Of Yr 86; MVP In Tennis 85 & 86.

WASSERMAN, DEBRA; Commack HS South; Dix Hills, NY; (Y); 30/367; Cmnty Wkr; Political Wkr; Yrbk Ed-Chief; VP Frsh Cls; VP Soph Cls; Pres Jr Cls; Mgr(s); Var Tennis; High Hon Roll; NHS; Princpls Awd 86; Stu Ldrshp Day 82-86; Presdntl Schlr 86; U Of Michigan; Pol Sci.

WASSERMANN, ANOUK; Eastchester HS; Eastchester, NY; (Y); Debate Tm; Pres French Clb; Ski Clb; SADD; VP Band; Concert Band; Mrchg Band; School Play; Ed Yrbk Stf; Rep Frsh Cls; All League All-Confnc Grls Tnns 85; 1st/2nd Iona Lang Contst 84-85; Loc/Reg Wnr Natl Frnch Exam 84-86.

WASSON, KELLY MICHAEL; Monroe HS; Rochester, NY; (Y); 19/176; Boy Scts; Cmnty Wkr; Latin Clb; Ski Clb; Band; Concert Band; Jazz Band; Mrchg Band; School Musical; Eagl Sct 85; Ithaca Coll Schlrshp Awd 86; Ithaca Coll; Pre-Med.

WASSON, MICHAEL T; Hunter College HS; New York, NY; (Y); Ed Lit Mag; Ntl Merit SF; Phlsphy.

WASZKIEWICZ, SALLY; Bainbridge-Guilford HS; Bainbridge, NY; (Y); Pres French Clb; Girl Scts; Band; Mrchg Band; Yrbk Stf; Cheerleading; Trk; Hon Roll; Niagra U; Acctng.

WATANABE, KIM A; School Of The Holy Child; Rye Brook, NY; (Y); Chorus; School Musical; Lit Mag; Cit Awd; High Hon Roll; NHS; Ntl Merit Ltr; Smith Bk Awd-Smith Coll 85; Brown U Clb Of Westcher-Rgnl Schlr 86; Yale U.

WATERS, DAVID; Newfane SR HS; Newfane, NY; (Y); 130/155; Church Yth Grp; Drama Clb; VICA; Band; Symp Band; Bsbl; Carpntry.

WATERS, FRANK; Ripley Central HS; Ripley, NY; (Y); Boy Scts; Church Yth Grp; Quiz Bowl; Band; Concert Band; Mrchg Band; Stat VP Bsktbl; Capt Golf; Hon Roll; NHS; Mth.

WATERS, LORI; Seton Catholic Central Schl; Johnson City, NY; (Y); Art Clb; Church Yth Grp; Trs VICA; School Musical; Stage Crew; Nwsp Rptr; VICA Ldrshp Awd 85; VICA 3rd Open/Clsng Ceremonies NYS 86; NC ST U; Csmtlgy.

WATERS, MICHAEL R; Monsignor Farrell HS; Staten Island, NY; (Y); 11/299; Computer Clb; Math Tm; Bsktbl; Bowling; Ftbl; Iona Coll Itln Awd 85; Mnhtn Coll Prsdntl Schlrshp Hnr Scty 86; NYS Rgnts Awd 86; Aerospc Engr.

WATERSTON, JENNIFER; Blind Brook HS; Rye Brook, NY; (Y); Pres AFS; Cmnty Wkr; Spanish Clb; Temple Yth Grp; Band; Jr Cls; Stu Cncl; Bsktbl; Hosp Aide; VP Fdrtn Temple Yth 86; Jr Yr Awd Vaggar Coll-Acdmc/Prsnl Qual & Cntrbtn HS 86.

WATIER, KEVIN; Lockport SR HS; Lockport, NY; (Y); Band; Mrchg Band; Symp Band; Trk; Hist.

WATKINS, KAREN; Immaculata HS; New York, NY; (Y); Computer Clb; Dance Clb; Office Aide; Political Wkr; Spanish Clb; Teachers Aide; Varsity Clb; Chorus; Yrbk Stf; Pres Soph Cls; 1st Pl Ldrshp Awd 86; Svc Awd 86; Long Island U; Physcl Thrpy.

WATKINS, SARAH; Attica HS; Attica, NY; (Y); AFS; Dance Clb; Spanish Clb; Band; Color Guard; Concert Band; Drill Tm; Mrchg Band; Nwsp Stf; Rep Frsh Cls.

WATROUS, DENNIS; Clyde-Savannah Central HS; Clyde, NY; (Y); Am Leg Boys St; Boy Scts; Ski Clb; Band; JV Bsbl; Var Bowling; L Ftbl; Var Trk; Hon Roll; Hon Engl; Comp Sci.

WATROUS, KAREN M; Schalmont HS; Schenectady, NY; (Y); 4/165; Quiz Bowl; Yrbk Stf; Stat Socr; Stat Trk; DAR Awd; High Hon Roll; Kiwanis Awd; NHS; Ntl Merit Ltr; Prfct Atten Awd; Coll Of William & Mary; Lib Art.

WATROUS, S KEITH; Hugh C Williams HS; Canton, NY; (Y); 45/145; Var Bsbl; JV Var Ftbl; Hon Roll; Prfct Atten Awd; Clarkson U; Arctctrl Engrng.

WATSON, CHERRISE; John Jay HS; Brooklyn, NY; (Y); JA; Office Aide; Teachers Aide; Yrbk Stf; Off Frsh Cls; Hon Roll; Prfct Atten Awd; Spnsh Schlrshp Awd 84; Sci Fair Awd 84; Achvt Awd 85.

WATSON, CINDA; Bainbridge-Guilford HS; Bainbridge, NY; (Y); Spanish Clb; Band; Color Guard; Orch; Pres Soph Cls; Stu Cncl; Bsktbl; Tennis; Trk; Coll St Rose; Elem Ed.

WATSON, DANNIELLE; Hoosic Valley Central HS; Schaghticoke, NY; (Y); High Hon Roll; Hon Roll; John J Simmons Awd 86.

WATSON, DEVIN; Grand Island HS; Grand Island, NY; (Y); Hosp Aide; Ski Clb; Yrbk Stf; Im Ftbl; Hon Roll; HS Acdmc Excllnc Awd; Acdmc Lttr; U Of Buffalo.

WATSON, EDWIN; Gates-Chili HS; Rochester, NY; (Y); Boy Scts; Church Yth Grp; JV Bsktbl; High Hon Roll; Hon Roll; Ntl Merit Ltr; Syracuse U; Elec Engrng.

WATSON, LINDA; Beacon HS; Beacon, NY; (Y); Mgr(s); Score Keeper; Stat Vllybl; Hon Roll; Les Soeurs Amiable Awd 86; Martin Luther King Awd 86; NY Inst Of Tech; Elec Engrng.

WATSON, MARK; Midwood HS; Brooklyn, NY; (Y); French Clb; Band; Church Choir; Wt Lftg; Arista 84; Frnch Hon Awd 84; Med.

WATSON, NICOLA; Prospect Heights HS; Brooklyn, NY; (S); Dance Clb; French Clb; Office Aide; Hon Roll; NHS; Prfct Atten Awd; Law.

WATSON, PAUL A; Byram Hills HS; Armonk, NY; (Y); Math Clb; Thesps; Band; Concert Band; Jazz Band; School Musical; School Play; Variety Show; Swmmng; High Hon Roll; Drtmth Bk Awd 86.

WATSON, PAUL J; Rome Free Acad; Rome, NY; (Y); 2/450; Intnl Clb; Ski Clb; Yrbk Rptr; Rep Soph Cls; Hon Roll; Jr NHS; NHS; Sal; Air Force ROTC Schlrshp 86; Class III Stu Pilot Cert 86; Syracuse U; Aerosp Engrg.

WATSON, ROYEN; H S Of Art & Design; Brooklyn, NY; (Y); Office Aide; Stage Crew; Variety Show; Yrbk Stf; Hon Roll; Prfct Atten Awd; Natl Fndtn Advncmnt Arts 85-86; Brd Ed Cty NY Cert Recgntn 86; Natl Yth Sports Pgm 81; Natl Acad Schl; Comm Art.

WATSON, SEAN; Hoosick Falls Central HS; Hoosick Falls, NY; (Y); Letterman Clb; Varsity Clb; Capt Ftbl; Var Wt Lftg; Capt Wrstlng; 1st Strng All Star Ftbl Tm 86; Outstndg Wrstlr 86; Cortland; Coach.

WATSON, VERONICA M; Roosevelt HS; Yonkers, NY; (Y); Syracuse U.

WATSON, WILLIAM J; Lockport SR HS; Lockport, NY; (Y); 20/411; Latin Clb; Capt L Bsbl; Capt L Ice Hcky; Capt L Socr; VP NHS; Outstndng Athl Cnty Awd, Athl Yr, Rgnt Schlrshp 86; Hobart Coll; Pre Law.

WATT, JACQUELINE M; Midwood HS; Brooklyn, NY; (Y); 155/638; Hosp Aide; Library Aide; Office Aide; Service Clb; Chorus; School Musical; Yrbk Stf; Lit Mag; Prfct Atten Awd; St Johns U; Chem.

WATTENSCHAIDT, KARLA; Herkimer SR HS; Herkimer, NY; (Y); 10/128; Pep Clb; Pres Band; Concert Band; Drm Mjr(t); Mrchg Band; Pep Band; School Musical; High Hon Roll; NHS; VFW Awd; Rgnts Schlrshp 86; Wells Coll; Psych.

WATTS, E DAVID; Northeastern Clinton Central HS; Mooers, NY; (Y); 8/160; Boy Scts; Church Yth Grp; Model UN; Quiz Bowl; Concert Band; Jazz Band; Mrchg Band; Nwsp Stf; Var Socr; High Hon Roll; Eagle Scout 86; Amer Lgn Schlrshp 86; Clinton Cmnty Clg Schlrshp 86; Army; Policework.

WATTS, STEPHANIE D; Horseheads HS; Horseheads, NY; (Y); Church Yth Grp; Dance Clb; VP Intnl Clb; Color Guard; Mrchg Band; Hon Roll; NHS; Drama Clb; SADD; Variety Show; Natl Spnsh Exam 84-86; Yth Cnty 85; Htl/Rstrnt Mgmt.

WATTSMAN, TERRI-ANN; Keveny Memorial Acad; Troy, NY; (S); Church Yth Grp; Math Clb; Math Tm; Spanish Clb; Var JV Bsktbl; Var JV Crs Cntry; Mgr(s); Var Sftbl; Var Vllybl; High Hon Roll; Girl Sct Silver Awd; Dr.

WATZ, CHRISTOPHER; Grand Island HS; Gr Island, NY; (Y); Drama Clb; Ski Clb; Varsity Clb; Chorus; Concert Band; Trs Madrigals; School Musical; School Play; L Socr; Vllybl; Rgnts Schlrp 86; Stanley Marcus Hmntrn Awd PTSA 86; Mst Val Frosh Chorus & Drama Clbs 82 & 83; Fairfield U; Bus Mgmt.

WAUGAMAN, MELISSA; Holland Central HS; Holland, NY; (Y); AFS; Am Leg Aux Girls St; Cmnty Wkr; VP Band; VP Concert Band; Jazz Band; VP Mrchg Band; Symp Band; Hon Roll; Jr NHS; Jeannie Blair Awd Hgh Achvmnt Engl Cmpstn 86.

WAUGH, BERNARD; Beaver River Central HS; Croghan, NY; (Y); Church Yth Grp; FFA; Wrstlng; Hon Roll; NHS; Awd Christian Conduct 86; Hist.

WAWRYK, KIMBERLY; Mercy HS; Sag Harbor, NY; (Y); 7/150; Math Clb; Yrbk Stf; L Bsktbl; Sftbl; Tennis; High Hon Roll; Hon Roll; Ntl Merit Ltr.

WAWRZONEK, SHARON; John F Kennedy HS; Sloan, NY; (Y); 13/135; Art Clb; Church Yth Grp; Pres FHA; GAA; Varsity Clb; JV Bsktbl; JV Var Socr; Im Vllybl; Im Wt Lftg; Hon Roll; Hnr Awd For Outstndng Svc-FHA 84-85; Hnr-Schltc Ability & Athltc Invlvmt 83-84.

WAY, AMY; Charles H Roth HS; Henrietta, NY; (Y); GAA; Latin Clb; Rep Jr Cls; JV Var Cheerleading; Mgr(s); Hon Roll; NHS; Church Yth Grp; German Clb; Rep Soph Cls; German Hon Soc; Highest Grd Pt Avg German; 99 Pct On Natl German Exam; ST Teacher Coll; Second Educ.

WAYMAN, BRENDA; Unatego JR SR HS; Otego, NY; (Y); #13 In Class; Cmnty Wkr; Ski Clb; Spanish Clb; Varsity Clb; Band; Chorus; Concert Band; Pep Band; School Musical; School Play; All Cty Band 86; Art Thrpy.

WAYMAN, JODI; Cato-Meridian HS; Cato, NY; (Y); VICA; Im Badmtn; Var Trk; JV Var Vllybl; Pre-Schl Tchr.

WAYMAN, STEVEN; Schoharie Central HS; Schoharie, NY; (Y); Boy Scts; Band; Crs Cntry; Trk; Cit Awd; High Hon Roll; Prfct Atten Awd; Pres Acdmc Ftns 85-86; Eagle Sct 84; Amer Lgn Amrcnsm Awd 85; Air Force.

WEAGLEY, CHRISTINE; James E Sperry HS; Henrietta, NY; (Y); Chorus; Hon Roll; Ski Clb; SADD; Acpl Chr; Off Soph Cls; Swmmng; Intershp Awd; Lib Arts.

WEATHERBORN, YANINA; Yonkers HS; Yonkers, NY; (Y); Church Yth Grp; Debate Tm; 4-H; Hosp Aide; Spanish Clb; Acctng.

WEATHERELL, JANIS; Friendship Central HS; Friendship, NY; (S); 4/30; Spanish Clb; Band; Chorus; School Play; Yrbk Bus Mgr; Yrbk Ed-Chief; High Hon Roll; NHS; Model UN; Mrchg Band; All Cnty Choirs 82-86; Monroe CC; Radlgy.

WEAVER, ALAN R; Alfred-Almond Central Schl; Alfred, NY; (Y); Boy Scts; Chess Clb; Church Yth Grp; Drama Clb; Exploring; Thesps; Band; Chorus; Concert Band; Mrchg Band; Alfred U; Archeology.

WEAVER, AMY; North Babylon SR HS; N Babylon, NY; (Y); 22/436; French Clb; Intnl Clb; Chorus; Cit Awd; French Hon Soc; High Hon Roll; Hon Roll; NHS; Fshn Merch.

WEAVER, CARIN; E J Wilson HS; Spencerport, NY; (Y); Am Leg Aux Girls St; Church Yth Grp; French Clb; Mathletes; Model UN; Symp Band; Frsh Cls; Crs Cntry; Trk; High Hon Roll; Engl Awd Outstndng Achvt 86; Band Outstndng Achvt 84; Phys Thrpy.

WEAVER, CASSONDRA LYNN; Auburn HS; Auburn, NY; (Y); Church Yth Grp; Varsity Clb; JV L Socr; JV L Sftbl; Var L Swmmng; Var L Timer; High Hon Roll; Hon Roll; Jr NHS; NHS; John J Pettigrass Mem Athletc Awd 86; MVP Soccer,Sftbl 85; Comp.

WEAVER, DANIEL; Hahn American HS; Lusk, WY; (Y); 4/76; Boy Scts; Model UN; VP Soph Cls; Pres Jr Cls; Rep Stu Cncl; Var L Crs Cntry; Var L Wrstlng; High Hon Roll; Hon Roll; Jr NHS; USAF Acad; Engrng.

WEAVER, DAWN; Lyndonville Central HS; Lyndonville, NY; (Y); 4-H; Spanish Clb; Chorus; Nwsp Rptr; Cit Awd; 4-H Awd; Awd Trips Cnties & ST 82-86; Anml Sci.

WEAVER, J PAUL; Alfred-Almond Central HS; Alfred, NY; (Y); Pres Aud/Vis; Drama Clb; Pres Exploring; JA; Thesps; School Musical; School Play; Pres Stage Crew; Var Crs Cntry; Regets Schlrshp 85-86; Audio-Visual Stage Crew Awd 84; Performing Artists Guild 84; Alfred U; Performing Arts.

WEAVER, JASON; Sackets Harbor Central HS; Sackets Harbor, NY; (Y); Camera Clb; Band; Chorus; Church Choir; Mrchg Band; School Musical; School Play; Stage Crew; Yrbk Phtg; Var Ftbl; Am Leg Poppy Poster Awd 84; NYSSMA Solo Comptn Awd Excllnt Outstndng 84-86; Various Art Awds 84-86.

WEAVER, JOYCE; Twin Tiers Baptist HS; Watkins Glenn, NY; (S); 2/18; Sec Church Yth Grp; Chorus; Sec Jr Cls; Var Bsktbl; Sftbl; NHS; Prfct Atten Awd; Acadmc All Amercn 85.

WEAVER, LORI; Chatham Central HS; Valatie, NY; (Y); 52/136; Trs Church Yth Grp; GAA; Ski Clb; Teachers Aide; Chorus; Yrbk Stf; Var JV Bsktbl; Var JV Socr; Var Sftbl; Stat Vllybl; Air Force.

WEAVER, MARY E; Carthage Central HS; Deferiet, NY; (Y); GAA; Spanish Clb; Rep Stu Cncl; JV Var Socr; Var Capt Vllybl; NYS Regents Nrsng Scholar 86; Jefferson CC; Nrsng.

WEAVER, TAMMY; G Ray Bodley HS; Fulton, NY; (Y); 38/260; High Hon Roll; Hon Roll; Bus Educ Awd Bst All-Arnd 86; Rcgntn Awd Bus 84; Central Aty Bus Inst; Exec Sec.

WEAVER, YOMO; Poughkeepsie HS; Poughkeepsie, NY; (Y); #54 In Class; Art Clb; Camera Clb; Hosp Aide; Office Aide; SADD; Y-Teens; Chorus; Variety Show; JV Var Cheerleading; High Hon Roll; Nrsg Altrntv Schrlshp Awd 86; Dutchiss CC; Acctng.

WEBB, ALLEN; Fairport HS; Fairport, NY; (Y); Boy Scts; Pres Model UN; Var Ski Clb; VP Stu Cncl; JV Crs Cntry; JV Var Tennis; High Hon Roll; NHS; Socr; Dartmouth Clg Bk Awd 86; Modl UN Bst Delg Hnbl Mntn Hilton Conv 85; Hstry.

WEBB, CEVITA; Herbert H Lehman HS; Bronx, NY; (Y); Science Clb; Yrbk Stf; Lit Mag; Prfct Atten Awd; Awd-Lang Arts 84; NY U; Pre-Med.

WEBB, DENNIS; Hutch Tech HS; Buffalo, NY; (Y); Church Yth Grp; Band; Jazz Band; Mrchg Band; Stu Cncl; Bsktbl; Socr; Hon Roll; Arch.

WEBB, NADJA M; Convent Of The Sacred Heart; Bronx, NY; (Y); Dance Clb; Debate Tm; Hosp Aide; Model UN; Ski Clb; Variety Show; Nwsp Rptr; Nwsp Stf; Yrbk Stf; Rep Frsh Cls; Cmps Mnstry Awd 85; Natl Hspnc Schlrs Awd 86; Hmnts.

WEBB, NEIL; Paul V Moore HS; Bernhards Bay, NY; (Y); German Clb; Ski Clb; JV Golf; Var Socr; JV Tennis; High Hon Roll; NHS; Pres Clsrm Young Am 86; Bus Mgmt.

WEBB, STEPHEN J; Canastota HS; Canastota, NY; (Y); 16/157; Chess Clb; Leo Clb; Science Clb; Service Clb; Var Socr; Var Tennis; Var Trk; High Hon Roll; Plattsburg ST; Comp Engr.

WEBBER, AMY; Northville Central HS; Benson, NY; (Y); Cmnty Wkr; Color Guard; JV Cheerleading; JV Chrldng Awd 85-86.

WEBER, EDWARD; Newburgh Free Acad; Newburgh, NY; (Y); Church Yth Grp; Spanish Clb; Hon Roll; Prfct Atten Awd.

WEBER, JANICE; L I Lutheran HS; West Babylon, NY; (S); 5/94; Band; Chorus; Jazz Band; School Musical; Sec Stu Cncl; Var Cheerleading; Var L Sftbl; Var L Vllybl; High Hon Roll; NHS; Music.

WEBER, KELLY; Mount Mercy Acad; W Seneca, NY; (Y); 21/196; Service Clb; Ski Clb; Spanish Clb; SADD; Chorus; Stage Crew; Rep Sr Cls; Var Stat Vllybl; Hon Roll; NHS; Fair Spnsh Prjct 2nd Pl 85; Music Fest In NYC Mt Mercy Slvr Medal 85; Second Educ.

WEBER, RICHARD; Manhasset HS; Manhasset, NY; (Y); Trs Chess Clb; Church Yth Grp; Computer Clb; Mathletes; Lit Mag; JV Socr; Bausch & Lomb Sci Awd; High Hon Roll; Pres NHS.

WEBER, STEPHEN; Roy C Ketcham HS; Wappingers Falls, NY; (Y); Pres Drama Clb; Thesps; School Musical; School Play; Stage Crew; Yrbk Stf; Stu Cncl; High Hon Roll; NHS; Ntl Merit Ltr; Prtcptn Smmr Schlrs Pgm Brd Coll 86.

WEBSTER, ANDREA; Grace Dodge Voc HS; Bronx, NY; (Y); Dance Clb; Hosp Aide; Chorus; Variety Show; Rep Soph Cls; Rep Jr Cls; Var Cheerleading; Prfct Atten Awd; Hnr Consumer Law 85; Howard U; Lawyer.

WEBSTER, CHRISTINA; Bradford Central HS; Painted Post, NY; (S); 2/30; FBLA; School Play; Ed Nwsp Stf; VP Rep Stu Cncl; Score Keeper; Mgr Sftbl; High Hon Roll; Im Socr; Capt Vllybl; Hon Roll; Math.

WEBSTER, COLLEEN; Notre Dame HS; Horseheads, NY; (Y); 21/88; French Clb; Lit Mag; Sftbl; High Hon Roll; Hon Roll; NHS; Crng Comm Coll; Erly Chldhd Ed.

WEBSTER, ERIC; Oneida HS; Oneida, NY; (Y); Am Leg Boys St; Trs Church Yth Grp; Varsity Clb; School Play; Yrbk Stf; Var L Socr; Var L Tennis; Var L Wrstlng; High Hon Roll; NHS; Natl Sci Merit Awd Wnnr 86; Presdntl Physcl Fitness Awd 84-86; Education.

WEBSTER, JEFFREY D; Medina SR HS; Medina, NY; (Y); 19/175; Church Yth Grp; Rep Stu Cncl; Var L Bsbl; Var Capt Golf; Var Capt Swmmng; High Hon Roll; Masonic Awd; NHS; 3 Yr Al-Leag Glfr Indvdl Al-Leag Chmpn 84; Gannon U; Mechncl Engr.

WEBSTER, NORMA; Solvay HS; Solvay, NY; (Y); French Clb; Math Clb; Yrbk Stf; Off Frsh Cls; Off Soph Cls; Off Jr Cls; Hon Roll.

WECHSLER, MARC; Herricks HS; Searingtown, NY; (Y); Quiz Bowl; Band; Swmmng; NHS; Mathletes; Temple Yth Grp; Concert Band; Mrchg Band; Hon Roll; Jr NHS; Hofstra Aquatic Clb 85-86; Tsunami Swm Clb 83-85; Bus.

WEDEMEYER, KRISTIN; William Nottingham HS; Syracuse, NY; (Y); Sec Latin Clb; Ski Clb; Acpl Chr; Chorus; School Musical; High Hon Roll; NHS; Ntl Merit Ltr; Swmmng; St Schlr; Wellesley Bk Awd 86; Magna Cum Laude Silver Mdl Ntl Latin Exam 85-86; Psych.

WEED JR, DONALD L; Immanuel Baptist Christian Schl; Moravia, NY; (S); 1/2; Computer Clb; Quiz Bowl; Chorus; Orch; VP Stu Cncl; Var Capt Bsktbl; Var Crs Cntry; Var Capt Socr; Var Capt Trk; Val; 1st Chr Strng Bass SC All ST Orch 83; Bob Jones U; Math.

WEED, ROBIN; St John Villa Acad; Staten Island, NY; (Y); 4/123; Art Clb; Math Tm; Yrbk Ed-Chief; Var Cheerleading; Engl Excllnce Awd 86; Pre-Calc Excllnce Awd 86; 1st Pl Wnnr NYC Prfrmg Art Lit Cont 85; Fash Inst Tech; Mrchndsg.

WEEDEN, RICHARD; Union Springs Acad; Middle Grove, NY; (Y); Boy Scts; Chess Clb; Church Yth Grp; Cmnty Wkr; Ski Clb; Im Bsbl; Im Bsktbl; Im Bowling; Im JV Ftbl; Im Socr; Elec.

WEEKES, STEPHANIE; Cold Spring Harbor HS; Huntington, NY; (Y); 47/127; Band; Var Sftbl; Capt Var Swmmng; Hon Roll; Schl Sprts Hall Fame Swmng 86; Mst Vlbl Swmmr 85-86; Mst Imprvd Sftbl Plyr 86.

WEEKS, DANIEL; Cato-Meridian HS; Weedsport, NY; (Y); 1/100; Trs Drama Clb; 4-H; Trs French Clb; Model UN; School Play; 4-H Awd; High Hon Roll; Jr NHS; NHS; Val; Hghst Achvt Engl, Soc Stds, Frgn Lang 84-86; Kirk Myrs Mem Awd Wnnr 85; Syracuse U; Pblc Cmnctns.

WEEKS, GABRIELLE M; Oneonta SR HS; Oneonta, NY; (Y); Art Clb; Hosp Aide; Key Clb; Varsity Clb; Chorus; Yrbk Stf; Stu Cncl; Vllybl; NHS; St Schlr; Farone Hnr Schlrshp 86; NY ST Rgnts Nrsg Schlrshp 86; Natl Hnr Soc 86; Marymount Coll Of VA; Nrsg.

WEEKS, JAMES; Erasmus Hall SR HS; Brooklyn, NY; (Y); Cmnty Wkr; Jr NHS; Operation Success 84-85; Part Time Coop 85-86; Excllnc Prog 85-86; Bklyn Coll; Gynecology.

WEEKS, MICHAEL W; Cooperstown Central Schl; Hartwick, NY; (Y); 18/105; Am Leg Boys St; Church Yth Grp; JV Var Socr; NHS; Schlrshp To NC Outward Bnd Schl 86; ENVRNMNTL Sci.

WEEKS, R SCOTT; Alfred-Almond Central Schl; Alfred Station, NY; (Y); 26/67; Church Yth Grp; Cmnty Wkr; JCL; Latin Clb; SADD; Concert Band; Var Bsbl; Var Socr; Var Wrstlng; Hon Roll; Clarkson U; Bio Med Engrng.

WEEMAN, MICHAEL; Cardinal O Hara HS; Grand Island, NY; (Y); Chess Clb; Computer Clb; Service Clb; Varsity Clb; Drm & Bgl; Var L Crs Cntry; Var L Trk; High Hon Roll; Hon Roll; IN Inst Tech; Comp Sci.

WEGENER, KARI; St Peters HS For Girls; Staten Island, NY; (Y); Cmnty Wkr; SADD; Chorus; Tennis; Trk; Vllybl; Prfct Atten Awd; Ntl Hstry & Govt Achvt Awd 86; Boston U; Med.

WEHLE, TINA; Nardin Acad; Buffalo, NY; (Y); Speech Tm; School Play; Swing Chorus; Lit Mag; Hon Roll; Cert Merit Regnts Eng III 85-86; Cert Merit Creat Wrtg 85-86.

WEHRBERGER, DAWN; Holy Trinity Diocesan HS; Plainview, NY; (S); 18/403; Math Clb; Ski Clb; JV Cheerleading; JV Gym; Mgr(s); Score Keeper; Hon Roll; NEDT Awd.

WEHRLE, MICHELLE; Sauquoit Valley Central HS; Sauguoit, NY; (Y); 20/99; SADD; Chorus; Yrbk Stf; Hon Roll; NHS; Prfct Atten Awd; Acad Scholar Johnson & Wales Coll 86; Colgate U Sem 84-86; SUNY Cobleskill; Travel.

WEI, LUCY; Fontbonne Hall Acad; Brooklyn, NY; (Y); Chess Clb; Math Clb; Teachers Aide; Varsity Clb; Pres Sr Cls; Tennis; Hon Roll; NHS; Prtl Schlrshp NY U 86-87; Hwrd Gldn Awd Achvmnt 86; Awd Chrctr Ldrshp & Achvmnts 86; NY U.

WEI, MARY; Fontbonne Hall Acad; Brooklyn, NY; (Y); 3/130; Chess Clb; Nwsp Rptr; Yrbk Rptr; Sec Soph Cls; Pres Jr Cls; Pres Stu Cncl; Tennis; High Hon Roll; NHS; Prfct Atten Awd; Mr Jenson Awd 85; Schl Schlrshp 84, 85&86; Boston Coll.

WEIBEL, BRIAN; Frentice Central HS; Blasdell, NY; (Y); #40 In Class; Trs Church Yth Grp; Sec German Clb; Math Tm; Science Clb; Var Crs Cntry; Var Trk; Hon Roll; NHS; Ntl Merit SF; NEDT Awd; Regents Schlrshp 86; Empire ST Schlrshp 86; Pres Schlrshp 86; Clarkson U; Chem Engr.

WEIDEN, ELIZABETH C; Franciscan HS; Yorktown Hts, NY; (Y); 10/50; Spanish Clb; School Musical; Chorus; Variety Show; Nwsp Rptr; Yrbk Stf; Var Stat Vllybl; NHS; Spanish NHS; Pres Schlrshp 86; Manhattan Clg; Eng Prof.

WEIGAND, DAVE; Long Island Lutheran HS; Glen Cove, NY; (S); Spanish Clb; Trs SADD; Yrbk Phtg; Yrbk Stf; JV Tennis; High Hon Roll; Jr NHS; NHS; Mrktg.

WEIGEL, JOHN F; Hillcrest HS; Glendale, NY; (Y); 48/801; Church Yth Grp; Computer Clb; Math Tm; Teachers Aide; High Hon Roll; St Schlr; NYS Regents Schlrshp 86; German Lit Scty Slvr Cert 85; Hofstra Dist Acad Schlrshp 86; Hofstra U; Med.

WEIGEL, JOYCE; Kenmore East HS; Tonawanda, NY; (Y); 72/330; GAA; Pep Clb; JV Var Vllybl; Hon Roll; NHS; Bryant & Straton Informtn Procsng Sectrl Schlrshp 85; Bryant & Stratton; Word Prcssng.

WEIGHTMAN, KELLY; Clayton A Bounton HS; Voorheesville, NY; (Y); French Clb; Intnl Clb; SADD; Chorus; Yrbk Stf; Lit Mag; Stu Cncl; Capt Bsktbl; Powder Puff Ftbl; Capt Socr; Bus Admin.

WEIGOLD, JOHN; Clarkstown South HS; New City, NY; (Y); Nwsp Stf; Capt Ice Hcky; Var Lcrss; Nwsp Rptr; Im Bsktbl; Bambergers Cmmnty Srv Awd 86; 4 Yrs Var Hcky Capt & All Cnty 82-86; 4 Yrs All Sec & MVP 84-86; Geneseo Coll.

WEIL, JOYCE; Christ The King R HS; Ridgewood, NY; (Y); 5/450; Math Tm; Office Aide; Yrbk Stf; Rep Stu Cncl; High Hon Roll; NHS; Ntl Merit Ltr.

WEILBACHER, DIANE; North Babylon SR HS; Babylon, NY; (Y); 80/485; French Clb; Intnl Clb; Chorus; Madrigals; School Musical; Swing Chorus; Gym; French Hon Soc; Jr NHS; NHS; PTA Cncl Schlrhsp 86; Elem PTA Schlrshp 86; PTSA Schlrshp Schlrshp 86; SUNY Farmingdale; Vet Sci Tech.

WEIN, JOE; Moosie Valley Central HS; Troy, NY; (Y); 4-H; VICA; Rep Stu Cncl; JV Var Score Keeper; Var Trk; Hon Roll; Prfct Atten Awd; Chef.

WEINBERG, ILAN J; White Plains HS; White Plains, NY; (Y); 10/500; Computer Clb; Math Clb; Math Tm; Stage Crew; JV Socr; Bausch & Lomb Sci Awd; Hon Roll; Pres Local Jets Clb 85-87; NY St Supv Assn Physics Awd 86; Rsrch Sci.

WEINER, AMY; Syosset HS; Syosset, NY; (Y); 56/492; Political Wkr; Rep Stu Cncl; Var Bsktbll; NHS; Prfct Atten Awd; NY ST Rgnts Schlrhsp 86; ST U Of NY-BNGHMTN; Mgmt.

WEINER, BILL; Jamesville De Witt HS; Fayetteville, NY; (Y); 2/250; Mathletes; Math Clb; Math Tm; Model UN; Political Wkr; Nwsp Stf; Engl Awd 85; Mth Awd 85 & 86; Sci Awd 84-86; Elec Engrng.

WEINER, ELAINE; Niskayuna HS; Schdy, NY; (Y); AFS; Cmnty Wkr; 4-H; French Clb; Hosp Aide; Chorus; Mrchg Band; Orch; School Play; Symp Band; Stdnt Wrtr Wk 85; Cert Achvt Candystrpng, Nrsg Hme Vltr 84; Guilford Coll.

WEINGARDT, KENNETH R; Edgemont HS; Scarsdale, NY; (Y); Boy Scts; Debate Tm; Ntl Merit Ltr; NY ST Rgnts Schlrshp 86; Cornell U; Hstry.

WEINGARTNER, KELLY; West Hempstead HS; Island Park, NY; (Y); FBLA; Var L Vllybl; Hon Roll; NHS; Bus Dynmcs Awd 83-84; Acctg, Bkkpg Awd 85-86; Spnsh Achvt Awd I, II, III 83-86; Bus Admn.

WEINHEIMER, LORNA; New Lebanon Central HS; Old Chatham, NY; (Y); 1/55; Trs Church Yth Grp; French Clb; Math Tm; Ski Clb; Yrbk Stf; Stu Cncl; Var Trk; High Hon Roll; NHS; Val; RPI Math & Sci Awd 85; Rgnts Schlrshp 86; Williams Coll Book Awd 85; Hamilton Coll; Med.

WEINMANN, LAURA; South Kortright Central HS; Hobart, NY; (Y); 1/25; Varsity Clb; Band; School Play; Sec Stu Cncl; Var Bsktbl; Var Socr; Var Capt Sftbl; High Hon Roll; Val; Outstndg & Excptnl Perf In Sci 86; Outstndg In Effrt & Achvt 86; Outstndg Achvt Math 86; Rensselaer Polytech Inst; Biol.

WEINREICH, ANDREW P; Edgemont HS; Scarsdale, NY; (Y); Latin Clb; Model UN; School Play; Stage Crew; Nwsp Rptr; Bsbl; JV Ice Hcky; Var Socr; Cum Laude Soc 86; U PA.

WEINSTEIN, BARBARA; Blind Brook HS; Rye Brook, NY; (Y); Drama Clb; Math Tm; VP Ski Clb; VP Temple Yth Grp; Acpl Chr; Chorus; School Musical; School Play; Yrbk Stf; Ed Lit Mag; Yale.

WEINSTEIN, DAN; The Harvey Schl; Rye, NY; (S); 1/44; Library Aide; Lit Mag; Var Crs Cntry; High Hon Roll; Frnch Awd 85; Dekadeis Soc 5th Pl Stu In Schl 86; Engl Lit.

WEINSTEIN, STEPHEN; Irondequoit HS; Rochester, NY; (Y); 25/380; Exploring; Hosp Aide; Mgr Radio Clb; Pres SADD; Temple Yth Grp; Jazz Band; Pep Band; School Musical; Yrbk Sprt Ed; Hon Roll; Northwestern; Adv.

WEINSTOCK, DAVID; Jericho HS; Jericho, NY; (Y); 49/200; SADD; Varsity Clb; Jazz Band; Mrchg Band; Nwsp Stf; Yrbk Stf; Bowling; Socr; Trk; NHS; Parent Tchr Stu Awd 86; U MI.

WEINSTOCK, MARK; W Hempstead HS; West Hempstead, NY; (Y); Cmnty Wkr; Computer Clb; German Clb; Temple Yth Grp; JV Bsktbl; Math.

WEINTRAUB, DANA L; Scarsdale HS; Scarsdale, NY; (Y); Varsity Clb; Var Fld Hcky; Var Capt Socr; NHS; Dartmouth Coll.

WEINTRAUB, MATTHEW; Auburn HS; Auburn, NY; (Y); 2/450; Computer Clb; Debate Tm; Model UN; Speech Tm; JV Tennis; JV Trk; High Hon Roll; NHS; Enrchd Engl Awd Excllnc 86; Top Score Natl Math Cntst 86; Excllnc Chem 86; Deep Springs Coll; Govt.

WEINTRAUB, STUART A; Lynbrook HS; Lynbrook, NY; (Y); Drama Clb; Thesps; Band; Yrbk Bus Mgr; Ice Hcky; Tennis; Hon Roll; Regnts Schlrshp 86; TUFTS U; Med Fld.

WEIR, ROBERT; Saugerties HS; Saugerties, NY; (S); 3/258; Pres Chess Clb; German Clb; Co-Capt Math Tm; Quiz Bowl; Concert Band; Mrchg Band; Symp Band; Cit Awd; High Hon Roll; Unltd Parameters Awd 85; 2nd Pl Natl Socl Studies Olympd 85; U Rochester; Astrnmy.

WEIR, SHERIE; Hoosic Valley Central Schl; Schaghticoke, NY; (S); 4/100; Church Yth Grp; 4-H; Teachers Aide; Chorus; Crs Cntry; Trk; Hon Roll; NHS; Ntl Merit Ltr; ST U; Chem.

WEIR, SONYA LYNN; Keshequa Central Schl; Nunda, NY; (Y); Church Yth Grp; Ski Clb; Varsity Clb; Mrchg Band; Nwsp Sprt Ed; Bsktbl; Socr; Trk; Bausch & Lomb Sci Awd; High Hon Roll; Pre-Med.

WEIRICH, DAVID M; Clarence Central HS; Clarence, NY; (Y); 15/276; Drama Clb; Varsity Clb; School Musical; School Play; Capt Golf; Tennis; High Hon Roll; Hon Roll; NHS; Mock Trl Tm 86; MI ST; Engrng.

WEIS, ANN MARIE; Newfield HS; Coram, NY; (Y); Camera Clb; Cmnty Wkr; SADD; Yrbk Ed-Chief; Yrbk Phtg; Yrbk Rptr; Yrbk Stf; High Hon Roll; Hon Roll; Prfct Atten Awd; Pblc Adm.

WEISBERG, AREL Y; Yeshiva Univ High Schl For Boys; Great Neck, NY; (Y); Math Tm; NY St Regnts Schlrshp 86; Bio Hnrs 82-83.

WEISBERG, BRETT; Valley Central HS; Walden, NY; (Y); Capt Aud/Vis; Pres Service Clb; Color Guard; Nwsp Rptr; Pres Frsh Cls; Rep Soph Cls; Var Golf; Var Socr; Hon Roll; Drama Clb; Mrtn G Hlprn Outstndg Schl Svc Awd 84; 1st Pl Engl Excllnc Cmptn 84; Law.

WEISE, MARY; Tri-Vballey Central HS; Claryville, NY; (Y); 2/70; Quiz Bowl; Band; Chorus; Pep Band; School Musical; School Play; Var Socr; High Hon Roll; VP NHS; Sal; NY ST Regnts Schrlshp; Cornell U; Microbio.

WEISENSALE, ANGELA; Fillmore Central HS; Portageville, NY; (S); 4/59; Office Aide; Nwsp Stf; High Hon Roll; NHS; Prfct Atten Awd; Sec Soph Cls; Hon Roll; Olean Bus Inst Schlrshp Awd 86; Olean Bus Inst; Scrtry.

WEISENSEEL, KIM; Baldwin SR HS; Baldwin, NY; (Y); Nassau Cc.

WEISGERBER, DENISE; Preston HS; Bronx, NY; (S); Capt JV Bsktbl; Var Sftbl; Im Vllybl; High Hon Roll; Hon Roll; NHS; NEDT Awd.

WEISGERBER, KEITH R; Mount Saint Michael Acad; Bronx, NY; (Y); 97/298; Im Bsktbl; Im Fld Hcky; Var Ftbl; Im Sftbl; Var Wt Lftg; Hon Roll; Regents Scholar; Manhattan Coll; Elec Engrng.

WEISMAN, CARLA J; Rye Country Day Schl; Scarsdale, NY; (Y); 4/86; AFS; Cmnty Wkr; French Clb; Model UN; Band; Orch; Nwsp Ed-Chief; Nwsp Rptr; Nwsp Stf; VP Capt Cheerleading; All Cnty Band, Orchestra & All ST Bnd 82-86; Natl French Cntst 85; Natl Sci Olympd Top 10 82-85; Yale U; Med.

WEISMAN, NATHAN E; Susan Wagner HS; Staten Island, NY; (Y); 2/460; Pres Key Clb; Office Aide; Quiz Bowl; Science Clb; Variety Show; Nwsp Rptr; Yrbk Rptr; Rep Stu Cncl; Gov Hon Prg Awd; High Hon Roll; Amer Chem Soc Awd 83-84; Brooklyn Coll; Bio.

WEISS, ANN MARIE; Holy Trinity HS; Wantagh, NY; (S); 53/403; Ski Clb; Var Cheerleading; Var Gym; JV Sftbl; Hon Roll; Fairfield; Bus.

WEISS, CHRISTINA; J C Wilson Magnet HS; Rochester, NY; (Y); 1/200; Math Tm; Ski Clb; Band; Chorus; Mrchg Band; Coach Actv; Mgr(s); Swmmng; Tennis; High Hon Roll; Klepper Awd-Outstndng Schlr/Athltc 84; Rensselaer Math & Sci Awd 86; Ec.

WEISS, ELYSSA; North Babylon SR HS; N Babylon, NY; (Y); 72/455; VP French Clb; GAA; Intnl Clb; Chorus; Sftbl; Vllybl; French Hon Soc; Jr NHS; Elem Tchr.

WEISS, MICHELLE; Roosevelt HS; Yonkers, NY; (Y); SADD; High Hon Roll; 90 Clb; Supts Awd.

WEISS, NICOLE; John H Glenn HS; E Northport, NY; (Y); Hosp Aide; Temple Yth Grp; Orch; Rep Frsh Cls; Rep Stu Cncl; Var Tennis; Hon Roll; NHS; Grad Hbrw HS 86; Acctg.

WEISS, WARREN M; West Babylon HS; Babylon, NY; (Y); Am Leg Boys St; CAP; Concert Band; Jazz Band; Mrchg Band; Mitchell & Earhart Awds 84 & 86; Elec Engr.

WEISSBERG, ANDREW; Commack HS North; Commack, NY; (Y); 45/390; Boy Scts; Temple Yth Grp; Y-Teens; Acpl Chr; Chorus; Swing Chorus; Nwsp Rptr; Nwsp Stf; High Hon Roll; Hon Roll, Rgnts Schlrshp 86; ST U NY Binghamton; Comnctns.

WEISSEND, MARK; Victor Central Schl; Victor, NY; (Y); 60/240; AFS; 4-H; Letterman Clb; Quiz Bowl; School Musical; School Play; Sec Jr Cls; Sec Sr Cls; Var JV Ftbl; Var L Golf; MVP JV Vllybl, Golf 85 & 86; Hstry Quz Bowl Rnr-Up 85 & 86; Military Acad; Engrng.

WEISSFELD, RACHEL; Williamsville North HS; Williamsville, NY; (S); DECA; Hosp Aide; Ski Clb; Temple Yth Grp; Yrbk Stf; Off Frsh Cls; Off Soph Cls; Stu Cncl; 1st Pl Rgnl Wnnr Gnrl Mrktg DECA 85; 2nd Pl ST Wnnr NY Fd Mrktng DECA 86; Vtg Dlgt Ntl Career Cnfr; Bus.

WEISSMAN, JILL; Kings Park SR HS; Northport, NY; (Y); DECA; Drama Clb; Radio Clb; Science Clb; Speech Tm; Chorus; School Musical; School Play; Rep Stu Cncl; NHS; Best All Arnd Drama Clb 86.

WEITMAN, NEAL; Commack H S North; E Northport, NY; (Y); 6/300; FBLA; Math Tm; Spanish Clb; High Hon Roll; NHS; Ntl Merit Ltr; Gold Mdl Metric Msrmnt Regnl Sci Olympd 86; Suffolk Cnty Mth Tchrs Exam 86; Engrng.

WEITZ, DANIEL; Riverdale Country Schl; Bronx, NY; (Y); Bsbl; Bsktbl; Socr; Pres SADD 86.

WEITZ, JIM; West Seneca West SR HS; Buffalo, NY; (Y); Boy Scts; German Clb; SADD; JV Wrstlng; Hon Roll; Jr NHS; Suny Buffalo; Arch.

WEITZ, WILLIAM; Bronx H S Of Science; Bronx, NY; (Y); Teachers Aide; Pres Temple Yth Grp; Lit Mag; Frontlashs Stat Liberty Essay Cont 3rd Pl 86; John Peter Zenger Mem Essay Cont Fnlst 85; Biol.

WEKLAR, PATRICK; Bishop Maginn HS; Albany, NY; (Y); 8/84; Art Clb; Pep Clb; School Musical; Variety Show; Nwsp Stf; Yrbk Stf; High Hon Roll; Coll Of St Rose; Art.

WELCH, BRADLEY A; Waterloo Central HS; Waterloo, NY; (Y); 4/168; Varsity Clb; Yrbk Sprt Ed; Pres Soph Cls; VP Sr Cls; Stu Cncl; JV Var Ftbl; Var L Trk; Bausch & Lomb Sci Awd; NHS; Model UN; Gold Key Awd 86; Rgnts Schlrshp 86; Engr.

WELCH, BRENDEN; Walt Whitman HS; Huntington Sta, NY; (Y); 38/580; Golf; Socr; High Hon Roll; Hon Roll; Jr NHS; Spanish NHS; Engrng.

WELCH, CHRIS; Union Endicott HS; Endicott, NY; (S); 28/450; Exploring; Key Clb; Varsity Clb; Bsbl; Ftbl; High Hon Roll; Hon Roll; NHS; Natl Cncl Yth Ldrshp Awd; Natl Phys Ed Awd; Biomed Engr.

WELCH JR, EDDIE; Burgard V HS; Buffalo, NY; (Y); Church Yth Grp; JA; Ftbl; Sevrl Merit Awds; Math Awd 78; Avtn Mech.

WELCH, ERIC; Schroon Lake Central HS; Schroon Lake, NY; (S); 3/25; French Clb; Trs Jr Cls; High Hon Roll; Hon Roll; NHS; Bio Awd 85; Engld & France Trip 85; Med.

WELCH, JANET L; Holland Patent Central HS; Rome, NY; (Y); 1/144; Church Yth Grp; Mathletes; Trs Spanish Clb; Concert Band; Drm & Bgl; Var L Trk; NHS; Ntl Merit Ltr; Chorus; Orch; Outstndg Stu Of Yr 86; Empire ST Schlrshp Of Excllnc 86; Smith Coll Bk Awd 85; Houghton Coll; Chemistry.

WELCH, MARK; Avon Central HS; Avon, NY; (Y); Church Yth Grp; Spanish Clb; Var Capt Bsbl; Var Capt Bsktbl; Var Capt Ftbl; High Hon Roll; Jr NHS; Lion Awd; NHS; Jr Athltc Cup; U Of Rochester; Bus Mgt.

WELCH, MARK; Lausingburgh HS; Troy, NY; (Y); Boy Scts; Ski Clb; JV Var Bsbl; JV Var Bsktbl; Im Mgr Ftbl; Im Mgr Wt Lftg; High Hon Roll; Hon Roll; Jr NHS; Med.

WELCH, SARAH; Honeoye Central Schl; Avon, NY; (S); Band; Jazz Band; Var Bsktbl; JV Var Socr; JV Var Sftbl; French Clb; Mrchg Band; Pep Band; Trs Frsh Cls; Trs Soph Cls; Intl Rltns.

WELCHER, ROBERT L; Sidney Central HS; Sidney, NY; (Y); 19/99; Drama Clb; Pres French Clb; Capt Chrmn Quiz Bowl; School Play; Var Capt Swmmng; High Hon Roll; Hon Roll; NHS; Ntl Merit Ltr; NYS Rgnts Scshlrshp 86; SUNY Potsdam; Math.

WELDON, SHELLEE; Frewsburg Central Schl; Jamestown, NY; (Y); 10/70; Church Yth Grp; Spanish Clb; Chorus; Yrbk Stf; Var Vllybl; Hon Roll; NHS; Sci.

WELKER, ANN M; Jamestown HS; Jamestown, NY; (Y); 23/390; French Clb; German Clb; Hosp Aide; Intnl Clb; Ski Clb; Spanish Clb; Band; Orch; Rep Stu Cncl; Hon Roll; Hugh O Bryan Yth Ldrshp Rep; Georgetown U; Intl Bus.

WELKLEY, SHERI; Victor Central HS; Victor, NY; (Y); 8/206; Art Clb; JV Var Crs Cntry; Im Gym; Socr; Var JV Trk; High Hon Roll; Pres Awd Physcl Ftns Tst 86; Geheseo; Bus.

WELLER, BRIAN P; Wayne Central HS; Walworth, NY; (Y); 7/197; Am Leg Boys St; Concert Band; Jazz Band; Mrchg Band; Pres Jr Cls; Pres Sr Cls; Capt Var Crs Cntry; Capt Var Trk; Hon Roll; NHS; Comp Sci.

WELLER, JENNIFER; Batavia SR HS; Batavia, NY; (Y); 1/205; Church Yth Grp; Concert Band; Mrchg Band; Var Swmmng; High Hon Roll; NHS; Band; Hon Roll; Outstndng Achvt Lang Arts; Engrg.

WELLER, MICHAEL; Lake George HS; Lake George, NY; (Y); 14/90; Aud/Vis; Boy Scts; Band; Chorus; Var Socr; Hon Roll; NHS; Pres Schlr; 3 Yr Army ROTC Schlrshp 86; NY ST Regnts Schlrshp 86; Norwich U; Civl Engrg.

WELLIN, ERIC; Charles O Dickerson HS; Trumansburg, NY; (Y); 1/120; Cmnty Wkr; Science Clb; Bausch & Lomb Sci Awd; High Hon Roll; JETS Awd; NHS; Hghst Avg Earth Sci 84, Bio 85, Chem 86; Rochester Inst Tech; Engrng.

WELLING, JENNIFER; Carmel HS; Carmel, NY; (Y); Am Leg Aux Girls St; Art Clb; 4-H; Pres French Clb; Hosp Aide; Ski Clb; SADD; Band; Concert Band; Mrchg Band; Eng.

WELLOTT, LESLIE; Bronxville HS; Bronxville, NY; (Y); Cmnty Wkr; Rep Stu Cncl; Var Fld Hcky; Var Tennis; High Hon Roll; Hon Roll.

WELLS, ELLEN; Riverhead HS; Riverhead, NY; (Y); 6/190; NHS; Gntcs.

WELLS, GLENN; Johnstown HS; Johnstown, NY; (Y); Var L Bsbl; Var L Bsktbl; Var L Ftbl; Hon Roll; Acctg.

WELLS, JOHN ELLIOT; Oneida HS; Oneida, NY; (S); Am Leg Boys St; Church Yth Grp; Varsity Clb; Band; Bsbl; Ftbl; Golf; Socr; Trk; Wt Lftg.

WELLS, KIMBERLY; Pierson HS; Sag Harbor, NY; (Y); 2/64; Math Tm; School Musical; Nwsp Rptr; Nwsp Stf; Var L Cheerleading; High Hon Roll; NHS; Hghst Aver Awd 84-86; Awd For Excllnc In Engl 84-86; Pre-Law.

WELLS, LINDA; Lansing HS; Lansing, NY; (Y); Spanish Clb; Nwsp Stf; JV Var Cheerleading; JV Var Sftbl; JV Var Vllybl; High Hon Roll; Hon Roll; Im Powder Puff Ftbl; Bus Acad Awds 84-85; Bus Exec.

WELLS, LISA; Linton HS; Schenectady, NY; (Y); 4/322; Intnl Clb; Key Clb; Yrbk Ed-Chief; Rep Frsh Cls; Rep Soph Cls; Rep Jr Cls; Var L Bsktbl; Hon Roll.

WELLS, MARY; Jamesville De Witt HS; Dewitt, NY; (Y); 44/245; Church Yth Grp; German Clb; Hosp Aide; Political Wkr; Bsktbl; Golf; Mgr(s); Socr; Sftbl; High Hon Roll; Francesca Emily Hannett Memrl Schlrshp 86; Boston Coll; Bus.

WELLS, SARAH; Jamesville-Dewitt HS; Dewitt, NY; (Y); Church Yth Grp; Hosp Aide; Key Clb; Political Wkr; SADD; JV Socr; JV Sftbl; Hon Roll; Law.

WELLS, TIMITHY; Avon JR SR HS; Avon, NY; (Y); 23/92; French Clb; Letterman Clb; Varsity Clb; VP Frsh Cls; VP Soph Cls; Bsktbl; Ftbl; Golf; Im Wt Lftg; High Hon Roll; U Of Dayton; Acctng.

WELSCH, MICHAEL E; Notre Dame-Bishop Gibbons HS; Schenectady, NY; (Y); 34/120; Service Clb; Stage Crew; Rep Stu Cncl; Var Crs Cntry; Var Ftbl; Var Trk; Hon Roll; Regents Schlrshp 85-86; Albany Schl Of Phrmcy; MD.

WELSH, LAURA; St Edmund HS; Brooklyn, NY; (Y); 35/208; Dance Clb; Yrbk Stf; Im Cheerleading; JV Sftbl; Hon Roll; Certf Awd Span I,II,III,Physcl Ed,Relgn 84-86; Outstndng Ldrshp Physcl Ed 86; St Francis Coll; Physcl Ed.

WELSH, PATRICIA; Bethpage HS; Gilford, NH; (Y); Camera Clb; Spanish Clb; Teachers Aide; Varsity Clb; Flag Corp; Mrchg Band; Var JV Cheerleading; Var Swmmng; Notre Dame Coll; Lib Arts.

WELSH, SEAN; Rice HS; New York, NY; (S); Boy Scts; Chess Clb; Quiz Bowl; ROTC; Scholastic Bowl; Band; Concert Band; Drm & Bgl; Mrchg Band; Orch; VI Sci Enrchmnt Pgm 84; Recmmnded Early Admssns Pgm 84-85; Bus Adm.

WELSH, TOBIATHA; John C Birdlebough HS; Phoenix, NY; (Y); #18 In Class; Color Guard; Trs Frsh Cls; Var Sftbl; JV Vllybl; High Hon Roll; Hon Roll; NHS.

WELTY, DARREN; Archbishop Molloy HS; Flushing, NY; (Y); 23/383; French Clb; Ed Lit Mag; Im Bsktbl; Im Ftbl; Im Sftbl; High Hon Roll; NHS; Wrtng.

WEMESFELDER, MIKE; Sodus Central HS; Sodus, NY; (Y); Varsity Clb; Var L Bsbl; Var L Bsktbl; Var L Socr; High Hon Roll; NHS; Prfct Atten Awd; Drtmth Bk Clb Awd 86; Bus Mgmnt.

WEMETTE, TODD; Franklin Acad; Malone, NY; (Y); Pep Clb; Ski Clb; Trs Spanish Clb; Varsity Clb; Var L Crs Cntry; Var L Trk; Hon Roll; Clarkson U; Comp Pgmr.

WENBORNE, JAYNE ROBERTA; Corcoran HS; Syracuse, NY; (Y); 2/250; Drama Clb; PAVAS; SADD; Color Guard; Yrbk Stf; Pres Soph Cls; Off Sr Cls; High Hon Roll; NHS; Sal; Cornell Bk Awd 85; Wellesley Coll Bk Wd 85; Vassar Coll.

WENDEL, AMY; Royalton-Hartland Central HS; Lockport, NY; (Y); Spanish Clb; Varsity Clb; VP Stu Cncl; Var Cheerleading; Dnfth Awd; Hon Roll; NHS; VP Frsh Cls; Pres Soph Cls; JV Trk; 4 Yr Hnr Stdnt, Outstndng Art Stdnt, Outstndng Acad Achvt Pres Acad Ftnss Awd 86; U MI; Grphc Dsgn.

WENDLER, JUAN MARTIN; St Agnes HS; New York, NY; (Y); 7/98; NHS; John F Kennedy Chptr Natl Hnr Socy 84; Hunter Coll; Optmtrst.

WENG, CHARLES T; John F Kennedy HS; Bronx, NY; (Y); JA; Scholastic Bowl; Science Clb; Nwsp Stf; Wrstlng; Hon Roll; NHS; NY Acad Hnr Cert For Intrnshp Sci Fair 85; Pre-Med.

WENNBERG, JENNIFER; York Central HS; Leicester, NY; (Y); Color Guard; School Musical; Stage Crew; Im Bsktbl; L Var Crs Cntry; Var Swmmng; L Var Trk; Im JV Vllybl; High Hon Roll; Clsrm Hnrs In Sci 86; Gld Ltr In X-Cntry 84; Acctng.

WENTLAND, LYNN; Hamburg SR HS; Hamburg, NY; (Y); 152/350; Hosp Aide; Library Aide; SADD; Chorus; Stage Crew; Nwsp Stf; Frsh Cls; Stu Cncl; Fld Hcky; Vllybl; Cornell; Vet.

WENTWORTH, CINDY; James A Beneway HS; Ontario, NY; (Y); French Clb; Girl Scts; Chorus; Var Bsktbl; Sftbl; Cit Awd; High Hon Roll; Hon Roll; NHS; Dlgnce Awd Bio 85; Trvl Bus.

WENTWORTH, STEPHEN F; Cicero-North Syracuse HS; N Syracuse, NY; (Y); Am Leg Boys St; Band; Concert Band; Jazz Band; Mrchg Band; Symp Band; JV Socr; JV Trk; NHS; Ntl Merit Ltr; 6 Coll Crdts Spnsh Adelphi U 86; US Serv Acad; Lbrl Arts.

WENZEL, LAURA M; Saint Marys Girls HS; Albertson, NY; (Y); Art Clb; Drama Clb; Pep Clb; PAVAS; Ski Clb; Chorus; School Musical; School Play; Stage Crew; Hon Roll; 2nd Pl C W Post Art Shw Wtr Clr Div 84-85; SUNY Oswego.

WERBOWSKY, GINA; East Hampton HS; Montauk, NY; (Y); VP FBLA; Girl Scts; Sec Trs Service Clb; SADD; Band; Chorus; Concert Band; Mrchg Band; JV Gym; Var Trk; Mst Imprvd Englsh Awd; Sclgy.

WERDANN, LORRAINE; Laguardia HS For Music & The Arts; New York, NY; (Y); 9/552; Cmnty Wkr; VP JA; Office Aide; Service Clb; Band; Concert Band; Orch; School Musical; Symp Band; Stu Cncl; Pride Yankees Princpls Awd 84; NYS Regnts Schlrshp 86; Dave Winfield Found Schlrshp 86; Manhattanville Coll; Music.

WERMUTH, DAVID J; Rye Neck HS; Mamaroneck, NY; (Y); 1/93; Am Leg Boys St; Key Clb; Band; Trs Sr Cls; Trs Stu Cncl; Ftbl; Wrstlng; NHS; Ntl Merit Ltr; Val; NYS Regnts Schlrshp 86.

WERNER, ERIC D; Clinton SR HS; Clinton, NY; (Y); Model UN; Pres SADD; Nwsp Rptr; Yrbk Stf; Var L Socr; Var Trk; Ntl Merit Ltr; Vassar Coll; History.

WERNER, JEFF; Linton HS; Schenctady, NY; (Y); Ski Clb; Var Socr; Var Tennis.

WERT, HANS; Bishop Scully HS; Amsterdam, NY; (S); 5/50; Latin Clb; Math Clb; Pres Soph Cls; JV Ftbl; Var Golf; High Hon Roll; NHS; Med.

WERTH, DOREEN; Niagara Wheatfield HS; North Tonawanda, NY; (Y); 31/293; Am Leg Aux Girls St; Church Yth Grp; German Clb; Chorus; Church Choir; High Hon Roll; Hon Roll; NHS; Prfct Atten Awd; Niagara Cnty Intern 85-86; Niagara U; Accntng.

WERTH-WAXMAN, ERIK; John Dewey HS; Brooklyn, NY; (Y); Cmnty Wkr; JA; Model UN; Office Aide; Political Wkr; Capt Quiz Bowl; Service Clb; Nwsp Bus Mgr; Rep Frsh Cls; Rep Soph Cls; NY Ynkees-Dly News Awd-Acadmc Achvt & Extrcrrclr Actvts June 85; Ivy Leag U; Law.

WERTHEIM, SUZANNE; Commack North HS; Commack, NY; (Y); 26/394; French Clb; Acpl Chr; Chorus; School Musical; Swing Chorus; Nwsp Stf; High Hon Roll; NHS; Ntl Merit Ltr; Pres Schlr; Duke U; Pol Sci.

WERTHMAN, TODD; Ilion Central HS; Ilion, NY; (Y); Boys Clb Am; Boy Scts; Spanish Clb; SADD; Im Bsbl; Capt JV Bsktbl; Capt Im Ftbl; JV Trk; Hon Roll; Amer Aux Poster Cont 84; Herkimer CC; Bus.

WERTS, EDWARD CHARLES; Depew HS; Depew, NY; (Y); 26/272; School Musical; JV Vllybl; JV Wrstlng; Hon Roll; NHS; NYS Regnts Schlrshp 86; Rochester Inst Of Tech; Biotech.

WESBY, RONALD; Bishop Loughlin Memorial HS; Brooklyn, NY; (Y); Boy Scts; Varsity Clb; JV Bsbl; Var Crs Cntry; Var Trk; Cit Awd; Law.

WESCOTT, JOHN; Cato-Meridian Central HS; Baldwinsvl, NY; (Y); Boy Scts; Computer Clb; French Clb; Model UN; Nwsp Phtg; Nwsp Rptr; Nwsp Stf; Var Crs Cntry; Hon Roll; Comp Literacy Cont 3rd Pl 85; Oceanogrphy.

WESELAK, JOANNE; Villa Maria Acad; Buffalo, NY; (Y); Trs Church Yth Grp; Pres French Clb; FBLA; Pep Clb; Yrbk Stf; Rep Stu Cncl; Bowling Proprietors Assn Of WNY Schlrshp 86; Bryant & Stratton Inst; Secrtry.

WESHNER, BRETT R; Hillcrest HS; Fresh Meadows, NY; (Y); Computer Clb; Debate Tm; Radio Clb; Ski Clb; SADD; Temple Yth Grp; Varsity Clb; Nwsp Phtg; Nwsp Rptr; Rep Sr Cls; SUNY Albany Bflo; Pltcl Sci.

WESLEY, MICHAEL D; Hornell HS; Hornell, NY; (Y); 2/1680; AFS; Am Leg Boys St; Dance Clb; 4-H; Latin Clb; Letterman Clb; Pep Clb; Y-Teens; Band; Chorus; Harvarda; Educ.

WESLEY, THOMAS; Aquinas Inst; Rochester, NY; (Y); French Clb; Var Bowling; JV Ftbl; Hon Roll; Frnch 84-86; Amer Studies 86; Engl 85; Frnch.

WESLINE, SHARON; Nazareth Academy; Rochester, NY; (Y); Trs Exploring; Library Aide; Spanish Clb; Speech Tm; SADD; School Play; Yrbk Stf; NHS; Yrbk Phtg; Stu Cncl; Nazareth Acad Schlrshp 82-83; Geneseo; Psych.

WESOLEK, TRACEY; St Marys HS; Depew, NY; (S); Church Yth Grp; Varsity Clb; Yrbk Stf; JV Var Cheerleading; Hon Roll; NHS; ST U NY Buffalo; Arch.

WEST, BRENDA C; Cobleskill Central Schl; Cobleskill, NY; (Y); Church Yth Grp; Cmnty Wkr; Drama Clb; Hosp Aide; Varsity Clb; Chorus; Trs Stu Cncl; Im Bsktbl; Var Vllybl; High Hon Roll; NYS Rgnts Schlrshp 86; NY ST U; Blgcl Tchnlgy.

WEST, BRIAN J; Seton Catholic Central HS; Binghamton, NY; (Y); Am Leg Boys St; Church Yth Grp; Cmnty Wkr; Key Clb; Ski Clb; Soroptimist; Spanish Clb; SADD; Nwsp Rptr; Rep Stu Cncl; Mock Trial Tm; Finance.

WEST, CATHI; Coxsackie-Athens HS; Coxsackie, NY; (Y); 1/100; German Clb; Ski Clb; Trs Jr Cls; JV Cheerleading; Var L Socr; JV Capt Vllybl; High Hon Roll; NHS; Acctng.

WEST, CHARLES; Midlakes HS; Phelps, NY; (Y); 19/155; Chess Clb; French Clb; Bowling; Hon Roll; Acctng.

WEST, CURTIS; Greenville HS; Medusa, NY; (Y); 20/84; Chess Clb; Sec Bsktbl; Var Golf; JV Var Mgr(s); JV Var Score Keeper; Hon Roll; Coll Of St Rose; Chem.

WEST, JUDITH; Frontier SR HS; Hamburg, NY; (Y); 25/460; Cmnty Wkr; Exploring; 4-H; French Clb; Science Clb; SADD; Teachers Aide; Varsity Clb; Drill Tm; Yrbk Rptr; Blsdll H S Schlrshp 86; Hmbrg Twp 86; ST U-Fredonia; Psychlgy.

WEST, KAREN; Frontier Central HS; Hamburg, NY; (Y); French Clb; FBLA; SADD; Teachers Aide; Hon Roll; Bus Mgmt.

WEST, MARK; Lake George HS; Lake George, NY; (Y); Art Clb; Band; Chorus; Jazz Band; Mrchg Band; Variety Show; JV Bsktbl; High Hon Roll; Hon Roll; NHS.

WEST, MICHELLE; New Rochelle HS; New Rochelle, NY; (Y); FBLA; JA; SADD; Pep Band; Off Jr Cls; Sftbl; MD; Bus.

WEST, STACY; John F Kennedy HS; Utica, NY; (Y); Church Yth Grp; FBLA; Key Clb; Spanish Clb; Rep Frsh Cls; Rep Soph Cls; Rep Jr Cls; Crs Cntry; Fld Hcky; Hon Roll; Educ.

WEST, SUSAN E; Le Roy Central Schl; Pavilion, NY; (Y); Am Leg Aux Girls St; Math Tm; Spanish Clb; Band; Chorus; School Musical; Yrbk Ed-Chief; Var L Cheerleading; High Hon Roll; NHS; Cornell U.

WESTAD, HEATHER; Burnt Hills-Ballston Lake HS; Schenectady, NY; (Y); Church Yth Grp; Orch; High Hon Roll; Schltc Silvr Mdl 84; Acadmc Achvt Awds Wnnr 85; Math.

WESTERFIELD, ERIC; Tupper Lake JR SR HS; Tupper Lk, NY; (Y); 5/100; Pep Clb; Frsh Cls; VP Sr Cls; Stu Cncl; JV Bsktbl; Capt Var Ftbl; Capt Var Golf; High Hon Roll; Hon Roll; NHS; Hghst Soc Stds Avg 84-85; Hghst Gr Soc Stds Rgnts Tst 85-86; Law.

WESTFALL, CHRISTOPHER T; Amsterdam HS; Amsterdam, NY; (Y); 14/329; Band; Concert Band; Mrchg Band; Var Golf; Var Trk; Hon Roll; NHS; Pre-Med.

WESTGATE, MARK; Monsignor Farrell HS; Staten Island, NY; (Y); French Clb; Im Bsktbl; Var L Socr; High Hon Roll; Natl Frnch Cntst 2nd Pl 85; Natl Frnch Cntst 86; Accntncy.

WESTHAUSER, LISE; New Hyde Park Memorial HS; New Hyde Park, NY; (Y); 1/246; Teachers Aide; Orch; School Musical; High Hon Roll; Jr NHS; NHS; Ntl Merit Schol; Pres Schlr; Val; All-ST Orch 85; Boston U; Msc.

WESTON, CINDY A; East Islip HS; Islip Terrace, NY; (Y); 66/425; Art Clb; Band; Concert Band; Mrchg Band; Orch; School Musical; Var Bsktbl; Hon Roll; 2nd Pl Suffolk Cnty DWI Poster Contest 85; Artst.

WESTON, KELLY; South Jefferson Central HS; Adams Center, NY; (Y); FFA; Varsity Clb; Band; Color Guard; Concert Band; Var Bowling; Capt Var Sftbl; Var Tennis; Cobleskill ATC; Agronomy.

WESTON, MICHAEL; Alfred G Berner HS; Massapequa Park, NY; (Y); 55/413; Key Clb; Pep Clb; Variety Show; Trs Stu Cncl; Ftbl; Lcrss; Wt Lftg; Hon Roll; U Vermont.

WESTPHAL, KAREN; Frontier Central HS; Hamburg, NY; (Y); 35/498; Church Yth Grp; German Clb; Color Guard; Hon Roll; NHS; Bus.

WESTWIG, ERIK; Corning-Painted Post West HS; Corning, NY; (Y); Thesps; Varsity Clb; School Musical; Stage Crew; Var Crs Cntry; Var Trk; NHS; Scholastic Bowl; Swmmng; High Hon Roll.

WETJEN, ERIC; Smithtown H S West; Smithtown, NY; (Y); VP Church Yth Grp; Exploring; Math Tm; Jazz Band; Symp Band; French Hon Soc; NHS; Ntl Merit Ltr.

WETMORE, JANINE M; Liverpool HS; Liverpool, NY; (Y); 67/816; Exploring; JV Bsktbl; JV Fld Hcky; JV Socr; Hon Roll; Jr NHS; NHS; NYS Rgnts Schlrshp 86; Le Moyne Coll; CPA.

WETMORE, STEVE; Harpursville HS; Nineveh, NY; (Y); 5/87; Nwsp Rptr; Nwsp Sprt Ed; Stu Cncl; Var Bsbl; Var Ftbl; Var Capt Vllybl; Var Capt Wrstlng; High Hon Roll; NHS; Prfct Atten Awd; U S Army Rsrv Natl Schlr/Athlt Awd 86; Var Bsbl Spirit Awd 86; Var Wrstlng Most Spirit Awd 85; Mohawk Valley; Adv.

WETTELAND, MICHELLE; West Babylon HS; W Babylon, NY; (Y); Cmnty Wkr; Leo Clb; Service Clb; SADD; Variety Show; Cheerleading; High Hon Roll; Hon Roll; Long Island Cheerldng Comptn-1st Pl 85.

WETTERAU, JAMES B; Hunter College HS; Flushing, NY; (Y); Church Yth Grp; Math Clb; Pres Service Clb; Band; NCTE Awd; Ntl Merit SF; Eng.

WETTERAU, KRISTINA; Dansville Central HS; Dansville, NY; (Y); 18/165; Pres Church Yth Grp; Drama Clb; Hosp Aide; Band; Stu Cncl; Cheerleading; NHS; YFU Exch Stdnt Ecuador 84; Yorkers JR Hstrcl Scty VP 85-86; Soclgy.

WETTJE, ELIZABETH; Middletown HS; Middletown, NY; (Y); Hon Roll; Bus.

WETTLAUFER, INGE; Skaneateles Central Schl; Skaneateles, NY; (Y); 8/150; Debate Tm; Off Jr Cls; Sec Sr Cls; Tennis; High Hon Roll; NHS; Rgnts Schlrshp 86; Olympcs Mind RFCA 84; Wellesley Coll.

WETZ, ROBERT; Monsignor Farrell HS; Staten Island, NY; (Y); Church Yth Grp; Cmnty Wkr; Church Choir; Im Bsktbl; Im Bowling; Hon Roll; NHS; Polc Dept Holy Name Soc Scholar 83; Mdl Outstndng Svc & Ldrshp 85; Cert Excllnce Engl 84; Rutgers; Phrmctcl Rsrchr.

WEYAND, DOUGLAS; Bishop Timon HS; Buffalo, NY; (S); 16/163; Computer Clb; Spanish Clb; Chorus; School Musical; School Play; Nwsp Stf; Yrbk Sprt Ed; Lit Mag; Trk; NHS; Bio Awd 83; U Of Buffalo; Cmmnctns.

WEYER, JEANETTE; Seton Catholic Central HS; Endwell, NY; (S); 6/162; Art Clb; Cmnty Wkr; French Clb; Girl Scts; Key Clb; High Hon Roll; NHS; Pres Schlr; Grl Scts Gld Awd 86.

WHALEN, COLLEEN; Mexico HS; Mexico, NY; (Y); JV Cheerleading; Var Socr; Var JV Sftbl; Acctg.

WHALEN IV, DANIEL A; Christian Brothers Acad; Albany, NY; (Y); 48/122; Am Leg Boys St; Cmnty Wkr; ROTC; Rep Sr Cls; Var Capt Crs Cntry; Var Capt Trk; Hon Roll; NEDT Awd; Army ROTC Scholar 86; Princpls Awd 86; Supr Cadet Awd 86; Marquette U; Bus Adm.

WHALEN, PAM; Williamsville East HS; Williamsvl, NY; (Y); Yrbk Stf; VP Sftbl; Hon Roll; Advrtsng.

WHALEY, ELIZABETH; Dover JR/Sr HS; Dover Plains, NY; (Y); Drama Clb; Girl Scts; Math Clb; Science Clb; Spanish Clb; SADD; Chorus; Swing Chorus; Socr; Vllybl; Pre-Law.

WHEATON, JAMES; Holland Central HS; S Wales, NY; (Y); 10/141; Boys Clb Am; Letterman Clb; Varsity Clb; Var L Bsbl; Var JV Bsktbl; Hon Roll; Var L Socr; 2nd Tm-All Star Bsktbl 85-86; Acctnt.

WHEATON, MICHELLE L; Odessa-Montour Central Schl; Montour Falls, NY; (Y); 23/86; Am Leg Aux Girls St; Pres Church Yth Grp; Hosp Aide; Library Aide; Sec SADD; Yrbk Ed-Chief; Sec Jr Cls; Sec Sr Cls; Sec Stu Cncl; Swmmng; Douglas P Clark Awd 86; NY ST Regnts Schlrshp 86; Nrsg.

WHEATON, STEVEN J; Jasper Central Schl; Jasper, NY; (Y); Drama Clb; Rptr 4-H; FFA; Varsity Clb; School Play; Socr; Trk; Wrstlng; 4-H Awd; Hon Roll; Wrstlng Trphy Outstndng Awd 85-86; Cstc Fbrsis Walk Mst Pldgs Trphy 85-86; 4h Bf Prod Jdgng Shwn Trph; Suny Alfred Wellsville; Auto Mc.

WHEATON, STUART; Hamburg SR HS; Hamburg, NY; (Y); 60/384; Var Lcrss; High Hon Roll; Hon Roll; Wrk Wth Tmrs 85-86; Bus.

WHEELER, AARON; Dundee Central HS; Himrod, NY; (Y); 4/80; Quiz Bowl; Ski Clb; Nwsp Ed-Chief; Tennis; High Hon Roll; Prfct Atten Awd; Dundee Tchrs Assoc Awd Chem,Comp,Am Studies 83-86.

WHEELER, ANNETTE; John F Kennedy HS; Cheektowaga, NY; (Y); 10/135; Trs Church Yth Grp; GAA; Natl Beta Clb; PAVAS; Yrbk Stf; Capt Var Bsktbl; Capt Var Crs Cntry; Var Socr; High Hon Roll; NHS; Sec.

WHEELER, BARBARA; Potsdam Central HS; Potsdam, NY; (S); 27/121; Band; Capt Cheerleading; Hon Roll; Most Imprvd Chrldr Awd Bsktbl 84; MV Chlrdr Ftbl 85-86; Potsdam; Bus.

WHEELER, EILEEN P; St Joseph Hill Acad; Staten Island, NY; (Y); 17/107; FTA; VP Library Aide; Teachers Aide; Yrbk Stf; JV Var Bsktbl; Var Tennis; Hon Roll; NHS; JV Sftbl; NEDT Letter Of Commendation; Natl Lang Arts Olympiad Ctf; Siena Coll.

WHEELER, ELLEN; Ft Plain Central HS; Ft Plain, NY; (S); 8/54; Am Leg Aux Girls St; Computer Clb; French Clb; SADD; Varsity Clb; Yrbk Sprt Ed; Pres Frsh Cls; VP Rep Stu Cncl; Elks Awd; Pres NHS; Board Of Eductn-Outstndng Undrclswmn Athlt 83-85; Capt-X Cntry, Soccer, Vllybl, Bsktbl & Sftbl 85-86; Pre-Med.

WHEELER, JEFF; Tully HS; Tully, NY; (Y); Varsity Clb; Band; Chorus; Crs Cntry; Trk; Awd Plaque Best Stu Rnnr 84; Broke 800 Meter Record 86; Hgst Scorer Track 86; Mech Engr.

WHEELER, LISA; Fabius-Pompey HS; Jamesville, NY; (Y); 4-H; Nwsp Stf; Yrbk Stf; Rep Stu Cncl; Vllybl; 4-H Awd; High Hon Roll; Hon Roll; NHS; Advrtsng.

WHEELER, LISA; Stissing Mt JR SR HS; Red Hook, NY; (Y); AFS; Yrbk Stf; Sec Frsh Cls; Stat Bsktbl; Capt Fld Hcky; Var Trk; High Hon Roll; Hon Roll.

WHEELER, LORIANN; Fairport HS; Fairport, NY; (Y); Church Yth Grp; Hosp Aide; Red Cross Aide; Yrbk Stf; High Hon Roll; Hon Roll; Monroe CC; Bus Admin.

WHEELER, MARIE A; Chateaugay Central HS; Burke, NY; (Y); 1/50; Chorus; Trs Stu Cncl; Bausch & Lomb Sci Awd; Hon Roll; NHS; Prfct Atten Awd; Val; 1st Pl Sci Cont 85; Rgnts Schlrshp; Clarkson U; Chem Engrng.

WHEELER, MARIE N; Poland Central Schl; Remsen, NY; (Y); 4/72; Am Leg Aux Girls St; Ski Clb; Varsity Clb; Band; VP Jr Cls; Rep Stu Cncl; Var L Socr; Cit Awd; Hon Roll; NHS; Acad Scholar 84-86; Biomed Engrng.

WHEELER, MARY ELIZABETH; Scotia-Glenville HS; Scotia, NY; (Y); Camera Clb; Church Yth Grp; Cmnty Wkr; Spanish Clb; Thesps; Chorus; Church Choir; JV Co-Capt Vllybl; Hon Roll; NHS; Psych.

WHEELER, MONIKA; Wilson Central HS; Wilson, NY; (Y); Chess Clb; Ski Clb; Y-Teens; Yrbk Stf; Powder Puff Ftbl; Var Sftbl; Var Vllybl; High Hon Roll; Hon Roll; All Wester NY Sftbll 85; All Wstrn NY 86; All Leag 86; U FL; Fshn Mrchndzng.

WHEELER, PATRICK; Berlin Central HS; Stephentown, NY; (S); 2/80; Band; VP Frsh Cls; Pres Soph Cls; Pres Jr Cls; JV Bsbl; Var Socr; Var Wrstlng; High Hon Roll; Hon Roll; Army Athltc Schlr Awd; Math.

WHEELER, RICHARD L; Herkimer HS; Herkimer, NY; (Y); 8/113; Boy Scts; Computer Clb; Exploring; Pres Radio Clb; Yrbk Phtg; Var L Trk; Cit Awd; NHS; NYS Empire St Games Alpine Skiing 86; 1st Pl Utica Coll Regnl Sci 86; Engr.

WHEELER, SHIRLEY; Christ The King R HS; Springfield Garde, NY; (Y); 63/455; Dance Clb; FNA; Teachers Aide; Yrbk Stf; Trk; Vllybl; Hon Roll; Nrsng.

WHEELER, STEFANIE L; Ravena-Coeymans-Selkirk HS; S Bethlehem, NY; (Y); 4/180; Pres VP 4-H; SADD; Elks Awd; High Hon Roll; NHS; Ntl Merit Ltr; Sec Soph Cls; Debate Tm; Key Clb; Pep Clb; Hnr Awds; Merit Schlrshp Colgate U 86; Regents Schlrshp 86; Colgate U; Pre Med.

WHEELOCK, CORINA; Poland Central Schl; Cold Brook, NY; (Y); 1/62; Cmnty Wkr; French Clb; Library Aide; Service Clb; SADD; Teachers Aide; Band; Concert Band; Mrchg Band; Orch; Acad Schlrshp 86-87; Ntl Scl Stud Olympiad Awd 85; Outstndg Muscnshp Awd 86; Niagara U; Trvl Agnt.

WHELAN, BRENDAN; Bishop Grimes HS; N Syracuse, NY; (S); 15/146; Boy Scts; Exploring; Math Clb; Model UN; Science Clb; Var Ftbl; Var Golf; Hon Roll; Ntl Merit Ltr; Engrng.

WHELAN, MICHAEL; Cardinal Spellman HS; Bronx, NY; (Y); German Clb; Hon Roll; Fordham U.

WHIPPLE, MICHELE; Canastota HS; Canastota, NY; (Y); Camera Clb; Dance Clb; Hosp Aide; Ski Clb; Yrbk Phtg; Cheerleading; Trk; Hon Roll; Money Regnl Schlstc Art Awd 86; ST U NY; Agricultural.

WHIPPLE, SHERI; Naples Central HS; Naples, NY; (Y); Aud/Vis; SADD; Chorus; Church Choir; Color Guard; Mrchg Band; Cheerleading; Socr; Drug & Alchl Awrnss 84-86; Stu Of Mnth 85-86; Better Your Own Bdy 85-86; Soc Wrk.

WHIPPLE, SUSAN; Averill Park HS; Averill Park, NY; (Y); Drama Clb; Pres Key Clb; Yrbk Ed-Chief; Yrbk Phtg; Trs Frsh Cls; Trs Soph Cls; Trs Jr Cls; Trs Sr Cls; God Cntry Awd; Hon Roll; Silver Ldrshp Awd; Rotary Exc Stu Spain; Pub Rel.

WHIPPLE, WENDY M; Dryden HS; Harford, NY; (Y); Drama Clb; School Play; Trs Jr Cls; Trs Sr Cls; Rep Stu Cncl; L Bsktbl; L Sftbl; L Swmmng; NHS; Otstndng SR Fml Athlt 86; DFA Awd 86; Rgnts Schlrshp 86; Rgnts Schlrshp 86; Lock Haven U Of PA; Athlt Trnr.

WHISPELL, TRACEY R; Trott Vocational & Technical HS; Niagara Falls, NY; (Y); 12/147; Office Aide; Sec Jr Cls; Sec Sr Cls; Rep Stu Cncl; Stat Ftbl; JV Trk; Hon Roll; Police Athltc Lg Outstndg Stu 86; Ngara Flls Bd Of Rltrs Outstndg Stu 85; Sntr Dlys Intrnshp Pgm 86; Niagara Cnty CC; Comp Sci.

WHITAKER, CARLA; Walton Central Schl; Walton, NY; (Y); #13 In Class; Pres Key Clb; Varsity Clb; JV Bsktbl; Var Fld Hcky; Var Sftbl; Var Vllybl; Cit Awd; High Hon Roll; NHS; Voice Dem Awd; CPA.

WHITAKER, KEN; Charles O Dickerson HS; Trumansburg, NY; (Y); Pres Church Yth Grp; Exploring; Church Choir; Hon Roll; Tompkins Crtlnd Coll; Arch.

WHITAKER, KEVIN J; Mc Quaid Jesuit HS; Rochester, NY; (Y); Cmnty Wkr; Tennis; Vllybl; Hon Roll; NHS; Ntl Merit Schol; Var Tnns 4 Yrs; 2nd Tm Natl Platform Tnns 85; All Co Vllybl 1st Tm 86; Union Coll NY.

WHITAKER, MICHELLE; Mont Pleasant HS; Schenectady, NY; (Y); Trs German Clb; Pep Clb; Yrbk Phtg; Yrbk Stf; Tennis; Hon Roll; NHS; Germn Hon Soc 85 & 86; Cmmrcl Art.

WHITAKER, SCOTT; Brighton HS; Rochester, NY; (Y); 1/325; Letterman Clb; Var Capt Bsbl; JV Var Ftbl; Church Yth Grp; Radio Clb; Ski Clb; All-Legue Ftbl Qb & Bsbl Ptchr 85-86; Princeton 1; Law.

WHITBECK, CARL; Lafayette HS; Buffalo, NY; (Y); Pres Computer Clb; Hon Roll; Harbison-Walker Awd 86; Camp Enterprise Bus Camp Rotary Clb Buffalo 86; Comp Sci.

WHITBURN, JENNIFER T; Laguardia HS Of Music & Arts; New York, NY; (Y); 132/437; Camera Clb; JA; Office Aide; Teachers Aide; Yrbk Phtg; Stu Cncl; Hon Roll; Msc & Art HS Art Exhbt Awd 83 & 84; Crnl U.

WHITCAVITCH, JULIA E; Johnstown HS; Johnstown, NY; (Y); Intnl Clb; Political Wkr; Rep Stu Cncl; JV Bsktbl; Var L Crs Cntry; Var L Fld Hcky; Var Powder Puff Ftbl; JV Trk; High Hon Roll; Hon Roll; St Lawrence U; Pol Sci.

WHITE, ADRIANE; New Rochelle HS; New Rochelle, NY; (Y); Sec Church Yth Grp; Debate Tm; Political Wkr; Teachers Aide; Variety Show; Prfct Atten Awd; Girl Scts; Chorus; Church Choir; Im Bsktbl; Guidance Cnslr Hlpr Awd 85; Negro Hstry Mnth Essy Cont Awd 86; Natl JR Leag 1st Pl Bwlng 86; Bus Admin.

WHITE, AMY L; Salmon River Central HS; Hogansburg, NY; (Y); Church Yth Grp; Cmnty Wkr; Ski Clb; Yrbk Stf; Rep Frsh Cls; Rep Soph Cls; Stu Cncl; JV Cheerleading; Var Crs Cntry; Im Lcrss; Syracuse U; Biology.

WHITE, ANNE B; Professional Childrens Schl; Shrub Oak, NY; (Y); Stu Cncl; Hon Roll; Jr NHS; Hnrb Mntn Natl Arts Recgntn & Tlnt Srch 85-86; Soloist-Dance Theatre In Westchester 84-86; Schl Of American Ballet NY.

WHITE, ANNIE; Belmont Central HS; Belmont, NY; (Y); Spanish Clb; Color Guard; Drill Tm; Nwsp Stf; Var Socr; Var Tennis; Var Vllybl; Psych.

WHITE, APRIL A; Fishers Island Union Free HS; Fishers Island, NY; (Y); 1/3; Drama Clb; Band; Chorus; School Musical; School Play; Stage Crew; Yrbk Phtg; Yrbk Rptr; Yrbk Stf; Sec Frsh Cls; NY ST Rgnts Schlrshp 86; Syracuse U.

WHITE, AUDREY; Buffalo Traditional HS; Buffalo, NY; (S); 19/120; Cmnty Wkr; Political Wkr; Band; Drill Tm; Var Capt Coach Actv; Var Capt Crs Cntry; Capt Var Trk; Hon Roll; Prfct Atten Awd; Syracuse U; Acctg.

WHITE, BERTRAND; Murry Bergtraum HS; Brooklyn, NY; (Y); JA; Band; Baruch; Mktg.

WHITE, BRIAN E; Liverpool HS; Liverpool, NY; (Y); 41/816; JCL; School Musical; Stage Crew; Stu Cncl; Im Bsbl; Im Lcrss; High Hon Roll; Jr NHS; NHS; Ntl Merit Ltr; NYS Regents Schlrshp Wnnr 85-8l; Engrng.

WHITE, CHERYLANN; Greenville Central HS; Greenville, NY; (Y); 19/77; Girl Scts; Pep Clb; Spanish Clb; Varsity Clb; Band; Color Guard; Concert Band; Jazz Band; Mrchg Band; Orch; Paul Smith; Trvl.

WHITE, CHRISTINE; Commack HS North; Commack, NY; (Y); 23/390; Exploring; Spanish Clb; SADD; Ed Nwsp Stf; Off Frsh Cls; Off Soph Cls; Off Jr Cls; Off Sr Cls; Var Badmtn; Var Tennis; Rgnts Schlrshp 86; Le Moyne Coll Acad Schlrshp 86; Le Moyne Coll; Pre-Med.

WHITE, CYNTHIA; Hutchinson Central Tech HS; Buffalo, NY; (Y); Church Yth Grp; Cmnty Wkr; Computer Clb; French Clb; Office Aide; Red Cross Aide; Nwsp Rptr; Nwsp Stf; Hon Roll; Outstndng Yth-N Buffalo YES Pgm 85; Sftbl Chmps-HNPYB 83; Beta Sigma Phi Girls Hnr Srrty 84-87; RIT; Comp Tech.

WHITE, DANIEL T; Wheatland-Chili HS; Scottsville, NY; (Y); Am Leg Boys St; VP 4-H; Band; Variety Show; Var Bsbl; Var Bsktbl; Var Socr; Hon Roll; Genesco ST; Bus.

WHITE, DAVID; Valley Central HS; Montgomery, NY; (Y); 9/260; Boy Scts; Natl Beta Clb; Cit Awd; Hon Roll; NHS; Prfct Atten Awd; Pres Schlr; Spanish NHS; Eagle Sct 86; Rgnts Schlrp 86; Knghts Of Col Awd; Rochester Inst Tech; Chem.

WHITE, DEANNA J; Cortland JR SR HS; Cortland, NY; (Y); 85/194; Aud/Vis; Drama Clb; Quiz Bowl; Radio Clb; Ski Clb; Thesps; Swing Chorus; Lit Mag; NHS; Ntl Merit Schol; ST U Coll-Cortland; Comm.

WHITE, DENISE R; Connetquot HS; Ronkonkoma, NY; (Y); Church Yth Grp; Computer Clb; Chorus; Church Choir; Rep Frsh Cls; Rep Stu Cncl; Mgr Sftbl; High Hon Roll; Hon Roll; Pres Scholar Mt St Marys Coll 86; Hnrs Pgm Southampton Post Scholar 86; Southampton Post; Pre-Law.

WHITE, DONNA; Holy Angels Acad; North Tonawanda, NY; (Y); 15/36; Pres Sec Church Yth Grp; Math Clb; Spanish Clb; Chorus; Church Choir; Nwsp Rptr; Nwsp Stf; Ed Lit Mag; Trs Frsh Cls; Sec Jr Cls; All Am Awd 85; Church Yth Of Yr 85; Yng Mssnry Of Yr 85; Spelman College; Pre Law.

WHITE, ED; Waterloo SR HS; Waterloo, NY; (Y); Am Leg Boys St; Cmnty Wkr; Key Clb; Band; Concert Band; Yrbk Bus Mgr; Var Golf; Var Wrstlng; Hon Roll; Debate Tm; Elmira Clg Key Awd 86; Pre-Med.

WHITE, FELICIA; Honeoye Central; Honeoye, NY; (S); Color Guard; VP Frsh Cls; VP Soph Cls; VP Jr Cls; VP Stu Cncl; JV Capt Bsktbl; Var Cheerleading; Var Capt Socr; JV Capt Sftbl; Flag Corp; Natl Hnr Soc 85; Psych.

WHITE, FRANK; Schoharie Central HS; Esperance, NY; (Y); Am Leg Boys St; Boy Scts; French Clb; Varsity Clb; School Musical; Nwsp Bus Mgr; Nwsp Ed-Chief; Var Crs Cntry; Var Wrstlng; Rep Frsh Cls; Eagle Scout Awd 85; Cmmnctns.

WHITE, HEATHER K; Wheatland-Chili HS; Scottsville, NY; (Y); 1/74; Am Leg Aux Girls St; Model UN; SADD; Jazz Band; School Musical; Pres Sr Cls; VP Stu Cncl; Var L Socr; NHS; Val; Awd Intrst Prsng Law 86; Vassar Coll; Psych.

WHITE, JOANNE; Onondaga Central HS; Nedrow, NY; (Y); Art Clb; Camera Clb; Math Clb; Ski Clb; Diving; Socr; Sftbl; Swmmng; Vllybl; Art Clb; Hgh Hnrs 84-85; Hnrs 86; NYS Coll; Sci.

WHITE, JUDITH; Springfield Gardens HS; Queens, NY; (Y); Church Yth Grp; Office Aide; SADD; Teachers Aide; Variety Show; Rptr Frsh Cls; Rptr Soph Cls; Capt Jr Cls; Vllybl; Rptr Stu Cncl; Psych.

WHITE, JULIE A; Brockport HS; Brockport, NY; (Y); 15/335; French Clb; Stage Crew; Yrbk Stf; High Hon Roll; NYS Regnts Schlrshp 86.

WHITE, KATY; Maple Hill HS; Castleton, NY; (S); 18/90; Drama Clb; Hosp Aide; Band; Concert Band; Mrchg Band; School Musical; School Play; Fld Hcky; Hon Roll; Music.

WHITE, KIMBERLY A; Cohocton Central Schl; Cohocton, NY; (Y); 1/27; French Clb; Band; Yrbk Stf; Trs Church Yth Grp; Tennis; Bausch & Lomb Sci Awd; DAR Awd; Sec NHS; Val; Bausch & Lomb Schlrshp U Of Rochester 86; U Of Rochester; Bio.

WHITE, LAURA A; Fairport HS; Fairport, NY; (Y); Church Yth Grp; Drama Clb; Ski Clb; Church Choir; School Musical; Yrbk Bus Mgr; Rep Stu Cncl; JV Var Tennis; Hon Roll; NHS; NY ST Rgnts Schlrshp 86; Wittenberg U; Polit Sci.

WHITE, LYNETTE; Addison Central HS; Cameron, NY; (Y); Sec Frsh Cls; Trs Jr Cls; High Hon Roll; NHS; Law.

WHITE, LYNN A; Haverling Central Schl; Bath, NY; (S); 14/138; Exploring; French Clb; JCL; Latin Clb; Math Clb; Ski Clb; Yrbk Stf; Rep Stu Cncl; Var Socr; High Hon Roll; Pharmcst.

WHITE, MARK; Knox Memorial Central HS; Russell, NY; (S); 5/30; Ski Clb; Varsity Clb; Band; Mrchg Band; School Play; Yrbk Sprt Ed; Pres Sr Cls; Capt Bsktbl; High Hon Roll; NHS; Area All-ST Orch 84-885; Marietta Coll; Petro Engr.

WHITE, MATTHEW; Pulaski JR SR HS; Pulaski, NY; (S); 5/150; Computer Clb; French Clb; Math Clb; Swmmng; Wt Lftg; Hon Roll; Schl Recog Awd 82; Stu Of Mnth 82; Oral Roberts U; Pedtrcn.

WHITE, MICHELLE IRENE; Rensselaer County Vo-Tec; Rensselaer, NY; (S); 2/14; Church Yth Grp; Spanish Clb; Church Choir; Nwsp Stf; Bsbl; Score Keeper; Gregg Typng Awd 85; Bay Path CC; Rtl Mgmt.

WHITE, OLIVIA; Bishop Loughlin M HS; Brooklyn, NY; (Y); 33/233; Pres Intnl Clb; Teachers Aide; Variety Show; Nwsp Rptr; Rep Frsh Cls; Rep Soph Cls; VP Sr Cls; Stu Cncl; High Hon Roll; NHS; Dist Attrny Elizabeth Holtzman Citatn Hnr 86; NHS Awd 83-86; Stu Cncl Awd 86; SUNY Buffalo; Frgn Lang.

WHITE, PATRICIA; Fairport HS; Fairport, NY; (Y); Church Yth Grp; Drama Clb; Intnl Clb; Key Clb; Model UN; Varsity Clb; Orch; School Play; Hon Roll; French Clb; Bst Italian Stu 87; Intl Bus.

WHITE, PENNY; Knox Memorial Central HS; Hermon, NY; (S); 2/28; VP French Clb; Yrbk Stf; Pres Frsh Cls; Trs Soph Cls; Trs Jr Cls; Cheerleading; High Hon Roll; Hon Roll.

WHITE, REGINALD; Brooklyn Tech HS; Brooklyn, NY; (Y); Chess Clb; Math Tm; Science Clb; Band; School Play; Trk; Wt Lftg; Ntl Merit Ltr; Rgnts Schlrshp; Cert Merit; Rensselaer Polytech Inst; Engr.

WHITE, RICK; East Hampton HS; Montauk, NY; (Y); 17/143; Am Leg Boys St; Church Yth Grp; School Play; Pres Stu Cncl; Var Bsbl; Capt Ftbl; Wt Lftg; Cit Awd; Hon Roll; Lion Awd; Wake Forest U; Bus.

WHITE, ROBERT; Sewanhaka HS; Bellerose, NY; (S); 76/345; Chess Clb; DECA; Nwsp Rptr; Nwsp Stf; 3rd Pl Overall NY ST Advertising & Display Svcs 86; 3rd Pl Indiv NY ST Sales Event 86; Nassau CC; Business.

WHITE, RONALD; Kenmore East SR HS; Tonawanda, NY; (Y); 66/350; Hosp Aide; Varsity Clb; Var JV Bsbl; NHS; U Of Buffalo; Phrmcy.

WHITE, SCOTT; Balton Central Schl; Bolton Landing, NY; (Y); 3/20; SADD; Yrbk Stf; Trs Frsh Cls; Trs Jr Cls; Rep Stu Cncl; Var L Bsbl; Var Capt Bsktbl; Im Coach Actv; Var L Socr; Hon Roll; Env Sci.

WHITE, SEAN; Mercy HS; Ridge, NY; (Y); Varsity Clb; Yrbk Stf; Capt L Bsbl; Capt L Bsktbl; Capt L Ftbl; Hon Roll; NHS; Amer Lgn Schl Awd Ldrshp & Srv 83; 110 Pct Awd Bsktbll 85; MVP Ftbll Offns 84.

WHITE, SHERRY L; Massena Central HS; Norfolk, NY; (Y); 55/246; Teachers Aide; Rep Frsh Cls; Rep Soph Cls; Rep Jr Cls; Rep Sr Cls; JV Crs Cntry; High Hon Roll; Hon Roll; Edctnl Secs Awd 86; Coop Work Stdy Pgm 84-86; Ltr Awd 86; Canton Ag & Tech Coll; Bus Admn.

WHITE, STEPHEN; Xavier HS; Brooklyn, NY; (Y); 22/240; ROTC; Nwsp Rptr; Off Frsh Cls; Off Soph Cls; Off Jr Cls; Off Sr Cls; Stu Cncl; Hon Roll; Ntl Merit Ltr.

WHITE, SUE; Webster HS; Webster, NY; (Y); 35/500; Pres Cmnty Wkr; High Hon Roll; Hon Roll; Jr NHS; Prfct Atten Awd; John A Regan Schlrshp 86; A R C Schlrshp 86; Spnsh Merit Awd 83; SUNY At Geneseo; Spec Ed.

WHITE, VALERIE; The Ursuline Schl; Eastchester, NY; (Y); Varsity Clb; JV Var Bsktbl; Hon Roll; Math Awd 85-86.

WHITE, WAYNE; Knox Memorial HS; Hermon, NY; (S); 3/28; Varsity Clb; School Play; Bsktbl; Socr; Vllybl.

WHITE, WENDY; West Genesee SR HS; Camillus, NY; (Y); 48/485; Camera Clb; Pep Clb; SADD; Nwsp Rptr; Nwsp Stf; Off Frsh Cls; Off Soph Cls; Off Jr Cls; Off Sr Cls; Stu Cncl; Crouse Irving Mem; Nrsng.

WHITECAVAGE, DIANE; Dominican Commercial HS; Woodhaven, NY; (S); Teachers Aide; Pres Stu Cncl; Hon Roll; Exec Bd Stdnt Cncl 86-87; Law.

WHITEHALL, RICHARD; Prospect Heights HS; Brooklyn, NY; (S); Debate Tm; FBLA; Rptr Nwsp Rptr; Pres Jr Cls; High Hon Roll; Hon Roll; NHS; Prfct Atten Awd; Engl Dept Stu Mnth 85; Nov Schlr 85; Acadmc Achvmnt Hnr Roll 86; Polytechnic Inst NY; Elec Engr.

WHITEHEAD, DANIEL; Bishop Cunningham HS; Oswego, NY; (Y); Church Yth Grp; French Clb; Variety Show; Var Bsbl; Var Bsktbl; Var Socr; Hon Roll; MVP Sccr Prsntd By US Army Ntl Sccr Cochs Assn 86; Bsbl 1st Tm Outfld 85 Ptchr 86; Bsktbl 85; Nazareth; Law.

WHITEMAN, WENDY E; Chatham HS; Chatham, NY; (Y); 2/129; Library Aide; Math Tm; SADD; Chorus; School Musical; Socr; Bausch & Lomb Sci Awd; Elks Awd; NHS; Sal; Clarkson U; Engrng.

WHITENS, TIMOTHY; Bishop Cunningham HS; Fulton, NY; (S); 5/31; JV Bsktbl; NHS.

WHITESIDE, CLAXTON J; Laquazdia HS Music And The Arts; Queens, NY; (Y); 156/437; Art Clb; PAVAS; Teachers Aide; Yrbk Stf; Prfct Atten Awd; FIT; Advrtsng.

WHITFIELD, ELIZABETH; Oyster Bay HS; Oyster Bay, NY; (Y); Art Clb; Spanish Clb; JV Bsktbl; Hon Roll; C W Post Cazenovia; Erly Chldhd.

WHITFORD, MATTHEW; Ticonderoga HS; Ticonderoga, NY; (Y); 2/100; JV Var Ftbl; Var Trk; Hon Roll; CORP Law.

WHITING, MELANIE; Olean HS; Olean, NY; (Y); 82/214; AFS; Ski Clb; Sec Varsity Clb; Chorus; Color Guard; School Musical; Yrbk Ed-Chief; Yrbk Stf; Cheerleading; Hon Roll; S W MO ST; Tourism.

WHITING, NOELLE; Pelham Memorial HS; Pelham Manor, NY; (Y); AFS; Chess Clb; Girl Scts; SADD; Chorus; School Musical; Stage Crew; Yrbk Stf; Rep Frsh Cls; Vet.

WHITLOW, ANTHONY; Wheatland Chili Central Schl; Rochester, NY; (Y); Chorus; Var L Bsktbl; Im Ftbl; Var L Socr; Hon Roll; Prfct Atten Awd; Hon Pass For 3rd & 4th Qtr 85-86; SUNY Geneseo; Accounting.

WHITMAN, BONNIE; Northville Central HS; Northville, NY; (Y); 6/54; 4-H; Hosp Aide; Library Aide; SADD; School Play; Yrbk Stf; Stu Cncl; Pres Schlr; Plattsbrgh Coll Found Schlrshp 86-87; Cnrd H & Anna Belle Schlrshp 86-87; BUNY Plattsburgh.

WHITMAN, SANDRA; Moriah Central HS; Mineville, NY; (Y); 14/88; French Clb; GAA; Ski Clb; Stu Cncl; Cheerleading; Hon Roll; SUNY Plattsburgh; Bus Mgmt.

WHITNEY, AMY; Hamburg SR HS; Hamburg, NY; (Y); 26/374; Church Yth Grp; German Clb; SADD; Band; Chorus; Church Choir; Concert Band; Lit Mag; High Hon Roll; NHS; Mst Outstndng Engl Stu Grds 7 Thru 9 84; Villa Maria Coll; Photogrphr.

WHITNEY, DEBORAH; Granville HS; Fort Edward, NY; (Y); 13/125; AFS; French Clb; Girl Scts; SADD; Chorus; Co-Capt Cheerleading; Fld Hcky; Score Keeper; High Hon Roll; Hon Roll; Chrng Schlrshp 84; Prfct Attndnc Awd 85; Mrt Hon Rl 83 & 84; U Buffalo; Bus.

WHITNEY, LYNN ANN; Valley Central HS; Wallkill, NY; (Y); Service Clb; Off Soph Cls; Hon Roll; SGA Srv Awd 86; Bus Mngmnt.

WHITNEY, NANCY; Union Endicott HS; Endwell, NY; (Y); Cmnty Wkr; Exploring; Hosp Aide; Ski Clb; SADD; Concert Band; Jazz Band; Yrbk Stf; Stat Sftbl; Hon Roll; SUNY Cortland; Hlth Sci.

WHITNEY, SARAH; Fairport HS; Fairport, NY; (Y); Church Yth Grp; Ski Clb; Spanish Clb; SADD; Band; Concert Band; Mrchg Band; Yrbk Ed-Chief; Yrbk Stf; JV Capt Diving; Diving Awd 84-85.

WHITNEY, WILLIAM P; Horseheads HS; Big Flats, NY; (S); 25/380; Boy Scts; Band; Jazz Band; Mrchg Band; Nwsp Stf; Yrbk Stf; Im Vllybl; NHS; Ntl Merit Ltr; Med.

WHITSON, LINDA F; Wayland Central HS; Wayland, NY; (Y); Varsity Clb; Chorus; JV Var Bsktbl; JV Mgr(s); JV Var Score Keeper; Var Capt Socr; JV Var Timer; JV Var Vllybl; FHA; FNA; Nice Kid Awd 85; Soccr All Star Tm 86; High Hnrs Charles G Maye Occup Ctr 86; Delhi; RN.

WHITTAKER, LAURA; Charlotte Valley C S; E Meredith, NY; (S); 3/40; GAA; Yrbk Stf.

WHITTLETON, PAM; L A Webber HS; Lyndonville, NY; (Y); VP Trs Church Yth Grp; Band; Chorus; Church Choir; Var Capt Bsktbl; Var JV Socr; Hon Roll; Lion Awd; Varsity Clb; Mrchg Band; Bub Mealand Mem Awd 86; Potential Tchr Awd 86; Roberts Wesleyan Coll; Acctng.

WHITTON, MELISSA; Potsdam HS; West Stockholm, NY; (Y); 32/144; French Clb; Varsity Clb; Yrbk Stf; Var JV Cheerleading; JV Socr; Var Sftbl; JV Vllybl; Hon Roll; Mst Imprvd Bsktbl Chrldr Trophy 84-85; Mst Valuable Hocky Chrldr Trophy 85-86; Cobleskill; Bus Adm.

WHITTON, MICHAEL; Sauquoit Valley Central Schl; Sauquoit, NY; (Y); Am Leg Boys St; Boys Clb Am; Exploring; Intnl Clb; Bowling; Golf; Hon Roll; Jr NHS; NHS; Rotary Awd; Prncpls Lst Pin Awd 85-86; Mohawk Vly CC; Engrng.

WHOLIHAN, SUSAN; St Peters HS For Girls; Staten Island, NY; (Y); 10/74; Trs FNA; Library Aide; Chorus; School Play; Sec Sr Cls; Hon Roll; Pres NHS; Generosa Pope Awd 86; St Johns U; Bus.

WHYTE, SHELLEY; Midlakes HS; Clifton Spgs, NY; (Y); VP Frsh Cls; VP Soph Cls; VP Jr Cls; JV Sftbl; JV Vllybl; Hon Roll; Arch Design.

WIANT, DAVID; Grand Island SR HS; Grand Isl, NY; (Y); JA; Varsity Clb; Variety Show; JV Bsktbl; Var JV Ftbl; Var Capt Ice Hcky; Var Lcrss; Bus Adm.

WICELINSKI, VINCENT; St Francis Prep; Flushing, NY; (Y); 52/653; Office Aide; SADD; Im Socr; Im Sftbl; Im Vllybl; Pres NHS; Math Clb; Im Bsktbl; Im Ftbl; Pres Schlr; NY U Racoosn Merit Schlrshp 86; Franciscan Sprt Awd 86; Amer Lgn Schl Awd 86; NY U; Bus.

WICHERN, CARYN; Northport HS; E Northport, NY; (Y); Office Aide; Radio Clb; Chorus; Mrchg Band; Stage Crew; Nwsp Stf; Yrbk Rptr; Lit Mag; Stat Bsktbl; Fld Hcky; Vrsty Fld Hcky Ltr 86.

WICHMAN, DARCY; Irondequoit HS; Rochester, NY; (Y); Church Yth Grp; Hosp Aide; Latin Clb; Ski Clb; Chorus; Church Choir; School Musical; Yrbk Phtg; Yrbk Stf; Pres Frsh Cls; Elem Tchr.

WICK, SCOTT; Rome Catholic HS; Rome, NY; (Y); Cmnty Wkr; School Musical; Yrbk Rptr; JV Var Bsktbl; JV Var Golf; Socr; DAR Awd; High Hon Roll; NHS; Bio Chem.

WICKENS, MARSHA; Vernon Verona Sherrill HS; Sherrill, NY; (Y); Church Yth Grp; 4-H; Girl Scts; SADD; Chorus; Church Choir; Orch; Cheerleading; 4-H Awd; Hon Roll.

WICKERT, CARRIE; Cicero-North Syracuse HS; Clay, NY; (S); 30/623; Church Yth Grp; Teachers Aide; Tchr.

WICKS, KEVIN GUY; Patchogue-Medford HS; Patchogue, NY; (S); Church Yth Grp; Band; Concert Band; Mrchg Band; Orch; Grumman Data Inst; Comp Oper.

WIDA, MICHELE; Elmira Southside HS; Pine City, NY; (Y); 24/335; French Clb; Pep Clb; Off Varsity Clb; Band; Chorus; Yrbk Stf; Rep Sr Cls; Sftbl; Capt Vllybl; Hon Roll; SUNY; Acctng.

WIDELSKI, MARY; Chateaugay Central HS; Chateaugay, NY; (Y); 4-H; Chorus; Church Choir; VP Jr Cls; VP Sr Cls; 4-H Awd; High Hon Roll; Hon Roll; NHS; Franklin Cnty Dairy Prncss Altrnt 86-87; X-Ray Tech.

WIDEN, CURTIS; Falconer Central HS; Jamestown, NY; (Y); 14/125; Boy Scts; Ski Clb; Band; Jazz Band; Yrbk Phtg; Tennis; God Cntry Awd; Hon Roll; NHS; Quiz Bowl; Boy Scts Eagle Awd 86; Jamestown CC; Engrng.

WIDMER, JOHN J; Naples Central Schl; Naples, NY; (Y); Am Leg Boys St; Stage Crew; Yrbk Stf; Trs Frsh Cls; Sec Jr Cls; Rep Sr Cls; Var Stat Bsktbl; JV Var Socr; JV Var Tennis; Hon Roll; Engrng.

WIDMER, RAE A; Arkport Central Schl; Arkport, NY; (Y); 7/56; Hosp Aide; Red Cross Aide; School Play; Yrbk Ed-Chief; Sec Yrbk Stf; Im Bowling; Var Timer; Stat Trk; Rgnts Schlrshp 86; Arkprt Acad Soc 85-86; SUNY; Psychology.

WIDOMSKI, KATHLEEN; West Seneca West SR HS; W Seneca, NY; (Y); Pres Debate Tm; Q&S; SADD; Orch; Nwsp Stf; Hon Roll; JC Awd; Jr NHS; NHS; Prfct Atten Awd; Assist Princpls Awd Svc Achvt Schlrshp 84; Outstndng Musician Yr 84; 3rd Pl PA Ad Desgn Comptn 84.

WIDRICK, TIMOTHY W; Beaver River Central Schl; Croghen, NY; (Y); 11/86; Am Leg Boys St; FFA; Varsity Clb; JV Bsbl; Score Keeper; Var L Wrstlng; Bausch & Lomb Sci Awd; High Hon Roll; Hon Roll; NHS; Rgnts Schlrshp; Canton ATC; Engr Sci.

WIECK, JOHN; Walt Whitman HS; Huntington Stat, NY; (Y); 8/477; Concert Band; Drm Mjr(t); Jazz Band; Mrchg Band; Pep Band; School Musical; Symp Band; Ger Spkg Awd 84; Bus.

WIECZOREK, GARY; Hutch Tech; Buffalo, NY; (Y); Chess Clb; Computer Clb; Teachers Aide; Stage Crew; Stu Cncl; Hon Roll; Prfct Atten Awd; Phrmcy.

WIECZOREK, MATT; John C Birdlebough HS; Phoenix, NY; (Y); SADD; Band; Concert Band; Jazz Band; Mrchg Band; School Musical; Yrbk Stf; JV Stat Bsktbl; JV Var Ftbl; Hon Roll; All-Cnty Cncrt Bnd 84-86; All-Cnty Jazz Bnd 86; JR All-Amer Hall Of Fame Bnd Hnrs 85-86; Physcl.

WIEDER, MARLA; John A Coleman HS; Kingston, NY; (S); Key Clb; Ski Clb; Stage Crew; Rep Frsh Cls; Bsktbl; Fld Hcky; Capt Trk; High Hon Roll; Hon Roll; NHS; Law.

WIEDRICH, HEATHER; Fayetteville-Manlius HS; Manlius, NY; (Y); JCL; Chorus; Nwsp Rptr; Yrbk Stf; Capt Sftbl; Capt L Trk; High Hon Roll; NHS; Elem Ed.

WIEGAND, ERICA; Niagara Wheatfield HS; Niagara Falls, NY; (Y); Am Leg Aux Girls St; Church Yth Grp; Pep Clb; Sec Spanish Clb; Mgr(s); Var Swmmng; High Hon Roll; Hon Roll; NHS; Dntstry.

WIEGMANN, GARY; Alfred G Berner HS; Massapequa, NY; (Y); Var Ftbl; Var JV Lcrss; High Hon Roll; Hon Roll; NHS; Coast Guard Acad; Engrng.

WIELAND, CHRIS; Horseheads HS; Horseheads, NY; (Y); JCL; Trs Latin Clb; Varsity Clb; Band; Concert Band; Jazz Band; Mrchg Band; Orch; School Play; Variety Show; Math.

WIELER, JENNIFER; Wantagh HS; Charlotte, NC; (Y); Band; Concert Band; Orch; School Musical; Nwsp Sprt Ed; Nwsp Stf; Ed Yrbk Stf; Var Badmtn; Var Capt Cheerleading; Var Tennis; Prsdntl Schlrshp High Pnt Coll 86; High Point Coll; Md Cmmnctns.

WIENECKE, RICHARD M; Walt Whitman HS; Huntington Sta, NY; (Y); #40 In Class; Boy Scts; Church Yth Grp; Trs Radio Clb; Pres Science Clb; Hon Roll; Jr NHS; NYS Rgnts Schlrshp 86; SUNY Stony Brook; Elec Engrng.

WIENER, ARYEH M; Veshiva Univ HS; Lawrence, NY; (Y); Temple Yth Grp; Band; Nwsp Stf; Var Bsktbl; Ntl Merit SF; Excl Frnch 83; Yeshiva U.

WIENER, GLENN; Sachem North HS; Holbrook, NY; (Y); 122/1558; Cmnty Wkr; Hon Roll; Bus.

WIENHOLZ, TISHA M; North Babylon Senior HS; No Babylon, NY; (Y); Computer Clb; Trs French Clb; Office Aide; Service Clb; Band; Sftbl; Vllybl; High Hon Roll; Jr NHS; NHS; Systms Anlyst.

WIERICH, PETER; Fordham Prep; Larchmont, NY; (Y); Model UN; Hon Roll; Ntl Merit Ltr.

WIESEL, ANDREA; Lawrence HS; Woodmere, NY; (Y); Pres VP DECA; Spanish Clb; Rptr Yrbk Stf; Hon Roll; NHS; Debate Tm; Mrktng Mnl 1T Pl NY ST; Arcon Ntl Servc Soc; Gvt In Actn; Bus Adm.

WIESNER, HEATHER; Heather Wiesner HS; Staten Island, NY; (Y); Hon Roll; Coopertv Educ Awd 86; Cobleskill; Bus Adm.

WIESNER, LAWRENCE; Binghamton HS; Binghamton, NY; (Y); Civic Clb; Ski Clb; Temple Yth Grp; Var Socr; Hon Roll.

WIEZALIS, JULIE; West Genesee SR HS; Syracuse, NY; (Y); Key Clb; Ski Clb; Spanish Clb; Sec Sr Cls; Rep Stu Cncl; Var Cheerleading; JV Var Socr; High Hon Roll; NHS; Opt Clb Awd; Le Moyne Acadmc Schlrshp 86; SUNY Binghamton; Pre Med.

WIGDOR, DOUGLAS H; E L Vandermuelen HS; Port Jefferson, NY; (Y); Aud/Vis; Spanish Clb; Pres Temple Yth Grp; Trs Varsity Clb; Nwsp Sprt Ed; Yrbk Ed-Chief; NHS; Var Bsktbl; Var Golf; Anncr Ftbl And Bsktbl 83-86; Regnts Schlrshp NYS 86; WA U St Louis; Ecnmcs.

WIGGERS, EDWIN M; Briarcliff HS; Briarcliff Manor, NY; (Y); Debate Tm; Mathletes; NFL; Nwsp Ed-Chief; Lit Mag; JV Crs Cntry; JV Trk; High Hon Roll; Hon Roll; NHS; Brown U Bk Awd Excllnce Wrttn & Spkn Exprssn 85; Columbia U Bk Awd Excllnce Soc Stud 85, Sci Hnr Pgm.

WIGGINS, NIGEL; William E Grady Vo Tech; Brooklyn, NY; (Y); Aud/Vis; Church Yth Grp; Computer Clb; Math Tm; Science Clb; Yrbk Stf; Comp.

WIGGINS, THERON; Mc Quaid Jesuit HS; Webster, NY; (Y); Im Bsktbl; Im Ftbl; Trk.

WIGHT, JENNIFER S; Naples Central Schl; Naples, NY; (Y); 23/64; Cmnty Wkr; 4-H; Quiz Bowl; VICA; Band; Concert Band; 4-H Awd; High Hon Roll; Merit Awd 83; Chef.

WIGHTMAN, BRENDA; West Genesee SR HS; Marcellus, NY; (Y); Church Yth Grp; Dance Clb; French Clb; Color Guard; Mrchg Band; Rep Jr Cls; Rep Sr Cls; Rep Stu Cncl; Var Capt Twrlr; Hon Roll; 2nd Pl Choreogrphy Dncng 83-84; Awd Frnch Spkng 84-85; Acctg.

WIGHTMAN, JENNIFER; De Ruyter Central HS; De Ruyter, NY; (S); Drama Clb; Concert Band; Mrchg Band; School Musical; Sec Jr Cls; JV Cheerleading; Hon Roll; Stu Mnth 84-85; Psych.

WIGHTMAN, MELISSA; South New Berlin Central HS; Norwich, NY; (Y); 8/38; Concert Band; Jazz Band; Mrchg Band; Pep Band; Yrbk Stf; Capt Bsktbl; Capt Socr; Lion Awd; NHS; Pres Acad Fitness Awd 86; US Marine Corp Distgshd Athlt Awd 86; Amer Leg Citiznshp Awd 86; SUNY Cortland; Bio.

WIGSTEN, TRACY; Mynderse Acad; Seneca Falls, NY; (S); 13/138; Church Yth Grp; FHA; Spanish Clb; Chorus; School Musical; Stage Crew; JV Var Socr; JV Trk; Cit Awd; High Hon Roll; Bus Mgmt.

WIKANDER, JOHN; Mercy HS; Sag Harbor, NY; (Y); 3/127; Pres Math Tm; Yrbk Stf; High Hon Roll; NEDT Awd; Outstndng Math Achvt 85-86; 3rd Pl Cthlc Leag Essy Cntst 86; Engrng.

WIKHEIM, JODY; Ramstein Am HS; Apo New York, NY; (Y); Hosp Aide; Band; Concert Band; Capt Drill Tm; Pep Band; Lit Mag; High Hon Roll; Outstndng Achvt Bio, Eng & Cosmtlgy 86; Best Attitude, All Around Capt Drill Tem 86; Hnr Band 84; AZ ST U; Bus.

WIKTORSKI, AMY; Buff Acad Of The Sacred Heart; Buffalo, NY; (Y); Cmnty Wkr; French Clb; Hosp Aide; Pep Clb; Red Cross Aide; Science Clb; Varsity Clb; Variety Show; Nwsp Rptr; Sec Frsh Cls; Psych.

WILBER, BRADLEY; Oneida SR HS; Oneida, NY; (S); Am Leg Boys St; Church Yth Grp; Debate Tm; Drama Clb; French Clb; Intnl Clb; Thesps; Chorus; School Play; Lit Mag; Guideposts Mag Yth Wrtng Cntst Hnrs 86; Creative Writing.

WILBER, TANYA; Pinecrest Christian Schl; Salisbury Center, NY; (S); 1/9; Sec Natl Beta Clb; Sec Jr Cls; VP Sr Cls; L Bsktbl; High Hon Roll; NHS; Val; Church Yth Grp; Debate Tm; ASCI Dstngshd HS Stu 85-86; Extrordnry Chrstn Amer Stu 85; Sci.

WILBER, TRACY; Chatham HS; Ghent, NY; (Y); 18/130; Church Yth Grp; Ski Clb; Band; Concert Band; Mrchg Band; Pep Band; Yrbk Stf; Rep Stu Cncl; Score Keeper; Hon Roll; Spcl Ed.

WILBUR, KIM; Vernon-Verona-Sherrill HS; Sherrill, NY; (Y); 9/210; GAA; Red Cross Aide; Rep Frsh Cls; Rep Soph Cls; Rep Jr Cls; Rep Stu Cncl; JV Fld Hcky; Score Keeper; Var Trk; High Hon Roll; Regents Schlrshp New York ST 86; Sherrill Rotory Schlrshp 86; Clarkson U; Accntng.

WILCOX, EDDIE; Port Jervis HS; Port Jervis, NY; (Y); 20/200; Church Yth Grp; Math Tm; Ski Clb; Yrbk Phtg; Yrbk Sprt Ed; Bowling; Ftbl; High Hon Roll; Hon Roll; NHS; SUNY; Elec Engrng.

WILCOX, EILEEN; Le Roy Central HS; Leroy, NY; (Y); French Clb; School Musical; Yrbk Stf; Hon Roll; NHS; Church Yth Grp; Church Choir; Leroy Hist Soc Volntr 85-87; Pres Chrch ST-WIDE Grls Clb 85-86; Kent ST U; Art.

WILCOX, KATHY; Potsdam Central HS; Potsdam, NY; (Y); 16/170; AFS; Math Clb; High Hon Roll; Hon Roll; NHS; Exploring; French Clb; Varsity Clb; Trk; Tlntd JRS 85-86; Clrksn U; Gntc Engr.

WILCOX, KEITH; Vestal SR HS; Vestal, NY; (Y); Church Yth Grp; Church Choir; Jazz Band; Pres Mrchg Band; Orch; Pep Band; Symp Band; Im Vllybl; High Hon Roll; 1st Rnr Up Rotary Yth Schlrshp 86; Elec Engrng.

WILCOX, LA TONYA; Nazareth Acad; Rochester, NY; (Y); Boys Clb Am; Church Yth Grp; Cmnty Wkr; Exploring; Political Wkr; SADD; Acpl Chr; Chorus; Church Choir; Stage Crew.

WILCOX, PATRICK; Valley Central HS; Walden, NY; (Y); 45/352; Acpl Chr; Band; Chorus; School Musical; Variety Show; JV Tennis; French Hon Soc; Hon Roll; NHS; Intl Bus.

WILCOX, REBECCA; Keshegua Central HS; Nunda, NY; (Y); Cmnty Wkr; Math Tm; Acpl Chr; Vllybl; NHS; Drama Clb; Mrchg Band; Bsktbl; High Hon Roll; Jr NHS; Am Leg Schltc Awd, Frgn Lang Awd Excllnce 84 & 85; NYSSMA Solo Comp Outstndg Ratgs 84-86; Geneseo ST; Pub Rel.

WILCZAK, PAMELA; Vernon-Verona-Sherrill HS; Vernon, NY; (Y); GAA; Girl Scts; VP Band; Concert Band; Mrchg Band; JV Var Cheerleading; JV Capt Fld Hcky; JV Capt Sftbl; High Hon Roll; NHS; Mst Outstndng Soph Band 84-85; Fld Hcky Bst Tm Plyr 85-86; NYSSMA Solo Comptn Piccolo 86; Phy Thrpy.

WILCZEK, LAURA; Frontier Central HS; Hamburg, NY; (Y); 23/480; Ski Clb; Concert Band; Var Socr; Var Tennis; Hon Roll; NHS; Rotary Awd; Art Clb; Latin Clb; Band; Arch.

WILCZEK, RENEE; West Seneca West SR HS; Cheektowaga, NY; (Y); 42/545; GAA; Church Choir; Color Guard; Orch; School Musical; Var Swmmng; High Hon Roll; NHS; Prfct Atten Awd; Church Yth Grp; Sci Schlrshp 86; Pres Acad Ftnss Awd 86; Southgate Plz Schlrshp 86; SUNY-BUFFALO; Med.

WILCZEK, SANDRA JEAN; Newburgh Free Acad; Newburgh, NY; (Y); High Hon Roll; Outstndng Sec Procdrs Stu 86; Presdntl Acad Fitns Awd 86; Sec.

WILCZEWSKI, DEBRA D; Eden SR HS; Eden, NY; (Y); 2/166; GAA; Concert Band; School Musical; Var JV Cheerleading; Var Capt Tennis; Im Vllybl; Hon Roll; Trs NHS; Sal; St Schlr; U Of Rochester Alumni Schlrshp 86; U Of Rochester; Pre Med.

WILDER, MICHELE; Saranac Lake HS; Saranac Lk, NY; (Y); Church Yth Grp; Cmnty Wkr; Girl Scts; Trs Frsh Cls; Rep Stu Cncl; Co-Capt Cheerleading; Cmmnctns.

WILDNER, CHRISTINE; Sachem HS North; Farmingville, NY; (Y); 149/1558; Sec VP Church Yth Grp; Pres French Clb; Band; Church Choir; Concert Band; Madrigals; Mrchg Band; Orch; School Musical; Symp Band; NY ST Schl Music Assn Mdls Flte & Voice; U Miami; Physcl Thrpy.

WILDSTEIN, ALLAN; Canarsle HS; Brooklyn, NY; (Y); Cmnty Wkr; Chorus; School Play; Bowling; Hon Roll; Sci Fair Awd 83-84; Pre Law.

WILENSKY, JOSEPH; Eastchester HS; Eastchester, NY; (Y); Aud/Vis; Drama Clb; Spanish Clb; School Musical; Nwsp Phtg; Ed Yrbk Phtg; Lit Mag; Hon Roll; NHS; Encllnc Phtgrphy 84.

WILENSKY, MARK E; Lindenhurst SR HS; Lindenhurst, NY; (Y); 1/550; Chess Clb; Math Tm; Ski Clb; Spanish Clb; JV Socr; Var Tennis; High Hon Roll; NHS; Sal; Quiz Bowl; NYS Rgnts Schlrshp 86; US Acdmc Dcthln 3rd Plc Sci 86; Johns Hopkins U; Med.

WILES, CHRISTIN A; Hamburg SR HS; Hamburg, NY; (Y); 32/387; Chorus; Madrigals; School Musical; School Play; Stage Crew; Nwsp Stf; High Hon Roll; NHS; Northeastern U; Phy Thrpy.

WILHELM, KIMBERLY; Fairport HS; Fairport, NY; (Y); Art Clb; Cmnty Wkr; Key Clb; Latin Clb; Ski Clb; Varsity Clb; Chorus; Yrbk Ed-Chief; Swmmng; Hon Roll; Acadia; Marine Bio.

WILHELM, PETER C; Our Lady Of Lourdes HS; Pleasant Valley, NY; (Y); Drama Clb; Nwsp Stf; Ftbl; Swmmng; NYS Regnts Schlrshp 85-86.

WILK, BRIAN D; John F Kennedy HS; Yonkers, NY; (Y); 10/873; JA; Office Aide; Teachers Aide; Hon Roll; Schlrshp Amer Inst Of CPA 86; NYS Regnts Schlrshp; ST U Of NY Binghampton; Acctg.

WILK, KAREN MARIE; Hauppauge HS; Hauppauge, NY; (Y); 48/491; Orch; Nwsp Rptr; Nwsp Stf; Yrbk Bus Mgr; Yrbk Stf; Var Cheerleading; High Hon Roll; NHS; Hosp Aide; JV Trk; Muhlenberg Coll; Ed.

WILKE, ERIC; Oneida SR HS; Oneida, NY; (S); 17/200; Boy Scts; Band; Jazz Band; Mrchg Band; School Musical; Symp Band; Yrbk Stf; Crs Cntry; High Hon Roll; NHS; Rgnts Schlrshp 86; Elec Engrng.

WILKIE, JAMES; Bellport HS; E Brookhaven, NY; (Y); 74/300; Drama Clb; Hosp Aide; Ski Clb; Spanish Clb; Varsity Clb; Stage Crew; Variety Show; Tennis; Trk; Mst Imprvd Plyr Tnns Tm 85; SUNY Binghinton; Pre-Med.

WILKIE, KARIN; Liverpool HS; Liverpool, NY; (Y); 120/860; ROTC; Color Guard; Drill Tm; Air Force Assoc Awd 86; Rtrd Affcrs Assoc Awd 86; AM Lgn Schlstc Excllnc Awd 86; Syracuse U; Elctrl Engnrng.

WILKINS, BARRONDIA; Buffalo Traditional HS; Buffalo, NY; (S); #20 In Class; Cmnty Wkr; Band; VP Sec Church Choir; Concert Band; Mrchg Band; Nwsp Stf; Hon Roll; Prfct Atten Awd; 2nd Pl Piano Comptn 83; Morris Brown; Law.

WILKINS, ERIC; Corinth Central HS; Corinth, NY; (Y); 13/100; Math Clb; Science Clb; Pres Jr Cls; Pres Sr Cls; High Hon Roll; Hon Roll; Jr NHS; NHS; Cmnty Wkr; Exploring; Math & Sci Hnr Soc 86; Bio.

WILKINS, MARK C; Nottingham HS; Syracuse, NY; (Y); 60/230; Boy Scts; Pres Civic Clb; Computer Clb; Var Ftbl; Var Capt Swmmng; Var Trk; High Hon Roll; Ntl Merit SF; Outstndng Elctrnc Stu Of Yr 85; Elctrnc Engrng.

WILKINS, TRACE; Wyandanch HS; Wyandanch, NY; (Y); 1/120; Dance Clb; Thesps; Band; Mrchg Band; Variety Show; Nwsp Stf; Yrbk Phtg; High Hon Roll; NHS; Val; Martin Luther King Schlrshp Awd 86; Frederick Douglass Schlr-Amer U 86; Pachman, Block Lgl Awd 86; American U; Econ.

WILKINSON, ANTHONY T; St Marys Boys HS; Old Brookville, NY; (Y); Computer Clb; Debate Tm; Drama Clb; School Musical; School Play; Nwsp Stf; Lit Mag; NYS Rgnts Schlrshp 86; American U; Cmmnctns.

WILKINSON, JENNIFER L; Pittsford Mendon HS; Pittsford, NY; (Y); Pres Church Yth Grp; Yrbk Ed-Chief; Yrbk Sprt Ed; Yrbk Stf; Lit Mag; Bsktbl; Sftbl; NHS; Math Clb; Quiz Bowl; NY St Rgnts Schlrshp 86; Prdcr & Mgr-Yrbk Sld Shw & & Sr Sld Shw 86; Syracuse U; Tv Prodctn.

WILKINSON, JODY; Berne-Knox-Westerio Central Schl; Berne, NY; (Y); Band; Chorus; Concert Band; Mrchg Band; Pep Band; School Musical; School Play; Variety Show; Hon Roll; NHS; Bus Adm.

WILKINSON, THEODORE; John F Kennedy HS; Utica, NY; (Y); Aud/Vis; Computer Clb; Debate Tm; Exploring; Math Clb; NFL; Ski Clb; Spanish Clb; Concert Band; Jazz Band; Applied Physics.

WILL, JULIE; Bishop Grimes HS; North Syracuse, NY; (S); Stu Cncl; JV Var Bsktbl; Hon Roll; Acad All Amer 86.

WILLARD, DIANNE C; Iroquois Central HS; Elma, NY; (Y); 112/300; Drama Clb; Chorus; Concert Band; Orch; School Musical; School Play; Stage Crew; Symp Band; Erie Cnty Orch 86; ST Sectnls Zone I Band 85; Slippery Rock U; Music Thrpst.

WILLARD, ELLERY T; Johnstown HS; Johnstown, NY; (Y); Band; Concert Band; Jazz Band; Mrchg Band; Variety Show; Capt L Bsktbl; Im JV Ftbl; Var L Trk; High Hon Roll; NHS; Mst Lkly To Succeed In Acad & Athltcs 83; MVP Varsty Bsktbl 86; Regents Schlrshp Wnnr 86; Colgate U; Econ.

WILLARD JR, JAMES T; Newark Valley HS; Berkshire, NY; (Y); 13/127; Pres Church Yth Grp; Varsity Clb; L Socr; Var Trk; Hon Roll; Tm Ldrshp Awd JV 84; Pilot.

WILLARD, KERRY B; Wayne Central HS; Ontario, NY; (Y); 4/200; Math Tm; Teachers Aide; Concert Band; Rep Stu Cncl; JV Cheerleading; Var Socr; Var Trk; Hon Roll; NHS; Pres Schlr; NYS Regnts Schlrshp 86; Ithaca Coll; Phy Thrpy.

WILLARD, ROBERT; Heuvelton Central Schl; Heuvelton, NY; (S); 1/60; Pres Trs 4-H; Band; Concert Band; 4-H Awd; Hon Roll; NHS; Ntl Merit Ltr; Bio Regents Hghst Schl Score 85; Hstry Hghst Cls Avg 85; Mth Hghst Schl Score 85; Attorney.

WILLETT, AMY; Northport HS; Northport, NY; (Y); Red Cross Aide; Capt Color Guard; Nwsp Ed-Chief; Ed Yrbk Stf; High Hon Roll; NHS.

WILLETT, FRANK; Olean HS; Olean, NY; (Y); 6/200; Quiz Bowl; Band; Concert Band; Jazz Band; Mrchg Band; Orch; Var Bsktbl; Hon Roll; NHS; Pres Frsh Cls.

WILLETT, SCOTT; Candor Central HS; Candor, NY; (Y); Am Leg Boys St; Boy Scts; Cmnty Wkr; Socr; High Hon Roll; Hon Roll; NHS; Church Yth Grp; 4-H; Chorus; Schlstc Art Awds; Ag Tech Alfred; Arch Dsgn.

WILLETTS, DAWN MARIE; Waterford-Halfmoon HS; Waterford, NY; (Y); 1/73; Math Tm; Trs SADD; Teachers Aide; Yrbk Ed-Chief; Bausch & Lomb Sci Awd; Elks Awd; NHS; Val; Math Clb; Yrbk Phtg; Rensselear Mdl Math & Sci 85; Regents Schlrshp 86; Stu Dir ASAP; JR Great Bk Dscssn Grp; Union Coll; Engrng.

WILLETTS, LAURA J; Wellsville HS; Wellsville, NY; (Y); 13/126; VP Pres FBLA; Key Clb; Nwsp Stf; Yrbk Stf; Sftbl; High Hon Roll; NHS; Sftbl; High Hon Roll; NHS; Rgnts Schlrshp 86; Rchstr Inst Of Tech; Acctng.

WILLEY, CHRIS; Ballston Spa HS; Ballston Spa, NY; (Y); 2/250; Am Leg Boys St; Boy Scts; Church Yth Grp; Debate Tm; Socr; Tennis; Bausch & Lomb Sci Awd; High Hon Roll; Trs NHS; Sal; NY ST Chem Awd 86; Chem.

WILLEY, DICK; Geneseo Central HS; Geneso, NY; (Y); Boy Scts; Band; Yrbk Phtg; Var L Swmmng; Var L Trk; Top Jewelry Awd Sibleys Schlstc Art Shw 86.

WILLIAMS, ADRIAN; Springfield Gardens HS; Jamaica, NY; (Y); 56/440; Computer Clb; Math Clb; Math Tm; Off Jr Cls; Hon Roll; Hnrb Mntn In Amer Inst Of Sci & Tech 86; Comp Prgmr.

WILLIAMS, AMY B; Letchworth Central HS; Warsaw, NY; (Y); 1/84; Band; Drm Mjr(t); Yrbk Stf; Bsktbl; Capt Vllybl; Cit Awd; High Hon Roll; Pres NHS; Ntl Merit Ltr; Val; NY ST Rgnts Schlrshp 86; Lng Islnd U Schlrs Awd 86; All Str Tm Bsktbl & Vllybl 86; Long Islnd U; Marine Bio.

WILLIAMS, ANDREA M; William H Maxwell HS; Brooklyn, NY; (Y); 36/228; Sec FBLA; High Hon Roll; Hon Roll; Prfct Atten Awd; Church Yth Grp; Band; Church Choir; Rep Sr Cls; Bernard M Baruch Coll; Comm Adv.

WILLIAMS, ANGELA; Uniondale HS; Uniondale, NY; (Y); Church Yth Grp; French Clb; Hosp Aide; Key Clb; Church Choir; VFW Awd; Wilberface; Hotel Mang.

WILLIAMS, ANNE; Earl L Vandernevlen HS; Mt Sinai, NY; (Y); FBLA; Girl Scts; JCL; Pep Clb; SADD; Band; Concert Band; Rep Stu Cncl; JV Var Cheerleading; Stat Mgr Ftbl; Latin Awd 84; Bus.

WILLIAMS, ANTOINE; Art & Design HS; New York, NY; (Y); Art Clb; Boys Clb Am; Cmnty Wkr; Drama Clb; French Clb; Speech Tm; SADD; Teachers Aide; Swmmng; Vllybl; Social Studies Awd 83-84; Cornell U; Arch.

WILLIAMS, ASIA; Centereach HS; Centereach, NY; (Y); Hon Roll; Prfct Atten Awd; Comp Sci.

WILLIAMS, AUDREY LYNN; Whitesboro SR HS; Marcy, NY; (Y); 147/354; Church Yth Grp; VP GAA; VP Band; Church Choir; Concert Band; Jazz Band; Mrchg Band; Orch; Stu Cncl; Stat Bsktbl; Charm Clb; Schlrshp Alumni Asso 86; Senter Cole Schlrshp; Central Oneida League 85; ST U Coll-Cortland; Bus Mgmt.

WILLIAMS, BARBARA; Schoharie Central HS; Schoharie, NY; (Y); Hst FHA; Pres Key Clb; SADD; Chorus; Yrbk Stf; Stu Cncl; JV Vllybl; Prfct Atten Awd; Acad All Amer Schlr Awd 85; Erly Chldhd Ed.

WILLIAMS, BILLY; Walter Panas HS; Peekskill, NY; (Y); FBLA; Im Vllybl; Hon Roll; Acctng.

WILLIAMS, BONNIE; Holland Patent Central HS; Barneveld, NY; (Y); 50/180; 4-H; GAA; Stage Crew; Nwsp Rptr; Rep Stu Cncl; JV Capt Bsktbl; Var Capt Cheerleading; JV Capt Fld Hcky; Var Sftbl; Hon Roll; Chrldng Awd Excell 84-86; Csmtlgy.

WILLIAMS, CAROL; Corinth Central HS; Corinth, NY; (Y); Drama Clb; French Clb; SADD; Teachers Aide; Varsity Clb; Fld Hcky; Tennis; Vllybl; NHS; Coll St Rose Albany; Lib Arts.

WILLIAMS, CASSANDRA; Emma Willard Schl; New York, NY; (Y); Chorus; Trk; NHS.

WILLIAMS, CATHY; Somers HS; Somers, NY; (Y); Pres AFS; Intnl Clb; SADD; Yrbk Stf; Crs Cntry; NHS; Spanish NHS; Soc Stu Stu Mnth 85; Adv Fabric Fshn 86.

WILLIAMS, CHRISTINE; Clara Barton For Health Prof; Brooklyn, NY; (Y); Church Yth Grp; Dance Clb; Debate Tm; Science Clb; Nwsp Stf; Hon Roll; NHS; Vassar U; Pre-Med.

WILLIAMS, COLLEEN; Cato Mediedin HS; Cato, NY; (Y); Art Clb; GAA; JA; Library Aide; SADD; Nwsp Phtg; Nwsp Rptr; Nwsp Stf; Yrbk Phtg; 1st Pl Halloween Athr Cont 85, Feb Athr Cont 86; 4th Pl Feb Athr Cont 86; Rider COLL; Engl.

WILLIAMS, CRAIG A; Town Of Webb HS; Woodgate, NY; (Y); Am Leg Boys St; Letterman Clb; Math Tm; Varsity Clb; Yrbk Stf; Pres Sr Cls; Rep Stu Cncl; Bsktbl; Mgr(s); Socr; Plattsburgh ST; Educ.

WILLIAMS, DANIELLE; Riverhead HS; Riverhead, NY; (Y); Hosp Aide; Key Clb; Band; Cheerleading; Psych.

WILLIAMS, DARIUS; Rice HS; New York, NY; (Y); SADD; Pres Jr Cls; Rep Stu Cncl; Computer Technology.

WILLIAMS, DARLENE; Cathedral HS; Ny, NY; (Y); 98/272; FNA; Yrbk Stf; Im Gym; Hon Roll; Prfct Atten Awd; Hafstra U; Comp Prgmmng.

WILLIAMS, DARRYL; Rice HS; Bronx, NY; (Y); Rep Jr Cls; Pres Sr Cls; Rep Stu Cncl; JV Var Bsktbl; Prfct Atten Awd; GQ Slb Pres 86; Stu Exchng Pgm 86; Stu Ldrshp 86.

WILLIAMS, DELLRECE; Sacred Heart Acad; Buffalo, NY; (Y); Hosp Aide; Red Cross Aide; Prfct Atten Awd.

WILLIAMS, DESIREE M; Bronx High School Of Science; Bronx, NY; (Y); Church Yth Grp; Key Clb; Office Aide; Teachers Aide; Band; Yrbk Stf; NHS; Ntl Merit SF; Schltc Achvt Ctatn Awd Gvrnrs Cmmtte 85-86; Bio-Chem.

WILLIAMS, DESMOND; Christopher Columbus HS; Bronx, NY; (Y); 69/671; Key Clb; Band; Yrbk Stf; High Hon Roll; NHS; Prfct Atten Awd; Sci Tech Found Honrbl Ment 86; Super Yth 84; Coop Gov 86; NY U; CPA.

WILLIAMS JR, DONALD; De Witt Clinton HS; Bronx, NY; (S); Boy Scts; Computer Clb; ROTC; Bsktbl; Var Ftbl; Socr; Sftbl; Trk; Math Awd 84; OH ST; Pro Ftbl.

WILLIAMS, DONNA; Jordan-Elbridge Central HS; Skaneateles Fls, NY; (Y); 15/143; Band; Mrchg Band; School Musical; Nwsp Stf; Yrbk Phtg; Var Capt Cheerleading; JV Sftbl; High Hon Roll; Jr NHS; NHS; Ntl Cmprs & Hkrs Assoc Schlrshp 86; ST U Of NY; Cmmnctns.

WILLIAMS, ELAINE; Sandy Creek Central HS; Pulaski, NY; (Y); 21/94; Drama Clb; French Clb; Office Aide; Band; Chorus; Concert Band; Mrchg Band; School Musical; JV Var Mgr(s); Hon Roll; 1st Plc ST Comptn HOSA 86; Dollars Schlrs Schlrshp 86; Jefferson CC; RN.

WILLIAMS, ELIZABETH L; Hunter College HS; New York, NY; (Y); Church Yth Grp; Girl Scts; Model UN; Church Choir; VP Stu Cncl; Mu Alp Tht; Ntl Merit SF; Prfct Atten Awd; Physcn.

WILLIAMS, GARY; Midlakes HS; Clifton Spgs, NY; (Y); Sec Aud/Vis; Chess Clb; Letterman Clb; Thesps; Varsity Clb; School Musical; School Play; JV Var Ftbl; L Mgr(s); Hon Roll; Comm.

WILLIAMS, GWENDOLINE W; Irvington HS; Ardsley On Hudson, NY; (Y); Church Yth Grp; Drama Clb; Varsity Clb; Chorus; School Musical; Swing Chorus; Lit Mag; Gym; Hon Roll; Schlrshp-New Ballt Schl Affltd Wth Feld Bllt 84-86; Theater.

WILLIAMS, HAL; Greece Athena HS; Rochester, NY; (Y); 6/330; Boy Scts; Chess Clb; German Clb; JA; Pep Clb; Science Clb; Band; Concert Band; Symp Band; Im Ftbl.

WILLIAMS, HEATHER; Valley Central HS; Walden, NY; (Y); 2/315; Concert Band; Mrchg Band; School Musical; Off Soph Cls; Off Jr Cls; Sec Stu Cncl; JV Var Vllybl; High Hon Roll; Trs NHS; Spanish NHS; Mst Imprvd Musician 85; RPI Sci & Math Awd 86; Sienna; Bio.

WILLIAMS, HUSSON; Hempstead HS; Hempstead, NY; (Y); English Clb; JA; Library Aide; Pep Clb; Pep Band; Yrbk Stf; Bsktbl; Wt Lftg; Prfct Atten Awd.

WILLIAMS, JACQUELINE; Alfred E Smith HS; Bronx, NY; (S); 5/217; Cmnty Wkr; VICA; Concert Band; Jazz Band; Nwsp Stf; Yrbk Stf; Hon Roll; JETS Awd; NHS; Prfct Atten Awd; Alg Awd 83; Eng Awds 83 & 85; Geom Awd 85; Law.

WILLIAMS, JANE A; Jamesville-De Witt HS; De Witt, NY; (Y); 43/245; Church Yth Grp; Pres German Clb; SADD; Yrbk Stf; VP Sr Cls; Cheerleading; High Hon Roll; NHS; Schltc Art Awd-2 Gld Kys 84-85; Outstndng Achvr & Ldrshp Awd 85; Med.

WILLIAMS, JASON; Bishop Bloughlin HS; Brooklyn, NY; (Y); Church Choir; Rep Frsh Cls; Coach Actv; JV Var Crs Cntry; Trk; Cit Awd; Otstndng MVR Trk & Fld 86; UCLA; Psych.

WILLIAMS, JENNIFER; Seton Catholic Central HS; Windsor, NY; (Y); 44/162; Key Clb; Ski Clb; Rep Stu Cncl; Var Trk; Actvties Clb Bldg Faity Comm 82-84; PA ST U; Hortculture.

WILLIAMS, JENNIFER ANN; Cazenovia Central Schl; Cazenovia, NY; (Y); 51/141; Acpl Chr; Band; Chorus; Church Choir; Concert Band; Madrigals; Mrchg Band; School Musical; School Play; Symp Band; Syracuse Schlrshp 86; Outstndng Achvt Music Awd 86; Hgst Achvt Soc Psychlgy Awd 86; Syracuse U; Music Ed.

WILLIAMS, JOE; Mc Quaid HS; Fairport, NY; (Y); 110/180; Boy Scts; Ski Clb; Varsity Clb; JV Bsbl; JV Var Bsktbl; Var Capt Ftbl; Var Im Trk; Hon Roll; Bus.

WILLIAMS, JOSEPH; G Ray Bodley HS; Fulton, NY; (Y); Am Leg Boys St; Latin Clb; Pres Jr Cls; Pres Sr Cls; Rep Stu Cncl; Var Golf; Var Ice Hcky; Var Socr; Dnfth Awd; High Hon Roll; Gene Mac Danil Mem Awd Intllgnc 84; Peter Lafrate Awd Ldrshp 86; Rchstr Inst Of Tech; Dntstry.

WILLIAMS, KAREEN; Buffalo Traditional HS; Buffalo, NY; (S); 4/116; Intnl Clb; Band; Concert Band; Jazz Band; Nwsp Rptr; Nwsp Stf; Trk; Hon Roll; NHS; Prfct Atten Awd; U Of South FL; Bus Adm.

WILLIAMS, KAREN L; Newburgh Free Acad; Newburgh, NY; (Y); Aud/Vis; Computer Clb; French Clb; Science Clb; Chorus; Stage Crew; Nwsp Ed-Chief; Var Score Keeper; JV Socr; Comp Sci.

WILLIAMS, KEITH; Berlin Central HS; Stephentown, NY; (Y); JV Var Wrstlng; Engl Jrnlsm.

WILLIAMS, KEITH R; Frontier Central SR HS; Blasdell, NY; (S); 44/444; Aud/Vis; Church Yth Grp; Exploring; FBLA; Library Aide; Office Aide; Teachers Aide; Hon Roll; Jr NHS; NHS; Daemen Coll; Bus Adm.

WILLIAMS, KELLY; Elmira Free Acad; Elmira, NY; (Y); Art Clb; Spanish Clb; Stat Bsktbl; Score Keeper; Vllybl; Hon Roll; Cert Achvt Art 86; Gold Key 86; Acctng.

WILLIAMS, KERRI S; Marcus Whitman JR SR HS; Naples, NY; (Y); 2/130; Church Yth Grp; Church Choir; Concert Band; High Hon Roll; Mrch Stu Of Mnth 86; Liberty U; Psychlgy.

WILLIAMS, KEVIN; Sanford H Calhoun HS; Merrick, NY; (S); 89/313; Boy Scts; DECA; VP Key Clb; Band; Nwsp Rptr; Rep Soph Cls; Rep Jr Cls; Rep Sr Cls; JV Bsktbl; Var Golf; Boy Scouts Of Amer Eagle Scout 86; Rapport Awd For Outstndng Svc In Cmnty 86; DECA 1st Pl 86; Geneseo Suny; Bus.

WILLIAMS, KIMBERLY; Truman HS; Bronx, NY; (Y); Cmnty Wkr; Office Aide; Teachers Aide; Band; Hon Roll; Spn Awd 86; Atten 85-86; Hunter Coll; Med.

WILLIAMS, KIMBERLY J; Ward Melville HS; Centereach, NY; (Y); 209/725; Church Yth Grp; Political Wkr; VICA; Band; Church Choir; Concert Band; Mrchg Band; Hon Roll; SUNY Buffalo; Engrng.

WILLIAMS, KRISTEN; Gates-Chili HS; Rochester, NY; (S); 14/446; Pres Church Yth Grp; Math Tm; Ski Clb; Rep Jr Cls; High Hon Roll; NHS; Ntl Merit Ltr; Brigham Young U; Bio.

WILLIAMS, KURT; Brockport HS; Clarkson, NY; (Y); Radio Clb; Ski Clb; Var L Crs Cntry; Var L Trk; Hon Roll; Commnctns.

WILLIAMS, LISA; Mohawk Central-Gregory B Jarvi Schl; Mohawk, NY; (Y); 3/100; Pres French Clb; Math Clb; Varsity Clb; Rep Stu Cncl; Var Cheerleading; VP Fld Hcky; Elks Awd; VP NHS; Drama Clb; Exploring; Empire St Schlrshp-Excllnc & Rgnts Schlrshp 86; Pres Schlr-St John Fisher Coll 6; St John Fisher Coll; Math.

WILLIAMS, LISA; Parishville Hopkinton HS; Colton, NY; (Y); Cmnty Wkr; Hosp Aide; SADD; Chorus; High Hon Roll; Hon Roll; Johnson-Wales Coll; Fd Srv Mgmt.

WILLIAMS, LORI; Pelham Memorial HS; Pelham, NY; (Y); AFS; Cmnty Wkr; Drama Clb; VP JA; Chorus; School Musical; School Play; Lit Mag; Hon Roll; Sec Trs NHS.

WILLIAMS, LYNDA M; La Salle SR HS; Niagara Falls, NY; (S); 17/250; Band; Church Choir; Concert Band; Jazz Band; Mrchg Band; Orch; School Musical; Hon Roll; NHS; Prfct Atten Awd; U S Band Dir Assn Awd 85; U Of Buffalo; Comp Sci.

WILLIAMS, MARTIN D; North Rose-Wolcott HS; Rose, NY; (Y); Band; Stu Cncl; Golf; NHS; Crss Cntry Ski Tm; Geneseo; Psychlgy.

WILLIAMS, MARYANNE; Our Lady Of Lourdes HS; Wappingers Fls, NY; (Y); 33/183; VP Church Yth Grp; Cmnty Wkr; Yrbk Ed-Chief; Yrbk Stf; Stu Cncl; Swmmng; Hon Roll; NHS.

WILLIAMS, MELANIE; Hillcrest HS; Jamaica, NY; (Y); Cmnty Wkr; Hosp Aide; Teachers Aide; Science Project With Merit 84; Med.

WILLIAMS, MICHAEL; Archbishop Walsh HS; Olean, NY; (Y); Ski Clb; Trs Frsh Cls; Pres Jr Cls; Stu Cncl; JV Var Ftbl; Hon Roll.

WILLIAMS, MICHAEL; Franklin Acad; Malone, NY; (Y); Church Yth Grp; Letterman Clb; Varsity Clb; Bsbl; Bsktbl; Ftbl; Socr; Trk; IN Inst Tech; Comp Engr.

WILLIAMS, MICHAEL; Rice HS; New York, NY; (Y); Hosp Aide; Bsktbl; Crs Cntry; Swmmng; Trk; Wt Lftg; Scholar 84; Baruch; Bus.

WILLIAMS, MICHELLE; Oriskany Central HS; Oriskany, NY; (Y); Am Leg Aux Girls St; Pres Key Clb; Spanish Clb; SADD; Varsity Clb; School Play; Var Cheerleading; Sftbl; High Hon Roll; NHS.

WILLIAMS, MONIQUE; Fashion Industries HS; Queens Vlg, NY; (Y); 128/335; Service Clb; Chorus; Hampton Inst; Comp Sci.

WILLIAMS, OTHNIEL; Andrew Jackson HS; Queens, NY; (Y); 32/539; Boy Scts; JA; Key Clb; Chorus; School Play; Socr; Swmmng; Hon Roll; Mu Alp Tht; Prfct Atten Awd; Outstndng Perf Math And Physcs 82-83; Excllnc Achvt Zoolgy 85-86; Excllnc Achvt Sci 85-86; Queens College; Comp Prog.

WILLIAMS, OVITA; Clara Barton HS; Brooklyn, NY; (Y); 4/487; Debate Tm; Color Guard; Nwsp Ed-Chief; Pres Soph Cls; Rep Sr Cls; Cheerleading; High Hon Roll; Hon Roll; NCTE Awd; NHS; Alpha Kappoa Alpha Srty Schlrshp 86; Gvrnrs Cmmtee Schlstc Achvmnt 86; 1st Awd Englch 86; Vassar Coll; Psych.

WILLIAMS, PATRICIA B; White Plains HS; White Plains, NY; (Y); 71/421; Exploring; Hosp Aide; Orch; Lit Mag; VP Sr Cls; Rep Stu Cncl; Cit Awd; Prfct Atten Awd; French Clb; Band; Stu Principals Planning Comm 85-86; All Am Hall Of Fame Band Hons 86; HO-AM Mem Awd 86; English.

WILLIAMS, PURCELL; Benjamin Franklin HS; Rochester, NY; (Y); High Hon Roll; Hon Roll; Rochester Blck Schlrs Cmmtte Urban League 85; Air Force.

WILLIAMS, REBECCA; Marlboro HS; Marlboro, NY; (Y); 5/150; Rep Church Yth Grp; Drama Clb; Girl Scts; Band; Chorus; Yrbk Ed-Chief; Cit Awd; NHS; Pres Schlr; Girl Scout Gold Awd 83; Area All ST Chorus 85-86; Rochester Inst Tech.

WILLIAMS, REGINA; Letchworth Central HS; Bliss, NY; (Y); 25/100; Library Aide; VICA; Sftbl; Hon Roll; Cert Cmpltn Yth Emplymnt Prep Prgm 84; Comp Prgrmng.

WILLIAMS, RHETT L; Skaneateles HS; Auburn, NY; (Y); 66/152; Boy Scts; Ski Clb; JV Bsktbl; Var Capt Ftbl; JV Lcrss; Cit Awd; God Cntry Awd; High Hon Roll; Hon Roll; Schlrshp-Ftbl Boostrs Best Overall Plyr 85; Cortland ST; Bus Mgmt.

WILLIAMS, ROSEMARIE; St Raymond Acad; Bronx, NY; (Y); 12/73; Computer Clb; Library Aide; Spanish Clb; Band; Bsktbl; Sftbl; Hon Roll; Cornell; Pediatrician.

WILLIAMS, SANDRA; Addison Central HS; Woodhull, NY; (Y); JCL; Sec Soph Cls; Rep Jr Cls; VP Sr Cls; Stu Cncl; Var Bsktbl; Var Socr; Var Sftbl; Hon Roll; NHS; Poli Sci.

WILLIAMS, SANDY; Hoosic Valley Central HS; Schaghticoke, NY; (Y); Teachers Aide; Band; Var JV Bsktbl; Var JV Fld Hcky; Var Mgr(s); Hudson Valley CC; Erly Chldhd.

WILLIAMS, SEAN L; Horseheads HS; Elmira, NY; (Y); Am Leg Boys St; JCL; Latin Clb; Science Clb; Ski Clb; Varsity Clb; Hst Sr Cls; Var L Swmmng; Hon Roll; Med.

WILLIAMS, SHENELLE RONETTE; De Witt Clinton HS; Bronx, NY; (Y); Key Clb; Office Aide; Chorus; JV Trk; Cit Awd; Gov Hon Prg Awd; Hon Roll; Jr NHS; NHS; Prfct Atten Awd; Good Gal Awd 85; VP Hlth Career Cls; Pedtrcn.

WILLIAMS, STACEY; Marcus Whitman HS; Rushville, NY; (Y); 8/109; Am Leg Aux Girls St; Ski Clb; Yrbk Stf; VP Frsh Cls; Sec Soph Cls; Sec Jr Cls; Sec Sr Cls; Sec Stu Cncl; Var Cheerleading; JV Var Tennis; MVP Tennis 85-86; Rotary Clb Stu Of Mnth 85; Congrssnl Yth Schlr To Washington DC 85; NH U; Hotel Adm.

WILLIAMS, STACI; Alexander Central HS; Darien, NY; (Y); Chorus; Color Guard; Mrchg Band; Spec Rcgntn Art Shw GCC 85; Cert Merit Sblys Art Shw 85 & 86; Cmrcl Art.

WILLIAMS, STEPHANIE; Hillcrest HS; Jamaica, NY; (Y); 409/800; Church Yth Grp; Cmnty Wkr; Girl Scts; Chorus; Church Choir; Orch; School Musical; School Play; Hon Roll; Prfct Atten Awd; La Guardia CC; Dental Hygnst.

WILLIAMS, STEVEN; Watertown HS; Watertwon, NY; (Y); Band; NHS; Electrnc Engr.

WILLIAMS, TANYA M; Cardinal Spellman HS; Bronx, NY; (Y); Girl Scts; Band; Concert Band; Mrchg Band; Howard U; Spnsh Mjr.

WILLIAMS, TERESA; Pulaski JR SR HS; Pulaski, NY; (S); VP GAA; Sec Band; Chorus; School Musical; Swing Chorus; Yrbk Stf; Var JV Socr; Vllybl; Hon Roll; NHS; Phys Thrpy.

WILLIAMS, TERRIE; Notingham HS; Syracuse, NY; (Y); Rochester.

WILLIAMS, TONY; Ravena-Coryman-Selkirk HS; Ravena, NY; (Y); Rep Frsh Cls; Rep Soph Cls; Rep Jr Cls; Var Bsktbl; Var Ftbl; Hon Roll.

WILLIAMS, TRINA; Grace Dodge Voc HS; Bronx, NY; (Y); Teachers Aide; Chorus; Hon Roll; Prfct Atten Awd; Sci Hnrs 85; Hstry Hnrs 85; Mth Hnrs 84.

WILLIAMS, VALERIE; John Dewey HS; Brooklyn, NY; (Y); Church Yth Grp; Library Aide; Chorus; Pre Med.

WILLIAMS, VALERIE; Murry Bergtraum HS; New York, NY; (Y); 124/601; JA; Chorus; Church Choir; School Musical; Elizabeth Setoncoll; Bus Adm.

WILLIAMS, VERA; Henninge HS; Syracuse, NY; (Y); Church Yth Grp; Cmnty Wkr; Library Aide; Church Choir; Hon Roll; Onondagg CC; Air Force.

WILLIAMS, VERONICA; Augsburg American HS; APO New York, NY; (Y); Dance Clb; Letterman Clb; Model UN; Bsktbl; Cheerleading; Crs Cntry; Socr; Trk; DAR Awd; Cameron U; Bus Adm.

WILLIAMS JR, WILLIE L; Bayshore HS; Bayshore, NY; (Y); Church Yth Grp; FBLA; Political Wkr; Spanish Clb; Teachers Aide; Mrchg Band; Capt Bsbl; Capt Bsktbl; Coach Actv; Gym; MVP JR Vrsty Bkstbl 83; Catp Vrsty Bsktbl 86-87; Hofstra U; Business Admin.

WILLIAMS, YOLANDA; St Pius V HS; Bronx, NY; (Y); 27/67; Hosp Aide; SADD; Yrbk Stf; Rep Stu Cncl; Capt Cheerleading; Swmmng; Trk; Hon Roll; Marymount Coll; Intr Dsgn.

WILLIAMSON, GREGORY S; Glen Cove HS; Glen Cove, NY; (Y); 20/270; Pres Drama Clb; Mathletes; Pres Thesps; Chorus; School Musical; School Play; Sec Soph Cls; Var Trk; Hon Roll; NHS; Rgnts Schlrshp Wnr 86; Vrsty Ltr Drma Clb 85; Vtd Mst Mscl SR Cls 85-86; Tufts U; Mechncl Engnrng.

WILLIAMSON, HEIDI; Copiague HS; Copiague, NY; (Y); German Clb; SADD; Sftbl; NHS; Band; Concert Band; Mrchg Band; Rep Frsh Cls; Germn Natl Hnr Socty 85; Bus Mgmt.

WILLIAMSON, MICHAEL D; Rush-Henrietta Charles H Roth HS; Rush, NY; (Y); 3/195; Am Leg Boys St; Boy Scts; Ski Clb; JV Socr; Var Tennis; French Hon Soc; NHS; AFROTC Scholar 86; Rochester Inst Tech; Elec Engr.

WILLIG, ANNE; Saugerties HS; Saugerties, NY; (Y); 16/244; 4-H; French Clb; Library Aide; High Hon Roll; Hon Roll; NHS.

WILLIG, SUE; Saugerties HS; Saugerties, NY; (Y); 15/244; 4-H; French Clb; High Hon Roll; Hon Roll; NHS.

WILLIS, BONNY M; Maryvale SR HS; Cheektowaga, NY; (Y); 175/305; GAA; Girl Scts; Library Aide; Spanish Clb; Varsity Clb; Bowling; JV VP Mgr(s); Var Capt Socr; JV Vllybl; Hon Roll; 2nd Tm All Stars Sccr 86; 1st Ping Pong Intrmrls 86; Libry Awd 86; Erie CC; Sec Sci.

WILLIS, CORINNE; Mahopac HS; Mahopac, NY; (Y); 121/383; Girl Scts; Library Aide; Band; Color Guard; Concert Band; Mrchg Band; Stage Crew; Symp Band; Hon Roll; Taylor U; Bus.

WILLIS, HEATHER; Groton Central HS; Groton, NY; (Y); Sec Drama Clb; Chorus; Concert Band; Jazz Band; Mrchg Band; School Musical; Swing Chorus; Hon Roll; Music.

WILLIS, PATRICIA; Naples Central Schl; Naples, NY; (S); VP DECA; Concert Band; Jazz Band; Mrchg Band; Var L Bsktbl; JV Var Vllybl; High Hon Roll; Hon Roll; VFW Awd; Voice Dem Awd; Bus.

WILLITT, TROY; Canaseraga Central Schl; Canaseraga, NY; (Y); 1/24; Am Leg Boys St; Band; Chorus; Jazz Band; School Play; Yrbk Ed-Chief; Pres Sr Cls; High Hon Roll; Pres NHS; Area All Cnty Chorus 86; Legl Stds.

WILLMANN, JENIFER R Q; Division Avenue HS; Levittown, NY; (S); 1/335; Off Math Clb; Political Wkr; Nwsp Ed-Chief; Rep Stu Cncl; Var Capt Badmtn; Var L Vllybl; Pres NHS; Ntl Merit Ltr; Val; Cmnty Wkr; Arista Chrtr; Steuben Grmn Excllnc Awd 83.

WILLMART, RANDY; Colton Pierrepont Central HS; Colton, NY; (Y); 1/25; French Clb; Quiz Bowl; VP Soph Cls; VP Jr Cls; Pres Sr Cls; Bausch & Lomb Sci Awd; Elks Awd; Hon Roll; Jr NHS; NHS; Clarkson U; Electrcl Engr.

WILLMOTT, MELISSA; Mercy HS; Riverhead, NY; (Y); 40/129; Drama Clb; Ski Clb; Color Guard; Drm & Bgl; School Musical; Stage Crew; Yrbk Ed-Chief; Var Timer; Awd Of Achvmnt Deaf Stu 85; Awd Of Achvmnt Drama 84-85; Aernautics.

WILLNER, ANITA; Blindbrook HS; Rye Brook, NY; (Y); Pres AFS; Computer Clb; French Clb; Math Tm; SADD; Iona Frnch Cntst-2nd Hnrs 84; Bio.

WILLOTH, LARA; Wayne Central HS; Ontario, NY; (Y); Var Capt Cheerleading; Var Gym; Var Socr; Var Sftbl.

WILLOUGHBY, KELLI; Freeport HS; Freeport, NY; (Y); Cmnty Wkr; Dance Clb; Teachers Aide; School Musical; Variety Show; Yrbk Stf; Rep Frsh Cls; Rep Soph Cls; Rep Jr Cls; Rep Stu Cncl; Dr Martin Luther King Scholar Awd 86; ST Scholar Dance Theatre Harlem 86; Perfrmng Arts.

WILLS, KRISTINE; Mexico Acad & Central Schl; Lycoming, NY; (Y); Sec Frsh Cls; Trs Soph Cls; Trs Jr Cls; Var Bsktbl; Var Capt Socr; Var Capt Sftbl; Charles Giovo II Macs Coaches Awd 85; Macs MVP Sftbl 86; Met Palmer Awd 3 Sprt Vrsty Athlt 86; Chemistry.

WILLSEY, TINA; Cicero-North Syracuse HS; N Syracuse, NY; (S); 54/667; Sec Church Yth Grp; Var Capt Swmmng; NHS; SUNY; Psych.

WILLSON, JEANNINE; St Marys HS; E Aurora, NY; (Y); Camera Clb; Church Yth Grp; Office Aide; Var Acad Achvt Awds 83-86; Early Chldhood Educ.

WILLSON, LEANNE; Camden Central HS; Camden, NY; (Y); 4-H; Band; School Play; JV Bsktbl; Var Trk; Cit Awd; 4-H Awd; Hon Roll; Sci.

WILMOT, DENNIS; Mc Quaid Jesuit HS; Rochester, NY; (Y); Cmnty Wkr; Hosp Aide; Letterman Clb; Varsity Clb; JV Capt Socr; Var JV Trk; High Hon Roll; Hon Roll; Jr NHS; NHS; People To People 86; Hospice Asst 85; Lib Arts.

WILMOT, LYNN; Union Springs HS; Aurora, NY; (Y); Band; School Play; Var Bsktbl; Var Coach Actv; Mgr Fld Hcky; Mgr(s); Sftbl; High Hon Roll; Hon Roll; Comp Tech.

WILMOTT, CLAYTON O; Roosevelt JR/SR HS; Hempstead, NY; (S); Art Clb; Science Clb; Var Socr; High Hon Roll; Hon Roll; NHS; Martin Luther King JR Achvt Awd 85; Elec Engr.

WILMS, JEFFREY; Schoharie Central HS; West Berne, NY; (S); Varsity Clb; Band; Concert Band; Var Bsbl; Var Bsktbl; Var Socr; High Hon Roll; Mst Imprvd Bsbl Plyr 83-84, Soccr 84-85; Cert Captl Dist Indstrl Arts Assn 85; 1st Cnty Socr Lg 84-85; HVCC; Indstrl Tech.

WILNER, STEWART K; Hastings HS; Hastings-On-Hudso, NY; (Y); 1/110; Model UN; Yrbk Ed-Chief; Capt JV Socr; High Hon Roll; NHS; Ntl Merit Ltr; Val; French Clb; Crs Cntry; Renssalaer Polytechnic Awd Math & Sci 85; NYS Sci Suprvsrs Assn Awd Chem 85; U Of Pennsylvania; Ecnmcs.

WILSEY, KELLEY; Unatego HS; Otego, NY; (S); 1/85; Drama Clb; Band; Chorus; Concert Band; Jazz Band; School Musical; School Play; High Hon Roll; NHS; Ntl Merit Ltr; Hghst Ovrl Aver Awd 83; Excel Chrl Singng Awd 84; Hghst Engl Rgnts Mark 85; Music.

WILSON, BRIAN; Saranac Central HS; Cadyville, NY; (S); 26/121; Drama Clb; Stage Crew; Yrbk Stf; Var L Trk; Hon Roll.

WILSON, CAMILLE; South Shore HS; Brooklyn, NY; (Y); Church Yth Grp; Service Clb; Hlth & Phys Ed Awd 86; Boston U; Law.

WILSON, CHAKA; Franklin Central Schl; Franklin, NY; (Y); Boy Scts; Drama Clb; FFA; Ski Clb; SADD; School Play; Var Bsktbl; Var Socr; Var Trk; Mst Val Trck 86; Mst Imprvd Plyr Bsktbl; Educ.

WILSON, CHANDRA; Erasmus Hall HS; Brooklyn, NY; (Y); Teachers Aide; Gym; Trk; Vllybl; Wt Lftg; Hon Roll; NHS; Prfct Atten Awd; Achvt Awd Word Proc 86; New York City Tech Coll; Bus.

WILSON, CHRISTIAN; Johnstown HS; Johnstown, NY; (Y); 18/160; Intnl Clb; Yrbk Stf; Pres Soph Cls; Rep Sr Cls; Trs Stu Cncl; JV Crs Cntry; JV Tennis; High Hon Roll; Hon Roll; NHS; Regnts Schlrshp 86; Le Moyne Coll; Math.

WILSON, DAHLIA; Alexander Hamilton HS; Elmsford, NY; (S); Hosp Aide; VP Intnl Clb; JA; Math Tm; Lit Mag; Pres Stu Cncl; Trk; High Hon Roll; Jr NHS; Ntl Merit Ltr; High Hnr Roll 83-85; Stu Govt Pres 84-86; Jr Achvt 83-84 & 85-86; Johns Hopkins U; Neurosurgery.

WILSON, DARREN; Brasher Falls Central HS; Brasher Falls, NY; (S); 6/105; French Clb; Letterman Clb; SADD; Varsity Clb; Band; Chorus; Concert Band; Jazz Band; Mrchg Band; Orch; Acdmc All Nrthn Hockey Tm 84-86; SUNY Canton; Eng Sci.

WILSON, ELIZABETH; Catholic Central HS; Cohoes, NY; (S); 9/179; Ski Clb; Band; High Hon Roll; NHS; Ntl Merit Ltr; Pres Schlr; Math Clb; Concert Band; RPI Medal-Math & Sci Excllnc 85.

WILSON, FELICIA; Adlai E Stevenson HS; Bronx, NY; (Y); 107/487; Orch; School Musical; Stage Crew; Bowling; Tennis; Prfct Atten Awd; NY ST Regents Schlrshp 86; Marymount Manhattan Stu Ldrshp Schlrshp 86; Comm.

WILSON, JAMES; Argyle Central HS; Argyle, NY; (Y); French Clb; Math Tm; Yrbk Rptr; Yrbk Stf; Var JV Bsbl; JV Bsktbl; Var JV Socr; Most Improved Sci 86; Elec Engrng.

WILSON, JAMES; Skaneateles HS; Skaneateles, NY; (Y); 10/156; Ski Clb; Ftbl; Wt Lftg; High Hon Roll; NHS; Ntl Merit SF; Rochester Inst Tech; Comp Sci.

WILSON, JASON G; New Rochelle HS; New Rochelle, NY; (Y); 52/600; SADD; Rep Jr Cls; Rep Sr Cls; Var L Trk; French Hon Soc; NHS; Cmnty Wkr; French Clb; Model UN; Ski Clb; Commend Stu Ntl Achvt Schrlshp 85; Regents Schrlshp 85; Lead Pgm Bus 85; Princeton U; Banker.

WILSON, JENNIFER; Mattituck HS; Mattituck, NY; (Y); 12/117; Am Leg Aux Girls St; Variety Show; Pres Frsh Cls; VP Soph Cls; Stu Cncl; Capt Cheerleading; Off Jr Cls; Off Sr Cls; Hon Roll; NHS; Amer Leg Aux Grls Ntn Rep 85; Rtry Stu Of Mnth 86; Lions Clb-Strwbrry Queen-Schlrshp 86; Lafayette Coll; Intl Affrs.

WILSON, JILL G; Cardinal Spellman HS; Bronx, NY; (Y); Capt Flag Corp; Nwsp Phtg; Yrbk Stf; Off Sr Cls; Trk; Hon Roll; Ntl Merit Ltr; PA ST U; Bio.

WILSON, JOE; G Ray Bodley HS; Fulton, NY; (Y); Church Yth Grp; Latin Clb; Political Wkr; Rep Frsh Cls; Rep Soph Cls; Rep Jr Cls; JV Lcrss; Im Wt Lftg; Hon Roll; Mass Media Comm.

WILSON, JOHN L; Oneida SR HS; Oneida Castle, NY; (Y); 20/210; Am Leg Boys St; Church Yth Grp; Letterman Clb; Varsity Clb; Jazz Band; Bsktbl; Socr; Trk; High Hon Roll; NHS; Natl Sci Merit Awd Chem 86; US Svc Acad; Aerontcl Engrng.

WILSON, JOHN M; Odgensburg Free Acad; Ogdensburg, NY; (Y); 1/184; Church Yth Grp; French Clb; Quiz Bowl; Band; Bausch & Lomb Sci Awd; High Hon Roll; NHS; Ntl Merit SF; Concert Band; Elec Engrng.

WILSON, KATHERINE; Lindenhurst HS; Lindenhurst, NY; (Y); 71/550; French Clb; Nwsp Stf; Yrbk Phtg; Hon Roll; NHS; Pres Acdmc Ftns Awd 86; Natl Hnr Soc Ofcr 85-86; Hofstra U; Eng Maj.

WILSON, KATHLEEN; Gates-Chili SR HS; Rochester, NY; (Y); Dance Clb; High Hon Roll; NHS.

WILSON, KELLY; Emma Willard HS; Albany, NY; (Y); Aud/Vis; Camera Clb; Teachers Aide; School Play; SUNY Albany.

WILSON, KIM; Munich American HS; Encinitas, CA; (Y); FBLA; Ski Clb; Yrbk Stf; Trs Soph Cls; Pres Jr Cls; Rep Stu Cncl; Trk; Hon Roll; NHS; Church Yth Grp; Intl Stu Ldrshp Inst 85; U Of CA; Psych.

WILSON, KRISTI LYNN; Liverpool HS; Liverpool, NY; (Y); 215/816; Church Yth Grp; JA; Color Guard; Mrchg Band; Stu Cncl; Powder Puff Ftbl; Twrlr; Hon Roll; Jr NHS; Hnr Awd 12th Grd Socl Stds 86; Onondaga CC; Bus.

WILSON, KRISTIN M; Gloversville HS; Gloversville, NY; (Y); 66/244; Church Yth Grp; Drama Clb; Teachers Aide; Chorus; School Play; Stage Crew; Powder Puff Ftbl; Var Sftbl; High Hon Roll; Hon Roll; Fltn Cnty Mntl Hlth Awd 86; Fulton Montgomery CC; Psych.

WILSON, LATONIA; South Shore HS; Brooklyn, NY; (Y); Art Clb; Dance Clb; Library Aide; Math Clb; PAVAS; Service Clb; SADD; Band; School Play; Yrbk Stf; Dance 86; Yrbk Stff 86; Math Clb 83; Comp Tech.

WILSON, LAURA; Northville Central Schl; Northville, NY; (Y); Yrbk Stf; Var Cheerleading; JV Socr; Hon Roll; NHS; Frnch Regents Awd 86.

WILSON, LAURA S; Newfane SR HS; Lockport, NY; (S); 10/181; Science Clb; JV Fld Hcky; Hon Roll; Mu Alp Tht; NHS; Hnr Awd Achvt Wood Wrk II & Mechncl Drwng I & II 84; U Of Buffalo; Physcl Thrpy.

WILSON, LINDA; Corning Painted-Post East HS; Corning, NY; (Y); 19/210; Ski Clb; Chorus; School Musical; Ed Yrbk Stf; Rep Soph Cls; Rep Jr Cls; Rep Sr Cls; Capt Pom Pon; High Hon Roll; NHS; 1st Pl Dance Camp 85; Acctg.

WILSON, LINDA H; Liverpool HS; N Syracuse, NY; (Y); 45/816; AFS; Art Clb; SADD; Stage Crew; Nwsp Stf; Hon Roll; NHS; St John Fisher Presdntl Schlrshp 86-87; NY ST Regents Schlrshp; St John Fisher Coll; Comm.

WILSON, LUANNE; Camden Central HS; Camden, NY; (Y); 34/211; Varsity Clb; Band; Concert Band; Jazz Band; School Musical; School Play; Yrbk Stf; Stat Bsbl; JV Var Bsktbl; JV Score Keeper; Herkimer; Med Lab Tech.

WILSON, MARY; Mount Saint Mary Acad; Kenmore, NY; (Y); Drama Clb; Pep Clb; Chorus; School Musical; School Play; Stage Crew; Swing Chorus; Variety Show; Rep Frsh Cls; Hon Roll; Travel/Trsm.

WILSON, MELISSA; Smithtown HS West; Smithtown, NY; (Y); Ski Clb; Orch; Off Soph Cls; Off Jr Cls; Off Sr Cls; Stu Cncl; JV Var Cheerleading; JV Var Fld Hcky; French Hon Soc; NHS; Bus.

WILSON, MICHELE; Catholic Central HS; Cohoes, NY; (S); 5/179; Math Clb; Math Tm; Teachers Aide; Concert Band; Bsktbl; Sftbl; Tennis; Timer; Trk; Holy Cross Bk Prz 85; Chem Awd, Math II Hnrs Awd 85; Engrng.

WILSON, PARA B; Glen Cove HS; Glen Cove, NY; (Y); Am Leg Boys St; ROTC; Varsity Clb; Color Guard; Var JV Bsbl; Var JV Ftbl; Var Wrstlng; Hon Roll; SAR Awd; Nrsng.

WILSON, PETER; Mc Quaid Jesuit HS; Rochester, NY; (Y); Aud/Vis; French Clb; Ski Clb; Band; Concert Band; Symp Band; Variety Show; Yrbk Phtg; Yrbk Stf; Lit Mag; 1st Battle Of Bands 86; Schlstc Achvt Awd 83; Penn ST U; Engrng.

WILSON, RACHEL; Dewitt Clinton HS; Bronx, NY; (Y).

WILSON, RICHARD; Saugerties HS; Mt Marion, NY; (Y); Hon Roll; NHS.

WILSON, ROBERT; Greece Athena HS; Rochester, NY; (Y); Computer Clb; French Clb; JA; Science Clb; Ski Clb; Hon Roll; MOLE Hnr Chem Clb 84-85; Elec Engrng.

WILSON, ROBERT P; Newfane SR HS; Newfane, NY; (Y); Boy Scts; Ski Clb; Regents Schlrshp 86; Fndtn Intl Coop 80-86; Austin Peay ST U; Corp Mgt.

WILSON, SCOTT; Auburn HS; Auburn, NY; (Y); JA; JV Var Ftbl; Var Score Keeper; Var Timer; JV Var Wt Lftg; Hon Roll; Prfct Atten Awd; Pres Schlr; NY ST Rgnts Schlrshp 86; Cayuga CC; Mktg.

WILSON, SHARON LYNN; Roy C Ketcham HS; Wappingers Fls, NY; (Y); 138/500; Stage Crew; Ed Yrbk Phtg; Var JV Cheerleading; High Hon Roll; Hon Roll; Prjct Advntr 82-83; IBM Co-Op 85-86; Bstn U Schlrshp 86-87; Boston U; Bus Admin.

WILSON, SHERISE; Central Islip SR HS; Central Islip, NY; (Y); 23/372; Band; Mrchg Band; Rep Sr Cls; Cheerleading; Sftbl; Trk; Suffolk Cnty Human Rights Commssn 85 & 86; Amer Assn Tchrs Spn & Portgs 84; NYS Schl Music Assn 84-86; Acctng.

WILSON, SHERWIN; Msgr Mcclancy Memorial HS; So Ozone Park, NY; (Y); 83/219; Cmnty Wkr; JA; ROTC; School Play; VP Jr Cls; Pres Sr Cls; JV Bsktbl; Im Crs Cntry; Var Score Keeper; Im Trk; Cert Merit Assmbly ST NY 86; St Johns ROTC Schlrshp 86; SR Achvt Awd 86; St Johns U; Pre-Law.

WILSON, TERESA JILL; Highland HS; Highland, NY; (Y); 17/124; Church Yth Grp; Varsity Clb; Concert Band; Mrchg Band; Var L Cheerleading; Var L Tennis; Var L Trk; High Hon Roll; NHS; Spanish NHS; Prsdntl Acad Ftnss Awd 86; HS Physcl Ftnss Awd 86; Cedarville Coll; Chem.

WILSON, TERRANCE L; Our Saviour Lutheran HS; Bronx, NY; (Y); 8/26; Yrbk Stf; Var Socr; Var Trk; Im Vllybl; Rgnts Schlrshp 86; Bnkg.

WILSON, TONYA; Washington Irving HS; Brooklyn, NY; (Y); Church Yth Grp; Girl Scts; Hosp Aide; Office Aide; Teachers Aide; Church Choir; Bsktbl; Cit Awd; Cert Of Hnr-Achvt In Acadmcs; Punctulty Hnr; Comp Pgmng.

WILTSEY, DONNA E; Union Endicott HS; Endicott, NY; (Y); 23/453; Key Clb; Mathletes; SADD; Sec Concert Band; Drill Tm; Nwsp Rptr; High Hon Roll; NHS; VA Tech; Cmptr Engrng.

WIMBERLY, CONSTANCE; Springfield Gardens HS; Queens Village, NY; (Y); 95/438; Office Aide; Band; Concert Band; Nwsp Ed-Chief; Nwsp Rptr; Yrbk Rptr; Yrbk Stf; Rep Jr Cls; VP Sr Cls; Capt Cheerleading; Blue Hnr Rl 83-84; VA ST U; Mass Cmmnctns.

WIMBERLY, SEBRINA; Midwood HS; Brooklyn, NY; (Y); Office Aide; Teachers Aide; Church Choir; Rep Stu Cncl; Bus.

WIMMER, PAUL; Sachem North HS; Holbrook, NY; (Y); 369/1560; Church Yth Grp; Cmnty Wkr; German Clb; Ski Clb; Church Choir; Jazz Band; Orch; Variety Show; Im Vllybl; Hon Roll; Bus Mgmt.

WINANS, STEPH; Ward Melville HS; Stony Brook, NY; (Y); Hosp Aide; Ski Clb; Variety Show; Stu Cncl; Cheerleading; Fld Hcky; Lcrss; Trk; High Hon Roll; Hon Roll; NYSSMA 82; 3 Sprt Awd 83; Hnr Cmpr Awd 83; U Of Amherst; Indstrl Psych.

WINCH, DEAN; Saranac HS; Cadyville, NY; (S); Ski Clb; Hon Roll.

WINCH, JEFFREY; Lake George JR & SR HS; Lake George, NY; (Y); Lit Mag; Im Socr; Game Warden.

WINCHELL, MARY; Cohoes HS; Cohoes, NY; (Y); Chorus.

WINDE, CHERYL; Villa Maria Acad; Lancaster, NY; (S); Computer Clb; FBLA; Pep Clb; Ski Clb; Yrbk Stf; Rep Jr Cls; Rep Stu Cncl; Hon Roll; AFS; Natl Rifle Assn 85-86; 2nd Pl Typng Awd 84-85; CPA.

WINDELS, ROBIN ANN; Westhampton Beach HS; E Quogue, NY; (Y); Church Yth Grp; Band; Chorus; Church Choir; School Musical; School Play; Off Stu Cncl; Tennis; Hon Roll; NHS; Hmptn Msc Eductrs Assoc Schlrshp 86; Nadine Mondini Memorial Awd 86; Katherine M Vastine Schlrshp 86; Susquehanna U; Music.

WINDERL, LISA; Bishop Ludden HS; Syracuse, NY; (S); JA; Model UN; Nwsp Stf; Var L Cheerleading; High Hon Roll; NHS; Certs In Frnch II & III 83-84; 1st Pl Art Cntst Wtr Clrs 83; Rochester Inst Of Tech.

WINDERS, JEFF; Mohonasen HS; Schenectady, NY; (Y); 2/175; Key Clb; Math Tm; Ski Clb; Varsity Clb; Var L Bowling; Var JV Ftbl; High Hon Roll; NHS; High Frnch Avrg 84; Rep Math Exam 86; High Bwlng Game 86; Robtcs.

WINDOVER, SUSAN; Union Springs Acad; Saranac, NY; (Y); Band; Chorus; Church Choir; Concert Band; Yrbk Stf; VP Soph Cls; Bsktbl; Score Keeper; Timer; Vllybl; Plyd Bassoon & Sang For NYSMA; Andrews U; Soc Wrkr.

WINDSOR, SEAN; Rocky Point HS; Rocky Pt, NY; (Y); Ski Clb; Varsity Clb; JV Bsktbl; Var Golf; Var JV Socr; Hon Roll; NY Rgnts Schrlshp Wnnr 86; Golf All Conf 86; Golf Mst Vlb Plyr All Lgue 83; SUNY At Plattsburgh; Bus.

WING, JOHN P; Pulaski HS; Richland, NY; (S); 21/98; Drama Clb; French Clb; Math Clb; Ski Clb; Band; Chorus; School Musical; Yrbk Stf; Hon Roll; Edward La Point Instrmntal Awd 85; SUNY Fredonia; Music Ed.

WING, KEITH; Gates Chili HS; Rochester, NY; (Y); Swmmng; Cit Awd; Hon Roll; Sibleys Art Show; Mltry; Art.

WINGARD, JAMES D; Springville Griffith Inst; Springville, NY; (Y); Church Yth Grp; Varsity Clb; Band; Concert Band; Jazz Band; Mrchg Band; Orch; Pep Band; School Musical; Stage Crew; NYS Athltc Assn Ftbl Champs Sec VI Div V 85; Coll Sci Explrtn 86; USAF; Engrng.

WINIATOWSKI, MICHELLE; Villa Maria Acad; Buffalo, NY; (S); 25/90; Computer Clb; Dance Clb; Debate Tm; Trs FBLA; Pep Clb; Yrbk Stf; Stu Cncl; Bsktbl; Swmmng; Hon Roll; Impromptu Spkg 2nd 85; Marian Medal Catholic Yth 84; Psych.

WINKELMAN, JENNIFER; Westfield Academy & Centrl; Westfield, NY; (Y); 9/65; Y-Teens; Band; Chorus; Mrchg Band; Off Sr Cls; Var Capt Bsktbl; Var L Sftbl; Var Capt Vllybl; High Hon Roll; NHS; Dean Schlrshp Daemen Coll, Dept Schlrshp Daemen Coll 86-87; Daemen Coll; Phys Ther.

WINKLER, KATHERINE; Hamburg SR HS; Orchard Park, NY; (Y); 48/374; Cmnty Wkr; French Clb; Hosp Aide; School Musical; Yrbk Phtg; Hon Roll; Bus.

WINKLER, THOMAS; St Peters Boys HS; Staten Isld, NY; (Y); 3/163; JV Bsbl; Im Bsktbl; Im Ftbl; Hon Roll; NHS; St John Baptist De La Salle Schlrshp; Engr.

WINKLEY, BETH; Mt Mercy Acad; East Aurora, NY; (Y); 48/166; Church Yth Grp; Pres Cmnty Wkr; French Clb; JA; Model UN; SADD; Co-Capt Trk; Hon Roll; Myrs Yth Ovrll Achvt Awd 86; Marist Coll; Cmnctns.

WINKOWSKI, SUSAN; Kenmore East SR HS; Tonawanda, NY; (Y); SADD; Band; Concert Band; Mrchg Band; Pep Band; Im Vllybl; Hon Roll; NHS; Fashion Inst Tech; Fshn Merch.

WINNERT, AMY; Eden SR HS; Eden, NY; (Y); Am Leg Aux Girls St; 4-H; GAA; Chorus; Im Badmtn; Var L Bsktbl; Var Im Vllybl; Hon Roll; NHS; Prfct Atten Awd; Engrng.

WINNICK, VALERIE; Brockport HS; Brockport, NY; (Y); 95/315; Sec Church Yth Grp; Pep Clb; Sec Spanish Clb; Teachers Aide; Yrbk Sprt Ed; Yrbk Stf; JV Var Cheerleading; Im Gym; JV Var Pom Pon; Stat Score Keeper; Soc Wrk.

WINNING, SHAREE; Gloversville HS; Gloversville, NY; (Y); 34/200; Pres Church Yth Grp; Hosp Aide; Ski Clb; Teachers Aide; Color Guard; Yrbk Stf; Var Crs Cntry; Var Powder Puff Ftbl; Var Trk; Hon Roll; Physcl Thrpy.

WINSLOW, JEAN; St John The Baptist HS; N Babylon, NY; (Y); Library Aide; Ski Clb; Socr; Sftbl; Trk; Hnrs Sci; Merit In Math Awd; Homecmng Comm; Regents Rcptn; :CPA.

WINSLOW, MICHAEL; H Frank Carey HS; Franklin Sq, NY; (Y); 22/228; VP Key Clb; VP Science Clb; Varsity Clb; JV Var Bsbl; High Hon Roll; Hon Roll; NHS; St Schlr; Stony Brook; Med.

WINSLOW, MICHAEL; Whitesboro Central HS; Utica, NY; (Y); 10/306; Varsity Clb; Im Coach Actv; Var Ftbl; Var Lcrss; Var Wrstlng; Hon Roll; NCTE Awd; NHS; Math Hall Fm 84.

WINSOR, ELLEN; Geneva HS; Geneva, NY; (S); 10/175; Am Leg Aux Girls St; Hosp Aide; Ski Clb; Concert Band; Mrchg Band; Tennis; High Hon Roll; Hon Roll; NHS; Band; Engl.

WINSPEAR, DAVID; Letchworth Central HS; Bliss, NY; (Y); Boy Scts; Chess Clb; 4-H; FFA; Varsity Clb; Var Ftbl; Mechncs.

WINSTON, DAVINA; Grover Cleveland HS; Buffalo, NY; (Y); Office Aide; Spanish Clb; Crs Cntry; Trk; Hon Roll; NHS; Accntnt.

WINTER, CAREY; Walt Whitman HS; Huntinton Sta, NY; (Y); Church Yth Grp; GAA; Key Clb; Office Aide; Orch; Yrbk Stf; Var Capt Fld Hcky; Socr; Trk; JV Vllybl; Girls Phy Ed Awd 83-84; Girls Ldrs 85-86; NYS Music Assc 83-84; Ball ST U; Phy Ed.

WINTERS, DEBRA; Dominican Commercial HS; Woodhaven, NY; (Y); 45/273; Pep Clb; Teachers Aide; Chorus; Rep Frsh Cls; Rep Soph Cls; Stu Cncl; High Hon Roll; Jr NHS; NHS; Pres Schlr; Endowed Merit Schlrshp 86-88; Schlstc Excllnc Awd 86; Accntng Achvt Awd 86; Queensborough Coll; Accntnt.

WINTERS, HEIDI; Niskayuna HS; Rexford, NY; (Y); Service Clb; Spanish Clb; Chorus; Timer; Niskayuna Inter-Cmmnty Svc Schlrshp Awd 87; Erly Chldhd Dvlpmnt.

WINTERS, KIMBERLEY; Wilson Central HS; Wilson, NY; (Y); Church Yth Grp; 4-H; Band; Church Choir; Pep Band; Yrbk Stf; Fld Hcky; Sftbl; Hon Roll; Varsity Clb; Spec Educ.

WINTERS, MATTHEW; Tupper Lake HS; Tupper Lake, NY; (Y); 3/117; Letterman Clb; Varsity Clb; Band; Concert Band; Jazz Band; Orch; Pres Frsh Cls; Pres Soph Cls; Pres Jr Cls; Stu Cncl; 1st Tm All Nrthnr Ftbl & Bsktbl 84-86; All Outstndnd Athlt & Schlr Athlt Awd; Yrly Ftbl Schlrshp Lafay; Lafayette Coll; Elec Engr.

WINTERS, MICHELLE; Tupper Lake JR SR HS; Tupper Lk, NY; (Y); Girl Scts; Chorus; School Musical; School Play; Sec Trs Sr Cls; Sec Stu Cncl; JV Var Bsktbl; JV Var Socr; Hon Roll; Jr NHS; Outstndng Achvt Sci Awd 83; Outstndng Bus Stu Awd 86; Bus Awd 86; Our Lady Of Victory Sec; Ex Sec.

WINTERS, PETER; Clarkstown North HS; New City, NY; (Y); Cmnty Wkr; Temple Yth Grp; Var Bsktbl; U Of S FL Tampa; Bus Mngmnt.

WIRTH, COLLEEN; Alden HS; Marilla, NY; (Y); Church Yth Grp; Trs 4-H; GAA; Letterman Clb; Mathletes; Math Clb; Trs Spanish Clb; Varsity Clb; Chorus; Rep Soph Cls; Natl Hstry Dy Cntst 85.

WIRTH, TINA; L A Webber JR SR HS; Lyndonville, NY; (Y); 10/88; Girl Scts; Teachers Aide; Band; Color Guard; Yrbk Bus Mgr; Yrbk Stf; Score Keeper; Jr NHS; NHS; CPA.

WIRTH, WENDY; Hilton HS; Hilton, NY; (Y); 11/299; Sec Frsh Cls; Sec Soph Cls; Sec Jr Cls; Pres Stu Cncl; Capt Cheerleading; Trk; NHS; Ntl Merit Ltr; Pres Schlr; Western NY Vol Firemans Assn Queen 84; NCA All Am Chrldr Awd 84; Top 5 Chrldrs Monroe Co 85-86; Ithaca Coll; Phys Ther.

WIRTZ, KRISTINA; James Sperry HS; Henrietta, NY; (Y); 2/271; Thesps; Band; Chorus; Orch; French Hon Soc; NHS; Ntl Merit Ltr; Sal; French Clb; School Musical; Molly Mulligan Schlrshp 84; Paideia Awd Excllnc Hmnts 85; HS Engl Dept Awd 86; Cornell U; Bio.

WISCH, BETH; South Side HS; Rockville Ctr, NY; (Y); Science Clb; Temple Yth Grp; Chorus; Hon Roll; Grad Hnr Grd & Ushr 86; Cmmnctns.

WISDO, CHRISTOPHER T; Roy C Ketcham HS; Wappingers Falls, NY; (Y); 5/400; Drama Clb; Chorus; Orch; Nwsp Stf; High Hon Roll; Jr NHS; NHS; Ntl Merit SF; Computer Clb; Math Clb; Ad Altare Dei 83; 2nd Pl-Dtchss Cnty Tlnt Srch 83; Brown; Engrng.

WISE, HOLLY; Westfield Acad & Central Schl; Westfield, NY; (Y); Church Yth Grp; 4-H; PAVAS; Yrbk Stf; Var L Trk; 4-H Awd; High Hon Roll; Hon Roll; NHS; Ntl Sci Merit Awd 84.

WISHANSKY, MARC A; Sachem North HS; Holbrook, NY; (Y); 31/1300; Office Aide; Science Clb; Ski Clb; Spanish Clb; Temple Yth Grp; Jr NHS; NHS; Ntl Merit Schol; Biomed Engr.

WISLOH, JO ANN; James Madison HS; Brooklyn, NY; (Y); 55/754; Yrbk Stf; Twrlr; Hon Roll; Arista & Archon; Regents Schlrshp; St Johns U; Math.

WISNIEWSKI, JUDITH; Villa Maria Acad; Cheektowaga, NY; (Y); Computer Clb; Girl Scts; Math Clb; Ski Clb; Chorus; Sec Soph Cls; VP Jr Cls; Rep Stu Cncl.

WISNIEWSKI, KRYSTYN; The Bronx HS For Science; Malba, NY; (Y); Church Yth Grp; Debate Tm; Hosp Aide; NFL; Teachers Aide; Varsity Clb; Concert Band; Capt Var Sftbl; Hon Roll; Prfct Atten Awd; Art Awd Music Dept 83-84; UFT NYC Art Tchr Assoc Pgm 84; Rensaleer Poly Tech; Pre-Med.

WISNIEWSKI, NORMAN A; West Seneca East SR HS; Cheektowaga, NY; (Y); 60/375; Aud/Vis; CAP; NY ST Rgnts Schlrshp Wnnr 86; Outstndng Achvt-NY ST Stu Enrgy Resrch Comp 85; Cvl Air Ptrl 84; Canisius Coll; Poltcl Sci.

WISNIEWSKI, ROBERT W; Niagara Wheatfield HS; Niagara Falls, NY; (Y); 1/291; Trs German Clb; Pres Math Clb; PAVAS; Stu Cncl; Capt Swmmng; High Hon Roll; NHS; Val; Rgnts Schlrshp 86; Crnll Natl Schlr Awd 86; Swmng Tm MVP 86; Cornell U; Elctrl Engr.

WISNIEWSKI, TAMARA EVETTE; Dunkirk SR HS; Dunkirk, NY; (Y); Am Leg Aux Girls St; Cmnty Wkr; Key Clb; Science Clb; Spanish Clb; Yrbk Ed-Chief; Stu Cncl; Hon Roll; Service Clb; Yrbk Phtg; RN.

WISNOCK, MICHAEL D; Newfane SR HS; Newfane, NY; (Y); 14/181; Am Leg Boys St; Drama Clb; Scholastic Bowl; Band; School Play; Stage Crew; Sr Cls; DAR Awd; Mu Alp Tht; NHS; NYS Regents Scholar; Boston U; Naval Aviatn Offcr.

WISOR, MICHAEL J; Wilson Central HS; Lockport, NY; (Y); Ski Clb; Varsity Clb; Var Capt Bsbl; Var Capt Bsktbl; Coach Actv; Var Capt Ftbl; FL ST; Ed.

WISSINGER, ANNE-LOUISE; Sacred Heart Acad; Garden City Park, NY; (S); 47/182; VP Church Yth Grp; Pres Trs Dance Clb; Office Aide; SADD; School Musical; Nwsp Rptr; Rep Jr Cls; Rep Sr Cls; Hon Roll; NHS; U S Stdnt Cncl Awds 85-86; Danc Thrpst.

WISZ, DAVID; Cardinal O Hara HS; Tonawanda, NY; (S); JV Bsbl; Cordinal Ohara One Yr Schlrshp 82; 5th Pl Coll Inst Math Cntst 82; Lawyer.

WITKIN, B J; The Knox Schl; N Babylon, NY; (Y); 3/41; Drama Clb; Library Aide; Thesps; School Play; Nwsp Ed-Chief; Nwsp Rptr; Lit Mag; Stu Cncl; Crs Cntry; Socr; Harvard Bk Awd 84-85; Bst Dramatic Prfrmnce 84-85; U S Naval Acad Fndtn Scholar 86-87; U S Naval Acad; Navl Aviatr.

WITKOP, JAMES; Catholic Central HS; Mechanicville, NY; (Y); Church Yth Grp; Math Clb; Ski Clb; Spanish Clb; SADD; JV Ftbl; High Hon Roll; NHS; Prfct Atten Awd; Air Force Acad; Pilot.

WITKOWSKI, LYNN; Villa Maria Acad; Buffalo, NY; (Y); GAA; Varsity Clb; Nwsp Stf; Capt Var Bowling; Var Capt Score Keeper; Hon Roll; All Cathlc 1st Tm Bwlng Hi Avg, MVP & Hi Set 86; Comp/Kybrdng Hi Avg 86; Math.

WITKOWSKI, LYNNE; Henninger HS; Syracuse, NY; (Y); 17/395; Cmnty Wkr; Intnl Clb; Key Clb; SADD; Acpl Chr; Chorus; Yrbk Stf; High Hon Roll; Hon Roll; Kiwanis Awd; Regents Schlrshp 86; Amer Lgn Schlrshp Awd 86; Onondaga CC; Chem.

WITMAN, SCOTT; Hamburg Central HS; Hamburg, NY; (Y); 42/385; Cmnty Wkr; Concert Band; Mrchg Band; Symp Band; Var Bsbl; Var Ice Hcky; JV Socr; Hon Roll; NHS; Band; Phy Ed Awd 84; MVP Bsbl 84; MVP Sccr 84.

WITMER, JOELLE; Fairport HS; Fairport, NY; (Y); Church Yth Grp; Dance Clb; Key Clb; Pep Clb; SADD; Chorus; School Musical; Rep Stu Cncl; Clara Abbott Fdn 86; Messiah Coll; Elem Educ.

WITT, MICHAEL D; Adirondack HS; Boonville, NY; (Y); 13/140; Am Leg Boys St; Boy Scts; Ski Clb; Acpl Chr; Band; Chorus; Church Choir; Concert Band; Jazz Band; School Musical; Enrnmt Sci.

WITTENBERG, ALEXANDER; Yeshiva University H S For Boys; Jackson Hts, NY; (Y); 22/108; Computer Clb; Hosp Aide; Science Clb; Nwsp Stf; Ntl Merit SF; Yeshiva U; Bio.

WITTER, GARY; Addison Central HS; Addison, NY; (Y); Church Yth Grp; Pres 4-H; Science Clb; Var Crs Cntry; Var Swmmng; Var Trk; Cit Awd; 4-H Awd; High Hon Roll; Hnr Society 86.

WITTINE, HEIDI M; St Francis Prep; Glendale, NY; (S); 30/693; German Clb; Service Clb; Teachers Aide; Chorus; NHS; Prncpls List 83-84; Optimate Soc 82; Trvl & Trsm.

WITTMAN, YVETTE; Akron Central HS; Akron, NY; (Y); 31/145; Church Yth Grp; Drama Clb; French Clb; Pep Clb; Band; Color Guard; Concert Band; Mrchg Band; School Musical; School Play; Alfred ST Coll; Nrsng.

WITTMEYER JR, RON; North Collins Central HS; Springville, NY; (Y); 4/68; Ski Clb; Yrbk Phtg; L Socr; Hon Roll; Jr NHS; NHS; Prfct Atten Awd; Educ Fndtn Schlrshp 86; ECIC 1st Tm All Star Sccr 85; SUNY-ALFRED; Mech Engrng.

WITTNER, JULIE; Martin Van Buren HS; New Hyde Pawrk, NY; (Y); 106/576; Service Clb; Yrbk Stf; Hon Roll; Nrsg.

WITTNER, MICHELE; Midwood HS; Brooklyn, NY; (Y); 129/667; Model UN; Band; School Musical; Lit Mag; Socr; Prfct Atten Awd; Svc League 86; Sci Hnr Rl 86.

WITTREICH, BETINA J; Brentwood HS; Brentwood, NY; (Y); 1/500; Drama Clb; German Clb; Hosp Aide; Radio Clb; School Play; Nwsp Ed-Chief; Yrbk Rptr; Sr Cls; Trs Stu Cncl; NHS; Brnz Medl-Engl, Germn I 83-84; Slvr Medls-Engl II, Physcs, Germn II, Adv Comp, Hnrs Amer Hstry 84-5; Adelphi U; Pre-Med.

WITZ, JOHN; Cicero N Syracuse HS; Clay, NY; (S); 17/667; VP Church Yth Grp; Math Clb; Math Tm; L JV Bsbl; Bsktbl; High Hon Roll; NHS; Prfct Atten Awd; Colgate U Schlrshp; Colgate U; Bus.

WITZEL, TOM; Horseheads HS; Horseheads, NY; (Y); 34/420; Am Leg Boys St; Spanish Clb; Nwsp Sprt Ed; Var Capt Socr; CC Awd; Hon Roll; Cmnty Bldrs Awd 85; Cornell; Htl Mtl Mgmt.

WIXSON, MARK; Bishop Grimes HS; North Syracuse, NY; (S); 3/200; Church Yth Grp; Cmnty Wkr; Hosp Aide; Latin Clb; Math Clb; Math Tm; Quiz Bowl; Science Clb; Trs Stu Cncl; High Hon Roll; Syracuse U; Premed.

WOD, BRETT C; Pittsford Mendon HS; Pittsford, NY; (Y); Ski Clb; Chorus; Yrbk Stf; Var Capt Lcrss; JV Socr; Hon Roll; ROTC Army Schlrshp 86; Ski Team; Cert Hnr DNA Lab U Of Rochester 85; St Lawrence U; Pre-Med.

WODZINSKI, JOYCE; Lackawanna SR HS; Lackawanna, NY; (Y); JA; Ski Clb; Powder Puff Ftbl; Trk; Cazenovia Coll; Intr Desgn.

WOELFEL, MARK; Frontier Central HS; Hamburg, NY; (Y); Trs Art Clb; VP Chess Clb; Drama Clb; VP Latin Clb; Radio Clb; School Play; Stu Cncl; Hon Roll; NHS; Bus Adm.

WOERTER, PATTY; Connetquot HS; Ronkonkoma, NY; (Y); 125/800; Chorus; Color Guard; Drill Tm; Yrbk Stf; Cheerleading; Fld Hcky; Sftbl; Twrlr; High Hon Roll; Hon Roll; Crtlnd ST U; Physcl Ed.

WOHLRAB, JULIE; Whitesboro SR HS; Utica, NY; (Y); 16/306; Lit Mag; Rep Frsh Cls; Rep Soph Cls; Rep Jr Cls; Rep Sr Cls; Rep Stu Cncl; Var JV Cheerleading; High Hon Roll; Hon Roll; Jr NHS.

WOICCAK, ROBERT; Seton Catholic Central HS; Endwell, NY; (Y); 3/162; Aud/Vis; Var Golf; Var Trk; NHS; Ntl Merit Ltr; Seton Schlr; Helios Prog; Clarkson U; Chem Engr.

WOJCIECHOWSKI, ANNMARIE; Villa Maria Acad; Buffalo, NY; (Y); Am Leg Aux Girls St; Church Yth Grp; Office Aide; Pep Clb; Yrbk Stf; Pres Jr Cls; JV Bsktbl; Bowling; Sftbl; Soc Wrk.

WOJCIK, DOUGLAS; Bishop Ludden HS; Liverpool, NY; (S); Boy Scts; Church Yth Grp; Computer Clb; Exploring; VP JA; Spanish Clb; Yrbk Stf; Lit Mag; High Hon Roll; NHS; Order Arrow Scouting Awd 84; Outstndng Accomplishments Span 84; Bio.

WOJCIK, GLENN; Kenmore West HS; Buffalo, NY; (Y); Math Clb; Math Tm; Var L Bowling; Var L Trk; Hon Roll; Ntl Merit Ltr; St Schlr; -Ny ST Bwlng Trnment 4th 83; Pepsi Hpsht 1st Pl 85 & 86; U Of Buffalo; Law.

WOJCIK, TAMMY; Frontier Central HS; Hamburg, NY; (S); 1/444; Hosp Aide; Ski Clb; Stu Cncl; JV Var Cheerleading; NHS; Ntl Merit Ltr; NEDT Awd.

WOJDYLA, STEVEN; Henninger HS; Syracuse, NY; (Y); 5/363; JV Capt Bsbl; JV Var Ftbl; Var Trk; High Hon Roll; NHS; Elctrcl Engr.

WOLD, EDWARD; Hahn American HS; Apo New York, NY; (Y); 4/75; Boy Scts; Letterman Clb; Varsity Clb; Rep Jr Cls; Rep Sec Stu Cncl; L Capt Ftbl; Var L Trk; Var Wrstlng; NHS; Arch Engrng.

WOLF, CHRIS; Sanford H Calhoun HS; Merrick, NY; (Y); Aud/Vis; Drama Clb; Chorus; Lcrss; Var Capt Socr; Capt Trk; Capt Wrstlng; Hon Roll; Presdntl Phys Fitness Awd 85 & 86; Best Attitude-Wrstlng 85; Boston Coll; Psych.

WOLF, DAWN M; Amherst Central SR HS; Snyder, NY; (Y); 26/292; Girl Scts; Ski Clb; Chorus; Madrigals; Swing Chorus; Capt Var Bowling; High Hon Roll; Hon Roll; NHS; Ntl Merit Ltr; NYU Buffalo; Pol Sci.

WOLF, EMILY; St Francis Prep Schl; Douglaston, NY; (Y); 350/750; Exploring; 4-H; Hosp Aide; SADD; Rep Frsh Cls; JV Vllybl; 4-H Awd; Jrnlsm.

WOLF, GEORGE J; Lakeland HS; Putnam Valley, NY; (Y); 56/348; Computer Clb; Ski Clb; SADD; Band; Concert Band; Jazz Band; Mrchg Band; School Musical; School Play; Yrbk Stf; Clarkson U; Comp Sci.

WOLF, JOSEPH M; St Marys HS; Depew, NY; (Y); 45/166; Computer Clb; Science Clb; Crs Cntry; Score Keeper; Trk; Canisius Coll Grnt 86-87; NYS Regnts Schlrshp 86-90; Canisius Coll NY; Comp Sci.

WOLF, KAREN; North Shore HS; Glen Head, NY; (Y); 28/210; Sec AFS; Dance Clb; Hosp Aide; Key Clb; Lit Mag; Rep Stu Cncl; Var Bsktbl; NHS; Glen Head Bus Assoc Schlrshp 86; Pres Acadmc Ftsns Awd 86; Sfst Comm Drv Awd 86; Delaware U; Comm.

WOLF, MARIE; St Marys HS; Depew, NY; (Y); Church Yth Grp; Ski Clb; SADD; Nwsp Stf; Cheerleading; Trk; High Hon Roll; NHS.

WOLF, NANCY L; West Seneca East SR HS; West Seneca, NY; (Y); 6/375; VP Trs Church Yth Grp; German Clb; Sec Pres GAA; Chorus; Nwsp Stf; Var Capt Bsktbl; Var Capt Fld Hcky; Var Capt Socr; Var Capt Vllybl; NHS; St Bonaventure U; Chem.

WOLF, PHILLIPS; Fairport HS; Fairport, NY; (Y); Computer Clb; Model UN; Lit Mag; Hon Roll; Ntl Merit Ltr; Spanish NHS.

WOLF, SARAH; Eldred Central Schl; Yulan, NY; (Y); 2/32; Trs SADD; Teachers Aide; Nwsp Stf; Trs Stu Cncl; L Socr; NHS; Sal; Hamilton Coll; Gvrnmt.

WOLF, SCOTT; Lansingburgh HS; Troy, NY; (Y).

WOLF, TERRI-LYNN; Geneva HS; Waterloo, NY; (Y); 54/192; 4-H; Red Cross Aide; Yrbk Phtg; JV Var Cheerleading; Cmnty Wkr; Drama Clb; Latin Clb; Model UN; Chorus; School Musical; 4-H Ambssdr 83-86; Red Crss Ldrshp 85; NY ST Yth 86; Outstndg Teenagr 85; Govt Rltns.

WOLFE, DOUG; Roslyn HS; Roslyn, NY; (Y); English Clb; Temple Yth Grp; Varsity Clb; Variety Show; Nwsp Rptr; Yrbk Stf; Stu Cncl; Var Bsbl; Capt Bowling; Var Ftbl; Roslyn Little Lg Schlrshp Awd 86; Regents Schlrshp 85; O W Post Bsbl Schlrshp Div 5 86; C W Post.

WOLFE, GARRET; Iona Prepatory Schl; Yonkers, NY; (Y); 52/204; Im Bowling; JV Crs Cntry; Im Ftbl; JV Trk; Hon Roll; 2nd Hrns 83-84; 1st Hnrs & 2nd Hnrs 84-85; 2nd Hrns 85-86; Engr.

WOLFE, HEATHER; Barker Central HS; Barker, NY; (Y); 17/107; Pres AFS; French Clb; FBLA; FHA; Spanish Clb; Varsity Clb; Chorus; School Musical; Nwsp Stf; Trs Soph Cls; Gregg Typng Awd 85; Gregg Typng Awd 86; Dstngsh Mrt Schlrshp 86; Niagara Cnty Comm Coll; Anthpg.

WOLFE, JENNIFER; Duanesburg JR SR HS; Quaker St, NY; (Y); 5/66; Pres Camera Clb; Church Yth Grp; Dance Clb; Drama Clb; GAA; Intnl Clb; SADD; Varsity Clb; Chorus; Color Guard; MVP Sccr 83-85; Hghst Avg Frnch II 85; Tlnt Amrc NYS Fnlst 86; Frgn Srvc.

WOLFE, MARYALICE; St Patricks CCHS; Catskill, NY; (Y); 12/26; Red Cross Aide; Yrbk Stf; JV Var Cheerleading; Hon Roll; Sullivan Co Cmnty Coll; Trvl.

WOLFE, THOMAS; Pine Plains HS; Red Hook, NY; (Y); 10/100; AFS; Varsity Clb; Band; JV Var Bsktbl; Var L Crs Cntry; Var L Trk; Hon Roll; Hnr Key 84-85; Crs Cntry Mst Imprvd Trphy 84; Cmnctns.

WOLFF, CINDY; Herricks SR HS; Roslyn, NY; (Y); Sec DECA; Temple Yth Grp; Varsity Clb; Nwsp Sprt Ed; Nwsp Stf; Var Capt Bsktbl; Var Sftbl; NHS; Voice Dem Awd; 1st Pl Wnr DECA ST Career Conf-Mktng Manual Evnt 86; Bus Mgmt.

WOLFF, DEBORAH; Liverpool HS; Liverpool, NY; (Y); 106/816; Church Yth Grp; Ski Clb; Chorus; Concert Band; Rep Stu Cncl; Powder Puff Ftbl; Capt Var Tennis; Hon Roll; NHS; MIP Awd Tennis 85; Springfield Coll; Physcl Thrpy.

WOLFLEY, SARAH; Alexander Central HS; Alexander, NY; (Y); Ski Clb; Bsktbl; Socr; Sftbl; Vllybl; Mst Imprvd Plyr JV Vllybl 83-84; MVP JV Vllybl 84-85; Mst Imprvd Plyr Var Soccr 84-85; MVP Var Socr; Cortland; Phys Ed.

WOLFORD, JOHN; Fairport HS; Fairport, NY; (Y); 106/600; Key Clb; Nwsp Sprt Ed; Pres Frsh Cls; Rep Stu Cncl; Var Capt Bsbl; Var Capt Swmmng; Hon Roll.

WOLFSON, TINA; Shulamith HS; Brooklyn, NY; (S); Cmnty Wkr; Dance Clb; Debate Tm; Math Tm; Quiz Bowl; Scholastic Bowl; Temple Yth Grp; Yrbk Stf; Lit Mag; Pres Stu Cncl; Frnch Awd 85; Awd Effrt 85; Good Char Awd 85.

WOLICKI, ARLENE; Villa Maria Acad; Buffalo, NY; (Y); Im Bowling; Im Vllybl; Hon Roll; Deans Schlrshp 86-87; Dept Schlrshp 86-87; Daemen Coll; Accntnt.

WOLIN, ANDREW; Norwich HS; Norwich, NY; (Y); 1/200; Math Tm; Jazz Band; Orch; Symp Band; Pres Frsh Cls; High Hon Roll; NHS; Ntl Merit SF; Val; Lbrl Arts.

WOLIN, WENDI; Pittsford Mendon HS; Pittsford, NY; (Y); 1/270; Drama Clb; Pep Clb; Scholastic Bowl; Rep Soph Cls; JV Socr; Hon Roll; NHS; Lat Awd; Fr Awd Cont; Gift & Tlnted Regents Scholar; SUNY Binghamton; Acctg.

WOLK, KAREN; Our Lady Of Victory Acad; Yonkers, NY; (S); 7/159; Science Clb; SADD; Yrbk Stf; Lit Mag; Pres Stu Cncl; Trs NHS; NEDT Awd; Spanish NHS; Part Scholar RPI Summr Chem Pgm 85; 1st Prz St Thomas Aguinas Coll Chem Cont 84; Eng Medl 84-85; Engrng.

WOLLE, KATHRYN; Chittenango HS; Katonah, NY; (Y); Church Yth Grp; Drama Clb; Library Aide; Model UN; School Play; Lit Mag; Bsktbl; 4-H Awd; NHS; Cmnty Wkr; NY ST Bar Assn Cert Of Hon 86; Yth Actvty Uni Cert Awd 83; Cert Of Awd For Acdmc Endeavors 86; Comp Law.

WOLLEN, GREG; Alden Central HS; Lancaster, NY; (Y); Letterman Clb; Ski Clb; JV Var Ftbl; Crimnl Justc.

WOLLER, ALLYSON; Tappan Zee HS; Tappan, NY; (Y); 22/245; Cmnty Wkr; Dance Clb; Intnl Clb; SADD; Chorus; Color Guard; School Play; Nwsp Rptr; NHS; Ntl Merit Ltr; Rgnts Schlrshp 86; Sqntl Math III Otstndng Achvmnt Awd 85; Cmprtv Jstc Smnr Lndn England 85; SUNY Binghamton; Accntng.

WOLLHEIM, MONICA; H Frank Carey HS; Franklin Square, NY; (Y); 7/256; French Clb; Church Choir; Yrbk Stf; Trk; French Hon Soc; High Hon Roll; NHS; Church Yth Grp; German Clb; Bsktbl; Newsdays Mst Outstndng Ecolgy Proj-LI Sci Cngrss 86; Tlntd/Gftd 85-86; Ecology Clb-Pres; Frgn Lang.

WOLOSEN, DEBBIE; Hoosic Valley Central HS; Schaghticoke, NY; (Y); Office Aide; Yrbk Stf; Trs Frsh Cls; Trs Soph Cls; Trs Jr Cls; Var JV Bsktbl; Var JV Fld Hcky; JV Sftbl; Hon Roll; NHS; Hudson Valley CC; Med Sec Sci.

WOLOSZYN, PATRICIA; Villa Maria Acad; Buffalo, NY; (S); Yrbk Stf; Stat Bsktbl; Bowling; Score Keeper; High Hon Roll; NHS; Prfct Atten Awd; Rlgn Awd; Bus Dynmcs Awd; SUNY-BUFFALO; Media Comm.

WOLTER, LAURA; John Marshall JR SR HS; Rochester, NY; (Y); Pres VP Church Yth Grp; Math Tm; Spanish Clb; Church Choir; Nwsp Rptr; Rep Stu Cncl; High Hon Roll; NHS; Nwsp Stf; Yrbk Stf; Rensselaer Math/ Sci Awd 86; Mock Trial Comp 86.

WOLTHAUSEN, HEIDI; Clinton SR HS; Clinton, NY; (Y); 7/136; Spanish Clb; Mrchg Band; Pep Band; Symp Band; Pres Stu Cncl; Var L Socr; Var Capt Sftbl; Bausch & Lomb Sci Awd; VP NHS; Opt Clb Awd; NYS Rgnts Schlrshp 86; NY Tele Co Schlrshp 86; U Of Rochester; Engrng.

WOMACK, MICHELLE; New Rochelle HS; New Rochelle, NY; (Y); Bsktbl; Trk; Wrd Prcsng.

WOMELSDORF, IRENE; Corning-Painted Post West HS; Addison, NY; (Y); Pres Exploring; Varsity Clb; Var Crs Cntry; Var Trk; Hon Roll; VA Wesleyan Coll.

WONDRACK, JIM; Cazenovia Central HS; Cazenovia, NY; (Y); Art Clb; Exploring; Pres Frsh Cls; Trs Soph Cls; Trs Jr Cls; Rep Sr Cls; Rep Stu Cncl; Var Capt Socr; Var L Trk; Lcrss; MONY Art Awd 83; Mst Imprvd Art Stu 86; Grphc Arts.

WONG, ALICE; Pichmond Hill HS; Richmond Hill, NY; (Y); 25/288; FBLA; Key Clb; Radio Clb; SADD; Bsktbl; Crs Cntry; Sftbl; Trk; Hon Roll; NHS; Spanish Ntl Hnr Scty 82-85; Bus Hnr Scty 83-86; Buruch; Pub Accntng.

WONG, ALVIN; Archbishop Molloy HS; New York, NY; (Y); 80/383; Art Clb; Cmnty Wkr; Intnl Clb.

WONG, AMY; Spackenkill HS; Poughkeepsie, NY; (Y); Debate Tm; Math Tm; Thesps; Band; Pep Band; Stage Crew; Nwsp Rptr; Nwsp Stf; Yrbk Ed-Chief; Yrbk Stf; RPI Math, Sci Awds 86; Spr Achvt Awd Ntl Grmn 84; SUPR Achvt NY Math Leag 85.

WONG, ANTHONY; Forest Hills HS; New York, NY; (Y); 90/826; Boy Scts; Debate Tm; FCA; Math Clb; Band; Orch; Ed Yrbk Stf; Capt Tennis; High Hon Roll; NHS; Army/ROTC Awd-Outstndng Athlt/Schlr 86; NY Regnts Schlrshp 86; Columbia U; Bioengrng.

WONG, ATHENA; Seward Park HS; New York, NY; (Y); Cmnty Wkr; Debate Tm; Nwsp Rptr; Yrbk Stf; Off Frsh Cls; Rep Jr Cls; Stu Cncl; Library Aide; Teachers Aide; Band; Cert Of Hnr-NY ST Bar Assn 86; Lincoln/Douglas Debates Schlrshp 86; City Cncl Studnt Svc Hnr Citn 84; Eng.

WONG, CINDY Y; Seward Park HS; New York, NY; (Y); 132/544; Trs Computer Clb; Hosp Aide; Office Aide; Service Clb; SADD; Teachers Aide; Band; Concert Band; Nwsp Rptr; Yrbk Rptr; Myrs Yth Svc Awd 86; Cprtn Govt Awd Slvr Mdl 86; Baruch Coll; Comp Info.

WONG, DANNY; Newtown HS; Middle Village, NY; (Y); 24/780; Service Clb; Acpl Chr; Chorus; Bowling; High Hon Roll; Hon Roll; Arista, Outstndng Achvt In Hstry 84; Bus.

WONG, DAVID; Valley Stream Central HS; Valley Stream, NY; (Y); Art Clb; PAVAS; Speech Tm; Badmtn; Bsbl; Fld Hcky; Sftbl; Tennis; Wt Lftg; Hon Roll.

WONG, FLORENCE; H S For The Humaniti; New York, NY; (Y); 13/170; Cmnty Wkr; Hosp Aide; Teachers Aide; Nwsp Stf; Co-Capt Bsktbl; Hon Roll; Hofstra U; Bus Mgmnt.

WONG, JAMES; Xavier HS; Brooklyn, NY; (Y); 1/205; Cmnty Wkr; Computer Clb; Latin Clb; Math Clb; Math Tm; Teachers Aide; Stu Cncl; Ntl Merit SF; NEDT Awd; Natl Hist & Gov Awd 86; Natl Latin Cntst Gold Mdl 84; Natl Latin Cntst Silver Mdl 83.

WONG, JASON; Xavier HS; Brooklyn, NY; (Y); Varsity Clb; Var Tennis; Hon Roll; Brown U; Med & Hlth Sci.

WONG, JODIE; Westhampton Beach HS; East Moriches, NY; (Y); 30/260; Fld Hcky.

WONG, JUDY; Cathedral HS; New York, NY; (Y); 12/277; Church Yth Grp; Cmnty Wkr; FCA; French Clb; FNA; Hosp Aide; Intnl Clb; Library Aide; Teachers Aide; Nwsp Stf; NY U; Mgt.

WONG, KAI SUI; Fort Hamilton HS; Brooklyn, NY; (Y); #8 In Class; Math Tm; Band; NHS; Regnts Schlrshp 86; UFT Coll Schlrshp Fnd 86; SUNY Buffalo; Elec Engr.

WONG, MANNAR; Fontbonne Hall Acad; Brooklyn, NY; (Y); Art Clb; PAVAS; SADD; Teachers Aide; Nwsp Stf; Yrbk Stf; Pratt Inst; Arch.

WONG, PAUL P; Seward Park HS; New York, NY; (Y); Art Clb; Computer Clb; Drama Clb; School Play; Yrbk Stf.

WONG, TANYA; Uniondale HS; Hempstead, NY; (Y); Nwsp Ed-Chief; Nwsp Rptr; Yrbk Stf; Rep Sr Cls; High Hon Roll; NHS; Bio Schlrshp Adelphi U 85; Chem Schlrshp Adelphi U 86; Pres Blck Stds Clb 86-87; Engl.

WONG, THERESA; Westhampton Beach HS; E Moriches, NY; (Y); 45/212; Nwsp Phtg; Nwsp Rptr; Yrbk Stf; Lit Mag; Trs Soph Cls; Var Gym; JV Var Vllybl; Hon Roll; FBLA; Ski Clb; Jrnlsm Awd 86; Gymnstc Awd Mst Imprvd 83; Geneseo; Comp.

WONG, TIN; John Dewey HS; Brooklyn, NY; (Y); Math Tm; Science Clb; Nwsp Bus Mgr; Capt Im Sftbl; Im Vllybl; Jr NHS; Prfct Atten Awd; I A Green Awd, Bus Ed Advsry Cmmssn Mdl 86; NY U; Fin.

WONG, WALTER; John Dewey HS; Brooklyn, NY; (Y); Computer Clb; Quiz Bowl; Scholastic Bowl; Science Clb; Concert Band; Nwsp Rptr; Yrbk Stf; Regnts Schlrshp 86; Sanford I Weill Schlrshp 86; Acad Finance 84-86; NYU; Finance.

WONG, YU FAY; Mabel Dean Bacon Vocation HS; New York, NY; (Y); Bsktbl; Bowling; Vllybl; Hon Roll; Prfct Atten Awd; Bio Awd 86; Phys Awd 86; Math Awd 86; NY U; Acct.

WONTROBSKI, KAREN PATRICIA; Floral Park Memorial HS; Floral Park, NY; (Y); 25/150; GAA; Varsity Clb; Variety Show; Var Cheerleading; Var Capt Gym; Var Socr; JV Sftbl; Var Trk; High Hon Roll; Hon Roll; Rgnts Schlrshp 86; High Hnr Rll 80-86; SUNY Cortlnd; Archtct.

WOO, KARYL; The Bronx HS Of Science; Flushing, NY; (Y); Red Cross Aide; Office Aide; Teachers Aide; Temple Yth Grp; Chorus; Rep Soph Cls; Rep Jr Cls; Var L Swmmng; Var L Trk; Hon Roll; Hlth.

WOO, KATHERINE; Guilderland Central HS; Schenectady, NY; (Y); Service Clb; Yrbk Stf; High Hon Roll; NHS; Harvard Prize Bk Harvard Alumni Assn 86; Am Leg Helderberg Awd 86; Alumni Assn Awd 86; Sci Rsrch.

WOO, TINA; Midwood HS; Brooklyn, NY; (Y); 7/556; Office Aide; NFL; Orch; Stage Crew; Nwsp Stf; Yrbk Stf; Lit Mag; Gov Hon Prg Awd; Ntl Merit Ltr; Hnrs Grp Westinghouse Sci Talent Search 86; U Of PA.

WOOD, ANDREA CLAIRE; Oyster Bay HS; Oyster Bay, NY; (Y); Church Yth Grp; Debate Tm; Hosp Aide; Model UN; SADD; Chorus; Nwsp Rptr; Lit Mag; Rep Jr Cls; Sec Stu Cncl; Jrnlsm Awd 86; Schlrshp To Atnd WA Wrkshps Cnfrnc 86; Vndrblt U; Pre-Med.

WOOD, ANN; Franklin Acad; Malone, NY; (Y); 90/264; Sec Trs 4-H; Pres Rep Spanish Clb; Chorus; Acadmc All Amer 82; Malone Fed Tchrs Schlrshp 86; Potsdam Coll; Tchr.

WOOD, BONNIE; Granville Central HS; Pawlet, VT; (Y); 4/125; VP French Clb; Intnl Clb; VP Key Clb; Math Tm; Chorus; High Hon Roll; NHS; Pres Awd 86; Frnch Awd 83-85; Interact Clb Awd 86; U Vermont; Psychlgy.

WOOD, BRYAN R; Saranac Lake HS; Saranac Lake, NY; (Y); 27/126; Capt Var Bsktbl; Ftbl; Trk; Hon Roll; NYS Rgnts Schlrshp 86; SUNY Geneseo; Bus.

WOOD, CHERYL; Cairo-Durham JR-SR HS; Durham, NY; (Y); Trs Sr Cls; Trs Stu Cncl; High Hon Roll; NHS; Pol Sci.

WOOD, CHRISTINE; Panama Central HS; Ashville, NY; (Y); 6/62; Quiz Bowl; Chorus; Sec Concert Band; Pep Band; School Musical; Nwsp Stf; Var L Swmmng; Hon Roll; NHS; NEDT Awd; Swmr Wk Locl Nwspr 84-85; Chosn Altrnt NY All ST Band 85; Chautauqua All Cnty Band 83-85; Nrsg.

WOOD, CLIFFORD J; Linton HS; Schenectady, NY; (Y); 26/338; Am Leg Boys St; Key Clb; Acpl Chr; Chorus; Concert Band; Jazz Band; Stu Cncl; Ftbl; Trk; Hon Roll; Poli Sci.

WOOD, CRAIG; Vernon HS; Sherrill, NY; (Y); Boy Scts; Cmnty Wkr; Exploring; Thesps; Orch; School Musical; Nwsp Rptr; Lit Mag; Bowling; Socr; Brdcst Jrnlsm.

WOOD, DAVID L; Anthony A Henninger HS; Syracuse, NY; (Y); Art Clb; Drama Clb; SADD; School Play; Yrbk Stf; Chrmn Jr Cls; Lcrss; High Hon Roll; NHS; Civic Clb; MONY Schltcs Art Awd Gold Key 86; Syracuse U; Grahic Desgn.

WOOD, ERIC; De Ruyter Central HS; Deruyter, NY; (S); Church Yth Grp; Drama Clb; Band; Concert Band; Jazz Band; Mrchg Band; Trs Jr Cls; Bowling; NHS.

WOOD, JEFFREY T; Middleburgh Central Schl; Middleburgh, NY; (Y); Rep Soph Cls; Trs Sr Cls; L Bsbl; L Bsktbl; NY ST Rgnts Schlrshp 86; UNY Oneonta; Elem Ed.

WOOD, KEVIN; Northville Central HS; Mayfield, NY; (Y); 12/46; Sec Pres Varsity Clb; Concert Band; Pres Jr Cls; JV Var Bsbl; JV Var Bsktbl; JV Var Socr; Ski Clb; SADD; School Play; Trs Soph Cls; Defensive Bsktbll Awd 86; Sccr Coach Awd 86; Sccr Tri-Vly Leag All-Star 86; St Bonaventure U; Arts.

WOOD, LISA; Bishop Ford Central Catholic HS; Brooklyn, NY; (Y); Aud/Vis; Yrbk Stf; Var Bsbl; Var JV Mat Maids; Var Score Keeper; Var Trk; Var Vllybl; Spn Cert Hnr, 2nd Hnrs 82-83; Pres Phys Fit Awd 82-83; 1st Hnrs, 2nd Hnrs 85-86; Cert Merit 85-86; Pace; Acctg.

WOOD, LISA; New Rochelle HS; New Rochelle, NY; (Y); Church Yth Grp; Drama Clb; PAVAS; School Musical; School Play; JV Socr; French Hon Soc; NHS; Ntl Merit Ltr; Actng.

WOOD, LYNETTE; Thousans Islands HS; Clayton, NY; (Y); Band; Chorus; Mrchg Band; School Play; Variety Show; Yrbk Stf; Vllybl; Hon Roll; Jfrsn Cnty Altrnt Dry Prncss 86-87; Jfrsn Cmnty Coll; Bus.

WOOD, MELISA; Grand Island HS; Grand Island, NY; (Y); Ski Clb; Spanish Clb; SADD; Varsity Clb; Chorus; Off Soph Cls; Rep Stu Cncl; JV Var Bsktbl; Var Socr; JV Sftbl; MIP Girls Vrsty Bsktbl 84-85; Miss Teen NY Genrl Awrns Test Awd 85; Law.

WOOD, MICHELLE; West Seneca East SR HS; Cheektowaga, NY; (Y); 2/375; Am Leg Aux Girls St; German Clb; School Musical; School Play; Var Capt Bsktbl; DAR Awd; High Hon Roll; JC Awd; NHS; Sal; Schl Lang Awds; UAW Schlrshp; SUNY Buffalo; Law.

WOOD, NATALIE; Hilton Central HS; N Greece, NY; (Y); Intnl Clb; Ski Clb; High Hon Roll; Hon Roll; Prfct Atten Awd; RIT; Accntnt.

WOOD, SUSAN; Eden Central HS; Eden, NY; (Y); Sec Church Yth Grp; GAA; Capt Var Bsktbl; Capt Var Crs Cntry; Var Trk; JV Vllybl; Div All Star Cross Cty 84; Schl Record Track 86; Checkers All Star Cross Cty 84-83.

WOOD, TERRY; Watkins Glen HS; Watkins Glen, NY; (S); 4/135; Letterman Clb; Math Clb; Trs Sr Cls; Rep Stu Cncl; Ftbl; Trk; French Hon Soc; Hgh Hon Roll; Hon Roll; NHS; Chem Bwl Fnlst; 2nd Pl Olympc Wghtlftng Cmptn; Mech Engrng.

WOODARD, DANNY; Alden Central HS; Alden, NY; (Y); Yrbk Stf; Var Capt Bsktbl; Im Ftbl; JV Golf; Var Tennis; Pres Schlr; Liberty U; Bus.

WOODARD, MARY HEATHER; Victor HS; Canandaigua, NY; (Y); 3/220; Art Clb; Ski Clb; Spanish Clb; Chorus; School Play; Stu Cncl; Cheerleading; Swmmng; Trk; High Hon Roll; Ontario Cty Bankers Assn Scholar 86; Pres Acad Fit Awd Pgm 86; Outstndng Schltc Achvt Hnr Awd 86; U FL Gainesville; Chem Engrng.

WOODCOCK, JAMES; Corinth Central HS; Corinth, NY; (Y); Spanish Clb; School Play; High Hon Roll; Hon Roll; Jr NHS; Hartwick Coll; Compu Sci.

WOODCOCK, MELISSA; Greenwich Central HS; Cossayuna, NY; (Y); 4-H; 4-H Awd; Grggs Typg Awd 40 WPM 86; Bus.

WOODFORD, WENDY; Uniondale HS; Uniondale, NY; (Y); FBLA; Intnl Clb; Key Clb; Acpl Chr; Chorus; Rep Sr Cls; Var Mgr(s); High Hon Roll; Hon Roll; Jr NHS; Ctznshp Hnr 85; Englsh.

WOODHOUSE, ELIZABETH; Cicero North Syracuse HS; Clay, NY; (S); 19/623; Church Yth Grp; Office Aide; Hon Roll; Acad All Amer 86; BYU; Engl.

WOODHOUSE, GWEN; Curtis HS; Staten Island, NY; (Y); Library Aide; Teachers Aide; Varsity Clb; Chorus; Var Swmmng; Hon Roll; S I & Di Champs Swm Tm 86; Close-Up Govt Prog 86; Coll Of Staten Islnd Pre Coll Isnt Prog 85; Comp Repair.

WOODHULL, CHRISTY; Greenville JR SR HS; Hannacroix, NY; (Y); 12/76; Sec FFA; Pres Latin Clb; Cit Awd; Hon Roll; NHS; NY St FFA Empire Degree; Polit Sci.

WOODRUFF, KEVIN; John H Glenn HS; Greenlawn, NY; (Y); 102/268; Boy Scts; JV Var Ftbl; FL Inst Tech; Ocn Engrng.

WOODRUFF, SEAN T; Midwood HS; Brooklyn, NY; (Y); 78/556; Computer Clb; Hosp Aide; Math Tm; Teachers Aide; Chorus; School Musical; Lit Mag; High Hon Roll; Hon Roll; Hgh Chrs Hnr 83; Med.

WOODS, BARBARA; Tapt HS; Bronx, NY; (Y); Cmnty Wkr; Library Aide; PAVAS; Band; Sftbl; Vllybl; NHS; Hnr Roll Cert 84; Attndnc 85.

WOODS, BENNETT; Victor SR HS; Victor, NY; (Y); Boy Scts; Debate Tm; Exploring; Model UN; Quiz Bowl; Science Clb; Chorus; Yrbk Phtg; JV Tennis; Cit Awd; Engrng.

WOODS, CHRISTINE; West Genesee SR HS; Camillus, NY; (Y); Concert Band; JV Bsktbl; Im Swmmng; Over 100 Trophies Irish Dancing; Trophies Mus & Art 85.

WOODS, CHRISTOPHER; Arch Bishop Molloy HS; Flushing, NY; (Y); 283/383; Church Yth Grp; Hosp Aide; SADD; Teachers Aide; Nwsp Rptr; Nwsp Stf; Yrbk Stf; Lit Mag; Bsktbl; Fld Hcky; Engl Lit.

WOODS, DEBRA; Union Endicott HS; Endicott, NY; (Y); Pres Church Yth Grp; Mathletes; Band; Church Choir; Concert Band; Mrchg Band; Mgr Stage Crew; High Hon Roll; Hon Roll; NHS; Rgnst Schlrshp 86; Potsdam Mert Schlrshp 86; Tutrng 82-86; Wnd Ensmbl 83-85; SUNY; Math.

WOODS, HEATHER; Ticonderoga HS; Ticonderoga, NY; (Y); 14/107; Drama Clb; French Clb; Trs Key Clb; Varsity Clb; School Musical; School Play; Var L Gym; High Hon Roll; Hon Roll; NHS; Elem Educ.

WOODS, LESSIE MICHELLE; Henninger HS; Syracuse, NY; (Y); Cmnty Wkr; Spanish Clb; Varsity Clb; Yrbk Stf; Off Stu Cncl; Socr; Hon Roll; NHS; Spanish NHS; Mnrty Mntr Pgm 83-84; Lmbda Kappa Mu Srty Jr High Incntv Awd 84; Alpha Kappa Acad Exsllnc 86; NC ST U; Pltcl Sci.

WOODS, MELANIE NECOLE; Central Islip SR HS; Central Islip, NY; (Y); 20/376; Teachers Aide; Chorus; Orch; School Musical; School Play; Jr Cls; Princpls Awd, Bst All Around Girl 83; Tempo Music Hnrs Soc 86; Acctg.

WOODS, PATTY; Mamaronock HS; Larchmont, NY; (Y); Sec Key Clb; JV Bsktbl; JV Mgr(s); JV Sftbl; Schl Psychlgy Awd 85; Trvl Agnt.

WOODWARD, RAYMOND; Linton HS; Schenectady, NY; (Y); Church Yth Grp; Computer Clb; JCL; Hon Roll; NHS; NY St Regents Schlrshp 86; W TX ST U.

WOODWARD, SCOTT; Canton Central HS; Canton, NY; (Y); 30/150; Var JV Bsbl; Var JV Socr; High Hon Roll; Hon Roll; Crmnl Jstc.

WOODWARD, THERESA; East Aurora HS; E Aurora, NY; (Y); Church Yth Grp; SADD; Yrbk Phtg; Yrbk Stf; JV Var Bsktbl; Var Capt Fld Hcky; Var Capt Sftbl; JV Var Vllybl; High Hon Roll; Hon Roll; Arch.

WOODWARD, WILLIAM; Gouverneur Central HS; Gouverneur, NY; (Y); Pres 4-H; Yrbk Ed-Chief; Yrbk Stf; Im Bowling; 4-H Awd; Hon Roll; Jr NHS; NHS; Band; Concert Band; Pub Spkng Medal 4 H 85; Star Breeder 84; Math.

WOODWORTH, JENNY; Churchville-Chili SR HS; North Chili, NY; (Y); Ski Clb; Chorus; Concert Band; Ed Yrbk Stf; Pres Sr Cls; Rep Stu Cncl; JV Sftbl; JV Var Swmmng; High Hon Roll; NHS; Area All State Bnd 81; NYSSMA Solo Awds 79-86; Ntl Hnr NFF Piano 83; Syracuse U; Med Doc.

WOODWORTH, STEVEN; Cahisteo Central HS; Hornell, NY; (Y); 12/76; Var Capt Ftbl; Var Capt Trk; Var Capt Wrstlng; Cit Awd; High Hon Roll; Coach Actv; Wt Lftg; 2 Time Sctnl Wnnr Wrstlng 85-86; Outstndng Wrstr Midlks Trnmnt 86; Lycoming Coll; Cvl Engrng.

WOOLCOCK, EDITH; Monsignor Scanlan HS; Bronx, NY; (Y); Library Aide; Rep Frsh Cls; Rep Soph Cls; Rep Jr Cls; Rep Stu Cncl; St Johns U; Psych.

WOOLEVER, CHARLES; Hornell HS; Hornell, NY; (Y); 20/168; Computer Clb; Math Clb; Band; Concert Band; Mrchg Band; Pep Band; Vllybl; Hon Roll; NHS; Regents Scholar 86; SUNY Binghamton; Comp Sci.

WOOLEVER, TERRI; Corning Painted Post West HS; Painted Post, NY; (Y); VP JA; Band; Concert Band; Mrchg Band; Pep Band; School Musical; JV Var Vllybl; High Hon Roll; NHS.

WOOLEY, JUANITA; Jamestown HS; Jamestown, NY; (Y); French Clb; Hosp Aide; Acpl Chr; Chorus; School Musical; Stu Cncl; Stat Var Bsktbl; Mgr(s); JV Sftbl; Acctg.

WOOLLEY III, ALBERT M; Riverhead HS; Aquebogue, NY; (Y); 14/200; Key Clb; Rep Latin Clb; Ski Clb; JV Capt Bsbl; Var Capt Ftbl; Hon Roll; NHS; Med.

WOOLSCHLAGER, WAYNE; Jamestown HS; Jamestown, NY; (Y); 126/400; VP Church Yth Grp; Lib Acpl Chr; Morrisville U; Bus Admn.

WOOLSON, ANN; Mexico Acad & Central Schls; Mexico, NY; (Y); Band; Rep Jr Cls; Rep Stu Cncl; Prfct Atten Awd; Bryant & Stratton; Sec.

WOOSTER, DAVID CHARLES; La Salle Insti; North Troy, NY; (Y); 9/83; Boy Scts; ROTC; Drill Tm; L Trk; High Hon Roll; NHS; Computer Clb; Service Clb; NYS Regnts, ROTC & Rens Polytech Inst Schlrshps 86; Rensselaer Polytech Inst; Engr.

WOOSTER, JULIE; Perry Central HS; Perry, NY; (Y); Varsity Clb; Band; Yrbk Stf; Rep Stu Cncl; Var L Bsktbl; Var L Sftbl; Cit Awd; Score Keeper; JV L Socr; Acad Achvt Awd 86; All-Star Sftbl & Bsktbl Team 86; Sunny Cobleskill; Lbrl Arts.

WOOTEN, CYNTHIA; Fayetteville-Manlius HS; Manlius, NY; (Y); Boy Scts; Church Yth Grp; Exploring; FBLA; Chorus; Church Choir; Variety Show; Badmtn; Wt Lftg; Hon Roll; NY U; Intl Bus.

WORMUTH, MICHELLE; Hancock Central HS; Hancock, NY; (Y); Library Aide; Spanish Clb; Chorus; School Play; JV Vllybl; Trs NHS; Ldrshp Cnfrnc Nrwch 86; Nrsng.

WORONIECKI, RENEE; Mount Mercy Acad; Orchard Park, NY; (Y); Computer Clb; Drama Clb; Science Clb; Spanish Clb; SADD; Nwsp Rptr; Ed Nwsp Stf; Ed Lit Mag; Cmnctns.

WORONKA, CHRISTINE; Eastport HS; Eastport, NY; (Y); 1/45; Band; Nwsp Ed-Chief; VP Frsh Cls; Var Sftbl; High Hon Roll; JP Sousa Awd; NHS; Rotary Awd; Val; Hofstra U.

WORRELL, CHRISTINE; Evander Childs HS; Bronx, NY; (Y); Math Tm; Bsbl; Crs Cntry; Gym; Score Keeper; Sftbl; Trk; SUNY; Compu Prg.

WORRELL, STELLA R; Julia Richman HS; New York, NY; (Y); 10/429; Church Choir; High Hon Roll; Hon Roll; NHS; Niagara U; Accntng.

WORTH, CASSANDRA; Charlotte HS; Rochester, NY; (Y); Office Aide; Teachers Aide; Cit Awd; Prfct Atten Awd; Prctcl Chem Awd 86; Outstndng Achvt In Engl Awd 84; Outstndng Achvt In Rdng Awd 84; Bflo ST Coll; Bus Admin.

WORTHINGTON, MAUREEN; Longwood HS; Medford, NY; (Y); Spanish Clb; SADD; Chorus; Variety Show; Nwsp Rptr; Nwsp Stf; High Hon Roll; Hon Roll; Cosmtlgst.

WORTHY, CHARMAINE; Dominican Commercial HS; Cambria Heights, NY; (Y); Cmnty Wkr; Drama Clb; Varsity Clb; Chorus; School Musical; School Play; Variety Show; Swmmng; Hon Roll; Mst Sprtd Awd Trphy Swm Tm 85; Arts.

WORTMAN, RACHEL; Williamsville East HS; Williamsvl, NY; (Y); French Clb; Pep Clb; Ski Clb; Stu Cncl; JV Var Sftbl; High Hon Roll; Hon Roll; Psych.

WOUTERS, DANIEL; Liverpool HS; Liverpool, NY; (Y); 16/880; Am Leg Boys St; ROTC; Drill Tm; Rep Frsh Cls; Var L Crs Cntry; Var L Trk; JV Wrstlng; High Hon Roll; Jr NHS; NHS.

WOZNA, SHEILA; Holland Patent HS; Holland Patent, NY; (Y); 40/160; Hon Roll; Mohawk Coll CC; Med Rcrds.

WOZNIAK, JOANNE; Lackawanna SR HS; Lackawanna, NY; (Y); Girl Scts; JA; Red Cross Aide; Trs Band; Mrchg Band; Pep Band; Symp Band; Nrsng.

WOZNIAK, JOHN; Frontier Central HS; Lake View, NY; (Y); Chess Clb; NHS; ST U Of NY; Engrng.

WRATE, SUSAN; Jamesville De Witt HS; Jamesville, NY; (Y); 30/235; SADD; School Musical; Swing Chorus; VP Frsh Cls; VP Soph Cls; Stat Bsbl; JV Cheerleading; High Hon Roll; NHS; Hon Roll; Fclty Serv Awd 86; Bus.

WREN, MYLES T; Ramapo SR HS; Monsey, NY; (Y); 118/529; Aud/Vis; German Clb; Radio Clb; Nwsp Stf; Trk; Hon Roll; Ntl Merit Ltr.

WRIGHT, ANTONIO; Baldwin SR HS; Freeport, NY; (Y); 136/476; Capt Crs Cntry; Capt Trk; Hon Roll; George A Craig Awd 85-86; Harris N Suerman Mrl Schlrshp Awd 86; Syracuse U.

WRIGHT, BARRY; Hannibal SR HS; Hannibal, NY; (Y); Boy Scts; Im JV Ftbl; JV VP Trk; Rgnts Coll Schlrshp 86; Eagle Scout 85; Oswego SUNY; Biolgcl Sci.

WRIGHT, BONITA; Sodus Central HS; E Williamson, NY; (Y); 34/112; French Clb; Letterman Clb; Science Clb; Varsity Clb; VICA; Chorus; Yrbk Stf; Rep Stu Cncl; Var L Trk; High Hon Roll; Stu Of Mth-May-Wayne Area Voc Ctr 86; Chef.

WRIGHT, CASSANDRA; Nyack HS; Nyack, NY; (Y); Band; Church Choir; Concert Band; Mrchg Band; Stu Cncl; Hon Roll; Clb Persnlty 86; Air Force; Astrnt.

WRIGHT, DALE; East Syracuss-Minda HS; Minoa, NY; (Y); Ski Clb; JV Bsbl; JV Var Socr; Var Tennis; High Hon Roll; Jr NHS; NHS; Achvt Awd Engl 85-86; Cptn Soccer Tm 86; Engrng.

WRIGHT, DAVID; St Amrys HS; Lancaster, NY; (Y); JV Ftbl; Capt Var Wrstlng; DAR Awd; Hon Roll.

WRIGHT, DAVID; Unions Springs Acad; Syracuse, NY; (S); 1/30; Chorus; Concert Band; Yrbk Phtg; Pres Frsh Cls; Stu Cncl; Var Bsktbl; Capt Vllybl; High Hon Roll; NHS; Loma Linda U; Bus.

WRIGHT II, DAVID; Victor Central SR HS; Macedon, NY; (Y); 1/238; JA; Science Clb; School Musical; Var Tennis; Bausch & Lomb Sci Awd; High Hon Roll; NHS; Ntl Merit Ltr; Pres Schlr; Rnsslr Polytech Inst Math & Sci Mdl 85; Glsn Mem Schlrshp 86; MA Inst Of Tech; Chem Engnrng.

WRIGHT, EDDIE; Charlotte HS; Rochester, NY; (Y); Trs Church Yth Grp; Cmnty Wkr; Ski Clb; Socr; Swmmng; Hon Roll; Ntl Yth Phys Ftnss Prog 84; Carpentry.

WRIGHT JR, ERNEST ALVIN; Iona Preparatory Schl; White Plains, NY; (Y); 38/191; Computer Clb; Science Clb; Nwsp Rptr; Crs Cntry; Socr; Trk; Hon Roll; Masonic Awd; Haverford Coll; Hist.

WRIGHT, FRED D; Chenango Forks HS; Binghamton, NY; (Y); 5/180; Am Leg Boys St; Ski Clb; Trs Frsh Cls; Trs Soph Cls; Trs Jr Cls; Trs Stu Cncl; Socr; NHS; Ntl Merit SF; Paleontlgst.

WRIGHT, JASON; Springville Griffith Inst HS; Springville, NY; (Y); Pres Frsh Cls; Pres Sr Cls; JV Var Ftbl; JV Var Trk; Var Wt Lftg; Pre-Law.

WRIGHT, KANDEE L; Dundee Central HS; Dundee, NY; (Y); 2/75; Am Leg Aux Girls St; Trs Ski Clb; Sec Pres SADD; Cit Awd; DAR Awd; High Hon Roll; Sec Pres NHS; Sal; French Clb; Sec Pres Science Clb; Schlrshp Rotary; Am Leg Bradley Jessop Awd; Alfred Ag Tech Coll; Chem Tech.

WRIGHT, KAREN; Lansingburgh HS; Troy, NY; (S); 1/185; Hosp Aide; Math Tm; Sftbl; High Hon Roll; Jr NHS; NHS; Val; Lois C Smith Chem Schlrshp 85; Awd Hgst Avg Math,Acctng I 83-85; Siena Coll; Acctng.

WRIGHT, KEVIN; Middletown HS; Middletown, NY; (Y); SADD; Var Bowling; Var Fld Hcky; Var Golf; Var Ice Hcky; Hon Roll; Arch Engr.

WRIGHT, KEVIN; Schoharie Central HS; Schoharie, NY; (Y); FFA; Varsity Clb; Bsbl; Bowling; Socr; Prfct Atten Awd; JR Prom Atten.

WRIGHT, KIM; Mt Mercy Acad; Buffalo, NY; (Y); 34/250; French Clb; Chorus; Lit Mag; Rep Soph Cls; Rep Sr Cls; Hon Roll.

WRIGHT, KIMBERLY E; Horace Mann HS; Bronx, NY; (Y); Sec Trs Dance Clb; Intnl Clb; Library Aide; VP Spanish Clb; Chorus; School Musical; School Play; Nwsp Rptr; Lcrss; Mgr(s); Ntl Merit Cmndtn For Outstndng Negro Stu 85-86; Maroon Key Awd For Exc 83-85; Tele Brdcstng Cmncts.

WRIGHT, LEIGH ANNE; Smithtown HS East; Smithtown, NY; (Y); Dance Clb; Drama Clb; SADD; Thesps; Chorus; School Play; Variety Show; Hon Roll; Fashn Merchandising.

WRIGHT, LYNDA G; Marcellus SR HS; Marietta, NY; (Y); 35/167; AFS; Church Yth Grp; Girl Scts; Teachers Aide; Chorus; Church Choir; High Hon Roll; Hon Roll; NY ST Rgnts Coll Schlrshp 86; US Navy; Comp Prcssng.

WRIGHT, MARCELINE; Far Rockaway HS; Far Rockaway, NY; (Y); Drama Clb; 4-H; Library Aide; Math Clb; Chorus; Sftbl; Tennis; Vllybl; 4-H Awd; Hon Roll; Nrsg.

WRIGHT, MAUREEN R; Kenmore East HS; Buffalo, NY; (Y); 6/330; Chorus; Concert Band; Mrchg Band; High Hon Roll; NHS; Commended Stu Innatl Merit Schlrshp Comtpn 85-86; Bryant Stratton Schlrshp; Regents Schlrshp; Bryant & Stratton; Sec.

WRIGHT, PATRICIA; Fairport HS; Fairport, NY; (Y); Math Tm; Model UN; Rep Stu Cncl; High Hon Roll; Hon Roll; 5th Pl Bryant & Stratton Typing Cntst 85; 2nd Pl Tm Shrthnd Cntst-MCBEA 86; Bio.

WRIGHT, RISI; New Rochelle HS; New Rochelle, NY; (Y); Church Yth Grp; Civic Clb; Cmnty Wkr; Variety Show; Hon Roll; NHS; Fine Arts.

WRIGHT, ROBERT; St Peters Boys HS; Staten Island, NY; (Y); 21/155; Boy Scts; Church Yth Grp; Cmnty Wkr; Im Bsktbl; Im Ftbl; Var L Tennis; High Hon Roll; Hon Roll; NHS; VMP Tnns 83-86; St Francis Acad Schlrshp 86-87; St Francis Coll PA; Acctg.

WRIGHT, ROLAND L; Canarsie HS; Brooklyn, NY; (Y); 150/500; Drama Clb; PAVAS; Service Clb; Acpl Chr; Band; Chorus; Concert Band; Madrigals; School Musical; School Play; Prtcptn 1st Brklyn Music Fstvl 86; Stu Of Mnth 85; Hope Ferrick Awd Exsllnc Music 86; U Of Hartford; Musical Thtr.

WRIGHT, SAMUEL C; Taconic Hills HS; Hudson, NY; (Y); 13/119; Computer Clb; Library Aide; Yrbk Stf; Socr; Trk; Hon Roll; MVP Sccr 85; Rgnts Schlrhsp 86; Elec Engrng.

WRIGHT, SANDRA; Erasmus Hall HS; Brooklyn, NY; (Y); Art Clb; Church Yth Grp; Dance Clb; Drama Clb; English Clb; FBLA; Key Clb; Temple Yth Grp; Church Choir; Capt Vllybl; Baruch Coll; Bus Adm.

WRIGHT, SCOTT E; Arlington HS; La Grangeville, NY; (Y); 50/560; Aud/Vis; Cmnty Wkr; Debate Tm; Teachers Aide; Hon Roll; VFW Awd; Rgnts Schlrshp & Hnr Key 86; Rnslr Poly Tech Inst; Nclr Engr.

WRIGHT, SEAN F; Au Sable Valley Central HS; Keeseville, NY; (Y); 6/130; Drama Clb; Band; Concert Band; Jazz Band; School Play; Stage Crew; Yrbk Stf; High Hon Roll; Hon Roll; NHS; Clarkson Trustee & 3 Yr Army ROTC & 4 Yr USAF ROTC Altrnt Schlrshps; Clarkson U; Comp Mgmt Sys.

WRIGHT, SHEILA; Ripley Central HS; Ripley, NY; (Y); 4/24; Church Yth Grp; Girl Scts; Library Aide; Quiz Bowl; Teachers Aide; Chorus; Hon Roll; Sec Trs NHS; Ntl Merit Ltr; ST U Coll Fredonia; Educ.

WRIGHT, SONDRA; Charlotte HS; Rochester, NY; (Y); Exploring; 4-H; Teachers Aide; Hon Roll; Foods & Ntrtn 85-86; Ntrtnal Awd Cty Schl Dist 85-86; Nazereth Coll; Acctnt.

WRIGHT, STACEY; Worth Rockland HS; Haverstraw, NY; (Y); Girl Scts; Pres Church Choir; Mgr JV Bsktbl; JV Mgr(s); Pre-Law.

WRIGHT, TARYN; John Dewey HS; Brooklyn, NY; (Y); Church Yth Grp; Dance Clb; Girl Scts; Chorus; Yrbk Phtg; Yrbk Rptr; Pres Frsh Cls; Pres Soph Cls; Pres Jr Cls; Pres Sr Cls; Hartwick Schlrshp 86; Exsllnc Awd In Coop Educ 86; Hartwick Coll; Mgmnt.

WRIGHT, TRICIA; Gloversville HS; Gloversville, NY; (Y); Church Yth Grp; Drama Clb; Girl Scts; Ski Clb; Teachers Aide; Chorus; Stage Crew; Swing Chorus; Yrbk Stf; Hon Roll; Nrsng.

WRIGHT, WAYNE; All Hallows HS; Bronx, NY; (S); 2/114; Computer Clb; Math Clb; School Play; Nwsp Rptr; Trk; Hon Roll; Lwyr.

WRINKLE, BILL; Haverling HS; Bath, NY; (Y); French Clb; Latin Clb; Letterman Clb; Math Tm; Ski Clb; Church Choir; Diving; Golf; Swmmng; Hon Roll; Rtry Frgn Exchng Brazil 85-86; Govt Ser.

WROBEL, GARY; Bishop Ludden HS; Syracuse, NY; (Y); JV Bsbl; Var Capt Ftbl; Var L Lcrss; Bus Adm.

WROBEL, MARK; Bishop Ludden HS; Syracuse, NY; (Y); Cmnty Wkr; Bsbl; Bsktbl; Coach Actv; Fld Hcky; Ftbl; Sftbl; Timer; Trk; Wt Lftg; Wagner Schlrshp, CW Post Grant 86; Wagner; Bus.

WROBEL, TERRY; Royalton-Hartland Central HS; Gasport, NY; (Y); 5/125; Sec Jr Cls; Sec Sr Cls; Var Cheerleading; JV Trk; Fin.

WROBLESKI, MICHAEL J; Eden SR HS; Hamburg, NY; (Y); 6/166; Model UN; Pres Varsity Clb; Rep Stu Cncl; Var Capt Bsbl; Bsktbl; Var Capt Ftbl; Hon Roll; NHS; Ntl Merit SF; Div All Star Bsbl Ftbl 86; Schlr Athlt Awd Bsktbl 85-86; Chem Engr.

WRONOSKI, KEVIN; Albany HS; Albany, NY; (Y); 105/580; Latin Clb; L Var Crs Cntry; Var Capt Wrstlng; Rep Frsh Cls; Rep Jr Cls; Cls VP 85; Cls Pres 86; Siena Coll; Bus Adm.

WU, JUDY; Half Hollow Hills HS East; Dix Hills, NY; (Y); Hosp Aide; Intnl Clb; Office Aide; SADD; Teachers Aide; Swing Chorus; French Hon Soc; High Hon Roll; NHS; Art Clb; NYSSMA Solo Awd Piano 83-86.

WU, MONITA; Southampton HS; Southampton, NY; (Y); Exploring; Service Clb; High Hon Roll; Hon Roll; Bus Mgmnt.

WU, ROBERT T; Hunter Collee HS; Flushing, NY; (Y); Var Bowling; Mu Alp Tht; Natl Sci Olynpiad, Physcs 84-85; Cornell U; Engrng.

WU, RONALD S; James Madison HS; Brooklyn, NY; (Y); 41/748; JA; School Play; Stage Crew; Lit Mag; Hon Roll; Prfct Atten Awd; NY ST Regents Scholar 86; Phys Fit Achvt Awd 85.

WU, SUSIE; Allegany Central Schl; Allegany, NY; (S); 5/104; Art Clb; Hosp Aide; Ski Clb; Yrbk Stf; Trs Stu Cncl; Capt Cheerleading; Var L Tennis; High Hon Roll; Sec NHS; Schlrshp Soc & Top 5% Of Cls 82-86; Communty Yth Salute-Leadrshp, Svc & Acadmcs 85.

WU, TAMMY L; Kingston HS; Kingston, NY; (Y); #47 In Class; Latin Clb; Ski Clb; Stu Cncl; Var L Cheerleading; High Hon Roll; Off Jr NHS; NHS; Pres Schlr; St Schlr; US Ath Awd; Cum Laude; SUNY Albany.

WU, TAOLAN CAROLYN; James Madison HS; Brooklyn, NY; (Y); 12/748; Computer Clb; Math Clb; Science Clb; Prfct Atten Awd; Achvmnt Sci Rsrch Brklyn Smmr Acad 85; Chem By Amer Chem Scty, Brklyn Sbsctn 86; Fnlst Sci Fair 86; Rensselaer Poly Tech; Elec Engr.

WULFF, KATHLEEN; St Dominic HS; E Norwich, NY; (Y); 3/118; Hosp Aide; Model UN; SADD; School Musical; Nwsp Bus Mgr; Stu Cncl; Capt Cheerleading; High Hon Roll; NHS; Ntl Merit Ltr; U Of VA; Bio.

WUNDERLICH, MICHELE; Sachem HS North HS; Holtsville, NY; (Y); 17/1600; Math Tm; Ski Clb; Mrchg Band; School Musical; Symp Band; Im JV Socr; Im Vllybl; Jr NHS; VP NHS; Biomed Engr.

WUREM, BARBARA M; Bronx School Of Science; Bronx, NY; (Y); Camera Clb; Office Aide; Teachers Aide; Temple Yth Grp; Concert Band; Hon Roll; NHS; SUNY Albany; Bus.

WURL, DERRICK; Niagara Wheatfield HS; Sanborn, NY; (Y); 2/300; Am Leg Boys St; Pres Latin Clb; Pres Math Clb; Quiz Bowl; Trs Frsh Cls; Stu Cncl; Var Capt Vllybl; High Hon Roll; VP NHS; Sal.

WURTZ, RICHARD; Walt Whitman HS; Huntington Sta, NY; (Y); 72/477; Drama Clb; Band; Concert Band; Mrchg Band; School Musical; School Play; Lit Mag; JV Trk; Im Wt Lftg; Mech Engr.

WUTZ, JENNIFER; Williamsville South HS; Williamsville, NY; (Y); Pep Clb; Nwsp Phtg; Yrbk Phtg; Rep Stu Cncl; L Swmmng.

WYANT, GRACE; Pine Bush HS; Bloomingburg, NY; (Y); 38/288; Pres Sec Church Yth Grp; Dance Clb; Band; Chorus; Drill Tm; Mrchg Band; School Musical; NHS; Library Aide; Pom Pon; Area All ST Band 85; Ornge Cnty Music Fstvl 84 & 85; Orange County CC; Ocptnl Thrpy.

WYANT, LISA; Frontier SR HS; Blasdell, NY; (Y); Sec Church Yth Grp; Drama Clb; French Clb; Hosp Aide; Pep Clb; Chorus; Church Choir; Stage Crew; Hon Roll.

WYANT, MATTHEW; Beacon HS; M D Beacon, NY; (S); 7/150; Math Clb; Math Tm; Science Clb; Varsity Clb; Im Bsktbl; Im Ice Hcky; Var JV Socr; High Hon Roll; Hon Roll; Jr NHS; All Conf All Str Sccr Plyr 85; Math & Sci Awds 84; Acad All Amer 85; Engrng.

WYBENGA, ERIC; Center Moriches HS; Center Moriches, NY; (Y); Cmnty Wkr; Debate Tm; Drama Clb; French Clb; Band; Chorus; Mrchg Band; School Musical; School Play; Nwsp Rptr; Princeton Book Awd Semifinal 86; Harvard Smmr Schl 86; 12 Acad Crdts Fshn Insti Of Tech 83-85; Harvard U; Politics.

WYDER, DAVE; Oakfield-Alabama HS; Basom, NY; (Y); Ski Clb; Stu Cncl; Var Tennis; Bus Mgmt.

WYDLER, STEVEN C; The Dalton Schl; New York, NY; (Y); Stu Cncl; Im Bsbl; Var Lcrss; Var Capt Wrstlng; Ntl Merit Ltr; Rgnts Schlrshp Cert 86; Dartmouth Coll; Hist.

WYGANT, KURT; Rome Free Acad; Rome, NY; (Y); Church Yth Grp; Intnl Clb; Key Clb; Y-Teens; Pres Frsh Cls; VP Stu Cncl.

WYLLIE, AARON T; Nazareth Regional HS; Brooklyn, NY; (Y); Computer Clb; High Hon Roll; Typng,Cpmo,Earth Sci Awd 86; Horseback Riding Cert 83-85; Math Awd 83; City Coll NY; Elect Engr.

WYMAN, HEATHER; Shenendehowa HS; Clifton Park, NY; (Y); Church Yth Grp; Cmnty Wkr; Key Clb; SADD; Band; Drill Tm; Drm & Bgl; Yrbk Stf; Hon Roll; Otstndng Acad Achvmnt Awd 84; Mrktng.

WYMAN, SEANA; Nardin Acad; Buffalo, NY; (Y); Dance Clb; Drama Clb; Latin Clb; School Musical; School Play; Nwsp Stf; Lit Mag; Rep Frsh Cls; Rep Soph Cls; Hon Roll; Denison U; Pre-Law.

WYMAN, TOM; Lindenhurst HS; Lindenhurst, NY; (Y); Boy Scts; SADD; Varsity Clb; Stage Crew; Rep Stu Cncl; Capt Crs Cntry; Capt Trk; MVP Wntr Trck 84-85; MVP 85-86; Don Seamen Awd 86; Mech Drftr.

WYMER, JOEL; Arch Bishop Walsh HS; Salamance, NY; (Y); Ski Clb; DAR Awd; High Hon Roll; Hon Roll.

WYNN, RENE; Greece Olympia HS; Rochester, NY; (Y); Trs DECA; Ski Clb; SADD; Trs Varsity Clb; Concert Band; Rep Frsh Cls; Rep Soph Cls; Rep Jr Cls; Rep Sr Cls; JV Var Cheerleading; DECA Rgnl Fnlst 85; Sctn V AAA Chmpn Chrldng 85&86; U Of Buffalo; Bus Mgmt.

WYNN, ROBIN; Whitesboro JR HS; Marcy, NY; (Y); 11/310; Drama Clb; Mathletes; Model UN; Speech Tm; Acpl Chr; School Musical; Lit Mag; Hon Roll; Jr NHS; NHS; Psych.

WYNN, ROXANNE; Sheepshead Bay HS; Brooklyn, NY; (Y); 11/429; Church Yth Grp; Cmnty Wkr; Hosp Aide; Nwsp Ed-Chief; Nwsp Rptr; Yrbk Rptr; Yrbk Stf; Sec Stu Cncl; NHS; Arista Ldrshp Awd Pin 86; Archon Pin 86; Elsbeth Kroeber Mem Awd Bio Sci 86; NY U; Jrnlsm.

WYNNE, SHARON A; Hillcrest HS; Cambria Heights, NY; (Y); Girl Scts; Hosp Aide; Teachers Aide; Band; JR Acad NY Acad Sci 82-86; Music Clb Pres 84-85; Asian Clb 85-86; Acad Olympc Tm Capt 84-86.

WYNTER, DEAN; Curtis HS; Staten Island, NY; (Y); Math Clb; Swmmng; Smmr Schlrshp 84.

WYRICK, JENNIFER; Peru Central JR SR HS; Plattsburgh, NY; (Y); Exploring; Hosp Aide; JA; Pep Clb; Spanish Clb; Chorus; JV Socr; U Of NC; Nrsng.

WYSONG, LARA; Fredonia HS; Fredonia, NY; (Y); Cmnty Wkr; Spanish Clb; Stage Crew; Nwsp Stf; Yrbk Stf; Lit Mag; Hon Roll; Hnrbl Mntn Oral Intrprtn Comp Spanish 86; Comm.

WYSZKOWSKI, JOY; Tonawanda JR SR HS; Tonawanda, NY; (Y); 30/220; Aud/Vis; Church Yth Grp; Band; Chorus; Jazz Band; School Musical; Cheerleading; Trk; Rgnts Nrsng 86; Acdmc Schlrshp 86; Roberts Wesleyan Coll; Nrsng.

XIKES, RENE; St Francis Preparatory HS; Flushing, NY; (Y); Church Yth Grp; Dance Clb; Hosp Aide; Band; Concert Band; Mrchg Band; Hon Roll; Arista 83-84; Bus.

XIPPOLITOS, KRISTIN; Smithtown East HS; Head Of The Harbr, NY; (Y); Aud/Vis; Church Yth Grp; Dance Clb; Key Clb; SADD; Yrbk Stf; Rep Stu Cncl; Hon Roll; Itln Hnr Soc; Intrct Clb; Cmmnctn.

XIXIS, SOPHIA; Bronx H S Of Science; Whitestone, NY; (Y); Teachers Aide; Orch; Nwsp Ed-Chief; Nwsp Rptr; Nwsp Stf; Yrbk Stf; Lit Mag; Im Vllybl; NHS; NYU; Jrnlsm.

YACOBUCCI, PETER; Canisius HS; Buffalo, NY; (Y); Model UN; Nwsp Stf; Var Capt Crs Cntry; Var Capt Trk.

YACONO, TOMLYNN; Bethlehem Central HS; Delmar, NY; (Y); Am Leg Aux Girls St; Cmnty Wkr; Model UN; Teachers Aide; Orch; Lit Mag; High Hon Roll; Rnsslr Inst Of Art 86.

YACOVELLO, BARBARA; Bishop Ford Central Catholic HS; Brooklyn, NY; (S); #15 In Class; Cmnty Wkr; Yrbk Stf; High Hon Roll; Hon Roll; NHS; Ldr Actvtes Cncl 84-85.

YAEGER, ROB; Smithtown H S West; Smithtown, NY; (Y); Camera Clb; Cmnty Wkr; German Clb; Ski Clb; Band; Im Bsktbl; Im Ftbl; JV Socr; JV Tennis; Im Wt Lftg; German Natl Hnr Soc 86-87.

YAGER, ELIZABETH; Frewsburg Central Schl; Frewsburg, NY; (Y); 4/50; FCA; Pres Sec 4-H; Hon Roll; 4-H Awd; Computer Clb; Jamestown Bus Coll Typg Cont 3rd Pl 86.

YAGER, ROBERT; Archbishop Stepinac HS; Yonkers, NY; (Y); 85/200; Boy Scts; Teachers Aide; Rep Sr Cls; Rep Stu Cncl; Im Fld Hcky; Var Tennis; Im Wt Lftg; Manhatten Clg; Engnrng.

YAGGIE, JOHN; Jamestown HS; Jamestown, NY; (Y); Church Yth Grp; French Clb; SADD; Band; Concert Band; Jazz Band; Mrchg Band; Orch; Pep Band; School Musical; RPI; Comp Engrng.

YAGUDAEV, ALEX; Hillcrest HS; Flushing, NY; (Y); 1/38; Band; Concert Band; Orch; Badmtn; Wt Lftg; High Hon Roll; Hon Roll; NHS; Prfct Atten Awd; Schlstc Awds Sci & Spnsh Math Eng Music 83-86; NYC Assoc Phys Ftns Achvmnt 83-84; Prestigious NY; Gnrl Dntrsty.

YAHN, CHRISTINE E; Cardinal Mooney HS; Rochester, NY; (Y); 18/305; Library Aide; Ski Clb; Nwsp Stf; Rep Soph Cls; Rep Jr Cls; Rep Sr Cls; Rep Stu Cncl; Var Capt Cheerleading; NHS; Spanish NHS; NYS Rgnts Schlrshp 86; Jr Var Chrldr Yr 84; Geneseo SUNY; Cmmnctns.

YAHN, MELISSA; Bishop Grimes HS; Fayetteville, NY; (S); 18/150; Cmnty Wkr; School Musical; Powder Puff Ftbl; High Hon Roll; Jr NHS; NHS; Natl Merit Awd Engl 85; Bio.

YAKAL, DAWN; Frontier HS; Hamburg, NY; (Y); French Clb; Math Clb; Pep Clb; Yrbk Stf; Socr; High Hon Roll; Hon Roll; NHS; Buffalo News Carrier Mnth 3rd Plc 85; UB; Comp.

YAN, BELINDA; John H Glenn HS; E Northport, NY; (Y); French Clb; Q&S; Service Clb; Varsity Clb; Nwsp Ed-Chief; Yrbk Sprt Ed; Var Trk; French Hon Soc; High Hon Roll; NHS; Bus Mgmt.

YAN, CARINA; John H Glenn HS; E Northport, NY; (Y); Nwsp Stf; Yrbk Stf; Rep Soph Cls; Rep Jr Cls; Trk; Vllybl; Hon Roll; NHS; Spanish NHS; Corp Law.

YANDER, CATHERINE; Lindenhurst SR HS; Lindenhurst, NY; (Y); School Play; Variety Show; Yrbk Stf; Trk; Hon Roll; Dance For Heart Top Seller 86; Sci Awd Cert Awd 84; Dist Art Fair 85; Nassau CC; Chld Psychlgst.

YANDO, LISA; Smithtown West HS; Smithtown, NY; (Y); Exploring; Concert Band; Mrchg Band; Stage Crew; Yrbk Stf; Socr; Vllybl; French Hon Soc; High Hon Roll; NHS; Rgnts Schlrshp 86; Pres Acad Ftns Awd 86; St Lawrence U; Gvrnmnt.

YANG, ALICE; New Town HS; Elmhurst, NY; (Y); Hon Roll; Sci.

YANG, ANGEL; Stuyvesant HS; New York, NY; (Y); 5/704; Intnl Clb; Math Tm; Science Clb; Orch; Nwsp Ed-Chief; Elks Awd; Ntl Merit Schol; Hosp Aide; Library Aide; Office Aide; SMGTM Essay Cntst 1st Pl 83 & 85; E C Hallbeck Schlrp 86; 2 JR Vlntr Awds S I Hosp 84 & 85; Harvard.

YANG, CHARLEEN; St Francis Prep; Flushing, NY; (S); 137/690; Girl Scts; Math Clb; Ski Clb; SADD; Concert Band; Rep Drm & Bgl; Mrchg Band; School Musical; NHS; Opt Clb Awd; Comp Pgrmr.

YANG, KYLE; Fairport HS; Fairport, NY; (Y); Model UN; Orch; High Hon Roll; Hon Roll; Prfct Atten Awd; Engrng.

YANTZ, CYNTHIA M; Nazareth Acad; Rochester, NY; (Y); 1/110; Pres Library Aide; Math Clb; Math Tm; Spanish Clb; Nwsp Ed-Chief; Lit Mag; Var Socr; Bausch & Lomb Sci Awd; High Hon Roll; NHS; Cngrssnl Yth Ldrshp Cncl 86; Scndry Educ.

YANUKLIS, KATHERINE EMILIE; Brewster HS; Houston, TX; (Y); Pres 4-H; Sec Girl Scts; Nwsp Rptr; Ed Lit Mag; 4-H Awd; NHS; Spanish NHS; Acad Recgntn Schlrshp 86; U Of Houston; Scndry Educc.

YANULAVICH, NANCY; Lake George HS; Glens Falls, NY; (Y); 29/90; Church Yth Grp; SADD; Chorus; Lit Mag; JV Bsktbl; Var Cheerleading; Var Powder Puff Ftbl; Var Sftbl; Hon Roll; Prfct Atten Awd; Cortland; Elem Educ.

YAPLE, DENISE; Alexander Central HS; Alexander, NY; (Y); Spanish Clb; Varsity Clb; Capt Color Guard; Stu Cncl; JV Bsktbl; Var Sftbl; JV Capt Vllybl; Hon Roll; Jr NHS; Drama Clb; Hmcng Prncss 85-86; Mst Imprvd Sftbll Plyer 85-86; Genesee CC; Bus Sec.

YARDE, TERENCE; Alexander Hamilton HS; Elmsford, NY; (S); 1/59; Pres Key Clb; Pres Science Clb; VP Spanish Clb; Band; Mrchg Band; Yrbk Stf; Pres Jr Cls; Pres Stu Cncl; Stat Bsktbl; Martin Luther King Yth Awd 85; Comp Sci.

YARDLEY, CRAIG; East Hampton HS; Amagansett, NY; (Y); 25/120; Am Leg Boys St; Civic Clb; Pep Clb; Rep Stu Cncl; JV Var Bsktbl; JV Var Ftbl; Var Golf; Hon Roll; Math Awd 82-83; Stu Ldrs 84-86; Stu Govt Awd 86; Elon Coll; Pub Adm.

YARDLEY, GWYN; Saranac Lake HS; Tupper Lk, NY; (Y); Band; VP Jr Cls; Rep Stu Cncl; Var Bsktbl; JV Var Socr; Var Sftbl; Var Trk; Hon Roll; NHS; Bsktbl Red Lttr Awd 86; Jrnlsm.

YARMUS, HEATH P; Centereach HS; Lake Grove, NY; (Y); 39/429; Pres Temple Yth Grp; Concert Band; Mrchg Band; Trs Soph Cls; Socr; High Hon Roll; NY ST Rgnts Schlrshp 86; Brnrd Coll; Englsh.

YARTER, DEBRA; Catholic Central HS; Cohoes, NY; (Y); Drama Clb; Math Clb; Spanish Clb; SADD; School Musical; School Play; Stage Crew; Yrbk Stf; Hon Roll; Soc Stds Awd 84; Bus.

YARTZ, ANDREW R; E Aurora HS; E Aurora, NY; (Y); Letterman Clb; Varsity Clb; Var Capt Crs Cntry; Var JV Swmmng; Var L Trk; Hon Roll; NY ST Chmpn Crs Cntry Tm 86; Cornell U; Micro Bio.

YARWOOD, JURENE; St Pius V HS; Bronx, NY; (Y); Cmnty Wkr; Spanish Clb; Nwsp Stf; Pres Frsh Cls; Pres Soph Cls; Sec Jr Cls; Hon Roll; Pres NHS; Chess Clb; Natl Soc Scndry Schl; Cert Merit Hghst Avg Sci, Engl & Afro-Asian 84; Awd Spnsh, Engl & Bio Awd 85-86; Pediatrian.

YARYURA, ADRIANA; Roslyn HS; Roslyn, NY; (Y); Church Yth Grp; Cmnty Wkr; Dance Clb; Hosp Aide; Y-Teens; Chorus; School Musical; School Play; Nwsp Rptr; Yrbk Stf; Runnr Up Nassau Cnty JR Poetry Cntst 85; U Of Toronto; Med.

YASKULSKI, ROBIN; Kendall JR SR HS; Kendall, NY; (S); 2/95; Spanish Clb; Concert Band; Mrchg Band; Rep Stu Cncl; JV Capt Bsktbl; Socr; Sftbl; Vllybl; High Hon Roll; NHS; RIT; Prodctn Engrng.

YASMIRL, MURRAY; Eastern District HS; Brooklyn, NY; (Y); Art Clb; Dance Clb; Debate Tm; Drama Clb; Spanish Clb; Nwsp Rptr; Nwsp Stf; Gym; Vllybl; Jrnlsm.

YATES, BRENDA A; Arkport Central Schl; Arkport, NY; (Y); 5/55; Varsity Clb; Band; School Play; Pres Jr Cls; Pres Stu Cncl; Var Capt Bsktbl; JV Capt Socr; Var Capt Sftbl; Var Capt Vllybl; High Hon Roll; Regnts Schlrshp 85-86; Ithaca Coll; Phy Thrpy.

YATES, DAVID; Onteora HS; Shokan, NY; (Y); 29/201; Math Tm; Chorus; School Musical; Tennis; High Hon Roll; Hon Roll; NHS; By Sct Egl Awd Rank 86; MVP Tnns Vrsty Tm 86; Rochester Inst ; Engr.

YATES, KAREN; Geneva HS; Geneva, NY; (S); 17/175; French Clb; Varsity Clb; Pres Sr Cls; Rep Stu Cncl; JV Var Cheerleading; Var Socr; Sftbl; Hon Roll; NHS; Mst Improved Plyr Var Sftbl 84-85; Big 6 Awd 3 Var Ltrs 84-85; William Smith Coll; Bio Sci.

YATES JR, RICHARD L; Cuba Central Schl; Cuba, NY; (Y); 7/55; Pres Church Yth Grp; Quiz Bowl; Band; Concert Band; Mrchg Band; Pep Band; Var L Trk; High Hon Roll; VP NHS; Rgnts Schlrshp 86; Houghton Coll; Comp Sci.

YATES, TAMMY; Greece Athena HS; Rochester, NY; (Y); Church Yth Grp; FBLA; Girl Scts; JA; Spanish Clb; SADD; Varsity Clb; JV Var Sftbl; MCC; Secy.

YATTEAU, JENNIFER; Our Lady Of Mercy HS; Rochester, NY; (Y); Hosp Aide; Ski Clb; Bowling; Sftbl; Monroe CC; Fashn Retlng/Merchn.

YAVORNITZKI, LISA; Oneida HS; Oneida, NY; (Y); Church Yth Grp; Drama Clb; 4-H; French Clb; Chorus; School Musical; School Play; Trs Sr Cls; Golf; Hon Roll; Stu Govt Prog 84; Jr Prom Queen 85; Area All St Choir 86; Buffalo ST Coll; Elem Ed.

YEAGER, BRENDA M; Convent Of The Sacred Heart HS; New York, NY; (Y); Cmnty Wkr; Dance Clb; Drama Clb; Math Tm; School Musical; Variety Show; Yrbk Phtg; Yrbk Stf; Ntl Merit SF; Lang.

YEANEY, ERIC; Westfield Central HS; Westfield, NY; (Y); 2/63; Boy Scts; Ski Clb; Trk; God Cntry Awd; NHS; Sal; Church Yth Grp; Key Clb; ROTC; Band; Ny St Rgnts Schlrshp Wnnr 86; Air Force ROTC Schlrshp Wnnr 86; Navy ROTC Schlrshp Wnnr 86; Rensselaer Polytech; Math.

YEARWOOD, JUAN; Freeport HS; Freeport, NY; (Y); High Hon Roll; Hon Roll; Law.

YEAVASIS, EVE; Syosset HS; Syosset, NY; (Y); 11/482; Cmnty Wkr; Dance Clb; Hosp Aide; Band; Jazz Band; School Musical; Nwsp Ed-Chief; Stu Cncl; Cit Awd; NHS; U Of VA; Med.

YEDDO, BRIDGETTE; Franklin Acad; Malone, NY; (Y); Cmnty Wkr; Rep Soroptimist; Hon Roll; Hnr Roll Awd 85-86; Epsilon Hnr Socty 84-87; Psych.

YEE, ALICE; James Madison HS; Brooklyn, NY; (Y); 1/748; Math Tm; Service Clb; Lit Mag; NHS; Prfct Atten Awd; Val; Office Aide; Science Clb; Teachers Aide; Hon Roll; Wstnghse Sci Tlnt Srch Cmptn 86; Otto P Burgdorf Sci & Math Rsrch Cmptn Fnlst 86; Massachusetts Tech Inst; Engrng.

YEE, BONDING; Port Chester HS; Port Chester, NY; (Y); 1/240; Trs Key Clb; Pres Spanish Clb; Mrchg Band; Trs Sr Cls; Rep Stu Cncl; Var L Crs Cntry; Mu Alp Tht; NHS; Ntl Merit SF; Rensselaer Mdl 85; Chem Engrng.

YEE, EUGENE P; Bayside HS; Whitestone, NY; (Y); 1/658; Math Tm; Science Clb; Ed Yrbk Stf; Gov Hon Prg Awd; NHS; Ntl Merit Ltr; Prfct Atten Awd; Val; Westinghouse Sci Tlnt Srch SF 86; Rensselaer Polytech Mdlst Math & Sci 85; Co-Capt Acad Olym Tm 86; Cornell U; Engrng.

YEE, JUDITH LYNN; Seward Park HS; New York, NY; (Y); 35/544; Computer Clb; Office Aide; Service Clb; Teachers Aide; Band; Yrbk Stf; Rep Sr Cls; Rep Stu Cncl; Hon Roll; Prfct Atten Awd; Baruch Coll; Indstrl Psych.

YEGIDIS, ROBERT; Middletown HS; Middletown, NY; (Y); 7/315; Jazz Band; Symp Band; Yrbk Stf; Tennis; High Hon Roll; NHS; NYSSMA Conf All ST Band 85; Zone 9 Area Music Festvl 84-85; All Cty Music Festvl 84-86.

YEH, ALICE; Ardsley HS; Ardsley, NY; (Y); 1/153; Mathletes; Yrbk Rptr; Var Swmmng; JV Trk; Ntl Merit SF; Val; JA; Chorus; Orch; Mnhtn Schl Of Msc Merit Schlrshp 85; Smth Coll Bk Awd 85; Astrphyscst.

YEH, LILY; Alfred G Berner HS; Massapequa, NY; (Y); French Clb; Capt Fld Hcky; Trk; Hon Roll; NHS; Ntl Merit Ltr; NYS Regnts Schlrshp 86; Wellesley Coll; Biochem.

YEH, SUSAN; Williamsville South HS; Williamsville, NY; (Y); Chorus; NHS.

YEHL, MICHAEL; Salamanca City Central Schl; Salamanca, NY; (Y); 5/150; Am Leg Boys St; Sec Drama Clb; Spanish Clb; Concert Band; Rep Soph Cls; Var Trk; NHS; Spanish NHS; Varsity Clb; Close Up Fndtn Trip Washington 86; Law.

YEKELL, NEIL; John Dewey HS; Brooklyn, NY; (Y); Boy Scts; Chess Clb; Computer Clb; English Clb; Capt Math Tm; Science Clb; Spanish Clb; Nwsp Rptr; John Hopkins U; Engr.

YEN, BENITA; Churchville-Chili HS; Rochester, NY; (Y); Ski Clb; Var Tennis; High Hon Roll; NHS; Bus Hnr Socty 86.

YENCER, DEBBIE; Alden HS; Alden, NY; (Y); Church Yth Grp; VP Sec French Clb; Letterman Clb; Ski Clb; Yrbk Stf; VP Pres Stu Cncl; Var Capt Tennis; Var Capt Trk; John Carroll U; Bus.

YENCER, JAMES; Perry Central HS; Perry, NY; (Y); 20/84; Math Tm; Chorus; Concert Band; Jazz Band; Mrchg Band; Yrbk Stf; Tennis; Masonic Awd; Boy Scts; Computer Clb; Eagl Sct; Rgnts Schlrshp; Vigil Hnr-Ordr Arrw; Monroe CC; Engrng Sci.

YEOMANS, DANIELLE; Greenville Central HS; Greenville, NY; (Y); 12/80; Church Yth Grp; Pep Clb; Spanish Clb; JV VP Cheerleading; VP Trk; Hon Roll; NHS; Art.

YERDON, JEANETTE M; Pulaski Acad & Central Schl; Pulaski, NY; (S); Drama Clb; French Clb; GAA; Math Clb; Pep Clb; Ski Clb; SADD; Band; Chorus; Mrchg Band; Teachng.

YERGENS, LISA A; Randolph Central Schl; Randolph, NY; (Y); 7/80; Drama Clb; French Clb; Sec Spanish Clb; VP Frsh Cls; Rep Stu Cncl; L Cheerleading; L Crs Cntry; L Trk; Hon Roll; Trs NHS; Big 30 Ftbl Chrldr 86; St Qualifiers For Cross Cntry & Track 84-85; Genessee CC; Travel.

YERVES, JANE; Smithtown HS East; St James, NY; (Y); Service Clb; SADD; School Play; Off Soph Cls; Chrmn Jr Cls; Trk; Rep French Hon Soc; Hon Roll; Frnch Hnr Scty 85; Bio.

YETMAN, CHRIS; Immaculate Heart Contral HS; Watertown, NY; (Y); Boy Scts; Letterman Clb; Science Clb; Varsity Clb; Yrbk Phtg; Pres Stu Cncl; Golf; Swmmng; Bausch & Lomb Sci Awd; Hon Roll; Eagle Scout; ST U NY; Bio Sci.

YICK, JANICE; William Cullen Bryant HS; Astoria, NY; (S); 132/623; Hosp Aide; Intnl Clb; Library Aide; Office Aide; Nwsp Rptr; Nwsp Stf; Hon Roll; Jr NHS; NHS; Acad Pin For Engl.

YINGLING, PAMELA; Wilson Central Schl; Newtone, NY; (Y); Sec Camera Clb; Church Yth Grp; Office Aide; Chorus; Cheerleading; Future Sectrys Assn 85-86; Busnss Clb 83-84 & 85-86; Niagra Cnty CC; Busnss.

YINGLING, RHONDA; Holley JR SR HS; Holley, NY; (Y); Am Leg Aux Girls St; Pres Spanish Clb; Chorus; Ed Nwsp Stf; Yrbk Stf; High Hon Roll; Hon Roll; NHS; Trphy For Hghst Avg In Spnsh III 86; Roberts Wesleyan Coll; Nrsng.

YIP, GEAYIN M; Richmond Hill HS; Richmond Hill, NY; (Y); 1/288; Key Clb; Pres Math Clb; French Hon Soc; Hon Roll; NHS; Val; Qns Coll Pres Awd Achvt 85 & 86; NY Newsday Hgh Hnrs Ldg Schltc Achvr 86; Govrs Schltc Achvt Schlrshp; MA Inst Of Tech; Engrng.

YIP, RENEE; Richmond Hill HS; Kew Gardens, NY; (Y); Key Clb; Library Aide; Office Aide; SADD; School Play; Lit Mag; Hon Roll; NHS; Frnch Hnr Rl 86; Engl Hnr Soc 85-86; Socl Stud Hnr Soc 86; St Johns U; Pharmacy.

YOCHIM II, BARRIE; Clymer Central Schl; Sherman, NY; (Y); 13/45; School Play; Var Capt Bsbl; Var Capt Bsktbl; Var L Ftbl; Hon Roll; Rgnts Schlrshp 86; Eric Mdsn Mem Sprtsmnshp Awd 86; Marietta Coll; Brdcstng.

YOCKEL, JIM; Naples Central Schl; Naples, NY; (Y); 6/63; Boy Scts; Drama Clb; French Clb; School Play; Rep Stu Cncl; Im Ice Hcky; Var L Socr; Var L Tennis; High Hon Roll; Prfct Atten Awd; CC Finger Lakes; Bus.

YOINGCO, ROCYNA; Dominican Commercial HS; Queens Village, NY; (Y); 70/250; Church Yth Grp; Cmnty Wkr; Hosp Aide; Teachers Aide; School Musical; Swmmng; Timer; Prfct Atten Awd; Cert Hnr NYS Bar Assn 86; Siena Clb 85-86; Princpls List 84-85; Princeton U; Cmmnctns.

YONATY, STEPHEN L; Binghamton HS; Binghamton, NY; (Y); 22/457; Am Leg Boys St; Debate Tm; Key Clb; Ski Clb; Trs SADD; Temple Yth Grp; Lit Mag; Rep Jr Cls; Rep Sr Cls; Rep Stu Cncl; Hstry Awd 86; Ky Clb 86; Hnr Soc 86; SUNY Binghamtom; Bus.

YOON, ARTHUR; Sweet Home Senior HS; Amherst, NY; (Y); Pres Latin Clb; Capt Quiz Bowl; Trs SADD; Chorus; Nwsp Rptr; Lit Mag; Pres Frsh Cls; Rep Jr Cls; JV VP Lcrss; Im Mgr Wt Lftg; Harvard Prize Book Awd 86; CAWNY Latin Awd 86; All ST Chorus 84; Med.

YOON, DAVID; Catholic Central HS; Troy, NY; (Y); French Clb; Math Clb; Math Tm; Stu Cncl; Tennis; NHS; Econ.

YOON, HELEN; Pelham Memorial HS; Pelham, NY; (Y); Science Clb; School Play; NHS; Fordham U; Law.

YOON, HONG; Eastchester HS; Tuckahoe, NY; (Y); Trs Latin Clb; Church Yth Grp; JA; Leo Clb; JV Var Bsktbl; Var Capt Socr; Trk; High Hon Roll; Jr NHS; NHS; Geomtry Rgnts Cert Of Merit 84; Int Alb Trig Rgnts European Studies 85; Engrng.

YORK, JEAN; Letchworth Central HS; Castile, NY; (Y); Drama Clb; L Band; Chorus; Yrbk Stf; Var L Vllybl; High Hon Roll; NHS; Am Leg Aux Girls St; Church Yth Grp; 4-H; Health Prof.

YORKE, CHRIS; St Francis Prep; Rego Pk, NY; (Y); Church Yth Grp; Cmnty Wkr; Speech Tm; SADD; Im Coach Actv; Im Mgr(s); Var Capt Swmmng; L Trk; Im Vllybl; Im Wt Lftg; Discplnry Exc 84-86; Math.

YOSH, PAM; Saugerties HS; Saugerties, NY; (S); Drama Clb; Pres French Clb; Ski Clb; School Musical; Yrbk Stf; Stat Socr; Hon Roll; Cmmnctns.

YOST, HEATHER; Gloversville HS; Gloversvl, NY; (Y); French Clb; Girl Scts; SADD; Yrbk Stf; Cheerleading; Mgr(s); Hon Roll; Med.

YOUMANS, BRENDA L; Wilson Magnet HS; Rochester, NY; (Y); JV Sftbl; Var Capt Vllybl; High Hon Roll; Hon Roll; Early Recog Blk Schlrs 86; Comp Sci.

YOUMANS, JODIE MICHELLE; Walton Central Schl; Walton, NY; (Y); 8/110; Key Clb; Chorus; Yrbk Stf; Cheerleading; Fld Hcky; Sftbl; High Hon Roll; Voice Dem Awd; Broome CC; Dntl Hygne.

YOUMANS, VIRGINIA; Addison Central HS; Addison, NY; (Y); Church Yth Grp; Sec Exploring; Trs Science Clb; Chorus; Color Guard; Drill Tm; Yrbk Stf; Bowling; Hon Roll; Cntrl City Bus Inst; Sec.

YOUNG, ALAN; Sodus Central Schl; Sodus, NY; (Y); Science Clb; Varsity Clb; Crs Cntry; Trk; High Hon Roll; Hon Roll; Denver Auto & Diesel Coll; Mech.

YOUNG, AMY; Mynderse Acad; Seneca Falls, NY; (S); 35/141; Cmnty Wkr; SADD; Band; School Musical; Yrbk Stf; Trs Stu Cncl; Var Capt Crs Cntry; Var Trk; Hon Roll; Stu Of Mth 83; St John Fisher Coll; Cmmnctns.

YOUNG, BRITTANY; Pine Valley HS; South Dayton, NY; (S); 4/60; AFS; Ski Clb; Pres Band; Drm Mjr(t); Jazz Band; Sec Jr Cls; Var Swmmng; Hon Roll; Jr NHS; NHS; All Cnty Music Fest Awds 85; Lwyr.

YOUNG, CAMILLE; St Barnabas HS; Bronx, NY; (Y); 38/189; Teachers Aide; Var JV Twrlr; Awd Rcgntn Bio 85; Acctg.

YOUNG, CHRISTOPHER; Geneseo Central HS; Geneseo, NY; (Y); 2/86; Drama Clb; Mathletes; Trs Spanish Clb; Band; School Musical; Yrbk Stf; Lit Mag; Tennis; High Hon Roll; NHS; Proj Close Up 86; Ranatra Fusca Crtvty Awd 85; Bio Resrch.

YOUNG, COLETTE; Buffalo Seminary HS; Buffalo, NY; (Y); Trs Camp Fr Inc; Sec Church Yth Grp; Dance Clb; Pep Clb; Chorus; Church Choir; School Musical; School Play; Variety Show; Badmtn; Judith Mc Dade Schlrshp 83; YPD Awd 86; Acctg.

YOUNG, DAVE; Marlboro HS; Middlehope, NY; (Y); Camera Clb; Band; Mrchg Band; Nwsp Stf; Yrbk Stf; Trk; Jrnlsm.

YOUNG, DEANNA; Nazareth Acad; Rochester, NY; (Y); Dance Clb; Drama Clb; Latin Clb; Radio Clb; Spanish Clb; SADD; Chorus; School Musical; Off Frsh Cls; Off Soph Cls; Phy Thrpy.

YOUNG, ELLEN; Mt St Ursula HS; Bronx, NY; (Y); 42/129; Drama Clb; Science Clb; SADD; Church Choir; School Musical; School Play; Rep Frsh Cls; Rep Stu Cncl; Regents Schlrshp 85-86; Potsdam ST; Drama.

YOUNG, ERIC; Morris HS; Bronx, NY; (Y); JA; Math Tm; Church Choir; Color Guard; Stage Crew; Nwsp Rptr; Yrbk Phtg; Crs Cntry; Trk; Hon Roll; Arista Trphy 83; Hnr Mdls 81; LIU; Bus Mgt.

YOUNG, GREGORY; St Marys Boys HS; Floral Pk, NY; (Y); Church Yth Grp; Civic Clb; Cmnty Wkr; Computer Clb; Dance Clb; Library Aide; Political Wkr; Radio Clb; Sci.

YOUNG, JACQUELINE L; Charles H Roth SR HS; Rochester, NY; (Y); 27/175; Drama Clb; Radio Clb; School Musical; School Play; Stage Crew; French Hon Soc; Spanish NHS; NY ST Smmr Schl Media Arts Almns 85; Schlstc Photo Awds Natl Awd 86; Video Art.

YOUNG, JEFFREY; Springville Griffith Inst; Springville, NY; (Y); Im Socr; Alfred ST Coll; Engrng.

YOUNG, JERRY; Mexico Academy & Central Schl; Mexico, NY; (Y); Ski Clb; Golf; Socr; Harry E King Schlrshp 86; Schlrshp For Diligence & Achvt 86; Canton ATC; Refrigeration.

YOUNG, JILL; St Josephs By The Sea HS; Staten Island, NY; (Y); Civic Clb; Dance Clb; Debate Tm; Drama Clb; French Clb; JA; Pep Clb; Chorus; School Musical; School Play; L Intertit Frnch Awd 85; Marymount Coll; Psychlgst.

YOUNG, JO-ANN; Woodlands HS; Hartsdale, NY; (Y); Off Church Yth Grp; Chorus; Church Choir; School Musical; Variety Show; Lit Mag; Hon Roll; NHS; Band; Stage Crew.

YOUNG, KEVIN; E J Wilson HS; Spencerport, NY; (Y); 1/250; Drama Clb; French Clb; Math Clb; School Play; Stage Crew; Variety Show; Yrbk Stf; Var Tennis; High Hon Roll; NHS; Bst Art Stu 83-85; Bst Engl Stu 85-86; U Of PA.

YOUNG, KRISTIN; Columbia HS; Rensselaer, NY; (Y); 3/407; Church Yth Grp; 4-H; Orch; School Musical; Symp Band; Vllybl; 4-H Awd; High Hon Roll; NHS; Ntl Merit SF; AlST Band, Orchestra NYSSMA 84 & 85; Frgn Lang.

YOUNG, LULU; Williamsville E HS; E Amherst, NY; (Y); 24/302; Computer Clb; Math Clb; Scholastic Bowl; Concert Band; Capt Socr; L Var Trk; High Hon Roll; NHS; Ntl Merit SF; Pep Band; Early Bach Awd Piano 83; Athl Yr Awd 83; Pre-Med.

YOUNG, MADELEINE; Bronx HS Of Science; Hillcrest, NY; (Y); Sec Camera Clb; Science Clb; Chorus; Lit Mag; NHS; Sm-Fnlst Westinghouse Sci Tlnt Srch 86; Fnlst St Johns Sympsm 86; Pres Acad Fi T Awd 86; Williams Coll; Biochem.

YOUNG, MATTHEW; Westfield Acad; Westfield, NY; (Y); Am Leg Boys St; Chess Clb; Drama Clb; English Clb; Quiz Bowl; Ski Clb; Chorus; School Play; Sec Sr Cls; Rep Stu Cncl; Englsh.

YOUNG, MELISSA; Fort Plain HS; Fort Plain, NY; (S); Varsity Clb; Yrbk Stf; VP Frsh Cls; Rep Jr Cls; Trs Stu Cncl; JV Var Cheerleading; JV Var Socr; Var Trk; Trs NHS; Math.

YOUNG, MICHAEL; Amsterdam HS; Amsterdam, NY; (Y); 47/316; JA; Band; Concert Band; Mrchg Band; Crs Cntry; Capt Swmmng; Aviation.

YOUNG, PAULA; George G Wingate HS; Brooklyn, NY; (Y); Psychology.

YOUNG, POLLY; Gloversville HS; Gloversvl, NY; (Y); Am Leg Aux Girls St; Hosp Aide; SADD; Band; School Musical; Sec Jr Cls; Sec Sr Cls; Cheerleading; Tennis; Hon Roll; Prom Ct 86; Hartwick; Nrsg.

YOUNG, SANDY; Bronx HS Of Science; Woodside, NY; (Y); Teachers Aide; School Musical; Trk; Trustees Schlrshp 86; Pres Acadmc Ftnss Awd Prog 86; NY U; Math.

YOUNG, STEPHEN C; Hunter College HS; Hollis, NY; (Y); French Clb; Math Clb; Ski Clb; Teachers Aide; School Play; Variety Show; Off Jr Cls; Off Sr Cls; Bowling; Ntl Merit Schol; Union Coll; Mth.

YOUNG, SUSAN; St Hildas And St Hughs Schl; Yonkers, NY; (Y); PAVAS; Fine Art.

YOUNG, TAMMY; Fort Plain Central HS; Fort Plain, NY; (S); 11/57; Girl Scts; Office Aide; Varsity Clb; Color Guard; Yrbk Stf; Off Sr Cls; Socr; Vllybl; Hon Roll; NHS; Acdmc Awrnss Among Stu 84-85; Cosmetlgy.

YOUNG, TAWYA; Midwood HS; Brooklyn, NY; (Y); Church Yth Grp; Church Choir; Color Guard; Yrbk Ed-Chief; Yrbk Stf; High Hon Roll; NHS; Teachers Aide; School Play; Wt Lftg; Arista Soc 84; Psych.

YOUNG, TOMARA; Jamesville-Dewitt HS; Dewitt, NY; (Y); Cmnty Wkr; Var L Trk; Hon Roll; Syracuse U Pre Coll Prog Schlrshp 86; Hampton U; Mrktng.

YOUNG, TONYA; Granville Central HS; Granville, NY; (Y); 3/124; SADD; Band; Concert Band; Mrchg Band; VP Soph Cls; Sec Sr Cls; Sec Stu Cncl; Var L Cheerleading; High Hon Roll; NHS; Mst Outstndng Hlth 85-86; Mst Outstndng Chmstry 85-86; Rochester Inst Of Tech; Math.

YOUNG, VICKI; Jordan Elbridge HS; Elbridge, NY; (Y); 35/143; Girl Scts; Band; Concert Band; L Mrchg Band; Var L Tennis; Var L Vllybl; High Hon Roll; Hon Roll; SR Banquet Chrprsn 86; SUNY At Alfred; Comp Science.

YOUNG, VIVIAN; Smithtown HS East; Nesconset, NY; (Y); DECA; Office Aide; SADD; Teachers Aide; Yrbk Stf; Stu Cncl; Hon Roll; Italian Hnr Scty 85-86; Cornell U; Med.

YOUNG, WAYNE XAVIER; Wyandanch Memorial HS; Wyandanch, NY; (Y); Science Clb; Band; Concert Band; Jazz Band; Mrchg Band; Yrbk Stf; High Hon Roll; Urbn Lg Ntl Schlrshp 87-90; U Rochester; Chmcl Engrng.

YOUNGBERG, MELISSA; Mahopac HS; Mahopac, NY; (Y); Cmnty Wkr; Leo Clb; Office Aide; JV Crs Cntry; JV Fld Hcky; Var Stat Score Keeper; Var Capt Socr; Var Vllybl; Var Stat Wrstlng; Hon Roll; MVP JV Sccr 84 & 85; Soc Wrk.

YOUNGERS, DENNIS; Letchworth Central HS; Warsaw, NY; (Y); 4-H; FFA; Math Tm; Spanish Clb; Cit Awd; High Hon Roll; Hon Roll; NHS; Geneseo ST U; Comp Sci.

YOUNGERS III, ROBERT JAMES; Hamburg SR HS; Hamburg, NY; (Y); Boy Scts; Church Yth Grp; 4-H; Chorus; Madrigals; School Musical; School Play; Socr; Wrstlng; Medal Merit BSA Meritorious Action 85; US Army; Law Enfrcmnt.

YOUNGHESE, MICHELE; St Johns Prep; Middle Vlg, NY; (Y); 27/458; Nwsp Stf; High Hon Roll; Hon Roll; NHS; Katharine Gibbs Schlrp 86; Bus Dept Awd 86; Ofc Procdrs Awd 86; Katharine Gibbs Sch; Bus.

YOUNGS, KAREN; Groton Central HS; Groton, NY; (Y); 14/90; Sec Drama Clb; Spanish Clb; SADD; Capt Color Guard; Yrbk Ed-Chief; Yrbk Rptr; Yrbk Stf; Sec Jr Cls; High Hon Roll; Hon Roll; Spd Typst 85; Plcmnt In Advncd Engl 86-87; Jrnlsm.

YOUNGS, TIMOTHY; Rocky Point JR SR HS; Rocky Point, NY; (S); 17/175; Church Yth Grp; JV Lcrss; Hon Roll; Mark Twain Lit Cont 85.

YOUSETT, KYLE; Wilson Central HS; Newfane, NY; (Y); Church Yth Grp; Cmnty Wkr; 4-H; SADD; Band; Pep Band; 4-H Awd; Niagara Cnty 4-H Schlrshp 86; Lockport Svgs Bk Bus Schlrshp 86; NY ST Rep Natl 4-H Clothing Revue 85; Bryant & Stratton; Bus Mgt.

YOUSSEF, DALIA; Moore Catholic HS; Staten Island, NY; (Y); Hon Roll; Honor Certificate In Geometry 85; Engrng.

YOVIENE, PAULA; Frontier Central HS; Hamburg, NY; (Y); 35/430; VP Art Clb; Girl Scts; Latin Clb; Pep Clb; SADD; Band; Stu Cncl; Hon Roll; NHS; Actn Learning Internshp Pgm 86; Interior Dsgn.

YOVINO, JEANINE; Hauppauge HS; Hauppauge, NY; (Y); 97/500; Aud/Vis; Mrchg Band; Orch; School Musical; Symp Band; High Hon Roll; Hon Roll; Music Schlrshp 86; Wnr NY ST Media Arts Shw 86; Outstndng Achvmnt In Band Awd 86; Susquehanna U; Music.

YOXALL, THOMAS; Rome Catholic HS; Whitesboro, NY; (Y); 8/68; Rep Stu Cncl; JV Ftbl; Capt JV Ice Hcky; High Hon Roll; NHS; Pres Schlr; Im Wt Lftg; NEDT Awd; NYS H S Hcky Chmpn 84-86; Mrns Athltc Schlr Awd 86; Coaches Athltc Awd 86; Canisius Coll; Phrmcy.

YSTUETA, SUSAN; Brentwood Ross HS; Brentwood, NY; (Y); 3/500; Cmnty Wkr; Co-Capt Scholastic Bowl; Symp Band; Pres Sr Cls; Var Capt Pom Pon; Cit Awd; High Hon Roll; NHS; Church Yth Grp; Drama Clb; Semi Fnlst Ntl Hispnc Schlrshp 86; MIT MITES Smmr Pgm 85; Bio.

YU, CATHERINE L; Bayside HS; Beechhurst, NY; (Y); 20/658; Trs Church Yth Grp; Teachers Aide; Orch; Ed Yrbk Stf; Ed Lit Mag; Hon Roll; Jr NHS; Trs NHS; Prfct Atten Awd; Columbia U.

YU, CHARLES; Brooklyn Technical HS; Elmhurst, NY; (Y); 57/1159; Cmnty Wkr; JA; Library Aide; Math Clb; Math Tm; Quiz Bowl; Service Clb; Lit Mag; High Hon Roll; Hon Roll; Regents Schlrshp 86; Cornell Grant 86; NY Acad Scie Resrch Pgm 85; Cornell U; Engrng.

YU, ELIZABETH K; Humanities HS; New York, NY; (Y); Computer Clb; Library Aide; Teachers Aide; Orch; Nwsp Rptr; Cit Awd; Merit Schlrshp 84; Art Gllry Squad 84; Mtrpd Awd 84; Aerontc Engrng.

YU, MEEI LING; High Schl For The Humanits; New York, NY; (Y); Cmnty Wkr; Computer Clb; Pres Dance Clb; Off Math Tm; Hon Roll; NHS; Arista Awd 85-86; Engr.

YU, PAK-LIM; Far Rockaway HS; Flushing, NY; (Y); 7/338; Math Tm; Office Aide; Teachers Aide; Stage Crew; Bowling; Capt Tennis; Acdmc Olympics/Schlstc Awd 85-86; Arista/Hon Soc Awd 85; Assoc Asst Principals Foreign Lang Awd 86; SUNY; Engrng.

YU, RANDOLPH; Shenedehowa HS; Clifton Park, NY; (Y); 8/675; Cmnty Wkr; French Clb; Math Tm; High Hon Roll; NHS; Ntl Merit Ltr; Prfct Atten Awd; Pres Schlr; Outstndng Acadmc Stu 82-83; Supr Hnr Rll 82-86; Cornell U; Engrng.

YU, SHEUNG FUNG; Newtown HS; Elmhurst, NY; (Y); 77/667; Math Tm; Office Aide; Teachers Aide; School Musical; School Play; Nwsp Stf; Yrbk Stf; Hon Roll; Prfct Atten Awd; SEHNAP Schlrshp 86; Molloy Schlrshp 86; Pace Schlrshp 86 NYU; Nrsng.

YUAN, ERHMEI; Commack High School South; Commack, NY; (Y); 4/370; Art Clb; Hosp Aide; Math Tm; Ed Nwsp Stf; Ed Yrbk Stf; Ed Lit Mag; Var Badmtn; NHS; Pres Schlr; NY ST Rgnts Schrlshp, Pres Acad Ftnss Awd 86; Columbia U; Fine Arts.

YUE, DIANE; New Dorp HS; Staten Island, NY; (Y); Intnl Clb; Office Aide; Teachers Aide; Hon Roll; Prfct Atten Awd; Pre-Med.

YUEN, JUDITH B; Farmingdale HS; Farmingdale, NY; (Y); 5/560; Chorus; Rptr Yrbk Stf; Hon Roll; NHS; Ntl Merit Ltr; Weldon E Howitt Physcs Awd 86; Socl Stu Achvt Awd 86; Regnts Schlrshp 86; Houghton Clg; Librl Arts.

YUEN, MAI; Bronx High School Of Science; Bronx, NY; (Y); Cmnty Wkr; Hosp Aide; Chorus; Nwsp Rptr; Nwsp Stf; Yrbk Stf; Prfct Atten Awd; Bus.

YUEN, MINDY; Fashion Industries HS; Ny, NY; (Y); 14/329; Art Clb; Computer Clb; Drama Clb; Hosp Aide; JA; Library Aide; Chorus; Tennis; Vllybl; Hon Roll; Spnsh & Englsh Hnr Awd 84-85; Bus Mngmnt.

YUEN, VICTORIA; Brooklyn Technical HS; New York, NY; (Y); 90/1159; Office Aide; Teachers Aide; Band; Yrbk Stf; Hon Roll; NCTE Awd; NHS; United Fedrtn Of Tchrs Schlrshp 86; YMCA Yth & Govt 82-85; Pol Athltc Leagues Story Wrtng Awd 86; Psych.

YUILLE, MELISSA; Schalmont HS; Schenectady, NY; (Y); Capt Color Guard; Mrchg Band; Rep Frsh Cls; Rep Jr Cls; Stat Bsbl; Stat Bsktbl; Capt Var Cheerleading; High Hon Roll; Hon Roll; NHS; Albany Coll Pharmacy; Phrmcst.

YULE, CATHERINE; Whiteboro SR HS; Utica, NY; (Y); 16/306; GAA; Service Clb; JV Var Bsktbl; Var Sftbl; Var Tennis; High Hon Roll; Hon Roll; NHS; Science Clb; School Musical; MVP JR Var Bsktbl Tm 85; All-Star Var Sftbl Tm 86; Area All ST Violin 84-85; Librl Arts.

YUN, MI SUM; Fairport HS; Fairport, NY; (Y); Pres Church Yth Grp; Cmnty Wkr; Intnl Clb; Chorus; Church Choir; Capt Flag Corp; Rep Frsh Cls; Rep Soph Cls; Rep Jr Cls; Rep Stu Cncl; Bus.

YUNA, GEORGE; Edison Vo-Tech; Rochester, NY; (Y); Boy Scts; Exploring; Bsbl; Golf; Swmmng; Hon Roll.

YUNAEV, EMIL; Midwoo HS; Brooklyn, NY; (Y); Socr; Prfct Atten Awd; Law.

YURACKO, KIM; Scarsdale HS; Scarsdale, NY; (Y); French Clb; Math Tm; Orch; Nwsp Sprt Ed; Var Capt Tennis; NHS.

YURCHAK, ELIZABETH; Nardin Acad; Hamburg, NY; (S); 14/85; Pres French Clb; Hosp Aide; Service Clb; Acpl Chr; School Musical; School Play; Lit Mag; Var Cheerleading; Var Tennis; Hon Roll; Govt.

YURMAN, JOANNE; Our Lady Of Perpetual Help HS; Brooklyn, NY; (Y); 14/155; Dance Clb; Gym; Hon Roll; NHS; The Wood Schl; Exec Sec.

YUSIM, ILYA; Franklyn D Roosevelt HS; Brooklyn, NY; (Y); 21/900; Math Clb; Math Tm; Scholastic Bowl; Science Clb; Service Clb; NHS; Prfct Atten Awd; Rnd 1 Wnnr-STWIDE Stu Enrgy Rsrch Comptn 86; Cert Of Hnr-Excllnc H S Math 86; Elec Engr.

YUVIENCO, NICOLE S; Smithtown H S East; Nesconset, NY; (Y); Hosp Aide; Off Frsh Cls; Off Soph Cls; Co-Capt Jr Cls; Co-Capt Sr Cls; High Hon Roll; Hon Roll; NHS; VP Spanish NHS; Ntl Hspnc Schlrshp Awds Pgm; Pre-Med.

YZAGUIRRE, CHARLES R; Mount St Michael Acad; Bronx, NY; (Y); 18/292; Service Clb; Yrbk Rptr; Stu Cncl; Var Capt Bowling; Hon Roll; NHS; Spanish NHS; Im Bsktbl; L Crs Cntry; Im Sftbl; Mt St Michael Outstndg Bwlr 85-86; Hi Series Bwlg Cty Champ 84-85; Dist Atty Bronx Cnty Svc & Ldrshp; Boston Coll; Acctg.

ZABATTA, LANCE; Riverhead HS; Baiting Hollow, NY; (Y); 17/200; Computer Clb; VP Latin Clb; Ski Clb; Im Ice Hcky; JV Var Socr; Var Tennis; VP Jr NHS; Pre-Med.

ZABELL, ARI; Oceanside HS; Oceanside, NY; (Y); 50/565; Mathletes; Thesps; Jazz Band; Orch; Variety Show; Hon Roll; NHS; Ntl Merit Ltr; Hopwood Schlrshp 86; Rutgers U; Vet Med.

ZABELNY, LISA M; Nazareth Acad; Rochester, NY; (Y); Hosp Aide; Latin Clb; Ski Clb; Chorus; School Musical; Stage Crew; Off Soph Cls; Off Jr Cls; Socr; NHS; Natl Latin Exam Magna Cum Laude 84; U Rochester.

ZABRISKIE, LAWRENCE; St Agnes HS For Boys; New York, NY; (Y); 4/106; Hon Roll; NHS; Columbia U.

ZABROUSKI, KARYN; St Francis Prep; Bayside, NY; (S); Art Clb; Science Clb; Rep Stu Cncl; Hon Roll; Opt Clb Awd; Grls ST Altrnt 85; Prsns Schl Of Dstn; Art.

ZABSKI, PAULA A; Herbert H Lehman HS; Bronx, NY; (Y); 6/385; Church Yth Grp; Jazz Band; Orch; Hon Roll; 2nd Teen Talnt 85; Membr H H Lehman H S Arista Soc 85; Acadmc Perfrmnc Awd 86; Long Island U; Chem.

ZACCARIA, RAFFAELLA; St John The Baptist Y HS; Greenlawn, NY; (Y); Art Clb; French Clb; Band; Bus.

ZACCHEA, JEANNE; Academy Of St Joseph HS; Sayville, NY; (Y); Dance Clb; Debate Tm; SADD; Church Choir; Nwsp Ed-Chief; Nwsp Phtg; Nwsp Rptr; Rep Stu Cncl; Crs Cntry; Var Mgr(s); Long Island Catholic Jrnlsm Awd 86.

ZACCHEA, MICHAEL; St Anthonys HS; Sayville, NY; (Y); 38/240; Boy Scts; Intnl Clb; Nwsp Stf; Lit Mag; JV Var Crs Cntry; JV Var Trk; French Hon Soc; High Hon Roll; NHS; Ntl Merit Ltr; NROTC Schlrshp; NYS Rgnts Schlrshp; Knghts Of Columbus Schlrshp; U Of Notre Dame.

ZACEK JR, BRADLEY P; Rome Free Acad; Rome, NY; (Y); 159/462; Aud/Vis; Cmnty Wkr; 4-H; SADD; Vllybl; 4-H Awd; Prfct Atten Awd; ST U NY Morrisville; Lndscpng.

ZACH, KYLE; Thousand Islands HS; Clayton, NY; (Y); #1 In Class; Am Leg Boys St; Cmnty Wkr; Varsity Clb; School Play; Trs Stu Cncl; JV Bsbl; Var L Ice Hcky; Var Capt Socr; Bausch & Lomb Sci Awd; High Hon Roll; Public Brdcstng TV Quiz Tm; Minor Hockey Ofcl; Engrng.

ZACH, VALERIE; Smithtown HS East; St James, NY; (Y); Mgr(s); Score Keeper; High Hon Roll; Hon Roll; Ntl Merit Ltr; Psych.

ZACHARIAH, NIMMY E; Tottenville HS; Staten Island, NY; (Y); 88/872; Church Yth Grp; Key Clb; Yrbk Rptr; Lit Mag; Cit Awd; Gov Hon Prg Awd; NHS; Ntl Merit Schol; SADD; Teachers Aide; NEH Resrch Awd Merit 85; NFC NSC Awds 86; NCTE Awd Merit 85; Eng.

ZACHER JR, JOHN J; La Salle SR HS; Niagara Falls, NY; (S); 2/259; Math Tm; Yrbk Stf; Stu Cncl; L Var Bsbl; L Var Bsktbl; L Var Ftbl; NHS; Ntl Merit Ltr; Sal; Library Aide; Wshngtn Wrkshps; Chem Engrng.

ZACHOLL, LISA; John C Birdlebough HS; Pennellville, NY; (Y); AFS; French Clb; SADD; Band; Concert Band; Mrchg Band; Nwsp Rptr; Nwsp Stf; Yrbk Stf; Var L Socr; Hgh Acdmc Achvt Sprts Prtcptn 84; SUNY Oswego; Sec Educ.

ZACK, TERRI; Lackawanna HS; Lackawanna, NY; (Y); 1/230; Spanish Clb; High Hon Roll; NHS; Awd Excllnc-Chem 85; Hghst Schltc Achvt 85 & 86; Awd Excllnc-Spnsh III 86; Bio Sci.

ZACKMAN, ODIN; Mameroneck HS; Larchmont, NY; (Y); Cmnty Wkr; SADD; Nwsp Rptr; Nwsp Stf; Lit Mag; Hon Roll.

ZADZILKA, EUGENE W; Lackawanna SR HS; Lackawanna, NY; (Y); 2/265; Am Leg Boys St; Scholastic Bowl; Stage Crew; Rep Stu Cncl; Var Bowling; Var Tennis; Var Vllybl; Bausch & Lomb Sci Awd; High Hon Roll; NHS; Knights Of Pythias-Outstndng Sr Awd 86; H J Doherty Mem Awd-Physics 85; U Of Buffalo; Elec Engrng.

ZADZILKA, JOYCE; West Seneca West SR HS; W Seneca, NY; (Y); 2/520; Mathletes; Quiz Bowl; Chorus; School Musical; School Play; High Hon Roll; JC Awd; Jr NHS; NHS; Pres Schlr; Acctg.

ZAFFARANO, VICTORIA; Frankfort-Schuyler HS; Frankfort, NY; (S); Yrbk Ed-Chief; Rep Frsh Cls; Rep Soph Cls; Rep Sr Cls; Stu Cncl; Capt Cheerleading; Var Vllybl; High Hon Roll; Trs NHS; Hmcmng Ct 85; SUNY Oswego; Mth.

ZAGAJESKI, KIM NOELL; Hicksville SR HS; Hicksville, NY; (Y); Var Bsktbl; Var Sftbl; Var Vllybl; Jr NHS; NHS; Empre ST Sftbl Team 86; All Cnty & MVP Sftbl Plyr 85 & 86; Prncpls List; Law.

ZAGAJESKI II, THOMAS A; Hicksville HS; Hicksville, NY; (Y); 46/456; Am Leg Boys St; FTA; Spanish Clb; Nwsp Sprt Ed; Yrbk Sprt Ed; Bsbl; Bsktbl; Trk; NHS; Hofstra U; Comp Sci.

ZAGAMI, STEVEN M; Willaimsville North HS; Williamsville, NY; (Y); 76/301; Church Yth Grp; Teachers Aide; Band; Chorus; Jazz Band; Pres Orch; Pep Band; School Musical; School Play; Pres Frsh Cls; Nw Englnd Msc Cnsrvtry; Orchsta.

ZAGARELLA, DONNA; Dominican Commercial HS; Cambria Hts, NY; (Y); 100/250; Yrbk Stf; Rep Stu Cncl; Coach Actv; Sftbl; Var Capt Vllybl; Hon Roll; Yrbk Rptr; Pres Sr Cls; Vllybl Tm Mst Vlble Plyr 84 & 86; Physcl Ed Awd 86; St Marys Vllybl Trnmnt Mst Vlble Plyr 83; Molloy Coll; Soc Wrk.

ZAGER, MARA K; Oceanside HS; Oceanside, NY; (Y); 139/531; Sec Computer Clb; L Chorus; Library Aide; Mathletes; Teachers Aide; Temple Yth Grp; Thesps; School Musical; School Play; Stage Crew; Rgnts Schlrsp 86; Flrnc Smth Memrl Tchng Schlrshp 86; U Of MA Amherst; Chldhd Educ.

ZAGO, JENNIFER; Newburgh Free Acad; Newburgh, NY; (Y); Church Yth Grp; Girl Scts; Spanish Clb; JV Var Cheerleading; High Hon Roll; Hon Roll; Prfct Atten Awd; TWA Flght Schl; Flght Attndnt.

ZAGREDA, ELZA; Academy Of Mt St Ursula; Yonkers, NY; (Y); Church Yth Grp; Drama Clb; School Play; Variety Show; Nwsp Rptr; Pres Soph Cls; Rep Jr Cls; Pres Stu Cncl; High Hon Roll; Exmptn All Final Exams 84; NYU; Drama.

ZAHM, CHARLENE; Frontier Central HS; Woodlawn, NY; (Y); Art Clb; Church Yth Grp; Drama Clb; Pep Clb; Spanish Clb; Chorus; School Musical; Stage Crew; Hon Roll; NHS; Med Fld.

ZAHORSKY, JOANNE; Saugerties HS; Saugerties, NY; (S); 1/250; Pres Boy Scts; Chess Clb; Sec 4-H; French Clb; Quiz Bowl; Scholastic Bowl; Pres Thesps; Band; Mrchg Band; Nwsp Rptr; All Cnty Bnd 84-86; Cornell U; Vet Med.

ZAHRADKA, DEAN; Bayport-Bluepoint HS; Bayport, NY; (Y); 23/210; Boy Scts; Key Clb; Yrbk Stf; Ftbl; Wt Lftg; JV Wrstlng; Hon Roll; NHS; U S Mrchnt Marine Acad; Engrng.

ZAIA, PHILIP D; Pittsford Sutherland HS; Pittsford, NY; (Y); Boy Scts; Chess Clb; Mgr Model UN; Var Crs Cntry; JV Trk; High Hon Roll; Hon Roll; Pres Schlr; X-Cntry Ski Cap Var 83-86; Exch Stu Pgm Japan 86; Intershp Judicial Process Comm 86.

ZAIFERT, MICHELLE; Allegany Central HS; Allegany, NY; (Y); Color Guard; Yrbk Bus Mgr; Yrbk Stf; Socr; High Hon Roll; Hon Roll; Prfct Atten Awd; Rochester Bus Inst; Accntnt.

ZAINEDDIN, MARK A; Thomas Alva Edison HS; Elmira, NY; (Y); Am Leg Boys St; Boy Scts; Model UN; Band; Rep Stu Cncl; Var L Tennis; High Hon Roll; Aud/Vis; Chess Clb; Church Yth Grp; Elmra Coll Key Awd & Schlrshp 86; U Thnt Awd Acdm Excllnc Mdl UN Bffl NY 86; Compltd WA Smmr Smnr; Intrntl Stds.

ZAINO, PINA; Lynbrook HS; Lynbrook, NY; (Y); French Clb; Sec Trs Key Clb; Hon Roll; Italian Club 84-86; Hofsta; Accntng.

ZAJAC, KARA; Onondaga Central HS; Syracuse, NY; (S); Church Yth Grp; German Clb; SADD; Band; Chorus; Capt Cheerleading; JV Socr; High Hon Roll; Hon Roll; NHS.

ZAJKOWSKI, KRISTA; Upton Lake Christian Schl; Hyde Park, NY; (Y); Dance Clb; 4-H; Capt Pep Clb; Chorus; Yrbk Stf; Capt Cheerleading; Capt Pom Pon; 4-H Awd; Hon Roll; Gordon Coll; Psych.

ZAK, JAMES J; Seneca Vocational HS; Buffalo, NY; (Y); 13/206; CAP; High Hon Roll; Hon Roll; Rgnts Schlrshp 86; Merit Roll 81-86; Alfred A&T; Comp Drftg.

ZAK, KRISTEN; Port Jervis HS; Montague, NJ; (Y); 7/185; Hosp Aide; Teachers Aide; Varsity Clb; Chorus; Trs Yrbk Stf; Trk; High Hon Roll; Trs NHS; Frnch Cert Merit 85; Spn Cert Merit 82-86; E Stroudsburg U PA; Psych.

ZAK, WALTER; Frontier Central HS; Blasdell, NY; (Y); Art Clb; Aud/Vis; Drama Clb; French Clb; SADD; School Musical; School Play; Stage Crew; Frsh Cls; Soph Cls; Cornell U; Hotl Mgmt.

ZAKEN, AVA MARIE; Cardinal O Hara HS; Tonawanda, NY; (Y); Drama Clb; Library Aide; Spanish Clb; School Play; Nwsp Stf; Rep Stu Cncl; Hon Roll; NHS; Gld Mdl In Prfcncy Rlr Dnc Sktng 86; Phrmcy.

ZAKLIKOWSKI, RENEE; Frontier Central HS; Hamburg, NY; (Y); DECA; FBLA; Bus.

ZAKOWSKI, KARI; Frontier SR HS; Blasdell, NY; (Y); Camp Fr Inc; Girl Scts; Hosp Aide; Pep Clb; Spanish Clb; Chorus; Church Choir; School Play; Yrbk Stf; JV Socr; UB; Math.

ZALE, ELIZABETH ANNE; Gates-Chili HS; Rochester, NY; (S); 4/446; French Clb; Math Tm; Ski Clb; Chorus; School Musical; School Play; Rep Frsh Cls; Rep Soph Cls; Rep Jr Cls; Rep Sr Cls; Engl.

ZALEWSKI, ELIZABETHANN M; Kenmore West HS; Tonawanda, NY; (Y); Pres Church Yth Grp; Girl Scts; Band; Concert Band; Mrchg Band; Hon Roll; NHS; D Youville Coll; Scl Wrk.

ZALKIN, STACEY; Liberty HS; Liberty, NY; (Y); Debate Tm; Library Aide; Speech Tm; SADD; Nwsp Ed-Chief; Yrbk Stf; Stu Cncl; Capt Tennis; Hon Roll; Rotary Awd; Sci Fr 1st Pl 85; Blr Smmr Schl Jrnlsm 86; Sfty Ptrl 85-87; Jrnlst.

ZALOOM, VALERIE MICHELLE; St John Villa Acad; Staten Island, NY; (Y); 9/125; Church Yth Grp; Math Tm; Spanish Clb; Yrbk Stf; Bsktbl; Cheerleading; Socr; NHS; Achvt Awd Spnsh, Rlgn, Geom, Trig, Chem, Amer Stds, Europ Stds 83-86; Law.

ZAM, SANDRA; Beach Channel HS; Belle Harbor, NY; (Y); Drama Clb; Chorus; School Play; Nwsp Rptr; Var L Bsktbl; Var Capt Cheerleading; JV Crs Cntry; Var Vllybl; Hon Roll; NHS; MVP Chrldng Sq 86; Mos Imprvd Plyr Bsktbl Tm 86; 2nd Pl Wnnr Essay Cntst 84; Drama.

ZAMENICK, JAMES; Marlboro HS; Marlboro, NY; (Y); #16 In Class; Cit Awd; High Hon Roll; Jr NHS; NHS; RIT; Engrng.

ZAMIR, RON; Hunter College HS; Forest Hills, NY; (Y); Boy Scts; Chorus; Madrigals; School Musical; Cit Awd; Ntl Merit Ltr; Semi-Fnlst Ntl Arts Recgntn & Tlnt Srch Comp 86; Eagle Scout 84; Music.

ZAMITES, CAROLLYNN; Our Lady Of Mercy HS; Rochester, NY; (Y); Church Yth Grp; Cmnty Wkr; Spanish Clb; Hon Roll; Rochester Inst Tech; Trvl Mgmt.

ZAMPI, CORINNA; Aquinas Inst; Rochester, NY; (Y); Band; Mrchg Band; Off Soph Cls; Off Jr Cls; Var Swmmng; High Hon Roll; Acdmc Schlrshp Aquinas 84-87; Accntng.

ZAMPINI, DEBRA; Bishop Ludden HS; Liverpool, NY; (Y); School Musical; Var Capt Cheerleading; Var Trk; High Hon Roll; Hon Roll; Schlstc Art Awd Gld Key 83-84; 2nd Pl NYS Rgnls Hmrs Intrp Spch 84.

ZANCHE, GABRIEL J; Mc Quaid Jesuit HS; Rochester, NY; (Y); Computer Clb; Socr; NY Rgnts Schlrshp 86.

ZANDER, INGRID; St Francis Prep; Jamaica, NY; (Y); Church Yth Grp; German Clb; Library Aide; Office Aide; Chorus; School Play; Hon Roll; Fshn Inst Tech; Fshn Byng & Mer.

ZANDIEH, PEYMAN S; St Francis Prep; Whitestone, NY; (S); 18/653; Sec Science Clb; Mgr Jazz Band; Mrchg Band; Pep Band; Symp Band; Im Vllybl; High Hon Roll; NHS; All Amer Awd; Ntl Sci, Ldrshp Merit Awd; Med.

ZANG, JANET; Thousand Island HS; Lafargeville, NY; (Y); 7/92; French Clb; Hon Roll; Lion Awd; NHS; Secy Practc.

ZANG, STEVEN; Arlington HS; Hopewell Junction, NY; (Y); 1/560; Am Leg Boys St; Var Capt Tennis; Val; Math Tm; Lion Awd; NCTE Awd; Ntl Merit Ltr; Natl Rnkg In Ten-Boys Undr 16 84; Harvard U; Biochem.

ZANGRANDI, PATRICIA; Cardinal Spellman HS; Bronx, NY; (Y); 1st & 2nd Hnrs.

ZANGRI, LUCY; Smithtown HS East; Nesconset, NY; (Y); GAA; Hosp Aide; Varsity Clb; Yrbk Stf; Stu Cncl; JV Bsktbl; Var Capt Fld Hcky; Sftbl; Var Vllybl; Hon Roll.

ZAPATA, JEANNIE; Fashion Industries HS; Queens, NY; (Y); 30/365; Dance Clb; Teachers Aide; Bsktbl; Gym; Vllybl; Fshn Dsgn.

ZAPFEL, RICHARD; Colonie Central HS; Albany, NY; (Y); 5/421; Yrbk Stf; JV Bowling; Var Tennis; High Hon Roll; NHS; Pres Schlr; St Schlr; Clarkson U Trustee Awd 86; Outstndng Acadmc Achvt Awd 86; Sarah Mahar Math Prz 86; Clarkson U; Elec Engrng.

ZAPOLSKI JR, RICHARD; Connetquot HS; Bohemia, NY; (S); 14/690; Church Yth Grp; Computer Clb; Math Clb; Chorus; Church Choir; School Musical; JV Var Ftbl; Var Capt Lcrss; High Hon Roll; NHS; NYS Regents Scholar 86; Cornell.

ZAPPA, JOANN; School Of The Holy Child; Malverne, NY; (S); 1/13; Debate Tm; Model UN; Quiz Bowl; Nwsp Bus Mgr; Nwsp Rptr; Yrbk Stf; Ed Lit Mag; Rep Jr Cls; Var Bsktbl; Var Socr; Hist Awd & Hghst Avg 84 & 85; Sci Awd 85; Prelaw.

ZAPPASODI, ROSALIE; Centereach HS; Selden, NY; (Y); FTA; Hosp Aide; Band; Concert Band; Mrchg Band; Pep Band; Yrbk Phtg; Yrbk Stf; Rep Frsh Cls; Rep Soph Cls; NYSSMA Achvt Awds Music 82-86; Svc Awds For Volntrng St Charles Hosp 83-86; Smmr Music Gftd/Tlntd Pro; Hlth Adm.

ZAPPIA, ANDREW; Newark HS; Newark, NY; (Y); 5/200; Am Leg Boys St; Latin Clb; Political Wkr; Service Clb; Nwsp Stf; Yrbk Ed-Chief; Rep Stu Cncl; High Hon Roll; NHS; Tufts; Poli Sci.

ZARANEK, JAMIE; St Marys HS; Cheektowaga, NY; (Y); Boy Scts; Chess Clb; Church Yth Grp; SADD; School Play; JV Bsbl; Var Bsktbl; Var Ftbl; Var Trk; Comp Sci.

ZARCO, LAURA; Bronx H S Of Science; Bronx, NY; (Y); Rgnts Schlrshp Awd 86-90; SUNY Albany; Lawyer.

ZARDEZED, YVONNE; Horseheads HS; Erin, NY; (S); 52/385; JCL; Speech Tm; Chorus; School Musical; School Play; Nwsp Rptr; Nwsp Stf; Rep Stu Cncl; Im Sftbl; Hon Roll; Fin Miss NY Natl Teen-Ager Pgnt 86; Mbr Of All-Cnty Choir 85-86; Mbr Of Yth Cnty 85; Bus Adm.

ZARELLI, STEVEN A; Mohonasen HS; Schenectady, NY; (Y); 11/174; Trs Frsh Cls; Trs Soph Cls; Trs Jr Cls; Trs Sr Cls; High Hon Roll; NHS; Ntl Merit Ltr; Drama Clb; Key Clb; Spanish Clb; NYS Regents Schlr 86; Cortland Frshmn Schlrshp 86-87; Cortland; Cmmnctns.

ZAREMBA, CHARLOTTE; Geneseo Central Schl; Geneseo, NY; (Y); 4/89; Trs Pres Drama Clb; French Clb; Science Clb; Chorus; School Musical; School Play; Variety Show; Yrbk Stf; JV Bsktbl; French Hon Soc; NY ST Rgnts Schlrshp 86; Binghampton ST; Chem.

ZARKOS, ANASTASIOS THOMAS; Bishop Ford Central Catholic HS; Brooklyn, NY; (Y); 190/400; Computer Clb; Math Clb; High Hon Roll; Hon Roll; Scndry Educ.

ZARNEKE, DAVID; Victor HS; Victor, NY; (Y); 17/228; Am Leg Boys St; Spanish Clb; Var L Bsktbl; Var L Crs Cntry; Var L Trk; Cit Awd; High Hon Roll; NHS; Acad All Amer 86; Mth.

ZARRELL, ANTHONY; Gloversville HS; Gloversville, NY; (Y); Frsh Cls; Soph Cls; Jr Cls; Socr; Prom Chrmn 86; Prom Crt 86; Fitness Awd 86; FMCC; Bus.

ZARROW, ANDREW; New Rochelle HS; Scarsdale, NY; (Y); Ski Clb; Spanish Clb; Band; Var Socr; Var Tennis; High Hon Roll; Hon Roll; NHS; Ntl Merit Ltr; Spanish NHS; Engr.

ZASADA, JOHN R; Chittenango Central Schl; Bridgeport, NY; (Y); 23/200; Am Leg Boys St; French Clb; Science Clb; Varsity Clb; Band; Concert Band; Jazz Band; Orch; School Musical; Rep Frsh Cls; Outstdng Achvt Awd Co-Curricular Actvs 85-86; Tri-Vlly All Star Tm Tnns 85-86; 2nd Intersctnl Tnns; Utica Coll; Bus Adm.

ZASTROW, MARY; Wilson Central HS; Ransomville, NY; (Y); Band; Jazz Band; School Play; Yrbk Sprt Ed; Yrbk Stf; Bsktbl; Fld Hcky; Sftbl; Hon Roll; Sci.

ZATORSKI, STEVEN; Xavier HS; Brooklyn, NY; (Y); Church Yth Grp; FCA; Teachers Aide; JV Var Ftbl; JV Trk; JV Var Wt Lftg; JV Wrstlng; Hon Roll.

ZAVALA, LEONARDO; Bashwick HS; Bronx, NY; (S); 26/255; Intnl Clb; Spanish Clb; Teachers Aide; Sec Sr Cls; Rep Stu Cncl; Bsbl; Bsktbl; Ftbl; Socr; Sftbl; Smmr Yth Prog Awd; US Navy; Flght Engr.

ZAVARELLA, LAURIE ANN; Yorktown HS; Yorktown Hgts, NY; (Y); 39/319; Cmnty Wkr; Trs Band; Chorus; School Musical; Trs Lit Mag; Hon Roll; NHS; Drama Clb; Trs Concert Band; Trs Pep Band; Putnam Symph Orch 85; All ST Chrs 85-86; First Nghtrs Chrs,Drma And Band Awds 85-86; Psych.

ZAWADZKI, TODD; West Seneca East SR HS; Cheektowaga, NY; (Y); Camera Clb; Chess Clb; Exploring; Radio Clb; SADD; VICA; Chorus; Stage Crew; Lit Mag; Diving; Schlstc Ldrshp Awd 86; Erie CC; Crmnl Sci.

ZAWAR, KAREN; West Seneca East SR HS; Buffalo, NY; (S); Band; Concert Band; Jazz Band; Mrchg Band; School Musical; NYSSMA Festival 85; Music Ed.

ZAYAS, KATHERINE; Monsignor Scanlan HS; Bronx, NY; (Y); Church Yth Grp; Cmnty Wkr; Political Wkr; Chorus; Church Choir; Nwsp Rptr; Nwsp Stf; VP Jr Cls; Rep Stu Cncl; Prfct Atten Awd; Berkley Bus Schl; Bus Adm.

ZAYATZ, PAUL D; North Tonawanda HS; N Tonawanda, NY; (Y); 31/365; Am Leg Boys St; Varsity Clb; Var Capt Bsbl; Coach Actv; Wt Lftg; Hon Roll; NHS; Cmnty Wkr; Letterman Clb; JV Bsktbl; Qlty Stu 85-86; Flcn Fndtn Schlr 86; NM Military Inst; Flght.

ZAYICEK, JIM; Broadalbin HS; Gloversville, NY; (Y); Am Leg Boys St; Pres Spanish Clb; SADD; VP Band; Concert Band; Mrchg Band; Stage Crew; Yrbk Stf; Rep Soph Cls; Rep Jr Cls; MVP Trck; Lndscp Archtctr.

ZAZYNSKI, PATTY; Horseheads HS; Horseheads, NY; (Y); Art Clb; Church Yth Grp; Pep Clb; Sftbl; Hon Roll; Cazenovia Coll; Socl Wrkr.

ZDIMAL, MICHELLE; Binghamton HS; Binghamton, NY; (Y); 19/456; VP Church Yth Grp; Hosp Aide; Key Clb; VP SADD; Varsity Clb; VP Stu Cncl; Socr; Vllybl; Cit Awd; NHS; Outstndng SR 86; Salute To Yth 85; Boston U; Phy Thrpy.

ZDRAHAL, KATERINA; Shenendehowa Central HS; Rexford, NY; (Y); 19/675; Sec English Clb; Intnl Clb; Ski Clb; SADD; Band; NHS; Superior Hnr Rll 82-86; Acad Achvt Awd 84-85; Pres Acad Ftnss Awd 85-86; Boston Coll.

ZEAFLA, DOREEN L; Pioneer HS; Yorkshire, NY; (Y); 7/230; Hon Roll; NHS; Utica Coll; Optmtry.

ZEBRASKI, PAUL J; Dunkirk SR HS; Dunkirk, NY; (Y); Ski Clb; Varsity Clb; Concert Band; Mrchg Band; School Musical; Rep Stu Cncl; Capt Var Golf; Var Socr; Bausch & Lomb Sci Awd; Trs NHS; NY ST Regnts Coll Schlrshp 86; Chem Proc & Sply Corp Wrk Stdy Prog 85; ST U Coll Fredonia; Chem Engr.

ZEBROWSKI, DANIEL; Mercy HS; Bridgehampton, NY; (Y); Drama Clb; Library Aide; Ski Clb; Varsity Clb; School Musical; School Play; Stage Crew; Yrbk Phtg; Yrbk Stf; Ftbl.

ZEFI, JON; Archbishop Molloy HS; Woodhaven, NY; (Y); 42/383; Boys Clb Am; Church Yth Grp; Cmnty Wkr; Hosp Aide; Intnl Clb; Pep Clb; Service Clb; High Hon Roll; Hon Roll; NHS; NY U; Bus.

ZEGARELLI, JOHN; Mt St Michael HS; Bronx, NY; (Y); 151/297; Political Wkr; School Play; Yrbk Bus Mgr; Off Soph Cls; CC Awd; Cit Awd; Gov Hon Prg Awd; Spanish NHS; Val; 4 Schl 2nd Hnr Awds Of Acad Avg 83-84; Ust Schl 2nd Hnr Awd For Acad Avg 84-85; Spnsh Accmplshmnt 84; Iona Coll; Bus Admin.

ZEH, ADRIENNE; Port Chester HS; Port Chester, NY; (Y); Yrbk Stf; Lit Mag; High Hon Roll; Hon Roll; Mu Alp Tht; NHS; Spanish NHS; Port Chester HS Sci Hnr Soc 86.

ZEH, REBECCA; Cohocton Central Sch; Cohocton, NY; (S); Trs Church Yth Grp; Pres 4-H; Chorus; School Musical; Stu Cncl; Cit Awd; 4-H Awd; High Hon Roll; Prfct Atten Awd; Bus.

ZEH, TRACEY; Southampton HS; Southampton, NY; (Y); Chorus; Hon Roll; NHS; Suffolk Cnty Math Cntst 84; Acctg.

ZEHLER, SUSAN; Attica Central HS; Varysburg, NY; (S); 8/145; Chorus; Church Choir; Hon Roll; Bus.

ZEHR, BRENDA; Beaver River Central HS; Castorland, NY; (Y); Am Leg Aux Girls St; Trs FHA; Var JV Sftbl; NHS; Ntl Merit SF; Church Yth Grp; Drama Clb; GAA; Spanish Clb; Chorus; GATE Pgm 83-86; Choraleers 86; Pre-Med.

ZEHR, DARIN J; Beaver River Central HS; Lowville, NY; (Y); Varsity Clb; L Bsbl; JV Ftbl; Var Wrstlng; Hon Roll; Rgnts Schlrshp 86; Oswego ST; Chmstry.

ZEHR, KATHERINE E; Beaver River Central Schl; Croghan, NY; (Y); Church Yth Grp; GAA; Chorus; School Musical; Yrbk Stf; JV Var Sftbl; High Hon Roll; Hon Roll; Goshen Coll; RN.

ZEIBAQ, REEMA; Sacred Heart Acad; Uniondale, NY; (Y); Drama Clb; English Clb; Band; Concert Band; Orch; School Musical; School Play; Lit Mag; Bus.

ZEIDNER, BRIAN; Morrisville-Eato HS; Weat Eaton, NY; (Y); Am Leg Boys St; Church Yth Grp; Library Aide; Ftbl; Hon Roll.

ZEISZ, EDDIE; Burgard HS; Buffalo, NY; (Y); Church Yth Grp; WY Tech Inst.

ZEITLIN, MICHAEL; Hendrick Hudson HS; Peekskill, NY; (S); 10/187; Debate Tm; NFL; VP Speech Tm; Nwsp Rptr; Var Socr; Trk; High Hon Roll; NHS; 4 Yr ROTC Schlrshp 85-86; 3rd Pl N Amrcn Orientrng Chmpnshps 83-86; Regnts Schlrshp 86; Cornell; Geolgy.

ZELASKO, JOHN; John F Kennedy HS; Cheektowaga, NY; (Y); 10/141; Art Clb; Cmnty Wkr; Debate Tm; Drama Clb; English Clb; Letterman Clb; PAVAS; Speech Tm; Varsity Clb; School Musical; Gifted & Tlntd Pgm 85-87; Bus.

ZELASKO, KATHLEEN A; Mount Mercy Acad; Buffalo, NY; (Y); 46/180; SADD; Yrbk Stf; Rep Stu Cncl; SR Essy Cntst 86; Bryant & Stratton; Word Process.

ZELAZNY, JON B; Penfield SR HS; Penfield, NY; (Y); 57/365; Sec Church Yth Grp; Cmnty Wkr; Pres Drama Clb; Pres Model UN; Sec Band; Chorus; Church Choir; Orch; Pep Band; School Musical; Army ROTC Schrlshp 86; Phs One Act Play Cntst 86; Geneseo Drama Festvl 84; Syracuse U; Pol Sci.

ZELAZNY, LINDA; Walt Whitman HS; Huntington Stat, NY; (Y); 4-H; Hosp Aide; Sprtsmnshp Awd Frm Pny Clb 85; Dfrnt Rbns For Cmptn In Hrs Shws 85-86; Outstndng Acdmc Imprvmt PTA Aw; St Johns; Lwyr.

ZELKO, MELISSA; Horseheads HS; Horseheads, NY; (Y); Art Clb; Cmnty Wkr; Library Aide; Ski Clb; Spanish Clb; Yrbk Stf; Stu Cncl; Var Trk; JV Var Vllybl; Hon Roll; Schlstc Art Awd 84; Fash Merch.

ZELLER, EILEEN; East Meadow HS; East Meadow, NY; (S); Key Clb; SADD; Var Bsktbl; Var Fld Hcky; JV Lcrss; Var Sftbl; Hon Roll; NHS; Hugh O Brien Schlrshp Cmptn Fnlst 84-85; Sci.

ZELLER, ROBERT A; Vernon-Verona -Sherrill Cntrl HS; Durhamville, NY; (Y); Am Leg Boys St; Intnl Clb; Stage Crew; Rep Stu Cncl; JV Var Ftbl; Var Trk; Var Capt Wrstlng; High Hon Roll; NHS; Rnsslr Plytchnc Inst Math & Sci Awd 86; Med.

ZEMANEK, LAURA; Johnstown HS; Johnstown, NY; (Y); Ski Clb; Band; Chorus; Concert Band; Mrchg Band; School Musical; School Play; Variety Show; Nwsp Stf; Tennis; Pltsbrg; Theatre.

ZENENBERG, ROBERT; Rye HS; Rye, NY; (Y); Red Cross Aide; Ftbl; Hon Roll; Physcn.

ZENOBIO, CRIS; St Marys Boys HS; Sand Point, NY; (S); 15/147; VP Capt Lcrss; NHS; Bus Mngmnt.

ZENON, MELISSA ANNE; Bishop Grimes HS; N Syracuse, NY; (S); Exploring; Girl Scts; Latin Clb; NFL; Speech Tm; Rep Frsh Cls; High Hon Roll; Drew U; Pre-Med.

ZENOSKI, MARK; Belmont Central HS; Belmont, NY; (Y); Am Leg Boys St; Yrbk Rptr; Yrbk Stf; VP Frsh Cls; VP Soph Cls; VP Jr Cls; Var Bsbl; JV Var Bsktbl; Var Socr; Hon Roll; JV Bsktbl MVP 84; Bill Fanton Memrl Bsebl Awd 85; Sprts Med.

ZENTZ, CYNTHIA; Warsaw Central HS; Warsaw, NY; (S); 3/92; Church Yth Grp; French Clb; Mathletes; Band; Chorus; Sec Stu Cncl; JV Capt Bsktbl; Var Capt Socr; Var JV Sftbl; High Hon Roll; Acctng.

ZEOLLA, KAREN; Westlake HS; Thornwood, NY; (Y); Am Leg Aux Girls St; Civic Clb; Girl Scts; Chorus; Nwsp Rptr; Hon Roll.

ZEPECKI, KATIE; Victor HS; Macedon, NY; (Y); 85/200; Camp Fr Inc; Ski Clb; Band; Concert Band; Mrchg Band; Rep Stu Cncl; Var JV Mgr(s); Score Keeper; Hon Roll; Prfct Atten Awd; Typing Awd.

ZEPLIN, MARC S; Oceanside HS; Oceanside, NY; (Y); #26 In Class; Cmnty Wkr; Key Clb; Latin Clb; Mathletes; Spanish Clb; Teachers Aide; Temple Yth Grp; Nwsp Rptr; Rep Soph Cls; Rep Jr Cls; Fnlst Christopher Cruhn Schlrshp 86; MBA Prgrm U MI 86; Regnts Schlrshp 86; U Of MI; Bus.

ZEPPETELLI, CAROL; Walter Panas HS; Peekskill, NY; (Y); FBLA; Girl Scts; Hosp Aide; Ski Clb; Chorus; Nwsp Stf; Yrbk Stf; Var Capt Fld Hcky; Hon Roll; Bus.

ZERAFA, ANDREA; Cardinal Spellman HS; Bronx, NY; (Y); Second Hnrs 84-86; Grace Inst; Bus.

ZERAY, MATTHEW; Hicksville HS; Hicksville, NY; (Y); Aud/Vis; Boy Scts; NHS; Egl Sct 86; Engrng.

ZERBE, TAMMY; Unatego JR SR HS; Otego, NY; (S); 10/82; Hosp Aide; Ski Clb; Spanish Clb; Church Choir; Concert Band; Orch; Var Cheerleading; Vllybl; High Hon Roll; NHS; Taylor U; Educ.

ZERBO, MICHAEL; Ossiming HS; Ossining, NY; (Y); 68/268; Cmnty Wkr; Letterman Clb; Varsity Clb; JV Var Bsbl; JV Coach Actv; JV Var Ftbl; Var Mgr(s); JV Var Wt Lftg; Hon Roll; Hudson Valley CC; Nvl Officer.

ZERBY, DANAE; Frontier SR HS; Hamburg, NY; (Y); Aud/Vis; Exploring; French Clb; German Clb; Girl Scts; Hosp Aide; Pep Clb; Red Cross Aide; Varsity Clb; Color Guard; Lk Shore Freman Ldies Auxlry Schlrshp 86; Suny At Brockport; Nrsng.

ZERNER, SCOTT B; The Bronx High School Of Science; Bellerose, NY; (Y); Library Aide; Political Wkr; Soph Cls; Jr Cls; Bowling; NHS; Ntl Merit Ltr; Cornell; Law.

ZERNONE, MICHELLE; Clarkstown North HS; New City, NY; (Y); Orch; Itln Clb; Tutoring Sqad; Law.

ZERRENNER, ANN MARIE; Preston HS; Bronx, NY; (Y); Nwsp Stf; Yrbk Stf; Ed Lit Mag; Hon Roll; Regents Schrlshp; Hunter Coll; Writing.

ZERVOUDAKES, JASON; W C Mepham HS; N Bellmore, NY; (Y); Debate Tm; Model UN; Political Wkr; Band; Concert Band; Jazz Band; Mrchg Band; Nwsp Rptr; Nwsp Stf; JV Ftbl; Ltr Bank 84-86; SUNY.

ZEVOS, IANTHE; Potsdame Central Schl; Potsdam, NY; (Y); French Clb; Math Clb; Band; Chorus; Pep Band; Stu Cncl; Cheerleading; Trk; Vllybl; NHS; Bstn U.

ZHANG, RONG; Sheepshead Bay HS; Brooklyn, NY; (Y); 33/439; Library Aide; Math Tm; Office Aide; NY ST Regents Schlrshps 86; Acad All-Amer 86; Accntng.

ZHOU, ZHEN H; Herbert H Lehman HS; Bronx, NY; (Y); 15/391; Computer Clb; Math Clb; Capt Science Clb; Mgr Nwsp Ed-Chief; Pres Frsh Cls; Socr; Tennis; Hon Roll; Prfct Atten Awd; Math Assn America Cntsts 1st Pl 84 & 85; Contntl Math Leag Comput Cntsts Wnr 85 & 86; Sci Fair Awds 86; Polytech U; Elec Engrng.

ZHU, JIASONG; Far Rockaway HS; Far Rockaway, NY; (Y); Math Tm; Office Aide; Teachers Aide; Polytech U Schlrshp 86; Polytch U Of NY; Engrng.

ZIAKAS, HELEN; Eastridge HS; Rochester, NY; (Y); 2/214; Sec French Clb; Pres Red Cross Aide; Capt Color Guard; School Musical; Fld Hcky; Vllybl; High Hon Roll; NHS; Sal; Paideia Awd 85; EITA Schlrshp 86; Dghtrss Of Penelope 86; U Of Rochester; Sci.

ZICARI, MARC T; Edison Tech & Occupational Ctr; Rochester, NY; (Y); 26/276; Mgr(s); NYS Rgnts Schlrshp Awd 86.

ZICCARDI, SHERI; Pembroke Central HS; Batavia, NY; (Y); 3/118; Chorus; Sec School Musical; Variety Show; Yrbk Stf; High Hon Roll; Hon Roll; NHS; VP Science Clb; Cmptv Rlr Sktng Chmpn-MVP 86; 99 Prct Spnsh Avg 85 & 86; Bus.

ZIEGLER, GREGORY; Valley Stream Central HS; Valley Stream, NY; (Y); AFS; Computer Clb; German Clb; Science Clb; Ski Clb; SADD; Chorus; Socr; Jr NHS; NHS.

ZIEGLER, JEFFREY; Palmyra Macedon HS; Palmyra, NY; (S); 1/175; Pres German Clb; Mathletes; Chorus; Rep Jr Cls; Rep Stu Cncl; Var Crs Cntry; Var Capt Tennis; High Hon Roll; NHS; All Lgu Tennis Plyr 85.

ZIEGLER, LAURA; W C Mepham HS; North Merrick, NY; (Y); Key Clb; Off Sr Cls; Twrlr; Hon Roll; Sec Ed.

ZIEGLER, MARCIA; Jamesville De Witt HS; Dewitt, NY; (Y); 24/250; Exploring; Teachers Aide; Band; Concert Band; Orch; School Musical; School Play; High Hon Roll; NHS; Cornell; Vet Med.

ZIEGLER, PETER; Carmel HS; Carmel, NY; (Y); Concert Band; JV Var Bsbl; JV Var Bsktbl; Im Vllybl; High Hon Roll; Hon Roll; Rochester Inst Of Tech; Archtct.

ZIELINSKI, JILL A; Manlius Pebble Hill HS; Liverpool, NY; (Y); Chorus; Orch; Swing Chorus; Yrbk Stf; Bausch & Lomb Sci Awd; NHS; Ntl Merit Ltr; School Musical; High Hon Roll; Jr NHS; James L Turrentine Schlrshp 86; Fredonia Freshmn Merit Schlrshp 86; Lila Acheson Wallace String Schlrs; SUNY Fredonia; Violin Perf.

ZIEMER, JENNIFER; West Seneca East SR HS; Cheektowaga, NY; (Y); DECA; Church Choir; Stage Crew; Soph Cls; Jr Cls; Cheerleading; Trk; Good News Camp Cnslr Awd 84-85; 1st Pl Erie Cnty Fair Chrldng Awds 84 & 85; Bus Adm.

ZIEMS, FREDERICK M; Earl L Vandermeulen HS; Mt Sinai, NY; (Y); Aud/Vis; Exploring; FCA; FBLA; Leo Clb; Letterman Clb; Ski Clb; Varsity Clb; Chorus; Yrbk Rptr; All Leag Wntrtk,Cnty Sprg Trck,Regnts Schlrshp 86; Lawyr.

ZIER, LINDA; Northville Central HS; Northville, NY; (Y); Church Yth Grp; Cmnty Wkr; GAA; Yrbk Bus Mgr; Yrbk Stf; Capt Var Bsktbl; Socr; High Hon Roll; Hon Roll; Sec NHS; Phys Ther.

ZIESE, SHARON; New Field HS; Selden, NY; (Y); 163/515; Aud/Vis; Computer Clb; FBLA; Service Clb; Hon Roll; Suffolk Cmnty Coll; Acctg.

ZIFF, LORI; Oyster Bay HS; Oyster Bay, NY; (Y); 18/122; Trs Spanish Clb; VP Temple Yth Grp; Pres Trs Band; Pres Trs Concert Band; Pres Trs Mrchg Band; JP Sousa Awd; NHS; Rotary Awd; Hon Roll; Faculty Cncl Awd; Mst Imprvd Plyr Fencing; U MA; Bus Adm.

ZIGADLO, MARK; Mc Quaid Jesuit HS; Rochester, NY; (Y); Boy Scts; Church Yth Grp; JA; Ski Clb; Varsity Clb; Yrbk Stf; Socr; Trk; Vllybl; Hon Roll; Regent Schlrshp Awd 86; George Mason; Bus Admn.

ZIGON, MARIANNE; Central Islip SR HS; Central Islip, NY; (Y); 51/400; Chorus; School Play; Ed Yrbk Stf; VP Frsh Cls; VP Soph Cls; Trs Jr Cls; Rep Sr Cls; Rep Stu Cncl; Stat Ftbl; JV Tennis; SUNY Plattsburg; Bus Adm.

ZILLER, CAROLYN; St Marys Girls HS; New Hyde Pk, NY; (Y); 35/170; Spanish Clb; High Hon Roll; Hon Roll; Southern VT Coll; Ofc Mgmt.

ZIMA, KAREN; Brockport HS; Churchville, NY; (Y); 26/330; Trs Church Yth Grp; French Clb; Yrbk Stf; Rep Soph Cls; JV Swmmng; High Hon Roll; NHS; Frnch II Awd 84-85; Frnch.

ZIMBRICH, URSULA; Greece Athena HS; Rochester, NY; (Y); 32/265; German Clb; Math Tm; Ski Clb; Chorus; High Hon Roll; Hon Roll; NHS; Pres Schlr; Amer Assn U Wmn 86; Rgnts Schlrshp 86; SUNY Geneseo; Scndry Ed-Math.

ZIMET, MARK; Hendrick Hudson HS; Peeskill, NY; (S); 21/180; Pres Debate Tm; Drama Clb; NFL; Speech Tm; Temple Yth Grp; Yrbk Stf; Var Tennis; NHS; Ntl Merit Ltr; WA U.

ZIMMER, CAROL E; Webster SR HS; Webster, NY; (Y); Drama Clb; Thesps; Chorus; School Musical; School Play; Swing Chorus; Yrbk Stf; Hon Roll; Natl Choral Awd 86; Webster Theatr Gld Schlrshp 86; Brighton Theatr Gld Schlrshp; Fredonia ST U; Music Ed.

ZIMMER, DAVID; Amherst SR HS; Snyder, NY; (Y); 7/392; Varsity Clb; L Bsbl; L Capt Bsktbl; L Ftbl; High Hon Roll; NHS; Cornell; Bio.

ZIMMER, STEVEN P; Prattsburg Central HS; Prattsburg, NY; (Y); 7/32; Am Leg Boys St; Band; Concert Band; Jazz Band; Mrchg Band; Bsktbl; Crs Cntry; Trk; Hon Roll; Pres Schlr; Marketing.

ZIMMER, TODD J; John H Glenn HS; East Northport, NY; (Y); Science Clb; Drm Mjr(t); Nwsp Stf; Lit Mag; SUNY Oneonta; Pre-Dent.

ZIMMERLI, LYN; Kendall JR-SR HS; Kendall, NY; (Y); 3/110; Trs Spanish Clb; Band; Concert Band; Mrchg Band; Capt Bsktbl; Co-Capt Sftbl; Sftbl; Vllybl; High Hon Roll; Pres Jr NHS; Med.

ZIMMERMAN, BRIAN; Susan Wagner HS; Staten Island, NY; (Y); Cmnty Wkr; JA; Office Aide; Political Wkr; Wt Lftg; Cit Awd; High Hon Roll; Hon Roll; Ephrm Bodine Mem Schlrshp 86; Coll Of Staten Islnd; Arch.

ZIMMERMAN, CHRISTINE; Midwood HS; Brooklyn, NY; (Y); 156/667; Church Yth Grp; Office Aide; Cheerleading; Nursing.

ZIMMERMAN, CHRISTINE; Ward Melville HS; S Setauket, NY; (Y); Gym; Mgr(s); Score Keeper; Superdance For MDA 84 & 85; Schl Nrs Ofc Hlpr 84; Elem Ed.

ZIMMERMAN, GLEN; Rye Neck HS; Mamaroneck, NY; (Y); 1/98; AFS; Am Leg Boys St; Key Clb; Varsity Clb; Rep Soph Cls; Rep Jr Cls; Off Sr Cls; Rep Stu Cncl; Var Bsktbl; Capt Var Socr; All League Hnrb Mntn-Soccer 85; Rye Neck HS Video Awd 86; Knghts Columbus Dist Free Throw Champ 84; Econ.

ZIMMERMAN, KAREN; Candor HS; Candor, NY; (Y); Trs Camera Clb; Quiz Bowl; Yrbk Ed-Chief; Yrbk Phtg; VP Soph Cls; High Hon Roll; Hon Roll; NHS; Score Keeper; Timer; Outstndng Stu Awd, Wrd Proc Svc Awd, Gldn Glln Awd 86; Tompkins Cortland CC; Cmnctns.

ZIMMERMAN, LORETTA; Cornwall Central HS; Cornwall, NY; (Y); Drama Clb; Exploring; School Musical; School Play; Church Yth Grp; Sec Girl Scts; Hosp Aide; Spanish Clb; Hon Roll; Law.

ZIMMERMAN, RONNIE; Our Lady Of Victory Acad; Tappan, NY; (S); 13/157; Church Yth Grp; Spanish Clb; NHS; Spanish NHS; Alpha Hnr Soc 85-86; Elem Educ.

ZIMMERMAN, UZI; East Meadow HS; East Meadow, NY; (S); 5/340; Debate Tm; Mathletes; Jazz Band; Mrchg Band; Symp Band; Bsbl; Var Crs Cntry; Var Tennis; High Hon Roll; NHS; All ST Jazz Ensemble 85; Mc Donalds Tri-ST Jaze Ensmbl Altrnt 85-86; All Cnty Jazz Ensmbl 85-86.

ZIMPFER, R DEAN; Canisius HS; Elma, NY; (Y); Church Yth Grp; Pep Clb; Yrbk Phtg; Yrbk Stf; Bsktbl; Ftbl; Vllybl; Var Wrstlng; High Hon Roll; Hon Roll; Comp Engr.

ZINCK, SHARYL; Palmyra-Macedon HS; Macedon, NY; (Y); Art Clb; Girl Scts; Office Aide; Band; Rep Frsh Cls; Var Mgr(s); Var Score Keeper; Hon Roll; Prfct Atten Awd; Katie-Gibbs; Bus.

ZINGARO, LINDA; Liverpool HS; Liverpool, NY; (Y); SADD; Hon Roll; Jr NHS; NHS; Pres Schlr; NY ST U Geneseo; Accntng.

ZINGEL, GABRIELA T; De Witt Clinton HS; Bronx, NY; (Y); 11/270; Church Yth Grp; Hosp Aide; Office Aide; Band; Nwsp Rptr; NHS; Regents Scholar 86; SUNY Binghampton; Med.

ZINGER, STEPHEN J; Palmyra Macedon Central HS; Palmyra, NY; (S); 1/180; Church Yth Grp; Math Tm; ROTC; Scholastic Bowl; Socr; High Hon Roll; NHS; Val; Cornell Alumni Prz 85; Chem Engr.

ZINK, TRACEY; Hauppauge HS; Hauppauge, NY; (Y); Art Clb; Exploring; Pep Clb; High Hon Roll; Hon Roll; Outstndng Art Achvt Awd 84; Farmingdale Coll; Bus Admin.

ZINKIN, DONNIEL; Shaarei Torah HS; Highland Park, NJ; (S); 1/25; Drama Clb; Thesps; School Play; Nwsp Stf; Yrbk Stf; Lit Mag; Rep Soph Cls; Pres Jr Cls; Hon Roll; JC Awd; Law.

ZINTER, KATHY; Brewster HS; Brewster, NY; (Y); Church Yth Grp; Nwsp Rptr; French Hon Soc; High Hon Roll; Hon Roll; Frnch I Asia/Africa 84; Comp Awareness Frnch II 85; Chem, Comp Prog II & Englsh II 86; Psych.

ZIPNICK, DEBORAH; Newfield HS; Selden, NY; (Y); 25/550; Camera Clb; Dance Clb; Temple Yth Grp; Chorus; School Musical; Cheerleading; Var Tennis; Hon Roll; VP NHS; Spanish NHS; Stgcoach Elem Schl Schlrshp 86; Pres Physcl Ftns Awd 85; AZ ST U; Brdcstng.

ZIPP, LEANNE; Wilson Central HS; Wilson, NY; (Y); Aud/Vis; GAA; Trs Concert Band; Pep Band; School Play; Capt JV Bsktbl; Capt JV Fld Hcky; JV Var Sftbl; JV Var Vllybl; High Hon Roll; All-Leag Fld Hock 84; Sftbl ST Chmpsns 86; Bus Mngmnt.

ZIRASCHI, MICHAEL; Aviation HS; Astoria, NY; (Y); Math Tm.

ZISER, BORIS; Port Richmond HS; Staten Island, NY; (Y); Hosp Aide; Office Aide; School Musical; School Play; NHS; Jewsh Publc Schl Yth 85; Med.

ZITO, DANIELLE; Centereach HS; Centereach, NY; (Y); SADD; Teachers Aide; Band; Mrchg Band; JV Mgr(s); Var JV Score Keeper; Stat Wrstlng; Hon Roll; Child Psych.

ZITO, JOHN; Batavia HS; Batavia, NY; (Y); Bsktbl; Ftbl; Golf; Socr; Golf 86; Bsktbl 86; Bus Managmnt.

ZITT, JONATHAN R; Syosset HS; Woodbury, NY; (Y); Aud/Vis; NFL; Acpl Chr; Chorus; Golf; Var Socr; Rgnts Schlrshp 86; Hobart/William Smith Coll; Law.

ZITTEL, KRISTEN; Eden Central HS; Eden, NY; (Y); AFS; Pres Church Yth Grp; 4-H; German Clb; GAA; Ski Clb; Concert Band; Symp Band; Sec Jr Cls; Stu Cncl; AFS Stu Exc Germany 86; Lib Arts.

ZIVIN, KAREN SUE; Mercy HS; Selden, NY; (Y); 31/125; Church Yth Grp; Hosp Aide; Ski Clb; Chorus; Variety Show; Fld Hcky; Hon Roll; NEDT Awd.

ZLOTY, JULIE; Hamburg SR HS; Hamburg, NY; (Y); Spanish Clb; Im JV Cheerleading; Hon Roll; Stu Of Catalina Clb 84-87.

ZMIJEWSKI, TINA; Catholic Central HS; Latham, NY; (Y); Math Clb; Spanish Clb; Pres SADD; Chorus; School Play; Rep Stu Cncl; JV Bsktbl; Var Pom Pon; High Hon Roll; NHS; Peer Ldrshp Awd 86; Bus Admin.

ZMOLIL, DIANE; Midwood HS; Brooklyn, NY; (Y); 255/526; Bus Mgmt Awd 86; Typng Awd 86; The Wood School; Bus.

ZOBEL, CHRIS; Lansing HS; Lansing, NY; (Y); 1/85; Boy Scts; Drama Clb; Letterman Clb; Scholastic Bowl; Spanish Clb; Concert Band; Jazz Band; Madrigals; Orch; School Musical; Dram Awds Bst Drmtc Perf 85-86.

ZOBRIST, TAMMY L; Kensington HS; Buffalo, NY; (Y); 20/238; Cmnty Wkr; Computer Clb; Trs FNA; Trs Science Clb; Yrbk Stf; Rep Stu Cncl; NYS Rgnts Schlrshp 86; Semi Fnlst-Modern Miss Phlsphy Pgnt 85; U Of AZ; Psych.

ZOCCOLILLO, SHARON; Bishop Grimes HS; N Syracuse, NY; (Y); 20/200; Capt Church Yth Grp; Cmnty Wkr; Drama Clb; Exploring; School Musical; Cheerleading; Socr; High Hon Roll; Hon Roll; NHS; Vet-Med.

ZOLADZ, JULIE; Frontier SR HS; Hamburg, NY; (Y); French Clb; Pep Clb; SADD; School Play; JV Crs Cntry; Var Tennis; Hon Roll; Chorus; Erie Cnty Chorus 84; NY ST Olimpiada Of Spoken Russian 86; VP Of Polish Clb 86-87; Lbrl Arts.

ZOLENGE, JODI; Commack South HS; Commack, NY; (Y); Cmnty Wkr; Office Aide; Service Clb; Temple Yth Grp; Yrbk Stf; Sec Jr Cls; VP Sr Cls; Mgr(s); Var Tennis; High Hon Roll; Ldrshp Day 86; Ldrs Corp 86; Forgn Langs.

ZOLLICOFFER, ANTHONY; Bishop Loughlin Memorial HS; Brooklyn, NY; (Y); Art Clb; Chess Clb; Computer Clb; Stage Crew; High Hon Roll; High Schltc Avrg 83; Irene Gilchrist Meml Awd 84; Silvr L High Avrg Awd 86; Pre Dntstry.

ZOLNOWSKI, JULIE; Mount Mercy Acad; Buffalo, NY; (Y); Computer Clb; JCL; Latin Clb; Math Clb; Ski Clb; Stage Crew; Im Bowling; Im Vllybl; Hon Roll; Jr NHS; Photo.

ZOLOTSKY, SCOTT; Topttenville HS; Staten Island, NY; (S); 16/950; Scholastic Bowl; Teachers Aide; Stage Crew; Var Capt Trk; High Hon Roll; NHS; Spanish NHS; Engrng.

ZONA, ROBERT; Monsignor Farrell HS; Staten Island, NY; (S); Cmnty Wkr; Dance Clb; Ski Clb; Teachers Aide; Yrbk Sprt Ed; VP Chess Clb; VP Stu Cncl; Bsbl; Bsktbl; Coach Actv; Bio.

ZONIN, JOSEPH; Walt Whitman HS; Huntington Stat, NY; (Y); 52/477; VP Soph Cls; Off Stu Cncl; Capt Lcrss; Socr; High Hon Roll; Scl Stds Awd; All Leag Lacrss; Capt Awd-Lacrss; Bus.

ZOOK, GINA M; Kingston City HS; Kingston, NY; (Y); Church Yth Grp; Band; Chorus; Church Choir; School Musical; Cheerleading; High Hon Roll; Spanish NHS; Regents Schlrshp Awd 86; Ulster County CC; Rocketry.

ZOOTA, HERB; Commack High School South; Commack, NY; (Y); 29/357; Boy Scts; Trs Exploring; Math Tm; High Hon Roll; NHS; Emory U.

ZOPPEL, JASON; Tottenville HS; Staten Island, NY; (Y); Am Leg Boys St; Pres SADD; Pres Stu Cncl; Var Wrstlng; Hon Roll; NHS; 123 Precinct Youth Cncl 86.

ZORN, JENNIFER; Frontier Central HS; Hamburg, NY; (Y); German Clb; Band; Mrchg Band; Var Socr; Var Tennis; Hon Roll; NHS; Marine Bio.

ZOTTO, NICHOLAS; Islip HS; Bay Shore, NY; (Y); 1/250; Am Leg Boys St; Mathletes; Nwsp Stf; Pres Stu Cncl; Bsbl; Ftbl; Cit Awd; High Hon Roll; NHS; Val; Rnslr Tech Inst; Biomed Engrng.

ZOULAS, CHRISTINA; Mont Pleasant HS; Schenectady, NY; (Y); Chorus; Co-Capt Color Guard; Mrchg Band; Off Soph Cls; Off Jr Cls; Off Sr Cls; Spanish NHS; Key Clb; Pep Clb; Service Clb; Symphonic Sngrs-Hnr Chorus 85-86; Schdy CC; Socl Sci.

ZSEDELY, ROBERT J; East Syracuse-Minoa HS; Minoa, NY; (Y); 78/333; JA; Hon Roll; Jr NHS; NHS; Regents Scholar 85-86; U Buffalo; Comp Sci.

ZUBER, CHRISTINA; Farmingdale SR HS; Massapequa Park, NY; (Y); 7/600; Band; Concert Band; Mrchg Band; Symp Band; Hon Roll; NHS; Hofstras Recgntn Schlrshp 86; Farmingdale Cncl Parent Tchr Assoc Merit Cert 86; Hofstra U; Math.

ZUBRZYCKI, TIMOTHY J; Lowville Acad & Central Schl; Lowville, NY; (Y); Pres 4-H; Pres FFA; Var L Bsbl; Capt L Bsktbl; 4-H Awd; Hon Roll; Regents Scholar Awd 86; Jefferson CC; Acctng.

ZUCARO, ANNMARIE C; St Francis Prep HS; Bayside, NY; (S); 178/750; Hosp Aide; SADD; Chorus; Stu Cncl; Sftbl; Vllybl; NHS; Opt Clb Awd; Adelphe U Nrsng Schl; Nrs.

ZUCHOWSKI, LYNN; Fredonia HS; Fredonia, NY; (Y); 1/182; VP 4-H; Sec Science Clb; SADD; Chorus; School Musical; Var Capt Cheerleading; Cit Awd; High Hon Roll; Val; Spnsh Excllnc Awds 84-85; Colgate U; Neurosci.

ZUCKER, BARBARA; Herkimer SR HS; Herkimer, NY; (Y); Pep Clb; Spanish Clb; Yrbk Stf; Off Frsh Cls; Off Soph Cls; Off Jr Cls; Gym; Sftbl; Pharm.

ZUCKERMAN, AVIVA C; Sara Schenirer HS; Brooklyn, NY; (Y); Nwsp Ed-Chief; Yrbk Rptr; Hon Roll; Rgnts Schlrshp.

ZUGAC, DEBBIE; Cazenovia Central HS; Chittenango, NY; (Y); 4-H; 4-H Awd; Canton ATC; Vet Sci Tech.

ZUIDEMA, JUDITH; Lansing HS; Lansing, NY; (Y); Spanish Clb; SADD; Orch; School Musical; Stage Crew; Trs Jr Cls; Trs Sr Cls; Pres Stu Cncl; Cheerleading; Diving; Otstndng Stu 86; Sr Orchstra Awd 85-86; Pres Acad Ftns Awd 86; Geneseo ST; Art Hist.

ZUKERMAN, AMY; Half Hollow Hills High Schl East; Melville, NY; (Y); FBLA; Leo Clb; Office Aide; SADD; Teachers Aide; Temple Yth Grp; Cheerleading; High Hon Roll; Jr NHS; NHS; Law.

ZULAWSKI, CHRISTINE; Eden SR HS; Eden, NY; (Y); 4-H; Sec FFA; Rep Stu Cncl; Stat Bsktbl; Erie Co Dairy Princess 86-87; Trocaire; X-Ray Tech.

ZULICK, JENNY; Saugerties HS; Saugerties, NY; (S); 70/249; Ski Clb; Var Bsktbl; Powder Puff Ftbl; JV Socr; Var L Trk; Im Vllybl; Trck Awd 85; Arch.

ZULLO, ANN MARIE; East Meadow HS; East Meadow, NY; (S); 33/340; FBLA; Key Clb; Band; Mrchg Band; Symp Band; Yrbk Stf; Cheerleading; Socr; Hon Roll; NHS; Bus Admin.

ZULLO, KARIN; Liverpool HS; Liverpool, NY; (Y); Ski Clb; Color Guard; Stu Cncl; JV Cheerleading; Powder Puff Ftbl; Trvl.

ZUMBO, CLAUDIA; Moore Catholic HS; Staten Island, NY; (Y); Art Clb; Hosp Aide; Teachers Aide; Yrbk Phtg; Yrbk Stf; Var Bowling; Gym; Hon Roll; Ntl Merit Ltr; Alisi Itln Lvl I Cntst 2nd Pl 85; Alisi Itln Level II Cntst 3rd Pl 86; Amrcn Assoc Tchrs Itln 85-86; FIT; Fshn Merch.

ZUMBOLO, BRIAN; Amsterdam HS; Amsterdam, NY; (Y); 51/316; Rep Frsh Cls; Rep Soph Cls; Var JV Ftbl; High Hon Roll; Law.

ZUNIGA, MONICA; Clarkstown HS North; New City, NY; (Y); Exploring; JA; Spanish Clb; Band; Chorus; Concert Band; Mrchg Band; Vllybl; High Hon Roll; Hon Roll; Spcl Olympcs Prtcptn Awd 86; Iona Coll Lang Cntst 2nd Hnrs 86; Ntl Hnr Roll Awd 86; Boston U; Ec Intl Bus.

ZUNTAG, MATTHEW; Tottenville HS; Staten Island, NY; (S); 16/850; Jazz Band; Rep Soph Cls; Rep Jr Cls; Rep Sr Cls; Var Bsktbl; Capt Golf; Cit Awd; High Hon Roll; NHS.

ZUPAN, KARIN; Vernon Verona Sherrill HS; Verona, NY; (Y); Church Yth Grp; Ski Clb; Yrbk Stf; JV Var Golf; High Hon Roll.

ZUSKIN, SHARI; Commack HS North; Commack, NY; (Y); 20/361; Spanish Clb; Off Frsh Cls; Off Soph Cls; Off Jr Cls; Off Sr Cls; High Hon Roll; VP NHS; Regnts Schlrshp 86.

ZVENYATSKY, OLGA; Christopher Columbus HS; Bronx, NY; (Y); #2 In Class; Debate Tm; Pres Key Clb; Yrbk Stf; Lit Mag; Trs Jr Cls; High Hon Roll; NHS; Prfct Atten Awd; Sal; Cornell U; Comp Sci.

ZWART, GAIL; Valley Central HS; Montgomery, NY; (Y); 19/288; Church Yth Grp; Band; School Musical; Yrbk Stf; Stat Bsbl; Capt Cheerleading; Hon Roll; NHS; Prfct Atten Awd; Spanish NHS; Schlrshp Chrldg Cmp 85; NY ST Schl Music Assn Meds 83 & 85; Orange County CC; Data Proc.

ZWARUN, LARA; The Wheatley Schl; Roslyn Hts, NY; (Y); Model UN; School Musical; School Play; Nwsp Rptr; Ed Nwsp Stf; Sec Soph Cls; Var Cheerleading; JV Var Socr; Ntl Merit Ltr; Latin Clb; Ntl Frnch Cntst 2nd Pl Regnly 84-85; WPIX Editrl Cntst 85-86; Engl.

ZWEIFEL, DAPHNE; The Stony Brook Schl; Chevy Chase, MD; (Y); 15/80; Church Yth Grp; Chorus; Var Cheerleading; Var Sftbl; Var Tennis; High Hon Roll; NHS; Piano Winnr 84-86; Gold Mdl Spnsh And Silvr Mdl Bio 84-85; Jones Art Awd 86; Bucknell U.

ZWETSCH, ERIC; Wilson HS; Spencerport, NY; (Y); High Hon Roll; Hon Roll; Rochester Inst Tech; Elect Engr.

ZWICKAU, OLAF; Williamsville South HS; E Amherst, NY; (Y); Ski Clb; SADD; Var L Ice Hcky; Var L Swmmng; Var L Tennis; High Hon Roll; Ski Races 80-82; Tenns Tm 84; Swm Tm 85-86; Cornell; Math.

ZWICKIS, LIZA; John Adams HS; Richmond Hill, NY; (Y); Church Yth Grp; Cmnty Wkr; Key Clb; Teachers Aide; NHS; Queens Coll.

ZWICKLBAUER, LIESL K; Guilderland Central HS; Altamont, NY; (Y); 33/370; Sec German Clb; Sec Sr Cls; Rep Stu Cncl; Var Capt Socr; High Hon Roll; NHS; Rotary Awd; Church Yth Grp; 4-H; Girl Scts; Prom/Hmcmng Courts 85; Hugh O Brien Yth Fndtn 84; Rotary Smmr Exch Stu Englang/Germany 84&85; Lafayette Coll; Chem Engrng.

ZYWIAK, RICHARD C; Whitesboro SR HS; Marcy, NY; (Y); Ski Clb; SADD; Hon Roll; Rgnts Schlrshp 86; Mohawk Valley CC; Comp Prgmg.

PUERTO RICO

ACOSTA, ROBERTO; San Jose College; Mayaguez, PR; (Y); Church Yth Grp; Debate Tm; Math Tm; Band; Concert Band; Orch; School Musical; Pres Frsh Cls; Rep Stu Cncl; Bsktbl; Croem.

ACOSTA, ZULMA; Colegio San Jose HS; San German, PR; (Y); Computer Clb; Hosp Aide; Political Wkr; Soph Cls; Bsktbl; Crs Cntry; Gym; Trk; Vllybl.

ADJUTANT, ANGELIQUE; Santa Rita HS; Bayamon, PR; (S); Drama Clb; Pres NFL; Science Clb; Ed Nwsp Stf; Pres Soph Cls; Prfct Atten Awd; Jrnlsm.

AGUILO-BRAU, JULIA J; Immaculate Conception Acad; Mayaguez, PR; (S); 1/92; Art Clb; Model UN; Spanish Clb; Yrbk Stf; NHS; Acdmc All-Amer 86; U Of Puerto Rico; Mrktng.

ALMODOVAR, JOSE I; Colegio San Ignacio De Loyola HS; Rio Piedras, PR; (Y); Boy Scts; Camera Clb; Chess Clb; Cmnty Wkr; Computer Clb; Math Clb; Model UN; Lit Mag; Egl Sct Awd 85; Ntl Hspnc Schlrshp Semifnlst 86; Nclr Med.

ALONSO, FERNANDO; Baldwin Schl; Rio Piedras, PR; (S); VP Math Clb; Math Tm; Science Clb; School Play; VP Soph Cls; Rep Stu Cncl; Cit Awd; High Hon Roll; Hon Roll; NHS; Sci Fair 2nd 84; Engrng.

ALVAREZ, DOROTHY; Colegio Ponceno HS; Ponce, PR; (Y); 5/76; Church Yth Grp; Dance Clb; Library Aide; Math Clb; High Hon Roll; NHS; Prfct Atten Awd; Hgh Hnr 83-86; Excllnt Cndct 83-86; 2nd Awd Litry Cntst-Essay 86; Krecinto U Mayaguez; Medcn.

ALVAREZ, JOSE L; Colegio Madre Cabrini HS; Rio Piedras, PR; (S); 2/45; Computer Clb; Science Clb; Bsktbl; Vllybl; NHS; Purdue; MD.

AMADEO, JAVIER; Antilles HS; Guaynabo, PR; (Y); 1/115; VP Key Clb; Concert Band; Mrchg Band; Var L Crs Cntry; Var L Trk; Var L Wrstlng; NHS; Ntl Merit SF; Pres Computer Clb; Trs Math Clb; Natl Hispnc Schlr SF 86; Yale U; Bio.

AQUINO-CLASS, MARIA; Eloisa Pascual Bairoa III; Caguas, PR; (S); DECA; Math Tm; NHS; Colegio U De Mayaguez; Chem Eng.

ARISSO, MARIA; Academia San Jose; Guaynabo, PR; (Y); 2/130; Camera Clb; Debate Tm; Drama Clb; French Clb; Yrbk Ed-Chief; Yrbk Phtg; Trs Frsh Cls; Hon Roll; NHS; NEDT Awd; Achvt Awds Hghst GPA Eng I 82-83; Spn II Geom Fr I Achvt Awds 83-84; Soclgy Fr II Achvt Awds 84-85; Elec Engrng.

AYALA, ADAN; Colegio San Jose HS; Rio Piedras, PR; (Y); 3/80; Model UN; Band; Yrbk Stf; Sec Sr Cls; High Hon Roll; NHS; Ntl Merit Ltr; Pres Schlr; Chess Clb; Church Yth Grp; Ntl Hspnc Schlr Semifnlst 86; Wndsrfg Instrctr 83-86; Biomdcl.

AYALA, MARIA ILEANA; Academia Santa Teresita; Carolina, PR; (Y); 1/60; Church Yth Grp; French Clb; FTA; Pres Mathletes; Sec Math Clb; Math Tm; Trs Natl Beta Clb; Church Choir; Nwsp Rptr; Rep Frsh Cls; Natl Soc Of Professional Engrs Schlrshp 86; Mdls Hons In Span, Hist, Eng, & Calculus 86; U Of PR; Computer Engr.

BAEZ, EDMA; Colegio San Jose HS; San German, PR; (Y); 4/45; Art Clb; Pres Church Yth Grp; Hosp Aide; Library Aide; Sec Jr Cls; Cmptr Engrng.

BARALT, DEIDRE; Antilles HS; Bayamon, PR; (Y); 27/106; Keywanettes; Sec Math Clb; Capt Drill Tm; School Musical; Swing Chorus; Yrbk Stf; VP Frsh Cls; Mgr Bsktbl; Hon Roll; NHS; Bus.

BARQUERO, JORGE; Academia San Jorge HS; Santurce, PR; (S); 3/59; Art Clb; Aud/Vis; JA; Library Aide; Stage Crew; Nwsp Stf; VP Soph Cls; VP Jr Cls; Rep Stu Cncl; Score Keeper; Spnsh Acad Comptn 3rd Pl 83-84; Cert Merit Svc 85; Cert Hnr Sci Fair 3rd Prz 85; RUM U; Elect Engr.

BATISTA, GIOVANNI; Antilles HS; Carolina, PR; (Y); Church Yth Grp; Computer Clb; FCA; Quiz Bowl; Teachers Aide; School Play; Var Bsbl; JV Var Wrstlng; High Hon Roll; Hon Roll.

BELINDA, LUGO; Inmmaculate Conception Acad; Anasco, PR; (Y); Model UN; Service Clb; Spanish Clb; Acadmc Excllnc-Spnsh Awd 84-86; U De PR; Jrnlst.

BELLOTTI, BERENICE; St Johns Schl; Hato Rey, PR; (Y); 1/38; Cmnty Wkr; VP Pres Computer Clb; VP Trs French Clb; Math Tm; Model UN; Office Aide; Science Clb; Service Clb; VP Spanish Clb; Teachers Aide; Semifnlst Ntl Hispanic Schlr Awd Prg & Hnr Soc Schlrshp Prg 86; Outstndg Achvt Amer Chem Soc Test 84; Chem.

BERRIOS ROMAN, MARISELY; Manuela Toro Moris HS; Caguas, PR; (S); 9/315; Church Yth Grp; Church Choir; 9th Grd Awd 84; Engl Awd 84; Phrmcy.

BIAGGI, PATRICIA; A I C HS; Mayaguez, PR; (Y); Drama Clb; School Play; Yrbk Phtg; Vllybl; Hon Roll; Prfct Atten Awd; Pres Clsrm; Pblcty.

BLASINI, ENID; Academia Santa Monica; Bayamon, PR; (S); 1/52; Church Yth Grp; Drama Clb; French Clb; JA; Church Choir; Nwsp Stf; Yrbk Stf; Rep Stu Cncl; Jr NHS; NHS; Prncpls Lst 83-85; U PR; Engrg.

BOLIVAR, JOSE; Colegio San Ignacio HS; Rio Piedras, PR; (Y); Cmnty Wkr; Varsity Clb; Bsktbl; JV L Trk; Vllybl; Natl Mert Hspnc Awd Semifnlst 85; Mechncl Engr.

BON, SAMUEL E; Jose Gautier Benitez HS; Caguas, PR; (Y); Science Clb; VP Frsh Cls; NHS; Pres Acadmc Fitns Awd 86; U Of MA; Zoology.

CALZADA-NAVARRO, RAMON LUIS; Academia Del Sagrado Corazon; Bayamon, PR; (S); 1/76; Drama Clb; English Clb; FHA; JA; Library Aide; Red Cross Aide; Science Clb; Spanish Clb; Speech Tm; Teachers Aide; 1 Pl ASC Ltrty Cntst Drama 85; Fnlst Intelecfual Compttns 83; 5 Pl Fnls Ntl Orration Leag 85; Med.

CANDELARIO, DAMARIS; Antilles HS; Rio Piedras, PR; (Y); 7/108; Computer Clb; Drama Clb; French Clb; Keywanettes; Drill Tm; Trs Frsh Cls; Rep Sr Cls; High Hon Roll; Sec NHS; 1st Prz Sci Fair 83; Ldrshp Awd 83; Engl Awd 84; U Of Capey; Dntstry.

CAPO, RAFAEL; Colegio Ponceno HS; Ponce, PR; (Y); 2/76; Church Yth Grp; Nwsp Ed-Chief; Pres Frsh Cls; Pres Soph Cls; Pres Stu Cncl; Hst NHS; Sal; 1st Plc Ltry Cntst 82-86; Schl Rep Intl Yth Assmbly Rome 85; Mst Dstngshd Grad & Ldrshp Awd 86; Cath U Of PR; Priest.

CARABALLO, LUIS; Colegio Santa Rita HS; Catano, PR; (S); Church Yth Grp; School Musical; Rep Jr Cls; High Hon Roll; NHS; Natl Honor Soc 84 & 85; U Of Puerto Rico; Jrnlsm.

CARBONELL, FEDERICO; Colegio San Jose HS; Hormigueros, PR; (Y); Church Yth Grp; Orch; Frshmn Of Yr Playing Bskbl; Engineer.

CARDONA, MARIBEL CRESPO; Manuel Mendez Liciaga HS; San Sebastian, PR; (Y); 8/400; English Clb; Library Aide; Pres Math Clb; Chorus; Outstndng Achvt Eng,Spnsh 83-85; Bests Punctutions Coll Bd Awd 86; Phrmcy.

CARDONA, NYDIA; Academia Sagrado Corazon HS; Santurce, PR; (S); Pres Jr Cls; Swmmng; NHS; Drama Clb; English Clb; JA; Red Cross Aide; Science Clb; 1st Clss Hnr 84-86; PR Mst Outstndg Yng People Awd 85; Med.

CARRASQUILLO PAGAN, IDALIZ; Manuela Toro Morice HS; Caguas, PR; (S); 1/315; Church Yth Grp; NHS; Engl, Math & Sci Awds 84; UPR; Med Tech.

CASTAING, PEDRO; Colegio Ponceno HS; Ponce, PR; (S); 1/68; Math Clb; Math Tm; Trs Jr Cls; Stu Cncl; NHS; Valedictorian 83; Med.

CASTILLO, LUIS J; Academia Perpetuo Socorro HS; Miramar, PR; (Y); Camera Clb; Chess Clb; Cmnty Wkr; Computer Clb; Dance Clb; Debate Tm; Hosp Aide; Model UN; Science Clb; School Musical; Natl Hspnc Schlr Awds Pgm Fnlst 86; Chem Engrng.

CASTILLO, ROSA; Inmaculate Conception HS; Mayaquez, PR; (Y); Art Clb; Drama Clb; Science Clb; Spanish Clb; Yrbk Stf; Sec Sr Cls; Stu Cncl; Inmaculate Cncptn Acad.

CASTILLO, SHARON J; Academia San Jose HS; Guaynabo, PR; (Y); French Clb; Acpl Chr; Trs Jr Cls; Rep Stu Cncl; Cheerleading; Hon Roll; NHS; Drama Clb; School Play; Amer U Grnt & Rstrctd Loan 86-87; Ethncs Awd & Engl Awd; Frnch Awd JR; Typg, Jrnlsm, Marrg Awds SR; The American U; Cmmnctns.

CASTRO, SANDRA I; Wesleyan Acad; Bayamon, PR; (Y); Church Yth Grp; Drama Clb; JA; Chorus; School Play; Nwsp Stf; Rep Soph Cls; Sec Stu Cncl; JV Bsktbl; JV Var Cheerleading; Perfect Attendence Awd 82-84; Hnr Roll 84-86; Jr Achvt 100 Dollar Club Awd 84; FL Inst Of Tech; Aeroncl Engrg.

CATALA, GLORISA; Baldwin School Of P R; Guaynabo, PR; (S); GAA; Yrbk Stf; VP Soph Cls; Capt Var Bsktbl; Capt Var Sftbl; Var Capt Vllybl; Cit Awd; Hon Roll; Jr NHS; Pres VP NHS; Bst Ath PR O J Simpson Awd 83-84; Natl Bsktbl Tm PR 84-85; Ath Of Yr 82-85; Vet Med.

CEREZO, DIANA E SOTOMAYOR; Colegio San Antonio HS; Aguadilla, PR; (S); 1/31; Art Clb; Civic Clb; Math Clb; Science Clb; Spanish Clb; Teachers Aide; Im Bsktbl; Im Sftbl; Im Vllybl; High Hon Roll; CAAM; Psych.

CHAPPUIS, JACQUES P; Baldwin Schl; San Juan, PR; (Y); Computer Clb; Debate Tm; Pres Math Clb; Math Tm; Model UN; Pres Soph Cls; Var L Socr; Var L Trk; JETS Awd; NEDT Awd; Geo Acad Awd Frnch Achvt Awd 83-84; Chem Achvt Awd 84-85; Physcs Acad Awd 85-86; Chem Engrng.

CIMADEVILLA, MARGARITA I; Acadmeia San Jose HS; Guaynabo, PR; (Y); 23/129; Church Yth Grp; Cmnty Wkr; Debate Tm; French Clb; NFL; L Chorus; NHS; NEDT Awd; Pres Schlr; Alg I Awd 82-83; Ntl Hispanic Schlrshp Awd 86; Bardley U Comp Camp Achvmnt Awds 84; Bus.

COLLAZO, NAYDA; Academia Perpetuo Socorro HS; Santurce, PR; (Y); 9/93; VP Art Clb; Camera Clb; Computer Clb; Science Clb; Pres Schlr; MA Coll Of Art; Grphc Dsgn.

COLON, ALBA; Inmaculate Conception HS; Mayaguez, PR; (S); 12/94; Church Yth Grp; Model UN; Pres Spanish Clb; Chorus; Nwsp Stf; Rep Stu Cncl; Cit Awd; VP NHS; Prfct Atten Awd; Stu Cncl Schlrshp 85-86; Lidershp Value Yr 85; Hall Fame 86; MECH Engr.

COLON, JOSE; Colegio Ponceno HS; Ponce, PR; (S); 21/77; Acpl Chr; Yrbk Stf; Var Bsktbl; Im Capt Vllybl; Hon Roll; U Of PR Mayaguez; Elec Engrng.

COLON RODRIGUEZ, MARISEL; Manuela Toro Morice HS; Caguas, PR; (S); 2/30; Church Yth Grp; Off Jr Cls; NHS; UPR; Ag.

CONCEPCION, GLORIMAR; Colegio San Antonio HS; Hato Rey, PR; (Y); 19/97; Church Yth Grp; Cmnty Wkr; English Clb; Church Choir; Nwsp Rptr; Nwsp Stf; High Hon Roll; NHS; Engls Awd 85; Acadmc Prgrs Awd 85; Svc Awd 85; U Of Detroit; Mgmnt.

CORDERO, INGRID M; Academia Perpetua Socorro HS; Rio Piedras, PR; (Y); 19/96; Cmnty Wkr; French Clb; Math Clb; Science Clb; Vllybl; NHS; Ntl Merit SF; Geo Awd 83; Comp Sci Awd 85; Bus.

CRUZ, MAGALY; Colegio San Jose HS; Lajas, PR; (Y); Civic Clb; Debate Tm; Intnl Clb; Inter Amer U; Crmnl Law.

CRUZ, MARIBEL; Inmaculate Conception Acad; Mayaguez, PR; (S); Dance Clb; Drama Clb; Sec Model UN; Science Clb; Service Clb; Nwsp Rptr; Rep Soph Cls; Sec Stu Cncl; Cit Awd; Trs NHS; Kodak Pctr Awd Sci Teria 86; Sci Teria 1st Pl 85; Jrnlsm.

CRUZ, YANIA; Antilles HS; Rio Piedras, PR; (Y); 3/110; Sec Keywanettes; Yrbk Stf; Capt Pom Pon; Capt Powder Puff Ftbl; Pres NHS; Ft Buchanans Offcrs Wives Clb Schlrshp 86; Acadmc All Amer 84-86; UPR Mayaguez; Engr.

CRUZ MARCANO, IVONNE; Manuela Toro Morice HS; Caguas, PR; (S); FHA; Library Aide; Teachers Aide; NHS; U Of Puerto Rico.

CRUZADO, WANDA; Colegio Santa Rita HS; Bayamon, PR; (S); Dance Clb; Drama Clb; School Musical; Var Cheerleading; NHS; Merit 84 & 85; U PR; Ortho.

CUEBAS, ILEANA; A I C HS; Mayaguez, PR; (S); 1/110; VP Pres Church Yth Grp; Math Tm; Science Clb; Pres Service Clb; Spanish Clb; Sec NHS; Opt Clb Awd; Yrbk Co Edtr 86-87; Chem Sci Tm 86; Stu Cncl 85-86; U PR Mayaquez; CPA.

DE GRACIA, CARLOS; Academia Santa Monica; Santurce, PR; (S); 2/67; Chess Clb; Varsity Clb; VP Frsh Cls; Im Bsktbl; Im Vllybl; Pre-Med.

DE HOYOS MARTINEZ, LOURDES; Manuela Toro Morice HS; Caguas, PR; (S); 1/30; NHS; VPR; Periodsm.

DE LA CRUZ, LYNNETTE; Colegio San Antonio HS; Isabella, PR; (S); 3/33; Church Yth Grp; Cmnty Wkr; Drama Clb; English Clb; Science Clb; Spanish Clb; School Play; Hon Roll; NHS; Stu Of Yr 83-84; Cooprtn Cert Daughters Of Mary 85; Soc Fair Awd 85; Chem.

DEL VALLE, JOAN I; Academy Of The Immaculate Cncptn; San German, PR; (Y); 5/49; Art Clb; Aud/Vis; Camp Fr Inc; Church Yth Grp; Civic Clb; Cmnty Wkr; Dance Clb; Debate Tm; Drama Clb; Hosp Aide; Church Awd 83; Bskbl Awd 82; PA ST U; Cmnctns.

DETRES, CESAR; Southwestern Educational Society; Mayaguez, PR; (Y); Boy Scts; Chess Clb; Computer Clb; Debate Tm; Drama Clb; JA; Model UN; Wt Lftg; Ntl Merit SF; Pres Schlr; 1st Prz Sci Fair PR-PHYSCS 84; Fnlst PR JR Sci & Humnties Sympsm 85; 1st Prz ICPR Wrtg Cntst 83; Law.

DETRES, LAURA; Southwestern Educational Soc HS; Mayaguez, PR; (S); Debate Tm; JA; Model UN; School Play; VP Frsh Cls; VP Jr Cls; VP Stu Cncl; Var Bsktbl; High Hon Roll; Pres NHS; Pres Clsrm Yng Am 86; Yrbk Layout Editor 86.

DIAZ, ANGEL L; Baldwin Schl; Gardens Rio Pdrs, PR; (S); Boy Scts; Computer Clb; Math Clb; Math Tm; Science Clb; Yrbk Stf; Trs Stu Cncl; Socr; Tennis; Hon Roll; 2nd Prz Sci Fr 84.

DIAZ, MARIA DEL PILAR; Colegio Ponceno HS; Ponce, PR; (S); Yrbk Stf; Pres Jr Cls; JV Trk; JV Vllybl; Jr NHS; NHS; Sal; Clb De Orientadores 84; Bary U; BBA.

EGOAVIL, VERONAICA; Immaculate Conception Acad; Mayaguez, PR; (Y); German Clb; GAA; Science Clb; Spanish Clb; Speech Tm; Nwsp Ed-Chief; Yrbk Stf; Capt Bsktbl; Capt Vllybl; Athlete Yr 83-84; Most Outstndng Stu Spch Clb 85-86.

EMMANUELLI, LUIS; Colegio Ponceno HS; Guayanilla, PR; (S); Boy Scts; School Play; Jr Cls; Bsbl; Bsktbl; Sftbl; Vllybl; Hnrs Night 81-85; Sci U Of PR; Doc.

ESCORIAZA, PHILLIP A; University Of P R Secondary Schl; Rio Piedras, PR; (Y); 1/86; Church Yth Grp; Drama Clb; Science Clb; Chorus; VP Sr Cls; Rep Stu Cncl; NHS; Natl Hispnc Schlrs Awd Pgm SF 86; Sci Awd 83; Hstry Awd 83; Med.

FERNANDEZ, ALEXANDRA; Academia San Jose; Bayamon, PR; (Y); 5/121; Camera Clb; Debate Tm; NFL; Q&S; Nwsp Rptr; Yrbk Stf; High Hon Roll; Pres NHS; Ntl Merit SF; Mst Dstngshd Stu 85086; Schmbrg Schlrshp; Frgn News Crspdnt.

FERRE, LINDA; Academia Perpetuo Socorro HS; Isla Verde, PR; (Y); 1/93; Math Clb; Math Tm; Science Clb; Speech Tm; Var Crs Cntry; Var Trk; High Hon Roll; Jr NHS; NHS; NEDT Awd; Chem Awd Am Chem Soc 85; SF Ntl Hispanc Pres Schlrshp Awd 85; Aerontcl Engr.

FIGUEROA, RAYMOND; Antilles HS; Levittown, PR; (Y); Key Clb; Var Bsbl; High Hon Roll; Hon Roll; NHS; Med.

FISCHBACH, KEVIN; Southwestern Educational Soc HS; Mayaguez, PR; (Y); 3/14; Cmnty Wkr; Drama Clb; School Play; Yrbk Bus Mgr; Pres Sr Cls; High Hon Roll; NHS; Outstndng Of Yr 85-86; Sci Bwl Tm-2nd Pl Regl Sci B 84-85; GA Inst Tech; Aerspc Engr.

FORTUNA, IVETTE; Southwestern Educational Society; Hormigueros, PR; (S); Drama Clb; JA; Model UN; Speech Tm; School Play; Yrbk Stf; Pres Jr Cls; Trs Stu Cncl; Trk; Cit Awd; Trk & Fld Awds; Natl Hnr Sco Plq 85.

FRY, DAVID; Robinson Schl; Santurce, PR; (S); 5/32; Trs Math Clb; Math Tm; Variety Show; Nwsp Phtg; Yrbk Ed-Chief; Yrbk Phtg; Rep Sr Cls; Var Capt Socr; Mu Alp Tht; NHS; UC San Diego; Chem.

FUENTES, NATALIA; Academia San Jorge HS; Santurce, PR; (Y); 1/47; Model UN; Political Wkr; Chorus; Yrbk Stf; VP Frsh Cls; Stu Cncl; Hon Roll; Pres Jr NHS; NHS; Val; Semi-Fnlst Natl Hspnc Schlr Awds 85-86; Semi-Fnlst Prsdntl Schlrs 85-86; Elec Engrng.

GALLETTI, FRANCISCO; Wesleyan Acad; Rio Piedras, PR; (Y); 1/50; Pres Spanish Clb; Trs Sr Cls; JV Var Socr; Var L Trk; Bausch & Lomb Sci Awd; High Hon Roll; VP NHS; Ntl Merit SF; Boy Scts; Crest Awd 85; Aerospace Engr.

GARCIA, CHRISTOPHER A; Saint Johns Schl; Santurce, PR; (Y); 7/40; Boy Scts; Nwsp Stf; Lit Mag; High Hon Roll; Hon Roll; Schlrshp Awds Bnningtn & Swrthmr 86; Bennington; Author.

GARCIA, ZULMA; Colegio San Jose HS; San German, PR; (Y); VP Girl Scts; JA; Chorus; School Musical; Var Bsktbl; Pres Clsssrm Yng Am 86; Engr.

GARCIA SEGARRA, IVELISSE; Manuela Toro Morice HS; Caguas, PR; (S); 1/315; NHS; Sci, Spnsh, Math Awds 84; UPR; Medcl Tchnlgy.

GARCIA VAZQUEZ, FERNANDO; Manuela Toro Morice HS; Caguas, PR; (S); 7/515; Chess Clb; Church Yth Grp; Library Aide; Red Cross Aide; Soroptimist; Church Choir; School Musical; Nwsp Phtg; Nwsp Rptr; Jr Cls; Natl Hnr Soc Chess Chmpn East Rgn 85; U PR; Med.

GARCIA-O FERRALL, YADIRA; Academia Santa Monica HS; Rio Piedras, PR; (S); Drama Clb; JA; Chorus; Yrbk Stf; Sec Frsh Cls; Rep Soph Cls; Rep Stu Cncl; 1st Hnr 83; 2nd Hnr 84; Princpls List 85; Tulane U; Comp Pgmmr.

GIBSON-ROSADO, ERICA MIGDALIA; Colegio Puertorriqueno De Nina HS; Rio Piedras, PR; (Y); 2/81; Rep Church Yth Grp; Pres SADD; Nwsp Rptr; Cit Awd; NHS; St Schlr; Rep Camera Clb; Rep Civic Clb; Rep Cmnty Wkr; Natl Hspnc Schlr Awds Prgrm Semifnlst 85-86; PR Mdcl Assn Prsdntl Awd 85-86; Hnrs Sci Rsrch U PR; Loyola U Of Chcgo; Ntrl Sci.

GIL, ALCIDES; Colegio San Ignacio De Loyola; Rio Piedras, PR; (Y); Computer Clb; Dance Clb; Drama Clb; Model UN; School Play; Spanish NHS; Emory U; Bio.

GOMEZ, IVETTE; Academia San Joage HS; Santurce, PR; (S); 4/47; Chorus; Var Vllybl; Hon Roll; VP Jr NHS; Pres NHS; Sr Vcl In Dscpln Cmtt; Pblc Adress Clb; Srv To Schl Trophie; Bus.

GONZALEZ, BRENDA DENISSE; Academia Santa Monica; Bayamon, PR; (S); 4/51; Church Yth Grp; Debate Tm; JA; Church Choir; Variety Show; Nwsp Stf; Yrbk Stf; Rep Soph Cls; Rep Stu Cncl; Tlnt Shw Dnc Awd 83; 1st Hnr 84; Princpls Lst 85; U PR; Law.

GONZALEZ, JULIO A; Academia Sagrado Corazon HS; Levittown, PR; (S); English Clb; Leo Clb; Science Clb; NHS; 2nd Hnr Frshmn 83-84; 2nd & 1st Hnr Awds 84-85; Aero Sp Engrng.

GONZALEZ, RICARDO; Colegio Ponceno Inc; Salinas, PR; (S); #17 In Class; Var Bsktbl; Im Vllybl; High Hon Roll; NHS; Hgh Hnr Trphy Bst Avg 83-84; Hgh Hnr Trphy Bst Avg 84-85; USAF Acad; Aeron Engr.

GONZALEZ, WALESKA; Antilles HS; Bayamon, PR; (Y); Art Clb; Drama Clb; French Clb; Girl Scts; Office Aide; Teachers Aide; Drill Tm; Rep Sr Cls; Powder Puff Ftbl; High Hon Roll; Marine Bio.

GONZALEZ RODRIGUEZ, AIXA M; Colegio Mdre Cabrini Ecarnacn Hs; Puerto Nuevo, PR; (S); 11/28; Chorus; Nwsp Rptr; Rep Jr Cls; NHS; Comp Engr.

GUERRA, ARLENE; Immaculate Conception HS; Mayaguez, PR; (S); Drama Clb; English Clb; Science Clb; VP Service Clb; Spanish Clb; Speech Tm; NHS; Most Dstngshd Mbr Of Sci Club 84-85; Secy Of Ecology Club 85-86; Engrng.

GUERRA, ZUIMDIE; Immaculate Conception HS; Mayaguez, PR; (S); Drama Clb; VP English Clb; Science Clb; Service Clb; Spanish Clb; Speech Tm; NHS; Most Distinguished Mbr Of Sci Club 84-85; Treasure Of Ecology Club 85-86; Engrng.

HERNANDEZ, CARMEN; Academia Sagrado Corazon; Guaynabo, PR; (S); 3/75; Civic Clb; Dance Clb; English Clb; High Hon Roll; Sec NHS; Prfct Atten Awd; U Of PR; BBA.

HERNANDEZ, CESAR; Ramon Powery Giralt HS; Juncos, PR; (Y); FFA; Bsbl; Bsktbl; Gym; Sftbl; Swmmng; Trk; Vllybl; Wt Lftg; U PR; Aviation Engrg.

HERNANDEZ, JOSE; Academia Sagrado Corazin; Guaynabo, PR; (S); Civic Clb; English Clb; Var Bsktbl; Score Keeper; High Hon Roll; NHS; Elec Engrng.

HERRERA-NIEVES, MARISOL; Academia San Jorge HS; Santurce, PR; (S); 1/55; Drama Clb; Speech Tm; Chorus; Sec Frsh Cls; Stu Cncl; Hon Roll; Jr NHS; Idioms.

HERRERO, VIVIAN; Immaculate Conception Acad; Mayaguez, PR; (S); 3/96; Pres Art Clb; Nwsp Stf; Yrbk Ed-Chief; Rep Soph Cls; Rep Stu Cncl; Gov Hon Prg Awd; NHS; Pres Clsrm Yng Amer 85 & 86; Acdmc All Am 85 & 86; Mayaguez U; Indstrl Engrng.

HIRALDO NERIS, MARIBEL; Manuela Toro HS; Caguas, PR; (S); NHS; Math, Sci Awds 84; UPR; Med.

HORNAN, LESLIE; Academia Inmaculada Concpn; Mayaguez, PR; (Y); Drama Clb; Pres GAA; Science Clb; School Play; Stage Crew; Stu Cncl; Var Capt Bsktbl; Var L Vllybl; Cls Athlte Awd & Exclnce Engl Cls 86; Schs Sci Fair Hnrb Mntn 85; Mayaguez Sftbl Tm Champ Awd 85; Engrng.

HUNT, JULIANNE; Southwestern Educational Society; Mayaguez, PR; (S); 1/14; Drama Clb; Model UN; School Play; Nwsp Ed-Chief; Yrbk Stf; VP Sr Cls; VP Stu Cncl; Sec NHS; Ntl Merit Schol; Math Tm; Hnbl Mntn Schlstc Wrtng Cont; Stu Yr; Harvard; Sci Rsrch.

IRIZARRY, JANICE MARIE; San Jose Parrochial School; Lajas, PR; (Y); Art Clb; Civic Clb; Drama Clb; Leo Clb; Off Frsh Cls; Rep Soph Cls; VP Jr Cls; VP Sr Cls; Pres Stu Cncl; Cheerleading; For Wnng 2nd Rnnr Up Miss Borinquen Tnn Or Miss US Tn PR & Wnng Title Miss Elegnc 86; USA U; Merchandising.

ISERN, REBECA; Antilles HS; Dorado Beach, PR; (Y); 23/107; High Hon Roll; Hon Roll; NHS; Prfct Atten Awd; VP Keywanettes; VP Library Aide; Chorus; Var L Tennis; Mst Imprvd Engl 84-85; TX A & M U Galveston; Mrn Biol.

JETTER, PATRICIA; Immaculate Conception Acad; Mayaguez, PR; (S); JA; Pres Model UN; Science Clb; Service Clb; Nwsp Rptr; Stu Cncl; Pres NHS; Drama Clb; Mdl UN Awd 83-84; Stu Cncl Awd 2nd Prz PR Sci Fr 84-85; Natl Hnr Scty Awd, Mdl UN Awd 85-86; Intl Rltns.

JHAVERI, RAKESH; Colegio Jponceno HS; Ponce, PR; (S); 17/77; Boy Scts; Chess Clb; Church Yth Grp; Drama Clb; Math Clb; Math Tm; Band; Chorus; Church Choir; Mrchg Band; Hnr Stu 81-84; U Of PR; Comp Engr.

JIMENEZ, LUIS B; Central De Artes Visuales HS; Rio Piedras, PR; (Y); 4/72; Pres Art Clb; Pres Camera Clb; Pres Church Yth Grp; Cmnty Wkr; Hosp Aide; Science Clb; Yrbk Bus Mgr; Yrbk Phtg; Yrbk Stf; Pres Sr Cls; 1st Prz-Drwg & Painting 83-84; 2nd Prz Painting-Hnrbl Mntn 84-85; 2nd Prz Paintg & Wtr Color 85-86; Loyola U Chgo IL; Doc.

JIMENEZ, MELISSA; Academia San Jorge HS; Santurce, PR; (S); 5/50; Church Yth Grp; Civic Clb; Drama Clb; Library Aide; Chorus; School Play; High Hon Roll; Jr NHS; NHS; U Of PR; Chem.

JIMENEZ DIAZ, CORALIE; Manuela Toro HS; Caguas, PR; (S); 3/257; Chess Clb; English Clb; Girl Scts; Math Tm; Chorus; Gym; Hon Roll; NHS; Psych.

JOHNSON, NORMA; Robinson HS; San Juan, PR; (S); 3/36; Natl Beta Clb; Spanish Clb; Sec Soph Cls; Rep Jr Cls; Var Bsktbl; Capt Cheerleading; Var Stat Sftbl; Var Vllybl; Jr NHS; NHS; Spn Medl 84-85; Biol Mdl 83-84; Med.

KUSHNER, MATTHEW; Academia Del Perpetuo Socorro HS; Santurce, PR; (Y); 19/101; Cmnty Wkr; Computer Clb; NFL; PAVAS; Ed Q&S; Speech Tm; Temple Yth Grp; Variety Show; Nwsp Ed-Chief; Nwsp Rptr; Ntl Hisp Awds Semi-Fnlst 85-86; Math.

LAFONT, ERIK; Santiago Veve Calzada HS; Fajardo, PR; (Y); English Clb; ROTC; Spanish Clb; Varsity Clb; Bsbl; High Hon Roll; Rotary Awd; U Of PR; Engrng.

LAGO, LORRAINE; Caribbean Schl; Ponce, PR; (Y); Drama Clb; Mathletes; Math Clb; Chorus; School Play; Pres Soph Cls; Pres Stu Cncl; JV Var Bsktbl; High Hon Roll; Jr NHS; Bio-Med Engrng.

LAZARUS, ANTHONY; Southwestern Educational Society; Mayaguez, PR; (S); JA; Model UN; Band; Concert Band; Jazz Band; Nwsp Ed-Chief; Yrbk Ed-Chief; Yrbk Phtg; Yrbk Stf; Rep Frsh Cls; Kodak & Eastman Awd Phtgrphy 85; 3rd Pl Schl & Regnl Sci Fair Chem 85; Brown U; Ind Mgr.

LEADER, IDA; Academia San Jose HS; Guaynabo, PR; (Y); French Clb; Girl Scts; Service Clb; Chorus; Hon Roll; Lion Awd; Trs NHS; Gld Awd Girl Scts 84; Outstndg Stu Yr 85; Honorary Egl Sct 84; Finance.

LOPEZ, EDGARDO; Colegio Marista HS; Guaynabo, PR; (Y); 1/82; Boy Scts; Church Yth Grp; Cmnty Wkr; NFL; Variety Show; Nwsp Stf; Rep Stu Cncl; NHS; Ntl Merit SF; Val; 1st Pl Marista Art Cntst 84-85; 1st Prz Poetry Maristas Lit Cntst 82-83; Col Maristas Stu Yr 86; Arch.

LOPEZ MARRERO, LUIS A; Eloisa Pascual HS; Caguas, PR; (S); DECA; Wt Lftg; NHS; Bus Adm.

LOYOLA, MARIO; Southwest Educational Society HS; Mayaguez, PR; (Y); Computer Clb; Debate Tm; Drama Clb; Model UN; Stage Crew; Nwsp Stf; Lit Mag; Semi Fnlst Ntl Hispnc Schlr Awd 85-86; Wrtr.

MADURO, GUILLERMO; Colegio San Ignacio De Loyola; Rio Piedras, PR; (Y); Trs Church Yth Grp; Cmnty Wkr; Drama Clb; NFL; School Play; Nwsp Ed-Chief; JV Var Socr; JV Trk; Ntl Merit SF; Pre-Med.

MALDONADO MORALES, GISELA; Manuela Toro HS; Caguas, PR; (S); 12/258; FHA; Acpl Chr; Vllybl; U Of Puerto Rico; Med.

MALPICA, GLADYS; Academia Sta Monica HS; Guaynabo, PR; (S); 6/51; Church Yth Grp; Temple Yth Grp; Church Choir; Lit Mag; Sr Cls; NHS; Library Awd 84; Pub Rltns.

MARCHANY, MARIA; Academia Inmaculada Concepcion HS; Mayaguez, PR; (Y); Art Clb; Drama Clb; English Clb; Model UN; Science Clb; Spanish Clb; Chorus; School Play; Nwsp Phtg; Natl Hnr Scty Ldrshp 84-86; Bst Stu MUN 86; Scnd Prz Marine Blgy 85; Bst Drama Clb 86; U Sagrado Corazon; Indstrl Psyc.

MARRERO, ARLENE; Colegio San Antonio HS; Rio Piedras, PR; (Y); 5/97; Church Yth Grp; English Clb; Sec NFL; Church Choir; Nwsp Ed-Chief; Rep Stu Cncl; High Hon Roll; NHS; Hnr Stu, Jrnlsm & Nwspr Awd, Schlrshp Awds 85-86; U Puerto Rico; Acctg.

MARTINEZ, EDITH; Colegio Ponceno HS; Ponce, PR; (Y); 4/76; Girl Scts; Yrbk Stf; Sec Stu Cncl; Cheerleading; Trk; NHS; Rotary Awd; Hgh Hnrs Awds; UPR; Bus Adm.

MARTINEZ, VICTOR M; Peupetuo Socorro HS; San Juan, PR; (Y); Camera Clb; Computer Clb; French Clb; Math Clb; Pep Band; Stage Crew; Yrbk Phtg; Vllybl; NEDT Awd 84 & 85; Geo-Physcs Srv Awd 86; Chem Engrng.

MARTINEZ, YAMILETTE; Academia Sagrado Corazon HS; Carolina, PR; (S); Drama Clb; JA; Speech Tm; Nwsp Stf; Rep Stu Cncl; Vllybl; NHS; 1st Hnr In Religion, Algebra I & Bio; Comp Engrng.

MARTINEZ-ACOSTA, JUAN A; Colegio Santa Rita HS; Bayamon, PR; (S); Off Jr Cls; NHS; U Of PR.

MARTINEZ-HERNANDEZ, CARMEN L; Academia Santa Monica; Bayamon, PR; (S); 7/51; Drama Clb; JA; Yrbk Stf; Rep Sr Cls; Princple List 83; 1st Hnr 85; 2nd Hnr 84; U Puert Rico; Bus Adm.

MARULL, SAMANTHA LUISA; Santa Rita Private HS; Bayamon, PR; (S); NFL; Off Frsh Cls; Off Soph Cls; Off Jr Cls; Rep Stu Cncl; NHS.

MEDINA-MUNIZ, RAUL E; Colegio Ponceno HS; Ponce, PR; (S); Math Clb; Band; Stage Crew; Aerntc Engr.

MELENDEZ, MEI-LING; Santa Rita HS; Bayamon, PR; (S); NFL; Teachers Aide; School Play; Sec Soph Cls; Sec Jr Cls; Score Keeper; Vllybl; Prfct Atten Awd; Stage Crew; Nwsp Stf.

MENDEZ, MARIA; Academia Sagrado Corazon HS; Levittown, PR; (S); Church Yth Grp; VP Red Cross Aide; Science Clb; NHS; Stdnt Mnth 85; CAAM; Concentrtn Mth.

MERCADO, LORNA GREGORY; Centro Oportuniadades Educativ; San German, PR; (Y); Church Yth Grp; JA; Leo Clb; Chorus; Church Choir; School Musical; Gym; Swmmng; Inter American U; Bio.

MERCADO RIVERA, LUZ M; Manuelatror Morrice HS; Caguas, PR; (S); 8/319; Library Aide; Hon Roll; NHS; Lbry Awd 84; Harvard U; Soc Sci.

MIRANDA, ANA; St Johns Schl; Guaynabo, PR; (Y); 2/38; Art Clb; French Clb; Model UN; NFL; Spanish Clb; School Play; Lit Mag; Score Keeper; High Hon Roll; Hon Roll; Natl Mrt Fnlst 86; Natl Hspnc Schlr Awds Smi-Fnslt 86; Harvard Coll; Intl Rltns.

MITCHELL, BRADLEY; Robinson Schl; Dorado, PR; (S); Nwsp Ed-Chief; Nwsp Rptr; Computer Clb; Math Clb; Math Tm; Scholastic Bowl; Yrbk Phtg; Pres Frsh Cls; Trs Stu Cncl; Var Golf.

MONSANTO, VIVIAN; Golegio Ponceno HS; Ponce, PR; (Y); 1/76; Sec Camera Clb; School Musical; Yrbk Rptr; High Hon Roll; NHS; Val; Hghst GPA 83-86; Grad Medls Hghst Avg Spnsh, Sci, Relgn, Socl Sci 86; Hgh Scr Coll Brd Tst 86; Georgetown U; Medcn.

MONTILLA, IVONNE; Academia Sagrado Corazon; Carolina, PR; (S); JA; VP Frsh Cls; VP Soph Cls; Rep Stu Cncl; NHS; Prfct Atten Awd; 1st Hnr Relgn, Alg, Biol, Engl,Span; Cooprtn Hist; U PR; Bus Adm.

MONTILLA, JORGE R; Colegio San Ignacio HS; Rio Piedras, PR; (Y); Cmnty Wkr; Computer Clb; Service Clb; Hon Roll; Ntl Merit SF; Hon Cert Tutrng Pgm 84 & 85; Big Brother Pgm 85-86; Mngmnt.

MORALES, GLADYMAR; Robinson HS; Guaynabo, PR; (S); 6/28; VP French Clb; Hosp Aide; NFL; Office Aide; Trs Spanish Clb; Hon Roll; Prfct Atten Awd; VP Frsh Cls; VP Soph Cls.

MORALES, GUSTAVO; Colegio Madre Cabrini HS; Rio Piedras, PR; (S); Pres Church Yth Grp; Rep Frsh Cls; Rep Soph Cls; VP Jr Cls; Off Sr Cls; VP Stu Cncl; Hon Roll; NHS; Medicine.

MORALES, JOSE A; Colegio San Antonio HS; Rio Piedras, PR; (Y); 15/97; Church Yth Grp; Teachers Aide; Chorus; Swing Chorus; Pres Stu Cncl; Hon Roll; NHS; Prncpls Svc Awd 85-86; Puerto Rico U; Dentistry.

MORALES, MIRKA; Academia San Jose; Guaynabo, PR; (Y); 3/128; School Play; Variety Show; Nwsp Rptr; Off Jr Cls; Rep Stu Cncl; Im Gym; NHS; Ntl Merit Schol; Sec Debate Tm; Trs Drama Clb; Pres Clssrm 86; Ballet 83-86; Natl Hispnc Schlr Awds Pgm SF 86; Harvard U; Intl Rltns.

MORALES, PEDRO FARINACCI; Colegio Ponceno HS; Ponce, PR; (S); 5/76; Pres Nwsp Phtg; Pres Yrbk Phtg; VP Jr Cls; Sr Cls; Off Bsktbl; Trk; NHS; Bst Acad Rank Sports 85-86.

MORALES GOMEZ, IRZA M; Elosia Paseual HS; Caguas, PR; (S); DECA; Teachers Aide; Church Choir.

MORAN, SCOTT; Colegio San Ignacio De Loyola HS; Rio Piedras, PR; (Y); Cmnty Wkr; Model UN; Temple Yth Grp; Var Capt Ftbl; Semi Fnlst-Ntl Hspncs Schlrshp Awd Pgm 85-86; 2nd Pl US Drwng Cntst 84; Trphs-Ftbl 85; Law.

MORENO, DEMETRIO; Antilles HS; Ft Buchanan, PR; (Y); Band; Jazz Band; Crs Cntry; Socr; Trk; High Hon Roll; Hon Roll; Jr NHS; NHS; Officer.

MUDAFORT, MARIA; Colegio Madre Cabrini HS; Guaynabo, PR; (S); Art Clb; Yrbk Stf; Jr NHS; NHS; 1st Pl Microbio Prjct Scintfc Fair 84; Spnsh, Engl, Bio Merits 84; Alg, Sci Merits 83; Cmnctns.

MUNOZ, IRMA M CURBELO; Colegio San Antonio HS; Quebradillas, PR; (S); 1/33; Drama Clb; English Clb; 4-H; Sec Leo Clb; Science Clb; Spanish Clb; Chorus; Pres Frsh Cls; Pres Soph Cls; Rep Stu Cncl; Sci Awds 84-85; Good Conduct Awds 80-85; Stu Cncl Awd 84-85; U Puerto Rico; Odontolgy.

NEGRON, DIANA; Baldwin Schl; Guaynabo, PR; (Y); Hosp Aide; Math Clb; Math Tm; Scholastic Bowl; Yrbk Stf; Pres Jr Cls; Pres Stu Cncl; Bsktbl; Cit Awd; High Hon Roll; Chem.

NUNEZ, ADALGISA RIVERA; Eloisa Pascual HS; Caguas, PR; (S); Church Yth Grp; DECA; Girl Scts; Math Clb; Speech Tm; Cheerleading; NHS; Arch.

OCASIO, WENDELL; Immaculate Conception Acad; Mayaguez, PR; (Y); 1/94; Nwsp Ed-Chief; Pres Stu Cncl; Ntl Merit Schol; Pres Schlr; Val; Boy Scts; VP JA; Model UN; Trs Science Clb; Nwsp Bus Mgr; Hall Of Fame 86; Fin Intl Sci & Engrng Fair 84; Harvard U; Physcn.

OCHOA-RODRIGUEZ, ISABENID I; Colegio Madre Cabrini HS; Rio Piedras, PR; (S); Chorus; Church Choir; Vllybl; NHS; Spanish NHS; 1st Pl Gold Mdl Sci Fair 84; Georgetown; Med.

OLAZAGASTI, MARIA T; Sagrado Corazon Acad; Carolina, PR; (S); 6/68; Speech Tm; Stage Crew; Nwsp Stf; NHS; Stu Of Mnth JR & Sphmr 85; Algbr Awd 85.

ORLANDI, JOSE A; Cupeyville Schl; Rio Piedras, PR; (Y); 2/54; VP Math Clb; Nwsp Stf; Tennis; Rep Jr NHS; Pres NHS; Sal; Val; Math Awd 83 & 86; Sci Awd 83; Pres Clsrm Yng Amer 85; Lehigh U; Engrng.

ORTIZ, ELKA; Colegio San Jose HS; San German, PR; (Y); Art Clb; Church Yth Grp; Cmnty Wkr; Girl Scts; Library Aide; Red Cross Aide; Scholastic Bowl; Science Clb; Chorus; School Musical; Coll Of Ag-Mech Art; Engr Comp.

ORTIZ, MANUEL; Academia Sagrado Corazon HS; Carolina, PR; (S); 1/68; VP Jr Cls; Rep Stu Cncl; Var Bsktbl; NHS; Spanish NHS; Fresh Stu Of Year 84; Spelling & Fire Drill Clb 85-86; U Of PR; Elec Engrng.

ORTIZ, MARIBEL; Colegio Santa Rita HS; Bayamon, PR; (S); Art Clb; Chorus; Nwsp Phtg; Nwsp Stf; Prfct Atten Awd; Schl Svc.

ORTIZ, ROSANA M; Saint Joseph Clg; Lajas, PR; (Y); Art Clb; Civic Clb; Leo Clb; Red Cross Aide; Off Soph Cls; Rep Stu Cncl; Wt Lftg; High Hon Roll; Phillips Acad Smmr Ssns Schlrshp At Andover Bstn 86; Princeton U; Snd Engrng.

OTERO, MARIA I; Academia Santa Monica; Santurce, PR; (S); 3/67; Chess Clb; French Clb; JA; Chorus; Spanish NHS.

OYOLA, MAUREEN; Colegio Nuestra Sra Del Pilar; Rio Piedras, PR; (Y); 1/179; Pres Math Clb; Math Tm; Service Clb; Yrbk Stf; High Hon Roll; Trs Jr NHS; NHS; Ntl Merit SF; Pres Schlr; Library Aide; Pres Acad Ftns Awd 86; Hgst Score PR PAA Test 85; Schls Tm Schlstc 85; Biomed.

PABON, ANTONIO; Inmaculate Conception Acad; Mayaquez, PR; (S); Church Yth Grp; Drama Clb; Model UN; Spanish Clb; School Play; Variety Show; Nwsp Rptr; Nwsp Stf; Yrbk Stf; Rep Frsh Cls; Stu Yr 84; Ntl Model Un 85; Pres Clsrm Yng Am 86; Psychlgy.

PADILLA, MARTA LUZ; Colegio Ponceno HS; Guayanilla, PR; (Y); Church Yth Grp; Office Aide; Band; Chorus; Church Choir; Concert Band; Mrchg Band; Variety Show; Rep Stu Cncl; Vllybl; Altrnt Rep Of Yr 86; Sngr Of Yr 86; Ms Smpthy-Schl-TV Pgm 86; Colegio Regional-UPR; Med Tech.

PADILLA, MYRIAM E RODRIGUEZ; Santa Rita Coll; Bayamon, PR; (S); Drama Clb; Math Clb; Teachers Aide; Jr NHS; NHS; U Puerto Rico; Med.

PADILLA, NATALIE; Colegio San Jose HS; San German, PR; (Y); Art Clb; Church Yth Grp; Civic Clb; Drama Clb; Letterman Clb; Teachers Aide; Varsity Clb; VP Soph Cls; VP Capt Bsktbl; Var Trk; Miss Co Legio By Stu Body 85-86; U Of Puerto Rico; Marine Bio.

PADILLA, OLGA; Inmaculate Conception Acad; Mayaguez, PR; (S); Drama Clb; English Clb; German Clb; JA; Spanish Clb; Yrbk Stf; Pres Soph Cls; Rep Stu Cncl; Pres NHS; AICS Hall Of Fame 86; Acad All Amer 86; Pres Clsrm Yng Amer 85.

PEDROSA, IVETTE; Sacred Heart Acad; Santurce, PR; (S); 10/71; Drama Clb; VP JA; NFL; Red Cross Aide; Teachers Aide; Chorus; Nwsp Stf; Stu Cncl; NHS; Philadelphia Clg; Fash Merch.

PENA, MARY; Academia San Jose HS; Guaynabo, PR; (Y); 7/128; Art Clb; Debate Tm; Drama Clb; French Clb; NFL; VP Speech Tm; NHS; School Play; Stage Crew; Cheerleading; Chem.

PEREZ, EULALIA; Colegio Madre Cabrini; Guaynabo, PR; (S); Art Clb; Drama Clb; Nwsp Stf; Yrbk Stf; Sec Frsh Cls; Jr NHS; Spn Sci & Eng 83; Sci Fair 1st Prz Spn 84; Comm.

PEREZ OYOLA, JOHANA; Manuela Toro Morice HS; Caguas, PR; (S); 5/258; NHS; Acad All-Amer 85; PR U; Mgr.

QUINONES, TERESITA; Rafael Aparicio Jimenez HS; Adjuntas, PR; (Y); Med.

RAFOLS, ALBERTO; Colegio San Antonio HS; Isabela, PR; (Y); 5/35; Art Clb; Boy Scts; Drama Clb; English Clb; Science Clb; Spanish Clb; Swmmng; Tennis; Cit Awd; Ordr Arrow 84; Scout Ldrshp Awd 84; Stu Yr 84-85; CAAM; CPA.

RAMIREZ, JOSE R; Colegio San Antonio HS; Isabela, PR; (Y); Chess Clb; Computer Clb; Debate Tm; Drama Clb; Intnl Clb; Math Clb; Math Tm; Science Clb; Spanish Clb; Variety Show; Hnr 86; Soc, Ed, Hnr, Spt & Artistc Awd 86; CAAM; Engrng.

RAMIREZ, VANESSA; Immaculate Conception Acad; Mayaguez, PR; (S); Model UN; Science Clb; Spanish Clb; School Musical; Variety Show; Cheerleading; Trk; High Hon Roll; Sec Frsh Cls; U Puerto Rico; Acctng.

RAMIREZ GUEVARA, JOSE R; Colegio San Antonio HS; Isabela, PR; (S); 1/5; Art Clb; Church Yth Grp; Debate Tm; Drama Clb; Math Clb; Science Clb; Variety Show; Sr Cls; Bsbl; Bsktbl; Hnr 82-85; Engr.

RAMOS, CALIR; Colegio Santa Rita HS; Rexville Bayamon, PR; (S); Church Yth Grp; Drama Clb; Office Aide; Teachers Aide; Church Choir; High Hon Roll; NHS; Lit Awd 85; U Puerto Rico; Med.

RASCO, MAILE; Academia Sagrado Cerazon; Santurce, PR; (S); 1/69; Drama Clb; JA; NFL; Speech Tm; School Play; Variety Show; Nwsp Rptr; Rep Stu Cncl; Jr NHS; NHS; Class Fav; Boston U; Diplmcy.

RESTITUYO, JOSE A; Colegio Santa Rita HS; Bayamon, PR; (S); 10/98; Math Clb; Var Bsktbl; NHS; Spanish NHS; U PR; Med.

REYES, EVELYN; Ramon Power Giralt HS; Las Piedras, PR; (Y); Church Yth Grp; FBLA; Chorus; MA; Airln Attndt.

RIERA, JOSE; Colegio San Ignacio De Loyola HS; Condado, PR; (Y); Church Yth Grp; Pres English Clb; Pres French Clb; Pres NFL; Spanish Clb; Stu Cncl; Capt Var Crs Cntry; Capt Var Trk; NHS; Sec Camera Clb; LEAD Pgm Bus 85; Georgetown U; Bus Adm.

RIOS, CARMEN; Antilles HS; Ft Buchanan, PR; (Y); Spanish Clb; Swing Chorus; Crs Cntry; Mgr(s); Powder Puff Ftbl; Trk; Hon Roll; NHS; Cptn Pwdr Puff 85-86; Cptn Trck 85-86; Cptn Crs-Cntry 85-86; Spts Med.

RIVERA, ALEXANDER; Antilles HS; Hato Rey, PR; (Y); 6/107; Key Clb; Library Aide; Scholastic Bowl; Band; Concert Band; Mrchg Band; Var Ftbl; Var Wrstlng; High Hon Roll; NHS; Natl Hspnc Schlr Awds Hnrb Mntn 86; PR Coll Board Tsts Top 100 Stu 86; Acad All-Amer; U Of PR; Elec Engr.

RIVERA, CARLOS A; Colegio San Antonio HS; Quebradillas, PR; (S); 4/31; Art Clb; Church Yth Grp; Math Tm; Science Clb; School Play; Trk; High Hon Roll; Hon Roll; Cooprtn Awd 85; Sci Fair Awd 82-84; Hstry Awd 83; NY Inst Tech; Aerosp Engrng.

RIVERA, GUSTAVO E; Colegio San Ignacio De Loyola HS; Gurabo, PR; (Y); Cmnty Wkr; Hosp Aide; Science Clb; Hon Roll; Ntl Merit SF; Pres Schlr; Amhrst Coll; Med.

RIVERA, ILEANA; Academia Inmaculada Concepc; Hormigueros, PR; (S); 17/92; Art Clb; Drama Clb; Spanish Clb; Chorus; Rep Frsh Cls; Sec Soph Cls; Rep Jr Cls; Sec Sr Cls; Stu Cncl; U Of PR; Mktg.

RIVERA, MILTON A; Immaculate Conception Acad; Mayaguez, PR; (S); 22/94; Boy Scts; Drama Clb; Pres JA; Spanish Clb; Chorus; Stu Cncl; Hon Roll; Trs NHS; Art Clb; 1st Pl VP Fin 84; Best Spkr Spnsh 85-86; Bus Adm.

RIVERA, SHEILA LEE; Southwestern Educational Society; Mayaguez, PR; (S); JA; Spanish Clb; Variety Show; Yrbk Stf; Trs Frsh Cls; Trs Soph Cls; Trs Jr Cls; Rep Stu Cncl; Hon Roll; 1st Prz Stu Govt Day 85; Spnsh Cmptn 1st Prz 84; Bus.

RIVERA, VALENTIN; Colegio Marista HS; Guaynabo, PR; (Y); 7/82; Cmnty Wkr; Computer Clb; Math Clb; Yrbk Phtg; Yrbk Stf; Var Bsktbl; Hon Roll; NHS; Spanish NHS; Engl, Sci, Conduct Mdls 86; 2nd Hnr Mdl 86; Cornell U.

RIVERA, WANDA; Ramon Power Givalt HS; Las Piedras, PR; (Y).

RIVERA-GIUSTI, JUAN ANGEL; Antilles HS; San Juan, PR; (Y); 46/115; Aud/Vis; Drama Clb; JA; Key Clb; Pep Clb; Q&S; Concert Band; Mrchg Band; Stage Crew; Lit Mag; Antilles Consldtd Schl System Comp Fair 1st Prz Graphics Category 85; Pabb Casais Museum 84; Arch.

RIVERO, LUIS RAUL; Academia Perpetuo Socorro; Rio Piedras, PR; (Y); 10/95; Art Clb; Cmnty Wkr; Computer Clb; French Clb; JA; Math Clb; Science Clb; Teachers Aide; Trs Frsh Cls; High Hon Roll; Stdnt Mnth Awd Sept 82; Hghst Grd Awd Frnch I, Bio, Engl 10 84; Hghst Grd Awd Chem I, Algbr II 85; Dentistry.

ROBLES, AWILDA; Luis Munoz Marin HS; Cabo Rojo, PR; (S); Church Yth Grp; Dance Clb; Pres DECA; Drama Clb; Pres FHA; Sec Jr Cls; Cit Awd; Masonic Awd; Yth Of Mnth Exchng Clb Cabo Rojo 84; Interamerican U Of PR; Dctrt.

ROBLES, JOSE JUAN; Colegio San Jose HS; San German, PR; (Y); Boy Scts; Rep Jr Cls; Rep Stu Cncl; Bsktbl; Swmmng; Hon Roll; Hnr Gmtry 86; Hnr Awd Algbr II & Algbr I 85; Hnr Awd Algb I 84; CCAM; Indstrl Engr.

RODRIGUEZ, EMILIA M; Academia Santa Monica; Puerto Nuevo, PR; (S); 4/51; Library Aide; Teachers Aide; Chorus; High Hon Roll; Cath Knights Ins Soc Schlrp 82-86; U PR; Nrsng.

RODRIGUEZ, LIZA I; Colegio Espiritu Santo HS; Rio Piedras, PR; (Y); 4/87; Church Yth Grp; Natl Beta Clb; Variety Show; Nwsp Stf; VP Stu Cncl; Var JV Sftbl; Var JV Vllybl; Hon Roll; Natl Hispnc Schnlrs Awd 85-86; A Pres Clsrm Yng Amer 86; ARTS Rcgntn & Tlnt Srch 85; U Of Puerto Rico; Comp Lit.

RODRIGUEZ, MARISOL; Wesleyan Acad; R P, PR; (Y); 24/50; Computer Clb; JA; Teachers Aide; School Musical; School Play; Yrbk Stf; Sftbl; Tennis; Hon Roll; Pres Schlr; Marquette Acad; Acctng.

ROLON, JOSE; Colegio San Jose HS; Rio Piedras, PR; (Y); 3/84; Cmnty Wkr; VP JA; Math Tm; Trs Model UN; Rep Stu Cncl; Crs Cntry; Pres Schlr; 1st Plc Schl Sci Fr 84; Spcl Chrctr Hnrs 85; Hnr Crtfct All Crs 84; Arspc Engnrng.

ROMAN, ISABEL M; Colegio San Antonio HS; Quebradillas, PR; (S); 1/26; Church Yth Grp; FHA; Math Clb; Chorus; Trs Frsh Cls; Pres Jr Cls; VP Sr Cls; Rep Stu Cncl; Hon Roll; Jr NHS; Sci Fair-2nd Pl Hlth 84; Natl Hnr Soc Sec 84; Natl Hnr Soc Histrn 85; U Of Bayamon; Psych.

ROMERO, YOLANDA; Colegio San Jose HS; Mayaguez, PR; (Y); Church Yth Grp; Debate Tm; Drama Clb; Girl Scts; Chorus; Church Choir; School Play; Rep Frsh Cls; Pres Soph Cls; Rep Stu Cncl; Coop Awd 86; 2nd Pl Awd Fld Day 86; U Of PR; Publ Rel.

ROSA, LILLIAN; Academia Santa Monica; Bayamon, PR; (S); 3/51; Church Yth Grp; Drama Clb; French Clb; Chorus; Yrbk Stf; Lit Mag; High Hon Roll; Hon Roll; Pres NHS; UC Berkeley; Chem Engrng.

ROSADO FLORES, LORNA M; Manuela Toro HS; Caguas, PR; (S); FHA; Pres Sr Cls; High Hon Roll; NHS; Math Awd; U De Puerto Rico; Lawyer.

ROSARIO, LUIS G; Central De Bellas Artes; Country Club, PR; (Y); Art Clb; English Clb; Arts Recog & Tlnt Srch Hnbl Mntn 85-86; Pratt Arch Natl Talnt Srch Fnlst 86; U Of Puerto Rico; Arch.

ROSARIO, SANDRA LEE ROSA; Manuela Toro Morice HS; Caguas, PR; (S); 8/258; FHA; Varsity Clb; Trk; Vllybl; NHS; U Sagrado Corazon; Strst.

ROSARIO, VELMA; Immaculada Concepcion HS; Mayaguez, PR; (Y); Church Yth Grp; English Clb; JA; Model UN; Speech Tm; Chorus; Variety Show; Pol Sci.

RUBIO, MILAGROS MARIA; Academia Santa Monica HS; Carolina, PR; (S); 8/51; Church Yth Grp; Drama Clb; Library Aide; Teachers Aide; Chorus; Church Choir; NHS; Library Clb Awd 84-85; U PR; Med.

RUIZ, CARMEN M; Colegio San Antonio HS; Quebradillas, PR; (S); 5/26; Church Yth Grp; Computer Clb; Science Clb; Acpl Chr; Church Choir; Bsktbl; 4-H Awd; NHS; Alto Hnr 84; High Hnr Relign Spn Prfct Asstnce & Major Promedis Mdls 83; CUTA; Med.

RUIZ, WILFRIDO; Bernardino Cordero Bernard HS; Ponce, PR; (Y); VICA; Acpl Chr; Band; Chorus; Church Choir; Concert Band; Jazz Band; Mrchg Band; Swing Chorus; Off Sr Cls; Mscn.

RUIZ SAN MILLAN, MINNKA; Robinson HS; Santurce, PR; (S); 3/32; Pres Math Clb; Var Bsktbl; JV Crs Cntry; JV Trk; Var Vllybl; High Hon Roll; Jr NHS; Trs NHS; Jesus Coll-Cambridge; Bio.

RUSSE, ZAHYRA; Academia Sagrado Corazon HS; Bayamon, PR; (S); 5/75; Computer Clb; Drama Clb; JA; Red Cross Aide; Chorus; Nwsp Stf; Rep Stu Cncl; Badmtn; Sec VP NHS; Intl Swmmng Compt-Puerto Rico 83-85; Grammar Awd 83; U Of Puerto Rico; Acctng.

SALLABERRY, CAROL; St Therese Acad; Santurce, PR; (Y); VP Art Clb; VP Drama Clb; Natl Beta Clb; Science Clb; Stage Crew; Cmnty Wkr; Sec Yrbk Stf; Sec Frsh Cls; Hon Roll; Ntl Merit SF; Lit Cntst 3rd Pl 85; Schlrshp Caparra Commrcl Corp 86; Creatv Wrtg.

SANABRIA-CARLO, DAVID I; Santa Rita HS; Bayamon, PR; (Y); 4/96; Math Clb; Yrbk Phtg; Yrbk Stf; Pres Sr Cls; VP Stu Cncl; NHS; Electrcl Engr.

SANCHEZ AGRINSONI, JUAN A; Manuela Toro Morice HS; Caguas, PR; (S); 5/315; Church Yth Grp; Pres Jr Cls; VP Stu Cncl; Bsbl; Bsktbl; Pres Schlr; Val; Ldrshp Awd 84; Church Awd 84; U Puerto Rico; Acctg.

SANCHEZ VEGA, MAGALY; Manuela Toro Morice HS; Caguas, PR; (S); 11/258; NHS; PR U; Pharm.

SANTIAGO, OLGA; Ramey Schl; Mayaguez, PR; (Y); 2/13; Church Yth Grp; NFL; Quiz Bowl; Yrbk Phtg; Sec Sr Cls; VP Stu Cncl; Mgr(s); Jr NHS; Sec NHS; Sal; Pres Schlr 86; Natl Hispnc Schlr Pgm 86.

SANTONI, ANGELES M; Inmaculada Concepcion Aced; Mayaquez, PR; (S); Drama Clb; GAA; Science Clb; Service Clb; School Musical; Variety Show; Off Soph Cls; Off Jr Cls; JV Gym; Stu Clss Of Yr Awd 85-86; U Of PR.

SANTOS, MARIA IVELISSE; Colegio Madre Cabrini HS; Levittown Lakes, PR; (S); Spanish Clb; Chorus; School Musical; School Play; Variety Show; Trs Frsh Cls; VP Jr Cls; Jr NHS; NHS; U Of Puerto Rico; Actg.

SANTOS SAURI, KARIN; Manuzla Toro HS; Caguas, PR; (S); Church Yth Grp; High Hon Roll; NHS; U Of PR.

SANZ, GABRIEL; Colegio Marista HS; Guaynabo, PR; (Y); 4/82; Cmnty Wkr; Model UN; Pres NFL; Nwsp Ed-Chief; Pres NHS; Boy Scts; Debate Tm; JA; Trs Spanish Clb; Speech Tm; Phlsphy.

SCHMELZ, CHARLES E; Baldwin Schl Of PR; Dorado, PR; (S); Cmnty Wkr; Math Tm; Science Clb; Yrbk Ed-Chief; High Hon Roll; NHS; Ntl Merit SF; Pres Schlr; VP Frsh Cls; VP Jr Cls; Geophyscs.

SEDA, AIDA; Imaculate Conception Acad; Mayaguez, PR; (S); 6/119; Church Yth Grp; Drama Clb; JA; Math Tm; Science Clb; Service Clb; Chorus; School Play; Mgr Jr Cls; NHS; Vet.

SEDA, ERICK; Immaculate Conception Acad; Hormigueros, PR; (S); JA; VP Science Clb; Sec Spanish Clb; Chorus; Pres School Musical; Nwsp Stf; Sec Stu Cncl; Cit Awd; Hon Roll; NHS; Hall Of Fame/Mst Outstndng Stu 85-86; Tlntd Mnrty Schlrshp To U MA 86-87; U MA; Htl/Rstrnt Adm.

SERRANO, LARISSA M; Academia San Jose; Rio Piedras, PR; (Y); 17/227; Debate Tm; Drama Clb; Sec Spanish Clb; Teachers Aide; Rep Stu Cncl; Hon Roll; Jr NHS; NHS; Math Concpts Schlrshp 86; TX Tech; Mktg.

SILVA, GUILLERMO; San Ignacio De Loyola Schl; Guaynabo, PR; (Y); Cmnty Wkr; Varsity Clb; Nwsp Rptr; Yrbk Sprt Ed; Sec Frsh Cls; Var Bsktbl; Var Capt Vllybl; Hon Roll; Camera Clb; Letterman Clb; Lead Pgm Wharton Schl U PA 85; Puerto Rico Athltc Alliance Vlybl All Star 85; SF Ntl Hispanic Pgm 85; Bio.

SMALLWOOD, JENNIFER; Robinson HS; Dorado, PR; (Y); Church Yth Grp; Drama Clb; Pres Latin Clb; Office Aide; Pep Clb; SADD; Church Choir; School Play; Nwsp Stf; Var Bsktbl; Outstndng Latin Stu 85; Outstndng Englsh Schlr 86; Englsh.

SOMOZA, RAFAEL; Immaculate Conception Acad; San Juan, PR; (S); JA; VP Model UN; Science Clb; Service Clb; Rep Jr Cls; VP Sr Cls; Rep Stu Cncl; Drama Clb; Variety Show; Im Bsbl; 2nd Prz Sci Fair 85; US Dept Engry Awd 85; Pres Clsrm Yng Am Proj 86; U PA; Bus.

SOSA CRUZ, CARMEN I; Manuela Toro Morice HS; Caguas, PR; (S); Science Clb; NHS; Math, Engl, Socl Stds, Spnsh & Sci Hnrs 84; Magna Cum Laude 84; Engrng.

SOTO, RAFAEL; Colegio Santa Rita HS; Sieerra Bayamon, PR; (S); Yrbk Rptr; Yrbk Stf; Im JV Bsktbl; 1st Pl Talent Show 84; Prsdntl Clssroom 85-86; U Of Puerto Rico; Engr.

SOTO PAZ, LUZ E; Alcides Fiqueroa HS; Anasco, PR; (Y); Dance Clb; Drama Clb; Leo Clb; Pgm Dir Plaque PR Island Ballet, Mst Outstndng Trophy 86; Arts Rcgntn /Tlnt Srch Cert 86; U PR.

TIRADO, MARITZA; Immaculate Conception Acad; Mayaguez, PR; (Y); Drama Clb; Model UN; Service Clb; Univeru Sagrado Corazon; Publcs.

TIRADO RIOS, NIDIA; Manuela Toro Morice HS; Caquas, PR; (S); 7/30; Science Clb; Teachers Aide; NHS.

TORO, GWENDOLYN; Colegio San Jose; San German, PR; (Y); JA; Colegio De Ag Arts Mcncs; Vet.

TORRES, SANDRA VAZQUEZ; Eloisa Pascual Bairoa 111 HS; Caguas, PR; (S); Church Yth Grp; DECA; Math Clb; Capt Vllybl; Arch.

TORRES MEJIAS, JANNETTE; Manvela Toro HS; Caguas, PR; (S); 5/257; Camera Clb; VP FHA; Science Clb; Chorus; VP Sr Cls; Hon Roll; NHS; 1st Prz Spllg Bee 83; Col De Mayaguez; Chem Engrg.

TRAXLER, DAVID KEVANE; Colegio San Ignacio De Loyola; Rio Piedras, PR; (Y); Drama Clb; NFL; Nwsp Ed-Chief; Yrbk Ed-Chief; Ntl Hispanc Merit Semifnlst 85; 3rd Pl Oratory-Forn Comptn 84; NY Jesuit 1 Act Ply Comp-Hnrbl Mntn 84.

TULLA, MIGUEL; Colegio Espiritau Santo HS; Hato Rey, PR; (Y); Church Yth Grp; Sec Debate Tm; Library Aide; Math Clb; Math Tm; Sec Model UN; Q&S; Science Clb; Chorus; School Play; GA Inst Of Tech; Elec Engr.

VALLE, JOSE; Colegie San Ignacio De Loyola HS; Rio Piedras, PR; (Y); 5/125; Boy Scts; Math Clb; Model UN; Varsity Clb; Rep Soph Cls; Im Stat Bsktbl; Bowling; Score Keeper; L Swmmng; Tennis; Pres Acadmc Fit Awd 86; Cornell U; Biomed Engrng.

VELAZQUEZ CALDERON, LIANABEL; Francisco Velazquez Flroes HS; Caguas, PR; (S); 8/319; Vllybl; Universidad; Contbldad.

VELEZ, CARMEN; Academia Santa Monica; Bayamon, PR; (S); 2/52; Church Yth Grp; Drama Clb; JA; Service Clb; Church Choir; NHS; Hgh Hnr Of Class 82; 1st Hnr 83; Princpls Lst 84-85; U PR; Pharm.

VELEZ, MAYRA; Academia Del Sagrado Corazon; Carolina, PR; (S); Aud/Vis; Church Yth Grp; Civic Clb; Library Aide; Science Clb; Stu Cncl; Roberto Clemente Prz-1st Hnr 84; Ldrshp, Hstry & Sci Medls-1st Hnr 84; 1st Hnr-Algbr, Bio & Eng 85; U Of PR; MD.

VELEZ GOMEZ, MARISOL; Manuela Toro Morice; Gurabo, PR; (S); 6/315; Church Yth Grp; NHS; U Turabo; Contable.

VIDAL, JOSE; Marista HS; Guaynabo, PR; (Y); 5/83; Cmnty Wkr; Computer Clb; Math Clb; Math Tm; Nwsp Stf; Jr NHS; NHS; Natl Hspnc Schlrshp 86; ITT Schlrshp 86; MA Inst Of Tech; Elect Engrng.

VIDAL, LUIS M; University Of Puerto Ricos HS; Rio Piedras, PR; (Y); 6/86; Band; Concert Band; School Play; Rep Frsh Cls; Im Vllybl; Hon Roll; NHS; Ntl Merit SF; Pres Schlr; Cornell U Smmr Coll Pgm Schlrshp 85; Arch.

YANG, WEI-LI; Robinson HS; Isla Verde, PR; (Y); 9/30; Church Yth Grp; Computer Clb; Math Clb; Math Tm; Variety Show; Var Cheerleading; Var Trk; Hon Roll; NHS; Robinson Schl Awd 86; P E Aeds 85-86; Spnsh Awd 84; Fairleigh Dickinson U.

ZABALA, SANDRA; Antilles HS; Ft Buchanan, PR; (Y); Pres Rep Drama Clb; Sec Sr Cls; Rep Stu Cncl; Var L Crs Cntry; Var L Trk; JV L Vllybl; High Hon Roll; Hon Roll; NHS; Minrty Intrdctn Engnrng-US Coast Guard Acad 86.

ZAYAS, ANA; Colegio San Jose HS; Mayaguez, PR; (Y); Hosp Aide; JA; Math Tm; OEA; Scholastic Bowl; Orch; Symp Band; Variety Show; Lit Mag; Bsktbl; RUM; Medicine.

RHODE ISLAND

ABATO, STACEY J; St Marys Acad; N Kingstown, RI; (Y); Girl Scts; Hosp Aide; Chorus; Church Choir; School Play; Variety Show; Rep Stu Cncl; High Hon Roll; Sci Expo 86; Robotics Proj 86; Acad Schlrshp; Pre-Law.

ABBATE, CHARLES; Bishop Hendricken HS; Warwick, RI; (Y); 18/240; Chess Clb; Cmnty Wkr; Math Tm; Teachers Aide; Rep Sr Cls; Im Mgr Bowling; JV Trk; High Hon Roll; NHS; Math Clb; Acptd Rswl Pk Smr Sci Prgm 86; Hmcmng Chrmn 86-87; Cls Mxr Chrmn 87; Dntstry.

ABBRUZZI, DIANA; Johnston HS; Johnston, RI; (S); 5/216; DECA; Co-Capt Drm Mjr(t); Yrbk Stf; French Hon Soc; High Hon Roll; Hon Roll; NHS; RI Hon Soc 86; Bio.

ABBY, TINA; Chariho Regional HS; Hope Valley, RI; (Y); Girl Scts; Hon Roll; Bus.

ABRAMES, HEATHER; St Mary Academy Bay View; Providence, RI; (Y); Drama Clb; French Clb; Math Tm; SADD; Stage Crew; Rep Stu Cncl; High Hon Roll; Hon Roll; NHS; NEDT Awd; Smith Coll Bk Awd 86; Acadmc Al-Amer 84; Bay Vw Hnr Soc 85; Art.

ABUELO, CHRISTINA; Barrington HS; Barrington, RI; (Y); French Clb; GAA; Pres Intnl Clb; Math Tm; Nwsp Rptr; Nwsp Stf; Yrbk Ed-Chief; Yrbk Phtg; Lit Mag; JV Fld Hcky; Math Lge Hghst Scrng Frshmn 84; Brown U.

ADAMO, KRISTEN; St Marys Academy Bayview; Warwick, RI; (Y); Exploring; Nwsp Rptr; Hon Roll; NHS; Itln Clb; Svc Awd Bay View 85-86; In Site 85; Jrnlsm.

ADAMS, ANNE-MARIE; Woonsocket SR HS; Woonsocket, RI; (Y); 1/460; VP Math Tm; High Hon Roll; NHS; Pres Schlr; St Schlr; Val; Holy Cross Bk Awd Eng 85; Germaine B Tougas Awd Frnch 83; Gold Medal Ntl Latin Ex 83; Brown U; Civil Engr.

ADAMS, GLEN; Pilgrim HS; Warwick, RI; (Y); Church Yth Grp; Computer Clb; Ski Clb; Bus.

ADAMS, JILL; Classical HS; Providence, RI; (Y); 11/261; Hon Roll; Cum Laude Soc 86; 3rd Ntl 10k Swm 85; ST Chmpn Rcrd Hldr 100 Yrd Bckstrk 84; South Coll; Bio.

ADRIANCE, HEATHER; North Kingstown SR HS; N Kingstown, RI; (Y); 20/359; Cmnty Wkr; Drama Clb; Hosp Aide; VP Service Clb; Color Guard; Mrchg Band; Rep Jr Cls; Rep Stu Cncl; JV Capt Vllybl; DAR Awd; RI Ambssdr Hgh O Brn Yth Fndtn 85; Bus.

AGUIAR, LORRI; Burrillville JR SR HS; Pascoag, RI; (Y); Ed Yrbk Stf; Stu Cncl; High Hon Roll; Hon Roll; Drftng.

AIDALA, RICHARD; Mt St Charles HS; Chepachet, RI; (S); 12/142; Math Clb; Rep Jr Cls; Rep Sr Cls; Var Capt Tennis; High Hon Roll; NHS; Providence Coll.

AKERS, RONALD; Rogers HS; Newport, RI; (Y); Chess Clb; 4-H; Red Cross Aide; Science Clb; Ftbl; High Hon Roll; NHS; Roger Williams Coll; Med.

ALEXANDER, WILLIAM; Portsmouth HS; Portsmouth, RI; (Y); 19/200; High Hon Roll; Hon Roll; NHS; Transcom Engrng Schlrshp 86; Work Exprnc Pgm 86; U Of RI; Comp Engrng.

ALFANO, NANCY; East Providence HS; E Prov, RI; (Y); Church Yth Grp; Girl Scts; Band; Chorus; VP Jr Cls; Stu Cncl; Var Cheerleading; NHS; Val; Hrvrd Book Awd 86; Archtchr.

ALLAM, AMY; Woonsocket HS; Woonsocket, RI; (Y); Am Leg Aux Girls St; Hosp Aide; Math Tm; Yrbk Rptr; High Hon Roll; Hon Roll; NHS; MA Coll Pharmacy; Phrmcy.

ALLAN, CATHERINE; South Kingstown HS; Wakefield, RI; (Y); 21/230; Cmnty Wkr; German Clb; Hosp Aide; SADD; Nwsp Rptr; Nwsp Stf; Yrbk Rptr; Yrbk Stf; Tennis; NHS; Excl Comptr Sci II 11th Grd; Chem.

ALLARD, R SCOTT; Mt St Charles Acad; Woonsocket, RI; (S); Band; Concert Band; Jazz Band; High Hon Roll; Bus.

ALLSWORTH, JENIFER; Pilgrim HS; Warwick, RI; (Y); VP JA; Math Clb; Math Tm; Ed Yrbk Stf; Off Frsh Cls; Off Soph Cls; Off Jr Cls; Stat Fld Hcky; High Hon Roll; Harvard Alum Bk Awd 86; RI Tchrs Italn Cert Merit 84-86; U RI Distngshd Faclty Schlrshp 86; Engrng.

ALMEIDA, AMYBETH; St Raphael Acad; Pawtucket, RI; (Y); Hosp Aide; Ski Clb; Spanish Clb; SADD; Yrbk Stf; Trs Frsh Cls; VP Jr Cls; Var Sftbl; Var Vllybl; Hon Roll; Providence Coll; Law.

ALMEIDA, JEAN; St Mary Acad Bay View; E Providence, RI; (Y); 85/210; Church Yth Grp; Exploring; French Clb; Girl Scts; Model UN; Ski Clb; Crs Cntry; Cit Awd; Hon Roll; Ctznshp Awd, Schl Svc Awd 85; Marine Bio.

AMALFITANO, JULIE; Cranston West HS; Cranston, RI; (Y); Cmnty Wkr; VP GAA; SADD; VP Stu Cncl; JV Var Bsktbl; Capt Crs Cntry; Var Fld Hcky; Sftbl; Capt Trk; Cit Awd; Ocean ST Girls Bsktbl-Outstndng Player 84 & 85; Psych.

AMARAL, RICK; Bristol HS; Bristol, RI; (Y); 30/200; JA; Math Tm; Ski Clb; SADD; Yrbk Bus Mgr; Var L Lcrss; Var L Tennis; High Hon Roll; Jr NHS; NHS; Embry-Riddle; Aeronaut Engrng.

AMARAL, TERRY; East Providence SR HS; E Providence, RI; (Y); Aud/Vis; Library Aide; Stage Crew; Trk; Wt Lftg; Hon Roll; URI Bk Awd 86; Magna Cum Laude 82; Med.

AMEDEO, RONALD; Pilgrim HS; Warwick, RI; (Y); Jr NHS.

ANDERSON, DEB; Barrington HS; Barrington, RI; (Y); GAA; Sec Trs Intnl Clb; Trs Chorus; Yrbk Stf; JV Socr; High Hon Roll; NHS; Solo Ensmble Piano; Natl Piano Plyng Audtns; Natl Music Hnr Soc; Pre-Med.

ANDREOZZI, LYNNE; Mt St Charles HS; N Providence, RI; (Y); Church Yth Grp; GAA; L Score Keeper; Stat Socr; JV Sftbl; High Hon Roll; NHS; Boston Coll; Psych.

ANDREWS, NANCY; Lincoln JR SR HS; Lincoln, RI; (Y); 41/195; Pres Church Yth Grp; Hosp Aide; Yrbk Stf; Hon Roll; Elem Ed Tchr.

ANGELL, SUSAN; St Mary Acad Bay View; Providence, RI; (Y); 23/202; Church Yth Grp; Debate Tm; Drama Clb; Pep Clb; Yrbk Stf; Rep Frsh Cls; Rep Soph Cls; Rep Jr Cls; Sr Cls; Rep Stu Cncl; American U; Pol Sci.

ANTONELLI, LISA MARIE; La Salle Acad; Johnston, RI; (Y); Church Yth Grp; Drama Clb; Girl Scts; School Play; Stage Crew; Nwsp Stf; Yrbk Stf; Off Stu Cncl; Hon Roll; Occptnl Ther.

ANZIVINO, JACQUELINE; Mount Saint Charles Acad; N Providence, RI; (Y); Church Yth Grp; High Hon Roll; Hon Roll; Jr NHS; NHS; Bryant Coll; Acctng.

ARCAND, ANGELA M; Lincoln JR SR HS; Manville, RI; (Y); 44/181; FBLA; Office Aide; Sec Band; Trs Concert Band; Pres Mrchg Band; High Hon Roll; Hon Roll; Church Yth Grp; Rep Stu Cncl; Pres Schlr; FBLA ST Comptn-2nd Pl Typng 3rd Pl Acctng 86; FBLA Natl Conf-4th Pl Typng 86; CC Of RI Pres Schlr; CC Of RI; Acctng.

ARCAND, HELENE; St Marys Academy Bayview; Coventry, RI; (Y); 8/202; French Clb; Hosp Aide; Math Clb; Orch; Nwsp Stf; French Hon Soc; NHS; Pres Schlr; Exploring; Pep Clb; Acad All Amer Schlr; Franco-Amer Frnch Awd; Holy Cross Coll.

ARENDT, WILLIAM; Scituat JR & SR HS; North Scituate, RI; (S); 12/114; Band; Concert Band; Jazz Band; Mrchg Band; School Musical; School Play; Bsktbl; Trk; Jr NHS; NHS.

ARONSON, ROBIN; Classical HS; Providence, RI; (Y); VP French Clb; School Play; Yrbk Ed-Chief; Hon Roll; Ntl Merit Ltr; St Schlr; Joel Sheman Schlr Awd 85; Nthan Resnick Mem Awd 86; Barnard Coll.

ASHLEY, KELLY; Mt Pleasant HS; Providence, RI; (Y); Church Yth Grp; Hosp Aide; JA; Library Aide; Cheerleading; Gym; Var Capt Vllybl; Hon Roll; Pedtrc Nrsng.

ASTON, GRETCHEN; North Kingstown HS; Jamestown, RI; (Y); 45/380; Cmnty Wkr; French Clb; Chorus; Nwsp Rptr; Yrbk Phtg; Fld Hcky; Socr; Sftbl; French Hon Soc; Hon Roll; RI Hnr Soc 85-86; U RI; Pre-Med.

AUBIN, JOHN; Lincoln Junior-Senior HS; Manville, RI; (Y); 22/210; Rep Soph Cls; Rep Jr Cls; Rep Sr Cls; JV Ftbl; High Hon Roll; Prfct Atten Awd; Nw Englnd Inst Tech; Electrncs.

AUBUT, DIANE; Mt St Charles Acad; Franklin, MA; (S); 21/141; Var Gym; Mgr(s); High Hon Roll; Hon Roll; NHS; MVP Gymnstcs Tm 83-84; USGF Cls I MA ST Champ 85; Franklins Jr Miss 86; UNH.

AUSLANDER JR, GEORGE L; Narragansett HS; Narragansett, RI; (Y); 7/135; Debate Tm; Math Tm; NFL; Speech Tm; Socr; French Hon Soc; High Hon Roll; Hon Roll; NHS; Mariner Schlr Awd 84-85; Tufts U; Pre-Med.

AVERY, JESSICA V; Lincoln Schl; Barrington, RI; (Y); 1/65; German Clb; Latin Clb; Math Tm; Im Crs Cntry; Ntl Merit SF; Pell Medal Amer Hist 85; Wheeler Schlrshp 85; Rensselaer Math & Sci 85; Bio.

BABIEC JR, JOSEPH R; Cumberland HS; Cumberland, RI; (Y); 2/410; Am Leg Boys St; Trs Church Yth Grp; School Musical; Yrbk Stf; Capt Socr; High Hon Roll; Pres NHS; Voice Dem Awd; Aud/Vis; Drama Clb; Century III Ldrshp Comp ST Fnlst; All ST Chrs; R I Mdl Legis Spkr Of Hse; Engrng.

BABLENIS, KAREN; Cranston HS; Cranston, RI; (Y); 113/417; Sec Trs Church Yth Grp; Ski Clb; Spanish Clb; Yrbk Stf; Lit Mag; DECA; URI.

BACON, MARY ANN; Woonsocket HS; Woonsocket, RI; (Y); JV Trk; Hon Roll; RI Hnr Soc 86; St Josephs Coll; Bio.

BAEZ, YAMIL; Classical HS; Providence, RI; (Y); Church Yth Grp; Chorus; Hon Roll; Times Pgm 83-86; Bus.

BAGLEY, WILLIAM; Johnston SR HS; Johnston, RI; (Y); Var L Ftbl; Var Trk; Hon Roll; Ntl Hist Day Cntst 85; Bus Mgmt.

BAILEY, DAVID ROBERT; Cranston High School East; Cranston, RI; (Y); 1/387; Capt Computer Clb; Math Tm; Q&S; Concert Band; Mrchg Band; Ed Nwsp Stf; Yrbk Ed-Chief; Yrbk Phtg; Rep Stu Cncl; Bausch & Lomb Sci Awd; Crnll U Ntl Schlr 86; IBM Wtsn Schlr 86; Cornell U; Engnrng.

BAILLARGEON, MICHELLE; North Smithfield JR SR HS; Slatersville, RI; (Y); French Clb; VP Intnl Clb; Letterman Clb; VP SADD; Var L Bsktbl; Var L Tennis; Var L Vllybl; Hon Roll; Mvp Bsktbl Cpt; Womens Sprts Fndtn High Sch All-Star Awd; Chemistry.

BAKER, HALLIE; Chariho Regional JR SR HS; Charlestown, RI; (Y); 22/250; Drama Clb; Acpl Chr; Band; Chorus; Concert Band; School Musical; School Play; Yrbk Stf; High Hon Roll; Hon Roll; All St-Chorus 86; 1st Prz-Assn Of Schl Principals Essy Cntst 85; Painting.

BALL, CAROLYN; Middletown HS; Newport, RI; (Y); Church Yth Grp; Drama Clb; JA; Math Tm; Speech Tm; School Play; Var JV Socr; Capt Vllybl; Jr NHS; Chem Engrg.

BALLARD, HEATHER; Warwick Veterans Memorial HS; Warwick, RI; (Y); SADD; Var L Fld Hcky; Var L Vllybl; Hon Roll; Jr NHS; Pres 4-H; Band; Rep Stu Cncl; PHYSCL Therapy.

BANAHAN, HEATHER; Charibe Regional HS; Rockville, RI; (Y); 15/250; Church Yth Grp; Girl Scts; Band; Chorus; Church Choir; Bsktbl; Crs Cntry; Capt Trk; High Hon Roll; Hon Roll; All S Cnty & All Div Crss Cntry & Trck 84-86; 1st Pl Voctnl Comptn Marn Tech 85; Natl Baptst Conv 84; U Of RI.

BANKAUSKAS, KAREN; Toll Gate HS; Warwick, RI; (S); Letterman Clb; Var Capt Cheerleading; Var L Trk; Sci Fair Wnnr 83; Track-Frshmn States 3rd Pl 82; All-City Cheerldr 85.

BARBER, KRISTYNE; Chariho Regional HS; Carolina, RI; (Y); CCRI; Acctng.

BARBIERI, JOANNE; La Salle Acad; Providence, RI; (Y); Trs Church Yth Grp; Drama Clb; Pep Clb; Quiz Bowl; Var Cheerleading; Sftbl; Im Vllybl; Hon Roll; Rhode Island Coll; Law.

BAUTISTA, KEVIN; Portsmouth Abbey HS; Brooklyn, NY; (Y); 17/60; Church Yth Grp; Math Tm; Radio Clb; Stage Crew; JV Bsbl; JV Ftbl; JV Wrstlng; Pan Amer Medal Spnsh 85; Natl Hspnc Schlr Awd Semi-Fin 86; Columbia U; Doc.

BEARD, ARETHA; Central HS; Providence, RI; (Y); Hon Roll; Svg Bnd Frm Ctzns Bnk 86; Bryant Coll; Bus CPA.

BEATTY, MONIQUE; Hope HS; Providence, RI; (Y); Office Aide; Cheerleading; Sftbl; Trk; Cit Awd; Hon Roll; Martin Luther King Jr Spirit Day Awd 85; Mst Imprvd Athltc Awd 86; Trck Coach Assn Awd 86; Nrs.

BEAUDOIN, PAMELA; North Smithfield JR SR HS; Woonsocket, RI; (Y); 28/150; Cmnty Wkr; Drama Clb; French Clb; Letterman Clb; SADD; Chorus; School Musical; School Play; Stage Crew; Variety Show; Pres Clsrm Young Amer Inc 86; Mst Imprvd Plyr Awd Sftbl 84; Cmmnctns.

BEAULIEU, TIMOTHY A; Bishop Hendricken HS; Warwick, RI; (Y); 5/236; Chess Clb; Math Tm; Service Clb; Nwsp Rptr; Elks Awd; High Hon Roll; NHS; Ntl Merit Schol; Herbert & Claiborne Pell Mdl Achvmnt Amer Hstry 85; Rhode Island Dstngshd Schlr 86; Brown U; Biochmstry.

BEAUSOLEIL, RITA; Woonsocket HS; Woonsocket, RI; (Y); Church Yth Grp; Quiz Bowl; SADD; Church Choir; Var Bsktbl; Var Sftbl; High Hon Roll; Relg Ed Coord.

BEAUVAIS, JAMES; La Salle Acad; East Providence, RI; (Y); Boys Clb Am; Chess Clb; Computer Clb; Key Clb; Model UN; Red Cross Aide; Teachers Aide; High Hon Roll; Hon Roll; Frank A Hopkins Memrl Awd 84-85; Comp Sci.

BELANGER, DAVID; North Smithfield JR SR HS; N Smithfield, RI; (Y); 40/144; Off Letterman Clb; L Bsbl; L Bsktbl; L Capt Ftbl; Unsung Hero-Ftbll 84; 2nd Tm All-Div Ftbll 85; North Eastern U; Engnrng.

BELANGER, KENNY; Coventry HS; Coventry, RI; (Y); JV Wrstlng; Hon Roll; Cert For Part In Ntnl Frnch Tst 85; Aviation.

BELCHER, DONNA; North Smithfield JR SR HS; Slatersville, RI; (Y); 17/155; French Clb; Intnl Clb; Letterman Clb; Band; Rep Jr Cls; Ed Stu Cncl; Var L Bsktbl; Var L Sftbl; Var L Tennis; Hon Roll; Rdlgy.

BELL, LISA; East Providence HS; E Prov, RI; (Y); Church Yth Grp; Quiz Bowl; Varsity Clb; Var Bsktbl; Var Crs Cntry; Var Sftbl; Trk; Prfct Atten Awd; Acctg.

BELL, WENDY; Coventry HS; Greene, RI; (Y); 17/330; Pep Clb; Ski Clb; Varsity Clb; Variety Show; Yrbk Stf; Stu Cncl; Stat Bsktbl; Stat Sftbl; Mcdnlds Schlrshp 86; Curry Coll; Elem Educ.

BENJAMIN, CAROL; Warwick Veterans Memorial HS; Warwick, RI; (Y); Hosp Aide; Math Tm; Var L Sftbl; French Hon Soc; High Hon Roll; Jr NHS; NHS; Ntl Merit Ltr; Cross-Age Tutorng 84-86; Wnnr Prov Jrnl Bk Revw Cont 85; Psych.

BENNETT, DONALD; Hope HS; Providence, RI; (Y); Cmnty Wkr; Letterman Clb; Office Aide; Radio Clb; Varsity Clb; Pres Jr Cls; Rep Stu Cncl; Wrstlng; Holy Cross Book Awd; Emerson; Mass Comm.

BENNETT, JO A; Middletown HS; Middletown, RI; (Y); Art Clb; Nwsp Rptr; Rep Frsh Cls; Trs Soph Cls; Trs Jr Cls; Sec Stu Cncl; Var Bsktbl; Var Crs Cntry; Capt Trk; St Schlr; Bread Loaf Yng Wrtrs Conf; Schl Exclence Awd; Pgm Rcgntn Intelectual Strngth Middletown; Western CT ST U; Jrnlsm.

BENNETT, KELLIE; Chariho Regional HS; Carolina, RI; (Y); 3/283; Math Tm; Science Clb; Chorus; Stu Cncl; Stat Crs Cntry; Stat Trk; High Hon Roll; Hon Roll; Jr NHS; NHS; Susan Farmer Ldrshp Awd 86; Prvdence Jrnl Acad Awd 86; Alliance Fran Gld Mdl Awd 86; U Of RI; Chem.

BENSON, LYNNE; Mt Pleasant HS; Providence, RI; (Y); 14/185; Hon Roll; NHS; Prfct Atten Awd; Outstndng Stu Italian 84-85.

BERARD, JEAN; Warwick Veterans Memorial HS; Warwick, RI; (Y); 26/283; Rep Stu Cncl; Var L Cheerleading; Var Capt Crs Cntry; High Hon Roll; Spanish NHS; RI Hnr Soc 86; U Of RI.

BERARD, MICHELE; Smithfield HS; Esmond, RI; (Y); Civic Clb; Girl Scts; Band; Concert Band; Jazz Band; Pep Band; Symp Band; Frsh Cls; Fld Hcky; Gym.

BERARD, SCOTT; Bishop Hendricken HS; W Warwick, RI; (Y); 76/240; French Clb; Rep Sr Cls; Rep Stu Cncl; Var JV Bsbl; Var JV Ice Hcky; French Hon Soc; High Hon Roll; Hon Roll; NHS.

BERGANTINO, LOUIS; Cranston West HS; Cranston, RI; (Y); Science Clb; Hon Roll; JV Ftbl; Outstndng Achvt In Italian 84 & 85; Chmcl Engrng.

BERTHIAUME, NORA; Community Christian HS; Mapleville, RI; (S); Camp Fr Inc; Church Yth Grp; French Clb; School Play; Yrbk Stf; Sftbl; Hon Roll; Psych.

BESSETTE, ARTHUR; Woonsocket SR HS; Woonsocket, RI; (Y); Church Yth Grp; Math Tm; Concert Band; Mrchg Band; Yrbk Phtg; Yrbk Stf; High Hon Roll.

BESSETTE, PAULA; East Providence SR HS; East Providence, RI; (S); 15/450; SADD; Chorus; Rep Jr Cls; Rep Sr Cls; Trs Stu Cncl; Capt Var Cheerleading; High Hon Roll; Jr NHS; NHS; Boston U; Pre Dntl.

BETTENCOURT, JOYCE; Charles E Shea SR HS; Pawtucket, RI; (Y); Library Aide; School Play; Sec Of SADD Club 85-86; RI Coll; Bus Admin.

BIAGETTI, JUSTINA; Burrillville JR SR HS; Harrisville, RI; (Y); Band; Concert Band; Mrchg Band; Yrbk Stf.

BIBEAULT, MICHELLE C; Woonsocket HS; Woonsocket, RI; (Y); Church Yth Grp; French Clb; Math Clb; Math Tm; Stu Cncl; Hon Roll; Var Crs Cntry; Var Trk; Hosp Schlrshp 86; Springfield Clg; Sprts Med.

BIGONETTE, ROBERT; Lincoln HS; Lincoln, RI; (Y); Letterman Clb; Varsity Clb; VP Capt Stu Cncl; Bsktbl; Golf; High Hon Roll; Hon Roll; NHS; Bus.

BILEZERIAN, KEITH; North Smithfield JR SR HS; N Smithfield, RI; (Y); Sec Pres Church Yth Grp; Trs Debate Tm; Concert Band; Mrchg Band; Orch; Nwsp Stf; Rep Stu Cncl; Socr; JA; RI All ST Music Fest; Solo & Ensmbl RIMEA; Govt Wrk.

BIROS, TRISH; Coventry HS; Coventry, RI; (Y); Hosp Aide; Stage Crew; Letterman Clb; Var Bsktbl; Var Cheerleading; Var Ice Hcky; Capt Sftbl; Hon Roll; NHS; Cornell; Pedtrcn.

BISBANO, BRUCE; Bristol HS; Bristol, RI; (S); Am Leg Boys St; Ski Clb; Band; Concert Band; Jazz Band; Mrchg Band; Stage Crew; Yrbk Stf; Stu Cncl; Bsktbl; Arch.

BISBANO, LARNEY JOHN; Bristol HS; Bristol, RI; (S); 8/194; Boy Scts; French Clb; Ski Clb; JV Bsktbl; Var Ftbl; Var Golf; Hon Roll; NHS; Var Score Keeper; Var Timer; Ftbl Schlr Awd 84-85; Iron Colt Awd 84-85; Boston Coll; Bus Adm.

BISCI, SHARON; North Providence HS; N Providence, RI; (Y); 12/230; Political Wkr; Band; Concert Band; Orch; Nwsp Ed-Chief; Yrbk Bus Mgr; Hon Roll; NHS; Miss Teen RI 85-86; Mount Holyoke Coll; Spnsh.

BISHOP, TRACY; North Providence HS; N Providence, RI; (Y); Cmnty Wkr; Office Aide; Teachers Aide; Lit Mag; Hon Roll; RIC; Chld Psych.

BLACKSON, TANYA P; Rogers HS; Newport, RI; (Y); Dance Clb; Hon Roll; Barbzn Schl Modlg 84-85; Prfrmg Danc 85-86; Afro Expernc 84-86; Johnson & Wales Coll; Fshn Mrch.

BLAIR, ROBBIE-LYNN; Prout Memorial HS; Coventry, RI; (Y); Sec Chorus; Concert Band; School Musical; Stage Crew; Variety Show; Nwsp Stf; Hon Roll; Acadmc Decathalon 86; Medcl Illustrtn.

BLAIS, ADAM; Warwick Veterans HS; Warwick, RI; (Y); Rep Stu Cncl; Hon Roll.

BLANCHETTE, JOANN; Coventry HS; Coventry, RI; (Y); Letterman Clb; Varsity Clb; Var Capt Cheerleading; JV Var Sftbl; Hon Roll; Paralgl.

BLOOM, LEONARD; Pilgrim HS; Warwick, RI; (Y); French Clb; VP JA; Math Clb; Soph Cls; Stu Cncl; French Hon Soc; High Hon Roll; Hon Roll; Jr NHS; NHS; Ntl Merit Ltr; Rensselaer Math, Sci Awd, U RI Bk Awd, 1st Cert Soc Sci Acad Dcthln 86; Pre Med.

BLYTHS, STEPHEN; Truerton HS; Tiverton, RI; (Y); Band; Concert Band; Jazz Band; Mrchg Band; Pep Band; School Musical; Stage Crew; Variety Show; All ST Bnd 83-84; Jazz Prfrmc.

BOBOLA, ROBERT; Lincoln SR HS; Lincoln, RI; (Y); 39/195; Church Yth Grp; CAP; VP Band; Concert Band; Jazz Band; Trk; Hon Roll; All-St Cncrt Bnd 86; Aerospc.

BOCHNER, INA; Pilgrim HS; Warwick, RI; (Y); French Clb; Math Tm; Sec Temple Yth Grp; VP Thesps; Yrbk Stf; Bausch & Lomb Sci Awd; French Hon Soc; High Hon Roll; Jr NHS; NHS; French Spelling Bee Winner 84,85,86; Soc Sci.

BOEDEKER, EDGAR; Classical HS; Providence, RI; (Y); 8/256; French Clb; Math Tm; Band; Nwsp Stf; Hon Roll; Pres Schlr; Alethe Weston Engl Awd 86; Wesleyan U.

BOFFI, ANGELA; Prout Memorial HS; Warwick, RI; (S); 3/77; Spanish Clb; Chorus; Color Guard; Jazz Band; School Musical; Nwsp Stf; Rep Jr Cls; High Hon Roll; Hon Roll; NHS.

BOGACZ, SABINA; Lincoln JR SR HS; Lincoln, RI; (Y); 6/195; Drama Clb; School Play; Stage Crew; Nwsp Stf; Hon Roll; NHS; Prfct Atten Awd; 3rd Grnt RI STA Sci Fair 84; 2nd Grnt RI STA Sci Fair 85; U Of RI Alumni Bk Awd 86.

BOHAN, THOMAS; La Salle Acad; Providence, RI; (Y); Church Yth Grp; Math Tm; Political Wkr; Nwsp Rptr; Bsktbl; Im JV Crs Cntry; Var L Trk; High Hon Roll; Hon Roll; NHS; Provdnce City Cncl Sportsmn Yr 85; Mt Pleasant Bsbl Coach 86; Natl Lang Arts Olympd Distnctn Awd 84; Boston Coll; Pre-Med.

BOISVERT, MICHELLE; Woonsocket SR HS; Woonsocket, RI; (Y); Church Yth Grp; SADD; Bsktbl; Vllybl; High Hon Roll; Hon Roll; Prfct Atten Awd; Highest French Avg For 4 Yrs 84; Jrnlsm.

BONGIARDO, TRACEY; North Providence HS; N Providence, RI; (Y); Yrbk Stf; Hon Roll; Drftng.

BOONE, JAMAL; Warwick Veterans Memorial HS; Warwick, RI; (Y); 4-H; SADD; School Play; Variety Show; JV Bsbl; JV Bsktbl; Var Ftbl; Hon Roll; Poetry Awd 83; Shrt Stories Awd 82; Cmnctns.

BOSCIA, RAYMOND; Bishop Thomas F Hendrickson HS; Cranston, RI; (Y); Church Yth Grp; Ski Clb; Trk; Wt Lftg; Hendricken Hnr Awd 84-86; Samaritan Tutorial Awd 85; Providence Coll; Lbrl Arts.

BOSCO, KATHY; Pilgrim HS; Warwick, RI; (Y); Art Clb; Flag Corp; Mrchg Band; Yrbk Stf; Cheerleading; Hon Roll; Jr NHS; Spanish NHS; PC; Cnslng.

BOSSDORF, TRACEY; Pilgrim HS; Warwick, RI; (Y); 21/305; Stage Crew; Yrbk Bus Mgr; High Hon Roll; Hon Roll; NHS; Mock Trial Trnmnt 85-86; U Of Bridgeport; Bus Law.

BOTELHO, BRIAN; Middletown HS; Middletown, RI; (Y); Art Clb; CAP; JV Bsbl; Im Ftbl; Hon Roll; Biocommunications.

BOTELHO, PAUL; East Providence SR HS; E Providence, RI; (Y); 31/528; Computer Clb; Stage Crew; Pres Acad Fit Awd 86; RI Hnr Soc 86; U Of RI; Elec Engrng.

BOUFFARD, KATHLEEN; St Raphael Acad; Pawtucket, RI; (Y); 6/176; French Clb; Model UN; SADD; Yrbk Stf; Stu Cncl; Co-Capt Tennis; French Hon Soc; Gov Hon Prg Awd; Hon Roll; VP NHS; Providence Coll Bk Awd; Congrsmn St Germain Awd; Century III Wnr; Simmons Coll; Librl Arts.

BOULEY, CHRISTINE; Woonsocket SR HS; Woonsocket, RI; (Y); VICA.

BOUMENOT, MICHAEL S; Chariho HS; Ashaway, RI; (Y); VICA; Var L Socr; Hon Roll; 2nd Tm All Div Sccr St 85; Sccr Bst Dfnsv Plyr & Gerald D Cahoon Sr Awd 85; New Eng Inst Tech; Mech Drftng.

BOURDEAU, MICHELLE; Central Falls HS; Central Falls, RI; (Y); Sec Church Yth Grp; Office Aide; Church Choir; Acctnt.

BOURQUE, THOMAS; North Smithfield HS; Woonsocket, RI; (Y); 70/142; Letterman Clb; Var L Bsbl; Var L Ice Hcky; Elks Awd; Bus Adm.

BOUSQUET, JEFF; Woonsocket HS; Woonsocket, RI; (Y); Crs Cntry; Trk; Hon Roll; St Schlr; Dennison MFG Co & RI ST Schlrshps 86; FL Inst Of Tech; Comp Engrng.

BOWERS, DARCI; Tiverton HS; Tiverton, RI; (Y); 82/190; Sec Church Yth Grp; Drama Clb; Girl Scts; ROTC; VP Band; Pres Chorus; Church Choir; VP Concert Band; Drm Mjr(t); Jazz Band; Schlrshp From RI Coll 86; Outstndg Music Stu Tvrtn High 86; Schlrshp From TEMPO; RI Coll; Music Ed.

BOYER, KELLI; Cumberland HS; Cumberland, RI; (Y); Boys Clb Am; Church Yth Grp; Spanish Clb; Chorus; Pep Band; Swing Chorus; Variety Show; High Hon Roll; Hon Roll; Sawyer Schl; Trvl & Trsm.

BRAGA, COLLEEN; La Salle Acad; Providence, RI; (Y); Church Yth Grp; Gym; Mgr(s); Sftbl; Trk; Hon Roll; Adv Life Saving & Water Sfty 86; Basic Life Supprt CPR 86; Multimedia Stndrd 1st Aid 86; RN.

BRANCEL, SARA; Middletown HS; Middletown, RI; (Y); 22/249; VP Spanish Clb; Concert Band; Jazz Band; Mrchg Band; Hon Roll; NHS; Spanish NHS; RI Hghr Educ Asstnce Auth Cert Of Hnr 86; Dr John Clarke Schlrshp 86; Navl Ofcrs Wvs Clb Schlrshp 86; Hofstra U; Bio.

BRASWELL, DAWN; Mount Pleasant HS; Providence, RI; (Y); Bsktbl; Vllybl; Prfct Atten Awd; Acad Dcthln 85-86; Gov Smmnr Pgm Sci, Math 85; Mst Prmsng Sci Mgnt Stdnt 83-84; Elec Engr.

BRAZELL, WILLIAM T; Portsmouth Abbey HS; Schenectady, NY; (Y); 12/67; Debate Tm; Drama Clb; Spanish Clb; Church Choir; School Play; Rptr Lit Mag; Pres Stu Cncl; Ntl Merit SF; Law.

BRENIZE, DIANA; Coverntry HS; Coventry, RI; (Y); #141 In Class; Dance Clb; Office Aide; Spanish Clb; Band; Chorus; Jazz Band; Mrchg Band; Pep Band; Cheerleading; Coach Actv; Hall Inst; Intr Design.

BRENNAN, MARJORIE A; Charino Reg HS; Rockville, RI; (Y); 23/289; Am Leg Aux Girls St; Girl Scts; Library Aide; Quiz Bowl; Service Clb; Chorus; School Musical; Hon Roll; Jr NHS; Ntl Merit SF; Girl Sct Slvr Awd 85; RI Acad Decath Slvr Mdl Eng Brnz Fine Art 85; RI Mod Leg Senatr 85; Intl Rel.

BRENTON, MELISSA JEANNE; St Mary Acad; Riverside, RI; (Y); 9/239; Sec Am Leg Aux Girls St; Pres Exploring; French Clb; Math Tm; Rep Jr Cls; Hon Roll; NHS; NEDT Awd; Cmnty Wkr; Stu Cncl; Acad Decathln Silver Cert Spch 86; Schl Svc Awds; Comm.

BRIDGE, MELISSA; Coventry HS; Coventry, RI; (Y); 9/450; Pres Church Yth Grp; French Clb; Letterman Clb; Trs Soph Cls; Off Soph Cls; Sec Stu Cncl; Var L Bsktbl; Var L Tennis; Var Capt Vllybl; Dely Natl Yth To Yth Conf Substance Abuse 85; 2nd Team All Div Vllybl 86; Teen Advclb Treas 85.

BRIEN, BRENDA LEE; William E Tolman SR HS; Pawtucket, RI; (Y); 26/236; French Clb; SADD; Yrbk Stf; French Hon Soc; High Hon Roll; Hon Roll; Jr NHS; NHS; Mrtn M Chase Mem Schlrshp 86; Kiwanis Schlrshp 86; Emrsn Coll; Sprtscstr.

BRIEN, THERESE; Woonsocket SR HS; Woonsocket, RI; (Y); Church Yth Grp; Library Aide; Math Tm; Office Aide; Teachers Aide; Band; Church Choir; Yrbk Stf; High Hon Roll; Hon Roll; Comp Sci.

BRISSETTE, TAMMY; Woonsocket SR HS; Woonsocket, RI; (Y); Band; Concert Band; Mrchg Band; High Hon Roll; Hon Roll; Prfct Atten Awd; 1st Girl Colt Lg 85; Chld Guidance.

BRITLAND, MICHAEL; Tiverton HS; Tiverton, RI; (Y); 22/189; ROTC; Nwsp Ed-Chief; Hon Roll; NHS; Presdntl Acad Fitnss Awd 86; 86 Outstndg NJ ROTC Cdt 86; TIVERTON NJ ROTC Unit Commndr 86; Citadel-Mltry Coll SC; Chem.

BROCATO, MARC; Charaibo Regional JR SR HS; Ashaway, RI; (Y); 44/258; Church Yth Grp; Ski Clb; Yrbk Sprt Ed; Var Bsktbl; Var Capt Tennis; Vllybl; Hon Roll; Prjct Close-Up 86; Sci & Math Providence Coll Prog 85; Cvl Engrng.

BROMAGE, DANIEL; Warwick Veterans Memorial HS; Warwick, RI; (Y); Cmnty Wkr; Letterman Clb; Service Clb; Yrbk Stf; L Wrstlng.

BROTHERS, BETTINA; Mount Saint Charles Acad; Johnston, RI; (S); High Hon Roll; NHS; Ntl Merit SF; Pediatrcn.

BROTHERS, MATTHEW; Mount Saint Charles Acad; N Smithfield, RI; (S); 11/190; Cmnty Wkr; Math Tm; Ski Clb; High Hon Roll; NHS; Ntl Merit Ltr.

BROUILLARD, BARBARA ANN; Lincoln JR SR HS; Manville, RI; (Y); 54/181; Trs Rptr FBLA; Hon Roll; NHS; RI ST Trea Awd Outstndng Prfrmnc Bus Stds 86; Lincoln HS Awd Outstndng Bus Stu 86; RI Hnr Soc 86; LA ST U; Bus.

BROUILLETTE, MICHELE; Prout Memorial HS; Coventry, RI; (S); 8/77; Exploring; Hosp Aide; Math Tm; Scholastic Bowl; Capt Varsity Clb; Color Guard; Yrbk Stf; Sec Sr Cls; Capt Vllybl; NHS; Prvdnc Coll Bk Awd 85; Nrs.

BROWN, DANIEL; Bishop Hendricken HS; Riverside, RI; (Y); 29/240; Boy Scts; Church Yth Grp; JV Ftbl; JV Trk; Hon Roll; NHS; Spanish NHS; Eagle Sct 86; Biol Engrg.

BROWN, DINA; St Marys Acad; Warwick, RI; (Y); Exploring; Spanish Clb; Hon Roll; Bus Adm.

BROWN, DONNA; Daviez Voc-Tech HS; Pawtucket, RI; (S); Church Yth Grp; Off FFA; Pep Clb; Chorus; 3rd Pl RI ST FFA Greenhd Publ Spkg 85; Chptr Frmr FFA 85; Str Greenhd 85; Plnt Care Bus.

BROWN, KERRIE; St Raphael Acad; Pawtucket, RI; (Y); Cmnty Wkr; Yrbk Stf; Hon Roll; Stone Hill Coll; Lbrl Arts.

BROWN, KRISTEN; Johnston SR HS; Johnston, RI; (Y); 22/260; Sec Dance Clb; Sec DECA; Yrbk Stf; Rep Soph Cls; Stu Cncl; Hon Roll; Frnch Acdmc Achvt 83-85; RI Coll; Elmntry Tchr.

BROWN, STEPHANIE; Coventry HS; Coventry, RI; (Y); Pres Church Yth Grp; French Clb; Pep Clb; Quiz Bowl; Spanish Clb; Varsity Clb; Var Stage Crew; Stu Cncl; Var Bsktbl; JV Crs Cntry; U Of RI; Phy Ed.

BRULOTTE, LAURIE; Tiverton HS; Tiverton, RI; (Y); Drama Clb; French Clb; SADD; Teachers Aide; Chorus; Church Choir; School Musical; Hon Roll; RI Music Ed Assn A Ensmbl 83; Southern MA U; Art.

BRYCE, KARIN; St Raphael Acad; Prov, RI; (Y); Pres Church Yth Grp; Quiz Bowl; Church Choir; Sftbl; Hon Roll; Pres Schlr; St Schlr; Sec Sr Cls; Leona Rogers Awd 86; Outstndng Svc Awd-Lady Aux 86; Natl Bus Soc 86; Bryant Coll; Mrktng.

BRYCE, MICHAELA; St Marys Academy Bay View; Seekonk, MA; (Y); Church Yth Grp; Exploring; French Clb; Orch; Soph Cls; Jr Cls; Var Sftbl; Hon Roll; NHS; NEDT Awd; Engl.

BRZOSTECKI, KRISTIN; West Warwick HS; West Warwick, RI; (Y); Pres French Clb; Math Tm; Concert Band; Mrchg Band; Variety Show; Bsktbl; Cheerleading; Sftbl; High Hon Roll; Hon Roll; Challenge Awd 85 & 86; Boston Coll; Bus Admn.

BUCCI, ERIK S; North Southfield JR SR HS; Slatersville, RI; (Y); 2/160; VP Church Yth Grp; Debate Tm; French Clb; Intnl Clb; Letterman Clb; Math Tm; Quiz Bowl; Pres Soph Cls; Pres Jr Cls; Rep Stu Cncl; U Of RI Bk Awd 87; Prsndtl Clssrm 87; MIT; Mechncl Engrng.

BUCKI, CAROLYNN; Mount Pleasant HS; Providence, RI; (Y); Art Clb; Library Aide; PAVAS; Yrbk Phtg; Yrbk Stf; Hon Roll; NHS; Anthny Mdl Excllnc Wrtg Awd; Excllnc Art/Pntng; Acdmc Decathln; RI Coll; Art.

BULLOCK, KIMBERLY; South Kingstown HS; W Kingston, RI; (Y); 9/205; Church Yth Grp; German Clb; Hosp Aide; Math Tm; Band; Variety Show; JV Var Fld Hcky; Trk; High Hon Roll; NHS.

BULSON, SUZANNE; Cumberland HS; Cumberland, RI; (Y); 17/369; Am Leg Aux Girls St; Church Yth Grp; Band; Color Guard; Flag Corp; Var Tennis; Var Vllybl; Hon Roll; Bus.

BUONACCORSI, JAMIE; St Mary Acad Bay View HS; Cranston, RI; (Y); 62/215; Exploring; French Clb; Math Clb; Pep Clb; Ski Clb; SADD; Sec Soph Cls; Rep Stu Cncl; Hon Roll; Cert Mrt Servc 84-86; Elem Ed.

BURATCZUK, MICHAELA; Warwick Veterans HS; Warwick, RI; (Y); Hosp Aide; SADD; Acpl Chr; Chorus; School Musical; High Hon Roll; Hon Roll; Jr NHS; NHS; Spanish NHS; PC; Pre-Med.

BURKINSHAW, MATTHEW; Woodsicket HS; Woonsocket, RI; (Y); 18/470; Boy Scts; Church Yth Grp; Band; Concert Band; L Capt Crs Cntry; L Capt Trk; Gov Hon Prg Awd; High Hon Roll; NHS; Ntl Merit Ltr; Boston Coll.

BURTON, MARY; Portsmouth HS; Portsmouth, RI; (Y); Pres FBLA; Band; Mrchg Band; Yrbk Stf; Var Capt Crs Cntry; Hon Roll; U Of RI; Fash Merch.

BUSALD, MARGE; St Raphael Acad; Pawtucket, RI; (Y); Drama Clb; SADD; School Musical; School Play; Stage Crew; Cheerleading; Tennis; Trk; Elem Educ.

BUTLER, CHRISTOPHER; Saint Raphael Acad; Lincoln, RI; (Y); Boy Scts; Hosp Aide; Variety Show; Hon Roll; Communications.

BYRNE, ELENA; St Marys Academy Bayview HS; Warwick, RI; (Y); 20/250; Cmnty Wkr; Sec Exploring; Service Clb; Spanish Clb; SADD; JV Var Vllybl; Hon Roll; Brown U Book Awd 86; 1st Pl RI Natl Spn Exam 86.

CABRAL, STEFANIE; Johnston HS; Johnston, RI; (S); 6/216; Am Leg Aux Girls St; JA; SADD; Yrbk Stf; Badmtn; Vllybl; High Hon Roll; Hon Roll; NHS; 1st Pl Natl Hstry Day ST Cmptn 83; RI Coll; Educ.

CABRAL, TRACI; Tiverton HS; Tiverton, RI; (Y); 18/189; High Hon Roll; Hon Roll; NHS; Johnson & Wales; Acctng.

CADY, DEBRA; La Salle Acad; Wyoming, RI; (Y); 30/285; Dance Clb; GAA; Girl Scts; Letterman Clb; Varsity Clb; Band; Concert Band; Mrchg Band; Yrbk Stf; Rep Frsh Cls; Med.

CAFARO, THOMAS; Burrillville HS; Glendale, RI; (Y); Boy Scts; Chess Clb; VP Church Yth Grp; 4-H; Letterman Clb; SADD; Varsity Clb; Band; Church Choir; Concert Band; Bus Adm.

CALEK, DANIEL; Rogers HS; Newport, RI; (Y); 9/233; ROTC; JV Bsbl; Var Bsktbl; Capt Bowling; Im Socr; French Hon Soc; High Hon Roll; Hon Roll; Spanish NHS; Boy Scts; RI ST Bwlng Champ & 8th Pl Ntl JR Bwlng Champ 86; Acadmc Excllnc Peoples Credit Union 85; CA U Davis; Vet.

CALISE, KRISTEN; North Providence HS; Cranston, RI; (Y); Hosp Aide; Drm Mjr(t); Nwsp Stf; Yrbk Stf; Twrlr; Jr NHS; NHS; Psych.

CAMPELLONE, GLENN; Charles E Shea SR HS; Pawtucket, RI; (Y); Boys Clb Am; Computer Clb; Ski Clb; Band; Concert Band; Jazz Band; Pep Band; JV Var Bsbl; JV Bsktbl; Im Vllybl; Acad All Amer Schlr Pgm 84; Bus.

CAMPINHA, JOAN; East Prov SR HS; E Prov, RI; (Y); Dance Clb; Hon Roll; NHS; Prfct Attndnc 83-85; Secrtry.

CANTONE, DONNA; North Providence HS; N Providence, RI; (Y); Chorus; Jazz Band; VP Jr Cls; VP Stu Cncl; Hon Roll; RI Coll; Comp Music.

CAPARCO, ANGELA; Cranston West HS; Cranston, RI; (Y); Chess Clb; Dance Clb; Variety Show; Jhnsn & Wales Coll; Accntng.

CAPORIZZO, MARIA; St Mary Acad Bay View; North Scituate, RI; (Y); 9/230; Am Leg Aux Girls St; Church Choir; Orch; VP Frsh Cls; Rep Soph Cls; Rep Sr Cls; VP Stu Cncl; Hon Roll; NHS; NEDT Awd; Wellesley Col Bk Awd 86; Sociolgy.

CAPOVERDE, MELISSA; Pilgrim HS; Warwick, RI; (Y); Hosp Aide; Spanish Clb; SADD; Stage Crew; Var Score Keeper; RDC; Nrs.

CARDIN, MARC; Woonsocket HS; Woonsocket, RI; (Y); Church Yth Grp; Cmnty Wkr; French Hon Soc; High Hon Roll; Hon Roll; NHS; Cert Of Awd 1st Hnrs 84; Schlrshp Awd 84; Cert Of Awd Bio 84; USAF Acad; Aero Engrg.

CARDIN, SHARON; North Smithfield JR/Sr HS; N Smithfield, RI; (Y); 25/145; Drama Clb; Pres 4-H; JA; Band; Mrchg Band; School Musical; School Play; Pres Acad Ftnss Awd 86; RI Hon Soc 86; ST Publc Spkg Cont 1st Pl 84; Bay Path JC; Acctg.

CAREY, JENNIFER; Narragansett HS; Narragansett, RI; (Y); 10/120; JA; Off Jr Cls; Trs Sr Cls; Stu Cncl; Var Socr; JV Vllybl; Hon Roll; NHS; Mainer Schlr Awd 85; Chem Engrng.

CARLONE, DAVID; Middletown HS; Little Compton, RI; (Y); Am Leg Boys St; VP JA; Concert Band; JV Ftbl; Var L Socr; Var L Trk; Var L Wrstlng; Hon Roll; Spanish NHS; Sports Med.

CARLOTTI, ALBERT; Bishop Hendricken HS; E Greenwich, RI; (Y); 20/273; Debate Tm; Letterman Clb; Spanish Clb; Jazz Band; Nwsp Rptr; Golf; High Hon Roll; NHS; Spanish NHS; Med.

CARLOTTO, JOHN; Barrington HS; Barrington, RI; (Y); Ftbl; JV Var Wrstlng; Envrnmnltlsm.

CARLTON, ANN; Burrillville HS; Pascoag, RI; (Y); Band; Concert Band; Mrchg Band; School Play; Yrbk Stf; JV Fld Hcky; Hon Roll; Fash Merch.

CARNEVALE, CHRISTINE; Bishop Francis P Keough Regnl HS; Johnston, RI; (S); Drama Clb; French Clb; Rep Model UN; School Play; Stu Cncl; Hon Roll; Ntl Merit Ltr; Bio.

CARNEY, LEIGH; East Greenwich HS; Exeter, RI; (Y); Cmnty Wkr; Chorus; School Musical; Variety Show; Var JV Vllybl; Hon Roll; Grad Barbizon Schl Mdlng 84; 2nd & 4th Rnnr Up Cndrlla Grl Schlrshp Pgnt & Miss Teen USA 84 & 85.

CARNEY, ROBERT; Charles E Shea HS; Pawtucket, RI; (Y); 34/225; Cmnty Wkr; Ed Nwsp Stf; Rep Soph Cls; Trs Jr Cls; Trs Sr Cls; L Tennis; Hon Roll; Model Leg & Rep & Sentr 84-86; RI Sec ST Awd 86; Frank Kleniewski Prnclpl Awd 86; RI Coll; Accntng.

CARR, DOUG; Coventry HS; Coventry, RI; (Y); Cmnty Wkr; Var Bsktbl; High Hon Roll; Acctnt.

CARR, JAYSON; Bishop Hendricken HS; Cranston, RI; (Y); 7/273; Sec Am Leg Boys St; Boy Scts; Sec French Clb; Nwsp Rptr; JV Crs Cntry; French Hon Soc; High Hon Roll; NHS; US Sentr Pell Mdl Amer Hstry 86; Samaritan Tutorng Svc 86; Biomed Engrng.

CARR II, PETER F; Bishop Hendricken HS; No Kingstown, RI; (Y); 10/240; Political Wkr; Ski Clb; Spanish Clb; Rep Soph Cls; Rep Stu Cncl; Var Bsbl; High Hon Roll; NHS; Spanish NHS; U Of RI Bk Awd 86.

CARREIRO, BETH; Tiverton HS; Tiverton, RI; (S); Concert Band; Mrchg Band; Pres Soph Cls; Sec Jr Cls; Var L Cheerleading; Var L Vllybl; Hon Roll; Hugh O Brian Yth Ldrshp Sem; Semi-Fnlst Cngrss-Bundestag Schlrshp Exch; Cent 3 Schlrshp Selctn Committ; Pub Rltns.

CARUSO, DOREEN; Pilgrim HS; Warwick, RI; (Y); 67/312; Dance Clb; Pep Clb; Ski Clb; Variety Show; Yrbk Stf; Capt Cheerleading; Itln Hnr Scty 85-86; Rhode Island Coll; Accntng.

CARVALHO, KAREN; Bristol HS; Bristol, RI; (Y); Lit Mag; Cheerleading; Powder Puff Ftbl; Sftbl; Journalism.

CARVISIGLIA, AMY; Prout Memorial HS; N Kingstown, RI; (S); 27/92; French Clb; Hosp Aide; Rep Stu Cncl; Var Bsktbl; Var Vllybl; DAR Awd; Advrtsng.

CARVISIGLIA, DIANE; Prout Memorial HS; N Kingstown, RI; (S); 11/96; Cmnty Wkr; French Clb; Hosp Aide; Office Aide; Acpl Chr; Chorus; Jazz Band; Rep Frsh Cls; Rep Soph Cls; Rep Jr Cls; Engl.

CASCI, KIM A; East Providence HS; E Prov, RI; (Y); Dance Clb; French Clb; PAVAS; Stage Crew; Nwsp Stf; Cheerleading; Hon Roll; Prjct Bus Cert 84; Sprltvs Ncst Arnd 84; U Rhode Island; Law.

CASEY, ANDREA; Cranston H S East; Cranston, RI; (Y); 7/380; Church Yth Grp; Sec Trs Q&S; Sec Spanish Clb; Flag Corp; Ed Nwsp Stf; Yrbk Bus Mgr; Rep Soph Cls; Rep Sr Cls; Rep Stu Cncl; Cit Awd; Wellesley Coll Bk Awd; Hugh O Brian Ldrshp Ambssdr; Spanish Hon Soc Awd Excllnc; Wheaton Coll.

CASTALDI, REBECCA; Woonsocket HS; Woonsocket, RI; (S); English Clb; PAVAS; Spanish Clb; Teachers Aide; Band; Color Guard; Concert Band; Drill Tm; Drm & Bgl; Drm Mjr(t); Wnter Guard Intl Clss A Champ 83; Providence Coll; Engl.

CASTON, JANEL; Portsmouth HS; Portsmouth, RI; (Y); 33/195; Sec FBLA; Band; Concert Band; Mrchg Band; Yrbk Stf; Hon Roll; RI Hnr Soc 85-86; Portsmouth Alumni Awd Schlrshp 86; U Of RI; Elec Engrng.

CATALDO, ROBERT M; Davies Vocational Technical HS; Pawtucket, RI; (Y); Cmnty Wkr; Political Wkr; VICA; Rep Sr Cls; JV Wrstlng; Hon Roll; RI Trade Shop Schl; Bus.

CATAURO, KRISTIN; Mt Saint Charles Acad; N Providence, RI; (S); 22/141; Hosp Aide; SADD; VP Sr Cls; Stu Cncl; Capt Cheerleading; Hon Roll; Jr NHS; NHS; Medcn.

CAVANAUGH, BETH; Classical HS; Providence, RI; (Y); Dance Clb; Math Tm; Political Wkr; Drm Mjr(t); Twrlr; High Hon Roll; Hon Roll; Bryant; Bus Admin.

CELONA, DAVID; Mount Saint Charles Acad; N Smith, RI; (S); 20/170; French Clb; Political Wkr; SADD; Rep Stu Cncl; VP Tennis; Im Wt Lftg; Jr NHS; HOBY Ldrshp Awd 85; NSSCA; U S Japan Sen Exch YFU 86.

CERESA, BRIAN; Chariho Regional HS; Hope Valley, RI; (Y); 11/287; Math Tm; Band; Yrbk Stf; Crs Cntry; Var Trk; NHS; Natl Hon Soc 86; Providence Coll Schlrshp 86-90; Collins & Aikman Merit Schlrshp 86-90; Providence Coll; Chem.

CERILLI, STEPHEN; Bishop Hendricken HS; Jamestown, RI; (Y); 65/257; Debate Tm; Var Swmmng; High Hon Roll; Hon Roll; NHS; Poli Sci.

CERRITO, CHANDRA; St Mary Acad Bay View; Cranston, RI; (Y); 1/202; Church Yth Grp; Exploring; Math Clb; Political Wkr; Trs Spanish Clb; SADD; High Hon Roll; NHS; Ntl Merit SF; Holy Cross Book Awd, Acdmc Achvt Awd AP Hist, Pre-Calc, Eng 86; NEDT Awd 85; Phys Ftns Awd 86.

CERULLO, SCOTT; Warwick Veterans HS; Warwick, RI; (Y); Computer Clb; Exploring; High Hon Roll; NHS; Spanish NHS; Brown Book Awd 86.

CERWONKA, DARA; Barrington HS; Barrington, RI; (Y); Pep Clb; SADD; Cheerleading; Hon Roll; American U; Crmnl Psychlgy.

CHA, THAI; Hope HS; Providence, RI; (Y); Church Yth Grp; Hon Roll; Upwrd Bnd Rhd Islnd Coll 86; Times 2 URI 85; Med Fld.

CHADWICK, DELAINE; Johnston HS; Johnston, RI; (Y); Nwsp Rptr; Hon Roll; Order Rainbow Girls Wrthy Advsr 85; RI Coll; Erly Ed.

CHAMPAGNE, ELISE; St Mary Acad; W Warwick, RI; (Y); 5/202; Math Clb; Nwsp Stf; Yrbk Stf; Var JV Cheerleading; Hon Roll; Jr NHS; NHS; Ntl Merit Ltr; NEDT Awd; RI Hnr Soc 85-86; URI Dstngshd Fclty Awd Schlrshp 86; U Of RI; Engnrng.

CHAPMAN, LORI; Warwick Veterans Memorial HS; Warwick, RI; (Y); Debate Tm; Hosp Aide; Letterman Clb; Math Tm; Yrbk Stf; Var L Tennis; French Hon Soc; High Hon Roll; NHS; Ntl Merit SF; Gov Summr Pgm Sci & Mth 86; Bronz Mdl Spch Acad Decthln 86; Ocean ST Wrtng Comptn Wnnr 86.

CHAPUT, RACHEL; Mount St Charles HS; Harrisville, RI; (Y); High Hon Roll; Hon Roll; Ntl Merit Ltr; George Washington U; Env Txclgy.

CHARETTE, JOSEPH; North Providence HS; N Providence, RI; (Y); Boy Scts; Band; Concert Band; Bsbl; Coach Actv; Wt Lftg; Hon Roll; Ntl Merit Ltr; Boy Scout Of Yr 83-84; West Point; Army.

CHARPENTIER, LINETTE; Prout Memorial HS; Coventry, RI; (S); 36/92; Math Tm; Jazz Band; Madrigals; School Musical; JP Sousa Awd; Chorus; Concert Band; Slo Ensmbl Fstvl Viola, Bartn Sax Scr A 85; Cert Awd Music 84 & 85; Cert Awd Alg I 84; Concrs Natl Fran.

CHARRON, ROBERT; Woonsocket SR HS; Woonsocket, RI; (Y); Sec Church Yth Grp; FCA; Var Crs Cntry; Var Trk; Hon Roll; Vllybl MVP St Josephs CYO 84; Moderate Awd Outstndng Svc St Josephs 84; Vllybl Unhrld St Josephs 85; Mktg.

CHECK, LAURA; Pilgrim SR HS; Warwick, RI; (Y); JA; Yrbk Stf; Rep Frsh Cls; Rep Soph Cls; Rep Jr Cls; French Hon Soc; High Hon Roll; Hon Roll; Jr NHS; NHS; Sth Providence Tuturl Cert Prfrmnc 84; FL Intl U; Clincl Psych.

CHEN, ALICE; North Smithfield JR SR HS; N Smithfield, RI; (Y); 1/150; Letterman Clb; Math Tm; Band; Stu Cncl; Capt Tennis; Vllybl; High Hon Roll; NHS; Val; Ntl Hon Soc Schlrshp 86; Grls Stu Athlt Awd 86fsec Of ST Ldrshp Awd 86; Brown U; Engrng.

CHEVIAN, LISA; Walwick Veterans Memorial HS; Warwick, RI; (Y); FBLA; Teachers Aide; Yrbk Stf; Hon Roll; Frshmn Exec, Soph Exec, JR Exec 83-86; Byrant; Acctg.

CHRISMAN, CARYN; N Smithfield HS; Forestdale, RI; (Y); #5 In Class; Letterman Clb; Math Tm; Var Capt Cheerleading; Sftbl; High Hon Roll; Hon Roll; NHS.

CHRISTIANSEN, KELI; N Providence HS; N Providence, RI; (Y); Hosp Aide; Nwsp Stf; Sec Sr Cls; VP Stu Cncl; Var Capt Cheerleading; High Hon Roll; Jr NHS; Ntl Merit Ltr; 3rd Grnt Ri ST Sci Fair 85; Nacel Frnch Cultural Exchng Partcpnt 86; Intl Rel.

CHRISTIE, KEITH; North Smithfield JR SR HS; North Smithfield, RI; (Y); Letterman Clb; Stu Cncl; L Var Bsbl; L Var Ftbl; L Var Ice Hcky; Hon Roll; All ST Ftbl Tm 1st Tm 84-85; All ST Ftbl 2nd Tm 85-86; Athltcs.

CICCONE, LISA; South Kingstown HS; Wakefield, RI; (Y); 3/211; Exploring; Hosp Aide; Chorus; Church Choir; Nwsp Stf; Mgr Fld Hcky; Lion Awd; NHS; High Hon Roll; Hon Roll; Silver Medal Spch 86; Top Frnch Stu 85; Exc Soclgy 86; Quinnipiac Coll; Physcl Thrpy.

CICERONE, DIANNE; North Providence HS; N Providence, RI; (Y); Hon Roll; Bryant Coll; Bus.

CINAMI, DINA; Lasalle Acad; Johnston, RI; (Y); 17/256; Library Aide; Church Choir; Hon Roll; NHS; Prfct Atten Awd; St Schlr; Hnr Soc, Pres Acad Ftns Awd, Merit Cert Spnsh SR Yr; Hgh Hnrs Wrld Hist & Engl Soph; Comms, Algb Frsh; RI Coll; Elem Ed.

CIRILLO, ALLISON; St Marys Acad; Warwick, RI; (Y); 14/220; French Clb; Math Tm; Trs Frsh Cls; Trs Soph Cls; Trs Jr Cls; Pres Stu Cncl; Hon Roll; NHS; Ntl Merit Ltr; Political Wkr; Hugh O Brien Ldrshp Cntst Rnr Up; Apprl Dsgn.

CIRILLO, PETER; Middletown HS; Little Compton, RI; (Y); Ski Clb; Bsktbl; Ice Hcky; Vllybl; Wt Lftg; Hon Roll.

CLARK, ANNA; Classical HS; Providence, RI; (Y); Drama Clb; French Clb; School Play; French Hon Soc; Schlastc Art Awd 86; RI Art Tchrs Cert Of Awd For Vsl Arts 86; Smth Coll Bk Awd 86; Art.

CLARK, CYNTHIA; Warwick Veterans Memorial HS; Warwick, RI; (Y); Letterman Clb; Off Soph Cls; Off Jr Cls; Sec Stu Cncl; Var Cheerleading; French Hon Soc; High Hon Roll; Hon Roll; RI Hnr Soc 85-86; Stu Cncl Schlrshp 86; Frnch Ntl Hnr Soc 83; U Of RI.

CLARK, JOANNE; Warwick Veterans HS; Warwick, RI; (Y); Yrbk Stf; Rep Frsh Cls; Rep Soph Cls; Rep Jr Cls; Rep Sr Cls; Var Capt Cheerleading; JV Var Crs Cntry; JV Var Trk; French Hon Soc; NHS; Bus Adm.

CLEARY, SHARON M; Cumberland HS; Cumberland, RI; (S); 6/387; SADD; Rep Jr Cls; Sr Cls; Var L Cheerleading; Var L Diving; Var L Trk; High Hon Roll; Hon Roll; Sec NHS; ST Diving Champ 84; Brown Intersclstc Diving Champ 85-86.

CLEMENT, MATTHEW; Bishop Hendricken HS; N Kingstown, RI; (Y); 36/237; Trs Pres Church Yth Grp; French Clb; Quiz Bowl; Var Capt Swmmng; High Hon Roll; Hon Roll; NHS; Ntl Merit Ltr; Ntl Merit Schlrshp 85-86; Bus Mgt.

CLEMENT, REGINA; Hope HS; Providence, RI; (Y); Boys Clb Am; Teachers Aide; Y-Teens; Chorus; School Musical; Variety Show; Stu Cncl; Howard U; Cmptr Sci.

COCCOLI, JESSICA; Mount Saint Charles Acad; Woonsocket, RI; (S); 15/166; Church Yth Grp; French Clb; Math Clb; SADD; Var Cheerleading; High Hon Roll.

COCKSHUTT, BARBARA; Pilgrim HS; Warwick, RI; (Y); Hon Roll; Secrtl.

CODERRE, THOMAS R; Saint Raphael Academy HS; Pawtucket, RI; (Y); Aud/Vis; Sec Computer Clb; Drama Clb; Exploring; Political Wkr; Stage Crew; Yrbk Stf; VP Stu Cncl; Hon Roll.

COELHO, KENNETH; East Prov SR HS; E Prov, RI; (Y); VICA; JV Ftbl; JV Trk; High Hon Roll; Hon Roll; NHS; Prfct Atten Awd; R I Chpt Of Amer Isnt Of Artahctct Awd Of Merit 86; Rgr Wlms Coll; Archtctr.

COIA, ROSEMARY A; Scituate JR SR HS; North Scituate, RI; (S); 11/119; Trs Am Leg Aux Girls St; Drama Clb; Trs FBLA; Yrbk Bus Mgr; Yrbk Stf; Stu Cncl; Stat Socr; Var Capt Vllybl; Cit Awd; Jr NHS; Hugh O Brian Yth Fndtn Ambassador 84; Vllybl All Div Hnrb Mntn 85; U Of RI Distngshd Fac Awd Prog 85; U Of RI; Bus Mngmnt.

COLINAN, JILL; Central Falls HS; Central Falls, RI; (Y); Am Leg Aux Girls St; Ed Yrbk Stf; Pres Frsh Cls; Sec Jr Cls; Trs Pres Stu Cncl; Var Capt Cheerleading; Hon Roll; U Of RI; Elem Tchr.

COLLARD, CLAIRE; Tiverton HS; Tiverton, RI; (Y); Trs Church Yth Grp; Off ROTC; SADD; Band; Mrchg Band; Orch; JV Vllybl; Hon Roll; The Retired Offcrs Assn Awd ROTC Medal 86; Miniture Boot Camp Orlando Fl 86; Accntng.

COLLETTE, MICHELLE M; St Raphael Acad; N Providence, RI; (Y); 8/178; Church Yth Grp; Dance Clb; Exploring; SADD; Rep Soph Cls; High Hon Roll; Hon Roll; NHS; Yrbk Lay Out Editor 85-86; Margaret Mc Gill Scholar Awd 86; RI Coll; Sec Ed.

COLOZZI, YVONNE; Chariho HS; Hope Valley, RI; (Y); OEA; Pep Clb; Chorus; Drill Tm; Variety Show; Off Jr Cls; Off Sr Cls; Stu Cncl; Score Keeper; Var Capt Cheerleading; Rhode Island U; Fshn Mdse.

COLUZZI, BETH; Tiverton HS; Tiverton, RI; (S); French Clb; Ski Clb; Band; Rep Stu Cncl; High Hon Roll; Hon Roll.

COLVIN, KIM; Pilgrim HS; Warwick, RI; (Y); Var Sftbl; Salve Regina Coll; Crmnl Jstc.

CONNELL, COLLEEN; Charino Regional HS; Charlestown, RI; (Y); 12/257; Church Yth Grp; SADD; Band; Yrbk Stf; Var Bsktbl; Var Fld Hcky; Trk; Hon Roll; Acdmc Decathlon 85-86; Stu Mnth 86; U RI; Engrng.

CONNOR, MARY; La Salle Acad; Providence, RI; (Y); Church Yth Grp; Cmnty Wkr; Library Aide; Band; Yrbk Stf; Rep Frsh Cls; Hon Roll; Rgnl CYO Ctr Rcgntn 86; Educ.

CONNORS, JOHN; Pilgrim HS; Warwick, RI; (Y); 59/307; Bsbl; Bsktbl; Socr; Trk; Spanish NHS; Bryant Coll; Mktg.

CONNORS, KAREN; St Raphael Acad; Cumberland, RI; (Y); Am Leg Aux Girls St; Church Yth Grp; Cmnty Wkr; SADD; Yrbk Stf; Score Keeper; Var Tennis; Hon Roll; NHS.

CONSTANTINEAU, LISA A; Burrillville JR SR HS; Mapleville, RI; (Y); 10/171; Math Tm; SADD; Band; School Play; Off Sr Cls; Stu Cncl; Stat Bsktbl; Var Fld Hcky; Hon Roll; NHS; Auren Jenks Schlrshp 86; Sec Of ST Ldrshp Awd 86; Stu Cncl Schlrshp 86; U Of NH; Nrsg.

CONTI, DOLORES; Classical HS; Providence, RI; (Y); Dance Clb; Math Clb; Math Tm; Orch; School Musical; Chorus; Hon Roll; Peabody Conserv Of Msc; Vlnst.

COOK, MELANIE A; The Wheeler Schl; Barrington, RI; (Y); 2/52; Math Tm; SADD; School Play; Stage Crew; Ed Lit Mag; Var Mgr(s); High Hon Roll; AFS; Var Score Keeper; NEDT Awd; Geneva, Switzerland Yth Understndng Exchng Stu 84-85; Cum Lande Soc 86; Highest Hnr Sci & Math Awd 86; Princeton U; Math.

COOK, STEVEN; Mt St Charles Acad; Millville, MA; (Y); 55/139; Cmnty Wkr; SADD; JV Bsbl; Im Bsktbl; JV Ice Hcky; Im Tennis; Hon Roll; Gold Medl-Hcky-Intl Trny 82; Cyclng, Bsbl & Hcky Awds 82-86; Anna Maria Col; Med Tech.

COONEY, KRISTEN; Mt St Charles Acad; Smithfield, RI; (Y); VP JA; Math Tm; Model UN; Ski Clb; Var L Sftbl; Var L Tennis; High Hon Roll; Hon Roll; NHS; All Div Tenns, Sftbl; Pre Law.

CORCORAN, GINA MARIE; N Providence HS; N Providence, RI; (Y); Church Yth Grp; Dance Clb; Girl Scts; Chorus; Church Choir; Sec Stu Cncl; Hon Roll; Bus.

CORCORAN, KATHLEEN; Charles E Shea HS; Pawtucket, RI; (Y); GAA; Capt Crs Cntry; Capt Trk; Hon Roll; Yrbk Stf; Trs Frsh Cls; Trs Soph Cls; Trs Jr Cls; Trs Stu Cncl; Bonnie Bell Cir Excllnc Certf Merit Crss Cntry 85-86; 2nd Tm All ST 1ST Tm All Div Crss Cnty 86; Graphic Ad.

CORDEIRO, ANTHONY; Bristol HS; Bristol, RI; (Y); 36/197; Boy Scts; Color Guard; Concert Band; Drill Tm; Drm & Bgl; Drm Mjr(t); Flag Corp; Jazz Band; Mrchg Band; Pep Band; Egle By Sct; U Of RI; Engr Elec.

CORDEIRO, BRIAN; Shea HS; Pawtucket, RI; (Y); Pres Church Yth Grp; Var Capt Ice Hcky; Var Capt Tennis; Hon Roll; Hnr Roll 85-86; U Of NH; Comp Engnr.

CORDEIRO, CHRISTINA; Shea HS; Pawtucket, RI; (Y); Library Aide; Hon Roll; NHS; RI Coll; Nrsng.

CORNACHIONE, LISA; Johnston SR HS; Johnston, RI; (Y); Nwsp Stf.

CORNELISON, CHRISTINA M; The Wheeler Schl; S Dartmouth, MA; (Y); Art Clb; Aud/Vis; Camera Clb; Drama Clb; Madrigals; Stage Crew; Nwsp Phtg; Nwsp Rptr; Lit Mag; Wt Lftg; Schlstc Art & Photo Awd 86; Roitman & Son Gold Key Wnnr 86; ARTS 86; RI Schl Dsgn; Apprl Dsgn.

CORRENTE, JEFFREY T; Barrington HS; Barrington, RI; (Y); 35/230; Computer Clb; VP Drama Clb; French Clb; Political Wkr; Nwsp Rptr; Im Bsktbl; Var Tennis; Im Vllybl; High Hon Roll; Math Clb; Mst Drmtc In Brrngtn 86; 3rd Grnt RI Sci Expo 85; Providence Coll; Pltcl Sci.

CORRENTE, LORI; Warwick Veterans HS; Warwick, RI; (S); Pres DECA; Hon Roll; 3 Awds In Finc & Crdt 85; ST VP & Chptr Pres Of DECA 85; Johnson & Whales Coll; Fshn Mrc.

CORRIGAN, KERRY; Mount Saint Charles Acad; N Providence, RI; (S); 2/162; Church Yth Grp; Cmnty Wkr; Dance Clb; SADD; Stu Cncl; Cheerleading; High Hon Roll.

CORSI, MICHAEL; La Salle Acad; Johnston, RI; (Y); Math Tm; Varsity Clb; Var L Ftbl; JV Var Trk; Hon Roll; NHS; Worcester Poly Inst; Engr.

CORVESE, ED; La Salle Acad; Johnston, RI; (Y); 15/296; Cmnty Wkr; Math Tm; JV Capt Bsbl; JV Bsktbl; Var L Ftbl; High Hon Roll; Hon Roll; Italian Cert Of Merit 83-85; Natl Lang Arts Olympiad Cert Of Distcntn 84.

CORY JR, DOUGLAS A; Tiverton HS; Tiverton, RI; (S); Variety Show; JV Var Socr.

COSTANTINO, HEATHER; Chariho Regional 4sr SR HS; Wyoming, RI; (Y); Pres Girl Scts; Math Tm; Science Clb; Var Bsktbl; Var Fld Hcky; Var Trk; High Hon Roll; Jr NHS; Gld Awd Hghst Grl Sct Hnr 85; Mrn Awd Cthlc Grl Sct Awd 84; Rdrs Dgst Cmnty Srvc Grnt 85; U Of RI.

COSTIGAN, JEFF; Lincoln HS; Manville, RI; (Y); 29/211; JV Var Bsbl; JV Var Ice Hcky; JV Var Socr; High Hon Roll; NHS; RI Hnr Socty 85-86; MA Inst Of Tech; Arch.

COTE, JENNIFER; Bristol HS; Bristol, RI; (Y); Art Clb; Cert Of Hnr In Indstrl Arts 85; Bryant Clg; Accntng.

COTE, MICHAEL R; N Smithfiels JR SR HS; N Smithfield, RI; (Y); French Clb; JA; SADD; Band; Hon Roll; RI Hnr Scty; RI Hrtg Assn Frnch Awd; N Smithfield Frnch Clb Comprhnsv Cntst Awd; Bryant Coll; Accntng.

COUTO, BERNADETTE; St Mary Acad; East Providence, RI; (Y); 14/215; Cmnty Wkr; Exploring; Pres French Clb; NHS; NEDT Awd; Fine Arts.

COUTU, NICOLLE; Scituate JR SR HS; N Scituate, RI; (Y); Chess Clb; Church Yth Grp; FFA; Concert Band; Mrchg Band; Pep Band; Nwsp Ed-Chief; Golf; Trk; Hon Roll; Clark; Sci.

COUTURE, MICHELLE ANN; Bishop Keough HS; Central Falls, RI; (S); VP Church Yth Grp; Drama Clb; Church Choir; School Play; Hon Roll; Brown U; Prelaw.

COUTURE, SHELLIE; Burrillville SR HS; Nasonville, RI; (Y); Church Yth Grp; Teachers Aide; Concert Band; Pep Band; Symp Band; High Hon Roll; Hon Roll; Broncette Figure Sktng Team Sec 86-87; Burrillville Fig Sktng Assn Mbr 83-86; Teaching.

COWETT, BETH; Classical HS; Providence, RI; (Y); French Clb; Hosp Aide; Teachers Aide; Temple Yth Grp; Hon Roll; Walter, Jen Z, Wally Sunbeam Awd 85.

CRANSHAW, CHRISTIN; St Marys Acad; Providence, RI; (Y); 50/198; Sec Trs Church Yth Grp; VP JA; Political Wkr; SADD; Church Choir; Hon Roll; NEDT Awd; Cmnty Wkr; Drama Clb; Exploring; U Of RI ST Sci Fair Spec Enrvnmtl Awd; Bst Actrs Awd-Pro N Rgnl CYO Drama Fstvl; ST Sci Fair Grnt; Psych.

CRETELLA, MICHELLE A; Barrington HS; Barrington, RI; (Y); Pres Church Yth Grp; French Clb; SADD; Lit Mag; Tennis; Vllybl; High Hon Roll; NHS; Art Clb; Dance Clb; Jrnl Bulletin Schltc Awd 86; East Bay CYO Yth Yr Awd 86; Pres Acad Fit Awd 86; Wesleyan U; Pre-Med.

CRIBB, RICHARD; Mount Saint Charles Acad; Smith, RI; (S); 1/149; Boys Clb Am; Cmnty Wkr; Math Tm; Ski Clb; School Play; High Hon Roll; NHS; Providence Jrnl Bulletin Schlrshp 85; Med.

CRISAFULLI, MARC; Mount Saint Charles Acad; Pawtucket, RI; (S); 17/143; Am Leg Boys St; Math Tm; Trs Soph Cls; Pres Stu Cncl; High Hon Roll; NHS; Most Spirited Stu; Century III Ldrs Awd; Polt Sci.

CROCKER, ANDREW; Lincoln HS; Lincoln, RI; (Y); Boy Scts; Trk; Vet Sci.

CROFT, ERIN; Warwick Vveterans Memorial HS; Warwick, RI; (Y); 18/298; Cmnty Wkr; Nwsp Stf; Stu Cncl; High Hon Roll; Yth-To-Yth Drg Free Yth; Puppt Shws For Chldrn Say No To Drgs; Exctive Cmmttee 4 Yrs Hlth Clb 10 11 12; Psych.

CRONIN, JOHN; Our Lady Of Providence HS; N Providence, RI; (Y); 18/100; Boy Scts; Church Yth Grp; Socr; Trk; Wrstlng; Hon Roll.

CRUGNALE, CHERYL; Tollgate HS; Warwick, RI; (S); Pep Clb; Spanish Clb; Chorus; Cheerleading; Gym; Pom Pon; Hon Roll; All Star Cheerldr 84-86; U Of RI; Pharmcy.

CRUZ, ANTONIO; Charles E Shea HS; Pawtucket, RI; (Y); 12/215; Hon Roll; NHS; Boys Clb Am; Ftbl; Socr; Trk; Vllybl; Stu Athlete Yr 86; Hall Inst; Drftng.

CULBERSON, PATRICIA; Tiverton HS; Tiverton, RI; (S); Drama Clb; French Clb; Ski Clb; Chorus; School Play; Stu Cncl; Var Cheerleading; Powder Puff Ftbl; High Hon Roll; Hon Roll; Vet Sci.

CULLEN, CHRISTIAN; Lincoln JR SR HS; Lincoln, RI; (Y); 3/211; Drama Clb; Math Tm; PAVAS; Chorus; School Play; JV Crs Cntry; Var Trk; Gov Hon Prg Awd; Pres Jr NHS; NHS; Ntl Merit Schlrshp 86; Engrng.

CULLEN, JOHN; Bishop Hendricken HS; No Kingstown, RI; (Y); 4/240; Church Yth Grp; Capt Quiz Bowl; Spanish Clb; Teachers Aide; Nwsp Rptr; Crs Cntry; Im Fld Hcky; Trk; High Hon Roll; Jr NHS; Holy Cross Coll JR Bk Awd 86; Jrnlsm.

CUNHA, MICHAEL; Warwick Vetrans Memorial HS; Warwick, RI; (Y); 40/298; Exploring; Math Tm; Drm Mjr(t); Rep Frsh Cls; Rep Soph Cls; Rep Jr Cls; Rep Sr Cls; Rep Stu Cncl; JV Bsbl; JV Socr; Ntl Itln Hnr Soc 85-86; RI Hnr Soc 85-86; RI Itln Hnr Soc; U Of RI; Pre-Vet.

CURE, MARTIN; Saint Raphael Acad; Cent Falls, RI; (Y); 81/186; Church Yth Grp; Cmnty Wkr; French Clb; Pep Clb; SADD; Im Bsbl; Im Bsktbl; JV Ftbl; Var Trk; Im Wt Lftg; Sci Awd 80 & 81; URI; Engrng.

CURRAN, JEFFREY M; N Smithfield JR SR HS; N Smithfield, RI; (Y); Boy Scts; Church Yth Grp; Debate Tm; SADD; Stat Concert Band; Jazz Band; Mrchg Band; Variety Show; Yrbk Stf; MVP Recrtnl Bsktbl NS Lg 85-86; Tchr.

CUSHMAN, JAMES; Woonsocket SR HS; Woonsocket, RI; (Y); Church Yth Grp; Quiz Bowl; Var Bsktbl; Var Trk; Hon Roll; Prfct Atten Awd; Bio.

CUSIMANO, MICHAEL D; Cumberland HS; Cumberland, RI; (Y); 15/369; Trk; Hon Roll; RI U; Mech Engr.

CYR, DEANNA; Woonsocket SR HS; Woonsocket, RI; (Y); Church Yth Grp; Math Tm; Capt Bsktbl; Var Cheerleading; Hon Roll.

CYR, JODI-LYNN; Woonsocket SR HS; Woonsocket, RI; (Y); Trs Church Yth Grp; Math Clb; Math Tm; Trk; High Hon Roll; Chrstn Sprtsmnshp Awd 84 & 85; Yth Svc Awd 84.

D ABATE, WENDY S; South Kingstown HS; Wakefield, RI; (Y); 21/210; Church Yth Grp; Cmnty Wkr; Debate Tm; Hosp Aide; Yrbk Stf; DAR Awd; Gov Hon Prg Awd; High Hon Roll; Hon Roll; NHS; U Of CT; Bus Fnc.

D ALENO, LENORA MARIE; Cov Entry HS; Coventry, RI; (Y); SADD; Jr Cls; High Hon Roll; Hon Roll; NHS; URI Alumni Bk Awd Ldrshp 86; Ntl Yth Convtn 85; Bus Adm.

D ORSI, DONNA; St Marys Acad Bayview; North Providence, RI; (Y); Church Yth Grp; Spanish Clb; VP Frsh Cls; Rep Soph Cls; Hon Roll; Pres Ftns Awd; Acctg.

DALY, KEARY; Prout Memorial HS; Kingston, RI; (S); 6/92; Math Clb; Math Tm; Stage Crew; Variety Show; Rep Jr Cls; Rep Stu Cncl; Var Crs Cntry; Hon Roll; High Hon Roll; U Of RI; Engrng.

DAM, CHIVENG; Hope HS; Providence, RI; (S); 10/163; Cmnty Wkr; English Clb; Off Sr Cls; Stu Cncl; Cit Awd; High Hon Roll; Hon Roll; Acad Ftnss Awd; NCCJ Awd; RI Coll; Intl Bus.

DAMBRA, ANGELIQUE; Central HS; Providence, RI; (Y); Sec Rep Jr Cls; Stu Cncl; Cheerleading; Hon Roll; Chrldng 84-85; Co-Capt Ftbl Chrldng 85; Capt Wrstlng; RIC; Bus.

DAMIANO, ANN MARIE; St Marys Acad; Providence, RI; (Y); Church Yth Grp; Exploring; Hosp Aide; Trk; NHS; Cert Awd Italian 3 86.

DANDENEAU, DIANE C; Cranston HS West; Cranston, RI; (Y); GAA; Spanish Clb; Soph Cls; Jr Cls; Sr Cls; Var Stu Cncl; Var Fld Hcky; Var Sftbl; Hon Roll; NHS; Sch Serv Awd; Engrg.

DAUPHINAIS, TINA; Cranston High School East; Cranston, RI; (Y); 40/373; Library Aide; School Play; Pres Frsh Cls; Hon Roll; NHS; Spanish NHS; Stu Mo 85; Wrld Ptry Hon Mntn 85; Pres Acdmc Awd 86; U Of Tampa; Psych.

DAVENPORT, LISA; Lincoln SR HS; Lincoln, RI; (Y); 52/181; JA; SADD; Variety Show; Cheerleading; Trs Frsh Cls; Trs Soph Cls; Trs Jr Cls; Trs Sr Cls; Rep Stu Cncl; Stat Vllybl; Cls Of 86 Schlrshp; U RI; Ed.

DAVENPORT, ROBERT; Lincoln SR HS; Lincoln, RI; (Y); 100/185; Variety Show; Mgr Bsbl; JV Var Bsktbl; Var Capt Ftbl; Trk; 1st Tm All-Div Ftbl 85; 2nd Tm All Call 84-85.

DAVIES, GREGG; Bishop Hendricken HS; Wakefield, RI; (Y); 101/240; Socr; French Hon Soc; Bus.

DAVIS, ERIN; Barrington HS; Barrington, RI; (Y); Intnl Clb; Soph Cls; Stu Cncl; Bsktbl; Crs Cntry; Vllybl; High Hon Roll; Hon Roll; Citzns Schrlshp Fund 1st Pl 84-85; Bio.

DAVIS, LINDA K; Rocky Hill Schl; Providence, RI; (Y); 3/30; Pres JCL; Latin Clb; Speech Tm; Band; Jazz Band; Orch; Cit Awd; High Hon Roll; Hon Roll; VP Jr Cls; Brown & Dartmouth Book Awds; Howland Msc Awd; Law.

DAVIS, THOMAS; Charles E Shea SR HS; Pawtucket, RI; (Y); 2/189; Computer Clb; Debate Tm; Jazz Band; Trs Jr Cls; Pres Sr Cls; JV Bsbl; DAR Awd; Elks Awd; Hon Roll; NHS; Sec Ed Intl Yth Yr Awd 85; Cong Yth Ldrshp Cncl 85; U RI; Phrmcy.

DAWES, TIMOTHY; Burrillville HS; Harrisville, RI; (Y); 28/180; School Play; VP Sr Cls; Var L Bsbl; Var L Bsktbl; Var L Ftbl; JV Socr; Hon Roll; All ST Ftbl 86; All Lg Bsktbl 86; West Point; Law Enfrcmnt.

DAY, PATRICK; Bishop Hendricken HS; W Kingston, RI; (Y); 27/240; Im Ice Hcky; Var Socr; High Hon Roll; Hon Roll; NHS; Spanish NHS; Pltcl Sci.

DE ANGELIS, ANTHONY; North Providence HS; N Providence, RI; (Y); Boys Clb Am; Yrbk Stf; Pres Frsh Cls; VP Soph Cls; JV Bsbl; Swmmng; Hon Roll; Jr NHS; Grand Lodge RH Sons Italy Amer 86.

DE CESARE, BRENDA; St Marys Academy Bay View; Warwick, RI; (Y); Exploring; Hosp Aide; Hon Roll; Pres Schlr; RI Hnr Soc 86; URI; Nrsng.

DE CRISTOFARO, CHARLES; Smithfield HS; Smithfield, RI; (Y); Church Yth Grp; Concert Band; Pep Band; JV Socr; Hon Roll; Sci.

DE GENOVA, KAREN; Pilgrim HS; Warwick, RI; (Y); 5/302; Drama Clb; Letterman Clb; Pep Clb; Quiz Bowl; Ski Clb; School Musical; Yrbk Stf; Capt Cheerleading; High Hon Roll; NHS; Itln Clb Pres; Wellesly Alumni Bk Awd 85; Boston College; Intl Rel.

DE LUCA, ANTHONY; Warwick Veterans Memorial HS; Warwick, RI; (Y); Boy Scts; Concert Band; Mrchg Band; Pep Band; JV Crs Cntry; Hon Roll; U Of RI.

DE MARCO, MARY C; Tiverton HS; Tiverton, RI; (S).

DE MAYO, LAURA; Mount Saint Charles Acad; Blackstone, MA; (S); 2/166; Church Yth Grp; JA; Math Tm; Ski Clb; Y-Teens; Orch; Swmmng; High Hon Roll; Jr NHS; MA Mdrn Miss 85-86; Acad All Amer 85; Natl Ldrshp & Serv Awd 85; Law.

DE MERCHANT, JEFF; Chariho Regional HS; Carolina, RI; (Y); 37/259; Boy Scts; VICA; High Hon Roll; Hon Roll; Comptr Sci.

DE ROSA, F ANTHONY; Mt St Charles Acad; N Attleboro, MA; (S); 19/166; Math Tm; Political Wkr; SADD; JV Var Ice Hcky; Var Trk; High Hon Roll; Hon Roll; Excelsior Awd Hgh Hnrs All Yr 84-85; U S Naval Acad.

DE SPIRITO III, ANTONIO; Barrington HS; Barrington, RI; (Y); 7/235; Boy Scts; Church Yth Grp; Computer Clb; Pres Debate Tm; Math Tm; NFL; Band; High Hon Roll; NHS; Century III Ldrshp Awd 86; U Of PA; Bus.

DEAN, LYNNE; North Smithfield JR SR HS; N Smithfield, RI; (Y); Drama Clb; French Clb; Chorus; School Play; Variety Show; Rep Frsh Cls; Rep Soph Cls; Rep Jr Cls; Hon Roll; All-ST Chors Membr 86; Tv Brodcstng.

DEANE, MICHELLE; Our Lady Of Fatima HS; Bristol, RI; (Y); 5/43; Dance Clb; Drama Clb; Ski Clb; School Play; Socr; Trk; High Hon Roll; NHS; U Of RI; Engnrng.

DEERING, NANCY; Warwick Veterans Memorial HS; Warwick, RI; (Y); Church Yth Grp; Cmnty Wkr; Letterman Clb; Spanish Clb; Varsity Clb; Gym; Timer; Hon Roll; Spanish NHS; St Schlr; Trinity Coll VT; Psych.

DEGNAN, DEBRA; St Raphael Acad; Central, RI; (Y); Var Capt Cheerleading; Var Pom Pon; Many Religious Retreats 84-86; CC RI; Secry.

DEITZ, APRIL; Smithfield HS; Greenville, RI; (Y); 17/208; Drama Clb; SADD; Ed Yrbk Ed-Chief; Rep Stu Cncl; NHS; St Schlr; Am Leg Aux Girls St; Camera Clb; Computer Clb; French Clb; Smithfield HS Schlrshp 86; U Of Tampa Pres Schlrshp 86; Lions Clb Schlrshp 86; U Of Tampa; Art.

DELANEY, KERRIN; Prout Memorial HS; N Kingstown, RI; (S); 15/76; Aud/Vis; Variety Show; Trs Frsh Cls; Rep Soph Cls; Trs Stu Cncl; JV Bsktbl; Var L Crs Cntry; Var Vllybl; Hon Roll; Ed.

DELEMONTEX, ELIZABETH; Pilgrim HS; Warwick, RI; (Y); Cmnty Wkr; Ski Clb; Spanish Clb; SADD; Flag Corp; School Play; Stage Crew; Yrbk Stf; Off Frsh Cls; Off Soph Cls; Bus Retl Mgnt.

DELGARDO, LA SHONNA; Mt Pleasant HS; Providence, RI; (Y); Church Yth Grp; Hosp Aide; Pep Clb; Cheerleading; Pom Pon; Hon Roll; Prfct Atten Awd; Boston Coll; Pedtrcn.

DEMATTEIS, ROBIN; St Mary Acad Bay View; Cranston, RI; (Y); Church Yth Grp; Cmnty Wkr; Exploring; French Clb; Hosp Aide; Quiz Bowl; Ski Clb; Hon Roll; Med Tech.

DEMERS, WENDY ANN; Woonsocket HS; Woonsocket, RI; (Y); Art Clb; SADD; RI School Design; Artst.

DENONCOURT, JAMES; Tolman HS; Pawtucket, RI; (Y); Computer Clb; Sec Frsh Cls; Cheerleading; Gym; 5th Pl All Around Gymnstcs Pgm 86; Keio U; Pre-Med.

DEROCHER, MICHELE; Coventry HS; Coventry, RI; (Y); Dance Clb; Spanish Clb; Variety Show; Yrbk Stf; Stu Cncl; Stat Socr; Stat Wrstlng; Hon Roll; Bus Mgmt.

DES MAISONS, EDWARD R; Toll Gale HS; Warwick, RI; (Y); 1/380; Math Tm; Q&S; School Play; Nwsp Ed-Chief; Lit Mag; Pres Stu Cncl; Capt Vllybl; NHS; Ntl Merit SF; Val; St Champ RI Acad Decathalon Tm 85; Harvard Book Awd; Pell US Hstry Awd; Stanford U.

DESCHENAUX, ROGER; Mt St Charles Acad; Blackstone, MA; (S); 8/142; Boy Scts; High Hon Roll; NHS; Worcester Poly Inst; Comp Sci.

DESIDERATO, LISA; Classical HS; Providence, RI; (Y); Cmnty Wkr; Hosp Aide; Political Wkr; Hon Roll.

DESMARAIS, EMILE; Woonsocket HS; Woonsocket, RI; (Y).

DESMARAIS, JACQUELINE; Woonsocket SR HS; Woonsocket, RI; (Y); 7/426; Dance Clb; French Clb; Yrbk Stf; Sec Jr Cls; Rep Stu Cncl; Var Cheerleading; High Hon Roll; Hon Roll; NHS; Schlrshp Frm Amrcn Bus Wmns Assoc 86; KI Mrt Schlr In Engl 86; Bentley Coll; Intl Bus Mgmt.

DESPLAINES, MICHAEL; St Raphael Acad; Pawtucket, RI; (Y); Cmnty Wkr; Drama Clb; Exploring; French Clb; Political Wkr; SADD; School Musical; School Play; Stage Crew; Elaine Coderre Awd Outstndg Srv 86; U Of RI; Plnt Sci.

DESROCHERS, ROLAND; St Raphael Acad; Riverside, RI; (Y); 3/181; Math Clb; Ftbl; Capt Trk; Wt Lftg; High Hon Roll; NHS; St Schlr; Val; Holy Crss Bk Prz 85; Annl HS Mathmtcs Ex Awd 85; DFA Schlrshp URI 85; U Rhode Island; Elec Engr.

DEXTRAZE, DARLENE; Woonsocket SR HS; Woonsocket, RI; (S); Math Tm; Color Guard; Drm Mjr(t); Mrchg Band; Yrbk Ed-Chief; Hon Roll; Surgcl Nrsng.

DI BIASE, ANN MARY; St Mary Academy Bay View; Cranston, RI; (Y); 5/230; Exploring; French Clb; Math Clb; Chorus; Hon Roll; Jr NHS; NEDT Awd; Acad Dcthln Mbr, URI Bk Awd, Natl Latn Exm Gld Mdl 85-86; Dr.

DI BIASIO, GINA; Coventry HS; Coventry, RI; (Y); 26/362; Hon Roll; Jr NHS; NHS; Keene ST Coll; Psychg.

DI CECCO, RHONDA; Central HS; Providence, RI; (Y); Nwsp Stf; Rep Jr Cls; Eng Awd In Upward Bound 86; Upward Bound Awd 85 & 86; Business Administration.

DI CHIARO, MICHAEL; Bishop Hendricken HS; Cranston, RI; (Y); 155/220; Boy Scts; Pres Church Yth Grp; Quiz Bowl; Ski Clb; VP Capt Swmmng; Biol.

DI MARZIO, DENISE M; North Providence HS; N Providence, RI; (Y); 8/226; Church Yth Grp; Nwsp Sprt Ed; Nwsp Stf; Yrbk Stf; Lit Mag; Jr NHS; NCTE Awd; NHS; Dr E A Ricci Itln Scholar 86; Fruit Hill Wmns Clb Scholar 86; RI Tchrs Itln Awd 84 & 85; RI Coll; Comm.

DI MASI, LISA; West Warwick SR HS; West Warwick, RI; (Y); 15/213; Am Leg Aux Girls St; Drama Clb; French Clb; Pep Clb; School Play; Variety Show; Yrbk Phtg; Yrbk Stf; Sec Frsh Cls; Pres Soph Cls; Stu Of Yr 83; Hugh O Brian Outstndng Awd 84; Stu Athlt Awd 86; U RI; Phrmcy.

DI NUNZIO, JOSEPH; North Smithfield HS; N Smithfield, RI; (Y); 8/149; Intnl Clb; JCL; Band; Chorus; Concert Band; Jazz Band; Lit Mag; JV Bsktbl; Var Golf; Hon Roll; All-St Band & Jazz Band 81-86; Natl Band Assn Jazz Band 86; Providence Coll.

DI PIPPO, GINA; Granston HS; Cranston, RI; (Y); 22/417; Debate Tm; Stage Crew; Lit Mag; Cheerleading; Hon Roll; NHS; Pres Schlr; St Schlr; Geo WA U.

DI PIPPO, GREGORY A; Classical HS; Providence, RI; (Y); Cmnty Wkr; Trs Latin Clb; Library Aide; Nwsp Stf; Lit Mag; Hon Roll; Ntl Merit SF; Slvr Mdl Natl Latin Cntst 83; Gold Mdl Natl Latin Cntst 85; Mc Gill U; Clscl Stu.

DICARLO, DEAN; Central HS; Providence, RI; (Y); Church Yth Grp; Navy; Cmmnctns Elec.

DICK, MARISSA; Warwick Veterans Memorial HS; Warwick, RI; (Y); 14/280; VP Church Yth Grp; Hosp Aide; Yrbk Ed-Chief; Capt Cheerleading; High Hon Roll; NHS; Spanish NHS; Hon Roll; Excel Frgn Lang, Ntl Hnr Soc Chrctr Schlrshps, Exec Comm Ldrshp Awd 86; Wheaton Coll; Elem Ed.

DILL, MATTHEW; Cranston High School West; Cranston, RI; (Y); 12/400; Church Yth Grp; Spanish Clb; Band; Variety Show; Hon Roll; NHS; Italian Hnr Scty 84-86; Music.

DIMASE, ROBERT; Lincoln HS; Lincoln, RI; (Y); 17/193; Varsity Clb; Variety Show; Bsktbl; Tennis; Bus.

DIPIPPO, MATTHEW; Middletown HS; Middletown, RI; (Y); #1 In Class; Drama Clb; Math Tm; Band; Concert Band; Mrchg Band; Stage Crew; High Hon Roll; Ntl Merit Ltr; Spanish NHS; Val; Holy Cross Book Awd 86; Claiborne Pell Awd-US Hstry Excllnc 86; Engrng.

DITUSA, LISA; Coventry HS; Coventry, RI; (Y); 40/362; Letterman Clb; Q&S; Rep Spanish Clb; Nwsp Rptr; Yrbk Stf; Trk; JV Vllybl; High Hon Roll; NHS; Grnt Tchrs Alliance & PTA Cncl 86; CCRI; Erly Chldhd.

DO COUTO, KATHLEEN; Tiverton HS; Tiverton, RI; (S); 16/187; Cmnty Wkr; Drama Clb; Girl Scts; School Play; Yrbk Stf; Sec Rep Stu Cncl; High Hon Roll; Hon Roll; NHS; Ntl Hnr Soc-Mst Outstndng Svc 85; Grl Sct Gld Awd 86; Advrtsng.

DOCHTERMAN, JOHN; Bishop Hendricken HS; North Kingstown, RI; (Y); 28/240; Church Yth Grp; Band; Concert Band; Mrchg Band; Pep Band; School Musical; Nwsp Rptr; High Hon Roll; NHS; Ntl Merit SF; Aernutcl Engr.

DOD, MARYPATRICIA; Our Lady Of Fatima HS; Barrington, RI; (Y); 4/43; Church Yth Grp; Drama Clb; School Play; Yrbk Stf; Sec Soph Cls; VP Jr Cls; Var Bsktbl; Var Crs Cntry; Civic Clb; St Schlr; Am Leg Warren RI Scholar 86; Salve Regina Newport; Sec Ed.

DODD, THOMAS; N Kingstown HS; N Kingstown, RI; (Y); 85/380; JV Wrstlng; Var Hon Roll; NHS; N Kingstwn Schl Srv Prsnl 86; Hall Inst Schlrshp 86; Fedrl Aid Frm 86; Hall Inst; Drftng.

DOLAN, WILLIAM J; Lincoln JR-SR HS; Lincoln, RI; (Y); 87/198; Pres Aud/Vis; Var Ftbl; Coll Of The Holy Cross; Pilot.

DONFRANCESCO, MICHAEL A; Lincoln HS; Lincoln, RI; (Y); 46/195; Am Leg Boys St; Var Capt Bsbl; Var Bsktbl; Hon Roll; Natl Hnr Soc 83; Junior Achvt 83; Math.

DONNELLY, PETER; Bishop Hendricken HS; N Kingston, RI; (Y); 77/237; Pres Church Yth Grp; Quiz Bowl; Ski Clb; Spanish Clb; Trk; Hon Roll; Mech Engrg.

DONNELLY, TIMOTHY; La Salle Acad; Johnston, RI; (Y); School Play; Ed Lit Mag; French Hon Soc; Gov Hon Prg Awd; High Hon Roll; Hon Roll; NHS.

DORCAS JR, TIMOTHY A; Classical HS; Providence, RI; (Y); Pres Exploring; School Musical; Lit Mag; Pres Sr Cls; VP Stu Cncl; Capt Var Trk; Hon Roll; Schlrshp Phillips Acad Smmrs 82-85; Citatn Providence Cty Cncl Hnr Rll & Trck Str Wk 84; Brown; Wrtr.

DOUGLAS, WILLIAM; Portsmouth HS; Portsmouth, RI; (Y); Pres FBLA; Band; Yrbk Stf; Rep Frsh Cls; Pres Soph Cls; Pres Jr Cls; Pres Sr Cls; Rep Stu Cncl; Mgr(s); Cit Awd; Am Leg Cert Schl Awd 86; Cngrssnl Medl Merit 86; Bryant Coll; Bus Mgmt.

DOWNEY, NICOLLE; Rogers HS; Newport, RI; (Y); Church Yth Grp; Cmnty Wkr; Cheerleading; Sftbl; Hon Roll; Hnr Rl 85-86; Sftbl Awd 84-85; Translator.

DRENNAN, MEREDITH; South Kingstown HS; Wakefield, RI; (Y); 80/220; Hosp Aide; SADD; Varsity Clb; Variety Show; Rep Sr Cls; Var Bsktbl; Var Capt Socr; Var Capt Trk; Hon Roll; Trs Frsh Cls; All ST Sccr 1st Tm Sweeper 83-85; All ST Track 2nd Tm 4x400 Relay 85; All ST Track 300 Hurdles 86; Accntng.

DUBE, CHRISTOPHER; Tiverton HS; Tiverton, RI; (S); Boys Clb Am; Socr; Hon Roll; Sakonnet Striders Schlrshp Rad Race 85; URI; Engrng.

DUBOIS, MARY ANNE LOUISE; North Smithfield JR SR HS; North Smithfield, RI; (Y); JA; Capt L Gym; High Hon Roll; Hon Roll; NHS; RI Hnr Soc 85-86; Dennison Mnfctrng Schlrshp Tpprwr 86; N Smith Vrsty Gym Tm MVP & Coch 84-85; Comm Coll RI; Chldhd Educ.

DUBOIS, MELISSA; Charitto Regional JR SR HS; Ashaway, RI; (Y); 1/275; Drama Clb; Hosp Aide; Math Tm; Science Clb; School Play; Bausch & Lomb Sci Awd; Jr NHS; NHS; Cmnty Wkr; High Hon Roll; Rensselaer Math & Sci Awd 86; Brown U Bk Awd 86; 1st Prz Watershed Area Essy Cont; Bus Law.

DUFF, DESIREE; Mount Pleasant HS; Providence, RI; (Y); Office Aide; Yrbk Stf; Var L Gym; Capt Score Keeper; Hon Roll; Outstndg Acctg I Awd 85-86; Outstndg Sclgy Awd 85-86; Outstndg Jrnlsm Awd 85-86; San Antonio Coll; Drg Rhbltn.

DUGAS, DANIELLE; N Smithfield HS; N Smithfield, RI; (Y); Church Yth Grp; French Clb; SADD; Wrtng.

DUGAS, SCOTT; La Salle Acad; Johnston, RI; (Y); Boy Scts; Var Debate Tm; Math Tm; Nwsp Rptr; Im Wt Lftg; JV Wrstlng; Hon Roll; Lion Awd; Sal; Debate Tm Ltr; Cert Hnr; Ntl Yth Physcl Ftns Pgm; Bryant Coll; Finance.

DUHAMEL, MARCEL C; N Smithfield HS; Forestdale, RI; (Y); 5/145; VP Debate Tm; VP SADD; Pres Jr Cls; Pres Sr Cls; DAR Awd; NHS; Ntl Merit Ltr; Am Leg Boys St; Boy Scts; Church Yth Grp; Cntry III Ldrshp ST Wnr 8; Boys Ntn 85; Eagle Scout 84; Case Wstrn Rsrv U; Lawyer.

DUMAIS, LYNN; Mt St Charles Acad; Woonsocket, RI; (S); 1/173; Church Yth Grp; Cmnty Wkr; Hosp Aide; Nwsp Stf; Trs Frsh Cls; VP Stu Cncl; High Hon Roll; Wntr Carnvl Qn 85; Dec Stdnt Mnth 85; Mst Spirtd Frshmn 84; Cmmnctns.

DUNBAR, KRISTA; Middletown HS; Little Compton, RI; (Y); 21/249; 4-H; Chorus; Yrbk Bus Mgr; Yrbk Sprt Ed; Lit Mag; High Hon Roll; Hon Roll; NHS; Spanish NHS; Pblshd 2 Ltrs Edtr 85; Natl Spnsh Hnr Soc 85-86; U Of RI; Bus Mngmnt.

DUNNINGTON, LYNDA; Narragansett HS; Narragansett, RI; (Y); Church Yth Grp; Hon Roll; U RI; Lndscpe Arch.

DUNPHY, MICHAEL; Saint Raphael Acad; Pawtucket, RI; (Y); Ftbl; Hon Roll; Bryant Coll; Acctnt.

DURDEN, CARLA; Woonsocket SR HS; Woonsocket, RI; (Y); Church Yth Grp; Cmnty Wkr; Church Choir; Concert Band; Fld Hcky; Var Sftbl; Ms N England Yth Wrkshp 86; Commnctn.

DURFEE, KEVIN; Narragansett HS; Narragansett, RI; (Y); 20/120; Ski Clb; Spanish Clb; Wrstlng; Hon Roll.

DWYER, KIMBERLY; Saint Raphael Acad; Pawtucket, RI; (Y); Drama Clb; Ski Clb; Spanish Clb; Stage Crew; Sec Sr Cls; Sftbl; Tennis; Tchr.

DWYER, TIMOTHY; St Raphael Acad; Pawtucket, RI; (Y); 20/181; Ski Clb; SADD; Pres Jr Cls; Stu Cncl; Bsbl; Bsktbl; Capt Ftbl; Trk; Dnfth Awd; NHS; Spn NHS; Hnr Rl; Boston U; Bus Adm.

EDGERTON, JOSEPH A; Bishop Hendricksen HS; N Kingston, RI; (Y); 151/231; Church Yth Grp; Ftbl; Ftbl Scholar U MA 86-87; Shotput Indr & Outdr ST Chmp 84-86; 2nd Pl New Englnd 85 & 86; U MA; Phys Ed.

EGAN, MARY; St Raphael Acad; Prov, RI; (Y); SADD; Sec Stu Cncl; JV Var Cheerleading; Hon Roll; NHS; Secty ST Ldrshp Awd 86; RI Hon Soc 86; Stonehill Coll; Bus.

EKLOF, DEAN; North Kingstown HS; N Kingstown, RI; (Y); Intnl Clb; Quiz Bowl; ROTC; Hon Roll; Master Councilor Of The Order Of De Molay 85; Model Legislature Rep 86; Engrng.

EKLUND, NICOLE; Middletown HS; Middletown, RI; (Y); Ski Clb; Yrbk Stf; Frsh Cls; Cheerleading; Crs Cntry; Powder Puff Ftbl; Trk; High Hon Roll; Hon Roll; Spanish NHS; Art Hnr Soc; U RI; Bus Mgmt.

ELDRIDGE, CHRISTINE; Mount St Charles Acad; Blackstone, MA; (S); French Clb; Concert Band; Mrchg Band; Cheerleading; High Hon Roll; Hon Roll; Jr NHS; RI All ST Band 86; Music Ed.

ENOS, MICHAEL; Classical HS; Providence, RI; (Y); Cmnty Wkr; Office Aide; Teachers Aide; School Play; Lit Mag; Hon Roll; Intl Bus.

ENOS, RUSSELL; Lincoln HS; Lincoln, RI; (Y); Variety Show; Var L Ftbl; Var L Trk; Law Enfrcmnt.

ERNST, LAURA; Prout Memorial Schl; Block Island, RI; (Y); 15/71; Am Leg Aux Girls St; Boy Scts; Cmnty Wkr; Computer Clb; Dance Clb; Debate Tm; Drama Clb; Exploring; French Clb; Political Wkr; Sccr Svc Awd 86; MIP Tnns 84; Pres Ftnss Awd 83-84; Rutgers U; Bus.

ESTEN, DAWN; St Marys Acad Bay View; Riverside, RI; (Y); Church Yth Grp; Exploring; French Clb; Girl Scts; Math Clb; Teachers Aide; Y-Teens; Church Choir; Gym; Hon Roll; Elem Educ.

ESTRADA, ELKIN; Central Falls JR SR HS; Central Falls, RI; (Y); Spanish Clb; Yrbk Stf; Socr; High Hon Roll; Jr NHS.

ESTRIN, ROBIN; Classical HS; Providence, RI; (Y); Cmnty Wkr; Latin Clb; Nwsp Ed-Chief; Nwsp Rptr; Yrbk Rptr; French Hon Soc; High Hon Roll; Ntl Merit Ltr; French Clb; Stage Crew; U Of PA Book Awd 86; 3rd Plc Amer Assoc Tchrs Frnch Cntst 85.

EUNIS, NATALIE; North Providence HS; Providence, RI; (Y); 34/250; High Hon Roll; Hon Roll; Acad Schlrshp Johnson & Wales 86; Johnson & Wales Coll; Fshn Merc.

FAGAN, CHRIS; Woonsocket SR HS; Woonsocket, RI; (Y); Boy Scts; Church Yth Grp; Quiz Bowl; Berklee Coll Of Music; Tchr.

FANTI, DONNA; St Raphael Acad; Riverside, RI; (Y); Cmnty Wkr; Drama Clb; French Clb; Intnl Clb; SADD; Stage Crew; French Hon Soc; Hon Roll; Pre-Med.

FARIA, SHARON; Lincoln JR SR HS; Lincoln, RI; (Y); 11/195; Variety Show; Sec Sr Cls; Rep Stu Cncl; JV Capt Bsktbl; Church Yth Grp; Dance Clb; Hon Roll; Jr NHS; NHS; Prfct Atten Awd; U Of VT; Phys Thrpst.

FARLEY, STEVEN; Saint Raphael Acad; Pawtucket, RI; (Y); 7/150; Chess Clb; CAP; French Clb; Math Clb; Math Tm; Stage Crew; French Hon Soc; High Hon Roll; NHS; 3rd Grant Sci Fair; Rep Schl Comp Pgm 85-86; Comp Sci.

FARRELL, LISA; Saint Raphael Acad; Lincoln, RI; (Y); 17/185; Cmnty Wkr; Hosp Aide; SADD; Capt Varsity Clb; Off Soph Cls; Off Jr Cls; Var Capt Cheerleading; Hon Roll; NHS; St Schlr; U RI; Psych.

FAUNCE, JULIE; Coventry HS; Coventry, RI; (Y); Hosp Aide; Y-Teens; Stat Bsktbl; Radio Clb; U Of RI; Law Enforcement.

FAUSTINO, NELSON; W M Davies Vo Tech; N Prov, RI; (Y); VICA; Concert Band; Mgr Bsbl; Mgr Socr; Wrstlng; Cit Awd; Hon Roll; NHS; Musicn Awd 86; Karate Actvty 85; North Eastern; Elctrncs Engrng.

FAWCETT, TRACY; Scituate JR SR HS; Foster, RI; (S); 5/112; Varsity Clb; Band; Jazz Band; Var Bsktbl; Var Sftbl; High Hon Roll; Jr NHS; NHS; NEDT Awd; Cert Musicianshp Awd Berklee Coll 85; RI All ST Bnd 86; Springfield Coll; Phys Ther.

FAY, COLLEEN; Warwick Veterans M HS; Warwick, RI; (Y); Hosp Aide; Mgr(s); Hon Roll; Italian Hon Soc; Elem Educ.

FAZIO, SARA; Warwick Vetgrans Memorial HS; Warwick, RI; (Y); #1 In Class; Debate Tm; Science Clb; Frsh Cls; Soph Cls; Jr Cls; Stu Cncl; Hosp Aide; Letterman Clb; Math Tm; Yrbk Stf; Hrvrd Bk Awd 86; Rnsslr Math & Sci Awd 86.

FELBER, STEVEN; Lincoln JR SR HS; Lincoln, RI; (Y); 14/181; Hon Roll; Jr NHS; NHS; Prfct Atten Awd; Pres Schlr; St Schlr; Durastone Flxcr Mfgs Schlrshp 86; Lncln Tchrs Assn Schlrshp 86; New Engld Inst Of Tech; Elec.

FENNESSEY, SUSAN; St Marys Acad -Bayview; Little Compton, RI; (Y); Church Yth Grp; Debate Tm; Drama Clb; Spanish Clb; Chorus; School Play; Bsktbl; Trk; VFW Awd; Voice Dem Awd; Commnctns.

FERREIRA, CORAL; Tiverton HS; Tiverton, RI; (S); 9/187; Hosp Aide; JV Cheerleading; High Hon Roll; Bridgewater ST Coll; Pre-Law.

FERREIRA, RICHARD; North Providence HS; N Providence, RI; (Y); Trs Church Yth Grp; JV Var Bsbl; JV Crs Cntry; Var Ftbl; Hon Roll; Jr NHS; Elect Tech.

FERRUCCI, STEVEN G; Cumberland HS; Cumberland, RI; (S); 11/389; JCL; JV Ftbl; JV Var Wrstlng; High Hon Roll; Hon Roll; VP NHS; St Schlr; Outstndg JV Wrstlr Awd 84-85; RI Readng Wk Bk Rvw Cont Wnr 86; Brandeis U; Pre-Med.

FERRY, HENRY; Mount St Charles Acad; Lincoln, RI; (S); 3/175; Ski Clb; VP Jr Cls; Rep Stu Cncl; JV Capt Bsbl; JV Capt Bsktbl; High Hon Roll; Jr NHS; Stdnt Mnth 85.

FINCK, BARRY; Classical HS; Providence, RI; (Y); Drama Clb; Latin Clb; Stage Crew; Yrbk Stf; Tennis; Hon Roll; Cert Honrbl Merit Cum Laude Natl Latin Exam 85 & 86; Gov Conf Drugs & Alcohol Rep 84; Economics.

FISHER, DAVID; Coventry HS; Coventry, RI; (Y); 12/350; French Clb; Science Clb; French Hon Soc; High Hon Roll; Hon Roll; Jr NHS; NHS; Ntl Merit Ltr; Engrng.

FISHER, GERALDINE; Woonsocket SR HS; Woonsocket, RI; (Y); High Hon Roll; Hon Roll; Prfct Atten Awd; St Schlr; French Awd 82-83; Tchrs Guild Schlrshp 86; Math Awd 82-83; RI Hnr Scty 86; U Of RI; Bus Adm.

FISHER, LOIS; St Marys Acad Bayview; Harrisville, RI; (Y); Church Yth Grp; Sec Exploring; Math Clb; Spanish Clb; Chorus; Hon Roll; Career Awarenss Explrng Pgm 84 & 85; Amateur Ath Union US Outstndng Achvt 84; Svc Cert Merit 85; Brown; Mth.

FITCH, MOLLY; Noah Kingstown HS; Jamestown, RI; (Y); 71/371; Church Yth Grp; Cmnty Wkr; Band; Concert Band; Mrchg Band; Var Capt Cheerleading; High Hon Roll; Hon Roll; Crwnd Suprmodl Of USA 86; Stu Of Wk 85; Emerson; Cmmnctns.

FITZPATRICK, ALAN; East Providence SR HS; Rumford, RI; (Y); Aud/Vis; VP Computer Clb; SADD; Stage Crew; Nwsp Phtg; Yrbk Phtg; L Crs Cntry; Trk; Bausch & Lomb Sci Awd; Jr NHS; Rep EPSH Acad Decathln 85-86; Embry Riddle; Astrnutcl Engr.

FLAD, JENNIFER; Portsmouth HS; Portsmouth, RI; (Y); 30/195; Band; Mrchg Band; Nwsp Phtg; Yrbk Phtg; Crs Cntry; Gym; Powder Puff Ftbl; Socr; Sftbl; Wt Lftg; X Cntry 2dn Tm All Divisn 82; Sccr Hon Mntn 85; Sftbl MVP 1st Tm All Divisn Capt 86; UNH; Bus Adm.

FLAGG, STEPHEN; Eat Providence HS; E Prov, RI; (Y); VICA; Prfct Atten Awd; Summa Cum Laude 83-84; Proj In-Site RI 83-84; MIT; Elec Engrng.

FLANAGAN, RICH; St Raphael Acad; Pawtucket, RI; (Y); 70/130; Boy Scts; Drama Clb; Concert Band; Variety Show; Var Crs Cntry; Var Trk; Hon Roll; Prfct Atten Awd; 3rd Hons June St Raphael Acad 85; 2nd Hons St Raphael Acad 86; SCI Arts.

FLEMING, LORI; St Marys Academy Bayview; Johnston, RI; (Y); 78/240; Cmnty Wkr; Drama Clb; Ski Clb; Spanish Clb; Yrbk Stf; Pres Frsh Cls; Rep Sr Cls; Rep Stu Cncl; Hon Roll; NEDT Awd; Mrktng.

FLOOD, KAREN L; Tolman HS; Pawtucket, RI; (Y); 11/276; Drama Clb; French Clb; Chorus; School Play; Yrbk Stf; Stu Cncl; Sftbl; Elks Awd; High Hon Roll; NHS; Outstndng French Stu; Hghst Avg Awd; Type Awd; URI; Pre-Med.

FLORU, STELLA; North Smithfield JR SR HS; N Smithfield, RI; (Y); Drama Clb; SADD; Comp.

FLUETTE, GERARD; Wood SR HS; Woonsocket, RI; (Y); Church Yth Grp; FCA; Library Aide; Band; Concert Band; Jazz Band; Mrchg Band; Hon Roll; URI; Comp Sci.

FOBER, PAMELA; Bishop Feehan HS; Pawtucket, RI; (Y); 120/241; Exploring; Hosp Aide; JV Cheerleading; Trk; Awd Outstndng Achvt Chem 86; Bus.

FOGARTY, JOHNNA; South Kingstown HS; Wakefield, RI; (Y); Dance Clb; Hosp Aide; SADD; Variety Show; Var Cheerleading; Var L Crs Cntry; Mgr(s); Var Trk; Hon Roll; All S Cnty Pos For X-Cntry 85; Law.

FOGERTY, JOHN; Pilgrim HS; Warwick, RI; (Y); 25/307; Stage Crew; Hon Roll; URI; Engl.

FOLLANSBEE, MICHELLE; Coventry HS; Coventry, RI; (Y); AFS; French Clb; JA; Chorus; Project Closeup 85; JA Offcr Yr Rnnr Up 83 & 84; JR Exec Awd 85; Exec Awd 85; Mngmnt Awd 84; Albertus Magnus Coll.

FOLLETT, KIMBERLY; Chariho JR SR HS; Ashaway, RI; (Y); 33/256; Chorus; Variety Show; Im Vllybl; Hon Roll; Pre Vet Med.

FONTAINE, JILL; St Mary Acad Bay View; Johnston, RI; (Y); Drama Clb; French Clb; JA; Ski Clb; Varsity Clb; VP Frsh Cls; Rep Soph Cls; Rep Jr Cls; Sec Sr Cls; Rep Stu Cncl; Intrschlstc Leag Dbls Titl 84; Presdntl Ftns Awd 86; Villanova; Poli Sci.

FONTAINE, LEO; Woonsocket SR HS; Woonsocket, RI; (Y); Church Yth Grp; Pep Clb; Jazz Band; Stage Crew; Variety Show; Rep Sr Cls; Rep Stu Cncl; Var Ice Hcky; High Hon Roll; Hon Roll; Athlcs Awd Ice Hcky; Svc Awd; Law.

FONTAINE, TANYA; Burrillview JRSR HS; Harrisville, RI; (Y); Varsity Clb; Band; Jazz Band; Mrchg Band; Pep Band; Stu Cncl; Var Cheerleading; Hon Roll; NCTE Awd; RI Music Edctrs Assn Solo-Ensmbl Mdl 84-85; Al-ST RI Band; Physcl Thrpy.

FORCIER, CHUCK; Lincoln JR SR HS; Manville, RI; (Y); 20/211; Chrmn Church Yth Grp; Quiz Bowl; Yrbk Stf; Rep Frsh Cls; Rep Soph Cls; Var Bsbl; JV Bsktbl; Hon Roll; Jr NHS; NHS; Comm.

FORGET, TODD; Woonsocket HS; Woonsocket, RI; (Y); Church Yth Grp; Pres Stu Cncl; Var Bsbl; Var Socr; Var Hon Roll; Bsbl ST Champ 86.

FORKIN, TRACY; La Salle Acad; Providence, RI; (Y); Hon Roll; NHS; Bus.

FORNARO, SUSAN LYNNE; St Mary Acad Bay View; Greenville, RI; (Y); 28/240; Sec Pres Exploring; Model UN; Spanish Clb; JV Crs Cntry; JV Var Sftbl; Hon Roll; NHS; Church Yth Grp; Pep Clb; NEDT Awd; Natl Latin Exam Cum Laude Cert; 1st Pl Latin Contst ; Hnrs Bio Dept Awd; Acad Svc Awd; Poltcl Sci.

FORTES, ANTONIO; Hope HS; Providence, RI; (S); 1/165; Capt Crs Cntry; JV Var Socr; Var Trk; Cit Awd; 4-H Awd; High Hon Roll; Hon Roll; Cross Cnty All ST 85; Excllnc Attnd & Schl Spirt Awd 83-86; All Cls Indr & Outdr Trck 85-86; Elec Engr.

FORTIER, MICHELE; Lincoln JR SR HS; Lincoln, RI; (Y); 42/195; Drama Clb; Chorus; JV Trk; RI All ST Chorus 85 & 86; Sec Schl Chorus 85-86; Hnr Rl 84-86; Bus Mgr.

FORTIN, LOUISE; Saint Raphael Acad; Pawtucket, RI; (Y); 68/181; Cmnty Wkr; Drama Clb; Girl Scts; SADD; School Musical; School Play; Stage Crew; Hon Roll; Drama Awd 84 & 86; RI Hnr Soc 86; Pres Acad Fit Awd 86; RI Coll; Studio Art.

FORTIN, MELISSA J; North Smithfield JR SR HS; Slatersville, RI; (Y); Drama Clb; VP French Clb; Concert Band; Jazz Band; Mrchg Band; Yrbk Ed-Chief; Stu Cncl; Vllybl; Hon Roll; Modlng.

FRAGOSE, JESSICA; North Providence HS; N Providence, RI; (Y); Cmnty Wkr; Hosp Aide; Office Aide; High Hon Roll; Hon Roll; Jr NHS; NHS.

FRAIOLI, SHARON; Bishop Keough Regional HS; Providence, RI; (S); 4/46; Stu Cncl; High Hon Roll; Hon Roll; NHS; URI Alumni Awd 85; Providence Coll; Med Tech.

FRANCIS, FRANK; Bristol HS; Bristol, RI; (Y); 11/200; Boy Scts; Scholastic Bowl; Ski Clb; Varsity Clb; Ftbl; Powder Puff Ftbl; Wrstlng; High Hon Roll; Jr NHS; NHS; U Of RI; Elec Engrng.

FRANCISCO, CELIA; La Salle Acad; East Providence, RI; (Y); Cmnty Wkr; Hosp Aide; High Hon Roll; Hon Roll.

FRANKLIN, KIMBERLY; Classical HS; Providence, RI; (Y); 47/261; Church Yth Grp; Hon Roll; Natl Itln Hnr Scty; Pres Acdmc Ftns Awd; Natl Mrt Schlrshp Tst Englsh; Rhode Island Coll; Psych.

FRANKLIN, PAM; St Marys Acad; Bristol, RI; (Y); 12/240; Am Leg Aux Girls St; Exploring; French Clb; Pep Clb; Yrbk Bus Mgr; JV Crs Cntry; JV Trk; Hon Roll; NHS; NEDT Awd; St Fnlst-Vs Japan Senate Exchng Pgm YFU 86; Schl US Hist Awd 86.

FREITAS, JOSE; Central Falls JR SR HS; Central Falls, RI; (Y); 14/120; Chess Clb; Latin Clb; Yrbk Stf; Socr; Wt Lftg; Wrstlng; Hon Roll.

FROMENT, NANCEY; Woonsocket SR HS; Woonsocket, RI; (Y); Church Yth Grp; Cmnty Wkr; Girl Scts; Pep Clb; Knigts Of Columbus Schlrshp 86; Bus Clb Schlrshp 86; Union St Jean Baptist 86; Nichols Coll; Child Socl Wrk.

FROST, ELIZABETH; St Mary Acad; Cranston, RI; (Y); 1/218; Math Clb; Science Clb; Ski Clb; Spanish Clb; Trs Jr Cls; Rep Stu Cncl; JV Crs Cntry; JV Trk; Bausch & Lomb Sci Awd; NHS; Contntl Mth Lg Awd 84; Dstngshd Faclty Scholar 86; Econ.

FUHR, MATTHEW; East Greenwich HS; East Greenwich, RI; (Y); Latin Clb; Office Aide; Science Clb; Teachers Aide; Concert Band; Mrchg Band; Pep Band; Var L Socr; Var Wrstlng; Hon Roll; NC ST Slct Sccr Tm 85; RI ST Slct Sccr Tm 86; Emory U; Intl Law.

FULTON, DAWN; Classical HS; Providence, RI; (Y); French Clb; Latin Clb; Math Tm; School Musical; French Hon Soc; High Hon Roll; Oberin Coll Bk Awd Exc Sci 86; Yng Keybd Artists Assoc Ntl Comptn SF 85; Ntl Latin Comptn Gold Medal; Music.

FURTIN, LESLEY; St Raphael Acad; Pawtucket, RI; (Y); Cmnty Wkr; Drama Clb; Spanish Clb; Yrbk Stf; Crs Cntry; Trk; Hon Roll; NHS; Spanish NHS; Acctg.

GABRIEL, CHRISTINE A; Lincoln JR SR HS; N Providence, RI; (Y); 40/181; Church Yth Grp; Sec Chorus; Variety Show; Yrbk Stf; Sec Jr Cls; Sec Sr Cls; Hon Roll; Jr NHS; Lincoln Cncl Arts Schlrshp 85-86; Lincoln Music Parents Assoc Schlrhps 85-86; Ed Found Schlrshp 85-86; Providence Coll; Music.

GAGNON, CLAUDINE; Warwick Veterans Memorial HS; Warwick, RI; (Y); 3/280; Letterman Clb; JV Sftbl; Var Tennis; Var Vllybl; DAR Awd; French Hon Soc; VP NHS; Rep Frsh Cls; Rep Soph Cls; Rep Jr Cls; Harvard Bk Awd 85; Worcester Polytechnic Inst.

GAGNON, PATRICIA; Burrillville HS; Harrisville, RI; (Y); Band; Mrchg Band; Pep Band; Stage Crew; Tennis; High Hon Roll; Hall Fm Hnrs Musc 86; Solo & Ensbl Fest Mdl Rcpnt 84-86; Msc Enthst Awd 86; U Of NH; Music.

GAINES JR, PAUL; Rogers HS; Newport, RI; (Y); Church Yth Grp; JA; Band; Drm Mjr(t); Mrchg Band; Var Ftbl; Var Capt Trk; 2 1st Tm Selectns Clss B Outdr Trck; 1 2nd Tm Selectn All ST Outdr Trck; Band Drum Mjr & VP; Podiatric Medicine.

GALAMAGA, PAUL; Bishop Hendricken HS; Warwick, RI; (Y); 30/230; Nwsp Rptr; VP Frsh Cls; Pres Soph Cls; Pres Jr Cls; Pres Sr Cls; JV Socr; JV Var Trk; High Hon Roll; NHS; Spec Awd For Distngshng Fire At Local Rest 85.

GALHARDO, LISA; Tiverton HS; Tiverton, RI; (S); 13/187; Stu Cncl; Score Keeper; High Hon Roll; Hon Roll; NHS; Bus Admin.

GALLAGHER, KELLY; St Marys Acad Bay View; Coventry, RI; (Y); 80/230; Exploring; Math Clb; Nwsp Rptr; Yrbk Stf; Trs Frsh Cls; Svc Project Insike Project Close-Up; Chld Psych.

GALLAGHER, MELISSA; Burrillville JR SR HS; Harrisville, RI; (Y); Church Yth Grp; Cmnty Wkr; Teachers Aide; Yrbk Stf; Stu Cncl; High Hon Roll; Hon Roll; St Schlr; Bst Bus Stu 85; Dudley Hall Inst Schlrshp 86; Dudley Hall Inst; Sec.

GALLEGO, LORI; East Providence HS; E Providence, RI; (Y); Cmnty Wkr; French Clb; JA; Quiz Bowl; SADD; French Hon Soc; High Hon Roll; Hon Roll; Wells Coll; Educ.

GAMACHE, JAMES; North Smithfield HS; N Smithfield, RI; (Y); 3/145; Boy Scts; French Clb; SADD; Yrbk Sprt Ed; Stu Cncl; JV Bsbl; High Hon Roll; Varsity Clb; St Schlr; U RI Distngshd Faclty Awd 86; RI Hnr Soc 86; Knghts Columbus Scholar 86; U RI; Elec Engrng.

GAMELIN, SUZANNE; Coventry HS; Coventry, RI; (Y); 110/365; Am Leg Aux Girls St; French Clb; Letterman Clb; Q&S; Variety Show; Nwsp Rptr; Yrbk Sprt Ed; Rep Jr Cls; Bsktbl; Vllybl.

GANUNG, SUSAN; Smithfield HS; Greenville, RI; (Y); 12/199; Band; Rep Jr Cls; Rep Sr Cls; Stu Cncl; Var Cheerleading; Hon Roll; Ntl Merit Ltr; Church Yth Grp; French Clb; Chorus; RI ST Band, RI Phlhrmnc Yth Orch 83-86; Scl Cmmtes 85-87; Lbrl Arts.

GARCEAU, DAWN; Chariho Regional JR SR HS; Hopkinton, RI; (Y); 14/252; Band; Hon Roll; High Level Study & Profcncy Span 84; Acctg.

GARDNER, SHERI; Smithfield HS; Smithfield, RI; (Y); 9/206; Off Jr Cls; Off Sr Cls; Off Stu Cncl; Hon Roll; NHS; Katharine Gibbs Dmnd Jubilee Schlrshp 86; RI Hnr Soc 86; RI Gen Trsrs Awd 86; Katharine Gibbs Schl; Exec Secy.

GARRIEPY, DAWN; Smithfield HS; Smithfield, RI; (Y); Drama Clb; JV Bsktbl; JV Fld Hcky; Var L Trk; Hon Roll; Bio.

GAUDREAU, BRIAN; Mount Saint Charles Acad; Woonsocket, RI; (Y); 31/178; Cmnty Wkr; VP Soph Cls; JV Bsbl; Var Capt Bsktbl; High Hon Roll; Hon Roll; NHS; Outstndng HS Athlts Of Amer; 1st Prsn To Scr 1000 Creer Vrsty Pnt-Bsktbl-HS.

GAULIN, KIM; Burrillville JR SR HS; Mapleville, RI; (Y); 83/181; Pres Church Yth Grp; Church Choir; Variety Show; Stu Cncl; Capt Bsktbl; Capt Vllybl; Fmly Of Yr 85; Sec.

GAUTHIER, JOYCE; Pilgrim HS; Warwick, RI; (Y); High Hon Roll; Hon Roll; Ldrshp Awd For Future Secrtries 86; Sec.

GAUTREAU, SUSAN; Borrillville JR SR HS; Pascoag, RI; (Y); Teachers Aide; Band; Mrchg Band; VP Frsh Cls; Rep Jr Cls; Stu Cncl; Var Bsktbl; Var Fld Hcky; Var Sftbl; Hon Roll.

GAYLORD, SCOTT W; Cumberland HS; Cumberland, RI; (S); 1/400; Church Yth Grp; JCL; Chorus; Rep Jr Cls; Rep Sr Cls; Var Stu Cncl; Var L Bsktbl; Var L Trk; NHS; Val; Commended Stu PSAT 86; Magna Cum Laude Ntl Latn League 85; Colgate U.

GEHRENBECK, DAVID; Classical HS; Providence, RI; (Y); 2/250; Boy Scts; Pres Latin Clb; Church Choir; School Musical; School Play; Rptr Lit Mag; Rep Stu Cncl; Var Trk; French Hon Soc; JV Crs Cntry; Hugh O Brian Yuth Fdtn 85; Harard Bk Awd 86.

GEISSER, BARBARA J; North Providence HS; N Providence, RI; (Y); 71/213; Church Yth Grp; GAA; Nwsp Stf; Yrbk Stf; Sftbl; Hon Roll; RI Coll; Elem Ed.

GELLIS, JENNY; Casskal HS; Providence, RI; (Y); Church Yth Grp; French Clb; JA; Latin Clb; Var Cheerleading; Hon Roll.

GENNARI, KAREN; East Providence SR High; East Providence, RI; (S); 10/523; Church Yth Grp; Cmnty Wkr; Dance Clb; Concert Band; Variety Show; Nwsp Rptr; Ed Nwsp Stf; NHS; Band; ST Ballet RI Apprentc 84-85; Wheaton Coll.

GEOFFROY, KIM; Woonsocket SR HS; Woonsocket, RI; (Y); Capt Cheerleading; Sftbl; Hon Roll.

GEORGE, BRIAN; North Providence HS; N Providence, RI; (Y); 57/260; JA; Ski Clb; Varsity Clb; Nwsp Rptr; VP Soph Cls; Pres Jr Cls; Pres Sr Cls; Trs Stu Cncl; VP Var Bsktbl; Hon Roll; Arctctrl Engr.

GERUSO, DONNA; North Smithfield JR SR HS; Slatersville, RI; (Y); Drama Clb; French Clb; Intnl Clb; Letterman Clb; SADD; Chorus; Yrbk Phtg; Yrbk Stf; Stu Cncl; Var Capt Cheerleading; Psych.

GERVASIO, RAUL; La Salle Acad; Smithfield, RI; (Y); Chess Clb; Computer Clb; Math Tm; Nwsp Rptr; Yrbk Ed-Chief; Yrbk Stf; Gov Hon Prg Awd; Hon Roll; NHS; Rensselaer Polytech Inst Medal 85-86; Biochmstry.

GIBBONS, BONNIE; Pilgrim HS; Warwick, RI; (Y); Spanish Clb; Drm & Bgl; Var Trk; Hon Roll.

GIBERTI, ELIZ; Classical HS; Providence, RI; (Y); Bsktbl; Sftbl; Providence Coll; Acctng.

GIBSON, MICHAEL; Portsmouth HS; Virginia Beach, VA; (Y); 44/212; FBLA; Math Tm; Band; Var L Ftbl; Wt Lftg; 2nd Pl ST FBLA Comp 86; TX A&M; Biol.

GIORGIANNI, CATHERINE; Bishop Keough HS; Providence, RI; (S); 3/46; Cmnty Wkr; Tennis; High Hon Roll; NHS; Holy Crs Book Prize Regln Awd 85; Frnch & Hstry Awd 83; Hstry Awd 84; RI Coll; Elem Ed.

GIRARD, GERIK; Narragansett HS; Narragansett, RI; (Y); German Clb; Ski Clb; Variety Show; Rep Stu Cncl; Var Capt Socr; Tennis; Wrstlng; Hon Roll; Cert Of Excllnc Awd Frnch; 1st Tm All Div Sccr.

GLASSCOCK, DAVID; Woonsocket HS; Woonsocket, RI; (Y); 30/430; Boy Scts; Library Aide; Yrbk Stf; Hon Roll; Prfct Atten Awd; Bryant Coll; Accntng.

GLEASON, DEBORAH; Prout Memorial HS; North Kingstown, RI; (Y); 16/71; Church Yth Grp; Hosp Aide; Band; Chorus; Color Guard; Concert Band; School Musical; Hon Roll; Rhode Islnd Hnr Soc 86; Northeastern U; Phy Thrpy.

GLOVER, ELIZABETH; Lincoln HS; Lincoln, RI; (Y); 19/192; Church Yth Grp; Drama Clb; JA; School Play; Variety Show; Stu Cncl; Cheerleading; Hon Roll; NHS; Pres Schlr; R I Distngshd Sr Awd 86; Colgate U.

GLUCKSMAN, DANIEL; Pilgrim HS; Warwick, RI; (Y); Trs Am Leg Boys St; Boy Scts; JA; Temple Yth Grp; Band; Nwsp Rptr; Pres Soph Cls; Stu Cncl; JV Socr; Hon Roll; 1st Rnnr Up Fine Arts Awd-Acad Decthln 86; ST Senate Yth Fnlst 85; Lester Aptel Awd Frm Synogogue 85; Mktg.

GOEBEL, KIM; Lincoln HS; Lincoln, RI; (Y); 61/195; Stage Crew; Stu Cncl; Var L Bsktbl; Var L Sftbl; Var L Tennis; Hon Roll; Mtrpltn Div Fast Pitch All Star Team 86; Physcl Thrpy.

GOFF, DONNA; North Smithfield HS; N Smithfield, RI; (Y); Dance Clb; Debate Tm; French Clb; Letterman Clb; Library Aide; Pep Clb; Band; JV Capt Cheerleading; Gym; Sftbl; Providence Coll Smmr Sci Prog 84-85; New Engl Jr Sci Sympsm U MA 85-86; Med.

GOLANSKI, CANDACE; Prout Memorial HS; N Kingstown, RI; (Y); 18/71; Drama Clb; Color Guard; Flag Corp; School Musical; Stage Crew; Nwsp Rptr; Hon Roll; Ntl Merit Ltr; Fordham U; Pre-Law.

GOLDITCH, JASON; Hope HS; Providence, RI; (Y); 22/133; Aud/Vis; PAVAS; Radio Clb; Teachers Aide; Dr Mrtn Lthr Kng Achvt Awds 85-86; Ooutstndng Media Stu Awd 86; Emrsn Coll; Mass Comm.

GOLDSTEIN, JENNIFER; South Kingstown HS; Peace Dale, RI; (Y); 11/211; Cmnty Wkr; Hosp Aide; Nwsp Rptr; JV Var Crs Cntry; JV Trk; CC Awd; High Hon Roll; Hon Roll; Pres NHS; URI Alumni Assoc Schlrshp, KSHS Exclnce French 86; SKHS Exclnce Span 85; U RI; Psych.

GOMES, MICHAEL; Saint Raphael Acad; Pawtucket, RI; (Y); 2/180; Math Tm; Political Wkr; Quiz Bowl; Var Crs Cntry; Var Tennis; French Hon Soc; High Hon Roll; Pres NHS.

GOMEZ, HOLLY; Middletown HS; Little Compton, RI; (Y); Church Choir; Cheerleading; Hon Roll; Nrsng.

GOODHART, GINA; Bishop Keough Reg HS; N Providence, RI; (S); Trs Jr Cls; High Hon Roll; Hon Roll; NHS; Ntl Merit Schol; Consistent Hard Working Awd 82; U RI; Pharm.

GOODWIN III, JOHN R; Chariho Regional HS; Charlestown, RI; (Y); 52/256; Boy Scts; Nwsp Rptr; VP Frsh Cls; Rep Soph Cls; Rep Jr Cls; Tennis; Spcl Frcs.

GOUGH, MARGARET; Prout Memorial HS; W Warwick, RI; (Y); 27/71; Exploring; Girl Scts; Math Tm; Pres Chorus; Flag Corp; Madrigals; School Musical; Stage Crew; Lit Mag; Hon Roll; Natl Schl Choral Awd 86; Parents Cncl Svc Awd 86; Rsprtry Thrpy.

GOUIN, LOUISE; Lincoln SR HS; Manville, RI; (Y); 2/195; Trs Frsh Cls; Trs Soph Cls; Trs Jr Cls; Trs Sr Cls; French Hon Soc; High Hon Roll; NHS; Biochem.

GOULD, ROBERT; Rogers HS; Newport, RI; (Y); Math Clb; Yrbk Stf; Rep Jr Cls; Stu Cncl; Tennis; French Hon Soc; Hon Roll; NEDT Awd; Engr.

GOULET, DAN; Burrillville HS; Pascoag, RI; (Y); JV Bsbl; JV Bsktbl; Var L Socr; Hon Roll; Golf; 1st Grant Sci Fair 84-85; ST Sci Fair 2nd Grand 84-85; Gov Pgm Mth & Sci 86; Comp Sci.

GOYETTE, PATRICIA; Wm M Davies Vo Tech; Pawtucket, RI; (Y); 10/163; Girl Scts; VICA; Band; Concert Band; Nwsp Ed-Chief; Yrbk Phtg; Rep Stu Cncl; Var Cheerleading; Var Swmmng; High Hon Roll; Bryant College; Acctg.

GRAY, KAREN; South Kingstown HS; West Kingston, RI; (Y); 21/211; Art Clb; Cmnty Wkr; Math Clb; Hon Roll; NHS; Mcdnlds Crew Schlrshp 86; RI Dstngshd Snr 86; U Of RI; Premed.

GRAY, LYNDA; Davies Voc Tech HS; Pawtucket, RI; (Y); Boys Clb Am; Computer Clb; Library Aide; Math Clb; Science Clb; SADD; VICA; Band; Yrbk Stf; Frsh Cls; Katherine Gibbs; Exec Sec.

GRAY, SCOTT; Bishop Hendricken HS; N Kingstown, RI; (Y); 2/240; Cmnty Wkr; Spanish Clb; School Play; Bsbl; High Hon Roll; NHS; Sal; Spanish NHS; Harvard Bk Awd 86; Med.

GRECO, WILLIAM; Woonsocket HS; Woonsocket, RI; (Y); Church Yth Grp; JA; JV Bsbl; JV Bsktbl; Var Socr; High Hon Roll; Hon Roll; Hnr Rll 84-86; Agrcltr.

GREEN, LISA CHRISTINE; Prout Memorial HS; Wakefield, RI; (S); Aud/Vis; Dance Clb; Stage Crew; Yrbk Stf; Rep Stu Cncl; High Hon Roll; Hon Roll; Zangrille Schlrshp 85; Dghtrs Isabella Schlrshp 83; U Of RI.

GREENE, TARA; Charing HS; Charlestown, RI; (Y); Camera Clb; Debate Tm; FBLA; Model UN; Ski Clb; SADD; School Musical; Var Bsktbl; Var Trk; High Hon Roll; Engrng.

GREENWOOD, JULIE; Johnston SR HS; Johnston, RI; (S); 12/216; DECA; Science Clb; Drm Mjr(t); Yrbk Stf; Hon Roll; NHS; Acad Decathlon 85; Intl Tchrs Italian Awd; Insite; Finance.

GRENIER, RAYMOND; Mount Pleasant HS; Providence, RI; (Y); Var Bsbl; Capt Var Ftbl; JV Var Score Keeper; Var Trk; Gov Hon Prg Awd; Hon Roll; Prfct Atten Awd.

GRENIER, RICHARD; Mount St Charles Acad; Franklin, MA; (Y); 45/168; Boy Scts; French Clb; Band; Church Choir; Concert Band; Mrchg Band; Hon Roll; Msc Awd 84-86; Vlntr Awd 84-86; Ordr Arrw 84-86; Bio.

GRIEVE, KERRIE; Charles E Shea SR HS; Pawtucket, RI; (Y); 14/220; Variety Show; Yrbk Stf; Rep Jr Cls; Rep Sr Cls; Pres Stu Cncl; Cit Awd; Hon Roll; Fernand St Germain Medl Merit 86; Martha Janes Schlrshp Awd 86; U Of RI; Dntl Hygn.

GRIFFITH, AMY; East Greenwich HS; E Greenwich, RI; (Y); 34/172; Hosp Aide; JA; Spanish Clb; Stage Crew; Variety Show; Cheerleading; VFW Awd; E Grnwch Frmns Schlrshp 86; Bryant Coll; Bus Admin.

GRILLI, GLENN; Johnston SR HS; Johnston, RI; (Y); Var Ftbl; Var Trk; Hon Roll; Ntl Hist Day ST Awd 84; Ntl Hist Day Ntl Fnlst 85; Psychlgy.

GROSSER, KRISTEN; Mt Saint Charles Acad; Bellingham, MA; (S); 9/169; Cmnty Wkr; Hosp Aide; Chrmn Stu Cncl; High Hon Roll.

GUAY, BRUCE; Mt St Charles HS; N Smithfield, RI; (S); 9/141; Computer Clb; Latin Clb; Math Tm; Political Wkr; Pres Jr Cls; Stu Cncl; Var Capt Ice Hcky; JV Socr; High Hon Roll; NHS; Notre Dame U; Med.

GUDAITIS, LEE; Barrington HS; Barrington, RI; (Y); Church Yth Grp; Key Clb; Stage Crew; Nwsp Rptr; Nwsp Stf; Yrbk Stf; Lit Mag; Eng.

GUERNON, MICHAEL; Burrillville HS; Glendale, RI; (Y); Am Leg Boys St; Church Yth Grp; SADD; Jazz Band; Nwsp Rptr; Pres Soph Cls; Pres Jr Cls; Pres Sr Cls; Stu Cncl; JV Var Socr; Tennis Tm 85-86; Theatr Co RI 83-85; RI Modl Legsltr 86-87; Providence Coll; Poltcl Sci.

GUERRA, LISA; Our Lady Of Fatima; Bristol, RI; (Y); 1/42; Drama Clb; Yrbk Stf; Jr Cls; Sr Cls; NHS; Prfct Atten Awd; Val; Providence Coll; Bio.

GUERTIN, PAMELA; E P SR HS; Riverside, RI; (Y); Lit Mag; Acctg.

GUIBEAU, CHRIS; East Providence HS; Rumford, RI; (Y); French Clb; JV Crs Cntry; Var Trk; Hon Roll; NHS; MIP Indoor Track 85-86; Worchester Polytech; Comp Engr.

GUILBAULT, BRIAN; Burrillville HS; Pascoag, RI; (Y); 2/180; Stu Cncl; Var L Bsbl; Var L Ice Hcky; Var L Socr; High Hon Roll; NHS; Math Tm; Varsity Clb; Band; Outstndng Acdmc Achvt Math & Frnch 85; RI Modl Legsltr 86; Engrng.

GUILBEAULT, JUDY; Smithfield HS; Smithfield, RI; (Y); 7/208; Church Yth Grp; GAA; Varsity Clb; Rep Stu Cncl; Var Sftbl; Elks Awd; NHS; Ntl Merit Ltr; Prfct Atten Awd; St Schlr; Cert Merit Englsh; RI Hon Soc; U CT; Phrmcy.

GUILLET, DONNA; Woonsocket SR HS; Woonsocket, RI; (Y); SADD; Yrbk Stf; Var Mgr Vllybl; High Hon Roll; NHS; Pres Schlr; Athletic Awd-Vllybll Mgr 86; Athletic Awd-Vllybll Vrsty 85.

GULINELLO, JAMES; Burrillville JR SR HS; Pascoag, RI; (Y); 30/174; Trs Church Yth Grp; Drama Clb; SADD; Church Choir; Concert Band; Jazz Band; Orch; Nwsp Stf; NHS; Mcdonalds All Amer Band 85; Hstry Buff Awd 84; Eastrn Nazarene Coll Alumni Bk Schlrshp-$100 86; Eastern Nazarene Coll; Bus Admi.

GUSTAFSON, CARL DAREN; William M Davies Jr Vo-Tech; N Providence, RI; (Y); SADD; VICA; Stu Cncl; Hon Roll; RI Coll; Marine Outbrd Mech.

GUSTAFSON, DEBORAH; Pilgrim HS; Warwick, RI; (Y); 87/307; Church Yth Grp; Ski Clb; Var Capt Fld Hcky; Var Gym; Var Sftbl; 1st Pl Frnch Spllg Bee 83; 2nd Pl Sci Fair 83; Fld Hcky All Div All Tourn 85; URI; Gen Bus.

GUSTAFSON, DEBRA L; Cranston HS East; Cranston, RI; (Y); 26/288; Band; Stu Cncl; Hon Roll; Jr NHS; NHS; Pres Schlr; RI Hnr Soc 86; Thunderbolt Band Awd 86; Dorothy P Cosale Mem Schlrshp 86; U Of CA; Spch & Hearing.

HADLEY JR, ROBERT G; Bishop Hendricken HS; Coventry, RI; (Y); 28/240; Ski Clb; Rep Jr Cls; Rep Stu Cncl; Var JV Socr; Elks Awd; High Hon Roll; Hon Roll; NHS; Spanish NHS; Bryant Coll; Bus Mgmt.

HAGAN II, WILLIAM JOHN; Classical HS; Providence, RI; (Y); Boy Scts; Debate Tm; Science Clb; Pres Speech Tm; Nwsp Stf; Off Jr Cls; Stu Cncl; French Clb; RI ST Wnnr Amer Lgn Nat HS Cntst 86; Ust Rnkd RI Lncoln-Douglas Dbt 85-86; Ust Pl Dbt Tm RI 85-86; Intl Affrs.

HAITZ, JEFFREY; Chariho Reginal HS; Charlestown, RI; (Y); Wrstlng; High Hon Roll; Hon Roll.

HALLIWELL, JON; Warwick Veterans Memorial HS; Warwick, RI; (Y); 13/298; Boy Scts; Stage Crew; Pres Stu Cncl; Var Ftbl; Var Trk; Wt Lftg; Hon Roll; Jr NHS; NHS; Spanish NHS; Eagl Sct 85; Bus.

HALLORAN, SUSAN; Lincoln HS; Lincoln, RI; (Y); 45/181; Library Aide; Nwsp Rptr; Crs Cntry; Denise Boulis Friends Of Lincoln Lbry Schlrshp 86; Twn & Cntry Trnsprtn Schlrshp 86; Providence Clg; Elem Educ.

HAMILTON, MATTHEW B; Providence County Day Schl; Providence, RI; (Y); 4/43; Sec Trs Drama Clb; Political Wkr; Rptr Nwsp Stf; Rptr Yrbk Stf; Rep Frsh Cls; Rep Soph Cls; Rep Sr Cls; Sec Stu Cncl; Ntl Merit Ltr; St Schlr; Membr Gum Laude Soc; Pell Medl For Exllnc US Hist; Richard S Stanzler Mem Prz For Excellnc Hmnts; U Of Chicago Coll; Librl Arts.

HANDRIGAN, BRIAN; East Providera SR HS; Rumford, RI; (Y); Boy Scts; Church Yth Grp; Computer Clb; French Clb; VP JA; Concert Band; Jazz Band; Mrchg Band; School Musical; Rep Jr Cls; RI All ST Concert Band 84; Medallist RI Solo Ensmbl Comp Alto Sax 84; U Of Miami; Communications.

HANRAHAN, WILLIAM; Coventry HS; Greene, RI; (Y); Intnl Clb; Letterman Clb; VICA; Drill Tm; Stage Crew; Var Golf; Hon Roll; Cmnty Srv In Grng 80-86; Clnry Inst Of Amer; Clnry Arts.

HARRINGTON, SEANNA; Burrillville HS; Pascoag, RI; (Y); JV Vllybl; Johnson & Wales; Clnry Arts.

HARRIS, THERESA; Tiverton HS; Tiverton, RI; (Y); French Clb; Band; Mrchg Band; Var L Vllybl; Fash Bus.

HARRISON, MARY JO; Lincoln HS; Lincoln, RI; (Y); 90/195; Church Yth Grp; Cheerleading; Prfct Atten Awd.

HART, JEANNE; Warwick Veterans HS; Warwick, RI; (Y); Church Yth Grp; Cmnty Wkr; Hosp Aide; Teachers Aide; Chorus; Rep Frsh Cls; Rep Soph Cls; Rep Jr Cls; Stu Cncl; High Hon Roll; Emerson Coll; Comm.

HARTMANN, LIZA; Barrington HS; Barrington, RI; (Y); AFS; Yrbk Ed-Chief; Var Bsktbl; JV Fld Hcky; Vllybl; High Hon Roll; NHS.

HARWOOD, JONATHAN; Warwick Veterans Memorial HS; Warwick, RI; (Y); AFS; Intnl Clb; Varsity Clb; Var Tennis; Hon Roll; Spanish NHS; Intl Stds.

HAWLEY, ALLISON; Smithfield HS; Greenville, RI; (Y); French Clb; Girl Scts; Band; Rep Frsh Cls; Rep Soph Cls; Rep Jr Cls; Rep Sr Cls; Rep Stu Cncl; Gym; Hon Roll; Medical.

HAXTON, RON; St Andrews Schl; Coventry, RI; (S); Church Yth Grp; Nwsp Rptr; Var Bsktbl; Var Crs Cntry; Capt Socr; High Hon Roll; Hon Roll; Sprtsmnshp Awd 84; Mst Imprvd Bsktbll Plyr 84.

HAYES, MARK; Lasalle Acad; Seekonk, MA; (Y); Ski Clb; Var Ice Hcky; Hon Roll; Wrkng Towrds Pilots Licns 87; Law.

HAYS, WENDY; Barrington HS; Barrington, RI; (Y); Church Yth Grp; Drama Clb; Letterman Clb; Yrbk Phtg; Var Cheerleading; Ice Hcky; Var Mgr(s); Socr; Var Vllybl; School Play; Keene ST Coll; Fn Arts.

HAZARD, JENNIFER; North Kingstown HS; N Kingston, RI; (Y); 60/453; Art Clb; Church Yth Grp; Rep Frsh Cls; Rep Soph Cls; Rep Soph Cls; Hon Roll; Spnsh I Excllnc Cert 84-85.

HEALEY, MATT; North Smithfield HS; Blackstone, MA; (Y); Boys Clb Am; Chess Clb; Var Crs Cntry; JV Socr; JV Wt Lftg; Lion Awd; Lions Clb Outstndng Stu Awd 82-83; U Of RI; Law.

HEBERT, AMY; La Salle Acad; Smithfield, RI; (Y); Math Tm; Stage Crew; French Hon Soc; High Hon Roll; Hon Roll; NHS; Acad Dcthln Gld Mdl Intrvw Cmptn 86.

HECTOR, DANETTE; Hope HS; Providence, RI; (S); Art Clb; Rep Stu Cncl; Var Trk; Cit Awd; High Hon Roll; Hon Roll; Prfct Atten Awd; The Harvard Prz Book; MLK JR-SPIRIT Day Awd; Mnrty Schlrshp Pre-Coll Pgm To RI Schl Of Dsgn; Prfsnl Phtgrphr.

HELLENDRUNG, MARK; E Providence HS; East Providence, RI; (S); 9/520; Trs Spanish Clb; Capt Bsbl; Ftbl; High Hon Roll; NHS; All-ST Ftbl 85; All-Div Bsebl 85; Dartmouth Bk Awd 85; Bio.

HELMBRECHT, TODD; Middletown HS; Middletown, RI; (Y); Temple Yth Grp; Variety Show; JV Bsbl; Var Trk; Var Wrstlng; Hon Roll; Computers.

HEON, MICHELLE; Woonsocket SR HS; Woonsocket, RI; (Y); #75 In Class; Pres Church Yth Grp; Drama Clb; Quiz Bowl; SADD; Teachers Aide; Nwsp Stf; Rep Trs Stu Cncl; Hon Roll; Elme Ed.

HERNANDEZ, DIANE; North Kingstown HS; N Kingstown, RI; (Y); 16/374; Orch; High Hon Roll; Hon Roll; NHS; Spanish I, II & III Awds 84-86; Dartmouth Book Awd 86; Boston Coll; Pre-Law.

HERNANDEZ, ELISA; Central Falls JR SR HS; Central Fls, RI; (Y); Spanish Clb; Chorus; Crs Cntry; Gym; Hon Roll; Jr NHS; NHS; Prfct Atten Awd; Spnsh Awd 86; Co-Op Awd 86; CCRI; Scl Wrkr.

HERVIEUX, SCOTT; Wm M Davies Technical HS; Pascoag, RI; (Y); Am Leg Boys St; SADD; Yrbk Stf; High Hon Roll; Hon Roll; In-Site RI 85; ITT; Data Prcsng.

HEWITT, PATRICIA; East Providence SR HS; Rumford, RI; (Y); 7/520; Church Yth Grp; French Clb; Girl Scts; Band; Chorus; Sec Jr Cls; Rep Stu Cncl; JV L Crs Cntry; L Trk; Jr NHS; Outstndng Band Dir Awd Band 84; Natl Schl Chorl Awd 84; Nrthrn Regnl & All ST Band 84; Phy Thrpy.

HICKEY, KAREN; Warwick Veterans Memorial HS; Warwick, RI; (Y); Sec Church Yth Grp; Letterman Clb; Math Tm; Var L Fld Hcky; Var L Sftbl; French Hon Soc; High Hon Roll; NHS; Yrbk Stf; Jr NHS; Dstngshd Fac Awd U Of RI 86; RI All ST Math Tm 84-86.

HIGGINBOTHAM, JULIE; Prout Memorial HS; Jamestown, RI; (S); 7/77; Aud/Vis; Church Yth Grp; Hosp Aide; Concert Band; School Play; Stage Crew; Spnsh Awd 83-84; Music Awd 82-85; Hnr Roll 82-85; Salve Regina; Law.

HIGGINS, JENNIFER; Cranston High School East; Cranston, RI; (Y); 22/360; Art Clb; Church Yth Grp; Chorus; Rep Jr Cls; Rep Stu Cncl; Hon Roll; Jr NHS; NHS; Pres Schlr; Schlstc Art Awd Hnbl Mntn 82; U Of RI; Bus.

HILL, KIMBERLY; St Mary Bay View Acad; Warwick, RI; (Y); Church Yth Grp; Cmnty Wkr; Exploring; 4-H; French Clb; Hosp Aide; Model UN; Pep Clb; Ski Clb; SADD; Comptitv Hrsbckrdng 85-86; Bayview Hnr Soc 84-85; Pres Physcl Ftns Awd 83-84; Comp Engrng.

HILLIKER, KATHLEEN; Woonsocket SR HS; Woonsocket, RI; (Y); 4/426; Drama Clb; JA; Math Tm; Stu Cncl; High Hon Roll; NHS; Pres Schlr; Church Yth Grp; Dartmouth Coll Schltc Awd 85; Tonehill Coll Hnrs Schlr 86; RI Dsgntd Schlr 86; Stonehill Coll; Hlth Admin.

HINCAPIE, MARIA-ELENA; St Raphael Acad; N Providence, RI; (Y); Church Yth Grp; Cmnty Wkr; Dance Clb; French Clb; Trk; French Hon Soc; Hon Roll; Jr NHS; NHS; Psych Bio.

HOBBS, BENN; Bristol HS; Bristol, RI; (Y); 15/227; JV Bsktbl; Var Tennis; Var Trk; NHS; Prfct Atten Awd; Lat Hnr Soc 85-86; Magna Cum Laude Natl Lat Exam 85-86; Cert Apprec Outstndg Tutor Wrk Chem 85-86; Arch Dsgn.

HOBIN, KARA M; West Warwick SR HS; W Warwick, RI; (Y); #45 In Class; Var Fld Hcky; Var Gym; High Hon Roll; Hon Roll; Salve Regina; Nrsng.

HOBIN, MICHAEL J; Warwick Veterans Memorial HS; Warwick, RI; (Y); Trs Frsh Cls; Trs Soph Cls; Pres Jr Cls; Pres Sr Cls; Var Vllybl; High Hon Roll; Hon Roll; Jr NHS; NHS; Spanish NHS; Prog Of Excllnc Awd; Crss Age Tutrg; No 1 Clb; Providence College; Acctg.

HOLDER JR, CHARLES M; Rogers HS; Newport, RI; (Y); Pres Church Yth Grp; Off Jr Cls; Var L Bsktbl; Var JV Ftbl; Stat Powder Puff Ftbl; Im Score Keeper; Im Sftbl; Var Trk; Hon Roll; Bus Mgmt.

HOLT, CURTIS; North Smithfield JR SR HS; N Smithfield, RI; (Y); Hon Roll; Hlth Clb 85-86; U RI; Marine Tech.

HOLT, PAMELA; North Smithfiels JR SR HS; N Smithfield, RI; (Y); Church Yth Grp; Drama Clb; French Clb; Girl Scts; Letterman Clb; Yrbk Stf; Stu Cncl; Bsktbl; Vllybl; Hon Roll; 2nd Team All Trnmnt Vllybl, Cls B Div Hon Mntn Vllybl 86; Excllnce Art 86; Intr Dsgn.

HOLTMANN, PATRICIA; Johnston SR HS; Johnston, RI; (S); 4/216; French Clb; Drm Mjr(t); Nwsp Stf; Ed Yrbk Stf; High Hon Roll; Hon Roll; NHS; Natl Hist Day Wnr; Proj In-Site; Bryant Coll; Bnkg.

HOPKINS, CHERYL; Smithfield HS; Greenville, RI; (Y); 15/200; Cmnty Wkr; French Clb; Office Aide; Band; Concert Band; Jazz Band; Hon Roll; Outstndng Achvmnt Typing I Bst Typst 84-85; Johnson & Wales Bus Sklls Mt 2nd Plc Typng 86; Katharine Gibbs Schl; Exec Sec.

HOPKINS, JENNIFER; Coventry HS; Coventry, RI; (Y); 5/450; French Clb; Pres Letterman Clb; Frsh Cls; Soph Cls; Var L Crs Cntry; Var L Trk; NHS; Acadmc Dec Tm; Poltc Sci.

HOPKINS, KATHRYN; Coventry HS; Coventry, RI; (Y); 11/400; French Clb; VP Letterman Clb; Q&S; Nwsp Stf; Rep Frsh Cls; Rep Soph Cls; Rep Jr Cls; JV Crs Cntry; Capt Vllybl; Hon Roll; Pltcl Sci.

HOPKINS, MELISSA; Woonsocket SR HS; Woonsocket, RI; (Y); Church Yth Grp; Girl Scts; Pep Clb; Spanish Clb; Yrbk Stf; Rep Stu Cncl; Capt Var Cheerleading; Prjct Close Up 86; Natl Conf Of Christians & Jews 85-86; Flcty Hnr Roll 85-86; Bentley; Bus.

HOPKINS, TINA M; Chariho Regional HS; Wyoming, RI; (Y); 16/289; Rptr Nwsp Stf; Var Crs Cntry; Capt Trk; Hon Roll; Jr NHS; RI Hnr Soc 86; Pres Acad Ftns Awd 85-86 Genevieve C Durfee Awd 86; Saint Michaels Coll; Elem Ed.

HORAN, MONICA; Mount Saint Charles HS; Pawtucket, RI; (S); Church Yth Grp; Model UN; Ski Clb; SADD; Trs Soph Cls; Chrmn Stu Cncl; Var Sftbl; Var Tennis; High Hon Roll.

HOULE, PAULA; North Smithfield JR SR HS; N Smithfield, RI; (Y); Drama Clb; French Clb; School Play; Hon Roll; Trvl Agnt.

HOWE, HOLLY; Coventry HS; Coventry, RI; (Y); Letterman Clb; Spanish Clb; Trs Frsh Cls; Soph Cls; Chrmn Jr Cls; Stu Cncl; Var JV Crs Cntry; JV Tennis; High Hon Roll; Jr NHS; Bus.

HRECZUCH, BELINDA; Woonsocket SR HS; Woonsocket, RI; (Y); 8/25; Spanish Clb; Chorus; Berkley; Music.

HUGHES, LYNN C; Lincoln JR SR HS; Lincoln, RI; (Y); 1/179; Pres Frsh Cls; Pres Soph Cls; Pres Jr Cls; Pres Sr Cls; Rep Stu Cncl; Capt L Cheerleading; L Trk; Capt L Vllybl; NHS; Val; Dghtrs Of Amer Rev 86; Elks MV Stu Awd 86; Cngrsmn Mdl Of Mrt 86; Brown U; Chem.

HULING, GEOFFREY; Warwick Veterans Memorial HS; Warwick, RI; (Y); Letterman Clb; Math Tm; Yrbk Stf; Bsbl; Ice Hcky; Socr; High Hon Roll; Jr NHS; NHS; Spanish NHS; 2nd Tm Al-Div Sccr 85; 3rd Tm Al-Div Bsbl 85 & 86; Bobby Orr Sportsmnshp Awd 83-84; Ivy League Schl; Law.

HURLEY, SEAN; South Kingstown HS; Wakefield, RI; (Y); Ski Clb; Spanish Clb; Variety Show; Stu Cncl; Wt Lftg; Hon Roll; NHS; Erth Sci Hnr Awd & Spnsh I Adv Hnr Awd 83-84.

HURTEAU, KEVIN; Woonsocket SR HS; Woonsocket, RI; (Y); JA; Nwsp Rptr; Var Bsbl; Ftbl; ST Bsbl Chmpns 86; Ftbll 12th Plyr Trphy 85; U Of RI; Cmptr Sci.

HUSSAIN, BILAL R; Moses Brown HS; Foxborough, MA; (Y); Computer Clb; Pres Spanish Clb; L Socr; L Tennis; Trk; Ntl Merit Schol; Ltr Vrsty Sqsh; John Hopkins U; Bio.

IACOBUCCI, LAURA; Lincoln HS; Lincoln, RI; (Y); 55/195; Church Yth Grp; Red Cross Aide; L Lib Band; L Lib Concert Band; Lib Mrchg Band; Var L Swmmng; Hon Roll; RI All-ST Tm Swmng 86; Rcgnzd As NE Outstndng Wmr 83-85; Band Srv Awd 86; Phys Thrpy.

IACONO, JANICE LEE; East Providence HS; E Providence, RI; (Y); Cmnty Wkr; Political Wkr; Hon Roll; Gld Key RI Rgnl Schlstc Art Awds 86; Cert Merit Vis Arts RI Art Tchrs Assoc, RI Yth Art Exhit Awds; Slave Regina Nwprt Collfpsych.

IANNAZZI, STEPHANIE; St Marys Academy- Bay View; Johnston, RI; (Y); Exploring; Math Clb; Nwsp Phtg; Nwsp Stf; Jr Cls; Stu Cncl; Hon Roll; NEDT Awd; Math Tm; Orch; Svc Awd 84; Hnr Soc 86; Hstry.

IANNUCCILLO, RITA; St Mary Academy Bay View HS; Bristol, RI; (Y); Boy Scts; Church Yth Grp; Exploring; Church Choir; Orch; Variety Show; NEDT Excllnc Awd 84; Rec Awds Vlntr Serv 84-85; Natl Latn Exm, Silv Mdl Magna Cum Laude 86; Vet Med.

IERVOLINO, MICHAEL; Bristol HS; Bristol, RI; (Y); Church Yth Grp; Off Jr Cls; Golf; Hon Roll; Vrsty Ltr In Golf 86; U RI; Elec Engrng.

IMPROTA, CHRISTINE; Pilgrim HS; Warwick, RI; (Y); 10/302; Church Yth Grp; Nwsp Ed-Chief; Cheerleading; High Hon Roll; Masonic Awd; Pres Schlr; St Schlr; RI Hnr Soc 86; RI Coll; Nrsng.

INGALL, ANDREW; Classical HS; Providence, RI; (Y); Drama Clb; French Clb; Latin Clb; School Musical; School Play; Off Soph Cls; Stu Cncl; Hon Roll.

IOVINI, SUSAN; La Salle Acad; Providence, RI; (Y); 73/244; Hon Roll; RI Honor Soc 86; RI Coll; Accntng.

ISA, JOSEPH; East Providence SR HS; E Providence, RI; (Y); Boys Clb Am; Church Yth Grp; French Clb; JA; Quiz Bowl; Varsity Clb; Jr Cls; Var Bsktbl; Var Trk; Hon Roll; Providence Coll.

ISSENBERG, LISA; Lincoln HS; Lincoln, RI; (Y); 8/211; Math Clb; Var Gym; Var Tennis; Var Vllybl; High Hon Roll; Hon Roll; Jr NHS; NHS; Arch.

JACHEM, CHRISTINA; Cumberland HS; Cumberland, RI; (Y); French Clb; SADD; Chorus; Variety Show; High Hon Roll; Hon Roll; Bryant Clg; Accntng.

JALBERT, RUSSELL; Bishop Hendricken HS; Coventry, RI; (Y); 75/240; French Clb; Im Bowling; Im Wt Lftg; French Hon Soc; Hon Roll; NHS; Bus.

JEFF, CROSS; Barrington HS; Barrington, RI; (Y); 18/200; Pres Debate Tm; Drama Clb; NFL; Speech Tm; School Musical; School Play; Yrbk Phtg; Lit Mag; Hon Roll; NHS; Brn U Book Awd 86; Top Spkr Lncln Dgls Debate & ST Chmpn 86.

JENKINS, BRETT; Middletown HS; Middletown, RI; (Y); Exploring; Var L Bsktbl; Im Coach Actv; Im Vllybl; Hon Roll; Spanish NHS; Engrng.

JOHANNIS, BETH; Narragansett HS; Narragansett, RI; (Y); Cmnty Wkr; Chorus; Gym; Sftbl; Hon Roll; Uri.

JOHNSON, CHRISTOPHER; Charles E Shea SR HS; Pawtucket, RI; (Y); Cmnty Wkr; Debate Tm; Drama Clb; French Clb; Letterman Clb; Nwsp Rptr; Stu Cncl; Bsbl; Bsktbl; Ftbl; U RI; Ind Engr.

JOHNSON, DIANE K; Pilgrim HS; Warwick, RI; (Y); 79/331; Church Yth Grp; Band; Orch; Nwsp Ed-Chief; Chrmn Soph Cls; Stat Vllybl; Hon Roll; Grnd Fdlty 84-85; Grnd Chrty 85-86; Dlgt Suprm Inspctr Intrntl; Ordr Rnbow Grls; Rhode Island Coll; Elem Educ.

JOHNSON JR, HENRY A; Tollgate HS; Warwick, RI; (Y); AFS; Debate Tm; German Clb; JA; NFL; Speech Tm; Stu Cncl; Trk; Hon Roll; MT ST U; Intl Lawyer.

JOHNSON, JENNIFER; Lincoln SR HS; Lincoln, RI; (Y); Chorus; Church Choir; Lit Mag; Crs Cntry; Swmmng; Vllybl; High Hon Roll; NHS; Prfct Atten Awd; Arch.

JOHNSON, KELLIE; Woonsocket HS; Greenville, RI; (Y); Church Yth Grp; Hosp Aide; Yrbk Stf; Sec Soph Cls; Stu Cncl; Var Cheerleading; Hon Roll; Nrsng.

JOHNSON, KIMBERLY K; Community Christiam Schl; Pascoag, RI; (Y); 1/75; Yrbk Stf; CC RI; RN.

JOHNSON, REBECCA; Narragansett HS; Narragansett, RI; (Y); 11/120; Hosp Aide; Library Aide; Vllybl; Hon Roll; Spanish NHS; Socl Wrk.

JOHNSON, RONALD E; Coventry HS; Coventry, RI; (Y); 5/362; Boy Scts; Pres Chess Clb; Computer Clb; Letterman Clb; Math Tm; Rep Science Clb; Trs Band; Rep Stu Cncl; Var L Crs Cntry; Var L Trk; Acad All-Amer 85; Natl Hnr Socy Schlrshp 86-87; Elks Most Valuable Stu Natl Schlrshp 86-87; Rensselaer Plytech Isnt; El Eng.

JOHNSON, TRACI; Woonsocket SR HS; Woonsocket, RI; (Y); Office Aide; SADD; Yrbk Stf; Hon Roll; Prfct Atten Awd.

JONES, JULIE; Barrington HS; Barrington, RI; (Y); Civic Clb; Drama Clb; GAA; Intnl Clb; School Musical; Nwsp Rptr; Yrbk Stf; Lit Mag; Var Capt Cheerleading; Ntl Merit Ltr; Peer Educ Awd; Var Lttrs Chrldng; Frgn/Pblc Rel.

JONES, KAREN; Central HS; Providence, RI; (Y); #1 In Class; High Hon Roll; Hon Roll; NHS; Val; Bryant RIC; Bus Tchr.

JOSEPH, ROBBIE; Mount St Charles Acad; Franklin, MA; (Y); 28/168; Boy Scts; Church Yth Grp; Cmnty Wkr; Key Clb; SADD; VP Frsh Cls; Rep Soph Cls; Trs Sr Cls; High Hon Roll; Hon Roll; Bus.

JOSLIN, BONNIE; Charino HS; Ashaway, RI; (Y); Pres VICA; Yrbk Stf; Rep Frsh Cls; Rep Soph Cls; Rep Jr Cls; Rep Sr Cls; Rep Stu Cncl; JV Var Sftbl; Hon Roll; Mst Outstndng Stndt Awd VICA 86; Bus Mgmnt.

JOUBERT, RENEE; Johnston SR HS; Johnston, RI; (S); 9/260; Hon Roll; NHS; Rhode Isl Tchrs Italian Hnr Soc 85-86; Providence Coll; Psychlgy.

JOURDENAIS, MARC; Coventry HS; Coventry, RI; (Y); 1/400; Trs French Clb; Radio Clb; Yrbk Ed-Chief; High Hon Roll; Jr NHS; Ntl Merit SF; Yrbk Stf; 2nd Degree Brown Belt Ki-Do-Ryu Jiu Kitsu 85; HOBY Awd 85; Brown Book Awd 86; Engrng.

JUTRAS JR, THOMAS; Smithfield HS; Smithfield, RI; (Y); 6/203; Computer Clb; Drama Clb; Rep Frsh Cls; Soph Cls; Im Capt Badmtn; Im Capt Vllybl; Im Wt Lftg; High Hon Roll; NHS; Pres Schlr; Jrnl Bulletin Schlstc Awd 86; Worcester Poly Tech Inst; Engr.

KADAK, CHRISTIAN; La Salle Acad; Barrington, RI; (Y); Church Yth Grp; Civic Clb; JA; Ski Clb; JV Var Lcrss; JV Socr; Hon Roll; 1st Grnt RI ST Sci Fair 84; 1st Pl Snfsh Sngl Rce 83-84; Bill Hntr Mem Race Brrngtn Ycht Clb 85; Union Coll Schenectady; Med.

KALIFF, KATHLEEN; St Mary Academy Bayview; E Providence, RI; (Y); 9/230; Debate Tm; Math Tm; Pep Clb; Pres Service Clb; Ski Clb; Chorus; Var Trk; NHS; Hghst JV Spkr Bates Coll Smmr Dleg Inst 86.

KALOOSKI, SCOTT; North Kingstown HS; Jamestown, RI; (Y); Boy Scts; Letterman Clb; Var Capt Bsbl; Var Ftbl; Most Desire Improve 85-86; Engrng.

KAMIN, ERICA; East Greenwich HS; E Greenwich, RI; (Y); 2/166; Drama Clb; Model UN; School Musical; School Play; Nwsp Bus Mgr; Lit Mag; High Hon Roll; Hon Roll; Sal; Wellesley Coll Bk Prz 85; Secy ST Ldrshp Awd 86; Providence Jrnl-Bulltn Schlstc Awd 86; U Of PA; Intl Rltns.

KAPLAN, BRUCE A; Cranston HS East; Cranston, RI; (Y); 27/400; Am Leg Boys St; Computer Clb; Math Tm; Q&S; Ed Nwsp Stf; Ed Lit Mag; Gov Hon Prg Awd; Hon Roll; Dartmouth.

KARCZ, DIANE; Warren HS; Warren, RI; (Y); 5/89; Office Aide; Band; Yrbk Stf; Trs Stu Cncl; Hon Roll; NHS; Outstndng Bus Stu 86; Jhnsn & Wls Coll; Secy.

KATZ, MICHELLE; Cranston West HS; Cranston, RI; (Y); 24/417; Debate Tm; Drama Clb; Exploring; GAA; Teachers Aide; Temple Yth Grp; Acpl Chr; School Musical; Lit Mag; Frsh Cls; Cranston Assoc Teachers Adm 86; Choir Schlrshp 86; Rhode Isl Hnr Soc 85-86; Boston U; Brdcstng.

KAYE, LISA; Cranston HS West; Cranston, RI; (Y); Dance Clb; Intnl Clb; Stage Crew; Variety Show; Yrbk Rptr; Lit Mag; Rep Jr Cls; Score Keeper; Timer; Hon Roll; Solo Dnce Wnnr 84; Excel Art Soc Stage Crw 83; RI Assn Schlrshp; RI Coll; Comm.

KEATING, SARA M; Prout Memorial HS; Warwick, RI; (Y); 45/71; Debate Tm; Girl Scts; Color Guard; Concert Band; School Musical; Variety Show; Arts Recgntn & Tlnt Srch 85-86; Comm.

KEENAN, CHRISTINE J; Rogers HS; Newport, RI; (Y); Church Yth Grp; Dance Clb; Ski Clb; Spanish Clb; Band; Church Choir; Concert Band; Mrchg Band; School Musical; Hon Roll; Mc Donalds Crew Schlrshp 86; Rogers HS Band Schlrshp 86; Mst Versatle Brd Mem Awd 86; U Of NH; Zoolgy.

KEENAN, KIM; Warwick Veterans Memorial HS; Warwick, RI; (Y); Cheerleading; Hon Roll; Psychol.

KEENE, DAVID; Pilgrim HS; Warwick, RI; (Y); Boy Scts; Pres Church Yth Grp; Spanish Clb; Varsity Clb; Frsh Cls; Soph Cls; Jr Cls; Crs Cntry; Trk; Hon Roll; US Mrchnt Mrn Acad; Nvgtn.

KEILUHN, JON; St Andrews HS; Barrington, RI; (S); 1/16; Yrbk Ed-Chief; Vllybl; High Hon Roll; Spanish NHS; U Of RI; Acctnt.

KELAGHAN, TARA; Lincoln JR SR HS; Lincoln, RI; (Y); 14/195; Drama Clb; Exploring; Chorus; School Musical; Variety Show; Rep Frsh Cls; Rep Soph Cls; Rep Jr Cls; Rep Sr Cls; Capt Cheerleading; All ST Chorus; Physcl Thrpy.

KELLERMAN, JENNIFER; St Mary Academy-Bay View; Bristol, RI; (Y); French Clb; Latin Clb; SADD; JV Crs Cntry; Var Swmmng; Hon Roll; C C Cirillo Awd YMCA Girl Of The Yr 84; James Dollins Sprtsmnshp Awd 84; George Jenleins 3rd Pl 84; Chld Psych.

KELLEY, PAULA; Coventry HS; Coventry, RI; (Y); Spanish Clb; Off Jr Cls; Trk; High Hon Roll; Jr NHS; NHS; Excllence In Spnsh 84-85; Providence Coll; Bio.

KENNEDY, KRISTEN; North Providence HS; N Providence, RI; (Y); Pres Sec Church Yth Grp; Dance Clb; Ski Clb; Band; Concert Band; Mrchg Band; Yrbk Stf; Co-Capt Crs Cntry; Trk; Hon Roll; Psychlgy.

KENNEDY, TIMOTHY J; Rogers HS; Jacksonville Bch, FL; (Y); ROTC; Jazz Band; Stage Crew; Exploring; Drill Tm; Socr; Hon Roll; Amer Lgn Mltry Exc Awd 85-86; Vrsty Ltr In Rfl Team 85-86; Vrsty Ltr Drill Team; U S Air Frc.

KENNY, ERIN; Classical HS; Providence, RI; (Y); Chess Clb; Drama Clb; Political Wkr; Thesps; School Musical; School Play; Stage Crew; Lit Mag; Hon Roll; Theatre.

KEOKHAW, BUNSONG; Hope HS; Providence, RI; (Y); Church Yth Grp; SADD; Yrbk Phtg; Off Stu Cncl; Socr; Vllybl; Cit Awd; Hon Roll; Nrsng.

KEORNEY, CATHLEEN; Narragansett HS; Narragansett, RI; (Y); 16/120; Hosp Aide; Ski Clb; SADD; Teachers Aide; Varsity Clb; Variety Show; Pres Frsh Cls; VP Soph Cls; VP Jr Cls; VP Sr Cls; Italian Hnr Soc 86; Intl Bus.

KEOUGH, MICHAEL P; La Salle Acad; No Providence, RI; (Y); 25/257; Pep Clb; Ski Clb; Spanish Clb; Band; JV Socr; Var L Tennis; Var L Trk; JV Wrstlng; Hon Roll; St Schlr; Le High U; Engrng.

KEOUGH, STACY; Central Falls HS; Central Fls, RI; (Y); 1/115; Church Yth Grp; Pep Clb; Var Capt Cheerleading; Cit Awd; High Hon Roll; Hon Roll; Jr NHS; NHS; Pres Schlr; Val; Garfield Soc Clb Scholart 86; Cntrl Falls Tchrs Union Scholar 86; Arabic Fndtn Scholar 86; Bryant Coll; Acctnt.

KETTLE, KATHY; Chariho Regional HS; W Kingston, RI; (Y); 22/284; 4-H; FFA; VICA; Bowling; 4-H Awd; High Hon Roll; Hon Roll; RI Hnrs Scty 86; Ntl 4-H Achvt Winr 85.

KIDD, BRANDON; Bishop Hendricken HS; East Greenwich, RI; (Y); 82/236; Chess Clb; Computer Clb; Band; Concert Band; Mrchg Band; Cataract Fire Schlrshp 86; New England Coll; Envrnmtl Sci.

KIERNAN, KEN; Pilgrim HS; Warwick, RI; (Y); Math Clb; Math Tm; Spanish Clb; High Hon Roll; Hon Roll; Spanish NHS; Arch.

KILEY, MELISSA; St Raphael Acad; Pawtucket, RI; (Y); 65/180; Spanish Clb; SADD; Yrbk Stf; Rep Soph Cls; Rep Jr Cls; Stu Cncl; Hon Roll; Spanish NHS; Mrktng.

KIM, SUN-HEE; North Providenc HS; N Providence, RI; (Y); 1/250; Library Aide; Math Tm; Quiz Bowl; Nwsp Ed-Chief; Nwsp Rptr; Lit Mag; High Hon Roll; Hon Roll; Jr NHS; NHS; Aerospc Engrng.

KING, JONATHAN A; N Kingstown HS; Jamestown, RI; (Y); Church Yth Grp; Cmnty Wkr; Red Cross Aide; ROTC; Drill Tm; Var L Ftbl; JV L Socr; JV L Trk; U Of FL; Pilot.

KING, SUSAN; Charles E Shea SR HS; Pawtucket, RI; (Y); Math Clb; SADD; Stu Cncl; High Hon Roll; Hon Roll; Harvard Bk Awd; Model Leg 86; Math.

KIPER, RICK; Coventry HS; Coventry, RI; (Y); 5/456; Church Yth Grp; Math Tm; Variety Show; Trs Stu Cncl; Var Crs Cntry; Var Trk; High Hon Roll; NHS; Art Clb; Camera Clb; RI Dstngshd Merit Sr Math 86; Schlstc Art Awd 84; Fl Inst Tech; Engrng.

KIRWAN, JOHN; Narragansett HS; Narragansett, RI; (Y); 14/180; Variety Show; Var Wt Lftg; Var Wrstlng; High Hon Roll; URI; Law.

KNEATH, THOMAS; Bristol HS; Bristol, RI; (Y); French Clb; Ski Clb; Rep Stu Cncl; Var L Tennis; High Hon Roll; Pres NHS; Ntl Merit Ltr; Prfct Atten Awd; Russo Awd 83-84; ST Sci Fair 84; 2nd Grant & Armd Forces Comm & Electrns Hnrb Mntn 84; Chem Engr.

KNUST, WENDY; Warwick Veterans Memorial HS; Warwick, RI; (Y); #27 In Class; Pep Clb; Spanish Clb; Yrbk Stf; JV Cheerleading; High Hon Roll; Hon Roll; Jr NHS; NHS; Spanish NHS; Blood Dr Comm; MAD; U RI.

KOBANI, PAUL; Woonsocket HS; Woonsocket, RI; (Y); JA; Nwsp Rptr; JV L Wrstlng; Johnson & Wales; Mtl Mgmt.

KOCIUBA, KARIN; Burrillville JR SR HS; Glendale, RI; (Y); French Clb; Girl Scts; SADD; School Play; Stu Cncl; Cheerleading; Gym; High Hon Roll; Hon Roll; Katherne Gibbs Schl; Sectrl Fld.

KOGUT, JENNIFER; Woonsocket SR HS; Woonsocket, RI; (Y); SADD; School Play; Yrbk Phtg; Yrbk Stf; Rep Stu Cncl; Trk; Hon Roll; Hnr Rll 85-86; Nat Cnfrnc Christians & Jews Cnfrnc Schlrshp 86; Salve Regina; Nrsng Admin.

KOPEL, SHERYL; Classical HS; Providence, RI; (Y); French Clb; Temple Yth Grp; Yrbk Phtg; Lit Mag; Gym; Hon Roll; Phtgrphy.

KORES, JUSTINE; Chariho Reg JR SR HS; Hopkinton, RI; (Y); Church Yth Grp; Chorus; Hon Roll; Diploma Exclnc Spnsh I 85-86; U Of RI; Psychlgy.

KORZENIOWSKI, HANK; Bishop Hendricken HS; Cranston, RI; (Y); 51/240; Am Leg Boys St; French Clb; Nwsp Stf; Yrbk Ed-Chief; Yrbk Stf; Crs Cntry; French Hon Soc; Hon Roll; NHS; Vet Sci.

KOSH, RANDY; La Salle Acad; Johnston, RI; (Y); 80/280; Rep Stu Cncl; L Ftbl; Hon Roll; NHS; Natl Honor Soc; U Of RI; Physcl Thrpy.

KOSIVER, MICHAEL; Coventry HS; Coventry, RI; (Y); Capt Bsktbl; Coach Actv; JV Trk; Hon Roll; Ntl Stdnt Cncl 84-85; Syracuse U; Bus Admn.

KOUNAVIS, ANGELA; Bishop Keough HS; Pawtucket, RI; (S); 7/46; Nwsp Rptr; Yrbk Rptr; Trs Sr Cls; Sftbl; High Hon Roll; Hon Roll; Engl Awd 84; Fairlawn All Star Sftbl Awd 84 & 85; Fairlawn Sftbl Awd 83-85; RI Coll.

KOWAL, JOHN; Coventry HS; Coventry, RI; (Y); 7/400; Bsbl; Bsktbl; High Hon Roll; NHS; RI Ntl Hnr Soc; Elect Engr.

KOZIOL, ROBERT; Coevntry HS; Coventry, RI; (Y); Yrbk Sprt Ed; Yrbk Stf; Hon Roll.

KRAEMER, SCOTT; Coventry HS; Coventry, RI; (Y); Hon Roll; U Of MA; Law.

KRALICKY, JOSEPH; Tiverton HS; Tiverton, RI; (S); Mrchg Band; JV Bsbl; Hon Roll; Comp Engrng.

KRETZER, DAWN; Narragansett HS; Narragansett, RI; (Y); Dance Clb; Drama Clb; School Play; Stage Crew; Variety Show; Soph Cls; Jr Cls; Sr Cls; Bsktbl; Var Capt Vllybl; Outstndng Stu Wk 86; Bus Educ Awd 86; Lt Richard R Zurcher Schlrshp Awd 86; RI CC; Law Enfrcmnt.

KUFFREY, CHERYL; Johnston HS; Warwick, RI; (Y); 10/212; DECA; Hosp Aide; Capt Wrstlng; Hon Roll; NHS; Quinnipc Schlrshp 86; Quinnipiac Clg; Phys Thrpy.

KUFFREY, CHERYL; Johnston SR HS; Johnston, RI; (S); 10/216; Hosp Aide; Hon Roll; NHS; Quinnipiac Coll; Phy Thrpy.

KUNSTMANN, KEVIN; Cranston East HS; Cranston, RI; (Y); 17/388; Var Capt Wrstlng; Cit Awd; Elks Awd; High Hon Roll; Jr NHS; NHS; Pres Schlr; St Schlr; Cmnty Wkr; Teachers Aide; Army Reserve Athlete/Schlr Awd 86; Sawin Engrng Schlrshp Awd 86; Cranstons Finest Awd; U Of AZ; Aerosp Engrng.

KUREK, KEITH; North Smithfield JR SR HS; Woonsocket, RI; (Y); Church Yth Grp; French Clb; Letterman Clb; Math Tm; Model UN; SADD; Band; Jazz Band; Mrchg Band; Yrbk Stf; Bryant Coll; CPA.

KURLAN, ELIZABETH J; Tiverton HS; Tiverton, RI; (Y); French Clb; Pep Clb; Ski Clb; School Musical; Yrbk Ed-Chief; Yrbk Phtg; Var Cheerleading; Var Pom Pon; Im Swmmng; Hon Roll; U RI.

KUROS, KRIS M; Bristol HS; Bristol, RI; (Y); 16/196; Yrbk Sprt Ed; Sec Church Yth Grp; VP Jr Cls; VP Sr Cls; Rep Stu Cncl; Capt Cheerleading; Capt Sftbl; Elks Awd; High Hon Roll; Trs NHS; RI ST Elks Scholar; RI CC; Radiogrphy.

KUT, STEPHEN; Lincoln SR HS; Lincoln, RI; (Y); 31/195; Church Yth Grp; Debate Tm; Stage Crew; Bsbl; Ice Hcky; Hon Roll; NHS; Engrng.

L HEUREUX, RACHEL ANN; Saint Raphael Acad; Cumberland, RI; (Y); Cmnty Wkr; Drama Clb; French Clb; Model UN; Stage Crew; Yrbk Stf; Sftbl; French Hon Soc; Hon Roll; NHS; Ed.

LA BADIE II, RICHARD; William Davies Vo-Tech; Pawtucket, RI; (Y); Boy Scts; Trs VICA; 2nd Pl Schl VICA Fair Indl Elec 86; URI; Indl Elec.

LA BELLE, LEANNE; South Kingstown HS; Kingston, RI; (Y); 55/170; Sec Drama Clb; Stu Cncl; Tennis.

LA CROIX, LISA; Prout Memorial HS; Slocum, RI; (S); GAA; Bsktbl; Vllybl; High Hon Roll; Hon Roll; Bio Awd & Hstry Awd Hghst Avg Clss 84; Vllybl All Div Awd Hnbl Mntn 85.

LA CROIX, RENEE; Warwick Veterans Memorial HS; Warwick, RI; (Y); 18/300; Rep Sr Cls; Rep Stu Cncl; High Hon Roll; Hon Roll; Spanish NHS; RI Hnrs Scty; Schl Htl Clb & Bld Drv Cmt; Ltr Of Rcgntn Fro Gvnr Di Prete As RI Schlr; RI Coll; Psychlgy.

LA PLANTE, CELESTE; West Warwick HS; West Warwick, RI; (Y); Church Yth Grp; Variety Show; Chrmn Soph Cls; Chrmn Jr Cls; Chrmn Sr Cls; Rep Stu Cncl; Var Cheerleading; Var Capt Trk; Johnson & Wales; Marktng.

LA ROSE, JOHN; Charles E Shea SR HS; Pawtucket, RI; (Y); Am Leg Boys St; Computer Clb; Letterman Clb; Var Capt Bsbl; Var Capt Bsktbl; Var Capt Ftbl; Hon Roll; Brown.

LA SCOLA, TODD; St Raphael Acad; Pawtucket, RI; (Y); 15/187; Boys Clb Am; JV Bsktbl; Var Capt Ftbl; Var Trk; Hon Roll; JC Awd; NHS; St Schlr; RIHEA Schlrshp 86; Hugh O Brien Yth Fndtn 84; WPI; Gntc Engrng.

LAFOND, CATHY; Woonsocket SR HS; Woonsocket, RI; (Y); Church Yth Grp; Girl Scts; Office Aide; Yrbk Stf; Hon Roll; Katharine Gibbs Schl Ldrshp Awd Future Sec 86; Katharine Gibbs Schl; Exec Sec.

LAGANA III, ANGELO J; Chariho Regional HS; W Kingston, RI; (Y); Church Yth Grp; Cmnty Wkr; VICA; Nwsp Stf; Pres Soph Cls; Presdntl Phy Ftns Awd 85; Coast Guard.

LAGASSE, ANNE MARIE; St Raphael Acad; Pawtucket, RI; (Y); Boys Clb Am; Exploring; JA; Math Clb; Tennis; Hon Roll; NHS; Cert Of Prfcncy Accntng 86; US Army Rsrv Nat Schlr Athlt Ad 86; Concours De Frangais 84; Bryant Coll; Accntng.

LALIBERTE, KATHLEEN; Narraganssett HS; Narragansett, RI; (Y); 10/120; Stage Crew; Variety Show; Yrbk Stf; Off Soph Cls; Off Jr Cls; Sec Sr Cls; Stu Cncl; Var Gym; Var Socr; Var Trk; Hnr Rll; Excllnc Frnch Awd; Phy Thrpy.

LALIBERTE, KRISTEN; Bishop Keough Regional HS; Pawtucket, RI; (S); Cmnty Wkr; Drama Clb; Model UN; Stage Crew; Sec Soph Cls; Tennis; High Hon Roll; NHS; Essy Cntst Prvdnc Jrnl 84; Govs Summer Pgm-Sci & Math 85; Eng Lit.

LALIBERTE, MICHAEL; Pilgrim HS; Warwick, RI; (Y); Church Yth Grp; French Clb; Stat Bsktbl; Var Tennis; Hon Roll; Bus Adm.

LAMBERT, KERRI; Warren HS; Warren, RI; (Y); 23/92; Church Yth Grp; Pres 4-H; JV L Crs Cntry; Var L Trk; 4-H Awd; RI ST Expo Sci Fr 1st Grnt RI Dntl Assoc Awd 83; Rdrs Dgst Ntl 4-H Ldrshp 2nd Altrnt Schlrshp 84; Johnson & Wales Coll; Htl Mgmt.

LAMBERT, LAURA; Woonsocket SR HS; Woonsocket, RI; (Y); Math Tm; Var Cheerleading; Var Crs Cntry; Var Trk; High Hon Roll; Hon Roll; Scndry Math Tm.

LAMOUREUX, DENISE; La Salle Acad; Cranston, RI; (Y); Rep Dance Clb; Rep Library Aide; Rep Office Aide; Rep Ski Clb; Rep Nwsp Stf; Off Frsh Cls; Off Soph Cls; Rep Stu Cncl; Hon Roll; Honors 85-86; Bryant Coll; Mgmt.

LANDOW, SHOSHANA; Classical HS; Providence, RI; (Y); Latin Clb; Library Aide; Math Tm; Nwsp Ed-Chief; Lit Mag; High Hon Roll; Hon Roll; Essay Cntst Japanese Govt Rep US Japan 84; Founded Womns Consiusns Grp 85-86; Bio Prof.

LANDRY, JOHANNA; Classical HS; Providence, RI; (Y); PAVAS; Science Clb; Stage Crew; Lit Mag; Pres Schlr; Cum Laude Hnr Soc-Alpha Delta Tau 87; Art.

LANDRY, MATHIEU; Davies Vo-Tech HS; Pawtucket, RI; (Y); Boy Scts; CAP; Hosp Aide; VICA; Band; Pres Soph Cls; Bsbl; Vllybl; VICA Bronz Medal Pub Spkg 85; URI; Technlgy.

LANE JR, BERNARD; Warwick Veterans Memorial HS; Warwick, RI; (Y); 53/270; Off Frsh Cls; Off Soph Cls; Off Jr Cls; Off Sr Cls; Bsktbl; JV Crs Cntry; Im Vllybl; St Schlr; Acdmc Dcthln 85; U Of RI; Accntng.

LANE JR, WILLIAM P; Moses Brown Schl; Cumberland, RI; (Y); Boy Scts; Church Yth Grp; French Clb; Ski Clb; Yrbk Stf; Var L Ice Hcky; JV Lcrss; JV Socr; High Hon Roll; Ntl Merit SF; Egl Sct 84.

LANGANKE, STEVEN W; Chariho Regional JR SR HS; Ashaway, RI; (Y); 5/278; Church Yth Grp; Var L Bsktbl; Co-Capt Trk; Hon Roll; NHS; RI Hnr Soc 85-86; RI Intrschltc Lg Mdl Trk 85 & 86; Pres Acad Fit Awd 85-86; Acad All Amer 85-86; URI; Bus.

LANGLOIS, JEFFREY; Wm M Davies JR Technical HS; Pawtucket, RI; (Y); VICA; $1000 Schlrshp-1st-ST VICA Comptn-Smll Applncs 86.

LANGUELL, CHRISTOPHER; Rogers HS; Newport, RI; (Y); Am Leg Boys St; German Clb; Math Tm; Off ROTC; Drill Tm; Var Trk; Hon Roll; Mu Alp Tht; Church Yth Grp; Germ Hnr Soc 86; Engrg.

LAREAU, DOUGLAS J; Burrillville JR SR HS; Pascoag, RI; (Y); 3/171; Math Tm; Model UN; Pres SADD; School Play; Pres Stu Cncl; Var Socr; DAR Awd; NHS; St Schlr; Sec Of State Leadership Awd 86; RI Honor Society 86; Cornell U; Animal Sci.

LARKIN, JENNIFER; Pilgrim HS; Warwick, RI; (Y); Hon Roll; RI Tchrs Of Italian 85 & 86; Italian Hon Soc 86.

LAROCQUE, HALLIE; Tiverton HS-NEWPORT Vo-Tech; Tiverton, RI; (S); Drama Clb; Hosp Aide; SADD; School Musical; School Play; Stage Crew; Rep Frsh Cls; Coach Actv; Hon Roll; Hghst Hnrs-Comp Pgmmng; URI; Comp Pgmmr.

LASSER, KAREN E; Wheeler Schl; Pawtucket, RI; (Y); VP SADD; Orch; School Musical; Ed Nwsp Stf; Lcrss; Tennis; Ntl Merit SF; Cum Laude 85; Harvard Book Awd 85; Soc Of Women Engrs Awd-Sci & Math 85.

LAVALLEE, DAWN; W Warwick HS; West Warwick, RI; (Y); Church Yth Grp; Drama Clb; Exploring; French Clb; Math Tm; Chorus; High Hon Roll; Hon Roll; Alg II, Typng Awds 84; Hnrs Awd 84-85; MVP Sftbl 85; URI; Nrs.

LAVERGNE, KEVIN; North Smithfield JR SR HS; N Smithfield, RI; (Y); Art Clb; Boy Scts; Camera Clb; Cmnty Wkr; Dance Clb; Teachers Aide; Yrbk Phtg; Yrbk Sprt Ed; Tennis; Wt Lftg; Boston; Director.

LAWRENCE, LEONARD A; Coventry HS; Coventry, RI; (Y); 5/404; Boy Scts; Chess Clb; Computer Clb; Math Clb; Math Tm; VP Science Clb; Spanish Clb; Stu Cncl; L Socr; Var L Trk; Sci Fair 1st Schl & 2nd ST 84-86; ST Chess Chmpn 5-86; ADRA Schlrshp 86; Christon Mc Kaulif Schlrshp; Worcester Polytech; Elec Engrng.

LE FEBVRE, DONNA; Pilgrim HS; Warwick, RI; (Y); Frsh Cls; Soph Cls; Jr Cls; High Hon Roll; Hon Roll; Providence Coll; Bus.

LEACH, KIM; Pilgrim HS; Warwick, RI; (Y); Var Sftbl; U Of RI; Bus Mgmt.

LEAMY, DEBORAH; La Salle Acad; Providence, RI; (Y); Band; Variety Show; Nwsp Stf; Hon Roll; NHS; Ntl Merit Ltr; Tuition Schlrshp Natl Acad Arts Smmr Session 86; Prof Dancer.

LEAVENE, ELIZABETH ANNE; North Kingstown SR HS; N Kingstown, RI; (Y); 55/380; Drama Clb; Intnl Clb; School Play; Stage Crew; Nwsp Stf; Yrbk Rptr; Yrbk Stf; High Hon Roll; Hon Roll; Vetrns Memrl Schlrshp 86; H S Chrties Schlrshp 86; RI Hnr Soc 82-86; U Of RI; Elem Educ.

LEBEAU, ESTELLE; Central Falls JR SR HS; Central Falls, RI; (Y); 2/125; VP JA; Office Aide; Science Clb; Yrbk Stf; Trs Jr Cls; Trs Stu Cncl; High Hon Roll; Jr NHS; 2nd Grnt ST Sci Fr; Chmcl Engr.

LEBEAU, JACQUELINE; Wm M Davies Jr Tech; Central Falls, RI; (Y); Johnson & Wales; Chef.

LEBLANC, KEVIN; St Raphael Acad; Central, RI; (Y); 58/160; Boy Scts; Cmnty Wkr; French Clb; Yrbk Stf; JV Ftbl; Hon Roll; Elec Tech.

LEDDY, KATHLEEN M; Smithfield HS; Smithfield, RI; (Y); 4/203; Church Yth Grp; Quiz Bowl; SADD; Trs Frsh Cls; Trs Soph Cls; Trs Jr Cls; Var L Bsktbl; Var L Fld Hcky; Var L Trk; High Hon Roll; Amer Lgn Ortrcl Cntst; 3rd Dist Lvl 86; Bsktbl All-St 2nd Tm; All USA Hnrbl Mntn 86; Acad Dcthln Cmp 86.

LEDOUX, MAUREEN; St Raphael Acad; Pawtucket, RI; (Y); Political Wkr; Spanish Clb; Yrbk Stf; Hon Roll; Spanish NHS.

LEE, NIGEL; Barrington HS; Barrington, RI; (Y); 1/240; Computer Clb; Math Tm; Concert Band; High Hon Roll; Jr NHS; Trs NHS; Ntl Merit SF; Rensselaer Polytechnic Inst Math & Sci Awd; R I Acad Decathlon-3 Mdls; Brown U; Math.

LEE, TRACEY; Smithfield HS; Smithfield, RI; (Y); Cmnty Wkr; Girl Scts; Speech Tm; Varsity Clb; Rep Soph Cls; Rep Jr Cls; Rep Stu Cncl; Var L Sftbl; Providence Coll; Bus Admin.

LEMAY, MICHELLE; North Smithfield JR SR HS; N Smithfield, RI; (Y); Church Yth Grp; Drama Clb; Trs French Clb; Letterman Clb; SADD; Band; Concert Band; Drm & Bgl; Drm Mjr(t); Sec Jazz Band; Most Imprvd Vrsty Gymnstcs 85; Cert & Lttr In Band 86; Cert Frnch Clb 86; Nrsng.

LEMIEUX, KELLIE; Ponaganset HS; Greenville, RI; (Y); 34/134; Letterman Clb; Pep Clb; Varsity Clb; Yrbk Stf; Cheerleading; Vllybl; High Hon Roll; Hon Roll; Pres Schlr; All Divisn 2nd Tm Vllybl 86; Unsung Hero Vllybll 86; Math.

LENDRUM, PETER; Rogers HS; Newport, RI; (Y); Am Leg Boys St; Church Yth Grp; Cmnty Wkr; Y-Teens; Var Bsbl; Bsktbl; Ice Hcky; Var Socr; Hon Roll; 2nd Tm Awd-Al Div Sccr 85-86; Mst Imprvd Plyr Awd Ice Hcky 86; Chrch Cncl Hnr 85-86; Physcl Ed.

LEONARDO, JOSEPH; Saint Raphael Acad; E Providence, RI; (Y); 1/178; French Clb; Math Clb; Quiz Bowl; Trs Jr Cls; Trs Sr Cls; French Hon Soc; High Hon Roll; Jr NHS; NHS; Pharmctcl Awd 85; Hosp Awd 85; Lwyr.

LEONE, KAREN; Mount Saint Charles Acad; Greenville, RI; (S); 12/170; Church Yth Grp; Model UN; Var Cheerleading; Var Tennis; High Hon Roll; Spanish NHS.

LESSMANN, JEREMY; Narragansett HS; Narragansett, RI; (Y); Band; Church Choir; Ftbl; Trk; High Hon Roll; Hon Roll; NHS; Church Yth Grp; Concert Band; Mrchg Band; Frdms & Ldrshp Yth Conf 86; 1st Pl Schl Sci Fair & 2nd ST 86; ST Rep Natl Luthern Yth Cnvtn 85; Chem.

LETENDRE, PETER; Lincoln SR HS; Lincoln, RI; (Y); 25/210; Boys Clb Am; Boy Scts; CAP; Math Tm; Political Wkr; Drill Tm; Variety Show; Swmmng; Hon Roll; NHS; Billy Mitchell Awd 84; Amelia Earhart Awd 85; 102nd Cmpst Squdrn Flyng Schlrshp 86; US Air Force Acad; Aerntcl Eng.

LETHBRIDGE, KERRIE; East Providence HS; East Providence, RI; (S); 12/523; Church Yth Grp; Concert Band; Jazz Band; Mrchg Band; Off Soph Cls; Off Jr Cls; Off Sr Cls; Stu Cncl; Tennis; NHS; Boston Coll; Lib Arts.

LETT, TARA; St Mary Acad; Smithfield, RI; (Y); Boys Clb Am; Exploring; French Clb; Library Aide; Hon Roll; Comp Rllrsktng Trophies 82-85; Cert Of Merit For Service St Mary Acad 85; 3rd Pl St Mry Acad Sci Fr 85; Real Estate.

LEVESQUE, CARRIE ANN; Tiverton HS; Tiverton, RI; (Y); Church Yth Grp; Pep Clb; Chorus; Concert Band; Mrchg Band; Sec Frsh Cls; Sec Soph Cls; Capt Cheerleading; Vllybl; Hon Roll; Var Let & 4 Var Pins Chrldng 86; 2 Ribbons Solo & Duet Bnd 84; Chld Psychlgst.

LEVESQUE, CARRIE-ANN; Tiverton HS; Tiverton, RI; (Y); Church Yth Grp; Chorus; Concert Band; Mrchg Band; Pep Band; Sec Frsh Cls; Sec Soph Cls; Capt Var Cheerleading; Coach Actv; Vllybl; Child Psych.

LEVESQUE, KRISTEN; Coventry HS; Coventry, RI; (Y); Ski Clb; Spanish Clb; Im Bsktbl; Im Tennis; CCRI; Mdcl Tech.

LEVESQUE, MICHAEL; La Salle Acad; North Providence, RI; (Y); Boy Scts; Church Yth Grp; Computer Clb; JA; Elks Awd; Hon Roll; NHS; Quiz Bowl; Concert Band; Jazz Band; Schlrshp To La Salle Acdmy 83; Egl Sct 84; Phy.

LEVESQUE, NADINE; Tiverton HS; Tiverton, RI; (S); Dance Clb; French Clb; Band; Concert Band; Mrchg Band; Im Badmtn; Im Bsktbl; Im Fld Hcky; Im Gym; Hon Roll.

LEWIS, ANDREW; Bishop Hendricken HS; Warwick, RI; (Y); 120/260; Church Yth Grp; Cmnty Wkr; Letterman Clb; Varsity Clb; Var Crs Cntry; Var Trk; Hon Roll; Prfct Atten Awd; Aerontcl Engrng.

LICCIARDI, SUSAN; St Mary Acad; Bristol, RI; (Y); French Clb; Ski Clb; Rep Soph Cls; Rep Jr Cls; Rep Stu Cncl; JV Cheerleading; JV Crs Cntry; JV Trk; Hon Roll; NEDT Awd; Stu Cncl Svc Awd 85-86; Pre-Med.

LIMOGES, MICHELE M; Warwick Veterans Memorial HS; Warwick, RI; (Y); 61/234; Boy Scts; French Clb; JA; Latin Clb; French Hon Soc; High Hon Roll; Hon Roll; Mdl Legsltr Awd To RI Coll 86; RI Coll; Soc Wrk.

LISI, CHRISTOPHER; Lincoln SR HS; Lincoln, RI; (Y); Stage Crew; Variety Show; Var Swmmng; RI Coaches All Strs Swmng Team, Prvdnce Jrnl All ST Swm Team, All Div Slctn 1st Team 86; Law.

LISI, CHRISTOPHER; North Providence HS; N Providence, RI; (Y); 66/223; Ski Clb; Var L Bsbl; Bsktbl; Var L Crs Cntry; Hon Roll; Edward Lanni Schlrshp 86; 2nd Tm All-ST X-Cnrty 10 Tm All-Div 84; RI Coll; Mass Media Comm.

LLAMAS, CRISTINA; Lincoln Schl; Manville, RI; (Y); VP Pres Church Yth Grp; Acpl Chr; Chorus; Church Choir; Madrigals; Lit Mag; French Clb; Stu Cncl; Tennis; High Hon Roll; Amy Wilson Hart Awd-Genl Acad Excllnc 83; Francis E Wheeler Awd-Genl Acad Excllnc 84-85; U Of PA.

LOFFREDO, JOE; Johnston HS; Johnston, RI; (Y); 8/212; JA; NHS; Pres Schlr; Bryant Coll; Bus.

LOH, DAVID; N Providence HS; N Providence, RI; (Y); 7/213; Scholastic Bowl; Stu Cncl; Var Stat Bsbl; Score Keeper; Gov Hon Prg Awd; High Hon Roll; NHS; Ntl Merit SF; Cornell U; Engrng.

LOMBARDI, REBECCA; St Raphael Acad; N Prov, RI; (Y); Church Yth Grp; French Clb; Sec SADD; VP Stu Cncl; Var Co-Capt Bsktbl; Var Co-Capt Sftbl; French Hon Soc; Hon Roll; NHS; Bskbl All ST Champs All Div All Tourney 86; Sft All Div Tm 86RI Hnr Soc 86; Vassar; Pre Law.

LOMBARDI, STEPHANIE; Mount Saint Charles Acad; N Smithfield, RI; (Y); 26/140; Chrmn Church Yth Grp; French Clb; Church Choir; School Musical; Stage Crew; Yrbk Phtg; Yrbk Stf; Var Tennis; Hon Roll; NHS; Providence Coll; Psychlgy.

LOMBARDI, VALERIE; Bishop Keough HS; N Providence, RI; (Y); 8/48; Church Yth Grp; Drama Clb; Girl Scts; School Play; Stage Crew; Yrbk Stf; Pres Stu Cncl; Cit Awd; Hon Roll; Charles De Blois Awd 86; Secy Of ST Ldrshp Awd 86; Natl Merit Awd Sci 85; Salve Regina; Librl Arts.

LONG, VANESSA; East Prov Senior HS; Riverside, RI; (Y); GAA; Chorus; Swing Chorus; Var Bsktbl; Capt Cheerleading; Var Crs Cntry; Var Trk; Var Vllybl; High Hon Roll; Hon Roll; Hnr Rll 84-86; Vrsty Bsktbll & Vllybll 84-86; URI.

LONGO, KATHLEEN; La Salle Acad; Providence, RI; (Y); Model UN; Ski Clb; Nwsp Stf; Yrbk Stf; Rep Soph Cls; Sftbl; High Hon Roll; NHS; Cum Laude Recog Natl Latin Exm 85; ST Acad Dcthln 86.

LONKART, KEVIN; St Rapahel Acad; N Scituate, RI; (Y); US Army.

LOPES, KEITH; East Providence SR HS; Riverside, RI; (Y); School Musical; French Clb; JA; SADD; Chorus; Church Choir; School Musical; Yrbk Stf; Jr Cls; Pres Stu Cncl; Cadmc Dcthln 86 & 87; Geo Wshngtn U; Physcn.

LOPES, WILLIAM G; Portsmouth HS; Portsmouth, RI; (Y); Boy Scts; Ski Clb; Band; Concert Band; Mrchg Band; Pep Band; Off Sr Cls; Stu Cncl; Bsktbl; Tennis; RI Hon Soc 86; Ntl Hon Soc 85-86; U Of RI; Comp Engrng.

LOPEZ, ANGELA; Charles E Shea HS; Pawtucket, RI; (Y); Art Clb; French Clb; Yrbk Ed-Chief; Frsh Cls; Stat Ice Hcky; Stat Socr; Vllybl; High Hon Roll; Hon Roll; Bio Frnch Albegra I 84; Boston Coll; Comp Engrng.

LOVETT, KIM; North Smithfield JR SR HS; Forestdale, RI; (Y); Letterman Clb; Stu Cncl; L Var Cheerleading; L Var Sftbl; L Var Tennis; Hon Roll; All-Star Wstrn Div 2nd Team Tennis Girls 84; Girls Tennis All Stars Hnrb Mntn Dbls 85; Elem Ed.

LOVETT, VALERIE ANN; Senior HS; Arlington, MA; (Y); Dance Clb; Debate Tm; Letterman Clb; Model UN; Varsity Clb; Color Guard; Rep Stu Cncl; Var Bsktbl; JV Trk; Hon Roll; Law.

LUCIAN, DIANNE; Prout Memorial HS; Wakefield, RI; (S); 1/71; Church Yth Grp; Exploring; Math Tm; Sec Chorus; Madrigals; School Musical; Nwsp Ed-Chief; High Hon Roll; NHS; Ntl Merit Ltr; Mc Gill U; Med.

LUNDGREN, JENNIFER; Charles E Shea HS; Pawtucket, RI; (Y); Chorus; Yrbk Ed-Chief; Sftbl; Vllybl; Hon Roll; Bus Cmmnctns.

LUZZI, ANGELO; Chariho Regional HS; Westerly, RI; (Y); Boy Scts; Trk; High Hon Roll; Hon Roll; CCRI; Art.

LYNCH, MATTHEW P; La Salle Acad; Woonsocket, RI; (Y); Math Tm; Ski Clb; Var L Bsbl; Var L Ftbl; Var L Swmmng; Var Trk; Hon Roll; NHS; Law.

LYNDEN, MADELEINE S; Barrington HS; Barrington, RI; (Y); 13/239; French Clb; Intnl Clb; Letterman Clb; Yrbk Bus Mgr; Tennis; NHS; NACEL Cltrl Exchng France 86; Acolyte St Johns Episcopal Church 81.

MACDOUGALL, CHRISTOPHER; East Providence SR HS; E Providence, RI; (Y); Spanish Clb; Band; Concert Band; Mrchg Band; Pep Band; JV Var Ftbl; Embry-Riddle Aerntcl U; Pilot.

MACHADO, SCOTT C; East Providence HS; Rumford, RI; (Y); French Clb; Band; Drm & Bgl; Mrchg Band; Stu Cncl; Hon Roll; Townie Awd 83-84; Psychlgy.

MACIOCIO, MICHAEL; North Providence HS; Providence, RI; (Y); 4-H; Boys Clb Am; Computer Clb; JA; Var L Bsbl; Var L Bsktbl; Im Crs Cntry; High Hon Roll; Engrng.

MAGGIACOMO, KAREN; Cranston West HS; Cranston, RI; (Y); Teachers Aide; Hon Roll; RI Tchrs Of Italian Awd 86; Human Svcs.

MAGLIONE, CHARLES; Mt Saint Charles Acad; N Smithfield, RI; (S); 6/141; VP JA; Math Tm; Rep Model UN; Political Wkr; Ski Clb; Socr; Elks Awd; High Hon Roll; NHS; Tulane U; Corp Law.

MAGUIRE, PATRICK; South Kingstown HS; Wakefield, RI; (Y); 16/285; Art Clb; Model UN; Trs Soph Cls; Trs Jr Cls; Trs Sr Cls; Stu Cncl; Capt Var Bsbl; Capt Var Socr; DAR Awd; High Hon Roll; Cls Treas; Stu Cncl 85-87; Soccer Capt; Hnr Rl 84-87; Arch.

MAHER JR, ROBERT R; N Providence HS; N Providence, RI; (Y); Boys Clb Am; Church Yth Grp; Band; Concert Band; Jazz Band; Yrbk Stf; Hon Roll; Msc Schlrshp 80; RI Schl Of Dsgn; Arctrcl Dsgn.

MAHONEY, JENNIFER A; Barrington HS; Barrington, RI; (Y); 1/235; Nwsp Stf; Ed Yrbk Stf; Rep Stu Cncl; Var Capt Tennis; NHS; Ntl Merit SF; All-St Tennis 83-86; Harvard Bk Clb Awd 85; Hugh O Brian Fdntn Ldrshp Awd 84.

MAIELLO, MICHAEL; La Salle Acad; Johnston, RI; (Y); 1/286; Math Tm; Var Wrstlng; High Hon Roll; NHS; Dartmouth Bk Awd 86; URI Dstngshd Fclty Awd Scholar 86; Schl Phys Fit Record 85.

MAINELLA, MARK; Barrington HS; Barrington, RI; (Y); Intnl Clb; Latin Clb; Letterman Clb; Varsity Clb; Ftbl; Trk; Wt Lftg; High Hon Roll; Hon Roll; Jr NHS; Tufts U; Medcl Prfsn.

MAKI, TINA; Chariho Regional HS; Kenyon, RI; (Y); 6/279; Band; Mgr(s); Trk; High Hon Roll; Hon Roll; NHS; Hnr Soc 86; Pres Acad Ftns Awd 86.

MALAFRONTE, CHRIS; Bristol HS; Bristol, RI; (Y); Computer Clb; French Clb; Ski Clb; Tennis; Pref Atten Cert 85; Fairfield U; Biomed.

MALIK, FARHANA; Woonsocket HS; Woonsocket, RI; (Y); Ski Clb; School Play; Yrbk Stf; Stu Cncl; Badmtn; Bsktbl; Gym; Sftbl; Trk; Vllybl; Badmintn Champnshp Trophy 83; Northeastern U; Pol Sci.

MALO, JODE; St Marys Academy Bay View; Seekonk, MA; (Y); Exploring; Chorus; Stage Crew; High Hon Roll; Bay View Hon Soc & Serv Awd 83-85; Cert For Volunteering Sctng 85-86; Nursing.

MALO, RONNY R; William Davies JR Vo Tech; Pawtucket, RI; (Y); VICA; High Hon Roll; Amer Assn Of Physics Tchrs Awd 86; Rotary Clb Of Pres Schlrshp Awd 86; Davies Paretn Fclty Org Awd 86; Hall Inst; Arch Drftng.

MANCINI, PAUL; La Salle Acad; Cranston, RI; (Y); 30/286; Sec Cmnty Wkr; Political Wkr; Bsktbl; Trk; 4-H Awd; R I Hnr Soc Awd 86; Citatn Ntl Hnr 86; Italian Achvt Awd 84-85; Boston Coll; Law.

MANIS, GEORGE; Barrington HS; Barrington, RI; (Y); 27/232; Boy Scts; Church Yth Grp; Nwsp Rptr; Nwsp Stf; Lit Mag; High Hon Roll; St Schlr; Pre-Med.

MANNING, LETICIA; Prout Memorial HS; West Warwick, RI; (S); 3/92; Variety Show; Nwsp Rptr; Pres Soph Cls; Pres Jr Cls; Var Bsktbl; Var Crs Cntry; Var L Sftbl; High Hon Roll; Hugh O Brien Leadrshp Awd 85; Govnrs Smmr Pgm In Sci & Math 85.

MANSOLILLO, JAY; Smithfield HS; Smithfield, RI; (Y); Band; Concert Band; Jazz Band; Var L Tennis; L Hon Roll; All Div Ten Tm 84; All ST Ten Tm 86; Engrng.

MARABELLO, CHERYL; Barrington HS; Barrington, RI; (Y); #1 In Class; VP Church Yth Grp; Sec GAA; Intnl Clb; Math Tm; Yrbk Stf; Var Socr; Var Vllybl; NHS; Hly Crss Bk Awd 86; 2nd Tm All-ST Sccr 86.

MARCELLO, MICHAEL; Scituate JR-SR HS; Scituate, RI; (S); 4/108; Yrbk Ed-Chief; Ed Yrbk Stf; Pres Soph Cls; Pres Jr Cls; Pres Sr Cls; Rep Stu Cncl; High Hon Roll; Jr NHS; Band; Pep Band; U S Snt Yth Pgm Delg 86; U S Sec Educ Intl Yth Yr Awd 85; Medcl Doc.

MARCHAND, JOHN; Cumberland HS; Cumberland, RI; (Y); Nwsp Stf; JV Bsktbl; JV Ftbl; Var L Trk; High Hon Roll; Hon Roll; CYO Bsktbl Asst Coac 83-86; Call All Area Trck Tm 86; All Nrthrn Div Trck 86; Spts Stu Corrspndnt 86; Sprts Jrnlsm.

MARNANE, DANA LYNNE; Middletown HS; Middletown, RI; (Y); 26/250; Drama Clb; Ski Clb; Spanish Clb; Band; Jazz Band; Mrchg Band; Pep Band; Socr; Swmmng; Hon Roll; Marist Coll; Spnsh.

MARS, CHRYSTAL; Charihe Regional HS; Kenyon, RI; (Y); 49/283; Church Yth Grp; High Hon Roll; Hon Roll; Outstndng Bus Stu 86; Johnson & Wales Sklls Meet Shrthnd Cmprhn 86; All Acad Stu Awd 86; Ocn ST Bus Inst; Exctve Sectry.

MARSH, DIANA; Classical HS; Providence, RI; (Y); Computer Clb; Drama Clb; Math Tm; Science Clb; Yrbk Phtg; Yrbk Sprt Ed; Lit Mag; JV Socr; French Hon Soc; High Hon Roll; Yale Bk Awd 86; 4th Prz ST AATF Frnch Cntst Lvl 4 86; Nationale Socte Frncs 86; Biomed Engr.

MARSHALL, DANIEL; North Providence HS; N Providence, RI; (Y); Church Yth Grp; Cmnty Wkr; JA; Ski Clb; Hon Roll; Jr NHS; Ntl Merit Ltr; RPI; Chem Engrng.

MARSIS, JENNIFER; Warwick Veterans Memorial HS; Warwick, RI; (Y); Dance Clb; Stu Cncl; JV Cheerleading; Hon Roll.

MARTEL, LISA ANN; St Raphael Acad; Cumberland, RI; (Y); 2/169; Church Yth Grp; Drama Clb; French Clb; Office Aide; Variety Show; Var JV Cheerleading; French Hon Soc; High Hon Roll; NHS; Yrbk Stf; Holy Cross Coll Bk Prz 86; RN.

MARTIN, ANN-MARIE; East Providence HS; East Providence, RI; (S); 26/528; Church Yth Grp; French Clb; Library Aide; Nwsp Rptr; Nwsp Stf; Hon Roll; RI Hnr Soc; RI Coll; Comp Pgm.

MARTIN, JOHN; Pilgrim HS; Warwick, RI; (Y); Band; Concert Band; Jazz Band; Mrchg Band; Orch; Pep Band; Hon Roll; Univ Of Rhode Isl; Mech Engrng.

MARTIN, MELANIE; Woon SR HS; Woonsocket, RI; (Y); Vllybl; High Hon Roll; Hon Roll.

MARTIN, RICHARD; Cranstons High West; Cranston, RI; (Y); Art Clb; Boy Scts; Computer Clb; Library Aide; Chorus; Stage Crew; Yrbk Stf; Lit Mag; Gov Hon Prg Awd; High Hon Roll; Bus.

MARTINELLI, DOMINICO; North Providence HS; N Providence, RI; (Y); Boys Clb Am; Ski Clb; JV Var Ftbl; Hon Roll; Jr NHS; Air Force; Jet Pilot.

MARTINELLI, MICHELE; St Marys Acad; Providence, RI; (Y); French Clb; Math Clb; Political Wkr; Rep Stu Cncl; Hon Roll; NHS; NEDT Awd; Law.

MARTINEZ, CHARLENE; St Mary Acad Bay View; Providence, RI; (Y); Debate Tm; Sec Exploring; French Clb; Math Clb; SADD; Chorus; Second Hnrs 85; Bus.

MARTINEZ, MARIA; Central Falls SR HS; Central Falls, RI; (Y); Rep Soph Cls; Stu Cncl; Prfct Atten Awd; Chem.

MARTINS, LISA; Tolman HS; Pawtucket, RI; (Y); 2/270; Yrbk Stf; Off Soph Cls; Off Jr Cls; Off Sr Cls; VP Stu Cncl; Var Swmmng; Var Tennis; Capt Var Vllybl; High Hon Roll; NHS; Hrvrd Bk Awd 85; Bst Fml Stu/Athlt 86; 1st Tm All-Div Vllybl & Tnns 86; Holy Cross; Law.

MARZOCCHI, ERIK; La Salle Acad; N Providence, RI; (Y); Art Clb; Boys Clb Am; Church Yth Grp; Cmnty Wkr; PAVAS; Band; Chorus; School Musical; Variety Show; Nwsp Stf; RISD; Actng.

MASELLI, STACEY; Bishop Keough Regional HS; Lincoln, RI; (S); Drama Clb; Library Aide; School Play; Variety Show; Nwsp Stf; Off Frsh Cls; Stu Cncl; Hon Roll; Ntl Merit Ltr; Eng Awd 85; Drama Awd 84; Hugh Obrien Ldrshp Smnr 85; Anthroplgy.

MASON, ROBERT; East Providence HS; E Prov, RI; (Y); Var Tennis; JV Wrstlng; Law.

MASSO, STEVEN; North Providence HS; N Providence, RI; (Y); Cmnty Wkr; Concert Band; Jazz Band; Mrchg Band; Lit Mag; Hon Roll; NHS; Rhode Isl Mock Trial Trnmnt 86; Depicted Evolution Of Music In Schl Mural 86; Law.

MASTANTUONO, LORI; Prout Memorial HS; Cranston, RI; (Y); 21/72; Aud/Vis; Computer Clb; Ski Clb; Rep Jr Cls; High Hon Roll; Hon Roll; NHS; RI Hnr Soc; RI Coll.

MASTERSON, TIMOTHY; Bishop Hendricken HS; Coventry, RI; (Y); 44/290; School Musical; Rep Jr Cls; Rep Sr Cls; Rep Stu Cncl; JV Var Bsbl; JV Stat Bsktbl; Score Keeper; Hon Roll; Jr NHS; NHS; Worcester Plytech Inst; Btchlgs.

MASTIN, LORENA; Coventry HS; Coventry, RI; (Y); #30 In Class; Letterman Clb; Pep Clb; Spanish Clb; Church Choir; Stu Cncl; Capt Cheerleading; Vllybl; Hon Roll; Spanish NHS; Ocptnl Thrpst.

MATHERS, ROBIN; East Providence HS; Riverside, RI; (Y); Church Yth Grp; Girl Scts; Hosp Aide; Yrbk Stf; Var JV Bsktbl; Var Capt Crs Cntry; Sftbl; Var Trk; High Hon Roll; Hon Roll; Marian Awd 84; Stu Athltc Awd 84; Girl Scts Slvr Awd 84; Nrsg.

MATHURIN, REBECCA; St Mary Academy Bay View; Warwick, RI; (Y); 1/200; Exploring; Math Tm; Spanish Clb; SADD; Orch; Hon Roll; Jr NHS; NHS; Acdmc All Am; Excllnce Eng Awd; Dartmouth Bk Awd; Cornell; Pre-Med.

MATIAS, FATIMA; Davies Voc Tech; Pawtucket, RI; (Y); Art Clb; JA; Church Choir; Gym; High Hon Roll; Hon Roll; Bestr Styled Manniquin Cntst 85; Best Hairstyle 1st Pl 86; Gen Sci Awd 84; Cosmetlgst.

MATOIAN, SANDRA; North Smithfield JR SR HS; Woonsocket, RI; (Y); French Clb; SADD; Band; Mrchg Band; Lit Mag; Stu Cncl; Hon Roll; Solo Ensmble Mdl Flute 84-85; Band Cert 84-85; Frgn Lang Artwrk Awd 84-85; Socl Wrk.

MATTEO, SHERI; Cumberland HS; Cumberland, RI; (Y); 34/389; Church Yth Grp; Math Tm; Powder Puff Ftbl; Var Sftbl; High Hon Roll; Hon Roll; NHS; Quiz Bowl; Thomas G King Mem Drftng Cntst 86; Prsdntl Drftng Awd 86; Cmbrlnd Police Dept Annl Schlrshp 86; Wentworth Inst Tech; Mech Dsgn.

MAURICIO, GINA; Johnston SR HS; Johnston, RI; (Y); DECA; Yrbk Stf; Hon Roll; Bus Mgmt.

MAYNARD, KEVIN J; Bishop Hendricken HS; Hope, RI; (Y); 4/240; French Clb; Yrbk Phtg; JV Trk; JV Wrstlng; French Hon Soc; High Hon Roll; NHS; Ntl Merit Ltr; Hon Roll; Dartmouth Coll Bk Awd 86; Ntl Engr Aptitude Srch Awd 84.

MAYNARD, WENDY; Warwick Veterans HS; Warwick, RI; (Y); Dance Clb; Math Clb; Math Tm; Drill Tm; Yrbk Stf; Off Frsh Cls; Off Soph Cls; Off Jr Cls; Off Sr Cls; Stu Cncl; Wheelock College; Erly Chldhd.

MAYNE, NANCY; Chariho Regional JR SR HS; Charlestown, RI; (Y); 1/279; Chorus; Var Vllybl; High Hon Roll; NHS; Pres Schlr; Val; Art Clb; Debate Tm; Library Aide; RI Hnr Socty; Pell Awd US Hstry; Johnson & Wales Clg Bkkpg Awd; PA ST U; Acctg.

MAZMANIAN, MARK C; Cumberland HS; Cumberland, RI; (S); 5/387; Art Clb; Church Yth Grp; Cmnty Wkr; Exploring; Hosp Aide; JA; Science Clb; JV Socr; Var Trk; High Hon Roll; Spnsh Diplma Merit 83; US Military Acad; Elect Engr.

MC ALISTER, CHRISTOPHER; N Smithfield JR SR HS; N Smithfield, RI; (Y); Boy Scts; French Clb; Math Tm; SADD; Concert Band; Rep Jr Cls; Rep Sr Cls; Rep Stu Cncl; High Hon Roll; Mathletes; Life Rnk Sctng 85; Ordr Arrow Awd 85; Law.

MC BRIDE, MARY BETH; North Smithfield HS; North Smithfield, RI; (Y); French Clb; Letterman Clb; SADD; Band; Concert Band; Mrchg Band; Pep Band; Var L Sftbl; Hon Roll; Ltr Band 86; Sprts Med.

MC CARTHY, COLLEEN; Saint Raphael Acad; Rumford, RI; (Y); 11/181; Political Wkr; Pres SADD; Yrbk Stf; Crs Cntry; Swmmng; Cit Awd; DAR Awd; French Hon Soc; Hon Roll; NHS; Boston College; Poltc Sci.

MC CARTHY, GARY; Rogers HS; Newport, RI; (Y); Var JV Bsbl; Im Bsktbl; Capt Socr; Var Trk; Hon Roll; NHS; 4th Knghts Columbus Schlrshp & Town - County Schlrshp; Bryant Coll RI; Bus.

MC CORMICK, GEORGE; Pilgrim HS; Warwick, RI; (Y); French Clb; JA; Math Tm; Varsity Clb; Var Capt Crs Cntry; Var Capt Trk; High Hon Roll; Hon Roll; Computer Clb; Letterman Clb.

MC CRAVE, MEREDITH; South Kingstown HS; Wakefield, RI; (Y); 67/172; Drama Clb; Band; Concert Band; Capt Flag Corp; Mrchg Band; School Musical; Variety Show; Mgr(s); Trk; Hon Roll; Travel.

MC CRILLIS, CHERYL; Coventry HS; Coventry, RI; (Y); French Clb; Political Wkr; VICA; Hon Roll; JR Vo-Tech Pres Food Servs 85-86; RI Islnd Schl Design; Clrnry.

MC CUMISKEY, TRACY; Chariho Regional HS; Ashaway, RI; (Y); 13/257; VICA; Pres Soph Cls; Pres Jr Cls; Pres Sr Cls; Sec Stu Cncl; Var Capt Bsktbl; Var Capt Fld Hcky; Var Sftbl; High Hon Roll; Hon Roll; Captn Bsktbl 85-86; 1st Team All Div 85-86; Colby Sawyer; Bus Adm.

MC DANIEL, STEVEN; Mount Saint Charles Acad; N Providence, RI; (S); Boys Clb Am; Chess Clb; Math Tm; High Hon Roll; Comp Prgmmr.

MC GAHERN, KATHLEEN; St Mary Academy Bay View; Prov, RI; (Y); 37/235; Pres Church Yth Grp; Exploring; Math Clb; Spanish Clb; Church Choir; Orch; Swmmng; Vllybl; Hon Roll; Natl Hnr Rll 86; Acctg.

MC GOWAN, TRACEY LYNN; East Providence SR HS; E Providence, RI; (Y); Church Yth Grp; JA; SADD; Hon Roll; Prfct Atten Awd.

MC GRATH, SUZANNE; Rogers HS; Newport, RI; (Y); 20/257; VP French Clb; Powder Puff Ftbl; French Hon Soc; High Hon Roll; Hon Roll; NHS; Sullivan Schlrshp 86; San Regina Coll; Lib Arts.

MC KENNA, BRIAN; Lincoln SR HS; Manville, RI; (Y); Boy Scts; Church Yth Grp; Quiz Bowl; Rep Soph Cls; Rep Jr Cls; Rep Stu Cncl; JV Bsbl; Var L Trk; Vllybl; Hon Roll.

MC KENNA, DEANA; Middletown HS; Middletown, RI; (Y); Church Yth Grp; Dance Clb; Yrbk Stf; Cheerleading; Powder Puff Ftbl; Score Keeper; Hon Roll.

MC KENNEY, KIM C; E Greenwich HS; E Greenwich, RI; (Y); 34/168; Church Yth Grp; Cmnty Wkr; GAA; Intnl Clb; Variety Show; Stu Cncl; Var L Bsktbl; Coach Actv; Var L Fld Hcky; Powder Puff Ftbl; 1st Tm All Div Sftbl 86; 1st Tm All ST Sftbl 86; E Greenwich Booster Clb & Fire Assn Scholr 86; AZ ST U; Exercise Tech.

MC KITCHEN, ERIN M; Tolman HS; Pawtucket, RI; (Y); Hosp Aide; Badmtn; Var Co-Capt Bsktbl; Sftbl; Swmmng; Var Tennis; Trk; Var Capt Vllybl; Tlmn High 7 Ltr Awd 86; 2nd Team All-Div Vllybl 86; 1 Total Vllybl Cmp Sprtsmnshp Awd 85; Sprgfld Coll; Phys Ed.

MC LAUGHLIN, SEAN; North Providence HS; North Providence, RI; (Y); Church Yth Grp; Crs Cntry; Var Lcrss; Hon Roll; Engr.

MC LOUGHLIN, HEATHER; Prout Memorial HS; Peace Dale, RI; (S); 2/79; Math Clb; Math Tm; Political Wkr; School Musical; Nwsp Ed-Chief; Yrbk Stf; Trs Sr Cls; JV Bsktbl; Var Cheerleading; High Hon Roll; Herbert Claiborne Pell Mdl US Hstry; Hghst Acadmc Avg Engl, Gym; Econmcs.

MC NAMARA, JENNIFER; Mt St Charles Acad; N Scituate, RI; (Y); Cmnty Wkr; SADD; Nwsp Rptr; Nwsp Stf; Stu Cncl; Wilkes Coll; Physcl Thrpy.

MC NEIL, MAUREEN; Mt Saint Charles Acad; Bellingham, MA; (Y); 60/168; Pres Church Yth Grp; Dance Clb; Drama Clb; Capt Quiz Bowl; Ski Clb; School Musical; JV Sftbl; Hon Roll; Chrch Yth Grp Mst Prmsng Yth & Bst Actrss 85; Soc Wrk.

MC VAY, ROBERTA; Charino Regional HS; Shannock, RI; (Y); 4-H; Cmnty Coll Of RI; Ocngrphy.

MECK, RICK; Rogers HS; Fairfax, VA; (Y); JV Bsktbl; Var Golf; Var Socr; Var Swmmng; High Hon Roll; US Air Force Acad.

MEDEIROS, DORENE L; Tiverton HS; Tiverton, RI; (S); Concert Band; Jazz Band; Mrchg Band; School Musical; VP Fld Hcky; Hon Roll; Band; JV Sftbl; RI All ST Band 84-85 & 85-86; Sthrn Regnl All ST RI 83-84; Yth Of Amer Europe Concrt Tour 85; Music.

MEEHAN, UNA; Prout Memorial HS; N Kingstown, RI; (S); Church Yth Grp; Hosp Aide; Var Capt Bsktbl; Socr; Var JV Sftbl; Hon Roll; Advrtsg.

MELILLO, LORI; Bishop Keough HS; N Providence, RI; (S); 5/46; Cmnty Wkr; Office Aide; Tennis; High Hon Roll; NHS; Sen Pell Hstry Awd 85; Providence Coll; Bio.

MELLO, JOHN; Lasalle Acad; Bristol, RI; (Y); 4-H; Socr; Hon Roll; 3rd Hnrs Sccr 1st Tm All Div; U Of CT; Bus Mgmt.

MELLO, LORI; Hope HS; Providence, RI; (Y); Art Clb; Office Aide; JV Fld Hcky; JV Golf; Var Sftbl; JV Vllybl; Hon Roll; Intl Schl Of Arts Miami; Art.

MELLOTT JR, JACK; North Kingstown HS; N Kingstown, RI; (Y); 42/380; Band; Mrchg Band; Hoftra U; Aerospc Engrg.

MELO, JANE; Bristol HS; Bristol, RI; (Y); Art Clb; Church Yth Grp; Cmnty Wkr; French Clb; Teachers Aide; Church Choir; School Play; Variety Show; Nwsp Stf; Yrbk Stf; Gnrl Awd Encllnc 82; Nrsng.

MENDES, GAIL L; William E Tolman SR HS; Pawtucket, RI; (Y); 1/280; Cmnty Wkr; Yrbk Ed-Chief; Rep Frsh Cls; Rep Soph Cls; Rep Jr Cls; Rep Sr Cls; Rep Stu Cncl; Stat Ftbl; DAR Awd; Elks Awd; Distngshd Merit Sr 86; ME U Orono; Forstry.

MENEZES, MONICA LYNN; Portsmouth HS; Portsmouth, RI; (Y); 27/212; FBLA; Math Clb; Math Tm; Pep Clb; Band; Chorus; Concert Band; Mrchg Band; Pep Band; Merrimack Coll; Math.

MENG, CHARIS; Portsmouth HS; Portsmouth, RI; (Y); 1/212; Dance Clb; Hosp Aide; Nwsp Stf; High Hon Roll; NHS; Rotary Awd; Spanish NHS; Val; Voice Dem Awd; Chorus; 3rd Pl ST Vc Of Dmcrcy 86; Carlton D Yates Mem Awd 86; Ruth B Franklin Awd 86; Brown U; Pre Med.

MERCER, HOLLY; Warwick Veterans HS; Warwick, RI; (Y); Church Yth Grp; Cmnty Wkr; Drama Clb; Hosp Aide; JA; Office Aide; Pep Clb; Service Clb; Chorus; Church Choir; URI; Psych.

MERCURIO, DEBBIE; St Mary Academy Bayview; Warwick, RI; (Y); Church Yth Grp; Exploring; JA; Math Clb; Nwsp Rptr; Nwsp Stf; Capt Var Cheerleading; Aud/Vis; Cmnty Wkr; Math Tm; 50 Pct Acdmc Schlrshp To Bayview 83-87; Jr Achvmnt Natl Merit Awd 84-85; Pre Law.

MERRILL, DAVID; Classical HS; Providence, RI; (Y); High Hon Roll; Prfct Atten Awd; Byrant Coll Smithfield RI; Bus.

METZ, JASON; Middletown HS; Middletown, RI; (Y); Chess Clb; Church Yth Grp; Drama Clb; JA; Math Clb; Math Tm; Quiz Bowl; Scholastic Bowl; Acpl Chr; Band; All-ST Bnd Blue & Red Rbbns Solo & Ensmble Achvt In Music 85-86; 1st Rnnr Up Bst Slsmn Spkr Yr 86; Bus.

MICHELSON, JERE; Coventry HS; Coventry, RI; (Y); Drama Clb; French Clb; Letterman Clb; Varsity Clb; Band; Concert Band; Mrchg Band; Bsbl; Socr; Hon Roll; Computer.

MILANO, CYNTHIA; Lasalle Acad; Providence, RI; (Y); Church Yth Grp; Rep Soph Cls; Hon Roll; Psych.

MILES, STEVEN; Tiverton HS; Tiverton, RI; (S); 18/187; Pres Trs Church Yth Grp; Letterman Clb; Ski Clb; Variety Show; Yrbk Stf; Trs Soph Cls; Stu Cncl; Socr; Tennis; Vllybl; Mst Lkly To Sccd 85; Chem.

MILLER, CAROL; Lincoln HS; Lincoln, RI; (Y); 60/195; Chrmn SADD; Variety Show; Yrbk Stf; VP Pres Stu Cncl; Gym; Hon Roll; Law.

MILLER, DAVID C; Bishop Hendricken HS; Warwick, RI; (Y); 14/237; VP Rep Church Yth Grp; French Clb; Service Clb; Im Bowling; French Hon Soc; High Hon Roll; NHS; Relgs Actvts Comm; URI Almn Bk Awd.

MILLS, AUDREY; Rogers HS; Newport, RI; (Y); Boys Clb Am; Pres Church Yth Grp; Drama Clb; French Clb; Math Tm; Chorus; Church Choir; School Musical; Lit Mag; French Hon Soc; A Ratg RI Solo Presntn Mozarts Allealia 85; A Locl Presntn Handels Messiah Wrk 85; Music.

MIRACLE, SHANNON; Smithfield HS; Greenville, RI; (Y); 7/203; Church Yth Grp; French Clb; Math Clb; Band; Concert Band; High Hon Roll; Hon Roll; Girl Scts; Mrchg Band; Oratoricl Cntst 85-86; Mthmtcs Tchr.

MITCHELL, ROBERT E; Classical HS; Providence, RI; (Y); Spanish Clb; Hon Roll; Ntl Merit SF; 3rd Pl Black Heritage Soc Essy 85; 3 Yr Schlrshp Prgm-Andover Smmr Sessn 83-85; Natl Conf Chrstn & Jew; Fin.

MOLLANDER, JULIE; Wm M Davies Vo Tech; Esmond, RI; (Y); Hosp Aide; SADD; VICA; Chorus; Rep Stu Cncl; Hon Roll; Awd Outstndg Cntrbtns IFSEA 85; Bus Mgmt.

MOLLOY, SUZANNE; Mt St Charles Acad; Bellingham, MA; (Y); Pres Church Yth Grp; Hosp Aide; Political Wkr; Ski Clb; Var Capt Gym; Hon Roll; Midge Palmer Mem Scholar 86; 1st Tm All ST Gymnstcs 86; 1st Tm Call All Stars 85-86; U MA; Bus.

MONGEAU, JILL A; Cumberland HS; Cumberland, RI; (S); 9/385; School Musical; Off Soph Cls; Off Jr Cls; Rep Sr Cls; Pres Stu Cncl; Var Capt Cheerleading; Var Fld Hcky; Var Score Keeper; DAR Awd; NHS; Hrvrd Bk Prz; Sec Of ST Ldrshp Awd; ST Sci Fair 2nd Grnt; Colby Coll; Bus.

MONGEON, DANIEL; Woonsocket HS; Woonsocket, RI; (Y); Church Yth Grp; Drama Clb; School Musical.

MONIZ, KELLY; Tiverton HS; Tiverton, RI; (S); Ski Clb; Chorus; Hon Roll.

MONTECALVO, DAVID; Bishop Hendricken HS; Coventry, RI; (Y); 131/248; Intnl Clb; Trk; Hon Roll; Bus.

MOODY, EMILY; Chariho Regional HS; Wyoming, RI; (Y); U Of RI; Socl Wrk.

MOODY, SCOTT; Classical HS; Providence, RI; (Y); Church Yth Grp; Science Clb; Church Choir; Socr; Var L Trk; Hon Roll.

MOREIRA, DAVID; Bristol HS; Bristol, RI; (S); 7/194; Drama Clb; Math Tm; Ski Clb; School Play; Stage Crew; Yrbk Ed-Chief; Rep Frsh Cls; Rep Soph Cls; Rep Jr Cls; Rep Sr Cls; Sci Dept Cert Of Hnr 85; Cvl Engrng.

MOREIRA, PAULO; Hope HS; Providence, RI; (S); Pres Intnl Clb; Nwsp Rptr; VP Frsh Cls; Sec Soph Cls; Pres Stu Cncl; Var Socr; Hon Roll; U S Stu Cncls Awd 86; Century III Ldrs Awd 86; Engrng.

MOREY, DENICE; Pilgrim HS; Warwick, RI; (Y); Hon Roll.

MORGAN, THOMAS M; Mount Saint Charles Acad; Johnston, RI; (Y); Ski Clb; JV Socr; High Hon Roll; Hon Roll; Law.

MORIN, CHRIS; Woonsocket HS; Woonsocket, RI; (Y); Teachers Aide; VP Jr Cls; Var Bsktbl; Var Socr; Im Swmmng; Hon Roll; CC Of Rhode Island; Acctg.

MORISSEAU, CHRISTINE; North Smithfield JR SR HS; N Smithfield, RI; (Y); French Clb; Hst Intnl Clb; Letterman Clb; Pep Clb; Chorus; Concert Band; Mrchg Band; Capt Cheerleading; Hon Roll; Drama Clb; Mst Val Bsktbl Chrldr Trphy 86; Cazenovia Coll; Med Asst.

MORRISSETTE, LORI; St Raphael Acad; Cumberland, RI; (Y); SADD; Stage Crew; Yrbk Stf; Hon Roll; Volntr Awd Svcs-Cumberlnd Pub Lib 86; Fshn Merchndsng.

MORRY, TERRI; North Providence HS; N Providence, RI; (Y); 21/260; Nwsp Rptr; VP Frsh Cls; Stu Cncl; Var L Bsktbl; High Hon Roll; Hon Roll; NHS; Providence Coll; Pltcl Sci.

MOTT, WARREN; Ogers HS; Newport, RI; (Y); French Clb; VICA; Crs Cntry; Trk; Hon Roll; Arch.

MOUSSEAU JR, ALBERT; Johnston SR HS; Johnston, RI; (S); 2/216; English Clb; Math Tm; Science Clb; SADD; Nwsp Rptr; Rep Frsh Cls; Rep Jr Cls; Rep Sr Cls; VP Stu Cncl; Var Bsbl; URI Alum Assn Bk Awd 84-85; Amer Hstry Day Natl Awd 82-83; Worcester Polytech; Aerspc Engr.

MOYER, LEANNE; North Kingstown HS; N Kingstown, RI; (Y); 5/364; Varsity Clb; Stu Cncl; Var Bsktbl; Var Fld Hcky; Var Vllybl; High Hon Roll; NHS; Ntl Merit Ltr; U S Hist Awd 86; Iberoam Culturl Exc Schlrshp 86; Engrng.

MOYER IV, TILGHMAN H; N Kingstown SR HS; N Kingston, RI; (Y); Church Yth Grp; Drama Clb; Political Wkr; Band; Concert Band; Drm Mjr(t); Jazz Band; Mrchg Band; Orch; Pep Band; Pre Law.

MULCAHY, KERIN; North Smithfield J S HS; Slatersville, RI; (Y); 20/142; Church Yth Grp; French Clb; JV Cheerleading; Hon Roll; Pres Schlr; RI Hnr Scty 86; RI Coll Grnt 86; RI Coll; Nrsng.

MULHEARN, CHRIS; Bishop Hendricken HS; W Warwick, RI; (Y); 42/240; Church Yth Grp; Intnl Clb; Model UN; Service Clb; Var Bsbl; Var Bsktbl; High Hon Roll; NHS; Rotary Awd; Italian Ntl Hnr Soc; Law.

MULLIGAN, BRIAN; Burrillville HS; Harrisville, RI; (Y); Computer Clb; Var Stu Cncl; Var Golf; JV Ice Hcky; High Hon Roll; Ski Clb; Hon Roll; Bus.

MUMFORD, ANN; St Mary Acad Bay View; Hope, RI; (Y); 4/200; Church Yth Grp; Drama Clb; French Clb; Math Clb; Ski Clb; Orch; School Play; Rep Stu Cncl; JV Crs Cntry; Sftbl; Wnnr RI Poetry Socty Cntst 85; Decath Acadmc 85; RI Solo Ensmbl 83-85; Dramtcs.

MURDOCCO, GAILYN; Prout Memorial HS; Wakefield, RI; (S); 31/92; Hosp Aide; Ski Clb; SADD; Variety Show; Yrbk Stf; Crs Cntry; Socr; Sftbl; Vllybl; Hon Roll; Holy Cross; Bus.

MURRAY, MELISSA; Woonsocket HS; Woonsocket, RI; (Y); Drama Clb; JA; Teachers Aide; Off Soph Cls; Off Jr Cls; Stat Bsktbl; Cheerleading; Stat Ice Hcky; High Hon Roll; Hnrs Pin 83; Vrsty Ltr Hcky Statstcn 85; RI Coll; Psychlgy.

MURRAY, TAMARA L; Cumberland HS; Cumberland, RI; (Y); 36/387; Church Yth Grp; Dance Clb; School Musical; Rep Jr Cls; Trs Sr Cls; Rep Stu Cncl; Var Capt Cheerleading; Hon Roll; Prfct Atten Awd; Rhode Island Hnr Soc 86; Rnnr Up Tlnt Amer Comptnt Dance Catgry 85; RI U.

MYERS, BRIAN J; Warwick Veterans Memorial HS; Warwick, RI; (Y); 5/298; Computer Clb; DECA; Math Tm; Stu Cncl; Tennis; Trk; Wrstlng; High Hon Roll; Hon Roll; Jr NHS; Penn; Fin.

NADEAU, DIANE; Ponaganset HS; Chepachet, RI; (Y); 51/120; FBLA; SADD; Teachers Aide; Sftbl; Trk; Hon Roll; Bus.

NADEAU, LISA; Mount Saint Charles Acad; Woonsocket, RI; (S); 1/175; French Clb; Hosp Aide; Math Tm; SADD; Rep Frsh Cls; Rep Soph Cls; Sec Jr Cls; Stu Cncl; Cheerleading; High Hon Roll; 1st Pl Natl Law Day Essay 85; Pre-Med.

NAYLOR, MICHAEL; Mt St Charles Acad; Pascoag, RI; (S); Computer Clb; French Clb; Math Clb; Math Tm; Quiz Bowl; Band; Jazz Band; Mrchg Band; Orch; Swmmng; Hnr Rll-Hgh Hnrs 81-86; Band-Music Awd 81-86; Schlrshp Parnts Cncl 84-87; Providence Coll; Pre-Med.

NEHRA, NEERJA; Pilgrim HS; Warwick, RI; (Y); French Clb; Spanish Clb; Band; Mrchg Band; Variety Show; Rep Stu Cncl; High Hon Roll; Hon Roll; Northeastern U; Engrng.

NESTELL, GERRI-LYN; Barrington HS; Barrington, RI; (Y); Am Leg Aux Girls St; GAA; JV Socr; JV Sftbl; Hon Roll; Social.

NEWMAN JR, RONALD; Warwick Veterans Memorial HS; Warwick, RI; (Y); Church Yth Grp; Ice Hcky; Hon Roll; Yth Ntl Conf 85-86; Hist.

NICHOLAS, KATHLEEN; Pilgrim HS; Warwick, RI; (Y); 83/304; Hon Roll; Spnsh Spellng Bee 2nd Pl 84; URI Schrlsh P85-86; U RI; Chem.

NIHILL, KAREN; Warren HS; Warren, RI; (Y); 9/93; SADD; Band; School Play; Rep Jr Cls; Rep Sr Cls; VP Stu Cncl; Cheerleading; Gym; Hon Roll; Capt Thomas A Corrcia Schlrshp 86; NEA/Warren Schlrshp 86; Amer Hmcmng Qun 1st Rnr-Up RI 86; NHS; Coll; Mrktng.

NOEL, JENNIFER; N Smithfield JR SR HS; N Smithfield, RI; (Y); French Clb; Letterman Clb; Lit Mag; Rep Soph Cls; Sec Jr Cls; Var JV Bsktbl; Hon Roll; NHS; Band; Concert Band; 2nd Pl Frnch Cmprhndn 86; 1st Pl Poem Cntst 86; All Clss, All Div Hon Ment Clss C Bsktbll 86; Cmmnctns.

NORDSTROM, JILL; N Kingstown HS; N Kingstown, RI; (Y); 2/430; Church Yth Grp; Drama Clb; French Clb; Mathletes; Ski Clb; School Musical; Stu Cncl; Var JV Swmmng; High Hon Roll; NHS; Chosn Residnt Hnrs Prog U Of Southern CA 86; Intl Bus.

NOTARANTONIO, JULIE; Woonsocket SR HS; Woonsocket, RI; (Y); 9/445; Debate Tm; Exploring; Math Tm; NFL; Rep Stu Cncl; High Hon Roll; Hon Roll; NHS; Pres Schlr; St Schlr; Mdl Legsltve Cmmtte Chrprsn 85-86; Providence Coll; Bus.

NOTARIANNI, MICHELE; Cranston HS West; Cranston, RI; (Y); 2/417; Trs Sec GAA; Math Tm; JV Bsktbl; Var Capt Crs Cntry; Var Capt Trk; Bausch & Lomb Sci Awd; Sal; Intnl Clb; Math Tm; High Hon Roll; Harvard Book Awd 84-85; Rensselaer Polytech Inst Awd 84-85; Amer Assn U Wmn Awd 85-86; Boston Coll.

NUNES, PAUL; Middletown HS; Middletown, RI; (Y); 20/228; Church Yth Grp; Rep Frsh Cls; JV Bsktbl; Var Ftbl; Im Ice Hcky; Powder Puff Ftbl; Im Vllybl; Im Wt Lftg; High Hon Roll; Bus.

O BRIEN, CHARYN; East Providence SR HS; Rumbord, RI; (Y); JA; Chorus; Yrbk Stf; Rep Jr Cls; Rep Sr Cls; Stu Cncl; Var L Swmmng; Hon Roll; Art Achvr 84; Bus Mgmt.

O BRIEN, WILLIAM; North Providence HS; N Providence, RI; (Y); Boys Clb Am; JV Bsbl; Var Capt Ftbl; Tennis; Jr NHS; Math Tchr.

O BRION, ANDREW; Middletown HS; Middletown, RI; (Y); Trk; High Hon Roll; Bus.

O DONNELL, LYNN MARIE; Cumberland HS; Cumberland, RI; (Y); Boys Clb Am; Church Yth Grp; Cmnty Wkr; Dance Clb; French Clb; SADD; Yrbk Stf; Var JV Cheerleading; Elem Ed.

O GARA, PATRICIA; East Providence HS; East Providence, RI; (S); 24/523; Church Yth Grp; PAVAS; SADD; Pres Chorus; Church Choir; School Musical; Variety Show; Capt Cheerleading; Cit Awd; NHS; Gvrnrs Essy Cntst 84; Tlnt Amer 1st Pl Voice Cmptn 83-85; Irving J Hicks Awd 83; Elem Educ.

O HARA, RUTH; Rogers HS; Newport, RI; (Y); Church Yth Grp; Political Wkr; SADD; Band; Pres Jr Cls; Var L Crs Cntry; Var Capt Trk; Hon Roll; AllST Crs Cntry Tm 82-85; AllST Trck Tm 83-85; New England Champ Crss Cntry Tm 85; Northeastern U; Crmnl Jstice.

O KEEFE, KEVIN; North Smithfield JR SR HS; N Smithfield, RI; (Y); VRI; Busnss.

O NEIL, PATRICIA; Central Falls SR HS; Central Falls, RI; (Y); 20/115; Drama Clb; Library Aide; SADD; School Play; Variety Show; Yrbk Ed-Chief; VP Stu Cncl; Hon Roll; Prfct Atten Awd; Stu Of Mnth 85; Rdio Brdcstng.

O SHEA, PAT; Warwick Veterans Memorial HS; Warwick, RI; (Y); JV Var Bsktbl; Accntng.

OCONNELL, DEBBIE; St Mary Academy Bayview; E Greenwich, RI; (Y); 28/215; Church Yth Grp; Math Clb; Chorus; Var JV Vllybl; Hon Roll; NHS; NEDT Awd; Brnz Mdl For Spch In Acdmc Dcthln 86; Law.

OCONNELL, JASON; Barrington HS; Barrington, RI; (Y); Chess Clb; Letterman Clb; Math Tm; Var L Tennis; JV Trk; Hon Roll; All ST Tenns 86; Physc.

OLAUSEN, KURT; Classical HS; Providence, RI; (Y); 12/261; Boy Scts; Church Yth Grp; Drama Clb; Exploring; Math Tm; School Musical; School Play; Stage Crew; Lit Mag; Var Crs Cntry; Cum Laude Soc 86; RITI Hnr Soc 84-86; Dickinson Coll; Intl Law.

OLIVEIRA, JEFF; Tiverton HS; Tiverton, RI; (S); Arch.

OLIVEIRA JR, JOHN; Tiverton HS; Tiverton, RI; (Y); 16/186; Church Yth Grp; Band; Hon Roll; NHS; Bethel Bptst Coll; Comp Sci.

OLIVEIRA JR, WILLIAM J; Tiverton HS; Tiverton, RI; (S); Church Yth Grp; Computer Clb; Socr; Bus.

OLIVERA, SUSAN; Tiverton HS; Tiverton, RI; (Y); Church Yth Grp; Ski Clb; Var JV Cheerleading; Psych.

OSBORNE, ELIZABETH; Tiverton HS; Tiverton, RI; (S); 3/187; Drama Clb; Sec French Clb; Band; Concert Band; Mrchg Band; School Musical; School Play; Variety Show; Yrbk Stf; High Hon Roll; Cent III Ldrshp Schlrshp 2nd Rnnr Up 85; All St Band/All Rgnl Band 1st Flute 82; Mst Contmpry 85; Chem Engrng.

OSBORNE, VIRGINIA; Coventry HS; Coventry, RI; (Y); 17/400; Pres Church Yth Grp; French Clb; SADD; Yrbk Stf; Stu Cncl; High Hon Roll; Jr NHS; NHS; Outstndg Achvt Spnsh I 84, Spnsh III 86; Cncl Of Mnstries/Chrch 85; Elem Educ.

OSTERBERG, LORI; Warwick Veterans Memorial HS; Warwick, RI; (Y); Church Yth Grp; Letterman Clb; Church Choir; Stu Cncl; JV Var Bsktbl; Var L Fld Hcky; Var L Sftbl; High Hon Roll; Hon Roll; NHS; Phy Educ.

OSTIGUY, LYNN; Lincoln HS; Lincoln, RI; (Y); 47/195; Drama Clb; Chorus; Twrlr; U Of FL.

OSTROWSKI, NATASHA; East Providence SR HS; Rumford, RI; (Y); Hosp Aide; Red Cross Aide; Chorus; Yrbk Stf; Cheerleading; Hon Roll; Rhode Island Hnr Soc 84-85; Fash Inst Of Tech; Fash Dsgn.

OWENS, GREGORY; Narragansett HS; Narragansett, RI; (Y); 19/130; Debate Tm; NFL; Concert Band; Jazz Band; Mrchg Band; Pep Band; Lit Mag; JV Golf; JV Tennis; Hon Roll; Mst Imprvd Debater Awd 85-86.

OWENS, LYNDA; St Mary Acad Bay View; Riverside, RI; (Y); Boys Clb Am; Exploring; Trs Girl Scts; Ski Clb; Spanish Clb; Var Crs Cntry; Var Swmmng; Var Trk; Hon Roll; Church Yth Grp; Slvr Awd Grl Scts 84; Cert Of Exc In NEDT Tst 84; Phrmcy.

OWRE, KRISTIN; North Smithfield JR SR HS; N Smithfield, RI; (Y); 11/143; French Clb; Intnl Clb; Trs Letterman Clb; Band; Yrbk Sprt Ed; Stu Cncl; Var Capt Cheerleading; Var Capt Gym; High Hon Roll; Hon Roll; Gym Champ 83-84; Regnl Tm Gym 82-84; Bronze Medal UCSF; U Connecticut; Athlt Reh.

PACHECO, TERESA; Shea SR HS; Pawtucket, RI; (Y); Drama Clb; French Clb; Var Crs Cntry; Vllybl; Music.

PAIVA, INES; Cranston High Schl East; Cranston, RI; (Y); French Clb; Library Aide; VICA; Nwsp Rptr; Lit Mag; Stu Cncl; French Hon Soc; Hon Roll; NEDT Awd; U RI; Math.

PAIVA, LALITA; La Sall Acad; Providence, RI; (Y); Camera Clb; Church Yth Grp; Drama Clb; School Play; Off Sr Cls; Sftbl; Vllybl; Art Clb; Dance Clb; Swmmng; Steubenville U; Psych.

PALLANTE, DEBORAH; West Warwick SR HS; West Warwick, RI; (Y); 32/213; Drama Clb; Var Socr; JV L Trk; Hon Roll; Brnz Hnrs 82-83; Typg Cert 83-84; Sprtsmnshp Awd; Hnr Rll Mdl And Ltr; Brian Messler Meml Schlrshp 85-86; Johnson & Wales Clg; Acctg.

PALLINI, JOHN; Mt St Charles Acad; Johnston, RI; (S); 11/166; Math Tm; Jazz Band; Golf; Yamaha Natl Elec Fstvl 1st Pl 84.

PALMER, BETH; Chariho Regional JR SR HS; Carolina, RI; (Y); 5/267; Yrbk Sprt Ed; Var Bsktbl; Var Socr; Var Sftbl; High Hon Roll; Prjct Close Up 86; Sci Tchrs Assoc Hnrbl Mntn Sci Expo 84; Hnrbl Mntn Lgu Ply Soccer & Bsktbl 85-86; Bio Sci.

PALMISCIANO, LYNNE; St Mary Acad Bayview; E Greenwich, RI; (Y); 1/202; Girl Scts; Math Clb; Orch; Yrbk Stf; Stu Cncl; Var JV Vllybl; Bausch & Lomb Sci Awd; High Hon Roll; NHS; Ntl Merit Ltr; Acad Decathln 85-86; Math Silver Medal 85; Harvard Bk Awd 85; Pre-Med.

PAOLANTONIO, MICHELLE; St Marys Academy Bay View; North Providence, RI; (Y); Debate Tm; Yrbk Ed-Chief; Rep Frsh Cls; Pres Soph Cls; Pres Jr Cls; Stu Cncl; Var Tennis; Cit Awd; Hon Roll; JC Awd; High O Brian Ldrshp Awd 85; Otstndng Sphmr Awd 85; Attnd Grls ST 86; Elct Gvrnr Grls ST 86; Bus Mgmnt.

PAPITTO, JOHN; Classical HS; Providence, RI; (Y); Hon Roll; Engrng.

PAQUETTE, STEVEN; Woon SR HS; Woonsocket, RI; (Y); Cmnty Wkr; Bsbl; Crs Cntry; Trk; Hon Roll; Prfct Atten Awd; Bryant CollBUS Mgmt.

PARK, NANCY E; Moses Brown Schl; Lincoln, RI; (Y); 1/84; French Clb; Hosp Aide; Nwsp Rptr; Nwsp Stf; Yrbk Stf; Lit Mag; Var JV Lcrss; Var JV Swmmng; Var Tennis; High Hon Roll; Cum Laude Soc; Alumni Brown U Bk Awd; John Milton Payne Awd Exclnce Eng; Pre-Med.

PARSONS, REGINA; Cranston High West; Cranston, RI; (Y); Off Soph Cls; Off Jr Cls; Hon Roll; Law.

PASSARELLI, CHERYL; Coventry HS; Coventry, RI; (Y); 2/456; VP Trs Spanish Clb; Varsity Clb; Off Frsh Cls; Off Soph Cls; Off Jr Cls; Pres Stu Cncl; Crs Cntry; Trk; Vllybl; High Hon Roll; Holy Crss Bk Awd 86; Pre-Med.

PATRICK, SHARON; Rogers HS; Newport, RI; (Y); 2/350; Bsktbl; JV Sftbl; Hon Roll; NHS; Citation Achvt Sftbl 85; Howard U; Pre-Law.

PECKHAM, APRIL; Central Falls JR SR HS; Central Falls, RI; (Y); 8/130; Boys Clb Am; JA; Capt Bsktbl; Score Keeper; Sftbl; Timer; Cit Awd; High Hon Roll; Hon Roll; NHS; Hoop Sht ST Chmp Elks Natl 81-83; Comptd Boston Garden Hot Shot 81-84; 2nd Tm All Vly 83-85; Socl Wrk.

PELOQUIN, MARY; Chariho HS; Ashaway, RI; (Y); 50/287; Church Yth Grp; Cmnty Wkr; FCA; Chorus; Pres Frsh Cls; Rep Soph Cls; Rep Jr Cls; Var Bsktbl; JV Fld Hcky; JV Sftbl; Bsktbl Awd All Div 3rd Tm 85-86; Bsktbl Chairho Str Awd Mvp 85-86; All S Cnty Bsktbl Tm 85-86; URI; Elem Ed.

PEPIN, SUSAN; Tollgate HS; Warwick, RI; (S); 18/348; French Clb; Yrbk Sprt Ed; Trs Jr Cls; Var Cheerleading; Var Gym; French Hon Soc; High Hon Roll; Jr NHS; NHS; Trs Sr Cls; JR Miss Dnc Of New Englnd 83.

PERALTA, MARLENE; St Mary Academy Bay View; Providence, RI; (Y); Exploring; Spanish Clb; Med.

PERRIN, HEIDI; Chariho Regional HS; Ashaway, RI; (Y); VP Frsh Cls; VP Soph Cls; VP Jr Cls; Var Bsktbl; Var Crs Cntry; Capt Trk; High Hon Roll; Hon Roll; Jr NHS.

PERRY, JAMES; Coventry HS; Warwick, RI; (Y); Boy Scts; Chess Clb; Computer Clb; French Clb; Math Clb; Math Tm; Quiz Bowl; Science Clb; Spanish Clb; SADD; FL Inst Of Tech; Engrng.

PERRY, MISSY; Middletown HS; Middletown, RI; (Y); Pres Church Yth Grp; Cmnty Wkr; Teachers Aide; Yrbk Stf; Rep Jr Cls; Rep Stu Cncl; Hon Roll.

PETERS, KURT; La Salle Acad; Smithfield, RI; (Y); 5/244; Chess Clb; Pres Computer Clb; Math Clb; Math Tm; Nwsp Sprt Ed; L Var Lcrss; L Var Socr; Hon Roll; NHS; St Schlr; URI Distngshd Fclty Awd 85-86; Pres Acad Ftns Awd 86; RI Distngshd Merit Awd Math 86; US Air Force Acad; Aerontcl.

PETERSON, DEBRA A; Tiverton HS; Tiverton, RI; (Y); 14/189; Pres Church Yth Grp; Intnl Clb; Band; Concert Band; Mrchg Band; School Musical; Var Vllybl; High Hon Roll; Hon Roll; NHS; URI; Comp Sci.

PETERSON, MARY; South Kingstown HS; Kingston, RI; (Y); JV Sftbl; Var Capt Tennis; Hon Roll; NHS; Pres Schlr; Physlgy Awd 86; Spnsh IV Awd 86; RI Hon Soc Exc Lng 86; Bstn Coll.

PETSCHING, PAUL; Mount Saint Charles Acad; N Scituate, RI; (S); 20/168; Church Yth Grp; Cmnty Wkr; High Hon Roll; Hon Roll; Spanish NHS; U Of CT; Civil Engr.

PETTIGREW, MARK; Cranston West HS; Cranston, RI; (Y); 18/417; Chess Clb; Trs Church Yth Grp; Pres Computer Clb; Math Tm; Hon Roll; NHS; NEDT Awd; RI ST Awd 86; Renselaer Polytech; Comp Engrng.

PHAN, NHUQUYNH; Central Falls HS; Central Fls, RI; (Y); Band; Variety Show; Nwsp Stf; French Hon Soc; Hon Roll; NHS; Engl Awd 86; RI Hnr Soc 86; Bryant Coll; Acctng.

PHELAN, SHELLEY; Mount St Charles Acad; Hopedale, MA; (S); 8/168; Dance Clb; French Clb; Girl Scts; Hosp Aide; Math Clb; SADD; Church Choir; Cheerleading; High Hon Roll; Genetic Engr.

PHILIPS, PHILIP A; Cumberland HS; Cumberland, RI; (S); 4/200; Church Yth Grp; Cmnty Wkr; Math Tm; Science Clb; Band; Concert Band; Mrchg Band; Tennis; High Hon Roll; NHS; Students Agnst Drunk Drvng; Best Latin & French Stu Awd; Med.

PHILLIPS, MISHELE; Bishop Francis P Keough Rgnl HS; Providence, RI; (S); Var Bsktbl; NHS; Intr Dsgn.

PICARD, CATHY; Mt St Charles Acad; Woonsocket, RI; (Y); 36/150; Pres VP Church Yth Grp; Cmnty Wkr; Quiz Bowl; Flag Corp; School Musical; Spirit Alive Awd 84; Bst Actrss Awd Rgnl Drama Fest 85; All ST Cast 85; Northeastern U; Theatre Arts.

PICERNO, TRACY; Warwick Vetrans Memorial HS; Warwick, RI; (Y); Pres Church Yth Grp; Dance Clb; FCA; Political Wkr; Yrbk Stf; Stu Cncl; Fld Hcky; Prfct Atten Awd; Soc Wrkr.

PIERCE, CHARLES; St Raphael Acad; Rumford, RI; (Y); 4/180; Church Yth Grp; Math Clb; Stu Cncl; High Hon Roll; NHS; Spanish NHS.

PIERCE, DAVID; Ponaganset HS; Chepachet, RI; (Y); 34/165; Boy Scts; Pres Ski Clb; Hon Roll; St Schlr; U Of Southern CA; Architecture.

PILLA, SHEILA; North Providence HS; N Providence, RI; (Y); Sftbl; Hon Roll.

PIMENTAL, DANIEL; Tiverton HS; Tiverton, RI; (Y); 68/189; Art Clb; Stage Crew; Variety Show; JV Var Bsbl; Ice Hcky; Score Keeper; JV Socr; Hon Roll; Prfct Atten Awd; Frgn Lang Awd 81; Hnr Rll 85; RI College; Bus.

PINAULT, SUZANNE; St Raphael Acad; Rumford, RI; (Y); Church Yth Grp; Cmnty Wkr; Drama Clb; Hosp Aide; Hon Roll; 2nd Hnrs JR Yr 85-86; RI Coll; Cld Psych.

PINCINCE, MICHELLE M; Cumberland HS; Cumberland, RI; (Y); 15/390; Dance Clb; Thesps; Chorus; School Musical; School Play; Variety Show; Yrbk Stf; High Hon Roll; Hon Roll; Elsa Heillich Kempe Awd 85; Psych.

PINE, MICHELLE ANNE; Cranston HS East; Cranston, RI; (Y); Church Yth Grp; Debate Tm; Library Aide; Office Aide; Political Wkr; Spanish Clb; Pres Jr Cls; Pres Sr Cls; Mgr(s); JV Tennis; ST Mock Trial Finals 86; Wheelock Coll; Elem Ed.

PINE, SHARON LOUISE; Cranston East HS; Cranston, RI; (Y); Church Yth Grp; German Clb; Office Aide; Political Wkr; Science Clb; Nwsp Stf; Ice Hcky; Var Sftbl; JV Tennis; Hon Roll; ST Sci Fair 3rd Grnt; Lasell JC; Law.

PITOCCHI, SUSAN M; Cranston HS West; Cranston, RI; (Y); Computer Clb; GAA; Yrbk Stf; Cheerleading; Sftbl; Var L Vllybl; High Hon Roll; JETS Awd; Jr NHS; Ntl Merit Ltr; Harvard Bk Awd, Acad Dcthln Essay Gld Mdl 86.

PLOUFFE, KEVIN M; Woonsocket SR HS; Woonsocket, RI; (S); Concert Band; Pres Mrchg Band; Orch; School Musical; Variety Show; Hon Roll; RI Solo & Ensemble Music Mdls 84-86; RI All St Band & Orchestra 84-86; Music Educ.

POCCIA, ELENA MARIE; Cranston High West; Cranston, RI; (Y); 55/417; GAA; Ski Clb; Variety Show; Off Soph Cls; Off Jr Cls; Off Sr Cls; Capt Cheerleading; Trk; Vllybl; Hon Roll; Schl Srvce Awd 84; URI.

POIRIER, RANDAL; Woon Socket SR HS; Woonsocket, RI; (Y); JA; Latin Clb; Spanish Clb; Band; School Musical; Off Frsh Cls; Var Ftbl; Trk; Wt Lftg; Hon Roll; Cert Accomplshmnt Proj Bus JA 83-84; Ath Awd Ftbl 86; Stock Mkt.

POISSON, RANDY; La Salle Acad; North Providence, RI; (Y); 28/289; Camera Clb; VP Aud/Vis; JA; Math Tm; Model UN; High Hon Roll; Hon Roll; Jr NHS; Cert Merit Brown U Smr HS 85; Renseller Poly Tech; Bus Mgmt.

POMPEI, GREGORY; La Salle Acad; Providence, RI; (Y); High Hon Roll; Hon Roll; Bryant; Acctg.

PONTBRIAND, CELESTE R; Lincoln JR SR HS; Manville, RI; (Y); 59/195; Pres Church Yth Grp; Quiz Bowl; SADD; Church Choir; Most Promising Yth Yr CYO 83-84; Tourism.

PONTBRIAND, RENEE; Lincoln HS; Manville, RI; (Y); 1/211; Trs Church Yth Grp; Math Clb; Model UN; Trs Yrbk Stf; Var L Bsktbl; Elks Awd; Hon Roll; NCTE Awd; NHS; Prfct Atten Awd; Sci Fair 1st Grant 85-86.

PONTE, MARIA; East Providence HS; East Providence, RI; (S); 21/530; Church Yth Grp; Exploring; French Clb; SADD; Chorus; Yrbk Stf; Cit Awd; High Hon Roll; Sec NHS; Ntl Merit Sci Awd 83; Providence Coll; Obstrcn.

POPE, CHRISTIAN; North Providence HS; Providence, RI; (Y); Church Yth Grp; Yrbk Stf; Lit Mag; High Hon Roll; Jr NHS; Comm.

POPIOLEK, DAWN; Chariho Regional HS; Charlestown, RI; (Y); 3/257; Church Yth Grp; Dance Clb; Band; Yrbk Stf; Var Cheerleading; JV Fld Hcky; Var Socr; High Hon Roll; Jr NHS; NHS; Harvard Bk Awd 86; Katherine Gibbs Ldrshp Awd 86; Comp.

POTEMRI, JOSEPH; Woonsocket HS; Woonsocket, RI; (Y); Church Yth Grp; Quiz Bowl; Variety Show; Yrbk Rptr; Sec Jr Cls; Rep Stu Cncl; Var L Bsbl; Var L Bsktbl; Var L Socr; High Hon Roll; Educ.

POULIOT, KAREN; Woonsocket SR HS; Woonsocket, RI; (Y); Variety Show; Yrbk Phtg; Yrbk Stf; Stu Cncl; Cheerleading; High Hon Roll; Jr NHS; Prfct Atten Awd.

PRENTISS, PAMELA ROYAL; Pilgrim HS; Warwick, RI; (Y); Dance Clb; Sec French Clb; JA; Ski Clb; SADD; Yrbk Stf; Rep Stu Cncl; Var L Tennis; Var Trk; Elem Ed.

PREST, STEPHANIE ROSE; North Providence HS; N Providence, RI; (Y); Aud/Vis; Library Aide; Hon Roll; Jr NHS; NHS.

PRISTAWA, STEVE; Woonsocket HS; Woonsocket, RI; (Y); Church Yth Grp; Quiz Bowl; Orch; Bsbl; Bsktbl; Tennis; Worcester Polytechnic; Cvl Engr.

PROULX, JENNIFER; Tiverton HS; Tiverton, RI; (Y); Intnl Clb; Chorus; Pres Jr Cls; Pres Sr Cls; Rep Stu Cncl; JV Var Cheerleading; High Hon Roll; Hon Roll; Prm Qun 86; Cert Merit RI Yth Art Exhibit 83; Sthestrn MA U; Art.

PROVENSAL, JAMES; N Smithfield JR SR HS; N Smithfield, RI; (Y); Church Yth Grp; French Clb; Letterman Clb; Varsity Clb; Chorus; Nwsp Stf; Yrbk Phtg; Yrbk Stf; Lit Mag; Crs Cntry.

PURDY, PATRICIA; Rogers HS; Newport, RI; (Y); Pres 4-H; Church Yth Grp; Drama Clb; German Clb; Sftbl; 4-H Awd; Hon Roll; Hugh O Brian Ldrshp Awd 83; 4-H Pres 2 Yrs 86; Vet.

PURNELL, DAVID; South Kingstown HS; Kingston, RI; (Y); Hosp Aide; JV Crs Cntry; Im Tennis; JV Trk; Hon Roll; Rhode Islnd Hon Soc 85-86; U Rhode Island; Engrng.

PURNELL, SARA BETH; South Kingstown HS; Kingston, RI; (Y); Cmnty Wkr; Variety Show; Nwsp Rptr; Tennis; Bus.

QUINN, PAUL; Lincoln JR SR HS; Lincoln, RI; (Y); 24/200; Church Yth Grp; Variety Show; Nwsp Stf; Yrbk Stf; Rep Frsh Cls; VP Bsbl; Stat Bsktbl; Coach Actv; Var Ice Hcky; Score Keeper; Bus.

QUINTANA, AMBER RAE; Rogers HS; Newport, RI; (Y); Intnl Clb; Flag Corp; School Musical; Yrbk Stf; Hon Roll; 3rd Pl Ntl Spnsh Exm; Soclgy.

RACOFSKY, JAMES; Covenrty HS; W Greenwich, RI; (Y); Bus Adm.

RADINSKY, SHIRA T; New England Acad Of Torah; Charleston, SC; (Y); Temple Yth Grp; Sec Pres Stu Cncl; JV Bsktbl; French Hon Soc; Ntl Merit SF; Natl Bible Cont 2nd Pl 84; Intl Bible Cont Part 85; Max Stem Schlrshp 85-89; Stern Coll For Women; Law.

RAINEY, NEAL; Warwick Vets HS; Warwick, RI; (Y); Var L Crs Cntry; Var L Trk; Hon Roll; Bryant Coll; Acctng.

RAMOS, ELCY; Mount Pleasant HS; Providence, RI; (Y); Church Yth Grp; Hosp Aide; Library Aide; Vllybl; Hon Roll.

RANDALL, MARK; Coventry HS; Coventry, RI; (Y); 52/350; French Clb; Library Aide; ROTC; H S Tchrs Allnc Schlrshp 86; AF Jnr ROTC Sprior Prfrmnc Awd 86; URI; Scndry Educ Tchr.

RAPOSO, ROBERT; Tiverton HS; Tiverton, RI; (Y); Boy Scts; Cmnty Wkr; Drama Clb; ROTC; Band; Concert Band; Mrchg Band; Pep Band; School Play; Stage Crew; Engrng.

RAVO, KRISTEN; Narragansett HS; Saunderstown, RI; (Y); 1/117; Hosp Aide; Variety Show; Yrbk Phtg; Yrbk Stf; Rep Frsh Cls; Rep Soph Cls; Rep Jr Cls; Rep Sr Cls; Rep Stu Cncl; Var Tennis; 1st Pl PTO Spec Awd Sci Fair; Alliance Francaise Awd; Red Owl Bio Awd; URI; Phrmcy.

RAVO, MICHEL; Cranston West HS; Cranston, RI; (Y); 3/417; Chess Clb; Letterman Clb; Math Tm; Soph Cls; Jr Cls; Bsbl; Bsktbl; Ftbl; High Hon Roll; NHS; Kenney Schlrshp Awd 86; All ST 2nd Tm Bsbl 86; MVP All Div Bsbl 86; U Of PA; Engineering.

RAWLINGS, DAVID; N Smithfield JR SR HS; N Smithfield, RI; (Y); Debate Tm; Drama Clb; Exploring; Math Tm; Scholastic Bowl; School Play; Lit Mag; JV Capt Bsktbl; Stat Ftbl; High Hon Roll.

RAWLINGS, KENNETH; North Smithfield JR SR HS; N Smithfield, RI; (Y); 16/145; Exploring; Intnl Clb; Letterman Clb; Mathletes; Math Tm; SADD; Var Bsbl; Var Capt Bsktbl; Var Crs Cntry; NHS; US Mrns Athltc Achvt Awd 86; RI Hon Soc 86; Pres Nrth Smthfld Chptr Ntl Hon Soc 86; Worchester Polytech Inst; Engr.

RAY, STEPHANIE ANN; Narragansett JR SR HS; Saunderstown, RI; (Y); 4/116; Church Yth Grp; Debate Tm; NFL; Speech Tm; Variety Show; Vllybl; High Hon Roll; NHS; Spanish NHS; Mariner Hnr Schlr 86; Natl Frnsc League 86; Concurrent Enrollment 86; RI Clg; Elem Educ.

RAY, STEVEN; Pilgrim HS; Warwick, RI; (Y); 63/313; Art Clb; Hon Roll; Cmmrcl Art.

REBECCHI, AMY; East Providence HS; East Providence, RI; (S); 4/523; Band; Jazz Band; School Musical; Nwsp Stf; Rep Soph Cls; Rep Jr Cls; Rep Sr Cls; Rep Stu Cncl; Capt Cheerleading; Gym; Wellesley Coll Bk Awd 86; Engl Ed.

REBELO JR, DENNIS J; St Raphael Acad; Cumberland, RI; (Y); 15/200; French Clb; Math Clb; Math Tm; Rep Frsh Cls; Rep Stu Cncl; JV Var Trk; French Hon Soc; High Hon Roll; JETS Awd; NHS; Brkhvn Ntl Lab Stdy Schlrshp; Armd Frcs Cmnctns & Elctrncs Awd; Ntl HS Hnrs Prgm; Physcs.

REED, CAROLINE; Tiverton HS; Tiverton, RI; (Y); Band; Rep Frsh Cls; Rep Soph Cls; Rep Jr Cls; Sec Sr Cls; Stu Cncl; Var Socr; Var Vllybl; Liberal Arts.

REGAN, SHAWN; Classical HS; Providence, RI; (Y); Art Clb; French Clb; Stage Crew; U RI; Engl.

REICH, NAOMI; Classical HS; Providence, RI; (Y); French Clb; Temple Yth Grp; Nwsp Rptr; French Hon Soc; Hon Roll; St Schlr; Brandeis U.

REID, ELISABETH; Community Christian Schl; Pascoag, RI; (S); Church Yth Grp; Yrbk Stf; Bsktbl; Fld Hcky; Sftbl; High Hon Roll; Outstndg Sci Stu Awd 84; Frsh Hgh Acad 90 Prcnt Avg Awd 84; Capt New England Chrch Quiz Tm 85; Liberty U; Chld Psych.

REILLY, JOHN; Cumberland HS; Cumberland, RI; (Y); FCA; Var Bsbl; Var Wrstlng; Hon Roll; Emerson; Bus.

REILLY JR, WILLIAM T; North Smithfield HS; N Smithfield, RI; (Y); Drama Clb; Spanish Clb; Band; Concert Band; Jazz Band; Mrchg Band; Swmmng; Hon Roll; William T Reilly; Bus Mgmt.

REKAS, COREY; Bishop Hendricken HS; Coventry, RI; (Y); 80/240; Boy Scts; French Clb; JA; JV Trk; JV Wrstlng; French Hon Soc; Hon Roll; Jr NHS; NHS; Nrthestrn U; Bus Adm.

REKAS, LINDA; Coventry HS; Coventry, RI; (Y); French Hon Soc; High Hon Roll; Hon Roll; Jr NHS; NHS; Law.

RENEHAN, GAIL; Middletown HS; Middletown, RI; (Y); Sec Church Yth Grp; Band; Rep Soph Cls; Rep Jr Cls; Sec Sr Cls; Rep Stu Cncl; Var L Trk; Hon Roll; ST Fnlst Japan-U S Senate Scholar 86; PRISM Gftd Pgm 84-85; Decor Comm 86; Biol.

RENZI, RENEE; Johnston SR HS; Johnston, RI; (Y); 71/250; DECA; Sec Soph Cls; Rep Jr Cls; Capt Powder Puff Ftbl; RI CC; Nrsg.

RESTIVO, ROBIN M; La Salle Acad; Providence, RI; (Y); 3/245; Math Tm; Church Choir; Pres Stu Cncl; High Hon Roll; Jr NHS; NHS; Pres Schlr; Rep Jr Cls; Rep Sr Cls; Ntl Latin Exam Awd Magna Cum Laude 83; Holy Cross Bk Awd 85; Sons Of Italy Schlrhsp 86; Providence Coll; Math.

REUTER, JEFF; Bishop Hendricken HS; E Greenwich, RI; (Y); 55/240; Letterman Clb; Varsity Clb; JV Bsbl; Ftbl; Wrstlng; French Hon Soc; High Hon Roll; Hon Roll; Jr NHS; NHS; Acad Ltr 85-86; Dntstry.

REYNOLDS, KERRY; Lincoln HS; Lincoln, RI; (Y); Church Yth Grp; Dance Clb; French Clb; Yrbk Stf; Hon Roll; CC Of RI; Nrsng.

REYNOLDS, SUZANNE; Smithfield HS; Greenville, RI; (Y); 48/204; Church Yth Grp; French Clb; Nwsp Rptr; Trs Sr Cls; Rep Stu Cncl; Var Bsktbl; Var Fld Hcky; Var Sftbl; JV Trk; Hon Roll; Stonehill Coll; Journlsm.

REYNOLDS, TRACEY; St Marys Acad; Cranston, RI; (Y); Cmnty Wkr; Math Clb; Pep Clb; Service Clb; Ski Clb; Spanish Clb; Var Cheerleading; Hon Roll; Career Awareness Awd, Hnr Rl Mbr; Chld Educ.

RHODES, PHILIP J; Rocky Hill Schl; Peacedale, RI; (Y); 2/32; Camera Clb; Computer Clb; JCL; Math Tm; Teachers Aide; Nwsp Ed-Chief; Yrbk Phtg; Lit Mag; Trs Frsh Cls; Trs Jr Cls; Engrng.

RICCI, DANA; Mt St Charles HS; Greenville, RI; (S); Trs French Clb; Rep Model UN; SADD; Rep Soph Cls; Rep Jr Cls; French Hon Soc; High Hon Roll; Hon Roll; Acad All Amer 85; Pre-Med.

RICCI, RHONDA; Cranston High School West; Cranston, RI; (Y); 42/417; Aud/Vis; Debate Tm; Intnl Clb; JA; Badmtn; Socr; Sftbl; Vllybl; Hon Roll; NHS; Merit Itln Lang 83-86; RI Hon Soc 86; URI; Acctg.

RICHARD, DAVID; N Smithfield JR SR HS; N Smithfield, RI; (Y); 4/160; Debate Tm; Letterman Clb; Math Tm; Sec Pres Stu Cncl; Var Bsktbl; Capt Socr; High Hon Roll; NHS; Am Leg Boys St; Quiz Bowl; All Div Hnrbl Mntn Socr 85; Hugh O Brian Yth Ldrshp Found Cadt 85; R I Delgt Boys Natn 86; Lwyr.

RIDGEWELL, STEVEN; Pilgrim HS; Warwick, RI; (Y); 148/303; Art Clb; Church Yth Grp; Letterman Clb; Pep Clb; Variety Show; JV Crs Cntry; Var L Ftbl; Var L Ice Hcky; JV Tennis; JV Trk; RI Coll.

RILEY, KRISTIN ANN; St Marys Acad Bay View; E Providence, RI; (Y); 42/215; Art Clb; Church Yth Grp; Cmnty Wkr; French Clb; Library Aide; Political Wkr; Elks Awd; Hon Roll; Bayview Hon Soc 85-86; Lesley Coll; Erly Chlhd Ed.

RINALDI, PATRICIA; Pilgrim HS; Warwick, RI; (Y); 48/304; Drama Clb; Letterman Clb; Pep Clb; Ski Clb; Hosp Aide; School Musical; School Play; Variety Show; Trs Sr Cls; Var Capt Cheerleading; Devison U; Theatre.

RISIO, ANDREW; Bishop Hendricken HS; Ashaway, RI; (Y); 74/240; Chess Clb; Church Yth Grp; French Clb; Band; Concert Band; VP Mrchg Band; French Hon Soc; Hon Roll; NHS; Ntl Merit Ltr; Worcester Poly Inst; Aero Engr.

RITACCO, SHELLY; Narragansett HS; Narragansett, RI; (Y); 53/125; Drama Clb; Hosp Aide; Teachers Aide; Chorus; Variety Show; Yrbk Phtg; Yrbk Sprt Ed; Yrbk Stf; Solo Ensmble 85; CCRI; Travel/Trsm.

RIVET, SCOTT; Burrillville JR/Sr HS; Burrillville, RI; (Y); Cmnty Wkr; Teachers Aide; JV Var Socr; Athl Awd 85-86; Bryant Coll; Acctg.

ROBBINS, SUSAN A; Bristol HS; Bristol, RI; (S); Art Clb; Dance Clb; DECA; Yrbk Stf; Cheerleading; Powder Puff Ftbl; Hon Roll; Fshn Merch.

ROBERT, CYNTHIA; Woonsocket SR HS; Woonsocket, RI; (S); Hosp Aide; Math Tm; Concert Band; Drm Mjr(t); Jazz Band; Sec Mrchg Band; Rep Stu Cncl; Sftbl; High Hon Roll.

ROBERT, NANCY A; Cumberland HS; Cumberland, RI; (S); 10/400; VP Church Yth Grp; Cmnty Wkr; French Clb; Math Tm; Thesps; Capt Flag Corp; Nwsp Rptr; Yrbk Stf; Lit Mag; Hon Roll; Ntl Assoc Of Tchrs Of Frnch Chptr Awd 83; Bst Feature Song 83-84; Quinnipiac Coll; Reg Occptnl.

ROBERTI, ANNE M; Classical HS; Providence, RI; (Y); 14/261; Drama Clb; Hosp Aide; School Musical; School Play; Var Socr; Hon Roll; NHS; VFW Awd; Voice Dem Awd.

ROBERTI, LISA; Classical HS; Providence, RI; (Y); French Clb; Yrbk Stf; Lit Mag; Hon Roll; Ntl Merit SF.

ROBICHAUD, ERIC; Mount Saint Charles Acad; Woonsocket, RI; (Y); 23/168; Nwsp Phtg; High Hon Roll; JETS Awd; NHS; Comp Engrng.

ROBICHAUD, SANDRA; Coventry HS; Coventry, RI; (Y); Hosp Aide; ROTC; Church Choir; Drill Tm; Sci Med Bio.

ROBIDEAU, DOREEN; Central Falls JR SR HS; Central Falls, RI; (Y); 6/123; Office Aide; Yrbk Stf; Rep Frsh Cls; VP Stu Cncl; Capt Cheerleading; Hon Roll; Jr NHS; NHS; Grl Of Mo 86; US Figr Sktng Assoc 85-86.

ROBINSON, MICHAEL; Bishop Hendricken HS; Coventry, RI; (Y); 12/243; Boy Scts; Jazz Band; Band; Concert Band; Jazz Band; Mu Alp Tht; Hon Roll; NHS; Spanish NHS; Pre-Med.

ROBINSON, MICHELLE; Portsmouth HS; Portsmouth, RI; (Y); 13/195; Pres SADD; Var Capt Bsktbl; Var Capt Crs Cntry; Var Capt Trk; Hon Roll; NHS; Army Rsrv Ntl Schlr/Athlt Awd 86; MVP Crs Cntry, Bsktbl, Trck & Fld 85-86; PA ST U; Archtctr.

ROCHA, ROSA; Classical HS; Providence, RI; (Y); Educ Field.

ROCHE, KELLIE ANN; Middletown HS; Middletown, RI; (Y); 66/218; Trs Sec 4-H; Hosp Aide; Stat JV Bsbl; Powder Puff Ftbl; 4-H Awd; Hon Roll; Knights Clmbs Schlrshp 86; Transcom Rcgntn Schlr Achvt 86; John & Wales Acad Schlrshp 86; Jhnsn & Wls Coll; Rcrtn Mngmnt.

RODRIGUES, CARLA; East Providence SR HS; E Pro, RI; (Y); JA; Library Aide; SADD; VICA; Yrbk Ed-Chief; Yrbk Stf; Rep Stu Cncl; High Hon Roll; Prfct Atten Awd; CYO Sec; Portuguese Clb; Psych.

RODRIGUEZ, MARISOL; Middletown HS; Middletown, RI; (Y); Girl Scts; Spanish Clb; Hon Roll; Spanish NHS; U MA Boston; Legal.

ROGERS, HEATHER; Warwick Veterans Memorial HS; Warwick, RI; (Y); 13/280; Sec Band; French Hon Soc; High Hon Roll; Ntl Merit Ltr; Cmnty Wkr; Teachers Aide; Concert Band; Mrchg Band; Yrbk Stf; Wheelock Coll; Chld Life Spclst.

ROGERS, SUZANNE; Lincoln JR SR HS; Lincoln, RI; (Y); Drama Clb; Chorus; Yrbk Stf; High Hon Roll; Hon Roll; NHS; Physcl Thrpy.

ROMER, BRYONY A; Classical HS; Providence, RI; (Y); 7/250; Drama Clb; VP French Clb; Latin Clb; Math Tm; School Musical; Stage Crew; Nwsp Stf; Lit Mag; French Hon Soc; High Hon Roll; Mbr Of Cum Laude Socy 86; Bard Coll Awd In Engl 86; Holy Cross Book Prize 85; Yale U.

ROONEY, LINDA; Narragansett HS; Narragansett, RI; (Y); 14/122; Camera Clb; Office Aide; Chorus; Variety Show; Off Jr Cls; Off Sr Cls; Hon Roll; Grade B Mdl Solo Chrs Comptn 84; Sec Treas Itln Clb 84-85; UCLA; Film.

ROSATI, DIANA-LYNN; Warwick Veterans Memorial HS; Warwick, RI; (Y); 30/283; Exploring; Letterman Clb; Yrbk Stf; Capt Cheerleading; High Hon Roll; NHS; Spanish NHS; U RI; Nrsng.

ROSSI, LAURIE; La Salle Acad; Johnston, RI; (Y); Stu Cncl; Hon Roll; Psych.

ROSSI, SUZANNE; Mt St Charles Acad; N Smith, RI; (S); 10/166; Rptr 4-H; Math Clb; Quiz Bowl; Ski Clb; Band; Concert Band; Mrchg Band; Symp Band; Hon Roll; US Frgn Lang Awd 85; All-Amer HS Stu Awd 84; Liberal Arts.

ROTHERMEL, ALISA; Middletown HS; Middletown, RI; (Y); Church Yth Grp; Band; Concert Band; Pep Band; Var Capt Cheerleading; Var Trk; JV Var Vllybl; Hon Roll; Spanish NHS; TX Chrst U; Law.

ROTHFUSS, MELISSA A; Pilgrim HS; Warwick, RI; (Y); Church Yth Grp; Hosp Aide; Church Choir; Mrchg Band; High Hon Roll; Spanish NHS; RI Coll; Nrs.

ROUNDS, NANCY; Charles E Shea HS; Pawtucket, RI; (Y); JA; School Play; Yrbk Bus Mgr; Yrbk Stf; Bsbl; High Hon Roll; Hon Roll; US Achvmnt Acad 83; Bus Mgmnt.

ROURKE, TODD; East Providence HS; Providence, RI; (Y); Aud/Vis; Debate Tm; Model UN; Political Wkr; Stage Crew; Variety Show; JV Trk; Bowdoin; Palntlgy.

ROUX, MARK ALLEN; Woonsocket HS; Woonsocket, RI; (S); Band; Concert Band; Drm & Bgl; Jazz Band; Mrchg Band; Orch; Pep Band; Symp Band; All ST 2 Yrs 84-86; Boston Yth Symphony 85; Music Tchr.

RUSSO, PAULA; Charino Regional HS; Hope Valley, RI; (Y); Church Yth Grp; Quiz Bowl; Rep Stu Cncl; Bsktbl; Var Fld Hcky; Var Mgr(s); Hon Roll; Sthrn RI CYO Sen Awd 85,VP 84-85; Athl Awds 83-85; Law.

RYAN, MICHAEL E; Portsmouth Abbey Schl; Barrington, RI; (Y); 1/60; Chess Clb; Ski Clb; Lit Mag; Var L Trk; NCTE Awd; Computer Clb; Math Clb; Speech Tm; Im Bsktbl; Im Socr.

RYAN, PATRICK; Barrington HS; Barrington, RI; (Y); Church Yth Grp; Church Choir; Nwsp Rptr; JV Ftbl; Trk; Hon Roll.

SABETTA, SHARON; St Mary Academy Bay View; Cranston, RI; (Y); 70/215; Exploring; Math Clb; Hon Roll; Cert Mrit Cmpltn Explrng Pgm 83-85; Cert Prtcptn Ntl Frnch Exm 84; Pre-Law.

SABITONI, LISA; Johnston HS; Johnston, RI; (Y); Drm Mjr(t); Powder Puff Ftbl; Twrlr; High Hon Roll; Prfct Atten Awd; Acdmc All Amer 85-86; Yth Cncl On Smkng 84-85; Majorettes 86-87; Lawyer.

SABOURIN, PAMELA; East Providence HS; East Providence, RI; (S); 20/526; Pres French Clb; Band; Chorus; School Musical; School Play; Cit Awd; High Hon Roll; Hon Roll; Hnrbl Mntn Essay-Value Free Press 83; NH U; Animal Sci.

SACKO, JULIUS; Classical HS; Providence, RI; (Y); Var Capt Bsktbl; Hon Roll; All St Bsktbl 84-85; LEAD Prgrm In Bus 86; Engrng.

SADOWSKI, MIKE; Central Falls HS; Central Fls, RI; (Y); 2/96; Var Capt Bsbl; Var Capt Bsktbl; Var L Ftbl; High Hon Roll; Hon Roll; Jr NHS; NHS; Prfct Atten Awd; Pres Schlr; Sal; Providence Jrnl Awd 86; Army Ntl Schlr Athlete Awd 86; Outstndng Sr In Math Awd 86; Bryant Coll; Accntng.

SALAZAR, CANDY; Bishop Keough HS; N Providence, RI; (S); Camera Clb; Church Yth Grp; Drama Clb; French Clb; School Play; Stu Cncl; High Hon Roll; NHS.

SALDEEN, BO; Hope HS; Providence, RI; (Y); 1/140; Bsktbl; Golf; Tennis; Vllybl; Martin Luther King Jr Rewrd 86; RI Hnr Soc Awd 86; Santa Fe Coll Gainesvl FL.

SALEM, DAVID; Lincoln SR HS; Lincoln, RI; (Y); 10/195; Art Clb; Boys Clb Am; Boy Scts; JA; Mathletes; Math Clb; Math Tm; Yrbk Stf; Rep Jr Cls; Trk; Sci.

SALERNO, SHERI; Pilgrim HS; Warwick, RI; (Y); Dance Clb; JA; Ski Clb; VP Frsh Cls; VP Soph Cls; Rep Jr Cls; Rep Stu Cncl; Cheerleading; Wellesly Bk Awd 86; Itln Hnr Scty 86; RI Tchrs Itln Hnr Scty 84-86.

SALLEY, DONNA; St Mary Acad Bay View; Foster, RI; (Y); Church Yth Grp; Math Clb; Stu Cncl; Ntl Italn Exam 85-86; Arch.

SAN ANTONIO, DOUGLAS J; Bishop Hendricken HS; Cranston, RI; (Y); 67/240; Aud/Vis; Chess Clb; Ski Clb; French Hon Soc; Hon Roll; Jr NHS; Arch.

SAN BENTO, TODD; Saint Raphael Acad; Pawtucket, RI; (Y); Varsity Clb; Trk; Wt Lftg; Hon Roll; Acctng.

SANTOS, BRENDA; Bristol HS; Bristol, RI; (Y); 52/200; Debate Tm; JCL; Latin Clb; Ski Clb; Acpl Chr; Chorus; Off Frsh Cls; Off Soph Cls; Off Jr Cls; Off Sr Cls; RI Hnr Soc Awd 86; Anthony P Iasielloa Wd 86; Bisbano Musc Awd 86; URI; Sec Ed.

SANTOS, MELISSA; East Providence HS; Rumford, RI; (Y); Drama Clb; JA; Teachers Aide; Cheerleading; Sftbl; Hon Roll; U Of RI.

SANTOS, STACEY ANNE; St Raphael Acad; East Providence, RI; (Y); Church Yth Grp; Exploring; Hosp Aide; Variety Show; High Hon Roll; Hon Roll; VP NHS; Spanish NHS; Dance Tchrs Clb Boston Margaret Rogers Tap Scholar 84; Grad Dance Tchrs Clb Boston Tchrs Trnng 86; Nrsg.

SARTINI, DAVID A; Cumberland HS; Cumberland, RI; (S); 3/400; Cmnty Wkr; Drama Clb; French Clb; Math Tm; Science Clb; School Play; High Hon Roll; Hon Roll; NHS; Frnch Exch Pgm 84; Bst Latin Stdnt Awd 83, 85; Phrmcy.

SAVARD, ROBT; North Smithfield JR SR HS; N Smithfield, RI; (Y); CAP; Exploring; JA; Hon Roll; Sthestrn MA U; Elec Engrng.

SAWYER, JACQUELINE M; Chariho HS; Wood River, RI; (Y); Capt Cheerleading; High Hon Roll; Jr NHS; Eng.

SCAMACCA, JEFFREY; Scituate HS; Scituate, RI; (Y); 8/117; Art Clb; Drama Clb; FBLA; Letterman Clb; Varsity Clb; School Play; Yrbk Stf; Ftbl; Tennis; Trk; Avon Found Schlrshpa Wd 86; R I Hghr Educ Athrty 86; Scituate Schlrshp Found 86; Boston U; Physc.

SCANLAN, ROBERT; East Providence SR HS; East Providence, RI; (S); 3/523; Var L Bsktbl; Var L Ftbl; High Hon Roll; NHS; Ntl Merit Ltr; Harvard Bk Awd 85; Most Lkly To Succeed 85.

SCANLAN, STEPHEN; East Providence SR HS; Riverside, RI; (Y); 8/500; Var Bsbl; Var Bsktbl; Var Capt Ftbl; High Hon Roll; NHS; Charles Bently Awd 86; Holy Cross Book Awd 86; Stu Ath Awd 84.

SCHNEIDER, BENJAMIN; Cranston HS West; Cranston, RI; (Y); Var Capt Debate Tm; VP JA; Var L Math Tm; Var Bsktbl; Var Crs Cntry; Var Trk; Hon Roll; Ntl Merit SF; Aud/Vis; Computer Clb; Acad Decthln Gold Mdl Sci, Silv Mth 86; Mth Lg ST Comptn 86; Mth Lg Top Indvdl Awd 86.

SCHNEIDER, ELEONORE E; South Kingstown HS; W Kingston, RI; (Y); 6/201; Am Leg Aux Girls St; Drama Clb; German Clb; Model UN; Band; Socr; Trk; NHS; Ntl Merit Ltr; St Schlr; Best Latn II Stu; RI Hnr Soc; Smith College; Govt.

SCHOBEL, DAVID; Pilgrim HS; Warwick, RI; (Y); JA; Letterman Clb; Ski Clb; SADD; School Musical; Yrbk Stf; Golf; Socr; Hon Roll; Spanish NHS; All Div Golf 86; Air Frc Acad; Pilot.

SCHROEDER, EMILY; Scituate JR SR HS; N Scituate, RI; (Y); Library Aide; Band; Chorus; School Play; Yrbk Rptr; Sec Frsh Cls; Rep Sr Cls; Stu Cncl; Bowling; Diving; Jrnlsm.

SCHROEDER, PAUL R; Bishop Thomas F Hendricken HS; Johnston, RI; (Y); 16/243; Spanish Clb; Im Crs Cntry; Var Trk; High Hon Roll; NHS; Ntl Merit Ltr; Spanish NHS; Pres Of Intract Clb 85-86; Tufts U; Med Bio.

SCHWANER, NANCY; Lincoln JR SR HS; Lincoln, RI; (Y); 84/195; Church Yth Grp; Flag Corp; Yrbk Ed-Chief; Rep Jr Cls; Hon Roll; Dntl Asst.

SCIOLTO, TONI K; Scituate JR SR HS; N Scituate, RI; (Y); 2/114; Concert Band; Jazz Band; Orch; Yrbk Stf; Var Tennis; Var Trk; Ntl Merit SF; Sal; JCL; Capt Quiz Bowl; Brwn Bk Awd 85; Ntl Schltc Art Awds Gld Key 85; Berkley Jazz Ensmbl Mscnshp Cert 85; Engrng.

SCOTTI, FRANCINE; Johnston SR HS; Johnston, RI; (Y); Drama Clb; Office Aide; Pep Clb; Chorus; Cheerleading; Crs Cntry; Powder Puff Ftbl; Trk; High Hon Roll; Hon Roll; MVP X-Cntry 82-83; Child Psych.

SCOTTI, THERESE; Johnston SR HS; Johnston, RI; (S); 11/200; Rep Stu Cncl; Var Cheerleading; Var Crs Cntry; Var Powder Puff Ftbl; Var Trk; Hon Roll; NHS; Itln Awd 85; MVP Trk 83; URI.

SEABERG, WENDY S; North Kingstown HS; N Kingstown, RI; (Y); 4/371; Pres Girl Scts; Intnl Clb; Teachers Aide; Chorus; Mrchg Band; High Hon Roll; NHS; Ntl Merit SF; Worthy Advsr Rainbow Girls 84-85; Girl Scout Gold Awd 84; Spnsh Achvt Awd 83-85; Math.

SEARLE, TAMMY LYNNE; East Providence HS; E Providence, RI; (Y); 39/527; Church Yth Grp; SADD; Pres Band; Off Soph Cls; Off Jr Cls; Off Sr Cls; Stu Cncl; Cit Awd; God Cntry Awd; Hon Roll; Ctznshp Schlrshp 86; Edward R Martin Schlrshp 86; Gordon Coll; Psych.

SEARS, LORI; Portsmouth HS; Portsmouth, RI; (Y); 50/220; French Clb; FBLA; JA; Nwsp Stf; Yrbk Phtg; Yrbk Stf; Gym; Hon Roll; URI; Elect Engrg.

SEDLOCK, ANNE; St Mary Acad; E Greenwich, RI; (Y); 4/201; Church Yth Grp; French Clb; Math Clb; Pep Clb; Teachers Aide; Yrbk Stf; High Hon Roll; Hon Roll; NHS; Ntl Merit Ltr; Career Poetry Awd; AP Calculus Schl Awd; U Of PA; Math.

SEKERES, MIKKAEL; Classical HS; Providence, RI; (Y); Sec Debate Tm; Drill Tm; Nwsp Rptr; Nwsp Stf; Lit Mag; Trk; High Hon Roll; Hon Roll; 1st Pl RI Novice Debate Champ 86; Dartmouth Bk Awd 86.

SENECAL, DESIREE; Warwick Veterans Memorial HS; Warwick, RI; (Y); Letterman Clb; Yrbk Stf; Sec Frsh Cls; Sec Soph Cls; Sec Jr Cls; Sec Sr Cls; Var Capt Tennis; Cit Awd; French Hon Soc; High Hon Roll; Scrtry Of St Ldrshp Awd 86; Mst Schl Spirit 86; Clb For Cmnty Cntrbtns 86.

SHAUGHNESSY, ANNE MARIE; Cranston High School West; Cranston, RI; (Y); 26/417; GAA; Spanish Clb; Var Stat Bsktbl; Var Capt Tennis; Var Capt Vllybl; Hon Roll; Jr NHS; NHS; NEDT Awd; Spanish NHS; Cranston Tchrs Alliance Schlrshp, John Christy Awd 86; Phys Ftns Awd; U RI; Math Tchr.

SHAW, KERRI; Pilgrim HS; Warwick, RI; (Y); Dance Clb; Ski Clb; Spanish Clb; Stage Crew; Variety Show; High Hon Roll; Hon Roll; Jr NHS; NHS; Prfct Atten Awd; URI; Dntl Hyg.

SHAW-FRYER, DIANA; Chariho HS; W Warwick, RI; (Y); 31/279; VICA; Chorus; High Hon Roll; Hon Roll; Jr NHS; Drama Awd 86; Community Coll; Nrsng.

SHEAHAN, MICHAEL; Mount Saint Charles Acad; N Smith, RI; (S); Cmnty Wkr; Ski Clb; VP Jr Cls; Stu Cncl; Socr; Tennis; High Hon Roll; NHS; Harvard Bk Awd Outstndg JR Cls 86; Lib Art.

SHERIDAN, COLLEEN; St Marys - Bay View Acad; Warwick, RI; (Y); Drama Clb; Exploring; Office Aide; Pep Clb; Nwsp Stf; Var Cheerleading; Hon Roll; Kiwanis Awd; Katherine Gibbs Sec Awd 85; Pres Acadmc Ftnss Awd 86; R I Hnr Soc 86; U Of RI; Bus.

SHINDELL, ROBERT C; Toll Gate HS; E Greenwich, RI; (Y); 24/346; Pres Church Yth Grp; German Clb; Band; Jazz Band; Mrchg Band; Nwsp Stf; Yrbk Stf; Rep Stu Cncl; Hon Roll; Ntl Merit SF; Rep Frsh Cls; Bston Coll Bk Awd 85; RI ST Chmpn Toll Gate Acad Dcthln Tm 85; U Of RI; Engrng.

SHOOT, WILLIAM; Pilgrim HS; Warwick, RI; (Y); Nwsp Stf; Yrbk Rptr; Spanish NHS; URI; Liberl Arts.

SHROYER, LAUREN; Johnston SR HS; Johnston, RI; (Y); VP JA; Co-Capt Drm Mjr(t).

SHURTLEFF, ROBIN; West Warwick HS; W Warwick, RI; (Y); 28/216; Stu Cncl; High Hon Roll; Hon Roll; U Of RI; Phych.

SICKSCH, LISA; Bishop Keough Regional HS; Providence, RI; (Y); FTA; German Clb; SADD; Ski Clb; Yrbk Stf; VP Frsh Cls; Hon Roll; Grmn Soc Schlrshp 86; RI Coll; Elem Ed.

SIDEL, PHILIP; East Greenwich HS; E Greenwich, RI; (Y); 10/184; Pres Trs Drama Clb; Q&S; Temple Yth Grp; School Musical; School Play; Nwsp Rptr; Yrbk Ed-Chief; Capt Tennis; High Hon Roll; NHS; Bio.

SIECZKIEWICZ JR, ROBERT A; La Salle Acad; North Providence, RI; (Y); Chess Clb; Drama Clb; School Musical; School Play; Stage Crew; Nwsp Rptr; Ed Lit Mag; NHS; Al-ST Actr/Edctnl Theatr Assn RI 85; RI ST Sci Fair 85; Engl.

SILVA, DANA; Warwick Veterans HS; Warwick, RI; (S); Church Yth Grp; Sec DECA; Letterman Clb; Rep Frsh Cls; Rep Soph Cls; Stu Cncl; JV Var Cheerleading; Hon Roll; No 1 Stu Awd 85; Mrktg.

SILVA, KIMBERLY A; Our Lady Of Fatima; Seekonk, MA; (Y); Drama Clb; Hosp Aide; Red Cross Aide; SADD; Sftbl; Hon Roll; Southeastern Acad; Trvl/Tourism.

SILVA, LISA; Saint Raphael Acad; Cumberland, RI; (Y); Church Yth Grp; Stu Cncl; Hon Roll; Cosm.

SILVERSTEIN, JON; Moses Brown Schl; Providence, RI; (Y); Cmnty Wkr; Drama Clb; Hosp Aide; Political Wkr; School Play; Nwsp Ed-Chief; Nwsp Phtg; Yrbk Stf; Pres Stu Cncl; Hon Roll; Stu Cncl Awd 86; Alg II Trig Awd 86; Pol.

SILVESTRI, JOHN; North Providence HS; N Providence, RI; (Y); 10/250; Office Aide; Nwsp Ed-Chief; Nwsp Stf; Yrbk Ed-Chief; Yrbk Phtg; Yrbk Stf; Hon Roll; Jr NHS; Church Yth Grp; Im Bsktbl; Hgh Obrn RI ST Ldrshp Smnr 85; URI Almni Dstngshd Merit Awd 86; Engrng.

SILVIA, IAN; Middletown HS; Little Compton, RI; (Y); VP Art Clb; Drama Clb; Socr; Wrstlng; Hnbl Mntn Schlstc Art & Phtgrphy Awd RI 83; Natl Art Hnr Socty VP 86; MA Art Inst; Commrcl Art.

SIMARD, SUSAN; Tiverton HS; Tiverton, RI; (S); 5/187; Drama Clb; Yrbk Stf; Elks Awd; High Hon Roll; Hon Roll; NHS; RI Coll; Psych.

SIMEONE, MATTHEW; Classical HS; Providence, RI; (Y); 86/261; Lit Mag; L Trk; Hon Roll; RI Tchrs Itln Merit Awd 85; Stu Exchng Svc 86; U RI; Chem Engr.

SIMOES, TRICIA; Bristol HS; Bristol, RI; (Y); Church Yth Grp; Ski Clb; Yrbk Stf; Stu Cncl; Capt Cheerleading; Gym; Powder Puff Ftbl; Sftbl; Hon Roll; RI Coll; Elem Schl Tchr.

SIMONELLI, ROBIN; Smithfield HS; Greenville, RI; (Y); Trs Church Yth Grp; Cmnty Wkr; Band; Concert Band; Stu Cncl; Cheerleading; Hon Roll; RI Clg Solo/Ensmbl Gld Med; Star In J Cafferty Music Video Sml Twn Grl; Alcohol Awrnss Pgm; Elem Educ.

SIMPSON, KEVIN; Cumberland HS; Cumberland, RI; (Y); 18/369; French Clb; JA; Mathletes; Math Clb; Science Clb; Band; Concert Band; Jazz Band; Mrchg Band; High Hon Roll; Bryant Coll; Accntng.

SKALAK, JO ANNA; Central Falls HS; Central Falls, RI; (Y); VP Church Yth Grp; JA; Office Aide; Church Choir; Hon Roll; Trvl Agnt.

SKEFFINGTON, ELIZABETH; La Salle Acad; N Scituate, RI; (Y); 24/300; Nwsp Sprt Ed; Rep Frsh Cls; Rep Soph Cls; Rep Jr Cls; Rep Sr Cls; Pres Stu Cncl; Stat Ftbl; Var Capt Socr; Tennis; Hon Roll; Holy Cross Bk Awd 86.

SKINNER, BRIAN; East Providence HS; E Prov, RI; (Y); Aud/Vis; Camera Clb; PAVAS; Teachers Aide; Varsity Clb; School Musical; Stage Crew; Variety Show; Score Keeper; Wrstlng; U Of RI; Marine Bio.

SKOG, KRISTEN; Coventry HS; Coventry, RI; (Y); French Clb; Q&S; Nwsp Rptr; Yrbk Rptr; Off Stu Cncl; JV Crs Cntry; JV Vllybl; Hon Roll; Jr NHS; Ntl Merit Ltr; Acdmc Decathalon Tm 86; Won RI Assc Of Schl Principals Wrtng Cntst 86; RI Coll Wrtng Cmpttn 86; NY U; Journlsm.

SLATTERY, CHRISTINE; Lincoln JR SR HS; Lincoln, RI; (Y); 25/180; Sec Church Yth Grp; Exploring; Girl Scts; JCL; Mathletes; Ski Clb; Variety Show; Nwsp Stf; Rep Frsh Cls; Rep Soph Cls; Russell Sage Coll Fndrs Scholar 86; Bonne Bell Circle Excllnce 85 & 86; All ST 2nd Tm Crs Cntry 85; Russell Sage Coll; Phys Ther.

SLOAT, KERRI; Bristol HS; Bristol, RI; (Y); Drama Clb; French Clb; Girl Scts; Ski Clb; School Play; Yrbk Ed-Chief; Yrbk Stf; Capt Cheerleading; Var Gym; Capt Powder Puff Ftbl; Gld & Slvr Ldrshp Awd; Marian Awd; Cmmnctns.

SLUSARSKI, KIMBERLY; Tiverton HS; Tiverton, RI; (S); Intnl Clb; Band; Concert Band; Mrchg Band; Orch; School Musical; Symp Band; Gov Hon Prg Awd; Hon Roll; Jr Div Al-ST 84; Sr Div Al-ST 85-86; Fin Art.

SMEDBERG, KAREN; East Providence SR HS; Riverside, RI; (S); 14/525; Pres Girl Scts; Band; Chorus; Concert Band; Mrchg Band; Capt Vllybl; High Hon Roll; Hon Roll; NHS; Prfct Atten Awd; Grl Sctng Gld Awd 86; U Of RI; Engrng.

SMITH, CHRISTOPHER; Smithfield HS; Greenville, RI; (Y); 23/208; Band; Concert Band; Jazz Band; Mrchg Band; Socr; Tennis; Hon Roll; Engrng.

SMITH, ERIC; South Kingstown HS; Peace Dale, RI; (Y); 47/201; Boy Scts; Teachers Aide; R I Hnr Scty 86; URI; Tchr.

SMITH, GRACE; St Mary Bay View Acad; Warwick, RI; (Y); Ski Clb; Spanish Clb; High Hon Roll; Hon Roll; NHS; NEDT Awd; Silvr Mdl Natl Latn Test 86; Law.

SMITH, SCOTT; Chariho HS; Hopkinton, RI; (Y); 20/250; Am Leg Boys St; Boy Scts; Church Yth Grp; Nwsp Stf; Yrbk Stf; JV Var Bsbl; JV Var Socr; JV Var Wrstlng; Hon Roll; U S Naval Acad; Engnrng.

SMITH, SCUDDER; Scituate JR SR HS; North Scituate, RI; (S); Varsity Clb; Concert Band; Jazz Band; Yrbk Phtg; Lit Mag; Bsktbl; Capt Socr; High Hon Roll; Jr NHS; Sal; Hallmark Awd 86; Gold Key 86; Schltc Art Awd 86; U RI Alumni Awd 85; Cert Muscnshp 85; Berklee Jazz Fest.

SMITH, TERRY; Smithfield HS; Greenville, RI; (Y); 30/203; French Clb; Quiz Bowl; Band; Concert Band; Mrchg Band; Var L Crs Cntry; Var L Trk; Elks Awd; U Of RI; Phrmcy.

SMOLAN, GREG; Lincoln HS; Lincoln, RI; (Y); 6/212; Var L Ice Hcky; Hon Roll; NHS; New Engl Jr Sci & Humanities Symposium 86.

SNOW, MARY; Tiverton HS; Tiverton, RI; (S); Church Yth Grp; Band; Concert Band; Mrchg Band; High Hon Roll; Hon Roll; Katharine Gibbs Schl; Accntnt.

SOARES, LENA; Bristol HS; Bristol, RI; (Y); Yrbk Stf; Hon Roll; NHS; Bus.

SOARES, NELLIE F; Shea HS; Pawtucket, RI; (Y); Yrbk Stf; Hon Roll; Johnson & Wales Coll; Bus Adm.

SOLITRO, CHRISTINE; St Mary Academy Bay View; Cranston, RI; (Y); Exploring; SADD; Chorus; Yrbk Phtg; Rep Stu Cncl; Hon Roll; Georgetown U; Pol Sci.

SOUSA, JULIANN; Bristol HS; Bristol, RI; (Y); Drama Clb; Yrbk Ed-Chief; Ed Yrbk Stf; Rep Frsh Cls; Rep Soph Cls; Rep Jr Cls; High Hon Roll; NHS; Natl Latin Hnr Soc 84-85; Frgn Lang Awd Portoguese IV 85-86.

SOUSA, KRISTIN; Bristol HS; Bristol, RI; (Y); Drama Clb; JCL; Latin Clb; Acpl Chr; School Musical; VP Jr Cls; Sec Stu Cncl; Hon Roll; Chorus; Madrigals; Latinam Hnrs Societatem 86; Cum Laude Ntl Lat Exam 86; English.

SOUSA, LISA ANN; Bristol HS; Bristol, RI; (Y); Church Yth Grp; Co-Capt Color Guard; Mrchg Band; Wt Lftg; Hon Roll; Prfct Atten Awd; Roger William Coll; Arch.

SOUSA, STEPHEN; Bristol HS; Bristol, RI; (Y); Church Yth Grp; Drama Clb; JCL; Pres Latin Clb; School Play; Stage Crew; Stat Ftbl; JV Ice Hcky; Hon Roll; Natl Latin Exam Bronze Mdl 84; Outstndng Achvt Latin 85.

SOUZA, LISA; Portsmouth HS; Portsmouth, RI; (Y); 80/212; Exploring; FBLA; Ski Clb; Y-Teens; Powder Puff Ftbl; Spanish NHS; U R I; Nrsng.

SOWERS, DANIEL; Rogers HS; Newport, RI; (Y); Exploring; Capt ROTC; Hon Roll; Comp Engr.

SPARKES, DEBORAH P; Cranston High School West; Cranston, RI; (Y); 5/417; Am Leg Aux Girls St; Pres Church Yth Grp; GAA; VP JA; Band; Stu Cncl; Capt Var Crs Cntry; Var Capt Swmmng; JV Vllybl; High Hon Roll; Holy Crs Bk Awd 85; RI Hnr Soc 86; U S Naval Acad; Sci.

SPAROZIC, ANNMARIE; North Kingstown HS; N Kingstown, RI; (Y); 63/465; Cmnty Wkr; Office Aide; Rep Soph Cls; Rep Jr Cls; High Hon Roll; Hon Roll; Achvt Awd-Prjct Create 84; $75 Cash Awd-Fundraiser Mst Sls 85; GE Walkman Fundraiser 2nd Mst Sls 86; Accntng.

SPECHT, FRED; Charles E Shea HS; Pawtucket, RI; (Y); Boy Scts; Church Yth Grp; Var L Bsbl; JV Ftbl; Var L Ice Hcky; Ross Simon Awd For Hcky & High Scorer 82; RI Good Sprtsmnshp Awd For Hocky 86; Kngs Crt JR Prm 86; Prvdnc Coll; Archtctr.

SPINA, STEVEN; La Salle Acad; Providence, RI; (Y); High Hon Roll; Hon Roll; Exc In Italn A Avg 84-86; US His 96 Avg & Engl 99 Avg 85-86; RI Coll; Hist.

SPINELLA, ELIZABETH; Mount St Charles Acad; Woonsocket, RI; (Y); 21/130; Sec Church Yth Grp; Quiz Bowl; SADD; Chorus; Flag Corp; Capt Cheerleading; Hon Roll; NHS; Whtn Coll; Bio-Chem.

SPRAGUE, ELIZABETH; East Providence HS; East Providence, RI; (S); 15/523; Chorus; Concert Band; Jazz Band; School Play; Variety Show; Capt Cheerleading; JV Var Vllybl; Stat Wrstlng; Hon Roll; VP NHS; Holy Cross Bk Awd 85; Elem Ed.

SQUADRITO, ELLEN M; Pilgrim HS; Warwick, RI; (Y); 14/330; Art Clb; Nwsp Stf; Ed Yrbk Stf; High Hon Roll; Jr NHS; NHS; RI Hnr Soc 86; RI Tchrs Italian Hnr Soc 84; RI Schl Desgn; Desgn.

ST JEAN, STEVEN; Woonsocket SR HS; Woonsocket, RI; (Y); 147/490; Computer Clb; Library Aide; Quiz Bowl; High Hon Roll; Hon Roll; Cum Laude Natl Latn Exam 83; U Of RI; Secndry Educ.

ST LAURENT, ARTHUR; N Smithfield JR SR HS; N Smithfield, RI; (Y); 23/145; Hon Roll; Rhode Islnd Hnr Soc 86; Bryant Coll.

ST PIERRE, GERARD; Central Falls SR HS; Central Falls, RI; (Y); 1/136; Computer Clb; Science Clb; SADD; Yrbk Ed-Chief; Pres Jr Cls; Rep Stu Cncl; High Hon Roll; Jr NHS; Voice Dem Awd; Chess Clb; Le Foyer Prix Dexcllnc Enfranc 86; Boy Mnth Dec 85; Air Force Acad; Sci.

STALLWOOD, TRACEY; Lincoln SR HS; Lincoln, RI; (Y); 44/195; Pep Clb; Temple Yth Grp; Variety Show; Sec Jr Cls; Var Capt Cheerleading; Var Fld Hcky; Var Gym; Var Sftbl; Bus Mgmt.

STAVELEY, RICK S; Classical HS; Bristol, RI; (Y); Aud/Vis; Hon Roll; U Of Miami; Accntn.

STEINER, SCOTT; Cranston High School West; Cranston, RI; (Y); Boys Clb Am; Spanish Clb; Temple Yth Grp; School Play; Hon Roll; Prfct Atten Awd; Bus.

STEPKA, LYNN; Johnston HS; Johnston, RI; (Y); Art Clb; Church Yth Grp; Hosp Aide; Yrbk Stf; High Hon Roll; Hon Roll; Itln Hon Awd 85-86; Acad Dcthln 85-86; Nrsng.

STEWART, JOSEPH F; Middletown HS; Middletown, RI; (Y); Debate Tm; JA; Library Aide; Teachers Aide; Stu Cncl; Var Bsktbl; Var Ftbl; Powder Puff Ftbl; Var Tennis; High Hon Roll; Bus.

STOCKWELL, MELISSA; La Salle Acad; Johnston, RI; (Y); 17/244; Aud/Vis; Camera Clb; Nwsp Rptr; Nwsp Stf; Hon Roll; NHS; Pres Schlr; Church Yth Grp; Library Aide; U Or RI Almni Mrt Schlrshp 86; US & Canadn Gld Mdlst Fgr Sktng; U Of RI; Englsh.

STOKELL, PAUL; North Kingstown HS; N Kingstown, RI; (Y); Political Wkr; ROTC; Chorus; Church Choir; Crs Cntry; Trk; US Navy; Pol Sci.

STREUBEL, HEIDI; Warwick Veterans Memorial HS; Warwick, RI; (Y); 9/298; Hosp Aide; Letterman Clb; Score Keeper; Var Capt Tennis; Stat Wrstlng; French Hon Soc; High Hon Roll; Sec NHS; Frshmn Ldrshp Awd-Mrymnt Coll 86; Acadmc Dcthln 85; Marymount Coll; Bio.

STUART, SHERSTINE; Narragansett HS; Narragansett, RI; (Y); 31/120; Dance Clb; Stage Crew; Variety Show; Off Sr Cls; Hon Roll; Art Clb; Church Yth Grp; Teachers Aide; Excllnc Hm Ec 85; URI; Elem Ed.

SUESS, MELISSA; Ponaganset HS; Chepachet, RI; (Y); 21/140; Church Yth Grp; French Clb; Band; Church Choir; Concert Band; Hon Roll; Math.

SULLIVAN, KELLY; Chariho Regional HS; Hope Valley, RI; (Y); Prvt Invstgtn.

SUMMERVILLE, JULIUS; Central HS; Providence, RI; (Y); Church Yth Grp; Cmnty Wkr; Var Socr; Hon Roll.

SUTHERLAND, SCOTT; North Smithfield HS; N Smithfield, RI; (Y); French Clb; Intnl Clb; Letterman Clb; SADD; Varsity Clb; Lit Mag; Var Bsktbl; Var L Socr; Var L Tennis; Awd Ntl Sccr Clnc Pgm 85; Good Stud Crdt Applctn For B Avg 85; Law.

SWEET, LISA; Warwick Veterans Memorial HS; Warwick, RI; (Y); 41/298; Letterman Clb; Off Frsh Cls; Off Soph Cls; Off Jr Cls; Off Sr Cls; Capt Bsktbl; Capt Crs Cntry; Capt Vllybl; Hon Roll; Kiwanis Awd; All-Div, All-City & All-ST Hon Men Vllybl 85; All-Div, All-Cls, All-Cty & All-ST 2nd Tm Vlybl 86; Rhode Island Coll; Psych.

SWEET, MONICA; Warwick Veterans Memorial HS; San Diego, CA; (Y); Debate Tm; Letterman Clb; Math Tm; Band; Chorus; Off Frsh Cls; Off Soph Cls; Off Jr Cls; Var Vllybl; French Hon Soc; UCLA; Med.

SWIERAD, MARIA; North Smithfield HS; N Smithfield, RI; (Y); French Clb; SADD; Chorus; Yrbk Stf; Lit Mag; Vllybl; Hon Roll; Excllnc Art 84-86; Art.

SYLVIA, CHERIE; North Providence HS; Providence, RI; (Y); Pres Church Yth Grp; Teachers Aide; Band; Concert Band; Crs Cntry; Vllybl; Hon Roll; Jr NHS; Arch.

SYLVIA, HOLLY; Tiverton HS; Tiverton, RI; (Y); Church Yth Grp; Drama Clb; French Clb; Pep Clb; Ski Clb; Sec Chorus; Church Choir; School Musical; Swing Chorus; Variety Show; Erly Chldhd Educ.

SYLVIA, KIMBERLY; Bristol HS; Bristol, RI; (Y); Girl Scts; Chorus; Color Guard; Cheerleading; Powder Puff Ftbl; Hon Roll; Hstry.

SZLASHTA III, PATRICK JOHN; St Raphael Acad; Lincoln, RI; (Y); 29/180; Drama Clb; Political Wkr; SADD; Ice Hcky; Wt Lftg; Wrstlng; Hon Roll; MED Fld.

TARTAGLIONE, LISA; Bishop Keough HS; N Providence, RI; (S); Drama Clb; School Play; High Hon Roll; NHS; Natl Jr Hnr Soc 82; RI Coll; Med Tech.

TAVARES, ANNABELLA; Charles E Shea SR HS; Lincoln, RI; (Y); 9/218; Boys Clb Am; Exploring; French Clb; Math Clb; Math Tm; Scholastic Bowl; Nwsp Ed-Chief; Ed Yrbk Stf; French Hon Soc; High Hon Roll; RI Hnr Soc 86; Pres Acdmc Ftns Awd 86; Boston U; Bio.

TAYLOR, BRYAN; Bishop Hendricken HS; Warwick, RI; (Y); 103/243; Teachers Aide; Band; Concert Band; Mrchg Band; Im Crs Cntry; Law.

TAYLOR, JANET; Barrington HS; Barrington, RI; (Y); 45/233; Varsity Clb; Capt Bsktbl; Fld Hcky; JV Socr; Sftbl; Capt Trk; Hon Roll; R I Hnr Soc 86; Hnr Rl 83-86; U CT; Physcl Thrpy.

TAYLOR, STEPHANIE; St Mary Academy Bay View; Johnston, RI; (Y); Exploring; French Clb; Chorus; Rep Frsh Cls; Rep Soph Cls; JV Trk; Hon Roll; NEDT Awd; Cmnty Wkr; Ski Clb; Srv Awd 84-85; Yth Ftnss Achvt Awd 84 & 86; Sprts Awd In Trk 86.

TEFFT, KEVIN; Coventry HS; Coventry, RI; (Y); High Hon Roll; NHS; RI ST Chem Tst 86; Comp Sci.

TELLIER, AMY; Woonsocket SR HS; Woonsocket, RI; (Y); Sec Trs Church Yth Grp; Drama Clb; Quiz Bowl; Chorus; School Musical; Nwsp Stf; Rep Frsh Cls; High Hon Roll; Hon Roll; Berklee Coll Music; Music.

TELLIER, RUSSELL; Charles E Shea SR HS; Pawtucket, RI; (Y); Boy Scts; Hosp Aide; JV Var Bsbl; Var L Swmmng; High Hon Roll; Hon Roll; Marine Bio.

TERRIEN, TINA; St Raphael Acad; Pawtucket, RI; (Y); Acctng.

TERRY, KEEVA L; Classical HS; Providence, RI; (Y); Cmnty Wkr; Math Tm; Political Wkr; Spanish Clb; Soph Cls; VP Sr Cls; Cheerleading; Hon Roll; Awd Acad Exc Provdnce NAACP 84; Stu Ntl Merit Schlrshp 85; Pgm Outstndng Negro Stu; CPA.

TESSIER, CHERIL; Smithfield HS; Smithfield, RI; (Y); 5/200; Cmnty Wkr; French Clb; Math Clb; Math Tm; Band; Jazz Band; Bowling; High Hon Roll; Hon Roll.

TESSIER, SHARON; North Smithfield JR SR HS; N Smithfield, RI; (Y); Church Yth Grp; Drama Clb; French Clb; SADD; Chorus; School Musical; School Play; Stu Cncl; Hon Roll.

TESTA, KIM; Johnston SR HS; Johnston, RI; (Y); Hon Roll; Fshn Desgnr.

TEXEIRA, TODNE; St Andrews Schl; E Providence, RI; (S); Library Aide; Drm & Bgl; Nwsp Rptr; Yrbk Phtg; Yrbk Stf; Stat Bsktbl; Var Crs Cntry; Var Sftbl; Var Vllybl; High Hon Roll; Athltc Sprtsmnshp Awd 84-85; Zest Live Awd 81-82; Bst Drmr-Drm/Bugl Corp 83-86; Srgcl Nrs.

THAUBALD, WILLIAM LEE; Rogers HS; Newport, RI; (Y); L Golf; Hon Roll; Meteorologist.

THEROUX, DONNA; Woonsocket HS; Woonsocket, RI; (Y); Church Yth Grp; SADD; Varsity Clb; Band; Concert Band; JV Var Bsktbl; JV Crs Cntry; High Hon Roll; Hon Roll.

THEROUX, WENDY; Smithfield HS; Smithfield, RI; (Y); 29/208; Church Yth Grp; Math Tm; SADD; School Play; Yrbk Stf; Rep Stu Cncl; Var Cheerleading; Stat Ftbl; Hon Roll; NHS; CA ST U; Mass Media.

THOMAS, THERESA; Bishop Keough Regional HS; Pawtucket, RI; (S); 6/46; Art Clb; SADD; Stage Crew; Lit Mag; Stu Cncl; Vllybl; High Hon Roll; NHS; Relign Awd 84; Hnr Roll 82-86; RI Coll; Engl.

THORN, LAURIE; Classical HS; Providence, RI; (Y); Band; JV Vllybl; Hon Roll; The Blue Stockings Clb 86; Bryant; Acctnt.

THORNTON, CAROLYN; Johnston SR HS; Johnston, RI; (S); 1/216; 4-H; Nwsp Rptr; Yrbk Ed-Chief; Capt Bsktbl; Crs Cntry; Capt Sftbl; High Hon Roll; NHS; Val; HOBY Rep 83-84; Brown Bk Awd Outstndg Eng Stu 84-85; RI Rep Natl Hstry Day 83-84; Brown U; Comm.

TOBIN, MARGARET; St Mary Acad; Providence, RI; (Y); Exploring; Spanish Clb; Hon Roll; NHS; NEDT Awd; Cert Awd DATS 84; Bus Educ.

TOLLEY, KIMBERLY; Tiverton HS; Tiverton, RI; (Y); 33/189; Dance Clb; Drama Clb; Pep Clb; Concert Band; Mrchg Band; School Play; Variety Show; Yrbk Phtg; Yrbk Stf; NHS; Pres Acad Ftnss Awds Pgm, Dram Awd, Tempo Schlrshp 86; Worcester ST Coll; Occup Thrpy.

TOMEI, JOHN; Saint Raphael Acad; Cumberland, RI; (Y); 6/180; Math Tm; Stage Crew; Im Bsktbl; Im Ice Hcky; French Hon Soc; High Hon Roll; NHS; URI Dstngshd Fclty Awd 86; 2nd Grnt ST Sci Fair 85; URI Bk Awd 86; Wrcstr Plytch Inst; Eltrcl Engr.

TORRES, KATHIE; Pilgrim HS; Warwick, RI; (Y); Boys Clb Am; Camp Fr Inc; Church Yth Grp; GAA; Girl Scts; JA; Yrbk Rptr; Yrbk Stf; JV Sftbl; Hon Roll; Acctg.

TOUPIN, DARLENE; Mount Saint Charles Acad; Woonsocket, RI; (S); 6/141; Cmnty Wkr; SADD; Capt Cheerleading; High Hon Roll; NHS; Pre-Med.

TRACEY, KRISTEN A; Tollgate HS; Warwick, RI; (S); Cmnty Wkr; Hosp Aide; Letterman Clb; PAVAS; SADD; Chorus; Cheerleading; Mgr Ftbl; Swmmng; Jr NHS; RI JR Hnr Soc 83; Psych.

TRACY, CHRISTINE; St Mary Academy Bay View; E Providence, RI; (Y); Art Clb; Church Yth Grp; Computer Clb; Exploring; Math Tm; Pep Clb; Ski Clb; Spanish Clb; SADD; Variety Show; Brothrhd Cntst Awd 84; RIC; Phys Thrpy.

TRACY, KATHLEEN; East Providence SR HS; E Providence, RI; (Y); 74/523; VP Chorus; Color Guard; Rep Sr Cls; Sec Stu Cncl; Acad Decathalon 86; Schlrshp Highest Level French 86; U RI; Bus Comm.

TRAHAN, LISA; La Salle Acad; Johnston, RI; (Y); Chess Clb; Drama Clb; Math Tm; School Play; Stage Crew; Rep Stu Cncl; High Hon Roll; NHS; Ntl Merit SF; Church Yth Grp; Harvard Bk Awd 86; RI Coll.

TRAHAN, MELISSA; East Providence HS; E Prov, RI; (Y); Drama Clb; Chorus; School Musical; School Play; Yrbk Ed-Chief; Stu Cncl; Im Trk; High Hon Roll; U Of RI; Med Tech.

TROOST, J LAURENS; Moses Brown Schl; Providence, RI; (Y); Pres Computer Clb; Drama Clb; Pres Science Clb; Spanish Clb; SADD; Chorus; Jazz Band; Nwsp Stf; Var L Ftbl; Ntl Merit SF; Thomas J Buttey Awd-Excllnc In Bio 84; Bio-Chem Reserch.

TROTTIER, SANDRA; Davies Vocational Tech HS; Pawtucket, RI; (Y); SADD; VICA; Hon Roll; Blood Tech.

TSAKONAS, DEMETRIOS; St Raphael Acad; Prov, RI; (Y); 10/173; Exploring; Math Tm; Quiz Bowl; Rep Frsh Cls; JV Socr; Hon Roll; NHS; Pres Schlr; Spanish NHS; St Champ-Quiz Bowl 85; Providence Coll; Bio.

TURCHETTI, DEBBIE; Johnston SR HS; Johnston, RI; (Y); Scholastic Bowl; Yrbk Ed-Chief; Capt Cheerleading; High Hon Roll; Hon Roll; Proj Insite 84; Porj Close Up 87; Psychlgy.

TURPIN, KAREN; Prout Memorial HS; N Kingstown, RI; (S); 12/71; VP JA; Math Clb; Scholastic Bowl; Capt Color Guard; Drill Tm; Nwsp Stf; Gov Hon Prg Awd; Hon Roll; NHS; Outstndng Clr Grd Awd 84-85; Hstry Awd 82-83; Med.

VACCHI, STEVEN R; Portsmouth HS; Portsmouth, RI; (Y); 7/195; Scholastic Bowl; Concert Band; Jazz Band; Mrchg Band; NHS; Pres Schlr; Rotary Awd; PAVAS; Band; Orch; Boston U Tanglwd Inst 85-86; Grtr Bstn Yth Sympny 84-86; Grtr Bstn Yth Symphny Estrn Europe Tr 85; Eastman Schl Of Msc; Appld Msc.

VALCOURT, CAROL; North Providence HS; N Providence, RI; (Y); Church Choir; Nwsp Ed-Chief; Yrbk Ed-Chief; Yrbk Stf; Lit Mag; Var Mgr(s); Gov Hon Prg Awd; Hon Roll; Jr NHS; NHS; Vrsty Lttr Mngr 86; Pre-Med.

VALCOURT, VAUGHN; Johnston HS; Johnston, RI; (S); 3/216; Boy Scts; SADD; Socr; Wrstlng; High Hon Roll; NHS; Ntl Merit Ltr; Bst ST Entry Natl Hstry Day 83; Comm.

VALE, VIKI; North Providence HS; N Providence, RI; (Y); Rep Soph Cls; VP Rep Jr Cls; Bsktbl; Sftbl; Hon Roll; NHS; Hnr Rll 84-85; Natl Hnr Socty 86; Bryant Coll; Htl Mgmt.

VALENCIA, PIEDAD S; Central Falls JR SR HS; Central Fls, RI; (Y); 6/120; Am Leg Aux Girls St; Church Yth Grp; JA; SADD; Rep Stu Cncl; Var L Bsktbl; Var Capt Sftbl; High Hon Roll; Hon Roll; Prfct Atten Awd; Ri Hnr Scty 86; Jr Achvmnt Schlrshp Awd $500 86; Model Leg, Excllnce In Fr Awd 86; Boston Coll; Bio.

VALLANTE, DAVID; Mt Pleasant HS; Providence, RI; (Y); Ed SADD; Var Bsbl; Var Bsktbl; Gov Hon Prg Awd; Hon Roll; Ntl Merit Ltr; Acad Decathalon Tm; Peer Educ Grp 4 Yrs; Comp Sci.

VALLEE, ROGER; Warwick Veterans Memorial HS; Warwick, RI; (Y); Cmnty Wkr; DECA; Teachers Aide; Stage Crew; High Hon Roll; Hon Roll; Jr NHS; Comp Progmr.

VELTRI, JOHN; North Providence HS; N Providence, RI; (Y); 15/200; Var JV Bsktbl; Hon Roll; Jr NHS; Northeastern U; Sports Med.

VENTURA, SUSANA; East Providence HS; East Providence, RI; (S); 11/523; Church Yth Grp; SADD; Band; Chorus; Yrbk Stf; Sr Cls; Stu Cncl; Capt Cheerleading; Trk; NHS; Bryant Coll; Bus Adm.

VERY, ELIZABETH; Mount St Charles Acad; Woonsocket, RI; (S); Cmnty Wkr; Dance Clb; VP French Clb; Teachers Aide; Mrchg Band; Tennis; High Hon Roll; Hon Roll; Tennis St Champ Cls B Tm 84-85; Bio.

VESCERA, LISA; St Marys Acad; Smithfield, RI; (Y); Hosp Aide; Hon Roll; NHS; NEDT Awd; Schl Svc Awd 85 & 86; Bryant; Acctng.

VIANA, MATTHEW J; Rogers HS; Newport, RI; (Y); Var Bsbl; Hon Roll; Engr.

VIEIRA, PAULO; La Salle Acad; Providence, RI; (Y); 45/286; Chess Clb; Mgr Computer Clb; Exploring; Mgr Church Choir; JV Var Score Keeper; JV Var Timer; High Hon Roll; Hon Roll; Awds For Comp & Chess Clubs 83-84 & 84-85; Awds For Comp & Mltry Explrers 85-86; Mech Engrng.

VILANDRIE, JEANNINE; St Mary Acad Bay View; Greenville, RI; (Y); Cmnty Wkr; Exploring; Var L Letterman Clb; Variety Show; Off Jr Cls; Coach Actv; Var L Swmmng; Svc Awd 86; Acctg.

VILBIG, MARK; Warwick Veterans Memorial HS; Warwick, RI; (Y); Chess Clb; Drama Clb; Acpl Chr; Chorus.

VILKER, LEE; Cranston H S West; Cranston, RI; (Y); 18/417; Am Leg Boys St; Math Tm; Political Wkr; SpanishClb; Trs Temple Yth Grp; Hon Roll; Jr NHS; NHS; Ntl Merit Ltr; Spanish NHS; Brandels U; Pre Med.

VILLANOVA, DONNA; Coventry HS; Coventry, RI; (Y); 24/441; French Clb; Yrbk Stf; Stu Cncl; Hon Roll; NHS; Cert Awd Stu Cncl 85-86; Cert De Merite Frnch Cls 83-85; Engrng.

VILLAREAL, LEOPOLDO; Portsmouth Abbey Schl; Elpaso, TX; (Y); 5/65; Dance Clb; Drama Clb; Key Clb; PAVAS; Spanish Clb; School Musical; School Play; Stage Crew; Yrbk Stf; Lit Mag; Deans Lst 85-86; URI Awd-Sci 84-85; Art Awd-Excllnc 84-85; Hspnc Schlrshp Awd 85-86; Ntl Hnr Soc 82-83; Yale.

VINAS, JACKIE; Central HS; Providence, RI; (Y); Art Clb; French Clb; JA; Pep Clb; Yrbk Rptr; Yrbk Stf; Sftbl; Swmmng; Tennis; Vllybl; URI Book Awd Eng Awd 86; Sci Fair Awd 86; RISD; Interior Designer.

VITULLO, SHERI; Our Lady Of Fatima HS; Warren, RI; (Y); 7/36; Ski Clb; Varsity Clb; Nwsp Phtg; Nwsp Stf; Yrbk Phtg; Yrbk Stf; Trs Frsh Cls; Trs Soph Cls; Trs Jr Cls; Trs Sr Cls; U Of ME Farmington; Phy Thrpy.

VIVEIROS, CRISTINA; St Raphael Acad; Central, RI; (Y); Dance Clb; Varsity Clb; Var Capt Cheerleading; Boston Coll; Pre-Med.

VIVEIROS, MARIA; East Providence HS; E Prov, RI; (Y); Cmnty Wkr; SADD; VICA; Band; Chorus; Concert Band; Mrchg Band; Yrbk Stf; Cit Awd; Hon Roll; E Providence Townie Awd 84; URI; Comp Engr.

VIVEIROS, SHERRI; Tiverton HS; Tiverton, RI; (Y); 9/190; Sec Jr Cls; Sec Sr Cls; VP Pres Stu Cncl; JV Var Cheerleading; DAR Awd; Elks Awd; NHS; Ski Clb; SADD; Variety Show; U Of RI Bk Awd; Stdnt Cncl Schlrshp; Southeastern MA U; Textl Tech.

VOWELS, THERESA; Coventry HS; Coventry, RI; (Y); 3/441; Hosp Aide; Math Tm; Chorus; Yrbk Stf; Capt Pom Pon; JV Trk; High Hon Roll; NHS; Hugh O Brian Awd 84-85; Cert Apprctn Tutor 85-86; Hnr Awds Acdmc Perf Span 83-86; Pre-Med.

WAGNER, CHRIS; Lincoln HS; Lincoln, RI; (Y); Pres Math Clb; Elks Awd; High Hon Roll; NHS; Prfct Atten Awd; Dstngshd Fclty Awd Of U Of RI 86; U Of RI; Mech Engnrng.

WAITE, WENDI; Chariho Regional HS; Hopkinton, RI; (Y); 4-H; SADD; Yrbk Stf; Stu Cncl; Bowling; Var JV Cheerleading; JV Var Fld Hcky; Hon Roll; TXTLS.

WALKER, BONNIE; Prout Memorial HS; Saunderstown, RI; (S); 1/92; Cmnty Wkr; English Clb; Library Aide; Teachers Aide; Chorus; School Musical; Nwsp Stf; High Hon Roll; Church Yth Grp; AATF Frnch Cntst 1st ST & 5th Regnl 85; Yng Peopl Inst Creatv Wrtg Wrkshp U Conn 84-85; Wrtg.

WALKER, JEFFREY; Classical HS; Providence, RI; (Y); Band; Hon Roll; Ntl Merit Ltr; Theatre.

WALSH, CHRISTINE; Warwick Veterans HS; Warwick, RI; (Y); Church Yth Grp; Sec VP JA; Teachers Aide; Yrbk Stf; Rep Jr Cls; Rep Stu Cncl; JV Sftbl; Hon Roll; Acctng.

WARDICK, JULIE A; Classical HS; Providence, RI; (Y); NHS; Natl Fndtn Advncmnt In Arts 86; St Judes Chldrns Rsrch Hosp 86; RI Coll; Nrsng.

WARE, JOHN; Pilgrim HS; Warwick, RI; (Y); 27/307; Trk; Cmnty Wkr; Hon Roll; Navl Cdts 81-85; Itln Hnr Soc 85-86; AZ ST U; Aero Engrg.

WARNER, MELANIE; Bayview Acad; Bristol, RI; (Y); 5/226; Am Leg Aux Girls St; French Clb; Orch; Rep Stu Cncl; Var L Bsktbl; Var L Crs Cntry; Var L Trk; Hon Roll; NHS; All ST Crs Cnty & Trk 85 & 86.

WARREN, BARBARA; Tiverton HS; Tiverton, RI; (S); 7/187; Sec Church Yth Grp; Girl Scts; Band; Drm Mjr(t); Mrchg Band; Yrbk Ed-Chief; Hon Roll; NHS; French Clb; Stu Cncl; Century III Schlrshp Schl Rep 85-86; U RI; Bio Sci.

WARRENER, TAMMY; Johnston SR HS; Johnston, RI; (S); 6/230; Ed Yrbk Stf; Pres Jr Cls; Pres Stu Cncl; L Bsktbl; Capt Sftbl; Var Trk; DAR Awd; High Hon Roll; Hon Roll; NHS; US Stu Cncl Awd; Cornell U; Engr.

WASHINGTON, COREY; Woonsocket DSR HS; Woonsocket, RI; (Y); Church Yth Grp; Church Choir; JV Bsktbl; JV Var Ftbl; Prfct Atten Awd; Tchrs Hnr Roll 85-86; Altrnt For Amrcn Legn Boys State 85-86.

WEED, LARINE; Chariho JR SR HS; Ashaway, RI; (Y); Computer Clb; Rep Frsh Cls; Rep Soph Cls; Rep Jr Cls; Rep Stu Cncl; Hon Roll; Ocn ST Bus Schl 85-86; Vica 84-85; Accntng.

WEIGOLD, SABRA; St Marys Academy Bay View; Cranston, RI; (Y); Art Clb; Sec VP Church Yth Grp; Cmnty Wkr; Exploring; JCL; Latin Clb; Math Clb; Office Aide; Teachers Aide; Sftbl; Gold Mdl JR Classcl Lg Latin Exam Lev 1 85, Cum Laude Lev 2 86; Schltc Art Awd Comptn 83; U RI; Latin Prof.

WESSELY, ERIN; Mt St Charles Acad; Johnston, RI; (S); 17/174; SADD; Variety Show; Var Score Keeper; Stat Socr; Var Timer; High Hon Roll; Secdry Ed.

WESTON, TODD; Coventry HS; Coventry, RI; (Y); High Hon Roll; Hon Roll; Jr NHS; NHS; Elect Engr.

WHEELER, ERICA LEIGH; Lincoln SR HS; Lincoln, RI; (Y); 7/211; Church Yth Grp; Var L Bsktbl; Var L Fld Hcky; Var L Sftbl; High Hon Roll; Jr NHS; NHS; All Vly Goalie Pawtucket Times Fld Hcky Tm Selection 85; Bio-Engrng.

WHEELER, JILL; St Marys Academy Bayview; Providence, RI; (Y); 14/213; Boy Scts; Hosp Aide; Spanish Clb; Orch; Rep Stu Cncl; Swmmng; Hon Roll; NHS; Mst Imprvd Clss A Grl Swm Tm 84-85; 7th Hgh Pt Scorer Swm Tm 84-85; RI Coll; Nrsng.

WHIPPLE, DEBRA; North Smithfield JR-SR HS; N Smithfield, RI; (Y); 55/150; French Clb; Letterman Clb; Pres Band; Concert Band; Jazz Band; Yrbk Ed-Chief; Pres Frsh Cls; Var Cheerleading; Sftbl; Tennis.

WHITE, ANDRE; Warwick Veterans Mem HS; Warwick, RI; (Y); 50/298; Cmnty Wkr; JA; Letterman Clb; Varsity Clb; Rep Stu Cncl; Var Capt Bsktbl; L Ftbl; Im Wt Lftg; Hon Roll; Lock Haven U.

WHITE, LISA JEAN; Coventry SR HS; Coventry, RI; (Y); Camp Fr Inc; Dance Clb; Letterman Clb; Q&S; Varsity Clb; Variety Show; Nwsp Rptr; Nwsp Stf; Stu Cncl; Var Cheerleading; 1st Rnnr Up Mod Miss Scholar Pag 85; URI; Lib Arts.

WHITE, RITA; Chariho HS; Ashaway, RI; (Y); 2/250; Camp Fr Inc; Math Tm; SADD; Band; Ed Yrbk Stf; Socr; Trk; High Hon Roll; Jr NHS; Prfct Atten Awd; YMCA Yth Of Mnth 86; URI Bk Awd 86; 2nd Pl Essy Cntst 86; Elem Ed.

WHITNEY, BRETT; South Kingstown HS; Wakefield, RI; (Y); 71/212; Bsktbl; Var Capt Trk; Hon Roll.

WHITTON, SANDRA; North Smithfield JR SR HS; Slatersville, RI; (Y); Church Yth Grp; French Clb; SADD; Chorus; Yrbk Stf; Stu Cncl; Hon Roll; French Pronunciation Awd 84; French Rdng Comprehension Awd 85-86; Interpretur.

WILDENHAIN, ANNMARIE; Davies Vo Tech; Pawtucket, RI; (Y); 20/157; VICA; Variety Show; Yrbk Stf; Stu Cncl; High Hon Roll; RI Hnr Soc Awd 86; Davies Prnt Fclty Awd 86; IFSEA Awd 85-86; Comm Coll; Erly Chldhd.

WILKINSON, DAVID; Burrillville HS; Harrisville, RI; (Y); SADD; Nwsp Rptr; Stu Cncl; Ftbl; Golf; Wt Lftg; High Hon Roll; Hon Roll; Prfct Atten Awd; Halls Inst; Drftng.

WILLIAMS, CHAD; Coventry HS; Coventry, RI; (Y); Boy Scts; Computer Clb; French Clb; Letterman Clb; Science Clb; Stage Crew; Variety Show; Nwsp Bus Mgr; Nwsp Phtg; Stu Cncl; Jrnlsm Awd; LA ST U; Law.

WILLIAMS III, HOWARD; Rogers HS; Newport, RI; (Y); 4/257; High Hon Roll; Hon Roll; NHS; Prfct Atten Awd; Hnrbl Mntn Resrc Mgmt 83; Comp Prgmmr.

WILLIAMS, PAUL; Tiverton HS; Tiverton, RI; (Y); Ski Clb; Rep Stu Cncl; Var Bsbl; Var Bowling; Var Ftbl; Hon Roll; Bus.

WILLIAMS, STEPHANIE; Charino Regional HS; Arlington, TX; (Y); Debate Tm; NFL; Spanish Clb; Band; Concert Band; Mrchg Band; Pep Band; Hon Roll.

WILMOUTH, RODNEY; Coventry HS; Coventry, RI; (Y); 40/367; Var L Ftbl; Var L Wrstlng; Hon Roll; NHS; RI Hnrs Soc 86; Barry U; Bus Managemnt.

WINTERS, ERIC; Hope HS; Providence, RI; (Y); PAVAS; Chorus; Variety Show; Var JV Bsktbl; Cit Awd; High Hon Roll; Hon Roll; Prfct Atten Awd; Schl Spirit 84-85; Berklee; Music.

WOJCIECHOWSKI, STEVEN; Narragansett HS; Narragansett, RI; (Y); 6/124; Aud/Vis; Camera Clb; Debate Tm; Hosp Aide; Math Tm; NFL; Stage Crew; CC Awd; NHS; Engrng.

WOLDU, GABRIEL ASFAHA; La Salle Acad; Providence, RI; (Y); Socr.

WOLFE, WILLIAM; La Salle Acad; Johnston, RI; (Y); Ftbl; Trk; Hon Roll; NHS; Pltcl Sci.

WOODS, KELLY ANN; Portsmouth HS; Portsmouth, RI; (Y); 40/220; Drama Clb; School Play; VP Frsh Cls; Rep Soph Cls; VP Jr Cls; VP Sr Cls; Rep Stu Cncl; Concert Band; Mrchg Band; Powder Puff Ftbl; Schlrshp Theresa Landry Sch Of Dance 85; Susan L Farmer Ldrshp Awd 86; Dramtcs Awd 86; U Of RI; Jrnlsm.

WOODS, SHELLEY; Classical HS; Providence, RI; (Y); Drama Clb; Intnl Clb; Math Clb; Science Clb; Spanish Clb; Hon Roll; Urbn Lg RI Outstndg Achvt Awd 84; Psych.

WRIGHT, JULIE Y; Prout Memorial HS; North Kingstown, RI; (Y); Church Yth Grp; Teachers Aide; Chorus; Stage Crew; Zangrelli Mem Schlrshp 84-85.

WRIGHT, SHERI; Prout Memorial HS; E Greenwich, RI; (S); 4/77; Teachers Aide; Sec Frsh Cls; VP Pres Soph Cls; Pres Jr Cls; VP Jr Cls; JV Var Bsktbl; Var Sftbl; Jr NHS; French Clb; Math Clb; Hghst Physcl Educ Awd 82-84; Hsghst Relgn Awd 83-84; Bentley Coll; Bus Adm.

WYMAN, DAVID; Warwick Veterans HS; Warwick, RI; (Y); Civic Clb; Band; Jazz Band; Mrchg Band; Hon Roll; USAF; Sci.

YEAW, THOMAS; Cranston HS West; Cranston, RI; (Y); Var Bsbl; Var Bsktbl; Hon Roll; NHS; Engrng.

YOUNG, CISSY S; Classical HS; Providence, RI; (Y); Computer Clb; French Clb; GAA; Math Clb; Science Clb; Yrbk Stf; Bsktbl; Socr; Vllybl; High Hon Roll; Classcl Chem Tm 1st Pl URI Chem Cntst 86; Brown U; Bio Med Engr.

YOUNG, MARK S; Portsmouth HS; Middletown, RI; (Y); 101/212; Art Clb; Boy Scts; Library Aide; Marine Corps Scholar Fndtn 86; Stacy Ann Sullivan Mem 86; Lyndon ST Coll; Meteorlgy.

YOUNG, TRACY; Chariho Regional HS; W Kingston, RI; (Y); 13/284; Trs 4-H; Trs FFA; VP Soph Cls; VP Jr Cls; VP Sr Cls; Capt Var Cheerleading; Capt Var Fld Hcky; Var Trk; Dnfth Awd; NHS; 4h Awd 85; Perfct Atten Awd 86; US Army Resrv Awd; RI Coll; Psych.

YOUNGREN, KRISTEN; Classical HS; Providence, RI; (Y); Church Yth Grp; Latin Clb; Var Trk; Hon Roll; Jrnlsm.

ZALEWSKI, RICHARD; Alternate Learning Project; Providence, RI; (S); Church Yth Grp; DECA; Nwsp Rptr; Nwsp Stf; Yrbk Stf; Rep Stu Cncl; Hon Roll; RI Coll; Bus.

ZALOUMIS, NICOLE; Rogers HS; Newport, RI; (Y); Powder Puff Ftbl; Yrbk Stf; Rep Sr Cls; Rep Stu Cncl; High Hon Roll; Rnnr Up Hmcmng Qun; Curry Coll; Librl Arts.

ZANGARI, KAREN; Bishop Keough Regional HS; N Providence, RI; (S); Dance Clb; Hosp Aide; Library Aide; Variety Show; Rep Stu Cncl; Cheerleading; Socr; Hon Roll; NHS; Relgious Stud Awd 85; Bryant Coll; Lwyr.

ZIENOWICZ, DAVID S; Bishop Hendricken HS; Cranston, RI; (Y); 11/242; Ski Clb; Jazz Band; School Musical; Symp Band; High Hon Roll; NHS; Ntl Merit SF; Biomed Engrng.

ZITO, STEPHANIE; Narragansett HS; Narragansett, RI; (Y); 16/130; Variety Show; Off Jr Cls; Off Sr Cls; Var L Tennis; Capt Var Vllybl; High Hon Roll; Hon Roll; NHS; Mariner Schlr Awd 85&86; Pt Judith Fshrman Schlrhsp 86; 1st Tm All Div Vllybl 86; Syracuse U; Italian Lang.

ZONA, KEVIN; Lincoln JR SR HS; Lincoln, RI; (Y); 34/195; Boys Clb Am; Boy Scts; Var Ice Hcky; Hon Roll; NHS; Wrcstr Polytech Inst; Elec Engr.

ZONFRILLO, LISA; Toll Gate HS; W Greenwich, RI; (S); Cmnty Wkr; DECA; Drama Clb; Pep Clb; School Play; VP Jr Cls; VP Sr Cls; Capt Cheerleading; Sftbl; DAR Awd; ,L/J; U RI.

ZUCKER, GEORGE; South Kingstown HS; Kingston, RI; (Y); 5/211; Am Leg Boys St; Debate Tm; Model UN; High Hon Roll; Hon Roll; NCTE Awd; NHS; Ntl Merit Ltr; Im Bsktbl; Im Swmmng; RI Coll Hnrbl Mntn Awd-Wrtg 85; Semi-Fnlst Century III Ldrshp Cmptn 85; Hmnties.

ZULETA, CESAR A; Central Falls HS; Central Fls, RI; (Y); Yrbk Phtg; Yrbk Stf; High Hon Roll; Hon Roll; RI Hnr Soc 86; NHS 86; Daniel Webster Coll; Plt.

ZULETA, MARIA; Central Falls JR HS; Central Falls, RI; (Y); Upwrd Bnd Pgm 86; Won Hnr For Excllnt Dscpln In Upwrd Bnd 86.

VERMONT

ABEL, TRACY; Mount St Joseph Acad; Mendon, VT; (Y); Am Leg Aux Girls St; GAA; Pep Clb; VP Ski Clb; Varsity Clb; Var Socr; Var Tennis; Boston U; Mktg.

ACHENBACH, ANNIS; Burr & Burton Seminary; Manchester, VT; (Y); Art Clb; Church Yth Grp; Hon Roll; Cert De Merite 86.

ACHILLES, ROBERT; St Johnsbury Acad; Saint Johnsbury, VT; (Y); Boy Scts; Church Yth Grp; Var L Ftbl; Var Trk; Var L Wrstlng; Wt Lftg; Hon Roll; Wrestlng Schlrshp 86; Vermont Tech Coll; Elect Engr.

ACKERMAN, WENDY; Chelsea HS; Chelsea, VT; (Y); Am Leg Aux Girls St; French Clb; FBLA; Varsity Clb; School Play; Trs Soph Cls; Trs Jr Cls; JV Bsktbl; Mgr(s); L Var Sftbl; Acctng.

ADAMS, JENNIFER; Hartford HS; White Rvr Jct, VT; (Y); Church Yth Grp; Drama Clb; GAA; Hosp Aide; Pep Clb; Ski Clb; Crs Cntry; Trk.

ADAMS, ROBERT; Vermont Acad; Walpole, NH; (Y); Band; Chorus; Concert Band; Mrchg Band; Var Ftbl; JV Ice Hcky.

ADOLFSSON, TINA; Mt St Joseph Acad; Pittsford, VT; (Y); 8/96; 4-H; Science Clb; Varsity Clb; Yrbk Ed-Chief; Var Cheerleading; Var Socr; Var Tennis; High Hon Roll; NHS; Ntl Merit Ltr.

ALBRYCHT, ELIZABETH; Mount Anthony Union HS; Bennington, VT; (Y); 9/273; Drama Clb; French Clb; SADD; Band; Jazz Band; School Musical; School Play; Sec Frsh Cls; NHS; Acad All Am 83-85; Boston U; Comm.

ALLEN, STEPHEN A; Essex Junction Educational Ctr; Essex Junction, VT; (Y); 15/350; Latin Clb; Concert Band; Orch; Lit Mag; Hon Roll; Ntl Merit SF; All State Bnd 85; VT Yth Orchestra 84-85; Political Discussion Clb 85; Teach.

ALNASRAWI, LEYLA; Champlain Valley Union HS; Shelburne, VT; (Y); Sec JA; Band; Concert Band; Jazz Band; Mrchg Band; Orch; School Musical; Variety Show; High Hon Roll; NHS; Hnr Rll 83-85; U Of VT; Music.

AMYOT, CAROL; Sacred Heart HS; Barton, VT; (Y); 12/24; Chorus; Yrbk Stf; Sec Frsh Cls; Sec Sr Cls; Socr; Eolo Johnson Wks Schlrshp, Sacred Heart Alumni Schlrshp 86; VT Coll Norwich U; Human Svcs.

ANCLIFFE, REBECCA; Chelsea HS; Corinth, VT; (Y); NFL; School Play; Nwsp Stf; Yrbk Phtg; High Hon Roll; Hon Roll; NHS; U Of VT.

ANTHONY, PATRICIA; Champlain Valley Union HS; Hinesburg, VT; (Y); 63/232; Church Yth Grp; Band; Cheerleading; Yrbk Orgnztns Editor 85-86; Mst Vlbl Chrldr In Soccer 85; Champlain Coll; Gen Bus.

ANTONICCI, CHRIS; Burlington HS; Burlington, VT; (Y); Boy Scts; Church Yth Grp; Math Tm; Var Bsbl; Bowling; Hon Roll; NHS; Math.

ARMSTRONG, EVE M; Essex Junction HS; Essex Junction, VT; (Y); Drama Clb; VP Intnl Clb; Political Wkr; SADD; School Play; Pres Frsh Cls; Rep Stu Cncl; JV Crs Cntry; NCTE Awd; Key Clb; Hnrs Comptn Writng Excllnc Schl Wnnr 85; Hugh O Brian Yth Fndtn Ldrshp Smnr 84; English.

ASHLINE, LISA M; Hartford HS; Hartland, VT; (Y); 13/107; 4-H; Teachers Aide; Yrbk Stf; Capt Bsktbl; High Hon Roll; Hon Roll; VFW Awd; Rotary Clb Schlrshp, Hartland Grange, Lad Aux Frgn Wars 86; VT Tech Coll; Ag Bus Mgmnt.

ASTRACHAN, PHILIP; Burke Mtn Acad; Intervale, NH; (Y); Ski Clb; JV Crs Cntry; Hon Roll; U CO; Bus.

ATHERTON, AMY; Burr & Burton Seminary; Bondville, VT; (Y); 9/95; Church Yth Grp; Drama Clb; French Clb; Cheerleading; High Hon Roll; Hon Roll; NHS; Cert Merit Hghst Hnr Sci-Math/Soc Wmn Engnrs 86; Wantastiquet Rotary Clb Schlrshp 86; JR Conf U VT; U Of VT; Bus Adm.

ATWOOD, MARK G; Northfield JR SR HS; Northfield, VT; (Y); 5/74; Pres Varsity Clb; Concert Band; Jazz Band; Var Bsbl; Var Ice Hcky; Var Socr; Elks Awd; Hon Roll; NHS; Ntl Merit Ltr; NHS Booster Clb Schlrshp 86; Max Sanborn Schrlshp 86; Elks Schlrshp 86; Norwich U; Civil Engr.

AUBUT, MIKE; Spaulding HS; Barre, VT; (Y); CAP; Drama Clb; SADD; Chorus; School Musical; School Play; Nwsp Rptr; JV Capt Ice Hcky; Mitchell Awd Cvl Air Ptrl 84; Earhart Awd Cvl Air Ptrl 86; Cdt Of The Yr Cvl Air Ptrl 85; Norwich U; Psych.

AUSTIN, WINIFRED M; Middlebury Union HS; Middlebury, VT; (Y); 7/158; Church Yth Grp; Church Choir; School Musical; Nwsp Rptr; Lit Mag; Tennis; Trk; High Hon Roll; Hon Roll; NHS.

BAILEY, KATHLEEN; Lake Region Union HS; Barton, VT; (Y); Hon Roll; Prfct Atten Awd; Cert Prfcncy Typng 40 WPM 85; Cert Achvt Miss TEEN Pgnt 84; Accntng.

BAKER, JILL A; Twinfield Union HS; Marshfield, VT; (Y); 4/36; Hosp Aide; SADD; VP Sr Cls; Rep Stu Cncl; Var Capt Bsktbl; Var Fld Hcky; Var Sftbl; Hon Roll; NHS; Pres Schlr; Pres Acad Ftnss Awd, Schlr-Athl Awd, Prncpls Awd Schlrshp 86; Trinity Coll.

BAKER, KIMBERLY; Mount Saint Joseph Acad; Rutland, VT; (Y); 31/75; SADD; Yrbk Stf; Rep Frsh Cls; Rep Soph Cls; Sec Sr Cls; L Socr; L Tennis; Hon Roll; Peom Pblshd Mountain Review 85; Rep Girls St 86; Var Ski Tm St Champs 84-86; Advrtsng.

BAKER, PAM; Mt Anthony Union HS; Pownal, VT; (Y); 50/328; Office Aide; SADD; Mrchg Band; Twrlr; Vllybl; High Hon Roll; Hon Roll; Cheerleading; Pownl Twrlng Cntst 1st Prz 86; UVM; Bus Mgmt.

BALL, FENNER; Green Mtn Union HS; Chester, VT; (Y); Art Clb; English Clb; Intnl Clb; Spanish Clb; JV Bsbl; NCTE Awd; Spanish NHS; Music.

BARNABY, CARMEN; Hartford HS; White River Jct, VT; (Y); DECA; GAA; Pep Clb; Var Capt Cheerleading; Hon Roll; Bus.

BARTLETT, CHRISTIANA; Twinfield HS; Plainfield, VT; (Y); Church Yth Grp; Trs Drama Clb; School Play; Stage Crew; Trs Jr Cls; NHS; Earth Sci.

BARTLETT, TAMARA; Burlington HS; Burlington, VT; (Y); Pres FBLA; VICA; High Hon Roll; NHS; Prfct Atten Awd; Outstndng Achvt Typng II, Offc Practc, Shrthnd II, FBLA Pres 86; Champlain Coll; Bus.

BARTLEY, BRENDA; Brattleboro Union HS; Putney, VT; (Y); 16/233; Pres VP FBLA; Model UN; Chorus; Yrbk Stf; Lit Mag; Hon Roll; NHS; Wndhm Fndtn Schlrshp 86; NH Coll; Admin Asst.

BASSETT, NANCY; Woodstock Union HS; Woodstock, VT; (Y); Am Leg Aux Girls St; SADD; Yrbk Stf; Var Capt Fld Hcky; Var Lcrss; Trs NHS; Debate Tm; French Clb; Latin Clb; Yrbk Phtg; Outstndng Engl I, Ltn II & Soc Studys; Boston Coll; Bus Mngmnt.

BATES, JENNIFER A; Middlebury Union HS; Middlebury, VT; (Y); 3/200; Am Leg Aux Girls St; Pres Chorus; Madrigals; Nwsp Ed-Chief; Nwsp Rptr; High Hon Roll; NHS; Ntl Merit SF; Fnlst UVM Writg Hnrs Comp 85; All-Eastrn Chorus 86; VT All-ST Chorus 83-85; Tchng.

BEAUCHEMIN, KELLY; Essex Junction Educational Ctr; Essex Jct, VT; (Y); Pres Church Yth Grp; Cmnty Wkr; Intnl Clb; SADD; Bsktbl; Fld Hcky; Trk; Merit Awd Cnfrmtn Tm Ldr 85; Fshn Mktg.

BEBO, DEANNA; Woodstock Union HS; Woodstock, VT; (Y); Cmnty Wkr; French Clb; SADD; Chorus; School Musical; School Play; Yrbk Stf; Var Capt Fld Hcky; Lcrss; Swmmng; UVM; Spec Ed.

BECK, JANET LYNN; Blue Mountain Union HS; Groton, VT; (Y); 5/38; Cmnty Wkr; SADD; Varsity Clb; Band; Chorus; Sec Sr Cls; Capt Bsktbl; Capt Socr; Hon Roll; Lion Awd; Lttr & Pins Sports 82-86; Julie Beck Mem Schlrshp 86; Vlntr Svc Awd Cystic Fbrs Fndtn 82-86; U Of VT; Social Wrk.

BECKER, ELENA; Rice Memorial HS; Shelburne, VT; (Y); Pep Clb; Rep Frsh Cls; Var Bsktbl; Var Socr; Var Tennis; JV Vllybl; Hon Roll; Med.

BECKETT, ONDREA; Mt Saint Joseph Acad; Mt Holly, VT; (Y); Trk; Hon Roll; Montserrat; Art.

BEENEN, PAMELA; Vergennes Union HS; Vergennes, VT; (Y); 7/125; Church Yth Grp; German Clb; Yrbk Stf; Var Bsktbl; Hon Roll; Acdmc All Amer Awd 86; RN.

BELL, SHERRY; Mt Anthony Union HS; Bennington, VT; (Y); 25/250; Pep Clb; High Hon Roll; NHS; Pres Schlr; Excllnc Engl 83-86; Dollars For Schlrs 86; U Of New Hampshire; Psych.

BELL, TINA; Rutland HS; Rutland, VT; (Y); High Hon Roll; Hon Roll.

BENJAMIN, MARTIN; Mount Anthony Union HS; N Bennington, VT; (Y); Cmnty Wkr; Debate Tm; Intnl Clb; Office Aide; Political Wkr; Spanish Clb; School Musical; Nwsp Stf; Lit Mag; High Hon Roll; Columbia Coll; Intl Lawyer.

BENOIT, AMY; St Johnsbury Acad; E St Johnsbury, VT; (Y); #4 In Class; Rep Am Leg Aux Girls St; Art Clb; Yrbk Stf; Sec Jr Cls; Pres Rep Stu Cncl; Var Fld Hcky; Var Pom Pon; Var Trk; High Hon Roll; NHS; Dartmouth; Marine Bio.

BENOIT, BRIAN H; Randolph Union HS; Randolph, VT; (Y); 25/96; AFS; Library Aide; Office Aide; Teachers Aide; Nwsp Sprt Ed; Im Badmtn; Im Bsktbl; Im Crs Cntry; Capt Var Socr; Wt Lftg; Boyds Travel Schl; Publ Rltns.

BENOIT, DARYL; Champlain Valley Union HS; Shelburne, VT; (Y); Aud/Vis; Camera Clb; Nwsp Phtg; Nwsp Rptr; Nwsp Stf; JV Trk; JV Wrstlng; Engrng.

BERGERON, SHELLEY; Missisquoi Valley Union HS; Swanton, VT; (Y); Nwsp Rptr; Nwsp Stf; Hon Roll; Alternatv ST Rep 85-86; Writing.

BERGEVIN, MICHAEL A; Middleburg Union HS; Middlebury, VT; (Y); 9/160; Band; Concert Band; Jazz Band; Mrchg Band; Pep Band; School Play; Var L Ftbl; Hon Roll; NHS; Worester Plytchncl Inst; Cvl En.

BERGSTEIN, LAURA; Colchester HS; Colchester, VT; (Y); Drama Clb; Chorus; School Play; Variety Show; Rep Frsh Cls; Rep Soph Cls; Rep Jr Cls; Rep Sr Cls; Rep Stu Cncl; Score Keeper; Sthestrn Acad; Trvl & Trsm.

BERIAU, MARY; Otter Valley Onion HS; Pittsford, VT; (Y); Am Leg Aux Girls St; Debate Tm; NFL; Concert Band; Jazz Band; School Musical; Pres Frsh Cls; High Hon Roll; Hon Roll; NHS.

BERNIER, SUZANNE M; Spaulding HS; Graniteville, VT; (Y); Trs Church Yth Grp; FBLA; Office Aide; SADD; Teachers Aide; Varsity Clb; VICA; Yrbk Stf; Rep Frsh Cls; Rep Soph Cls; Good Kid Awd; Bus Schlrshp; Middle Hnrs; Champlain Coll; Exec Sec.

BERRY, KEVIN; Hartford HS; White River Jct, VT; (Y); 20/110; Ski Clb; Band; Concert Band; Jazz Band; Madrigals; Pep Band; Crs Cntry; Lcrss; Hon Roll; JP Sousa Awd; Dean JC; Communications.

BETIT, MICHELLE; Mount Anthony Union HS; Bennington, VT; (Y); French Clb; SADD; Chorus; Drm Mjr(t); Yrbk Stf; NHS; Prfct Atten Awd.

BETTIS, WENDY A; Hartford HS; White Rvr Jct, VT; (Y); 15/97; GAA; Office Aide; Pep Clb; Teachers Aide; Yrbk Stf; Var Ftbl; Var Sftbl; Hon Roll; NHS; Cmnty Wkr; Dr Norman Tenney Schlrshp, Chester Burnham Schlrshp, John Gates Awd Athl Tm Plyr 86; VT Tech Coll; Vet Assist Pgm.

BEYOR, LISA; Missisquoi Valley Union HS; Franklin, VT; (Y); Church Yth Grp; Teachers Aide; Band; Concert Band; Mrchg Band; Symp Band; Variety Show; Stat Mgr(s); High Hon Roll; Hon Roll; Chmpln Coll; Lgl Secy.

BHATTACHARYYA, MAITRAYEE; Essex Junction Educational Center; Essex Junction, VT; (Y); 3/338; Math Tm; Pres Frsh Cls; Pres Soph Cls; Sec Trs Stu Cncl; JV Var Socr; Var L Trk; NHS; Intnl Clb; Latin Clb; Math Clb; Hnrbl Mntn All Am 84; Schlrshp Unitd Natns Pilgrmg 86; Gold Mdlst Natl Latn Exm 86.

BIGRAS, DIANE; Spaulding HS; Barre, VT; (Y); Cmnty Wkr; Drama Clb; French Clb; Hosp Aide; Rep Frsh Cls; Rep Soph Cls; Rep Jr Cls; Capt Cheerleading; Trk; Hon Roll.

BIRD, STACEY; Otter Valley U HS; Forestdale, VT; (Y); French Clb; Yrbk Sprt Ed; VP Soph Cls; Pres Jr Cls; Stu Cncl; Capt Bsktbl; Fld Hcky; Sftbl; DAR Awd; Hon Roll; Psych.

BISHOP, PENNY; Middlebury Union HS; E Middlebury, VT; (Y); Sec AFS; Drama Clb; School Musical; School Play; Nwsp Rptr; VP Frsh Cls; Rep Soph Cls; Sec Stu Cncl; High Hon Roll; Hon Roll; Prsdntl Yth Exchng Intiatv Schlrshp 85-86; Williams Amherst.

BISSEX, PAUL L; Twinfield HS; Plainfield, VT; (Y); Boy Scts; Drama Clb; French Clb; Band; Chorus; Madrigals; School Play; Hon Roll; Ntl Merit SF; NEDT Awd.

BISSON, JULIE; Mt Anthony Union HS; North Pownal, VT; (Y); 20/262; Art Clb; Yrbk Stf; High Hon Roll; Hon Roll; NHS; NEDT Awd; Breadloaf Wrtrs Conf, Gov Inst Arts, Peer Cnslng Grp/Training Help Line 86; Psych.

BIZZOZERO, CHARLES; Spaulding HS; Barre, VT; (Y); Key Clb; Var Lcrss; JV Var Socr; JV Trk; Acctng.

BLACKMER, MELISSA; Rutland HS; N Clarendon, VT; (Y); Church Yth Grp; Library Aide; Math Clb; Science Clb; Nwsp Rptr; High Hon Roll; Hon Roll; NHS; Ntl Merit Ltr; Pres Schlr; U Of VT; Engl.

BLAIS, NICOLE; Sacred Heart HS; Newport, VT; (S); Am Leg Aux Girls St; FCA; VP Frsh Cls; Sec Jr Cls; Rep Stu Cncl; Var Capt Bsktbl; L Var Socr; Var Sftbl; Hon Roll; NHS; Math, Alg I & II Achvt 84-85; Ntl Hnr Rll, Ctznshp Ldrshp Awds 85; Hlth Sci.

BLAKE, COURTLAND; Spaulding HS; Barre, VT; (Y); 3/245; Am Leg Boys St; Key Clb; Var L Ice Hcky; Var L Socr; Var Tennis; High Hon Roll; NHS; Rotary Awd; U Of Vermont; Engr.

BLAKE, CRAIG; Spaulding HS; East Barre, VT; (Y); 20/270; Am Leg Boys St; Cmnty Wkr; Yrbk Rptr; Yrbk Stf; Var Lcrss; Hon Roll; NEDT Awd; Top 10 Pct UVM Prize Math Exam 86; Governors Inst On Sci & Tech 85; U Of Vermont; Comp Sci.

BLAKE, SHANNON B; Essex Junction HS; St Albans, VT; (Y); 112/325; Bsbl; JV Capt Ftbl; Var L Wrstlng; Hon Roll; Wrstlg ST Champ & Schl Recrd Mst Wins 117, 100 Win Clb Coaches Assn, 4 Yr Vrst Awd 85-86; Springfield Coll; Bus.

BLISS, KRISTEN; Barre U 32 HS; Barre, VT; (Y); Dance Clb; Teachers Aide; Yrbk Stf; Sr Cls; Bowling; Sftbl; Hon Roll; Stu Cncl; Champlain Coll; Secy.

BLUMEN, DEBRA; Champlain Valley Union HS; Shelburne, VT; (Y); 2/240; Teachers Aide; Var Capt Bsktbl; Var L Fld Hcky; Var L Sftbl; High Hon Roll; NHS; Band; Mrchg Band; Simmonds Precsn Spec Schlrshp 86; U S Army Resrv Natl Schlr Athl Awd 86; U Of NH Hnr Schlrshp 86; U Of NH; Secdry Ed.

BOERI, JENNIFER; Woodstock Union HS; Woodstock, VT; (Y); Concert Band; Mrchg Band; Pep Band; School Musical; Yrbk Sprt Ed; Yrbk Stf; Var Fld Hcky; Var Sftbl; Hon Roll; Mst Outstndng US Hstry Stu 86.

BOHN, ELIZABETH; Twinfield HS; Marshfield, VT; (Y); Am Leg Aux Girls St; Art Clb; Drama Clb; Math Tm; Acpl Chr; Chorus; VP Frsh Cls; Pres Soph Cls; Hon Roll; NHS; JR Conf U Of VT 86; Eng.

BOLTZ, JEFFREY; Otter Valley HS; Brandon, VT; (Y); Am Leg Boys St; Church Yth Grp; Var Wrstlng; Hon Roll; NHS; U VT; Pre-Med.

BOOMER, LAURA; Lake Region Union HS; Irasburg, VT; (Y); Drama Clb; Hosp Aide; Chorus; Color Guard; Mgr Bsktbl; Fld Hcky; Hon Roll; NHS; Engl Awd Rsrch Wrtng 85-86; Awd Achvt Frnch I 85-86; Psych.

BOSE, PAT; Missisiquoi Valley HS; Swanton, VT; (Y); Am Leg Boys St; SADD; School Musical; School Play; Variety Show; Bsbl; Bsktbl; Socr; High Hon Roll; Hon Roll.

BOUCHARD, PATRICIA E; Mount Mansfield Union HS; Richmond, VT; (Y); 2/187; Sec Church Yth Grp; Band; Orch; Crs Cntry; Elks Awd; Gov Hon Prg Awd; NHS; Sal; Balfour Awd 86; Colby Coll Bk Prz 85; U Vermont; Biochem.

BOUCHER, PATRICK; Missisquoi Valley Union HS; Highgate, VT; (Y); 30/160; Rep Church Yth Grp; Rep French Clb; School Play; Stage Crew; Variety Show; Yrbk Stf; VP Jr Cls; Pres Stu Cncl; JV Bsbl; Hon Roll; Comp Sci.

BOUDREAU, ANN L; Missisquoi Valley Union HS; Franklin, VT; (Y); Art Clb; Church Yth Grp; Library Aide; Office Aide; Teachers Aide; Band; Concert Band; Mrchg Band; Yrbk Stf; High Hon Roll; Cert Of Awd Libry Aide 86; Awd Chrldng 86; Champlain Bus Coll.

BOWEN, SHELLY; Mount St Joseph Academy; Mendon, VT; (Y); 27/98; Varsity Clb; Capt Bsktbl; Socr; Hon Roll; Jr NHS; Kiwanis Awd; NHS; U Of VT; Psychlgy.

BOWER, JENNIFER; Mount Anthony Union HS; Bennington, VT; (Y); 8/360; Church Yth Grp; English Clb; French Clb; Nwsp Stf; Yrbk Stf; Lit Mag; High Hon Roll; NHS; Dollars For Schlrs Awd 86; Grove City Clg; Eng.

BOWMAN, ROSEMARY; Winooski HS; Winooski, VT; (Y); Drama Clb; Spanish Clb; Band; Chorus; School Musical; School Play; Bsktbl; Fld Hcky; Nrsng.

BRAMBLETT, JOHN; Harwood Union HS; Waterbury, VT; (Y); Am Leg Boys St; Boy Scts; Church Yth Grp; Chorus; VP Frsh Cls; Sec Sr Cls; Off Stu Cncl; Im Badmtn; Capt JV Bsbl; Im Bsktbl; Govnr Boys ST 86; Delg Boys Natn 86; Top 7 Metr Intrmdt Hurdls 86; Advtsg Comm.

BRAMMAN, BETHANY; Spaulding HS; Barre, VT; (Y); 86/262; Pres Church Yth Grp; Church Choir; School Play; Lit Mag; Crs Cntry; Trk; Hon Roll; Prfct Atten Awd; UVM; Psych.

BRATCHER, CHERYL; Mount Anthony Union HS; Pownal, VT; (Y); VP Band; Chorus; VP Concert Band; Madrigals; Mrchg Band; High Hon Roll; Hon Roll; Prfct Atten Awd; Natl Acad All Amer 85; North Adams ST; Bus Adm.

BREER, TABITHA; Harwood Union HS; Waitsfield, VT; (Y); Art Clb; Aud/Vis; Cmnty Wkr; Political Wkr; Lit Mag; Crs Cntry; High Hon Roll; Hon Roll; Prfct Atten Awd; Outstndng Bio Stu 84-85; Psychlgy.

BRIDGES, KATHRYN; Mount Saint Josephs Acad; Killington, VT; (Y); #2 In Class; SADD; Var Socr; Var Sftbl; Hon Roll; NHS; Sal; LUVM JR Cnfrnc 87; Grl Sst Altrnt 87; :Accntnt.

BRIEN, KAREN; Mount Anthony Union HS; Bennington, VT; (Y); 6/276; Rep Stu Cncl; Stat Bsbl; Var Fld Hcky; High Hon Roll; NHS; NEDT Awd; Prfct Atten Awd; UVM Math Awd 86.

BRIGGS, CHAD; Peoples Acad; Morrisville, VT; (Y); 12/61; Boy Scts; Ski Clb; Band; Concert Band; Mrchg Band; School Play; Hon Roll; NHS; Ntl Merit Ltr.

BROMIRSKI, ANN; Mt Anthony Union HS; Bennington, VT; (Y); Model UN; Stu Cncl; Var JV Bsktbl; Var JV Fld Hcky; High Hon Roll; Hon Roll; Excllnc Engl 86.

BROOKS, SONIA; Spaulding HS; East Barre, VT; (Y); 31/251; Church Yth Grp; Office Aide; Teachers Aide; Church Choir; Hon Roll; Latin Hnr Soc; Girl JR Champ VT ST In Rifle; Physcl Thrpy.

BROPHY, JULIE; Burr & Burton Seminary; E Dorset, VT; (Y); 13/93; Sec Frsh Cls; Stat Bsktbl; JV Ice Hcky; High Hon Roll; Lion Awd; Sec NHS; Natl Ldrshp & Svc Awd 86; Acadmc All Amer Awd 85; Coll Of St Joseph VT; Acctg.

BROTHERS, THOMAS; Windsor HS; Windsor, VT; (Y); Band; Concert Band; Mrchg Band; Trs Frsh Cls; Var Ftbl; High Hon Roll; Hon Roll; NEDT Awd; U Of VT; Agriculture.

BROWN, HEIDI; North Country Union HS; Newport, VT; (Y); 4-H; Chorus; Crs Cntry; 4-H Awd; Hon Roll; Bk Of Knwldg Awd; UVM.

BROWN, JENNIFER; Essex Junction HS; Westford, VT; (Y); AFS; SADD; Chorus; Co-Capt Flag Corp; Crs Cntry; Math.

BROWN, KATHY; St Johnsbury Acad; Saint Johnsbury, VT; (Y); 29/150; Church Yth Grp; Bsktbl; Socr; JV Sftbl; Trk; Hon Roll; Bus Mgmt.

BROWN, TAIRITA; Green Mtn Union HS; Cavendish, VT; (Y); 6/65; Art Clb; French Clb; Spanish Clb; Teachers Aide; School Musical; School Play; Elks Awd; Hon Roll; Church Yth Grp; Drama Clb; VT JR Miss 86 Schlrshp 86; VT Spriti Of JR Miss 86 Schlrshp 86; Springfield Comm Plyrs 85 & 86; USA; Anesthetist.

BROWNELL, CHRIS; Mount Anthony Union HS; N Pownal, VT; (Y); 37/300; Am Leg Aux Girls St; Spanish Clb; Yrbk Ed-Chief; Yrbk Stf; Cit Awd; DAR Awd; High Hon Roll; Hon Roll; NHS; Excllnc Engl; Rensselaer Polytechnic Inst.

BRYANT, SUE; Otter Valley Union HS; Brandon, VT; (Y); Cmnty Wkr; Hosp Aide; Pres VP Band; Concert Band; Orch; Hon Roll; NHS; French Clb; Library Aide; Mrchg Band; Bay Path JC; Medcl Asst.

BUELL, SARAH E; Essex Jct HS; Essex Junction, VT; (Y); Sec Church Yth Grp; Band; Chorus; Concert Band; Mrchg Band; Pep Band; School Musical; Var L Cheerleading; Frnch.

BULLENT, HEATHER; Otter Valley Union HS; Brandon, VT; (Y); Band; Concert Band; Mrchg Band; Pep Band; NHS; Big Sistr Camp Day Brk Emotnly Distrbd Chldrn 86; Medcl Tech.

BULLOCK, KIMBERLY L; Bellows Free Acad; Milton, VT; (S); 34/225; Am Leg Aux Girls St; Pres Sec DECA; 4-H; VP VICA; JV Bsktbl; Var L Fld Hcky; Var JV Sftbl; Hon Roll; NHS; Ntl Hnr Roll; Outstndng JR Conf; Champlain Coll; Rtl Mgmt.

BURGBACHER, WENDY; Green Mtn Union HS; Proctorsville, VT; (Y); 1/80; Am Leg Aux Girls St; Capt Ski Clb; Chorus; Concert Band; Sec Frsh Cls; Sec Soph Cls; Sec Jr Cls; Fld Hcky; Capt Trk; DAR Awd.

BURGESS, EDWARD; Chelsea HS; Chelsea, VT; (Y); Debate Tm; Chorus; Stage Crew; Yrbk Stf; Rep Jr Cls; Crs Cntry; High Hon Roll; NHS; UVM Mathmtcs Awd 84-85 & 85-86; Engrng.

BURK, JENNIFER; St Johnsbury Acad; Barnet, VT; (Y); 20/140; Sec FBLA; Stu Cncl; JV Bsktbl; Var Socr; High Hon Roll; Hon Roll; NHS; Hgh Obrn Awd 85; X-Cntry Skng Vrsty; UVM; Bnkng.

BUSH, MICHELE; Leland & Gray Union HS; Newfane, VT; (Y); 3/50; Yrbk Stf; Var Capt Cheerleading; Mgr(s); Var Capt Sftbl; Elks Awd; High Hon Roll; NHS; Mary Meyer Bus Awd 86; Hnrb John Barrett Awd 86; Ted Fisher Mem Awd 86; AZ ST U; Bus Mngmnt.

BUZEMAN, ANDREA; Vergennes HS; Vergennes, VT; (Y); Church Yth Grp; Computer Clb; Drama Clb; 4-H; German Clb; Chorus; School Musical; School Play; Variety Show; All New England Chorus 86; All ST Chorus 84; 1 Act VT ST Actrss Awd 86; Calvin Coll; Compu.

BUZZELL, KEITH; Mount Saint Joseph Acad HS; Rutland, VT; (Y); Am Leg Boys St; Drama Clb; SADD; Varsity Clb; Stage Crew; Yrbk Phtg; Yrbk Stf; JV Var Ftbl; Var L Ice Hcky; Rep Frsh Cls; U Of Lowell; Elec Engrng.

BUZZELL, PAUL; North County Union HS; Newport, VT; (Y); French Clb; Trs Key Clb; School Play; Variety Show; Bsktbl; Tennis; NHS; Frnch Dept Awd 83-85; Math Awd 84-86; 4.0 Avg 85-86; U Of VT; Pre Vet Sci.

CACIOPPI, TED; Mt St Joseph HS; Rutland, VT; (Y); 16/75; Debate Tm; Science Clb; Varsity Clb; Ftbl; Lcrss; Wt Lftg; Gov Hon Prg Awd; Hon Roll; Ntl Merit Ltr; JR Ski Ptrlr Of Yr 85; Poetry Awd 86.

CALDERARA, BRIAN; Spaulding HS; Barre, VT; (Y); 10/256; Am Leg Boys St; Church Yth Grp; Political Wkr; Service Clb; Im Badmtn; JV Bsbl; JV Bsktbl; Im Bowling; Im Ftbl; Im Golf; US Navl Acad; Engr Sci.

CALLAHAN, KATIE; Mt Anthony Union HS; Bennington, VT; (Y); Dance Clb; Spanish Clb; Variety Show; Off Frsh Cls; Off Soph Cls; Off Jr Cls; Off Sr Cls; Stu Cncl; Var Bsktbl; Var Fld Hcky; Boston Coll; Med.

CAMPBELL, CRICKET; Harwood Union HS; Waterbury, VT; (Y); 1/100; Am Leg Aux Girls St; Aud/Vis; Teachers Aide; Stage Crew; JV Var Bsktbl; JV Var Socr; JV Sftbl; Cit Awd; Hon Roll; Pres NHS; Tp JR Awd 86; Outstndng Sci, Frnch Stdnt 83-86; Cngrssnl Art Shw 83; Stanford U; Sci Rsrch.

CAMPBELL, SUSAN; Lake Region HS; Orleans, VT; (Y); Camera Clb; Church Yth Grp; DECA; Drama Clb; School Musical; School Play; Stage Crew; Nwsp Stf; Hon Roll; Awd Cert Of Exc In Algbra I 84; Awd Cert For Drama 85; 1st Pl For Pblc Spkng ST Cmpttn For Deca 86.

CAMPION, CHRISTOPHER; Winooski HS; Winooski, VT; (Y); 10/52; Am Leg Boys St; Debate Tm; Drama Clb; French Clb; Math Tm; Scholastic Bowl; Acpl Chr; Band; Chorus; Jazz Band; VT All ST Chorus 83; VT Chfs Police Schlrshp 86; Winooski Police Assc Schlrshp 86; U Of AZ; Crmnl Jstc.

CAMPOS, TERRY; Harwood Union HS; Waterbury, VT; (Y); High Hon Roll; Hon Roll; Mrkng Prd Englsh Ii Hnrs Awd 84-85; Typng I Awd 84-85; U Of FL; Elec Engr.

CANO, KIM; Spaulding HS; Barre, VT; (Y); 67/246; Sec FBLA; Hosp Aide; Office Aide; Spanish Clb; Rep Stu Cncl; Hon Roll; Schlrshp Barre Bus & Pro Wmns Clb 86; 3rd Pl Bus Englsh, 1st Pl Entrprnrshp 85; Champlain Coll; Acctg.

CARLSEN, LAURA; Mount Anthony Union HS; Shaftsbury, VT; (Y); 64/250; Church Yth Grp; Teachers Aide; Off Jr Cls; Stu Cncl; Trk; Hon Roll; Engl Awd 83-4; Socl Studies.

CASAGRANDE, ROBYN; Otter Valley Union HS; Pittsford, VT; (Y); 1/102; Sec French Clb; JA; Trs Concert Band; Mrchg Band; High Hon Roll; NHS; Pres Schlr; Val; U Of Vermont; Psych.

CASEY, KAREN; Spaulding HS; Barre, VT; (Y); 7/269; Am Leg Aux Girls St; Pres Frsh Cls; Pres Soph Cls; Pres Jr Cls; Pres Sr Cls; Rep Stu Cncl; Capt Var Cheerleading; Trk; Hon Roll; Band; HOBY Ldrshp Fdtn 85; Home Ec.

CASEY, TRICIA; Burlington HS; Burlington, VT; (Y); Varsity Clb; Chorus; Symp Band; Var L Bsktbl; Var L Socr; Var L Sftbl; Var L Trk; Letterman Clb; Band; Mrchg Band; VT Lk Div All Str Goalie 85; VT Div I ST Dscs Chmpn 86; Nw Englnd Rnnrup Dscs 86; U Vermont; Physcl Educ.

CASSANI, DOMENIC; Spaulding HS; Barre, VT; (Y); JV Var Socr; Var Tennis; Hon Roll; Phrmcy.

CASSANO, SCOTT; Woodstock Union HS; Killington, VT; (Y); Aud/Vis; School Musical; Stage Crew; Variety Show; Stu Cncl; Co-Capt Ftbl; Ice Hcky; Lcrss; Hon Roll; Off & Def Plyr Wk 86.

CASSESE, CATHERINE; Mt St Joseph Acad; Rutland, VT; (Y); 12/97; Church Yth Grp; Drama Clb; SADD; School Play; Yrbk Ed-Chief; NHS; Presdntl Acadmc Fitness Awd 86; Quinnipiac Coll; Intl Bus.

CASSIDY, LEA; Vergennes Union HS; Vergennes, VT; (Y); 25/130; Sec VP 4-H; French Clb; FBLA; Library Aide; School Musical; Yrbk Stf; Bsktbl; 4-H Awd; Hon Roll; Bus Adm.

CHAMBERS, CHRISTOPHER; St Johnsbury Acad; Saint Johnsbury, VT; (Y); 6/120; Computer Clb; Ntl Merit SF; Worcester Polytech Inst; Comp.

CHAPPELL, MARK; Mt Anthony Union HS; Bennington, VT; (Y); Computer Clb; German Clb; Model UN; Rep Frsh Cls; Hon Roll; NHS; Pres Schlr; Dollars For Schlrs Awd 86; Hudson Vly CC; Aerntcl Engr.

CHARRON, DENISE; Rice Memorial HS; Burlington, VT; (Y); Sec Church Yth Grp; School Musical; JV Fld Hcky; Hon Roll; Job-Work Local Ice Sktg Arena Snack Bar Attendant 85-86; Lib Arts.

CHENEY, KITTY; Williamstown JR-SR HS; Williamstown, VT; (Y); Trs FBLA; Office Aide; VP SADD; Teachers Aide; Chorus; Champlain Coll; Bus Mgmt.

CHESAUX, MATTHIEU; Calais U 32 HS; Calais, VT; (Y); 9/120; Church Yth Grp; High Hon Roll; Ltr Of Cmmndtn Prfrmnc PSAT/NMSQT 84; Arch.

CHEVALIER, ERIC; Missisquoi Union HS; Swanton, VT; (Y); Teachers Aide; School Play; Wt Lftg; Hon Roll; VT Maple Fest Blue Ribbon Maple Sugar 85; Acmplshd Stu Poem 86.

CHICOINE, ANDREA; Lake Region Union HS; Irasburg, VT; (Y); 40/87; Am Leg Aux Girls St; French Clb; Intnl Clb; Pep Clb; Science Clb; Teachers Aide; Chorus; Church Choir; JV Bsktbl; Hon Roll; Marlboro College; Bio.

CHILDERS, PAULA; Vergennes Union HS; Vergennes, VT; (Y); Church Yth Grp; SADD; Band; Mrchg Band; Hon Roll; Champlain Committee Col6; Acctg.

CHILDS, APRIL; Mount Saint Joseph Acad; Rutland, VT; (Y); Pep Clb; Ski Clb; Varsity Clb; Variety Show; Var Socr; Var Tennis; Hon Roll; 1st Womns Slaln 86.

CHIRIATTI, AMY; Mount Mansfield Union HS; Richmond, VT; (Y); 20/187; Chorus; Stage Crew; Capt L Crs Cntry; Capt L Trk; High Hon Roll; Hon Roll; Outstndng JR Conf 85; Ithaca Coll; Physcl Ed.

CHOQUETTE, ANNE; Sacred Heart HS; Newport, VT; (Y); FCA; Band; Drill Tm; Trs Frsh Cls; Crs Cntry; Sftbl; High Hon Roll; Hon Roll; NHS; Acad Achvt Awd 85-86; Spch Thrpy.

CHOQUETTE, MICHELLE; Lake Region Union HS; Barton, VT; (Y); Drama Clb; French Clb; Intnl Clb; Pep Clb; Chorus; School Play; Yrbk Phtg; Yrbk Rptr; Sec Soph Cls; Sec Jr Cls; Flight.

CHRISTIANSEN, JOAN; Essex Jct Educational Ctr; Burlington, VT; (Y); 117/328; Cmnty Wkr; Intnl Clb; Latin Clb; Red Cross Aide; Band; Concert Band; Mrchg Band; Pep Band; Hon Roll; Psych.

CICCOTELLI, LISA; Mt St Joseph Acad; Rutland, VT; (Y); 5/97; Pep Clb; Lit Mag; Stu Cncl; Cheerleading; High Hon Roll; Hon Roll; NHS; Rtland SO Rtry Schlrshp, US Pres Acdmc Ftns Awd 86; Fairfield U.

CIOFFI, ROBERT; Bellows Free Acad; St Albans, VT; (Y); 11/198; Am Leg Boys St; Drama Clb; Political Wkr; Quiz Bowl; Yrbk Ed-Chief; Bsbl; Bsktbl; Ftbl; Hon Roll; NHS; Amer Legion Boys Nation 85; U VT; Pol Sci.

CLARK, CAROLYN; Mt Mansfield Union HS; Underhill, VT; (Y); Church Yth Grp; Civic Clb; Band; Chorus; School Musical; School Play; Lit Mag; NHS; High Hon Roll; Hon Roll; Potsdam Merit Schlrshp 86; VT Yth Orchstra 84-86; Al-ST, Al-New Englnd Music Fstvl 86; Crane Schl Of Music; Music.

CLARK, PAM; Vergennes Union HS; Vergennes, VT; (Y); Band; Concert Band; Mrchg Band; Pep Band; Stage Crew; Variety Show; Hon Roll; Champlain Coll; Bus Mgt.

CLARK, SUZANNE; Woodstock Union HS; Woodstock, VT; (Y); 5/95; Camera Clb; Church Yth Grp; Cmnty Wkr; Dance Clb; English Clb; French Clb; Latin Clb; PAVAS; SADD; Varsity Clb; Cathlc Yth Dely; Am Leg Schlrshp; Cllrs For Schlrs Schlrshp; U VT.

COBLE, LISA M; Essex Educational Ctr; Essex Junction, VT; (Y); Cmnty Wkr; Drama Clb; Intnl Clb; Latin Clb; SADD; Chorus; Orch; School Play; Stage Crew; Hon Roll; Fnlst-Congrs-Bundestag Schlrshp Cmptn 85; Magna Cum Laude Cert Ntl Ltn Prz Exm 85; Baldwin-Wallace Coll; Piano.

COHEN, KARA; Mount Anthony U HS; Bennington, VT; (Y); 9/300; Drama Clb; French Clb; Model UN; Spanish Clb; Speech Tm; Yrbk Bus Mgr; Im Vllybl; High Hon Roll; NHS; Pres Schlr; Lions Clb Awd 86; UVM; Hstry.

COLBY, JAMES; Hartford HS; White Rvr Jct, VT; (Y); Boy Scts; Im JV Bsktbl; Var Capt Crs Cntry; Trk.

COLBY, KELLY; Chelsea HS; Chelsea, VT; (S); Am Leg Aux Girls St; Debate Tm; NFL; Rep Stu Cncl; Var Capt Bsktbl; Var L Fld Hcky; High Hon Roll; VFW Awd; French Clb; Varsity Clb; Athl Yr 83-84; Hustle Awd Bsktbl 85; Math.

COLEMAN, AMY; Missiquoi Valley Union HS; Swanton, VT; (Y); GAA; Office Aide; Red Cross Aide; Teachers Aide; Variety Show; Yrbk Stf; Bsktbl; Socr; High Hon Roll; Prfct Atten Awd; Champlain Clg; Legal Scrtry.

COLLINS, AMANDA; Enosburg Falls HS; Enosburg Falls, VT; (Y); Am Leg Aux Girls St; French Clb; FHA; Ski Clb; Chorus; Nwsp Ed-Chief; Yrbk Ed-Chief; VP Jr Cls; JV Bsktbl; Sec NHS; U VT.

COLLINS, MARGARET; Black River HS; Ludlow, VT; (S); 6/36; Am Leg Aux Girls St; Pep Clb; Rep Frsh Cls; Rep Soph Cls; Rep Jr Cls; Rep Sr Cls; Sec Stu Cncl; Capt Bsktbl; Cit Awd; DAR Awd; DAR Good Ctzn Awd 85-86; NHS 85-86; Champlain Coll; Bus Mngmnt.

COMBES, SHARON; Black River HS; Ludlow, VT; (S); 1/39; School Play; Yrbk Ed-Chief; Pres Sr Cls; Rep Stu Cncl; Capt Var Bsktbl; Capt Var Socr; Var JV Sftbl; Cit Awd; High Hon Roll; Pres NHS; Proj Wnnr VT Ntl Hist Proj 84; 2nd Pl Dist Amer Lgn Oratrcl Cntst 84; 1st Pl Schlessay Ex Wrtng 85; Georgetown U; Govt & Law.

COMEAU, RACHAEL; Missisqudi Valley Union HS; Swanton, VT; (Y); 14/143; Am Leg Aux Girls St; Church Yth Grp; Cmnty Wkr; GAA; Church Choir; School Play; Nwsp Rptr; Rep Frsh Cls; Rep Soph Cls; Rep Jr Cls; Green Mountain Teen Inst 86; All New England Yth Tm 86; Close-Up 86; Jrnlst.

COON, HEATHER; Bellows Free Acad; St Albans, VT; (Y); 38/249; Hosp Aide; Band; JV Var Cheerleading; High Hon Roll; Hon Roll; Cntstnt VT Teen USA Pagnt 85; Math.

COOPER, TRULA A; Missisquoi Valley Union HS; Franklin, VT; (Y); 8/131; Church Yth Grp; 4-H; FBLA; Yrbk Ed-Chief; High Hon Roll; Hon Roll; NHS; Teachers Aide; School Play; Stage Crew; Close Up; Prsdntl Acdmc Ftnss Awd; Trnty Coll Prsdntl Schlrshp; Trinity Coll Of VT; Acctg.

COPP, LISA; Concord HS; N Concord, VT; (S); 2/20; Trs 4-H; Math Tm; Office Aide; Scholastic Bowl; SADD; Yrbk Stf; Cheerleading; Dnfth Awd; 4-H Awd; NHS; 4-H Ctznshp Awd 83; Class Marshall 85.

CORBITT, ROY; St Johnsbury Acad; St Johnsbury, VT; (Y); Ski Clb; Var Crs Cntry; U Of Lowell; Plastic Engrng.

COTA, ROXANNE; St Johnsbury Acad; Saint Johnsbury, VT; (Y); Spanish Clb; Bus Mgmt.

COTE, DANIELLE; North Country Union HS; Beebe Plain, VT; (Y); 20/253; Am Leg Aux Girls St; French Clb; Acpl Chr; Chorus; School Musical; Rep Stu Cncl; Var Fld Hcky; High Hon Roll; NHS; St Schlr; Ntl Schl Choral Awd 86; Hnr Stu 86; U Of VT; Psych.

COTE, TOD; Enosburg Falls HS; Enosburg Falls, VT; (Y); Church Yth Grp; Office Aide; SADD; Off Jr Cls; Hon Roll; Ntl Merit Ltr; Prfct Atten Awd; Hghst Grd In Bio & Geo 84-85; Svc To Schl 85-86; Physics.

COWANS, ROBERT; Proctor HS; Proctor, VT; (Y); 2/56; Boy Scts; Concert Band; Jazz Band; Pres Jr Cls; Pres Sr Cls; Var Capt Ice Hcky; Var Capt Socr; High Hon Roll; NHS; Sal; Eagle Sct 86; VT All St Band 85-86; Hugh Obrien Yth Fndtn 85; Mcgill U.

CRANE, REBECCA; Mt Abraham Union HS; Bristol, VT; (Y); Am Leg Aux Girls St; Drama Clb; Band; Chorus; Pres Frsh Cls; JV Var Bsktbl; JV Var Fld Hcky; Var Trk; NHS; Quiz Bowl; Dartmouth Book Awd 86; UVM Mth Hnrb Mntn 86; Tech Wrtng.

CRAWFORD, THOMAS; Missisquoi Valley Union HS; St Albans, VT; (Y); Aud/Vis; Boy Scts; Church Yth Grp; Library Aide; School Musical; Variety Show; Rep Soph Cls; Rep Jr Cls; Hon Roll; Rotary Awd; Law.

CROLL, NORA S; Middleburg Union HS; Ripton, VT; (Y); Art Clb; Drama Clb; English Clb; Band; School Musical; School Play; Stage Crew; Variety Show; Nwsp Stf; Lit Mag; Lit.

CROSS, JENNEFER JANE; Essex Jct Educational Ctr; Essex, VT; (Y); 30/336; AFS; Am Leg Aux Girls St; French Clb; Intnl Clb; Latin Clb; Ski Clb; Acpl Chr; Chorus; Orch; Stu Cncl; VT Yth Orchstra 84-86; Mgzn Drive Chrprsn 85-86; All-Star, All-ST, & Twin-ST Sccr; Wllsly Coll; Music.

CROSS, TARA; Saint Johnsbury Acad; Saint Johnsbury, VT; (Y); 13/110; Trs Church Yth Grp; Dance Clb; Drama Clb; Pres FBLA; Nwsp Rptr; Rep Stu Cncl; JV Var Cheerleading; Var Pom Pon; High Hon Roll; NHS; Mgmt.

CROWLEY, WILLIAM; Mt Saint Josephs Acad; Mendon, VT; (Y); 6/76; Am Leg Boys St; Ski Clb; SADD; Varsity Clb; Rep Stu Cncl; Var Bsbl; Var Crs Cntry; Var Ftbl; Var Tennis; High Hon Roll; Skig Vrsty ST Champs.

CRUZ, VINCE; Burlington HS; Burlington, VT; (Y); French Clb; Spanish Clb; JV Ftbl; JV Var Tennis; Arch.

CUMMING, DOUGLAS; Spaulding HS; Barre, VT; (Y); 10/245; Am Leg Boys St; Computer Clb; Nwsp Ed-Chief; Yrbk Phtg; Lit Mag; Hon Roll; Chess Clb; Church Yth Grp; Civic Clb; Drama Clb; Pro Merito 86; U Of VT; Comp Engr.

CUNNINGHAM, CHRISTINE; Mount Anthony Union HS; Bennington, VT; (Y); 1/267; Church Yth Grp; Girl Scts; Spanish Clb; Chorus; Madrigals; Orch; Var Fld Hcky; High Hon Roll; Val; DAR US Hstry Awd 86; Yale U; Bio.

CURRAN, PAUL; Mount Saint Joseph Acad; Mendon, VT; (Y); 5/100; SADD; Yrbk Stf; Rep Stu Cncl; L Var Bsbl; Var JV Ftbl; L Var Ice Hcky; NHS; Varsity Clb; High Hon Roll; Hon Roll; VT ST All-Str Hcky Tm 85; Strt Hcky & Bsbll 84-87; Vt Chmps 85-86; Bus.

CUTTING, HEATHER; Brattleboro Union HS; Guilford, VT; (Y); Math Clb; Church Yth Grp; Cmnty Wkr; Model UN; Yrbk Phtg; Yrbk Stf; Rep Soph Cls; Rep Jr Cls; Sktng Clb Of Amhrst Merit Awd 85-86; Slvr Mdl For Sktng 85; Fgr Sktng Amateur Coaching Awd 85-86; Nrs.

DA GROSA, JOHN; Vermont Acad; Tequesta, FL; (S); 5/85; SADD; Varsity Clb; JV Bsbl; Var Capt Bsktbl; Var Ftbl; Var Trk; Var Wt Lftg; High Hon Roll; Hon Roll; Boy Scts; Colgate.

DALE, JULIE; Otter Valley Union HS; Brandon, VT; (S); Pres French Clb; Rep Latin Clb; Rep Leo Clb; Lit Mag; VP Frsh Cls; Sec Jr Cls; Rep Stu Cncl; JV Var Bsktbl; Var Fld Hcky; Var Sftbl; Fld Hcky-Cntrl VT Grls Athltc Leag All Oppnent Tm 85-86; CVGAL All Oppnent Tm-Sftbl 85; Dartmouth; Poltcl Sci.

DAVIES, JANINE; Peoples Acad; Morrisville, VT; (Y); 22/70; Church Yth Grp; Cmnty Wkr; Pep Clb; Varsity Clb; Mrchg Band; Yrbk Stf; Cheerleading; Pom Pon; NHS; Prfct Atten Awd; VT Excel 85-86; Johnson ST Coll.

DELUCIA, STEPHEN; Mt Anthony Union HS; Bennington, VT; (Y); French Clb; Soph Cls; Jr Cls; Trk; Hon Roll; Ntl Merit SF; Prfct Atten Awd; Physcs.

DEMKO, PETER J; Essex Jct Educational Center; Essex Junction, VT; (Y); 31/326; Boy Scts; VP Pres Church Yth Grp; Pres Exploring; ROTC; SADD; Color Guard; Drill Tm; Lit Mag; Hon Roll; Ntl Merit SF; Outstndng Cdt AFJROTC 83; PA ST U; Elec Engrng.

DEREPENTIGNY, BRENDA; Otter Valley Union HS; Whiting, VT; (Y); 7/103; FBLA; Nwsp Stf; Yrbk Ed-Chief; Trs Jr Cls; Hon Roll; Trs NHS; Eugenia T Ladam Mem Schlrp 86; Marie Crovot Schlrp 86; Champlain Coll; Accntg.

DESAUTELS, JULIE; Richford HS; Richford, VT; (Y); 8/30; French Clb; Natl Beta Clb; Band; Chorus; School Musical; School Play; Yrbk Stf; JV Var Score Keeper; Hon Roll; NHS; Pres Acad Fit Awd 86; Scholar Grace Casavant 86; Champlain Coll; Acctng.

DESJARDINS, LEE ROBERT; Woodstock Union HS; S Pomfret, VT; (Y); Letterman Clb; School Musical; School Play; Var L Bsbl; Var L Ftbl; Hon Roll; NHS; Prfct Atten Awd; Ftbll All Lgu Tm 85; Insprtnl Ldr Awd Ftbl & Bsbl 85-86; Norwich U; Chem.

DESROCHERS JR, JOHN; Mississquoi Valley Union HS; Swanton, VT; (Y); 45/140; Church Yth Grp; Yrbk Ed-Chief; Var Capt Ice Hcky; Var Capt Trk; High Hon Roll; Hon Roll; Mst Imprvd-Trck 85-86; U S Navy; Nclr Proplsns.

DICKEY, AARON; Vermont Acad; N Adams, MA; (Y); 15/70; Church Yth Grp; Debate Tm; Ski Clb; Teachers Aide; Ice Hcky; Lcrss; Socr; High Hon Roll; Hon Roll; Real Est.

DIEMER, KRISTIN; St Johnsbury Acad; Saint Johnsbury, VT; (Y); Church Yth Grp; Chorus; Nwsp Rptr; Nwsp Stf; Stu Cncl; Cheerleading; Fld Hcky; Trk; Hon Roll; Nrsg.

DILL, HEIDI; Harwood Union HS; Waterbury Center, VT; (Y); Church Yth Grp; Cmnty Wkr; Red Cross Aide; Teachers Aide; Concert Band; School Musical; Lit Mag; Mgr(s); Socr; Hon Roll; Finrs Rainbw Musc 84; Wind Ensmbl 84-86; Winooski Vlly Fest 85; Tchr Ed.

DINSMORE, MARK; St Johnsbury Acad; Barnet, VT; (Y); Math Clb; Spanish Clb; JV Wrstlng; Air Force; Comp.

DION, JOSEPH; Woodstock Union HS; South Woodstock, VT; (Y); Am Leg Boys St; Stu Cncl; Capt Var Ftbl; Var L Lcrss; Bausch & Lomb Sci Awd; High Hon Roll; NHS; St Schlr; Math Tm; Concert Band; Hugh O Brian Yth Fndtn-Outstndg Stu 85; Outstndg Stu In Sci 86; Prncpls Clb-All A-4 Consetv Terms 85-6; Mech Engr.

DITTRICH, ERIK; Burlington HS; Burlington, VT; (Y); Am Leg Boys St; French Clb; Latin Clb; Ski Clb; Band; Concert Band; Pep Band; Golf; Hon Roll; NHS; Captain Ski Tm 85-87; Bio.

DOBBINS, SARITA; Oxbow HS; Bradford, VT; (Y); 11/90; AFS; French Clb; Band; Mrchg Band; Trs Frsh Cls; Trs Soph Cls; Trs Jr Cls; Trs Sr Cls; Capt Bsktbl; Capt Fld Hcky; Hme Eco Awd 84; U Of VT; Dntl Hygn.

DORWART, RICHARD WILSON; Burlington HS; Burlington, VT; (Y); AFS; Trk; NHS; Coaches Awd Trck 86; Colbt Coll; Soc Studies.

DUARTE, CARLA; Burlington HS; Burlington, VT; (Y); 7/249; AFS; Pres Spanish Clb; Yrbk Stf; Rep Stu Cncl; Var Trk; Hon Roll; Jr NHS; NHS; Ntl Merit Ltr; Pres Schlr; Tufts U; Intl Rel.

DUARTE, NATASHA; Burlington HS; Burlington, VT; (Y); AFS; Am Leg Aux Girls St; Latin Clb; Sec VP Spanish Clb; Rep Stu Cncl; Spn II & III 84-86; Lang.

DUFFY, SARAH; Rice Memorial HS; S Hero, VT; (Y); 32/160; Political Wkr; School Musical; Stage Crew; Rep Soph Cls; Rep Jr Cls; Trk; Wt Lftg; Frshmn Orntatn; Chrstn Ldrshp; U Of Chicago; Econ.

DUFIELD, GLORIA; Green Mountain Union HS; Chester Depot, VT; (Y); 7/74; Latin Clb; SADD; NHS.

DUFRESNE, MONIQUE; Twinfield HS; Marshfield, VT; (Y); 1/36; Rep Mgr Am Leg Aux Girls St; Rep SADD; Pres Jr Cls; Sec Rep Stu Cncl; Var Cheerleading; Var Sftbl; Elks Awd; Pres NHS; St Schlr; Val; U VT; Dental Hygn.

DUNN, DANIELLE; Woodstock Union HS; S Royalton, VT; (Y); Drama Clb; French Clb; Capt Ski Clb; Concert Band; Socr; Sftbl; Hon Roll; Jr NHS; Debate Tm; Math Tm; VT Hnrs Comptn Excllnce Wrtng Rnnr Up 86; U VT JR Conf 86; Arch.

DUSTIN, APRIL; Wilmington HS; Wilmington, VT; (Y); Scholastic Bowl; Band; Chorus; School Musical; Yrbk Stf; Var Capt Cheerleading; JV Var Fld Hcky; Var Mgr(s); Hon Roll; Mock Trial Tm-JV/Vrsty 83-86; VT Hnrs Comptn For Excllnc In Wrtng-Locl Lvl Wnnr 86; U Of CT; Law.

DUTTON, DONNIE; Lake Region Union HS; Brownington, VT; (Y); Pres Church Yth Grp; Band; Chorus; Church Choir; Bsbl; Hon Roll.

EAGAN, JOHN; Mount Saint Josephs Acad; Bomoseen, VT; (Y); 7/85; Am Leg Boys St; Boy Scts; Pres Church Yth Grp; Key Clb; Letterman Clb; Scholastic Bowl; SADD; Varsity Clb; Yrbk Stf; Ftbl; Harvard College; Lwyr.

EDQUID, FRED; Winooski HS; Winooski, VT; (Y); 3/61; Am Leg Boys St; Math Tm; Concert Band; School Play; Yrbk Stf; Var Bsbl; Var Ftbl; Elks Awd; High Hon Roll; JP Sousa Awd; Carregie Mellon U; Engrng.

EGGLESTON, MICHELLE; Mount Saint Joseph HS; Rutland, VT; (Y); Varsity Clb; Capt Var Bsktbl; Var L Socr; Var Capt Sftbl; Hon Roll; NHS; Prsdntl Schlrshp Lyndn ST Coll 86; Lyndon ST Coll; Cmmnctns.

ELLISON, KIMBERLY JAY; Rutland HS; Manchester Ctr, VT; (Y); 85/221; Church Yth Grp; CAP; Drama Clb; FBLA; Orch; Nwsp Stf; Rutland Area Votech Ctr; Acctnt.

ELWOOD, ROMONA; Enosburg Falls HS; Enosburg Falls, VT; (Y); FFA; FHA; Teachers Aide; Yrbk Stf; JV Bsktbl; JV Sftbl; Stwrds.

ELZINGA, TENA; Vergennes Union HS; Vergennes, VT; (Y); 6/101; Church Yth Grp; German Clb; Var Capt Bsktbl; NHS; Marie Crovat Schlrshp 86; Natl Secndry Educ Cncls Acad All-Amer Schlr 85; Gordon Coll; Sprts Med.

ENGEL, MARIGRACE; Rice Memorial HS; Burlington, VT; (Y); School Musical; Socr; Hon Roll; Hofstra U; Jrnlsm.

ENGLERT, HILARY; Woodstock Union HS; Woodstock, VT; (Y); 10/109; Model UN; Concert Band; Jazz Band; School Musical; NHS; Debate Tm; Sec Drama Clb; French Clb; Mrchg Band; Orch; Brown U Book Awd 86; U VT JR Conf 86; Gov Inst Arts 86; Outstndng Engl Stu 85 & 86; Hamilton; Engl.

ESTERBROOK, KRISTIN; Proctor HS; Rutland, VT; (Y); #4 In Class; French Clb; SADD; Chorus; Hon Roll; NHS.

EVERTS, MEGAN; Winooski HS; Winooski, VT; (Y); 1/60; Am Leg Aux Girls St; Church Yth Grp; Var JV Bsktbl; Var JV Sftbl; Bausch & Lomb Sci Awd; High Hon Roll; NHS; Var Crs Cntry; Im Vllybl; Hon Roll; Fres Athlt Of Yr Feml 83-84; Publc Green Mt Revw 85; Comp Prgmmg.

FAIVRE, SAM; Otter Valley Union HS; Brandon, VT; (S); 23/108; Am Leg Boys St; Church Yth Grp; VP Sr Cls; Rep Stu Cncl; Co-Capt Crs Cntry; Var Trk; High Hon Roll; ST Champ 84-86; Trk Champ 85; Sprts Illstrtd 86; Springfield Clg; Sprts Med.

FANTINI-CESPEDES, ALVINO MARIO; Brattleboro Union HS; Brattleboro, VT; (Y); 26/244; Art Clb; Ed Lit Mag; Stu Cncl; Hon Roll; NHS; Ntl Merit Ltr; VFW Awd; Intnl Clb; Model UN; Stage Crew; Natl Hispnc Schlr Awds Prog SF 85; Century III Ldrshp Cntst 1st Locl Rnnr Up 85; Anthrop.

FARNUM, TONY; Brattleboro Union HS; Brattleboro, VT; (Y); Boy Scts; Church Yth Grp; Cmnty Wkr; Model UN; SADD; Band; Concert Band; Mrchg Band; Pep Band; Hon Roll; Outstndng Svc, Ldrshp & Imprvmnt-Band 85-86; Engrng.

FEARY, ELIZABETH; Woodstock Union HS; Woodstock, VT; (Y); Church Yth Grp; Drama Clb; Teachers Aide; Mgr Stage Crew; Yrbk Stf; VP Soph Cls; Rep Stu Cncl; Var Lcrss; Pres NHS; Intrl Bus.

FEDOR, KIRK; Burrt Burton Seminary HS; Manchester, VT; (Y); 9/100; Am Leg Boys St; Var L Bsktbl; Var Capt Golf; Hon Roll; Prfct Atten Awd; Bus Mgt.

FISHER, HEATHER; Missisquoi Valley Union HS; Highgate, VT; (Y); 4-H; Intnl Clb; Yrbk Stf; Rep Frsh Cls; Stu Cncl; Stat Bsktbl; JV Var Socr; Wt Lftg; Hon Roll; Gov Inst Intl Affrs 86; William & Mary; Law.

FISHER, HEIDI; Burlington HS; Burlington, VT; (Y); Church Yth Grp; Varsity Clb; JV Cheerleading; Var Capt Gym; JV Mgr Sftbl; Hon Roll; NHS; Excllnc In Acctng I, Data Prcsng, Typng II, & Advncd Ofc Prcdrs 86; Chmpln Coll; Info Prcssng.

FLANNERY, MAUREEN; Mount Saint Joseph Acad; Rutland, VT; (Y); 1/76; Am Leg Aux Girls St; Church Yth Grp; SADD; Stage Crew; Yrbk Stf; VP Frsh Cls; Socr; Trk; High Hon Roll; Hon Roll; Stu Govt Green Key Awd 84; Sci Fair Slvr Medal 84; Dartmouth Clb Bk Awd 86; Sci.

FLETCHER, ANGELA; Proctor JR SR HS; Proctor, VT; (Y); 1/53; Am Leg Aux Girls St; Band; Chorus; Yrbk Stf; Pres Stu Cncl; High Hon Roll; NHS; Ntl Merit Ltr; Amer Lg Aux Grls Natn Delg 86.

FLETCHER, DEBORAH; Mt Anthony HS; Shaftsbury, VT; (Y); 15/265; Chess Clb; CAP; Pres Leo Clb; Science Clb; Church Choir; Drill Tm; Lit Mag; Hon Roll; NHS; VICA; 1st VT Hnrs Comp Exclnce Wrtng; US Army; Intlgnce Corp.

FLETCHER, SHERI; Green Mountain Union HS; Chester, VT; (Y); Am Leg Aux Girls St; Pres French Clb; Latin Clb; Trs Frsh Cls; Trs Soph Cls; Trs Jr Cls; Trs Sr Cls; Var JV Fld Hcky; Trs NHS; Chorus; Excllnc Frnch 84-86; Excllnc Latin 84-85; Sprtsmnshp Vrsty Fld Hcky 85-86; Pre Law.

FONTAINE, CARMEN; Otter Valley Union HS; Whiting, VT; (Y); Math Tm; Teachers Aide; Acpl Chr; Chorus; School Musical; School Play; Sec Soph Cls; Rep Stu Cncl; Hon Roll; NHS; Air Frc CC.

FOREST, DIANE; Concord HS; Concord, VT; (S); 3/22; Am Leg Aux Girls St; French Clb; Radio Clb; Scholastic Bowl; Band; Var Bsktbl; Var Socr; Var Sftbl; Hon Roll; Prfcncy Typng I & II Awds 85-86; Olympc Natl Schltc Typng Cntst Schl Wnnr 86; Frnch II Prfcncy Awd; Soc Wrk.

FOURNIER, MOLLY; Missisquoi Valley Union HS; Swanton, VT; (Y); 4-H; School Play; Yrbk Stf; High Hon Roll; Hon Roll; Cmmnctns.

FOURNIER, PAULA; Sacred Heart HS; Newport, VT; (Y); Am Leg Aux Girls St; SADD; Pres Soph Cls; Rep Stu Cncl; JV Bsktbl; Var Sftbl; High Hon Roll; Hon Roll; NHS; Early Chldhd Ed.

FREDERICK, SARAH A; Vermont Acad; Saxtons River, VT; (S); 1/65; Math Tm; Speech Tm; Lit Mag; Rep Soph Cls; Rep Jr Cls; Var Lcrss; JV Var Socr; High Hon Roll; School Musical; 1st Alt In Japan-U S Senate Schlrshp Prog 86; Cum Laude Hnr Scty 86.

FRENCH, SUSAN; Burlington HS; Burlington, VT; (Y); Church Yth Grp; Dance Clb; French Clb; Var Powder Puff Ftbl; Var Trk; Im Vllybl; Hon Roll; NHS; Awd Exclnc Typng; U Of Vermont; Lbrl Arts.

FROST, ERIC B; Lake Region Union HS; W Glover, VT; (Y); 11/89; Rep Am Leg Boys St; FFA; Math Tm; Pres Science Clb; Ski Clb; Hon Roll; NHS; Camera Clb; Cmnty Wkr; Intnl Clb; Pres Acadmc Fitns Awd 86; 1st Pl UVM Math Cont 85-86; 1st ST Dairy Prodcts Judg 86; Rennselaer Polytech; Engrng.

GAFFNEY, DONALD; Rice Memorial HS; Williston, VT; (Y); 8/144; Am Leg Boys St; Boy Scts; Debate Tm; Math Clb; Scholastic Bowl; JV Bsktbl; Var Ftbl; Var Trk; High Hon Roll; NHS; Phrmclgy.

GAGE, JENNIFER REID; Burr & Burton Seminary; Manchester Center, VT; (Y); 13/65; Church Yth Grp; Ski Clb; Var Socr; JV Tennis; JV Trk; Im Vllybl; High Hon Roll; Hon Roll; Cert Of Merit In Frnch 84 & 85; Rcgntn By Gvrnr Of VT For Attndg Camp Dybrk 85-86.

GAGNE, GLENN D; Spaulding HS; Graniteville, VT; (Y); Am Leg Boys St; Pres Chess Clb; Church Yth Grp; Office Aide; Mrchg Band; Nwsp Rptr; Nwsp Stf; Lit Mag; JV Socr; JV Trk; Governors Inst Of Intl Affairs 85; St Michaels Coll; Polit Sci.

GAGNON, RICHARD; Woodstock Union HS; Woodstock, VT; (S); Boy Scts; SADD; Yrbk Stf; NHS; Ntl Merit SF; Ovrll Bst Lang Stu 83-84; Frgn Exch Stu Fr; U Of AZ; Lang Mjr.

GALLAGHER, BRIAN; Lyndon Inst; Lyndonville, VT; (Y); Church Yth Grp; Cmnty Wkr; Bsktbl; Crs Cntry; Trk; Hon Roll; Prfct Atten Awd; Ski Patrl 84-87; Close-Up Clb 86.

GALLO, PAULA; Mount Saint Joseph Acad; Rutland, VT; (Y); 22/75; Church Yth Grp; Dance Clb; Drama Clb; Latin Clb; Spanish Clb; SADD; Stage Crew; Yrbk Stf; Elks Awd; Hon Roll; Psychlgy.

GALLUZZO, SARA; Chelsea HS; Corinth, VT; (Y); French Clb; FBLA; JV Bsktbl; 2nd Pl Bus Mth & ST FBLA Convntn 86; Acctg.

GAMMELL, PEGGY; St Johnsbury Acad; Saint Johnsbury, VT; (Y); Cmnty Wkr; French Clb; Girl Scts; Sftbl; Lyndon ST Coll; Elem Ed.

GARAND, BRIAN; Spaulding HS; Barre, VT; (Y); 59/259; Key Clb; Rep Frsh Cls; Var Lcrss; Var Tennis; Hon Roll; Top 10 Pct UVT Mth Tst 86; VT All Star Rifle Tm 86; U VT; Mth.

GARAND, MARK A; Spaulding HS; Barre, VT; (Y); Am Leg Boys St; VP Key Clb; Var L Socr; Var JV Trk; Hon Roll; Law.

GARANT III, HERVE I; Colchester HS; Colchester, VT; (Y); 1/210; Varsity Clb; Var Capt Crs Cntry; Var Capt Trk; Gov Hon Prg Awd; High Hon Roll; NHS; Val; Crs Cntry Ski Var Capt 82-86; Dartmouth Coll; Engrng.

GARDINER, CLAIRE C; Burlington HS; S Burlington, VT; (Y); #2 In Class; AFS; Aud/Vis; Drama Clb; Model UN; School Musical; School Play; Ftbl; Latin Clb; Trk; High Hon Roll; Howard Ed Prz 86; Quinn Lascoumes Awd In Frnch 86; Thomas J Watson Mem Schlrshp 86; U Of Stirling Scotland; Cmp Sci.

GARDNER, MATT; Mt Anthony Union HS; Pownal, VT; (Y); 4-H; FFA; Ftbl; Hon Roll; UVM; Vet.

GARMON, YVETTE; Woodstock Union HS; Woodstock, VT; (Y); Church Yth Grp; SADD; Stage Crew; Var JV Cheerleading; Var Diving; Var Gym; Var JV Socr; Var Swmmng; Var Trk; Phys Educ Ftns Awd 83-84; CT Coll; Councing.

GARROW, LESLIE; Richford JR SR HS; Richford, VT; (Y); 10/28; Am Leg Aux Girls St; FHA; Chorus; Concert Band; Nwsp Stf; Yrbk Ed-Chief; Pres Jr Cls; Pres Sr Cls; VP Rep Stu Cncl; Var L Bsktbl; Miss VT Teen Pgnt 84; VT Stu Asstnce Corp 82-86; Disabld Amer Schlrshp 86; Wright Stetsn Schlrshp 86; U Of NH; Math.

GATES, CHERYL; Bettows Free Acad Fairfax; Fairfax, VT; (Y); 7/53; Am Leg Aux Girls St; Yrbk Stf; VP Pres Stu Cncl; Var Capt Bsktbl; Var Capt Fld Hcky; Var Capt Sftbl; High Hon Roll; NHS; Dance Clb; Varsity Clb; MVP Field Hockey & Bsktbl 85-86; Mst Ath; BFA Clb Scholar; Stu Cncl Awd; Pro Wmns Clb Awd 86; Sthrn CT ST U; Phys Ed.

GATES, SCOTT; Enousburg Falls HS; Bakersfield, VT; (Y); Am Leg Boys St; FBLA; Rep Frsh Cls; Rep Soph Cls; Rep Jr Cls; Rep Stu Cncl; JV Var Bsbl; JV Var Bsktbl; Socr; Hon Roll; Stu Advsry 83-85; Amer Lgn Boys St; Future Bus Ldrs Of Amer; Fresh,Soph,& JR Cls Rep; Stu Cncl; Hnr Roll.

GAULIN, BRENDA; Rice Memorial HS; S Burlington, VT; (Y); Church Yth Grp; Varsity Clb; Chorus; Variety Show; Socr; Sftbl; Trk; St Michaels; Accntnt.

GAWRYS, BRENDA; Rutland HS; Rutland, VT; (Y); Church Yth Grp; 4-H; Chorus; JV Golf; Var Sftbl; Hon Roll; NHS; Queens Coll; Fshn Dsgn.

GEBO, MELISSA; Mount Abraham UHS HS; Bristol, VT; (Y); 32/118; Drama Clb; VP Pres SADD; Band; Chorus; Off Soph Cls; Var Trk; High Hon Roll; Church Yth Grp; Teachers Aide; Concert Band; Hugh O Brien Yth Found 85; GMTI Comptn 84-85; Adv Plcmnt Engl 86; Theatre Arts.

GELBAR, EDWARD; Mt St Josephs HS; Rutland, VT; (Y); Varsity Clb; Band; Concert Band; Variety Show; JV Var Ftbl; NHS; Key Clb; Science Clb; Pep Band; Hon Roll; Gold Medl VT ST Sci Fair 85; Law Enfrcmnt.

GERACE, DONNA; Burlington HS; Burlington, VT; (Y); Band; Var L Bsktbl; Var L Socr; Var L Trk; ST Chmp 400m Sprnt Trck 85&86; Service Acad; Geolgy.

GERVIA, MATT; Colchester HS; South Hero, VT; (Y); Art Clb; Boy Scts; 4-H; FFA; Socr; Trk; Farmng.

GINGRAS, PAULA; Williamstown JR SR HS; Williamstown, VT; (Y); Am Leg Aux Girls St; VP FBLA; Chorus; Church Choir; School Play; Pres Jr Cls; JV Bsktbl; Mgr(s); High Hon Roll; Hon Roll; Green Mount Teen Inst Drugs And Alchl 84; Close Up 85; Elem Ed.

GOFF, F LEWIS; Woodstock Union HS; Woodstock, VT; (Y); 15/95; Am Leg Boys St; Boy Scts; Church Yth Grp; Debate Tm; Model UN; Scholastic Bowl; Pres Soph Cls; Pres Jr Cls; Stu Cncl; Var Ice Hcky; Class Of 1922 Schlrshp 86; St Lawrence U; Engl.

GOGLIA, MIKE; Rice Memorial HS; Shelburne, VT; (Y); 70/150; Boy Scts; JV Var Ftbl; Var Ftbl; Mgr(s); Var Trk; Harvard; Bus.

GOLDBERG, LISA; Rochester HS; Lynchburg, VA; (Y); Camera Clb; FBLA; Teachers Aide; Varsity Clb; Chorus; School Play; Yrbk Phtg; Yrbk Stf; Cheerleading; Sftbl; Hugh O Brian Yth Fndtn 85; Gvrnr Yth Ldrshp Conf Alchl & Sfty 85; Fshn Mrch.

GOLDING, KARL; Lyndon Inst; Lyndonville, VT; (Y); French Clb; Red Cross Aide; Spanish Clb; Ftbl; Trk; VICA & MVP Ftbl 85-86; ST Troopr.

GOODMAN, CHRISTINE; Black River HS; Ludlow, VT; (S); 6/40; Drama Clb; Trs Pep Clb; Chorus; Mrchg Band; Variety Show; Mgr Yrbk Stf; Trs Sr Cls; Capt Var Bsktbl; Capt Var Socr; Trs NHS; All-State VT Sccr Team 84-85; All-Oppnt Team Bsktbll 85; All-Oppnt Team Sftbll 85; UVM; Bus.

GOULD, LORI; Windsor HS; Windsor, VT; (Y); 9/65; Pep Clb; Ski Clb; Color Guard; Yrbk Stf; Stu Cncl; Fld Hcky; Sftbl; Hon Roll; NHS; Champlain Coll; Bus Mgmt.

GRABOWSKI, JILL; Mount Anthony Union HS; Bennington, VT; (Y); Ski Clb; Cheerleading; Fld Hcky; Sftbl; Trk; Hon Roll; NHS; NEDT Awd; Educ.

GRAVELLE, ASHLEY; Windsor HS; Windsor, VT; (Y); 5/56; Am Leg Aux Girls St; 4-H; Ski Clb; Concert Band; Mrchg Band; Sec Sr Cls; VP Stu Cncl; Capt Var Fld Hcky; Capt Var Timer; Elks Awd; Stu Mnth Nal Hnr Soc; Ani Sci.

GRAY, CHERYL; North Country Union HS; Newport, VT; (S); 14/260; VP DECA; Score Keeper; Socr; Trk; High Hon Roll; VP NHS; 1st Ovrll Gen Mktg DECA 85; Acctg 85; 3rd Tm Disply DECA 85; New Hampshire Coll; Acctg.

GRAY, TRAVIS; St Johnsbury Acad; St Johnsbury, VT; (Y); 16/160; Drama Clb; French Clb; SADD; School Musical; School Play; Stage Crew; Variety Show; Nwsp Rptr; Yrbk Stf; High Hon Roll; Hotel Mgmt.

GREENE, LAURA; Mount Anthony Union HS; Shaftsbury, VT; (Y); 6/305; Church Yth Grp; Cmnty Wkr; 4-H; GAA; Spanish Clb; Varsity Clb; Trk; 4-H Awd; Hon Roll; NHS; Spn Awd 86; Eng Awd 86; Lat Awd 86.

GREENE, MISSY; Mount Anthony Union HS; Shaftsbury, VT; (Y); French Clb; Ski Clb; Yrbk Stf; Rep Jr Cls; Rep Stu Cncl; Var Fld Hcky; Var Trk; Hon Roll; VT ST Long Jump Champ 85; Fld Hcky, Molly Stark Lg All Str 85; MVP Fld Hockey, High Scorer 84.

GREENIP, TRICIA; Green Mountain Union HS; Chester, VT; (Y); Library Aide; Band; Chorus; Concert Band; Rep Frsh Cls; Var Cheerleading; JV Var Fld Hcky; JV Var Sftbl; Hon Roll; Slvr GM 86; Recrtnl Mgmt.

GRIGGS, JENNIFER; Woodstock Union HS; Woodstock, VT; (Y); 14/106; Am Leg Aux Girls St; Math Tm; Teachers Aide; Yrbk Stf; Var L Socr; High Hon Roll; Hon Roll; Jr NHS; NHS; Jhnsn & Wales Coll; Bus Mngmnt.

GUMIENNY, JULIE; Rice HS; Shelbourne, VT; (Y); 20/144; Am Leg Aux Girls St; Chorus; Yrbk Stf; Var Capt Tennis; Frshmn Orntatn Pgm; Chrstn Ldrshp.

HADDEN, KATHERINE S; Vermont Acad; Grafton, VT; (S); 4/60; Chorus; Yrbk Stf; Ed Lit Mag; Var Socr; Var Tennis; Var Trk; High Hon Roll; Hon Roll; NCTE Awd; Breadloaf Wrtrs Conf Prtcpnt 86; Gvrnrs Arts Inst Prtcpnt 85; Wrtr.

HALL, SUELLEN; Montpelier U 32 HS; Montpelier, VT; (Y); VP 4-H; Office Aide; Concert Band; JV Var Cheerleading; JV Var Sftbl; Hon Roll; Central VT Rotary Scholar 86; Outstndng Contribtn Band 86; Champlain Coll; Legal Sec.

HAMEL, DARCIE; Lyndon Inst; Lyndonville, VT; (Y); Church Yth Grp; French Clb; Var Fld Hcky; Var Trk; High Hon Roll; Hon Roll; NHS.

HAMILTON, ANDREW J; Middlebury Union HS; Middlebury, VT; (Y); Nwsp Stf; Ed Lit Mag; Capt Trk; NHS; Ftbl; JV Socr; Grinnell Coll; Engl.

HAMMERLUND, ERIK; Brattleboro Union HS; Brattleboro, VT; (Y); Am Leg Boys St; Pres VICA; VP Ftbl; Var L Trk; Hon Roll.

HANCOCK, CYNTHIA J; North Country Union HS; Newport, VT; (Y); 16/256; Church Yth Grp; German Clb; Varsity Clb; Band; Chorus; Mrchg Band; Pep Band; Bsktbl; Hon Roll; NHS; BPW Schlrshp, Am Leg Schlrshp, Schlrshp Pin 86; Castleton ST Coll; Acctg.

HARDY, CHRISTOPHER; Mt Anthony Union HS; N Bennington, VT; (Y); 9/300; French Clb; Ski Clb; Rep Stu Cncl; Var Bsbl; High Hon Roll; NHS; Prfct Atten Awd; Engrng.

HARDY, CHRISTOPHER; North Country Union HS; Newport, VT; (Y); Aud/Vis; Key Clb; Band; Chorus; Mrchg Band; Stage Crew; Rep Stu Cncl; Bk Knwldg Pn 85; SR All-Amer Hl Fm Bnd Hnrs 86; Msc Ltr 86; Music.

HARLOW, KELLY; Woodstock Union HS; Woodstock, VT; (Y); Cmnty Wkr; GAA; SADD; School Play; Yrbk Stf; Fld Hcky; Mgr(s); Var Sftbl; Im Vllybl; Hon Roll; Outstndng Spnsh II & III Stud 81-86; Mdl Cngrss 85-86; Spnsh.

HARRINGTON, BRENDA; Woodstock Union HS; N Pomfret, VT; (Y); Pres Band; Jazz Band; Mrchg Band; Pep Band; Capt Bsktbl; Capt Socr; Sftbl; High Hon Roll; Hon Roll; NHS; Robert E Dailey Athl & Gary Hersey Memrl Athl Schlrshps 86; Sccr MVP Awds 85-8l; Hofstra U; Comp Sci.

HARRINGTON, FRANK; Mt Anthony Union HS; Bennington, VT; (Y); 11/273; Ski Clb; Spanish Clb; Trs SADD; Jazz Band; Pres Soph Cls; VP Jr Cls; Rep Stu Cncl; JV Golf; Hon Roll; NHS; Elec Engrng.

HARRINGTON, JAMES; Jesgennes Union HS; Vergennes, VT; (Y); Chess Clb; CC Of VT Archtctrl 85; VR Tech Coll; Engrng.

HARRINGTON, JEFFREY S; Vermont Acad; Saxtons River, VT; (S); 3/70; French Clb; Math Tm; Var Bsbl; Var Ice Hcky; Capt Socr; High Hon Roll.

HART, KIM; Fair Haven Union HS; Castleton, VT; (Y); Drama Clb; SADD; Band; Chorus; Concert Band; Mrchg Band; Pep Band; Hon Roll; Air Force Acad; Jrnlst.

HATCH, WILLIAM; Rice Memorial HS; S Burlington, VT; (Y); 35/155; Variety Show; Sec Trs Sr Cls; Ftbl; Var Golf; Var Ice Hcky; Mgr(s); Hon Roll; U Of VT; Educ.

HAYNES, JULIE; Mt Anthony Unionm HS; Bennington, VT; (Y); Cmnty Wkr; French Clb; Model UN; Political Wkr; Ski Clb; SADD; Chorus; Stu Cncl; Mgr(s); Hon Roll; Close Up 84-87; Met Pres Regan Sem 86; Congrssnl 84; Pol Sci.

HAYNES, MARK; Mt Anthony Union HS; Shaftsbury, VT; (Y); 31/350; Spanish Clb; Var L Bsktbl; Var Golf; Var Capt Socr; Vllybl; Wt Lftg; High Hon Roll; Hon Roll; NHS; Envrnmntl Sci.

HAZELTINE, TAMMIE; Green Mountain Union HS; Chester, VT; (Y); Church Yth Grp; Drama Clb; Pres 4-H; Concert Band; Swing Chorus; Rep Stu Cncl; Socr; Sftbl; 4-H Awd; Hon Roll; Bronze Medalst Olympiada Cntst Spkn Russian 84; Physcl Therpy.

HEATON, GARDNER; Harwood Union HS; Warren, VT; (Y); Am Leg Boys St; Art Clb; Ski Clb; Crs Cntry; Socr; Trk; High Hon Roll; NHS; Williams Ski Trhpy 84; Outstndng Physcl Sci Stud 84; Bio Chem 85-86.

HEBERT, JENNIFER; Mt Saint Joseph Acad; Rutland, VT; (Y); 11/75; SADD; Varsity Clb; Yrbk Stf; Var Cheerleading; Trk; NHS; Drama Clb; Key Clb; Science Clb; Jazz, Tap Dancr; Psych.

HECHT, DEBORA; Rice Memorial HS; Winooski, VT; (Y); Pep Clb; Pres Science Clb; Spanish Clb; Variety Show; Stat Bsktbl; Ftbl; Var L Trk; JV Vllybl; High Hon Roll; NHS; Bradley Spec Scholar 86; Bradley U; Bus Adm.

HEINECKEN, DAWN M; Middlebury Union HS; Middlebury, VT; (Y); 8/165; Am Leg Aux Girls St; Scholastic Bowl; School Musical; Lit Mag; Var L Fld Hcky; Var L Trk; DAR Awd; NHS; Aud/Vis; Drama Clb; Films Studies.

HEMENWAY, CLYSTA; Missisquoi Valley Union HS; Santon, VT; (Y); Office Aide; Teachers Aide; School Play; Nwsp Rptr; Nwsp Stf; Yrbk Ed-Chief; Yrbk Stf; Hon Roll; Boyd Schl; Journlsm.

HEPBURN, LU ANNE; Williamstown HS; Williamstown, VT; (Y); Cmnty Wkr; Computer Clb; French Clb; VP Ski Clb; Teachers Aide; Pres VICA; Stu Cncl; JV Fld Hcky; Mgr Score Keeper; Cit Awd; Alumni Awd 86; Comp Awd Coop 86; Vermont CC; Sys Oper.

HERRLICH, KATHERINE; Colchester HS; Colchester, VT; (Y); 3/210; Art Clb; Math Tm; Model UN; Band; Pep Band; School Play; Trk; Sal; Vermont Schlrs Awd 86; Raymond R Mooney Awd 86; U VT; Hist.

HILL, KATHERINE; Burlington HS; Burlington, VT; (Y); 1/257; Latin Clb; Math Tm; Stu Cncl; Var L Crs Cntry; Var L Trk; Bausch & Lomb Sci Awd; High Hon Roll; NHS; Church Yth Grp; Model UN; Rensselaer Mdl 86; VT ST Math Cntst 3rd 86; Soc Of Womn Engrs Awd 86.

HILL, KRISSY; Spaulding HS; Barre, VT; (Y); 45/262; Stu Cncl; Powder Puff Ftbl; Score Keeper; Good Kid Awd 86.

HOAGUE JR, RONALD; Missisquoi Valley Union HS; Swanton, VT; (Y); Teachers Aide; Yrbk Stf; JV Bsbl; Var Wt Lftg; Hon Roll; Graphic Dsgnr.

HOARD, THERESA; Mt Anthony Union HS; Bennington, VT; (Y); 56/274; FBLA; Band; Drm Mjr(t); Mrchg Band; Var Capt Cheerleading; High Hon Roll; Hon Roll; Prfct Atten Awd; Bay Path JC; Trvl Adm.

HODGDON, CYNTHIA; Hartford HS; White River Jct, VT; (Y); Hon Roll; Mildred Kingsbury Awd 86; Best Sch Typst 86; High Schlrshp Sec 86; Hesser College; Sec.

HOLME, CHRIS; Green Mounain Union HS; Chester, VT; (Y); 2/70; Church Yth Grp; Drama Clb; Political Wkr; School Musical; Rep Stu Cncl; JV Bsktbl; JV Var Socr; JV Tennis; Jr NHS; NHS.

HOLT, STEVE; Woodstock Union HS; Woodstock, VT; (Y); Intnl Clb; Latin Clb; Letterman Clb; Variety Show; Yrbk Stf; Var Ftbl; Capt Swmmng; Trk; Hon Roll; UVM.

HON, DEBBIE; Arlington Memorial HS; Arlington, VT; (Y); Dance Clb; Chorus; School Musical; School Play; Variety Show; Yrbk Stf; High Hon Roll; Hon Roll; Prfct Atten Awd; U Of Vermont; Sci.

HOVEY, GREGORY; Concord HS; N Concord, VT; (S); 3/20; Am Leg Boys St; Debate Tm; Math Clb; Math Tm; Model UN; Scholastic Bowl; Yrbk Stf; Pres Soph Cls; Dnfth Awd; NHS; Acad All Amer 85-86; U Of VT; Wldlfe Bio.

HOVEY, SAMANTHA; Concord HS; Panama City Beach, FL; (Y); 5/20; FBLA; Teachers Aide; Varsity Clb; Bsktbl; Socr; Sftbl; Elks Awd; High Hon Roll; Pres Clsrm Wash DC 85; Yth Ldrshp Conf 86; Roger Sorrell Awd 86; Gulf Coast Coll; Accntng.

HOWARTH, DEBBIE; Chelsea HS; Corinth, VT; (Y); Church Yth Grp; French Clb; FBLA; JV Bsktbl; Bus.

HOWE, JEFF; Mt Anthony Union HS; Bennington, VT; (Y); Church Yth Grp; French Clb; SADD; Var Socr; Vllybl; Chem Engr.

HOWLAND, ANGELA; Hartford HS; Morgan, VT; (Y); 2/102; AFS; Am Leg Aux Girls St; Hosp Aide; Teachers Aide; Rep Stu Cncl; High Hon Roll; Hon Roll; NHS; Pres Schlr; Sal; Awd Excllnc Frgn Lang 86; Middlebury Coll; Spnsh.

HUDSON, CHARLES; Rice Memorial HS; Cambridge, VT; (Y); Church Yth Grp; Drama Clb; Chorus; Church Choir; School Musical; School Play; Variety Show; Nwsp Rptr; Nwsp Stf; High Hon Roll; New Englnd JR Sci & Hmntys Sympsm 86; Archlgy.

HUFFMAN, JACOB N; Burlington HS; Burlington, VT; (Y); Art Clb; French Clb; Model UN; Ski Clb; Trk; Hon Roll; NHS; 1st WVMT Arts Cntst 85; Cheap Art Enclave 85-86; Tufts Schl; Fine Art.

HULL, PAMELA; Enosburg Falls HS; Enosburg Falls, VT; (Y); FFA; FHA; Variety Show; Yrbk Stf; Trs Jr Cls; Stu Cncl; JV Var Bsktbl; JV Var Sftbl; High Hon Roll; Prfct Atten Awd; Exc In Sci; Achvt Typg I; Exc Frnch III.

HUNT, TAMMY; Bellows Free Acad; Fairfield, VT; (Y); French Clb; Office Aide; SADD; Rep Stu Cncl; Bsktbl; Cheerleading; Sftbl; Trk; Cit Awd; Hon Roll; Salem Coll; Mdcl Tech.

HUNTER, LINDA; Brattleboro Union HS; Brattleboro, VT; (Y); Church Yth Grp; Model UN; SADD; Band; Drill Tm; Jazz Band; Mrchg Band; Pep Band; School Musical; School Play; Lib Arts.

HUNTOON, SHANIN; Oxbow HS; Bradford, VT; (Y); Office Aide; Teachers Aide; Hon Roll; Prfct Atten Awd; Champlain Coll; Sec.

HUTCHINS, KEVIN; Milton HS; Milton, VT; (Y); 1/141; Computer Clb; Drama Clb; Band; Chorus; School Musical; Rep Stu Cncl; High Hon Roll; Hon Roll; Ntl Merit SF.

HUTCHINS, NANCY; Vengennes Union HS; Vergennes, VT; (Y); 17/125; 4-H; Jr Cls; Sr Cls; Socr; Sftbl; Cit Awd; 4-H Awd; Hon Roll; Peer Cnslr 85-87; U VT; Phys Ther.

HUTTON, JACQUELINE; Brattleboro Union HS; Brattleboro, VT; (Y); Exploring; French Clb; German Clb; Red Cross Aide; Speech Tm; School Musical; Pres Frsh Cls; Capt Tennis; Hon Roll; Ntl Merit Ltr; Accntnt.

HYZER, GARY; Mill River U HS; Wallingford, VT; (Y); 3/129; Am Leg Boys St; Drama Clb; Band; Chorus; NHS; Ntl Merit Ltr; St Schlr; Thesps; Concert Band; Jazz Band; William E G & Helen B Mitchell Awd; Arion Music Fndtn Awd; VT ST Music Scholar; IN U; Music.

JABLONSKI, VICTORIA M; Mill River Union HS; Clarendon, VT; (Y); 17/131; Drama Clb; Library Aide; Band; Stage Crew; Yrbk Phtg; Yrbk Stf; Hon Roll; NHS; Ntl Merit Ltr; U Of VT; Politc Sci.

JACOBS, PAMELA; Richford JR SR HS; Richford, VT; (Y); 15/27; Camera Clb; Church Yth Grp; Model UN; Church Choir; Nwsp Phtg; Yrbk Phtg; Yrbk Stf; Socr; Hon Roll; Prfct Atten Awd; Lgsltv Art Awd 85; John Colver Awd 86; Chmpln Coll; Exec Scrtry.

JACOBSON, BRITT; Burlington HS; Burlington, VT; (Y); Church Yth Grp; Cmnty Wkr; Intnl Clb; Latin Clb; Ski Clb; Teachers Aide; Varsity Clb; Yrbk Stf; Sec VP Stu Cncl; Var Tennis; Psych.

JAFFE, PAUL; Burlington HS; Burlington, VT; (Y); Jazz Band; Ice Hcky; Hon Roll; Lgl Study Awd 86; Boston U; Law.

JERRY, JOHN; Enosburg Falls HS; Sheldon, VT; (Y); Exploring; VICA; Band; Jazz Band; Mrchg Band; JV Bsbl; JV Socr; Vrmnt Tech Coll; Crpntry.

JODOIN, STEPHANIE; Burlington HS; Burlington, VT; (Y); Spanish Clb; JV Var Bsktbl; JV Sftbl; Var Trk; High Hon Roll; Hon Roll; NHS; Acctg & Data Proc I & Ofc Proc 84-85; Acctg II & Adv Ofc Proc 85-86; Plymouth ST Coll; Acctg.

JOHNSON, JEANETTE; Essex Junction HS; Essex Jct, VT; (Y); Church Yth Grp; Hon Roll; Erly Chldhd Ed.

JOHNSON, KATHY M; Lake Region Union HS; Orleans, VT; (Y); 1/88; Church Yth Grp; English Clb; Pep Clb; Band; Mrchg Band; Off Soph Cls; Off Jr Cls; Mgr Sftbl; Bausch & Lomb Sci Awd; Gov Hon Prg Awd; Ltr Commndtn Natl Merit Scholar Pgm 84; U VT; Nrsng.

JONES, CHRISTINE; Fair Haven Union HS; Fair Haven, VT; (Y); 13/132; Am Leg Aux Girls St; Cmnty Wkr; Ski Clb; Spanish Clb; SADD; Yrbk Phtg; Rep Stu Cncl; Capt Cheerleading; Cit Awd; NHS; U VT; Bus Admin.

JOSEPH, CINDY; North Country Union HS; Derby Line, VT; (Y); 3/249; Am Leg Aux Girls St; Band; Var Crs Cntry; JP Sousa Awd; Pres NHS; Ntl Merit Schol; SADD; Concert Band; Mrchg Band; Frdrc Chpn Awd 86; Engl Hon 86; 2nd Pl Nrth Cntry Ntl Math Tst 86; Wellesley Coll; Biochem.

JURGIEWICH, MIKE; Mt Anthony Union HS; Bennington, VT; (Y); 25/263; French Clb; Ski Clb; Socr; High Hon Roll; NHS; NEDT Awd; 2nd Pl Natl Fld Archrs Assoc ST Chmpnshp 86; U ME Orono; Frstry Engrg.

KALLEM, TIMOTHY S; South Burlington HS; S Burlington, VT; (Y); Key Clb; Stage Crew; Variety Show; Nwsp Rptr; Nwsp Sprt Ed; Vllybl; Hon Roll; NHS; Ntl Merit SF; U VT; Hist Georgraphy.

KARDAS, SHANNON; Burr & Burton Seminary HS; Dorset, VT; (Y); #4 In Class; SADD; Band; Concert Band; Jazz Band; Yrbk Stf; Var Cheerleading; Var Fld Hcky; JV Mgr(s); JV Sftbl; Vllybl; Hugh Obrien Yth Ldr Semnr 85-86; Act 51 Comtee 85-86; Grn Mtn Teen Inst 85; Pol Sci.

KAYHART, STEPHEN E; Vergennes Union HS; Vergennes, VT; (S); 33/101; 4-H; FFA; Ski Clb; Band; Mrchg Band; Bsbl; L Wrstlng; Hon Roll; ST FFA Ofcr 85-86; Natl FFA Dry Shwmnshp Gld Emblm Wnr 83-84; Virginia Tech; Dairy Sci.

KEEP, CYNDEE; Hartford HS; Quechee, VT; (Y); 20/100; French Clb; Teachers Aide; High Hon Roll; Hon Roll; Lion Awd; Tchrs Assn Schlrshp 86; Acad All-Amer Schlrs Awd 85; Former Wmns Clb Schlrshp 86; U VT; Early Chldhd Ed.

KEITH, MICHAEL JAMES; Otter Valley Union HS; Brandon, VT; (Y); Church Yth Grp; Drama Clb; Ski Clb; Thesps; Off Frsh Cls; Bsbl; Bsktbl; Socr; Prfct Atten Awd; Plymouth ST; Bus.

KELLEY, CHRIS; Rice Memorial HS; Burlington, VT; (Y); 25/155; Nwsp Rptr; Nwsp Sprt Ed; Rep Sr Cls; JV Stat Bsktbl; Var Mgr Ftbl; Mgr(s); Var Trk; Hon Roll; Cmnctns.

KELLEY, MATTHEW; St Johnsbury Acad; Saint Johnsbury, VT; (Y); Am Leg Boys St; Nwsp Ed-Chief; Nwsp Rptr; Stu Cncl; JV Bsbl; Var Bsktbl; High Hon Roll; NHS; Bus.

KELLEY, NAAMA; Twinfield Union HS; Plainfield, VT; (Y); Sec Pres Art Clb; French Clb; Chorus; Variety Show; Yrbk Phtg; Hon Roll; NHS; NEDT Awd; New England Yng Wrtrs 86; 2nd Prize Norwich U Art Show 86; Hnrb Mntn Poetry Trumbull Arts Fest 84.

KEMP, DAVID; St Johnsbury Acad; Saint Johnsbury, VT; (Y); Am Leg Boys St; Pres Church Yth Grp; Cmnty Wkr; Letterman Clb; Spanish Clb; Variety Show; Var L Bsbl; Var L Bsktbl; Var L Ftbl; Wt Lftg; Crmnl Jstice.

KENNEDY, CAROL; Chelsea HS; Chelsea, VT; (Y); Debate Tm; NFL; Varsity Clb; Band; School Play; Rep Soph Cls; Rep Jr Cls; Var Fld Hcky; Mgr(s); Hon Roll; Excllnc Algbr II 85-86; Hghst Achvmnt Stdy Soc Stds 85-86; Math.

KENNEDY, HEATHER; Mt Anthony Union HS; Bennington, VT; (Y); Ski Clb; Yrbk Phtg; Trs Frsh Cls; Crs Cntry; Fld Hcky; Church Yth Grp; Drama Clb; Model UN; Pep Clb; Chorus; JR Nastar Alipine Skiing 8th Pl Wnnr All VT 84-85; Vts Mst Imprvd Field Hockey 83; Arctctr.

KENYON, AMY; Mt Anthony Union HS; N Bennington, VT; (Y); 24/270; Camera Clb; Church Yth Grp; Chorus, Nwsp Stf; Yrbk Stf; High Hon Roll; Hon Roll; NHS; Dolalrs Schlrs Schrlshp 86; Catherine Groran Awd 86; Clarion U; Acctng.

KINNEY, JILL; Richford HS; W Berkshire, VT; (Y); 15/30; Camera Clb; Cmnty Wkr; Computer Clb; Debate Tm; Drama Clb; FHA; Chorus; Mrchg Band; School Play; Nwsp Stf; Chmstry Acad Awd 3rd Pl 85; FHA Ckng Awd 85; Champlain Coll.

KINSMAN, JENNIFER; Mt St Joseph HS; Rutland, VT; (Y); SADD; Yrbk Stf; JV Var Bsktbl; JV Crs Cntry; Elks Awd; Bus.

KIRBY, DAVID; Burlington HS; South Hero, VT; (Y); Boy Scts; Church Yth Grp; CAP; Spanish Clb; Mgr Ftbl; Trk; Aerospc Engrng.

KLITTICH, DEBORAH; Champlain Valley Union HS; Shelb0rne, VT; (Y); 24/245; Am Leg Aux Girls St; Church Yth Grp; Key Clb; Chorus; Church Choir; Var Capt Crs Cntry; Var L Trk; High Hon Roll; Kiwanis Awd; NHS; Liberty U; Tele Comm.

KNAPP, STEVE; Arlington Memorial HS; Arlington, VT; (Y); Church Yth Grp; Band; Chorus; Church Choir; Jazz Band; School Musical; Variety Show; Yrbk Phtg; Socr; High Hon Roll; Wrote & Sang A Professionally Recorded Song That Was Played By Many Radio Stas In VT, NY, & Boston.

KOVOLICK, KATE; Otter Valley HS; Pittsford, VT; (Y); 34/104; Am Leg Aux Girls St; 4-H; Chorus; Madrigals; Rutland Cnty Coll St Joseph Scholar 86; Brandon Aux Scholar 86; Pittsford Wmns Clb Scholar 86; Coll St Joseph; Med Asst.

KRAMER, DOUGLAS; Rutland HS; Rutland, VT; (Y); 5/193; Boy Scts; Church Yth Grp; Debate Tm; Science Clb; SADD; Rep Frsh Cls; Pres High Hon Roll; NHS; Excllnc Eng 82; Pres Acadmc Ftnss Awd 86; Castleton ST Clg; Acctg.

KRAMER, SUSAN; Harwood Union HS; Waitsfield, VT; (Y); Pres German Clb; Teachers Aide; Var Diving; Var Socr; Var Swmmng; Var Tennis; High Hon Roll; Hon Roll; Exchng Ldr-Grmny 85 & 86; Outstndng Grmn Awd 86; FL Isnt Tech; Marine Bio.

KREIDEL, THOMAS; Chelsee HS; Tunbridge, VT; (Y); Debate Tm; FBLA; Rep Jr Cls; Pres Stu Cncl; Bus.

LA BORIE, DARREN; St Johnsbuury Acad; Mc Indoe Falls, VT; (Y); Am Leg Boys St; Debate Tm; Scholastic Bowl; School Musical; Nwsp Rptr; Rep Stu Cncl; Var Socr; NHS; Drama Clb; Math Clb; Natl Latn Exm 84; New England Math Leag Cert Merit 87; Dartmouth.

LA ROSE, DOMINIQUE; Blue Mountain Schl; Groton, VT; (Y); Church Yth Grp; Cmnty Wkr; FHA; Teachers Aide; Band; Chorus; Concert Band; Mrchg Band; Trs Frsh Cls; Swaggart U; Tchng.

LABANOWSKI, KURT; Mt Anthony Union HS; Bennington, VT; (Y); Ski Clb; Var Capt Ftbl; Var Trk; Wt Lftg; Ftbll MVP; All St Shrn Tm ST All Star 85-86; Trck UT ST Shotput Qulfld New Englnd; Albany ST U; Lbrl Arts.

LACEY, DANIELLE; S Burlington HS; S Burlington, VT; (Y); 48/200; SADD; Band; Chorus; Variety Show; Var Capt Cheerleading; French Hon Soc; Hon Roll; NHS; Mst Spirit Awd Chrldng 85-86.

LAFAYETTE, ROBIN; Rice Memorial HS; Burlington, VT; (Y); Chorus; Church Choir; Yrbk Stf; Cheerleading; Hon Roll; U Of Vermont; Engr.

LAMARCHE, JULIE; Sacred Heart HS; Irasburg, VT; (S); FCA; Band; Jazz Band; Mrchg Band; Rep Stu Cncl; Var Bsktbl; Var Socr; Var Sftbl; Hon Roll; NHS; Elem Ed.

LAMBERT, BRUCE; Rice Memorial HS; Burling, VT; (Y); Boy Scts; Church Yth Grp; Letterman Clb; Pep Clb; Varsity Clb; Variety Show; Var Bsbl; Var L Ftbl; MVP Defense Ftbll 86-87; Ftbll Coaches Awd Mst Outstndg Plyr 86-87; Capt Ftbll Tm 86-87; FL ST U.

LAMELL, ROBERT; Peoples Acad; Morrisville, VT; (Y); 4/57; Scholastic Bowl; Trs Jr Cls; Trs Sr Cls; Pres Stu Cncl; Capt Bsbl; Capt Bsktbl; Capt Socr; DAR Awd; Trs NHS; VT Schlr 86; U Of VT; Acctng.

LAMONT, TAMMY; Lyndon Inst; West Burke, VT; (Y); Church Yth Grp; FHA; Hosp Aide; Ski Clb; Teachers Aide; Church Choir; Cheerleading; Sftbl; High Hon Roll; Hon Roll; Captain Of Jv Chrldng 82; Hmcmng Queen Frshmn Class 82; Captain Of Varsity Sftbl 85; Bankng.

LAMORE, MARTHA E; Drury SR HS; Stamford, VT; (Y); 24/180; Church Yth Grp; Cmnty Wkr; Chorus; Church Choir; Nwsp Rptr; Sec Stu Cncl; Trs Pom Pon; Hon Roll; NHS; Rotary Awd; U VT.

LANDON, TODD; Proctor HS; Proctor, VT; (Y); 15/53; Art Clb; Aud/Vis; Church Yth Grp; Cmnty Wkr; 4-H; FBLA; JV Var Bsktbl; Var Golf; 4-H Awd; Kiwanis Awd; Cnty & St Wnnr Petroleum Power & Forestry 85, Ctznshp 86; Engrng.

LANEUVILLE, KARA C; Rice Memorial HS; N Williston, VT; (Y); Church Yth Grp; Cmnty Wkr; Red Cross Aide; Sec Frsh Cls; Sec Soph Cls; Sec Jr Cls; Sec Stu Cncl; Fld Hcky; High Hon Roll; NHS; Real Est.

LANG, DEANNA; Worcester U 32 HS; Worcester, VT; (Y); 9/120; Church Yth Grp; Dance Clb; Drama Clb; Chorus; School Musical; High Hon Roll; Hon Roll; Chesamore Hnrs Schrlshp 86-87; Johnson ST Coll; Bus.

LANOUE, AMY; Lake Region HS; Barton, VT; (Y); Var DECA; Rep Soph Cls; Rep Jr Cls; Rep Stu Cncl; JV Fld Hcky; O Briens; Csmtlgy.

LAROCHE, REBECCA; Bellows Free Acad; Fairfax, VT; (Y); 1/52; Sec Drama Clb; French Clb; Pres Jr Cls; Pres Sr Cls; Sec NHS; Ntl Merit Ltr; Pres Schlr; Val; Math Tm; Sec Thesps; Watson Schol 86; VT Schol VSAC 86; Fraternal Coll Schlrshp 86; Govnrs Inst On Intl Affairs 85; Bates Coll; Poli Sci.

LARSON, ALFRED; Essex Junction Educational Center; Westford, VT; (Y); Var Ftbl; JV Trk; JV Wrstlng; VT Tech Coll; Archtctrl Dsgn.

LAVALLEE, KIM J; Champlain Valley Union HS; Richmond, VT; (Y); 179/231; Trs Church Yth Grp; Pres 4-H; Trs Girl Scts; Var Capt Cheerleading; Score Keeper; 4-H Awd; Hon Roll; Most Valuble Chrldr 86; Poller Bronze Medal 83; Vermont Costemotolgy; Hari Dres.

LAVOIE, MARLENE; Woodstock Union HS; Killington, VT; (Y); 16/95; SADD; Band; School Musical; Yrbk Stf; Var Lcrss; Var Socr; Hon Roll; Jr NHS; NHS; Spnsh I Awd For Being Bst In Clss Grde Wse 85-86; UVM Coll; Dntl Hygne.

LAWRENCE, NOEL; Essex Junction HS; Essex Jct, VT; (Y); 123/332; Aud/Vis; Computer Clb; Library Aide; Pres Political Wkr; Ski Clb; Trs Nwsp Stf; Ed Lit Mag; JV Tennis; JV Wrstlng; Creatv Wrtg Awd-Govr Of VT 85; Century III Ldrshp Schlrshp Wnnr 86; Polit Sci.

LAWSON, KELLY; Mt Anthony Union HS; Pownal, VT; (Y); 12/263; Off Am Leg Aux Girls St; Yrbk Stf; Stu Cncl; Stat Socr; Elks Awd; High Hon Roll; Lion Awd; NHS; Prfct Atten Awd; John R Wilson Scholar Trust 86; Pres Acad Fit Awd 86; Peer Cnslng 84-86; Cornell U; Pre-Law.

LAWYER, KIMBERLY; Enoxburg Falls HS; Enosburg Falls, VT; (Y); Am Leg Aux Girls St; FHA; Office Aide; Teachers Aide; Nwsp Ed-Chief; Yrbk Ed-Chief; Yrbk Stf; Frsh Cls; Stu Cncl; Mgr(s); Champlain Coll; Fash Merch.

LE BEAU, MICHAEL; Missisquoi Valley Union HS; Swanton, VT; (Y); Church Yth Grp; Debate Tm; Wt Lftg; USC; Chem.

LE BOEUF, MARY; Vergennes Union HS; Vergennes, VT; (Y); 2/100; Am Leg Aux Girls St; Band; Drm Mjr(t); School Musical; Pres Stu Cncl; JV Var Bsktbl; Var Tennis; High Hon Roll; Hon Roll; NHS; Darmouth Bk Clb Awd 86; U VT; Health.

LE CLAIR, COLLEEN; Windsor HS; Windsor, VT; (Y); Sec 4-H; French Clb; Ski Clb; Color Guard; Fld Hcky; Capt Sftbl; Chld Psych.

LEACH, ROSEMARY; Twinfield Union HS; Plainfield, VT; (Y); Dance Clb; French Clb; GAA; Acpl Chr; Chorus; Madrigals; Variety Show; Socr; Hon Roll; NHS; VT St Hnrs Wrtng 3rd Pl Wnr 85; All St Music Chorus 85; All New Engl Chorus 86.

LEBEL, TERI; Bellows Free Acad; St Albans, VT; (Y); JV Var Cheerleading; Hon Roll; Trinity Coll; Librl Arts.

LEBERT, MELISSA; Mt Anthony Union HS; North Benningto, VT; (Y); Church Yth Grp; Chorus; School Musical; Nwsp Rptr; Lit Mag; Trk; Hon Roll; NHS; Vrsty Trck Ltr 85-86; Acdmc Achvt Excllnc Engl 86; Acdmc Achvt Excllnc Frnch I 85; Jrnlsm.

LEBLANC, KIMBERLEE; Sacred Heart HS; Tampa, FL; (Y); 5/20; Drama Clb; Acpl Chr; Band; Chorus; Church Choir; Concert Band; Jazz Band; Madrigals; Mrchg Band; Trs Sr Cls; Outstndng Chrl Awd 86; Grad Hnrs 86; Rcvng Solos NE & All ST Msc Fest 84-86; U Of Southern FL; Msc Perf.

LECLERC, JOANNE; Spaulding HS; Barre, VT; (Y); French Clb; FBLA; JA; Teachers Aide; JV Bsktbl; Powder Puff Ftbl; JV Sftbl; Hon Roll; Bus Mgr.

LEMAY, JOANNE; Lyndon Inst; Lyndon, VT; (Y); Drama Clb; School Play; Yrbk Stf; Wrthy Stu Awd C Elis Lbby Awd 86; Schlrshp Pin 86; Champlain Coll; Exec Secty.

LEMIEUX, TODD; Champlain Valley Union HS; Williston, VT; (Y); Var Bsbl; Var Ice Hcky; Hon Roll; Bus Mgmt.

LENAHAN, JOE; St Johnsbury Acad; St Johnsbury, VT; (Y); Cmnty Wkr; French Clb; Pep Clb; Ski Clb; Band; Concert Band; Jazz Band; Mrchg Band; Orch; Pep Band; Poltcl Sci.

LENO, ANNE MARIE; Mount Saint Joseph Acad; Rutland, VT; (Y); 13/99; Drm Mjr(t); Nwsp Stf; JV Bsktbl; Twrlr; High Hon Roll; Hon Roll; NHS; Champlain Coll; Acctng.

LEVINS, KIM; Mt St Joseph Academy; Rutland, VT; (Y); 5/75; Pep Clb; SADD; Varsity Clb; Stu Cncl; Bsktbl; Crs Cntry; Socr; Tennis; High Hon Roll; Hon Roll; Sprts Med.

LEWIS, ALEXANDRA; Woodstock Union HS; Woodstock, VT; (Y); French Clb; Ski Clb; SADD; Yrbk Stf; JV Fld Hcky; Var Socr; Im Swmmng; High Hon Roll; Hon Roll; NHS; Outstndng Alge II Awd 86; Coachs Awd Swmmng 85; Law.

LEWIS, GREGORY; Woodstock Union HS; Woodstock, VT; (Y); 1/100; Am Leg Boys St; Math Tm; Scholastic Bowl; Jazz Band; School Musical; Yrbk Stf; Rep Stu Cncl; Bsbl; High Hon Roll; NHS; Rensselaer Polytech Inst Math/Sci Awd & Mdl 86; US Nvl Acad Smmr Prg 86; Bst In Schl Cert 86.

LIBBY, KRISTIE; Stowe HS; Stowe, VT; (Y); 5/43; Cmnty Wkr; Girl Scts; Red Cross Aide; Ski Clb; Stage Crew; Yrbk Sprt Ed; Sec Frsh Cls; Pres Sr Cls; Rep Stu Cncl; JV Var Bsktbl; Wmns Clb Cmmnty Svc Awd 86; Tchrs Assoc Schlrhsp Awd 86; Rtry Schlrshp Awd 86; Cntry III Ldrs Awd 86; Syracuse U; Radio Brdcstng.

LISCINSKY, JOSEPH; Mount St Joseph Acad; Rutland, VT; (Y); 24/78; Am Leg Boys St; Pres SADD; VP Soph Cls; VP Jr Cls; VP Sr Cls; Badmtn; Capt Ftbl; Cmnty Wkr; Varsity Clb; Variety Show; Ftbl All ST Hnrb Mntn 85; Green Key Awd 85-86; VT Stu Asst Corp Srch Pgm 86; Med.

LIU, ANNA; Mt Anthony Union HS; Bennington, VT; (Y); Church Yth Grp; Latin Clb; Ski Clb; Band; Fld Hcky; Trk; Hon Roll; U VT.

LOLATTE, KRISTEN; Brattleboro Union HS; Brattleboro, VT; (Y); Intnl Clb; Model UN; SADD; Yrbk Phtg; Yrbk Stf; Var Trk; High Hon Roll; Hon Roll; NHS; Drama Clb; Albertus Magnus; Marine Bio.

LONDON, TAMARA; Rice Memorial HS; Shelburne, VT; (Y); Computer Clb; Chorus; Yrbk Stf; JV Var Bowling; Bus Admin.

LONGE, RONALD; Enosburg Falls JR SR HS; Sheldon Spgs, VT; (Y); 1/70; Drama Clb; Teachers Aide; Nwsp Ed-Chief; VP Soph Cls; High Hon Roll; Trs NHS; Val; Am Leg Boys St; School Musical; School Play; Close-Up Fndtn 86; Hugh O Brien Yth Fndtn 84; U Of ME Almni Schlr 86; U Of ME Farmington; Scndry Edu.

LORD, MICHAEL JAY; Fair Haven Union HS; Bomoseen, VT; (Y); 2/120; Am Leg Boys St; Yrbk Bus Mgr; Capt Var Bsktbl; Var L Socr; Var L Trk; Hon Roll; VP NHS; Sal; Pres Acadmc Fit Awd 86; Natl Schlr Athl Awd 86; U Of VT; Comp Sci.

LOSO, PAMELA SUE; Union-32 HS; E Montpelier, VT; (Y); VICA; Chorus; Yrbk Stf; Var L Sftbl; Hon Roll; Amer Legn Post 3 Schlrshp 86; Buddy Pgm Awd 86; Most Spirited Sftbl Playr Awd 83; Trinity Coll; Math Tchr.

LOVE, SCOTT C; Vermont Acad; Englewood, CO; (Y); Camera Clb; School Play; Nwsp Rptr; Yrbk Ed-Chief; Yrbk Phtg; Ed Lit Mag; Ice Hcky; Lcrss; Var Trk; Hon Roll; CO Coll.

LOZON, HEATHER; Rice Memorial HS; Colchester, VT; (Y); 7/144; Am Leg Aux Girls St; High Hon Roll; Hon Roll; NHS; Pre-Law.

LUCIER, MICHELLE; Vergennes Union HS; N Ferrisburg, VT; (Y); 3/100; Am Leg Aux Girls St; Var Capt Socr; Var Tennis; NHS; Library Aide; High Hon Roll; Hon Roll; Athlt And Schlr Of Yr 86; 3rd Hnrs 86; U Of VT; Pro Nrsg.

LUSIGNAN, JODY; Burlington HS; Burlington, VT; (Y); Church Yth Grp; French Clb; Powder Puff Ftbl; Hon Roll; NHS; Comp Pgmr.

LYONS II, DONALD J P; Spaulding HS; Graniteville, VT; (Y); VICA; Tennis; Hon Roll; Engrng.

MAC ARTHUR, SUSAN W; Williamstown JR SR HS; Graniteville, VT; (Y); 3/36; Trs Band; Chorus; School Play; Nwsp Rptr; Yrbk Stf; Var Bsktbl; Var Capt Crs Cntry; Hon Roll; JP Sousa Awd; VP NHS; Acad Achvt Awds 85-86; U Of MA-AMHERST; Htl Admin.

MAC DONALD, SAMANTHA; Twinfield HS; Plainfield, VT; (Y); Dance Clb; Drama Clb; SADD; Thesps; Acpl Chr; Chorus; School Play; Variety Show; Yrbk Stf; Hon Roll; Nw Engln Math Leag Cert Of Merit 82; JR Hgh Fld Hcky 82; Psych.

MAILLET, AMY; Mount Anthony Union HS; Pownal, VT; (Y); 15/273; 4-H; Yrbk Stf; Trk; Twrlr; Cit Awd; 4-H Awd; Hon Roll; NEDT Awd; Ntl 4-H Awds 84-85; VT 4-H Hnr Soc 85; Phys Thrpy.

MANCINI, LISA; Rutland HS; Rutland, VT; (Y); Am Leg Aux Girls St; Art Clb; Computer Clb; VP Debate Tm; French Clb; Key Clb; Science Clb; SADD; Teachers Aide; Nwsp Bus Mgr; NHS 85-86; Girls ST Dely 85; Castleton ST Coll; Chld Psych.

MARRION, JULIE; Mant Anthony HS; Bennington, VT; (Y); Model UN; Ski Clb; Spanish Clb; Band; Concert Band; Mrchg Band; Trs Frsh Cls; Capt Cheerleading.

MARSH, MICHAEL G; Montpelier HS; Barre, VT; (Y); 7/111; Am Leg Boys St; CAP; Drama Clb; Latin Clb; Varsity Clb; School Musical; School Play; Trs Stu Cncl; Var Crs Cntry; Var L Trk.

MARSHALL, RICHARD; Mount St Joseph Acad; Rutland, VT; (Y); SADD; Varsity Clb; Yrbk Stf; Pres Frsh Cls; Pres Soph Cls; Pres Jr Cls; Pres Sr Cls; JV Bsbl; JV Var Bsktbl; Var Capt Ftbl; HOBY 84.

MARSHIA, KERRY; Enosburg Falls HS; Bakersfield, VT; (Y); Am Leg Aux Girls St; Church Yth Grp; Drama Clb; French Clb; Office Aide; SADD; Teachers Aide; Band; Pres Soph Cls; Rep Stu Cncl; Stu Of Mo Oct 84-85; Elem Educ.

MARTIN, ANDREW; Champlain Valley Union HS; Hinesburg, VT; (Y); Boy Scts; Capt Var Bsbl; Capt Var Bsktbl; JV Var Crs Cntry; Vermont Tech Schl; Elec Engrng.

MASON, JUDY; Enosburg Falls JR SR HS; Enosburg, VT; (Y); Am Leg Aux Girls St; Sec 4-H; Band; Concert Band; Mrchg Band; Stu Cncl; 4-H Awd; High Hon Roll; Hon Roll; Rep Vermont In 4-H Cngrs In Chicago 86; All St Band 84; Alternate For Girls St 86; Flight Attndnt.

MATTHEWS, TIMOTHY D; Colchester HS; Colchester, VT; (Y); 12/210; Am Leg Boys St; Capt Quiz Bowl; Pres Band; Var Socr; Var Capt Wrstlng; JP Sousa Awd; NHS; Ntl Merit Ltr; Pres Acadmc Ftnss Awd 86; U Of VT; Engrg.

MAXWELL, ODIN; St Johnsburg Acad; St Johnsburg, VT; (Y); Church Yth Grp; Exploring; Math Tm; Quiz Bowl; Rep Stu Cncl; Golf.

MAYNARD, BRENDA; Enosburg Falls HS; Bakersfield, VT; (Y); Sec FBLA; FFA; Ski Clb; SADD; Teachers Aide; Trs Jr Cls; Stu Cncl; JV Var Cheerleading; Hon Roll; Prfct Atten Awd; GMTI Drug & Alchl Prev Cnclr 85-86; Stu Advsr 82-84; June Dairy Dy Schlrshp Pgnt 86; Champlain Coll; Lgl Sec.

MC CAFFREY, SHARON; Essex Educational Center; Essex Junction, VT; (Y); 150/347; Yrbk Stf; Var Cheerleading; JV Fld Hcky; JV Trk; Johnson & Wales; Fash Retlg.

MC CLALLEN, GREG; Mount Saint Joseph Acad; Rutland, VT; (Y); Church Yth Grp; Ski Clb; SADD; Varsity Clb; JV Bsbl; JV Ftbl; Var L Golf; Coaches Awd Mt St Joseph Ski Team 85; ST Champ Skiing 84-86; All ST Ski Team 85-86.

MC CORMACK, JOHN; Burlington HS; Burlington, VT; (Y); Latin Clb; L Socr; L Trk; Hon Roll; NHS; Natl Latin Exam-Magna Cum Laude 85; Natl Latin Exam-Cum Laude 86; Excllnce In Writing Comp Clss Wnr 85; Physics.

MC COSTIS, PETER; Burr & Burton Seminary HS; Dorset, VT; (Y); Exploring; Ski Clb; JV Var Bsbl; Swmmng; Outwrd Rnd-MN 84; Close-Up Prgm Wash DC 86; U CO Boulder; Bio.

MC CULLOUGH, BILLI R; Vermont Acad; Walpole, NH; (S); Church Yth Grp; 4-H; Math Tm; Chorus; Lcrss; Socr; Swmmng; High Hon Roll; Cum Laude Soc 86.

MC DERMOTT, TAMMIE; Arlington Memorial HS; Arlington, VT; (Y); Dance Clb; 4-H; Girl Scts; Pep Clb; Ski Clb; Chorus; School Play; Variety Show; Yrbk Ed-Chief; Cheerleading.

MC KEON, PATRICK DANIEL; Spaulding HS; Barre, VT; (Y); 15/246; Church Yth Grp; Spanish Clb; Nwsp Rptr; Trk; Hon Roll; Knights Of Clmbs Schrlshp 86; Spldng HS Mem Schlrshp 86; St Michaels Coll; Jrnlsm.

MC LEOD, HEATHER PAGE; St Johnsbury Acad; Branford, CT; (Y); Church Yth Grp; Drama Clb; Girl Scts; Political Wkr; Band; Chorus; Concert Band; Mrchg Band; Pep Band; Im Bowling; Paramedic.

MC NALLY, ANGI; Missisquoi Valley Union HS; Highgate Ctr, VT; (Y); Teachers Aide; Yrbk Ed-Chief; Yrbk Phtg; Rep Frsh Cls; Rep Soph Cls; Capt Cheerleading; JV Socr; High Hon Roll; Hon Roll; Prfct Atten Awd; Springfield Coll; Phys Ther.

MEARS, SHELLIE; Spaulding HS; Barre, VT; (Y); Drama Clb; Sec French Clb; Yrbk Bus Mgr; Yrbk Stf; Stu Cncl; Hon Roll; Bryant Coll Pres Schlrshp 86; Spaulding Mem Schlrshp 86; Bryant Coll; Mrktng.

MELLETT JR, RICHARD; Montpelier HS; Montpelier, VT; (Y); Am Leg Boys St; Ski Clb; Yrbk Phtg; JV Capt Bsbl; Var Ftbl; Var Golf; JV Socr; Cit Awd; High Hon Roll; NHS; Engrng.

MENARD, DANIEL R; Montpelier HS; Montpelier, VT; (Y); 1/107; Am Leg Boys St; Rep Stu Cncl; JV Var Crs Cntry; JV Trk; High Hon Roll; NHS; Ntl Merit SF; VT Hstrcl Scty Wrtng Cntst ST Wnr 85; Elec Engr.

MENARD, LYNNE; Craftsbury Acad; Craftsbury, VT; (S); 1/11; Am Leg Aux Girls St; Nwsp Ed-Chief; Yrbk Bus Mgr; Trs Stu Cncl; Co-Capt Bsktbl; Capt Socr; Var Sftbl; DAR Awd; High Hon Roll; Pres NHS; Sccr CVL; Boston U; Comm.

MERCIER, JEFFERSON; Burr & Burton Seminary; Manchester Ctr, VT; (Y); 16/80; CAP; German Clb; Pres Soph Cls; Stu Cncl; Vllybl; Rotary Awd; VFW Awd; Voice Dem Awd; Var Bsktbl; Var JV Socr; Eagles Clb Schlrshp; Outstndng Bio Stu; Unsng Hero Bsktbl Awd; U Vermont; Engrng.

MESH, ELIZABETH; Chelsea HS; Chelsea, VT; (Y); Debate Tm; Drama Clb; FBLA; NFL; Varsity Clb; Yrbk Phtg; Bsktbl; Fld Hcky; Hon Roll; NHS; Pres Ftns Awd 86; Athltcs Schrlshp 86; Carl Jsln Mem Schlrshp 86; Ithaca Coll.

MESSIER, MATT; Rice Memorial HS; Underhill, VT; (Y); Boy Scts; FCA; Band; JV Ftbl; Var Tennis; Var Trk; Hon Roll; Best Attitude Awd Tennis Team 86; U Of VT.

METCALF, RHONDA; Bellaus Free Acad; St Albans, VT; (Y); 6/22; Art Clb; VICA; Hon Roll; Nrs.

MEYETTE, SONJA; Lyndon Inst; East Haven, VT; (Y); Pep Clb; School Play; Stage Crew; Nwsp Stf; Yrbk Stf; Mgr(s); VP Sftbl; Hon Roll; Prfct Atten Awd; Champlain Coll; Bus Adm.

MIGLORIE, DARIN; Mount St Joseph HS; Center Rutland, VT; (Y); 5/76; JV Bsktbl; Var L Tennis; Hon Roll; NHS; Yrbk Edtr 86-87.

MILLER, SONYA; Middlebury Union HS; Middlebury, VT; (Y); 2/165; AFS; Debate Tm; Math Tm; Orch; High Hon Roll; NHS; Ntl Merit Ltr; Cert Top 10% Audtns All-Nw-Engld Orch 85; Chsn For VT Gvrnrs Inst Arts 85; Cert Merit HS Math ExmVT; Mt Holyoke Coll; Astrophyscst.

MILLER, SUTHERLAND I; Burlington HS; Burlington, VT; (Y); Drama Clb; Model UN; School Musical; Nwsp Phtg; Nwsp Rptr; Nwsp Stf; Ntl Merit SF; Aud/Vis; Off Latin Clb; Chorus; 3rd Pl Poetry Awd 85; 1st Pl Essay 85; Book Review Awd 84; Brown; Jrnlsm.

MILLER, WENDY; Vergennes Union HS; Ferrisburg, VT; (Y); #5 In Class; 4-H; Math Clb; Sec VICA; Stage Crew; JV Socr; JV Sftbl; Hon Roll.

MILLETT, LAURA; Proctor HS; Rutland, VT; (Y); Am Leg Aux Girls St; Drama Clb; German Clb; SADD; School Play; Variety Show; Church Yth Grp; Cmnty Wkr; Band; Chorus; New Englnd Yng Wrtrs Cnfrnc-Breadloaf 86; Govs Inst Arts 86; Green Mtn Tn-Age Inst 85; Musicl Theatr.

MILLS, KENDRA; Saint Johnsbury Acad; Peacham, VT; (Y); Church Yth Grp; Cmnty Wkr; 4-H; French Clb; Girl Scts; Intnl Clb; Political Wkr; Rep Stu Cncl; Var L Fld Hcky; Hon Roll; Aviation.

MILLS, VANESSA; Otter Valley Union HS; Florence, VT; (Y); 42/104; 4-H; Teachers Aide; Chorus; Variety Show; Lit Mag; Var L Fld Hcky; 4-H Awd; Citznshp-Washington Focus 84; VT ST Capital Bldg-Poetry Exhibitn 86; Berklee Coll Of Music; Music.

MILLS, VICKY; Vergennes Union HS; N Ferrisburg, VT; (Y); Art Clb; French Clb; Hon Roll; Prfct Atten Awd; Cmrcl Art.

MOLINAROLI, KAREN; St Johnsbury Acad; Saint Johnsbury, VT; (Y); 4/130; Sec French Clb; Service Clb; Rep Stu Cncl; Capt Cheerleading; Var L Fld Hcky; High Hon Roll; NHS; Anthro Clb 83-84; Williams Clg Bk Awd 85-86.

MOORS, DONNA J; Mt Anthony Union HS; Bennington, VT; (Y); 32/285; Church Yth Grp; Model UN; Band; Mrchg Band; School Musical; Yrbk Sprt Ed; JV Var Bsktbl; NHS; Rotary Awd; Pres Acad Ftnss Awd 85-86; David Hugger Saeur Senice Awd 85-86; Acad All Am Schlr 84-85; Lesley Coll; Human Srvcs.

MORIN, ERIC; Richford HS; Richford, VT; (Y); 3/28; Am Leg Boys St; Model UN; Nwsp Stf; Yrbk Bus Mgr; Bsktbl; Socr; Hon Roll; NHS; U Vermont Math Awd 86; Prsdntl Acdmc Ftns Awd 86; U Of Vermont; Cmptr Sci.

MORRISON, KIMBERLY; Windsor HS; Windsor, VT; (Y); Am Leg Aux Girls St; Band; Mrchg Band; Var JV Fld Hcky; JV Sftbl; High Hon Roll; NHS; Balfour Awd Math 84-86; Balfour Awd Hstry 86.

MORRISSETTE, JOSEPH; Randolph Union HS; Raudolph Ctr, VT; (S); 25/90; Pres FFA; JV Bsktbl; Mgr(s); Hon Roll; FFA Str Grnhnd Awd 85; Vrsty Sccr Mgr Vrsty Lttr 85; VT Tech Coll Tech-Prep Pgm 86; VT Tech Coll; Dry Frm Mgmt.

MORTENSON, DALE; Otter Valley Union HS; Rutland, VT; (Y); 31/103; Var Crs Cntry; Capt Wrstlng; VT ST Rnr-Up In Wrstlng 85-86; U Of TX Arlngtn; Psych.

MOUNT, AMY B; Vermont Acad; Saxtons River, VT; (S); 5/66; Chorus; Yrbk Stf; Var Capt Bsktbl; Var Lcrss; Var Socr; High Hon Roll; Hon Roll; Pre-Med.

MULLGAN, JAMES L; Spaulding HS; Barre, VT; (Y); Trs Key Clb; Rep Soph Cls; Golf; Ice Hcky; Var L Socr; Hon Roll; Ntl Merit SF; Bus Admin.

MUNGER, VIKKI; Fair Haven Union HS; Benson, VT; (Y); 8/119; French Clb; Band; Rep Soph Cls; Rep Jr Cls; Rep Sr Cls; Var Fld Hcky; JV Sftbl; Hon Roll; Lion Awd; NHS; Bertha R Franke Awd 86; U VT; Bus Admin.

MUZZIO, JOHN; Burr & Burton HS; Manchester, VT; (Y); 22/93; Am Leg Boys St; SADD; VP Frsh Cls; Stu Cncl; Var L Bsbl; Var L Bsktbl; Var L Socr; Im Vllybl; Cross U; Bus.

MYERS, JENNIE; Mt Anthony Union HS; Bennington, VT; (Y); 63/269; Church Yth Grp; French Clb; Pep Clb; SADD; Band; Concert Band; Pep Band; Yrbk Stf; Fld Hcky; Trk; Dollars Schlrs 86; Knights Columbus 86; Tchrs Scholar 86; Keene ST Coll; Elem Ed.

NADLER, KRISSY; Mount St Joseph Acad; W Rutland, VT; (Y); 13/87; Cmnty Wkr; Key Clb; Library Aide; Service Clb; SADD; Ed Nwsp Ed-Chief; Nwsp Rptr; Yrbk Stf; Hon Roll; NHS; Chrmn For Cystc Fbrsis Bk-A-Thn 85-86; Fndr Of Teen Ctr In Rtlnd VT 86-87; Smth Coll; Engl.

NAPOLITANO, ANTHONY; Mount Anthony Union HS; Bennington, VT; (Y); 10/263; Latin Clb; Nwsp Rptr; Socr; Capt Trk; High Hon Roll; Lion Awd; NHS; Pres Schlr; Rotary Awd; Spanish NHS; Hugh Obrien Yth Ldrshp Fndtn Rep; Balfour Awd; VT ST Trck Cham 100 M,200 M,400m Relay; U VT; Bio.

NASH, ELIZABETH; North Country Union HS; West Charleston, VT; (S); DECA; German Clb; Yrbk Stf; Bsktbl; Trk; Hon Roll; US Army; Bust.

NATIVI, LISA; Spaulding HS; Barre, VT; (Y); 1/245; Nwsp Sprt Ed; VP Stu Cncl; Var L Bsktbl; Var L Fld Hcky; Var L Sftbl; Pres NHS; Pres Schlr; Val; Am Leg Aux Girls St; Office Aide; RIP Medal 85; Top 10 Pct Math Test; Schlstc; Dartmouth Coll; Pre-Med.

NEILY, JESSICA; Windsor HS; Windsor, VT; (Y); 2/56; Am Leg Aux Girls St; Drama Clb; French Clb; Pep Clb; Band; Concert Band; Mrchg Band; Pep Band; School Play; Yrbk Sprt Ed; Balfr Awds-Spch, Bio, Pre-Calcls, Calcls & Physcs; Boston U; Engrng.

NESSEN, R PETER; Middlebury Union HS; Middlebury, VT; (Y); 15/160; Am Leg Boys St; Math Clb; Math Tm; Scholastic Bowl; Chorus; School Musical; School Play; Hon Roll; Ntl Merit SF; Pres Schlr; ACDA Estrn Hnrs Choir 85-86; New Engl Math Supr Achvt Awd 84-85; High Scr U VT Math 85; Vassar Coll; Math.

NEWQUIST, DEBORAH; St Johnsbury Acad; St Johnsbury, VT; (Y); 2/157; Pres Church Yth Grp; Drama Clb; Math Tm; School Musical; School Play; Yrbk Stf; Rep Sr Cls; High Hon Roll; NHS; Spanish Clb; U VT Math Awd 86; 1st Pl Leag Math Awd 84.

NICHOLSON, DAREN; Arlington Memorial HS; Arlington, VT; (Y); 1/44; Am Leg Boys St; Band; Pres Stu Cncl; Var Bsbl; Var Bsktbl; Var Socr; Gov Hon Prg Awd; NHS; U S Sen Schlrshp Recpnt 86.

NIQUETTE, KIM; Burlington HS; Burlington, VT; (Y); Am Leg Aux Girls St; Varsity Clb; Concert Band; Orch; Yrbk Stf; Rep Stu Cncl; Var Crs Cntry; Var Trk; Hon Roll; NHS.

NOBLE, AARON S; Colchester HS; Colchester, VT; (Y); 28/189; Boy Scts; Church Yth Grp; Var Capt Bsbl; JV Capt Bsktbl; Var L Socr; Grad Hnrs; VT Tech Coll; Cvl Engrng.

O BRIEN, THOMAS P; Mill River Union HS; North Clarendon, VT; (Y); 16/133; Am Leg Boys St; Drama Clb; Chorus; Madrigals; School Play; Stu Cncl; JV Bsbl; JV Bsktbl; Var JV Socr; DAR Awd; All NE Cst 85; All NE Chrs 86; U Of Vermont.

O BRYAN, MELISSA; Proctor JR-SR HS; Chittenden, VT; (Y); Computer Clb; French Clb; Hosp Aide; Red Cross Aide; Mrchg Band; Off Jr Cls; JV Bsktbl; Hon Roll; RN.

O HARA, MARGARET; Enosburg Falls HS; Enosburg Falls, VT; (Y); Church Yth Grp; Drama Clb; Ski Clb; Sec SADD; Jazz Band; Orch; Yrbk Stf; Mgr Bsktbl; JV Socr; Pres NHS; Castleton ST Comp Camp Scholar 84; VT Grls ST 86; Fin Congrss-Bundestag Yth Exch 85.

OBRIEN, CHRIS; Burlington HS; Burlington, VT; (Y); Church Yth Grp; Latin Clb; Spanish Clb; Concert Band; Mrchg Band; Yrbk Stf; Stu Cncl; JV Capt Bsbl; JV Var Bsktbl; Var Socr; MVP Bsbl 84; MVP Vrsty Sccr-1st Tm Al-Leag 85-86; Excllnc Hstry 83-84; Sprts Medcn.

OLSON, LANCE; Missisquoi Valley Union HS; Swanton, VT; (Y); 3/140; Math Clb; Math Tm; School Play; Rep Jr Cls; Rep Sr Cls; High Hon Roll; Hon Roll; NHS; Boys ST 86; Aero.

OLSZANSKYJ, SERGE J; Essex Junction Educational Center; Guilford, CT; (Y); 1/330; Capt Math Tm; Capt Scholastic Bowl; School Play; Stage Crew; Nwsp Stf; NHS; Ntl Merit SF; Yrbk Stf; Hon Roll; Val; Rensslr Mdl Math & Sci 85; 2nd Pl Olympcs Of Mind Wrld Fnls 83; Dartmth Coll Bk Awd 85; Natl Merit Schl.

PALLINI, LISA; Mt Anthony Union HS; Scottsdale, AZ; (Y); Drama Clb; Model UN; Bsbl; Bsktbl; Crs Cntry; Socr; Trk; Vllybl; Wt Lftg; High Hon Roll; U Of A; Clncl Psych.

PALLMAN, TRECIA; Mount Anthony Union HS; Shaftsbury, VT; (Y); 3/273; Chorus; Jazz Band; Madrigals; School Musical; Symp Band; Variety Show; Yrbk Stf; Lion Awd; NHS; U VT; Music.

PALUMBO, DAWN; Winooski HS; Winooski, VT; (Y); Computer Clb; Debate Tm; 4-H; Hosp Aide; Library Aide; OEA; Spanish Clb; SADD; Cheerleading; Sftbl; Libr Awd & Volunteer Awd; UVM; Med.

PARENT, CLAUDE; Enosburg Falls JR SR HS; Enosburg Falls, VT; (S); 8/65; Am Leg Boys St; FFA; Ski Clb; Hghst In Chem; ST Rptr FFA; Vermont Tech Coll; Elec Engrng.

PARISEAU, MICHAEL; Enosburg Falls JR SR HS; Enosburg Falls, VT; (Y); Am Leg Boys St; FBLA; School Play; Yrbk Stf; Sec Rep Soph Cls; Sec Rep Jr Cls; High Hon Roll; Hon Roll; NHS; Mgr(s); Svc To Schl; U Vermont; Bus.

PARKER, CATHY; Burlington HS; Burlington, VT; (Y); FBLA; Var Gym; Var Socr; NHS; Exclnce Typ I 84-85; Data Proc/Acctg I Exclnce 85-86; Champlain Coll; CPA.

PARKMAN, RYAN; Mount St Joseph Acad; Rutland, VT; (Y); Yrbk Stf; Var Ftbl; Var Tennis; Elks Awd; Hon Roll; Music.

PARRY, LAURA; Montpelier HS; Montpelier, VT; (Y); 15/110; Hosp Aide; Yrbk Stf; Crs Cntry; Ftbl; Mgr(s); Powder Puff Ftbl; Trk; High Hon Roll; VT Coll Full Tuition Scholar 86; VT Coll; Med Tech.

PATEL, KAMLESH; Mt Anthony Union HS; Bennington, VT; (Y); 17/276; Computer Clb; Model UN; JV Var Ftbl; NHS; RPI; Comp Engrng.

PATERSEN, ANDREW; Spaulding HS; Barre, VT; (Y); Am Leg Boys St; Key Clb; Bsktbl; Var Lcrss; Var Capt Socr; Hon Roll.

PATNO, JACQUELINE; Burlington HS; Burlington, VT; (Y); AFS; Chorus; Hon Roll; NHS; U Of VT; Bio.

PAULMAN, LYNETTE; Burlington HS; Burlington, VT; (Y); Rep Am Leg Aux Girls St; Church Yth Grp; Cmnty Wkr; Dance Clb; VP DECA; Drama Clb; 4-H; Girl Scts; Library Aide; Office Aide; Outstndng Achvt Mrktng 86; Fash Merch.

PAUSTIAN, JAMES; Arlington Memorial HS; W Arlington, VT; (Y); Church Yth Grp; Cmnty Wkr; Var Bsbl; High Hon Roll; Hon Roll; Golden Pencil Awd Indstrl Arts 84 & 86; Aviatn.

PEARSON, BETH; Twinfield Union HS; Plainfield, VT; (Y); Pres Art Clb; Drama Clb; French Clb; Chorus; Madrigals; School Play; Stage Crew; Variety Show; Socr; High Hon Roll; 3rd Pl Wood Art Gallery Regnl Art Show 86; All ST Chorus 85.

PEELER, KRISTINE; Woodstock Union HS; Hartland, VT; (Y); Latin Clb; Varsity Clb; Chorus; School Musical; Fld Hcky; Lcrss; High Hon Roll; Hon Roll; Psych.

PERCY, MICHAEL; St Johnsbury Acad; St Johnsbury, VT; (Y); 45/165; Church Yth Grp; Cmnty Wkr; Var JV Bsbl; Var JV Ftbl; Hon Roll; Darab Batmanglidj Mem Prz 86; F X Ryan Mem Prz 86; St Anselms Coll; Comp Sci.

PERRAS, PAMELA; Missisquoi Valley Union HS; Swanton, VT; (Y); Teachers Aide; VICA; Chorus; Yrbk Phtg; Yrbk Stf; Elem Tchr.

PETERS, STEPHANNIE; Mount Anthony Union HS; Bennington, VT; (Y); German Clb; Band; Concert Band; Mrchg Band; Pep Band; Lit Mag; High Hon Roll; NHS; NEDT Awd; Pres Acadmc Ftnss Awd; Southern VT Coll; Crmnl Jstce.

PEZDIRTZ, KRISTA; St Johnsbury Acad; Saint Johnsbury, VT; (Y); 23/120; Rep Church Yth Grp; French Clb; FBLA; Stu Cncl; Bsktbl; Var Socr; High Hon Roll; Hon Roll; Chld Psych.

PHILION, VALERIE B; Middlebury Union HS; Shoreham, VT; (Y); 33/170; Am Leg Aux Girls St; Frsh Cls; Pres Jr Cls; Im Bsbl; Var Bsktbl; Var Capt Fld Hcky; JV Sftbl; Hon Roll; Jim Jette Tiger Awd 85-86; JR Marshal 85; Peer Cnslng & Peer Tutoring 85-86; Johnson ST Coll; Elem Educ.

PILZ, LAURA; Arlington Memorial HS; Arlington, VT; (Y); Church Yth Grp; Chorus; Variety Show; Yrbk Bus Mgr; Sec Soph Cls; Rep Jr Cls; Cheerleading; Hon Roll; Nursing.

PINARD, MARY BETH; Spaulding HS; Barre, VT; (Y); 1/278; Am Leg Aux Girls St; JCL; Pres Varsity Clb; Lit Mag; Sec Frsh Cls; Sec Soph Cls; Stu Cncl; Var Bsktbl; Var Fld Hcky; Var Sftbl; Fnlst US Japan Senate Schlrshp 85-86; Grn Mtn Teen Inst 86; Schl 1st Rnnr Up Hugh O Brien 84; Pol Sci.

PIXLEY, COLLEEN; Green Mountain Union HS; Cavendish, VT; (Y); Church Yth Grp; Drama Clb; Spanish Clb; Sec SADD; Band; Var JV Fld Hcky; Var Trk; NHS; New Englnd Yng Wrtrs Conf 86; Heroditus Awd Hist, Gov Inst Intl Affairs 86; U VT; Hist Tchr.

PLANTE, JENNIFER; Spaulding HS; Barre, VT; (Y); 3/259; Am Leg Aux Girls St; Service Clb; Varsity Clb; VP Frsh Cls; VP Soph Cls; Stu Cncl; Bsktbl; Fld Hcky; Sftbl; High Hon Roll; Dartmouth JR Bk Awd 85-86; Biochmstry.

PLOOF, CHERYL; Richford HS; East Berkshire, VT; (Y); 13/28; Drama Clb; Rptr FHA; Band; Chorus; Jazz Band; Mrchg Band; School Play; Nwsp Bus Mgr; Nwsp Rptr; Yrbk Bus Mgr; Commrcl Awd; Alumni Schlrshp; Charles Lenard Mem Schlrshp; Champlain Coll; Bus Mgmt.

POULEN, CHARLES; Mount Anthony Union HS; Bennington, VT; (Y); German Clb; Math Clb; SADD; Chorus; Madrigals; Socr; Vllybl; Hon Roll; NHS; Prfct Atten Awd.

POULIOT, CAROLE D; North Country U HS; Newport, VT; (S); 24/244; DECA; Chorus; JV Socr; JV Trk; High Hon Roll; Hon Roll; X Cntry Skiing 82; CLOSE-UP 84; Typng I-Outstndng Achvt Plaque 84; Accntng I & Distrbtv Ed I Plq 85; Ins Agnt.

PRIBRAM, SARAH; Green Mountain Valley HS; Auburn, ME; (Y); Pres SADD; Varsity Clb; Yrbk Stf; Var L Crs Cntry; Var L Fld Hcky; Var L Trk; Cit Awd; High Hon Roll; NHS; All ST Ski Tm 83-85; Ctznshp & Acdmc Hnrs Awds 83; Middlebury Coll.

PROFERA, JEFFREY; Spaulding HS; Barre, VT; (Y); 15/250; Key Clb; VICA; L Bsbl; L Bsktbl; L Socr; High Hon Roll; Hon Roll; VT Tech Coll; Archt Bus.

PROVENCHER, TINA; Spaulding HS; Barre, VT; (Y); Church Yth Grp; Cmnty Wkr; Intnl Clb; Var Rep Soph Cls; Var Rep Jr Cls; Var Stu Cncl; Trk; High Hon Roll; Hon Roll; Bus Mgmt.

PUCHRIK, AMY; Rice Memorial HS; Burlington, VT; (Y); Chorus; Yrbk Stf; Tennis; Katherine Gibbs Schl; Bus Admin.

PUTTLITZ, ERIK A; Mount Mansfield Union HS; Underhill, VT; (Y); 2/185; Orch; School Musical; Var L Tennis; French Hon Soc; High Hon Roll; NHS; Sal; Dartmth Bk Clb Awd 85; UVM Jr Conf 85; IBM Watson Schlrshp 86; UVM; Engrg.

PUTVAIN, TAMARA; Peoples Acad; Wolcott, VT; (Y); 6/59; Quiz Bowl; Pres SADD; School Musical; Pres Frsh Cls; Pres Jr Cls; Pres Sr Cls; Rep Stu Cncl; Bsktbl; Cheerleading; Socr; Merit Lit Awd 83-84 & 86; NHS Scholar 86; U VT; Phys Thrpy.

RABOIN, LAURIE; Spaulding HS; Barre, VT; (Y); 20/263; Office Aide; Chorus; JV Sftbl; Im Trk; Hon Roll; 3rd Pl U VT Wrtng Cntst 85-86; Spcl Olympcs Bstr Clb 85-86; Bus Mngmnt.

RABOW, LINDA; Black River HS; Ludlow, VT; (S); Temple Yth Grp; Band; Chorus; Yrbk Stf; Socr; Hon Roll; NHS; AFS; Pep Clb; SADD; Tzfn Rgn Exctv VP; Abraham Joshua Heschel Natl Hnr Soc; Ludlow JR Miss Pgnt 1st Rnnr Up; Lbrl Arts.

RAYMOND, TONYA; Missisquoi Valley Union HS; Swanton, VT; (Y); Church Yth Grp; FFA; Office Aide; Chorus; Church Choir; Yrbk Phtg; Yrbk Rptr; Yrbk Stf; Prfct Atten Awd; Bus Mgmt.

RAYNAK, JENIFER; Missisquoi Valley Union HS; Franklin, VT; (Y); 1/150; Am Leg Aux Girls St; Church Choir; Jazz Band; School Musical; Sec Stu Cncl; Bausch & Lomb Sci Awd; High Hon Roll; NHS; Prncpls Clb 85-86; VT All-ST Jzz Bnd Brtn Sax 85-86; Msc.

READ, CHRISTOPHER; Burr & Burton Semnry; E Dorset, VT; (Y); 3/100; Band; Concert Band; Mrchg Band; Orch; Yrbk Stf; High Hon Roll; Hon Roll; Math.

REBIDEAU, JACQUELINE; Woodstock Union HS; Plymouth, VT; (Y); Math Tm; Yrbk Ed-Chief; Trs Jr Cls; Trs Sr Cls; High Hon Roll; Hon Roll; NHS; JV Socr; Jr NHS; Outstndng Acclrtd Advncd Math Stu 86; Outstndng Geo Stu 85; Outstndng Alg I Stu 84; Math.

RECZEK, MICHAEL; Mount St Joseph HS; Rutland, VT; (Y); Drama Clb; School Play; Var Bsbl; Var Mgr(s); Hon Roll; VT Hnrs Cmptn Excllnc Wrtng 85 & 86; USC; Filmmkr.

REESE, LYNN; Winooski HS; Winooski, VT; (Y); 2/60; Am Leg Aux Girls St; JV Var Cheerleading; Var Coach Actv; JV Var Fld Hcky; JV Var Score Keeper; Var Trk; High Hon Roll; Hon Roll; Jr NHS; Art Clb; Outstndng Achvt Chem 86; Data Proc.

REIL, MARYELLEN; Williamstown HS; Williamstown, VT; (Y); Yrbk Stf; Var Socr; Hon Roll; Trinity Coll; Liberal Arts.

REISE, LYNN A; Essex Jct HS; Essex Jct, VT; (Y); 7/316; Church Yth Grp; Girl Scts; ROTC; Color Guard; Drill Tm; Flag Corp; NHS; Ntl Merit SF; Avon GS Ldrshp Schlrshp 85; Physics.

REMAILY, NEISHA; Twinfield HS; Marshfield, VT; (Y); Art Clb; Camera Clb; Dance Clb; Drama Clb; French Clb; Acpl Chr; Chorus; Madrigals; School Play; Variety Show; Trvl.

RESCH, ELIZABETH; Mount Anthony Union HS; North Benningto, VT; (Y); Art Clb; Drama Clb; Band; Chorus; Mrchg Band; School Play; Symp Band; Hon Roll; Visual Arts.

REYNOLDS, DAVID; Mt Anthony Union HS; Pownal, VT; (Y); #72 In Class; French Clb; Model UN; SADD; Stu Cncl; Var JV Socr; JV Trk; Var Wrstlng; 1st New England Tu Ldrshp Conf 85; Commendation In Eng 84; Sccr Schlrshp Keen ST Owl Sccr Camp 84; Castleton ST Coll; Commun.

RHOAD, STEPHANIE; Windsor HS; Windsor, VT; (Y); 5/71; Am Leg Aux Girls St; Band; Yrbk Bus Mgr; Yrbk Stf; Pres Sr Cls; VP Sec Stu Cncl; Var Capt Bsktbl; Var Capt Fld Hcky; High Hon Roll; NHS; Stu Of Month 86; Compu.

RHODES, STEPHANIE; North Country Union HS; Newport, VT; (Y); 11/259; French Clb; Varsity Clb; Fld Hcky; Trk; Elks Awd; High Hon Roll; NHS; Scholar Ltr & Pins 84-86; Pres Fit Awd 83; Amer Lg Aux Scholar 86; U VT; Bus Adm.

RICCIUTI, JENNIFER; Misiquoi Valley Union HS; Swanton, VT; (Y); Yrbk Sprt Ed; High Hon Roll; Hon Roll; Education.

RICHARDSON, REBECCA S; Lyndon Inst; Sheffield, VT; (Y); 3/117; Church Yth Grp; Band; Church Choir; Concert Band; Jazz Band; Mrchg Band; Pep Band; Var Mgr(s); Var Score Keeper; High Hon Roll; Christopherson Music Awd 86; Dane-Keniston Schlrshp 86; Awd For 87 Or Better Ave For 4 Yr 86; Cedarville Coll; Elemtry Ed.

RIVARD, DANIELLE; Hartford HS; Hartford, VT; (Y); 29/141; Church Yth Grp; 4-H; Sec GAA; Office Aide; Band; Chorus; School Play; Yrbk Phtg; Hon Roll; NHS; Sec.

ROGERS, DEBRA JEAN; Rattleboro Union HS; Brattleboro, VT; (Y); 38/240; Pres Church Yth Grp; SADD; Mrchg Band; Yrbk Ed-Chief; Capt Twrlr; Hon Roll; NHS; French Clb; FBLA; Hosp Aide; Psychlgy.

ROUSSEAU, DAVID H B; St Johnsbury Acad; Saint Johnsbury, VT; (Y); 49/157; Sec Boy Scts; Drama Clb; School Play; Variety Show; Var Cheerleading; Var Wrstlng; Elks Awd; God Cntry Awd; Debate Tm; French Clb; Eagle Scout 86; Dsgn Several Patches Scout Camps 84-85; Dsgn Chld Sfty Prog Illustrated Chld Sfty Bk; Adv.

ROY, RENE; North Country Union HS; West Charleston, VT; (Y); 11/262; Drama Clb; Pres FFA; Chorus; Church Choir; School Musical; School Play; Sr Cls; Trs Stu Cncl; High Hon Roll; NHS; Top Grad Acdmcs, Ldrshp Sprvsd Experience 86; Ldrshp Cup, FFA Dist Star Farmer 86; U VT; Ag Tech.

ROY, SUSAN; Mount Anthony Union HS; Bennington, VT; (Y); 35/286; Am Leg Aux Girls St; Church Yth Grp; Model UN; Band; Var Capt Bsktbl; Var Capt Fld Hcky; Var Capt Sftbl; Im Vllybl; NHS; Pres Schlr; Natl Army Rsrv Schlr-Athlt 86; Springfield Coll; Bio.

ROYER, JOEY; Lake Region Union HS; Orleans, VT; (Y); English Clb; Intnl Clb; Math Tm; Band; Chorus; Church Choir; School Musical; Stu Cncl; Mgr(s); JV Socr; Comp Prgmmg.

RUSSELL, JEANNINE; Burlington HS; Burlington, VT; (Y); AFS; Church Yth Grp; Band; Chorus; Church Choir; Concert Band; Mrchg Band; Pep Band; Trk; Hon Roll; Nyack Coll; Music.

SAMPLE, KAREN; Hartford HS; Wilder, VT; (Y); GAA; Pep Clb; Cheerleading; Crs Cntry; Pom Pon; Trk; SADD; Band; Drill Tm; Mrchg Band.

SAMUELS, SHOSHANA L; Twinfield Union HS; Plainfield, VT; (Y); 8/37; Pres Drama Clb; Pres French Clb; Off SADD; VP Band; School Play; Nwsp Ed-Chief; Rep Stu Cncl; Hon Roll; Ntl Merit SF; NEDT Awd; Tri-M-Hnr Soc; Gov Inst Sci; Proj Excel; Cmmnctns.

SANCIBRIAN, JULIE; Spaulding HS; Barre, VT; (Y); Cmnty Wkr; Computer Clb; Hosp Aide; Rep Frsh Cls; Rep Soph Cls; Rep Jr Cls; Stu Cncl; JV Var Bsktbl; Score Keeper; Stat Sftbl; Psych.

SANDILLO, ANTOINETTE; Mount Saint Joseph Acad; Rutland, VT; (Y); Church Yth Grp; Drama Clb; Ski Clb; Varsity Clb; Chorus; Stage Crew; Rep Stu Cncl; JV Sftbl; Child Dvlpmnt.

SANVILLE, RONALD; Craftsbury Acad; Craftsbury, VT; (Y); Pres Church Yth Grp; FBLA; Concert Band; Mrchg Band; Rep Stu Cncl; Var Bsbl; Var Bsktbl; Var Socr; Hon Roll; Am Leg Boys St; Jr Conf 86; Bus.

SARGENT, BETH; Spaulding HS; Barre, VT; (Y); VP Church Yth Grp; Hosp Aide; Office Aide; Rep Jr Cls; JV Stat Bsktbl; Mgr(s); Hon Roll; Psych.

SAULNIER, TRICIA; Twinfield HS; Marshfield, VT; (Y); Church Yth Grp; German Clb; Chorus; Concert Band; Drm Mjr(t); Flag Corp; Mrchg Band; Rep Frsh Cls; Var L Cheerleading; Hon Roll; Intl Bus.

SCHAAD, SUZANNE; Mt Anthony Union HS; Bennington, VT; (Y); Drama Clb; 4-H; French Clb; Ski Clb; SADD; Band; Fld Hcky; Vllybl; High Hon Roll; Hon Roll; Arch.

SCHLEEDE, LYNNE; Burlington HS; Burlington, VT; (Y); Pres Church Yth Grp; Drama Clb; Latin Clb; Chorus; Church Choir; Madrigals; School Musical; Kiwanis Awd; NHS; Letourneau Educ Schlrshp 86; UVM; Biolgy.

SCHUCK, SUSAN; Vermont Acad; Newfane, VT; (Y); Debate Tm; Drama Clb; Teachers Aide; VP Frsh Cls; L Var Bsktbl; JV Var Lcrss; JV Var Socr; Hon Roll; Georgetown U; Hstry.

SCOTT, CONSTANCE K; Essex Jct HS; Essex Jct, VT; (Y); 16/332; Boy Scts; Pres Church Yth Grp; Ski Clb; Var L Ftbl; JV Tennis; High Hon Roll; NHS; Ski Clb; Trk; Hon Roll; 1 Of 3 Top Frnch III Stu 84-85; Unsng Hro Awd Hrd Wrk Ftbl 85; Schlr Athlt Hnr 86; U Of VT; Bus Adm.

SECOY, RAINY; Burr & Burton Seminary; Route 2 Box 175, VT; (Y); 6/90; Am Leg Aux Girls St; JA; Spanish Clb; Var Bsktbl; Var Crs Cntry; Var Trk; Cit Awd; Var High Hon Roll; Var NHS; VFW Awd; Pres Physcl Ftnss Awd 84; Scty Of Wmn Engnrs 86; Hdmstrs List 86; Physcl Thrpy.

SENDAK, MICHELLE; Colchester HS; Colchester, VT; (Y); 6/220; High Hon Roll; Hon Roll; Jr NHS; NHS; Prsdntl Acdmc Ftnss Awd; St Mchls Coll Chttndn Cnty Hnr Tuitn Schlrshp 86; St Michaels Coll; Bus Admin.

SHEPARD, RAYMOND; Rochester HS; Rochester, VT; (Y); 2/14; Am Leg Boys St; Varsity Clb; Rep Frsh Cls; Rep Soph Cls; Rep Jr Cls; Var Bsbl; Var Bsktbl; Var Capt Socr; High Hon Roll; NHS.

SHERMAN, LISA; Burlington HS; Burlington, VT; (Y); Var Cheerleading; Coachs Awd Var Chrldng 85; U Of VT; Elem Ed.

SHERWIN, ALLISON GWEN; Mount Anthony Union HS; Shaftsbury, VT; (Y); 1/270; SADD; Pres Frsh Cls; Rep Soph Cls; Rep Jr Cls; Sec Sr Cls; Im Badmtn; Im Vllybl; Bausch & Lomb Sci Awd; Cit Awd; DAR Awd; Dartmouth Bk Awd; Ruth Adler Exclnc In Math Awd; Rensselaer; Aerontcl Engrg.

SHROPSHIRE, TODD; Harwood Union HS; Waitsfield, VT; (Y); Am Leg Boys St; Boy Scts; Church Yth Grp; Cmnty Wkr; Concert Band; Var Bsktbl; Var Socr; Var Trk; High Hon Roll; Hon Roll; Air Force Acad; Comp Sci.

SIEGEL, ERIC; Burlington HS; Burlington, VT; (Y); Chess Clb; Drama Clb; Band; Chorus; Church Choir; Madrigals; Mrchg Band; School Musical; School Play; Computer Science.

SILVIA II, KENNETH A; Spaulding HS; Barre, VT; (Y); 8/278; Am Leg Boys St; Church Yth Grp; Stat Ice Hcky; Var Lcrss; JV Trk; High Hon Roll; Hon Roll; NEDT Awd; Ntl Latin Hnr Sco 85-86; Med.

SIPLEY, LISA; Vergennes Union HS; Vergennes, VT; (Y); 17/98; Trs Church Yth Grp; Rptr FBLA; German Clb; OEA; JV Bsktbl; Fred A Vann Mem Schlrshp 86; I Dare You Awd 86; Ofc Persnl Schlrshp 86; Chowan Coll; Exec Sec.

SKUMLIEN, MICHAEL; Chelsea HS; Chelsea, VT; (Y); Church Yth Grp; French Clb; FBLA; JV Bsktbl; High Hon Roll; Armed Svcs.

SLATTERY, MICHAEL J; Essex Junction Educational Ctr; Essex Junction, VT; (Y); 3/326; Church Yth Grp; Math Tm; ROTC; Ski Clb; Color Guard; Drill Tm; Ed Yrbk Stf; Im Bsktbl; Var L Tennis; DAR Awd; AFJROTC Air Force Assn Awd 85; Top Frnch III Stu 84; Top Frnch Adv Plcmnt I 85; Princeton U; Physics.

SMALL, WINFORD; Stowe HS; Stowe, VT; (Y); Computer Clb; English Clb; Latin Clb; SADD; Yrbk Stf; Bowling; High Hon Roll; Hon Roll.

SMITH, ANDREA; Harwood Union HS; Moretown, VT; (Y); 2/130; Am Leg Aux Girls St; Acpl Chr; Lit Mag; Frsh Cls; Stu Cncl; Crs Cntry; Trk; All New Englander Cross Cty Rnng 82-85; U VT Schlr 86; Dartmouth Bk Awd 85; U VT.

SMITH, DIANA; Missiquoi Valley Union HS; Highgate Ctr, VT; (Y); Cmnty Wkr; Intnl Clb; Band; Concert Band; Mrchg Band; Hon Roll; US Air Force; Pilot.

SMITH, KIMIKO; Green Mountain Union HS; Proctorsville, VT; (Y); 9/75; Am Leg Aux Girls St; GAA; Varsity Clb; Off Jr Cls; Off Sr Cls; Stu Cncl; Bsktbl; Socr; Sftbl; Hon Roll; Secy Stdnt Govt 86-87; Proj Excel 86; Prom Qn 86; Syracuse U; Cmmnctns.

SMITH, STACEY; Mount St Joseph Acad; Rutland, VT; (Y); Drama Clb; Varsity Clb; Chorus; Bsktbl; Powder Puff Ftbl; Sftbl; Hon Roll; ST Michaels Coll; Elem Educ.

SNOW, BRADFORD; Arlington Memorial HS; E Arlington, VT; (Y); Trs Church Yth Grp; Im Golf; Im Socr; Hon Roll; Close-Up Pgm WA DC 86; Plt Comp.

SOARES, SEAN; Burr & Burton Seminary; Manchester, VT; (Y); Letterman Clb; Varsity Clb; Golf; Socr; Vllybl; Hon Roll; Accntng.

SOLZHENITSYN, YERMOLAY; Green Mountain Union HS; Cavendish, VT; (Y); French Clb; Scholastic Bowl; Nwsp Rptr; Tennis; High Hon Roll; Hon Roll; NHS.

SORRENTINO, TINA; Fair Haven Union HS; Castleton, VT; (Y); FHA; Teachers Aide; Chorus; Hon Roll; Castleton ST Coll; Acctng.

SOUTHWICK, PATRICIA C; Middlebury Union HS; Middlebury, VT; (Y); Chorus; Gym; Hon Roll; Prfct Atten Awd; Outstndg Secy Stu Sprg & Fall 85; Champlain Coll; Exec Secy.

SPAFFORD, JENNIFER W; Burlington HS; Burlington, VT; (Y); 32/244; Am Leg Aux Girls St; Drama Clb; Varsity Clb; Band; Chorus; Yrbk Stf; Pres Stu Cncl; Capt Fld Hcky; Hon Roll; NHS; Alumnae Svc Awd, Exclnce Sr Sem Hist, Outstndng Svc Stu Cncl-Pres 86; Bryn Mawr Coll.

SPANGLER, PAULA SUE; Mt Anthony Union HS; Pownal, VT; (Y); 41/270; Latin Clb; Ski Clb; Band; Mrchg Band; VP Frsh Cls; Var Fld Hcky; Var Sftbl; Hon Roll; NHS; Dllrs For Schlrs 86; Bnnngtn Pttrs Excllnc Crmcs Awd 86; U Of VT; Biochem.

SPENCER, JULIE C; Vergennes Union HS; Vergennes, VT; (Y); 8/125; Drama Clb; Band; Jazz Band; Mrchg Band; School Musical; School Play; Variety Show; High Hon Roll; Hon Roll; Ntl Merit Ltr; Acad All Amer Schlr 86; Gov Inst Arts 84; Pre-Med.

SPENO, LEE; St Johnsbury Acad; Hamilton, NY; (Y); French Clb; Hosp Aide; Chorus; School Musical; Swing Chorus; Variety Show; VP Stu Cncl; Var JV Cheerleading; Var Pom Pon; Hon Roll; Best All Season 1st Pl 85; Dance Awd 85-86; Singing Awd 85-86; Drama.

SPROUT, LESLIE A; Burlington HS; Burlington, VT; (Y); 1/240; AFS; Trs Church Yth Grp; Latin Clb; Math Tm; Orch; Im Ftbl; High Hon Roll; VP NHS; Ntl Merit SF; Val; Ancnt Hist.

STEELE, KIMBERLY; Otter Valley Union HS; Sudbury, VT; (Y); 26/107; 4-H; SADD; Teachers Aide; Yrbk Stf; Stu Cncl; Cheerleading; Fld Hcky; Springfield Coll; Lib Arts.

STEWART, MARK; Burlington HS; Burlington, VT; (Y); Church Yth Grp; FCA; German Clb; Church Choir; JV Bsbl; Var L Bsktbl; Var L Ftbl; JV Trk; NHS; Cmmnctns.

STONE, KAREN; Enosburg Falls HS; E Fairfield, VT; (Y); Rptr FBLA; Teachers Aide; Chorus; Cheerleading; High Hon Roll; Hon Roll; Exc Typng I 84; Most Imprvd Awd Chrldng 83; Cert Achvt Sec Practice 86.

STOWE, EMILY; St Johnsbury Acad; Saint Johnsbury, VT; (Y); 9/120; Am Leg Aux Girls St; Drama Clb; French Clb; Ski Clb; Church Choir; School Musical; School Play; JV Var Fld Hcky; High Hon Roll; NHS.

STUART, CINDY; Concord HS; Concord, VT; (S); 3/20; Drama Clb; Math Clb; Model UN; Pres Jr Cls; Pres Sr Cls; Bsktbl; Socr; Sftbl; Hon Roll; NHS; HOBY Ldrshp Sem 83; Rnnr-Up VT Bundestag Yth Exchg Pgm 85; JR Conf 85; St Anselm; Pre-Law.

STUDER, LORETTA; North Country Union HS; W Charleston, VT; (Y); Cmnty Wkr; Dance Clb; Hosp Aide; Band; Chorus; Mrchg Band; Pep Band; School Play; L Bsktbl; L Socr; Trinity Coll; Lib Arts.

STURTEVANT, KATHY; Enosburg Falls HS; Enosburg, VT; (Y); 4-H; FFA; Teachers Aide; Chorus; Variety Show; High Hon Roll; Hon Roll; Awds Exc Chorus,Acctng,Achvt Family Livng 86; Champlain Coll; CPA.

SULLIVAN, GAIL; Rutland SR HS; Rutland, VT; (Y); Pres Church Yth Grp; SADD; Drm & Bgl; Yrbk Stf; Hon Roll; Clss Artst 86; Vermont Tech Coll; Artchtcture.

SULLIVAN, WINIFRED; Mt Mansfield Union HS; Underhill, VT; (Y); Cmnty Wkr; Quiz Bowl; Teachers Aide; High Hon Roll; NHS; Seymour Awd 86; Pro Merito 86.

SULVA, PAUL; Burlington HS; Burlington, VT; (Y); Am Leg Boys St; Boy Scts; Church Yth Grp; Computer Clb; Exploring; Math Tm; JV Socr; JV Tennis; Hon Roll; NHS; Excllnc In Wstrn Cvlztns & US Hstry Awd 84-86; Elctrcl Engrng.

SWAN, JEFFREY; Missisquoi Valley Union HS; Highgate Ctr, VT; (Y); Rep Stu Cncl; JV Var Bsktbl; High Hon Roll; Hon Roll; NHS; Am Leg Boys St; Boy Scts; French Clb; JV Ftbl; Clrksn Col6; Math.

SWARTOUT, JENNIFER; Burlington HS; Burlington, VT; (Y); 4-H; SADD; Flag Corp; Var L Bsktbl; L Crs Cntry; Var L Trk; 4-H Awd; Hon Roll; NHS; Honorable Mention Natl Track All-Am 85; Nuclear Engrng.

SWENOR, TOM; Vergennes Union HS; Vergennes, VT; (Y); AFS; SADD; Band; Concert Band; Mrchg Band; Pep Band; School Musical; Pres Bowling; Hon Roll.

SWIATEK, JEFFREY C; Burlington HS; Burlington, VT; (Y); 3/247; AFS; German Clb; Math Tm; Scholastic Bowl; Teachers Aide; Varsity Clb; Yrbk Stf; Var Capt Tennis; Pres NHS; Natl Merit Fnlst 86; Dartmouth Coll; Intl Bus.

SYEDA, HUMERA; Montpelier HS; Montpelier, VT; (Y); 2/108; Yrbk Stf; Cit Awd; High Hon Roll; NHS; Pres Schlr; Val; Century III Awd 85; NH JR Sci & Hmnts Sympsm 85; Outstndg Stu 85; Wesleyan U; Pre Med.

TAFT, ALISON; Harwood Union HS; Waterbury, VT; (Y); 2/130; Am Leg Aux Girls St; Church Yth Grp; Political Wkr; Service Clb; Yrbk Phtg; Yrbk Stf.

TALBOT, MICHAEL; Winooski HS; Winooski, VT; (Y); 3/60; Am Leg Boys St; Var Capt Bsbl; Var Capt Ftbl; Hon Roll; NHS; Coachs Awd Frsmn Bsbl, Frsmn Athlt Awd, Led Trm In Hitting 84; Ralph Lapointe Athltc Awd 85; U Of VT; Pre-Med.

TALLMAN JR, STEVEN E; Lamoille Union HS; Hyde Park, VT; (Y); 15/107; AFS; Boy Scts; JV Crs Cntry; Hon Roll; Voctnl Graphic Arts Outstndng Achvt Awd 86; Intl Fine Arts; Cmmnctn Desgn.

TATRO, PAMELA; Enosburg Falls HS; Enosburg Fls, VT; (Y); FHA; Pep Clb; Variety Show; Nwsp Stf; Yrbk Stf; Mgr(s); Score Keeper; Sftbl; High Hon Roll; Prfct Atten Awd; Hghst Frnch Achvmnt.

TAYLOR, BETH; Spaulding HS; Barre, VT; (Y); 12/250; Am Leg Aux Girls St; Varsity Clb; Yrbk Rptr; Sec Frsh Cls; Sec Soph Cls; Sec Jr Cls; Pres Stu Cncl; Var Capt Cheerleading; Hon Roll; Kiwanis Awd; Memrl Schlrshp 86; Hilda Allan Taplin Memrl Schlrshp 86; U Of Vermont; Adm.

TAYLOR, SHAWN FRANK; Whitingham HS; Jacksonville, VT; (Y); Spanish Clb; Teachers Aide; Varsity Clb; Band; Chorus; Rep Frsh Cls; VP Sr Cls; Var JV Bsbl; Var JV Bsktbl; Im Gym; MVP-SOCCER Awd 85-86; Natl Acadmc-Athltc Awd 85-86; US Army; Spec Forces.

TEDESCO, GUY; Mount Saint Joseph Acad; Rutland, VT; (Y); FBLA; SADD; Varsity Clb; Trs Frsh Cls; Trs Soph Cls; Trs Jr Cls; Trs Sr Cls; Var Capt Bsktbl; High Hon Roll; NHS; U VT JR Conf 86; New England Booksllrs Assn Book Review Wnnr 84; Advrtsng Campgn Bst Flat Ad Wnnr 84; Bus.

TERRIEN, AMY M; Rice Memorial HS; Burlington, VT; (Y); #8 In Class; Art Clb; Cmnty Wkr; Drama Clb; GAA; Chorus; Variety Show; Yrbk Bus Mgr; Yrbk Ed-Chief; Yrbk Rptr; Yrbk Stf; Miss HS All Around Girl 86; Schlr/Athlete 86; VT Schlrs Stu 86; Soc Wmns Engrs Schlrshp Awd 86; Dartmouth Coll.

TESSIER, CHAD; Windsor HS; Brownsville, VT; (Y); Am Leg Boys St; VP Church Yth Grp; Band; Drm Mjr(t); Mrchg Band; Yrbk Phtg; Lit Mag; Pres Soph Cls; Rep Sr Cls; Trk; Pol Sci.

TETREAULT, LYNNE; Bellow Free Acad; Fairfield, VT; (Y); 3/209; Am Leg Aux Girls St; Pres SADD; VP Jr Cls; Trs Sr Cls; Pres Stu Cncl; High Hon Roll; NHS; Church Yth Grp; Drama Clb; Giftd Talntd Pgm 84-86; U VT; Med.

THANASSI, DAVID G; South Burlington HS; South Burlington, VT; (Y); 2/190; Am Leg Boys St; Mathletes; Band; Chorus; Concert Band; Jazz Band; Orch; Symp Band; Variety Show; NHS; Renslr Awd Math & Sci 85; VT ST Brass Comptnt 1st Pl 85; Yth Orchstr Pres 85; Sci.

THATCHER, LAURA; Proctor HS; Rutland, VT; (Y); 7/54; French Clb; SADD; Chorus; Yrbk Sprt Ed; Yrbk Stf; Trs Sr Cls; Hon Roll; Bus Mgmt.

THOMAS, KARL; St Johnsbury Acad; Saint Johnsbury, VT; (Y); 2/120; Church Yth Grp; Intnl Clb; Latin Clb; VP Math Tm; Ski Clb; Yrbk Ed-Chief; Stat Bsbl; Var Crs Cntry; High Hon Roll; NHS; Rensselaer Mth & Sci Awd 86; Maxima Cum Laude Natl Latin Exam 84-85; Rsrch.

THOMPSON, GARY; Blue Mountain Union HS; Mc Indoe Falls, VT; (Y); Am Leg Boys St; Capt Bsbl; Capt Bsktbl; Capt Socr; High Hon Roll; Hon Roll; NHS; Excllnc Engl Awd; Engrng.

THOMPSON, GERI; Springfield HS; Springfield, VT; (Y); 9/152; Varsity Clb; Chorus; Variety Show; Var VP Bsktbl; JV Var Fld Hcky; JV Var Sftbl; Var Swmmng; High Hon Roll; Hon Roll; NHS; Champlain Coll; Bus Adm.

THOMPSON, KELLI; Chelsea HS; Bradford, VT; (Y); Church Yth Grp; VP FBLA; School Play; Rep Soph Cls; Rep Stu Cncl; Var Cheerleading; JV Sftbl; Hon Roll; Trvl Agent.

THOMPSON, THERESA; Burr & Burton Seminary; Manchester, VT; (Y); 8/100; Spanish Clb; Yrbk Stf; Var JV Cheerleading; Var JV Fld Hcky; Var Mgr(s); Var Mgr Sftbl; Hon Roll; NHS; Prfct Atten Awd; Spnsh Exchng 85; Fshn Merch.

TILLEY, PATRICIA; Colchester HS; Colchester, VT; (Y); 8/208; Var Crs Cntry; Var Socr; Var Trk; Trs Debate Tm; X-Cntry Skiing 82-86; U Of VT; Engrng.

TILLOTSON, LEIF; Enosburg Falls HS; Bakersfield, VT; (Y); Am Leg Boys St; VP Church Yth Grp; FFA; Band; Concert Band; Mrchg Band; Orch; Yrbk Stf; High Hon Roll; Hon Roll; Engl Excllnce Awd 84; Hofstra U; Cmmnctn Arts.

TODD, BECKY; Proctor HS; Chittenden, VT; (Y); 14/37; Art Clb; Church Yth Grp; French Clb; Var Mgr(s); Var Score Keeper; Var L Sftbl; Hon Roll; Natl Art Awd 86; St Josephs VT; Accntng.

TOMCZAK, KATHY; Burlington HS; Burlington, VT; (Y); Letterman Clb; Band; Concert Band; Mrchg Band; Yrbk Stf; Gym; Co-Capt Socr; Trk; Hon Roll; Outstndng Stu Data Proc & Accntng 86; U Of Southern CA; Bus.

TOWER, D MARTIN; Vermont Acad; Rindge, NH; (S); 15/85; SADD; Varsity Clb; Band; Chorus; School Play; Yrbk Stf; Var Bsktbl; Var Ftbl; Var Lcrss; Hon Roll.

TOWNSEND, HOWARD; Lyndon Institute HS; Lyndon Center, VT; (Y); Boy Scts; Church Yth Grp; Latin Clb; Church Choir; Var L Bsbl; Var L Bsktbl; Hon Roll; Elec Engr.

TREAT, DANNY; Burr & Burton Seminary; Manchester, VT; (Y); Boy Scts; Church Yth Grp; Ski Clb; L Crs Cntry; JV Trk; Hon Roll; Prfct Atten Awd.

TREMBLAY, CHRISTOPHER; Hartford HS; Wilder, VT; (Y); School Musical; JV Var Ice Hcky; JV Var Socr; Hon Roll; Coaches Awd-Soccer 84.

TREMBLAY, NORMAN; Missisquoi Valley U HS; Highgate Ctr, VT; (Y); Math Clb; School Play; Pres Jr Cls; JV Bsbl; Hon Roll; NHS; Prfct Atten Awd; Brdcstng.

TROMBLEY, RONALD; Burlington HS; Burlington, VT; (Y); JV Var Bsktbl; JV Var Ftbl; JV Im Lcrss; Im Wt Lftg; Hon Roll; UNC; Sports Med.

TROMBLEY, SALYNN; Peoples Acad; Barre, VT; (Y); 5/60; French Clb; Ski Clb; Variety Show; Yrbk Sprt Ed; Sec Stu Cncl; Capt Bsktbl; Golf; Capt Socr; Amer Legn Certft Schl Awd 86; Copley Hosp Schlrshp Asso 86; Sharon Brown Memrl Awd; U VT; Physcl Therpy.

TRUDEAU, DONALD J; Mt Anthony Union HS; Pownal, VT; (Y); 5/273; Am Leg Boys St; Church Yth Grp; French Clb; Ed Lit Mag; Stu Cncl; L JV Socr; Var L Tennis; High Hon Roll; VP NHS; Ntl Merit Ltr; Knights Columbus ST Cncl Scholar 86; Knights Columbus Greatest Achvt Awd 86; Williams Coll; Physics.

TRUDEAU, EDWARD; Mount Anthony Union HS; Pownal, VT; (Y); 2/270; Rep Am Leg Boys St; Church Yth Grp; CAP; JV Socr; High Hon Roll; NHS; Ntl Merit SF; RPI Medl Wnnr 85-86; Colby Bk Awd Wnnr 85-86; Brown Bk Awd Wnnr 85-86; Aerospc Engr.

TRUDELL, KELLY; Peoples Acad; Morrisville, VT; (Y); Dance Clb; Drama Clb; Hosp Aide; SADD; Thesps; Band; Color Guard; Concert Band; Mrchg Band; Orch; 2nd Pl Govs Natl Hist Day 85; VT Excel Prog Norwich U 85-86; U Of VT; Nutrition.

TRUDELL, MARY MARGARET; Peoples Acad; Morrisville, VT; (Y); 12/64; Dance Clb; Band; Mrchg Band; Variety Show; Sec Soph Cls; High Hon Roll; Hon Roll; Sec NHS; Art Clb; Drama Clb; Co-Oprnts Frnch Awd 1st Pl ST 84; 2nd Pl Govs Natl Hist Day 85; VT Excel Norwich U 2 Sems 85-86; Art.

TRUEMAN, DAVID J; Vergennes Union High; No Ferrisburg, VT; (Y); 12/101; Concert Band; Jazz Band; Mrchg Band; Pep Band; Yrbk Stf; Golf; NHS; Church Yth Grp; German Clb; Band; All ST Brass Schlrshp 2nd Pl 86; Boston U Tanglewd Inst 85; Vergennes Area Rescue Sq; Wake Forest U; Bio.

TULER, ANGELA; Montpelier HS; Montpelier, VT; (Y); 36/101; Pres Debate Tm; Pres VP 4-H; French Clb; Latin Clb; Band; Mrchg Band; Yrbk Stf; Mgr Trk; 4-H Awd; High Hon Roll; Exch Prog Swtzrlnd 86; Silvr M; U Of VT; Psych.

TULLAR, JEFFREY; Chelsea HS; Corinth, VT; (Y); Church Yth Grp; Cmnty Wkr; FBLA; School Play; VP Frsh Cls; VP Soph Cls; Var Capt Bsbl; Var Capt Bsktbl; Var Socr; Husson Coll.

TURNER, CHARLENE; Rutland HS; Rutland, VT; (Y); Color Guard; Drm & Bgl; Flag Corp; Yrbk Stf; High Hon Roll; Hon Roll; Colorguard Person Of Yr 85; Freedom Knight Of Yr 85; Bus.

TURNER, EDWARD A; Harwood Union HS; Waitsfield, VT; (Y); Teachers Aide; Rep Sr Cls; JV Var Bsbl; JV Bsktbl; JV Var Mgr(s); JV Var Score Keeper; Var Socr; NHS; Pres Schlr; Coaches Awd-Outstndg Svcs To Athls 86; U Of VT; Engl.

TWISS, NANCY; Whitingham Schl; Whitingham, VT; (Y); 10/21; Drama Clb; Spanish Clb; SADD; Teachers Aide; Chorus; School Musical; JV Var Cheerleading; JV Fld Hcky; Var Score Keeper; Champlain Coll; Chldhd Ed.

USHER, KARL; Rice Memorial HS; Colchester, VT; (Y); 5/144; Am Leg Boys St; Church Yth Grp; Spanish Clb; Band; Concert Band; Jazz Band; Pep Band; School Play; Var Golf; High Hon Roll; Tech Engnrng.

VALCOUR, MAURICE; Peoples Acad; Morrisville, VT; (Y); Pres Aud/Vis; Boy Scts; Trs Church Yth Grp; Drama Clb; Band; Chorus; Jazz Band; Mrchg Band; School Musical; School Play; Diesel/Auto Mech.

VALENTINE, MICHAEL; Mt St Josephs Acad; Rutland, VT; (Y); Debate Tm; Drama Clb; English Clb; Quiz Bowl; Scholastic Bowl; Varsity Clb; School Play; Stage Crew; Yrbk Sprt Ed; Yrbk Stf; Coachs Awd Tnns 86; Juror Mock Trial 86; ST Ftbl Champ 86; Darthmouth; Bio.

VALZ, JENNIFER; Vergennes Union HS; Vergennes, VT; (Y); 1/130; Pres Trs 4-H; Lib Chorus; Rep Frsh Cls; VP Soph Cls; VP Jr Cls; JV Var Bsktbl; JV Var Crs Cntry; 4-H Awd; Rnnr Up Japan US Sen Schlrshp Pgm 85-86; Hugh O Brian Ldrshp Conf 84; Outstndg JR Conf; U Of VT; Pre Med.

VANDEWEERT, JEAN; Vergennes Union HS; Ferrisburg, VT; (Y); 21/97; Church Yth Grp; German Clb; Church Choir; Yrbk Stf; JV Var Bsktbl; Im Tennis; Hon Roll; Bus Schlrshp 86; Crvt Trst Fnd 86; Liberty U; Acctg.

VARGO, GERALD L; Whitcomb HS; Bethel, VT; (Y); 7/28; CAP; Band; Jazz Band; Mrchg Band; Trs Sr Cls; Bsktbl; Socr; Bausch & Lomb Sci Awd; High Hon Roll; Hon Roll; FL Inst Tech; Aviatn Flght Tec.

VERAGUTH, DONNA; Brattleboro Union HS; W Dover, VT; (Y); Art Clb; Church Yth Grp; Intnl Clb; Model UN; Ski Clb; Yrbk Phtg; Hon Roll; Excllnc In Art Awd; Rookie Of The Yr Awd-Ski Tm; Photo.

VERCHEREAU, JOAN; Montpelier U 32 HS; Montpelier, VT; (Y); 30/120; Varsity Clb; Nwsp Rptr; Nwsp Stf; Off Frsh Cls; Off Soph Cls; Off Jr Cls; Off Sr Cls; Var VP Bsktbl; Var Fld Hcky; Hon Roll; Lyndon ST Coll Pres Schlrshp, Acctg I Bst Stu Awd, Fld Hcky Unsung Heroine Awd 86; Lyndon ST Coll; Rec Ther.

VIENS, CARMEN; Enosburg Falls HS; Enosburg Falls, VT; (Y); 6/65; Red Cross Aide; Variety Show; Yrbk Stf; Trs Frsh Cls; Trs Soph Cls; VP Jr Cls; Off Stu Cncl; Bsktbl; Capt Socr; Capt Sftbl; VT All St Sccr, New Eng All St Sccr, Schlrshp Pgnt USAC Hnr Schlrshp 85-86; Dean Blaisdell Awd; Champlain Coll; Fshn Merch.

VIENS, JOHANNE; Enosburg Falls HS; Enosburg Fls, VT; (Y); French Clb; Pep Clb; SADD; Nwsp Stf; VP Soph Cls; JV Var Bsktbl; Var Score Keeper; Var Socr; Var Sftbl; Phy Ed.

VIERZEN, JELTINA; Vergennes Union HS; Vergennes, VT; (Y); 24/121; Church Yth Grp; 4-H; Intnl Clb; Red Cross Aide; Rep Jr Cls; VP Sr Cls; JV Bsktbl; High Hon Roll; Hon Roll; Frgn Rltns.

VINCENT, JEFFREY; Rice Memorial HS; Burlington, VT; (Y); 25/130; VP Church Yth Grp; Chorus; Church Choir; Trs Stu Cncl; JV Bsbl; JV Var Bsktbl; Trk; Hon Roll; Scl Wrk.

VITAGLIANO, SALVATORE; Mt Saint Joseph Acad; Rutland, VT; (Y); Debate Tm; Drama Clb; FBLA; SADD; Varsity Clb; School Play; Variety Show; Var L Bsbl; Var L Bsktbl; Var L Ftbl; Dentstry.

VOGHELL, SCOTT; Hartford HS; Hartland, VT; (Y); Boy Scts; Prfct Atten Awd; Otstndng Stu 86; Elec.

VOSS, BARRY; Rice Memorial HS; Shelburne, VT; (Y); 6/108; Trs VP Church Yth Grp; Computer Clb; School Play; Rep Stu Cncl; Stat Score Keeper; Var Capt Socr; Trk; Hon Roll; NHS; Ski Clb; Dartmouth Book Awd 85; Jim Of Mnth Awd For Nwpr Carrier 86; Clarkson U; Engrng.

WADE, MATT; Arlington Memorial HS; E Arlington, VT; (Y); 7/50; Am Leg Boys St; Boy Scts; Church Yth Grp; Band; Chorus; Var Bsbl; Var Bsktbl; Var Socr; UT NH Lions Clb Soccer JR Mgr; Ntl Hnr Soc.

WADKINS, JIM; Chelsea HS; Washington, VT; (Y); VP Computer Clb; Sec FFA; Var Bsbl; VT Tech Coll; Elec Engr.

WAGNER, GRETCHEN; Burlington HS; Burlington, VT; (Y); AFS; Am Leg Aux Girls St; GAA; Latin Clb; Band; Concert Band; School Musical; Yrbk Stf; Stu Cncl; Var Trk; All-ST Bnd 85-86; NE Bnd 86; Williams Coll Bk Awd 86; Jrnlsm.

WALBRIDGE, LISA; Burington HS; Burlington, VT; (Y); AFS; Church Yth Grp; Drama Clb; SADD; Chorus; Orch; Symp Band; Trk; Hon Roll; NHS; Educ.

WALKER, STEVEN; Burlington HS; Burlington, VT; (Y); Psych.

WALLER, LYNN; Champlain Valley HS; Charlotte, VT; (Y); AFS; Am Leg Aux Girls St; Church Yth Grp; Cmnty Wkr; Drama Clb; Key Clb; Political Wkr; Teachers Aide; Acpl Chr; Chorus; Kathy M Sringer Devost Memrl Schlrshp Awd 86; Skidmore Coll.

WALSH, BRANDON; Vermont Acad; Miami, FL; (Y); God Cntry Awd; US Open Jr Snwbrdng Co-Chmpn 85-86; 3rd Pl Salom & Giant Slalom -Wrld Snwbrdng Classic 86.

WALSH, MINDY; Brattleboro Union HS; Brattlebro, VT; (S); DECA; Art Clb; Drama Clb; FBLA; Model UN; SADD; Chorus; Variety Show; Rep Frsh Cls; Rep Stu Cncl; Mrktng.

WARDEN, ALICE; St Johnsbury Acad; Barnet, VT; (Y); Drama Clb; 4-H; French Clb; SADD; JV Bsktbl; JV Fld Hcky; High Hon Roll; Ntl Merit Ltr; Top 10 Score Schl UVM Math Tst; Arch.

WARREN, KAREN; Harwood Union HS; Waterbury, VT; (Y); Teachers Aide; JV Var Cheerleading; High Hon Roll; Hon Roll; NHS; Pep Clb; Varsity Clb; Acctng Awd 85-86; Hnr Rl Awd 84-86; Steno Awd 85-86; Champlain Coll; Acctng.

WARWICK, WAYNE; Brattleboro Union HS; Brattleboro, VT; (Y); Model UN; Band; Chorus; Concert Band; Jazz Band; Mrchg Band; Pep Band; School Musical; Variety Show; MA U Amherst; Music.

WASHBURN, BRENDA; Windsor HS; Windsor, VT; (Y); 8/64; AFS; Band; Church Choir; Concert Band; Mrchg Band; NHS; Pep Clb; Chorus; Jazz Band; School Play; Fshn Merch.

WASHBURN, LISA; Peoples Acad; Morrisville, VT; (Y); 7/57; Church Yth Grp; Hosp Aide; SADD; Band; Chorus; Church Choir; Mrchg Band; School Musical; NHS; Prfct Atten Awd; Ntl Hnr Soc Schlrshp 86; Pro Merito Hnr Stu 86; Champlain Coll; Acctng.

WATERHOUSE, LAURIE; Craftsbury Acad; Craftsbury, VT; (Y); 3/13; Am Leg Aux Girls St; Chorus; Church Choir; Variety Show; Yrbk Bus Mgr; Yrbk Stf; VP Soph Cls; Var Bsktbl; Var Mgr(s); Var Socr; Paul Smiths Coll; Pre-Med.

WAY, LAURIE A; South Burlington HS; S Burlington, VT; (Y); 19/184; Church Yth Grp; French Clb; Intnl Clb; Pep Clb; SADD; Chorus; Nwsp Rptr; Nwsp Stf; Var Capt Cheerleading; Hon Roll; Volnteer Fndraisng Public TV 85; Spec Olymp Volnteer 85; Wrtg.

WEAVER, RACHEL; Bellowo Free Acad; St Albans, VT; (Y); 40/249; Cmnty Wkr; Hosp Aide; Spanish Clb; SADD; Sec Jr Cls; Stat Bsbl; JV Var Cheerleading; JV Var Crs Cntry; Var Pom Pon; Var Stat Trk; VT Miss TEEN Pgnt-5th Rnnr Up 84; USA TEEN Miss Pgnt-1st Rnnr Up 85; VT TEEN USA Fnlst 85; Middlebury Coll; Spansh Tranltr.

WEBSTER, ERIC; Randolph Union HS; Randolph, VT; (Y); 12/90; Am Leg Boys St; Boy Scts; Church Yth Grp; Band; Jazz Band; Mrchg Band; Yrbk Stf; Hon Roll; NHS; Stu Of Mnth 85; Franklin Pierce Coll; Bus Adm.

WELLS, KIM; Mississquoi Valley HS; Sheldon, VT; (Y); Art Clb; Church Yth Grp; Teachers Aide; Variety Show; Yrbk Stf; Sec Frsh Cls; Sec Soph Cls; Rep Jr Cls; Sec Sr Cls; Stu Cncl; Skit Night Awd 84; Art Mgmt.

WELLS, MICHELLE C; Vermont Acad; Westminster West, VT; (S); Math Tm; Var Ski Clb; Rep Jr Cls; Var L Bsktbl; Var Capt Lcrss; Var L Socr; Hon Roll; Peer Supprt Grp 83-86; Hugh O Brian Yth Org 85.

WELLS, TRICIA; Calais U 32 HS; Calais, VT; (Y); 6/120; Drama Clb; Pres Frsh Cls; Pres Soph Cls; Off Jr Cls; Bsktbl; Cheerleading; Fld Hcky; High Hon Roll; NHS; U Of VT; Engrng.

WERNECKE, JENNIFER; Northfield J 32 HS; Northfield, VT; (Y); 2/112; Dance Clb; French Clb; Varsity Clb; Yrbk Stf; Lit Mag; Var Gym; JV Sftbl; Var Capt Trk; High Hon Roll; NHS; U VT; Psych.

WEST, TONYA; Essex Jct Educational Ctr; Essex Junction, VT; (Y); Mgr French Clb; Mgr Yrbk Stf; JV Var Sftbl; Lyndon ST Coll; Comm Arts.

WESTER, BETH; Mount Anthony Union HS; Bennington, VT; (Y); Drama Clb; French Clb; Pres SADD; Chorus; School Musical; School Play; Variety Show; Fld Hcky; Vllybl; Hon Roll; Tchr Hrng Imprd.

WESTNEY, CRAIG; Windsor HS; Taftsville, VT; (Y); 8/58; Am Leg Boys St; French Clb; Ski Clb; Rep Stu Cncl; Var L Ftbl; Hon Roll; NHS; Syracuse U; Mech Engrng.

WHEELER, BRENDA M; Lake Region Union HS; Albany, VT; (Y); 16/88; Sec DECA; Pep Clb; Yrbk Sprt Ed; VP Soph Cls; Trs Jr Cls; Rep Sr Cls; VP Capt Cheerleading; Hon Roll; NHS.

WHEELER, ERIK; Mount Saint Joseph Acad; Pittsford, VT; (Y); 10/90; Drama Clb; Science Clb; Band; Chorus; Jazz Band; Mrchg Band; Yrbk Phtg; Var Crs Cntry; Var Lcrss; Wt Lftg; Psych.

WHITE, REBECCA; Arlington Memorial HS; Arlington, VT; (Y); Yrbk Stf; Hon Roll; Yrbkk Staff Art Edtr 85-86; London Schl Art; Art.

WHITLEY, PATRICK; Rochester JR SR HS; Rochester, VT; (Y); Am Leg Boys St; Varsity Clb; School Play; Trs Frsh Cls; Trs Soph Cls; Rep Jr Cls; L Var Socr; Hon Roll; Vermont Hnrs Comptn Exclnc Wrtng 85-86; Cert Prof Century 21 Accntng Typng 85-86; Accntng.

WHITNEY, CATHERINE E; Montpelier HS; Montpelier, VT; (Y); 14/115; Sec Spanish Clb; Trs Sr Cls; Var Capt Bsktbl; Var Crs Cntry; Var Fld Hcky; Var Capt Sftbl; Im Vllybl; High Hon Roll; Montpelier Womens Clb Schlrshp 86; Ct St Augustine No 976 Catholic Daughters Of Amer Schlrshp 86; U Of VT; Phys Thrpy.

WHITNEY, SARAH; Emsburg Falls HS; E Fairfield, VT; (Y); FFA; FHA; Band; Concert Band; Mrchg Band; Yrbk Stf; Off Stu Cncl; JV Var Bsktbl; JV Var Socr; Hon Roll; Outstndng Achvt Wind Ensmbl Cncrt Band 84; Mst Prffcnt Band Stu 84; Achvt Hist & Engl; Champlain Coll; Accntng.

WICK, JEFF; Burlington HS; Burlington, VT; (Y); Cmnty Wkr; Jazz Band; Var Ice Hcky; Hon Roll; NHS; Ntl Merit Ltr; VT Gov Inst Arts 86.

WILKINS, CAROL; Saint Johnsbury Acad; Saint Johnsbury, VT; (Y); 12/167; French Clb; Band; Concert Band; Jazz Band; Mrchg Band; Pep Band; Var L Trk; High Hon Roll; Hon Roll; NHS; U VT; Agri.

WILLARD, SCOTT; Spaulding HS; Barre, VT; (Y); 46/259; Key Clb; VICA; Var Lcrss; High Hon Roll; Hon Roll; Schl Spnsrd Athltc Actvty Rflry JV; Comp.

WILLEY, KIM; Lyndon Inst; St Johnsbury, VT; (Y); Capt Fld Hcky; High Hon Roll; Hon Roll; Prfct Atten Awd; Champlain; Sec Sci.

WILLIAMS, ANNE MARIE; Otter Valley Union HS; Brandon, VT; (Y); 15/102; Latin Clb; Band; Church Choir; Concert Band; Jazz Band; Mrchg Band; School Musical; Variety Show; NHS; Semper Fidelis Awd Musicl Exc 86; Summa Cum Laude Latin 85; Spcl Recgntn Exc Adv Band 86; Music.

WILLIAMS, DIANA; Windsor HS; Windsor, VT; (Y); Pep Clb; Band; Concert Band; Mrchg Band; JV Var Cheerleading; JV Fld Hcky; NHS; NEDT Awd.

WILLIAMS, KAREN; Arlington Memorial HS; Arlington, VT; (Y); Variety Show; Var Bsktbl; Stat Fld Hcky; JV Var Sftbl; High Hon Roll; Hon Roll; Prfct Atten Awd; US Am Frgn Lang Assn Hon Roll 85; Business.

WILLIAMS, RHONDA; Whitingham Schl; Whitingham, VT; (S); 3/25; GAA; Spanish Clb; Concert Band; Yrbk Ed-Chief; Trs Sr Cls; Trs Stu Cncl; Fld Hcky; Leo Clb; Teachers Aide; Band; Yth Of Amer Europe Tour Concrt Band 85; All ST Music Fest-Band 83 & 84; All New England Music Fest 84; Putnam Mem Schl Of Prac Nursng.

WILSON, GEORGIANA; Vermont Acad; Lake Placid, NY; (Y); Intnl Clb; Key Clb; Ski Clb; Varsity Clb; Yrbk Stf; Lit Mag; Pres Frsh Cls; Rep Jr Cls; Stu Cncl; Capt Socr; Gold Ltr Awd Skiing; MVP Soccer.

WINTERS, MICHAEL; Missisquoi Valley Union HS; Swanton, VT; (Y); Church Yth Grp; Ski Clb; Var Crs Cntry; Var Trk; High Hon Roll; Hon Roll; NHS.

WITT, SHERI; Arlington Memorial HS; Arlington, VT; (Y); Varsity Clb; Band; School Play; Stage Crew; Lit Mag; Sec Jr Cls; Var L Bsktbl; Var L Fld Hcky; Var L Sftbl; Hon Roll.

WOLCOTT, LINDA D; Vermont Acad; Saxtons River, VT; (S); Spanish Clb; Acpl Chr; Chorus; School Musical; School Play; Variety Show; Lit Mag; Pres Soph Cls; Rep Jr Cls; Im Badmtn; Hdmstrs List Acad Hnrs 83-87; MIP Area Smmr Swim Team 84.

WOODARD, CHRISTINA; North Country Union HS; Newport Center, VT; (Y); 33/254; Flag Corp; High Hon Roll; Lion Awd; Book Of Knowldg Awd-A Avg 83-85; Schlrhsp Ltr-A Avg 85-86; Champlain Coll; Accntng.

WRIGHT, DEAN; Enosburg Falls HS; Enosburg Falls, VT; (S); 4-H; FFA; Band; Var Bsktbl; 4-H Awd; ST FFA VP 85-86; 2nd Pl Dairy Jdgng Tm Natl FFA 85; VT Tech Coll; Ag.

WRIGHT, JAY; St Johnsbury Acad; Saint Johnsbury, VT; (Y); 1/130; Am Leg Boys St; Math Clb; Quiz Bowl; Var L Bsktbl; Var Capt Crs Cntry; Var L Trk; Bausch & Lomb Sci Awd; High Hon Roll; NHS; Prfct Scr Natl Latn Exm 86; Bankng.

WRIGHT, STEPHEN; Craftsbury Acad; Craftsbury Common, VT; (S); 3/11; Am Leg Boys St; FBLA; Ski Clb; Capt Bsbl; Var Bsktbl; Var Socr; High Hon Roll; Hon Roll; VP NHS; Top 10 Pct UVM Math Cntst 85-86; Wrtg Publshd Mt Review 83; U Of VT; Geolgy.

WYLLIE, SUSAN; St Johnsbury Acad; Saint Johnsbury, VT; (Y); 18/150; Church Yth Grp; FBLA; Spanish Clb; SADD; Var Bsktbl; Var Socr; Var Trk; High Hon Roll; NHS; Bus Mgmnt.

WYMAN, MICHELLE; Arlington Memorial HS; Arlington, VT; (Y); Am Leg Aux Girls St; Pres Church Yth Grp; Yrbk Sprt Ed; Sec Frsh Cls; Var Bsktbl; Var Fld Hcky; Var Sftbl; High Hon Roll; Hon Roll; NHS; Math.

WYMAN, SUE; Otter Valley Univ HS; Brandon, VT; (S); French Clb; GAA; Latin Clb; Trs Frsh Cls; Trs Soph Cls; VP Jr Cls; Rep Stu Cncl; Var L Bsktbl; Var L Fld Hcky; Hon Roll; CVGAL Grls Athl All Leag Goalie 84-85; Stdnt Mnth 85; Mst Dedctd Fld Hcky 84; Exercs Sci.

YAGER, PETER; Arlington Memorial HS; Arlington, VT; (Y); Ski Clb; Yrbk Stf; Bsbl; Bsktbl; Socr; Indstrl Arts Awd 85-86; Art Awd 85-86; Engrng.

YOUNG, ANDREA; Lake Region Union HS; Glover, VT; (Y); Church Yth Grp; DECA; Pep Clb; VP Jr Cls; Trs Stu Cncl; JV Bsktbl; Socr; Hon Roll; DECA Fd Serv 2nd & 4th Pl 86; Trvl.

YOUNG, BRAD; Twinfield HS; Plainfield, VT; (Y); Church Yth Grp; Drama Clb; FFA; Band; Chorus; Church Choir; Madrigals; Ftbl; Hon Roll; NHS; US Marine Corps; Med.

YOUNG, MARILYN; Lyndon Inst; Lyndonville, VT; (Y); 12/105; High Hon Roll; Hon Roll; NHS; Oreanna Merriam Awd 86.

YOUNG, STEPHANIE; Enosburg Falls HS; Enosburg Falls, VT; (Y); 15/67; Am Leg Aux Girls St; FHA; Ski Clb; Teachers Aide; Yrbk Ed-Chief; Trs Var Stu Cncl; Var Capt Socr; Cit Awd; DAR Awd; Hon Roll; Stu Of Mnth 85; Chmpln Coll; Trvl.

ZAHLER, REUBEN; Champlain Valley Union HS; Charlotte, VT; (Y); Drama Clb; Model UN; School Musical; School Play; Var Wrstlng; High Hon Roll; Hon Roll; NHS; Amer Assn Of Spnsh & Prtguese Awd 86; Mohandas Gandhi Awd 86; Engl Awd 83; Cornell U; Hist.

ZEHLE, MONIKA; Essex Jct Educational Ctr; Essex Ject, VT; (Y); French Clb; Intnl Clb; Latin Clb; Varsity Clb; Nwsp Stf; Yrbk Sprt Ed; Stat Var Ice Hcky; Var L Tennis; Pres YMCA Ldrs Club 85-86; Tm Ldr Supercamp 86; Mktg.

VIRGIN ISLANDS

BAILEY, CARON; Antilles Schl; St Thomas, VI; (Y); Dance Clb; Office Aide; Trs Spanish Clb; Chorus; School Musical; Yrbk Stf; Pres Jr Cls; Trs Stu Cncl; JV Var Sftbl; Co-Capt Vllybl; Albrt Keep Awd 84-85; Mst Outstndng Mscl Stu 85-86; Tchrs Awd; Bus.

CALDERON, CELINDA; Central HS; Christiansted, VI; (Y); Art Clb; Dance Clb; English Clb; Exploring; Girl Scts; Math Clb; ROTC; Spanish Clb; Chorus; Sec Frsh Cls; Med.

CALLWOOD, CONCHA; Charlotte Amalie HS; St Thomas, VI; (S); Pres Church Yth Grp; Office Aide; Service Clb; Spanish Clb; Lit Mag; Rep Sr Cls; Var Sftbl; High Hon Roll; Jr NHS; NHS; 2nd Interschltc Indl Arts Drftg Comptn 83; 1st Pl Locl Natl Spnsh Exm 85; 2nd Pl Grp Entry Sci Fair 85; U Of Tampa; Socl Sci.

CHARLTON, JENNIE; Charlotte Amalie HS; St Thomas, VI; (Y); Church Yth Grp; Drama Clb; English Clb; French Clb; FHA; Spanish Clb; Church Choir; Cit Awd; High Hon Roll; NHS; Acad All Amer Awd 83-86; Rgnl Spllng Bee Chmpn 78; Nat Ldrshp Awd 85-86; PA Sst U; Med.

CONNOR, RYAN; Antilles HS; St Thomas, VI; (Y); 3/17; Church Yth Grp; Debate Tm; Quiz Bowl; Teachers Aide; Band; Yrbk Phtg; Yrbk Stf; L Ftbl; L Var Socr; Var L Sftbl; Intrschltc Athltc Assoc Awd 86; Pilot.

CORNISH, BEN M; Antilles Schl; St Thomas, VI; (Y); Quiz Bowl; Trs Jr Cls; Pres Sr Cls; Var L Ftbl; Capt L Tennis; Hon Roll; NHS; Law.

COTTO, SANDRA; St Croix Central HS; Kingshll-St Croix, VI; (Y); Dance Clb; FBLA; Girl Scts; Pep Clb; Spanish Clb; School Musical; Variety Show; Cheerleading; Hon Roll; Prfct Atten Awd; Bus Mgr.

DAVIS, SHARMANE P; Antilles Schl; St Thomas, VI; (Y); 2/18; Debate Tm; English Clb; Spanish Clb; Chorus; Nwsp Stf; Yrbk Stf; Lit Mag; Pres Frsh Cls; Sec Stu Cncl; High Hon Roll; Fclty Schlrshp 85-86; Natl Jr Hnr Soc Schlrshp 85-86; Crmnlgy.

DUGGINS, DESHONE; Charlotte Amalie HS; St Thomas, VI; (S); Church Yth Grp; Dance Clb; Office Aide; Sec Chorus; Church Choir; Jazz Band; Stu Cncl; Cheerleading; Hon Roll; NHS; Englsh Awd & Majorette Of Yr 83; Miss Sop Sweetheart , Miss Intellct & Miss Popularity 84; FLA A&M U; Sec Educ Hstry.

GARDNER, CAROLYN; Charlotte Amalie HS; St Thomas, VI; (S); Boy Scts; Church Yth Grp; Drama Clb; Exploring; French Clb; Hosp Aide; Math Tm; Radio Clb; Teachers Aide; School Play; De Paul U; Pre-Med.

GUTH, HEIDI; Antilles Schl; St Thomas, VI; (Y); Library Aide; Quiz Bowl; Nwsp Stf; Lit Mag; Trs Stu Cncl; Jr NHS; NHS; Spanish Clb; Trs Frsh Cls; Sec Jr Cls; Hdmstrs Awd 86; Outstndng Englsh Stu 85-86; Dartmouth; Wrtr.

HAMILTON, ALISA F; St Joseph HS; Christiansted, VI; (Y); 3/73; Sec FBLA; Trs Pep Clb; Church Choir; Pres Frsh Cls; VP Jr Cls; Pres Sr Cls; Score Keeper; Var Vllybl; High Hon Roll; Sec Church Yth Grp; Tulane U; Bio.

HEIKKILA, ERIK; Antilles Schl; St Thomas, VI; (Y); Yrbk Phtg; Yrbk Stf; Var Socr; Virgin Islnds Olympic Gymnstc Tm 84-86; Outstndng Phy Ed Stu 86; Brnz Mdl Gyn Hgh Bar Puerto Rico 85.

JOSEPH, DARCY; Charlotte Amalie HS; St Thomas, VI; (S); Sec Spanish Clb; Rep Jr Cls; Pres Sr Cls; Rep Stu Cncl; Var Vllybl; High Hon Roll; Hon Roll; Pres NHS; US Art Awd 85-86; Outstndng Svc Awd 85-86; NC A&T ST U; Bus Educ.

LAWRENCE, DERRICK; Antilles Schl; St Thomas, VI; (Y); 1/18; Quiz Bowl; Spanish Clb; High Hon Roll; Jr NHS; NHS; Prfct Atten Awd; Mrtn Lthr Kng Essay Cntst 86; Med.

LIDICKER, ERIC C; Antilles Schl; St John, VI; (Y); Quiz Bowl; Spanish Clb; Nwsp Bus Mgr; Nwsp Rptr; Nwsp Sprt Ed; Lit Mag; Pres Soph Cls; Rep Stu Cncl; Scl Sci Awd 85; American U Wash DC; Jrnlsm.

MATTHEW, JULIEN; Charlotte Amalie HS; St John, VI; (S); FBLA; Varsity Clb; Nwsp Ed-Chief; Nwsp Rptr; Stu Cncl; Tennis; Trk; Vllybl; Natl VP FBLA 85-86; Chmbr Commrc Advsry Cncl 82-86; U CT New Haven; Htl Mngmnt.

MILLER, JOHANN; Antilles Schl; St Thomas, VI; (Y); Spanish Clb; Lit Mag; Pratt; Art And Dsgn.

MORON, JACKIE; Charlotte Amalie HS; St Thomas, VI; (Y); Cmnty Wkr; Leo Clb; Pep Clb; Political Wkr; Radio Clb; Spanish Clb; Teachers Aide; Cheerleading; Hon Roll; Poetry Awd 83; Cert Poliana Mdlng Schl 84; Cert Couture Mdlng Schl 85; Intl Coll Fine Arts; Fshn Mrchn.

NESTOR, STEPHEN; St Croix Central HS; Kingshill, VI; (Y); 1/480; Computer Clb; Radio Clb; School Play; Rep Sr Cls; Rep Stu Cncl; High Hon Roll; Hon Roll; Pres Spanish NHS; Val; Upward Bnd Stu Of The Yr Awd 85-86; Pres Clsrm Stu Awd 85; Mc Donalds Outstndng Stu Awd 83; Boston U; Engrng.

OWEN, GEMAINE; St Croix Central HS; Christiansted, VI; (Y); Church Yth Grp; Quiz Bowl; Radio Clb; Orch; Rep Stu Cncl; Hst NHS; Spanish NHS; Val; Hovic Merit Awd 86; AFT Schlrshp 86; Johns Hopkins U; Biomed Engr.

PICKERING, JEFFREY; Charlotte Amalie HS; St Thomas, VI; (S); 32/417; Church Yth Grp; Office Aide; Radio Clb; Spanish Clb; Teachers Aide; Church Choir; Stage Crew; Nwsp Ed-Chief; Nwsp Rptr; Nwsp Stf; Guidnc Aid & Chem Awds 84-85; VI Leg Page Cert 8k; Coll Of VI; Acctg.

SMALL, MAVIS; Charlotte Amalie HS; St Thomas, VI; (S); Church Yth Grp; Hon Roll; NHS; Acadmc All Amer 85; Natl Ldrshp & Svc Awd 86; Coll Of The Virgin Islands; Law.

SUTHERLAND, IAN; Antilles HS; St Thomas, VI; (Y); Quiz Bowl; Lit Mag; High Hon Roll; Hon Roll; Jr NHS; NHS; Spnsh Quiz Bwl 85; Bus.

TORRENS, MARISOL; St Croix Central HS; C Sted St Croix, VI; (Y); Pres Church Yth Grp; French Clb; Spanish Clb; School Play; French Hon Soc; Hon Roll; NHS; Spanish NHS; Svc Awd Of Natl Hnr Socy 85-86; Bilingual Tutorial Awd 85-86; U Of Turabo; Bio.

TURNBULL, MARIO; Charlotte Amalie HS; St Thomas, VI; (S); 53/417; Office Aide; Chorus; Concert Band; Yrbk Stf; Pres Frsh Cls; Pres Soph Cls; Pres Jr Cls; Pres Stu Cncl; Hon Roll; NHS; Charlotte Amalie-Outstndg Ldrshp 83 & 84; 1st Pl Cmmnctn Arts Show Case 86; Prncpls Awd 84-85; Coll Of The VI; Math Tchr.

WALTERS, WAYNE N; Charlotte Amalie HS; St Thomas, VI; (Y); Church Yth Grp; JA; Math Tm; Band; Concert Band; Pres Jazz Band; Mrchg Band; Pep Band; Symp Band; Variety Show; Mst Imprvd Frshmn & Soph 82-84; Outstndng JR Solo 84-85; Music.

ZIMNEY, RICHARD; Charlotte Amalie HS; Fairfield, AL; (S); Trs Chess Clb; Math Tm; Quiz Bowl; Pres Drill Tm; Concert Band; Jazz Band; Mrchg Band; Hon Roll; NHS; Ntl Merit SF; Rider Coll; Bio.

FOREIGN COUNTRIES

AIELLO, JOSEPH M; Bitburg HS; Apo Ny, NY; (Y); Rep Stu Cncl; High Hon Roll; Computer Clb; Office Aide; School Play; Stage Crew; Rep Frsh Cls; Powder Puff Ftbl; Socr; Hon Roll; Elctrncs, US Hstry, Spnsh I & II Outstndng Achvt Awds 85-86; Elec Engr.

AKAGI, KAI; Munich American HS; Apo New York, NY; (Y); Band; Jazz Band; JV Bsktbl; JV Tennis; Hon Roll; VP NHS; UCLA; Sci.

ALEWINE, PAULETTE; Vilseck American HS; APO New York, NY; (Y); Art Clb; Church Yth Grp; Band; Concert Band; Jazz Band; Mrchg Band; School Play; Symp Band; Yrbk Phtg; Chrmn Frsh Cls; Outstndng Soloist Awd 83-84; Outstndng Bandsmn 83-84; Lee Christian Coll; Ed.

ALLINSON, KATHERINE; Bitburg American HS; Apo Ny, NY; (Y); German Clb; Teachers Aide; Band; Concert Band; Rep Stu Cncl; Hon Roll; Cert Proficiency.

AMENS, LEANN; Ramstein Amer HS; Apo New York, NY; (Y); Church Yth Grp; Dance Clb; Teachers Aide; Variety Show; Jr NHS; Prodtn Mgr Fshn Shw 84-85; Bus.

BARKER, JOSH; Torrejon American HS; Apo, NY; (Y); Aud/Vis; Boy Scts; Church Yth Grp; Yrbk Sprt Ed; Yrbk Stf; Var L Bsktbl; Var L Crs Cntry; Var L Ftbl; Var L Trk; High Hon Roll; Cross Cntry All Spain All Conf 85; West Point; Military Sci.

BEESON III, GILBERT WARD; Seoul American HS; Apo San Francisco, CA; (Y); 17/100; Church Yth Grp; Spanish Clb; Var Capt Bsktbl; L Trk; Hon Roll; NHS; NEDT Awd; Spanish NHS; Seoul Area Off Wvs Clb Schlrshp 86; Huntngdn Schlr Awd 86; Pres Acdmc Fit Awd 86; Huntingdon Coll; Pre Law.

BERNACCHI II, JAMES; North Park Secondary Schl; Canada; (Y); Pep Clb; Varsity Clb; Rep Jr Cls; Rep Stu Cncl; Var L Ftbl; Capt Powder Puff Ftbl; Var L Wrstlng; Bus Admin.

BLANCHARD, JAMES; Ramstein American HS; Apo New York, NY; (Y); Art Clb; Outstndng Achvt Adv Art Awd 85-86; Comm Art.

BOGGS, CHRISTINE; W T Sampson HS; Norfolk, VA; (Y); DECA; FBLA; Spanish Clb; Powder Puff Ftbl; Hon Roll; Jr NHS; Evie Mansfield Schl Modelng Ltd Diploma 86; Old Dominion U; Fshn Dsgn.

BOLET, MONICA; Evangelical Christian Acad; Spain; (Y); 1/6; VP Church Yth Grp; Chorus; Church Choir; School Musical; High Hon Roll; NHS; Prfct Atten Awd; Bible Memoriztn Awd 83-84; Bible Baptist Coll; Engl.

BOLSER, STEPHEN; Dalat Schl; Hamilton, OH; (Y); 1/19; Computer Clb; Math Clb; High Hon Roll; Mu Alp Tht; Pres Schlr; Purdue U; Aero Engr.

BOOZER, SABRINA; Hahn HS; Apo New York, NY; (Y); Pres Chorus; Rep Stu Cncl; Bowling; Powder Puff Ftbl; L Trk; L Vllybl; Ntl Schl Chrl Awd 84-85; Bus.

BORIES, SEAN; Ramstein American HS; San Antonio, TX; (Y); Boy Scts; Drama Clb; German Clb; Model UN; School Musical; School Play; Stage Crew; Nwsp Stf; Hon Roll; Arch Dsgn.

BOWMAN, PAUL G; Evangelical Christian Acad; Waterman, IL; (Y); 1/6; Chorus; Church Choir; School Play; Yrbk Stf; Stu Cncl; Socr; High Hon Roll; NHS; Drama Clb; Quiz Bowl; Outstndg JR SR Assoc Christn Schls Intl 84-85; Schl Music Awd Evang Chrstn Acad 85-86; U Of Madrid ; Fgn Missionary.

BRENNAN, ERIN; Ramstein American HS; Apo New York, NY; (Y); Ski Clb; Spanish Clb; Band; Yrbk Stf; Var L Cheerleading; Var L Tennis; Hon Roll; NHS; Bio.

BRYANT, TONJA; Izmir American HS; APO, NY; (Y); 4/15; Computer Clb; Teachers Aide; Nwsp Stf; Rep Jr Cls; $500 Schlrshp/Scl Clb 86; U Of Florida; Accntng.

CALE, STERLING R; Bonn American HS; Apo, NY; (Y); Boy Scts; Model UN; Science Clb; Spanish Clb; Band; Chorus; School Musical; Var Crs Cntry; Var Swmmng; Hon Roll; CA Mntr Prjct Schlr 83-85; Engrng.

CANNON, LESLIE; Balboa HS; Washington, DC; (Y); 56/285; Church Yth Grp; Computer Clb; Pres Girl Scts; Hosp Aide; Pres Spanish Clb; Nwsp Rptr; Nwsp Stf; Hon Roll; Natl Hispnic Scholar Pgm Semi-Fin 86; Corp Law.

CARR, WILL L; Nuernberg HS; Apo New York, NY; (Y); 45/390; Am Leg Boys St; JV Crs Cntry; Var Mgr(s); JV Trk; Hon Roll.

CASE, CHRISTINE; Ramstein HS; Apo New York, NY; (Y); Church Yth Grp; Cmnty Wkr; Drama Clb; Teachers Aide; Chorus; School Musical; School Play; Stage Crew; Teachers Aide; Hon Roll; Riding Clb Hnr Awd 83-84; Algebra I Achvt Awd 85-86; Auburn U; Bio Sci.

CHARLTON, MARIA; Robert D Edgren HS; APO San Fran, CA; (Y); 4/60; Drama Clb; JA; Math Clb; Math Tm; Hon Roll; Mu Alp Tht; NHS; Kitty Hawk Hnr Soc 85; Outstndng Cadet ROTC 85; Econ.

CLAYTON, ROBERT TAYLOR; Hanau American HS; West Germany; (Y); 2/280; Var L Golf; Var L Tennis; High Hon Roll; Hon Roll; NHS; Outstndng Golfer Yr 85-86; Schlr Athlt Yr 85-86; Sci Excllnc Awd 86; Math Excllnc Awd 85; Med Prof.

COCHRAN, CHARLES; W HH Arnold HS; Apo, NY; (Y); Church Yth Grp; Cmnty Wkr; German Clb; ROTC; Stage Crew; Yrbk Stf; Rep Frsh Cls; Im Tennis; Im Wt Lftg; ROTC Rifle Team 83-86; Evergreen ST U; Militar Svc.

COTTRILL, EDWARD A; Berlin American HS; Apo New York, NY; (Y); 8/57; Debate Tm; Model UN; ROTC; Spanish Clb; VP Frsh Cls; Var L Ftbl; Var L Socr; Pres Acad Ftnss Awd, All Cnf Sccr, HS Math Awd 86; Mary Washington Coll; Pol Sci.

DAUZAT, SARAH M; Torrejon HS; Apo New York, NY; (Y); 2/103; Girl Scts; Spanish Clb; Church Choir; Tennis; High Hon Roll; Trs NHS; NHS Outstndng Schlrshp 86; Consistent Efford & Achvmnt In Eng Cert 85; Awd Outstndng Achvmnt French 85; Saint Louis; Bus.

DAVIS, MARTHA; Hanau American HS; Apo, NY; (Y); 9/100; Pres Church Yth Grp; Office Aide; Varsity Clb; Off Sr Cls; Stu Cncl; Mgr(s); Vllybl; Hon Roll; Masonic Awd; Trs NHS; Panther Educ Asst Pgm 86; Darmstadt Womens Clb Schlrshp 86; U SC; Bus Admin.

DE ROSIA, MARGARET; Univeristy Of Winnipeg Collegia; Saginaw, MI; (Y); Art Clb; Dance Clb; PAVAS; Orch; Hon Roll; Hist Awd Hgst Mark Cls 84-85; Stu Distnctn 85-86; Schlrshp Royal Winnipeg Ballet Prof Schl 84-86; Royal Winnipeg Ballet; Dancer.

DELBOY, FREDERICK W; Gen H H Arnold American HS; A P O New York, NY; (Y); 2/167; Boy Scts; Pres Church Yth Grp; Computer Clb; Debate Tm; Library Aide; Model UN; Pep Clb; Quiz Bowl; Scholastic Bowl; Band; Pres Clsrm Cntst Wnnr Essay Cntst 86; 1st Prz Drug Alcohol Abuse Cntst 83; Bio.

DEMING, MIKE; Kaiserslautern Amer HS; APO, NY; (Y); Var Bsktbl; Var Ftbl; Var Trk; Hon Roll; Prfct Atten Awd; Hmcmng Page 83; Coach Awd Trck 86; Ftbl-Al-Cnfrnc, Al-Europn Dfnsv End 85; Blck Hls ST Coll SD; Acctng.

DENENBERG, KIMBERLY; Pardess Hanna HS; Encino, CA; (Y); Speech Tm; Temple Yth Grp; Nwsp Ed-Chief; Off Frsh Cls; Off Soph Cls; Off Jr Cls; Pres Stu Cncl; Cit Awd; High Hon Roll; Schlrshp Stdy Abrd Jwsh Fedrtn 85-86; Stu Ldrshp Awd 85-86; Northwestern; Jrnlsm.

DENUSTA, DIDI; John F Kennedy HS; Dededo, GU; (S); DECA; Library Aide; Office Aide; Teachers Aide; Church Choir; Pres Frsh Cls; Rep Soph Cls; Pres Trs Sr Cls; VP Trs Stu Cncl; Bowling; 4th Pl Awd-Apparel & Accesories DECA Comptn 86; 5th Pl Awd-Ovrall Comptn DECA 86; Bus.

DIBBLE, GWENDOLYN; Helene Lange Gymnasium HS; Kingsport, TN; (Y); Congress Bundestag Schlrshp-Yth Undrstndng 85-86; UNC Chapel Hill; Psych.

DICKINSON, KRISTY LYNN; Ramstein HS; APO New York, NY; (Y); Varsity Clb; Lit Mag; VP Frsh Cls; Var L Bsktbl; Var Capt Cheerleading; Var L Gym; Var Trk; Outstndng Achvt Aerobcs/Dance 85-86; Var Ltr Trck 83-84; Lit Mag Wrkr 85-86; Fash Merch.

DOWHAN, DAVID W; Aiglon HS; Houston, TX; (Y); Boy Scts; Church Yth Grp; Debate Tm; Church Choir; Madrigals; School Musical; Nwsp Rptr; L Socr; High Hon Roll; Gold Awds Actg Excllnc 85-86; Stanford; Math.

DRILON, REUEL; Guam Adaventist Acad; Agat, GU; (Y); Band; Chorus; Church Choir; School Musical; School Play; Variety Show; Cit Awd; High Hon Roll; Hon Roll; Jr NHS; Bst Actor Awd 84-85; Knights Altar Grand Knight Awd 84; Mens Shot Put Awd 4th Pl Overall 86; UC Berkeley; Lit.

DUNLAP, VALERIE; Munich American HS; Apo New York, NY; (Y); FBLA; Hon Roll; Piano Cmpttns Superior Rtngs 83-84; U MD; Compu Sci.

ELLIOTT, TODD; Pine Grove Acad; Waco, TX; (Y); 1/18; Church Yth Grp; Nwsp Ed-Chief; Pres Stu Cncl; Capt Bsktbl; Var L Socr; High Hon Roll; Drama Clb; Key Clb; Spanish Clb; Rep Frsh Cls; Pres Scholar Baylor 86-87; Val 85-86; Baylor U; Bus Adm.

ESCUE, PETER; Alconbury American HS; Apo, NY; (Y); 5/75; Pres Church Yth Grp; Debate Tm; Model UN; NFL; Sec Speech Tm; Var Ftbl; Var Tennis; Hon Roll; NHS; Ntl Merit SF; Optmst Clb Awd 84-85; U S Smmr Sci Semnr 86; U Of Southern CA; Elctrcl Engr.

EWING, MARC; American Schl In London; England; (Y); Library Aide; Math Tm; Thesps; Band; Concert Band; Jazz Band; Pep Band; School Musical; School Play; Stage Crew; Comptrs.

FAIRCHILD, MIKE; Bitburg American HS; Apo Ny, NY; (Y); Exploring; French Clb; Spanish Clb; Rep Soph Cls; Rep Jr Cls; Badmtn; Tennis; Trk; Hon Roll; Boy Scts; U ID; Chem.

FARMER, MARIA; American School Of Lima Peru; APO Miami, FL; (Y); 14/92; Varsity Clb; Yrbk Phtg; Yrbk Sprt Ed; Var Capt Trk; NHS; Variety Show; JV Crs Cntry; JV Socr; High Hon Roll; Ntl Hspnc Schlr Awds Pgm Schlrshp Semi Fnlst 85; Outstndng JR Awd 85; Diplm De Paris-Fnch Exm 85.

FELKER, JEFFREY; Ramstein American HS; Apo New York, NY; (Y); Computer Clb; Exploring; Band; Concert Band; JV Trk; VA Tech; Aero Engrng.

FOLSE, KATHERINE; Bitburg HS; Apo Ny, NY; (Y); 3/124; Church Yth Grp; Sec Model UN; Scholastic Bowl; Church Choir; Nwsp Ed-Chief; VP Frsh Cls; Pres Jr Cls; Pres Stu Cncl; L Capt Cheerleading; Hon Roll; Prom Prncss 86; Hmcmng Crt 84; Chrstms Qn 85; Intl Fshn Dsn.

FORGEY, ELISA; The American School In Japan; Washington, DC; (Y); Chorus; Madrigals; School Musical; Nwsp Rptr; High Hon Roll; NHS; Sal; Yale Book Awd 86; Best Actress 84; Hnrbl Mntn In The Martin Luther King Peace Prz Essy Cntst 85; Writer.

FROMME, ERIK K; St Stephens Schl; Italy; (Y); French Clb; Math Tm; Lit Mag; Trs Sr Cls; Stu Cncl; Im Bsktbl; Im Tennis; Im Wt Lftg; High Hon Roll; Ntl Merit SF; Stillwater Brd Ed Distngshd Achvt Awd 85; Schl Scholar 85; 1st Rnnr Up Samsbury Engl Prize 85.

FULFORD, SHANNON; Wagner HS; Fredericksburg, VA; (Y); 26/120; Church Yth Grp; Drill Tm; Lit Mag; Rep Civic Clb; Rep Sr Cls; Stu Cncl; Var Capt Cheerleading; Hon Roll; All Star Chrldr 84-85; Spirit Stick NCA Chrldng Camp 85; Accntnt.

GARCIA, PHILIP; Ramstein American HS; Apo, NY; (Y); Cmnty Wkr; Drama Clb; Variety Show; Crs Cntry; Ftbl; Trk; Hon Roll; Mdlng Cls V-Pres/Exclnc Ldrshp 1st Rnr Up Mdl Yr Shw 85-86; Hnrd Crtng Fnd Rsr Yrbk 85-86; Perf.

GIANNARIS, WILLIAM; Torrejon HS; APO New York, NY; (Y); Aud/Vis; PAVAS; Yrbk Phtg; Ftbl; Tennis; High Hon Roll; Ntl Merit Ltr; U Of FL; Visual Arts.

GILLETTE, DANIEL; Chrsitiansen Acad; Venezuela; (Y); Chorus; Yrbk Phtg; JV Var Bsktbl; JV Var Socr; JV Sftbl; Hon Roll; Moody Bible Inst; Bible Ed.

GILLIS, NANCY; Hahn HS; Virginia Beach, VA; (Y); Dance Clb; Drama Clb; German Clb; Stage Crew; Variety Show; High Hon Roll; Jr NHS; Trs Sec NHS; USAF; Pol Sci.

GOBIN, ALLAN A; Hanau American HS; Apo, NY; (Y); 10/132; Computer Clb; Office Aide; Teachers Aide; Nwsp Bus Mgr; Nwsp Ed-Chief; Im Gym; Im Wt Lftg; Var L Wrstlng; Cit Awd; Hon Roll; ROTC; Comp Sci.

GULLIKSON, CARESSA; J F K Schl; Little Rock, AR; (Y); AFS; French Clb; German Clb; Intnl Clb; Natl Beta Clb; Chorus; Church Choir; School Musical; School Play; Stage Crew.

GUZIK, PATRICK R; Berlin American HS; Apo, NY; (Y); 2/74; Model UN; Quiz Bowl; Varsity Clb; Var Socr; Var Tennis; High Hon Roll; Pres Schlr; Sal; ROTC 86; GA Inst Of Tech; Engrng.

GUZZO, LINDA; Alpha Secondary Schl; Canada; (Y); English Clb; JA; Pep Clb; SADD; School Musical; Nwsp Rptr; VP Stu Cncl; Cheerleading; Cit Awd; High Hon Roll; Hghst Stu Avg 84-85; Invlvd Stu Awd 85-86; UBC; Med.

HAMMOND, SEAN; Roger B Chaffee HS; C/O Fpo, NY; (Y); 9/21; Art Clb; Church Yth Grp; School Play; Yrbk Phtg; Yrbk Stf; Rep Frsh Cls; Var L Vllybl; Cit Awd; Hon Roll.

HARPER, WADE; Lord Beaverbrook HS; Canada; (Y); Boy Scts; Exploring; Ski Clb; Teachers Aide; Band; Concert Band; Drm Mjr(t); Jazz Band; Mrchg Band; Orch; CO ST U; Bus.

HEAPY, TODD; Nuernberg American HS; Apo New York, NY; (Y); 16/100; Art Clb; FCA; German Clb; Key Clb; Yrbk Ed-Chief; Yrbk Phtg; JV Socr; Hon Roll.

HEFLIN, LE ANNE; Bethel Christain Schl; Lubbock, TX; (Y); Church Yth Grp; Dance Clb; Drama Clb; English Clb; Sec French Clb; Office Aide; Speech Tm; Teachers Aide; Acpl Chr; Chorus; TX Tech U; Spch Path.

HERGET, ROBIN L; Seoul American HS; San Fran Apo, CA; (Y); Art Clb; French Clb; Scholastic Bowl; Ski Clb; Yrbk Bus Mgr; VP Jr Cls; Rep Stu Cncl; Var Capt Cheerleading; Mgr(s); Powder Puff Ftbl; U Of FL; Visual Arts.

HERNDON, MIKE; Hahn American HS; Apo New York, NY; (Y); Yrbk Phtg; Yrbk Sprt Ed; Var L Bsbl; Var L Ftbl; Var L Trk; Hon Roll; Acdmc All Amer In Ftbl 84-85; Benanor Cnfrnc Chmpnshp In Track 85-86; Cmnctns.

HINER, BRANDON; American Shcool Of Brasilia; APO Miami, FL; (Y); Camera Clb; CAP; Library Aide; ROTC; Varsity Clb; Yrbk Stf; Bsbl; Bsktbl; Socr; Hon Roll; Dadln Achvt Awd ROTC 85; TX A & M; Heronautical Engrng.

HOLLENBECK, CARTER; Bitburg American HS; Apo Ny, NY; (Y); Aud/Vis; Letterman Clb; Varsity Clb; Band; Jazz Band; Pep Band; Var Capt Ftbl; Powder Puff Ftbl; Var Wrstlng; Hon Roll; U NE; Crimnl Justice.

JASPER, JARROD E; Assumption College Schl; Detroit, MI; (Y); Hosp Aide; VP JA; Pres Political Wkr; Band; Jazz Band; Orch; Symp Band; Yrbk Phtg; Stu Cncl; Hon Roll; Engrng Dsgn Awd U Windsor 86; Boston U; Psychtry.

KEARNEY, SUZANNE; Bitburg American HS; Apo Ny, NY; (Y); Church Yth Grp; Trs Jr Cls; Trs Sr Cls; Crs Cntry; Hon Roll; Mst Imrpvd & Vlbl X-Cntry Rnr 84-85; U Of Reno NV; Bus Mgmt.

KEARNS, BOONDA; Hahn American HS; APO, NY; (Y); #8 In Class; Church Yth Grp; Library Aide; Red Cross Aide; School Musical; Variety Show; Nwsp Ed-Chief; Nwsp Rptr; Hon Roll; NHS; MD U Hrnrs Prog Schlrshp 86; Hahn AFB Schlrshp 86; Top 10 Hnr Grad 86; MD U; Comp Sci.

KILBACK, DENISE; Alpha Secondary HS; Canada; (Y); Dance Clb; Drama Clb; School Musical; School Play; Variety Show; Stu Cncl; Cheerleading; Coach Actv; Swmmng; Hon Roll.

KILE, KENTON; Hanau Amrican HS; Apo Ny, NY; (Y); Letterman Clb; Teachers Aide; Varsity Clb; Band; Concert Band; Jazz Band; JV Var Ftbl; Var JV Trk; Var Wrstlng; Hon Roll; Outstndng Muscnshp Bnd; Acdmc Exclnc Comp Pgmng; U Of Maryland.

KILPATRICK, BRITTA-LYN; Heidelberg HS; Apo New York, NY; (S); 28/149; JA; Varsity Clb; Nwsp Sprt Ed; VP Sr Cls; Capt L Bsktbl; Hon Roll; VFW Awd; Teachers Aide; Rep Frsh Cls; Rep Jr Cls; Athlete Of The Yr; 1st Tm All-Europe Bsktbl; 2nd Seed Am Ten Plyr In Europe; FL ST U; Bus Adm.

KOCHANIEWICZ, HEATHER; Heidelberg HS; APO, NY; (Y); Drama Clb; 4-H; Girl Scts; SADD; Chorus; School Musical; School Play; Var L Trk; God Cntry Awd; Hon Roll; Girl Scout Silver Awd 83; 3rd Pl Earth Sci Scholastic Awd 84; 3rd Pl Pony Club Know Down 84; Languages.

LA JOIE, MARK; Bitburg American HS; Apo Ny, NY; (Y); Am Leg Boys St; Boy Scts; Rep Frsh Cls; Rep Soph Cls; Rep Jr Cls; VP Stu Cncl; Var L Crs Cntry; Var L Trk; High Hon Roll; Hon Roll; USAFA.

LAMBERT, CINDY; Dalat HS; Malaysia; (Y); Natl Beta Clb; Pep Clb; Gym; Vllybl; Art Dept Awd 85-86; Gymnastic Most Hard Working 84-85; Dntl Fld.

LEISHMAN, THERESA; Jin Ai Girls HS; Traverse City, MI; (Y); English Clb; Hosp Aide; Intnl Clb; Pep Clb; SADD; Variety Show; Rep Jr Cls; Stu Cncl; NHS; Rotary Awd; NW MI Coll; Bus.

LENSCH, KAREN; The American HS; Mexico D F; (Y); Model UN; SADD; Nwsp Sprt Ed; Socr; JV Trk; Var Vllybl; High Hon Roll; Hon Roll; NHS; Spanish NHS; Outstndng Achvmnt In Bio 84-85; Bradford Coll; Comm Art.

LENSCH, SARA; American HS; Dallas, TX; (Y); Dance Clb; Drama Clb; Model UN; Pres SADD; Concert Band; School Musical; School Play; Stage Crew; Nwsp Rptr; Nwsp Stf; Cert Of Merit-Strtng SADD-MXICO 86; Cert Of Merit-Drama 86; Awd-Hghst Engl Lit Avg 84; Shenandoah Cnsrvtry-Music; Dram.

LEPRE, BRENDA M; Escola Americana De Brasilia; Manassas, VA; (Y); 3/32; FBLA; Chorus; Ed Nwsp Ed-Chief; Nwsp Rptr; Ed Yrbk Ed-Chief; Var Cheerleading; High Hon Roll; Hon Roll; NHS; Pres Schlr; Lttrd Hnr; Bst All Arnd SR Cls; VA Tech; Pol Sci.

LETENDRE, SCOTT; Carol Morgan HS; APO Miami, FL; (Y); Aud/Vis; Boy Scts; Computer Clb; Drama Clb; L Trk; Hon Roll; TX A&M; Elec Engr.

LIMON, LUIS; Heidelberg American HS; A P O New York, NY; (Y); 22/149; Drama Clb; Library Aide; Speech Tm; Teachers Aide; Thesps; School Play; Stage Crew; Nwsp Stf; Lit Mag; Jr NHS; Ntl Hspnc Schlrshp Awd Semifnlst 86; Law.

MARIMON, CLAUDIO; Torrejon American HS; Apo, NY; (Y); Chess Clb; Computer Clb; Band; Var Socr; Var Wrstlng; Hon Roll; NHS; Elec Engr.

MARTIN, LIANNE; General Planet SR HS; Canada; (Y); 1/75; JV Cheerleading; JV Var Crs Cntry; JV Var Trk; JV Vllybl; High Hon Roll; Hon Roll; Jr NHS; All Amer NCA Chrldr & Aloha Bwl NCA Spirtldr 85-86; Royal Military Coll; Engrng.

MAY, KATHERINE E; Ramstein American HS; Apo, NY; (Y); 21/230; Latin Clb; Math Clb; Math Tm; Concert Band; Drill Tm; Yrbk Stf; Capt Crs Cntry; High Hon Roll; NHS; St Schlr; Prncpl Nmntn USAF Acad By IL Rep K Gray; Elec Engr.

MC DONALD, ANTHONY; Lajes HS; Apo New York, NY; (Y); JV Bsktbl; Var Socr; JV Trk; Hon Roll; Southern IL U-Edwardsvle; Math.

MC ELROY, ELIZABETH ANNE; Mannheim American HS; Apo, NY; (S); VP Church Yth Grp; Church Choir; Yrbk Stf; High Hon Roll; NHS; Octagon Clb 83-85; Hghst Grd Amer Hstry Awd 85; Yrbk Stf Awd-Hghst Grd 85; U Of AR Fayettevl; Phy Thrpy.

MEKELBURG, THEODORE; Bitburg American HS; Apo Ny, NY; (Y); Boy Scts; Model UN; Band; Concert Band; Trs Frsh Cls; Mgr(s); High Hon Roll; Hon Roll; NHS; Score Keeper; Bst Alg II Stu 86; Aerontcl Engr.

MOONEYHAM, SCOTT; Torrejon HS; Apo, NY; (Y); Key Clb; Rep Frsh Cls; Trs Soph Cls; VP Stu Cncl; Var L Bsktbl; Var L Crs Cntry; Var L Golf; Var L Tennis; French Hon Soc; NHS; USAF Acad; Engrng.

MOREHOUSE, STACEY; Escola Americana HS; Oakland, CA; (Y); Dance Clb; Drama Clb; Hosp Aide; SADD; Drill Tm; School Musical; Nwsp Stf; Yrbk Ed-Chief; Hon Roll; Stu Cncl; Prncpls Awd; UCLA; Bio Sci.

MORGAN, RAUL; Balboa HS; Apo Miami, FL; (Y); 8/287; Computer Clb; French Clb; Spanish Clb; Bsktbl; Tennis; Hon Roll; NHS; Hispnc Natl Merit Fin 85; All Isthmian Ten 85; Panama Canal Coll; Indstrl Engr.

MUMBAUER, ANNE; Munich American HS; Apo New York, NY; (Y); ROTC; Teachers Aide; Color Guard; Stage Crew; Yrbk Stf; Lit Mag; Hon Roll; NHS; Execellance JROTC Awd 85; Superior Cadet Awd 85; :Edu.

MYLES, HOPE; Robert D Edgren HS; APO San Francisc, CA; (Y); Church Yth Grp; Girl Scts; JA; Library Aide; Church Choir; Nwsp Rptr; Nwsp Stf; Var Bsktbl; L Sftbl; Var L Trk; Grambling ST U.

NAYS, LANA; Torrejon HS; Apo, NY; (Y); Art Clb; Church Yth Grp; Drama Clb; Pep Clb; Teachers Aide; Band; Church Choir; Concert Band; Mrchg Band; Pep Band; TX U; Bus.

NICK, ROBYN; David Glasgow Farragut HS Dodds; FPO NY, NY; (Y); 3/50; Church Yth Grp; FBLA; Latin Clb; Im Swmmng; High Hon Roll; High Hon Roll; NHS; Natl Clsscl Hnr Soc 84-85; Ubrary Awd 85; U Of WI Madison; Jrnlsm.

NOBLE, GREG; Colegio Nueva Granada HS; Arvada, CO; (Y); Chorus; Stage Crew; Rep Stu Cncl; Im Coach Actv; JV Ftbl; Im Mgr(s); Var Trk; Var Wrstlng; High Hon Roll; Hon Roll; Accntng.

NOBLE, JOSHUA Y; Seoul American HS; Apo San Francis, CA; (Y); 8/101; Camera Clb; Ski Clb; Yrbk Ed-Chief; Yrbk Rptr; Rep Soph Cls; Rep Stu Cncl; JV Var Bsktbl; Capt Var Crs Cntry; JV Ftbl; Var Socr; US Army ROTC Scholar 86; KS ST Hnr Stu 83; The Citadel; Pol Sci.

OSBORNE, CATHY; Ramstein American HS; Apo New York, NY; (Y); Church Yth Grp; VP Church Choir; Off Frsh Cls; Sec Soph Cls; Trs Jr Cls; Cheerleading; Trk; Vllybl; High Hon Roll; Hon Roll; Coachs Awd Vllybl 84; Marine Bio.

PAPADOPOULOS, TINAMARIE; American Community Schl; Medway, MA; (Y); Church Yth Grp; Cmnty Wkr; Drama Clb; Girl Scts; Library Aide; Office Aide; Speech Tm; SADD; Teachers Aide; Chorus; Clg Acad Summr Sch 80; RI Sch Of Design; Dsgn Clothg.

PARKER, JEFFREY; Alconbury American HS; APO New York, NY; (Y); 33/80; Church Yth Grp; Trs Exploring; Model UN; Stage Crew; Nwsp Ed-Chief; Yrbk Sprt Ed; Rep Stu Cncl; Capt Var Socr; Hon Roll; Eagle Sct 84; TX Tech U; Brdcstg.

PARRIS, ISABEL MARIA; General H H Arnold HS; Apo, NY; (Y); 16/160; Church Yth Grp; French Clb; Trs Key Clb; Yrbk Stf; Lit Mag; Var Mgr(s); High Hon Roll; Hon Roll; NHS; Gen H H Arnold Schlrshp 86; JR Mrshl 85; U Of MD Munich.

PASCHAL, KELLEIGH; Hahn HS; Apo New York, NY; (Y); Computer Clb; Girl Scts; Political Wkr; Yrbk Stf; Powder Puff Ftbl; Swmmng; Vllybl; NM ST U; Psych.

PATTERSON, KRISTIN; Bitburg HS; APO Ny, NY; (Y); Church Yth Grp; Letterman Clb; Science Clb; Tennis; Hon Roll; U MD; Pltcl Sci.

PIETROWSKI, PAMELA; Ramstein American HS; Apo New York, NY; (Y); Church Yth Grp; Computer Clb; DECA; FBLA; German Clb; GAA; Red Cross Aide; Spanish Clb; Speech Tm; SADD; Physcl Educ Awd 84; Bus Admn.

PLANJE, CHRISTINA; Munich American HS; Apo New York, NY; (Y); 1/115; Cmnty Wkr; 4-H; Scholastic Bowl; Spanish Clb; Teachers Aide; Var L Swmmng; High Hon Roll; Trs NHS; Spanish NHS; All-Amer Swmmr All-ST 84-85; Mary Lee Nemic Schltc Awds Bio & Algbra II 84-85; SS Achvt Awd 85-86; Med.

PRICE, PENNY; Ramstein American HS; Apo New York, NY; (Y); Church Yth Grp; FBLA; Pep Clb; Varsity Clb; Concert Band; Yrbk Stf; Stat Bsktbl; Var Cheerleading; JV Socr; Var Trk; Comp Prgrm.

PRIMAS, ARTHUR; Ramstein American HS; Apo New York, NY; (Y); Yrbk Phtg; Yrbk Stf; Im Bsktbl; Im JV Ftbl; High Hon Roll; Hon Roll; Air Force Acad; Mltry Pilot.

RAMIREZ, BRIAN; Fulda American HS; Apo, NY; (Y); Boy Scts; German Clb; Pep Clb; Ski Clb; Chorus; Yrbk Stf; Ftbl; Wt Lftg; Hon Roll; U TX El Paso.

RAMSEY, JO; Bitburg HS; Apo Ny, NY; (Y); Church Yth Grp; Cmnty Wkr; FHA; Yrbk Stf; Hon Roll; Outstndng Meal Plnng Awd 86; Girls Missnry Assoc 83-84; Real Estate.

RAYOS, MARIBEL; Kinnick HS; FPO Seattle, WA; (Y); 5/75; Church Yth Grp; FBLA; Natl Beta Clb; Yrbk Bus Mgr; Mgr Ftbl; High Hon Roll; NHS; Spanish NHS; Office Aide; Service Clb; Yokohama Schlrshp 86; U MD Schrlshp 86; U W FL; Hosp Adm.

REXRODE, STEPHANIE; Leysin American Schl; Marshall, MI; (Y); 4-H; French Clb; Latin Clb; Q&S; School Musical; School Play; Nwsp Ed-Chief; Nwsp Stf; 4-H Awd; Hon Roll; Air Force; Admin.

REYNOLDS, MELISSA D; Fulda HS; Apo, NY; (Y); Girl Scts; Library Aide; Math Tm; Chorus; High Hon Roll; Hon Roll; Temple Yth Grp; Bus.

RITZ, STEPHANIE; Munich American HS; Apo New York, NY; (Y); Cmnty Wkr; Model UN; VP Soph Cls; VP Stu Cncl; High Hon Roll; NHS; German Clb; VP Intnl Clb; ROTC; Varsity Clb; JROTC Schlrshp Awd Nurnberg W Germany 84; Highest Achvt Engl Awd 86; International Studies.

SAAVEDRA, LUIS R; Collegio Maristas HS; Monterey, CA; (Y); Ftbl; Tennis; Wt Lftg; Bst Rsrch Wrk HS Metallurgic Engrng 86; Cnvntn Venezuelah Yth Sci Assoc 86; Comp Elec.

SALVADORE, NICOLE; Ramstein American HS; Apo New York, NY; (Y); Drama Clb; Teachers Aide; Varsity Clb; Drill Tm; School Play; Powder Puff Ftbl; Var Socr; Im Swmmng; Hon Roll; All Conf Soccr 86; All Trnmnt Soccr 86.

SAMPSON, DANIELLE; W T Sampson HS; Tucson, AZ; (Y); Drama Clb; Office Aide; Teachers Aide; Chorus; School Play; Lit Mag; VP Sr Cls; Rep Stu Cncl; Powder Puff Ftbl; High Hon Roll; Awd For Typng Aide 86; Awd For Spndrft Ltrary Edtn 86; Prima Coll; Comp.

SANOWSKI, TONJA RACHELE; Braidwood Central Schl; Stayton, OR; (Y); AFS; Drama Clb; 4-H; FFA; Key Clb; Spanish Clb; School Play; Bsktbl; Tennis; 4-H Awd; Acad AFS Exch Scholar 86; Vet.

SASSEVILLE, ANDREW; Country Day Schl; Apo Miami, FL; (Y); 4/33; Boy Scts; Drama Clb; Sec Sr Cls; Trs Stu Cncl; Var Socr; Var Wrstlng; High Hon Roll; Ntl Merit SF; Church Yth Grp; Intnl Clb; Arrw Ordr Boy Scts 82; St Michael U; Mltry Ofcr.

SCHWAB, ELIZABETH; Kubasaki HS; FPO Seattle, WA; (Y); Church Yth Grp; FBLA; Band; Church Choir; Concert Band; Ed Yrbk Stf; JV Socr; Jr NHS; NHS; All Cnty Band 84 & 85; Pensacola JC; Pre-Med.

SCOTT, PAULA; Ramstein HS; Apo New York, NY; (Y); Outstndng Achvt Awd US Hist 85-86; Secy.

SEIBERT, SUSAN LYNN; Puraquequara HS; Jersey Shore, PA; (Y); 1/9; Church Yth Grp; Band; Chorus; Church Choir; School Musical; School Play; Rep Frsh Cls; Rep Sr Cls; Sec Stu Cncl; Var Capt Bsktbl; Hon Soc Awd 85; MVP Awd Bsktbll 85-86; Schl Drama Awd 86; Cedarville Coll; Scndry Ed.

SMITH, AMY; Christian Alliance Acad; Ecuador; (Y); 2/30; Church Yth Grp; Drama Clb; Band; Church Choir; Concert Band; Mrchg Band; School Musical; School Play; Variety Show; Cheerleading; Wheaton Coll IL; Music.

SMITH II, DANIEL M; London Central HS; Burke, VA; (Y); 5/113; Model UN; Thesps; Chorus; Jazz Band; School Musical; School Play; Stage Crew; Symp Band; Variety Show; Nwsp Rptr; Marine Semper Fidelus Musician Awd 86; Intl Hnr Band 85-86; Rice U; Music.

SNIDER, MELISA M; Taegu American Schl; Indianapolis, IN; (Y); 1/23; Nwsp Ed-Chief; Sec Soph Cls; VP Jr Cls; Pres Stu Cncl; Var Capt Cheerleading; NHS; Ntl Merit Ltr; Pres Schlr; Val; Cmnty Wkr; Stars & Stripes Outstndg Citzn Awd 86; U AZ; Elem Ed.

SOLER, JUAN; Torrejon American HS; Apo, NY; (Y); Aud/Vis; French Clb; Spanish Clb; Yrbk Phtg; Yrbk Stf; Var Socr; High Hon Roll; Hon Roll; Jr NHS; NHS; Sci.

SPENCER, CHRISTINE; Yokota HS; APO Sn Francisco, CA; (Y); Exploring; JA; Library Aide; Pep Clb; Red Cross Aide; Spanish Clb; Teachers Aide; Yrbk Ed-Chief; Var Trk; Hon Roll; UCLA; Med.

SULLIVAN, DAVID; Tasis HS; England; (Y); Cmnty Wkr; Debate Tm; Drama Clb; Nwsp Stf; Rep Stu Cncl; Var Crs Cntry; Ntl Merit Ltr; Bio Chem.

TACKER, DAVID; Intl Schl Of Islamabad HS; Cambria, CA; (Y); 3/27; AFS; Boy Scts; Chess Clb; Computer Clb; Scholastic Bowl; Spanish Clb; Acpl Chr; Band; Chorus; Concert Band; Amer Wmns Clb Scholar Awd 86; Outstndg U S Hstry Stu 85; CSF 83-84; Lewis & Clark Coll.

THOMPSON, ERIKA A; Wurzburg American HS; Apo, NY; (Y); VP German Clb; Service Clb; Tennis; Hon Roll; NHS; Outstndng Anchr-Anchr Clb 83-85; Florida ST U; Htl Mngmnt.

TORRE, ANDY; American School Of London; England; (Y); Church Yth Grp; French Clb; Pres German Clb; JV Socr; JV Tennis; JV Wrstlng; Hon Roll; NHS; Rugby Vrsty 85-86; Bucknell; Pre Med.

TOWNSEND, MELISSA; Augsburg American HS; APO, NY; (Y); Cmnty Wkr; German Clb; Girl Scts; Office Aide; Pep Clb; Sec Soph Cls; Sec Jr Cls; Bsktbl; Gov Hon Prg Awd; Hon Roll; Spoke Conf-Lsvll KY 85; Western KY U; Comp Sci.

TRUE, LISA; Ballarat HS; Las Vegas, NV; (Y); Church Yth Grp; Debate Tm; NFL; School Play; JV Gym; Hon Roll; U NE Las Vegas; Pblc Relations.

TUCKER, CARIE; Yokota HS; Apo San Francisco, CA; (Y); Chrmn Church Yth Grp; Cmnty Wkr; Debate Tm; Drama Clb; SADD; Teachers Aide; Chorus; Church Choir; Nwsp Ed-Chief; Rep Frsh Cls; Frdm Fndtn Of Vly Frg Yth Ldrshp Smnr 85; Strs & Strps Ctznshp Awd 86; Pltcl Sci.

VAN BRAMER, JOHN W; American Schl Of The Hague; The Netherlands; (Y); 9/80; Model UN; Varsity Clb; Var L Bsbl; Var L Bsktbl; Var L Ftbl; Var L Vllybl; Hrns Rope One Top Cls 86; OH ST U; Elec Engrng.

VAN KLOMPENBERG, LORI; Numonohi HS; Hudsonville, MI; (Y); 1/10; Trs Church Yth Grp; Teachers Aide; Yrbk Ed-Chief; Yrbk Phtg; Yrbk Rptr; Yrbk Stf; Trs Sr Cls; High Hon Roll; Val; Scholar Awd 85-86; Elem Ed.

VANN, CINAMON; Knoxville College HS; Lakeport, CA; (Y); Debate Tm; Drama Clb; GAA; Pep Clb; School Musical; School Play; Hon Roll; Kiwanis Awd; Ntl Merit SF; Acad Dcthln Hgh Scre 85; Berkeley U Of CA; Frgn Rltns.

VAROLI, JOHN; International Schl Of Brussels; A P O, NY; (Y); 15/272; Cmnty Wkr; Drama Clb; Political Wkr; Nwsp Ed-Chief; Rep Soph Cls; Var Swmmng; French Hon Soc; High Hon Roll; School Musical; School Play; Natl Hispnc Schlr Awd 85-86; Bst Actr Yr 84; NROTC Scholar 85-86; Cornell U; Intl Bus.

VOS, JOLENE; Lycee Louis Barthou HS; Bowling Green, KY; (Y); FCA; French Clb; Concert Band; Mrchg Band; Orch; Symp Band; Hon Roll; NHS; E F Intl Stud Of Arts Schlrshp To France 85-86; Frnch III Awd 84-85.

WAGNER, TANYA; Munich American HS; APO New York, NY; (Y); Sec Jr Cls; Off Sr Cls; Stu Cncl; JV Var Bsktbl; Powder Puff Ftbl; Var Tennis; NHS; Pe Acad Excellence Awd 84; U Of CA-SANTA Cruz; Intl Affrs.

WAITES, HOUSTON C; Cairo American Coll; Ft Worth, TX; (Y); Pres Debate Tm; Drama Clb; Pres Spanish Clb; Pres Speech Tm; Thesps; School Musical; School Play; Swing Chorus; VP Sr Cls; Bsbl; TX A & M; Intl Bus.

WALKER, JENNIFER; Kubasaki HS; Apo SF, CA; (Y); Pep Clb; Spanish Clb; Teachers Aide; Concert Band; Mrchg Band; Pep Band; School Musical; Weber ST Coll; Psych.

WALKER, KIMBERLY A; Lakenheath American HS; Apo New York, NY; (Y); 22/92; Pep Clb; Teachers Aide; Yrbk Stf; Bowling; Cheerleading; Vllybl; Hon Roll; Jr NHS; St Schlr; NY ST Rgnts Schlrshp 86; Paul Smth Coll Fo Art; Htl Mngm.

WALKER, NATASCHA; Munich American HS; Apo New York, NY; (Y); 7/113; French Clb; FBLA; German Clb; Math Tm; Natl Beta Clb; Mat Maids; Gov Hon Prg Awd; Hon Roll; NHS; Pres Schlr; Acad Excllnce-German 84; Engrng.

WEAVER, ROBERT; Bitburg HS; Apo Ny, NY; (Y); Church Yth Grp; Cmnty Wkr; Var Bsbl; Im Bsktbl; Var Ftbl; Im Trk; Hon Roll; Prfct Atten Awd; U FL; Phys Ed.

WHITE, PATRICK; Ecole Internationale De Geneve HS; Switzerland; (Y); Acpl Chr; Chorus; Madrigals; School Musical; Stage Crew; JV Ftbl; Socr; U IA; Law.

WHITMAN, KATHERINE; Wiesbaden HS; APO New York, NY; (Y); Church Yth Grp; Cmnty Wkr; Hosp Aide; Keywanettes; Service Clb; Chorus; School Play; Ed Yrbk Stf; Rep Stu Cncl; Wt Lftg; Jefferson Comm 85-86; Keyette Hnry Awd 85-86; Editor Keyette Scrpbk 85-86; VA Tech; Law.

WILLIAMS JR, STEVE A; Wuerzburg American HS; Apo New York, NY; (Y); 1/108; Church Yth Grp; FBLA; Math Clb; Ntl Beta Clb; Var L Wrstlng; Cit Awd; High Hon Roll; NHS; Pres Schlr; Val; Notre Dame Schlr 86; Notre Dame; Arts.

WILLIAMS, TAMI; Torrejon American HS; Apo, NY; (Y); Aud/Vis; School Play; Stage Crew; Sec Jr Cls; Off Stu Cncl; Var Capt Cheerleading; Var Swmmng; L Trk; High Hon Roll; NHS; Outstndg Achvmnt Grp Actng 1st Pl; 1st Pl HS Annual Csmtlgy Cmpttn; Hon Engl; U Of CA; Mass Media.

WILLIAMS, WILLARD; Ramstein American HS; Apo New York, NY; (Y); Church Yth Grp; FBLA; ROTC; Drill Tm; Nwsp Stf; Im Ftbl; Im JV Wrstlng; Hon Roll; Excel Achvt Bus Lab 84-85; Vrsty Wrstlng Ltr 86; 2nd Pl FBLA ST Ldrshp Conf Awd Wrd Proc 86; U Of Cntrl FL; Cmmnctns.

WING, DAN; Frankfort American HS; Apo New York, NY; (Y); 51/253; FBLA; German Clb; Ski Clb; Computer Clb; Intnl Clb; Red Cross Aide; Teachers Aide; Nwsp Rptr; Hon Roll; Natl Ski Patrl 85-86; Comp Sci.

WISEMAN, CARLA; American International Schl; Poughquag, NY; (Y); 16/50; Yrbk Bus Mgr; Pres Frsh Cls; Pres Soph Cls; Pres Stu Cncl; Var Bsktbl; Var Fld Hcky; Var Capt Sftbl; Deans List 84-86; Messiah Coll; Nrsng.

WITHERSPOON, DAVID; American Community Schl; Webb City, MO; (Y); 3/43; Am Leg Boys St; Math Tm; Trs Stu Cncl; High Hon Roll; NHS; Ntl Merit SF; Pres Schlr; Sal; Hon Roll; Prfct Atten Awd; The Outstndg Sr 86; Michael Ochogavia Sci Awd 86; Princeton U; Engrg.

WOYTOWICH, MICHELLE; Ramstein HS; Apo New York, NY; (Y); Church Yth Grp; Cmnty Wkr; Drama Clb; Pep Clb; Concert Band; Hon Roll; Auburn; Bus.

YI, TRACEY; Alpha SR Secondary HS; Canada; (Y); Church Yth Grp; Trs Jr Cls; Rep Sr Cls; Trs Stu Cncl; JV Bsktbl; Var Cheerleading; Var Pom Pon; JV Tennis; High Hon Roll; BCYPS; U Of British Columbia; Pol Sci.

ZENTS, ALICIA; Ivory Coast Acad; Ivory Coast; (Y); English Clb; Temple Yth Grp; Chorus; Church Choir; School Musical; Sec Frsh Cls; Vllybl; High Hon Roll; Hon Roll; Top Engl Studnt Awd 84-85; Awd Recgntn In Hnr World Hstry 84-85; Awd From Hnrs Engl II 84-85.

CONNECTICUT

Abbott, Gina
Sacred Heart Acad
New Haven, CT

Abbott, Susan L
Greens Farms Acad
Southport, CT

Achilli, Beth
Lewis S Mills HS
Burlington, CT

Adae, Nana
Shelton HS
Shelton, CT

Adamczyk, Donna L
North Branford HS
Northford, CT

Adshade, Gordon
Southington HS
Milldale, CT

Agarwal, Poornima
Tolland HS
Tolland, CT

Agasi, David
Manchester HS
Manchester, CT

Agria, Carolyn M
Bunnell HS
Stratford, CT

Aiken, John M
Fairfield College
Preparatory Schl
Shelton, CT

Akerlind, Kris
Avon HS
Avon, CT

Akerson, Valerie
Bethel HS
Bethel, CT

Akoury, Lisa
Masuk HS
Monroe, CT

Alascia, Vincent
Bullard Havens
Tech HS
Bridgeport, CT

Albright, Wendy
Norwich Free Acad
Brooklyn, CT

Alcazar, Nicole
Greenwich HS
Greenwich, CT

Alexander, Bruce
New Canaan HS
New Canaan, CT

Alexander, David
Joseph A Foran HS
Milford, CT

Aloi, Jr Joseph Allen
Hamden HS
Hamden, CT

Amato, Jim
Emmett Obrien RV
Tech Schl
Bethany, CT

Amicucci, Mary
Stamford Catholic
Stamford, CT

Ancona, James
Ridgefield HS
Ridgefield, CT

Anderson, Laura
Stamford HS
Stamford, CT

Anderson, Michele
G
Mercy HS
Middletown, CT

Andreana, Cristina
Sacred Heart Acad
Stamford, CT

Angelastro, Terese
Marie
Kent HS
W Nyack, NY

Anglace, Wayne
St Joseph HS
Ansonia, CT

Ansart, John
Simsbury HS
Simsbury, CT

Anstett, Christina
East Hapton HS
East Hampton, CT

Antonucci, Brian
Vinal Regional
Vocational Tech
Portland, CT

Anzivine, Deanna
Crosby HS
Waterbury, CT

Apice, Anthony D
Fairfield Prep
Fairfield, CT

Arciola, III Samuel
P
Staples HS
Westport, CT

Ariyan, Stephan A
Branford HS
Branford, CT

Arning, Lisa
Greenwich HS
Cos Cob, CT

Asch, David
Brookfield HS
Brookfield Ctr, CT

Ashby, Karen
The Masters Schl
West Hartford, CT

Augustine, Tracy
St Joseph HS
Stratford, CT

Ault, Jonathan
Farmington HS
Farmington, CT

Austin, John A
Northwestern
Regional HS
New Hartford, CT

Austin, Sherral
William H Hall HS
W Hartford, CT

Avanzino, Jr
Kenneth C
New Canaan HS
New Canaan, CT

Avitabile,
Christopher G
West Haven HS
West Haven, CT

Ayazides, Alexandra
Torrington HS
Torrington, CT

Bacik, Timothy
Shelton HS
Shelton, CT

Baginski, Andrew G
Wolcott HS
Wolcott, CT

Baker, Kristen
Norwich Free Acad
Norwich, CT

Banatoski, Jill
Lewis S Mills HS
Burlington, CT

Banton, Jennifer
Bassick HS
Bridgeport, CT

Barnes, Kim
Glastonbury HS
Glastonbury, CT

Barry, Christopher J
St Bernard HS
Preston, CT

Bartlett, Valerie
East Hartford HS
E Hartford, CT

Bassett, Jennifer
Danbury HS
Danbury, CT

Bayendor, Holly
Greenwich HS
Old Greenwich, CT

Beaulac, Beth Ann
Tolland HS
Tolland, CT

Becher, Thomas
Greenwich HS
Greenwich, CT

Beck, David
Naugatuck HS
Naugatuck, CT

Beck, Stacy
Plainfield HS
Moosup, CT

Beckmann, Deborah
E
Guilford HS
Guilford, CT

Bell, Heather
Northhaven HS
North Haven, CT

Bellitto, Jr Robert B
Fairfield Prep
Fairfield, CT

Belmonte, Susan
Torrington HS
Torrington, CT

Benedetto, Louis
Fairfield
Preparatory Schl
Fairfield, CT

Bennett, Amy
East Lyme HS
E Lyme, CT

Bennett, Scott
Branford HS
Branford, CT

Bennett, Yvonne
Weaver HS
Hartford, CT

Benoit, Dawn M
Putnam HS
Putnam, CT

Berube, Tara
Southington HS
Southington, CT

Bessette, Debra
Plainfield HS
Plainfield, CT

Bezio, Twila
Bristol Central HS
Bristol, CT

Binder, Darren
Todd
Avon HS
Avon, CT

Birdsell, Mary
Seymour HS
Seymour, CT

Blake, Charlie
Berlin HS
Berlin, CT

Blank, Randall
Cheshire HS
Cheshire, CT

Blayney, Michelle
Danbury HS
Danbury, CT

Bobbitt, III John T
Ridgefield HS
Ridgefield, CT

Bodak, Michelle
St Joseph HS
Ansonia, CT

Bodie, Beth
Branford HS
Branford, CT

Bogan, Jack
Ridgefield HS
Ridgefield, CT

Boganski, Christine
Horace Wilcox
Technical Schl
Meriden, CT

Bogart, Kris
The Morgan HS
Clinton, CT

Bognar, Christine
Saint Joseph HS
Shelton, CT

Boissoneau, Michelle
Berlin HS
Kensington, CT

Boivin, Denise
St Joseph HS
Stratford, CT

Bonhage, John
Brien Mc Mahon
Norwalk, CT

Bonito, Ronald R
Derby HS
Derby, CT

Bontempo, Pamela
Marie
Daniel Hand HS
Madison, CT

Booker, Dorothea
E Hartford HS
East Hartford, CT

Boos, Scott
Fairfield College
Preparatory Schl
Fairfield, CT

Borchetta, Peter M
St Marys HS
Greenwich, CT

Bossone, Virginia
Brien Mc Mahon
S Norwalk, CT

Botet, Alfredo
Bullard Hayens
Bridgeport, CT

Bowers, Ray K
Derby HS
Derby, CT

Brandolini, Jodi
Cheshire HS
Cheshire, CT

Brandon, Cynthia A
Thomas Snell
Weavee HS
Hartford, CT

Brayton, James
Southington HS
Marion, CT

Brecher, Jennifer
Greenwich HS
Greenwich, CT

Brinkley, Paul
Tourtellotte
Memorial HS
N Crosvnordal, CT

Bristol, Hilary
Nathan Hale-Ray
East Haddam, CT

Brooks, Lori L
Emmanuel Christian
Hartford, CT

Brown, Andrea
St Josephs HS
Stratford, CT

Brown, Elizabeth
Lyme-Old Lyme HS
Lyme, CT

Brown, Kim
Danbury HS
Danbury, CT

Brown, Kimberly
Saint Joseph HS
Trumbull, CT

Brown, Leanne
Amity HS
Bethany, CT

Brown, Matt
East Lyme HS
Niantic, CT

Browning, Kathleen
Killingly HS
Danielson, CT

Bruck, Nicole
Greenwich HS
Riverside, CT

Bruder, Eric
Shelton HS
Shelton, CT

Bruno, Stephen
Wilton HS
Wilton, CT

Budihas, Alexa A
Glastonbury HS
Glastonbury, CT

Bugbee, Debby
East Hartford HS
E Hartford, CT

Burdo, Michael
Bullard Havens R V
T S HS
Bridgeport, CT

Burke, Colleen E
Andrew Warde HS
Fairfield, CT

Burns, Jennifer
Seymour HS
Seymour, CT

Burns, Joel E
Seymour HS
Oxford, CT

Burrell, Tishema
Cooperative HS
New Haven, CT

Butera, Susan
Stamford HS
Stamford, CT

Butkiewicz, Kristin
West Haven HS
W Haven, CT

Byam, Lorraine
Holly Cross HS
Naugatuck, CT

Cahalan, Eva
Wilton HS
Wilton, CT

Calabro, Maria
Bristol Central HS
Bristol, CT

Caldarola, Charles
St Mary HS
Greenwich, CT

Camarco, Michele
Jonathan Law HS
Milford, CT

Camp, Dedra
Crosby HS
Waterbury, CT

Campailla, Melinda
Mary Immaculate
New Britain, CT

Camuso, Matthew
Kent Schl
Ridgefield, CT

Candelora, John
Shelton HS
Shelton, CT

Cardarelli, Michael
Branford HS
Branford, CT

Carlascio, Keith
Kaynor Tech Schl
Waterbury, CT

Carlson, Allen
Cheshire HS
Cheshire, CT

Carlson, Jane
Nathan Hale-Ray
SR HS
East Haddam, CT

Carroll, Jonathan
Fairfield College
Shelton, CT

Carsten, Mike
Branford HS
Branford, CT

Carter, Allison
Andrew Warde HS
Fairfield, CT

Carter, Kelli
Joseph A Foran HS
Milford, CT

Cascia, Jona
Enfield HS
Enfield, CT

Casciano, Scott
Mark T Sheehan HS
Wallingford, CT

Castro, Deborah
Lynn
Bassick HS
Bridgeport, CT

Catanzaro, Ruth
The Morgan Schl
Clinton, CT

Celentano, Michael
Notre Dame HS
New Haven, CT

Chan, Angel
Norwalk HS
Norwalk, CT

Chapman, Yolanda
Stamford HS
Stamford, CT

Chemacki, Tim
Daniel Hand HS
Madison, CT

Cheng, Leslie
Trumbull HS
Trumbull, CT

Chiang, Darryl D
Edwin O Smith Schl
Mansfield Center, CT

Christos, Chris
Brookfield HS
Brookfield Center, CT

Ciak, Shari
Erkico Fermi HS
Enfield, CT

Cieri, Debra
Morgan HS
Clinton, CT

Cioppa, Julie Lynn
Wilton HS
Wilton, CT

Ciosek, Tracy
Southington HS
Southington, CT

Clapp, Jamie
Shelton HS
Shelton, CT

Clark, Alicia
Maloney HS
Meriden, CT

Clark, Andrew
Canton HS
Collinsville, CT

Clark, Francis
R E Fitch SR HS
Groton, CT

Clark, Todd C
Putnam HS
Putnam, CT

Clark, Tracy
Newington HS
Newington, CT

Clemens, David
Fairfield College
Fairfield, CT

Coakley, Richard
Wilby HS
Waterbury, CT

Cochrane, Heather
Ridgefield HS
Ridgefield, CT

Cockfield, Celia
Staples HS
Westport, CT

Cohen, Heidi
Bethel HS
Bethel, CT

Colgan, Danielle
Immaculate HS
Newtown, CT

Colla, Jr Raymond A
Windsor HS
Windsor, CT

Colon, Charles
Norwalk HS
Norwalk, CT

Colucci, Anthony R
Saint Joseph HS
Ansonia, CT

Comar, Jennifer
Bloomfieldm SR HS
Bloomfield, CT

Coniff, Melissa Ann
Daniel Hand HS
Madison, CT

Connor, Brian
East Catholic HS
Manchester, CT

Conroy, Michael
Lewis S Mills HS
Harwinton, CT

Consolini, Tracey
Housatonic Valley
Regional HS
Falls Village, CT

Contadino, Anna
Greenwich HS
Riverside, CT

Cook, Emily Jane
Low-Heywood
Thomas Schl
Wellesley, MA

Cook, Polly
Griswold HS
Jewett City, CT

Coon, Andrea
Simsbury HS
W Simsbury, CT

Cordani, Joe
Simsbury HS
Weatogue, CT

Cordery, Jeremy
Wilton HS
Wilton, CT

Correia, Lois Ann
St Bernard HS
Mystic, CT

Cosciello, Matthew
St Joseph HS
Ansonia, CT

Costa, John
Crosby HS
Waterbury, CT

Cowenhoven, Jr
Michael V
Fairfield College
Prep Schl
Redding Ridge, CT

Coyne, David
The Morgan Schl
Clinton, CT

Craig, Peter
Fairfield College
Norwalk, CT

Crane, Amanda
Wethersfield HS
Wethersfield, CT

Craw, III Kenneth G
Norwalk HS
Norwalk, CT

Crew, Janet
Avon HS
Avon, CT

Crew, Sheri
Sheehan HS
Wallingford, CT

Crowley, Robert
Staples HS
Westport, CT

Cruz, Alvin P
Manchester HS
Manchester, CT

Cuccinello, Lisa M
Newtown HS
Sandy Hook, CT

Cunha, Todd
Rockville HS
Vernon, CT

Cureton, II John P
Fairfield College
Shelton, CT

Curi, Sarah E
The Taft Schl
Goshen, CT

Czeczotka, Stefanie
Plainfield HS
Plainfield, CT

D Amato, Elizabeth
Wilby HS
Waterbury, CT

D Angelo, William
Robert
Newington HS
Newington, CT

D Auteuil, Monique L
William H Hall HS
West Hartford, CT

Dake, Robin
Staples HS
Westport, CT

Dalesio, Scott
Holy Cross HS
Waterbury, CT

Dalton, John
Shelton HS
Shelton, CT

Daniels, Kathi
Bethel HS
Bethel, CT

Darragh, Stacey
Norwalk HS
E Norwalk, CT

Daughters, Caroline
Ridgefield HS
Ridgefield, CT

Davidson, III
William F
Faifield College
Prep Schl
Stratford, CT

De Angelo, Deann
Ansonia HS
Ansonia, CT

De Capua, Sarah
Shelton HS
Shelton, CT

De Freitas, Scott
King Schl
Darien, CT

De Palma, Mark
St Paul Catholic HS
Bristol, CT

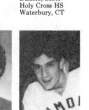
De Podesta, Craig
Hamden HS
Hamden, CT

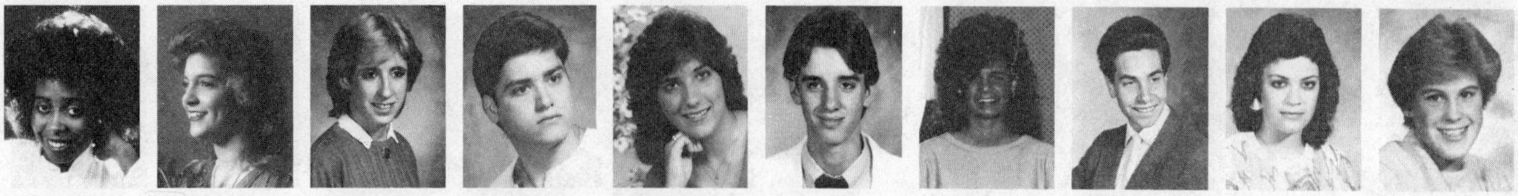

Dean, Adrienne
Sacred Heart HS
Waterbury, CT

Debo, Sylvia
Mary Immaculate
New Britain, CT

Defeo, Renee
Windham HS
W Willington, CT

Demce, Aslan
Plainfield HS
Moosup, CT

Dempsey, Dawn
Torrington HS
Torrington, CT

Depascale, Michael
St Joseph HS
Huntington, CT

Dery, Kelly
Putnam HS
Putnam, CT

Desena, Paul
Holy Cross HS
Waterbury, CT

Desmangles, Michelle
Conard HS
W Htfd, CT

Despathy, Danielle
St Bernard HS
Norwich, CT

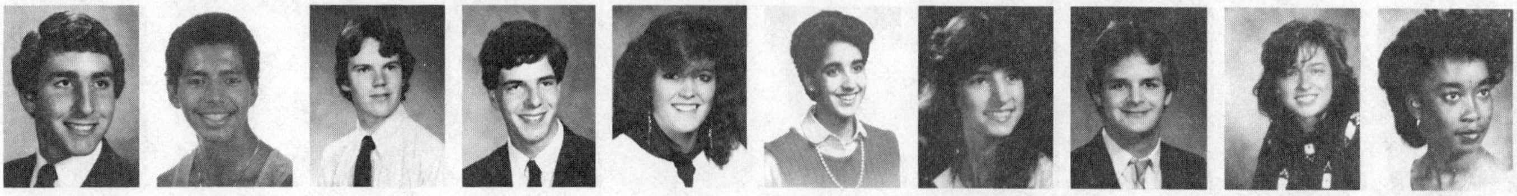

Di Dominic, Jr Dominic
Joseph F Foran HS
Milford, CT

Diaz, Wilfred
New Britain HS
New Britain, CT

Dickson, William
South Windsor HS
S Windsor, CT

Dies, Jason
Fairfield College
Fairfield, CT

Dione, Janine
The Morgan Schl
Clinton, CT

Doliveira, Roberta
Holy Cross HS
Waterbury, CT

Dollak, Melissa
William H Hall HS
W Hartford, CT

Dombrowski, Walter
St Bernard HS
Jewett City, CT

Donagher, Kelly
Farmington HS
Farmington, CT

Donaldson, Michelle
St Marys HS
W Haven, CT

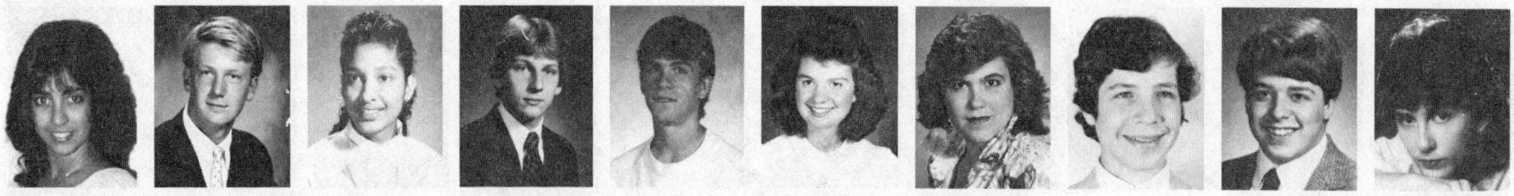

Donato, Deanna M
Holy Cross HS
Oxford, CT

Dorr, Marshall M
Kingswood-Oxford
Simsbury, CT

Douglas, Kathy
Westhill HS
Stamford, CT

Doukas, David
Mark T Sheehan HS
Wallingford, CT

Dowden, Nate
Granby Memorial
Granby, CT

Doyle, Elizabeth
St Marys HS
West Haven, CT

Draper, Mary Lynn
Branford HS
Branford, CT

Dreselly, Jim
Bolton HS
Bolton, CT

Dresen, Joe
Wilton HS
Wilton, CT

Drezek, Dawn
Windsor Locks HS
Windsor Locks, CT

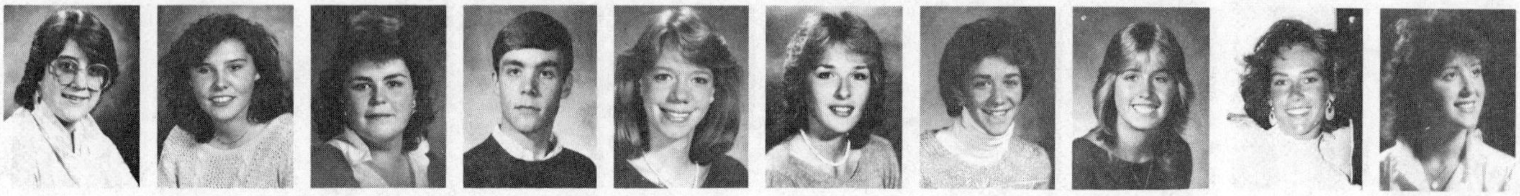

Drinkard, Lisa J
Waterford HS
Waterford, CT

Drugan, Danielle Elizabeth
Lyme-Old Lyme HS
Old Lyme, CT

Drugan, Margaret M
Lyme-Old Lyme HS
Old Lyme, CT

Dryburgh, Douglas
Staples HS
Westport, CT

Du Bay, Paulett
Stamford HS
Stamford, CT

Ducharme, Kelly
Parish Hill HS
N Windham, CT

Duchesneau, Nicole
Windham HS
Willimantic, CT

Duggan, Marnie
East Hartford HS
East Hartford, CT

Dunn, Marie
Conard HS
W Hartford, CT

Dunnack, Kerry Christine
R H A M SR HS
Andover, CT

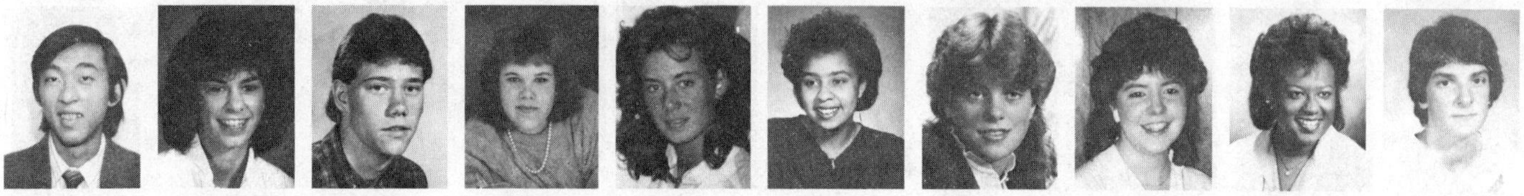

Duong, Duc Minh
Hartford Public HS
Hartford, CT

Dupont, Susanne
Thomaston HS
Thomaston, CT

Dupont, Wes
Kellingly HS
Danielson, CT

Durkin, Rachel
Conard HS
W Hartford, CT

Eckersley, Peir
Cheshire HS
Cheshire, CT

Edwards, Jenine
James Hillhouse HS
New Haven, CT

Eldridge, Tricia
Killingly HS
Sterling, CT

Ellis, Debbie
Danbury HS
Danbury, CT

Eppright, Elizabeth A
Ledyard HS
Gales Ferry, CT

Epstein, Steven
Conard HS
West Hartford, CT

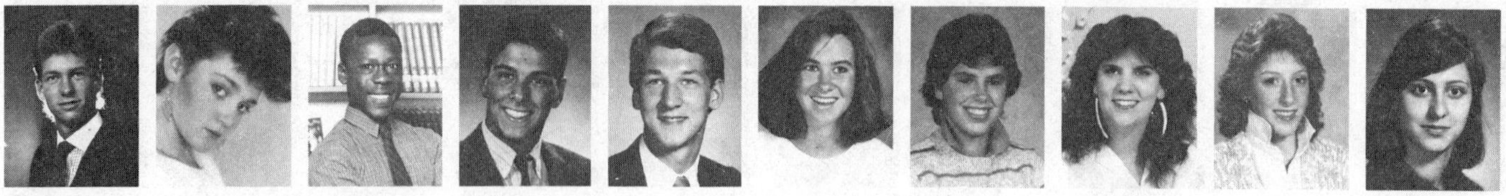

Erickson, Troy
Wethersfield HS
Wethersfield, CT

Esposito, Jill
Jonathan Law HS
Milford, CT

Etienne, Jr Gabriel
King Schl
Stamford, CT

Evans, Eric
St Bernard HS
Norwich, CT

Eveland, Jeffrey
Greenwich HS
Riverside, CT

Falsey, Ellen
Sacred Heart Acad
New Haven, CT

Farkas, Linda
Trumbull HS
Trumbull, CT

Fassio, Terri
Torrington HS
Torrington, CT

Fauxbel, Shannon
Plainfield HS
Plainfield, CT

Fazzari, Kirsten
Wilton HS
Wilton, CT

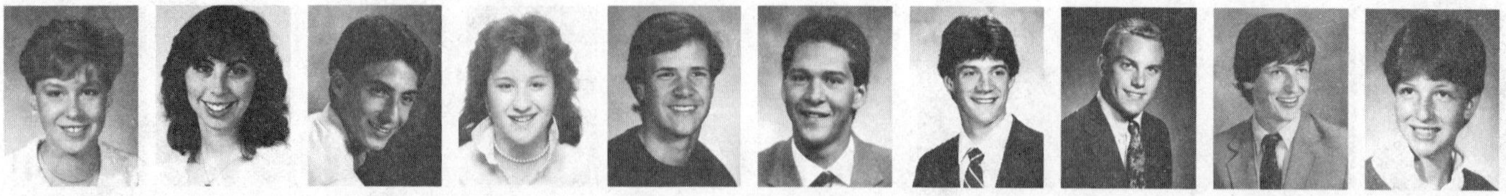

Fedeli, Kimberly
St Bernard HS
Norwich, CT

Feldman, Rachel
Hamden HS
Hamden, CT

Ferri, Jeffrey
Amity SR HS
W Haven, CT

Ferrillo, Heather Ann
Holy Cross HS
Oxford, CT

Fesko, Nick
Greenwich HS
Greenwich, CT

Fishberg, Mitchell
Newington HS
Newington, CT

Fitzgerald, John G
Fairfield Prep
Norwalk, CT

Fitzpatrick, Paul
New Canaan HS
New Canaan, CT

Flynn, Chris
Fairfield College Preparatory Schl
Wilton, CT

Flynn, Coreen
St Bernard HS
Uncasville, CT

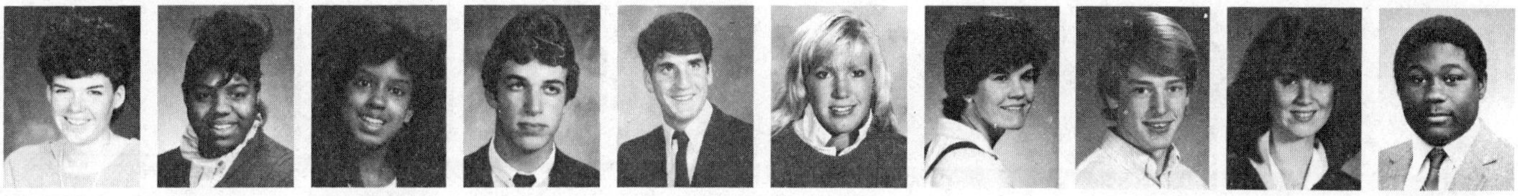

Foran, Susan
St Marys HS
Hamden, CT

Ford, Robin
Brian Mc Mahon
Norwalk, CT

Forster, Jacqueline
Miss Porters Schl
The Woodlands, TX

Forte, Stephen
Saint Joseph HS
Shelton, CT

Fortuna, Mike
Fairfield Prep
Fairfield, CT

Foss, Julie
Old Saybrook SR
Old Saybrook, CT

Fowler, Tara
Masuk HS
Monroe, CT

Fox, Benjamin
Brien Mc Mahon
Norwalk, CT

Foy, Laura
Norwalk HS
E Norwalk, CT

Fraklin, Jeffrey
Crosby HS
Waterbury, CT

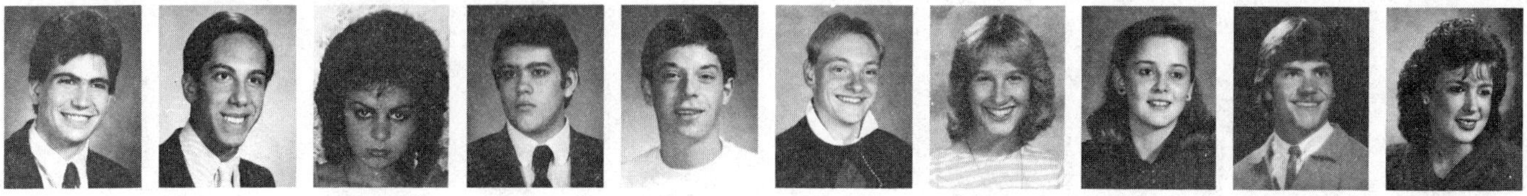

Franco, James
Notre Dame HS
Orange, CT

Frattarola, Mark W
Greenwich HS
Greenwich, CT

Frederick, Anna
Tourtellotte
Memorial HS
N Grosvnordal, CT

Freeman, Jr Jeffrey
Windham R V T S
Baltic, CT

Freundlich, Joel S
Weston HS
Weston, CT

Friedel, Stephan
Trumbull HS
Trumbull, CT

Fritsche, Cheryl
Danbury HS
Danbury, CT

Fritz, Suzanne
Ridgefield HS
Ridgefield, CT

Futtner, Jeff
East Hartford HS
E Hartford, CT

Gagne, Bernadette
Jonathan Law HS
Milford, CT

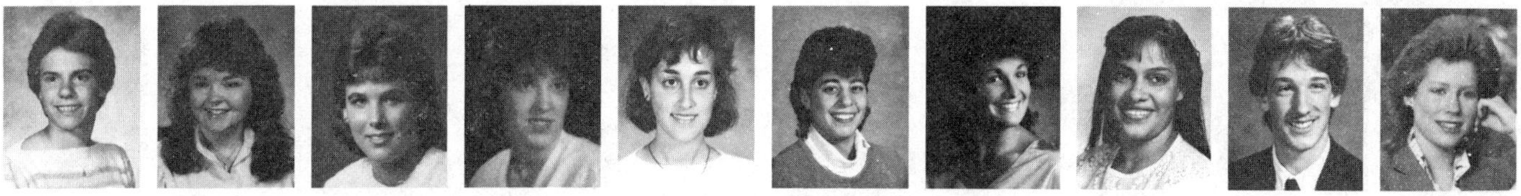

Gallagher, Edith
Brookfield HS
Brookfield Ctr, CT

Gallagher, Kathy
Jonathan Law HS
Milford, CT

Gallegos, Nena
Valley Regional HS
Deep River, CT

Gallery, Danielle
East Hartford HS
E Hartford, CT

Gambardella, Lee
Sacred Heart Acad
Hamden, CT

Gambino, Stephanie
St Mary HS
Harrison, NY

Garcia, Beatrice
Plainville HS
Plainville, CT

Garcia, Norma
Bassick HS
Bridgept, CT

Garlitz, Keith
Naugatuck HS
Ellicott City, MD

Garner, Alana
Plainfield HS
Central Village, CT

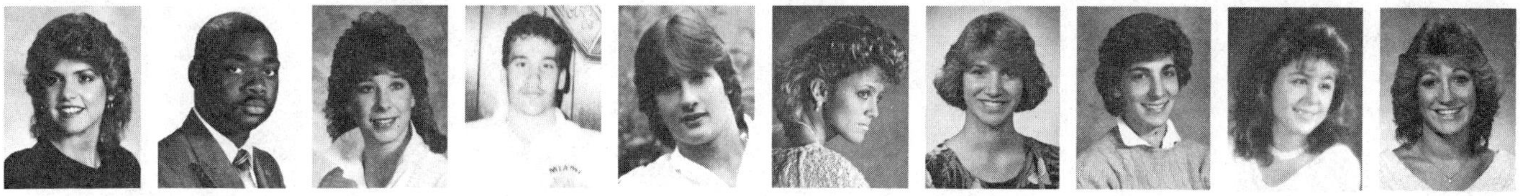

Garofalo, Joleen
Immaculate HS
Danbury, CT

Gaskins, Richard
Wilbur Cross HS
New Haven, CT

Gaudreau, Michelle
East Windsor HS
Broad Brook, CT

Gault, Kevin Donald
Francais
St Lukes HS
Stamford, CT

Genest, Scott
Sheehan HS
Wallingford, CT

Gentile, Sylvia
Holy Cross HS
Waterbury, CT

Gesseck, Stefanie
Lynn
St Margarets-Mc
Ternan HS
Cheshire, CT

Giannattasio,
Sandra
St Mary HS
Old Greenwich, CT

Giannelli, Diane
St Marys HS
New Haven, CT

Giannelli, Kara
Southington HS
Southington, CT

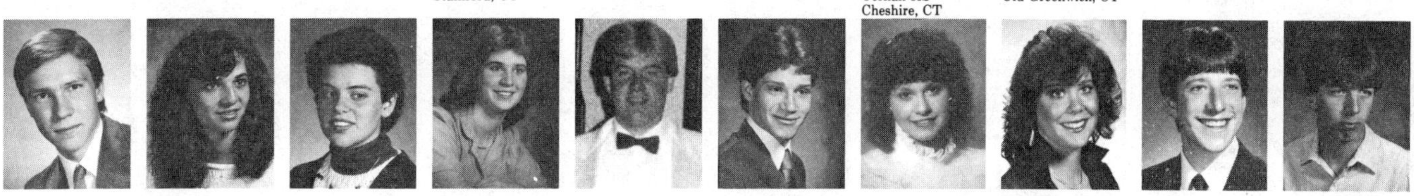

Gibb, James
Greenwich HS
Greenwich, CT

Gibbons, Angie
The Morgan Schl
Clinton, CT

Gilchrist, Kristin
Norwalk HS
Norwalk, CT

Gill, Virginia
Bloomfield HS
Bloomfield, CT

Gillette, Matthew
Holy Cross HS
Watertown, CT

Ginsburg, Mitchell
Bloomfield HS
East Windsor, CT

Giordano,
Antonietta
Ansonia HS
Ansonia, CT

Giordano, Sarah
Kolbe Cathedral HS
Bridgeport, CT

Glenn, Geofry
Shelton HS
Shelton, CT

Glidden, Thomas
Manchester HS
Manchester, CT

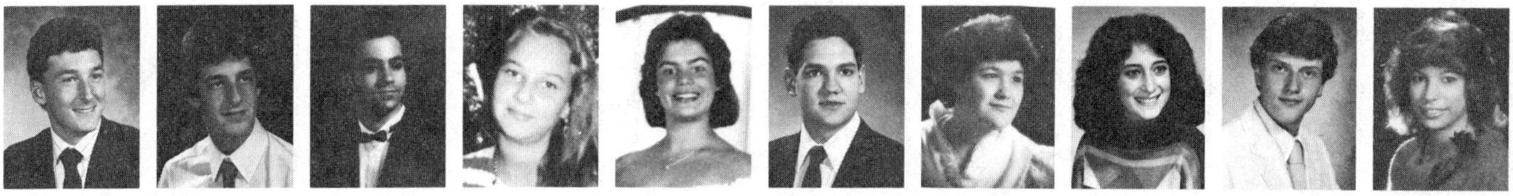

Godley, Mark
Amity HS
Woodbridge, CT

Goldbaum, David
West Haven HS
W Haven, CT

Goldin, Joshua
Jonathan Law HS
Milford, CT

Goldstein, Deidre J
Miss Porters Schl
Woodmere, NY

Gomes, Kelly
Crosby HS
Waterbury, CT

Good, Kelly
Danbury HS
Danbury, CT

Gordon, Cheri Ann
Stratford HS
Stratford, CT

Gostanian, Danielle
Ridgefield HS
Ridgefield, CT

Gostyla, Jeffrey
Berlin HS
Berlin, CT

Grady, Amy
New Fairfield HS
New Fairfld, CT

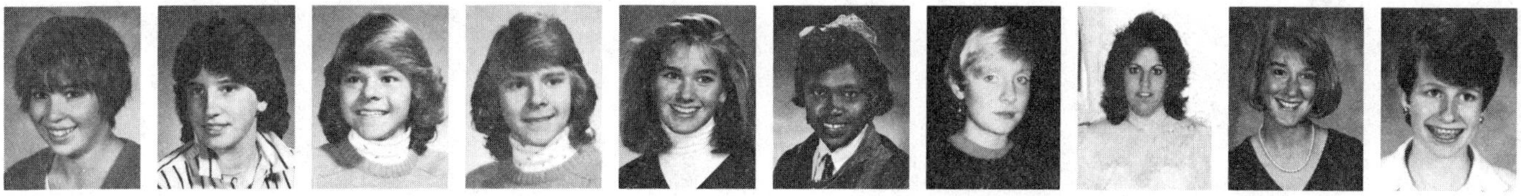

Grant, Jeanne
Robert E Gitch HS
Groton, CT

Grasso, Christina
Norwalk HS
Norwalk, CT

Gratrix, Elaine M
Trumbull HS
Trumbull, CT

Gratrix, Karen A
Trumbull HS
Trumbull, CT

Graves, Cameron
Greenwich HS
Riverside, CT

Gray, Dian
Guilford HS
Brooklyn, NY

Grazioso, Claudia
Hopkins Day
Prospect Hill Schl
New Haven, CT

Greco, Joyce
Crosby HS
Waterbury, CT

Greco, Noelle
Sacred Heart Acad
Hamden, CT

Greeley, Leonora
Sacred Heart Acad
Orange, CT

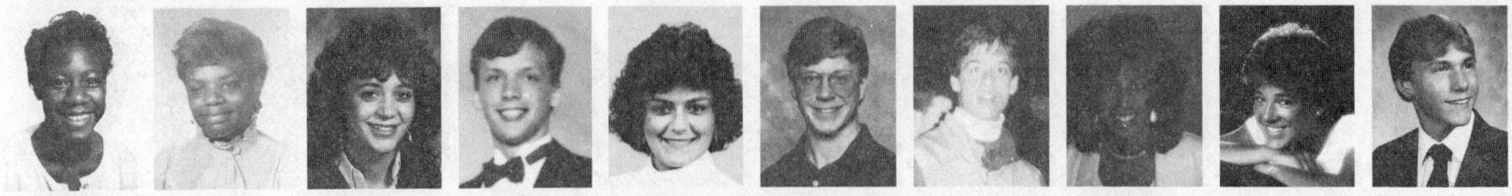

Green, Kelly
Choate Rosemary
Wallingford, CT

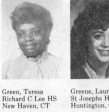

Green, Teresa
Richard C Lee HS
New Haven, CT

Greene, Lauren
St Josephs HS
Huntington, CT

Griffiths, Richard
Guilford HS
Guilford, CT

Grimaldi, Heather
Southington HS
Southington, CT

Gross, Christopher M
Brookfield HS
Brookfield, CT

Grow, Tom S
South Kent HS
Chatham, NJ

Guidi, Christina Marie
The Morgan HS
Clinton, CT

Guiel, Mindy
Enrico Fermi HS
Enfield, CT

Guliuzza, David
Seymour HS
Seymour, CT

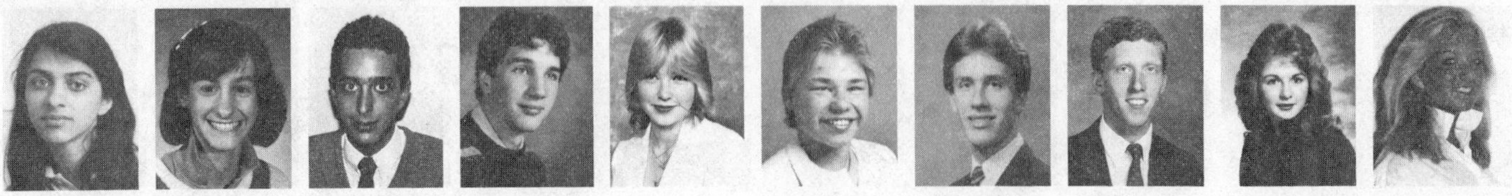

Gupta, Julie
Greenwich HS
Greenwich, CT

Guttmann, Lilian
Staples HS
Westport, CT

Haddad, William
Windham HS
Willimantic, CT

Hadfield, Andrew
Plainfield HS
Moosup, CT

Hadman, Julia
Vinal Regional
Cromwell, CT

Hale, Chris
Nonnewaug HS
Ansonia, CT

Hales, Scott
New Fairfield HS
New Fairfield, CT

Haley, Michael
Fairfield Coll Prep
Milford, CT

Hames, Mary Ellen
Shelton HS
Shelton, CT

Hamilton, Jennifer
Lauralton Hall HS
Stratford, CT

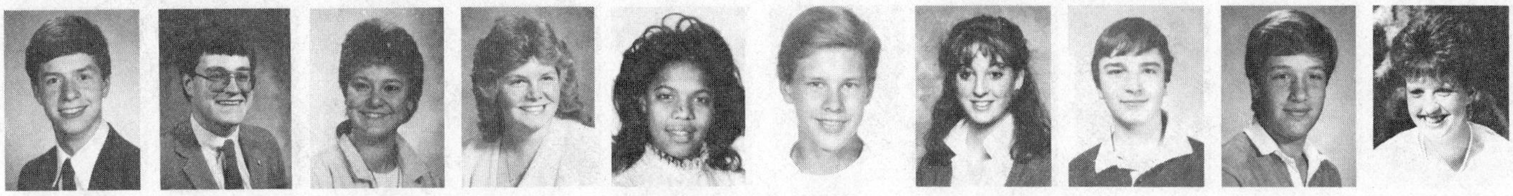

Hanratty, Mark G
Greenwich HS
Greenwich, CT

Hansen, James C
Ellat Grasso-SE Reg Voc Tech Schl
Groton, CT

Haray, Jamie
Kolbe Catherdral
Bridgeport, CT

Harper, Kim
Naugatuck HS
Naugatuck, CT

Harris, Dina
Hillhouse HS
New Haven, CT

Hartigan, Dennis
The Hotchkiss Schl
Ormond Bch, FL

Hartmann, Jennifer
Brookfield HS
Brookfield, CT

Hausmann, Daniel
East Granby HS
E Granby, CT

Havranek, Bill
Greenwich HS
Greenwich, CT

Hawk, Mary Ellen
Stamford Catholic
Stamford, CT

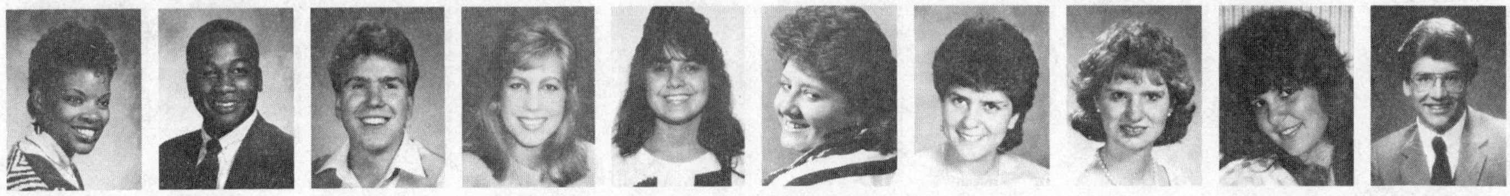

Head, Lisa
St Marys HS
New Haven, CT

Heard, Derek M
Fairfield Coll Preparatory Schl
Trumbull, CT

Hedding, Richard J
Enfield HS
Enfield, CT

Helmers, Kristen
Miss Porters Schl
Spartanburg, SC

Henclik, Theresa
Mark T Sheehan HS
Wallingford, CT

Henderson, Linda
Kaynor Tech HS
Waterbury, CT

Hernandez, Helena
Joseph A Foran HS
Milford, CT

Herold, Karen
East Catholic HS
Vernon, CT

Hesselbach, Cathrine
St Bernard HS
Norwich, CT

Hetzel, Rod
Mark T Sheehan HS
Wallingford, CT

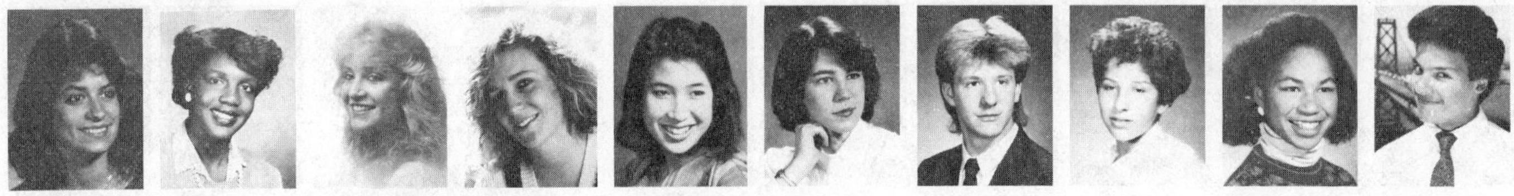

Heuser, Tammy
Shelton HS
Shelton, CT

Hillman, Regina L
Rockville HS
Vernon, CT

Hirtle, Robin
Newington HS
Bloomfield, CT

Hoban, Heather
Wykeham Rise Schl
West Haven, CT

Hodge, Kim
Coventry HS
Coventry, CT

Holbrook, Susan N
Holy Cross HS
Cheshire, CT

Holterman, III Henry F
New Fairfield HS
New Fairfield, CT

Holzman, Dara
Stamford HS
Stamford, CT

Horsey, Erika
Avon HS
Avon, CT

Howe, Alberto
New London HS
New London, CT

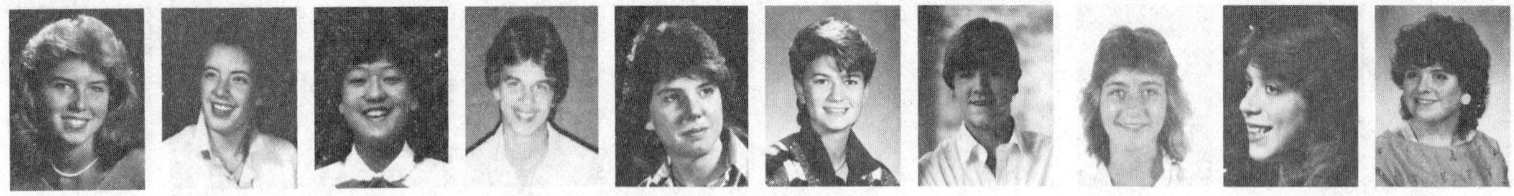

Howe, Alison
Lyman Hall HS
Wallingford, CT

Hrynchuk, Christine
New Britain HS
New Britain, CT

Huang, Juliet
Daniel Hood HS
Madison, CT

Hudson, John Barbour
Oliver Wolcott Tech
Harwinton, CT

Hughes, Renee
Jonathan Law HS
Milford, CT

Hughes, Tonya
Stamford HS
Stamford, CT

Hugo, Mark E
M T Sheehan HS
Wallingford, CT

Hulme, Nancy
Kingswood Oxford
Manchester, CT

Hunt, Tecia-Lue
Emmett O Brien RVT Schl
Beacon Falls, CT

Hunter, Maureen
Rham HS
Amston, CT

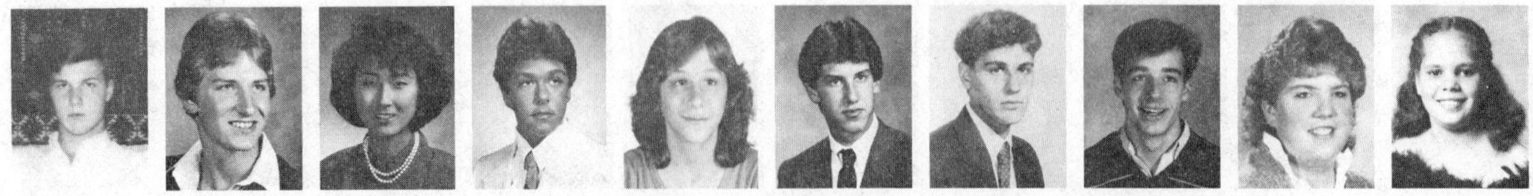

Hupe, Kurt
The Taft School
New York, NY

Huzi, Richard
Seymour HS
Seymour, CT

Hwang, Helen
Glastonbury HS
Glastonbury, CT

Hyzy, Christopher M
Brien Mc Mahon
S Norwalk, CT

Iacurci, Diane
Trumbull HS
Trumbull, CT

Ilardo, Michael
Fairfield College Prep Schl
Easton, CT

Imbimbo, Steven
Holy Cross HS
Cheshire, CT

Ireland, Matthew
Ridgefield HS
Ridgefield, CT

Irish, Julie
Killingly HS
Brooklyn, CT

Irizarry, Glorimar
Hartford HS
Hartford, CT

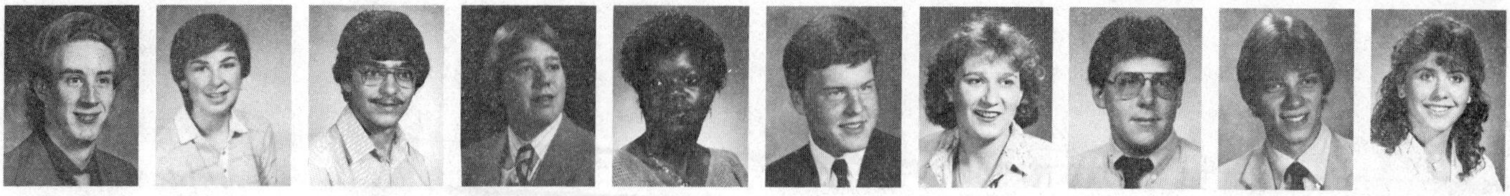

Irvine, Paul
The Morgan HS
Clinton, CT

Irving, Paula D
Ridgefield HS
Ridgefield, CT

Isfahani, Kazim
Greenwich HS
Riverside, CT

Jackson, Brian
Danbury HS
Danbury, CT

Jackson, Nancy
James Hillhouse HS
New Haven, CT

Janke, Bob
Fairfield College
Fairfield, CT

Jankowska, Renata
Norwalk HS
Norwalk, CT

Jankowski, Jr
Ronald L
Windsor HS
Windsor, CT

Janosko, Jr Paul A
Fairfield Prep
Bridgeport, CT

Jarrett, Christine
Stamford HS
Stamford, CT

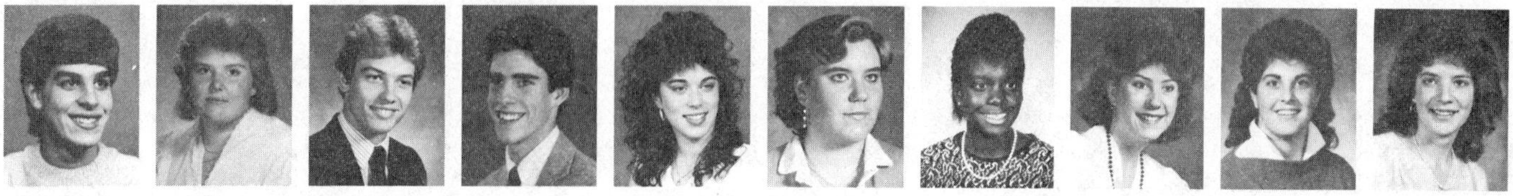

Jasminski, Robert
Wethersfield HS
Wethersfield, CT

Jelliffe, Marie
Louise
West Haven HS
W Haven, CT

Jenkin, Mark C
The Morgan Schl
Clinton, CT

Jennings, Gregory
Fairfield College
Fairfield, CT

Jensen, Melissa
West Haven HS
W Haven, CT

Johns, Marnee
Ridgefield HS
Ridgefield, CT

Johnson, Dwinette
The Loomis Chaffee
West Hartford, CT

Johnson, Elizabeth
Plainfield HS
Central Village, CT

Johnson, Jacquelyn
Rham HS
Amston, CT

Johnson, Karen
Rockville HS
Somers, CT

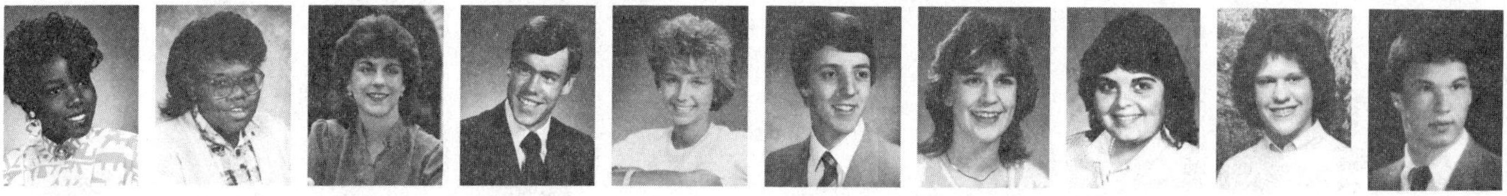

Johnson, Sharon
Stamford HS
Stamford, CT

Johnson, Terri
Wilby HS
Waterbury, CT

Joly, Michelle
Killingly HS
Danielson, CT

Joseph, Michael
Westhill HS
Stamford, CT

Jussaume, Julie
Killingly HS
Dayville, CT

Kaczor, Charles
Berlin HS
Kensington, CT

Kamm, Debra
East Hartford HS
E Hartford, CT

Kane, Darlene
Derby HS
Derby, CT

Kaptinski, Nancy
Lyman Hall HS
Wallingford, CT

Karasevich, David
M
St Bernard HS
Uncasville, CT

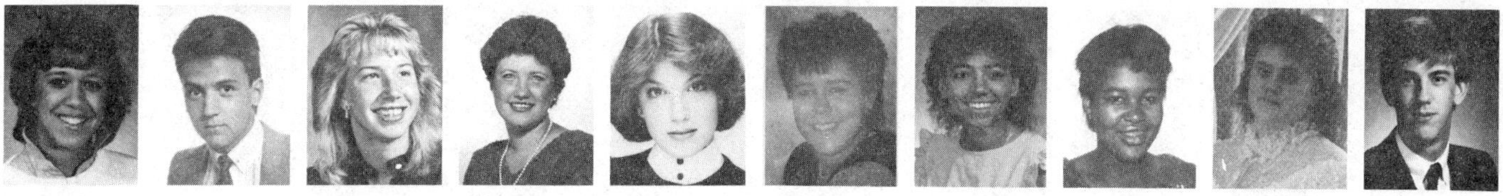

Karazin, Deborah
Staples HS
Westport, CT

Katreczko,
Alexander J
St Joseph HS
Huntington, CT

Katrick, Meta
Joseph A Foran HS
Milford, CT

Katrick, Wendy
Foran HS
Milford, CT

Kaufman, Rebecca
Miss Porters Schl
Ventnor, NJ

Kawecki, Lisa
Ft Maloney HS
Meriden, CT

Kearns, Heather
Rham HS
Hebron, CT

Keeling, Charlene
Miss Porters Schl
Bronx, NY

Kellett, Mary Jane
Shelton HS
Shelton, CT

Kelly, Mark
Wilton HS
Wilton, CT

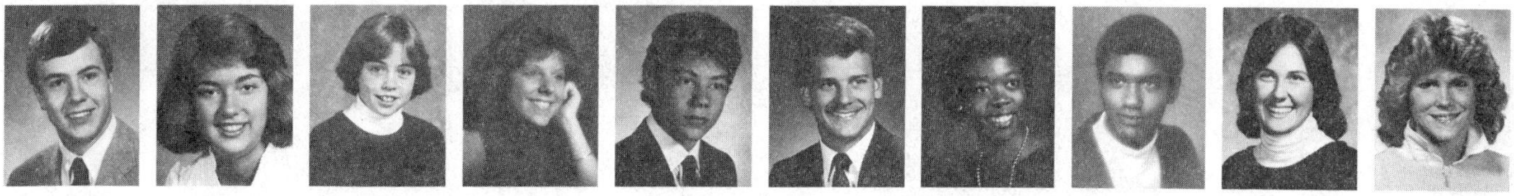

Kendall, Leigh
William H Hall HS
W Hartford, CT

Kendra, Caryn
Marie
Notre Dame
Catholic HS
Fairfield, CT

Kennedy, Shannon
Lee
Mary Immaculate
New Britain, CT

Kenyon, Kimberly
Mark T Sheehan HS
Wallingford, CT

Khalifa, Aly G
Greenwich HS
Riverside, CT

Kieras, Scott
Shelton HS
Shelton, CT

Kiganda, Mary
Edna
Academy Of The
Holy Family HS
Gaithersburg, MD

King, IV George
Ridgefield HS
Ridgefield, CT

Kissam, Barbara
Avon HS
Avon, CT

Kittredge, Courtney
Southington HS
Southington, CT

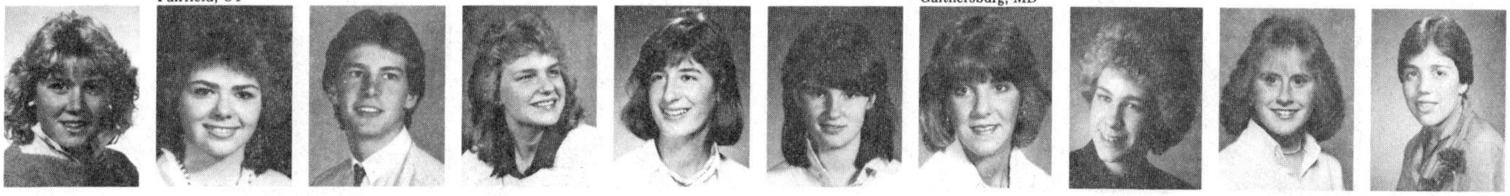

Kjos, Rachel
Norwich Free Acad
Canterbury, CT

Kneeland, Kimberly
East Hampton HS
E Hampton, CT

Koch, Peter
Central HS
Bristol, CT

Koerkel, Holly
Seymour HS
Seymour, CT

Komarowska,
Agnieszka
Norwalk HS
Norwalk, CT

Komarowska, Kasia
Norwalk HS
Norwalk, CT

Koperwhats, Kathy
Stratford HS
Stratford, CT

Kordys, Cynthia
Southington HS
Southington, CT

Kormanik, Kelley
Brookfield HS
Brookfieldcenter,
CT

Koutroubis,
Christina
Norwalk HS
Norwalk, CT

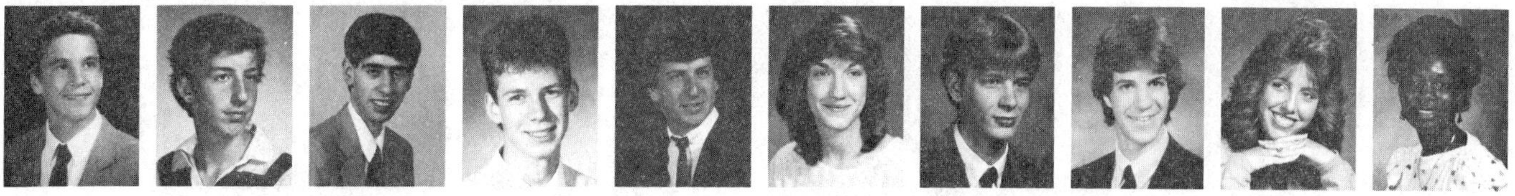

Kowack, Eric P
St Bernard HS
N Stonington, CT

Kowalchik, Richard
M
Trumbull HS
Trumbull, CT

Kreonides, Nicholas
C
Litchfield HS
Litchfield, CT

Kromish, Zane
Pham HS
Amston, CT

Kronenwetter, John
East Catholic HS
South Windsor, CT

Krysiak, Karen
Platt Regional
Vocational Tec
Milford, CT

Kulas, Donald
Granby Memorial
Granby, CT

Kusmik, William
Aldo
E Catholic HS
Manchester, CT

Kuziak, Jacquelyn
Shelton HS
Shelton, CT

Kwakye, Gladys
Hartofrd Public HS
Hartford, CT

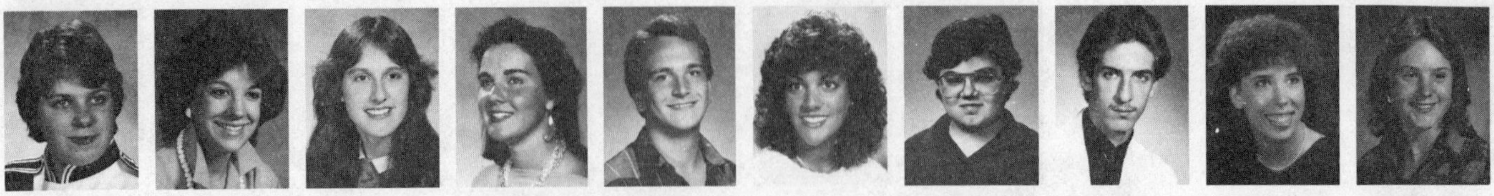

Labonte, Gabrielle
Putnam HS
Woodstock Valley, CT

Lahaie, Sherri
Plainfield HS
Sterling, CT

Lallier, Michelle
Conard HS
W Hartford, CT

Landers, Deirdre
Farmington HS
Farmington, CT

Landers, William M
Stamford HS
Stamford, CT

Landino, Sandra Elise
Sacred Heart Acad
New Haven, CT

Landy, Brett
Bethel HS
Bethel, CT

Lane, Tim
Bullard-Havens Reg
Stratford, CT

Lang, Marcia A
St Bernard HS
Lebanon, CT

Lange, Shelley
Cheshire Acad
Wallingford, CT

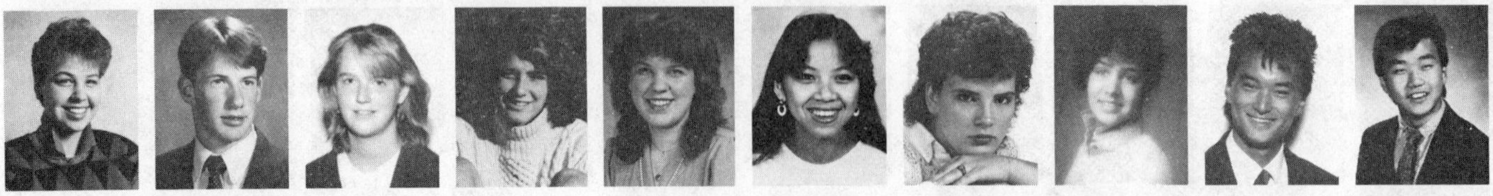

Lasher, Laura
Our Lady Of The Angels Acad
Enfield, CT

Lawlor, IV James R
Holy Cross HS
Waterbury, CT

Lawlor, Mary Patricia
Canterbury Schl
Waterbury, CT

Lawrence, Tonya
Pomfret Schl
Pomfret Center, CT

Lazeren, Cheryl
Rockville HS
Vernon, CT

Le, Trang
Central HS
Bridgeport, CT

Le Blanc, Catherine E
Putnam HS
Putnam, CT

Lee, Anja
Tolland HS
Tolland, CT

Lee, Charles
Shelton HS
Shelton, CT

Lee, Richard
East Catholic HS
S Windsor, CT

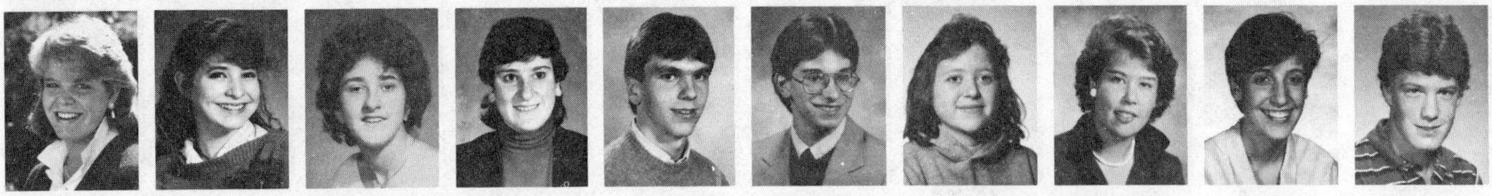

Lefko, Christine
Low Heywood Thomas Schl
Stamford, CT

Lefkowitz, Eva S
Wilton HS
Wilton, CT

Leggo, Heather
Ansonia HS
Ansonia, CT

Leheny, Cara
Ridgefield HS
Danbury, CT

Lemanowicz, Kevin
Killingly HS
Danielson, CT

Leonard, Andrew J
Hamden HS
Hamden, CT

Lepoutre, Christine
Stamford Catholic
Stamford, CT

Lesnick, Nancy
Ansonia HS
Ansonia, CT

Lev, Roslyn
Cheshire HS
Cheshire, CT

Levy, David
Norwalk HS
Norwalk, CT

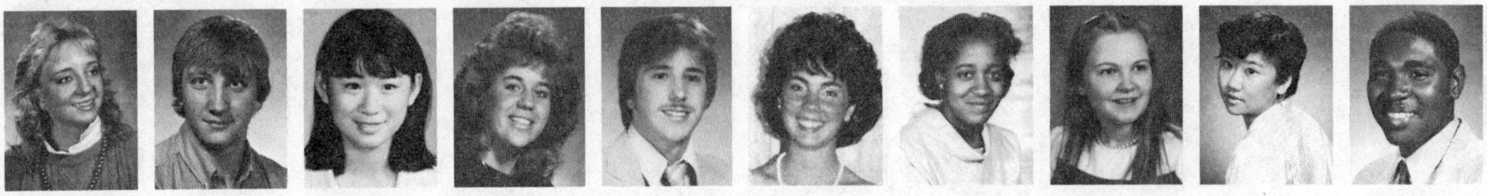

Lewis, Dawn Lucille
Henry Abbott Tech
Bethel, CT

Lewis, Jonathan
Southington HS
Southington, CT

Li, Jiaming
Choate Rosemary Hall HS
Wallingford, CT

Li Volsi, Amy
Stamford HS
Stamford, CT

Light, Allen
Danbury HS
Danbury, CT

Limato, Paulette
Holy Cross HS
Cheshire, CT

Liptrot, Melanie
Richard C Lee HS
New Haven, CT

Ljunggren, Deborah
St Marys HS
N Haven, CT

Lo, Wendy
Stamford HS
Stamford, CT

Lockett, Jeffrey
Hillhouse HS
New Haven, CT

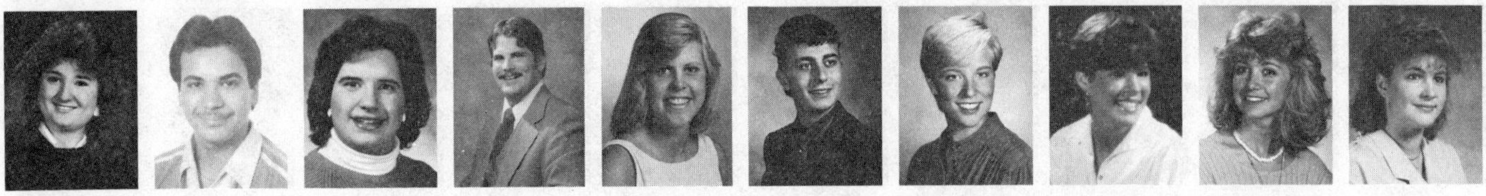

Lohenitz, Susan
Seymour HS
Oxford, CT

Lombardi, John
Kaynor Technical
Waterbury, CT

Lombardo, Nancy
New Britain HS
New Britain, CT

Lombardo, Philip
Wethersfield HS
Wethersfield, CT

Long, Lisabeth
The Taft Schl
Watertown, CT

Longo, Marco
Holy Cross HS
Naugatuck, CT

Lorimier, Kimberly M
New Canaan HS
New Canaan, CT

Lovetere, Caroline
Glastonbury HS
Glastonbury, CT

Lowrey, Jennifer K
Bristol Eastern HS
Bristol, CT

Lucas, Suzanne
Farmington HS
Unionville, CT

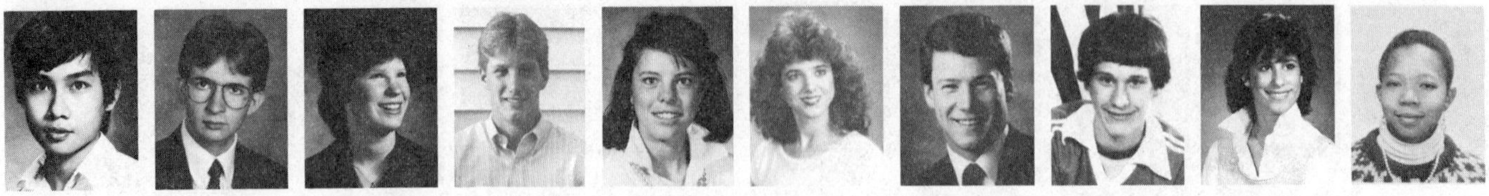

Luu, Thuan P
Hartford Public HS
Hartford, CT

Lyskowski, Kevin
Fairfield College Preparatory Schl
Ansonia, CT

Mac Calmont, Terry L
Nathan Hale-Ray
Colchester, CT

Mac Kay, Gregory
Holy Cross HS
Waterbury, CT

Mac Kay, Kerry
East Lyme HS
Niantic, CT

Maciejak, Donna
East Haven HS
East Haven, CT

Mackay, Bryan
Holy Cross HS
Waterbury, CT

Mackenzie, Robert
Putnam HS
Putnam, CT

Magid, Cheri A
Joel Barlow HS
Easton, CT

Magubane, Zine
Edwin O Smith HS
Storrs, CT

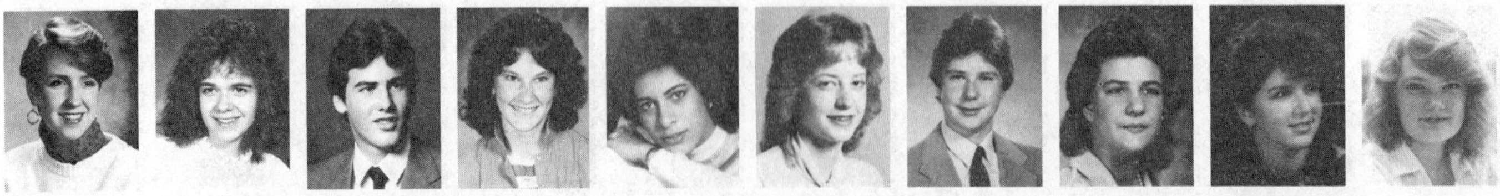

Mahoney, Karin L
Amity Regional SR
Orange, CT

Mailhot, Rose
St Marys HS
New Haven, CT

Makowicz, David
Ellington HS
Rockville, CT

Malenda, Kathy
Sacred Heart Acad
W Haven, CT

Mancini, Donna
Notre Dame Catholic HS
Bridgeport, CT

Mandrona, Melissa
Heritage Christian
Seymour, CT

Marchesseault, Donald
South Windsor HS
South Windsor, CT

Marcucci, Jennifer
St Marys HS
E Haven, CT

Marino, Mary Ann
St Paul Catholic HS
Farmington, CT

Markey, Jennifer
Pomperang HS
Southbury, CT

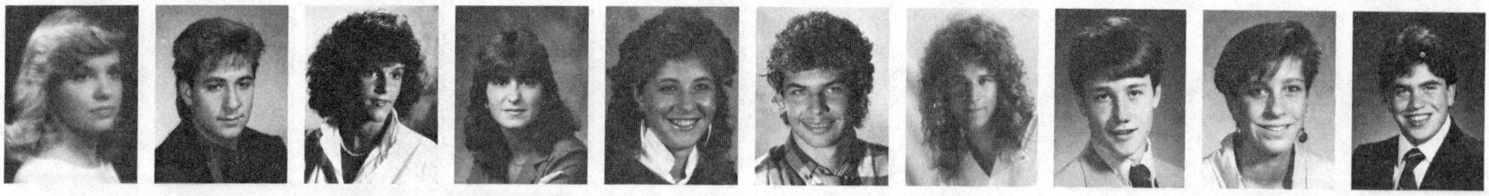

Martin, Jennifer J
New Fairfield HS
New Fairfield, CT

Marzullo, Scott
St Mary HS
Stamford, CT

Masto, Jennifer A
Amity Regional SR
West Haven, CT

Mastors, Alyssa
Wethersfield HS
Wethersfield, CT

Mathews, Kathy
Watertown HS
Watertown, CT

Mathieu, Richard
Marianapolis
Preparatory Schl
N Grosvenordale,
CT

Mattson, John
East Haven HS
East Haven, CT

Matz, David
Norwalk HS
Norwalk, CT

Mazzalupo, Christy
Notre Dame Acad
Waterbury, CT

Mazzaro, Vincent
Shelton HS
Shelton, CT

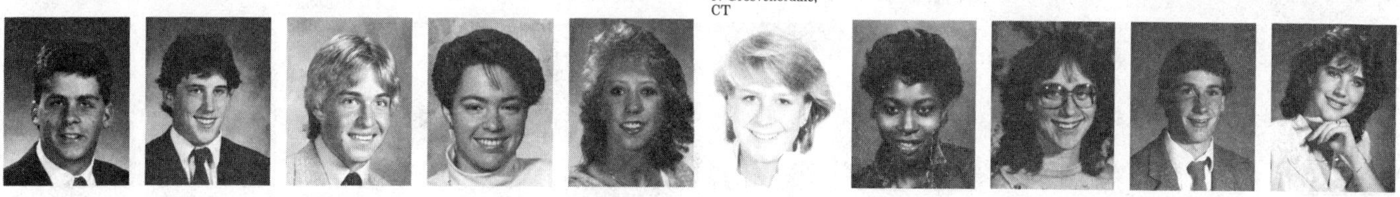

Mc Bride, Jr David
F
St Bernard HS
Lisbon, CT

Mc Cain, Thomas
St Josephs HS
Trumbull, CT

Mc Cart, Mike
Fairfield College
Prep Schl
Shelton, CT

Mc Carthy, Meghan
Sacred Heart Acad
Stamford, CT

Mc Cauley, Theresa
West Haven HS
West Haven, CT

Mc Connell, Melanie
Gwen
Greenwich HS
Old Greenwich, CT

Mc Cown, Tonia
James Hillhouse HS
New Haven, CT

Mc Curdy, Patricia
New Britain HS
New Britain, CT

Mc Dougall, Jerry
St Lukes Schl
Trumbull, CT

Mc Ewen, Rhonda
Shelton HS
Shelton, CT

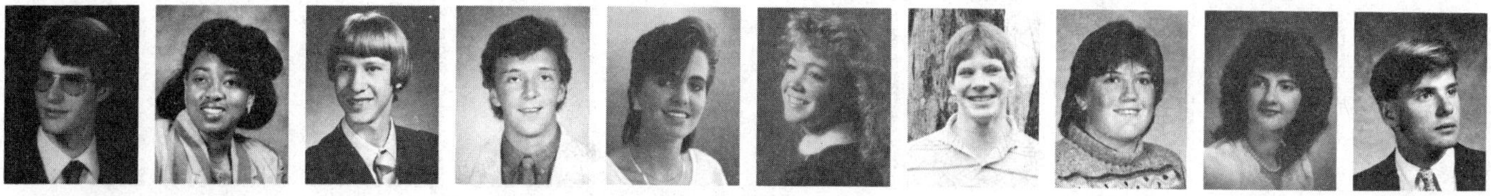

Mc Farland, Robert
Simsbury HS
Simsbury, CT

Mc Gee, Dana R
Rockville HS
Vernon, CT

Mc Girr, John
Norwalk HS
Norwalk, CT

Mc Graw, Patrick N
The Loomis Chaffee
Maplewood, NJ

Mc Guire, Laura
Brien Mc Mahon
Norwalk, CT

Mc Hugh, Joanne P
Glatonbury HS
Glastonbury, CT

Mc Intyre, Kevin
Weston HS
Newkirk, OK

Mc Knight, Jane
Kathryn
Joseph A Foran HS
Milford, CT

Mc Laughlin, Tara
Rockville HS
Rockville, CT

Mc Leod, Robert
Morgan Schl
Clinton, CT

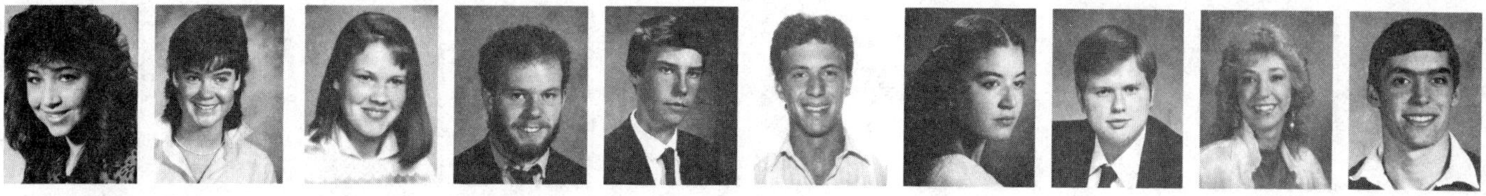

Mc Mahon, Cheryl
Vinal Regional
Technical Schl
N Branford, CT

Mc Mahon, Deborah
St Joseph HS
Shelton, CT

Mc Nair, Lindsay A
St Margarets-Mc
Ternan HS
Waterbury, CT

Mc Namee, John
St Mary HS
Greenwich, CT

Mc Tigue, Keith
Fairfield College
Huntington, CT

Meehan, Kevin
Holy Cross HS
Waterbury, CT

Mendez, Maria
New London HS
Waterford, CT

Merritt, Robert
Southington HS
Southington, CT

Merton, Jennifer
Rockville HS
Rockville, CT

Meyer, Gary
Ridgefield HS
Ridgefield, CT

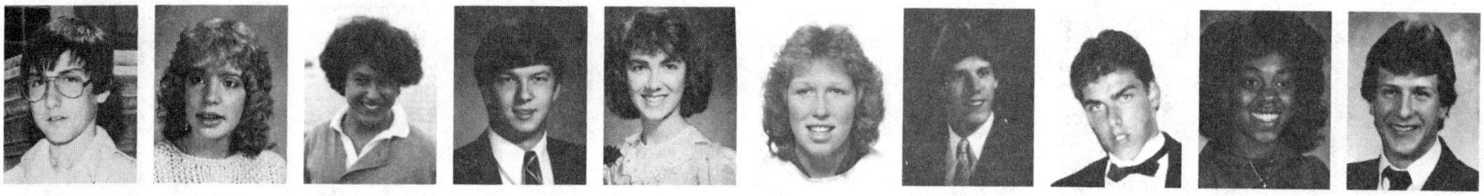

Meyer, Olivier S
Stamford HS
Stamford, CT

Michaud, Louise
Manchester HS
Manchester, CT

Migliaccio, Kristen
Conard HS
West Hartford, CT

Mihaly, Matthew
Trumball HS
Trumbull, CT

Milewski, Yvonne
Stamford Catholic
Stamford, CT

Miller, Denyse
Holy Cross HS
Seymour, CT

Miller, Jeremy
Danbury HS
Danbury, CT

Minahan, Timothy
Danbury HS
Danbury, CT

Minor, Stephany
Sacred Heart Acad
New Haven, CT

Mirando, Richard
H C Wilcox
Technical Schl
Plantsville, CT

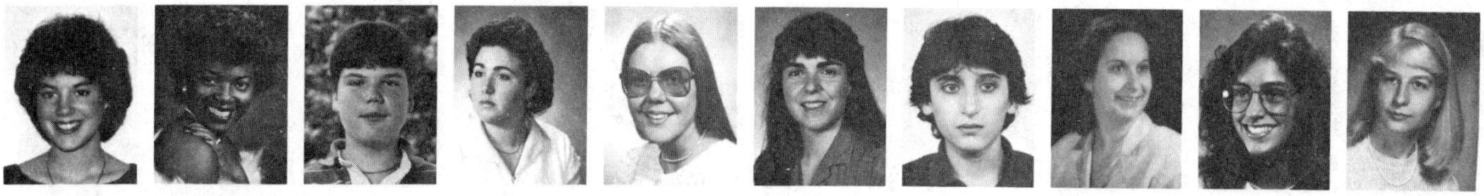

Mirto, Wendy
Lauralton Hall HS
Huntington, CT

Mitchell, Debbie
Ann
Seymour HS
Seymour, CT

Mitchell, Jeff
Wilton HS
Wilton, CT

Mitchell, Wendy
East Haven HS
E Haven, CT

Mizeski, Suzanne
Naugatuck HS
Union City, CT

Molinaro, Gioia
Conard HS
Farmington, CT

Montanaro,
Maurizio
Bullard-Havens
Bridgeport, CT

Montigny, Jessica A
Norwich Free Acad
Norwich, CT

Moore, Tracey
New Milford HS
New Milford, CT

Morin, Kelly Anne
Litchfield HS
Litchfield, CT

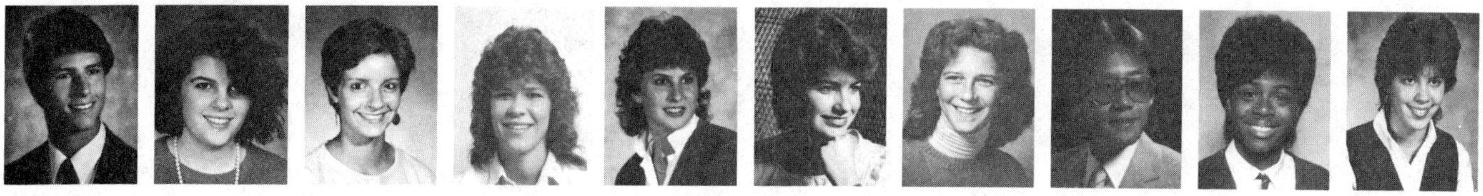

Mormino, Richard
Paul
Enrico Fermi HS
Enfield, CT

Morris, Elizabeth
Sacred Heart Acad
Guilford, CT

Morrissette, Susan
Conard HS
W Hartford, CT

Morus, Meredith
Greenwich HS
Greenwich, CT

Mosimann, Kristin
Thomaston HS
Thomaston, CT

Moskal, Michelle E
Mary Immaculate
New Britain, CT

Mountain, Kimberly
Canton HS
Collinsville, CT

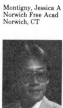

Moy, Wayne
Danbury HS
Danbury, CT

Moye, Kasandra
Farmington HS
Hartford, CT

Mudrick, Maryellen
St Joseph HS
Stratford, CT

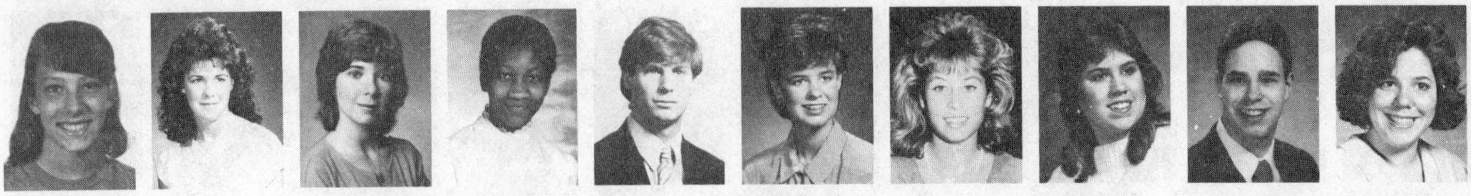

Mueller, Emily
Loomis Chaffee Schl
Hartford, CT

Munch, Lisa
Shelton HS
Shelton, CT

Mundell, Maribeth
Kingswood-Oxford
Wethersfld, CT

Murrell, Nicole
Richard C Lee
Education Ctr
New Haven, CT

Mushkin, Scott
Kent HS
Bennington, RI

Myers, Amy
Shelton HS
Shelton, CT

Myerson, Nancy
Kingswood-Oxford
W Hartford, CT

Naro, Tanya
Plainfield HS
Plainfield, CT

Navickas, John M
Rham HS
Marlborough, CT

Needs, Penny
Farmington HS
Farmington, CT

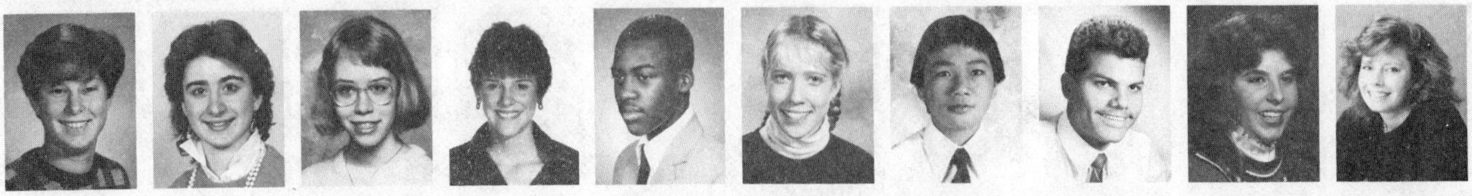

Nelson, Heather
Greenwich HS
Riverside, CT

Nemeth, Kristine
Torrington HS
Torrington, CT

Nemetz, Laurice
Brookfield HS
Brookfield, CT

Newman, Christy
Griswold HS
Jewett City, CT

Newton, Derick
Brien Mc Mahon
S Norwalk, CT

Newton, Lavinia
Coginchaug HS
Durham, CT

Ng, Richmond
Torrington HS
Torrington, CT

Nieves, Azarel
Bulard Havens
Bridgeport, CT

Niezelski, Laura
Morgan HS
Clinton, CT

Nilsson, April
Windsor HS
Windsor, CT

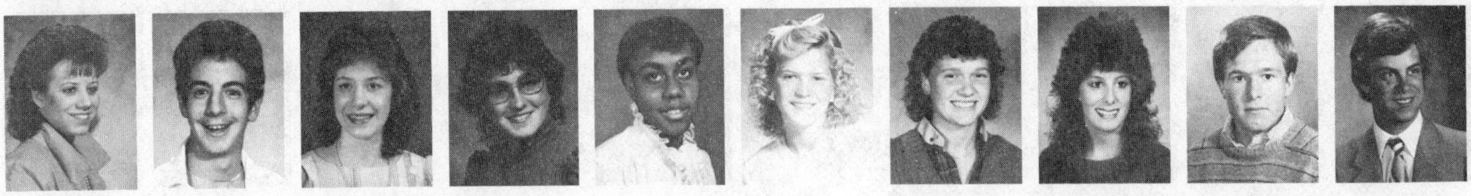

Niquette, Lisa
Wilby HS
Waterbury, CT

Nobile, Frank
Bollard-Havens
Tech HS
Stratford, CT

Nolan, Kathleen
East Catholic HS
Glastonbury, CT

Noll, Beth
Seymour HS
Oxford, CT

Nonnon, Annique
Watertown HS
Oakville, CT

Nopanen, Crissie
Shelton HS
Shelton, CT

Nordin, Christine
Shelton HS
Shelton, CT

Normile, Amy E
Enfield HS
Enfield, CT

Norris, Christopher
B
Nonnewaug HS
Woodbury, CT

Novak, Robert
St Josephs HS
Shelton, CT

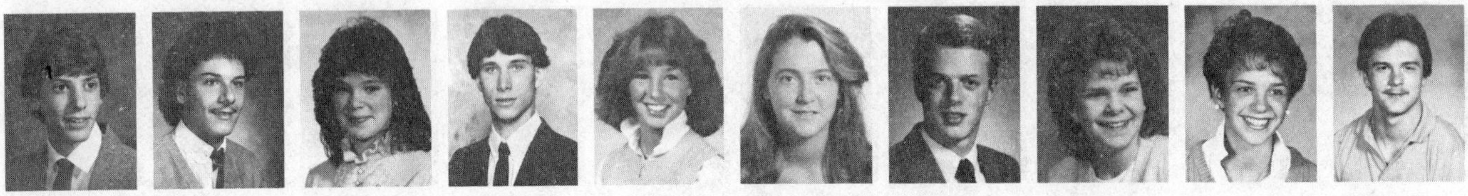

Nucifora, Salvatore
Vinal Regional
Vocational Tec
East Hampton, CT

Nunziante,
Ferdinando
Bristol Central HS
Bristol, CT

O Brien, Amy
Ansonia HS
Ansonia, CT

O Brien, Sean
Brookfield HS
Brookfield, CT

O Connell, Kathy
Glastonbury HS
Glastonbury, CT

O Hearn, Mary
Miss Porters Schl
New York, NY

Olbrich, Gregory
Wilton HS
Wilton, CT

Oldham, Sharon
Plainfield HS
Plainfield, CT

Olmsted, Erika
Sacred Heart Acad
Ansonia, CT

Orloski, Steven
Bullard Havens
Tech HS
Stratford, CT

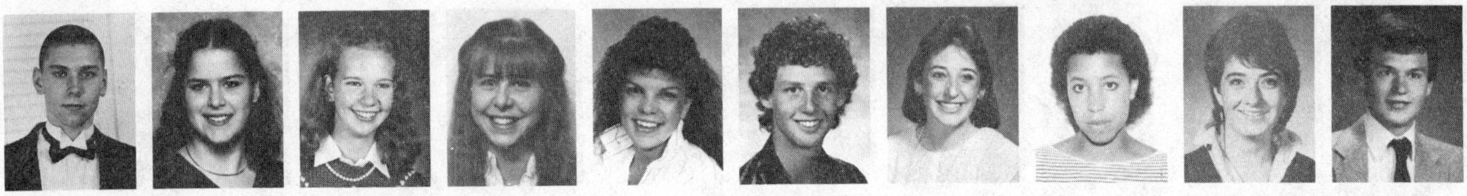

Ortega, Damon
High School In The
New Haven, CT

Oshman, Andra
Brookfield HS
Brookfield, CT

Osullivan, Maureen
Sacred Heart Acad
Hamden, CT

Oudin, Caroline A C
Pomfret HS
Pomfret, CT

Ouellette, Cathleen
Crsoby HS
Waterbury, CT

Page, Andrew
Southington HS
Southington, CT

Pagliaro, Petrea
Central Catholic HS
Norwalk, CT

Pahaham, Cheryl
Wooster Schl
Danbury, CT

Palmer, Dawna J
Rham HS
Hebron, CT

Palmer, Douglas
St Mary HS
Pt Chester, NY

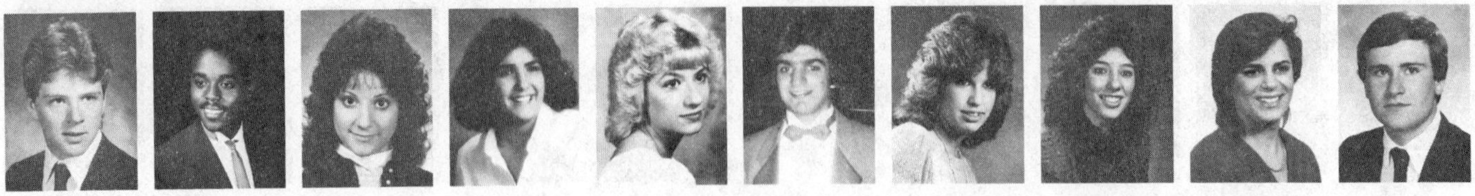

Palmer, Shawn
Rocky Hill HS
Rocky Hill, CT

Palmer, Timothy
Hamden HS
Hamden, CT

Palmieri, Cheryl
Southington HS
Southington, CT

Palumbo, Tracey
St Thomas Aquinas
New Britain, CT

Panaroni, Donna
Seymour HS
Seymour, CT

Panayotou, Nick
New Fairfield HS
New Fairfield, CT

Papallo, Anne
Platt HS
Meriden, CT

Pappalardo, Nella
East Hartford HS
E Hartford, CT

Paquette, Michelle
Farmington HS
Farmington, CT

Parent, Scott
Fairfield College
Fairfield, CT

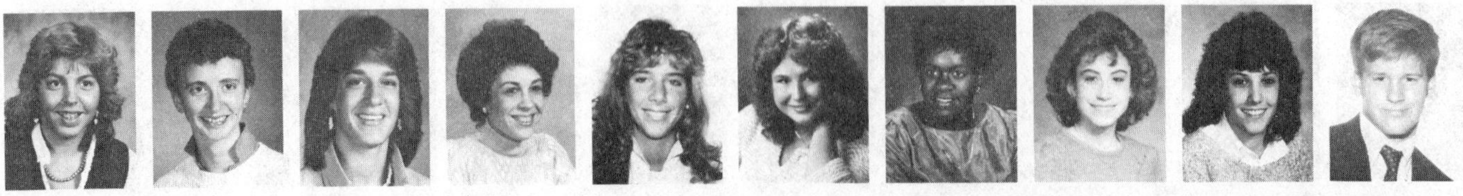

Parker, Leslie
St Joseph HS
Shelton, CT

Parkhurst,
Catherine M
Ridgefield HS
Ridgefield, CT

Paruta, Tina
Housatonic Valley
Regional HS
E Canaan, CT

Pastore, Shirley
Seymour HS
Seymour, CT

Pastorick, Denise
Cheshire HS
Cheshire, CT

Patry, Sherry
O H Platt HS
Meriden, CT

Payne, Morganna
St Marys HS
New Haven, CT

Pearson, Caroline
Hamden HS
Hamden, CT

Peccerillo, Kiersten
Derby HS
Derby, CT

Peck, Randall
Avon Old Farms
Houston, TX

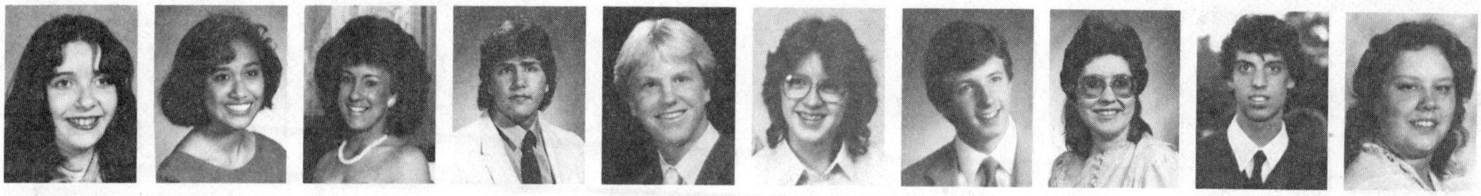

Peebles, Marion
Trumbull HS
Bridgeport, CT

Pelaez, Gina L
Greenwich HS
Greenwich, CT

Pelletier, Maureen
W F Kaynor
Regional Tech HS
Prospect, CT

Pensiero, Joe
Stamford HS
Stamford, CT

Pepsoski, Tony
Daniel Hand HS
Madison, CT

Perlot, Christine
Southington HS
Southington, CT

Perlot, David
Southington HS
Southington, CT

Perreault, Jane
Mary
Plainfield HS
Moosup, CT

Perri, Kevin
Bristol Centeral HS
Bristol, CT

Perrott, Stephanie
Nonnewaug HS
Seymour, CT

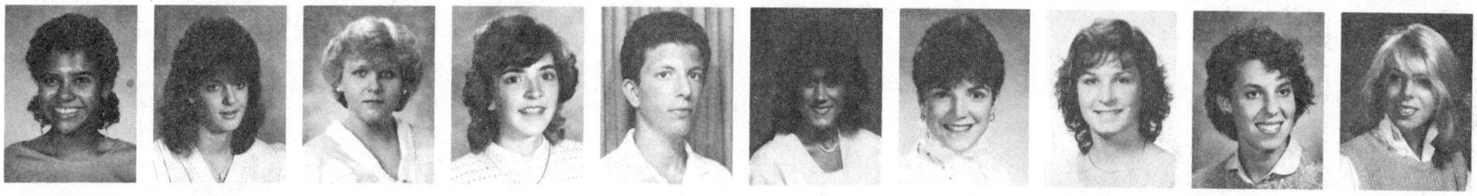

Pertillar, Tammy L
Loomis Chaffee HS
Hartford, CT

Petrowski, Jill
Academy Of The
Holy Family
Bozrah, CT

Petterson, Sonja
Tourtellotte
Memorial HS
Quinebaug, CT

Pettersson, Janice
Old Saybrook SR
Old Saybrook, CT

Philippopoulos,
Evan
St Basil Prep Schl
Stamford, CT

Pieger, Dana
Trumbull HS
Bridgeport, CT

Pike, Sandra
East Lyme HS
Salem, CT

Pikul, Dawn
Danbury HS
Danbury, CT

Pinsky, Shari
Hamden HS
Hamden, CT

Piper, Francesca L
Stamford HS
Stamford, CT

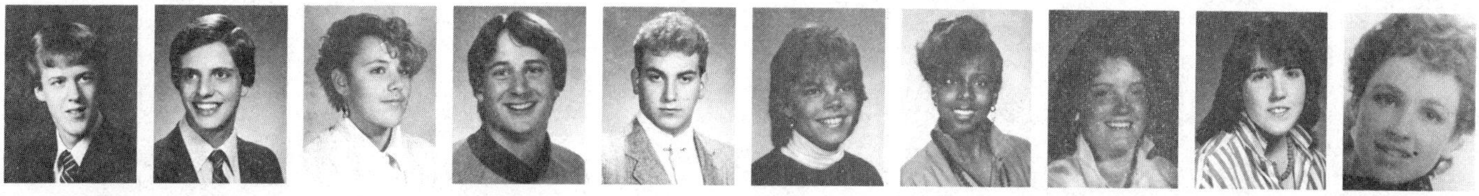

Pohorylo, Brian
Windsor Locks HS
Windsor Locks, CT

Poisson, Todd
Frank Scott Bunnell
Stratford, CT

Poklemba, Audrey
Trumbull HS
Trumbull, CT

Porada, Chris
Southington HS
Plantsville, CT

Porter, Richard A
Bethel HS
Bethel, CT

Pote, Nicole
New Canaan HS
New Canaan, CT

Powell, Karron
West Haven HS
Brooklyn, NY

Powell, Robyn
Thomaston HS
Thomaston, CT

Powers, Sheila C
Central Catholic HS
Westport, CT

Pratviel, Maryalice
Norwich Free Acad
Norwich, CT

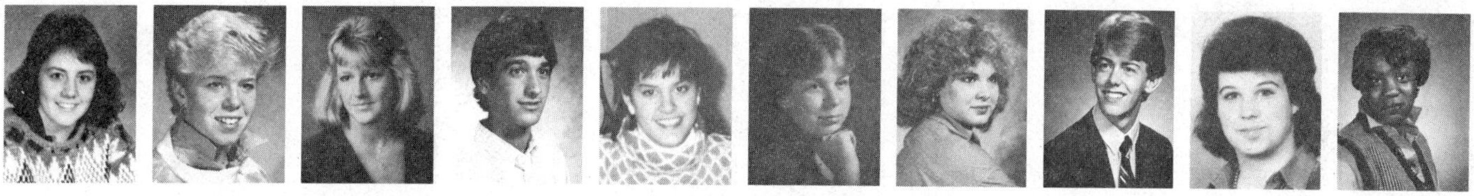

Pray, Judy
Shelton HS
Shelton, CT

Prescott, Erin
Manchester HS
Manchester, CT

Price, Jacqueline
North Haven HS
N Haven, CT

Primini, David
Watertown HS
Oakville, CT

Proctor, Courtney
Ridgefield HS
Ridgefield, CT

Provencal, Robin
Manchester HS
Manchester, CT

Pucci, Kathleen
Seymour HS
Oxford, CT

Puckett, Kelley B
Roger Ludlowe HS
Southport, CT

Pudlinski, Jill
Torrington HS
Torrington, CT

Pugh, Tricia
Norwalk HS
So Norwalk, CT

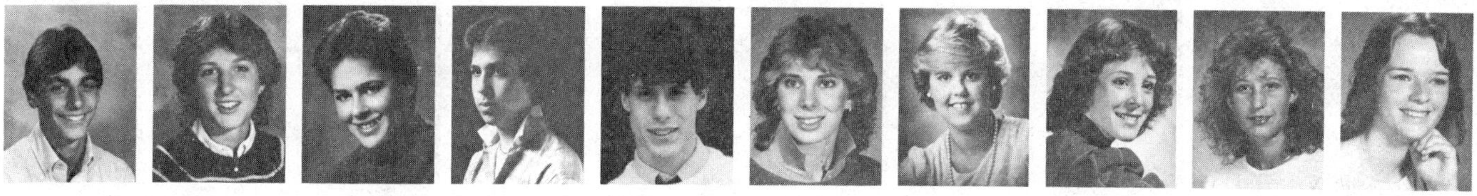

Pye, Richard
Plainfield HS
Moosup, CT

Quercia, Kaleen
Marianapolis Prep
Thompson, CT

Quinley, Matthew
Coginchaug Regional
Durham, CT

Ragaglia, Joseph
Holy Cross HS
Waterbury, CT

Raymond, David
Holy Cross HS
Waterbury, CT

Reardon, Gail
Windsor HS
Windsor, CT

Redden, Denise N
Naugatuck HS
Naugatuck, CT

Redinger, Paula
Rockville HS
Vernon, CT

Redman, Kristen
Bristol Central HS
Bristol, CT

Reed, April
Trumbull HS
Trumbull, CT

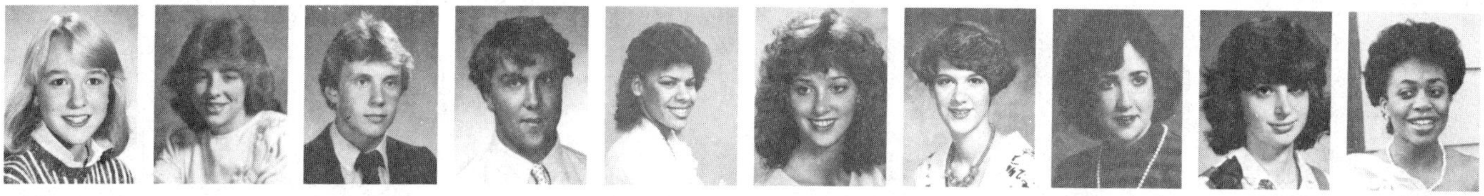

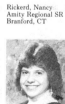

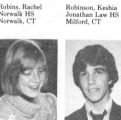

Reitenbach, Claudia
Greenwich HS
Cos Cob, CT

Rek, Laura
Naugatuck HS
Naugatuck, CT

Renda, Craig
Danbury HS
Danbury, CT

Renola, Matthew
Edward
Guilford HS
Guilford, CT

Rice, Etta
Oliver Wolcott Tech
RV HS
Winsted, CT

Rickerd, Nancy
Amity Regional SR
Branford, CT

Rideout, Bethany
Berlin HS
Kensington, CT

Riley, Mary
Christine
Miss Porters Schl
Larchmont, NY

Robins, Rachel
Norwalk HS
Norwalk, CT

Robinson, Keshia
Jonathan Law HS
Milford, CT

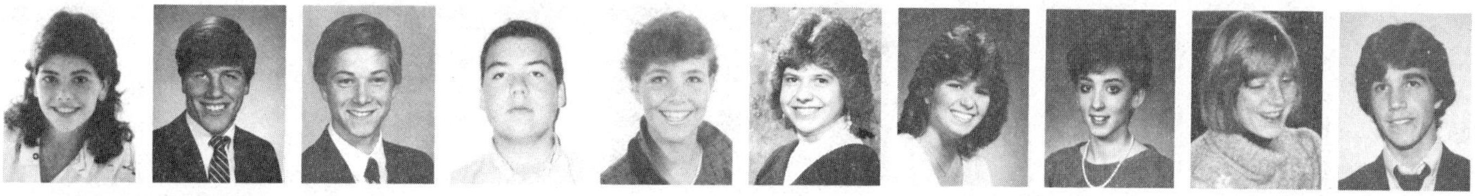

Rodrigues, Elizabeth
M
South Catholic HS
Rocky Hill, CT

Rogdan, Andrew
Greenwich HS
Greenwich, CT

Rogers, Tim
New Canaan HS
New Canaan, CT

Rojas, Matias
Kent HS
Kent, CT

Rolzhausen, Yvonne
Academy Of Our
Lady Of Mercy
Fairfield, CT

Roman, Lynda
Mary Immaculate
New Britain, CT

Romano, Dawn
Shelton HS
Huntington, CT

Romano, Gayle
The Morgan Schl
Clinton, CT

Romary, Mary Ellen
Staples HS
Westport, CT

Romeo, Frank
Kingswood Oxford
Newington, CT

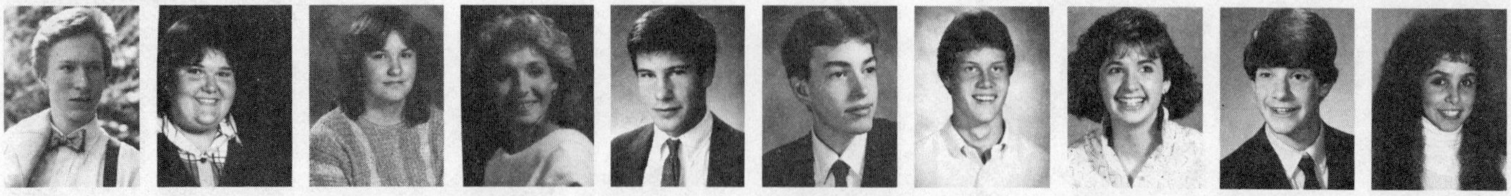

Rommey, Todd
Wilton HS
Wilton, CT

Root, Renee
Old Saybrook SR
Old Saybrook, CT

Rose, Pauline
Griswold HS
Voluntown, CT

Ross, Betsy
Danbury HS
Danbury, CT

Rottenberg, Jonathan A
Ridgefield HS
Ridgefield, CT

Rousseau, Michael
Lewis S Mills HS
Burlington, CT

Rowe, Gordon
Avon HS
Avon, CT

Rudnick, Cheryl
Trumbull HS
Trumbull, CT

Rudof, Michael
Hopkins HS
Orange, CT

Ruggiero, Kimberly A
The Morgan Schl
Clinton, CT

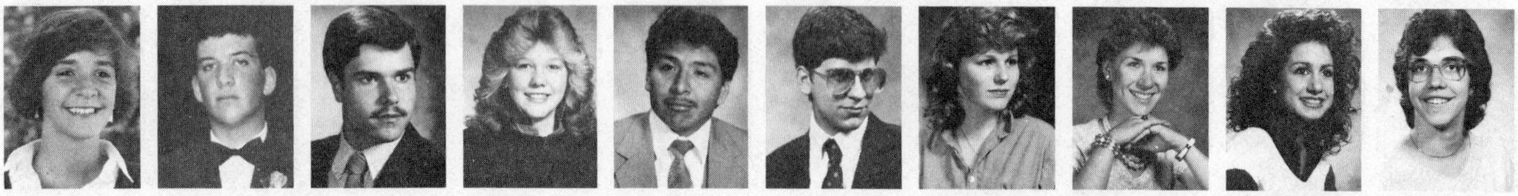

Russo, Nancy
Wilton HS
Wilton, CT

Ryan, Anthony J
Staples HS
Westport, CT

Sabo, Michael
Joesph A Foran HS
Milford, CT

Saksa, Dawn
Shelton HS
Shelton, CT

Salazar, Francisco
Derby HS
Derby, CT

Salvestrini, Matthew
Fairfield College Prep Schl
Ridgefield, CT

Samul, Cynthia A
New London HS
New London, CT

Sanders, Jennifer
E C Goodwin Tech
Forestvile, CT

Santarsiero, Gina
Holy Cross HS
Waterbury, CT

Santino, Michele
West Haven HS
W Haven, CT

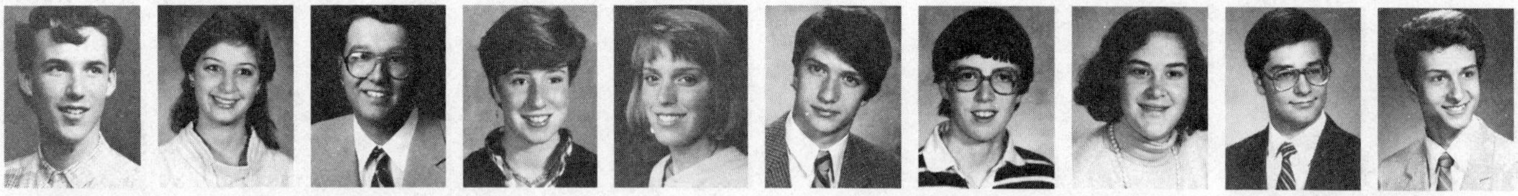

Sautter, Robert
Holy Cross HS
Oxford, CT

Savinelli, Christine
Sacred Heart Acad
Northford, CT

Sawyer, Timothy
Windsor Locks HS
Windsor Locks, CT

Schlegel, Kristin
Ridgefield HS
Ridgefield, CT

Schmerl, Amy
Edwin O Smith HS
Storrs, CT

Schneider, Jr David E
Fairfield Prep
Monroe, CT

Schuster, Wendi
Derby HS
Derby, CT

Schwartz, Karen
Greenwich HS
Old Greenwich, CT

Schweighofer, Peter
Ridgefield HS
Ridgefield, CT

Scinto, Ronald Louis
Shelton HS
Shelton, CT

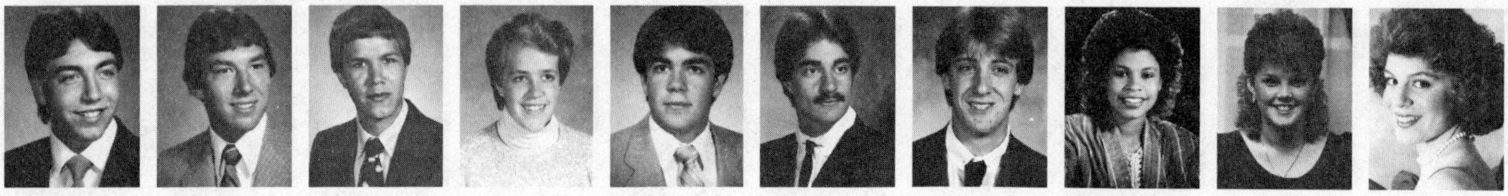

Sciortino, Michael J
Trumbull HS
Trumbull, CT

Seifert, John
Trumbull HS
Trumbull, CT

Semsel, III John S
Greenwich HS
Greenwich, CT

Senf, Stephanie
Ridgefield HS
Ridgefield, CT

Serrambana, Jr Victor
East Catholic HS
Vernon, CT

Sesto, Vincenzo
Bristol Central HS
Bristol, CT

Shannon, Michael
Saint Joseph HS
Stratford, CT

Shaw, Christine
Enrico Fermi HS
Enfield, CT

Shea, Colleen
Holy Cross HS
Waterbury, CT

Sheridan, Laura
South Catholic HS
Hartford, CT

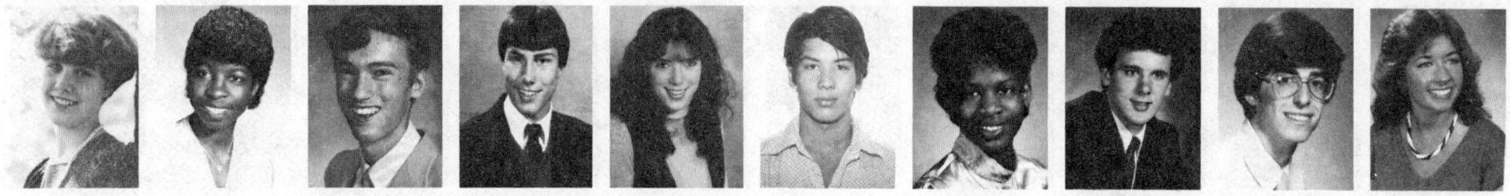

Sherman, Carolyn E
Wilton HS
Wilton, CT

Sherman, Mercedes
Hopkins HS
New Haven, CT

Shilberg, Nathan
Bristol Central HS
Bristol, CT

Shively, T Deloe
Avon Old Farms HS
Harwinton, CT

Shook, Jennifer
Oliver Wolcott Reg VT Schl
Kent, CT

Shotz, Geoff
Taft Schl
Tarzana, CA

Shular, Carol A
Norwalk HS
Norwalk, CT

Siebold, Mel
Manchester HS
Manchester, CT

Siegle, Greg
Stamford HS
Stamford, CT

Silva, Michelle L
Henry Abbott RVTS HS
Danbury, CT

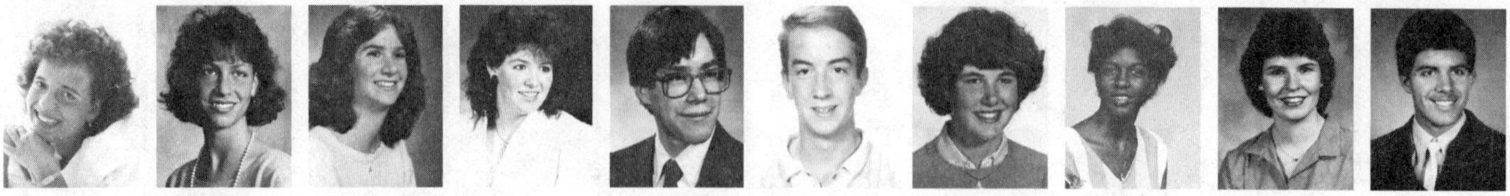

Silva, Rosa M
South Catholic HS
Newington, CT

Simonovich, Laura
Immaculate HS
Danbury, CT

Sloan, Sharon
Manchester HS
Manchester, CT

Smith, Diane
St Marys HS
New Haven, CT

Smith, Everett V
Norwich Free Acad
Canterbury, CT

Smith, Gerard
New Fairfield HS
New Fairfield, CT

Smith, Jessica
Amity Regional HS
Woodbridge, CT

Smith, Kimble
Cheshire HS
Cheshire, CT

Smith, Laureen
Seymour HS
Seymour, CT

Smith, Richard C
Howell Cheney Tech
Manchester, CT

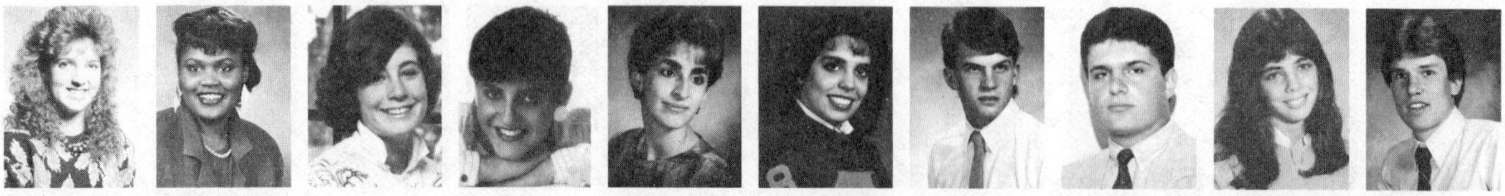

Smith, Sharai E
Amity Regional SR
Orange, CT

Smith, Stacy
New Britain SR HS
New Britain, CT

Smith, Tara
Miss Porters Schl
Keene, NH

Sodel, Melissa
O H Platt HS
Meriden, CT

Solomon, Julie
Cheshire HS
Cheshire, CT

Sorce, Michelle
Seymour HS
Seymour, CT

Soucy, Brett
Conard HS
W Htfd, CT

Sperduto, Vito
Greenwich HS
Greenwich, CT

Spezzano, Elizabeth
Andrew Warde HS
Stamford, CT

Spielman, Fred
Rockville HS
Ellington, CT

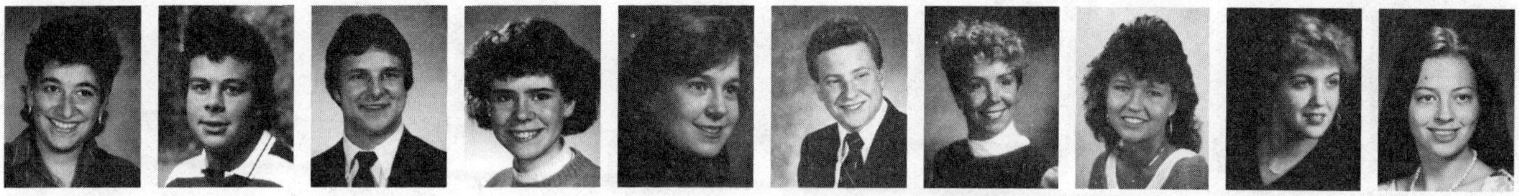

Spino, Carla
Sacred Heart Acad
Hamden, CT

Sponza, John
Wilton HS
Wilton, CT

St Georges, III George W
East Catholic HS
Broad Brook, CT

St Lawrence, Kelly
Norwich Free Acad
Norwich, CT

Staback, Tracey
Cheshire Acad
Meriden, CT

Stack, Jr Ronald W
Berlin HS
East Berlin, CT

Staley, Beth A
Cheshire HS
Cheshire, CT

Stanek, Janina T
Mary Immaculate
New Britain, CT

Starzec, Michele
Nathan Hale-Ray
East Haddam, CT

Steigerwald, Jessica G
Westhill HS
Stamford, CT

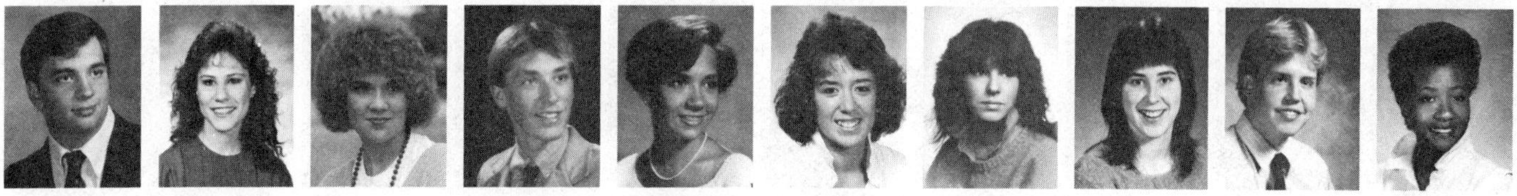

Stenz, Christopher
Fairfield College Prep Schl
Norwalk, CT

Stephens, Laura
Southington HS
Southington, CT

Stockman, Debora
Bristol Central HS
Britol, CT

Stoddard, Andrew
St Bernard HS
N Stoninston, CT

Stolfi, Dawn M
Holy Cross HS
Waterbury, CT

Stolfi, Janet
Southington HS
Southington, CT

Story, Chris
Nonnewaug HS
Woodbury, CT

Stratton, Stacey
Brien Mc Mahon
Norwalk, CT

Stuart, James
Coventry HS
Coventry, CT

Suber, Gail
West Haven HS
W Haven, CT

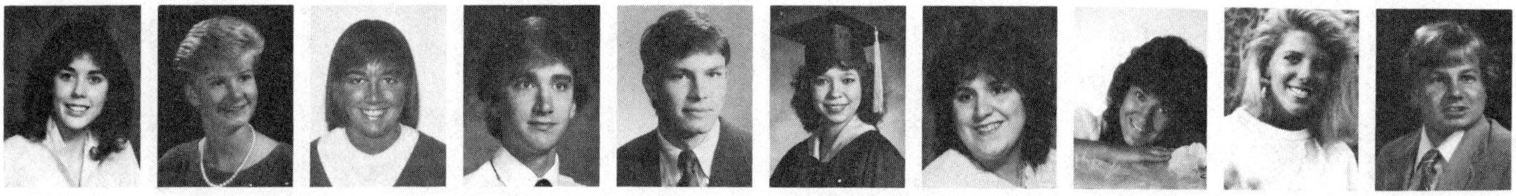

Suhie, Karen
Manchester HS
Manchester, CT

Sweeney, Kathryn
Danbury HS
Danbury, CT

Sweeney, Tricia
The Taft Schl
Oakville, CT

Sweet, Kevin
Morgan HS
Clinton, CT

Sweeting, Andrew C G
Avon Old Farms
Bahamas

Swindle, Honey
New London HS
New London, CT

Taliercio, Ann Elizabeth
Central Catholic HS
Norwalk, CT

Tangney, Lisa
Southington HS
Southington, CT

Taylor, Amanda
Miss Porters HS
Atlanta, GA

Telford, Jr Bob
Daniel Hand HS
Madison, CT

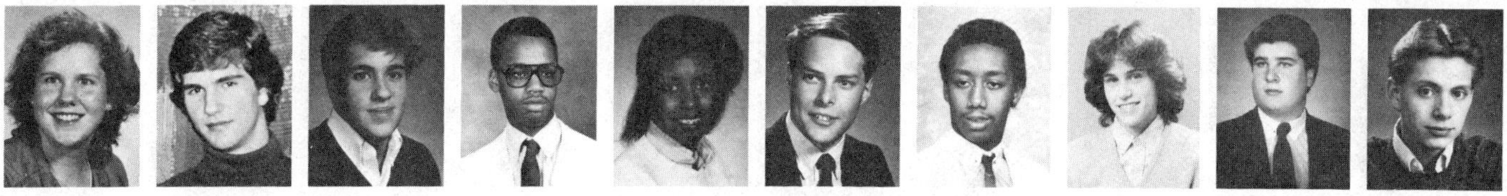

Terkelsen, Sandra
Greenwich HS
Greenwich, CT

Terry, Brett C
The Williams Schl
Mansfield Ctr, CT

Tesei, Peter
Greenwich HS
Greenwich, CT

Thomas, Ronald
Fairfield College Preparatory Schl
Bridgeport, CT

Thompson, Annette
Brien Mcmahon HS
Norwalk, CT

Thompson, Jason
Shelton HS
Shelton, CT

Thompson, II Richard L
Xavier HS
Middletown, CT

Thornton, Sharlene
Parish Hill HS
Hampton, CT

Thurz, Michael
East Catholic HS
Glastonbury, CT

Thyne, III John Joseph
Ridgefield HS
Ridgefield, CT

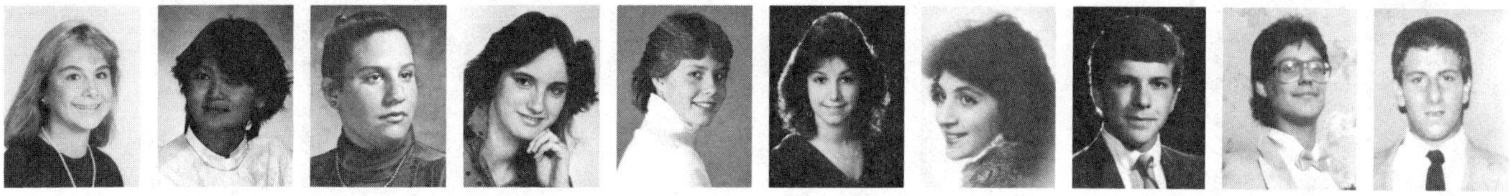

Tilley, Angela
Miss Porters Schl
Ft Worth, TX

Tinh, Nguyet
New Britain HS
New Britian, CT

Titus, Maro
Farmington HS
Farmington, CT

Toback, Lisa
Brookfield HS
Brookfield, CT

Tobeler, Tracy
East Catholic HS
Vernon Rockville, CT

Tolomeo, Elvira
North Haven HS
North Haven, CT

Tomatore, Karen
Shelton HS
Shelton, CT

Tomolonis, Paul
East Windsor HS
Broad Brook, CT

Tonner, Kristofer
Newfairfield HS
New Fairfld, CT

Torello, Jeff
Branford HS
Branford, CT

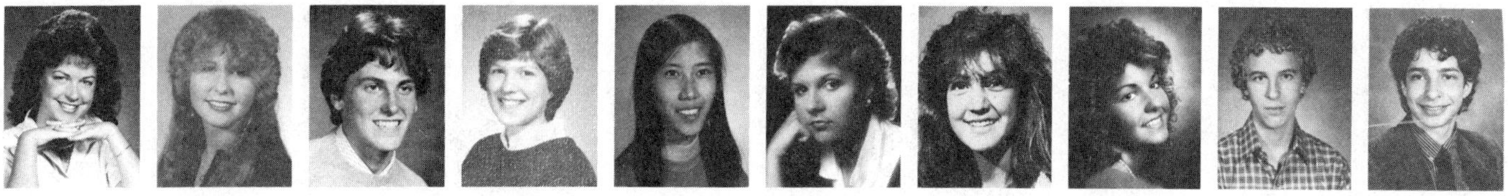

Torpey, Diane
Shelton HS
Shelton, CT

Toth, Cheryl Ann
New Britain HS
New Britain, CT

Tracy, Todd
Lewis S Mills HS
Harwinton, CT

Traisci, Leigh Ann
New Fairfield HS
New Fairfield, CT

Tsoi, Louisa
Greenwich HS
Greenwich, CT

Turek, Deborah A
Our Lady Of The Angels Acad
Suffield, CT

Turnquist, Kirsten
Stratford HS
Stratford, CT

Turro, Susan
Middletown HS
Middletown, CT

Ulisse, Christian
Jonathan Law HS
Milford, CT

Valente, Michael
Notre Dame HS
New Haven, CT

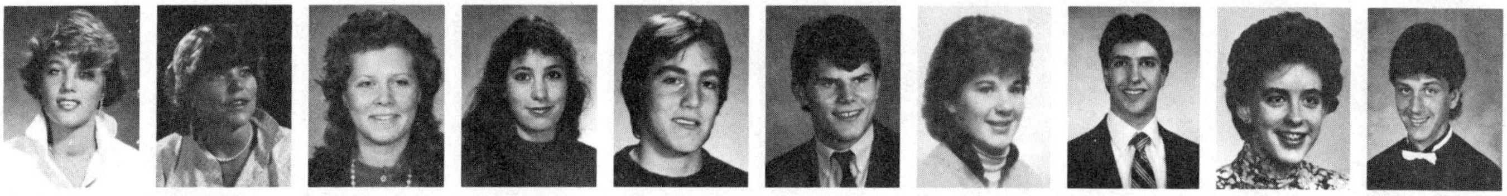

Valentine, Wendy A
Andrew Warde HS
Fairfield, CT

Valiante, Donna
Staples HS
Westport, CT

Van Dykes, Cynthia
East Catholic HS
Manchester, CT

Van Ness, Holly
Southington HS
Southington, CT

Vanghele, Nick
Andrew Warde HS
Fairfield, CT

Varga, Gregory
Fairfield College Prep Schl
Easton, CT

Veech, Michelle
Nonnewaug HS
Woodbury, CT

Vegiard, Roland Lee
East Catholic HS
E Hartford, CT

Vella, Andrea
Bethel HS
Bethel, CT

Verbitsky, Joseph
Bristol Central HS
Bristol, CT

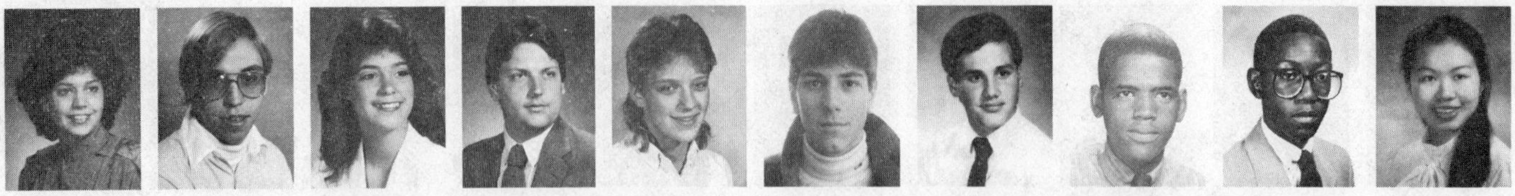

Viadella, Cynthia
Shelton HS
Shelton, CT

Vierps, Peter
Oliver Wolcott Tech
Torrington, CT

Vittorio, Michelle
Shelton HS
Shelton, CT

Voytek, Allan
Shelton HS
Shelton, CT

Wakefield, Tammy
Killingly HS
Dayville, CT

Waldman, David
St Lukes HS
Westport, CT

Waldron, Jr Dale
St Bernard HS
Preston, CT

Walker, Jr James L
Bassick HS
Bridgeport, CT

Walton, Jr Luther
Dean
Fairfield College
Preparatory Schl
Bridgeport, CT

Wang, Hsiu-Hui
New Britain HS
West Hartford, CT

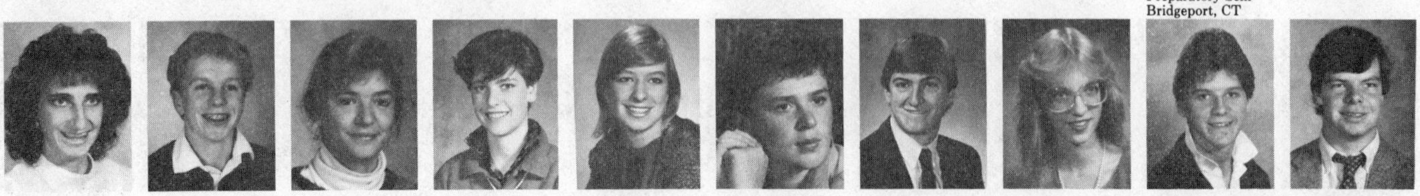

Watson, Dana
Killingly HS
Dayville, CT

Watson, Marty
Watertown HS
Oakville, CT

Waugh, Diana
Housatonic Valley
Regional HS
Sharon, CT

Weber, Jennifer
Ridgefield HS
Ridgefield, CT

Wedemeyer, Laura
Greenwich HS
Riverside, CT

Welkes, Dorota
Bullard-Havens Rvts
Bridgeport, CT

Welles, Ward
Kent Schl
Cold Spring Harbo,
NY

Werkheiser, Lora
Shelton HS
Shelton, CT

White, Christopher
Oliver Wolcott
Regnl Voc Tec
Winsted, CT

Wholey, Robert
Saint Mary HS
Pt Chester, NY

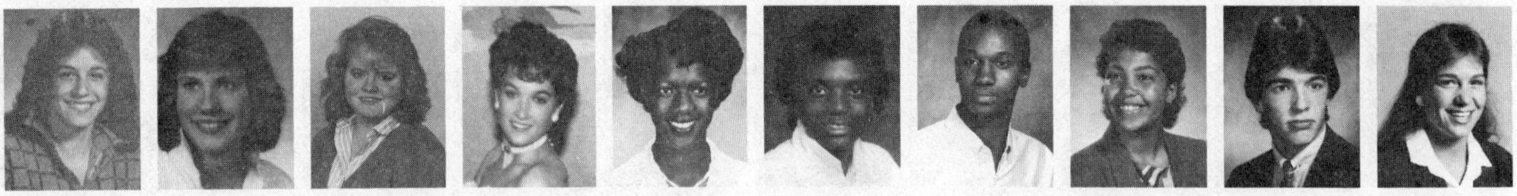

Wiederlight, Lisa M
Stamford HS
Stamford, CT

Wilcox, Caroline
Torrington HS
Torrington, CT

Wilcox, Sharon
Torrington HS
Torrington, CT

Will, Gabrielle
Ridgefield HS
Los Altos Hills, CA

Williams, Angela
Sacred Heart Acad
New Haven, CT

Williams, Charlene
Anissa
Northwest Catholic
Bloomfield, CT

Williams, Clarence
Hartford Public HS
Hartford, CT

Williams, Dawn
William H Hall HS
W Hartford, CT

Williams, Ronald
Cheshire HS
Cheshire, CT

Willis, Kim
Heritage Christian
Naugatuck, CT

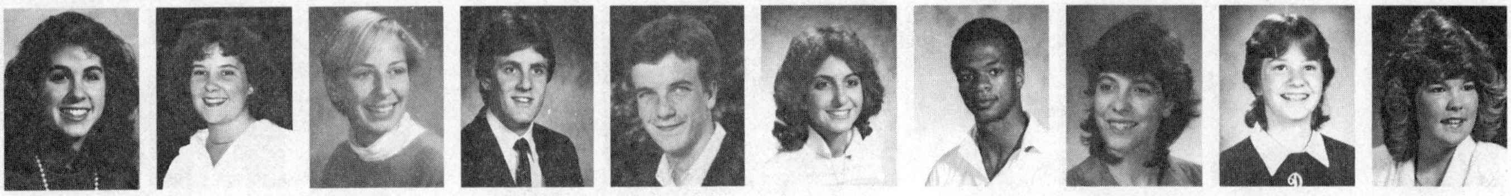

Wilson, Bethany
Maloney HS
Meriden, CT

Wilson, Cynthia A
Hamden HS
Hamden, CT

Wilton, Amy A
Litchfield HS
Litchfield, CT

Winakor, David
Nathan Hale-Ray
East Haddam, CT

Winn, Paul
Wilton HS
Wilton, CT

Winslow, Elizabeth
Watertown HS
Oakville, CT

Wofford, David
Bullard Havens
Tech Schl
Bridgeport, CT

Wojtowicz, Lisa
Northwest Catholic
Hartford, CT

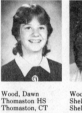

Wood, Dawn
Thomaston HS
Thomaston, CT

Wood, Kristen
Shelton HS
Shelton, CT

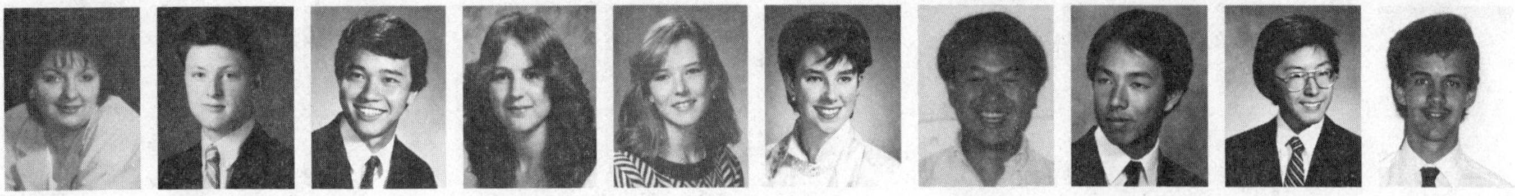

Woods, Sara
Stratford HS
Stratford, CT

Wozniak, John
Hamden HS
Hamden, CT

Yanagisawa, Ray
Hopkins Grammar
Day Prospect HS
Woodbridge, CT

Yanke, Dawn
Farmington HS
Farmington, CT

Yannuzzi, Paige
Greenwich HS
Greenwich, CT

Young, Jennifer
Wilton HS
Wilton, CT

Yu, Michael
Taft Schl
Waterbury, CT

Yu, Ronald W
Fairfield College
Trumbull, CT

Yun, James J
Hopkins Grammar
Orange, CT

Zak, Edward
Southington HS
Southington, CT

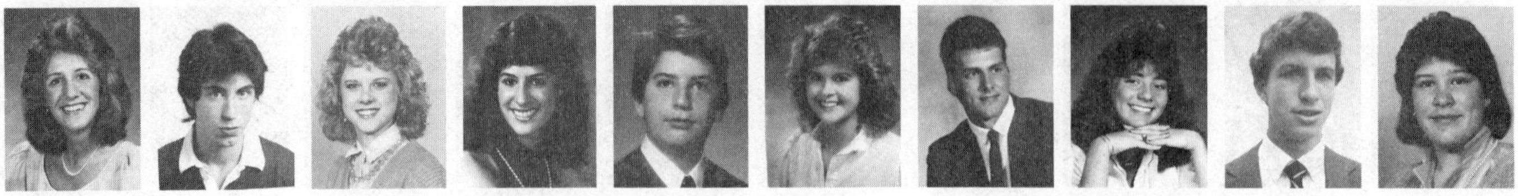

Zak, Rebecca
Southingotn HS
Southington, CT

Zalinger, Keith
Branford HS
Branford, CT

Zampaglione,
Glenna
Torrington HS
Torrington, CT

Zappola, Janine
East Catholic HS
Vernon Rockville,
CT

Zappone, Richard
Holy Cross HS
Waterbury, CT

Zawacki, Karen
Marie
Danbury HS
Danbury, CT

Zeller, James
Torrington HS
Harwinton, CT

Zeolla, Lisa
Shelton HS
Shelton, CT

Zschunke, Greg
Brookfield HS
Brookfield Center,
CT

Zubrowski, Diana
Torrington HS
Torrington, CT

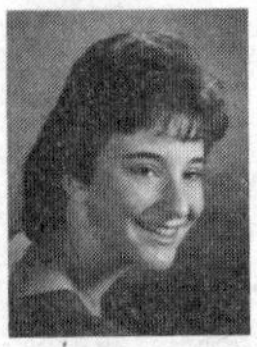

Zurolo, Mary
Sacred Heart Acad
Hamden, CT

MAINE

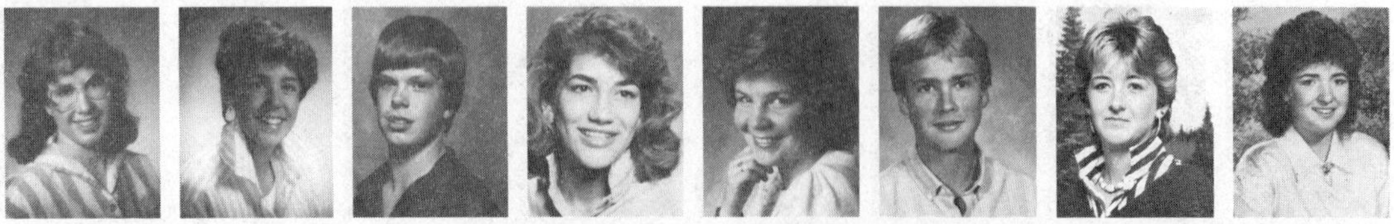

Allard, Nancy Anne
Noble HS
N Berwick, ME

Allen, Charline
Westbrook HS
Westbrook, ME

Alley, Kevin
Washington Acad
Jonesboro, ME

Anastasoff, Jennifer
Cape Elizabeth HS
Cape Elizabeth, ME

Arsenault, Wendy L
Cape Elizabeth HS
Cape Elizabeth, ME

Bartlett, John
Wells HS
Wells, ME

Beal, Heidi
Jonesport-Beals HS
Beals, ME

Berce, Wendy
Foxcroft Acad
Dover, ME

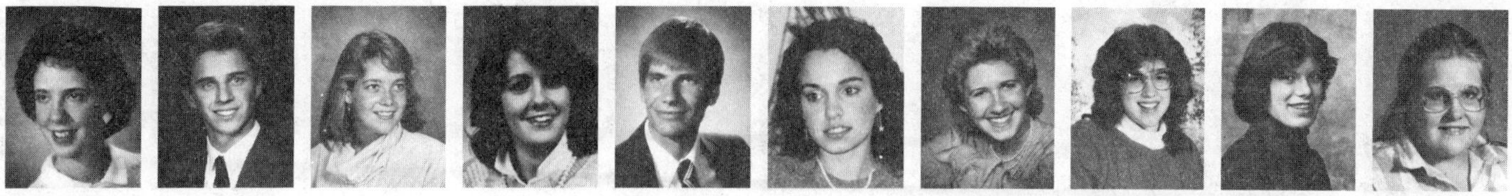

Bernier, Debbie
Windham HS
Windham, ME

Berube, John
Edward Little HS
Auburn, ME

Bisbee, Susan W
Berwick Acad
Rochester, NH

Boileau, Danielle
Livermore Falls HS
Livermore Falls, ME

Bolles, Thomas M
Gorham HS
Gorham, ME

Bourgoin, Debby
Lewiston HS
Lewiston, ME

Bragg, Margaret S
Ellsworth HS
Ellsworth, ME

Burleigh, Pamela
Central HS
E Corinth, ME

Buzzell, Felancy
Skowhegan Area HS
Skowhegan, ME

Byam, Jennifer
Rumford JR SR HS
Rumford Point, ME

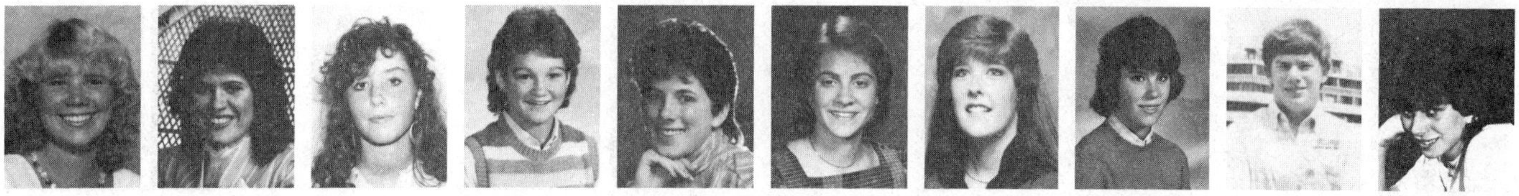

Campbell, Cheryl Ann
Edward Little HS
Auburn, ME

Campbell, Kim
Pendoscot Valley
Howland, ME

Campbell, Laurie
South Portland HS
S Portland, ME

Caron, Michele Lynn
Washburn District
Washburn, ME

Carver, Jean Denise
Narraguagus HS
Addison, ME

Caswell, Ginger
Edward Little HS
Auburn, ME

Charczynski, Lynne
Jonesport-Beals HS
Beals, ME

Chase, Deborah Rae
Greenville HS
Greenville, ME

Clement, Kevin
Bucksport HS
Bucksport, ME

Connell, Angela
Oxford Hills HS
So Paris, ME

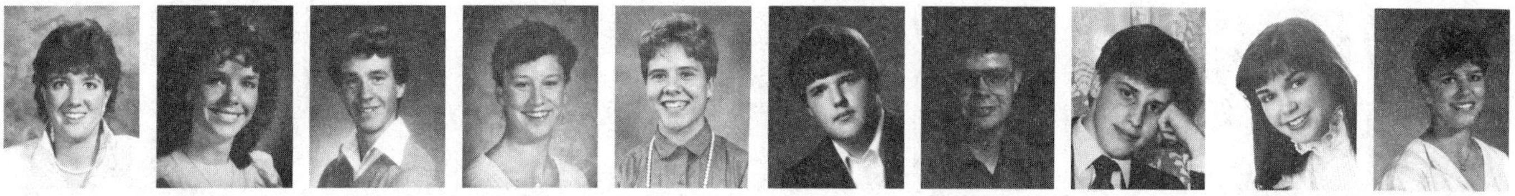

Cook, Shana
Mt Blue HS
Farmington, ME

Cookson, Lyla
Westbrook HS
Westbrook, ME

Cookson, Lyle
Westbrook HS
Westbrook, ME

Cooper, Rebecca Suzanne
Saint Domincs Regional HS
Lewiston, ME

Cousineau, Kathryn
Westbrook HS
Raymond, ME

Cousins, Caleb E
Narragnogus HS
Milbridge, ME

Cronkright, Dewayne
Fort Fairfield HS
Ft Fairfield, ME

Cushing, Webber
Bangor HS
Bangor, ME

Cutter, Mary
Edward Little HS
Auburn, ME

Daigle, Ginger
Community HS
Winterville, ME

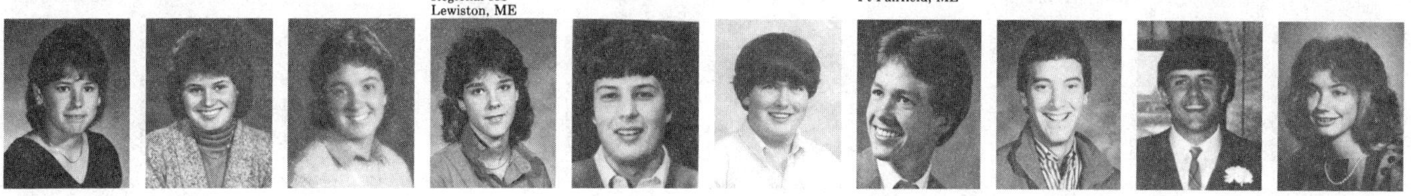

Desjardins, Donna M
Fort Kent Community HS
Fort Kent, ME

Doherty, Erin
Wells HS
Wells, ME

Doughty, Patricia L
Woodland HS
Baileyville, ME

Dow, Erin
Wells HS
Wells, ME

Doyle, Brendan
Cony HS
Augusta, ME

Dreher, Russell
Georges Valley HS
Thomaston, ME

Drisko, Arthur A
Scarborough HS
Scarborough, ME

Duane, III Herbert Tobias
Fryeburg Acad
Braintree, MA

Dube, Edward
Ashland Community
Portage Lake, ME

Duguay, Laura
Rumford HS
Rumford, ME

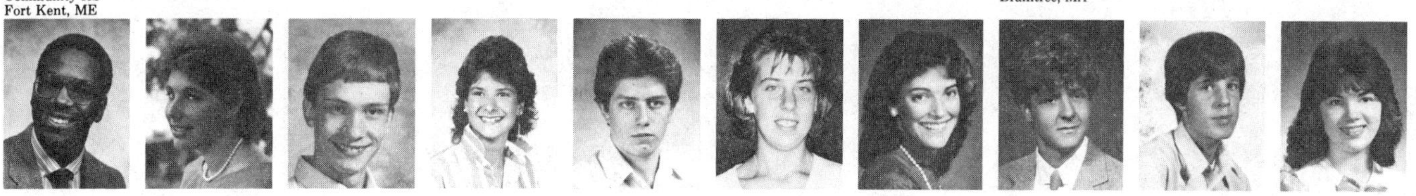

Duncan, III Lawrence
Cheverus HS
Brunswick, ME

Durgin, Wendy
Windham HS
S Casco, ME

Durost, Anthony Todd
Central Aroostook
Mars Hill, ME

Dyer, Vicki
Catherine Mc Auley
Portland, ME

Fahy, Thomas
Marshwood HS
S Berwick, ME

Flacke, Julia S
Belfast Area HS
Morrill, ME

Fournier, Doreen
Jay HS
Jay, ME

Giguere, Steven
Lewiston HS
Lewiston, ME

Giordano, Shawn
Piscataquis Community HS
Dexter, ME

Glidden, Deborah
Deering HS
Portland, ME

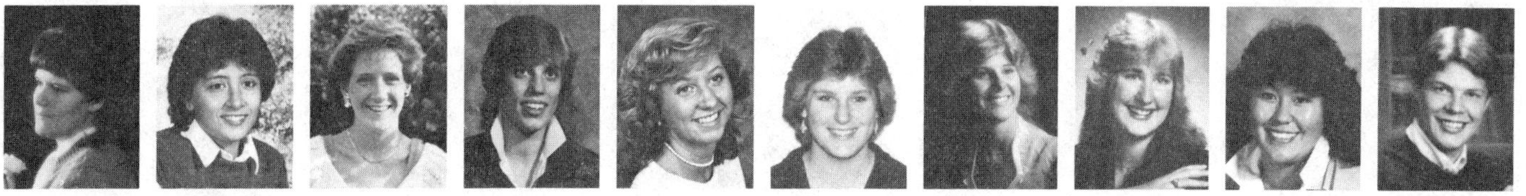

Golden, Karen
Woodland HS
Woodland, ME

Goodridge, Sherri
Piscataquis Comm
Sangerville, ME

Green, Christi
Deering HS
Portland, ME

Grindle, Christie
Mt Abram Regional
Eustis, ME

Hammond, Tracy
Bangor HS
Bangor, ME

Harriman, Jessica Jean
Medomak Valley HS
Union, ME

Haskell, Kerri
Edward Little HS
Auburn, ME

Hatt, Joan
Westbrook HS
Westbrook, ME

Havey, Wendy
Sumner Memorial
W Sullivan, ME

Hawksley, Thomas W
Bangor HS
Bangor, ME

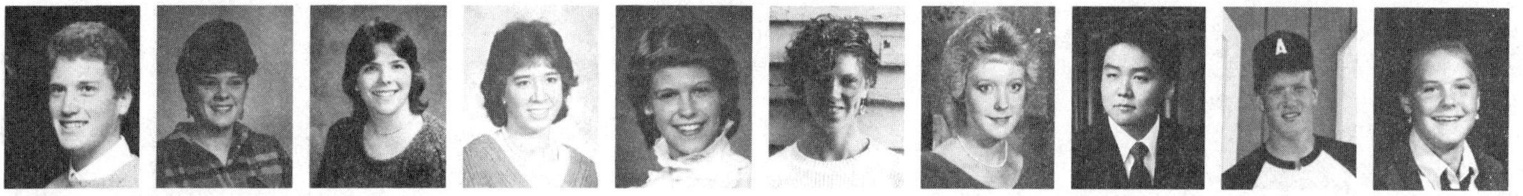

Hodgkinson, David
Jonesport-Beals HS
Jonesport, ME

Hovey, Shannon
Skowhegan Area HS
Skowhegan, ME

Hulsey, Diana J
Greely HS
Cumberland Center, ME

Hurley, Lynn
Sacopee Valley HS
W Baldwin, ME

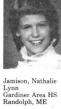

Jamison, Nathalie Lynn
Gardiner Area HS
Randolph, ME

Jenkins, Andrea
Mount Desert Island
Bar Harbor, ME

Jones, Melissa
Woodland HS
Princeton, ME

Kang, Robert Y
Cony HS
Togus, ME

Kelly, C Terrance
Ashland Community
Ashland, ME

Kent, Melissa
Rumford HS
Rumford, ME

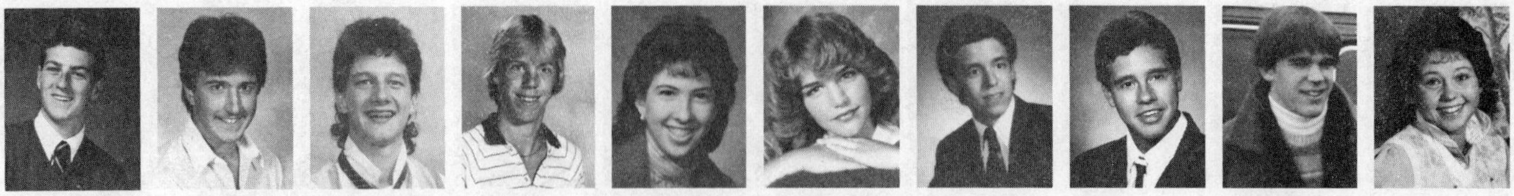

King, Steven
Deering HS
Portland, ME

Kokoszka, Kenneth
Fort Fairfield HS
Ft Fairfield, ME

Lammert, Piet
Georges Valley HS
Thomaston, ME

Larkin, John
Woodland HS
Waite, ME

Le Clair, Victoria
Gardiner Area HS
Gardiner, ME

Leary, Rhonda
Lawrence HS
Fairfield, ME

Lehane, Christopher
Kennebunk HS
Kennebunk, ME

Levesque, Juan
Bucksport HS
Bucksport, ME

Libby, Jeffrey
Edward Little HS
Poland, ME

Lincoln, Lori
Woodland HS
Woodland, ME

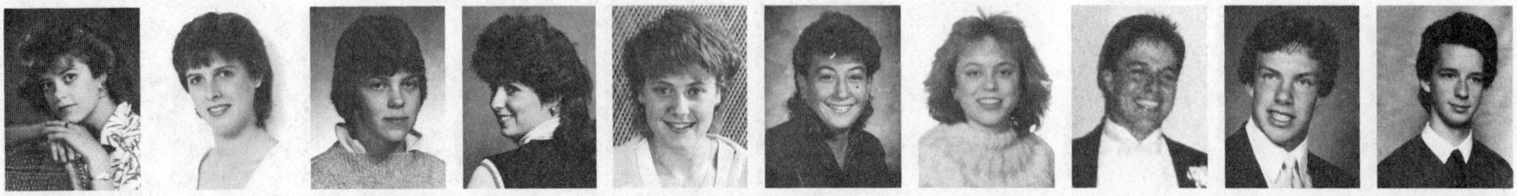

Lizotte, Kim
Wisdom HS
Madawaska, ME

Lowe, Greta A
Sumner Memorial
Corea, ME

Luce, Stephanie
North Yarmouth
Cumberland, ME

Mac Kinnon, Katherine
Rumford HS
West Peru, ME

Madore, Karen
Van Buren District
Van Buren, ME

Mailhot, Darlene
St Dominics Regional HS
Lewiston, ME

Major, Elizabeth
Catherine Mc Auley
Scarborough, ME

Mangino, Samuel
Falmouth HS
Falmouth, ME

Mann, Thomas
Bucksport HS
Bucksport, ME

Mansur, Kenneth
Edward Little HS
Auburn, ME

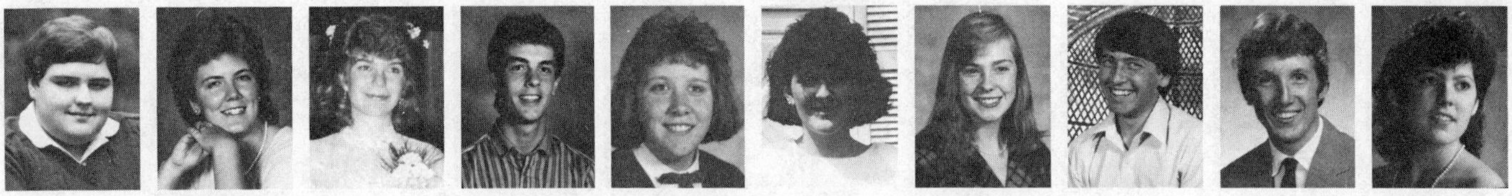

Marin, Joseph P
Community HS
Fort Kent, ME

Marston, Cheryl
Bangor HS
Bangor, ME

Martin, Lisa
Fort Kent Community HS
Fort Kent, ME

Masters, Eric
Lincoln Acad
Medomak, ME

Mc Allister, Althea
Fryeburg Acad
Center Lovell, ME

Mc Carthy, Colleen
Catherine Mc Auley
Portland, ME

Mc Cue, Aimee E
Fryeburg Acad
Bridgton, ME

Mc Intire, Carroll
Bonny Eagle HS
W Buxton, ME

Mc Leod, Troy
Lee Acad
Lee, ME

Mentas, Michelle Colleen
Mt Ararat Schl
Bowdoinham, ME

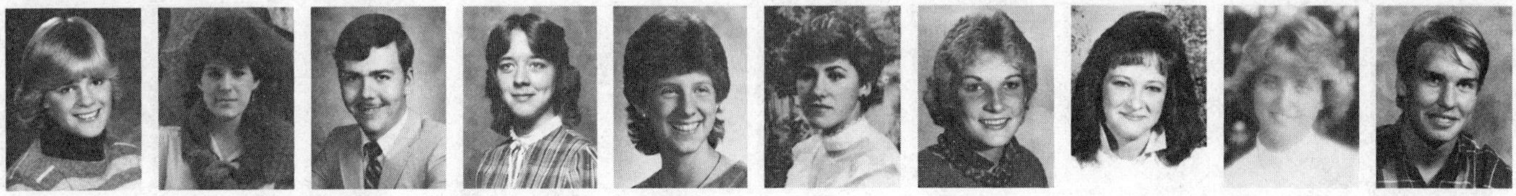

Merwin, Carol
Wells HS
Wells, ME

Messier, Patricia
Wells HS
Wells, ME

Michaud, Jr Robert P
Wisdom HS
St Agatha, ME

Mills, Christine
Bucksport HS
Bucksport, ME

Morin, Celeste
St Dominic Regional
Lewiston, ME

Mudgett, Stacie
Bangor HS
Glenurn, ME

Myler, Marlene
Woodland HS
Princeton, ME

Nadeau, Kimberly
Caribou HS
Caribou, ME

Nickerson, Kelly J
Presque Isle HS
Mapleton, ME

Noble, Scott
Mt Abram Regional
Stratton, ME

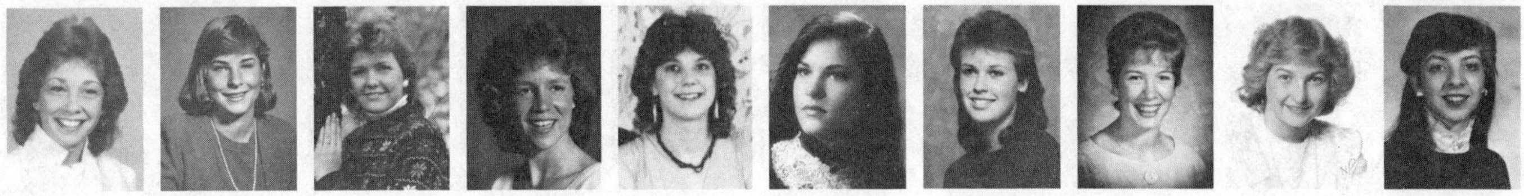

Norman, Julie
Woodland HS
Woodland, ME

Norris, Lee Ann
Rumford HS
Rumford, ME

Norton, Paula F
Washington Acad
Jonesboro, ME

O Bryan, Bridget Ann Patricia
Lincoln Acad
Damariscotta, ME

Oliva, Tracey
Calais Mem HS
Charlotte, ME

Oliver, Melissa
Catherine Mc Auley
Scarborough, ME

Ovellette, Karen
Jonesport-Beals HS
Jonesport, ME

Pelletier, Anne-Marie
St Dominic Regional
Lewiston, ME

Phinney, Angel
Bangor Baptist
Bangor, ME

Pratt, Gretchen
Lawrence HS
Clinton, ME

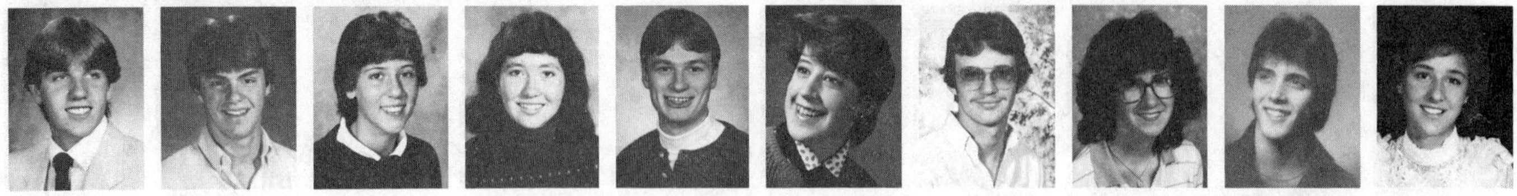

Radziszewski, Gregory
Edward Little HS
Poland Spring, ME

Raymond, Steve
Fort Kent HS
Fort Kent, ME

Read, Susan
Belfast Area HS
Belfast, ME

Reddy, Kathleen Michele
Brunswick HS
Brunswick, ME

Rich, Larry
Orono HS
Bangor, ME

Riley, Deborah
Windham HS
Raymond, ME

Robbins, Bruce
Easton HS
Easton, ME

Robbins, Kathleen
Sacopee Valley JR SR HS
East Baldwin, ME

Rodrigue, Rusty
Lewiston HS
Lewiston, ME

Rogers, Katy
Catherine Mc Auley
S Windham, ME

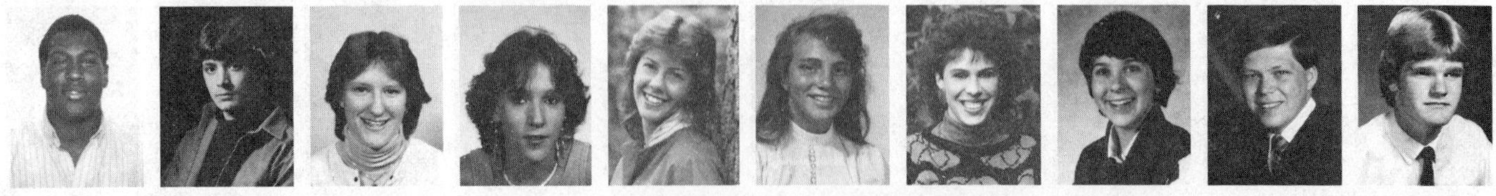

Rose, Wayne A
Fryeburg Acad
New York, NY

Ross, Troy
Mt Abram HS
Strong, ME

Rowe, Tracy
Edward Little HS
Mechanic Falls, ME

Roy, Annie
Lewiston HS
Lewiston, ME

Rublee, Vikki
Penquis Valley HS
Milo, ME

Rutherford, Patricia
South Portland HS
S Portland, ME

Saban, Kathy
Erskine Acad
Palermo, ME

Sandvoss, Dana
Waynflete Schl
Kennebunkport, ME

Saucier, Gary
Ft Fairfield HS
Ft Fairfield, ME

Savage, William
Bonny Eagle HS
W Buxton, ME

Sawyer, Dawn
Sacopee Valley HS
E Baldwin, ME

Small, Dorian
Skowhegan Area HS
Skowhegan, ME

Smith, Katie
Ashland Community
Ashland, ME

Sorel, David
Fryeburg Acad
Seekonk, MA

Southern, Jessica
Livermore Falls HS
Livermore Falls, ME

St Pierre, Suzanne
Van Buren Dist
Secondary Schl
Van Buren, ME

Sult, Tina
Lisbon HS
Lisbon, ME

Tabb, Jayme
Telstar HS
Andover, ME

Tetenman, Scott
Eduward Little HS
Poland Springs, ME

Theriault, Valerie
Caribou HS
Caribou, ME

Thompson, Robert
A
Brunswick HS
Brunswick, ME

Thorne, Judy
Edward Little HS
Auburn, ME

Timpany, Catherine
Edward Little HS
Auburn, ME

Traister, Michael
Edward Little HS
Auburn, ME

Treiber, John
Morse HS
Honolulu, HI

Walch, Jennifer
Westbrook HS
Westbrook, ME

Ward, Russell
Fryeburg Acad
Wareham, MA

Watts, Curt
Leavitt Area HS
Turner, ME

Wentworth, Donna
Fryeburg Acad
Fryeburg, ME

Wentworth, Erika
Fryeburg Acad
Fryeburg, ME

West, Terisia L
Mt Ararat Schl
Topsham, ME

Mass-chusetts

White, Angela
Traip Academy HS
Mesa, AZ

White, Kristopher D
Bucksport HS
Stockton Spgs, ME

White, Peter
Gorham HS
Scarborough, ME

Wight, Donald
Westbrook HS
Westbrook, ME

Wilburn, II Edward
J
Yarmouth HS
Yarmouth, ME

Wilson, Melissa
Bonny Eagle HS
Steep Falls, ME

Woodward, Karen S
Sumner Memorial
Gouldsboro, ME

Worthley, Carol
Rumford HS
W Peru, ME

Wright, Kenton
Nokomis Regional
Newport, ME

MASSA-CHUSETTS

York, Jody
Houlton HS
Houlton, ME

Abraham, Lisa
Boston Technical
Jamaica Pl, MA

Adams, April
Duxbury HS
Duxbury, MA

Adams, Edward A
Watertown HS
Watertown, MA

Adriano, Darci L
Grtr New Bedford
Rgnl Vo-Tech HS
New Bedford, MA

Affonso, George D
Somerset HS
Somerset, MA

Agostini, Paula
Bishop Feehan HS
Seekonk, MA

Ahern, Deborah
Burlington HS
Burlington, MA

Ahern, Michael E
Dennis-Yarmouth
Reg HS
W Yarmouth, MA

Alberque, Lisa
Marianhill CC HS
Spencer, MA

Almeida, Karen
New Bedford HS
New Bedford, MA

Aloisi, Robert
Burlinton HS
Burlington, MA

Along, Anthony
Dennis-Yarmouth
Regional HS
Yarmouthport, MA

Altieri, John
Cardinal Spellman
Brockton, MA

Altman, Wayne J
North Andover HS
North Andover, MA

Alukonis, Karen
Classical HS
Lynn, MA

Aluxek, Dawn
Holyoke Catholic
Holyoke, MA

Amaral, Greg
Westport HS
Westport, MA

Amicangioli, Linda
Our Ladys Newton
Catholic HS
Newton, MA

Anderson,
CarrieANN
Methuen HS
Methuen, MA

Anderson, Matthew
D
Marian HS
Framingham, MA

Anderson, Rhonda
Deniece
Boston Technical
Roxbury, MA

Andrade, Rebecca
B M C Durfee HS
Fall River, MA

Andreassen, Carolyn
Groton Dunstable
Regional HS
Groton, MA

Andress, Wayne
Dennis-Yarmouth
Regional HS
E Dennis, MA

Andrews, Jennifer
Westfield HS
Westfield, MA

Antonellis, Michael
Watertown HS
Watertown, MA

Antonucci, Eva
St Bernards Central
Catholic HS
Leominster, MA

Aponte, Madeline
Jamaica Plain HS
Roxbury, MA

Applin, Susan
Reading Memorial
Reading, MA

Arcieri, Joel
Boston College HS
Milton, MA

Armento, Cassandra
Stoneleigh-Burnham
Brattleboro, VT

Arnold, III William
P
Longmeadow HS
Springfield, MA

Arnum, Michael
Lincoln Sudbury
Regional HS
Sudbury, MA

Arruda, Keith J
Somerset HS
Somerset, MA

Arsenault, Cari-Ann
B M C Durfee HS
Fall River, MA

Arseneau, Sandra
Gardner HS
Gardner, MA

Asgeirsson, Jon
Greater Boston
Reading, MA

Ash, George
St Dominic Savio
Revere, MA

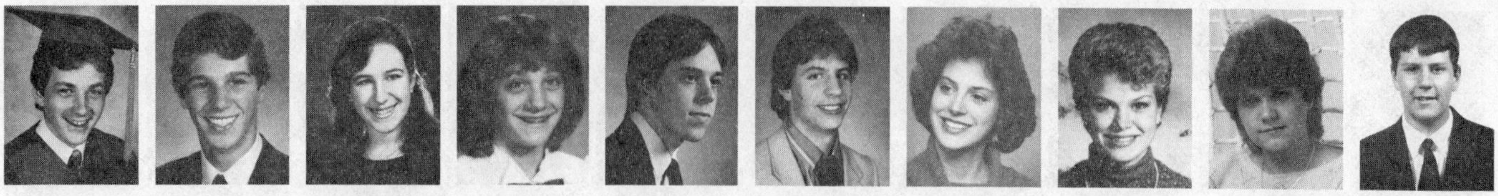

Ashman, Paul
East Boston HS
E Boston, MA

Athanasia, Chris T
Wilmington HS
Wilmington, MA

Atwood, Deborah
Natick HS
Natick, MA

Atwood, Paula
Somerville HS
Somerville, MA

Austin, John
Central Catholic HS
Tewksbury, MA

Ayles, Robert J
St Bernards Central
Catholic HS
Leominster, MA

Ayotte, Audra
King Philip
Regional HS
Norfolk, MA

Babinski, Heidi
Westfield HS
Westfield, MA

Bacon, Amy Mae
Palmer HS
Palmer, MA

Baikewicz, John A
Newburyport HS
Newburyport, MA

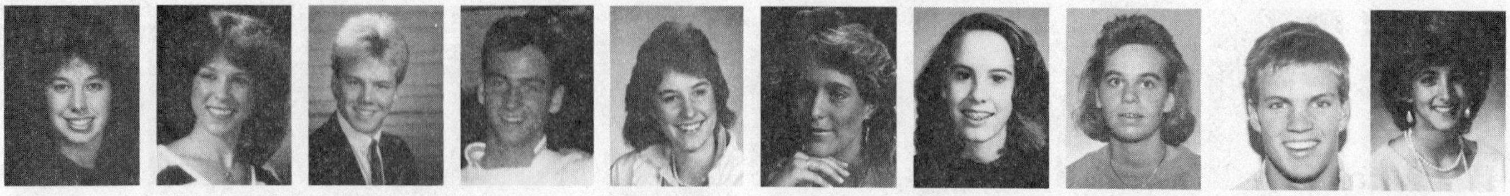

Baird, Lori Ann
Clinton HS
Clinton, MA

Baldi, Diane M
Bridgewater-Raynha
m Regional HS
Raynham, MA

Balutis, John M
Cardinal Spellman
Bridgewater, MA

Banks, Bryan
Boston Latin Schl
Boston, MA

Banks, Cheryl
Fitchburg HS
Fitchburg, MA

Barkhouse, Lee-Ann
Franklin HS
Franklin, MA

Barnes, Heather
Walnut Hill Schl Of
Performing Arts
Westfield, MA

Barrett, Patricia
North Quincy HS
Quincy, MA

Barringer, Scott B
Belmont HS
Wellesley, MA

Barron, Laura M
Norwell HS
Norwell, MA

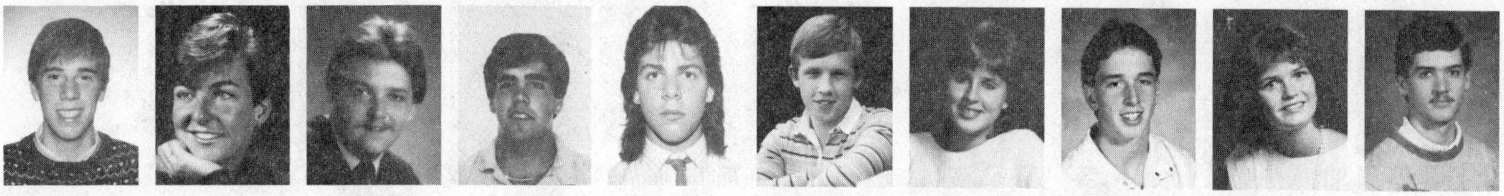

Barry, Christopher
Boston College HS
Wollaston, MA

Barry, Diane Marie
Scituate HS
Scituate, MA

Barry, John E
Everett HS
Everett, MA

Barry, William P
Watertown HS
Watertown, MA

Barsam, Charles
Belmont HS
Belmont, MA

Barstow, Thomas J
Falmouth HS
Teaticket, MA

Bartkus, Paula
North HS
Worcester, MA

Bartolomei, Thomas
Shepherd Hill
Regional HS
Dudley, MA

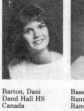

Barton, Dani
Dand Hall HS
Canada

Bass, David R
Randolph HS
Randolph, MA

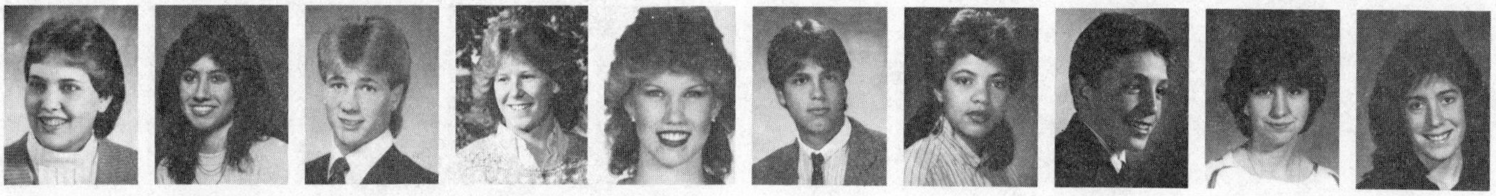

Bastiaans, Sally
Easthampton HS
Easthampton, MA

Bastianelli, Lisa
Marie
St Clare HS
Roslindale, MA

Bateman, Timothy
Charles
Xaverian Brothers
Marshfield, MA

Bator, Melissa
Ludlow HS
Ludlow, MA

Bauchman, Lori
Methuen HS
Methuen, MA

Baxendale, Greg
Bishop Connally HS
Swansea, MA

Beato, Rosa
English HS
Boston, MA

Beauchesne, P
Jonathan
Central Catholic HS
Methuen, MA

Beaumier, Sandra
Uxbridge HS
Uxbridge, MA

Becker, Diane
Uxbridge HS
N Uxbridge, MA

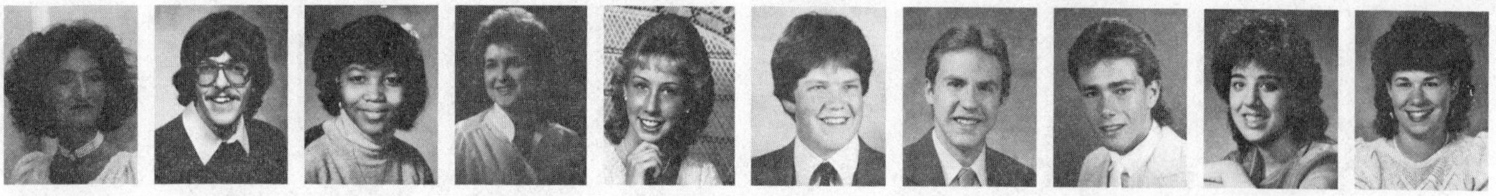

Beckett, Sally
Dennis Yarmouth
S Dennis, MA

Beland, Brian D
Wachusett Regional
Sterling, MA

Belizaire, Renette
English HS
Boston, MA

Bell, Marlene
Dracut SR HS
Dracut, MA

Belliveau, Tracey
Fairhaven HS
Fairhaven, MA

Benard, Robert
Chicopee
Comprehensive HS
Chicopee, MA

Benbenek, Michael
S
Narragansett
Regional HS
Templeton, MA

Benedict, Joseph P
Plymouth-Carver
Plymouth, MA

Benevides, Denise M
Somerset HS
Somerset, MA

Benoit, Susan
Somerville HS
Somerville, MA

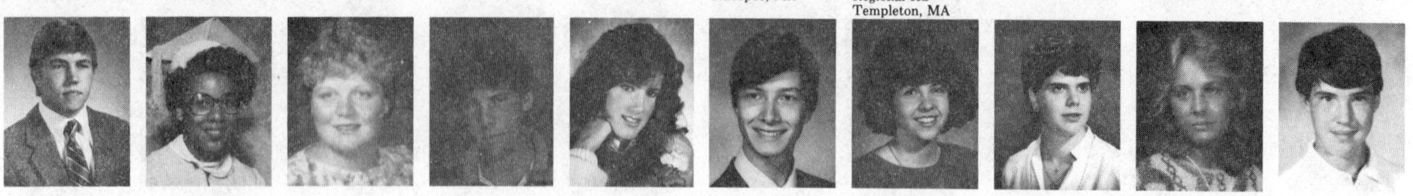

Benson, Steve
Northfield Mount
Hermon HS
E Walpole, MA

Bentley, Rhonda
Boston Latin Acad
Jamaica Plain, MA

Berens, Jodi
B M C Durfee HS
Fall River, MA

Berkowitz, Jeremy
Sharon HS
Sharon, MA

Berman, Marisa
Cathedral HS
Holyoke, MA

Bermann, Joseph
Newton North HS
Newton, MA

Bernard, Cheryl
Uxbridge HS
Uxbridge, MA

Bernier, Anne Marie
Bartlett HS
Webster, MA

Bernier, Jeanne
Simonne
Bishop Connolly HS
Fall River, MA

Berry, William
Boston College HS
Canton, MA

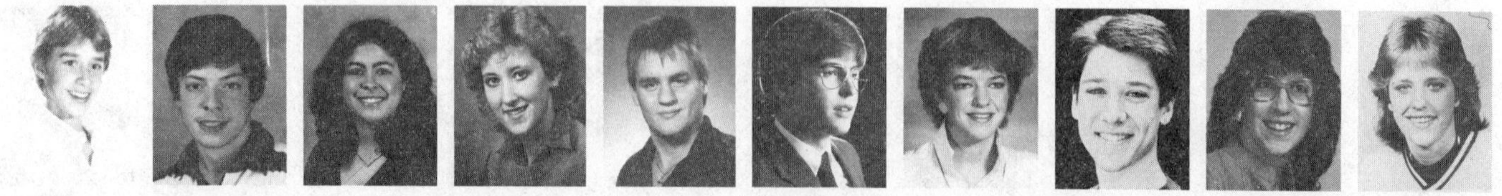

Berthiaume, Scott
Quaboag Regional
Warren, MA

Bertone, Salvatore
Franklin HS
Franklin, MA

Bettencourt, Sharon
Silver Lake Regional
Kingston, MA

Bialy, Beth
Bartlett HS
Webster, MA

Bickford, Mark R
Winthrop HS
Winthrop, MA

Bing-Zaremba,
Adrian Charles
St Marys HS
Southwick, MA

Birch, Kristen
West Ford Acad
Westford, MA

Birnschein, Timothy
A
Watertown SR HS
Watertown, MA

Bisbee, Mary E
Smith Voc-Agri HS
Chesterfield, MA

Bishop, Rachel
St Peter Marion HS
Worcester, MA

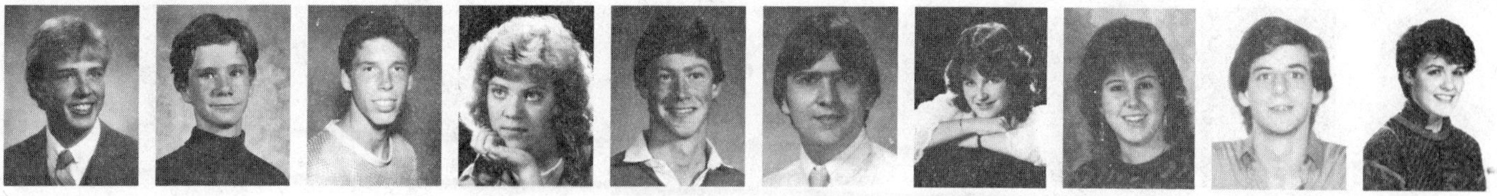

Bissaillon, Gary M
Hoosac Valley HS
Adams, MA

Blackburn, III
James R
Scituate HS
Scituate, MA

Blair, Richard
Chelsea HS
Chelsea, MA

Blake, Sandra
Norwell HS
Norwell, MA

Blanchard, James
Tantawqua Regional
SR HS
Sturbridge, MA

Blanchard, Michael
New Bedford HS
New Bedford, MA

Blanchard, Robin
Cape Cod Regional
Technical HS
South Yarmouth,
MA

Blood, Rebecca
Academy Of Notre
Pepperell, MA

Blumenthal, Jeremy
Sharon HS
Sharon, MA

Bobala, Louanne
Hampshire Regional
Westhampton, MA

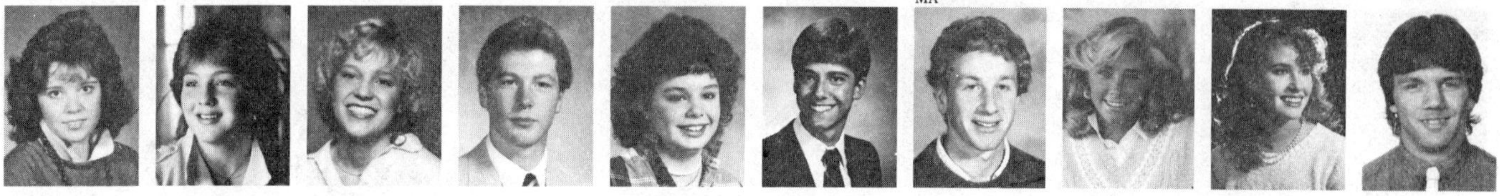

Bodemer, Sarah L
King Phillip
Regional HS
Wrentham, MA

Boisvere, Sally
Chicopee HS
Chicopee, MA

Bolton, Christina
Wayland HS
Wayland, MA

Bond, IV George W
Leominster HS
Leominster, MA

Boraccini, Patricia
Auburn SR HS
Auburn, MA

Borrelli, Joel L
Methuen HS
Methuen, MA

Bortman, Mark
Winchester HS
Winchester, MA

Bosler, Paula
Williston
Northampton Schl
Forth Worth, TX

Bouchard, Louisa
May G
Minnechaug
Regional HS
Wilbraham, MA

Bousquet, David
Andre
Methuen HS
Methuen, MA

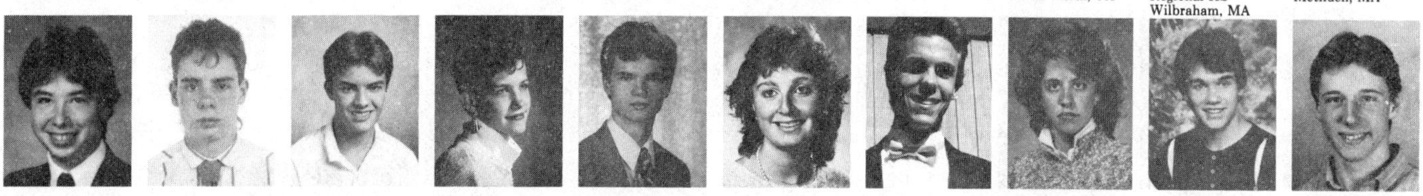

Bowen, Jr Joseph S
Melrose HS
Melrose, MA

Bower, Patrick
Methuen HS
Methuen, MA

Bowles, Steven M
Rockland HS
Rockland, MA

Bowman, Stacy
BMC Durfee HS
Fall River, MA

Boyle, John
Pope John XXIII
Central HS
Everett, MA

Boyle, Kelly Ann
Taconic HS
Pittsfield, MA

Bradanese, Marc
Medford HS
Medford, MA

Bradford, Lauren
Devra
Reading Memorial
Reading, MA

Bradley, Frank
Lawrence HS
Lawrence, MA

Bradley, John
Silver Lake Regional
Kingston, MA

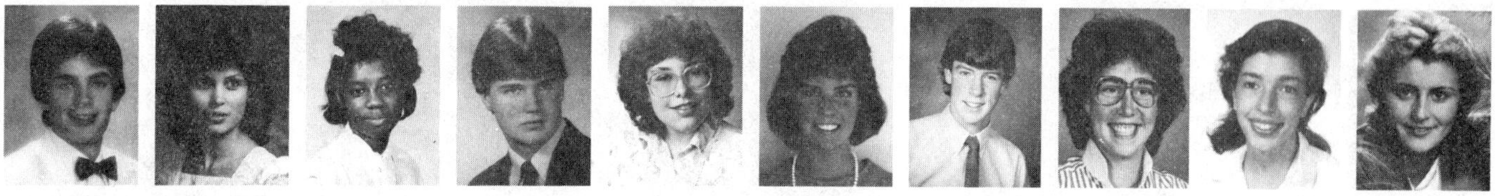

Brait, Jeffrey M
Catholic Memorial
Dedham, MA

Branco, Eve Marie
BMC Durfee HS
Fall River, MA

Brandon, Kerla
Jeremiah & Burke
Dorchester, MA

Brazil, Jr David M
Bridgewater-Raynha
m HS
Bridgewater, MA

Breault, Debbie
Attleboro HS
Attleboro, MA

Brenneman, Susan
Bishop Feehan HS
Foxboro, MA

Brice, Sean J
Old Rochester
Regional HS
Marion, MA

Brissette, Michelle
Fitchburg HS
Fitchburg, MA

Britto, Micaila
Taunton HS
Taunton, MA

Brogie, Maureen
Marlborough HS
Marlborough, MA

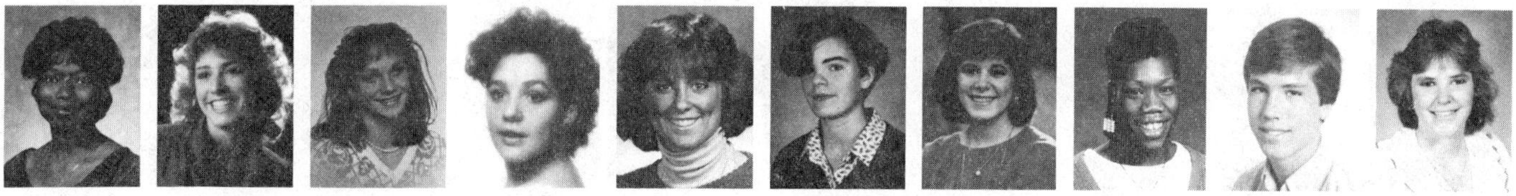

Brooks, Sheila
Jamaica Plain HS
Dorchester, MA

Brown, Courtney
Northfield Mount
Hermon HS
Abington, MA

Brown, Dianne
King Philip
Regional HS
Norfolk, MA

Brown, Elaine
Andrea
Coyleland Cassidy
Raynham, MA

Brown, Joann
Marblehead HS
Marblehead, MA

Brown, Liisa
St Bernards Central
Catholic HS
W Townsend, MA

Brown, Pamela
Notre Dame Acad
Canton, MA

Brown, Ramona
Mario Umana
Technical HS
Dorchester, MA

Bruen, Liam
Boston Coll HS
Sherborn, MA

Bruneau, Joanne
King Philip
Regional HS
Wrentham, MA

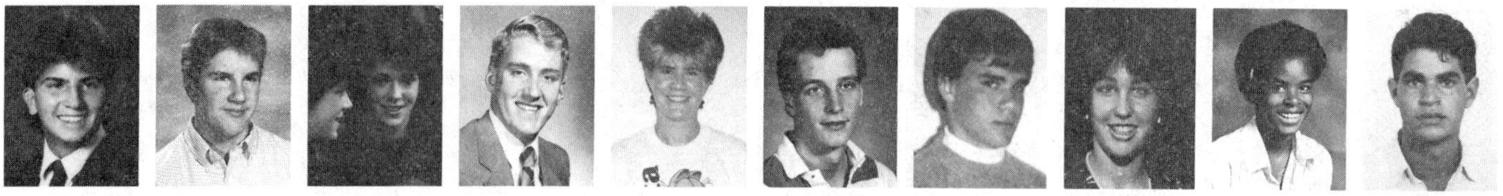

Bruno, David
Revere HS
Revere, MA

Bruno, Peter A
Mahar Regional HS
Orange, MA

Bubas, Tracey
Milton HS
Milton, MA

Buckley, Kevin
Woburn SR HS
Woburn, MA

Bufalino, Cara
Swampscott HS
Swampscott, MA

Burdick, Max
Shepherd Hill Reg
Charlton, MA

Burdick, Thomas
Mc Cann Tech
Florida, MA

Burstein, Judy
Longmeadow HS
Longmeadow, MA

Burton, Carla A
Milton Acad
Chester, PA

Bustamante, Alberto
Northfield Mount
Hermon HS
Ecuador

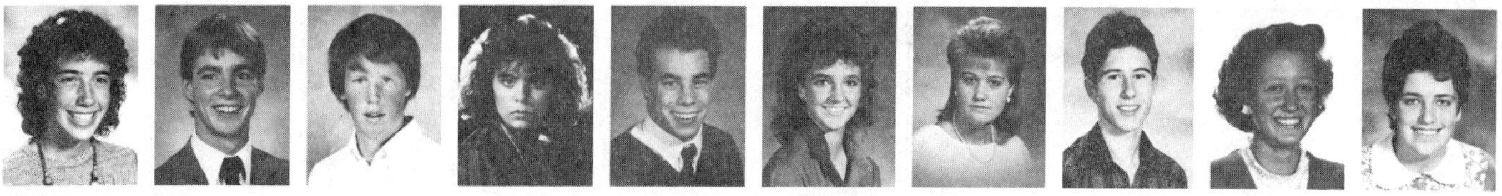

Butterworth,
Christine
Masconomet
Regional HS
Boxford, MA

Byers, James
Tewksbury
Memorial HS
Tewksbury, MA

Byrne, Michael
Bishop Connolly HS
Newport, RI

Cabral, Charlene
Bishop Connolly HS
Somerset, MA

Cabral, III R P
Middleboro HS
Middleboro, MA

Cabrini, Carrie
East Longmeadow
E Longmeadow, MA

Caci, Melissa
Winchester HS
Winchester, MA

Cahill, Jim
Salem HS
Salem, MA

Cahill, Joan
Fontbonne Acad
Quincy, MA

Cahill, Maureen
Notre Dame
Braintree, MA

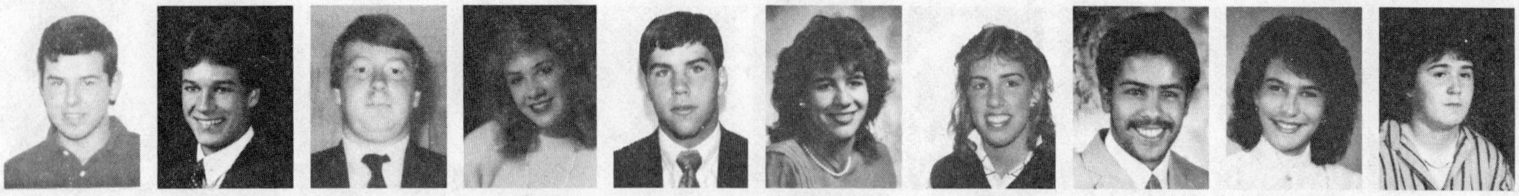

Calef, III Fred J
Quincy HS
Quincy, MA

Callahan, Kerry Patrick
Leominster HS
Leominster, MA

Callahan, Michael
Austin Prep
Burlington, MA

Cameron, Christine
Notre Dame Acad
South Weymouth, MA

Candelet, Kevin
Attleboro HS
N Attleboro, MA

Canellos, Diane
North Quincy HS
N Quincy, MA

Caputo, Kara Rogers
Belmont HS
Belmont, MA

Caraballo, Efrain
Holyoke HS
Holyoke, MA

Carabillo, Terri Lee
Concord-Carlisle HS
Concord, MA

Carbonneau, Michelle
Southwick HS
Sowick, MA

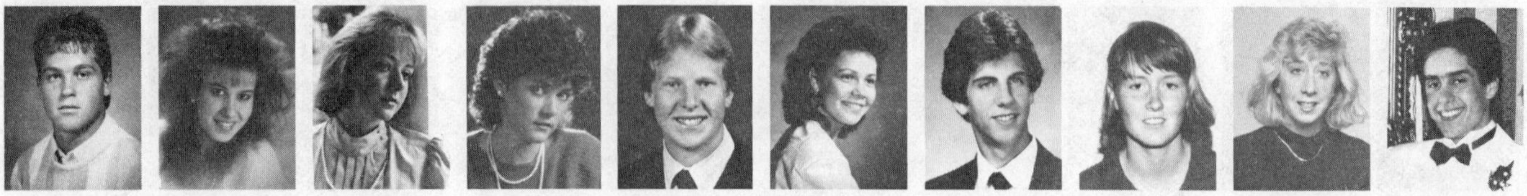

Carelli, John
St Peter-Marian HS
Worcester, MA

Carino, Chrisanne M
Pope John XXIII
Medford, MA

Caron, Cynthia
St Bernards Central Catholic HS
Fitchburg, MA

Caron, Lisa
Agawam HS
Feeding Hls, MA

Carpenter, William
Silver Lake Regional
Pembroke, MA

Carreiro, Lucy
B M C Durfee HS
Fall River, MA

Carreiro, Steven H
New Bedford HS
New Bedford, MA

Carrigg, Lisa
Governor Dummer
N Hampton, NH

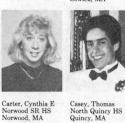

Carter, Cynthia E
Norwood SR HS
Norwood, MA

Casey, Thomas
North Quincy HS
Quincy, MA

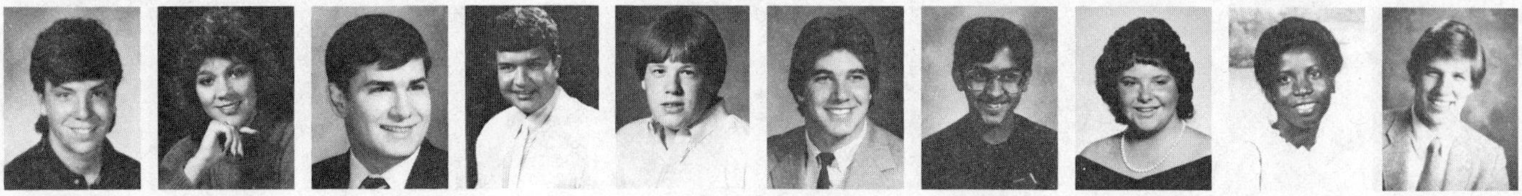

Casey, Thomas F
Boston College HS
Hanover, MA

Cassidy, Laura Jean
Mansfield HS
Mansfield, MA

Cavallaro, Richard
Central Catholic HS
Andover, MA

Celona, Stephen
Fitchburg HS
Fitchburg, MA

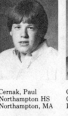

Cernak, Paul
Northampton HS
Northampton, MA

Cestrone, Albert
Central Catholic HS
Lawrence, MA

Chakravarty, Ananda
Georgetown JR SR
Georgetown, MA

Chasse, Deanne Marie
Lawrence HS
Lawrence, MA

Chery, Carline
English HS
Cambridge, MA

Chesnicka, Daniel J
Westfield HS
Westfield, MA

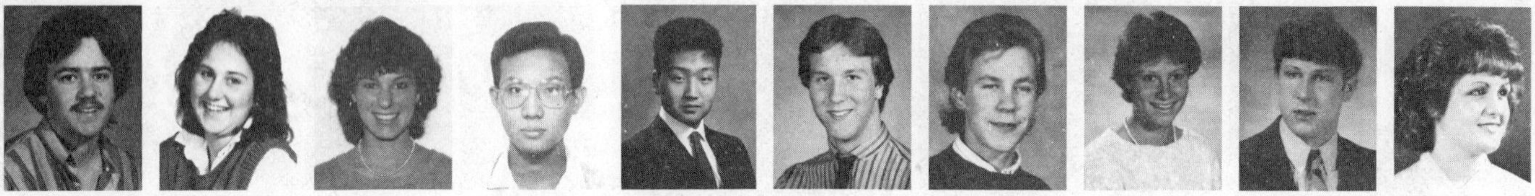

Chester, John
Uxbridge HS
Uxbridge, MA

Chiricotti, Jennifer
Westwood HS
Westwood, MA

Chorney, Michelle
Sharon HS
Sharon, MA

Chow, Herbert
Somerville HS
Somerville, MA

Chung, Pierre
Hingham HS
Hingham, MA

Ciccolini, Christopher
Fitchburg HS
Fitchburg, MA

Ciccone, Jonathan
Medway JR/SR HS
Medway, MA

Ciesla, Tammy
Frontier Regional
S Deerfield, MA

Ciosek, Richard F
Bishop Connolly HS
Swansea, MA

Ciulla, Julie
Everett HS
Everett, MA

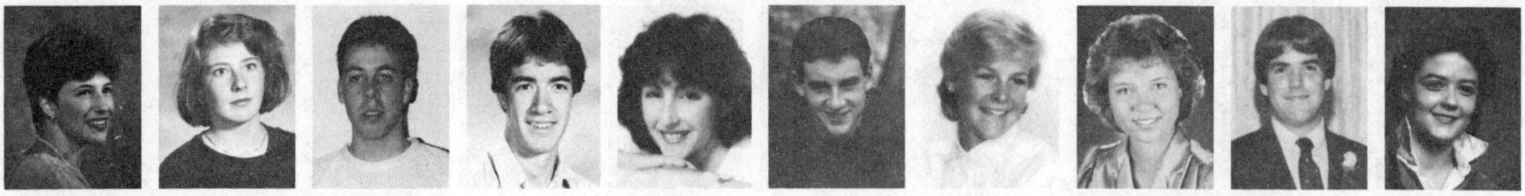

Ciulla, Rose Anne
Bishop Fenwick HS
Gloucester, MA

Clancy, Susan A
Bedford HS
Bedford, MA

Clark, Billy
St Dominic Savio
Revere, MA

Clark, Gordon
Athol HS
Athol, MA

Clark, Kara
Our Lady Of Nazareth Acad
Wilmington, MA

Clark, Mike
Barnstable HS
Centerville, MA

Clark, Stephanie
Norwell HS
Norwell, MA

Clark, Theresa
Holyoke Catholic
S Hadley, MA

Clarke, Kevin
Swampscott HS
Swampscott, MA

Claveau, Jeannine L
Bishop Fenwick HS
Salem, MA

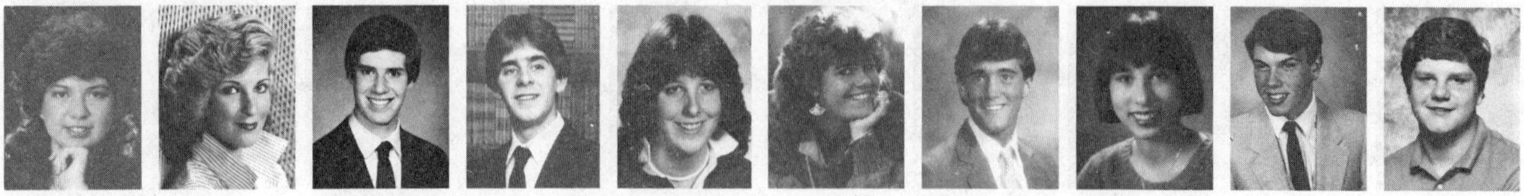

Clement, Jennifer
B M C Durfee HS
Fall River, MA

Co-Wallis, Gwen Marie
Silver Lake Regional
Halifax, MA

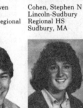

Cohen, Stephen N
Lincoln-Sudbury Regional HS
Sudbury, MA

Cokerdem, Shayne
Salem HS
Salem, MA

Colbath, Elisabeth Ann
Bedford HS
Bedford, MA

Colbert, Patricia
Norwell HS
Norwell, MA

Coleman, Christopher
Braintree HS
Braintree, MA

Colligan, Sharon
Lincoln-Sudbury Reg HS
Sudbury, MA

Collins, Neal O
Stoneham HS
Stoneham, MA

Colombo, Michael
Marian HS
Framingham, MA

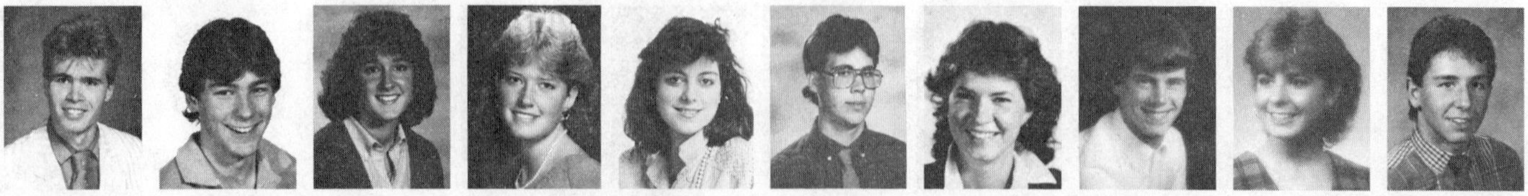

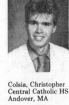

Colsia, Christopher
Central Catholic HS
Andover, MA

Comeau, III William J
Foxboro HS
Foxboro, MA

Como, Kristin
Frontier Regional
S Deerfield, MA

Conaty, Cathleen
King Philip Reg HS
Wrentham, MA

Condon, Marylee K
Silver Lake Reegional HS
Kingston, MA

Condron, Christopher
Southwick HS
Southwick, MA

Conley, Carey Ann
Northampton HS
Florence, MA

Connelly, Chris
Danvers HS
Danvers, MA

Connor, Jeanne D
Tewisbury Memorial
Tewksbury, MA

Consalvi, III Anthony J
St Dominic Savio
Revere, MA

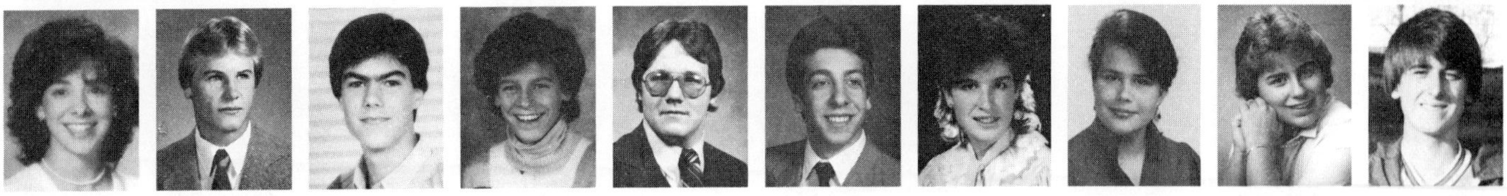

Constantine, Jennifer
New Bedford HS
New Bedford, MA

Cook, Jr Harland L
Walpole HS
Walpole, MA

Coombs, David L
Whitman-Hanson Regional HS
Whitman, MA

Cooney, Carolyn
Acad Of Notre
Lowell, MA

Cootey, Stephen
Central Catholic HS
Salem, NH

Coppeta, Greg
Central Catholic HS
Methuen, MA

Coppola, Rebecca C
Holy Name Central Catholic HS
Douglas, MA

Corbett, Ann E
Briegewater-Raynham Regional HS
Bridgewater, MA

Corbett, Kelley
Attleboro HS
Attleboro, MA

Corbosiero, Michael J
Cushing Acad
Winchendon, MA

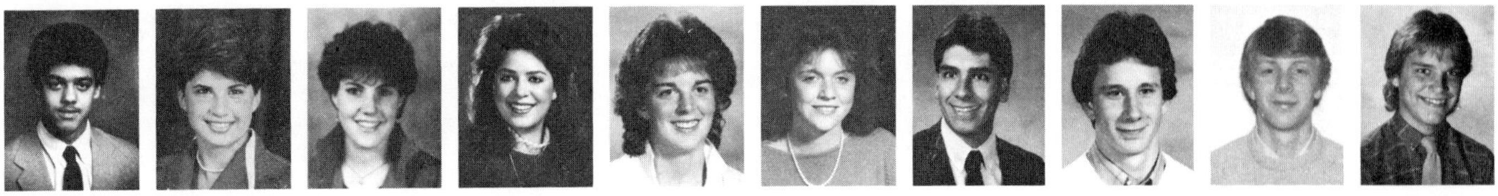

Cordes, Vaughn Michael H
Groton Schl
Bronx, NY

Cormier, Jennifer
New Bedford HS
Acushnet, MA

Corriveau, Melissa
Bourne HS
Pocasset, MA

Costa, Susan
Natick HS
Natick, MA

Costello, Jill
Bedford HS
Bedford, MA

Cote, Christina
Chelmsford HS
Chelmsford, MA

Coumounduros, Peter
St Johns Prep Schl
Stoneham, MA

Coveney, Edward
Marlbobo HS
Marlboro, MA

Cox, Jeff
Barnstable HS
Marstons Mills, MA

Cramstorff, Chris
Shepherd Hill Regional HS
Dudley, MA

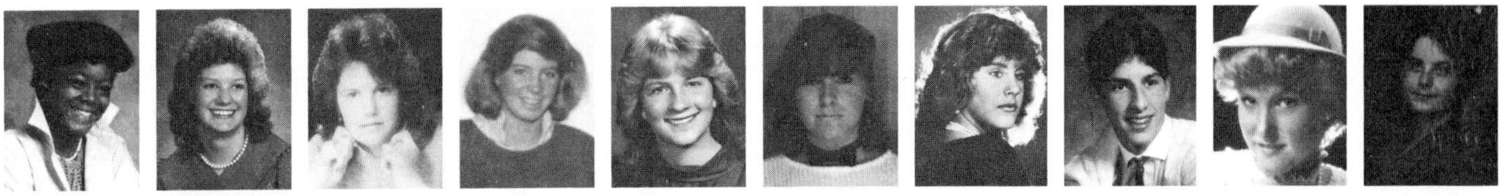

Crestwell, Robin S
Phillips Acad
Washington, DC

Cridge, Patti
Westford Acad
Reston, VA

Crocker, Amy
St Josephs Regional
Lowell, MA

Cronin, Elisabeth
Westwood HS
Westwood, MA

Crowell, Jerelyn J
Woburn SR HS
Woburn, MA

Cullen, Elizabeth
Bishop Feehan HS
Foxboro, MA

Cuneo, Paula
The Bromfield Schl
Harvard, MA

Cunha, Gary
Malden HS
Malden, MA

Cunniff, Susan
St Joseph Regional
Lowell, MA

Cunningham, Caroline
Miss Halls Schl
Lagrangeville, NY

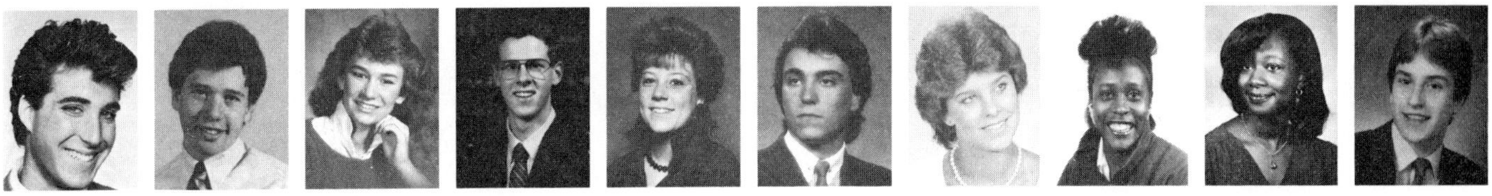

Curley, Austin
Revere HS
Revere, MA

Currie, Peter
Newton Catholic HS
Waltham, MA

Curtis, Kelley
Shawsheen Val Tech
Tewksbury, MA

D Espinosa, John V
Tri-County Reg Voc Tech Schl
Walpole, MA

D Itria, Dayna
Our Lady Of Nazareth Acad
Revere, MA

Da Cruz, John
Ludlow HS
Ludlow, MA

Dagilus, Linda
Turners Falls HS
Montague, MA

Daley, Simone
Mount Saint Joseph
Boston, MA

Daley, Tracey L
Boston Latin Schl
Dorchester, MA

Dalterio, John
St Johns HS
Hyannisport, MA

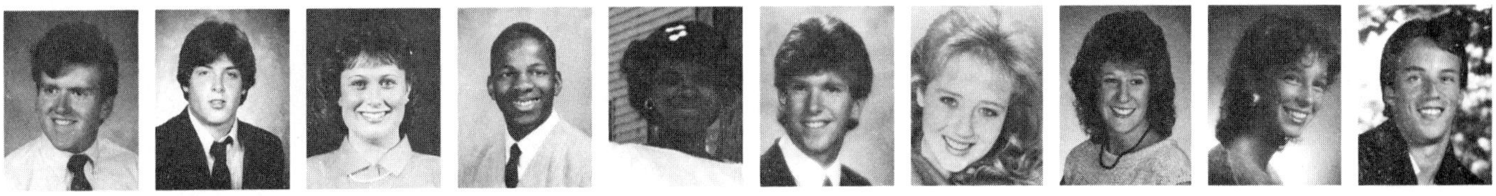

Daly, Michael T
Boston Latin Acad
West Roxbury, MA

Dandini, Michael P
St Bernards CC HS
Fitchburg, MA

Dangelo, Lisa
Everett HS
Everett, MA

Daniel, Kelly
Madison Park HS
Boston, MA

Daniel, Saudonya
Madison Park HS
Dorchester, MA

Dauphinais, Kevin
Braintree HS
Abington, MA

Davidson, Laura
Brockton HS
Brockton, MA

Davis, Donna
Groton-Dunstable Rgnl Secondry Schl
Dunstable, MA

Davis, Erika
Newburyport HS
Newburypt, MA

Davis, Steve
Old Rochester Regional HS
Marion, MA

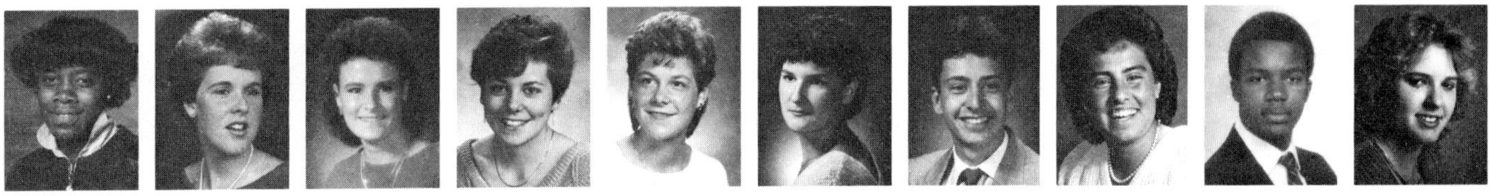

Daway, Loretta A
Newton Cntry Day/ Sacred Heart HS
Roxbury, MA

De Courcy, Cheryl
Wakefield HS
Wakefield, MA

De Fillippo, Teresa J
Hull HS
Hull, MA

De Hetre, Michelle
Triton Regional HS
Byfield, MA

De Luca, Keley Ann
Wilmington HS
Wilmington, MA

De Martino, Andrea D
Pittsfield HS
Pittsfield, MA

De Rossi, Scott S
New Bedford HS
Acushnet, MA

De Teso, Lori-Ann
Winchester HS
Winchester, MA

De Veaux, Darrell E
Arlington HS
Arlington, MA

Deary, Kim
Bartlett HS
Webster, MA

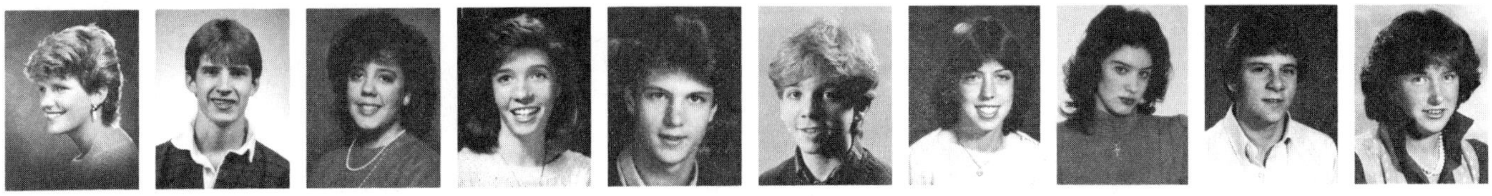

Dechene, Laurie
Bourne HS
Buzzards Bay, MA

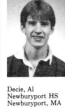

Decie, Al
Newburyport HS
Newburyport, MA

Del Greco, Adriana
Our Lady Of Nazareth Acad
Revere, MA

Del Tufo, Rose T
Dedham HS
Dedham, MA

Dellovo, Victor
St Peter Marian HS
Worcester, MA

Demello, IV Antone C
New Bedford HS
Middleboro, MA

Demeo, Jean
Waltham HS
Boston, MA

Demogenes, Stephanie
Concord Carlisle HS
Carlisle, MA

Den Boggende, Jerry
Marlboro HS
Marlboro, MA

Deroche, Deanna
Haverhill HS
Haverhill, MA

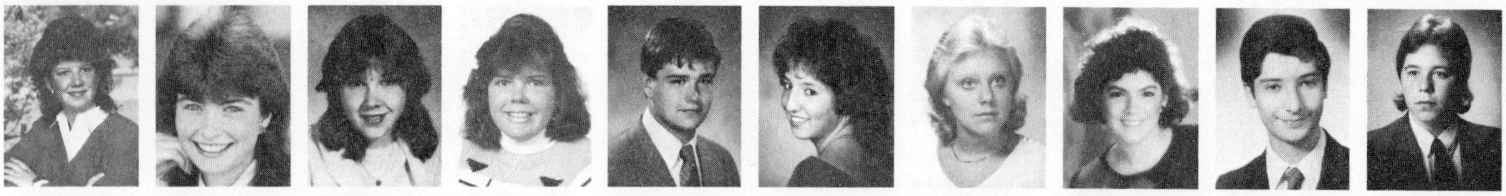

Deshaies, Lori
Lawrence HS
Lawrence, MA

Desmond, Jennifer
Lowell HS
Lowell, MA

Desper, Helen
King Philip
Regional HS
Plainville, MA

Desrosiers, Simone
Taunton HS
East Taunton, MA

Devine, Jr Joseph M
Arlington SR HS
Arlington, MA

Di Giacomo, Julie
Medford HS
Medford, MA

Di Mascio, Kristen
Duxbury HS
Duxbury, MA

Di Napoli, Leah
Braintree HS
Braintree, MA

Di Palermo, Joseph
Arlington HS
Arlington, MA

Di Russo, Anthony
S
Leominster HS
Leominster, MA

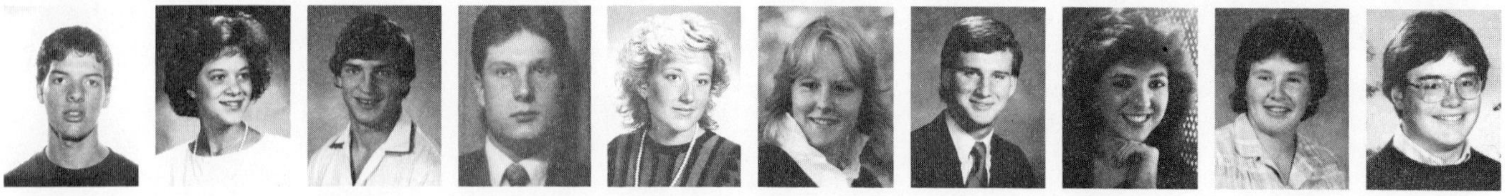

Di Tomasso, John C
Northampton HS
Northampton, MA

Dialessi, Gina
Agawam HS
Agawam, MA

Diatchenko, Dimitri
Newton North HS
Newtonville, MA

Dicologero, Anthony
Saugus HS
Saugus, MA

Dicorcia, Kathleen
Old Rochester
Regional HS
Rochester, MA

Digan, Stacey Ann
Dennis-Yarmouth
Regional HS
S Yarmouth, MA

Dillingham, Steven
G
Burlington HS
Burlington, MA

Dillon, Dawn
Billerica Memorial
Billerica, MA

Dimuzio, Angela
Rockland HS
Rockland, MA

Disque, Eric J
Belchertown HS
Belchertown, MA

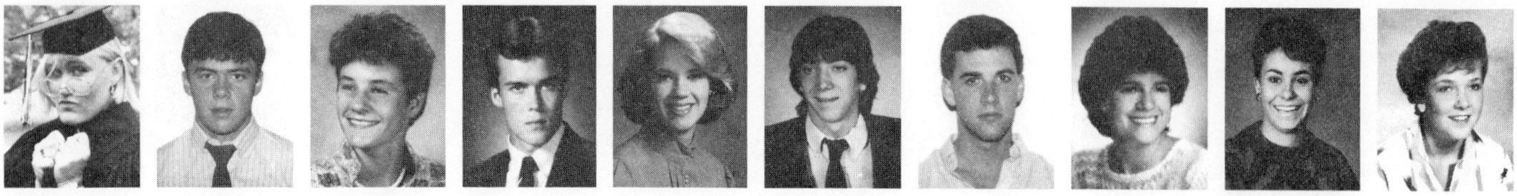

Dixon, Kristi
Northfield Mt
Hermon HS
Chatham, MA

Doherty, David R
Wakefield HS
Wakefield, MA

Dolan, Franci
Winthrop HS
Winthrop, MA

Donavan, William
Bridgewater-Raynha
m Regional HS
Bridgewater, MA

Donnelly, Jennifer
Notre Dame Acad
Weymouth, MA

Donofrio, Michael W
Saint Bernards HS
Winchendon, MA

Doran, David J
Norwood HS
Norwood, MA

Doucette, Darlene L
Newburyport HS
Newburyport, MA

Doucette, Heather
Fairhaven HS
Fairhaven, MA

Dow, Kelley
Westfield HS
Westfield, MA

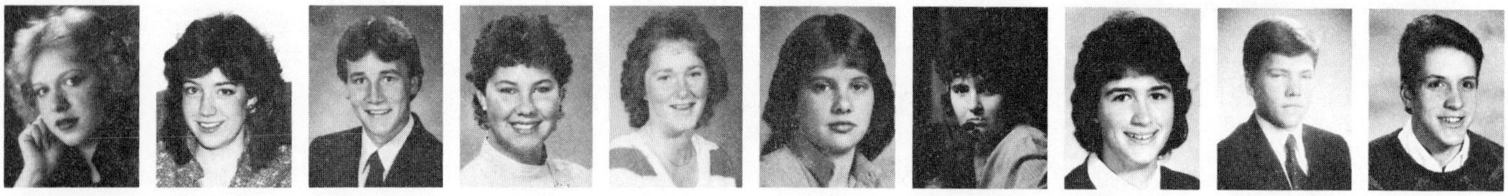

Downs, Nicole Y
Tantasqua Regional
Sturbridge, MA

Doyle, Catherine M
Cathedral HS
Wilbraham, MA

Doyle, Craig M
Waltham HS
Waltham, MA

Doyle, Michelle P
Newton North HS
Newtonville, MA

Doyle, Sarah
King Philip
Regional HS
Norfolk, MA

Drescher, Sandra
Lynn
Ayer SR HS
Ayer, MA

Dresser, Stephanie
Walnut Hill Schl Of
Performing Arts
Durham, NH

Drewniak, Kris
Somerset HS
Somerset, MA

Driscoll, Mark M
Saint Patricks HS
Watertown, MA

Du Mont, Joseph
Westfield HS
Westfield, MA

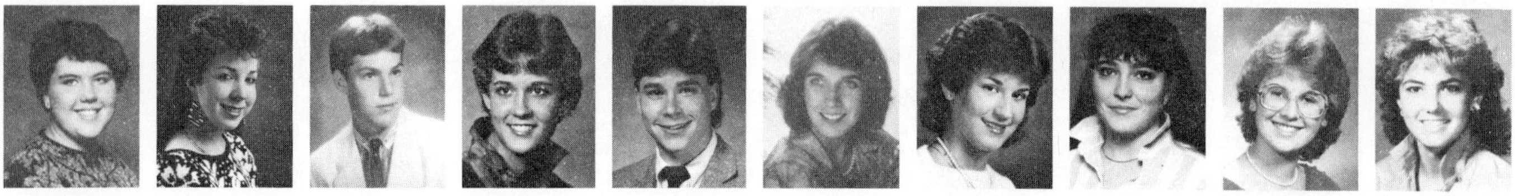

Ducey, Kathleen
Our Lady Of
Nazareth Acad
Wilmington, MA

Duchesneau, Amy B
West Springfield HS
W Springfield, MA

Dudek, Martin J
Pathfinder Regional
Tech Vo
Belchertown, MA

Dudley, Elizabeth
Old Rochester
Regional HS
Marion, MA

Dufault, Timothy M
Holy Name C C H S
Worcester, MA

Duffy, Mary Kate
Marian HS
Natick, MA

Dultz, Tina Marie K
West Springfield SR
West Springfield,
MA

Dumont, Stacie
Attleboro HS
Attleboro, MA

Dunn, Annemarie
Burlington HS
Burlington, MA

Dunn, Kelly
Taunton HS
Taunton, MA

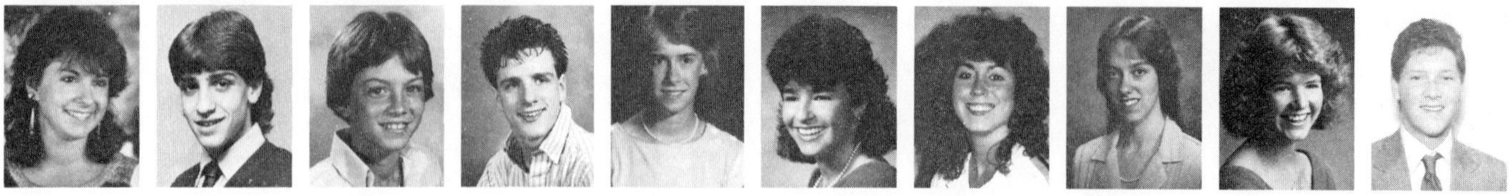

Duquette, Marie L
Chicopee HS
Chicopee, MA

Dustin, Craig
St Dominic Savio
Everett, MA

Duval, Mark
Haverhill HS
Haverhill, MA

Dye, Michael
Brockton HS
Brockton, MA

Earles, Trina
Concord-Carlisle HS
Concord, MA

Ecker, Amy Beth
Salem HS
Salem, MA

Edgerly, Cynthia
Wilmington HS
Wilmington, MA

Edwards, Diana
Beverly HS
Beverly, MA

Egan, Joanna Leigh
Dennis-Yarmouth
Regional HS
W Yarmouth, MA

Egan, Timothy
Boston College HS
Braintree, MA

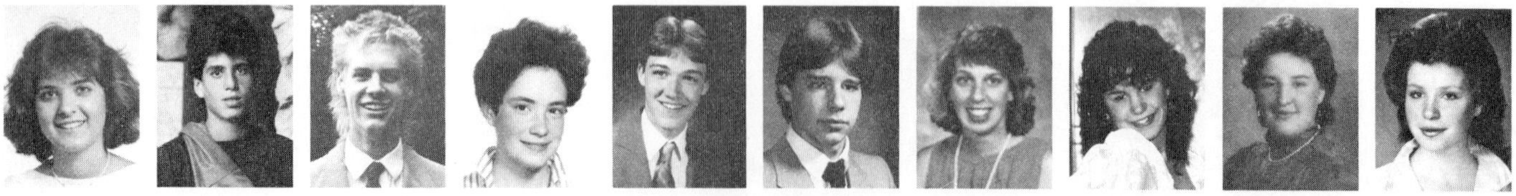

Eldridge, Barbara
Marian HS
Framingham, MA

Ellerin, Todd
Lynnfield HS
Lynnfield, MA

Ellis, Erik
Reading Mem HS
Reading, MA

Emery, Anne
The Waring Schl
Manchester, MA

Enos, Eric Scott
Taunton HS
Taunton, MA

Enzian, Thomas
Central Catholic HS
Dracut, MA

Eringi, Kristine
Fitchburg HS
Fitchburg, MA

Evans, Heather
North Midlesex
Regional HS
Pepperell, MA

Evans, Noreen
Fontbonne Acad
Quincy, MA

Eversoll, Rhonda
Murdock HS
Winchendon, MA

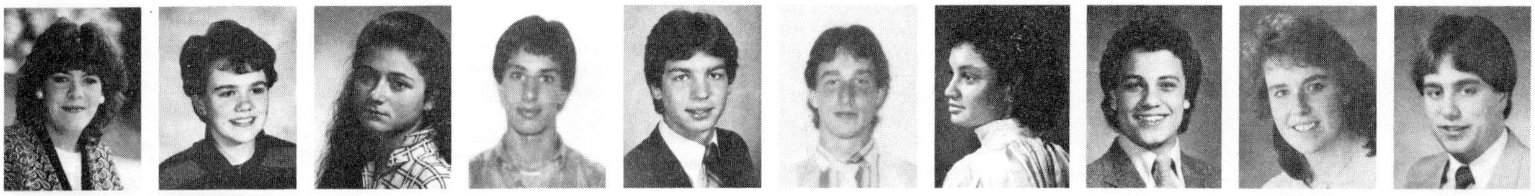

Fagan, Heidi
Mount Alvernia HS
West Roxbury, MA

Falvey, Kerry
Frontier Regional
S Deerfield, MA

Farberov, Inna
Marblehead HS
Marblehead, MA

Farinha, Jr Paul W
Taunton HS
E Taunton, MA

Farivar-Sadri, Kamran
Milford HS
Milford, MA

Farley, Sean M
Noble & Greenough
Charlestown, MA

Faro, Gina
Presentation Of Mary Acad
Atkinson, NH

Faro, Joseph
Central Catholic HS
Atkinson, NH

Farrand, Karen
Southbridge HS
Southbridge, MA

Farrell, Mark
Xaverian Brothers
Stoughton, MA

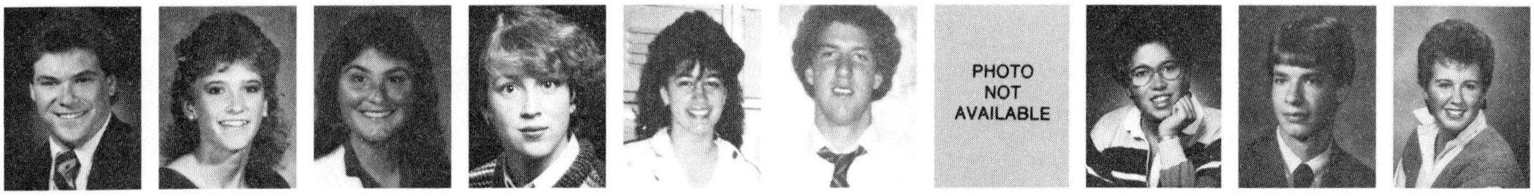
PHOTO
NOT
AVAILABLE

Farrell, Stephen J
Holy Name C C HS
North Grafton, MA

Farren, Lisa
Plymouth-Carver
Plymouth, MA

Favazza, Mary
Gloucester HS
Gloucester, MA

Fazekas, Karen
Newton Country Day Schl
Needham, MA

Fazio, Giovanna
Waltham HS
Waltham, MA

Fedor, Christopher
St Johns HS
Sterling, MA

Felder, Jr Ronald E
Milton Acad
Cincinnati, OH

Ferguson, Paula M
Shrewsbury HS
Shrewsbury, MA

Ferrantino, David
Ware HS
Ware, MA

Ferrari, Donna
Norwood HS
Norwood, MA

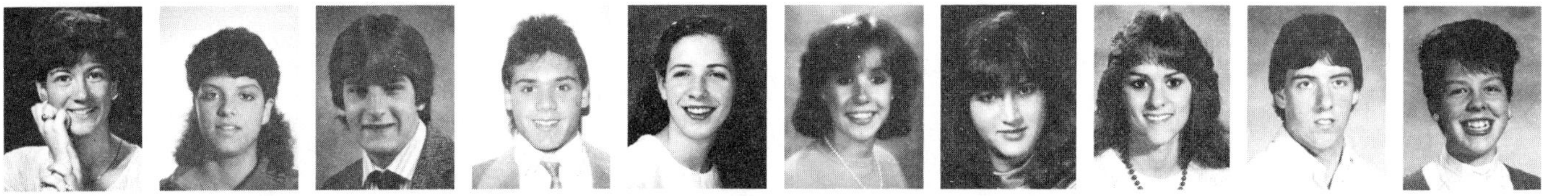

Ferrari, Lisa A
Medway JR SR HS
Medway, MA

Ferreira, Elizabeth
New Bedford HS
New Bedford, MA

Ferreira, Mark
Bishop Connolly HS
Westport, MA

Filetti, Sal
Austin Prep Schl
Methuen, MA

Fineberg, Donna G
Dartmouth HS
Fairhaven, MA

Fiore, Lisa Marie
Fontbonne Acad
Hyde Park, MA

Fischler, Melissa Sue
Westwood HS
Westwood, MA

Fitzgerald, Lisa
North Middlesex Regional HS
Townsend, MA

Fitzhenry, Bob
Foxborough HS
Foxboro, MA

Fitzmaurice, Michele
Notre Dame Acad
Holbrook, MA

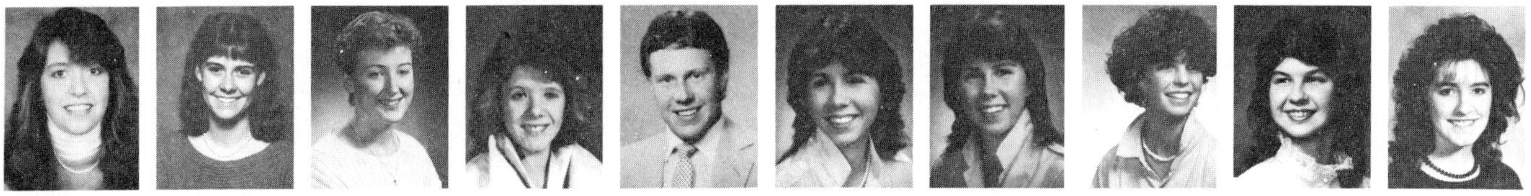

Flagg, Beverly
Brackton Christian Regional HS
Wareham, MA

Flaherty, Deirdre
Marian HS
Hopkinton, MA

Flaherty, Maureen Elizabeth
Notre Dame Acad
N Quincy, MA

Flamand, Charlene
Ware HS
Ware, MA

Flavin, Leo
Austin Prep
Billerica, MA

Fleming, Linda
Billerica Memorial
Billerica, MA

Fleming, Mary
Billerica Memorial
Billerica, MA

Fletcher, Jennifer
Marblehead HS
Marblehead, MA

Fleury, Linda
Bellingham Memorial JR/SR HS
Bellingham, MA

Flewelling, Chris
Haverhill HS
Haverhill, MA

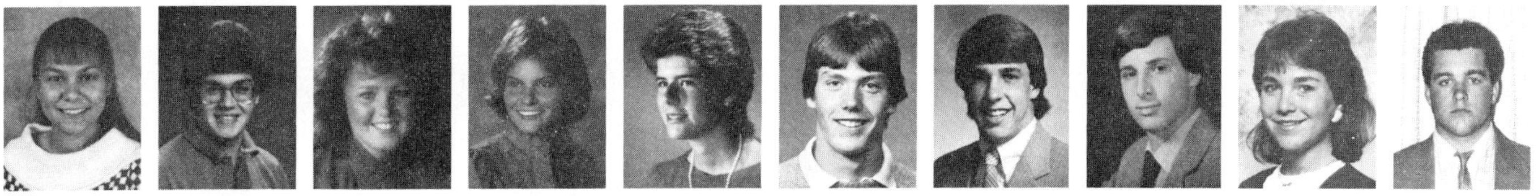

Flores, Rebecca
Acad Of Notre
Concord, NH

Flynn, Sean P
Saint Johns HS
Worcester, MA

Foley, Carolyn
Braintree HS
Braintree, MA

Foley, Kelly
Quaboag Regional
West Brookfield, MA

Follansbee, Caroline J
Ipswich HS
Ipswich, MA

Forbes, Michael
Wahconah Regional
Windsor, MA

Ford, Jr John K
St Peter-Marian CC
Worcester, MA

Formisano, Paul
Joseph Case HS
Swansea, MA

Fortin, Annette
Cardinal Spellman
Bridgewater, MA

Fortner, Frank
Bellingham JR SR Memorial HS
Bellingham, MA

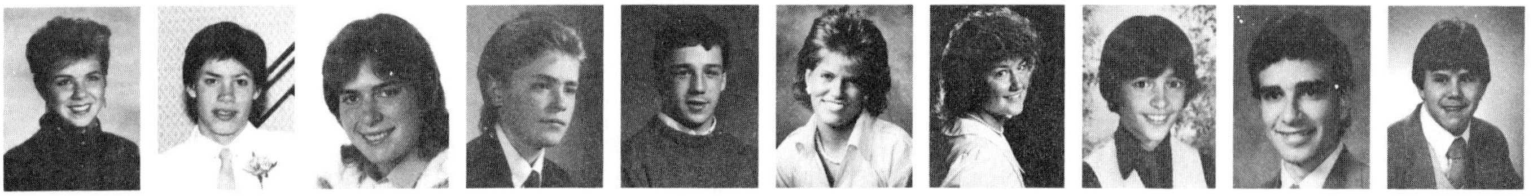

Forziati, Gina
Easthampton HS
Easthampton, MA

Foster, Jon
Bishop Feehan HS
Attleboro, MA

Foster, Lynn
Shepherd Hill Regional HS
Dudley, MA

Fournier, Steven
Central Catholic HS
Lowell, MA

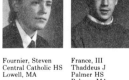

France, III Thaddeus J
Palmer HS
Palmer, MA

Francis, Kimberly
New Bedford HS
New Bedford, MA

Francis, Stephanie
North Quincy HS
Quincy, MA

Franco, Dickson E
Westfield HS
Westfield, MA

Franco, Michael
Taunton HS
Taunton, MA

Frenette, Glenn R
Athol HS
Athol, MA

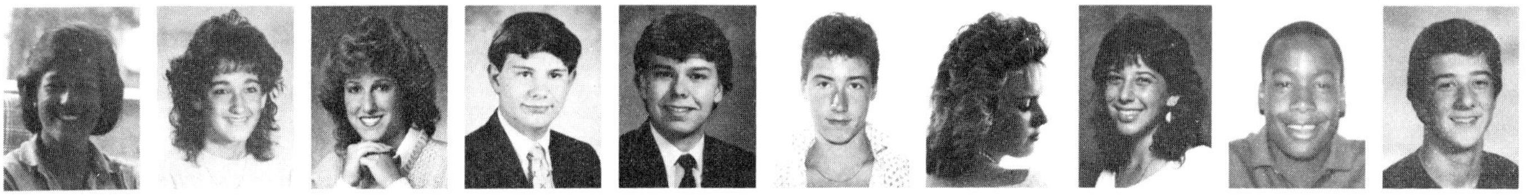

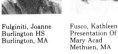

Fulginiti, Joanne
Burlington HS
Burlington, MA

Fusco, Kathleen
Presentation Of Mary Acad
Methuen, MA

Fyrberg, Denise M
David Prouty HS
Spencer, MA

Gagnon, Greg
Cathedral HS
Springfield, MA

Gagnon, Joel
Central Catholic HS
N Andover, MA

Gagnon, William
Easthampton HS
Easthampton, MA

Gahan, Patricia Ann
Holy Name C C HS
Worcester, MA

Gai, Alisa Nina
Marian HS
Holliston, MA

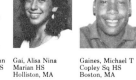

Gaines, Michael T
Copley Sq HS
Boston, MA

Gale, Daniel
Athol HS
Athol, MA

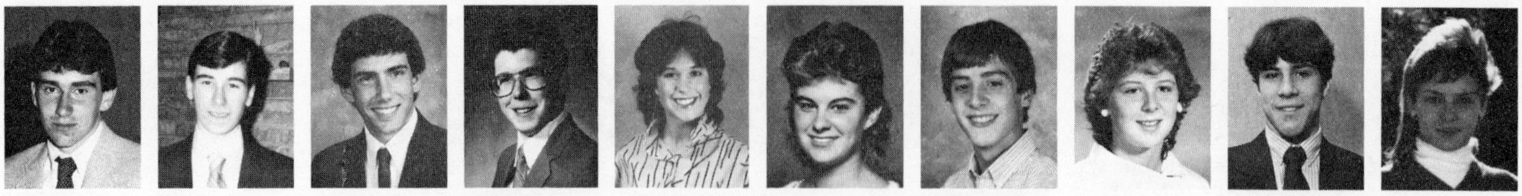

Gallagher, Matthew
Waltham HS
Boston, MA

Gallant, Steven L
Pentucket Regional
Merrimac, MA

Garabedian, Jr
Leonard M
Hopedale JR/SR HS
Hopedale, MA

Gariepy, David
Ludlow HS
Ludlow, MA

Garnett, Rachael
Westport HS
Westport, MA

Garrett, Melissa
Our Lady Of
Nazareth Acad
Revere, MA

Gastall, John Ryan
B M C Durfee HS
Fall River, MA

Gatherum, Karen
Dracut HS
Dracut, MA

Gattuso, Marc
Drury SR HS
North Adams, MA

Gaulin, Michelle
Southbridge HS
Southbridge, MA

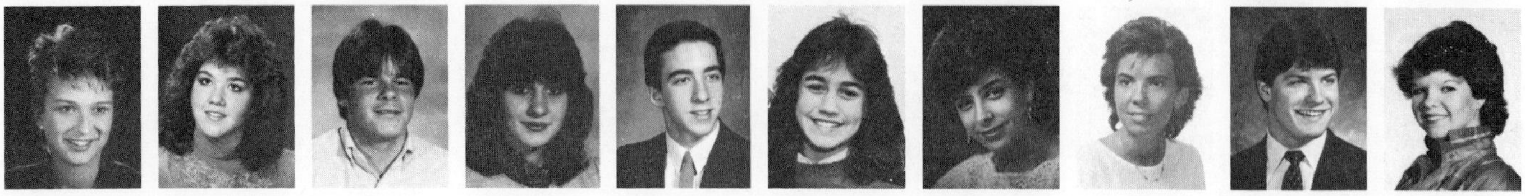

Gaunt, Kelly
S Hadley HS
S Hadly, MA

Gelineau, Lisa
Blackstone-Millville
Regional Schl
Blackstone, MA

Gennell, Eric
Central Catholic HS
Dracut, MA

Georgiadis, Pamela
Presentation Of
Mary Acad
Haverhill, MA

Gerroir, Steven
Central Catholic HS
Andover, MA

Getson, Julie
Framingham South
Framingham, MA

Giakoumis, Tina
Bartlett HS
Webster, MA

Giannandrea, Italia
Archbishop Williams
Quincy, MA

Giargiari, Robert P
Natick HS
Natick, MA

Gibbons, Deborah
Westwood HS
Westwood, MA

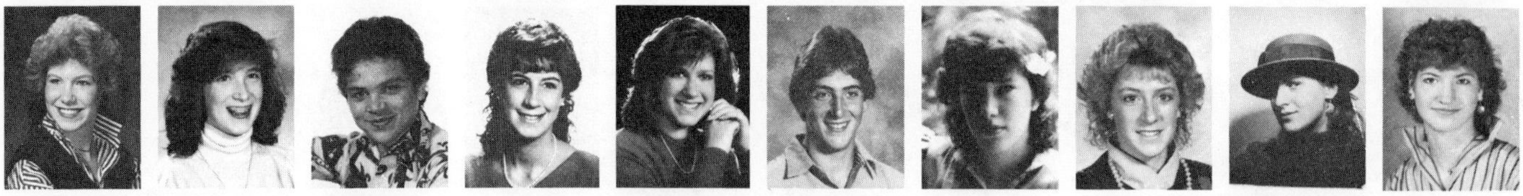

Giguere-Stellmack,
Donna
Blackstone-Millvl
Rgnl JR SR HS
Virginia Bch, VA

Gilbert, Lisa
Drury HS
N Adams, MA

Gilchrist, Miles
Fitchburg HS
Fitchburg, MA

Gillespie, Kristine
Randolph HS
Randolph, MA

Gillooly, Vanessa
Drury SR HS
N Adams, MA

Gilman, Pippin
Georgetown HS
Georgetown, MA

Ginsburg, Jessica L
Northfield Mount
Hermon Schl
Shelburne, VT

Girard, Bonnie
Haverhill HS
Bradford, MA

Girdis, Jaime S
Hampshire Regional
Goshen, MA

Girelli, Tammie
Norton HS
Norton, MA

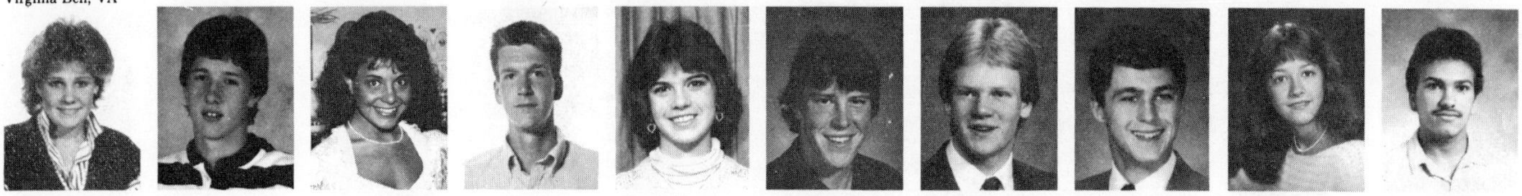

Girouard, Caroline
Holyoke Catholic
Chicopee, MA

Giuliano, Jr
Anthony
Hopedale JR SR HS
Hopedale, MA

Glavickas, Catherine
Easthampton HS
Easthampton, MA

Gleason, Jonathan P
Newton South HS
Newton, MA

Glenn, Tonya
Natick HS
Natick, MA

Gliniecki, Corey
Shepherd Hill
Regional HS
Dudley, MA

Glowik, Timothy J
St Mary Regional
Lynn, MA

Goldstein, Damon
Medford HS
Medford, MA

Golembewski,
Melissa Beth
North Attleboro HS
N Attleboro, MA

Gonzalez, Julio
Bay Pathe RVT HS
Southbridge, MA

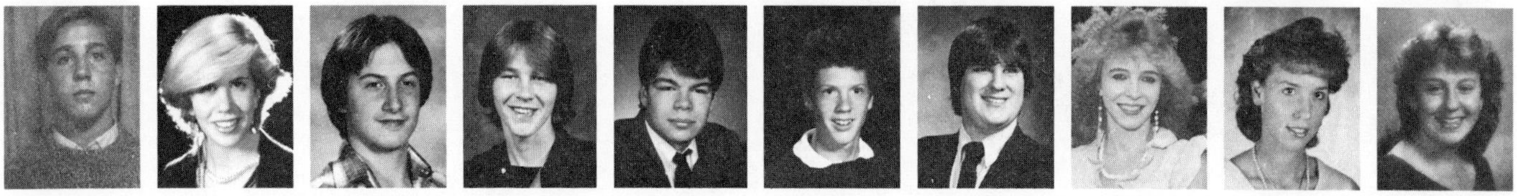

Goodman, Eric
Michael
North Quincy HS
Quincy, MA

Goodwin, Sandra
Wakefield HS
Wakefield, MA

Gordon, Andrew
Methuen HS
Methuen, MA

Gordon, Michael
Greater Lowell
Tygnsboro, MA

Gordon, Michael A
Murdock HS
Winchendon, MA

Gordon, Shawn J
David Prouty HS
Spencer, MA

Goudreau, John
Central Catholic HS
Salem, NH

Goulart, Maureen
Bristol Plymouth
Reg Tech Voc Schl
Taunton, MA

Grabiec, Tina
Hopkins Acad
Hadley, MA

Grady, Patricia
Mount Saint Joseph
E Boston, MA

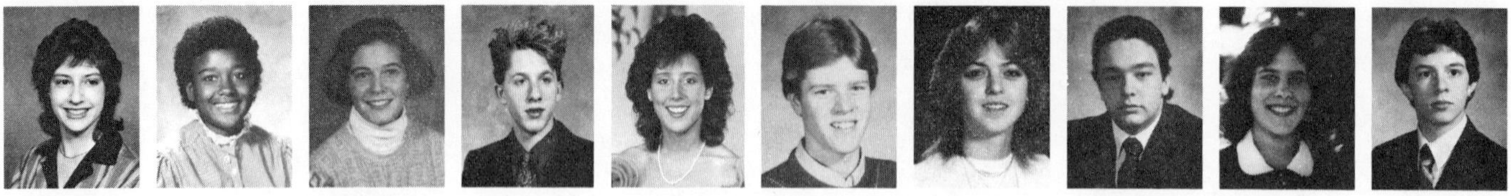

Greb, Christina
Wahconah Regional
Hinsdale, MA

Greenidge, Andrea
Sharon HS
Sharon, MA

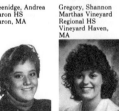

Gregory, Shannon
Marthas Vineyard
Regional HS
Vineyard Haven,
MA

Grigelevich, III
Joseph M
Bishop Feehan HS
N Attleboro, MA

Grimley, Karen
Maynard HS
Maynard, MA

Grinnell, Todd
Foxborough HS
Foxborough, MA

Grubb, Andrea
Danvers HS
Danvers, MA

Guarino, Daniel P
St Dominic Savio
Revere, MA

Guarnieri, Michelle
Mount Alvernia HS
Wellesley, MA

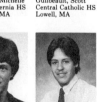

Guilbeault, Scott
Central Catholic HS
Lowell, MA

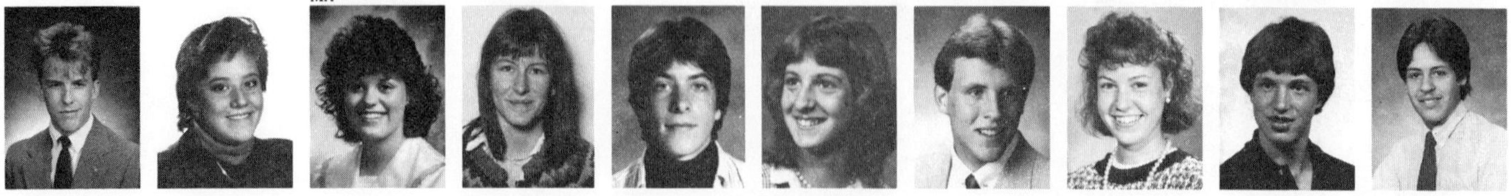

Guin, Michael
Bellingham
Memorial JR HS
Bellingham, MA

Gunn, Katy
Frontier Regional
Sunderand, MA

Gurry, Renee
North Quincy HS
Quincy, MA

Guzowski, Kimberly
Ann
Phillips Acad
Andover, MA

Gyles, Trevor
Masconomet
Regional HS
Boxford, MA

Hackett, Angelique
Drury SR HS
North Adams, MA

Hagerty, Stephen
Attleboro HS
Attleboro, MA

Hale, Carolyn
Wilmington HS
Wilmington, MA

Hale, Timothy K
Thayer Academy
Plymouth, MA

Hall, Jason M
Worcester
Vocational Tech
Spencer, MA

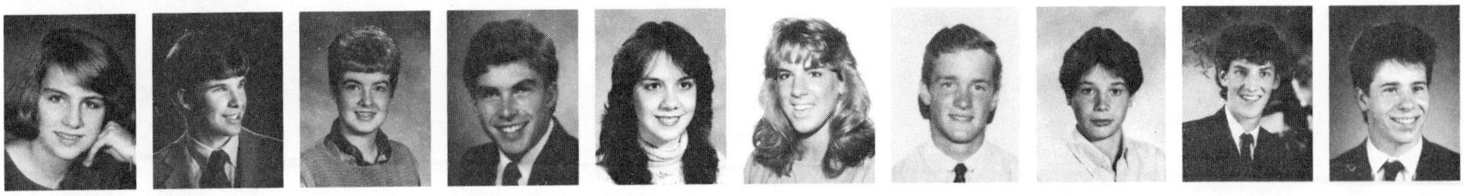

Hammond, Alysa D
Lincoln-Sudbury
Reg HS
Sudbury, MA

Hamre, John T
Cathedral HS
W Springfield, MA

Hand, Cathy
Sharon HS
Sharon, MA

Hannabury, John
Malden Catholic HS
Malden, MA

Hanson, Martha
Apponequet
Regional HS
Lakeville, MA

Hanssen, Karen
King Philip HS
Norfolk, MA

Harney, Michael
Walpole HS
Walpole, MA

Harper, David M
Northbridge JR SR
Whitinsville, MA

Harrington, Brian
Cathedral HS
Springfield, MA

Harrington, Michael
Cathedral HS
Somers, CT

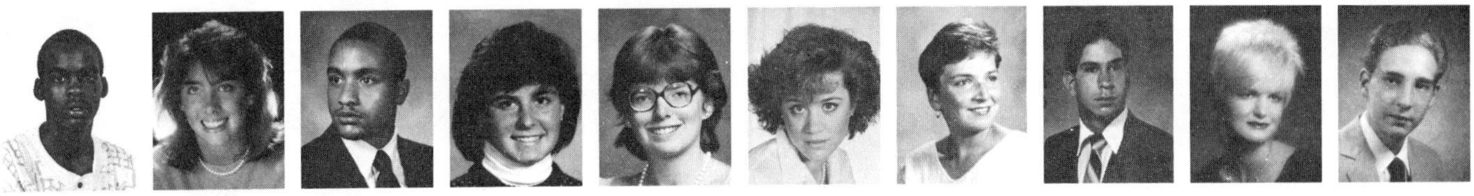

Harris, Phillip L
Jamaica Plain HS
Roxbury, MA

Harris, Sarah
Framingham North
Framingham, MA

Hart, Joseph
West Roxbury HS
Boston, MA

Hart, Patricia M
Notre Dame Acad
Hingham, MA

Harvey, Katherine
Elizabeth
Littleton HS
Littleton, MA

Hasche, Tina
Lincoln-Sudbury
Regional HS
Sudbury, MA

Hatch, Carolyn
Monument
Mountain Rgnl HS
W Stockbridge, MA

Hatem, Neil M
Newton North HS
Newton, MA

Hauser, Joni
Oliver Ames HS
North Easton, MA

Hayes, Bryon
Nauset Regional HS
N Eastham, MA

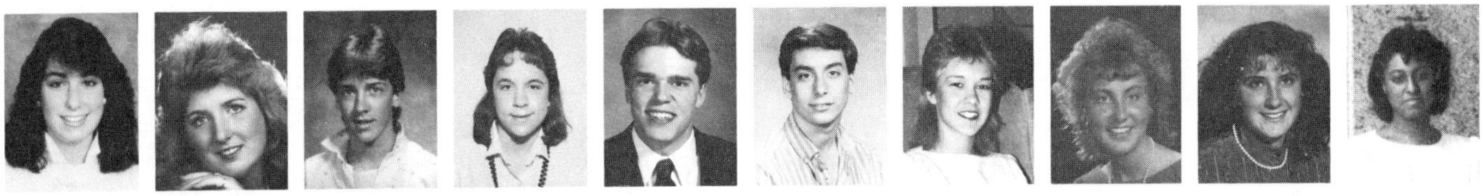

Hayes, Maureen
Brockton Christian
Regional HS
E Bridgewater, MA

Healy, Coleen
Wakefield Memorial
Wakefield, MA

Healy, Jay
Malden HS
Malden, MA

Healy, Mary Beth
Bishop Feehan HS
Attleboro, MA

Heaton, Andrew P
Central Catholic HS
Groveland, MA

Hebert, Jeffrey M
Grafton Memorial
SR HS
S Grafton, MA

Hebert, Patrice
Gr Lawrence
Technical HS
Lawrence, MA

Hennessey, Joan P
Arlington Catholic
Arlington, MA

Henry, Maureen
Methuen HS
Methuen, MA

Herbert, Clestine
Milton HS
Randolph, MA

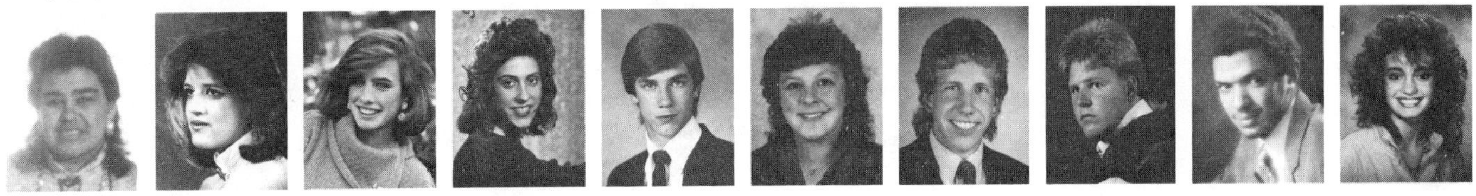

Hernandez, Maria
Greater Lawrence
Lawrence, MA

Herson, Nanci Sue
Natick HS
Natick, MA

Hesse, Alicia C
Noble & Greznovott
Weston, MA

Higgins, Maria
Medford HS
Medford, MA

Higgins, Randy
Monument
Mountain Regiona
Great Barrington,
MA

Hilditch, Pamela
Hepedale HS
Hopedale, MA

Hill, Michael
Chicopee HS
Chicopee, MA

Hill, Michael
Old Colony Regional
Carver, MA

Hill, Scott C
Uxbridge HS
Uxbridge, MA

Hill, Tiffany
Bishop Stang HS
Wareham, MA

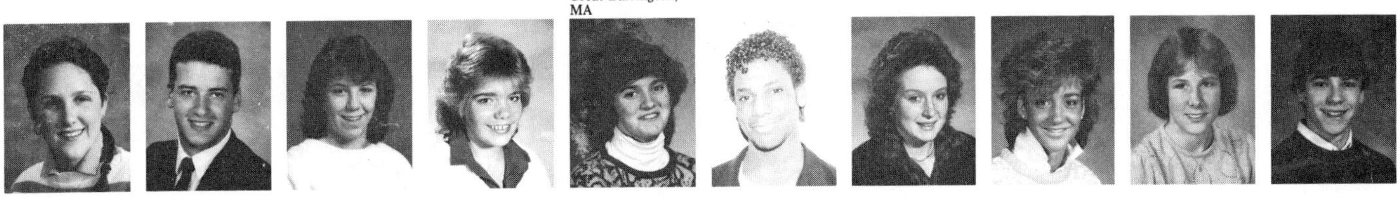

Hilliard, Catherine
Hopedale JR SR HS
Hopedale, MA

Hines, David
Lynn English HS
Lynn, MA

Hitchcock, Lynn
Palmer HS
Palmer, MA

Hoffman, Jennifer
Presentation Of
Mary Acad
Methuen, MA

Holding, Kelly
Uxbridge HS
Uxbridge, MA

Holman, Kyva
Reading Memorial
Boston, MA

Holohan, Sheila
Northmiddlesex
Regional HS
Townsend, MA

Hoover, Andrea
E Longmeadow HS
E Longmeadow, MA

Horgan, Beth
Arlington HS
Arlington, MA

Hosker, Michael
Newburyport HS
Newburyport, MA

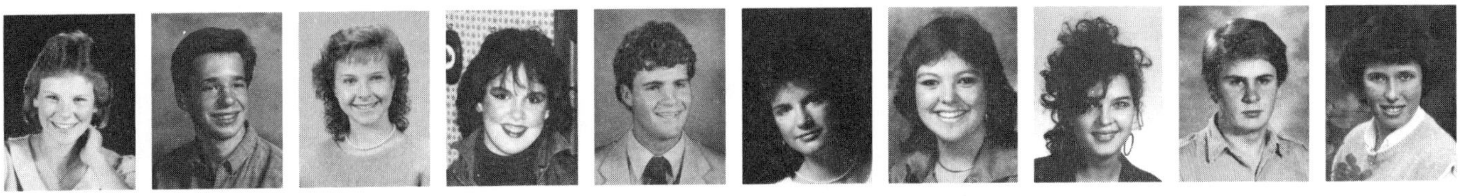

Houle, Karen
Chicopee
Comprehensive HS
Chicopee, MA

House, Bryan E
Longmeadow HS
Longmeadow, MA

Hovey, Cheryl
Franklin HS
Franklin, MA

Howard, Laurie
Hampshire Regional
Southampton, MA

Howard, IV Thomas
J
Cathedral HS
W Springfield, MA

Howe, Regina M
Wareham HS
W Wareham, MA

Hume, Shannon
St Marys Regional
Lynn, MA

Hunsaker, Lee
Walnut Hill HS
Roanoke, VA

Hunt, Christopher
Westfield HS
Westfield, MA

Hunt, Jodie
Triton Regional HS
Salisbury, MA

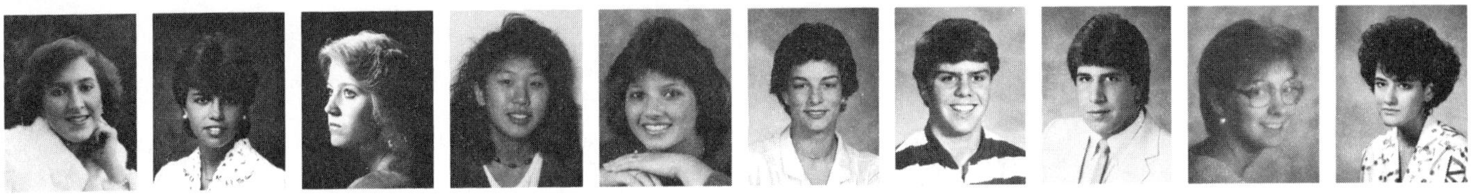

Hutchins, Deirdre
Littleton HS
Littleton, MA

Hutchinson,
Jennifer
Westford Acad
Westford, MA

Hutnak, Stephanie
Douglas Memorial
Douglas, MA

Hwang, Christine S
Phillips Acad
Carthage, MO

Iacovelli, Lisa
Abington HS
Abington, MA

Iannaco, Juliane
Woburn SR HS
Woburn, MA

Idzal, Thomas P
Wellesley HS
Wellesley, MA

Iellamo, Paul
Cathedral HS
Springfield, MA

Ievins, Lydia H
Walnut Hill School
Of Performg Arts
Binghamton, NY

Ioakimidis,
Elizabeth
West Roxbury HS
West Roxbury, MA

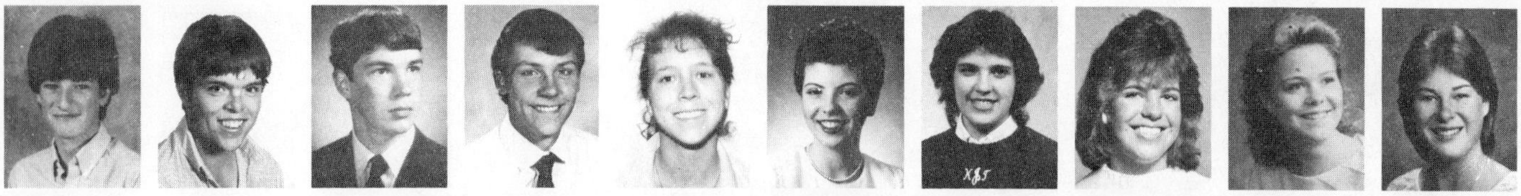

Ireland, Christopher J
Ayer HS
Ft Devens, MA

Jackman, Andrew
Turners Falls HS
Turners Fls, MA

Jackman, Christopher M
Newburyport HS
Newburyport, MA

Jakimczyk, John
Arlington Catholic
Medford, MA

James, Arlene T
Hingham HS
Hingham, MA

James, Christine
B M C Durfee HS
Fall River, MA

James, Kathryn
Silver Lake Regional
Kingston, MA

Jarvis, Janine
Masconomet Regional HS
Boxford, MA

Jarvis, Kimberly
Burncoat SR HS
Worcester, MA

Jedraszek, Paula
Beverly HS
Beverly, MA

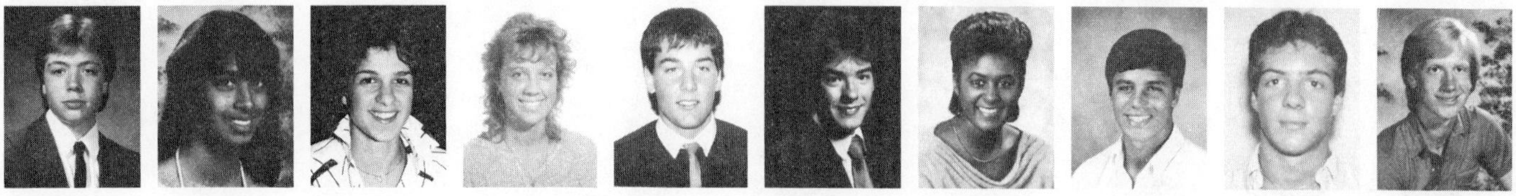

Jennings, Paul
Bristol Plymouth Tech HS
Taunton, MA

Jhaveri, Mona M
Apponequet Reg HS
Lakeville, MA

Jilian, Zovig
Watertown HS
Watertown, MA

Johnson, Caroline
Arlington Catholic
Arlington, MA

Johnson, Christopher E
Norwood HS
Norwood, MA

Johnson, James V
Greater Lowell Regionl Voca HS
Lowell, MA

Johnson, Michelle Renee
Auburn SR HS
Auburn, MA

Joncas, David W
Bishop Connolly HS
Fall River, MA

Jones, Allan P
Austin Preparatory
Burlington, MA

Jones, Darin R
Wachusett Regional
Rutland, MA

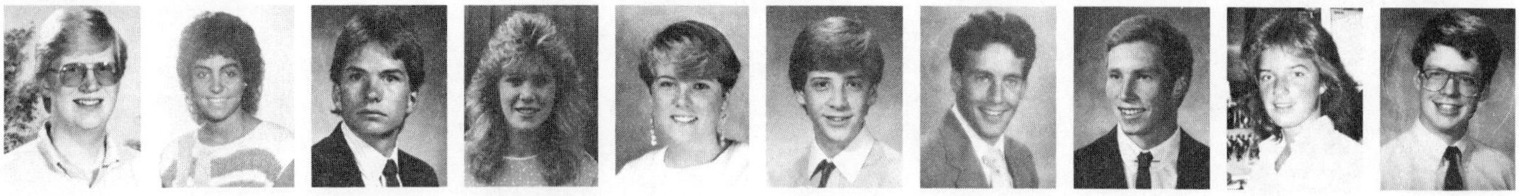

Jones, Jonathan
Pittsfield HS
Pittsfield, MA

Jones, Laurie
Bishop Feehan HS
Seekonk, MA

Jones, Michael
Westford Acad
Westford, MA

Jones, Sharon Alane
Greater Lowell Regnl Vo Tec
Dunstable, MA

Jordan, Carolyn
Norton HS
Norton, MA

Jorgensen, Luke R
Brockton HS
Brockton, MA

Joyce, Christopher
Braintree HS
Braintree, MA

Joyce, John
Don Bosco Tech
Dorchester, MA

Joyce, Meralee
Wilbraham & Monson Acad
Springfield, MA

Joynt, III Ernest H
Bishop Stang HS
East Wareham, MA

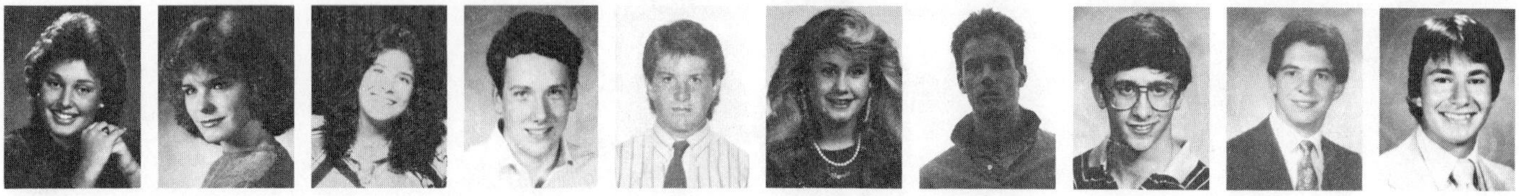

Jump, Kerri-Lynn
Academy Of Notre
Lowell, MA

Jurgelewicz, Stacy L
Middleboro HS
Wareham, MA

Kalman, Heidi
Malden HS
Malden, MA

Kalns, Andrew
Boston Coll HS
Pembroke, MA

Kane, Christopher
Newton Catholic HS
Brookline, MA

Kaplan, Rhonda
Newton South HS
Newton, MA

Kasper, S Andrew
Waltham HS
Waltham, MA

Katz, Daniel
Sharon HS
Sharon, MA

Katz, Robert L
New Bedford HS
New Bedford, MA

Keamy, Matthew
Methuen HS
Methuen, MA

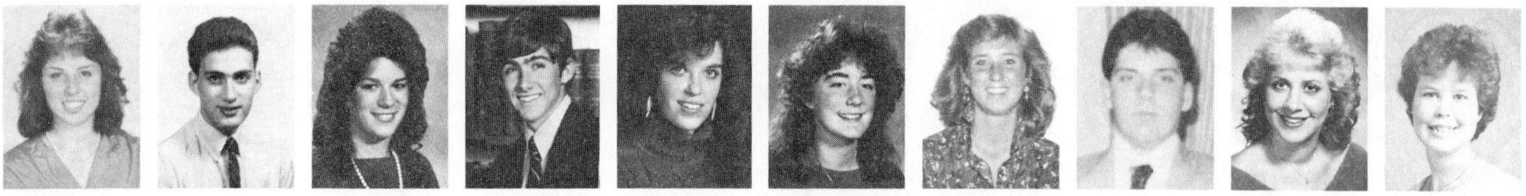

Keane, Mary Frances
Wakefield Memorial
Wakefield, MA

Keaney, Sean
North Quincy HS
Milton, MA

Kearns, Sharon
Marlboro HS
Marlboro, MA

Keeley, Matthew J
Tabor Acad
Tampa, FL

Kelley, Colleen
St Peter-Marion HS
Worcester, MA

Kelley, Jennifer
Arlington Catholic
Arlington, MA

Kelley, Maureen A
Westwood HS
Westwood, MA

Kelley, William
Milford HS
Milford, MA

Kelly, Amanda
Andover HS
Andover, MA

Kelly, Mary Teresa
Walpole HS
E Walpole, MA

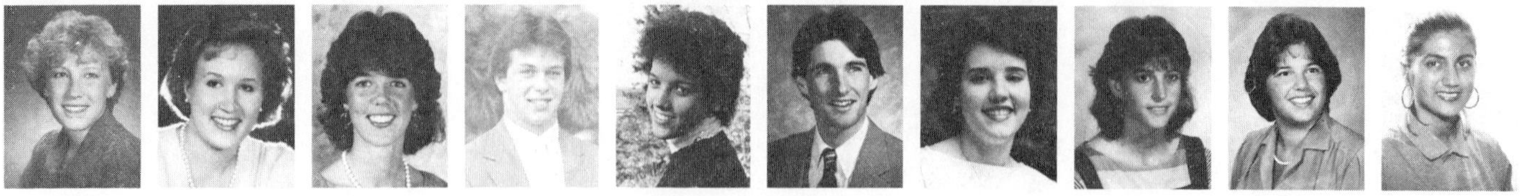

Kelly, Tracy
Bishop Feehan HS
Pawtucket, RI

Kemp, Kimberly
Lunenburg JR SR
Lunenburg, MA

Kench, Heather
St Marys Regional
Lynn, MA

Kenn, Robert
E Bridgewater HS
E Bridgewater, MA

Kennard, Donna M
Phillips Acad
St Albans, NY

Kennealy, Richard
Natick HS
Natick, MA

Kenny, Erin Marie
Thayer Acad
Milton, MA

Kerrigan, Shannon
Haverhill HS
Haverhill, MA

Khambaty, Murriam Jean
Gloucester HS
Gloucester, MA

Khatak, Nabeela
Mac Duffie Schl
S Hadley, MA

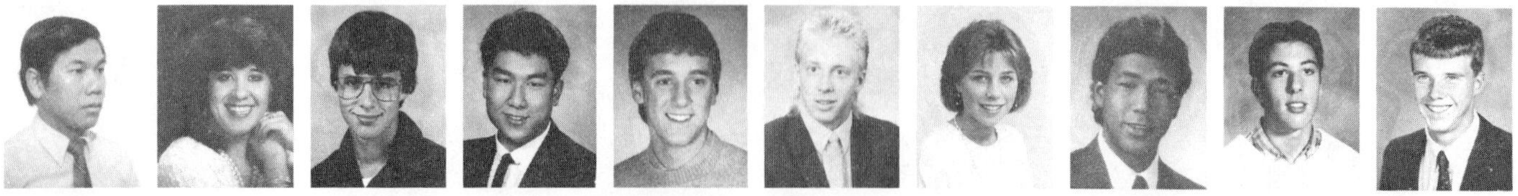

Khuc, Tan H
Somerville HS
Somerville, MA

Killizli, Mary
Boston Technical
Roslindale, MA

Kilmer, Charlie
Bourne HS
Pocasset, MA

Kim, Andrew D
Malden Catholic HS
Medford, MA

Kimbrough, M Scott
St Bernards Central Catholic HS
Ft Devens, MA

King, Edward A
Leominster HS
Leominster, MA

King, Kim
Frontier Regional
S Deerfield, MA

Kingman, Eamon R
East Bridgewater
East Bridgwater, MA

Kirwan, John M
Masconomet Regional HS
Middleton, MA

Kirwin, Jr James P
Wellesley SR HS
Wellesley, MA

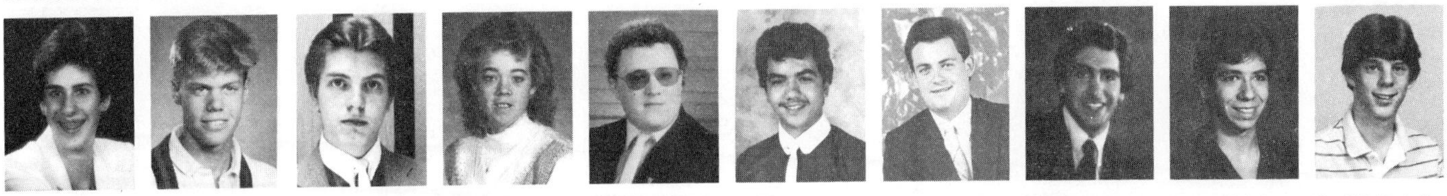

Kirwin, Laura Ann
Brainbree HS
Braintree, MA

Kline, Travis
Berkshire Schl
Hudson, NY

Knospins, Robert J
Boston Tech HS
Jamaica Plain, MA

Kociur, Joanne
Ware HS
Ware, MA

Kofton, Brandt
Brockton HS
Brockton, MA

Kolokithas, Demetrios
St Marys HS
Lynn, MA

Koloski, James M
Sandwich JR SR HS
E Sandwich, MA

Konowitz, Jeffrey Chip
Northfield Mt Hermon HS
Dover, DE

Kontos, Nicholas
Waltham HS
Waltham, MA

Kovalski, Kevin C
Smith Vocational Agricultural HS
Hatfield, MA

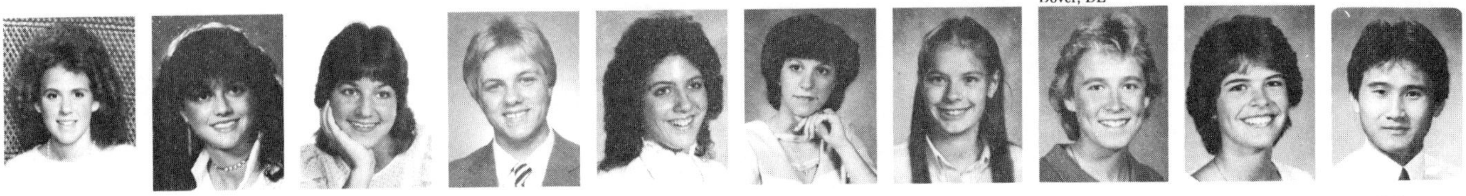

Kozlowski, Debra
Bartlett HS
Webster, MA

Kozuch, Karie
Fairhaven HS
Worcester, MA

Kruzewski, Tanya
Quaboag Regional
W Brookfield, MA

Krygowski, Tom
Marlborough HS
Marlboro, MA

Ksen, Denise
Quaboag Regional
W Warren, MA

Ksiazyk, Lori Ann
Medford HS
Medford, MA

Kulkkula, Jane E
Fitchburg HS
Fitchburg, MA

Kuta, Lisa
King Philip HS
Wrentham, MA

Kuza, Kathy
King Phillip Regional HS
Plainville, MA

Kwan, Hubert Shuman
Brookline HS
Brookline, MA

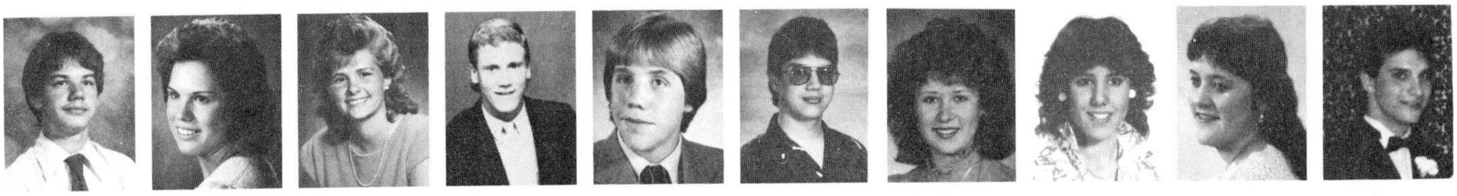

La Baire, William
Bartlett HS
Webster, MA

La Fland, Tracey
Our Lady Of Nazareth Acad
Methuen, MA

La Porte, Renee
Seekonk HS
Seekonk, MA

La Rochelle, Christopher
Sandwich HS
E Sandwich, MA

La Rochelle, Steven
Chicopee Comp HS
Chicopee, MA

La Verda, David
Pittsfield HS
Pittsfield, MA

Laberge, Amy
St Bernards HS
Lunenburg, MA

Lafleur, Jennifer
Walpole HS
E Walpole, MA

Lafontaine, Kimberly A
Drury SR HS
Clarksburg, MA

Laham, Bruce
Boston Technical
Boston, MA

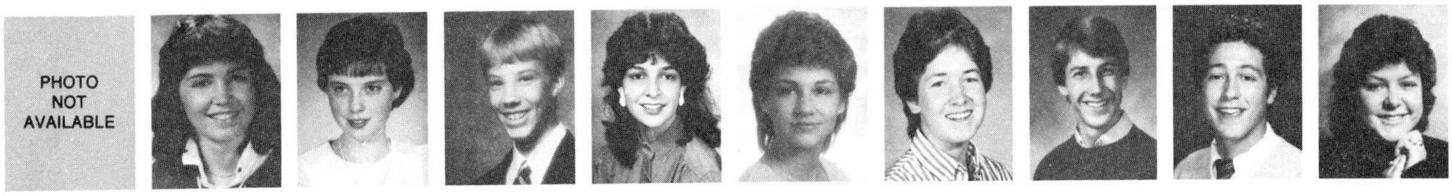
PHOTO
NOT
AVAILABLE

Lamarre, Denise
Mansfield HS
Mansfield, MA

Lambert, Donna
Bishop Connolly HS
Somerset, MA

Lambert, Kimberly A
Saint Bernards HS
Leominster, MA

Lamphier, John
Wakefield HS
Wakefield, MA

Lampros, Elena M
Lynn English HS
Lynn, MA

Lando, Diana
Watertown HS
Watertown, MA

Lang, Patricia
King Philip Regional HS
Norfolk, MA

Langille, Stephen
Taunton HS
Taunton, MA

Lanni, Keith Adam
North Attleboro HS
North Attleboro, MA

Lanucha, Susan
Easthampton HS
Easthampton, MA

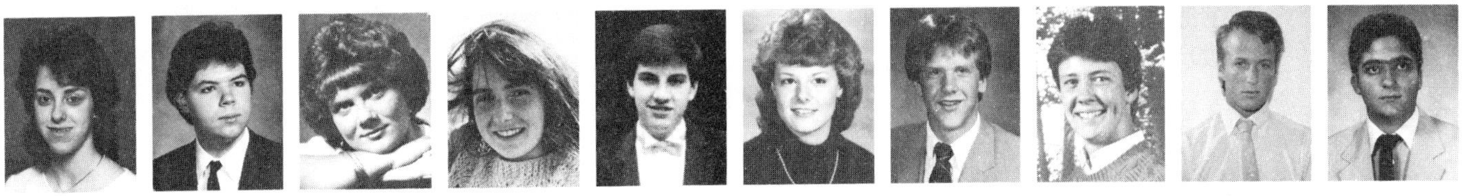

Lanzetta, Lisa
Attleboro HS
Attleboro, MA

Lara, Al
Central Catholic HS
Lawrence, MA

Lariviere, Cristie
Gardners HS
Gardner, MA

Lariviere, Kris
Barnstable HS
Hyannis, MA

Larkin, Bill
Bedford HS
Bedford, MA

Lashway, Deborah M
Hampshire Regional
Goshen, MA

Latch, Scott
Westford Acad
Westford, MA

Latham, Edward A
Sandwich HS
Sandwich, MA

Latham, William
Sandwich HS
Sandwich, MA

Lauletta, Anthony
Boston Latin Schl
Boston, MA

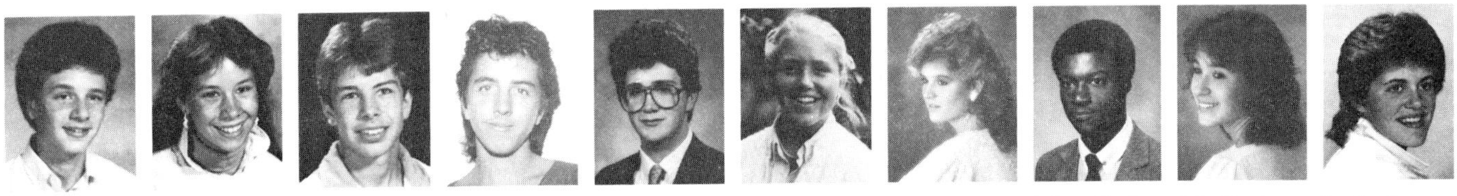

Lavan, Derek
Lynnfield HS
Lynnfield, MA

Le Bel, Kelly
Salem HS
Salem, MA

Le Blanc, III Raymond G
Salem HS
Salem, MA

Le May, Steven
Methuen HS
Methuen, MA

Le Noir, David A
Reading Memorial
Reading, MA

Le Roy, Elizabeth
Miss Halls Schl
Laconia, NH

Leboeuf, Melissa
Tantasqua HS
Southbridge, MA

Ledgister, Floyd
Randolph HS
Randolph, MA

Leduc, Pamela
Southbridge HS
Southbridge, MA

Lee, Brenda
Easthampton HS
Easthampton, MA

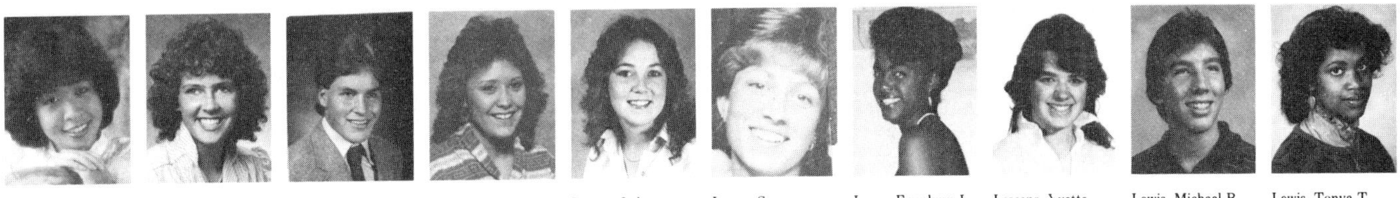

Lee, Linda T
Brookline HS
Cupertino, CA

Leinomen, Charlene M
David Prouty HS
Spencer, MA

Leistritz, Michael
Holy Name Central Catholic HS
Worcester, MA

Lemaire, Laurie
Mc Cann Tech Voc
Clarksburg, MA

Lemar, Jody
Westport HS
Westport, MA

Leone, Suzanne
Natick HS
Natick, MA

Leroy, Emmlynn L
North Cambridge Catholic HS
Somerville, MA

Lescano, Yvette
Matignon HS
Cambridge, MA

Lewis, Michael R
Burlington HS
Burlington, MA

Lewis, Tonya T
Boston Latin Acad
Dorchester, MA

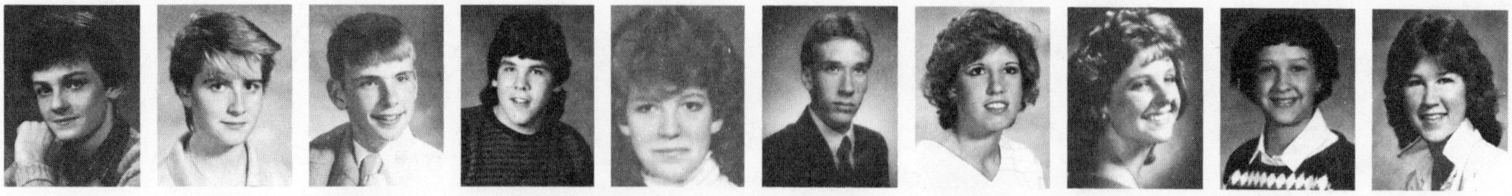

Lichoulas, Theodore
Reading Memorial
Reading, MA

Licht, Jennifer
Wellesley SR HS
Wellesley, MA

Liljegren, Erik K
Shawsheen Valley
Voc Tech HS
Tewksbury, MA

Linberg, Gregory
Fairhaven HS
Fairhaven, MA

Linde, Laura
Hanover HS
Hanover, MA

Lingerman, Eric
Newburyport HS
Newburyport, MA

Linker, Deborah
Athol HS
Athol, MA

Linscott, Julie
Newburyport HS
Newburyport, MA

Lis, Jennifer
Ware HS
Ware, MA

Litchfield, Brenda
Burncoat SR HS
Worcester, MA

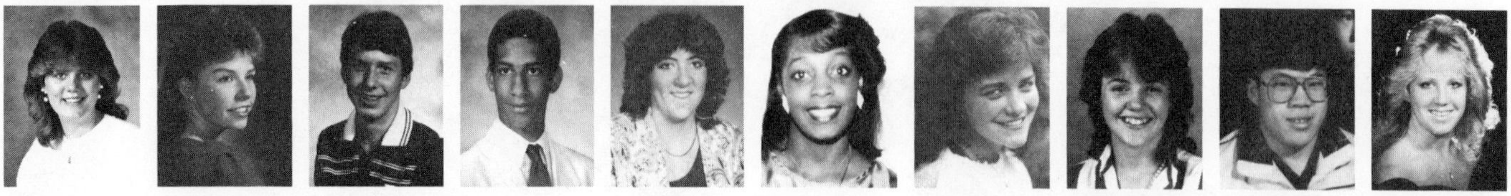

Litherland, Shannon
Monument
Mountain Regiona
Housatonic, MA

Livingston, Loree
Lynn Classical HS
Lynn, MA

Llewelyn, Frederick
G
Pioneer Valley
Regional HS
Northfield, MA

Lloyd, Glynn T
Sharon HS
Sharon, MA

Lobo, Paula
Shepherd Hill
Regional HS
Dudley, MA

Lodge, Sherra
Hyde Park HS
Dorchester, MA

Logan, Keri
Bishop Feehan HS
Attleboro, MA

Long, Deborah
Bourne HS
Buzzards Bay, MA

Louie, Derek
Norwood SR HS
Norwood, MA

Lovellette, Shelli
Taconic HS
Pittsfield, MA

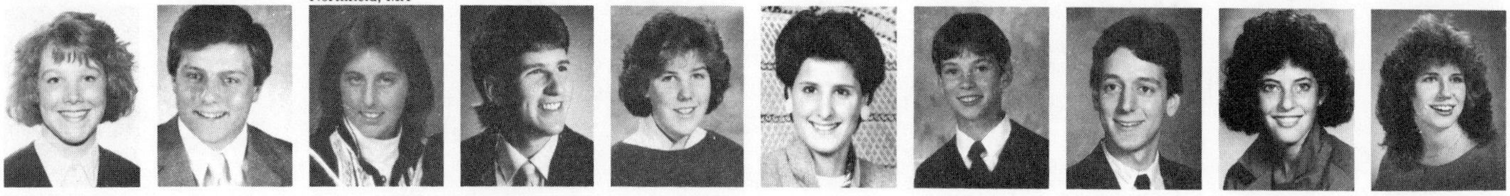

Lowenhagen, Tracy
Cohasset SR HS
Cohasset, MA

Lubold, Mark
Holyoke HS
Holyoke, MA

Lumpkin, Deborah
Sandwich JR SR HS
East Sandwich, MA

Lunardini, Matthew
Chicopee
Comprehensive HS
Chicopee, MA

Lyle, Ann
Hampshire Regional
Southampton, MA

Lyonnais, Nicole
Old Rochester.
Regional HS
Mattapoisett, MA

Lyons, John
Boston Latin HS
Boston, MA

Lyons, Michael
Central Catholic HS
Lowell, MA

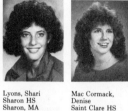

Lyons, Shari
Sharon HS
Sharon, MA

Mac Cormack,
Denise
Saint Clare HS
Boston, MA

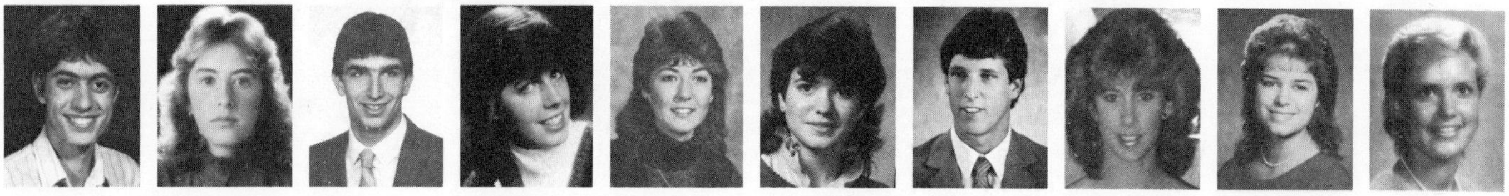

Mac Donald,
Christopher
Revere HS
Revere, MA

Mac Donald,
Deborah Lynn
Braintree HS
Braintree, MA

Mac Donald,
Stephen J
St Patricks HS
Waltham, MA

Mac Dougall, Kelley
Marshfield HS
Marshfield, MA

Mac Gregor, Dawn
Medway JR SR HS
Medway, MA

Mac Innis, Margaret
Holy Name CC HS
Douglas, MA

Mac Kay, Robert D
Hopkins Acad
Hadley, MA

Mac Leod, Kristen
Holyoke Catholic
Easthampton, MA

Macdonald, Melinda
Wakefield HS
Wakefield, MA

Maceachern, June
Mt St Joseph Acad
Boston, MA

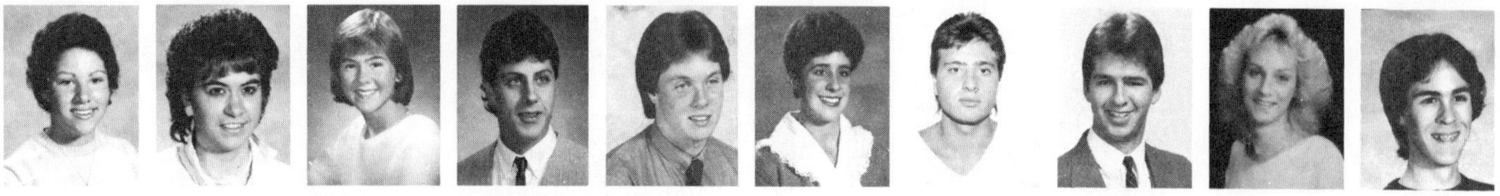

Macero, Jean Marie
St Clement HS
W Somerville, MA

Machnik, Michele
Presentation Of
Mary Acad
Salem, NH

Mackinnon, Lori
Bishop Feehan HS
Walpole, MA

Macrina, Richard C
Oliver Ames HS
S Easton, MA

Maddock, Thomas
More
Berkshire Schl
Camillus, NY

Madigan, Erin
Dover-Sherborn
Sherborn, MA

Maffeo, Anthony
East Boston HS
E Boston, MA

Mahoney, Gerald J
Cardinal Spellman
Brockton, MA

Makowski, Lisa
Greater Lawrence
Technical HS
N Andover, MA

Mallory, Michael
Quaboag Regional
Warren, MA

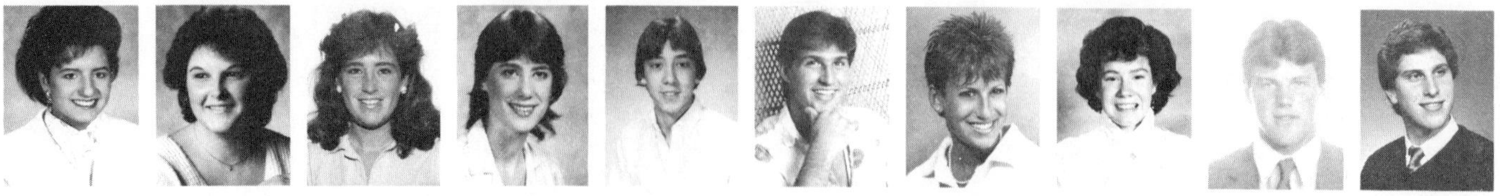

Maloney, Deborah
Ursuline Acad
Dedham, MA

Mann, Kim Marie
Oxford HS
Oxford, MA

Manning, Susan
Hingham HS
Hingham, MA

Mantelli, Lynn
Shepherd Hill
Regional HS
Dudley, MA

Marchessault, Scott
New Bedford HS
New Bedford, MA

Marciano, James
Westfield HS
Westfield, MA

Marcus, Greta
Randolph HS
Randolph, MA

Marescalchi, Cindi
Beverly HS
Beverly, MA

Marggraf, Jeffrey P
Central Catholic HS
Methuen, MA

Margolis, Gary J
Sharon HS
Sharon, MA

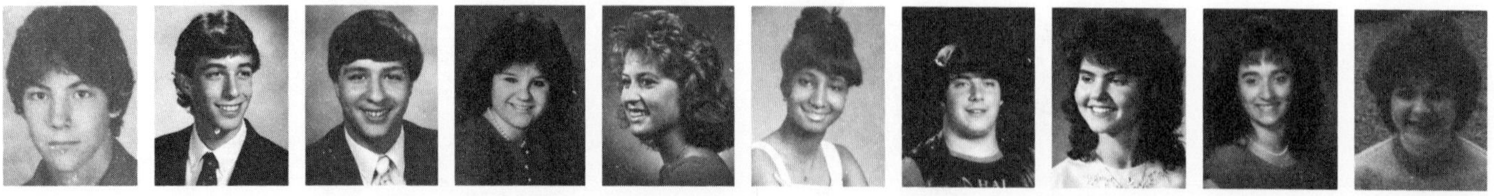

Markey, Glen G
Rockland HS
Rockland, MA

Marmer, Mark
Andover HS
Andover, MA

Marrone, Philip
Malden Catholic HS
Everett, MA

Martin, Darlene
New Bedford HS
New Bedford, MA

Martin, Maryanne C
Foxboro HS
Foxboro, MA

Martinez, Elizabeth
O
St Gregory HS
Dorchester, MA

Martinoli, II Bill
Haverhill HS
Methuen, MA

Martins, Luiza
Ludlow HS
Ludlow, MA

Martins, Sandra
B M C Dufee HS
Fall River, MA

Masciarelli, Lisa
Medford HS
Medford, MA

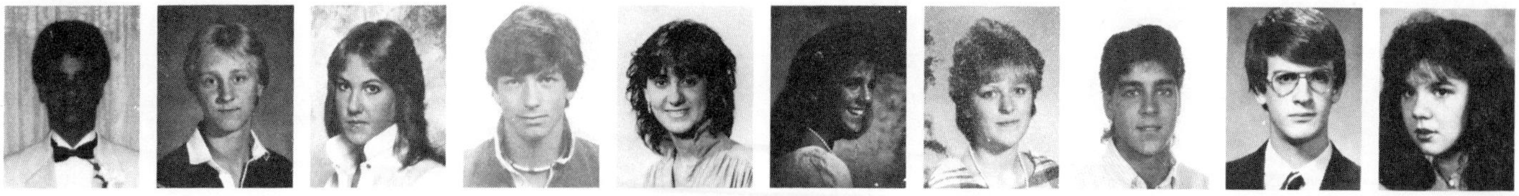

Massa, Neil
Winthrop HS
Winthrop, MA

Massicotte, Mark
Shepherd Hill
Regional HS
Dudley, MA

Masson, Laurie
Marian HS
Holliston, MA

Mastin, IV
Theodore H
Dennis-Yarmouth
Regional HS
East Dennis, MA

Matos, Milena
New Bedford HS
New Bedford, MA

Matrundola,
Jennifer
Winchester HS
Winchester, MA

Matson, Caroline
North Middlesex
Regional HS
Townsend, MA

Mauceri, David
North Reading HS
N Reading, MA

Mauger, David J
Wayland HS
Wayland, MA

Maxwell, Kimberly
A
Natick HS
Natick, MA

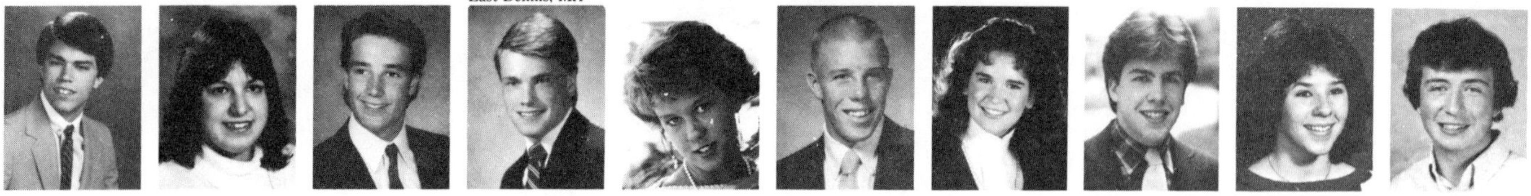

Maynard, James M
Brockton HS
Brockton, MA

Maziarz, Christine
Ludlow HS
Ludlow, MA

Mc Auley, Jr Daniel
Medford HS
Medford, MA

Mc Carthy, John D
Boston College HS
Scituate, MA

Mc Carthy, Kristen
Duxbury HS
Duxbury, MA

Mc Carthy, Michael
W
Taunton HS
Taunton, MA

Mc Cook, Noel
Wilbraham &
Monson Acad
Springfield, MA

Mc Donald, Gregory
Northfield Mt
Herman Schl
Boston, MA

Mc Gann, Sheila
Waltham HS
Boston, MA

Mc Gathey, James
Hingham HS
Hingham, MA

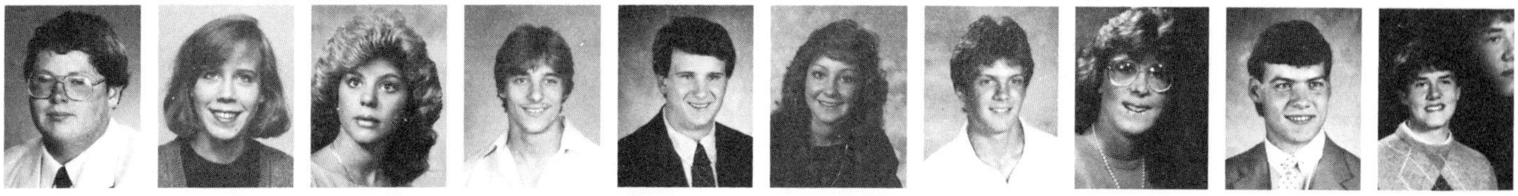

Mc Gonagle,
Michael D
Sandwich JR SR HS
Sandwich, MA

Mc Guirk, Lynda
Leominster HS
Leominster, MA

Mc Innis, Kelli Ann
South High
Community Schl
Worcester, MA

Mc Intyre, John D
Fitchburg HS
Fitchburg, MA

Mc Kay, Scott
Wilbraham &
Monson Acad
Shutesbury, MA

Mc Kinnon, Monica
M
Stoughton HS
Stoughton, MA

Mc Kinnon,
Timothy
Belchertown HS
Belchertown, MA

Mc Laughlin,
Christine
Tridon Regional HS
Salisbury, MA

Mc Lean, Scott
Chicopee
Comprehensive HS
Chicopee, MA

Mc Millan, Greg
Maynard HS
Maynard, MA

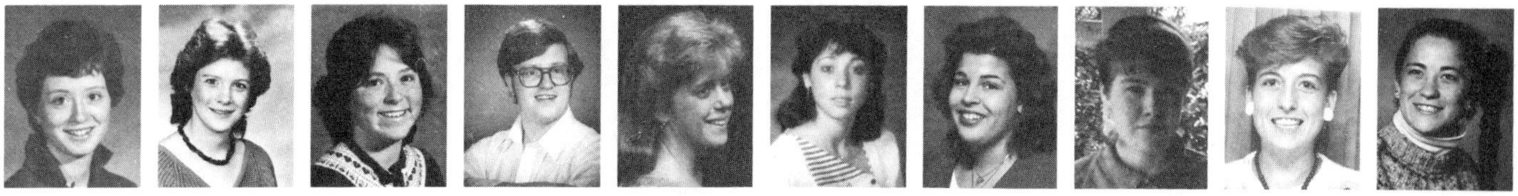

Mc Millan,
Wednesday
Mansfield HS
Mansfield, MA

Mc Nall, Heather L
Leominster HS
Leominster, MA

Mc Neely, Dawn
Plymouth-Carver
Plymouth, MA

Meador, III Thomas
D
Montachusett
Regional Vo Tec
Gardner, MA

Medailleu, Karen
Walpole HS
Walpole, MA

Medeiros, Raquel
B M C Durfee HS
Fall River, MA

Medugno, Jeanette
Girls Catholic HS
Malden, MA

Meegan, Joanne
Boston Latin Acad
Roslindale, MA

Meeker, Ann Marie
Wilmington HS
Wilmington, MA

Mello, Janis
Greater New
Bedford Regiona
New Bedford, MA

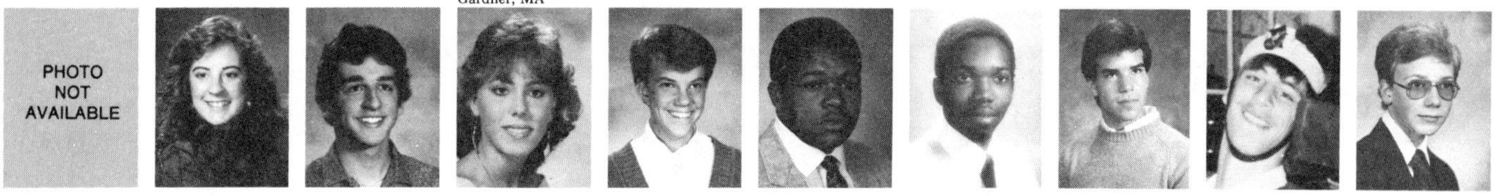

Mendelson, Kim G
Brookline HS
Brookline, MA

Mendes, Stephanie
Somerset HS
Somerset, MA

Mendonca, Edward
St Josephs Regional
Lowell, MA

Meredith, Deirdre
Bishop Stang HS
New Bedford, MA

Merrigan, Maribeth
Notre Dame
Milton, MA

Merrilles, Anthony
Randolph HS
Randolph, MA

Messam, Conrad
Hyde Park HS
Mattapan, MA

Metcalf, Robert
Salem HS
Salem, MA

Metro, Wesley
Newton North HS
Newton, MA

Miarecki, Paul
Palmer HS
Palmer, MA

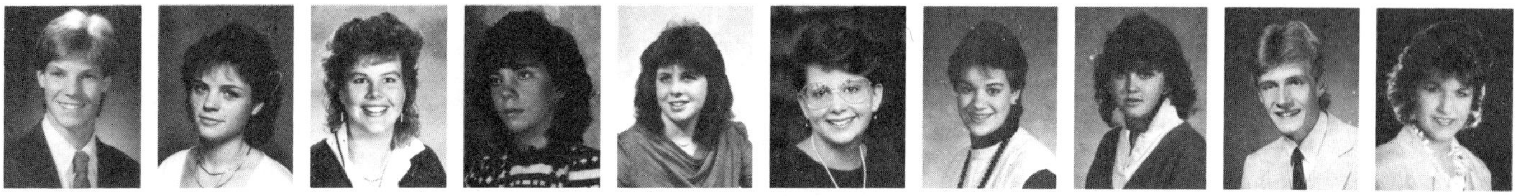

Michalewich,
Richard
Bishop Connolly HS
Somerset, MA

Middleton, Jane
Marian HS
Holliston, MA

Miller, Tara
Presentation Of
Mary Acad
Haverhill, MA

Millett, Martha
Academy Of Notre
Tewksbury, MA

Milner, Julie
Plymouth Carver
Plymouth, MA

Minasian, Lynn
St Mary HS
Haverhill, MA

Mirabile, Carmen
Ware HS
Ware, MA

Mitchell, Dina
Tantasqua Regional
Sturbridge, MA

Mitchell, John J
Archbishop Williams
Quincy, MA

Mokrzycki, Kerry J
West Springfield SR
W Springfield, MA

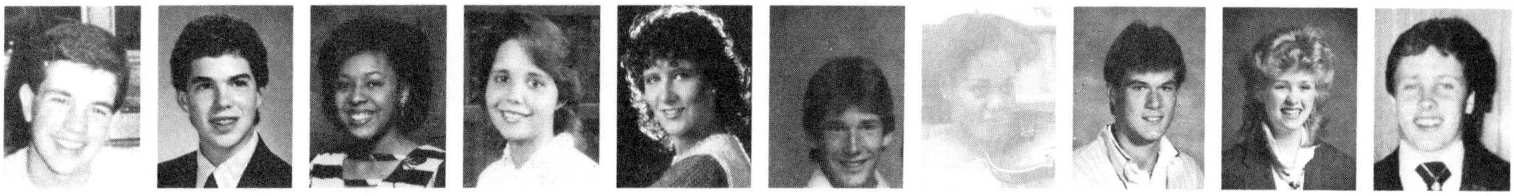

Monahan, Jr Josepn
M
Cathedral HS
Longmeadow, MA

Montanari, Michael
A
Wellesley SR HS
Wellesley, MA

Monteiro, Catarina
Boston Latin Acad
Roxbury, MA

Monteiro, Etelvina
St Gregory HS
Hyde Park, MA

Montesi, Michelle
Agawam HS
Feeding Hills, MA

Montgomery, Thos
Winthrop HS
Winthrop, MA

Moody, Karen L
Madison Park HS
Boston, MA

Moore, Scott B
Nauset Regional HS
East Dennis, MA

Moore, Valerie
Pittsfield HS
Pittsfield, MA

Moorehouse, John
Lynn Classical HS
Lynn, MA

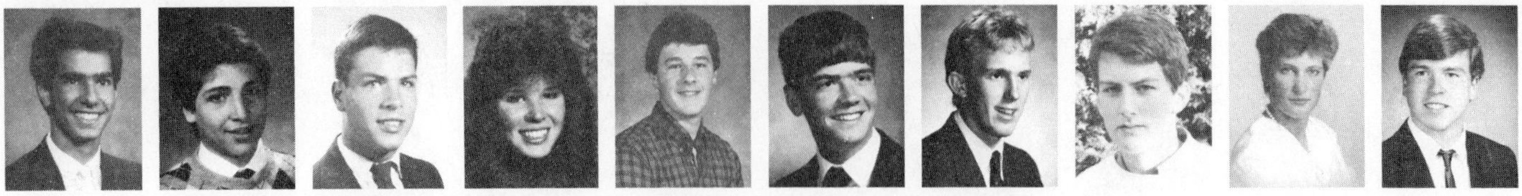

Mootafian, Stephen H
Peabody Veterans Memorial HS
Peabody, MA

Morad, Stephen S
Don Bosco Tech
Quincy, MA

Moran, Stephen W
Canton HS
Canton, MA

Moriarty, Kara
Westfield HS
Westfield, MA

Moriarty, Jr Michael J
Ware HS
Ware, MA

Moriarty, Thomas M
Quabbin Regional JRSR HS
Gilbertville, MA

Morin, Paul A
Westfield HS
Westfield, MA

Morris, Anthony
Concord Acad
Concord, MA

Morris, Jennifer
Dennis-Yarmouth Regional HS
W Yarmouth, MA

Morris, Kenneth J
Oakmont Regional
Westminster, MA

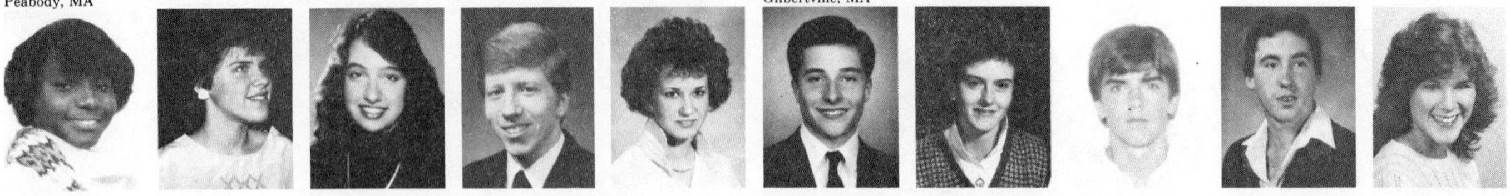

Morrison, Joy C M
Hyde Park HS
Dorchester, MA

Morse, Kerri
Academy Of Notre
Westford, MA

Moscaritolo, Kara
Melrose HS
Melrose, MA

Mularella, Glen
Gardner HS
Gardner, MA

Mull, Kim
Old Colony Reg Vo Tech HS
Rochester, MA

Mullaney, Stephen
St Bernards Central Catholic HS
Leominster, MA

Mulligan, Kristen
Fontbonne Acad
Hyde Park, MA

Mulligan, Richard
Westwood HS
Westwood, MA

Munro, Jr John C
Gloucester HS
Gloucester, MA

Murphy, Maureen
Silver Lake Regional
Plympton, MA

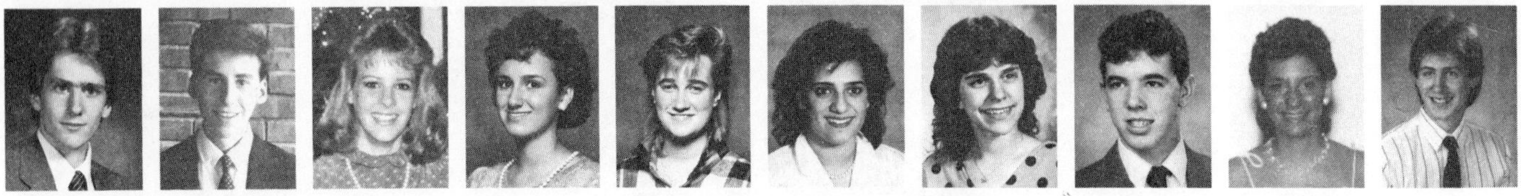

Murphy, Robert A
Austin Preparatory
Medford, MA

Murphy, Sean
Concord-Carlisle HS
Carlisle, MA

Murray, Marlene
Hingham HS
Hingham, MA

Nader, Kim
Our Lady Of Nazareth Acad
Andover, MA

Nahil, Kaitlin
Our Lady Of Nazareth Acad
North Andover, MA

Najjar, Deborah M
Westwood HS
Westwood, MA

Nardi, Kim
Agawam HS
Feeding Hills, MA

Nardone, Mark A
Lynn English HS
Lynn, MA

Natale, Danielle
West Roxbury HS
Roslindale, MA

Natale, William
Somerville HS
Somerville, MA

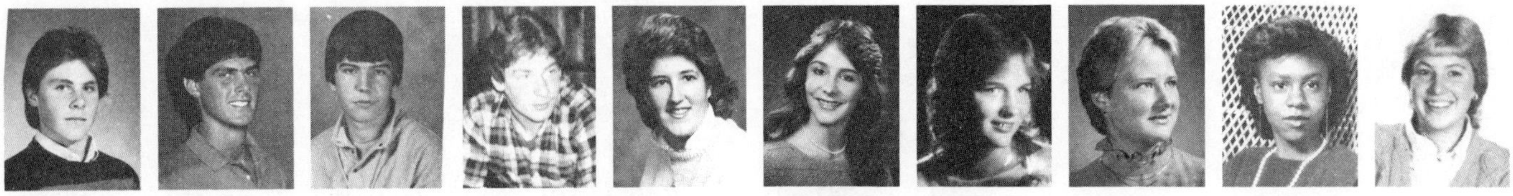

Nawn, Christopher D
Arlinton HS
Arlington, MA

Nelson, Brian
Bishop Feehan HS
Plainville, MA

Nelson, Brian D
East Bridgewater
East Bridgewater, MA

Nelson, Christopher
Natick HS
Natick, MA

Nelson, Deborah Lee
Holy Name C C HS
Worcester, MA

Nelson, Karen
King Philip HS
Plainville, MA

Nesbitt, Caitlin
Classical HS
Springfield, MA

Neuber, Susan
Walpole HS
Walpole, MA

Neville, Sheila M
Wayland HS
Roxbury, MA

Newbegin, Tracey
Dracut HS
Dracut, MA

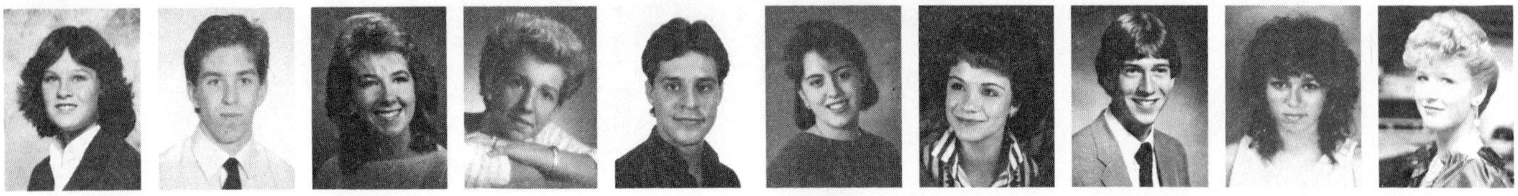

Newton, Sheryl
Cardinal Spellman
Hanson, MA

Neylon, Joseph
Saint Clement HS
Somerville, MA

Niebrzydowski, Susan L
Peabody Vets Mem
Peabody, MA

Nieuwenhoff, Cindy
Trantasqua Regional
Brookfield, MA

Nikolopoulos, Chris
Boston Latin Acad
Roslindale, MA

Noel, Deborah
Medford HS
Medford, MA

Noga, Christine S
Chicopee HS
Chicopee, MA

Nooonan, Todd M
N Andover HS
N Andover, MA

Normandin, Melody
Bishop Connolly HS
Somerset, MA

Norris, Pam
Melrose HS
Melrose, MA

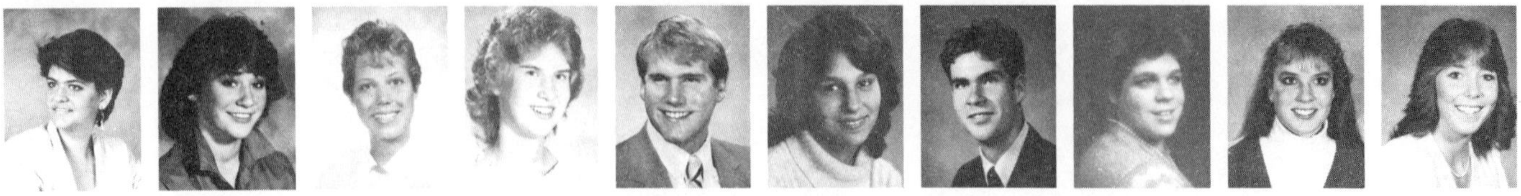

Northrop, Beth
Monument Mountain HS
Gt Barrington, MA

Norton, Danielle
Bartlett HS
Webster, MA

Norton, Kristine
Apponequet Regional HS
Assonet, MA

Novak, Pamela
Presentation Of Mary Acad
Methuen, MA

Noyes, Douglas Evan
Tewksbury Memorial HS
Tewksbury, MA

Nuttall-Vazquez, Kim Hellaine
Newton North HS
Newton, MA

O Brien, Daniel G
Hudson Catholic HS
Hudson, MA

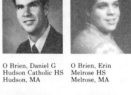

O Brien, Erin
Melrose HS
Melrose, MA

O Brien, Jennifer
Ursuline Acad
Norwood, MA

O Brien, Judyane M
King Philip Regional HS
Norfolk, MA

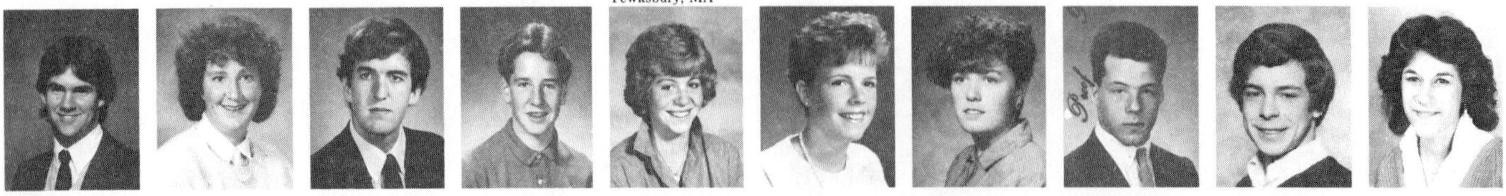

O Brien, Michael C
Hudson Catholic HS
Hudson, MA

O Brien, Michelle A
Boston Latin HS
West Roxbury, MA

O Brien, Sean M
Wellesley HS
Wellesley, MA

O Brien, Thomas M
Boston College HS
Braintree, MA

O Connell, Deirdre
Lynnfield HS
Lynnfield, MA

O Connell, Kristin
Notre Dame Acad
Norwell, MA

O Donnell, Julie
Msgr Ryan Memorial HS
Dorchester, MA

O Donnell, Paul
Milton HS
Milton, MA

O Neil, Christopher W
Bishop Feehan HS
Mansfield, MA

O Shea, Erin
Norton HS
Norton, MA

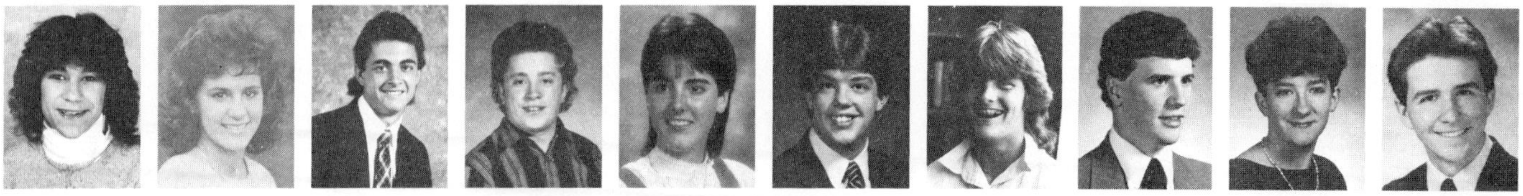

O Shea, Kelly
Norton HS
Norton, MA

Oconnell, Pamela
Haverhill HS
Haverhill, MA

Ohear, Kevin J
Sandwich HS
E Sandwich, MA

Olson, James J
Randolph HS
Randolph, MA

Omalley, Mary
Mt St Joseph Acad
Boston, MA

Orrall, Norman
Appohequet
Regional HS
Lakeville, MA

Ostroskey, Karen
Uxbridge HS
Uxbridge, MA

Ouellette, Eric G
Wilmington HS
Wilmington, MA

Ouellette, Julie
Marblehead HS
Marblehead, MA

Ouellette, Robert
Bishop Connolly HS
Westport, MA

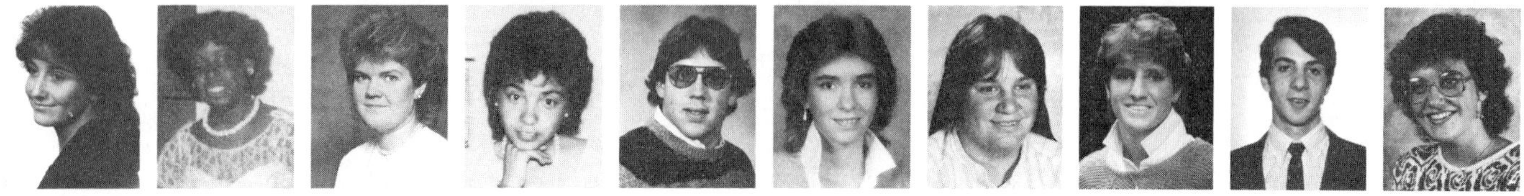

Owczarski, Christina
Mac Duffie Schl For
Agawam, MA

Owens, Martha
Jeremiah E Burke
Dorchester, MA

Pacewicz, Heidi
Cardinal Spellman
Brockton, MA

Pagan, Hilda Maria
Hayoke HS
Holyoke, MA

Pagliuca, David
Taunton HS
Taunton, MA

Pagnotta, Paula
Brockton Christian
Reginal HS
Brockton, MA

Paige, Kellie
Bedford HS
Bedford, MA

Pailes, Ann Marie
Triton Regional HS
Rowley, MA

Papagiannis, Dino
Belmont HS
Belmont, MA

Papleacos, Maria
Notre Dame Acad
Tewksbury, MA

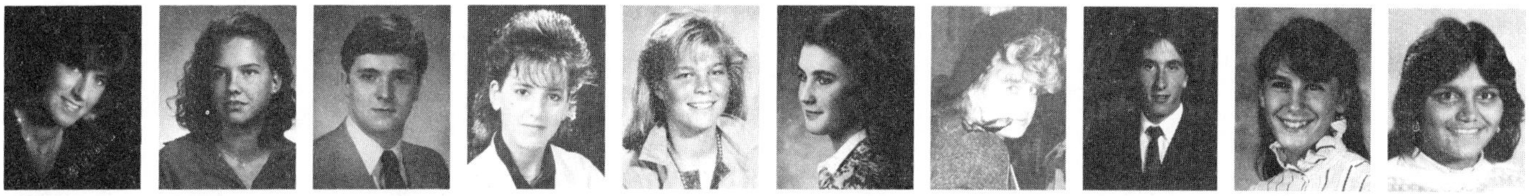

Pappathanasi, Kym
Swampscott HS
Swampscott, MA

Paquette, Danielle
Marblehead HS
Marblehead, MA

Parent, Albert
New Bedford HS
New Bedford, MA

Paris, Deborah A
Fitchburg HS
Fitchburg, MA

Parker, Alyssa Beth
Winchester HS
Winchester, MA

Partenheimer, Ann
M
Leicester HS
Leicester, MA

Partyka, Melanie
Williston
Northampton Schl
Chicopee, MA

Pasciuto, Paul
Winchester HS
Winchester, MA

Pastorello, Theresa
Our Lady Of
Nazareth HS
Saugus, MA

Patel, Pratiksha
Wachusett Regional
Holden, MA

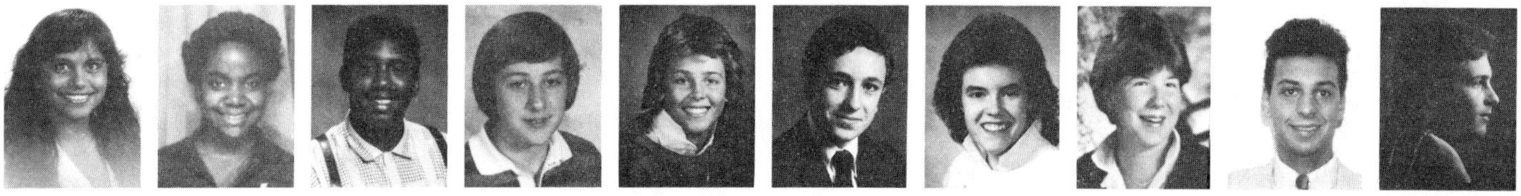

Patel, Vibha
Braintree HS
Braintree, MA

Patterson, Natalie
Phillips Acad
Chicago, IL

Patton, Clarence
Middlesex Schl
Ithaca, NY

Pavao, Joseph
Winchester HS
Winchester, MA

Pawlik, Patricia
Presentation Of
Mary Acad
No Andover, MA

Peachey, John
Westbridge HS
Littleton, MA

Pelletier, Jill E
Salem HS
Salem, MA

Peloquin, Tina
Marie
Easthampton HS
Easthampton, MA

Penta, Pasquale
Medford HS
Medford, MA

Pepka, David
Bartlett HS
Webster, MA

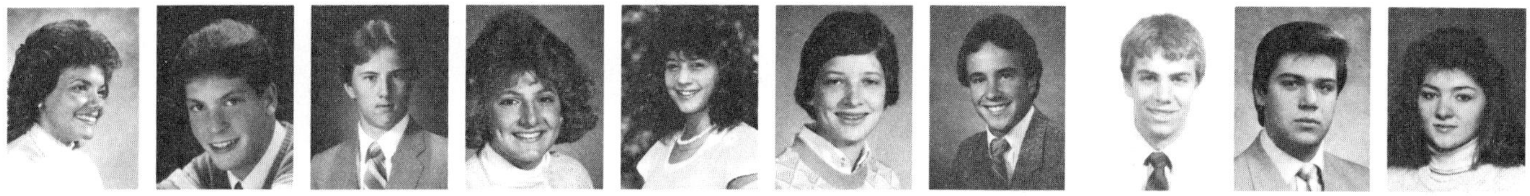

Pergakis, Nicole
Westford Acad
Westford, MA

Perillo, Paul
Everett HS
Everett, MA

Perry, Kevin A
Bridgewater
Rayham Regiona
Bridgewater, MA

Perry, Tamatha
Shepherd Hill
Regional HS
Dudley, MA

Persuitte, Karen
Montachusett
Regional Vo-Tec
Fitchburg, MA

Peters, Marie
Tantasqua Regional
SR HS
Brimfield, MA

Peterson, Thomas A
Shrewesbury SR HS
Shrewsbury, MA

Peto, Jeffrey
Clinton HS
Clinton, MA

Petruccelli, Richard
St Dominics Savio
E Boston, MA

Petruzziello, Iva
Saint Clare HS
Dedham, MA

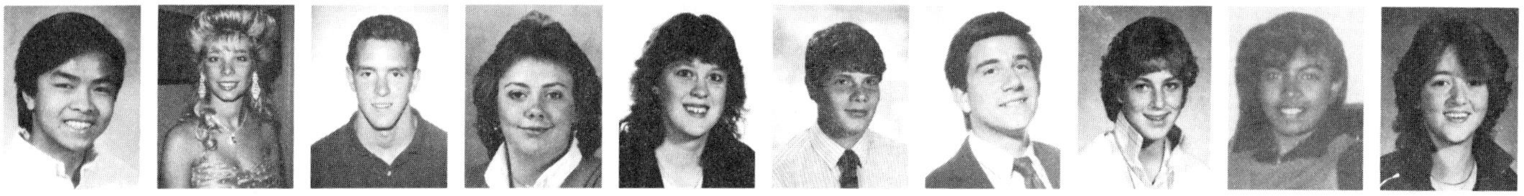

Pham, Son
Dedham HS
Dedham, MA

Phelan, Jacquelyn
Mount Alvernia HS
Roslindale, MA

Phelan, James
North Quincy HS
Quincy, MA

Phetteplace, Judith
Stoughton HS
Stoughton, MA

Phetteplace, Laura
Westfield HS
Westfield, MA

Pierce, Darren
Amherst Regional
Amherst, MA

Pierre, Michael
St Johns Prep Schl
Prides Crossing, MA

Pignatare, Judith N
Agawam HS
Agawam, MA

Pinet, Lillian
Madison Park HS
Boston, MA

Piteo, Marcy Ann
East Longmeadow
E Longmeadow, MA

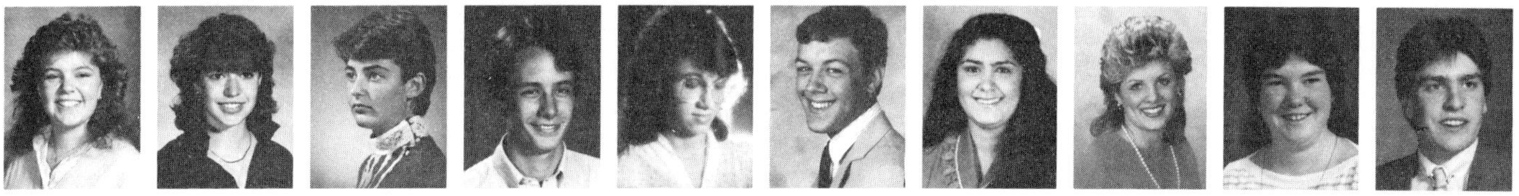

Pizziconi, Melissa
Leominster HS
Leominster, MA

Plunkett, Beth
Wellesley HS
Wellesley, MA

Plunkett, Mary
Wellesley HS
Wellesley, MA

Plutnicki, Paul
Marlboro HS
Marlboro, MA

Podosek, Paula Jean
Cathedral HS
Ludlow, MA

Pomeroy, Robert D
Manchester JR SR
Manchester, MA

Popat, Alka
Norton HS
Norton, MA

Porcaro, Paula J
Medford HS
Medford, MA

Pottle, Jennifer
Lynn
Blackstone Valley
Reg Vo Tech
Milford, MA

Potvin, Alan
Central Catholic HS
Lawrence, MA

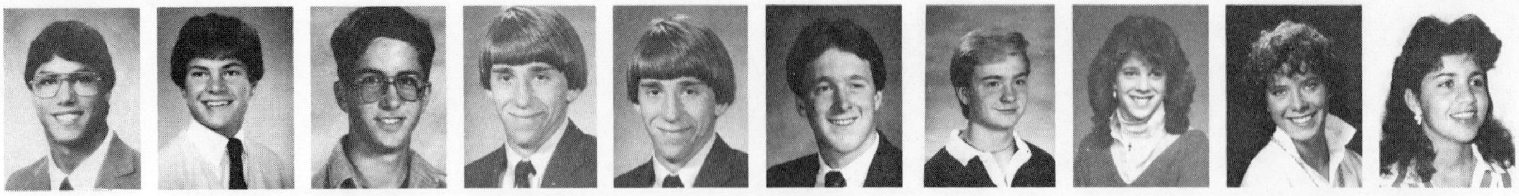

Potvin, Andrew F
Drury SR HS
North Adams, MA

Powell, Michael
Monument
Mountain Regiona
Gt Barrington, MA

Powell, Steven
Georgetown JR SR
Georgetown, MA

Power, Sandra
Salem HS
Salem, MA

Powers, Brian
Taunton HS
Taunton, MA

Powers, Craig R
North Brookfield
N Brookfield, MA

Pralinsky, Scott D
Athol HS
Athol, MA

Pratt, Gayle
Natick HS
Natick, MA

Prescott, Elizabeth
Franklin HS
Franklin, MA

Press, Sue
Hudson HS
Hudson, MA

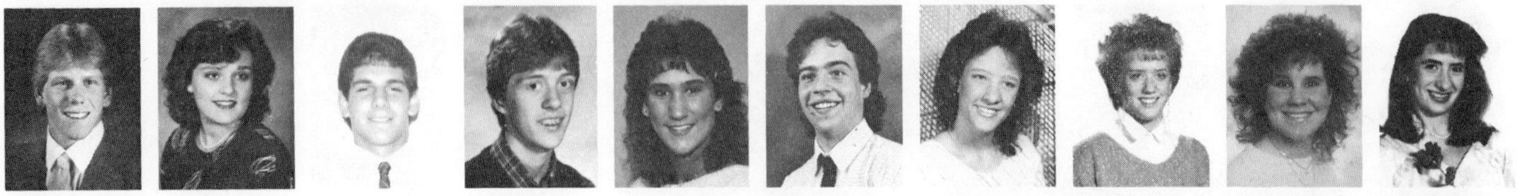

Preston, David J
Belchertown HS
Belchertown, MA

Previte, Gail
Kristina
Matignon HS
Lexington, MA

Proia, Mark M
Attleboro HS
Attleboro, MA

Proulx, Christopher
Southbridge HS
Southbridge, MA

Puglielli, Lisa
Waltham HS
Waltham, MA

Purcell, Glenn
Marianhill HS
Southbridge, MA

Pysczynski, Linda
Bedford HS
Bedford, MA

Quigley, Denise
Westwood HS
Westwood, MA

Quinlan, Colleen
Matignon HS
Somerville, MA

Quintiliani, Dawn
Matignon HS
Watertown, MA

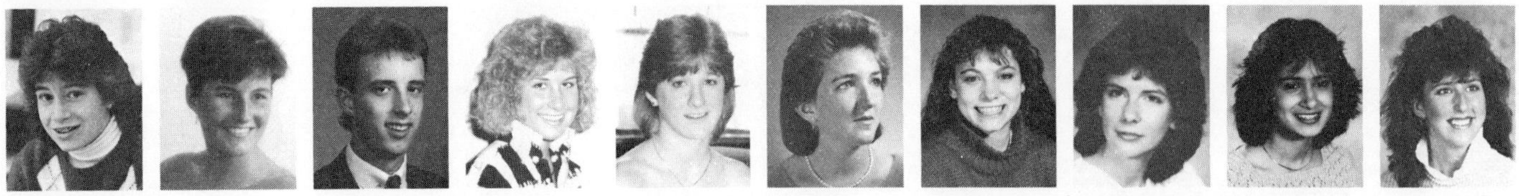

Quirk, Jenifer
Lunenburg HS
Lunenburg, MA

Quirk, Kristin A
Belmont HS
Belmont, MA

Racicot, Mark
Bartlett HS
Webster, MA

Raczkowski, Amy
Tantasqua Regional
Sturbridge, MA

Radula, Sandra J
South High
Community Schl
Worcester, MA

Raffoni, Cynthia
St Clare HS
Roslindale, MA

Rainville, Crystal
Attleboro HS
Attleboro, MA

Rajaniemi, Sherry
Lynn
Murdock HS
Winchendon, MA

Rao, Varsha
Framingham South
Framingham, MA

Rauscher, Heidi
Monument
Mountain Regiona
Glendale, MA

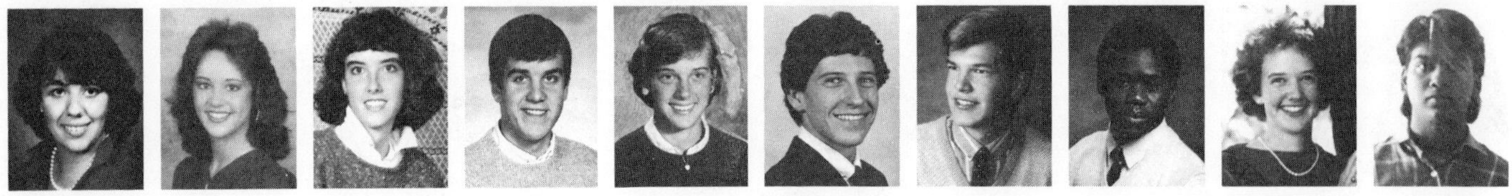

Rawding, Bridget
Haverhill HS
Ward Hill, MA

Raynard, Yvonne
Eastbridgewater HS
E Bridgewater, MA

Reardon, Amy
Old Rochester
Regional HS
Marion, MA

Reardon, John C
Walpole HS
Walpole, MA

Reece, Charlotte
Winchester HS
Winchester, MA

Regan, III Richard
P
Old Rochester
Regional HS
Mattapoisett, MA

Rego, James R
New Bedford HS
New Bedford, MA

Reid, Romeo
Boston Latin HS
Mattapan, MA

Reidy, Susan E
Notre Dame Acad
Shrewsbury, MA

Rekula, Venkat
Marlboro HS
Marlboro, MA

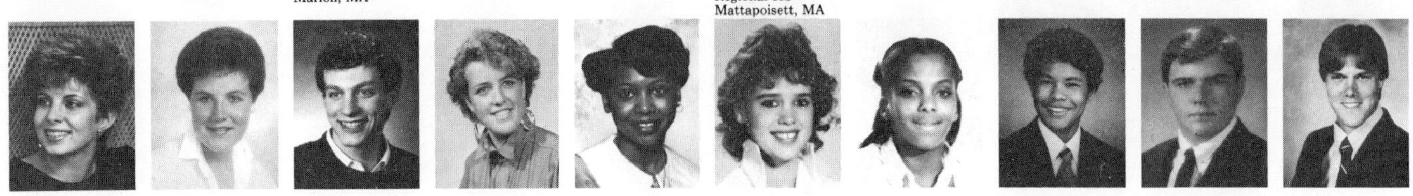

Renihan, Lauren M
Shrewsbury HS
Shrewsbury, MA

Reynolds, Tracy A
Mt Saint Joseph
Brighton, MA

Rezendes, Chris
BMC Durfee HS
Fall River, MA

Ribeiro, Juraci
New Bedford HS
New Bedford, MA

Rice, Letitia
Boston Latin Acad
Mattapan, MA

Richards, Wendy
David Hale Fanning
Trade HS
Worcester, MA

Richardson, Ami
Fontbonne Acad
Hyde Park, MA

Richardson, Stephen
Kye
Ayer HS
Shirley, MA

Richardson, Steven
Hull HS
Hull, MA

Rieke, Neil
Lee HS
Lee, MA

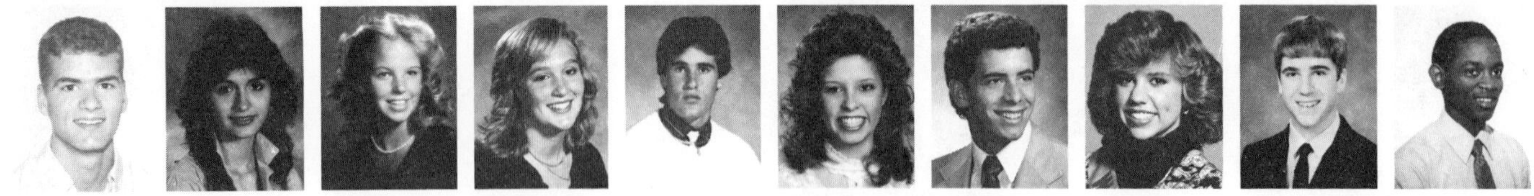

Riel, Matthew
Hampshire Regional
Southampton, MA

Rigney, Rachel
Fanning Trade HS
Worcester, MA

Rihm, Noel N
Minnecdhaug
Regional HS
Wilbraham, MA

Riley, Sandra
Winchester HS
Winchester, MA

Ripley, Ralph E
Wareham HS
Wareham, MA

Riutankoski,
Maureen S
Fitchburg HS
Fitchburg, MA

Rivela, Steve
Woburn SR HS
Woburn, MA

Roberts, Amy
Westford Acad
Westford, MA

Roberts, William M
Acton-Boxborough
Regional HS
Acton, MA

Robinson, Mark
Greater Boston
Milton, MA

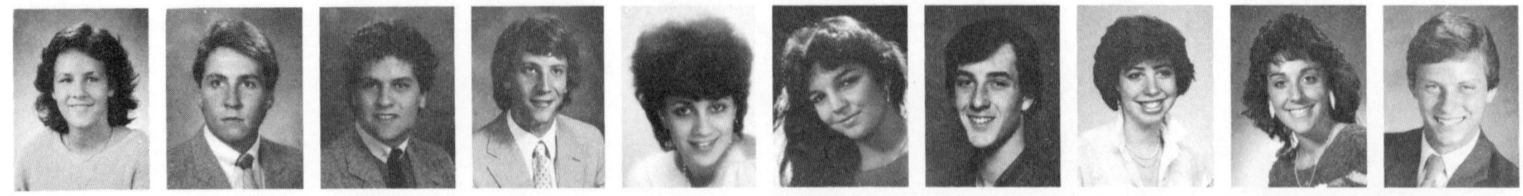

Roche, Kerry
Westwood HS
Westwood, MA

Rockwell, Steven
Tewksbury
Memorial HS
Tewksbury, MA

Rodericks, Ron
Brockton HS
Brockton, MA

Rohde, Peter F
North Andover HS
North Andover, MA

Romano, Lisa
Medford HS
Medford, MA

Romeo, Jennifer
Bishop Connolly HS
Fall River, MA

Roney, Stephen
Bishop Fenwick HS
Lynn, MA

Roover, Melissa
Natick HS
Natick, MA

Rosenberg, Lisa
Winthrop HS
Winthrop, MA

Rosenblum, William
The Lawrence Acad
S Hadley, MA

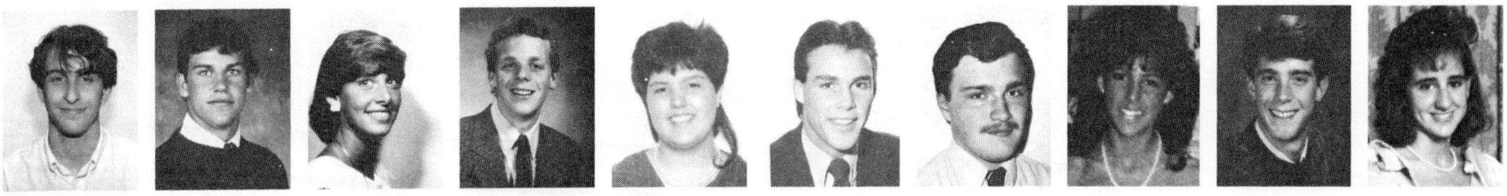

Ross, Douglas
Hingham HS
Hingham, MA

Ross, Michael G
Grafton HS
Grafton, MA

Rossiter, Renee
Easthampton HS
Easthampton, MA

Rothera, Matthew
Westford Acad
Westford, MA

Rotondo, Andrea
Reading Memorial
Reading, MA

Roy, John A
Brockton HS
Brockton, MA

Roy, Paul
New Bedford HS
New Bedford, MA

Rozman, Jill
Haverhill HS
Haverhill, MA

Rummo, Paul
Marian HS
Milford, MA

Rumsey, Suzanne
Braintree HS
Braintree, MA

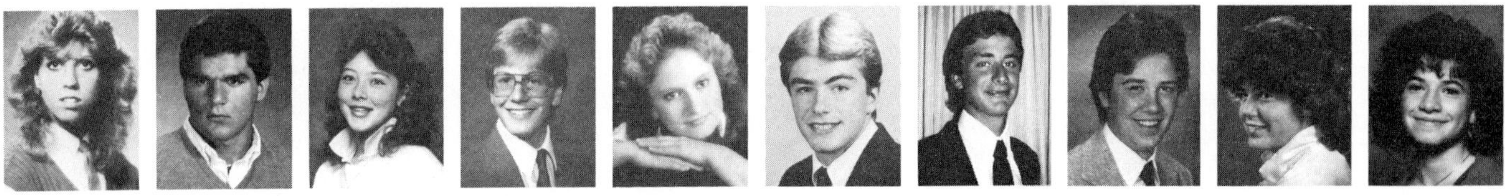

Russell, Christine
Milford HS
Burlington, MA

Russo, Domenic
Michael
Hudson HS
Hudson, MA

Russo, Rebecca
Girls Catholic HS
Revere, MA

Rutka, Timothy F
Pittsfield HS
Pittsfield, MA

Ryan, Dawn
Blackstone Valley
Reg Voc Tech HS
Bellingham, MA

Ryan, John C
Plymouth Carver
Carver, MA

Saad, Richard J
Boston College HS
Avon, MA

Saart, David
Hudson HS
Hudson, MA

Saart, Michelle
Hudson HS
Hudson, MA

Sabella, Marianne
Our Lady Of
Nazareth HS
Revere, MA

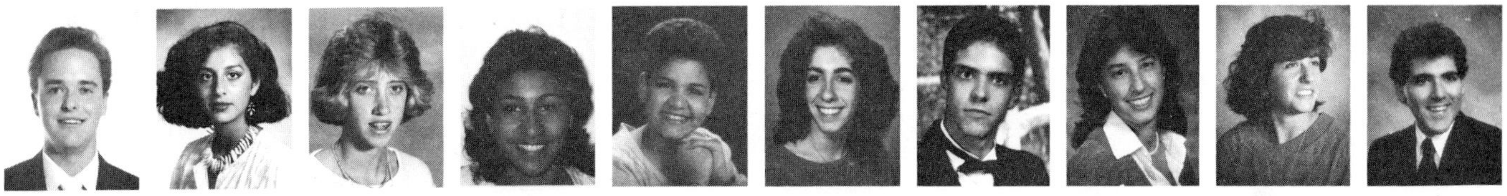

Saletnik, Michael J
Ludlow HS
Ludlow, MA

Saliby, Wafaa
Lawrence HS
Lawrence, MA

Salmonsen, Julie
Danvers HS
Danvers, MA

Santana, Carmen
Viviana
South High
Community Schl
Worcester, MA

Santiago, Wanda
Madison Park HS
Dorchester, MA

Santoro, Angela
East Boston HS
E Boston, MA

Santos, Louis Melo
Diman Regional
Vo-Tech HS
Fall River, MA

Santos, Patricia
Plymoth-Carver HS
Plymouth, MA

Saporito, Laura
Ipswich HS
Ipswich, MA

Sarkis, Anthony M
Drury SR HS
North Adams, MA

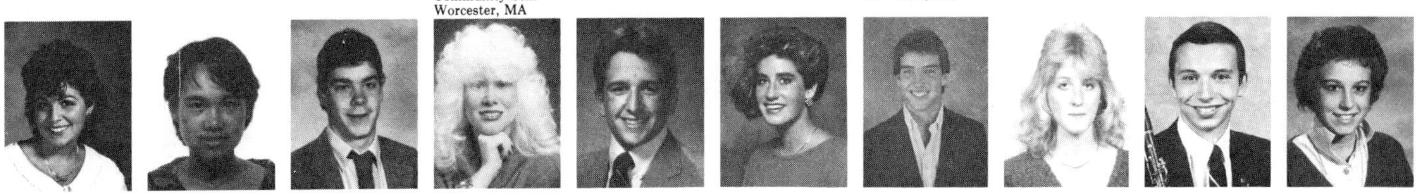

Sarkis, Susan
Lawrence HS
Lawrence, MA

Sarnsethsiri,
Naripun
Mac Dufie HS
Bloomfield Hills, MI

Saucier, Edward T
Holy Name CCHS
Worcester, MA

Sawyer, Tisha Lee
Doherty Memorial
Worcester, MA

Scampoli, David
Dedham HS
Dedham, MA

Scannell, Andrea
Sacred Heart HS
Bourne, MA

Scesny, James F
Saint Bernards
Central Catholi HS
Westminster, MA

Schatzel, Kristen
Old Rochester
Regional HS
Stanton, NJ

Scheufele, Matthew
Silver Lake Regional
Pembroke, MA

Schiappa, Susan
Notre Dame Acad
Hull, MA

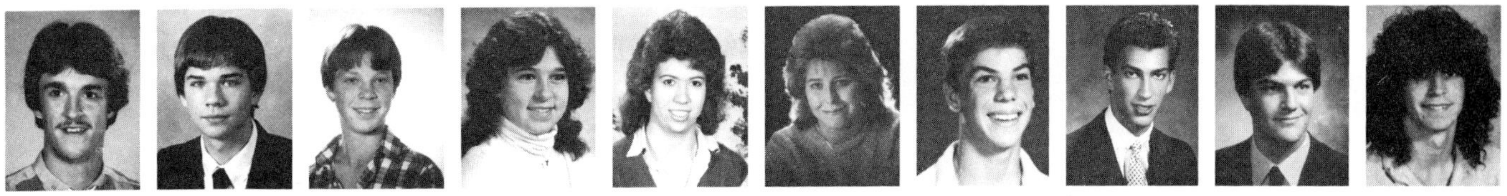

Schlicke, Kevin S
Narragansett
Regional HS
Phillipston, MA

Schmergel, Greg E
Roxbury Latin HS
Wellesley, MA

Schnopp, Kevin M
Wahconah Regional
Dalton, MA

Scholtz, Tabitha
Triton Regional JR/
SR HS
Salisbury, MA

Schonberg, Amy
Tahanto Regional
Boylston, MA

Schwab, Kristen
Marian HS
Framingham, MA

Schwalm, Mark
Reading Memorial
Reading, MA

Schwartz, Neil D
Newton South HS
Newton, MA

Sciola, Kirk M
Saugus HS
Saugus, MA

Scivoletto, John C
Salem HS
Salem, MA

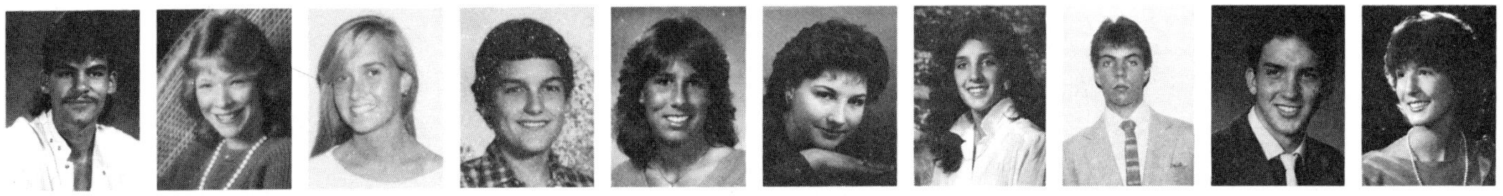

Segarra, Edwin
Greater Lowell
Regional Vo Tech
Lowell, MA

Selfe, Susan
Masconomet HS
Lock Haven, PA

Selinga, Kathleen A
Middlesex Schl
Fitchburg, MA

Sequeira, Anthony
Tahanto Regional
Boylston, MA

Sera, Laurie
Newton North HS
Newton, MA

Sergel, Theresa C
Bartlett HS
Webster, MA

Servidio, Maria
Minnechaug HS
Wilbraham, MA

Shannon, John H
Swampscott HS
Nahant, MA

Sharp, Gary
Bishop Stang HS
N Dartmouth, MA

Shatzer, Susan E
Ludlow HS
Ludlow, MA

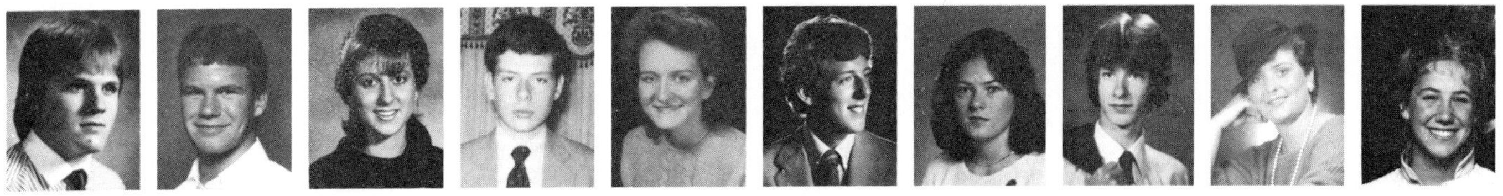

Shea, Stephen
Central Catholic HS
Pelham, NH

Shea, Terrence
Marian HS
Framingham, MA

Shedd, Susan
Notre Dame Acad
Weymouth, MA

Sheehan, Edward
St Dominic Savio
Prep HS For Boys
Revere, MA

Sheehy, Suzanne
Archbishop Williams
Quincy, MA

Shellito, Michael
Pioneer Valley
Regional Schl
Northfield, MA

Shepard, Steven
Methuen HS
Methuen, MA

Sheppard, Margaret
Fitchburg HS
Fitchburg, MA

Sheridan, Melissa
Clinton HS
Clinton, MA

Sherriff, Missy
Bishop Fenwick HS
Peabody, MA

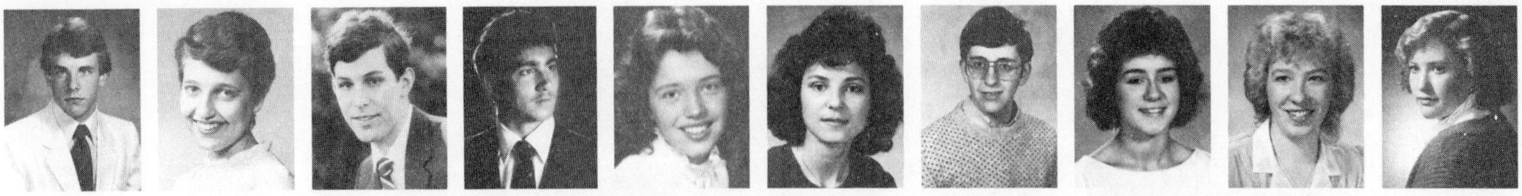

Shields, Matthew Jon
Hudson HS
Hudson, MA

Shlyam, Rose
Algonquin Regional
Northboro, MA

Shumway, David C
Duxbury HS
Duxbury, MA

Sibley, Glenray
Holyoke HS
Holyoke, MA

Silva, Cheryl L
Dighton-Rehoboth Regional HS
Rehoboth, MA

Silva, Luciana
New Bedford HS
New Bedford, MA

Silveira, Steven
Bristol Plymouth Regional HS
Taunton, MA

Simone, Bobbi Jean
Arlington Catholic
Arlington, MA

Simonis, Brenda
Brockton HS
Brockton, MA

Sinkiewich, Lynda M
Pittsfield HS
Pittsfield, MA

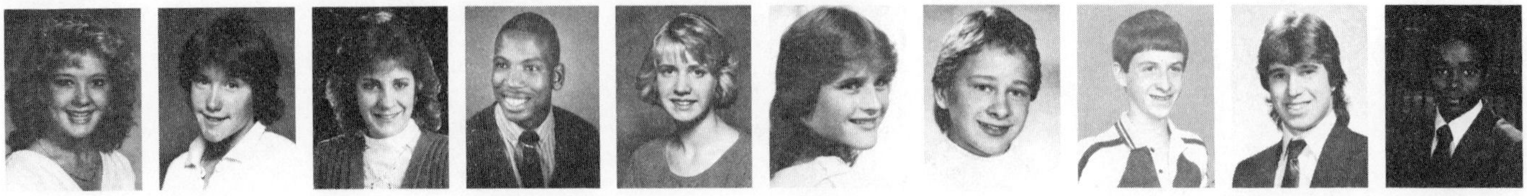

Skelton, Sarah
Sharon HS
Sharon, MA

Skinnion, Mary
Marian HS
Sudbury, MA

Slepecki, Diane M
Ludlow HS
Ludlow, MA

Slocumb, Damon
Classical HS
Springfield, MA

Slomba, Elizabeth
Marion HS
Milford, MA

Slowick, Renee
Cathedral HS
W Springfield, MA

Smarz, Jr George
Smith Acad
Hatfield, MA

Smith, Austin
Tri-County Voc Tech HS
Medfield, MA

Smith, Bruce C
Belchertown JR SR
Belchertown, MA

Smith, Christopher E
Bedford HS
Bedford, MA

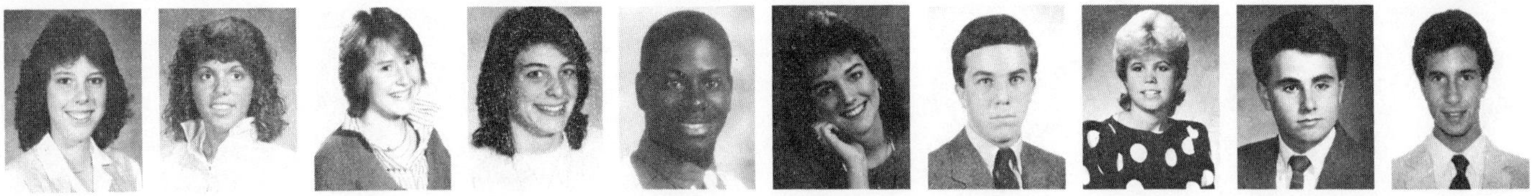

Smith, Claire
King Philip Regional HS
Norfolk, MA

Smith, Kerri
Bishop Feehan HS
Attleboro, MA

Smith, Kimberley
Reading Memorial
Reading, MA

Smith, Laura
Westwood HS
Westwood, MA

Smith, Parrish
Boston Technical
Boston, MA

Smith, Shannon M
Cardinal Spellman
Whitman, MA

Smith, Tom
Westwood HS
Westwood, MA

Snow, Lisa
Sharon HS
Sharon, MA

Soares, Jeffrey M
B M C Durfee HS
Fall River, MA

Sohmer, Bradley
Brockton HS
Brockton, MA

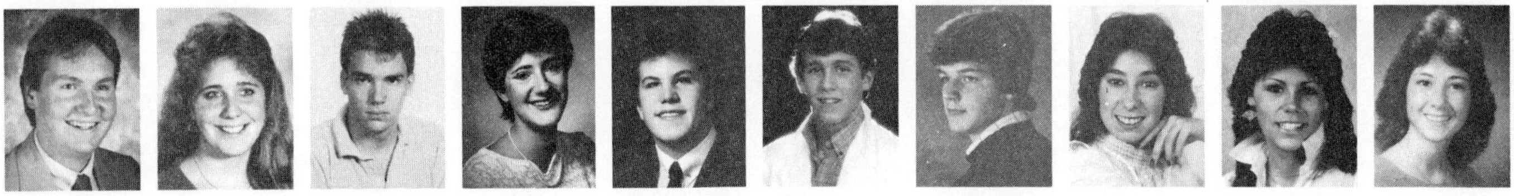

Sokol, Michael
Wilbraham & Monson Acad
Sturbridge, MA

Solovieff, Tracy
Fanning Trade HS
Worcester, MA

Somppi, Jr James L
Westfield HS
Westfield, MA

Sonier, Julie J
Notre Dame Acad
Rutland, MA

Soucy, Robert
North HS
Worcester, MA

Sousa, Lawrence W
Brockton HS
Brockton, MA

Southern, Michael
Tantasqua Regional
Alpharetta, GA

Souza, Barbara
Bellingham Memorial HS
Franklin, MA

Souza, Heidi Alcobia
Westport HS
Westport, MA

Spagone, Michelle
East Bridgewater
E Bridgewater, MA

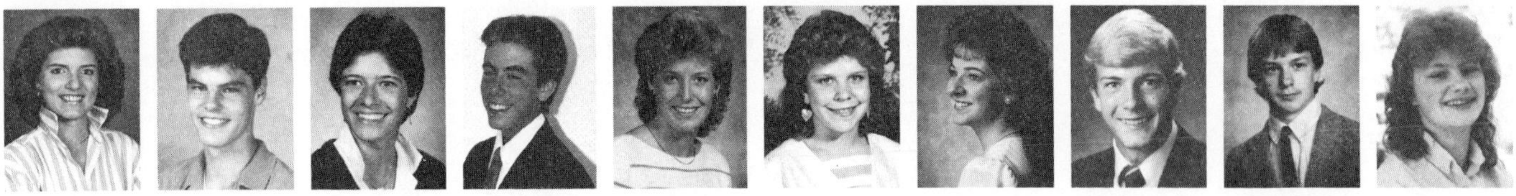

Spannagel, Carole
Hingham HS
Hingham, MA

Sparks, David
Hopedale HS
Hopedale, MA

Speliotes, Elizabeth K
Newton North HS
W Newton, MA

Spiewak, Brian
Pittsfield HS
Pittsfield, MA

Springer, Julie Christine
Shepherd Hill Regional HS
Dudley, MA

Squires, Debra A
Plymouth-Carver
Plymouth, MA

St John, Laura
Marianhill CCHS
Spencer, MA

St Pierre, James F
Attleboro HS
South Attleboro, MA

St Pierre, Thomas R
Fitchburg HS
Fitchburg, MA

Stachowicz, Linda
Ware HS
Ware, MA

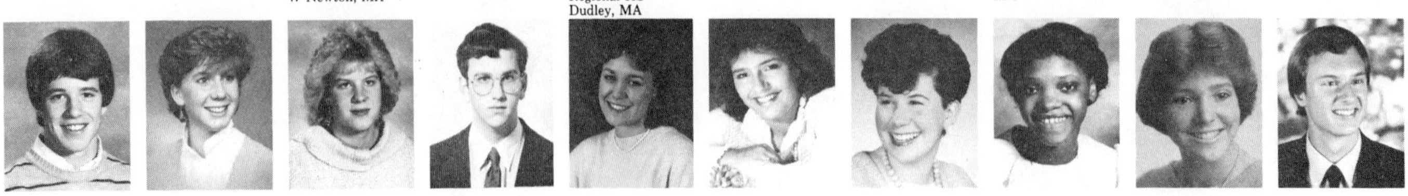

Stanley, Scott
Danvers HS
Danvers, MA

Stebbins, Kristen
Notre Dame Acad
Scituate, MA

Stefanik, Audra
Westfield HS
Westfield, MA

Stephens, Christopher J
Groton Schl
New York, NY

Sterczala, Beth
Bartlett HS
Webster, MA

Stetson, Melissa
Frontier Regional
S Deerfield, MA

Stevens, Shanon
Marlboro HS
Marlboro, MA

Stillwell, Titia
Mario Umaria Tech
Roxbury, MA

Stoehr, Marna
Dennis-Yarmouth Regional HS
S Dennis, MA

Strachota, Dan
Greenfield HS
Greenfield, MA

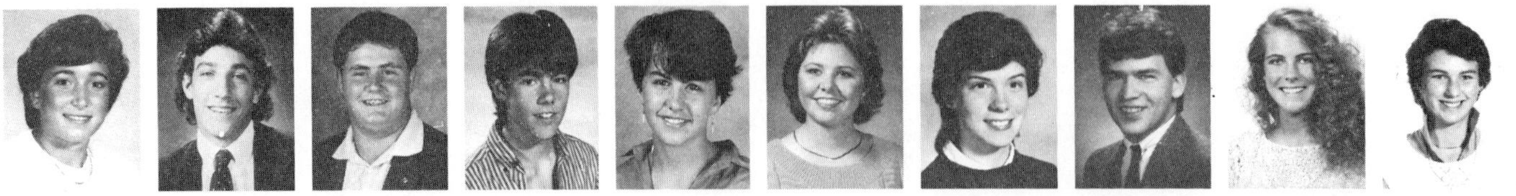

Strazzullo, Leslie
Winchester HS
Winchester, MA

Strout, Matthew
Auburn HS
Auburn, MA

Sulfaro, Jr Domenic
St Dominic Savio
S Boston, MA

Sullivan, Bradford
Apponequet Regional HS
Lakeville, MA

Sullivan, Colleen
Bishop Connolly HS
Westport, MA

Sullivan, Karen
Medfield HS
Medfield, MA

Sullivan, Sherri
Easthampton HS
Northampton, MA

Sullivan, Timothy
Billerica Memorial
Billerica, MA

Summerford, Candace
Leominster HS
Leominster, MA

Surowiec, Dorothy
Easthampton HS
Easthampton, MA

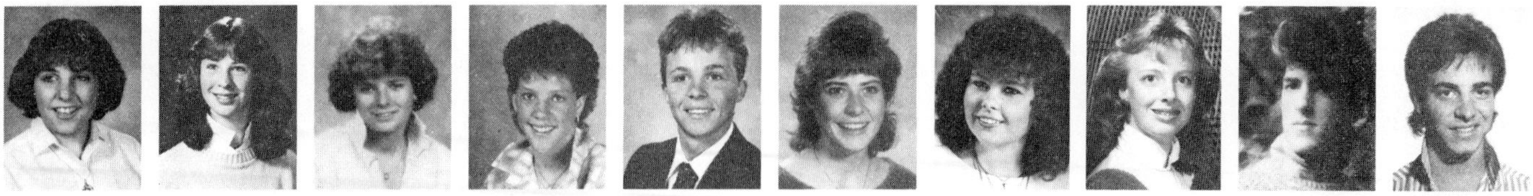

Sutera, Gina
Gloucester HS
Gloucester, MA

Svendsen, Kristen
North Attleboro HS
N Attleboro, MA

Swahn, Patricia
Simons Rock College
Delaware, NJ

Sweeney, Melissa
Bishop Connolly HS
Fall River, MA

Swenson, Daniel F
Waltham HS
Waltham, MA

Swenson, Deborah R
Danvers HS
Danvers, MA

Swiecanski, Marcia M
Cathedral HS
Indian Orchard, MA

Sylvia, Bobbi
New Bedford HS
New Bedford, MA

Sylvia, Edward
Middleborough HS
Middleboro, MA

Sylvia, Kevin
Old Colony Vocational Tech
Acushnet, MA

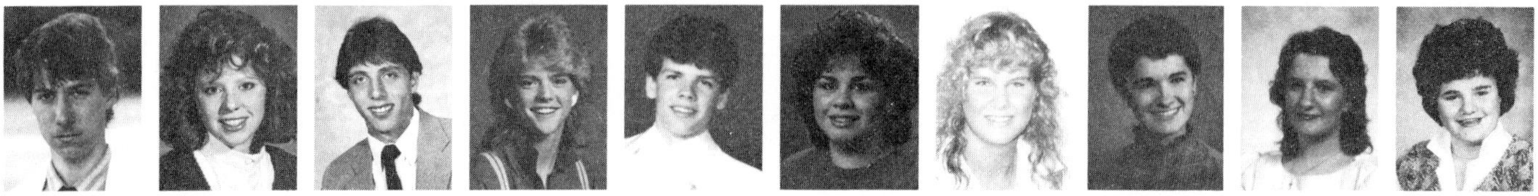

Tallman, Todd M
Narragansett Regional HS
Phillipston, MA

Tambolleo, Nikki
Sheperd Hill Regional HS
Charlton, MA

Tammaro, John
Stoughton HS
Stoughton, MA

Tassinari, Janeen
Palmer HS
Palmer, MA

Tattrie, Christopher
Franklin HS
Franklin, MA

Tavares, Nancy
B M C Durfee HS
Fall River, MA

Taylor, Catherine
Milford HS
Milford, MA

Teague, Andrea
Beverly HS
Beverly, MA

Tefts, Valerie A
Holyoke Catholic
Easthampton, MA

Tessi, Ann-Margaret
St Bernards Central Catholic HS
Fitchburg, MA

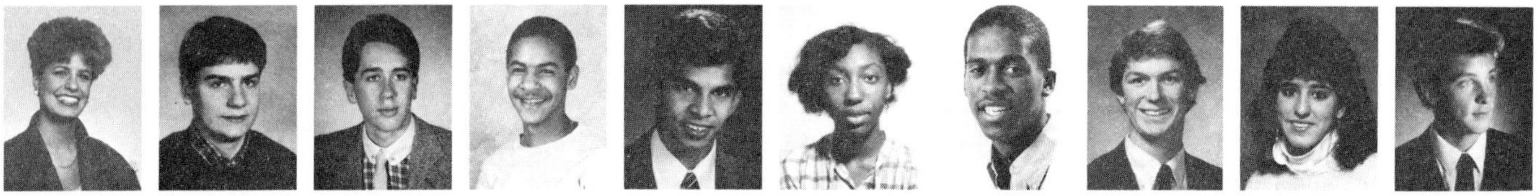

Theo, Paula
Danvers HS
Danvers, MA

Theodore, Stefan E
Westwood HS
Westwood, MA

Therrien, Christopher
St Bernards C C HS
Fitchburg, MA

Thimas, John U
Silver Lake Regional
Kingston, MA

Thirumalaisamy, Pillan K
Newton South HS
Newton, MA

Thomas, Gisel
Boston Technical
Dorchester, MA

Thomas, Todd
Williston-Northampton Schl
Springfield, MA

Thompson, Chris
Westwood HS
Westwood, MA

Thompson, Kathleen Marie
Hudson Catholic HS
Hudson, MA

Thompson, Richard E
Wilbram & Honson
Westfield, MA

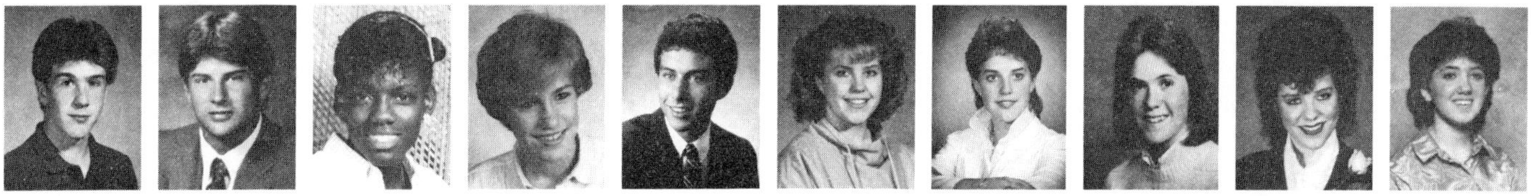

Thurber, Neil D
Westborough HS
Westborough, MA

Tibbetts, John
Wakefield Memorial
Wakefield, MA

Tilman, Teressa
Bedford HS
Boston, MA

Timmermeister, Karin
Stoneleigh-Burnham
Lima, OH

Todres, Jonathan
Dennis-Yarmouth Regional HS
South Yarmouth, MA

Toner, Bettina
Mansfield HS
Mansfield, MA

Tonry, Tammy
Montochusett Regional HS
Fitchburg, MA

Toomey, Patricia M
Danvers HS
Danvers, MA

Toone, Jennifer A
Marlborough HS
Marlboro, MA

Tortora, Debbie
Medford HS
Medford, MA

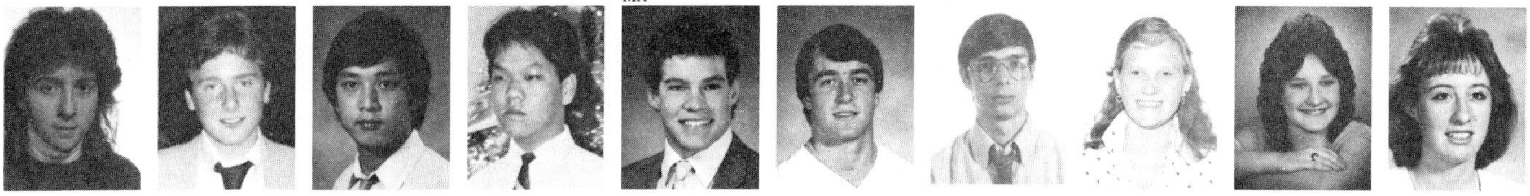

Touponce, Dawn
Lee HS
Lee, MA

Trachtman, Jonathan
Natick HS
Natick, MA

Tran, Hiep
Newton North HS
Newton, MA

Tran, Khiem T
Clinton HS
Fitchburg, MA

Traub, Stephen J
Xaverian Brothers
Sharon, MA

Traupe, Eric H
Ashland HS
Ashland, MA

Trayers, III Frederick
Saint Johns Preparatory School
Peabody, MA

Tremblay, Patricia
Billerica Memorial
N Billerica, MA

Trick, Juli
Montachusett Regional Vo Tech
Lunenburg, MA

Tripp, Doris
Marlboro HS
Marlboro, MA

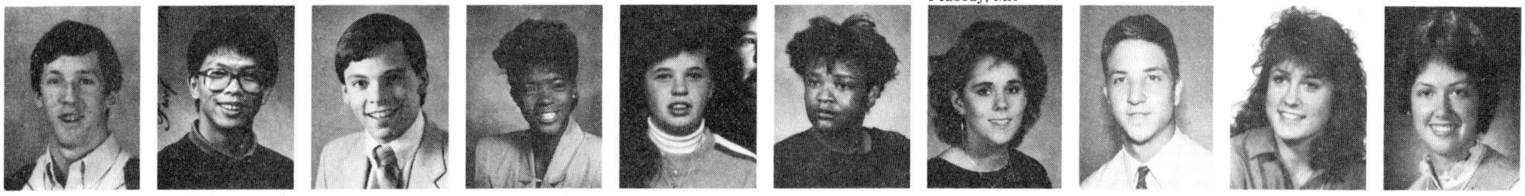

Troup, Kenneth
Silver Lake Regional
Halifax, MA

Truong, Tuong
West Roxbury HS
Dorchester, MA

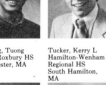

Tucker, Kerry L
Hamilton-Wenham Regional HS
South Hamilton, MA

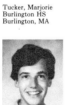

Tucker, Marjorie
Burlington HS
Burlington, MA

Tucker, Paula
Girls Catholic HS
Malden, MA

Tucker, Tanya M
Boston Latin Acad
Mattapan, MA

Tudor, Paula
Plymouth-Carver
Plymouth, MA

Tulli, Stephen M
Franklin HS
Franklin, MA

Tumas, Sharon
Shrewsbury HS
Shrewsbury, MA

Tuttle, Anne
Norwell HS
Norwell, MA

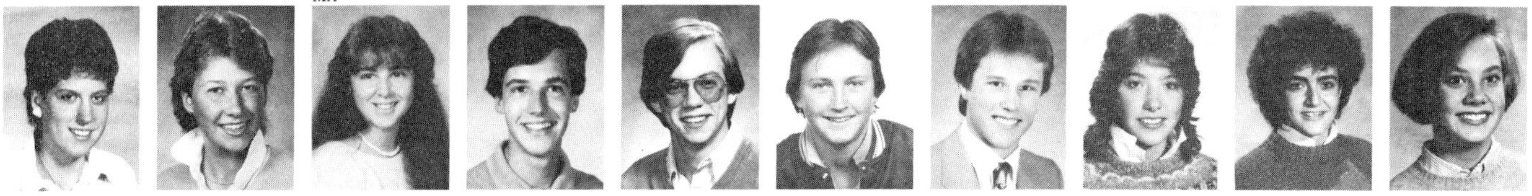

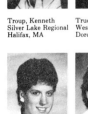

Tyler, Carrie
Commerce HS
Springfield, MA

Urda, Julianne
Acton-Boxborough Regional HS
Acton, MA

Vadala, Marie Theresa
Gloucester HS
Gloucester, MA

Valante, James
Boston College HS
Quincy, MA

Valatka, III Joseph A
Wilmington HS
Wilmington, MA

Valente, Christine
BMC Durke HS
Fall River, MA

Valkanas, Michael A
Xaverian Brothers
Dedham, MA

Vanasse, Karen
Holyoke Catholic
Northampton, MA

Vardis, Maria T
Apponequet Regional HS
Lakeville, MA

Varitimos, Nina
Presentation Of Mary Acad
Methuen, MA

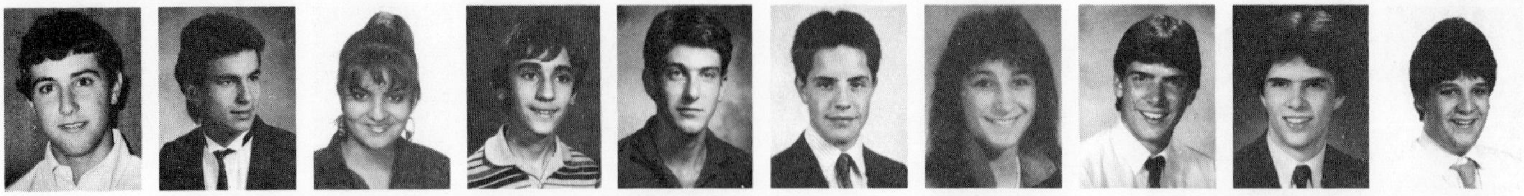

Vartabedian, Ara
Haverhill HS
Haverhill, MA

Vasques, Roy
Lawrence HS
Lawrence, MA

Vega, Elizabeth
Phillips Acad
Los Angeles, CA

Velella, Albert
Waltham HS
Boston, MA

Ventura, James S
Malden HS
Medford, MA

Verga, Joe
Plymouth Carver
Plymouth, MA

Verna, Christine
King Philip
Regional HS
Wrentham, MA

Vicino, John
Bishop Stang HS
Wareham, MA

Viera, Stephen
Bristol-Plymouth
Technical HS
Taunton, MA

Vincequere, Thomas
Anthony
Holy Name Catholic
Worcester, MA

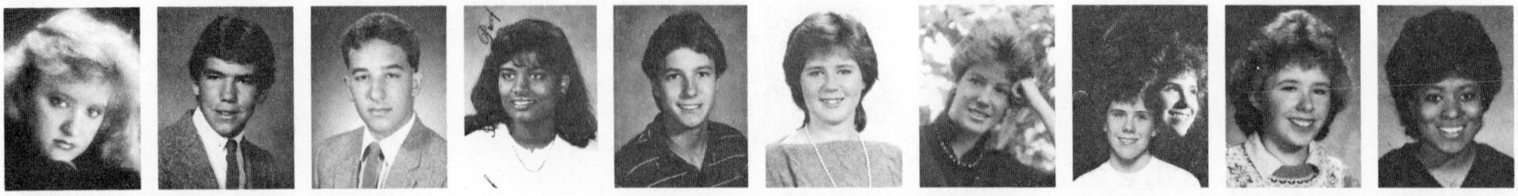

Vitukevich, Vicki L
Melrose HS
Wakefield, MA

Viveiros, John
Old Rochester
Regional HS
Rochester, MA

Volpe, Robert
Boston College HS
Quincy, MA

Vyravanathan, Indra
Somerville HS
Somerville, MA

Wahlstrom, Erik
Shepherd Hill
Regional HS
Charlton, MA

Walenty, Margaret
Uxbridge HS
Uxbridge, MA

Walker, Jennifer L
Plymouth-Carver
Plymouth, MA

Walker, Nancy
Cardinal Spellman
Brockton, MA

Walker, Noralee
Medford HS
Medford, MA

Walker, Stephanie
M
Randolph HS
Randolph, MA

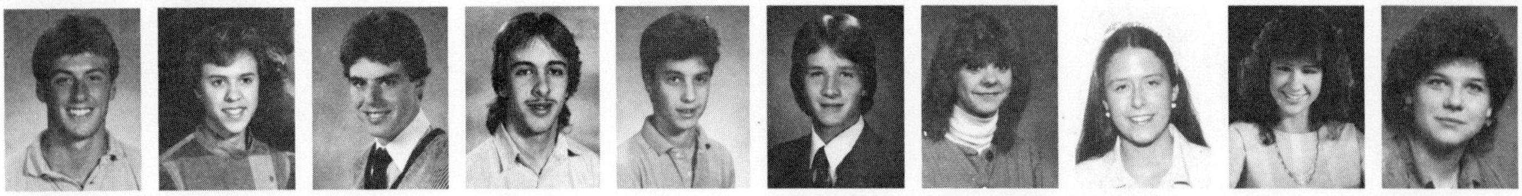

Ward, John Jerry
Lexington HS
Lexington, MA

Wasson, Laura J
Walpole HS
Walpole, MA

Wedge, James
Pope John XXIII
Revere, MA

Wedge, Jason
Methuen HS
Methuen, MA

Weene, Daniel S
Brockton HS
Brockton, MA

Welch, Laurence J
Methuen HS
Methuen, MA

Welch, Meredith
Whitman-Hanson
Reg HS
Whitman, MA

Wells, Jennifer
Walnut Hill Schl
Cranston, RI

Wells, Lisa
Easthampton HS
Easthampton, MA

Wells, Lisa
Winthrop HS
Winthrop, MA

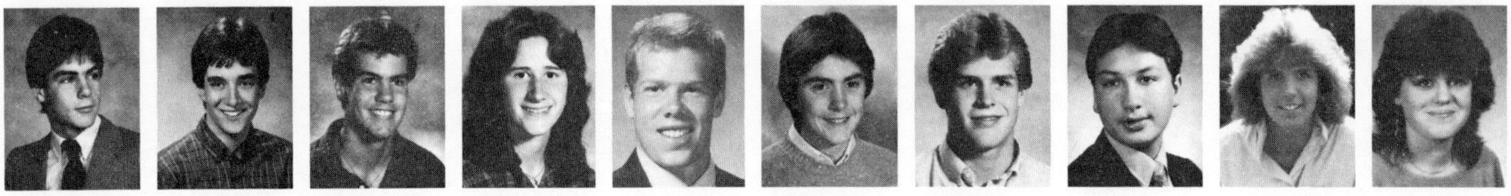

Wenz, Craig
Monument
Mountain Regiona
W Stockbridge, MA

Wereta, Richard
Dedham HS
Dedham, MA

Whalen, Kevin
Beverly HS
Beverly, MA

Wheeler, Linnea
Quaboag Regional
W Warren, MA

Wheeler, Roger J
Medfield HS
Medfield, MA

White, Cami
Athol HS
Athol, MA

White, Christopher
Westfield HS
Westfield, MA

White, Christopher
A
Bladstone Vly
Regional Voc Te
Millbury, MA

White, Kristen
Faith Christian
W Dennis, MA

White, Mary
Brockton HS
Brockton, MA

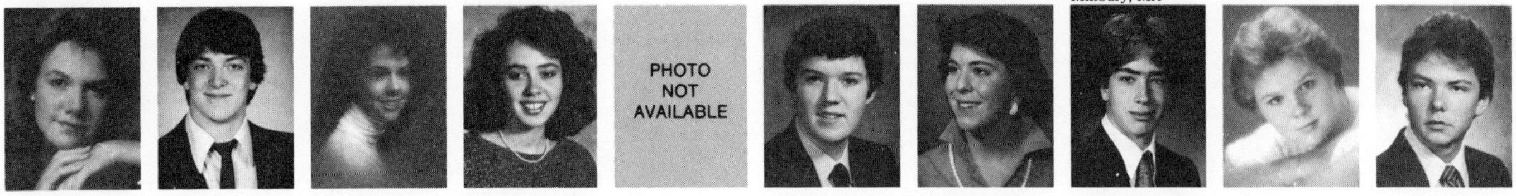
PHOTO
NOT
AVAILABLE

Whitehead, Janice
Wakefield HS
Wakefield, MA

Whitehead, Richard
St Bernards HS
Rindge, NH

Whitney, Jennifer
Natick HS
Natick, MA

Whiton, Kristina
Fontbonne Acad
W Roxbury, MA

Whittemore,
Rebecca
Quaboag Regional
Warren, MA

Whoriskey, Michael
Central Catholic HS
Plaistow, NH

Wicks, Patricia S
Haverhill HS
Haverhill, MA

Wiedl, Craig J
Middleborough HS
Middleboro, MA

Wierbowicz, Paula
Everett HS
Everett, MA

Wilder, Lance W
Chelmsford HS
Chelmsford, MA

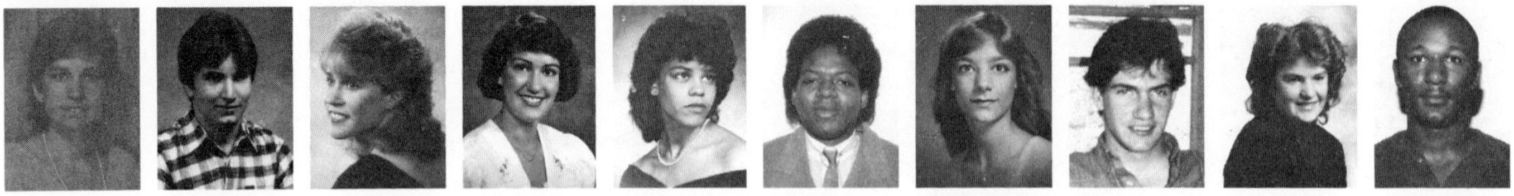

Wilhelmsen,
Heather
North Middlesex
Regional HS
Townsend, MA

Wilkinson, II Dennis
J
New Bedford HS
New Bedford, MA

Williamson, Debra
Hoosac Valley HS
Adams, MA

Wilson, Catharine L
Hamilton Wenham
Regional HS
S Hamilton, MA

Wilson, Marguerite
Mac Duffie Schl For
Norfolk, VA

Wilson, Mark C
Boston HS
Roxbury, MA

Winslow, Elaine P
Walpole HS
Walpole, MA

Winston, Padraic
Lenox Memorial HS
Lenox, MA

Wirtz, Lila
Katherine B
Auburn HS
Auburn, MA

Wise, Khalid
Boston Latin Acad
Boston, MA

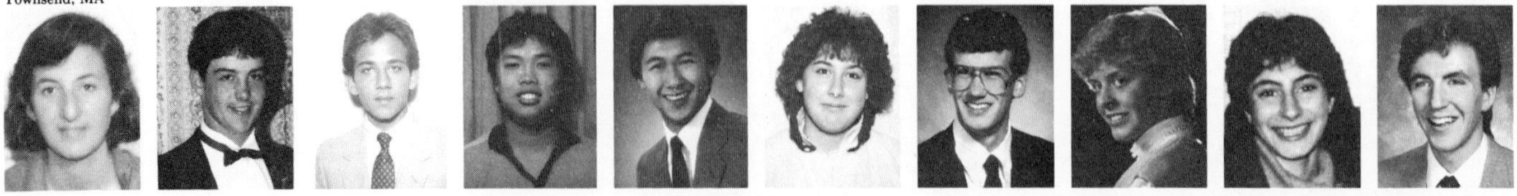

Wise, Sara
Marthas Vineyard
Regional HS
Chilmark, MA

Wojcik, John
Cathedral HS
Springfield, MA

Wolf, Scott I
Canton HS
Canton, MA

Wong, Henry
Saugus HS
Saugus, MA

Wong, Hubert S
Drury SR HS
N Adams, MA

Woodruff, Mary
Elizabeth
Plymouth-Carver
Plymouth, MA

Wright, Dave
Berkshire Schl
Skaneateles, NY

Wrona, Marguerite
Ludlow HS
Ludlow, MA

Yampolsky, Sasha
Newton North HS
Newton, MA

Yanover, Michael
Natick HS
Natick, MA

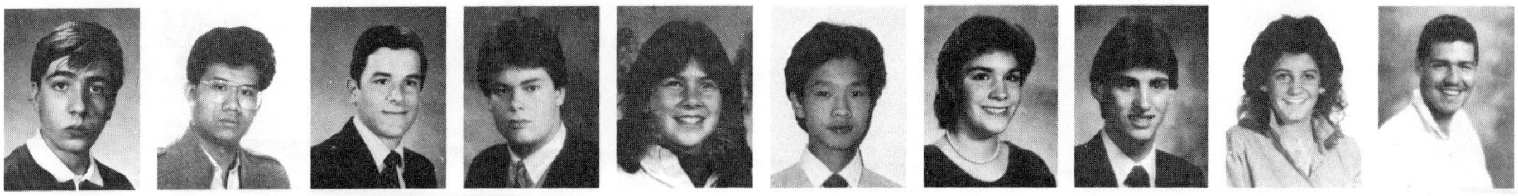

Yantosca, Robert
Boston College HS
E Boston, MA

Yee, Andrew
Boston Latin Acad
Allston, MA

Yocco, Stephen
Milton HS
Milton, MA

Young, Jason D
Scituate HS
N Scituate, MA

Young, Sharon
Pittsfield HS
Pittsfield, MA

Yung, Alan
Brookline HS
Brookline, MA

Zachara, Kathy
Bartlett HS
Webster, MA

Zamagni, Andy
Malden HS
Malden, MA

Zangari, Rebecca
Haverhill HS
Haverhill, MA

Zayas, Gerardo
Madison Park HS
Boston, MA

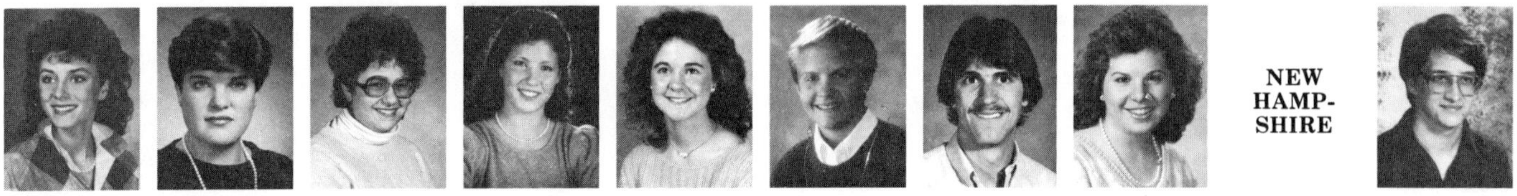

Zecha, Anne Therese
Chelsea HS
Chelsea, MA

Zenofsky, Amy
Foxborough HS
Foxboro, MA

Zimmerman, Rhonda
Randolph HS
Brockton, MA

Zokowski, Margaret
Smith Acad
Hatfield, MA

Zommer, Lora
Norton HS
Norton, MA

Zukowsky, Kathryn
Tantasqua Regional SR HS
Fiskdale, MA

Zumpfe, Christopher
Shepherd Hill Regional JR SR HS
Dudley, MA

Zygouras, Helen
Milton HS
Milton, MA

NEW HAMPSHIRE

Abberton, Michael
Alvirne HS
Hudson, NH

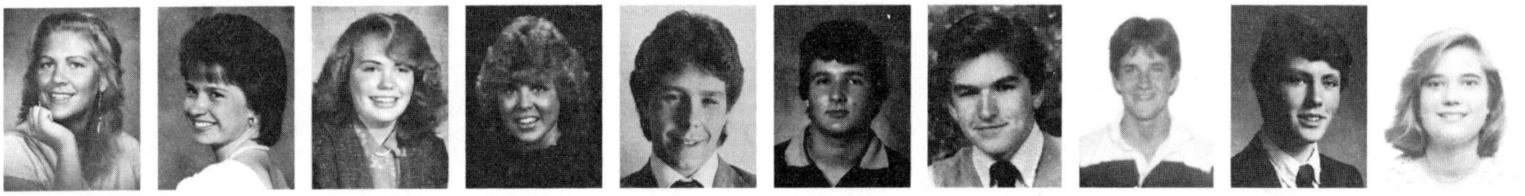

Abele, April
Alvirne HS
Hudson, NH

Allen, Bonnie Lynn
Newport HS
Newport, NH

Allen, Mary E
Spaulding HS
Rochester, NH

Allen, Vicki
Concord HS
Concord, NH

Alty, Joe
Dover HS
Dover, NH

Arevalo, Carlos
The Phillips Exeter
Mesquite, TX

Arsenault, Anthony James
Gilford Middle HS
Lanconia, NH

Arthur, Jonathan B
Keene HS
Alstead, NH

Ashton, Ken
Kearsarge Regional
Bradford, NH

Ayotte, Lynne Ann
Keene HS
Keene, NH

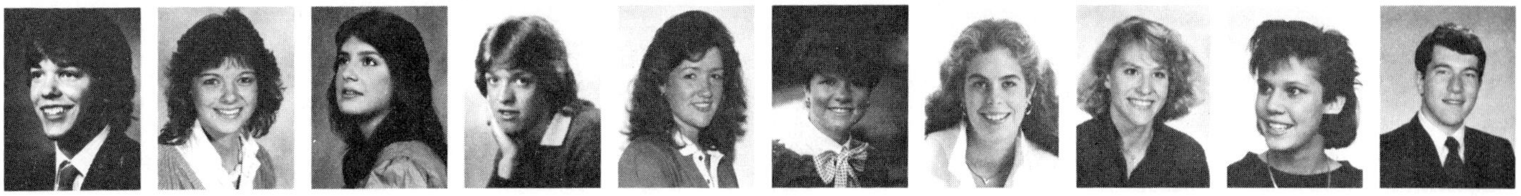

Bakanec, Bradley S
Londonderry HS
Londonderry, NH

Barnes, Doreen
Alvirne HS
Hudson, NH

Bartz, Margo
Franklin JR SR HS
Franklin, NH

Bassett, April
Alton Central HS
Alton, NH

Bechard, Deborah
Mount Saint Mary
Nashua, NH

Bechard, Kathi
Londonderry HS
Londonderry, NH

Belletete, Nancy
Conant HS
Jaffrey, NH

Bennett, Cynthia
Manchester Central
Manchester, NH

Bennett, Marcia
Memorial HS
Manchester, NH

Berger, Jonathan
Manchester HS
Bedford, NH

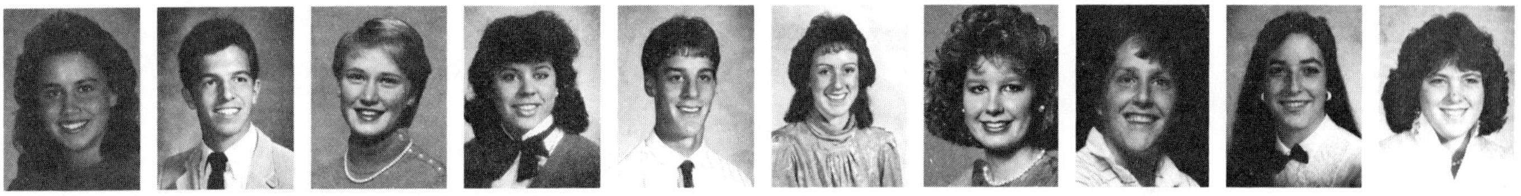

Bergeron, Tammy
Memorial HS
Manchester, NH

Bernarducci, Marc
Bishop Guertin HS
Hudson, NH

Bickford, Joanna
Inter-Lakes HS
Center Harbor, NH

Biello, Stephany
Merrimack HS
Merrimack, NH

Bisaillon, Steven
Spaulding HS
Rochester, NH

Blecharczyk, Pamela
Pelham HS
Pelham, NH

Bodnar, Sandra
Manchester Memorial HS
Manchester, NH

Boehle, Kathy
Laconia HS
Laconia, NH

Bossi, Amy
Bishop Brady HS
Contoocook, NH

Boudreau, Tammy
Spaulding HS
Rochester, NH

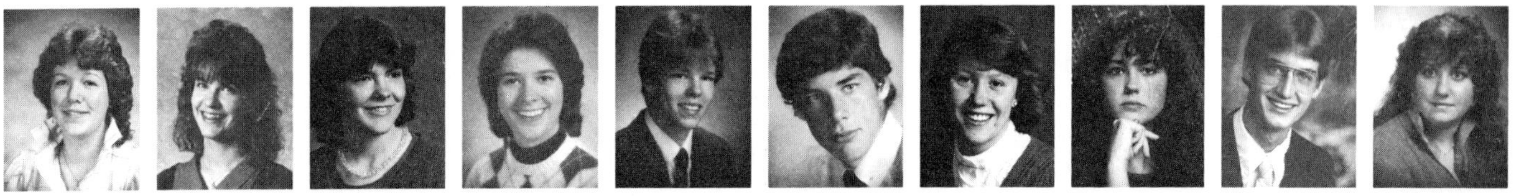

Bourassa, Lisa
Berlin HS
Berlin, NH

Bradley, Karen
Newport JR & SR
Newport, NH

Brown, Christine A
Kearsarge Regional
Wilmot Flat, NH

Brown, Heather
Belmont HS
Canterbury, NH

Brown, Keith
Berlin HS
Stratford, CT

Brown, Keith
Coe-Brown Acad
Ctr Strafford, NH

Bruce, Theresa
Lebanon HS
Lebanon, NH

Burbank, Barbara
Spaulding HS
Rochester, NH

Burke, Darin M
Alton Central HS
Alton, NH

Butler, Michelle
Coe-Brown Northwood Acad
Deerfield, NH

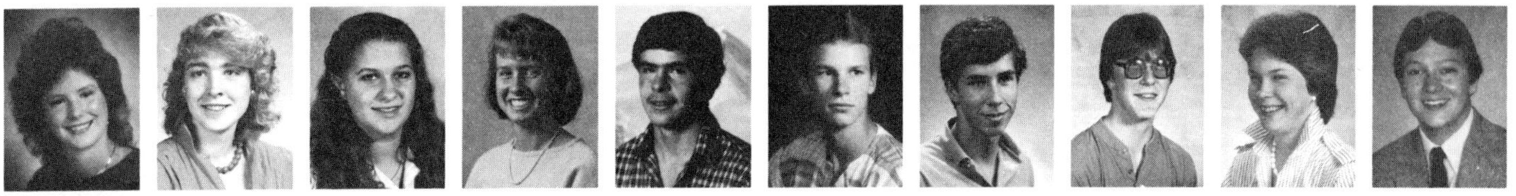

Buttrick, Melanie Lee
Concord HS
Bow, NH

Callum, Rhonda
Stevens HS
Newport, NH

Carey, Malialou
Alvirne HS
Hudson, NH

Carignan, Nicole
Manchester Memorial HS
Manchester, NH

Caron, Craig
Newport JR SR HS
Goshen, NH

Carr, Troy D
Newmarket Central
Newmarket, NH

Carter, Brian
Concord HS
Bow, NH

Casselberry, Richard
Spaulding HS
Rochester, NH

Chapman, Martha
Weare HS
Weare, NH

Charron, David Reginald
Manchester HS
Manchester, NH

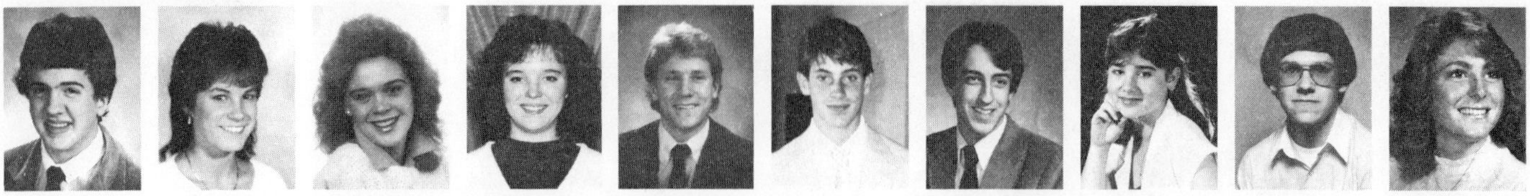

Charron, John
Bishop Guertin HS
Nashua, NH

Choate, Jo-Ellen
Alvirne HS
Hudson, NH

Clark, Rebecca
Alvirne HS
Hudson, NH

Cloutier, Jacqueline
Manchester H S
Manchester, NH

Coate, Thomas
Bishop Guertin HS
Windham, NH

Cochrane, Donald P
Pinkerton Acad
Windham, NH

Cooper, Gregory
Bishop Guertin HS
Merrimack, NH

Cormack, Janine
Kennett HS
Conway, NH

Costanzo, Glenn A
Farmington HS
Farmington, NH

Cram, Stephanie
Alvirne HS
Litchfield, NH

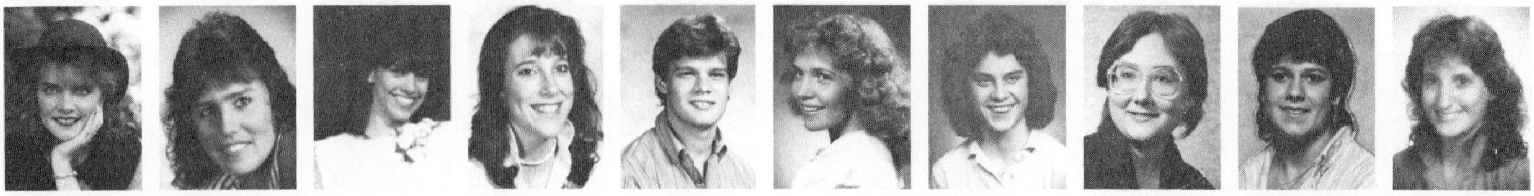

Crowley, Lisa
Newport HS
Newport, NH

Cunningham, Lynn
Salem HS
Salem, NH

Cunningham, Mary Ann
Pinkerton Acad
Windham, NH

Currier, Kelly
Central HS
Manchester, NH

Cusanelli, Michael
Stevens HS
Claremont, NH

Daigle, Frances
Goffstown HS
Goffstown, NH

Davis, Jennifer Sara
Nashua HS
Nashua, NH

De Grandpre, Betsy J
Conant HS
Jaffrey, NH

Deblois, Carolyn
Crosby Kennett HS
Conway, NH

Debutts, Patricia
Coe Brown
Northwood Acad
W Nottingham, NH

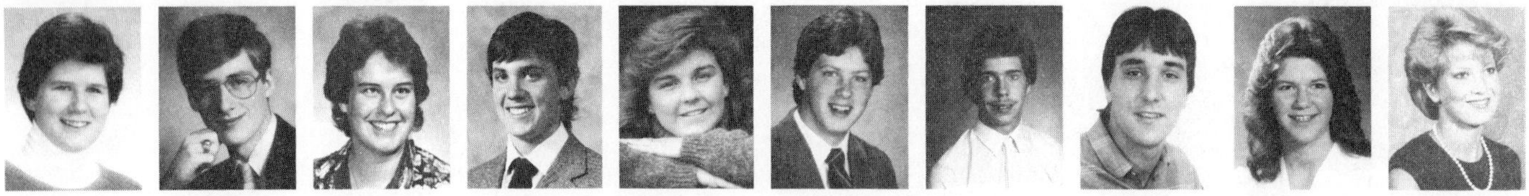

Decareau, Maria F
Milford Area SR HS
Amherst, NH

Demeritt, Edward
Coe-Brown
Northwood Acad
Barrington, NH

Demers, Lisa
Stevens HS
Claremont, NH

Demers, Matthew J
Memorial HS
Manchester, NH

Denis, Debbie
Nashua HS
Nashua, NH

Desruisseaux, Michael
Manchester HS
Manchester, NH

Dillon, James P
Nashua HS
Nashua, NH

Dimascola, Mike
Lebanon HS
Lebanon, NH

Dion, Lori A
Pelham HS
Pelham, NH

Dodd, Barbra
Inter-Lakes JR & SR HS
Ctr Sandwich, NH

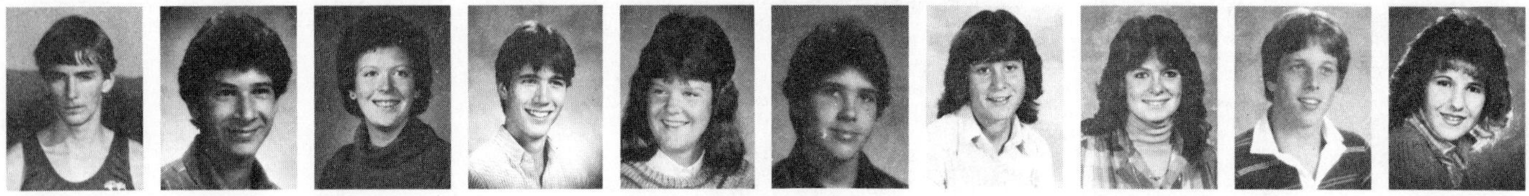

Doneski, James S
Plymouth Area HS
Plymouth, NH

Doubek, Greg J
Winnacunnet HS
Hampton, NH

Drescher, Lisa
Mt St Mary
Nashua, NH

Dubreuil, James L
Somersworth HS
Somersworth, NH

Dumas, Rebecca Lee
Mt St Mary
Seminary HS
Hudson, NH

Dupuis, Marc
Berlin HS
Berlin, NH

Dutton, Amy S
Alvirne HS
Hudson, NH

Enman, Doreen
Spaulding HS
Rochester, NH

Ennis, Chris
Belmont HS
Canterbury, NH

Faulhaber, Sherry
Spaulding HS
Rochester, NH

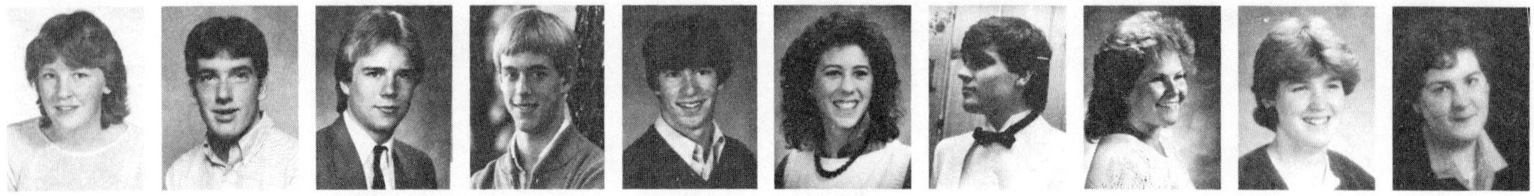

Felch, Leisa
Manchester Central
Hooksett, NH

Fickett, Andrew R
Kennett HS
Conway, NH

Field, Ken A
Pinkerton Academy
Windham, NH

Fillio, Christopher P
Exeter Area HS
East Kingston, NH

Fisher, Michael
Kingswood Regional
Ossipee, NH

Fleming, Ellen
Timberlane Regional
Atkinson, NH

Foley, Patrick E
Keene HS
Keene, NH

Fortier, Deirdre A
Alton Central HS
Laconia, NH

Fortin, Jennifer
Belmont HS
Belmont, NH

Forward, Debbie
Hanover HS
Hanover, NH

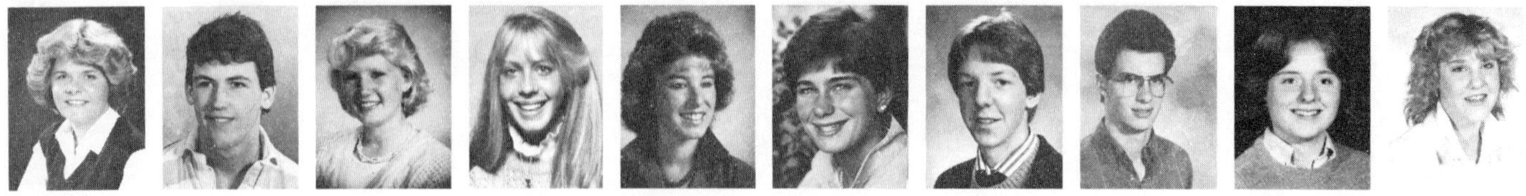

Foster, Kelly J
A Crosby Kennett
Fryeburg, ME

Frank, Karl Thomas
The Tilton Schl
Laconia, NH

Frechette, Ann
Merrimack HS
Merrimack, NH

Fuchslocher, Anita
Fall Mountain
Regional HS
Charlestown, NH

Gagne, Christine
Salem HS
Salem, NH

Gagner, Dael
Kingswood Regional
Wolfeboro Falls, NH

Garvey, Brian
Bishop Guertin HS
Dracut, MA

Gendron, Jeffrey
Alvirne HS
Hudson, NH

Germain, Suzanne
Alvirne HS
Hudson, NH

Gilbert, Debbie
Central HS
Manchester, NH

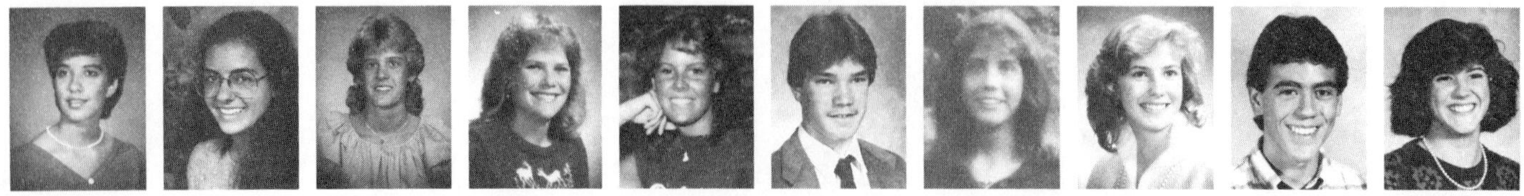

Gilbert, Jennifer Leigh
White Mountains
Regional HS
Twin Mountain, NH

Glidden, Janet
Spaulding HS
E Wakefield, NH

Godzyk, Melanie
Colebrook Acad
Colebrook, NH

Goelzer, Beth P
Timberlane Regional
Atkinson, NH

Goulet, Kelly Ann
Nashua SR HS
Nashua, NH

Gruca, Robert
Bishop Guertin HS
Lowell, MA

Haffer, Gretchen
Concord HS
Concord, NH

Hahn, Carol L
Timberlane Regional
Atkinson, NH

Haigis, Mark
Alvirne HS
Hudson, NH

Hale, Patricia
Spaulding HS
Rochester, NH

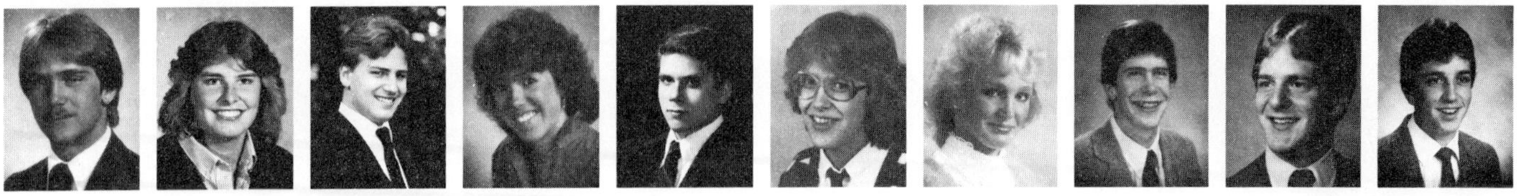

Hamel, Gary J
Goffstown Area HS
New Boston, NH

Hamilton, Gayle
Spaulding HS
Rochester, NH

Hansen, VI Otto E
Wilton-Lyndeboroug
h Coop
Wilton, NH

Harmon, Tammy
Concord HS
Manchester, NH

Haskell, Chris
Epping HS
Epping, NH

Hastings, Darlene
Newport JR SR HS
Newport, NH

Hayden, Wendy
Hopkinton HS
Contoocook, NH

Hayes, Jr John R
Bishop Guertin HS
Pelham, NH

Hazelton, III Robert
G
Londonderry HS
Manchester, NH

Hebert, Paul
Bishop Guertin HS
Nashua, NH

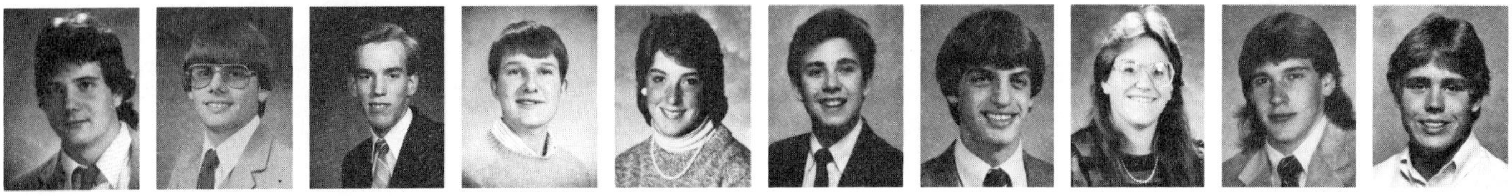

Heffernan, Patrick
Bishop Guertin HS
Nashua, NH

Henrikson, Scott A
Conant HS
Rindge, NH

Higgins, Stephen
Coe-Brown
Northwood Acad
Barrington, NH

Hillsgrove, Jr James
A
Milford Area SR HS
Amherst, NH

Hjulstrom, Katrina
Stevens HS
Claremont, NH

Hoffman, Jason
Concord Christian
Laconia, NH

Holloran, Gary
Bishop Quertin HS
Lowell, MA

Holmes, Jeannie
Pinkerton Acad
Chester, NH

Holt, Timothy
Mancheste Central
Manchester, NH

Hopkins, II
Wightman B
Moultonborough
Center Harbor, NH

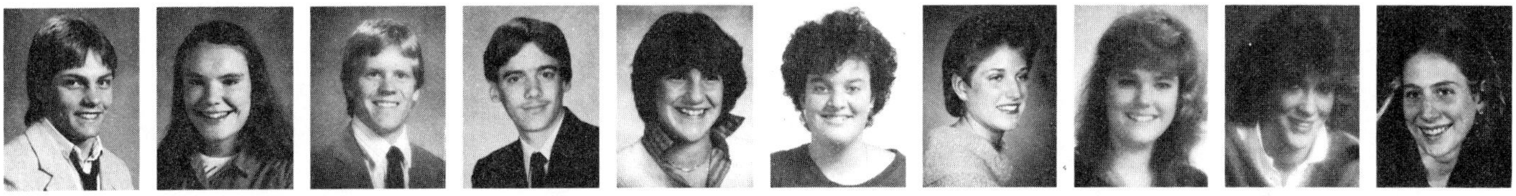

Howard, Clint
Spaulding HS
Rochester, NH

Howorth, Joanna K
Mount St Marys HS
Nashua, NH

Huntington, Neal
Milford Area SR HS
Amherst, NH

Hutchins, William K
Raymon JR/SR HS
Candia, NH

Ingersoll, Ann
Plymouth Area HS
Plymouth, NH

Ingraffia, Celeste
Phillips Exeter Acad
Pearl River, LA

James, Lora
Oyster River HS
Madbury, NH

Jeffrey, Marla L
Milford Area SR HS
Amherst, NH

Johnson, Kristin
Pinkerton Acad
Derry, NH

Johnson, Laurie Ann
Sunapee JR SR HS
Sunapee, NH

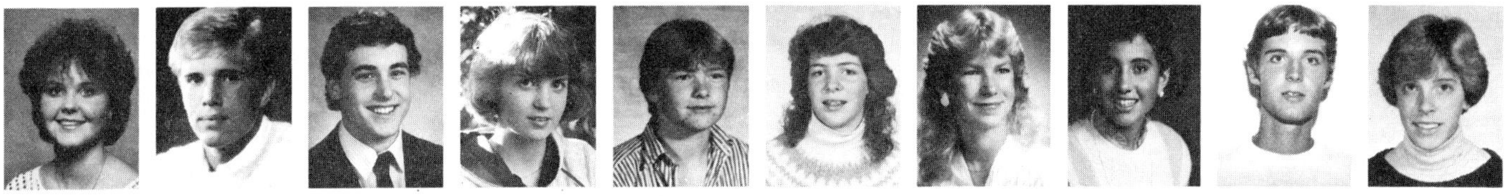

Jones, Kim
Inter-Lakes HS
Meredith, NH

Kaczmarek, Thomas
D
Phillips Exeter Acad
Inverness, IL

Karavasilis, Taki
Bishop Guertin HS
Nashua, NH

Kearns, Kristin
Phillips Exeter Acad
Exeter, NH

Kelsey, II Donald
Spaulding HS
Rochester, NH

Kidder, Heather
Central HS
Hooksett, NH

King, Lara D
Somersworth HS
Rollinsford, NH

King, Sherri
Mascoma Valley HS
Enfield, NH

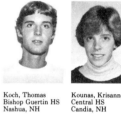

Koch, Thomas
Bishop Guertin HS
Nashua, NH

Kounas, Krisanne
Central HS
Candia, NH

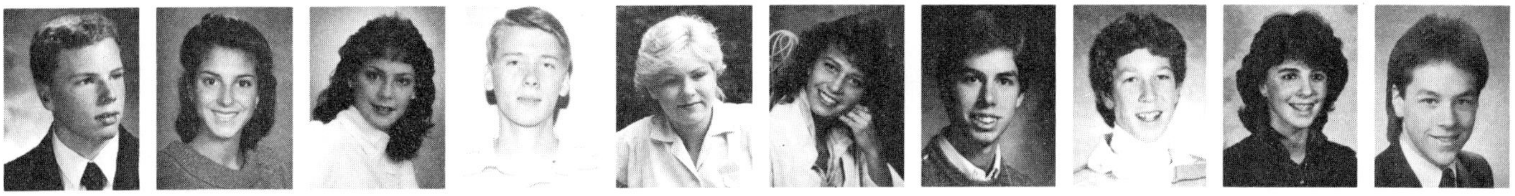

La Plante, Troy
Franklin JR SR HS
Franklin, NH

La Rocca, Denise
Manchester HS
Bedford, NH

Labranch, Susan
Pelham HS
Pelham, NH

Lammers, Steve
Portsmouth SR HS
Portsmouth, NH

Langley, Amy Jo
Keene HS
Marlborough, NH

Langlois, Tyhise
Dover HS
Barrington, NH

Lataille, Michael R
Alvirne HS
Hudson, NH

Lavigne, Kevin
Gorham HS
Gorham, NH

Lavigne, Michelle
Nashua HS
Nashua, NH

Le Blanc, Jeff
Manchester
Memorial HS
Manchester, NH

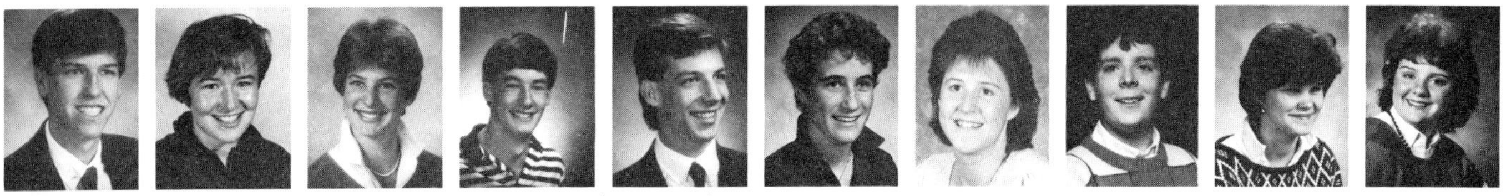

Le Duc, Todd
Bishop Guertin HS
Lowell, MA

Lee, Carrie
Alvirne HS
Hudson, NH

Lehman, Kimberley
S
Hopkinton HS
Contoocook, NH

Lempner, Michael S
Milford Area SR HS
Amherst, NH

Lombardi, Vince
Milford Area SR HS
Amherst, NH

Lord, Kelly D
Hopkinton HS
Contoocook, NH

Luck, Christine
Lynn
Newport HS
Newport, NH

Lyon, Jason
Newfound Memorial
Bristol, NH

Mackenzie, Diana
Concord HS
Concord, NH

Macri, Lisa
Alvirne HS
Hudson, NH

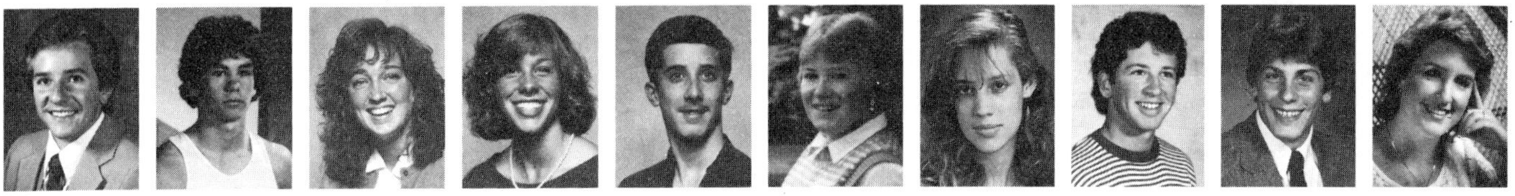

Majoros,
Christopher P
Newport HS
Guild, NH

Manderach, Frank
Salem HS
Salem, NH

Marsden, Julie
Kennett HS
N Conway, NH

Marshall, Kim
Kennett HS
Conway, NH

Martin, John
Inter-Lakes HS
Meredith, NH

Mason, Deborah
Littleton HS
Littleton, NH

Mathews, Kimberly
Henniker HS
Henniker, NH

Matos, Michael
Portsmouth SR HS
Portsmouth, NH

Matte, Peter J
Nashua SR HS
Nadshue, NH

Mayhew, Karen
Milford Area SR HS
Amherst, NH

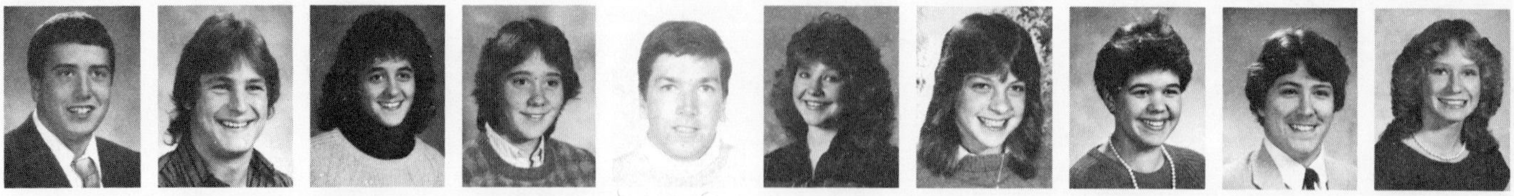

Mc Cann, Martin
Bishop Guertin HS
Lowell, MA

Mc Cormack, Brian
Pembroke Acad
Epsom, NH

Mc Gee, Kim
Spaulding HS
Rochester, NH

Mc Kinney, Melissa
Alvirne HS
Litchfield, NH

Mc Laughlin, Mark W
Exeter Area HS
E Kingston, NH

Mc Namara, Erin
Newport HS
Newport, NH

Mc Namara, Melissa
Pelham HS
Pelham, NH

Mejia, Micaela
Concord HS
Concord, NH

Mendolusky, Joel
Bishop Guertin HS
Amherst, NH

Messer, Cynthia
Keene HS
Keene, NH

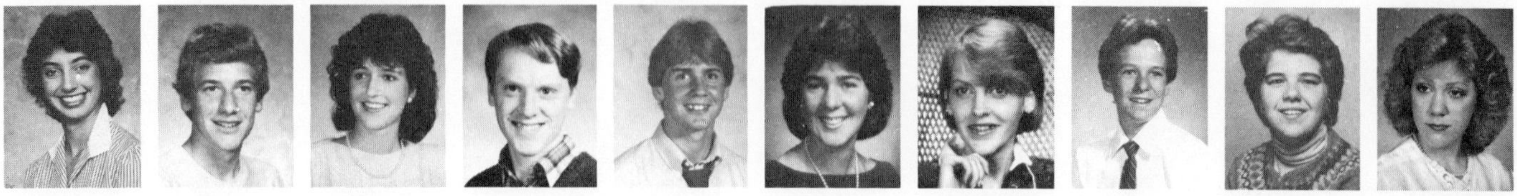

Messina, Donna Jean
Salem HS
Salem, NH

Michaud, Peter A
Hollis HS
Hollis, NH

Mikulis, Elizaeth A
Mt St Mary
Nashua, NH

Miner, Jonathan
Hopkinton HS
Hopkinton, NH

Minickiello, Scott
Keene HS
Keene, NH

Mone, Lisa Marie
Dover HS
Dover, NH

Morgan, Maureen Molly
Spaulding SR HS
Rochester, NH

Moriarty, Joe
Portsmouth HS
Rye, NH

Moulton, Christine
Laconia HS
Lakeport, NH

Mullane, Sheryl Ann
Mount St Mary
Nashua, NH

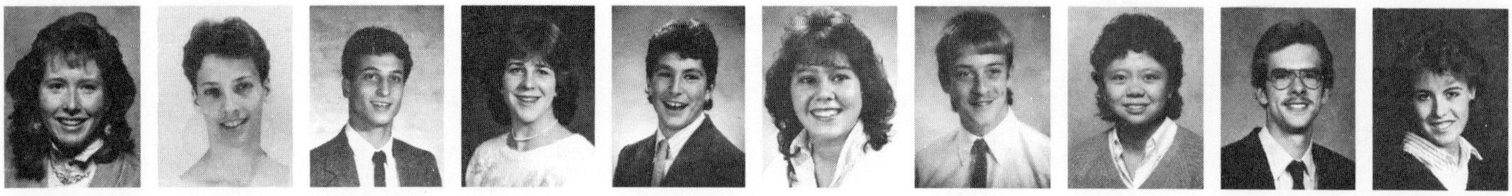

Murphy, Kirsten
Kennett HS
Intervale, NH

Neal, Philip Hawkins
Saint Pauls Schl
Richmond, VA

Negm, Robert S
St Thomas Aquinas
Portsmouth, NH

Neister, Kristen
Kingswood Regional
Barnstead, NH

Neveu, Mike
Bishop Guertin HS
Nashua, NH

Neveux, Traci
Concord HS
Concord, NH

Newell, III Ronald
Pembroke Acad
Suncook, NH

Ng, Siu
Laconia HS
Laconia, NH

Noble, Jeff
Franklin JR SR HS
Franklin, NH

Norris, Carmen
Mascoma Valley Regional HS
Enfield Ctr, NH

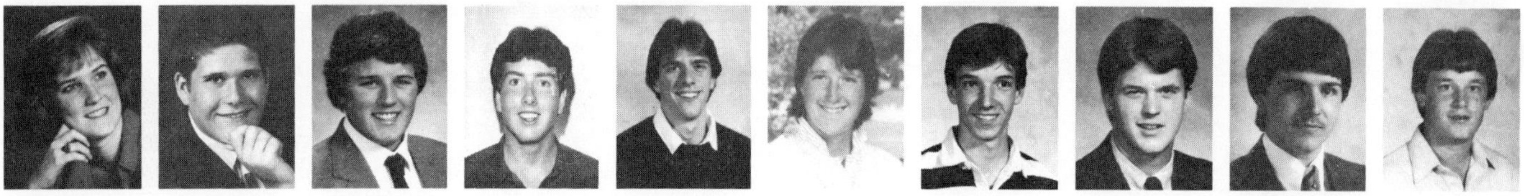

O Connor, Patricia
Portsmouth SR HS
New Castle, NH

O Rourke, II Gerard P
Alton Central HS
Laconia, NH

Oconnell, Bill
Bishop Brady HS
Concord, NH

Odum, Craig
Portsmouth HS
Portsmouth, NH

Ostergaard, Pete
Pelham HS
Pelham, NH

Patch, Suzanne
Stevens HS
Claremont, NH

Patrick, Mark
Portsmouth HS
Portsmouth, NH

Peters, Dan
Alvirne HS
Hudson, NH

Phillips, Jeffrey
Pembroke Acad
Suncook, NH

Phippard, Mark
Keene HS
Keene, NH

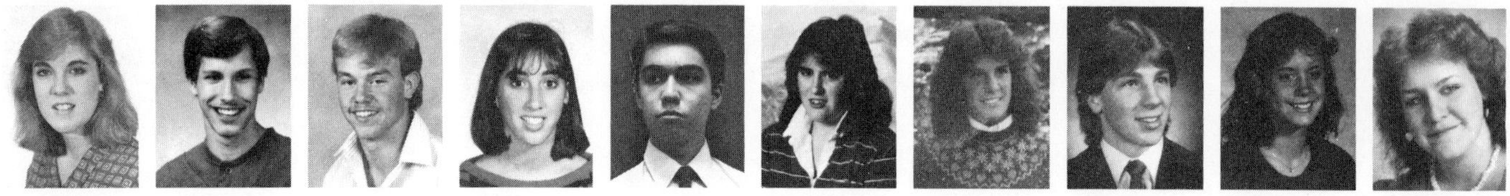

Pierce, Kimberly
Hanover HS
Hanover, NH

Pinard, Andrew
Pembroke Acad
Pittsfield, NH

Pitkin, Mark
Newport HS
Newport, NH

Platt, Paige
Central HS
Manchester, NH

Plautz, John P
St Thomas Aquina
Portsmouth, NH

Poisson, Loretta
Newport HS
Newport, NH

Porter, Stephanie
Contoocook Valley
Temple, NH

Potter, Mark
Salem HS
Salem, NH

Potvin, Julie
Portsmouth SR HS
Portsmouth, NH

Preve, Christina W
Concord HS
Penacook, NH

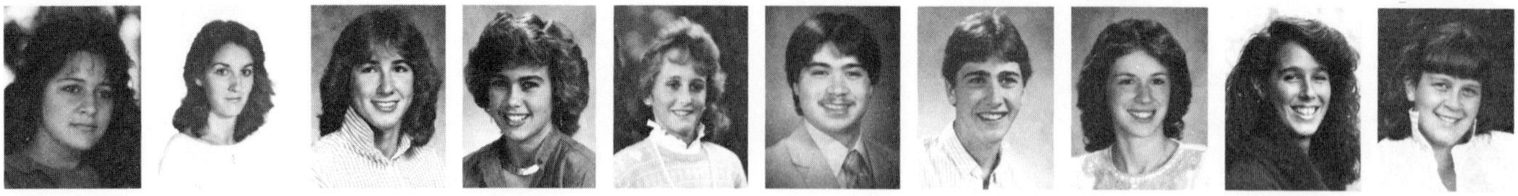

Prevel, Melina
Nashua SR HS
Nashua, NH

Quirk, Kimberly
Presentation Of Mary Acad
Dracut, MA

Ray, Kimberly
Dover HS
Dover, NH

Reed, Angela
Belmont HS
Canterbury, NH

Reed, Jennifer
Alvirne HS
Hudson, NH

Remington, Patrick Paul
Londonderry HS
Londonderry, NH

Reynolds, D Scott
Concord HS
Bow, NH

Rheault, Patricia
Manchester Central
Manchester, NH

Ricci, Christina M
Tilton Schl
Haverhill, MA

Rice, Kristen
Portsmouth HS
Portsmouth, NH

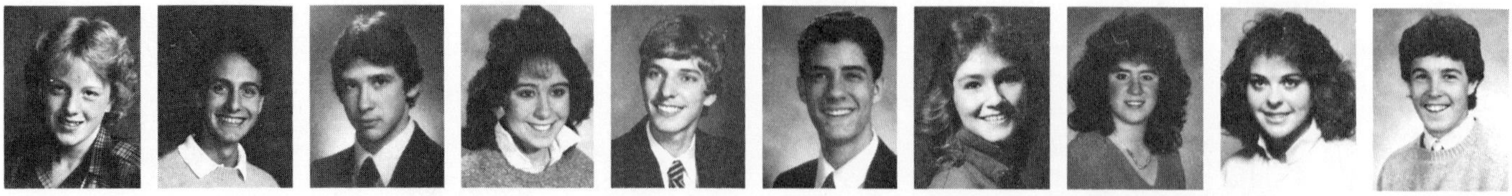

Rogers, Tara
Lebanon HS
W Lebanon, NH

Rohde, Monty
Mascoma Valley Reg
Canaan, NH

Rose, Todd J
Berlin HS
Dummer, NH

Rousseau, Kim
Alvirne HS
Hudson, NH

Routhier, Michael R
Nashua HS
Nashua, NH

Row, Christopher D
Bishop Guertin HS
Amherst, NH

Rowe, Diane
Thayer HS
Winchester, NH

Roy, Jannel A
Manchester H S
Bedford, NH

Russo, Nina
Nute HS
Milton, NH

Ryan, Timothy P
Bishop Brady HS
Canterbury, NH

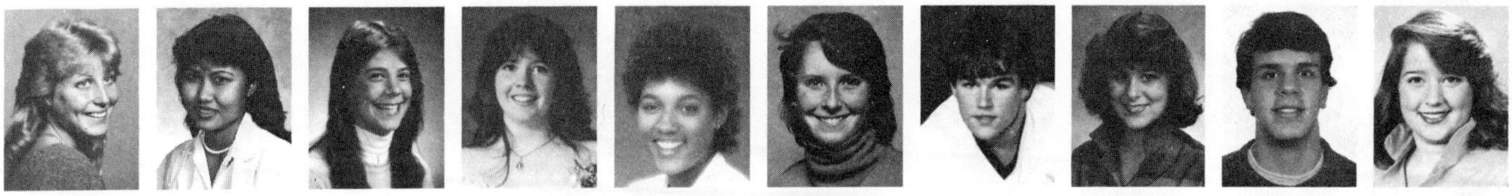

Sackos, Stacey
Alton Central HS
Alton Bay, NH

Sang, Somana Oum
Dover HS
Dover, NH

Schaltenbrand, Victoria
Tiberlane Regional
Atkinson, NH

Shepard, Julie
Keene HS
W Swanbey, NH

Sherman, Stephanie
Dover HS
Dover, NH

Shuff, Christen
Kennett HS
N Conway, NH

Sisk, Mark
Concord HS
Concord, NH

Smith, Laura
Bishop Brady HS
Penacook, NH

Smoot, David M
Phillips Exeter Acad
Raleigh, NC

Speer, Wendy
Merrimack HS
Merrimack, NH

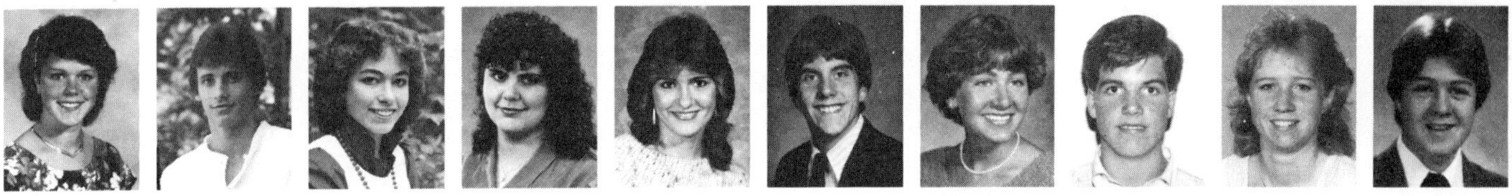

Srybny, Jennifer
Presentation Of Mary Acad
Haverhill, MA

Stallings, Carlton
Alvirne HS
Hudson, NH

Stevens, Betsy
Farmington HS
Middleton, NH

Strino, Sharon M
Alvirne HS
Manchester, NH

Styles, Jodi
Spaulding HS
Barrington, NH

Sullivan, James Joseph
Bishop Guertin HS
Lowell, MA

Swakla, Christine
Nashua HS
Newburyport, MA

Swan, III Thomas J
St Pauls Schl
Boston, MA

Tasker, Judi
Dover HS
Dover, NH

Tate, Jeffrey
Bishop Guertin HS
Hudson, NH

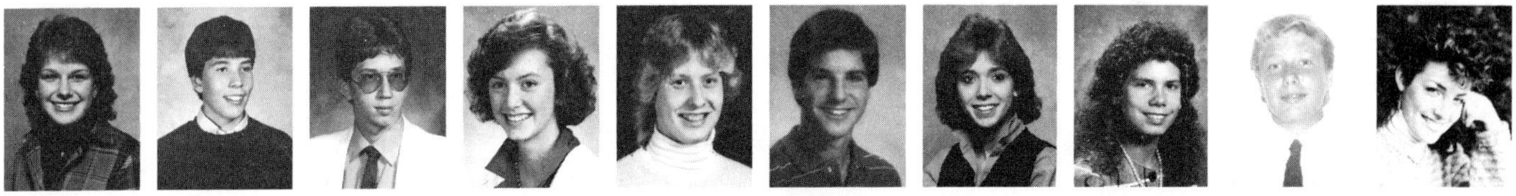

Taylor, Marcy L
Groveton HS
Groveton, NH

Tilton, John
Portsmouth HS
Portsmouth, NH

Topping, Noel
Nashua HS
Nashua, NH

Towle, Michele
Belmont HS
Canterbury, NH

Tracy, Donna
Pelham HS
Pelham, NH

Trask, Anthony
Winnacunnet HS
N Hampton, NH

Travis, Bonnie
Epping JR SR HS
Epping, NH

Tremblay, Jacqueline
Portsmouth SR HS
New Castle, NH

Troadec, Jean-Marc
High Mowing Schl
New London, CT

Trotter, Kim
Alvirne HS
Hudson, NH

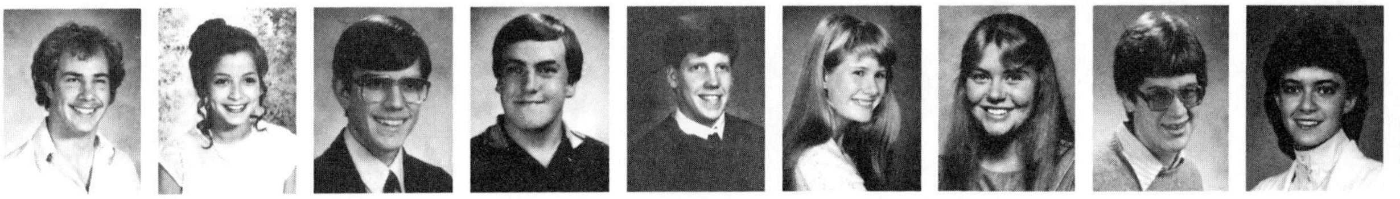

Vaas, Jeffrey
Spaulding HS
Rochester, NH

Vaillancourt, Josee
Alvirne HS
Hudson, NH

Vaillancourt, Ray
Bishop Guertin HS
Nashua, NH

Van Der Linde, Robert
Hillsboro-Deering Cooperative HS
Deering, NH

Van Mullen, William F
Trinity HS
Manchester, NH

Voll, S Layla
Oyster River HS
Durham, NH

Von Gillern, Heather
Fall Mountain Regional HS
Charlestown, NH

Waite, David
Concord HS
Concord, NH

Wallace, Susan L
Franklin HS
Franklin, NH

PHOTO NOT AVAILABLE

Wallin, Ian
Centeral HS
Candia, NH

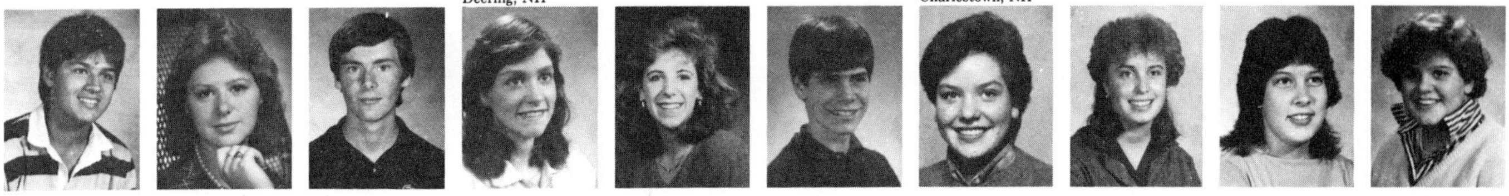

Ward, Dennis M
Spaulding HS
Rochester, NH

Washburne, Denise
Spaulding HS
Rochester, NH

Watson, Donald
Hollis HS
Hollis, NH

Wayman, Tricia
Concord HS
Concord, NH

Welch, Sonja
Concord Christian
Concord, NH

Wheeler, Jesse
Concord HS
Concord, NH

Wilbur, Karen
Dover HS
Dover, NH

Wilder, Kate
Keene HS
Keene, NH

Wilder, Lorri
Spaulding HS
Rochester, NH

Williams, Heather
Concord HS
Concord, NH

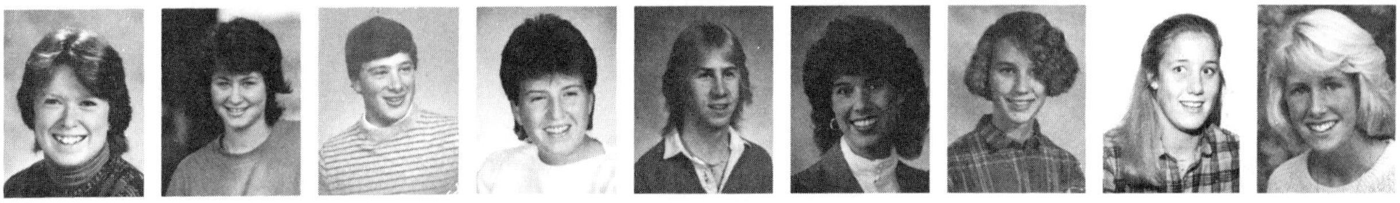

Williams, Kathleen
Belmont HS
Belmont, NH

Williams, Laura
Fall Mountain Regional HS
Walpole, NH

Williams, Robert
Manchester West
Bedford, NH

Wilt, Michelle
Lebanon HS
Hampton, NH

Woods, Ken
West HS
Bedford, NH

Woodwell, Lori
Keene HS
Keene, NH

Wozniak, Ann Marie
Presentation Of Mary Acad
Hduson, NH

Wyman, Anne B
St Pauls Schl
Quogue, NY

Young, Kimberly B
Kingswood Regional
Wolfeboro, NH

NEW YORK

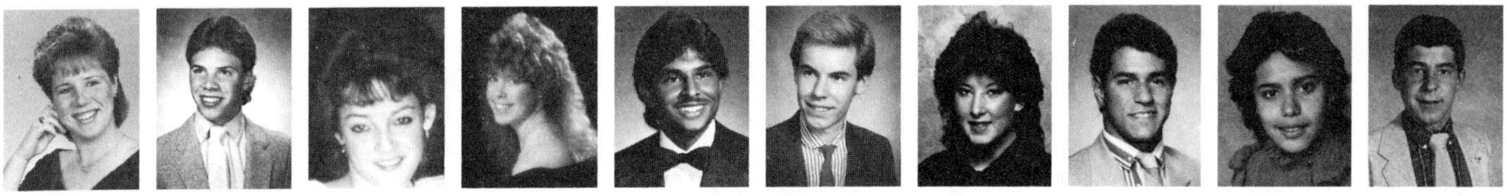

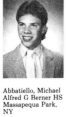

Abbate, Kathleen
Curtis HS
Staten Island, NY

Abbatiello, Michael
Alfred G Berner HS
Massapequa Park, NY

Abbatiello, Regina
St Raymond Academy For Girls
Bronx, NY

Abbott, Lisa
Cobleskill HS
Cobleskill, NY

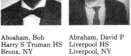

Aboaham, Bob
Harry S Truman HS
Bronx, NY

Abraham, David P
Liverpool HS
Liverpool, NY

Abrams, Debbie
Monroe Woodbury
Monroe, NY

Acampora, Kenneth
Sachem North Campus HS
Lk Ronkonkoma, NY

Acevedo, Giselle
Beach Channel HS
Richmond Hill, NY

Ackerman, Brian M
Curtis HS
Staten Island, NY

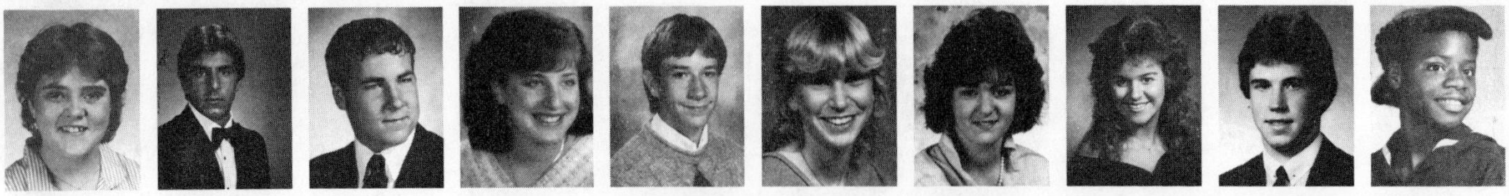

Ackler, Denise
Gowanda Central
Gowanda, NY

Acocella, Frank X
Iona Prep
Scarsdale, NY

Adair, Kevin J
Wayne Central HS
Ontario, NY

Adams, Barbara
Pittsford Sutherland
Pittsford, NY

Adams, Brian Burke
Columbia HS
Rensselaer, NY

Adams, Debbie
Henninger HS
Syracuse, NY

Adams, Kelly
N Tonawanda SR
N Tonawanda, NY

Adams, Michelle
Mont Pleasant HS
Schenectady, NY

Adams, II Peter W
Union Springs Acad
Andover, NJ

Adams, Terry
Yonkers HS
Yonkers, NY

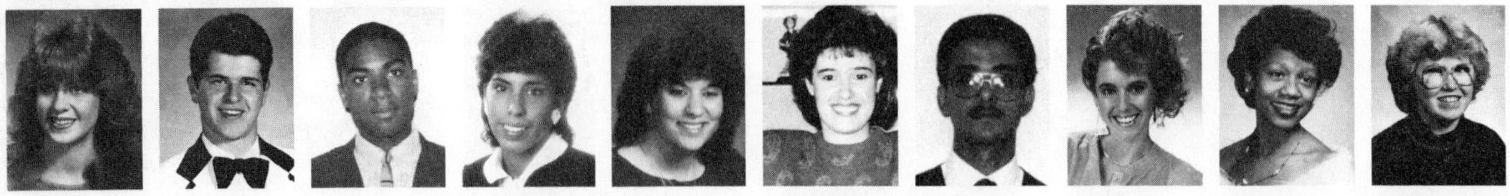

Adderley, Joanne
Watertown HS
Watertown, NY

Adinolfi, Michael T
Msgr Farrell HS
Staten Island, NY

Adolph, Anthony
Northeastern Acad
Jamaica, NY

Aggrippino, Jeanne
Hudson HS
Hudson, NY

Agnello, Joanna
Gates-Chili SR HS
Rochester, NY

Aguiar, Ana O
St Francis Prep
Jackson Hts, NY

Ahuja, Ajay
Newton HS
Rego Park, NY

Ainbinder, Ivy J
Oceanside SR HS
Oceanside, NY

Akers, Daria
Trott Vocational HS
Niagara Falls, NY

Akley, Helen
Canton Hugh C
Williams HS
Canton, NY

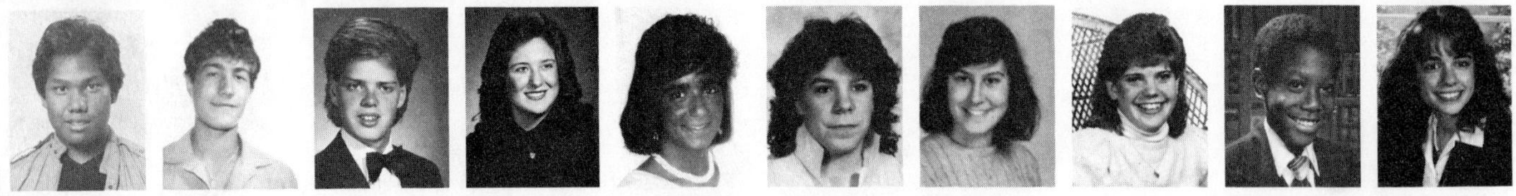

Alama, Rommel S
St Francis Prep
Rosedale, NY

Albanese, David
Archbishop Stepinac
N Tarrytown, NY

Albanese, Kevin
Iona Prep Schl
Yonkers, NY

Albano, Valerie A
Eastchester HS
Eastchester, NY

Albergo, Gia Lyn
Comsewogue HS
Pt Jeff Station, NY

Alberti, Laurie
Gates-Chili HS
Rochester, NY

Alduino, Leeanne
Central Islip HS
Central Islip, NY

Alexander, Julie
Thousand Islands
Cape Vincent, NY

Alexander, Michael
Bishop Ford
Catholic HS
Brooklyn, NY

Alexatos, Joyce
Archbishop Iakovos
Bayside, NY

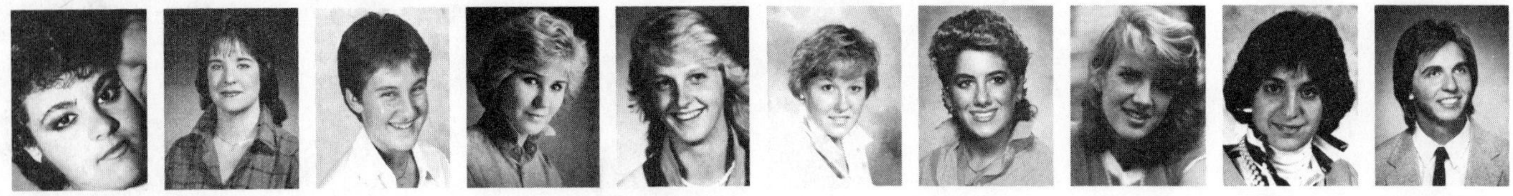

Aliotta, Dina
Washingtonville HS
Salisbury Mls, NY

Allen, Kathleen M
Sacred Heart Acad
Baldwin, NY

Allen, Lara
P V Moore HS
Bernhards Bay, NY

Allen, Mary
East
Syracuse-Minoa HS
Minoa, NY

Allen, Meredith L
Walton Central HS
Walton, NY

Allen, Shannon
Linton HS
Schenectady, NY

Allocco, Andrea
North Babylon SR
North Babylon, NY

Allport, Linda C
Irvington HS
Tarrytown, NY

Aloian, Patricia
North Tonawanda
SR HS
North Tonawanda,
NY

Alongi, Paul Robert
Plainedge HS
Massapequa, NY

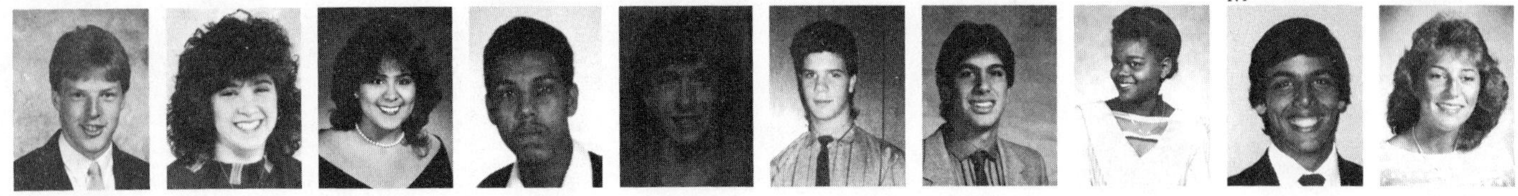

Altamuro, Paul
Frankfort-Schuyler
Frankfort, NY

Altschul, Ilene
Port Richmond HS
Staten Island, NY

Alvarado, Arlene
John F Kennedy HS
Bronx, NY

Alvarez, Domingo
Eastern District HS
Brooklyn, NY

Amann, Ken
Pelham Memorial
Pelham Manor, NY

Amarosa, Ricci
Mount Saint
Michael Acad
Bronx, NY

Amato, Frank
Archbishop Stepinac
White Plains, NY

Ambrose, Victoria
Nyack HS
Nyack, NY

Ambrosino, Allen
Albertus Magnus
New City, NY

Ames, Nanci
Massena Central HS
Massena, NY

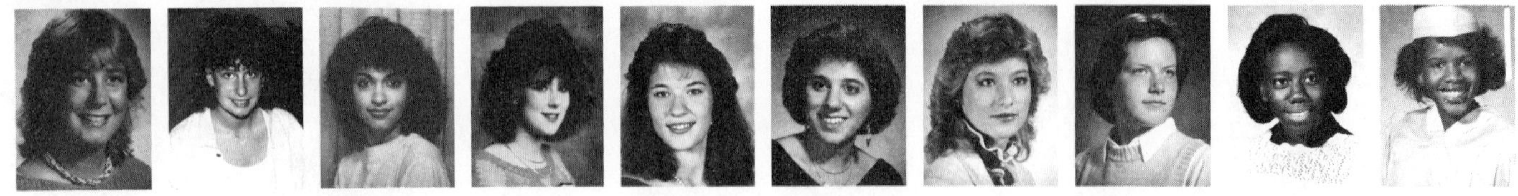

Amidon, Shellean R
Waterloo Central
Waterloo, NY

Amiel, Sarina
Haftr HS
Island Park, NY

Amores, Lizette
Cardinal Spellman
New York, NY

Amorosi, Anne
Brewster HS
Mount Vernon, NY

Amrhein, Eleanor
St Johns Prep
Middle Vlg, NY

Ancona, Lara Jean
Earl L
Vandermeulen HS
Mt Sinai, NY

Anderlik, Joelle
Cicero-North
Syracuse HS
Clay, NY

Anderson, Allie
Falconer Central HS
Conewango Vly, NY

Anderson, Arlene
Evander Childs HS
Bronx, NY

Anderson, Chanda
A Philip Randolph
Campus HS
New York, NY

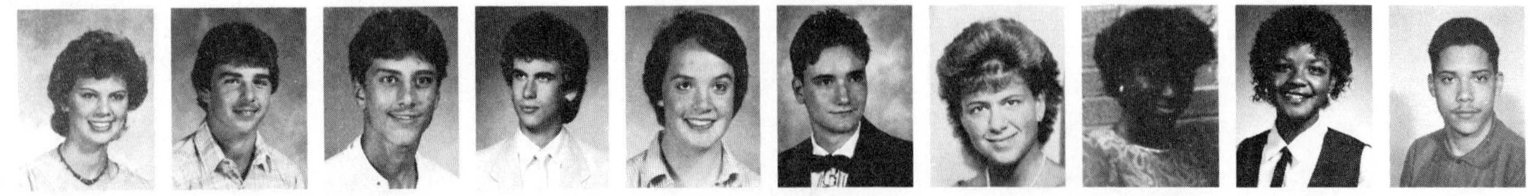

Anderson, Christine
Fairport HS
Fairport, NY

Anderson,
Christopher
Falconer Central HS
Kennedy, NY

Anderson, Jr Garth
Allan
York Central Schl
York, NY

Anderson, Gustav C
Centereach HS
Lk Ronk, NY

Anderson, Judith
Panama Central HS
Niobe, NY

Anderson, Michael
St Johns Prep
Long Island Cty,
NY

Anderson, Michele
West Islip HS
W Islip, NY

Anderson, Michele
Patrice
De Witt Clinton HS
Bronx, NY

Anderson, Telia
St Joseph HS
Brooklyn, NY

Andino, Luis
Alfred E Smith HS
Bronx, NY

Andrews, Jay
Fayetteville-Manlius
Manlius, NY

Andrews, Sean
Hahn American HS
Apo New York, NY

Androff, Amy Jo
Mount Mercy Acad
Lackawanna, NY

Andrzejewski, Susan
Liverpool HS
Liverpool, NY

Andujar, Ebelise
Grace Dodge Voc
Bronx, NY

Anello, Angelo P
La Salle SR HS
Niagara Falls, NY

Angerhofer, Todd E
Pittsford-Mendon
Pittsford, NY

Anghel, Marina
St Agnsen Academic
Elmhurst, NY

Angileri, Angela
Islip HS
Islip, NY

Angioli, Mark A
Iona Prep
Yonkers, NY

Anglero, Angel
Uniondale HS
Hempstead, NY

Anschultz,
Christopher
Shenendehowa HS
Ballston Lake, NY

Antes, Tanya
Croughton HS
Apo, NY

Antonovich, David
Union Springs Acad
Woodside, NY

Antoun, Nicholas
Vestal HS
Binghamton, NY

Anuth, James
Monsignor Farrell
Staten Island, NY

Apiado, Michelle
Commack HS South
Dix Hills, NY

Aptaker, Lisa G
The Spence Schl
New York, NY

Aquino, Denise
Niagara Catholic HS
Niagara Fls, NY

Arbelo, Albert L
Dewitt Clinton HS
Bronx, NY

Argersinger, Donald
Amsterdam HS
Amsterdam, NY

Arginteanu, Marc S
Tottenville HS
Staten Island, NY

Arias, Eliana
Christ The King HS
Maspeth, NY

Arleth, Erika K
Midwood HS
Brooklyn, NY

Armenia, Jo Ann
Tonawanda SR HS
Tonawanda, NY

Armison, Diane
Fillmore Central HS
Fillmore, NY

Armstrong, Austin
John A Coleman HS
Saugerties, NY

Armstrong, Michael
Vernon Verona
Sherrill Central Schl
Verona, NY

Arnold, Jennifer
Cicero-North
Syracuse HS
Mattydale, NY

Arricale, Frances J
M
Saint Francis Prep
Bayside, NY

Arrindell, Lisa C
High School Of
Performing Arts
Brooklyn, NY

Asdal, Kristin
Susan E Wagner HS
Staten Island, NY

Ash, Christina
Paul V Moore HS
Cleveland, NY

Asher, Debra
Canarsie HS
Brooklyn, NY

Ashraf, Saba
Bethpage HS
Bethpage, NY

Asif, M Kamil
Port Jervis HS
Sparrow Bush, NY

Aspecada, Maria
Dominican
Commercial HS
Jamaica, NY

Aspromonti, Vincent
Smithtown HS West
Smithtown, NY

Atherton, Duane
Bolivar Central Schl
Little Genesee, NY

Atherton, Kimberly
Greenwood Central
Canisteo, NY

Atkin, Andrew
Rocky Point HS
Rocky Point, NY

Atkinson, Scott
Pulaski JR SR HS
Pulaski, NY

Attico, Derek
William Howart
Taft HS
Bronx, NY

Attzs, Beverley
St Raymonds
Bronx, NY

Atwater, Bob
Liverpool HS
Liverpool, NY

Audouin, Elizabeth
Nazareth Regional
Brooklyn, NY

Augstein, Karen
Greenville Central
Greenville, NY

Ault, Charles
Torrejon American
Blytheville AFB, AR

Ausbon, Lenora H
The Fieldston Schl
New Rochelle, NY

Austin, Eustenia
Erasmus Hall HS
Brooklyn, NY

Avallone, Regina
H Frank Carey HS
Franklin Square,
NY

Avellanosa, Kristen
Nardin Acad
Williamsville, NY

Avery, Andrew
Horseheads HS
Horseheads, NY

Avery, David
Sherburne-Earvlle
Central HS
Earlville, NY

PHOTO
NOT
AVAILABLE
Avery, Michelle J
Morris HS
Bronx, NY

Avino, Mary
Mt Saint Mary Acad
Tonawanda, NY

Avril, Norma
Catherine Mcauley
Queens Village, NY

Axel, Lorey
Lawrence HS
Cedarhurst, NY

Ayala, Ayde
Msgr Scanlan HS
Bronx, NY

Ayotte, Thomas G
Smithtown West HS
Hauppauge, NY

Babbitt, Karen Beth
Belfast Central Schl
Caneadea, NY

Babrowicz, Wendy
Herkimer HS
Herkimer, NY

Bacchetta, Carlo
Angle American HS
Forest Hills, NY

Bacon, Andrew
Sachem HS North
Lake Ronkonkoma,
NY

Bacsardi, Paul P
Monroe-Woodburg
Central HS
Chester, NY

Baehr, Lisa
Duanesburg HS
Delanson, NY

Baginski, Jocelyn
Bishop Ford C C HS
Brooklyn, NY

Baglin, Marci
Greece Athena HS
Rochester, NY

Baguio, Miriam
The Stony Brook
Setauket, NY

Baiamonte, Rosalia
Bayside HS
Bayside, NY

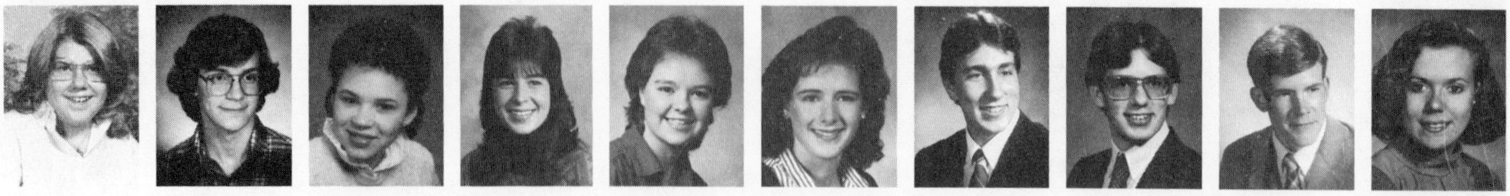

Bailey, Helen
Catholic Central HS
Troy, NY

Bailey, James
Livonia HS
S Lima, NY

Bailey, Jeanna
Baldwin SR HS
Roosevelt, NY

Bailey, Jodi
Avon JR SR HS
Avon, NY

Bailey, Kimberly R
Elmira Southside
Wellsburg, NY

Bailey, Rebecca
Clymer Central HS
Clymer, NY

Bailey, Shaune M
Jamestown HS
Jamestown, NY

Bailie, James
Saratoga Springs SR
Saratoga Sprgs, NY

Baker, Andrew J
East Aurora HS
E Aurora, NY

Baker, Heidi M
John Jay SR HS
South Salem, NY

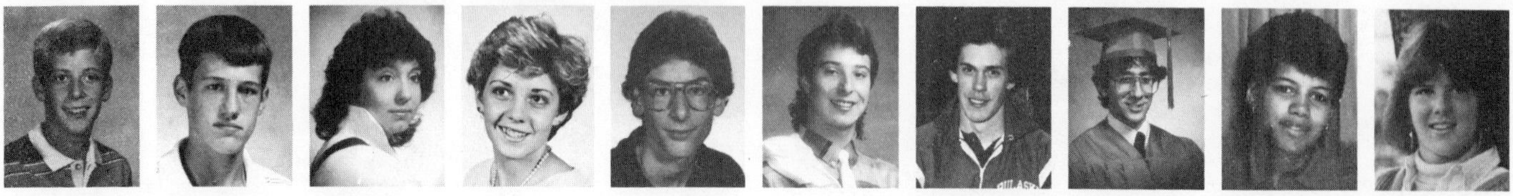

Baker, Robert
Sherburne-Earlville
Central HS
North Norwich, NY

Baker, Sean
Cazenovia HS
Cazenovia, NY

Baker, Shannan
Warsaw Central HS
Warsaw, NY

Baker, Tina
Hancock Central HS
Equinunk, PA

Balbera, Todd
Newfield HS
Selden, NY

Balcom, G Todd
South Glens Falls
SR HS
S Glens Falls, NY

Balcom, Thomas
Pulaski HS
Pulaski, NY

Balian, John
Nottingham HS
Syracuse, NY

Balines, Mitzy
Evander Childs HS
Bronx, NY

Ballard, Doreen
Milford Central Schl
Milford, NY

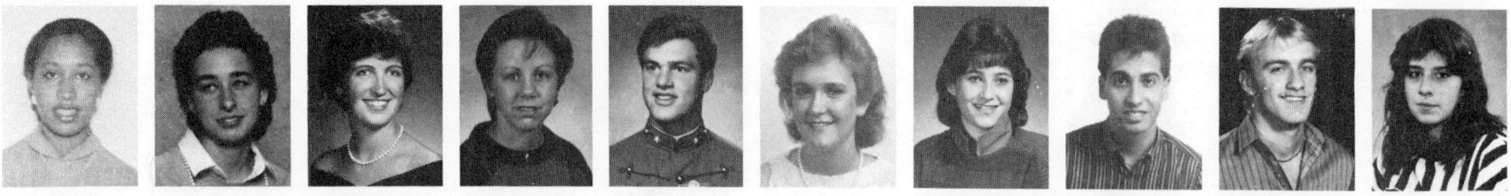

Banerjee, Rukmini
Clara Barton HS
Brooklyn, NY

Banks, Cynthia
Eunice
Hancock Central HS
Fishs Eddy, NY

Bannon, Elizabeth C
Our Lady Of
Lourdes HS
Poughkeepsie, NY

Barabas, Monica
Alden SR HS
Alden, NY

Baratta, Christopher
La Salle Military
E Islip, NY

Barauskas, Lisa A
Eastport HS
Eastport, NY

Barba, Jennifer
Roy C Ketcham SR
Poughkeepsie, NY

Barba, John M
Monsignor Farrell
Staten Island, NY

Barber, Kyle
Ticonderoga HS
Ticonderoga, NY

Barbera, Laura J
James Madison HS
Brooklyn, NY

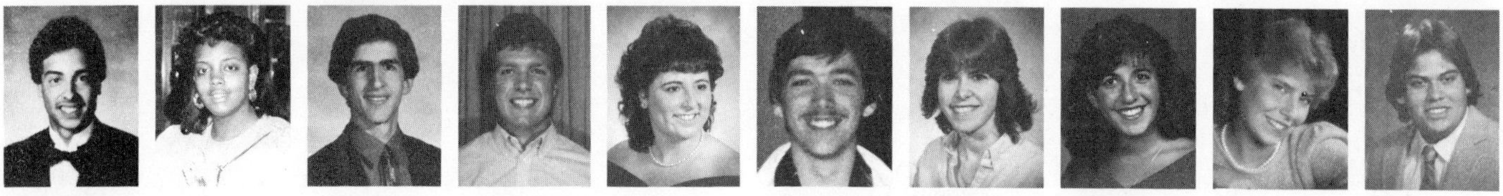

Barbosa, Stephen
Central Islip SR HS
Central Islip, NY

Barbour, Rachel
Dominican
Commercial HS
St Albans, NY

Barcia, Jr Salvatore
Monsignor Farrell
Staten Island, NY

Barden, Christopher
M
South Glens Falls
Gansevoort, NY

Bardon, Kelly L
Columbia HS
Castleton, NY

Barish, Eric M
Baldwin SR HS
Baldwin, NY

Barker, Wendy M
Scotia-Glenville HS
Scotia, NY

Barkett, Barbara
New Hartford
Central HS
Clinton, NY

Barner, Kristin M
Brockport Central
Hamlin, NY

Barnes, Jr Garry E
Marlboro HS
Marlboro, NY

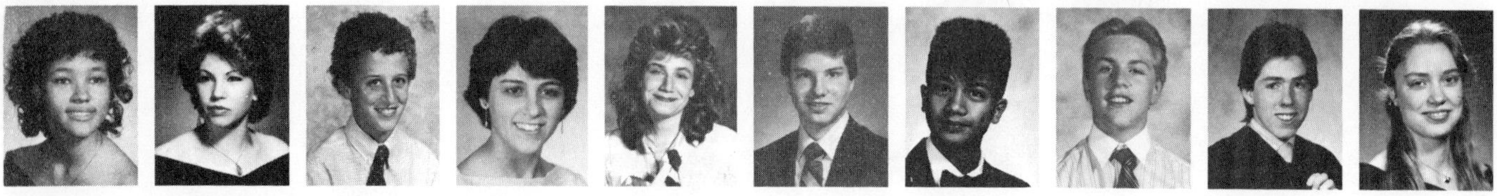

Barnes, Melissa
Bishop Loughlin
Memorial HS
Brooklyn, NY

Barnes, Priscilla
Minisink Valley
Central Schl
Howells, NY

Baroncelli, Craig A
Christian Brothers
Cazenovia, NY

Barone, Anne
Kenmore West SR
Kenmore, NY

Barone, Danielle
St John Villa Acad
Staten Island, NY

Barresi, III Anthony
V
Hendrick Hudson
Croton On Hudson,
NY

Barrion, Antonio
Archbishop Molley
S Ozone Park, NY

Barry, Jr James J
Minisink Valley HS
Middletown, NY

Barry, John
Clarkstown S HS
Bardonia, NY

Barry, Kristen
St Barnabas HS
Bronx, NY

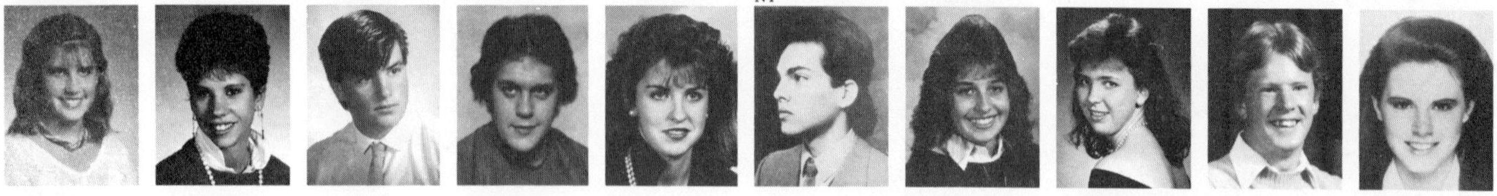

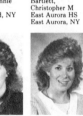

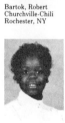

Bartel, Cheryl
Long Island
Lutheran HS
Garden City, NY

Bartkow, Bonnie
Curtis HS
Staten Island, NY

Bartlett,
Christopher M
East Aurora HS
East Aurora, NY

Bartok, Robert
Churchville-Chili
Rochester, NY

Bartokvich, Vicki
Hamburg SR HS
Hamburg, NY

Bartolomeo, Andrew
High School Of Art
& Design
Brooklyn, NY

Barton, Dena
Notre Dame-Bishop
Gibbons HS
Clifton Park, NY

Barton, Ivy
Hendrick Hudson
Peekskill, NY

Barton, Robert P
Red Jacket Central
Shortsville, NY

Bartow, Cheryl
Academy Of Saint
Bayport, NY

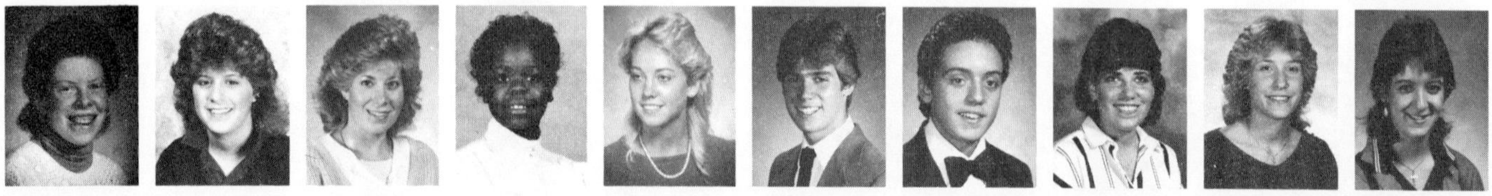

Bashford, Katie A
Averill Park HS
W Sandlake, NY

Basi, Maryrose
Frankfort Schuyler
Frankfort, NY

Basile, Marie
Grand Island HS
Grand Island, NY

Baskin, Dawn
Springfield Gardens
Springfield Grdns,
NY

Bassage, Denise
Wayne Central HS
Walworth, NY

Basso, Robert D
Peekskill HS
Peekskill, NY

Basulto, Dean
Fordham
Preparatory Schl
Bronx, NY

Batemarco, Lynn
Clarkstown High
School South
Nanuet, NY

Bates, Kristen
Greece Athena HS
Rochester, NY

Bates, Staci
Kendall SR SR HS
Holley, NY

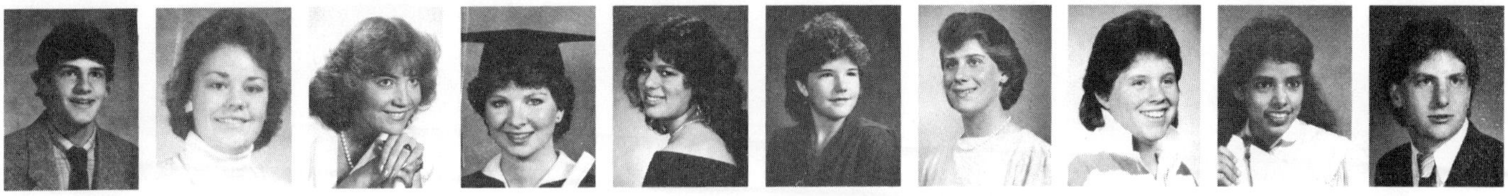

Battista, Michael
Archbishop Stepinac
Hawthorne, NY

Bauer, Natalie R
North Collins HS
Springville, NY

Bauer, Tammy
Marcus Whitman
Stanley, NY

Bauer, Vicki
Frankfurt American
APO New York, NY

Baum, Rachel
Hendrick Hudson
Croton On Hudson, NY

Beach, Melissa M
Little Falls HS
St Johnsville, NY

Beasley, Tamara L
Herkimer SR HS
Herkimer, NY

Beaulieu, Renee
Colonie Central HS
Albany, NY

Becerril, Deborah
John Dewey HS
Brooklyn, NY

Bechtel, Trevor M
Homer Central HS
Homer, NY

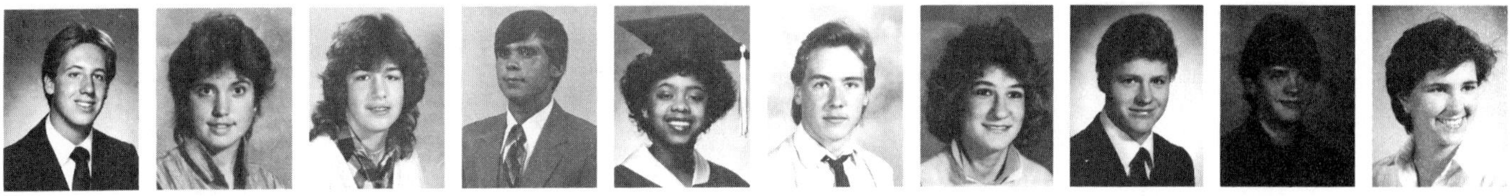

Becker, Charles E
Ward Melville HS
Centereach, NY

Becker, Laura
Jordan-Elbridge HS
Elbridge, NY

Becker, Stacey
Glen Cove HS
Glen Cove, NY

Beckwith, Kyle J
Granville Central
Granville, NY

Bedford, Cheryl
St John The Baptist D HS
Amityville, NY

Begin, Kenneth
Berlin Central HS
Berlin, NY

Begy, Karen
Wayne Central HS
Ontario, NY

Behari, Jr Joseph
Savona Central Schl
Savona, NY

Belden, Mark
Hudson Falls SR
Hudson Falls, NY

Belfay, Ann
Liverpool HS
Liverpool, NY

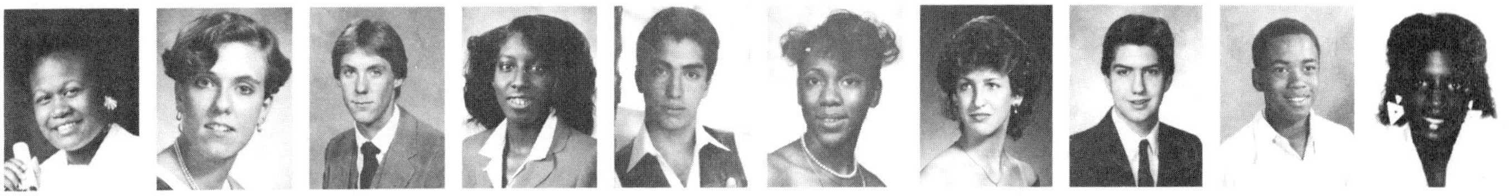

Belizaire, Guirlaine
Midwood H S At Brooklyn College
Brooklyn, NY

Bell, Amy M
Our Lady Of Mercy
Penfield, NY

Bell, Michael J
Perry Central HS
Perry, NY

Bell, Vanecia
Greater N Y Acad
Central Islip, NY

Bellantoni, Rory J
Blind Brook HS
Rye Brook, NY

Bellinger, Pamela
Hillcrest HS
Jamaica, NY

Bellisario, Stephanie
Sacred Heart HS
Yonkers, NY

Belmonte, John B
Patchogue-Medford
Patchogue, NY

Belton, David
Lafayette HS
Buffalo, NY

Belton, Tanya
White Plains HS
White Plns, NY

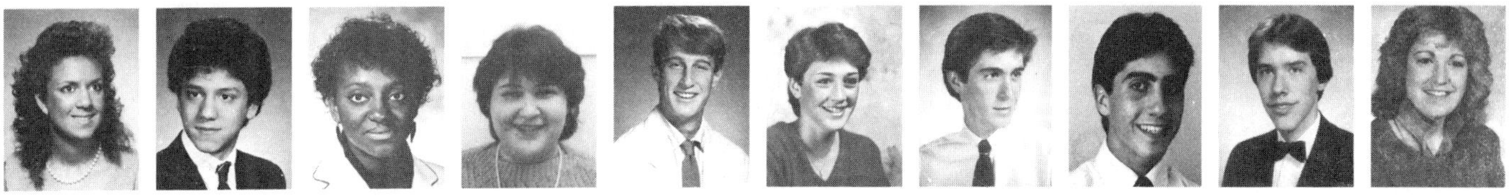

Beltrani, Annmarie
Sachem HS
Farmingville, NY

Ben-Dor, Eldad
Suffern SR HS
Monsey, NY

Benbow, Curin
The Knox Schl
East Setauket, NY

Benedict, Lael
Bainbridge-Guilford Central HS
Bainbridge, NY

Benerofe, Jeff
Harrison HS
Purchase, NY

Beninati, Nancy
Bay Shore HS
Bay Shore, NY

Benjamin, Scott S
Oswego HS
Oswego, NY

Bennati, Brian
Vernon-Verona-Sherrill HS
Sherrill, NY

Benner, Michael J
Canisius HS
Cheektowaga, NY

Bennett, Deborah
Victor Central HS
Macedon, NY

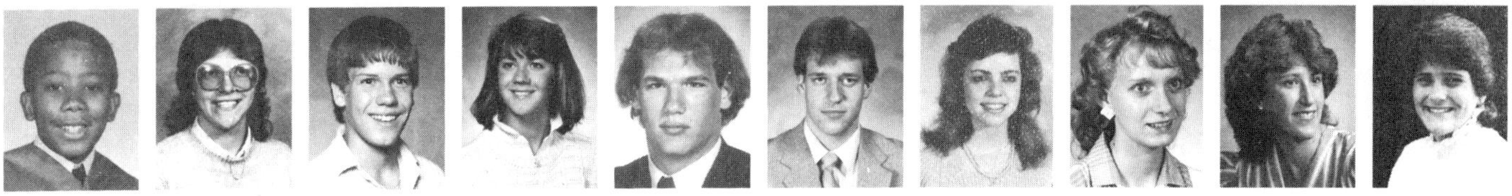

Bennett, Derrick C
Adlai E Stevenson
Bronx, NY

Bennett, Heather
Warsaw Central
Warsaw, NY

Bennett, James
Rome Free Acad
Rome, NY

Bennett, Kerry A
Baldwin HS
Baldwin, NY

Bennink, Michael J
East Syracuse-Minoa HS
East Syracuse, NY

Benns, Jr George
Burgard Vocational
Buffalo, NY

Benson, Donna
Curtis HS
Staten Island, NY

Benson, Yvette
Cattaraugus Central
Cattaraugus, NY

Bentley, Julie L
Panama Central
Niobe, NY

Benwitz, Candace
Newark SR HS
Newark, NY

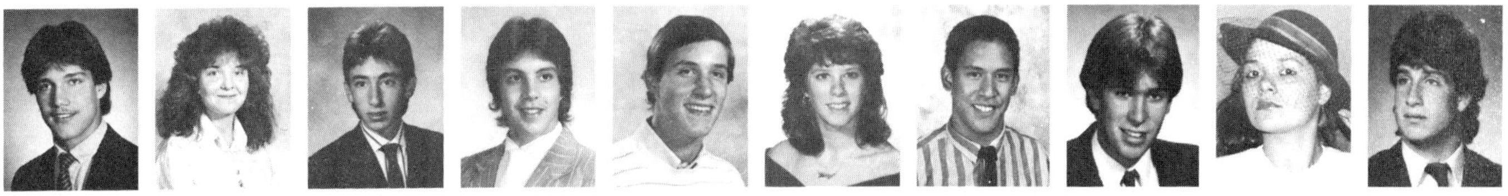

Benzinger, Andrew X
Glen Cove HS
Glen Cove, NY

Beraud, Kelly
New Dorp HS
Staten Isl, NY

Berg, Jonathan D
General Douglas Mac Arthur HS
Wantagh, NY

Berger, Chris
John F Kennedy HS
Mahopac, NY

Berkenfield, James
Woodlands HS
Hartsdale, NY

Berliner, Theresa
Lindehurst HS
Lindenhurst, NY

Bernales, Clark G
Christian Brothers
Fayetteville, NY

Berns, Jon
Mamaroneck HS
Mamaroneck, NY

Bernstein, Veronica
Onteora Central HS
West Shokan, NY

Bersin, Scott A
Oceanside HS
Oceanside, NY

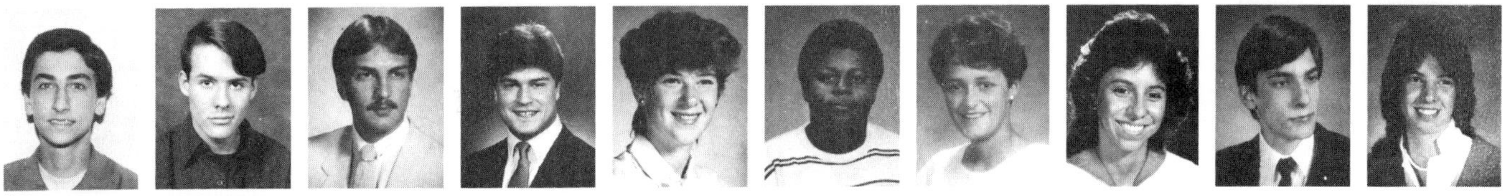

Bertoldo, Jon
Monsignor Farrell
Staten Island, NY

Bertoletti, Robert A
St Francis Prep
Douglaston, NY

Bertucci, Thomas J
Dunkirk SR HS
Dunkirk, NY

Bertuccio, Michael J
St Anthonys HS
Tanglewood Hills, NY

Besemer, Eliese
Union-Endicott HS
Endicott, NY

Bess, Jamey
Jamestown HS
Jamestown, NY

Besse, Kimberly
Queensbury HS
Glens Falls, NY

Betancourt, Gloria E
Uniondale HS
Uniondale, NY

Betrus, Marc
Rome Catholic HS
Rome, NY

Beverly, Kerry
Oakfield-Alabama Central HS
Oakfield, NY

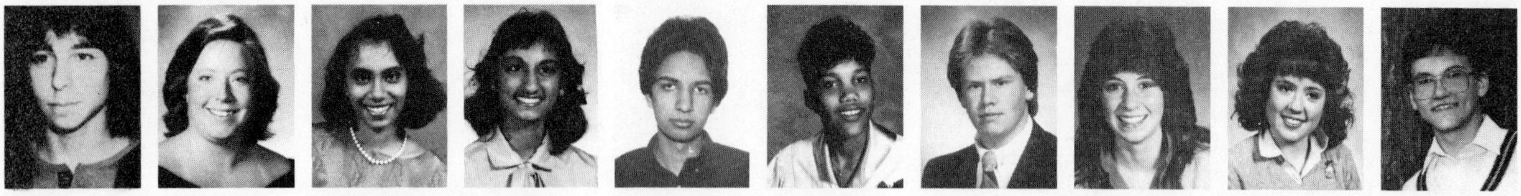

Bevilacqua, John
West Genesee HS
Syracuse, NY

Beyer, Beth M
Northport HS
Northport, NY

Bhagwan, Sharon
Stuyvesant HS
New York, NY

Bhalla, Anju
Fairport HS
Fairport, NY

Bhatnager, Ashu
Pleasantville HS
Pleasantville, NY

Bice, Towanna
St Catharine Acad
Bronx, NY

Bidak, Dean
Lewiston-Porter SR
Youngstown, NY

Bielemeier, Erica
Marie
Cornwall Central HS
Cornwall, NY

Bier, Elizabeth M
Bishop Ludden HS
Syracuse, NY

Bierer, Matthew K
Sodus Central HS
Williamson, NY

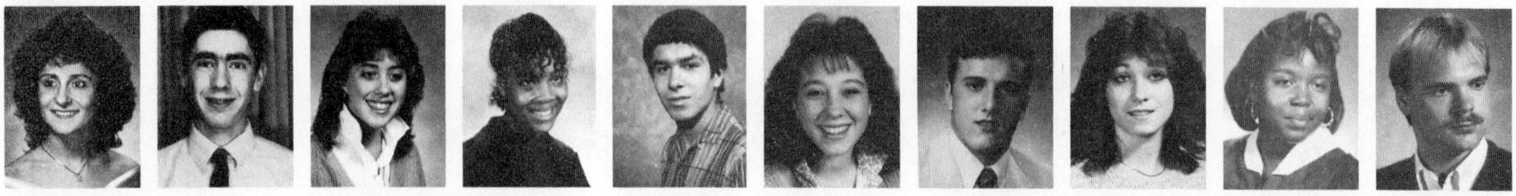

Bifulco, Maryanne F
The Mary Louis
S Ozone Park, NY

Bigley, John
Mount St Michael
Mount Vernon, NY

Billittier, Mary Beth
Mt Mercy Acad
Hamburg, NY

Billups, Tangela
Jaquet
Irondequoit HS
Rochester, NY

Binenti, Douglas
Mount Vernon HS
Mt Vernon, NY

Bionda, Danielle
Northport HS
Northport, NY

Birmingham, Brian
S
Penn Yan Acad
Penn Yan, NY

Birrittella, Patricia
Roy C Ketcham SR
Wappinger Falls,
NY

Bishop, Chanda
Nazareth Regional
Brooklyn, NY

Bishop, Jeffrey
Anthony A
Henninger SR HS
Syracuse, NY

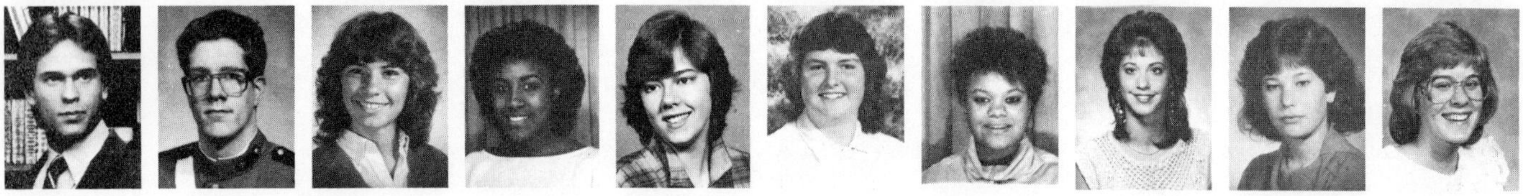

Biswanger, Jr
Robert
Liverpool HS
Liverpool, NY

Black, David
Thuney
Albany Acad
Albany, NY

Black, Joy L
Seton Catholic
Central HS
Apalachin, NY

Blackwood, Ariella
St Edmund HS
Brooklyn, NY

Blaetz, Elke Monika
Canajoharie HS
Canajoharie, NY

Blaize, Carolyn
Mont Pleasant HS
Schenectady, NY

Blake, Shantel
St Catharine Acad
Bx, NY

Blam, Holly R
East Islip HS
Great River, NY

Blanchard, Suzanne
Clayton A Bouton
JR SR HS
Voorheesville, NY

Blann, Stephanie
Faith Heritage Schl
Baldinsville, NY

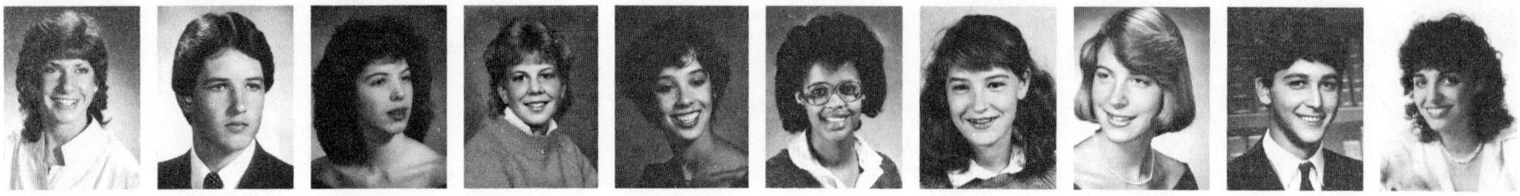

Blau, Cheryl
Massapequa HS
Massapequa Park,
NY

Blecha, Mark D
Pioneer Central HS
Machias, NY

Blish, Stefanie G
Ravena Coeymans
Selkirk HS
S Bethlehem, NY

Bliss, Denise
Kendall JR SR HS
Hamlin, NY

Blocker, Wendy Jill
Kingston HS
Lake Katrine, NY

Blount, Christina
Sperry HS
Rochester, NY

Blumenauer,
Christine
Bay Shore HS
Bay Shore, NY

Blumenauer,
Kathleen A
Bay Shore HS
Bay Shore, NY

Blumenfeld, Brad
Roslyn HS
Roslyn, NY

Blumreich, Janna
Barker Central HS
Barker, NY

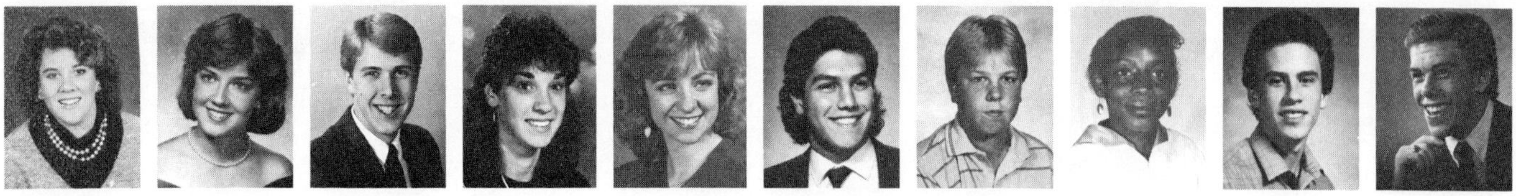

Bly, Jennifer
Southside HS
Pine City, NY

Boate, Christine
Connetquot HS
Bohemia, NY

Boatwright, Michael
W
Horseheads HS
Horseheads, NY

Bobis, Melissa
Clarkstown HS
New City, NY

Bobo, Tracey
Ramstein American
Apo, NY

Boccia, Vincent
Oceanside HS
Oceanside, NY

Bock, Duane Philip
East Hampton HS
E Hampton, NY

Boddie, Dana
Morris HS
New York, NY

Bogaczyk, David
Union-Endicott HS
Endicott, NY

Bohanan, Todd
Liverpool HS
Liverpool, NY

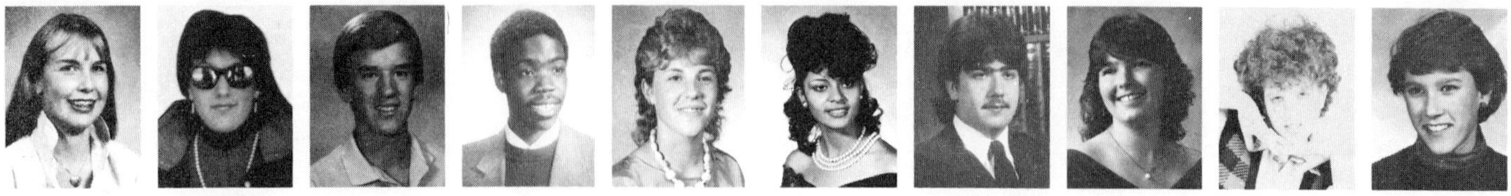

Bohli, Margaret
Bishop Ludden HS
Syracuse, NY

Boice, Christina
Margaretville
Central HS
Margaretville, NY

Boice, Randy
Sherburne-Earlville
Norwich, NY

Bolden, Jr Vernie
James E Sperry HS
Henderson, NC

Boldt, Diane C
West Seneca West
SR HS
W Seneca, NY

Bolivar, Aura
Jane Addams VHS
Bronx, NY

Bolognese, Patrick J
West Seneca West
SR HS
West Seneca, NY

Bolton, Amy L
Oneida HS
Oneida, NY

Boltz, Ann
South Park HS
Buffalo, NY

Boltz, Catherine L
Hamberg SR HS
Hamburg, NY

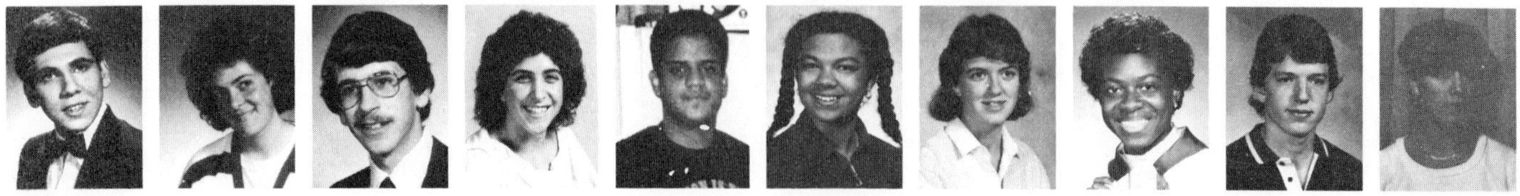

Bonanno, Vincent J
Regis HS
New York, NY

Bonasia, Dolores
Sewanhaka HS
Elmont, NY

Boncaro, David
Colonie Central HS
Albany, NY

Bonello, Jeanine
Sachem H S North
Holbrook, NY

Bonilla, Jr Rene
Eastern District HS
Brooklyn, NY

Boone, Darlene N
Midwood HS
Brooklyn, NY

Boone, Melissa
Bishop Grimes HS
Manlius, NY

Boothe, Lisa
Andrew Jackson HS
St Albans, NY

Borer, Robert
Portville Central
Portville, NY

Borges, Lucy
St Catharine Acad
Bronx, NY

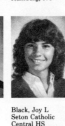

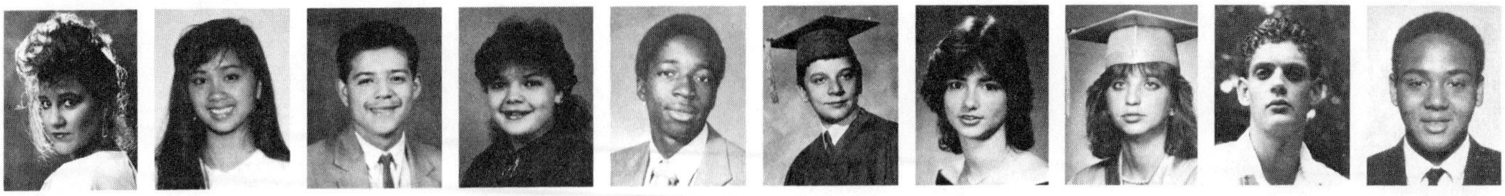

Borgesano, Theresa
Saint John The
Baptist HS
Lindenhurst, NY

Borja-Gorre, Jessica
Half Hollow Hills
HS East
Dix Hills, NY

Borjas, Astor
Cardinal Hayes HS
Bronx, NY

Boschen, Rachel
Acad Of Mt St
Bronx, NY

Boswell, Orville
Allhallows Inst
New York, NY

Botschagow, Alex
Archbishop Molloy
Richmond Hill, NY

Bott, Marcella
St Barnabas HS
Bronx, NY

Bottitta, Grace E
Bayport-Blue Point
Blue Point, NY

Bouchard, John
New Lebanon
Central HS
New Lebanon, NY

Bouey, III Benkai
Edward H
HS For The
New York, NY

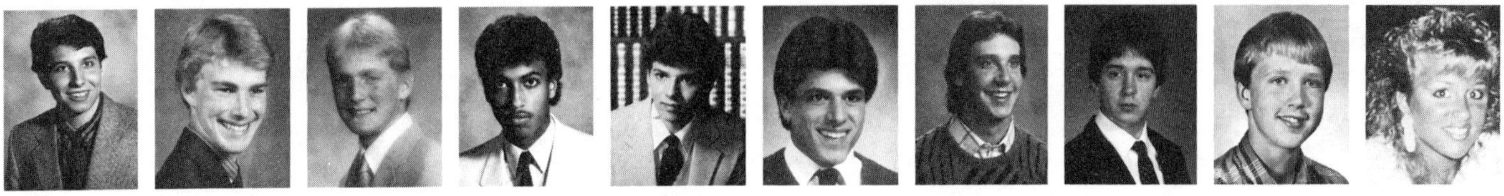

Bougiamas, John S
Bronx HS Of
Syosset, NY

Boule, Aaron E
Whitehall HS
Whitehall, NY

Boule, Eugene
Fort Ann Central
Ft Ann, NY

Bourdony, Michael
R
The Bronx HS Of
Bronx, NY

Bourgault, Brian
Tamarac HS
Troy, NY

Bousselot, Brian
Liverpool HS
Liverpool, NY

Bouton, Chris
Rome Free Acad
Rome, NY

Bouza, George Louis
Herricks HS
New Hyde Prk, NY

Bova, Shawn
Frewsburg Central
Frewsburg, NY

Bova, Susan
St Edmund HS
Brooklyn, NY

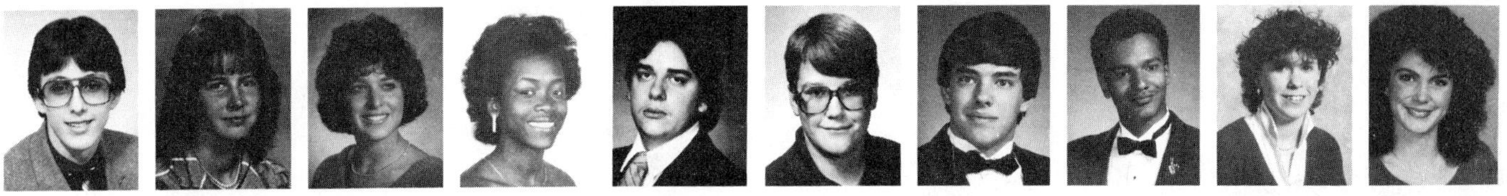

Bowen, Jay
Newfane HS
Newfane, NY

Bowman, Deborah L
Faith Heritage Schl
Clay, NY

Boyack, Sharon
Gates Chili SR HS
Rochester, NY

Boyd, Quanda
Deirdra
Mount Vernon HS
Mt Vernon, NY

Boyd, Stephen
Long Island
Lutheran HS
Westbury, NY

Boyd, Tim
West Seneca West
W Seneca, NY

Boynes, Thomas M
Cathedral
Preparator
Bronx, NY

Bozan, Erik David
Cardinal Hayes HS
New York, NY

Bozzey, Leann
Seton Catholic
Central HS
Endwell, NY

Brabazon, Tara
Bellport HS
Bellport, NY

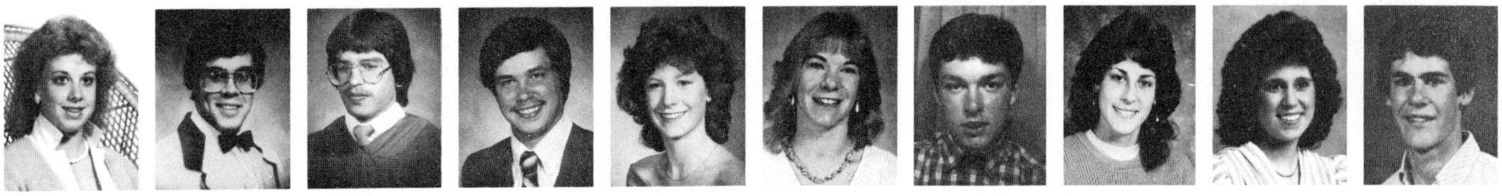

Brace, Monica
Watkins Glen HS
Burdett, NY

Brache, Amiro
Mc Quaid Jesuit HS
Fairport, NY

Brackman, Jr James
Ellenville HS
Napanoch, NY

Bradley, Michael
La Fayette HS
Lafayette, NY

Bradt, Linda J
Schalmont HS
Schenectady, NY

Bradway, Kimberly
G Ray Bodley HS
Fulton, NY

Brady, Kevin
All Hallows HS
New York, NY

Brady, Noreen
Mynderse Acad
Seneca Falls, NY

Brady, Tara
Hicksville SR HS
Hicksville, NY

Brahm, James E
Naples Central Schl
Canandaigua, NY

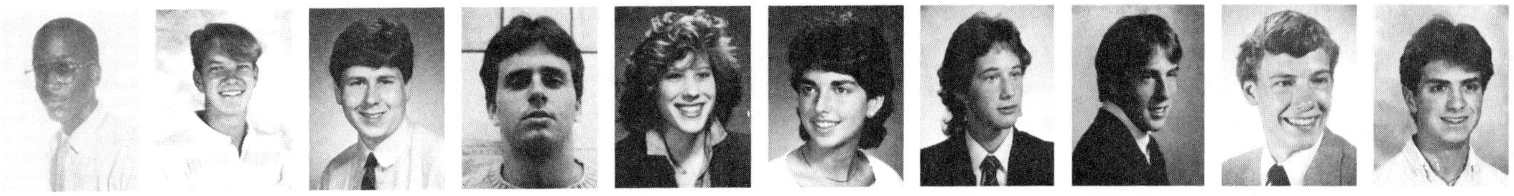

Branch, Dwayne
Riverhead HS
Riverhead, NY

Branch, Scott
Th Stony Brook
Stony Brook, NY

Brand, Terrance A
F D Roosevelt HS
Clinton Corners, NY

Brandman, Andrew
Polytechnic
Presparatory CDS
Brooklyn, NY

Brandt, Erika
Walt Whitman HS
Huntington Stat,
NY

Braslow, Michele
White Plains HS
White Plains, NY

Brasser, John C
Churchville-Chili SR
Rochester, NY

Brayton, Stephen G
Glens Falls HS
Glens Falls, NY

Breed, II Charles L
Chittenango HS
Chittenango, NY

Breitenstein, David
Duansburg Central
Delanson, NY

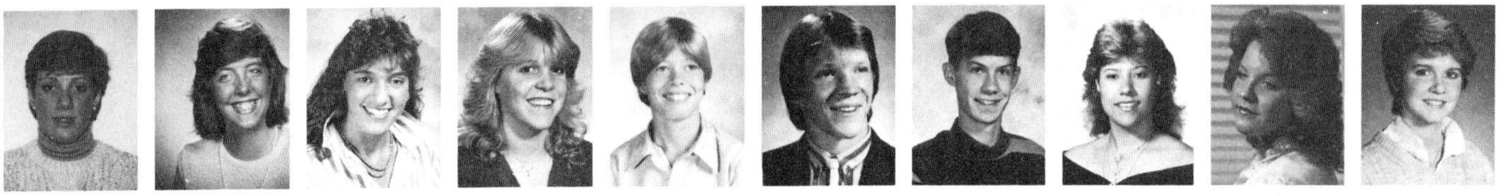

Brennan, Heather
Clayton A Bouton
JR SR HS
New Scotland, NY

Brennan, Maureen
Our Lady Of Merch
Fairport, NY

Brennan, Michelle
Brockport HS
Brockport, NY

Brenner, Crissy
Miller Place HS
Miller Place, NY

Bressler, Larry
Herbert H Lehman
Bronx, NY

Brethen, Patrick S
Red Creek Central
Red Creek, NY

Breunig, Michael D
Sidney Central HS
Sidney, NY

Brewington, Maretta
Copiague HS
Copiague, NY

Bridge, Karen
Alexander Central
Batavia, NY

Bridgeford, Erin
Cornwall Central HS
Cornwall, NY

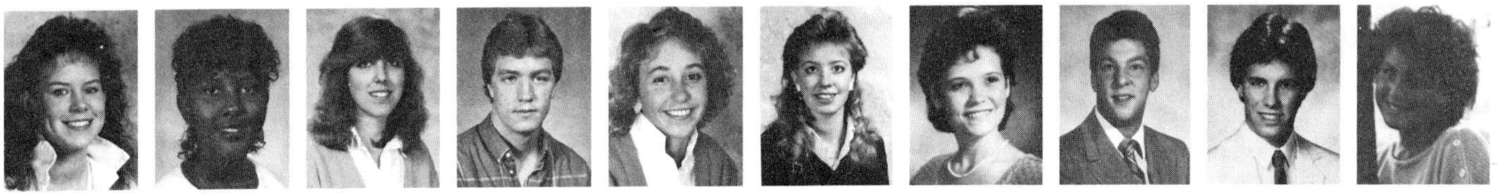

Briggs, Michele
Mexico Acad HS
Parish, NY

Briggs, Yvette
Trott Vocational HS
Niagara Falls, NY

Brinkley, Christine
Archbishop Lakovos
Jamaica, NY

Brinn, Mark
Penn Yan Acad
Penn Yan, NY

Brissette, Michelle
Liverpool HS
Liverpool, NY

Brite, Holly
Upper Room
Christian Schl
Lindenhurst, NY

Broadhead, Wendy
S
Falconer Central HS
Falconer, NY

Brocato, Frank
Monsignor Farrell
Staten Island, NY

Brocks, William R
Wellington C
Mepham HS
N Bellmore, NY

Brod, Melissa A
Irvington HS
Tarrytown, NY

Brodersen, Lisa
H Frank Carey HS
Franklin Square, NY

Brodkin, Tara L
Edgemont HS
Scarsdale, NY

Brodman, David
Bronx H S Of
Riverdale, NY

Brodsky, Geri
Canarsie HS
Brooklyn, NY

Bromirski, Judy
St Marys Academy
Hoosick Falls, NY

Bromirski, Timothy
Hoosick Falls
Central Schl
Hoosick Falls, NY

Bromley, Heather
Pine Valley Central
Cherry Creek, NY

Broncato, Buffy
Mt St Mary Acad
Tonawanda, NY

Bronson, Peggy Sue
Clymer Central HS
Clymer, NY

Brooks, Anne Marie
Amsterdam HS
Amsterdam, NY

Brooks, Kent
Northern
Adirondack HS
Ellenburg Depot,
NY

Brothers, III Alfred
S
Plattsburgh HS
Newtonville, MA

Brothers, Amy
Madrid-Waddington
Central HS
Madrid, NY

Brown, Amy
Wyoming Central
Wyoming, NY

Brown, Amy
Elizabeth
Arlington Central
Poughkeepsie, NY

Brown, Babette
Campbell Central
Campbell, NY

Brown, Baron
Mercy HS
Coram, NY

Brown, Charla
Walton Central Schl
Walton, NY

Brown, Charles
Dewitt Clinton HS
Bronx, NY

Brown, Charles
Dundee Central Schl
Dundee, NY

Brown, Cheryl
James Madison HS
Brooklyn, NY

Brown, Cheryl
Notre Dame Acad
Staten Island, NY

Brown, Chris
Hendrickson HS
Peekskill, NY

Brown, Corey
Dewitt Clinton HS
New York, NY

Brown, Dwayne
Anthony
Rice HS
New York, NY

Brown, Glenn C
Hamburg SR HS
Hamburg, NY

Brown, Jeffery R
Gilboa-Conesville
Central HS
Gilboa, NY

Brown, Kelly
Amityville Memorial
Amityville, NY

Brown, Kelly
Sherburne-Earlville
Earlville, NY

Brown, Lavell B
Bronx HS Of Sci
New York, NY

Brown, Lisa
Haldane HS
Cold Spring, NY

Brown, Michael
Rice HS
Bronx, NY

Brown, Rene F
Hampton Bays HS
Hampton Bays, NY

Brown, Sheryll
Springfield Gardens
Rosedale, NY

Brown, Stephania M
The Masters Schl
Ardsley, NY

Brown, Sylvett
Amityville Memorial
Amityville, NY

Browne, Mimi
East Hampton HS
E Hampton, NY

Browne, Ursula A
Hillcrest HS
Jamaica, NY

Brozgul, Evelina
H S Of Art &
Long Island Cty,
NY

Brueckner, Debbie
Onteora HS
Glenford, NY

Bruggemann, Jr
Robert H
William Cullen
Bryant HS
Astoria, NY

Brundage, Bobbi Jo
Haverling JR SR
Bath, NY

Brunner, Dolores
Jane Addams
Vocational HS
Bronx, NY

Brunner, Melissa J
Morristown Central
Morristown, NY

Bruno, Brenda
St Barnabas HS
Bronx, NY

Brust, Carolyn
Sachem North HS
Farmingville, NY

Bryant, Toshar
Cathedral HS
Ny, NY

Bryceland, Charles
Fordham Prep Schl
Bronx, NY

Buckalew, Lee
North Rose-Wolcott
Wolcott, NY

Buckley, Timothy
Alfred G Berner HS
Massapequa Park,
NY

Buckner, Stephannie
Barker Central HS
Appleton, NY

Buckstad, Erik
Washingtonville SR
Washingtnvle, NY

Buddendeck, Kelly
Victor Central HS
Macedon, NY

Budhi, Ronald
New Dorp HS
Staten Isl, NY

Budries, Mark
Mahopac HS
Carmel, NY

Bueti, Grace E
Pleasantville HS
Pleasantville, NY

Bui, Hong
Mineola HS
Mineola, NY

Bulger,
Deanna-Lynn
Bishop Maginn HS
Albany, NY

Bullaro, Stephanie A
Stella Maris HS
Howard Bch, NY

Bullock, Kimberly A
Dominican
Commercial HS
Jamaica, NY

Bullock, Mary Jo M
G Ray Bodley HS
Fulton, NY

Bunk, Benson
Cuba Central Schl
Belfast, NY

Buono, Denise
Bishop Maginn HS
Rensselaer, NY

Burch, Jill A
West Seneca SR HS
Cheektowaga, NY

Burg, Amy
Penn Yan Acad
Penn Yan, NY

Burg, Karen
Grand Island HS
Grand Island, NY

Burgess, Nancy A
Lakeshore Central
Old Saybrook, CT

Burgin, Cecilia
The Berkeley
Carroll Street Schl
Brooklyn, NY

Burke, Daniel C
Sachem HS
Holbrook, NY

Burke, Timothy
Glens Falls SR HS
Glens Falls, NY

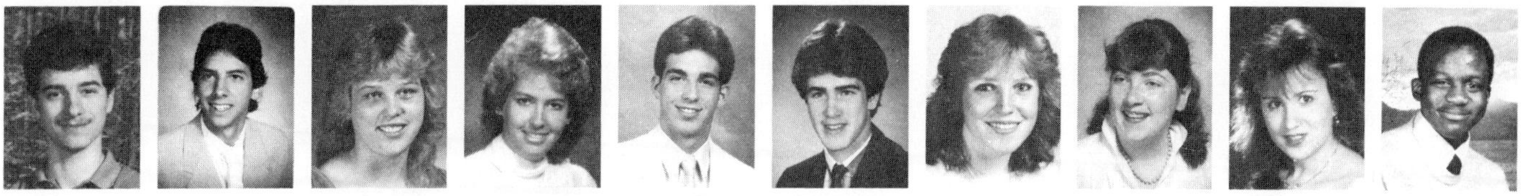

Burl, Tracy
Salmon River
Central HS
Ft Covington, NY

Burlew, Kip
Mynderse Acad
Seneca Falls, NY

Burlingame, Janet
Churchville-Chili SR
Churchville, NY

Burmeister, Karen
Fairport Central HS
Fairport, NY

Burnam, Scott M
St Johns Acad
Plattsburgh, NY

Burns, Bradley
Gouverneur SR HS
Gouverneur, NY

Burns, Brandi
Lindenhurst SR HS
Lindenhurst, NY

Burns, Patricia L
Westhill SR HS
Syracuse, NY

Burns, Rosemary
Hendrick Hudson
Verplanck, NY

Burnside, Derrick
De Witt Clinton HS
Bronx, NY

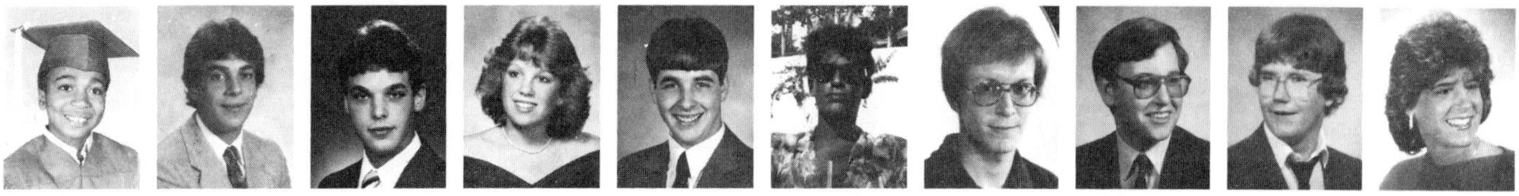

Burton, Mark
De Witt Clinton HS
Bronx, NY

Busacca, Anthony
Monsignor Farrell
Staten Island, NY

Busch, Gregory H
St Anthonys HS
Ronkonkoma, NY

Busch, Stacey
Connetguoh HS
Bohemia, NY

Busche, Stephen M
South Kortright
Central HS
South Kortright, NY

Bushell, Craig
York Prep Schl
New York, NY

Bushey, David
Northern
Adirondack Centra
Lyon Mt, NY

Bushnell, Jr
Timothy
Victor SR HS
Farmington, NY

Busseno, William
Amsterdam HS
Amsterdam, NY

Bussjager, Rebecca
East
Syracuse-Minoa HS
Minoa, NY

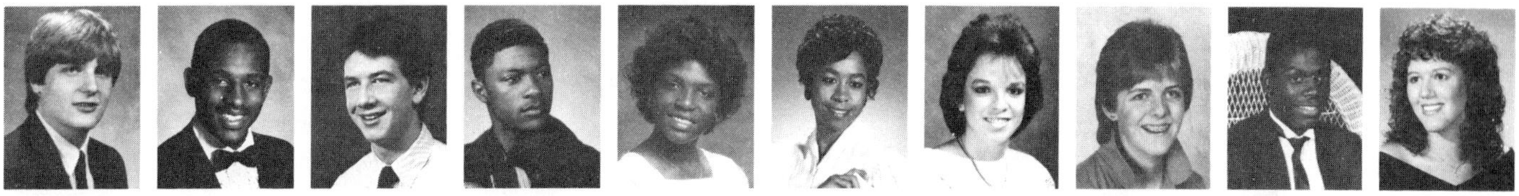

Butcher, Marc
Pine Valley Central
S Dayton, NY

Butler, Alan
Rice HS
Jamaica, NY

Butler, Brian
Westhill HS
Syracuse, NY

Butler, Jr Donald
Uniondale HS
Hempstead, NY

Butler, Kenyetta S
St Nicholas Of
Tolentine HS
Bronx, NY

Buxton, Lisa
Newburgh Free
Newburgh, NY

Buzzetta, Catherine
Adelphi Acad
Brooklyn, NY

Byers, Tammy
Paul V Moore HS
Constantia, NY

Byrd, David J
South Park HS
Buffalo, NY

Caballero, Michele
Bishop Kearney HS
Brooklyn, NY

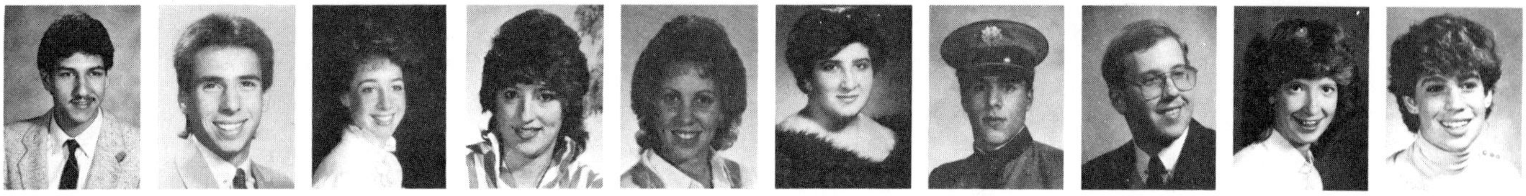

Cabarcos, Orlando
Bronx High School
Of Science
New York, NY

Caccuitto, III
Michael J
Scotia-Glenville SR
Scotia, NY

Caggiano, Pamela
Holy Trinity D/ HS
East Meadow, NY

Cagle, Tracey
Bradford Central
Savona, NY

Cahill, Jennifer
Northport HS
E Northport, NY

Caivano, Nancy
St Barnabas HS
Bronx, NY

Calabria, Troy
La Salle Military
Acad HS
Dix Hills, NY

Calaman, Keith
Oswego HS
Oswego, NY

Caldwell, Andrea
Honeoye Falls-Lima
Central Schl
Mendon, NY

Caldwell, Danielle
Eden SR HS
Boston, NY

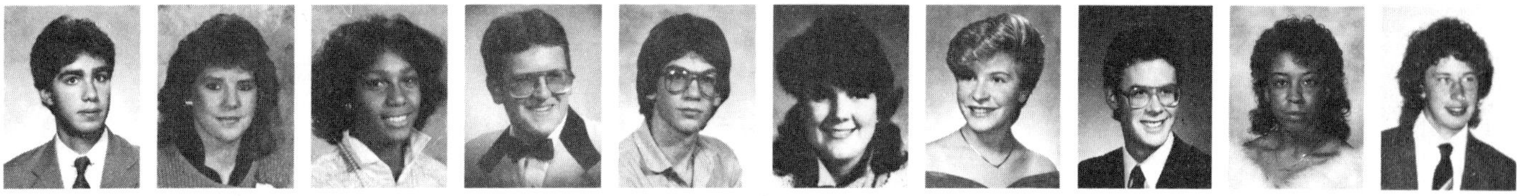

Cali, III Joseph L
Sayville HS
Sayville, NY

Call, Melissa
Liverpool HS
Liverpool, NY

Callender, Natalie
Dover JR SR HS
Wingdale, NY

Callery, Jr Patrick
Bishop Kearney HS
Rochester, NY

Camelio, Carmen J
Irondequait HS
Rochester, NY

Cameron, Heather
Auburn HS
Auburn, NY

Cameron, Patti
William Floyd HS
Mastic Beach, NY

Camillone, Michael
V
Eastchester HS
Scarsdale, NY

Campbell, Anissa
Central Islip SR HS
Central Islip, NY

Campbell, Bryan
St Marys Boys
Floral Pk, NY

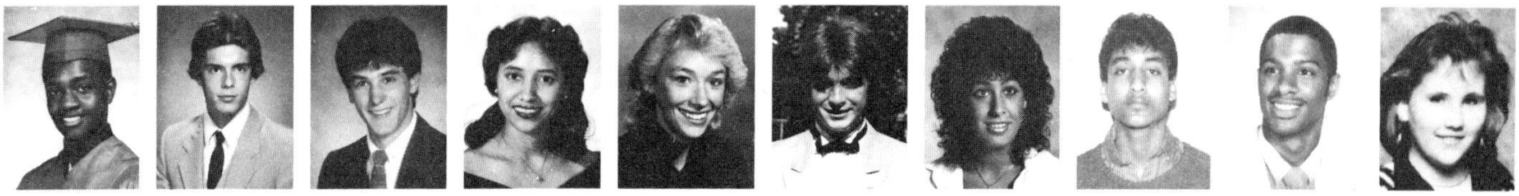

Campbell, Isaac R
Midwood High Schl
At Brooklyn College
Brooklyn, NY

Campoli, James
Valley Central HS
Montgomery, NY

Campolo, Phil
Bishop Grimes HS
E Syracuse, NY

Canales A, Haydee
E
St Pius V HS
Bronx, NY

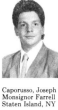

Canell, Tammy
Thousand Islands
Clayton, NY

Canfora, John L
John H Glenn HS
E Northport, NY

Cannavo, Jacqueline
St John Villa Acad
Staten Island, NY

Canton, Demetrious
St John The Baptist
Holbrook, NY

Canty, Kevin
Nottingham HS
Syracuse, NY

Caparis, Laurie
Pelham Memorial
Pelham, NY

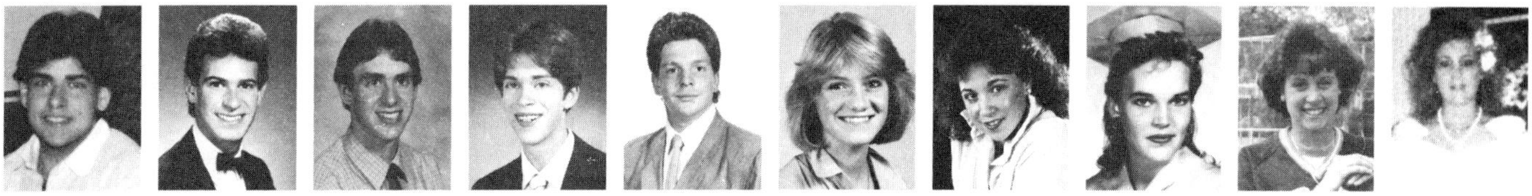

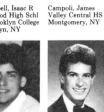

Capasso, James
Fordham Prepartory
Scarsdale, NY

Capellupo, Anthony
J
Mount St Michael
Bronx, NY

Capone, Harry
Faith Heritaghe HS
Canastota, NY

Capone, John J
Hampton Bays HS
Hampton Bays, NY

Caporusso, Joseph
Monsignor Farrell
Staten Island, NY

Cappiello, Stephanie
Bay Shore HS
Bay Shore, NY

Caputo, Johanna
W Seneca E SR HS
West Seneca, NY

Caputo, Karen
South Shore HS
Brooklyn, NY

Caracci, Corinna
James Madison HS
Brooklyn, NY

Caravello, Dawn
Centereach HS
Centereach, NY

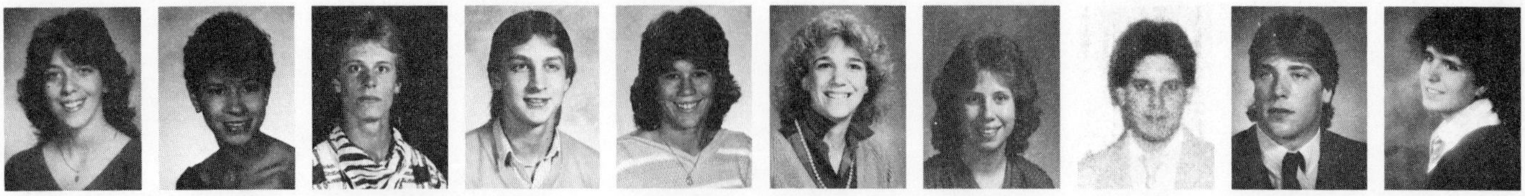

Carberry, Lisa
Dryden Central HS
Etna, NY

Carbone, Nina
Mt Vernon HS
Mount Vernon, NY

Carey, Richard
Minisink Valley HS
Port Jervis, NY

Cargnoni, Jim
Victor Central Schl
Shortsville, NY

Carlough, Colleen
Center Morickes HS
Center Moriches, NY

Carlsen, Lynn
Union Endicott HS
Endicott, NY

Carlton, Beth
Jefferson HS
Rochester, NY

Carluzzo, Edward J
Susan E Wagner HS
Staten Island, NY

Carmichael, Kevin
Le Roy Central HS
Leroy, NY

Carnevale, Anne Marie
Our Lady Of Mercy
Rochester, NY

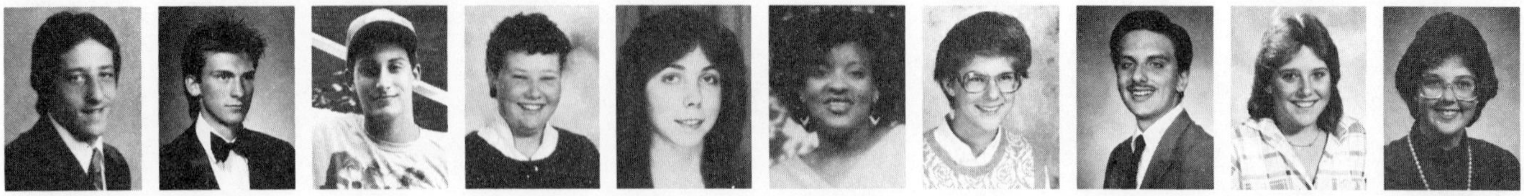

Carniello, Glenn
Noth Babylon SR
North Babylon, NY

Carobene, Christopher S
St Francis Prep Schl
Douglaston, NY

Carollo, Jim
Rome Free Acad
Rome, NY

Carpenter, Sara
Keveny Acad
Cohoes, NY

Carpinella, Lisa
Sachem HS North
Lake Ronkonkoma, NY

Carr, Carmen
Fayetteville Manlius Central Schl
Cleveland, OH

Carr, Colleen
Liverpool HS
Liverpool, NY

Carr, Craig A
Westfield Acad And Cen Schl
Westfield, NY

Carr, Donna
Centereach HS
Lk Ronkonkoma, NY

Carr, Kathleen
Liverpool HS
Liverpool, NY

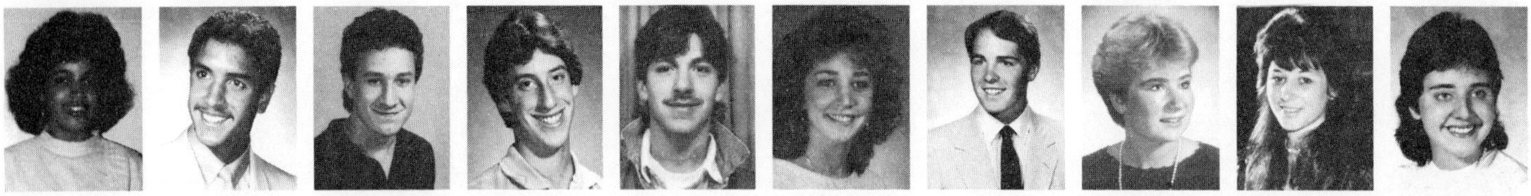

Carrasco, Ruth M
Eastern District HS
Brooklyn, NY

Carrasquillo, Carlos L
Bay Shore HS
Bay Shore, NY

Carreras, Matthew
Bayport Blue Point
Bayport, NY

Carrier, Michael
Tuckahoe HS
Bronxville, NY

Carrigan, Brian
Corcoran HS
Syracuse, NY

Carroll, Michele
Mount St Mary
Buffalo, NY

Carroll, Paul
East Islip HS
East Islip, NY

Carroway, Kathleen
Liverpool HS
Liverpool, NY

Carruba, Lisa
Domininican Commercial HS
S Ozone Park, NY

Carson, Mary
New Rochelle HS
New Rochelle, NY

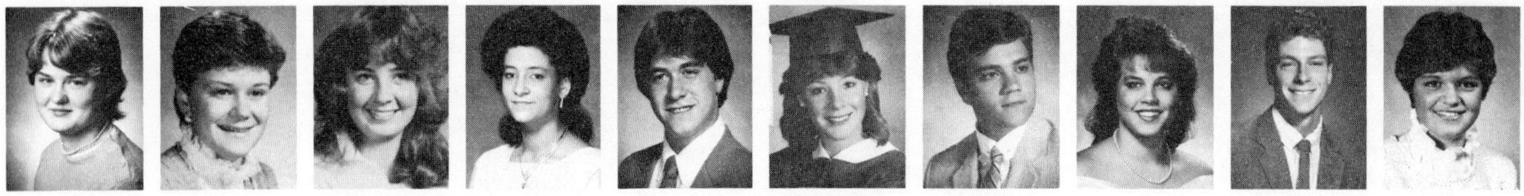

Carson, Monica
Geneva HS
Geneva, NY

Carswell, Rhonda
Vestal SR HS
Vestal, NY

Carter, Annmarie
Vernon-Verona-Sherrill HS
Sherrill, NY

Carter, Jamie Alissa
Long Island Lutheran HS
Roosevelt, NY

Carter, John
East Syracuse Minoa HS
E Syracuse, NY

Carter, Kim
Holy Trinity HS
Levittown, NY

Cartini, Jay
Bishop Grimes HS
Jamesville, NY

Caruso, Teri-Ann
John H Glenn HS
E Northport, NY

Cary, Sean
Albertus Magnus
Pearl River, NY

Casamento, Ann Marie
Niagara Wheatfield
Niagara Falls, NY

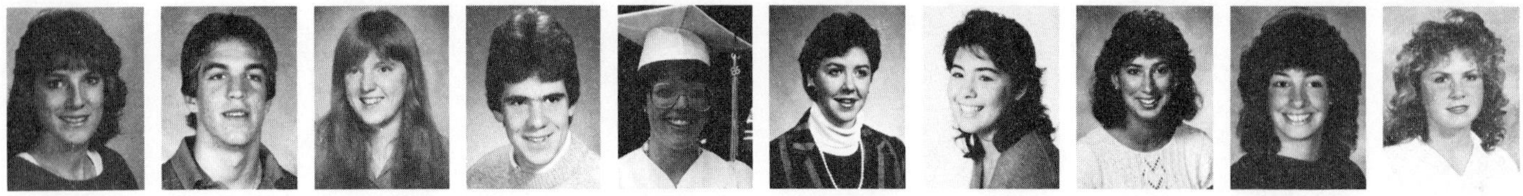

Casey, Debbie
Huntington HS
Huntington, NY

Casey, James
Lake George HS
Glens Falls, NY

Casey, Kristine A
Fayetteville-Manlius
Manlius, NY

Casko, Stephen F
Stuyvesant HS
New York, NY

Casler, Christine
Canastota HS
Canastota, NY

Casler, Maureen
Corcoran HS
Syracuse, NY

Casoni, Dava
Amherst Central HS
Amherst, NY

Cassani, Margaret M
General Douglas Mac Arthur HS
Levittown, NY

Cassella, Christine
Lake George HS
Glens Falls, NY

Castaldo, Lisa
Niskayuna HS
Schenectady, NY

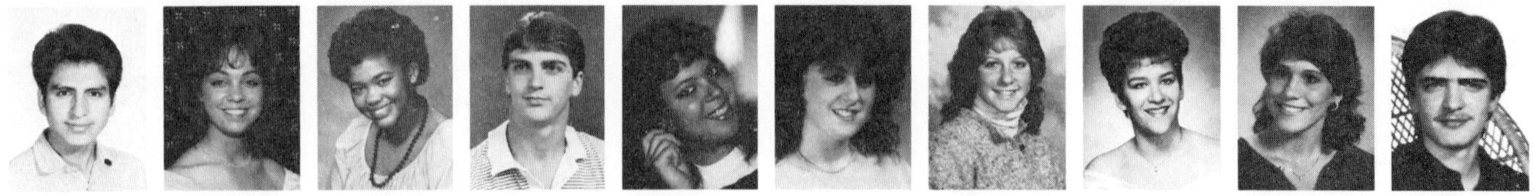

Castaneda, Eddie
Cardinal Hayes HS
Bronx, NY

Castelluzzo, Diane
Plainedge HS
N Massapequa, NY

Castro, Chea
Westbury SR HS
Westbury, NY

Castronovo, Tony
Whitesboro SR HS
Whitesboro, NY

Casul, Maria
S Shore HS
Brooklyn, NY

Catani, Michelle
Mt St Mary Acad
Buffalo, NY

Cater, Beth
Scotia Glenville SR
Scotia, NY

Cavagliere, Nadia M
Half Hollow Hills HS West
Farmingdale, NY

Cavallaro, Kathy A
Corning-Painted Post East HS
Corning, NY

Cavic, Rade
Richfield Springs Central Schl
Richfield Spgs, NY

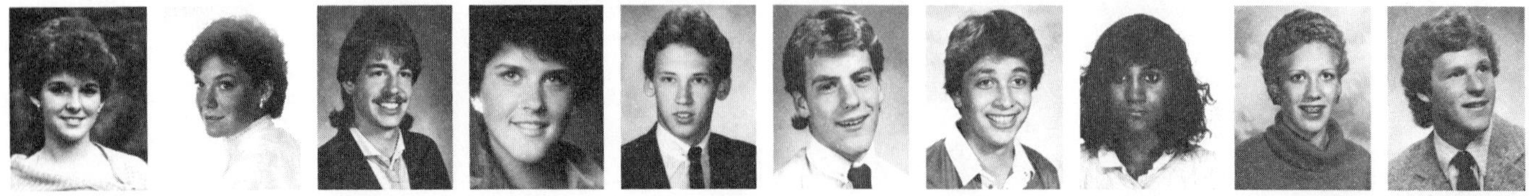

Cavoli, Nancy
Scotia-Glenville HS
Scotia, NY

Cayea, Christine
Geneva HS
Geneva, NY

Cecil, Richard A
South Jefferson Central HS
Adams Center, NY

Cella, Christina
Eldorado HS
Las Vegas, NV

Cerasuolo, Anthony J
Patchogue-Medford
Patchogue, NY

Cerrone, Mike
Eden SR HS
Eden, NY

Cesare, Anthony
John Glenn HS
E Northport, NY

Cestero, Tricia
St Raymond Acad
Bronx, NY

Chaloner, Jennifer
Coxsackie Athens Central HS
Coxsackie, NY

Chamberlain, Dave
Gloversville HS
Gloversville, NY

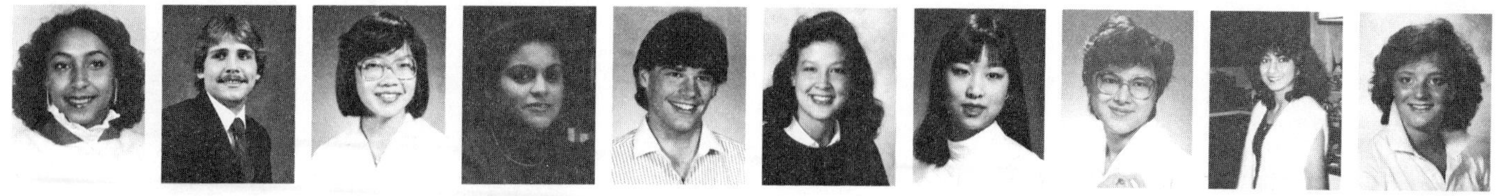

Chamberlain, Michelle Christopher
Columbus Bronx
Bronx, NY

Champlin, James E
Auburn HS
Auburn, NY

Chan, Paula
Preston HS
Bronx, NY

Chancey, Denise
Freeport HS
Freeport, NY

Chandler, Jim
Alexander Central
Darien, NY

Chang, Claudia
Huntington HS
Huntington, NY

Chang, Janice M
Walter Panas HS
Peekskill, NY

Chang, Jerry
Pt Joseph HS
Brooklyn, NY

Chani, Harshila
Forest Hills HS
Forest Hills, NY

Chanin, Debbie
Jericho HS
Westbury, NY

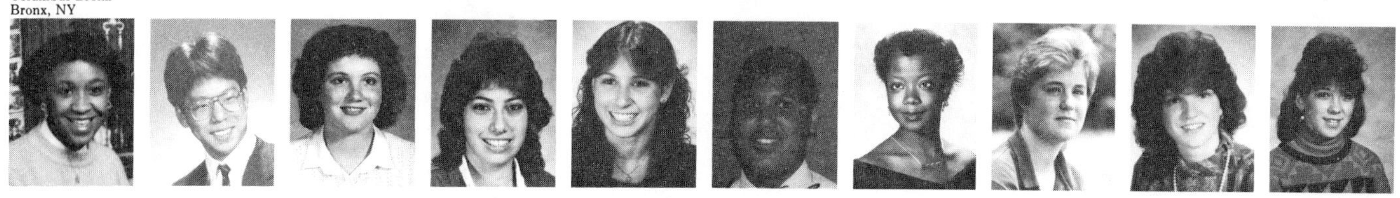

Channell, Tonya
Murry Bergtraum
Brooklyn, NY

Chao, Jerome D
Sleepy Hollow HS
Scarborough, NY

Charak, Roberta
Uniondale HS
Uniondale, NY

Charbonneau, Lisa
G Ray Bodley HS
Fulton, NY

Charette, Jacqueline R
East Syracuse Minoa HS
East Syracuse, NY

Charlemagne, Jr James M
James Monroe HS
Bronx, NY

Charles, Madonna N
Catherine Mc Auley
Brooklyn, NY

Chase, Catherine
Spacenkill HS
Poughkeepsie, NY

Chase, Jennifer D
Liverpool HS
Liverpool, NY

Chase, Robin
Potsdam Central HS
Potsdam, NY

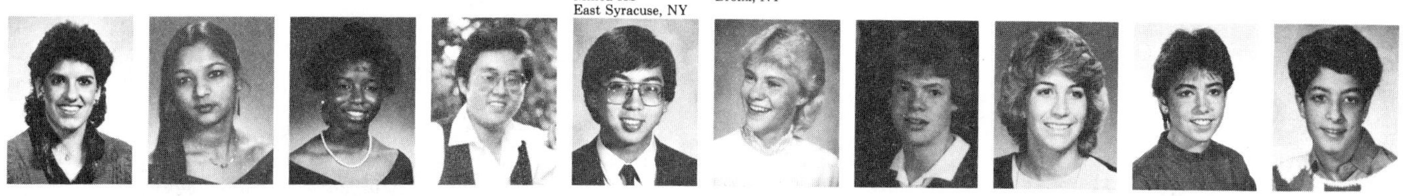

Chatt, Jill
Batavia HS
Batavia, NY

Chauhan, Archana
Monsignor Scanlam
Bronx, NY

Cheatham, Dianne A
Manhattan Center For Science & Math
New York, NY

Chen, David
Arlington HS
Poughkeepsie, NY

Chen, Humphrey D
Bronx High Schl Of
New York, NY

Chenaille, Jeanette
Massena Central HS
Massena, NY

Chernosky, Walt
Smithtown East HS
Smithtown, NY

Chesner, Constance
Portville JR SR HS
Olean, NY

Chiafolo, Christina
Hauppauge HS
Hauppauge, NY

Chianese, Joanne M
W Tresper Clarke
Westbury, NY

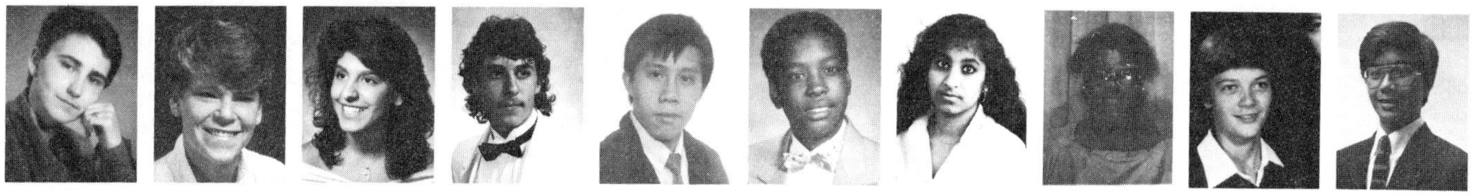

Chiarenza, Cara-Antonia M
Our Lady Of Mercy
Henriatta, NY

Chido, Linda
Cheektowaga Central HS
Cheektowaga, NY

Chiello, Christine
The Mary Louis
Ridgewood, NY

Chille, Ralph A
Niagara Falls HS
Niagara Falls, NY

Chin, Bryan
Archbishop Molloy
Sunnyside, NY

Chin, Cedric
Bishop Loughlin Memorial HS
Brooklyn, NY

Chirumamilla, Sree
Oneida HS
Oneida, NY

Chisolm, Bernadette
De Witt Clinton HS
Bronx, NY

Chisum, Criag
Franklin Acad
Malone, NY

Chiu, Victor
Locust Valley HS
Bayville, NY

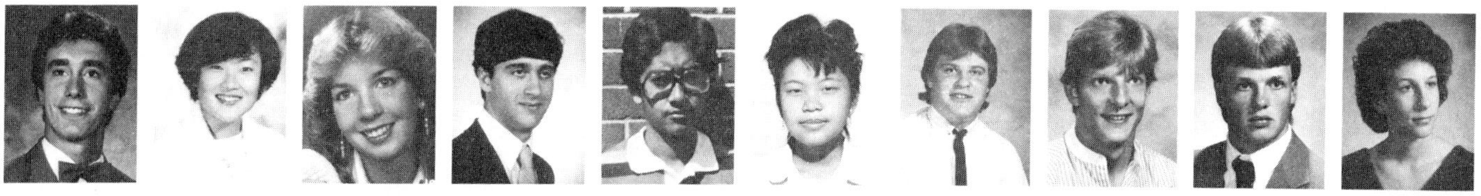

Chivily, Philip S
Lakeland HS
Putnam Valley, NY

Cho, Jennie
Niskayuna HS
Schenectady, NY

Chorazak, Jennifer
Frontier Central SR
Blasdell, NY

Chottiner, Jeffrey E
Jamesville-De Witt
De Witt, NY

Choudhury, Sayeed
Jamesville-De Witt
Jamesville, NY

Chow, Bernice
HS Of Art & Design
New York, NY

Christian, David
Beacon HS
Beacon, NY

Christian, Rick
Windsor JR SR HS
Kirkwood, NY

Christiansen, Matthew
Penn Yan HS
Penn Yan, NY

Christino, Paula A
Westhill SR HS
Syracuse, NY

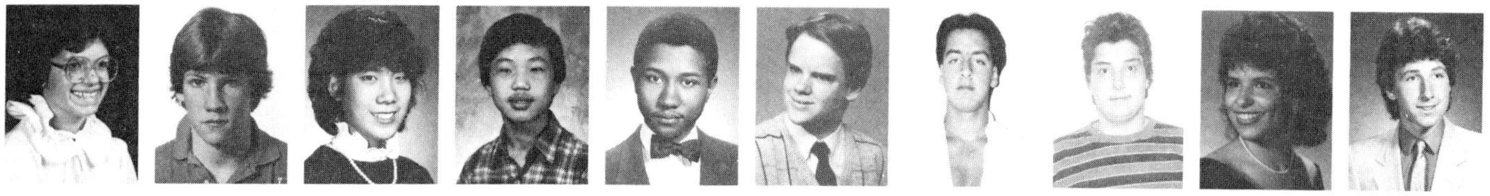

Christman, Amy
Duanesburg Central
Delanson, NY

Christy, Scott
Bitburg HS
Apo Ny, NY

Chu, Victoria W
Stuyvesant HS
Flushing, NY

Chung, Eun Soo
St Francis Prep
Flushing, NY

Chung-A-Fung, Ronald Arthur
Regis HS
Brooklyn, NY

Church, Glenn Alan
Onondaga Central
Syracuse, NY

Ciacciarelli, Michael
Port Richmond HS
State Island, NY

Ciafone, John J
Long Island City HS
Long Is Cty, NY

Cianciotta, Laurie
Bishop Kearney HS
Brooklyn, NY

Cianflone, Anthony
Carmel HS
Stormville, NY

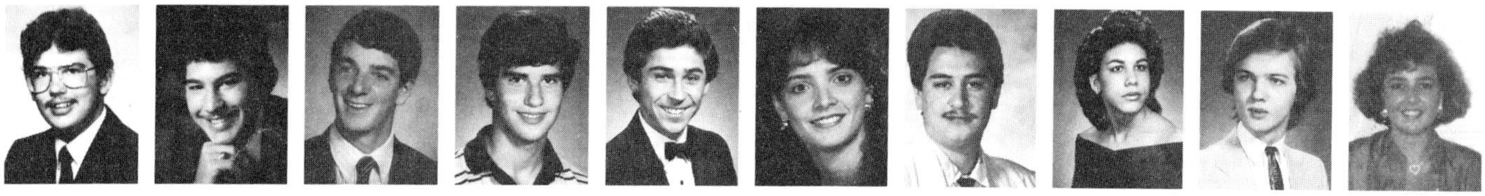

Ciavatta, Michael
Connetquot HS
Oakdale, NY

Ciccarella, Mark
Maryvale SR HS
Depew, NY

Cicci, Stephen A
Fayetteville-Manlius
Fayetteville, NY

Ciferri, Rod
Our Lady Of Lourdes HS
Millbrook, NY

Cintron, Richard P
Mt St Michael Acad
Bronx, NY

Cipolla, Kim
Union Endicott HS
Endicott, NY

Cipriani, Michael
Copiague SR HS
Copiague, NY

Cirillo, Donna L
Cardinal Spellman
Bronx, NY

Cisek, Paul E
Carmel HS
Carmel, NY

Ciuitano, Susan
Ursuline HS
New Rochelle, NY

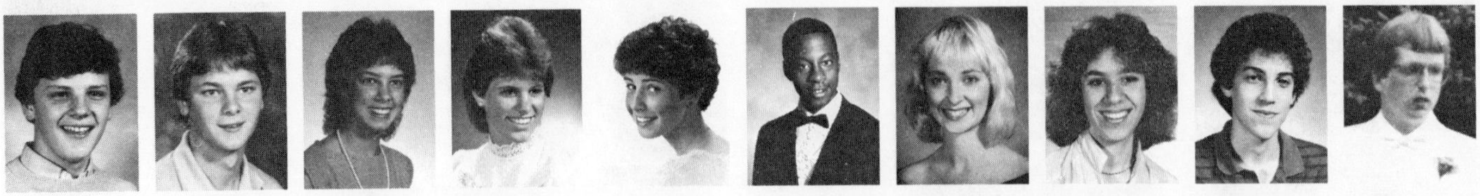

Clabeaux, Robert
Hutchinson Central
Technical HS
Buffalo, NY

Clapp, Brian
Clarkstown HS
New City, NY

Clar, Suzanne
Our Lady Of Mercy
Webster, NY

Clark, Cheryl
Waverly JR-SR HS
Waverly, NY

Clark, Christine
Geneva HS
Geneva, NY

Clark, Earl
Rice HS
New York, NY

Clark, Judith A
Owego Free Acad
Apalachin, NY

Clark, Ronalyn
Hornell HS
Hornell, NY

Clark, Tom
West Genesee HS
Syracuse, NY

Clark, Zachary
Lake Placid HS
Lake Placid, NY

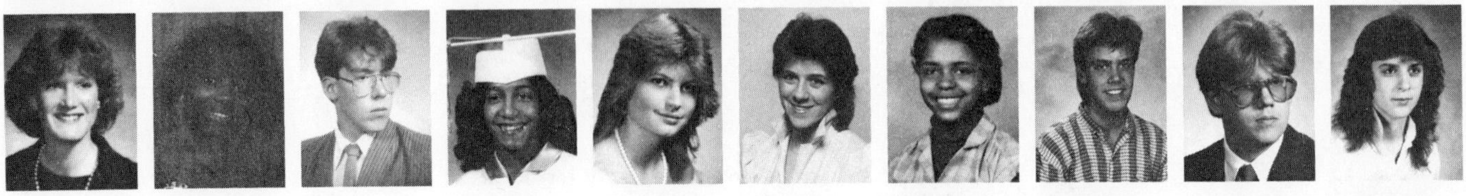

Clarke, Amy J
Earl L
Vandermeulen HS
Mt Sinai, NY

Clarke, Janneth
Jane Addams HS
Bronx, NY

Clatyon, Gregory
Shaker HS
Latham, NY

Clayton, Janeen
St Catharine Acad
Bx, NY

Clayton, Judith
Trott Vocational &
Tech Schl
Niagara Falls, NY

Clemente, Lena
Solvay HS
Solvay, NY

Clermont,
Frederique
Bronx H S Of
Queens Village, NY

Cline, Brad
East Hampton HS
E Hampton, NY

Clive, Jeffrey M
Ilion HS
Ilion, NY

Cloen, Lynnette
Hutchinson Central
Buffalo, NY

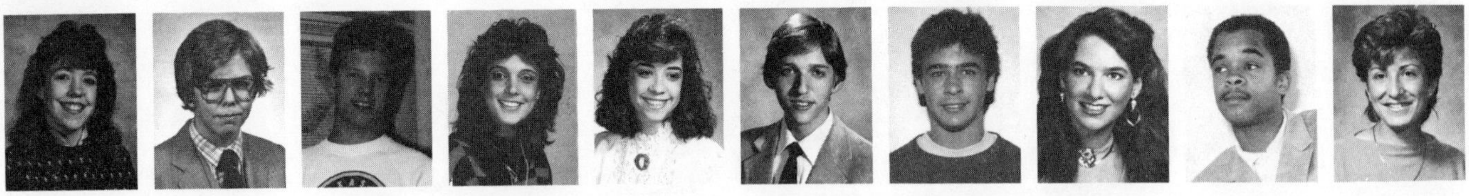

Close, Kathryn M
Johnstown HS
Johnstown, NY

Closser, Mike
Charles H Roth HS
Rochester, NY

Clow, Derrick
Trumansburg HS
Trumansburg, NY

Cluna, Jamie
Farmingdale HS
Farmingdale, NY

Cody, Jennifer
Charles H Roth HS
W Henrietta, NY

Cohen, Daniel E
The Bronx High
School Of Science
Jackson Heights,
NY

Cohen, Darin E
Ward Mehville HS
South Setauket, NY

Cohen, Dawn S
Midwood HS
Brooklyn, NY

Cohen, Gregory
Newtown HS
Cambria Hgts, NY

Cohen, Nanci A
Clarkstown North
New City, NY

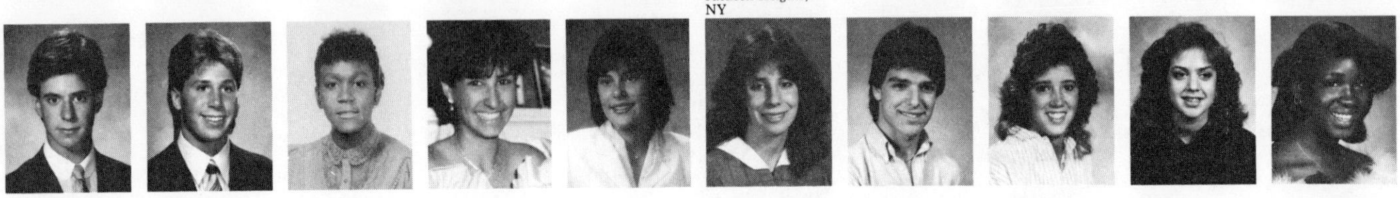

Cohen, Scott P
Gen Douglas Mac
Arthur HS
Levittown, NY

Cohen, Seth H
Lynbrook HS
E Rockaway, NY

Coke, Jacqueline
James Monroe HS
Bronx, NY

Colabella, Dorine
New Rochelle HS
New Rochelle, NY

Colandro, Tinamarie
New Hyde Pk
Memorial HS
New Hyde Pk, NY

Colangelo, Christine
Notre Dame Acad
Staten Island, NY

Colantino, Chris
Eden SR HS
Eden, NY

Colasante, Dana
Mahopac HS
Mahopac, NY

Colasanti, Mary
Patricia
Bishop Ludden HS
Liverpool, NY

Colbert, Ilene
St Barnabas HS
Bronx, NY

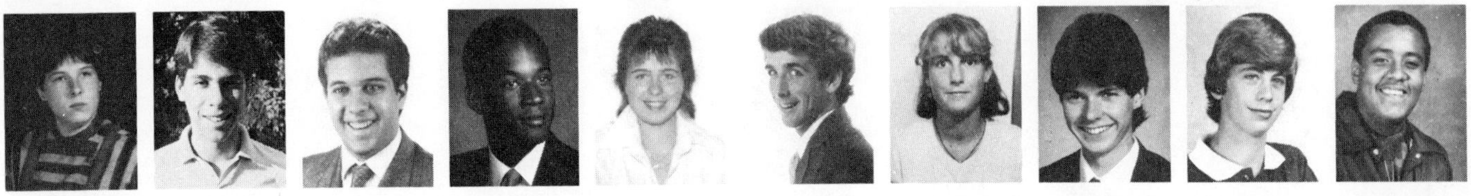

Cole, Amy
Livonia Central HS
Lima, NY

Cole, Craig
Middletown HS
Circleville, NY

Cole, Jonathan
Port Chester SR HS
Port Chester, NY

Coleman, Mark H
Vestal SR HS
Binghamton, NY

Colic, Michele
Dominican
Commercial HS
Brooklyn, NY

Collins, Craig
Clifton
Cobleskill Central
Cobleskill, NY

Collins, Elizabeth
The Ursuline Schl
Yonkers, NY

Collins, Michael S
Nottingham HS
Syracuse, NY

Collura, Scott
Bay Shore HS
Bay Shore, NY

Colon, Alex Xavier
All Hallows Inst
New York, NY

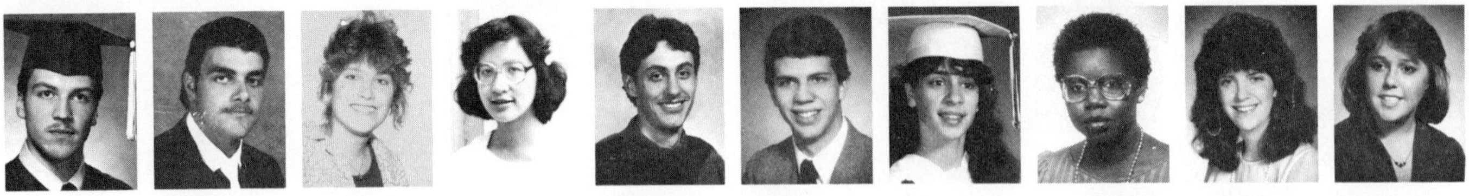

Colon, Edwin
St John The Baptist
Wyandanch, NY

Colon, Gregory
All Hallows HS
Bronx, NY

Combatti, Margaret
Patchogue-Medford
Patchogue, NY

Compas, Pam
Academy Of St
Joseph HS
Holbrook, NY

Compolo, Frank
Herkimer SR HS
East Herkimer, NY

Compson, Jr
Richard G
Clinton Central Schl
Clinton, NY

Conceicao,
Ermelinda
Charles E Gorton
Yonkers, NY

Coney, E Christine
T J Corcoran HS
Syracuse, NY

Conley, Kelly
Frankfort-Schuyler
Frankfort, NY

Conn, Renee M
Ballston Spa HS
Ballston Spa, NY

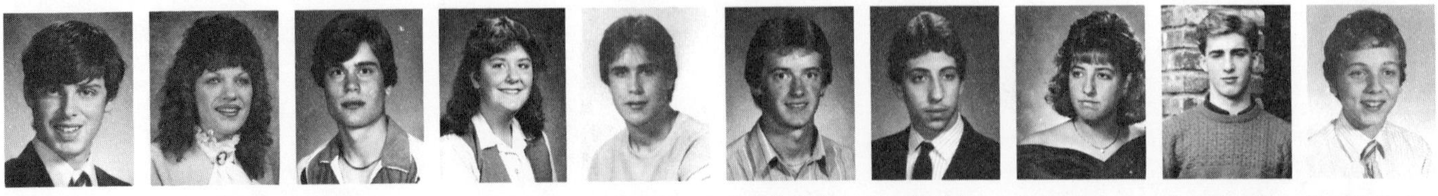

Connell, Thomas A
Delaware Valley
Central Schl
North Branch, NY

Connolly, Dianne
James Madison HS
Brooklyn, NY

Consaga, Tony
Ossinging HS
Ossining, NY

Consavage, Jennifer
Sacred Heart HS
Yonkers, NY

Considine, William J
Fordham Prep
Bronx, NY

Constable, Michael
Walton HS
Walton, NY

Constable, Seth
Wallkill SR HS
Newburgh, NY

Constantine,
Kimberly A
Babylon HS
Babylon, NY

Constantino, III
Michael
Friends Acad
Glen Cove, NY

Conte, Christopher
Uniondale HS
Uniondale, NY

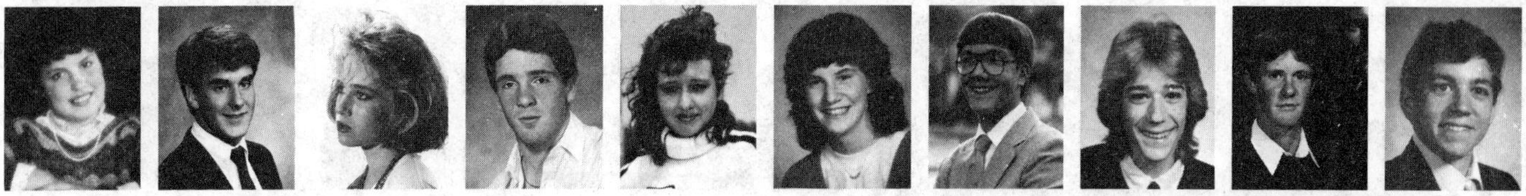

Converse, Carri
Irondequoit HS
Rochester, NY

Convey, Maurice J
Garden City HS
Garden City, NY

Conviser, Lenore
Pelham Memorial
Pelham, NY

Cooke, Stephen
Saugerties HS
Saugerties, NY

Cooke, Winifred
Lafayette HS
Brooklyn, NY

Cookhouse, Faye
Fayetteville-Monlius
Manlius, NY

Coolidge, Gary
Waverly JRSR HS
Waverly, NY

Coombs, Brian E
Bishop Ludden HS
Clay, NY

Coon, Dale L
Madison Central HS
Oriskany Falls, NY

Cooney, Brian
Lyons Central Schl
Lyons, NY

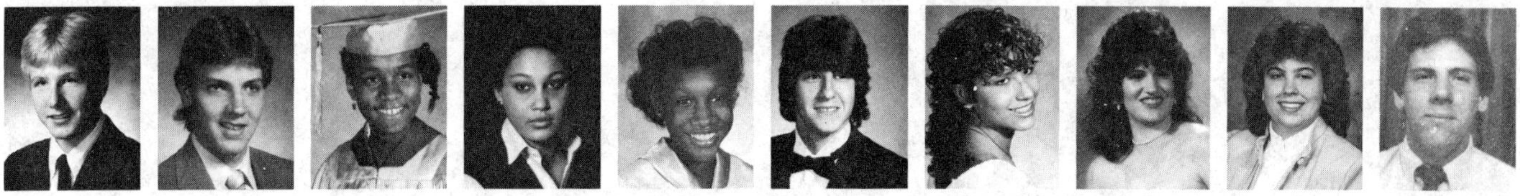

Cooney, Michael
Jude
Lansingburgh HS
Troy, NY

Coons, Bradford
Pine Plains Central
Pine Plains, NY

Cooper, Karen M
Queen Of The
Rosary Acad
Amityville, NY

Cooper, Zara
The Dwight Schl
New York, NY

Copeland, Janique
Half Hollow Hills
East HS
Wheatley Hts, NY

Coppa, Steven J
Park West HS
Bronx, NY

Corbet, Jennifer
Tottenville HS
Staten Island, NY

Corchia, Linda A
St Francis Prep
Astoria, NY

Corcoran, Courtney
Lyn
Medina SR HS
Medina, NY

Corcoran, Jason
Henninger High HS
Syracuse, NY

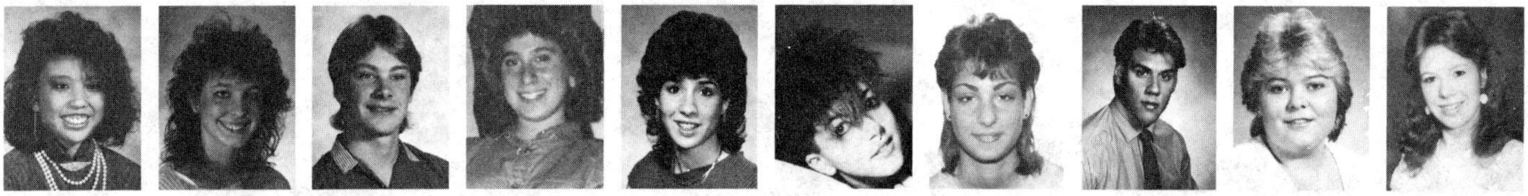

Cordova, Vivian
Shaker HS
Latham, NY

Corneles, Karen
Waterloo SR HS
Waterloo, NY

Cornell, Kenneth
Perry Central HS
Perry, NY

Cornwall, Christine
A
St Francis Prep
Little Neck, NY

Corradino, Michelle
Sachem North HS
Holbrook, NY

Corrigan, Claudia
A G Berner HS
Massapequa Park,
NY

Cortina, Lisa
St Mary Girls HS
New Hyde Park, NY

Corvato, Mike
Bay Shore HS
Bayshore, NY

Coss, Darnell
Whitesboro Central
Marcy, NY

Costa, Deborah
North Babylon HS
North Babylon, NY

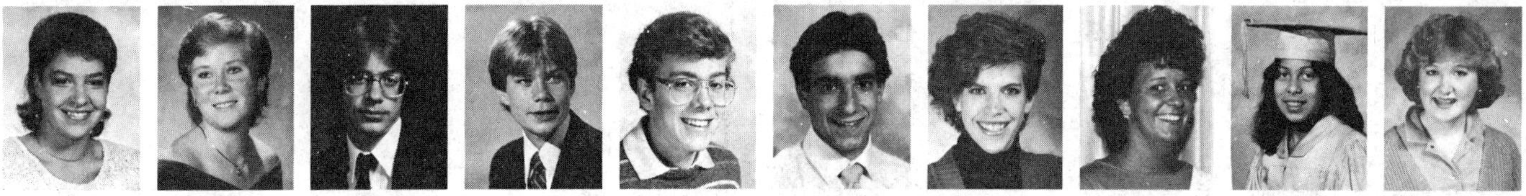

Costantini, Valerie
Fairport HS
Fairport, NY

Costello, Theresa
Our Lady Of
Perpetual Help
Brooklyn, NY

Costic, Kenneth
Port Jervis HS
Port Jervis, NY

Costley, Scott J
Horseheads HS
Horseheads, NY

Cothran, David
Onondaga HS
Nedrow, NY

Cotugno, Aaron
Amsterdam HS
Amsterdam, NY

Couch, Debra
Grand Island HS
Grand Island, NY

Coulsting, Marian K
Smithtown HS West
Smithtown, NY

Cousin, Lolita
Sacred Heart Acad
Cambria Hts, NY

Cousins, Mary Lynn
Brockport HS
Brockprot, NY

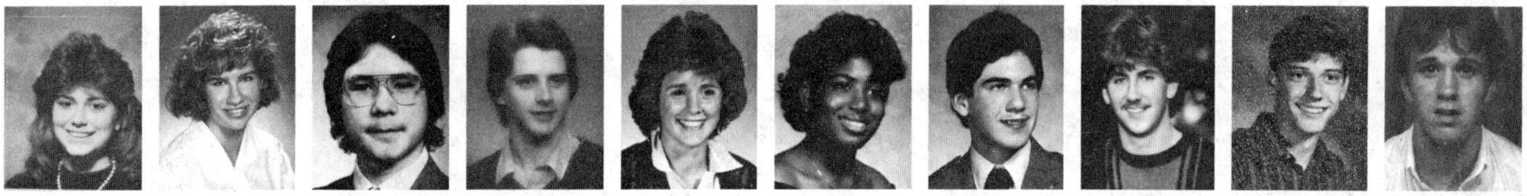

Coutant, Lynda
John A Coleman HS
Ruby, NY

Covert, Barbara A
Newburgh Free
Newburgh, NY

Covey, Lonn C
Arthage Central HS
Carthage, NY

Cowen, Mark
Randolph Central
Conewango Valley,
NY

Cowie, Kim
Alexander Central
Alexander, NY

Cox, Cheryl
Hillcrest HS
Sp Gdns, NY

Cox, Geoffrey
Nyack HS
Nyack, NY

Cramer, Richard T
Red Jacket Central
Palmyra, NY

Crane, Jeff
Haverling HS
Bath, NY

Craner, Fran
Catholic Central HS
Cohoes, NY

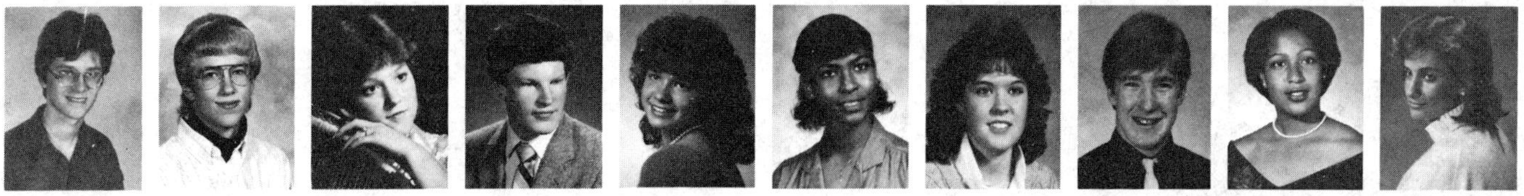

Craner, Garren T
North Shore HS
Glenwood Landg,
NY

Craner, John
Jamesville Dewitt
Jamesville, NY

Craney, Brenda
Tamarac HS
Troy, NY

Crawford, Chris R
Elmont Memorial
Elmont, NY

Crawford, Stacey L
Johnson City HS
Binghamton, NY

Crawford, Wanda L
Flushing HS
Cambria Heights,
NY

Cregan, Karen
West Genesee SR
Camillus, NY

Cremean, Michael
North Rose-Wolcott
Central HS
Wolcott, NY

Creque, Patricia
Adlai E Stevenson
Bronx, NY

Criscuolo, Paula
Mamaroneck HS
Larchmont, NY

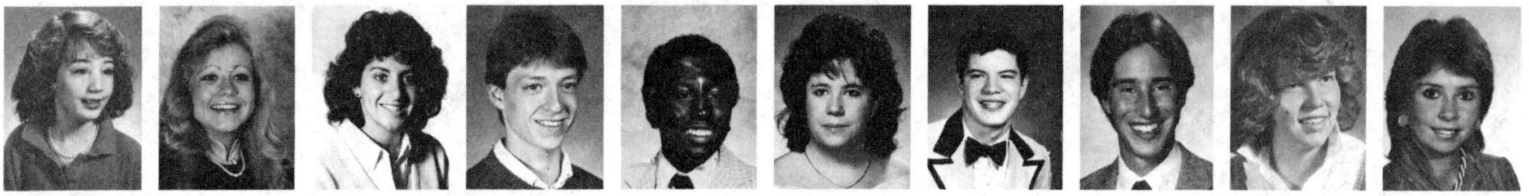

Cristodero, Christine
H Frank Carey HS
Franklin Square,
NY

Crobar, Kimberley L
Liverpool HS
Liverpool, NY

Croce, Carla
Hamburg HS
Hamburg, NY

Crolle, James
Westfield Central
Westfield, NY

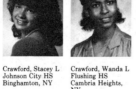

Cromartie, Joseph
Far Rockaway HS
Far Rockaway, NY

Cronin, Elizabeth
Dominican
Comercial HS
Bellerose, NY

Cronin, James
Sacred Heart HS
Yonkers, NY

Cronin, Joseph P
Wellington C
Mepham HS
Merrick, NY

Cronin, Michelle
Lafayette HS
Nedrow, NY

Cronin, Susan
Sachem HS
Farmingville, NY

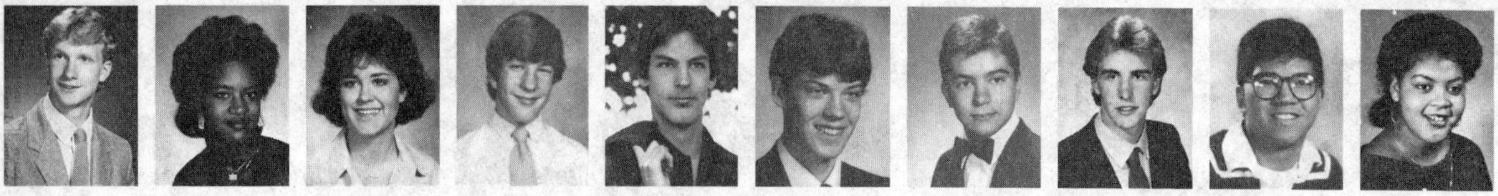

Cropley, Ralph
Dover JR SR HS
Windgale, NY

Crosby, Dawn
Ossining HS
Ossining, NY

Cross, Colleen Sheehan
Cardinal Mooney
Rochester, NY

Cross, Mark
John Marshall HS
Rochester, NY

Crossan, Sean
Rhinebeck Central
Rhinebeck, NY

Crossway, Matthew B
Hamilton Central
Hamilton, NY

Crowley, Dennis
Regis HS
Wilton, CT

Crowley, Robert N
Bellport SR HS
Bellport, NY

Cruces, Robert
Woodlands HS
Hartsdale, NY

Crump, Sonya
Buffalo Traditional
Buffalo, NY

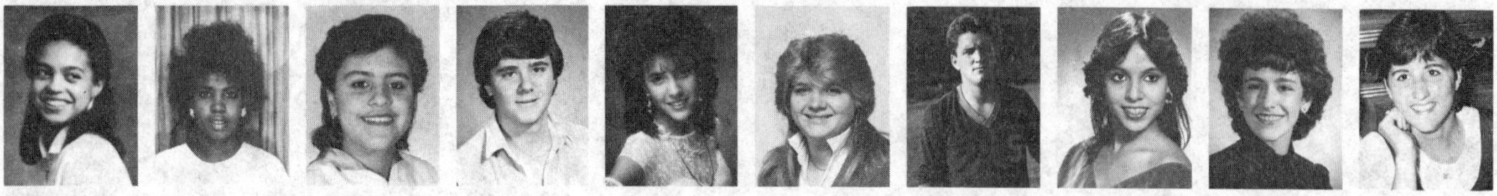

Cruz, Evelyn
Sheepshead Bay HS
Brooklyn, NY

Cruz, Jeannette
Grace H Dodge Voc
New York, NY

Cruz, Lucesita
Herbert H Lehman
Bronx, NY

Cucchiara, Donald
Valley Central HS
Newburgh, NY

Cuccia, Michele
Sacred Heart Acad
Garden City, NY

Cuddeback, Carolyn
Union Springs Central HS
Cayuga, NY

Cuddy, William
Trinity Pawling HS
Pawling, NY

Cuevas, Evelyn
Erasmus Hall HS
Brooklyn, NY

Cuffaro, Catherine
Union-Endicott HS
Endicott, NY

Cuiffo, Deborah
The Masters Schl
Bronxville, NY

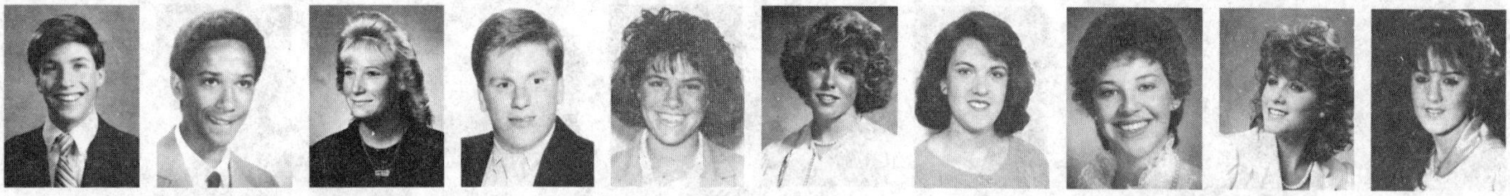

Cullen, Anthony
St Pauls Schl
Garden City, NY

Culley, Matthew P
Alfred-Almond Central Schl
Alfred, NY

Cullinan, Terri-Ann
Sachem HS
Holtsville, NY

Cullon, Joseph
The Wheatley Schl
E Williston, NY

Cumella, Jean
Sacred Heart Acad
Westbury, NY

Cummings, Christine A
E L Vandermeulen
Port Jeff Station, NY

Cunningham, Geraldine
Bronx HS Of
Bronx, NY

Cunningham, Karla
Aquinas Inst
Rochester, NY

Cunningham, Rebecca L
Southside HS
Horseheads, NY

Curanaj, Theresa Ucaj
St Catharine Acad
Bx, NY

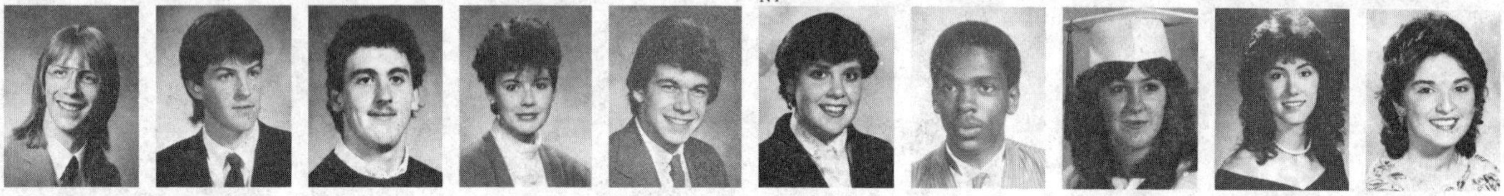

Curns, Dan
Elmira Free Acad
Elmira, NY

Curran, Christopher
Saranac Lake Central HS
Saranac Lk, NY

Currier, Edward
Auburn HS
Auburn, NY

Curry, Alicia
Walt Whitman HS
Huntington, NY

Curry, Christopher J
Goshen Central HS
Florida, NY

Curry, Frances
Ichabod Crane HS
Stuyvesant, NY

Curry, Jonathan
Edison HS
Rochester, NY

Cusack, Cathy
Acad Of St Jsph
Kings Pk, NY

Cusato, Kristen
Pine Bush HS
Pine Bush, NY

Cutaia, Anna
Mahopac HS
Mahopac, NY

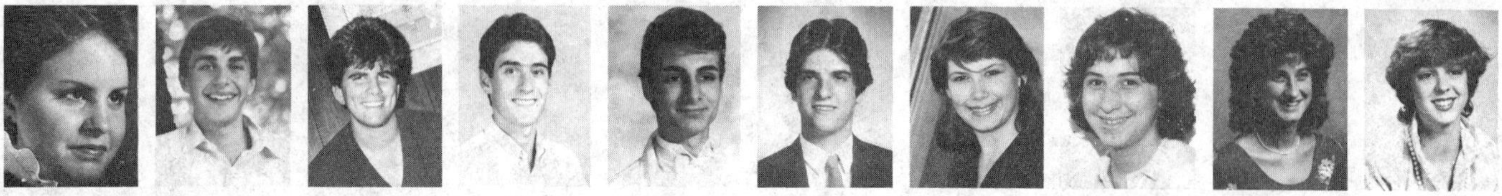

Cutler, Beth A
Norwood-Norfolk Central HS
Norwood, NY

Cutler, Jr Kenneth B
Bronxville HS
Bronxville, NY

Cutrona, Michael A
La Salle Military
Brooklyn, NY

Cutter, Christian
Bellport HS
Brookhaven, NY

Czamara, Kenneth J
Gates Chili SR HS
Buffalo, NY

Czarniak, Jr David F
Depew HS
Depew, NY

Czerwinskyj, Chrystina D
Marymount School Of New York
Bronx, NY

D Amelio, Michelle
St Marys Girls HS
Port Washington, NY

D Arpino, Carla
St Marys Girls HS
Roslyn Heights, NY

D Arrigo, Elizabeth
Williamsville East
Williamsvl, NY

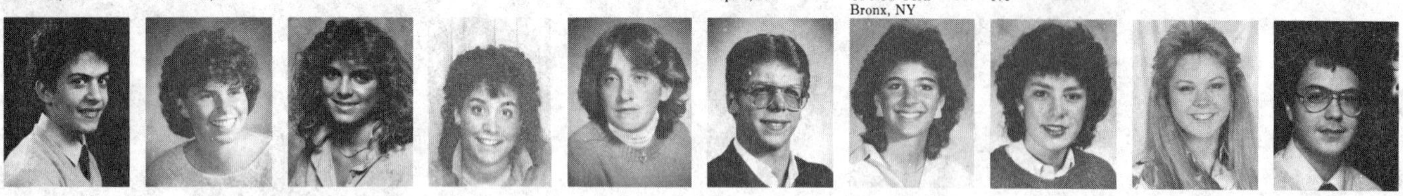

D Elia, Gian
Archbishop Molloy
Glendale, NY

D Isabel, Deborah L
Niskayuna HS
Schenectady, NY

D Onofrio, Toniann
Pelham Memorial
Pelham Manor, NY

D Urso, Rosanna
Sacred Heart Acad
New Hyde Park, NY

Daby, Donna
Lake Placid Central
Lake Placid, NY

Daddabbo, Nick
Auburn HS
Auburn, NY

Daddesa, Lisa A
Tottenville HS
Staten Island, NY

Dahl, Julie
Frontier Central HS
Lake View, NY

Dahl, Sheree
Bonanza HS
Las Vegas, NV

Dailey, Craig East
Syrcause-Minoa HS
E Syracuse, NY

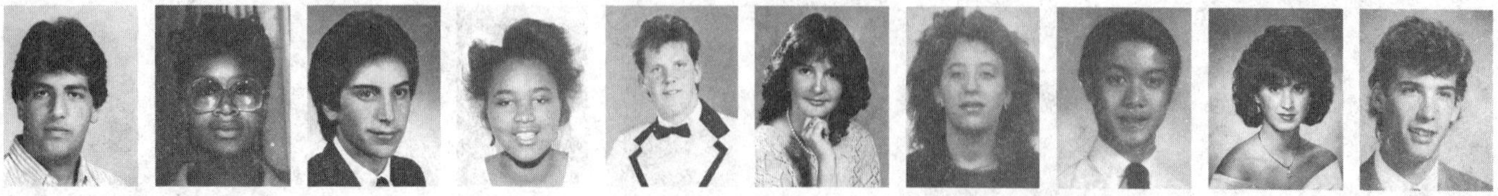

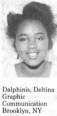

Daleo, Roy
Westhampton Beach
Mastic, NY

Daley, Desrene
De Witt Clinton HS
Bronx, NY

Dall, Marc S
Warsaw Central
Warsaw, NY

Dalphinis, Deltina
Graphic Communication
Brooklyn, NY

Dalton, Sean
Msgr Farrell HS
Staten Island, NY

Daly, Eileen Mary
Floral Park Memorial HS
Floral Park, NY

Damkohler, Lisa
St Francis Prep
Whitestone, NY

Dang, Anh Steve
Williamsville South
Williamsville, NY

Daniello, Michele
St Francis Prep
Howard Bch, NY

Dann, Michael P
Liverpool HS
Liverpool, NY

Danoski, Jeffrey R
Chenango Valley JR
SR HS
Binghamton, NY

Dantuono, Beth
Liverpool HS
Liverpool, NY

Dao, Linh T
Norman Thomas HS
New York, NY

Darling, Dane M
Perth Central HS
Johnstown, NY

Daube, Kathleen
Holland Patent
Central HS
Marcy, NY

Dauer, Julie
Brockport HS
Brockport, NY

Daumen, Michael J
Canisius HS
Buffalo, NY

Davey, Jr Robert
Auburn HS
Auburn, NY

David, Kendall B
Geneva HS
Geneva, NY

Davidson, Carla
Chautauqua Central
Mayville, NY

Davidson, Cathleen
Clarkstown SR High
School South
New City, NY

Davidson, Craig
Wallkill Central HS
Walden, NY

Davies, Anna
Wilson Magnet HS
Rochester, NY

Davies, Brian F
Williamson SR HS
Williamson, NY

Davies, Taffy
Middletown HS
Middletown, NY

Davis, Andrea R
Uniondale HS
Hempstead, NY

Davis, Bertha Ann
Monticello HS
Monticello, NY

Davis, Corey
All Hallows Inst
New York, NY

Davis, II Donald T
Mc Graw HS
Marathon, NY

Davis, La Shan
Newburger Free
New Windsor, NY

Davis, Lashawn
Grace Dodge Voc
Bronx, NY

Davis, Marie
Riverhead HS
Riverhead, NY

Davis, Melanie
Nazareth Acad
Rochester, NY

Davis, Melissa
Neward Senior HS
Newark, NY

Davis, Paul M
Hillcrest HS
Cambria Heights,
NY

Davis, Robert
Babylon HS
Babylon, NY

Davis, Scott
Corning-Painted
Post West HS
Painted Post, NY

Davis, Vickie
Avoca Central Schl
Avoca, NY

Davitt, John
Westhill HS
Syracuse, NY

Dawson, III John F
Northeastern
Clinton Central HS
Champlain, NY

Day, Dawn Marie
Central Islip SR HS
Central Islip, NY

Day, Jenny
Shenendehowa
Central HS
Clifton Park, NY

Day, Jim
Midlakes HS
Phelps, NY

De Almeida, Nellie
H Frank Carey HS
Franklin Square,
NY

De Aveiro, Robert
Lafayette HS
Brooklyn, NY

De Badts, Richard
K
North Rose-Wolcott
Wolcott, NY

De Bella, Stephen
Bishop Ford
Brooklyn, NY

De Celestino, Blase
Herbert Lehman HS
Bronx, NY

De Clercg, Patricia
John Marshall HS
Rochester, NY

De Filippo,
Elizabeth
John Jay SR HS
Hopewell Junction,
NY

De Franco, Laura
Massena Central HS
Massena, NY

De Iasi, Lisa M
Floral Park
Memorial HS
Bellerose, NY

De Jager, Philip
Riverdale Country
Bronx, NY

De La Rosa, Lynn
Division Ave HS
Levittown, NY

De Leon, Rachel A
St Francis Prep
Jamaica Estates, NY

De Lucia, Maria
St Agnes HS
Westbury, NY

De Marco, Jr
Anthony L
Newark SR HS
Newark, NY

De Marzio, Kim
West Seneca West
SR HS
West Seneca, NY

De Miguel, Carlos
John A Coleman HS
Kingston, NY

De Moors, Tamara
Weedsport Central
Weedsport, NY

De Rosa, Stephen V
Bronx HS Of
Whitestone, NY

De Rue, Shane
Palmyra Macedon
SR HS
Macedon, NY

De Socio, Nicolette
Auburn HS
Auburn, NY

De Steno, David A
Highland HS
Highland, NY

De Tore, Tammy
Frankfort Schuyler
Central HS
Frankfort, NY

De Touche, Amelia
C
Dominican
Commercial HS
Jamaica, NY

De Vincenzi,
Elizabeth
Franklin Delano
Roosevelt HS
Brooklyn, NY

De Vito, Michael A
St Marys Boys HS
Rockville Ctr, NY

De Vito, Sina
Bishop Kearney HS
Brooklyn, NY

De Vivio, Lori
South Shore HS
Brooklyn, NY

De Water, Michael
Southside HS
Elmira, NY

Deaton, Brantley
Pulaski Acad &
Central Schl
Pulaski, NY

Decambre, Tracia
Mount Vernon HS
Mt Vernon, NY

Deck, Pamela
Fairport HS
Fairport, NY

Decker, Brenda
Lynn
Mynderse Acad
Seneca Falls, NY

Decker, Dawn
Port Jervis HS
Huguenot, NY

Deegan, Mary
Our Lady Of Mercy
Sea Cliff, NY

Deegan, William P
Huntington HS
Huntington, NY

Deforest, Evette
Hamburg Central
Boston, NY

Defranco, Douglas A
The Wheatley Schl
Old Westbury, NY

Degelleke, Jenell
Clyde-Savannah HS
Lyons, NY

Deidan, Diana J
St Francis Prep
Woodside, NY

Del Casale, Karen
St Catharine Acad
Bronx, NY

Del Eveille, Lori
Andrew Jackson HS
Hollis, NY

Del Negro, Susan
Albertus Magnus
Garnerville, NY

Del Popolo, Jr
Joseph
Manlius Pebble Hill
Liverpool, NY

Del Rio, Michael
Stuyvesant HS
New York, NY

Del Rosario, Marc
Valley Stream
Central HS
Valley Stream, NY

Delaney, Stacey
Berne-Knox-Westerl
o HS
Glenmont, NY

Delgado, Rafael E
Adela Stevenson HS
Bronx, NY

Delillo, Mark
Monsignor Farrell
Staten Island, NY

Delli Pizzi, Ann
Marie
St Catherines Acad
Bronx, NY

Delongchamp,
James
Bishop Scully HS
Amsterdam, NY

Delsoin, Marc A
Springfield Gardens
Rosedale, NY

Delsoin, Pierre
John Dewey HS
Brooklyn, NY

Deluca, Debby
Tottenville HS
Staten Isld, NY

Delwo, Kristi
Herkimer HS
Herkimer, NY

Demarco, Matthew
Archbishop Stepinac
Harrison, NY

Demaria, Linda
Amsterdam HS
Amsterdam, NY

Demirjian, Janet
Christopher
Columbus HS
Bronx, NY

Dempsey, Caroline
Moore Catholic HS
Staten Island, NY

Dempsey, Paula
Oceanside HS
Oceanside, NY

Dendy, David
Valley Central HS
Montgomery, NY

Denero, Joseph A
Bishop Grimes HS
Syracuse, NY

Denger, Lynn
Seaford HS
Seaford, NY

Denko, Julie
Granville Central
Pawlet, VT

Denmark, Becky
Waterloo Central
Waterloo, NY

Dennis, Jodie Ann
Roy C Ketcham HS
Poughkeepsie, NY

Depew, Jr Robert D
Geneva HS
Geneva, NY

Depferd, Michelle
Brockport HS
Brockport, NY

Depina, Sabrina
Cathedral HS
Ny, NY

Deraco, Lorenzo
Nyack HS
Nyack, NY

Derella, Michael
Mohawk Central
Mohawk, NY

Derienzo, Dawn
Northport HS
East Northport, NY

Derr, Robyn
Penn Yan Acad
Bellona, NY

Desai, Ravi
Vestal SR HS
Binghamton, NY

Desnoyers, Philip
Lansingburgh HS
Troy, NY

Desormeaux,
Michelle
Berlin Central HS
Stephentown, NY

Despaigne, Luis A
Manhattan Center
For Science & Math
Bronx, NY

Dessibourg, Ursula
St Johns Prep
Astoria, NY

Devita, Charles
Brooklyn Technical
Flushing, NY

Devlen, Nancy
Groton Central Schl
Groton, NY

Devoe, Christy
Shenendehowa
Central HS
Clifton Park, NY

Devoe, Craig
Hauppauge HS
Hauppauge, NY

Devries, Jennifer
John Jay HS
Wappingers Fls, NY

Dewey, David K
St Francis HS
Eden, NY

Deyette, David
Glens Falls SR HS
Glens Falls, NY

Deyette, John
Scotia-Glenville HS
Scotia, NY

Deyette, Michelle A
Shenendehowa HS
Round Lake, NY

Deza, Patrice
Dominican
Commercial HS
Jamaica, NY

Di Benedetto,
Andrea Kim
Earl L
Vandermeulen HS
Pt Jeff Sta, NY

Di Bernardo, Lisa
Bethlehem Central
Glenmont, NY

Di Cristofaro, David
P
Linton HS
Schenectady, NY

Di Gennaro, David J
East Syracuse
Minoa HS
Minoa, NY

Di Giacomo, Jr
Vincent Paul
Gloversville HS
Gloversville, NY

Di Giorgio, Paul
Warwick Valley HS
Warwick, NY

Di Ioia, Steven
Cortland JR SR HS
Dryden, NY

Di Iulio, Renee
Ou Lady Of Mercy
Fairport, NY

Di Maria, Jr Joseph
F
Mc Quaid Jesuit HS
Fairport, NY

Di Meglio, Lori
Port Jervis HS
Port Jervis, NY

Di Natale, Anthony
New Dorp HS
Staten Island, NY

Di Santo, Sue Anne
Clyde-Savannah HS
Clyde, NY

Di Virgilio, Sarah E
St Johns
Preparatory HS
Astoria, NY

Diadema, Debra
Paul D Schreiber
Port Washington,
NY

Diamond, Dina
Smithtown High
School West
Smithtown, NY

Diana, Patricia
Fayetteville-Manlius
Manlius, NY

Diaz, Omar
Cardinal Spellman
Bronx, NY

Dicerbo, Cheri
Manhasset HS
Manhasset, NY

Dickhaus, Deborah
L
Auburn HS
Auburn, NY

Dickler, Philip S
Valley Stream South
Valley Stream, NY

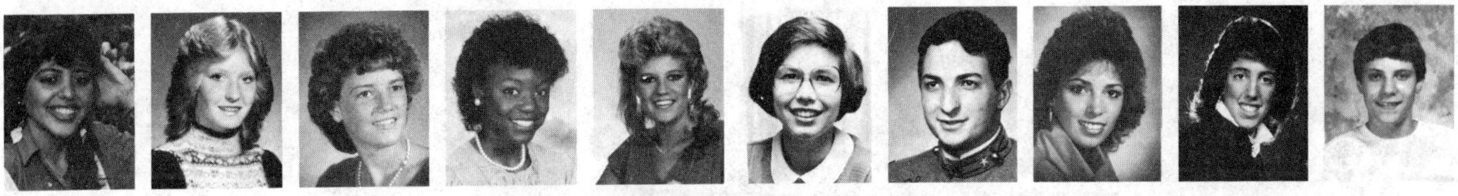

Dicosola, Lisa A
St Catharines Acad
Bronx, NY

Diekman, Stacy
North Salem HS
N Salem, NY

Diffendorf, Mary
Susquehanna Valley
Kirkwood, NY

Diggs, Kelly
Middletown HS
Middletown, NY

Dillillo, Linda
Susan E Wagner HS
Staten Is, NY

Dillon, Julia E
Spring Valley SR
Nanuet, NY

Dimaggio, Rosario
La Salle Military
Flushing, NY

Dimitrov, Barbara
Bishop Kearney HS
Rochester, NY

Dio Guardi, Sarah
Mt Morris Central
Mt Morris, NY

Dioguardi, Thomas
Avon JR SR HS
Avon, NY

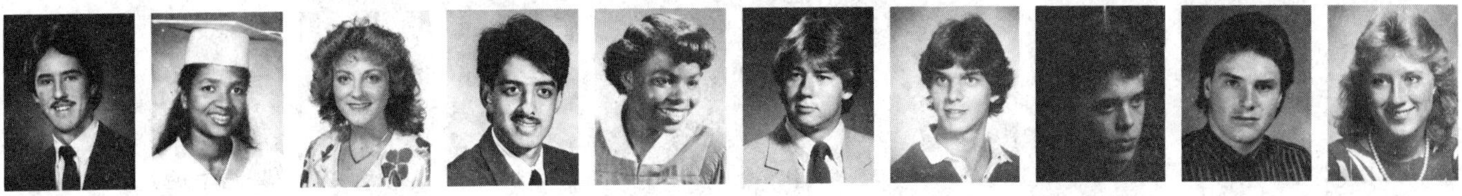

Dion, David A
Northeastern
Clinton Central Schl
Rouses Point, NY

Diptee, Angeline R
The Mary Louis
Jamaica, NY

Diskin, Lee
St John The Baptist
N Babylon, NY

Dixit, Sanat
Tottenville HS
Staten Island, NY

Dixon, Patricia
Erasmus Hall HS
Brooklyn, NY

Dlhosh, William J
Royt C Ketcham HS
Wappingers Falls,
NY

Dlugolenski,
Thomas J
Liverpool HS
Liverpool, NY

Dobbins, Evan
Greece Athena HS
Rochester, NY

Dobles, Jeff
E J Wilson HS
Spencerport, NY

Dobosiewicz,
Elizabeth J
Depew HS
Depew, NY

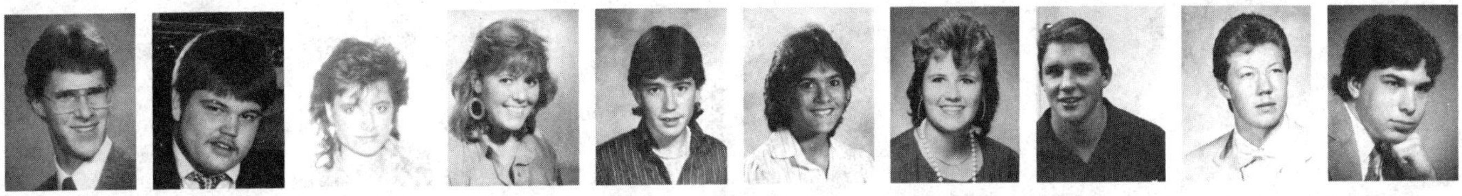

Dobransky, Eric R
Maine-Endwell SR
Johnson City, NY

Dobrasz, Stanley J
La Salle SR HS
Niagara Falls, NY

Dobry, Emily
The Mary Louis
Jamaica Estates, NY

Dockendorf, Pamela
Bitburg HS
Apo Ny, NY

Dodge, Michael
Maryvale HS
Cheektowaga, NY

Doggett, Kerry
Saugerties HS
Saugerties, NY

Doherty, Erin Anne
East Meadow HS
East Meadow, NY

Dolan, Jack
Niskayuna HS
Schenectady, NY

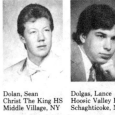

Dolan, Sean
Christ The King HS
Middle Village, NY

Dolgas, Lance
Hoosic Valley HS
Schaghticoke, NY

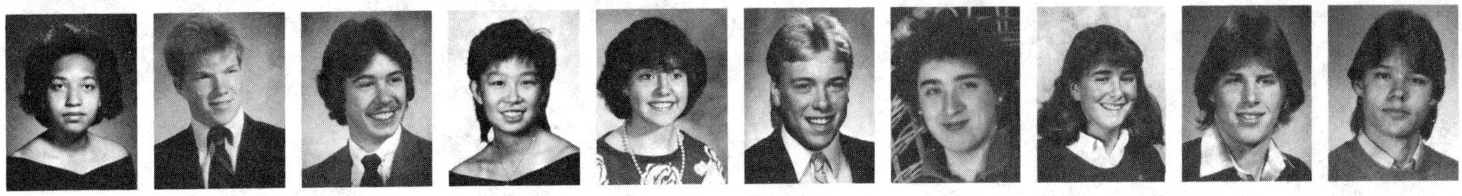

Dolson, Fay Ann
Minisink Valley HS
Otisville, NY

Dombrow, Russell
W
Bishop Ludden HS
Syracuse, NY

Donati, Michael J
Shaker HS
Latham, NY

Dong, Helen H
Hillcrest HS
Briarwood, NY

Donlon, Lynee
Waterville HS
Waterville, NY

Donnelly, Gerard J
Kings Park SR HS
Kings Park, NY

Donofrio, Anna
Mynderse Acad
Seneca Falls, NY

Dopsovic, Beth
Bay Shore HS
Brightwaters, NY

Dorlon, III Daniel A
Amsterdam HS
Amsterdam, NY

Dorney, Chris
Kendall JR SR HS
Hamlin, NY

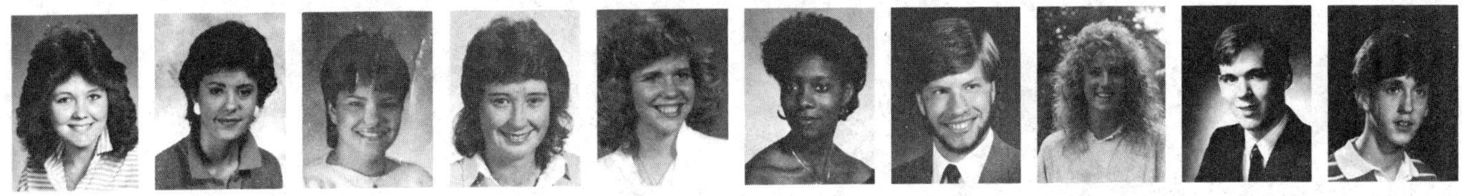

Dorsey, Christine
John Jay HS
Fishkill, NY

Dotegowski, Tracy
Gowanda Central
Collins, NY

Doty, Stephanie
Cortland JR SR HS
Cortland, NY

Doud, Michelle
Twin Tiers Baptist
Lawrenceville, PA

Dougher, Wendy
Queensbury HS
Glens Falls, NY

Douglas, Tracey
Bishop Loughlin HS
Queens, NY

Douros, Timothy J
Oyster Bay HS
Oyster Bay, NY

Dowd, Meghan
Bellport HS
Bellport, NY

Dowling, Joseph A
Watervliet HS
Watervliet, NY

Downey, Mark J
John S Burke
Catholic HS
Montgomery, NY

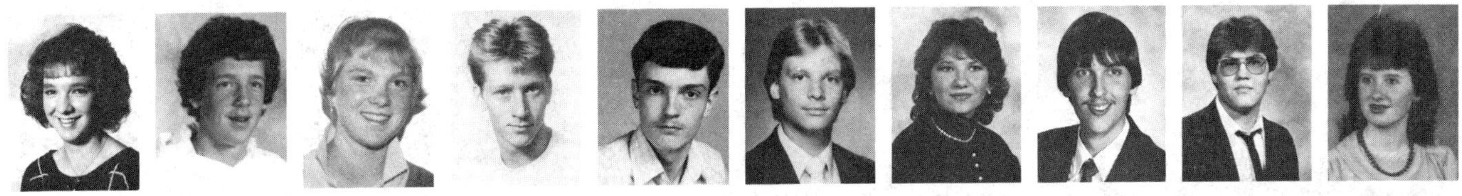

Doyka, Denise
Hamburg SR HS
Hamburg, NY

Doyle, Jim
Pine Bush HS
Pine Bush, NY

Doyle, Patty
St Marys Girls HS
Port Washington,
NY

Drake, Andrew J
Clinton Central HS
Clinton, NY

Drawbridge, Tim
Riverhead HS
Baiting Hollow, NY

Drazka, Frank J
Sanford H Calhoun
Merrick, NY

Dreaney, Teresa
Amsterdam HS
Amsterdam, NY

Drengers, Andrew
St Agnes HS
Bayside, NY

Drews, Hans W
Little Falls JR SR
St Johnsville, NY

Drum, Margaret
St Marys Acad
Glens Falls, NY

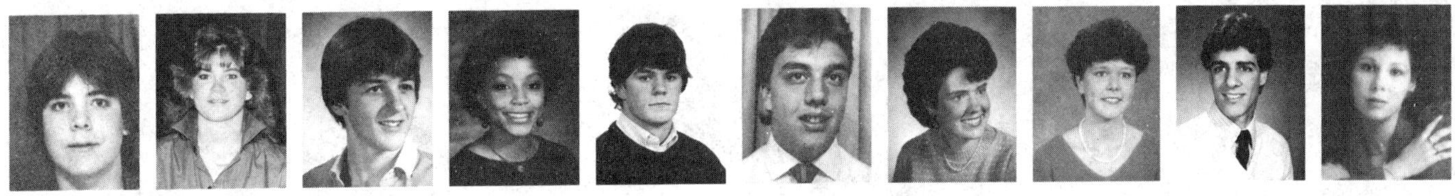

Drum, Michael T
Garden City HS
Garden City, NY

Drusin, Cami L
Clarkstown High
School North
New City, NY

Du Bois, II Thomas
E
G Ray Bodley HS
Fulton, NY

Du Vernay, Janine
Haverling HS
Bath, NY

Dubel, Mark
Canisius HS
Lancaster, NY

Duca, John
Henninger HS
Syracuse, NY

Dudash, Sheila
Bishop Ludden HS
Liverpool, NY

Duell, Kimberly
Corinth Central Schl
Corinth, NY

Duffy, Patrick J
Franklin D
Roosevelt HS
Hyde Park, NY

Dufresne, Elizabeth
M
Arlington HS
Pleasant Valley, NY

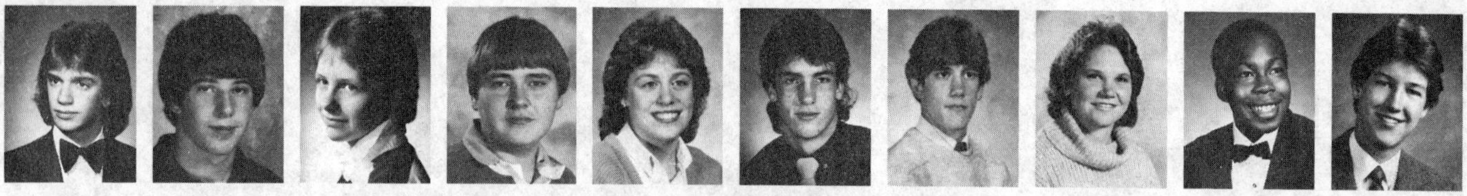

Dugan, James C
St Francis Prep
College Point, NY

Dugan, Mark
Fayetteville-Manlius
Fayetteville, NY

Duke, Samantha
Mandy
Troy HS
Troy, NY

Dumas, Arthur
Franklin Acad
Malone, NY

Dumas, Tracey
G Ray Bodley HS
Fulton, NY

Duncan, Glen
Aquinas Inst
Rochester, NY

Duncan, James
Hutchinson Central
Technical HS
Buffalo, NY

Duncan, Lisa
Dover JR SR HS
Dover Plains, NY

Dungie, Chris D
Mt St Michael Acad
Bronx, NY

Dunn, Daniel P
Oneida HS
Oneida, NY

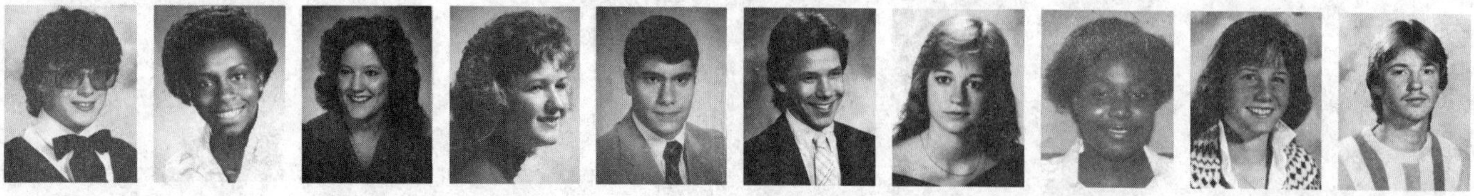

Dupee, Tami
Northeastern
Clinton Central HS
Champlain, NY

Dupree, Carole
Roosevelt HS
Yonkers, NY

Durand, Paula
Cicero North
Syracuse HS
N Syracuse, NY

Durkin, Darlene
Ann
Depew HS
Depew, NY

Duskas, William
Hugh C Williams
Canton, NY

Dutzer, Thomas M
Garden City SR HS
Garden City, NY

Dyckes, Micheline
St Dominic HS
Huntington, NY

Dyett, Michelle
George Washington
Brooklyn, NY

Dykeman, Karin
Stissin Mt JR SR
Red Hook, NY

Dyksen, James R
Ichabod Crane HS
Stuyvesant, NY

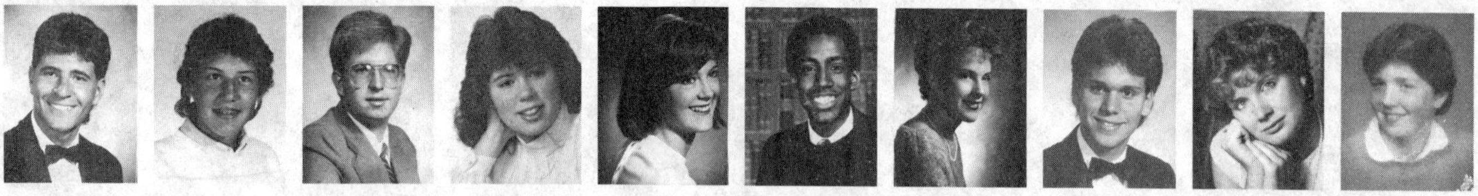

Dzielski, Mark
Canisius HS
Grand Island, NY

Dzierzanowski,
Lynette
Alexander Central
Darien Ctr, NY

Eades, Jr Richard E
Dansville HS
Dansville, NY

Eagen, Lynnette A
Arlington HS
Poughkeepsie, NY

Eager, Tiffanny E
Jamestown HS
Jamestown, NY

Eatman, Timothy K
Mt Pleasant
Christian Acad
New York, NY

Eaton, Carolyn J
Troy HS
Troy, NY

Eberle, Dean
Canisius HS
Amherst, NY

Ebert, Michelle
Lynn
Brockport SR HS
Brockport, NY

Eckberg, Kelley S
Southwestern
Central HS
Jamestown, NY

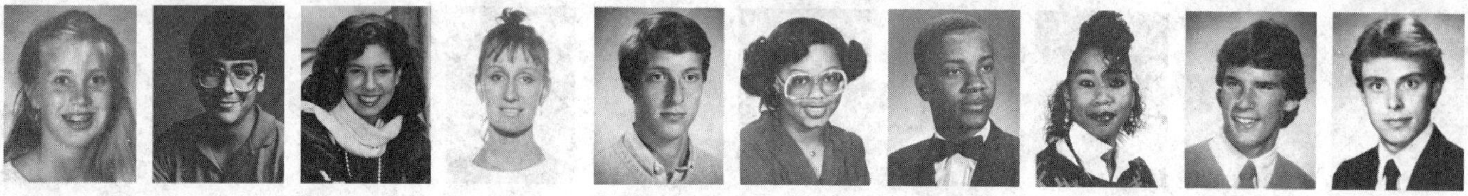

Eckerlin, Suzanne
Tully Central HS
Tully, NY

Eckes, David
Port Jervis HS
Sparrow Bush, NY

Edesess, Marie E
Convent Of The
Sacred Heart
New York, NY

Edgar, Victoria
Smithtown East HS
St James, NY

Edinger, Henry F
Corcoran HS
Syracuse, NY

Edmondson, Jill
Uniondale HS
Hempstead, NY

Edwards, Jr Arthur
L
Regis HS
Brooklyn, NY

Edwards, Charlaina
Turner-Carroll HS
Buffalo, NY

Edwards, Dennis C
East Syracuse
Minoa HS
Minoa, NY

Edwards, V Franklin
G
West Islip HS
West Islip, NY

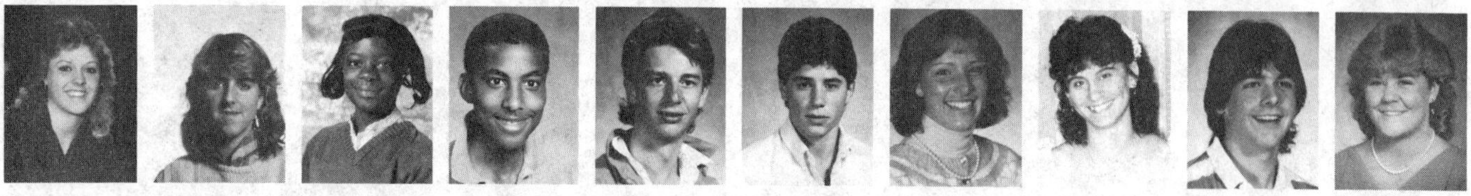

Edwards, Jennifer
Letchworth HS
Castile, NY

Edwards, Laura
Southampton HS
Southampton, NY

Edwards, Myrei
Brooklyn Technical
Brooklyn, NY

Edwards, Scott
John Jay Sr HS
Wappingers Fls, NY

Edwards, Sean
Southwestern
Central Schl
Lakewood, NY

Ehjem, Tony
Whitesboro SR HS
Whitesboro, NY

Ehlers, Christina
Tully Central HS
Tully, NY

Ehrlich, Jodie
Schoharie Central
Schoharie, NY

Eipp, Billy
Northville Central
Northville, NY

Eipp, Marianne
Lafayette HS
Lafayette, NY

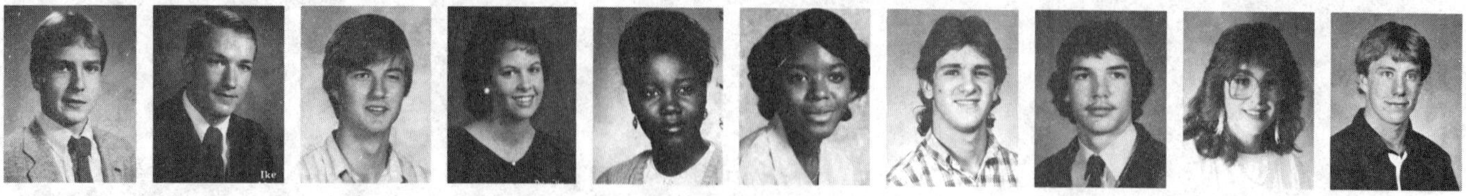

Eiselen, Karl
Mc Quaid Jesuit HS
Rochester, NY

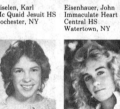

Eisenhauer, John
Immaculate Heart
Central HS
Watertown, NY

Ekeland, Tor B
Fairport HS
Fairport, NY

Ekholm, Jennifer L
Cortland SR HS
Cortland, NY

Eliacin, Patricia
John Dewey HS
Brooklyn, NY

Elliott, Althea
East Meadow HS
East Meadow, NY

Elnasser, Farris M
Fredonia HS
Fredonia, NY

Elswick, Richard
Torrejon HS
APO, NY

Emeny, Suzanne
Fabius-Pompey HS
Fabius, NY

Emerson, Michael
Penn Yan Acad
Penn Yan, NY

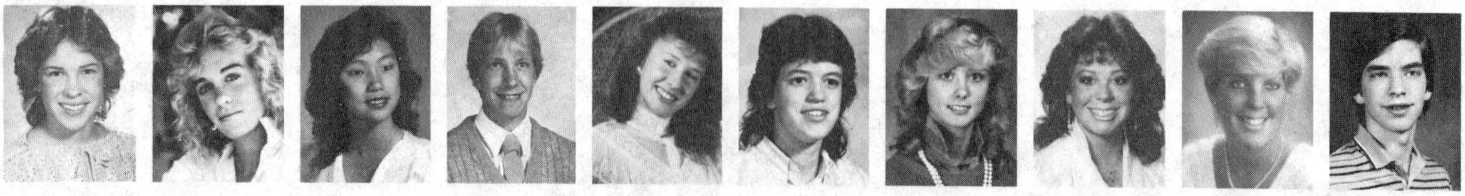

Emery, Lynette
Pioneer Central Schl
Delevan, NY

Emrich, Meg
Spackenkill HS
Poughkeepsie, NY

Eng, Joan
Hicksville HS
Hicksville, NY

Engel, Michael
Hahn American HS
Apo New York, NY

Engelfried, Debora
A
Pittsford HS
Pittsford, NY

Engelhardt, Kristin
Guilderland HS
Voorheesville, NY

Engle, Robin
Albion Central HS
Albion, NY

Englesberg, Bari Sue
Newfield HS
Coram, NY

Enkvist, Kristine A
Pittsford Mendon
Pittsford, NY

Ennis, David L
DansvilleSR HS
Dansville, NY

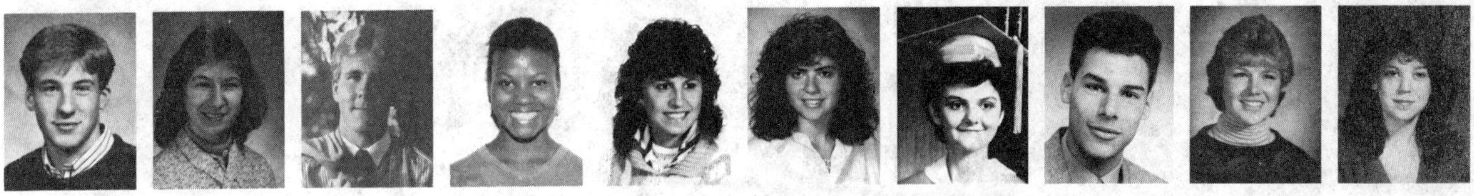

Enserro, Robert
Jamestown HS
Jamestown, NY

Enslow, Tracy
Waterloo SR HS
Waterloo, NY

Epperson, Lloyd
Hahn Americna HS
Apo New York, NY

Epps, Kimberly Y
Bronx HS Of
New York, NY

Epps, Marjorie
Franklin Central
Oneonta, NY

Epstein, Alyse K
Syosset HS
Jericho, NY

Ergin, Aysegul
Greece Olympia HS
Rochester, NY

Erian, Neil
Liverpool HS
Liverpool, NY

Erickson, Suzanne
Cairo-Durham HS
E Durham, NY

Erkenbeck, Marie
Valley Central HS
Walden, NY

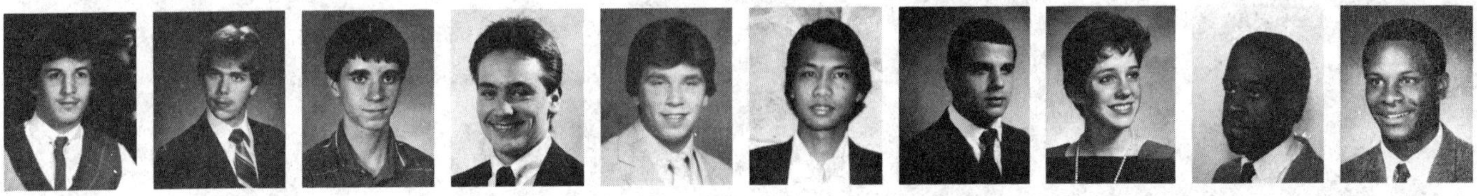

Ernst, Joseph
Maryvale SR HS
Cheektowaga, NY

Errichetti, Chris
Washingtonville HS
Rock Tvn, NY

Erskine, John
Westfield Central
Westfield, NY

Erway, Victor M
Cherry Valley HS
Cherry Valley, NY

Esposito, Jr Thomas P
Saratoga Springs HS
Saratoga Springs, NY

Estilo, Alvin E
St Francis Prep Schl
Howard Beach, NY

Etoll, Thomas M
Bishop Ludden HS
Syracuse, NY

Ettinger, Katherine L
John S Burke Catholic HS
Monroe, NY

Eugene, Jude E
Polytechnic Prep Country Day Schl
Elmont, NY

Eure, Joseph D
Poly Prep CDS
Brooklyn, NY

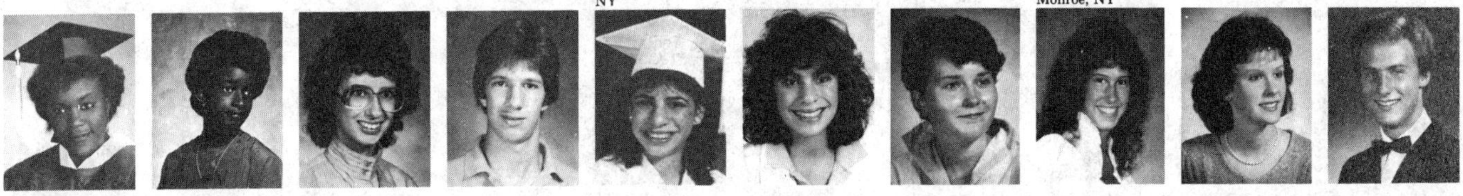

Evans, Camille Lititia
Holy Trinity Diocesan HS
Uniondale, NY

Evans, Sabrina
Midwood HS
Brooklyn, NY

Ewert, Heather
Wayland Central
Wayland, NY

Excell, Charles
Brockport HS
Hamlin, NY

Exelbert, Michelle
Half Hollow Hills East HS
Dix Hills, NY

Exelbert, Renee
Half Hollow Hills HS East
Dix Hills, NY

Exton, Mary Jo
Palmyra-Macedon
Palmyra, NY

Fabiano, Denise
Saugerties HS
Saugerties, NY

Fagnan, Karen
Cardinal Mooney
Rochester, NY

Fahey, Jonathan T
Half Hollow Hills High School East
Melville, NY

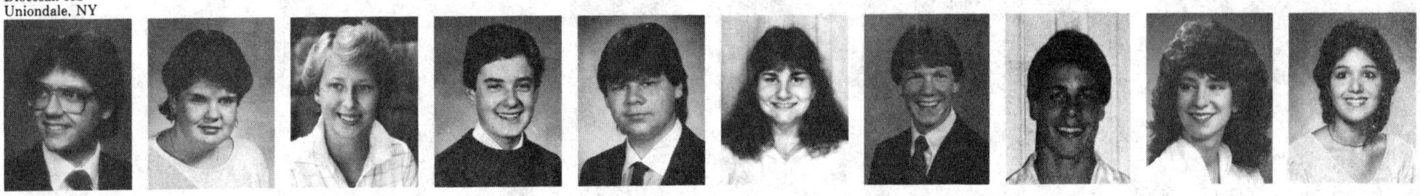

Fairbanks, John Daniel
Union Springs Acad
Jamestown, NY

Faircloth, Suzanne
Eden SR HS
Eden, NY

Falkowski, Agatha
Ichabod Crane HS
Valatie, NY

Falvey, Scott P
Penn Yan Acad
Penn Yan, NY

Fanara, Peter J
West Seneca West SR HS
West Seneca, NY

Fanos, Deirdre
St Marys Girls HS
Floral Pk, NY

Farbaniec, David
Glens Falls SR HS
Glens Falls, NY

Farber, Darren
Liberty HS
Liberty, NY

Farber, Sharon
Herkimer SR HS
Herkimer, NY

Farina, Karen
Smithtown HS
Smithtown, NY

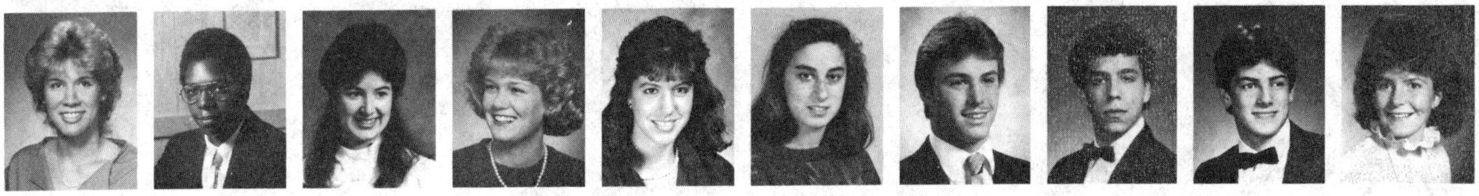

Farley, Jo Ann D
Centereach HS
Centereach, NY

Farley, Jonathan
Brockport HS
Brockport, NY

Farr, Samara
Horseheads HS
Big Flats, NY

Farr, Virginia H
Auburn HS
Auburn, NY

Farrell, Deborah
Brockport HS
Brockport, NY

Farrington, Karen
Bellport HS
E Patchogue, NY

Farruggio, Thomas P
Lancaster Central
Depew, NY

Farrugia, Joseph G
Xavier HS
New York, NY

Fasciglione, Joseph P
Mount St Michael
Bronx, NY

Faulkner, Denise
Clymer Central Schl
Clymer, NY

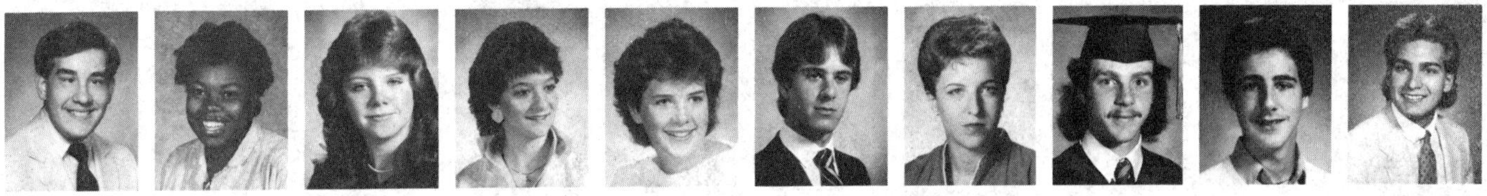

Fauls, Brian
Smithtown HS West
Smithtown, NY

Faust, Carletta
Uniondale HS
Baldwin, NY

Fay, Margaret
Liverpool HS
North Syracuse, NY

Fazio, Kristen
Frankfort Schuyler Central HS
Frankfort, NY

Feagles, Judy
St Johnsville Central HS
St Johnsville, NY

Federico, Carmen J
Liverpool HS
Liverpool, NY

Fedynak, Stephanie A
Wellington C Mepham HS
North Bellmore, NY

Fein, Gene F
The Bronx HS
Bronx, NY

Fekler, David
Union Endicott HS
Endicott, NY

Felakos, James G
Somers HS
Granite Springs, NY

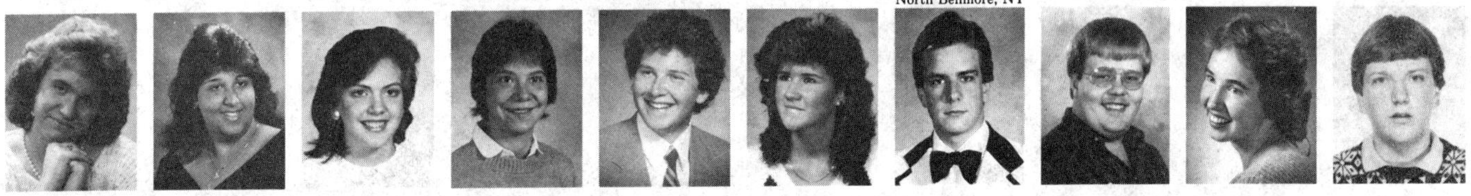

Feldman, Nicole
Broadalbin Central
Johnstown, NY

Felicello, Mia
Marlboro HS
Marlboro, NY

Felso, Alice
Lyndonville Central
Medina, NY

Fennell, Christine
Kenmore East HS
Kenmore, NY

Fenocchi, Michael G
Liverpool HS
Liverpool, NY

Feola, Michelle
Central HS
Valley Stream, NY

Ferguson, Alfred
Monsignor Farrell
Staten Island, NY

Ferguson, Jeffrey
Oppenheim Ephiatah Centra
St Johnsville, NY

Ferguson, Patrice L
Williamson SR HS
Williamson, NY

Ferguson, Patrick
Msgr Mc Clancy HS
Long Islnd City, NY

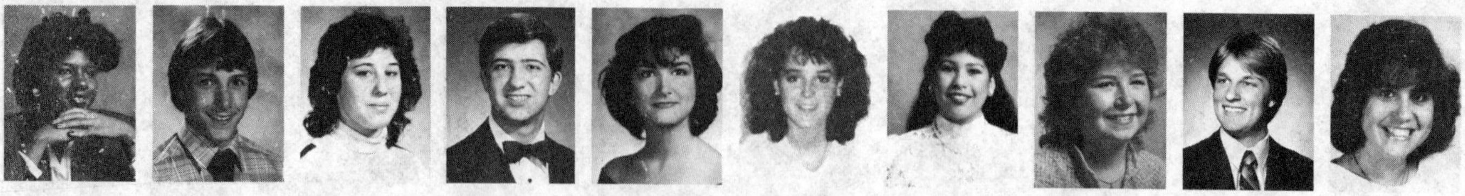

Ferguson, Tanya
Bishop Kearney HS
Rochester, NY

Fermon, Dan
Penfield HS
Penfield, NY

Fernandes, Dawn
Brewster HS
Brewster, NY

Fernandes, Jr
Manuel D
Iona Prep
Yonkers, NY

Fernandez, Francine
HS Of Art And
Astoria, NY

Fernandez, Vicky
St Francis Prep
College Point, NY

Fernandez, Zenia C
St Agnes Acad
Littleneck, NY

Fernsebner, Karen
Depew HS
Cheektowaga, NY

Ferrante, Michael
Long Beach HS
Long Beach, NY

Ferrara, Anna
The Wheatley Schl
E Williston, NY

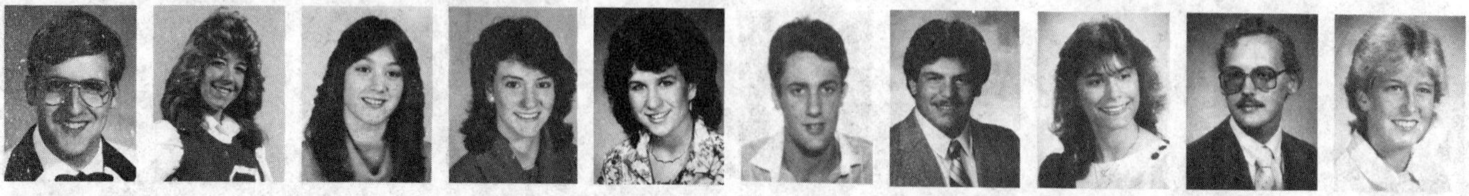

Ferrara, Daniel J
Monsignor Farrell
Staten Island, NY

Ferraro, Jean
Central HS
Valley Stream, NY

Ferraro, Julie
Saugerties HS
Saugerties, NY

Ferrer, Monica
The Barnard Schl
Bronx, NY

Ferrera, Doreen E
Walt Whitman HS
Huntington Sta, NY

Ferrero, Vincent M
Newburgh Free
Newburgh, NY

Ferretti, III Paul F
Lindenhurst SR HS
Lindenhurst, NY

Ferretti, Theresa
Shenendehowa HS
Clifton Park, NY

Ferris, Lee M
Fonda-Fultonville
Central Schl
Fultonville, NY

Ferris, Samantha L
Liverpool HS
Liverpool, NY

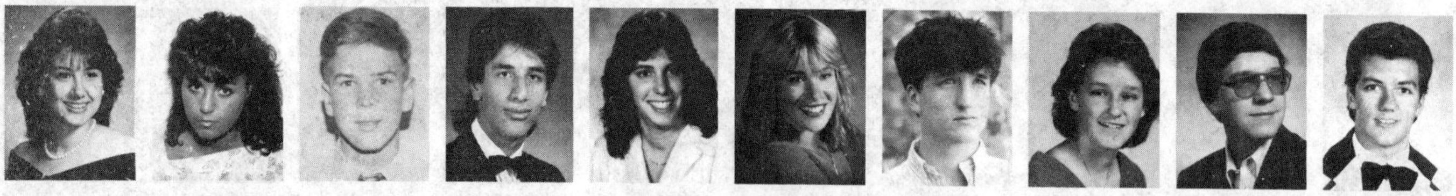

Ferro, Laurieann
Pine Bush HS
Middletown, NY

Ferro, Maria
Christ The King R
Middle Village, NY

Ferrone, George
Archbishop Molloy
Flushing, NY

Ferruggia, Michael
A
Half Hollow Hills
HS East
Melville, NY

Feuerman, Mary
Riverhead HS
Riverhead, NY

Feuerstein,
Kimberly
Niskayuna HS
Schenectady, NY

Fey, Daniel R
Briarcliff Manor HS
Briarcliff Manor,
NY

Fey, Kimberly
Sachem HS
Lake Ronkonkoma,
NY

Fiebke, Kevin M
Columbia HS
East Greenbush, NY

Figari, Jack N
Msgr Farrell HS
Staten Island, NY

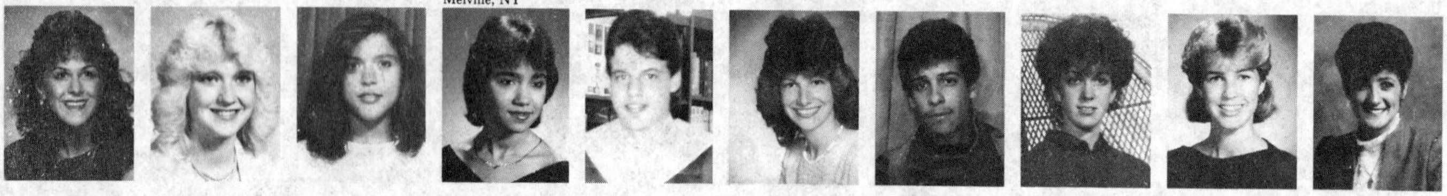

Figlioli, Diane
Valley Stream
Central HS
Valley Stream, NY

Figlow, Jodi
Batavis SR HS
Batavia, NY

Figueroa, Johanna
St Pius V HS
Bronx, NY

Figueroa, Lizbeth
Monsignor Scanlan
Bronx, NY

Figueroa, Sean
Central Islip HS
Central Islip, NY

Filingeri, Andrea
Franckfort-Schuyler
Central Schl
Frankfort, NY

Filipe, Steven
La Salle Acad
New York, NY

Filippetti, Mia
Watkins Glen HS
Watkins Glen, NY

Filipski, Dorie
Springville Griffith
Colden, NY

Filosa, Jennifer
Anne
Sachem HS
Farmingville, NY

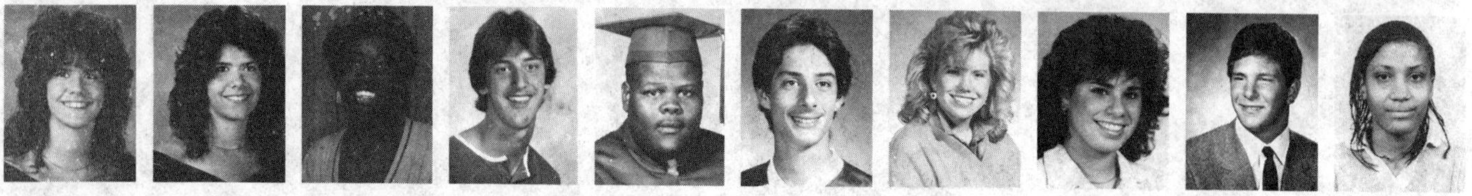

Finan, Cathleen M
Stella Maris HS
Belle Harbor, NY

Finan, Colleen M
Stella Maris HS
Belle-Harbor, NY

Finch, Janice
Murry Bergtraum
Bronx, NY

Finch, Jr John A
Hannibal Central
Sterling, NY

Findlay, Lancelot
Christopher
Columbus HS
Bronx, NY

Finelli, Christopher
M
Roy C Ketcham HS
Poughkeepsie, NY

Finister, Lisa
Brewster HS
Brewster, NY

Fink, Shari
Commack HS
Commack, NY

Finkelstein, Adam
Long Beach HS
Lido Beach, NY

Finlay, Michelle
Evander Childs HS
Bronx, NY

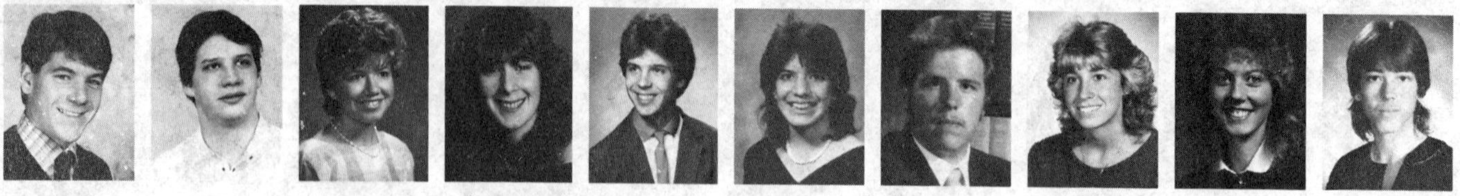

Finney, David
West Genesee HS
Syracuse, NY

Fiore, Anthony
Christ The King HS
Ridgewood, NY

Fiore, Katerina
Herkimer SR HS
Herkimer, NY

Fiore, Katherine M
Tuxedo HS
Greenwood Lake,
NY

Fiore, Michael J
Sachem North HS
Farmingville, NY

Fiorello, Christine
Westlake HS
Hawthorne, NY

Fischer, Peter
Dunkirk HS
Dunkirk, NY

Fischer, Sharon
Wayne Central HS
Ontario, NY

Fiser, Loretta
Port Jervis HS
Pt Jervis, NY

Fisher, David
Marion Central Schl
Marion, NY

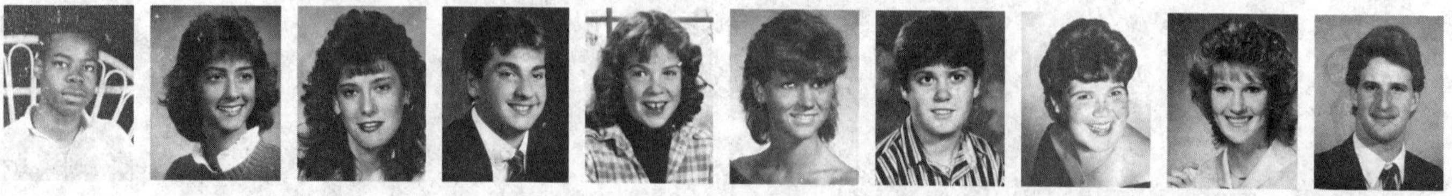

Fisher, Emanuel
Burgard Voc HS
Buffalo, NY

Fisher, Kimberly
Amsterdam HS
Amsterdam, NY

Fisher, Suzette
Greenwich Central
Greenwich, NY

Fiske, Gregg
Cortland HS
Cortland, NY

Fitzgerald, Dorothy
A
John Jay SR HS
Katonah, NY

Fitzgerald,
Geraldine
Lincoln HS
Yonkers, NY

Fitzgerald, John
Clarkstown HS
New City, NY

Fitzgerald, Kathleen
M
Fontbonne Hall
Brooklyn, NY

Fitzpatrick,
Jacqueline
Dominican
Commercial HS
Woodhaven, NY

Fitzsimmons, II
Patrick J
Saugerties HS
Saugerties, NY

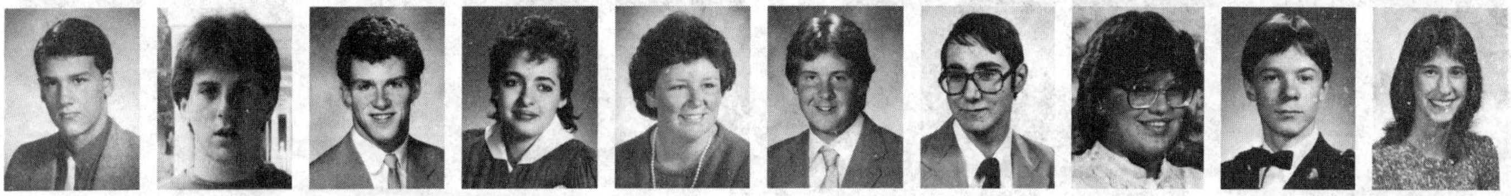

Fix, Matthew
East Aurora HS
East Aurora, NY

Fixler, Mitchell
David
Somers HS
Tarrytown, NY

Flaherty, Michael F
General Douglas
Mac Arthur HS
Levittown, NY

Flashburg, Sandra
Sheepshead Bay HS
Brooklyn, NY

Fleming, Christine A
Westhill HS
Syracuse, NY

Fleming, Michael A
Huntington HS
Huntington Sta, NY

Fletcher, Jeffrey
Naples Central HS
Naples, NY

Fletcher, Jennie
Columbia HS
Nassau, NY

Fletcher, Thomas
Xavier HS
Brooklyn, NY

Flierl, Stacy
Frontier Central HS
Blasdell, NY

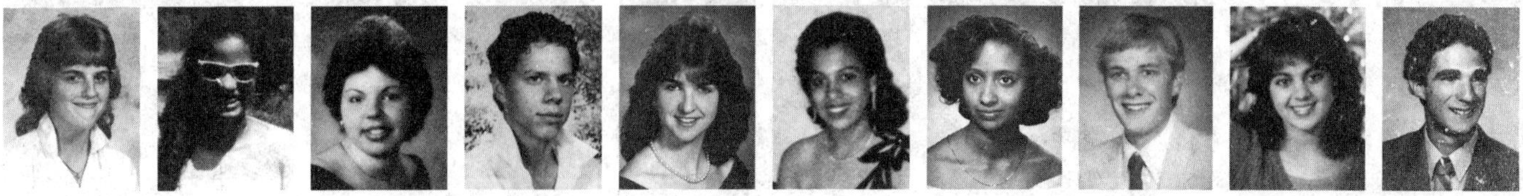

Flint, Shannon
Hannibal Central
Hannibal, NY

Flores, Dennisse
Academy Of Mt St
Ursula HS
Bronx, NY

Focarile, Christina
North Rockland HS
Van Alstyne, TX

Foley, Roger W
Gregory B Jarvis
Mohawk, NY

Foley, Shioban M
Goshen Central HS
Goshen, NY

Fontanes, Lillian
Dominican
Commercial HS
Jamaica, NY

Fontenelle, Michelle
A
Bishop Ford Central
Catholic HS
Brooklyn, NY

Foote, John H
La Fayette HS
Lafayette, NY

Forastiero, Donna
Cicero-North
Syracuse HS
Clay, NY

Foray, Stephen
Connetquot HS
Oakdale, NY

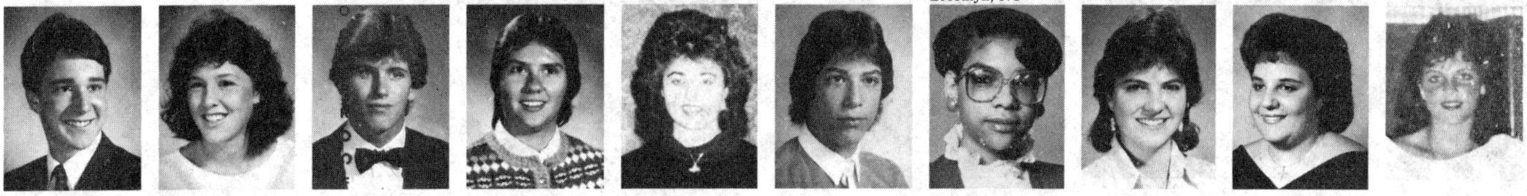

Forbes, Sean C
Susquehanna Valley
Binghamton, NY

Ford, Melissa
Honeoye Falls-Lima
Honeoye Falls, NY

Ford, Robert
Fordham Prep Schl
Yonkers, NY

Ford, Sharon
Palmyra-Macedon
Macedon, NY

Ford, Valerie C
Susan E Wagner HS
Staten Island, NY

Forster, Mike
Liverpool HS
Liverpool, NY

Forster, Samantha
Midwood MSI HS/
BROOKLYN Coll
HS
Brooklyn, NY

Forsyth, Melissa
Valley Central HS
Montgomery, NY

Forte, Anne Marie
St Joseph Hill HS
Staten Island, NY

Forte, Ethel
Christ The King
Regional HS
Middle Village, NY

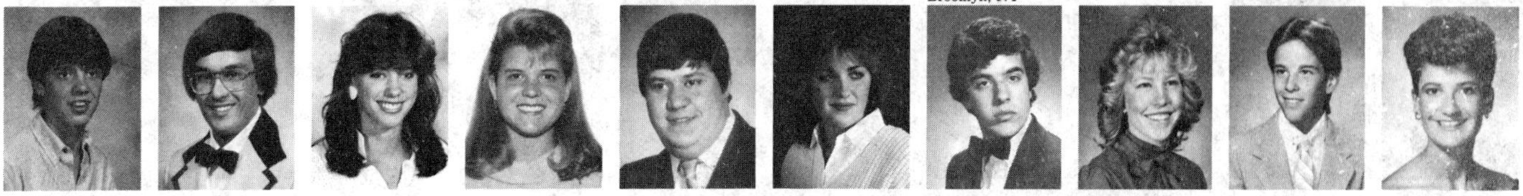

Fortin, Robert
Bishop Grimes HS
N Syracuse, NY

Forys, Albert
Bishop Kearney HS
Rochester, NY

Foster, Jeanette
Keveny Memorial
Clifton Park, NY

Foster, Johanna
Arlington HS
Wappingers Falls,
NY

Foster, Steven R
New Berlin Central
New Berlin, NY

Fotino, Gia
Warwick Valley
Central HS
Warwick, NY

Fox, Armando
Regis HS
Rego Park, NY

Fox, Bethany
Pine Valley Central
Conewango Valley,
NY

Fox, Eric J
Centereach HS
Centereach, NY

Fraccalvieri,
Maryanna
Lindenhurst HS
Lindenhurst, NY

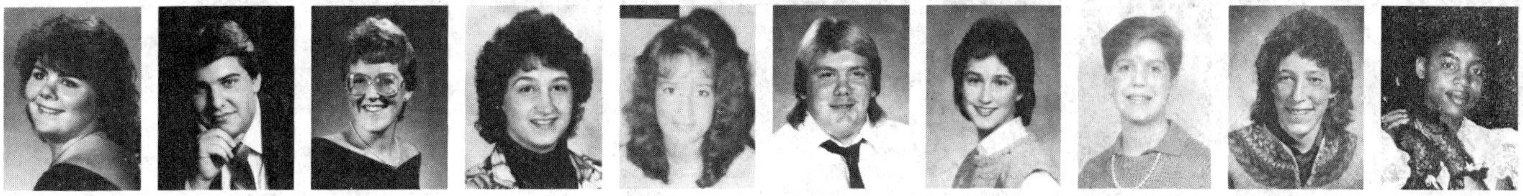

Fracentese, Mary
Bishop Kearney HS
Brooklyn, NY

Fradella, Henry F
The Searing Schl
Morganville, NJ

Fraleigh, Kimberly J
Our Lady Of
Lourdes HS
Poughkeepsie, NY

Fraliegh, Laurie
Dover JR SR HS
Dover Plains, NY

Frampton, Bonnie
Sachem HS
Holtsville, NY

France, Christian R
Hornell HS
Hornell, NY

Franceschelli, Carol
Auburn HS
Auburn, NY

Franchetti, Suzanne
P
St Franics Prep
Manhasset, NY

Francia, Lisa
Norwood Norfolk
Central HS
Norfolk, NY

Francis, Beatrice
St Edmund HS
Brooklyn, NY

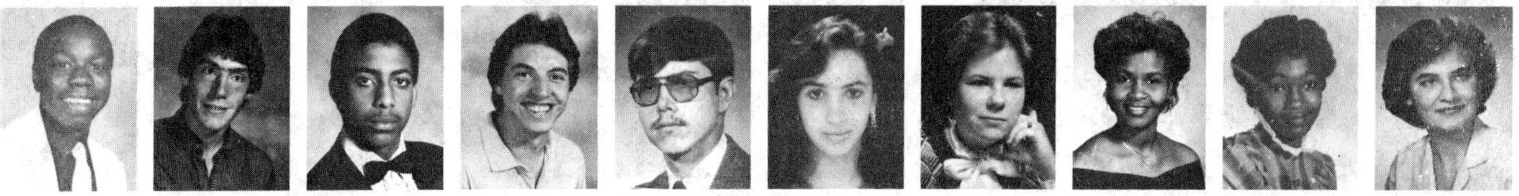

Francis, Dwayne
William E Grady
Brooklyn, NY

Francis, Michael M
Haverling Central
Bath, NY

Francis, Omar
Rice HS
Bronx, NY

Frank, Jr Dominick
G
Amsterdam HS
Amsterdam, NY

Frank, Jeff
Mayfield Central HS
Mayfield, NY

Frank, Samantha
The High Schl Of
Music & Art
New York, NY

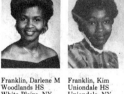

Frankino, Nancy
St Marys HS
Buffalo, NY

Franklin, Darlene M
Woodlands HS
White Plains, NY

Franklin, Kim
Uniondale HS
Uniondale, NY

Franklin, Patricia A
West Islip HS
W Islip, NY

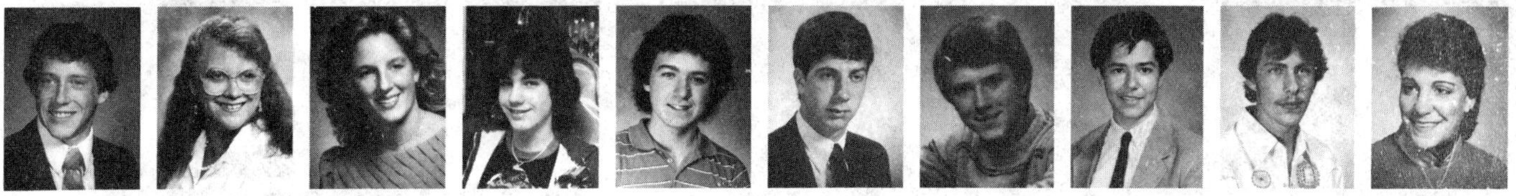

Franks, Tom M
Maine Endwell HS
Endwell, NY

Franz, Pamela S
Garden City HS
Garden City, NY

Franzese, Julie
Watkins Glen HS
Watkins Glen, NY

Franzitta, Jack
Valley Stream
Central HS
Valley Stream, NY

Fraser, David
Mynderse Acad
Seneca Falls, NY

Fraser, Thomas G
Lewiston-Porter SR
Youngstown, NY

Frasier, Gary
Gloversville HS
Gloversville, NY

Frattura, II David E
Archbishop Stepinac
Yonkers, NY

Frazier, Jeffrey
Fillmore Central HS
Fillmore, NY

Frederick, Michelle
R
Morris Central HS
Morris, NY

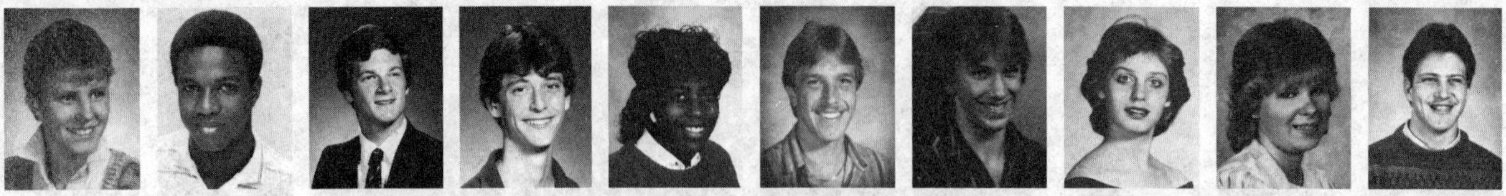

Frederick, Pamela
Johnstown HS
Johnstown, NY

Frederick, Jr
Schimeon
Thomas Edison HS
Rosedale, NY

Freed, Andrew
White Plains HS
White Plains, NY

Freeman, Charlie
North Salem HS
Purdys, NY

Freeman, Jacqueline
M
Grover Dleveland
Buffalo, NY

Freer, III Roy
Cairo-Durham JR
SR HS
Leeds, NY

Freligh, John
Saugerties HS
Saugerties, NY

French, Cynthia J
Art & Design HS
New York, NY

French, Sue Ann
Haverling Central
Bath, NY

Fresch, Joseph
G Ray Bodley HS
Fulton, NY

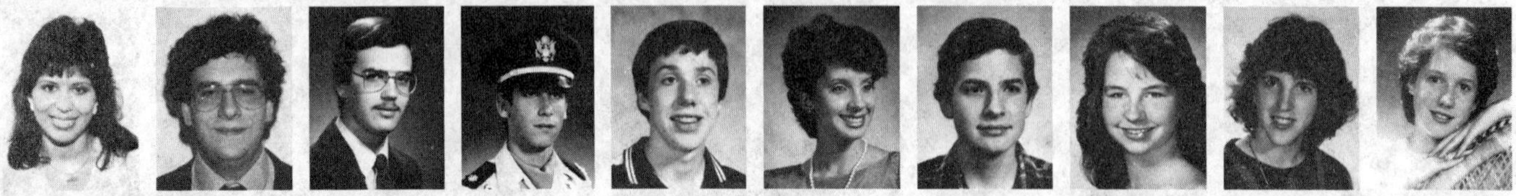

Frey, Diana
Dominican
Commercial HS
Brooklyn, NY

Frey, Scott
John F Kennedy HS
Bellmore, NY

Friday, Matt
Walter Panas HS
Peekskill, NY

Friello, Stephen A
Aviation HS
Richmond Hill, NY

Frisbee, Michael P
Guilderland Central
Schenectady, NY

Fritz, Jill M
E J Wilson HS
Rochester, NY

Fritzmeier, David S
Hugh C Williams
Canton, NY

Froude, Sharon E
Bay Shore HS
Bay Shore, NY

Fruehwirth,
Elizabeth
Bellport HS
E Patchogue, NY

Fry, Laurie J
Pavilion Central HS
East Bethany, NY

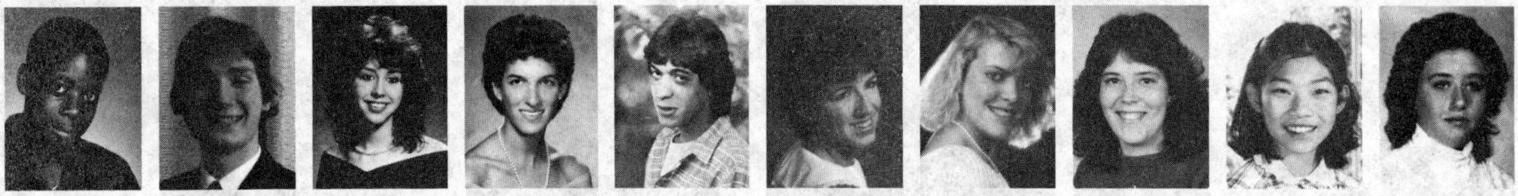

Fryar, Michael
Poughkeepsie HS
Poughkeepsie, NY

Fryscak, Francis M
Roosevelt HS
Crestwood, NY

Fuchek, Carolyn
Walter Panas HS
Peekskill, NY

Fuchs, Pamela Ivy
Centereach HS
Lake Grove, NY

Fuentes, Alberto
David
Charlotte Valley HS
East Meredith, NY

Fuierer, Tristan A
Holley JR SR HS
Holley, NY

Fullagar, Molly
Penn Yan Acad
Penn Yan, NY

Fuller, Barbara
Gouverneur Central
Gouverneur, NY

Fung, Audrey S
Sacred Heart Acad
Westbury, NY

Funk, Michelle
Lansingburgh HS
Troy, NY

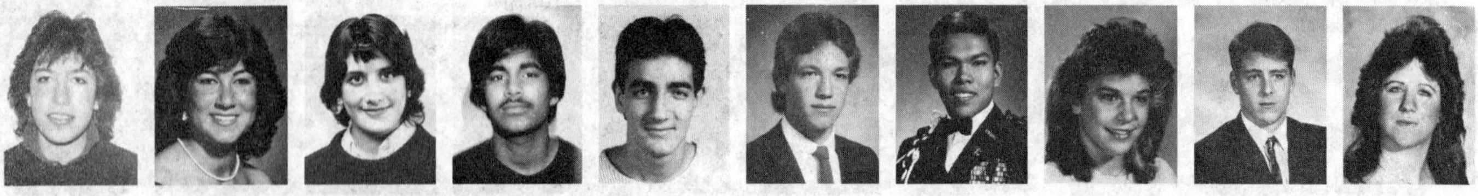

Furman, Nancy
Blind Brook HS
Rye Brook, NY

Fussteig, Robin L
Somers HS
Katonah, NY

Gabay, Jacqueline E
Stuyvesant HS
Rego Park, NY

Gabbur, Nagaraj
The Wheatley Schl
E Williston, NY

Gabizon, Guy
South Shore HS
Brooklyn, NY

Gabriel, James V
Liverpool HS
Liverpool, NY

Gabriel, Nick H
Xavier HS
Brooklyn, NY

Gabriele, Kathleen
Glen Cove HS
Glen Cove, NY

Gaeta, Mark E
Msgr Farrell HS
Staten Island, NY

Gaffney, Eileen M
St Catharine Acad
Bronx, NY

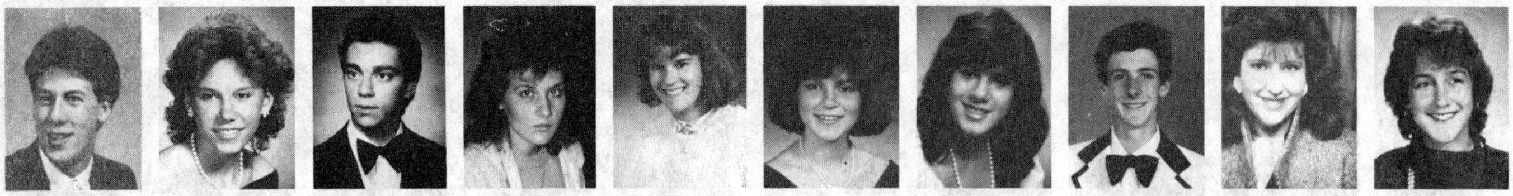

Gagnier, Paul
Chittenango HS
Chittenango, NY

Gailis, Linda
Pine Bush Central
Circleville, NY

Gaiso, Michael A
Saint Francis Prep
Howard Beach, NY

Gajdos, Alena
John Dewey HS
Brooklyn, NY

Galanakis,
Alexandra
The Stony Brook
Stony Brook, NY

Galanty, Carol A
Hampton Bays HS
Hampton Bays, NY

Galarza, Sane C
Southside HS
S Hempstead, NY

Gallagher, Timothy
A
Monsignor Farrell
Staten Island, NY

Gallello, Kathleen
Dominican
Commercial HS
Queens Village, NY

Galler, Sheryl Beth
Yeshivah Of
Flatbush HS
Brooklyn, NY

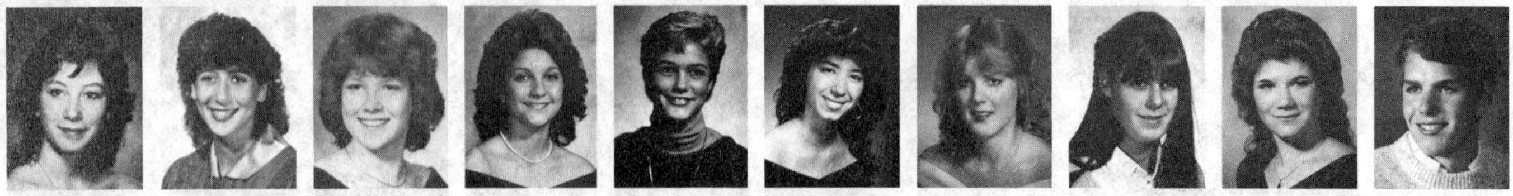

Gallery, Dawn
St Agnes Acad
Queens Village, NY

Galletta, Jacqueline
Bishop Ford CC HS
Brooklyn, NY

Galligan, Maureen
Clarkstown South
New City, NY

Gallo, Frances
Mahopac HS
Mahopac, NY

Gallo, Lisa
Iroquois Central HS
Lancaster, NY

Galura, Donna
Sacred Heart HS
Yonkers, NY

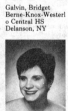

Galvin, Bridget
Berne-Knox-Westerl
o Central HS
Delanson, NY

Galvin, Sue
Mount Saint Joseph
Buffalo, NY

Gama, Lisa
St Joseph By The
Sea HS
Staten Island, NY

Gamache, Lawrence
W
Warwick Valley HS
Warwick, NY

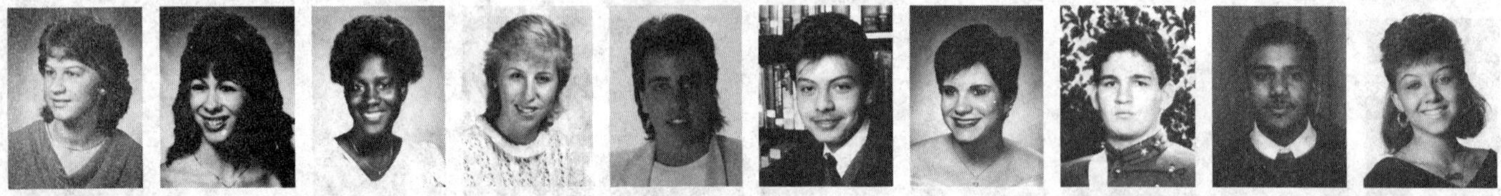

Gandini, Christine
East Meadow HS
E Meadow, NY

Gandolfo, Angela
Dominican
Commercial HS
Glendale, NY

Gandy, Tonia L
White Plains HS
White Plains, NY

Ganey, Christine
Frontier Central HS
Hamburg, NY

Gang, David
Lawrence HS
Woodmere, NY

Ganjian, Emil
Anglo American HS
Forest Hills, NY

Garafalo, Julie
Bishop Ford Central
Brooklyn, NY

Garcia, Andrew
La Salle Military
Bayonne, NJ

Garcia, David
Evander Childs HS
Bronx, NY

Garcia, Denise
Murry Bergtraum
Brooklyn, NY

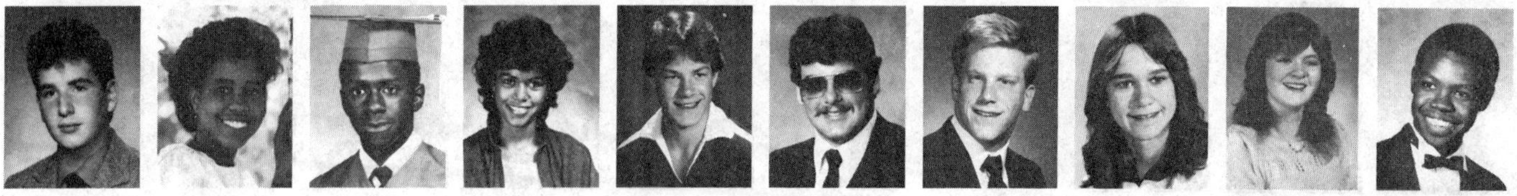

Garil, Scott E
Martin Van Buren
Queens Village, NY

Garran, Christina
Spackenkill HS
Poughkeepsie, NY

Garrett, Derrick
Archbishop Molloy
Queens Vlg, NY

Garrett, Eufaula K
The Harley Schl
Rochester, NY

Gates, Collin
Honeoye Central HS
Honeoye, NY

Gates, Daniel J
Eden SR HS
Eden, NY

Gates, Doug
Spackenkill HS
Poughkeepsie, NY

Gavey, Barbara C
Albertus Magnus
Spring Valley, NY

Gawronski, Kelly
Mount Mercy South
Park & BVTC
Buffalo, NY

Gayle, Eric
Evander Childs HS
Bronx, NY

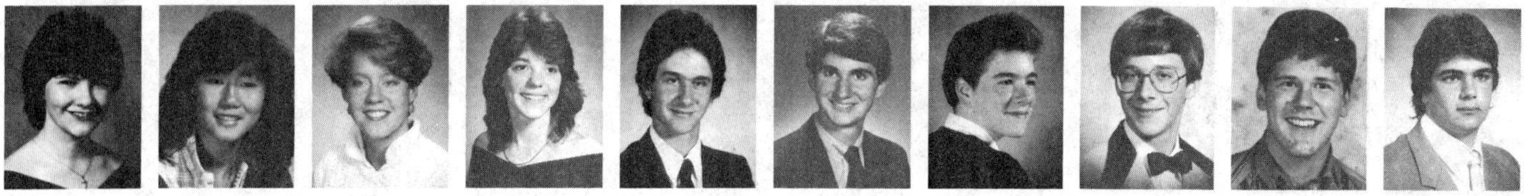

Geary, Katherine M
St Joseph Hill Acad
Brooklyn, NY

Gee, Stacey
Herricks SR HS
New Hyde Park, NY

Gehan, Mary
Our Lady Of Mercy
Rochester, NY

Geiselman, Ann
Marie
Pine Bush HS
Middletown, NY

Gelfuso, Thomas J
Frankfort Schuyler
Frankfort, NY

Geller, Paul S
Lawrence HS
Cedarhurst, NY

Gennarelli, Holly
Chenango Forks HS
Binghamton, NY

Genova, Andrew
Bishop Kearney HS
Rochester, NY

Gens, John Scott
Liverpool HS
Liverpool, NY

Gentile, Jr Joseph B
Oswego HS
Oswego, NY

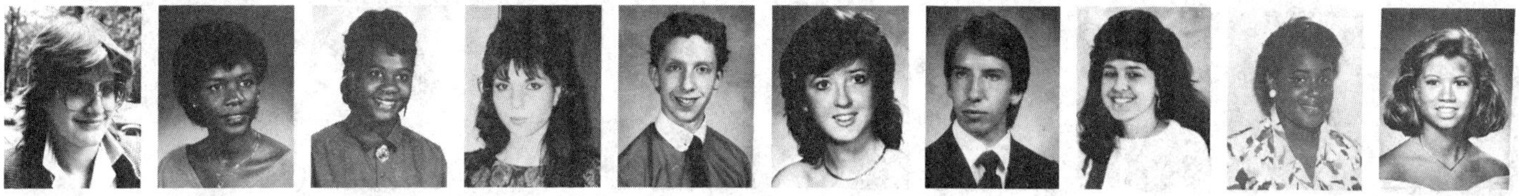

Gentile, Wendy
Roosevelt HS
Yonkers, NY

George, Ann
Margaret
George Wingate HS
Brooklyn, NY

George, Teressa
Nazareth Acad
Rochester, NY

Georgis, Venice
Garden Schl
Woodside, NY

Gerace, III Thomas
P
Lake Shore Central
Irving, NY

Gergen, Jennifer A
Amityville Memorial
Massapequa, NY

Gerwig, R S
Williamsville North
Kenmore, NY

Gerwin, Elizabeth
Port Richmond HS
Staten Island, NY

Ghartey, Mbiabah
Lisa
Mount Vernon HS
Mt Vernon, NY

Ghingo, Lauren E
St Francis Prep
Flushing, NY

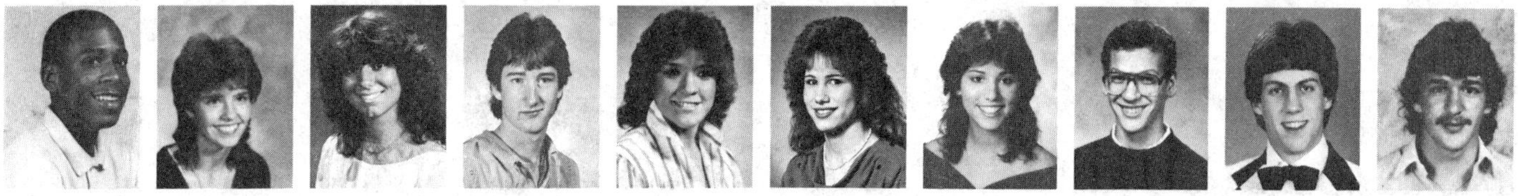

Gholson, Ronald L
Bridgehampton HS
Bridgehampton, NY

Giambra, Trish
Franklin Central
Oneonta, NY

Giannakis, Anna
Archbishop Jakovos
Bayside, NY

Gibson, David
Charles H Roth HS
W Henrietta, NY

Gibson, Sharon
Livingston Manor
Central Schl
Livingston Manor,
NY

Giglia, Cheryl
St Dominic HS
Huntington, NY

Giglia, Deborah
St Dominics HS
Huntington, NY

Gilebarto, Philip J
Jamestown HS
Jamestown, NY

Gill, Donald C
Msgr Farrell HS
Staten Island, NY

Gillen, Nelson
Frankfort-Schuyler
Central HS
Frankfort, NY

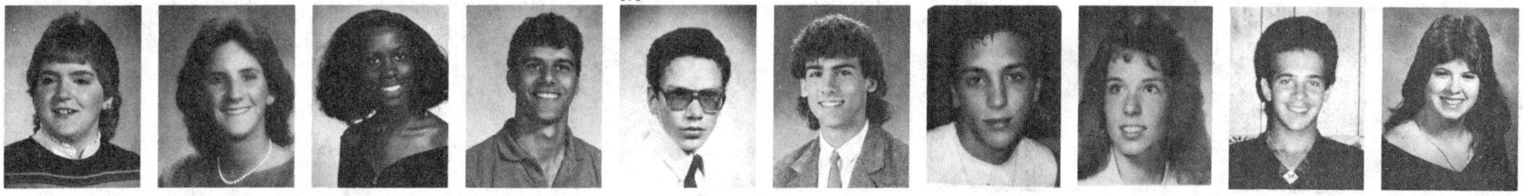

Gillette, Carrie M
C-Pp East HS
Corning, NY

Gilligan, Marybeth
Glens Falls HS
Glen Falls, NY

Gills, Karen
Bishop Loughlin HS
Brooklyn, NY

Gilman, Lynly
Norwood Norfolk
Central HS
Raymondville, NY

Gilmore, Louis
Oswego HS
Oswego, NY

Gioffre, Tony
Blind Brook HS
Rye Brook, NY

Giordano, Andrew
South Shore HS
Brooklyn, NY

Giris, Janet J
Plainedge HS
N Massapequa, NY

Giuliano, Anthony
Beach Channel HS
Howard Beach, NY

Giunta, Joanne
Marlboro Central
Marlboro, NY

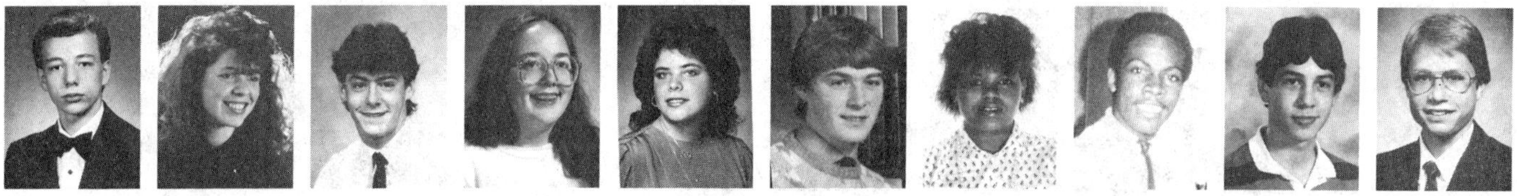

Gjelaj, George
Cardinal Spellman
Bronx, NY

Glatt, Shira
Yeshiva University
High Schl For Grls
Flushing, NY

Glatz, Jamie
Jamestown HS
Jamestown, NY

Glave, Suzette
Auburn HS
Auburn, NY

Glazer, Kim F
Walt Whitman HS
Huntington, NY

Glazier, Daniel
Sandy Creek Central
Lacona, NY

Glover, Marjorie
New Dorp HS
Staten Island, NY

Glover, Rodell H
La Guardia Schl For
Performing Arts
New York, NY

Godinez, Bradley
Franklin Acad
Malone, NY

Godsen, Michael
Westhill SR HS
Syracuse, NY

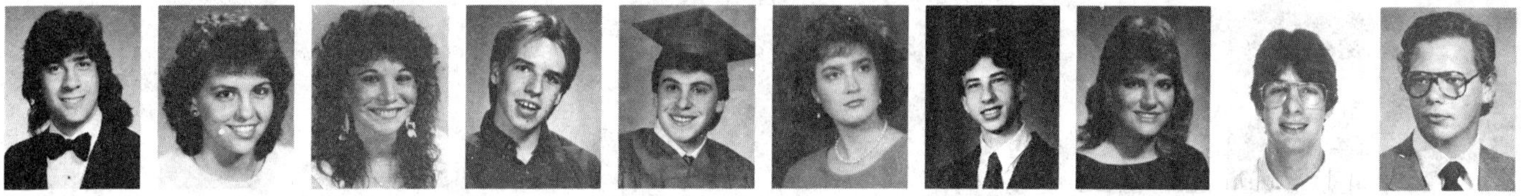

Goetz, Robert
Lincoln HS
Yonkers, NY

Gold, Jennifer
Roy C Ketcham HS
Wappingers Falls,
NY

Goldberg, Lori
Central Islip HS
Central Islip, NY

Goldblatt, Michael
Valley Central HS
Newburgh, NY

Goldfeder, Steven
Abraham Lincoln
Brooklyn, NY

Goldman, Elizabeth
E
Kenmore East HS
Tonawanda, NY

Goldman, Jeffrey D
Clarkstown HS
New City, NY

Goldstein, Brook J
E L Vandermeulen
Pt Jefferson Sta,
NY

Goldstein, David J
Lakeland HS
Yorktown Hts, NY

Goldstein, Gregory
M
Mc Kee Vocational
& Technical HS
Staten Island, NY

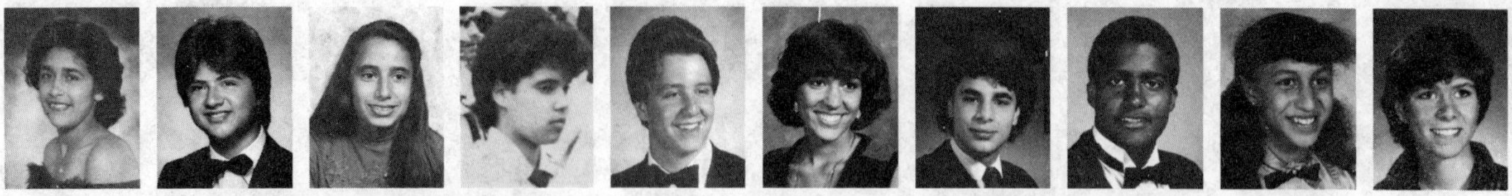

Gomez, Alicia
John Dewey HS
Brooklyn, NY

Gomez, Freddy
Sachem North HS
Ronkonkoma, NY

Gomez, Marybel
John Dewey HS
Brooklyn, NY

Gomez, Tanya
De Witt Clinton HS
Bronx, NY

Gongora, Rafael C
Christian Brothers
Syracuse, NY

Gonzales, Michele
Fairport HS
Fairport, NY

Gonzalez, James R
Valley Stream South
Valley Stream, NY

Goodloe, Paul
Archbishop Stepinac
New Rochelle, NY

Goodson, Tracey
Freeport HS
Freeport, NY

Goodwin, Deidre
Pittsford Sutherland
Rochester, NY

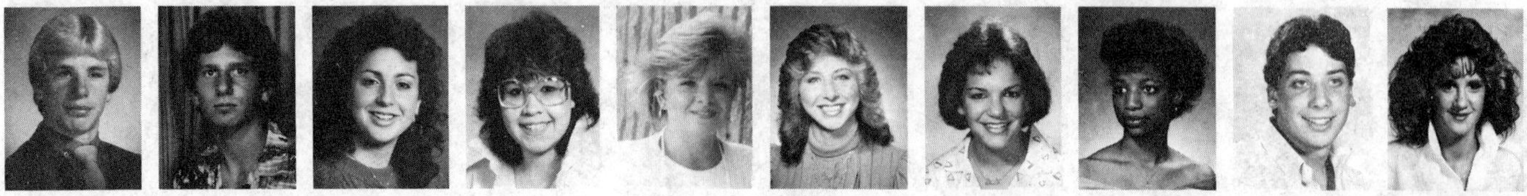

Gooley, Jody
Newark Valley HS
Owego, NY

Gorddard, Jeffrey P
Farmingdale HS
Farmingdale, NY

Gordon, Corinne
Ward Melville HS
Stony Brook, NY

Gordon, Lisa
John Jay SR HS
Fishkill, NY

Gordon, Wendy
Middletown HS
Middletown, NY

Gorman, Patricia
East Meadow HS
East Meadow, NY

Gottesman, Linda
Mac Arthur HS
Seaford, NY

Gourdine, Natasha
Paulette
Dominican
Commercial HS
Cambria Heights

Graber, Michael
John H Glenn HS
Greenlawn, NY

Grabiec, Jennifer
Turner-Carroll HS
Buffalo, NY

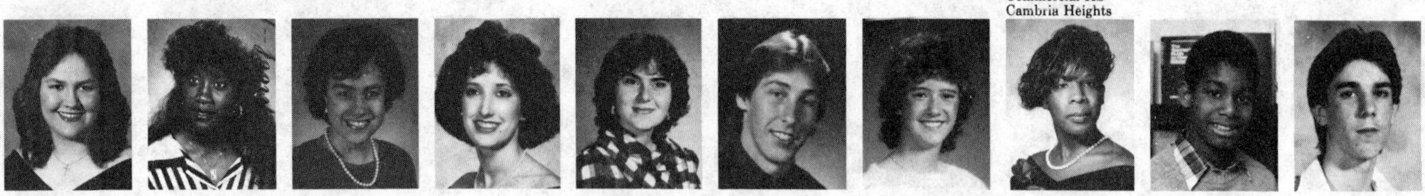

Grabowski, Lynda J
St Joseph Hill Acad
Staten Island, NY

Gracia, Roselyne
John Dewey HS
Brooklyn, NY

Graef, Christine M
Mount St Mary
Buffalo, NY

Graham, Courtney
Middletown HS
Middletown, NY

Graham, Sharon
Tri-Valley Central
Grahamsville, NY

Granbois, Tom
Weedsport HS
Weedsport, NY

Graney, Patricia M
E J Wilson SR HS
Rochester, NY

Grant, Alicia R
La Guardia H S Of
Music & The Arts
New York, NY

Grant, Carl
Springfield Gardens
Laurelton, NY

Grant, Daniel
Patrick
Minisink Valley HS
Middletown, NY

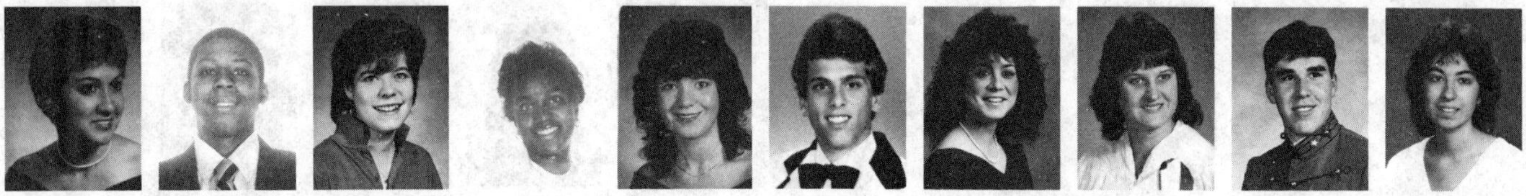

Grant, Diane
Columbia HS
Castleton, NY

Grant, Jr Thomas
Rice HS
New York, NY

Gray, Ameena
Fayetteville-Manlius
Manlius, NY

Gray, Michelle
Immaculata HS
New York, NY

Gray, Stacy
Whitesboro SR HS
Whitesboro, NY

Graziano, Anthony
M
MSGR Farrell HS
Staten Island, NY

Graziano, Mildred
Nazareth HS
Brooklyn, NY

Greaney, Laura
Hicksville HS
Hicksville, NY

Greco, Jason
La Salle Military
Huntington, NY

Greco, Patricia R
Rome Free Acad
Rome, NY

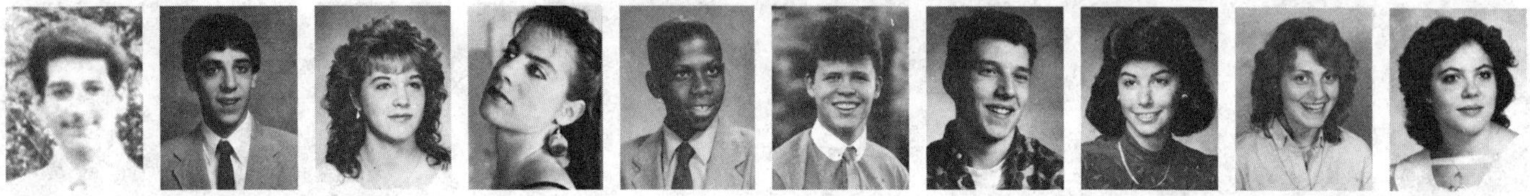

Greco, Richard
Pelham Memorial
Pelham Manor, NY

Greco, Vito J
Rome Free Acad
Rome, NY

Gredder, Darleen J
Baldwin SR HS
Baldwin, NY

Green, Cynthia
John Jay HS
Katonah, NY

Green, Darrin
Cardinal Hayes HS
New York, NY

Green, David C
Franklin Delano
Roosevelt HS
Hyde Park, NY

Green, Jamie
Auburn HS
Auburn, NY

Green, Lauren H
Walt Whitman HS
Melville, NY

Green, Marah
Middletown HS
Middletown, NY

Green, Michelle A
James Madison HS
Brooklyn, NY

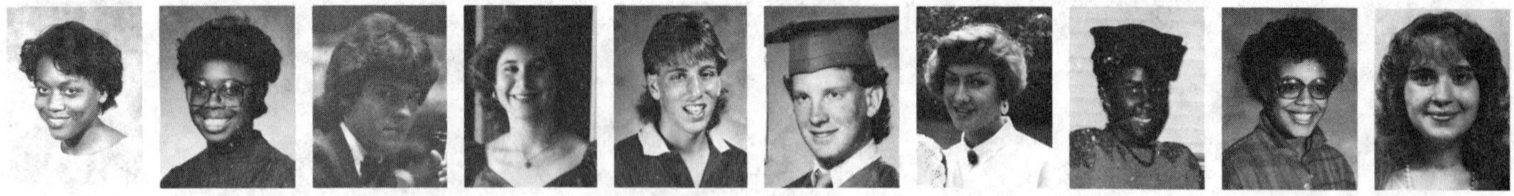

Green, Wendy
Sophia
Mt Vernon HS
Mount Vernon, NY

Greenaway, Andrea
Northeastern Acad
Jamaica, NY

Greenberg, Jay
Tottenville HS
Staten Island, NY

Greenberg, Loren
Tottenville HS
Staten Island, NY

Greenblatt, Rick
Churchville-Chili
Spencerport, NY

Greene, Chris
John H Glenn HS
E Northport, NY

Greene, Erinn
Fayetteville-Manluis
Manlius, NY

Greene, Karen
Uniondale HS
Hempstead, NY

Greene, Laura M
Martin Luther HS
St Albans, NY

Gregor, Susan
Villa Maria Acad
Buffalo, NY

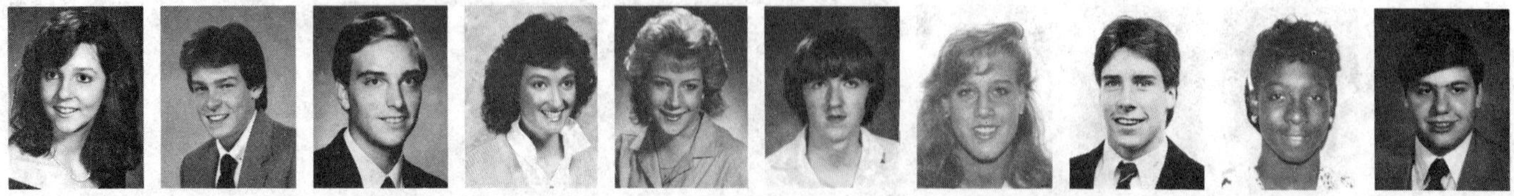

Gresis, Tracy
Somers HS
Somers, NY

Gresock, Gregory G
Horseheads HS
Horseheads, NY

Greubel, Kirk
S H Calhoun HS
Merrick, NY

Grey, Tara
Frankfort - Schuyler
Frankfort, NY

Gribbins, Jean A
Floral Park
Memorial HS
Floral Park, NY

Gridley, Toby
Addison Central HS
Addison, NY

Grieco, Danielle
Manhasset HS
Manhasset, NY

Griffith, Joseph W
Garden City HS
Garden City, NY

Griffith, Leasiah
Franlyn Delano
Roosevelt HS
Brooklyn, NY

Grigoli, John
Oneonta SR HS
Oneonta, NY

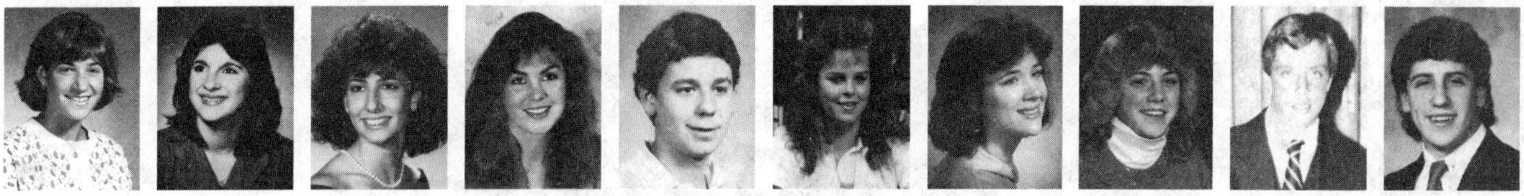

Griles, Allyson
Brewster HS
Brewster, NY

Grimaldi, Angela
Bethpage HS
Bethpage, NY

Grimaldi, Margaret M
Bishop Kearney HS
Brooklyn, NY

Grismore, Dana
Liverpool HS
Liverpool, NY

Groat, John
T J Corcoran HS
Syracuse, NY

Grohovac, Doris
Freeport HS
Freeport, NY

Grose, Jenna E
Ballston Spa HS
Ballston Spa, NY

Gross, Christine
Scotia-Glenville HS
Amsterdam, NY

Gross, Garrett
Lafayette HS
Brooklyn, NY

Gross, Ronald
Spring Valley SR
Spring Valley, NY

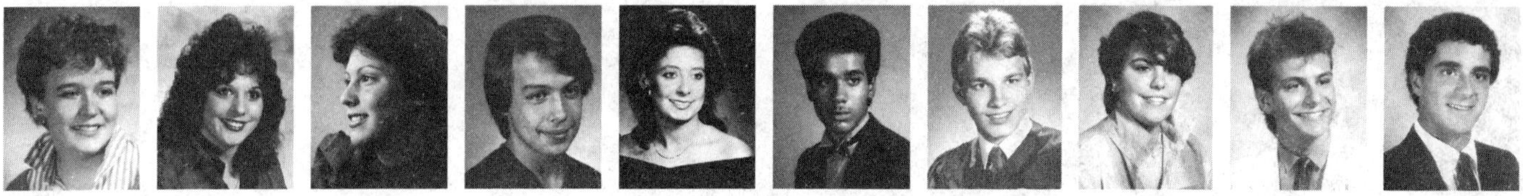

Gross, Trina
Eastridge HS
Rochester, NY

Grossi, Julianne
Webster HS
Webster, NY

Groth, Kristina A
Liverpool HS
Liverpool, NY

Grover, Steve
York Central Schl
Leicester, NY

Grubiak, Mary
Sacred Heart HS
Yonkers, NY

Grullon, Cesar A
All Hallows Inst
Bronx, NY

Grzesik, Joseph C
Massapequa HS
Massapequa, NY

Gualtieri, Catherine A
Anthony A Henninger HS
Syracuse, NY

Gualtieri, Eugene
Anthony A Henninger HS
Syracuse, NY

Gualtieri, Thomas P
Fayetteville-Manlius
Manlius, NY

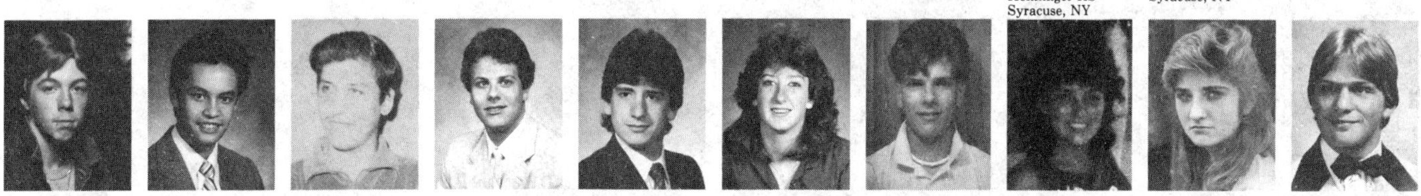

Guanciale, W Scott
Solvay HS
Syracuse, NY

Guarin, Marc F
Bayside Latin Honor Schl
Whitestone, NY

Guarino, James F
Park West HS
New York, NY

Guarino, Michael
Jamestown HS
Jamestown, NY

Guarino, Paul
Clarkstown South
Nyack, NY

Gubernick, Holly
Cornwall Central HS
Highland Mills, NY

Gubin, Vincent
St John The Baptist
Holbrook, NY

Gucciardo, Annette
Port Richmond HS
Staten Island, NY

Guchek, Lea Ann
Fontbonne Hall
Brooklyn, NY

Guenther, David
Kensington HS
Buffalo, NY

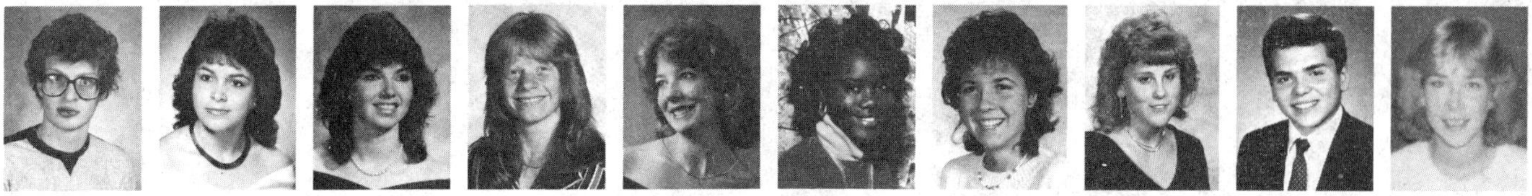

Guerin, Peter
Connetquot HS
Bohemia, NY

Guerrero, Sandra
The Mary Louis
Flushing, NY

Guiney, Patrice
Mahopac HS
Mahopac, NY

Guli, Stacey
St John Villa Acad
Staten Island, NY

Gulick, Joann A
Oneida SR HS
Oneida, NY

Gumbs, Rhonda J W V
Hillcrest HS
St Albans, NY

Gunning, Nancy
Herricks HS
Williston Prk, NY

Gunning, Teresa
Odessa-Montour Central HS
Trumansburg, NY

Gurel, Ozan
Stuyvesant HS
New York, NY

Gustum, Tammy
Rome Free Acad
Gunter AFS, AL

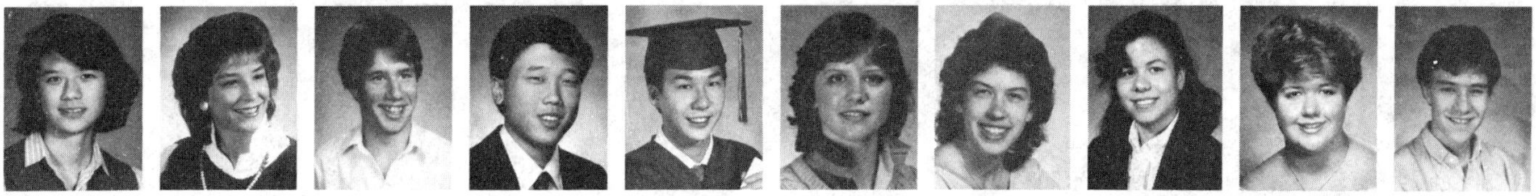

Guyburu, Silvia
Ossining HS
Ossining, NY

Guyton, Tracie
Carthage Central
Carthage, NY

Gwinn, Robert J
Averill Park Central
Troy, NY

Ha, Glen Jungho
Bethpage HS
Plainview, NY

Ha, Julian
The Bronx HS Of
New York City, NY

Habberfield, Karen
Scio Central HS
Wellsville, NY

Haber, Elizabeth A
Kingston HS
Kingston, NY

Hacker, Candice
St Hildas & St Hughs HS
New York, NY

Hadlow, Christine
St Agnes Academic
Flushing, NY

Hagenah, John
Brockport HS
Brockport, NY

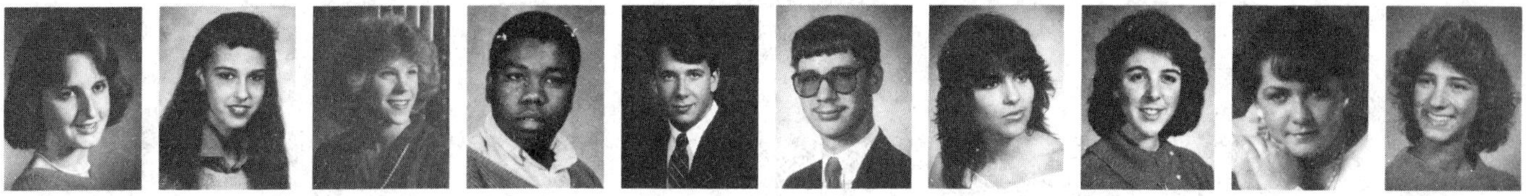

Haggerty, Kathleen A
Shenendehowa HS
Clifton Park, NY

Hagipadelis, Maria S
Abraham Lincoln
Brooklyn, NY

Hahn, Lori
Byron-Bergen HS
Bergen, NY

Hairston, John
Hutchison Central Technical HS
Buffalo, NY

Halbfinger, David
Baldwin SR HS
Freeport, NY

Hales, John
Albion HS
Albion, NY

Halfin, Marcia Alexandra
Colonie Central HS
Albany, NY

Hall, Anjeanette
Vestal SR HS
Vestal, NY

Hall, Colleen M
Johnson City HS
Johnson City, NY

Hall, Denise D
Amsterdam HS
Amsterdam, NY

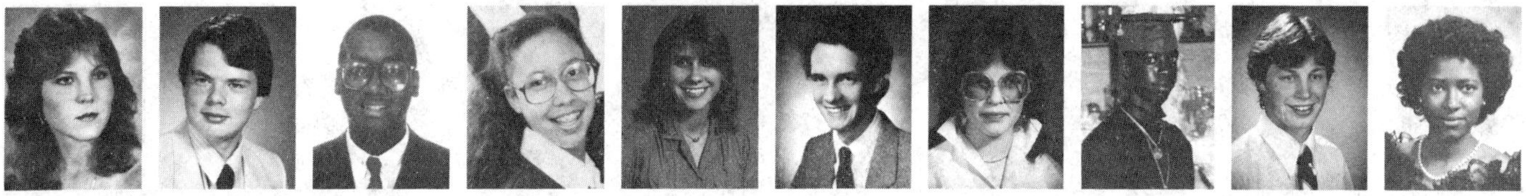

Hall, Donna
St Johns Prep HS
Middle Vlg, NY

Hall, Hugh
Dover JR SR HS
Dover Plains, NY

Hall, Kenneth
Polytechnic Prep County Day Schl
Brooklyn, NY

Hall, Vanessa
Mount Vernon HS
Mt Vernon, NY

Hall, Wendy Lynn
Canastota HS
Canastota, NY

Halloran, John J
Troy HS
Troy, NY

Hamblin, Penny L
Addison Central HS
Cameron Mills, NY

Hamilton, Ashley
Nazareth Regional
Brooklyn, NY

Hamilton, II David Brian
Gouverneur Central
Gouverneur, NY

Hamilton, Montrese
Niagara Falls HS
Niagara Falls, NY

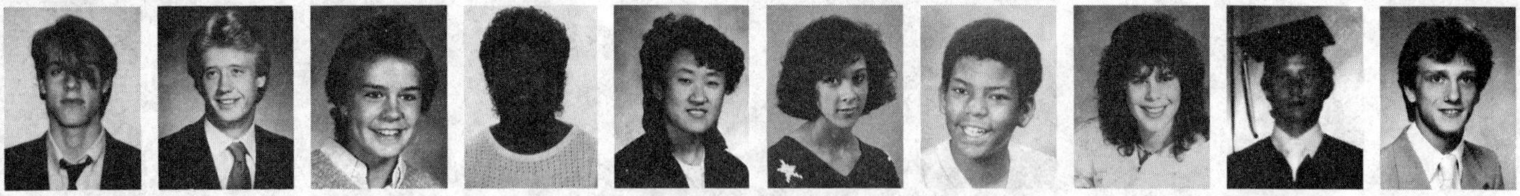

Hamilton, Randy
The Anglo American
New York, NY

Hamm, Joel L
Oakfield Alamba HS
Oakfield, NY

Hammond, Brenda
Avoca Central Schl
Cohocton, NY

Hampton, Tracy
Saint John The
Baptist HS
Amityville, NY

Han, Hye Sun
Flushing HS
Flushing, NY

Hanachi, Essya
Mercy HS
East Hampton, NY

Hancock, Ira A
Poughkeepsie HS
Poughkeepsie, NY

Handel, Jacqueline
M
Bronx HS Of
Flushing, NY

Haney, Stephen
Franklin Delanor
Roosevelt HS
Brooklyn, NY

Hanlon, Doug
Centereach HS
Lake Ronkonkoma,
NY

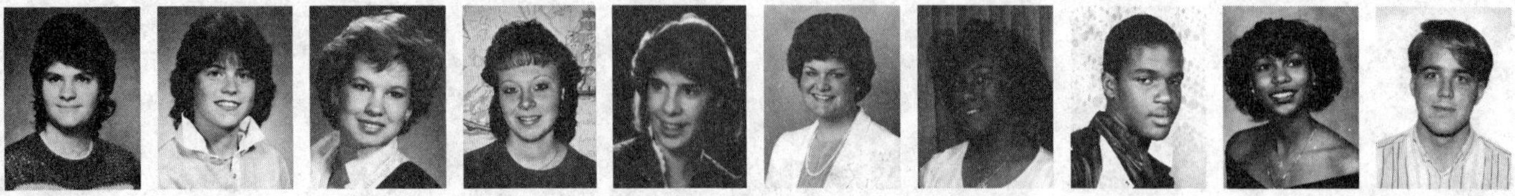

Hanlon, Frances
Longwood HS
Middle Island, NY

Hannan, Keli
Cornwall HS
Cornwall Hudson,
NY

Hansen, Karen-Lee
Washingtonville HS
New Windsor, NY

Hansen, Kristin
Queen Of The
Rosary Acad
Bellmore, NY

Hanson, Cynthia
Potsdam Central HS
Potsdam, NY

Hapeman, Donna
Horseheads SR HS
Horseheads, NY

Harbour, Janice
Midwood HS
Brooklyn, NY

Hargrave, Kyle
Charles H Roth HS
Rochester, NY

Hargraves, Deidra E
Hillcrest HS
St Albans, NY

Harley, Jr Colin
Emile
The Anglo-American
New York, NY

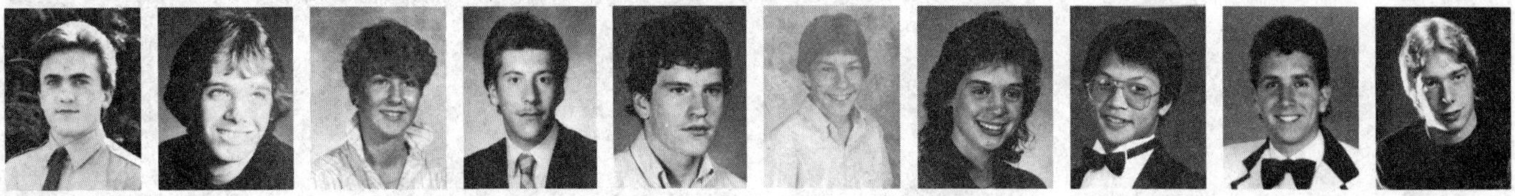

Harmer, Terry
Spackenkill HS
Poughkeepsie, NY

Harnick, Joel
Baldwin HS
Baldwin, NY

Harnly, Ann Marie
Fairport HS
Fairport, NY

Harow, Jay Scott
Brentwood Ross HS
Brentwood, NY

Harper, James
Westfield Central
Westfield, NY

Harper, II Robert W
Norwood-Norfolk
Central HS
Norwood, NY

Harriger, Shelley
Dundee HS
Dundee, NY

Harrington, Jr
Bruce E
Robert St JR SR
Canastota, NY

Harrington, Christop
J
MSGR Farrell HS
Staten Island, NY

Harrington, Scott
Naples Central Schl
Naples, NY

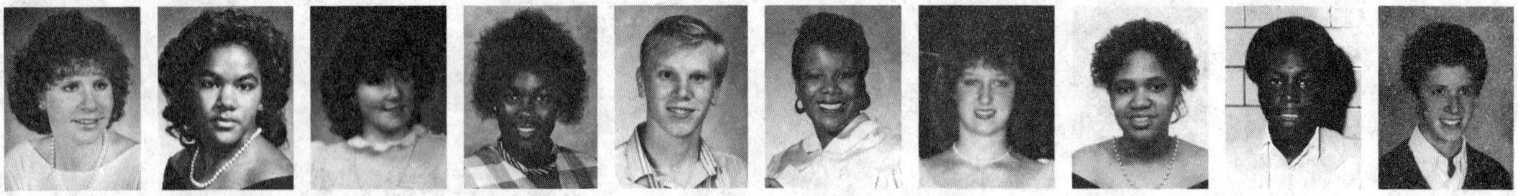

Harris, Benedicte
Paul V Moore HS
Constantia, NY

Harris, Donyale K
Notre Dame Schl
New York, NY

Harris, Katrina
Penn Yan Acad
Penn Yan, NY

Harris, Patrice R
Bitburg HS
Apo Ny, NY

Harris, Rexford M
Mayville Central
Mayville, NY

Harris, Sharon N
A Philip Randolph
Campus HS
New York, NY

Harris, Tami
Newark SR HS
Newark, NY

Harris, Tracie
Mt Vernon HS
Mt Vernon, NY

Harris, Troy
Morris HS
Bronx, NY

Harrison, Daniel A
Niskayuna HS
Schenectady, NY

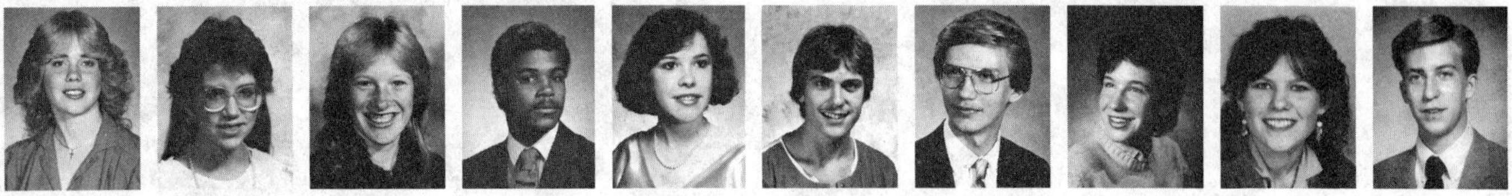

Hart, Laura
Ossining HS
Ossining, NY

Hart, Lucinda
Watkins Glen HS
Beaver Dams, NY

Hart, Rachael
Scotia-Glenville HS
Scotia, NY

Hart, Raymond L
Peekskill HS
Peekskill, NY

Harte, Kathleen
St John The Baptist
Lk Grove, NY

Hartel, Paul
Frontier Central HS
Blasdell, NY

Hartell, Mark
Susan E Wagner HS
Staten Is, NY

Hartmann, Lori C
Brockport HS
Brockport, NY

Hartmann, Winifred
Bellport HS
Bellport, NY

Hartung,
Christopher
Fayetteville-Manlius
Manlius, NY

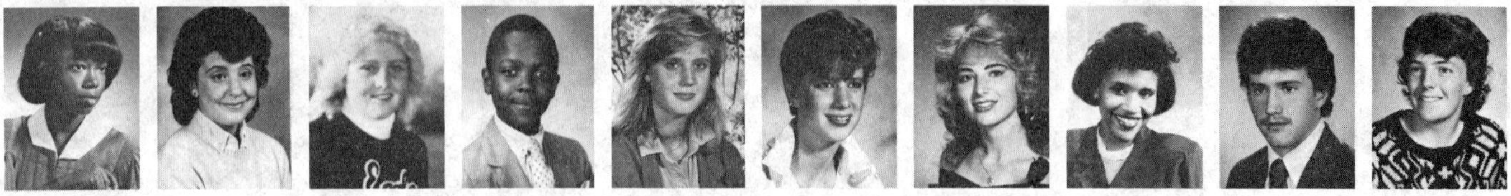

Harvey, Audrey
Erasmus Hall HS
Brooklyn, NY

Hasbrouck, Wendy
Hutchinson Central
Tech HS
Buffalo, NY

Haskins, Terri
Midlakes HS
Phelps, NY

Hatcher, Richard
Uniondale HS
Hempstead, NY

Haug, Andrea
The Waldorf Schl
Oceanside, NY

Havens, Martha
Pulaski Acad
Pulaski, NY

Hawkins, Jenifer
Minisink Valley HS
Middletown, NY

Hawthorne,
Adrienne
Uniondale HS
Hempstead, NY

Hawthorne, Michael
J
Harrisville Central
Harrisville, NY

Hayes, Polly
Union Endicott HS
Endicott, NY

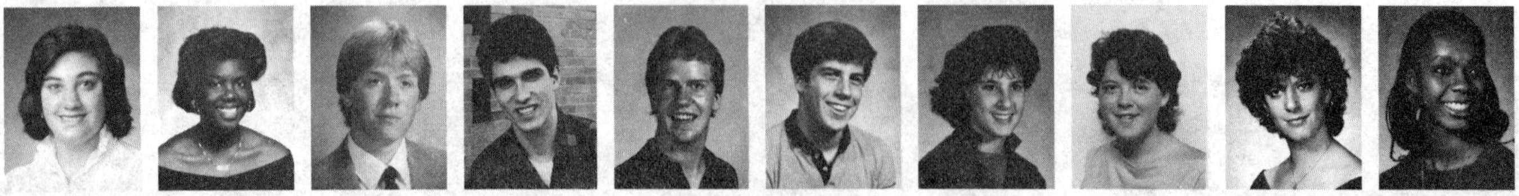

Haymes, Jennifer
Alfred-Almond
Central Schl
Almond, NY

Haynes, Sonja
Hillcrest HS
Cambria Hgts, NY

Hazard, Jr Edwin
Gates Chili HS
Rochester, NY

Healey, Mark
Holy Cross HS
Flushing, NY

Healy, Tom
Schem North
Farmingville, NY

Heaphy, Timothy
Corcoran HS
Syracuse, NY

Hebert, Nadine
Lansignburgh HS
Troy, NY

Heffernan, Ann
Fabius-Pompey HS
Fabius, NY

Hefke, Jennifer
Bay Shore HS
Bay Shore, NY

Heggins, Amy N
Laguardia H S Of
Performing Arts
Jamaica, NY

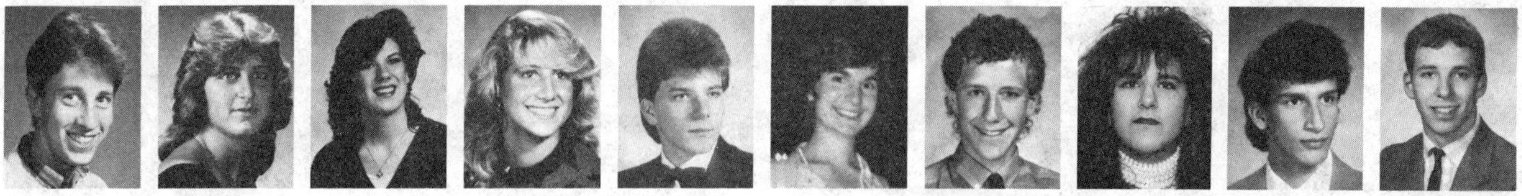

Heier, Jeffrey
Mepham HS
N Bellmore, NY

Hein, Carolyn
St Joseph
By-The-Sea HS
Staten Island, NY

Hein, Christina K
Rocky Point JR SR
Sound Bch, NY

Heinrich, Suzanne A
Scarsdale HS
Scarsdale, NY

Heiser, Travis M
Christian Brothers
Fayetteville, NY

Held, Jo Anne
Polytechnic Prep
Brooklyn, NY

Helenbrook, Brian
Grand Island HS
Gr Island, NY

Helfert, Michelle A
Nortre Dame Ny
Utica, NY

Heller, Dennis M
Mechanicville HS
Mechanicville, NY

Heller, Matthew
Hauppauge HS
Hauppauge, NY

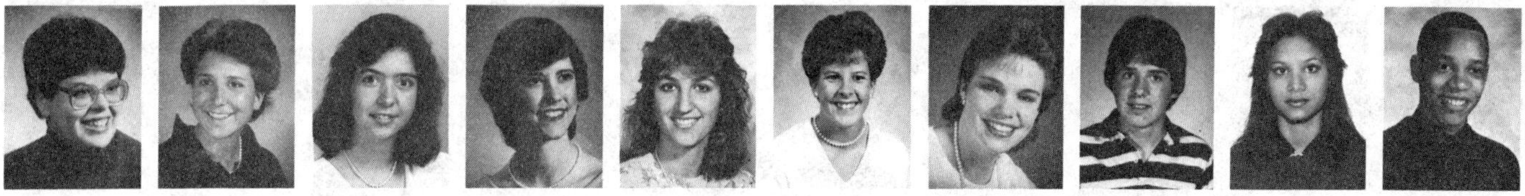

Henderson, Sue
Tully Central Schl
Tully, NY

Hendricks,
Stephanie L
Maine-Endwell SR
Endwell, NY

Henke, Susan
Bayport-Blue Point
Blue Pt, NY

Henkel, Carol A
Our Lady Of Mercy
Rochester, NY

Hennel, Deborah
Scotia-Glenville HS
Scotia, NY

Hennessey, Susan
Bishop Ludden HS
Syracuse, NY

Henry, Jennifer B
West Seneca West
SR HS
Cheektowaga, NY

Henry, Michael
Stuttgart American
Apo, NY

Henry, Nicole A
St Francis Prep Schl
S Ozone Park, NY

Henry, Robert
Gates-Chili SR HS
Rochester, NY

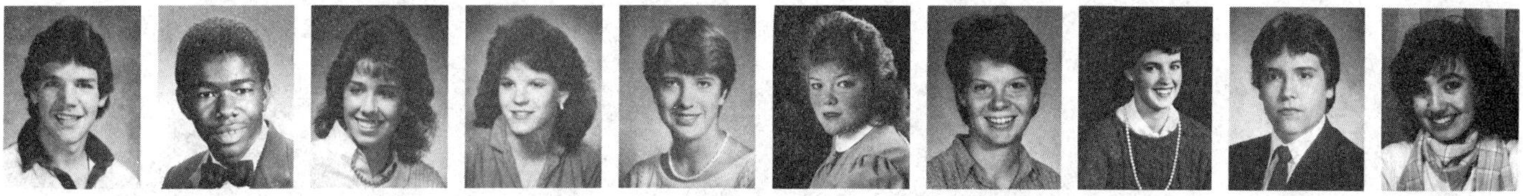

Henry, Timothy J
Caledonia-Mumford
Central Schl
Caledonia, NY

Henry, Wayne A
Erasmus Hall HS
Brooklyn, NY

Henshaw, Tammy
Campbell Central
Campbell, NY

Herbert, Christine
West Hempstead
Island Pk, NY

Herendeen, Deborah
M
Royalton-Hartland
Central HS
Gasport, NY

Herholz, Kelly
Marie
Sharon Springs
Central HS
Sharon Springs, NY

Herko, Suzanne
Ossining HS
Ossining, NY

Herlihy, Karen M
W Melville SR HS
Stony Brook, NY

Hermans, David J
Cardinal Mooney
Rochester, NY

Hernandez, Diana
Bronx High School
Of Science
Queens, NY

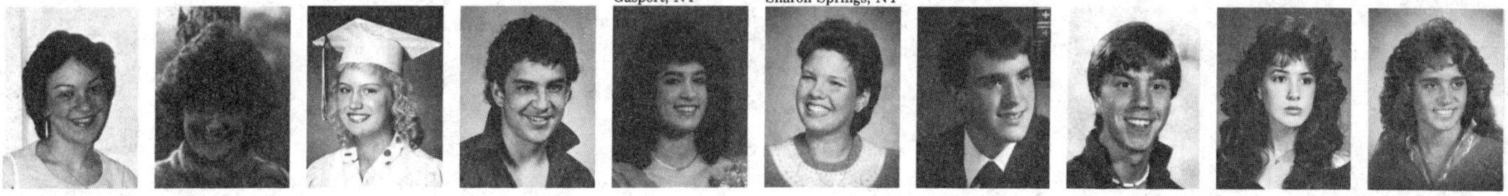

Hernandez, Maria P
St Francis Prep
Jackson Heights,
NY

Herow, Andrea J
Newfield HS
Terryville, NY

Herr, Cindy
L I Lutheran HS
E Northport, NY

Herrera, Brian
Charles H Roth HS
Henrietta, NY

Herrero, Marie
White Plains HS
White Plns, NY

Herrick, Nancy
Hamilton Central
Hamilton, NY

Herriman, Eric E
Wayne Central HS
Walworth, NY

Hershon, Andrew
Niskayuna HS
Schenectady, NY

Herson, Anne
Saint Barnabas HS
Bronx, NY

Hertig, Heidi A
Westhill SR HS
Syracuse, NY

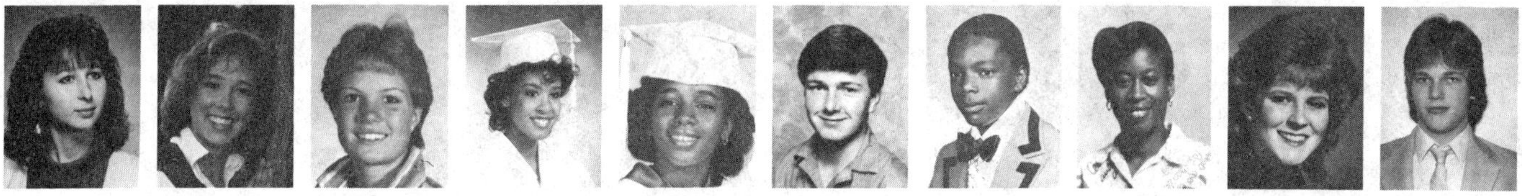

Herzog, Denise
Smithtown HS
Smithtown, NY

Hespenheide, Amy
L
Arlington HS
Poughkeepsie, NY

Hess, Kristin
Commack High
School North
E Northport, NY

Hester, Donna
Albany HS
Albany, NY

Heyward, Charese
St Chatharine Acad
Bx, NY

Hickey, John
Tappan Zee HS
Blauvelt, NY

Hickman, Darin
August Martin HS
Springfield Grdns,
NY

Hickman, Vivian C
St Jean Baptiste HS
Jamaica, NY

Hicks, Shelley D
Hammondsport
Central HS
Hammondsport, NY

Hiddessen, Mark
Holy Trinity HS
Seaford, NY

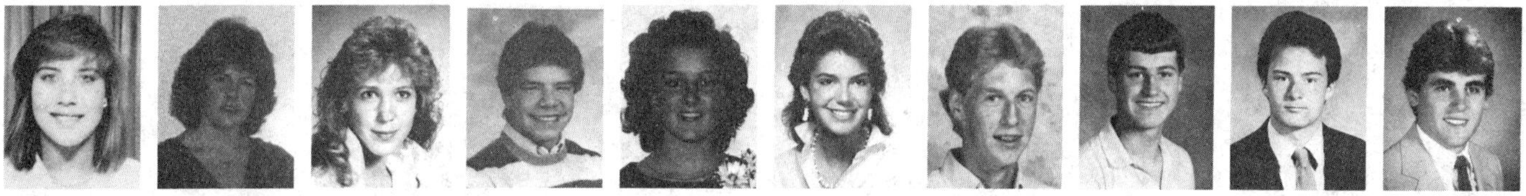

Hieber, Jennifer
Garden City HS
Garden City, NY

Higgins, Mary
Dominican
Commercial HS
Richmond Hill, NY

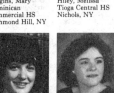

Hiley, Melissa
Tioga Central HS
Nichols, NY

Hill, Jason
Letchworth Central
Silver Springs, NY

Hill, Kristine C
East Islip HS
Great River, NY

Hill, Maria
Bayport Blue Point
Blue Point, NY

Hill, Tim
Camden Central HS
Camden, NY

Hillabrandt, Jr
Larry L
Honeoye Falls Lima
Central HS
Honeoye Falls, NY

Hillen, Brian
Moore Catholic HS
Staten Island, NY

Hills, Jerry
Union-Endicott HS
Endicott, NY

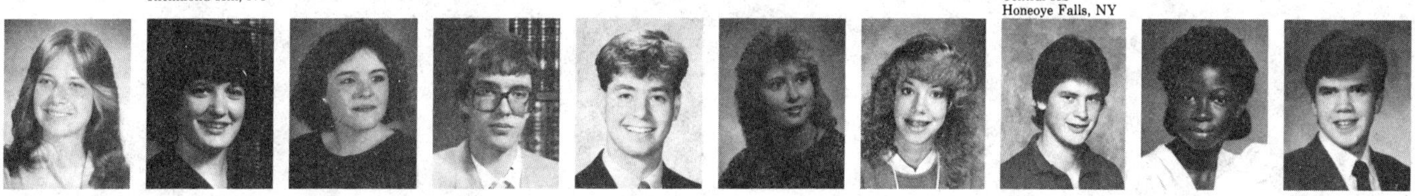

Hiltbrand, Lisa M
Liverpool HS
Liverpool, NY

Hine, Wendy
Fredonia HS
Fredonia, NY

Hinkley, Jodi Lynne
Susquehanna Valley
Kirkwood, NY

Hinz, Timothy F
Alexander Central
Batavia, NY

Hirshberg, Jay
Hebrew Acad Of
The Five Towns
W Hempstead, NY

Hladik, Melissa L
Johnstown HS
Johnstown, NY

Hoak, Susan J
Notre Dame HS
Byron, NY

Hocker, John D
Southold HS
Southold, NY

Hodge, Edith
St Joseph HS
Brooklyn, NY

Hodne, Thomas
Clarkstown HS
New City, NY

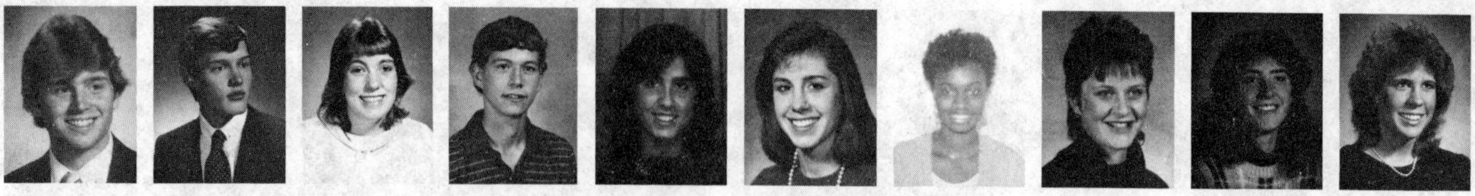

Hoerbelt, Mark D
Batavia HS
Batavia, NY

Hoffman, Glen L
Floral Park
Memorial HS
Floral Park, NY

Hoffman, Heidi
Valley Central HS
Montgomery, NY

Hoffman, John P
Marcus Whitman
Central HS
Gorham, NY

Hoffman, Julie
South Shore HS
Brooklyn, NY

Hoffman, Maureen
Tappanzee HS
Orangeburg, NY

Hoffman, Memray
New Rochelle HS
New Rochelle, NY

Hoffmann, Pauline
Alden Central HS
E Aurora, NY

Hohn, Rebecca
Hoosick Falls
Central Schl
Hoosick Falls, NY

Hoke,
Heather-Marie
Owen D Young HS
Jordanville, NY

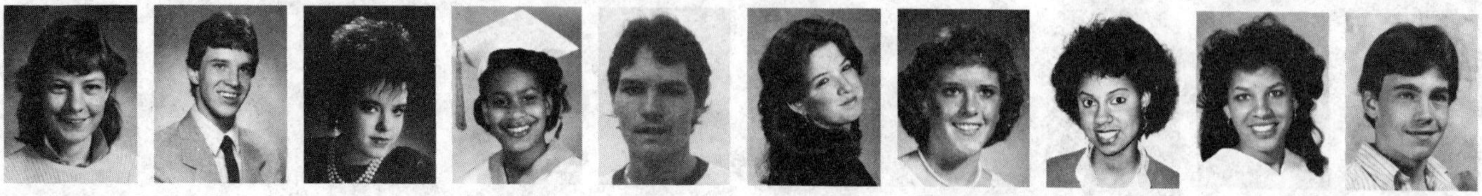

Holcomb, Dawn
Auburn HS
Auburn, NY

Holden, Greg M
Shoreham Wading
River HS
Shoreham, NY

Holder, Cheryl Anne
Chenango Forks HS
Binghamton, NY

Holder, Stacy O
Westbury HS
Westbury, NY

Holland, Michael
Franklin Acad
N Bangor, NY

Hollander, Stacey
Tohenville HS
Staten Island, NY

Holleran, Bethann
Vestal Senior HS
Apalachin, NY

Holloway, Victoria
Woodlands HS
White Plains, NY

Holman, Tania M
Norman Thomas HS
Flushing, NY

Holmes, Brennan
Bay Shore HS
Brightwaters, NY

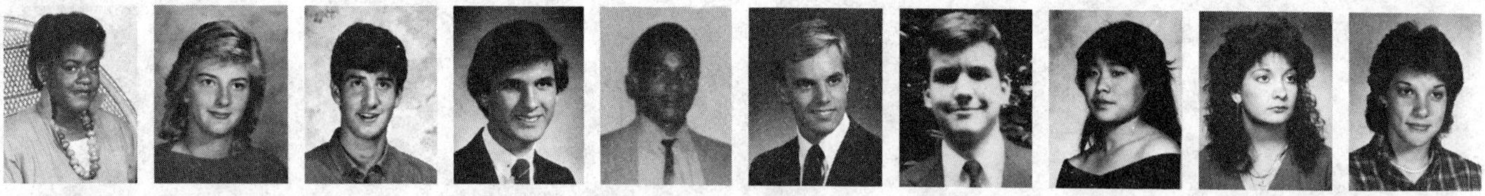

Holmes, Felicia
Romulus Central
Romulus, NY

Holmes, Linda
Warsaw Central
Warsaw, NY

Holowka, James
Orchard Park HS
Orchard Park, NY

Holt, Jack
Aquinas Inst
Rochester, NY

Holt, Shaun Dasselle
De Witt Clinton HS
Bronx, NY

Homa, David E
The Stony Brook
Selden, NY

Homin, Paul V
Newburgh Free
New Windsor, NY

Hong, May
Jamaica HS
Queens Village, NY

Honigmann, Gloria
Marie
Bethpage HS
Bethpage, NY

Hopkins, Joann
G Ray Bodley HS
Fulton, NY

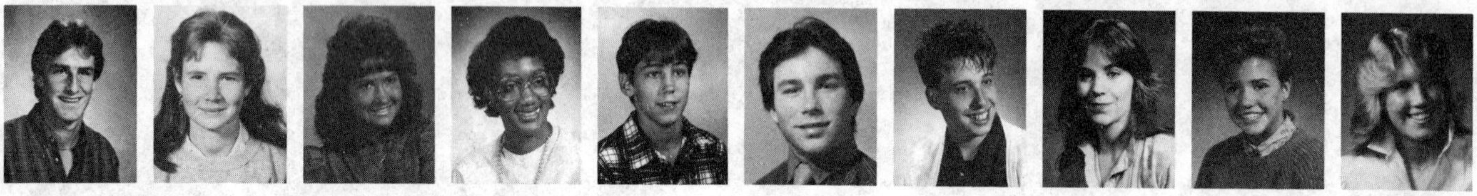

Hopko, Joe
Union-Endicott HS
Endicott, NY

Hopler, Carrie
Mercy HS
Shelter Island, NY

Horboychuk, Debbie
Arlington HS
Hopewell Jct, NY

Hordge, Cynthia
G Ray Bodley HS
Fulton, NY

Hordines, Carl
Cohoes HS
Cohoes, NY

Hosey, Brian
Valley Stream
Central HS
Valley Stream, NY

Hotaling, Richard
Newburgh Free
New Windsor, NY

Hotchkiss, Tracy L
West Seneca West
SR HS
W Seneca, NY

Houk, Rachel
Plainview-Old
Bethpage HS
Plainview, NY

Houle, Fawn
Penn Yan Acad
Pennyan, NY

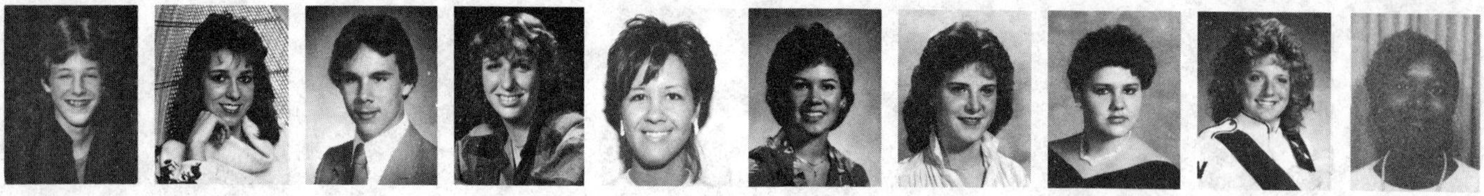

Housel, Todd
Marion JR SR HS
Marion, NY

Houseman, Jill J
Williamsville North
East Amherst, NY

Houser, Joseph
Cicero-North
Syracuse HS
Clay, NY

Hover, Kathy
Hornell HS
Hornell, NY

Howansky, Petrusia
Roosevelt HS
Yonkers, NY

Howard, Arlene
Cardinal O Hara HS
Kenmore, NY

Howard, Justine
South Jefferson
Central HS
Adams, NY

Howard, Margaret S
Midwood HS
Brooklyn, NY

Howard, Melissa M
Chenango Valley HS
Port Crane, NY

Howard, Sophia
Fowler HS
Syracuse, NY

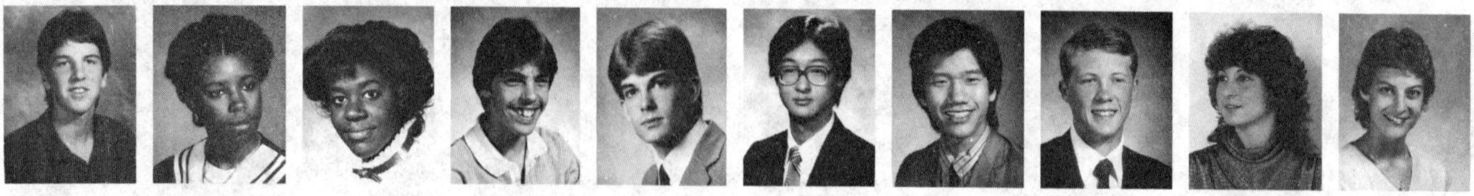

Howe, Craig A
Oneida SR HS
Oneida, NY

Howell, Detrel
Uniondale HS
Hempstead, NY

Howell, Lilli
Northeastern Acad
White Plains, NY

Howlan, Christopher
Colonie Central HS
Albany, NY

Hoyt, Rick
Elmira Free
Elmira, NY

Hsu, Hank
Edward R Murrow
Brooklyn, NY

Hsu, Kenneth D
Newtown HS
Elmhurst, NY

Huckabee, Andy
Lafayette HS
Jamesville, NY

Hudson, Gloria A
Patchoque-Medford
Patchogue, NY

Huffer, Bobbi
Kendall JR-SR HS
Hamlin, NY

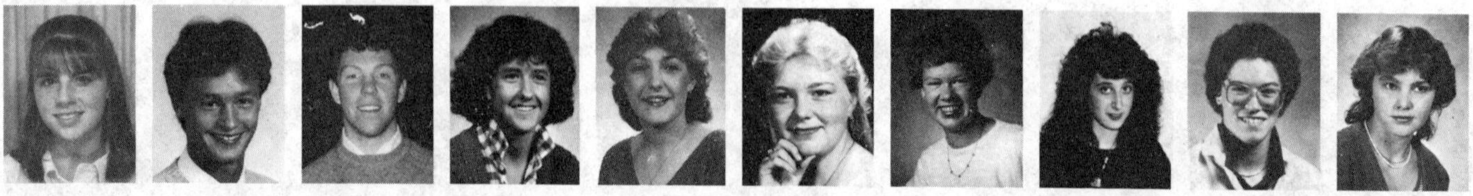

Hughes, Carolyn
St Dominic HS
N Bellmore, NY

Hughes, Patrick
Twin Tiers Baptist
Lawrenceville, PA

Hughes, IV Richard
J
La Salle Military
Massapequa, NY

Hughes, Sara
Bishop Ludden HS
Syracuse, NY

Hughner, Lisa
Naples Central Schl
Naples, NY

Hull, Michelle E
Belfast Central Schl
Caneadea, NY

Hulse, Beth
Greenwood Central
Greenwood, NY

Hulsen, Christine
North Babylon HS
N Babylon, NY

Humbert, Sheri
North Rose Wolcott
Clyde, NY

Humig, Katherine
Hutch Tech
Buffalo, NY

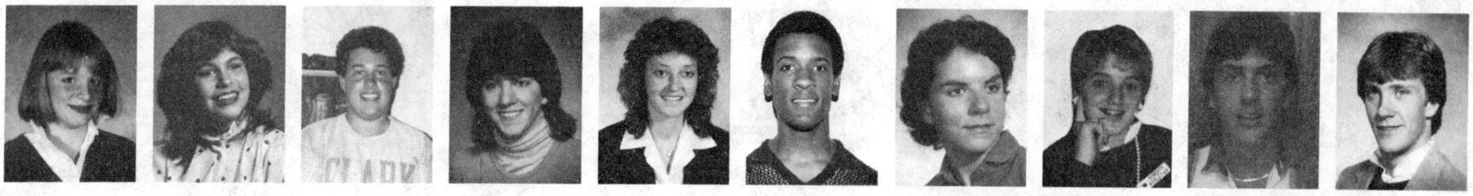

Humphrey, Shay
Lake George HS
Lake George, NY

Humphries, Patricia R
Julia Richman HS
Glendale, NY

Hundemer, Brett D
Midwood HS
Brooklyn, NY

Hunt, Chrisann
Auburn HS
Auburn, NY

Hunt, Noreen
Moore Catholic HS
Staten Island, NY

Hunt, Ronald
George W Wingate
Brooklyn, NY

Hunter, Joanne
Hoosic Valley
Central Schl
Johnsonville, NY

Huntington, Sally
Wilson Central HS
Ransomville, NY

Hunzinger, Scott
Deer Park HS
Deer Park, NY

Hurlburt, David A
Pioneer Central HS
Arcade, NY

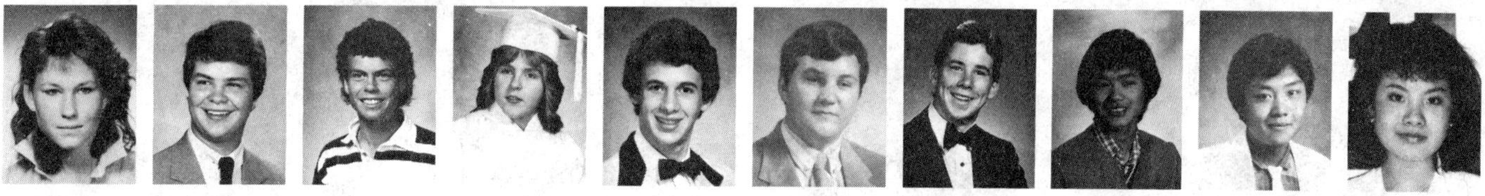

Hurley, Christine
Valley Stream North
Malverne, NY

Hurst, Matthew
Commack High Schl
Commack, NY

Hurtgen, Matthew T
Dunkirk HS
Dunkirk, NY

Hussey, Kathleen
Monticello HS
Monticello, NY

Huston, Todd W
Mc Quaid Jesuit HS
Rochester, NY

Huttleston, Timothy
Greene Central HS
Smithville Flats, NY

Huvane, Patrick
Cardinal Spellman
Bronx, NY

Huynh, Hung
Susan E Wagner HS
Staten Island, NY

Hwang, David H
Cortland JR SR HS
Cortland, NY

Hwang, Emmie
Hauppauge HS
Smithtown, NY

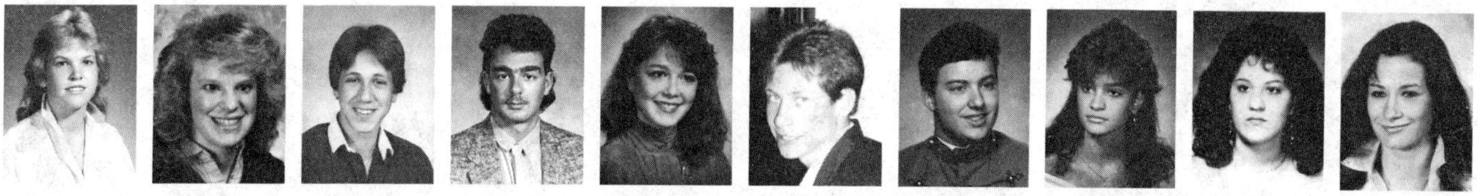

Hyde, Mariann
Hendrick Hudson
Peekskill, NY

Hyser, Heather
Frontier Central HS
Lancaster, PA

Iacovelli, Vincent
Commack South HS
Commack, NY

Iafe, George A
Tottenville HS
Staten Island, NY

Iannone, Lisa A
Shenendehowa HS
Waterford, NY

Ibelli, Stephen
Eastchester HS
Eastchester, NY

Ibietatorremendia, Jose
La Salle Military
W New York, NJ

Iglesias, Margarita
The Mary Louis
Jackson Heights, NY

Ignazio, Gina-Maria
Bishop Ford Ctl
Catholic HS
Brooklyn, NY

Ilardo, Mary Bea
Hamburg SR HS
Hamburg, NY

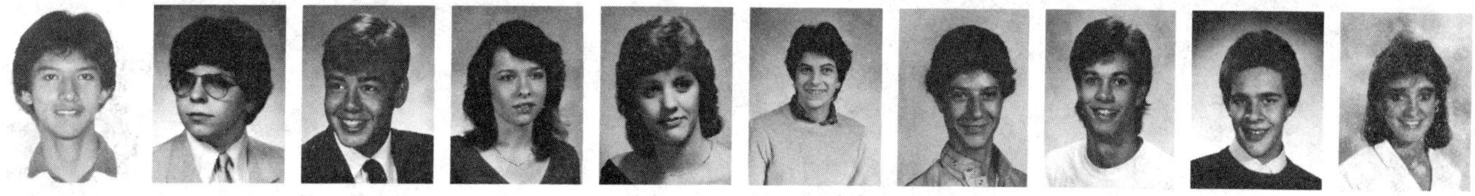

Immanuel, David
St Pauls Schl
Mineola, NY

Incorvaia, Joseph S C A
Bishop Ford HS
Brooklyn, NY

Infante, Jose
Mamaroneck HS
Larchmont, NY

Ingersoll, Melissa R
Alden Central HS
Alden, NY

Ingerson, Amy L
Kensington HS
Buffalo, NY

Ingher, Stacy
Commack HS South
Commack, NY

Intini, Frank
Sachem HS
Farmingville, NY

Intrieri, Thomas
Walt Whitman HS
Huntington Statio, NY

Inzana, Anthony
Aquinas Inst
Rochester, NY

Ioele, Sarah
Gloversville HS
Gloversvl, NY

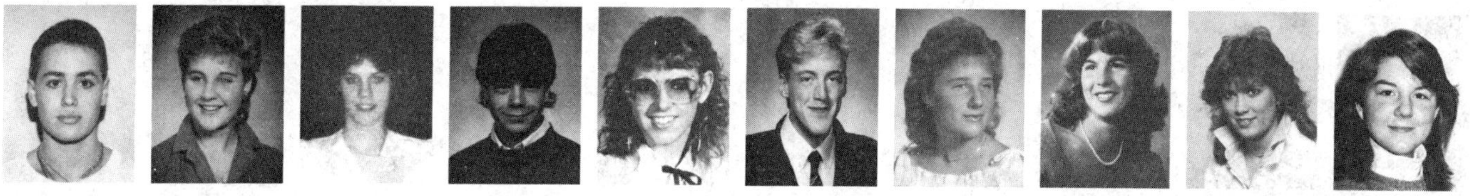

Ippolito, John M
Tottenville HS
Staten Island, NY

Irbe, Aina
Lafayette SR HS
Jamesville, NY

Irvine, Ann
Watervliet HS
Watervliet, NY

Isaacson, Todd
Jamestown HS
Jamestown, NY

Isaman, Annette
Perry Central HS
Perry, NY

Ivers, Kevin D
East Islip HS
Great River, NY

Izzo, Darcy Lynn
Northville Central
Northville, NY

Jabbs, Stephanie A
Liverpool HS
Liverpool, NY

Jackowski, Michelle
Solvay HS
Solvay, NY

Jackson, Catherine
Riverdale Country
New York, NY

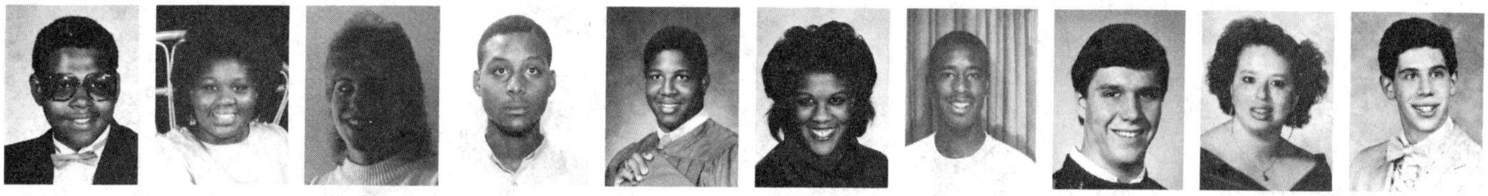

Jackson, Fred T
Norman Thomas
Commercial HS
Brooklyn, NY

Jackson, Jeuanita
South Park HS
Buffalo, NY

Jackson, Julie
Frontier Central HS
Blasdell, NY

Jackson, Junior R
North Babylon SR
North Babylon, NY

Jackson, Matthew
Pelham Memorial
Pelham, NY

Jackson, Phyllis H
Sonderling HS
Brentwood, NY

Jackson, Reginald
Mt Vernon HS
Bronx, NY

Jackson, Jr Richard E
Saugerties HS
Saugerties, NY

Jacobs, Brenda
Springfield Gardens
Jamaica, NY

Jacobs, Leonard A
Jamaica HS
Flushing, NY

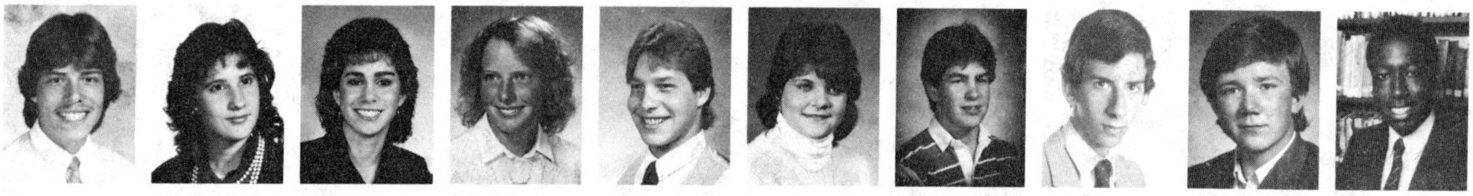

Jacobs, Robert
P V Moore HS
Cleveland, NY

Jacobson, Amy
Waterville Central
Deansboro, NY

Jacobson, Cheryl
Commack HS
Commack, NY

Jaeger, Lynda J
Baldwin SR HS
Baldwin, NY

Jagodzinski, Andrew J
Brockport Central
Hamlin, NY

Jakubczyk, Lisa
Mount Mercy Acad
Lackawanna, NY

Jakuc, Peter A
Shenendehowa
Central HS
Clifton Park, NY

James, Brian
West Hempstead
Long Island, NY

James, John H
Poland Central Schl
Poland, NY

James, Jr Ralph L
Archbishop Molloy
West Hempstead, NY

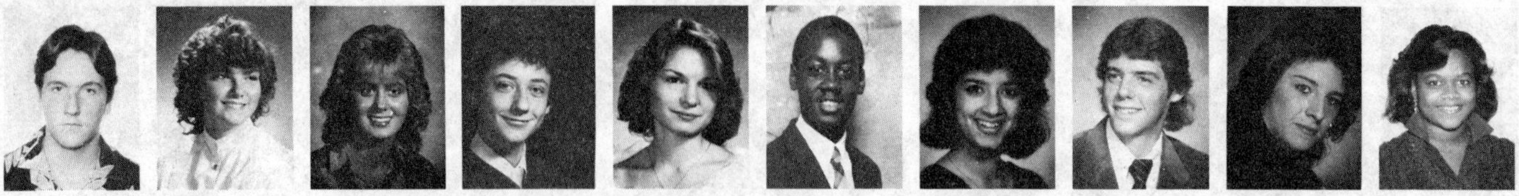

Jamieson, Donnie D
Newburgh Free
Newburgh, NY

Jannotti, Julianne
Newburgh Free
Newburgh, NY

Jaqueway, Deborah
Schoharie Central
Schoharie, NY

Jaroker, Jon
Susan E Wagner HS
Staten Island, NY

Jarosz, Jennifer A
Trott Vocational HS
Niagara Falls, NY

Jarvis, Ernesto
Art & Design HS
Brooklyn, NY

Javed, Zarqa
Eastport HS
Eastport, NY

Jaworski, Scott M
Westhill HS
Syracuse, NY

Jayne, Lora E
Dundee Central Schl
Dundee, NY

Jean-Felix, Diane
St Francis Prep
Laurelton, NY

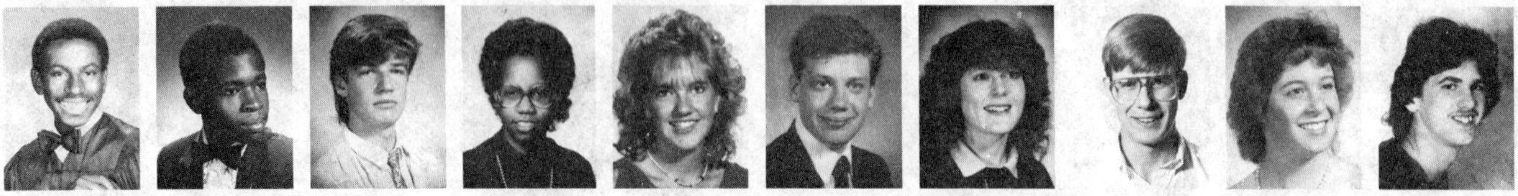

Jean-Romain, Djeno
Nazareth Regional
Brooklyn, NY

Jeanbaptiste, Rigal
Eramus Hall HS
Brooklyn, NY

Jedlicka, Paul J
Greece Athena HS
Rochester, NY

Jefferson, Denise
Patchogue-Medford
Medford, NY

Jeffries, Jennifer
Maryvale HS
Cheektowaga, NY

Jenkins, Michael D
Maple Hill HS
Castleton, NY

Jensen, Julie
Northville HS
Northville, NY

Jenson, Mark
Greenville Central
Greenville, NY

Jerge, Jeanne M
Grand Island SR HS
Grand Island, NY

Jesmer, Robert
Jordan-Elbridge SR
Jordan, NY

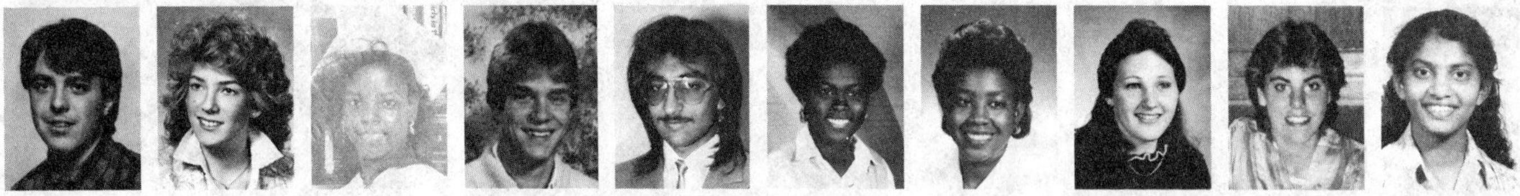

Jewett, Gregory
Solvay HS
Solvay, NY

Jezick, Jeanette
Sachem HS
Holtsville, NY

Jiggetts, Sabrina
De Witt Clinton HS
Bronx, NY

Jinks, Robert
Gloversville HS
Gloversvl, NY

Jivraj, Hanifmohamed
Forest Hills HS
Elmont, NY

Joachim, Junie
Holy Trinity HS
Hempstead, NY

Jocelyn, Carine
Elmont Memorial
Elmont, NY

Johaneman, Kelly
Livingston Manor Central HS
Livingston Manor, NY

Johansen, Patrice N
Dominican Commercial HS
Woodhaven, NY

John, Jolly
Yonkers HS
Yonkers, NY

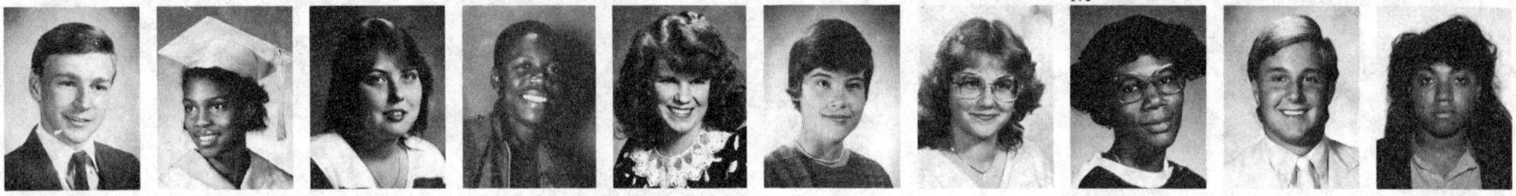

Johnson, Christopher
Newark Valley HS
Willseyville, NY

Johnson, Claudine
Dminican Commercial HS
Brooklyn, NY

Johnson, Cynthia A
Camden Central HS
Westdale, NY

Johnson, Derrick
Hanau American HS
Jackson, MS

Johnson, Jennifer
Middleburgh Central HS
Middleburgh, NY

Johnson, Julia L
Chittenango Central
Chittenango, NY

Johnson, Karin
Saugerties HS
Saugerties, NY

Johnson, Lynn
Poughkeepsie HS
Poughkeepsie, NY

Johnson, Michael R
Carle Place HS
Carle Place, NY

Johnson, Michelle A
St Francis Prep
Hollis, NY

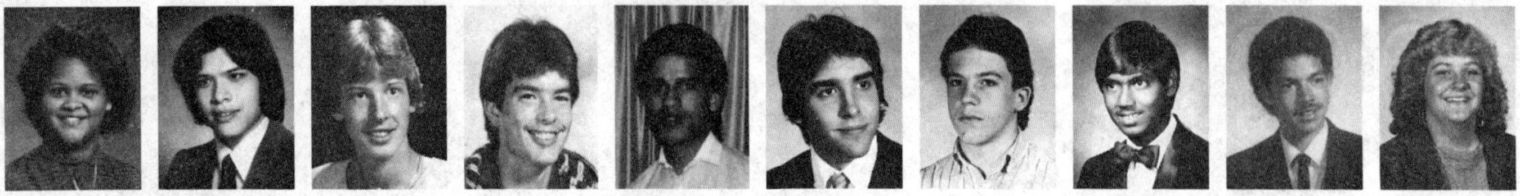

Johnson, Nicole
Mount Vernon HS
Mt Vernon, NY

Johnson, Wayne
Cicero North Syracuse HS
Syracuse, NY

Johnston, Christian E
Way Land Central
Wayland, NY

Johnston, Damian P
Arlington North Campus HS
Lagrangeville, NY

Johnston, Ian
Sewanhaka HS
Elmont, NY

Johnston, Robert
Tottenville HS
Staten Island, NY

Johnston, Rodney
Marlboro Central
Marlboro, NY

Jokhan, Larry V
St Francis Prep
Queens Village, NY

Jones, Adrian
Buffalo Traditional
Buffalo, NY

Jones, Dana
Plattsburgh HS
Plattsburgh, NY

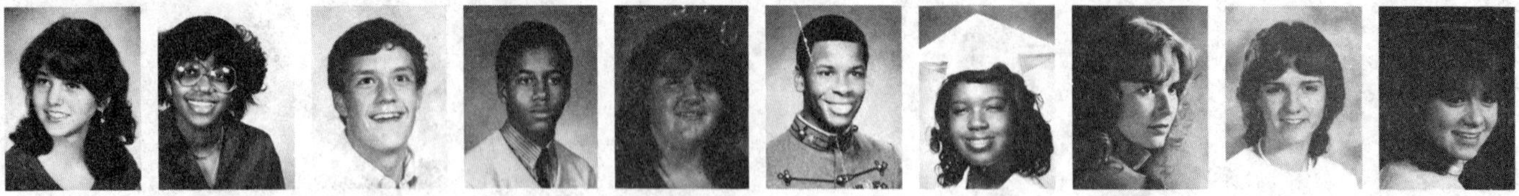

Jones, Darcy
La Fayette HS
Manlius, NY

Jones, Dionne
Hempstead SR HS
Hempstead, NY

Jones, Gary
Jamesville De Witt
Jamesville, NY

Jones, George P
Williamsville South
Williamsville, NY

Jones, Joelle
Waterloo SR HS
Waterloo, NY

Jones, Kenneth
La Salle Military
Queens, NY

Jones, Kimmarie
Dominican Commercial HS
St Albans, NY

Jones, Lynn G
Cambridge Central
Buskins, NY

Jones, Michelle
Franklin Acad
Malone, NY

Jones, Sandi Marie
Newfane Central HS
Lockport, NY

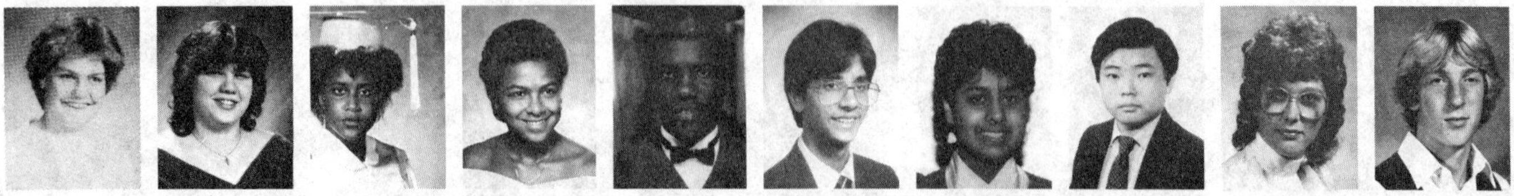

Joost, Inger
Saranac Lake HS
Paul Smiths, NY

Jordan, Veronica M
Nortre Dame HS
New York Mills, NY

Jordan, Yvette
A Philip Randolph
Brooklyn, NY

Jorif, Darlene
William Floyd HS
Moriches, NY

Joseph, Julio
George W Wingate
Brooklyn, NY

Joshi, Sanjay S
Shaker HS
Latham, NY

Joshi, Sunita A
Greece Athena HS
Rochester, NY

Jou, Peter
St Agnes HS
New York, NY

Jowdy, Lynne
Wilson Central HS
Lockport, NY

Joy, III Robert A
Morris Central HS
Morris, NY

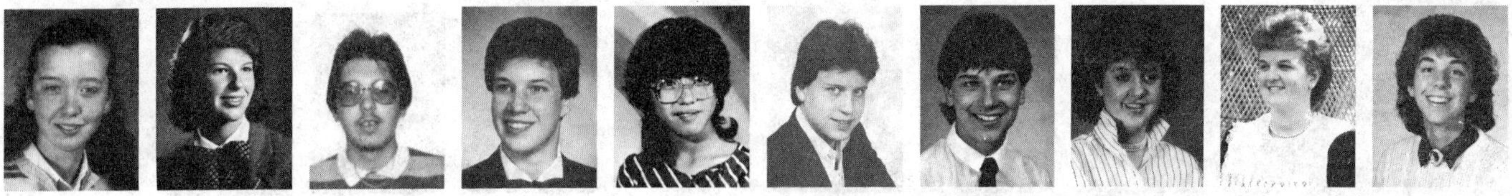

Joyce, Colleen
Mount Saint Mary
Tonawanda, NY

Judson, Kathryn
Ichabod Crane HS
Niverville, NY

Juhasz, Michael
St Francis Prep
Astoria, NY

Julian, Michael J
Christian Brothers
Fayetteville, NY

Julian, Stephanie
Holy Trinity HS
Hicksville, NY

Jurgens, Bruce W
Cairo-Durham JR SR HS
Cairo, NY

Juron, Jason R
Niagara Catholic HS
Niagara Falls, NY

Juskiewicz, Diane
Mt Mercy Acad
W Seneca, NY

Kaban, Renee
Lowville Academy And Central Schl
Lowville, NY

Kabasinskas, Marisa
Herricks SR HS
Williston Park, NY

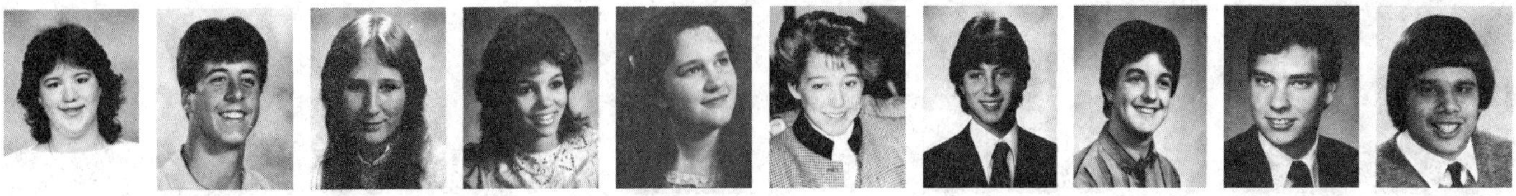

Kacprzak, Teresa
John Marshall HS
Rochester, NY

Kahn, Rick
Mahopac HS
Mahopac, NY

Kaiser, Christine E
Scio Central Schl
Scio, NY

Kalafarski, Carol
G Ray Bodley HS
Fulton, NY

Kalbfleisch, Kathryn
James E Sperry HS
Rochester, NY

Kalmus, Jackie
Acad Of St Joseph
Centereach, NY

Kaminsky, Andrew
Syosset HS
Plainview, NY

Kanaley, Timothy
Thomas J Corcoran
Syracuse, NY

Kanas, William S
Walt Whitman HS
Huntington Stn, NY

Kane, George
Whitestone Acad
Whitestone, NY

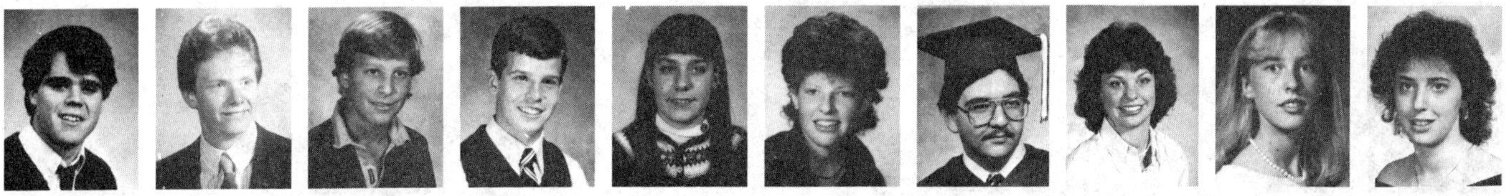

Kane, John
Bishop Ludden HS
Syracuse, NY

Kane, Kevin
Gates-Chili SR HS
Rochester, NY

Kaplan, Danny
Jamesville-Dewitt
Syracuse, NY

Karb, Michael
St Marys HS
Lancaster, NY

Karl, Deanna
Allegany Central HS
Allegany, NY

Kaskel, Pamela
Syosset HS
Jericho, NY

Kass, Mitchell
Flushing HS
Flushing, NY

Kasson, Mary L
Mercy HS
Albany, NY

Kats, Irina
Fox Lane HS
Mount Kisco, NY

Katz, Beth
Canarsie HS
Brooklyn, NY

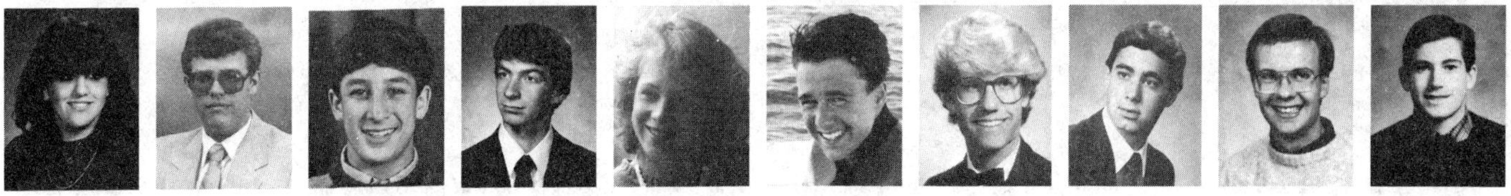

Katz, Jamie L
Eastchester HS
Eastchester, NY

Kaufinger, Gregory G
Horseheads HS
Elmira, NY

Kaufman, Eric
East Hampton HS
E Hampton, NY

Kaufman, Jody L
Ward Melville HS
Stony Brook, NY

Kaufmann, Kimberly
New Rochelle HS
New Rochelle, NY

Kay, IV William H
Arlington HS
Pleasant Valley, NY

Kazmierczak, III Thomas T
St Josephs Collegiate Inst
Cheektowaga, NY

Keagle, Jeffrey S
Horseheads SR HS
Horseheads, NY

Kearney, Jeffery
Jamestown HS
Jamestown, NY

Kearns, Michael P
Bishop Timon HS
Buffalo, NY

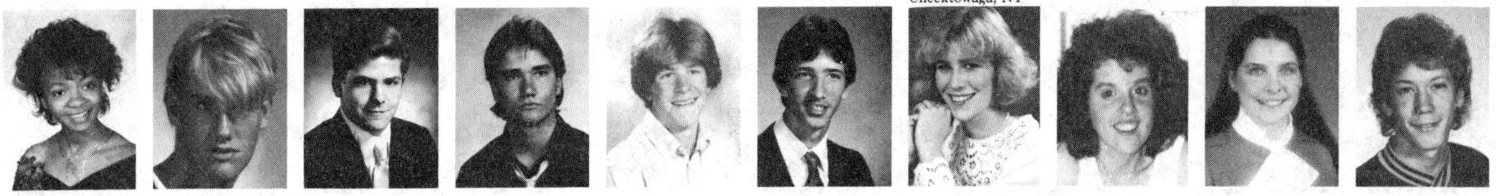

Kearse, Robin
Norman Thomas HS
Brooklyn, NY

Keaveny, Patrick
Williamsville North
W Amherst, NY

Keefe, Michael
Lansingburgh HS
Troy, NY

Keefe, Richard T
Greenport HS
Greeport, NY

Keenan, Kevin
Carmel HS
Carmel, NY

Keene, Dennis B
John F Kennedy HS
Mahopac, NY

Keene, Megan E
Waterloo HS
Waterloo, NY

Kekoler, Nancy
Abraham Lincoln
Brooklyn, NY

Kelchlin, Nancy
Mt Mercy Acad
Buffalo, NY

Keliher, John
Sachem North HS
Holbrook, NY

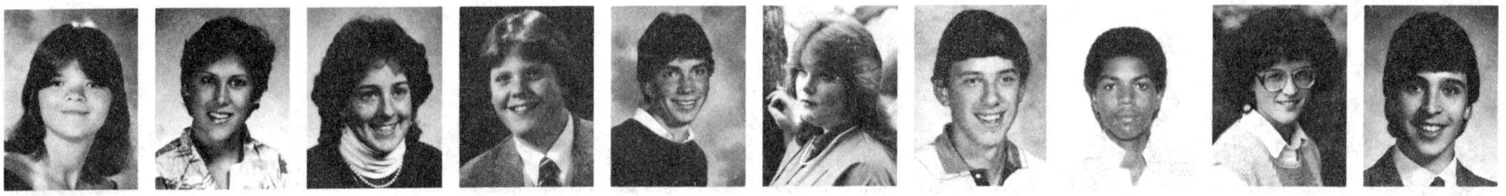

Kelleher, Helen C
Stella Maris HS
Rockaway Beach, NY

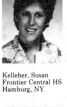

Kelleher, Susan
Frontier Central HS
Hamburg, NY

Keller, Kimberly
Hugh C Williams
Canton, NY

Kelley, James A
Sayville HS
Sayville, NY

Kelley, Joseph
Burnt Hills Ballston Lake HS
Ballston Lake, NY

Kelley, Lisa
Clifton-Fine Central
Oswegatchie, NY

Kelley, Michael
Newark SR HS
Newark, NY

Kellman, Karl
South Side HS
Rockville Centre, NY

Kelly, Althea
Delaware Acad
Hamden, NY

Kelly, Brian A
John S Burke Catholic HS
Pine Bush, NY

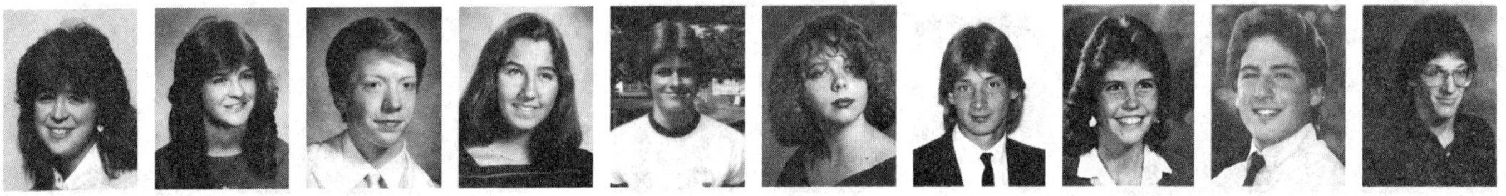

Kelly, Cindy
Solvay HS
Solvay, NY

Kelly, Deirdre
North Babylon HS
North Babylon, NY

Kelly, James
Cairo-Durham HS
Purling, NY

Kelly, Mary E
Liverpool HS
Liverpool, NY

Kelly, Matthew
Ward Melville HS
E Setauket, NY

Kelly, Michele P
Kingston HS
Kingston, NY

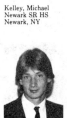

Kelly, Robert M
Amsterdam HS
Amsterdam, NY

Kelly, Veronica
Clarkstown North
New City, NY

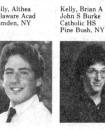

Kelner, Michael J
Arlington HS
Poughkeepsie, NY

Kelsey, Kenneth Lee
Wayne Central HS
Ontario, NY

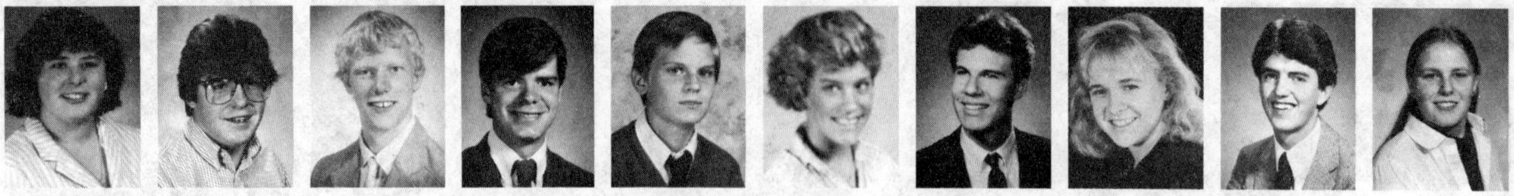

Kencik, Amy
Mount St Mary
Williamsville, NY

Kennedy, Chris
Hutchinson
Technical HS
Buffalo, NY

Kennedy, Dennis E
Tully Central Schl
Tully, NY

Kennedy, Eric
Waterville Central
Waterville, NY

Kennedy, James
Bishop Ludden HS
Syracuse, NY

Kennedy, Jennifer
Mineola HS
Mineola, NY

Kennedy, Kevin J
South Side HS
Rockville Centre, NY

Kennedy, Lynn
Smithtown HS West
Smithtown, NY

Kennedy, Michael R
Pine Bush HS
Middletown, NY

Kennedy, Samantha
Tottenville HS
Staten Island, NY

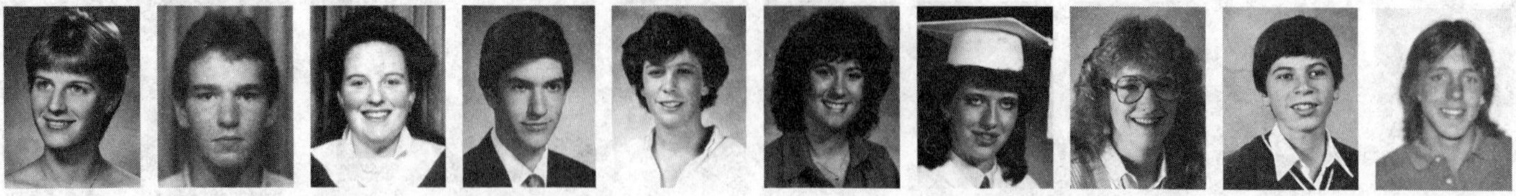

Kenney, Lisa
Babylon HS
Babylon, NY

Kenney, Michael
Susan E Wagner HS
Staten Island, NY

Kenny, Linda
Dominican
Commercial HS
Hollis, NY

Kenward, Michael L
Medina SR HS
Medina, NY

Keough, Debra
Barker Central HS
Appleton, NY

Keough, Elizabeth
Faith Heritage HS
Syracuse, NY

Kernaghan, Donna
Deer Park HS
Deer Park, NY

Kershner, Nancy
Candor Central HS
Owego, NY

Kesisian, Edward
Aviation HS
Staten Island, NY

Keyes, Bradley
Clarkstown HS
New City, NY

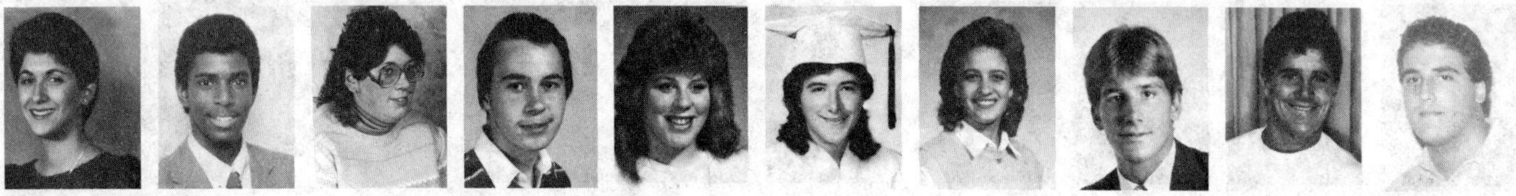

Khawly, Marianne
The Ursuline Schl
Eastchester, NY

Khealie, Darwin
High School For
The Humaniti
New York, NY

Kidder, Connie
Mexico Central Schl
Fulton, NY

Kieniksman, Andrew
Copiague HS
Copiague, NY

Kiernan, Lisa
Beacon HS
Beacon, NY

Kiernan, Patricia
Patchogue-Medford
Medford, NY

Kilburn, Kimberly
Dannemora HS
Elizabethtown, NY

Kiley, James D
Saint Francis Prep
Bayside, NY

Kilgannon, Kery F
Alfred G Berner HS
Massapequa, NY

Killerlane, James
Clarkstown South
W Nyack, NY

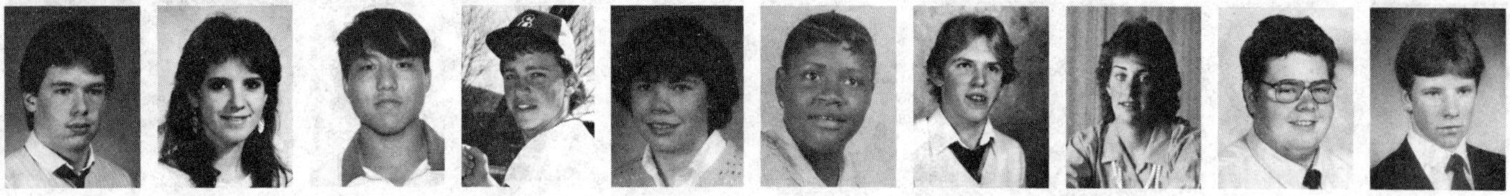

Killock, Rob
Pine Valley Central
S Dayton, NY

Kilthau, Joanna
Batavia HS
Batavia, NY

Kim, Kee
John Dewey HS
Brooklyn, NY

Kimball, Jr La Mott Tymer D
Corning East HS
Corning, NY

Kimber, Kathleen A
Genesco Central HS
Geneseo, NY

Kiner, Janiene
Canarsie HS
Brooklyn, NY

King, Alan
Bishop Ludden HS
Syracuse, NY

King, Lori
Paul V Moore HS
Central Sq, NY

King, Randy
Keveny Memorial
Watervliet, NY

King, Robert
Niskayuna SR HS
Scotia, NY

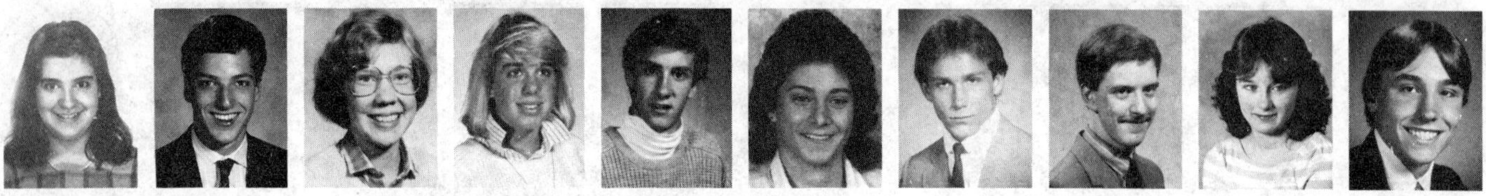

Kinkela, Katherine A
The Ursuline Schl
Bronxville, NY

Kinory, Adam D
Bronx Science
New York, NY

Kinyon, Mary Lou
Sweet Home SR HS
Williamsville, NY

Kiresen, Michelle
Our Lady Of Mercy
Webster, NY

Kirisits, Todd A
Southwestern HS
Lakewood, NY

Kirkby, Karen
Liverpool HS
Liverpool, NY

Kirkby, Robert
Liverpool HS
Liverpool, NY

Kirpatrick, Robert
Wallkill HS
Walden, NY

Kissane, Mairead
Monticello HS
Monticello, NY

Kissel, David N
West Seneca West SR HS
West Seneca, NY

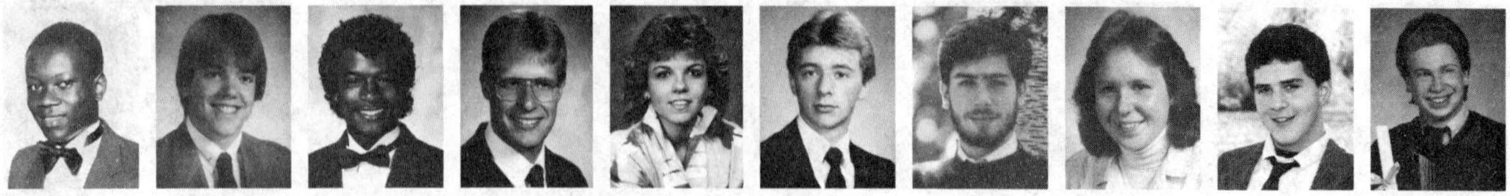

Kissi, Evans
Yonkers HS
Yonkers, NY

Kitchen, William
Vernon-Verona-Scherrill Centrl Schl
Vernon Ctr, NY

Kittles, Vincent
Central Islip HS
Central Islip, NY

Klafehn, David
Kendall JR SR HS
Kendall, NY

Klatt, Tina K
Medina SR HS
Medina, NY

Klein, Erik
Berlin Central HS
Berlin, NY

Klein, Jason M
Blind Brook HS
Rye Brook, NY

Klein, Kathryn T
Cheektowaga
Central HS
Cheektowaga, NY

Klein, Mitchell
The Harvey Schl
Armonk, NY

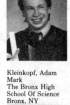

Kleinkopf, Adam Mark
The Bronx High School Of Science
Bronx, NY

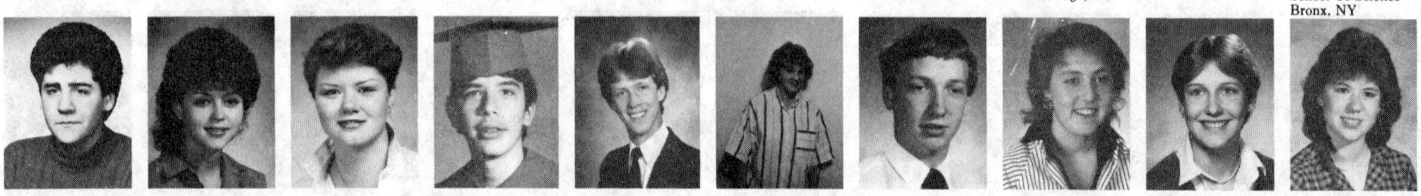

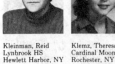

Kleinman, Reid
Lynbrook HS
Hewlett Harbor, NY

Klemz, Theresa
Cardinal Mooney
Rochester, NY

Klimaszewski, Mary
Villa Maria Acad
Buffalo, NY

Klimovich, Joseph
Herbert H Lehman
New York, NY

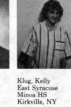

Klimpel, Eric R
Kingston HS
Tillson, NY

Klug, Kelly
East Syracuse Minoa HS
Kirkville, NY

Knapp, Christopher
Soranac Lake HS
Lake Clear, NY

Knapp, Nicole
Fabius-Pompey HS
Fabius, NY

Kneidl, Cathleen M
Shoreham Wading River HS
Wading River, NY

Knibbs, Tracey
Beacon HS
Beacon, NY

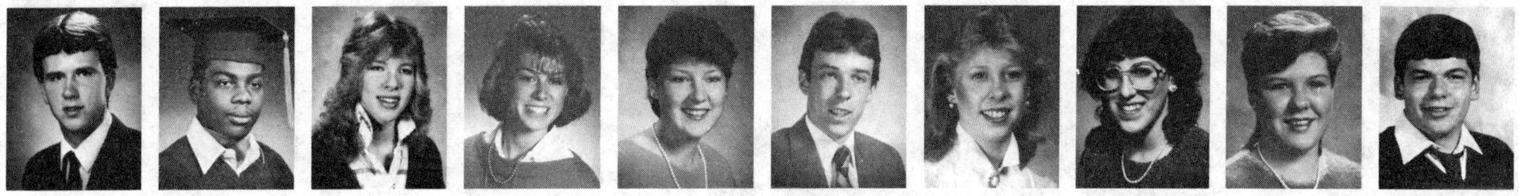

Knifley, John
Geneva HS
Geneva, NY

Knight, George D
Aviation HS
Flushing, NY

Knisley, Rachelle
Hutch Tech HS
Bufflao, NY

Knoll, Danielle T
Massapequa HS
Massapequa, NY

Knoll, Katherine
Eden Central HS
Eden, NY

Koch, John C
Seton Catholic
Central HS
Endwell, NY

Koehler, Suzanne
Mount Mercy Acad
Buffalo, NY

Kogut, Gail
Bishop Ludden HS
Syracuse, NY

Kolch, Kimberly A
Rome Free Acad
Rome, NY

Kolodziej, Jeffrey
Bishop Scully HS
Amsterdam, NY

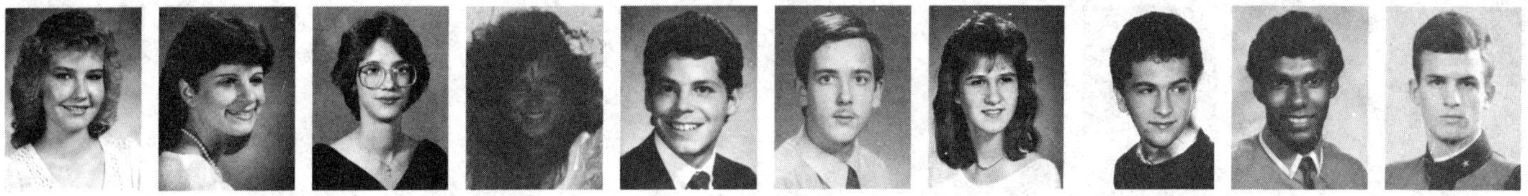

Kompalla, Sharon
West Seneca East
SR HS
Cheektowaga, NY

Konecky, Karen
Union-Endicott HS
Endicott, NY

Kopczynski, Mary E
St Joseph Hill Acad
Staten Island, NY

Kopf, Ann
Sweet Home SR HS
Tonawanda, NY

Kops, Mitch
Earl L
Vandermeulen HS
Pt Jefferson, NY

Kordana, Kevin
Roy C Ketcham HS
Poughkeepsie, NY

Kordolemis, Haroula
Stuyvesant HS
Long Island Cty,
NY

Korothy, John
Hicksville HS
Hicksville, NY

Koshy, Jay
Faith Heritage Schl
Syracuse, NY

Kosinski, Henry
La Salle Military
Rye, NY

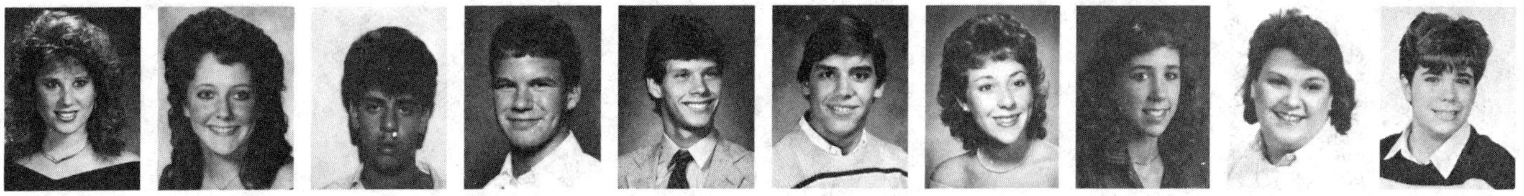

Kosko, Laura
Preston HS
Bronx, NY

Koszalka, Joan
Copiague HS
Copiague, NY

Kotenoglou,
Demetrios
Lynbrook HS
Lynbrook, NY

Koukoulas, Demetra
Fontbonne Hall
Brooklyn, NY

Kovac, Ivan J
Glen Cove HS
Glen Cove, NY

Kowalczyk, Don
St Marys HS
W Seneca, NY

Kowalinski, Lisa A
St Francis Prep
Maspeth, NY

Kowalski, Jennifer
Cortland SR HS
Cortland, NY

Kozlowski, Jeanne
Westmoreland
Central HS
Rome, NY

Kramer, Kristina A
St Francis Prep
Bayside, NY

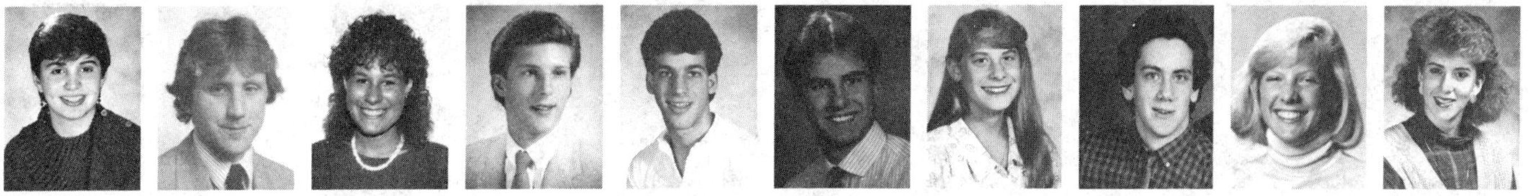

Krassas, Nicole R
Bronx High School
Of Science
Bronx, NY

Krauss, Todd
Smithtown East HS
St James, NY

Kraut, Julie
W C Mepham HS
Bellmore, NY

Krawczyk, J Mark
Liverpool HS
Liverpool, NY

Kreiswirth, Barry
Commack High Schl
E Northport, NY

Krempl, Gary M
Kingston HS
Lake Katrine, NY

Kresel, Tobey
Jamesville-Dewitt
Dewitt, NY

Kresock, David M
Elba Central Schl
Elba, NY

Kresse, Claire
Buffalo Seminary
Orchard Pk, NY

Kreutzer, Lynn
West Seneca East
SR HS
Cheektowaga, NY

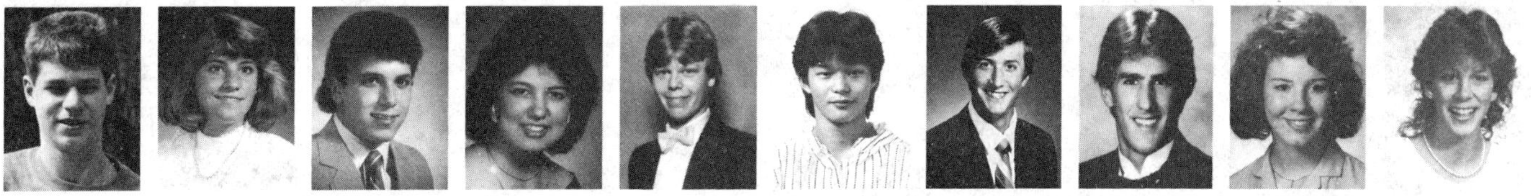

Krochtengel, Brian
South Shore HS
Brooklyn, NY

Kroslow, Michele
The Stony Brook
Stony Brook, NY

Krupa, Michael
Cardinal Mooney
Rochester, NY

Krywe, Stephanie
Somers HS
Katonah, NY

Krzyminski, John
St John The Baptist
Seaford, NY

Kubo, Ryu
Tottenville HS
Staten Isld, NY

Kucher, Philip
Port Chester HS
Port Chester, NY

Kucza, Michael J
Brentwood
Sorderling HS
Brentwood, NY

Kugler, Rosemary E
Syosset HS
Woodbury, NY

Kuhen, Kelli
Tonawanda HS
Tonawanda, NY

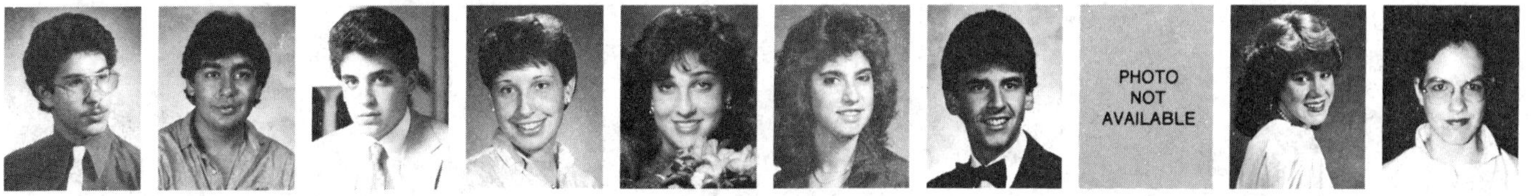
PHOTO
NOT
AVAILABLE

Kulesa, Thomas C
Cicero-North
Syracuse HS
North Syracuse, NY

Kumrah, Praveen
Churchville Chiu HS
Rochester, NY

Kunken, Jeffrey
Friends Acad
Upper Brookville,
NY

Kurylo, Natalie
Spackenkill HS
Poughkeepsie, NY

Kushner, Susan M
Williamsville East
E Amherst, NY

Kusterer, Jennifer
Tuckahoe HS
Bronxville, NY

Kuzler, Robert
Archbishop Molloy
Maspeth, NY

Kwasnik, John
Sherburne-Earville
Central HS
Sherburne, NY

Kyrillidis, Helen C
St Francis
Preparatory Schl
Flushing, NY

La Borne, Kathleen
M
East Islip HS
E Islip, NY

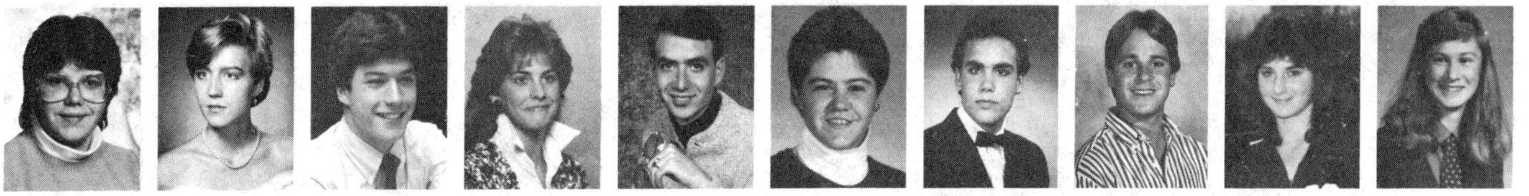

La Brake, Terri
Colton-Pierrepont
Central Schl
Potsdam, NY

La Croix, Noelle C
St Francis
Prepartory Schl
Flushing, NY

La Fave, Thomas
Arlington HS
Poughkeepsie, NY

La Fountain, Lisa
Northern
Adirondack Centra
Altona, NY

La George, Peter
North Spencer
Christian Acad
Candor, NY

La Plante, Kimberly
Lansingburgh HS
Troy, NY

La Rocca, Anthony
Brooklyn Acad
Brooklyn, NY

La Rocca, Mark
Greenville JR/SR
Medusa, NY

La Rocco, Angela
Le Roy Central HS
Leroy, NY

La Rose, Nikki
Dannemora Union
Free HS
Dannemora, NY

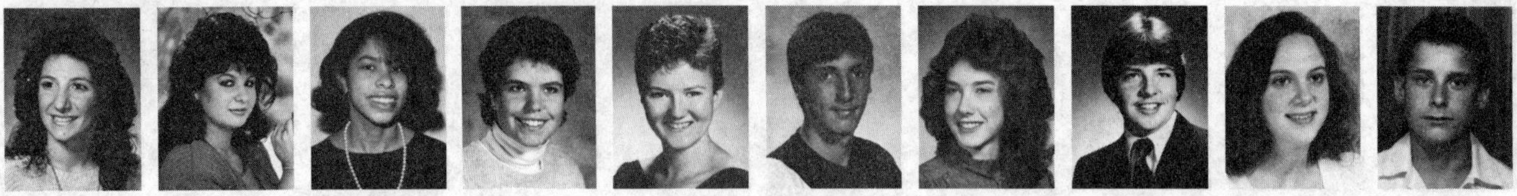

La Salla, Gina Marie
Bethpage HS
Bethpage, NY

La Scala, Michelle
The Ursuline Schl
City Island, NY

La Taillade, Jaslean J
Bronx H S Of Sci
New York, NY

La Varnway, Michelle L
Haverling Central
Bath, NY

Labashinsky, Eileen F
St Michaels HS
Brooklyn, NY

Lacarrubba, Sal
East Hampton HS
Amagansett, NY

Lacomis, Ellen
Shenendehowa HS
Clifton Park, NY

Lacon, Thomas S
H Frank Carey HS
Franklin Sq, NY

Ladd, Darla
Paul V Moore HS
Central Sq, NY

Laforte, Alex
New Dorp HS
Staten Island, NY

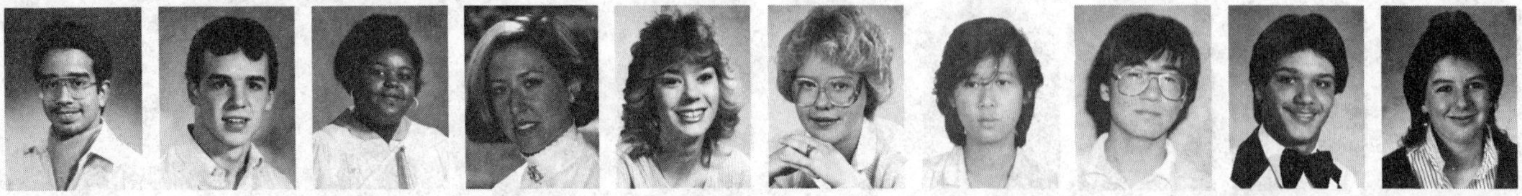

Lagomarsini, Alex
Aviation HS
Bronx, NY

Laing, Andrew
Sherburne-Earlville
Earlville, NY

Laing, Kim
St Raymond Acad
Bronx, NY

Laires, Michelle C
Marymount Schl
City Island, NY

Lalka, Susan
Lackawanna SR HS
Lackawanna, NY

Lally, Tammy J
Midlakes HS
Clifton Springs, NY

Lam, Cam
HS Of Fashion Inds
Jackson Heights, NY

Lam, Noah
St John The Baptist
Great Rvr, NY

Lamazza, Lonnie M
Monsignor Farrell
Staten Island, NY

Lamb, Lynette
Fabius-Pompey HS
Pompey, NY

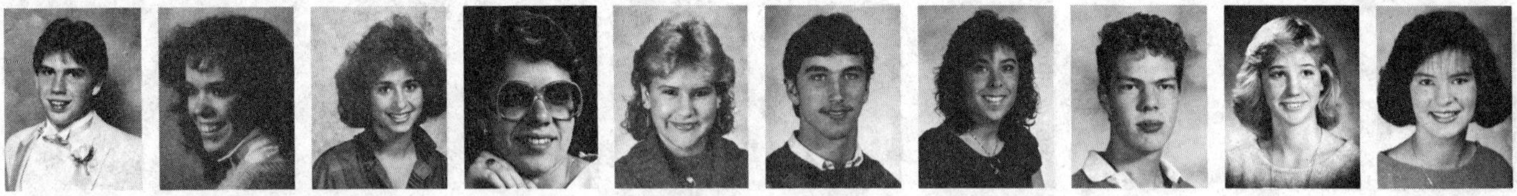

Lambert, Thomas W
John F Kennedy HS
Yorktown Heights, NY

Lamica, Shayne
Glens Falls HS
Colens Falls, NY

Lamonica, Lisa
Frankfort Schyler
Central Schl
Frankfort, NY

Landers, Kim
Royalton-Hartland
Gasport, NY

Landers, Tricia
Churchville-Chili
Rochester, NY

Landess, Brad
Marcus Whitman
Gorham, NY

Landman, Geri
Half Hollow Hills
West HS
Dix Hills, NY

Landstrom, Scott
Tottenville HS
Staten Island, NY

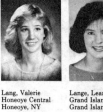

Lang, Valerie
Honeoye Central
Honeoye, NY

Lange, Leanne
Grand Island HS
Grand Island, NY

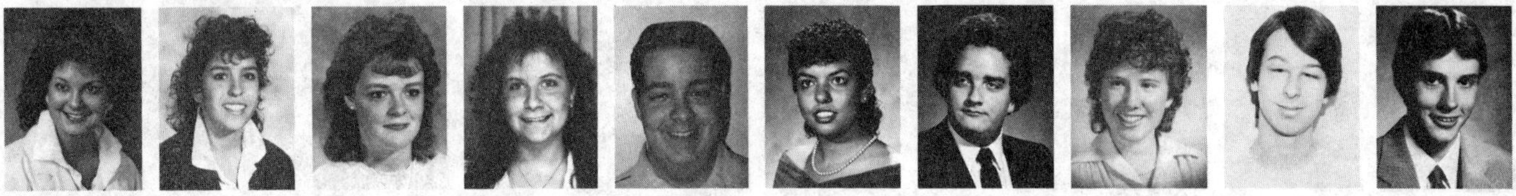

Langlie, Heather M
Johnson City HS
Binghamton, NY

Langsam, Lili
Burnt Hills-Ballston
Lake HS
Schenectady, NY

Lanthier, Darcy
Tupper Lake HS
Tupper Lk, NY

Lantz, Jacqueline Ann
Lincoln HS
Yonkers, NY

Lanzisera, Joseph
Roy C Ketcham HS
Poughkeepsie, NY

Lao, Danira
Our Lady Of
Perpetual Help
Brooklyn, NY

Lape, Jr Robert E
Walter Panas HS
Peekskill, NY

Laragy, Molly
Bishop Kearney HS
Rochester, NY

Laraia, Bo
Byram Hills HS
Armonk, NY

Laraway, Wesley D
Middleburgh
Central HS
Middleburgh, NY

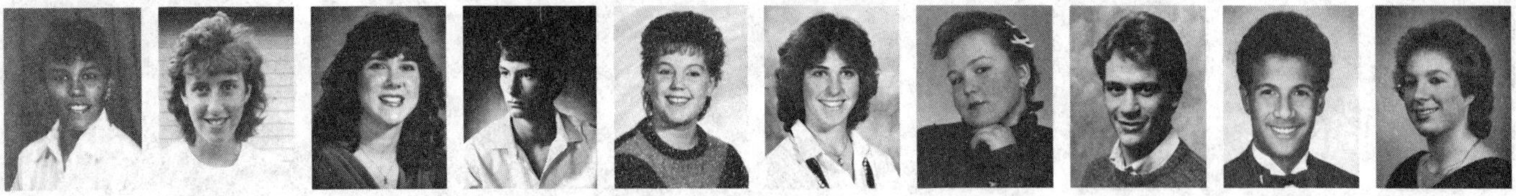

Large, Patricia
Grace Dodge Voc
Bronx, NY

Lariviere, Susan
Fayetteville-Manlius
SR HS
Chittenango, NY

Larkin, Amy
Shenendehowa HS
Clifton Park, NY

Larkin, James
Lansingburgh HS
Troy, NY

Larsen, Ann
Susan E Wagner HS
Staten Island, NY

Larson, Karen
Maple Hill HS
Castleton, NY

Larson, Michelle
Ralph R Mc Kee
Staten Island, NY

Larson, Timothy
John A Coleman HS
Ulster Park, NY

Lasalle, Hector D
Brentwood High
Ross Center
Bay Shore, NY

Lasher, Marie
Dolgeville Central
Dolgeville, NY

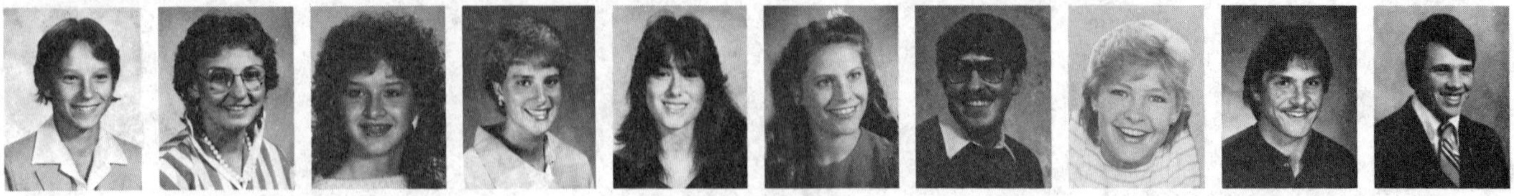

Latenberger, Kyle
E J Wilson HS
Rochester, NY

Lathrop, Monica
Canisteo Central HS
Hornell, NY

Lauenborg, Kim
Newfield HS
Selden, NY

Laux, Michele
Buffalo Acad Of
The Sacred Hrt HS
Buffalo, NY

Lavas, Michele
New Dorp HS
Staten Island, NY

Lavery, Elizabeth
Springville Griffith
Springville, NY

Law, George
George W Fowler
Syracuse, NY

Law, Shari
Tonawanda JR SR
Tonawanda, NY

Lawton, Bruce
Wayland Central HS
Perkinsville, NY

Layman, Dennis A
West Seneca West
SR HS
West Seneca, NY

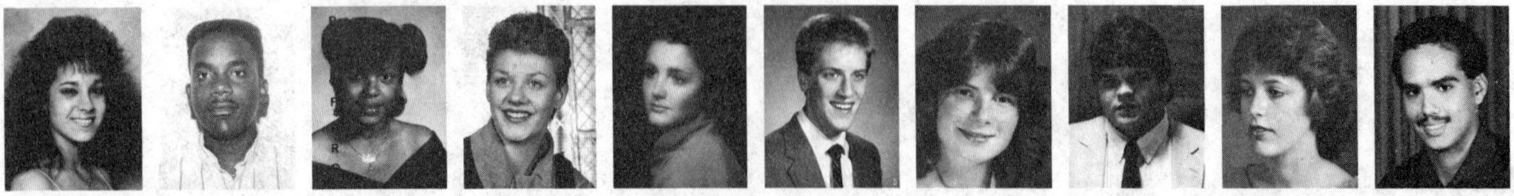

Lazaro, Debra
Moore Catholic HS
Staten Island, NY

Lazarus, Assad
Uniondale HS
Greenbelt, MD

Lazarus, Selina B
Bishop Loughlin HS
Brooklyn, NY

Le Baron, Roberta L
Cassadaga Valley
Central Schl
Sinclairville, NY

Le Blanc, Jennifer L
Ballston Spa HS
Ballston Spa, NY

Le Febvre, David M
John F Kennedy HS
Carmel, NY

Le May, Laurel Lynn
Tri-Valley Central
Neversink, NY

Le Pre, Doug
Riverhead HS
Huntington, NY

Leach, Patricia
Sodus Central HS
Alton, NY

Leal, Fernando
St Agnes HS
New York, NY

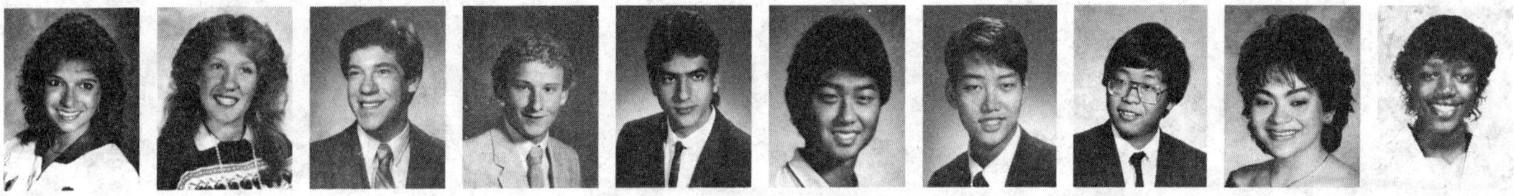

Leanza, Elisa
Our Lady Of Victory
Eastchester, NY

Leatbers, Suzanne
Greece Athena SR
Rochester, NY

Lebish, Craig L
Centereach HS
Lake Grove, NY

Lechner, Steven E
Saugerties HS
Saugerties, NY

Lecusay, Jr Dario A
Elmont Meorial HS
Elmont, NY

Lee, Benjamin
Vestal Senior HS
Apalachin, NY

Lee, David
Benjamin N
Cardozo HS
Bayside, NY

Lee, Eugene
John H Glenn HS
E Northport, NY

Lee, Gina
St Catherine Acad
Bronx, NY

Lee, Rosalind
Benjamin Franklin
Rochester, NY

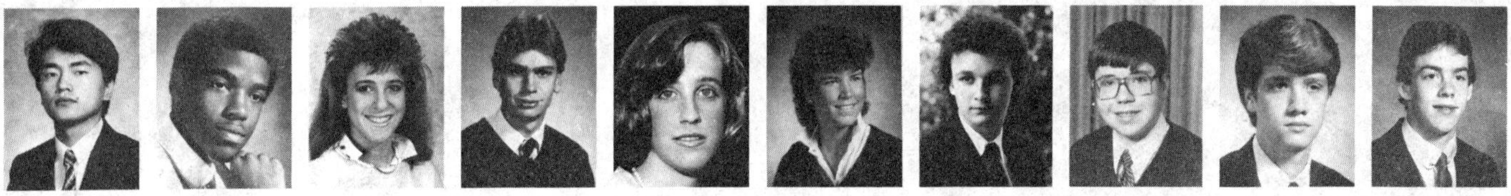

Lee, Woo
Hillcrest HS
Woodside, NY

Leeper, Jonathan
Jamestown HS
Jamestown, NY

Leff, Bonnie
Commack HS North
Commack, NY

Leffers, John W
Whitesboro SR HS
Utica, NY

Lefkowitz, Julie
Scarsdale HS
Scarsdale, NY

Legg, Marjorie
La Fayette HS
La Fayette, NY

Lehrer, Scott E
Woodmere Acad
Hewlett Harbor, NY

Leibensperger, Dale
B
Elmira Christian
Painted Post, NY

Leidich, Raymond
Union Springs Acad
Middletown, NY

Leirey, James E
Kingston HS
Kingston, NY

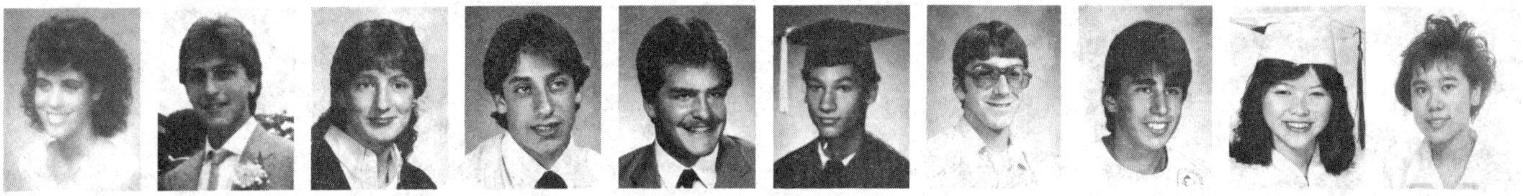

Lemmo, Lisa Ann
Cornwall Central HS
Cornwall, NY

Lenczewski, Vincent
Archbishop Molloy
Middle Vlg, NY

Leonard, Tonia
Watkins Glen
Central HS
Watkins Glen, NY

Leone, Michael
Niagara Catholic HS
Niagara Fls, NY

Leotta, Jr Frank A
E Islip SR HS
East Islip, NY

Leser, Steven H
Alfred G Berner HS
Massapequa Park,
NY

Lester, Gary
Mechanicville HS
Mechanicville, NY

Leta, Kurt
Lyndonville HS
Waterport, NY

Leung, Jeanie
Farmingdale Senior
Massapequa Park,
NY

Leung, Judy
H S Of Art &
New York City, NY

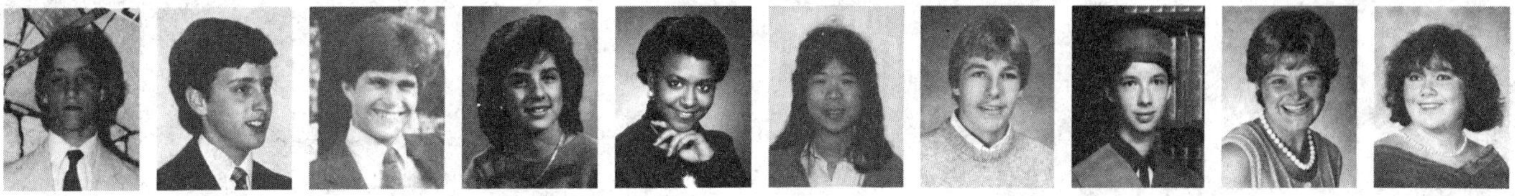

Levine, Craig
Earl L Von Der
Meulen HS
Mt Sinai, NY

Levine, Richard A
Valley Stream South
Valley Stream, NY

Levy, David J
Baldwin SR HS
Baldwin, NY

Levy, Susan
New Rochelle HS
New Rochelle, NY

Levy, Tanya
Peter Stuyvesant
Brooklyn, NY

Lew, Shirley
Greece Athena HS
Rochester, NY

Lewandoski, Donald
J
Red Creek Central
Sterling, NY

Lewandowski,
Gerald
St Marys HS
Depew, NY

Lewis, Bethann
Notre Dame HS
Elmira, NY

Lewis, Maureen Ann
Saint Saviour HS
Brooklyn, NY

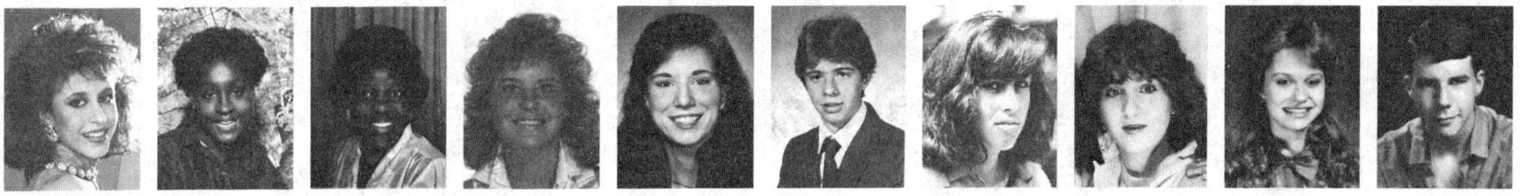

Lewis, Michelle
Susan E Wagner HS
Staten Island, NY

Lewis, Novada
Hillcrest HS
Queens, NY

Lewis, Patricia
Park West HS
New York, NY

Lewis, Victoria
Fontbonne Hall
Brooklyn, NY

Lezaja, Dorothy
Bethpage HS
Bethpage, NY

Librader, Erik A
Valhalla HS
North White Plain,
NY

Lichstein, Amy
Scarsdale HS
Scarsdale, NY

Licitra, Gina
Canarsie HS
Brooklyn, NY

Licursi, Tammy
St Marys HS
Cheektowaga, NY

Liddle, Roger
Naples Central Schl
Naples, NY

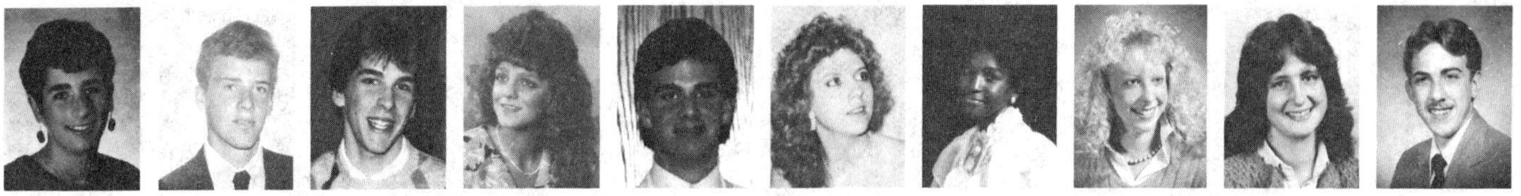

Lidestri, Amy
Waterloo SR HS
Waterloo, NY

Liegey, II Mark I
Archbishop Molloy
Far Rockaway, NY

Lieval, Michael
Nanuet HS
Nanuet, NY

Lindahl, Dawn
Aileen
James E Sperry/
Greece Athena HS
Rochester, NY

Lindner, John F
South Shore HS
Brooklyn, NY

Lindsay, Jean E
Centereach HS
Centereach, NY

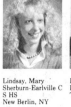

Lindsay, Makeba G
A Philip Randolph
Campus HS
Brooklyn, NY

Lindsay, Mary
Sherburn-Earlville C
S HS
New Berlin, NY

Linendoll, Kimberly
Lansingburgh HS
Troy, NY

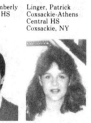

Linger, Patrick
Coxsackie-Athens
Central HS
Coxsackie, NY

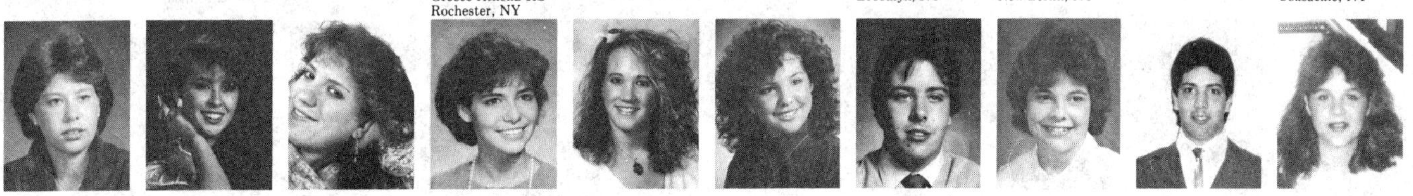

Link, Gail Ann
Bishop Kearney HS
Webster, NY

Link, Kimiko
Arlington HS
Poughquag, NY

Lino, Josette Marie
Margaretville
Central HS
Arkville, NY

Lipinsky, Stephanie
Ogdensburg Free
Ogdensburg, NY

Lippe, Wendy A
Great Neck South
SR HS
Great Neck, NY

Lirio, Pamela J
Niskayuna HS
Schenectady, NY

Little, Donald
Henninger HS
Syracuse, NY

Little, Lorna R
Bitburg American
Apo New York, NY

Liuzzo, John P
St Francis Prep
Whitestone, NY

Liveo, Mary Ann
New Utrecht HS
Brooklyn, NY

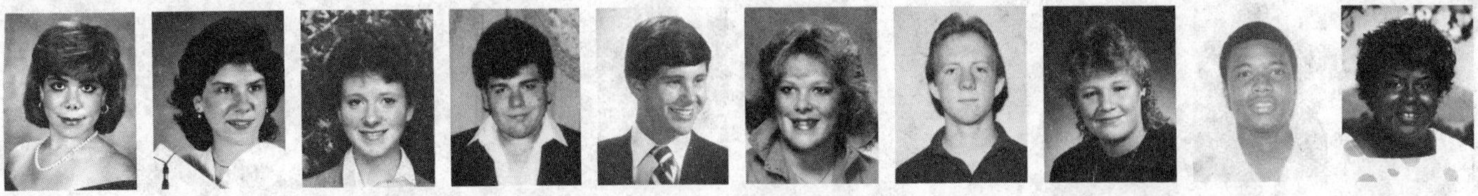

Llano, Frances
St Johns Prep
Elmhurst, NY

Lo Gatto, Jeanne
Marie
Hicksville HS
Hicksville, NY

Loan, Dawn
Central Square-Paul
V Moore HS
Cleveland, NY

Locascio, Andrew
John Adams HS
Ozone Park, NY

Lockwood, Michael
Hilton Central Schl
Rochester, NY

Lodge, Jennifer J
East Islip HS
Great River, NY

Loeffler, Michael
Monsingnor Farrell
Staten Island, NY

Loesch, Carol Ann
Deer Park HS
Deer Park, NY

Loftin, Larry
South Shore HS
Brooklyn, NY

Logan, Beverly
Midwood HS
Brooklyn, NY

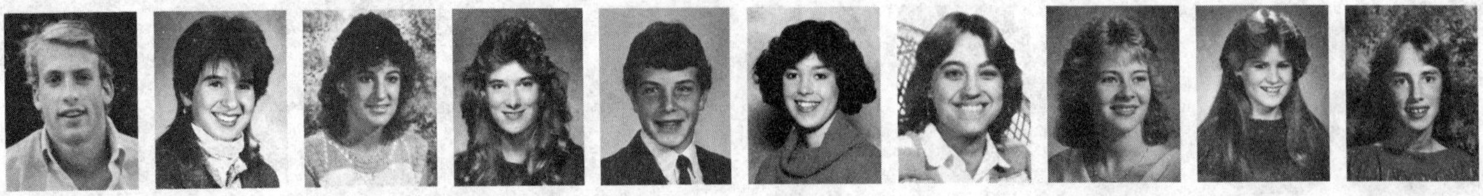

Logue, Chris
Williamsville South
Williamsville, NY

Long, Andrea
Hutchinson Central
Buffalo, NY

Long, Jennifer
Middletown HS
Middletown, NY

Long, Jeri Lynn
Longwood HS
Middle Island, NY

Longhouse, John
Lansing HS
Freeville, NY

Longoria, Jill
Woodbridge
American HS
A P O New York,
NY

Longway, Jill
Thousand Islands
Clayton, NY

Longwell, Lisa E
Waterloo SR HS
Waterloo, NY

Lonigan, Jennifer
Valley Central HS
Montgomery, NY

Looman, Cynthia
Oppenheim Epratah
Dolgeville, NY

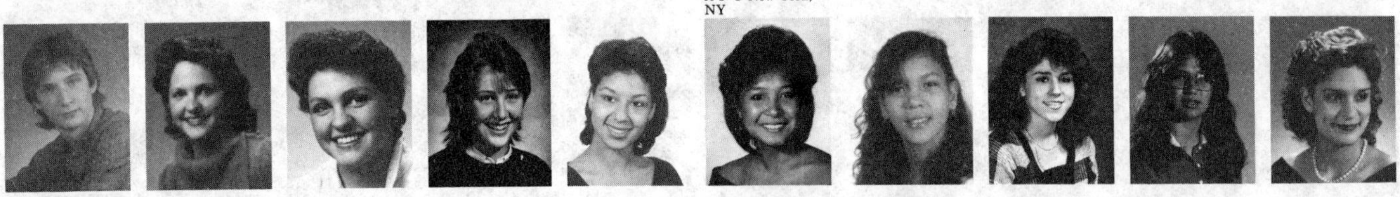

Loomis, Chris
Salem Washington
W Rupert, VT

Loomis, Kathryn
Liverpool HS
Liverpool, NY

Loomis, Kristin
Liverpool HS
Liverpool, NY

Loomis, Susan
Bishop Maginn HS
Albany, NY

Loperena, Maria
St Pius V HS
Bronx, NY

Lopez, Debbie
St Dominic HS
Bayville, NY

Lopez, Martha
Newtown HS
Jackson Heights,
NY

Lopez, Olivia
Adelphi Acad
Brooklyn, NY

Lopez, Rita
Jaqueline
Wheatley HS
Mineola, NY

Lopez, Wanda
Monsignor Scanlan
Bronx, NY

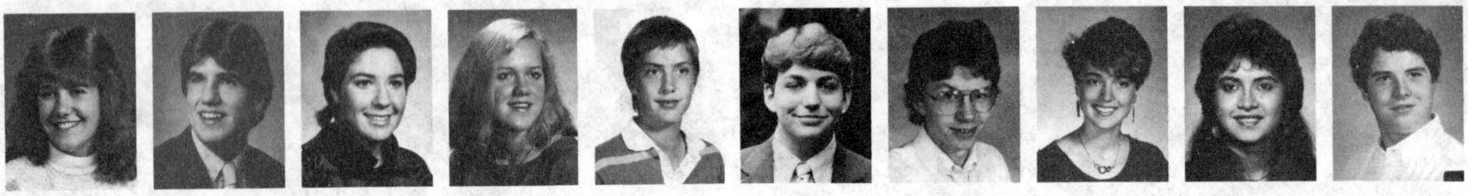

Lopitz, Amanda
Canastota HS
Canastota, NY

Losito, John
Elmira Free Acad
Elmira, NY

Louis, Tina
Thomas J Corcoran
Syracuse, NY

Louit, Anne
Mamaroneck HS
Larchmont, NY

Loverde, Nick
Sweet Home Central
Williamsville, NY

Loverro, Ian
Herricks HS
Carlsbad, CA

Lowery, Michael
Perry Central HS
Perry, NY

Loysen, Kathleen
Our Lady Of Mercy
Rochester, NY

Lozano, Teresa
Freeport HS
Freeport, NY

Lucas, Marshall
Commack HS North
Commack, NY

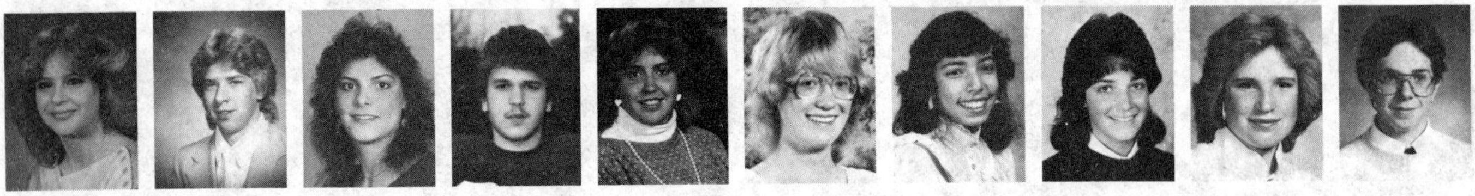

Lucca, Joey
City Honors HS
Buffalo, NY

Luce, Paul M
Gowanda Central
Gowanda, NY

Luci, Maureen
Amsterdam HS
Amsterdam, NY

Lucia, Jeffrey
Onondaga Central
Syracuse, NY

Lucido, Elizabeth
Amsterdam HS
Amsterdam, NY

Lufkin, Camille A
Cambridge Central
Cambridge, NY

Lugo, Sandy
Seaford HS
Seaford, NY

Luizzi, Beth
Mercy HS
Rensselaer, NY

Luke, Michele
J C Birdlebough HS
Phoenix, NY

Lumb, Jeff
Auburn HS
Auburn, NY

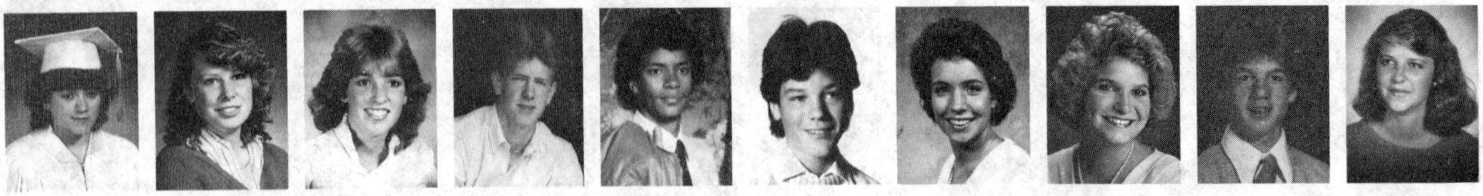

Luna, Zulma
Manhattan Center/
Sci P Math HS
New York, NY

Lund, Anne-Marie
Spackenkill HS
Poughkeepsie, NY

Lunden, Stephanie
Northstar Christian
Churchville, NY

Lundy, Scott
New Lebanon JR
SR HS
Old Chatham, NY

Lungu, James
Dansville Central
Dansville, NY

Lupica, Daniel
Hamburg HS
Hamburg, NY

Lustyik, Sara
Lake George HS
Lk George, NY

Luther, Laura Lee
Frankfort-Schuyler
Frankfort, NY

Luther, Legg
Ravena-Coeymans-S
elkirk HS
South Bethlehem,
NY

Lutz, Laura M
Westhill HS
Syracuse, NY

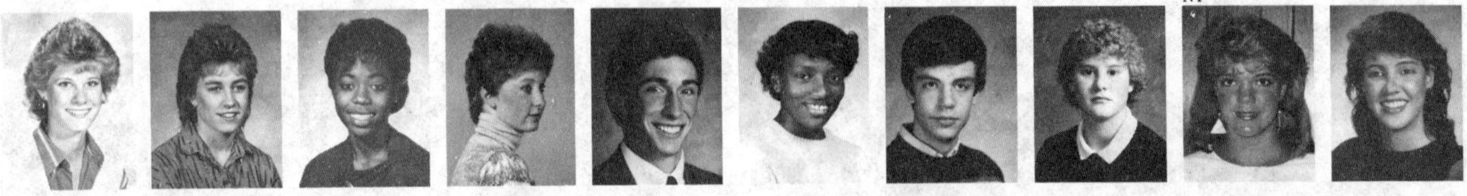

Luyster, Carrie
John H Glenn HS
Huntington, NY

Lydell, Diann
Frewsburg Central
Frewsburg, NY

Lynch, Dionne
North Eastern Acad
Jamaica, NY

Lynch, Margaret
Horseheads SR HS
Horseheads, NY

Lynch, Michael
Binghamton HS
Binghamton, NY

Lynch, Monica
Burgard Vocational
Buffalo, NY

Lynch, Tom
Grand Island HS
Grand Island, NY

Lynn, Kerri
Port Jervis HS
Montague, NJ

Mac Adam, Heather
Chittenango HS
Brideport, NY

Mac Donald,
Melissa A
Liverpool HS
Liverpool, NY

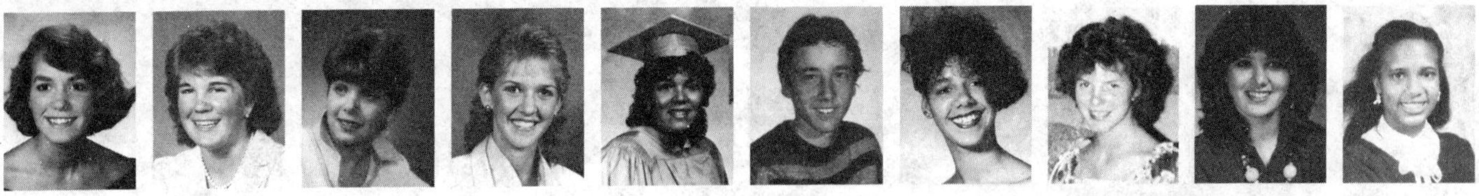

Mac Gregor, Elisabeth
Northport HS
Northport, NY

Mac Intyre, Kimberley
Delaware Academy & Central HS
Delhi, NY

Mac Neal, Stacey R
Waterloo HS
Waterloo, NY

Mac Whinney, Melissa
Ramstein Am HS
Apo New York, NY

Macaluso, Christina
South Shore HS
Brooklyn, NY

Macey, Andrew L
Farmingdale HS
Farmingdale, NY

Macias, Lissette
La Guardia HS Of Music And Arts
Elmhurst, NY

Maciborka, Julianne
William Cullen Bryant HS
Jackson Heights, NY

Mack, Kristina
West Seneca East SR HS
Cheektowaga, NY

Mack, Pamela D
Thomas A Edison Tech Voc HS
Long Island City, NY

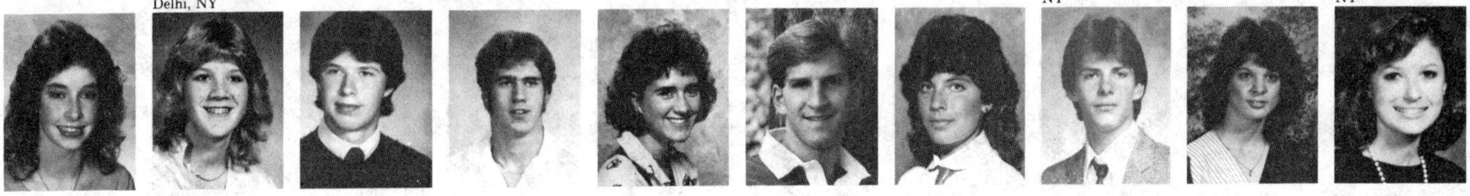

Mackenzie, Laura
Earl L Vandermeulen HS
Mt Sinai, NY

Macknik, Jacqueline
West Genesee HS
Warners, NY

Macner, Gerald J
Utica Free Acad
Remsen, NY

Macomber, III John H
Greenport HS
Greenport, NY

Macort, Shannon
Monroe Woodbury
Monroe, NY

Macray, Dennis J
Heidelberg American HS
Apo, NY

Macrini, Elizabeth
St Joseph By-The-Sea HS
Staten Island, NY

Macry, James A
James Madison HS
Brooklyn, NY

Madden, Elizabeth
Johnstown HS
Johnstown, NY

Maddock, Tara L
West Genesee SR
Camillus, NY

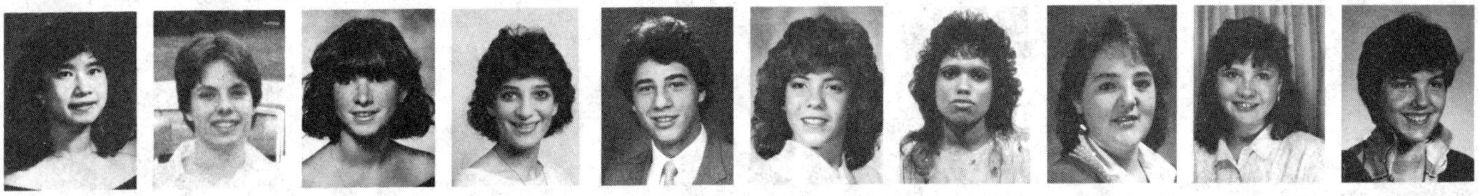

Madrigal, Elma
Cheryl Sarreal
Albertus Magnus
Orangeburg, NY

Maggio, Frank
Sachem HS
Farmingville, NY

Magistrali, Karin
Northport HS
Northport, NY

Magliocco, Laurie
Binghamton HS
Binghamton, NY

Magrino, John
St Anthonys HS
Smithtown, NY

Magro, Carol
Clarkstown South
New City, NY

Mahadeo, Sharon
John Adams HS
Richmond Hill, NY

Maher, Diane
Waterloo SR HS
Waterloo, NY

Maher, Joanne P
Massapequa HS
Massapequa Park, NY

Mahler, Elizabeth
Our Lady Of Mercy
Fairport, NY

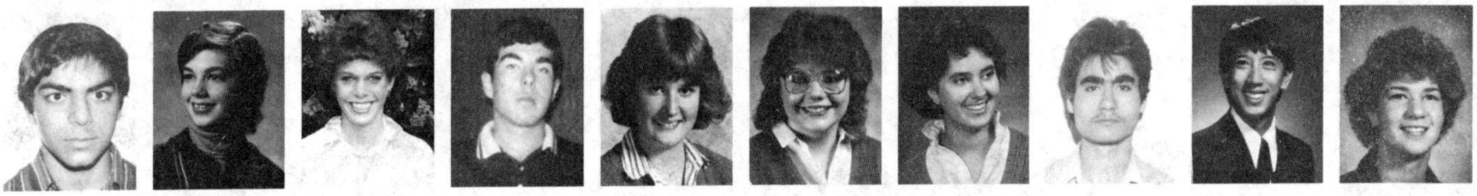

Mahmud, Urooj
Xavier HS
New York, NY

Mahoney, Amy L
Ogdensburg Free
Ogdensburg, NY

Mahoney, Danielle
Harpursville HS
Harpursville, NY

Mahoney, Kevin P
Regis HS
Brooklyn, NY

Mahoney, Margaret
Onondaga Central
Syracuse, NY

Majkowski, Lynne
West Seneca East SR HS
W Seneca, NY

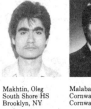

Makeyenko, Lauren
Hamburg SR HS
Hamburg, NY

Makhtin, Oleg
South Shore HS
Brooklyn, NY

Malabanan, Ariel O
Cornwall Central HS
Cornwall, NY

Malachowski, Elizabeth
Shenendehowa HS
Clifton Park, NY

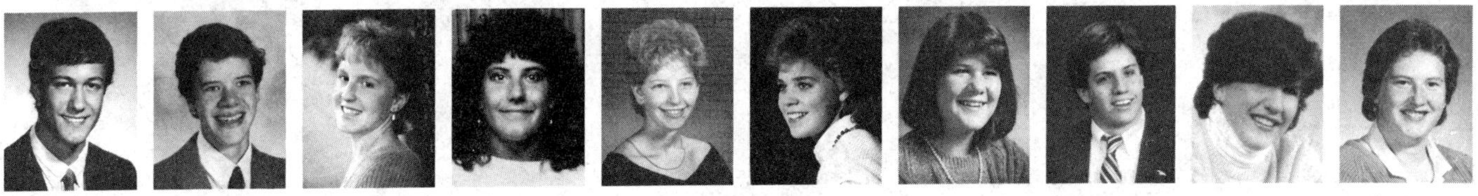

Maldonado, Thomas
Scarsdale HS
Scarsdale, NY

Maleady, Thomas
Monsignor Farrell
Staten Island, NY

Malek, Andrea R
Lyons JR & SR HS
Lyons, NY

Malin, Serena
Commack North HS
Commack, NY

Malkin, Diane L
John F Kennedy HS
Bronx, NY

Mallow, Karen L
Horseheads HS
Horseheads, NY

Malloy, Kathleen
East Syracuse-Minoa HS
Minoa, NY

Maloney, Dennis M
Arlington HS
Poughkeepsie, NY

Maloney, Erin C
Our Lady Of Mercy
Pittsford, NY

Maloney, Karen
Brewster HS
Brewster, NY

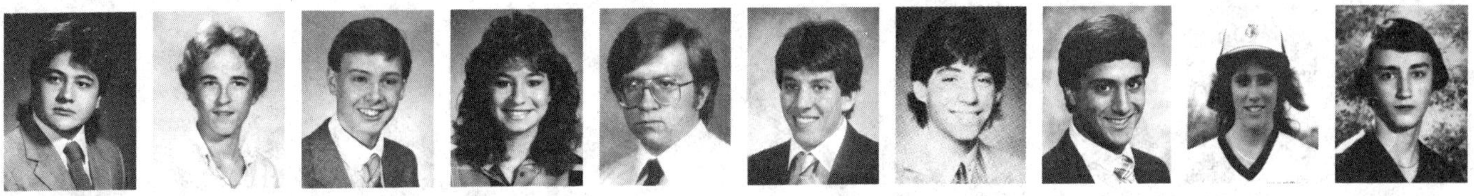

Malvarosa, Vincent M
Port Chester HS
Port Chester, NY

Mammina, Joseph
Miller Place HS
Miller Place, NY

Manchester, John I
Springville-Griffith
Springville, NY

Mancuso, Carolyn
T R Proctor HS
Utica, NY

Mandigo, James Robert
St Marys Academy Of The Nort
Corinth, NY

Maney, Patrick T
Columbia HS
Rensselaer, NY

Manfredi, Christian
Niagara Catholic HS
Lewiston, NY

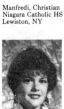

Mangano, Kenneth
Garden City SR HS
Garden City, NY

Mangone, Lori
Mamaroneck HS
Mamaroneck, NY

Manley, John
Schroon Lake Central HS
Severance, NY

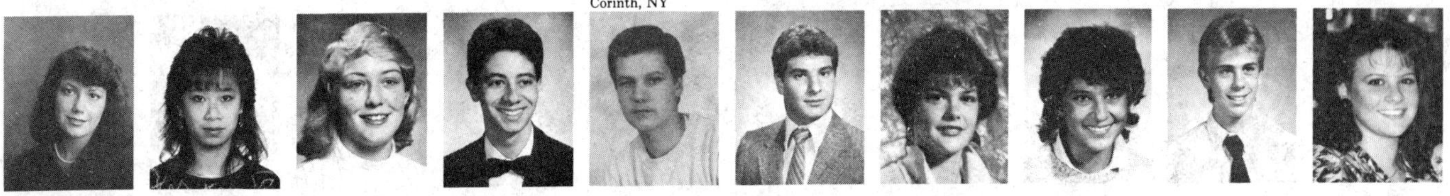

Mann, Deborah
Onondaga HS
Syracuse, NY

Manna, Lu
Seward Park HS
New York, NY

Manning, Lieann
Massena Central HS
Massena, NY

Manno, Lawrence L
St Josephs Collegiate Inst
Wmsvl, NY

Manoli, III Victor R
Cairo-Durham HS
Acra, NY

Manthey, Jeffrey
Peekskill HS
Peekskill, NY

Manus, Laura
Duanesburg Central
Delanson, NY

Manuse, Deana J
Bishop Kearney HS
Rochester, NY

Manwaring, Derek W
Oswego HS
Oswego, NY

Manzo, Gina M
St Francis Prep
W Hempstead, NY

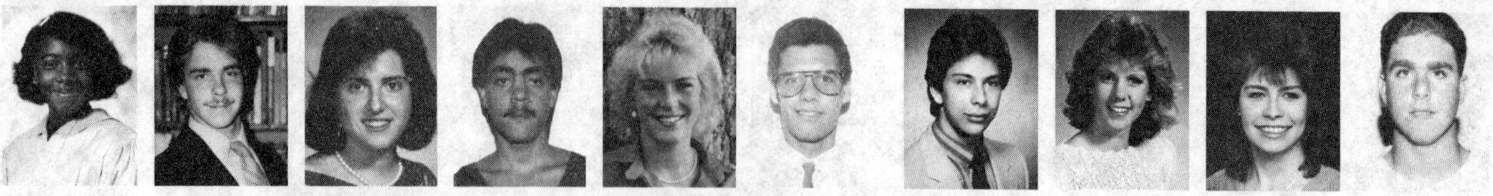

Mapp, Vanessa
Mount Saint Ursula
Bronx, NY

Marani, Jeffrey
George W Fowler
Syracuse, NY

Marans, Michelle C
Scarsdale HS
Katonah, NY

Marceda, Robert
Tottenville HS
Staten Island, NY

Marchese, Kersten C
F D Roosevelt HS
Salt Point, NY

Marchesi, Giancarlo
Westbury HS
Westbury, NY

Marchetti, Michael
Bishop Ford Central
Cath HS
Brooklyn, NY

Marciniak, Deborah
Ann
Whitesboro SR HS
Marcy, NY

Marczewski, Daena
Bennett HS
Buffalo, NY

Mare, Stephen D
Mepham HS
N Bellmore, NY

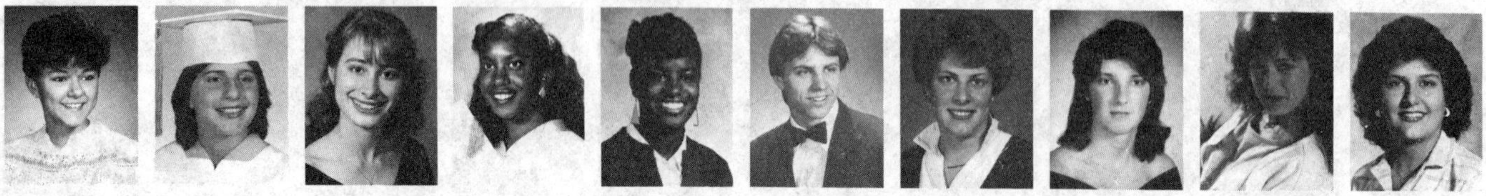

Marin, Patricia
Stuyvesant HS
Rego Park, NY

Marino, Elizabeth
Sacred Heart Acad
Malverne, NY

Marino, Virginia C
St Joseph Hill Acad
Staten Island, NY

Mark, Sonia
Catherine Mc Auley
Brooklyn, NY

Markhaim, Stefanie
Mercy HS
Albany, NY

Markowski,
Christopher
Regis HS
Maywood, NJ

Marks, Christine
Saratoga Central
Catholic HS
Gansevoort, NY

Markus, Rebecca S
Whitesboro SR HS
Utica, NY

Marlin, Melissa A
Cultural Arts HS
Westbury, NY

Marotte, Rosemarie
St John Villa Acad
Staten Island, NY

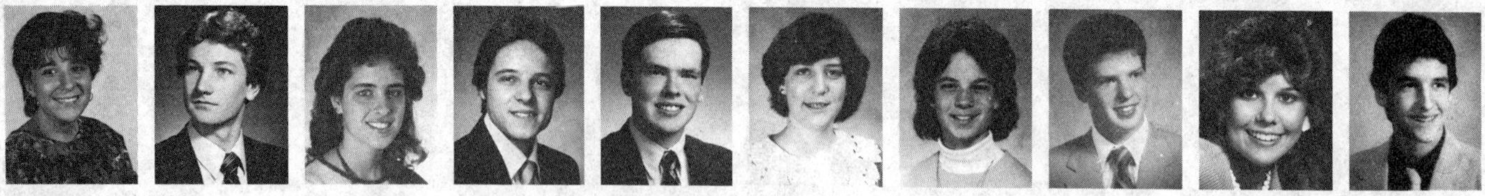

Marques, Anabella
Mineola HS
Mineola, NY

Marquette, IV
Charles
Walter Panas HS
Peekskill, NY

Marr, Susan
Waterloo SR HS
Waterloo, NY

Marriott, John
Walt Whitman HS
Huntington Sta, NY

Marsch, Peter M
Liverpool HS
Liverpool, NY

Marsh, Kelly
Brockport HS
Adams Basin, NY

Marsh, Robin S
Randolph Central
Kennedy, NY

Marsh, Steve
Massena Central HS
Massena, NY

Marshall, Michelle
Cardinal O Hara HS
Buffalo, NY

Marshall, Timothy J
Gates-Chili SR HS
Rochester, NY

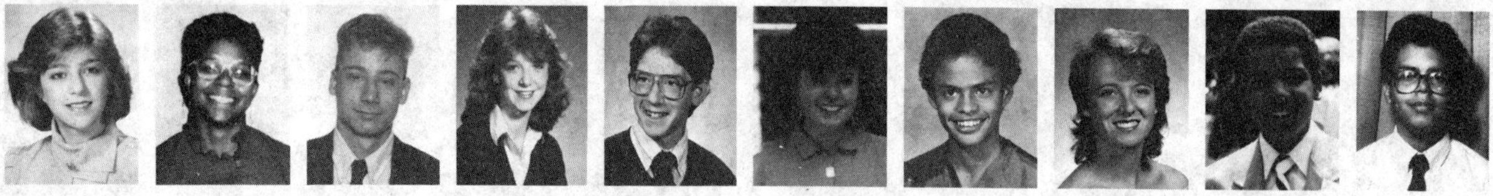

Martin, Carol A
Patchogue-Medford
Patchogue, NY

Martin, Dawn R
Hillcrest HS
Jamaica, NY

Martin, James
Saint Marys Boys
Mineola, NY

Martin, Patricia
Sacred Heart HS
Yonkers, NY

Martin, Travis L
S New Berlin
Central HS
New Berlin, NY

Martinez, Diana
St Johns Prep
Jackson Hts, NY

Martinez, Juan
Eastern District HS
Brooklyn, NY

Martinez, Melissa
Droger B Chaffer
FPO New York, NY

Martinez, Rueben
Bronx HS Of Sci
Laurelton, NY

Martinez, Sergio
Art & Design HS
New York, NY

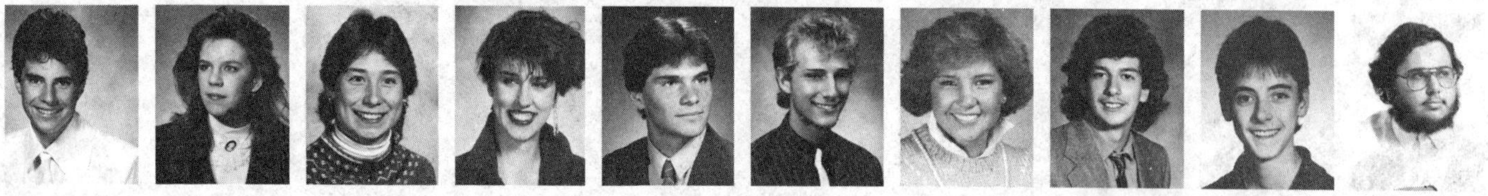

Martinez, Vincent
Lindenhurst HS
Lindenhurst, NY

Martone, Christina
A
Smithtown East
Nesconset, NY

Marvin, Rebecca
Lake Placid Central
Lake Placid, NY

Marx, Stephanie
Tonawanda SR HS
Tonawanda, NY

Mascetta, Robert
Carmel HS
Holmes, NY

Masiello, Douglas S
Allendale Columbia
Rochester, NY

Maslona, Serena
West Seneca East
SR HS
W Seneca, NY

Massa, David S
Bayside HS
Whitestone, NY

Mastandrea, Peter
East Meadow HS
East Meadow, NY

Masterov, Michael
Bronx HS Of
Tenafly, NJ

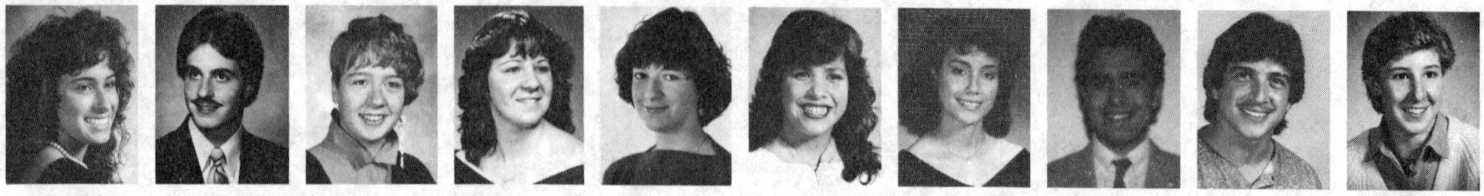

Mastronardi,
Corinne
Chenango Valley HS
Binghamton, NY

Mataragas, Kenneth
J
Babylon JR SR HS
W Babylon, NY

Mater, J Christine
Newark SR HS
Newark, NY

Matis, Theresa
St Barnabas HS
Bronx, NY

Matloft, Ellen
Geneva HS
Geneva, NY

Matos, Haydee
Msgr Scanlan HS
Bronx, NY

Matos, Zoila Yudith
Washington Irving
New York, NY

Mattas, Louis C
Patchogue-Medford
Patchogue, NY

Mattera, Richard
Sachem North HS
Holbrook, NY

Matteson, Jody
Waterville JRSR HS
Deansboro, NY

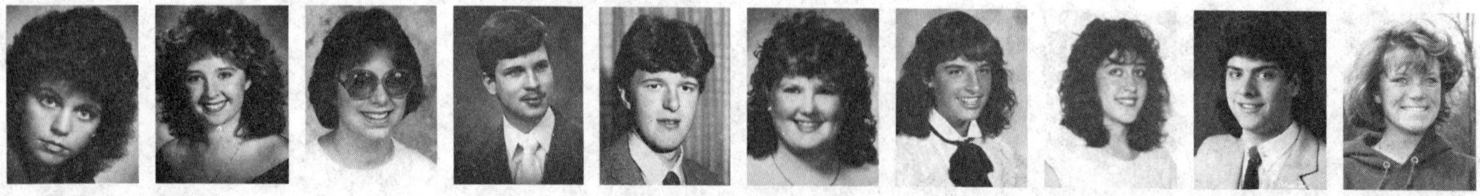

Matteson, Margaret
Gates-Chili HS
Rochester, NY

Matthews, Nancy
Lee
Grand Island HS
Grand Island, NY

Matthie, Patricia
Madrid-Waddington
JR SR HS
Lisbon, NY

Matthys, Jack
Sodus Central Schl
Sodus, NY

Mattison, Scott
Ogdensburg Free
Ogdensburg, NY

Mau, Christine
Bishop Ford HS
Brooklyn, NY

Mauro, Gina
John H Glenn HS
Huntington, NY

Mavromichalis,
Patty
H Frank Carey HS
Garden City S, NY

Maxwell, Mark K
Cortland JR SR HS
Cortland, NY

Mayer, Casey
Ward Melville HS
Stony Brook, NY

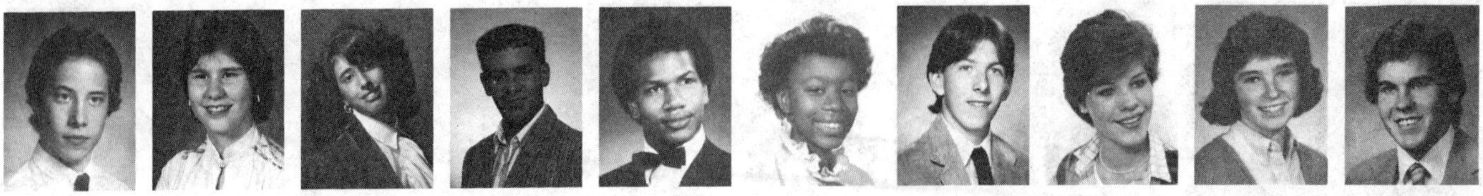

Mayer, Sonny
Cicero North
Syracuse HS
N Syracuse, NY

Mazourek, Roberta
Newfield Central
Newfield, NY

Mazza, Jennifer
Tottenville HS
Staten Island, NY

Mazzarvlli, Paul V
John Jay HS
Katonah, NY

Mc Adoo, Keith
Anthony
Half Hollow Hills
East HS
Wheatley Heights

Mc Allister, Kim
Yvette
Uniondale HS
Uniondale, NY

Mc Ardle, Thomas
M
St Marys Boys HS
Floral Park, NY

Mc Cabe, Caitlin
Roy C Ketcham HS
Poughkeepsie, NY

Mc Caffery, Jeanne
North Salem HS
Brewster, NY

Mc Carthy, Daniel
Lynn
Thomas A Edison
JR SR HS
Elmira Hts, NY

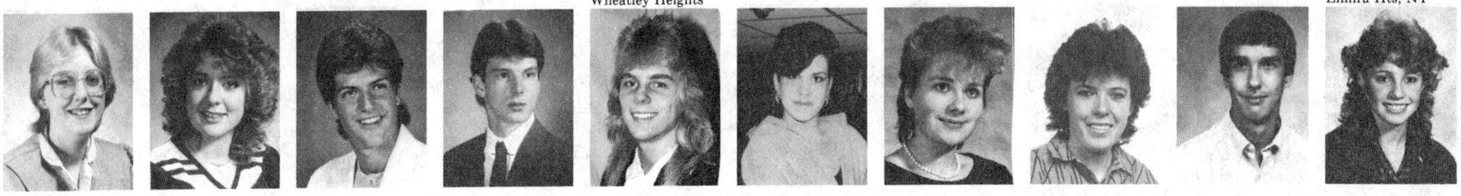

Mc Carthy, Jennifer
Cazenovia HS
Erieville, NY

Mc Carty, Sheila
Aquinas HS
Rochester, NY

Mc Carty, Skip
Odessa-Montour
Central HS
Montour Falls, NY

Mc Cauley, Thomas
G
Vestal SR HS
Binghamton, NY

Mc Closky, Mark
Scotia-Glenville HS
Scotia, NY

Mc Cord, Christine
Francis Schl
Staten Island, NY

Mc Cormack,
Elizabeth A
Pleasantville HS
Pleasantville, NY

Mc Crann, Traci A
A G Berner HS
Massapequa, NY

Mc Cullough, James
A
Jamestown HS
Jamestown, NY

Mc Cully, Kathleen
Dryden JR SR HS
Dryden, NY

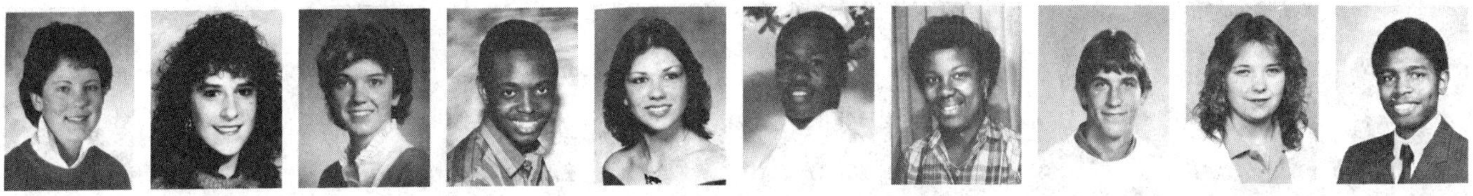

Mc Dermott, Debbie
Waterloo SR HS
Waterloo, NY

Mc Dermott,
Kimberly
Catholic Central HS
Cohoes, NY

Mc Donough,
Michele
Corning-Painted
Post West HS
Corning, NY

Mc Eachin, Andrew
Mount Vernon HS
Mt Vernon, NY

Mc Erlean,
Genevieve
Connetquot HS
Ronkonkoma, NY

Mc Fadden, Craig B
East HS
Rochester, NY

Mc Farlane, Barbara
Dominican
Commercial HS
Jamaica, NY

Mc Gayhey, Sean P
Shelter Island Union
Free Schl
Shelter Is, NY

Mc Ginnis, Melinda
John Marshall JR
SR HS
Rochester, NY

Mc Girt, Eugene A
William H Maxwell
Brooklyn, NY

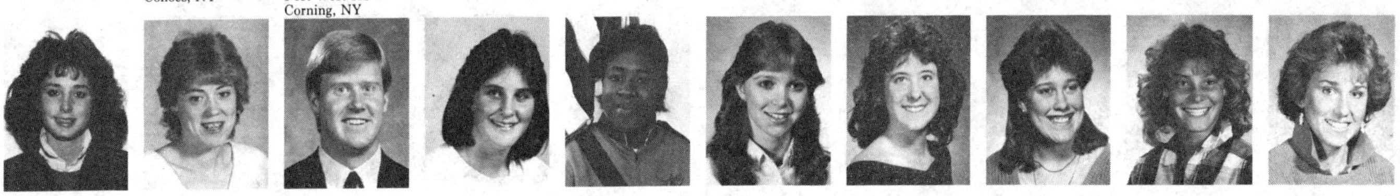

Mc Gorry, Amy
St Francis Prep
Bayside, NY

Mc Grath, Colleen
New Lebanon HS
W Lebanon, NY

Mc Grath, Timothy
St Pauls HS
Valley Stream, NY

Mc Grath, Wendi
Sachem HS
Farmingville, NY

Mc Guinness,
Lauren
Mt Vernon HS
Mt Vernon, NY

Mc Intyre, Dawn
Frewsburg Central
Jamestown, NY

Mc Intyre, Eileen
Carmel HS
Carmel, NY

Mc Kain, Mari A
Miller Place HS
Miller Pl, NY

Mc Kay, Brenda
Corning-Painted
Post West HS
Painted Post, NY

Mc Kee, Cara
Brewster HS
Brewster, NY

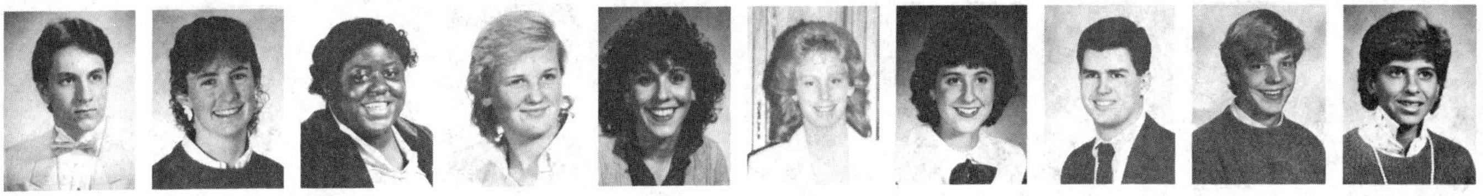

Mc Kee, Todd
West Seneca West
West Seneca, NY

Mc Kenna, Tricia
Waterloo SR HS
Waterloo, NY

Mc Kenzie, Sarah
The Franciscan
Syracuse, NY

Mc Kinnon, Mary
Cato-Meridian HS
Cato, NY

Mc Laughlin,
Carllene
Susquehanna Valley
Kirkwood, NY

Mc Laughlin,
Kathleen
Centereach HS
Centereach, NY

Mc Leod, Susan
Northstar Christian
Rochester, NY

Mc Liverty, Keith
Archbishop Molloy
Forest Hills, NY

Mc Mahon, David J
Pierson HS
Sag Harbor, NY

Mc Mahon,
Kathleen
Bishop Ludden HS
Camillus, NY

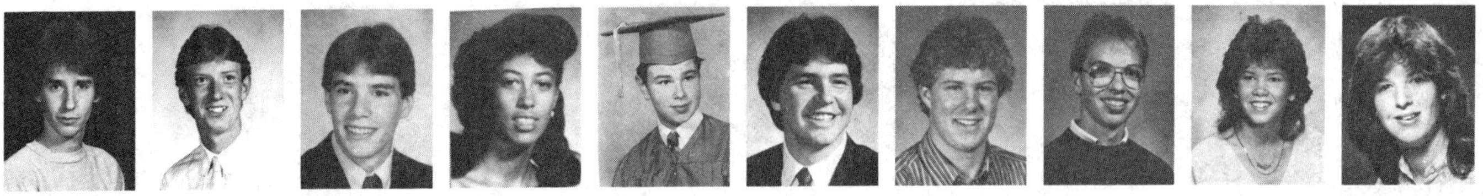

Mc Monagle, Gary
John C Birdlebough
Pennellville, NY

Mc Mullan, Jeremy
F
Rocky Pt JR SR HS
Rocky Point, NY

Mc Namara, Kerry
Saranac Lake HS
Saranac Lk, NY

Mc Near, Diana
Lynn
Acad Of Mt St
Bronx, NY

Mc Neil, Daniel
Tottenville HS
Staten Island, NY

Mc Neil, Jeff
Greece Athena HS
Rochester, NY

Mc Neil, Mark
Alden HS
Alden, NY

Mc Neill, Andrew
Geneseo Central HS
Geneseo, NY

Mc Neill, Dina
Valley Stream
Central HS
Valley Stream, NY

Mc Neill, Patricia
Lawrence HS
Inwood, NY

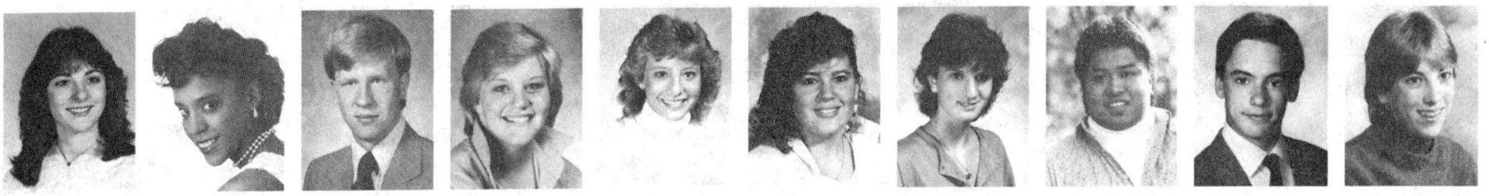

Mc Nicholas,
Rosemarie
Sacred Heart Acad
Valley Stream, NY

Mc Watt, Leslie
Malvern HS
Rockville Ctr, NY

Mead, John C
Oxford Acad
Oxford, NY

Meadowcroft,
Deanna
Stamford Central
Stamford, NY

Means, Kimberly
Brockport HS
Spencerport, NY

Meca, Kelly Anne
Amsterdam HS
Amsterdam, NY

Mech, Terri
Brockport HS
Spencerport, NY

Medalla, Apolinario
Briarcliff HS
Briarcliff, NY

Mehl, Richard R
W C Mepham HS
N Bellmore, NY

Mehlenbacher,
Connie
Charles O Dickerson
Trumansburg, NY

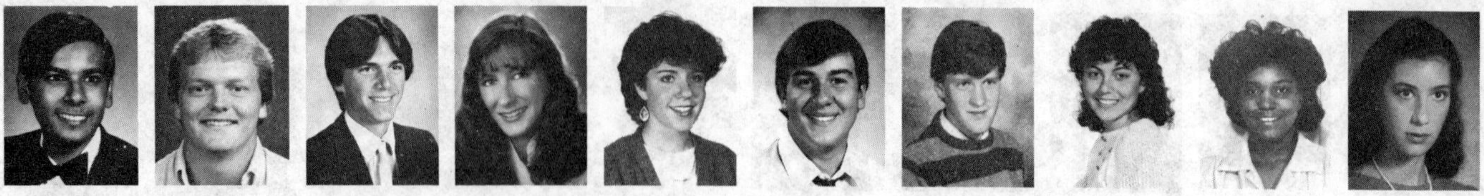

Mehta, Sujan
East Chester HS
Scarsdale, NY

Meigs, Brian
Cazenovia Central
Cazenovia, NY

Meindl, Gregory
Holy Trinity HS
Malvern, NY

Meisenzahl, Jennifer E
Our Lady Of Mercy
E Rochester, NY

Meisner, Amy
Hamburg SR HS
Hamburg, NY

Meleca, Jr Thomas J
Bishop Kearney HS
Walworth, NY

Meleco, Vincent
Catholic Central HS
Waterford, NY

Melita, Nancy
Notre Dame Bishop Gibbons HS
Schenectady, NY

Mellieon, Lisa
Bishop Loughlin
Brooklyn, NY

Meltzer, Marna Denise
Jamesville De Witt
Dewitt, NY

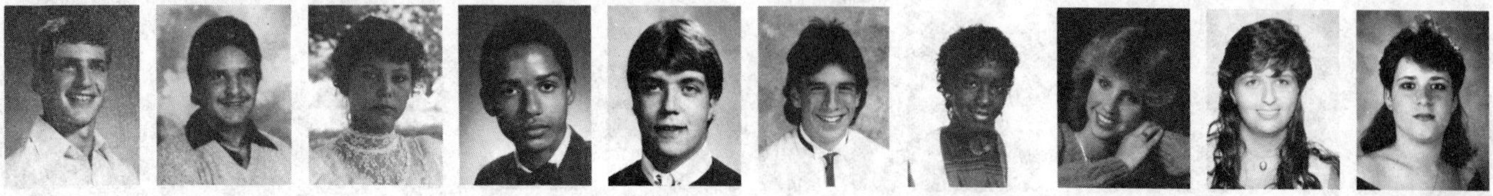

Mendel, Brett D
Vestal SR HS
Vestal, NY

Mendez, David
Amsterdam HS
Hagaman, NY

Mendez, Jo Antoinette
Julia Richman HS
Brooklyn, NY

Mendez, Trevor
Erasmus Hall HS
Brooklyn, NY

Mendy, Jr Paul B
Lackawanna SR HS
Lackawanna, NY

Menickelli, Todd
Liverpool HS
Liverpool, NY

Menifee, Kimberly
Corcoran HS
Syracuse, NY

Mensching, Sharon
Roy C Ketcham SR
Wappingers Fls, NY

Menting, Diane
Mercy HS
Shirley, NY

Menzies, Melissa M
Stella Maris HS
Far Rockaway, NY

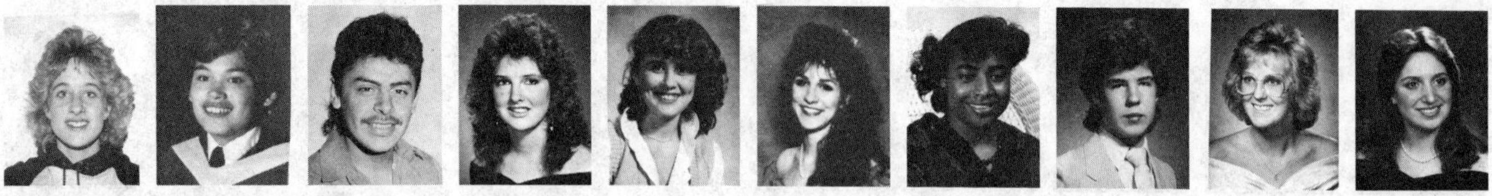

Mercado, Ana Maria
St Joseph By The Sea HS
Staten Island, NY

Mercado, Carlos
Rice HS
Bronx, NY

Merino, Armando
William Howard Taft HS
Bronx, NY

Merkel, Bonnie E
Somers HS
Purdys, NY

Merkle, Melissa
Cardinal O Hara HS
Tonawanda, NY

Merlino, Jeanette
Moore Catholic HS
Staten Island, NY

Merritt, Darlene
Wilson Magnet HS
Rochester, NY

Merritts, Danny
Walter Panas HS
Peekskill, NY

Merz, Christine A
St Francis Prep
Glendale, NY

Meschi, Nancy L
St Anthonys HS
Smithtown, NY

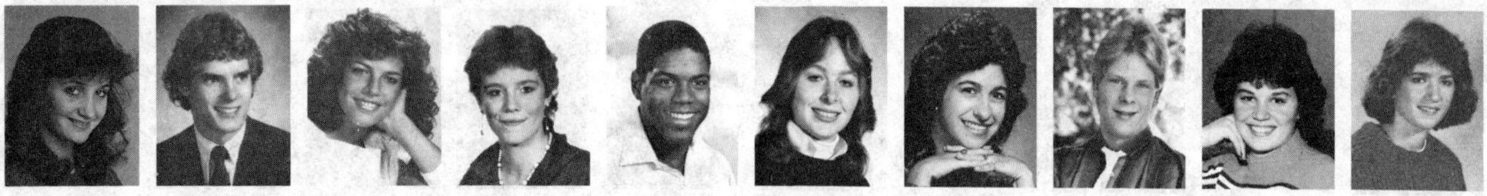

Mesler, Stacey
Monroe-Woodbury SR HS
Newburgh, NY

Mesolella, Gregory A
Greece Athena HS
Rochester, NY

Messineo, Alessandra M
John Jay HS
Hopewell Jct, NY

Mettler, Stepanie
Cato Meridian HS
Meridian, NY

Metz, Lloyd M
Horace Greeley HS
Chappaqua, NY

Meyer, Diane
Lafayette HS
Buffalo, NY

Miano, Tina M
Pine Bush HS
Bullville, NY

Micalizzi, Larry
Division Ave HS
Levittown, NY

Michalas, Christine
Warwick HS
Warwick, NY

Michaleas, Alexia
Glen Cove HS
Glen Cove, NY

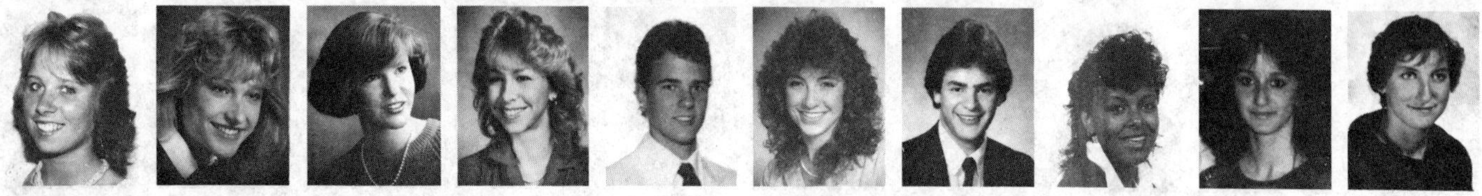

Mickoliger, Tammy
Riverhead HS
Riverhead, NY

Mielens, Melissa A
Columbia HS
E Greenbush, NY

Miett, Catherine M
Bishop Grimes HS
East Syracuse, NY

Mikolajczak, Bernadette
Immaculata Acad
Hamburg, NY

Mikula, Matthew
Plainedge Public HS
Massapequa, NY

Milborrow, Michele
Greece Athena HS
Rochester, NY

Milch, Stewart
Newfield HS
Coram, NY

Milden, Sonja R
Riverhead HS
Riverhead, NY

Mileo, Lisa A
St Francis Prep
Bellerose, NY

Miller, Cheryl
Frontier Central HS
Hamburg, NY

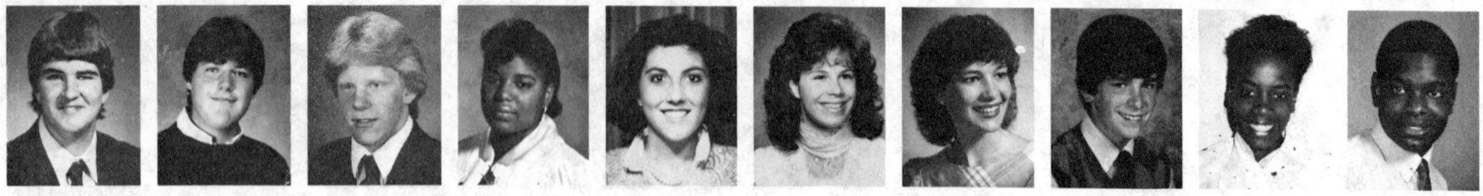

Miller, Christian
Valley Central HS
Montgomery, NY

Miller, II Dennis B
Mynderse Acad
Seneca Falls, NY

Miller, Eric W
Odessa-Montour C S
Cayuta, NY

Miller, Jeanine
Bronx H S Of
Brooklyn, NY

Miller, Jennifer
Sacred Heart Acad
Rockville Centre, NY

Miller, Joanne
Smithtown HS East
Smithtown, NY

Miller, Kimberly
Cicero North Syracuse HS
Clay, NY

Miller, Mark
Bishop Ludden HS
Syracuse, NY

Miller, Nicole L
The Bronx H S Of
Bronx, NY

Miller, Robert
Arlingotn HS
Billings, NY

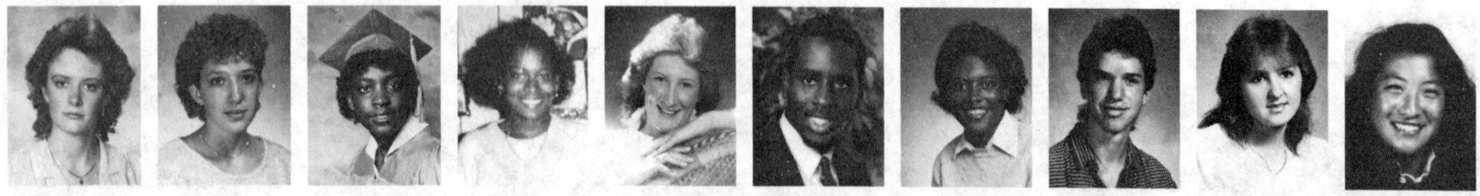

Miller, Robin
Newfield HS
Selden, NY

Miller, Sarah
Cazenovia HS
Cazenovia, NY

Miller, Stacey
St Raymond Acad
Bronx, NY

Millien, Saadiah
St Michael HS
Brooklyn, NY

Milligan, Tammie L
Pavilion Central HS
Pavilion, NY

Millington, Chris
Lafayette HS
Brooklyn, NY

Mills, Gayon
Erasmus Hall HS
Brooklyn, NY

Millward, Kevin J
Southwestern Central HS
Jamestown, NY

Milosich, Mary
Lockawanna SR HS
Lackawanna, NY

Min, Julie Elizabeth
East Islip HS
East Islip, NY

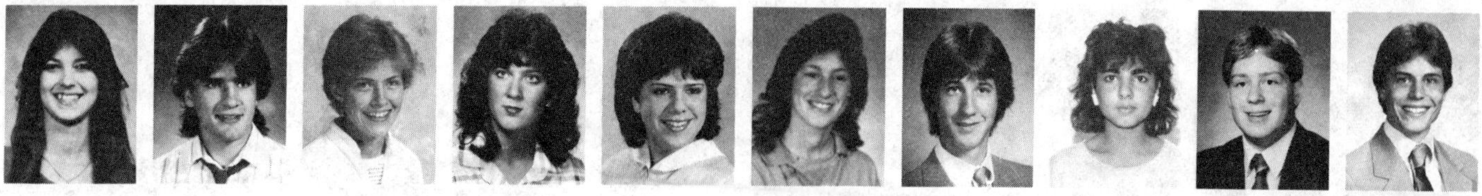

Mineo, Melanie
Depew HS
Depew, NY

Miner, II Marvin C
Palmyra-Macedon
Macedon, NY

Miner, Michele
Liverpool HS
Liverpool, NY

Minucci, Susan
Sachem HS
Ronkonkoma, NY

Mirabile, Dina
Christ The King HS
Howard Beach, NY

Miranda, Joelle
Cleveland Hill HS
Cheektowaga, NY

Mirguet, Peter S
Greece Athena HS
Rochester, NY

Mirza, Samira
New Rochelle HS
New Rochelle, NY

Misita, Jr Robert M
East Islip HS
East Islip, NY

Miska, Steven M
Greenport HS
Greenport, NY

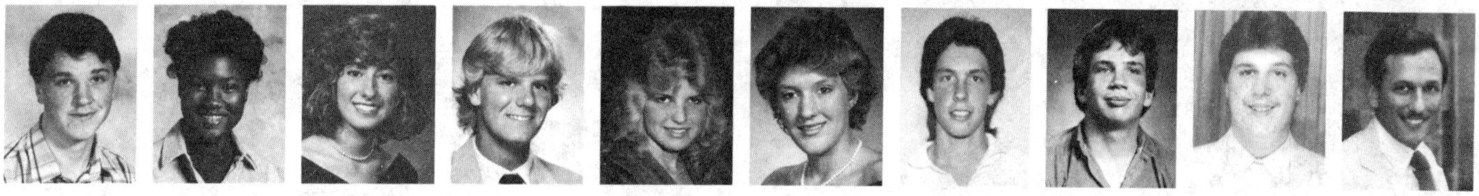

Missana, Mark
Burnt Hills Ballston Lake HS
Scotia, NY

Mitchell, Joy
Ward Melville HS
Stony Brook, NY

Mitchell, Lorelei B
Tappan Zee HS
Sparkill, NY

Mitola, Daniel
Islip HS
Islip, NY

Mittak, Micheline M
Newark SR HS
Newark, NY

Moak, Kris
Ravena-Coeymans-Selkirk HS
Ravena, NY

Moakley, John
Tottenville HS
Staten Island, NY

Modugno, Robert Anthony A
Henninger HS
Syracuse, NY

Moffitt, II Thomas J
N Babylon SR HS
N Babylon, NY

Mohr, David J
Arlington HS
Poughkeepsie, NY

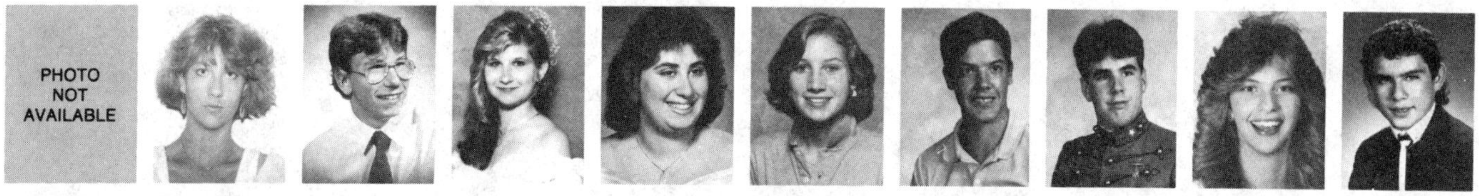
PHOTO
NOT
AVAILABLE

Molea, Anthony J
Iona Prep
New Rochelle, NY

Molenda, Janice
Jamesville-Dewitt
Dewitt, NY

Molesworth, Keith
Onondaga Central
Syracuse, NY

Molinelli, Kim
Tottenville HS
Staten Island, NY

Mollo, Dina M
St Francis Preparatory HS
Fresh Meadows, NY

Monachino, Jennifer L
Pelham Memorial
Pelham Manor, NY

Monaco, Keith Dwight
Hampton Bays HS
Hampton Bays, NY

Monahan, Daniel
La Salle Military
College Pt, NY

Mondrick, Patty
Mexico Academy &
Oswego, NY

Monks, Jr Joseph
Elmont Memorial
Valley Stream, NY

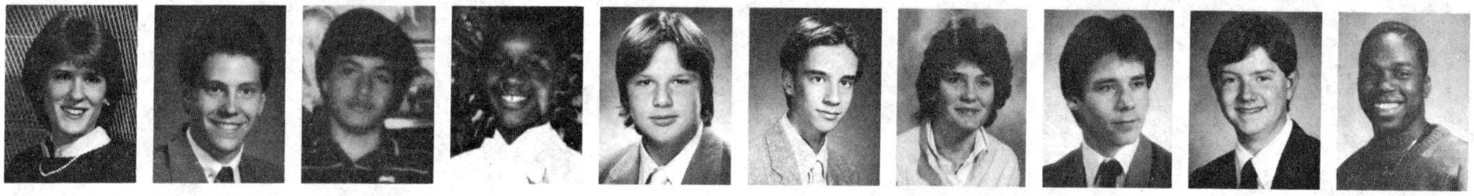

Monroe, Dorie
Schuylerville Central
Gansevoort, NY

Monroe, Jeffery D
Batavia HS
Batavia, NY

Montalvo, Robert
HS For The
New York, NY

Montgomery, Charles
Turner/Carroll HS
Buffalo, NY

Montilli, T J
Lawrence HS
Cedarhurst, NY

Montross, William
Rhinebeck Central
Rhinebeck, NY

Moonen, Jill
Vernon-Verona-Sherrill HS
Verona, NY

Moonen, Peter
Vernon Verona Sherrill Central Schl
Verona, NY

Moore, Alec T
Utica Free Acad
Utica, NY

Moore, Charles
Uniondale HS
Uniondale, NY

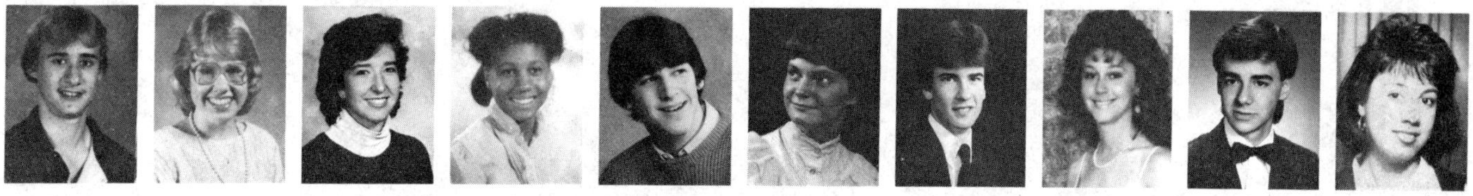

Moore, Daniel
Schenectady Christian Schl
Alplaus, NY

Moore, Julie
Greece Olympia HS
Rochester, NY

Moore, Maureen
Jamesville-De Witt
De Witt, NY

Moore, Patty
Woodlands HS
White Plains, NY

Moore, Richard
Norman Howard
Pittsford, NY

Moore, Susan
Charles H Roth HS
Rochester, NY

Morabito, Thomas C
Lewis C Obourn HS
East Rochester, NY

Moraci, Jennifer
Centereach HS
Centereach, NY

Morales, Albert
Regis HS
Englewood Cliff, NJ

Morales, Milagros
St Raymond Acad
Bronx, NY

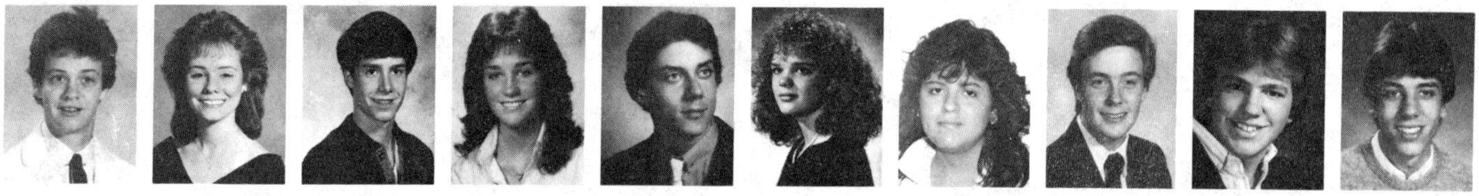

Moran, Brian
Monsingnor Farrell
Staten Island, NY

Moran, Donna
St Peters HS For
Staten Island, NY

Moran, Joseph D
Sidney Central HS
Sidney, NY

Moran, Maria M
Our Lady Of Mercy
Massapequa Park, NY

Moran, Michael
Victor Central HS
Victor, NY

Moran, Michelle N
Mamaroneck HS
Larchmont, NY

Moran, Roxana E
Lynbrook HS
Lynbrook, NY

Morel, John J
Monsignor Farrell
Staten Island, NY

Moreland, Michael R
Owego Free Acad
Owego, NY

Morell, John
Pal-Mac HS
Palmyra, NY

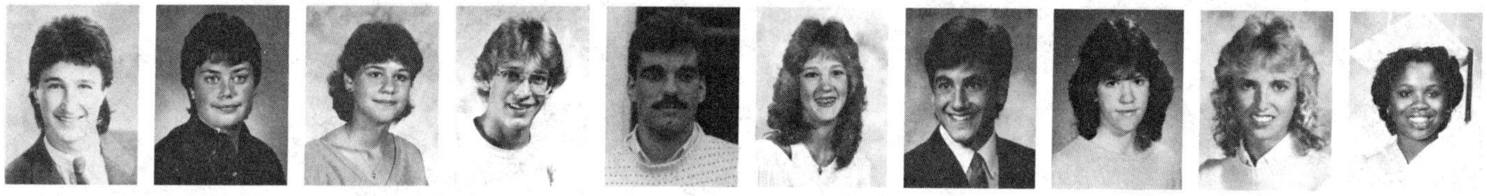

Morelli, Joseph Peter
Bishop Grimes HS
Syracuse, NY

Morgan, Elizabeth
York Central HS
Linwood, NY

Morgan, Michelle
Greece Athena SR
Rochester, NY

Morgante, Pat
Frontier SR HS
Hamburg, NY

Moriarty, Brenden S
Millbrook Prep Schl
Millbrook, NY

Morreale, Kelly
Amsterdam HS
Amsterdam, NY

Morreale, Matthew G
Garden City SR HS
Garden City, NY

Morris, April
Valley Central HS
Montgomery, NY

Morris, Carol
Minisink Valley HS
Middletown, NY

Morris, Lyssa Michelle
Hillcrest HS
Jamaica, NY

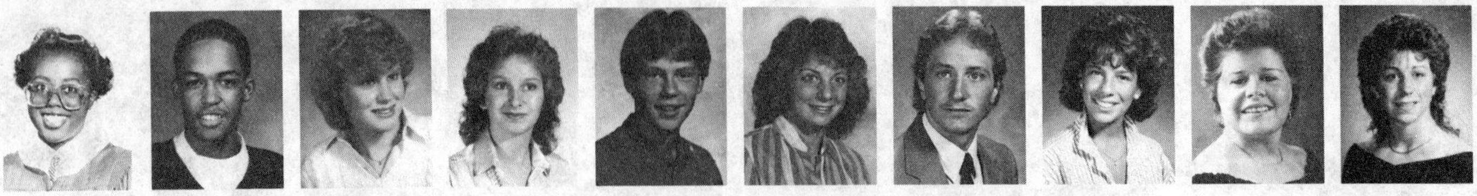

Morris, Marsedean
Evander Childs HS
Bronx, NY

Morris, Shawn
Churchville Chili HS
Rochester, NY

Morrow, Vangie Jill
Churchville-Chili SR
Rochester, NY

Morse, Adrienne
Alexander Central
Alexander, NY

Morse, Richard
Groton JR SR HS
Groton, NY

Mortillaro, Denise
Clarkstown Nroth
Congers, NY

Mosack, Philip
Pine Valley Central
S Dayton, NY

Moses, Michele
John F Kennedy HS
Plainview, NY

Mosier, Carmen
La Salle SR HS
Niagara Falls, NY

Mosunic, Lisa
Lakeland HS
Yorktown Hts, NY

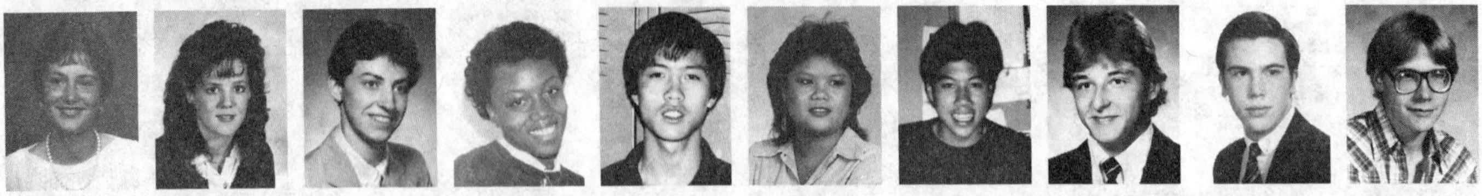

Mott, Andrea
Harpursville JR-SR
Port Crane, NY

Moulin, Andrea
Moore Catholic HS
Staten Island, NY

Moulton, Steven B
Sachem HS
Lk Ronkonkoma, NY

Moultrie, Mercedes Y
Wilson Magnet HS
Rochester, NY

Moy, Edward
Seward Park HS
New York, NY

Moy, Helen
Wagner HS
Staten Island, NY

Moy, Robert J
South Shore HS
Brooklyn, NY

Mueller, Rob
Baldwin HS
Baldwin, NY

Mulet, Jr Luis
Garden Schl
Flushing, NY

Mulford, Todd
Windham-Ashland
Jewett Central HS
Windham, NY

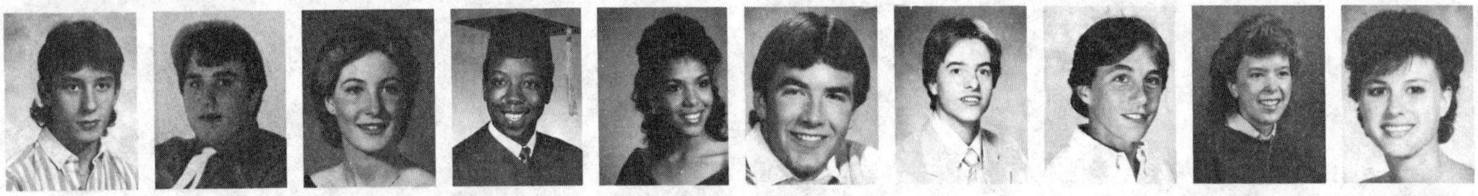

Mulhall, John
Odessa Montour Cntrl HS
Montour Falls, NY

Mulholland, Daniel
Bishop Ford Central Catholic HS
Brooklyn, NY

Mulvehill, Ann M
St Joseph Hill Acad
Brooklyn, NY

Mungin, Melvin
Mount Vernon HS
Mount Vernon, NY

Muniz, Yolanda
Maria Regina HS
Yorktown Hghts, NY

Munroe, II James
Marcus Whitman
Canandaigua, NY

Munyak, John
Smithtown High School East
Nesconset, NY

Mura, Jr John
Paul V Moore HS
Brewerton, NY

Muralt, Gina
Ramstein HS
Apo New York, NY

Muraski, Michelle
Guilderland Central
Schenectady, NY

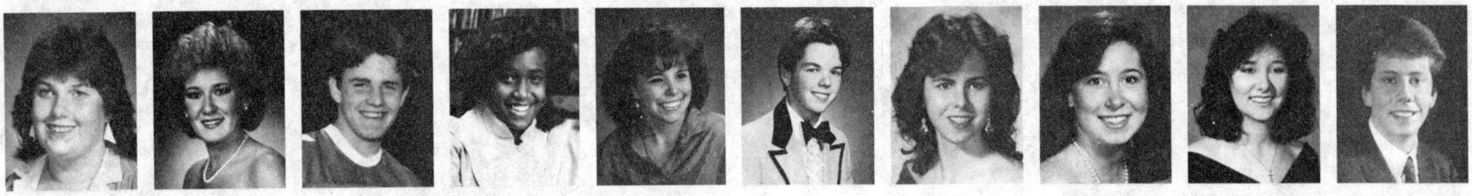

Murdock, Ronda
Mynderse Acad
Seneca Falls, NY

Murney, Joell
Waterloo SR HS
Clyde, NY

Murphy, Brian H
St Francis Prep
Fresh Meadows, NY

Murphy, Celeste Michele
Freeport HS
Freeport, NY

Murphy, Christine
Roosevelt HS
Yonkers, NY

Murphy, Edward
Sacred Heart HS
Yonkers, NY

Murphy, Linda
West Babylon SR
W Babylon, NY

Murphy, Melisa
Somers HS
Granite Spgs, NY

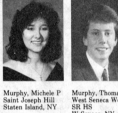

Murphy, Michele P
Saint Joseph Hill
Staten Island, NY

Murphy, Thomas
West Seneca West SR HS
W Seneca, NY

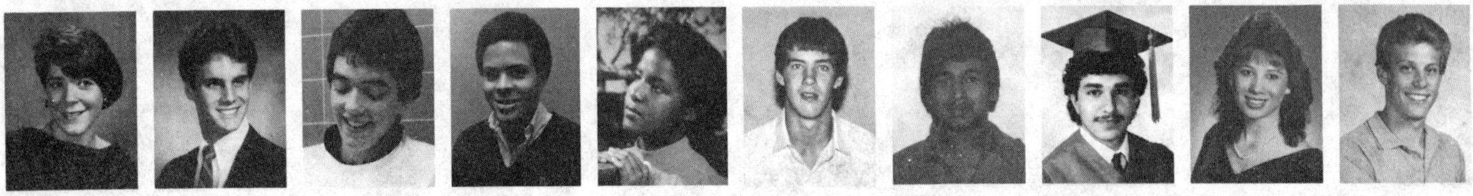

Murray, Cynthia
Ramstein American
Apo New York, NY

Murray, Robert W
Guilderland Central
Guilderland, NY

Murray, Jr Thomas N
Eastchester HS
Scarsdale, NY

Murray, Tracy
Edison Technical & Industrial HS
Rochester, NY

Murray, Uwada
Midwood
Atbrooklyn Colleg
Brooklyn, NY

Murtaugh, Jeff
Holland Patent Central HS
Holland Patent, NY

Musa, Rhajkumar
Amityville Memorial
Amityville, NY

Mustafa, Bekir S
T A Edison Voc Tech HS
Beechhurst, NY

Muszynski, Graceann
Monsignor Scanlan
Flushing, NY

Muth, Eric R
Binghamton HS
Binghamton, NY

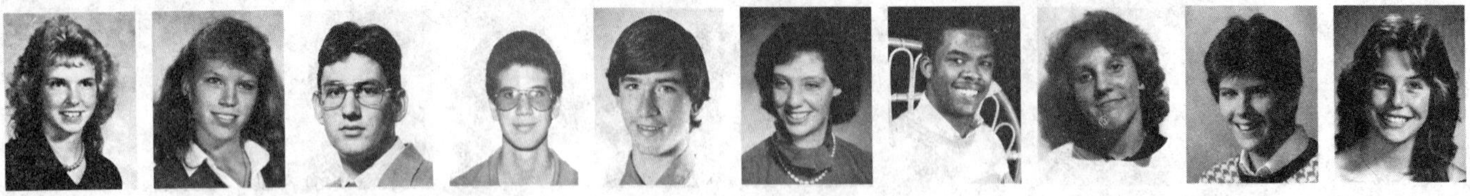

Muth, Tamara
Windham-Ashland-Jewett Central HS
E Jewett, NY

Muthig, Susan
Fairport HS
Fairport, NY

Myer, Darren
Sargerties HS
Saugerties, NY

Myers, Allan
New Rochelle HS
Scarsdale, NY

Myers, Daniel
St Agnes HS
Long Island City, NY

Myers, Kristin
Owego Free Acad
Owego, NY

Myree, Troy
Buffalo Tradional
Buffalo, NY

Mytko, Dodie
Sachem North HS
Lake Ronkonkoma, NY

Nacy, Karolyn
Hudson Falls HS
Hudson Falls, NY

Nagle, Kelly Ann
Lakeland HS
Yorktown Hts, NY

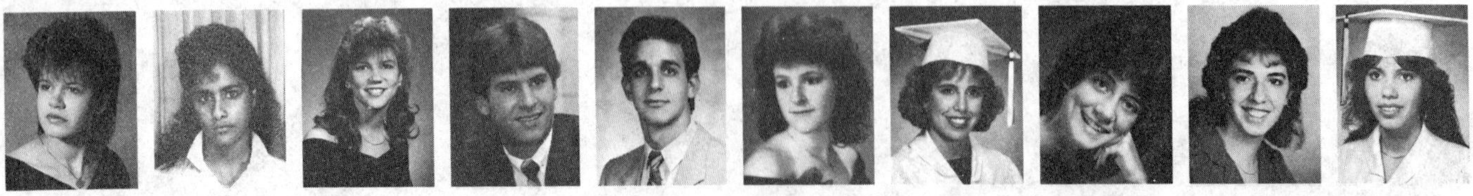

Napoli, Theresa M
St Joseph Hill Acad
Staten Island, NY

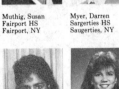

Naraindat, Aheliya
Amityville Memorial
Amityville, NY

Nash, Karen
Carmel HS
Carmel, NY

Naso, Mark W
Highland HS
Highland, NY

Nasoulis, Demetrios
Flushing HS
College Point, NY

Nass, Rachael
Lafayette HS
Brooklyn, NY

Nastri, Annmarie
Plainedge HS
N Massapequa, NY

Naum, Tamra
East Syracuse HS
East Syracuse, NY

Navarra, Christina
New Lebanon Central School
E Nassau, NY

Nazario, Michelle
W Hempstead HS
West Hempstead, NY

Neal, Victoria
John C Birdlebough
Phoenix, NY

Neale, Kelly
Sharon Springs
Central Schl
Sharon Springs, NY

Neddo, Tammy
Auburn HS
Auburn, NY

Nee, Samantha
St Vincent Ferrer
Jackson Hts, NY

Neger, Marybeth
St John The Baptist
Smithtown, NY

Negus, Douglas
Westhill HS
Syracuse, NY

Nejman, Rachel
Clarkstown HS
New City, NY

Nelson, Charles A
Lake Shore HS
Angola, NY

Nemec, Nancy
Schoharie Central
Central Bridge, NY

Nemeth, Gary
Newfield HS
Selden, NY

Nentwich, Kevin M
Sachem HS
Holbrook, NY

Neri, John
Corinth HS
Corinth, NY

Neri, Philip
North Babylon HS
No Babylon, NY

Neron, Sabita
Walton HS
Bronx, NY

Nesbitt, Tanya
Jane Addams HS
Bronx, NY

Nester, M Noel
Long Beach HS
Lido Beach, NY

Neumann, Roberta
York Central HS
Leicester, NY

Nevins, Grace
Onteora Central HS
Boiceville, NY

Newburg,
Bernadette T
St Joseph Hill Acad
Staten Island, NY

Newkirk, Nisa
Newburgh Free
Newburgh, NY

Newman, Betina
Rose
George W Fowler
Syracuse, NY

Newman, Dina
Jamesville-De Witt
Dewitt, NY

Newman, Jennifer
Poughkeepsie HS
Poughkeepsie, NY

Newman, Kathe
Carmel HS
Carmel, NY

Newmark, Scott
H Frank Carey HS
W Hempstead, NY

Ng, Debbie
James Madison HS
Brooklyn, NY

Nguyen, Jeanne
Diep
Roy C Ketcham HS
Wappingers Fls, NY

Nguyen, Theresa T
H
The Mary Louis
Mineola, NY

Nguyen, Yun
Roy C Ketcham HS
Wappinger Fls, NY

Nichols, Amy
Canaseraga Central
Swain, NY

Nicholson, Jason
Penn Yan Acad
Bluff Point, NY

Nickerson, Michael
Dover JR SR HS
Wingdale, NY

Nicklaus, James J
Southern Cayuga
Central Schl
Genoa, NY

Nickles, Timothy C
Jamestown HS
Jamestown, NY

Niclas, Tania
Mohonasen SR HS
Schenectady, NY

Nicolellis, Kevin J
Longwood HS
Yaphank, NY

Nicosia, Joseph
Greenville HS
Climax, NY

Niedzielski, Robert
J
Kingston HS
Kingston, NY

Nikolaus, Lisa
Sharon Springs
Central Schl
Sharon Springs, NY

Nikstenas, Joseph E
Amsterdam HS
Amsterdam, NY

Nikstenas, Judianne
Amsterdam HS
Amsterdam, NY

Niles, Bill
Port Jervis HS
Port Jervis, NY

Nilsen, Joanne
St Anthonys HS
Massapequa, NY

Nin, Carol Noell
Victor Central HS
Condado, PR

Nirenberg, Melissa J
Ardsley HS
Dobbs Ferry, NY

Nisanian, Anahid
Jaquelline
Forest Hills HS
Sunnyside, NY

Nitkin, Angela
Christopher
Columbus HS
Bronx, NY

Nitkowski, Denise E
Cheektowaga
Central HS
Cheektowaga, NY

Nitto, Pam
Susquehanna Valley
Binghamton, NY

Nittolo, Francine E
Bishop Kearney HS
Brooklyn, NY

Noah, Robert
Brewster HS
Patterson, NY

Noble, Denise
Hugh C Williams
Canton, NY

Nobre, Elizabeth
Dominican
Commercial HS
Jamaica, NY

Noga, IV Joseph L
Mcquiad Jesuit HS
Rochester, NY

Nolan, Courtney
Notre Dame HS
New York, NY

Nolan, Robert S
Christian Brothers
Liverpool, NY

Nolan, Teresa
The Mary Louis
Bellerose, NY

Noldan, Nancy
Fayetteville-Manlius
Fayetteville, NY

Noles, Charles B
City Honors Schl
Buffalo, NY

Noll, Nancy M
Jamesville-Dewitt
Fayetteville, NY

Nolletti, Natasha
Munich American
Apo New York, NY

Nolte, Laura
Lakeland SR HS
Mohegan Lake, NY

Norden, Paul
Msgr Farrell HS
Staten Island, NY

Norris, Susan
West Irondequoit
Rochester, NY

Norwood, Consuelo
Uniondale HS
Uniondale, NY

Noval, Tara L
Allendale Columbia
Pittsford, NY

Novelle, Monica
Margaretville
Central HS
Arkville, NY

Novosat, Deanna
North Tonawanda
SR HS
N Tonawanda, NY

Nowack, Cynthia
Buffalo Seminary
E Aurora, NY

Nowak, Gregory
Depew HS
Depew, NY

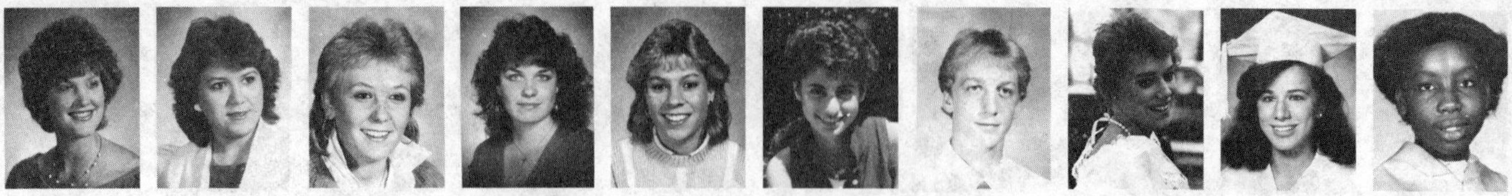

Nowak, Julie
Albion Central HS
Albion, NY

Nowak, Kathleen
Frontier Central HS
Blasdell, NY

Nowhitney, Lisa
Franklin Central
Franklin, NY

Nowyj, Donna M
Westhill HS
Syracuse, NY

Noyes, Gretchen
G Ray Bodley HS
Fulton, NY

Nugget, Hope
Centereach HS
Centereach, NY

Numssen, Erik
Saugerties HS
Saugerties, NY

Nunziato, Marisa
Ravena-Coeymans-S
elkirk HS
Ravena, NY

Nur, Peggy
The Mary Louis
Sunrise, FL

Nwankpa, Onyinye
Dewitt Clinton HS
Bronx, NY

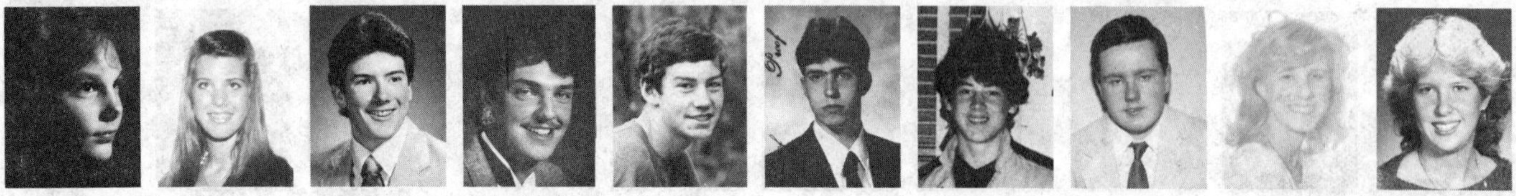

O Brien, Cassandra
Oneida SR HS
Oneida, NY

O Brien, Jennifer
Smithtown H S East
Saint James, NY

O Brien, Kevin
Walter Panas HS
Peekskill, NY

O Brien, Patrick
Michael
Mynderse Acad
Seneca Falls, NY

O Connell, John J
St Peters Boys HS
Staten Island, NY

O Connor, Denis J
Copiague HS
Copaigue, NY

O Connor, Jr
Edmund A
Mount Saint
Michael Acad
Bronx, NY

O Connor, Sean P
St Francis
Prepartatory Schl
New York, NY

O Donnell, Kerry
Sacred Heart Acad
East Meadow, NY

O Donnell, Mary T
Floral Park
Memorial HS
Floral Park, NY

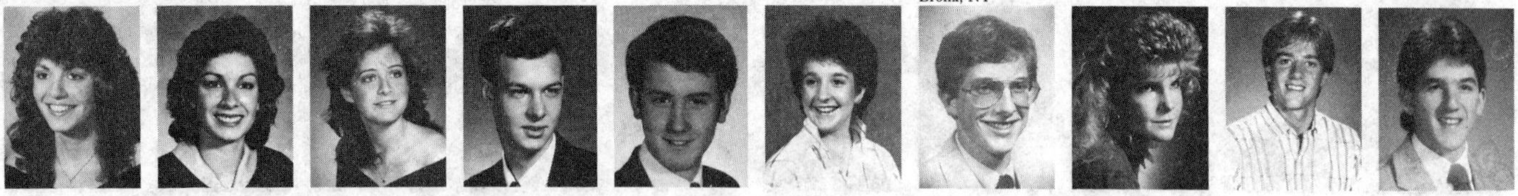

O Donnell, Phyllis
Marie
St Joseph
By-The-Sea HS
Staten Island, NY

O Hanlon, Denise
New Dorp HS
Staten Island, NY

O Hara, Kathleen
Saint Barnabas HS
Bronx, NY

O Hara, Jr Peter W
F D Roosevelt HS
Hyde Park, NY

O Hearn, Brendan
Northport HS
Northport, NY

O Leary, Kelly
Whitesboro SR HS
Whitesboro, NY

O Leyar, Stephen C
Irondequoit HS
Rochester, NY

O Malley, Theresa
Lee
Troy HS
Troy, NY

O Neil, Sean
Michael
Our Lady Of
Lourdes HS
Newburgh, NY

O Neil, Timothy B
North Tonawanda
N Tonawanda, NY

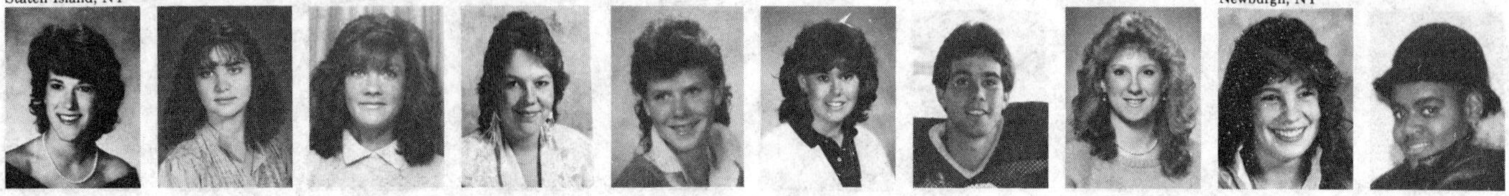

O Neill, Christa
West Babylon SR
West Babylon, NY

O Shea, Janet M
Yorktown HS
Yorktown Height,
NY

O Shea, Karen
Moore Catholic HS
Staten Island, NY

Ochsner, Vicki
Onodaga HS
Lafayette, NY

Oconnell, Loraine
Deposit Central Schl
Deposit, NY

Oconnell, Pattie
Commack HS North
Commack, NY

Oconnor, John
St John The Baptist
Selden, NY

Oconnor, Loren
Smithtown HS East
Nesconset, NY

Oconnor, Michelle
Mahopac HS
Carmel, NY

Odom, Kelsey
Bishop Loughlin HS
Brooklyn, NY

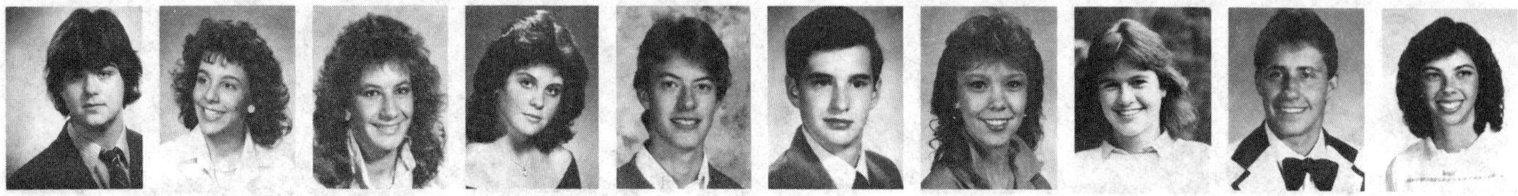

Odonnell, Patrick
Linton HS
Schenectady, NY

Oelcher, Shannon
Smithtown HS East
Saint James, NY

Ogden, Eleanor
Centereach HS
Selden, NY

Ohalloran, Patricia
M
St Barnabas HS
Bronx, NY

Ohland, Mark
Liverpool HS
Liverpool, NY

Ohmann, Kyle
Saranac Lake HS
Saranac Lk, NY

Okal, Cheryl
Alden Central HS
Alden, NY

Olds, Elizabeth M
The Fieldston Schl
New York, NY

Olender, Jeffrey J
Msgr Farrell HS
Staten Island, NY

Olivari, Susan
Rocky Point JR SR
Rocky Point, NY

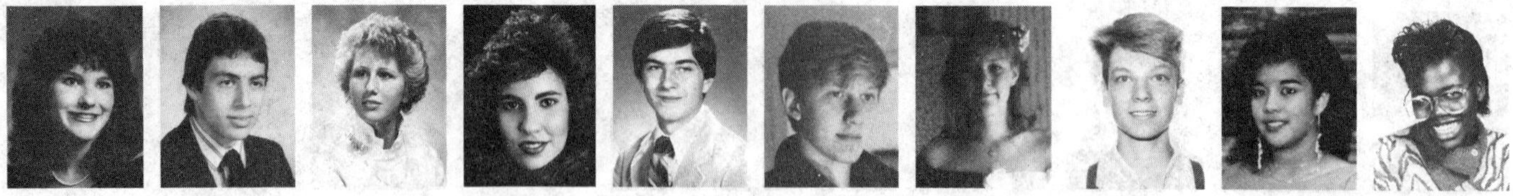

Olivella, Suzanne M
Notre Dame HS
Utica, NY

Oliver, Jason R
Livonia HS
Lakeville, NY

Oliver, Karen D
Canaseraga Central
Canaseraga, NY

Olivier, Michele
Jericho SR HS
Jericho, NY

Oliviero, Anthony J
Lawrence HS
Cedarhurst, NY

Olsen, Garrick
John Jay SR HS
Goldens Bridge, NY

Olsen, Lori
Bayport-Blue Point
Bayport, NY

Olson, John
Archbishop Molloy
Bellerose, NY

Ongjoco, Roxanne C
S
Perry Central HS
Perry, NY

Onyeije, Iheoma U
Liverpool HS
Liverpool, NY

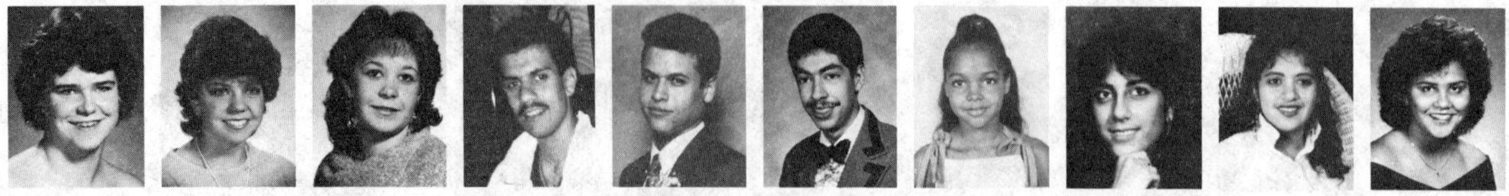

Orange, Joann
Roy C Ketcham HS
Hughsonville, NY

Orchard, Julie
Byron Bergen
Central HS
Bergen, NY

Oricchio, Janice
Saunder Trades &
Technical HS
Yonkers, NY

Orlando, Nicky
Tottenville HS
Staten Isld, NY

Ortega, Jr Jose
Bishop Ford Central
Catholic HS
Brooklyn, NY

Ortega, Luis F
August Martin HS
Brooklyn, NY

Ortiz, Carmen A
Bushwick HS
New York, NY

Ortiz, Christine
The Acad Of St
Pt Jeff Sta, NY

Ortiz, Diane
South Park HS
Buffalo, NY

Ortiz, Gloria I
Cardinal Spellman
Bronx, NY

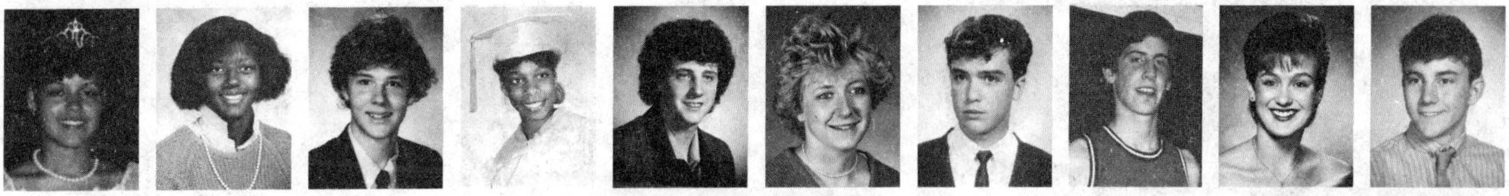

Ortiz, Jeanette
Murry Bergtraum
Brooklyn, NY

Osa-Yande, Cadisa
Sweet Home SR HS
North Tonawanda, NY

Osborne, David P
East Hampton HS
East Hampton, NY

Osbourne, Alethia
Bishop Laughlin Memorial HS
Brooklyn, NY

Osinski, James
Cicero-North Syracuse HS
N Syracuse, NY

Osinski, Mary
Eden Central HS
Eden, NY

Osmond, Thomas A
East Aurora HS
E Aurora, NY

Osterman, Jeff
Archbishop Stepinac
White Plains, NY

Osterwald, Anne Marie
Dominican Commercial HS
Queens Village, NY

Ostrander, Brent
Paul V Moore HS
Central Sq, NY

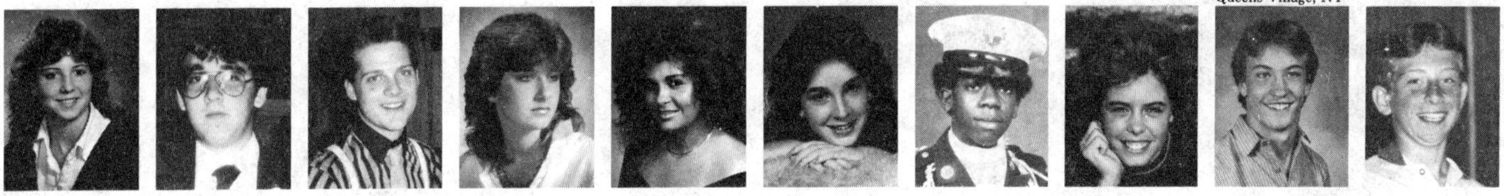

Ostrander, Joanne
Onteora Central HS
Willow, NY

Ostrow, Alex
West Hempstead
Island Park, NY

Ottaviano, Mark
Martin Van Buren
New York, NY

Ottman, Kristen A
G Ray Bodley HS
Fulton, NY

Ottuso, Maria
Preston HS
Bronx, NY

Ovady, Elizabeth
Stamford Central
S Kortright, NY

Owens, Edward V
Xavier HS
New York, NY

Owens, Stacy
Holland Patent HS
Holland Patent, NY

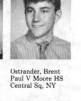

Paar, Sean
Olean HS
Olean, NY

Paciorek, Steven
Southside HS
Elmira, NY

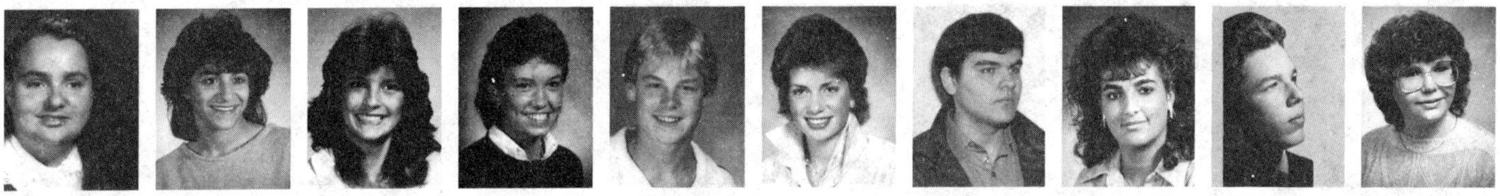

Padlovsky, Esther M
Newtown HS
Jackson Hts, NY

Pagan, Elsa Iris
Thomas R Proctor
Utica, NY

Pagano, Kimberly Ann
Charles E Groton
Yonkers, NY

Page, Judy
Bishop Maginn HS
Albany, NY

Page, Michael
E J Wilson HS
Spencerport, NY

Paino, Cynthia L
Norwich HS
Norwich, NY

Pais, Salvatore
Brooklyn Technical
Jackson Heights, NY

Palazzotto, Maria B
Deer Park HS
Deer Park, NY

Palestrant, Christopher W
Newtown HS
Elmhurst, NY

Palicki, Tracy A
Depew HS
Depew, NY

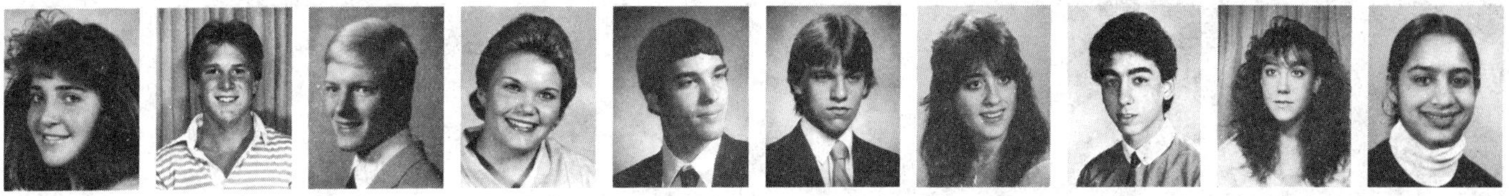

Palladino, Dana
Notre Dame Academy HS
Staten Island, NY

Palmer, David J
Alfed G Berner HS
Massapequa Pk, NY

Palmer, Douglas D
Hartford Central
Granville, NY

Palmer, Elaine
Schoharie Central
Sloansville, NY

Palmer, Joseph Patrick
Canajoharie HS
Canajoharie, NY

Palmer, Joseph W
Depew HS
Depew, NY

Palmieri, Francine
Marlboro HS
Marlboro, NY

Panagakos, Peter
Arch Bishop Iakajos
Jamaica, NY

Panella, Elizabeth
Saugerties HS
Saugerties, NY

Pannu, Harpreet Kaur
Albany Academy For Girls
Cohoes, NY

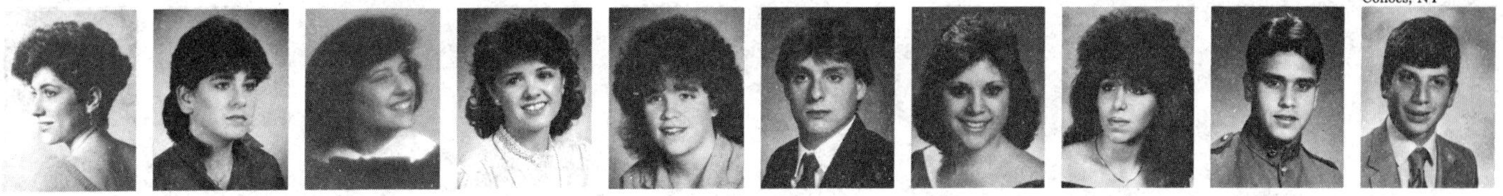

Paolantonio, Jo Ann
Sewanhaka HS
Stewart Manor, NY

Paolone, Elizabeth A
Shaker HS
Latham, NY

Paolozzi, Maryrose
Whitesboro SR HS
Utica, NY

Papelino, Jeannine M
Notre Dame HS
Utica, NY

Papp, Mary
West Genesee SR
Camillus, NY

Paradise, Steven
Myndersz Acad
Seneca Falls, NY

Parascandola, Patricia
St Agnes Cathedral
Rosedale, NY

Pardo, Mary
Canarsie HS
Brooklyn, NY

Pardo, Walter
New York Military
Ridgewood, NJ

Parente, John
Monsignor Farrell
Staten Island, NY

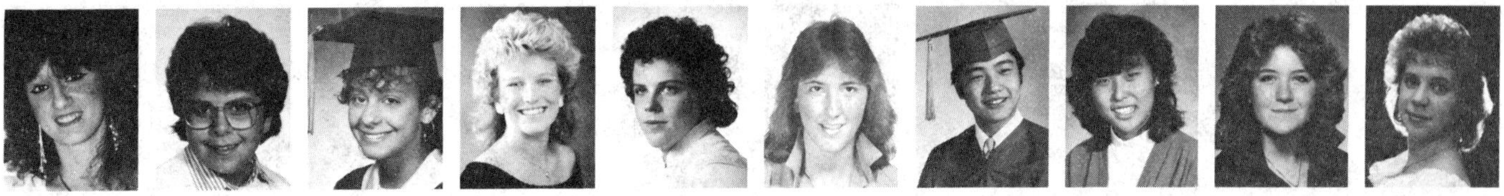

Parente, Michele
Dominican Commercial HS
Richmond Hill, NY

Parenti, Christine
Farmingdale SR HS
Farmingdale, NY

Pares, Nayda
John Dewey HS
Brooklyn, NY

Parfitt, Candace E
La Salle SR HS
Niagara Falls, NY

Pargeter, Rachel S
Warwick Valley HS
Warwick, NY

Parisian, Nicole
Massena Central HS
Massena, NY

Park, Chun Sae
New Town HS
Elmhurst, NY

Park, Sujin
Bayside HS
Flushing, NY

Parker, Stacy
Sachem HS
Lake Ronkonkoma, NY

Parodi, Melissa
Sachem High Schl
Ronkonkoma, NY

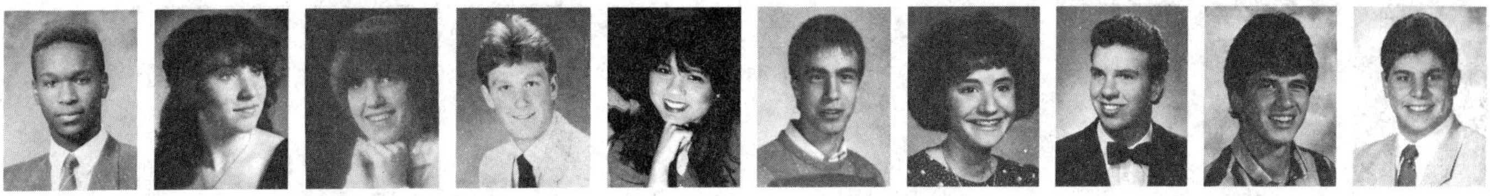

Parris, James
HS Of Art And
Hollis, NY

Parrish, Laura
Cicero-North Syracuse HS
Clay, NY

Parzych, Melissa A
Horseheads HS
Horseheads, NY

Pascale, Peter
Port Chester HS
Port Chester, NY

Pascual, Veronica
Sacred Heart Acad
Uniondale, NY

Pasieczny, William
Hahn American HS
Apo New York, NY

Passalaris, Tina
Herricks SR HS
New Hyde Park, NY

Passaretti, Chris
St John The Baptist
N Babylon, NY

Passaro, Anthony
Greenville Central
Greenville, NY

Pastore, John V
Patchogue-Medford
Hampton Bays, NY

Patellis, Sophia
Herricks SR HS
New Hyde Park, NY

Paternoster,
Christopher L
East Islip HS
E Islip, NY

Patino, Oscar
La Salle Military
Uniondale, NY

Patrick, Brian
Ricardo
Sachem North HS
Holbrook, NY

Patrick, William
Frankfurt American
Apo, NY

Patten, Jennifer
Jane Addams
Bronx, NY

Pattengill, Vikki
South New Berlin
Central HS
S New Berlin, NY

Patterson, Thomas
Minisink Valley HS
Middletown, NY

Paul, Joseph Wesley
Nazareth Regional
Brooklyn, NY

Pauley, Michelle
Randolph Central
Randolph, NY

Pavlik, Tony J
Corning East HS
Corning, NY

Pavlin, Jordan M
Wheatley Schl
Albertson, NY

Pawloski, Mark
Canisins HS
Elma, NY

Payne, Sabrina
Bishop Kearney HS
Brooklyn, NY

Payton, Lance
Cardinal Hayes
Memorial HS
New York, NY

Pearson, Eileen
Rebecca
Amsterdam HS
Amsterdam, NY

Peck, Katrina
Webster HS
Webster, NY

Peck, Lara
Fairport HS
Fairport, NY

Peck, Renee
Fairport HS
Fairport, NY

Pedalino, Peter
Monsignor Farrell
Staten Island, NY

Peek, Chad Evan
Brockport HS
Brockport, NY

Peets, Carlene
Port Jervis HS
Port Jervis, NY

Peinkofer, Brian
Saint Josephs
Collegiate Inst
Eggertsville, NY

Pelczynski, Darleen
Villa Maria Acad
Buffalo, NY

Pellegrini, Christine
Half Hollow Hills
HS East
Dix Hills, NY

Pellegrino,
Samantha Y
Gorton HS
Yonkers, NY

Pellicci, Lisa P
St Francis Prep
College Point, NY

Pena, Elbert
Central Islip SR HS
Central Islip, NY

Pena, Francis
Archbishop Molloy
Elmhurst, NY

Penk, Timothy
Ravena-Coeymans-S
elkirk HS
Selkirk, NY

Pennachio, Robert
St Marys Boys HS
Douglaston, NY

Pennell, Deena
Mohonasen HS
Schenectady, NY

Penning,
Christopher
South Glens Falls
Central Schl
S Glens Falls, NY

Pensa, Gina
Commack HS North
East Northport, NY

Peralta, Ivelisse
Dominican
Commercial HS
Ozone Park, NY

Percely, Adam
Minisink Valley HS
Westtown, NY

Percy, Jacqueline
John H Glenn HS
Huntington, NY

Perez, Blanca
John Dewey HS
Brooklyn, NY

Perez, Edgar
Bay Shore HS
Bay Shore, NY

Perez, Edwin
Saint Agnes HS
New York, NY

Perez, Rosalyn
St Raymond Acad
Bronx, NY

Perkins, Christopher
J
Wayland Central HS
Dansville, NY

Perkins, Ross
Camden SR HS
Camden, NY

Perl, Andrea
York Preparatory
New York, NY

Perna, Jr Anthony J
Middletown HS
Middletown, NY

Perrin, Michelle
Alexander Central
Alexander, NY

Perry, David
Spencerport HS
Spencerport, NY

Perry, James M
Maine-Endwell SR
Endwell, NY

Perry, Renard
Rice HS
New York, NY

Perry, Ruby Ellen
Morgan
Portville Central HS
Portville, NY

Perry, III Zollie
Thomas
Smauel Gompers HS
Bronx, NY

Person, Anthony
Earl
Bishp Ford Central
Catholic HS
Brooklyn, NY

Peryea, Deborah A
Ausable Valley
Central HS
Keeseville, NY

Pesiri, Barbara
St John The Baptist
Amityville, NY

Peter, Joseph
St Marys HS
Depew, NY

Peterman, Renee
Valley Stream
Central HS
Valley Stream, NY

Peters, Brian M
Newburgh Free
Newburgh, NY

Peters, Jan M
Bethelem Central
Delmar, NY

Petersdorf, Lisa
South Park HS
Buffalo, NY

Petersen, Lisa
Sacred Heart Acad
Malverne, NY

Peterson, Noelle
Cicero-North

Peterson, Sharon L
Vestal SR HS

Peterson, Zane
Paul V Moore HS

Petit Michel, Marie
Newfield HS

Petraglia, Scott
North Babylon HS

Petramale, Francis
R

Petramale, Patricia
Saugerties HS

Petrosky, Andrew J

Petrucco, Claudia

Petry, Craig J

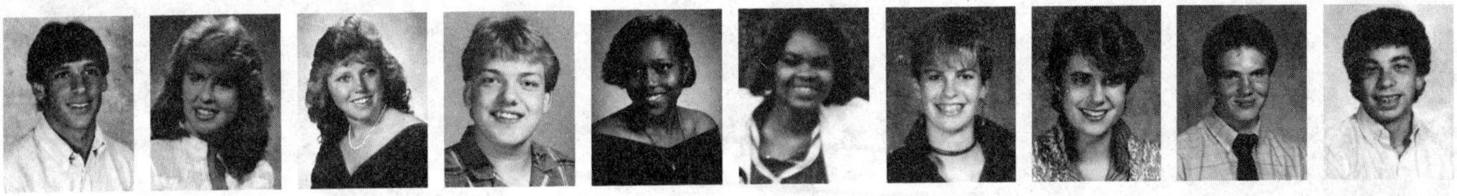

Pettinelli, Neal
P V Moore HS
Brewerton, NY

Pettit, Daphne
Gloversville HS
Gloversville, NY

Pettit, Elizabeth
West Islip HS
W Islip, NY

Petzold, Keith
Farmingdale HS
Farmingdale, NY

Philippe, Liliane
Pine Bush HS
Middletown, NY

Phillips, Pamela
Park W HS
Manhattanville, NY

Phillips, Shanda
The Harley HS
Rochester, NY

Phillips, Teresa
Avon Central HS
Honeoye Falls, NY

Phillips, Todd
Faith Heritage HS
Syracuse, NY

Phillips, William A
Whitney Point
Central Schl
Binghamton, NY

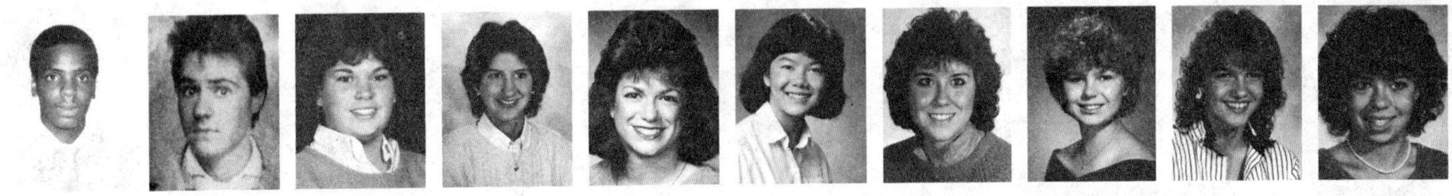

Phills, Darryl
St Francis Prep
St Albans, NY

Pianka, Joseph
St John The Baptist
W Islip, NY

Picard, Amy
Catholic Central HS
Clifton Pk, NY

Piccirillo, Karen
Mohonasen HS
Schenectady, NY

Picozzi, Janette
Walt Whitman HS
Huntington Sta, NY

Pien, Grace
Elmira Southside
Pine City, NY

Pierce, Lisa
Commack North HS
Commack, NY

Pierce, Paula
Minisink Valley HS
New Hampton, NY

Piercynski, Kristin
Earl L
Vandermeulen HS
Mt Sinai, NY

Pierson, Michelle
Corning-Painted
Post West HS
Painted Post, NY

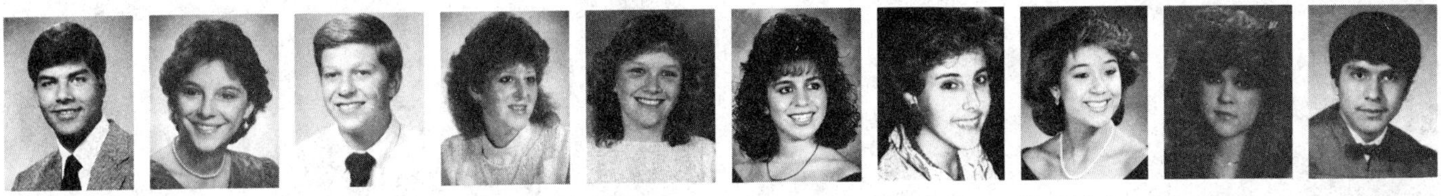

Pieters, Kevin
Amherst Central SR
Snyder, NY

Pietraszewski,
Denise M
Cheektowaga
Central HS
Cheektowaga, NY

Pignone, Frank
South Park HS
Buffalo, NY

Pike, Ameigh
Cicero-North
Syracuse HS
Clay, NY

Pike, Tracey
Cicero North
Syracuse HS
N Syracuse, NY

Pilarinos, Georgia
St Johns Prep
Astoria, NY

Pilpel, Patricia
Sacred Heart Acad
New Hyde Park, NY

Pimentel, Sarita
John F Kennedy HS
Bronx, NY

Pina, Betty
Msgr Scanlan HS
Jackson Heights,
NY

Pineda, Freddy
Alfred E Smith HS
Bronx New York,
NY

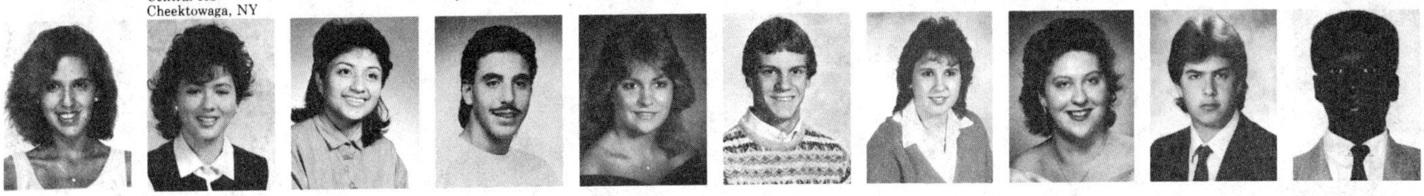

Pinilla, Leslie
Evander Childs HS
Bronx, NY

Pino, Tracy
Upper Room
Christian HS
Smithtown, NY

Pinto, Vilma
Dominican
Commercial HS
New York, NY

Pinzone, Vincent
John
Valley Stream North
Valley Stream, NY

Piotrowski, Paula
Mont Pleasant HS
Schenectady, NY

Pirko, Kevin
Dyrden HS
Dryden, NY

Pistilli, Valerie
Moore Catholic HS
Staten Island, NY

Pistone, Lisa Ann
Dominican
Commercial HS
Brooklyn, NY

Pitschi, John P
Patchogue Medford
Patchogue, NY

Pitters, Douglas
Bronx HS Of
Bronx, NY

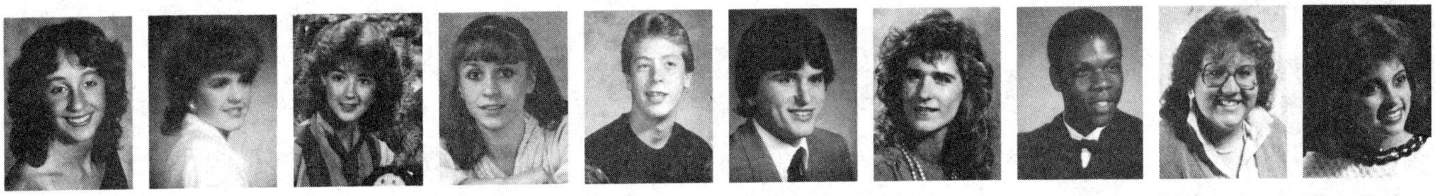

Pizzi, Ann Marie
Delli
St Catharine Acad
Bronx, NY

Pizzi, Jolie A
Cardinal Mooney
Rochester, NY

Plaisted, Donna
Waverly JR SR HS
Chemung, NY

Plimi, Tonia C
Long Beach HS
Long Beach, NY

Plimley, Mark
Beacon HS
Beacon, NY

Pluff, Michael
Altmar-Parish-Willi
amstown HS
Parish, NY

Podolec, Tiffani
Johnstown HS
Johnstown, NY

Poe, Darrell D
Julia Richman HS
Flushing, NY

Polakiewicz, Anne
Marie
Frontier Central HS
Blasdell, NY

Polanco, Mary
Adlar E Stevenson
Bronx, NY

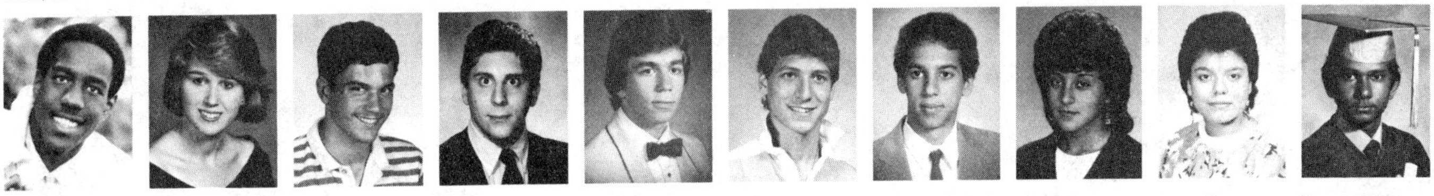

Poland, Gregory A
Spackenkill HS
Poughkeepsie, NY

Poletto, Valentina K
Saugerties HS
Saugerties, NY

Poli, Jr David R
Torrejon HS
APO, NY

Pollak, Arthur
General Douglas
Mac Arthur HS
Levittown, NY

Polsinelli, Vito
Mont Pleasant HS
Schenectady, NY

Polvino, James M
Gates Chili SR HS
Rochester, NY

Polvino, Jr James R
Charles H Roth HS
W Henrietta, NY

Poma, Mireille
Mamaroneck HS
Larchmont, NY

Ponce, Alyssa
Yonkers-Lincoln HS
Yonkers, NY

Pooran, Nakechan
F D Roosevelt HS
Brooklyn, NY

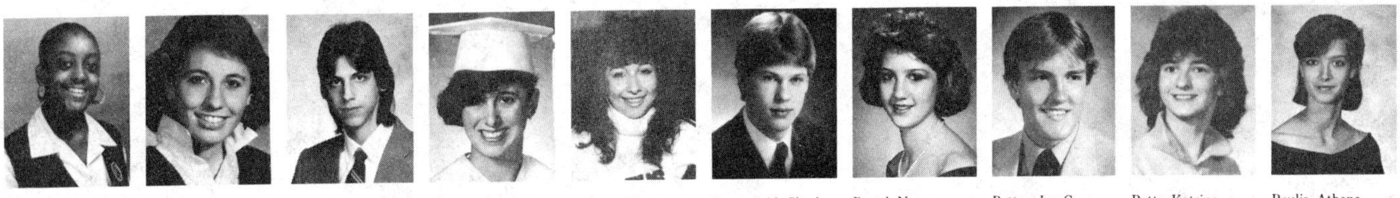

Pope, Tyann
Cathedral HS
Ny, NY

Popiel, Amy
Potsdam Central HS
Potsdam, NY

Poplawski, Thomas
J
Middletown HS
Middletown, NY

Poppiti, Kimberly D
New Field HS
Lelden, NY

Porpora, Tracey
Ann
Tohenville HS
Staten Isld, NY

Porterfield, Charles
A
Vestal Central HS
Apalachin, NY

Postel, Nancy
Hendrick Hudson
Montrose, NY

Potter, Jon C
Skaneateles HS
Skaneateles, NY

Potts, Katrina
Clarkstown South
Bardonia, NY

Poulis, Athena
Hillcrest HS
Jamaica, NY

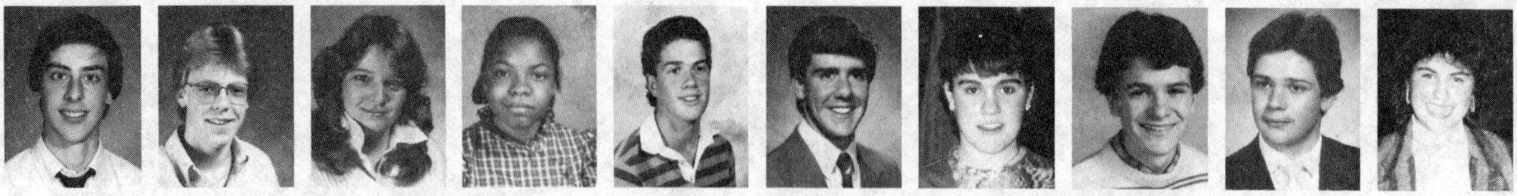

Pouloutides, John
Ossinging HS
Ossining, NY

Powalowski, Brian
St Marys HS
Cheektowaga, NY

Powell, Shannon
Stamford Central
Stamford, NY

Powell, Teresa
Westbury HS
Westbury, NY

Power, Brian
Mahopac HS
Mahopac, NY

Powers, Joseph E
Babylon HS
Babylon, NY

Powers, Kathryn
Babylon HS
Babylon, NY

Powers, Michael
Center Moriches HS
Center Moriches, NY

Powers, Stephen J
West Seneca West SR HS
West Seneca, NY

Pozin, Dina
Valley Stream North
Malverne, NY

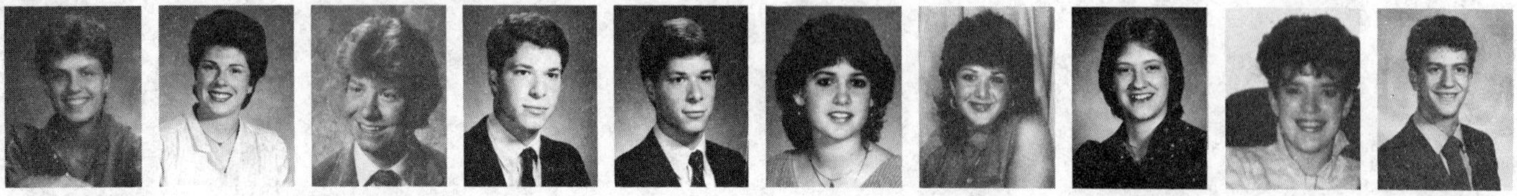

Pratt, Melissa M
Granville Central
Middle Granville, NY

Prefer, Kathleen A
Susan E Wagner HS
Staten Island, NY

Premock, Brian P
Owego Free Acad
Apalachin, NY

Press, Alan L
Ardsley HS
Ardsley, NY

Press, David L
Ardsley HS
Ardsley, NY

Preston, Dariann
Ossining HS
Ossining, NY

Prettitore, Gina
St Francis Prep
Flushing, NY

Price, Carolyn E
Poland Central Schl
Barneveld, NY

Price, Kiera
St Francis Prep
College Pt, NY

Priolo, Peter
Monsignor Farrell
Staten Island, NY

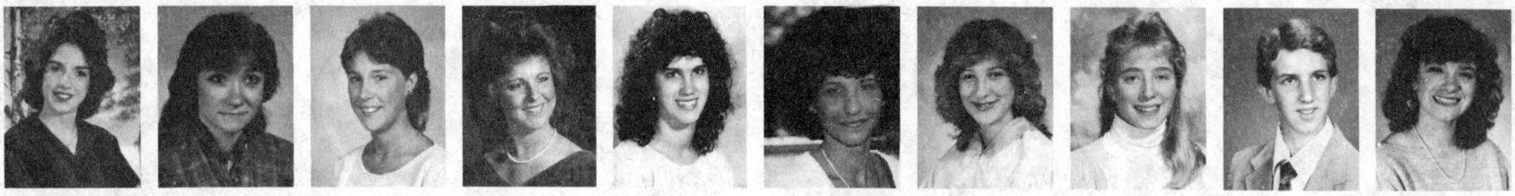

Pritchard, Denise
Frankfort-Schuyler
Frankfort, NY

Pritchette, Patricia
Riverside HS
Buffalo, NY

Pritty, Penny
Gouverneur HS
Gouverneur, NY

Profeta, Adrianne
Maria Regina HS
Yonkers, NY

Profeta, Denise
Mahopac HS
Mahopac, NY

Prokup, Lee Ann
St John Villa Acad
Staten Island, NY

Prosseda, Kelly
Fontebonne Hall
Brooklyn, NY

Pruiksma, Janice
Coxsackie-Athens
Coxsackie, NY

Prusinowski, Daniel P
Moravia Central
Locke, NY

Przepasniak, Mary Jo
Mount Mercy Acad
Buffalo, NY

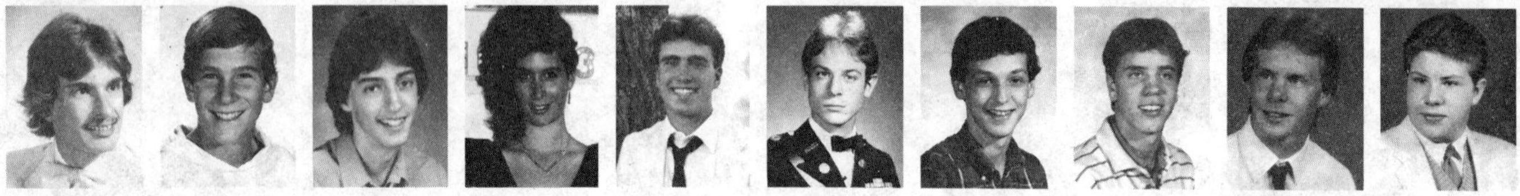

Przybysz, Kenneth P
Hutchison Central Technical HS
Buffalo, NY

Puccio, Gerard
Manhasset HS
Manhasset, NY

Puchebner, Ron
Greece Olympia HS
Rochester, NY

Puleo, Josephine
Dominican Commercial HS
Ozone Park, NY

Pullaro, Raymond G
F D Roosevelt HS
Poughkeepsie, NY

Purcell, Michael
Xavier HS
Brooklyn, NY

Purcell, Todd
Pittsford Mandon
Pittsford, NY

Purves, Todd
Fairport HS
Fairport, NY

Putnam, Todd
Queensbury HS
Glens Falls, NY

Putorti, Freddy
Whitehall JR SR
Whitehall, NY

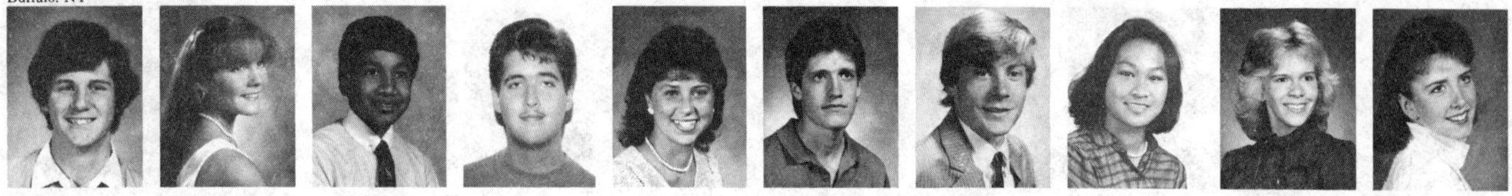

Pyke, James M
G Ray Bodley HS
Fulton, NY

Pylyshenko, Katja
Brockport HS
Brockport, NY

Pynadath, David V
Johnstown HS
Johnstown, NY

Pytluk, Scott
John Dewey HS
Brooklyn, NY

Quattrone, Tracy
Olean HS
Olean, NY

Quibell, Matthew D
Dansville SR HS
Dansville, NY

Quiett, D Eric
Barker Central HS
Barker, NY

Quijano, Aimee
The Wheatley HS
Roslyn Hts, NY

Quinn, Christine
White Plains HS
White Plains, NY

Quinn, Kathleen
Saratoga Central Catholic HS
Ballston Spa, NY

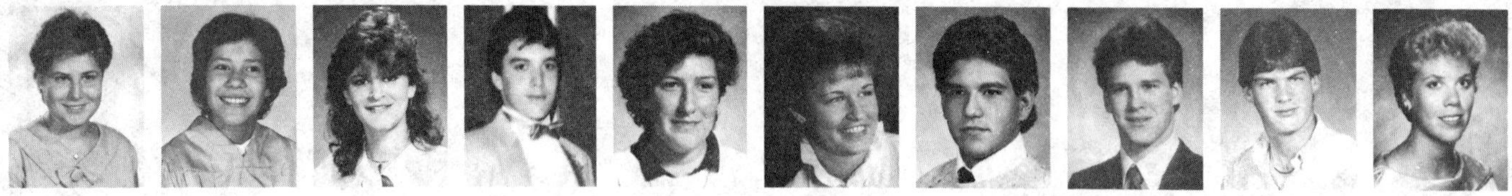

Quinn, Kathryn Ealr L
Vandermeulen HS
Mt Sinai, NY

Quintero, Alissa
Adlai E Stevenson
Bronx, NY

Quirke, Deirdre
Cardinal Spellman
Bronx, NY

Racano, Anthony
Cardinal Spellman
Bronx, NY

Racht, Andrea Anthony A
Henninger HS
Syracuse, NY

Rackmyre, Christina
Gloversville HS
Gloversville, NY

Radesi, Jr Felix J
York Central HS
Lercester, NY

Radliff, Bryan
Shenendehowa HS
Clifton Park, NY

Radonis, Richard
East Meadow HS
East Meadow, NY

Radziejewski, Christine
Plainedge HS
N Massapequa, NY

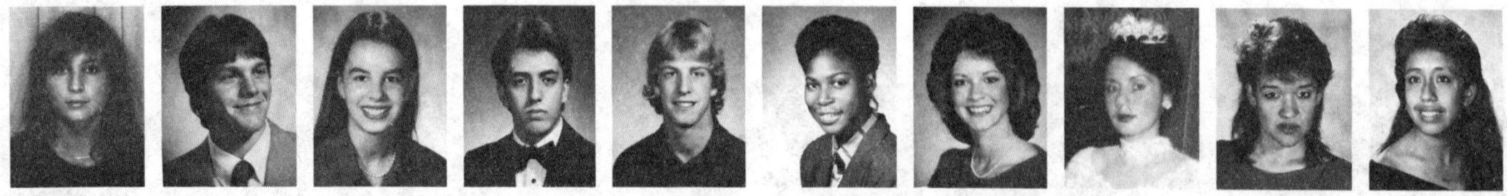

Radziewicz, Alisa
Sacred Heart Acad
Garden City, NY

Raemore, Michael C
Corning East HS
Corning, NY

Raffe, Melinda J
Riyerhead HS
Riverhead, NY

Ragone, Anthony P
Salesian HS
Bronx, NY

Rakoske, Eric
Cobleskill Central
Cobleskill, NY

Ralph, Jacqueline S
Northeastern Acad
Bronx, NY

Ralston, Larraine
Massena Central HS
Massena, NY

Ramirez, Magda
John Jay HS
Brooklyn, NY

Ramirez, Margaret
Bronx High School Of Sci
New York, NY

Ramos, Liz
Catherine Mc Auley
Brooklyn, NY

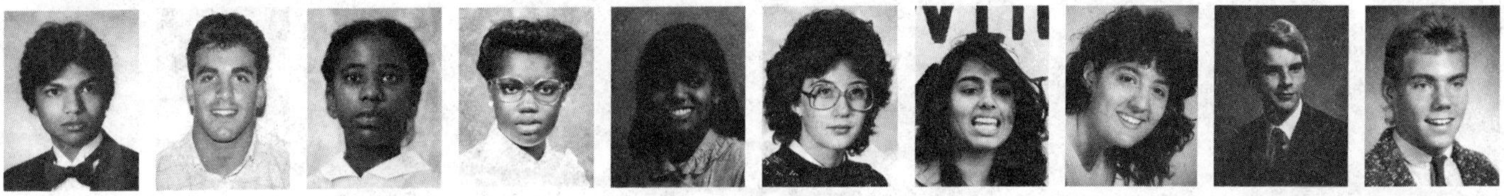

Ramotar, Valmiki
Brentwood HS
Brentwood, NY

Rampulla, Andrew
St John The Baptist
Massapequa, NY

Randall, Kwafi J
High School Of Art
And Design
Bronx, NY

Randall, Trina
Long Island City HS
Long Is Cty, NY

Rangaiah,
Thejomani
Scarsdale HS
Scarsdale, NY

Rankin, Denise K
Hamburg SR HS
Hamburg, NY

Rao, Anjali
Jericho HS
Syosset, NY

Rappazzo, Rosanna
Albany HS
Albany, NY

Rasha, Kyle W
Rome Free Acad
Lee Center, NY

Rask, Kurt
Shaker HS
Latham, NY

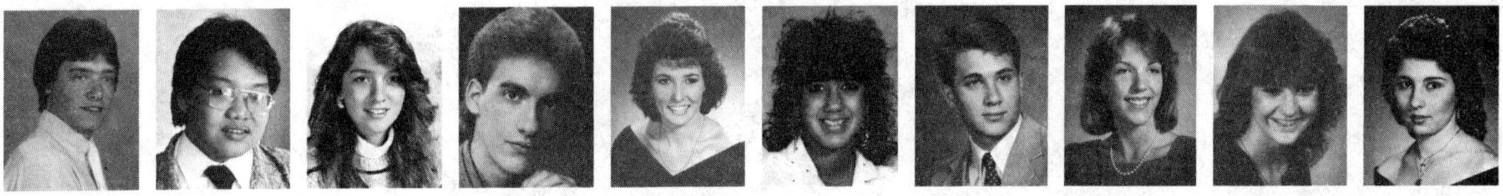

Rath, Randall G
Glens Falls HS
Glens Falls, NY

Ratunil, Ludemo
Mc Quaid Jesuit HS
Mt Morris, NY

Raus, Kim
Onondaga HS
Syracuse, NY

Ravert, Jr W John
Southside HS
Elmira, NY

Ray, Diane Patricia
Monsignor Scanlan
Flushing, NY

Raychaudhuri,
Renee
Ossining HS
Ossining, NY

Rea, Robert K
Saugerties Central
Saugerties, NY

Reagan, Michelle D
Bethlehem Central
Delmar, NY

Realmuto, Athena
Williamsville North
Getzville, NY

Reardon, Joann
Saint Barnabas HS
Bronx, NY

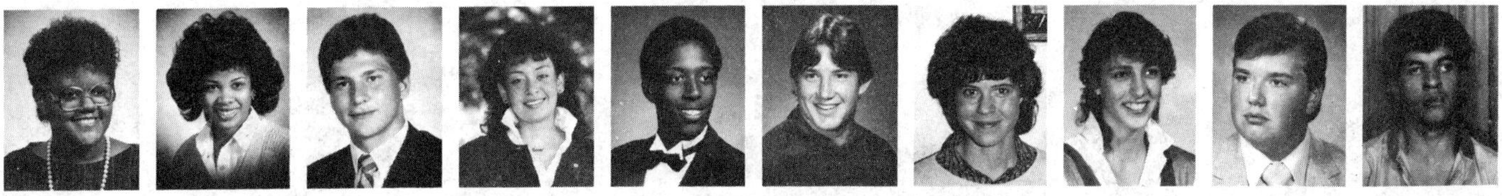

Reaves, Angela
Nottingham SR HS
Syracuse, NY

Reaves, Anita Dawn
Elsworth J Wilson
Rochester, NY

Rebuck, Paul S
Liverpool HS
Liverpool, NY

Recalde, Consuelo
Division Avenue HS
Levittown, NY

Recall, Leslie A
Cathedral
Preparator
Bronx, NY

Recher, Tim
Byram Hills HS
Armonk, NY

Reed, Stacey
Cambridge Central
Cambridge, NY

Reeves, Christine
Saugerties HS
Saugerties, NY

Reeves, Daniel
Valley Stream HS
Valley Stream, NY

Reeves, Dominic
South Shore HS
Brooklyn, NY

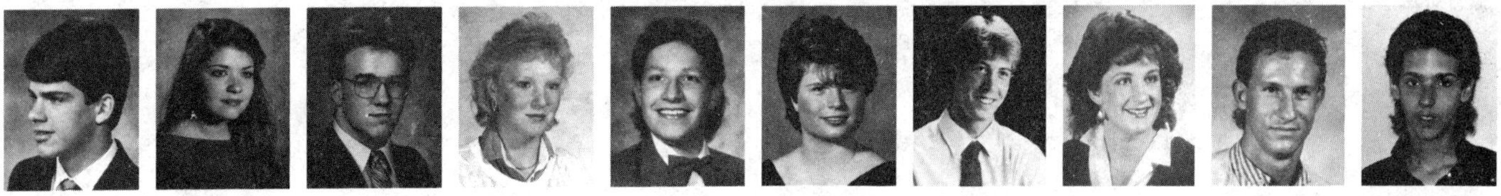

Regan, Robert F
Garden City SR HS
Garden City, NY

Regenhard,
Christina
Bronx High School
Of Science
Bronx, NY

Regulski, Peter A
Binghamton HS
Binghamton, NY

Rehbein, Jessica
Johnstown HS
Johnstown, NY

Reif, Richard P
Lakeland HS
Mohegan Lake, NY

Reilly, Lynn
St Joseph Hill Acad
Staten Island, NY

Reilly, III Paul V
Herkimer SR HS
Herkimer, NY

Reilly, Ruth
La Fayette Central
Manlius, NY

Reiman, Patrick
Fredonia HS
Fredonia, NY

Reines, Jeff
Longwood HS
Ridge, NY

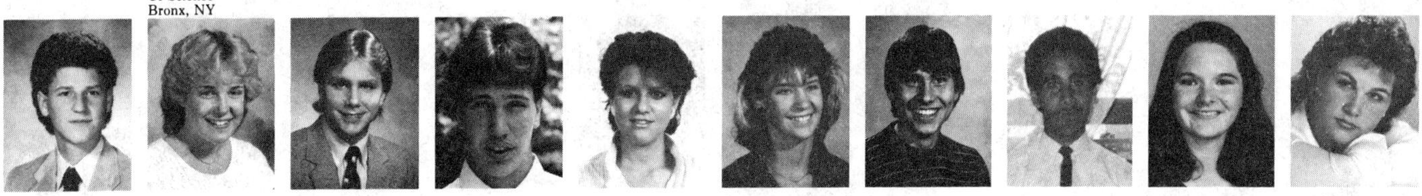

Reinhardt, Hal D
W Trespar Clarke
Westbury, NY

Reisner, Kimberly
Notre Dame-Bishop
Gibbons HS
Schenectady, NY

Remsen, Anthony
Williamsville East
Williamsville, NY

Rench, Adam
John Adams HS
Howard Beach, NY

Resko, Jody
Bronx High School
Of Science
Glendale, NY

Reuter, Shannon
Johnstown HS
Johnstown, NY

Reyes, George
Peru Central HS
Plattsburgh, NY

Reyes, Jose
William Howard
Taft HS
Bronx, NY

Reynolds, Christine
Lindenhurst SR HS
Lindenhurst, NY

Reynolds, Christine
Marlboro Central
Marlboro, NY

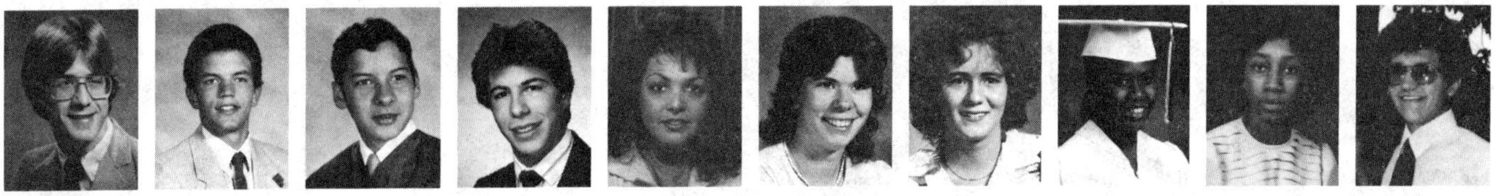

Reynolds, Mark D
Hamburg SR HS
Hamburg, NY

Rhodes, III Stephen
Monsignor Farrell
Staten Island, NY

Ribeiro, Sergio
Oyster Bay HS
Mill Neck, NY

Ricchiuti, Michael
West Islip HS
W Islip, NY

Ricciardi, Ann
Moore Catholic HS
Staten Island, NY

Rice, Cheryl
Haverling Central
Bath, NY

Richard, Gina M
Henninger HS
Syracuse, NY

Richards, Ella Jean
L
Midwood At
Brooklyn Coll
Brooklyn, NY

Richards, Laverda
Springfield Gardens
Rosedale, NY

Richards, Todd
Salmon River
Central Schl
Ft Covington, NY

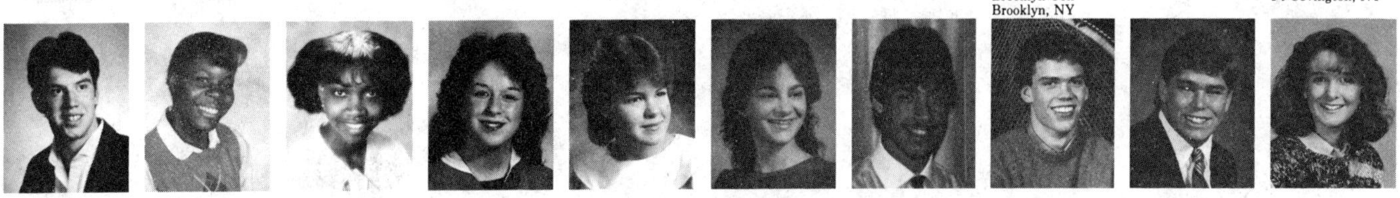

Rickard, Eric G
Poland Central Schl
Boonville, NY

Ricketts, Raquel
Uniondale HS
Uniondale, NY

Ricks, Juanita M
North Rockland HS
Pomona, NY

Ricupero, Vanessa
Abraham Lincoln
Brooklyn, NY

Riddell, Rosemarie
Brockport HS
Brockport, NY

Rigatti, Amy L
Amsterdam HS
Amsterdam, NY

Riggio, Louis
Lafayette HS
Buffalo, NY

Riggs, John
Matthew
Mexico Acad
Mexico, NY

Riker, Matthew D
Saratoga Springs HS
Gansevoort, NY

Riley, Kim
Mepham HS
Bellmore, NY

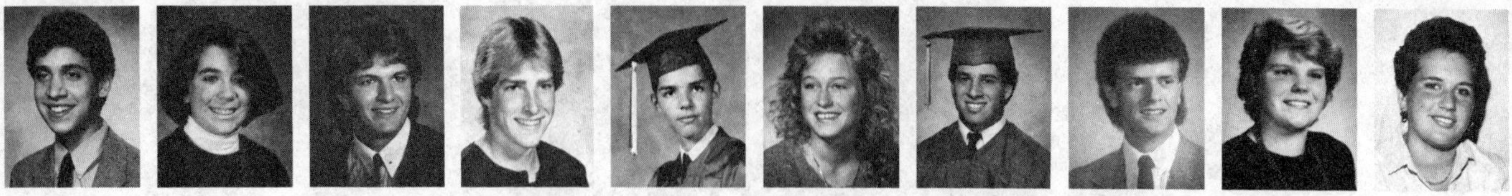

Rinaldi, John
St John The Baptist
Deer Park, NY

Ringle, Leslie
Nardin Acad
Buffalo, NY

Rion, Jr Frederick J
Kingston HS
Kingston, NY

Riordan, Mike
John H Glenn HS
E Northport, NY

Rios, Jose
John Dewey HS
Brooklyn, NY

Ripke, Karen
Bethpage HS
Bethpage, NY

Ripps, Andrew S
Baldwin SR HS
Baldwin, NY

Ristich, Tommy
Gates Chili HS
Rochester, NY

Rittenhouse, Michelle
Union-Endicott HS
Endicott, NY

Rituno, Randi
Masters Schl
Rye, NY

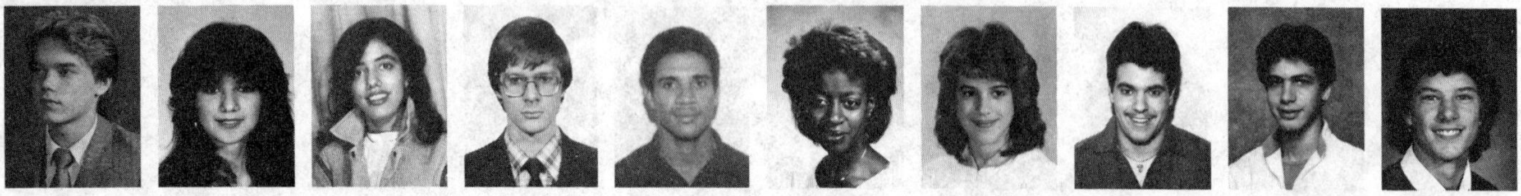

Ritvanen, Seppo
Saugerties HS
Saugerties, NY

Rivera, Bernadette
Adlai E Stevenson
Bronx, NY

Rivera, Elizabeth
Jane Addams Vocational HS
Bronx, NY

Rivera, Marcos
Mount St Michael
Bronx, NY

Rivera, Jr Miguel A
Nazareth Regional
Brooklyn, NY

Rivers, Melissa
Charles H Roth HS
W Henrietta, NY

Rizzi, Antoinette
St Edmund HS
Brooklyn, NY

Rizzo, John
St Francis Prep
Ozone Park, NY

Rizzo, Victor P
Pelham Memorial
Pelham, NY

Roach, Daniel Joseph
O Neil HS
Walton, NY

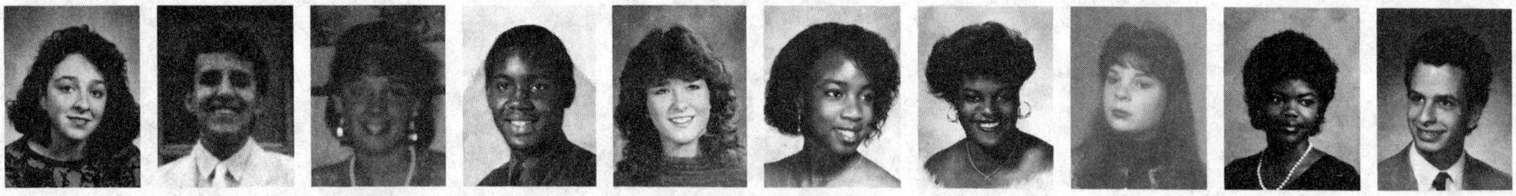

Roach, Jennifer
Bishop Ludden HS
Syracuse, NY

Robayo, Alex
Newfield HS
Selden, NY

Robben, Dawn
The Ursuline Schl
Rye, NY

Robbins, Gene B
August Martin HS
Jamaica, NY

Roben, Debra R
Island Trees HS
Levittown, NY

Roberson, Karon Marie
Jamaica HS
E Elmhurst, NY

Roberson, Patrina
Central Islip HS
Central Islip, NY

Robert, Tammi
Massena Central HS
Massena, NY

Roberts, Cheri La Rae
Sacred Heart Acad
West Hempstead, NY

Roberts, David P
Baldwin SR HS
Baldwin, NY

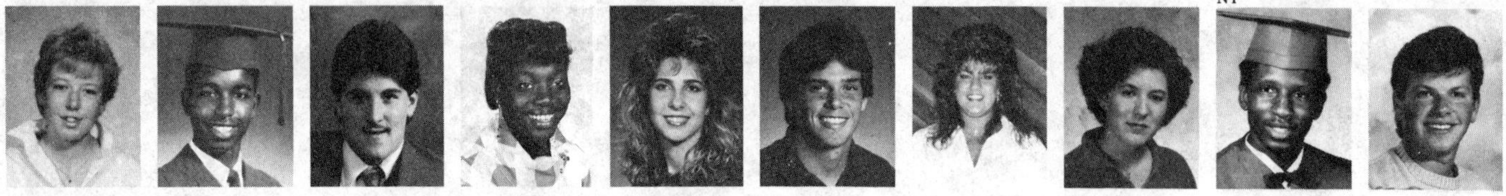

Roberts, Lisa
Sharon Springs Central Schl
Sharon Springs, NY

Roberts, Paul
The Stony Brook
Wenham, MA

Roberts, Sean
Franklin K Lane HS
Woodhaven, NY

Roberts, Sophia
John H Glenn HS
Greenlawn, NY

Robin, Marni R
Edgemont HS
Scarsdale, NY

Robinson, Colby
Bitburg American
Apo Ny, NY

Robinson, Donna
Lindenhurst HS
Encinitas, CA

Robinson, Jennifer
Frontier HS
Hamburg, NY

Robinson, Lloyd
Alfred E Smith HS
Bronx, NY

Robinson, Richard
Stissing Mt JR SR
Stanfordville, NY

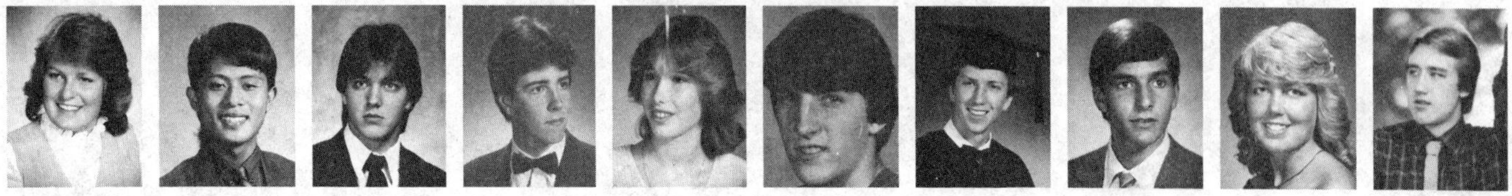

Robinson, Shelli M
Walton Central Schl
Walton, NY

Robles, Rudolph Gilbert
Mc Quaid Jesuit HS
Pittsford, NY

Rocco, Gary R
Flushing HS
College Point, NY

Roche, Michael
Regis HS
New York, NY

Rockow, Bobbi L
Wheatland Chili Central Schl
Scottsville, NY

Rocque, Marshall G
Whitehall Central
Whitehall, NY

Rode, David W
Half Hollow Hills East HS
Dix Hills, NY

Roden, Alan J
Scarsdale HS
Armonk, NY

Roderick, Denise
North Salem HS
N Salem, NY

Rodgers, Andrew T
F D Roosevelt HS
Hyde Park, NY

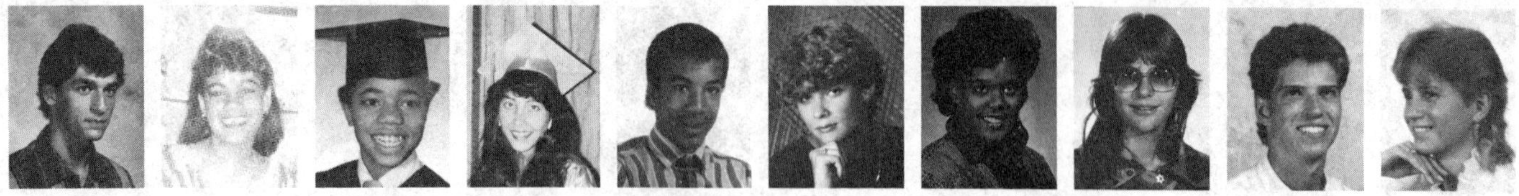

Rodriguez, Dennis
Bishop Grimes HS
Clay, NY

Rodriguez, Elizabeth
Queens Vocational
Astoria, NY

Rodriguez, Errol
Cardinal Hayes HS
New York, NY

Rodriguez, Nelly I
John Jay HS
Brooklyn, NY

Rodriguez, Robert
Woodlands HS
Elmsford, NY

Roemer, Kimberly A
Mayville Central
Dewittville, NY

Rogers, Crystal
Niagara Catholic HS
Niagara Fls, NY

Rogers, Lauren
Connetquot HS
Ronkonkoma, NY

Rogers, Todd
East Islip HS
East Islip, NY

Rogowski, Julie G
West Seneca West SR HS
S Cheektowaga, NY

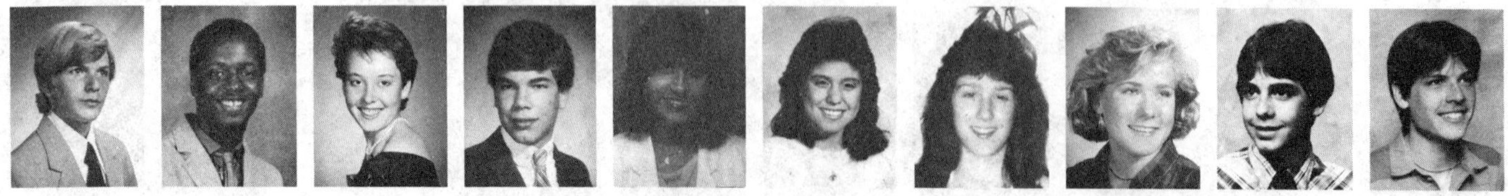

Roher, Michael A
Madison Central HS
Bouckville, NY

Rolston, Leon
All Hallows Inst
Bronx, NY

Romaine, Joan
Valley Central HS
Walden, NY

Romer, Randall J
Columbia HS
East Greenbush, NY

Romero, Lisa
Park West HS
New York, NY

Romero, Nancy
New Dorp HS
Staten Island, NY

Romito, Denise Marie
Comsewogue HS
Pt Jefferson Sta, NY

Romyn, C Rachel
Corning-Painted Post East HS
Corning, NY

Ronacher, Michael
Paul V Moore HS
Central Sq, NY

Roncone, Paul
South Park HS
Buffalo, NY

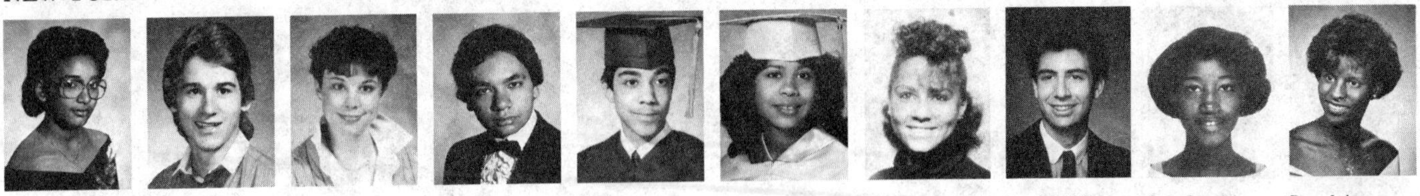

Rondon, Cherrie Ann Marie
Franklin D Roosevelt HS
Brooklyn, NY

Roode, Steve
Roy C Ketcham HS
Poughkeepsie, NY

Root, Kimberly
Brockport HS
Brockport, NY

Rosado, David
Rice HS
New York, NY

Rosado, Josue J
Fiorello H La Guardia HS
New York, NY

Rosado, Tabetha
Herbert H Lehman
Bronx, NY

Rosario, Angelica
Seward Park HS
New York, NY

Rose, David S
Walt Whitman HS
Huntington Sta, NY

Rose, Georgia
Mt Vernon HS
Mt Vernon, NY

Rose, Jody
Dominican Commercial HS
New York, NY

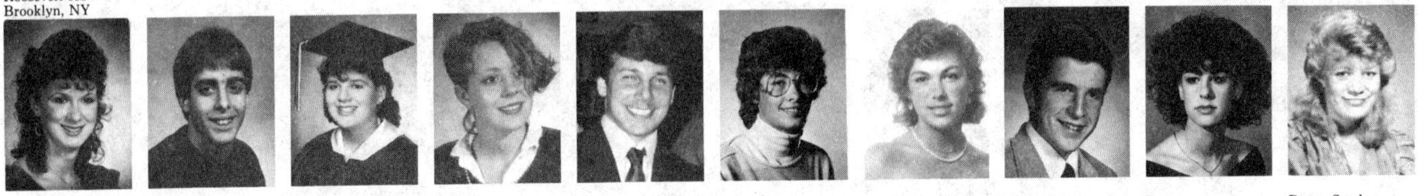

Rosekrans, Christine
Catholic Central HS
Troy, NY

Rosen, Corey D
Jamestown HS
Jamestown, NY

Rosen, Robin
Sachem HS North
Bayside, NY

Rosenbach, Virginia Anne
Franciscan Acad
Parish, NY

Rosenfeld, Steven M
Flushing HS
College Point, NY

Rosenhahn, Wendy
Kenmore East HS
Kenmore, NY

Rosenow, Racquel
South Park HS
Buffalo, NY

Rosenthal, Joseph A
Bayshore HS
Bayshore, NY

Rosenwasser, Christine K
St Joseph Hill Acad
Staten Island, NY

Roser, Sandra
Valley Central HS
Walden, NY

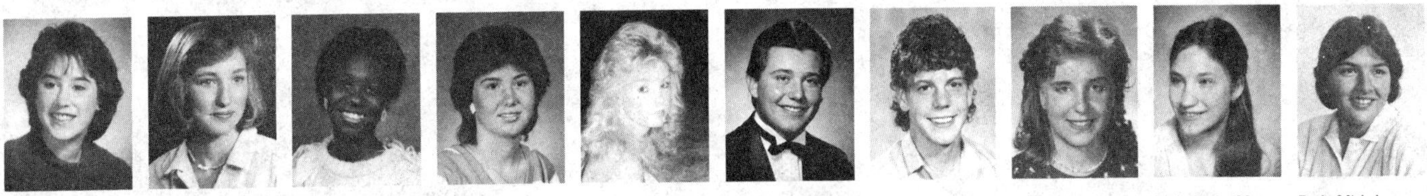

Rosewater, Karen
Bethlehem Central
Delmar, NY

Ross, Kathryne
Ichabod Crane HS
Valatie, NY

Ross, Toni
Morris HS
Bronx, NY

Ross, Tracy
West Seneca West SR HS
Buffalo, NY

Rossi, Joanne
Blind Brook HS
Rye Brook, NY

Rossini, Anthony David
St Francis Prep Schl
Beechhurst, NY

Rotella, Jeff
Shoreham-Wading River HS
Shoreham, NY

Roth, Barbara A
Huntington HS
Huntington Sta, NY

Roth, Janice M
Elba Central Schl
Elba, NY

Roth, Michele
Middletown HS
Middletown, NY

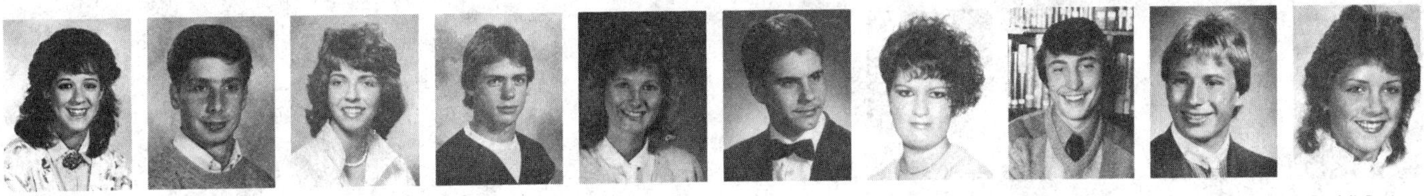

Rothman, Ellyn
Mc Kee Technical
Staten Island, NY

Roux, II Gerard
Broadalbin Central
Broadalbin, NY

Rowe, Jennifer
Smithtown H S East
Smithtown, NY

Rowinski, Jeff
Notre Dame-Bishop Gibbons HS
Schenectady, NY

Rowley, Victoria
Falconer Central HS
Kennedy, NY

Roxbury, Bernard
Regis HS
New York, NY

Rozenberg, Lana
Midwood HS
Brooklyn, NY

Rozenfeld, Yuri
The Anglo-American
Brooklyn, NY

Rubeck, Christopher
Hamburg SR HS
Hamburg, NY

Rubendall, Denise
St John The Baptist
N Massapequa, NY

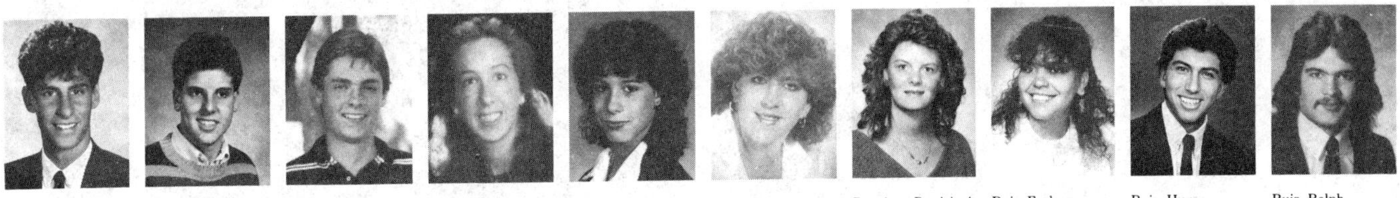

Rubenstein, Kenneth
Yeshira University
Suffern, NY

Rubenstein, Michael
West Genesee SR
Syracuse, NY

Rubin, Andrew
Blind Brook HS
Tuckahoe, NY

Rubin, Heidi
Uniondale HS
Uniondale, NY

Rubino, Lisa
Notre Dame Acad
Staten Island, NY

Ruff, Sherry
Holy Angels Acad
Buffalo, NY

Ruggiero, Patricia A
Sachem North HS
Holbrook, NY

Ruiz, Evelyn
John Dewey HS
Brooklyn, NY

Ruiz, Hugo
Saint Anthonys HS
Long Beach, NY

Ruiz, Ralph
Central Islip HS
Central Islip, NY

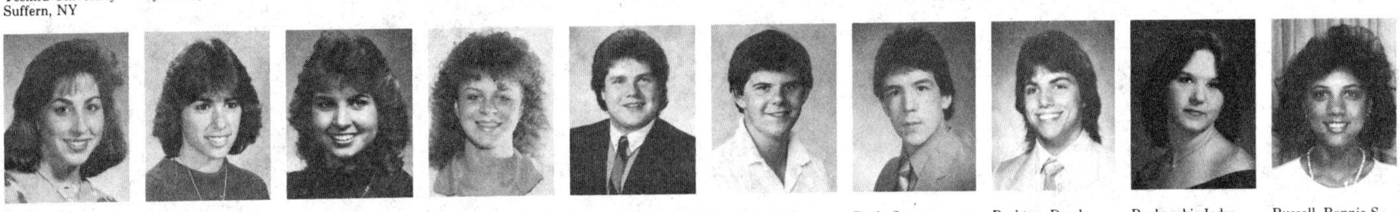

Rulli, Jeanette
Brewster HS
Brewster, NY

Rummo, Valerie
Glen Cove HS
Glen Cove, NY

Runo, Jocelyn M
John F Kennedy HS
Cheektowaga, NY

Ruocco, Josephine
Hauppauge HS
Smithtown, NY

Ruoso, Otello G
Huntingston HS
Huntington Statn, NY

Rupp, Jeff
Hugh C Williams
Canton, NY

Rush, Steven
New Amsterdam HS
Amsterdam, NY

Rushton, Derek
Bishop Ford Central Catholic HS
Brooklyn, NY

Ruskouski, Jody
Dover JR SR HS
Wingdale, NY

Russell, Bonnie S
Westbury SR HS
Westbury, NY

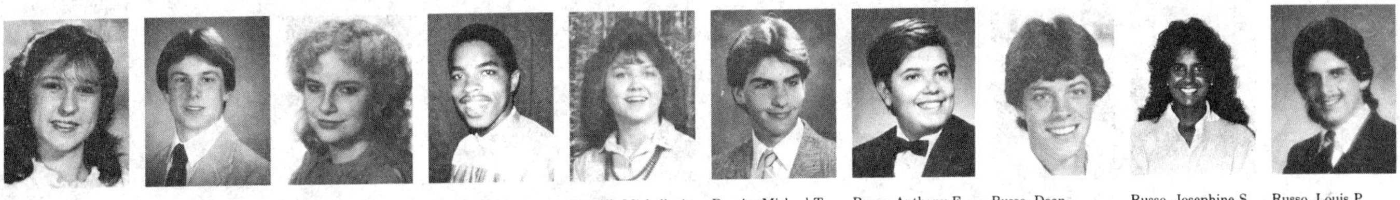

Russell, Christine H
Mohonasen SR HS
Schenectady, NY

Russell, John B
Vestal Central Schl
Vestal, NY

Russell, Laura
St Joseph By-The-Sea HS
Staten Island, NY

Russell, Michael
Dewitt Clinton HS
Bronx, NY

Russell, Michelle A
Salmon River Central HS
Brushton, NY

Russin, Michael T
Marlboro Central
Milton, NY

Russo, Anthony E
Mount Saint Michael Acad
Bronx, NY

Russo, Dean
Savgerties JR SR
W Camp, NY

Russo, Josephine S
White Plains HS
White Plns, NY

Russo, Louis P
Ft Edward Union Free HS
Ft Edward, NY

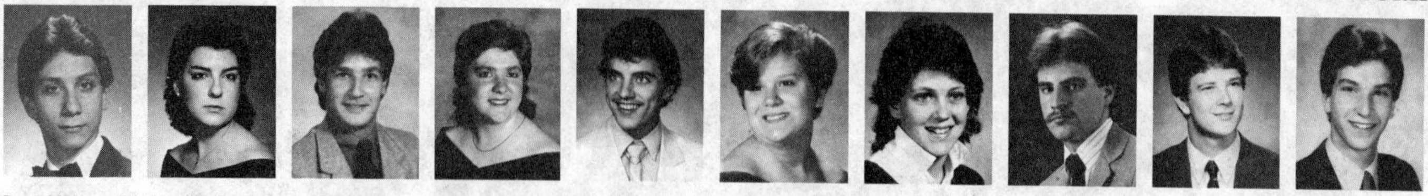

Russo, Martin
Regis HS
Middle Village, NY

Russo, Nancy
Academy Of The
Resurrection HS
Port Chester, NY

Russo, Stephen
Monsignor Farrell
Staten Island, NY

Russo, Susan A
St Catharine Acad
Bronx, NY

Rutigliano, James
Sachem North HS
Holtsville, NY

Ruvolo, Kristina
Marie
Our Lady Of
Perpetual Help
Brooklyn, NY

Ruwet, Diane
Auburn HS
Auburn, NY

Ruzewski, Robert M
Cheektowaga
Central HS
Cheektowaga, NY

Ryan, James A
Babylon HS
Babylon, NY

Ryan, James J
Bellport SR HS
Bellport, NY

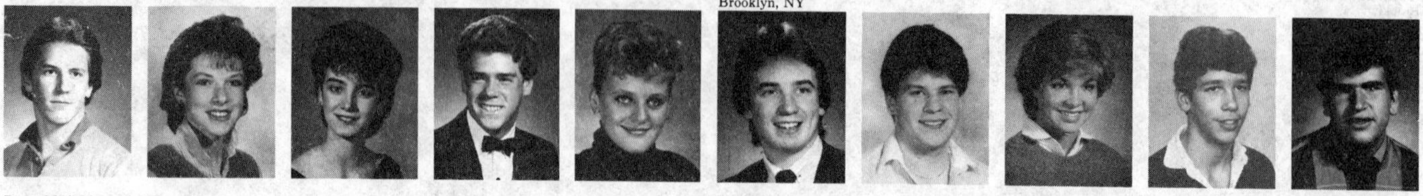

Ryan, Michael
Spackenkill HS
Poughkeepsie, NY

Ryan, Michele
Mohonasen HS
Schenectady, NY

Ryan, Patricia A
St Joseph Hill Acad
Staten Island, NY

Ryan, Robert W
Mount St Michael
Bronx, NY

Ryan, Sally
Nardin Acad
Orchard Park, NY

Ryan, III Thomas
Vincent
Walter Panas HS
Peekskill, NY

Ryan, Timothy J
Canajoharie HS
Canajoharie, NY

Rymarchyk,
Gretchen
La Fayette Central
Jamesville, NY

Rysedorph, Troy T
Columbia HS
Nassau, NY

Saar, James
Susquehanna Valley
Conklin, NY

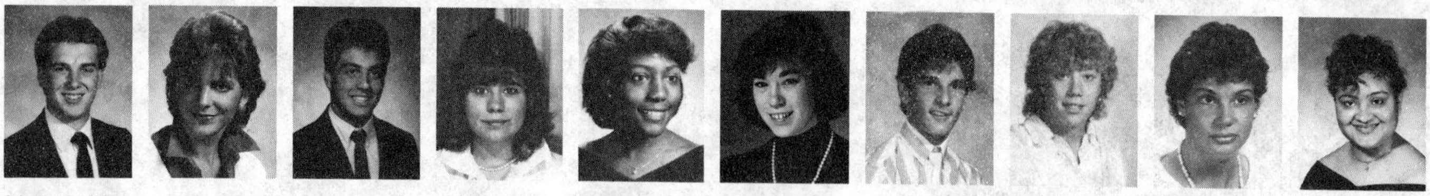

Sabados, Peter
Msgr Farrell HS
Staten Island, NY

Sabo, Christie
Mount Mercy Acad
W Seneca, NY

Sabol, Joseph E
Baldwin HS
Baldwin, NY

Saccomanno, Krista
Sacred Heart Acad
Floral Park, NY

Sadler, Tracy
Msgr Scanlan HS
New York, NY

Safarik, Irene M
Academy Of St
Huntington, NY

Salamino, Joseph
Bishop Grimes HS
Syracuse, NY

Salbego, Andrea
Watkins Glen HS
Watkins Glen, NY

Salerno, Amy
East-Syracuse-Mino
a HS
East Syracuse, NY

Salicrup, Madeline
Jane Addams
Vocational HS
Bronx, NY

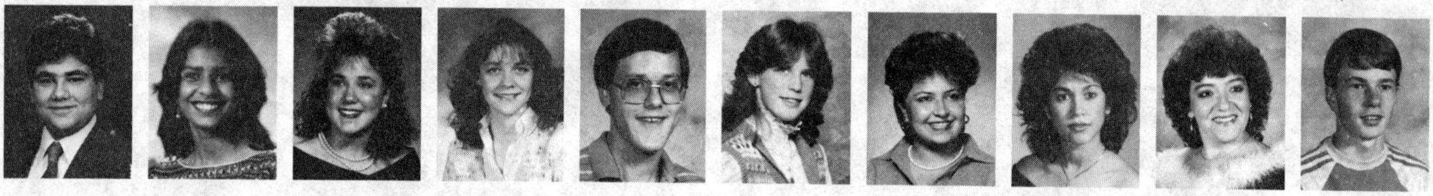

Salierno, Joseph
St Anthonys HS
Centereach, NY

Salim, Sarwat
Franklin Delano
Roosevelt HS
New York, NY

Salisbury, Edith N
Cardinal Spellman
Bronx, NY

Salley, Danielle
C- PP West HS
Corning, NY

Salva, Thomas J
Rome Free Acad
Rome, NY

Salzer, Christine
Freeport HS
Freeport, NY

Salzman, Randi
Commack H S
Dix Hills, NY

Samaroo, Denise
Mt St Ursula HS
Yonkers, NY

Samiou, Evelyn
Long Island City HS
Long Island Cty,
NY

Samokar, Scott
Dover JR SR HS
Dover Plains, NY

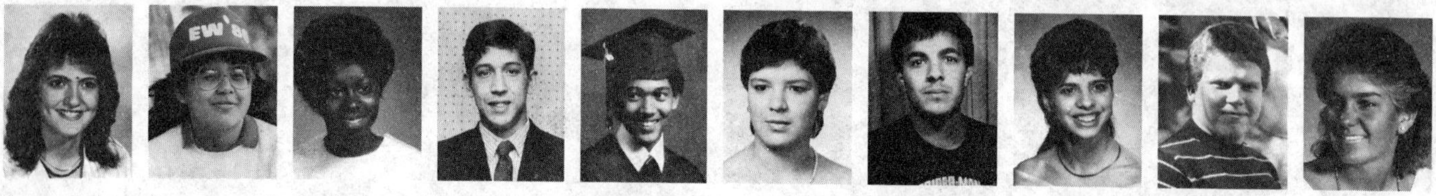

Sampson, Carol
Lynn
Mahopac HS
Mahopac, NY

Samson, Rosanne M
Emma Willars Schl
Loudonville, NY

Samuels, Dionne
Groton HS
Yonkers, NY

San Miguel,
Alejandro
The Browning Schl
Tenafly, NJ

Sanchez, Johnny
William Howard
Taft HS
Bronx, NY

Sanchez, Kathleen
Dominican
Commercial HS
Jamaica, NY

Sanchez, Philip A
Scarsdale HS
Scarsdale, NY

Sanchez, Yvette
The Mary Louis
Floral Park, NY

Sander, Henry
Delaware Academy
And Central HS
Delhi, NY

Sandklev, Jennifer
Susan E Wagner HS
Staten Island, NY

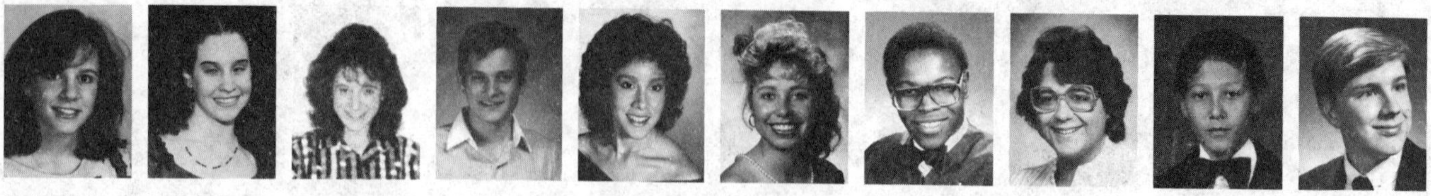

Sandler, Marlo
Huntington HS
Huntington, NY

Sands, Jill R
Sanford H Calhoun
Merrick, NY

Sanelli, Pina C
St Francis Prep HS
Maspeth, NY

Sanfilippo, Robert F
Orchard Park HS
Orchard Park, NY

Sangurima, Jessica
E
Fontbonne Hall
Brooklyn, NY

Sangvic, Harriet
Lindenhurst HS
Lindenhurst, NY

Sanon, Edison
Nazareth Regional
Brooklyn, NY

Santacesaria, Nancy
Greece Olympia HS
Rochester, NY

Santiago, Abel
Hempstead HS
Hempstead, NY

Santomero, Steven
P
Floral Park
Memorial HS
Floral Park, NY

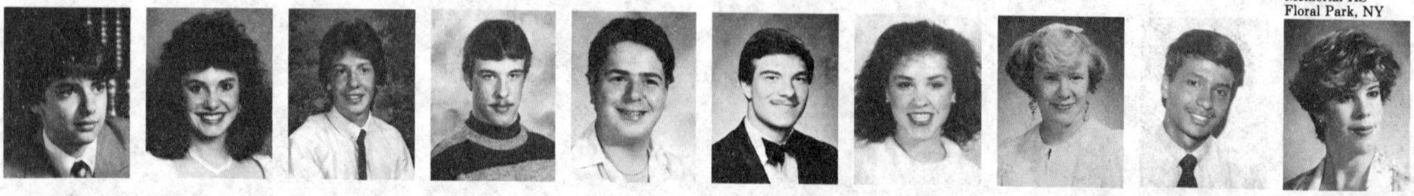

Santora, Jason M
Watervliet HS
Watervliet, NY

Santore, Gina
Moore Catholic HS
Manalapan, NJ

Santy, Daryle
Bishop Grimes HS
Syracuse, NY

Santy, Joel
Franklin Acad
Malone, NY

Sapirman, Louis
Tottenville HS
Staten Island, NY

Saponara, Nicholas
R
St Francis Prep
Whitestone, NY

Sapone, Carol
Scotia Glenville HS
Scotia, NY

Saravia, Mary
Roy C Ketcham HS
Wappingers Falls,
NY

Sarfati, Peter
Newtown HS
Elmhurst, NY

Sarles, Kimberly M
Roscoe Central HS
Roscoe, NY

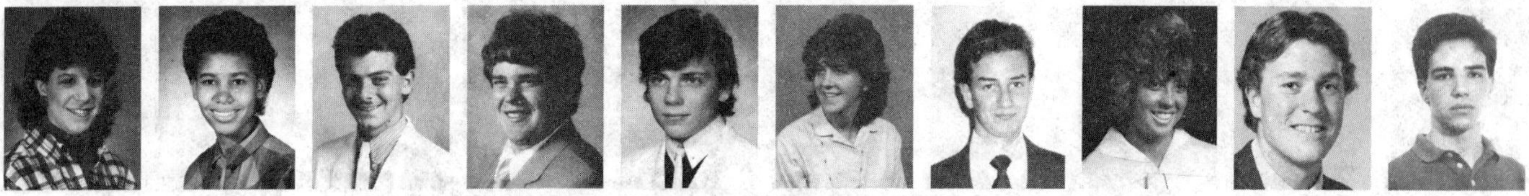

Sarra, Jamie
Mount Mercy Acad
W Seneca, NY

Saunders, Tracy
Northeastern Acad
New York, NY

Savastano, Michael
North Babylon HS
N Babylon, NY

Saville, Russell
Hudson Falls HS
Hudson Falls, NY

Savona, Anthony W
Sachem North HS
Centereach, NY

Sawn, Dale
Queensbury HS
Glens Falls, NY

Scaduto, Matthew
Smithtown HS West
Smithtown, NY

Scafide, Lisa
Smithtown HS
Hauppauge, NY

Scalise, Don
Grand Island HS
Grand Island, NY

Scanlon, Jr Thomas J
Our Lady Of
Poughkeepsie, NY

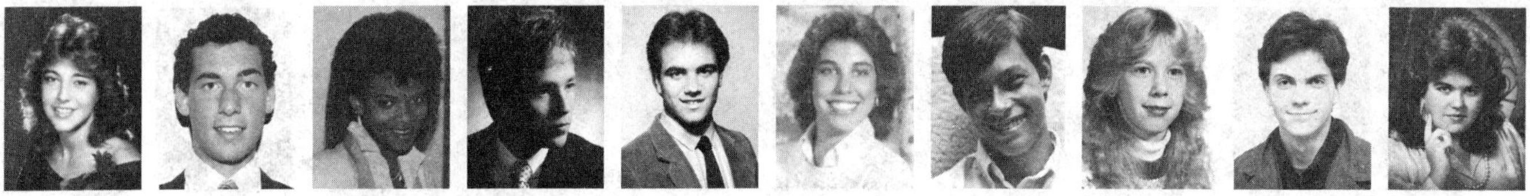

Scano, Nicole
F D Roosevelt HS
Poughkeepsie, NY

Scarantino, Stephen
Garden City SR HS
Garden City, NY

Scarborough, Janel
Freeport HS
Freeport, NY

Scarton, H James
Troy HS
Troy, NY

Scavone, Peter
St John The Baptist
Massapequa, NY

Schaefer, Catherine M
Villa Maria Acad
Sloan, NY

Schaefer, Frank
John Jay SR HS
Goldens Bridge, NY

Schaeffler, Lisa
Corcoran HS
Syracuse, NY

Schajer, Robert W
Professional
Childrens Schl
New York, NY

Schalk, Nadine
Royalton-Harhand
Central HS
Middleport, NY

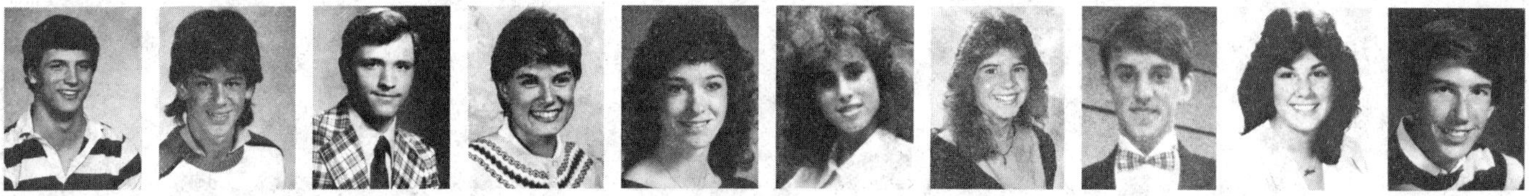

Schallert, Daniel
Cooperstown
Centeral HS
Hartwick, NY

Schang, Tim
Hahn American HS
Apo New York, NY

Schanz, Rodney
Middleburgh
Central Schl
Middleburgh, NY

Schauer, Beth
East Islip HS
Islip Terrace, NY

Schauer, Lynn
Altmar Parish
Willmstwn Cntrl HS
Parish, NY

Schechter, Basya
Shulamith HS For
Brooklyn, NY

Schechter, Lisa
Mahopac HS
Mahopac, NY

Scheffler, Eric
Fox Lane HS
Bedford, NY

Scheiman, Kara
Newfield HS
Selden, NY

Schell, George A
Mc Quaid Jesuit HS
Fairport, NY

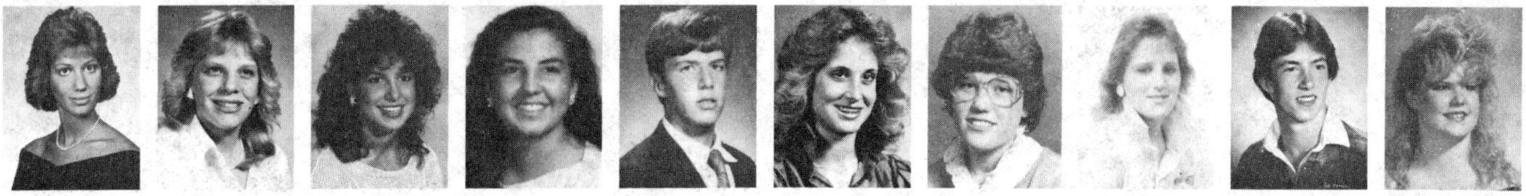

Scher, Cara F
Wantagh HS
Wantagh, NY

Scherer, Michelle
Susquehanna Valley
Conklin, NY

Schiavone, Lynn
Mahopac HS
Mahopac, NY

Schiavone, Shannon
Marlboro HS
Marlboro, NY

Schiffer, Chris
Iona Prep Schl
Valhalla, NY

Schihl, Dawn
Cardinal O Hara HS
Buffalo, NY

Schmidt, Connie
Hancock Central
Lakewood, PA

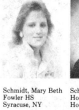

Schmidt, Mary Beth
Fowler HS
Syracuse, NY

Schmidt, Michael
Honeoye Central HS
Honeoye, NY

Schmitt, Jennifer
Mahopac HS
Mahopac, NY

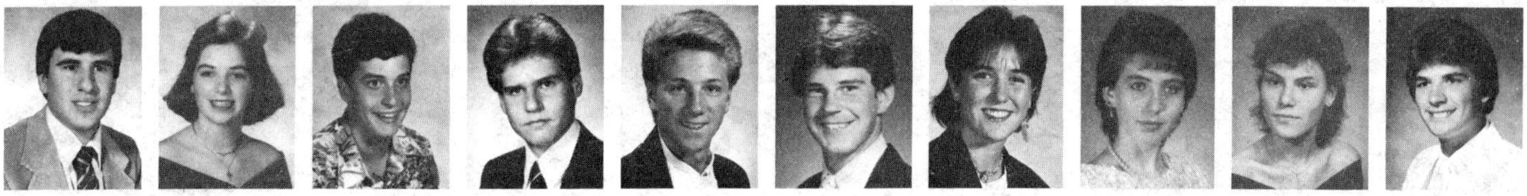

Schmulson, Louis J
Christopher
Columbus HS
Bronx, NY

Schnabel, Deidrea M
West Babylon HS
W Babylon, NY

Schnakenberg, Robt
John H Glenn HS
E Northport, NY

Schnall, Scott
Bay Shore HS
Bay Shore, NY

Schnauber, Glenn
Churchville Chili SR
Rochester, NY

Schnaudigel, Kevin
Carmel HS
Carmel, NY

Schneid, Megan
Commack HS North
Commack, NY

Schneider, Emilie
Mount Saint Mary
Buffalo, NY

Schneider, Erika
Coxsackie-Athens
W Coxsackie, NY

Schneider, Laurence S
Commack HS
Commack, NY

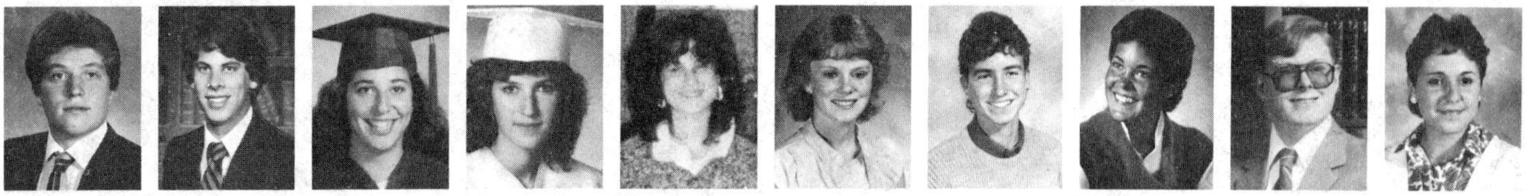

Schneider, Lawrence
Tottenville HS
Staten Island, NY

Schnipper, Eric
Roslyn HS
Roslyn, NY

Schoemaker, Lisa
George W Fowler
Syracuse, NY

Schoendorf, Susan
Brentwood Ross HS
Brentwood, NY

Schoffel, Hilary
Sheepshead Bay HS
Brooklyn, NY

Schofield, Samantha A
Churchville-Chili
Churchville, NY

Schofield, Stephen J
Chester HS
Chester, NY

Schoppe, Karen
Wayne Central HS
Ontario, NY

Schrader, Bert A
Amsterdam HS
Amsterdam, NY

Schraer, Lynann
Minisink Valley HS
Middletown, NY

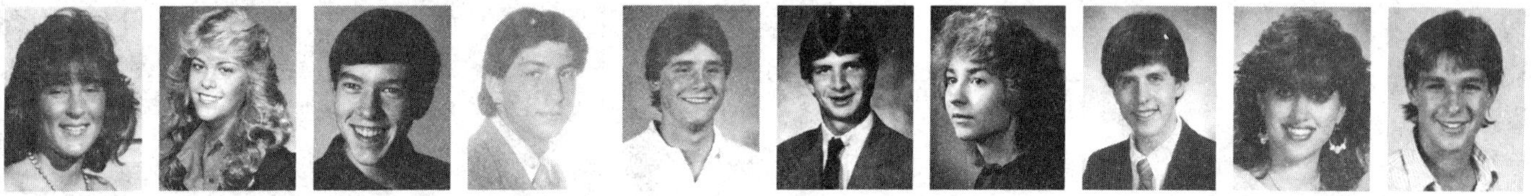

Schrager, Lara S
Vincent Smith HS
Lattingtown, NY

Schrimpe, Kristen
Long Island
Lutheran HS
Farmingdale, NY

Schroeder, Scott A
Floral Park
Memorial HS
Floral Park, NY

Schtierman, Irwin
East Meadow HS
East Meadow, NY

Schuck, IV John
Archbishop Walsh
Hinsdale, NY

Schultheis, David F
W T Clarke HS
Westbury, NY

Schultz, Cindy
Coxsackie Athens
JR SR HS
W Coxsackie, NY

Schultz, Eric W
Lewiston-Porter HS
Lewiston, NY

Schultz, Maryanne P
Lewiston-Porter HS
Lewiston, NY

Schumacher, Todd
Bay Shore HS
Brightwaters, NY

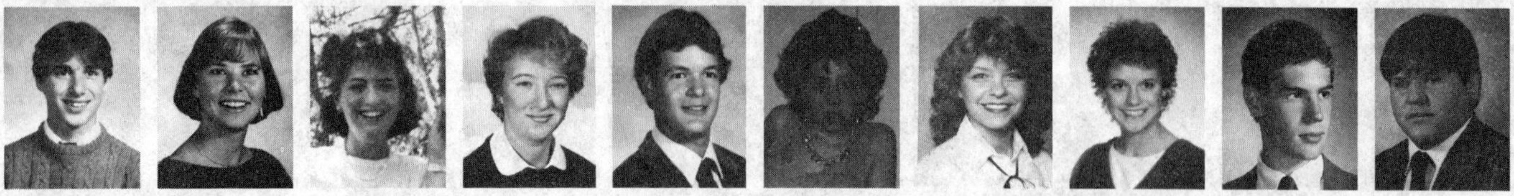

Schwabl, Craig
Bishop Timon HS
W Seneca, NY

Schwabl, Jill
Mt Mercy Acad
Buffalo, NY

Schwartz, Orit
Shulamith HS
Staten Island, NY

Schwartz, Renee
Hamburg SR HS
Hamburg, NY

Schwarzrock, Stephen
Monsignor Farrell
Staten Island, NY

Schweitzer, Jill D
Woodmere Acad
North Woodmere, NY

Scibilia, Regina
Niagara Catholic HS
Niagara Fls, NY

Sciera, Chrissy
Wheatland-Chili HS
Scottsville, NY

Sciortino, Jeffrey J
Honeoye Falls-Lima
Honeoye Falls, NY

Scism, III James H
Rondout Valley HS
Kingston, NY

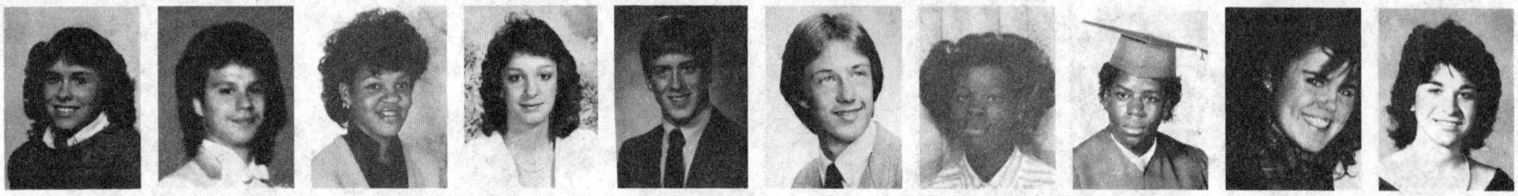

Scobell, Kimberly A
George W Fowler
Syracuse, NY

Scocca, Michael A
St John The Baptist
Copiayne, NY

Scott, Dawn
Liverpool HS
Liverpool, NY

Scott, Dawn Marie
Hannibal Central
Hannibal, NY

Scott, Gary
Pelham Memorial
Pelham, NY

Scott, Jeffrey W
Savona Central HS
Savona, NY

Scott, Patricia
Roosevelt JR SR HS
Roosevelt, NY

Scott, Patrick
Christopher Columbus HS
Bronx, NY

Scott, Shannon
Academy Of St
Coram, NY

Scotto, Michele
St Joseph By The Sea HS
Staten Island, NY

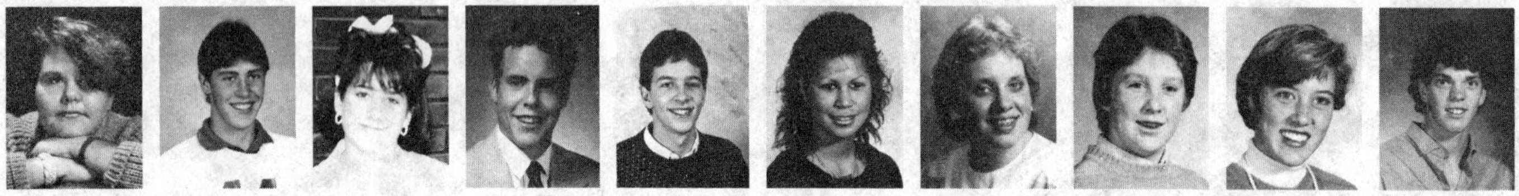

Scoville, Jennifer
Geneseo Central HS
Geneseo, NY

Scozzafava, Thomas
Gouverneur HS
Gouverneur, NY

Scragg, Sandra
St Joseph By-The-Sea HS
Staten Island, NY

Scutt, Christopher M
Troupsburg Central
Troupsburg, NY

Seamans, Jonathan D
Chittenango HS
Chittenango, NY

Sebayan, Elizabeth
Tottenville HS
Staten Isld, NY

Sebesta, Lia
Solvay HS
Solvay, NY

Secaur, Mark
Auburn HS
Auburn, NY

Seefeldt, Hilary
Tottenville HS
Staten Isld, NY

Seeley, John M
Midlakes HS
Phelps, NY

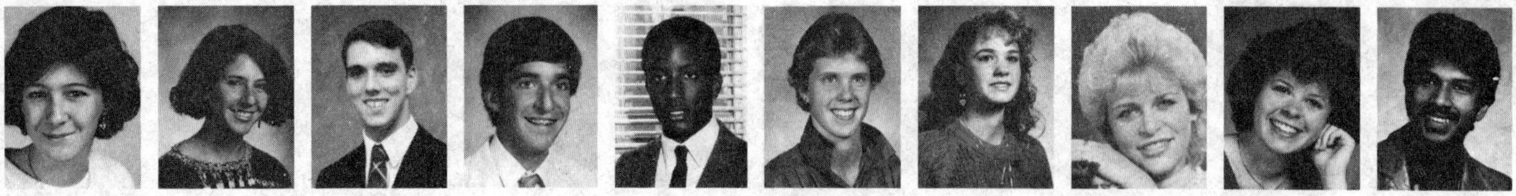

Seewaldt, Virginia
The Wheatley Schl
E Williston, NY

Segal, Michelle
The Masters HS
Beaverton, OR

Segall, Kevin
Baldwin SR HS
Baldwin, NY

Seidberg, Daniel R
Fayetteville-Manlius
Jamesville, NY

Selassie, Sengal M
Collegiate Schl
New York, NY

Selden, Jo Lynne
Panama Central
Ashville, NY

Seminski, Amy
Union Endicott HS
Endwell, NY

Semmler, Kimberly
Hilton Central HS
Hilton, NY

Senecal, Julie
Paul V Moore HS
Parish, NY

Seobarrat, Rejendra
Midwood H S At Brooklyn College
Richmond Hill, NY

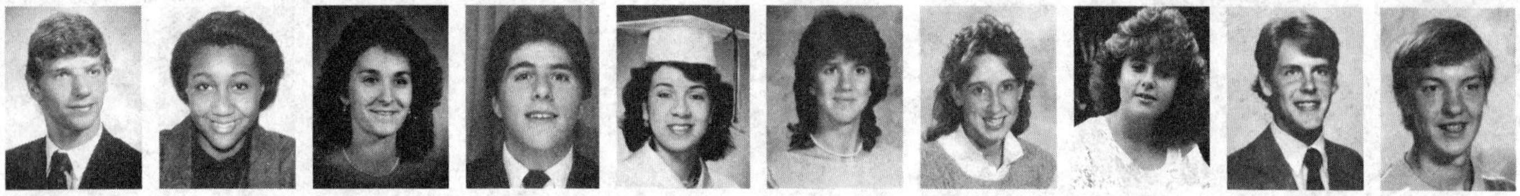

Sepanic, Tom
Buffalo Traditio
Buffalo, NY

Sequeira, Janice
Greater New York
Brooklyn, NY

Serafini, Lisa M
Mohonasen SR HS
Schenectady, NY

Serino, Carmine
North Babylon SR
N Babylon, NY

Serrano, Teresita
West Hempstead JR SR HS
Island Pk, NY

Sessler, Catherine
Bishop Grimes HS
Syracuse, NY

Settembrini, Elizabeth
Mahopac HS
Mahopac, NY

Severance, Heidi
Chatham Central
Canaan, NY

Severance, Steve
West Seneca Christian Schl
Orchard Park, NY

Severson, Kenneth
Saint Marys Acad
Schenectady, NY

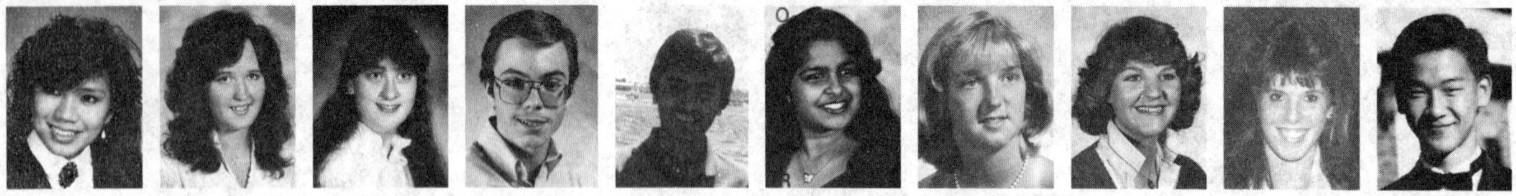

Sevilla, Armi
Stuyvesant HS
Elmhurst, NY

Sexton, Joan
Earl L Vandermeulen HS
Mt Sinai, NY

Seymour, Angela
Northstar Christian
Spencerport, NY

Shafer, Jeremy
Churchville Chili SR
N Chili, NY

Shah, Himanshu
Newtown HS
Elmhurst, NY

Shah, Sejal
W C Bryant HS
New York, NY

Shanahan, Ellen J
Nardin Acad
Kenmore, NY

Shanahan, Jennifer
Fairport HS
Fairport, NY

Shand, Christine
Herbert H Lehman
Bronx, NY

Shang, Tom
Oyster Bay HS
E Norwich, NY

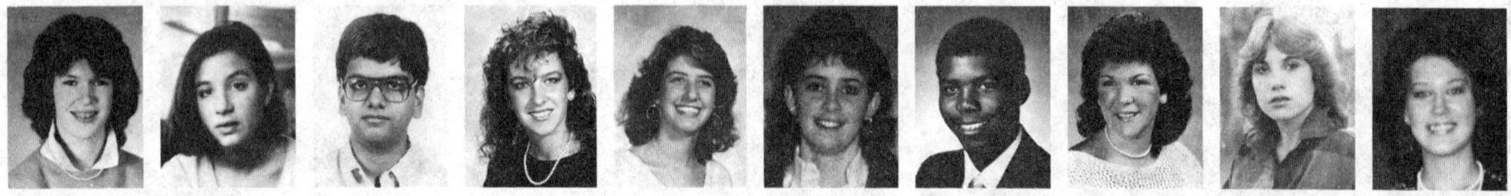

Shanks, Kathleen
Fillmore Central HS
Freedom, NY

Shapiro, Abigail
The Chapin Schl
New York, NY

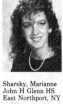

Sharma, Devindra
John Adams HS
S Ozone Park, NY

Sharsky, Marianne
John H Glenn HS
East Northport, NY

Shaulinski, Shelly
Fairport HS
Fairport, NY

Shaw, Heather
Paul V Moore HS
W Monroe, NY

Shaw, Richard
Bay Shore SR HS
Bay Shore, NY

Shawl, Heidi
Friendship Central
Friendship, NY

Shay, Susan
F D Roosevelt HS
Poughkeepsie, NY

Shea, Cynthia
Mont Pleasant HS
Schenectady, NY

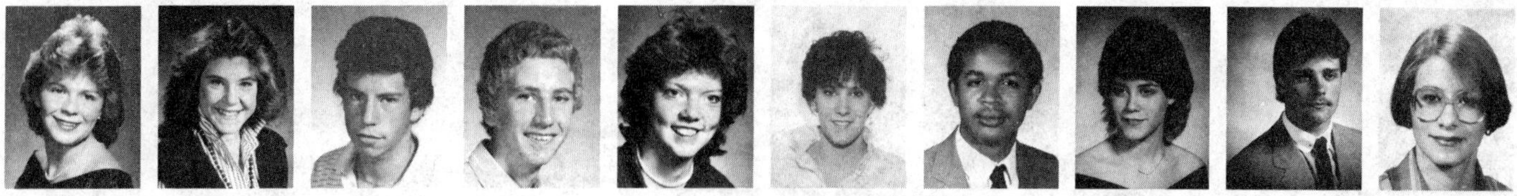

Sheedy, Karen A
Walter Panas HS
Peekskill, NY

Sheets, Christine M
Red Jacket Central
Shortsville, NY

Sherer, Brian A
Lawrence HS
Cedarhurst, NY

Sheridan, Chris
Brewster HS
Brewster, NY

Sheridan, Laurie Anthony A
Henninger HS
Syracuse, NY

Sheridan, Michelle
Cornwall Central HS
Cornwall, NY

Sheriff, Darin
New Rochelle HS
New Rochelle, NY

Sherman, Lisa
Notre Dame-Bishop Gibbons HS
Schenectady, NY

Sherman, Theodore J
G Ray Bodley HS
Fulton, NY

Sherwin, Carol S
Manhasset HS
Floral Park, NY

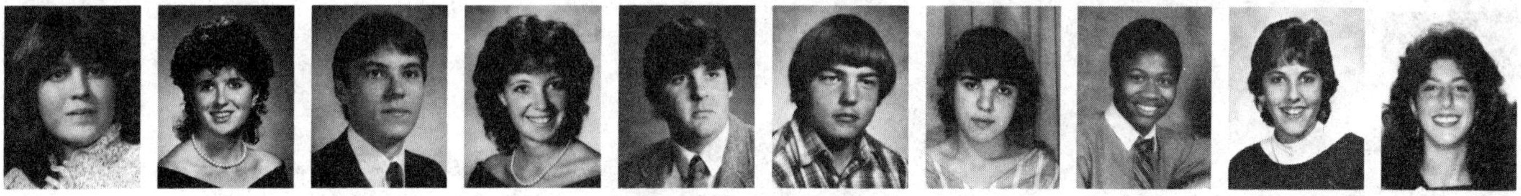

Sherwood, Shelly
Cato-Meridian HS
Cato, NY

Shevlin, Debra
Cornwall Central HS
Cornwall Hudson, NY

Sheweli, William
Aquinas Inst
Rochester, NY

Shields, Debra Anne
Northport HS
Northport, NY

Shirhall, Scott C
Whitney Point Central Schl
Richford, NY

Shirley, Thomas Edward Michael
Massena Central
Massena, NY

Shishmanian, Loretta
W C Bryant HS
New York, NY

Shivers, Eric
Mercy HS
Middle Island, NY

Shlefstein, Debbie L
Midwood HS
Brooklyn, NY

Shortino, Kristen
E J Wilson HS
Spencerport, NY

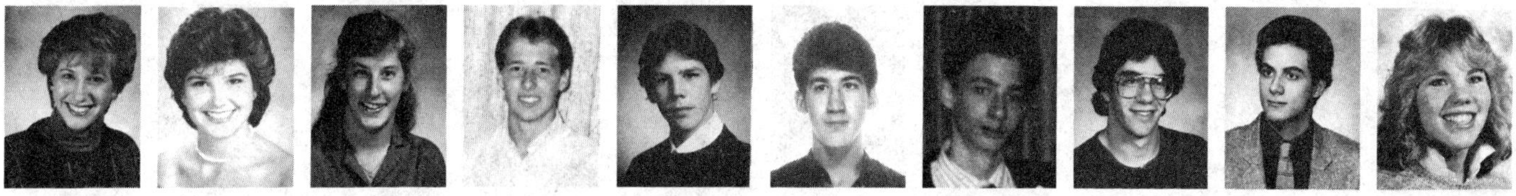

Shubert, Jennifer
Grand Island HS
Grand Island, NY

Shubert, Traci
Grand Island HS
Grand Island, NY

Shuemaker, Jennifer
Sacred Heart Acad
East Amherst, NY

Shuey, David
Webster Christian
Webster, NY

Shults, Dale
Canajoharie Central
Canajoharie, NY

Shumsky, David
Bethpage HS
Plainview, NY

Shustrin, Jarrett
South Shore HS
Brooklyn, NY

Shutes, Edward
Hornell HS
Hornell, NY

Siciliano, James
Sachem High Schl North Campus
Lake Ronkonkoma, NY

Sickler, Danielle
Stissing Mt JR SR
Stanfordville, NY

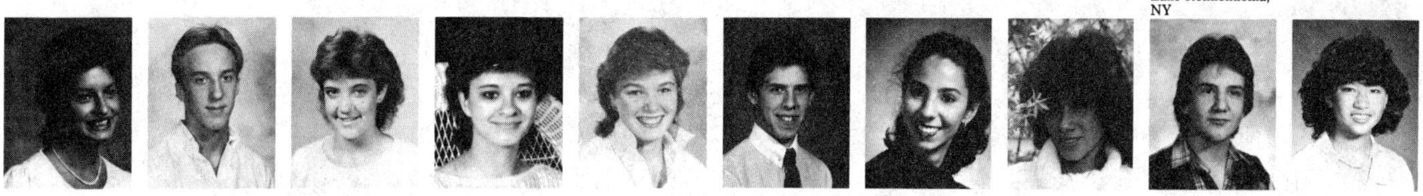

Side, Suzanne M
Newark SR HS
Newark, NY

Sidle, David
Odessa-Montour HS
Alpine, NY

Siebert, Kathryn
Batavia HS
Batavia, NY

Sieg, Kellie
South Park HS
Buffalo, NY

Siegel, Debbie
Middletown HS
Middletown, NY

Sifert, Eric
Saratoga Central Catholic HS
Schuylerville, NY

Sikorski, Julie
Cardinal Mooney
Rochester, NY

Silberman, Stacy
Newfield HS
Coram, NY

Silivestro, Michael
Gates-Chili HS
Rochester, NY

Silverio, Cynthia
Franklin Delano Roosevlet HS
Poughkeepsie, NY

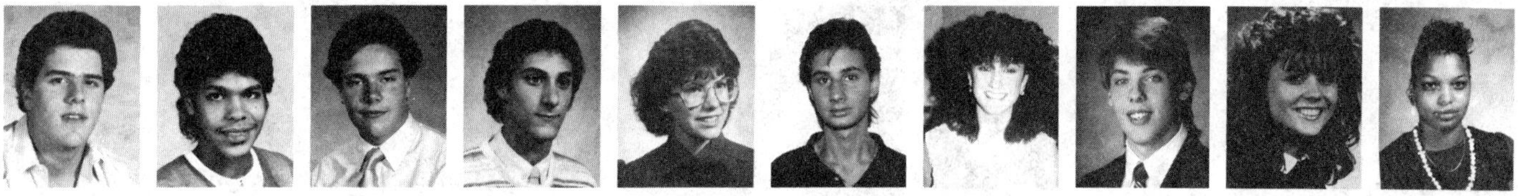

Silverman, Doug
Commack HS North
Commack, NY

Silvestri, Jr Pedro
Bay Shore HS
Bay Shore, NY

Simeone, Paul T
Tottenville HS
Staten Island, NY

Simicle, Michael
Bishop Ludden HS
Syracuse, NY

Simmons, Amanda
G Ray Bodley HS
Fulton, NY

Simon, Matthew
John Dewey HS
Brooklyn, NY

Simoncini, Tinamarie
St John Villa Acad
Staten Island, NY

Simonds, Timmie
Binghamton HS
Binghamton, NY

Simpson, Jacqueline
Notre Dame Acad
Staten Island, NY

Sims, Melissa Denise
Grand Island HS
Gr Island, NY

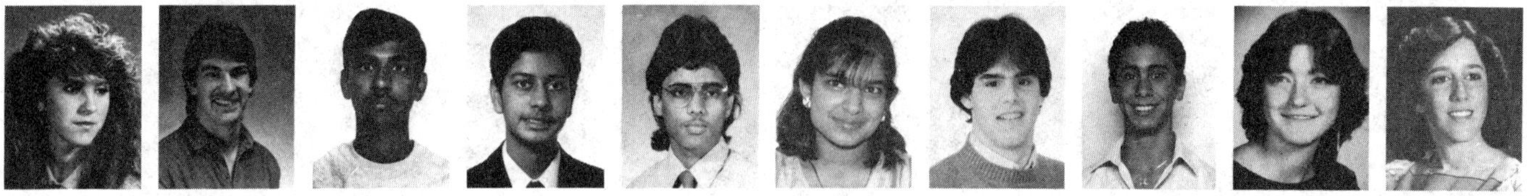

Sinclair, Alyson
Lawrence HS
Lawrence, NY

Sines, Roger
Bainbridge-Guilford
Bainbridge, NY

Singal, Ajay
Newtown HS
Elmhurst, NY

Singh, Navin
Stuyvesant HS
Woodside, NY

Singh, Subash
Mount Vernon HS
Mount Vernon, NY

Sinha, Vinceta
The Harley Schl
Pittsford, NY

Sinicropi, Michael
Amsterdam HS
Amsterdam, NY

Sinigaglia, Nicholas
Archbishop Molloy
Flushing, NY

Sink, Jennifer
Royalton Hartland Central HS
Sumpter, SC

Sinrod, Alysia L
Massapequa HS
Massapequa, NY

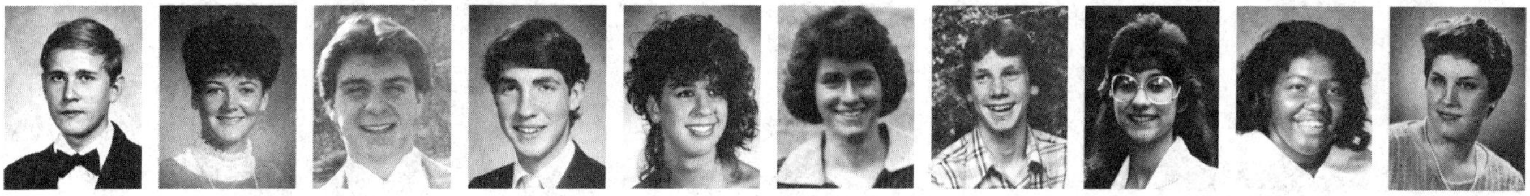

Sinyavich, Igor
Archibishop Molloy
Astoria, NY

Sipperly, Amy
Academy Of The Holy Names
Loudonville, NY

Sirico, Michael
Warwick Valley HS
Warwick, NY

Sisk, Steven H
Greece Athena HS
Rochester, NY

Sisley, Colleen
Whitesboro SR HS
Whitesboro, NY

Sisson, Christie
Victor Central HS
Macedon, NY

Sisson, Ken
Cassadaga Valley
Sinclairville, NY

Skelton, Kirstina
Aquinas Inst
Webster, NY

Skerritt, Stefanie Y
Adlai Ewing Stevenson HS
Bronx, NY

Skerry, Maura K
St Johns Acad
Plattsburgh, NY

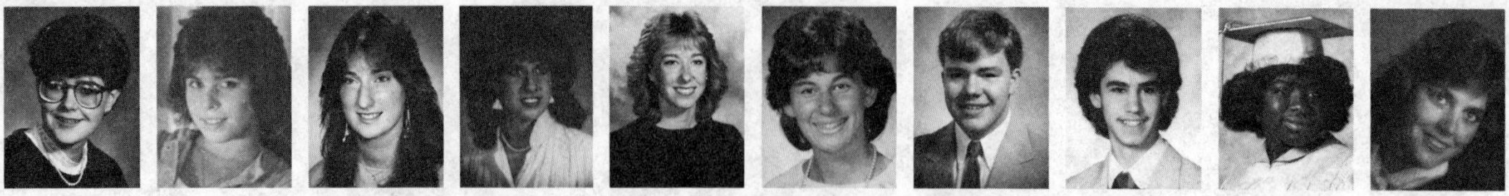

Skinkis, Inta A
Bayside HS
Bayside, NY

Skobel, Shari
Walter Paras HS
Peekskill, NY

Skolnik, Ursula N
Plainedge HS
Massapequa, NY

Slapelis, Linda
Bishop Kearney HS
Webster, NY

Slaski,
Anne-Christine
Scotia-Glenville HS
Scotia, NY

Slavkin, Deborah
Bay Shore HS
Bay Shore, NY

Slowik, Paul
Thomas
Lancaster Central
Lancaster, NY

Smalkin, Eric N
Patchogue-Medford
Patchogue, NY

Small, Maxine
Margaret
Grace Dodge Voc
Bronx, NY

Smart, Tracey
Newark Valley HS
Berkshire, NY

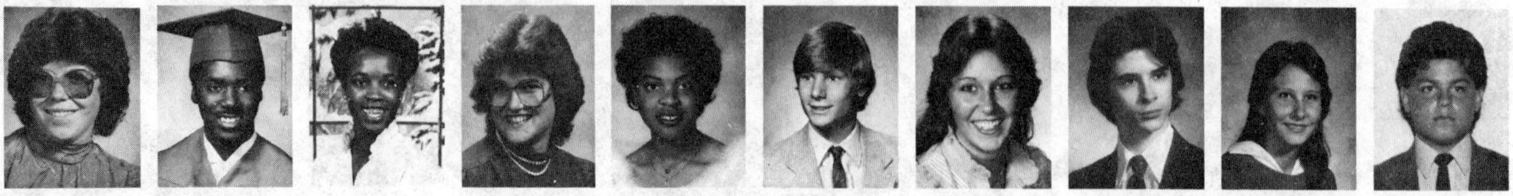

Smedley, Pamela
Bainbridge-Guilford
Bainbridge, NY

Smith, Ainsworth
Hempstead HS
Hempstead, NY

Smith, Angela
Newburgh Free
Newburgh, NY

Smith, Beth A
Letchworth Central
Portageville, NY

Smith, Carolyn
Hempstead HS
Hempstead, NY

Smith, Charles E
Sachem HS
Holtsville, NY

Smith, Christine
Rivearhead HS
Riverhead, NY

Smith, Christopher
S
Pine Plains Central
Ancram, NY

Smith, Cynthia
Onteora Central HS
Olivebridge, NY

Smith, Dennis
Smithtown East HS
Nesconset, NY

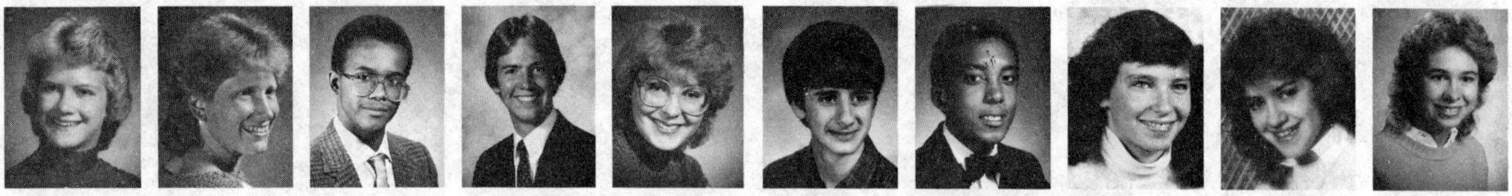

Smith, Doreen M
E J Wilson HS
Spencerport, NY

Smith, Edna
Susquehanna Valley
Harpursville, NY

Smith, Francisco
Stuyvesant HS
Brooklyn, NY

Smith, Gregory C
Huntington HS
Huntington Bay,
NY

Smith, Heather L
Newfane Central
Newfane, NY

Smith, Jason
Corning-Painted
Post West HS
Painted Post, NY

Smith, Jerome
New Rochelle HS
New Rochelle, NY

Smith, Jill
Bay Shore HS
Brightwaters, NY

Smith, Josie A M
Ogdensburg Free
Ogdensburg, NY

Smith, Kelly A
Cheektowaga
Central HS
Cheektowaga, NY

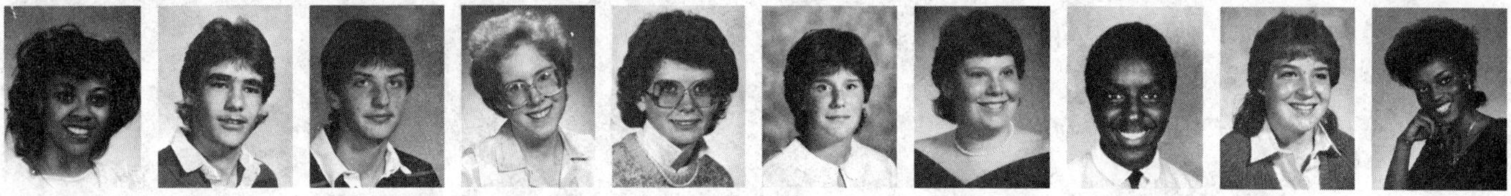

Smith, Kensala A
Buffalo Acad Fo V S
& Perf Arts
Cheektowaga, NY

Smith, Kraig
Dryden HS
Dryden, NY

Smith, Kyle V
Campbell Central
Campbell, NY

Smith, Linda S
Newburgh Free
New Windsor, NY

Smith, Lisa M
Marcus Whitman
JR-SR HS
Middlesex, NY

Smith, Liza
Cleveland Hill HS
Cheektowaga, NY

Smith, Maureen
Notre Dame Bishop
Gibbons HS
Ballston Lk, NY

Smith, Michael
Westbury HS
Westbury, NY

Smith, Michelle
Guilderland HS
Albany, NY

Smith, Patricia
New Dorp HS
Staten Island, NY

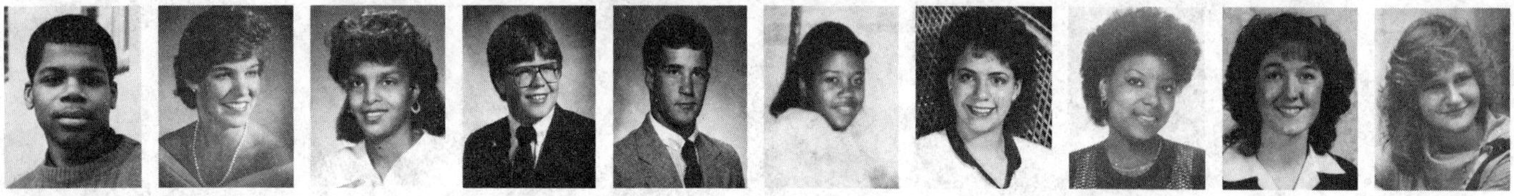

Smith, Jr Ranson
Hunter College HS
Brooklyn, NY

Smith, Rebecca
Mohonasen HS
Schenectady, NY

Smith, Sabrina
Cardinal Spellman
Bronx, NY

Smith, Scott G
Owego Free Acad
Apalachin, NY

Smith, Shane R
Baldwin SR HS
Baldwin, NY

Smith, Sharmaine
Immaculata HS
New York, NY

Smith, Sherrie
Addison Central HS
Addison, NY

Smith, Sonja E C
St John The Bapt
Wyandanch, NY

Smith, Susan
El-Lynn
Upper Room
Christian Schl
Central Islip, NY

Smith, Susan M
Arlington HS
Pleasant Valley, NY

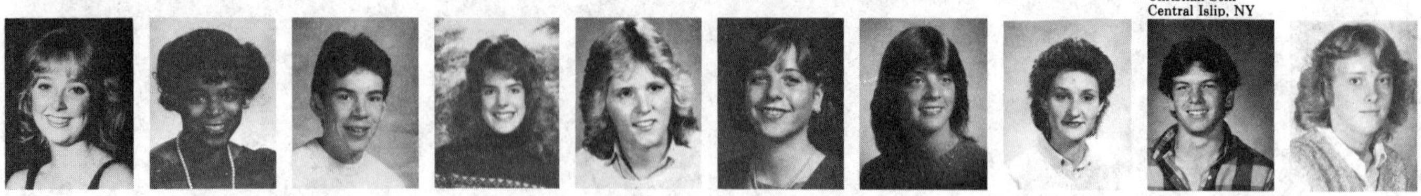

Smith, Suzanne
Sacred Heart Acad
Manhasset, NY

Smith, Sylvia
Gates-Chili SR HS
Rochester, NY

Smith, Thomas
Francis
George F Baker HS
Greenwood Lake,
NY

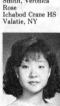

Smith, Veronica
Rose
Ichabod Crane HS
Valatie, NY

Smyth, Kelly Ann
Hicksville HS
Hicksville, NY

Snellinger, Andrea
Port Jervis HS
Pt Jervis, NY

Snow, Cindy
Union Endicott HS
Endicott, NY

Snyder, Deborah
Batavia HS
Batavia, NY

Snyder, Jammathon
J P
Milford Central HS
Maryland, NY

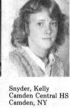

Snyder, Kelly
Camden Central HS
Camden, NY

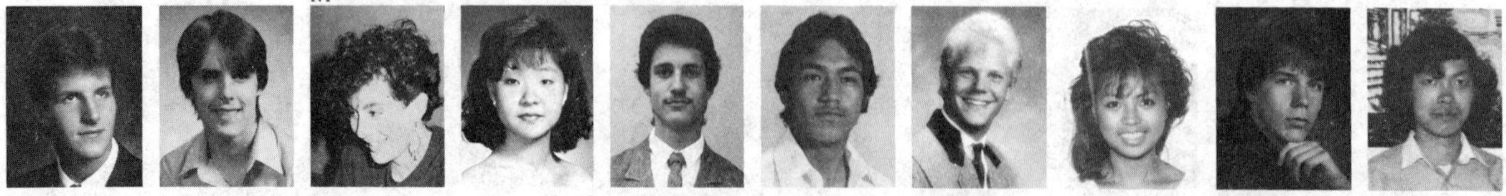

Snyder, Michael S
Brockport HS
Brockport, NY

Snyder, Robert
Riverside HS
Buffalo, NY

Sodos, Nadja S
Hunter College HS
Flushing, NY

Sohng, Heidi U
Our Lady Of
Lourdes HS
Wappingers Falls,
NY

Solak, Scott
Ossining HS
Ossining, NY

Solano, Louis
Mount Vernon HS
Mt Vernon, NY

Solberg, Robert S
Queensburg HS
Glens Falls, NY

Solomon, Barbra
St Agnes Acad
Flushing, NY

Soloski, Shane D
Catholic Central HS
Schaghticoke, NY

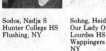

Son, Srane
Edison Tech HS
Rochester, NY

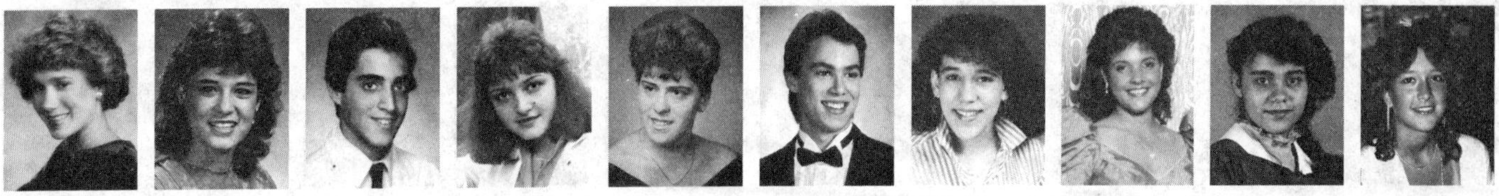

Soothcage, Terry Ann
Whitehall JR SR
Whitehall, NY

Sorce, Maria F
Niagara Wheatfield
Niagara Falls, NY

Sorgie, Jr Joseph G
William Floyd HS
Mastic Beach, NY

Sorkin, Diana
F D R HS
Brooklyn, NY

Sorrell, Shelley
Northern Adirondack Centra
Ellenburg Depot, NY

Sorrentino, II Gerald
St Francis HS
West Seneca, NY

Sosa, Tara
Monroe HS
Rochester, NY

Soskind, Pamela
Bronx HS Of
Flushing, NY

Soto, Myra
George Wingate HS
Brooklyn, NY

Soule, Debbie
W C Mepham HS
N Bellmore, NY

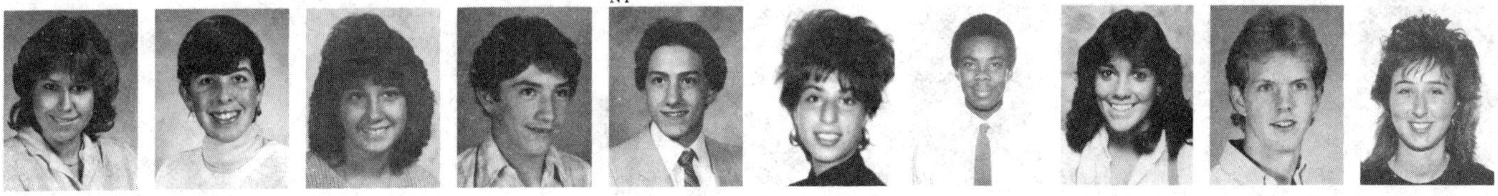

Soule, Kim
Hilton HS
Brockport, NY

Southwick, Cathy
Williamsville South
Williamsville, NY

Spado, Gina
Frankfort-Schuyler
Frankfort, NY

Spagnola, Brian
Amsterdam HS
Amsterdam, NY

Spagnolo, Anthony
Spring Valley HS
Spring Vly, NY

Spanakos, Helen
Garden City SR HS
Garden City, NY

Spence, Caple
Smithtown HS West
Smithtown, NY

Spence, Ruth
Pelham Memorial
Pelham, NY

Spencer, Daniel R
Maple Grove JR Sr
Bemus Point, NY

Spera, Patricia
Port Richmond HS
Staten Island, NY

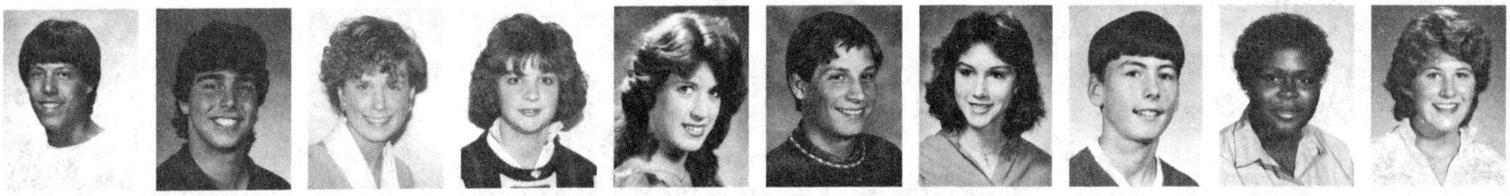

Speter, Andrew
Walt Whitman HS
Huntington Sta, NY

Speziale, Lance
Dunkirk HS
Dunkirk, NY

Spiegel, Katherine
Academy Of St
Sayville, NY

Spiegelglass, Joy
Patchogve-Medford
Medford, NY

Spithogianis, Despina
Whitestone Acad
Whitestone, NY

Spitz, Steven
Pierson HS
Sag Harbor, NY

Sprenz, Valerie M
Alfred G Berner HS
Massapequa, NY

Squiers, Kevin
Hoosick Falls Central HS
Eagle Bridge, NY

St Cyr, Patricia
Huntington HS
Huntington, NY

St Germain, Katherine A
Our Lady Of Lourdes HS
Verbank, NY

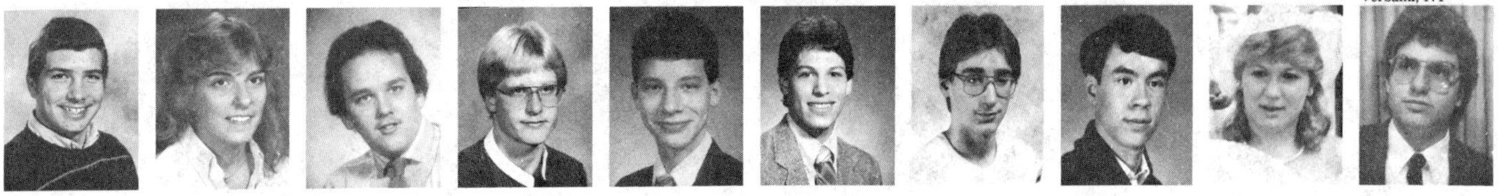

St John, Mark L
Canajoharie Central
Palatine Bridge, NY

St Louis, Julie A
Carthage Central
Deer River, NY

St Onge, Scott
Hoosic Valley Central HS
Schagticoke, NY

St Peter, Matthew
Sherburne-Earlville
Sherburne, NY

St Pierre, Christian
Cohoes HS
Cohoes, NY

Stabile, Thomas J
Ardsley HS
Ardsley, NY

Stacy, Ron
North Tonawanda SR HS
N Tonawanda, NY

Staffa, James A
Eden SR HS
Eden, NY

Stafford, Denise
Sharon Springs Central Schl
Sharon Springs, NY

Stahlin, Bruce
Fayetteville-Manlius
Manlius, NY

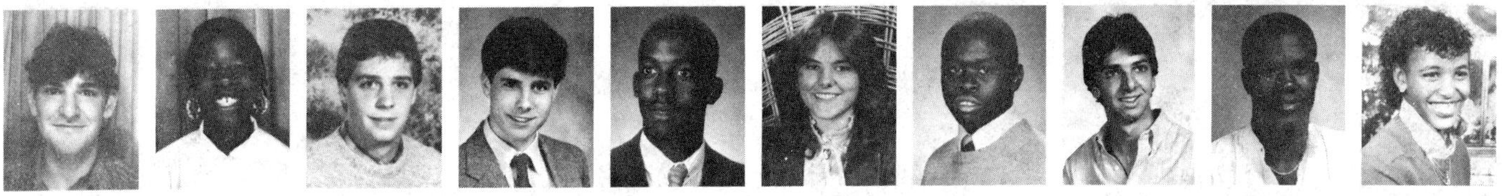

Staiman, Ari
Bronx Science HS
New York, NY

Staley, Jeannette E
Dewitt Clinton HS
Bronx, NY

Stalker, Mark D
Chatham HS
East Chatham, NY

Stamp, Michael
Canisius HS
Amherst, NY

Stanford, Derrick
Uniondale HS
Uniondale, NY

Stangle, Kathy
Perth Central HS
Amsterdam, NY

Stanley, II William
Valley Central HS
Walden, NY

Stanojevic, John
Rocky Point JR SR
Rocky Pt, NY

Staples, Ronald
Riverside HS
Buffalo, NY

Staples, Shaniqua
Newburgh Free
Newburgh, NY

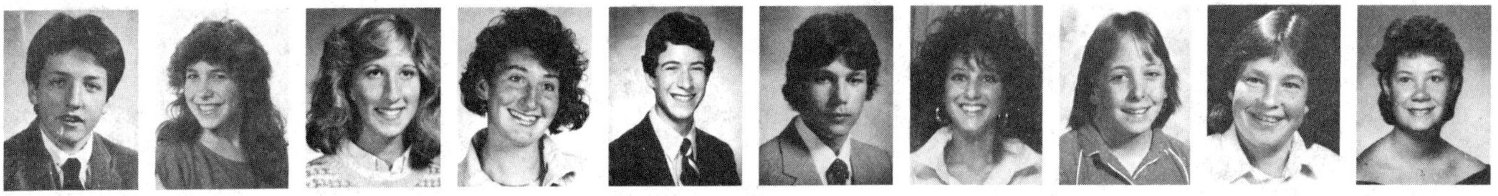

Stapleton, Michael
Mc Quaid Jesuit HS
Fairport, NY

Stark, Rachel
Susan Wagner HS
Staten Island, NY

Stark, Susan Allison
Roy C Ketcham HS
Poughkeepsie, NY

Starkman, Elisabeth Kerr
Half Hollow Hills High School West
Dix Hills, NY

Starkman, Scott D
Alfred G Berner HS
Massapequa, NY

Starowitz, Jr Leo
Byron-Bergen HS
Elba, NY

Stasio, Lisa
Connetquot HS
Oakdale, NY

Stearns, Patricia
Mont Pleasant HS
Schenectady, NY

Steck, Lori Anne M
Buff Acad For Visual & Perfmn
Buffalo, NY

Steele, Elaine
Connetquot HS
Oakdale, NY

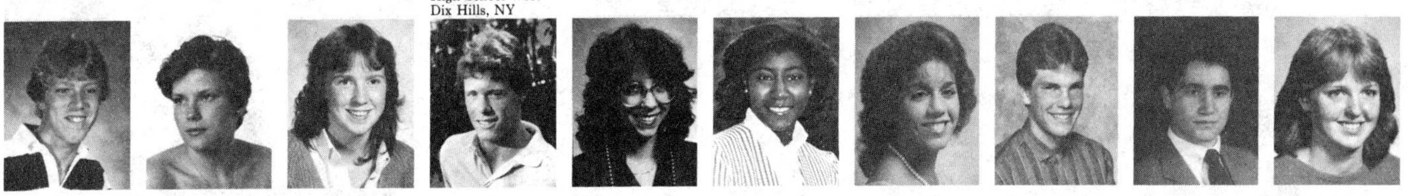

Steele, Todd
Pittsford-Menden
Fairport, NY

Steffens, Barbara
Newtown HS
Elmhurst, NY

Steiger, Maureen
Sweet Home SR HS
N Tonawanda, NY

Stein, David
Rockland Country Day HS
New City, NY

Stephan, Lisa
Cardinal O-Hara HS
Amherst, NY

Stephen, Lynnea Y
Convent Of The Sacred Heart HS
New York, NY

Stephens, Laura L
Depew HS
Depew, NY

Stepnowsky, Jr Carl J
Southold HS
Southold, NY

Stevens, Edward T
Liverpool HS
Liverpool, NY

Stevens, Heather
Batavia HS
Batavia, NY

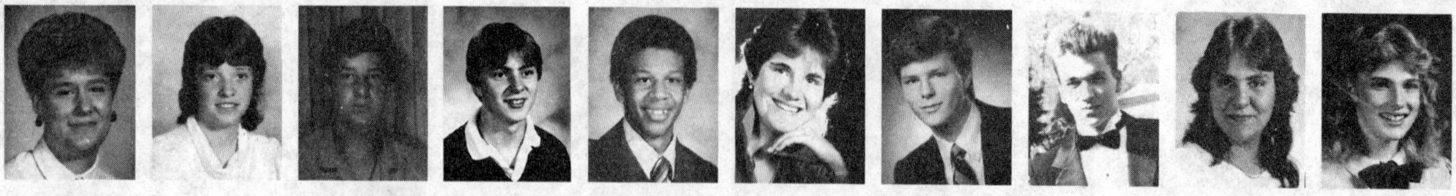

Stevens, Kathleen
Hoosick Falls
Central Schl
Hoosick Falls, NY

Stevenson, Margaret
Watkins Glen HS
Burdett, NY

Stewart, Matthew
South Shore HS
Brooklyn, NY

Stewart, Milton
Pulaski JR-SR HS
Richland, NY

Stewart, Paul
Cairo-Durham HS
E Durham, NY

Stillwell, Doreen
Tully JR-SR HS
Tully, NY

Stirlen, W
Christopher
Sutherland HS
Rochester, NY

Stock, Eric
Mc Quaid Jesuit HS
Rochester, NY

Stock, Pamela
Cleveland Hill HS
Cheektowaga, NY

Stockwell, Kimberly
Frewsburg Central
Frewsburg, NY

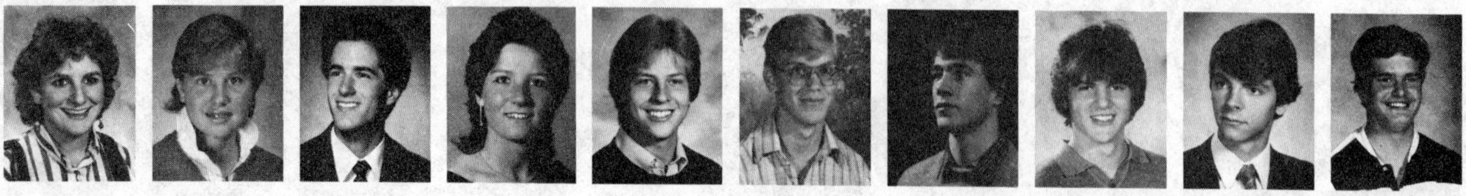

Stocum, Linda
Tupper Lake HS
Tupper Lake, NY

Stoecker, Amy
Cazenovia Central
Cazenovia, NY

Stoff, Matthew
Oceanside HS
Oceanside, NY

Stoffers, Carol
St Peters HS For
Staten Isl, NY

Stoltie, David
Potsdam Central HS
Potsdam, NY

Stone, Gregory
Minisink Valley HS
Pt Jervis, NY

Stonecipher, Allan
Skaneateles Central
Skaneateles, NY

Storen, Ken
Mahopac HS
Mahopac, NY

Stornelli, Marcus A
Red Creek Central
Martville, NY

Stoutenburg, Jeffrey
Onteora JR SR HS
West Hurley, NY

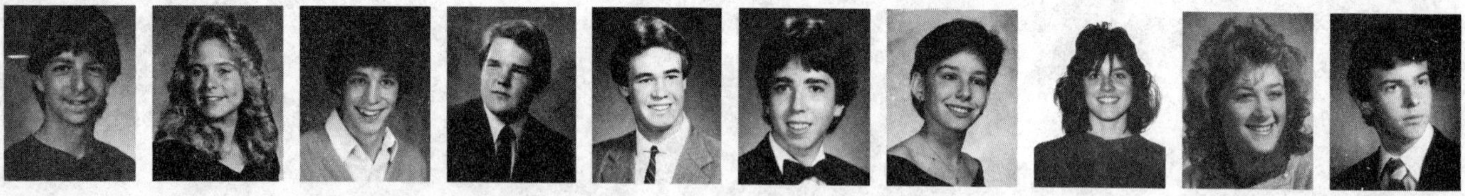

Stoyle, Shawn J
Dunkirk SR HS
Dunkirk, NY

Strahm, Diane
New Dorp HS
Staten Island, NY

Strandberg, David C
Brockport SR HS
Brockport, NY

Strange, Rodney J
Southside HS
Elmira, NY

Stranzl, Steven E
Cardinal Spellman
Bronx, NY

Strassberg, Adam
Franklin
Ramapo SR HS
Monsey, NY

Straus, Sherry
Jamaica HS
Jamaica, NY

Strazza, Claudine
Michele
Cardinal Spellman
Bronx, NY

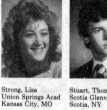

Strong, Lisa
Union Springs Acad
Kansas City, MO

Stuart, Thomas R
Scotia Glenville HS
Scotia, NY

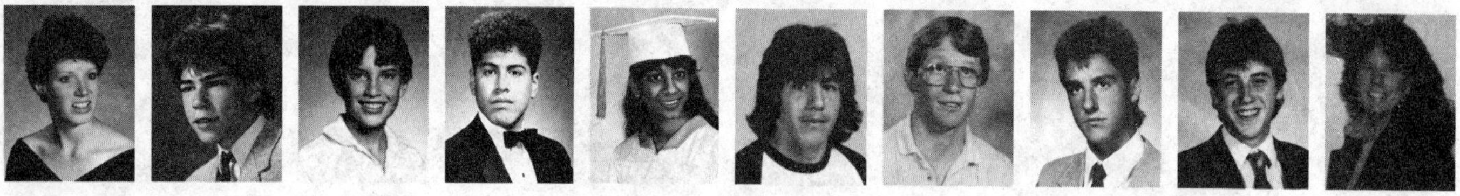

Stucin, Laura A
Tottenville HS
Staten Island, NY

Stulmaker, Jeffrey
M
Herkimer HS
Herkimer, NY

Sturman, Daniel
Niskayuna HS
Schenectady, NY

Suarez, Robert
Xavier HS
Brooklyn, NY

Sukhdeo, Alicia
Newtown HS
Elmhurst, NY

Sulli, Mike
Farmingdale HS
Farmingdale, NY

Sullivan, Brian
Carmel HS
Carmel, NY

Sullivan, John W
East Islip HS
Islip Terrace, NY

Sullivan, Sean
Monsignor Farrell
Staten Island, NY

Sullivan, Shannon
Sacred Heart Acad
Lynbrook, NY

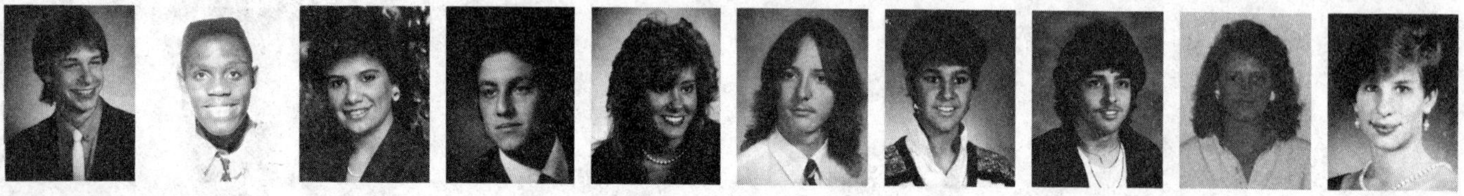

Sullivan, William
Johnstown HS
Johnstown, NY

Sumner, Stephen
Northport HS
East Northport, NY

Sumowicz,
Alessandra M
Convent Of The
Sacred Heart HS
Jackson Heights

Suozzi, Joseph P
Batavia HS
Batavia, NY

Supley, Lucinda L
Tully Central HS
Tully, NY

Surento, Timothy J
Amsterdam HS
Amsterdam, NY

Suriani, Susan F
Hornell HS
N Hornell, NY

Surowiec, Chuck
Wayne Central HS
Ontario, NY

Suslik, Michelle
Auburn HS
Tabb, VA

Sussman, Randi B
John F Kennedy HS
Riverdale, NY

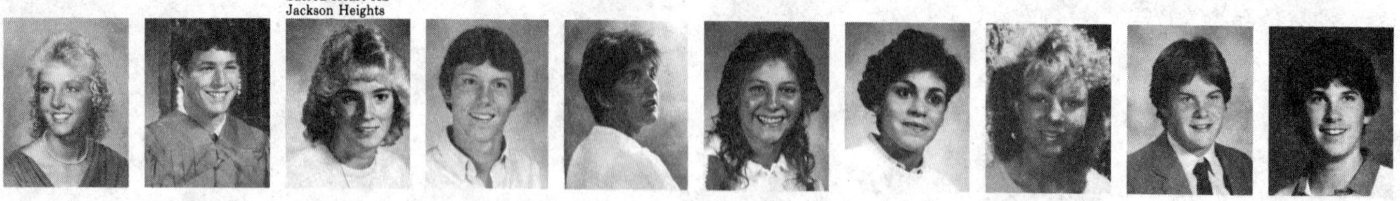

Suszczynski, Jean E
Commack HS South
Commack, NY

Sutfin, Mike
East Syracuse
Minoa HS
Kirkville, NY

Sutherland, Melody
Pulaski JR SR HS
Pulaski, NY

Swan, Jeff
Newfane SR HS
Newfane, NY

Swanson, Elizabeth
Avon Central HS
Avon, NY

Swartwood, Melissa
Dundee Central HS
Rock Stream, NY

Swartz, Stephanie
Bishop Ludden HS
Syracuse, NY

Swedish, Kristen
Harborfields HS
Centerport, NY

Sweeney, Douglas
Monsignor Farrell
New York, NY

Sweeney, Mark T
Kingston HS
Kingston, NY

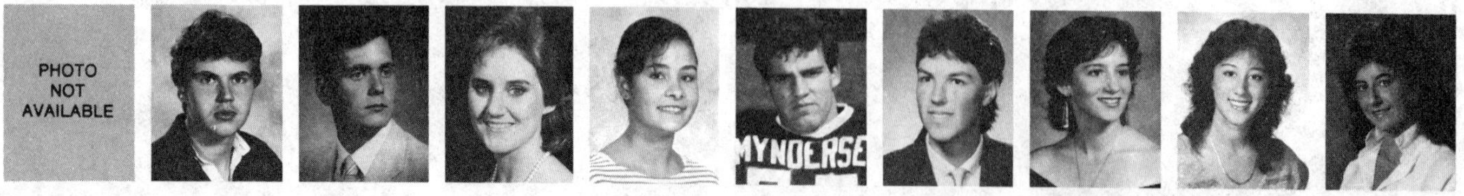
PHOTO
NOT
AVAILABLE
MYNDERSE

Sweeney, Orville R
Uniondale HS
Uniondale, NY

Sweeney, Steve
Gloversville HS
Gloversville, NY

Sweeney, Jr William
R
Amsterdam HS
Hagaman, NY

Sweet, Chandy
Alden Central HS
Alden, NY

Swender, Jennifer
Jamesville-De Witt
Dewitt, NY

Swenson, Scott
Mynderes Acad
Seneca Falls, NY

Swenton, Jr William
F
Smithtown West HS
Hauppauge, NY

Swick, Jr Sigrid
Jamaica HS
New York, NY

Swiss, Carissa Leigh
Huntington HS
Huntington, NY

Switzer, Michele
Rome Free Acad
Rome, NY

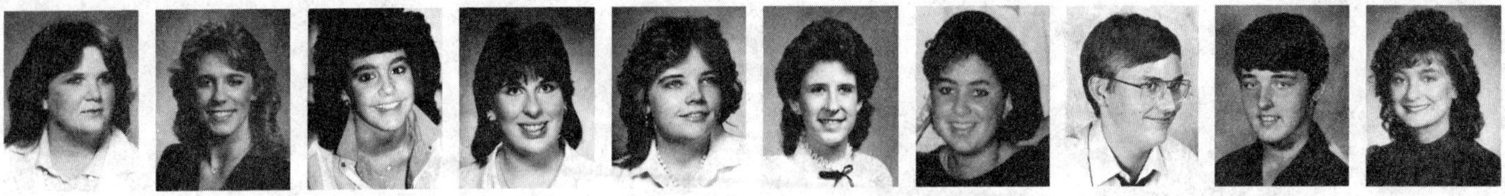

Sykes, Debbie
Smithtown East HS
Nesconset, NY

Sylka, Wendy
Villa Maria Acad
Buffalo, NY

Sylvander, Jennifer
St John The Baptist
Lindenhurst, NY

Sylvester, Laura
Bethpage HS
Bethpage, NY

Symes, Cheryl
Centor Moriches HS
Center Moriches, NY

Szalasny, Denise
John F Kennedy JR SR HS
Cheektowaga, NY

Szalkowski, Kelley
Whitesboro SR HS
Utica, NY

Szmal, Paul M
Paul V Moore HS
W Monroe, NY

Szokoli, John
John Glenn HS
Greenlawn, NY

Szymko, Shelley Ann
Whitesboro SR HS
Marcy, NY

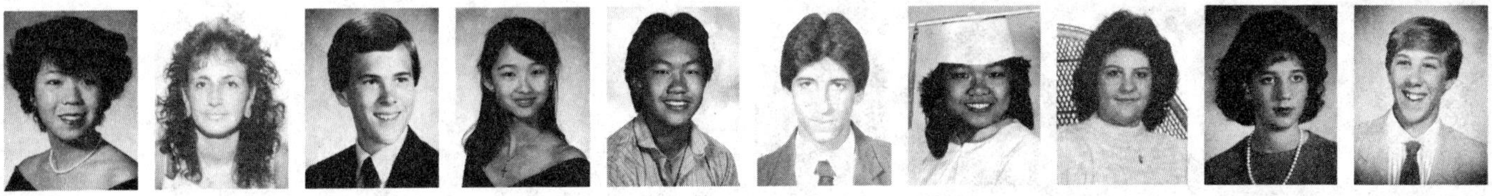

Takeishi, Christine Y
Laguardia HS Of Music & The Arts
New York, NY

Talbot, Geraldine
Saint Francis Prep
Bayside, NY

Tallant, Stephen
Liverpool HS
Liverpool, NY

Tam, Alice
La Guardia High Schl Of Musi
New York, NY

Tam, Ed
John Glenn HS
E Northport, NY

Tamarazo, Frank
Mckee Technical HS
Staten Island, NY

Tamayo, Mayvelyn G
St Francis Prep
Jamaica, NY

Tamburrino, Sharon
Herkimer HS
E Herkimer, NY

Tamer, Bonnie L
Utica Free Acad
Utica, NY

Tanner, David
Sandy Creek Central
Lacona, NY

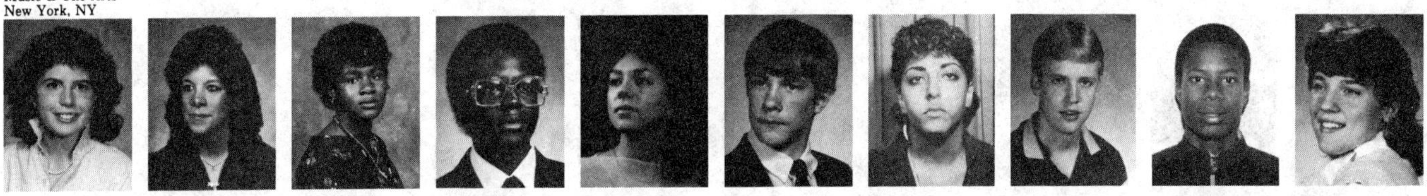

Taranto, Anne C
Lynbrook SR HS
Lynbrook, NY

Taranto, Lynda
Central HS
Valley Stream, NY

Tarver, Phyllis
Bishop Grimes HS
Syracuse, NY

Tarver, III Walter L
Henninger HS
Syracuse, NY

Tarzia, Michele
Liverpool HS
Clay, NY

Tavernia, Lee
Franklin Acad
Malone, NY

Tawil, Khouloud
Yonkers HS
Yonkers, NY

Taylor, D Jay
North Rose-Wolcott
Wolcott, NY

Taylor, Daivery
Freeport HS
Freeport, NY

Taylor, Karla M
Marathon Central
Cortland, NY

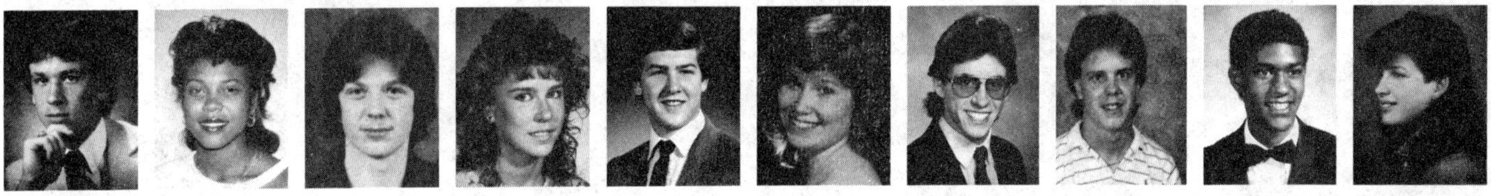

Taylor, Kevin A
New Fane SR HS
New Fane, NY

Taylor, Octavia Trinette
The Garden Schl
Laurelton, NY

Taylor, Scott
Wyoming Central
Wyoming, NY

Taylor, Stephanie
Walton Central HS
Walton, NY

Teague, Stephen S
Stony Brook Schl
Port Jefferson, NY

Tears, Natalie
Wallkill SR HS
Wallkill, NY

Tedd, II Michael T
Goshen Central HS
Goshen, NY

Tedford, Eric
Chittenango HS
Chittenango, NY

Tejera, Peter
Christian Brothers
Syracuse, NY

Tekmitchov, Sophia
Bolton Central HS
Bolton Landing, NY

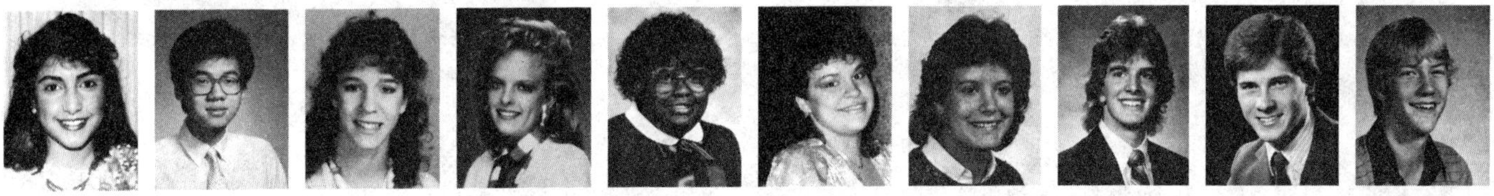

Tellalian, Sabrina
Bethpage HS
Plainview, NY

Teng, Eric
Herricks SR HS
New Hyde Park, NY

Terranova, Lisa
Newfield HS
Coram, NY

Terry, Amy
The Masters Schl
Dallas, TX

Terry, Michelle
Nazareth Acad
Rochester, NY

Tersy, Angelina
Dominican Commerical HS
Flushing, NY

Tessier, Barbara
Niagara Wheatfield SR HS
Sanborn, NY

Tewes, Eric M
Phelham Memorial
Pelham, NY

Thacher, Jeffrey T
Potsdam Central HS
Potsdam, NY

Thierling, Curtis
New Lebanon Central Schl
Canaan, NY

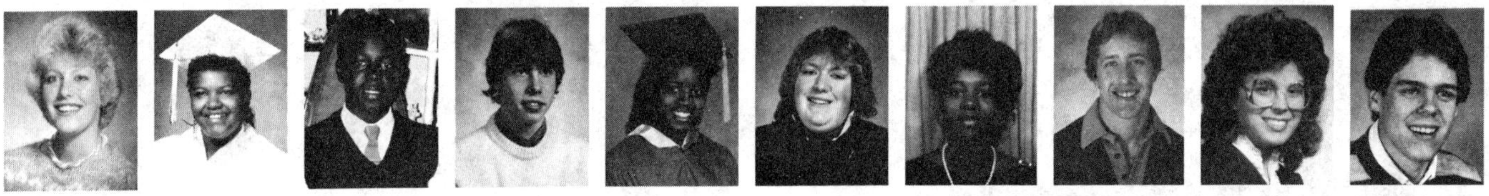

Thillman, Lori M
Waterloo SR HS
Waterloo, NY

Thomas, Dayana
Commack HS South
Dix Hills, NY

Thomas, George
Murry Bergtraum
Brooklyn, NY

Thomas, Jerry
Canton HS
Canton, NY

Thomas, Karen
Fashion Industries
Staten Island, NY

Thomas, Karen
G Ray Bodley HS
Fulton, NY

Thomas, Katrina
George Fowler HS
Syracuse, NY

Thomas, Maurice P
Claude C Doxtator
Waterloo, NY

Thomas, Patti
Union Springs Acad
Blossvale, NY

Thomas, Robert
South Park HS
Buffalo, NY

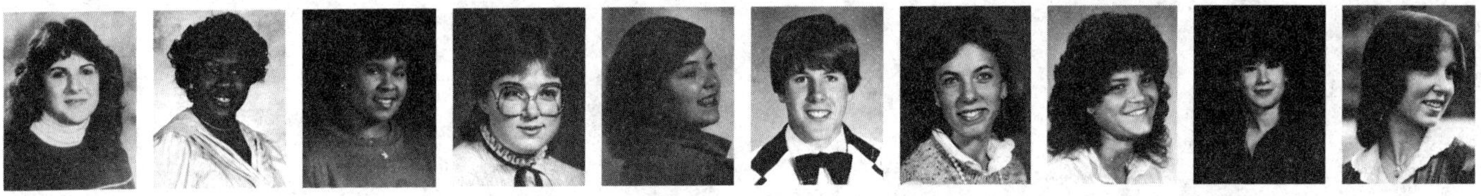

Thomas, Robin
Franklin Acad
Malone, NY

Thomas, Yvondria
Edison Technical
Rochester, NY

Thompson, Carla
Wheatland Chili JR SR HS
Scottsville, NY

Thompson, Connie
Addison Central
Addison, NY

Thompson, Donna
Windham-Ashland-Jewett Central HS
Jewett, NY

Thompson, Edward D
Msgr Farrell HS
Staten Island, NY

Thompson, Jennifer
Schuylerville Central
Schuylerville, NY

Thompson, Renee
Liberty Central HS
Liberty, NY

Thompson, Tammi
Midlakes HS
Phelps, NY

Thompson, Teresa
Charles D Amico
Albion HS
Albion, NY

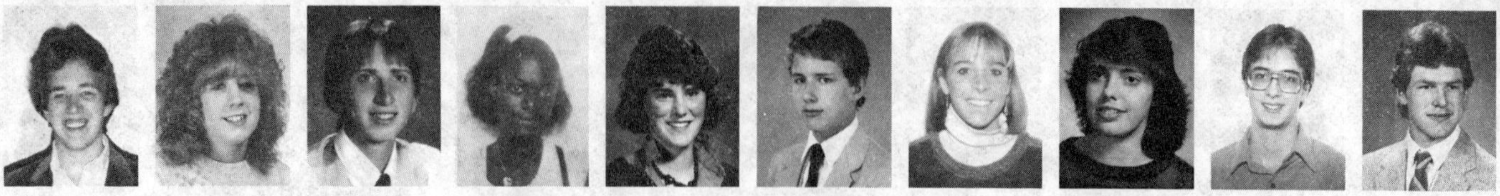

- Thorne, Gary / Seaford HS / Wantagh, NY
- Thornton, Kim / Cazenovia HS / Manlius, NY
- Thorp, Mark Andrew / Gananda HS / Walworth, NY
- Thorpe, Dashia A / John Jay HS / Brooklyn, NY
- Thune, Kelly / Thousand Islands / Cape Vincent, NY
- Thurlow, David K / Horseheads HS / Horseheads, NY
- Tietgen, Margaret / Honeoye Falls-Lima / Honeoye Falls, NY
- Tiffany, Teresa / Victor Central HS / Farmington, NY
- Tilenius, Eric W / Walt Whitman HS / Huntington Sta, NY
- Tillotson, John W / Marathon Central / Marathon, NY

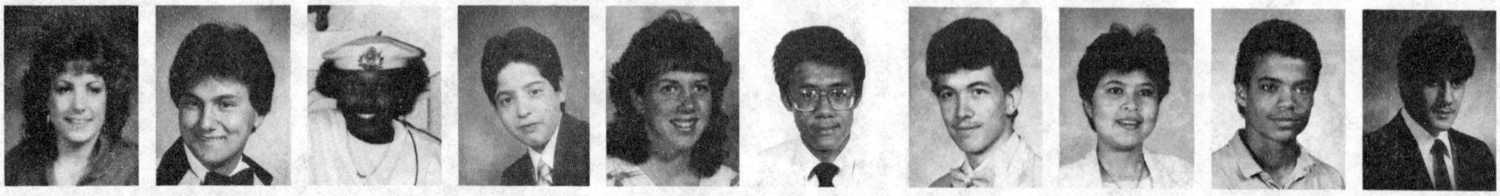

- Timberlake, Sandra / Frankfurt American / Apo New York, NY
- Tindale, Tomas M / Bishop Kearney HS / Rochester, NY
- Tinsley, Tywanda / Mount Vernon HS / Mt Vernon, NY
- Tiralongo, Frank / Bishop Ford CC HS / Brooklyn, NY
- Tittemore, Sharon / Mahopac HS / Mahopac, NY
- To, Edward Ha / Brooklyn Technical / Elmhurst, NY
- Tobin, Kevin / Wm E Grady / Brooklyn, NY
- Toch, Siphanny / Seward Park HS / New York, NY
- Tolliver, Joel E / Charles H Roth HS / W Henrietta, NY
- Toma, Michael / Mechanicville HS / Mechanicville, NY

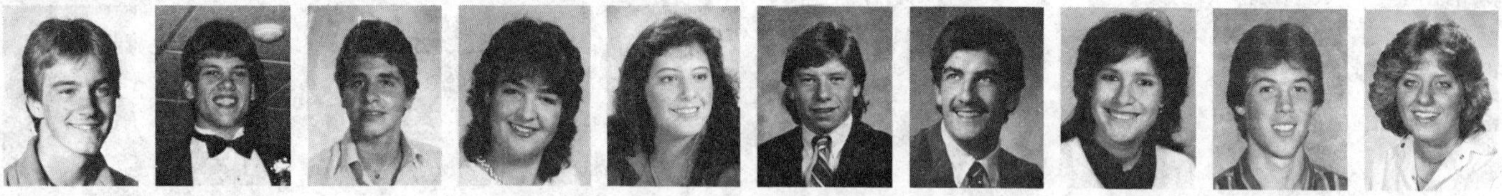

- Tomaka, Rich / Hamburg SR HS / Hamburg, NY
- Tomkosky, Michael / Charles H Roth HS / Henrietta, NY
- Tommaso, Ralph / Moore Catholic HS / Staten Island, NY
- Tomossonie, Robin / Westhampton Beach SR HS / East Moriches, NY
- Tooley, Laurie A / Liverpool HS / Liverpool, NY
- Topalovich, Stefan / St Pauls Schl / Garden City, NY
- Topping, Dave / Edison HS / Elmira Hts, NY
- Toquica, Claudia / Bellport HS / Bellport, NY
- Torebka, Thomas / Bolton Central HS / Bolton Landing, NY
- Torick, Carla / Hauppauge HS / York, PA

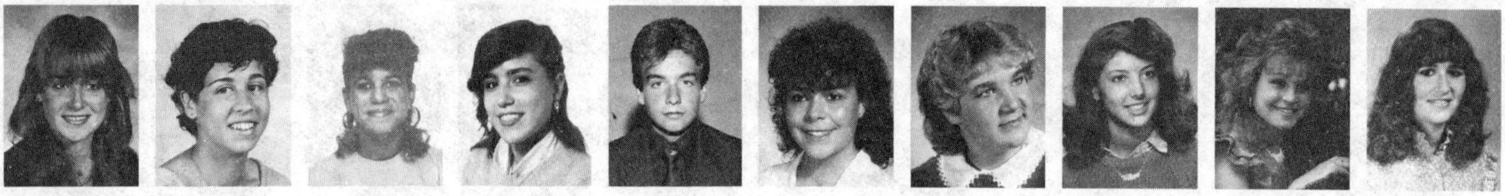

- Tormey, Megan Garry / Cold Spring Harbor / Lloyd Harbor, NY
- Torres, Christine / Bay Shore HS / Bay Shore, NY
- Torres, Eileen / Cardinal Spellman / Ny, NY
- Torres, Michele / John F Kennedy HS / New York, NY
- Torretta, Thomas John / St Peters Boys HS / Staten Island, NY
- Toscano, Ann Marie / John Marshall HS / Rochester, NY
- Tostanoski, Tina M / Corning Painted Post West HS / Corning, NY
- Tovo, Kathie / Smithtown High School East / Saint James, NY
- Tracey, Sheila / Arlington HS / Poughkeepsie, NY
- Trapini, Annette / Scotia-Glenville HS / Scotia, NY

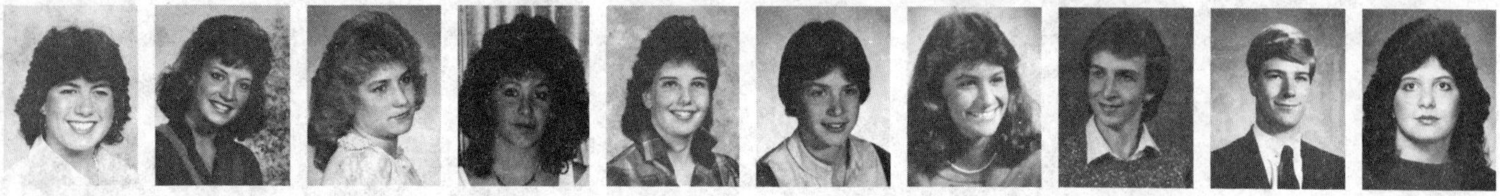

- Traverse, Kara / Ballston Spa HS / Ballston Spa, NY
- Travis, Claudeen / Sherburne-Earlville / Sherburne, NY
- Travis, Tammie / Westfield Academy & Central Schl / Westfield, NY
- Trazoff, Shari / Tottenville HS / Staten Island, NY
- Tretiak, Sandi / Frankfort-Schuyler / Frankfort, NY
- Triandafils, Richard / Ward Melville HS / Setauket, NY
- Tringali, Tiffany / Liverpool HS / Liverpool, NY
- Tripp, Craig / Bolton Central HS / Bolton Landing, NY
- Tripp, James L / Mc Quaid Jesuit HS / Pittsford, NY
- Trizzino, Daphna / John Dewey HS / Brooklyn, NY

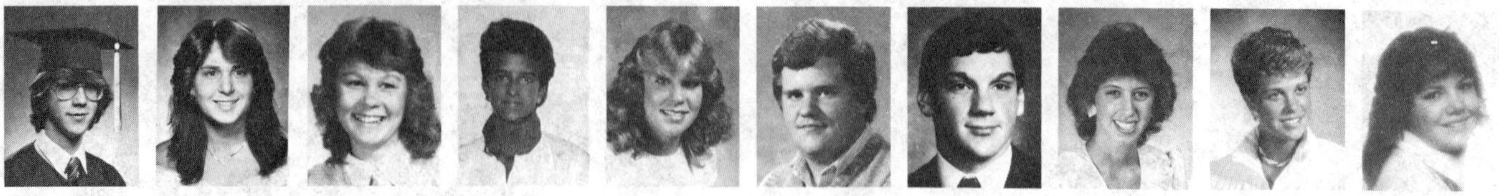

- Troch, Rodney / Center Moriches HS / Center Moriches, NY
- Trocha, Ingrid M / St Francis Prep Schl / Glendale, NY
- Trofinoff, Barbara J / Beacon HS / Beacon, NY
- Troisi, Dawn / Wantagh HS / Wantagh, NY
- Trojanovic, Silvia / Frontier SR HS / Lakeview, NY
- Trombly, Michael / Ogdensburg Free / Rensselaer Falls, NY
- Tronolone, Jr Michael F / Norwich HS / Norwich, NY
- Troutman, Teri / Churchville-Chili / Rochester, NY
- True, Laurie / Saranac Central HS / Saranac, NY
- Truman, Tracy / Afton Central HS / Nineveh, NY

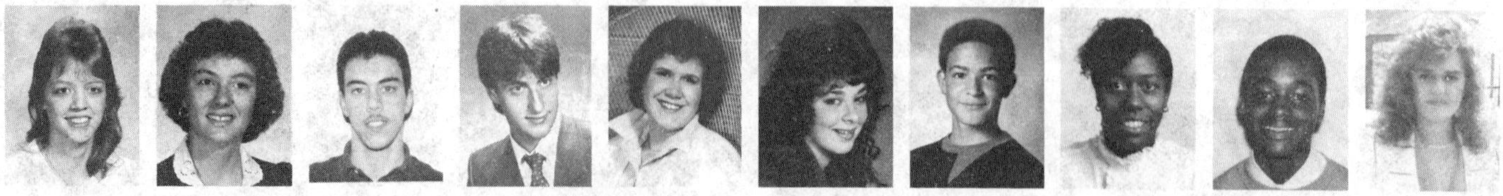

- Trumbauer, Tammy / Herkimer SR HS / Herkimer, NY
- Tryt, Krystina / Our Lady Of Mercy / Rochester, NY
- Tsatsaronis, Chris / St Francis Prep / Flushing, NY
- Tsekerides, Ted E / Sleepy Hollow HS / N Tarrytown, NY
- Tubbs, Joy / Saratota Central Catholic HS / Saratoga Springs, NY
- Tuccillo, Gail / Cornwall Central HS / Highland Mills, NY
- Tuck, Michael / New Rochelle HS / New Rochelle, NY
- Tucker, Joy Celeste / Hempstead HS / Hempstead, NY
- Tucker, Mark / Edmundian Ignatius Rice HS / New York, NY
- Tufarielli, Gia-Cynthia / St Edmund HS / Brooklyn, NY

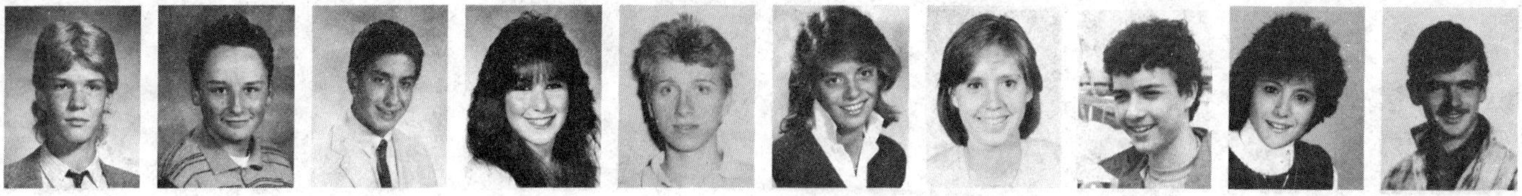

Tully, William T
John S Burke Chs
Chester, NY

Tunnicliff, Jeffrey
Addison Central HS
Cameron, NY

Turco, Jon Scott
Monsignor Farrell
Staten Island, NY

Turer, Joleen Georgi
New Rochelle HS
New Rochelle, NY

Turk, Kevin
Msgr Farrell HS
Staten Island, NY

Turnbull, Tracey
Mahopac HS
Mahopac, NY

Turner, Keren
Liverpool HS
Baldwinsville, NY

Turque, Theo
H S For The
New York, NY

Turturro, Nancy
Bellport HS
E Patchogue, NY

Tuttle, Kevin
Waterville Central
Waterville, NY

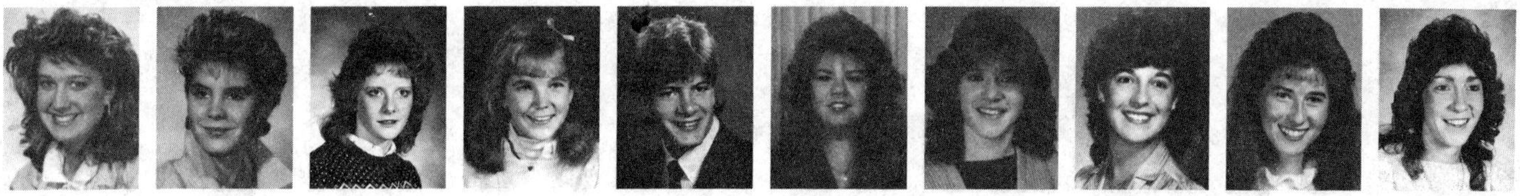

Tyndall, Kimberly
Walt Whitman HS
Hunt Station, NY

Tyndell, Jennifer
Corning Painted
Post West HS
Beaver Dams, NY

Tyner, Melinda
Avoca Central Schl
Avoca, NY

Tyo, Suzanne
Red Jacket Central
Shortsville, NY

Uhl, Lawrence
Kingston HS
Kingston, NY

Ulrich, Victoria
Westbury SR HS
Westbury, NY

Umbriaco, Melanie
Trott Vocation &
Niagara Falls, NY

Ungaro, Donna
Tuckahoe HS
Bronxville, NY

Unitas, Carolyn
Patchogue-Medford
Medford, NY

Upcraft, Vicky
Oswego HS
Oswego, NY

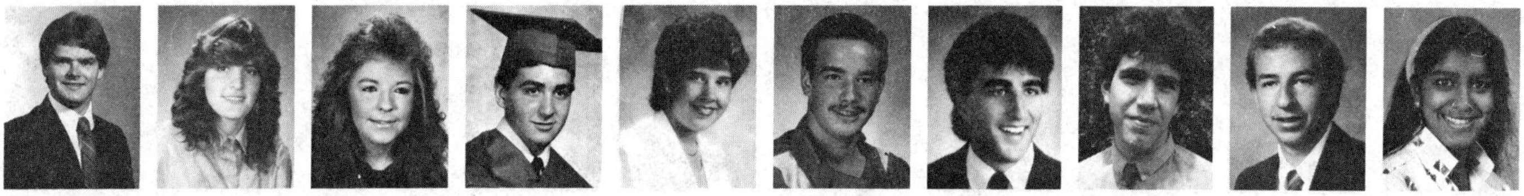

Upson, Roy D Jr
Grove St HS
Mohawk, NY

Urban, Sherene
Uniondale HS
Uniondale, NY

Urbanski, Denise
Hutchinson Central
Technical HS
Buffalo, NY

Useloff, Andrew
Jamaica HS
Fresh Meadows, NY

Usher, Stephanie L
Queensbury HS
Glens Falls, NY

Utter, Chris
Kendall JR SR HS
Kendall, NY

Vacanti, Charles J
Pittsford Mendon
Pittsford, NY

Vaccaro, Todd
Blind Brook HS
Rye Brook, NY

Vaccaro, Jr Victor
W
Rome Free Acad
Rome, NY

Vaidyanathan, Usha
Springville-Griffith
Inst HS
Springville, NY

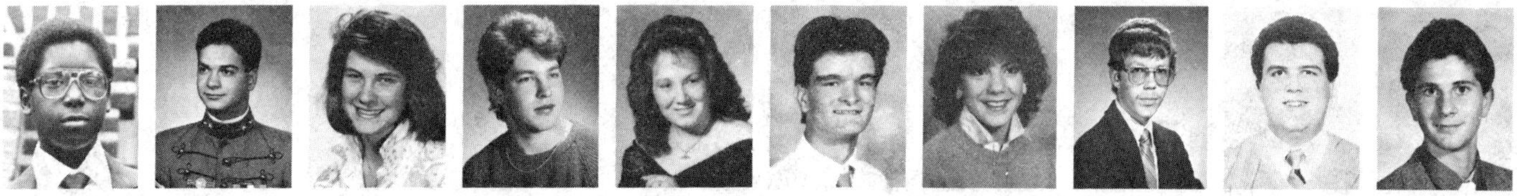

Valbrune, Alphonse
Midwood HS At
Brooklyn College
Brooklyn, NY

Valdes, Delvis
La Salle Military
Staten Island, NY

Valeika, Cheryl
Walt Whitman HS
Huntington Stat,
NY

Valensi, Philip
Sheepshead Bay HS
Brooklyn, NY

Valente, Angela
Herbert H Lehman
Bronx, NY

Valente, Jr
Theodore J
Catholic Central HS
Wynantskill, NY

Valentine, Jessica
Niskayuna HS
Schenectady, NY

Valle, David
Roy C Ketcham SR
Poughkeepsie, NY

Valleriani, Perry
Bishop Ludden HS
Baldwinsville, NY

Vallone, Robert
Msgr Farrel HS
Staten Island, NY

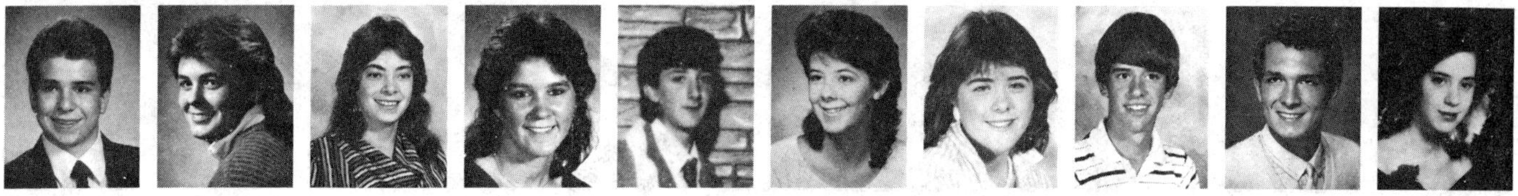

Valone, Jeffrey M
Gates-Chili HS
Rochester, NY

Van Aller, Jo Anne
Middleburgh
Central Schl
Middleburgh, NY

Van Bumble, Jolene
Notre Dame Bishop
Gibbons HS
Duanesburg, NY

Van Lare, Tammy
Marion Central HS
Marion, NY

Van Nostrand, Judd
North Babylon SR
North Babylon, NY

Van Nostrand, Lara
L
North Babylon HS
North Babylon, NY

Van Ryn, Caroline
Mahopac HS
Mahopac, NY

Van Slyke, Chip
Maple Hill HS
Castleton, NY

Vance, Beaumont
Fairport SR HS
Fairport, NY

Vancura, Sharon M
Ramapo SR HS
Pomona, NY

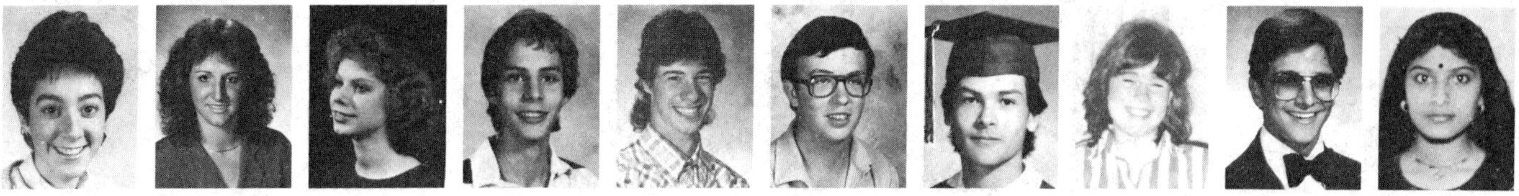

Vandenheuvel,
Michelle
Center Moriches HS
Ctr Moriches, NY

Vandenthoorn, Jill
E
Riverhead HS
Riverhead, NY

Vander Veen,
Kristen
Paul V Moore HS
Central Sq, NY

Vanderhoek, Mark
Jamesville Dewitt
Jamesville, NY

Vandermark, Jeffrey
Bainbridge-Guilford
Bainbridge, NY

Vanhorn, Charles
Nottingham HS
Syracuse, NY

Vanichpong, Somsak
Clarkstown HS
New City, NY

Vanora, Judi
H Frank Carey HS
Franklin Square,
NY

Varela, Julio
Fordham
Preparatory Schl
Bronx, NY

Varkey, Sherin
East Syracuse
Minoa HS
Minoa, NY

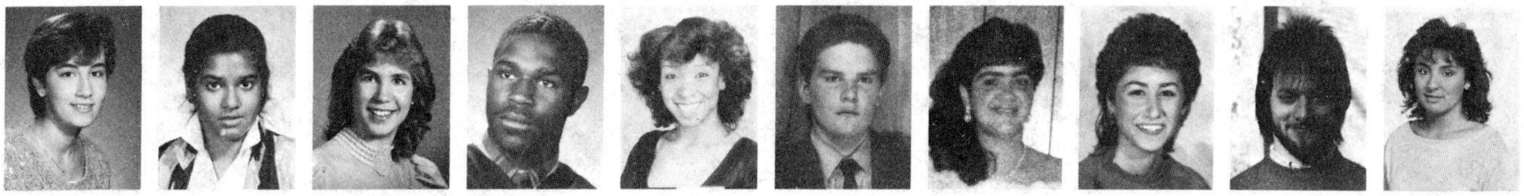

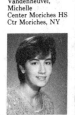

Varlamos, Cynthia
Harrison HS
Harrison, NY

Varma, Sarita
Yonkers HS
Yonkers, NY

Varuzzo, Lisa M
Arlington HS
Lagrangeville, NY

Vaughn, Arthur
Uniondale HS
Uniondale, NY

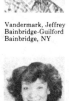

Vaughn, Erika J
Laguardia High Schl
Of Music & Arts
Cambria Heights,
NY

Vazquetelles, Daniel
All Hallow Inst
Bronx, NY

Vazquez, Gloria
William Howard
Taft HS
Bronx, NY

Vecchiariello,
Victoria
Mahopac HS
Mahopac, NY

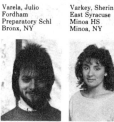

Veenstra, Alexander
Ali
Polytechnic Prep
Country Day Schl
Brooklyn, NY

Vega, Christine
The Mary Louis
Flushing, NY

Velez, Darren
Kings Park SR HS
Fort Salonga, NY

Velez, Renelle L
St Francis
Preparatory HS
New York, NY

Velia, Keith
Smithtown High
School West
Smithtown, NY

Vella, Adrienne
Dominican
Commercial HS
Baldwin, NY

Vellucci, Lynne
Fort Hamilton HS
Brooklyn, NY

Vellutino, Gian
Carlo
Hackley HS
Thornwood, NY

Venegas-Giron,
Ricardo A
Christian Brothers
Liverpool, NY

Venezia, Mike
New Dorp HS
Staten Island, NY

Vennochi, Leslie
New Rochelle HS
New Rochelle, NY

Vera, Steve Luis
De Witt Clinton HS
Bronx, NY

Verbjar, Michelle
Hilton Central HS
Hilton, NY

Verbocy, John
Buffalo Vocational
Technical Center
Buffalo, NY

Verdura, Andrea
Saint Francisx
Preparatory HS
Flushing, NY

Vermeulen, David E
Newfane SR HS
Newfane, NY

Vesely, Lisa
Islip HS
Islip, NY

Vesely, Liv
Sachem HS
Nesconset, NY

Vetrano, Gino
Archbishop Molloy
Ozone Park, NY

Vettorino, August
Tuckahoe HS
Tuckahoe, NY

Viana, Connie Garay
Mamaroneck HS
Mamaroneck, NY

Vicchiullo, Dominick
Minisink Valley HS
Port Jervis, NY

Villano, John P
Miller Place HS
Miller Plaze, NY

Villano, Mindi
East Meadow HS
East Meadow, NY

Villanueva, Rodney
Monsignor Farrell
Staten Island, NY

Villaruel, Mervyn
George Wingate HS
Brooklyn, NY

Vinciguerra, Scott
Paul V Moore HS
Brewerton, NY

Viniski, Tod M
Fairport HS
Fairport, NY

Violante, David A
Wallkill SR HS
Clintondale, NY

Virzera, Diane L
A G Berner HS
Massapequa, NY

Visciano, Carolyn
Commack HS North
Commack, NY

Vissuskus, Chris
Roy C Ketcham HS
Wappingers Falls,
NY

Vitale, Timothy
Unatego JR Ssr HS
Unadilla, NY

Vito, James
Cardinal Mooney
Rochester, NY

Vittorio, Melodie
Liverpool HS
Liverpool, NY

Vogel, Shoshana
Curtis HS
Staten Island, NY

Vogt, Amy
Lafayette HS
Lafayette, NY

Volan, Christopher J
La Fayette Central
Jamesville, NY

Volk, Christine J
Kingston HS
Kingston, NY

Volkers, Nancy E
Williamson SR HS
Williamson, NY

Volpe, Thomas
Archbishop Molloy
Flushing, NY

Voltmann, Kimberly
Lancaster Central
SR HS
Alden, NY

Von Bevern,
Michael
Msgr Farrell HS
Statenisland, NY

Von Bothmer, Maria
E
Spence HS
New York, NY

Vulin, Christine
The Mary Louis
Kew Gardens, NY

Wachman, Allyson
Clarkstown North
New City, NY

Wachspress,
Jonathan
Shaarei Torah Of
Rockland Cty HS
New York, NY

Wadler, Jeffrey R
Margaretville
Central Schl
Fleischmanns, NY

Wager, Jerry
Gates-Chili SR HS
Rochester, NY

Wagner, Ken
Seaford HS
Seaford, NY

Wagner, Traci
North Rose-Wolcott
Wolcott, NY

Wainio, Michael D
Liverpool HS
Liverpool, NY

Waldrop, June
Amsterdam HS
Amsterdam, NY

Walker, Clarence D
Brighton HS
Rochester, NY

Walker, Colleen
Hoosic Valley
Central HS
Melrose, NY

Walker, Ginevra
La Guardia H S Of
Music & The Arts
New York, NY

Walker, Gregory W
Lewiston-Porter SR
Lewiston, NY

Walker, Lea
E J Wilson HS
Spencerport, NY

Wall, Jeffrey
E Syracuse-Mina
E Syracuse, NY

Wallace, Bonnie M
Valley Central HS
Montgomery, NY

Wallace, Deborah
Uniondale HS
Uniondale, NY

Wallace, Jennifer P
Ward Melville HS
Setauket, NY

Wallace, Rhonda
Jean
Geneseo Central HS
Geneseo, NY

Wallace, Stacey A
St Joseph Hill Acad
Staten Island, NY

Wallach, Pam H
Scarsdale HS
Scarsdale, NY

Walley, David
O Neill HS
Walton, NY

Wallingford,
Victoria
Geneseo Central HS
Geneseo, NY

Wallshein, Nori E
Ward Melville HS
Selden, NY

Walpole, Gregory L
Dannemora HS
Dannemora, NY

Walpole, Katie
Donnemora Union
Free HS
Dannemora, NY

Walrod, Laura
Southwestern HS
Lakewood, NY

Walsh, Kevin P
Bronx High School
Of Science
Bronx, NY

Walsh, Thomas
Archbishop Stepinac
Bronx, NY

Walter, Bruce J
Walt Whitman HS
Huntington, NY

Walter, Seth L
Edward R Murrow
Brooklyn, NY

Walters, Brenda
Baldwin SR HS
Baldwin, NY

Walters, David N
Marcus Whitman
Penn Yan, NY

Walters, Maria
Patchogue Medford
Patchogue, NY

Walther, Evelyn A
Dominican
Commercial HS
Glendale, NY

Wambach, Beth
Our Lady Of Mercy
Pittsford, NY

Wanda, Diaz
Eastern District HS
Brooklyn, NY

Wang, Bobby
Ellenville Central
Phillipsport, NY

Wang, Marcy
Farmingdale HS
Farmingdale, NY

Wangelin, Sandy
Holland Central HS
Holland, NY

Wappman, Robert
Frontier Central HS
Hamburg, NY

Ward, Barbara A
Oneida SR HS
Oneida, NY

Ward, David
Trott Vocational HS
Niagara Falls, NY

Ward, Jill
Brushton Moira
Central HS
Moira, NY

Ward, Keith
Corcoran HS
Syracuse, NY

Ward, Sharon
Ward Melville HS
Setauket, NY

Ward, Suzanne M
R-H Roth HS
Honeoye Falls, NY

Ward, Timothy
La Salle Military
Southampton, NY

Wardrop, Matthew
Briarcliff HS
Briarcliff Manor,
NY

Ware, Oba N
Nazareth Regional
Brooklyn, NY

Waring, Keisha
Fashion Indstrs
New York, NY

Warner, Joan
De Witt Clinton HS
Bronx, NY

Warner, Timothy J
Notre Dame HS
E Bethany, NY

Warner, Wendy
Riverhead HS
Calverton, NY

Warnock,
Christopher A
Massapequa HS
Massapequa Pk, NY

Warren, Allyson
Amsterdam HS
Amsterdam, NY

Wartell, Bruce E
Irondequoit HS
Rochester, NY

Washington,
Stephanie
Queen Of The
Rosary Acad
Wyandanch, NY

Washinski, Anne
Marie
Bishop Ludden HS
Syracuse, NY

Wasnik, Renee
Cato Meridian HS
Cato, NY

Wasserman, Debra
Commack HS South
Dix Hills, NY

Wasson, Kelly
Michael
Monroe HS
Rochester, NY

Waszkiewicz, Sally
Bainbridge-Guilford
Bainbridge, NY

Waterston, Jennifer
Blind Brook HS
Rye Brook, NY

Watson, Dannielle
Hoosic Valley
Central HS
Schaghticoke, NY

Watson, Paul J
Rome Free Acad
Rome, NY

Watson, Royen
H S Of Art &
Brooklyn, NY

Watson, Sean
Hoosick Falls
Central HS
Hoosick Falls, NY

Watt, Jacqueline M
Midwood HS
Brooklyn, NY

Watts, E David
Northeastern
Clinton Central HS
Mooers, NY

Way, Amy
Charles H Roth HS
Henrietta, NY

Wayman, Brenda
Unatego JR SR HS
Otego, NY

Weaver, Cassondra
Lynn
Auburn HS
Auburn, NY

Webb, Neil
Paul V Moore HS
Bernhards Bay, NY

Weed, Robin
St John Villa Acad
Staten Island, NY

Weeks, R Scott
Alfred-Almond
Central Schl
Alfred Station, NY

Weiden, Elizabeth C
Franciscan HS
Yorktown Hts, NY

Weigel, John F
Hillcrest HS
Glendale, NY

Weigold, John
Clarkstown South
New City, NY

Weingardt, Kenneth
R
Edgemont HS
Scarsdale, NY

Weinstock, Mark
W Hempstead HS
West Hempstead,
NY

Weis, Ann Marie
Newfield HS
Coram, NY

Weiss, Warren M
West Babylon HS
Babylon, NY

Weissfeld, Rachel
Williamsville North
Williamsville, NY

Weitz, William
Bronx H S Of
Bronx, NY

Welch, Mark
Lausingburgh HS
Troy, NY

Welsch, Michael E
Notre Dame-Bishop
Gibbons HS
Schenectady, NY

Weng, Charles T
John F Kennedy HS
Bronx, NY

Werbowsky, Gina
East Hampton HS
Montauk, NY

Werdann, Lorraine
Laguardia HS For
Music & The Arts
New York, NY

Werthman, Todd
Ilion Central HS
Ilion, NY

Wesby, Ronald
Bishop Loughlin
Memorial HS
Brooklyn, NY

Wesley, Thomas
Aquinas Inst
Rochester, NY

West, Curtis
Greenville HS
Medusa, NY

Westad, Heather
Burnt Hills-Ballston
Lake HS
Schenectady, NY

Weston, Cindy A
East Islip HS
Islip Terrace, NY

Weston, Michael
Alfred G Berner HS
Massapequa Park,
NY

Wetterau, Kristina
Dansville Central
Dansville, NY

Wetz, Robert
Monsignor Farrell
Staten Island, NY

Whalen, IV Daniel
A
Christian Brothers
Albany, NY

Wheeler, Eileen P
St Joseph Hill Acad
Staten Island, NY

Wheeler, Marie N
Poland Central Schl
Remsen, NY

Wheelock, Corina
Poland Central Schl
Cold Brook, NY

Whipple, Michele
Canastota HS
Canastota, NY

Whipple, Sheri
Naples Central HS
Naples, NY

Whitbeck, Carl
Lafayette HS
Buffalo, NY

White, Adriane
New Rochelle HS
New Rochelle, NY

White, Amy L
Salmon River
Central HS
Hogansburg, NY

White, Anne B
Professional
Childrens Schl
Shrub Oak, NY

White, Audrey
Buffalo Traditional
Buffalo, NY

White, Daniel T
Wheatland-Chili HS
Scottsville, NY

White, Deanna J
Cortland JR SR HS
Cortland, NY

White, Ed
Waterloo SR HS
Waterloo, NY

White, Olivia
Bishop Loughlin M
Brooklyn, NY

Whitecavage, Diane
Dominican
Commercial HS
Woodhaven, NY

Whitehead, Daniel
Bishop Cunningham
Oswego, NY

Whitton, Melissa
Potsdam HS
West Stockholm,
NY

Whitton, Michael
Sauquoit Valley
Central Schl
Sauquoit, NY

Wichern, Caryn
Northport HS
E Northport, NY

Wicks, Kevin Guy
Patchogue-Medford
Patchogue, NY

Widmer, John J
Naples Central Schl
Naples, NY

Widmer, Rae A
Arkport Central
Arkport, NY

Widomski, Kathleen
West Seneca West
SR HS
W Seneca, NY

Wiedrich, Heather
Fayetteville-Manlius
Manlius, NY

Wiesel, Andrea
Lawrence HS
Woodmere, NY

Wiesner, Lawrence
Binghamton HS
Binghamton, NY

Wikander, John
Mercy HS
Sag Harbor, NY

Wikheim, Jody
Ramstein Am HS
Apo New York, NY

Wilber, Tanya
Pinecrest Christian
Salisbury Center,
NY

Wilcox, Keith
Vestal SR HS
Vestal, NY

Wildner, Christine
Sachem HS North
Farmingville, NY

Wilhelm, Peter C
Our Lady Of
Lourdes HS
Pleasant Valley, NY

Wilke, Eric
Oneida SR HS
Oneida, NY

Wilkie, Karin
Liverpool HS
Liverpool, NY

Wilkinson, Anthony
T
St Marys Boys HS
Old Brookville, NY

Williams, Andrea M
William H Maxwell
Brooklyn, NY

Williams, Anne
Earl L Vandernevlen
Mt Sinai, NY

Williams, Billy
Walter Panas HS
Peekskill, NY

Williams, Bonnie
Holland Patent
Central HS
Barneveld, NY

Williams, Carol
Corinth Central HS
Corinth, NY

Williams, Cathy
Somers HS
Somers, NY

Williams, Jr Donald
De Witt Clinton HS
Bronx, NY

Williams, Elizabeth
L
Hunter College HS
New York, NY

Williams, Gary
Midlakes HS
Clifton Spgs, NY

Williams, Jennifer
Seton Catholic
Central HS
Windsor, NY

Williams, Kevin
Sanford H Calhoun
Merrick, NY

Williams, Lynda M
La Salle SR HS
Niagara Falls, NY

Williams, Maryanne
Our Lady Of
Lourdes HS
Wappingers Fls, NY

Williams, Patricia B
White Plains HS
White Plains, NY

Williams, Sean L
Horseheads HS
Elmira, NY

Williams, Jr Willie
L
Bayshore HS
Bayshore, NY

Willmann, Jenifer R
Q
Division Avenue HS
Levittown, NY

Willoughby, Kelli
Freeport HS
Freeport, NY

Willsey, Tina
Cicero-North
Syracuse HS
N Syracuse, NY

Wilmot, Dennis
Mc Quaid Jesuit HS
Rochester, NY

Wilson, Camille
South Shore HS
Brooklyn, NY

Wilson, Chaka
Franklin Central
Franklin, NY

Wilson, Jill G
Cardinal Spellman
Bronx, NY

Wilson, Joe
G Ray Bodley HS
Fulton, NY

Wilson, Kim
Munich American
Encinitas, CA

Wilson, Linda H
Liverpool HS
N Syracuse, NY

Wilson, Robert
Greece Athena HS
Rochester, NY

Wilson, Robert P
Newfane SR HS
Newfane, NY

Wilson, Sherise
Central Islip SR HS
Central Islip, NY

Wilson, Sherwin
Msgr Mcclancy
Memorial HS
So Ozone Park, NY

Wimberly, Sebrina
Midwood HS
Brooklyn, NY

Wimmer, Paul
Sachem North HS
Holbrook, NY

Winde, Cheryl
Villa Maria Acad
Lancaster, NY

Windels, Robin Ann
Westhampton Beach
E Quogue, NY

Winkley, Beth
Mt Mercy Acad
East Aurora, NY

Winnert, Amy
Eden SR HS
Eden, NY

Winslow, Jean
St John The Baptist
N Babylon, NY

Winters, Heidi
Niskayuna HS
Rexford, NY

Wirth, Tina
L A Webber JR SR
Lyndonville, NY

Wisniewski, Tamara
Evette
Dunkirk SR HS
Dunkirk, NY

Wisnock, Michael D
Newfane SR HS
Newfane, NY

Witkowski, Lynn
Villa Maria Acad
Buffalo, NY

Witman, Scott
Hamburg Central
Hamburg, NY

Woelfel, Mark
Frontier Central HS
Hamburg, NY

Wojcik, Douglas
Bishop Ludden HS
Liverpool, NY

Wojdyla, Steven
Henninger HS
Syracuse, NY

Wolf, Chris
Sanford H Calhoun
Merrick, NY

Wolfe, Doug
Roslyn HS
Roslyn, NY

Wolfe, Thomas
Pine Plains HS
Red Hook, NY

Wolff, Cindy
Herricks SR HS
Roslyn, NY

Wolff, Deborah
Liverpool HS
Liverpool, NY

Wolle, Kathryn
Chittenango HS
Katonah, NY

Wong, Yu Fay
Mabel Dean Bacon
Vocation HS
New York, NY

Wood, Bonnie
Granville Central
Pawlet, VT

Wood, Christine
Panama Central HS
Ashville, NY

Wood, Clifford J
Linton HS
Schenectady, NY

Wood, Craig
Vernon HS
Sherrill, NY

Wood, David L
Anthony A
Henninger HS
Syracuse, NY

Wood, Jeffrey T
Middleburgh
Central Schl
Middleburgh, NY

Wood, Lisa
Bishop Ford Central
Catholic HS
Brooklyn, NY

Wood, Melisa
Grand Island HS
Grand Island, NY

Woodcock, James
Corinth Central HS
Corinth, NY

Woodhouse, Gwen
Curtis HS
Staten Island, NY

Woods, Barbara
Tapt HS
Bronx, NY

Woods, Melanie
Necole
Central Islip SR HS
Central Islip, NY

Woolcock, Edith
Monsignor Scanlan
Bronx, NY

Woolever, Terri
Corning Painted
Post West HS
Painted Post, NY

Wooster, David
Charles
La Salle Insti
North Troy, NY

Worrell, Christine
Evander Childs HS
Bronx, NY

Worth, Cassandra
Charlotte HS
Rochester, NY

Worthy, Charmaine
Dominican
Commercial HS
Cambria Heights,
NY

Wrate, Susan
Jamesville De Witt
Jamesville, NY

Wright, Antonio
Baldwin SR HS
Freeport, NY

Wright, Barry
Hannibal SR HS
Hannibal, NY

Wright, Dale
East
Syracuss-Minda HS
Minoa, NY

Wright, Fred D
Chenango Forks HS
Binghamton, NY

Wright, Kandee L
Dundee Central HS
Dundee, NY

Wright, Kevin
Schoharie Central
Schoharie, NY

Wright, Kimberly E
Horace Mann HS
Bronx, NY

Wright, Lynda G
Marcellus SR HS
Marietta, NY

Wright, Risi
New Rochelle HS
New Rochelle, NY

Wright, Roland L
Canarsie HS
Brooklyn, NY

Wright, Scott E
Arlington HS
La Grangeville, NY

Wright, Sean F
Au Sable Valley
Central HS
Keeseville, NY

Wright, Taryn
John Dewey HS
Brooklyn, NY

Wright, Wayne
All Hallows HS
Bronx, NY

Wrobel, Gary
Bishop Ludden HS
Syracuse, NY

Wrobel, Mark
Bishop Ludden HS
Syracuse, NY

Wu, Judy
Half Hollow Hills
HS East
Dix Hills, NY

Wu, Tammy L
Kingston HS
Kingston, NY

Wu, Taolan Carolyn
James Madison HS
Brooklyn, NY

Wydler, Steven C
The Dalton Schl
New York, NY

Wyman, Heather
Shenendehowa HS
Clifton Park, NY

Wymer, Joel
Arch Bishop Walsh
Salamance, NY

Wynn, Robin
Whitesboro JR HS
Marcy, NY

Xixis, Sophia
Bronx H S Of
Whitestone, NY

Yaeger, Rob
Smithtown H S
Smithtown, NY

Yager, Robert
Archbishop Stepinac
Yonkers, NY

Yarwood, Jurene
St Pius V HS
Bronx, NY

Yates, Jr Richard L
Cuba Central Schl
Cuba, NY

Yavornitzki, Lisa
Oneida HS
Oneida, NY

Yee, Alice
James Madison HS
Brooklyn, NY

Yeh, Alice
Ardsley HS
Ardsley, NY

Yoon, Arthur
Sweet Home Senior
Amherst, NY

Youmans, Jodie
Michelle
Walton Central Schl
Walton, NY

Young, Brittany
Pine Valley HS
South Dayton, NY

Young, Deanna
Nazareth Acad
Rochester, NY

Young, Lulu
Williamsville E HS
E Amherst, NY

Young, Stephen C
Hunter College HS
Hollis, NY

Youngers, Dennis
Letchworth Central
Warsaw, NY

Youngers, III Robert
James
Hamburg SR HS
Hamburg, NY

Yousett, Kyle
Wilson Central HS
Newfane, NY

Yoxall, Thomas
Rome Catholic HS
Whitesboro, NY

Yu, Catherine L
Bayside HS
Beechhurst, NY

Yu, Elizabeth K
Humanities HS
New York, NY

Yule, Catherine
Whiteboro SR HS
Utica, NY

Yurchak, Elizabeth
Nardin Acad
Hamburg, NY

Yurman, Joanne
Our Lady Of
Perpetual Help HS
Brooklyn, NY

Yusim, Ilya
Franklyn D
Roosevelt HS
Brooklyn, NY

Yzaguirre, Charles R
Mount St Michael
Bronx, NY

Zabell, Ari
Oceanside HS
Oceanside, NY

Zaffarano, Victoria
Frankfort-Schuyler
Frankfort, NY

Zagajeski, Kim Noell
Hicksville SR HS
Hicksville, NY

Zagajeski, II Thomas
A
Hicksville HS
Hicksville, NY

Zahm, Charlene
Frontier Central HS
Woodlawn, NY

Zaken, Ava Marie
Cardinal O Hara HS
Tonawanda, NY

Zale, Elizabeth Anne
Gates-Chili HS
Rochester, NY

Zamites, Carollynn
Our Lady Of Mercy
Rochester, NY

Zarneke, David
Victor HS
Victor, NY

Zarrell, Anthony
Gloversville HS
Gloversville, NY

Zarrow, Andrew
New Rochelle HS
Scarsdale, NY

Zavala, Leonardo
Bashwick HS
Bronx, NY

Zebraski, Paul J
Dunkirk SR HS
Dunkirk, NY

Zeh, Tracey
Southampton HS
Southampton, NY

Zeibaq, Reema
Sacred Heart Acad
Uniondale, NY

Zelasko, John
John F Kennedy HS
Cheektowaga, NY

Zenobio, Cris
St Marys Boys HS
Sand Point, NY

Zerrenner, Ann
Marie
Preston HS
Bronx, NY

Zervoudakes, Jason
W C Mepham HS
N Bellmore, NY

Zevos, Ianthe
Potsdame Central
Potsdam, NY

Ziegler, Jeffrey
Palmyra Macedon
Palmyra, NY

Ziems, Frederick M
Earl L
Vandermeulen HS
Mt Sinai, NY

Ziese, Sharon
New Field HS
Selden, NY

Ziff, Lori
Oyster Bay HS
Oyster Bay, NY

Zimet, Mark
Hendrick Hudson
Peeskill, NY

Zimmerman, Brian
Susan Wagner HS
Staten Island, NY

Zito, Danielle
Centereach HS
Centereach, NY

Zito, John
Batavia HS
Batavia, NY

Zitt, Jonathan R
Syosset HS
Woodbury, NY

Zivin, Karen Sue
Mercy HS
Selden, NY

Zmijewski, Tina
Catholic Central HS
Latham, NY

Zobrist, Tammy L
Kensington HS
Buffalo, NY

Zoladz, Julie
Frontier SR HS
Hamburg, NY

Zook, Gina M
Kingston City HS
Kingston, NY

Zotto, Nicholas
Islip HS
Bay Shore, NY

Zullo, Ann Marie
East Meadow HS
East Meadow, NY

Zuniga, Monica
Clarkstown HS
New City, NY

Zuntag, Matthew
Tottenville HS
Staten Island, NY

Zuskin, Shari
Commack HS North
Commack, NY

Zywiak, Richard C
Whitesboro SR HS
Marcy, NY

PUERTO RICO

Acosta, Roberto
San Jose College
Mayaguez, PR

Adjutant, Angelique
Santa Rita HS
Bayamon, PR

Almodovar, Jose I
Colegio San Ignacio
De Loyola HS
Rio Piedras, PR

Alvarez, Jose L
Colegio Madre
Cabrini HS
Rio Piedras, PR

Amadeo, Javier
Antilles HS
Guaynabo, PR

Ayala, Adan
Colegio San Jose HS
Rio Piedras, PR

Ayala, Maria Ileana
Academia Santa
Carolina, PR

Baez, Edma
Colegio San Jose HS
San German, PR

Barquero, Jorge
Academia San Jorge
Santurce, PR

Bellotti, Berenice
St Johns Schl
Hato Rey, PR

Biaggi, Patricia
A I C HS
Mayaguez, PR

Calzada-Navarro,
Ramon Luis
Academia Del
Sagrado Corazon
Bayamon, PR

Carbonell, Federico
Colegio San Jose HS
Hormigueros, PR

Cardona, Nydia
Academia Sagrado
Corazon HS
Santurce, PR

Castillo, Luis J
Academia Perpetuo
Socorro HS
Miramar, PR

Castillo, Sharon J
Academia San Jose
Guaynabo, PR

Catala, Glorisa
Baldwin School Of
Guaynabo, PR

Chappuis, Jacques P
Baldwin Schl
San Juan, PR

Collazo, Nayda
Academia Perpetuo
Socorro HS
Santurce, PR

Colon, Jose
Colegio Ponceno HS
Ponce, PR

Concepcion,
Glorimar
Colegio San Antonio
Hato Rey, PR

Cruzado, Wanda
Colegio Santa Rita
Bayamon, PR

De La Cruz,
Lynnette
Colegio San Antonio
Isabella, PR

Del Valle, Joan I
Academy Of The
Immaculate Cncptn
San German, PR

Detres, Cesar
Southwestern
Educational Society
Mayaguez, PR

Detres, Laura
Southwestern
Educational Soc HS
Mayaguez, PR

Diaz, Angel L
Baldwin Schl
Gardens Rio Pdrs,
PR

Diaz, Maria Del
Pilar
Colegio Ponceno HS
Ponce, PR

Emmanuelli, Luis
Colegio Ponceno HS
Guayanilla, PR

Figueroa, Raymond
Antilles HS
Levittown, PR

Fischbach, Kevin
Southwestern
Educational Soc HS
Mayaguez, PR

Fortuna, Ivette
Southwestern
Educational Society
Hormigueros, PR

Fuentes, Natalia
Academia San Jorge
Santurce, PR

Galletti, Francisco
Wesleyan Acad
Rio Piedras, PR

Garcia, Zulma
Colegio San Jose HS
San German, PR

Garcia-O Ferrall,
Yadira
Academia Santa
Monica HS
Rio Piedras, PR

Gibson-Rosado,
Erica Migdalia
Colegio
Puertorriqueno De
Rio Piedras, PR

Gil, Alcides
Colegio San Ignacio
De Loyola
Rio Piedras, PR

Gonzalez, Julio A
Academia Sagrado
Corazon HS
Levittown, PR

Guerra, Arlene
Immaculate
Conception HS
Mayaguez, PR

Guerra, Zuimdie
Immaculate
Conception HS
Mayaguez, PR

Herrera-Nieves,
Marisol
Academia San Jorge
Santurce, PR

Herrero, Vivian
Immaculate
Conception Acad
Mayaguez, PR

Hornan, Leslie
Academia
Inmaculada Concpn
Mayaguez, PR

Jhaveri, Rakesh
Colegio Jponceno
Ponce, PR

Johnson, Norma
Robinson HS
San Juan, PR

Lago, Lorraine
Caribbean Schl
Ponce, PR

Lopez, Edgardo
Colegio Marista HS
Guaynabo, PR

Loyola, Mario
Southwest
Educational Societ
Mayaguez, PR

Maduro, Guillermo
Colegio San Ignacio
De Loyola
Rio Piedras, PR

Marchany, Maria
Academia
Inmaculada Concepc
Mayaguez, PR

Martinez, Edith
Colegio Ponceno HS
Ponce, PR

Martinez-Acosta,
Juan A
Colegio Santa Rita
Bayamon, PR

Marull, Samantha
Luisa
Santa Rita Private
Bayamon, PR

Mercado, Lorna
Gregory
Centro
Oportuniadade
San German, PR

Miranda, Ana
St Johns Schl
Guaynabo, PR

Monsanto, Vivian
Golegio Ponceno HS
Ponce, PR

Montilla, Jorge R
Colegio San Ignacio
Rio Piedras, PR

Morales, Mirka
Academia San Jose
Guaynabo, PR

Moran, Scott
Colegio San Ignacio
De Loyola HS
Rio Piedras, PR

Mudafort, Maria
Colegio Madre
Cabrini HS
Guaynabo, PR

Munoz, Irma M
Curbelo
Colegio San Antonio
Quebradillas, PR

Negron, Diana
Baldwin Schl
Guaynabo, PR

Ortiz, Elka
Colegio San Jose HS
San German, PR

Ortiz, Rosana M
Saint Joseph Clg
Lajas, PR

Oyola, Maureen
Colegio Nuestra Sra
Del Pilar
Rio Piedras, PR

Pabon, Antonio
Inmaculate
Conception Acad
Mayaquez, PR

Pena, Mary
Academia San Jose
Guaynabo, PR

Perez, Eulalia
Colegio Madre
Guaynabo, PR

Ramirez, Vanessa
Immaculate
Conception Acad
Mayaguez, PR

Ramirez Guevara,
Jose R
Colegio San Antonio
Isabela, PR

Riera, Jose
Colegio San Ignacio
De Loyola HS
Condado, PR

Rios, Carmen
Antilles HS
Ft Buchanan, PR

Rivera, Carlos A
Colegio San Antonio
Quebradillas, PR

Rivera, Sheila Lee
Southwestern
Educational Society
Mayaguez, PR

Rivera-Giusti, Juan
Angel
Antilles HS
San Juan, PR

Rivero, Luis Raul
Academia Perpetuo
Rio Piedras, PR

Robles, Awilda
Luis Munoz Marin
Cabo Rojo, PR

Robles, Jose Juan
Colegio San Jose HS
San German, PR

Rodriguez, Liza I
Colegio Espiritu
Santo HS
Rio Piedras, PR

Rolon, Jose
Colegio San Jose HS
Rio Piedras, PR

Roman, Isabel M
Colegio San Antonio
Quebradillas, PR

Romero, Yolanda
Colegio San Jose HS
Mayaguez, PR

Rosado Flores, Lorna M
Manuela Toro HS
Caguas, PR

Ruiz, Carmen M
Colegio San Antonio
Quebradillas, PR

Ruiz, Wilfrido
Bernardino Cordero Bernard HS
Ponce, PR

Sallaberry, Carol
St Therese Acad
Santurce, PR

Santiago, Olga
Ramey Schl
Mayaguez, PR

Sanz, Gabriel
Colegio Marista HS
Guaynabo, PR

Silva, Guillermo
San Ignacio De Loyola Schl
Guaynabo, PR

Somoza, Rafael
Immaculate Conception Acad
San Juan, PR

Soto Paz, Luz E
Alcides Fiqueroa HS
Anasco, PR

Tirado, Maritza
Immaculate Conception Acad
Mayaguez, PR

Traxler, David Kevane
Colegio San Ignacio De Loyola
Rio Piedras, PR

Valle, Jose
Colegie San Ignacio De Loyola HS
Rio Piedras, PR

Vidal, Luis M
University Of Puerto Ricos HS
Rio Piedras, PR

RHODE ISLAND

Abato, Stacey J
St Marys Acad
N Kingstown, RI

Abbate, Charles
Bishop Hendricken
Warwick, RI

Abbruzzi, Diana
Johnston HS
Johnston, RI

Adriance, Heather
North Kingstown SR HS
N Kingstown, RI

Andrews, Nancy
Lincoln JR SR HS
Lincoln, RI

Arcand, Angela M
Lincoln JR SR HS
Manville, RI

Arendt, William
Scituat JR & SR HS
North Scituate, RI

Babiec, Jr Joseph R
Cumberland HS
Cumberland, RI

Barbieri, Joanne
La Salle Acad
Providence, RI

Beaudoin, Pamela
North Smithfield JR SR HS
Woonsocket, RI

Bennett, Jo A
Middletown HS
Middletown, RI

Berard, Michele
Smithfield HS
Esmond, RI

Berard, Scott
Bishop Hendricken
W Warwick, RI

Bilezerian, Keith
North Smithfield JR SR HS
N Smithfield, RI

Biros, Trish
Coventry HS
Coventry, RI

Blackson, Tanya P
Rogers HS
Newport, RI

Bobola, Robert
Lincoln SR HS
Lincoln, RI

Brancel, Sara
Middletown HS
Middletown, RI

Brennan, Marjorie A
Charino Reg HS
Rockville, RI

Bridge, Melissa
Coventry HS
Coventry, RI

Brien, Brenda Lee
William E Tolman SR HS
Pawtucket, RI

Brothers, Bettina
Mount Saint Charles
Johnston, RI

Cady, Debra
La Salle Acad
Wyoming, RI

Cafaro, Thomas
Burrillville HS
Glendale, RI

Calek, Daniel
Rogers HS
Newport, RI

Caporizzo, Maria
St Mary Acad Bay
North Scituate, RI

Cardin, Sharon
North Smithfield JR/SR HS
N Smithfield, RI

Carney, Leigh
East Greenwich HS
Exeter, RI

Carney, Robert
Charles E Shea HS
Pawtucket, RI

Carr, II Peter F
Bishop Hendricken
No Kingstown, RI

Casci, Kim A
East Providence HS
E Prov, RI

Charpentier, Linette
Prout Memorial HS
Coventry, RI

Colinan, Jill
Central Falls HS
Central Falls, RI

Corcoran, Gina Marie
N Providence HS
N Providence, RI

Cornelison, Christina M
The Wheeler Schl
S Dartmouth, MA

Couture, Shellie
Burrillville SR HS
Nasonville, RI

Cranshaw, Christin
St Marys Acad
Providence, RI

Cullen, Christian
Lincoln JR SR HS
Lincoln, RI

D Aleno, Lenora Marie
Cov Entry HS
Coventry, RI

Damiano, Ann Marie
St Marys Acad
Providence, RI

Davenport, Lisa
Lincoln SR HS
Lincoln, RI

De Rosa, F Anthony
Mt St Charles Acad
N Attleboro, MA

Desiderato, Lisa
Classical HS
Providence, RI

Di Chiaro, Michael
Bishop Hendricken
Cranston, RI

Di Pippo, Gina
Granston HS
Cranston, RI

Ditusa, Lisa
Coventry HS
Coventry, RI

Do Couto, Kathleen
Tiverton HS
Tiverton, RI

Dodd, Thomas
N Kingstown HS
N Kingstown, RI

Donnelly, Peter
Bishop Hendricken
N Kingston, RI

Dunnington, Lynda
Narragansett HS
Narragansett, RI

Dwyer, Kimberly
Saint Raphael Acad
Pawtucket, RI

Eklof, Dean
North Kingstown
N Kingstown, RI

Estrada, Elkin
Central Falls JR SR
Central Falls, RI

Fawcett, Tracy
Scituate JR SR HS
Foster, RI

Ferrucci, Steven G
Cumberland HS
Cumberland, RI

Fisher, Lois
St Marys Acad
Harrisville, RI

Follansbee, Michelle
Coventry HS
Coventry, RI

Fontaine, Tanya
Burrillview JRSR
Harrisville, RI

Fornaro, Susan Lynne
St Mary Acad Bay
Greenville, RI

Fortes, Antonio
Hope HS
Providence, RI

Franklin, Kimberly
Classical HS
Providence, RI

Gabriel, Christine A
Lincoln JR SR HS
N Providence, RI

Gagnon, Patricia
Burrillville HS
Harrisville, RI

Gaines, Jr Paul
Rogers HS
Newport, RI

Galamaga, Paul
Bishop Hendricken
Warwick, RI

Geoffroy, Kim
Woonsocket SR HS
Woonsocket, RI

Geruso, Donna
North Smithfield JR SR HS
Slatersville, RI

Gomes, Michael
Saint Raphael Acad
Pawtucket, RI

Gough, Margaret
Prout Memorial HS
W Warwick, RI

Gould, Robert
Rogers HS
Newport, RI

Gray, Karen
South Kingstown
West Kingston, RI

Gray, Lynda
Davies Voc Tech HS
Pawtucket, RI

Greene, Tara
Charing HS
Charlestown, RI

Guernon, Michael
Burrillville HS
Glendale, RI

Gustafson, Deborah
Pilgrim HS
Warwick, RI

Hagan, II William John
Classical HS
Providence, RI

Hamilton, Matthew B
Providence County Day Schl
Providence, RI

Hanrahan, William
Coventry HS
Greene, RI

Hayes, Mark
Lasalle Acad
Seekonk, MA

Hazard, Jennifer
North Kingstown
N Kingston, RI

Heon, Michelle
Woonsocket SR HS
Woonsocket, RI

Holder, Jr Charles M
Rogers HS
Newport, RI

Hopkins, Tina M
Chariho Regional
Wyoming, RI

Hussain, Bilal R
Moses Brown HS
Foxborough, MA

Iacobucci, Laura
Lincoln HS
Lincoln, RI

Iacono, Janice Lee
East Providence HS
E Providence, RI

Iannazzi, Stephanie
St Marys Academy-
Johnston, RI

Jalbert, Russell
Bishop Hendricken
Coventry, RI

Johannis, Beth
Narragansett HS
Narragansett, RI

Johnson, Diane K
Pilgrim HS
Warwick, RI

Johnson, Kellie
Woonsocket HS
Greenville, RI

Jutras, Jr Thomas
Smithfield HS
Smithfield, RI

Kaplan, Bruce A
Cranston HS East
Cranston, RI

Kelaghan, Tara
Lincoln JR SR HS
Lincoln, RI

Kiper, Rick
Coventry HS
Coventry, RI

Kneath, Thomas
Bristol HS
Bristol, RI

Kobani, Paul
Woonsocket HS
Woonsocket, RI

Kogut, Jennifer
Woonsocket SR HS
Woonsocket, RI

Korzeniowski, Hank
Bishop Hendricken
Cranston, RI

La Croix, Renee
Warwick Veterans Memorial HS
Warwick, RI

Lambert, Kerri
Warren HS
Warren, RI

Langanke, Steven W
Chariho Regional JR SR HS
Ashaway, RI

Languell, Christopher
Rogers HS
Newport, RI

Lareau, Douglas J
Burrillville JR SR
Pascoag, RI

Lawrence, Leonard A
Coventry HS
Coventry, RI

Lemieux, Kellie
Ponaganset HS
Greenville, RI

Lonkart, Kevin
St Rapahel Acad
N Scituate, RI

Lopes, Keith
East Providence SR
Riverside, RI

Lynch, Matthew P
La Salle Acad
Woonsocket, RI

Martin, Ann-Marie
East Providence HS
East Providence, RI

Martinelli, Dominico
North Providence
N Providence, RI

Martins, Lisa
Tolman HS
Pawtucket, RI

Mastin, Lorena
Coventry HS
Coventry, RI

Maynard, Kevin J
Bishop Hendricken
Hope, RI

Mayne, Nancy
Chariho Regional JR SR HS
Charlestown, RI

Mc Bride, Mary Beth
North Smithfield
North Smithfield, RI

Mc Crave, Meredith
South Kingstown
Wakefield, RI

Mc Grath, Suzanne
Rogers HS
Newport, RI

Mc Kenna, Deana
Middletown HS
Middletown, RI

Mc Namara, Jennifer
Mt St Charles Acad
N Scituate, RI

Mc Neil, Maureen
Mt Saint Charles
Bellingham, MA

Medeiros, Dorene L
Tiverton HS
Tiverton, RI

Meehan, Una
Prout Memorial HS
N Kingstown, RI

Melo, Jane
Bristol HS
Bristol, RI

Mercurio, Debbie
St Mary Academy
Warwick, RI

Miller, Carol
Lincoln HS
Lincoln, RI

Mollander, Julie
Wm M Davies
Esmond, RI

Moreira, Paulo
Hope HS
Providence, RI

Morry, Terri
North Providence
N Providence, RI

Moyer, IV Tilghman H
N Kingstown SR HS
N Kingston, RI

Mulligan, Brian
Burrillville HS
Harrisville, RI

Mumford, Ann
St Mary Acad
Hope, RI

Murdocco, Gailyn
Prout Memorial HS
Wakefield, RI

Newman, Jr Ronald
Warwick Veterans Memorial HS
Warwick, RI

Nunes, Paul
Middletown HS
Middletown, RI

Olausen, Kurt
Classical HS
Providence, RI

Osborne, Virginia
Coventry HS
Coventry, RI

Owre, Kristin
North Smithfield JR SR HS
N Smithfield, RI

Perry, James
Coventry HS
Warwick, RI

Phelan, Shelley
Mount St Charles
Hopedale, MA

Pierce, Charles
St Raphael Acad
Rumford, RI

Pincince, Michelle M
Cumberland HS
Cumberland, RI

Pouliot, Karen
Woonsocket SR HS
Woonsocket, RI

Proulx, Jennifer
Tiverton HS
Tiverton, RI

Ray, Steven
Pilgrim HS
Warwick, RI

Reich, Naomi
Classical HS
Providence, RI

Rekas, Linda
Coventry HS
Coventry, RI

Reuter, Jeff
Bishop Hendricken
E Greenwich, RI

Ridgewell, Steven
Pilgrim HS
Warwick, RI

Rinaldi, Patricia
Pilgrim HS
Warwick, RI

Robbins, Susan A
Bristol HS
Bristol, RI

Robichaud, Sandra
Coventry HS
Coventry, RI

Robinson, Michelle
Portsmouth HS
Portsmouth, RI

Rogers, Suzanne
Lincoln JR SR HS
Lincoln, RI

Rooney, Linda
Narragansett HS
Narragansett, RI

Rothermel, Alisa
Middletown HS
Middletown, RI

Rourke, Todd
East Providence HS
Providence, RI

Roux, Mark Allen
Woonsocket HS
Woonsocket, RI

Ryan, Michael E
Portsmouth Abbey
Barrington, RI

Salazar, Candy
Bishop Keough HS
N Providence, RI

Saldeen, Bo
Hope HS
Providence, RI

Scamacca, Jeffrey
Scituate HS
Scituate, RI

Schroeder, Paul R
Bishop Thomas F Hendricken HS
Johnston, RI

Schwaner, Nancy
Lincoln JR SR HS
Lincoln, RI

Shindell, Robert C
Toll Gate HS
E Greenwich, RI

Silverstein, Jon
Moses Brown Schl
Providence, RI

Silvestri, John
North Providence
N Providence, RI

Simonelli, Robin
Smithfield HS
Greenville, RI

Slattery, Christine
Lincoln JR SR HS
Lincoln, RI

Snow, Mary
Tiverton HS
Tiverton, RI

Soares, Lena
Bristol HS
Bristol, RI

Spinella, Elizabeth
Mount St Charles
Woonsocket, RI

Squadrito, Ellen M
Pilgrim HS
Warwick, RI

Stockwell, Melissa
La Salle Acad
Johnston, RI

Streubel, Heidi
Warwick Veterans Memorial HS
Warwick, RI

Taylor, Stephanie
St Mary Academy
Johnston, RI

Tefft, Kevin
Coventry HS
Coventry, RI

Terry, Keeva L
Classical HS
Providence, RI

Tomei, John
Saint Raphael Acad
Cumberland, RI

Tracey, Kristen A
Tollgate HS
Warwick, RI

Tracy, Kathleen
East Providence SR
E Providence, RI

Turpin, Karen
Prout Memorial HS
N Kingstown, RI

Valencia, Piedad S
Central Falls JR SR
Central Fls, RI

Villanova, Donna
Coventry HS
Coventry, RI

Vinas, Jackie
Central HS
Providence, RI

Waite, Wendi
Chariho Regional
Hopkinton, RI

Wardick, Julie A
Classical HS
Providence, RI

Warrener, Tammy
Johnston SR HS
Johnston, RI

Whipple, Debra
North Smithfield JR-SR HS
N Smithfield, RI

White, Lisa Jean
Coventry SR HS
Coventry, RI

White, Rita
Chariho HS
Ashaway, RI

Williams, Stephanie
Charino Regional
Arlington, TX

Wilmouth, Rodney
Coventry HS
Coventry, RI

Wright, Julie Y
Prout Memorial HS
North Kingstown, RI

Young, Mark S
Portsmouth HS
Middletown, RI

Young, Tracy
Chariho Regional
W Kingston, RI

Zienowicz, David S
Bishop Hendricken
Cranston, RI

Zonfrillo, Lisa
Toll Gate HS
W Greenwich, RI

Zuleta, Cesar A
Central Falls HS
Central Fls, RI

Zuleta, Maria
Central Falls JR HS
Central Falls, RI

VERMONT

Anthony, Patricia
Champlain Valley
Union HS
Hinesburg, VT

Antonicci, Chris
Burlington HS
Burlington, VT

Armstrong, Eve M
Essex Junction HS
Essex Junction, VT

Atwood, Mark G
Northfield JR SR
Northfield, VT

Aubut, Mike
Spaulding HS
Barre, VT

Bartley, Brenda
Brattleboro Union
Putney, VT

Beauchemin, Kelly
Essex Junction
Educational Ctr
Essex Jct, VT

Bettis, Wendy A
Hartford HS
White Rvr Jct, VT

Bhattacharyya, Maitrayee
Essex Junction
Educational Center
Essex Junction, VT

Blake, Shannon B
Essex Junction HS
St Albans, VT

Bliss, Kristen
Barre U 32 HS
Barre, VT

Blumen, Debra
Champlain Valley
Union HS
Shelburne, VT

Boucher, Patrick
Missisquoi Valley
Union HS
Highgate, VT

Boudreau, Ann L
Missisquoi Valley
Union HS
Franklin, VT

Brown, Tairita
Green Mtn Union
Cavendish, VT

Casey, Karen
Spaulding HS
Barre, VT

Cassidy, Lea
Vergennes Union
Vergennes, VT

Chevalier, Eric
Missisquoi Union
Swanton, VT

Coon, Heather
Bellows Free Acad
St Albans, VT

Cooper, Trula A
Missisquoi Valley
Union HS
Franklin, VT

Cross, Tara
Saint Johnsbury
Saint Johnsbury, VT

Demko, Peter J
Essex Jct
Educational Center
Essex Junction, VT

Desjardins, Lee Robert
Woodstock Union
S Pomfret, VT

Dill, Heidi
Harwood Union HS
Waterbury Center, VT

Dion, Joseph
Woodstock Union
South Woodstock, VT

Duffy, Sarah
Rice Memorial HS
S Hero, VT

Dustin, April
Wilmington HS
Wilmington, VT

Eggleston, Michelle
Mount Saint Joseph
Rutland, VT

Farnum, Tony
Brattleboro Union
Brattleboro, VT

Fedor, Kirk
Burrt Burton
Seminary HS
Manchester, VT

Fournier, Molly
Missisquoi Valley
Union HS
Swanton, VT

French, Susan
Burlington HS
Burlington, VT

Gammell, Peggy
St Johnsbury Acad
Saint Johnsbury, VT

Garand, Brian
Spaulding HS
Barre, VT

Garrow, Leslie
Richford JR SR HS
Richford, VT

Gawrys, Brenda
Rutland HS
Rutland, VT

Gebo, Melissa
Mount Abraham
UHS HS
Bristol, VT

Gerace, Donna
Burlington HS
Burlington, VT

Greene, Laura
Mount Anthony
Union HS
Shaftsbury, VT

Hardy, Christopher
Mt Anthony Union
N Bennington, VT

Hatch, William
Rice Memorial HS
S Burlington, VT

Hebert, Jennifer
Mt Saint Joseph
Rutland, VT

Heinecken, Dawn M
Middlebury Union
Middlebury, VT

Hoard, Theresa
Mt Anthony Union
Bennington, VT

Howland, Angela
Hartford HS
Morgan, VT

Jablonski, Victoria M
Mill River Union
Clarendon, VT

Jodoin, Stephanie
Burlington HS
Burlington, VT

Jones, Christine
Fair Haven Union
Fair Haven, VT

Jurgiewich, Mike
Mt Anthony Union
Bennington, VT

Kennedy, Heather
Mt Anthony Union
Bennington, VT

Kirby, David
Burlington HS
South Hero, VT

Klittich, Deborah
Champlain Valley
Union HS
Shelb0rne, VT

Kramer, Susan
Harwood Union HS
Waitsfield, VT

La Rose, Dominique
Blue Mountain Schl
Groton, VT

Landon, Todd
Proctor HS
Proctor, VT

Laroche, Rebecca
Bellows Free Acad
Fairfax, VT

Lawson, Kelly
Mt Anthony Union
Pownal, VT

Lebel, Teri
Bellows Free Acad
St Albans, VT

Leblanc, Kimberlee
Sacred Heart HS
Tampa, FL

Lemieux, Todd
Champlain Valley
Union HS
Williston, VT

Libby, Kristie
Stowe HS
Stowe, VT

Lolatte, Kristen
Brattleboro Union
Brattleboro, VT

Lozon, Heather
Rice Memorial HS
Colchester, VT

Mac Arthur, Susan W
Williamstown JR SR
Graniteville, VT

Marrion, Julie
Mant Anthony HS
Bennington, VT

Marshia, Kerry
Enosburg Falls HS
Bakersfield, VT

Martin, Andrew
Champlain Valley
Union HS
Hinesburg, VT

Mc Leod, Heather
Page
St Johnsbury Acad
Branford, CT

Mears, Shellie
Spaulding HS
Barre, VT

Mellett, Jr Richard
Montpelier HS
Montpelier, VT

Menard, Daniel R
Montpelier HS
Montpelier, VT

Miller, Wendy
Vergennes Union
Ferrisburg, VT

Millett, Laura
Proctor HS
Rutland, VT

Mount, Amy B
Vermont Acad
Saxtons River, VT

Mullgan, James L
Spaulding HS
Barre, VT

Nadler, Krissy
Mount St Joseph
W Rutland, VT

Nativi, Lisa
Spaulding HS
Barre, VT

O Hara, Margaret
Enosburg Falls HS
Enosburg Falls, VT

Pallini, Lisa
Mt Anthony Union
Scottsdale, AZ

Paustian, James
Arlington Memorial
W Arlington, VT

Peters, Stephannie
Mount Anthony
Union HS
Bennington, VT

Pilz, Laura
Arlington Memorial
Arlington, VT

Ploof, Cheryl
Richford HS
East Berkshire, VT

Pouliot, Carole D
North Country U
Newport, VT

Raboin, Laurie
Spaulding HS
Barre, VT

Reynolds, David
Mt Anthony Union
Pownal, VT

Rogers, Debra Jean
Rattleboro Union
Brattleboro, VT

Rousseau, David H
B
St Johnsbury Acad
Saint Johnsbury, VT

Saulnier, Tricia
Twinfield HS
Marshfield, VT

Sipley, Lisa
Vergennes Union
Vergennes, VT

Slattery, Michael J
Essex Junction
Educational Ctr
Essex Junction, VT

Studer, Loretta
North Country
Union HS
W Charleston, VT

Swenor, Tom
Vergennes Union
Vergennes, VT

Talbot, Michael
Winooski HS
Winooski, VT

Tetreault, Lynne
Bellow Free Acad
Fairfield, VT

Thompson, Gary
Blue Mountain
Union HS
Mc Indoe Falls, VT

Thompson, Theresa
Burr & Burton
Manchester, VT

Trudeau, Donald J
Mt Anthony Union
Pownal, VT

Tullar, Jeffrey
Chelsea HS
Corinth, VT

Turner, Edward A
Harwood Union HS
Waitsfield, VT

Valz, Jennifer
Vergennes Union
Vergennes, VT

Vargo, Gerald L
Whitcomb HS
Bethel, VT

Walsh, Brandon
Vermont Acad
Miami, FL

Weaver, Rachel
Bellowo Free Acad
St Albans, VT

Webster, Eric
Randolph Union HS
Randolph, VT

Woodard, Christina
North Country
Union HS
Newport Center, VT

Wright, Stephen
Craftsbury Acad
Craftsbury Common, VT

Wyman, Sue
Otter Valley Univ
Brandon, VT

Zehle, Monika
Essex Jct
Educational Ctr
Essex Ject, VT

VIRGIN ISLANDS

Charlton, Jennie
Charlotte Amalie
St Thomas, VI

Cornish, Ben M
Antilles Schl
St Thomas, VI

Cotto, Sandra
St Croix Central HS
Kingshll-St Croix, VI

Gardner, Carolyn
Charlotte Amalie
St Thomas, VI

Joseph, Darcy
Charlotte Amalie
St Thomas, VI

Lawrence, Derrick
Antilles Schl
St Thomas, VI

Moron, Jackie
Charlotte Amalie
St Thomas, VI

Owen, Gemaine
St Croix Central HS
Christiansted, VI

Pickering, Jeffrey
Charlotte Amalie
St Thomas, VI

Small, Mavis
Charlotte Amalie
St Thomas, VI

Turnbull, Mario
Charlotte Amalie
St Thomas, VI

Walters, Wayne N
Charlotte Amalie
St Thomas, VI

Zimney, Richard
Charlotte Amalie
Fairfield, AL

FOREIGN COUNTRIES

Allinson, Katherine
Bitburg American
Apo Ny, NY

Barker, Josh
Torrejon American
Apo, NY

Blanchard, James
Ramstein American
Apo New York, NY

Boggs, Christine
W T Sampson HS
Norfolk, VA

Bories, Sean
Ramstein American
San Antonio, TX

Bowman, Paul G
Evangelical
Christian Acad
Waterman, IL

Brennan, Erin
Ramstein American
Apo New York, NY

Bryant, Tonja
Izmir American HS
APO, NY

Cale, Sterling R
Bonn American HS
Apo, NY

Charlton, Maria
Robert D Edgren
APO San Fran, CA

Cottrill, Edward A
Berlin American HS
Apo New York, NY

Dauzat, Sarah M
Torrejon HS
Apo New York, NY

Delboy, Frederick W
Gen H H Arnold
American HS
A P O New York,
NY

Deming, Mike
Kaiserslautern Amer
APO, NY

Denusta, Didi
John F Kennedy HS
Dededo, GU

Dickinson, Kristy
Lynn
Ramstein HS
APO New York, NY

Drilon, Reuel
Guam Adaventist
Agat, GU

Farmer, Maria
American School Of
Lima Peru
APO Miami, FL

Folse, Katherine
Bitburg HS
Apo Ny, NY

Fulford, Shannon
Wagner HS
Fredericksburg, VA

Gobin, Allan A
Hanau American HS
Apo, NY

Guzzo, Linda
Alpha Secondary
Canada

Hammond, Sean
Roger B Chaffee HS
C/O Fpo, NY

Herget, Robin L
Seoul American HS
San Fran Apo, CA

Herndon, Mike
Hahn American HS
Apo New York, NY

Jasper, Jarrod E
Assumption College
Detroit, MI

Kearney, Suzanne
Bitburg American
Apo Ny, NY

Kearns, Boonda
Hahn American HS
APO, NY

Kilback, Denise
Alpha Secondary HS
Canada

Kilpatrick,
Britta-Lyn
Heidelberg HS
Apo New York, NY

Kochaniewicz,
Heather
Heidelberg HS
APO, NY

La Joie, Mark
Bitburg American
Apo Ny, NY

Martin, Lianne
General Planet SR
Canada

May, Katherine E
Ramstein American
Apo, NY

Mc Elroy, Elizabeth
Anne
Mannheim
American HS
Apo, NY

Mekelburg,
Theodore
Bitburg American
Apo Ny, NY

Mooneyham, Scott
Torrejon HS
Apo, NY

Noble, Joshua Y
Seoul American HS
Apo San Francis,
CA

Price, Penny
Ramstein American
Apo New York, NY

Primas, Arthur
Ramstein American
Apo New York, NY

Ramsey, Jo
Bitburg HS
Apo Ny, NY

Saavedra, Luis R
Collegio Maristas
Monterey, CA

Salvadore, Nicole
Ramstein American
Apo New York, NY

Sanowski, Tonja
Rachele
Braidwood Central
Stayton, OR

Sasseville, Andrew
Country Day Schl
Apo Miami, FL

Smith, Amy
Christian Alliance
Ecuador

Snider, Melisa M
Taegu American
Indianapolis, IN

Townsend, Melissa
Augsburg American
APO, NY

True, Lisa
Ballarat HS
Las Vegas, NV

Van Bramer, John
W
American Schl Of
The Hague
The Netherlands

Vann, Cinamon
Knoxville College
Lakeport, CA

Waites, Houston C
Cairo American Coll
Ft Worth, TX

Walker, Kimberly A
Lakenheath
American HS
Apo New York, NY

Williams, Tami
Torrejon American
Apo, NY

Williams, Willard
Ramstein American
Apo New York, NY

Woytowich, Michelle
Ramstein HS
Apo New York, NY

Yi, Tracey
Alpha SR Secondary
Cananda

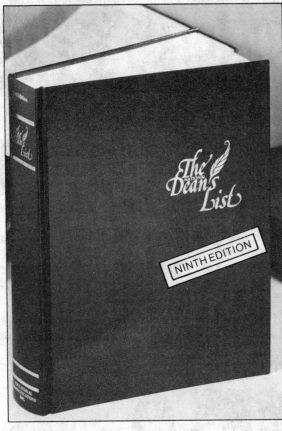